THE OXFORD ENGLISH DICTIONARY

SECOND EDITION

THE OXFORD ENGLISH DICTIONARY

First Edited by

JAMES A. H. MURRAY, HENRY BRADLEY, W. A. CRAIGIE
and C. T. ONIONS

COMBINED WITH

A SUPPLEMENT TO THE OXFORD ENGLISH DICTIONARY

Edited by

R. W. BURCHFIELD

AND RESET WITH CORRECTIONS, REVISIONS
AND ADDITIONAL VOCABULARY

THE OXFORD ENGLISH DICTIONARY

SECOND EDITION

Prepared by

J. A. SIMPSON *and* E. S. C. WEINER

VOLUME VIII

Interval–Looie

CLARENDON PRESS · OXFORD

1989

Oxford University Press, Walton Street, Oxford OX2 6DP
Oxford New York Toronto
Delhi Bombay Calcutta Madras Karachi
Petaling Jaya Singapore Hong Kong Tokyo
Nairobi Dar es Salaam Cape Town
Melbourne Auckland
and associated companies in
Berlin Ibadan

Oxford is a trade mark of Oxford University Press

British Library Cataloguing in Publication Data
Oxford English dictionary.—2nd ed.
1. English language-Dictionaries
I. Simpson, J. A. (John Andrew), 1953-
II. Weiner, Edmund S. C., 1950-
423
ISBN 0-19-861220-6 (vol. VIII)
ISBN 0-19-861186-2 (set)

Library of Congress Cataloging-in-Publication Data
The Oxford English dictionary.—2nd ed.
prepared by J. A. Simpson and E. S. C. Weiner
Bibliography: p.
ISBN 0-19-861220-6 (vol. VIII)
ISBN 0-19-861186-2 (set)
1. English language—Dictionaries. I. Simpson, J. A.
II. Weiner, E. S. C. III. Oxford University Press.
PE1625.087 1989
423—dc19   88-5330

Data capture by ICC, Fort Washington, Pa.
Text-processing by Oxford University Press
Typesetting by Filmtype Services Ltd., Scarborough, N. Yorks.
Manufactured in the United States of America by
Rand McNally & Company, Taunton, Mass.

KEY TO THE PRONUNCIATION

THE pronunciations given are those in use in the educated speech of southern England (the so-called 'Received Standard'), and the keywords given are to be understood as pronounced in such speech.

I. *Consonants*

b, d, f, k, l, m, n, p, t, v, z *have their usual English values*

g as in *g*o (gəʊ)

h ... *h*o! (həʊ)

r ... *r*un (rʌn), te*rr*ier ('tɛrɪə(r))

(r) ... he*r* (hɜː(r))

s ... *s*ee (siː), su*cc*ess (sək'sɛs)

w ... *w*ear (wɛə(r))

hw ... *wh*en (hwɛn)

j ... *y*es (jɛs)

θ as in *th*in (θɪn), ba*th* (bɑːθ)

ð ... *th*en (ðɛn), ba*the* (beɪð)

ʃ ... *sh*op (ʃɒp), di*sh* (dɪʃ)

tʃ ... *ch*op (tʃɒp), di*tch* (dɪtʃ)

ʒ ... vi*s*ion ('vɪʒən), dé*j*euner (deʒøne)

dʒ ... *j*udge (dʒʌdʒ)

ŋ ... si*ng*ing ('sɪŋɪŋ), thi*n*k (θiŋk)

ŋg ... fi*ng*er ('fɪŋgə(r))

(FOREIGN AND NON-SOUTHERN)

ʎ as in It. serra*gli*o (ser'raʎo)

ɲ ... Fr. co*gn*ac (kɔɲak)

x ... Ger. a*ch* (ax), Sc. lo*ch* (lɒx), Sp. fri*j*oles (fri'xoles)

ç ... Ger. i*ch* (ıç), Sc. ni*ch*t (nıçt)

ɣ ... North Ger. sa*g*en ('zaːɣən)

c ... Afrikaans baardmanne*tj*ie ('baːrtmanəci)

ɥ ... Fr. c*u*isine (kɥizin)

Symbols in parentheses are used to denote elements that may be omitted either by individual speakers or in particular phonetic contexts: e.g. *bottle* ('bɒt(ə)l), *Mercian* ('mɜːʃ(ı)ən), *suit* (s(j)uːt), *impromptu* (ım'prɒm(p)tjuː), *father* ('fɑːðə(r)).

II. *Vowels and Diphthongs*

SHORT	LONG	DIPHTHONGS, etc.
ɪ as in p*i*t (pɪt), -n*e*ss, (-nɪs)	iː as in b*ea*n (biːn)	eɪ as in b*ay* (beɪ)
ɛ ... p*e*t (pɛt), Fr. s*e*pt (sɛt)	ɑː ... b*ar*n (bɑːn)	aɪ ... b*uy* (baɪ)
æ ... p*a*t (pæt)	ɔː ... b*or*n (bɔːn)	ɔɪ ... b*oy* (bɔɪ)
ʌ ... p*u*tt (pʌt)	uː ... b*oo*n (buːn)	əʊ ... n*o* (nəʊ)
ɒ ... p*o*t (pɒt)	ɜː ... b*ur*n (bɜːn)	aʊ ... n*ow* (naʊ)
ʊ ... p*u*t (pʊt)	eː ... Ger. Schn*ee* (ʃneː)	ɪə ... p*eer* (pɪə(r))
ə ... *a*nother (ə'nʌðə(r))	ɛː ... Ger. F*äh*re ('fɛːrə)	ɛə ... p*air* (pɛə(r))
(ə) ... beat*e*n ('biːt(ə)n)	aː ... Ger. T*ag* (taːk)	ʊə ... t*our* (tʊə(r))
i ... Fr. s*i* (si)	oː ... Ger. S*oh*n (zoːn)	ɔə ... b*oar* (bɔə(r))
e ... Fr. b*é*b*é* (bebe)	øː ... Ger. G*oe*the ('gøːtə)	
a ... Fr. m*a*ri (mari)	yː ... Ger. gr*ü*n (gryːn)	aɪə as in f*ie*ry ('faɪərɪ)
ɑ ... Fr. b*â*timent (bɑtimɑ̃)		aʊə ... s*our* (saʊə(r))
ɔ ... Fr. h*o*mme (ɔm)	NASAL	
o ... Fr. *eau* (o)	ɛ̃, æ̃ as in Fr. f*in* (fɛ̃, fæ̃)	
ø ... Fr. p*eu* (pø)	ɑ̃ ... Fr. fr*an*c (frɑ̃)	
œ ... Fr. b*oeu*f (bœf) c*oeu*r (kœr)	ɔ̃ ... Fr. b*on* (bɔ̃)	
u ... Fr. d*ou*ce (dus)	œ̃ ... Fr. *un* (œ̃)	
ʏ ... Ger. M*ü*ller ('mʏlər)		
y ... Fr. d*u* (dy)		

The incidence of main stress is shown by a superior stress mark (') preceding the stressed syllable, and a secondary stress by an inferior stress mark (ˌ), e.g. *pronunciation* (prəˌnʌnsɪ'eɪʃ(ə)n).

For further explanation of the transcription used, see *General Explanations*, Volume I.

LIST OF ABBREVIATIONS, SIGNS, ETC.

Some abbreviations listed here in italics are also in certain cases printed in roman type, and vice versa.

a. (in Etym.)	adoption of, adopted from
a (as a 1850)	ante, 'before', 'not later than'
a.	adjective
abbrev.	abbreviation (of)
abl.	ablative
absol.	absolute, -ly
Abstr.	(in titles) Abstract, -s
acc.	accusative
Acct.	(in titles) Account
A.D.	Anno Domini
ad. (in Etym.)	adaptation of
Add.	Addenda
adj.	adjective
Adv.	(in titles) Advance, -d, -s
adv.	adverb
advb.	adverbial, -ly
Advt.	advertisement
Aeronaut.	(as label) in Aeronautics; (in titles) Aeronautic, -al, -s
AF., AFr.	Anglo-French
Afr.	Africa, -n
Agric.	(as label) in Agriculture; (in titles) Agriculture, -al
Alb.	Albanian
Amer.	American
Amer. Ind.	American Indian
Anat.	(as label) in Anatomy; (in titles) Anatomy, -ical
Anc.	(in titles) Ancient
Anglo-Ind.	Anglo-Indian
Anglo-Ir.	Anglo-Irish
Ann.	Annals
Anthrop., Anthropol.	(as label) in Anthropology; (in titles) Anthropology, -ical
Antiq.	(as label) in Antiquities; (in titles) Antiquity
aphet.	aphetic, aphetized
app.	apparently
Appl.	(in titles) Applied
Applic.	(in titles) Application, -s
appos.	appositive, -ly
Arab.	Arabic
Aram.	Aramaic
Arch.	in Architecture
arch.	archaic
Archæol.	in Archæology
Archit.	(as label) in Architecture; (in titles) Architecture, -al
Arm.	Armenian
assoc.	association
Astr.	in Astronomy
Astrol.	in Astrology
Astron.	(in titles) Astronomy, -ical
Astronaut.	(in titles) Astronautic, -s
attrib.	attributive, -ly
Austral.	Australian
Autobiogr.	(in titles) Autobiography, -ical
A.V.	Authorized Version
B.C.	Before Christ
B.C.	(in titles) British Columbia
bef.	before
Bibliogr.	(as label) in Bibliography; (in titles) Bibliography, -ical
Biochem.	(as label) in Biochemistry; (in titles) Biochemistry, -ical
Biol.	(as label) in Biology; (in titles) Biology, -ical
Bk.	Book
Bot.	(as label) in Botany; (in titles) Botany, -ical
Bp.	Bishop
Brit.	(in titles) Britain, British
Bulg.	Bulgarian
Bull.	(in titles) Bulletin
c (as c 1700)	circa, 'about'
c. (as 19th c.)	century
Cal.	(in titles) Calendar
Cambr.	(in titles) Cambridge
Canad.	Canadian
Cat.	Catalan
catachr.	catachrestically
Catal.	(in titles) Catalogue
Celt.	Celtic
Cent.	(in titles) Century, Central
Cent. Dict.	Century Dictionary
Cf., cf.	confer, 'compare'
Ch.	Church
Chem.	(as label) in Chemistry; (in titles) Chemistry, -ical
Chr.	(in titles) Christian
Chron.	(in titles) Chronicle
Chronol.	(in titles) Chronology, -ical
Cinemat., Cinematogr.	in Cinematography
Clin.	(in titles) Clinical
cl. L.	classical Latin
cogn. w.	cognate with
Col.	(in titles) Colonel, Colony
Coll.	(in titles) Collection
collect.	collective, -ly
colloq.	colloquial, -ly
comb.	combined, -ing
Comb.	Combinations
Comm.	in Commercial usage
Communic.	in Communications
comp.	compound, composition
Compan.	(in titles) Companion
compar.	comparative
compl.	complement
Compl.	(in titles) Complete
Conc.	(in titles) Concise
Conch.	in Conchology
concr.	concrete, -ly
Conf.	(in titles) Conference
Congr.	(in titles) Congress
conj.	conjunction
cons.	consonant
const.	construction, construed with
contr.	contrast (with)
Contrib.	(in titles) Contribution
Corr.	(in titles) Correspondence
corresp.	corresponding (to)
Cotgr.	R. Cotgrave, Dictionarie of the French and English Tongues
cpd.	compound
Crit.	(in titles) Criticism, Critical
Cryst.	in Crystallography
Cycl.	(in titles) Cyclopædia, -ic
Cytol.	(in titles) Cytology, -ical
Da.	Danish
D.A.	Dictionary of Americanisms
D.A.E.	Dictionary of American English
dat.	dative
D.C.	District of Columbia
Deb.	(in titles) Debate, -s
def.	definite, -ition
dem.	demonstrative
deriv.	derivative, -ation
derog.	derogatory
Descr.	(in titles) Description, -tive
Devel.	(in titles) Development, -al
Diagn.	(in titles) Diagnosis, Diagnostic
dial.	dialect, -al
Dict.	Dictionary; spec., the Oxford English Dictionary
dim.	diminutive
Dis.	(in titles) Disease
Diss.	(in titles) Dissertation
D.O.S.T.	Dictionary of the Older Scottish Tongue
Du.	Dutch
E.	East
Eccl.	(as label) in Ecclesiastical usage; (in titles) Ecclesiastical
Ecol.	in Ecology
Econ.	(as label) in Economics; (in titles) Economy, -ics
ed.	edition
E.D.D.	English Dialect Dictionary
Edin.	(in titles) Edinburgh
Educ.	(as label) in Education; (in titles) Education, -al
EE.	Early English
e.g.	exempli gratia, 'for example'
Electr.	(as label) in Electricity; (in titles) Electricity, -ical
Electron.	(in titles) Electronic, -s
Elem.	(in titles) Element, -ary
ellipt.	elliptical, -ly
Embryol.	in Embryology
e.midl.	east midland (dialect)
Encycl.	(in titles) Encyclopædia, -ic
Eng.	England, English
Engin.	in Engineering
Ent.	in Entomology
Entomol.	(in titles) Entomology, -logical
erron.	erroneous, -ly
esp.	especially
Ess.	(in titles) Essay, -s
et al.	et alii, 'and others'
etc.	et cetera
Ethnol.	in Ethnology
etym.	etymology
euphem.	euphemistically
Exam.	(in titles) Examination
exc.	except
Exerc.	(in titles) Exercise, -s
Exper.	(in titles) Experiment, -al
Explor.	(in titles) Exploration, -s
f.	feminine
f. (in Etym.)	formed on
f. (in subordinate entries)	form of
F.	French
fem. (rarely f.)	feminine
fig.	figurative, -ly
Finn.	Finnish
fl.	floruit, 'flourished'
Found.	(in titles) Foundation, -s
Fr.	French
freq.	frequent, -ly
Fris.	Frisian
Fund.	(in titles) Fundamental, -s
Funk or Funk's Stand. Dict.	Funk and Wagnalls Standard Dictionary
G.	German
Gael.	Gaelic
Gaz.	(in titles) Gazette
gen.	genitive
gen.	general, -ly
Geogr.	(as label) in Geography; (in titles) Geography, -ical

Geol.	(as label) in Geology; (in titles) *Geology, -ical*	masc. (*rarely* m.)	masculine
Geom.	in Geometry	*Math.*	(as label) in Mathematics; (in titles) *Mathematics, -al*
Geomorphol.	in Geomorphology	MDu.	Middle Dutch
Ger.	German	ME.	Middle English
Gloss.	Glossary	*Mech.*	(as label) in Mechanics; (in titles) *Mechanics, -al*
Gmc.	Germanic	*Med.*	(as label) in Medicine; (in titles) *Medicine, -ical*
Godef.	F. Godefroy, *Dictionnaire de l'ancienne langue française*	med.L.	medieval Latin
Goth.	Gothic	*Mem.*	(in titles) *Memoir, -s*
Govt.	(in titles) *Government*	*Metaph.*	in Metaphysics
Gr.	Greek	*Meteorol.*	(as label) in Meteorology; (in titles) *Meteorology, -ical*
Gram.	(as label) in Grammar; (in titles) *Grammar, -tical*	MHG.	Middle High German
Gt.	Great	midl.	midland (dialect)
		Mil.	in military usage
Heb.	Hebrew	*Min.*	(as label) in Mineralogy; (in titles) *Ministry*
Her.	in Heraldry		
Herb.	among herbalists	*Mineral.*	(in titles) *Mineralogy, -ical*
Hind.	Hindustani	MLG.	Middle Low German
Hist.	(as label) in History; (in titles) *History, -ical*	*Misc.*	(in titles) *Miscellany, -eous*
hist.	historical	mod.	modern
Histol.	(in titles) *Histology, -ical*	mod.L	modern Latin
Hort.	in Horticulture	(Morris),	(quoted from) E. E. Morris's *Austral English*
Househ.	(in titles) *Household*	*Mus.*	(as label) in Music; (in titles) *Music, -al; Museum*
Housek.	(in titles) *Housekeeping*		
Ibid.	*Ibidem*, 'in the same book or passage'	*Myst.*	(in titles) *Mystery*
		Mythol.	in Mythology
Icel.	Icelandic		
Ichthyol.	in Ichthyology	N.	North
id.	*idem*, 'the same'	n.	neuter
i.e.	*id est*, 'that is'	*N. Amer.*	North America, -n
IE.	Indo-European	*N. & Q.*	*Notes and Queries*
Illustr.	(in titles) *Illustration, -ted*	*Narr.*	(in titles) *Narrative*
imit.	imitative	*Nat.*	(in titles) *Natural*
Immunol.	in Immunology	*Nat. Hist.*	in Natural History
imp.	imperative	*Naut.*	in nautical language
impers.	impersonal	N.E.	North East
impf.	imperfect	*N.E.D.*	*New English Dictionary*, original title of the *Oxford English Dictionary* (first edition)
ind.	indicative		
indef.	indefinite		
Industr.	(in titles) *Industry, -ial*		
inf.	infinitive	*Neurol.*	in Neurology
infl.	influenced	neut. (*rarely* n.)	neuter
Inorg.	(in titles) *Inorganic*	NF., NFr.	Northern French
Ins.	(in titles) *Insurance*	No.	Number
Inst.	(in titles) *Institute, -tion*	nom.	nominative
int.	interjection	north.	northern (dialect)
intr.	intransitive	Norw.	Norwegian
Introd.	(in titles) *Introduction*	n.q.	no quotations
Ir.	Irish	N.T.	New Testament
irreg.	irregular, -ly	*Nucl.*	Nuclear
It.	Italian	*Numism.*	in Numismatics
		N.W.	North West
J., (J.)	(quoted from) Johnson's *Dictionary*	*N.Z.*	New Zealand
(Jam.)	Jamieson, *Scottish Dict.*	obj.	object
Jap.	Japanese	obl.	oblique
joc.	jocular, -ly	*Obs., obs.*	obsolete
Jrnl.	(in titles) *Journal*	*Obstetr.*	(in titles) *Obstetrics*
Jun.	(in titles) *Junior*	occas.	occasionally
		OE.	Old English (= Anglo-Saxon)
Knowl.	(in titles) *Knowledge*		
		OF., OFr.	Old French
l.	line	OFris.	Old Frisian
L.	Latin	OHG.	Old High German
lang.	language	OIr.	Old Irish
Lect.	(in titles) *Lecture, -s*	ON.	Old Norse
Less.	(in titles) *Lesson, -s*	ONF.	Old Northern French
Let., Lett.	letter, letters	*Ophthalm.*	in Ophthalmology
LG.	Low German	opp.	opposed (to), the opposite (of)
lit.	literal, -ly		
Lit.	Literary	*Opt.*	in Optics
Lith.	Lithuanian	*Org.*	(in titles) *Organic*
LXX	Septuagint	orig.	origin, -al, -ally
		Ornith.	(as label) in Ornithology; (in titles) *Ornithology, -ical*
m.	masculine		
Mag.	(in titles) *Magazine*	OS.	Old Saxon
Magn.	(in titles) *Magnetic, -ism*	OSl.	Old (Church) Slavonic
Mal.	Malay, Malayan	O.T.	Old Testament
Man.	(in titles) *Manual*	*Outl.*	(in titles) *Outline*
Managem.	(in titles) *Management*	*Oxf.*	(in titles) *Oxford*
Manch.	(in titles) *Manchester*		
Manuf.	in Manufacture, -ing	p.	page
Mar.	(in titles) *Marine*	*Palæogr.*	in Palæography

Palæont.	(as label) in Palæontology; (in titles) *Palæontology, -ical*
pa. pple.	passive participle, past participle
(Partridge),	(quoted from) E. Partridge's *Dictionary of Slang and Unconventional English*
pass.	passive, -ly
pa.t.	past tense
Path.	(as label) in Pathology; (in titles) *Pathology, -ical*
perh.	perhaps
Pers.	Persian
pers.	person, -al
Petrogr.	in Petrography
Petrol.	(as label) in Petrology; (in titles) *Petrology, -ical*
(Pettman),	(quoted from) C. Pettman's *Africanderisms*
pf.	perfect
Pg.	Portuguese
Pharm.	in Pharmacology
Philol.	(as label) in Philology; (in titles) *Philology, -ical*
Philos.	(as label) in Philosophy; (in titles) *Philosophy, -ic*
phonet.	phonetic, -ally
Photogr.	(as label) in Photography; (in titles) *Photography, -ical*
phr.	phrase
Phys.	physical; (*rarely*) in Physiology
Physiol.	(as label) in Physiology; (in titles) *Physiology, -ical*
Pict.	(in titles) *Picture, Pictorial*
pl., plur.	plural
poet.	poetic, -al
Pol.	Polish
Pol.	(as label) in Politics; (in titles) *Politics, -al*
Pol. Econ.	in Political Economy
Polit.	(in titles) *Politics, -al*
pop.	popular, -ly
Porc.	(in titles) *Porcelain*
poss.	possessive
Pott.	(in titles) *Pottery*
ppl. a., pple. adj.	participial adjective
pple.	participle
Pr.	Provençal
pr.	present
Pract.	(in titles) *Practice, -al*
prec.	preceding (word or article)
pred.	predicative
pref.	prefix
pref., Pref.	preface
prep.	preposition
pres.	present
Princ.	(in titles) *Principle, -s*
priv.	privative
prob.	probably
Probl.	(in titles) *Problem*
Proc.	(in titles) *Proceedings*
pron.	pronoun
pronunc.	pronunciation
prop.	properly
Pros.	in Prosody
Prov.	Provençal
pr. pple.	present participle
Psych.	in Psychology
Psychol.	(as label) in Psychology; (in titles) *Psychology, -ical*
Publ.	(in titles) *Publications*
Q.	(in titles) *Quarterly*
quot(s).	quotation(s)
q.v.	*quod vide*, 'which see'
R.	(in titles) *Royal*
Radiol.	in Radiology
R.C.Ch.	Roman Catholic Church
Rec.	(in titles) *Record*
redupl.	reduplicating
Ref.	(in titles) *Reference*
refash.	refashioned, -ing
refl.	reflexive
Reg.	(in titles) *Register*

reg.	regular	str.	strong	*Trop.*	(in titles) *Tropical*
rel.	related to	*Struct.*	(in titles) *Structure, -al*	Turk.	Turkish
Reminisc.	(in titles) *Reminiscence, -s*	*Stud.*	(in titles) *Studies*	*Typog., Typogr.*	in Typography
Rep.	(in titles) *Report, -s*	subj.	subject		
repr.	representative, representing	*subord. cl.*	subordinate clause	ult.	ultimately
Res.	(in titles) *Research*	subseq.	subsequent, -ly	*Univ.*	(in titles) *University*
Rev.	(in titles) *Review*	subst.	substantively	unkn.	unknown
rev.	revised	*suff.*	suffix	*U.S.*	United States
Rhet.	in Rhetoric	superl.	superlative	U.S.S.R.	Union of Soviet Socialist Republics
Rom.	Roman, -ce, -ic	Suppl.	Supplement		
Rum.	Rumanian	*Surg.*	(as label) in Surgery; (in titles) *Surgery, Surgical*	usu.	usually
Russ.	Russian	s.v.	*sub voce,* 'under the word'	v., vb.	verb
S.	South	Sw.	Swedish	var(r)., vars.	variant(s) of
S.Afr.	South Africa, -n	s.w.	south-western (dialect)	*vbl. sb.*	verbal substantive
sb.	substantive	*Syd. Soc. Lex.*	Sydenham Society, *Lexicon of Medicine & Allied Sciences*	*Vertebr.*	(in titles) *Vertebrate, -s*
sc.	*scilicet,* 'understand' or 'supply'	syll.	syllable	*Vet.*	(as label) in Veterinary Science; (in titles) *Veterinary*
Sc., Scot.	Scottish	Syr.	Syrian	*Vet. Sci.*	in Veterinary Science
Scand.	(in titles) *Scandinavia, -n*	*Syst.*	(in titles) *System, -atic*	viz.	*videlicet,* 'namely'
Sch.	(in titles) *School*			*Voy.*	(in titles) *Voyage, -s*
Sc. Nat. Dict.	Scottish National Dictionary	*Taxon.*	(in titles) *Taxonomy, -ical*	*v.str.*	strong verb
Scotl.	(in titles) *Scotland*	techn.	technical, -ly	*vulg.*	vulgar
Sel.	(in titles) *Selection, -s*	*Technol.*	(in titles) *Technology, -ical*	*v.w.*	weak verb
Ser.	Series	*Telegr.*	in Telegraphy		
sing.	singular	*Teleph.*	in Telephony	W.	Welsh; West
Sk.	(in titles) *Sketch*	(Th.),	(quoted from) Thornton's *American Glossary*	wd.	word
Skr.	Sanskrit			Webster	*Webster's (New International) Dictionary*
Slav.	Slavonic	*Theatr.*	in the Theatre, theatrical		
S.N.D.	Scottish National Dictionary	*Theol.*	(as label) in Theology; (in titles) *Theology, -ical*	*Westm.*	(in titles) *Westminster*
Soc.	(in titles) *Society*	*Theoret.*	(in titles) *Theoretical*	WGmc.	West Germanic
Sociol.	(as label) in Sociology; (in titles) *Sociology, -ical*	Tokh.	Tokharian	*Wks.*	(in titles) *Works*
Sp.	Spanish	tr., transl.	translated, translation	w.midl.	west midland (dialect)
Sp.	(in titles) *Speech, -es*	*Trans.*	(in titles) *Transactions*	WS.	West Saxon
sp.	spelling	*trans.*	transitive		
spec.	specifically	*transf.*	transferred sense	(Y.),	(quoted from) Yule & Burnell's *Hobson-Jobson*
Spec.	(in titles) *Specimen*	*Trav.*	(in titles) *Travel(s)*	*Yrs.*	(in titles) *Years*
St.	Saint	*Treas.*	(in titles) *Treasury*		
Stand.	(in titles) *Standard*	*Treat.*	(in titles) *Treatise*	*Zoogeogr.*	in Zoogeography
Stanf.	(quoted from) *Stanford Dictionary of Anglicised Words & Phrases*	*Treatm.*	(in titles) *Treatment*	*Zool.*	(as label) in Zoology; (in titles) *Zoology, -ical*
		Trig.	in Trigonometry		

Signs and Other Conventions

Before a word or sense

† = obsolete
‖ = not naturalized, alien
¶ = catachrestic and erroneous uses

In the listing of Forms

1 = before 1100
2 = 12th c. (1100 to 1200)
3 = 13th c. (1200 to 1300), etc.
5-7 = 15th to 17th century
20 = 20th century

In the etymologies

* indicates a word or form not actually found, but of which the existence is inferred
:— = normal development of

The printing of a word in SMALL CAPITALS indicates that further information will be found under the word so referred to.

.. indicates an omitted part of a quotation.

‐ (in a quotation) indicates a hyphen doubtfully present in the original; (in other text) indicates a hyphen inserted only for the sake of a line-break.

PROPRIETARY NAMES

THIS Dictionary includes some words which are or are asserted to be proprietary names or trade marks. Their inclusion does not imply that they have acquired for legal purposes a non-proprietary or general significance nor any other judgement concerning their legal status. In cases where the editorial staff have established in the records of the Patent Offices of the United Kingdom and of the United States that a word is registered as a proprietary name or trade mark this is indicated, but no judgement concerning the legal status of such words is made or implied thereby.

interval ('ɪntəvəl), *sb.* Forms: α. 3 enterwal, 8 (sense 4) enterval(l. β. 4–5 intervalle, 7 -vall, 7– interval. See also INTERVALE. [Ultimately ad. L. *intervallum*, orig. 'space between palisades or ramparts', later 'interval of space or of time', f. *inter* between + *vallum* rampart. In F. the word appears as *entreval, antreval* (13th c.), *entrevale, -valle* (14–16th c.), *intervalle* masc. from 14th c. The earliest Eng. example represents the first of these; the 14–16th c. *intervalle* was evidently also immediately from F.

The appearances of the word till the beginning of the 17th c. are quite sporadic, having little or no historical connexion with each other.]

1. a. The period of time between two events, actions, etc., or between two parts of an action, performance, or sitting, two sessions of parliament, etc.; a period of cessation; a pause, break.

Often used more or less specifically of a recognized short pause in the course of some otherwise continuous action, e.g. in the course of school hours, between the parts of a musical or dramatic performance, etc. In Scotland, the ordinary name for the short space between the morning and afternoon service at church. Applied by A. Wood (*c* 1660–5) to the period of the Commonwealth.

a **1300** *Cursor M.* 22444 (Cott.) Queþer þai [signs of Doomsday] sal hal on ran bitide, or enterwal [*Edin. MS.* enterwall, **13..** *Gött.* enter-vale] bituix þam bide. *c* **1386** CHAUCER *Melib.* ¶ 567 Whan the defense is doon anon withouten Interualle or with-outen tariyng or delay. *c* **1430** *Pilgr. Lyf. Manhode* I. cliii. (1869) 76 With oute jnterualle alle thing enoyeth; bothe the faire weder, and thilke of reyn. **1611** COTGR., *Intervalle*, an Interual, intermedium, respit, pawse or space betweene. [Not in Minsheu or Florio, in rendering *intervalo, intervallo*.] **1647** CLARENDON *Hist. Reb.* I. §7 Whoever considers the Acts of power and injustice.. in those intervals of Parliament. **1660** WOOD *Life* (O.H.S.) I. 356 Habits much neglected in the late intervall. **1664** *Ibid.* 31 Dec II. 26 John Hall..bred in the interval; a presbyterian. **1667** PEPYS *Diary* 12 Aug., I..talked to them all the intervals of the play. *a* **1715** BURNET *Own Time* (1724) I. III. 389 So matters were most in his hands during the intervals of Parliament. **1853** C. BRONTË *Villette* xvi, In the interval, between the two acts, I 'fell on sleep'. **1871** BLACK *Daughter of Heth* (1872) 36 After the 'interval', as it was technically called, they had to go to church again.

b. *spec.* The space of time intervening between the beginning of one febrile paroxysm and that of the ensuing one (*Syd. Soc. Lex.*), or between any fits or periods of disease. ***lucid interval***: see LUCID.

1634 W. TIRWHYT tr. *Balzac's Lett.* (vol. I) 70 The interuals or good dayes of a Tertian Ague. **1713** SWIFT *Frenzy J. Denny* Wks. 1755 III. I. 142 If the patient on the third day have an interval. **1771** WESLEY *Serm.* ii. div. i. §9 Even this poor wretch, in his sober intervals, is able to testify, *Oderunt peccare boni.* **1887** in *Syd. Soc. Lex.*

2. a. The space of time intervening between two points of time; any intervening time. Formerly often ***interval of time***.

1616 BULLOKAR, *Interuall*, a distance of time or place. **1664** POWER *Exp. Philos.* I. 62 In all which interval of time, there is a palpable and sensible heat produced. **1676** I. MATHER *K. Philip's War* (1862) 113 In this interval of time, the town of Mendam..was burnt down by the Indians. **1802** MAR. EDGEWORTH *Moral T.* (1816) I. 240 There was no interval of time between his receiving the vase and his putting it into the fire. **1809** A. HENRY *Trav.* 2 The surrender of Montreal..followed that of Fort de Levi, at only the short interval of three days. **1847** GROTE *Greece* II. xlvii. (1862) IV. 155 An interval of more than sixty years. **1883** C. J. WILLS *Mod. Persia* 159 After a decorous interval the bishop enters.

b. Phr. ***at*** (†***by***) ***intervals***, now and again, not continuously. Also † ***by intervals***, alternately.

1588 A. KING tr. *Canisius' Catech.* I iij, Yat..ye cowrse of ye moone may haiff by interualles now 29. now 30. dayes. **1744** A. DOBBS *Hudson's Bay* 12 The Month of February was variable..at Intervals warm, and then sharp Weather. **1760** WASHINGTON *Writ.* (1889) II. 153 The Rain continued by intervals through the night. **1835** POE *Adv. Hans Pfaall* Wks. 1864 I. 10 A drizzling rain falling at intervals. **1860** TYNDALL *Glac.* I. xi. 85 In spite of cold and hard boards, I slept at intervals.

c. *Physics.* A quantity *ds*, invariant under the Lorentz transformation, that represents the separation of two events in space-time and is defined by $ds^2 = dx^2 + dy^2 + dz^2 - c^2dt^2$ (or by the negative of the right-hand side), where *dx, dy, dz*, and *dt* are the differences in the space and time coordinates of the events and *c* is the speed of light.

1918 A. S. EDDINGTON *Rep. Relativity Theory Gravitation* ii. 15 In the four-dimensional continuum the interval δs between two point-events..is unaffected by any rotation of the axes, and is therefore invariant for all observers. **1929** W. C. D. DAMPIER-WHETHAM *Hist. Sci.* ix. 422 Just as the distance between two points in the continuous space of Euclidean geometry is the same however measured, so, in the new continuum of space-time, two events may be said to be separated by an 'interval', involving both space and time. **1952** C. MØLLER *Theory of Relativity* iv. 99 This expression for the line element or the interval defines the geometry in (3 + 1)-space. **1959** J. AHARONI *Special Theory of Relativity* i. 25 When the interval is time-like it is always possible to find a system of coordinates in which the events appear in the same place.

3. a. An open space lying between two things or two parts of the same thing; a gap, opening. Also, an intervening portion *of* something.

1489 CAXTON *Faytes of A.* I. xxiv. 73 The interualle or dystance that ought for to be betwix euery rowe. **1656** tr. *Hobbes' Elem. Philos.* Wks. 1839 I. 178 There cannot be more than one least interval or length between the same points. **1667** MILTON *P.L.* VI. 105 Now 'Twixt Host and Host but narrow space was left, A dreadful interval. **1717** DE FOE *Hist. Ch. Scot.* II. 49 He was driven back..by half the Number of the Scots Cavalry, with Musketeers in their Intervals. **1791** W. BARTRAM *Travels* 316 One continued rapid, with some short intervals of still water. **1833** *Regul. Instr. Cavalry* I. 10 Open Interval is taken by each recruit stretching out his right arm so as to touch the shoulder of his right hand man, and keeping that distance from him. **1837** BREWSTER *Magnet.* 361 The intervals which separate the ultimate atoms of material bodies.

b. Phr. ***at intervals***, here and there; at some distance from each other.

1812 BRACKENRIDGE *Views Louisiana* (1814) 91 These villages..are situated at intervals along the river. **1834** MEDWIN *Angler in Wales* I. 288 The spearsmen took their posts at intervals in the shallows.

4. In N. America: = INTERVALE 3.

1684 in Hudson *Hist. Sudbury* (1889) 66 All the lands within said bounds of hills, vallies, planes, intervalls, meadows, swamps. **1725** S. WILLARD *Jrnl.* in *Appalachia* (Boston, 1881) II. 343 This morning we came on some Entervalls and plain land. *Ibid.*, A still stream..with plenty of Enterval, and old planting land of yᵉ Indians. **1784** J. BELKNAP in *B. Papers* (1877) II. 181 The intervals are excellent, and the uplands very good. **1843** PRESCOTT *Mexico* I. v. (1864) 42 A natural opening in the forest, or a rich strip of interval. *a* **1862** THOREAU *Yankee in Canada* i. (1866) 4 A remarkably large and level interval like the bed of a lake.

5. *Mus.* The difference of pitch between two musical sounds or notes, either successive (in melody) or simultaneous (in harmony).

1609 DOULAND *Ornith. Microl.* 17 An Interuall..is the distance of a base and high sound. *Ibid.*, The vsuall Interuals are in number 9. **1676** tr. *Guillatiere's Voy. Athens* 308 At a distance that agreed exactly with the intervals and modulation of the Musick. **1807** ROBINSON *Archæol. Græca* v. xxiii. 534 In music the Greeks distinguished sounds, intervals, concords [etc.]. **1855** BAIN *Senses & Int.* II. ii. §8 Although in music no less intervals than a semitone are admitted, the ear can distinguish still smaller differences.

6. *fig.* Distance between persons in respect of position, endowments, beliefs, etc., or between things in respect of their qualities.

1839 MACAULAY *Hist. Eng.* ii. I. 186 The interval between the Episcopalian and the Presbyterian seemed to vanish, when compared with the interval which separated both from the Papist. *Ibid.* ix. II. 450 The interval was immense between discontent and rebellion. **1855** BAIN *Senses & Int.* II. ii. §19 (1864) 144 From turtle to stale oat-cakes, or a piece of black bread, what a mighty interval!

7. *Math.* **a.** A range between one number and another; *spec.* that between successive values of the argument in a mathematical table.

1838 *Penny Cycl.* XII. 508/2 The smaller the tabular interval, the more correctly will a given number of differences serve to make the interpolation. **1911** *Encycl. Brit.* XIX. 862/2 The actual calculation of the number of primes in a given interval may be effected by a formula constructed and used by D. F. E. Meissel. **1928** [see INTERPOLATE *v.* 6]. **1946** *Nature* 12 Oct. 504/1 The basic sequence is the integration procedure for one interval of the integration, which is a sequence of operations starting from the initial values for that interval and giving final values which become the initial values for the next interval. **1968** FOX & MAYERS *Computing Methods for Scientists & Engineers* i. 8 If $1{\cdot}5 \leqslant x \leqslant 2{\cdot}5$, then $y = x^{10}$ is in the approximate interval $57{\cdot}6 \leqslant y \leqslant 9536{\cdot}7$. **1974** *Nature* 26 Apr. 739/1 The grain temperature..is determined by the emissivity between 4 and 15 μm. We have carried out calculations..over this spectral interval.

b. A set composed of all the numbers between two given numbers, which may be either included in the set (a *closed interval*) or excluded (an *open interval*); an analogously defined subset of any partially ordered set.

The distinction made in quot. 1949 is not usual.

1902 *Encycl. Brit.* XXVIII. 545/2 This domain may be an 'interval', i.e., it may consist of two terminal numbers, all the numbers between them and no others. **1949** S. LEFSCHETZ *Introd. Topology* i. 27 If the real line *L* is parameterized by means of a parameter *u*, then an interval is a set: $a < u < b$, and a segment is a set $a \leqq u \leqq b$, $a < b$. **1962** B. H. ARNOLD *Intuitive Concepts Elem. Topology* viii. 164 It is easy to see that a set $A \subset R$ is an interval if and only if it contains all points which lie between any two of its members. **1965** A. ABIAN *Theory of Sets* iv. 184 Let $(P, \leqq)$ be a partially ordered set. For every two elements *a* and *b* of *P*, the set of all elements of *P* such that $a \leqq x \leqq b$ is called a closed interval and is denoted by $[a, b]$, and the set of all elements *x* of *P* such that $a < x < b$ is called an open interval and is denoted by (a, b).

8. *attrib.* and *Comb.*, as (sense 1) ***interval issue, man, music, prose, time, way***; (sense 3) ***interval distance***; (sense 4) ***interval land***. **interval running**, in *Athletics*, a method of training by running set distances at pre-determined speeds (opp. FARTLEK); so **interval training; interval signal** *Broadcasting* (see quot. 1941).

1796 *Instr. & Reg. Cavalry* (1813) 143 In open column the leading division of each squadron preserves the interval distance from the one before. **1652** BENLOWES *Theoph.* Pref., In reviewing these Intervall Issues of spiritual Recreation. **1683** in Temple & Sheldon *Hist. Northfield* (1875) 95 That every person that has 60 acres granted of interval land, shall settle two inhabitants upon it. **1771** J. ADAMS *Diary* 7 June, Wks. 1850 II. 271 The road is three quarters of a mile from the river, and the interval land lies between. **1805** LADY HUNTER in *Sir. M. Hunter's Journ.* (1894) 223 Except an island..and the interval lands, the rest is very bad land. **1660** WOOD *Life* (O.H.S.) I. 356 To encourage others, especially the intervall men..and make the intervall way.. neglected and ridiculous..just antipodes to the intervall time. **1951** *Catal. of Exhibits, South Bank Exhib., Festival of Britain* 176 Recordings for Interval Music. **1967** *Daily Tel.* 12 May 20/6 The unchanging interval-music. **1970** *Listener* 8 Jan. 60/2 The material..provided interval prose of just the right emotional tone between two parts of a good concert. **1957** *Oxf. Pocket Bk. Athletic Training* (ed. 2) 22 *Interval running*,..a series of runs over a particular distance each in a certain time..linked up by jogging between each. **1932** *B.B.C. Year Bk.* 373 The sudden failure of the programme ..is likely to cause the listener to think his set has become faulty. The radiation of the interval signal relieves all anxieties on this account. **1941** *B.B.C. Gloss. Broadcasting Terms* 16 *Interval Signal*, particular sequence of sounds used by a broadcasting organization to fill short intervals between programmes, and to enable listeners to identify its transmissions. Interval time [see *interval man* above]. **1962** *Times* 9 Apr. 5/7 Oxford's application of interval training, on the other hand, may have been at fault. Interval way [see *interval man* above].

interval ('ɪntəvəl), *v. rare.* [f. prec. sb.]

†**1.** *intr.* **a.** To come between or in an interval. **b.** To form an interval: in **'intervalling** *ppl. a.*

1630 JAMES RATRAY in *J. Taylor's* (Water P.) *Wks.* 245 If clouds doe interuall, Apolloes face Is but a figur'd shape. **1632** LITHGOW *Trav.* VI. 254 This Lake is foure score miles in length, and according to its intervalling Circuite, sometimes two..or five miles in breadth. *Ibid.* 255 To drowne their situations and intervalling plaines with water.

2. *trans.* (in *pass.*) †**a.** To separate by an interval (*obs.*). †**b.** To administer at intervals (*obs.*). **c.** To break or interrupt at intervals. Hence **'interval(l)ed** *ppl. a.*

1659 D. PELL *Impr. Sea* Proœm. C, England wants not.. intercourse with various..Nations, how far intervall'd soever. **1716** M. DAVIES *Athen. Brit.* II. To Rdr. 10 The sharp acid Cathartick of Sal Mirabile..being occasionally premis'd or intervall'd. **1883** RUSKIN *Fors Clav.* VIII. xcii. 208 A march of infinite light..intervaled indeed with eddies of shadow. **1899** *Daily News* 10 Mar. 5/5 To harass the Sirdar's long intervalled line of outposts on the Nile.

intervale ('ɪntəveɪl). Now *Amer.* Forms: 4 entervale, 7 intervale, -vail; (sense 3) 7 entervail(e, -vale, intervayle, 8 intervail, 7– intervale. [In former English use, only a rare variant or collateral form of INTERVAL: cf. OF. *entreval* and *entrevale, -valle*, and the 14–16th c. Eng. *intervalle*. But by Lithgow in 1632, and from 17th c. in New England, associated with *vale*, in the specific American sense 3.

It is not clear whether the association with *vale, valley*, was, in the first place, one of popular etymology, favoured perhaps by the partial survival of the old variant form in *-vale* (cf. *intervail* in sense 2), or whether this was in New England a natural development of the sense, arising from the fact that the chief *intervals* in the primaeval forest were the bottoms of the river valleys, and giving rise to an association with *vale*, as used in English in such names as the Vale of Clwyd, Vale of Llangollen, Vale of the Yarrow, etc. It is possible that both principles operated together; and it is to be noted that, in this specific sense, *intervale* has not, even in American use, ousted *interval*.]

†**1.** Of time: = INTERVAL *sb.* 1. *Obs.*

13.. [see INTERVAL *sb.* 1]. *a* **1661** FULLER *Worthies* I. (1662) 65 In that intervale after the Sun is set..and before candles are set up. **1682** *Conn. Col. Rec.* (1859) III. 113 This Court in the intervales of the Generall Court doe desire and impower the Governour and Assistants [etc.].

†**2.** Of space: = INTERVAL *sb.* 3. *Obs.*

1683 *New Jersey Archives* (1880) I. 431 Be sure that..no Street be laid close to the back of another without an Intervale of at least a pair of Butts. **1684** *Scanderbeg Rediv.* vi. 144 The Army in Three Lines, all closed, without any Intervails.

3. In N. America: A low level tract of land, esp. along a river; = INTERVAL *sb.* 4. Also *attrib.*

Orig. in New England, but now used in some other parts of U.S. and in Canada. The sense is the same as that of *haugh* in Scotland.

[**1632** LITHGOW *Trav.* VIII. 365 This City of Fez is situate upon the bodies and twice double devalling faces..of two hills..; the intervale, or low valley betweene both..being the Center.] **1653** *Early Rec. Lancaster, Mass.* (1884) 27 Thirty acors of uppland and fortie acors of Entervale land. **1659** in Nourse *Hist. Harvard* (1894) 16 Still Riuer farm bounded Southwest by the enteruail. *a* **1704** W. HUBBARD *Hist. New Eng.* iii. (1815) 18 Fruitfull spots of land, such as they call intervail land, in levells and champain ground.. neere the banks of great rivers. **1792** BELKNAP *Hist. New Hampsh.* III. Pref. 6 Another word..which perhaps is not more known in England, viz. *intervale*..is well understood in all parts of New-England to distinguish the low-land adjacent to the fresh rivers, which is frequently overflowed by the freshets. **1794** S. WILLIAMS *Vermont* 35 By intervales we mean those low lands which are adjacent to the rivers. **1856** WHITTIER *Mary Garvin* i, From the heart of Waumbek Methna, from the lake that never fails, Falls the Saco in the green lap of Conway's intervales. **1884** DAWSON *Handbk. Dom. Canada* 108 The spring freshets flood these wide valleys, and produce what is called 'intervale' land of great fertility.

intervallary (ɪntə'vælərɪ), *a. rare.* [See INTERVALLIC *a.* and -ARY².] = INTERVALLIC *a.*

c **1864** G. M. HOPKINS *Jrnls. & Papers* (1959) 76 The division then is of abrupt and gradual,..of intervallary and chromatic..and qualitative beauty. **1889** *London Med. Recorder* 20 Aug. 310/2 Herr Pfeiffer recommends in the intervallary treatment of gout the Wiesbaden baths.

intervallic (ɪntəˈvælɪk), *a.* Also -valic. [f. L. *intervall-um* + -IC.] Of or pertaining to an interval or intervals.

1847 J. HALLIDAY *Rustic Bard* 61 The streamlet shows a summer visage clear, As its intervalic gushes fall in music on the ear. **1883** *Grove's Dict. Mus.* III. 613 Until the end of the 16th century the common characteristics of the chorale.. were..a diatonic intervallic progression. **1887** *Century Mag.* XXXV. 318 The intervalic relation of tones.

‖**interˈvallum.** *Obs.* Pl. -valla, -vallums. [L.; see INTERVAL *sb.*] = INTERVAL *sb.* 1, 2.

1574 GRINDAL *Let. to Burleigh* 13 Nov. in *Rem.* (Parker Soc.) 351 My fits of colic, stone, and strangury are very grievous when they come; but God sendeth me some *intervalla.* **1597** SHAKS. *2 Hen. IV*, v. i. 90 He shall laugh with Interuallums. **1622** MABBE tr. *Aleman's Guzman d'Alf.* I. 57 Not allowing me the least *intervallum* of time or any space or respit..to take any rest. **1644** CHILLINGW. *Serm. bef. his Majesty* 19 In one of these *Intervalla*, one of these sober moodes. **1647** N. BACON *Disc. Govt. Eng.* I. lvi. 102 They were not always of such sad influence, but had their *lucida intervalla.*

intervalometer (ɪntəvəˈlɒmɪtə(r)). *Photogr.* [f. INTERVAL *sb.* + -OMETER.] An attachment for a camera that enables photographs to be taken automatically at set intervals.

1933 *Discovery* Feb. 60/1 The photographer works out the intervals that he must allow between exposures, so as to secure a 60 per cent. overlap, and sets the required interval on the intervalometer on the remote control. **1971** *Amat. Photographer* 13 Jan. 51/3 Time-lapse devices known as Intervalometers (repeating timers giving various ranges of delays between 0·2 sec. and 10 min.). With these the camera can be left unattended for indefinite periods (for motion analysis of such things as plant growth, etc.).

inter-valve: see INTER- *pref.* 5.

intervalvular (ɪntəˈvælvjʊlə(r)), *a.* [INTER- 4 a.] Situated between valves.

1830 LINDLEY *Nat. Syst. Bot.* 15 Those fruits which are said to have intervalvular placentæ.

inter-varietal: see INTER- *pref.* 6.

intervarsity, -vary: see INTER- *pref.* 5, 1 b.

intervascular (ɪntəˈvæskjʊlə(r)), *a. Anat.* [INTER- 4 a.] Situated or occurring between the vessels of an animal or plant, esp. between blood-vessels.

1849–52 TODD *Cycl. Anat.* IV. 1219/2 The.. intervascular spaces are variable in number. **1885** G. H. TAYLOR *Pelvic & Hern. Therap.* 122 The intervascular fluids of the whole pelvic region.

intervein (ɪntəˈveɪn), *v.* Also 7 -veyne. [f. INTER- 1 a + VEIN *sb.* or *v.*]

1. *trans.* To intersect with or as with veins.

1615 BARGRAVE *Serm.* E iv, If I interveyne our Earles honours with his wives vertues. **1671** MILTON *P.R.* III. 257 Two rivers flow'd..and left between Fair Champain with less rivers interveind. **1810** WORDSW. *Scenery of Lakes* i. (1823) 29 The broom..interveins the steep copses with its golden blossoms. **1814** CARY *Dante, Purg.* XXIX. 110 White the rest With vermeil intervein'd. **1858** DE QUINCEY *S. Parr* Wks. 1862 V. 116 Richly interveined with political allusions and sarcasms.

2. (In *pass.*) To place in alternate veins.

1811 PINKERTON *Petral.* II. 30 In the same interesting isle marble and steatite are reciprocally interveined. **1842** FABER *Styrian Lake*, etc. 307 The streaks of green turf shine with the black olive-gardens interveined.

inter-veinal: see INTER- *pref.* 6.

intervene (ɪntəˈviːn), *v.* Also 7 entervene, interveyn, *Sc.* -vein. [ad. L. *interven-īre*, f. *inter* between + *venīre* to come. Cf. F. *intervenir* (earlier *entrevenir*, 1363 in Hatz.-Darm.).]

1. *intr.* To come in as something extraneous, in the course of some action, state of things, etc.

1605 BACON *Adv. Learn.* I. iv. §1 Those errours and vanities, which haue interueyned amongst the studies themselues of the learned. **1646** SIR T. BROWNE *Pseud. Ep.* III. viii. 122 When during the discourse the partie or subject interveneth, and there ensueth a sudden silence, it is usually said, *Lupus est in fabulâ.* **1667** MILTON *P.L.* IX. 222 For while so near each other thus all day Our task we choose, what wonder if so near Looks intervene and smiles. **1799** WORDSW. *Ruth* xxiv, In his worst pursuits..sometimes there did intervene Pure hopes of high intent. **1825** SCOTT *Talism.* i, Labour and danger were doomed to intervene ere the horse or horseman reached the desired spot.

2. Of an event or occurence: To happen or take place between other events, or between certain points in time; to occur in the meanwhile.

a **1610** SIR J. SEMPLE in *S. Ballatis* (1872) 242 Suche strange events hes interveinit sensyne That I dare not avow [etc.]. **1730** A. GORDON *Maffei's Amphith.* 81 Some of which were upon a certain Occasion, which then interven'd, destroyed. **1784** *New Spectator* No. 20. 4/2 It so intervened, that Capt. T—— was left, unprotected, to the three heroes. **1824** LAMB *Elia* Ser. II. *Poor Relation*, Some argument had intervened between them. **1850** CARLYLE *Latter-d. Pamph.* iii. 12 If some cleaning of the Augis stable have not intervened for a long while.

3. Of a person, party, or state: To come between in action; to interfere, interpose; also, to act as intermediary; †to take a share *in* (*obs.*).

1646 J. HALL *Horæ Vac.* 193 These Inventions are most quick..and full of life, wherein there doe not intervene any other persons but mortall. **1669** TEMPLE *Wks.* (1731) II. 197 In all the Negotiations where he has intervened for eight or nine Months past. **1750** CARTE *Hist. Eng.* II. 88 When his own brother..came to intervene in the affair with very unbecoming menaces. **1846** TRENCH *Mirac.* xxix. (1862) 396 He intervenes with mighty help, but not till every other help ..has seemed utterly to have failed. **1874** GREEN *Short Hist.* ix. §7. 664 A formal invitation to William to intervene in arms..was signed by these leaders. **1880** J. F. BRIGHT *Hist. Eng.* III. (1884) 1397 It was necessary that England should intervene with clean hands, and as the friend of both parties [Greece and Turkey]. **1883** *Wharton's Law Lex.* (ed. 7) 429 The Queen's proctor, or any other person, may intervene in any suit, for the dissolution of marriage, on the ground that the parties have been guilty of collusion, or that material facts have been suppressed.

b. Of a thing: To come in or between so as to affect, modify, or prevent a result, action, etc.

1649 BP. HALL *Cases Consc.* IV. vi. 458 Many things may intervene betwixt this engagement..and that full and compleate solemnization, which may breake off the match. **1671** R. BOHUN *Wind* 54 The motions of Winds..are..in right lines; if nothing intervene to check and retard their course. **1744** SARAH FIELDING *David Simple* (ed. 2) II. 125 People who let their Pride intervene with their Tenderness ...to make them quarrel with their Friends. **1828** D'ISRAELI *Chas. I*, II. xi. 285 Between our intentions and our practices, our little and our great passions may intervene. **1873** M. ARNOLD *Lit. & Dogma* (1876) 178 The materialising conceptions of the writer do yet evidently intervene..to hinder a perfectly faithful mirroring of the thought of Jesus.

4. a. Of a thing: To be placed or situated locally *between* other things; to come or lie between.

c **1709** [see INTERVENING below]. **1728** DYER *Grongar Hill* 43 No clouds, no vapours intervene. **1799** KIRWAN *Geol. Ess.* 55 Distant climates, betwixt which and Siberia mountains above nine thousand feet high intervene. **1859** KINGSLEY *Misc.* (1860) I. 229 Between the next two cantos intervenes the well known cradle song. **1882** DANA *Elem. Geol.* II. 206 Beds of shale in many places intervene.

b. Of space or time: To extend or lie *between* places or events.

1621 LD.-KPR. WILLIAMS in *Fortescue P.* (Camden) 165 The intervening of eight dayes well permitting that the Certificate may bee brought from Exeter. *a* **1732** ATTERBURY *Serm. Matt.* xxvii. 25 (Seager) A greater tract of time than intervened from the first building of their temple by Solomon to its final destruction by Titus. **1837** WHEWELL *Hist. Induct. Sc.* (1857) I. 140 The vast spaces which intervene between the celestiall luminaries. **1860** TYNDALL *Glac.* I. xxiv. 175 Scarcely five minutes.. intervened between every two successive peals.

†**5.** *trans.* To come between; to intercept; to interfere with; to prevent, hinder. *Obs.*

1588 A. KING tr. *Canisius' Catech.* H j, Pape pius quintus ..being interueneit by daith, left ye same to pape gregore his successor to be accompleseit. **1651** W. G. tr. *Cowel's Inst.* 234 So as there are fifteen dayes intervene each Writ. **1658–9** *Burton's Diary* (1828) III. 232 Nothing ought to intervene a fundamental order of the House. **1839** DE QUINCEY *Recoll. Lakes, Grasmere* Wks. 1863 II. 2 Woodlands of birch..and hazel, that meander through the valley, intervening the different estates with natural sylvan marches.

Hence **interˈvening** *vbl. sb.*

1605 BACON *Adv. Learn.* II. viii. §2 Many parts of nature can neither be inuented..nor demonstrated..without the aide and interueyning of the Mathematicks. **1665** BOYLE *Occas. Refl.* IV. iii. (1848) 184 Prevented by the intervening of Eusebius.

[**intervene** *sb.*, in J. (whence in later dicts.), founded on an obvious misprint for INTERVIEW in one of its 17th c. spellings.]

interˈvenent. [irreg. f. INTERVENE *v.* + -ENT; the etymological form is *intervenient.*] = next.

1802 A. BROWNE *Civ. Law & Law Admiralty* (ed. 2) II. 428 The intervenent must give security by fidejussors, to ratify the acts of his proctor.

intervener[1] (ɪntəˈviːnə(r)). Rarely -or. [f. prec. vb. + -ER[1].] One who intervenes or exercises intervention; *spec.* in *Law*, one who intervenes in a suit to which he was not originally a party.

1621 BP. MOUNTAGU *Diatribæ* I. 200 Christ was hee..the Interuener betweene the Lawe and Grace. **1854** PHILLIMORE *Internat. Law* I. 434 Where the interest of the intervener is not immediately..affected. **1870** *Daily News* 18 Oct., The intervener thinks one belligerent a brute and the other a coward, or incapable of taking care of himself. **1883** *Wharton's Law Lex.* (ed. 7) 429/1 An intervener must take the cause as he finds it at the time of his intervention. **1890** *Law Times* LXXXIX. 164/1 An appeal by certain intervenors in a damage action from a decree of Judge Benedict.

interˈvener[2]. *Law.* [f. INTERVENE *v.*, after *interpleader*, *determiner*, etc.] (See quot. 1847.)

1847 CRAIG, *Intervener*, In Law, the interposition or interference of a person in a suit in the ecclesiastical court in defence of his own interest is so termed, and a person is at liberty to do this in every case in which his interest is affected either in regard of his property or his person. **1870** *Daily News* 1 June, Before the decree was made absolute, Colonel L.——, a relation of the latter [the co-respondent], appeared and entered an intervener.

†**interˈvenience.** *Obs. rare.* [f. INTERVENIENT: see -ENCE.] The fact of intervening; intervention; a coming between.

a **1626** W. SCLATER *Exp. 4th Chapt. Rom.* (1650) 177 In respect of that frequent intervenience of sins, destroying the value of other works. **1657** W. MORICE *Coena quasi Κοινὴ* Diat. ii. 105 To retrench all intervenience of time. *a* **1677** HALE *Prim. Orig. Man.* IV. v. 335 The intervenience of more successive instrumental Causes. **1814** COLERIDGE in Jos. Cottle *Early Recoll.* (1837) II. 230 Without intervenience.. of any interest, sensual or intellectual.

†**interˈveniency.** *Obs. rare.* [f. next: see -ENCY.] = prec.

1660 S. FISHER *Rusticks Alarm* Wks. 431 Its far from coming immediately from God, sith it is not without the Interveniency of the hands of..innumerable.. Transcribers. **1664** POWER *Exp. Philos.* II. 111 No Contiguity..in dry Bodies..can exclude the interveniency of Ayr. **1668** HOWE *Bless. Righteous* (1825) 190 This internal discovery is made by the mediation and interveniency of the external.

intervenient (ɪntəˈviːnɪənt), *a.* (*sb.*) [ad. L. *intervenient-em*, pr. pple. of *intervenīre* to INTERVENE.]

1. That intervenes or comes in between; that comes in as something incidental, secondary, or extraneous.

1605 BACON *Adv. Learn.* II. viii. §2 In the mathematics, that use which is collateral and intervenient is no less worthy than that which is principal and intended. **1612** —— *Ess., Judicature* (Arb.) 458 When there is matter of Law interuenient in businesse of State. *a* **1656** USSHER *Ann.* (1658) 855 Detained with contrary winds, or by some intervenient delay. **1678** WANLEY *Wond. Lit. World* v. i. §97. 468/1 The Protestants, whose patience and perseverance with intervenient crosses abated his edge at last. **1805** WORDSW. *Prelude* II. 201, I hasten on to tell How Nature, intervenient till this time And secondary, now at length was sought For her own sake. **1850** *Tait's Mag.* XVII. 166/2 Grieved that any intervenient sorrow should check the calm current of their bliss.

2. a. Situated between other things or between points in space; intervening.

1626 BACON *Sylva* §104 Now there bee interuenient in the Rise of Eight (in Tones) two Beemolls or Halfe notes. **1776** G. CAMPBELL *Philos. Rhet.* (1801) I. I. v. 110 Some intervenient object. **1807** G. CHALMERS *Caledonia* I. I. iii. 110 A pleasant bank, which gives them an extensive prospect of the frith, and the intervenient country. **1837** WORDSW. *Musings near Aquapendente* 18 On the horizon's verge, O'er intervenient waste, through glimmering haze.

b. Occurring between certain points of time or events; happening in or occupying an interval.

1618–29 in Rushw. *Hist. Coll.* (1659) I. 20 The Statute of 1 E. 6. chap. 12. takes away all intervenient Statutes which declared new Treasons. *c* **1640** J. SMYTH *Lives Berkeleys* (1883) I. 297 Spent many intervenient days in huntings hawkings and other sports of the feild. *c* **1674** *Scotl. Grievances under Lauderdale* 3, I need not use any long deduction of the intervenient changes, to lead us unto the present posture of our affairs. **1748** RICHARDSON *Clarissa* (1811) IV. xxi. 112 The settlements might be drawn and engrossed in the intervenient time. **1817** BYRON *Beppo* xxiv, Unless within the period intervenient, A well-timed wedding makes the scandal cool.

3. Intervening in action; intermediary.

1651 HOBBES *Leviath.* I. vi. (1839) 48 If the intervenient appetites, make any action voluntary; then..all intervenient aversions, should make the same action involuntary. **1778** JOHNSON *Let. Dr. Wheeler* 2 Nov., He would not want any intervenient solicitation to obtain the kindness of one who loves learning and virtue. **1884** SYMONDS *Shaks. Predecess.* ii. 80 An absence of any intervenient medium.

B. *sb.* One who intervenes, an intervener. *rare.*

1620 WOTTON in *Reliq.* (1672) 505 Silently inferring, that the German Princes were the properest intervenients. **1871** LE FANU *Checkmate* II. xxvii. 250 It was only prudent to keep his temper with this lucky intervenient.

interˈvening, *ppl. a.* [f. INTERVENE *v.* + -ING[2].]

1. *gen.* That intervenes.

1646 H. LAWRENCE *Comm. Angells* 50 All the intervening Mediums. *c* **1709** PRIOR *Charity* 37 As through the artist's intervening glass Our eye observes the distant planets pass. **1783** WATSON *Philip III* (1839) 57 In the intervening night a dreadful storm arose. **1880** HAUGHTON *Phys. Geog.* vi. 304 Separated from each other by deep intervening oceans.

2. *Psychol.*, ***intervening variable***, a factor, such as individual memory, desire, or habit, which may affect the results of psychological tests or experiments in a way which is hard to predict.

1935 E. C. TOLMAN in *Philos. of Sci.* II. 365 The nature of this their resulting behavior is determined by a set of intervening variables to be conceived as lying in the organism... The molar behaviorist seeks to state the intervening variables as specific types of behavior-readiness. **1951** *Mind* LX. 50 The methodological device of the 'intervening variable' (drive, habit, demand, etc.). **1963** A. PAP *Introd. Philos. of Sci.* v. xx. 383 Human behavior also has mental determinants, such factors as memories, expectations, desires, [etc.]. But since these 'intervening variables' were supposed to be inaccessible to scientific investigation, the tendency developed to interpret them as certain *dispositions* to overt behavior.

intervenor, legal var. of INTERVENER[1].

†**interˈvent,** *v. Obs. rare.* [f. L. *intervent-*, ppl. stem of *intervenīre* to INTERVENE: cf. *prevent.*] *trans.* To come between, obstruct, thwart. Hence **interˈventing** *vbl. sb.* and *ppl. a.*

1593 T. BELL *Motives Rom. Faith* (1605) 31 Perfect satisfaction is that, whose valour and price wholly proceedeth from the debtour, without either preuenting or interuentinge grace of the creditour. **1600** *Dr. Dodypoll* II. iii. in Bullen *O. Pl.* (1884) III. 119 Some harshe chaunce To intervent the joye of the successe. **1647** WARD *Simp. Cobler* 51, I trust there is both day and meanes to intervent that bargaine.

†**intervent**, *sb. Obs. rare*⁻¹. [ad. L. *intervent-us* sb., f. ppl. stem of *intervenīre*: see prec.] = INTERVENTION 2 b.

1657 TOMLINSON *Renou's Disp.* 532 Its Inventor.. describes it without the intervent of honey.

intervention (ɪntəˈvɛnʃən). [ad. late L. *interventiōn-em*, n. of action f. *intervenīre* to INTERVENE. Cf. F. *intervention* (15th c.).]

1. a. The action of intervening, 'stepping in', or interfering in any affair, so as to affect its course or issue. Now freq. applied to the interference of a state or government in the domestic affairs or foreign relations of another country.

c **1425** *Found. St. Bartholomew's* (E.E.T.S.) 44 That whatsumeuer..be denayid me of mercy may be fulfillid yn tyme to come by thyn interuencioun and merytys. **1619** VISC. DONCASTER in *Eng. & Germ.* (Camden) 201 Though our master's intervention were at first sincerely desired [etc.]. **1692** DRYDEN *St. Euremont's Ess.* 184, I know how much the intervention of the Gods is necessary to an Epick Poem. **1831** J. W. CROKER in *C. Papers* (1884) II. xvi. 103 The Whigs erected their administration on three legs—non-intervention, retrenchment, reform; they are..at this moment as deep in intervention as any Government ever was. **1866** BRANDE & COX *Dict. Science* II. 238 The intervention of the allied powers between Greece and Turkey in 1827. **1868** G. DUFF *Pol. Surv.* 44 We need either a direct intervention of the foreign Powers, or a domestic revolution.

b. *Law.* The action of one, not originally a party, who intervenes in a suit.

1860 *Act 23 & 24 Vict.* c. 144 §7 The said Proctor..may ..intervene in the Suit, alleging such Case of Collusion.. and it shall be lawful for the Court to order the Costs.. arising from such Intervention, to be paid by the Parties. **1864** G. BROWNE *Treat. Princ. & Pract. Court for Divorce & Matrimonial Causes* 152 There are two kinds of intervention, one 'by any person' under the first branch of the section, the second by the Queen's proctor under the latter branch... It appears that at any time before a decree for dissolution of marriage is made absolute, it is competent for one of the public to intervene. *Ibid.* 153 The Court will not act on an intervention, when satisfied that it is made at the instance of the respondent or co-respondent. **1883** [see INTERVENER¹]. **1952** *Stroud's Judicial Dict.* (ed. 3) II. 1500 Intervention in divorce proceedings (generally by the King's Proctor) is for (*a*) collusion, or (*b*) suppression of a material fact.

2. Intermediate agency; the fact of coming in or being employed as an intermediary. **a.** Of persons.

1659 PEARSON *Creed* (1839) 156 Adam was framed immediately by God, without the intervention of man or woman. **1768** BLACKSTONE *Comm.* III. xvii. 255 Injuries to the rights of property can scarcely be committed by the crown without the intervention of it's officers. **1818** JAS. MILL *Brit. India* II. v. ii. 366 The Supreme Council resolved to treat with the ministers at Poona by an agent of their own, without the intervention of the Presidency of Bombay. **1856** KANE *Arct. Expl.* I. xxxii. 441 Then by the intervention of Petersen, I called on Kalatunah for his story.

b. Of things.

1665 BOYLE *Occas. Refl.* III. ii, Loggs, on which the Fire could take no hold, but by the intervention of..smaller Sticks. **1756** BURKE *Subl. & B.* IV. i, Things which cause pain operate on the mind by the intervention of the body. **1881** WESTCOTT & HORT *Grk. N.T.* Introd. §17 A text was constructed..without the intervention of any printed edition.

3. a. The fact of coming or being situated between in place, time, or order.

1645 BOATE *Irel. Nat. Hist.* (1652) 165 The heat never being very great, and..often interrupted by the intervention of the foul weather. **1671** R. BOHUN *Wind* 84 The Trade Winds..are frequently impeded by the intervention of Islands, and Crosse Winds. **1776** ADAM SMITH *W.N.* I. III. xi. (1869) I. 211 Notwithstanding the intervention of one or two dear years. **1797** M. BAILLIE *Morb. Anat.* (1807) 367 Such masses..are connected with it loosely, by the intervention of cellular membrane. **1875** RENOUF *Egypt. Gram.* 8 The intervention of a vowel must be understood.

b. An intervening thing, event, or period of time.

a **1677** HALE *Contempl.* II. 127 The Publick Imployments, that..have been put upon me, and many other Interventions. **1800** W. TAYLOR in *Monthly Mag.* VIII. 597 Not..to entirely read them, but to turn them over with interventions of study.

Hence **inter'ventional** *a.*, of or pertaining to intervention; **inter'ventionism**, the principle or policy of intervening, esp. in international and economic affairs; **inter'ventionist**, one who approves of intervention, esp. in international affairs; one who favours a doctrine of intervention; one who favours intervention with the course of a disease on medical grounds (*Cent. Dict.*); also as *adj.*

1829 BENTHAM *Justice & Codif.* 61 Under every system, appeal is for cause assigned, namely mis-decision, either ultimate or interlocutory, or say interventional. **1839** *Morn. Herald* 23 Apr., Changing the character and offices of mediators into those of warlike interventionists. **1899** *Contemp. Rev.* Oct. 476 There have been interventionists and anti-interventionists in South Africa. **1915** *Morning Post* 19 Apr. 8/4 Interventionist, and, in some places, neutralist meetings were held yesterday at Milan. **1921** *Glasgow Herald* 22 July 7 M. Tchitcherin sees in this fact another 'interventionist' manœuvre. **1923** *Ibid.* 29 Mar. 5 The methods of interventionism..are contrary to the spirit of cooperation. **1930** *Times Lit. Suppl.* 14 Aug. 648/2 The 'interventionist' conception of miracle has passed out of fashion. **1940** *Economist* 6 July 2/2 It was not primarily because of this advocacy of support for Britain that Mr. Willkie was nominated... We cannot go further than to say that Mr. Willkie's interventionism did not prevent his success. Moreover, there are severe limitations on interventionism even of the Willkie type... For example, there is the almost universal qualification that aid must stop 'short of war'. **1945** K. R. POPPER *Open Soc.* II. xvii. 117 We must demand that *laissez-faire capitalism* give way to an *economic interventionism*. *Ibid. Notes* 318, I suggest using the name *laissez-faire capitalism* for that period which Marx analysed..and the name *interventionism* for our own period. The name 'interventionism' could indeed cover the three main types of social engineering in our time: the collectivist interventionism of Russia; the democratic interventionism of Sweden and the 'Smaller Democracies' and the New Deal in America. **1962** *Listener* 20 Dec. 1040/1 The long-standing tradition [*sc.* in France] of an active, confident, and interventionist civil service. **1967** *Economist* 30 Sept. 1162/1 The new interventionism is an economic theory that came into vogue with some Labour intellectuals about three years ago, and with some core of justification. Its kernel was the entirely true argument that the governments of some countries with successful postwar economic records (e.g. France, Japan, Italy) have had greater scope for influencing the course of major industrial investment than have the less successful governments of postwar Britain. **1969** *Observer* 26 Jan. 8/4 America has never swung back..to isolationism and Russia has never regressed to all-out revolutionary interventionism. **1970** *Times* 2 July 8/3 It will not be easy to persuade the country to prefer government interventionism to the freedom which is Mr. Heath's aim. **1971** *Physics Bull.* June 261/2 Interventionists such as Joan of Arc, Ralph Nader, Ghandi [*sic*] and Sir Alan Herbert. **1973** *Financial Times* 28 Feb. 27/2 The contrast between the philosophy of the Conservative Government that believed so earnestly in the miraculous powers of laissez-faire in 1970 and the interventionist Conservative Government of today.

interventive (ɪntəˈvɛntɪv), *a.* [f. as INTERVENT *v.* + -IVE. Cf. F. *interventif* (Littré).]

Characterized by or tending to intervention.

1890 J. MARTINEAU *Author. Relig.* IV. ii. 394 Their function was not creative, but only interventive.

interventor (ɪntəˈvɛntə(r)). [a. L. *interventor*, agent-n. f. *intervenīre* to INTERVENE.]

1. *Eccl.* = INTERCESSOR 3 (q.v.).

2. *U.S.* A mine-inspector (*Cent. Dict.*).

interventricular (ˌɪntəvɛnˈtrɪkjʊlə(r)), *a. Anat.* [INTER- 4 a.] Situated between the ventricles (of the heart, or of the brain).

1836–9 TODD *Cycl. Anat.* II. 977/2 The inter-ventricular valve..separates each chamber from that which follows it. **1879** *St. George's Hosp. Rep.* 257 Heart. A small abscess in inter-ventricular septum.

†**inter'venture.** *Obs. rare*⁻¹. [f. as INTERVENT *v.* + -URE; cf. *venture.*] = INTERVENTION 2.

1578 BANISTER *Hist. Man* I. 23 By the interuenture of Cartilages, and Ligamentes..safe connected and bound together.

†**intervenue.** *Obs. rare*⁻¹. [a. obs. F. *inter-*, *entrevenue* (Godef.), f. *inter-*, *entrevenir* to INTERVENE: cf. *avenue*, *revenue.*] Intervention, coming between.

1636 SIR H. BLOUNT *Voy. Levant* 125 This Crowne hath now had five weake Princes, without intervenue of any one active.

inter'verbal, *a. rare*⁻¹. [INTER- 4 a.] Placed between words.

1866 *Pall Mall G.* 24 Aug. 10 The interverbal translation ..is, in many respects, admirable.

†**inter'version.** *Obs. rare*⁻¹. [ad. late L. *interversiōn-em*, n. of action f. *intervertĕre*: see next.] Embezzlement: cf. next, 1 b.

1755 CARTE *Hist. Eng.* IV. 623 The Sophi knew nothing of this interversion of the money.

†**inter'vert**, *v. Obs.* [ad. L. *intervert-ĕre*, f. *inter* between + *vertĕre* to turn. Cf. F. *intervertir* (Cotgr., in sense 1).]

1. To divert another way, or put to a use other than that intended; to alienate, misapply, misuse.

1603 HOLLAND *Plutarch's Mor.* 1092 The good never intervert, nor miscognize the favour and benefit which they have received. **1611** SPEED *Hist. Gt. Brit.* IX. xxiv. §42. 1142 With an intent to interuert the inheritance and honour of the O-Neale another way. **1648** *Acts Gen. Assembly* (1682) 477 Where the collection is more, it is hereby specially inhibited and discharged that any part thereof be retained or interverted to any other use whatsomever.

b. *esp.* To divert to one's own use or profit; to appropriate, embezzle.

1600 HOLLAND *Livy* III. lxxii. 138 Yet would there not be so much gained and gotten by comming thus betweene, and interverting the land [*agro intercipiendo*]. **1647** TRAPP *Comm. Titus* i. 10 Interverting, embezeling their masters estates. **1691** RAY *Words* Pref. 2 Lest I..should defraud him, and intervert any part thereof. **1850** *Fraser's Mag.* XLI. 529 Bentley was the first among modern critics—though his adversaries accused him herein of 'interverting' Neveletus—to discover the merits of the poet.

2. To give a different turn to; to change, invert.

a **1638** WOTTON *Life Dk. Buckhm.* in *Reliq.* (1651) 99 The Duke getting knowledge..interverted the bargain, and gave the poor Widow for them five hundred pounds. **1792** GOUV. MORRIS in Sparks *Life & Writ.* (1832) II. 261 The Cordeliers know well the danger of interverting the order of succession. **1825** JEFFERSON *Autobiog.* Wks. 1859 I. 61 Interverted, abridged, mutilated, and often reversing the sense of the original.

Hence †**inter'verting** *vbl. sb.*

1614 RALEIGH *Hist. World* II. (1634) 488 The interverting of some Treasures by Belosus. **1660** in Crookshank *Hist. Suffer. Ch. Scot.* (1749) I. Introd. 59 The prejudice the church doth suffer by the interverting of the vaking stipends.

intervertebral (ɪntəˈvɜːtɪbrəl), *a. Anat.* [INTER- 4 a.] Situated between vertebræ.

1782 A. MONRO *Anat. Bones, Nerves*, etc. 140 The intervertebral cartilages sooner shrivel. **1881** MIVART *Cat* 36 The adjoined concavities..of two adjacent vertebræ, constitute a rounded opening termed an intervertebral foramen.

Hence **inter'vertebrally** *adv.*, between vertebræ.

1888 ROLLESTON & JACKSON *Anim. Life* 415 Intercrural cartilages which are placed intervertebrally.

intervesicular: see INTER- 4 a.

†**inter'vesting, -'vesture.** *Obs. rare*⁻⁰. [INTER- 2.] (See quot.)

1611 COTGR., *Entravestissement*, an interuesting, or interuesture; a mutuall possession, or ioint possessing of.

interview (ˈɪntəvjuː), *sb.* Forms: α. 6 entervewe, -vieu(e, 6–7 -vew, -viewe, 6–8 enterview; β. 7 intervieu, 7– interview. [a. F. *entrevue* (earlier *entreveue*, 1498 in Godef. *Compl.*), verbal sb. from *entrevoir* to have a glimpse of, *s'entrevoir* to see each other, f. *entre-* (ENTER-) + *voir*:—L. *vidēre* to see. (Mod.F. has taken *interview* from English in sense 1 c.)]

1. a. A meeting of persons face to face, esp. one sought or arranged for the purpose of formal conference on some point.

In early times, esp. a formal or ceremonial meeting of princes or great persons, such as that of Henry VIII and Francis I at the Field of the Cloth of Gold.

α. **1514** DK. SUFFOLK in Ellis *Orig. Lett.* Ser. II. I. 248 Your Grace understode how well mynded and desirous he was for th' Enterview to be had, betwixt your Highnes and hym. *a* **1548** HALL *Chron., Hen. VI* 84 b, John duke of Bedforde, Philip duke of Burgoyn, & John duke of Britayn, made an assemble & frendly entervewe in the citee of Amias. **1603** FLORIO *Montaigne* I. xiii. *title*, Of Ceremonies in the enterview of Kings. *Ibid.* I. xiii. (1898) 67 At the enterview, prepared at Merceilles betweene Pope Clement the seventh and Francis the first. **1703** ROWE *Fair Penit.* II. i. 455 This one Enterview shall end my Cares.

β. **1623** MEADE in Ellis *Orig. Lett.* Ser. I. III. 137 Some opportune place where..they might have an interview. *a* **1626** BACON *New Atl.* (1650) 24 They have ordained that none doe intermarry, or contract, untill a Moneth be past from their first inter-view. *a* **1714** BURNET *Hist. Ref.* I. II. 203 He passed the seas, and had an interview with the French king. **1769** ROBERTSON *Chas. V*, VI. Wks. 1813 VI. 77 He proposed an interview between the two monarchs at Nice. **1856** FROUDE *Hist. Eng.* I. v. 378 She had an interview with Henry on his return through Canterbury. **1871** B. TAYLOR *Faust* (1875) I. Notes 226 The interview of Satan with the Lord in the first and second chapters of Job.

†**b.** The action or fact of meeting or conferring together. *Obs. rare.*

1540–1 ELYOT *Image Gov.* 19 Beyng sore shaken with many sweete woordes and longe entervieu, they yeld at the laste. **1609** BP. W. BARLOW *Answ. Nameless Cath.* 64 Not Christian onely for enteruiew and Salutation.

c. *spec.* in recent use: A meeting between a representative of the press and some one from whom he seeks to obtain statements for publication. Similarly in broadcasting.

1869 *Nation* (N.Y.) 28 Jan. 67 The 'interview', as at present managed, is generally the joint product of some humbug of a hack politician and another humbug of a newspaper reporter. **1884** *Pall Mall G.* 31 Dec. 3/1 Among the permanent gains of the year the acclimatization of the 'interview' in English journalism certainly should be reckoned. **1897** *Westm. Gaz.* 2 Jan. 7/1 It is claimed for him [Joseph M'Cullagh, of St. Louis] that he was the inventor of the modern newspaper interview. **1956** B. PAULU *Brit. Broadcasting* vii. 176 The BBC prefers straight talks to interviews, believing that talks are more apt to be carefully worked out. **1965** *Listener* 18 Feb. 260/2 The right interview ..has to be used in the right place with the right person if the programme is to be craftsmanlike. **1974** *Radio Times* 21 Feb. 5/5 The background to my interviews is firmly in my head, though I still face the interviewer's perennial problem of..when to change the topic.

†**2.** Mutual view (*of* each other). *Obs. rare.*

1603 HOLLAND *Plutarch's Mor.* 328 They cannot endure the enterview one of another againe. **1667** H. MORE *Div. Dial.* III. xxxiv. (1713) 273 Able to take a mutual interview of one another at such a distance. **1667** MILTON *P.L.* VI. 555 At interview both stood A while.

†**3. a.** Looking into, inspection, examination.

c **1555** HARPSFIELD *Divorce Hen. VIII* (Camden) 117 We will..make a short enterviewe of those authors which they have brought forth for their purpose. **1579** J. STUBBES *Gaping Gulf* E ij, Yet doe I not gladly medle with thys particular, but wil also refer it to hir Maiesties enteruieue. **1586** FERNE *Blaz. Gentrie* II. 119 That they should make an enter-uew into the doinges of their judges and iustices.

†**b.** A view, glance, glimpse (*of* a thing). *Obs.*

1610 HEALEY *St. Aug. Citie of God* VI. x. (1620) 241 If one had time to take enter-view of their actions, hee should see [etc.]. **1613** PURCHAS *Pilgrimage* V. xiv. 440 Superstition, whose Owlish eyes cannot endure the enterview of Truth. **1638** PENKETHMAN *Artach.* C iij, All the sorts of Bread [are] presented by every paire of Pages lying open at one Enterview. **1704** NORRIS *Ideal World* II. iii. 112, I have a confuse interview of this involved secret, like the glimmering light that trims the edges of a dark cloud. **1719**

YOUNG *Revenge* II. i, Let me not see him now; But save us from an interview of death.

4. ***interview room*** (in a police station or prison).

1967 E. GRIERSON *Crime of one's Own* xvi. 135 Donald was called..to the interview room on the ground floor [of the prison]. **1969** J. GARDNER *Compl. State of Death* v. 76 Interview room. Usual. Stone walls and glossy paint. Table. Three chairs. **1974** J. WAINWRIGHT *Evidence I shall give* xxxiii. 188 He..left the Murder Room and found a telephone in one of the Interview Rooms, where he couldn't be overheard.

†**interview**, *v.*[1] *Obs.* Also 6 entervieu, -vew, 6-7 -view. [ad. F. *entrevoir*, *s'entrevoir*, pa. pple. *entrevu*, on analogy of prec. or of VIEW *v.*]

1. a. *trans.* To have a personal meeting with (each other). **b.** *intr.* To meet together in person.

a **1548** HALL *Chron. Hen. VI* 175 b, Their mutuall frendes ..exhorted theim..to mete and entervieu, in some place. *Ibid., Edw. IV* 230 b, That the .ij. princes..for the continuaunce of amitie should entervew eche other, in some place moste expedient. *Ibid.* 233 b, That the two Princes shoulde enterview, and mete in a place by both parties to be appoynted.

2. *trans.* To catch a glimpse of, get a view of; to glance at, view.

1592 G. HARVEY *Four Lett.* Sonn. vi, Oh, let me live to interview the face Of fair humanity and bounteous grace. **1611** FLORIO, *Interuedere*, to interuiew or see. **1624** F. WHITE *Repl. Fisher* 521 Enteruiewing the places, you shall perceiue, that the Fathers..speake of obtention and impetration.

interview (ˈɪntəvjuː), *v.*[2] [f. INTERVIEW *sb.*] *trans.* To have an interview with (a person); *spec.* on the part of a representative of the press: to talk with or question so as to elicit statements or facts for publication; similarly, to talk with or question (a person) for a programme broadcast on radio or television.

1869 *Nation* (N.Y.) 28 Jan. 66 'Interviewing' is confined to American journalism. **1869** *Daily News* 17 Dec., The *Sun* interviews Corbin, Fisk..and whoever else has any story to tell or axe to grind. **1870** LONGF. in *Life* (1891) III. 144 A northwest newspaper, in which I have been 'interviewed', and private conversation reported to the public. **1877** E. FITZGERALD *Lett.* I. 409, I was the intelligent Friend who interviewed Squire. **1880** *Daily News* 13 Nov., The American custom of 'interviewing' people of notoriety and of 'drawing' them for opinions on all topics. **1933** *Radio Times* 14 Apr. 96/1 Three speakers..will interview experts in design before the microphone on behalf of listeners. **1957** G. HARDING *Along my Line* xvi. 159 One or two of the guests whom I had agreed to interview had gone to the trouble to notify their friends and relations across the width and breadth of Canada. **1974** *Radio Times* 21 Feb. 41/2 Robin Day interviewing those making the news.

Hence ˈ**interviewed** *ppl. a.*; ˈ**interviewing** *vbl. sb.* Also **interˈviewable** *a.*, capable of or open to being interviewed.

1869 *Daily News* 17 Dec., A portion of the daily newspapers of New York are bringing the profession of journalism into contempt, so far as they can, by a kind of toadyism or flunkeyism, which they call 'interviewing'. **1878** *N. Amer. Rev.* CXXVII. 65 The interviewed..with great facility changes his positions. **1880** GRANT WHITE *Every-Day Eng.* 307 It must have got about that I was an interviewable man (interviewable, although never used before, I believe, is an excellent word). **1949** *Radio Times* 15 July 9/2 As compère, Brian Reece returns to the job in which he first showed his flair for radio—that of interviewing, 'gagging', and knitting a programme together. **1960** *20th Cent.* May 458 There is no substitute for direct contact through intimate interviewing. **1968** *Guardian* 26 Apr. 9/1, I wish I had some interviewing officers who could interview.

interviewee (ˌɪntəvjuːˈiː). [f. INTERVIEW *v.*[2] + -EE[1].] One who is interviewed, esp. by a member of the press or a broadcasting organization.

1884 *Pall Mall G.* 31 Dec. 3 Interviewing is an instance of the division of labour. The 'interviewee'..supplies the matter; the interviewer the form. **1886** *Sat. Rev.* 1 May 595/2 The interviewer seems to have been worthy of the interviewee. **1959** F. GRISEWOOD *My Story of B.B.C.* xii. 190 The laborious business of discovering exactly how many ..interviewees watched or listened to each of more than a hundred programmes a day. **1965** *Listener* 20 May 756/2 It [*sc.* a radio programme] seemed to have caught some of the town-hall atmosphere, tersely described by a teenage interviewee as 'dead'. **1970** *Nature* 8 Aug. 641/1 Hammerton might contemplate the exact nature of the questions he asked his interviewees. **1973** *Guardian* 17 Apr. 15/1 The interviewee usually remembers the one-to-one relationship with the reporter.

interviewer (ˈɪntəvjuːə(r)). [f. INTERVIEW *v.*[2] + -ER[1].] One who interviews; *spec.* a journalist who interviews a person with the object of obtaining matter for publication; similarly, a person employed by a broadcasting organization to perform a similar function.

1869 *Nation* (N.Y.) 28 Jan. 67 The correspondent, whether interviewer or not. **1872** LOWELL *Milton* Pr. Wks. 1890 IV. 68 Let the seventeenth century, at least, be kept sacred from the insupportable foot of the interviewer! **1880** L. STEPHEN *Pope* iv. 88 Twickenham villa..became of course a centre of attraction for the interviewers of the day. **1886** *Pall Mall G.* 11 May 14/1 The interview is the worst feature of the new system—it is degrading to the interviewer, disgusting to the interviewee, and tiresome to the public. **1939** *Radio Times* 25 Aug. 20/2 'Come and be televised.' Interviewer, Elizabeth Cowell. **1941** *B.B.C. Gloss. Broadcasting Terms* 16 *Interviewer*, person whose role is to interrogate a broadcaster at the microphone and to elicit his story. **1969** *Times* 24 Nov. 17/3 Praise the Lord for a television interviewer who does not ram his personality down our throats. **1974** [see INTERVIEW *sb.* 1 c].

†**interˈvigilant**, *a. Obs. rare*$^{-0}$. [ad. pr. pple. of L. *intervigilāre*: see next.]

1656 BLOUNT *Glossogr.*, *Intervigilant*, that is watchful, or that awakes now and then, or between whiles.

†**interˈvigilate**, *v. Obs. rare*$^{-0}$. [f. L. *intervigilāt-*, ppl. stem of *intervigilāre* to watch between whiles.] (See quot.) Hence †**intervigiˈlation**.

1623 COCKERAM, *Interuigilate*, to watch now and then. *Ibid.* II, Watchfulnes, *interuigilation*. **1658** PHILLIPS, *Intervigilation*, a watching between whiles.

inter-village, -villous: see INTER- *pref.* 5, 4 a.

intervisceral (-ˈvɪsərəl), *a. rare*$^{-0}$. [INTER- 4 a.] Situated between or among the viscera. Hence **interˈviscerally** *adv.*

1870 ROLLESTON *Anim. Life* 231 Below the funnel are seen the gills, and between them and the rectum one of the inter-viscerally placed ganglia.

intervisible: see INTER- *pref.* 2 a.

Intervision (ˈɪntəvɪʒən). [f. *Inter*national tele*vision*.] (See quot. 1962[2].)

1961 *Listener* 2 Nov. 729/2 Other countries in the Intervision (East European) network. **1962** *Ibid.* 20 Dec. 1042/2 It [*sc.* the speech] was also carried by Intervision for viewers in Finland, Denmark, and Sweden. **1962** *B.B.C. Handbk.* 25 International co-operation between BBC engineers, Eurovision, and its Eastern counterpart, Intervision.

interˈvisit, *sb. rare.* [f. INTER- 2 a + VISIT *sb.*] An intermediate visit.

1846 in WORCESTER (citing *Qu. Rev.*).

intervisit (ɪntəˈvɪzɪt), *v.* [ad. F. *entrevisiter* (15th c. in Littré), f. *entre-* (INTER- 1 b) + *visiter* to VISIT.] *intr.* To exchange visits.

1609 DANIEL *Civ. Wars* VIII. xc, After hauing finisht all the rite Of complement and interuisiting. **1686** tr. *Bouhours' Ignatius* II. 117 He obliged them often to intervisit. **1814** W. TAYLOR in *Monthly Rev.* LXXIII. 51 He could intermarry and intervisit with the family of General Halifax, without rendering his loyalty suspicious. **1830** —— *Hist. Surv. Germ. Poetry* II. 80 The minister Bernstorff intervisited with the Stolbergs.

intervital (ɪntəˈvaɪtəl), *a. rare.* [INTER- 4.] Existing between two lives or stages of existence.

1850 TENNYSON *In Mem.* xliii, If..every spirit's folded bloom Thro' all its intervital gloom In some long trance should slumber on. **1878** FARRAR *Eternal Hope* (1879) 12 [There] comes no faintest whisper from the intervital gloom.

inter vivos: see INTER L. prep.

intervocal (ɪntəˈvəʊkəl), *a.* [INTER- 4 a + L. *vocāl-is* vocal, a vowel.] Occurring between vowels. So **intervoˈcalic** *a.*, (more usual) in same sense; **intervoˈcalically** *adv.*

1887 *Amer. Jrnl. Philol.* VIII. 490 Showing..that intervocalic *i* of the Provencal MSS. should not invariably be reproduced as *j*. **1891** A. L. MAYHEW *O.E. Phonol.* §405 OE. b = Vulgar Latin b = L. p (intervocal). **1896** BRACHET & TOYNBEE *Hist. Gram. French* 89 A medial consonant may be..intervocal (i.e. placed between two vowels). *Mod.* The loss of Latin intervocalic *t* and *d* in Old French, as in *rota, roue, sūdare, suer*. **1950** D. JONES *Phoneme* 22 Double k occurs only inter-vocalically. **1964** R. H. ROBINS *Gen. Ling.* viii. 327 Cockney speakers often have glottalized stops inter-vocalically. **1972** *Language* XLVIII. 465 Whatever analysis is adopted, the patterning of these segments is admittedly anomalous. They occur only intervocalically.

intervolute (ɪntəˈvɒljuːt). *Arch.* [INTER- 3.] The space between the volutes or scrolls in Ionic, Corinthian, and Composite capitals.

1831 *Fraser's Mag.* IV. 281 Arising from the different proportions of the necking itself, and of the volutes and intervolute, or the interval between them.

intervolution (ɪntəvəʊˈl(j)uːʃən). [n. of action from next.] Intervolved condition; a winding.

1850 HAWTHORNE *Scarlet L.* iii. (1879) 72 Making one little pause, with all its wreathed intervolutions in open sight. **1885** L. OLIPHANT *Sympneumata* xiii. 192.

intervolve (ɪntəˈvɒlv), *v.* [f. L. type **intervolvĕre*, f. *inter* (INTER- 1) + *volvĕre* to roll, wind; cf. *involve*, etc.]

1. *trans.* To wind or roll up (things) within each other; to wind or involve (something) within the coils of something else.

1667 MILTON *P.L.* v. 623 Mazes intricate, Eccentric, intervolv'd, yet regular Then most, when most irregular they seem. **1820** SHELLEY *Witch Atl.* vi, The sly serpent, in the golden flame Of his own volumes intervolved. **1849** MISS MULOCK *Ogilvies* xxvii. (1875) 205 Intercepting and intervolving him wherever he moves. **1884** *Nonconf. & Indep.* 1 May 422 His panel of 'A Wood Nymph'..in which a girl and the leafage of background are intervolved.

2. *intr.* To wind within each other.

1886 W. ALEXANDER *St. Augustine's Holiday*, etc. 48 Now intervolving richly type by type, Reticulated sounds with sounds enlace.

Hence **interˈvolved** *ppl. a.*; **interˈvolving** *vbl. sb.* and *ppl. a.*

1667 [see 1 above]. **1742** YOUNG *Nt. Th.* IX. 1322 This exquisite machine, with all its wheels, Tho' intervolv'd, exact. **1858** G. MACDONALD *Phantastes* iv. 38 Entwining every complexity of intervolved motion. **1896** G. MEREDITH *Amazing Marriage* v. 47 Trees, whose round intervolving roots grasped the yellow roadside soil. **1896** *Academy* 11 Jan. 27/3 This 'intervolving' of the landscape with the mind of a person is peculiarly characteristic of Mr. Meredith.

ˈ**intervolve**, *sb. rare.* [f. prec. vb.] An act of intervolving; intertwining.

1898 T. HARDY *Wessex Poems* 266 Of wise contrivance, deeply skilled In every intervolve of high and wide.

inter-war, *a.* [INTER- 5.] Of a period occurring between wars; *spec.* of the period 1919 to 1939 between the two world wars.

1939 O. LANCASTER *Homes Sweet Homes* 74 The inter-war period through which we have just passed. **1944** W. TEMPLE *Church looks Forward* v. 39 There must be no slipping back into the self-seeking and self-indulgence of the interwar years. **1959** *Encounter* Aug. 47/1 In the inter-war period [in Hungary] a limited number of Government and Opposition newspapers could be printed. **1973** *Listener* 25 Jan. 104/3 *Mein Kampf* is a vital document of the inter-war period.

interweave (ɪntəˈwiːv), *v.* Also 6-7 enter-. Pa. t. -wove, pa. pple. -woven (7-8 -wove); also 7-8 -weaved. [f. INTER- 1 b + WEAVE *v.*]

1. *trans.* To weave together, as the warp and woof of a fabric; to interlace; to intertwine.

1578 [see INTERWEAVING *vbl. sb.*]. **1598** FLORIO, *Intertessere*, to interweaue, to weaue or worke betweene, as tinsell or striped canuasse is. **1649** MILTON *Eikon.* xvii. Wks. (1851) 460 Heer we may see the very dark roots..how they twine and interweave one another in the Earth. **1725** POPE *Odyss.* v. 617 Two Olives..With roots intwin'd, and branches interwove. **1778** *England's Gazetteer* (ed. 2) s.v. *Isle*, Those floats, called coracles,..are of a form almost oval, and made of split sallow twigs interwoven. **1870** ROCK *Text. Fabr.* Introd. I. 34 Attalus's name was bestowed upon a new method of interweaving gold with wool or linen. **1870** ROLLESTON *Anim. Life* Introd. 33 Muscular fibres are ordinarily interwoven..with its substance.

2. *transf.* and *fig.* To intermingle (thoughts, ideas, relations, etc.) as if by weaving; to interlink or intertwine intricately; to blend intimately.

1589 [see INTERWEAVING *vbl. sb.*]. **1612** DRAYTON *Polyolb.* To Rdr. A iij, Those Prophecies out of Merlin sometime interwouen. **1628** LE GRYS tr. *Barclay's Argenis* 304 When he did interweaue the course of affaires, the causes and euents together. **1647** DENHAM *Commend. Verses Fletcher*, None Can say here Nature ends, and Art begins But mixt like th' Elements, and borne like twins, So interweav'd, so like, so much the same. **1665** HOOKE *Microgr.* 70 Uniting and interweaving it self with some other body that is already joyn'd with the tinging particles. **1736** BUTLER *Anal.* II. i. Wks. 1874 I. 168 The moral law is..interwoven into our very nature. **1749** FIELDING *Tom Jones* IV. viii, He cheered the rural nymphs and swains, when upon the green they interweaved the sprightly dance. **1820** W. IRVING *Sketch Bk.* I. 28 He has interwoven the history of his life with the history of his native town. **1874** GREEN *Short Hist.* viii. §1. 448 The common phrases, which we owe to great authors.. which unconsciously interweave themselves in our ordinary talk.

b. *intr.* for *refl.*

1827 DE QUINCEY *Goethe* Wks. 1863 XV. 167 Such subjects..interweave one into another. **1892** ASHBY STERRY *Lazy Minstrel* 48 Drifting down on the dear old River, O, the music that interweaves!

Hence **interˈweaved** *ppl. a.*, interwoven; **interˈweaving** *ppl. a.* Also **interˈweavement**, interweaving. **interˈweaver**, one who interweaves. **interˈweavingly** *adv.*, by way of interweaving.

1598 FLORIO, *Intertessitore*, an interweauer [**1611** enterweauer]. **1665** HOOKE *Microgr.* 139, I could not so plainly perceive their joints, or their manner of interweaving. **1700** BLACKMORE *Job* 31 All his interweaving roots. **1820** *Mair's Tyro's Dict.* (ed. 10) 384 *Contextim* (adv.), of one piece, interweavingly. **1843** *For. & Col. Q. Rev.* II. 339 Its majestic interweavement with a cosmogony matchless and divine. **1898** *Daily News* 24 Nov. 2/2 Some space of lattice work..with its interweaved greenery.

interˈweaving, *vbl. sb.* [f. prec. vb. + -ING[1].] The action or process of weaving together or intermingling intricately; intertexture; quasi-*concr.*, an interwoven texture or structure.

1578 BANISTER *Hist. Man* IV. 63 One Muscle, hauyng..a sharpe end, and enterweauynges of diuers Fibres. **1589** PUTTENHAM *Eng. Poesie* II. x[i]. (Arb.) 102 The twelfth..by reason of his largenesse receiuing moe compasses and enterweauings. **1641** [see INTERWORKING]. **1797** BEWICK *Brit. Birds* (1847) I. 84 Covering the whole upper part with an interweaving of thorny twigs. **1868** MRS. WHITNEY *P. Strong* xiv. 162 Marvellous interweavings of glorious color.

interwed: see INTER- *pref.*

interweft (ˈɪntəwɛft). *rare.* [f. INTER- 2 a + WEFT *sb.*[1]] = INTERWEFTAGE.

1927 R. FRY *Cézanne* 80 In nature such a scene gives an effect of a confused interweft. **1939** —— *Last Lectures* 19 We begin to yield ourselves to the rhythmical movements of Botticelli's linear design, to its mazy interweft of curves.

†**interˈweftage.** *Obs.* [f. INTER- 2 a + WEFTAGE.] Interweaving; interwoven work.

1673 GREW *Anat. Roots* iv. §19 A..sight of these Fibres, and of their Interweftage, by splitting a Vine-Root, or a piece of Oak, may..be obtained.

interweld, -wend, -whiff, -while, -whistle: see INTER- *pref.*

interwind (ɪntəˈwaɪnd), *v.* Pa. t. and pple. **-wound** (-ˈwaʊnd). [INTER- 1 b.] *trans.* To wind (things) into or through each other; to wind together; to wind (one thing) through the windings of another; to intertwine, intertwist. Also *fig.*

1693 *Phil. Trans.* XVII. 895 Narrowing it by Piles drove down and inter-wound with Branches of Trees. **1844** MRS. BROWNING *Brown Rosary* I. xvii, Her speaking is so interwound Of the dim and the sweet. **1897** *Christian Herald* (N.Y.) 4 Aug. 592/1 A great many of these threads are interwound.

b. *intr.* (for *refl.*)

1876 G. MEREDITH *Beauch. Career* II. x. 178 Circumstances will often interwind with the moods of simply irritated men. **1879** E. S. PHELPS *Sealed Orders*, etc. 94 Uncounted sails which..pass and repass, wind and interwind.

Hence **interˈwinding, interˈwound** *ppl. adjs.*

1827 MONTGOMERY *Pelican Island* v. 28 Small isles, By interwinding channels linked yet sundered. **1877** FAIRBAIRN *Stud. Philos. Relig. & Hist.* 263 Interwound branches do not make two trunks one tree.

interwish, -word: see INTER- *pref.*

interwork (ɪntəˈwɜːk), *v.* Also 7 **enter-**. Pa. t. & pple. **-wrought** (-ˈrɔːt), **-worked** (-ˈwɜːkt). [INTER- 1 b.] *trans.* To work one thing into and through another to combine by interpenetration.

1603 FLORIO *Montaigne* II. ix, They had..certaine armes so curiously enter-wrought as they seemed to be made like feathers. *a* **1618** RALEIGH *Maxims St.* in *Remains* (1661) 9 The several States are sometimes mixed, and inter-wrought one with the other. **1882** MASSON in *Athenæum* 25 Feb. 251/2 Results from all these are interwrought with facts from Mr. Page's narrative and documents.

b. *intr.* To work upon each other; to interact.

1855 MILMAN *Lat. Chr.* (1883) I. I. ii. 92 The Roman character did not interwork into the general Christianity alone. **1876** W. ALEXANDER *Bampton Lect.* (1877) 216 Where various laws meet and interwork harmoniously. **1877** E. R. CONDER *Bas. Faith* ii. 53 Two divers sets of causes are ever interworking and counterworking in the tangled web of human affairs.

Hence **interˈworking** *vbl. sb.* and *ppl. a.*; **interˈwrought** *ppl. a.*

1641 MILTON *Reform.* II. (1851) 36 What interweavings or interworkings can knit the Minister and the Magistrate in their several Functions, to the regard of any precise correspondency? **1836** J. GILBERT *Chr. Atonem.* vii. (1852) 201 Circumstances, possessing..no moral interworking energies. **1895** *Chamb. Jrnl.* XII. 780 This way and that they lurched, with interwrought limbs.

inter-world, -worry: see INTER- *pref.*

†**interwound** (ɪntəˈwuːnd), *v. Obs.* [INTER- 1 b.] *trans.* To wound mutually. Hence †**interˈwounding** *ppl. a.*

1599 DANIEL *Musophilus* lxxiii, Hence interwounding Controversies spring. **1605** SYLVESTER *Du Bartas* II. iii. IV. *Captaines* 823 With their owne arms themselves to interwound.

interwound (-ˈwaʊnd), *ppl. a.*: see INTERWIND *v.*

interwoven (ɪntəˈwəʊv(ə)n), *ppl. a.* [pa. pple. of INTERWEAVE *v.*] Woven together; interlaced; intricately mingled or entangled.

1647 H. MORE *Poems* 6 Farre more fine Then interwoven silk with gold or silver twine. **1698** FRYER *Acc. E. India & P.* 6 Another Island..whose interwoven barren Mountains are as impossibly exprest as Stoneheng numbred. **1796** WITHERING *Brit. Plants* (ed. 3) III. 292 Capsule.. composed of interwoven fibres. **1818** JAS. MILL *Brit. India* (1858) I. 347 He has..printed the interwoven expressions of the commentator in italics. **1859** KINGSLEY *Misc.* (1860) I. 144 Its lacework of interwoven light and shade.

Hence **interˈwovenly** *adv. rare.*

a **1693** URQUHART *Rabelais* III. l. 401 The Fingers of both her hands interwovenly clenched together. **1880** G. MEREDITH *Tragic Com.* iii. (1892) 28 Amply-flowing, vivacious, interwovenly the brook, the stream, the torrent.

interwrap: see INTER- *pref.* 1 b.

interwreathe (-ˈriːð), *v.* [INTER- 1 b.] *trans.* To wreathe together; to intertwine into, or as in, a wreath. Hence **interˈwreathed** *ppl. a.*

a **1658** LOVELACE *Posthuma, To Mr. E. R.* 10 Happy youth, crown'd with a heav'nly ray Of the first Flame, and interwreathed bay. **1726** LEONI *Alberti's Archit.* Life 4 Foliages..very curiously interwreathed together. **1828** MISS MITFORD *Village* Ser. III. (1863) 517 Interwreathed and intertwisted by bramble and brier. **1866** J. B. ROSE *Virgil* 52 Thus sung thy bard, Pierides divine, What time he interwreathed the osier bine.

interˈwrought, *ppl. a.*: see INTERWORK *v.*

interxylary: see INTER- *pref.* 6.

interzoecial: see INTER- *pref.* 6.

interzonal (ɪntəˈzəʊnəl), *a.* [INTER- 4 a, c.] Existing or carried on between zones.

1881 E. L. MARK in *Bull. Mus. Compar. Zool. Harvard* VI. II. 198 When seen lengthwise of the spindle, the numerous ..thickenings appear arranged..in the form of a ring... Between the two zones of thickenings are stretched delicate nearly parallel threads, which I shall designate as interzonal filaments. **1920** L. DONCASTER *Introd. Study Cytol.* iii. 32 As the chromosomes travel to the poles, the interzonal spindle-fibres are seen still running continuously from pole to pole. **1956** *Ann. Reg. 1955* 229 In interzonal trade [in Germany] the volume reached little more than half the target figure for the year. **1959** *Ann. Reg. 1958* 263 Dr Adenauer..warned the East Germans that interzonal trade..would meet with difficulties if there were any interference with West Berlin's supplies.

inter-zone, -zygapophysial, -zygomatic: see INTER- *pref.*

†**intestaˈbility.** *Obs. rare.* [f. next: see -ITY.] The quality or state of being 'intestable'.

1590 SWINBURNE *Testaments* 55 The exception of intestabilitie, may be opposed against the probate of the testament. **1622** DONNE *Serm.* clvi. (Alford) VI. 235 The worst degree of intestability is not to be believed, not to be admitted to be a Witness of any other.

†**inˈtestable**, *a. Obs.* [ad. late L. *intestābilis*, f. *in-* (IN-^{3}) + *testābilis*, f. *testārī*: see INTESTATE. Cf. F. *intestable* (16th c. in Godef. *Compl.*).]

1. Legally incapable of making a will or of benefiting by a will.

1590 SWINBURNE *Testaments* 47 Albeit the testament be made before the mariage, yet she being intestable at the time of her death, by reason her husband is then liuing, the testament is voyd. **1726** AYLIFFE *Parergon* 289 After a Person has been thus excommunicated, he is rendered Infamous and Intestable both Actively and Passively. **1767** BLACKSTONE *Comm.* II. xxxii. 497 Such persons, as are intestable for want of liberty or freedom of will.

2. Disqualified from being a witness or giving evidence.

a **1631** DONNE *Serm.* lxxxvi. (Alford) IV. 81 He was intestable, so as that he could not testify, he should not be believed in the behalf of another. —— in *Select.* (1840) 268 A Christian in profession, that is not a Christian in life, is intestable so, he discredits Christ, and hardens others against him. **1656** BLOUNT *Glossogr.*, *Intestable*..that cannot be taken in witness, not to be believed.

Hence †**inˈtestableness**, intestability (Bailey, 1727).

intestacy (ɪnˈtɛstəsɪ). *Law.* [f. INTESTATE *a.*: see -ACY.] The condition or fact of dying intestate or without having made a will.

1767 BLACKSTONE *Comm.* II. xxxii. 491 Mention is made of intestacy, in the old law before the conquest, as being merely accidental. **1827** JARMAN *Powell's Devises* II. 197 The construction was not induced by the motive of avoiding an intestacy. **1876** FAWCETT *Pol. Econ.* II. vi, The only occasion in which the eldest son is necessarily preferred to the younger children is in the case of intestacy. **1880** GLADSTONE *Sp. Ho. Com.* 15 Mar., I am of opinion..that the present irregular scale of duty upon intestacy is excessive.

†**inˈtestant**, *a. Obs. rare*$^{-1}$. [app. f. IN-^{3} + L. *testānt-em*, pr. pple. of *testārī*: see next.] = INTESTATE *a.* 1.

1673 *Rhode Island Col. Rec.* (1857) II. 507 Every person's estate that dyeth intestant in the said towne.

intestate (ɪnˈtɛstət), *a.* and *sb.* [ad. L. *intestāt-us*, f. *in-* (IN-^{3}) + *testātus*, pa. pple. of *testārī* to bear witness, to make a will. Cf. F. *intestat* (13th c. in Godef. *Compl.*).]

A. *adj.* **1.** Of a person: Not having made a will.

1377 LANGL. *P. Pl.* B. xv. 134 Curatoures of holy kirke.. dyeth intestate, and þanne þe bisshop entreth [etc.]. **1553** T. WILSON *Rhet.* 24 b, Al bequestes and goodes of suche his frendes as dyed intestate. **1760** JOHNSON *Idler* No. 98 ¶7 He was the less mindful of his dissolution, and died intestate. **1872** MISS BRADDON *R. Ainsleigh* I. xvii. 314 My benefactress died intestate, without care or thought for the orphan youth she had adopted.

fig. **1594** SHAKS. *Rich. III*, IV. iv. 128 (Qo. 1597) Windie atturnies to your Client woes, Aerie succeeders of intestate [*1st Fol.* intestine] ioies.

b. *transf.* (after L. *intestāta senectūs*, Juvenal i. 144).

1615 G. SANDYS *Trav.* 69 Hence sudden deaths, and age intestate spring. **1693** DRYDEN *Juvenal* (1697) 17 Repletions, Apoplex, intestate Death.

2. Of things: Not disposed of by will; belonging to the estate of an intestate.

1538 STARKEY *England* I. iv. 127 The prerogatyfe gyuen to the same Byschope of Cantorbury, wherby he hath..the admynystratyon of intestate godys. **1774** BP. HALLIFAX *Anal. Rom. Civ. Law* (1795) 48 The Roman Law concerning Intestate Succession. **1828** WEBSTER s.v., An intestate estate.

†**3. a.** 'That no man will take for a witness' (Blount *Glossogr.* 1656). **b.** 'Not proved by witness' (Phillips, 1678). *Obs.*

1635 A. STAFFORD *Fem. Glory* Ep. Ded., Sure I am if you have infirmities, they are intestate, unlesse you place your owne Conscience for a witnesse.

B. *sb.* One who dies without making a will.

1658 tr. *Coke's Rep.* 38 b, The next and most faithful friends of the intestate. **1670** BLOUNT *Law Dict.* s.v., There are two kinds of Intestates; one that makes no Will at all; another that makes a Will and Executors, and they refuse. **1747** CARTE *Hist. Eng.* I. 483 We find in Glanvil's time, all the goods and chattels of intestates belonged to the king or immediate lord. **1865** *Sat. Rev.* 7 Jan. 18/1 Intestates of this class.

intestation (ɪntɛˈsteɪʃən). *rare*$^{-1}$. [f. IN-^{3} + TESTATION, after *intestable*, *intestate*.] Deprivation of the right of making a will.

1833 WADDINGTON *Hist. Ch.* ix. 128 They menaced the contumacious with confiscation, intestation, exile.

†**inteˈstator.** *Obs. rare*$^{-1}$. [f. IN-^{3} + TESTATOR.] = INTESTATE *sb.*

1699 *Col. Rec. Pennsylv.* I. 557 Where y^e s^d testators or intestators personal estates are sufficient.

†**inˈtestement.** *Obs. rare*$^{-1}$. Will; testament.

1463 *Bury Wills* (Camden) 42 Alle suche goodes that they reseyve of mine by vertu of this myn intestement.

intestinal (ɪnˈtɛstɪnəl), *a.* [ad. med. or mod.L. *intestīnāl-is*, f. *intestīnum* an intestine; cf. F. *intestinal* (Paré, 16th c.).]

1. a. Of or pertaining to the intestines; found in or affecting the intestines.

1599 A. M. tr. *Gabelhouer's Bk. Physicke* 320/1 For intestinalle woundes, take onlye the pouldre of redde Beetes. **1646** SIR T. BROWNE *Pseud. Ep.* III. iii. 109 Their dung and intestinall excretions. **1797** M. BAILLIE *Morb. Anat.* (1807) 192 Another supposition,..that intestinal worms are really formed from the matter contained in the intestines. **1851** CARPENTER *Man. Phys.* (ed. 2) 267 In Man, the whole length of the intestinal tube is about thirty feet.

fig. **1794** SULLIVAN *View Nat.* II. 124 Ætna, Vesuvius, and other burning mountains, in this manner,..throw off their intestinal superfluities. **1945** *N.Y. Times Mag.* 21 Oct. 18/4 (*caption*) Edgar Bergen—'That guy has a lot of intestinal fortitude.' Charlie McCarthy—'I know a quicker way to say that.' **1961** J. S. MAYER *Restorative Art* (ed. 4) 21 This is the time for intestinal fortitude and determination.

b. Having an intestine or enteron: opposed to ANENTEROUS.

2. = INTESTINE *a.* 1. *rare.*

a **1861** MRS. BROWNING *Sword Castruccio* v, In that strife of intestinal hate.

intestine (ɪnˈtɛstɪn), *a.* [ad. L. *intestīnus* internal, f. *intus* within. Cf. F. *intestin* (14th. c. in Littré).] Internal, belonging to the interior.

1. Internal with regard to a country or people; domestic, civil: usually said of war, feuds, or troubles, also of enemies.

1535 STEWART *Cron. Scot.* III. 374 Till armour all [the Douglasses] drew syne, With dalie stryfe and battell intestyne. **1547** J. HARRISON *Exhort. Scottes* B iv b, The inhabitauntes..haue euer sithe been vexed with intestine warres and ciuill discorde. **1596** SHAKS. *1 Hen IV*, I. i. 12 The intestine shocke, And furious cloze of ciuill Butchery. **1672** MARVELL *Reh. Transp.* I. 122. **1706** PRIOR *Ode glorious Success* 248 Their own intestine feuds and mutual jars. *a* **1764** LLOYD *Henriade* Poet. Wks. 1774 II. 237 Laws abus'd by foul intestine foes. **1869** RAWLINSON *Anc. Hist.* 396 Intestine division made the very name of Hellas a mockery.

fig. **1602** MARSTON *Ant. & Mel.* I. Wks. 1856 I. 16 The rocks gron'd At the intestine uprore of the maine. **1633** P. FLETCHER *Pisc. Ecl.* VII. xiii, The seas..Thou softly charm'st, and windes intestine ire..Thou quiet laid'st.

†**2.** Internal with regard to human nature or the nature of things; inward, innate. *Obs. rare.*

1583 STUBBES *Anat. Abus.* I. (1877) 24 The intestine malice of our owne hearts. *a* **1656** USSHER *Ann.* VII. (1658) 864 Caius..for a time dissembled his intestine anger to Petronius. **1678** CUDWORTH *Intell. Syst.* I. i. §1. 3 Everything Naturally labours under an Intestine Necessity.

†**3.** Internal with regard to the body; seated in the bowels; intestinal. *Obs.*

1613 R. CAWDREY *Table Alph.* (ed. 3), *Intestine*,.. belonging to the inward parts. **1616** BULLOKAR, *Intestine*, bred in the bowels. *a* **1619** FOTHERBY *Atheom.* I. xiii. §3 (1622) 140 His plague was seated into his bowells, which tormented him with an intestine torture. **1727** SWIFT *Gulliver* IV. vi, Human bodies..every part, external and intestine, having diseases appropriated to itself.

4. Internal with reference to any thing or place. *Obs.* (exc. as *fig.* from 1 or 3).

1664 EVELYN *Sylva* (1776) 290 With Fir, we likewise make all intestine Works as Wainscot, floors [etc.]. **1671** R. BOHUN *Wind* 33 Those suddain tumors, which happen in the rivers..neer Bourdeaux, seem to be the effects of intestine winds. **1784** COWPER *Task* VI. 139 It sleeps; and the icy touch Of unprolific winter has impress'd A cold stagnation on the intestine tide.

b. ***intestine motion***: Motion entirely within, or among the molecules of, a body.

1664 POWER *Exp. Philos.* Pref. 11 If the very nature of fluidity consist in the Intestine motion of the parts of that Body call'd fluid. **1692** BENTLEY *Boyle Lect.* iv. 116. **1717** J. KEILL *Anim. Oecon.* (1738) 111 If the attracting Corpuscles are elastick, they must necessarily produce an intestine Motion. **1853** KANE *Grinnell Exp.* (1856) 546 The polar basin is not only the seat of an active supply and discharge, but of an intestine circulation independent of either. **1862** H. SPENCER *First Princ.* II. xiii. §100 (1875) 291 When the atoms are kept in a state of intestine agitation.

Hence **inˈtestineness** (Bailey vol. II, 1727).

intestine (ɪnˈtɛstɪn), *sb.* Also 7 **intestin**, and in L. form **inteˈstinum**, *pl.* **-a.** [ad. L. *intestīnum* sb., neuter of *intestīnus* adj.: see prec.]

1. The lower part of the alimentary canal, from the pyloric end of the stomach to the anus, constituting what are popularly called the bowels or guts. In ordinary use, commonly pl. *intestines*; the singular is applied to each of the two distinct parts, ***the small intestine*** (comprising the duodenum, jejunum, and

ileum), and the *large intestine* (comprising the cæcum, colon, and rectum), and also, in scientific use, to the canal as a whole; in biology, it is often extended to include the whole alimentary canal from the mouth downward, especially in invertebrate animals. **a.** *plural.*

1597 A. M. tr. *Guillemeau's Fr. Chirurg.* 20/2 The intestines or entralls beinge verye ill disposed and ill at ease. **1625** B. JONSON *Staple of N.* v. v, *Alm.* We shall see thorow him. *P. sen.* And his gut colon, tell his intestina. **1649** T. WATSON *God's Anat.* 2 The Priest did divide the Beast in peeces, and so the *intestina*, the inward parts, were made visible. **1656** RIDGLEY *Pract. Physick* 1 The Cause is..the shortness of the Intestins. **1695** tr. *Colbatch's New Lt. Chirurg. put out* 38 Both Liver and Intestines were wounded. **1767** GOOCH *Treat. Wounds* I. 116 A total division of the small intestines, is to be looked upon as a mortal wound. **1800** *Med. Jrnl.* IV. 518 The contents of the stomach and intestines were of a similar nature. **1869** HUXLEY *Physiol.* vi. §21.

b. *singular.*

1651 *Raleigh's Ghost* 219 Their hindermost intestine or gut became putrified. **1681** COTTON *Wond. Peak* (ed. 4) 49 The Subterranean People ready stand..To guide, who are to penetrate inclined The *Intestinum Rectum* of the Fiend. **1803** *Med. Jrnl.* X. 248 The intestine, which alone formed the hernia, was of a deep red colour. **1807–26** S. COOPER *First Lines Surg.* (ed. 5) 437 Wounds of the abdomen, attended with injury of the intestine. **1869** HUXLEY *Physiol.* vi. §21 The *duodenum*..is..that part of the small intestine which immediately succeeds the stomach... The *rectum*..is that part of the large intestine which opens externally. **1884** M. MACKENZIE *Dis. Throat & Nose* II. 221 The cephalic portion of the intestine originates from the epiblast.

†**2.** *fig.* The inmost part or member. *Obs. rare.*

a **1533** LD. BERNERS *Gold. Bk. M. Aurel.* (1546) E iv b, The frend, whiche is the intestyne of the heart.

intestiniform (ɪntɛ'staɪnɪfɔːm), *a. Anat.* [f. L. *intestīn-um* INTESTINE *sb.* + -(I)FORM.] Having the shape of an intestine.

1859 TODD *Cycl. Anat.* V. 705/1 The resemblance to a mesentery is more obvious in the..intestiniform uterus of the mammalia.

intestino-vesical (ɪntɛˌstaɪnəʊ'vɛsɪkəl), *a.* [f. *intestino-*, taken as combining form of L. *intestīnum* INTESTINE *sb.* + L. *vēsīca* bladder + -AL[1].] Relating to the intestine and the bladder.

1867 *New Syd. Soc. Biennial Retrosp.* 314 Sufferings produced by an intestino-vesical fistula.

intestinule (ɪn'tɛstɪnjuːl). *rare.* [f. L. *intestīn-um* + dim. -ULE.] A small or minute intestine.

1836–9 TODD *Cycl. Anat.* II. 423/1 These organs..are invariably composed of intestinules or branched cæca.

intewne, obs. variant of ENTUNE *v.*

†**in'tex**, *v. Obs. rare*⁻¹. [ad. L. *intexĕre* to weave in.] *trans.* To weave in.

1599 R. LINCHE *Fount. Anc. Fict.* G iij, There might you see with greatest skill intexed. *Ibid.* K iij, A foot cloth wherein is wrought and intexed diuerse strange workes.

intexine, *Bot.*: see INTEXTINE.

†**'intext**, *sb. Obs. rare*⁻¹. [? ad. L. *intextus* an interweaving, or ? f. IN *adv.* 12 + TEXT *sb.*: cf. TEXT, CONTEXT.] The text or matter of a book.

1648 HERRICK *Hesp., To his Closet-gods*, I had a book which none Co'd reade the intext but my selfe alone.

†**in'text**, *v. Obs. rare*⁻¹. [f. L. *intext-*, ppl. stem of *intexĕre*: see INTEX.] *trans.* = INTEX; *transf.* to work in, to incorporate in the text.

1563–87 FOXE *A. & M.* (1596) 282/1 Which [epistle]..I thought meet here to intext and place.

intextine (ɪn'tɛkstɪn). *Bot.* Also **intexine**. [f. L. *int-us* within + EXTINE.] An inner coating of the pollen grain within the extine.

1835 LINDLEY *Introd. Bot.* (1848) I. 359 [Fritzche] speaks of four coatings to the pollen of Clarkia elegans, calling the fourth, which is near the extine, the Intexine. **1885** GOODALE *Phys. Bot.* (1892) 428 *note*, Oenothera, where the extine separates into a true extine and an intextine.

†**in'texture**, *sb. Obs. rare*⁻¹. [f. L. *intext-*, ppl. stem (see INTEXT *v.*) + -URE, after *texture*.] A weaving in, blending.

1607 TOPSELL *Four-f. Beasts* (1658) 232 Camerarius commendeth a certain colour called in Latine, *Varius*.. because of the divers in-textures of colours.

in'texture, *v. rare*⁻⁰. [f. as prec.] *trans.* To weave or work in. Hence **in'textured** *ppl. a.*

1856 WEBSTER, *Intextured.* **1882** OGILVIE, *Intexture.*

in-thing: see IN *a.* 2.

inthirsted, variant of ENTHIRSTED.

inthral(l, etc., obs. var. of ENTHRAL, etc.

†**in'thring**, *v. Sc. Obs.* Pa. t. inthrang. [f. IN-[1] + THRING *v.*] *intr.* To press in.

a **1500** *Colkelbie Sow* 419 Curris, kenseis and knavis Inthrang and dansit in thravis. **1508** DUNBAR *Tua Mariit Wemen* 13 In haist to the hege so hard I inthrang.

inthrone, -ment, obs. var. ENTHRONE, -MENT.

†**in'throng**, *v. Obs.* [f. IN-[1] + THRONG *v.*] *intr.* To throng in; to press or crowd in.

1600 FAIRFAX *Tasso* XV. xli, How the seas betwixt those iles inthrong, And how they shouldred land from land away. *Ibid.* XIX. xxxvii, His people like a flowing streame inthrong.

inthronise, -yse, obs. forms of ENTHRONIZE.

†**inthro'nistic**, *a.* and *sb. Obs.* [ad. med.L. **inthronisticus* (*-um*), ad. eccl. Gr. ἐνθρονιστικός (*-όν*) inaugural, f. ἐνθρονίζειν to ENTHRONIZE. Cf. med.L. *inthroniasticum* a gift to an ordaining bishop.] **a.** *adj.* Pertaining to ecclesiastical ordination. **b.** *sb.* A gift made to a bishop for ordination or installation.

1685 BURNET *Life William Bedell* 82 When the Metropolitan [etc.]..came and ordained the Bishop..it was but reasonable that their expence should be discharged; and this came to be rated to a certain Summ, and was called the Inthronistick. **1725** tr. *Dupin's Eccl. Hist. 17th C.* I. v. 113 That Right which Justinian calls Inthronistick, which his Predecessor Julian has called by the Term Cathedratick, which was given, not for the Ordination, but for that which we call the Installation.

†**in'thronizate**, *ppl. a. Obs.* Also -tron-. [ad. late L. *int(h)ronizāt-us*, pa. pple of *int(h)ronizāre* to ENTHRONIZE.] *trans.* To enthrone.

c **1470** HARDING *Chron.* XLIX. i, Maryus, his soonne, was then intronizate. *Ibid.* LII. i, Seuerus To Britayn come and was intronizate. **1577** HOLINSHED *Chron.* II. V v/2 In the feast of all Saintes, the Archbishop Bonifacius was inthronizate at Canterburie.

Hence †**inthroni'zation**, obs. var. of ENTHRONIZATION.

inthrough ('ɪn'θruː), *prep.* and *adv. Sc.* Also **inthrow** (-'θrʌu). [f. IN *adv.* + THROUGH.]

A. *prep.* In and through; through (a place) from the outside; in towards the centre of.

16.. *Lord's Trumpet* 7 (Jam. Suppl.), I would rather have one of yon sufferers that is bred in Christ's school inthrow Clydesdale yonder, than a hundred of you to join with me. **1699** T. BOSTON *Art Man-fishing* (1900) 33 When thou preachest doctrine, so as wicked men may run out-through and in-through it. **1825–80** JAMIESON s.v., *To gae inthrow and outthrow any thing*, to examine or try it in every direction. *Angus.*

B. *adv.* In towards the centre; towards the fireside.

1825–80 in JAMIESON.

†**in'thrust**, *v. Obs. rare*⁻¹. [f. IN-[1] + THRUST *v.*] *trans.* To thrust in; to intrude.

1605 CAMDEN *Rem.* 122 Those..of strange base parentage were forbidden..to insert, or inthrust themselves into noble and honest families.

'inthrust, *ppl. a. rare.* [IN *adv.* 11 b.] Thrust in.

1658 A. FOX *Wurtz' Surg.* III. v. 232 The inthrust tent will melt in the wound. **1885** G. H. TAYLOR *Pelvic & Hern. Therap.* 89 Adhesion of the inthrust parts to the borders of the hernial ring.

intice, -ment, obs. variants of ENTICE, -MENT.

‖**intichiuma** (ɪntɪtʃɪ'uːmə). Pl. **intichiuma**. [Native name.] Sacred ceremonies performed by some Central Australian Aborigines with the purpose of increasing the totemic plants or animals, and thus ensuring a good food supply.

1899 SPENCER & GILLON *Native Tribes Cent. Austral.* vi. 170 It sometimes happens that the members of the totem, such as..the rain or water totem, will hold their *Intichiuma* when there has been a long drought and water is badly needed. **1911** J. G. FRAZER *Golden Bough* (ed. 3) I. iii. 85 The general result supposed to be accomplished by these magical totemic ceremonies, or *intichiuma*, as the Arunta call them, is that of supplying the tribe with food and other necessaries. **1950** J. STRACHEY tr. *Freud's Totem & Taboo* iv. 139 The *intichiuma* ceremonies of the Central Australian tribes.

intier, -ty, obs. variants of ENTIRE, -TY.

in'till, intil, *prep. Sc.* and *north. dial.* Forms: (3 in tel), 3–5 in til, 4–5 intill(e, in tyl, 4– intil, (-till), (8– intul). [f. IN *adv.* + TILL *prep.* in its northern sense of *to*. Cf. UNTIL. In early use the two elements were often written separately.]

1. Of motion, direction, change of condition: = INTO. *Sc.* and *north. dial.*

1258 *Eng. Proclam. Hen. III*, And al on þo ilche worden is isend in to æurihce oþre shcire.., and ek in tel Irelonde. *a* **1300** *Cursor M.* 5042 In til egypte son come þai. *c* **1375** *Lay Folks Mass Bk.* (MS. B.) 32 Intil englishe þus I draw hit. *c* **1386** CHAUCER *Knt.'s T.* 1204 (Harl.) Ther sawȝh I dyane turned in til a tree [*Ellesm.* yturned til, *so 3 others*; *Heng. & Petw.* to]. *c* **1400** MAUNDEV. (Roxb.) ii. 7 He was ledd in til a gardyne. **1490** CAXTON *Eneydos* xlv. 136 Vysus dyde putte hym self in tyl a path and was soone goon. **1562** J. HEYWOOD *Prov. & Epigr.* (1867) 142 The mids he lept in till. **1562** A. SCOTT *Poems* (S.T.S.) i. 210 Prent þe wordis Intill this bill. **1596** DALRYMPLE tr. *Leslie's Hist. Scot.* II. 141 He fell intill al kynde of lust. **1797** MRS. WHEELER *Westmld. Dial.* i. 37 They baith lowpt intulth Cart. **1834** M. SCOTT *Cruise Midge* (1863) 190 She was a..gude wife..before she fell away intil that evil propensity. **1893** *Northumbld. Gloss.* s.v., Put them in till a poke.

†**b.** = UNTO, TO. (Cf. TILL.) *Obs.*

a **1300** *Cursor M.* 13459 (Gött.) Iesus clamb vp intill a fell. *c* **1340** HAMPOLE *Prose Tr.* 13 At the comynge of Criste intill hyme. **1340** —— *Pr. Consc.* 4508 Þai sal turne thurgh Goddes myght þe fadirs hertes intil þe sons right.

2. Of place, position, condition, state, time: = IN. (Cf. INTO 22.) Only *Sc.* (*central* and *north-east.*)

1375 BARBOUR *Bruce* I. 186 Bath castell and toune War intill his possessioune. *Ibid.* 340 As to the gud Erle of Artayis, Robert, befell intill his dayis. *c* **1425** WYNTOUN *Cron.* VIII. x. 174 [He] tretyd hym in-til þat case; As ay þe Dewyle dois in Falase. **1535** STEWART *Cron. Scot.* I. 533 Thair wes richt few Or nane that tyme that he mycht traist in till. **1567** *Gude & Godly B.* (S.T.S.) 137 In till ane myrthfull Maij morning Quhen Phebus did vp spring. *a* **1572** KNOX *Hist. Ref.* Wks. 1846 I. 228 The said Maister James and Johne Knox being intill one galay. **1861** WHYTE MELVILLE *Tilbury Nogo* 244 There's just naething at a' intill him but what he puts in wi' the spune.

intilted ('ɪntɪltɪd), *ppl. a.* [IN *adv.* 11 b.] Tilted inwards.

1940 F. SMYTHE *Adventures Mountaineer* viii. 117 At the base of the buttress lay a big intilted granite slab. **1956** M. STEWART *Wildfire at Midnight* x. 87 He climbed..easily, making for the next stance, which was an in-tilted ledge some fifteen feet above him.

‖**'intima.** *Biol.* [Short for L. *tunica intima* = inmost coating.] The inmost coating or membrane of a part or organ, *esp.* of a vein or artery.

1873 T. H. GREEN *Introd. Pathol.* (ed. 2) 333 Under the microscope, the cells of the intima and of the middle and external coats are found to be considerably increased in number. **1876** tr. *Wagner's Gen. Pathol.* 192 The intima appears slightly clouded, as if covered with a fine dust.

intimacy ('ɪntɪməsɪ). [f. INTIMATE *a.*: see -ACY.] The quality or condition of being intimate.

1. a. The state of being personally intimate; intimate friendship or acquaintance; familiar intercourse; close familiarity; an instance of this.

1641 J. JACKSON *True Evang. T.* III. 180 Any other noble, and lawfull familiarities of intimacie, and deerenesse. **1675** BAXTER *Cath. Theol.* II. IX. 201 That they did dissemble.. my own intimacy with them assured me. **1709** MRS. MANLEY *Secret Mem.* (1736) IV. 169 A Friend of mine that was of their Intimacy. **1800** MRS. HERVEY *Mourtray Fam.* III. 140 The closest intimacy was immediately struck up between them. **1814** JANE AUSTEN *Mansf. Park* II. iii, Sir Thomas, drawing back from intimacies in general. **1898** A. W. W. DALE *Life R. W. Dale* iii. 43 Intimacy and affection ..have turned the dead volumes into living friends.

b. *euphem.* for sexual intercourse.

1676 tr. *Guillatiere's Voy. Athens* 70 Having a mutual desire to continue their intimacy. **1879** FROUDE *Cæsar* xii. 151 Cæsar was accused of criminal intimacy with many ladies of the highest rank. **1889** *Daily News* 23 Jan. 2/6 The defendant..did not however have intimacy with her. He had never been intimate with her. **1906** B. WEBB in S. Hynes *Edwardian Turn of Mind* (1968) iv. 114 Friendship between particular men and women..is practically impossible.. without physical intimacy... There remains the question whether, with all the perturbation caused by such intimacies, you would have any brain left to think with? **1907** *Westm. Gaz.* 14 Dec. 11/2 She stayed the night with Wood at his father's house... Intimacy took place on that occasion. **1963** A. HERON *Towards Quaker View of Sex* 71 *Intimacy*, close friendship, but also as a synonym for sexual intercourse.

c. Closeness of observation, knowledge, or the like.

1714 HEARNE *Duct. Hist.* I. Advt. 3rd ed. 2 The Observations..had not enter'd with intimacy enough into that Subject. **1817** CHALMERS *Astron. Disc.* ii. (1852) 42 There is a something in the intimacy of a man's own experience.

2. Intimate or close connexion or union. *rare.*

1720 WATERLAND *Eight Serm.* 137 The Union and Intimacy between Father and Son is such, that they are not two Gods, but one God. **1870** H. SPENCER *Princ. Psychol.* (ed. 2) I. §35. 85 Explosions occur only..where the elements concerned are..distributed among one another molecularly, or, as in gunpowder, with minute intimacy.

†**3.** Inner or inmost nature; an inward quality or feature. *Obs.*

1660 HEXHAM, *Inwendigheydt*, Inwardnesse, or Intimacie. **1771** P. H. *View 2 last Parlts.* 118 Every one that had the Honour to be acquainted with the Intimacies of this Gentleman's Skill and Address, knew him form'd for the Prime Management in whatever he undertook.

†**intimado** (ɪntɪ'mɑːdəʊ). *Obs.* [An alteration of INTIMATE *sb.*, after Sp. words in -ADO, q.v.] = INTIMATE *sb.* 2.

1682 T. FLATMAN *Heracl. Ridens* (1713) II. 125 Whitlock ..was his Lordship's Intimado. **1683** CAVE *Ecclesiastici* App. 31 Which he had left with a woman; a prime *intimado* and zealous confident of his Party. **1690** E. GEE *Jesuit's Mem.* 46 As great Intimado's as if they had been of the same Society. **1748** RICHARDSON *Clarissa* (1811) VII. 359 A gentleman of no good character (an *intimado* of Mr. Lovelace). **1823** LAMB *Elia* Ser. II. Pref., His *intimados*, to confess a truth, were in the world's eye a ragged regiment.

intimal ('ɪntɪməl), *a. Biol.* [f. INTIM(A + -AL.] Of the intima.

1907 *Buck's Handbk. Med. Sci.* (rev. ed.) II. 98/2 A ligated vessel may be occluded by intimal proliferation without thrombosis taking place. **1961** *Lancet* 22 July 187/1 Numerous small systemic arteries can be seen and some of these show intimal hypertrophy.

intimate ('ɪntɪmət), *a.* and *sb.* [ad. L. *intimāt-us*, pa. pple. of *intimāre*, f. *intimus* inmost,

deepest, profound or close in friendship, as *sb.* a close friend, f. *int-us* within: see INTIMATE *v.*]

A. *adj.* **1. a.** Inmost, most inward, deep-seated; hence, Pertaining to or connected with the inmost nature or fundamental character of a thing; essential; intrinsic. Now chiefly in scientific use.

1632 SHERWOOD, Intimate (or inward), *intime.* **1647** H. MORE *Song of Soul* IV. xxxi, This faculty is very intimate And near the Centre. **1678** HOBBES *Decam.* iv. 44 The true and intimate Substance of the Earth. **1830** HERSCHEL *Stud. Nat. Phil.* III. iv. (1851) 291 Its necessary connection with the intimate constitution of the substance. **1878** STEWART & TAIT *Unseen Univ.* iii. §92. 100 With regard to the intimate structure of matter and ether.

b. Entering deeply or closely into a matter.

1817 COLERIDGE *Biog. Lit.* iv. (1894) 42 A more intimate analysis..matured my conjecture into full conviction.

2. Pertaining to the inmost thoughts or feelings; proceeding from, concerning, or affecting one's inmost self; closely personal.

1671 MILTON *Samson* 223 They knew not That what I motioned was of God; I knew From intimate impulse, and therefore urged The marriage on. **1702** *Eng. Theophrast.* 218 Justice..is nothing but an intimate fear of losing one's own. **1863** GEO. ELIOT *Romola* ix, He had an intimate sense that Romola was something very much above him. **1871** R. ELLIS *Catullus* xxxv. 5 Some particular intimate reflexions One would tell thee.

3. a. Close in acquaintance or association; closely connected by friendship or personal knowledge; characterized by familiarity (with a person or thing); very familiar. Said of persons, and personal relations or attributes. Also *transf.* of things, Pertaining to or dealing with such close personal relations.

1635 J. HAYWARD tr. *Biondi's Banish'd Virg.* 106 A Knight who was an intimate friend of his. **1659** D. PELL *Impr. Sea* 117 They are bound by the Laws..of Heaven..to maintain no intimate, or delightful converse with the wicked. **1700** S. L. tr. *Fryke's Voy. E. Ind.* 91 Sorry at the fate of one of 'em ..being one of my intimate acquaintance. **1754** RICHARDSON *Grandison* I. xxviii. 205 Kindred minds will be intimate at first sight. **1784** COWPER *Task* IV. 139, I crown thee [winter] king of intimate delights. **1831** LYTTON *Godolph.* xxxvi, Our losses are not intimate and household. **1841** MISS MITFORD in L'Estrange *Life* (1870) III. viii. 124 My friends the Carys ..are very intimate with Mr. Newman. *a* **1870** T. ERSKINE *Spir. Order* (1876) 14 The family relation is a more intimate one than the political, and makes more demands on the heart and inner life. **1897** A. UPWARD *Secr. Crts. Europe* 157 Another anecdote..is, perhaps, a little too intimate for general repetition.

b. *euphem.* of sexual intercourse.

1889 [see INTIMACY 1 b]. **1926** R. MACAULAY *Crewe Train* II. vi. 139 Some of them were..what newspapers call intimate together, without having undergone marriage. **1963** 'E. MCBAIN' *Ten Plus One* (1964) xiv. 162 Do you mean that you and the other two girls were *intimate* with these boys? **1969** *Times* 15 Nov. 3/2, I ripped her dress off. She was lying on her face. I was intimate with her.

c. Familiarly associated; closely personal.

1884 H. JAMES *Little Tour* 214 These diminutive intimate things bring one near to the old Roman life. **1898** *Daily News* 8 Aug. 6/1 Writers like Mr. Henry James, Mr. Howells, and Miss Wilkins, students and observers only of the minute, the delicate, and the intimate.

d. Used allusively of women's underclothing.

1904 P. GIBBON *Souls in Bondage* i. 5 Clothes hung on lines in all directions, intimate linen flapped in the wind. **1970** *Globe & Mail* (Toronto) 28 Sept. 32/4 (Advt.), Next week we'll be highlighting panti hose and the week after it will be Intimate Apparel week in our Foundations Departments. **1973** *Tucson* (Arizona) *Daily Citizen* 22 Aug. 10 (Advt.), Intimate Apparel, mall level.

e. Of a theatrical performance, esp. a revue: that aims at establishing familiar and friendly relations with the audience. Also of a theatre itself.

1915 H. K. MODERWELL *Theatre To-Day* xvi. 309 The [Manchester Repertory] theatre happens to work mostly with the modern 'intimate' or 'realistic' play, and so is enabled to get along with one company of actors, albeit a large one. **1919** A. HORNBLOW *Hist. Theatre Amer.* II. xxxi. 343 The new method is to build a smaller house, or *théâtre intime*, allowing of an auditorium with limited capacity so that no seat will be very far from the stage. Among these theatres may be mentioned..the Maxine Elliott, one of the first of the intimate theatres. **1929** *N.Y. Times* 1 May 28/5 The Little Show. An intimate revue in two acts and twenty-seven scenes. **1930** *Nation* (N.Y.) 24 Sept. 331/1 The place and the popularity of the intimate music show is assured. People are delighted if it sounds like an impromptu affair. **1948** *Penguin Music Mag.* VI. 51 A series of intimate opera to be given at La Scala with a small audience seated on the stage. **1952** GRANVILLE *Dict. Theatr. Terms* 102 *Intimate revue*, a smart, topical revue played in a small (*intimate*) theatre. **1959** *Times* 22 Jan. 3/2 Intimate revue, at a glance, appears to be the theatre's gift to television. **1961** A. BERKMAN *Singers' Gloss. Show Business* 52 The Intimate Position of the head is that in which both the face and the eyes are directed squarely toward the other person. **1974** *Times* 27 Aug. 8/5 That quiet British archness which put the phrase Intimate Revue into the language.

4. Of knowledge or acquaintance: Involving or resulting from close familiarity; close.

a **1680** BUTLER *Rem.* (1759) I. 211 Challenge intimate Acquaintance With all the learned Moderns, and the Ancients. **1771** *Junius Lett.* liv. 286 My abhorrence..arises from an intimate knowledge of his character. *Mod.* One who has an intimate acquaintance with parliamentary procedure.

5. Of a relation between things: Involving very close connexion or union; very close.

1692 SOUTH *12 Serm.* (1697) I. 502 Pride..is of such Intimate, and even Essential Connexion with Ingratitude. **1831** LARDNER *Pneumat.* v. 286 Such pressure only renders the contact of the valve more intimate. **1839** MURCHISON *Silur. Syst.* I. xxxi. 415 This grit is made up of an intimate mixture of fine grains of white quartz and pink felspar. **1860** EMERSON *Cond. Life* vi. (1861) 127 There is an intimate interdependence of intellect and morals. **1876** *Clin. Soc. Trans.* IX. 153 The adhesions were most intimate over the upper lobe.

B. *sb.* †**1.** One who intimately belongs to something; a typical representative or example. *Obs.*

1607 WALKINGTON *Opt. Glass* xi. 124 For the intimates of this complexion [the Phlegmatic]..are always pale coloured; slow pac'd; drowsie Headed.

2. A person with whom one is intimate; a very close friend or associate.

1659 *Gentl. Calling* (1696) 118 The other sort of power that which they have over their Friends and intimates. **1670** *Devout Commun.* (1688) 169 Make the liveliest of them my most intimates, and..improve their fellowship to the best advantage. **1712** STEELE *Spect.* No. 515 ⁋1 To procure from that Intimate of hers one of her Letters. **1828** SCOTT *F.M. Perth* xx, Henry..only remembered that Oliver had been his friend and intimate. **1888** BURGON *Lives 12 Gd. Men* I. III. 344 The variety and extent of his knowledge..often astonished his intimates.

intimate ('ɪntɪmeɪt), *v.* Pa. pple. **intimated**; also 6–7 **intimate**. [f. late L. *intimāt-*, ppl. stem of *intimāre* to put or bring into, drive or press into, to make known, announce, notify by legal process, f. *intim-us* inmost. Cf. F. *intimer* (1325 in Godef. *Compl.*).]

1. *trans.* To make known formally, to notify, announce, state; †formerly, to communicate (knowledge), to declare (war).

1538 BALE *Thre Lawes* 1490 What fashyon vse ye, to vs here intymate. *a* **1548** HALL *Chron., Hen. IV* 17 He incontinente did proclaime and intimate open warre. *Ibid., Hen. VII* 34 b, Assone as the commynge of ye Mayre was intymate and knowen to the ryotous persones, they fledde. **1614** in *Vicary's Anat.* (1888) App. III. 145 Their humble peticion..Intymating..that the said Hospitall hath bin chardged with the keeping of three Children. **1629–39** SIR W. MURE *Ps.* xix. 2 Day speaks to day and night to night Doth knowledge intimate. **1759** ROBERTSON *Hist. Scot.* VI. Wks. 1813 I. 418 This resolution she intimated to the leaders of both factions. **1816** SCOTT *Introd. 1st Ser. Tales My Landlord*, I have only further to intimate, that Mr Peter Pattieson..hath more consulted his own fancy than the accuracy of the narrative. **1884** *Manch. Exam.* 19 Feb. 4/7 The coalmasters..have posted a notice..intimating a reduction of ten per cent in the wages of miners.

†**b.** To designate as something. *Obs. rare.*

1799–1805 S. TURNER *Anglo-Sax.* (1836) I. III. xi. 255 *note*, It was Athelstan..that may, with the greatest propriety, be entitled *primus monarcha Anglorum*; and accordingly Alured of Beverley so intimates him.

2. To make known or communicate by any means however indirect; hence, to signify, indicate; to imply, to suggest, to hint at.

1590 SPENSER *F.Q.* III. ix. 30 To her he sought to intimate His inward griefe, by meanes to him well knowne. **1634** SIR T. HERBERT *Trav.* 69 Till Easter day, when they take up the representative Bodie, intimating thereby his Resurrection. **1660** JER. TAYLOR *Worthy Commun.* ii. 14 The Apostle expresses one duty and intimates another. **1728** YOUNG *Love Fame* v. 74 Her darling china, in a whirlwind sent, Just intimates the lady's discontent. **1814** SCOTT *Wav.* viii, The open avowal of what the others only ventured to intimate. **1876** MOZLEY *Univ. Serm.* vi. 135 The Great Spirit, speaking by dumb representation to other spirits, intimates and signifies to them something about Himself.

b. To mention indirectly or in passing.

1634 CANNE *Necess. Separ.* (1849) 74 We do deny that those here intimated are true ministers. **1661** BRAMHALL *Just Vind.* x. 275 This is the treatise of Schisme intimated in my answer to Monsieur de la Militiere. **1800** *Asiat. Ann. Reg., Proc. E. Ind. Ho.* 85/1 He had intimated another subject, which could not be brought forward without fourteen days notice.

†**3.** To make intimate, to familiarize. *Obs.*

1642 ROGERS *Naaman* 362 The Lord intimated his heart with this thought. **1654** WHITLOCK *Zootomia* 451 For two of a Profession (that are not intimated by nearenesse of Friendship) to give one another a good word is Candidnesse miraculous.

Hence **'intimated** *ppl. a.* Also **'intimater**, one who intimates.

1606 FORD *Honour Triumph, Monarchs Meet.* xi, A goodly view of majestie it was To see such intimated league betwixt them. **1611** FLORIO, *Indittore*, an inditer, a denouncer. Also an intimater. **1850** W. IRVING *Goldsmith* xxvii. 274 Goldsmith treasured up the intimated hope.

intimately ('ɪntɪmətlɪ), *adv.* [f. INTIMATE *a.* + -LY².] In an intimate manner.

1. Very deeply or inwardly; In a way that affects one's inmost self or moves the deepest feeling.

1637 BP. HALL *Remedy Prophaneness* I. §1. 10 We apprehend him [God]..intimately present to us, with us, in us. **1662** SPARROW tr. *Behme's Rem. Wks., 1st Apol. Balth. Tylcken* 8 If some people fearing God, had not intimately.. entreated for it, I had not given it to any at all. *a* **1677** HALE *Prim. Orig. Man.* I. i. 43 When I deeply and intimately consider these things. **1712** STEELE *Spect.* No. 290 ⁋2, I shall not act it as I ought, for I shall feel it too intimately to be able to utter it. **1774** GOLDSM. *Grecian Hist.* II. 240 Alexander..proved how intimately he was affected with the unhappiness of a prince who deserved a better fate.

2. In a manner involving close acquaintance; so as to be very familiar.

1645 MILTON *Tetrach.* ad fin., Lest..they expose themselves rather to be pledg'd up and down by men who intimately know them. **1697** DAMPIER *Voy.* I. 60 Being intimately acquainted with him, I know the course of his Travels. **1838** DICKENS *Nich. Nick.* iii, 'I know her circumstances intimately, ma'am', said Ralph.

3. In a way that involves or effects a very close connexion or union of parts or elements.

1665 HOOKE *Microgr.* 70 By uniting more intimately either with some particular corpuscles..or with all of them. **1722** QUINCY *Lex. Physico-Med.* (ed. 2) 11 Thereby the Blood [is] more intimately broken and divided, so that it becomes fitter for the more fluid Secretions. **1756** C. LUCAS *Ess. Waters* III. 129 These two salts are so intimately mixed, as to be in a manner inseparable. **1773** FRANKLIN *Lett.* Wks. 1887 V. 134 Lightning..by penetrating intimately the hardest metals..has separated the parts in an instant. **1873** TRISTRAM *Moab* Pref. 1 A country..intimately connected with Jewish history.

'intimateness. *rare.* [f. as prec. + -NESS.] = INTIMACY.

1642 T. GOODWIN *Heart Christ in Heaven* 7 A word denoting the greatest nearnesse, dearnesse, and intimatenesse. **1649** BP. REYNOLDS *Hosea* v. 44 This accurate fitnesse and intimatenesse of the parts with one another. **1659** D. PELL *Impr. Sea* 66 Take heed of too much intimateness and familiarity with Sea-men.

intimation (ɪntɪ'meɪʃən). [a. F. *intimation* (1394 in Godef. *Compl.*), ad. late L. *intimātiōn-em* (in med.L. *spec.* judicial notification), n. of action from *intimāre* to INTIMATE.]

1. The action of intimating, making known, or announcing; formal notification or announcement; †formerly, declaration (of war).

1442–3 *Rec. Coldingham Priory* (Surtees) 148 Discorde heirupon raysit..I made til hym intimacion of my richts be ȝour lettres. *a* **1548** HALL *Chron., Hen. VIII* 174 The defiaunce, dooen by your Herault as a paremptory intimacion of warre. **1603** HOLLAND *Plutarch's Mor.* 1316 They made an edict, with an intimation, that whosoever killed a storke should be banished. **1697** DAMPIER *Voy.* I. 518, I therefore give this intimation, because it is the interest of the Nation..to be informed of abuses in their Factories. **1816** SCOTT *Old Mort.* Introd., As soon as his body was found, intimation was sent to his sons at Balmaclellan. **1858** MRS. CARLYLE *Lett.* II. 393 My acknowledgement of the intimation of her uncle's death. **1861** W. BELL *Dict. Law Scot.* 471 Intimation is a step necessary in certain circumstances for the complete transference of a right.

b. *Law.* Notification of a requirement made by law, coupled with an announcement of the penalty that will be incurred in case of default. ? *Obs.*

1632 *High Commission Cases* (Camden) 263 Elizabeth Holland a woman of ill reporte and her husband were called upon an intimation of 100 *l.* **1752** J. LOUTHIAN *Form of Process* (ed. 2) 59 Craving Precepts or Letters of Intimation, for intimating to his Majesty's Advocate..to fix a Day for his Trial, within sixty Days next after the Intimation, under the Pains and Certifications contained in the Statute.

2. The action of making known or expressing merely; an expression by sign or token, an indication; a suggestion, a hint.

1531 ELYOT *Gov.* I. xxi, The associatinge of man and woman in daunsing..was nat begonne without a speciall consideration, as well for the necessarye coniunction of those two persones, as for the intimation of sondry vertues. **1662** STILLINGFL. *Orig. Sacr.* I. iii. §9 Where he doth give the least intimation of Manetho being elder then Alexander, I am yet to seek. **1793** BEDDOES *Calculus* 23 He..felt from time to time some slight pains or intimations of pain. **1807** WORDSW. (*title*), Intimations of Immortality from Recollections of Early Childhood. **1875** JOWETT *Plato* (ed. 2) I. 432, I have often had intimations in dreams.

†**'in-,timber.** *Obs.* In 5 *Sc.* intymmyr. [IN *adv.* 10 a.] Inner or inside timber; 'boards to line the inside of a vessel'.

1497 *Acc. Ld. High Treas. Scot.* I. 378 Item, for tymmyr, to be intymmyr and dwangis to hir mast..xxxs.

'intime (ɛ̃tim), *a.* (*sb.*) Also **-tim, -tymme.** [ad. L. *intim-us* inmost: perh. immediately a. F. *intime* (14th c. in Godef. *Compl.*).] **a.** = INTIMATE *a.* **b.** Now only as the French word revived in modern English use.

a **1618** SYLVESTER *Job Triumphant* II. 260 Mine Intimemost, Those that I loved best, Abhor mee all. **1629** C. POTTER *Consecr. Serm.* 69 His intime friend and familiar. **1644** DIGBY *Nat. Bodies* v. (1658) 45 An intime application of the Agents. **1675** E. WILSON *Spadacr. Dunelm.* 56, I sharpened the water to divers degrees for its more intim penetration and dissolution. **1678** GALE *Crt. Gentiles* III. 22 So that ἐνεργεία signifies God's intime presence. **1857** W. BAGEHOT in *National Rev.* V. 411 The real, rougeless, *intime* Flicflac we know not. **1947** *Ballet Ann.* I. 73 *Ballet intime* bears the same relation to *Ballet Russe* as chamber music bears to a symphony. **1963** J. WIESENFARTH *Henry James* iii. 60 Another carriage ride introduces Maisie to an intime relationship between her father and her governess. **1968** W. GARNER *Deep, Deep Freeze* vii. 87 She..patted the sofa, 'Come and sit here. It is more *intime.*' **1973** *New York* 26 Mar. 21/2 Intime restaurant with continental cuisine.

c. *sb.* The inmost part.

1657 *Divine Lover* 278 Wound the intymme of my soule with the remembrance of thy wounds.

Hence †**'intimely** *adv.*, intimately.

1657 *Divine Lover* 303 A gratious guift by which wee sweetelie and intimmelie aspire to God. **1678** GALE *Crt. Gentiles* III. 114 God workes intimely in al things.

intimidate (ɪn'tɪmɪdeɪt), *v.* [f. med.L. *intimidāt-*, ppl. stem of *intimidāre*, f. *in-* (IN-²) +

timid-us TIMID: see -ATE³, and cf. F. *intimider* (16th c. in Godef. *Compl.*).] *trans.* To render timid, inspire with fear; to overawe, cow; in modern use *esp.* to force to or deter from some action by threats or violence.

1646 H. LAWRENCE *Comm. Angells* 121 Nothing intimidates more than ignorance. *a* **1714** BURNET *Hist. Ref.* an. 1553 (R.) When a government is firm, and factions are weak, the making some public examples may intimidate a faction otherwise disheartened. **1759** ROBERTSON *Hist. Scot.* v. Wks. 1813 I. 377 She hoped that such a discovery of her sentiments would intimidate Mary. **1769** *Junius Lett.* xv. 62 Unless you can find means to corrupt or intimidate the jury. **1844** H. H. WILSON *Brit. India* III. 431 Advantage was taken of the presence of the regular troops..to intimidate the Grasia chiefs into acquiescence. **1878** JEVONS *Prim. Pol. Econ.* viii. §52. 68 To allow one holder of goods to intimidate and prevent other holders from selling to the public.

Hence **in'timidated, in'timidating** *ppl. adjs.*

1727 BAILEY vol. II, *Intimidated*, put into Fear, disheartened. **1795–1814** WORDSW. *Excursion* VII. 837 (ed. 1), Why do ye quake, intimidated Thrones? *a* **1812** A. M. LEAN *Comm. Hebr.* (1847) I. 121 Every temptation to apostasy, whether of the alluring or intimidating kind.

intimidation (ɪntɪmɪ'deɪʃən). [n. of action from prec.: cf. F. *intimidation* (16th c. in Godef. *Compl.*).] The action of intimidating or making afraid; the fact or condition of being intimidated; now, *esp.* the use of threats or violence to force to or restrain from some action, or to interfere with the free exercise of political or social rights.

1658 PHILLIPS, *Intimidation*, a making timorous or fearful. **1721** in BAILEY. **1785** PALEY *Mor. Philos.* VI. vii. (1830) 397 The king carried his measures in parliament by intimidation. **1817** LADY MORGAN *France* Pref., I offer the following work to public notice, with feelings of great intimidation and distrust. **1829** J. W. CROKER in *Diary* 29 Mar. (1884), What was denied to reason and policy is surrendered to intimidation. **1833** HT. MARTINEAU *Manchester Strike* iv. 44, I am sorry to see this parade, which looks too much like intimidation. **1856** FROUDE *Hist. Eng.* (1858) I. iii. 274 In Italy, intrigue was used against intimidation.

intimidator (ɪn'tɪmɪdeɪtə(r)). [agent-n. in L. form, from *intimidāre* to INTIMIDATE.] One who intimidates or exercises intimidation.

1857 H. H. WILSON tr. *Rig-veda* III. 346. **1860** MILL *Repr. Govt.* (1865) 85/2 The intimidator could see the extorted obedience rendered irrevocably on the spot. **1871** *Daily News* 27 June, By enabling a man to shelter his vote from the intimidator we were going to enact immorality, and to give national sanction to lying. **1884** *St. James's Gaz.* 17 July 3/2 We must do our best at once to intimidate the intimidators.

in'timidatory, *a. rare.* [f. as prec. + -ORY.] Of intimidating nature or tendency.

a **1846** SIR J. GRAHAM cited by Worcester. **1858** GLADSTONE *Homer* III. 138 The vehemence with which he spoke produced the same intimidatory effect upon the gods as did the great speech of Achilles upon the envoys.

intimism ('ɪntɪmɪz(ə)m). Also ‖**intimisme.** [ad. F. *intimisme.*] (See quot. 1959.)

1903 *Daily Chron.* 19 Dec. 3/2 The great result of the emancipation of French art from Italian influence is what he [*sc.* C. Mauclair] calls 'intimism'. **1959** P. & L. MURRAY *Dict. Art & Artists* 164 *Intimisme*, a form of Impressionist technique applied to the depiction of everyday life in domestic interiors rather than to landscape. The work of Bonnard and Vuillard is usually meant. **1960** *Times* 16 Feb. 14/7 To paint a group of television viewers would be a caricature of 'intimisme'.

Hence **'intimist,** ‖**'intimiste** *a.*, relating to intimism. Also *transf.* Also as *sb.*, a painter following the principles of intimism.

1903 P. G. KONODY tr. *Mauclair's French Impressionists* ix. 196 Simon Bussy is decidedly the most personal of that young generation of 'Intimists' who seem to have retained the best principles of the Impressionist masters. **1937** *Times* 7 Oct. 12/3 In artistic slang they [*sc.* Bonnard and Vuillard] are grouped together as 'intimists', and the name serves well enough to describe..their habit of dwelling upon their material so as to extract from it the last possibilities in subtle colour relationships. **1959** *Listener* 21 May 898/1 The modified impressionism of Vuillard, a style especially suitable for such *intimiste* themes. **1967** *Ibid.* 18 May 654/1 Károly Ferenczy's 'Sunny Morning' of 1905 and the *intimiste* paintings of about the same period by..an associate of Bonnard in Paris. **1968** *Ibid.* 23 May 680/1 Jiri Menzel has everywhere been praised, like other Czech directors, as *intimiste.* **1973** *Times* 20 Mar. 9/7 The gallery shows a mixture of contemporary art and regular *Paris-Londres* exhibitions together with minor impressionists and intimists.

intimity (ɪn'tɪmɪtɪ). [f. L. *intim-us* inmost, deepest, intimate + -ITY: cf. F. *intimité* (1735 in Hatz.-Darm.), whence app. the current sense 2.]

†**1.** Close friendship or acquaintance, INTIMACY.

1617 COLLINS *Def. Bp. Ely* Ep. Ded. 3 The Historian, that alleadges friendship..and some intimitie with him.

2. Intimate quality or nature; inwardness; the quality of being very private; privacy.

1889 *Sat. Rev.* 30 Nov. 620/1 We owe her..one of the very best pictures of a decorous kind of a Court 'in intimity' that exists. **1897** *Ibid.* 16 Oct. 423 When the veil of intimity was lifted by Mrs. Orr and others, it was found that Browning had an excellent reason for his discretion. **1896** MRS. H. WARD *Sir G. Tressady* (1898) 402 It gave him a delicious passionate sense of intimity.

†**'intimous,** *a. Obs.* [f. L. *intim-us* (see INTIMATE *a.*) + -OUS.] = INTIMATE *a.* Hence †**'intimously** *adv.*, intimately.

1619 W. SCLATER *Exp. 1 Thess.* (1630) 553 To bee Companions with Drunkards, and of their intimous Familiars. **1629** H. BURTON *Babel no Bethel* 71 Is hee so intimously acquainted with Romes minde? **1657** TOMLINSON *Renou's Disp.* 401* Vitriol..roborates the intimous parts. *a* **1665** J. GOODWIN *Filled w. the Spirit* (1867) 233 In an intimous, serious, and affectionate converse with those glorious overtures of comfort [etc.].

†**in'tinct,** *sb. Obs.* [ad. L. *intinct-us* a dipping in, sauce, f. *intingĕre*: see INTINCT *v.*] A dye.

1657 TOMLINSON *Renou's Disp.* 77 Which they call the green intinct of some Greeks.

†**in'tinct,** *ppl. a. Obs.* [ad. L. *intinct-us*, pa. pple. of *intingĕre*: see next.] Wetted, suffused.

13.. in *Minor Poems fr. Vernon MS.* (E.E.T.S.) 139 Of a whyth corporaus..in-tync wit red wyn. **1432–50** tr. *Higden* (Rolls) VII. 91 The nexte day folowynge a wedrede tree intincte with his bloode wexede grene.

†**in'tinct,** *v. Obs.* [f. L. *intinct-*, ppl. stem of *intingĕre*, *-guĕre* to dip in, f. *in-* (IN-²) + *ting(u)ĕre* to wet, moisten, dye, TINGE.] *trans.* To moisten, dye, suffuse.

1547 BOORDE *Brev. Health* lxxxvii. 35 b, Intincte blacke wol in it and put it into the eare. **1654** GAYTON *Pleas. Notes* IV. xviii. 263 His Ill-favour'd face was not easily to be intincted with a blush.

intinction (ɪn'tɪŋkʃən). [ad. late L. *intinctiōn-em*, n. of action from *intingĕre*: see prec.]

†**1.** The action of dipping in, esp. in something coloured; a dyeing; the liquid in which something has been dipped, an infusion. *Obs.*

1559 MORWYNG *Evonym.*, Quench the dros of iron in hony and drinck the intinction. **1658** PHILLIPS, *Intinction*, a dying, a dipping into any coloured liquor.

2. *Eccl.* The action of dipping the bread in the wine in the administration of the Eucharist, in order that the communicant may receive both kinds; esp. as practised in the Oriental Churches.

1872 O. SHIPLEY *Gloss. Eccl. Terms* s.v., In the West intinction is retained at mass. **1881** F. E. WARREN *Liturgy Celt. Ch.* 165 *note*, This custom of intinction in the West between the seventh and twelfth centuries. **1887** J. W. KEMPE *Reserv. Sacram.* 130 If..upon..sufficient grounds, the two kinds cannot be reverently conveyed separately, they may be administered conjointly by intinction. **1890** GASQUET & BISHOP *Edw. VI & Bk. Com. Prayer* 213 *note*, The 'intinction', or purely oriental rite.

†**intinc'tivity.** *Obs. rare*⁻¹. [Compounded of IN-³ + L. *tinct-*, ppl. stem of *tingĕre* to dye + -IVE + -ITY: prob. after *inactivity*.] The quality of not communicating colour.

1794 KIRWAN *Elem. Min.* I. 200 Fullers earth is distinguished from..colorific earths, by its intinctivity.

†**in'tincture.** *Obs. rare*⁻¹. [f. L. *intinct-*, ppl. stem of *intingĕre* (see INTINCT *v.*) + -URE: cf. *tincture.*] Suffusion.

1634 PEACHAM *Gentl. Exerc.* I. xxiii. 72 It [earth] seemeth blacke, brownish, and of other colours, by reason of the intincture and commixture of other elements.

intine ('ɪntɪn). *Bot.* [f. L. *int-us* within + -INE.] The inner membrane of the pollen grain.

1835 LINDLEY *Introd. Bot.* (1848) I. 359 Fritzche asserts that these plants have both an extine and an intine. **1870** BENTLEY *Bot.* 254 The intine is the first formed layer, and appears to be of the same nature and appearance in all pollen-cells. **1885** GOODALE *Phys. Bot.* (1892) 428 The membrane..being generally composed of two coats—an outer, the extine..and an inner, the intine.

intire, intisce, -tise, intitle, obs. forms of ENTIRE, ENTICE, ENTITLE.

†**in'titulate,** *v. Obs.* Chiefly *Sc.* Also 7 **en-**. [f. *intitulāt-*, ppl. stem of late L. *intitulāre*: see INTITULE. First used in pa. pple. *intitulat*, ad. L. *intitulātus*.] *trans.* = INTITULE, ENTITLE.

1560 ROLLAND *Crt. Venus* II. 547 As in this bill it is Intitulat. **1582–8** *Hist. Jas. VI* (1804) 274 By the lettres, he was not intitulat King. **1632** LITHGOW *Trav.* x. 500 In my last Worke Intitulated Scotlands welcome to King Charles. **1641** *Vind. Smectymnuus* iv. 56 All Pastors be they intitulated Bishops or Priests have equall authority. **1675** tr. *Camden's Hist. Eliz.* II. (1688) 198 In a Paper of his which he entitulated The Chameleon.

intitulation (ɪntɪtjuː'leɪʃən). Also 9 **en-**. [n. of action from prec.; perh. a. obs. F. *intitulation* (1399 in Godef.), or ad. med.L. or L. type **intitulātiōn-em.*]

1. The action of entitling or furnishing with a title or superscription; a superscription, title.

1517 H. WATSON *Shyppe of Fooles* Argt. A j, The fyrste auctoure dyde delyte hym in the newe intytulacyon of this present boke. **1533** UDALL *Flowres* 94 (R.) Valerius Maximus, in the third boke, maketh an intitillacion—*De fiducia sui.* **1638** PENKETHMAN *Artach.* D iij b, Their severall Intitulations or words on the heads of each part or columne. **1866** *Reader* No. 158. 14/2 With the intitulation in letters of gold. **1888** *Bookseller's Catal.*, The Seven Planets..eight copper-engravings..with Freitag in the intitulation.

2. The action of bestowing a title; a designation.

1586 FERNE *Blaz. Gentrie* II. 63 It were absurde that..in the intitulation of stiles &c. he should derogate any thing from that which the ancestor vsed. **1892** *Cornh. Mag.* July 2 That Mr. Physic..had never learned that one canon of social intitulation. **1892** *Blackw. Mag.* Sept. 392 The high-sounding entitulation confers only a fictitious importance.

intitule (ɪn'tɪtjuːl), *v.* Also 5–8 **en-**. [a. OF. *en-*, *intituler* (1285 in Godef. *Compl.*), mod.F. *intituler*, ad. late L. *intitulāre* (Rufinus *c* 400), f. *in-* (IN-²) + *titulus* TITLE. Cf. ENTITLE.]

1. *trans.* To furnish (a book or document) with a heading or superscription; to give a designation to (a book, etc.); = ENTITLE 1. Now chiefly used technically in reference to Acts of Parliament.

1490 CAXTON *Eneydos* Prol. 10 This present boke compyled by virgyle Intytuled Eneydos. **1553** EDEN *Treat. Newe Ind.* (Arb.) 5 A sheete of printed paper, entytuled Of the newe founde landes. **1591** SPENSER *Ruines Time* Ded., This small Poeme, intituled by a generall name of The Worlds Ruines. **1648** *Art. Peace* c. 14 An Act..Intituled, An Exemplanation of the Act made in a Session of this Parliament for [etc.]. **1727** SWIFT *Poison. E. Curll* Wks. 1755 III. I. 148 A satyrical piece, entituled Court Poems. **1793** SMEATON *Edystone L.* §27 A book..entituled The Storm. **1866** WHITTIER *Marg. Smith's Jrnl.* Prose Wks. 1889 I. 65 It proved to be a Latin Treatise, by a famous Papist, intituled, 'The Imitation of Christ'. *Mod. Notice*, Pursuant to the Statute of 22nd and 23rd Vic. cap. 35 intituled 'An Act to further Amend the Law of Property and to relieve Trustees' [etc.].

†**b.** To ascribe (a book) *to* a person as its author; = ENTITLE 1 c. *Obs.*

a **1555** LATIMER *Serm. & Rem.* (Parker Soc.) 283 The book is open to be read, and is entituled to one which is Bishop of Gloucester. **1559** *Homilies* I. *Faith* I. (1859) 37 Written in a book intituled to be of Didymus Alexandrinus. **1563–87** FOXE *A. & M.* (1596) 60/2 These decretall epistles suspiciously intituled to the names of the fathers of the primitive church. **1579** FULKE *Heskins' Parl.* 208 Whether it be rightly intituled to him, I will not contende.

†**c.** To prefix *to* a book the name of a person as its patron to whom it is dedicated; = DEDICATE *v.* 3, with construction inverted. *Obs.*

1664 EVELYN tr. *Freart's Archit.* Ep. Ded., I intituled Your Majesty to a Work. **1677** W. HUBBARD *Narrative* Pref., The entituling so many names of worth to the patronage of so small and inconsiderable a Volume. **1691** tr. *Emilianne's Observ. Journ. Naples* Ded. A iv a.

†**2.** To dedicate *to* by name or title; to name after some one. *Obs.*

1483 CAXTON *Gold. Leg.* 235 b/1 Thys moneth of Auguste ..The peple entituled it to hys name & callyd it Augustus. **1667** *Decay Chr. Piety* xvi. ¶4 He refutes their factions entituling themselves to Paul and Apollos. **1707** J. CHAMBERLAYNE *St. Gt. Brit.* III. iv. 288 The Society [of the Garter] is entituled to St. George.

3. To give a (specified) title or designation to; = ENTITLE 2. *arch.*

1568 GRAFTON *Chron.* II. 743 The Lady Elizabeth, entituled Dolphinesse of Vien. **1597** HOOKER *Eccl. Pol.* v. xxv. §2 Our Lord himselfe hath..sanctified his own Temple, by entituling it *the house of Prayer.* **1601** HOLLAND *Pliny* I. 117 Where be nations entituled with many and sundry names. **1647** N. BACON *Disc. Govt. Eng.* I. iv. (1739) 9 The Romans intituled the Coasts of Norfolk and Suffolk the Saxons Coasts. **1869** BLACKMORE *Lorna D.* ii, Enough that they who made the ring intituled the scene a 'mill' [= pugilistic encounter].

†**b.** With inverted construction: To give as a title or designation (*to* something.) *Obs.* (Cf. 5.)

a **1654** SELDEN *Table-t.* (Arb.) 112 The Third Person is made of his own Frenzy, Malice, Ignorance and Folly, by the Roundhead (to all these the Spirit is intituled).

†**4.** To furnish (a person) with a 'title' *to* an estate. Hence *gen.* to give (a person or thing) a rightful claim *to* a possession, privilege, designation, etc., or *to be, have,* or *do* something; = ENTITLE 4. *Obs.*

1584 POWEL *Lloyd's Cambria* 237 Every one is intituled to the name of Bardh. **1642** tr. *Perkins' Prof. Bk.* v. §383. 166 She was once entituled to have dower. **1655** FULLER *Ch. Hist.* VI. iii. 317 The insuing story intituleth it self to as much probability as any other. **1670** BAXTER *Cure Ch. Div.* 112 The profession of Christianity which entituleth men to Church Communion. *a* **1797** H. WALPOLE *Mem. Geo. III* (1845) II. x. 230 Our merchants at home had..asked less for themselves than they were intituled to.

†**b.** To invest with an office, function, etc.; = ENTITLE 4 c. *Obs.*

1570–6 LAMBARDE *Peramb. Kent* (1862) 307 The Monks.. seeing that they themselves could not prevaile intituled their Archbishop Edmund. **1600** HOLLAND *Livy* 356 As if the Patritij were entirely alone intituled and invested in the prerogative of Sacerdotall Dignities.

†**c.** To furnish with a TITLE to ordination; = ENTITLE 4 b. *Obs.*

1720 WHITE *Monit. Clergy Peterb.* I. 16 Persons so intituled to any Curacy, shall actually enjoy the Right and immediate Possession of it.

†**5.** *trans.* To represent (something) as the cause of a particular action or effect. (Const. *to.*) = ENTITLE 5. *Obs.* (The converse of b.)

1663 J. SPENCER *Prodigies* (1665) 377 So neither may we infer the sin from the punishment, intituling some great evil of sin to such a great kind of suffering. **1706** DE FOE *Jure Div.* v. 21 *note*, Some People are very fond of intituling the Glory

and Honour of God to all their Actions, and to pretend to act for him.

†**b.** To impute or ascribe *to*; = ENTITLE 5 c.

1651 HOBBES *Govt. & Soc.* iii. §32. 56 The bad actions, which please them, are ever entituled to some Vertue.

Hence **in'tituling** *vbl. sb.*

1523 FITZHERB. *Surv.* Prol., A boke in parchement, bearyng a certayne date, after the maner and forme as I shall make an intytulynge.

into ('ɪntʊ), *prep.* and *a.* Also 1 in tó, 2–3 (*Orm.*) innto, 2–6 **in to**. [Orig. the two words, *in* adv., *to* prep., as in the similar collocations *out to*, *up to*, *down to*, *away to*, *off to*, *on to*, *in from*, *out from*, *away from*, *out of*, etc., in which the adv. expresses the general direction of motion, and the prep. specifies or has reference to a particular point or place. In the case of *in to*, the two words may refer to the same space, as in 'he went *in to* the house', or the *to* may refer to something which is *in* the space entered, as in 'he went *in* to the patient'; it is from the former of these that the combined *into* has arisen; in the latter the words are still written separate. But in early MSS. and editions this is often neglected; not only are the words often written separate when the sense is combined, but they are sometimes written in one, when the sense is the unconnected *in to* (a person, etc.). In *in to*, the *n* is long; in *into* the *n* is shortened by its rapid passage into the allied mute, *t*.]

General Sense:—The preposition expressing motion from without to a point within limits of space, time, condition, circumstance, etc.; the motion which results in the position expressed by IN, or which is directed towards that position.

In the Teutonic languages, as in Latin, this was originally expressed by the prep. *in* followed by the accusative or case of direction, and so distinguished from the simple notion of position expressed by *in* with the locative (or dative); but, when the case-endings were becoming weakened or lost in OE., so that the language was losing the power of making the distinction expressed in Latin by *in aquā*, *in aquam*, the periphrasis *in tó*, *intó*, was substituted for the latter. The other Teutonic langs., having retained the inflexions, esp. in the article and demonstrative words, have not required a parallel formation: cf. Ger. *in dem (im) wasser*, *in das (ins) wasser*. In OE. *intó* was usually, like the simple *tó*, construed with the dative; but also, not infrequently, with the accusative, like the simple *in* (*on*) which it superseded, or the L. *in* which it rendered: see sense 1.

As the prep. *in*, partly from its OE. blending with *on* (see IN *prep.* 2), partly from its identification with L. *in*, had various uses now usually expressed by other prepositions, so *into* was formerly used in senses now properly expressed by *unto*, *upon*, *towards*, *against*, etc.: see II.

The earlier use of *in* to express motion died out gradually, so that there long remained (and still remain) phrases and constructions in which *in* has the sense of *into* (see IN *prep.* 31); conversely, in some dialects, and esp. in Central and North-eastern Scotch, *into* was extended to express position, and thus took the sense of *in* (cf. F. *en*, *dans* in, into): see III.

A. *prep.* **I.** Of motion or direction: ordinary uses.

1. a. Expressing motion to a position within a space or thing: To a point within the limits of; to the interior of; so as to enter. In reference to a space or thing having material extension. Regularly after verbs of going, coming, bringing, putting, sending, and the like.

a **1000** *O.E. Chron.* (Parker MS.) an. 876 Her hiene bestæl se here into Werham. *Ibid.* an. 877 Her cuom se here into Escan ceastre from Werham. *c* **1000** ÆLFRIC *Gen.* vii. 7 Noe eode into þam arce. *c* **1000** *Ags. Gosp.* Matt. iv. 24 Ða ferde hys hlisa into ealle Syriam. —— Mark xvi. 15 Farað into ealne middan-eard. *a* **1100** *O.E. Chron.* (Laud MS.) an. 1016 þa ferdon hi in to Stæfford scire & into Scrobbes byriȝ & to Leȝeceastre. *Ibid.* an. 1083 Sume urnon in to cyrcean .. & hi ferdon æfter heom into þam mynstre. **11..** *Ibid.* an. 1100 Se cyng .. þone biscop .. into þam ture on Lundene let ȝebringon. *c* **1175** *Lamb. Hom.* 85 Þe corne þe me scal don in to þe gernere þet is in to heuene. *c* **1200** ORMIN 8706 Helyas forrþrihht anan þær stah innto þatt karrte. **1297** R. GLOUC. (Rolls) 2700 He fley in to walis. *a* **1300** *Cursor M.* 7552 (Gött.) Wid þis he went in to þe place. *c* **1340** *Ibid.* 13459 (Trin.) Ihesus clomb vp into a hille [*v.rr.* vn till, intill, vn to a fell(e)]. **1382** WYCLIF *Matt.* xxviii. 7 Lo he schal go bifore ȝou in to Galilee. *c* **1450** *Merlin* 17 They entred in to a chamber. **1535** COVERDALE *Gen.* vi. 18 Thou shalt go in to the Arcke. **1652** J. WRIGHT tr. *Camus' Nature's Paradox* 319 Beeing come into the presence of him, whom hee had so dearely loved. **1658** W. SANDERSON *Graphice* 81 Strike into the brick or stone-wall, stumps of head-nails. **1759** *Chron.* in *Ann. Reg.* 63/1 No rascally piccaroon, or pirate, could have fired worse stuff into us. **1821** KEATS *Isabella* viii, I may speak my grief into thine ear. **1839** THIRLWALL *Greece* I. VI. 215 He made an expedition into Samaria, to punish the Samaritans. **1855** TENNYSON *Maud* I. xxii. 1 Come into the garden, Maud.

b. Also with verbs in which the idea of motion is not explicitly expressed.

971 *Blickl. Hom.* 79 Hi .. wið feo sealdon [þæt folc] wide into leodscipas. *c* **1205** LAY. 29631 þu scalt .. in to hefneriche. *c* **1250** *Kent. Serm.* in *O.E. Misc.* 33 For to here [= hire] werkmen in-to his winyarde. ? *a* **1500** *Chester Pl.* x. 274 Upon myne asse shalt thou now sit, into Egipt till we hytt. **1503–4** *Act 19 Hen. VII*, c. 34 *Preamble*, The seid Piers Werbek .. aryved into this Land. **1622** LAUD *Wks.* (1853) III. 141, I wrote to my Lord of Buckingham into Spain. *a* **1641** BP. MOUNTAGU *Acts & Mon.* 327 In 749, he was employed into Pannonia, against the rebels. **1657** R. LIGON *Barbadoes* (1673) 103 That the girders be strong, and very well Dove-tayld, one into another. **1703** MOXON *Mech. Exerc.* 206 A Pin .. to fit hard and stiff into the round Hole. **1728** SCHEUCHZER in *Phil. Trans.* XXXV. 588 It .. looses itself jointly with that River into the Adriatick Gulf. **1843** *Blackw. Mag.* LIV. 779 He .. bit into it with the furious eagerness of a wolf. **1895** SIR A. KEKEWICH in *Law Times Rep.* LXXIII. 663/1 A sensible limitation which can easily be read into deed or will.

c. With the verb understood by ellipsis, or expressed in a verbal sb. or other word.

c **1489** CAXTON *Sonnes of Aymon* ix. 227 The one waye was towarde Fraunce, the other in to Spayne, the other in to Galyce, and the fourth in to Gascoyn. **1610** *Chester's Tri.* Particulars (Chetham Soc.) 1 [He] stood upon his hands with his feet into the Ayre. **1670** BAXTER *Cure Ch. Div.* 356 What influence it may have into our conclusions. *a* **1677** HALE *Prim. Orig. Man.* II. iv. 157 Which may be the material constituents or ingredients into Artificial Structures. **1691** RAY *Acc. Err.* in *Collect. Words* 160 That *D* is an ingredient into it Children do easily discern. **1852** MRS. CARLYLE *Lett.* II. 195 Darwin is into his new house. **1887** *Pall Mall G.* 28 Dec. 2/1 Establishing special tariffs for the sole benefit of German exports into Russia. **1892** R. KIPLING *Barrack-r. Ballads, East & West* 13 At dusk he harries the Abazai—at dawn he is into Bonair.

2. Pregnant uses. **a.** = Into the possession of.

a **1100** *O.E. Chron.* (Laud MS.) an. 675 Nu ȝife ic Sce Peter to dæi in to his minstre .. þas landes. *Ibid.* an. 852 To þæt forewearde þæt æfter his dæi scolde þæt land in to þe minstre. **1872** E. W. ROBERTSON *Hist. Ess.* 195 *note*, In the following year [998] Leofwine, Wulfstan's son, willed some lands 'into Westminster'. **1883** *Law Times Rep.* L. 192/2 There were alternative modes of getting the legal estate into the same person.

b. The name of the thing or place after *into* often includes or means its action or function. Cf. IN *prep.* 1 b, 7.

1382 WYCLIF *Jas.* v. 4 The cry of hem entride in to the erys of the Lord of hoostis. **1535** COVERDALE *Gen.* xiv. 20 God .. hath delyuered thine enemies in to thy handes. **1553** T. WILSON *Rhet.* (1580) 216 Reason might beate thus muche into our heades. **1606** SHAKS. *Ant. & Cl.* v. ii. 22 Y'are falne into a Princely hand. **1625** LAUD *Wks.* (1847) I. 116 When he first came into the throne. **1659** D. PELL *Impr. Sea* 20 Not fit to put into the place of government. **1674** tr. *Martiniere's Voy. N. Countries* 90 Our Elks being harnessed, and put into the Sledges. **1849** MACAULAY *Hist. Eng.* v. I. 540 An Earl of Devonshire could not engage to bring ten men into the field.

c. Used with collectives, it frequently expresses entrance or admission to membership or participation. Cf. IN *prep.* 3, 7.

a **1548** HALL *Chron.*, *Edw. IV* 231 b, I will neither enter into your league, nor take truce with the Frenche kyng. **1613** PURCHAS *Pilgrimage* (1614) 619 They would admit none into their Societie, but such as were learned. **1643** MARSHALL *Let. Vind. Ministry* 27 Proclamations .. that no Papists should be entertained into His Majesties Army. **1709** STEELE *Tatler* No. 15 ¶2 It was one of the most wealthy Families in Great Britain into which I was born. *a* **1715** BURNET *Own Time* (1823) I. 332 Many .. ingenious men went into the society for natural philosophy. **1840** MACAULAY *Ess.*, *Ranke* (1887) 584 Marrying his son into one of the great continental houses. **1849** —— *Hist. Eng.* i. I. 39 A class into which his own children must descend. **1878** MORLEY *Condorcet* 47 Condorcet was elected into the Academy.

3. In reference to non-physical realms, regions of thought, departments or faculties of the mind, etc., treated as having extension or content. Cf. IN *prep.* 8.

1513 MORE in Grafton *Chron.* (1568) II. 777 These things .. beaing beaten into the Dukes minde. **1568** GRAFTON *Chron.* II. 757 Richarde .. began .. to chalenge the Crowne, puttyng his clayme into the Parliament. **1601** R. JOHNSON *Kingd. & Commw.* (1603) 258 To pierce .. into the secrete counsels of the king of Spaine. *a* **1656** HALES *Gold. Rem.* (1688) 73, I will therefore recall into your memories so much of my former meditations. **1875** JOWETT *Plato* (ed. 2) III. 275 We shall have to take Damon into our counsels. **1887** L. CARROLL *Game of Logic* iv. 93 That lets me into a little fact about you!

4. a. In reference to a state or condition.

c **1000** *Ags. Gosp.* Matt. xxv. 21 Ga into þines hlafordes blisse. *c* **1175** *Lamb. Hom.* 67 Ne led us noht in to costnunga. *c* **1230** *Hali Meid.* 5 Nis ha witerliche akast & in to þeowdom idrahen. **1340** *Ayenb.* 117 We ziggeþ 'Lyene uader, ne led ous naȝt in-to uondinge, þet is ne þole naȝt þet we go in-to consentinge'. *c* **1400** MAUNDEV. xi. (1839) 89 He fell in to seknesse. **1513** MORE in Grafton *Chron.* (1568) II. 756 Many of them .. growen into his favor. **1551** T. WILSON *Logike* (1580) 16 When men knowe not, thei .. fall into errour. **1589** R. HARVEY *Pl. Perc.* (1860) 19 He put those lies into print vnlawfully. **1644** LAUD *Wks.* (1854) IV. 152, I grew into want. **1671** LADY MARY BERTIE in *12th Rep. Hist. MSS. Comm.* App. v. 23 Wee are all goeing into mourning for the Dutchesse of York. **1731** *Gentl. Mag.* I. 391/1 This put Bluster into such a Passion. **1831** CARLYLE *Sart. Res.* III. xii, An ambrosial joy as of over-weariness falling into sleep. **1849** MACAULAY *Hist. Eng.* vi. II. 117 The Scottish treasury was put into commission. **1885** S. COX *Expos.* Ser. I. iii. 37 He was before the first Adam, and called him into being. **1895** *Law Times Rep.* LXXIII. 21/2 [He] got into difficulties and he became bankrupt in 1880.

b. The state or condition may be expressed by a concrete sb. (Akin to 2 b.)

1716 [see BURST *v.* 6 c]. **1766** GOLDSM. *Vic. W.* xxv, They now seemed all repentance and, melting into tears, came [etc.]. **1802** MAR. EDGEWORTH *Moral T.*, *Angelina* iv, Angelina burst into tears. **1860** DICKENS *Uncom. Trav.* xiii, Folk who come unexpectedly into a little property.

5. In reference to occupation or action.

c **1475** *Rauf Coilȝear* 90 Into sic talk fell thay. **1576** FLEMING *Panopl. Epist.* 228 Fell into an exceeding great laughter. **1635** J. HAYWARD tr. *Biondi's Banish'd Virg.* 65 The Prince afterwards falling into discourse of the generall affaires. **1711** STEELE *Spect.* No. 49 ¶2 What Measures the Allies must enter into. **1712** BUDGELL *Spect.* No. 365 ¶11 Since I am got into Quotations, I shall conclude this Head with Virgil's Advice to young People. **1843** *Blackw. Mag.* LIV. 806 The crowd burst into yells of applause. **1885** *Manch. Exam.* 26 June 5/3 To coax or cajole the Pope into making an appointment. **1887** A. BIRRELL *Obiter Dicta* Ser. II. 174 Burke flung himself into farming.

6. a. Introducing the substance or form into which anything turns or grows, or is changed, moulded, fashioned, or made.

c **1250** *Kent. Serm.* in *O.E. Misc.* 29 [The water] hasteliche was i-went into wyne. *c* **1350** *Will. Palerne* 4105 Sche chaunged my sone In to a wilde werwolf. **1387** TREVISA *Higden* (Rolls) I. 165 Sche .. kutte þe hyde into a þong þat was ful long and ful smal. *c* **1400** MAUNDEV. Prol. (1839) 5, I haue put this boke out of latyn into frensch, and translated it aȝen out of Frensch into englyssch. *Ibid.* (Roxb.) v. 15 Þe water .. congelez in to gude salt. **1513** MORE in Grafton *Chron.* (1568) II. 801 The King and the Queene chaunged their robes into cloth of Golde. **1568** GRAFTON *Chron.* I. 34 That one vowell may be chaunged in a word, and specially, A into O, which in some mannes mouth soundeth oftentymes lyke. **1617** MORYSON *Itin.* III. 115 Fresh curds newly pressed, and made into little cheeses. **1657** R. LIGON *Barbadoes* (1673) 72 The Indians .. spin it into fine thred. **1658** W. BURTON *Itin. Anton.* 26 Valleys exalted into Mountaines, and great Hills abased into Valleys. **1792** *Hist.* in *Ann. Reg.* 10/2 Anarchy, according to the nature of extremes, ran into despotism. **1835** W. IRVING *Tour Prairies* 74 The twilight thickened into night. **1865** HOOK *Lives Abps.* IV. xiii. 205 They .. had formed themselves into a school. **1875** JOWETT *Plato* (ed. 2) I. 214 If we knew how to convert stones into gold. *Mod.* The stalks and leaves are collected into heaps and burned.

b. Introducing the condition or result brought about by some action.

c **1540** *Pilgr. T.* 283 in *Thynne's Animadv.* (1865) App. i. 85 To teache men in-to better lyf. **1621** BURTON *Anat. Mel.* III. ii. VI. i. (1651) 547 Till he be fully wained from anger .. and habituated into another course. **1678** BUTLER *Hud.*, *Lady's Answer* 40 The motives which t' induce, Or fright us into love, you use. **1742** YOUNG *Nt. Th.* VI. 697 All dies into new life. **1780** COWPER *Table-talk* 546 Neglected talents rust into decay. **1813** BYRON *Br. Abydos* I. xi, I will kiss thee into rest. **1849** MACAULAY *Hist. Eng.* v. I. 538 The Covenanters had been persecuted into insurrection. **1890** L. STEPHEN in *Dict. Nat. Biog.* XXI. 251/1 Birched into Latin grammar by his master.

7. Introducing the parts produced by division, breaking, folding, and the like.

1382 WYCLIF *1 Sam.* xv. 33 Samuel hewide hym into gobbetis before the Lord. **1390** GOWER *Conf.* III. 244 His mantel .. He kut it into pieces twelve. **1551** T. WILSON *Logike* (1580) 15 The whole is divided into his partes, as .. The bodie is divided into the hedde, beallie, handes and feete. **1676** tr. *Guillatiere's Voy. Athens* 116 The Shore .. bends into three several bows, which do make so many Harbours. **1798** W. YONGE in *Beddoes' Contrib. Phys. & Med. Knowl.* (1799) 300 A cambric handkerchief, folded into six or eight doubles. **1815** W. H. IRELAND *Scribbleomania* 192 *note*, The antique was broken into several pieces. **1886** SIR N. LINDLEY in *Law Rep.* 32 Ch. Div. 28 The authorities .. are divisible into two classes. **1892** *Law Times* XCIII. 417/1 The area of the City .. is partitioned into twenty-eight wards.

8. Used technically with the vb. MULTIPLY, q.v.

e.g. Two numbers multiplied into each other.

9. As an addition or accession to: as ***into the bargain, into the boot*** (cf. BARGAIN 7, BOOT *sb.*[1] 1). [Perh. = 'in, to the bargain', 'in, to boot': cf. IN *adv.* 4.]

1646 *Suckling's Poems* (ed. 2) Pref. 2 A man may buy the reputation of some Authours into the price of their Volume. **1659** WILLSFORD *Scales Comm.*, *Archit.* 14 The spar-feet and Eaves-board, are in common building, measured into the whole Roof. **1775** SHERIDAN *Rivals* II. ii, I'll make her the best husband in the world, and Lady O' Trigger into the bargain. **1885** ANSTEY *Tinted Venus* x. 121 A son-in-law with whom she had nothing in common, and who was a hairdresser into the bargain.

10. Expressing direction without actual motion of the agent after such verbs as *turn*, *look*, *search*.

1605 SHAKS. *Macb.* I. iii. 58 If you can looke into the Seedes of Time. **1634** SIR T. HERBERT *Trav.* 216 The Ile .. gives a large prospect into the Ocean. **1676** tr. *Guillatiere's Voy. Athens* 311 That you must .. search deeply into the merits of the Cause. **1783** WATSON *Philip III* (1839) 203 They did not take time to inquire into their number. **1823** J. F. COOPER *Pioneers* xxxvii, He examined into every fissure in the crags. **1891** *Law Times* XCII. 105/1 [They] inquire minutely into the evidence.

11. Introducing a period of time to the midst of which anything advances or continues.

1594 SHAKS. *Rich. III*, v. iii. 234 How farre into the Morning is it Lords? **1861** DICKENS *Gt. Expect.* lii, We had now got into the month of March. **1861** M. PATTISON *Ess.* (1889) I. 47 This obligation they discharged far down into Protestant and peaceful times. **1885** *Manch. Exam.* 10 Sept. 5/5 The drizzling rain .. continued far into the night. **1886** RUSKIN *Præterita* I. viii. 249 Far on into life [we] were glad when any chance brought us together again. **1890** FENN *Double Knot* III. xi. 154 It was well into the next season before they were back.

II. Obsolete senses, related to ME. uses of *in*, or rendering L. *in* with accus.

†**12.** Unto, even unto, even to (a place or point); to the very... *Obs.*

c **1205** LAY. 4298 Belin ȝef his leue broþer anne dal of his londe .. to halden norð in to þare sæ. *Ibid.* 14099 Heo hatieð þe swiðe in to þan bare dæðe. **13..** *K. Alis.* 777 Bulsifal neied so loude, That hit schrillith into the cloude. **1525** LD. BERNERS *Froiss.* II. cxxxvii. [cxxxiii.] 382 In the chapell he was vnarmed of all his peces into his doublet. *a* **1548** HALL *Chron.*, *Hen. VIII* 63 [They] came wel appareled to Westmynster, and sodeynly stryped them into their shertes.

†**13.** Towards, in the direction of. *Obs.* (Cf. 10.)

c **1290** *S. Eng. Leg.* I. 345/11 Abouten ei3te hondert mile Engelond long is Fram þe South into þe North. *a* **1300** *Cursor M.* 3384 (Gött.) þai held..þe landes þat lay in to þe est. *c* **1430** LYDG. *Min. Poems* (Percy Soc.) 61 Youre hertis ye lyft up into the est, And al your body and knees bowe a-downe. **1568** GRAFTON *Chron.* I. 56 The first of these foure wayes was named Fosse, the which stretcheth out of the South, into the North. **1652** NEEDHAM tr. *Selden's Mare Cl.* 38 A streight line drawn..from the North-East into the South.

†**14.** Unto, until, on to, up to (a time or date).

c **1380** *Sir Ferumb.* 1420 Fro þat day in to þys myn herte haþ he yraft. *c* **1380** WYCLIF *Last Age Chirche* p. xxvi, Fro þe by-gynnynge of ebrew lettris in to Crist..weren two and twenty hundriddis of yeeris. *c* **1449** PECOCK *Repr.* 86 Into tyme that thei schulden falle into fi3ting. *c* **1450** tr. *De Imitatione* III. xx. 86 Fro þe houre of my birþe into the daie of my goynge oute of þis worlde. **1534** MORE *on Passion* Wks. 1314/1 Hee loued theym in to the ende.

†**15.** To the number of, as many as. *Obs.*

c **1400** MAUNDEV. (1839) xviii. 191 He hath also in to a xiiij mil Olifauntz or mo. **1441** *Plumpton Corr.* (Camden) p. lvi, Sir William Plompton with other officers came to Burghbrig ..& with him into xxiiij persons.

†**16.** Unto, to (a thing or person). *Obs.*

1382 WYCLIF *Ps.* cxxxiii[i]. 2 Heueth vp 3oure hondis in to holi thingis. *c* **1440** *Jacob's Well* (E.E.T.S.) 2 3oure soule, in þis pytt of corrupte watyr, nedyth to cry in-to god. *c* **1449** PECOCK *Repr.* 181 Sche dide a good werk into him. *Ibid.* II. xx. 267 If..the freend come into him personali. **1609** BIBLE (Douay) *Jer.* xliii. 11 He shal strike the Land of Ægypt: those that into death, into death..and those that into the sword, into the sword. **1611** SHAKS. *Cymb.* I. vi. 167 That he enchants Societies into him.

†**17.** Unto (a purpose or result); in order to, with a view to. *Obs.*

1382 WYCLIF *Matt.* xxvi. 28 My blood..whiche shal be shed out for many in to remissioun of synnys. *c* **1400** *Apol. Loll.* 4 He..leuiþ to wirke, & doþ contrarily directly, & in to þe harme of his maistir. *c* **1449** PECOCK *Repr.* II. vii. 181 Sche did it into the mynde of him and..into the biriyng of him. **1502** *Bury Wills* (Camden) 95 Into witnesse herof..I haue put my seale.

†**18.** In order to be; for; as: after *choose, elect, take*, etc. *Obs.*

1382 WYCLIF *Ps.* cxxxi[i]. 13 He ches it in to dwelling to hym. *c* **1400** *Apol. Loll.* 4 If ani chosun of God Himselue & of þe puple, in to pope or prelate, & ordend in to vicar of Crist [etc.]. **1422** tr. *Secreta Secret., Priv. Priv.* 162 Agage the kynge of amalech into his prysoner he toke.

†**19.** Upon on: of motion or direction. *Obs.*

c **1375** *Sc. Leg. Saints, Egyptiane* 703 In-to þe floure þan done fel I. *c* **1380** *Antecrist* in Todd *Three Treat. Wyclif* (1851) 116 Hise y3en shule loke in to pore men. *c* **1380** WYCLIF *Sel. Wks.* III. 351 Certes synne of siche children turneþ in to heed of þer fadir. *c* **1449** PECOCK *Repr.* I. xvii. 97 That 3e bileeue in to him which he sende.

†**20.** To, among (a number). *Obs.* Cf. 7.

1551 ROBINSON tr. *More's Utop.* II. i. (1895) 119 The worke beyng diuyded into so great a numbre of workemen.

†**21.** Defining the particular part of anything in which it is penetrated, pierced, etc. Cf. IN *prep.* 5.

1523 LD. BERNERS *Froiss.* I. ccxlii. 356 Kyng Henry.. strake kyng Dampeter into the body. *a* **1548** HALL *Chron., Hen. VI*, 186 b, Putting of his gorget, sodainly wᵗ an arrowe [he] was stricken into the throte. **1641** J. JACKSON *True Evang. T.* III. 201 John James..with a rusty dagger..did stab into the breast Peter Heywood. **1719** DE FOE *Crusoe* I. ii, I..fired again, and shot him [a lion] into the head. **1788** *New Lond. Mag.* 8 He was shot into the shoulder.

III. 22. Of position: = IN. (After 1400 characteristically *Sc.*)

971 *Blickl. Hom.* 205 Michael..himsylfa þæt tacn [*MS.* tanc] þæs si3es 3esette & 3ecyðde into þy swiðan slæpe. **1297** R. GLOUC. (Rolls) 10540 Worre was in to al þis lond. *c* **1330** *Assump. Virg.* 772 (B.M.MS.) Tho wist þe apostles, I-wis, The bodi was in to paradis. **1375** BARBOUR *Bruce* I. 602 The Kyng sat into parleament. *c* **1380** *Sir Ferumb.* 4948 He suffreþ my worschip spille in tal þys countre wyde. *a* **1400** *Octouian* 60 In Parys was y-feld ech a sale Into all the toun. *c* **1470** HENRYSON *Mor. Fab.* (Mait. Cl.) 56 The same season into ane soft morning. **1508** DUNBAR *Tua Mariit Wemen* 315 Mercy in to womanheid is a mekle vertu. **1552** LYNDESAY *Monarche* 1216 Bot, in to rest, schorte tyme indurit his ryng. **1552** ABP. HAMILTON *Catech.* (1884) 26 Ane man that behaldis his bodaly face into ane myrrour. *a* **1572** KNOX *Hist. Ref.* Wks. 1846 I. 73 Deuouring woulves into sheip skynnes. **1585** JAS. I *Ess. Poesie* (Arb.) 25 Her nyne-voced mouth resembled into sound The daunce harmonious making heauen resound. **1606** G. W[OODCOCKE] tr. *Hist. Ivstine* 81 a, He came to Siracuse, into which Citty he was entertained as amongst other inhabyters. **1626** JAS. HAIG in J. Russell *Haigs* vii. (1881) 178 Nothing..whereof into your letter you did assure me she had written. **1658** *Kirk Sess. Rec.* in Campbell *Balmerino* (1899) 409 The hous..free and sufficient for dwelling into. *a* **1776** *'Get up and bar the door'*. (Herd's Coll.) 'What ails ye at the puddin' bree, That boils into the pan?' *Mod. north-east Sc.* 'He's bidin' into a new hoose.'

23. Interested or involved in; knowledgeable about. *colloq.*

1969 *Rolling Stone* 28 Jan. 19/1, I tend to like the stuff the rock groups are doing because they're creative and original, and that's something I'm very much into. **1969** *Down Beat* 20 Mar. 17/1 She is a Libra, for those of you who are into that. **1969** *It* 4–17 July 15/3 He was basically into being a hustler, which he was very, very good at. **1971** *Ink* 12 June 19/1 This should have been the high-light of the evening, but the audience just wasn't into it. **1971** *New Yorker* 11 Sept. 48 First I was into Zen, then I was into peace, then I was into love, then I was into freedom, then I was into religion. Now I'm into money. **1973** *Listener* 15 Feb. 209/1 Margaret is 'into' astrology, and consults the *I-Ching* each morning.

B. *adj. Math.* Used to designate a mapping (of one set 'into' another (INTO *prep.* 6 a)) that is not necessarily 'onto'.

1949 S. LEFSCHETZ *Introd. Topology* 215 (Index), Into transformation. **1958** K. S. MILLER *Elem. Mod. Abstr. Algebra* i. 21 Since the mapping is into, there may exist elements in $\bar{S}$ which have no preimage in *S*. **1968** E. T. Copson *Metric Spaces* vii. 85 Every 'onto' mapping is 'into' but not all 'into' mappings are 'onto'.

in-toed ('ɪnˌtəʊd), *a.* [IN *adv.* 13.] Having the toes turned inwards.

1835 *Fraser's Mag.* XII. 489 To which large in-toed feet are as regularly attached. **1884** *Good Words* Nov. 746/2 Their in-toed feet encased in sandals [in Shetland].

intolerability (ɪnˌtɒlərəˈbɪlɪtɪ). Also 6 -toll-. [f. next + -ITY: in late L. *intolerābilitās*, obs. F. *intollerabilité* (Godef.).] The quality of being intolerable; intolerableness.

1597 A. M. tr. *Guillemeau's Fr. Chirurg.* 48/1 Accompanied with bitinge payn, with intollerabilitye, and with a continuall commotion. **1813** SHELLEY *Q. Mab* Poet. Wks. (1891) 48/2 Notes, If the mind sinks beneath the weight of one, is it an alleviation to increase the intolerability of the burthen? *a* **1849** POE *Marginalia* Wks. 1864 III. 485 The goodness of your true pun is in direct ratio of its intolerability.

b. An intolerable thing.

1602 DEKKER *Satirom.* Wks. 1873 I. 242 Make him proove these intolerabilities.

intolerable (ɪnˈtɒlərəb(ə)l), *a.* (*adv.*) Also 5–8 intoll-. [ad. L. *intolerābilis* that cannot bear, that cannot be borne, f. *in-* (IN-[3]) + *tolerābilis* TOLERABLE: cf. F. *intolérable* (13th c. in Littré).]

1. That cannot be tolerated, borne, or put up with; unendurable, unbearable, insupportable, insufferable. **a.** physically.

1435 MISYN *Fire of Love* 89 þa sall criste scharp & intollerabyll to þer eyne for þam þer hartis in þis lyfe felt hym neuer sweet. **1483** CAXTON *Cato* I v, Payne and tormente eternalle intollerabile and wythoute ende. **1564** GOLDING *Justine* 65 (R.) He was tormented with so intollerable paine, that he desired to haue a sworde to ridde him selfe out of it wythall. **1607** E. GRIMSTONE tr. *Goulart's Mem. Hist.* 336 [They] committed the innocent Sonne to prison, where the intollerable torment of the torture made him confesse that [etc.]. **1756** BURKE *Subl. & B.* II. xxi, No smells or tastes can produce a grand sensation, except excessive bitters, and intolerable stenches. **1803** *Med. Jrnl.* X. 483 Patients chiefly suffer from the intolerable itching. **1861** ALFORD in *Life* (1873) 311 The glorious Coliseum itself, basking in a cloudless, intolerable sun.

b. mentally or morally.

1494 FABYAN *Chron.* VII. ccxxxv. 272 For yᵉ intollerable dedis of yᵉ Iewes. **1513** MORE in Grafton *Chron.* (1568) II. 792 The king..was..every where over all the realme intollerable. **1593** SHAKS. *2 Hen. VI*, I. i. 175 Yet let vs watch the haughtie Cardinall, His insolence is more intollerable Then all the Princes in the Land beside. **1692** SOUTH *12 Serm.* (1697) I. 231 A blind man sitting in the Chimney corner is pardonable enough, but sitting at the Helm he is Intolerable. **1759** ROBERTSON *Hist. Scot.* IV. Wks. 1813 I. 269 To a woman, and a queen, such behaviour was intolerable. **1796** BURKE *Regic. Peace* iii. Wks. VIII. 366 The intolerable licence with which the newspapers break.. the rules of decorum. **1883** FROUDE *Short Stud.* IV. I. iii. 31 The conduct of the lower class of clergy was..growing daily more intolerable.

†**c.** In loose sense, as a strong intensive: Excessive, extreme, exceedingly great. (Cf. *awful.*)

1544 *Act 35 Hen. VIII*, c. 12 His maiestie..hath taken intollerable paines, travaile studye and laboure, in his owne moste royall persone. **1596** SHAKS. *1 Hen. IV*, II. iv. 592 O monstrous, but one halfe penny-worth of Bread to this intollerable deale of Sacke? **1600** J. PORY tr. *Leo's Africa* II. 378 Their Ganga, who now gave out intolerable brags. **1725** *Wodrow Corr.* (1843) III. 224 In our Highlands and Islands the parishes are extremely large, some twenty, thirty, some more, miles in length... Ministers..are..able to do little in such spacious and intolerable parishes.

2. That cannot be withstood, irresistible. *rare.*

1432–50 tr. *Higden* (Rolls) I. 91 Thei scholde be intollerable and invincible, if they my3hte haue the vertu of perseueraunce after theire impetuosite. **1614** RALEIGH *Hist. World* IV. iii. §i. (1634) 487 Their force was intolerable, but for want of good guidance, ineffectual. **1878** *Harper's Mag.* Feb. 439 To..scourge away the remnant of Hassan's men with intolerable musketry.

†**B.** as *adv.* Intolerably, insufferably; also, as a strong intensive, Exceedingly, extremely. *Obs.*

1592 CHETTLE *Kinde-hart's Dr.* (1841) 23 This, taken at a draught before the fit, is intollerable good. **1596** SHAKS. *Tam. Shr.* I. ii. 89 Her onely fault..Is, that she is intollerable curst. **1645** BP. HALL *Remedy Discontents* 29 How intolerable tedious would it prove in the fruition? **1716** C'TESS COWPER *Diary* (1864) 100 Dr. Dunster preached an intolerable dull Sermon.

intolerableness (ɪnˈtɒlərəb(ə)lnɪs). [-NESS.]

1. The quality or condition of being intolerable; unbearableness.

1579 TWYNE *Phisicke agst. Fort.* II. cxiv. 304 b, Yf..vnto the intollerablenesse of the payne, there be added some farther greefe. **1668** R. STEELE *Husbandm. Call.* vi. (1672) 179 The intolerableness of that fire that is never quenched. **1851** H. MELVILLE *Whale* xiii, Such is the endlessness, yea, the intolerableness of all earthly effort. **1853** RUSKIN *Stones Ven.* III. iii. §67. 158 Of the grotesque in our own Shakespeare I need hardly speak, nor of its intolerableness to his French critics.

†**2.** Incapacity of endurance; intolerance. *Obs.*

1597 A. M. tr. *Guillemeau's Fr. Chirurg.* 17 b/2 Throughe the intollerablenes and greate dolore or payne of the patient. **1598** FLORIO, *Intoleranza*, intolerablenes, impacience.

intolerably (ɪnˈtɒlərəblɪ), *adv.* [f. as prec. + -LY[2].] In an intolerable manner or degree; so as to be intolerable; unbearably, insufferably.

1482 *Monk of Evesham* (Arb.) 52 Y haue ben caste downe hed longe into a grete hepe of brennynyng money amonge the whiche y brente ful intolerably. **1600** J. PORY tr. *Leo's Africa* II. 208 It is..so intolerably cold, that onely that side therof is habitable which looketh towards Fez. **1687** A. LOVELL tr. *Thevenot's Trav.* III. 104 It is intollerably hot there from March till July. **1710** T. FULLER *Pharm. Extemp.* 164 The Pain rages intollerably. **1824** DIBDIN *Libr. Comp.* 744 These cantos became intolerably dull. **1856** KANE *Arct. Expl.* I. xxxii. 445 The transition..to 46° below zero..was intolerably trying.

†**b.** As a strong intensive: Excessively, extremely, 'awfully'. *Obs.*

1768 STERNE *Sent. Journ.* (1778) II. 110 (*Case Conscience*), I..cannot say I was intolerably out of temper with the man. **1821** *Examiner* 1 Apr. 205/1 Her voice and eye were intolerably pleasant.

intolerance (ɪnˈtɒlərəns). [ad. L. *intolerāntia* impatience, unendurableness, f. *intolerānt-em* INTOLERANT: cf. F. *intolérance* 'impatiencie' (Cotgr.).] The fact or quality of being intolerant.

1. The fact or habit of not tolerating or enduring (something); inability, or unwillingness, to tolerate or endure some particular thing; incapacity of endurance. Const. *of.*

1765 LOWTH *Lett. to Warburton* 62 You, my Lord, is it You of all men living, that stand forth to accuse another of Intolerance of Opinions! **1844** H. H. WILSON *Brit. India* I. 237 In his intolerance of supposed official peculation, [he] inflicted severe punishment before its justice was undeniably established. **1844** DUFTON *Deafness* 81 Attended with tinnitus aurium, and great intolerance of sound.

2. *spec.* Absence of tolerance for difference of opinion or practice, esp. in religious matters; denial of the right to differ; narrow-minded or bigoted opposition to dissent.

1790 BURKE *Fr. Rev.* Wks. V. 209 Nothing was wanted but the power of carrying the intolerance of the tongue and of the pen into a persecution which would strike at property, liberty, and life. **1809–10** COLERIDGE *Friend* (1865) 20 If any temptation can provoke a well-regulated temper to intolerance, it is the shameless assertion, that truth and false-hood are indifferent in their own natures. **1838** THIRLWALL *Greece* xxxii. IV. 273 Intolerance, as usual, kept pace with superstition and fanaticism. **1857** BUCKLE *Civiliz.* I. iv. 171 The great antagonist of intolerance is not humanity, but Knowledge.

†**in'tolerancy.** *Obs. rare.* [ad. L. *intolerāntia*: see prec. and -ANCY.] = prec.

1623 COCKERAM, *Intolerancie*, impatiencie. **1768** *Woman of Honor* II. 104 Too supercilious an intolerancy of fools. **1798** PENNANT *Hindoostan* I. 56 Mahometan persecution and intolerancy.

intolerant (ɪnˈtɒlərənt), *a.* (*sb.*) [ad. L. *intolerānt-em*, f. *in-* (IN[3]) + *tolerānt-em*, pr. pple. of *tolerāre* to bear, endure, TOLERATE. Cf. F. *intolérant* (1732 Dict. Trév.).] **A.** *adj.* Not tolerant; wanting in tolerance or toleration.

1. a. Not having the habit or capacity of tolerating (something); unable, or unwilling, to tolerate or endure (something specified). Const. *of.*

a **1735** ARBUTHNOT (J.), The powers of human bodies being limited and intolerant of excesses. **1864** BURTON *Scot Abr.* I. v. 275 At one period aristocracy and government are intolerant of the poor and of liberty—at another, the populace are intolerant of rank and order. **1874** SYMONDS *Sk. Italy & Greece* (1898) I. i. 4 We are intolerant of everything that is not simple. **1896** *Spectator* 31 Oct. 583/1 You..hear physicians say that this or that man's constitution is 'intolerant' of this or that drug, intolerant, say, of quinine or iron.

b. *Ecol.* Of trees or other plants: unable to flourish in deep shade.

1898 G. PINCHOT *Adirondack Spruce* 5 The Poplar, a tree very intolerant of shade..rapidly takes possession of the soil. *Ibid.* 22 If the intolerant species can get the start, being often rapid of growth, they may hold their position by growing above the other trees about them. **1929** WEAVER & CLEMENTS *Plant Ecol.* xiv. 320 The leaves of intolerant trees can not make food in weak, diffuse light. **1952** P. W. RICHARDS *Tropical Rain Forest* iii. 42 Of the young trees in this patch of undergrowth the more light-demanding (intolerant) species respond more quickly than the shade-bearing (tolerant) species. **1965** G. L. CLARKE *Elem. Ecol.* (rev. ed.) vi. 233 Plants that require strong illumination and will not survive or develop in reduced light are referred to as intolerant species.

2. *spec.* That does not tolerate opinions or practices different from one's own, esp. in religious matters; that denies or refuses to others the right to differ or dissent; disposed to persecute those who differ.

1765 LOWTH *Lett. to Warburton* 62 Why then am I branded, as an intolerant Zealot? **1794** PALEY *Evid.* (1825) II. 250 The national temper of the Jews was intolerant. **1849** MACAULAY *Hist. Eng.* ii. I. 167 The House of Commons.. showed a strong disposition to check the intolerant loyalty of the Cavaliers. **1878** MORLEY *Crit. Misc.* Ser. I. *Carlyle* 200 Holding one or other of the rival creeds in its most extreme, exclusive and intolerant form.

B. *sb.* An intolerant person.

1765 LOWTH *Lett. to Warburton* 61 You might as well have concluded, that I was a Jew, or a Mahometan, as an Intolerant and a Persecutor. **1827** *Blackw. Mag.* XXII. 404 They are finished intolerants and exclusionists. **1881** PALGRAVE *Vis. Eng.* 159 Rival intolerants each 'gainst other flamed.

intolerantly (ɪnˈtɒlərəntlɪ), *adv.* [f. prec. + -LY[2].] In an intolerant manner or spirit; without tolerance.

1765 *Hist. Eur.* in *Ann. Reg.* 4/1 The most intolerantly zealous members of the persuasions they respectively belong to. **1874** GEO. ELIOT *College Breakf. P.* in *Jubal*, etc. 237 He gave five puffs Intolerantly sceptical, then said [etc.]. *Mod.* He spoke vehemently and intolerantly.

†**inˈtolerate,** *v. nonce-wd.* [IN-[3]. Cf. L. *intolerāre* not to bear, to take ill (*Notæ Tiron.*).] *trans.* Not to tolerate; to treat with intolerance.

1767 CHESTERF. *Lett.* (1792) IV. 251, I would have all intoleration intolerated in its turn.

†**inˈtolerating,** *a. Obs.* [IN-[3].] = INTOLERANT.

1710 SHAFTESB. *Charac.* (1737) III. Misc. II. ii. 86 They who..had once experienc'd this intolerating Spirit, cou'd no longer tolerate on their part. **1777** ROBERTSON *Hist. Amer.* II. VIII. 350 Many authors have represented the intolerating spirit of the Roman Catholic religion, as the cause of exterminating the Americans. **1839** J. ROGERS *Antipopopr.* I. ii. 67 When we contemplate popery upheld by intolerating persecution.

intoleration (ɪntɒləˈreɪʃən). *rare.* [IN-[3].] Want of toleration; intolerance.

1611 FLORIO, *Insopportanza*, intoleration. **1753** CHESTERF. *Lett.* (1792) IV. 34 This noise against the Jew bill proceeds from narrow mob-spirit of intoleration in religious ..matters. **1861** MUSGRAVE *By-roads* 73 To shock the mind of humanity by similar excesses of bigotry and merciless intoleration.

†**ˈin-toll.** *Sc. Obs.* [f. IN *adv.* 12 + TOLL.] A payment made to the bailie upon entering into possession of burghal property. Cf. IN-PENNY.

1872 C. INNES *Sc. Legal Antiq.* 91 In our older burgh usages, burghal subjects were transferred by the bailie taking a penny for in-toll and a penny for out-toll.

†**inˈtollerous,** *a. Obs. rare.* [f. stem of *intolerable*, etc. + -OUS.] Intolerable; insufferable.

1594 *Register Stationers' Comp.* in *N. & Q.* 3rd Ser. III. 3 An excellent newe ballad, declaringe..the intollerous pride nowe-a-daies used.

intomb(e, obs. form of ENTOMB.

‖**intombi** (ɪnˈtɒmbiː). [Xhosa, Zulu *i-ntombi* maiden.] (See quot. 1913.)

1809 R. COLLINS *Jrnl.* in D. Moodie *Record: Papers Native Tribes S. Afr.* (1842) v. 46 Cattle are never given for a Tumbee, but her father or brother is supplied with assagays by her keeper. **1833** S. KAY *Trav. Caffraria* xviii. 470 'That,' said he, 'contains the body of an *intombi* (young woman) who was killed by lightning from heaven, about two years ago.' **1855** J. W. COLENSO *Ten Weeks in Natal* 26 There is another special one [*sc.* reason] for the young men wishing to go home from time to time—namely, to make acquaintance with the *intombies*, or young women, whom they will one day acquire for wives. **1913** C. PETTMAN *Africanderisms* 228 *Intombi*,..a girl or young unmarried woman. **1947** L. HASTINGS *Dragons are Extra* vi. 118 The little girls, the intombis, were busy with bunches of twigs tidying up the huts.

intonable (ɪnˈtəʊnəb(ə)l), *a.* [f. INTONE *v.* + -ABLE.] Capable of being intoned; in quot. applied to a 'voiced' or sonant consonant.

1864 MAX MÜLLER *Sc. Lang.* Ser. II. iii. (1868) 133 The letter 'sh' as heard in 'sharp', and..'j' in the French 'jamais'; the former mute, the latter intonable.

‖**intonaco, -ico** (ɪnˈtəʊnəkəʊ, -ɪkəʊ). [It. *intonico*, formerly also *intonaco* plaster, f. *intonicare* to cover with plaster, L. type **intunicāre*, f. *tunica* coat, TUNIC.] The final coating of plaster spread upon a wall or other surface, esp. for fresco painting.

1806 J. DALLAWAY *Obs. Eng. Archit.* 216 Palladio, who.. so happily adopted intonaco or plaster. **1855** BROWNING *Men & Wom., Old Pict. in Florence* xxvi, But are you too fine, Taddeo Gaddi, To grant me a taste of your intonaco? **1883** C. C. PERKINS *Ital. Sculpt.* I. iii. 46 *note*, Ugolino's picture..was painted..on the 'intonaco', or plaster surface.

†**ˈintonate,** *v.*[1] *Obs. rare.* [f. ppl. stem of L. *intonāre* intr., to thunder, thunder forth, f. *in-* (IN-[2]) + *tonāre* to thunder.] *trans.* To thunder forth; to utter with a loud voice like thunder.

1626 DONNE *Serm.* xlvi. 467 God intimates, God interminates, God intonates with such a vehemency ..'Earth, earth, earth, heare the Word of the Lord'. **1739** S. HARRIS *53rd Ch. Isaiah* App. 262 So then, the great τετελέσται shall be intonated by the general Voice of the whole Host of Heaven.

intonate (ˈɪntəʊneɪt), *v.*[2] [f. ppl. stem of med.L. *intonāre* = It. *intonare*, F. *entonner*, f. *in-*, F. *en-* (IN-[2]) + *tonus*, F. *ton* TONE.]

1. *trans.* To recite in a singing voice; to INTONE.

1795 ROSCOE *Lorenzo* (1796) II. 270 Savonarola.. intonating with a tremendous voice, the psalm *Exurgat Deus.* **1858** DE QUINCEY *Th. Grk. Trag.* Wks. IX. 74 The recitation..was undoubtedly much more sustained, and intonated with a slow and measured stateliness. **1864** SIR F. PALGRAVE *Norm. & Eng.* III. 631 As little intelligible to his auditors, as if Caedmon..were to intonate his glee at an oratorio in Hanover Square.

2. To utter or pronounce with a particular tone; to give a specified or indicated intonation to.

1823 *New Monthly Mag.* VIII. 18 'Thus' is intonated comparatively high. **1824** *Blackw. Mag* XV. 589 The Italian naturally intonates his language with greater violence, and change of tone and emphasis, than an English-man does. **1867** MACFARREN *Harmony* i. 7 The Easter and Southern nations..habitually intonate smaller musical intervals than semitones.

3. *Phonetics.* To emit or pronounce with sonant vibration; to 'voice'. *rare.*

1875 WHITNEY *Life Lang.* iv. 66 The *l* sets the tip of the tongue against the roof of the mouth, but leaves the sides open for the free escape of the intonated breath.

intonation[1] (ɪntəʊˈneɪʃən). [n. of action from med.L. *intonāre* to INTONE: cf. F. *intonation* (14th c. in Godef. *Compl.*).]

1. In *Church Music.* The opening phrase of a plain-song melody, preceding the Reciting-note, and usually sung either by the priest alone, or by one or a few of the choristers; the recitation of this. In quot. 1620 *fig.*

1620 BRENT tr. *Sarpi's Hist. Counc. Trent* (1676) 673 It was replyed that he might have suffered others to make the intonation, and not to have been the Author himself of that prejudice. **1696** PHILLIPS (ed. 5), *Intonation*, the giving the Tune or Key by the Chanter to the rest of the Quire. **1852** HOOK *Ch. Dict.* (1871) 399 Intonation is, properly speaking, the recitation by the chanter..of the commencing words of the psalm or hymn, before the choir begins. **1880** W. S. ROCKSTRO in Grove *Dict. Mus.* II. 12 Some of the most important Intonations in general use are those proper to the Gregorian Tones. *Ibid.*, Handel, in 'The Lord gave the word', from 'The Messiah', uses the Intonation of the First Tone, transposed a fourth higher, with wonderful effect.

2. The action of intoning, or reciting in a singing voice: esp. the musical recitation of psalms, prayers, etc. in a liturgy, usually in monotone.

1788 GIBBON *Decl. & F.* xlviii, The conspirators.. expected, as the signal of murder, the intonation of the first psalm by the emperor himself. **1794** MATHIAS *Purs. Lit.* (1798) 233 Her bolder notes the willing muse should swell In lyrick intonation grave and deep. **1795** MASON *Ch. Mus.* ii. 90 These were all sung not merely in simple intonation or chaunt, but in this mode of figurate discant. **1862** F. HALL *Hindu Philos. Syst.* 68 The recitation and intonation of hymns of praise from the Veda.

3. The utterance or production (by the voice, or an instrument, etc.) of musical tones: in reference to manner or style, esp. to exactitude of pitch or relation to the key or harmony.

fixed intonation, that of instruments, such as keyboard instruments, in which the pitch of each note is fixed, not variable at the will of the performer.

1776 BURNEY *Hist. Mus.* I. Pref. 14 The Organ..has it no imperfections? Yes. It wants expression and a more perfect intonation. **1845** E. HOLMES *Mozart* 104 She has a beautiful voice—neither strong nor weak, but very pure and good in the intonation. **1874** SYMONDS *Sk. Italy & Greece* (1898) I. xiv. 294 A most extraordinary soprano..and true to the least shade in intonation. **1878** *Grove's Dict. Mus.* I. 459 On instruments of fixed intonation C × = D ♮ [etc.].

attrib. **1852** SEIDEL *Organ* 137 To set a pipe right again which has been bent,..use an intonation-iron.

4. Manner of utterance of the tones of the voice in speaking; modulation of the voice; accent.

1791 NEWTE *Tour Eng. & Scot.* 201 The people of Inverness..are not only free from that unfortunate intonation of Aberdeenshire..but speak the English language with greater purity than they do in any other part in Scotland. **1843** LYTTON *Last Bar.* I. ii, There was a marked distinction in the intonation, the accent, the modulation of voice. **1873** BLACK *Pr. Thule* (1874) 4 That peculiar and pleasant intonation that marks the speech of the Hebridean who has been taught English in the schools. **1935** M. SCHUBIGER *Role of Intonation in Spoken Eng.* 2 Word-order can remain unaltered, and then the different intonation, the rising instead of the falling tune, is the sole bearer of the interrogative relation. **1965** W. S. ALLEN *Vox Latina* 6 It is important to distinguish tone from intonation. The former refers to the pitch-patterns operative within individual words, whereas 'intonation' refers to the pitch-pattern operative over the whole clause or sentence.

5. *attrib.* and *Comb.*, as ***intonation change, morpheme***; **intonation contour**, a succession of levels of pitch extending over an utterance; **intonation curve**, the rising and falling of pitch within an utterance; **intonation pattern**, a pattern of variations in pitch; **intonation phoneme** = INTONEME; **intonation tune** (see quot. 1964); **intonation turn**, the point, usually at a prominent part of an utterance, at which the intonation rises or falls.

1964 C. BARBER *Present-Day Eng.* iii. 50 There are intonation-changes inside the syllable which require a certain length of vowel to manifest themselves. **1946** K. L. PIKE *Intonation Amer. Eng.* iii. 20 All speakers of the language use basic pitch sequences in similar ways under similar circumstances. These abstracted characteristic sentence melodies may be called *Intonation Contours.* **1960** [see ATTITUDINAL *a.*]. **1964** R. A. HALL *Introd. Ling.* xix. 114 An intonation contour does not..make any difference in the 'dictionary meaning' of an utterance. **1970** Intonation contour [see CONTOUR *sb.* 1 e]. **1936** H. MULDER *Cognition & Volition in Lang.* ii. 65 Wishes, commands, and questions introduced by interrogative pronouns, can be communicated on the same intonation-curve as plain statements. **1965** *Language* XLI. 498 In refusing to consider intonation-curves as subject to division into significant units, Martinet alleges that every modification..of a melodic curve brings with it a corresponding modification of meaning. **1953** *Internat. Jrnl. Amer. Ling.* XIX. ii. Suppl. 29 Hjelmslev requested a metalinguistic analysis of the English intonation morphemes which Smith had demonstrated earlier so as to make clear the difference between differential meaning and the meaning in general of the intonation patterns. **1966** G. N. LEECH *Eng. in Advertising* ii. 18 The relationship of apposition between elements is marked in speech by tone-concord, or equivalent intonation patterns on each element. **1971** D. CRYSTAL *Ling.* Interlude 134 A noun phrase may not have any separate intonation pattern at all. **1948** Intonation phoneme [see INTONEME]. **1934** J. J. HOGAN *Outl. Eng. Philol.* I. v. 31 Its [*sc.* a verse's] accompanying intonation-tune suffers modification by the regular tune which is what the line always retains of its character as a sentence or clause. **1964** R. H. ROBINS *Gen. Ling.* iv. 148 Intonations or intonation *tunes*, as they are often called, are regular sequences of pitch differences coextensive with a whole sentence or with successive parts thereof, and constituting an essential feature of normal spoken utterance. **1935** M. SCHUBIGER *Role of Intonation in Spoken Eng.* 9 If the psychological predicate consists of several words the most important gets the intonation turn.

Hence **intoˈnational** *a.*, relating to intonation; **intoˈnationally** *adv.*, in an intonational manner.

1895 J. OSGOOD in *Forum* June 503 The misused intonational 'twist', technically noted as the circumflex inflection. **1949** E. A. NIDA *Morphol.* (ed. 2) 62 In English the sentence-final glides which follow the last intonationally stressed syllable constitute morphemes. **1952** *Trans. Philol. Soc.* 91 Differences of intonational relationship between stem and ending. **1957** *Publ. Amer. Dial. Soc.* XXVIII. 6 We might start intonationally with Qs [*sc.* questions] classed as upmoving and downmoving. **1958** C. F. HOCKETT *Course in Mod. Ling.* 45 Certain types of speech..show..a total loss of intonational contrasts. **1964** R. H. ROBINS *Gen. Ling.* iii. 112 The different ways in which pitch differences are exploited intonationally and tonally. *Ibid.* iv. 149 In English ..stressed syllables carry more intonational weight than unstressed syllables. **1971** D. CRYSTAL *Ling.* 133 The intonational movement over the noun phrase as a whole must be indicated.

intoˈnation[2]. *rare*$^{-0}$. [n. of action from INTONATE *v.*[1]] A thundering; a roaring or rumbling as of thunder.

1658 PHILLIPS, *Intonation*, a thundering or making a terrible noise. **1755** in JOHNSON. **1855** MAYNE *Expos. Lex.*, Term applied to the gurgling noise produced by the movement of flatus in the bowels: intonation.

intonator (ˈɪntəʊneɪtə(r)). [agent-n. in L. form from *intonāre* to INTONE.] A monochord for the study of musical intervals, furnished with a diagram indicating the divisions of the string necessary for the production of the notes of the scale in exact intonation.

1875 STAINER & BARRETT *Dict. Mus. Terms. Intonator*, a monochord, or single string stretched across a flat soundboard.

intone (ɪnˈtəʊn), *v.* Also 5-6, 9 entone [ad. med.L. *intonā-re* to intone; in form *entone*, prob. immed. a. OF. *entoner* (13th c.).]

1. *trans.* To utter in musical tones; to sing, chant; *spec.* To recite in a singing voice (esp. a psalm, prayer, etc. in a liturgy); usually to recite in monotone.

c **1485** *Digby Myst.* (1882) IV. 1498 Now may thou entone a mery songe. *Ibid.* 1620 Entone sum ermonye. **1513** DOUGLAS *Æneis* VII. xii. 5 ȝe Musis now..Entone [*ed.* 1555 intone] my sang, and till endyt me leyr. **1805** SOUTHEY *Madoc* II. v, No choristers the funeral dirge intoned. **1833** MRS. BROWNING *Prometh. Bd.* Poet. Wks. 1850 I. 158 All the mortal nations..Are a dirge entoning. **1853** CDL. WISEMAN *Ess.* III. 84 The canons hastened..to the crowded cathedral, to intone the usual song of praise. **1868** MILMAN *St. Paul's* i. 12 The Clergy began to intone their Litany.

b. *absol.* or *intr.*

1849 *Blackw. Mag* LXV. 681 [They] join in the most wonderful responses, in a set key, which they call entoning. **1870** DICKENS *E. Drood* iv, He has even tried the experiment of slightly intoning in his pulpit. **1886** BESANT *Childr. Gibeon* II. x, I can intone of course, but I cannot sing.

2. To sing the opening phrase of a plain-song melody at the beginning of a chant, canticle, etc., usually as a solo or semichorus: see INTONATION[1] 1.

1880 W. S. ROCKSTRO in Grove *Dict. Mus.* II. 12 *Intoning*, the practice of singing the opening phrase of a Psalm, Canticle, or other piece of Ecclesiastical Music, not in full chorus, but as a solo or semi-chorus, assigned either to a single Priest, or to one, two, or four leading Choristers. *Ibid.* 15 The first clause [of the Introit] is intoned when the Celebrant approaches the Altar, by one, two, or four Choristers, according to the solemnity of the Festival: which done, the strain is taken up by the full Choir.

3. To utter with a particular tone or intonation: = INTONATE *v.*[2] 2.

1860 MARSH *Eng. Lang.* xiii. 292 A clear, appropriate and properly intoned and emphasized pronunciation, in reading aloud, is one of the rarest as well as most desirable of social accomplishments. **1866** ENGEL *Nat. Mus.* ii. 27 With some uncivilized nations the ear is so little cultivated that the intervals are very rudely and indistinctly intoned.

4. *intr.* To utter tones, as in singing or speaking; 'to make a slow protracted noise' (J.).

1728 POPE *Dunc.* II. 253 So swells each wind-pipe; Ass intones to Ass; Harmonic twang! of leather, horn, and brass.

5. *fig.* (*trans.*) To imbue with a particular tone of feeling; to tone. *rare.*

1883 MAUDSLEY *Body & Will* II. iv. 156 Every one is penetrated and intoned, so to speak, by the social atmosphere of the particular medium in which he lives.

Hence **in'toned** *ppl. a.*; **in'toning** *vbl. sb.* and *ppl. a.*

1854 MILMAN *Lat. Chr.* VIII. v. 361 His was not..the richly-intoned voice swelling the full harmony of the choir. **1863** OUIDA *Held in Bondage* (1870) 2 We had prayers at eight, which he read in a style of intoning peculiar to himself. **1900** *Westm. Gaz.* 13 Feb. 2/1 No hush of a church listening to some intoning clergyman could have been greater.

in'tone, *sb.* [f. INTONE *v.*]

†**1.** Something intoned; a song or chant. *Obs.*

?*a* **1550** in *Dunbar's Poems* (1893) 324 The potent Prince ..is, of angellis with a sweit intone, Borne of the most chest Virgyn Mary bricht.

2. The action of intoning; the tone of voice used in intoning.

1886 N. SHEPPARD *Before an Audience* v. 67 The intone is easier to speak and easier to be heard. But it is equally natural for us to fall into the intone as a habit without reference to the contingency.

intoneme (ɪnˈtəʊniːm). [Short for *intonation phoneme*: see -EME.] An intonation pattern that contributes to the meaning of an utterance.

1948 K. L. PIKE *Tone Lang.* v. 60 One may choose to call the key pitches *intonation phonemes* or *intonemes*. **1965** *Language* XLI. 498 Intonation-curves..can nevertheless be classified into contrasting units (call them 'tonemes' or 'intonemes' if you like). **1967** *Word* XXIII. 473 To turn again to my son's efforts to communicate, it was possible to isolate at the age of four months two intonemes, the one for desiderative and the other for deictic purposes. **1968** *Language* XLIV. 82 These two intonemes operate in the high range in the intonation system.

intonement (ɪnˈtəʊnmənt). *rare.* Also en-. [f. INTONE *v.* + -MENT.] The action of intoning; intonation; chanting.

1849-53 ROCK *Ch. of Fathers* IV. xii. 137 Each took his own side of the choir for the entonement of the antiphons. **1857** *Chamb. Jrnl.* VIII. 48 Where hymns were said In musical intonements and rich chimes.

intoner (ɪnˈtəʊnə(r)). [f. as prec. + -ER[1].] One who intones.

1865 *Testimonial*, In addition to his other eminent qualifications, he is musical and a practised intoner. **1890** *Pall Mall G.* 23 Oct. 4/2 When the celebrated assault case between the intoners and sayers of the Litany was before the Westminster police-court. **1900** *Daily Chron.* 25 June 3/3 As an intoner he [Tom Stevens] was more appreciated, and was said to get the phrase 'caterpillars innumerable' into a single syllable.

'in-,toothed, *a.* [IN *adv.* 13.] Having the teeth directed or growing inward.

1829 *Blackw. Mag.* XXVI. 915 A miserable, gaunt, in-toothed, half-penny-a-day growl.

†**in'topiaried**, *ppl. a. Obs. rare.* [f. IN-[2] + L. *topiāria* ornamental gardening, *topiārium* topiary-work + -ED[1].] Ornamentally planted and arranged.

1592 R. D. *Hypnerotomachia* 67 Conuenyent garden pots in the which in stead of growing plantes, euerie one was of pure glasse..intopiaried boxe the rootes and stalkes of golde [etc.].

intorsion (ɪnˈtɔːʃən). [a. F. *intorsion*, ad. L. *intortiōn-em*, n. of action f. *intorquēre*: see INTORT *v.*] The action of twisting; *spec.* in *Bot.* the twisting of the stem of a plant; in *Ophthalm.* (see quots.).

1760 J. LEE *Introd. Bot.* III. xiv. (1765) 202 Intorsion, Winding, is the Flexion or Bending of any Part of a Plant towards one Side. **1794** MARTYN *Rousseau's Bot.* xxxi. 485 The intorsion or manner of bending in the stems. **1855** in MAYNE *Expos. Lex.* **1887** *Syd. Soc. Lex.*, *Intorsion*, applied by Linnæus to the phenomenon presented by certain plants which twine around a support by means of their flexible stalks. **1899** A. DUANE tr. *Fuchs's Text-bk. Ophthalm.* (ed. 2) xiv. 578 It [*sc.* the superior rectus muscle] also rolls the eye in such a way that the upper extremity of its vertical meridian is inclined inward (intorsion). **1964** [see EXTORSION].

†**'intort**, *sb. Obs.* [f. L. *intort-us* twisted: see next.] A pipe or tube twisted in circles.

1657 TOMLINSON *Renou's Disp.* 678 A Pipe..with turning gyres like a Serpent, whence called an Intort.

†**in'tort**, *ppl. a. Obs. rare.* [ad. L. *intort-us*, pa. pple. of *intorquēre*: see next.] Twisted or thrust in.

c **1420** *Pallad. on Husb.* II. 344 Sette hem transuerse, oon side intort the grounde [*ut latus..figatur in terra*].

intort (ɪnˈtɔːt), *v.* Now *rare.* [f. L. *intort-*, ppl. stem of *intorquēre*, f. *in-* (IN-[2]) + *torquēre* to twist.] *trans.* To twist or curl inwards. Perh. only in the pa. pple. **in'torted**, twisted or curled inwards; twisted, wreathed, involved. *lit.* and *fig.*

1615 CROOKE *Body of Man* 244 The vessels of seede..are writhen and intorted with wonderfull art, and implicated or foulded vp in many boughts and circumuolutions. **1616-61** HOLYDAY *Persius* 324 The truth Of thy rule well apply'd,.. Shew'd me intorted manners. **1633** T. ADAMS *Exp. 2 Peter* iii. 3 The secrets of God's providence are curled and intorted, we cannot unfold them. **1657** TOMLINSON *Renou's Disp.* 503 Rowls intorted like ropes. **1725** POPE *Odyss.* III. 555 With reverend hand the king presents the gold, Which round the intorted horns the gilder roll'd. **1839** *New Monthly Mag.* LVII. 32 How tedious then was the surplusage of awkward and intorted phrases! **1892** STEVENSON & L. OSBOURNE *Wrecker* 208 The loose topsail.. swayed and sang in the declining wind, a raffle of intorted cordage.

intortell, -tle, var. ENTORTILL *v.*, to entwine.

†**in'tortillage.** *Obs. rare*[−1]. [ad. F. *entortillage*: see ENTORTILL and -AGE.] An involved intertwisting.

1809 COLERIDGE *Let.* (Sotheby's Catal. 1-4 Dec. 1896, 28), 'The Friend'..is partly chargeable with..an intortillage or intertwisting both of the thoughts and sentences.

†**in'tortive**, *a. Obs. rare*[−1]. [f. L. *intort-*, ppl. stem of *intorquēre* + -IVE.] Of intorted or twisted nature; in quot. *fig.*

1560 ROLLAND *Crt. Venus* II. 963 Bandownit with baill and full of brukilnes, With diuers faltis and wordis Intortiue.

‖**in toto**: see IN *Lat. prep.*

Intourist (ˌɪnˈtʊərɪst). [Russ. *Inturist*, abbrev. of *inostránnyĭ turíst* foreign tourist.] Name of the State Travel Bureau of the U.S.S.R. Also *attrib.*

1932 *Intourist's Pocket Guide to Soviet Union* 581 The State Joint-Stock Company for Foreign Tourists—*Intourist* —was established in 1929 jointly by the People's Commissariat for Foreign and Domestic Trade, the People's Commissariat for Ways and Communications and the Soviet Mercantile Fleet. **1935** N. MITCHISON *We have been Warned* II. 194 All arrangements in the competent hands of the Intourist Office, who undertook all Russian travel. **1940** H. G. WELLS *Babes in Darkling Wood* III. ii. 251, I suppose they were packing off most of the Intourist people. **1949** F. MACLEAN *Eastern Approaches* I. iii. 35, I walked into the local branch of Intourist and informed the seedy little Armenian clerk behind the counter that I wished to book a passage across the Caspian to Central Asia. **1952** M. MCCARTHY *Groves of Academe* (1953) ix. 169 He took you through that session like a regular Intourist guide with a party of dumb fellow-travellers. **1958** J. GUNTHER *Inside Russia Today* i. 29 You go to any travel agency that has an arrangement with Intourist, the official Russian agency.. and apply for a tourist visa. **1973** T. ALLBEURY *Choice of Enemies* xix. 95 The failed ballerinas seconded to Intourist as easy lays for Western salesmen.

†**in'tower**, *v. Obs. rare.* Also 7 en-. [IN-[2].] *trans.* To confine or imprison in a tower. Hence **in'towering** *vbl. sb.*

1592 WARNER *Alb. Eng.* VIII. xl. (1612) 195 Yeat was he taken and in-tow'rd, and lost his head for this. *a* **1649** DRUMM. OF HAWTH. *Answ. Object.* Wks. (1711) 214 The entowering of Henry the VI. **1649** EVELYN *Mem.* (1857) III. 42 The unexpected surprisal and intowering of John Lilburne, proclaiming him traitor.

'in-,town *sb.*, *a.*, (and *adv.*) [f. IN *adv.* + TOWN.] **1.** *Sc.* = INFIELD. Chiefly *attrib.*, as *intown pasture*; **intown multure** = INSUCKEN *multure*; **intown weed**, 'a weed common in pastures, an annual weed' (Jam. 1880).

1538 *Aberd. Reg.* V. 16 (Jam.) Ane pleucht of the intowne of Ardlayr. **1812** J. HENDERSON *Agric. Surv. Sutherl.* vi. 62 The milk cows are fed on the *in-town* pasture, until the farmer removes them..to distant shealings. **1818** SCOTT *Hrt. Midl.* xiii. *note*, The lock and gowpen, or small quantity and handful, payable in thirlage cases, as intown multure. **1820** —— *Monast.* xiii, The cultivators of each barony or regality..in Scotland, are obliged to bring their corn to be grinded at the mill of the territory, for which they pay a heavy charge, called the 'intown multures'.

2. *adj.* and *adv.* Within (the central part of) a town.

1817 J. KEATS *Let.* 16 May (1958) I. 147, I am glad to hear of Mr T's health and of the Wellfare of the In-town-stayers. **1941** W. STEVENS *Let.* 25 Mar. (1967) 388 Today, as I walked in-town, I heard..song sparrows. **1958** S. SPENDER *Engaged in Writing* i. 24 A concourse of canals that formed a minute intown harbour. **1967** *Boston Herald* 1 Apr. 22/1 Three intown congregations..will join in worship here at 11 a.m. Sunday.

in'toxicable, *a. rare.* [f. L. *intoxicā-re* to INTOXICATE + -ABLE.] Liable to be intoxicated.

a **1734** NORTH *Exam.* II. iv. §156 (1740) 314 The People not so intoxicable as to fall in with their brutal Assistance.

intoxicant (ɪnˈtɒksɪkənt), *a.* and *sb.* [ad. med.L. *intoxicānt-em*, pr. pple. of *intoxicāre* to INTOXICATE: see -ANT.]

A. *adj.* Intoxicating.

1882 TRAILL *Sterne* vi. 89 Written,..we can clearly see, under the full intoxicant effect which a bewildering succession of new sights and sounds will produce.

B. *sb.* An intoxicating substance or liquor.

1863 *Glasgow Morn. Jrnl.* 28 Apr., Eight o'clock morning is early enough to begin drinking or selling intoxicants. **1874** CARPENTER *Ment. Phys.* II. xvii. (1879) 643 A somewhat similar experience from another intoxicant, is recorded of himself by Dr. Laycock. **1883** C. J. WILLS *Mod. Persia* 316 The habit of indulging in intoxicants.

intoxicate (ɪnˈtɒksɪkət), *ppl. a.* (*sb.*) Also 5 en-. [ad. med.L. *intoxicāt-us*, pa. pple. of *intoxicāre*: see next. In later use treated as shortened form of *intoxicated*.]

†**1. a.** Impregnated, steeped in, or smeared with poison; rendered poisonous: empoisoned. *Obs.*

1412-20 LYDG. *Chron. Troy* III. xxiv. (MS. Bodl. 230) lf. 119/2 An arwe The hede of wiche wt venym was enoint Intoxycat at the square poynt. **1494** FABYAN *Chron.* VI. clxv. 160 He toke a pocion of a physycion..whiche was intoxicat, by meane of which venemous pocion, he dyed shortlye after. **1567** *Satir. Poems Reform.* xi. 34 To sla with dart Intoxicat. **1632** I. L. *Womens Rights* 350 To drinke vp the said drinke so intoxicate. **1637** GILLESPIE *Eng. Pop. Cerem.* Ep. A iv, Simple ones..doe sucke from the intoxicate dugs of Conformity, the foster-milke which makes them grow in Error.

†**b.** Poisoned; killed by poison. *Obs.*

1471 RIPLEY *Comp. Alch.* III. ix. in Ashm. (1652) 141 But no man shall be by hyt intoxycate, After the tyme yt ys into Medycyne Elevate. **1480** CAXTON *Ovid's Met.* XI. xxii, The fayre Esperie..was by a venemous serpente pricked on the foot. She was entoxicat and enpoysoned in suche wyse that she felle doun deed. **1555** EDEN *Decades* 325 In such sorte qualyfyinge the maliciousnesse therof [poison], that none shall therby bee intoxicate. **1607** TOPSELL *Four-f. Beasts* (1658) 198 It is also good against those that are intoxicate with poison.

†**c.** Of a disease, etc.: Caused by poison. *Obs.*

1607 TOPSELL *Four-f. Beasts* (1658) 204 The bloud being dryed and decocted with marrow, is good against all intoxicate passions.

2. Inebriated: = INTOXICATED 2.

1581 J. BELL *Haddon's Answ. Osor.* 188 In that blynde denne of your intoxicate braynes. **1601** HOLLAND *Pliny* I. 185 His head was intoxicate with the strong sauor of the incense,..and so being beside himself, wist not what he did. **1610** BP. HALL *Apol. Brownists* 39 Drunk and intoxicate with the Whores cuppe. **1845** HIRST *Com. Mammoth*, etc. 164 Like one intoxicate with scents.

3. *fig.* = INTOXICATED 3.

c **1500** MERSAR *Perrell in Paramours*, With tressone so intoxicait Are mennis mowthis at all ouris. **1531** FRITH *Judgm. Tracy* (1829) 247 Their mind is so intoxicate, that there is nothing but they will note it with a black coal. **1671** MILTON *P.R.* IV. 328 Deep versed in books and shallow in himself, Crude or intoxicate, collecting toys, And trifles for choice matters, worth a sponge. **1805** WORDSW. *Prelude* XIII. 29 The mind intoxicate With present objects. **1879** J. TODHUNTER *Alcestis* 22 Such sun and air make me intoxicate With a strange passion.

B. *sb.* One who is intoxicated or inebriated.

1760 H. WALPOLE *Corr.* (1837) II. 33 The fair intoxicate turned round and cried, 'I am laughed at!—Who is it?'

intoxicate (ɪnˈtɒksɪkeɪt), *v.* [f. ppl. stem of med.L. *intoxicāre*, f. *in-* (IN-[2]) + *toxicāre* to smear with poison, f. *toxicum* = Gr. τοξικόν poison.]

†**1.** *trans.* To poison. *Obs.*

1530 PALSGR. 592/2, I intoxycat, I poyson with venyme. **1537** LATIMER *Serm. bef. Convoc.* 9 June an. 1536 A v b, Meate I say, and not poyson. This dothe intoxicate and slee the eater, that fedeth and nourysheth him. **1584** R. SCOT *Discov. Witchcr.* III. iii. (1886) 34 He [the devil] supplieth their wants of powders and roots to intoxicate withall. **1684** tr. *Bonet's Merc. Compit.* VI. 206 If one be intoxicated with a poisonous Animal.

2. To stupefy, render unconscious or delirious, to madden or deprive of the ordinary use of the senses or reason, with a drug or alcoholic liquor; to inebriate, make drunk.

1598 HAKLUYT *Voy.* I. 97 It..goeth downe very pleasantly, intoxicating weake braines. **1613** PURCHAS *Pilgrimage* (1614) 830 They intoxicate the fish with a strong sented wood called Ayaw, whereby they easily take them on the top of the water. **1635** SWAN *Spec. M.* vi. §2 (1643) 215 It filleth and intoxicateth the brain, as wine doth. **1693** LUTTRELL *Brief Rel.* (1857) III. 90, 2 or 3 men..forced a potion down his mouth, which intoxicated him. **1775** BOSWELL *Let.* 12 Aug., I run wild but did not get drunk. I was however intoxicated and very ill next day. *a* **1803** *Sir Hugh le Blond* viii, in Child *Ballads* III. lix B. (1885) 47/1 He intoxicate the leper-man, With liquors very sweet. **1894** A. ROBERTSON *Nuggets*, etc. 87 His mind and tongue were sober, but his legs were intoxicated.

b. *absol.* To cause or produce intoxication.

1687 A. LOVELL tr. *Thevenot's Trav.* I. 277 They put Lime to it to make it intoxicate. **1746** BERKELEY *2nd Let. Tar-water* §9 Cordials, which heat and intoxicate. **1811** A. T. THOMSON *Lond. Disp.* (1818) 414 When new it is flatulent, debilitating, and purgative, and intoxicates sooner than old wine.

3. *fig.* †**a.** To 'poison'; to corrupt morally or spiritually. *Obs.*

a **1529** SKELTON *Col. Clout* 704 Suche maner of sysmatykes And halfe heretykes..That wolde intoxicate,.. That wolde contaminate..The Church's hygh estates. **1680** BUNYAN *Mr. Badman* Wks. 1767 I. 738 They are intoxicated with the deadly poison of sin. **1860** PUSEY *Min. Proph.* 421 The woe falls on all, who in any way intoxicate others with flattering words or feigned affection, mixing poison under things pleasant, to bring them to shame.

b. To stupefy or excite as with a drug or alcoholic liquor; to render unsteady or delirious in mind or feelings; to excite or exhilarate beyond self-control.

1591 SYLVESTER *Du Bartas* I. i. 663 With grace of Princes, with their pomp, and State, Ambitious Spirits he doth intoxicate. **1640-4** CHAS. I in Rushw. *Hist. Coll.* III. (1692) I. 732 So new a Power will undoubtedly intoxicate Persons who were not born to it. *a* **1680** BUTLER *Rem.* (1759) I. 241 Authority intoxicates..The Fumes of it invade the Brain, And make Men giddy, proud, and vain. *a* **1716** SOUTH (J. s.v. *Stupefy*), The fumes of his passion do as really intoxicate his discerning faculty, as the fumes of drink discompose and

stupify the brain. **1718** *Freethinker* No. 87 ¶10 It too often happens, that a Man..is..intoxicated with Pride and Self-Conceit. **1863** Mrs. Oliphant *Salem Ch.* vi. 100 Those smiles..which intoxicated for the moment every man on whom they fell.

Hence **in'toxicating** *vbl. sb.*

1712 tr. *Pomet's Hist. Drugs* I. 138 Imployed chiefly for intoxicating of Birds and Fish.

in'toxicated, *ppl. a.* [f. prec. + -ED[1].]

†**1.** Imbued with poison; poisoned. *Obs.*

1558 Warde tr. *Alexis' Secr.* (1568) 20a, If a man be.. hurte with anie intoxicated weapon, ye must wryng wel the bloud out of the wounde. **1610** R. Abbot *Old Way* 9 To Suger the brims of their intoxicated Cups, that men the more greedily..may drinke those venimous potions. **1636** Brathwait *Lives Rom. Emp.* 291 By an intoxicated medicine..he suddenly dyed at Mantua.

2. Stupefied or having the brain affected with a drug or alcoholic liquor; inebriated, drunk.

1576 Fleming *Panopl. Epist.* 290 Some so full of wine, and intoxicated with Bacchus berries. **1607** E. Grimstone tr. *Goulart's Mem. Hist.* 311 Being at table in his lodging, and his head some-what intoxicated, he spake so rudely of the Pope..that he was arrested. **1802** Surr *Splendid Misery* III. 31 [Lying] in a state of intoxicated insensibility. **1860** Tyndall *Glac.* I. iii. 31 A guide, who, though partly intoxicated, did his duty well.

3. *fig.* Excited or roused in mind as if with alcoholic liquor; inebriated.

1692 Dryden *St. Euremont's Ess.* 296 When a Man intoxicated with reading, makes his first Step in the World, 'tis usually a false one. **1770** *Junius Lett.* xxxix. 202 Intoxicated with pleasure. **1798** Washington *Lett.* Writ. 1893 XIV. 22, I cannot believe..that the Directory of France, intoxicated and abandoned as it is, will have the folly to invade our territorial rights. *a* **1890** J. Brown *Serm.* (1892) 224 Men long held in spiritual slavery began to breathe and to be intoxicated with the air of freedom.

Hence **in'toxicatedly** *adv.*, in an intoxicated manner; like one who is intoxicated.

1883 Miss Broughton *Belinda* III. iii. viii. 46 He rows slowly on in a dream, his eyes intoxicatedly watching that pendent hand.

in'toxicating, *ppl. a.* [f. as prec. + -ING[2].] That intoxicates: see the vb.

1634 Brereton *Trav.* (Chetham Soc.) 40 Hemlock, which he said was of a most venomous, somnifying, stupifying, and intoxicating quality. **1645** Milton *Tetrach.* Wks. (1851) 196 (*Deut.* xxiv. 1, 2) Men might..live happily and healthfully, without the use of those intoxicating licors. **1748** Smollett *Rod. Rand.* vi. (1804) 22 An intoxicating piece of good fortune. **1848** A. Tod *Disc.* 102 Beware of the intoxicating cup. **1894** Sir E. Sullivan *Woman* 115 Of all the good gifts ..the love of woman has been the most delicious, the most intoxicating, and even the least deceitful.

Hence **in'toxicatingly** *adv.*

1892 *Sat. Rev.* 30 July 127/1 They will drink deeply, intoxicatingly, of the Pierian streams.

intoxication (ɪntɒksɪ'keɪʃən). Also 5 en-. [n. of action f. INTOXICATE *v.*; cf. F. *intoxication* (1408 in Hatz.-Darm.), in sense 1.]

1. The action of poisoning; administration of poison; killing by poison; the state of being poisoned; an instance of this. *Obs.* exc. *Med.*

1548 Hall *Chron.*, *3 Rich. III* (1809) 407 Either by.. pensyvenes of hearte, or by intoxicacion of poison..within a few daies the Quene departed oute of this transitorie lyfe. **1607** Topsell *Four-f. Beasts* (1658) 103 His bloud..being drunk in Wine, it is good against poisoned wounds and all intoxications. **1842** E. P. Davis in *Med. News* I. 310 (Cent.) It has been supposed that only in the case of abraded surfaces could intoxication with solutions [of corrosive sublimate] of 1 to 1000 and 1 to 2000 occur. **1896** *Allbutt's Syst. Med.* I. 720 The palsy which occasionally appears in or after enteric fever is..due to diphtheria intoxication. *attrib.* **1897** *Allbutt's Syst. Med.* II. 949 Schweinitz maintains that it is an intoxication-amblyopia similar to that caused by tobacco. **1898** P. Manson *Trop. Diseases* Introd. 14 There is a class of intoxication diseases which depend on toxins generated by germs whose habitat is the soil, water, or other external media.

2. The action of rendering stupid, insensible, or disordered in intellect, with a drug or alcoholic liquor; the making drunk or inebriated; the condition of being so stupefied or disordered.

1646 Sir T. Browne *Pseud. Ep.* II. vi. 101 The prevalent intoxication is from the spirits of drink dispersed into the veynes and arteries. **1780** Bentham *Princ. Legisl.* xiii. §4 The English law does not admit intoxication as a ground of excuse. **1817** Miss Mitford in L'Estrange *Life* (1870) II. i. 12 He [Coleridge] had for some time relinquished his English mode of intoxication by brandy and water for the Turkish fashion of intoxication of opium. **1875** Jowett *Plato* (ed. 2) V. 34 In Sparta..any one found in a state of intoxication is severely punished.

b. Intoxicating quality. *rare.*

1674 tr. *Martiniere's Voy. N. Countries* 32 A certain grain which gives it [strong water] the same strength and intoxication as ours.

c. *concr.* An intoxicating draught. *rare.*

1799 E. King *Munim. Antiqua* I. Pref. 19 Proudly quaffing a vile intoxication from the excavated skull of his enemy.

3. *fig.* †**a.** The 'poisoning' of the moral or mental faculties; a cause or occasion of this. *Obs.*

1494 Fabyan *Chron.* VII. 551 The..insypient drynkyth the swete and delycious wordis vnauysydly, and perceyuyth not entoxycacion whiche they ben myngyd or myxte with. **1605** Bacon *Adv. Learn.* II. xxv. §15 Whatsoever knowledge reason cannot at all worke upon and conuert, is a meere intoxication and indangereth a dissolution of the minde and understanding. **1660** *Eng. Monarchy freest State in World* 11 Being extricated and quitted from the poysonous intoxications of some very viperous Spirits. **1728** Morgan *Algiers* I. Pref. 5 They are prejudiced, even to intoxication, against the whole world besides.

b. The action or power of exhilarating or highly exciting the mind; elation or excitement beyond the bounds of sobriety.

1712 Addison *Spect.* No. 351 ¶15 That secret Intoxication of Pleasure. **1752** Young *Brothers* II. i. 17 He's ever warbling nonsense in her ear With all the intoxication of success. **1796** Burke *Regic. Peace* I. Wks. VIII. 104 This plan of empire was not taken up in the first intoxication of unexpected success..it was projected. **1835** Thirlwall *Greece* I. vi. 194 The intoxication of wealth and power, in which men forget their weakness and mortality. **1875** Jowett *Plato* (ed. 2) IV. 279 He is going out of his mind in the first intoxication of a great thought.

intoxicative (ɪn'tɒksɪkeɪtɪv), *a. rare.* [f. as INTOXICATE *v.* + -IVE.]

1. Tending to intoxicate; †poisonous; inebriating.

1632 I. L. *Womens Rights* 350 A certaine drinke..mixed and compounded with powders and intoxicatiue spices. **1797** *London Art of Cookery* 216 Malt is a wholesome nutritious grain..but by no means intoxicative, except used in very large quantities.

2. Pertaining to or characteristic of intoxication.

1896 *Allbutt's Syst. Med.* I. 879 The sterile products of choleraic cultures administered to a guinea-pig will cause distinct intoxicative symptoms.

in'toxicator. *rare.* [agent-n. from INTOXICATE.] One who intoxicates; †a poisoner.

1744 Lewis *Pecocke* 242 That most impious intoxicator, who had imbibed the poison of perfidiousness. **1830** *Fraser's Mag.* I. 209 Our friend the Intoxicator is an Irishman.

intoximeter (ɪn'tɒksɪmiːtə(r)). orig. *U.S.* Also Intoximeter. [f. INTOXI(CATION + -METER.] A device for measuring the alcohol content of a person's breath, esp. in cases of suspected drunken driving.

Orig. a proprietary name in the U.S.

1950 *Official Gaz.* (U.S. Patent Office) 1 Aug. 28/2 Intoximeter. For apparatus for determining the alcohol-carbon dioxide ratio in the alveolar air of a person. ..Claims use since June 22, 1946. **1955** [see DRUNKOMETER]. **1983** *Times* 20 Apr. 4/1 One of the machines, the Lion Intoximeter 3000..resembles a standard microcomputer, with keyboard, plus a bottle containing a measured solution of alcohol, through which the breath sample passes. *Ibid.* 16 Sept. 3/1 The intoximeters, as they are called, were introduced on May 6. **1984** *Daily Tel.* 20 Mar. 19/8 One of four intoximeters tested by the Government before the device was introduced for detecting drink-drivers was faulty.

intra ('ɪntrə), *prep.* [L., = within.] **1.** In phr. ***intra vires***, within the powers or legal authority (*of* a person, etc.). Cf. ULTRA *prep.* 1.

1877 S. Brice *Treat. Doctrine Ultra Vires* (ed. 2) II. ii. 56 It will be best to retain the secondary use of the term Ultra Vires, and..to deal only with those proceedings which are bad in reference to matters admitted to be Intra Vires in both meanings. **1884** *Law Times* LXXVIII. 110 (Stanford), If this were *intra vires*, the other securities which they had accepted were not *bonâ fide* ones. **1930** A. Palmer *Company Secretarial Pract.* 185 Excess borrowing *intra vires* of the company but *ultra vires* of the directors may be ratified by ordinary resolution. **1966** *Rep. Comm. Inquiry Univ. Oxf.* I. 256 We have already explained..the methods by which this power may be kept *intra vires*. **1970** *Internat. & Compar. Law Q.* 4th Ser. XIX. II. 244 It would seem that, at least in New Zealand municipal law, if the Antarctica Act is *intra vires*, the Dependency includes the high seas south of 60° S.

2. intra vitam, during life; while still living. Freq. *attrib.*, = INTRAVITAL *a.*

1881 *Bull. Mus. Compar. Zool. Harvard* VI. II. 264 Whether the intranuclear network was present as a structure *intra vitam*. **1898** *Jrnl. Microsc. Soc.* 133 Herr A. M. Przesmycki has made a long series of experiments on *intra-vitam* staining. **1965** *Acta Med. Scand.* CLXXVIII. 155 (*heading*) Intra-vitam diagnosis of oxalosis.

intra- (ɪntrə), *prefix*, repr. L. *intrā* 'on the inside, within', used in numerous recent formations, chiefly adjectival. This use of *intra-* does not occur in classical L., and only a few examples appear in late and med.L. But it is largely used in modern times, esp. in biological terms, where it is often naturally opposed to EXTRA-. It is sometimes confused with INTER-.

1. In adjectives (properly, and most frequently, of Latin origin) in which it stands in prepositional relation to the sb. implied in the second element.

intra-ab'dominal, situated or occurring within the abdomen; **intra-acinous** (-'æsɪnəs), occurring within an acinus or racemose gland; **intra-al'veolar**, occurring within the alveoli or air-cells of the lungs; **intra-amni'otic**, taking place, situated, or administered within the amnion; so **intra-amni'otically** *adv.*, within the amnion; **intra-ar'terial**, occurring within an artery; also, administered into an artery; **intra-ar'terially** *adv.*, (by injection) into an artery; **intra-ar'ticular**, situated within or passing into a joint of the body; **intrabranchial** (-'bræŋkɪəl), situated within the branchiæ or gills; **intrabronchial** (-'brɒŋkɪəl), occurring within the bronchi; **intra'buccal** [L. *bucca* cheek], situated within or on the inside of the cheek: **intraca'licular**, situated within the calicle of a polyp; **intraca'nonical**, relating to what is included in the canon of Scripture; **intraca'pillary**, existing within a blood capillary; **intra'capsular**, situated or occurring within a capsule, or within the capsular ligament of a joint; **intra'cardiac, -'cardial** [Gr. καρδία heart], situated or occurring within the heart (= ENDOCARDIAL a); **intra'cardially** *adv.*, into the heart; **intra'carpellary** *Bot.*, situated within a carpel; also (*erron.*) between or among carpels (properly *intercarpellary*); **intracartilaginous** (-'ædʒɪnəs), situated or occurring within the substance of cartilage; **intra'cavital**, occurring within the cavities, *e.g.* of the stem of a plant; **intra'cellular** *Biol.*, situated or occurring within the substance of a cell (as digestion in Protozoa); hence **intra'cellularly** *adv.* **intracephalic** (-sɪ'fælɪk) [Gr. κεφαλή head], situated or occurring within the head; **intra'cerebral**, situated or occurring within the cerebrum or brain (*Syd. Soc. Lex.* 1887); **intra'cerebrally** *adv.*, in or into the cerebrum; **intraci'sternal**, occurring within or (of an injection) administered into a cistern of the body, esp. one in the brain; hence **intraci'sternally** *adv.*; **intracloacal** (-kləʊ'eɪkəl), situated within the cloaca; **intracœlomic** (-siː'lɒmɪk), situated within the cœlome; **intra'coastal**, situated close to the coast; **intraconti'nental**, situated within, or in the interior of, a continent; **intra'coronal** *Dentistry*, placed or performed within the crown of a tooth; hence **intra'coronally** *adv.*; **intracor'poreal**, situated or occurring within the body; **intracor'puscular**, occurring within corpuscles (*e.g.* those of the blood); **intra'cortical**, situated or occurring within the cortex of the brain; **intra'cosmical**, existing within the cosmos or universe; **intra'crustal** *Geol.*, situated within the earth's crust; **intra'crystalline** *Min.*, occurring within a crystal; **intra'cultural**, occurring within a culture; hence **intra'culturally** *adv.*; **intracu'taneous** = *intradermal* (below); hence **intracu'taneously** *adv.*; **intracystic** (-'sɪstɪk), occurring within a cyst; **intracyto'plasmic**, situated or occurring within the cytoplasm of a cell; **intra-depart'mental**, done or occurring within a department; **intra'dermal, -'dermic**, situated or applied within the skin; hence **intra'dermally** *adv.*; **intradi'visional**, done within a division; **intra'ductal**, situated or applied within a duct (of a breast); **intra'dural**, situated or performed within the dura mater; hence **intra'durally; intra-ecclesi'astical**, existing or occurring within a church; **intraepi'dermal, -epi'dermic**, situated or occurring within the epidermis; **intra-epi'thelial**, situated within the substance of the epithelium; **intra-Euro'pean**, occurring or carried on within Europe; **intra-experi'ential**, within experience; **intrafa'scicular** *Bot.*, situated within a vascular bundle; **intrafor'mational** *Geol.*, formed or occurring within a geological formation; **intra'fusal** [L. *fusus* spindle], situated or occurring within a muscle spindle; **intra'gastric**, applied, existing, or situated within the stomach; hence **intra'gastrically** *adv.*, into the stomach; **intrage'neric**, occurring or existing within a genus or between individuals of a single genus; **intra'genic** [GENIC *a.*], occurring within a gene; **intra'glacial** = ENGLACIAL *a.*; also, lying upon or within, or being, the terrain formerly occupied by a glacier or ice-sheet; **intra'glandular**, existing or carried out within a gland; **intraglu'teal**, administered into the gluteal muscles; **intragovern'mental**, occurring within the institutions or branches of a government; **intra'gyral** (-'dʒaɪrəl), situated within a gyrus or convolution of the brain; **intrahe'patic** [Gr. ἧπαρ liver], situated or occurring within the substance of the liver; **intra-im'perial**, carried on within the (British) Empire; **intra'lamellar**, situated within the lamellæ, *e.g.* of the 'gills' of a fungus; **intralaryngeal** (-lə'rɪndʒiːəl), situated or performed within the larynx; hence **intrala'ryngeally** *adv.* **intralen'ticular** *Ophthalm.*, situated within the lens of the eye; **intraliga'mentous**, occurring within the substance of a ligament; **intra-'lingual**, (*a*)

Med., situated or occurring in the substance of the tongue (*New Syd. Soc. Lex. Med.* 1888); (*b*) of communication, etc.: within a given language; within the bounds of language; **intra-lin'guistic** = *intra-lingual* (*b*); **intra'locular**, situated within the loculi or chambers of some structure; **intra'logical**, within the boundaries of logic. **intra'luminal**, existing within a lumen, esp. that of the intestine; **intra'mammary**, existing or applied within a breast; **intraman'dibular**, situated within the mandible; **intra'marginal**, situated on the inner side of the margin, *e.g.* of a leaf; **intra'matrical** *Bot.*, situated or growing within a matrix, as a parasitic plant; hence **intra'matrically** *adv.* **intra'medullary** [see MEDULLA], situated within the substance of the spinal cord, or of the medulla oblongata (*Syd. Soc. Lex.*); **intra'membranous**, 'within the substance of a membrane, or enclosed by membrane' (*Syd. Soc. Lex.*); **intrameningeal** (-miːˈnɪndʒiːəl), situated or occurring within the investing membranes of the brain; **intra-'mental**, occurring within the mind; so **intra-men'tality**; **intramer'curial, -ian** *Astron.*, situated within the orbit of Mercury; **intrametro'politan**, situated within the metropolitan boundary; **intra'montane**, situated within a mountain; **intramor'phemic**, occurring or existing within a morpheme; **intra'muscular**, situated or taking place within the substance of a muscle; also, administered into a muscle; hence **intra'muscularly** *adv.*, (by injection) into a muscle; **intra'nasal**, situated or occurring within the nose; **intra'nasally** *adv.*, through, in, or into the nose; **intra'natal**, taking place at the time of birth; **intra'national**, occurring or carried on within a nation-state; **intra'neural**, situated or occurring within a nerve; **intra'nuclear**, situated within the nucleus of a cell; **intranucleolar** (-njuːklɪˈəʊlə(r)), (-njuːˈkliːələ(r)), situated or occurring within a nucleolus; **intra-'oral** [L. *ōs*, *ōr-* mouth], situated within the mouth; **intra-'orbital**, situated or occurring within the orbit of the eye; **intra-or'ganic, -orga'nismal, -orga'nismic**, within an organism; **intra-'osseous** [L. *os*, *oss-* bone], situated within the substance of a bone; also **intra-'osteal** [Gr. ὀστέον bone], in same sense; **intra-'oval** [L. *ōvum* egg], taking place within the egg; **intra-o'varian**, contained or remaining in the ovary; **intrapara'central**, situated within the paracentral convolution of the brain; **intrapara'sitic**, existing in the substance of a parasitic organism; **intrapa'rochial**, existing or occurring within a parish; **intra'pelvic**, situated or occurring within the pelvis; **intraperi'cardiac, -al**, situated within the pericardium; **intraperito'neal**, situated or taking place within the cavity of the peritoneum; hence **intraperito'neally** *adv.*; **intra-'personal**, occurring inside a person's mind or character; **intraphilo'sophic**, that is within the limits of philosophy; **intra'plantar** [L. *planta* sole of the foot], situated on the inner side of the sole of the foot; **intra'pleural**, situated within the pleural cavity; **intra'polar**, situated within, i.e. between, the poles, e.g. of a galvanic battery (more properly INTERPOLAR); **intraproto'plasmic**, situated or occurring within the substance of protoplasm; **intra-'psychic, -'psychical**, occurring or existing within the psyche; **intra'pulmonary** [L. *pulmōn-es* lungs], situated or taking place within the lungs; **intrapul'monic** = *intrapulmonary*; **intra'racial**, within, or occurring within, a race; **intra'rectal**, situated within the rectum; **intra'regional**, occurring within a region; **intra'retinal**, situated within the substance of the retina; **intraseg'mental** *Zool.* and *Linguistics*, occurring within a 'segment'; **intra'seminal** *Bot.*, occurring or existing within a seed; **intra'semital**, situated within a semita of an echinoderm; **intra'serous**, existing or taking place within the serum of the blood; **intraso'matic** [Gr. σῶμα body], situated or occurring within the body; **intra'spinal**, situated or occurring within the spinal column or spinal cord; **intra'spinally** *adv.*, within the spinal cord; **intra'stromal**, situated within the stroma or connective tissue of an organ or structure; **intra-sub'jective**, of a reaction, response, etc., which occurs within a person; **intra'tarsal**, situated on the inner side of the tarsus; **intraterri'torial**, situated or contained within a territory; **intrate'sticular**, existing or carried out within, or administered into, a testicle; hence ˌ**intrate'sticularly** *adv.*; **intra'thecal**, (*a*) contained or enclosed in the theca (*e.g.* of a polyp), (*b*) going into or occurring within the spinal theca; hence **intra'thecally** *adv.*; **intratho'racic**, situated or occurring within the thorax; **intra'tracheal**, within the trachea or windpipe; **intra'tracheally** *adv.*, within the trachea; **intra'tubal**, **intra'tubular**, contained or occurring within a tube or tubule, esp. of the animal body; **intra-'typical**, occurring within one type; **intra-um'bilical**, situated within the umbilicus; **intra-'urban** [L. *urbs* city], carried on within a city; **intra-u'rethral**, situated within the urethra; **intrava'ginal**, (*a*) situated within the vagina. (*b*) *Bot.*, within the sheath of a leaf; **intra'valvular**, situated within or between valves (more properly *intervalvular*). **intrava'rietal**, occurring or existing within a variety (VARIETY 6 b), or between individuals of the same variety; **intrave'hicular**, of, pertaining to, or used within a space vehicle; **intra'verbal**, within a word; **intra'vertebral**, situated within a vertebra; hence **intra'vertebrally** *adv.* **intra'vesical** [L. *vēsīca* bladder], situated or occurring within the urinary bladder or the gall-bladder; **intravi'telline** [L. *vitellus* yolk], occurring within the yolk of an egg; **intraxylary** (-ˈzaɪlərɪ) *Bot.*, situated within the xylem or woody tissue, as the soft bast in the *Combretaceæ*.

1887 *Syd. Soc. Lex.*, *Intra-abdominal. **1897** *Allbutt's Syst. Med.* III. 975 The cæcum in an adult may be in any of its successive intra-abdominal positions. **1879** T. BRYANT *Pract. Surg.* II. 245 The *intra-acinous collections of them correspond to the structure of medullary cancer. **1873** T. H. GREEN *Introd. Pathol.* (ed. 2) 307 Cases in which the pulmonary consolidation is mainly due to a catarrhal *intra-alveolar growth. **1960** *Biol. Abstr.* XXXV. 1865/2 (*heading*) The lipids in the coating layer of the epidermis during the *intra-amniotic life. **1973** *Nature* 26 Jan. 280/1 The observed periodicity in response to the intra-amniotic injection of PGF_{2a} must..be related to endocrine and/or other rhythmic metabolic changes. **1961** *Lancet* 5 Aug. 279/1 If the endocrine condition of one uterine horn is altered experimentally (..by injecting progesterone *intra-amniotically into one horn) the two horns deliver at different times. **1973** *Nature* 26 Jan. 280/1 Intra-amniotically injected PGF_{2a} appears to be slowly transferred from the amniotic compartment. **1897** *Allbutt's Syst. Med.* IV. 389 Signs..of *intra-arterial tension. **1946** *Ibid.* 17 Aug. 238/1 Buchtal and Kahlson have pointed out that the close intra-arterial injection of 5 μgm. acetylcholine after introduction of adenosine triphosphate increases the intensity and duration of the mechanical response of muscle. **1962** *Lancet* 29 Dec. 1338/1 Substances given by intra-arterial infusion. **1938** *Coll. Papers Mayo Clinic* XXIX. 533 Histamine phosphate..and acetyl β-methylcholine..were injected *intra-arterially. **1964** W. G. SMITH *Allergy & Tissue Metabolism* ii. 26 Doses of antigen given intra-arterially or intravenously. **1890** BILLINGS *Med. Dict.* I. 711/1 *Intra-articular. **1908** *Practitioner* Apr. 516 There was much intra-articular effusion into both knee-joints. **1961** *Lancet* 29 July 266/2 Intra-articular cartilage is avascular. **1878** BELL *Gegenbaur's Comp. Anat.* 321 The water is streaming..into the branchial plates or the *intrabranchial cavity. **1898** *Allbutt's Syst. Med.* V. 31 Cases of *intrabronchial hæmorrhage. **1899** RENDEL HARRIS in *Contemp. Rev.* Dec. 810 We will leave on one side such cases as are *intra-canonical. **1879** *Jrnl. Physiol.* II. 336 The relation which exists between the *intracapillary pressure and the degree of dilation of these delicate tubes. **1961** *Lancet* 16 Sept. 664/2 A higher intracapillary hydrostatic pressure is presumably related to a greater leakage of protein and fluid. **1879** *St. George's Hosp. Rep.* IX. 324 Of the 8 cases of fracture of the *cervix femoris*, six occurred in females, and were *intracapsular. **1887** *Syd. Soc. Lex.*, **Intracardiac.* **1897** *Allbutt's Syst. Med.* IV. 389 It [the first heart-sound] is intracardiac and not muscular. **1917** *Jrnl. Immunol.* II. 141 Römer..injected guinea pigs sensitized to horse serum *intracardially with diphtheria antitoxin. **1958** *Immunology* I. 104 Injections were made intracardially. **1876** tr. *Wagner's Gen. Pathol.* (ed. 6) 160 The *intra-cardial nerve-centres. **1874** R. BROWN *Man. Bot.* Gloss., **Intracarpellary*, among or interior to the carpels. **1887** *Syd. Soc. Lex.*, **Intracartilaginous.* **1897** *Allbutt's Syst. Med.* III. 119 So far the description refers to intra-cartilaginous ossification. **1876** tr. *Wagner's Gen. Pathol.* 154 *Intra-cellular. **1883** S. WAINWRIGHT *Sci. Sophisms* vii. 109 An enclosed nucleus with surrounding intracellular matrix or matter. **1887** *Amer. Naturalist* XXI. 419 Brought into harmony with the phenomena of intra-cellular digestion. **1881** E. R. LANKESTER in *Jrnl. Microsc. Sc.* Jan. 122 In many Cœlentera the *intra-cellularly digestive cells are limited in number and position. **1896** *Allbutt's Syst. Med.* I. 519 Although most enzymes are discharged outwards, that is, are secreted, and act extracellularly, some of them effect their fermentative action intra-cellularly. **1881** G. SIGERSON tr. *Charcot's Lect. Dis. Nervous System* II. 281 An *intra-cerebral focus of hæmorrhage. **1890** W. JAMES *Princ. Psychol.* I. iii. 100 He found very regularly an immediate deflection of the galvanometer, indicating an abrupt alteration of the intra-cerebral temperature. **1964** S. DUKE-ELDER *Parsons' Dis. Eye* (ed. 14) xxxiii. 530 They spread slowly within the sheaths, and death is due to intracerebral extension. **1910** *Jrnl. Exper. Med.* XII. 253 Inoculated *intracerebrally with spinal cord. **1937** *Jrnl. Path. & Bacteriol.* XLIV. 418 The strain of fowl pest virus..was only very slightly pathogenic for mice when inoculated intraperitoneally or even intracerebrally. **1970** *European Jrnl. Cancer* VI. 173/1 Inbred Swiss/Ry-female mice were inoculated intracerebrally with Ehrlich carcinoma. **1932** DORLAND & MILLER *Med. Dict.* (ed. 16) 642/1 **Intracisternal*, within a cistern, especially the cisterna magna. **1958** *Technology* Jan. 384/3 By intracisternal injection *nor*-morphine was rather more active than morphine. **1964** G. H. HAGGIS et al. *Introd. Molecular Biol.* v. 141 One hour after the first meal following starvation.. the endoplasmic reticular cavities of the basal zone..are distended and contain small granules (intracisternal granules). **1934** *Physiol. Abstr.* XIX. 481 Histamine.., acetylcholine, and padutin have no influence upon the blood pressure when injected *intracisternally. **1971** *Nature* 5 Mar. 54/1 Intracisternally injected radioactive noradrenaline. **1928** *Daily Tel.* 26 June 10/6 Houston['s].. hinterland is shortly to be widened by the construction of the *intra-coastal canal from New Orleans. **1964** *Times Rev. Industry* Mar. 86/1 Between Jacksonville and Palatka.. there is a navigable channel in the St. Johns River forming part of the Atlantic Intracoastal waterways. **1972** *Countryman* Winter 41 Fifty miles along the intracoastal canal to the Aransas wildlife sanctuary [in Texas]. **1888** F. E. BEDDARD in *Proc. Zool. Soc.* (London) 20 Mar. 217 Annelid of Genus Æolosoma..*Intracœlomic muscular bands. **1940** S. D. TYLMAN *Theory & Pract. Crown & Bridge Prosthesis* xix. 177 Retainers are classified into three types: The first is the *intracoronal, or inlays... As the name indicates, the prepared cavity and its cast retainer lie largely within the body of the coronal portion of the tooth. **1963** C. R. COWELL et al. *Inlays, Crowns & Bridges* ii. 4 A gold inlay is an intracoronal restoration for a vital tooth. *Ibid.* vi. 60 Tooth substance may have been lost to such an extent that a restoration cannot be retained *intracoronally. **1898** P. MANSON *Trop. Dis.* i. 4 Each variety or species of the *intra-corporeal plasmodium has its special and more or less definite life-span of twenty-four hours. **1897** *Allbutt's Syst. Med.* II. 724 The *intra-corpuscular amœboid form, to which they gave the name *plasmodium.* **1890** W. JAMES *Princ. Psychol.* II. xix. 128 The normal forward irradiation of *intra-cortical excitement through association-paths is checked. **1970** *Jrnl. Physiol.* CCX. 57P (*heading*) Relation of movements induced by intracortical stimulation to receptive fields of points in the perirolandic and parietal cortex of the monkey. **1865** GROTE *Plato* I. i. 58 He did not proclaim his Nous to be..an *intra-cosmical..instinct. **1933** *Intracrustal [see BYSMALITHIC *a.*]. **1921** *Sci. Papers U.S. Bureau of Standards* XVI. 215 The fracture of normal material is, in general, *intra-crystalline; that is, it consists of a break across the grains rather than of a separation between them. **1955** *Soil Sci.* LXXX. 425 The intracrystalline swelling of montmorillonite. **1973** *Nature* 3 Aug. 277/1 The increase in intra-crystalline slip..may lead to the elongation of the recrystallized grains. **1937** R. H. LOWIE *Hist. Ethnol. Theory* (1938) xiii. 237 As soon as functionalism is reduced to what it is—a worthy programme for ascertaining what *intracultural bonds may exist—the neglect of other methods appears as solely a matter of personal preference. **1956** GARVIN & MATHIOT in J. A. Fishman *Readings Social. of Lang.* (1968) 366 In intra-cultural terms, different segments of a speech community can be compared as to the degree to which the standard language has penetrated them, just as different subcultures of the same culture can be compared in terms of different degrees of penetration by urban elements. **1956** LENNEBERG & ROBERTS *Language of Experience* 4 Not all hypotheses can be verified *intra-culturally. **1972** *Jrnl. Social Psychol.* LXXXVII. 13 The study of values both intraculturally and cross-culturally has a long, and..distinguished history. **1885** M. HAY tr. *H. von Ziemssen's Handbk. Gen. Therapeutics* II. 391 We may characterise all such procedures, in contradistinction to the epidermic method, as the endermic or *intracutaneous administration of remedies. **1905** HYDE & MONTGOMERY *Pract. Treat. Dis. Skin* (ed. 7) 96 Hypodermatic and intracutaneous injections. **1956** D. M. PILLSBURY et al. *Dermatol.* xv. 139 Scratch or intracutaneous tests are routinely employed to detect the presence of skin-sensitizing antibodies. **1925** *Jrnl. Immunol.* X. 729, 0·1 cc. was the amount *intracutaneously injected in each case. **1927** *Proc. Soc. Exper. Biol. & Med.* XXV. 97 An injection..was given intracutaneously. **1961** *Jrnl. Amer. Med. Assoc.* 29 July 279/2 Alum-precipitated toxoids were injected intracutaneously. **1878** T. BRYANT *Pract. Surg.* I. 101 An *intra-cystic growth may project from it as a fungus. **1916** *Jrnl. R. Microsc. Soc.* 307 The chromatic margin of the undulating membrane represents an *intracytoplasmic posteriorly-directed flagellum. **1971** *Biol. Abstr.* LII. 2029/1 In other organs..secretory granules may undergo intracytoplasmic lysis without destruction of their limiting membrane. **1961** P. FLEMING *Bayonets to Lhasa* xxiii. 291 The fruits of *intradepartmental research. **1967** A. BATTERSBY *Network Analysis* (ed. 2) iii. 42 The single activity..might well be a summary of an intra-departmental arrow diagram. **1900** DORLAND *Med. Dict.* 327/2 *Intradermal. **1946** *Nature* 31 Aug 311/2 The intradermal test [for tuberculosis] is conceded to be eminently satisfactory in cattle. **1964** W. G. SMITH *Allergy & Tissue Metabolism* i. 8 A patient who developed a local reaction to an intradermal injection. **1926** *Amer. Year Bk.* *1925* 951/1 The time required for the disappearance of *intradermally injected salt solution. **1937** *Jrnl. Path. & Bacteriol.* XLIV. 410 Four rhesus monkeys were inoculated intradermally on the inner side of the left thigh with 0·2 c.c. of a 20 per cent. suspension of mouse brain. **1962** *Lancet* 26 May 1107/2 Sarcoid tissue..was..inoculated intradermally into 4 patients with suspected sarcoidosis. **1888** *Syd. Soc. Lex.* III, *Intradermic. **1966** *Amer. Jrnl. Vet. Res.* XXVII. 541/1 The cervical region of cattle is the most responsive site for applying intradermic tuberculin tests. **1873** *Daily News* 11 Aug.,. *Intradivisional sham fights are more interesting and instructive than fights in which one division is pitted against another. **1953** L. C. DE LEBORGNE tr. *R. A. Leborgne's Breast in Roent. Diagn.* i. 14 When contrast mammography shows *intraductal lesions..we collect the liquid that has been injected, by softly expressing the breast (intraductal rinse). **1961** *Lancet* 29 July 241/2 Prolactin activity was detected and assayed semiquantitatively by the localised lactogenic response of the mammary gland of the pseudo-pregnant rabbit to intraductal injections. **1971** *Amer. Jrnl. Obstetr. & Gynecol.* CX. 505/1 In our study of 20 intraductal papillomas of the breast, the similarity of these lesions to the papillary hidradenoma of the vulva was striking. **1890** BILLINGS *Med. Dict.* I. 711/1 *Intradural. **1901** J. COLLINS in Hektoen & Riesman *Text-bk. Path.* xi. 618 Intradural

tumors arise either from the inner surface of the dura or the pia. **1950** *Jrnl. Neurosurg.* VII. 1 Intradural granulomas are very rare and may be intramedullary or extramedullary. **1971** *Ibid.* XXXIV. 378/1 We therefore think that the intradural approach..is not more hazardous than the extradural approach. **1944** *Brit. Jrnl. Ophthalm.* XXVIII. 328 Some surgeons again approach the ganglion *intradurally. **1960** *Cleveland Clinic Q.* XXVII. 198 When this extradural treatment fails..we have injected corticosteroids intradurally by lumbar puncture. **1971** *Jrnl. Neurosurg.* XXXIV. 378/2 No facial palsy occurred in more than 1000 patients, most of whom were operated on intradurally. **1840** G. S. FABER *Regen.* 50 The Translation of a man, from his natural or extra-ecclesiastical state in fallen Adam, to an acquired or *intra-ecclesiastical State in Christ, the second Adam. **1861** BERESF. HOPE *Eng. Cathedr. 19th C.* 252 We all know that intramural and intra-ecclesiastical interment is now illegal. **1904** F. P. FOSTER *Appleton's Med. Dict.* 1161 *Intraepidermal. **1951** J. J. & W. D. ELLER *Tumors Skin* (ed. 2) vii. 336 (*heading*) Intra-epidermal and superficial carcinomatous changes. **1971** *Dermatologica* CXLII. 29 (*heading*) On benign intra-epidermal follicular acanthomas. **1904** F. P. FOSTER *Appleton's Med. Dict.* 1161 *Intraepidermic. **1910** *Practitioner* June 871 An intra-epidermic abscess. **1949** *Time* 11 Apr. 39 They had launched the Intra-European Payments plan also as 'the little ECA'. **1962** H. O. BEECHENO *Introd. Business Stud.* i. 4 The European countries felt that there was no further danger of another intra-European War. **1967** *Guardian* 15 May 6/6 Intra-European bilateral contacts continue to proliferate benignly. **1973** *Nature* 16 Mar. 150/2 Designed for intra-European communication the satellite will handle telephone, telegram, telex and television channels. **1881** *Jrnl. Microsc. Sc.* Jan. 108 [This] may be spoken of as an *intraepithelial vesicle. **1895** W. JAMES *Meaning of Truth* (1909) ii. 45 Mental images..are one phenomenal fact; the tigers are another; and their pointing to the tigers is a perfectly commonplace *intra-experiential relation. **1909** W. M. URBAN *Valuation* vi. 188 For Ehrenfels the real test of the rationality of the desire is not an intra-experiential test. **1900** B. D. JACKSON *Gloss. Bot. Terms* 137/1 *Intrafascicular (*fasciculus*, a bundle), within a bundle. **1914** M. DRUMMOND tr. *Haberlandt's Physiol. Plant. Anat.* ii. 97 So-called fascicular or intrafascicular cambium forms a strip which extends tangentially right across the bundle. **1917** *Ann. Bot.* XXXI. 45 The existence of this vestigial, intrafascicular cambium indicates that Monocotyledons have been derived from a dicotyledonous stock. **1960** W. B. R. LAIDLAW *Guide Brit. Hardwoods* 228 *Interfascicular*, between bundles..(cp. intrafascicular—cambium inside a bundle). **1894** C. D. WALCOTT in *Bull. Geol. Soc. Amer.* V. 192 An *intra-formational conglomerate is one formed within a geologic formation of material derived from and deposited within that formation. **1938** HATCH & RASTALL *Petrol. Sedimentary Rocks* (ed. 3) iv. 76 Remarkable beds of intraformational breccia and conglomerate are found in some limestone and dolomite formations. **1940** E. S. HILLS *Outl. Structural Geol.* i. 15 When a slumped mass slides down on to undisturbed sediments it may later be covered by younger deposits. Severely disturbed beds will then be found between undisturbed strata, an arrangement that is known as intraformational contortion or corrugation. **1963** D. W. & E. E. HUMPHRIES tr. *Termier's Erosion & Sedimentation* x. 194 False unconformities and intraformational unconformities can often be explained by the effect of 'creep'. **1894** C. S. SHERRINGTON in *Jrnl. Physiol.* XVII. 240 Its own contained muscle-fibres, or as they may be termed the *intrafusal muscle-fibres, always however run parallel with the long axis of the spindle itself. **1905** J. S. FERGUSON *Normal Histol.* ix. 136 The bundle of intrafusal muscle fibres is again surrounded by a delicate axial sheath of connective tissue. **1968** PASSMORE & ROBSON *Compan. Med. Stud.* I. xxiv. 12/2 A muscle spindle.. contains a few short and very slender striated muscle cells; these are the intrafusal fibres which contrast with the main mass of extrafusal fibres. The intrafusal fibres receive motor nerve terminals. **1970** F. J. SCHULTE in U. Stave *Physiol. Prenatal Period* II. xxv. 805 In kittens, the intrafusal activity ..seems to be less tonic than in adult cats. **1900** DORLAND *Med. Dict.* 327/2 *Intra-gastric. **1903** G. HERSCHELL *Man. Intragastric Technique* vii. 107 The intragastric needle-douche..may be described as the application of fine jets of fluid under considerable pressure to the interior of the stomach. **1926** J. A. RYLE *Gastric Function* I. i. 15 When the stomach is filled and the intragastric tension thereby raised, the tension..quickly falls again. **1972** *Nature* 21 Apr. 385/2 Contractions of the body of the stomach of an anaesthetized rat measured from pressure changes in an intragastric balloon. **1959** *Proc. Amer. Assoc. Cancer Res.* III. 63/2 (*heading*) Relationship of dose of *intragastrically administered methylcholanthrene to incidence of breast cancer in rats. **1971** *Nature* 16 Apr. 461/1 Propane sultone administered intragastrically at two dose levels gave rise chiefly to gliomas. **1947** *Biol. Abstr.* XXI. 2107/2 The role of *intra- and inter-generic hybridization in the breeding of cultivated plants. **1971** *Nature* 22 Oct. 526/1 They approach the limits of intrageneric relationship when compared with other fish taxa. **1937** *Ibid.* 30 Oct. 760/2 These are changes of 'balance', and rank with *intra-genic changes and position changes as one of the three effective means of variation. **1971** *Ibid.* 10 Dec. 337/1 One or more amino-acids have been deleted, probably during intragenic crossing over. **1895** J. D. DANA *Man. Geol.* (ed. 4) 957 Nearly all transported debris of the glacier was confined at first to its lower part... It was *intraglacial, as now in Greenland. *Ibid.*, The term englacial..is not here adopted because it is half Greek. Intraglacial accords with Latin usage. **1896** *Amer. Geologist* XVIII. 153 Intraglacial..is here used for drift deposited in the field occupied by the ice, in contradistinction to extraglacial drift which has come to rest on ground not actually covered by the ice when it was deposited. According to Prof. Dana's use of this term, however, it would be synonymous with englacial, as Prof. Chamberlin designates the drift enclosed in the lower part of the ice-sheet. **1898** *Q. Jrnl. Geol. Soc.* LIV. 205 The débris-bands and intraglacial material with which the lower part of the glacier is so richly charged. **1966** *Geogr. Abstr.* A. 287 In the intraglacial zone are found: forms of marginal dissection, numerous eskers and kames. **1892** *Amer. Jrnl. Med. Sci.* CIII. 466 The author believes that in circumscribed growths, in the future, the only operation that will be admissible will be the bloodless *intra-glandular method. **1909** *Practitioner* Nov. 682 Intraglandular enucleation.. should be performed. **1969** *Cancer* XXIV. 765/2 The intraglandular dissemination of thyroid cancer was seen in a very high proportion in follicular adenocarcinoma. **1940** BECKER & OBERMAYER *Mod. Dermatol. & Syphilol.* xlviii. 798/1 *Intragluteal injection should be made in the upper outer quadrant of the buttock. **1961** *Lancet* 29 July 268/2 They were given 125 units of chorionic gonadotrophin daily by deep intragluteal injection. **1964** P. WORSLEY in I. L. Horowitz *New Sociol.* 388 The institutional norms..*intra-governmental and intra-social. **1967** *Time* 10 Feb. 58 An ugly intragovernmental feud over the creation of an electronics and broadcasting giant. **1887** *Syd. Soc. Lex.*, **Intra-hepatic*. **1897** *Allbutt's Syst. Med.* IV. 28 The intrahepatic bile-ducts. *Ibid.* 82 Increased viscidity of bile, consequent on intrahepatic catarrh. **1896** *Current Hist.* (U.S.) VI. 916 *Intra-Imperial Communication. **1872** COHEN *Dis. Throat* 107 Chronic inflammation of the vocal cords and other *intra-laryngeal structures. **1897** *Allbutt's Syst. Med.* IV. 828, 8216 [cases] had been operated on *intra-laryngeally. **1944** *Amer. Jrnl. Ophthalm.* XXVII. 1427/1 A case of *intralenticular foreign body is presented. **1962** HARRIS & GRUBER in A. Pirie *Lens Metabolism Rel. Cataract* 383 If..there are capsular and intralenticular barriers to diffusion..localized accumulation of fluid could occur. **1900** *Brit. Med. Jrnl.* No. 2040. 261 A specimen of *intraligamentous myoma removed by cœliotomy. **1937** O. JESPERSEN *Analytic Syntax* II. xxix. 109 In the case of..the German or Latin masculine the correspondence with the extralingual quality 'male sex' is far from being pure: here the extralingual and the *intralingual are inextricably mingled. *Ibid.*, When the preterit is used for 'the shifted present time' in indirect speech this cannot in the same way be said to refer to something outside the linguistic expression: it is intralingual. **1956** J. WHATMOUGH *Lang.* 63 For intralingual purposes (i.e. communication within a single language) every language is a good language for those who actually use it. **1964** E. A. NIDA *Toward Sci. Transl.* i. 3 'Intralingual' translation..consists essentially in rewording something within the same language. **1965** *Language* XLI. 505 Meaning refers to the intralingual relations contracted by linguistic units. **1937** J. R. FIRTH *Tongues of Men* iii. 34 For the vast majority of mankind clicks are extra-linguistic sounds, but for..Zulus they are *intra-linguistic—that is to say, they form part of grammatical words. **1945** *Mind* LIV. 149 Morris' 'syntactics'..deals only with relations among expressions in a language and thus with an entirely intra-linguistic subject-matter. **1962** U. WEINREICH in Householder & Saporta *Probl. Lexicogr.* 35 Over-schematized though it may be, ad hoc intralinguistic considerations suggest that 'c_1 and c_2' should have been considered a single condition. **1847-9** TODD *Cycl. Anat.* IV. 133/1 The *intra-locular matter is in itself soft. **1833** SIR W. HAMILTON *Discuss.* (1852) 152 Syllogism and enthymeme being distinguished as two *intralogical forms of argumentation. **1936** STEDMAN *Med. Dict.* (ed. 13) 555/2 **Intraluminal*, intra-tubal. **1943** *Jrnl. Clin. Invest.* XXII. 225/1 The clinical importance of intra-luminal pressure measurements in hollow viscera is well exemplified by the syndromes of hyper- and hypotension in the cardiovascular system. **1961** *Lancet* 30 Sept. 738/2 This flora may have utilised a relatively large part of the intraluminal nutrients during their logarithmic rate of growth. **1971** *Gut* XII. 268 Intraluminal pressure measurements may be a useful guide for the treatment of achalasia by pneumatic dilatations. **1892** *Amer. Jrnl. Med. Sci.* CIV. 96 (*heading*) The treatment of *intra-mammary abscesses. **1960** *Farmer & Stockbreeder* 8 Mar. 107/1 His vet bill was too high... The balance was for drugs—almost entirely expensive intra-mammary antibiotics. **1971** *Jrnl. Endocrinol.* LI. p. xiii, The myoepithelial cells of the mammary gland contract in response to oxytocin and this results in a rise in intra-mammary pressure. **1846** WORCESTER cites LOUDON for **Intramarginal*. **1875** BENNETT & DYER tr. *Sachs' Bot.* 361 The sori..are placed on an intramarginal anastomosing bend of the veins, and covered with a cup-shaped indusium. **1884** BOWER & SCOTT *De Bary's Phaner.* 383 Those parts of Phanerogamic Parasites which are developed inside the host, (*intramatrically), as well as their *haustoria*, behave differently. **1879** *St. George's Hosp. Rep.* IX. 395 *Intra-meningeal hæmorrhage. **1904** *Jrnl. Philos., Psychol. & Sci. Methods* I. 300 The *intra-mental and the extra-mental objects..differ only in position and in relational context. **1935** *Mind* XLIV. 356 Purely intra-mental causation. **1958** Intra-mental [see *extra-mental* (EXTRA- 1)]. **1946** *Mind* LV. 372 Notwithstanding his insistence on the *intra-mentality of objects, he keeps 'what is in the mind "intirely distinct" from the mind itself'. **1878** NEWCOMB *Pop. Astron.* III. iii. 286 The supposed *intra-Mercurial planets. **1898** *Westm. Gaz.* 29 Sept. 9/3 [He] says: 'The East London Company give a constant supply to the whole of their *intra-Metropolitan and all their extra-Metropolitan area, with the exception of a small portion near Buckhurst Hill. **1864** *Reader* 5 Mar. 302 A deep, precipitous, *intramontane chasm, forming the basin of a profound lake—viz., the 'Dead Sea'. **1962** A. TIETZE in Householder & Saporta *Probl. Lexicogr.* 272 It has no *intra-morphemic changes. **1973** A. H. SOMMERSTEIN *Sound Pattern Anc. Greek* ii. 22 Words containing intramorphemic clusters /pm bm p^hm/.. all, historically, underwent assimilation. **1874** BARKER tr. *Frey's Histol.* § 183 *Intramuscular. **1878** T. BRYANT *Pract. Surg.* I. 500 The intramuscular veins are sometimes affected without the subcutaneous. **1946** *Nature* 17 Aug. 242/2 The present data..cover some twenty-six treatment schedules with intra-muscular penicillin. **1962** LUNTZ & WRIGHT in A. Pirie *Lens Metabolism Rel. Cataract* 317 These persons,.. when given a desensitizing course of intramuscular injections.., rapidly improved. **1909** *Practitioner* Dec. 871 Digalen..can be used by the mouth, by the rectum, intravenously, *intramuscularly, and hypodermically. **1933** *Discovery* Jan. 4/2 This could be safely injected intramuscularly and intravenously. **1961** *Ann. N.Y. Acad. Sci.* XCIV. 917 A carcinoma had been transplanted intramuscularly, intraperitoneally, or into the lungs. **1886** *Med. News* 21 Aug. 213 (*Heading*) Neurotic asthma and other neurotic maladies in their relations to *intranasal disease. **1897** *Allbutt's Syst. Med.* IV. 684 Cases of intra-nasal lupus. **1933** *Jrnl. Amer. Med. Assoc.* 24 June 2014/1 These agents were given *intra-nasally. **1961** *Lancet* 23 Sept. 680/2 Swiss white mice..were infected intranasally with..egg cultures of influenza viruses. **1971** *Infection & Immunity* IV. 738 Statolon..when instilled intranasally (IN) protects mice infected with lethal doses of influenza virus. **1902** *Encycl. Brit.* XXXI. 304/1 The causes of the high death-rate among infants, whether due to ante-natal, *intra-natal, or neo-natal conditions, come under.. observation. **1922** *Rep. Public Health & Med. Subjects* (Ministry of Health) No. 7. 8 Death during labour—intra-natal fœtal death. **1963** D. G. W. CLYNE *Textbk. Gynaecol. & Obstetr.* xxxvii. 875 The intranatal care of the premature infant has been summarized. **1923** G. O'BRIEN *Ess. Econ. Effects Reformation* iv. 179 It is an institution at once *intranational and international. **1940** A. HUXLEY *Let.* 15 Dec. (1969) 464 Two satisfactory alternatives, either voluntary international and intranational co-operation, or balance of power. **1901** *Buck's Handbk. Med. Sci.* (rev. ed.) II. 110/1 Foci of degeneration in the nerves were found to correspond to nodules upon *intraneural arterial branches. **1936** H. MULDER *Cognition & Volition in Lang.* iii. 118 A bit of intra-neural behavior in the brain of the man who coined it. **1954** ZACHARY & ROAF in H. J. Seddon *Peripheral Nerve Injuries* II. 73 Complete palsies have been caused by the accidental intraneural injection of a noxious substance. **1887** *Syd. Soc. Lex.*, **Intranuclear network*, a delicate system of protoplasmic fibres traversing the nucleus of cells. **1879** *Jrnl. R. Microsc. Soc.* II. 138 Finally, the ordinary *intranucleolar network is produced, marking the completion of the division process and the entrance of the nuclei into a state of quiescence. **1970** *Jrnl. Cell Biol.* XLV. 584 (*heading*) Aberrant intranucleolar maturation of ribosomal precursors in the absence of protein synthesis. **1880** *Jrnl. Linn. Soc.* XV. 106 Inner lip..rising into a tooth on the first *intraoral thread. **1887** *Syd. Soc. Lex.*, **Intra-orbital aneurysm*, aneurysm occurring within the orbit, and therefore affecting one of the branches of the ophthalmic artery. **1894** A. C. FRASER in Locke *Hum. Und.* II. iv. xi. 327 An odd and inadequate illustration; for 'writing' and 'moving the hand', although *intraorganic, as much need to have their reality indicated as the sight of black or white does. **1962** S. K. LANGER *Philos. Sk.* i. 9 Sentience is a phase of vital process itself, a strictly intraorganic phase, i.e., an appearance which is presented only within the organism in which the activity occurs. **1941** J. S. HUXLEY *Uniqueness of Man* xi. 241 Analogy may very readily mislead. Weismann sought to apply this same analogy of *intra-organismal struggle and selection to the units of heredity; but the analogy happens not to hold good. **1952** *Brit. Jrnl. Psychol.* XLIII. 245 The production of a neurosis in a cat by a method that is of special interest in that a difficult discrimination of intraorganismal cues was involved. **1955** *Intraorganismic [see *extra-organismic* (EXTRA- 1)]. **1835-6** TODD *Cycl. Anat.* I. 61/1 Oleaginous matter is deposited in the *intra-osseous tissue. **1898** J. HUTCHINSON *Archives Surg.* IX. 295 What appeared to be a very large *intra-osteal cartilaginous tumour. **1897** *Allbutt's Syst. Med.* II. 1035 The embryo though visible, has not quite completed its *intra-oval development. **1898** P. MANSON *Trop. Dis.* iii. 74 The identity of the *intra-parasitic pigment and that found in the tissues. **1858** *Lit. Churchman* IV. 257/1 The best methods of what we may call *intra-parochial organization. **1887** *Syd. Soc. Lex.*, **Intrapelvic*. **1893** A. S. ECCLES *Sciatica* 5 The probability of intrapelvic pressure being the predisposing, if not the exciting, cause of the sciatic pain. **1879** *St. George's Hosp. Rep.* IX. 405 *Intra-pericardiac aneurism of the aorta. **1875** HAYDEN *Dis. Heart* 9 The *intra-pericardial portions of the pulmonary artery, aorta, and superior vena cava. **1835-6** TODD *Cycl. Anat.* I. 19 The viscera have..been distinguished..by the names *intra-peritoneal and extra-peritoneal. **1881** ERICHSEN in *Times* 4 Aug. 11/5 The operative treatment of intraperitonæal tumours. **1897** *Allbutt's Syst. Med.* II. 700 When inoculated *intraperitoneally into guinea-pigs, it causes, in from 11 to 20 days, a paresis of the hind limbs. **1909** W. M. URBAN *Valuation* x. 286 The terms of estimation are..wholly *intra-personal, within the ego. **1935** G. K. ZIPF *Psycho-Biol. of Lang.* (1936) 297 The occasions of inter-personal conflict are often occasions for intra-personal conflict as well. **1955** R. JAKOBSON in H. Werner *On Expressive Lang.* 79 A competition of both devices is manifest in any symbolic process, either intrapersonal or social. **1878** S. H. HODGSON *Philos. of Reflect.* I. iii. § 1. 167 What is the nature of this or that existence in the supra-scientific but *intra-philosophic region? **1898** *Allbutt's Syst. Med.* V. 380 If the opening be ..free, air passes out of the pleural sac as well as into it, and there may be *intrapleural tension. **1878** *Rep. Smithsonian Inst.* 365 With a very strong polarizing current the whole *intra-polar portion of the nerve is put into a state of anelectrotonus. **1887** *Syd. Soc. Lex.*, *Intrapolar region*, Pflüger's term for the part of an electrotonic nerve through which an exciting current is passing, being that between the poles of the battery. **1917** C. R. PAYNE tr. *Pfister's Psychoanal. Method* viii. 169 The sleeping state lowers the power of the *intra-psychic censor. **1954** J. A. C. BROWN *Social Psychol. of Industry* ix. 252 Frustration, whether intrapsychic or due to external factors. **1935** *Mind* XLIV. 215 The interplay of conflicting *intra-psychical forces. **1898** *Allbutt's Syst. Med.* V. 65 Instances of sustained *intra-pulmonary pressure. **1923** *Amer. Jrnl. Physiol.* LXV. 229 Blood pressure changes are..complicated by the increased *intrapulmonic pressure interfering with filling of the heart. **1968** *Biol. Abstr.* XLIX. 2076/2 Excess intrapulmonic pressure in the abdominal and thoracic cavities. **1903** *Biometrika* Feb. 152 The interracial correlation of the mean numbers of stamens and pistils is very much greater than the mean *intraracial correlation between stamens and pistils. **1922** JOYCE *Ulysses* 717 Intraracial inhibition. **1957** *Antiquity* XXXI. 196 These two groups [of early Man] are in effect intra-racial variants. **1893** A. S. ECCLES *Sciatica* 56 Cases in which *intra-rectal electrization is adopted. **1964** *Ann. Reg. 1963* 204 *Intra-regional trade increased. **1966** *B.B.C. Handbk.* 51 These intra-regional services are directed..to the region as a whole. **1909** WEBSTER, *Intrasegmental. **1940** *Chambers's Techn. Dict.* 456/2 *Intrasegmental*, said of vertebrae which arise by the fusion of the cranial and caudal elements of the same somite. **1953** C. E. BAZELL *Ling. Form* 3 It is to be noted however that the intra-segmental range of a suprasegmental phoneme has normally no distinctive relevance. **1972** *Language* XLVIII. 46 In intra-segmental variation, as has been seen, different values for a feature are distributed over different portions of one and the same segment. **1895** S. H. VINES *Students' Text-bk. Bot.* II. III. 440 The *intra-seminal stage includes the whole of the development which the embryo undergoes during the conversion of the ovule into the ripe seed. **1902** *Nature* 3

Apr. 519/1 Seeds from infected plants are entirely free from disease, thereby proving fairly conclusively the impossibility of intra-seminal sources of infection. **1930** *Ann. Bot.* XLIV. 772 The germination of the seed [of *Garrya elliptica*] is reported as 'intra-seminal'. **1835–6** TODD *Cycl. Anat.* I. 59/1 The *intra-serous sebaceous fat. **1896** *Allbutt's Syst. Med.* I. 244 Drugs may be introduced.. by Intraserous Injection. **1932** H. H. PRICE *Perception* viii. 257 The revival of kinaesthetic and other *intra-somatic data..is..far less common. **1938** [see EXTRASOMATIC *a.*]. **1939** *Mind* XLVIII. 517 His treatment of intrasomatic sense-perception is equally precise. **1948** *Mind* LVII. 246 Any 'map' which may be elaborated at this level has a purely 'intrasomatic' significance. **1840** G. V. ELLIS *Anat.* 158 The *intra-spinal veins are very numerous. **1906** *Jrnl. Physiol.* XXXIV. 31 The reflex arcs from separate areas of the receptive field are closely knit together *intraspinally. **1970** *Biol. Abstr.* LI. 7775/1 (*heading*) Clinical trials with the use of 5% phenol intraspinally in the treatment of cancer pain. **1847–9** TODD *Cycl. Anat.* IV. 118/2 All growths possess vessels which..permeate..*intrastromal substances. **1914** MYERS & VALENTINE in *Brit. Jrnl. Psychol.* VII. I. 72 Bullough's..physiological aspect has here been extended to include not merely the sensory effects and the changes in feeling..but also the experiences of self-activity which the sounds may produce in the subject; in consequence, the word '*intra-subjective' will be substituted for this aspect. **1921** E. BULLOUGH *Ibid.* XII. I. 86 After the experiments of C. S. Myers..I would adopt the term 'intra-subjective' proposed by him, in place of 'physiological', which..was found by him to be too narrow, when applied to musical experiences. **1955** *Times* 26 May 3/4 Bruckner was a late romantic and as such was concerned with intra-subjective emotion as the material of his art. His fondling of an idea, then dropping it, at a silent pause and picking up another involves no incongruity. **1959** W. V. QUINE in R. A. Brower *On Translation* II. 159 Intrasubjective synonymy..is intrasubjective in that the synonyms are joined for each subject by sameness of stimulus meaning for him;.. intrasubjective synonymy is in principle just as objective, just as discoverable by the outside linguist, as is translation. **1888** *Syd. Soc. Lex.*, *Intratesticular. **1921** *Brain* XLIV. 168 In case XXIX an intratesticular injection of 3 c.c. [was given]. **1958** *Immunology* I. 4 For intratesticular grafting, the right testis was delivered through the smallest possible incision in the scrotum. **1970** *Sci. Jrnl.* June 68/2 The spermatozoa..are transferred through an uninterrupted system of ducts which originate from a complex network of intratesticular ducts. **1942** *Cancer Res.* II. 288 After the blood examinations had been concluded, the animals were inoculated *intratesticularly with the Brown-Pearce tumor. **1971** *Lipids* VI. 706/1 Fatty acid synthesis was studied in testes of young and adult rats either injected intratesticularly or incubated with 1–^{14}C acetate. **1887** G. C. BOURNE in *Q. Jrnl. Microsc. Sc.* Aug. 31 In the *intrathecal parts of the polyp the endoderm cells are entirely converted into a parenchymatous tissue. **1921** *Brain* XLIV. 168 In Case III an intrathecal injection of 1·5 c.c. cerebrospinal fluid was given. **1960** P. W. DAYKIN *Vet. Appl. Pharmacol. & Therapeutics* iv. 36 Administration by the intrathecal route involves the penetration of the dura mater, and the route is not frequently used in veterinary practice. **1971** *Jrnl. Path.* CIV. 141 An intrathecal lipoma of the filum terminale..was found in a 2-yr-old female infant dying from extensive burns. **1928** L. E. H. WHITBY *Med. Bacteriol.* xxiii. 236 The most popular method is to inject 500 units *intrathecally immediately the diagnosis is made. **1972** *Lancet* 30 Dec. 1401/2 An account of the toxicity of antifolate drugs given intrathecally. **1862** H. W. FULLER *Dis. Lungs* 17 Instances in which the lung is compressed by *intra-thoracic tumours. **1879** *St. George's Hosp. Rep.* IX. 195 Seven cases of intrathoracic aneurism. **1898** *Allbutt's Syst. Med.* V. 326 *Intra-tracheal injections of menthol. **1923** *Jrnl. Exper. Med.* XXXVII. 793 (*caption*) Protocols of rabbits treated *intratracheally and intraperitoneally with killed cultures of hog-cholera bacillus. **1930** *Jrnl. Laboratory & Clin. Med.* XVI. 87 (*heading*) A new apparatus for administering volatile anesthetics intratracheally without tracheotomy. **1973** *Nature* 16 Mar. 203/2 Turkey poults were inoculated intratracheally. **1887** *Syd. Soc. Lex.*, **Intratubal*, within a tube, as the Eustachian or the Fallopian tube. **1898** *Allbutt's Syst. Med.* V. 27 The occasional intratubal mucous inspissations of acute bronchitis. **1858** THUDICHUM *Urine* 245 The presence in the urine of *intratubular hyaloid casts indicates a chronic disease of the kidneys. **1934** *Mind* XLIII. 74 An *intra-typical variable is a variable all of whose arguments are of one type. **1959** P. F. STRAWSON *Individuals* I. i. 53 The cases in which this intra-typical identification is possible are severely restricted. For they require that the parties to an identifying reference should be operating with one and the same type-homogeneous referential framework. **1881** WATSON in *Jrnl. Lin. Soc.* XV. No. 85. 261 Slightly nicked by the *intraumbilical furrow. **1886** *Edin. Rev.* July 15 The telephone is coming more and more into use for short distances and *intra-urban communications. **1887** *Syd. Soc. Lex.*, **Intra-urethral*. **1898** J. HUTCHINSON *Archives Surg.* IX. 362 He comes to me in June with an intra-urethral ulcer. **1857** BULLOCK *Cazeaux' Midwif.* 57 The neck..in its *intra-vaginal portion. **1900** I. B. BALFOUR tr. *Goebel's Organogr. Plants* II. 359 The intravaginal squamules are organs which secrete mucilage for the protection of the bud. **1951** MCLEAN & IVIMEY-COOK *Textbk. Theoret. Bot.* I. xxii. 993 The first [leaf structures] are called intravaginal scales because they appear in the axil within the leaf sheath or vagina of certain Monocotyledons... They take the form of small tooth-like scales. **1866** *Treas. Bot.*, **Intravalvular*, placed within valves, as the dissepiments of many crucifers. **1916** *Mem. N.Y. Bot. Garden* VI. 352 The marked self-sterility of individual plants, the *intra-varietal sterility, and the cases of inter-varietal sterility are not due to 'any inherent weakness of either ovaries or pollen grains'. **1970** *Euphytica* XIX. 382 (*heading*) Intra-varietal variation of yield in two varieties of *Lolium perenne* L. **1969** *Encycl. Sci. Suppl.* (Grolier) 329 The *intravehicular space suit consists of: fecal containment subsystem, constant wear garment, [etc.]. **1970** N. ARMSTRONG et al. *First on Moon* iii. 62 There were two kinds of suits... Mike Collins had the lighter 'intravehicular' version. **1909** WEBSTER, *Intraverbal. **1953** C. E. BAZELL *Ling. Form* 87 On the level of the sememe itself, all such facts as congruence, rection, extra-verbal as opposed to intra-verbal formation, are excluded. **1957** B. F. SKINNER in Saporta & Bastian *Psycholinguistics* (1961) 229/2 A comparable minimal repertoire was found to be lacking in intraverbal behavior. **1855** R. G. MAYNE *Expos. Lex. Med. Sci.* (1860) 535/2 *Intra-vertebral chord. **1896** *Phil. Trans. R. Soc.* B. CLXXXVII. 10 One of the last changes of importance is the appearance of intra-vertebral cartilage. *Ibid.* 12 In all Amphibia and Amniota each spinal nerve lies intravertebrally, *i.e.* issues behind the dorsal arch of its vertebra. **1887** *Syd. Soc. Lex.*, **Intravesical*. **1897** *Allbutt's Syst. Med.* IV. 438 It [a stone in the ureter] may be arrested by the narrow intravesical portion.

2. Prefixed to sbs., forming adjs., with the sense 'Situated, occurring, carried on, etc. within...'; as ***intra-station***; **intra-class, -party, -state**, occurring within a class, political party, state. Also **intracloud**, within a cloud; **intra-day**, occurring within one day; **intra-list** *Psychol.*, occurring between lists (of words, numbers, etc.) within a test situation; **intra-sentence**, occurring within a sentence. (Cf. ANTI- 4, INTER- 5.)

1950 Intra-class [see *inter-class* (INTER- 5)]. **1971** *Jrnl. Gen. Psychol.* Apr. 306 The intraclass correlation was significant but small. **1970** *Sci. News* 28 Mar. 320 Zeroing in on intracloud lightning. **1973** J. L. MARSHALL *Lightning Protection* iii. 31 The higher frequency radiation is dominant in intracloud discharges. **1972** *Daily Tel.* 11 Nov. 17/4 The previous intra-day high for this most illustrious of all stock market indices was 1,001·11 which was reached more than six-and-a-half years ago on Feb. 9, 1966. **1972** *Korea Times* 16 Nov. 3/5 The Dow topped 1,000 on an intraday basis—a compilation of the day's highs for all component issues. **1942** *Jrnl. Exper. Psychol.* XXX. 185 (*heading*) Intra-list generalization as a factor in verbal learning. **1958** G. A. MILLER in Saporta & Bastian *Psycholinguistics* (1961) 213/2 The redundant strings show greater intralist similarity. **1970** *Jrnl. Gen. Psychol.* Oct. 256 The last letter being thus the only characteristic by which the entire series was to be differentiated..would reduce the level of intralist interference. **1971** *Ibid.* Apr. 194 Overt intralist intrusions were scored as if stimuli had been clustered for both groups. **1923** *Glasgow Herald* 24 Apr. 8/4 Mr Harding proposed to the Senate that the United States should accept membership of the Court of International Justice at The Hague... Present indications are that he will refuse to retreat, and will make participation in the Court the issue of the preliminary intra-party campaign. **1963** *Economist* 20 July 257/1 This is nothing less than an intraparty revolt. **1969** *Sunday Statesman* (Calcutta) 27 July 12/3 The intra-party quarrel of the SSP deepens. **1969** *Computers & Humanities* IV. 129 Investigation of intra-sentence parallelism in present-day American prose. **1903** E. JOHNSON *Amer. Railway Transportation* 370 In 1886 the Supreme Court in the Wabash decision..limited the authority of the State strictly to the intrastate traffic and excluded that moving from one State to another. **1969** *Jane's Freight Containers 1968–69* 37/2, 101 inter- and intra-state motor freight lines serving the Port of Toledo. **1971** M. TAK *Truck Talk* 90 *Intrastate shipping*, any transportation of goods that has its origin and destination within the same state. **1888** *Pall Mall G.* 9 May 4/1 Better mechanical appliances for coupling and uncoupling waggons, improved methods of working intra-station traffic.

3. Prefixed, in adverbial relation, to nouns of action, as in **intra-susception**, the action of taking into its own substance (cf. *intussusception*).

1666 J. SMITH *Old Age* 160 Parts of the Body..nourished by the intra-susception of enlivened aliment.

intra-abdominal to **intra-articular**: see INTRA- *pref.* 1.

,intra-a'tomic, *a.* [INTRA- 1.] Occurring or existing within an, or the, atom.

1904 *Nature* 16 June 151/2 Enormous orbital velocities due to intra-atomic rearrangement. **1946** *Nature* 23 Nov. 726/1 For 'chemical process' is suggested the definition: 'a process in which a product is formed by a re-arrangement or re-distribution of atoms of chemical elements present in the starting materials, or by intra-atomic change'. **1955** *Bull. Atomic Sci.* Mar. 92/1 The possibility of releasing very large reserves of intra-atomic energy appeared suddenly a few months after the discovery by Hahn and Strassmann of the neutron fission of uranium atoms. **1971** B. A. LENGYEL *Lasers* (ed. 2) iii. 212 The general laws of emission and absorption of radiation are as valid for recombinations [of electrons and holes in semiconductors] as they are for ordinary intra-atomic transitions.

intra-capillary to **intracortical**: see INTRA- *pref.* 1.

†in'tracer. *Obs. rare.* [f. IN-^{1} + TRACER, after L. *investīgātor*.] One who searches into anything.

1432–50 tr. *Higden* (Rolls) VI. 359 Alured a ȝiffer of almes ..the intracer [*investigator*] of artes not knowen.

intracerebral to **intracloud**: see INTRA- *pref.*

intraclitellian (-klɪ'tɛlɪən), *a.* (*sb.*) *Zool.* [f. mod.L. *Intraclitelliāni*, f. *intrā* within + CLITELLUM.] Belonging to that division of Earthworms in which the male genital apertures are situated within the clitellum or thickened band. **b.** as *sb.* An earthworm of this division.

1888 F. E. BEDDARD in *Encycl. Brit.* XXIV. 683/2 Perrier divided earthworms into three groups:—(1) *Preclitellians*..; (2) *Intraclitellians*..where the male pores are within the clitellum; and (3) *Postclitellians*.

So **intraclitelline** (-klɪ'tɛlaɪn) *a.*, situated within the clitellum.

intracloacal, to **-cosmical**: see INTRA- *pref.*

intracranial (-'kreɪnɪəl), *a.* [f. INTRA- 1 + *cranium* skull: cf. *cranial*.] Situated or occurring within the cranium or skull. Hence **intra'cranially** *adv.*, in or within the cranium.

1847–9 TODD *Cycl. Anat.* IV. 509/1 A sensation is excited, provided the intracranial portion of it [the brain] be in a normal state. **1878** A. HAMILTON *Nerv. Dis.* 35 The other arises from some intracranial cause. **1908** *Practitioner* Aug. 296 Rabbits were inoculated intracranially with the fluid. **1971** *Biol. Abstr.* LII. 7922/2 A large stick remained intracranially for a long time without clinical neurological deficit.

intracrustal, intracrystalline: see INTRA- *pref.*

intractability (ɪn,træktə'bɪlɪtɪ). [f. next: see -ITY.] The quality of being intractable; intractableness: **a.** of persons or animals.

1579 FENTON *Guicciard.* I. (1599) 17 Virginio, to whose intractabilitie and obstinacie, he referred the chief occasion of all these disorders. **1816** J. SCOTT *Vis. Paris* (ed. 5) p. xix, It is not to be regretted..that something of intractability should manifest itself. **1890** 'L. FALCONER' *Mlle. Ixe* i. (1891) 33 The incapacity of the teachers or the intractability of the pupils.

b. Of things.

1738 WARBURTON *Div. Legat.* II. App., Wks. 1811 II. 219 The greater portions of the physical system may, from the intractability of Matter, be subject to some inconsiderable irregularities. **1828** W. SEWELL *Oxf. Prize Ess.* 5 Barrenness and intractability of soil. **1879** *St. George's Hosp. Rep.* IX. 588 His observation as to the intractability of advanced laryngeal phthisis.

intractable (ɪn'træktəb(ə)l), *a.* (*sb.*) [ad. L. *intractābil-is*, f. *in-* (IN-^{3}) + *tractābilis* TRACTABLE: cf. F. *intractable* (15th c.).] Not tractable.

1. Of persons and animals: Not to be guided; not manageable or docile; uncontrollable; refractory, stubborn.

1545 JOYE *Exp. Dan.* i. 14 b, Preseruing the good and iuste a lyue, and the intractable and incurable to suppresse them. **1548** HOOPER *Declar. 10 Commandm.* Pref., They were a stiff-necked people, and intractable. **1579** FENTON *Guicciard.* I. (1599) 22 Ferdinand was not intractable to this marriage. **1769** ROBERTSON *Chas. V*, IX. (1796) III. 149 They..found Charles more haughty and intractable than before. **1837** M. DONOVAN *Dom. Econ.* II. 117 The Dshikketaei, or Wild Mule..is a timid animal, yet indocile and intractable. **1849** MACAULAY *Hist. Eng.* i. I. 84 He convoked a second Parliament, and found it more intractable than the first. **1878** DOWDEN *Studies Lit.* 162 Lesson after lesson of experience was wasted upon his intractable will.

2. Of things: Not to be manipulated, wrought, or brought into any desired condition; not easily treated or dealt with; resisting treatment or effort.

1607 TOPSELL *Four-f. Beasts* (1658) 152 The teeth of those elephants..are so smooth and hard as they seem intractable. **1756–7** tr. *Keysler's Trav.* (1760) I. 148 Its iron is..so hard and intractable in the fire, that, without some other iron ore, it cannot be brought to a fusion. **1774** WARTON *Hist. Eng. Poetry* I. i. 2 A language extremely barbarous, irregular and intractable. **1861** TULLOCH *Eng. Purit.* i. 73 Lands..of a boggy, intractable character. **1899** ARNOLD WHITE *Modern Jew* ii. 37 When Russia became the chief accomplice in the murder of Polish liberty.., the poisonous Jewish Question infected her life-blood. She acquired the disease in a peculiarly intractable form.

B. *sb.* An unmanageable person.

1883 *Spectator* 1 Sept., If they refuse, opinion will punish them as Intractables.

Hence **in'tractableness**, the quality of being intractable; intractability. **in'tractably** *adv.*, in an intractable manner.

1664 H. MORE *Myst. Iniq.* 242 The halting of the Horse.. and his contumacy and intractableness. **1802** PALEY *Nat. Theol.* v. §1 (1819) 50 To expose some intractableness and imperfection in the materials. **1824** LANDOR *Imag. Conv.* Wks. 1846 I. 23 When the leading stag..is intractably wild ..he ought to be hamstrung. **1860** MILL *Repr. Govt.* (1865) 21/1 The impediments opposed to the most salutary public improvements by the ignorance, the indifference, the intractableness, the perverse obstinacy of a people.

†in'tracted, *ppl. a. Obs.* [f. L. *intract-us*, *intrahĕre* to drag along + -ED^{1}; the sense is conformed to IN *adv.*] Drawn in; retracted inwards.

1584 HUDSON *Du Bartas' Judith* III. 229 Fostred on that burning sand, With hot intracted tongue, and sonken een.

intractile (ɪn'træktɪl, -aɪl), *a. rare.* [IN-^{3}.]

†1. Not tractile; incapable of being drawn out in length; not ductile. *Obs.*

1626 BACON *Sylva* §§839–40 The Consistences of Bodies are very diuers..Flexible, Inflexible; Tractile, or to be drawne forth in length, Intractile; Porous, Solid.

2. = INTRACTABLE *a.* 2.

1880 *Daily News* 18 Oct. 3/1 Poor intractile clays, wrought by tillage excessive in its cost and hazardous in its return.

†in'tractive, *a. Obs. rare*$^{-0}$. [f. IN-^{3} + L. *tract-*, ppl. stem of *trahĕre* to draw + -IVE. Cf. *attractive*.] = INTRACTABLE *a.*

1623 COCKERAM II, Stubborne, *Intractiue*.

intracultural to **intracystic**: see INTRA- *pref.*

intrada (ɪn'trɑːdə). *Mus.* [Modified f. It. *intrata*, older form of *entrata* entry, prelude.] An introduction or prelude; = ENTRÉE 3 b.

1740 J. GRASSINEAU *Mus. Dict.* 113 *Intrada*, an entry, much the same as prelude, or overture. **1801** BUSBY *Dict. Mus.*, *Intrada*, the old Italian name for an opera overture, or prelude. **1883** GROVE *Dict. Mus.* III. 756/1 In Purcell's suites, for instance, which date from the last 10 or 20 years of the 17th century, besides the Allemande and Courante.. in one case the group also comprises a Sarabande, Cebell, Minuet, Riggadoon, Intrade, and March. **1954** *Grove's Dict. Mus.* (ed. 5) IV. 525/1 These intradas usually form part of a suite of dances. The term is seldom found after the middle of the 17th century, being replaced by the French term *entrée*, though Bach, Mozart.. and Beethoven.. still used it.

intra-day: see INTRA- *pref.* 2.

†**in'trade**. *Obs.* [a. F. *intrade* (Rabelais, 16th c.), ad. Sp. *intrada*: see INTRADO and -ADE.] = INTRADO 2.

1656 HEYLIN *Surv. France* 182 His intrade about 6000 crowns a year.

intra-departmental to **intradivisional**: see INTRA- *pref.* 1.

†**in'trado**. *Obs.* [ad. Sp. *entrada* entry = late L. *intrāta* entry (Du Cange), f. L. *intrāre* to enter: see ENTRADA and -ADO 2.]

1. A formal entry.

1656 BLOUNT *Glossogr.*, *Intrado* or *Entrado*, an income or yeerly revenue; also an entrance. **1665** SIR T. HERBERT *Trav.* (1677) 98 With great Pomp he made his Intrado into Agra. **1716** *Gentl. Instructed* (ed. 6) I. 117 Now my Lady makes her *Intrado*, and begins the great Work of the Day.

2. Income; revenue.

1640 H. PARKER *Case Ship Money* 16 His ordinary private rights, and intradoes. **1652–62** HEYLIN *Cosmogr.* III. (1673) 38/2 The *Intrado* of the Crown must needs amount constantly to a Million and a half yearly if it were not more. **1672** W. DE BRITAINE *Interest Eng. Dutch War* 18 Their *Intrado* would never support their ordinary charges.

3. An entering upon (any business).

1654 H. L'ESTRANGE *Chas. I* (1655) 122 The earl finding the *intrado* of his negotiation like to come to nothing.. returned home.

intrados (ɪn'treɪdɒs). *Arch.* [a. F. *intrados*, f. L. *intrā* within + F. *dos* the back.] The lower or interior curve of an arch; *esp.* the lower curve of the voussoirs or stones which immediately form the arch. Cf. EXTRADOS.

1772 C. HUTTON *Bridges* iii, The relations between their intrados and extrados. **1823** P. NICHOLSON *Pract. Build.* 283 Design of a bridge in which the intrados is the arc of a circle. **1879** SIR G. SCOTT *Lect. Archit.* II. 141 We have hitherto supposed our arches to be of moderate depth from extrados, or outer line, to intrados, or inner line.

intraductal to **intrafascicular**: see INTRA- *pref.*

intrafoliaceous (-'fəʊlɪeɪʃəs), *a. Bot.* [f. INTRA- 1 + L. *folium* leaf: see FOLIACEOUS.] Situated on the inner side of a leaf.

1760 J. LEE *Introd. Bot.* III. xvi. (1765) 210 Stipulæ.. Intrafoliaceous, on the Inside of the Leaves, in Ficus and Morus. **1870** BENTLEY *Bot.* 171 If such stipules cohere.. so as to form a sheath which encircles the stem above the leaf, they form what is termed an ochrea or intrafoliaceous stipule.

intraformational to **intragovernmental**: see INTRA- *pref.*

intragroup ('ɪntrəgruːp), *a.* [INTRA- 2.] Existing or occurring within a group or between the members of a group.

1918 *Genetics* III. 477 Intra-group competition. **1952** C. P. BLACKER *Eugenics* iv. 90 If we owe as much to the social instincts and co-operativeness of our forebears as to their competitive success in a struggle for existence, how far, we may ask, is the continued strife between man and man necessary for the further development of the race? Diverse answers were given by the controversialists of the period, and discussion turned much on the effects of two kinds of struggle—that *inside* social groups and that *between* social groups—or, as they were called *intra*-group and *inter*-group struggle. **1958** W. J. H. SPROTT *Human Groups* ix. 141 The organized group displayed much more intra-group aggression than did the unorganized group. **1963** C. S. JOHNSON in M. M. Grossack *Mental Health & Segregation* 44 For the Negro youth, the tensions inherent in the intra-group class struggle become extremely important. **1965** *Math. in Biol. & Med.* (*Med. Res. Council*) III. 86 The degree of variation within the groups was estimated by the average intragroup distance. **1972** *Accountant* 23 Mar. 384/1 The accounting practice persists whereby we defer profits on all intra-group sales and chalk up another defeat for reality.

intragyral, -hepatic, etc.: see INTRA- *pref.*

†**intraict, -trait**, obs. ff. ENTREAT *v.*, to treat.

1588 A. KING tr. *Canisius' Catech.* 184 It war ane lang thing to intraict now sewerallie of thir gifts.

intrail(e, intral, intrel, obs. ff. ENTRAIL.

intra-imperial to **intraligamentous**: see INTRA- *pref.*

intra-list: see INTRA- *pref.* 2.

intralobular (ɪntrə'lɒbjʊlə(r)), *a. Anat.* [f. INTRA- 1 + LOBULE; cf. *lobular*.] Situated or occurring within the lobes of an organ or structure. *intralobular bile-vessels*, the biliary capillaries.

1839–47 TODD *Cycl. Anat.* III. 172/2 The intralobular veins pour their current into the sublobular veins. **1881** MIVART *Cat* 188 The blood.. collects in the commencements of the hepatic vein, which are called intralobular veins. **1887** *Syd. Soc. Lex.*, Intralobular bile-vessels.

intralocular to **intramercurial**: see INTRA- *pref.*

intramolecular (-məʊ'lɛkjʊlə(r)), *a.* [INTRA- 1.] Situated, existing, or occurring within a molecule or the molecules of a body or substance. Hence **intramo'lecularly** *adv.*, within a molecule.

1884 A. DANIELL *Princ. Physics* xiii. 323 Intramolecular work [is] done within each several molecule [in the] production of intramolecular vibrations. **1885** GOODALE *Phys. Bot.* (1892) 371 The chemical processes which cause the production and evolution of carbonic acid in the absence of free oxygen are grouped by Pflüger under the term intramolecular respiration. **1893** BALL *Story of Sun* 261 The rapidity with which these intra-molecular oscillations are effected. **1936** G. M. KLINE *Organic Plastics* (U.S. Bureau of Standards Circular C411) 6 Condensations may take place intramolecularly, as in the case of the formation of phthalic anhydride from phthalic acid, or intermolecularly. **1962** WALKER & STRAW *Spectroscopy* II. 181 Dipole attachment occurs between the intramolecularly hydrogen bonded and the solvent molecule. **1964** N. G. CLARK *Mod. Org. Chem.* x. 195 It undergoes a Cannizzaro reaction with sodium hydroxide; this occurs intramolecularly, i.e. within the same molecule. **1971** *Biochemistry* (Easton, Pa.) X. 925/1 Is the S–S polylysine intramolecularly or intermolecularly cross-linked?

intramontane to **intramorphemic**: see INTRA- *pref.* 1

intramundane (-'mʌndeɪn), *a.* [f. INTRA- 1 + L. *mund-us* world: cf. *mundane*.] Situated or existing within the world (i.e. this world, or the material or created world).

1839 BAILEY *Festus* xxxiii. (1852) 542 Like a bolt Of thunder forged in intramundane air. **1894** *Thinker* VI. 348 The intramundane cause of the uncreated world.

intramural (ɪntrə'mjʊərəl), *a.* [f. INTRA- 1 + L. *mūr-us* wall: cf. *mural*, also in same sense, late L. *intrāmūrānus*.]

1. Situated, existing, or performed within the walls of a city or building.

1846 GROTE *Greece* II. ii. II. 343 That expansion of the social and political feelings to which protected intra-mural residence and increased numbers gave birth. **1868** M. PATTISON *Academ. Org.* v. 316 If any proof could convince the advocates of intramural residence of the futility of 'college discipline'. **1881** *Macm. Mag.* Feb. 299 The practice of intramural interment which made the family hearth almost literally a tombstone.

2. *Anat.*, *Path.*, and *Biol.* Situated within the substance of the wall of a hollow organ, or of a cell.

1879 *St. George's Hosp. Rep.* IX. 455 An intramural fibroid discovered; ergot administered. **1884** BOWER & SCOTT *De Bary's Phaner.* 206 Since the intra-mural glands, .. when regarded purely histologically, are merely a special case of schizogenetic secretory cavities in the epidermis.

intramurally (-'mjʊərəlɪ), *adv.* [INTRA- 1.] Within the walls or boundaries; inside a particular community, institution, etc.

1927 [see EXTRAMURALLY *adv.*]. **1952** *Facilities for Advanced Study Univ. Oxf.* 29 Research studies in all branches of agricultural economics have been conducted both 'in the field', extra-murally, and intra-murally by means of records. **1968** *Sat. Rev.* (U.S.) 2 Nov. 32 Older families, with their own special and intramurally recognized ways of walking, talking and thinking.

intramuscular to **intranasal**: see INTRA- *pref.* 1.

intrance, obs. form of ENTRANCE.

in'traneous, *a. rare.* [f. late L. *intrāneus* that is within, inner (Cassiodorus): cf. *extraneous*.] That is within; internal.

1656 BLOUNT *Glossogr.*, *Intraneous*,.. that is within, inward. **1864** A. LEIGHTON *Myst. Leg. Edinburgh* (1886) 86 Money, commonly said to be extraneous, is often so far in its influences intraneous, that it changes the feelings and motives.

intraneural: see INTRA- *pref.*

intranquillity (ɪntræŋ'kwɪlɪtɪ). [IN-³.] Lack of tranquillity; inquietude; restlessness.

1689–90 TEMPLE *Ess.*, *Health & Long Life* Wks. 1731 I. 282 To relieve that Intranquillity which attends most Diseases. **1710** *Acc. Last Distemper Tom Whigg* I. 3 He lived not far from Westminister Abbey, within hearing of the choir, which perhaps did not a little contribute to his Intranquillity.

intranscalency (ɪntrɑːn'skeɪlənsɪ, -æ-). [f. next: see -ENCY.] Imperviousness to heat.

1864 E. FRANKLAND in *Philos. Mag.* Ser. IV. XXVII. 334 This extraordinary intranscalency of aqueous vapour to rays issuing from water has been conclusively proved by Tyndall.

intranscalent (ɪntrɑːn'skeɪlənt, -æ-), *a.* [f. IN-³ + TRANSCALENT; after *transparent*.] Impervious to heat.

1846 WORCESTER cites TURNER. **1861** E. FRANKLAND in *Jrnl. Chem. Soc.* XIV. 113 Water is intranscalent to rays of obscure heat.

intransferable (ɪn'trɑːnsfərəb(ə)l, -æ-, ɪntrɑːns'fɜːrəb(ə)l, -æ-), *a.* [IN-³.] Not transferable; incapable of being transferred.

1853 MISS SHEPPARD *Ch. Auchester* viii. (1875) 32 The power they possess—innate, unalienable, intransferable—of suffering all they feel. **1865** *Pall Mall G.* 24 Nov. 10 Selection of hymns with intransferable tunes for Church use. *a* **1898** J. CAIRD *Fundamental Ideas Christianity* (1899) II. xv. 151 The moral acts of each involving a personal responsibility intransferable to the other.

intransferrible (ɪntrɑːns'fɜːrɪb(ə)l, -æ-), *a.* [f. IN-³ + TRANSFERRIBLE: cf. *inferrible*.] = prec.

1873 H. ROGERS *Orig. Bible* viii. (1878) 267 Its chief excellences are in that case intransferrible.

intrans'formable, *a.* [IN-³.] Not transformable; incapable of transformation.

1887 J. SULLY in *Mind* Jan. 118 The transformable gives place to the intransformable.

intrans'fusible, *a. rare.* Also **-able**. [IN-³.] That cannot be transfused.

1804 ANNA SEWARD *Mem. Darwin* 209 The perhaps intransfusable felicities of verbal expression.

intransgressible (ɪntrɑːns'grɛsɪb(ə)l, -æ-), *a.* [IN-³.] That cannot or may not be transgressed.

1603 HOLLAND *Plutarch's Mor.* 1049 That Fatall destinie is a divine reason or sentence intransgressible and inevitable. **1837** *Chamb. Jrnl.* 22 July 206 It was the well-nigh intransgressible law of the amphitheatre.

†**in'transible**, *a. Obs. rare*⁻⁰. [ad. late L. *intransibilis* impassable, f. *in-* (IN-³) + **transibilis*, f. *transīre* to pass away.] That cannot be passed over. Hence †**in'transibly** *adv.*, impassably.

1654 VILVAIN *Theorem. Theol.* ii. 63 The term of life is intransibly fixd.

†**in'transient**, *a. Obs.* [IN-³.] Not passing over; not passing to another by succession.

1650 R. HOLLINGWORTH *Exerc. Usurped Powers* 2 The peoples constitution of their Governors may.. be individuall, or intransient, as in those Kingdomes, or States which are called.. Elective. **1657–83** EVELYN *Hist. Relig.* (1850) I. 221 His [God's].. essential properties.. are intransient and incommunicable. **1717** KILLINBECK *Serm.* v. 93 This man, because he continueth for ever, hath an unchangeable ἀπαράβατον Ἱερωσύνην, an intransient, an indefeasible Priesthood.

in'transigeance. *rare.* [Fr.] = INTRANSIGENCE.

1899 J. W. MACKAIL *Life W. Morris* II. 291 Socialism.. from extreme intransigeance.. had swung back to something approaching opportunism. **1909** *Daily Chron.* 20 July 3/2 The loves of Jeanne-Jeannette and the young man from Montpellier are threatened by the intransigeance of their respective ancestors.

intransigeantly (ɪn'trɑːnsɪdʒəntlɪ, -æ-), *adv.* [f. F. *intransigeant* (see INTRANSIGENT *a.* and *sb.*) + -LY².] Uncompromisingly.

1921 *Contemp. Rev.* Sept. 331 The peasants are intransigeantly anti-Karlist. **1925** *Glasgow Herald* 17 Mar. 8 The advocates of an intransigeantly nationalist policy.

intransigence (ɪn'trɑːnsɪdʒəns, -æ-). [f. as next: see -ENCE.] = next.

1882 *Sat. Rev.* 19 Aug. 255/2 Such tyranny.. was almost wholly due to the stubborn intransigence of the Italian revolutionists.

intransigency (ɪn'trɑːnsɪdʒənsɪ, -æ-). [f. next: see -ENCY.] The quality of being intransigent; uncompromising hostility; irreconcilability.

1890 BP. STUBBS *Primary Charge* 49 The intransigency of the one party forced the conservatism of the other into an attitude of inflexible resistance.

intransigent (ɪn'trɑːnsɪdʒənt, -æ-), *a.* and *sb.* Also **-eant**. [a. F. *intransigeant* (ɛ̃trɑ̃siʒɑ̃) in Littré *Suppl.*, from Sp. *los intransigentes*, applied to the party of the Extreme Left in the Spanish Cortes, and in 1873–74 to the extreme Republicans in Spain; f. L. *in-* (IN-³) + *transigent-em*, pr. pple. of *transigĕre* to come to an understanding, f. *trans* across + *agĕre* to act. Also used in F. spelling.]

A. *adj.* That refuses to come to terms or make any compromise (in politics); uncompromising, irreconcilable.

α. **1883** *Guardian* 18 Apr. 554/2 He saw the moderate portion of the Republican party submerged by the advancing tide of *intransigeant* radicalism. **1893** *Nation* (N.Y.) 6 July 6/1 Richter and his friends.. have always been as *intransigeant* as Liebknecht and his associates. **1899** *Daily News* 5 July 8/3 The President is as intransigeant as ever on the franchise question.

β. **1881** *Daily News* 23 Dec. 5/5 The intransigent attitude of the Judges [who opposed altering the system of judicial vacations]. **1894** *Speaker* 14 July 44/2 Christian XVI. is a

king of intransigent principles, a king with a faith in his providential mission; zealous, rigid, narrow.

B. *sb.* An irreconcilable (in politics); an uncompromising Republican.

1879 M. PATTISON *Milton* xi. 122 The party of anti-Oliverian republicans, the Intransigentes, became one of the greatest difficulties of the Government. **1883** *19th Cent.* Sept. 539 It is quite right to have an eye over the Intransigeants and the Royalists. **1899** *Q. Rev.* Oct. 514 Certain of the Intransigents..are averse to a reconciliation between Italy and the Papal See.

Hence **in'transigentism**, the principles of intransigents. **in'transigentist**, an intransigent.

1882 GOLDW. SMITH in *Pop. Sci. Monthly* XX. 757 Communism, intransigentism, and nihilism are not well represented in scientific reunions. **1893** —— *Ess.* 2 Satanism manifests itself in different countries under various forms and names, such as Nihilism, Intransigentism, Petrolean Communism. **1898** *Daily News* 11 Mar. 5/3 The only real enemy the Progressive cause has to fear is a spirit of intolerance and intransigentism within its own ranks.

in-'transit, intransit, *a.* [f. IN *prep.* 18 + TRANSIT *sb.*] Of or pertaining to people, goods, etc., that are in transit; being in transit.

1918 JOHNSON & HUEBNER *Princ. Ocean Transportation* III. xx. 309 The granting of in-transit privileges on all-rail routes. **1951** *Manila Daily Bulletin* 26 Mar. 1-P, The ship had seven intransit passengers and around 1,741 tons of transit cargo. **1967** V. S. NAIPAUL *Mimic Men* III. vii. 279 There were no aeroplanes..that day... Sixteen intransit hours awaited me. **1969** *Jane's Freight Containers 1968–69* 102/2 The in-transit time between UK/Europe and the Far East could be considerably reduced by transporting containers by rail across the North American continent. **1971** *Jamaican Weekly Gleaner* 17 Nov. 38/4 Miss Milford Rohrbaugh, 53, an American tourist slipped and fell in the intransit lounge of the Palisadoes Airport yesterday on her way to board an aircraft to Miami, Florida.

intransitable (ɪn'trɑːnsɪtəb(ə)l, -æ-), *a. rare.* [f. IN-[3] + TRANSIT + -ABLE.] Unavailable for transit.

1838 'TEXIAN' *Mexico v. Texas* 9 In that singular region of Mexico..there extends..a desert..so utterly devoid of water and vegetation as to be intransitable. **1889** *Times* 24 Dec. 5/2 Its lands are tropical..and there is a gigantic, often intransitable, river system. **1897** *Geogr. Jrnl.* X. 64 A road along the coast would become lost in intransitable gorges of the coast range of mountains.

intransitive (ɪn'trɑːnsɪtɪv, -æ-), *a.* (*sb.*) [ad. L. *intransitīvus* not passing over (Priscian), f. *in-* (IN-[3]) + *trans-īre* to pass over. Cf. F. *intransitif.*]

1. *Gram.* Of verbs and their construction: Expressing action which does not pass over to an object; not taking a direct object. (See TRANSITIVE, NEUTER.)

1612 BRINSLEY *Lud. Lit.* 129 This Verbe *Sum es*, is a Verbe Substantiue intransitiue, not a transitiue; and therefore will haue such case after it as it hath before it. *a* **1638** MEDE *Apost. Latter Times* II. i. Wks. (1672) III. 675 The syntax of the words in the Greek is uncapable of such an intransitive construction. **1711** J. GREENWOOD *Eng. Gram.* 154 Those verbs whose action does not pass on any other Thing, are called Intransitive. **1861** MASON *Eng. Gram.* §177 Many verbs which denote actions are used sometimes as transitive, sometimes as intransitive verbs.

b. as *sb.* An intransitive verb.

1824 L. MURRAY *Eng. Gram.* (ed. 5) I. 108 Verbs neuter may properly be denominated *intransitives*, because the effect is confined within the subject, and does not pass over to any object: as, 'I sit, he lives, they sleep'.

2. That does not pass on to another person, or beyond certain limits (specified or implied). *rare.*

a **1641** BP. MOUNTAGU *Acts & Mon.* (1642) 129 So is that Righteousnesse indefatible [? indefectible], and intransitive to any other State. **1664** JER. TAYLOR *Dissuas. Popery* II. II. vi. (R.), And then it is for the image sake, and so far is intransitive; but whatever is paid more to the image is transitive, and passes further. **1780** BENTHAM *Princ. Legisl.* vii. §13. **1856** VAUGHAN *Mystics* (1860) I. 29 The mysticism of St. Bernard..the intransitive mysticism of the cloister.

3. *Logic.* Of a relation: such that if the relation holds between a first and a second item, and also between the second and third, it cannot hold (or more widely, does not hold) between the first and the third.

1870 C. S. PEIRCE in *Mem. Amer. Acad.* (1873) IX. 369 Repeating relatives may be divided (after De Morgan) into those whose products into themselves are contained under themselves, and those of which this is not true. The former are well named by De Morgan transitive, the latter intransitive. **1881** J. VENN *Symbolic Logic* xix. 403 Relations ..may be divided into those which are 'transitive' and those which are 'intransitive'. **1903** B. RUSSELL *Princ. Math.* xxvi. 218 Relations which do not possess the second property I shall call not transitive; those which possess the property that *xRy*, *yRz* always exclude *xRz* I shall call intransitive. All these cases may be illustrated from human relationships. .. *Spouse* is symmetrical but intransitive; ..*father* is both asymmetrical and intransitive. **1930** L. S. STEBBING *Mod. Introd. Logic* vii. 113 Symmetry and transitiveness..are independent, so that relations can be symmetrical and either transitive or intransitive; asymmetrical and either transitive or intransitive. **1964** E. BACH *Introd. Transformational Gram.* vii. 155 *Equal, Smaller* are transitive; *Father* is an intransitive relation; *Friend* is non-transitive if you are my friend and have friends who are not my friends.

4. *Math.* Of a group: not transitive (see TRANSITIVE *a.* (*sb.*) 6 and quot. 1889).

1889 *Amer. Jrnl. Math.* XI. 195 If a substitution-group *I* is intransitive, the letters upon which it operates can be distributed into 'systems of intransitivity', $x_1, x_2 \ldots; y_1, y_2 \ldots; z_1, z_2 \ldots$ such that the substitutions of *I* interchange among each other only the letters $x_1, x_2 \ldots$; the letters $y_1, y_2 \ldots$; the letters $z_1, z_2 \ldots$, and so on, and connect transitively the letters of each system. **1940** D. E. LITTLEWOOD *Theory Group Characters* iii. 42 In an intransitive group the symbols are divided into transitive sets, the symbols of each set being permuted amongst themselves. **1971** POWELL & HIGMAN *Finite Simple Groups* vii. 234 If the union of these is Ω, they form a fixed trio, and if not, the group is intransitive.

Hence **in'transitively**, in an intransitive manner.

a **1638** MEDE *Apost. Latter Times* II. i. Wks. (1672) III. 675 It is usually translated intransitively, with reference to the persons expressed in the former verse. **1656** JEANES *Fuln. Christ* 32 Saith Eckard, the divine properties are communicated to the humanity, not transitively, but intransitively. **1762** LOWTH *Eng. Gram.* (1838) 49 *note*, The difference between Verbs absolutely neuter and intransitively active is not always clear. **1884** *New Eng. Dict.* Introd. 19.

intransitivity (ˌɪntrɑːnsɪ'tɪvɪtɪ, -æ-). [f. INTRANSITIV(E *a.* + -ITY.] The property or quality of being intransitive (in any sense).

1889 [see INTRANSITIVE *a.* 4]. **1933** CHAPMAN & HENLE *Fund. Logic* 3 We have chosen four logical properties of certain relations—transitivity and intransitivity, symmetry and asymmetry. **1950** W. V. QUINE *Methods of Logic* (1952) 177 A dyadic relative term is called..intransitive.. according as it fulfils:..(x) (y) (z) (Fxy.Fyz. ⊃ – Fxz) (intransitivity). **1971** *Archivum Linguisticum* II. 104 Aspect, as well as transitivity, intransitivity, expression of cause, wish, etc., are secondary developments and more recent than the use of *s* to denote tense or mood.

intransitivize (ɪn'trɑːnsɪtɪvaɪz, -æ-), *v. Gram.* [f. INTRANSITIV(E *a.* + -IZE.] *trans.* To make intransitive. Chiefly as **in'transitivizing** *ppl. a.*

1949 E. A. NIDA *Morphol.* (ed. 2) iii. 68 In Tzeltal there is an intransitivizing verbal infix -h-. **1964** *Language* XL. 76 The intransitivizing stem formative -di.

in transitu: see IN *Lat. prep.*

intranslatable (ɪntrɑːn'sleɪtəb(ə)l, -æ-), *a.* [IN-[3].] That cannot be translated; untranslatable.

1690 LOCKE *Hum. Und.* III. v. §8 *marg.*, The intranslatable Words of divers Languages. **1860** ADLER *Fauriel's Prov. Poetry* xviii. 420 A number of pieces intranslatable..on account of their unbounded licentiousness.

intransmissibility (ˌɪntrɑːnsmɪsɪ'bɪlɪtɪ, -æ-). [f. INTRANSMISSIBLE *a.* + -ITY.] The state or quality of being intransmissible.

1913 H. GOUDY in P. Vinogradoff *Ess. Legal Hist.* 225 The passive intransmissibility of actions of Debt and Account.

intransmissible (ɪntrɑːns'mɪsɪb(ə)l, -æ-), *a.* [IN-[3].] Not transmissible; that cannot be transmitted.

1656 JEANES *Fuln. Christ* 48 An intransmissible Priesthood, which passeth not from one unto another. **1837** LOCKHART *Scott* lxiv, The greatly higher but intransmissible rank of a Privy-Councillor.

intransmutable (ɪntrɑːns'mjuːtəb(ə)l, -æ-), *a.* [IN-[3].] Not transmutable; that cannot be transmuted into something else; unchangeable. Hence **intransmuta'bility**, unchangeableness.

1691 RAY *Creation* I. (1692) 89 Some of the most learn'd and experienc'd Chymists do affirm Quick-silver to be intransmutable. **1692** —— *Dissol. World* III. v. (1732) 387 This Fixedness and Intransmutability of Principles secures the Universe from Dissolution. **1794** SULLIVAN *View Nat.* I. 139 Were colour in the atoms themselves, says Lucretius, it would be as intransmutable as they are.

†**intrans'natable**, *a. Obs.* [ad. med.L. *intransnatābilis*, f. *in-* (IN-[3]) + *transnatā-re* to swim across; cf. *natābilis*, f. *natāre* to swim.] That cannot be swum across.

c **1450** tr. *De Imitatione* III. xv. 83 O weight unmeasurable, o see intransnatable.

intransparency (ɪntrɑːn'spɛərənsɪ, -æ-, -'pær-). [f. INTRANSPARENT *a.*: see -ENCY.] The quality of being opaque; also, an instance of this.

1902 *Encycl. Brit.* XXXI. 570/1 This intransparency caused by a mere infiltration generally clears away in the course of time. *Ibid.*, Centrally placed intransparencies, which cover the pupil, are relatively the most disturbing.

intransparent (ɪntrɑːn'spɛərənt, -træns-, -'pær-), *a.* [IN-[3].] Not transparent; incapable of being seen through.

1842 PRICHARD *Nat. Hist. Man* 100 The cortical part appeared in both almost equally thick and intransparent.

intrant ('ɪntrənt), *sb.* and *a.* Chiefly *Sc.* See also ENTRANT. [ad. L. *intrānt-em*, pr. pple. of *intrāre* to enter.]

A. *sb.* **1.** One who enters: **a.** One who comes in, as into a room; an incomer (*rare*).

1663 SIR G. MACKENZIE *Relig. Stoica* xx. (1685) 162 That curious Painter; who having drawn an excellent face..did thereafter dash it afresh upon the suggesion of each intrant. *a* **1834** COLERIDGE *Lit. Rem.* (1838) III. 275 A pleasure garden, in which the intrants having presented their *symbolum portæ*..walk at large.

b. One who enters a college or institution, or an association or body.

1560 in Spottiswood *Hist. Ch. Scot.* III. (1677) 163 The Beddale shall have for his stipend 2*s*. Scots, of every Intrant and Suppost of the University. **1831** SIR W. HAMILTON *Discuss.* (1852) 427 The 'Excerpta Statutorum' which the intrant receives at matriculation. **1859** MASSON *Milton* I. 87 The school in which the intrant had been previously educated is specified. **1879** GLADSTONE *Gleanings* VII. 202 The door was barred against intrants, and there was consequently no succession to maintain the school.

c. One who enters into holy orders.

1637–50 ROW *Hist. Kirk* (1842) 19 Some..did afterwards compell Ministers and intrants to subscryve to the verie contrair Conclusions. **1730** *Wodrow Corr.* (1843) III. 466 We have much reason to pray earnestly for intrants to the ministry. **1761–2** HUME *Hist. England* liii. (1806) IV. 120 A new oath was arbitrarily imposed on intrants, by which they swore to observe the articles of Perth, and submit to the liturgy and canons.

d. One who makes legal entry; one who enters into the possession of land, etc.

1592 *Sc. Acts Jas. VI* (1814) III. 623/2 Quhilk pensioun wes disponit..to the said williame for all the dayis of his lyftyme be provisioun furth of þe court of Rome, w[t] consent of the intrant. **1880** MUIRHEAD *Ulpian* i. §21 Nor is such a gift valid if introduced between two institutions, and both the heirs enter; but it was, according to the old rule, if the sole intrant was the heir first instituted.

†**2.** Formerly, in the University of St. Andrews; a student chosen by each nation for the election of the Rector. *Obs.*

1806 FORSYTH *Beauties Scot.* IV. 92 Each nation [of the university of St. Andrews] chooses an intrant, and the four intrants name the rector. **1819** T. M[c]CRIE *Melville* I. iv. 213 These elected annually four intrants or electors by whom the rector was chosen.

B. *adj.* Entering; that enters.

1828 WEBSTER, *Intrant*, entering, penetrating.

intranuclear to **intranucleolar**: see INTRA- *pref.* 1.

intra-ocular (ɪntrə'ɒkjʊlə(r)), *a.* [f. INTRA- 1 + L. *ocul-us* eye: cf. *ocular.*] Situated or occurring within the eyeball. (In quot. 1826 erron. used for INTEROCULAR.)

1826 KIRBY & SP. *Entomol.* IV. 315 *Stemmata*..Intra-ocular..when placed in the space between the eyes. **1872** DARWIN *Emotions* vi. 160 During violent expiration the intra-ocular..vessels of the eye are all affected in two ways. **1879** *St. George's Hosp. Rep.* IX. 492 The usefulness of the left eye was irreparably destroyed by intraocular hæmorrhage.

intra-oral to **intra-ovarian**: see INTRA- *pref.*

†**in'trap**, *sb. Obs.* [f. *intrap*, ENTRAP *v.*] An act of entrapping; a stratagem.

1550 W. LYNNE tr. *Carion's Cron.* 113 Bellisarius, enclosyng in Wittichus by an intrap, toke him.

intrap, obs. form of ENTRAP *v.*

intraparietal (ˌɪntrəpə'raɪɪtəl), *a.* [f. INTRA- 1 + L. *pariet-em* partition-wall: cf. *parietal.*]

1. 'Situated or happening within walls or within an inclosure; apart from public view'.

1882 in ANNANDALE *Imperial Dict.* Suppl.

2. *Anat.* 'Situated in the substance of the walls of an organ' (*Syd. Soc. Lex.*).

1887 tr. *Heitzmann's Anat. Descr.* II. 97 Limited posteriorly by the intra-parietal fissure.

intraparochial to **intrapelvic**: see INTRA- *pref.*

intrapetalous (ɪntrə'pɛtələs), *a.* [f. INTRA- 1 + late L. *petal-um* PETAL + -OUS: cf. *apetalous*, etc.]

1. *Zool.* Situated within, or at the inner part of, the petaloid ambulacra of an echinoderm.

1877 HUXLEY *Anat. Inv. Anim.* ix. 574 Others surround the outer extremities of the petaloid ambulacra, and are termed peripetalous, or, when they encircle the inner terminations of their ambulacra, intrapetalous.

2. *Bot.* Situated within, or on the inner side of, the petals of a flower.

1887 *Syd. Soc. Lex.*, *Intrapetalous*, within the petals.

intrapetiolar (ɪntrə'pɛtɪələ(r)), *a. Bot.* [f. INTRA- 1 + PETIOLE: cf. *petiolar.*] Situated within, or on the inner side of, the petiole or leaf-stalk; applied **a.** to an axillary bud formed immediately under the base of the petiole and surrounded by it so as not to appear until the leaf has fallen; **b.** to a stipule, or pair of confluent stipules, between the petiole and the axis. Also **intra'petiolary** *a.* (Cooke *Man. Bot. Terms* 1862).

1864 WEBSTER, *Intrapetiolar*. **1875** BENNETT & DYER *Sachs' Bot.* 562 In woody plants the axillary buds..are not unfrequently so completely surrounded by the base of the leaf-stalk that they are not visible until the leaf has fallen off, as in..Platanus, &c., and are then called Intrapetiolar Buds. **1897** WILLIS *Flowering Plants* II. 330 The stipules..stand ..between the petiole and the axis (*intrapetiolar*).

intraphilosophic to **intrapleural**: see INTRA- *pref.*

intrapluvial (ɪntrə'pluːvɪəl), *a.* and *sb.* [f. INTRA- 1 + PLUVIAL *a.*] **A.** *adj.* Of, pertaining to, or designating relatively short, drier periods

(less marked than interpluvials) that may have occurred during pluvials. **B.** *sb.* An intrapluvial period.

1934 E. J. WAYLAND in *Jrnl. R. Anthrop. Inst.* LXIV. 344 In each of them [*sc.* pluvials] there is a break, or intrapluvial period. **1939** T. P. O'BRIEN *Prehist. Uganda* i. 9 The evidence in support of the intrapluvial in Pluvial I was provided by local, though not intense, soil reddening, selenite beds within Pluvial I deposits and by talus accumulations. **1940** *Geogr. Jrnl.* XCVI. 333 There have been very long wet and dry phases, the so-called pluvials and interpluvials; there have been shorter intrapluvials and epipluvials; and there have been short-period oscillations... The intrapluvial oscillations are measured in terms of one hundred years. **1946** F. E. ZEUNER *Dating Past* viii. 247 The succession of pluvials with intrapluvials and separated by interpluvials, however, appears at present to be somewhat uncertain.

intrapolar: see INTRA- *pref.*

intrapolation (ɪnˌtræpəˈleɪʃən). [f. INTRA- 3 + *-polation*, after *extrapolation*.] = INTERPOLATION 3; also more widely, (an) inference within the scope or framework of what is known.

1923 C. D. BROAD *Sci. Thought* xi. 428 Like all extrapolations, this argument is weaker than an intrapolation. **1949** KOESTLER *Insight & Outlook* xxv. 352 The listener is forced to complete its pattern himself, by a process of intrapolation and extrapolation. **1956** E. H. HUTTEN *Lang. Mod. Physics* v. 195 This intrapolation between observations is not, as such, required as support for the theory. **1969** D. F. HORROBIN *Sci. is God* iv. 49 This is known as intrapolation because.. the process operates only within the range.. actually measured.

So **inˈtrapolate** *v.* = INTERPOLATE *v.* 6.

1956 E. H. HUTTEN *Lang. Mod. Physics* v. 189 In classical mechanics we are able to intrapolate between observations and to say that, between the space-time points where it is observed, the particle follows a definite path.

intraprotoplasmic to **intraretinal**: see INTRA- *pref.* 1.

intrarious (ɪnˈtrɛərɪəs), *a. rare.* [f. late L. *intrāri-us* (f. *intrā* within + *-āri-us*, -ARY) + -OUS. Cf. F. *intraire*.] (See quot.)

1855 MAYNE *Expos. Lex.*, *Intrarius*, applied by L. C. Richard to the embryo, when it is contained in the albumen: intrarious.

†**intraˈrupt**, *a. Obs.* [var. of INTERRUPT, with confusion of prefixes: cf. It. *intrarompere* to interrupt (Florio, 1611).] = INTERRUPTED.

c **1440** *Partonope* 5600 Hit shall be intrarupt for me.

intrasegmental to **intra-sentence**: see INTRA- *pref.*

intraseptal (ɪntrəˈsɛptəl), *a.* [f. INTRA- 1 + L. *sept-um* partition + -AL[1].] Situated within a septum or partition; said *esp.* of the chambers enclosed by each pair of mesenteries in *Anthozoa*.

1888 ROLLESTON & JACKSON *Anim. Life* 725 When the mesenteries [in *Anthozoa*] are paired, the two members of every pair inclose a space which is known as intra-septal, the spaces between adjacent pairs being termed inter-septal.

intraserous to **intrasomatic**: see INTRA- *pref.*

intraˈspecies, *a.* [INTRA- 2.] = next.

1927 *Techn. Bull. N.Y. State Agric. Exper. Stat.* No. 127. 5 During the past 18 years many intra- and inter-species crosses of *Prunus* have been made. **1953** *New Biol.* XIV. 9 Intraspecies fighting is different from interspecies fighting. **1963** *Language* XXXIX. 461 The whistles, squeals, chirps, clicks, rasps, and other noises of marine mammals have suggested three areas of inquiry: orientation by echolocation, intraspecies communication, and interspecies communication. **1973** *Sci. Amer.* Aug. 29/1 This interspecies difference contrasts with remarkable intraspecies similarity.

intraspeˈcific, *a.* [f. INTRA- 1 + SPECIFIC *a.*, as adj. from *species*.] Produced, occurring, or existing within a (taxonomic) species or between individuals of a single species.

1919 *Genetics* IV. 501 (*heading*) An analysis of certain cases of intraspecific sterility. **1929** *Hereditas* XIII. 185 Partial sterility in intra- and interspecific crosses. **1937** A. HUXLEY *Ends & Means* xiv. 265 Progress is dependent on the preponderance of intra-specific co-operation over intra-specific competition. **1953** N. TINBERGEN *Herring Gull's World* x. 88 Species are known in which the reproductive season brings much intraspecific strife. **1966** M. LATZKE tr. *Lorenz's On Aggression* iii. 18 The survival value of inter-specific fights is much more evident than that of intra-specific contests. **1968** R. D. MARTIN tr. *Wickler's Mimicry* xvi. 227, I have given the term intra-specific mimicry to this form of self-imitation within a species. **1969** *Daily Tel.* 13 Feb. 22/4 Mankind's allegedly instinctive affection for weaponry and intraspecific killing has been a selling subject.

intraspinal to **intra-state**: see INTRA- *pref.*

†**inˈtraste**, *v. Obs.* [f. IN *adv.* + *trast*, TRUST.] *trans.* To trust in. (Perh. to be read as two words.)

c **1460** *Towneley Myst.* xxv. 182, I byd the noght abaste, bot boldly make you bowne, With toyles that ye intraste, And dyng that dastard downe.

intrastitial (ɪntrəˈstɪʃəl), *a. Phys.* [From *interstitial* with intentional change of prefix.] Occurring within the ultimate microscopical cells or fibres which compose an organ.

1873 T. H. GREEN *Introd. Pathol.* (ed. 2) 55 These two processes.. go hand in hand together, the interstitial infiltration inducing the intrastitial degeneration.

intrastromal to **intrasusception**: see INTRA- *pref.*

†**ˈintrat.** *Obs.* [a. L. *intrat* '(he) enters', 3rd sing. pres. ind. of *intrāre* to enter. Cf. *exit*.] An entrance of a character upon the stage.

a **1652** J. SMITH *Sel. Disc.* vi. 300 Exits and intrats upon this prophetical stage being made.. in an invisible manner.

intratarsal: see INTRA- *pref.*

†**ˈintrate.** *Obs.* [var. of ENTRATE: cf. It. *entrata* income, and INTRADO.] Income, revenue.

1538 STARKEY *England* II. ii. 186 To make a rekenyng and count.. of al hys intrate, rentys, and reuenewys.

intratelluric (-tɛˈl(j)ʊərɪk), *a. Geol.* [f. INTRA- 1 + L. *tellus*, *tellūr-em* earth (cf. *telluric*). Anglicized immediately from Ger. *intratellurisch*, Rosenbusch *Mikrosk. Physiogr. Mineral.* (ed. 2) II. 8.] Occurring, taking place, or formed in the interior of the earth; hypogene; ***intratelluric period***, a period or stage of crystallization, etc., passed under the surface of the earth.

1889 *Nature* 17 Jan. 273/2 After their slow development in the magma during an intra-telluric period.

intraterritorial to **intratracheally**: see INTRA- *pref.*

intratropical (-ˈtrɒpɪkəl), *a.* [INTRA- 1.] Situated or occurring within the tropics; = INTERTROPICAL, TROPICAL.

1811 *Edin. Rev.* XIX. 184 The Cerealia are not cultivated in the intra-tropical part of Mexico. **1880** *Nature* 1 Jan. 210/1 During extensive intra-tropical rains.

intratubal, -umbilical: see INTRA- *pref.*

intraunce, obs. form of ENTRANCE *sb.*

intra-urban, -urethral: see INTRA- *pref.*

intra-uterine (ɪntrəˈjuːtərɪn, -aɪn), *a.* Also **intrauterine.** [f. INTRA- 1 + L. *uterus*: cf. *uterine*.] Situated, occurring, or passed within the uterus or womb; relating to this stage of an animal's life. Applied *spec.* to contraceptive devices for placing in the uterus.

1835-6 TODD *Cycl. Anat.* I. 69/2 In the early periods of intra-uterine life. **1862** H. SPENCER *First Princ.* II. xii. §93 (1875) 279 An intra-uterine biography beginning with him as a microscopic germ. **1931** F. W. S. BROWNE tr. *T. H. van de Velde's Fertility & Sterility in Marriage* xiv. 354 The intra-uterine appliances were based on the same principle as the vaginal; but they soon completely changed their mechanism and structure. **1969** N. W. PIRIE *Food Resources* 15 The contraceptive ideal is a treatment of some sort that makes one or other sex infertile until it is reversed. The closest approach to this ideal so far is the intrauterine device. **1972** *Guardian* 10 July 9/2 Asking, at a Family Planning Association branch, for an intra-uterine device.

intravaginal to **intravarietal**: see INTRA- *pref.*

intravasation (ɪnˌtrævəˈseɪʃən). *Path.* [f. INTRA-, after EXTRAVASATION.] The entrance into vessels of matters formed in the surrounding tissues.

1674 C. GOODALL *Coll. Physic. Vind.* (1676) 82 What is said of extravasation and intravasation in deaths approaches. **1887** *Syd. Soc. Lex.*, *Intravasation*, the entrance of pus or other morbid product into a blood-vessel or a lymphatic through an aperture made in it by an abscess or an ulcer.

intravascular (-ˈvæskjʊlə(r)), *a. Anat.* and *Path.* [f. INTRA- 1 + L. *vascul-um* vessel: cf. *vascular*.] Situated or occurring within a vessel of an animal or plant, esp. within a blood-vessel. (In quot. 1876 app. erron. for INTERVASCULAR.) Hence **intraˈvascularly** *adv.*, within the vascular system.

1876 tr. *Wagner's Gen. Pathol.* 154 The spleen, liver, and marrow of bones contained cinnabar in the intravascular tissues at nearly the same time and in equal degrees. **1887** *Syd. Soc. Lex.*, *Intravascular clotting*, the production of a blood-clot within the blood-vessels. **1906** [see ANTI-[1] 6 c]. **1971** *Nature* 5 Feb. 412/2 For preservation, dog brain was perfused intravascularly with 3% glutaraldehyde for 5–20 min.

intravehicular: see INTRA- *pref.* 1.

intravenous (ɪntrəˈviːnəs), *a.* and *sb.* [f. INTRA- 1 + L. *vēn-a* vein: cf. *venous*. Cf. F. *intraveineux* (Littré *Suppl.*).] Existing or taking place within a vein or the veins. Also as *sb.*, an intravenous injection or feeding.

1847-9 TODD *Cycl. Anat.* IV. 102/1 Intra-venous Formations are produced by evolution of absorbed elements. **1876** HARLEY *Mat. Med.* (ed. 6) 110 Intravenous injections of ammonia have also been suggested. **1898** P. MANSON *Trop. Diseases* viii. 167 They then immunised a horse by intravenous injections of living virulent cultures. **1960** J. G. BALLARD in D. Knight *100 Yrs. Sci. Fiction* (1969) 355 Took me half an hour to steady myself enough for an intravenous. **1970** *New Yorker* 21 Nov. 66/2 You have intravenouses going in both your hands.

Hence **intraˈvenously** *adv.*

1897 *Allbutt's Syst. Med.* II. 821 When the venom is intravenously introduced there is an extraordinary and immediate diminution of the white cells.

intraventricular (-vɛnˈtrɪkjʊlə(r)), *a. Anat.* [f. INTRA- 1 + L. *ventricul-us*, *-um* VENTRICLE; cf. *ventricular*.] Situated or contained within a ventricle of the brain or heart. Hence **intravenˈtricularly** *adv.*, into or within a ventricle.

1882 *Pop. Sci. Monthly* XXII. 173 The intraventricular portion of the left *corpus striatum*. **1887** *Syd. Soc. Lex.*, *Intraventricular fluid*, the fluid contained within the ventricles of the brain or heart. **1951** *Year Bk. Drug Therapy* 218 Trial of streptomycin intraventricularly.. seems indicated. **1955** *Brit. Jrnl. Pharmacol.* X. 373/1 Bulbocapnine, when injected intraventricularly, produces its characteristic effects in doses a fraction of those effective on subcutaneous injection. **1961** *Lancet* 22 July 178/1 The sodium salt of polymyxin B methane sulphonic acid.. is well tolerated intraventricularly. **1972** *Science* 29 Sept. 1213/2, 6-HDA administered intraventricularly can produce several aspects of the classical lateral hypothalamic syndrome.

intraverbal: see INTRA- *pref.* 1.

intraversable (ɪnˈtrævəsəb(ə)l), *a.* Also **intraversible.** [IN-[3].] That cannot be traversed or crossed.

1803 W. TAYLOR in *Ann. Rev.* I. 442 It is then shut up as a sea-port by intraversable gulfs of ice. **1900** W. JAMES *Let.* 26 Sept. (1920) II. 137 It must seem strange to you that the way from the mind to the pen should be as intraversable as it has been in this case of mine. **1923** R. F. HORTON *Mystical Quest Christ* III. xxiv. 255 The vast universe seems so homeless, so comfortless; its spaces of darkness so intraversible.

†**inˈtraverse**, *v. Obs.* [? f. IN-[2] + TRAVERSE *v.*] *trans.* ? To cross, intersperse.

1607 WALKINGTON *Opt. Glass* Pref. (1664) 15 That I should intraverse, and interlard my speeches with lively conceits.

intravertebral, -vertebrally: see INTRA- *pref.* 1.

intraˈvertebrate, *a. Zool. rare*[−0]. [ad. mod.L. *intrāvertebrātus*, used by Geoffrey St. Hilaire as below: see INTRA- and VERTEBRATE.] Having an internal bony skeleton; = VERTEBRATE. Also **intraˈvertebrated** *a.*

1855 MAYNE *Expos. Lex.*, *Intravertebratus*, applied by Geoffrey St. Hilaire, who restores to a similar type of organization the articulated and the vertebrated animals, to those having their osseous covering within the body, in distinction from those in which it is exterior: intravertebrated.

1887 *Syd. Soc. Lex.*, *Intravertebrate.*

intravesical: see INTRA- *pref.*

intravital (ɪntrəˈvaɪtəl), *a. Biol.* [f. INTRA- 1 + VITAL *a.*, perh. suggested by *intra vitam* (see INTRA *prep.* 2).] Performed on, applied to, or occurring in something alive.

1890 in BILLINGS *Med. Dict.* 712/1. **1922** *Proc. R. Soc.* B. XCIV. 138 On intra-vital staining by polychrome methylene blue, some of these granules are stained blue, others red. **1938** *Biochem. Jrnl.* XXXII. 381 The distribution of the lyochromes in the kidneys of frogs and rats was studied by intravital microscopy. **1963** *Lancet* 19 Jan. 152/2 The technique of intravital staining of the motor end plate.. is of limited diagnostic value.

Hence **intraˈvitally** *adv.*, during life, in a living organism.

1930 *Biol. Abstr.* IV. 3299/3 (Index), Iron lactate, storage intravitally. **1937** *Acta Med. Scand.* XCI. 350 It has been demonstrated intravitally in retinal vessels in cases of stasis provoked by pressure on the eye.

intra vitam: see INTRA *prep.* 2.

intravitelline, -xylary: see INTRA- *pref.*

in-tray (ˈɪntreɪ). [Cf. IN *adv.* 12 a.] In an office, etc.: a tray for incoming correspondence and other papers; = IN-BASKET. Cf. OUT-TRAY.

Sometimes written as two separate words with *in* regarded adjectivally.

1941 *Punch* 25 June 602/2, I found the first one lying quietly in my IN tray (or IN wire-basket). **1943** W. S. CHURCHILL *Second World War* (1951) IV. 852 A habit of having secret papers placed in 'In' or 'Out' trays on the desks of important officers. **1958** *New Statesman* 25 Jan. 112/3, I hope some copies reach the In-trays of the Indian officials who refused to support him at Oxford. **1968** P. MCKELLAR *Experience & Behaviour* vi. 163 In an office, some item waiting to be dealt with in the older man's in-tray may seem to him to wait only a short time. **1970** *New Scientist* 30 Apr. 239/1 The issue of industrial noise is finding its way to the political in-trays.

†**inˈtrayl**, obs. f. ENTRAIL *v.*, to entwine. Hence **inˈtrayling** *ppl. a.*

a **1548** HALL *Chron.*, *Hen. VIII* 73 The pyllers wrapped in a wrethe of golde curiously wroughte and intrayled. **1622** WITHER *Mistr. Philar.* Wks. (1633) 621 In those faire curled snares They are hampred unawares; And compeld to sweare a duty To her sweet intrayling beauty.

ˈintrayle, obs. form of ENTRAIL *sb.*^{1}
c **1440** *Promp. Parv.* 262/2 Intrayle, or yssu of a dede beeste, *intesti[n]um, et alia infra in issu.*

†**inˈtrayn**, obs. f. ENTRAIN *v.*^{1}, to draw on or in.
1605 SYLVESTER *Du Bartas* II. iii. IV. *Captaines* 379 Still faining so, Till (politick) he hath in-trayn'd the Foe Right to his Ambush.

intrazonal (ɪntrəˈzəʊnəl), *a. Soil Sci.* [a. F. *intrazonal* (N. Sibirtsev 1897, in *Compt. Rend. de la VIIe Session, Congr. géol. internat.* (1899) II. III. v. 83): see INTRA- 1 and ZONAL *a.*]
Designating any soil which occurs within a major soil zone but differs from the characteristic soil of that zone owing to the overriding influence of relief, parent material, or other local factor.
[**1908** *Jrnl. Agric. Sci.* III. 84 In all these zones also certain interzonal soils are sure to occur, which owe their peculiarities to special conditions of topography alone. *Ibid.*, Such soils constitute the six..interzonal types enumerated by Sibirtzev.] **1927** C. F. MARBUT tr. *Glinka's Great Soil Groups* 28 Intrazonal soils originate, according to Sibirceff, where local soil forming forces predominate over the general or zonal forces. **1946** LUTZ & CHANDLER *Forest Soils* xi. 385 Intrazonal soils have more or less well-defined characteristics which reflect the dominating influence of some local factor, such as relief, parent material, or age, over the normal effect of climate and vegetation. **1965** B. T. BUNTING *Geogr. Soils* i. 18 The soils of the world have been considered as belonging to one of the three major orders—zonal, azonal and intrazonal—each divisible into many groups.

intreague, obs. form of INTRIGUE.

intreasure, variant of ENTREASURE *v.*

intreat, obs. or arch. form of ENTREAT.

†**inˈtreatable**, *a.*^{1} *Obs.* [ad. F. *intraitable* (16th c. in Littré), f. *traiter* to treat, after L. *intractābilis*: see INTRACTABLE.] That cannot be treated with; inexorable.
1509 BARCLAY *Shyp of Folys* (1874) II. 115 No thynge we muse on deth: but despyse his furour intretable whiche sure shall come. **1514** —— *Cyt. & Uplondyshm.* (Percy Soc.) p. lxxi, Fearefull is Labour..a monster intreatable. **1598** BERNARD *Terence, Phormio* III. ii. 420 So intreatable, as that you can be appeased neither by piety nor by prayer.

inˈtreatable, *a.*^{2}, obs. f. ENTREATABLE, easy to be entreated.

intreatance, -treater, -treaty, etc., obs. ff. ENTREATANCE, etc.

intredite, obs. form of INTERDICT.

intrel, obs. form of ENTRAIL *sb.*

†**inˈtrembled**, *ppl. a. Obs. rare.* [f. IN-^{2} + TREMBLE + -ED^1; after OF. *entremblé* 'agité comme par un tremblement' (Godef.).] Shaken with fear, trembling. So **inˈtrembling** *ppl. a.* (an attempt to conform the word to *trembling*).
1627 FELTHAM *Resolves* II. [I] xiii. (1628) 37 Into what a trepidation of the soule, does feare decline the Coward? how it Downes the head in the intrembled bosome? [*So edd.* **1636, 1647, 1661**; *edd.* **1677, 1696** intrembling.]

†**intreˈmendous**, *a. Obs. rare.* [IN-^{3}.] Erron. used for: Devoid of fear.
1659 D. PELL *Impr. Sea* 220 None..can be found..resembling this intremendous and fearless creature [the Whale].

intremet, variant of ENTERMETE, *Obs.*

intrench (ɪnˈtrɛnʃ), *v.* [f. IN-^{1} + TRENCH.]
1. *trans.* To make a trench in; to furrow.
1754 P. H. *Hiberniad* 37 Intrench'd her Forehead, horrent stands her Hair. **1871** L. STEPHEN *Playgr. Europe* vi. (1894) 144 Towers of ice intrenched by deep crevasses.
2. Variant of ENTRENCH *v.*, q.v.

†**inˈtrenchant**, *a.*^{1} *Obs. rare*$^{-1}$. [f. IN-^{3} + TRENCHANT *a.*; but the passive sense, in Shaks., is irregular.]
1. Not trenchant or cutting. *rare*$^{-0}$.
2. Incapable of being cut.
1605 SHAKS. *Macb.* v. viii. 9 Thou loosest labour, As easie may'st thou the intrenchant Ayre With thy keene Sword impresse, as make me bleed.

intrenchant (ɪnˈtrɛnʃənt), *a.*^{2} *rare*$^{-1}$. [f. IN *adv.* 1 or 2 + TRENCHANT: the passive sense is irregular.] Cutting in, penetrating.
1833 *New Monthly Mag.* XXXVII. 37 What fearful gashes, what deep intrenchant scars, succeeded to this!

intrencher (ɪnˈtrɛnʃə(r)). *rare.* [f. INTRENCH, ENTRENCH *v.* + -ER^1.] One who makes trenches.
1884 *Century Mag.* Nov. 102/1 Their fighting redeemed well their shortcomings as intrenchers.

intrenching, -ment: see ENTRENCHING, -MENT.

intrepid (ɪnˈtrɛpɪd), *a.* [ad. L. *intrepid-us*, f. *in-* (IN-^{3}) + *trepidus* alarmed; cf. F. *intrépide* (16th c. in Littré).] Of persons and personal qualities: Fearless; undaunted; daring; brave.
1697 DRYDEN *Virg. Æneid* Ded. (R.), That quality [valour], which signifies no more than an intrepid courage. *Ibid., Georg.* IV. 122 The two contending Princes..Intrepid thro' the midst of Danger go. **1738** GLOVER *Leonidas* I. 214 Three hundred more compleat th' intrepid band. **1766** GOLDSM. *Vic. W.* xxviii, 'Where, sir, is your fortitude?' returned my son with an intrepid voice. **1833** HT. MARTINEAU *Fr. Wines & Pol.* iii. 42 Is there to be no pride in intrepid patriotism? **1854** WISEMAN *Fabiola* II. xxv. 288 She stood intrepid and unmoved before him.

intrepidity (ɪntrɪˈpɪdɪtɪ). [f. as prec. + -ITY. Cf. F. *intrépidité* (17th c. in Hatz.-Darm.).] The quality of being intrepid; fearlessness; firmness of mind in the presence of danger; courage, boldness.
1704 *Lond. Gaz.* No. 4058/2 The Intrepedity of Your Admiral. **1764** REID *Inquiry* ii. §6. 108 It required an uncommon degree of philosophical intrepidity. **1803** MACKINTOSH *Def. Peltier* Wks. 1846 III. 242 Intrepidity in the discharge of professional duty is so common a quality at the English Bar. **1865** CARLYLE *Fredk. Gt.* XVI. iii. (1872) VI. 162 He [Saxe] had perfect intrepidity; not to be flurried by any amount of peril or confusion.

intrepidly (ɪnˈtrɛpɪdlɪ), *adv.* [f. INTREPID + -LY^2.] In an intrepid manner; fearlessly, boldly.
a **1720** SHEFFIELD (Dk. Buckhm.) *Wks.* (1753) I. 161 Yet Cæsar, still intrepidly serene, Goes proudly on, despising us, and danger. **1868** MILMAN *St. Paul's* 129 Those brothers who so intrepidly resisted. **1888** A. T. PIERSON *Evang. Work* vi. 60 Intrepidly indifferent to either compliment or censure.

intrepidness (ɪnˈtrɛpɪdnɪs). [f. as prec. + -NESS.] The quality of being intrepid; intrepidity.
1627 DONNE *Serm.* xlvii. 473 No apprehensions of Death removed him from his holy intrepidnesse, and religious Constancy. **1741** RICHARDSON *Pamela* (1824) I. lxxvii. 432 You told me, sir, last night, of your intrepidness: I think you are the boldest man I ever met with.

intres(s, var. of ENTRESS *Obs.*, entrance.

intress, var. of INTERESS *Obs.*, interest.

intrete, -er, obs. forms of ENTREAT, -ER.

ˈin-ˈtriangle. *Math.* [Cf. IN-CIRCLE.] A triangle inscribed in a circle or other figure.

†**intriˈbution.** *Obs. rare*$^{-0}$. [ad. L. *intribūtiōn-em*, from *intribuĕre* to contribute.]
1656 BLOUNT *Glossogr.*, *Intribution*, contribution or lot-mony paid for Lands.

†**ˈintricable**, *a. Obs.* [a. obs. F. *intricable* (14th c. in Godef.), f. L. type **intrīcābilis*, f. *intrīcāre* to entangle: see INTRICATE.] Entangling, perplexing; entangled, intricately involved.
a **1540** BARNES *Wks.* (1573) 278/1 Now here haue I aunswered, to an intricable doubt. **1612** SHELTON *Quix.* III. vii. 182 They shall remaine captiue, and intangled in the intricable amorous net. **1621** BURTON *Anat. Mel.* Democr. to Rdr. 64 A labyrinth of intricable questions, unprofitable contentions..one calls it [School divinity].

intricacy (ˈɪntrɪkəsɪ). [f. next: see -ACY.]
1. The quality or state of being intricate; complexity; complicated or involved condition.
1602 WARNER *Alb. Eng.* Epit. (1612) 366 Our..Method wherein we now execute lawes and dispatch, with lesser intricacie, the Collections and businesses for the Weale publike. **1619** NAUNTON in *Fortesc. Papers* (Camden) 107 It is a buisines of much intricasie. **1697** DRYDEN *Virg. Georg.* (1721) I. Ess. 201 It often puzzles the Reader with the Intricacy of its Notions. **1711** ADDISON *Spect.* No. 39 ¶3 The modern Tragedy excels that of Greece and Rome, in the Intricacy and Disposition of the Fable. **1753** HOGARTH *Anal. Beauty* v. 28 The beauty of a composed intricacy of form. **1830** HERSCHEL *Stud. Nat. Phil.* 247 The mathematical theory of the propagation of sound..is one of the utmost intricacy. **1866** ROGERS *Agric. & Prices* I. xx. 512 The lock must have varied in value, according to its size and to the intricacy of its workmanship.
2. quasi-*concr.* An instance of this condition; a complication; an entangled or involved state of affairs; a perplexing difficulty.
1611 COTGR., *Intrique*, an intricacie, Laborinth, Maze,..difficultie. **1628** LE GRYS tr. *Barclay's Argenis* 255 Cut off these intricacies: set downe a time, beyond which no controuersie shall depend in Court. *a* **1661** FULLER *Worthies* (1840) II. 487 Because the sun doth not so much dry the intricacies of such flowers which are duplicated. **1796** MORSE *Amer. Geog.* II. 606 Twelve palaces, and 1000 houses, the intricacies of which occasion its name. **1821** SCOTT *Kenilw.* viii, He conducted Tressilian..through a long intricacy of passages. **1874** L. STEPHEN *Hours in Library* (1892) I. ix. 316 Every intricacy was plainly mapped out in his own mind.

intricate (ˈɪntrɪkət), *a.* (*sb.*) (In 5 **interkat.**) [ad. L. *intrīcāt-us*, pa. pple. of *intrīcāre* to entangle, perplex, embarrass, f. *in-* (IN-^{2}) + *trīcæ* trifles, toys, quirks, tricks, perplexities, *trīcārī* to raise difficulties, play tricks.]
1. Perplexingly entangled or involved; interwinding in a complicated manner.
1579 E. K. *Ded. Spenser's Sheph. Cal.*, The words them selues being so auncient, the knitting of them so short and intricate. **1601** HOLLAND *Pliny* II. 569 The wonderful intricat winding of the serpents, clasping and knitting them about. **1632** LITHGOW *Trav.* v. 190 Wrestling amongst intricate paths of Rockes: two..broke their neckes. *a* **1667** COWLEY *Wish* Wks. 1711 III. 43 Tho' he sit upon the Place of Judgment with a learned Face Intricate as the Law. **1703** MAUNDRELL *Journ. Jerus.* (1732) 79 From this place you proceed in an intricate way amongst Hills and Valleys. **1822** SCOTT *Nigel* iii, At the end of one of those intricate and narrow lanes. **1892** STEVENSON *Across the Plains* I Mount St. Helena..looks down on much green intricate country.
b. *Entomol.* Of markings; see quot.
1826 KIRBY & SP. *Entomol.* IV. 274 *Intricate*. When depressions or elevations so run into each other as to be difficult to trace.
2. Of thoughts, conceptions, statements, etc.: Perplexingly involved or complicated in meaning; entangled; obscure.
c **1470** HENRYSON *Fables* xii. (*Wolff and Lamb*) 121 (Bannatyne MS.) O man of law lat be thy sutelte, With wys jympis, and frawdis interkat. **1529** MORE *Dyaloge* I. Pref. A j b/1 Fyndyng oure treatye so dyuerse and so long, and sume tyme such wyse intrycate that my self could not wythout labour call it orderly to mind. **1599** *Life More* in Wordsw. *Eccl. Biog.* (1853) II. 52 Now is the common-lawe of this realme so intricate..as it would requier a whole and entire man, all his life tyme..to come to anye excellencie therein. **1683** CHALKHILL *Thealma & Cl.* 95 He..could clear The doubts that puzzle the strong working brain, And make the intricat'st anigmas plain. **1719** YOUNG *Revenge* II. i, Give me your maze Of gloomy thought, and intricate design. **1849** MACAULAY *Hist. Eng.* vi. II. 25 According to the intricate and subtle rule which was then in force.
†**3.** = INTRICATED. Const. *with, in. Obs.*
1526 *Pilgr. Perf.* (1531) 58 Be thou neuer..intricate, busyed or troubled in the defautes or offences of other. **1528** ROY *Rede Me* (Arb.) 91 They kepe none of all the thre [vows] With mundane affections intricate.
†**B.** *sb.* Something intricate; an intricacy. *Obs.*
1655 GURNALL *Chr. in Arm.* I. 127 Satan labours to puzzle the Christian with nice questions, that meeting with such intricates in his Christian course..he may be made, either to give over, or go on heavily.

intricate (ˈɪntrɪkeɪt), *v.* Now *rare*. Also 6 **en-**. [f. L. *intrīcāt-*, ppl. stem of *intrīcāre* to entangle: see prec. Cf. ENTRIKE.]
1. *trans.* To render intricate; to make (a thing) involved or obscure; to complicate.
1564 *Brief Exam.* A ij, Such [questions] as be intricated with great controuersies amongest godly men. **1624** HEYWOOD *Gunaik.* IV. 168 This Labyrinth..being a house so intricated with windings and turnings this way and that way. **1649** BP. HALL *Cases Consc.* vi. (1654) 45 How ever the matter may be intricated by passing through many perhaps unknowing hands. **1671** R. BOHUN *Wind* 278 Woods, thus [with wonderful entanglings] rent asunder and intricated. **1688** *Vox Cleri Pro Rege* 43 Why does he..labour to perplex and intricate the meaning of Dr. Sherlock's plain Words? *c* **1748** VOLTAIRE in W. Bayne *James Thomson* ix. (1898) 150 Mr. Thomson's tragedies seem to me wisely intricated and elegantly writ. **1900** *Dundee Advertiser* 8 June 4 It so intricated peace desires with war menaces as to begin the campaign on a scale of disastrous military inefficiency.
2. To entangle or ensnare (an animal or person); to involve in toils; to embarrass, perplex.
1548 *Act 2 & 3 Edw. VI*, c. 21 § 1 They myght..be lesse entricated and troubled withe the Chardge of householde. **1566** PAINTER *Pal. Pleas.* (Marsh) I. 189, I am so intricated in the Labarinthe of my unbrideled will. **1579** FENTON *Guicciard.* v. (1599) 227 The Frenchmen beginning to intricate and intangle themselues, fell to flying. **1649** JER. TAYLOR *Gt. Exemp.* III. Ad Sect. xvi. 134 Like wilde beasts intricating themselves by their impatience. *a* **1734** NORTH *Exam.* (1740) 57 This speculum of his own ignorance..did so intricate and embarrass his understanding.
Hence **ˈintricated** *ppl. a.*, entangled, involved in toils; **ˈintricating** *vbl. sb.*, entanglement.
1565–73 COOPER *Thesaurus*, *Contortulus*,..wrested, wrethed, intricated, conclused. **1628** DONNE *Serm.* cxxxiv. V. 407 Intricated entangled conscience! **1632** LITHGOW *Trav.* II. 66, I left the turmoyling dangers of the intricated Iles of the Ionean and Adriaticall seas. **1649** JER. TAYLOR *Gt. Exemp.* II. Disc. ix. §22. 117 To the intricating of the judgement, to the dishonour of Religion. **1798** PENNANT *Hindoostan* II. 340 The various great rivers which form so many intricated windings.

intricately (ˈɪntrɪkətlɪ), *adv.* [f. INTRICATE *a.* + -LY^2.] In an intricate manner or state; complicatedly; with intricacy or perplexity. In *Entomol.* With intricate sculpture or markings.
1552 HULOET, Intricately, *perplexe.* **1593** NASHE *Christ's T.* (1613) 140 They labour not to speake properly, but intricately. **1601** DANIEL *Civ. Wars* VI. lxxiv, The sword..Must cut this knot so intricately tyde. **1656** *Burton's Diary* (1828) I. 181 Upon the accounts of subsidies this gentleman leaves it very intricately. **1768–74** TUCKER *Lt. Nat.* (1834) I. 473 Through a thousand intricately-winding channels.

ˈintricateness. [f. as prec. + -NESS.] The quality of being intricate; intricacy.
a **1586** SIDNEY *Arcadia* (1622) 54 Therin he found such intricatenesse, that he could see no way to lead him out of the maze. **1633** BP. HALL *Hard Texts* 441 Then doe also appear a certaine intricatenesse and a perplexity in the proceedings thereof. **1685** BOYLE *Enq. Notion Nat.* iv. 72 The intricateness and importance of the subject hindered me from making it shorter.

†**intriˈcation.** *Obs.* [ad. med.L. *intrīcātiōn-em*, n. of action from *intrīcāre* (see INTRICATE *a.*); cf. F. *intrication* (14th c. in Godef.).] The action of intricating or condition of being intricated; complication, entanglement.
1432–50 tr. *Higden* (Rolls) I. 9 Attendenge the intricacion inextricable [*inextricabilem attendens intricationem*] of this

labor presente as of the mase of Dedalinus. **1532** MORE *Confut. Tindale* Wks. 615/2 For the auoydyng of all intricacion wherof, I purposelye forbare to putte in the Pope as parte of the diffinicyon of the church. **1548** PATTEN *Exp. Scot.* in Arb. *Garner* III. 120 It should be too much an intrication to the matter. **1579** TWYNE *Phisicke agst. Fort.* II. Ep. Ded. 160a, The indissoluble knottes and intrications of matters. **1661** BOYLE *Examen* Wks. 1772 I. 240, I do not see how the *motus circularis simplex* should need to be superadded to the contact or intrication of the cohering firm corpuscles, to procure a cohesion. **1773** J. ROSS *Fratricide* III. 732 (MS.) Much delay'd, Thus dark, by intrications in their way, And many a mazy Labyrinth.

†**intri'cator.** *Obs. rare*⁻⁰. [agent-n. in Lat. form f. *intricāre* to entangle: see INTRICATE *a.*] An entangler; one who complicates.

1611 COTGR., *Embarasseur*, an intricator, pesterer. *Ibid.*, *Trigaut*, an intricator, intangler, perplexer of a businesse.

intrick, var. ENTRIKE *Obs.*: see INTRIKE.

‖**in'trico.** *Obs.* [It. *intrico* (Florio, 1598): see INTRIGUE.] An intricacy; a maze.

a **1670** HACKET *Abp. Williams* I. (1692) 12 The potions of School Divinity wrought easily with him, so that he was not lost a whit in their *Intricoes* any further than they lose themselves.

†**in'trie,** *v. Obs. rare*⁻¹. [f. IN-¹ + *trie*, TRY *v.*] *trans.* To put in, introduce, add.

c **1420** *Pallad. on Husb.* IV. 355 To cley & chalk the firthe part intrie Of gipse [L. *si argillæ et cretæ quartam partem gypsi misceas*].

intrigant, -ante: see INTRIGUANT, -ANTE.

‖**in'trigo.** *Obs.* Also intriego, intriguo. [It. *intrigo*: see INTRIGUE.] = INTRIGUE *sb.*

1648 *King's Gracious Messages for Peace* 110 The deep subtilty and *intrigo* of it was not then apparent. **1656** EARL MONM. *Advt. fr. Parnass.* 243 How to explain..all the cunning intriegoes used in times of peace and war, in the government of their states. **1665** SIR T. HERBERT *Trav.* 225 The Intrigo's of State. **1676** SHADWELL *Virtuoso* I. 6, I have indeed to night an *Intriguo* with a Lady.

b. *spec.* The plot of a play; = INTRIGUE *sb.* 3.

1672 VILLIERS (Dk. Buckhm.) *Rehearsal* I. (Arb.) 29 The Plot..the Intrigo's now quite out of my head. **1672** MARVELL *Reh. Transp.* I. 11.

intriguant, -gant ('ɪntrɪgənt, F. ɛ̃trigɑ̃), *sb.* and *a.* [a. F. *intriguant*, pr. pple. of *intriguer* to INTRIGUE; also *intrigant*, ad. It. *intrigante.*]

A. *sb.* An intriguer.

1781 BENTHAM *Wks.* (1843) X. 93 One of the busiest and most successful of *intriguants.* **1794** *Amer. St. Papers, For. Relat.* (1832) I. 403 (Stanf.) Putting off the character of minister to put on that of *intriguant.* **1809** WELLINGTON in Gurw. *Desp.* (1837) IV. 507 [He] has certainly the mind and manners of an *intrigant.* **1846** MRS. GORE *Eng. Char.* (1852) 25 The appearance of Farren in the part of the ambitious intriguant. **1886** *Century Mag.* Nov. 33/1 Illiterate intriguants..insisted on shaping legislation according to their own fancy.

B. *adj.* Intriguing; scheming.

1897 *African Critic* 21 Aug. 224 The most unscrupulous and intriguant amongst the Continental oligarchies.

‖**intriguante, -gante** (ɪntri'gɑːnt, -æ-, F. ɛ̃trigɑ̃t). [F. *intriguante, -gante*, fem. of *intriguant, -gant*: see prec.] A woman who intrigues.

1806 MAR. EDGEWORTH *Leonora* (1832) 54 Mdᵉ. de P—— is a perfect specimen of the combination of an *intrigante* and an *élégante.* **1823** BYRON *Juan* XIV. lxiii, Her Grace too pass'd for being an *intrigante*.. One of those pretty, precious plagues, which haunt A lover with caprices soft and dear. **1829** LYTTON *Devereux* III. vii, My Mistress was the greatest *intriguante* of her party. **1856** VAUGHAN *Mystics* VIII. iv. (1860) II. 51 That he must toil in obscurity..to subserve the ambition of an implacable *intriguante.*

intrigue (ɪn'triːg), *sb.* Also 7 in-, entreague, intregue, -iegue; intrique, -eque. [a. F. *intrigue*, formerly *intrique* (16–17th c.), ad. It. *intrigo, -ico*, f. *intrigare, -care* to intricate, entangle, entrap:—L. *intricāre*: see INTRICATE *a.*]

†**1.** Intricacy, complexity; a complicated contrivance; a maze, a labyrinth. *Obs.*

1656 BLOUNT *Glossogr.*, *Intrique*, an intricacy, labyrinth, maze, incumbrance, difficulty. *Cressy.* **1660** *Chas. II.'s escape fr. Worcester* in *Select. fr. Harl. Misc.* (1793) 382 His majesty was had to his lodging, and the intrigues of it shewn him. **1673** RAY *Trav.* (1738) I. 419 A famous engine to raise up water..There is so little of it remaining that it is impossible thence to find out all the contrivance and intrigue of it. **1686** GOAD *Celest. Bodies* I. iv. 11 No finite Knowledge can be comprehensive of an Effect..in every minute Intrigue of Nature.

†**b.** *fig.* An intricate or complicated state of affairs; an involved mode of action. *Obs.*

1660 JER. TAYLOR *Duct. Dubit.* (L.), There are so many certain but indiscernible fallibilities, so many intrigues of fancy in the disputers. **1693** SOUTH *Serm.* 332 To look into the little intrigues of matter and motion. **1704** HEARNE *Duct. Hist.* (1714) I. 106 To unravel (if I may say so) all the Intreagues betwixt God and Man.

2. The exertion of tortuous or underhand influence to accomplish some purpose; underhand plotting or scheming.

1668 E. HOWARD *Usurper* Ep. A ij b, Intregue (the true Soul and Genius of the Stage). **1769** ROBERTSON *Chas. V*, VI. Wks. 1813 VI. 107 A spirit of action and intrigue is infused into all its members. **1818** JAS. MILL *Brit. India* II. IV. iii. 110 A complicated scene..of plotting and intrigue.

b. (with *pl.*) A plot to accomplish a purpose by tortuous or underhand influence.

1647 CLARENDON *Hist. Reb.* I. §23 According to the mysteries and intrigues of State. **1692** DRYDEN *St. Euremont's Ess.* 345 He was made Cardinal by Intrigues, Factions, and Tumults. **1767** *Junius Lett.* xv. 63 You have fairly confounded the intrigues of opposition. **1869** FREEMAN *Norm. Conq.* III. xii. 121 It is also quite possible that the Primate of Normandy himself had a share in his brother's intrigues.

†**3.** The plot of a play, poem, or romance. *Obs.*

1651 DAVENANT *Gondibert* Pref. 23 The third [act] makes a visible correspondence in the under-walks (or lesser intrigues) of persons; and ends with an ample turn of the main design. **1676** COLES, *Entreague*,..also a story (after many entangled passages) brought to a calm end. **1678** PHILLIPS (ed. 4) s.v. *Intricacy*, Also *Intrigue* or *Intreague*, the various and subtle intercourse of passages in the Plot of a Play. **1725** POPE *Odyss.* I. *View Epic Poem* p. xv, As these Causes are the Beginning of the Action, the opposite Designs against that of the Hero are the Middle of it, and form that Difficulty or *Intrigue* which makes up the greatest part of the Poem.

4. Clandestine illicit intimacy between a man and a woman; a liaison.

1668 CHARLETON *Ephes. & Cimm. Matrons.* II. Pref., She in like manner falls into an Intrigue (as they now adays call it). **1673** DRYDEN *Marr. à la Mode* II. i. Wks. 1883 IV. 279 Intrigue, Philotis! that's an old phrase; I have laid that word by; amour sounds better. **1712** STEELE *Spect.* No. 276 ⁋1 Taken in an Intrigue with another Man's Wife. **1883** C. J. WILLS *Mod. Persia* 276 In Shiraz, where intrigues among married women are very rife.

b. *transf.* The combination of queen and knave in certain games of cards.

1830 'EIDRAH TREBOR' *Hoyle made familiar, Pope Joan* 82 Matrimony is the king and queen, and Intrigue the knave and queen of trumps; the players of these cards take the pools belonging to them. *Ibid.* 83 The game [of Matrimony] consists of five chances, viz. *Matrimony*, which is king and queen: *Confederacy*, king and knave; *Intrigue*, queen and knave [etc.]. **1887** *All Year Round* 5 Feb. 66 There was Intrigue, that unhallowed flirtation between Queen and Knave.

intrigue (ɪn'triːg), *v.* Also 7 intreag. [a. F. *intrigue-r*, ad. It. *intrigare*:—L. *intricāre*: see INTRICATE *a.* OF. had *entriquer, intriquer*, whence ENTRIKE, INTRIKE.]

1. *trans.* To trick, deceive, cheat; to embarrass, puzzle, perplex. Now *rare.*

1612 *Trav. Four Englishm.* 68 He that trusteth to a Greeke, Shall be intreaged, and still to seeke. **1703** MAUNDRELL *Journ. Jerus.* (1721) 135 Who..were basely intrigu'd by the People..and forc'd to redeem their Lives at a great Sum of Money. **1794** S. WILLIAMS *Vermont* 40 To intrigue and baffle a brave and meritorious people out of their rights and liberties. **1894** *Month* May 122.

2. To entangle, involve; to cause to be entangled or involved, to implicate. Now *rare.*

a **1677** BARROW *Wks.* (1686) II. Serm. xxiii. 338 It doth not seem worth the while..with more subtilty to intrigue the Point. **1681** J. SCOTT *Chr. Life* I. iv. (R.), How doth it perplex and intrigue the whole course of your lives, and intangle ye in a labyrinth of knavish tricks and collusions. **1690** CHILD *Disc. Trade* Pref. (1694) 43 The way..is not..hidden from us in the dark, or intrigued with difficulties. **1899** *Speaker* 4 Feb. 152/2 This intrigues us against his Holiness.

3. *intr.* To carry on a secret amour or illicit intimacy; to have a liaison.

1660 PEPYS *Diary* 10 Dec., He and others had intrigued with her often. **1666** *Ibid.* 15 Oct., All the people..do make no scruple of saying that the King do intrigue with Mrs. Stewart. **1710** E. WARD *Vulgus Brit.* II. 28 So Jilts wed those they ne'er affected, Purely t'intrigue the less suspected. **1879** FROUDE *Cæsar* xi. 119 He had intrigued with a Vestal virgin.

4. a. *intr.* To carry on underhand plotting or scheming; to employ secret influence for the accomplishment of designs; to make an intrigue.

a **1714** BURNET *Hist. Ref.* an. 1527 (R.) That the cardinal of York was not satisfied to be intriguing for the popedom after his death, but was aspiring to it while he was alive. **1791** GOUV. MORRIS in Sparks *Life & Writ.* (1832) I. 354 They tell me that the Queen is now intriguing with Mirabeau. **1849** MACAULAY *Hist. Eng.* vi. II. 155 That fortnight Rochester passed in intriguing and imploring. **1874** GREEN *Short Hist.* ii. §8. 104 At Rome, at Paris the agents of the two powers intrigued against each other.

†**b.** *trans.* To plot; to scheme for. *Obs.*

1747 H. WALPOLE *Lett. to Mann* 26 June, The Duchess of Queensberry has at last been at court; a point she has been intriguing these two years.

c. To bring or get by intrigue.

1673 O. WALKER *Educ.* II. vii. (ed. 2) 277 Whose designs are to intrigue themselves into business. **1839** *Standard* 15 May in *Spirit Metropol. Conserv. Press* (1840) I. 378 The charge against Lord Canterbury, that he had intrigued out Lord Melbourne. **1839** *John Bull* 28 July ibid. II. 253 A bill for giving a charter to Birmingham was shamefully smuggled and intrigued through. **1844** DISRAELI *Coningsby* I. ii. 12 Rigby, who had already intrigued himself into a subordinate office. **1864** SALA in *Daily Tel.* 26 Feb., He would have been ousted or intrigued out of office some years ago.

5. *trans.* To excite the curiosity or interest of; to interest so as to puzzle or fascinate. Also *absol.* (A modern gallicism.)

1894 *Month* May 122 The publishers often become so intrigued by these claims of authorship, that we find them at times passing by the matter altogether. **1896** *Westm. Gaz.* 1 May 2/1 The authorship of the piece..attributed by Mr. W——, intent upon intriguing the public, to a 'Member of Parliament'. **1900** *Westm. Gaz.* 5 Dec. 2/2 We do agree most heartily, but the observation intrigues us not a little. **1909** H. G. WELLS *Ann Veronica* iii. 78 The New Woman and the New Girl intrigue me profoundly. **1918** A. QUILLER-COUCH *Stud. in Lit.* 1st Ser. 147 These theological poets and preachers of the seventeenth century..were intrigued..by man's lapse from a state of innocence. **1924** W. M. RAINE *Troubled Waters* xxi. 225 The conspiracy she proposed intrigued his interest. **1957** PARTRIDGE *English gone Wrong* i. 9 Such words as..'to be *intrigued*' for 'deeply or much interested'..have degenerated from definite sense to indefinite nonsense.

intriguer (ɪn'triːgə(r)). [f. prec. + -ER¹. Cf. F. *intrigueur* (17th c.).] One who intrigues; one who carries on a tortuous or underhand plot; a secret schemer or manœuvrer, esp. in politics.

1667 PEPYS *Diary* 28 Oct., He never was an intriguer in his life, nor will be. **1710** STEELE *Tatler* No. 193 ⁋3 A Gentleman of the Inns of Court, and a deep Intriguer. **1796** BURKE *Regic. Peace* ii. Wks. VIII. 240 All the intriguers in foreign politicks, all the spies, all the intelligencers..acted solely upon that principle. **1844** KINGLAKE *Eothen* vi. (1878) 85 They [the Greeks] were intriguers-general of S.W. Asia.

b. One who carries on an intrigue or liaison.

a **1719** ADDISON (J.), I desire that intriguers will not make a pimp of my lion, and convey their thoughts to one another. **1775** SHERIDAN *Rivals* II. i, He..was in his youth a bold intriguer and a gay companion.

intriguery (ɪn'triːgərɪ). *rare.* [f. prec. + -Y³. Cf. -ERY 1 b.] The practice of intriguing.

1815 BYRON *Let. to Moore* 2 Feb., Tell me what is going on in the way of intriguery.

†**in'triguess.** *Obs.* [f. INTRIGU(ER + -ESS. (Perh. after F. *intrigueuse* (17th c.); but the proper Eng. form would be *intrigueress.*] A female intriguer.

a **1734** NORTH *Lives* (1826) I. 180 His lady being a most violent intriguess in business. —— *Exam.* (1740) 297 The Wife..was a compleat Intriguess. [**1809** MAR. EDGEWORTH *Tales Fash. Life* III. *Manœuvring* i. 4 *note.*]

intriguing (ɪn'triːgɪŋ), *vbl. sb.* [f. INTRIGUE *v.* + -ING¹.] The action of the verb INTRIGUE.

1813 (*title*) Suppressed Evidence or Royal Intriguing, being a History of the Courtship [etc.] of the Princess of Wales. **1840** DICKENS *Barn. Rudge* xii, Not lying. Only a little management, a little diplomacy, a little—intriguing, that's the word. **1890** *Athenæum* 4 Oct. 441/2 There is much intriguing and some play of character.

attrib. **1801** MRS. CROFFTS *Salvador* II. 71 A noble English Lord of intriguing memory.

in'triguing, *ppl. a.* [f. as prec. + -ING².] That intrigues; forming secret plots or schemes. Also, that excites interest or curiosity; fascinating.

1682 TATE in *Dryden's Abs. & Achit.* II. 521 Intriguing fops, dull jesters, and worse pimps. **1790** BURKE *Fr. Rev.* Wks. V. 41 A man much connected with literary caballers, and intriguing philosophers. **1895** *United Service Mag.* July 377 Turks..governed by a lot of intriguing women. **1909** *Daily Chron.* 29 Apr. 3/2 A brisk, intriguing, and entertaining story. **1920** *Isis* (Oxf.) 27 Oct. 2/1 Edited..by three members of Oriel..with a longish and intriguing introduction by Mr. John Masefield. **1935** W. S. MAUGHAM *Don Fernando* x. 190, I would say boldly then that no great artist is more intriguing than El Greco. **1974** *Observer* 10 Feb. 32/8 Even more intriguing than the sociology of fashion is its psychology.

Hence **in'triguingly** *adv.*, in an intriguing manner; with secret machinations.

1742 RICHARDSON *Pamela* III. 329 Having been thus tempted, thus try'd, by the Man she hated not, pursued, not intriguingly pursuing. **1755** in JOHNSON. **1922** *Blackw. Mag.* June 778/2 The line of alders on the far bank was intriguingly punctuated with squatting figures. **1970** *Daily Tel.* (Colour Suppl.) 30 Oct. 15/1 She was a mine of intriguingly useless information.

intriguish (ɪn'triːgɪʃ), *a. rare*⁻¹. [f. INTRIGUE *sb.* + -ISH¹.] Somewhat of the nature of intrigue.

a **1734** NORTH *Exam.* (1740) 293 Considering the Assurance and Application of Women, especially to Affairs that are intriguish, we must conclude that the chief Address was to Mrs. Wall.

intriguist (ɪn'triːgɪst). *rare*⁻¹. [f. INTRIGUE + -IST.] A professional or habitual intriguer.

1830 AMELIA OPIE *Let.* 5 Nov. in *Life* xvii. (1854) 255 If I were a royalist, and an intriguist.

†**intrike, intryke, intrick,** variants of ENTRIKE, *Obs.*, to entangle.

c **1440** *Promp. Parv.* 262/2 Intrykyn, or snarlyn, *intrico, illaqueo.* **1524** *St. Papers Hen. VIII*, IV. 270 We have bene intriked with some comberous and paynfull busynes. **1533** MORE *Debell. Salem* xvii. Wks. 1004/2 As wililye as those shrewes that beguyle hym haue holpe hym to inuolue and intryke the matter. *a* **1548** HALL *Chron., Rich. III* 54b, In what doubtful perell we be now intricked.

†**in'trince,** *a. Obs.* Also intrinse. [perh. abbreviated from INTRINSICATE (used in same sense); cf. *reverb* for *reverberate* in *Lear* I. i. 155. (Godef. has OF. *intrincé*, var. f. *intrinqué, intriqué* intricate.)] Intricate, entangled, involved.

1605 SHAKS. *Lear* II. ii. 81 Such smiling rogues as these, Like Rats oft bite the holy cords a twaine, Which are t' intrince t' vnloose. [**1895** H. H. FURNESS *Pref. Mids. Nt's. Dr.* 6 A knot too intrinse to unloose.]

intrine (ɪnˈtraɪn), *v. rare.* [f. IN-² + TRINE, after It. *intreare.*] *trans.* To unite in a group of three.
1892 C. E. NORTON *Dante's Par.* XIII. 84 The Love which with them is intrined [l. 57, *l'Amor che in lor s'intrea*].

intrinsec, -secal, etc.: see INTRINSIC, etc.

intrinsic (ɪnˈtrɪnsɪk), *a.* (*sb.*) Forms: 5–7 **intrinsique,** (5 **-tryn-**), 6 **intrynsyke,** 7 **intrinsike, -sicke, -seque, -sec(k,** 7–8 **-sick,** 7– **intrinsic.** [a. F. *intrinsèque* (13–14th c. in Godef. *Compl.*), ad. med.Schol.L. *intrinsec-us* adj. (Fr. Mayron *a* 1325; Herveus Natalis *a* 1322 has an adv. *intrinsece*: Prantl), f. L. *intrinsecus* adv. inwardly, inwards. The ending was from the beginning confounded with the adj. suffix -IC, but the etymological *-eque, -ec(k* occurs in 17th c. Cf. EXTRINSIC, to which this is in all senses opposed.]

A. *adj.* † **1. a.** Situated within; interior, inner. *Obs.* (exc. as in b.)
1490 CAXTON *Eneydos* xxv. 91 Occupyed for to make the palayces and other edyfices intrinsique of yᵉ cyte. **1541** R. COPLAND *Guydon's Quest. Chirurg.* C ij b, How many maners of skynnes or lether are there?.. Two, one is extrynsyke or outforth.. The other is intrynsyke. **1665** SIR. T. HERBERT *Trav.* (1677) 253 The Waters.. mixing with it [[the earth] in the most intrinsique places.

b. *Anat.* Applied to a muscle of a member or organ which has its origin and insertion within that organ; so in *Path.* to a morbid growth arising in the part or tissue in which it is found.
1839–47 TODD *Cycl. Anat.* III. 111/2 The intrinsic muscles of the larynx.. determine its form. **1874** ROOSA *Dis. Ear* 56 The auricle has also a set of muscles which are contained in its structure, intrinsic muscles, as they are called by several authors. **1890** *Nature* 11 Sept., Structures which, like the outer digits of the horse's leg, or the intrinsic muscles of the ear of a man, are present in the adult in an incompletely developed form, and in a condition in which they can be of no use. **1897** *Allbutt's Syst. Med.* IV. 834 The intrinsic variety [of laryngeal cancer] including the growths originating from the vocal cords.

† **2. a.** Inward, internal (in *fig.* sense); secret, private. *Obs.* (passing into sense 3).
1490 CAXTON *Eneydos* xix. 71 By gret yre gadred by inmense sorow intrynsique wythin her hert. **1605** BACON *Adv. Learn.* I. iv. § 12 There are.. other.. peccant humors.. not so secret and intrinsike, but that they fall vnder a popular obseruation. **1658** *Hist. Mem. K. James* 66 Not only .... the publick but most intrinsick actions of the State. **1689** BURNET *Tracts* I. 16 When there are Intrinsic diseases in a state.

† **b.** Intimate. *Obs.*
1613 SHERLEY *Trav. Persia* 65 We must haue a more intrinsicke acquaintance to perfect that knowledge. **1651** *Life Father Sarpi* (1676) 53 The General of the Servi.. being an intrinsick friend of the Fathers.

3. a. Belonging to the thing in itself, or by its very nature; inherent, essential, proper; 'of its own'.
intrinsic mode: see INTRINSICAL 3.
1642 HOWELL *For. Trav.* (Arb.) 46 If one would go to the intrinsique value of things. **1661–98** SOUTH *Twelve Serm.* III. 57 As if every such single Act could by its own Intrinsick Worth merit a glorious Eternity. **1691** LOCKE *Money* Wks. 1727 II. 67 The intrinsick Value of Silver consider'd as Money, is that Estimate which common Consent has placed on it. **1692** BENTLEY *Boyle Lect.* 221 By an intrinseck principle of gravity or attraction. **1725** WATTS *Logic* [see INTRINSICAL 3]. **1758** BLACKSTONE *Comm.* I. Introd. 14 The civil and canon laws, considered with respect to any intrinsic obligation, have no force or authority in this kingdom. **1835** THIRLWALL *Greece* I. iv. 84 Confirmed as well by high authority as by intrinsic probability. **1859** KINGSLEY *Misc.* (1860) II. 167 Then came out the intrinsic rottenness of the whole system. **1861** W. BELL *Dict. Law Scot.*, *Intrinsic* is a term applied to circumstances.. so intimately connected with the point at issue that they make part of the evidence afforded by the oath, and cannot be separated from it.

b. Const. *to.*
1850 GLADSTONE *Homer* II. II. 153 Latona.. remains all alone without any meaning or purpose intrinsic to herself. **1873** L. FERGUSON *Disc.* 159 The flower has no beauty that is not its own,.. that is not intrinsic and native to it.

c. *Math.* ***intrinsic equation of a curve***: an equation expressing the relation between its length and curvature (and so involving no reference to external points, lines, etc., as in equations referred to co-ordinates).
1849 WHEWELL in *Camb. Phil. Trans.* VIII. 660 The intrinsic equation to the circle is $s = a\phi$, *a* being the radius. **1862** WALTON in *Q. Jrnl. Math.* V. 260 (*title*) On the Discontinuity of the Intrinsic Equations to Curves.

d. ***intrinsic factor***, a substance (perhaps a mucoprotein) which is secreted in the gastric juice and makes possible the absorption by the body of vitamin B_{12} ('extrinsic factor').
1930 [see EXTRINSIC *a.* 3c]. **1961** *Lancet* 26 Aug. 483/2 Vitamin-B_{12} deficiency through lack of intrinsic factor (I.F.), as in pernicious anæmia, has stimulated efforts to purify and isolate I.F. **1965** A. DOSCHERHOLMEN *Stud. Metabolism Vitamin B_{12}* 4 The intrinsic factor has not yet been isolated in pure form.., but it is believed to be a mucoprotein or mucopolypeptide.... The purpose of the intrinsic factor is to bring about the absorption from the food, by some mechanism still unknown.., of the small amount of cyanocobalamin needed.

e. *Physics.* Of a semiconductor: owing its electrical conductivity to thermally excited electrons from the principal substance present, rather than to electrons from impurity atoms. Hence applied to conduction that arises in this way.
1933 R. H. FOWLER in *Proc. R. Soc.* A. CXL. 507 Semi-conductors without impurities owe their conductivity and other electrical properties to thermal excitation of electrons from band 2 to band 1. These we shall refer to as intrinsic semi-conductors. **1945** *Jrnl. Appl. Physics* XVI. 562/2 The atoms of the bulk material hold their valence electrons at low temperatures but become thermally ionized at elevated temperatures. An electronic conductivity of this type is called intrinsic. **1948** TORREY & WHITMER *Crystal Rectifiers* iii. 47 Intrinsic semiconduction occurs in materials that have a band structure similar to that of insulators.. but with the difference that the gap in energy between the highest filled band and the lowest empty band is relatively small. **1962** SIMPSON & RICHARDS *Physical Princ. Junction Transistors* viii. 167 The region near the collector is practically intrinsic and under proper operating conditions the transition region (depletion region) of the collector barrier occupies the whole of it. **1966** C. R. TOTTLE *Sci. Engin. Materials* ii. 46 Intrinsic semiconductors.. are insulators below a given temperature and conductors with a negative temperature coefficient above it. Silicon and germanium are examples of this type of semiconductor.

† **B.** as *sb.* (*ellipt.* for 'inmost part', 'intrinsic value', 'intrinsic quality': see 3.)
1665 SIR T. HERBERT *Trav.* (1677) 88 To visit and search the intrinsique of that precious piece of Earth which [etc.]. **1716** COLLIER tr. *Panegyrick*, etc. 96 We should be better prepar'd to examine the Intrinsick. *a* **1734** NORTH *Lives* (1826) III. 168 It is no other than a token, or leather money, of no intrinsic. —— *Exam.* III. vi. §78 (1740) 481 Then the Merchants tumbled them in for the Gain by the Intrinsic. **1751** WARBURTON *Notes Pope's Dunc.* II. 187 Let our English at least escape, whose intrinsic is scarce of marble so solid, as not to be impaired or soiled by such rude and dirty hands.

intrinsical (ɪnˈtrɪnsɪkəl), *a.* (*sb.*) Now *rare.* Forms: 6 **intryncicall,** 6–8 **intrinsecal(l,** (**-icall**), 7–9 **-ical.** [f. med.L. *intrinsec-us* (see prec.) + -AL¹. The etymological *-ecal* was usual till *c* 1710.]

† **1.** = prec. 1. *Obs.*
1571 DIGGES *Pantom.* IV. v. V iij a, The semidimetient of the intrinsicall circle. **1580** G. HARVEY *3 proper Lett.* 14 That small skill I have in extrinsecall and intrinsecall physiognomie. **1650** BULWER *Anthropomet.* 83 For their intrinsecal operation, they used little hollow Pipes. **1688** R. HOLME *Armoury* II. 16/2 The Intrinsical.. are all such Lines or Circles, as ly inward.

† **2.** = prec. 2. *Obs.*
a **1548** HALL *Chron., Hen. VI* 172 b, After this apparant concord, and intrinsecall discord. **1631** R. S. tr. *Drexelius' Nicetas* II. 385 Those that are cast into outward darknes shal neuer be illuminated with any intrinsecall light. **1640** BP. HALL *Chr. Moder.* (ed. Ward) 24/2 Besides that intrinsical mischief, which it works upon a man's own heart. **1654–66** LD. ORRERY *Parthen.* (1676) 545 His external as well as intrinsecal sufferings.

† **b.** = prec. 2 b. *Obs.*
1600 W. WATSON *Decacordon* (1602) 99 How intrinsecall soeuer they two were together. **1602** T. FITZHERBERT *Apol.* 40 b, Without the consent or knowledg of any of his superiours, yea or of any intrinsecal frend of theirs. *a* **1639** WOTTON *Life Dk. Buckhm.* in *Reliq.* (1651) 77 He falls into intrinsecall society with Sir John Greham. *Ibid.*, *Char. Grand Duke Tuscany* 363 He had a close and Intrinsecall Favourite. **1879** tr. *Guizot's Cromwell* III. 149 There may be a more intrinsical and mutual interest of each in other.. for the good of both.

3. = prec. 3.
intrinsical mode, with the Scotist school of mediæval philosophers, an attribute (such as *existence*) which, while predicated of a subject in itself, and not merely in relation to something else, and having no independent character of its own, yet neither formed part of, nor followed from, nor in any way affected, the definition of its subject. (By later logicians used in a more general sense: cf. quot. 1725.)
1550 BALE *Image Both Ch.* II. Pref. 2 b, Vnsauerye sophysmes, problemes.. subtiltees, seconde intencyons, intrinsecall moodes. **1627** BP. HALL *Best Bargaine* Wks. 515 There is an intrinsecall or formall truth in things truly existing. *a* **1661** FULLER *Worthies, Wiltshire* III. (1662) 150 Though the same in noise and number, not the same in intrinsecal valuation. **1691** RAY *Creation* I. (1692) 163 That Learning.. hath in it this intrinsical Imperfection. **1725** WATTS *Logic* I. ii. §4 The third division of modes shews us, they are either *intrinsical* or *extrinsical*. Intrinsical modes are conceived to be in the subject or substance, as when we say, a globe is round, or swift, rolling, or at rest; or when we say a man is tall or learned, these are intrinsic modes. **1865** *Reader* 4 Feb. 128/1 The position which Austria has taken in the Peninsula has neither augmented nor consolidated her intrinsical power.

b. Const. *to, unto.*
1638 WILKINS *New World* xiv. (1707) 117 The heaviness of a Body.. is not any absolute Quality intrinsical unto it. **1690** LOCKE *Hum. Und.* II. i. §24 Impressions that are made on our Senses by outward Objects that are extrinsecal to the Mind; and its own Operations, proceeding from Powers intrinsical and proper to itself.

c. With a descriptive noun: That is such intrinsically, or by its very nature.
1821 BYRON in Moore *Life* (1866) 537 All men are intrinsical rascals and I am only sorry that not being a dog I can't bite them.

† **B.** *sb.* (*pl.*) Inward qualities, feelings, etc.; internal or essential character. *Obs.*
c **1645** HOWELL *Lett.* IV. xi. (1650) I. 449 This history will display the very intrinsicals of the Castilian, who goes for the prime Spaniard. *Ibid.* xxxvi. 472 There is none knows my intrinsecals better then you. **1676** *Phil. Trans.* XI. 554 The external difference seems easy for vulgar observation, the intrinsecals were intricate.

Hence **intrinsiˈcality** = INTRINSICALNESS.
1852 ROGET *Thesaurus* § 5.

intrinsically (ɪnˈtrɪnsɪkəlɪ), *adv.* [f. as prec. + -LY².] In an intrinsic manner or relation.

† **1.** Internally, inwardly, within (*lit.* and *fig.*).
1584 R. SCOT *Discov. Witchcr.* IV. iv. (1886) 61 Intrinsecallie they represse the courage. *a* **1639** WOTTON *Life Dk. Buckhm.* in *Reliq.* (1651) 106 The lesse he shewed without, the more it wrought intrinsecally, according to the nature of suppressed passions. **1667** *Obs. Burn. Lond.* in *Select. fr. Harl. Misc.* (1793) 456 Which, if it be not dried up, doth moisten all porous things intrinsically.

2. By, or in relation to, the inner nature of the thing: in itself; inherently, essentially.
1602 T. FITZHERBERT *Apol.* 46 a, The which kind of worship by publik sacrifice.. proceedeth so intrinsecally from the very grounds and principles of nature it selfe. **1644** BP. MAXWELL *Prerog. Chr. Kings* xvi. 176 This Law is a transcendent Law, for it is found intrinsecally in all Lawes. **1711** SHAFTESB. *Charac.* (1737) I. I. i. 172 Do I only make a fair show, and am intrinsecally no better than a Rascal? **1712** *Spect.* No. 292 ¶1 A Diamond may want polishing, though the Value be still intrinsically the same. **1871** L. STEPHEN *Playgr. Europe* iv. II. 310 We know the protection to be intrinsically worthless. **1875** STUBBS *Const. Hist.* II. xvi. 508 *note*, There is nothing intrinsically improbable in it.

inˈtrinsicalness. *rare.* [f. as prec. + -NESS.] The state or quality of being intrinsic.
1676 H. MORE *Remarks* Contents a v b, All the directions of Motion in water as to Primitiveness and Intrinsecalness are of one kind. **1727** BAILEY vol. II, *Intrinsicalness*, inwardness.

† **inˈtrinsicate,** *a. Obs.* Also **intrinsecate.** [app. f. It. *intrinsecato, -sicato* familiar, confused in sense with *intricato* intricate.] = INTRICATE, involved, entangled.
1560 WHITEHORNE *Arte Warre* (1573) 40 a, Seeming unto them.. partly an intrinsicate matter [*viluppo*] whiche they understande not. **1599** B. JONSON *Cynthia's Rev.* v. ii, I confesse you to be of an apted and docible humour; yet there are certain puntilioes, or (as I may more nakedly insinuate them) certain intrinsecate strokes and wards, to which your activitie is not yet amounted. **1599** MARSTON *Sco. Villanie* (To iudiciall Perusers), I knowe hee will vouchsafe it, some of his new-minted Epithets, (as Reall, Intrinsecate, Delphicke). **1606** SHAKS. *Ant. & Cl.* v. ii. 307 [To the Asp]: Come thou mortal wretch, With thy sharpe teeth this knot intrinsicate Of life at once vntye: Poore venomous Foole, Be angry, and dispatch.

† **inˈtrinsicate,** *v. Obs.* [f. It. *intrinsecare*, †*-sicare*, refl. *intricarsi* 'to become familiar, friendly, or inward with one' (Florio), f. *intrinseco*, †*-ico* intimate, familiar: see -ATE³.] *intr.* ? To enter intimately.
1603 H. CROSSE *Vertues Commw.* (1878) 82 To heare how some such clouting beetles rowle in their loblogicke, and intrinsicate into the maior of the matter, with such hide-bound reasons.

inˈtrippe, obs. corrupt form of INTERRUPT *v.*

intrique, obs. form of INTRIGUE.

† **ˈintrite.** *Min. Obs.* [? f. L. *intrā* within + -ITE.] A general name given by Pinkerton to rocks consisting of crystalline or other particles embedded within a matrix.
1811 PINKERTON *Petral.* I. 132 The rocks here called Intrites, because crystals or particles are imbedded in a paste, are distinguished from Glutenites, in which the particles coalesce together with little or no visible cement. *Ibid.* 220 Mode XIII. Siliceous intrite.

intro, intro., colloq. abbrev. of INTRODUCTION.
1923 *Daily Mail* 17 July 12 (Advt.), It's extraordinary the number of fellows who.. write to us.. thanking me for the intro! **1928** *Melody Maker* Feb. 195/3 The sixth and eighth bars of the intro. worried me a little. **1929** J. B. PRIESTLEY *Good Companions* III. ii. 515 You'd never see him if you hadn't an intro, but when you do see him, 's'business. **1949** L. FEATHER *Inside Be-Bop* ii. 17 The intro and coda of *Ko-ko.* **1964** *Listener* 17 Dec. 987/2 The intro film's symbols.. appear to be so dully strange that they induce an uneasy feeling. **1968** *Blues Unlimited* Dec. 6 Al Smith compered. Not very imaginatively, in fact he started off two intros word for word the same. **1973** J. JONES *Touch of Danger* xx. 116 Fred Tarkoff.. gave me a letter of intro to her. **1974** *Melody Maker* 13 Apr. 50/2 There are guitar intros and solos.

intro- (ɪntrəʊ), *prefix.* L. *intrō* adv. 'to the inside', used with verbs and their derivatives, as *intrōdūcĕre* to lead in, introduce, *intrōspicĕre* to look within. Hence in English words derived from L. or formed of L. elements, the more important of which will be found in their alphabetical places. The following are of less frequent use:

intro-ˈactive *a.*, having the property of acting within, internally active; in quot. 1876 *loosely*, Mutually active, INTERACTIVE. **introˈceptive** *a.* [L. *capĕre* to take; cf. *receptive*], adapted to receive something within itself. **introcession** (-ˈsɛʃən) *rare*⁻⁰ [mod.L. *intrōcessio*: cf. L. *intrōcēdĕre* to go in, enter]: see quots. † **introˈclude** *v. Obs. rare*⁻⁰ [ad. late L. *intrōclūdĕre*], 'to shut within' (Blount *Glossogr.* 1656). **introconˈversion** *Chem.*, the conversion of either of two compounds into the other by change of internal molecular structure without

change of ultimate composition; so **introconverti'bility**, the capability of being thus converted. **intro'digitate** *v. intr.* = INTERDIGITATE 1. **introflexed** (-ˈflɛkst) *ppl. a.* [see FLEX *v.*], bent or curved inwards; so **introflexion** (-ˈflɛkʃən), an inward bending or curvature. **intromo'lecular** *a.*, subsisting within a molecule, or between its constituent atoms (distinguished from *intermolecular*). **intro-'mutative** *a.* [L. *mūtāre* to change], applied by R. C. Temple to languages in which the inflexional changes are within the words. †**intro'pression** *Obs.*, pressure inwards. **intro'pulsive** *a.* [L. *puls-*, ppl. stem of *pellĕre* to drive; cf. *impulsive*, *repulsive*], having the quality of driving inwards. **introre'ception**, the action of receiving within. **intro'ruption** *rare*⁻⁰ [f. L. type **intrōruptiōn-em*, f. *intrōrumpĕre* to burst in], a bursting or breaking in, irruption. **intro'sensible** *a.*, capable of being inwardly perceived or felt. **intro'sentient** *a.*, perceiving within. **intro'suction**, the action of sucking inwards. **intro'traction** [see TRACTION], the action of drawing inwards. **introvision** (-ˈvɪʒən), a seeing or looking within; inward or mental vision. †**intro'voke** *v. Obs. rare*⁻⁰ [ad. L. *intrōvocāre*], 'to call in' (Cockeram, 1623).

1855 BROWNING *Cleon* 212 A quality..within his soul, which, *intro-active..may view itself, And so be happy. *a* **1876** M. COLLINS *Th. in Garden* (1880) I. 200 To serve and be served are introactive functions: the nation serves its king, the true king serves his nation. *c* **1818** BRITTON *Lincolnshire* 600 The pipes..have no insertions, but are joined by an exterior ring..with an *introceptive process of strong cement, like the bed in which the pipes are laid. [**1811** HOOPER *Med. Dict.*, Introcessio.] **1823** CRABB *Technol. Dict.*, **Intro-cession* (*Med.*), a depression or sinking of any parts inwards. **188.** *Amer. Chem. Jrnl.* IX. 371 The reactions and *introconvertibility of maleic and fumaric derivatives cannot be brought in harmony with the assumption. **1870** ROLLESTON *Anim. Life* 130 Five pairs of accessory.. dissepiments, *introdigitating along their interior. **1846** WORCESTER, **Introflexed*, bent inward. *Smith.* **1866** *Treas. Bot.*, *Introcurvus, Introflexus, Introflexed*, curved inwards. **1849** W. H. HARVEY *British Marine Algæ* 12 Small, spherical chambers, formed by the *introflexion of the walls of the receptacle. **1895** STORY-MASKELYNE *Crystallogr.* vi. §152 Not merely the relative distribution *inter se*—the *intermolecular* distribution—of the chemical molecules.., but also the *intromolecular arrangement of the atoms, whereof the molecules are composed. **1899** R. C. TEMPLE *Univ. Gram.* 7 Since affixes may be prefixes, infixes, or suffixes..languages are..divisible into (1) pre-mutative, or those that prefix their affixes; (2) *intro-mutative, or those that infix them; and (3) post-mutative, or those that suffix them. **1758** BATTIE *Madness* x. 74 Fracture, *intropression, and concussion of the head occasion such pressure. **1825** COLERIDGE *Aids Refl.* (1858) I. App. C 408 The *intropulsive force, that sends the ossification inward. **1896** *Allbutt's Syst. Med.* I. 314 Compressed air exercises an intropulsive influence. *a* **1660** HAMMOND *Wks.* (1683) IV. 564 Were but the love of Christ to us, ever suffered to come into our hearts, as Species to the eye by *introreception. **1683** E. HOOKER *Pref. Pordage's Mystic Div.* 64 Hee..came to the reception, perception and cognition, or rather introspection, intuition and introreception of the præmentioned..by the pure Revelation of the..Spirit of God. **1656** BLOUNT *Glossogr.*, **Introruption* (*introruptio*), an entring or rushing in by violence. **1857** T. E. WEBB *Intellect. Locke* iv. 73 Sensible Ideas..restricted to the Sensible Qualities of Matter and the *Intro-Sensible Operations of Mind. **1842** J. STERLING *Ess.*, etc. (1848) I. 450 [The] *introsentient part of man. **1663** POWER *Exp. Philos.* II. 97 Then draw back the Squirt staff, and the Syringe will appear a Vacuity (which will pain your finger by an *Introsuction of it in at the Orifice). **1670** *Phil. Trans.* V. 1083 He examines the Torricellian Experiment, not admitting that to be an Instance of Vacuity, but esteeming, that a great force of Introsuction (so he calls it) makes temporary pores and pervious passages. **1843** *Blackw. Mag.* LIV. 653 The touch ..brings the sight within..the sphere of vision. But somewhat less directly..the sight operates the same *introtraction (pardon the coinage) upon itself. **1861** LYTTON *Str. Story* II. 300 How the mesmerists would account for this phenomenon of hygienic *introvision and clairvoyance. **1869** *Contemp. Rev.* XII. 623 An energetic mind cut off..from active communication with the material world, and so driven to an introvision..the more intense as his outward sense became dimmed.

intro-active, -ceptive, -cession, -digitate, etc.: see above in INTRO- *pref.*

introduce (ɪntrəʊˈdjuːs), *v.* Also 5-6 **-duyse**. [ad. L. *intrōdūcĕ-re* to lead or bring in, bring forward, institute, originate, f. *intrō* within + *dūcĕre* to lead, bring. Cf. F. *introduire* (13th c. in Littré).] *General Sense*: To lead or bring in (a person or thing) into a place, position, state, condition, or relation to something, or into a circle or series of persons or things; to cause, by any kind of direct action, (a person or thing) to enter or be included or comprised within any sphere or circle; to insert, interpose, etc. Hence, to bring (a person) into the circle of the knowledge, acquaintance, or recognition of another or others.

1. *trans.* To lead or bring into a place, or into the inside or midst of something; to bring in, conduct inwards. (In quots. 1698 with double obj.)

1639 T. BRUGIS tr. *Camus' Mor. Relat.* 216 He used such meanes that he introduced himselfe into this Castle. **1698** FRYER *Acc. E. India & P.* 151 We were introduced the Vice-Roys Presence. *Ibid.* 398 Alighting they are introduced the Guest-Chamber. **1756** P. BROWNE *Jamaica* 231 This shrub has been but lately introduced to, or cultivated in Jamaica. **1834** MEDWIN *Angler in Wales* I. 25 Byron gave orders to Tita to introduce the monkey and bulldog. **1873** TRISTRAM *Moab* i. 4 The Adwân..whose inability to introduce any one into the Highlands of Moab I had experienced.

b. To put or place in from without, to insert.

1695 WOODWARD *Nat. Hist. Earth* (1702) 20 Sparry and Flinty Matter being then soft, or in..solution..when it was thus introduced into these shelly-Moulds. **1807** T. THOMSON *Chem.* (ed. 3) II. 379 He..reduced it to powder, and introduced it while yet warm into a retort. **1869** TYNDALL *Notes Lect. Light* 44 If two or more metals be introduced into the flame at the same time.

c. To usher or bring (a person) into a society or body; also, †into a state or condition (*obs.*).

1532 MORE *Confut. Tindale* Pref., Wks. 341/2 Then haue ye his introduccion into Sayncte Poules pistle, with whiche he introduceth and bringeth his reders into a false vnderstanding of saynt Poule. **1766** GOLDSM. *Vic. W.* xvi, This was considered by us all as an indication of his desire to be introduced into the family. **1844** MACAULAY *Ess.*, *Earl of Chatham* (1887) 824 On the same day..Bute was not only sworn of the Privy Council, but introduced into the Cabinet.

2. To bring (a thing) into some sphere of action or thought; to bring in in the course of some action or in a literary or artistic composition; to add or insert as a feature or element. Sometimes with the notion of bringing in for the first time or as a new feature.

1559 W. CUNNINGHAM *Cosmogr. Glasse* 82 The Poets in their tragedies, introduce persons comming out from under th' earth and call that place Hell. **1647-8** COTTERELL *Davila's Hist. Fr.* (1678) 31 Abuses that were introduced into the Government. **1661** BRAMHALL *Just Vind.* ii. 11 They introduced unlawful rites into the Liturgies of the Church. **1676** tr. *Guillatiere's Voy. Athens* 268 In the action of those heroick parts it is impossible the Comœdian should introduce that baseness of Gesture. **1783** BLAIR *Rhet.* II. xxx. 130 If that thought..does not anticipate any thing that is afterwards to be introduced in a more proper place. **1849** MACAULAY *Hist. Eng.* v. I. 583 Amendments were introduced which greatly mitigated the severity of the bill. **1883** C. J. WILLS *Mod. Persia* 288 The gentle-man on the mention of the word..would instantly introduce the quotation.

3. To bring into use or practice; to bring into vogue or fashion; to institute (a law, custom, etc.).

1603 FLORIO *Montaigne* III. i. (1897) V. 18 Witoldus Prince of Lituania, introduced an order with that nation.. that the party condemned to die, should with his owne handes make himselfe away. **1615** G. SANDYS *Trav.* 171 Upon the Twelfth day, they rebaptize yearely;..a custome introduced not past a hundred yeares since. **1775** JOHNSON *Journ. West. Isl.*, *Ostig* 243 The principle upon which extemporary prayer was originally introduced, is no longer admitted. **1805** *Edin. Rev.* VI. 82 *note*, Hudson..introduced ..these anglicised botanic names. **1868** LOCKYER *Elem. Astron.* v. (1879) 205 The Julian calendar was introduced in the year 44 B.C. **1874** PARKER *Goth. Archit.* I. iii. 32 The Norman style was introduced into England in the time of Edward the Confessor.

†**4.** To bring on, bring about, give rise to, occasion, induce. *Obs.*

1605 BACON *Adv. Learn.* II. xx. §11 Introducing such an health of mind, as was that health of body of which Aristotle speaketh of Herodicus. **1641** J. JACKSON *True Evang. T.* II. 102 Grace of Regeneration..introduceth gracious habits of sweetnesse, peace and love. **1651** HOBBES *Govt. & Soc.* iii. §11. 45 To hurt another without reason introduces a warre. **1692** LOCKE *Educ.* (J.), Whatsoever introduces habits in children deserves the care and attention of their governors.

5. To usher in (a time, action, matter, etc.); to bring forward with preliminary or preparatory matter; to start, open, begin.

1667 MILTON *P.L.* III. 368 With Præamble sweet Of charming symphonie they introduce Thir sacred Song. **1708** *Tatler* No. 116 ¶3 To introduce the second argument, they begged leave to read a petition of the rope-makers. **1727** A. HAMILTON *New Acc. E. Ind.* II. xliv. 140 Tornadoes, or Squalls of Wind and Rain, introduced with much Thunder and Lightning. **1816** SCOTT *Antiq.* xxxv, This discussion served to introduce the young soldier's experiences. **1824** L. MURRAY *Eng. Gram.* (ed. 5) I. 291 When adverbs are emphatical, they may introduce a sentence.

†**6.** To bring (a person) into the knowledge of something; to initiate; to teach, instruct. *Obs.*

1475 *Bk. Noblesse* (Roxb.) 79 And over this that they be lerned and introduced in the drede of God. *c* **1477** CAXTON *Jason* 67 b, He introduced the archadyens for to liue honestly. *c* **1500** *Melusine* 37 Wel I wote that wel ye haue hold alle that I introduysed, or taught you of.

7. To bring into personal acquaintance; to make known to a person or to a circle. **a.** orig. ***to introduce into*** or ***to the acquaintance of***; hence, ***to introduce to***: to make known in person, esp. in a formal manner, with announcement of name, title, or other identification.

1659 EVELYN *Mem.* 26 Nov. (1857) I. 352, I was introduced into the acquaintance of divers learned and worthy persons. **1739** W. RICHARDSON in *Swift's Lett.* (1768) IV. 227, I will endeavour to introduce Mr. Swift to the acquaintance of some persons before I leave this. **1766** GOLDSM. *Vic. W.* iii, I begged the landlord would introduce me to a stranger of so much charity as he described. **1768** STERNE *Sent. Journ.* (1778) I. 70 (*In the Street*) He introduced himself to my acquaintance. **1786** SUSANNAH HASWELL *Victoria* I. 80 Give me leave to introduce you the amiable Lady C—ne. **1849** MACAULAY *Hist. Eng.* vi. II. 48 He had been introduced to Charles and James..as a man fit and ready for the infamous service of assassinating the Protector. **1875** JOWETT *Plato* (ed. 2) IV. 159 Let me introduce some countrymen of mine, I said. **1889** RUSKIN *Præterita* III. ii. 92 He prayed permission to introduce his mother and sister to us. **1900** *Corresp.* The English rule is that the (conventionally) inferior is introduced to the superior (*not* the superior to the inferior).

b. To conduct formally into a person's presence; to present formally, as at court, or in an assembly, as the House of Lords or Commons, a society, etc.

1685 WOOD *Life* 25 Mar. (O.H.S.) III. 136 Cambridge presented verses to the King. Their Chancellor (Albemarle) would not introduce them. **1687** A. LOVELL tr. *Thevenot's Trav.* I. 69 When he gives Audience, it being their part also to introduce others into the Princes presence. **1718** LADY M. W. MONTAGU *Let. to C'tess [Bristol]* 12 Sept., The Chevalier ..with great civility, begged to introduce us at court. **1817** *Parl. Deb.* 3 July 1750 Lord Colchester was introduced by Lords Redesdale and Dynevor, and took the oaths and his seat. **1891** *Law Times* XCII. 124/2 When a new representative Peer of Ireland has been elected, he is not introduced, but simply takes and subscribes the oath.

c. To bring out into society; *spec.*, in modern use, to bring (a young lady) 'out'.

1708 STEELE *Tatler* No. 127 ¶7 He is always promising.. to introduce every man he converses with into the world. **1814** JANE AUSTEN *Mansf. Park* i, Give a girl an education, and introduce her properly into the world, and ten to one but she has the means of settling well. **1828** *Light & Shades* II. 307-8 We have daughters to introduce. **1888** F. HUME *Mad. Midas* I. i, Curtis introduced her to society.

d. To bring to the knowledge of, or make acquainted with, a thing, by actual contact, by experience, description, representation, etc. Const. *to*.

1741 E. ERSKINE *Serm.* Wks. 1871 III. 1, I shall not consume time in introducing myself to these words. **1834** MEDWIN *Angler in Wales* II. 167, I name Shelley first..I will introduce you to them [Shelley and Byron] presently. **1849** JAMES *Woodman* iv, I must now introduce the reader to a scene then very common in England.

8. †**a.** To present (an address or the like) formally. *Obs.*

1698 FRYER *Acc. E. India & P.* 338 At hand to introduce all Addresses that concern his Office to represent.

b. To bring to the notice or cognisance of a person, etc.; to bring a bill or measure before parliament, etc.

1766 GOLDSM. *Vic. W.* viii, To have an opportunity of introducing to the company a ballad. **1817** *Parl. Deb.* 911 It was his wish that the bills should proceed through the House, *pari passu*. Only the two he had now introduced were yet ready. **1879** *Cassell's Techn. Educ.* IV. 70/2 Finely chopped turnips, meal, etc., which it soon begins to relish if they are properly introduced to its notice.

Hence **intro'duced** *ppl. a.*; **intro'ducing** *vbl. sb.*; also *attrib.*, as †**introducing house** *Obs.* exc. *Hist.* (see quots.).

1657 *Divine Lover* 13 Expulsion of Vicious Habits and inclinations, and an answerable introducing of vertuousnesse. *a* **1711** KEN *Serm.* Wks. (1838) 166 The introducing of the images of saints and martyrs into churches. **1846** *Swell's Night Guide* 41 French introducing houses. These accommodation cribs have become so numerous, that it requires some tact and *nous* to discover them. **1857** W. ACTON *Prostitution* vii. 97 The establishments of certain procuresses..vulgarly called 'introducing houses'..are worth notice as the leading centres of the more select circles of prostitution here. **1861** MAYHEW *Lond. Labour* (1862) Extra vol. 214/1 Under this head [*sc.* brothels] we must include introducing houses, where the women do not reside, but merely use the house as a place of resort in the daytime. **1877** W. S. GILBERT *Foggerty's Fairy* (1892) 223 The introduced scene with the guinea-pig and the hair-oil. **1884** D. MORRIS *Rep.* in Moloney *Forestry W. Afr.* (1887) 8 Indigenous and introduced trees. **1955** C. PEARL *Girl with Swansdown Seat* ii. 36 The Victorian 'introducing house' where the pleasant ceremony of introducing wealthy amateurs to willing girls was carried out with dignity and delicacy.

ˌintrodu'cee. [f. INTRODUCE + -EE.] One who is introduced.

1831 *Fraser's Mag.* III. 413 The introducer and introducee are thus placed on nearly the same footing.

†**intro'ducement.** *Obs.* [f. as prec. + -MENT.] The action of introducing; an introduction.

1536 *Plumpton Corr.* 232, I send you a godly New Testament..Yf it wil please you to read the introducement, ye shal se marvelous things hyd in it. *a* **1639** WOTTON in *Reliq.* (1685) 474 Your Sir Jacob Ashby is grown a great man at Court in private introducements to the King. **1647** CLARENDON *Hist. Reb.* VII. §82 Most believed it rather a dislike of some Churchmen, and of some introducements of Theirs. **1651** DAVENANT *Gondibert* Pref., The second [act] begins with an introducement of new persons. *c* **1785** BENTHAM *Comm.-pl. Bk.* Wks. 1843 X. 141 The introducement of a mischief greater than the benefit.

introducer (ɪntrəʊˈdjuːsə(r)). [f. as prec. + -ER¹.]

1. One who introduces (in senses of the vb.).

1626 *Impeachm. Dk. Buckhm.* in Rushw. *Hist. Coll.* (1659) I. 342 He was not the onely introducer and first bringer in of this. **1647** CLARENDON *Hist. Reb.* II. §18 The Women and Ladies of the best Quality..made war upon the Bishops, as introducers of Popery and Superstition. **1677** *Govt. Venice* 121 He has a kind of Introducer of Embassadors, call'd, *il Cavalier del Doge.* **1771** SMOLLETT *Humph. Cl.* 5 June, Mr. Barton..undertook to be our introducer. **1832** LYTTON *Eugene A.* II. iv, One of the first introducers of the polished

fashion of France. **1885** *Manch. Weekly Times* 6 June 5/5 The introducer of the Bill rose to reply.

2. An instrument for introducing; *spec.* one for fixing an intubation tube in position.

1891 *Ann. Univ. Med. Sc.* VI. Sect. G. 5 W. H. L. Staveley describes a modification of O'Dwyer's introducer.

introducible (ɪntrəʊˈdjuːsɪb(ə)l), *a.* Also -ceable. [f. INTRODUCE + -IBLE.] Capable of being introduced or brought in.

1673 O. WALKER *Educ.* x. 120 Whether introducible amongst us..it is not for me to determine. **1685** R. L'ESTRANGE *Observator Def.* 4 A violation of some more soveraigne good introduceable. **1768-74** TUCKER *Lt. Nat.* (1834) II. 649 They must be..introducible by other channels. **1862** CARLYLE *Fredk. Gt.* VIII. v. (1872) III. 27 Proposals of improvement introducible at the said Carzig. **1890** *Athenæum* 10 May 611/3 Picturesque costumes, variety of attitude, action, and character..were introduceable at the artist's pleasure.

†**introˈduct,** *ppl. a. Obs. rare.* [ad. L. *intrōduct-us*, pa. pple. of *intrōdūcĕre* to INTRODUCE.] Introduced, brought in. (Construed as pa. pple.)

1432-50 tr. *Higden* (Rolls) I. 123 Men of Assyria were introducte whiche admitte oonly the lawe of Moyses. **1496** *Dives & Paup.* (W. de W.) ii. 22/2 Seculer or cyuyle lord-shyppe Introducte by occasyon of synne.

†**introduct,** *sb. Obs. rare*$^{-0}$. [f. L. type **intrōductus*, f. ppl. stem *intrōduct-*: see next.] Introduction.

1570 LEVINS *Manip.* 182/24 Introduct, *introductio.*

†**introˈduct,** *v. Obs.* Also 5-6 -duyte. [f. L. *intrōduct-*, ppl. stem of *intrōdūcĕre* to INTRODUCE. The form *introduyte* was f. F. *introduit, -ite*, pa. pple. of *introduire* cf. *conduct, conduyte, -duite.*]

1. *trans.* To teach, instruct.

1481 BOTONER *Tulle on Old Age* (Caxton) 3 b (R. Suppl.), They that be introducted and enfourmed in sciences and vertue. **1489** CAXTON *Faytes of A.* I. x. 25 In all the forsaid vsages the nobles auncyent introducted and taught theyr children. *c* **1500** *Melusine* 190, I wyl teche & introduyte you for your wele & honour.

2. To introduce; to bring in.

1570 LEVINS *Manip.* 182/23 Introduct, *introducere.* **1594** O. B. *Quest. Prof. Concern.* 18 a, To introduct and make me afterwards to stand in his good opinion. **1604** T. WRIGHT *Passions* v. §2. 159 To introduct musicke among them. **1615** G. SANDYS *Trav.* 83 The manner of their lamentings..may appeare by this ironicall personating of a father following the exequies of his sonne, introducted by Lucian. *a* **1670** HACKET *Abp. Williams* I. (1693) 29 The Chaplains full and absolute Parts did introduct him to this Love and Liking.

introduction (ɪntrəʊˈdʌkʃən). Forms: 4-6 introduccion, 4-5 -ccioun, 5 -xion, (6 -ctyon), 6- introduction. [a. F. *introduction* (14th c. in Hatz.-Darm.), ad. L. *intrōductiōn-em*, n. of action from *intrōdūcĕre* to INTRODUCE: cf. also OF. *entroduction* teaching, instruction (15th c. in Godef.).]

1. a. The action of introducing; a leading or bringing in; a bringing into use or practice, bringing in in speech or writing, insertion, etc.

1651 HOBBES *Leviath.* II. xxiv. 128 The Introduction of Propriety is an effect of Common-wealth. **1710** STEELE *Tatler* No. 127 ¶3 If we consult the Collegiates of Moorfields, we shall find most of them are beholden to their Pride for their Introduction into that magnificent Palace. **1829** in Willis & Clark *Cambridge* (1886) III. 104 The Lecture Room..must be so placed, as to admit the introduction of the Sun's light for two or three hours in the middle of the day. **1871** R. F. WEYMOUTH *Euph.* 3 The mere introduction of new words was not an object of Lilie's ambition. **1875** JOWETT *Plato* (ed. 2) IV. 228 There is no reason for the introduction of such a digression. **1879** LUBBOCK *Sci. Lect.* v. 155 The period immediately before the introduction of metal.

b. Something introduced; a practice or thing newly brought in, etc.

1603 FLORIO *Montaigne* I. xliii. (1897) II. 173 Others like new-fangled and vicious introductions [*aultres pareilles introductions*]. **1866** ROGERS *Agric. & Prices* I. xxiv. 615 This fish was a late introduction.

†**c.** An inference. *Obs. rare.*

1632 LITHGOW *Trav.* III. 107 Many other introductions flow from his shallow base-branded apprehension which I purposely omit.

d. The issuing of new shares by a company not directly to the public but through the medium of the Stock Exchange.

1929 *Economist* 27 July 175/1 The Stock Exchange 'introduction' (as distinct from the issue by prospectus or offer for sale) will fill an increasingly important *rôle.* **1966** P. A. S. TAYLOR *New Dict. Econ.* 152 *Introduction*, the offer of a new issue to the public, not directly but through the Stock Exchange... This method does away with part of normal new issue procedure, but necessitates that there should be a large body of shareholders, securities available to start the market, and no large 'deal' involved in the marketing of the securities. **1970** G. D. NEWBOULD *Business Finance* III. 193 Two less common techniques are the public issue and the introduction... The *introduction* is unique, since there is no formal issue of shares... The introduction can be used only where there are a sufficient number of shareholders to ensure a market when quotation is granted. **1971** J. BATES *Financing Small Business* (ed. 2) vi. 95 The Stock Exchange introduction is effectively an application by the issuing house on behalf of the shareholders for shares to be quoted on a Stock Exchange.

†**2.** The action or process of leading to or preparing the way for something; that which leads on to some result; a preliminary or initiatory step or stage. *Obs.*

c **1386** CHAUCER *Can. Yeom. Prol. & T.* 833 Thus maketh he his introduccion To brynge folk to [hir] destruccion. *a* **1450** *Fysshynge w. Angle* (1883) 24 The barbyll..is a quasy meete and a peryllous for mannys body. For comynly he yeuyth an introduxion to þe Febres. *a* **1548** HALL *Chron., Rich. III* 42 b, Bondes and pactes..betwene princes..are the cause efficient and especiall introduction that their realmes and countries are fortified..with a double power. **1660** R. COKE *Power & Subj.* 133 Obedience is..the first and only introduction to all virtues Theological and Moral.

†**3.** Initiation in the knowledge of a subject; instruction in rudiments, elementary teaching. *Obs.*

c **1430** *Art Nombryng* (E.E.T.S.) 1 Algorisme..is had ofe en or in, and gogos that is introduccioun, and Rithmus nombre, that is to say Interduccioun of nombre. *c* **1477** CAXTON *Jason* 124 b, Peleus had a wil for to be Reduyte into yong age as the king your fadre is by myn Introduccion. **1559** W. CUNNINGHAM *Cosmogr. Glasse* 13, I wyll give you some introduction into the celestiall sphere. **1597** HOOKER *Eccl. Pol.* v. xviii. §3 For the first introduction of youth to the knowledge of God, the Jews even till this day have their Catechisms. **1702** R. MORDEN (*title*) Introduction to Astronomy, Geography, Navigation and other Mathematical Sciences made easy, by the Description and Uses of the Cœlestial and Terrestial Globes.

4. That which leads to the knowledge or understanding of something. †**a.** In early use, That which initiates in a subject, a first lesson; in *pl.*, rudiments, elements (*obs.*).

c **1530** L. COX *Rhet.* (1899) 87 This shall be sufficyent for an introductyon to yonge begynners, for whom all-onely this boke is made. **1561** T. NORTON *Calvin's Inst.* III. ii. (1634) 257 They which are not yet instructed in the first introductions. **1643** SIR T. BROWNE *Relig. Med.* II. §11 He that understands not thus much, hath not his introductions or first lesson. **1671** MILTON *P.R.* III. 247 The monarchies of the earth, their pomp and state, Sufficient introduction to inform Thee, of thyself so apt, in regal arts.

b. A preliminary explanation prefixed to or included in a book or other writing; the part of a book which leads up to the subject treated, or explains the author's design or purpose. Also, the corresponding part of a speech, lecture, etc.

1529 MORE *Suppl. Soulys* Wks. 291/2 He so deuyseth his introduccion, as all hys purpose shoulde haue a gret face of charitie, by that he speaketh all in the name of the pore beggars. **1531** in *Pol. Rel. & L. Poems* 35 The Newe testament in englissh, with a Introduction to the Epistle to the Romaynes. **1559** W. CUNNINGHAM *Cosmogr. Glasse* 1 An Isagoge, or Introduction unto the hole worke. **1617** MORYSON *Itin.* III. 181 Of the..Bohemians Commonwealth, under which title I containe an Historicall introduction; the Princes pedegrees [etc.]. **1749** FIELDING *Tom Jones* Contents I. i, The Introduction to the Work, or Bill of Fare to the Feast. **1860** TYNDALL *Glac.* II. i. 224 A few remarks on the nature of sound will form a fit introduction. **1861** *Sat. Rev.* 7 Dec. 587 Mr. Wright's Introduction is what an Introduction of this sort should be..a commentary on the pieces edited, and nothing more.

c. A text-book or treatise intended as a manual for beginners, or explaining the elementary principles of a subject.

1540 (*title*) An Introduction to Wysedome, made by Ludouicus Viues, and translated into Englyshe by Rycharde Morysine. **1546** (*title*) An Introduction for to lerne to reckon with the Pen, or with the Counters [etc.]. **1603** HOLLAND *Plutarch's Mor.* 58 When their books, and pettie introductions are laid out of their hands..a man shall find them as raw as other. **1769** PRIESTLEY (*title*) An Introduction to the Study of Electricity. **1849** PARKER (*title*) Architectural Manual: An Introduction to the Study of Gothic Architecture. **1894** A. J. BALFOUR *Found. Belief* Prelim. 1 Sometimes, by an Introduction to a subject is meant a brief survey of its leading principles.

d. A course of study preliminary and preparatory to some special study; matter introductory to the special study of some subject, e.g. of a book or document of the Bible; isagoge.

1874 J. FERGUSSON *Hist. Archit.* (ed. 2) I. I. IV. i. 283 The study of Etruscan art is a necessary introduction to that of Roman. **1883** BRIGGS *Bibl. Study* iv. 76 The dogmatical method of Biblical Introduction is contrary to the genius of biblical study. **1899** *Expositor* Jan. 1 To sift preliminary questions such as are dealt with in 'Introductions' is outside my present purpose.

5. a. The action of introducing or making known personally; *esp.* the formal presentation of one person to another, or of persons to each other, with communication of names, titles, etc.

1711 POPE *Let. to H. Cromwell* 21 Dec., I would willingly return Mr. Gay my Thanks for the Favour of his Poem..I ..shou'd have been very glad to have contributed to it's Introduction into the World. **1766** GOLDSM. *Vic. W.* v, He seemed to want no introduction, but was going to salute my daughters as one certain of a kind reception. **1814** JANE AUSTEN *Mansf. Park* II. ii, Maria saw with delight and agitation the introduction of the man she loved to her father. **1873** J. H. NEWMAN *Hist. Sk.* II. Pref. 6 To you..I owe my introduction to a large circle of friends. **1876** MRS. WHITNEY *Sights & Ins.*, My first introduction to her,—I do not mean the naming of our names by a third person.

b. *letter of introduction*, or ellipt. *introduction*: a letter given by one person to another, introducing him to the acquaintance of a third person.

1801 C. WILMOT *Let.* 13 Dec. in *Irish Peer* (1920) 14 Mr. Holcroft, to whom Lady Mount Cashell had a letter of introduction. **1816** 'QUIZ' *Grand Master* I. 24 The youth.. Receives..A letter, too, of introduction. **1816** JANE AUSTEN *Emma* II. xiv. 267 The idea of her being indebted to Mrs. Elton for what was called an *introduction*—of her going into public under the auspices of a friend of Mrs. Elton's. **1827** LYTTON *Pelham* x, I lost no time in presenting my letters of introduction. **1832** G. DOWNES *Lett. Cont. Countries* I. 529, I had an introduction to M. Charles Vernet, but of course refrained from delivering it. **1885** A. EDWARDES *Girton Girl* III. xv. 267 It was well for her, she said, to..look at Newnham and Girton from without, before delivering her letters of introduction. **1949** *Radio Times* 15 July 6/3 The BBC's New York office has given me introductions to the broadcasting people in Montreal. **1969** L. HELLMAN *Unfinished Woman* vii. 81, I had sent off a few letters of introduction, but..they weren't answered.

c. The process of becoming acquainted, or that makes one acquainted, with a thing.

1808 JANE AUSTEN *Let.* 26 June (1952) 200 They have nice weather for their introduction to the Island. **1888** J. INGLIS *Tent Life Tigerland* 344 My first introduction to one of these horrid holes was nearly making an end of me altogether.

6. *Mus.* A preparatory passage or movement at the beginning of a piece of music.

1880 C. H. H. PARRY in *Grove's Dict. Mus.* II. 13/2 In great orchestral works, such as symphonies, Haydn usually commences with a set and formal Introduction in a slow tempo.

7. *attrib.*, as ***introduction piece, stage, writer.***

1887 *Pall Mall G.* 17 June 3/1 Its manner is perhaps a trifle too florid to be of good example to the other introduction writers of the series. **1898** *Westm. Gaz.* 14 Feb. 1/2 In the introduction stage still greater difficulties arise. The member..may possibly name a date for second reading which is probably fatal to the progress of the measure.

introductive (ɪntrəʊˈdʌktɪv), *a.* [ad. L. type **intrōductīv-us*, f. ppl. stem of *intrōdūcĕre* to INTRODUCE (see -IVE): perh. after F. *introductif, -ive* (1520 in Hatz.-Darm.).] = INTRODUCTORY.

1. Serving to introduce or bring in; causing or promoting the introduction *of* something.

1659 J. ARROWSMITH *Chain Princ.* 321 Paul..shews how introductive it is of all the rest. **1662** PETTY *Taxes* (1769) 15, I pitch upon all these particulars..as introductive of new trades into England. **1765** BLACKSTONE *Comm.* I. i. 126 Laws, when prudently framed, are by no means subversive but rather introductive of liberty. **1861** W. S. PERRY *Hist. Ch. Eng.* I. vi. 257 They [tithes] were only declarative of a divine, and not merely introductive of a human right.

2. Leading on *to* something that follows.

1638 PENKETHMAN *Artach.* I, The course of penning introductive Preambles. **1644** PRYNNE & WALKER *Fiennes's Trial* 28 The three first Articles, being but introductive to the impeachment. **1668** HOWE *Bless. Righteous* (1825) 189 This is a counsel leading and introductive to the rest. **1843** J. CLASON *Serm.* x. 172 The judgment seat to which he knows death to be introductive.

Hence **introˈductively** *adv.*, in a manner serving to introduce.

1856 in WEBSTER.

introˈductor. *arch.* [a. late L. *intrōductor*, agent-n. from *intrōdūcĕre* to INTRODUCE: cf. F. *introducteur* (16th c. in Godef. *Compl.*).] One who or that which introduces; an introducer.

1638 BAKER tr. *Balzac's Lett.* (vol. II.) 221, I should not be his worst introductor. **1655** STANLEY *Hist. Philos.* I. (1701) 3/1 Institutor of the Magi, and Introductor of the Chaldaick Sciences amongst the Persians. **1751** *Phil. Trans.* XLVII. 300, Fig. 2. The same canula improved..which I name introductor. **1852** HAWTHORNE *Tanglewood Tales, Wayside* (1879) 10 Not..that there was any real necessity for my services as introductor.

b. One whose office it is to introduce persons at court; esp. ***introductor of ambassadors*** (F. *introducteur des ambassadeurs*): see quot. 1706.

1651 EVELYN *Diary* 15 Sept., We were accompanied both going and returning by yᵉ Introductor of Ambassadors and Ayd of Ceremonies. **1662** J. DAVIES *Olearius' Voy. Ambass.* v. 271 Jesaul Senhobet, who is as it were the Introductor, or Master of the Ceremonies. **1706** PHILLIPS s.v., *An Introductor of Ambassadors*,..a Master of Ceremonies, that brings them to Audience in a Prince's Court. **1774** H. SWINBURNE in *Crts. Europe Close last Cent.* (1841) I. 9 About eleven, the introductors gave notice of the king's levee being ready, and so..we trudged up stairs. **1788** GIBBON *Decl. & F.* liii. (1846) V. 246 The introductor and interpreter of foreign ambassadors were the great Chiaous and the Dragoman. **1834** BECKFORD *Italy* II. 344 You must come with me immediately to the Infanta and Don Gabriel..I am to be your introductor.

introductorily (ɪntrəʊˈdʌktərɪlɪ), *adv.* [f. INTRODUCTORY + -LY².] In an introductory manner; by way of introduction.

1846 in WORCESTER citing BAXTER. **1880** G. MEREDITH *Tragic Com.* (1881) 13 As far as she can be portrayed introductorily, she is not without exemplars in the sex.

introˈductoriness. *rare*$^{-0}$. [f. next + -NESS.] The quality of being introductory.

1727 BAILEY vol. II, *Introductoriness*, introducing.

introductory (ɪntrəʊˈdʌktərɪ), *a.* and *sb.* [ad. late L. *intrōductōrius* (*intrōductōrii libri* Cassiod.), f. ppl. stem of *intrōdūcĕre* to INTRODUCE: see -ORY, and cf. F. *introductoire* (Godef.).]

A. *adj.* †**1.** Serving to introduce or bring in; introductive *of. Obs.*

1605 COKE *Rep.* v. I. 8 a, The said Act..was not a Statute introductorie of a new law, but declaratorie of the old. **1717** L. HOWEL *Desiderius* (ed. 3) 108 They are not only good in

themselves, but are introductory of all other virtues. **1800** ADDISON *Amer. Law Rep.* 48 Such testimony is dangerous and introductory of fraud.

2. Introducing *to* something that follows; leading up to or on to something; preliminary.

1660 WILLSFORD *Scales Comm.* a, Merchants Accounts epitomised;..here being both the Introductory part and Practicall. *a* **1661** FULLER *Worthies, General* xi. (1662) 34 I place Schools before Colledges, because they are introductory thereunto. **1749** FIELDING *Tom Jones* XVII. i. *heading,* Containing a portion of introductory Writing. **1875** JOWETT *Plato* (ed. 2) I. 115 In the introductory scene Plato raises the expectation.

3. Serving to introduce personally.

1787 M. CUTLER in *Life, Jrnls. & Corr.* (1888) I. 203 Dr. Willard..favored me with a number of introductory letters to gentlemen at the southward. **1812** SHELLEY *Lett.* Pr. Wks. 1880 III. 343, I considered the motives which actuated me in writing the inclosed sufficiently introductory to authorize me in sending you some copies.

B. *sb.* †**1.** An introductory treatise or text-book.

c **1391** CHAUCER *Astrol.* Prol., The .5. partie shal ben an introductorie aftur the statutz of owre doctours, in which thow maist lerne a gret part of the general rewles of theorik in Astrologie. *c* **1532** DU WES in Palsgr. 890 (*title*) An Introductorie for to lerne..to speke French Trewly. **1552** HULOET, Introductory, *isagogicon.*

2. A step leading on to something further; a preliminary step.

1646 E. F[ISHER] *Mod. Divinity* 137 Sometimes the name of repentance is given to those preparatory beginnings and introductories thereof. **1882–3** SCHAFF *Encycl. Relig. Knowl.* II. 1164 A propitious introductory to a union between the Protestant churches in Germany and England.

introductress (ɪntrəʊˈdʌktrɪs). [f. INTRODUCTOR + -ESS.] A female introducer.

1657 EARL MONMOUTH tr. *Paruta's Pol. Disc.* 176 Experience being the best introductress. *a* **1747** HOLDSWORTH *Rem. Virgil* (1768) 266 The Sibyl herself was a Goddess: and as such required an introductress to her. **1835** *Blackw. Mag.* XXXVII. 201 We were indebted to our youthful introductress for hurrying us through the first forms of a meeting.

introessive (-ˈɛsɪv), *a. Gram.* [f. L. *intrō* within + *esse* to be + -IVE.] Designating the case which expresses 'motion into'.

1903 *Amer. Anthropologist* Jan.–Mar. 13 Besides a general locative some of the most frequently occurring are inessive, superessive, introessive, ablative, and terminative.

introflexed, -flexion: see INTRO- *pref.*

introgress (ɪntrəʊˈgrɛs), *v. Biol.* [Back-formation from next.] *intr.* To be transferred by introgression *into* another species. So **introˈgressed** *ppl. a.*, (*a*) transferred in this way; (*b*) produced as a result of introgression; **introˈgressing** *ppl. a.*

1958 F. C. ELLIOTT *Plant Breeding & Cytogenetics* ix. 267 Genes from one species introgress into another. **1963** E. MAYR *Animal Species & Evolution* vi. 124 Introgressing hybrid swarms. *Ibid.*, They are introgressing hybrid populations between *D. middendorfiana, D. schoedleri,* and *D. pulex.* **1965** D. ZOHARY in Baker & Stebbins *Genetics Colonizing Species* 415 Introgressed types are quickly fixed by self-pollination. **1968** J. A. SERRA *Mod. Genetics* III. xx. 198 This introduction of alien loci or introgressed loci may be of as much interest as the introduction of entire alien chromosomes. **1972** *Science* 22 Sept. 1076/2 Where the introgressed maize at Tehuacán came from is not known.

introˈgression (-ˈgrɛʃən). [f. L. type **intrōgressiōn-em*, f. *introgredī* to step in.]

1. A going or coming in, entrance, incoming.

1656 BLOUNT *Glossogr., Introgression* (*introgressus*), a going in. **1845** STOCQUELER *Handbk. Brit. India* (1854) 136 Instead of being jostled out of employment by the introgression of Europeans.

2. *Biol.* The transfer of a small amount of genetic material from one (usu. plant) species to another as a result of hybridization between them and repeated back-crossing.

1938 ANDERSON & HUBRICHT in *Amer. Jrnl. Bot.* XXV. 399 We conclude that there is a strong introgression of *T. canaliculata* into *T. occidentalis.* **1950** G. L. STEBBINS *Variation & Evolution in Plants* vii. 265 In this instance, therefore, frequent interspecific hybridization is not accompanied by introgression of genes across the barrier formed by partial sterility of the F_1 hybrid. **1963** LEWIS & JOHN *Chromosome Marker* IV. iv. 373 Low sterility and open pollination will favour introgression. **1971** V. GRANT *Plant Speciation* iv. 52 If the introgression goes far enough, it may obliterate the morphological and ecological distinctions between the original species.

introgressive (ɪntrəʊˈgrɛsɪv), *a. Biol.* [f. INTROGRESS(ION + -IVE.] Characterized by, bringing about, or resulting from introgression; ***introgressive hybridization***, introgression; hybridization leading to introgression.

1938 ANDERSON & HUBRICHT in *Amer. Jrnl. Bot.* XXV. 396 We have therefore given it a distinctive name, introgressive hybridization. *Ibid.* 398 The introgressive effect of *T. canaliculata.* **1950** G. L. STEBBINS *Variation & Evolution in Plants* vii. 263 The habitat provides an ecological niche for the establishment of the introgressive types. **1968** J. A. SERRA *Mod. Genetics* III. xx. 199 The introgressive introduction of some loci of *Nicotiana plumbaginifolia* into *N. tabacum.* **1970** *Watsonia* VIII. 85 (*heading*) Introgressive hybridisation between British annual *Senecio* species. **1971** V. GRANT *Plant Speciation* iv. 51 Such bridging populations of hybrid origin fall into two general classes: hybrid swarms and introgressive populations. **1971** G. L. STEBBINS *Chromosomal Evolution Higher Plants* v. 149 The phenomenon of introgressive hybridization or introgression is a sequence of three processes: hybridization, back crossing, and natural selection of back cross derivatives in a habitat where they are superior to either of the original parents.

introit (ˈɪntrɔɪt, ɪnˈtrəʊɪt), *sb.* [a. F. *introït*, in 14th c. (in sense 2) *introïte* (Hatz.-Darm.), ad. L. *introitus* entering, entrance, f. *introīre* to go within, enter.]

†**1.** The action, or an act, of going in; entrance.

1481 BOTONER *Tulle on Old Age* (Caxton) D vij (R. Suppl.), By the introites and entrees of the sonne in to the vii signes of the yere. **1693** URQUHART *Rabelais* III. xvii, Heraclitus..was nothing astonished at his Introit into such a course and paultry Habitation. **1716** M. DAVIES *Athen. Brit.* II. 171 From the Transit and Introit of the Saxons hither, to the Year 1153.

†**b.** *fig.* Introduction. *Obs.*

1583 STUBBES *Anat. Abus.* I. (1877) 154 A preparatiue to wantonnes, a prouocatiue to vncleanes, and an introite to al kind of leuedenes.

2. *Eccl.* An antiphon or psalm sung while the priest approaches the altar to celebrate mass or Holy Communion. Also, the first two or three words of the office appropriated to a particular day and formerly sometimes used to describe or denote it. See quot. 1833.

1483 CAXTON *Gold. Leg.* 133 b/2 Two yong angellis began the Introyte of the masse. *Ibid.* 412/1 Saynt gregory ordeyned thyntroyte of the masse to be songen. *c* **1532** DU WES *Introd. Fr.* in Palsgr. 1069 The raymentes belongyng to the servyce of the masse, unto the introite of the same. **1548–9** (Mar.) *Bk. Com. Prayer, Communion* Rubric, Then shall the Clerkes syng in Englishe for the office, or Introite, (as they call it) a Psalme appointed for that daie. **1754** HUME *Hist. Eng.* I. 401 He had previously ordered the introit to the communion service should begin with these words, Princes sat and spake against me. **1833** SIR H. NICOLAS *Chron. Hist.* Pref. 17 Ecclesiastics in the middle ages..describe a day by the 'introit', or commencement of the service appointed by the church to be performed there-on. *Ibid.* 111/2 Circumdederunt, the introit and name of Septuagesima Sunday. **1867** C. WALKER *Ritual Reason Why* 147 The Introit is one or more verses sung at the entrance of the clergy into the sanctuary.

†**introit,** *ppl. a. Obs. rare.* [ad. L. *introitus*, pa. pple. of *introīre*: see prec.] Entered. (Const. as *pa. pple.*)

1432–50 tr. *Higden* (Rolls) II. 179 If a member..be owte of his place naturalle, and a straunge thynge haue introite in to hit [*et intraverit alienum*], the body is troublede.

inˈtroitive, *a. rare.* = next.

See UNINTROITIVE.

†**inˈtroitory,** *a. Obs.* [ad. late or med.L. *introitōri-us* (Gloss. Philox.) of or belonging to entrance, f. *introit-us* INTROIT.] Pertaining to an entrance or beginning; introductory.

1652 URQUHART *Jewel* Wks. (1834) 180 In this introitory discourse.

introject (ɪntrəʊˈdʒɛkt), *v. Psychol.* [Back-formation f. INTROJECTION.] *trans.* To incorporate an inward image of (an external object, or the values and attitudes of others) into oneself. Cf. INTROJECTION 2, 3. Hence **introˈjective** *a.*, that is introjected; **introˈjected** *ppl. a.*

1925 J. RIVIERE et al. tr. *Freud's Coll. Papers* IV. 78 The objects presenting themselves, are absorbed by the ego into itself, 'introjected'. **1932** *Brit. Jrnl. Psychol.* Oct. 156 Between the ages of 1 and 2¼ his [the child's] mentality alternates between an introjective psychotic pattern..and a projective psychotic pattern. **1935** *Internat. Jrnl. Psycho-Anal.* XVI. 145 From the beginning the ego introjects objects 'good' and 'bad', for both of which the mother's breast is the prototype—for good objects when the child obtains it and for bad when it fails him. **1937** 'C. CAUDWELL' *Illusion & Reality* viii. 158 A blue rose, which was in the *speaker's* perceptual world,..has been formed in the common perceptual world and introjected into the hearer's perceptual world. **1952** W. J. H. SPROTT *Social Psychol.* ix. 169 We are familiar with a theory that we 'introject' our version of our parents. **1962** *Sci. & Psychoanal.* V. 74 Second, the problem was said to be related to the *cathexis* of a deceased sister now existing as an 'introjected object'. **1964** GOULD & KOLB *Dict. Social Sci.* 353/2 It is more probable that as a result of the powerful oral medium of the initial object-relations, identification may assume a more or less oral-cannibalistic, incorporative, and therefore introjective terminology. **1967** M. ARGYLE *Psychol. Interpersonal Behaviour* vii. 123 Children introject their parents' love and admiration of themselves. If they are never loved they will come to reject themselves and suffer from low self-esteem in later life.

introjection (ɪntrəʊˈdʒɛkʃən). [L. *jacĕre* to throw; cf. *projection, interjection.* In senses 2 and 3, ad. G. *introjektion.*]

1. The action of throwing in; in quot. of 'throwing oneself into' or entering eagerly upon, some course or pursuit.

1866 BLACKMORE *Cradock Nowell* xxix. (1883) 154 She had so much self-abandonment, such warm introjection.

2. *Philos.* A theory whereby external objects are images of elements within the consciousness of the individual. Hence **introˈjectionism,** belief in a theory of introjection, **introˈjectionist** *a.*, pertaining to introjection.

1899 J. WARD *Naturalism & Agnosticism* II. xvi. 172 The term 'introjection' we owe..to the late Richard Avenarius of Zurich. *Ibid.*, Thus while my environment is an external world for me, his experience is for me an internal world in him. This is introjection. **1903** A. E. TAYLOR *Elem. Metaphysics* II. i. 81 Subjectivism is thus the last step in the development of the fallacy which begins with what Avenarius calls 'introjection'. *Ibid.* IV. i. 304 To translate it into the introjectionist psychology. **1912** *Mind* XXI. 10 The theory appears..to be really a piece of lingering introjectionism. **1931** G. F. STOUT *Mind & Matter* 291 Ward finds this in a supposed process..which, following Avenarius, he calls Introjection.

3. a. *Psycho-analysis.* A term used by S. Ferenczi (1909 *Jahrb. f. Psychoanalyt. Forschungen* I. 422–57) to denote the forming of a subjective image of an object and the transfer to it of emotional energy previously given to the object itself.

1916 E. JONES tr. *Ferenczi's Contrib. Psycho-Anal.* ii. 40 One might give to this process, in contrast to projection, the name of *Introjection.* **1917** C. R. PAYNE tr. *Pfister's Psychoanal. Method* xii. 387 In the projection, one feels subjective processes producing discomfort as influences of the outer world; in the introjection, inversely, processes of the outer world as one's own. **1922** J. STRACHEY tr. *Freud's Group Psychol.* 65 First, identification is the original form of emotional tie with an object; secondly, in a regressive way it becomes a substitute for a libidinal tie, as it were by means of the introjection of the object into the ego. **1946** *Mind* LV. 83 This growth of the super-ego has four main features, 'narcissism', 'introjection', 'nemesism', and 'sado-masochism'. **1963** *Listener* 7 Mar. 431/2 The ego has incorporated (by means of introjection..) certain fantasy figures acquired in infancy (such as the image of the breast).

b. *Psychol.* The forming of an inward image of the attitudes, values, and expectations of people or groups by whom one is anxious to be accepted.

1931 J. C. FLÜGEL in W. Rose *Outl. Mod. Knowl.* ix. 384 An introjection into the self of the earliest external moral forces, i.e. the moral attitudes and precepts of parents. **1955** M. KLEIN *New Directions in Psycho-Anal.* i. 21 External and internal situations are always interdependent, since introjection and projection operate side by side from the beginning of life. **1962** *Listener* 21 June 1055/2 When a child's parents have habitually reacted to his behaviour in a certain way—for instance, being shocked if he cheats—then after a time the child begins to react in this way towards himself. This is the process sometimes described as 'introjection'. **1967** M. ARGYLE *Psychol. Interpersonal Behaviour* vii. 121 A process of *introjection*, whereby children adopt the perceptions, attitudes, and reactions to themselves of parents and others.

†**introˈmeddle,** *v. Obs. rare.* [For *intermeddle*, with confusion of prefix.] To interfere, intermeddle. So †**intromeddle** *sb.*, interference.

1524 WOLSEY in *St. Papers Hen. VIII*, IV. 89 That therle of Angwishe do not entre Scotland, ne intromedle therwith. *Ibid.*, The Quene in no wise wolde that thErle of Angwishe shulde have any intromedle herin, or entre into Scotland.

intromissible (ɪntrəʊˈmɪsɪb(ə)l), *a. rare.* [f. L. *intromiss-*, ppl. stem of *intrōmitt-ĕre* to INTROMIT + -IBLE.] Capable of being intromitted; admissible. Hence **intromissiˈbility**, capability of being intromitted.

1808 HERSCHEL in *Phil. Trans.* XCIX. 268 A modification which takes effect at the outside of the prism at very oblique angles of incidence, and may be called a different intromissibility. *Ibid.* 269 By the lawes of the different refrangibility of light, the red rays are intromissible at *a.*

intromission (ɪntrəʊˈmɪʃən). [n. of action from L. *intrōmittĕre* to INTROMIT: perh. immed. a. F. *intromission* (Paré, 16th c.).] The action of intromitting.

1. The action of sending, letting, or putting in; insertion, introduction; admission, admittance.

1601 BP. W. BARLOW *Defence* 152 The Nouatians..denie to those that relapse..any hope of..intromission into the church. **1613** JACKSON *Creed* II. xvi. §4 They draw a curtaine ..least further intromission of such beames might interrupt their pleasant sleepe. **1634** PEACHAM *Gentl. Exerc.* I. xviii. 59 If sight be caused by intromission, or receiving in, the forme of that which is seene, contrary species or formes should be received confusedly together. **1667** *Phil. Trans.* II. 519 A Moderate Intromission of Blood had well succeeded. **1727** SWIFT *Gulliver* IV. vi, For nature..intended the..orifice only for the intromission of solids and liquids. **1834** M'MURTRIE *Cuvier's Anim. Kingd.* 415 A tube..is open at both ends for the intromission of water. **1836–9** TODD *Cycl. Anat.* II. 411/2 The reciprocal introduction of the organs of intromission into the vulvæ. **1883** SCHAFF *Encycl. Rel. Knowl.* 2271 What he [Swedenborg] claims to have seen and heard during his intromission into the spiritual world.

2. Intermeddling, interference: esp. in or from *Sc. Law*, the action of intermeddling with the effects of another, the assuming of the possession and management of the property of another, either with or without legal authority; in the latter case called ***vicious intromission***. Also, generally, the transactions of an agent or subordinate with the money of his employer or principal.

1567 *Renunciation Mary Q. Scots* (Holinshed), And be thir our letteris freelie, of our awin motiue will renuncis..all intromission and dispositioun of onie casualiteis, properties [etc.]. *c* **1575** *Balfour's Practicks* (1754) 41 Ony spuilzie or

wrangous intromissioun with the saidis gudis. *a* **1639** SPOTTISWOOD *Hist. Ch. Scot.* II. (1677) 33 The Monks who had been trusted.. with the intromission of the rents, were charged to uplift the same. **1682** BURNET *Rights Princes* vi. 200 Willing to discharge the Guardian for his Intromission. **1773** ERSKINE *Inst. Law Scot.* III. ix. §49. 626 Vitious intromission.. consists in apprehending the possession of, or using any moveable goods belonging to the deceased unwarrantably, or without the order of law. **1808** W. TENNANT *Ind. Recreat.* (ed. 2) III. 75 His duties extend to .. customs and excise.. as well as to the collection of the land rents. For all these intromissions, he was strictly accountable to government. **1833** *Act 3 & 4 Will. IV*, c. 46 §59 Such collector and treasurer.. shall.. grant bond.. for their intromissions, and for the just and faithful execution of their office. **1884** *Contemp. Rev.* Feb. 268 Keeping wisely aloof from all ill-timed intromission in the interior affairs.

b. quasi-*concr.* (*Sc. Law.*) *pl.* Proceeds of such transactions. (Cf. *earnings*.)

1792 *Spalding's Troub. Chas. I*, II. 146 The monies.. which the collector and his depute shall be bound to pay to them out of the first of his intromissions [*original* intromissioun] thereof. **1807–8** R. BELL *Dict. Law Scot.* s.v., Should the intromitter be obliged to impute his intromissions to the preferable title.. then all his intromissions must go to extinguish the preferable debts.

intromissive (-ˈmɪsɪv), *a.* [f. L. *intrōmiss-*, ppl. stem of *intrōmittĕre* (see next) + -IVE.] Having the quality or effect of intromitting or letting in (e.g. rays of light); connected with intromission.

1808 HERSCHEL in *Phil. Trans.* XCIX. 279 As in fig. 8 and 9, the intromissive separation was produced by the horizontal side, so it is, in these figures, effected by the vertical one.

intromit (ɪntrəʊˈmɪt), *v.* Forms: α. 5 intromete, 5–7 *Sc.* intromet, 6 *Sc.* intromeit, intrommet, 6–7 *Sc.* intromett; β. 5–6 intromitte, 6 -myt, 6– intromit. [ad. L. *intrōmitt-ĕre* to send in, let in or into, introduce, f. *intrō* + *mittĕre* to send. In part a refashioning after L. of the earlier ENTERMETE (*entremet, entromyt*) q.v.]

1. *trans.* To cause or allow to enter; to put in, introduce, interpose, insert; to send or let in, admit. Now *rare*.

1582–8 *Hist. Jas. VI* (1804) 27 Shoe was perswadit be these that were hir keeperis, and vthers intromettit for that purpois. **1612** R. CARPENTER *Soules Sent.* 74 Shall wee presumptuouslie intromit our ouer-weening curiosity? **1615** CROOKE *Body of Man* 945 The fourth hole.. intromitteth the Iugular veine. **1647** H. MORE *Poems, Cupid's Confl.* lxxvii, Whether our reasons eye be clear enough To intromit true light. **1747** *Gentl. Mag.* 528 Indeed, some diseases not cutaneous may be intromitted thro' the skin. **1895** B. F. BARRETT *Quest. Answ.* 119 This is the way.. in which he [Swedenborg] was himself intromitted into the spiritual world.

†**2.** *refl.* To interfere (*with* or *in* something).

1492 *Plumpton Corr.* 201, I desire and pray you noe further to intromete you with the sayd land and right of his church. **1531** CRANMER *Wks.* (Parker Soc.) II. 229 Wherefore he had never pleasure to intromit himself in this cause. **1535** COVERDALE *Isa.* xxx. 10 They darre saye to the prophetes: Intromitte youre selues with nothinge. **1657** TWYSDEN *Vind. Ch.* (1847) 100 [He] did then intromit himself and his agents in the raising of it and so did convert some good proportion to his own use.

3. *intr.* for *refl.* To interfere, intermeddle, have to do *with*. (Now only *Sc.*)

1432–50 tr. *Higden* (Rolls) IV. 153 The lawe of feldes.. that þe senate scholde not intromitte of the feldes of eny man dyenge whom he hade afore in his lyfe. **1492** *Plumpton Corr.* 264 Willinge and desyreinge you, therefore, that.. yee will in noe wise further intromete or deale with the said land. **1540** *Act 32 Hen. VIII*, c. 20 §3 No sheryffe.. shall in any wyse intromyt or medel in, with, or vpon any of yᵉ premisses. **1560** in Calderwood *Hist. Kirk* (1843) II. 3 Nor yitt sall intromett.. anie maner of way with the querrells and discords of the lords. **1572** *Act 14 Eliz.* c. 5 §38 The Justices.. within any County.. shall not intromit or enter into any City.. where be any Justice.. for any such City. **1623** W. SCLATER *Tythes* 197 He would.. intromit in a quaestion proper to a higher profession. **1814** SCOTT *Wav.* x, A whiggish mob.. plundered his dwelling-house of four silver spoons, intromitting also with his mart and his meal-ark. **1833** L. RITCHIE *Wand. by Loire* 197 Saint Felix who intromitted so improperly with the loves of his niece and Monsieur Pappolen. *a* **1847** CHALMERS *Posth. Wks.* I. 61 It is patent from these verses that God intromitted with Jacob on the matter of his leaving Laban.

b. *Sc. Law.* To have (pecuniary) dealings, to deal *with*; *esp.* to deal with property or effects; either *legally* as administrator, agent, etc., or *viciously* without legal right.

1522 in Balfour *Practicks* (1754) 51 The Provest.. and communitie of Edinburgh, hes gude richt, title and power to buy, sell, or utherwayis to intromet with schipis of weirfair .. within the read, havin or port of Leyth. **1569** in Row *Hist. Kirk* (1842) 40 That the poore labourers may intromett with their awin teindis upon a reasonable composition. **1609** SKENE *Reg. Maj.* 25 The wife.. may not take vp [the dowrie], nor intromet with the frutes thereof, induring her husbands lifetime, bot her husband sall intromit therewith, for sustentation of his wife and familie. **1664** J. CARSTARES in R. H. Story *W. Carstares* (1874) 373, I leave my loving and faithfull spouse.. my sole executrix, to intromett with my goods and gear. **1772** JOHNSON in *Boswell* Argt. case vicious Intromission, He who never intromits at all will never intromit viciously. **1880** MUIRHEAD *Gaius* II. §163 If an heir who has the right of abstaining have once intromitted with hereditary effects,.. he has not the power of afterwards relinquishing the inheritance.

Hence **intro'mitted** *ppl. a.*; **-'mitting** *vbl. sb.*

1450–70 *Golagros & Gaw.* 1171 And alse the meryest on mold has intrometting. **1706** J. SERGEANT *Acc. Chapter* (1853) 109 The new intromitted jurisdiction took place and governed. **1831** BREWSTER *Newton* (1855) I. viii. 189 Certain rays of the intromitted pencil are absorbed or lost. **1853** HERSCHEL *Pop. Lect. Sc.* vi. §23 (1873) 239 This intromitted portion is single.

intromittent (ɪntrəʊˈmɪtənt), *a.* [ad. L. *intrōmittent-em*, pr. pple. of *intrōmittĕre*: see prec.] That intromits or introduces; having the function of intromission.

Chiefly in *Zool.* and *Physiol.*, ***intromittent apparatus, organ***, the male copulatory organ.

1836–9 TODD *Cycl. Anat.* II. 411/2 In the Earthworm.. the intromittent apparatus is deficient. **1870** ROLLESTON *Anim. Life* Introd. 47 All male Mammalia have an intromittent organ. **1880** GÜNTHER *Fishes* 157 The males of most.. are provided with copulatory or intromittent organs.

intromitter (ɪntrəʊˈmɪtə(r)). Forms: 6 intromettar, 6–7 -mettor(e, 7 -meter, -mittor, 8– intromitter. [f. INTROMIT + -ER[1]; cf. the earlier *entermeter*, F. *entremetteur*.] One who intromits; *spec.* in *Sc. Law*, One who interferes or deals with the property of another.

c **1575** *Balfour's Practicks* (1754) 27 That the takaris and intromettaris with the Landis.. be callit. **1640–1** *Kirkcudbr. War-Comm. Min. Bk.* (1855) 95 The schyreffes, baillies.. and uther intrometers with His Majesty's rentes. *Ibid.* 171 He.. appoyntes Robert Ewart, his sone, and Helene Ewart, his dochter, his onlie executores and intromettores with his haile goodes and geir. **1696** *Lond. Gaz.* No. 3228/2 Act anent Vitious Intromettors. **1773** ERSKINE *Inst. Law Scot.* III. ix. §51. 627 An intromitter incurs no passive title, if one has been, previously to the intromission, confirmed executor to the deceased. **1861** W. BELL *Dict. Law Scot.* s.v. *Intromission*, A confirmation as executor puts an end to the vitious intromission, since it infers an intention on the part of the intromitter to account for his intromissions.

intromolecular, -mutative: see INTRO-.

intron (ˈɪntrɒn). *Genetics.* [f. *intr(agenic* adj. s.v. INTRA- + -ON[1]: see quot. 1978.] A segment of an RNA molecule which is excised during or soon after its transcription from DNA and takes no part in forming the eventual gene; a segment of a DNA molecule which codes for this. Cf. EXON[2].

1978, etc. [see EXON[2]]. **1980** *Sci. Amer.* Sept. 87/3 A similar explanation could account for introns, the noncoding sequences that interrupt coding sequences in many eukaryotic genes. **1980** *Amer. Jrnl. Trop. Med. & Hygiene* XXIX. 1034/1 These results show that VSG genes are not riddled with introns. **1981** [see EXONIC *a.*]. **1982** P. N. GRAY in T. M. Devlin *Textbk. Biochem.* xviii. 910 The nucleotide sequences of the intron-exon borders have some similarities that appear to be common for several species. Introns in RNA generally begin with.. pGpU.. and end with.. pApG. **1985** B. LEWIN *Genes* (ed. 2) xx. 362 Many of the long introns in these genes have open reading frames in register with the preceding exon; at least in some cases, there is evidence for translation of the intron.

Hence **in'tronic** *a.*

1978 *Nature* 9 Feb. 501/1 The gene is a mosaic: expressed sequences held in a matrix of silent DNA, an intronic matrix. **1980** *Ann. N.Y. Acad. Sci.* CCCXLIII. 430 The middle of the hybridized strand.. was looped out, presumably because the intronic sequence was spliced out from the mRNA. **1985** *Science* 20 Sept. 1264/3 The abundance of this repeat in nuclear RNA of the rat and mouse is roughly proportional to the copy number of the sequence in the respective genomes. This is consistent with the notion of random intronic distribution and transcription of this repeat.

†**intro'nificate**, *v. nonce-wd. Obs.* [f. obs. F. *intronificqu-er*, Rabelais (f. the stem part of late L. *inthron-izāre*, F. *intron-iser* + L. *-ficāre*: see -FY) + -ATE[3].] *trans.* To enthrone.

1653 URQUHART *Rabelais* I. xix, The substantifick quality of the elementary complexion, which is intronificated in the terrestreity of their quidditative nature.

intronise, -ize, etc., obs. var. of ENTHRONIZE, etc.

intronizate, var. INTHRONIZATE *v.*, *Obs.*

†**intronization**, obs. var. ENTHRONIZATION.

1470–85 MALORY *Arthur* v. xii, Thenne the senatours maade redy for his Intronysacyon.

†**in'troop**, variant of ENTROOP, *Obs.*

1611 FLORIO, *Infrottare*, to introupe, to insquadron.

intropression, -pulsive, etc.: see INTRO-.

intropunitive (ɪntrəʊˈpjuːnɪtɪv), *a. Psychol.* Also intrapunitive. [f. L. *intrō* inwardly (cf. INTRO-) + PUNITIVE *a.*] Blaming oneself rather than other people or events; of or pertaining to an unreasonable feeling of responsibility for frustrations or the like. Contrasted with EXTRAPUNITIVE *a.* and IMPUNITIVE *a.*

1938 S. ROSENZWEIG in H. A. Murray *Explorations in Personality* vi. 587 He may react with emotions of guilt and remorse and tend to condemn himself as the blameworthy object. This type of reaction may be termed 'intropunitive'. **1954** G. W. ALLPORT *Nature of Prejudice* xxvii. 437 This inwardness and ability to know and to laugh at oneself make for the intropunitive tendency that we examined... Self-blame takes the place of projected external blame. **1958** [see IMPUNITIVE *a.*]. **1965** B. I. MURSTEIN *Handbk. Projective Techniques* xxxii. 575 These criteria included diagnostic council ratings.., Rosenzweig Extrapunitive and Intrapunitive Scores, and the self-ratings of the subject. **1969** [see EXTRAPUNITIVE *a.*].

Hence **intro'punitiveness**, the condition of being intropunitive.

1943 *Psychol. Abstr.* XXVII. 99/2 Nonhypnotizability is associated with other defense mechanisms.., and with other reactions to frustration, such as intropunitiveness and extrapunitiveness. **1958** M. ARGYLE *Relig. Behaviour* xii. 161 There is no evidence concerning the intropunitiveness or private religious activities of sect members, but the above three findings confirm the application of the reduction of guilt theory to sects. **1969** M. D. VERNON *Human Motivation* ix. 145 One of the most frequently occurring types of intropunitiveness is anxiety.

introreception: see INTRO- *pref.*

introrsal (ɪnˈtrɔːsəl), *a. Bot.* [f. as next + -AL[1].] = next.

1831 MACGILLIVRAY tr. *Richard's Elem. Bot.* 421 The stamina.. are introrsal and nearly sessile.

introrse (ɪnˈtrɔːs), *a. Bot.* [ad. L. *intrors-us*, from *introversus* (turned) inwards (in ancient L. only adv.).] Turned or directed inwards; of an anther which opens towards the centre of the flower.

1842 BRANDE *Dict. Sci.* etc. 609/2 In most plants the anthers are introrse, being turned towards the style. **1870** HOOKER *Stud. Flora* 238 Apocyneæ.. Anthers basifixed, dehiscence introrse.

Hence **in'trorsely** *adv.*, in an inward direction.

introruption: see INTRO- *pref.*

introscope (ˈɪntrəʊskəʊp). [f. INTRO- + -SCOPE.] An instrument designed to be inserted into tubes so as to permit a visual examination of their interiors, and provided with a light source and some kind of optical system.

1937 *Nature* 27 Feb. 380/2 Charles Baker showed an 'introscope', an instrument for inspecting the interiors of boiler tubes, ship shaftings, oxygen bottles and aeroplane spars, etc. By means of this instrument, it is possible to illuminate and examine microscopically surfaces which cannot easily be inspected in other circumstances. **1958** *Ann. Rep. Chief Insp. Factories for 1957* (Cmnd. 521) 27 Entry into the reactor vessel itself will not be possible. Accordingly,.. great attention is being given to the developments of introscopes.. which will allow remote inspection of internal surfaces. **1962** *Punch* 18 Apr. 604/2 There are men who spend their best years bending pipes;.. others who peer inside them, with the aid of introscopes and boroscopes capable of seeing round four or five corners. **1973** A. PARRISH *Mech. Engineer's Ref. Bk.* viii. 3 Introscopes, Endoscopes, Borescopes, etc. (The Trade name depending on the manufacturer) are forms of rigid, narrow, long industrial telescopes which introduce light and permit visual examination through small apertures e.g. down a small bore tube. They range from 2–50 mm in diameter and, in special cases, may be made from small sections up to 50 m long.

introsensible, -sentient: see INTRO- *pref.*

introspect (ɪntrəʊˈspɛkt), *v.* [f. L. *intrōspect-*, ppl. stem of *intrōspicĕre* to look into, or f. L. *intrōspectāre*, freq. of this.]

1. *trans.* To look into, esp. with the mind; to examine narrowly or thoroughly. Now *rare*.

1683 E. HOOKER *Pref. Pordage's Mystic. Div.* 66 There to view, introspect and comprehend, as wel as apprehend, the Wonders of Jehovah Ælohim. **1723** *Trickology* 15 The Drum.. look into it, there is nothing; so beware they do not introspect you. **1885** L. OLIPHANT *Sympneumata* xi. 167 The records of the intellect introspecting human nature cannot evince a perfect understanding.

2. *intr.* or *absol.* To look within; to examine one's own thoughts or feelings.

1884 *Pop. Sci. Monthly* XXV. 257 We can not cogitate without examining consciousness, and when we do this we introspect. **1896** *Daily News* 18 Feb. 6/1 No man went further in introspection than all the world's chartered libertine, Mr. Pepys. But Mr. Pepys 'introspected' with a single mind! He never, we think, defends his conduct.

Hence **intro'spected, intro'specting** *ppl. adjs.*

1881 J. SULLY *Illusions* 18 Introspected facts being known only in relation to perceived facts. **1882** HALL CAINE *Recoll. D. G. Rossetti* 212 [Rossetti had] large grey eyes with a steady introspecting look.

introspectible (ɪntrəʊˈspɛktɪb(ə)l), *a.* Also -able. [f. INTROSPECT *v.* + -IBLE.] Of a thought, sensation, experience, or other mental phenomenon: capable of being examined by introspection.

1925 C. D. BROAD *Mind & its Place* ix. 419 How little of this.. is introspected or is introspectible! **1937** *Mind* XLVI. 22 We must include, under the psychological responses which the words tend to produce, not only immediately introspectable experiences, but *dispositions* to react in a given way with appropriate stimuli. **1940** *Philosophy* Jan. 10 Show me the impression, the sensible or introspectible datum.., from which your general symbol derives its meaning. **1959** A. J. AYER *Logical Positivism* 17 The prevailing view was that these [elementary] statements referred to the subject's introspectible or sensory experiences. **1971** A. QUINTON in A. Bullock *20th Cent.* 257/2 The introspectible facts of mental life.

introspection (ɪntrəʊˈspɛkʃən). [n. of action from L. *intrōspicĕre* (see INTROSPECT *v.*); cf. *inspection*.]

1. The action of looking into, or under the surface of, things, esp. with the mind; close

inspection or examination *of* something. ? *Obs.* exc. in reference to one's own thoughts or feelings: see 2.

a **1677** HALE *Prim. Orig. Man.* I. ii. 55 The actings of the Mind or Imagination it self, by way of reflection or introspection of themselves. **1683** E. HOOKER *Pref. Pordage's Mystic. Div.* 64 Hee, as a Philosopher..came to the reception, perception and cognition, or rather introspection, intuition and introreception of the præmentioned. **1794** G. ADAMS *Nat. & Exp. Philos.* III. xxxv. 456 The heavenly bodies..are too remote for his [man's] introspection. **1870** J. H. NEWMAN *Gram. Assent* II. vii. 209 Introspection of our intellectual operations is not the best of means for preserving us from intellectual hesitations.

2. *spec.* (with no object expressed): The action of looking within, or into one's own mind; examination or observation of one's own thoughts, feelings, or mental state.

[**1695** DRYDEN *Parall. Poetry & Paint.* (R.), So that I [Guido Reni] was forced to make an introspection into mine own mind.] **1807** KNOX & JEBB *Corr.* I. 324 The introspection, the spirituality, and, if we may so speak, the heavenward views which one meets with in every page. **1850** GLADSTONE *Homer* II. 17 In Homer's time..the human self-consciousness was scarcely awakened, introspection had not begun its work. **1863** COWDEN CLARKE *Shaks. Char.* x. 246 An apparently hopeless passion has taught her reflection, introspection, and humility of spirit.

introspectionism (ɪntrəʊˈspɛkʃənɪz(ə)m). *Psychol.* [f. INTROSPECTION + -ISM.] Introspective psychology (see INTROSPECTIVE *a.*); also, more generally, = INTROSPECTION 2.

1922 R. S. WOODWORTH *Psychol.* ii. 21 Without caring to attach ourselves exclusively to either introspectionism or behaviourism. **1931** *Psyche* Jan. 68 Straightforward introspectionism, on the whole, judged by the contents of this book, has very little status in modern psychology. **1965** N. CHOMSKY *Aspects of Theory of Syntax* 193 Introspectionism—should one make use of introspective data in the attempt to ascertain the properties of these underlying systems? **1967** *Lancet* 11 Nov. 1050/1 Behaviourism..arose as a reaction to the even less fruitful introspectionism of the late 19th century.

introˈspectionist. [f. prec. + -IST.] **a.** One who practises introspection or self-examination. **b.** One who adopts the method of introspection in psychological inquiry. **c.** *attrib.* or as *adj.*

1881 J. OWEN *Evenings with Skeptics* I. iv. 312 As a rule Skeptics..are keen introspectionists. **1883** MAUDSLEY *Body & Will* I. vi. 91 Little favour will these discussions have, and little will they weigh, with the introspectionist, who in the end does not fail to fall back dogmatically upon the direct intuition of freedom. **1899** *Expositor* Oct. 316 Spurgeon is not so much of a practical analyst as a self-introspectionist. **1934** WEBSTER, *Introspectionist* adj. **1949** KOESTLER *Insight & Outlook* xiii. 184 Behaviourism has rendered a service to science by its puritan intolerance towards introspectionist debauch.

introspectioˈnistic, *a.* = prec.

1943 *Mind* LII. 133 The methodologically correct use..of introspectionistic terms..is not impugned.

introspective (ɪntrəʊˈspɛktɪv), *a.* [f. L. *intrōspect-*, ppl. stem of *intrōspicĕre* to INTROSPECT + -IVE: cf. *inspective, respective*, etc.] Having the quality of looking within; examining into one's own thoughts, feelings, or mental condition, or expressing such examination; of, pertaining to, characterized by, or given to introspection. ***introspective psychology***, psychology based on introspection and on the direct observation of one's own mental states.

1820 SOUTHEY *Lett.* (1856) III. 171 Whom I..well remember as a mild, melancholy, introspective man. **1878** W. JAMES in R. B. Perry *Tht. & Char. W. James* (1935) II. LIII. 29 Those whose highest flights are articles in the *Popular Science Monthly* will talk of the exploded superstitions of introspective psychology. **1887** SAINTSBURY *Hist. Elizab. Lit.* i. 10 With Wyatt and Surrey English poetry became at a bound the most personal and..the most 'introspective' in Europe. **1891** E. PEACOCK *N. Brendon* I. 118 She was very young, and not in the least introspective. **1931** R. S. WOODWORTH *Contemp. Schools Psychol.* ii. 17 What we do find..is..more precise formulation of the aim of introspective psychology. *a* **1942** B. MALINOWSKI *Sci. Theory of Culture* (1944) vii. 71 Whether we use introspective psychology, and say that understanding means identification of the mental processes, or whether, as behaviourists, we affirm that his response to the integral stimulus of the situation follows lines familiar to us from our own experiences, does not change the argument profoundly. **1951** E. E. EVANS-PRITCHARD *Social Anthropol.* iii. 44 Other anthropologists were later left in a similar way in the fashion of introspective psychology.

Hence **introˈspectively** *adv.*; **introˈspectiveness; introˈspectivism** *nonce-wd.* [see -ISM]; **introˈspector**, one who practises introspection.

1855 H. SPENCER *Princ. Psychol.* (1872) I. II. i. 164 Each feeling..which when introspectively contemplated appears to be homogeneous. **1874** *Contemp. Rev.* XXIII. 960 A..girl, whose self-condemning grief has something of the introspectiveness wrongly imputed to all Mr. Browning's characters. **1884** SEELEY in *Contemp. Rev.* Nov. 667 Is it, then, true that Christianity is a system of morbid and melancholy introspectiveness? **1893** MORRIS & BAX *Socialism* iii. 58 The individualistic introspectivism of the Christianity of the decaying empire.

introsuction: see INTRO- *pref.*

†**introˈsume,** *v. Obs.* [f. INTRO- + L. *sūmĕre* to take.] *trans.* To take in; to take (medicine) internally; to absorb (nutriment).

1657 TOMLINSON *Renou's Disp.* 109 Those antidota which introsumed help many grievous affections. **1664** EVELYN *Sylva* (1776) 38 As their vessels enlarge and introsume more copious nourishment, [trees] often starve their neighbours.

So †**introˈsumption**, the action of 'introsuming'; †**introˈsumptive** *a.*, relating to or adapted for 'introsumption'.

1657 TOMLINSON *Renou's Disp.* 599 Cordial Powders..may be..mixed with introsumtive medicaments. **1706** PHILLIPS, *Introsumption*, the taking in of the Alimentary or nourishing Particles, whereby living Bodies are encreas'd.

introsuscept (ˌɪntrəʊsəˈsɛpt), *v.* [f. INTRO- + L. *suscipĕre* to take up: cf. SUSCEPTIBLE.] *trans.* = INTUSSUSCEPT. Hence **introsuˈscepted** *ppl. a.*

1835–6 TODD *Cycl. Anat.* I. 184/2 A portion of the large intestine..must have become..introsuscepted. **1858** COPLAND *Dict. Med.* I. 553 The introsuscepted portion.

introsusception (ˌɪntrəʊsəˈsɛpʃən). [f. INTRO- + L. *susceptiōn-em* a taking, SUSCEPTION, f. *suscipĕre*: in mod.L. *intrōsusceptio*. Cf. *intra-susception* in INTRA- *pref.* 3 and the erron. INTERSUSCEPTION.] The action of taking up or receiving within; intussusception.

1. *Phys.* and *Biol.* = INTUSSUSCEPTION 2.

1816 KEITH *Phys. Bot.* II. 90 The intro-susception of non-elastic fluids. **1827** STEUART *Planter's G.* (1828) 221 These act as so many superadded mouths, to take up, by means of introsusception, the food proper for the nourishment of the plant.

2. *Path.* = INTUSSUSCEPTION 3.

1786 J. C. LETTSOM (*title*) The history of an extraordinary introsusception... With an account of the dissection. By..Whately. **1794–6** E. DARWIN *Zoon.* (1801) III. 253 This malady is occasioned sometimes by an introsusception of a part of the intestine into another part of it. **1822–34** *Good's Study Med.* (ed. 4) I. 160 One portion of the affected intestine, constringed and lessened in its diameter, has fallen into another portion below it, and thus produced what is called an introsusception. **1857** BERKELEY *Cryptog. Bot.* §123. 150 In many instances, the inner membrane of each cell is singularly depressed at either end by a sort of introsusception, and sometimes it protrudes into the neighbouring cell.

3. = INTUSSUSCEPTION 1, 1 b.

a **1834** COLERIDGE in *Fraser's Mag.* (1835) XII. 494 The organising forces..must subsist in some such bond or..introsusception..as will warrant us in the conclusion that they are at once one and many. **1841** J. H. NEWMAN *Tracts for Times* No. 90. 50 He thus opposes the doctrine of introsusception, which the spiritual view of the Real Presence naturally suggests. **1857** DE QUINCEY *Goldsmith* Wks. VI. 222 Law and arms..through their essential functions..opened for themselves a permanent necessity of introsusception into the organism of the state.

introtraction: see INTRO- *pref.*

‖**introuvable** (ɛ̃truvabl), *a.* [Fr.] Unfindable, undiscoverable; *spec.* of books. Also as *sb.*

1824 *Edin. Rev.* Mar. 2 We are by no means of opinion that it [*sc.* a correct standard of national prosperity] is really *introuvable.* **1856** *Newsp. & Gen. Reader's Compan.* II. §1436 Give me a mere *annonce* of any thing, that can tell me of your *introuvable* friend. **1895** H. B. FORMAN in Nicoll & Wise *Lit. Anecdotes 19th Cent.* I. 67 The almost introuvable tract *Prothanasia and other Poems.* **1963** *Times Lit. Suppl.* 15 Feb. 116/3 A potential *introuvable* to future collectors.

†**introˈvenient,** *a. Obs. rare*$^{-1}$. [ad. L. *intrōvenient-em*, pr. pple. of *intrōvenīre* to come in, f. INTRO- + *venīre* to come.] Coming in.

1646 SIR T. BROWNE *Pseud. Ep.* IV. x. 201 The commixture of introvenient nations either by commerce or conquest.

introverse (ɪntrəʊˈvɜːs), *a. rare.* [ad. L. *intrōvers-us* (turned) inwards (in L. only adv.).] = INTROVERTED 2 b.

1879 FARRAR *St. Paul* II. 200 *note*, The figure of speech is called *Chiasmus*, or introverse parallelism.

introversible (ɪntrəʊˈvɜːsɪb(ə)l), *a.* [f. **intrōvers-*, ppl. stem of assumed L. **intrōvertĕre* + -IBLE: cf. *reversible.*] Capable of being introverted or drawn within, as the finger of a glove.

1883 E. RAY LANKESTER in *Encycl. Brit.* XVI. 652/1 (*Mollusca*) An alternately introversible and eversible tube connected with an animal's body. **1885** *Ibid.* XIX. 432/1 (*Polyzoa*) Muscular fibre-cells..are attached at three different levels to the soft introversible portion of the body, and by their retraction pull it in three folds or telescopic joints into the capacious hinder part of the body.

Hence **introversiˈbility.**

1885 E. RAY LANKESTER in *Encycl. Brit.* XIX. 439/2 The telescopic introversibility of the anterior region of the body is greatly developed.

introversion (ɪntrəʊˈvɜːʃən). [ad. mod.L. *intrōversiōn-em*, n. of action from **intrōvertĕre*: see INTROVERT *v.*]

1. a. The action of turning the thoughts inwards, i.e. to one's own mind or soul, or to the contemplation of inward or spiritual things.

1654 GATAKER *Disc. Apol.* 68 Their..Fastings, Prayings, ..Introversions,..Humiliations, Mortifications. **1678** R. BARCLAY *Apol. Quakers* XI. §16. 380 They plentifully assert this inward Introversion and Abstraction of the Mind..from all Images and Thoughts. **1788** WESLEY *Wks.* (1872) VI. 451 The attending to the voice of Christ within you is what they [the Mystics] term Introversion. **1870** LOWELL *Study Wind.* 214 Hamlet, who so perfectly typifies the introversion and complexity of modern thought as compared with ancient.

b. The tendency to turn psychic energy inwards and to withdraw from the external world; opp. EXTRAVERSION 2, EXTROVERSION 3.

1912 *Psychol. Bull.* IX. 159 So that when in later life there occurs an introversion (in the sense of Jung), it consists of a harking back to regressive, reminiscent, infantile material. **1915**, etc. [see EXTRAVERSION 2]. **1935** C. G. JUNG *Analytical Psychol.* (1968) ii. 41 The psychological mechanism of introversion of the conscious mind into the deeper layers of the unconscious psyche. **1955** *Sci. News Let.* 19 Mar. 185/2 Patients with this disease are at times completely withdrawn from the world around them and give the picture of the very extreme of introversion. **1964** M. ARGYLE *Psychol. & Social Probl.* vi. 75 Eysenck has suggested the three dimensions of neuroticism, psychoticism and introversion-extraversion.

2. a. The action of (physically) turning inwards, esp. of withdrawing an outer part into the interior; the condition of being so turned inwards.

1794–6 E. DARWIN *Zoon.* (1801) III. 297 This disease is sometimes produced by the introversion of the edge of the lower eyelid. **1883** E. RAY LANKESTER in *Encycl. Brit.* XVI. 652/1 (*Mollusca*) The process of incomplete introversion of that simple rostrum. *Ibid.*, The process either of introversion or of eversion of the tube may be arrested at any point.

b. Of lines of verse: see INTROVERTED 2 b.

1896 R. G. MOULTON *Lit. Study Bible* I. 50 Such introversion is merely a matter of form.

introversive (ɪntrəʊˈvɜːsɪv), *a.* [f. stem **intrōvers-* of **intrōvertĕre* (see next) + -IVE.] **a.** Having the quality or effect of turning inwards. **b.** Characterized by turning the mind or thought inwards upon itself.

1866 TATE *Brit. Mollusks* iv. 86 The worms are caught alive, being drawn into the mouth by the introversive action of the tongue. **1884** *Pop. Sci. Monthly* XXV. 267/2 When we come to mental derangements, introversive study is obviously fruitless.

c. Characterized by introversion (sense 1 b).

1923, 1932 [see EXTROVERSION 3]. **1970** *Jrnl. Gen. Psychol.* July 65 Rorschach writes:..all of these findings indicate a more introversive type. **1972** *Daily Tel.* (Colour Suppl.) 25 Aug. 31/1 Indoor flying is one of the world's most esoteric and introversive hobbies.

introvert (ɪntrəʊˈvɜːt), *v.* [f. L. type **intrōvertĕre* (prob. in mod.L.), f. INTRO- + *vertĕre* to turn: cf. L. *intrōversus* adv.] To turn inwards.

1. *trans.* To turn (the mind, thought, etc.) inwards upon itself; to direct (one's thinking or effort) to that which is internal or spiritual.

1669 WOODHEAD *St. Teresa* I. Pref. 28 The Soul being straight, introverted..into itself, and easily conforming to God's will and time. **1822** HAZLITT *Table-t., Prejudice* (1852) 85 The less we look abroad, the more our ideas are introverted, and our habitual impressions..grow together into a kind of concrete substance. **1830** H. N. COLERIDGE *Grk. Poets* (1834) 26 The mind of the old poets was rarely introverted on itself.

2. To turn or bend inwards (physically); in *Zool.* to turn (a part or organ) inwards upon itself; to withdraw a part within its own tube or base, as the finger of a glove may be withdrawn.

1784 [see INTROVERTED 2]. **1883** E. RAY LANKESTER in *Encycl. Brit.* XVI. 652/2 (*Mollusca*) It cannot be completely everted owing to the muscular bands, nor can it be fully introverted owing to the bands which tie the axial pharynx to the adjacent wall of the apical part of the introvert.

introvert (ˈɪntrəʊvɜːt), *sb. Zool.* [f. prec. vb.: cf. *convert* sb.] **1.** A part or organ that is or can be introverted.

1883 E. RAY LANKESTER in *Encycl. Brit.* XVI. 652/1 (*Mollusca*) Important distinctions which obtain amongst the various 'introverts' or intro- and e-versible tubes so frequently met with in animal bodies. **1885** *Ibid.* XIX. 431/1 (*Polyzoa*) The anterior portion of the body of the polypide can be pulled into the hinder part as the finger of a glove may be tucked into the hand. It is, in fact, an 'introvert'.

2. *Psychol.* A person characterized by introversion; a withdrawn or reserved person; opp. EXTROVERT *sb.* Also *attrib.* and as *adj.* Also **ˈintrovertish** *a.*, said of such a person, his activities, etc.

1918, etc. [see EXTROVERT *sb.* (and *a.*)]. **1925** C. FOX *Educational Psychol.* 254 The introvert abstracts from the object and deals with it by concepts concentrating upon the inner world of thought. **1934** *Brit. Jrnl. Psychol.* July 26 They were noticeably more introvert, schizoid and desurgent in temperament. **1946** R. P. BASLER in W. S. Knickerbocker *20th Cent. English* III. 392 In the snugness of introvertish isolation, there is always time, an eternity for continual deception and indecision. **1955** L. LANGSTROTH *Struct. of Ego* vii. 82 This question of the relative strength of the social and biological selves suggests at once Jung's broad division of personalities into two main types: the introvert and the extrovert. **1957** H. J. EYSENCK *Dynamics Anxiety & Hysteria* vi. 213 The introvert, as we have seen, is socialized. **1960** *Encounter* XV. 47 The introvert-intellectual is the hero of several of Buchan's works. **1967** M. ARGYLE *Psychol. Interpersonal Behaviour* iii. 50 Experiments with schoolchildren show that introverts respond better to praise.

introverted (ɪntrəʊ'vɜːtɪd), *ppl. a.* [f. INTROVERT *v.* + -ED¹.] Turned inwards.

1. Of the mind or thought: Directed inwards upon itself, or upon that which is inward or spiritual. Also *transf.* of a person: Given to introversion of mind (esp. in *Psychol.*).

1781 COWPER *Conversation* 365 Self-searching with an introverted eye. **1847** EMERSON *Repr. Men, Swedenborg* Wks. (Bohn) I. 313 In modern times, no such remarkable example of this introverted mind has occurred, as in Emanuel Swedenborg. **1856** VAUGHAN *Mystics* (1860) I. 16 So that his mysticus is emphatically the enclosed, self-withdrawn, introverted man. **1866** MRS. STOWE *Lit. Foxes* 125 In morals, in religion, too, the same introverted scrutiny detects only errors and evils, till all life seems to them a miserable, hopeless failure. **1915** [see EXTRAVERSION 2]. **1916** C. E. LONG tr. *Jung's Coll. Papers Analytical Psychol.* 348 The introverted type is characterised by the fact that his libido is turned towards his own personality to a certain extent. **1923** [see EXTROVERT *sb.* (and *a.*)]. **1957** H. J. EYSENCK *Dynamics Anxiety & Hysteria* i. 31 We may take dysthymics on the one hand, and hysterics and psychopaths on the other, as examples of our introverted and extroverted groups. **1968** C. RYCROFT *Critical Dict. Psychoanal.* 48 There is a tendency to equate 'introverted' with 'withdrawn' or 'schizoid'. **1974** *Country Life* 17 Jan. 76/3 Dorothy Osborne... This witty and introverted girl.

2. a. Turned or bent inwards (physically).

1784 COWPER *Task* IV. 633 His awkward gait, his introverted toes, Bent knees, round shoulders, and dejected looks. **1855** H. SPENCER *Princ. Psychol.* (1872) I. I. ii. 25 The skin, including those introverted portions of it which form the receptive area of the special senses.

b. Applied to an arrangement of words, lines of verse, etc. in which two corresponding elements (*e.g.* lines riming with each other) form the inner or middle part of the whole.

1896 R. G. MOULTON *Lit. Study Bible* I. 50 In the Quatrain Reversed or Introverted, the first line corresponds with the fourth.

intro'vertive, *a.* [f. as prec. + -IVE.] = INTROVERSIVE.

1864 S. WILBERFORCE *Ess.* (1874) I. 358 With the introvertive tendency which we have ascribed to him, was joined .. an ambitious temper. **1875** DORA GREENWELL *Liber Human.* 146 A cultivated, introvertive, reflective era. **1882** *Chicago Advance* 23 Nov., The church is to be congratulated on the change from the introvertive to the active.

introvision, -voke: see INTRO- *pref.*

introvolution (ˌɪntrəʊvəʊ'l(j)uːʃən). *rare.* [f. INTRO- + *-volution* in *evolution, involution*, etc. (n. of action f. L. *volvĕre* to roll).] The process of involving one thing within another.

1829 LAMB *Let. to Robinson* 17 Apr. in Talfourd *Final Mem.* (1848) II. 63 *Per se*, it is good, to show the introvolutions, extravolutions of which the animal frame is capable. **1858** DE QUINCEY *Th. Grk. Trag.* Wks. IX. 56 There are cases occasionally occurring in the English drama and the Spanish, where a play is exhibited within a play .. at every step of the *introvolution* (to neologise a little in a case justifying a neologism), something must be done to differentiate the gradations, and to express the subordinations of life.

intrude (ɪntruːd), *v.* Also 6 entrude, -trewde, 7 intrud. [ad. L. *intrūdĕre* (doubtful in Cic.), f. *in-* (IN-²) + *trūdĕre* to thrust. Cf. OF. *intruire, -ure* (1479 in Godef.) and pa. pple. *intrus.*]

1. a. *trans.* To thrust, force, or drive (any thing) in; to introduce by force. Const. *into*, †*in.*

1563-83 FOXE *A. & M.* 1455/2 Yᵉ marrowbones of the masse, which .. you by force, might, and violence intrude in sound of wordes in some of the scripture. **1597** A. M. tr. *Guillemeau's Fr. Chirurg.* xvii. b/2 When as we intrude the same [point of a knife] in anye fistle. **1674** GREW *Causes Mixt.* iv. §3 Their parts are wedged and intruded one into another. **1695** WOODWARD *Nat. Hist. Earth* IV. (1723) 202 We .. find some few of these fossil Shells, .. with Iron-Ore .. intruded into their Pores. **1860** TYNDALL *Glac.* II. xxxi. 410 As if air had intruded itself between the separated surfaces. **1886** WILLIS & CLARK *Cambridge* II. 467 When the new Kitchen was built it was intruded into the area of the old Hall.

†**b.** *intr.* for *refl.* To thrust oneself; to come or make one's way by force. *Obs.*

1562 PHAER *Æneid.* IX. Ffjb, Vnprudent man, yᵗ whan the Rutill king did through intrude Coulde him not entring spye. **1770** GOLDSM. *Des. Vill.* 342 To distant climes .. Where half the convex world intrudes between .. they go.

2. *trans.* To thrust or bring in without leave; to force (something unwelcome) *on* or *upon* a person.

1586 A. DAY *Eng. Secretary* II. (1625) 15 Upon whose absence and departure .. you seeke to intrude the summe of all your unhappinesse and misfortune. **1653** BAXTER *Chr. Concord* 56 They were not Ordained and placed in void places, but intruded into Churches that had lawfull Bishops. *a* **1786** W. HASTINGS in Burke *Articles* XVII. xxix, You must forbid any person of that nation to be intruded into your presence, without his introduction. **1842** *Claim & Protest of Ch. Scotl.* in *State Trials* (N.S.) IV. (1892) 1401 Ordaining a Church Court to .. admit to the office of the holy ministry .. a probationer .. and to intrude him also on the congregation, contrary to the will of the people. **1849** R. BUCHANAN *Ten Years' Conflict* xi. II. 205 Prepared to intrude ministers against reclaiming congregations, and that, if need were, at the point of the bayonet. **1864** BRYCE *Holy Rom. Emp.* vii. (1875) 95 The tendency which intruded earthly Madonnas and saints between the worshipper and the spiritual Deity.

†**3.** *refl.* and *intr.* To thrust oneself into any benefice, possession, office, or dignity to which one has no title or claim; to usurp *on* or *upon*: cf. INTRUSION 2. Passing into 4. *Obs.*

1534 *Act 26 Hen. VIII*, c. 3 §5 Dignities benefices or other spirituall promocions wherein they shal so enter and entrewde before the paiment of the saide firste fruites. *a* **1548** HALL *Chron., Hen. VI* 178 Duryng whose .. captivitie he wrongfully usurped and entruded upon the royall power and high estate of this Realme. **1563** ABP. PARKER *Articles* §6 Item, whether ther be any parsons that intrude them selfe .. without imposition of handes and ordinary authoritie. **1592** WARNER *Alb. Eng.* VIII. xliii. (1612) 206 He gave the Liuers dwellings, lesse than where they since intru'de. **1602** MARSTON *Ant. & Mel.* II. Wks. 1856 I. 25, I pree thee intrude not on a dead mans right. **1628** COKE *On Litt.* I. 277 a, He that entreth vpon any of the Kings Demesnes, and taketh the profits, is said to Intrude vpon the Kings possession. **1682** BURNET *Rights Princes* i. 14 If he went violently to intrude himself into other Parishes.

4. To thrust oneself in without warrant or leave; to enter or come where one is uninvited or unwelcome. Also *transf.* and *fig.* of things, and in non-material relations. Const. *into*, †*in* (a place, company, etc.), *on, upon* (a person, something personal or private, etc.).

a. *refl.* **1573** G. HARVEY *Letter-bk.* (Camden) 48 M. Hoult intrudid himself as his accustomid manner is. **1659** D. PELL *Impr. Sea* 116 To what end shouldst thou intrude thy self unwarrantably into their companies? **1769** *Junius Lett.* iii. 20 And do you .. presume to intrude yourself, unthought of, uncalled for, upon the patience of the public? **1874** L. STEPHEN *Hours in Library* (1892) I. viii. 286 The strangest freaks of fancy intrude themselves into his sublime contemplations.

b. *intr.* **1588** SHAKS. *Tit. A.* II. i. 27 Thy wit wants edge And manners, to intru'd where I am grac'd. *a* **1601** ? MARSTON *Pasquil & Kath.* II. 275 Shee wonders at your rudenesse, that intrudes Vpon the quiet of her mornings rest. **1635** J. HAYWARD tr. *Biondi's Banish'd Virg.* 20 The Count thought it unfitting to intrude (as then) into their company. **1709** STEELE *Tatler* No. 62 ¶6 A very odd Fellow, who would intrude upon us. **1786** tr. *Beckford's Vathek* (1883) 143 This was the only sound that intruded on the silence of these doleful mansions. **1836** MARRYAT *Japhet* lxxii, I perceived that my presence was not welcome, and I would no further intrude. **1879** *Cassell's Techn. Educ.* IV. 70/1 There is a tendency for certain dominant and improved races of live stock to intrude into districts up to this time occupied by native breeds.

5. *trans.* †**a.** To enter forcibly. *Obs. rare.*

1593 SHAKS. *Lucr.* 848 Why should the worm intrude the maiden bud; Or hateful cuckoos hatch in sparrows' nests?

b. *Geol.* To be forced or thrust into.

1925 J. JOLY *Surface-Hist. Earth* viii. 130 Both these [series], together with a series mainly of basaltic eruptives .., were finally intruded by vast uprisings of granites (largely batholithic). **1932** W. H. EMMONS et al. *Geol.* xii. 361 This sill intrudes limestone, is nearly flat lying, and in general is almost parallel to the beds it intrudes. **1955** *Econ. Geol.* L. 715 Four locations where sills, dikes, and stocks intrude or cut off the phosphate-bearing beds. **1957** *Mineral. Mag.* XXXI. 588 This block is intruded by three stock-like masses of fine-grained granite. **1966** C. O. DUNBAR *Earth* iv. 61 Remnants of the oldest sedimentary formations were intensively deformed and intruded by the underlying granite. **1971** I. G. GASS et al. *Understanding Earth* ii. 48/2 A small igneous intrusion .. which intruded a fossiliferous sediment.

intruded (ɪn'truːdɪd), *ppl. a.* [f. prec. + -ED¹.]

1. Thrust or forced in, introduced forcibly or unwarrantably, crowded in, etc.: see prec.

1562 WINȜET (*title*) The Last Blast of the Trumpet .. agains the usurpit auctoritie of Iohne Knox and his Caluiniane brether intrudit Precheouris. **1665** HOOKE *Microgr.* xxv. 144 Corroded by the pungent .. pores of the intruded liquor. **1890** *Athenæum* 8 Nov. 623/2 The intruded minister who succeeded him [under the Commonwealth] was so ignorant as to be scarcely able to write his name. **1893** FOWLER *Hist. C.C.C.* (O.H.S.) 219 The newly appointed, or, as they were called by their antagonists, 'intruded' members of the College.

2. *spec.* **a.** *Entom.* (See quot. 1826.) **b.** *Bot.* = INTRUSE *a.* **c.** *Geol.* = INTRUSIVE 2 b.

1826 KIRBY & SP. *Entomol.* IV. 306 *Intruded*, when the head is nearly withdrawn within the trunk. **1830** LINDLEY *Nat. Syst. Bot.* 218 They approach Rubiaceæ .. in .. their intruded style, and valvate æstivation. **1833** LYELL *Princ. Geol.* III. 105 The intruded mass then cooled down at a certain distance below the uplifted surface. **1854** HOOKER *Himal. Jrnls.* I. ii. 33 Some hills of intruded greenstone.

intruder (ɪn'truːdə(r)). Also 7 (in legal use) -or. [f. as prec. + -ER¹.] One who intrudes.

1. One who intrudes into an estate or benefice or usurps on the rights or privileges of another; *spec.* one who, after the determination of a life-tenancy, enters before the remainderman or reversioner, or who trespasses in any way on crown lands. Now only in legal use.

1534 *Act 26 Hen. VIII*, c. 3 §5 Euery suche person .. shalbe accepted and taken an entrewder vppon the Kinges possessions. **1628** COKE *On Litt.* I. 194 a, Where there bee two ioynt Abators or Intrudors which come in meerely by wrong. **1635** N. R. *Camden's Hist. Eliz.* I. an. 9. 72 Joh. Mason .. a great intruder into Ecclesiasticall livings. **1648** in Gross *Gild Merch.* (1890) II. 78 Diuers and many Intrudors .. as also diuers other strangers and forinors. **1865** NICHOLS *Britton* II. 2 The law allows such intruders to be ejected while the intrusion is fresh by the right heirs.

2. One who thrusts himself in in an encroaching manner or without invitation or welcome.

1588 SHAKS. *Tit. A.* II. iii. 65 Vnmannerly Intruder as thou art. **1693** W. BOWLES in *Dryden's Juvenal* v. (1697) 100 Will you a bold Intruder, ever learn To know your Basket, and your Bread discern? **1751** JOHNSON *Rambler* No. 127 ¶6 Others .. consider every man who fills the mouth of report with a new name, as an intruder upon their retreat, and disturber of their repose. **1876** T. HARDY *Ethelberta* (1890) 93, I felt always like an intruder and a bondswoman, and had wished myself out of the Petherwin family a hundred times.

3. An aeroplane (or its pilot) that invades the enemy's aerodromes to interfere with his operations. Also *attrib.*, as ***intruder attack, raid.***

1941 *Aeroplane Spotter* 9 Oct. 174 *The Intruder.* 'Night intrusion' is the name of one type of operation on which Douglas Havocs are earning distinction. The Havocs fly out over enemy aerodromes when the night bombers are returning and shoot them down over their home stations. *Ibid.* 6 Nov. 205 Messerschmitt Me 110 two-motor fighters are now being used with Ju 88s for night defence over Germany and 'intruder' work over Great Britain. **1943** *Times* 22 Dec. 4/5 R.C.A.F. intruders destroyed two enemy aircraft. **1944** *Times* 6 Nov. 4/4 Night fighters and intruder aircraft of Bomber Command supported the bombers. **1966** M. R. D. FOOT *SOE in France* iv. 82 But 418 was an ordinary Canadian intruder squadron.

in'truding, *ppl. a.* [f. INTRUDE *v.* + -ING².] That intrudes.

1602 SHAKS. *Ham.* III. iv. 31 Thou wretched, rash, intruding foole, farewell. **1830** ALFORD in *Life* (1873) 53 The rampant and intruding brier. **1867** FREEMAN *Norm. Conq.* I. ii. 18 The intruding nation altogether supplanted the elder nation.

Hence **in'trudingly** *adv.*, in an intruding manner.

1704 STEELE *Lying Lover* I. 10, I thrust my self intrudingly upon you.

in'trudress. *rare.* [f. INTRUDER + -ESS.] A female intruder.

1650 FULLER *Pisgah.* III. x. 402 As if foreseeing .. that .. a distressed Prince .. should .. recover his rightfull throne from the unjust usurpation of .. an Idolatrous intrudress thereinto.

intrumpcioun, intrupcion, obs. ff. INTERRUPTION.

†**in'trunk**, *v. Obs. rare*⁻¹. [f. IN-² + TRUNK *sb.*] *trans.* To enclose in or as in a trunk.

1633 FORD *Love's Sacr.* v. iii, Had eager lust intrunk'd my conquer'd soul, I had not buried living joys in death.

intruse (ɪn'truːs), *a. Bot.* [ad. L. *intrūs-us*, pa. pple. of *intrūdĕre* to INTRUDE.] Having a form as if pushed or thrust inwards.

1870 HOOKER *Stud. Flora* 51 Siléne conica .. calyx .. intruse at the base.

†**in'truse**, *v. Obs.* Chiefly *Sc.* [f. L. *intrūs-*, ppl. stem of *intrūdĕre* to INTRUDE.] = INTRUDE *v.*

c **1470** HENRYSON *Mor. Fab.* XII. (*Wolf & Lamb*) xii, Thow wald intruse ressoun, Quhair wrang and reif suld dwell in propertie. ? **1535** BOORDE *Let.* 12 Aug. in *Introd. Knowl.* (1870) Forewords 48, I amonges yow intrusyd in a close ayre, myȝth neuer haue my helth. **1554** LATIMER *Disput. Oxon.* Wks. (Parker Soc.) II. 482 Which indeed you may by violence, might, and power, thrust and intruse into sound of words of some places of scripture. *c* **1570** *Schort Somme 1st Bk. Discipl.* §4 No minister suld be intrused upon any particular kirk without thair consent.

Hence †**in'trused** *ppl. a.*, intruded.

1535 STEWART *Cron. Scot.* II. 577 Thus endit he [who] wes bot intrusit king.

†**in'trusery.** *Obs.* [f. as prec. + -ERY.] Intrusive action; intrusion.

c **1470** HARDING *Chron.* CLXXXI. ii, Philyp of Valoyes .. Kyng of Fraunce was by intrusery.

intrusion (ɪn'truːʒən). [ME. a. OF. *intrusion*, in med.(Anglo-)L. *intrūsio* (Bracton, *c* 1250), n. of action f. *intrūdĕre* to INTRUDE.] The action of intruding.

1. a. The action of thrusting or forcing in, or fact of being thrust in; also *concr.* something thrust in, a forcible or unwelcome addition.

1639 WOODALL *Wks.* Pref. (1653) 10 This Work .. free from .. imperfect and ridiculous errours, and impertinent intrusions. **1665** HOOKE *Microgr.* xvii. 109 By this intrusion of the petrifying particles, this substance also becomes hard. **1842** A. COMBE *Physiol. Digestion* (ed. 4) 130 There is something more in the constitution of the stomach .. which renders the too early intrusion of new food hurtful. **1873** MIVART *Elem. Anat.* ii. 53 The neural spine .. may .. be separated from its centrum by the intrusion of the skull wall. **1886** WILLIS & CLARK *Cambridge* II. 14 This porch, however, is a subsequent intrusion.

b. *spec.* in *Geol.* The influx of rock in a state of fusion into fissures or between strata; a portion of intruded rock.

1839 R. I. MURCHISON *Silurian Syst.* v. 78 This intrusion having taken place on a line of ancient volcanic eruption, the origin of which cannot be understood without a previous acquaintance with the history of the Silurian System, the account of this new red trap dyke is necessarily deferred. **1849** MURCHISON *Siluria* viii. 167 At certain distances from such granitic intrusions. **1875** LYELL *Princ. Geol.* II. II. xxxii. 211 Regions where .. the intrusion of igneous matter into fissures [was] once most frequent. **1896** *Pop. Sci. Jrnl.* L. 242 The rocks composing such intrusions [are] the densest of igneous rocks.

2. a. The action of thrusting oneself into a vacant estate or ecclesiastical benefice to which

one has no title or claim; *spec.* the entry of a stranger after the determination of a particular estate of freehold (as a life-tenancy) before the remainder-man or reversioner; also, a trespass on the lands of the crown. Hence, by extension, violent or unjust entrance into or seizure of land or rights belonging to another; invasion; usurpation. (The earliest sense in Eng.; now only in legal use.)

information of intrusion: see INFORMATION 5 b (*c*).

[**1292** BRITTON III. i. §3 Intrusioun est torcenous abatement vacaunt le soil, taunt cum nul neest en seisine.] **1387–8** T. USK *Test. Love* I. i. (Skeat) I. 17 Straunge hath by way of intrucioun made his home there me shulde be, yf reason were herde as he shulde. **1433** LYDG. *St. Edmund* III. 469 He dradde.. Lyst newe Intrusioun [of Danes] brouhte in ydolatrie. *c* **1460** CAPGRAVE *Chron.* Ded. (Rolls) 4 He that entered by intrusion vas Henry the Fourte. **1516** *Plumpton Corr.* 217 Ther is a suyt against your mastership in the Excheker for introshon. **1540** *Act 32 Hen. VIII*, c. 46 To make aunswer for his or their intrusion vpon the kinges possession. **1579** FULKE *Ref. Rastel* 766 They had taken part with Nouatus, which would be a bishoppe by intrusion. **1661** COWLEY *Verses & Ess.*, *Cromwell* (1669) 62 All power is attained either by the Election and Consent of the people, and that takes away your objection of forcible intrusion. **1691** LUTTRELL *Brief Rel.* (1857) II. 244 An information of intrusion is brought by the atturny general against the old archbishop of Canterbury and 2 others, for wrongfully detaining and intruding upon the king's possession of Lambeth house. **1765** T. HUTCHINSON *Hist. Mass.* I. iii. 369 Writs of intrusion were brought against some.. who refused to petition for patents. **1883** *Wharton's Law Lex.* (ed. 7), *Intrusion*, the entry of a stranger after a particular estate of freehold is determined before him in reversion or remainder.

b. The settlement of a minister of the Church of Scotland contrary to the will or without the consent of the congregation: see INTRUSIONIST, NON-INTRUSION. Also *attrib.* in reference to the Non-intrusion conflict.

1849 R. BUCHANAN *Ten Years' Conflict* ix. II. 137 A threat which the Marquis of Tweeddale had lately thrown out at an intrusion meeting in East Lothian. **1878** T. BROWN *Annals Disrupt.* iii. (1884) 23 They would give no promise to refrain from the intrusion of Mr. Edwards, and.. the Church was resolved to protect the people from such intrusion.

3. The action of thrusting oneself in in an encroaching manner, or of introducing something inappropriately; uninvited or unwelcome entrance or appearance; encroachment on something possessed or enjoyed by another. *spec.* in contexts of Journalism.

1592 SHAKS. *Rom. & Jul.* I. v. 92, I will withdraw, but this intrusion shall Now seeming sweet, conuert to bitter gall. **1667** MILTON *P.L.* XII. 178 Frogs, Lice and Flies must all his Palace fill With loath'd intrusion, and fill all the land. **1725** POPE *Odyss.* I. 115 The bold intrusion of the Suitor-train. **1783** BURKE *Sp. E. India Bill* Wks. IV. 5 It has been a little painful to me to observe the intrusions into this important debate of such company as *quo warranto*, and *mandamus*, and *certiorari*. **1850** GLADSTONE *Glean.* V. xiii. 182 If the reply be a correct one, my intrusion upon your Lordship's time may be excused. **1883** FROUDE *Short Stud.* IV. II. v. 230 His feelings had been.. embittered by the intrusion of religious discord into families. **1896** *Speaker* 3 Oct. 351/2 [George Fox's] intrusion of himself into assemblies where he was not wanted. **1958** *Spectator* 18 July 110/3 Newspaper intrusion into private lives. **1960** *New Statesman* 15 Oct. 556/2 The intrusion and impertinence of some of the gossip writers.

Hence **in'trusional** *a.*, pertaining to intrusion (Webster 1864, and in recent Dicts.).

in'trusionist. [f. prec. + -IST.] One who practises or supports intrusion.

During the controversy regarding the intrusion of ministers in the Established Church of Scotland, which resulted in the Disruption of 1843, applied by those who called themselves *non-intrusionists* to their opponents. So **intrusionism**.

1841 in R. Buchanan *Ten Years' Conflict* xii. (1849) II. 313 Even the callous-hearted people that sat in the pew, the only pew representing *intrusionism* and forced settlements, were moved. **1849** *Ibid.* xi. II. 203 He was not by any means an out-and-out intrusionist.

intrusive (ɪn'truːsɪv), *a.* and *sb.* [f. L. *intrūs-*, ppl. stem of *intrūdĕre* to INTRUDE + -IVE.]

A. *adj.* **1.** Of intruding character; characterized by coming or entering in an encroaching manner, or without invitation or welcome; done or carried out with intrusion.

1647 M. HUDSON *Div. Right Govt.* II. iv. 98 Every Polarchical action in the Polarchs.. being rebellious and intrusive. **1735** THOMSON *Liberty* I. 299 No mighty moles the big intrusive storm, From the calm stations roll resounding back. **1813** SCOTT *Rokeby* I. xxx, Still he turned impatient ear From Truth's intrusive voice severe. **1891** E. PEACOCK *N. Brendon* I. 175 He was not shy, but did not wish to be intrusive.

2. a. That has been intruded or thrust in.

1862 MARSH *Eng. Lang.* ii. 34 An intrusive element in a language is confined to the vocabulary and minor grammatical forms. **1897** *Allbutt's Syst. Med.* IV. 476 Large quantities of this intrusive substance strangling the secreting textures. **1900** I. TAYLOR in *N. & Q.* 9th Ser. V. 483/1 The *n* in Pentland Firth is intrusive, while the Pentland Hills were Penland, the *t* being intrusive and the *n* radical.

b. *Geol.* Of an igneous rock: Forced, while in a state of fusion, into cavities or fissures of other rocks.

1844 DARWIN *Geol. Obs.* (1876) II. 513 The number and bulk of the intrusive masses of different coloured porphyries .. is truly extraordinary. **1858** GEIKIE *Hist. Boulder* xii. 241 The intrusive traps occur in the form of walls and veins. **1876** PAGE *Adv. Text-bk. Geol.* iv. 85 When igneous matter appears to have thrust itself between certain strata in wedge-shaped or sheet-like masses, it is spoken of as intrusive.

3. Inward-thrusting. *rare.*

1847 R. WILLIS tr. *Harvey's Wks.* 383 (*Generat. Animals* lii.), I straightway perceived a certain protuberant fleshy part, affected with an alternating extrusive and intrusive movement.

B. *sb. Geol.* An intrusive rock or rock mass.

1895 A. HARKER *Petrol.* vii. 87 Acid intrusives. The acid intrusive rocks embrace a considerable range of varieties. **1925** N. E. ODELL in E. F. Norton *Fight for Everest, 1924* 300 Yet the character of the former [*sc.* the limestone series] may be entirely due to its proximity to the hard crystalline rocks and its alteration brought about by pressure against them, if not also by their igneous intrusives. **1962** W. T. HUANG *Petrol.* iii. 51 It [*sc.* magma] may be solidified at great depth, forming such large intrusives as batholiths, stocks, and lopoliths. **1968** J. GILLULY et al. *Princ. Geol.* (ed. 3) xviii. 435 (*caption*) Devil's Tower, Wyoming, probably a volcanic plug, but perhaps part of a roofed intrusive.

intrusively (ɪn'truːsɪvlɪ), *adv.* [f. prec. + -LY².] In an intrusive manner; so as to intrude.

1847 in CRAIG. **1869** CARLYLE *Let. Jean Aitken* 11 Mar. in *Athenæum* (1895) 2 Feb. 149/2 Mrs. Grote in a chair intrusively close to Majesty. **1882** J. HAWTHORNE *Fort. Fool* I. xxix, It was intrusively apparent.. that Sir Stanhope loved the girl without stint.

intrusiveness (ɪn'truːsɪvnɪs). [f. as prec. + -NESS.] The quality of being intrusive.

1847 in CRAIG. **1860** MOTLEY *Netherl.* (1868) II. x. 69 He was much addicted.. to.. general intrusiveness. **1874** HELPS *Soc. Press.* vii. (1875) 84 The Intrusiveness which is innate in mankind.

†**in'trusor.** *Obs.* Forms: 4 intrewsar, 5 intrusour, 5–6 -ore, 6 *Sc.* -ar. [a. AF. *en-*, *intrusour*, in med.(Anglo-)L. *intrūsor* one who usurps a possession, office, or dignity, agent-n. from *intrūdĕre* to INTRUDE.] = INTRUDER I.

[**1292** BRITTON III. i. §2 Qe ceux entrusours pusent estre engettez freschement apres la intrusioun. *Ibid.* §4 Bon est qe teus brefs i soint ordinez, qe plus chacent les intrusours a respouns.] *c* **1400** *Apol. Loll.* 77 Or ellis þat clerkis now are .. fals intrewsars. **1430–40** LYDG. *Bochas* VIII. i. (1554) 177 b, An intrusour, one called Julian, Thestate usurping to reigne there began. **1594** *Sc. Acts. Jas. VI* (1816) IV. 69/1 The personis intrusaris of thame selffis in sic possessioun, delayis the mater. **1599** W. WATSON in *Archpr. Controv.* (Camden) I. 91 Parsons and Blackwell, intrusores into our haruest.

intrust, var. form of ENTRUST *v.*

†**in'trycar.** *Obs.* [f. *intryke*, INTRIKE, ENTRIKE *v.* + -AR².] = INTRIGUER.

a **1529** SKELTON *Image Ipocr.* II. 142, I thinke that suche frykars Be not Christes vickars, But crafty intrycars.

intryke, var. ENTRIKE: see INTRIKE.

†**intu'baceous**, *a. Bot. Obs.* [f. L. *intubus* endive + -ACEOUS.] Akin to endive; = CICHORACEOUS.

1657 TOMLINSON *Renou's Disp.* 243 Wild Lettices, and all intubaceous Plants.

intubate ('ɪntjuːbeɪt), *v.* [f. IN-² + L. *tūba* TUBE + -ATE³.]

†**1.** *trans.* To form into tubes. *Obs.*

1612 STURTEVANT *Metallica* (1854) 102 When this impasted oare is.. Intubated and formed into pipes, as if it were clay or loame.

2. *Med.* To treat by inserting a tube into an aperture, esp. into the larynx in the case of certain throat diseases: see next. Also *absol.*

1889 *Year-Bk. Treatment for* 1888. 188 [The child was] intubated again at 12.30 p.m. **1890** *Braithwaite's Retrosp. Med.* CI. 45 The amount of practice required to intubate fairly well. **1891** *Ann. Univ. Med. Sc.* IV. Sect. G. 1 Of those tracheotomized 30.3 per cent. recovered, while of those intubated 35.3 per cent. recovered.

intubation (ɪntjuː'beɪʃən). [n. of action from prec.: see -ATION.] The insertion of a tube; esp. ***intubation of the larynx***, the insertion of a tube into the glottis to keep it open, in diphtheria, etc.: see prec. 2.

1887 *Braithwaite's Retrosp. Med.* XCV. 176 Intubation is destined, I think, to be employed more generally than tracheotomy. **1896** *Allbutt's Syst. Med.* I. 752 The use of tubage or intubation of the glottis is a topic which hardly needs to be discussed with reference to diphtheritic laryngitis. **1897** *Ibid.* III. 376 In the earlier stages of malignant stricture Symonds advocates intubation of the stricture.

†**'intube**, *sb. Obs. rare.* [ad. L. *intubus* (*intybus*, *intibus*), ad. Gr. ἔντυβον.] = ENDIVE, q.v.

1657 TOMLINSON *Renou's Disp.* 243 The sative Succory, or Intube.

intube (ɪn'tjuːb), *v.* [f. IN-² + TUBE.] *trans.* To place in a tube. Hence **in'tubed** *ppl. a.*

1688 J. SMITH *Baroscope* 61 Just equal to the Top of the intubed Mercury.

intue (ɪn'tjuː), *v. rare.* [ad. L. *intuē-rī*: see INTUITION.] *trans.* To know, perceive, or recognize by intuition; to intuit.

1860 W. G. WARD *Nat. & Grace* I. 40 We will further use the word 'intue', as corresponding in every respect with the substantive 'intuition', and the adjective 'intuitive'. **1869** *Life M. M. Hallahan* (1870) 124 It was a part of her religious sense, something which, to borrow a word of modern coinage, she had from the first intued. **1874** *Contemp. Rev.* Dec. 69 Dr. Ward attempts to leap off his own shadow by all manner of strange phrases about necessary truth and contingent truth, 'cognizing', 'intuing', 'ontologism'. **1888** J. MARTINEAU *Study Relig.* I. I. iv. 115 These two related terms, the intuent act and the thing intued were, in the view of the Greek Realist, only one.

intuem ('ɪntjuːɛm). *rare.* [erron. from prec., after *theorem*, etc.] (See quot.)

1860 W. G. WARD *Nat. & Grace* I. 40 Let us coin the word 'intuem'.. I will define an 'intuem', then, 'a truth legitimately intued'. *Ibid.* 41 If I 'intue' unsoundly, the thing intued is not a *real* 'intuem'.

†**'intuence.** *Obs.* [f. L. type **intuēntia*, f. *intuēnt-em*: see next and -ENCE.] A looking into; insight; reflection.

1616 J. LANE *Contn. Sqr.'s T.* (1887) 63/358 Certifie, with industrious intuence, With manlie presence, willinge dilligence.

intuent ('ɪntjuːənt), *a.* [ad. L. *intuēnt-em*, pr. pple. of *intuērī*.] That knows by intuition.

1865 GROTE *Plato* (1867) II. xxvi. 329 You do not, by producing this fact of innate mental intuitions, eliminate the intuent mind. **1888** J. MARTINEAU *Study Relig.* I. I. i. 68 Reaching to the intuent self. *Ibid.* iv. 115 [see INTUE *v.*].

intuit (ɪn'tjuːɪt, 'ɪn-), *v.* Also -ite. [f. L. *intuit-*, ppl. stem of *intuērī*: see INTUITION.]

†**1.** *trans.* ? To tutor, to instruct. *Obs. rare.*

1776 *Adventures of a Corkscrew* 15 Scarce.. a sharper or gambler but what could freely take his lordship by the hand; intuited by such company, it was in vain his mother now attempted to remonstrate.. against his proceedings.

2. a. *intr.* or *absol.* To receive or assimilate knowledge by direct perception or comprehension.

1840–1 DE QUINCEY *Rhetoric* Wks. 1859 XI. 42 God must see; he must intuit, so to speak; and all truth must reach him simultaneously. **1895** *Thinker* VIII. 448 Anselm does not attempt to intuit, but only to prove. **1968** J. C. HOLMES *Nothing more to Declare* 105 You had to be able to intuit on the bias, to hear music *being* music.

b. *trans.* To know anything immediately, without the intervention of any reasoning process; to know by intuition.

1858 BUSHNELL *Nat. & Supernat.* ii. (1862) 28 *note*, He is a being.. who by the eternal necessity even of his nature, intuits everything. **1872** H. SPENCER *Princ. Psychol.* II. VII. iv. 359 *note*, If space and time are forms of intuition they can never be intuited; since it is impossible for anything to be at once the *form* of intuition and the *matter* of intuition. **1874** LEWES *Probl. Life & Mind* I. 419 The mind intuites what the eye cannot see. **1881** SULLY *Illusions* 33 Our other senses are also avenues by which we intuit and recognize objects. **1926** A. HUXLEY *Two or three Graces* 85 You intuit things that aren't there at all. **1968** *Times* 13 Jan. 20/3 We may intuit his reality, but we cannot share it. **1972** *Times Lit. Suppl.* 18 Feb. 178/1 What Johnson intuited and asserted in 1765, that of the Folios only the first had any textual authority, was demonstrated by Malone in 1790.

intuitable (ɪn'tjuːɪtəb(ə)l), *a.* [f. INTUIT *v.* + -ABLE.] That can be known by intuition.

1887 G. T. LADD tr. *Lotze's Outl. Logic* §64 'Abstraction' makes the content of the concept intuitable only as a whole. **1904** J. H. MUIRHEAD in J. E. Hand *Ideals of Sci. & Faith* 91 If the mere absence of intuitable continuity were the only difficulty in the way of assimilation, we might ignore it. **1932** H. H. PRICE *Perception* vi. 168 The intuitable characteristics of the sense-datum now sensed. **1971** R. HARROD *Sociol.* 51 In the case of lying, there is no question of its having a certain innate intuitable quality.

intuited (ɪn'tjuːɪtɪd), *ppl. a.* [f. INTUIT *v.* + -ED¹.] Arrived at or known by intuition.

1886 A. WEIR *Hist. Basis Mod. Europe* xii. 481 The mathematical sciences.. drew their conclusions from intuited figures and series. **1890** W. JAMES *Princ. Psychol.* I. 630 Meanwhile, the specious present, the intuited duration, stands permanent, like the rainbow on the waterfall, with its own quality unchanged by the events that stream through it. **1924** H. J. W. HETHERINGTON *Life & Lett. Sir H. Jones* I. 64 Even intuited truth is not reality. **1967** *Listener* 4 May 593/1 Some felt or intuited absolute ethical standard. **1973** S. HENDERSON *Understanding New Black Poetry* 10 Fidelity to the observed or intuited truth of the Black Experience in the United States.

intuition (ɪntjuː'ɪʃən). [a. F. *intuition*, ad. late or med.L. *intuitiōn-em*, n. of action from *intuērī* to look upon, consider, contemplate, f. *in-* (IN-²) + *tuērī* to look. Cf. L. *intuitus*.]

†**1.** The action of looking upon or into; contemplation; inspection; a sight or view. (= L. *intuitus*.) *Obs.*

1497 BP. ALCOCK *Mons Perfect.* B iij, That they myght have a perpetuall intuycion & fruycion of his Infynyte Joye. **1627–77** FELTHAM *Resolves* II. lvi. 275 A Looking-glass.. becomes spotted and stained from their only intuition. **1649** JER. TAYLOR *Gt. Exemp.* II. Disc. ix. §36. 126 His disciples must not onely abstain from the act of unlawfull concubinate, but from the impurer intuition of a wife of another man. **1664** EVELYN tr. *Freart's Archit.* 123 To remove, uncover, and take in pieces, for the intuition of every Contignation.

†**2.** The action of mentally looking at; contemplation, consideration; perception, recognition; mental view. *Obs.*

1628 T. Spencer *Logick* 10 Which hath..a power, aptitude, or fitnes, to bring the thing, objected unto our understanding, into the knowledge, and intuition thereof. **1652** Benlowes *Theoph.* ii. 15 She is wholly taken up with Intuition of supercœlestial Excellencies. **1755** B. Martin *Mag. Arts & Sc.* ii. xii. 253 That the Employment of Time to endless Ages will consist in an uninterrupted Intuition and Contemplation of [an infinite Scene of the Operations of divine Power and Wisdom].

†**3.** The action of mentally looking to or regarding as a motive of action; ulterior view; regard, respect, reference. ***with intuition to*** (*of*), with reference to; ***in intuition to***, in respect to, in view of, in consideration of. *Obs.*

1612–15 Bp. Hall *Contempl., O.T.* xx. x, God doth not always strike with an intuition of sin: sometimes he regards the benefit of our trial, sometimes the glory of his mercy in our cure. **1637** —— *Serm. Consecr. Buriall-place* 81 Praying for the dead..but not the Romish: that is, not with an intuition to their fained Purgatory. **1650** Fuller *Pisgah* ii. iii. 91 This Countrey was conferred upon them in Intuition to their valour. **1659** Pearson *Creed* iv. (1662) 214 The recompence of the reward was set before him, and through an intuition of it he chearfully underwent whatsoever was laid upon him. **1667** *Decay Chr. Piety* v. ¶16 For he that sues upon the naked intuition of recovering his right, without any aspect of revenge on the invader; has as fully the benefit of the law. **1718** Hickes & Nelson *J. Kettlewell* iii. §72. 381, I do it with Affectionate intuitions of doing Honour to Religion.

4. *Scholastic Philos.* The spiritual perception or immediate knowledge, ascribed to angelic and spiritual beings, with whom vision and knowledge are identical.

1652 Benlowes *Theoph.* i. i, Might souls converse with souls, by Angel-way Enfranchis'd from their pris'ning clay What strains by Intuition would they then convey. **1660** Jer. Taylor *Worthy Commun.* i. §5. 97 St. Pauls faith did not come by hearing, but by intuition and revelation. **1711** Addison *Spect.* No. 162 ¶4 Our Superiors are guided by Intuition, and our Inferiors by Instinct. **1690** Baxter *Kingd. Christ* ii. (1691) 44 As if the Intuition of Spirits and Spiritual Bodies, were not a more eminent discerning than our Eyesight. *a* **1720** Sheffield (Dk. Buckhm.) *Wks.* (1753) I. 122 Their [i.e. Angels'] thoughts are communicated to one another by what the schoolmen call intuition. **1836** J. Gilbert *Chr. Atonem.* iv. (1852) 101 For a creature to know an infinite Being by intuition is plainly impossible.

5. a. *Mod. Philos.* The immediate apprehension of an object by the mind without the intervention of any reasoning process; a particular act of such apprehension.

a **1600** Hooker (in Cottle *Coleridge* II. 217) An intuition, that is, a direct beholding or presentation to the mind through the senses or imagination. **1782** Priestley *Matter & Spir.* I. xi. 134 What we *feel*, and what we *do*, we may be said to know by intuition. **1840–1** De Quincey *Rhetoric* Wks. 1859 XI. 42 An *intuition* is any knowledge whatsoever, sensuous or intellectual, which is apprehended *immediately*. **1860** Abp. Thomson *Laws Th.* §47. 74 Notions of single objects are called Intuitions, as being such as the mind receives when it simply attends to or inspects (*intuetur*) the object.

b. Immediate apprehension by the intellect alone; a particular act of such apprehension.

1659 *Gentl. Calling* (1696) 20 This is that Tree of Knowledge..which instructs not..by sad and costly experience, but by fair and safe intuitions. *a* **1677** Hale *Prim. Orig. Man.* i. i. 2 There seems to be a third means, which is a kind of intuition; there are some truths so plain and evident, and open, that need not any process of ratiocination to evidence or evince them. **1695** Locke *Hum. Und.* iv. ii. §1 The Mind perceives, that White is not Black, That a Circle is not a Triangle, That Three are more than Two, and equal to One and Two. Such kind of Truths the Mind perceives at the first sight of the Ideas together, by bare Intuition, without the intervention of any other Idea. **1841** Myers *Cath. Th.* iii. §1. 2 Such laws and precepts as the reasonings and intuitions and sentiments of men have agreed to pronounce the wisest and worthiest. **1846** Mill *Logic* Introd. §4 The truths known by intuition are the original premises from which all others are inferred. **1850** McCosh *Div. Govt.* (1852) 487 *note*, The real intuitions of the human soul are just the human faculties and feelings acting according to their fundamental principles. **1856** Dove *Logic Chr. Faith* Introd. §5. 17 God would be a primary of intuition. **1865** Lecky *Ration.* II. iv. 67 The intuition by which we know what is right and what is wrong, is clearer than any chain of historic reasoning. **1877** E. R. Conder *Bas. Faith* iv. 157 Primary judgments (such as that every change must have a cause) are often called beliefs, though 'intuitions' would be a better term.

c. Immediate apprehension by sense; a particular act of such apprehension.

Esp. in reference to Kant, who held that the only intuition (*anschauung, intuitus*) possible to man was that under the forms of sensibility, space, and time.

1796 F. A. Nitsch *Gen. View Kant's Princ. concerning Man* 75 Those ideas which immediately arise in consequence of our external sense being affected are external perceptions or external intuitions. **1819** Richardson tr. *Kant's Proleg. to Metaph.* 53 All our intuition however takes place by means of the senses only. **1855** H. Spencer *Princ. Psychol.* ii. i. 78 *note*, Sir William Hamilton..restricts the meaning of intuition to that which is known by external perception. **1864** Bowen *Logic* i. 1 Such acts are called Intuitions or Presentations. *Ibid.*, In receiving Intuitions, the mind exerts no conscious activity. *Ibid.* ii. 40 Derived from processes of observation or intuition.

6. In a more general sense: Direct or immediate insight; an instance of this.

1762–71 H. Walpole *Vertue's Anecd. Paint.* (1789) IV. 152 It is..a proof of his intimate intuition into nature. **1851** Hawthorne *Fr. & It. Jrnls.* II. 234 A miraculous intuition of what ought to be done just at the time for action. *a* **1862** Buckle *Misc. Wks.* (1872) I. 40 That peculiar property of genius which, for want of a better word, we call intuition. **1866** Dk. Argyll *Reign Law* ii. (ed. 4) 111 The intuitions of genius unconscious of any process. **1879** Froude *Cæsar* xxiii. 410 Rashness if it fails is madness, and if it succeeds is the intuition of genius.

intuitional (ɪntjuːˈɪʃənəl), *a.* [f. prec. + -al[1].]

1. Of, pertaining to, or derived from intuition; of the nature of intuition.

1860 W. G. Ward *Nat. & Grace* i. §1. 39 Were it not for this '*intuitional* light', we should be shut up..in the dreary region of actually present consciousness. **1861** E. H. Browne in *Aids Faith* vii. 309 No elevation of the intuitional consciousness can account for such fore-knowledge. **1863** M. Pattison *Ess.* (1889) II. 267 The masses require either an intuitional religion..or a ceremonial of drill and parade. **1883** A. Barratt *Phys. Metempiric* 138 Acts of mental vision, Relations and groups of Relations with like escort.. are intuitional, like the intuition of distance or of causal relations.

2. Possessed of intuition. (Cf. *rational.*)

1877 T. Sinclair *Mount* 59 They are so sympathetic, intuitional, calm, and womanlike in their practical wisdom.

3. Pertaining to that theory, or philosophical school, which bases certain elements of knowledge on intuition (see prec. 5 b).

1865 *Reader* 20 May 563/2 Whether or no the intuitional metaphysicians will have anything to reply on behalf of their own theory, is another question. **1879** Lewes *Study Psychol.* i. 5 We still hear of the Intuitional Psychology and the Sensational School. **1879** H. Spencer *Data Ethics* iii. §14. 38 By the intuitional theory I here mean..the theory which regards such feelings as divinely given, and as independent of results experienced by self or ancestors.

Hence **intu'itionally** *adv.*, by intuition; intuitively.

1872 T. W. Fowle in *Contemp. Rev.* Nov. 866 An undeviating law of conduct intuitionally apprehended.

intu'itionalism. [f. prec. + -ism.] The doctrine or theory of the intuitional school; the doctrine that the perception of truth, or of certain truths, is by intuition.

1850 McCosh *Div. Govt.* (1852) 486 The rationalism which was felt to be insufficient for any one practical purpose whatsoever..has become a more pretending intuitionalism. **1864** *Theol. Rev.* Mar. 71 What might easily become the not less positive or offensive dogmatism of Intuitionalism.

intu'itionalist. [f. as prec. + -ist.]

1. One who holds the doctrine of intuitionalism.

1856 Vaughan *Mystics* (1860) I iii. iii. 71 All these intuitionalists profess to evolve from their depths very much more than those simplest ethical perceptions. **1871** Calderwood in *Contemp. Rev.* Jan. 238 Being myself an intuitionalist in morals. **1891** *Athenæum* 29 Aug. 283/1 He [Herbert Spencer] has a morality quite as distinct from mere expediency and policy as that of any Intuitionalist.

2. = intuitionist 1.

1869 *Contemp. Rev.* XI. 258 Hutcheson, Reid..Wilson and Hamilton..were all, more or less distinctively, intuitionalists.

intuitionism (ɪntjuːˈɪʃənɪz(ə)m). [f. intuition + -ism.]

1. The doctrine of Reid and other philosophers of the Scottish school, that in perception, external objects are known immediately, without the intervention of a vicarious phenomenon.

1847 *Blackw. Mag.* LXII. 243 Representationism could not possibly be avoided, neither could intuitionism be possibly fallen in with, on the analytic road which he took. **1874** W. G. Ward *Ess.* (1884) I. 204 He [Mill] accounted the controversy between intuitionism and phenomenism far more fundamental than any other, in matters no less of social than of strictly philosophical speculation. **1896** G. M. Sloane *Life James M'Cosh* viii. 103 His philosophic creed, being the intuitionism of the Scottish School.

2. = intuitionalism.

1874 Sidgwick *Meth. Ethics* i. 9 What we may call *Intuitionism.* **1884** *Athenæum* 11 Oct. 461/3 Prof. Sidgwick ..showed his strong preference for utilitarianism over the other two methods, egoism and intuitionism, which completed his trio of possible schemes of ethical study by logical processes.

3. *Math.* The theory put forward by L. E. J. Brouwer (1908) that mathematics is founded on extra-linguistic constructs based on pure intuition (in the Kantian sense, cf. intuition 5 c); that space geometry is reducible to arithmetic and that therefore the law of the excluded middle, applying to finite classes, might not be valid for infinite classes. Cf. formalism 3.

1913 tr. L. E. J. Brouwer in *Bull. Amer. Math. Soc.* XXV. 86 From the present point of view of intuitionism..all mathematical sets of units..can be developed out of the basal intuition, and this can only be done by combining a finite number of times the two operations: 'to create a finite ordinal number' and 'to create the infinite ordinal number ω'. **1940** [see formalism 3 a]. **1941** Courant & Robbins *What is Math.?* i. 87 Some distinguished mathematicians have recently advocated the more or less complete banishment from mathematics of all non-constructive proofs... The school of 'intuitionism', which has adopted this program, has met with strong resistance. **1959** E. W. Beth *Found. Math.* xv. 413 One of the most spectacular features in Brouwer's intuitionism is..his rejection of the unrestricted application of the principle of the excluded third in mathematical reasoning. **1965** Kleene & Vesley *Found. Intuitionistic Math.* i. 1 Modern intuitionism, founded by Brouwer, constitutes a vigorous manifestation of the constructive tendency. **1973** *Sci. Amer.* Mar. 103/2 Three modern schools of mathematical thought: logicism, formalism and intuitionism.

intu'itionist, *sb.* (and *a.*) [f. as prec. + -ist.] One who holds the theory of intuitionism.

1. An adherent of the doctrine of Reid concerning immediate perception: see prec. 1. Also *attrib.*

1872 Mill *Exam. Hamilton's Philos.* (ed. 4) xiv. 339 This ..is the staple of the Intuitionist argument. **1890** in *Cent. Dict.*

2. a. = intuitionalist 1. Used esp. in *Math.* Cf. intuitionism 3.

1855 Miss Cobbe *Intuit. Mor.* 76 Where the Deductive Science of the Intuitionist stops, there the Inductive Science of the Experimentalist meets it. **1865** Mill *Exam. Hamilton* 208 The most strenuous Intuitionist does not include this among the things that I know by direct intuition. **1879** H. Spencer *Data Ethics* iv. §20. 55 Nor is it otherwise with the pure intuitionists, who hold that moral perceptions are innate in the original sense. **1913** *Bull. Amer. Math. Soc.* XXV. 86 The intuitionist can never feel assured of the exactness of a mathematical theory by such guarantees as the proof of its being non-contradictory, the possibility of defining its concepts by a finite number of words or the practical certainty that it will never lead to a misunderstanding in human relations. **1926** *Proc. London Math. Soc.* 2nd Ser. XXV. 339 Apart from formalism, there are two main general attitudes to the foundation of mathematics: that of intuitionists or finitists..and that of the logicians. **1933** M. Black *Nature of Math.* 195 The intuitionist recognises only the existence of denumerable sets. **1941** [see formalist 5]. **1952** R. M. Hare *Lang. Morals* iii. 30 The word 'good' is treated in the fashion that many intuitionists have treated it. **1959** E. W. Beth *Found. Math.* xv. 421 The intuitionist..can point to the edifice of intuitionistic mathematics which has been built alongside classical mathematics. **1967** S. C. Kleene *Math. Logic* §36. 196 To prove an existence statement $\exists x A(x)$, an intuitionist insists that it be shown how to find an x such that $A(x)$. **1973** *Sci. Amer.* Mar. 103/2 As for intuitionists, they have in effect returned to the Pythagorean position that the natural numbers must be accepted without further analysis as the foundation of mathematics.

b. *attrib.* or as *adj.* Of or pertaining to intuitionism.

1885 *Athenæum* 8 Aug. 170/3 He gives to the intuitionist theory as strong a position as can well be given to it. **1926** [see formalist B]. **1933** M. Black *Nature of Math.* 11 Intuitionist doctrines require the larger part of mathematics to be rewritten. *Ibid.*, The intuitionists..are beginning to produce an intuitionist formal logic. **1960** S. Körner *Philos. of Math.* vi. 131 The intuitionist logic is a *post factum* record of the principles of reasoning which have been employed in mathematical constructions. *Ibid.*, *Every* intuitionist proposition *p*, whether or not the (intuitionist-)negation occurs in it, is the record of a construction. **1970** A. Kino et al. *Intuitionism & Proof Theory* 19 That is the general way of accepting-on-faith in the domains of religion and philosophy, and in traditional intuitionist or constructivist mathematics also.

Hence **intuitio'nistic** *a.*, holding the theory of intuitionism; also **intuitio'nistically** *adv.*, in an intuitionistic manner.

1882 W. G. Ward *Ess.* (1884) II. 155 And this criticism of Intuitionistic philosophers suggests a more general remark. **1940** *Mathematical Rev.* Nov. 323/1 The treatment is 'intuitionistic' in the sense that it is purely algebraic, involving reference to order, absolute value, boundedness, etc., but not to limiting processes. **1942** D. D. Runes *Dict. Philos.* 150 The resulting disjunction becomes intuitionistically acceptable. **1944** *Mathematical Rev.* Sept. 198/2 The author proves intuitionistically seven theorems concerning the full product of a finite or denumerable number of virtually ordered sets, generalizing some results of Brouwer concerning the full products of sets of integers. **1945** E. T. Bell *Devel. Math.* (ed. 2) xxiii. 560 The 'objects' with which intuitionistic mathematics is concerned are said to be immediately apprehended in thought. **1946** *Nature* 7 Sept. 323/1 Nevertheless, if ethics is to be scientific in this sense, some possible theories, particularly those commonly called intuitionistic, are excluded. **1957** *Encycl. Brit.* XV. 82B/1 Most theorems of classical arithmetic can be established intuitionistically. **1962** B. Meltzer tr. *Gödel's On formally Undecidable Propositions* 60 The following is demonstrated in an intuitionistically unobjectionable way. **1965** Kleene & Vesley (*title*) The foundations of intuitionistic mathematics. **1967** S. C. Kleene *Math. Logic* §44. 257 The consistency proof by a truth definition can even be managed intuitionistically. **1971** R. Schock *Quasi-Connectives* vi. 58 The resulting quasi-connectives satisfy all the axioms of the intuitionistic sentential calculus, but not the principle of the excluded middle.

intuitionless (ɪntjuːˈɪʃənlɪs), *a.* [f. as prec. + -less.] Devoid of intuition.

1856 Vaughan *Mystics* (1860) I. iii. iii. 72 You dispute with Schelling, and he waves you away as a profane and intuitionless laic.

intuitive (ɪnˈtjuːɪtɪv), *a.* (and *sb.*) [ad. med.L. *intuitīv-us*, f. *intuitus* intuition; cf. F. *intuitif, -ive.*]

A. *adj.* † **1. a.** Beholding, seeing. *Obs.*

1644 Bulwer *Chirol.* 82 If therefore we but cast an intuitive eye upon those memorials.

†**b.** Of sight or vision: That consists in direct and immediate looking upon an object, and sees it as it is. *Obs.*

1594 HOOKER *Eccl. Pol.* II. vii. §5 The greatest assurance generally with all men, is that which we haue by plaine aspect and intuitiue beholding. **1656** BLOUNT *Glossogr.* s.v., An intuitive Vision is a cleer sight of a thing, as it is in itself.

†**2.** Said esp. of the kind of 'vision' or immediate perception ascribed to angelic and spiritual beings. (See INTUITION 4.) *Obs.* (or merged in 3).

1594 HOOKER *Eccl. Pol.* I. xi. §6 Faith..beginning here with a weak apprehension of things not seen, endeth with the intuitive vision of God in the world to come. *a* **1619** FOTHERBY *Atheom.* II. iii. §1 (1622) 212 We may ascend.. vnto the very presence, and intuitiue vision of God. **1643** SIR T. BROWNE *Relig. Med.* I. §33 If they [spirits] have that intuitive knowledge, whereby..they behold the thoughts of one another.

3. a. Of knowledge or mental perception: That consists in immediate apprehension, without the intervention of any reasoning process.

c **1645** HOWELL *Lett.* (1650) II. 67 Being faithfull eywitnesses of those things which other receive but in trust, whereunto they must yeeld an intuitive consent, and a kind of implicit faith. **1690** LOCKE *Hum. Und.* IV. i. §9 Intuitive Knowledge, where the Ideas themselves by an immediate View, discover their Agreement or Disagreement one with another. **1698** NORRIS *Pract. Disc.* (1707) IV. 143 Intuitive [Intellectual Sight] when we perceive the Agreement or Disagreement of one Idea with another immediately and by themselves, without the Mediation of any other Idea. **1704** —— *Ideal World* II. iii. 146 Immediate knowledge, or knowledge of the principle, we may call intuitive, because the mind then in one and the same view that it perceives the ideas, perceives also their relations. **1849** ROBERTSON *Serm.* Ser. I. i. 9 The intuitive vision comes like an inspiration.

b. Of a truth: Apprehended immediately or by intuition.

1833 MILL *Let.* 5 July (1910) I. ii. 54, I conceive that most of the highest truths are..intuitive; that is, they need neither explanation nor proof, but if not known before are assented to as soon as stated. **1872** BAGEHOT *Physics & Pol.* (1876) 118 The truths of Arithmetic, intuitive or not, certainly cannot be acquired independently of experience.

c. Of any faculty or gift: Not acquired by learning; innate.

1621 BP. MOUNTAGU *Diatribæ* Introd. 32 Hauing not the gift of Prophesie, nor Intuitiue knowledge of what you would one day vndertake. **1845** E. HOLMES *Mozart* 9 The musical faculty appears to have been intuitive in him.

4. Of the mind or reason, or a mental act or process: That acts by intuition or immediate apprehension; opposed to *discursive*.

1667 MILTON *P.L.* v. 488 Whence the soule Reason receives, and reason is her being, Discursive, or Intuitive. **1790** BURKE *Fr. Rev.* Wks. V. 159 The first intuitive glance, without any elaborate process of reasoning, would shew, that this..would justify every extent of crime. **1865** DICKENS *Mut. Fr.* I. ix, Mr. Boffin, who had a deep respect for his wife's intuitive wisdom. **1879** FARRAR *St. Paul* (1883) 63 The swift power of intuitive discernment was not yet theirs.

5. Of persons: Possessing intuition.

1652 BENLOWES *Theoph.* Pref., Super-cœlestials are Intelligencies..excellent in their Beings, intuitive in their Conceptions. **1660** BURNEY *Κέρδ. δῶρον* (1661) 115 When Kings are as Intuitive Angels, to support and set a living pattern. **1851** GALLENGA *Italy* i. 5 Hardly a deep, intuitive poet, like Dante, in the fourteenth century.

6. Of or pertaining to the school of moral philosophy that holds the first principles of ethics to be apprehended immediately or by intuition.

1852 MILL in *Westm. Rev.* LVIII. 362 If it is alleged that the intuitive school require, as an authority for the feeling, that it should *in fact* be universal, we deny it. **1861** —— *Utilit.* 4 The intuitive school affirm as strongly as the inductive, that there is a science of morals. **1869** LECKY *Europ. Mor.* I. i. 2 The intuitive moralist..believes that the utilitarian theory is profoundly immoral.

7. Obvious to the senses; directly visible. *rare.*

1801 FUSELI in *Lect. Paint.* iii. (1848) 434 It is placed beyond all doubt by the glorious apparition above; it is made nearly intuitive by the uplifted hand and finger of the Apostle in the centre. *c* **1811** *Ibid.* iv. 450 It may be more than doubted whether the resignation of Alcestis can ever be made intuitive..the Art can show no more than Alcestis dying.

B. *sb.* One who works by intuition.

1907 *Westm. Gaz.* 28 Nov. 2/1 Poincaré divides mathematicians into analysts and geometers—i.e., into logicians and 'intuitives'. **1927** A. HUXLEY *Proper Stud.* 207 Intellectuals and intuitives.

in'tuitively (-ɪvlɪ), *adv.* [f. prec. + -LY².]

†**1.** By direct and immediate vision; esp. by that ascribed to angelic and spiritual beings, which gave immediate knowledge. *Obs.*

1597 HOOKER *Eccl. Pol.* v. xlii. §7 That..which Angels and glorified Saints doe intuitiuely behold. **1655** BAXTER *Quaker Catech.* 9 Nor have I seen him in glory intuitively, or as the glorified in heaven do. **1677** GALE *Crt. Gentiles* III. 83 Thus much seems acknowledged by Plato..'Are there not very few.. who are able to know and contemplate beautie it self (i.e. God) according to himself' i.e. intuitively?

2. By intuition; by immediate perception or direct mental apprehension; without the aid of intermediate ideas.

1608 D. T. *Ess. Pol. & Mor.* 108 God himselfe (the searcher of all hearts, and who alone intuitivelie knowes all things). **1736** BUTLER *Anal.* II. v. Wks. 1874 I. 210 It is by no means intuitively certain how far these consequences could possibly..be prevented. **1755** JOHNSON *Pref. to Dict.* ¶43 As nothing can be proved but by supposing something intuitively known, and evident without proof, so nothing can be defined but by the use of words too plain to admit a definition. **1814** D. STEWART *Philos. Hum. Mind* II. ii. §1. 96 The truth of mathematical axioms has always been supposed to be intuitively obvious; and the first of these, according to Euclid's enumeration, affirms, That if A be equal to B, and B to C, A and C are equal. **1856** MISS MULOCK *J. Halifax* 105 We both intuitively supplied the noun to that indefinite personal pronoun. **1877** E. CAIRD *Philos. Kant* I. 172 That very correlation of all substances which as intuitively apprehended in perception we call space.

3. *Logic.* By, or to, unaided reflection; without the use of any technique of logic.

1942 J. C. COOLEY *Primer of Formal Logic* vi. 218 Most of the statements excluded by the theory of types would probably be avoided intuitively because they do not make sensible English sentences.

intuitiveness (ɪn'tju:ɪtɪvnɪs). [f. as prec. + -NESS.] The quality of being intuitive.

1. Capability of being intuitively recognized as true.

1841 TRENCH *Parables* (1860) 36 That this or that circumstance was merely added for the sake of giving intuitiveness to the narrative. **1873** M. ARNOLD *Lit. & Dogma* (1876) 264 The winning simplicity and limpid intuitiveness which make the charm of *epieikeia*.

2. Intuitive apprehension or faculty; insight.

1873 W. S. MAYO *Never Again* vii. 88 She had no intuitiveness. She looked only at the surface.

intuitivism (ɪn'tju:ɪtɪvɪz(ə)m). [f. as prec. + -ISM.]

1. The doctrine that the fundamental principles of ethics are matters of intuition.

a **1866** J. GROTE *Exam. Utilitarian Philos.* (1870) i. 21 That doctrine, hostile to utilitarianism, to which he has given the name of 'intuitivism'. **1874** SIDGWICK *Meth. Ethics* I. ix. 99 The difference between the two phases of Intuitivism in which these notions are respectively prominent, is purely formal: their practical prescriptions are never found to conflict.

2. = INTUITIVENESS 2.

1883 *Century Mag.* 479 They depend for their significancy on the words themselves as related to the appreciative intuitivism of the reader. **1886** J. B. MAYOR *Metre* 50 What I should call the principle of aesthetic intuitivism.

in'tuitivist, *a.* [f. as prec. + -IST.] One who holds the doctrine of intuitivism; one who believes in the intuitive character of ethical ideas. Also *attrib.* Holding, or pertaining to, this doctrine.

a **1866** J. GROTE *Exam. Utilitarian Philos.* (1870) x. 168 The..description of conscience which Mr. Mill gives.. seems to me, if anything is, intuitivist. **1870** J. L. DAVIES in *Contemp. Rev.* Aug. 94 There is more of reference to the will of God..in those publicans the Utilitarians, than in most of the 'intuitivist' philosophers. **1874** SIDGWICK *Meth. Ethics* i. 3 Many of the school called Intuitivist. **1886** J. B. MAYOR *Metre* 49 This aesthetic or intuitivist way of regarding metrical questions.

intumb, obs. form of ENTOMB *v.*

intumesce (ɪntju:'mɛs), *v.* [ad. L. *intumēscĕre* to swell up, f. *in-* (IN-²) + *tumēscĕre*, inceptive of *tumēre* to be tumid, to swell.] *intr.* To swell up, become tumid; to bubble up.

1796 KIRWAN *Elem. Min.* (ed. 2) I. 276 Treated by the blow pipe, it intumesces, and gives a frothy mass. **1860** MAURY *Phys. Geog. Sea* (Low) xi. §513 The appearance of an immense caldron, boiling, and bubbling, and intumescing in the upper air.

intumescence (ɪntju:'mɛsəns). [a. F. *intumescence* (Cotgr. 1611), f. L. *intumēscĕre*: see prec. and -ENCE.]

1. The process of swelling up.

1656 BLOUNT *Glossogr.*, *Intumescence*, a swelling, puffing or uprising. **1660** BOYLE *New Exp. Phys. Mech.* iv. (1682) 27 A farther and sufficient manifestation, whence the intumescence of the bladder proceeds. **1671** *Phil. Trans.* VI. 2141 The Lungs are dilated..; upon their Dilatation follows the Intumescence of the Diaphragme as of a Sail. **1755** JOHNSON *Pref. to Dict.* ¶86 As much superiour to human resistance, as the revolutions of the sky, or intumescence of the tide. **1872** W. S. SYMONDS *Rec. Rocks* i. 15 Its intumescence forces it to exude through a crack or hole in the cover of the vessel.

b. *fig.* in reference to language.

1893 F. HALL in *Nation* (N.Y.) LVI. 274/2 The flatulent intumescence of Dr. Parr.

2. *Physiol.* A swelling of the tissue of any organ or part of the body, or of a plant. Also *concr.*

1822–34 *Good's Study Med.* (ed. 4) IV. 178 Producing a kind of general intumescence of the abdomen on the right side. **1839–47** TODD *Cycl. Anat.* III. 313/1 The compression made by the intumescence of the muscles. **1858** CARPENTER *Veg. Phys.* §391 A little swelling or intumescence, formed of very spongy cellular tissue, and containing a great deal of fluid. **1861** F. H. RAMADGE *Curab. Consumpt.* 76 In consequence of mucous bronchial intumescence.

3. The bubbling up of a fluid or molten mass.

1661 BOYLE *Spring Air* III. xx, The intumescence of it might proceed from small parcels of air..harboured in the body of that liquor. **1696** W. COWPER in *Phil. Trans.* XIX. 234 This Intumescence and agitation of the matter is made in the Stomach. **1796** HATCHETT *ibid.* LXXXVI. 287 The mixture melted without intumescence. **1879** RUTLEY *Study Rocks* x. 112 Before the blowpipe sodalite fuses with intumescence to a colourless glass.

b. *fig.* Excited spirit or feeling.

1775 JOHNSON *Tax. no Tyr.* 20 The intumescence of nations would have found its vent, like all other expansive violence, where there was least resistance.

†**intu'mescency.** *Obs.* [f. as prec.: see -ENCY.] Intumescent quality or condition.

1650 SIR T. BROWNE *Pseud. Ep.* VII. xiii. (1686) 300 Parts disposed to intumescency at the bottom. **1663** POWER *Exp. Philos.* II. 139 If..the Bladder's intumescency..did proceed from the forced extension of the Ayr in the Receiver. **1696** W. COWPER in *Phil. Trans.* XIX. 234 Hence it is we have less Appetite some time after eating (when this Intumescency is made) than we had immediately after.

intumescent (ɪntju:'mɛsənt), *a.* [ad. L. *intumēscent-em*, pr. pple. of *intumēscĕre*: see INTUMESCE.] Swelling up; becoming tumid.

1870 ROLLESTON *Anim. Life* 119 The integument is.. thickened and intumescent. **1875** LYELL *Princ. Geol.* II. II. xxvii. 68 The..lava..appears to have been a long time in an intumescent state.

†**in'tumil**, *v. Obs.* [f. L. type **intumul-āre* to bury (see INTUMULATE), prob. in late or med.L.; cf. OF. *entumuler*, *entombeler* (Godef.).] *trans.* = INTUMULATE.

c **1540** tr. *Pol. Verg. Eng. Hist.* (Camden) I. 199 His corpes was carried to Winchester, and there, with honorable buriall, intumiled.

†**in'tumilated**, *ppl. a. Obs. rare*$^{-0}$. [f. L. *intumulāt-us* not buried (IN-³) + -ED¹.]

1623 COCKERAM, *Intumilated*, not buried.

†**in'tumulate**, *v. Obs.* Also 6 -ilate. Pa. pple. -at(e and -ated. [f. ppl. stem of L. type **intumulāre* to bury (see INTUMIL), f. *in-* (IN-²) + *tumulus* burial mound.] *trans.* To place in a tomb: to entomb, bury.

(In earlier use only in pa. pple. *intumulate*. *Intumulit* in quot. 1535, may be pa. pple. of *intumule* = INTUMIL.)

1535 STEWART *Cron. Scot.* III. 271 Intumulat in Drumfermling wes syne. *Ibid.* 443 And syne in Scone intumulit wes he. *a* **1548** HALL *Chron.*, *Edw. IV* 250 Whose corps was..princely enterred and intumulate. *Ibid.*, *Hen. VI* (1809) 303 He was removed to Winsore and there in a new vawte newly intumilate. **1584** B. R. tr. *Herodotus* 45 The dead bodyes of their countrimen..they never bury or intumulate. **1598** ROUS *Thule* II. I. xiv, His ioy intumulated in the graue. **1606** BIRNIE *Kirk-Buriall* xix. F iij, What tombe could intumulate any entyre race of folks?

Hence †**in,tumu'lation**, entombment, burial.

1658 PHILLIPS, *Intumulation*, a throwing a heap upon, a burying.

†**in'tunable**, *a. Obs.* [IN-³.] = UNTUNABLE.

1706 in PHILLIPS.

intune, variant of ENTUNE *v.*, *Obs.*

†**in'turbidate**, *v. Obs. rare.* [f. IN-² + ppl. stem of late L. *turbidāre* to confuse, f. *turbidus* confused.] *trans.* To render turbid; to disturb, confuse.

1684 R. WALLER *Nat. Exper.* 134 A little white Cloud.. which by shaking, diffuses it self through all the Liquor, and inturbidats it. *a* **1834** COLERIDGE *Lit. Rem.* (1838) III. 147 The confusion of ideas and conceptions under the same term painfully inturbidates his theology.

inturgescence (ɪntɜ:'dʒɛsəns). *rare.* [f. late L. *inturgēsc-ĕre* to swell up (f. *in-*, IN-² + *turgēscĕre*, inceptive of *turgēre* to be swollen) + -ENCE.] The action of swelling up; a swollen condition.

1755 in JOHNSON. In mod. dicts.

†**intur'gescency.** *Obs.* [f. as prec. + -ENCY.] The quality of being swollen; *concr.* a swelling.

1650 SIR T. BROWNE *Pseud. Ep.* (ed. 2) VII. xiii. 312 Inturgescencies caused first at the bottome, and carrying the upper part before them.

inturn ('ɪntɜ:n), *sb.* [IN *adv.* 11 d.]

†**1.** An inward turn, bend, or curve. *Obs.*

1690 J. BANISTER in *Phil. Trans.* XVII. 671 And in the middle of the Entry on the Inturn of the Shell, grows a small white Tooth.

2. The turning in of the toes; also, a step in dancing.

1599 MASSINGER, etc. *Old Law* III. ii, (*Dancing-Master*) Now here's your in-turn, and your trick above ground. **1860** WRAXALL tr. *Kohl's Wand. Lake Superior* 5 The women turn their toes in slightly..a bent and heavily-laden body always produces an inturn of the feet.

†**3.** In wrestling: The act of putting a leg between the thighs of an opponent and lifting him up. Hence ***to get the inturn***, ***to hold a person upon the inturn***: to succeed in applying this device in wrestling. Also *fig. Obs.*

1602 CAREW *Cornwall* 76a, Many Sleights and tricks appertaine hereunto..such are the Trip, fore-Trip, Inturne, the Faulx. **1652** BENLOWES *Theoph.* XI. xiii, If Bacchus th' Inturn gets, down conscience goes and all. **1683** E. HOOKER *Pref. Pordage's Mystic Div.* 90 An handfull it is, as it were, of wrastling Saincts, who..have got within Him and hold Him..upon the In-turn, and wil not let Him go, but there keep him. **1690** D'URFEY *Collin's Walk* II. 74 By Strength or'e buttock cross to hawl him, And with a trip i' th' Inturn maul him.

4. *Curling.* An inward turn of the elbow made in delivering a stone.

1890 [see OUT-TURN c]. **1897** *Encycl. Sport* I. 262/1 The inturn is made when the curl is to be toward the right. **1923** G. RAE *Langsyne in Braefoot* iv. 42, I want the inturn, an' I

want ye here. Dinna lie back for ony sake. **1969** R. WELSH *Beginner's Guide Curling* xi. 83 Almost all beginners are taught first to play the in-turn.

†**in'turn**, *v. Obs. rare.* [f. IN *adv.* + TURN *v.*, after L. *invertĕre.*] *trans.* To invert, to turn round.

1573 TWYNE *Æneid* XI. Hhjb, Til moystie night..the heauen inturnd [*invertit cœlum*] and whole with starres replenisht had.

inturned ('ɪn,tɜːnd), *ppl. a.* [IN *adv.* 11 b.] Turned inward.

1858 J. BROWN *Horæ Subs.* (1863) 122 His broad, simple, childlike, in-turned feet. *a* **1900** *Mod. Newsp.*, Those in-turned toes. **1906** R. H. BENSON *Queen's Tragedy* III. iv. 367 She..touched the palms of her hands with her in-turned fingers. **1923** D. H. LAWRENCE *Birds, Beasts & Flowers* 6 The fig-fruit: Involved, Inturned, The flowering all inward and womb-fibrilled. **1967** *Antiquaries Jrnl.* XLVII. 256 The ditch as now defined with its right-angle turn near the western corner of the Arbour and its possible inturned entrance is best interpreted as the defence or boundary work of a Belgic *oppidum*.

†**in'turnement.** *Obs.* [Deriv. of *turnement*, TOURNAMENT; the pref. appears to be incorrect and meaningless.] = TOURNAMENT.

c **1440** *Partonope* 5148 Thus here shall be thys Inturnement And I am assented to here entent. *Ibid.* 5275, I shall make hem leve her entent And anulle all this Inturnement.

inturning ('ɪn,tɜːnɪŋ), *vbl. sb.* [IN *adv.* 11 c.] A turning in. Also *attrib.*

1382 WYCLIF *Gen.* xlii. 27 That he myȝte ȝyue to his beest meete in an inturnyng place to reste [Vulg. *in diversorio*]. **1897** *Allbutt's Syst. Med.* III. 821 The in-turning of the bowel wall is in the direction of the anus.

†**'intuse.** *Obs. rare*⁻¹. [f. L. *intūs-um*, pa. pple. of *intundĕre* to bruise.] A bruise.

1590 SPENSER *F.Q.* III. v. 33 And, after having searcht the intuse deepe, She with her scarf did bind the wound, from cold to keepe.

intussuscept (,ɪntəssə'sɛpt), *v. Path.* [f. L. *intus* within + *suscept-*, ppl. stem of *suscipĕre* to take up: after next.] *trans.* To take up within itself or some other part; to introvert, to invaginate: said spec. of part of a bowel. Hence **intussu'scepted** *ppl. a.*

1802 *Med. & Physical Jrnl.* VII. 36 The part of the intestine inflated by Mr. Muir, was an intus-suscepted portion. **1835** GREGORY *The. Med.* (ed. 4) VII. v. 542 The intussuscepted portion of intestine sloughing off. **1897** *Allbutt's Syst. Med.* III. 711 A case in which the ileum below Meckel's diverticulum became intussuscepted into the diverticulum. *Ibid.* 874 The strangulated loop, or the intussuscepted gut may become gangrenous.

intussusception (,ɪntəssə'sɛpʃən). [f. L. *intus* within + *susceptiōn-em* a taking up, f. *suscipĕre* to take up: cf. F. *intussusception* (1705 in Hatz.-Darm.) and INTROSUSCEPTION.]

1. a. A taking within; absorption into itself.

1707 *Curios. in Husb. & Gard.* 29 Plants..receive their Nourishment by *Intus-susception*. **1836–9** TODD *Cycl. Anat.* II. 317/2 Intus-susception of one germ within another. **1881** HUXLEY *Sc. & Cult.* xi. 278 A particle of dry gelatine may be swelled up by the intussusception of water.

b. *transf.* and *fig.* The taking in of things immaterial; e.g. of notions or ideas into the mind.

1860 O. W. HOLMES *Prof. Breakf.-t.* x. (Paterson) 224 This intussusception of the ideas of inanimate objects. **1861** MAX MÜLLER *Sc. Lang.* I. 325, I..take this view of the gradual formation of language by agglutination, as opposed to intussusception. **1888** E. SALTUS *Tristrem Varick* (1889) 151 Resuscitations of hope, and intussusceptions of her presence. **1898** *Month* June 595 Like language, dogma is modified by desuetude, by intussusception, by neology.

2. *Phys.* and *Biol.* The taking in of foreign matter by a living organism and its conversion into organic tissue. In *Veg. Phys.* (see quot. 1882), opposed to apposition, or the deposition of new particles in layers on the inner side of the cell-wall.

1764 PLATT in *Phil. Trans.* LIV. 40 The Belemnite seems to be formed by apposition, and the Aculeus or Spine by protrusion, or, as Mr. Reaumur calls it, by intus-susception. **1771** *Phil. Trans.* LXI. 239 Some will have them [shells] increase by intussusception, and others by juxtaposition. **1835–6** TODD *Cycl. Anat.* I. 123/2 Increase in the unorganized world happens through *juxta-position*, in the organic through *intus-susception*. **1875** BENNETT & DYER *Sachs' Bot.* 31 The growth also of such thicknesses as project outwardly, like the combs and spines of pollen-grains, &c., can only be explained by intussusception, not by apposition. **1881** MIVART *Cat* 167 The intimate way in which assimilation takes place, is named intussusception. **1882** GILBURT in *Jrnl. Quekett Club* Ser. II. No. 1. 23 Growth of the cell-wall takes place by intussusception, i.e. the intercalation or insertion of new molecules between those already existing.

3. *Path.* **a.** The inversion of one portion of intestine and its reception within an adjacent portion; invagination; introversion; an instance of this. Also, the mass of intestine involved in this.

1802 *Med. & Physical Jrnl.* VII. 36 Intestinal intus-susceptions vary much in their extent, situation, and other circumstances. **1811** HOOPER *Med. Dict.*, *Intus-susception*, a disease of the intestinal tube, and most frequently of the small intestines; it consists in a portion of gut passing for some length within another portion. **1827** ABERNETHY *Surg. Wks.* II. 241 An irritable and striving action of the bowel, which produces a kind of intussusception. **1838** *Guy's Hosp. Rep.* III. 332 There were four intus-susceptions of the small intestines. **1878** T. BRYANT *Pract. Surg.* I. 627 Intussusceptions may occur at any period, though more common in infancy and child-life. **1960, 1970** [see INTUSSUSCEPTUM]. **1970** H. M. SPIRO *Clin. Gastroenterol.* xxii. 356/1 At laparotomy, the intussusception is easily recognized and reduced or..resected.

b. An insertion resembling an intestinal intussusception.

1811–31 BENTHAM *Logic* iv. Wks. 1843 VIII. 257 There has been framed a whole nest of physical aggregates, one within another, in a long chain or series of intus-susceptions or enclosures. **1836–9** TODD *Cycl. Anat.* II. 877/1 Each segment of the insect forms a slight intussusception.

intussusceptive (,ɪntəssə'sɛptɪv), *a.* [f. as INTUSSUSCEPT + -IVE.] Characterized by or of the nature of intussusception.

1882 S. H. VINES in *Nature* XXVI. 595/2 Naegeli.. believed that the mode of growth [of cell-walls] was intussusceptive with subsequent differentiation of layers.

intussusceptum (,ɪntəssə'sɛptəm). *Med.* [mod.L., neut. sing. of *intussusceptus*: see INTUSSUSCEPT *v.*] The middle and the innermost tubes of intestine (taken together) of the three present in an intussusception; also (less commonly), the innermost tube alone.

1857 DUNGLISON *Dict. Med. Sci.* (rev. ed.) 507/2 It [sc. *intussusceptio*] means the introduction of one part of the intestinal canal—*intussusceptum*—into another, which serves it as a sort of vagina or sheath. Generally, it is the upper part of the small intestine, which is received into the lower—*intussuscipiens*—when the intussusception is said to be progressive. **1884** F. TREVES *Intestinal Obstructions* viii. 168 The external of the three layers is known as the intussuscipiens, the sheath, or the receiving layer... The innermost cylinder is known as the entering layer..and the middle one as the returning layer... Taken together, these two layers form the intussusceptum. **1960** JONES & GUMMER *Clin. Gastroenterol.* iii. 93 An intussusception when fully developed is made up of three layers of intestine. The innermost or entering portion of the gut is called the intussusceptum... The middle or returning layer..is referred to as the resceptum and the outermost or ensheathing layer is the intussuscipiens. **1965** LUMSDEN & TRUELOVE *Radiol. Digestive Syst.* xv. 497 The barium may penetrate between the intussuscipiens and the intussusceptum, thus outlining the apex of the intussusceptum. **1970** H. M. SPIRO *Clin. Gastroenterol.* xxii. 353/2 Intussusception is the telescoping of the wall of one segment of the bowel into the adjacent distal portion... In formal circles, the invaginated segment is known as the intussusceptum, the receiving segment is the intussuscipiens.

intussuscipiens (,ɪntəssə'sɪpɪɛnz). *Med.* [mod.L., pres. pple. of *intussuscipere*: cf. prec.] The outermost of the three tubes of intestine which are present in an intussusception, and into which the other two are inserted.

1857, etc. [see prec.].

in-twa, in-two, in-twain, in-twin, in-twyn: see TWO, TWAIN, TWIN.

intwight, variant of ENTWIT(E *v.*, *Obs.*

†**in'twin**, *v. Obs. rare*⁻¹. [IN-².] *trans.* To couple, pair.

1613–16 W. BROWNE *Brit. Past.* I. iv, And to the Period of her sad sweet key Intwinn'd her case with chaste Penelope.

intwine, intwist, var. ENTWINE, ENTWIST.

†**'intybe.** *Obs. rare*⁻¹. [f. L. *intyb-us*, ad. Gr. ἔντυβον endive, succory.] Chicory.

1666 W. BOGHURST *Loimographia* (1894) 58 Gowrds, Dates, Figs, Intybes.

†**'intybous**, *a. Bot. Obs. rare*⁻¹. [f. as prec. + -OUS.] Cichoraceous.

1676 GREW *Anat. Flowers* ii. §12 In Scorzonera, Cichory, and all the Intybous Kind.

†**intyce, -tyse**, etc., obs. forms of ENTICE, etc.

1483 *Cath. Angl.* 197/1 Intysynge, *jncitans. Ibid.*, An Intysynge, *jncitacio.* **1552** HULOET, Intysement, *illicium.* **1560** J. DAUS tr. *Sleidane's Comm.* 183 No man that is of an other jurisdiction oughte to be intysed to theyr Religion.

intyre, intytle, obs. ff. ENTIRE, ENTITLE.

inuart, obs. Sc. form of INWARD.

†**inuch, -t**, obs. Sc. forms of ENOUGH.

c **1375** *Sc. Leg. Saints, Petrus* 502 Schame Inucht had he. *Ibid., Mathias* 345 It for lof Inuch suld be.

†**inu'dation.** *Obs. rare*⁻¹. [n. of action f. late L. *inūdāre* to wet, moisten.] The collection or accumulation of moisture.

1597 LOWE *Chirurg.* (1634) 80 By pressing on it [a tumour] with the two thombes, wee find it soft with great inudation.

inuendo, erron. form of INNUENDO.

inuert, inugh, obs. ff. INWARD, ENOUGH.

Inuit, var. INNUIT.

‖**inula** ('ɪnjʊlə). [L.: see ELECAMPANE.] A plant so called by Pliny, Columella, and other Roman writers; identified by mediæval herbalists with Elecampane (*Inula Helenium* Linn.); hence, in *Bot.*, the name of the large genus of *Compositæ* to which the elecampane belongs.

[**1813** T. BUSBY *Lucretius* II. Comm. xix, The inula was a sweet sauce made by the Romans from the herb of the same name.] **1822–34** *Good's Study Med.* (ed. 4) I. 445 The officinal inula of our own day, does not appear to be that of the Latins..let the quality of the Roman inula be what it may, we do not seem to possess this plant in the almost tasteless and inert root, employed under this name in our own day.

Hence **inu'laceous** *a. Bot.*, allied to or typified by the genus Inula. **inulic** ('ɪnjuːlɪk) *a. Chem.*, of or pertaining to inula: in *inulic acid*, a crystalline substance obtained by heating inulol (*Syd. Soc. Lex.* 1887). **'inulin** [-IN¹] *Chem.*, a white starchy substance ($C_6H_{10}O_5$), obtained from the roots of elecampane and other *Compositæ*. **'inuloid**, a soluble modification of inulin, occurring in the roots of Jerusalem artichoke, dahlia, etc. **'inulol**, a yellowish peppermint-smelling liquid ($C_{15}H_{20}O_2$), obtained from the root of Inula.

1813 SIR H. DAVY *Agric. Chem.* iii. (1814) 118 Inulin is so analogous to starch that it is probably a variety of that principle. **1866** *Treas. Bot.* 624/1 Starchy material called inulin, which differs from ordinary starch in being coloured yellow by iodine. **1875–9** WATTS *Dict. Chem.* 2nd Suppl. 670 *Inuloid*,..this is a soluble modification of inulin..Dried over sulphuric acid it has the composition $C_{12}H_{20}O_{10}$. $2H_2O$. **1876** BENNETT & DYER *Sachs' Bot.* 629 In some tubers (as the dahlia, artichoke, &c.), the starch is replaced by inulin.

inulase ('ɪnjuleɪz, -s). *Biochem.* [f. INUL(IN + -ASE.] An enzyme which hydrolyses inulin to fructose, found esp. in some fungi.

1893 J. R. GREEN in *Ann. Bot.* VII. 90 This transformation has been found to be due to a special enzyme, to which the name inulase may be given. It is a different body from diastase, for it has no action upon starch-paste. **1931** E. C. MILLER *Plant Physiol.* xi. 628 Inulase may occur with diastase but has no action whatsoever upon starch. **1965** FLORKIN & STOTZ *Comprehensive Biochem.* (ed. 2) XIII. 136 Systematic name: β-2, 1-Fructan fructanohydrolase. Recommended trivial name: Inulase.

†**in'ulcerated**, *a. Obs. rare*⁻¹. [IN-².] Ulcerated.

1632 J. HAYWARD tr. *Biondi's Eromena* 117 To fester an old long sithence inulcerated sore.

†**in'umbrate**, *v. Obs.* [f. ppl. stem of L. *inumbrāre*, f. *in-* (IN-²) + *umbrāre* to shade, f. *umbra* shade, shadow.] *trans.* To cast a shadow upon; to shade; to overshadow, put in the shade.

1623 COCKERAM, *Inumbrate*, to cast a shadow. **1762** tr. *Busching's Syst. Geog.* III. 43 The shores are bordered with charming walks and alleys, inumbrated with interlaced vine branches. **1802** J. JAMIESON *Use Sacr. Hist.* I. II. 441 How much more delightful to be inumbrated by the glory of the Lord. **1822** T. TAYLOR *Apuleius* 251 Her private parts were inumbrated by a thin silken garment.

Hence †**inum'bration**, overshadowing, shading.

1603 HOLLAND *Plutarch's Mor.* 1172 The obstruction and inumbration [in an eclipse] beginneth on that side on which that commeth first that maketh the said inumbration. **1658** PHILLIPS, *Inumbration*, a casting a shadow upon.

†**i'nuncate**, *v. Obs. rare*⁻⁰. [f. ppl. stem of L. *inuncāre*, f. *in-* (IN-²) + *uncus* a hook.] *trans.* To hook or entangle. Hence †**inun'cation.**

1623 COCKERAM, *Inuncate*, to incroach, to hooke, to intangle. **1721** BAILEY, *Inuncate*, to hook or entangle. **1730–6** —— (folio), *Inuncation*, a hooking into.

inunct (ɪ'nʌŋkt), *v. rare.* [f. L. *inunct-*, ppl. stem of *inunguĕre*, f. *in-* (IN-²) + *unguĕre* to smear, anoint.] *trans.* To anoint; to besmear (arrows) with poison; to anoint with ointment.

1513 DOUGLAS *Æneis* IX. xii. 106 To graith and til invnct a castyng dart, And with vennom to garnys the steil hedis. *Ibid.* X. iii. 47 Thow Ismarus..eik thar mycht men the se, Invnctand venemus schaftis. **1623** COCKERAM, *Inuncted*, anoynted. **1897** *Allbutt's Syst. Med.* II. 76 The patients.. were compelled to inunct themselves in a most thorough manner.

inunction (ɪ'nʌŋkʃən). Also 6 **en-**. [ad. L. *inunction-em*, n. of action f. *inunguĕre*: see prec.]

1. The action of anointing; smearing with, or rubbing in of, oil or ointment.

1621 BURTON *Anat. Mel.* II. v. III. i. (1676) 248/2 Fomentations, irrigations, inunctions, odoraments, prescribed for the head. **1663** BOYLE *Usef. Exp. Nat. Philos.* II. v. x. 211 Quicksilver, which by inunction may be made as well to salivate, as if it were swallowed down. **1756** C. LUCAS *Ess. Waters* III. 176 Celsus recommends..bathing, with or without inunction with oil. **1875** H. C. WOOD *Therap.* (1879) 392 The advantage claimed for inunction is that the digestion is less apt to be disturbed than when the drug is exhibited by the mouth. **1898** *Allbutt's Syst. Med.* V. 315 Mercurial inunction was ordered.

b. The anointing with oil in consecration and other religious rites. Cf. UNCTION. *Obs.* or *arch.*

1483 *Wardr. Acc.* in *Antiq. Rep.* (1807) I. 38 A coyfe to be put on the Kyngs heede after his inunction. **1509** in Maskell

Mon. Rit. III. 73 *note*, For the consecration, envnction, and coronation of the seid moost excellent Prince Henry. **1537** *Inst. Chr. Man* 1 b, They dyd call it..extreme unction, bycause it is the last in respecte of the other inunctions whiche be ministred. **1610** HOLLAND *Camden's Brit.* II. 145 Upon some small gift or oblation at the Baptisme, Inunction and Burial. **1686** AGLIONBY *Painting Illustr.* 247 The Sacred Inunction of King Francis the First..by this Pope Leo the Tenth.

2. *concr.* An ointment, liniment, or unguent.
1601 HOLLAND *Pliny* XX. xiii. II. 58 Many haue vsed an inunction thereof [Rue] to their eies.

3. *attrib.*
1898 *Q. Rev.* July 6 He proceeded to Aachen to be present at the inunction and coronation ceremony. **1899** J. HUTCHINSON *Archives Surg.* X. 137 On each occasion the inunction treatment had promptly cleared away all symptoms.

†**i'nunctment.** *Obs. rare*$^{-1}$. [f. INUNCT *v.* + -MENT: cf. ANOINTMENT.] Ointment.
1513 DOUGLAS *Æneis* XII. Prol. 146 Precyus invnctment, salve or fragrant pome.

†**inunctu'osity.** *Obs. rare*$^{-1}$. [Cf. next.] The quality of being inunctuous.
1794 KIRWAN *Elem. Min.* I. 198 Porcelain clay is distinguished from Fuller's earth, by colour, degree of cohesion and inunctuosity.

†**in'unctuous,** *a. Obs. rare*$^{-1}$. [IN-^{3}.] Not unctuous; without oil or grease.
1634 T. JOHNSON *Parey's Chirurg.* X. xxxii. (1678) 263 These things which are to be outwardly applied, are inunctuous Baths.

†**i'nund,** *v. Obs.* Chiefly *Sc.* [ad. L. *inund-āre*: see INUNDATE. Cf. OF. *enunder* (12th c.), *inonder* (13th c. in Hatz.-Darm.).] *trans.* To inundate, flood. *lit.* and *fig.* Hence **i'nunding** *vbl. sb.* and *ppl. a.*
1628 SIR W. MURE *Spir. Hymn* 195 Of ire what hudge, inunding spaite, had quenchde our of-spring weake? **1628** —— *Doomesday* 586 What ouerflowing spaite, Inunding this Theater great. **1631-2** *Acc. Burgh Peebles* (Rec. Soc.) 417 The schoole flore whilk wes invndit with the water. **1632** LITHGOW *Trav.* I. 13 Tyber..impetuously inunding his bankes. *Ibid.* VII. 317 Such inunding can not be called cherishings. **1659** FULLER *App. Inj. Innoc.* II. 18 Those Sholes of People..came into Jiutland, and thence Inunded the most of Europe.

i'nundable, *a. rare.* [f. L. *inundāre*: see -ABLE.] Liable to inundation.
1821 W. TAYLOR in *Monthly Rev.* XCV. 18 Dividing it [the country] into inundable and hilly districts.

inundant (ɪ'nʌndənt), *a.* [ad. L. *inundānt-em*, pr. pple. of *inundāre*: see INUNDATE *v.* and -ANT.] Overflowing, inundating, flooding.
1629 *Drayner Conf.* B iv b, The River (whose naturall Current, as it is most plentifull, so his excesse is most inundant). **1634** HEYWOOD & BROME *Witches Lanc.* v. Wks. 1874 IV. 252 It is in vaine to guesse at this my griefe 'Tis so inundant. **1635** HEYWOOD *Hierarch.* VIII. 530 A Torrent.. in the Spring and Winter inundant and raging. *c* **1750** SHENSTONE *Economy* I. 173 Thy voice, hydropic Fancy! calls aloud For costly draughts, inundant bowls of joy. **1874** PUSEY *Lent. Serm.* 346 What measure we bring thither of faith to hold, so much of the inundant tide of grace do we receive within us.

inundatal ('ɪnəndeɪtəl), *a. Ecol.* [irreg. f. INUNDATE *v.* + -AL.] Of plants: growing in areas subject to flooding.
1847 H. C. WATSON *Cybele Britannica* I. 65 Inundatal. Plants of places liable to be inundated in wet weather, but often dry in summer. **1897** G. C. DRUCE *Flora Berkshire* 575 Water Whorl Grass... Native. Inundatal. On the muddy margins of ditches, ponds, &c. **1926** *Nat. Hist. Oxford District* 88 Paludal flora (including uliginal and inundatal species).

inundate ('ɪnʌndeɪt, ɪ'nʌndeɪt), *v.* [f. ppl. stem of L. *inundāre* (f. *in-* (IN-^{2}) + *undāre* to flow): see -ATE^{3}.
The stress is now mostly on the first syllable, though this is not found in the dictionaries before *c* 1880; later dicts. still give preference to *i'nundate*. See note to CONTEMPLATE.]

1. *trans.* To overspread *with* a flood of water; to overflow, flood.
1791 W. BELOE *Herodotus* II. Note 39. 240 During the period when the Nile inundates Ægypt. **1796** H. HUNTER tr. *St.-Pierre's Stud. Nat.* (1799) I. 169 To produce an annual overflow of the Amazon..and to inundate a great part of Brasil. **1898** T. B. MACLACHLAN *Mungo Park* viii. 64 The rivers were overflowing their banks and inundating the land.

2. *transf.* and *fig.* To fill with an overflowing abundance or superfluity; to overwhelm, 'swamp'.
1623 COCKERAM, *Inundated*, ouerwhelmed. **1667** WATERHOUSE *Fire Lond.* 67 God has..strengthened the sphere and activity of the Fire to inundate things sacred and civil. **1798** WASHINGTON *Lett.* Writ. 1893 XIV. 60, I was inundated with letters, describing the crisis. **1831-3** E. BURTON *Eccl. Hist.* xi. (1845) 266 That strange mixture of opinions which were now inundating the world under the name of Gnosticism. **1849** COBDEN *Speeches* 80, I say inundate Ireland with Indian corn and good wheat.

Hence **inundated** *ppl. a.*, flooded.
1875 LYELL *Princ. Geol.* II. III. xl. 395 Columbus and other navigators, who first encountered these banks of Algae, compared them to vast inundated meadows.

inundation (ɪnʌn'deɪʃən). Also 7 en-. [ad. L. *inundātiōn-em*, n. of action f. *inundāre*: see prec. and -ATION. OF. had *inundacion* in 12-14th c. (perh. the immediate source); mod.F. *inondation* (Paré, 16th c.).]

1. The action of inundating; the fact of being inundated with water; an overflow of water; a flood.
1432-50 tr. *Higden* (Rolls) I. 35 The firste age began from the creation of man; the secunde of a meruellous invndacion of water [HIGDEN *inundatione diluvii*, TREVISA Noes flood]. *a* **1548** HALL *Chron., Rich. III* 39 The ryver rose so high that yt overflowed all the countrey..By this inundacion the passages were so closed that [etc.]. **1599** HAKLUYT *Voy.* II. 203 This place hath a great pond caused by the inundation of Nilus. **1607** MARKHAM *Caval.* I. (1617) 6 Free from all enundation or ouer-flowe of waters. **1726** CAVALLIER *Mem.* IV. 347, I embarked..on flat Boats, on which we were two Hours a crossing that inundation. **1834-47** J. S. MACAULAY *Field Fortif.* (1851) 86 The waters should be retained by dams, that they may accumulate in front of the intrenchment, and thus form an inundation. **1880** HAUGHTON *Phys. Geog.* iv. 192 Rich plains, which are fertilized by their periodic inundations.

2. *transf.* and *fig.* An overspreading or overwhelming in superfluous abundance; overflowing, superabundance.
1589 PUTTENHAM *Eng. Poesie* I. vi. (Arb.) 27 Then aboutes began the declination of the Romain Empire, by the notable inundations of the Hunnes and Vandalles. **1592** SHAKS. *Rom. & Jul.* IV. i. 12 And in his wisedome, hasts our marriage, To stop the inundation of her teares. **1607** E. GRIMSTONE tr. *Goulart's Mem. Hist.* 571 At last this inundation of earth stayed it selfe against 2. houses..which were covered up halfe way the walles. **1654** tr. *Martini's Conq. China* 64 By reason of a great inundation of Locusts which devoured all. **1659** *Gentl. Calling* viii. ¶27 By a steady opposing himself against the inundation of profaneness and licentiousness. **1767** *Woman of Fashion* II. 138 [They] let in an Inundation of impertinent Visitors. **1798** PENNANT *Hindoostan* II. 21 A Brahmin..by the most pathetic supplications endeavoured to avert this inundation of pollution. **1860** EMERSON *Cond. Life, Behaviour* Wks. (Bohn) II. 384 What inundation of life and thought is discharged from one soul into another through them [eyes]!

inundator ('ɪnʌndeɪtə(r)). *rare.* [agent-n. in L. form, from INUNDATE.]
1794 T. TAYLOR tr. *Pausanias' Descr. Greece* II. 377 [They] may be called the parricides and inundators of Greece. **1803** G. S. FABER *Dissert. Myst. Cabiri* I. 91 The Argives..built a temple to Neptune the Inundator.

inundatory (ɪ'nʌndətərɪ), *a. rare*$^{-1}$. [f. as INUNDATE + -ORY.] Tending to inundate or flood.
1860 tr. *Hartwig's Sea & Wond.* i. 9 The endeavours of the Dutch to protect their flat land by dykes against the inundatory waters.

†**inunder'standing,** *a. nonce-wd.* [IN-^{3}.] Not understanding; without apprehension.
1659 PEARSON *Creed* xi. 747 That such inunderstanding souls should..be furnished with bodies.

†**i'nungate,** *v. Obs. rare*$^{-1}$. [irreg. f. stem of L. *inungu-ĕre* to anoint + -ATE^{3}.] To inunct or anoint. Hence †**i'nungation,** inunction, anointing.
1599 A. M. tr. *Gabelhouer's Bk. Physicke* 42/1 In the 3 yeare this inungation is needles, and inutile. *Ibid.* 45/2 Theron inungate him with oyle olive.

†**inun'variable,** *a. Obs. rare*$^{-1}$. = INVARIABLE.
1535 TINDALE *Tracy's Test.* Wks. (1573) 432/1 Nothyng that hath happened sence hath chaunged the purpose of the inunuariable God.

†**i'nurance.** *Obs.* Also 6 enurance. [f. INURE *v.* + -ANCE.] The action of inuring or fact of being inured; habituation.
1571 GOLDING *Calvin on Ps.* xl. 6 His woorkes..by continewall enurance, doo far surmount the capacitie of man. **1659** STANLEY *Hist. Philos.* XIII. (1701) 624/2 Nothing doth asswage Pain more than constancy, and inurance to suffering.

inurbane (ɪnɜː'beɪn), *a.* [ad. L. *inurbān-us*, f. *in-* (IN-^{3}) + *urbānus* URBANE.] Not urbane; unpolished; esp. impolite, discourteous.
1623 COCKERAM, *Inurbane*, rusticall. **1818** J. BROWN *Psyche* 198 And by her inurbane behaviour, Half broke a heart. **1873** M. ARNOLD *Lit. & Dogma* (1876) 186 Just would this be, and by no means inurbane; but hardly, perhaps, Christian. **1881** *Scribner's Mag.* XXII. 101 The inurbane exaggeration of his [Carlyle's] violence of diction.

Hence **inur'banely** *adv.*, in a manner not urbane; without civility or polish; discourteously. **inur'baneness,** inurbanity (Bailey vol. II, 1727).
1610 BP. CARLETON *Jurisd.* 221 After his [Alexander's] death Vrbanus dealt very inurbanely: for hee drewe Mamphred in, excluding my selfe the true heyre. *a* **1687** PETTY *Pol. Arith.* (1690) 73 The very same People shall.. spend more than when they lived more sordidly and inurbanely.

inurbanity (ɪnɜː'bænɪtɪ). [IN-^{3}. Cf. F. *inurbanité* (Littré), It. *inurbanita* (Florio, 1598).] Lack of urbanity; rude or unpolished manner or deportment; esp. incivility, discourtesy.
1598 FLORIO, *Inurbanita*, inurbanitie, rudenes, discourtesie, clownishnes, vnmannerlines. **1629** (*title*) An Answer to Pope Vrban his Invrbanity, expressed in a Breve sent to Lowis the French King..Written in Latine by Ioseph [Hall]..Translated in English by B. S. **1645** MILTON *Colast.* Wks. (1851) 368 Such idle stuff..as his own servile inurbanity forbeares not to put into the Apostles mouth. **1728** MORGAN *Algiers* I. Pref. 6 The Algerines.. want nothing but less Pride and Inurbanity. **1799** W. TAYLOR in Robberds *Mem.* I. 250, I hope he attributes to me no inurbanity. **1825** *New Monthly Mag.* XVI. 253 The proverbial inurbanity of these official Cerberi.

inure, enure (ɪ'njʊə(r), ɛ'njʊə(r)), *v.*^{1} [f. EN-^{1}, IN-^{2} + URE, work, operation, exercise, use, a. F. *œuvre* work.
The form *inure* has now largely superseded *enure*; the latter, however, has a long independent history, and has been given separate treatment at ENURE *v.*, q.v.]

1. *trans.* To bring (a person, etc.) by use, habit, or continual exercise to a certain condition or state of mind, to the endurance of a certain condition, to the following of a certain kind of life, etc.; to accustom, habituate. **a.** Const. *to* (†*unto*), *inf.*
α. *c* **1489-1837** [see ENURE *v.* 2].
β. **1519** *Interl. Four Elem.* (Percy Soc. 1848) 5 But man to knowe God is a dyffycultè, Except by a meane he hym-selfe inure, Whiche is to knowe Goddes creaturys that be. *a* **1568** ASCHAM *Scholem.* II. (Arb.) 155 Who..could neuer inure their tong to wise speaking. **1616** DRUMM. OF HAWTH. *Bless. Faithf. Souls* in Farr *S.P. Jas. I* (1848) 20 Let vs each day inure ourselues to dye. **1649** MILTON *Eikon.* ii. 21 We see to what easie satisfactions..he had inur'd his conscience. **1700** PRIOR *Carmen Sec.* 435 Inure them in feign'd camps to real arms. **1781** COWPER *Hope* 7 The poor, inured to drudgery and distress. **1859** SMILES *Self-Help* iii. (1860) 61 He was early inured to work.

†**b.** Const. *with, in. Obs.*
1509-1561 [see ENURE *v.* 2 b]. **1528** ROY *Rede me* (Arb.) 56 The devils with coursses are invred, As authours there of with out fayle. **1556** ROBINSON tr. *More's Utop.* I. (Arb.) 40 The Frenche souldiours, which from their youth haue ben practised and inured in feates of armes. **1612** BRINSLEY *Lud. Lit.* iii. (1627) 13, I am well inured with this grievance, which you speak of. **1654** tr. *Scudery's Curia Pol.* 92 The Queen..had a soul so inured with afflictions.

†**2.** *intr.* for *refl.* To accustom or habituate oneself. *Obs. rare.*
1598 Q. ELIZ. tr. *Plutarch De Curios.* xii. 1 Let us invre if by an others hous we go Not to Louk in, nor rolle our yees to that wiche is within.

†**3.** *trans.* To put into exercise or operation; to exercise, to practise, to commit (a crime). *Obs.* (Chiefly in form *enure*: see ENURE *v.* 1.)
α. **1549-1667** [see ENURE 1].
β. *a* **1577** GASCOIGNE *Herbs, Voy. Holland* Wks. (1587) 172 The best almost in all their land..Wil (as men say) inure the same sometime.

4. *intr.* Chiefly *Law.* To come into operation; to operate; to be operative; to take or have effect. Often in form *enure*: see ENURE *v.* 3.
α. **1607-1888** [see ENURE *v.* 3 a].
β. **1589** PUTTENHAM *Eng. Poesie* II. xi[i]. (Arb.) 116 It inureth as a wish by way of resemblaunce in [*Simile dissimile*]. **1622** CALLIS *Stat. Sewers* (1824) 275, I suppose this release shall inure to both. **1651** G. W. tr. *Cowel's Inst.* 137 This Legacy shall inure not only to A. but to B. and his Heires also. **1718** HICKES & NELSON *J. Kettlewell* App. 4 The Decree of Deprivation doth not inure, 'till a Judicial Sentence passeth further upon us. **1850** GLADSTONE *Homer* II. 497 We are dealing with a relation that was not governed by rules, and that might virtually inure by usage only. **1879** PARKMAN *La Salle* 92 The results..were to inure, not to the profit of the producers, but to the building of churches.

Hence **i'nuring** *vbl. sb.*
1606 [see ENURING]. **1885** R. W. DIXON *Hist. Ch. Eng.* III. 472 The passing and inuring of the Second Act for Uniformity.

†**i'nure,** *v.*^{2} *Obs.* [ad. L. *inūr-ĕre* to burn in, f. *in-* (IN-^{2}) + *ūrĕre* to burn. Cf. INUST.]

1. *trans.* To burn in, brand in or upon something, impress by burning.
a **1619** FOTHERBY *Atheom.* I. iv. §1 (1622) 20 They.. would neuer haue lefte it vnnoted vpon any generall nation, if they could haue inured any such vpon them. **1646** GAULE *Cases Consc.* 59 He himselfe impresses or inures the Marke of the Beast, the Devills Flesh-brand, upon one or other part of the body. **1679** PRANCE *Addit. Narr. Pop. Plot* 14 The brands of infamy justly inured upon their Persons.

2. To burn in a flame, expose to the direct action of fire.
1709 ADAMS in *Phil. Trans.* XXVII. 25 Inuring each of the Ends into the purest part of the Flame.

†**i'nure,** *a. Obs.* [attrib. use of phrase *in ure*, in operation, exercise, or habitual use: see URE *sb.*] Accustomed, habituated; practised (*in* something).
1475 *Bk. Noblesse* (Roxb.) 62 By reason and by inure deliberacion of hymsilf and of the wise senatoure. *c* **1485** *Digby Myst.* (1882) III. 2102 þou blyssyd woman, invre In mekenesse.

inured (ɪ'njʊəd), *ppl. a.* [f. INURE *v.*^{1} + -ED^{1}.] Accustomed, habituated (see the verb); rendered or become habitual.
a **1619** FOTHERBY *Atheom.* I. ix. §5 (1622) 65 He.. deseruеth that inured note of Tullie (*Capitalis Euripides*). **1864** *Fine Arts Q. Rev.* III. 14 There is death in her very calm of inured insensibility. **1874** PUSEY *Lent. Serm.* 12 Why should not the habit of youth be that of middle age, and the wont of middle age be the inured custom of advanced age?

Hence **i'nuredness.**
1682 H. MORE *Annot. Glanvill's Lux O.* 32 Long inuredness to those Celestial Objects.

inurement (ɪˈnjʊəmənt). Also 7 en-. [f. INURE *v.* + -MENT.] The action of inuring, or state of being inured; habituation.

1586 A. DAY *Eng. Secretary* II. (1625) 44 An allurement and inurement to unthriftines. **1611** [see ENUREMENT]. *a* **1639** WOTTON *Educ.* in *Reliq.* (1651) 319 Education being nothing else but a constant plight and Inurement. **1828** P. CUNNINGHAM *N.S. Wales* (ed. 3) II. 301 Our feelings, at first melted by the sight of every moving spectacle, defy by gradual inurement the most horrific! **1874** PUSEY *Lent. Serm.* 264 Awakening the soul from the hopeless inurements in sin.

†**i'nurled,** *ppl. a. Obs.* [f. IN-² + *urle*, var. of ORLE, border.] Adorned with an 'orle' or border; bordered.

1599 T. M[OUFET] *Silkwormes* 49 An azur'd cloth of state ..with twelue braue signes and glistring stars inurld.

inurn (ɪˈnɜːn), *v.* Also 7 en-. [IN-².] *trans.* To put (the ashes of a cremated body) in an urn; hence *transf.*, to entomb, bury, inter. Also *fig.* Hence **i'nurned** *ppl. a.*, **i'nurning** *vbl. sb.*; **i'nurnment**, the process of placing the ashes of a cremated body into an urn.

1602 SHAKS. *Ham.* I. iv. 49 Why the Sepulcher Wherein we saw thee quietly enurn'd, Hath op'd his ponderous and Marble iawes, To cast thee vp againe? *a* **1711** KEN *Hymns Festiv.* Poet. Wks. 1721 I. 350 Thither he return'd In his Birth-place to be inurn'd. **1715-20** POPE *Iliad* VII. 451 Let a truce be ask'd, that Troy may burn Her slaughter'd heroes, and their bones inurn. **1766** MRS. GRIFFITH *Lett. Henry & Frances* III. 160 Like the inurned Ashes, or embalmed Heart. **1819** BYRON *Juan* I. iv, There's no more to be said of Trafalgar, 'Tis with our hero quietly inurn'd. **1839** MRS. BROWNING *Sabbath Morn. at Sea* vi, I oft had seen the dawnlight..break Through many a mist's inurning. **1845** HIRST *Com. Mammoth*, etc. 117 If thou wilt but inurn, love, The ashes of the past. **1861** *Sat. Rev.* 7 Sept. 253 The body was sometimes burnt and inurned, but sometimes buried. **1934** *Amer. Speech* IX. 317/1 Olivet Memorial Park provides every service for Entombments, Inurnments, Interments. **1948** E. WAUGH *Loved One* 36 Normal disposal is by inhumement, entombment, inurnment or immurement, but many people..prefer insarcophagusment.

inusitate (ɪˈnjuːzɪteɪt), *a.* Now *rare.* [ad. L. *inūsitāt-us*, f. *in-* (IN-³) + *ūsitātus*, pa. pple. of *ūsitārī* to use often.] Unwonted, unusual, out of use.

1546 *St. Papers Hen. VIII*, XI. 95 A thing very strange and inusitate. **1624** F. WHITE *Repl. Fisher* 439 Bread may be called the bodie of Christ by an inusitate forme of speaking. **1656** BRAMHALL *Replic.* i. 59, I finde some inusitate expressions. **1881** *Academy* 19 Nov. 381/1 The word 'despicion' is dangerously inusitate.

Hence **i'nusitateness**, the state of being unused.

1888 *Sat. Rev.* 15 Dec. 706/2 Careful indications of the line which separates actual inelegancy or worse from mere 'inusitateness' [of words].

inusi'tation. *rare.* [f. as prec.: see -ATION.] The action of not using or the condition of being unused; disuse.

1802 PALEY *Nat. Theol.* xxiii. (1827) 529/1 The mammæ of the male have not vanished by inusitation.

†**i'nust,** *a. Obs. rare.* [ad. L. *inust-us*, pa. pple. of *inūrĕre*: see INURE *v.*²] Burnt in, branded.

1634 T. JOHNSON *Parey's Chirurg.* XII. ix. (1678) 298 The fire which is internal and inust into the part. **1647** H. MORE *Song of Soul* II. iii. III. lxix. That furious hot inust impression Doth so disturb his veins, that [etc.].

†**i'nustion.** *Obs.* [n. of action f. L. *inūrĕre, inust-*: see prec. and -TION.]

1. Burning.

1618 T. ADAMS *Serm. Bad Leaven* Wks. 1862 II. 354 A kingdom brought him to tyranny, tyranny to..inustion of other countries, among which Israel felt the smart in the burning of her cities and massacring her inhabitants.

2. The action of burning in or branding with fire. Also *fig.*

1647 H. MORE *Song of Soul* Notes 429 That memory that is seated in the Mundane spirit of man, by a strong impression, or inustion of any phantasme..upon that spirit.

3. Cauterization.

1684 tr. *Bonet's Merc. Compit.* XIX. 711 The Chinese.. undertake to cure almost all Diseases by Inustion. **1765** *Univ. Mag.* XXXVII. 237/2 It may be..done by.. scarification, or by inustion. **1822-34** *Good's Study Med.* (ed. 4) III. 288 The latter..recommending that inustion should follow the application of the knife, instead of preceding it.

†**in'usual,** *a. Obs. rare*⁻¹. [IN-³.] = UNUSUAL.

1609 DOULAND *Ornith. Microl.* 25 Inusuall and forbidden Moodes.

in utero: see IN *Lat. prep.*

inutile (ɪnˈjuːtɪl), *a.* Also 5-6 -yle, 7 -ill. [a. F. *inutile*, ad. L. *inūtil-is*, f. *in-* (IN-³) + *ūtilis* useful. Orig. prob. stressed *inu'tile*, but *i'nutile* in A. Hume 1590.

It appears to have gone out of use, except as an occasional Gallicism, before 1700, and is marked as obsolete in Dicts.; but of recent years it has come into use again, perh. as a re-adoption from French.]

Useless, of no service, unprofitable.

1484 CAXTON *Fables of Æsop* III. vii, Despreyse and flee al synne and vyce, Whiche ben inutyle harmeful and dommageable. **1490** —— *Eneydos* iv. 19 This is but lytyll prowesse to the..vpon a deed corps to take vengeaunce soo Inutyle. *a* **1533** LD. BERNERS *Gold. Bk. M. Aurel.* (1546) Kkb, They haue aredyed the mylle, and..left it inutile. **1590** A. HUME *Hymns*, etc. (1832) 5 And did the tung inutile heill Of Zacharie that was dum. **1649** EVELYN *Liberty & Servit.* iv. Misc. Writ. (1805) 19 Their journey was not altogether inutill. **1677** GALE *Crt. Gentiles* IV. Pref., I am no friend to those vexatiose, contentiose, and inutile Disputes of these times. **1756** GRAY *Lett.* xci. (1819) II. 10 (Stanf.) Having been in a very listless, unpleasant, and *inutile* state of mind. **1862** MRS. H. WOOD *Mrs. Hallib.* II. xxiv. 288 Before she could oppose any answering, but most inutile [*ed.* 1890 useless] argument. **1884** *Evangelical Mag.* Feb. 49 Are our Christian temples..beautiful but inutile? **1894** *Daily News* 12 June 5/6 Another..member rising to carry on an obviously inutile conversation.

Hence **i'nutilely** *adv.*, uselessly.

1491 CAXTON *Vitas Patr.* (W. de W. 1495) II. 247 b/1 The moneye whiche was alredy inutylly spende.

inutility (ɪnjuːˈtɪlɪtɪ). [a. F. *inutilité* (1416 in Hatz.-Darm.), or It. *inutilità* (Florio), ad. L. *inūtilit-ās*, f. *in-* (IN-³) + *ūtilitās* UTILITY: see prec. and -ITY.] The quality or state of being useless; want of utility; uselessness, unprofitableness.

1598 FLORIO, *Inutilita*, disprofit, inutilitie, vnprofitablenes. **1603** —— *Montaigne* I. li. (1632) 165 The Mahometans, by reason of it's inutilitie, forbid the teaching of it [Rhetoric] to their children. **1651** *Life Father Sarpi* (1676) 11 The vanity and inutility thereof he did always and absolutely despise. **1731** LD. BOLINGBROKE in *Swift's Lett.* (1766) II. 135 The absolute inutility I am of to those whom I should be the best pleased to serve. **1786** BURKE *Art. Hastings* Wks. 1842 II. 132 The moral impossibility, as well as inutility in point of profit, of forcing a son to greater violence and rigour against his mother. **1825** LYTTON *Falkland* 14 To teach me, like Faustus, to find nothing in knowledge but its inutility.

b. An instance of uselessness; a thing or person that is useless.

1802 W. TAYLOR in Robberds *Mem.* I. 433 Give me the spot where victories have been won over the inutilities of nature by the efforts of human art. **1813** E. S. BARRETT *Heroine* (1815) II. 68 One of the beautiful Inutilities, who sits in sweet stupidity, [and] plays off the small simpers. **1884** HUNTER & WHYTE *My Ducats & My Dau.* xxviii. (1885) 438 Constantly engaged in the purchase of inutilities or superfluities.

i'nutilized, *a. rare.* [IN-³.] Not utilized; not made use of.

1874 W. CROOKES *Dyeing & Calico-print.* I. x. 80 The application [of native ultramarine] remained inutilised for several years.

in'utterable, *a.* Now *rare.* [IN-³.] That cannot be uttered; unutterable.

1603 DEKKER *Wonderfull Yeare* C iv, The dreadfulnesse of such an houre is in-vtterable. **1667** MILTON *P.L.* II. 626 Nature breeds, Perverse, all monstrous, all prodigious things, Abominable, inutterable. **1729** T. COOKE *Tales, Proposals*, etc. 30 Agenor feels inutterable Woes. **1859** TENNYSON *Vivien* 884 Kill'd with inutterable unkindliness.

invaccinate (ɪnˈvæksɪneɪt), *v. rare.* [IN-².] *trans.* To introduce into the system by vaccination.

1880 *Daily News* 12 June 2/5 An absolute guarantee against the propagation of those human diseases occasionally invaccinated with humanised lymph.

Hence **in'vaccinated** *ppl. a.*; also **invacci'nation**, introduction or implanting by vaccination.

1897 *Allbutt's Syst. Med.* II. 561 Noticed in cases of invaccinated syphilis. *Ibid.* 562 Lupus of the vaccination scars is discussed under Invaccinated Tubercle. **1899** *Daily News* 16 July 6/6 The supporters of vaccination..denied.. the very possibility of the invaccination of syphilis.

in vacuo: see IN *Lat. prep.*

in'vadable, *a. rare.* Also 7 -ible. [f. INVADE + -ABLE.] Capable of being invaded.

1611 COTGR., *Invasible*, inuasible, inuadible. **1755** H. WALPOLE *Lett. H. Mann* (1834) III. 108 The season has been the wettest that ever has been known, consequently the roads not very invadeable.

†**inva'dation,** erroneous form for INVASION.

a **1607** T. BRIGHTMAN *Revelation* (1615) 214 Inuadations by showers, and horrible tempests did spoile all things.

invade (ɪnˈveɪd), *v.* Also 6-7 en-. [ad. L. *invādĕre*, f. *in-* (IN-²) + *vādĕre* to go, walk.]

1. *trans.* To enter in a hostile manner, or with armed force; to make an inroad or hostile incursion into.

1494 FABYAN *Chron.* IV. lxi. 41 The Pictes and other Enemyes, which dayly inuaded the Lande. **1534** MORE *Comf. agst. Trib.* III. Wks. 1236/2 God shall not suffer the Turkes to enuade this lande. **1543** GRAFTON *Contn. Harding* 603 The kyng of Scottes..inuad Englande with an hoste of an hundred thousande menne. **1630** WADSWORTH *Pilgr.* viii. 80 When the Spaniards saw the King of France to enuade the Valtoline. **1728** NEWTON *Chronol. Amended* 36 Asserhadon invades Babylon. **1847** EMERSON *Poems, Blight*, We invade them impiously for gain; We devastate them unreligiously. **1858** FROUDE *Hist. Eng.* III. xii. 32 For a subject to invite a foreign power to invade his country is the darkest form of treason.

2. *transf.* and *fig.* To enter or penetrate after the manner of an invader. **a.** Of a physical agent.

1605 SHAKS. *Lear* I. i. 146 Let it fall rather, though the forke inuade The region of my heart. *Ibid.* III. iv. 7 This contentious storme Inuades vs to the skin. **1671** R. BOHUN *Wind* 218 An Island; which being invaded on all sides by the Sea-vapors and Winds, seldome enjoys [etc.]. **1753** SMOLLETT *Ct. Fathom* (1784) 53/1 Ferdinand..was actually invaded to the skin, before he could recollect himself so far as to quit the road. **1804** W. TENNANT *Ind. Recreat.* (ed. 2) II. 381 The deer invade the crops in such numbers. **1860** TYNDALL *Glac.* I. xviii. 123 The blue firmament..was more and more invaded by clouds.

b. Of sounds, diseases, feelings, etc.

a **1548** HALL *Chron., Hen. VII* 3 b, A deadly and burnyng sweate invaded their bodyes. **1602** MARSTON *Ant. & Mel.* IV. Wks. 1856 I. 54 A sodden horror doth invade my blood. **1673** *Lady's Call.* I. ii. §17 The tongue..in its loudest clamors can naturally invade nothing but the ear. **1738** JOHNSON *Van. Hum. Wishes* 151 Should no disease thy torpid veins invade. **1865** M. ARNOLD *Ess. Crit.* iv. (1875) 173 A sense of loss, of loneliness invades her.

3. *intr.* or *absol.* To make an invasion or attack. Const. *on* (*upon, into*), and with *indirect pass.*

1491 *Act 7 Hen. VII*, c. 11 §1 Ye verily intendyng..to invade upon your and our auncien ennemyes with an Armee roiall. **1534** WHITINTON *Tullyes Offices* II. (1540) 107 Of late this mischefe inuaded in to this commenwelthe of Rome. **1598** GRENEWEY *Tacitus, Ann.* I. ix. (1622) 16 Germanicus feared so much the more, because he knew the enemy would not faile to inuade, as soone as he vnderstood..that the riuers side was vndefended. **1733** POPE *Ess. Man* III. 298 Made To serve, not suffer, strengthen, not invade. **1814** *Spaniards* v. iii, 'T is for our monarch's realm, invaded on.

4. *trans.* To intrude upon, infringe, encroach on, violate (property, rights, liberties, etc.).

1514 BARCLAY *Cyt. & Uplondyshm.* (Percy Soc.) p. lxv, Why doest thou invade my part and portion? **1647** COWLEY *Mistr., Spring* v, You did their Natural Rights invade. **1648** *Eikon Bas.* iv. 20 Those Tumults..spared not to invade the Honour and Freedom of the two Houses. **1768** BLACKSTONE *Comm.* III. xvii. 255 Whenever..the crown hath been induced to invade the private rights of any of it's subjects. **1835** I. TAYLOR *Spir. Despot.* v. 218 That liberty of private judgment which cannot be invaded without crushing the human mind. **1852** CONYBEARE & H. *St. Paul* (1862) I. ii. 54 The jurisdiction of the Sanhedrin was invaded by the most arbitrary interference.

†**b.** To usurp, seize upon, take possession of.

1617 MORYSON *Itin.* I. 93 At this day the family of Este being extinct, the Bishop of Rome hath invaded this Dukedome. **1635** PAGITT *Christianogr.* III. (1636) 13 Having murthered his Soveraigne Lord Constance, invaded his Crowne. **1712** BERKELEY *Pass. Obed.* Wks. III. 137 By virtue of the duty of non-resistance we are not obliged to submit the disposal of our lives and fortunes to the discretion either of madmen, or of all those who by craft or violence invade the supreme power.

†**5.** To make an attack upon (a person, etc.); to set upon or asssault. *lit.* and *fig. Obs.*

1513 DOUGLAS *Æneis* IX. x. 2 Ascanyus..That wont was wyth his schot bot to invaid The wild bestis. **1526** TINDALE *Acts* xviii. 10 Noo man shall invade the that shall hurt the. *c* **1540** tr. *Pol. Verg. Eng. Hist.* (Camden) I. 53 The Brittons ..of a sodaine invaded the seventhe parte of the legion which was sente for the purveyance of corne. **1553** EDEN *Treat. Newe Ind.* (Arb.) 16 When this beast attempteth to inuade the Elephant. *a* **1578** LINDESAY (Pitscottie) *Chron. Scot.* (S.T.S.) I. 15 Thay dreid to prouock grettar troubillis ..give thay wold invaid so gret ane man. **1647** N. BACON *Disc. Govt. Eng.* I. lxvii. (1739) 169 No Free-man shall be.. outlawed, or banished, or invaded, but by the Law of the Land, and Judgement of his Peers. **1697** DRYDEN *Virg. Georg.* IV. 643 Audacious Youth, what Madness cou'd provoke A Mortal Man t'invade a sleeping God? **1753** *Scots Mag.* Sept. 469/2 James Miln..was indicted for invading and wounding, on the high-way, William Bennet.

†**6.** (Latinisms): **a.** To enter. *lit.* and *fig.* **b.** To go, traverse, or accomplish (a distance). **c.** To rush or enter hurriedly into (a struggle, etc.).

1590 SPENSER *F.Q.* II. x. 6 The venturous Mariner..Gan more the same frequent, and further to invade. *Ibid.* III. vi. 37 Matter..Which, whenas forme and feature it does ketch, Becomes a body, and doth then invade The state of life out of the griesly shade. **1598** GRENEWEY *Tacitus, Ann.* XI. iii. (1622) 143 Bardanes, who being a man of action and able to go thorow great enterprises, in two daies inuaded three thousand Stadia, and chased out Gotarzes..not one dreaming of his comming. **1700** DRYDEN *Pal. & Arc.* III. 519 Nor (captives made) Be freed, or arm'd anew the fight invade.

Hence **in'vaded** *ppl. a.*; **in'vading** *vbl. sb.* and *ppl. a.*

1598 FLORIO, *Inuaso*, inuaded or assailed. **1601** R. JOHNSON *Kingd. & Commw.* (1603) 173 By invading of their neighboures, procured unto themselves..most spacious kingdomes. **1634** SIR T. HERBERT *Trav.* 224 A defensive Warre..against the insatiate and invading Spaniard. **1720** WELTON *Suffer. Son of God* II. xxix. 750 To whom Leprosie itself, and all other Invading Sicknesses..submit themselves. **1837** CARLYLE *Fr. Rev.* III. I. i, You gathering in on her..with your..invadings and truculent bullyings. **1855** MACAULAY *Hist. Eng.* xiii. III. 333 Food for an invading army was not to be found in the wilderness of heath and shingle.

†**in'vade,** *sb. Obs. rare*⁻¹. [f. prec. vb.] The act of invading; invasion.

1591 *Troub. Raigne K. John* II. (1611) 107 Only the heart impugnes with faint resist The fierce inuade of him that conquers Kings.

†**in'vadent,** *a. Obs. rare*⁻¹. [ad. L. *invādent-em*, pr. pple. of *invādĕre* to INVADE: see -ENT.] Invading.

1655 DIGGES *Compl. Ambass.* 402 Upon any invasion..the confederates are mutually to proclaim the said King invadent, enemy.

invader (ɪnˈveɪdə(r)). Also 6–7 -or, 7 -our. [f. INVADE *v.* + -ER[1].]

1. One who invades or enters in a hostile manner.

1549 COVERDALE, etc. *Erasm. Par. Eph.* vi. 14 b, They make ready to beate backe the inuader. **1579–80** NORTH *Plutarch* (1676) 972 He..coming upon the Invadors, fought with them, and drave them beyond the Rhine. **1637** BP. HALL *Remedy Prophanen.* ii. §15. 207 The Tartars..are better invaders of other mens possessions, than keepers of their owne. **1651** R. SAUNDERS *Plen. Possess.* 19 They may resist an Invadour. **1748** *Anson's Voy.* III. x. 414 It continues exposed..to the ravages of every petty Invader. **1855** MACAULAY *Hist. Eng.* xix. IV. 314 Such an army as might be sufficient to repel any invader who might elude the vigilance of her fleets.

fig. **1728** YOUNG *Love Fame* v. 2 Nor reigns Ambition in bold man alone; Soft female hearts the rude Invader own.

2. One who intrudes or encroaches.

1637 BASTWICK *Answ. Inform. Sir J. Banks* 18 They are invaders of his Prerogative. **1698** FRYER *Acc. E. India & P.* 194 The Moguls are the Invaders of their Liberties and Properties, ruling tyrannically. **1709** STEELE *Tatler* No. 76 ¶1 Every Invader upon his Time, his Conversation, and his Property. **1871** FREEMAN *Hist. Ess.* i. 39 To see in the great Edward no reckless invader of other men's rights.

b. One who seizes or takes possession.

1651 HOBBES *Govt. & Soc.* xvii. §9. 305 That it may be known by Right to belong to the Receiver, Invader, or Possessour.

†**inˈvadiate**, *v.* *Obs.* *rare*[−0]. [f. ppl. stem of med.L. *invadiāre* to engage, f. *in-* (IN-[2]) + med.L. *vadiāre* = vulgar L. *wadiāre*, *guadiāre*, f. *vadium*, *wadium*, *guadium*, from Teutonic: cf. Goth. *wadi*:— OTeut. **wadjo*[m] pledge, GAGE; the spelling with *v* being due to association with L. *vas*, *vad-em* pledge.] 'To engage or mortgage land, etc.'

1706 in PHILLIPS. **1730–6** in BAILEY (folio).

inˈvaginable, *a.* *rare.* [f. INVAGINATE *v.*: see -BLE.] Susceptible of invagination.

1888 E. RAY LANKESTER in *Encycl. Brit.* XXIV. 187/2 The great proboscis of *Balanoglossus* may well be compared to the invaginable organ similarly placed in the Nemertines.

inˈvaginate, *a.* *rare.* [ad. mod.L. type **invagināt-us*, pa. pple. of **invagināre*: see next.] INVAGINATED.

1887 *Amer. Naturalist* XXI. 422 Invaginate gastrula.

invaginate (ɪnˈvædʒɪneɪt), *v.* [f. mod.L. type **invagināre*, f. L. *in-* (IN-[2]) + *vagīn-a* sheath: see -ATE[3]. Cf. mod.F. *invaginer* (Littré).]

1. *trans.* **a.** To put in a sheath; to sheathe. **b.** *Phys.* To turn or double (a tubular sheath) back within itself; to introvert.

1656 BLOUNT *Glossogr.*, *Invaginate*, to sheath or put into a sheath. **1835–6** [see INVAGINATED *ppl. a.*]. **1861** HULME tr. *Moquin-Tandon* II. III. iii. 136 The pseudo chrysalis..is half invaginated in the cast-off skin of the second larval form. **1882** H. S. BOASE *Creat. & Evol.* vi. 138 The wall of the planula is next pushed in on one side, or invaginated, whereby it is converted into a double sac with an opening. **1885** H. O. FORBES *Nat. Wander. E. Archip.* ii. 93 In some cases the rostellum (the upper margin of the stigma) is not invaginated down the stylary canal.

2. *intr.* To become invaginated.

1887 *Amer. Naturalist* XXI. 422 The endoderm cells.. will no longer immigrate one at a time, but will invaginate in a body, and thus in a more direct way establish a gastric cavity.

invaginated (ɪnˈvædʒɪneɪtɛd), *ppl. a.* [f. prec. + -ED[1].] **a.** Inserted or received into a sheath; sheathed. **b.** Turned into a sheath. **c.** Introverted.

1835–6 TODD *Cycl. Anat.* I. 184/2 A portion of the large intestine..must have become invaginated. **1857** DUNGLISON *Med. Lex.* 508 The invaginated or slit and tail bandage, is one in which strips or tails pass through appropriate slits or button-holes. **1878** T. BRYANT *Pract. Surg.* I. 627 When the invaginated portion of intestine becomes strangulated, the symptoms are acute. **1897** *Allbutt's Syst. Med.* II. 1013 This cyst contains the spirally rolled and much-wrinkled invaginated cestrode head.

invagination (ɪnvædʒɪˈneɪʃən). [n. of action from INVAGINATE *v.*: so in mod.F. (Littré).] The action of sheathing or introverting; the condition of being sheathed or introverted: intussusception.

1658 PHILLIPS, *Invagination*, a putting into a sheath or scabbard. **1822–34** *Good's Study Med.* (ed. 4) I. 167 Some writers represent the bowels as exhibiting after death a remarkable diminution in their diameter; some have met with invaginations. **1847–9** TODD *Cycl. Anat.* IV. 27/1 These little animals..recede into themselves by a kind of invagination of their own bodies. **1879** tr. *Haeckel's Evol. Man* I. viii. 221 The Gastrula..was originated by an inversion or invagination of the Blastula.

inˈvaginator. *Med.* [agent-n. in L. form from INVAGINATE *v.*] 'The wooden or other cylinder used for thrusting the skin into the canal in the operation for the radical cure of hernia' (*Syd. Soc. Lex.* 1887).

invaid, invaie, invail, invain, obs. ff. INVADE, INVEIGH, INVEIL, INVEIN.

in vain *phr.*: see VAIN.

†**inˈvale**, *v.* *Obs.* *rare*[−1]. [f. IN-[1] or [2] + VALE *sb.* Cf. It. *invallare* 'to enter or come into a valley' (Florio 1611).] *trans.* To convey into a valley; *refl.* to occupy a valley.

1612 DRAYTON *Poly-olb.* xiv. 229 What fountaine send they forth (That finds a river's name, though of the smallest worth) But it invales it selfe.

invalescence[1] (ɪnvəˈlɛsəns). *rare.* [f. IN-[3] + -*valescence* in *convalescence*.] The state or condition of being an invalid; ill health.

1730–6 BAILEY (fol.), *Invalescence*, want of health. **1895** 'J. O. HOBBES' in *Daily News* 24 Jan. 6/6 My long days and hours of invalescence have allowed me the leisure to read more than many of those who mainly write.

invalescence[2] (ɪnvəˈlɛsəns). *rare.* [f. L. *invalēscĕre* to grow strong, inceptive of *invalēre* to be strong against: see -ENCE.] Strength; health; force (J.).

1755 in JOHNSON. **1828** in WEBSTER. **1887** *Syd. Soc. Lex.*, *Invalescence*, recovery from weakness or disease.

†**inˈvaletude.** *Obs.* *rare*[−1]. Also 7 -itude. [ad. L. *invaletūdo*, *-tūdin-em*, f. *in-* (IN-[3]) + *valetūdo* health.] Ill health, sickness, bodily infirmity.

1623 COCKERAM, *Inualiditie, Inualitude*, weaknesse. **1647** R. BARON *Cyprian Acad.* 7 Paris..being plagued with an almost generall infection or invalitude. **1742** BAILEY, *Invalescence, Invaletude*, Want of Health.

†**invaletudiˈnarian**, *sb.* *Obs.* *rare*[−1]. In 8 invalit-. [f. as next + -AN.] A sickly, infirm, or feeble person, a weakling: cf. VALETUDINARIAN.

1762 *London Mag.* XXXI. 612 The present race of young invalitudinarians..this spurious, effeminate, mushroom breed.

†**invaleˈtudinary**, *a.* *Obs.* *rare.* [ad. med.L. *invaletūdināri-us*. f. *invaletūdin-em*: see prec., INVALETUDE, and -ARY.] Wanting health or strength; weak, infirm, invalid.

1661 *Papers on Alter. Prayer Bk.* 126 Whether usually the most studious laborious Ministers, be not the most invaletudinary and infirm? **1661** R. L'ESTRANGE *State Divinity* 42 This Point will be the Death of the Invaletudinary Ministers, (as our Ciceronians expresse it).

invalid (ɪnˈvælɪd), *a.*[1] Also 7 -ide. [ad. L. *invalid-us* not strong, infirm, weak, inadequate; f. *in-* (IN-[3]) + *validus* strong.] Not valid.

†**1.** Of no power or strength; weak, feeble. *Obs.*

1635 J. GORE *Well-doing* Ded. 1 The beames of the Moone are too weake and too invalid to ripen a tender grape. **1651** BIGGS *New Disp.* ¶281 If a remedy be invalid and not able to charge a disease. **1708** *Brit. Apollo* No. 14. 2/2 His Studies are barren, invalid his Pains. **1822–34** *Good's Study Med.* (ed. 4) III. 476 As though..the proportions belonging to the organ whose outlet is invalid, were distributed among the other organs.

2. Of no force, efficacy, or cogency; *esp.* without legal force, void.

1635 J. SWAN *Spec. M.* ii. §3 (1643) 33 The Chaldee Paraphrast..is so much the more invalid. **1651** HOBBES *Leviath.* I. xiv. 70 A Covenant to accuse ones selfe, without assurance of pardon, is..invalide. **1656** BRAMHALL *Replic.* viii. 340 That which was invalid from the beginning, cannot become valid by prescription or tract of time. **1768** BLACKSTONE *Comm.* III. vi. 84 The privileges granted therein..were of so high a nature, that they were held to be invalid. **1837–8** SIR W. HAMILTON *Logic* xxi. (1866) I. 427 The inference, though valid in itself, is logically,—is scientifically, invalid. **1844** LD. BROUGHAM *Brit. Const.* xiv. (1862) 202 The marriage with Catherine was declared invalid in the face of the whole facts of the case. **1874** SIDGWICK *Meth. Ethics* xiii. 352 His method will be declared invalid.

invalid (ɪnvəˈliːd, ˈɪnvəliːd, -lɪd) *a.*[2] and *sb.* Also -ide. [f. as prec., with modification of pronunciation after F. *invalide* (1549 in R. Estienne), ad. L. *invalidus*.

The early pronouncing Dictionaries (e.g. Bailey 1727) give this as *inˈvalid*; so that it appears to have been orig. only a special sense of INVALID *a.*[1], conformed in 18th c. in stress (rarely in spelling) to F. *invalide*. *Invaˈlides* (rime *deeds*) occurs in Prior (*a* 1721), and J. 1755 has *invaˈlide*, as *sb.* Webster 1828 has *ˈinvalid*, and this pronunciation (given in most American Dicts.), is commonly heard in England also, esp. in attrib. use, as 'an invalid sister'.]

A. *adj.* Infirm from sickness or disease; enfeebled or disabled by illness or injury. Now only as attrib. use of the sb.

1642 JER. TAYLOR *Episc.* (1647) 150 Narcissus Bishop of Ierusalem, was invalid and unfit for government by reason of his extreame age. **1696** PHILLIPS (ed. 5), *Invalid*,.. wounded, maimed, sickly. **1714** *Lond. Gaz.* No. 5193/4 Sir John Gibson's Company of Invalid Serjeants. **1748** LADY LUXBOROUGH *Lett. to Shenstone* 12 Dec., Because of the death and burial of one of the invalid servants. **1756–82** J. WARTON *Ess. Pope* (ed. 4) I. vii. 371 Men that were..grown invalid with age and thereby past all military action. **1865** M. ARNOLD *Ess. Crit.* viii. 263 That the donkey exists in order that the invalid Christian may have donkey's milk. **1869** SIR J. T. COLERIDGE *Mem. Keble* viii. 140 His invalide and suffering sister.

B. *sb.* **1.** An infirm or sickly person.

1709 *Tatler* No. 16 ¶2 Bath is..always as well stow'd with Gallants as Invalids. **1748** LADY LUXBOROUGH *Lett. to Shenstone* 23 Aug., It is well I am an *invalid*. **1775** ABIGAIL ADAMS in *J. Adams' Fam. Lett.* (1876) 126 'Tis late for me, who am much of an invalid. **1808** PIKE *Sources Mississ.* II. (1810) 199 Thus those poor lads are to be invalids for life. **1875** STUBBS *Const. Hist.* III. xviii. 71 He was for years a miserable invalid.

b. *transf.* and *fig.* Anything damaged, dilapidated, or the worse for wear.

1860 W. H. RUSSELL *Diary in India* I. x. 158 The carriages were old second-class invalids of English lines.

2. A soldier or sailor disabled by illness or injury for active service; formerly often employed on garrison duty, or as a reserve force.

1707 J. CHAMBERLAYNE *Pres. St. Gt. Brit.* III. 672 Her Majesty's Royal Hospital at Chelsea..26 Officers, 32 Serjeants..and 336 Private Soldiers, Invalides. **1715** *Lond. Gaz.* No. 5310/3 The invallids of each Regiment. **1731** *Gentl. Mag.* I. 355 —— Dobson, Gent. made Ensign of an independent Company of Invalids in Garrison at Portsmouth. **1748** *Anson's Voy.* I. i. 6 Five hundred invalids to be collected from the out-pensioners of Chelsea college. **1808** FORSYTH *Beauties Scotl.* V. 139 Fort Charlotte..is garrisoned by a small detachment of invalids. **1840** MARRYAT *Poor Jack* xxxv, There was the sergeant of the invalids.

b. *Invalides*, the *Hôtel des Invalides*, a hospital or home for old and disabled soldiers in Paris.

a **1721** PRIOR *Written in Mezeray's Hist.* ii, Yet for the fame of all these deeds, What Beggar in the Invalides,.. Wish'd ever decently to die? **1833** ALISON *Europe* (1849–50) I. iv. §97. 535 The invalids in the garrison of the Invalides refused to point their guns on the people.

3. *attrib.* **a.** (See A.) **b.** Of or for invalids.

1822 M. EDGEWORTH *Let.* 28 May (1971) 402 Her own invalid breakfast as she called it, a glass of Seltzer-water and milk! **1845** STOCQUELER *Handbk. Brit. India* (1854) 198 Persons belonging to the invalid establishment. **1847** W. M. THACKERAY *Vanity Fair* (1848) xli. 375 Sir Pitt's invalid-chair was wheeled away into a tool-house in the garden. **1859** DICKENS in *N.Y. Ledger* 27 Aug. 5/5 The hand-carriage was spinning away..at a most indecorous pace for an invalid vehicle. **1861** MRS. BEETON *Bk. Househ. Managem.* 893 (*heading*) Invalid cookery... A few rules to be observed in cooking for invalids. **1862** *Illustr. London News* 1 Nov. 473/1 An elongated invalid-chair is shown which is capable of being arranged as an ordinary easy-chair and of being extended into a camp bedstead. **1873** C. M. YONGE *Pillars of House* I. iii. 38 Wilmet could..do invalid cookery. **1875** KNIGHT *Dict. Mech.* 1193/2 The invalid-chair which has traveling arrangements is known as a perambulator. **1876** C. M. YONGE *Three Brides* II. xiv. 259 He diverged to the invalid-carriage he had secured. **1880** Invalid furniture [see *carrying-chair* (CARRYING *vbl. sb.* 4)]. **1893** *Daily News* 27 Mar. 5/5 Each year,..about October, certain sailing vessels which have the name of being 'invalid ships' leave England for Australia. **1899** *Price List.* Invalid furniture of every description. Invalid feeding cups. **1902** 'MARK TWAIN' *Let.* 23 Oct. in C. Clemens *Mark Twain* (1932) 95 We brought Mrs. Clemens through successfully in an invalid car. **1911** *Daily Colonist* (Victoria, B.C.) 27 Apr. 6/1 (Advt.), Wiese & Brohn's Oporto Invalid Port, best on the market. **1934** T. S. ELIOT *Rock* I. 15 And political religion is like invalid port: you calls it a medicine but it's soon just a 'abit. **1953** 'N. BLAKE' *Dreadful Hollow* I. ii. 28 She's got an electric invalid-carriage. **1967** *Guardian* 12 June 6/4 As an Oxford undergraduate with a muscular dystrophy, I am grateful for a Ministry of Health invalid tricycle. **1972** K. BONFIGLIOLI *Don't point that Thing at Me* i. 1 Invalid Port of an unbelievable nastiness. **1972** *Guardian* 4 Sept. 11/8 The middle-aged spina bifida sufferer who, after having saved to buy an invalid car, lost his job.

invalid (ɪnˈvælɪd), *v.*[1] Now *rare.* [f. INVALID *a.*[1]: cf. F. *invalider* (R. Estienne, 1549), and INVALIDATE *v.*] *trans.* To render invalid; to invalidate.

1643 PRYNNE *Sov. Power Parl.* I. (ed. 2) 42 Ergo this unlawfull Action of theirs..must nullifie, or at least invalid ..the lawfull proceedings of those worthy faithfull members who continue in it. **1660** *Trial Regic.* 180 If you have any-thing to say to invalid these witnesses. **1727** *Philip Quarll* 143 A way to invalid her Deposition. **1827** O. W. ROBERTS *Centr. Amer.* 171 If I assisted in repulsing her, I would, in some measure, invalid that impression.

invalid (ɪnvəˈliːd, ˈɪn-), *v.*[2] Also 9 -ide. [f. INVALID *a.*[2]]

1. *trans.* To affect with disease or sickness; to make an invalid; to 'lay up' or disable by illness or injury. (Chiefly in *passive*.)

1803 BEDDOES *Hygëia* ix. 208 To avoid being incommoded and invalided. **1837** COL. HAWKER *Diary* (1893) II. 123 The Queen..was invalided at Windsor. **1865** CARLYLE *Fredk. Gt.* xx. i. (1872) IX. 14, 200 of Daun's men died..300 more were invalided for life. **1898** *Dict. Nat. Biog.* LIV. 83/1 Receiving some severe wounds, which invalided him several months.

2. To enter on the sick-list, to treat as an invalid; to report (a soldier or sailor) as unfit for active service; to remove or discharge from active service on account of illness or injury.

1787 NELSON 8 Feb. in Nicolas *Disp.* (1845) I. 212 Mr. William Lewis, who was invalided to go to England for the establishment of his health. **1816** A. C. HUTCHISON *Pract. Obs. Surg.* (1826) 172 Bradley continued to state..that..he was no longer fit for the service, and hoped I would invalid him. **1836** E. HOWARD *R. Reefer* xxxvii, My duty..will not permit me to invalide you. **1882** MRS. CROKER *Proper Pride* II. iii. 77 He was invalided home, sorely against his will.

3. *intr.* To become an invalid or unfit for active work through illness; of a soldier or a sailor: To go on the sick-list; to leave the service on account of illness or injury.

1829 MARRYAT *F. Mildmay* xvii, I have invalided for them [fits] four times. **1834** M. SCOTT *Cruise Midge* xx, Poor Mr Donovan has had to invalid. **1850** R. W. SIBTHORP in J. Fowler *Life* (1880) 111, I cannot conceal from myself that I am invaliding, getting worn out. **1885** *Spectator* 10 Jan. 36/1 The conscripts die fast, they invalid at an inexplicable rate.

†**in'validable,** *a. Obs. rare.* [f. as next + -ABLE.] Of no force or effect; ineffective.

1634 SIR T. HERBERT *Trav.* 109 Some attempts he used but invalidable; to shoot darts or arrowes at it was one with ayming at the moone. **1638** *Ibid.* (ed. 2) 315 The wals.. are reasonable strong; but invalidable against.. Cannon.

invalidate (ɪn'vælɪdeɪt), *v.* Also 7 -vallidate. [f. L. type **invalidāre*, perh. after F. *invalider* (R. Estienne, 1549): see -ATE^{3} 7.] *trans.* To render invalid; to destroy the validity or strength of (an argument, contract, etc.); to render of no force or effect; *esp.* to deprive of legal efficacy; to make null and void.

1649 SIR E. NICHOLAS in *N. Papers* (Camden) 143 Concessions.. which they can insist on without evident invallidating yᵉ Regall power. **1651** G. W. tr. *Cowel's Inst.* 182 The omission.. doth not invalidate the Obligation. **1674** tr. *Scheffer's Lapland* vi. 17 This doth not at all invalidate our arguments. **1759** FRANKLIN *Ess.* Wks. 1840 III. 486 We found the governor had enacted a law there, invalidating the acts of the other colonies. **1801** *Med. Jrnl.* V. 169 To invalidate the evidence of Jane Waters, he calls her a poor ignorant creature. **1866** CRUMP *Banking* v. 107 Any alteration made with the consent of an acceptor does not invalidate the instrument.

Hence **in'validated** *ppl. a.*; **in'validating** *vbl. sb.* and *ppl. a.*

a **1716** SOUTH *Twelve Serm.* (1717) V. 195 It is again alledged for the invalidating of the Report made by the Disciples.

invalidation (ɪnvælɪ'deɪʃən). [n. of action from INVALIDATE *v.*: cf. F. *invalidation* (1642 in Hatz.-Darm.).] The action of invalidating or rendering invalid.

1771 BURKE *Powers Juries Prosec. Libels* Wks. 1877 VI. 160 The thirty-four confirmations [of Magna Charta] would have been only so many repetitions of their absurdity, so many new links in the chain, and so many invalidations of their right. **1863** A. GILCHRIST, etc. *W. Blake* I. 266 It is no invalidation of this high claim. **1891** *Law Rep.* Weekly Notes 122/2 The decision.. was subject to appeal, and the vote subject to invalidation.

invalidator (ɪn'vælɪdeɪtə(r)). [agent-n. in L. form from INVALIDATE *v.*] One who invalidates.

1869 *Contemp. Rev.* X. 133 The latest and most formidable invalidator of the genuineness of this letter.

invalided (ɪnvə'li:dɪd), *ppl. a.* [f. INVALID *v.*^{2} + -ED^{1}.] Made or accounted an invalid; 'laid up' or disabled by illness or injury; removed from service on account of infirmity.

1837 DICKENS *Pickw.* xlv, Mr. Pickwick cut the matter short by drawing the invalided stroller's arm through his, and leading him away. **1859** LANG *Wand. India* 26 Invalided officers who reside at the sanatarium during the summer.

b. Of things: Fallen into disrepair; damaged so as to be unserviceable.

1855 MOTLEY *Corr.* (1889) I. vi. 179 It looks like a hospital for invalided or incurable furniture. **1860** DICKENS *Uncom. Trav.* vi, Where five invalided old plate-warmers leaned up against one another under a discarded old melancholy side-board.

invalidhood (ɪnvə'li:dhʊd, 'ɪn-). [f. INVALID *sb.* + -HOOD.] The condition of being an invalid.

1863 *Reader* 16 May 477 [He] knocks him into confirmed invalidhood and paralysis with a brass candlestick. **1883** MISS BROUGHTON *Belinda* III. IV. i. 154 On the sofa, by right of her invalidhood, Belinda is lying.

invaliding (ɪnvə'li:dɪŋ), *vbl. sb.* [f. INVALID *v.*^{2} + -ING^{1}.] Removing or discharging from service on account of sickness or injury. Also *attrib.*

1796 NELSON 2 Aug. in Nicolas *Disp.* (1845) II. 229 Those made since him in invaliding vacancies, are confirmed. **1797** *Ibid.* Apr. 324 In the Sick List, three men, objects for invaliding. **1869** E. A. PARKES *Pract. Hygiene* (ed. 3) 536 There is invaliding also; that is, men with fatal diseases are discharged. **1897** HUGHES *Medit. Fever* i. 3 Though the rate of mortality is very low, the invaliding rate is high.

invalidish (ɪnvə'li:dɪʃ, 'ɪn-), *a.* [f. INVALID *sb.* + -ISH.] Of the nature or character of an invalid; resembling an invalid, somewhat of an invalid.

1855 *Cornwall* 299 [They] envelope their faces and throats in handkerchiefs, so as to present something of an invalidish appearance. **1873** GEO. ELIOT in Cross *Life* III. 221 We have been invalidish lately.

invalidism (ɪnvə'li:dɪz(ə)m, 'ɪn-). [f. as prec. + -ISM.] The state or condition of being a recognized or confirmed invalid; chronic infirmity or ill health that prevents activity.

1794 ANNA SEWARD *Lett.* 25 Oct. (1811) IV. 19 Social and melodious exertions, trying enough to invalidism. **1843** *Blackw. Mag.* LIII. 704 The solitary hours of his invalidism put an end to his folly. **1862** HOLMES *Hunt after Captain* in *Old Vol. Life* (1891) 28 He piped his grievances to me in a thin voice, with that finish of detail which chronic invalidism alone can command.

invalidity (ɪnvə'lɪdɪtɪ). [f. L. type **invaliditās*, f. *invalid-us* INVALID *a.*: cf. *validity*, and F. *invalidité* (16th c. in Littré).]

1. [Related to INVALID *a.*^{1}] The quality of being invalid; want of force or cogency; *esp.* want of legal validity.

c **1550** *Life Fisher* in *F.'s Wks.* (E.E.T.S.) II. p. lviii, By bringing in question the validitie or invaliditie of this maryage. **1586** A. DAY *Eng. Secretary* II. (1625) 8 To advertise you of the.. invaliditie of your conjectures. **1678** CUDWORTH *Intell. Syst.* I. v. 767 To shew the Invalidity of the Atheistick Argumentations, against an Incorporeal Deity. **1711** *Lond. Gaz.* No. 4861/2 The Invalidity of their Passports. **1841** MYERS *Cath. Th.* IV. §19. 280 Suspicion of the invalidity of the evidence. **1884** LD. BLACKBURN in *Law Rep.* 9 App. Cases 553 It was quite unnecessary.. to say anything about the validity or invalidity of a rule giving a borrowing power.

†**2.** Want of strength or efficacy; weakness, incapacity. *Obs.*

1589 J. PROCTOR *Ep. Ded. R. Robinson's Gold. Mirr.* A ij b, The vnstablenesse and inualiditie of riches in comparison to vertue. **1659** D. PELL *Impr. Sea* 485 All their helps have an invalidity in them. **1698** FRYER *Acc. E. India & P.* 88 The ill managing of which Penalties formerly, or the Invalidity to inflict them, may [etc.].

3. a. [Related to INVALID *a.*^{2}] Want of bodily strength or health; condition of being an invalid; bodily infirmity.

a **1698** TEMPLE (J.), He ordered.. that none who could not work, by age, sickness, or invalidity, should want. **1755** JOHNSON, *Invalidity*.. 2. Want of bodily strength. This is no English meaning. **1782** S. PEGGE *Cur. Misc.* 272 A Litter upon wheels.. adapted both to State and invalidity among the higher orders. **1808** DR. BURNEY in *Mad. D'Arblay's Diary & Lett.* VI. 335 During my invalidity at Bath. **1813** W. TAYLOR *Eng. Synom.* 292 Invalidity is a temporary infirmity, a constitutional deficiency of health or strength. **1891** T. E. YOUNG *Germ. Law Insur.* 18 Allowances for both invalidity and old age.

b. *attrib.*

1906 *Daily Chron.* 18 Nov. 3 A State scheme of invalidity insurance would lead to the destruction of the successful voluntary system. **1907** *Ibid.* 15 July 3/2 [Germany] The invalidity pensions go to all those of any age who are unfitted for relief. **1908** *Ibid.* 16 June 5/7 There is a great deal to be said for the German invalidity scheme. **1969** *Daily Tel.* 25 July 23 The new 'invalidity pension' will be introduced as part of the proposed earnings related retirement pension scheme.. due to come into force in 1972. *Ibid.*, The new invalidity pension is designed to take over after a person has been away from work through illness for more than 28 weeks.

invalidly (ɪn'vælɪdlɪ), *adv.* [f. INVALID *a.*^{1} + -LY^{2}.] So as to be invalid, without validity.

1705 HEARNE *Collect.* 23 Nov. (O.H.S.) I. 93 The invalidly deprived Fathers. **1834** CHITTY in *West. Morn. News* 30 Oct. 6/6 If the moneys.. were paid invalidly, the payments out.. were also invalid.

in'validness. [f. as prec. + -NESS.] The quality of being invalid; invalidity.

a **1630** DONNE *Serm.* xcix. IV. 304 And brings the subtlest plots.. not only to an invalidness and ineffectualness but to a Derision. **1727** in BAILEY vol. II. **1828** in WEBSTER, etc.

†**in'validous,** *a. Obs.* [f. L. *invalid-us* INVALID *a.*^{1} + -OUS. Cf. *validous*.] = INVALID I.

1611 SPEED *Hist. Gt. Brit.* x. i. §20. 1225 For Confirmation.. as if the Sacrament of Baptisme were thereby confirmed, and were inualidous without it. **1642** SIR E. DERING *Sp. on Relig.* 24 That the late Canons are invalidous. *Ibid.* 31 See how inconsistent and invalidous they are.

inva'lidship. *rare.* [f. INVALID *sb.* + -SHIP.] The condition or status of an invalid.

1830 BENTHAM *Constit. Code* Wks. 1843 IX. 418 Diminution is never produced by other causes than invalidship or death.

invalidy ('ɪnvəli:dɪ), *a. colloq.* [f. INVALID *sb.* + -Y^{1}.] Of the nature of an invalid.

1894 MRS. H. WARD *Marcella* III. 9 She's fussy, you know, and invalidy, and has to be wrapped up in shawls. **1912** 'R. DEHAN' *Between two Thieves* 626 We invaded the Crimea with a weakly, invalidy, or crippled army.

†**in'valley,** *v. Obs. rare.* [f. IN-^{2} + VALLEY *sb.*] **a.** *intr.* (See quot. 1611.) **b.** *trans.* To furnish or mark with valleys.

1611 FLORIO, *Inuallare*, to inually, to enter or come into a vally. **1627** FELTHAM *Resolves* II. [I.] lxxxvi. (1628) 250 Lest his fluid waters Mace, Creeke broad Earths invallyed face.

invalorous (ɪn'vælərəs), *a. rare.* [IN-^{3}.] Not valorous, cowardly.

a **1846** O'CONNELL cited in Worcester.

invaluable (ɪn'vælju:əb(ə)l), *a.* (*sb.*) [IN-^{3}.]

1. That cannot be valued; above and beyond valuation, of surpassing or transcendent worth or merit; priceless, inestimable.

1576 FLEMING *Panopl. Epist.* 172 *note*, Honest and faithful friends are an invaluable jewel. **1622** R. AYLETT in Farr *S.P. Jas. I* (1848) 203 This most rich inualewable treasure. **1652** KIRKMAN *Clerio & Lozia* 92 A Box wherein was her Pourtraiture of an invaluable worth. **1707** NORRIS *Treat. Humility* vi. 262 A good name.. is a valuable, or if you will, an invaluable thing, not to be valued by money. **1741** BUTLER *Serm. Ho. Lords* Wks. 1874 II. 268 A free government.. is an invaluable blessing. **1850** CARLYLE *Latter-d. Pamph.* IV. 29 All men know.. that to men and Nations there are invaluable values which cannot be sold for money at all. **1879** M. ARNOLD *Ess., Democr.* 37 Its negative intellectual action.. has been invaluable.

†**b.** Too great to be estimated; incalculable.

a **1694** TILLOTSON *Serm.* (1744) XI. 4818 In contemplation of his sufferings, and of their own invaluable loss. **1704** HEARNE *Duct. Hist.* (1714) I. 150 Books.. which do in some measure make amends for the otherwise invaluable Loss.

2. Without value, valueless.

1640 *Treaty at Ripon* (1869) p. xiv, The money I have received is so invaluable a sum that I have forborne as yet to pay it in. **1803** G. COLMAN *John Bull* III. i, I flattered myself I might not be altogether invaluable to your lady-ship. **1865** T. WRIGHT in *Intell. Observ.* No. 47. 385 An interesting and far from an invaluable labour.

Hence **in'valuableness,** inestimableness; **in'valuably** *adv.*, beyond valuation, inestimably.

a **1601** ? MARSTON *Pasquil & Kath.* II. 208 Loue, invaluably precious. **1625** BP. HALL *Serm. Thankskgiv.* Jan. Wks. 1634 II. 301 That invaluably precious blood of the Sonne of God. *a* **1656** —— *Satan's Fiery Darts quenched* II. (R.), Deny, if thou canst, the invaluablenesse of this heavenly gift.

†**in'value,** *v.*^{1} *Obs. rare*$^{-1}$. [f. IN-^{3} + VALUE *v.*] *trans.* To reckon of no value or worth.

1673 *Rhode Island Col. Rec.* (1857) II. 502 Other wayes the witness noe wayes to be invallued because an Indian.

†**in'value,** *v.*^{2} *Obs. rare*$^{-0}$. [f. IN-^{2} + VALUE *v.*] *trans.* To make valuable; to give value to.

1611 FLORIO, *Inualidare*, to inualue or make forcible.

†**in'valued,** *a. Obs. rare.* [IN-^{3}.] Of which the value has not been reckoned; *poetic* for Invaluable.

1603 DRAYTON *Bar. Wars* VI. xv, To Nottingham the Norths emperious eye.. Closely conuaies this great in-valued spoile. **1612** —— *Poly-olb.* xiii. 220 And with th' invalewed prize of Blanche the beautious crown'd. **1773–83** HOOLE *Orl. Fur.* XVII. 585 No vulgar price th' invalu'd treasure bought. **1806** T. MAURICE *Fall Mogul* I. iii. (Jod.), With rapture I accept The invalued boon.

†**in'vapour,** *v. Obs. rare*$^{-1}$. [f. IN-^{2} + VAPOUR *sb.*] *trans.* To turn into vapour.

c **1566** J. ALDAY tr. *Boaystuau's Theat. World* P vij b, All those that are invapored in the ayre, all those that the fier hath consumed.

Invar ('ɪnvɑ:(r)). Also **invar**. [a. F. *invar* (M. Thury *Nouveau Pendule Compensateur* (1897) 4), f. *invar(iable* invariable.] The proprietary name of an alloy of iron or steel (about 64%) and nickel (about 36%), which has a very small coefficient of expansion.

1902 *Encycl. Brit.* XXXIII. 805/2 For ordinary standards of length Guillaume's alloy (invar) of nickel (35·7 per cent.) and steel (64·3 per cent.) is used, as it is a metal that can be highly polished, and is capable of receiving fine graduations. **1928** J. E. HASWELL *Horology* iii. 29 The more recent discovery of the nickel-steel alloy, 'Invar', by Dr. C. E. Guillaume has, however, to a considerable extent revolutionised compensated pendulums. **1929** J. A. RATCLIFFE *Physical Princ. Wireless* iii. 50 The oscillating system.. is not an electrical circuit, but is a tuning-fork made of 'invar' metal, whose frequency remains very constant under all conditions. **1955** [see GRAVIMETER 2]. **1962** J. G. TWEEDDALE *Metall. Princ. for Engineers* iv. 106 Nickel may be used to reduce the coefficient of thermal expansion of steel, 36% reducing the coefficient practically to zero at room temperature when the carbon is 0·2% and manganese 0·5% (this alloy is sold in this country under trade names such as 'Invar' and 'Nilo 36'). **1971** R. J. P. WILSON *Land Surveying* viii. 134 Invar tapes are more delicate than steel tapes and cannot stand up to everyday survey use. Also the degree of accuracy they can provide is unnecessary on most survey work. However, they are invaluable on precise base measurements, all the British bases being measured with 100-ft invar tapes.

invariability (ɪn,vɛərɪə'bɪlɪtɪ). [f. next: see -ITY. Cf. F. *invariabilité* (1717 in Hatz.-Darm.).] The quality or condition of being invariable; unchangeableness; constancy.

1644 DIGBY *Nat. Bodies* xxxvii. (1645) 399 This invariability in the birds operations must proceed from a higher intellect. *a* **1771** R. WOOD *Ess. Homer* (1775) 145 To inquire, how such an invariability in the modes of life should be peculiar to that part of the world. **1830** HERSCHEL *Stud. Nat. Phil.* 275 The researches of Laplace and Lagrange have demonstrated the absolute invariability of the mean distance of each planet from the sun. **1864** BOWEN *Logic* x. 326 The assumed invariability of what are called 'the laws of nature' rests upon no foundation whatever but uniform experience. **1885** F. TEMPLE *Relat. Relig. & Sc.* i. 24 Having discovered invariability in any given case, we presume causation even when we cannot yet show it.

invariable (ɪn'vɛərɪəb(ə)l), *a.* (*sb.*) [f. IN-^{3} + VARIABLE, or a. F. *invariable* (Oresme, 14th c.; Cotgr. 1611 has '*Invariable* vnvariable'); so It. *invariabile* (Florio, 1611).]

Not subject to variation or alteration; unchangeable, unalterable; remaining ever the same, unchanging, constant; occurring alike in every case, unvarying.

1607 TOPSELL *Four-f. Beasts* 137 Their common properties of nature, such as.. remaine like infallible and invariable truths in euery kinde and country of the world. **1696** WHISTON *The. Earth* IV. (1722) 339 The Heat on the Face of the Earth would still be equal and invariable. **1709** BERKELEY *Th. Vision* §66 If there was one only invariable and universal language in the world. **1747** HERVEY *Medit.* II. 93 Clear as the Sun, the greater and invariable Luminary. **1770** *Phil. Trans.* LX. 364, I used an invariable pendulum which M. de la Condamine got constructed at Quito. **1825** MᶜCULLOCH *Pol. Econ.* II. ii. 141 The value of gold and silver is certainly not invariable, but, generally speaking, it changes only by slow degrees. **1841** MYERS *Cath. Th.* III. §5. 16 The conscience of man is no invariable and definite endowment, the same in all men everywhere and always. **1868** FREEMAN *Norm. Conq.* II. ix. 395 Banishment was the invariable sentence. **1871** C. DAVIES *Metr. Syst.* I. 17 Every system of weights and measures must have an invariable unit for its base.

†**b.** Of a person. *Obs. rare.*

1696 PHILLIPS (ed. 5), *Invariable*, firm, resolute, constant. **1718** HICKES & NELSON *J. Kettlewell* III. §86. 409 He persisted Invariable to his Principles.

c. *Math.* Of a quantity: Constant. Of a point, line, etc.: Fixed.

1704 HAYES *Fluxions* 77 By the Property of the [Logarithmic] Curve, the Subtangent PT is equal to an invariable Quantity. **1807** HUTTON *Course Math.* II. 304 In the algebraic expression $a^2 - bx$, where a and b denote constant or invariable quantities, and x a flowing or variable one. **1820** HERSCHEL *Examp. Finite Diff.* 126 This equation is to be integrated on the hypothesis of $y_2 \frac{dy_2}{dx_2}$ being invariable by the change of z to $z + 1$. **1828** MINCHIN *Unipl. Kinemat.* 44 An equation between the radius vector drawn to the instantaneous centre from an invariable point (or particle) in the moving body, and the angle which this radius vector makes with fixed line (or invariable row of particles) in the body.

B. *sb. Math.* An invariable quantity, a constant.

1864 in WEBSTER. **1885** in *Cassell's Encycl. Dict.*

invariableness (ɪnˈvɛərɪəb(ə)lnɪs). [f. prec. + -NESS.] The quality of being invariable; unchangeableness, constancy.

1654 W. MOUNTAGUE *Devout Ess.* II. ii. §3. 32 From the dignity of their [angels'] intellect, arises the invariableness of their wills. **1768–74** TUCKER *Lt. Nat.* (1834) I. 514 A variety of dispensations [may] be consistent with an invariableness of design. **1864** BOWEN *Logic* x. 324 We are compelled to infer its existence from the invariableness of the sequence in time between the two events. **1871** tr. *Hartwig's Subterr. W.* v. 43 The constant invariableness of their temperature.

invariably (ɪnˈvɛərɪəblɪ), *adv.* [f. as prec. + -LY².] In an invariable manner; without variation, unchangingly, constantly; without exception, in every case alike.

1646 SIR T. BROWNE *Pseud. Ep.* VI. vii. 307 Computing by these as invariably as by the other. **1751** JOHNSON *Rambler* No. 141 ⁋2 We come forth..invariably destined to the pursuit of great acquisitions, or petty accomplishments. **1797** MRS. RADCLIFFE *Italian* xvii, They were almost invariably silent. **1871** FREEMAN *Norm. Conq.* IV. xviii. 225 The usual, but invariably fatal, mistake was made.

invariance (ɪnˈvɛərɪəns). *Math.* [f. next: see -ANCE.] **1.** The character of remaining unaltered after a linear transformation; the essential property of an invariant. Hence applied to a similar property with respect to any transformation or operation. Also *attrib.* and **inˈvariancy.**

1878 SYLVESTER in *Amer. Jrnl. Math.* 77 It thus appears that every given homogeneous graph has an intrinsic character of capability or incapability of respondence to algebraical in- or co-variance. **1895** ELLIOTT *Algebra of Quantics* 6 There are in fact irrational and fractional functions which have the property of invariancy and covariancy. **1910** [see GALILEAN *a.*² b]. **1919** A. N. WHITEHEAD *Enquiry Princ. Nat. Knowl.* 41 This invariance, with these formulae for transformation, does not extend to Maxwell's equations for the electromagnetic field. **1941** COURANT & ROBBINS *What is Math.?* iii. 159 A particular consequence of the invariance of angle under inversion is that two circles or lines that are orthogonal, i.e. that intersect at right angles, remain orthogonal after an inversion. **1969** *Observer* 13 Apr. 1 These rules [*sc.* conservation laws of physics] are based on much more fundamental ideas about nature, called invariance principles. *Ibid.* 2/6 The conservation of energy is a direct result of the principle of 'time invariance'. This says that the laws of nature do not change with time.

2. *gen.* The property of remaining unaltered or of being the same in different circumstances; an instance of this, an invariant.

1939 *Mind* XLVIII. 50 This (heuristic) principle of ethical invariance is what I wish to oppose to the principle of ethical relativity. **1956** JAKOBSON & HALLE *Fund. of Lang.* iii. 28 The study of invariances within the phonemic pattern of one language must be supplemented by a search for universal invariances in the phonemic patterning of language. **1962** F. I. ORDWAY et al. *Basic Astronautics* xiii. 525 Drugs..might also minimize the psychological problems of space flight by reducing the tensions associated with sensory deprivation or invariance. **1964** *Language* XL. 202 Concepts concerning the invariance of linguistic units. **1973** [see INVARIANT *a.* a].

invariant (ɪnˈvɛərɪənt), *a.* and *sb.* [f. IN-³ + VARIANT.]

A. *adj.* **a.** Unvarying, invariable.

1874 LEWES *Probl. Life & Mind* I. 95 Each cause is invariant; it is only the phenomena that are variable. **1957** G. E. HUTCHINSON *Treat. Limnol.* I. ix. 634 The relatively invariant climatic conditions of the equatorial regions. **1964** M. ARGYLE *Psychol. & Social Probl.* i. 14 These so-called 'first-order factors' are not a satisfactory final solution, since they will reflect the numbers of tests of different kinds which have been used, and fail to yield a stable or 'invariant' set of factors. **1966** [see sense B. 2 below]. **1973** *Sci. Amer.* Feb. 26/1 The locations of nerve cells, the trajectories of nerve fibers and the spatial arrays of synaptic connections are invariant in all individuals of the same species. This invariance is termed neuronal specificity.

b. *Physical Chem.* Having no degrees of freedom (see FREEDOM 10 b).

1899 R. A. LEHFELDT *Text-bk. Physical Chem.* v. 208 Such systems may conveniently be called invariant, univariant, divariant, &c., according as they possess no, one, two, &c., degrees of freedom. **1923** A. C. D. RIVETT *Phase Rule* i. 25 When $F = 0$ the system is said to be invariant, since none of its variables may be altered at will without destroying the system in the sense of altering the number of coexisting phases. **1971** F. A. BETTELHEIM *Exper. Physical Chem.* xxvii. 259 Phase diagrams of ternary systems that are plotted on a triple co-ordinate graph have two important features: an invariant point, *O*, and the solubility curves.

c. *Math.* and *Physics.* Unchanged by a specified transformation or operation. Const. *under.*

1908 H. HILTON *Introd. Theory Groups of Finite Order* v. 62 If every element of a group G transforms an element g of G into itself, so that g is permutable with every element of G, g is called a normal, self-conjugate, or invariant element of G... Similarly, if every element of G transforms a subgroup H into itself, H is called a normal, self-conjugate, or invariant subgroup of G. **1914** L. SILBERSTEIN *Theory of Relativity* iv. 111 The principle of relativity excludes all such laws as are not invariant with respect to the Lorentz transformation. **1919** A. N. WHITEHEAD *Enquiry Princ. Nat. Knowl.* 39 They [*sc.* Newton's equations] are invariant for the spatio-temporal transformations from one such set to another within the Newtonian group. **1941** BIRKHOFF & MACLANE *Survey Mod. Algebra* vi. 153 A subgroup S of a group G is normal (in G) if and only if it is invariant under all inner automorphisms of G (i.e., contains with any element all its conjugates). **1955** W. PAULI *Niels Bohr* 34 The theory is invariant with respect to space or time reflection separately. **1968** [see COVARIANT B].

B. *sb. Math.* **1. a.** A function of the coefficients of a quantic such that, if the quantic be linearly transformed, the same function of the new coefficients is equal to the first function multiplied by some power of the modulus of transformation. Also *attrib.*

1851 SYLVESTER in *Philos. Mag.* Nov., The remaining coefficients are the two well-known hyperdeterminants, or, as I propose henceforth to call them, the two Invariants of the form $ax^4 + 4bx^3y + 6cx^2y^2 + 4dxy^3 + ey^4$. *Ibid.*, If $I(a, b, ..l) = I(a', b', ..l')$, then I is defined to be an invariant of f. **1873** H. SPENCER *Study Sociol.* (1882) 223, I learn that the Theory of Invariants and the methods of investigation which have grown out of it constitute a step in mathematical progress larger than any made since the Differential Calculus. **1908** J. E. WRIGHT *Invariants of Quadratic Differential Forms* Pref., The aim of this tract is to give..an account of the invariant theory connected with a single quadratic differential form. **1940** J. L. COOLIDGE *Hist. Geom. Methods* II. ii. 156 The invariant idea, thus launched, was eagerly seized on, especially..by the great twin brethren, Cayley and Sylvester.

b. Any quantity or expression which is invariant under a specified transformation or operation.

1908 H. HILTON *Introd. Theory Groups of Finite Order* vii. 99 An expression is an invariant of [a substitution-group] G if it is not altered when we perform on it every one of a set of substitutions which generate G. **1914** L. SILBERSTEIN *Theory of Relativity* iv. 112 It may be expressed shortly by saying that $x^2 + y^2 + z^2 - c^2t^2$..is a relativistic invariant. **1956** E. M. PATTERSON *Topology* i. 11 Such entities are called topological invariants, because they are the same for all topologically equivalent spaces. **1959**, **1967** [see COVARIANT].

2. *gen.* An invariant property or feature.

1939 *Mind* XLVIII. 39 There is a widespread view that the sole invariant of morals is their sociological function to secure the preservation and welfare of a social group. **1960** E. DELAVENAY *Introd. Machine Transl.* iii. 28 In 1949 Weaver pointed out that..one discovers statistical invariants, as found in cryptography.., semantic invariants, ..and logical invariants. **1966** J. J. KATZ *Philos. of Lang.* ii. 9 The study of language in general provides us with generalizations expressing the invariant features of language which we may particularize as the requirement that an empirically correct description of a natural language represents such invariants.

invariantive (ɪnˈvɛərɪəntɪv), *a. Math.* [f. prec. B. + -IVE.] Belonging to an invariant; not altered by a linear transformation of the original quantic. Hence **inˈvariantively** *adv.*

1853 SYLVESTER in *Phil. Trans.* CXLIII. I. 543 A form invariantively connected with a given form or system of forms. **1878** CAYLEY in *Encycl. Brit.* VI. 722/1 A curve $u = 0$ may have some invariantive property, viz., a property independent of the particular axes of coordinates used in the representation of the curve by its equation.

invaried (ɪnˈvɛərɪd), *a. rare.* [IN-³.] Not varied; unvaried.

a **1677** HALE *Prim. Orig. Man.* II. vi. 174 Their constant uninterrupted and invaried Motion. **1727** BLACKWALL *Sacr. Classics* I. 136 (T.) Change of the particles, or the lesser invaried words, that add to the signification of nouns and verbs. **1826** SCOTT *Diary* 4 Mar. in *Lockhart*, I daresay the young Duke would do the same for the invaried love I have borne his house.

†**invaˈriety.** *Obs. rare*⁻⁰. [IN-³.]

1611 FLORIO, *Inuarieta*, inuariety, constancy.

invaroid (ɪnˈvɛərɔɪd). *Math.* [f. after INVARIANT *sb.*, with termination *-oid*, after *criticoid*, etc.] (See quot.)

1884 R. HARLEY in *Proc. R. Soc.* XXXVIII. 57 But we have not in general ultra-critical functions, or, as it is proposed to call them, Invaroids... Sir James Cockle suggests that in a limited number of cases it may be possible by means of semicritical relations to form invaroids, that is, ultra-critical functions of the calculus analogous to the invariants or ultra-critical functions of algebra.

invasible (ɪnˈveɪzɪb(ə)l), *a. rare.* [a. OF. *invasible* offensive, of attack (14–16th c. in Godef. and in Cotgr. 1611).] Offensive, used in attack.

1489 CAXTON *Faytes of A.* IV. xiv. 273 They may go with diffensable armes and not inuasible..as to a cas of deffense and not for to enuayshe. **1501** DOUGLAS *Pal. Hon.* I. xlviii, Euerie inuasibill wapon on him he bair. **1611** COTGR., *Invasible*, inuasible, inuadible.

invasion (ɪnˈveɪʒən). [a. F. *invasion* (12th c. in Hatz.-Darm., frequent from 14th c.), ad. late L. *invāsiōn-em*, n. of action f. *invādĕre* to INVADE.]

1. a. The action of invading a country or territory as an enemy; an entrance or incursion with armed force; a hostile inroad.

1539 TONSTALL *Serm. Palm Sund.* (1823) 74 If they shal persyst in their pestilent malice to make inuasyon into this realme [etc.]. **1548** HALL *Chron., Hen. VIII* 174 b, No prince could hurte hym by warre or invasion. **1611** BIBLE *1 Sam.* xxx. 14 Wee made an inuasion vpon the South of the Cherethites. **1671** MILTON *P.R.* III. 365 The Parthian.. Found able by invasion to annoy Thy country. **1790** BEATSON *Nav. & Mil. Mem.* I. 145 The Spaniards..made a powerful invasion upon the infant colony of Georgia. **1851** D. WILSON *Preh. Ann.* (1863) II. III. ii. 32 A foe ever watching the opportunity for invasion and spoil. **1856** EMERSON *Eng. Traits, Race* Wks. (Bohn) II. 32 In the Danish invasions, the marauders seized upon horses where they landed.

b. *fig.* A harmful incursion of any kind, e.g. of the sea, of disease, moral evil, etc.

c **1566** J. ALDAY tr. *Boaystuau's Theat. World* Q vij b, Savegarde, and defende him, aswell from the invasions of wicked spirites as of other snares of the fleshe and the worlde. **1613** PURCHAS *Pilgrimage* (1614) 41 The Earth.. being freed from the tyrannicall invasion and usurpation of the Waters. **1665** BOYLE *Occas. Refl.* II. xiv, The fore-runners..of the Cold fit of an Ague, the first Invasion of that Disease having been preceded by the like Distempers. *a* **1735** ARBUTHNOT (J.), What demonstrates the plague to be endemial to Egypt, is its invasion and going off at certain seasons. **1847** H. ROGERS *Ess.* I. v. 257 It by no means appears that a momentary invasion of doubt, or even of scepticism, is inconsistent with a prevailing and habitual faith.

attrib. **1897** *Allbutt's Syst. Med.* II. 396 The usual symptoms of the invasion stage.

c. *Path.* The spreading of pathogenic microorganisms or malignant cells that are already in the body to new sites.

1891 F. P. FOSTER *Med. Dict.* III. 2011/2 *Invasion*, the process by which a particular organ or part becomes affected with disease or parasites existing elsewhere in the organism. **1892** G. M. STERNBERG *Man. Bacteriol.* III. i. 221 The invasion of the blood which occurs in anthrax and in various forms of septicæmia in the lower animals, induced by subcutaneous inoculation with pure cultures of certain pathogenic bacteria, does not generally immediately follow the inoculation. **1924** R. MUIR *Text-bk. Path.* xii. 332 Incision of the capsule may permit of renewed invasion by the tumor. **1949** H. T. KARSNER *Human Path.* (ed. 7) 312/2 Although certain normal cells may infiltrate into neighboring structures,..yet infiltration and invasion are properties of neoplastic cells. **1965** T. F. NEALON *Managem. Patient with Cancer* i. 13/2 Extension or invasion is the spread of a cancer by direct involvement of surrounding structures, lymphatics, or blood vessels.

2. Infringement by intrusion; encroachment upon the property, rights, privacy, etc of any one. Esp. in phr. ***invasion of privacy.***

1650 in W. S. Perry *Hist. Coll. Amer. Col. Ch.* (1860) I. 1 Suffer no Invasion in matters of Religion. **1736** NEAL *Hist. Purit.* III. 514 His government for almost fifteen years was one continued..invasion upon the civil liberties of his subjects. **1769** ROBERTSON *Chas. V*, VIII. Wks. 1813 III. 102 A voluntary invasion of the rights of his kinsman and ally. **1844** LD. BROUGHAM *Brit. Const.* xiii. (1862) 182 There were ..many invasions of the constitution. **1890** *Harvard Law Rev.* 15 Dec. 198 The common law recognizes and upholds a principle applicable to cases of invasion of privacy. **1912** KIPLING *Divers. Creatures* (1917) 2 Any complaint of invasion of privacy needs immediate investigation. **1967** H. MCCLOY *Further Side of Fear* i. 3 He would have no motive for coming by stealth... Besides, it was impossible to associate Mr. Erskine with any invasion of privacy.

†**3.** Assault, attack (upon a person, etc.). *Obs.*

1591 SPENSER *M. Hubberd* 1090 The Tygre, and the Bore ..raged sore In bitter words, seeking to take occasion Upon his fleshly corpse to make invasion. **1661–98** SOUTH *Twelve Serm.* III. 186 An House built out of the Road is exposed to the Invasion of Robbers. **1757** W. WILKIE *Epigoniad* I. 11 Prepares, by swift invasion, to remove Your virgin bride.

4. *Ecology.* The spread of a plant or animal population into an area formerly free of the species concerned.

1905 F. E. CLEMENTS *Res. Methods Ecol.* iv. 210 By invasion is understood the movement of plants from an area of a certain character into one of a different character, and their colonization in the latter. **1932** FULLER & CONARD tr. *Braun-Blanquet's Plant Sociol.* xiii. 308 The colonization of new unoccupied land by plant disseminules may be either by centrifugal or by marginal invasion. **1940** H. F. WITHERBY et al. *Handbk. Brit. Birds* I. 31 The slender-billed nutcracker... Not confined to conifer woods in its 'invasions' of Europe. **1958** C. ELTON *Ecol. of Invasions* vi. 111 We have to accept the proposition that invasions of animals and plants and their parasites—and *our* parasites —will continue. **1964** GOULD & KOLB *Dict. Social Sci.* 354/1 The process which occurs when one kind of population begins to occupy a territory (or an occupational niche) already occupied by another, or it increases its rate of occupancy... In human ecology *invasion* is restricted to this ..meaning.

5. *attrib.*

1915 MRS. BELLOC LOWNDES *Let.* 10 Mar. (1971) 57 No, I do *not* believe in either Zeppelins or an invasion... There is an invasion scare but I don't believe in that. **1923** W. S. CHURCHILL *World Crisis* (1938) I. xix. 404 An invasion scare took a firm hold of the military and naval authorities. **1941** *Times* (Weekly ed.) 15 Oct., One of the heaviest attacks of the war was made on the invasion coast. **1942** *R.A.F. Jrnl.* 3 Oct. 8 The men..who would fly tomorrow's dawn patrol

along the invasion coast. *Ibid.* 18 A tradition which was.. renewed in France in 1939..; over the 'invasion ports' of Northern France in 1940 and 1941.

Hence **inˈvasionist**, one who advocates or believes in an invasion; also *attrib.*

1853 COBDEN 1793 & 1853, Pol. Writ. (1878) 196 The other argument of the invasionists.. will be successful. *Ibid.* 210 These invasionist writings.

invasive (ɪnˈveɪsɪv), *a.* [a. F. *invasif, -ive* (15–16th c. in Godef.), in med.L. *invāsīv-us*, f. *invās-*, ppl. stem of *invādĕre*: see -IVE.]

1. Of, pertaining to, or of the nature of, invasion or attack; offensive.

a **1520** BARCLAY *Jugurth* (1557) 21 b, Ingines inuasiue to his enemies and defensiue to his company. **1570–6** LAMBARDE *Peramb. Kent* (1826) 301 Sallet, Shield, Sword, and so many other partes of defensive and invasive furniture. **1601** R. JOHNSON *Kingd. & Commw.* (1603) 178 Nothing so much hindereth the invasive ambition of this Prince, as the nature of places. **1788** *Hist. Eur.* in *Ann. Reg.* 47/1 The first campaign of an invasive war. **1880** A. FORBES in *19th Cent.* VII. 219 These premisses being set down, what course of invasive action did it behove Lord Chelmsford to pursue?

2. a. Characterized by or addicted to invasion; invading.

1598 DRAYTON *Heroic Ep., Mortimer & Isabel* (ed. Smethwick) 49 Guyne and Aquitan.. Charles by invasive arms again shall take And send the English forces o'er the lake. **1602** WARNER *Alb. Eng.* Epit. (1612) 365 As of their.. often fights with the inuasiue Danes. **1741** SHENSTONE *Judgm. Hercules* 13 If none check th' invasive foe's designs. **1858** CARLYLE *Fredk. Gt.* II. i. (1872) I. 50 He.. made truce with the Hungarians, who were excessively invasive at that time. **1881** SWINBURNE *Mary Stuart* IV. i. 135 A deadlier stroke and blast of sound more dire Than noise of fleets invasive.

b. *transf.* and *fig.*

a **1763** SHENSTONE *Economy* I. 32 Thy fell approach, like some invasive damp, Breath'd thro' the pores of earth from Stygian caves. **1830** I. TAYLOR *Unitar.* 127 That Christianity is essentially an invasive, expansive doctrine.

c. *Path.* Of, exhibiting, or characterized by invasiveness.

1926 H. T. KARSNER *Human Path.* xii. 332 It is probable that nearly all tumors begin originally as a somewhat invasive growth... The invasive character depends very largely upon the multiplication of the cells in the margin of the tumor. **1948** R. A. WILLIS *Path. Tumours* ix. 148 While proliferation is an important factor in invasive growth, it is certainly not the only or even the most essential one. **1970** [see INVASIVENESS]. **1971** *Brit. Med. Bull.* XXVII. 4/2 The attempt is made to relate the number of cases of carcinoma-in-situ entering a population to the number leaving it to become cases of invasive cancer.

3. Tending to intrude upon the domain or to infringe the rights of another; intrusive, encroaching.

1670 COTTON *Espernon* I. IV. 150 They rather chose.. to submit themselves to his invasive Government, than to acknowledge, and obey their own lawful, and natural Prince. **1724** SWIFT *Drapier's Lett.* Wks. 1755 V. II. 50 In no manner derogatory or invasive of any liberty or privilege of his subjects. **1875** MAINE *Hist. Inst.* vi. 163 As a proceeding invasive of tribal rights and calculated to infeeble them. **1881** G. MACDONALD *Mary Marston* xlviii, Sepia found her companion distrait and he felt her a little invasive.

invasiveness (ɪnˈveɪzɪvnɪs). *Path.* [f. INVASIVE *a.* + -NESS.] The ability of pathogenic microorganisms or malignant cells that are already in the body to spread to new sites.

1937 R. W. FAIRBROTHER *Text-bk. Med. Bacteriol.* vii. 69 The term *invasiveness* is sometimes erroneously used as synonymous with virulence; it, however, applies strictly to the power of the organism to invade the tissues of the host. **1949** *Cancer Res.* IX. 559/1 Evidence was found indicating that the invasiveness of the cancer cells depended on their lessened adhesiveness. **1967** R. A. WILLIS *Path. Tumours* (ed. 4) ix. 149 The factors determining invasiveness are still uncertain. Continued excessive proliferation is one of them. **1970** PASSMORE & ROBSON *Compan. Med. Stud.* II. xviii. 28/1 Virulence may involve invasiveness or toxigenicity; some pathogenic organisms are typically invasive, e.g. the causative organisms of typhoid fever.

†inˈvasor. *Obs. rare.* Also 5 *Sc.* -ar, 6 -our. [a. late L. *invāsor*, agent-n. from *invās-*, ppl. stem of *invādere* to INVADE; perh. immed. ad. OF. *invaseur* (15–16th c. in Godef.).] An invader.

1443 *Sc. Acts Jas. II* (1814) II. 33/1 Notour spulȝearis, distrubillaris, or inuasaris [**1566** inuasouris] of haly kirk. **1524** HEN. VIII *Instruct. Pace* in Strype *Eccl. Mem.* I. App. xiii. 27 To geve an assistence ayenist the invasour. **1536** BELLENDEN *Cron. Scot.* (1821) I. 132 The invasour of the common weill. **1602** H. ELY in *Archpriest Controv.* (1898) II. 196 To wᵗhstand and fyght against such invasors whatsoeuer.

invassal, -el, -alage, var. ENVASSAL, -AGE.

invay(e, invayle, inveagle, obs. ff. INVEIGH, INVEIL, INVEIGLE *vbs.*

[**inveccyde,** *sb.* and *a. Sc.*, app. misprint for *invectyve*, INVECTIVE.

1586 *Satir. Poems Ref.* (S.T.S.) xxxvi. title, and l. 15.]

invecked (ɪnˈvɛkt), *ppl. a.* Also 5 inveckit, 6 envecked. [f. *inveck* for *invect*, L. *invect-us*, pa. pple. of *invehĕre* (see INVEIGH) + -ED: cf. INVECTED.] Bordered by or consisting (as an edge) of a series of small convex lobes (see quot. 1610). Chiefly in *Her.*

1496 *Bk. St. Albans, Her.* C iv b, *Portat vnam crucem planam inuectam de coloribus albis et nigris*.. He beareth.. a cros of Siluer and Sable inuekkyt. *Ibid.* D iij a, The wich.. ar calde armis quarterit inueckit or of colowris inueckyt, for in them.. oon colowre is inuehit in to an othir. **1562** LEIGH *Armorie* (1579) 31 b, He beareth sable, a crosse enuecked Argent. **1610** GUILLIM *Heraldry* I. v. (1660) 27 As the former [ingrailed] doth dilate itself by way of incroaching into the Field, contrariwise this doth contract itself by inversion of the points into itself; in regard whereof.. it.. is called Invecked. **1677** PLOT *Oxfordshire* 144 These leaves of ours being all invecked, whereas the Trachelia are all indented. **1836** BAINES *Hist. Lancs.* III. 183 The eastern window [of Whalley Church].. is invecked with ramified tracery. **1889** *N. & Q.* 7th Ser. VII. 97/1 It.. reveals an under coat of pale blue with invecked edges.

inveckee (ɪnˈvɛkeɪ, -kɪ), *a. Her.* Also 6–7 enveckie, -y. [f. as prec. with F. *-é, -ée* = Eng. -ED.] Consisting of two or three arcs or semicircles meeting in cusps: said of lines and edges.

1572 BOSSEWELL *Armorie* II. 27 b, The most auncient bearing of twoo Colours.. is to beare the same plaine, and neither engralee, rasie, enueckie, or dentillie. **1634** PEACHAM *Gentl. Exerc., Drawing* 148 The single line is sometime indented envecky, wavey, embatteled.

†inˈvect, *v. Obs.* [f. L. *invect-*, ppl. stem of *invehĕre*: see INVEIGH. Cf. med.L. *invect-āre*, freq.]

1. *trans.* To bring in, import, introduce.

1548 UDALL *Erasm. Par. Luke* Pref. 4 They see now.. the beaste of romishe abominacion.. had inuected into Christes Churche and holy congregacion, al thynges that were contrary to Christe.

2. *intr.* To inveigh, utter invectives.

1614 R. TAILOR *Hog Hath Lost His Pearl* Prol. in Hazl. *Dodsley* XI. 427 Invecting Much at our city vices. *a* **1625** BEAUM. & FL. *Faithf. Friends* III. iii, Fool that I am thus to invect against her!

invected (ɪnˈvɛktɪd), *ppl. a.* [f. L. *invectus*, pa. pple. of *invehĕre* (see INVEIGH) + -ED¹.] Brought in, introduced; *spec.* in *Her.* = INVECKED.

a **1641** BP. MOUNTAGU *Acts & Mon.* (1642) 397 By their invented and invected Traditions they are charged to have made Gods word.. of none effect. *a* **1657** SIR W. MURE *Hist. Rowallane* Wks. (S.T.S.) II. 240 Borders, borne of a divers fashion, as plane, invected, engrailed, indented. **1706** PHILLIPS, *Invecked*, or *Invected*. **1864** BOUTELL *Her. Hist. & Pop.* 113 It was.. invected or jagged at the bottom.

†inˈvection. *Obs.* [ad. L. *invectiōn-em* bringing in, importation; in late L., attacking with words, n. of action from *invehĕre* to INVEIGH.]

1. The action of inveighing; an invective.

1590 DAVIDSON *Repl. Bancroft* in *Wodrow Soc. Misc.* 505 A bitter invection against the godlie brethren. **1622** H. SYDENHAM *Serm. Sol. Occ.* (1637) 151 No touch of malecontentedness or spirit of invection. **1651** C. CARTWRIGHT *Cert. Relig.* I. 84 Who can thinke.. his invections, a depravement, when he belches forth such blasphemies?

2. Carrying or bringing in, importation.

1603 STOW *Surv.* (1842) 20 Invection, by the which commodities are gathered into the city, and dispersed from thence into the country by land. **1623** COCKERAM, *Inuection*, a carying. **1658** PHILLIPS, *Invection*, a carrying in.

†inˈvectivate, *v. Obs. rare*⁻¹. [f. next + -ATE³.] *intr.* To utter invectives.

1624 DARCIE *Birth of Heresies* Ep. to Rdr., Some do Inuectiuate and Inueigh against it.

invective (ɪnˈvɛktɪv), *a.* and *sb.* Also 6 en-. [a. F. *invectif, -ive* adj., *invective* sb. (14–15th c. in Hatz.-Darm.), ad. late L. *invectīvus* 'reproachful, abusive', in med.L. *invectīva* (sc. *ōrātio*) as sb., f. ppl. stem of *invehĕre*: see INVECT and -IVE.]

A. *adj.* **1.** Using or characterized by denunciatory or railing language; inclined to inveigh; expressing bitter denunciation; vituperative, abusive. Now *rare*.

1430–40 LYDG. *Bochas* VI. xv. (MS. Bodl. 263) 336/2 He .. Compiled hadde an Invectiff scripture Ageyn Antoyne. **1576** A. HALL *Acc. Quarrell* (1815) 35 Divers invective speeches.. had passed in the same. **1591** GREENE *Disc. Coosnage* (1859) 58 What is the matter good wife (quoth I) that you use such invective words against the collier? *a* **1661** FULLER *Worthies, Cambr.* I. (1662) 153 He was.. always devoted to Queen Mary, but never invective against Queen Elizabeth. **1716** *Wodrow Corr.* (1843) II. 120 They kept a fast to pray for success to the Pretender's arms, and a thanksgiving for his arrival.. and were very invective and bitter. **1741** MIDDLETON *Cicero* I. vi. 471 Cicero.. made a reply to him on the spot in an Invective speech, the severest perhaps, that was ever spoken by any man. **1866** *Athenæum* No. 2001. 299/3 What we may call invective history. **1890** E. JOHNSON *Rise Christendom* 368 William, the invective opponent of the.. friars.

†2. Carried or borne in (against something). *Obs.*

1603 FLORIO *Montaigne* II. xii. (1632) 244 As hugh rocks doe regorge th' invective waves.

B. *sb.* **1.** A violent attack in words; a denunciatory or railing speech, writing, or expression.

1523 SKELTON *Garl. Laurel* 96 Iuuenall was thret parde for to kyll For certayne enuectyfs, yet wrote he none ill. **1546** *Supplic. Poore Commons* (E.E.T.S.) 84 Theyr sermons were lytle other then inuectiues agaynst vsery. **1640** BP. HALL *Episc.* II. xvii. 183 This it is that fills.. Pamphlets with spightfull invectives. **1781** GIBBON *Decl. & F.* xxvii. (1869) II. 82 Their satirical wit degenerated into sharp and angry invectives. **1839** JAMES *Louis XIV*, IV. 342 The duke, in going down stairs, poured forth volleys of invectives upon the Chief President. **1844** THIRLWALL *Greece* lxii. VIII. 177 Cleomenes.. sent a letter to the assembly, containing bitter invectives against Aratus.

2. (Without *pl.*) Denunciatory or opprobrious language; vehement denunciation; vituperation.

1602 FULBECKE *2nd Pt. Parall.* 26 Yet the Græcians did not alwaies suffer this licentious rage and inuectiue of Poets. *a* **1770** JORTIN *Serm.* (1771) V. xix. 401 The book of Proverbs is full of invective and indignation against.. those profligates. **1839** KEIGHTLEY *Hist. Eng.* II. 27 He burst out into a torrent of invective.

inˈvectively, *adv.* Now *rare.* [f. INVECTIVE *a.* + -LY².] In an invective manner; with inveighing or denunciation.

1549 *Compl. Scot.* vii. 70 Sche began to reproche them inuectyuely of ther neclegens, couuardeis ande ingratitude. **1600** SHAKS. *A.Y.L.* II. i. 58 Thus most inuectiuely he pierceth through The body of Countrie, Citie, Court. **1717** *New Hampshire Prov. Papers* (1869) III. 678 They are pleased to reflect invectively on those members of the Councill lately appointed.

inˈvectiveness. *rare.* [f. as prec. + -NESS.] The quality of being invective.

a **1661** FULLER *Worthies, Hantshire* II. (1662) 14 Some wonder at his invectiveness; I wonder more, that he inveigheth so little. **1694** PENN *Trav. Holland* 183, I related to them the bitter Mockings and Scornings that fell upon me,.. the Invectiveness and Cruelty of the Priests.

†inˈvectiver. *Obs. rare.* [f. **invective* vb. (a. F. *invectiver* Cotgr.) + -ER¹.] One who utters invectives; a railer.

1596 H. CLAPHAM *Briefe Bible* I. 77 Let therefore Invectivers against Brethren.. Smite their thigh.

inˈvectivist. *rare.* [f. INVECTIVE *sb.* + -IST, after *satirist*, etc.] One who practises invective.

1862 *Independent* (N.Y.) 12 June (Cent.), It is the work of a very French Frenchman, of a.. powerful satirist and invectivist.

†inˈvector. *Obs.* [a. late L. *invector*, agent-n. from *invehĕre*: see INVEIGH.] An inveigher.

1654 GAYTON *Pleas. Notes* IV. xxiii. 276 This is the very life of all books,.. it is their guard and security from the mouths of scandalous invectors.

†inˈvectory, *a. Obs. rare*⁻¹. [f. L. *invect-*, ppl. stem of *invehĕre*: see -ORY.] Invective.

1608 T. MORTON *Preamb. Encounter* 33 An eloquent and inuectory style of writing.

†inˈvecture. *Obs.* [f. as prec. + -URE.] The action of inveighing; the use of invective.

1633 T. ADAMS *Exp. 2 Peter* ii. 5, I have no thought of invecture against the creature.

invegel, -vegle, obs. forms of INVEIGLE.

inveigh (ɪnˈveɪ), *v.* Forms: α. 5–6 inveh, 6 invei(e, -vai(e, (invee, -veihe, -veygh, inwey), 6–7 invey(e, -vay(e, 6– inveigh. β. 6 enveh, -vei(e, -vey(e, 6–8 enveigh, (6 -veygh). [ad. L. *invehĕre* to carry or bear to or into, bring in, *invehī* to be borne, carry oneself, or go into, to attack, to assail with words, f. *in-* (IN-²) + *vehĕre* to carry, bear. (For the spelling compare *conveigh*, 16–18th c. form of CONVEY, also *weigh*.)]

I. With literal notion of *carry*.

†1. *trans.* To carry in, introduce. *Obs. rare.* Cf. INVECKED.

1486 *Bk. St. Albans, Her.* D iij a, In them ar ij colowris quarterli put: yᵉ toon in to the othir, & so oon colowre is inuehit in to an othir.

†2. To bring in (to use); to introduce. *rare.*

1550 GARDINER *Let. to Ld. Protector* 6 June in Foxe *A. & M.* (1583) II. 1346/2 They.. shoulde so soone.. aduise to enuey such matter of alteration.

†3. To carry or draw mentally by influence or allurement; to entice, inveigle. *Obs.*

1649 EVELYN *Liberty & Servit.* iii. Misc. Writ. (1805) 13 She.. being altogether inveighed by inclination.. towards the person where she hath placed her affections. **1670** G. H. *Hist. Cardinals* I. III. 97 They endeavour to obtain the favour of the Cardinals they serve, by inveighing him to dishonesty. *a* **1680** BUTLER *Rem.* (1759) II. 443 He is a Spirit, that inveighs away a Man from himself.

†4. To carry away (*to* a place). *Obs. rare.*

1878 R. W. DIXON *Hist. Ch. Eng.* I. ii. 137 The Lords and Commons.. represented that the age and infirmity of many of the prelates rendered it likely that other large sums would be inveighed to Rome anon.

II. To speak vehemently.

5. *intr.* To give vent to violent denunciation, reproach, or censure; to rail loudly. Const. *against* (†*at, of, on, upon*). The current sense.

α. **1529** MORE *Dyaloge* 115 b/2 The author inueheth agaynst the most pestylent secte of these Lutheranys. **1540** MORYSINE *Vives' Introd. Wysd.* I vij, Thou shalte immoderately invee ageynst no man. **1563** WINȜET *Wks.* (1890) II. 28 Quhow vehementlie inweys the blissit Apostil Paul contrare certane men. **1567** *Triall Treas.* (1850) 6 Sir, in this you seme against me to inuaye. **1573** TWYNE *Æneid.* XI. Argt., Drances and Turnus vpon auncient hatred inueigh one at the other. **1584** R. SCOT *Discov. Witchcr.* I. v. (1886) 9 He would not have pretermitted to invaie against their presumption. **1619** H. HUTTON *Follie's Anat.* 27 Good is but good; and no man can more say; To praise the bad

makes satyrists invay. **1655** FULLER *Hist. Camb.* viii. §16. 149, I can hardly inhold from inveighing on his memory. **1666** PEPYS *Diary* 4 July, He much inveighs upon my discoursing of Sir John Lawson's saying heretofore, that sixty sail would do as much as one hundred. **1673** MARVELL *Reh. Transp.* II. 45 To invey against them and trample upon them. **1741** MIDDLETON *Cicero* I. ii. 122 This was irregular and much inveighed against. **1828** D'ISRAELI *Chas. I*, I. viii. 271 Williams inveighed against Laud as a Papist. **1882** FROUDE in *Fortn. Rev.* CCXXIX. 742 The leadership passed to popular orators, who rose to power by inveighing against property.

β. **1531** R. MORICE in *Lett. Lit. Men* (Camden) 24 Secretly he envehed against thair doctrine. *a* **1540** BARNES *Wks.* (1573) 318/1, I haue taken vpon mee, not to enuey agaynst any person. **1553** T. WILSON *Rhet.* (1567) 62 b, I might enueigh thus, O shamefull deede. **1561** DAUS tr. *Bullinger on Apoc.* Pref. (1573) 5 To enueygh against the Popish clergie. **1655** FULLER *Ch. Hist.* IV. i. §15 The Arch-Bishop of Canterbury enveigh'd as bitterly of the Franchises infringed, of the Abby-Church of Westminster.

† **6.** *trans.* To attack or assail with words. *rare.*

1670 G. H. *Hist. Cardinals* II. III. 201 It may well stand in competition with any that enveighs it.

Hence **in'veighing** *vbl. sb.* and *ppl. a.* (in sense 5); **in'veigher**, one who inveighs, a denouncer.

1568 SIR F. KNOLLYS in Ellis *Orig. Lett.* Ser. I. II. 245 The Quene of Skottes..fell into hyr ordinarye invaying agaynst my Lord of Murraye. **1584** HOOKER *Descr. Excester* (1765) 83 A sharp Inveigher against the one, and an earnest Maintainer of the other. **1634** SIR T. HERBERT *Trav.* 79 This inveighing discourse..prevailed with credulous youth-full Temeriske. **1669** R. MONTAGU in *Buccleuch MSS.* (Hist. MSS. Comm.) I. 421 The rest of the conversation passed with great inveighing on his side against the Dutch. **1687** in *Magd. Coll. & Jas. II* (O.H.S.) 229 *note*, A bitter inveigher of the Church of Rome.

inveigle (ɪnˈviːg(ə)l, ɪnˈveɪg(ə)l), *v.* Forms: *α.* 6 envegel, -vegle, (-veugle), 6–8 enveigle, (6 -veighle, 7 -veygle), 7–8 enveagle. *β.* 5 invegel, 6–7 -vegle, 6–8 -veagle, (7 inveighle), 6– inveigle. [In 15–16th c. *envegle* (rarely *enveugle*), app. a corruption of an earlier **avegle*, *aveugle*, a. F. *aveugler* to blind, f. *aveugle*, OF. also *avuegle*:—late pop.L. *aboculum*, f. *ab-* away from, without + *ocul-us* eye. The word appears to have been analysed as *a-vegle*, and this by exchange of prefixes, made *en-vegle*, as in some other words: cf. *enbraid* = *abraid*, *enorn* = *aorn*, *adorn*; cf. esp. L. *exemplum*, OF. *essample*, ME. **esaumple*, *asaumple*, corruptly *ensample*. It is probable that some analogy suggested the prefix *en-*, whence the Latinized *in-*. The stem-vowel *ē* is normal: cf. *people* = F. *peuple*, L. *populus*.]

† **1.** *trans.* To blind in mind or judgement; to beguile, deceive, cajole. *Obs.*

α. **1522** MORE *De Quat. Noviss.* Wks. 79/1 Thus enueigleth he them that either be good, or but metely badde. **1609** HOLLAND *Amm. Marcell.* xxx. vi. 385 They..enveagle and deceive by their subtile orations the integritie of Iudges. **1611** FLORIO, *Ciecare*, to blinde, to enueagle. *a* **1709** ATKYNS *Parl. & Pol. Tracts* (1734) 390 Your rhetorical Flourishes in a Case of Innocent Blood, which contributed in an high Degree to enveagle the Jury, and bring that Noble Lord to the Scaffold.

β. **1494** FABYAN *Chron.* VII. 668 The sayd duke of Glouceter inuegelyd so the archbysshop of Caunterbury.. that he went with hym to the quene. **1552** LATIMER *3rd Serm. Lord's Prayer* Wks. (Parker Soc.) I. 357 He [the devil] intendeth to inveigle even very kings, and to make them negligent in their business and office. **1579** LYLY *Euphues* (Arb.) 87 So it is that loue hath as well inuegled me as others. **1594** HOOKER *Eccl. Pol.* I. vii. §7 The subtiltie of Satan inueagling vs, as it did Eue. **1646** SIR T. BROWNE *Pseud. Ep.* I. vii. 28 The Chymistes, overmagnifying their preparations, inveigle the curiosity of many.

2. a. To gain over or take captive by deceitful allurement; to entice, allure, seduce.

α. *c* **1540** tr. *Pol. Verg. Eng. Hist.* (Camden) I. 75 The Pictes..were more envegeled with the desier of fraye then inflamed with the ambition of imperie. **1549** LATIMER *4th Serm. bef. Edw. VI* (Arb.) 128 Other there be that enuegle mennes daughters..and go about to marrye them wythoute theyr [fathers] consente. **1674** OWEN *Holy Spirit* (1693) 212 She had no Baits or Allurements..to enveagle the minds of Corrupt and Sensual Men.

β. **1558** BP. WATSON *Sev. Sacram.* xxix. 188 Let not the flattering face of worldlye wealthe inueigle and deceyue you. **1589** GREENE *Menaphon* (Arb.) 36 Thinking with the sight of his flockes to inueigle her. **1601** HOLLAND *Pliny* I. 291 These birds..take a great delight to inveagle others, and to steale away some pigeons from their owne flocks. **1634** MILTON *Comus* 538 Yet have they many baits, and guileful spells To inveigle and invite the unwary sense. **1663** BUTLER *Hud.* I. ii. 588 As Indians with a Female Tame Elephant inveigle the Male. **1687** SHADWELL *Juvenal* 49 She stood at the door to inveagle Passengers. **1766** FORDYCE *Serm. Yng. Wom.* (1767) I. iii. 115 Poltrons..inveigle the affections of virtuous women. **1840** DICKENS *Barn. Rudge* xxxi, I don't want to inveigle you. **1860** MOTLEY *Netherl.* (1868) I. ii. 44 An organised system of harlotry, by which the soldiers and politicians of France were inveigled.

† **b.** To entrap, ensnare, entangle. *Obs.*

1551 T. WILSON *Logike* (1567) 80 b, One maie easely be enueigled and brought to an inconuenience, before he be ware. **1647** SANDERSON *Serm.* II. 216 To enveigle and entangle his necessitous neighbour..till he have got a hank over his estate. **1707** SLOANE *Jamaica* I. 235 The branches are inveigled among one another, spreading themselves on every hand. *Ibid.* II. 196 They [webs of a certain spider] are so strong as to give a man inveigled in them trouble for some time.

c. With complemental extension: To draw (any one) by guile *into* (*to*, *from*, etc.) action, conduct, a place, etc.; *away*, *in*; †*to do* something.

1539 TAVERNER *Gard. Wysed.* I. 35 a, He myght be.. inuegled by the force & power of frendes to do any thing otherwyse, then the tenour of iustyce & honesty requyred. **1564** GOLDING *Justine* (1570) 175 His sonne Comanus..was inuegled ageinst the Massiliens, by one of his Lordes. **1616** SURFL. & MARKH. *Country Farme* 38 Neuer attempting to inueagle or draw away any of their men servants or maids from them. **1643** SIR T. BROWNE *Relig. Med.* I. §7, I never ..endeavoured to enveagle any mans belief unto mine. **1663** WOOD *Life* Mar. (O.H.S.) I. 471 Inveighling Dr. Thomas Jones..to be false to his trust. **1663** COWLEY *Cutter Colman St.* I, Ye shall no more..inveigle into Taverns young Foremen of the Shop. **1682** H. MORE *Annot. Glanvill's Lux O.* 105 A soul enveigled in vitiousness. **1754** RICHARDSON *Grandison* (1781) I. xxiii. 161 The chairmen..were inveigled away to drink somewhere. **1768–74** TUCKER *Lt. Nat.* (1834) I. II. xxvi. §35. 573 Many of them are inveigled to enlist by drink, or by bounty money. **1774** PENNANT *Tour Scot. in 1772.* 139 To enveigle him from his father and friends. **1875** JOWETT *Plato* (ed. 2) I. 111 Socrates, who inveigles him into an admission that everything has but one opposite. **1876** GLADSTONE *Glean.* (1879) II. 281 The Natives are inveigled on board to look at axes or tobacco.

d. In good or neutral sense: To beguile.

a **1720** SHEFFIELD (Dk. Buckhm.) *Wks.* (1753) II. 219 My garden..has nothing in it to inveagle one's thoughts.

e. *colloq.* To cajole one out of something.

1849 E. E. NAPIER *Excurs. S. Africa* II. 107 He managed to 'inveigle' me out of sixpence and a roll of tobacco, before we parted.

f. To force (something) *upon* a person by cajolery, etc. *rare.*

1788 MAD. D'ARBLAY *Diary* 3 Jan., She had distressed me ..by inveigling, rather than forcing upon me, a beautiful.. new year's gift.

Hence **in'veigled** *ppl. a.* (in quot. in sense 'inveigling'), **in'veigling** *vbl. sb.* and *ppl. a.*

1572 FORREST *Theophilus* 318 in *Anglia* VII, Bllynded by Sathans enveglynge. **1590** MARLOWE *Edw. II*, I. ii. 266 That sly inveigling Frenchman we'll exile. *a* **1610** HEALEY *Cebes* (1636) 153 To passe by them speedily, and stop the earres unto their inveygled perswasions. **1672** MARVELL *Reh. Transp.* I. 57 It looks all so like subterfuge and inveagling. **1692** DRYDEN *St. Euremont's Ess.* 227 An invegling, self-interessed Widow.

inveiglement (ɪnˈviːg(ə)lmənt, -ˈveɪ-). [f. prec. + -MENT.] The action, process, or means of inveigling; cajolery, allurement, enticement.

1653 H. MORE *Conject. Cabbal.* (1713) 238 There is no way better that I know to be freed from such inveiglements. **1660** tr. *Amyraldus' Treat. conc. Relig.* III. i. 312 They are the invegleme nts to incontinence. **1768–74** TUCKER *Lt. Nat.* (1834) II. v. §16. 52 The fall of Troy is ascribed to the inveiglements of Paris and elopement of Helen. **1865** *Cornh. Mag.* Nov. 533 He..would try even not to think upon the female inveiglement in which he believed.

inveigler (ɪnˈviːglə(r), -ˈveɪ-). [f. as prec. + -ER[1].] One who inveigles; an enticer, seducer, cajoler.

1549 *Latimer's 4th Serm. bef. Edw. VI* (Arb.) 128 *marg.*, The inueglers of mens doughters ar[e] notyd. **1661** K. W. *Conf. Charac., Courtier* (1860) 20 The court minions (those paramours of lust, and inveaghlers to debauchery). **1782** MISS BURNEY *Cecilia* IV. 273 Thou thing of fair professions! thou inveigler of esteem! **1883** *Leisure Hour* 615/1 The portrait of an 'inveigler' [Thug].

† **in'veil**, *v. Obs.* Also 6–7 -vail, -vayl. [f. IN-[1] or [2] + VEIL *v.*: cf. ENVEIL.] *trans.* To cover or shroud with or as with a veil; to enveil.

1592 DANIEL *Delia* xl, Think the same becomes thy fading best, Which then shall most inuaile, and shadow most. **1613–16** W. BROWNE *Brit. Past.* I. v, Invailed with a sable weed she sate. **1625** JACKSON *Creed* v. I. §4 [*tr.* Seneca] Thy heart is not invailed; thou art free from avarice. *a* **1763** ? SHENSTONE in Dodsley *Descr. Leasowes* ¶41 And while the sight inveils a part Let fancy paint the rest.

in'vein, *v. rare.* Also 6 envayn. [f. IN-[2] (EN-[1]) + VEIN *v.*] *trans.* To streak or diversify with or as with veins.

a **1529** SKELTON *'Knoledge, aquayntance'* 17 Saphyre of sadnes, enuayned with indy blew. **1826** *New Monthly Mag.* XVI. 404 Carpets wove Of purple grain with gold inveined.

inve(l)lop(e, obs. forms of ENVELOP *v.*

invendible (ɪnˈvɛndɪb(ə)l), *a. rare.* [IN-[3].] Not vendible; unsaleable. Hence **in,vendi'bility**, **in'vendibleness**, unsaleableness.

1706 PHILLIPS, *Invendible*,..unsaleable. **1727** BAILEY vol. II, *Invendibleness*, unsaleableness. ? **17..** BROME To Rdr. (R.), The author may be laughed at, and the stationer beggared by the book's invendibility. **1789** JEFFERSON *Writ.* (1859) II. 566 It had already begun to render our oils invendible in the ports of France.

† **in'venemated**, *ppl. a. Obs. rare*[−1]. [For **invenenated*, f. L. *in-* (IN-[2]) + *venēnum* poison, *venēnātus* poisoned: after *inveneme*, ENVENOM.] *trans.* To envenom.

1716 M. DAVIES *Athen. Brit.* II. To Rdr. 40 Enemies of the most invenemated Viperin or rather Draconick kind.

inveneme, -im, -om(e, -omous, obs. ff. ENVENOM, -OMOUS.

c **1440** *Promp. Parv.* 263/1 Invenymyn, *veneno.* *a* **1533** LD. BERNERS *Gold. Bk. M. Aurel.* Let. ix. (1559) E e viij b, Take heede..that our loue be not inuenimed with vnkindnes.

invenient (ɪnˈviːnɪənt), *a. rare.* [ad. L. *invenient-em*, pr. pple. of *invenīre* to come upon.] Coming on, oncoming.

1854 DOBELL *Balder* xxvii. 187 Bound and prone, expatiate with nice art To the invenient honor.

invent (ɪnˈvɛnt), *v.* [f. L. *invent-*, ppl. stem of *invenīre* to come upon, discover, find out, devise, contrive, f. *in-* (IN-[2]) + *venīre* to come. Cf. F. *inventer* (1539 in R. Estienne).]

† **1.** *trans.* To come upon, find; to find out, discover. (*Obs.* exc. in reference to the *Invention of the Cross*: see INVENTION 1 b.)

(Often implying 'to find out or discover by search or endeavour', and so passing into the later senses.)

c **1475** *Songs & Carols* (Percy Soc.) 64 Syns that Eve was procreat owt of Adams syde, Cowd not such newels in this lond be inventyd. **1541** R. COPLAND *Galyen's Terapeut.* 2 C j, They shuld inuent and knowe that there be two fyrste dyfferences of the functions and actions of medycyne. **1546** LANGLEY *Pol. Verg. De Invent.* II. xii. 68 Gold..Cadmus, as Plinie affyrmeth, found it in the mount Pangeus, in Thrace; or as some thynke, it was Thoas and Eaclis that inuented it in Panchaia. *a* **1548** HALL *Chron., Hen. VII* 34 b, Because none of their Masters were invented culpable of thys naughtye acte, the kynge..restored them to their libertie. **1590** SPENSER *F.Q.* III. v. 10 Florimell..vowed never to returne againe Till him alive or dead she did invent. **1668** CULPEPPER & COLE *Barthol. Anat.*, At the beginning of the Colon, a Valve is placed..invented by Baubinus. **1717** J. KEILL *Anim. Oecon.* Pref. (1738) 11 Inventing many Propositions concerning the Motion of the Blood. **1887** ATHELSTAN RILEY *Athos* v. 71 *note*, According to the popular belief amongst the Greeks it was in a bed of this tender herb [sweet basil] that Our Lord's Cross was invented.

2. To find out or produce by mental activity.

† **a.** To devise, contrive; to plan, plot. *Obs.*

1539 *Lisle Papers* 9 Aug. V. 26 (MS.) He will invent all means he can to be stayed here. **1596** DALRYMPLE tr. *Leslie's Hist. Scot.* v. 288 Throw counsell of his wyf he inuented the kings slauchtre. **1641** J. JACKSON *True Evang. T.* III. 199 A plot..invented, one would imagine, not by men, but by Cacodæmons. **1750** JOHNSON *Rambler* No. 77 ¶14 For laboured impiety, what apology can be invented? **1821** KEATS *Lamia* 315 And there had led Days happy as the gold coin could invent Without the aid of love.

† **b.** To compose as a work of imagination or literary art; to treat in the way of literary or artistic composition. *Obs.* or merged in c or 3.

1576 FLEMING *Panopl. Epist.* 323 *note*, Your braine or your wit, and your pen, the one to invent and devise: the other to write. **1600** SHAKS. *A. Y. L.* IV. iii. 29, I say she neuer did inuent this letter, This is a mans inuention, and his hand. *a* **1683** OLDHAM *Art Poetry* Wks. (1686) 20 Take a known Subject and invent it well. **1697** DRYDEN *Æneid* Ded. (R.), A poet is a maker, as the word signifies: and he who cannot make, that is, invent, hath his name for nothing.

c. To devise something false or fictitious; to fabricate, feign, 'make up'.

1535 COVERDALE *Susanna* 43, I neuer dyd eny soch thinges, as these men haue maliciously inuented agaynst me. *a* **1548** HALL *Chron., Edw. IV* 237 b, He invented a cause of his commyng,..to pertracte the tyme, till his men [etc.]. **1676** tr. *Guillatiere's Voy. Athens* 74 [She] confessed that she had invented the news. **1791** MRS. RADCLIFFE *Rom. Forest* x, She directed Peter to invent some excuse for his absence. **1849** MACAULAY *Hist. Eng.* vi. II. 158 The calumnies which ..he had invented to blacken the fame of Anne Hyde. **1871** FREEMAN *Norm. Conq.* IV. xviii. 137 His real history is well-nigh as marvellous as anything that legend could invent.

3. To find out in the way of original contrivance; to create, produce, or construct by original thought or ingenuity; to devise first, originate (a new method of action, kind of instrument, etc.). The chief current sense.

1538 STARKEY *England* I. i. 12 We schal see infynyte strange artys and craftys inuentyd by mannys wyt. **1546** LANGLEY *Pol. Verg. De Invent.* III. x. 78 b, Dædalus..firste inuented the art of Carpentrie with these instrumentes folowyng, the Sawe, Chippe axe, and Plumline. **1568** GRAFTON *Chron.* I. 54 Esdras..invented the same Hebrew Charectes which are used at this day. **1601** R. JOHNSON *Kingd. & Commw.* (1603) 27 They invented the art of printing. **1665** R. HOOKE *Microgr.* Pref. b ij b, There may be yet invented several other helps for the eye. **1783** BLAIR *Rhet.* I. x. 195 Galileo invented the telescope. **1882** PEBODY *Eng. Journalism* xiii. 94 The *Morning Chronicle* had the credit..of inventing the leading article. **1883** HUXLEY in *Academy* 24 Nov., I only said I invented the word 'agnostic'.

† **4.** To originate, introduce, or bring into use formally or by authority; to found, establish, institute, appoint. *Obs.*

1546 LANGLEY *Pol. Verg. De Invent.* VII. iv. 139 Dominicke..inuented a newe fraternite named Dominicans, black Friers, or Friers preachers. **1577** NORTHBROOKE *Dicing* (1843) 44 Festiual dais in old time were inuented for recreation. **1613** PURCHAS *Pilgrimage* (1614) 589 Who first invented the order of the Mamalukes. **1665** MANLEY *Grotius' Low C. Warres* 926 That all Taxes invented during the War should be abolished. **1692** DRYDEN *St. Euremont's Ess.* 6 The first Tarquin to give more Dignity to the Senate..invented Ornaments, and gave marks of Distinction.

† **5.** With *inf.* (in senses 2–4): To plan, plot, devise, contrive, find out how (*to do* something).

a **1548** HALL *Chron., Edw. IV* 238 When as kyng Edward sought, invented and studied dayly and howerly to bryng hym selfe to quietnesse. **1563** SHUTE *Archit.* B j b, The Tuscanes..inuented to buylde stronglye after the maner aforsayde. **1660–1** PEPYS *Diary* 8 Feb., If they do invent to bring their masters in so much a week by their industry or theft. **1661** FELTHAM *Lusoria*, etc. (1696) 64 What Pliny said of him that first invented to saw stones. **1729** BUTLER *Serm. Govt. Tongue* Wks. 1874 II. 41 They will invent to engage your attention.

†**invent**, *sb. Obs.* [ad. L. *invent-um*, sb. use of neut. of *inventus*, pa. pple of *invenīre*: see prec.]

1. Something invented; a device, contrivance: = INVENTION 6, 9.

1555 ABP. PARKER *Ps.* cvi. 308 But they more oft rebeld: With theyr inuentes and so for sinne they were but iustly feld. **1623** LISLE *Ælfric on O. & N. Test.* To Rdr. 4 Many notable inuents, and works of old time, haue perished.

2. Inventive faculty: = INVENTION 4.

a **1605** MONTGOMERIE *Sonn.* xxix, Thy Homers style, thy Petrarks high invent, Sall vanquish death, and live eternally.

†**in'vent**, *ppl. a. Obs.* [ad. L. *invent-us*, pa. pple. of *invenīre* to INVENT.] Found out, discovered, INVENTED. (Const. as *pa. pple.*)

a **1500** *Colkelbie Sow* 680 The king..a cornar of a cuntre seuerall, Nocht than invent, inhabit as it lay, Gaif him be seile heretable for ay. *a* **1520** BARCLAY *Jugurth* (Pynson, ed. 2) 46 b, For at that tyme..they were nat yet inuent.

inventable: see INVENTIBLE.

†'**inventar, -aire.** Chiefly *Sc. Obs.* [a. OF. *inventaire* (1344 in Godef.), ad. late L. *inventārium*, lit. a list of what is found, f. *invenīre, invent-* to find: see INVENT.] = INVENTORY *sb.*

1435 *E.E. Wills* (1882) 103 The seyd godes in the Inuentare. **1616** W. HAIG in J. Russell *Haigs* vii. (1881) 160 That trunk was packed according to the inventaire. **1633** *Sc. Acts Chas. I* (1870) V. 14/2 The pairties vpgivers of the saids inventars. **1640–1** *Kirkcudbr. War-Comm. Min. Bk.* (1855) 45 Ane rentall of the dewties of the lands thairin contained, with ane inventar.

Hence †**inventar** (**-ir, -ure**) *v.*, to inventory.

1663 *Inventory Ld. J. Gordon's Furnit.*, The insight of the place of Greenlaw is inventired beffoir the persones following. **1756** MRS. CALDERWOOD *Jrnl.* 292 They have first been shown, and inventured and valued at the custom-house here.

inventar, obs. Sc. form of INVENTOR.

inventarize, obs. var. INVENTORIZE *v.*

†'**inventary, -arie**, *sb. Obs.* [Variant f. INVENTORY, after L. *inventārium.*] = INVENTORY *sb.*

a **1529** SKELTON *Image Ipocr.* II. Wks. 1843 II. 427/2 Of inventaries [*printed* inventataries], Of testamentaries, And of mortuaries. **1568** GRAFTON *Chron.* II. 10 After an Inventary taken thereof, caused the same to be brought into his treasurie. **1641** *Termes de la Ley* 190 b, An Inventary is a catalogue or recitall in writing of all the goods and chattels of one that is dead, with the valuation of them by foure credible persons, which every Executor and Administrator ought to exhibite to the Ordinary at the time appointed him. **1703** [see next]. **1763** WHEELOCK *Serm.* 30 June (1767) 23 If I omit any thing in their inventary.

†**b.** *loosely.* A plan or specification. *Obs.*

1608 WILLET *Hexapla Exod.* 850 In publike buildings.. the workmen haue a certaine inuentarie or plot giuen them, which they follow in their worke.

†'**inventary**, *v. Obs.* = INVENTORY *v.*

1590 SWINBURNE *Testaments* 220 First of all the moueable goodes were inuentaried and praised, as houshold stuffe, corne, and cattell, &c. then the immoueable, as leases of groundes or tenements. **1703** *Providence* (U.S.) *Rec.* (1894) V. 144 All those Moveable goods the which are inventaried in the inventarey of my late husband his Estate.

†**in'ventative**, *a. Obs. rare.* [f. INVENT *v.* + -ATIVE.] = INVENTIVE.

1541 *Act 33 Hen. VIII*, c. 9 §1 Many subtill inuentatiue and crafte persons.

invented (ɪn'vɛntɪd), *ppl. a.* [f. INVENT *v.* + -ED[1].] Discovered, found out (*obs.*); devised, contrived; made up, fabricated, feigned.

1541 R. COPLAND *Galyen's Terapeut.* 2 E iv, To the good and ryght vsage of inuented thynges. **1561** T. NORTON *Calvin's Inst.* I. 5 New inuented formes of worshipping God. **1667** MILTON *P.L.* II. 70 Mixed with Tartarean Sulphur, and strange fire, His own invented Torments. **1726** LAW *Serious C.* xv. (1729) 267 Those antick and invented motions which make fine dancing. **1828** WHATELY *Rhetoric* in *Encycl. Metrop.* I. 253/1 Aristotle, in his Rhetoric, has divided Examples into *Real* and *Invented.*

inventer: see INVENTOR.

in'ventful, *a. rare.* [f. INVENT *v.* (or *sb.*) + -FUL.] Full of invention; showing inventiveness.

1797 J. GIFFORD *Rem.* in *Resid. France* (T.), The genius of the French government appears powerful only in destruction, and inventful [*ed.* 2 I. Pref. 29 inventive] only in oppression. **1856** RUSKIN *Mod. Paint.* III. IV. x. §21 We have enough, and to spare, of noble inventful pictures.

inventi'bility, -a'bility. *rare.* [f. next: see -ITY.] **a.** Capability of being invented. †**b.** (In quot.) Capacity of inventing, inventiveness.

1662 J. SPARROW tr. *Behme's Rem. Wks., Theos. Lett.* 15 In the Power of the Divine Vision, Inventibility, and Perceptibility.

in'ventible, -able, *a. rare.* [f. INVENT *v.* + -IBLE, -ABLE. The form in *-ible* is on L. analogy from *invent-*, ppl. stem of *invenīre.*] Capable of being invented.

1641 LD. J. DIGBY *Sp. Trienn. Parl.* 13 There can be no cause colourably inventable, wherunto to attribute them. **1650** A. B. *Mutat. Polemo* 7 Which our party did assay by all inventible means to bring him to. **1655** MRQ. WORCESTER *Cent. Inv.* lxvii. (T.), When first I gave my thoughts to make guns shoot often, I thought there had been but one only exquisite way inventible. **1892** *Chicago Advance* 14 Jan., If only there were invented, or inventible, some sort of 'Keeley-cure'.

Hence **in'ventibleness** (Craig, 1847).

invention (ɪn'vɛnʃən). [a. OF. *invencion, envention* (1270–97 in Godef. *Compl.*), ad. L. *invention-em* n. of action from *invenīre*: see INVENT *v.*]

I. The action, faculty, or manner of inventing.

1. The action of coming upon or finding; the action of finding out; discovery (whether accidental, or the result of search and effort). *Obs.* or *arch.*

a **1350** *St. Stephen* 212 in Horstm. *Altengl. Leg.* (1881) 30 Saynt Steuyn inuencioun: þat es þe finding of his body. **1526** *Pilgr. Perf.* (W. de W. 1531) 258 In the inuencyon of the body of saynt Stephan. **1538** STARKEY *England* I. iv. 116 For no study nor desyre of victory, but only for the inventyon of the truth and equyte. **1594** HOOKER *Eccl. Pol.* II. i. §3 That judicial method which serveth best for the invention of truth. **1665–6** *Phil. Trans.* I. 14, I have..reason to believe, that the Invention of Longitudes will come to its perfection. **1691** RAY *Creation* II. (1692) 45 Nature hath provided..four..Channels to convey it into the Mouth, which are of late invention, and called by Anatomists, *Ductus Salivales.* **1728** NEWTON *Chronol. Amended* i. 166 The invention and use of the four metals in Greece. **1850** NEALE *Med. Hymns* (1867) 104 But that thirst Thou wouldst express For lost man's invention. **1867** FREEMAN *Norm. Conq.* (1877) I. v. 440 *note*, His tomb must have been removed on the Invention of Arthur in the time of Henry the Second.

b. *Invention of the Cross*: the reputed finding of the Cross by Helena, mother of the Emperor Constantine, in A.D. 326 (see CROSS *sb.* 2); hence, the church festival observed on the 3rd of May in commemoration of this.

1451 *Paston Lett.* I. 211 The Sonday next after the Fest of the Invencion of the Cros, the ix. day of May. **1587** HOLINSHED *Scot. Chron.* (1805) II. 65 On the Holy Rood-day, called the invention of the Cross. **1698** FRYER *Acc. E. India & P.* 281 On the same day they commemorate St. Helen's Invention of the Cross at Jerusalem. **1709** *Lond. Gaz.* No. 4539/1 Yesterday being the Feast of the Invention of the Holy Cross, the Emperor, the two Empresses.. performed their Devotions in the Church of the Jesuits. **1897** J. T. TOMLINSON *Prayer Book, Art. & Hom.* I. 14 The *Invention of the Cross*..'has not been disproved',—a faint praise, which might be applied to many other doubtful 'inventions'.

†**c.** Finding out, solution (of a problem). *Obs.*

1484 CAXTON *Fables of Alfonce* (1889) 3 A subtyle Inuencion of a sentence gyuen upon a derke and obscure cause. **1571** DIGGES *Pantom.* IV. xxiv. Ee iij a, Rules for the inuention of his capacitie superficiall and Solide. **1621** BURTON *Anat. Mel.* III. iv. I. iii. (1651) 667 Pythagoras offered an hundred Oxen for the invention of a Geometrical Probleme.

d. *Rhet.* The finding out or selection of topics to be treated, or arguments to be used.

1509 HAWES *Past. Pleas.* VIII. (Percy Soc.) 29 The fyrste of them is called Invencion, Whiche surdeth of the most noble werke Of v. inward wittes. **1531** ELYOT *Gov.* I. xiv, Whiche is the fyrste parte of Rhetorike, named Inuention. **1659** O. WALKER *Oratory* 1 The Parts of Oratory are Invention, taking care for the Matter; and Elocution, for the Words and Style. **1725** WATTS *Logic* III. ii. §7 By some logical Writers this Business of Topics, and Invention is treated of in such a manner with mathematical Figures and Diagrams, filled with the barbarous technical Words, *Napcas, Nipcis, Ropcos, Nosrop*, etc. *a* **1886** J. KER *Lect. Hist. Preach.* xiv. (1888) 251 His sermons are remarkable for the skill displayed in what the French call 'invention' or the raising of topics.

2. The action of devising, contriving, or making up; contrivance, fabrication.

1526 *Pilgr. Perf.* (W. de W. 1531) 2 These thynges, whiche be not of myne inuencion, but with great labour gathered. **1551** P'CESS MARY in Ellis *Orig. Lett.* Ser. I. II. 163 To use alteracyons of theyr owne Invencyon. **1695** WOODWARD *Nat. Hist. Earth* (1702) 92 Carrying rather an appearance of Figment and Invention..than of Truth and Reality. **1704** SWIFT *T. Tub* Ded., This proceeding is not of my own invention. **1722** DE FOE *Plague* (1754) 1 Printed News-Papers..to spread Rumours and Reports of Things; and to improve them by the Invention of Men. *Mod.* Who is credited with the invention of this fable?

3. The original contrivance or production of a new method or means of doing something, of an art, kind of instrument, etc. previously unknown (see INVENT *v.* 3); origination, introduction.

1531 ELYOT *Gov.* I. xxvi, They that write of the firste inuentions of thinges, haue good cause to suppose Lucifer.. to be the first inuentour of dise playinge. **1604** JAS. I *Counterbl.* (Arb.) 99 The first inuention of Tobacco taking. **1651** HOBBES *Leviath.* I. iv. 12 The Invention of Printing.. compared with the invention of Letters. **1781** GIBBON *Decl. & F.* xxxviii. (1869) II. 429 The military art has been changed by the invention of gunpowder. **1857** BUCKLE *Civiliz.* I. xiv. 820 All half civilized nations have made many great inventions, but no great discoveries. **1873** HAMERTON *Intell. Life* VII. iv. (1876) 247 The extreme rarity of inventions due to women.

b. In art and literary composition: The devising of a subject, idea, or method of treatment, by exercise of the intellect or imagination; 'the choice and production of such objects as are proper to enter into the composition of a work of art' (Gwilt *Archit. Gloss.*).

1638 F. JUNIUS *Paint. of Ancients* 234 The Painter being loath to spoyle the naturall beautie..with an Artificiall bridge, fetcheth a sudden Invention out of..Palme-trees. **1666** DRYDEN *Pref. Ann. Mirab.* Wks. (Globe) 40 The first happiness of the poet's imagination is properly invention, or finding of the thought. **1769** SIR J. REYNOLDS *Disc.* ii. (1876) 317 Invention..is little more than a new combination of those images which have been previously gathered and deposited in the memory. **1843** RUSKIN *Mod. Paint.* I. II. VI. iii. §23 All so-called invention is in landscape nothing more than appropriate recollection.

4. The faculty of inventing or devising; power of mental creation or construction; inventiveness.

c **1480** HENRYSON *Test. Cres.* 67, I wait nocht gif this narratioun Be authoreist, or fenyeit of the new Be sum poeit, throw his inventioun. **1576** FLEMING *Panopl. Epist.* Ep. A ij, I commende your wit and invention. **1638** F. JUNIUS *Paint. of Ancients* 226 Wee must rather give our Invention the full raines. **1793** SMEATON *Edystone L.* §100 He was not a man of much invention. **1838** PRESCOTT *Ferd. & Is.* (1846) I. iii. 156 His invention was ever busy in devising intrigues.

†**5.** The manner in which a thing is devised or constructed; invented style, fashion, design. *Obs.*

1513 BRADSHAW *St. Werburge* I. 1787 Your garmentes.. Euery yere made after a newe inuencyon. **1711** ADDISON *Spect.* No. 115 ¶6 Guns of several Sizes and Inventions. **1715** LEONI *Palladio's Archit.* (1742) I. 59 The Chambers.. are..painted in grotesque of a very fine Invention.

II. The thing invented.

6. Something devised; a method of action, etc. contrived by the mind; a device, contrivance, design, plan, scheme. (Now merged in 8 and 9.)

1513 MORE in Grafton *Chron.* (1568) II. 786 The weight of all that invention rested in thys. **1516** *Life St. Bridget* in *Myrr. our Ladye* (1873) Introd. 53 There was a knyght that alway studyed to fynde newe inuencyons amonge the people. **1593** SHAKS. *3 Hen. VI*, IV. i. 35 What, if both Lewis and Warwick be appeas'd, By such inuention as I can deuise? **1602** WARNER *Alb. Eng.* XIII. lxxvii. (1612) 318 To worship meare Inuentions, yea inferior Things of nought. **1611** BIBLE *Eccl.* vii. 29 God hath made man vpright: but they haue sought out many inuentions. **1665** BOYLE *Occas. Refl.*, *Disc. Occas. Medit.* IV. ii, True Preachers..mingle not their own Inventions, or humane Traditions, with that pure and sincere Light of Revelation. **1819** BYRON *Juan* II. cxxiii, Those soft attentions, Which are (as I must own) of female growth, And have ten thousand delicate inventions.

†**b.** A discovery. *Obs.*

1613 PURCHAS *Pilgrimage* (1614) 36 Another of stone, in both which they writ their inventions of Astronomy. **1666** J. SMITH *Old Age* To Rdr. A vij b, The Circular Motion of the Bloud; the best and most useful Invention of this Latter Age.

†**7.** A work or writing as produced by exercise of the mind or imagination; a literary composition. *Obs.*

1484 CAXTON *Fables of Æsop* 3 She gaf to hym the yefte of speche for to speke dyuerse fables and Inuencions. **1593** NASHE *4 Lett. Confut.* 32 In al other my inuentions thou [Aristophanes] interfusest delight with reprehension. **1601** SHAKS. *Twel. N.* V. i. 341 Or say, tis not your seale, not your inuention.

8. A fictitious statement or story; a fabrication, fiction, figment.

1500–20 DUNBAR *Poems* ix. 125 In fowll disceptionis, in als inventionis breiding. **1601** SHAKS. *All's Well* III. vi. 105 None in the world, but returne with an inuention, and clap vpon you two or three probable lies. **1698** FRYER *Acc. E. India & P.* 233 It may more probably be an Invention to fright Passengers. **1748** F. SMITH *Voy. Disc.* I. 179 The Story which they had related..was all meer Invention. **1898** W. M. RAMSAY *Was Christ born in Bethlehem?* v. 102 The extreme school of critics reject the tale as an invention.

9. Something devised or produced by original contrivance; a method or means of doing something, an instrument, an art, etc. originated by the ingenuity of some person, and previously unknown; an original contrivance or device.

1546 LANGLEY *Pol. Verg. De Invent.* III. v. 70 b, Tyle and slate to couer houses were the inuencion of Sinyra. **1585** T. WASHINGTON tr. *Nicholay's Voy.* I. xix. 21 b, Gabions..in forme of Baskets..a very commodious invention, for the shot..can doe no hurt nor dammage. **1644** EVELYN *Diary* 2 May, We entered by the draw-bridge, which has an invention to let one fall, if not premonished. **1781** W. BLANE *Ess. Hunt.* (1788) 7 Barometer..this instrument, though a fine invention, is still imperfectly understood. **1821** J. Q. ADAMS in C. Davies *Metr. Syst.* III. (1871) 215 The French system..is in design the greatest invention of human ingenuity since that of printing. **1856** EMERSON *Eng. Traits, Race* Wks. (Bohn) II. 20 The English..have made or applied the principal inventions.

†**10.** Something formally or authoritatively introduced or established; an institution. *Obs.*

1639 GENTILIS *Servita's Inquis.* (1676) 844 The Cardinal yielding to necessity went away, and the new inventions were revoked. **1672** TEMPLE *Ess., Govt.* (R.), Being forced to supply the want of authority by wise inventions, orders, and institutions.

11. *Mus.* A short piece of music in which a single idea is worked out in a simple manner.

1880 GROVE *Dict. Mus.*, *Invention*, a term used by J. S. Bach, and probably by him only, for small pianoforte pieces —15 in 2 parts and 15 in 3 parts—each developing a single idea, and in some measure answering to the Impromptu of a later day.

III. †**12.** Coming in, arrival. *Obs. rare.*

1612 DRAYTON *Poly-olb.* i. 3 And whilst green Thetis Nymphes..Sing our Invention safe unto her long-wisht Bay.

inventional (ɪn'vɛnʃənəl), *a. rare*$^{-0}$. [f. prec. + -AL^1.] Of, pertaining to, or of the nature of invention.
In recent Dicts.

†**in'ventioner.** *Obs. rare*$^{-1}$. [f. as prec. + -ER^1.] One who produces an invention; an inventor.
1612 S. STURTEVANT *Metallica* (1854) 7 The inuentioner by his study, industrie and practise, hath already brought to passe and published diuerse projects, and new deuises.

in'ventionless, *a. rare.* [f. as prec. + -LESS.] Devoid of invention.
1887 E. GURNEY *Tertium Quid* II. 77 Musical material, even in its most inventionless combinations, may have more emotional quality than marble.

†**in'ventious,** *a. Obs.* [f. INVENTION, as if on a L. type **inventiōsus*: see -OUS.] Having or showing a power of invention; inventive.
1591 F. SPARRY tr. *Cattan's Geomancie* 107 The man is wise and inuentious, and especially about warres. **1599** B. JONSON *Cynthia's Rev.* II. ii, Thou art a fine inventious Rogue. **1609** HEYWOOD *Brit. Troy* I. xiv, Persuaded such a high inuentious straine Could not proceed from any Mortals braine. **1656** W. D. tr. *Comenius' Gate Lat. Unl.* §277. 75 Hee that easily apprehendeth a thing [is] ingenious; hee that deviseth, inventious.

inventive (ɪn'vɛntɪv), *a.* [a. OF. *inventif, -ive* (15th c. in Godef. *Compl.*) = It. *inventivo*; ad. L. type **inventīv-us*, f. *invent-*, ppl. stem of *invenīre* to INVENT: see -IVE.]
1. Having the faculty of invention; apt or quick to invent; original in contriving or devising.
c **1450** LYDG. *Secrees* 144 Alle othir Reemys in philosophye It doth excelle and of hih Reson Is moost inventyff. ?*c* **1470** G. ASHBY *Active Policy* 12 A personne, lerned and Inuentif. *a* **1568** ASCHAM *Scholem.* II. (Arb.) 115 Those that haue ye inuentiuest heades. **1662** EVELYN *Chalcogr.* 34 Never hit upon among the Greeks and inventive Romans. **1765** BURKE *Hints Drama* Wks. 1842 II. 500 By the inventive genius, I mean the creator of agreeable facts and incidents. **1879** H. GEORGE *Progr. & Pov.* x. iii. (1881) 473 No slaveholding people were ever an inventive people.
b. Const. *of.*
1603 HOLLAND *Plutarch's Mor.* 252 He was passing ingenious and inventive of matter. **1834** HT. MARTINEAU *Demerara* iv. 46 Not a slave on the plantation was so inventive of excuses. **1869** *Adam Smith's W.N.* I. I. vi. 50 *note,* This labour..is inventive of mechanical expedients.
2. Characterized by invention; produced by or showing original contrivance.
1601 HOLLAND *Pliny* II. 535 A notable picture..the deuise whereof was passing full of wit, and verie inuentiue. **1816** SCOTT *Old Mort.* xxxv, Treated with every circumstance of inventive mockery and insult. **1856** RUSKIN *Mod. Paint.* III. IV. iii. §21 The last characteristic of great art is that it must be inventive, that is, be produced by the imagination.
†**3.** Invented, made up, fictitious. *Obs.*
1612 WARNER (*title*) Albion's England; a continued historie of the same Kingdome..not barren in varietie of inventive and historicall intermixtures. **1673** [R. LEIGH] *Transp. Reh.* 42 The absurdity of his inventive Divinity.

inventively (ɪn'vɛntɪvlɪ), *adv.* [f. prec. + -LY^2.] In an inventive manner; in a way characterized by invention.
1847 in CRAIG. **1868** RUSKIN *Time & Tide* vi, The Japanese masks..were inventively frightful, like fearful dreams. **1898** *Link* Mar. 4/3 Those..who are inventively minded.

inventiveness (ɪn'vɛntɪvnɪs). [f. as prec. + -NESS.] The quality of being inventive; power or faculty of invention; aptitude in inventing.
1668 WILKINS *Real Char.* III. vii. 441 Inventiveness. **1727** BAILEY vol. II, *Inventiveness,* Aptness to invent. **1819** FOSTER *Pop. Ignor.* (1834) 114 An incessant multifarious inventiveness in making almost every sort of information offer itself in..attractive forms. **1882** H. SPENCER in *Standard* 31 Oct. 5/7 The inventiveness which, stimulated by the need for economising labour, has been so wisely fostered among us.

inventor (ɪn'vɛntə(r)). Also 6 -our, (-ure), *Sc.* -ar, 6–9 -er. [a. L. *inventor*, agent-n. from *invenīre* to come upon, INVENT. Cf. F. *inventeur* (1454 in Hatz.-Darm.).] One who invents.
†**1.** One who finds out, a discoverer (whether by chance, or by investigation and effort). *Obs.*
1509 BARCLAY *Shyp of Folys* 7 b (8 a), Esculapius which was fyrst Inuentour of Phesyke. **1541** R. COPLAND *Galyen's Terapeut.* 2 F iij b, To shewe that Hippocrates hath ben inuentour..of all other thynges that is for to be knowen to hym that ought to hele an vlcere well. **1546** LANGLEY *Pol. Verg. de Invent.* I. xvii, The inuentours of Herbes medicinable. **1570** BILLINGSLEY *Euclid* I. xv. 24 Thales Mileseus..was the first inuenter of this Proposition. **1684** RAY *Corr.* (1848) 139, I am not sure that Mr. Newton was the first inventor of that plant. **1726** FREIND *Hist. Med.* II. 315 Dr. Willis, the first inventor of the nervous system.
2. One who devises or contrives; a contriver, designer; now, usually, One who devises something fictitious or false, a fabricator. †Formerly, also, a founder, institutor (*obs.*).
1513 MORE in Grafton *Chron.* (1568) II. 807 Although king Richarde harde often of these..malicious saiyngs..he durst not wyth strong hande be on the first inventors revenged. **1552** HULOET, Inuentour of false accusations, and tales, *sycophanta.* **1557** N. T. (Genev.) *Rom.* I. 30 Inuenters of euyl thynges, disobedient to father and mother. **1570** BUCHANAN *Admonit.* Wks. (1892) 24 Counsalours of tratouris, inuentaris of tressoun. **1594** T. B. *La Primaud. Fr. Acad.* I. 353 Some say that the Lydians were the first inventers of games. **1613** PURCHAS *Pilgrimage* (1614) 586 Heere also lived the first Heremites (the first..of which was Antony, an Egyptian, inventor of this order). **1685** STILLINGFL. *Orig. Brit.* i. 8 These Inventers of History have still given out, that they met with some Elder Writers, out of whom they have pretended to derive their Reports. **1882** SPURGEON *Treas. Dav.* Ps. cxix. 23 When we suffer from a libel it is better to pray about it than..even to demand an apology from the inventor.
3. One who devises or produces something new (as an instrument, an art, etc.) by original contrivance; the originator of a previously unknown method or means of doing something; 'the first finder-out'. (The prevailing sense.)
1555 EDEN *Decades* To Rdr. (Arb. 49), Of the mazes cauled Labyrinthi, or of horryble great Images cauled Colossi..and..other portentous inuentions, the which..brynge rather a fame to theyr inuentoures, then trewe glorye. **1570** DEE *Math. Pref.* 34 A certaine Instrument: which by the Inuenter and Artificer..was solde. **1623-4** *Act 21 Jas. I*, c. 3 §6 [*Statute of Monopolies*] Lettres Patente..to the true and first Inventor and Inventors of such Manufactures. **1738** WARBURTON *Div. Legat.* I. Ded. 6 Applauses due to the Inventers of the Arts of Life. **1798** FERRIAR *Illustr. Sterne* ii. 26 Its author is no more thought of than the inventor of the compass. **1827** HARE *Guesses* Ser. I. (1847) 34 Xerxes promist a great reward to the inventer of a new pleasure. *a* **1859** MACAULAY *Hist. Eng.* xxiii. V. 37 He was the inventor of Exchequer Bills; and they were popularly called Montague's notes.

inventorial (ɪnvɛn'təːrɪəl), *a. rare.* [f. L. type **inventōri-us* (f. *inventor*) + -AL^1.] Pertaining to, or having the character of, an inventory; detailed. Hence **inven'torially** *adv.*, in the manner of an inventory, in detail.
1604 SHAKS. *Ham.* V. ii. 118 (Qo. 2) To deuide him inuentorially, would dosie th' arithmaticke of memory. **1830** S. MAUNDER *Dict. Eng. Lang., Inventorial.* **1871** H. B. FORMAN *Living Poets* 378 An ingenious and inventorial minuteness of circumstance.

inventories (ɪn'vɛntərɪz), *sb. pl. colloq.* [f. INVENT or INVENTOR, after *Fisheries*, the name of a previous exhibition: cf. COLINDERIES, HEALTHERIES.] A name familiarly given to the Inventions Exhibition held in London in 1885.
1885 *Pall Mall G.* 31 Mar. 3/1 The 'Fisheries', the 'Healtheries', or the 'Inventories'. **1885** DINSDALE (*title*) Sketches at the 'Inventories'.

inventorize (ɪn'vɛntəraɪz), *v.* Also 7 -arize. [f. INVENTORY (or INVENTARY) + -IZE.] **a.** *trans.* To make an inventory of; to record in detail; to catalogue. **b.** *intr.* To make an inventory.
1601 J. WHEELER *Treat. Comm.* 42 He commanded also the ships and goods of all the English Merchants..to be attached, and inuentarised. **1708** MOTTEUX *Rabelais* IV. xlix. (1737) 199 Strictly mustering up, and inventorising your Sins. **1846** MRS. MARSH *Emilia Wyndham* viii. I. 193 He sat down, and began inventorizing, examining, and noting, and was soon lost in business.

inventory ('ɪnvəntərɪ), *sb.* [ad. med.L. *inventōri-um*, for cl.L. *inventāri-um* (see INVENTAR, INVENTARY): cf. OF. *inventoire, inventore.*]
1. A detailed list of articles, such as goods and chattels, or parcels of land, found to have been in the possession of a person at his decease or conviction, sometimes with a statement of the nature and value of each; hence any such detailed statement of the property of a person, of the goods or furniture in a house or messuage, or the like.
[**1483**: see INVITORY *sb.*^{2}] **1523** FITZHERB. *Husb.* §151, I haue sene..inuentories made after theyr decease of theyr appareyll. **1577** HELLOWES *Gueuara's Chron.* 137 He caused them to giue an inuentorie, of their owne proper goods. **1582** in Hakluyt *Voy.* (1600) III. 755 You shall make a iust and true inuentorie..of all of the tackle [etc.]. **1590** SWINBURNE *Testaments* 101 b, Euerie tutor ought..to make a true inuentorie of al the goods and cattelles of his pupil. **1613** SHAKS. *Hen. VIII*, III. ii. 451 There take an Inuentory of all I haue, To the last peny, 'tis the Kings. *a* **1714** BURNET *Hist. Ref.* an. 1553 (R.) Visitors were..appointed to examine what church-plate, jewels, and other furniture, was in all cathedrals and churches; and to compare their account with the inventories made in former visitations. **1769** *Junius Lett.* xxix. 133 *note,* The..duke..ordered an inventory to be taken of his son's wearing apparel. **1855** PRESCOTT *Philip II*, I. III. iii. 345 The duke's emissaries were active in making inventories of the property of the suspected parties.
2. a. *gen.* or *fig.* from 1. A list, catalogue; a detailed account.
1589 *Pappe w. Hatchet* D iv, I haue taken an inuentorie of al thy vnciuill..tearmes. **1607** E. GRIMSTONE (*title*) A General Inventorie of the History of France from the beginning of the Monarchie unto 1598. By I. de Serres. **1641** MILTON *Ch. Govt.* I. vi. Wks. (1851) 126 What sects? What are their opinions? give us the Inventory. *a* **1708** BEVERIDGE *Priv. Th.* I. (1730) 56 All He hath is briefly summed up in this short Inventory; whatsoever is in Heaven above, or in the Earth beneath, is His. **1856** EMERSON *Eng. Traits, Ability* Wks. (Bohn) II. 40 Sir John Herschel..at the Cape of Good Hope, finished his inventory of the southern heaven. **1857** TRENCH *Defic. Eng. Dict.* 5 The lexicographer is making an inventory; that is his business;..his task is to make his inventory complete.
b. *spec.* in *Linguistics.*
1945-49 *Acta Linguistica* V. 88 The graphemes become manifested in concrete letters and letter-attributes... These items make up what may be called the graphic inventory of the given language, which has..its counterpart in the phonic inventory of the same language. **1954** U. WEINREICH in *Word* X. 394 One thing is certain: In the study of language contact and interference..a clear picture of differences in inventory is a prerequisite. *Ibid.* 395 We are not told whether in the phoneme inventory of Southeastern American English, the /æy/ of *pass* does or does not correspond as an inventory item to the /æ/ of other varieties. **1971** B. MAFENI in J. Spencer *Eng. Lang. W. Afr.* 109 It is possible that a number of nasalised vowel phonemes may be included in the vowel inventories of some of the conservative varieties of Nigerian Pidgin spoken in certain parts of the country.
3. a. *transf.* The lot or stock of goods, etc., which are or may be made the subject of an inventory.
1691 NORRIS *Pract. Disc.* 5 Those who have duly prized and valued the whole Inventory of this World's goods. **1784** COWPER *Task* IV. 401 All the care Ingenious Parsimony takes, but just Saves the small inventory, bed, and stool, Skillet, and old carv'd chest, from public sale. **1890** E. F. KNIGHT *Cruise of 'Alerte'* ii. 30 She was provided..with new sails..and an excellent inventory throughout. **1895** *Daily News* 30 Nov. 3/4 Paying all outgoings, which included a heavy inventory.
b. *spec.* The quantity of material, etc., in use or held in stock in an installation at any one time. Also *attrib.*
1955 *Proc. Internat. Conf. Peaceful Uses Atomic Energy* (United Nations) III. 4/2 The inventory is the total of all separated fissile fuel supplied to the reactor or system other than produced internally in the reactor, less the amount assignable to the steady rate of make-up. **1963** *Chem. Engineer* 292/1 Returns..may range from inventory statements to quality control rights. *Ibid.*, The problem of maintaining minimum inventories at minimum cost to the company. **1970** *New Scientist* 25 June 628/2 Freezing also wins over evaporating as the 'heat inventory' is far lower —the latent heat of fusion is far less than the latent heat of evaporation. **1970** *Supervisor* XXI. 65/2 Vehicles are built for inventory in slack sales periods in anticipation of the peak sales periods. Production hours can thus be stored as physical inventory.
4. *attrib.*
1529 in *10th Rep. Hist. MSS. Comm.* App. IV. 532 The Inventory Bylle wrytten by Richard Thurketill parishe prest of Eye. **1906** *Daily Chron.* 1 Feb. 5/1 An attempt to enforce the inventory clause of the new separation law was responsible for serious conflict between the police and the people in many quarters of Paris to-day. **1927** CARR-SAUNDERS & JONES *Survey Social Struct. Eng. & Wales* 107 There is a distinction between what we may call the 'going concern' and the 'inventory' methods of estimating wealth. **1943** N. J. SILBERLING *Dynamics of Business* xviii. 443 Manufacturing and mining industries are now able to operate more freely on a rational inventory-valuation method that unquestionably will introduce greater stability in income statements. *Ibid.* xvi. 367 Speculation in raw materials or merchandise or what is known as 'inventory write-up'. **1951** A. H. HANSEN *Business Cycles & National Income* II. ix. 122 What is happening..to inventory accumulation..throws light on how business activity, employment, and income are likely to unfold. **1958** *Spectator* 7 Feb. 186/1 One would expect the present cyclical-type recession [in the U.S.A.] to last longer than the previous inventory-type recession of twelve to sixteen months. **1962** A. BATTERSBY *Guide to Stock Control* p. vii, Not only do excessive stocks immobilize our capital resources: they can generate the so-called 'inventory recession'. **1969** J. ARGENTI *Managem. Techniques* 137 That aspect of inventory control concerned with how large a consignment of any given item one puts into stock at a time.

inventory ('ɪnvəntərɪ), *v.* See also INVENTARY. [f. prec. sb.] **1.** *trans.* To make an inventory or descriptive list of; to enter in an inventory, to catalogue: **a.** goods, etc.
[**1526**: see INVITORY.] **1622** SIR R. BOYLE in *Lismore Papers* (1886) II. 40 Sir Lawrence Parsons..was to inventory all the wrytings. **1649** EVELYN *Diary* 2 Apr., To London, and inventoried my moveables. **1721** *Lond. Gaz.* No. 5986/3 Any such Estate not inventoried. **1762-71** H. WALPOLE *Vertue's Anecd. Paint.* (1786) II. 110 Certain commissioners were..appointed to inventory, secure and appraise the said goods. **1881** M. A. LEWIS *2 Pretty Girls* I. 2 All his possessions were being inventoried for sale.
b. *gen.* or *fig.* (Cf. *to take stock of.*)
1601 SHAKS. *Twel. N.* I. v. 264 It [my beauty] shal be inuentoried and euery particle and vtensile labell'd to my will. **1645** MILTON *Colast.* Wks. (1851) 345 The lerned Author himself is inventoried, and summ'd up, to the utmost value of his Livery cloak. **1730** T. BOSTON *View Covt. Grace* (1771) 228 This trust makes the unsearchable riches of Christ, not to be particularly inventoried by us, since they are unsearchable. **1889** C. D. WARNER *Lit. Journ. World* vii, When she had scanned and thoroughly inventoried Margaret.
2. *intr.* and *trans.* To amount to or be worth (so much) on an inventory.
1902 G. H. LORIMER *Lett. Merchant* ix. 113 The last time I saw her, she inventoried about $10,000 as she stood. **1905** *Springfield* (Mass.) *Weekly Republ.* 20 Oct. 12 The late Senator Platt left an estate which inventories at $20,880.

inventress (ɪn'vɛntrɪs). [f. INVENTOR + -ESS.] A female inventor.
1586 T. B. *La Primaud. Fr. Acad.* 71 The inventresse of lawes, and the mistres of maners and discipline. **1697** DRYDEN *Alexander's Feast* 162 At last divine Cecilia came, Inventress of the vocal frame. **1744** ELIZA HEYWOOD *Female Spectator* II. 132 The ingenious inventress of it had made them call at Rome. **1862** RAWLINSON *Anc. Mon.* I. viii. 216 Chaldæa stands forth as the great parent and original inventress of Asiatic civilisation.
†**b.** A female finder or discoverer. *Obs. rare.*

1790 Pennant *London* (1813) 614 The Holy Cross, and its inventress Helena.

†**inven'trice.** *Obs.* [F. fem. of *inventeur* INVENTOR.] = prec.

1509 Barclay *Shyp of Folys* (1874) II. 104 Pouerte of all the lawes was Inuentryce, Mother vnto vertue, confonderes of vyce. **1546** Langley *Pol. Verg. de Invent.* III. i. 63 Virgyll wytnesseth that Ceres was firste inuentrice of it.

in'ventrix. ? *Obs.* [L. fem. of INVENTOR.] = prec.

1604 Parsons *3rd Pt. Three Convers. Eng.* Relat. Trial 108 This inuentrix of grace, this mediatrix of Saluation. **1678** Wanley *Wond. Lit. World* IV. li. §10. 453/2 Together with Ide the Inventrix and Contriver of this mischief. **1744** Paterson *Comm. Milton's P.L.* 327 She was the inventrix of corn and husbandry.

†**in'ventuary.** *Obs.* [irreg. var. of INVENTARY.] = INVENTORY *sb.*

1494 Fabyan *Chron.* VII. 504 Inuentuaryes [were] made of suche goodys as than remayned. **1529** *Act 21 Hen. VIII*, c. 5 The probacion of any testament and inventuary.

in'venturous, *a. rare.* [IN-³.] Not venturous.

1863 F. Cerny [Griffiths] *The Jew* 41 The boat which hugs the shore, Creeping inventurous from point to port.

†**inve'nust,** *a. Obs. rare*⁻¹. [f. L. *invenustus*, f. *in-* (IN-³) + *venustus* lovely.] Unlovely.

1623 Cockeram II, Not to bee Beloued, *Inuenust, Inamiable.* **1712** Oldisworth tr. *Odes Horace* I. 9/2 How Hungry, Dry and Invenuste is the Sentence.

‖**inver.** *Obs.* [a. Gael. *inbhir* (f. *in* prep. 'in' + root *ber-*, Gael. *beir* to bear, carry), freq. in place-names, as INVERNESS.] The mouth of a river; the point where one river enters another.

1615 *Burgh Rec. Aberdeen* (1848) II. 324 The first marche ..at the inver of the Blind burne quhair the same enteris in the Blackburne..direct forganes or anent the said inver.

inveracious (ɪnvəˈreɪʃəs), *a.* [IN-³.] Untruthful.

1885 F. Hall in *Nation* (N.Y.) XL. 256/3 Her..editor.. represents her as having been most disingenuous and inveracious. **1894** *Chicago Advance* 28 June, Inveracious and contradictory excuses.

inveracity (ɪnvəˈræsɪtɪ). [IN-³.] Untruthfulness; an untruth, a false statement.

1864 J. H. Newman *Apol.* App. 17 Where you may let your imagination play revel to the extent of inveracity. **1873** F. Hall *Mod. Eng.* 145 Its loathsome spawn of shams and inveracities. **1881** *Philad. Rec.* No. 3413 If any successful curb can be put upon its inveracity.

†**in'verecund,** *a. Obs.* [ad. L. *inverēcundus* shameless, f. L. *in-* (IN-³) + *verēcundus* reverent, modest, f. *verērī* to revere. Cf. 16th c. F. *inverecond* (Godef.).] Unabashed.

1657 Tomlinson *Renou's Disp.* 465 Female Vipers are.. of an inverecund and fierce aspect.

†**in'verge,** *v. Obs.* [f. IN-² + VERGE *sb.*] *trans.* To border. **a.** To furnish with a verge or border. **b.** To form a border to.

1611 Speed *Hist. Gt. Brit.* VIII. iii. §14. 385 To expiate the sinnes of his Father..hee inuerged the same with a deepe ditch, and offered vp his Crown vpon the Martyrs Tombe. —— *Theat. Gt. Brit.* xix. (1614) 37/2 The Devils Ditch.. made for a defence..against the east Angles, whose kingdome it inverged. *Ibid., Wales* iii. 111/2 This trench doth likewise inverge her west side so farre as the river.

inverisimilitude (ɪnˌverɪsɪˈmɪlɪtjuːd). [IN-³.] Lack of verisimilitude; unlikeness to truth; unlikelihood; improbability.

a **1834** Coleridge *Shaks. Notes* in *Rem.* (1836) II. 161 The events are too well and distinctly known to be, without plump inverisimilitude, crowded together in one night's exhibition. **1836** J. W. Donaldson *Theat. Greeks* (ed. 4) 366 An inverisimilitude which is only found out by dissection was to them none at all.

inverminate (ɪnˈvɜːmɪneɪt), *v. nonce-wd.* [f. IN-² + L. *vermināre*: see INVERMINATION.] *trans.* To infest like worms; to swarm or burrow in.

1830 Coleridge *Ch. & St.* (ed. 2) 225 The visible globe, that we inverminate.

invermination (ɪnˌvɜːmɪˈneɪʃən). [f. IN-² + L. *verminātiōn-em* the disease of worms, f. *vermināre* to have worms, f. *vermis* a worm.] The condition of being infested with (intestinal) worms.

1808 *Char.* in *Ann. Reg.* 116 Liable..to polysarcia, atrophy, and above all, to invermination. **1822–34** *Good's Study Med.* (ed. 4) IV. 500 Varieties of helminthea or invermination.

†**in'vermine,** *v. Obs. rare*⁻⁰. [f. It. *inverminare* (Florio), f. L. *in-* (IN-²) + *vermināre* to have worms; cf. OF. *envermer.*] *intr.* To breed worms.

1611 Florio, *Inuermicare*, to inuermine, to fill with or grow to wormes.

inver'nacular, *a. rare.* [IN-³.] Not vernacular.

1880 F. Hall *Doctor Indoctus* 10 The English translation of the invernacular phrase italicized is 'fall under consideration'.

Inverness (ɪnvəˈnɛs). [a. Gael. *Ionar-* or *Inbhirnis* mouth of the (river) Ness: see INVER.] The name of a town in the Highlands of Scotland. Hence ***Inverness cloak, overcoat***, name of an overcoat with a removable cape (***Inverness cape***).

1865 *Morning Star* 8 Mar., Two Inverness capes were also found. **1885** *Fortn. in Waggonette* 44 A thick Inverness cape covers the most of his person. **1888** *Cambridge* (Mass.) *Tribune* 24 Nov., These 'Inverness' overcoats are close-fitting, and when worn without the cape have the appearance of an ulsterette.

inveron, -oun, obs. ff. ENVIRON *v.* and *adv.*

inversatile (ɪnˈvɜːsətɪl, -aɪl), *a.* [IN-³.] Not versatile. *Entom.* Of antennæ: Not moving on their supports.

1890 in *Cent. Dict.*

inverse (ɪnˈvɜːs, ˈɪnvɜːs), *a.* and *sb.* [ad. L. *invers-us* inverted, pa. pple. of *invertĕre*, f. *in-* (IN-²) + *vertĕre* to turn: orig. sense app., To turn outside in. Cf. F. *inverse.*]

A. *adj.* **1.** Turned upside down; inverted.

a **1658** Cleveland *News fr. Newcastle* 86 A Coal-pit is a Mine of every thing..An inverse Burse, an Exchange under Ground. **1661** Lovell *Hist. Anim. & Min.* 345 Also things seeme inverse, by reason of the mutation of the site of the crystalline humour. **1703** Moxon *Mech. Exerc.* 256 Make from these Piers inverse Arches. **1709** Berkeley *Th. Vision* §100 Whether objects were erect or inverse. *a* **1845** Hood *Two Swans* ii, A tower builded on a lake, Mock'd by its inverse shadow.

2. Inverted in position, order, or relations; that proceeds in the opposite or reverse direction or order; that begins where something else ends, and ends where the other begins.

1831 Brewster *Newton* (1855) II. xxii. 298 The first who gave the analysis of the inverse truth, without supposing the direct one to be already known. **1848** Clough *Amours de Voy.* IV. 32 What shall I do?..Go on..Seeking, an inverse Saul, a kingdom to find only asses. **1868** Lockyer *Guillemin's Heavens* (ed. 3) 65 The same appearances are observed, but in an inverse order. **1869** J. Martineau *Ess.* II. 19 It must follow an inverse order.

3. *Math.* **a.** *Arith.* and *Alg.* Of such a nature in respect to another operation, relation, etc. that the starting-point or antecedent of the one is the result or conclusion of the other, and *vice versa*; opposite in nature or effect. Opp. to *direct*; e.g. *Inverse Method of Fluxions*: see quot. 1807.

inverse ratio: (*a*) a ratio related to another ratio in the way defined above, i.e. one in which the terms are reversed; (*b*) the ratio of two quantities which vary inversely, i.e. one of which increases in the exact proportion in which the other decreases, and *vice versa*; so ***inverse proportion***. (In popular language often loosely extended to the case of two things one of which decreases, or is less, as the other increases, or is greater.) ***inverse square***: often used for the relation of two quantities one of which varies inversely as the square of the other. ***Rule of Three Inverse***: that case of the Rule of Three in which the antecedent of each of the ratios corresponds to the consequent of the other.

1660 Barrow *Euclid* v. Def. xiii, Inverse ratio is when the consequent is taken as the antecedent and so compared to the antecedent as the consequent. **1790** Burke *Fr. Rev.* 139 The operation of opinion being in the inverse ratio to the number of those who abuse power. **1793** Beddoes *Math. Evid.* 19 A balance of which one arm should be ten inches, and the other one inch long, and each arm should be loaded in an inverse proportion to its length. **1806** Hutton *Course Math.* I. 44 Rule of Three Inverse, is when more requires less, or less requires more. **1807** *Ibid.* II. 279 The direct method [of fluxions] consists in finding the fluxion of any proposed fluent..; and the inverse method..consists in finding the fluent of any proposed fluxion. **1816** Playfair *Nat. Phil.* II. 295 The attraction of a spheroid, in the plane of its equator, does not decrease exactly in the inverse ratio of the square of the distance. **1816** tr. *Lacroix's Diff. & Int. Calculus* 547 By substituting for *x* the inverse function of *a* (*x*), by which is understood that function which written instead of *x* in the expression of *a* (*x*) produces *x* as the final result. *Ibid.*, e^x and log *x* are inverse functions of each other, since log (e^x) = *x*. **1834** Mrs. Somerville *Connex. Phys. Sc.* viii. (1849) 70 The inverse problem had now to be solved. **1865** Fred. Oakeley *Historical Notes* 51 The ratio of its extent appeared to be inverse with the degree in which it was sought. **1882** Minchin *Unipl. Kinemat.* 161 Matter attracting according to the law of the inverse square of distance.

b. *Geom.* ***inverse point, line, curve***, etc., one related to another point, line, curve, etc. in the way of geometrical inversion (see INVERSION 3 b).

1873 B. Williamson *Diff. Calc.* (ed. 2) xii. §181 By aid of this property the tangent at any point on a curve can be drawn, whenever that at the corresponding point of the inverse curve is known. *Ibid.* xvii. §227 If two curves be inverse to each other with respect to any origin. **1881** Casey *Sequel to Euclid* 95 If *X* be a circle, *O* its centre, *P* and *Q* two points on any radius such that the rectangle *OP*. *OQ* = square of the radius, then *P* and *Q* are called inverse points with respect to the circle.

4. *Cryst.* Opposed to *direct*: see quot.

1878 Gurney *Crystallogr.* 65 The second class of rhombohedrons may be called inverse..The unequal index is algebraically less than the other two. **1895** Story-Maskelyne *Crystallogr.* 141 and 312.

5. ***inverse spelling***, an unetymological spelling based on the spelling of another word containing an element that is no longer pronounced, e.g. *limb* from OE. *lim* after *lamb* (from OE. *lamb*).

1933 L. Bloomfield *Lang.* xvii. 294 So-called inverse spellings tell the same story... When we find the word *deleite*..spelled *delight*, then we may be sure that the [χ] was no longer spoken in words like *light*. **1956** N. E. Eliason *Tarheel Talk* v. 194 Occasionally inverse spellings occur, for example *forks* for *folks*,..and *polk* for *pork*.

6. *Cryst.* Designating a spinel structure, $B[AB]O_4$, in which half the B (trivalent) cations are in tetrahedral holes and the A (bivalent) cations together with the other half of the B cations are in octahedral holes in the array of oxide ions (in contrast to the normal structure $A[B_2]O_4$).

[**1947** Verwey & Heilmann in *Jrnl. Chem. Physics* XV. 175/2 For the sake of convenience, the first arrangement will be indicated as characteristic for 'normal spinels', the Barth and Posnjak arrangement as that of 'inversed spinels'.] **1957** *Jrnl. Physics & Chem. Solids* III. 313 These energies..may be sufficient to determine whether a given spinel shall be normal or inverse. **1970** R. G. Burns *Mineral. Applications Crystal Field Theory* vi. 112 Ni^{2+} and Cu^{2+} have a strong tendency to form inverse spinels. Ions such as Fe^{3+} and Mn^{2+}, which have zero octahedral site preference energies, form both normal and inverse spinels.

B. *sb.* **1.** An inverted state or condition; that which is in order or direction the direct opposite of something else; thus *CBA* is the inverse of *ABC*.

1681 tr. *Willis' Rem. Med. Wks.* Vocab., *Inverse*, a turning inside out, or outside in, upside down, quite contrary. **1794** G. Adams *Nat. & Exp. Philos.* IV. lii. 456 Rain, which is the inverse of evaporation. **1823** H. J. Brooke *Introd. Crystallogr.* 74 Proceeding in an order the inverse of that by which the modified crystal has been formed. **1891** Gladstone *Sp.* 2 Oct., The foreign policy of the present Administration has been well-nigh the inverse and the reverse to that of the Administration of Lord Beaconsfield.

2. The result of inversion: **a.** *Math.* A ratio, proportion, or process in which the antecedents and consequents are interchanged. Also, short for ***inverse function***.

1695 Alingham *Geom. Epit.* 101 By the other two, the inverses of both are proved, for as *a*: *A*::*b*:*B*, also as *b*:*a*::*B*:*A*. **1839** *Penny Cycl.* XIII. 5 From all the inverses of a function $\phi\chi$..we separate that one, $a\chi$, which gives both $\phi a\chi = \chi$ and $a\phi\chi = \chi$, and call it the convertible inverse.

b. *Geom.* Short for ***inverse curve, point***, etc.

1873 B. Williamson *Diff. Calc.* (ed. 2) xii. §180 If on any radius vector *OP*, drawn from a fixed origin *O*, a point *P′* be taken, such that the rectangle *OP*, *OP′* is constant, the point *P′* is called the inverse of the point *P*; and if *P* describe any curve, *P′* describes another curve called the inverse of the former. **1887** R. A. Roberts *Integ. Calc.* I. 315 The central inverse of a conic.

c. *Logic.* The proposition obtained by inversion.

1896 [see INVERSION 2 e].

3. *Rouge et Noir.* The section at the end of the table in which are placed bets wagering that the colour of the card that wins the coup will not be the same as that first dealt for a colour.

1850 *Bohn's Hand-bk. Games* 343 If the player..be determined to try his luck on the inverse, he must place his money on a yellow circle, or rather a collection of circles, situated at the extremity of the table. *Ibid.*, The punters place on the Rouge, the Noir, the Couleur, or the Inverse, the sum they wish to risk. **1909** [see COULEUR 2]. **1950** *Hoyle's Games Modernized* (ed. 20) 291 The *tailleur* never mentions the words 'Black' or 'Inverse', but always says that Red wins or Red loses, and that the colour wins or the colour loses.

4. *Math.* An element which, when combined with a given element by a given operation, produces the identity element for that operation.

E.g. the inverse of any number with respect to multiplication is the reciprocal of that number, and with respect to addition the negative of it.

1900 *Ann. Math.* II. 48 For every element T_κ exists an element (denote it by T_κ^{-1}) such that $T_\kappa T_\kappa^{-1} = T_\kappa^{-1} T_\kappa = 1$. T_κ^{-1} is called the inverse of T_κ. **1905** *Trans. Amer. Math. Soc.* VI. 187 The identity, *z*, of this group, is called the zero-element of the field, and is denoted by 0; while the inverse of an element *a* is here called the negative of *a*, and is denoted by $-a$. **1951** N. Jacobson *Lect. Abstr. Algebra* I. i. 22 If the operation in $\mathfrak{G}$ is denoted as +, we denote the identity as 0. The inverse of *a* if it exists is written as $-a$. **1953** Birkhoff & MacLane *Survey Mod. Algebra* (ed. 2) vi. 122 Hence $\phi\psi = I$ and ψ is a right-inverse of ϕ. **1965** Patterson & Rutherford *Elem. Abstr. Algebra* i. 19 Let $\wedge$ be the closed binary operation in R defined by $x \wedge y = x + y - 2x^2y^2$... Show..that every..non-zero element *x* of R such that $x > -\frac{1}{2}$ has two inverses but that if $x < -\frac{1}{2}$, then *x* has no inverse.

inverse (ɪnˈvɜːs), *v.* Now *rare.* [f. prec. or f. *invers-*, ppl. stem of *invertĕre*: cf. *reverse* vb.] *trans.* To turn upside down; to invert; to reverse in order or direction.

1611 Florio, *Inuersare*, to inuert, to inuerse. **1663** Power *Exp. Philos.* II. 115 We therefore fill'd our Glass-Tubes.. half with Water, and the rest with Ayr, and afterwards invers'd it into a pail of water. **1694** *Loyal Satirist* in Somers *Tracts* VII. 68 You would think the church as well as religion, were inversed, and the anticks which were used to be without were removed into the pulpit. *a* **1701** Sedley *Happy Pair* Wks. 1766 I. 17 From hence the baffled world has been inverst, Princes involv'd in war, and people curst. **1849** C. Brontë *Shirley* vii, Inversing the natural order of insect existence.

inversed (ɪnˈvɜːst), *ppl. a. rare.* Also **inverst.** [f. as INVERSE *a.* + -ED¹, -T.]

1. Inverted; turned upside down.

1603 SIR C. HEYDON *Jud. Astrol.* v. 158 Hauing had the world inuerst presented to their imagination in their sleepe. **1664** POWER *Exp. Philos.* I. 5 The supportance of her self, though with her back downwards and perpendicularly invers'd to the Horizon. **1703** MOXON *Mech. Exerc.* 256 To turn Arches inversed, or upside down.

b. Reversed; with reverted sequence.

1581 SAVILE *Tacitus, Hist.* Annot. (1591) 52 Liuy, in describing these Centuries, seemeth to vse an inuersed kinde of speech. **1657** J. SMITH *Myst. Rhet.* 117 *Antimetabole* is a sentence inverst, or turn'd back.

2. Turned inward.

1584 R. SCOT *Discov. Witcher.* XIII. xix. (1886) 258 Diverse sorts of glasses..the round, the cornerd, the inversed, the eversed.

Hence **inversedly** (ɪn'vɜːstlɪ, -'sɛdlɪ), *adv. rare.* = next.

1753 *Phil. Trans.* XLVIII. 83 That the gravity at any point of the earth is inversedly as the distance from the center.

inversely (ɪn'vɜːslɪ), *adv.* [f. INVERSE *a.* + -LY².] In an inverse manner or order; as the inverse; by inversion.

1660 BARROW *Euclid* v. xxi, Because *D.E::B.C.* therefore inversely *E.D.* **1695** ALINGHAM *Geom. Epit.* 19 If *A* : *B* :: *C* : *D* : then inversly as *B* : *A* :: *D* : *C*. *a* **1738** HELSHAM *Lect. Nat. Phil.* i. (1739) 4 Why the water rises to heights which are inversly as the distances of the glasses. **1766** tr. *Beccaria's Ess. Crimes* xxvi. (1793) 92 It seems as if the greatness of a state ought to be inversely as the sensibility and activity of the individuals. *c* **1860** FARADAY *Forces Nat.* ii. 46 Two bodies attract each other inversely as the square of the distance. **1868** LOCKYER *Guillemin's Heavens* (ed. 3) 129 At the Last Quarter we get a phase like that presented at the first quarter, but inversely situated.

b. Invertedly; upside down; as ***inversely conical***, conical with the vertex downward.

1776–96 WITHERING *Brit. Plants* (ed. 3) I. 122 Petals 2, inversely heart-shaped. *Ibid.* II. 197 Root wood-like, inversely conical at the crown. **1849** MURCHISON *Siluria* vii. 133 Of an inversely pyramidal shape.

inversion (ɪn'vɜːʃən). [ad. L. *inversiōn-em* an inverting, n. of action from *invertĕre* to INVERT; cf. F. *inversion* (1570 in Hatz.-Darm.).] The action of inverting, the condition of being inverted.

I. 1. a. A turning upside down.

1598 FLORIO, *Inuersione*, an inuersion, a turning inside out, or upside downe, a misplacing. **1604** R. CAWDREY *Table Alph.*, *Inuersion*, turning vpside downe, turning contrariwise. **1663** POWER *Exp. Philos.* II. 111 After inversion of the Tube into the vessel'd Quicksilver. **1860** TYNDALL *Glac.* I. iv. 36 They often mistook this aërial inversion for the reflection from a lake.

b. *Geol.* The folding back of stratified rocks upon each other, so that older strata overlie the newer.

1849 MURCHISON *Siluria* iv. 72 A great fault was.. supposed to intervene, to account for this apparent inversion. **1882** GEIKIE *Text Bk. Geol.* IV. IV. 518 Individual mountains..present stupendous examples of inversion, great groups of strata being folded over and over each other.

2. a. A reversal of position, order, sequence, or relation.

1599 H. BUTTES *Dyets drie Dinner* M ij, We may now a dayes use Plinies wordes, with an inversion of the sense. **1639** FULLER *Holy War* II. xiv. (1647) 63 The inversion of order bringeth all to confusion. **1646** SIR T. BROWNE *Pseud. Ep.* I. iii. 9 A reciprocation, or rather an Inversion of the creation, making God one way, as he made us another; that is, after our Image, as he made us after his owne. **1695** WOODWARD *Nat. Hist. Earth* (1702) 61 Without Inversion or Variation of the ordinary Periods, Revolutions, and Successions of things. *a* **1716** SOUTH *Serm.* (1737) VI. x. 395 If, by an odd inversion of the command, all that we do is first to pray against a temptation, and afterwards to watch for it. **1855** BAIN *Senses & Int.* III. i. §42 (1864) 397 When we dress by a mirror we perform a series of inversions, very difficult at first. **1876** T. HARDY *Ethelberta* (1890) 133 'Tis an unnatural inversion of the manners of society.

†**b.** *Rhet.* The turning of an opponent's argument against himself; = ANTISTROPHE 3 b. *Obs.*

1551 T. WILSON *Logike* (1567) 34 b, You maye confute the same by inuersion, that is to saie, tournyng his taile cleane contrary. **1657** J. SMITH *Myst. Rhet.* 125 Inversion is a figure, whereby the Orator or speaker reasons, or brings in a thing for himself, which was reported or alleadged against him.

c. *Gram.* Reversal of the order of words; = ANASTROPHE.

1586 A. DAY *Eng. Secretary* II. (1625) 82 *Anastrophe*, a preposterous inversion of words besides their common course, as..faults, no man liveth without. **1620** T. GRANGER *Div. Logike* II. 229 Inversion is when the Consequent, or bond, is placed before the Antecedent. **1791** BOSWELL *Johnson* an. 1750, The structure of his sentences..often has somewhat of the inversion of Latin. **1875** JOWETT *Plato* (ed. 2) IV. 279 Any arbitrary inversion of our ordinary modes of speech is disturbing to the mind.

d. *Mus.* The action of inverting an interval, chord, phrase, or subject (see INVERT *v.* 2 e); also, the interval, chord, etc. so produced (in relation to the original one).

first, second, etc. ***inversions*** (of a chord): the chords produced by taking the successive higher notes of the original chord respectively as the lowest note.

1806 CALLCOTT *Mus. Gram.* II. i. 100 When any lower Note of an Interval is placed an Octave higher, or the higher Note an Octave lower, the change thereby produced is called *Inversion.* **1838, 1875** [see INVERT *v.* 2 e]. **1869** OUSELEY *Counterp.* xix. 159 Sometimes..the answer is made by contrary motion, constituting a 'fugue by inversion'. **1880** W. S. ROCKSTRO in Grove *Dict. Mus.* II. 16 [In] Double Counterpoint in the Octave..the Inversion is produced by ..transposing the upper part an octave lower, or [*vice versa*]. But the Inversion may take place in any other Interval. *Ibid.* 17 The Chord of the 6-3 is called the First Inversion of the Common Chord; and the Chord of the 6-4, the Second. **1889** E. PROUT *Harmony* vi. §150 A triad, which consists of three notes, has two inversions, because it contains two notes besides its root, and either of these notes can be placed in the bass.

e. *Logic.* A form of immediate inference in which a new proposition is formed whose subject is the negative of that of the original proposition.

1896 WELTON *Manual of Logic* (ed. 2) III. iii. §102 Inversion is the inferring, from a given proposition, another proposition whose subject is the contradictory of the subject of the original proposition. The given proposition is called the Invertend, that which is inferred from it is termed the Inverse... The rule for Inversion is: Convert either the Obverted Converse or the Obverted Contrapositive.

f. *Meteorol.* In full, ***temperature inversion***. An increase of temperature with height in part of the atmosphere (the reverse of the usual situation); a layer of air having such a temperature gradient; also, more widely, an analogous deviation from the normal temperature gradient in bodies of water.

1902 *Sci. Abstr.* V. 285 There are instances of temperature inversion, ascribed to insulation of the clouds. **1903** *Sci. Abstr.* A. VI. 491 Temperature inversions were observed.. mostly between altitudes 200 and 1,500 m. **1906** W. MARRIOTT *Hints to Meteorol. Observers* (ed. 6) 66/2 *Inversion of temperature*, a warmer stratum of air above a colder one. **1928** D. BRUNT *Meteorol.* vi. 59 An inversion is most readily produced during a clear night in winter. **1957** G. E. HUTCHINSON *Treat. Limnol.* I. vii. 487 Slight temperature inversions of the order of 0·1° to 0·2°C often occurred in the temperature curves at the bottom of two Austrian lakes. **1969** *Courier-Mail* (Brisbane) 16 Sept. 2/3 New York's skyscraper skyline is now badly clouded..only when the city is trapped under what is called an 'inversion'. **1971** *Nature* 26 Feb. 583/2 It is only a decade since old people in their hundreds were killed off in northern cities when sulphur dioxide and other noisome products were trapped beneath inversion layers.

g. Philol. ***inversion-compound***, a compound place-name in which the second element is a personal name, or a word designating a person, in the genitive (or genitive-equivalent) case, as the property-name *Kuikobba* (in Kirkwall), f. ON. *kví Kobba* sheep-pen of Kobbi.

1918 E. EKWALL *Scandinavians & Celts in N.-W. Eng.* i. 15 In inversion-compounds the second element is a necessary ingredient, which can be absent only owing to ellipsis. **1963** C. MATRAS in Brown & Foote *Early Eng. & Norse Stud.* xii. 148 'Inversion-compounds' can serve as a criterion for classifying a settlement as Norwegian (as distinct from Danish).

h. *Biol.* A reversal of the order of the genes in a chromosome segment as compared with the corresponding segment of a normal homologous chromosome; a chromosome segment exhibiting such a reversal.

1921 A. H. STURTEVANT in *Proc. Nat. Acad. Sci.* VII. 236 The simple inversion of a section of a normal chromosome. **1939** C. H. WADDINGTON *Introd. Mod. Genetics* iv. 93 Pairing may be more nearly complete in flies heterozygous for very long inversions. **1964** G. H. HAGGIS et al. *Introd. Molecular Biol.* x. 258 The term mutation embraces stable chromosomal variations..including..the turning of an interstitial segment back to front (inversion). **1969** G. W. BURNS *Sci. Genetics* xii. 221 Inversions act chiefly as so-called crossover suppressors. **1972** W. V. BROWN *Textbk. Cytogenetics* xiv. 204/2 In most interbreeding populations inversions are eliminated because of the numerous types of inviability they produce. *Ibid.* 205/1 *Drosophila pseudoobscura* is unusual for the number of different inversions within especially the third chromosome of the species.

i. *Electr.* The conversion of direct current into alternating current: the opposite of rectification.

1926 L. B. W. JOLLEY *A.C. Rectification* (ed. 2) xix. 443 The problem of inversion, viz. the conversion from direct to alternating current. **1964** *New Scientist* 2 Apr. 25/1 Thyristors can also be used to convert d.c. to a.c.—a process known as 'inversion'. **1967** F. G. SPREADBURY *Electr. Inverters* i. 2 The choice of a current converter for inversion purposes will, of course, depend on the magnitude of the output voltage, current and frequency required.

j. *Telecommunications.* Reversal of the order of the component frequencies of a signal: cf. INVERT *v.* 2 g.

1930 *Engineering* 14 Nov. 625/3 Though the simple inversion..is satisfactory on short waves, it is not so effective on long waves, since, as only one side band is present, it is immaterial whether the transmission is inverted or not, provided the oscillator at the receiving end injects a local carrier of the correct frequency. **1933** K. HENNEY *Radio Engin. Handbk.* x. 273 To insure secrecy of transmission, frequency inversion or frequency scrambling methods are used. **1967** D. H. HAMSHER *Communication Syst. Engin. Handbk.* x. 23 A reduction in interfering energy of about 3 db is realized by frequency inversion.

k. *Computers.* The conversion of either of the two binary digits or signals into the other; negation.

1955 R. K. RICHARDS *Arithmetic Operations in Digital Computers* ii. 32 The 'not' operation, or inversion, is symbolized by a block labeled with the letter *I.* **1970** O. DOPPING *Computers & Data Processing* ii. 39 The number that is somewhat inappropriately called the 1-complement of x is obtained simply by inversion, i.e. by substituting zeroes for all ones and vice versa. **1972** B. H. VASSOS *Analog & Digital Electronics for Scientists* viii. 207 There are two other basic gates.., called NOR and NAND, respectively. They cannot be implemented by simple diode logic, because inversion is required, which can only be produced by an active device.

l. *Physics.* In full ***population inversion***. A transposition of the relative numbers of atoms or molecules occupying certain energy levels.

1961 *Physical Rev. Lett.* VI. 106/1 Population inversions are achieved between several Ne levels by means of excitation transfer. **1968** E. L. STEELE *Optical Lasers in Electronics* iv. 135 In the limit when total inversion occurs the ground state is entirely empty. **1973** *Sci. Amer.* Feb. 92/3 The condition of having more atoms in the upper state is called a population inversion (because it goes against the normal processes of nature, which tend to keep more electrons at lower energies than at higher energies).

3. *Math.* **a.** *Arith.* and *Alg.* The reversal of a ratio by interchanging the positions of the antecedent and consequent.

1660 BARROW *Euclid* v. xx, Because *E.F::B.C* by inversion shall be *F.E::C.B.* **1695** ALINGHAM *Geom. Epit.* 102 The Alternations and Inversions of which, follow from what was before proved. **1827** HUTTON *Course Math.* I. 327 If four quantities be proportional; they will be in proportion by inversion, or inversely. **1837–8** SIR W. HAMILTON *Logic* xv. (1866) I. 272 These two quantities stand to each other..in a determinate ratio—the ratio of inversion.

b. *Geom.* A transformation in which for each point of a given figure is substituted another point in the same straight line from a fixed point (called the ***origin*** or ***centre of inversion***), and so situated that the product of the distances of the two points from the centre of inversion is constant (***cyclical*** or ***spherical inversion***). Also extended to similar transformations involving a more complex relation of corresponding points or lines, as ***quadric inversion***, ***tangential inversion***.

1873 B. WILLIAMSON *Diff. Calc.* (ed. 2) xii. §182 If the focus [of a conic] be the origin of inversion, the inverse is a curve called the Limaçon of Pascal. **1885** WATSON & BURBURY *Math. The. Electr. & Magn.* I. 125 According as the centre of inversion is without or within the original sphere.

c. *Math.* The process of finding a function $g(y)$ which either (*a*) yields a variable x when its argument is a given function $y = f(x)$ of that variable, or else (*b*) yields a given function when transformed by a given transformation.

1880 *Encycl. Brit.* XIII. 66/2 We have mentioned..the problem of inversion which leads to elliptic functions, viz., that if $u = \mathrm{F}(\kappa, \phi)$, then $\phi = \mathrm{am}\, u$. **1934** *Trans. Amer. Math. Soc.* XXXVI. 107 $f(x) = \int_0^\infty e^{-xt} d\alpha(t)$... By the inversion of the integral we mean the determination of the function $\alpha(t)$ in terms of the function $f(x)$. **1962** D. R. COX *Renewal Theory* i. 11 Suppose that we have calculated the Laplace transform $k^*(s)$ of an as yet unknown function $k(x)$. The problem of finding $k(x)$ from $k^*(s)$ is called the inversion problem. *Ibid.* 13 We shall commonly find that, although we can find a quite simple expression for the Laplace transform, $k^*(s)$, of the function $k(x)$ in which we are interested, the inversion cannot be done explicitly in simple terms. **1968** P. A. P. MORAN *Introd. Probability Theory* vi. 250 $\phi(t)$ [$= \int_{-\infty}^{\infty} e^{itx} dF(x)$] is uniquely determined by $F(x)$. We shall show that the reverse is true by obtaining an explicit expression, the inversion formula, for $F(x)$ in terms of $\phi(t)$.

4. *Mil.* An evolution by which ranks are converted into files.

1635 BARRIFFE *Mil. Discip.* xxxi. (1661) 38 Inversion doth alwayes produce file or files; and Conversion, rank or ranks. **1650** R. ELTON *Mil. Art* (1668) 32 My subject in this Chapter shall be of Ranks filing, and Files filing, and Ranks ranking, and Files ranking, which are by some called Inversion and Conversion. **1832** [see INVERT *v.* 3].

5. *Chem.* **a.** A decomposition of certain carbohydrates into two different substances, as of cane-sugar into dextrose and lævulose, whereby the direction of the optical rotatory power is reversed. (Cf. INVERTED 6.)

1864–72 WATTS *Dict. Chem.* II. 863 A solution of cane-sugar left to itself, or warmed with dilute acids, loses its dextro-rotatory power, and acquires a lævo-rotatory power, which, when the transformation, or *inversion*, is complete, amounts to 38° for every 100° of the original rotation to the right.

b. In full, ***Walden inversion*** [tr. G. *Walden'sche umkehrung* (E. Fischer 1906, in *Ber. d. Deut. Chem. Ges.* XXXIX. 2895), named after P. von *Walden* (1863–1957), Latvian chemist]. Originally, the reversal of the direction of optical rotation observed in certain substitution reactions. Now interpreted as a change of configuration (from D to L or vice versa) occurring when a reactant enters along the axis of the bond between a central atom and the leaving group and causes the other substituents on the central atom to pass through a plane perpendicular to this axis; hence extended to other substitution reactions in which there is such a reversal of configuration, regardless of whether the molecule is optically active or the direction of activity reversed.

1899 *Jrnl. Chem. Soc.* LXXVI. II. 540 If..the sign of the rotatory power alone is considered, then optical inversion

occurs in the action of phosphorus pentachloride and pentabromide..and the only 'normal' action in which no inversion occurs is the hydrolysis by means of silver oxide. **1911** *Ann. Rep. Progr. Chem.* VIII. 64 Most cases of the Walden inversion have been observed in transformations of α-substituted acids and their derivatives. **1937** F. C. WHITMORE *Org. Chem.* xxi. 480 In the Walden inversion, the process takes place on a *single* carbon atom instead of with a system of several atoms. **1962** E. L. ELIEL *Stereochem. Carbon Compds.* xiii. 375 In most cases the covalent attachment occurs from the side opposite to the one from which X had departed..and the stereochemical course is therefore predominantly inversion. **1964** D. A. SHIRLEY *Org. Chem.* ix. 202 The molecule of methyl bromide is said to undergo inversion in its conversion to methyl alcohol. **1966** MORRISON & BOYD *Org. Chem.* (ed. 2) xiv. 473 Paul Walden..discovered the phenomenon of inversion in 1896 when he encountered one of the exceptional reactions in which inversion [of configuration] does *not* take place. **1968** J. MARCH *Adv. Org. Chem.* x. 254 The Walden inversion has been found at a primary carbon atom..and at a sulfur (in sulfoxides), a silicon, and a phosphorus atom.

†**6.** = METAPHOR. *Obs.*

1552 HULOET, Inuersion of wordes, *allegoria, est quædam figu.* **1553** T. WILSON *Rhet.* (1567) 88a, An Allegorie, or inuersion of wordes. **1589** PUTTENHAM *Eng. Poesie* III. xvi[i]. (Arb.) 190 In these verses the inuersion or metaphore, lyeth in these words, *saw, harbourd, run.*

7. *Physical Chem.* A transformation of a substance, esp. an enantiotropic one, from one solid form to another; **inversion temperature**, the temperature at which the two forms can coexist in equilibrium.

1903 M. H. FISCHER tr. *Cohen's Physical Chem.* vii. 111 This temperature, above which the Glauber's salt is transformed into the anhydride, is designated the inversion temperature of the Glauber's salt. **1904** A. FINDLAY *Phase Rule* iii. 34 If the vapour phase [of sulphur] is absent and the system maintained under a constant pressure..there will also be a definite temperature at which the two solid forms are in equilibrium... This temperature..is known as the transition temperature or inversion temperature. **1928** *Jrnl. Physical Chem.* XXXII. 1205 When quartz is subjected to a uniform hydrostatic pressure..the temperature of its high-low inversion is raised. **1947** R. H. BOGUE *Chem. Portland Cement* vii. 125 The α-β inversion temperature of C_2S was found to be 1456°. **1966** W. A. DEER et al. *Introd. Rockforming Min.* 129 It [*sc.* pigeonite] then later inverts to an orthorhombic pyroxene and the inversion is accompanied by the exsolution of a second generation of augite lamellae.

II. 8. *Her.* See INVERTED 7.

1638 GUILLIM *Heraldry* III. xv. (ed. 3) 202, I say that the Eversion of the taile of the Lyon is an expresse token of his placabilitie or tractablenesse, as contrariwise the Inversion of his taile is a note of his wrath and fury, especially if he doe beate the backe therewith.

9. a. A turning outside in, introversion; a turning inside out. *spec.* in *Path.*

[**1598**: see I.] *a* **1784** *Med. Observ. & Inq.* IV. (*heading*) History of a Fatal Inversion of the Uterus and Rupture of the Bladder. **1851–6** WOODWARD *Mollusca* iv. 25 The snail ..draws in its eye-stalks, by a process like the inversion of a glove-finger. **1856–8** W. CLARK *Van der Hoeven's Zool.* I. 92 The anterior part..retractile within the posterior by inversion. **1887** *Syd. Soc. Lex., Inversion of bladder*, the condition in which the bladder is prolapsed through the urethra, either partially or completely.

b. A turning out of the contents.

1822–34 *Good's Study Med.* (ed. 4) II. 558 The dose [of an emetic] should have its power limited, as nearly as may be, to a single inversion of the stomach.

c. *Anat.* (See quots.)

1869 G. V. ELLIS *Demonstrations Anat.* (ed. 6) ix. 762 In inversion the great toe is adducted, the inner border of the foot is shortened, and is raised from the ground so that the sole looks inwards, whilst the outer border is depressed. **1902** D. HEPBURN in D. J. Cunningham *Text-bk. Anat.* 304 By inversion we mean the raising of the inner border of the foot so that the sole looks inwards, while the toes are depressed towards the ground. **1971** D. L. KELLEY *Kinesiology* vi. 75 Inversion lifts the medial border of the foot to turn the sole inward.

III. †**10.** Diversion to an improper purpose; perversion. *Obs.*

1711 *Light to Blind* II. iii. §33 in *10th Rep. Hist. MSS. Comm.* App. v. 115 Who..would object unto the King an inversion of the lawes of the land? For he left the courts of judicature to run their usual course. **1755** YOUNG *Centaur* vi. Wks. 1757 IV. 276 What a terrible inversion is this of the high favours of heaven!

11. In full, ***sexual inversion***. Homosexuality (see also quot. 1958).

1895 A. BEARDSLEY *Let.* 15 May (1971) 85 [*To André Raffalovitch*] Your study of inversion is I think quite brilliant. **1897** H. ELLIS *Stud. Psychol. Sex* I. ii. 27 In Italy, also, Ritti, Tamassia, Lombroso, and others began to study these phenomena, and it seems to have been in Italy that the convenient term 'sexual inversion' was first used. When the matter was taken up in France, the same term was used. **1901** J. A. GODFREY *Sci. Sex* v. 206 Sexual inversion—that is, the turning-in of the sex instinct towards individuals of the same sex—is an abnormal phenomenon. **1927** *Scots Observer* 1 Oct. 15/3 It will help to approach the problems of inversion with knowledge and charity. **1958** *Amer. Jrnl. Orthopsychiatry* XXVIII. 424 Many workers fail to distinguish between homosexuality and sexual inversion, or more accurately, sex-role inversion. Freud..himself.. equated the two terms. *Ibid.*, The following distinction is offered: homosexuality refers to sexual activity or the desire for such activity between two members of the same sex, while the criterion of inversion is a personality in which a person's thinking, feeling, and acting are typical of the opposite sex. **1965** J. MARMOR (*title*) Sexual inversion.

IV. 12. Special Comb.: **inversion temperature**, (*a*) *Physics*, the temperature (for any particular gas) at which the Joule-Thomson effect changes sign, so that the gas is neither heated nor cooled when allowed to expand without doing any work; (*b*) (see sense 7 above).

1902 *Phil. Mag.* III. 536 It had been deduced by Wilkowski..by assuming the thermodynamic coincidence of the inversion temperatures for hydrogen and for air. **1940** S. GLASSTONE *Text-bk. Physical Chem.* iv. 285 The inversion temperature, as derived from the van der Waals equation, should be twice the Boyle point... The observed inversion temperature for hydrogen is about 190°K. **1971** *Nature* 20 Aug. 519/1 For every gas, however, there is at a given pressure an inversion temperature above which throttled expansion results in a temperature increase. (The inversion temperature decreases with increasing pressure.)

inversive (ɪnˈvɜːsɪv), *a.* [f. L. *invers-*, ppl. stem of *invertĕre* to INVERT + -IVE: cf. mod.F. *inversif, -ive* (Littré).] Characterized by inversion.

1875 *Spiritualist* 25 June, The deadly self-hoods of sects, of inversive human society, or of clans, hordes [etc.]. **1893** J. PULSFORD *Loyalty to Christ* II. 333 This..process of making all things new will go on and on, until the self-seeking and self-sufficient man of the world's inversive civilisation has disappeared.

in'verso-, mod. comb. form of L. *inversus* INVERSE, used in sense 'inversely—': as in **in'verso-bino-'annular** *a.* [L. *bīnī* two each + *annul-us* ring: ANNULAR]; **in'verso-e'marginate** *a.* [EMARGINATE] (see quots.).

1855 MAYNE *Expos. Lex., Inverso-Binoannularis*, applied by Haüy to a variety of the regular hexahedral prism, of which the base is surrounded by a row of facets disposed in a ring, resulting from the decrease by two rows in height on the margins of the same base..*inversobinoannular. Ibid., Inverso-Emarginatus*,..applied by Haüy to a variety of carbonated lime which presents the form of the inverse, emarginated at the superior edges by the primitive facets, and at the inferior edges by those of a hexahedral prism: *inversoemarginate.*

inversor (ɪnˈvɜːsə(r)). [agent-n. in L. form from *invertĕre, invers-* to overturn, INVERT.] An instrument for reversing an electric current; a commutator; = INVERTOR 1.

1839 G. BIRD *Nat. Philos.* 246 This instrument, which I propose to call the *inversor.*

invert (ɪnˈvɜːt), *v.* [f. L. *invert-ĕre*, f. *in-* (IN-²) + *vertĕre* to turn; *lit.* to turn in, to turn outside in, hence to turn the opposite way.]

I. 1. a. *trans.* To turn upside down.

1613 BEAUM. & FL. *Coxcomb* I. v, What an she were inverted, With her heels upward like a traitor's coat? **1641** J. JACKSON *True Evang. T.* I. 44 Others inverted with feet upward, and head downward, and a fire being underneath, were so smoaked and suffocated to death. **1665** HOOKE *Microgr.* Pref. c b, I invert the Frame, placing the head downwards. *a* **1763** SHENSTONE *Elegies* xix. 1 Again the lab'ring hind inverts the soil. **1800** tr. *Lagrange's Chem.* I. 47 If you place a card on a glass filled with water, and invert the glass, the water will not escape. **1860** TYNDALL *Glac.* I. iv. 35 The coast line was inverted by atmospheric refraction.

†**b.** *fig.* To overthrow, upset; to subvert. *Obs.*

1588 J. UDALL *Diotrephes* (Arb.) 22 Al that I saye or desire, is not to inuert any thing in the state that is good. **1648** *Hunting of Fox* 36 The designe to invert and subvert both Church and Commonwealth. **1695** FOUNTAINHALL in M. P. Brown *Suppl. Decis.* (1826) IV. 279 The Lords.. would not summarily invert the Town of Edinburgh's possession. **1706** DE FOE *Jure Div.* Pref. 7 Who shall invade the Property of the Subject, invert the publick Justice, or overthrow the Religion and Liberty of England.

2. a. To reverse in regard to position, order, or sequence; to turn in an opposite direction.

1533 MORE *Debell. Salem* Wks. 985/2 Whyche thys good man dissembleth here and inuerteth here thorder for the nonce. **1614** SELDEN *Titles Hon.* 67 In the Scripture you haue the very name [Hannibal] but inverted: Baal-Hanan in Gen. cap. xxxvi. **1620** T. GRANGER *Div. Logike* 285 An inverted Syllogisme..Wherein the conclusion is sometimes put in the first place. **1651** HOBBES *Leviath.* IV. xlvii. 384 The way is the same, but the order is inverted. **1824** L. MURRAY *Eng. Gram.* (ed. 5) I. 221 This sentence may be inverted without changing a single word. **1869** J. MARTINEAU *Ess.* II. 21 Dr. Whewell..inverts this order of processes.

b. *fig.* To reverse the relations of, so as to produce an opposite meaning, state of affairs, etc.

1552 ASCHAM in *Lett. Lit. Men* (Camden) 12 The fallax of composicion and division..do sometyme so invert the sentence as in the self same words thus joyned or so separated. **1586** A. DAY *Eng. Secretary* I. (1625) 67 To invert the good also that in such a person may be..unto a worser sense. **1613** PURCHAS *Pilgrimage* (1614) 631 Thus is all inverted, many Kings, and few subjects. **1665** BOYLE *Occas. Refl.* III. vi, He may..invert the Profession of Saint Paul, and say, that he preaches not Christ crucify'd, but himself. **1710** STEELE *Tatler* No. 225 ¶1 A set of People who invert the Design of Conversation. **1822** HAZLITT *Table-t.* Ser. II. xviii. (1869) 368 The principle of economy is inverted. **1874** L. STEPHEN *Hours Library* (1892) I. vi. 221 The old-fashioned canons of poetical justice are inverted. **1881** WESTCOTT & HORT *Grk. N.T.* Introd. §35 The relative attractiveness of conflicting readings becomes inverted by careful study.

†**c.** *Rhet.* To retort an argument upon an opponent. *Obs.*

1631 J. BURGES *Answ. Rejoined* 221 The recrimination which..the Replyer inverts vpon our Bishops, hath more shew then substance. **1796** BURKE *Regic. Peace* I. Wks. 1808 VIII. 173 They inverted, and retaliated the impiety.

†**d.** To transfer (words) from their literal meaning; to use in a metaphorical sense. *Obs.*

1589 PUTTENHAM *Eng. Poesie* III. xvi[i]. (Arb.) 190 Ye see that these words, *source, shop, flud, sugred*, are inuerted from their owne signification to another, not altogether so naturall, but of much affinitie with it.

e. *Mus.* To change the relative position of the notes of (an interval or chord) by placing the lowest note higher, usually an octave higher; also, to modify (a phrase or subject) by inverting the intervals between the successive notes, i.e. by reversing the direction of its motion.

1838 *Penny Cycl.* XI. 3/1 Fugue by Inversion..In this the theme is inverted. **1875** OUSELEY *Harmony* ii. 22 If the lower of the two notes forming any interval be changed into its upper octave,..the interval is said to be inverted, or, in other words, the new interval thus formed, is an inversion of the former. **1880** W. S. ROCKSTRO in Grove *Dict. Mus.* II. 17 A Chord is said to be Inverted, when any note, other than its Root, is taken in the lowest part.

f. *Logic.* To obtain the inverse of (a proposition): see INVERSION 2e. (In quot. *intr.* for *pass.*)

1896 WELTON *Man. Logic* (ed. 2) III. iii. §102 *marg.*, *SeP* inverts to *SiP* by converting the Obv[erte]d Converse.

g. *Telecommunications.* To subject (a signal) to a heterodyning process that reverses the order of the component frequencies (either completely or in a restricted range) prior to modulation for transmission, those at the two extremes being interchanged.

1930 *Engineering* 14 Nov. 625/1 The risk of important conversations being overheard..has still further been reduced by using a complex heterodyning process, which inverts and mixes the signals. *Ibid.* 626/1 The original speech-frequency range is divided into a number of bands. .. These bands can then be inverted as explained above, and re-arranged in transposed bands. **1933** K. HENNEY *Radio Engin. Handbk.* x. 274 To obtain an intelligible signal at the receiving end, it is necessary to again invert the modulation frequencies by the reverse process. **1966** *McGraw-Hill Encycl. Sci. & Technol.* X. 624/2 The first method employs equipment for inverting speech to make overseas telephone conversations unintelligible to the casual listener.

h. *Math.* To transform by inversion; to obtain the inverse of: see INVERSE *sb.* 2, INVERSION 3.

3. *Mil.* See quot. and cf. INVERSION 4.

1832 *Regul. Instr. Cavalry* III. 46 *Inversion*—A Regiment is said to be inverted when the Squadrons are not in their natural order, but the right Squadron on the left, and the left on the right, as for instance when the Squadrons entire have wheeled to the right or left about. *Ibid.* 113 It will be better to invert by Regiments.

4. *Chem.* To break up (cane-sugar) into dextrose and lævulose: see quot. s.v. INVERTED 6.

1864–72 WATTS *Dict. Chem.* II. 856 Honey..contains cane-sugar (which is gradually inverted by keeping), inverted sugar, and an excess of dextroglucose. **1899** J. CAGNEY tr. *Jaksch's Clin. Diagnosis* v. 162 Hoffman has availed himself of the property which HCl. possesses of inverting cane-sugar, i.e. of breaking it up into dextrose and lævulose.

†**5.** *intr.* To change to the opposite. *Obs.*

1615 CHAPMAN *Odyss.* XVII. 61 Double not needless passion on a heart Whose joy so green is, and so apt t' invert. **1813** T. BUSBY *Lucretius* II. *Comment.* xli, Till their natures change, and their order of operation invert.

6. *intr.* Of a substance: to undergo inversion.

1887 [see CARAMEL *v.*]. **1933** *Amer. Jrnl. Sci.* XXV. 284 It would..be possible for β-solid solutions to invert to the γ-form. **1966** [see INVERSION 7].

II. †**7.** *trans.* To divert from its proper purpose; to pervert to another use. *Obs.*

1587 HARRISON *England* II. xix. (1877) I. 309 They inuerted his intent herein to another end. **1603** HOLLAND *Plutarch's Mor.* 930 Neither could any man..accuse him for robbing the State, or inverting any thing to his own use. **1670** R. COKE *Disc. Trade* 18 In being committed prisoners, the means which is thereby spent in paying Fees to Jaylors, is inverted from that end to which it might have been imployed towards the Payment of his Debts.

III. †**8.** *trans.* To turn in or inward. *Obs.*

1645 G. DANIEL *Poems* Wks. 1878 II. 78 Invert thy Eyes and see Its State, and thy degree. **1646** SIR T. BROWNE *Pseud. Ep.* V. i. 234 The bill..is flat and broad, and somewhat inverted at the extreame.

9. a. To turn outside in, or inside out; *spec.* in *Path.*

1615 CROOKE *Body of Man* 249 A kinde of yard..which they say is the necke of the wombe if it be inuerted. **1638** SIR T. HERBERT *Trav.* (ed. 2) 16 Skin of a Lyon, Leopard..or Sheep (the haire inverted) is as a roabe put about their shoulders. **1656** RIDGLEY *Pract. Physick* 131 The Ey-lid inverted may be rubbed with Fig-leaves. **1800** *Med. Jrnl.* III. 463 If a portion is strongly adherent to the uterus, we may by this force invert the uterus.

b. *trans.* To empty (the stomach) by means of an emetic.

1822–34 *Good's Study Med.* (ed. 4) I. 134 The asarum.. at the same time that it inverts the stomach, acts powerfully on the olfactory nerves.

10. *Geom.* (*intr.*) To be transformed by inversion *into*.

1865 R. TOWNSEND *Chapters on Mod. Geom.* II. xxiv. 384 Every two circles invert into two whose radii have a constant ratio from every point on any third circle coaxal with themselves. **1916** J. L. COOLIDGE *Treat. Circle & Sphere* i. 22 Points within the circle of inversion other than the centre will invert into points without, points without will always invert into points within. **1966** J. H. CADWELL *Topics in Recreational Math.* v. 42 Hence the locus..is a circle centre C_1. We note that C_1 is not the inverse of C, i.e. centres do not invert into each other.

Hence **in'verting** *vbl. sb.* and *ppl. a.*

1579 FULKE *Heskins' Parl.* 25 This is no inuerting of Gods order. 1665 HOOKE *Microgr.* 60 Reflection being nothing but an inverting of the Rays. 1894 *Athenæum* 4 Aug. 165/3 To represent the objects as they would be seen in an inverting telescope. 1899 J. CAGNEY tr. *Jaksch's Clin. Diagnosis* v. 172 The chief are the tryptic, fat-splitting and emulsifying..and inverting ferments.

invert (ˈɪnvɜːt), *sb.* [f. INVERT *v.*] **1.** An inverted arch, as at the bottom of a canal or sewer. Also *attrib.*

1838 *Pub. Wks. Gt. Brit.* 22 The tunnel..being supported by a brick invert or counter arch. 1862 SMILES *Engineers* III. 314 These walls were further supported by a strong invert,—that is, an arch placed in an inverted position under the road,—thus binding together the walls on both sides. 1882 *Worcester Exhib. Catal.* III. 16 Invert blocks for the bottom of sewers. 1885 *Times* (weekly ed.) 18 Sept. 9/1 The bottom of the sewer or 'invert', is also defective.

2. *Psychol.* One whose sex instincts are inverted. (Cf. INVERSION I I; INVERTED *ppl. a.* 3 c.)

1897 H. ELLIS *Stud. Psychol. Sex* I. 12 Caesar was proud of his physical beauty, and like many modern inverts he was accustomed carefully to shave his skin. *Ibid.* 144 The sexual invert is specially liable to suffer from a high degree of neurasthenia. 1911 R. W. CHAMBERS *Common Law* i. 29 This world is full of pale, enraptured artists;..full of unwashed little inverts. 1957 L. DURRELL *Justine* II. 96 At least the invert escapes this fearful struggle to give oneself to another. 1957 *Observer* 1 Sept. 11/5 For once, the hero is not wrongly but rightly accused: he is an irrevocable invert. 1971 R. REISNER *Graffiti* (1974) viii. 115 The inverts (a word preferred by homosexuals to perverts) attempt to win converts.

ˈinvert, *a.* [Short for INVERTED: see sense 6.]

a. In **invert sugar**: Sugar formed by the breaking up of cane-sugar into dextrose and lævulose. Also *ellipt.*

1880 *Libr. Univ. Knowl.* (U.S.) VIII. 846 A mixture of these two sugars [dextrose and lævulose] constitutes *fruit sugar*, or, as sometimes called, *invert sugar.* 1885 LANDOIS & STIRLING *Text-bk. Hum. Phys.* I. 296 The saliva of the horse which can also convert cane-sugar into invert sugar. 1910 *Encycl. Brit.* IV. 508/2 This method is more suited to the preparation of invert in the brewery itself than the acid process. 1940 H. L. HIND *Brewing* II. xxii. 545 The sugars must be pale in colour and carefully selected in accordance with the flavour required in the beer. No. 1 and No. 2 inverts and other sugars of somewhat similar character are suitable. 1971 J. S. HOUGH et al. *Malting & Brewing Sci.* xi. 296 The solid invert can be added directly to the copper or dissolved in liquor before addition.

b. invert soap [tr. G. *invertseife* (Kuhn & Bielig 1940, in *Ber. d. Deut. Chem. Ges.* LXXIII. 1080)]. A soap whose surface-active ion is a cation (rather than the more usual anion): a cationic detergent.

1941 *Chem. Abstr.* XXXV. 3596 K. and B. intended to study the mechanism of the bactericidal action of Zephirol (mixt. of alkyldimethylbenzylammonium chlorides) and other quaternary ammonium, sulfonium and phosphonium salts by means of expts. on the interaction of these 'invert soaps'..with proteins, chromoproteids, ferments, symplexes and genes. 1947 CONANT & BLATT *Chem. Org. Compounds* (ed. 3) x. 213 Another group of detergents consists of the invert soaps... These are quaternary ammonium salts containing at least one large alkyl group. 1966 SMITH & CRISTOL *Org. Chem.* xl. 765 Cationic detergents or invert soaps are used mainly for germicidal properties.

invertant (ɪnˈvɜːtənt), *a. Her.* [f. INVERT + -ANT[1].] = INVERTED 7.

1828–40 BERRY *Encycl. Herald.* I. Gloss., *Invertant*, or *Inverted*, turned the wrong way: wings, when the points are downward, are termed *inverted.* 1889 in ELVIN *Dict. Heraldry.*

invertase (ˈɪnvɜːt-, ɪnˈvɜːteɪz, -s). *Biochem.* [f. INVERT(IN + -ASE.] = INVERTIN.

1887 *Jrnl. Chem. Soc.* LI. 60 Solutions of invertase and diastase were prepared from Mr. O'Sullivan's specimens. 1949 [see FICIN]. 1964 N. G. CLARK *Mod. Org. Chem.* xvi. 330 Hydrolysis is also brought about by the enzyme, invertase. 1970 *Sci. Jrnl.* Mar. 19/3 A 1 ml sample of this water is then treated with the enzyme invertase, which converts any of the sugar sucrose..into a mixture of glucose and fructose.

invertebracy (ɪnˈvɜːtɪbrəsɪ). [f. INVERTEBRATE: see -ACY.] The quality of being invertebrate; want of 'backbone'.

1886 *New York Semi-weekly Tribune* 24 Dec. (Cent. Dict.), A person may reveal his hopeless invertebracy only when brought face to face with some critical situation. 1899 HORTON in *Chr. World Pulpit* 8 Nov. 297/1 It is said..that invertebracy of thought is the great characteristic of the closing years of this century.

invertebral (ɪnˈvɜːtɪbrəl), *a. rare.* [f. IN-[3] + VERTEBRAL, as a repr. of F. *invertébré*: see INVERTEBRATE.] = INVERTEBRATE *a.*

1816 J. SCOTT *Vis. Paris* (ed. 5) App. 298 The invertebral animals are chiefly deposited in cases in the middle of the apartments. 1822–34 *Good's Study Med.* (ed. 4) III. 7 A nervous cord without a brain, answering the purpose of a spinal marrow in most invertebral animals. 1828 [see next].

‖**Invertebrata** (ɪnvɜːtɪˈbreɪtə), *sb. pl.* [mod.L., = *animālia invertebrāta*, corresp. to F. *animaux invertébrés*, invertebrate animals: see INVERTEBRATE.] A name given to all animals except the *Vertebrata* or back-boned animals; originally introduced as correlative with the latter term, but now recognized as containing numerous sub-kingdoms, as distinct from each other as from the Vertebrata, and therefore retained only as a convenient negative term compehending all groups below the Vertebrata.

1828 STARK *Elem. Nat. Hist.* II. *Invertebrata* 2 The Invertebral animals..are arranged by Cuvier into three great divisions. 1841 T. R. JONES *Anim. Kingd.* i. §2 Animals ..corresponding to the invertebrata of more recent Zoologists. 1842 BRANDE *Dict. Sci.* 610/2 Lamarck's primary division of the animal kingdom into *Vertebrata* and *Invertebrata* corresponds with that proposed by Aristotle into *Enaima* and *Anaima.* 1843 OWEN *Lect. Comp. Anat.* 12 Lamarck proposed, therefore, the name of *Vertebrata* for the one class and *Invertebrata* for the other. 1849 MURCHISON *Siluria* i. (1867) 8 Crustaceans, Mollusks, and other invertebrata. 1879 *Cassell's Techn. Educ.* I. 4 Invertebrata, or animals destitute of a cranium or skull, and a vertebral column.

invertebrate (ɪnˈvɜːtɪbrət), *a.* and *sb.* [ad. mod.L. *invertebrāt-us*, in neuter pl. INVERTEBRATA, corresp. to F. *invertébrés* (see below), f. L. *in-* (IN-[3]) + *vertebra* joint, esp. of the spine: see VERTEBRATE.

The classification of Vertebrate and Invertebrate Animals was primarily due to Lamarck; but in his *Système des animaux sans vertèbres*, 1801, he does not use the word *invertébrés*, which occurs however in his *Philosophie Zoologique* of 1809; it had been used by Cuvier and Duméril in 1805 (Cuvier *Leçons d'Anatomie compar.* I, Table I), and by Duméril, in 1806, in his *Zoologie analytique*, 3, Table I.]

A. *adj.* Not having a backbone or spinal column.

1838 *Penny Cycl.* XII. 488/1 Invertebrate animals are divided by Lamarck into two great groups, which he calls 'animaux apathiques', and 'animaux sensibles'. 1858 GEIKIE *Hist. Boulder* v. 72 The higher tribes of the invertebrate animals. 1877 W. THOMSON *Voy. Challenger* I. i. 7 Even at that depth the invertebrate sub-kingdoms are still fairly represented.

b. *fig.* Without moral 'backbone'; wanting strength, firmness, or consistency.

1879 *Fortn. Rev.* No. 187. 910 Running a man whose political creed is vague and invertebrate. 1889 *Times* 29 Mar. 9/4 The House..has voted for an invertebrate measure supported by flabby arguments. 1896 *Eclectic Mag.* Apr. 507 Nor is the affection for the invertebrate parent secured by the indulgences.

B. *sb.* An animal without a backbone or spinal column; any animal not belonging to the vertebrate sub-kingdom.

1826 KIRBY & SP. *Entomol.* IV. xlv. 239 In this particular differing from the majority of Invertebrates. 1879 *Cassell's Techn. Educ.* IV. 123/2 Wall-cases and floor-cases are best suited for the display of the vertebrate classes, and table-cases for the invertebrates. 1880 HAUGHTON *Phys. Geog.* iii. 78 Animals of higher organisation than the Invertebrates.

b. *fig.* A man without strength of character or principles.

1869 *Spectator* 22 May 620 Indifference as to the fate of such political invertebrates. 1884 *Pall Mall G.* 29 Feb. 1/1 Nerveless invertebrates..whose only conception of statesmanship is that of divining how the cat will jump.

Hence **invertebrateness** (ɪnˈvɜːtɪbrətnɪs), the quality of being invertebrate.

1884 *Punch* 23 Feb. 87 There's no spell In sheer invertebrateness.

invertebrated (ɪnˈvɜːtɪbreɪtɪd), *a.* [f. as prec. + -ED[2].] = INVERTEBRATE.

1829 J. & C. BELL *Anat. Hum. Body* (ed. 7) II. 10 *note*, The oviparous mammalia, fishes, and the invertebrated animals. 1831 YOUATT *Horse* v. (1867) 106 The first division of animals is into vertebrated and invertebrated.

inverted (ɪnˈvɜːtɪd), *ppl. a.* [f. INVERT *v.* + -ED[1].]

I. 1. a. Turned upside down.

1598 FLORIO, *Inuerso*, inuerted. 1609 DOULAND *Ornith. Microl.* 75 There be that ascribe an inuerted semicircle to this proportion. 1665 HOOKE *Microgr.* 11 A fit Vessel for this purpose, will be an inverted Glass Syphon. 1766 CAVENDISH in *Phil. Trans.* LVI. 178 The air remaining unabsorbed in the inverted bottle of sope leys. 1806 *Naval Chron.* XV. 106 They had no covering but an inverted boat. 1824 J. JOHNSON *Typogr.* II. iii. 58 Inverted commas owe their origin to Mons. Guillemet, a Frenchman. 1838 and 1857 Inverted commas [see COMMA 4]. 1842–76 GWILT *Archit.* §1885 In foundations where..there would be a liability, from uneven bearing, to partial failure, it has been the practice..to turn inverted arches, to catch on their springing the weight to be provided against. 1869 TYNDALL *Notes Lect. Light* 22 Dove has applied the 'reversion prism' to render erect the inverted images of the astronomical telescope.

b. *Mus.* Of chords or intervals: Having the lowest note transposed an octave higher.

1811 BUSBY *Dict. Mus.* (ed. 3), *Inverted*, a term applicable to certain positions of any subject or chord. 1889 E. PROUT *Harmony* i. §26 An inverted 5th becomes a 4th.

c. Applied to a letter whose sound is produced by inverting the tongue against the hard palate. Also *absol.* as *sb.*

1879 SWEET in *Philol. Soc. Trans.* 468, *rn*, etc. represent single inverteds. 1888 —— *Eng. Sounds* 26 The inverteds are ..represented in Sanskrit under the name of cerebrals. 1902 [see CACUMINAL *a.*]. 1918, 1934 [see CEREBRAL *a.* 2].

2. Reversed in position or order; turned in the opposite direction.

1620 T. GRANGER *Div. Logike* 230 Defects are to be supplied;..and the inverted parts are to be placed in order. 1796 BURKE *Let. Noble Ld.* Wks. VIII. 47, I live in an inverted order. They who ought to have succeeded me are gone before me. 1851 MAURICE *Patriarchs & Lawg.* xviii. (1867) 327 This is the inverted order of Paganism.

3. a. Reversed in relations.

1702 STEELE *Funeral* Prol., But we, still kind to your inverted sense, Do most unnatural things once more dispense. 1709 STEELE *Tatler* No. 127 ¶1 This inverted Idolatry, wherein the Image did Homage to the Man. 1786 BURKE *Art. Hastings* Wks. 1842 II. 181 All the true and substantial powers of government were in an inverted relation and proportion to the official and ostensible authorities. 1863 KINGLAKE *Crimea* (1876) I. xii. 193 The mere inverted Jesuitism of a man resolved to do good that evil might come.

b. Reversed in meaning.

1646 SIR T. BROWNE *Pseud. Ep.* I. iv. 14 Intended expressions receiving inverted significations. 1663 J. SPENCER *Prodigies* (1665) 97 Were I inclined to an Observation of Omens and Prodigies, I should..make an inverted use of the words of the Reverend Publisher.

c. *Psychol.* spec. of the sex instincts.

1897 H. ELLIS *Stud. Psychol. Sex* I. 16 The painter Bazzi seems to have been radically inverted. *Ibid.* 156 Social opinion is most amply adequate to deal with the manifestations of inverted sexuality. 1958 *Amer. Jrnl. Orthopsychiatry* XXVIII. 428 Inverted females would be expected to show..a relatively complete identification with the masculine role. 1974 *Times Lit. Suppl.* 1 Feb. 109 A telling parody of inverted sexist trends in our own society.

4. *Mil.* See INVERT *v.* 3.

1832 *Regul. Instr. Cavalry* III. 84 An Inverted Line can change its Front.

5. *Math.* = INVERSE *a.* 3.

1885 WATSON & BURBURY *Math. The. Electr. & Magn.* I. 125 Every sphere in the original system becomes another sphere in the inverted system.

6. *Chem.* Of cane-sugar: see quots.

1864–72 WATTS *Dict. Chem.* II. 855 Dextroglucose occurs abundantly in sweet fruits..and always with such a quantity of lævorotatory fruit-sugar that the mixture exhibits lævorotatory power, and is thence called inverted sugar. *Ibid.* 863 The mixture of [dextroglucose and lævoglucose] in equal numbers of atoms constitutes fruit sugar, or inverted sugar, which is itself lævo-rotatory, because the specific rotatory power of lævoglucose is greater than that of dextroglucose.

II. 7. *Her.* Turned inwards or towards the middle of the field: said of animals or their members: see quots.

1610 GUILLIM *Heraldry* III. xvii. (1611) 159 The field is Ruby, two wings Inuerted and conioined Topaz. 1661 MORGAN *Sph. Gentry* I. v. 67 When fishes are borne swimming you shall say Naiant..when respecting each other, Inverted. 1864 BOUTELL *Her. Hist. & Pop.* x. 64 If the tips of the wings droop downwards they are inverted.

8. *Path.* Introverted; turned inside out.

1787 R. CLEGHORN in *Med. Commun.* II. 241 Sometimes the inversion is so partial, that no part of the inverted uterus descends below it's mouth. 1822–34 *Good's Study Med.* (ed. 4) IV. 110 The womb is inverted, when at the same time that it is displaced or has fallen down, it is turned inside out.

9. Special collocations: ***inverted comma*** (see also COMMA 4), ***engine*** (see quot. 1961), ***loop***, ***pleat***; **inverted snob**, one who dislikes, or avoids contact or association with, the upper classes; one who tries to appear to be a member of, or sympathetic to, the lower classes; so ***inverted snobbery***, ***snobbism***; **inverted spelling** = *inverse spelling* (INVERSE *a.* 5).

1789 J. ROBERTSON *Ess. Punctuation* 130 Two inverted commas are generally placed at the beginning of a phrase or a passage, which is quoted or transcribed from some author, in his own words. 1927 R. B. MCKERROW *Introd. Bibliogr.* 316 Inverted commas were, until late in the seventeenth century, frequently used at the beginnings of lines to call attention to sententious remarks... They were not especially associated with quotations until the eighteenth century. 1933 *Week-End Rev.* 28 Oct. 439/1 'Dunky Fitlow'! What a name! One could hardly ask for it without embarrassment, without qualifying it by inverted commas in the voice. 1956 A. S. C. Ross in M. Black *Importance of Lang.* (1962) 95 It is non-U to place the name of a house in inverted commas. 1963 AUDEN *Dyer's Hand* 520 One has a sense, and nowhere more strongly than in the songs [of *Twelfth Night*], of there being inverted commas around the 'fun'. [1885 *List of Subscribers, Classified* (United Telephone Co.) (ed. 6) 236 High-class..stationary engines. Beam, Compound Condensing, Inverted, Vertical.] 1933 *Meccano Mag.* Feb. 109/2 It is fitted with three de Havilland 'Gipsy III' inverted engines. 1961 WEBSTER, *Inverted engine*, an engine whose crankshaft is above the cylinders. 1940 *Chambers's Techn. Dict.* 458/1 *Inverted loop*, a manœuvre of an aeroplane consisting of a complete revolution about a lateral axis, with the normally upper surface of the machine on the outside of the path of the loop. Must be commenced while flying inverted. 1915 *T. Eaton & Co. Catal.* Spring & Summer Suppl. 1/2 The smart patch pockets are finished with stitched inverted pleats. 1964 *McCall's Sewing* ii. 30/1 *Inverted pleat*, two side pleats which turn toward each other. 1971 'D. HALLIDAY' *Dolly & Doctor Bird* iii. 29 For golf, I have always worn an Orkney tweed skirt with a low inverted pleat at the back. 1943 N. MARSH *Colour Scheme* vi. 99 Don't call me Mr. Bell. I'm afraid you're an inverted snob. 1955 KOESTLER *Trail of Dinosaur* II. 87 Only an inverted snob will pretend..that 'the aristocracy'..is devoid of value. 1966 *Guardian* 14 May 7/6 But, gosh, don't be an inverted snob! Subculture is fun! 1883 R. L. STEVENSON *Silverado Squatters* 176 His book.. was a capital instance of the Penny Messalina school of literature; and there arose from it..a rank atmosphere of.. sickening, inverted snobbery. 1930 R. LEHMANN *Note in Music* III. 108 Inverted-snobbery complex, Clare would have called it. 1937 L. BROMFIELD *Rains Came* I. xxxviii. 159 It was that eternal, inverted snobbery of his, that hatred of anyone born with the things he had never achieved. 1958 *Times* 25 Jan. 7/3 Inverted snobbery, we are told, is rampant in Cambridge. 1971 *Lancet* 23 Apr. 918/2 The curious inverted snobbery of the use of 'Mr.' by surgeons (even if

they have an M.D. or a PH.D. as well as their M.B.),..with all its regional and specialty variations, is well worth the attention of a sociologist. **1939** A. THIRKELL *Before Lunch* vi. 160 The inverted snobbism that at once overcame her against her will. **1958** G. L. BROOK *Hist. Eng. Lang.* v. 102 Another contributory cause of the confusion of Modern English spelling is to be found in what are called inverted spellings. **1970** B. M. H. STRANG *Hist. English* II. v. 291 Inverted spellings, e.g. *y* for *e* in districts suspected to be *y*-less, are as revealing as direct *e* for *y* spellings.

in'vertedly, *adv.* [f. prec. + -LY^2.] In an inverted manner; upside down; with inversion of order.

1682 SIR T. BROWNE *Chr. Mor.* III. §14 'Tis but to live invertedly, and with thy Head unto the Heels of thy Antipodes. **1794** G. ADAMS *Nat. & Exp. Philos.* II. xv. 183 The lens..by refraction, depicts them invertedly on the screen. **1886** T. HARDY *Mayor Casterbridge* I. xxii. 287 Miss Templeman..talked up at Elizabeth-Jane invertedly across her forehead and arm.

invertend ('ɪnvətɛnd). *Logic.* [ad. L. *invertend-us*, gerundive of *invertĕre* to INVERT.] The proposition from which another proposition (the *inverse*) is obtained by inversion.

1896 [see INVERSION 2 e].

in'verter. [f. INVERT *v.* + -ER^1.] **1.** One who inverts. *rare.*

1611 FLORIO, *Inuertore*, an inuerter, a peruerter. **1621** BP. MOUNTAGU *Diatribæ* 44 It was a rare thing then to finde a Cain, a Iudas, an Inuerter, Detayner, Vsurper of Gods Right.

2. That which inverts, or produces inversion. **a.** *Electr.* Also **invertor**. Any apparatus which converts direct current into alternating current.

1926 L. B. W. JOLLEY *A.C. Rectification* (ed. 2) xix. 444 In an inverter such as is shown in Fig. 324 a direct current generator G is supplying a steady current to two three-electrode valves and the primary of a transformer. **1947** P. KEMP *Alternating Current Electr. Engin.* (ed. 7) xxviii. 498 Inverters are used for regenerative braking on electric railways. **1961** *Listener* 9 Nov. 773/1 The valve serves not only as a rectifier..but—at the other end of the direct current link—as an invertor, turning direct current into alternating current. **1962** A. SHEPARD in *Into Orbit* 103 Inverters are used to convert the DC current which comes from the batteries into the AC current required to power some of the systems in the booster. **1970** J. SHEPHERD *Higher Electr. Engin.* (ed. 2) xxv. 817 D.C. links (with a rectifier at one end and an invertor at the other end of the link) are now commonly used to connect two a.c. power distribution systems together. **1973** *Wireless World* June 27 (Advt.), Models 107A and B are precision built inverters providing 240 volts a.c. from 12 and 24 volt battery systems.

b. *Telecommunications.* A device that inverts a signal (see INVERT *v.* 2 g).

1930 *Engineering* 14 Nov. 625/3 The inverter is usually inserted at the point where the transmitting and receiving signals are combined.

c. *Computers.* A device which converts either of the two binary digits or signals into the other.

1955 R. K. RICHARDS *Arithmetic Operations in Digital Computers* ii. 32 If the input to an inverter is *A*, the output is *Ā*. **1960** T. C. BARTEE *Digital Computer Fund.* iv. 63 Because of its high input resistance, low output resistance, and voltage- and current-gain characteristics, the inverter is one of the most commonly used transistor configurations in digital systems. **1972** MILLMAN & HALKIAS *Integrated Electronics* vi. 164 The output of an inverter is relatively more positive if and only if the input is relatively less positive.

†**invertible** (ɪn'vɜːtɪb(ə)l), *a.*^{1} *Obs.* [ad. late L. *invertibil-is* (4th c., Hilary), f. *in-* (IN-^{3}) + *vertĕre* to turn: see -BLE.] That cannot be turned or reversed.

1534 CRANMER *Let. to Cromwell* 17 Apr. in Strype *Mem.* (1812) 694 An indurate and invertible conscience. **1633** T. ADAMS *Exp. 2 Peter* ii. 4 The will of the devil is still invertible.

in'vertible, *a.*^{2} [f. INVERT *v.* + -IBLE. Cf. OF. *invertible.*] **1. a.** That can be inverted. **b.** That tends to invert the usual order. *rare.*

1881 MACFARREN *Counterp.* ii. 4 This interval is not invertible. **1892** *Fortn. Rev.* LI. 521 There is a sort of invertible quality in the Japanese..which makes them train their horses to gallop uphill.

2. *Math.* Of an element of a set: having an inverse in the set (*spec.* an inverse for multiplication).

1956 C. CHEVALLEY *Fund. Concepts Algebra* ii. 27 Let *G* be the set of all invertible elements of a monoid *A*. **1963** G. D. MOSTOW et al. *Fund. Struct. Algebra* vi. 141 Invertible elements are divisible only by invertible elements. *Ibid.* xii. 341 An element *a* is called invertible if there is an element *a'* in *A* such that $aa' = a'a = e$. **1965** PATTERSON & RUTHERFORD *Elem. Abstract Algebra* iv. 122 An element $x \in R$ is said to be invertible if it has an inverse with respect to multiplication: that is, if there exists *y* such that $xy = e = yx$.

Hence **inverti'bility.**

1963 H. B. CURRY *Found. Math. Logic* v. 249 Ketonen..showed the invertibility of his classical propositional rules. **1973** J. J. ZEMAN *Modal Logic* iii. 50 The number of rules we must examine for invertibility.

in'vertile, *a. rare.* [f. L. *invertĕre* to INVERT: see -ILE. (Cf. *retractile.*)] Capable of being turned inside out.

1856 GOSSE *Marine Zool.* II. 18 Polyzoary plant-like, horny, tubular..the extremity flexible and invertile.

invertin (ɪn'vɜːtɪn, 'ɪnvətɪn). *Chem.* [f. INVERT *v.* + -IN^1.] A chemical ferment, obtained as a white powder from yeast desiccated in air; it is the constituent which produces the inversion of sugar.

1879 WATTS *Dict. Chem.* VIII. 784 *Invertin*—Donath..obtains this substance by treating yeast according to Zulkowsky and König's method..It is obtained in the form of a powder, a very small quantity of which is sufficient to bring about the inversion of cane-sugar. **1896** *Allbutt's Syst. Med.* I. 519 Invertin, an enzyme capable of changing cane-sugar into dextrose, is found in internal bacilli.

invertor (ɪn'vɜːtə(r)). [f. INVERT *v.* + -OR (here unetymological).] **1.** An instrument for reversing an electric current; a commutator.

In mod. Dicts.

2. *Anat.* A muscle which turns a part (as the foot) inwards.

1903 [see EVERTOR]. **1967** ROWE & WHEBLE *Conc. Textbk. Anat. & Physiol.* (ed. 2) v. 258 The invertors of the foot are:—*Tibialis posterior* [and] *Tibialis anterior*. **1969** MACCONAILL & BASMAJIAN *Muscles & Movements* xiii. 254 The tibialis posterior is an invertor in non-weightbearing movements of the foot.

3. *Electr.* var. INVERTER 2 a.

invertuate, var. of INVIRTUATE *v.*, *Obs.*

invest (ɪn'vɛst), *v.* Also 6 en-. [ad. L. *invest-īre*, f. *in-* (IN-^{2}) + *vestīre* to dress, clothe. Cf. F. *investir* (14–15th c. in Hatz.-Darm.); also OF. *envestir*. Sense 9 is from It. *investire.*]

I. 1. a. *trans.* To clothe, robe, or envelop (a person) *in* or *with* a garment or article of clothing; to dress or adorn.

1583 STUBBES *Anat. Abus.* I. (1879) 38 He..could haue inuested them in silks, veluets [etc.]. **1598** F. MERES *Palladis Tamia* 280 The English tongue is..gorgeouslie invested in rare ornaments. **1612** DRAYTON *Poly-olb.* xv. 241 Ile show you, how the Bride, faire Isis, they invest. **1691** WOOD *Ath. Oxon.* II. 493 In the jollity of that humour he invested George Wither..in the royal habiliments. **1850** MRS. JAMESON *Leg. Monast. Ord.* (1863) 25 Murillo has represented the Virgin and two angels about to invest the kneeling saint, with the splendid chasuble.

b. Of an article of dress: To clothe, cover, adorn.

1704 SWIFT *T. Tub* II. (1709) 38 They held the Universe to be a large suit of clothes which invests every thing. **1710** PARNELL *Hermit* 176 Fair rounds of radiant points invest his hair. **1820** SCOTT *Ivanhoe* iv, The high cap no longer invested his brows.

c. To put on as clothes or ornaments; to don.

1596 SPENSER *F.Q.* IV. v. 18 So faire a crew..Cannot find one this girdle to inuest. **1628** DONNE *Serm.* xxix. 289 He needed not to have invested and taken the forme of a tongue. **1629** *Ibid.* xxiv. 240 Bound to that Religion that he had invested in Baptisme. **1850** MRS. BROWNING *Poems* II. 177 Meek angels ye invest New meeknesses to hear such utterance rest On mortal lips.

2. *transf.* **a.** To cover or surround as with a garment. Const. *with.*

1548 UDALL *Erasm. Par. Luke* iii. 46 b, Y^e holy ghost being of himself..inuisible, but for ye time enuested and clad with a figure or likenesse visible. **1592** DAVIES *Immort. Soul* cclxviii, The fables..others did with brutish forms invest. **1651** *Raleigh's Ghost* 197 Those Soules, which while they were here invested with their bodies, did live wickedly. **1772** *Hist. Rochester* 13 The king is said to have invested Rochester with a wall. **1777** COCKIN in *Phil. Trans.* LXX. 159 Where the sun shone the bushes were each invested with a mist. **1860** MAURY *Phys. Geog. Sea* (Low) i. 1 Our planet is invested with two great oceans.

b. To cover, envelop, or coat, as a garment does.

1632 LITHGOW *Trav.* VIII. 376 Thus with the Torrid Zone, am I oppress, And lock't twixt Tropickes Two, which me invest. **1660** BOYLE *New Exp. Phys. Mech.* xxi. 152 The thin film of water that invests and detains it [the air in bubbles]. **1832** LYELL *Princ. Geol.* II. 11 A belief..that the primeval ocean invested the whole planet long after it became the habitation of living beings. **1861** MISS PRATT *Flower. Pl.* III. 184 Thread-like down which invests the plant. **1873** MIVART *Elem. Anat.* vii. 236 The skin of man invests his body pretty closely.

c. To embed in or surround *with* investment (sense 2 b).

1892 C. HUNTER *Man. Dental Laboratory* viii. 107 We..apply the little plaster-mould to the face of the model and settle the tooth in it, cement tooth to auxiliary plate, then carefully remove from denture, invest and solder. **1946** *Foundry* Aug. 85/1 Precision casting is a somewhat abused term often employed to designate the lost wax investment casting process... Properly, the phrase *investment casting* is the most suitable for use in defining the lost wax investment casting process since it is characterized primarily by the use of a molding material which completely enrobes or invests an expendable pattern. **1964** S. CRAWFORD *Basic Engin. Processes* xii. 255 This casting process involves the use of a heat-disposable wax pattern which is invested with refractory material forming a mould (or shell).

3. *fig.* **a.** To clothe or endue with attributes, qualities, or a character. Const. *with*, also *in*, *into*.

1604 SHAKS. *Oth.* IV. i. 40 Nature would not inuest her selfe in such shadowing passion, without some Instruction. **1610** HOLLAND *Camden's Brit.* (1637) 8 The tales of Arthur..he hath invested into the goodly title of an Historie. **1713** STEELE *Englishm.* No. 21. 139 They are invested with the Character of Ambassadors from Heaven. **1855** PRESCOTT *Philip II*, II. ix. (1857) 305 The mystery thus thrown around the fate of the unhappy sufferer only invested it with an additional horror. **1871** B. TAYLOR *Faust* (1875) I. i. 31 Bliss hath invested him. **1877** R. W. DALE *Lect. Preach.* v. (1878) 122 To invest with interest subjects which in themselves are uninteresting.

†**b.** *refl.* (const. *into*). *Obs.*

1592 WYRLEY *Armorie* 12 Both of them..relinquished their deuise of vndie, and inuested themselues into ridels. *Ibid.* 14 Into one of these kind of differings could I wish our yoonger brothers..to invest themselues.

4. To clothe *with* or *in* the insignia of an office; hence, *with* the dignity itself; to install *in* an office or rank with the customary rites or ceremonies.

1533–4 *Act 25 Hen. VIII*, c. 20 §1 That euery Archbishop and Bishop, being..consecrated and inuested shall be installed accordingly. *a* **1548** HALL *Chron., Hen. VII* 36 The lord Thomas Stanley he invested with the swoorde of the countie of Darby. **1600** HOLLAND *Livy* IV. vii. 144 They were invested both in the jurisdiction, and also in the ornaments of the Consuls. **1670** G. H. *Hist. Cardinals* I. III. 77 The day the Pope is invested they do so too. **1765** BLACKSTONE *Comm.* I. xi. (1809) 380 If such arch-bishop or bishop do refuse to confirm, invest, and consecrate such bishop elect, they shall [etc.]. **1855** MILMAN *Lat. Chr.* (1864) II. IV. iii. 255 Theodorus, who had been invested in the metropolitan dignity at Rome. **1864** BRYCE *Holy Rom. Emp.* xii. (1875) 187 Richard was at the same time invested with the Kingdom of Arles by Henry VI.

5. To establish (a person) in the possession of any office, position, property, etc.; to endow or furnish with power, authority, or privilege. Const. *in*, *with* (also †*of*, *into*, *unto*).

1564 GOLDING *Justine* 150 (R.) Alexander..began..to mocke and despyse Ptolomie himselfe, by whome he was put in and inuested in that kyngdome. **1581** SAVILE *Tacitus' Agric.* (1622) 197 The end of Britannie is found, not by fame and report, but we are with our armes and pauilions really inuested thereof. **1608** D. T. *Ess. Pol. & Mor.* 61 His..end, was to invest a creature of his owne with that charge and dignitie. **1617** HIERON *Wks.* I. 112 To bee by faith ingraffed into Christ is the true honour; this doth inuest a man into that royalty, which is in the person of Christ. **1632** LITHGOW *Trav.* VIII. 346 A brother of the one Baron, and a sister of the other, were instantly invested in their Lands. **1710** PRIDEAUX *Orig. Tithes* i. 3 God..invested Man in a full property of all things. **1796** MORSE *Amer. Geog.* I. 271 This body is invested with the spiritual government of the congregation. **1836** J. GILBERT *Chr. Atonem.* vii. (1852) 204 The innocent being is by law invested with the right to enjoy security. **1855** MILMAN *Lat. Chr.* XIV. i. (1864) IX. 5 They were invested in a kind of omniscience. **1861** M. PATTISON *Ess.* (1891) I. 35 Rudolf [agreed] to invest Hartmann with lands to the capital value of 10,000*l.*

6. a. To settle, secure, or vest (a right or power) in (a person). Const. *in* (†*with*, †*upon*).

1590 SWINBURNE *Testaments* 49 b, For that which is the wiues, is by reason of the mariage her husbandes, and being inuested in him..cannot bee giuen from him without his licence or consent. **1610** GUILLIM *Heraldry* V. i. (1611) 253 The inheritance aswell of the possessions as of the coat armour are inuested in them and their posterity. *a* **1641** BP. MOUNTAGU *Acts & Mon.* (1642) 88 Then..was the Scepter..invested upon the Tribe of Iudah. **1646** H. LAWRENCE *Comm. Angells* 67 Some reasons why God gives this ministery to the Divells, why it is invested in them by God. **1794** S. WILLIAMS *Vermont* 300 The powers invested in Congress were in effect. **1800** *Ann. Reg.* 56 The supreme magistracy was to be invested in a grand elector.

†**b.** *intr.* To settle itself, vest *in* some possessor.

1602 WARNER *Alb. Eng.* Epit. (1612) 393 How..the Crowne-right of the House of Edward the first inuested in the Familie of York, and from whom they claimed, and in whome their claime effected.

7. *Milit.* To enclose or hem in with a hostile force, so as to cut off approach or escape; to lay siege to; to besiege, beleaguer; †to attack.

1600 HOLLAND *Livy* V. vi. 183 No wearisomnesse of long siege & assault..is able to raise the Romane armie from any towne once by them invested. **1653** H. COGAN tr. *Pinto's Trav.* i. 2 They discovered a ship, vnto which they gave chase all the night,..having fetcht her up by break of day, they gaue her a volley of three pieces of Ordnance, and presently invested her with a great deal of courage. **1726–31** TINDAL *Rapin's Hist. Eng.* (1743) II. XVII. 112 The Earl not having sufficient forces to besiege the Fort contented himself with investing it. **1810** WELLINGTON in Gurw. *Desp.* (1838) VI. 41 Astorga is invested, but has not been vigorously attacked. **1840** MACAULAY *Ess., Clive* (1887) 534 Rajah Sahib proceeded to invest the fort of Arcot, which seemed quite incapable of sustaining a siege.

†**8.** To occupy or engage, to absorb. *Obs. rare.*

1601 R. JOHNSON *Kingd. & Commw.* (1603) 62 The one [prince] was invested in the war of Persia, the other in the commotions of the Low countries.

II. [after It. *investire* '..also, to laie out or emploie ones money vpon anie bargaine for aduantage' (Florio, 1598). This sense is exemplified as early as 1333 in *Vocab. della Crusca*. It prob. passed through the Levant or Turkey Company into the East India Company's use.]

9. a. To employ (money) in the purchase of anything from which interest or profit is expected; now, esp. in the purchase of property, stocks, shares, etc., in order to hold these for the sake of the interest, dividends, or profits accruing from them.

1613 T. ALDWORTH *Let. to E. India Co.* Surat, 25 Jan. (MS., Orig. Corr. 102), Hauinge left with vs in goods and monies to be inuested in Commodities fitt for Englande..to the vallew of 4000 li. **1615** T. ELKINGTON *Let. to E. India Co.* 25 Feb. (Orig. Corr. 251), To invest itt in Indico to bee in Surrat before the raynes. **1616** SIR T. ROE *Jrnl.* 28 May (Hakl. Soc.), This is yearly theyr Custome at this season to bring goodes, and so to goe for Agra and invest in Indico. **1710** in *Peere Williams' Rep.* I. (1792) 141 The primary Intent of the Testator in carrying abroad the Money was to

invest it in Trade. **1740** *Ibid.* 140 The..captain..had 800 dollars on board the ship, which he intended to invest in trade. **1757** *Herald* (1758) I. v. 66 By investing in the stocks so much of their incomes and gains as they do not spend. **1804** EARL LAUDERD. *Publ. Wealth* (1819) 157 That portion of capital invested in a plough, supplants the necessity..of the labour of five diggers. **1833** HT. MARTINEAU *Loom & Lugger* I. i. 3 There was little encouragement to invest his remaining capital. **1840** MACAULAY *Ess., Clive* (1887) 562 Many of them even invested their property in India stock. **1878** JEVONS *Primer Pol. Econ.* v. 45 To invest capital.. means to turn circulating into fixed capital, or less durable into more durable capital.

fig. **1837** HT. MARTINEAU *Soc. Amer.* III. 45 He has most profitably invested his time and energy in the anti-slavery cause. **1872** BAGEHOT *Physics & Pol.* (1876) 49 Every intellectual gain..was invested and taken out in war.

b. *absol.* or *intr.* To make an investment, to invest capital; *colloq.* to lay out money, make a purchase. (So in It.)

1864 WEBSTER s.v., To invest in stocks. **1868** MONTGOMERIE in *Proc. R. Geog. Soc.* 15 July 155 The Pundit had invested in a wooden bowl. **1870** ROGERS *Hist. Gleanings* Ser. II. 146 Men invested in a parliamentary seat as they did in any kind of speculative stock. **1883** *Wharton's Law Lex.* s.v., When a trustee, executor, or administrator is not expressly forbidden to invest in real securities, in the United Kingdom. *Mod. colloq.* To invest in a penny time-table.

c. To lay out money in betting on a horse race, or in football pools, etc.

1951 'H. CECIL' *Painswick Line* ix. 107 He went to the £5 tote windows and invested (as they euphemistically call it) £100 on Maiden Aunt. **1958** *Punch* 27 Aug. 265/1 Your skill can put you on top of the world when it's invested with——'s [Pools]. **1973** *Times* 21 Apr. 12/1 In bookie parlance, one does not bet on a horse; one invests.

Hence **in'vested** *ppl. a.*

Mod. Eager for news of the relief of the invested town.

†**in'vest**, *sb. Obs. rare*⁻¹. [f. prec. vb.] A payment made to the Pope or Head of the church by a bishop or the like at his investiture.

1533-4 *Act 25 Hen. VIII*, c. 20 § 1 Yeldyng vnto the kinges highnes..all suche dueties, rightes, and inuestes, as before time hath ben accustomed to be paid for any such Archbishopricke or Bishopricke.

in'vestable, *a.* [f. INVEST *v.* + -ABLE.] Capable of being invested.

1896 *Chicago Advance* 17 Dec. 857 Any person having investable capital.

†**inve'station.** *Obs. rare*⁻¹. Bad form of **investition* or *investion*.

1665 R. HEAD *Eng. Rogue* xxvi. 86 An Oath, which every young Thief must observe..at his investation into the honour of one of the Knights of the Road.

inve'stee. *Law. rare.* [f. INVEST *v.* + -EE.] One who is invested with a right, property, etc.

1610 W. FOLKINGHAM *Art of Survey* III. vi. 77 Fee-Farme is a Fee, and importeth a perpetuity to the Inuestee and his heires.

investible, *a.* [f. INVEST *v.* + -IBLE.] = INVESTABLE *a.*

1931 *Economist* 18 July 110/2 Central Banks..should take steps..to counteract any tendency which their own nationals may show either to keep their investible resources excessively liquid or to undertake excessive long-term commitments. **1968** *Daily Tel.* 21 Nov. 3 These funds form a pool of investible money.

†**in'vestient**, *a. Obs.* [ad. L. *investient-em*, pr. pple. of *investīre* to INVEST: see -ENT.] Investing, coating, enveloping, enfolding.

1695 WOODWARD *Nat. Hist. Earth* v. (1702) 232 Freed from its investient Shell. **1757** A. COOPER *Distiller* III. xxv. (1760) 186 The Nutmeg..is separated from..its investient Coat the Mace, before it is sent over to us. **1762** A. CATCOTT *Treat. Deluge* (1768) 291 *note*, Stones that are worn to a roundness, which was not natural to them,..have never any coat or investient crust.

investigable (ɪn'vɛstɪgəb(ə)l), *a.*¹ [ad. late L. *investīgābil-is* that may be searched into, f. *investīgāre*: see INVESTIGATE and -ABLE.] Capable of being investigated, traced out, or searched into; open to investigation, inquiry or research.

1594 HOOKER *Eccl. Pol.* I. vii. § 7 In doing euill, we prefer a lesse good before a greater, the greatnesse whereof is by reason inuestigable and may bee knowne. **1637** GILLESPIE *Eng. Pop. Cerem.* III. viii. 138 It is investigable by the very light and guidance of naturall reason. **1738** WARBURTON *Div. Legat.* I. 439 Had the Doctrine been investigable by human Reason. **1838** *Blackw. Mag.* XLIV. 586 [It] places me in a world which has real infinitude, but is investigable only to the understanding.

†**in'vestigable**, *a.*² *Obs.* [ad. late L. *investīgābil-is* (Vulg.), f. *in-* (IN-³) + **vestīgābilis*, f. *vestīgāre* to track, trace: cf. in same sense OF. *investigable* (14–15th c. in Godef.).] Incapable of being traced; undiscoverable, unsearchable.

c **1510** BARCLAY *Mirr. Gd. Manners* (1570) E v, Inclose thee in cauernes or place inuestigable,..Our Lorde all beholdeth. **1513** DOUGLAS *Æneis* x. Prol. 101 O Lord, thy ways beyn investigabill! **1530** PALSGR. 316/2 Investygable nat able to be serched, *ineustigable*. **1654** GAYTON *Pleas. Notes* IV. ii. 183 Whose estate was incredible, and investigable by his executor. **1701** S. SEWALL *Diary* 30 June (1879) II. 38 The Providence of our Sovereign Lord is very investigable.

investigate (ɪn'vɛstɪgeɪt), *v.* [f. L. *investīgāt-*, ppl. stem of *investīgāre*, f. *in-* (IN-²) + *vestīgāre* to track, trace out.]

1. *trans.* To search or inquire into; to examine (a matter) systematically or in detail; to make an inquiry or examination into.

c **1510** BARCLAY *Mirr. Gd. Manners* (1570) B iij, This learning..cleare, playne and open, it selfe ready to shewe To suche as it searcheth, or will inuestigate. **1675** BAXTER *Cath. Theol.* II. I. 16 This is the only necessary and the sufficient method of Gods Decrees, which Man can investigate. **1772** *Junius Lett.* lxviii. 337 To investigate a question of law, demands some labour and attention. **1863** MRS. OLIPHANT *Salem Ch.* I. xiii. 223 Vincent proceeded to investigate the Directory. **1874** HELPS *Soc. Press.* iii. 40 Such was the belief of those persons who..investigated the matter.

†**b.** To trace out, to track. *Obs.*

1774 BP. HALLIFAX *Anal. Rom. Law* (1795) 52 The degrees of Consanguinity, by which the next of Kin are investigated.

2. *intr.* To make search; to reconnoitre, to scout; to inquire systematically, to make investigation.

c **1510** BARCLAY *Mirr. Gd. Manners* (1570) D vj, If he take a drinke intoxicate, Soon doth he for phisike and ayde investigate. **1581** STYWARD *Mart. Discipl.* II. 119 Thy light horsemen going before inuestigating and spieng where they maie passe. **1714** MANDEVILLE *Fab. Bees* (1723) 395, I intend now to investigate into the nature of Society. **1864** MRS. CARLYLE *Lett.* III. 237, I have investigated, and found all true.

Hence **in'vestigating** *vbl. sb.* and *ppl. a.*; also **in'vestigatingly** *adv.*, in an investigating manner; inquiringly, questioningly.

1833 J. H. NEWMAN *Arians* II. v. (1876) 221 Controversialists, who thought that truth was gained by disputing instead of investigating. **1856** OLMSTED *Slave States* 222 The report of the investigating commission was never made public. **1883** MISS BROUGHTON *Belinda* II. III. i. 173 Her sister's eyes flash investigatingly upon her. **1891** E. CASTLE *Consequences* I. II. ii. 208 The veteran eyed him investigatingly.

investigation (ɪnvɛstɪ'geɪʃən). [a. F. *investigation*, OF. *-acion* (14–15th c. in Hatz.-Darm.), ad. L. *investīgātiōn-em*, n. of action from *investīgāre* to INVESTIGATE.]

1. The action of investigating; the making of a search or inquiry; systematic examination; careful and minute research.

1436 *Pol. Poems* (Rolls) II. 195 Yf they [his statutes and decrees] were welle kepte in alle cuntrees. Of these he made subtile investigacioun. *a* **1548** HALL *Chron., Rich. III* 41 They..knewe not in what parte of the worlde to make investigacion or searche for hym. **1602** FULBECKE *1st Pt. Parall.* Introd. 1 They may perhaps prouoke others to the inuestigation of the truth. **1740** CHEYNE *Regimen* Pref. 8 There is scarce a Geometer, but has his own Method of Investigation. **1855** PRESCOTT *Philip II*, I. II. xii. 281 He made strict investigation into the causes of the late tumult.

attrib. **1897** *Daily News* 21 Oct. 7/7 Criminal investigation staffs in the provinces have been instructed to ascertain what persons may be missing within their several jurisdictions. **1899** *Westm. Gaz.* 20 Feb. 8/1 It is proposed to ask the shareholders..to contribute 6*d.* in the pound towards an investigation fund.

b. With *an* and *pl.*

1795 BURKE *Corr.* IV. 318 Characters which require a long investigation to unfold. **1816** KIRBY & SP. *Entomol.* (1828) I. Pref. 12 Technological investigations. **1832** LEWIS *Use & Ab. Pol. Terms* iv. 36 A full investigation of the different meanings. **1853** J. H. NEWMAN *Hist. Sk.* (1876) II. II. v. 260 The Romans..had neither time nor inclination for abstruse investigations.

2. The tracking of (a beast). *rare.*

1822 T. TAYLOR *Apuleius* 167 The dogs, destined to the sagacious investigation of savage animals.

investigational (ɪnvɛstɪ'geɪʃənəl), *a.* [f. INVESTIGATION + -AL.] Of or pertaining to investigation.

1905 *Science* 29 Sept. 387/1 Investigational apparatus of great importance. **1930** *Aberdeen Press & Jrnl.* 4 Sept. 7/3 An unprecedented demand for botanical specialists to fill investigational and advisory posts. **1946** *Nature* 12 Oct. 522/1 This would be sufficient for the investigational purposes now envisaged by the Board. **1971** *Mod. Law Rev.* XXXIV. VI. 651 What..is to be the future of the social sciences as part of the normal decisional or investigational equipment of lawyers?

investigative (ɪn'vɛstɪgeɪtɪv, -gətɪv), *a.* [f. L. *investīgāt-* (see INVESTIGATE *v.*) + -IVE.]

a. Characterized by or inclined to investigation.

1803 S. PEGGE *Anecd. Eng. Lang.* 251 When money was in his pocket, he [Johnson] was more deliberate and investigative. **1873** M. COLLINS *Squire Silchester* II. iv. 37 When he suddenly found himself in the very heart of a mystery, his old investigative temper rekindled. **1877** STUBBS *Lect. Hist.* (1886) 75 The exercise of the investigative instinct. **1925** [see FLAIR¹ 2]. **1955** *Sci. News Let.* 16 Apr. 249/2 The pathologists can and will assume their part in this investigative obligation and I'm sure that practicing physicians will do likewise. **1975** *Times* 24 Jan. 14/5 Some suggest that I should turn my investigative powers to other vanishing drinks.

b. Designating journalism or broadcasting which actively investigates and seeks to expose malpractice, miscarriage of justice, etc.; also applied to those who conduct this type of research; as *investigative journalism, journalist, reporter, reporting.* orig. *U.S.*

1951 *Editor & Publisher* 8 Dec. 20/2 'Newspapers must turn more and more to great reporters,' declared Mr. Walters. 'They will be known as investigative reporters.' *Ibid.* Investigative reporting has as its goal the stimulation of sufficient indignation to force a new code of ethics on the public officeholder. **1964** N. COPPLE *Depth Reports* iii. 19 *Investigative reporting* is almost self-explanatory... Usually it describes writing that results from digging out facts beneath the surface... There is no opinion in truly investigative reporting. **1972** *Village Voice* (N.Y.) 1 June 37/1 What is vitally needed is more investigative reporting on this growing national phenomenon. **1975** *Economist* 5 July 132 Lincoln Steffens has a good claim to be regarded as the father of modern investigative journalism.., of the carefully researched inquiry into political, social and economic issues. **1976** *Latin Amer.* 15 Oct. 318/2 The bait has been thrown to the United States investigative journalists. If they find further evidence of Carter's involvement..it will be extremely damaging to his electoral chances. **1986** *Daily Tel.* 13 June 14/2 Mr Lewis's classic piece of investigative reporting..into the plight of the Indians in the Brazilian rainforest..is journalism of a very high order.

investigator (ɪn'vɛstɪgeɪtə(r)). [a. L. *investīgātor*, agent-n. f. *investīgāre* to INVESTIGATE. Cf. F. *investigateur* (15–16th c. in Hatz.-Darm.).] One who (or that which) investigates; one who makes close research.

1552 HULOET, Inuestigatour, or expounder, *disquisitor*. Inuestigatours, or crafty searchers, *coryces*. **1608** TOPSELL *Serpents* (1658) 706 The investigators of nature do say that they have fifteen teeth of a side. **1751** WARBURTON *Notes Pope's Ep. Bathurst* 105 (Jod.) The high court of Chancery, the most unerring investigator of truth and falsehood. **1794** SULLIVAN *View Nat.* II. xliv. 271 Father Simon, an accurate investigator, will have it, that they..were written by some Jewish Scribes. **1812** SIR H. DAVY *Chem. Philos.* 25 The principal early chemical investigators. **1971** *Nature* 15 Oct. 469/2 Other investigators who have scanned the North Polar spur and portions of other galactic spurs..at large solar zenith angles have not observed any enhancement at soft X-ray energies. **1972** *Daily Tel.* 21 Jan. 7/1 Department of Employment investigators, only 30 for the whole country, are too few to catch offenders.

in,vestiga'torial, *a. rare.* [f. L. type **investīgātōri-us*: see next and -AL¹.] Pertaining to or characteristic of an investigator.

1808 BENTHAM *Sc. Reform* 69 *Investigation* or *investigatorial procedure*, a new and necessary name, for a practice in common use, but not as yet sufficiently distinguished. *Investigatorial power*, power for tracing out evidence, in the way of investigatorial procedure.

investigatory (ɪn'vɛstɪgətərɪ), *a.* [f. L. type **investīgātōri-us*, f. *investīgātor*: see above and -ORY.] Of investigating nature or character.

1836 *New Monthly Mag.* XLVIII. 71 The world has been growing..so wondrously philosophical and investigatory. *c* **1885** RUSKIN in *Daily News* 18 June 6/3 To estimate the quantity of careful and investigatory reading. **1966** *Punch* 23 Feb. 276/3 During his editorship, Sam Campbell, as he was known to most of Fleet Street, added more than one and a half million paying readers to his paper by sustained crusading investigatory journalism of a kind unequalled since W. T. Stead. **1969** *Listener* 27 Mar. 436/2 *World in Action* has an aggressive investigatory policy. **1969** *Daily Tel.* 31 Oct. 1/4 The judges said they believed it was desirable to have the inquest kept secret to 'protect its integrity, investigatory character and effectiveness'. *Ibid.*, Inquest proceedings are not accusatory and..they should be regarded as investigatory.

†**in,vesti'gatrix.** *Obs. rare*⁻⁰. [L. fem. of *investīgātor*: cf. F. *investigatrice.*] A female investigator.

1623 COCKERAM, *Inuestigatrix*, she which tracketh.

in'vesting, *vbl. sb.* [f. INVEST *v.* + -ING¹.] The action of the verb INVEST.

1598 FLORIO, *Investitura*,..an inuesting. **1622** BACON *Hen. VII* 189 New Commissions, for the Discouerie and inuesting of vnknowne Lands. **1711** *Light to Blind* II. vii. § 76 in *10th Rep. Hist. MSS. Comm.* App. v. 167 The Prince.. did not judge the investing of Lymerick..to hasten the surrender of the town.

in'vesting, *ppl. a.* [-ING².] That invests.

a. Enveloping or surrounding like clothing.

1646 SIR T. BROWNE *Pseud. Ep.* III. xiv. 139 Materialls.. call'd by the name of Salamanders wooll; which many too literally apprehending, conceive some investing part, or tegument of the Salamander. **1796** KIRWAN *Elem. Min.* (ed. 2) II. 188 [Green martial Earth] commonly found investing, or incumbent. **1800** *Med. Jrnl.* IV. 509 The investing membranes of the brain.

b. *Milit.* Beleaguering.

1828 J. M. SPEARMAN *Brit. Gunner* (ed. 2) 44 The arrangement usually made for the reception of the investing corps. **1872** YEATS *Growth Comm.* 269 They were, however, obliged to abandon the siege by Robert Clive, who subsequently defeated the investing army.

†**in'vestion.** *Obs. rare.* [ad. med.L. *investiōn-em* for **investītiōn-em*, n. of action f. *investīre* to INVEST.] The action of investing; investment.

1586 MARLOWE *1st Pt. Tamburl.* I. i, We knew, my lord, before we brought the Crown, Intending your investion so near The residence of your despised brother. **1632** LITHGOW *Trav.* VIII. 359 The Turkes investion of it [Tremizen].

investitive (ɪnˈvɛstɪtɪv), *a.* [f. ppl. stem of L. *investīre* to INVEST + -IVE.] Having the property or function of investing.

1780 BENTHAM *Princ. Legisl.* xviii. §35 *note*, What is meant by payment, is always an act of investitive power. 1809 *Edin. Rev.* XV. 102 The non-performance of investitive acts. 1875 POSTE *Gaius* III. (ed. 2) 359 Civil obligations..(1) those to which the title or investitive fact is a contract; and (2) those to which the title or investitive fact is a delict.

inˈvestitor. *rare.* [f. L. type **investītor, investītōr-em*, agent-n. from *investīre* to INVEST; cf. It. *investitore* 'an investor,..an enrober' (Florio).] One who or that which invests.

1850 L. HUNT *Autobiog.* viii. (1860) 148 Evil itself.. probably is but..the increaser, nay the very adorner and splendid investitor of good.

investiture (ɪnˈvɛstɪtjʊə(r)). [ad. med.L. *investitūr-a*, f. *investīre* to INVEST; It. *investitura* 'an enstalment, enrobing, endowrie, imploiment, investing' (Florio, 1598); F. *investiture* (1564).]

1. The action of clothing or robing; *concr.*, that which clothes or covers. Chiefly *fig.*

1651 JER. TAYLOR *Serm. for Year* I. xviii. 225 By the resurrection of the body, and a new investiture of the soul, with the same upper garment clarified. 1660 —— *Duct. Dubit.* II. ii. rule 6 §16 The bodily shape was the usual investiture of God's messengers in their appearances. 1855 SINGLETON *Virgil* I. Pref. 5 To dress the sovereign in a linsey-woolsey garb would be seen at once to be a very unsuitable investiture. *a* 1871 ALFORD *Gen. & Ex. Eng. Rdrs.* Ex. xix. 9 The darkness of clouds is the accustomed investiture of the Divine presence.

2. The action or ceremony of clothing in the insignia of an office; the ceremonial, official, or formal investing of a person with an office or rank; the formal putting (a person) in possession of a fief or benefice. Often, spec., the livery and seizin of the temporalities of a bishopric or other ecclesiastical dignity, the right of which was keenly contested between the papacy and the temporal powers during the Middle Ages.

1387 TREVISA *Higden* (Rolls) V. 289 He ordeyned þat no clerk schulde fonge þe investiture of his benefys [*investituram sui beneficii*], noþer of his offys, of a lewed man his hond. 1494 FABYAN *Chron.* VI. cliv. 142 He grauntyd vnto hym inuestiture of benefycis spirituall. 1530 TINDALE *Pract. Prelates* Wks. (Parker Soc.) II. 294 He had compelled him..to deliver up the investiture or election of bishops unto St. Peter's vicar, which investiture was of old time the king's duty. 1642 FULLER *Holy & Prof. St.* IV. xx. 343 We find him to be the first Prince of Wales, whose charter at this day is extant, with the particular rites of investiture, which were the Crownet, and ring of gold, with a Rod of Silver. 1757 BURKE *Abridgem. Eng. Hist.* III. iv, The king..gave the bishop the investiture, or livery and seizin of his temporalities, by the delivery of a ring and staff. 1845 J. SAUNDERS *Cabinet Pict. Eng. Life, Chaucer* 66 Investiture was the formal giving into the tenant's hands the lands granted, and which was done, as far as possible, literally by the lord or his deputy, or symbolically by the delivery..of a turf, a stone, or some other of the ninety-eight prevalent modes enumerated by Du Cange. 1852 MISS YONGE *Cameos* I. xii. 76 The tokens of investiture were the pastoral staff, fashioned like a shepherd's crook, and the ring by which the Bishop was wedded to his See.

3. Clothing in or enduement with attributes or qualities; establishment in any state of privilege or honour.

1626 BP. ANDREWES *Serm.* (1856) I. 62 Our freeing from under the Lawe, our investiture into our new adopted state. *a* 1631 DONNE in *Select.* (1840) 241 The appropriation and investiture of an actual and applying faith. 1833 LAMB *Elia* Ser. II. *Barrenness Imag. Faculty*, One incapable of investiture with any grandeur. *a* 1899 J. CAIRD *Fund. Ideas Chr.* II. xix. 246 His investiture with external power and glory.

4. The hostile investment of a place; = INVESTMENT 4. Now *rare.*

1649 EVELYN *Let. to Sir R. Browne*, Supposing that Paris is now free of the investiture. 1898 *Daily News* 4 Nov. 5/4 A commander..consents to break the line of investiture only when a favourable chance offers.

†**5.** = INVESTMENT 5. *Obs.*

1757 *Herald* (1758) I. v. 66 Augmented by so facile an investiture of savings. *Ibid.* II. xvi. 11 Investitures of money. 1805 W. TAYLOR in *Ann. Rev.* III. 308 The investiture of additional capitals in the purchase of corn. 1832 CHALMERS *Pol. Econ.* 315 Capital would find a fresh field for its investiture. 1845 *N. Brit. Rev.* III. 333 It tells us of the impossibility, at present, to get a profitable investiture for a poor man's savings.

[**investive,** *a.* Explained as: Encircling, enclosing. Error for INFESTIVE *a.*, troublesome, annoying.

[1610 *Englands Eliza* in *Mirr. Mag.* 829 Th'horrid fire all mercilesse did choake The scorched wretches with infestiue smoake.] 1818 TODD [quoting this as 'investive']. Hence in some later Dicts.]

investment (ɪnˈvɛstmənt). [f. INVEST *v.* + -MENT. Cf. the earlier VESTMENT.]

1. The act of putting clothes or vestments on; *concr.* clothing; robes, vestments. Also *fig.*

1597 SHAKS. *2 Hen. IV*, IV. i. 45 You, Lord Arch-bishop ..Whose white Inuestments figure Innocence. 1602 —— *Ham.* I. iii. 128 His vowes..they are Broakers, Not of the eye, which their Inuestments show: But meere implorators of vnholy Sutes. 1794 MATHIAS *Purs. Lit.* (1798) 37, I now present myself..clothed in the robes of their hereditary priesthood..But if, unworthy of this hallowed investment and interior ministry, the door of the sanctuary is closed upon me; I shall [etc.]. 1854 M. J. ROUTH in Burgon *Lives 12 Gd. Men* (1888) I. 101 No persons would spend their time in a leisurely disposal of the investments, after having taken them from the body.

2. *transf.* **a.** An outer covering of any kind; an envelope; a coating.

1646 SIR T. BROWNE *Pseud. Ep.* III. xiv. 140 Crocodiles, are without any haire, and have no covering part or hairy investment at all. 1796 KIRWAN *Elem. Min.* (ed. 2) I. 298 Some assert that these are only investments of other crystallized stones that have since decayed. 1804 ABERNETHY *Surg. Obs.* 27 Their capsules afford a striking instance of an investment acquired simply by a condensation of the surrounding cellular structure. 1874 LUBBOCK *Orig. & Met. Ins.* iv. 67 The hard and horny dermal investment of insects.

b. Refractory material which can be used to embed or surround an object and then is allowed to harden, so that soldering can be carried out (in *Dentistry*) or a mould made from it; freq. *attrib.*, as ***investment material***; **investment casting**, a technique for making small, accurate castings from alloys having high melting points, the mould being made by investing a pattern of wax or similar material that can be removed from the investment by melting it.

1892 C. HUNTER *Man. Dental Laboratory* viii. 115 If the new tooth must be soldered, an hour-and-a-half, from the time the case is ready to be put in the investment, is not too much for its safe accomplishment. 1942 *Iron Age* 9 July 39 Production of castings..by a modern modification of the lost-wax process is described herein. This method utilizes a refractory investment which makes possible the casting of stainless and other alloy steels. 1946 Investment casting [see INVEST *v.* 2c]. 1947 J. C. RICH *Materials & Methods Sculpture* vi. 140 For the solid casting of small bronze statuettes, the Greeks employed a simple technique. The work was modeled in wax and incased in a containing negative mold composed of sand and earth-clay. When this investment material was dry, an opening was made and the entire mass was heated until the wax ran off. 1956 J. N. ANDERSON *Appl. Dental Materials* xvii. 191 A wax pattern may be expanded directly by using warm water to mix the investment. 1963 C. R. COWELL et al. *Inlays, Crowns & Bridges* ii. 3 Modern inlay waxes and investment techniques make dimensional control possible. 1964 S. CRAWFORD *Basic Engin. Processes* xii. 255 Precision casting, investment casting, and the lost-wax process, are various names given to the process by which small intricate castings can be produced to a high grade of dimensional accuracy and surface finish in materials which prove difficult or impossible to cast and subsequently machine by the more traditional methods... The principle of the process..has been in use in the jewellery and dental trades for many years.

3. The action of investing or fact of being invested with an office, right, or attribute; endowment; = INVESTITURE 2, 3.

1649 MILTON *Eikon.* xviii. Wks. (1851) 470 The investment of that lustre, Majesty, and honour, which for the public good,..redounds from a whole Nation into one person. 1654 tr. *Scudery's Curia Pol.* 112 The Bassawes.. would have..prevented the said Kings investment, an Inauguration unto the Kingdom of Hungary. 1885 CLODD *Myths & Dr.* I. iv. 61 The investment of the powers of nature with personal life and consciousness.

4. *Milit.* The surrounding or hemming in *of* a town or fort by a hostile force so as to cut off all communication with the outside; beleaguerment; blockade. Also *attrib.*

1811 WELLINGTON in Gurw. *Desp.* (1838) VII. 214 You will likewise have heard of the surrender of Olivença and of the subsequent investment of Badajoz. 1868 KINGLAKE *Crimea* (1877) IV. x. 246 To draw the investment closer. 1884 *Mil. Engineering* (ed. 3) I. II. 7 Secrecy and speed are secured, in the investment of an inland fortress, by the use of an advanced force of cavalry and horse artillery, which conceals the march of the main body. *Ibid.* 17 Some distance in rear of the investment line.

5. *Comm.* The investing of money or capital. (Not in J. or T.) **a.** In early use in the East India trade, for the employment of money in the purchase of Indian goods.

1615 E. HOLMDEN *Let. to Governor E.I. Co.* 7 Mar. (MS., Orig. Corr. 262), For further aduyse in particulerising of the sayls of the Companies goods and Investment of that and of ther monies. 1618 SIR T. ROE *Let. to E.I.C.* 14 Feb. (Hakl. Soc. 473), Not to defer investmentes till our shippes arriuall and the Indicoes sweept away. 1675 *Let.* in Fryer *Acc. E. India & P.* (1698) 86 The Factors are sent to over-see the Weavers, buying up the Cotton-yarn to employ them all the Rains, when they set on foot their Investments. 1698 C. DAVENANT *Disc. Publ. Revenues* II. 345 (E.I. Trade) If the prime Cost of the respective Investments or Parcels of Goods, were truly valued and stated by judicious and disinterested Persons, a Judgment might from thence be made somewhat nearer the Truth. 1783 BURKE *9th Rep. Aff. India* Wks. XI. 51 A certain portion of the revenues of Bengall has been..set apart to be employed in the purchase of goods for exportation to England, and this is called the *Investment. Ibid.* 53 The practice of an Investment from the Revenue began in the year 1776. *Ibid.* 54. *Ibid.* 57 When an account is taken of the intercourse (for it is not commerce), which is carried on between Bengal and England, the pernicious effects of the system of Investment from Revenue will appear in the strongest point of view. 1791 ROBERTSON *India* IV. 151 To these staples, the natives of all the different regions in the eastern parts of Asia brought the commodities which were the growth of their several countries..and with them the ships from Tyre and from Egypt completed their investments. 1844 H. H. WILSON *Brit. India* III. 521 To sell and buy various articles, including pepper, which it was his business to provide for the Company's investments.

b. *gen.* The conversion of money or circulating capital into some species of property from which an income or profit is expected to be derived in the ordinary course of trade or business.

Distinguished from *speculation*, in which the object is the chance of reaping a rapid advantage by a sudden rise in the market price of something which is bought merely in order to be held till it can be thus advantageously sold again.

1740 *Peere Williams' Rep.* I. (1792) 140 The plaintiff insisted on the profits produced in trade, and the several investments that had been made therewith. *a* 1804 A. HAMILTON (Webster 1828), Before the investment could be made, a change of the market might render it ineligible. 1845 MᶜCULLOCH *Taxation* (1852) 398 Any feeling of insecurity is a most formidable obstacle to the investment of capital. 1858 J. B. NORTON *Topics* 203 An inducement for the investment of capital in the land. 1868 ROGERS *Pol. Econ.* vi. (1876) 54 When the profitable investment of saving is discouraged or diminished, capital is less eagerly accumulated.

c. An amount of money invested in some species of property; also, A form of property viewed as a vehicle in which money may be invested.

1837 HT. MARTINEAU *Soc. Amer.* III. 45 A friend..made some inquiries about investments in the region where his host lived..'I do not put myself in the way of hearing about profitable investments'. 1855 MACAULAY *Hist. Eng.* xx. (1889) II. 484 So popular was the new investment, that on the day on which the books were opened three hundred thousand pounds were subscribed. 1878 JEVONS *Prim. Pol. Econ.* ii. 23 If they put their wealth into banks and other good investments, they do great service in increasing the capital of the nation. 1888 F. HUME *Mad. Midas* I. i, Mrs. Villiers sold out all the investments which she had.

fig. 1873 BURTON *Hist. Scot.* VI. 63 He discovered a good investment for his skill, sagacity, and endurance in Poland. 1873 HAMERTON *Intell. Life* I. v. (1876) 28 Sacrifice to bodily well-being, the best of all possible investments.

d. *attrib.* and *Comb.* Also **investment currency**, the currency resulting from the sale of foreign securities or used for their purchase when such transactions are controlled and channelled through a market separate from the market in foreign exchange; **investment trust**, a trust (TRUST *sb.* 7a) whose business is the investment of money; also *attrib.*

1883 *Daily News* 8 Oct. 2/3 Consols and various other high class investment stocks are firm. 1885 *List of Subscribers, Classified* (United Telephone Co.) (ed. 6) 213 American Investment Trust Co. 1895 *Daily News* 21 Mar. 5/3 Regret is expressed that the special investment business of some of these savings banks is practically suspended. 1899 *Westm. Gaz.* 13 July 6/1 A lot of investment money seeking employment. 1924 B. D. NASH *Investment Banking in Eng.* 3 The function of investment banking is to gather together the savings and surplus capital of individuals and companies and to turn this accumulation into the hands of others for use in the construction of fixed plants. 1924 L. M. SPEAKER *Investment Trust* 3 The investment trust in its characteristic form is an institution mainly of British origin. It is essentially a corporation, the business of which consists chiefly of judicious investment of its capital. 1929 *Observer* 17 Nov. 2/3 Among the many high-class securities which have had to be sold to meet the demand for money caused by the depressed conditions have been the junior stocks of the large investment trust companies. 1933 B. ELLINGER *This Money Business* iv. 33 There are a number of firms and brokers connected with trust and investment companies. 1935 *Economist* 5 Jan. 23/1 The extent of the..movement may be appreciated from the following table of representative values and yields based on the Actuaries' Investment Index. 1951 R. W. JONES *Thomson's Dict. Banking* (ed. 10) 346/1 Investment Ledger. A separate account is opened in this ledger for each different investment. 1961 'E. LATHEN' *Banking on Death* (1962) iii. 21 Robichaux had..surprised his friends and relations by becoming an astute and competent investment banker. 1963 *Listener* 31 Jan. 191/1 Bankers have looked with jaundiced or favourable eye on the investment bank. 1965 D. GREENWALD et al. *McGraw-Hill Dict. Mod. Econ.* 274 The first real investment trust was the Foreign and Colonial Trust, which was established in London in 1868. Its purpose was to give small investors the same advantage, diversification, that large capitalists had. 1967 *Spectator* 21 July 85/3 Investment trusts are closed portfolios. Selling or buying shares in such trusts neither increases nor decreases the size of the portfolio. 1969 *Times* 30 Apr. 30/6 Investment companies qualify, so do unit trusts, and a company is eligible for relief if the interest would have been eligible when payable by an individual. 1969 *Times* 5 May (Suppl.) p. vi/5 Now the insurance companies have joined the fight for this part of the investment dollar. 1971 *Mod. Law Rev.* XXXI. VI. 699 The second chapter..contains a detailed practical account of the work of American investment bankers. 1972 D. LEES *Zodiac* 117 He's among the top six investment consultants in the world today. 1973 *Country Life* 12 July 120/3 It is necessary to buy what is known as investment currency, which is a pool of funds created by the sale of British investments abroad. 1973 *Times* 17 Dec. 14/3 Investment funds..went too much into property or overseas, too little into productive industry.

investor (ɪnˈvɛstə(r)). Also 6 -er. [f. INVEST *v.* + -OR.]

1. a. One who clothes or invests. **b.** One who invests with a military force.

1586 MARLOWE *1st Pt. Tamburl.* v. ii, Investers of thy royal brows Even with the true Egyptian diadem. 1870 *Pall Mall G.* 3 Oct. 5 The French..choosing their own moment for sortie, are of course far less hurt by this sort of work than their investors.

2. a. One who invests money or makes an investment.

1862 *Lond. Rev.* 16 Aug. 136 This numerous class of investors are ready to accept the guidance of any competent

authority which will tell them what stocks to choose and what to avoid. **1868** Peard *Water-farm.* x. 105 The stock of each investor would represent £20.

b. One who bets on a horse race, or in football pools, etc. Cf. invest *v.* 9c.

1958 [see banker[2] 5].

c. **investor relations** [after *public relations*], the establishment and maintenance of good relations between a company and its investors; the department of a company responsible for this. Freq. *attrib.* orig. *U.S.*

1959 *Public Utilities* 26 Mar. 477/1 This communication..should be undertaken at many levels under a carefully developed and fully maintained investor relations program. **1959** *Amer. Business* May 25/1 For small companies this uniformity of product is the most significant factor in investor relations. **1963** R. R. Augsburger in *Investor Relations* (Amer. Managem. Assoc.) iv. 127 We have in professional investor relations a new and growing area of financial management. **1970** *Harvard Business Rev.* Nov.–Dec. 122/2 In times of crisis the lot of the investor relations executive is not a very happy one. **1985** *Investors Chron.* 8–14 Nov. 6/2 British Petroleum has hired an investor relations man.

†**in'vestry.** *Obs. rare*[−1]. [f. invest *v.* + -ry.] = investiture.

1642 W. Bird *Mag. Honor* 30 The manner of solemnity used in the admittance and investry of Marquesses.

investure (ɪn'vɛstjʊə(r)), *sb.* [f. invest + -ure. (Not on L. analogies.)] = investiture, investment.

1577–87 Holinshed *Chron.* I. 69/1 Heerein he did no more than manie other would haue doone, neither yet after his inuesture did so much as was looked for at his hands. **1586** Ferne *Blaz. Gentrie* 161 To violate the holye rites, or inuestures of the Fæcials. **1601** R. Johnson *Kingd. & Commw.* (1603) 265 The investure of Placentia was not graunted to the house of the Farnesi but only to the fourth descendencie. *a* **1714** Burnet *Hist. Ref.* an. 1531 (R.), [The kings of England] did at first erect bishopricks, grant investures in them [etc.]. **1825** *Blackw. Mag.* XVII. 285 We were informed of the issue of the battles of the Pyrenees, and of the investure of St. Sebastian's. **1882** *Daily News* 24 Nov. 5/8 The Queen will hold an investure of several orders of Knighthood at Windsor Castle this afternoon.

†**in'vesture,** *v. Obs. rare.* [Partly f. prec. sb.; partly f. in-[1] or [2] + vesture.]

1. *trans.* To invest *in* an estate or dignity.

1552 Ascham *Germany* (1570) 16 He..hath made hym his heyre, and hath already inuestured hym in the Dukedome of Prusia.

2. To clothe, to habit. Hence †**in'vesturing** *vbl. sb.*, habit, vesture.

1593 Nashe *Christ's T.* (1613) 41 Those ruddy inuesturings, and scarlet habilements..shall they exhalingly quintessence. *a* **1661** Fuller (Webster, 1864), Our monks investured in their copes.

inveteracy (ɪn'vɛtərəsɪ). [f. next: see -acy.]

1. The quality of being inveterate; the state of being strong or deep-seated from long persistence.

a **1719** Addison (J.), The inveteracy of the people's prejudices compelled their rulers to make use of all means for reducing them. **1748** *Anson's Voy.* II. i. 114 The disease seemed to have acquired a degree of inveteracy which was altogether without example. **1794** G. Adams *Nat. & Exp. Philos.* I. i. 6 All those vulgar errors cherished from age to age by the blindness of prejudice, and inveteracy of habit. **1807** Jefferson *Writ.* (1830) IV. 86 Their boldness has betrayed an inveteracy of criminal disposition. **1822–34** *Good's Study Med.* (ed. 4) I. 489 Where habit has given inveteracy to the recurrence of the paroxysms.

2. In pregnant sense: Deep-rooted prejudice, hostility, or hatred; enmity of old standing.

1691 tr. *Emilianne's Frauds Rom. Monks* 54 He judged with an inveteracy of heart, what belongs alone to God to judge of. **1698** Fryer *Acc. E. India & P.* 350 The Turks, who disown that..Caliphship with the same Inveteracy to each others Claims, as among us Papists and Protestants. **1703** S. Parker tr. *Eusebius* 69 He shews the great Inveteracy of the Jews against the Christians. **1782** Paine *Let. Abbé Raynal* (1791) 69 Where is the impossibility..of England forming a friendship with France and Spain, and making it a national virtue to renounce for ever those prejudiced inveteracies it has been her custom to cherish? **1796** Nelson 3 July in Nicolas *Disp.* (1845) II. 201, I shall not fail to sow as much inveteracy against the French as is possible. **1861** May *Const. Hist.* (1863) II. xvi. 535 A fierce conflict arose between the orangemen and defenders,..which increased the inveteracy of the two parties.

inveterate (ɪn'vɛtərət), *a.* (*sb.*) Also 6–7 **-at.** [ad. L. *inveterāt-us* become old, of long standing, chronic, pa. pple. of *inveterāre* to render old, to give age to, f. *in-* (in-[2]) + *veterāre* to make old.]

1. That has existed or continued for a long time; of old standing; aged. (*Obs.* or blended with 2.)

1597 A. M. tr. *Guillemeau's Fr. Chirurg.* 41 b/1 Take ashes which are burned of the inveterate sydes of a wyne-pipe, two pownde. **1599** —— tr. *Gabelhouer's Bk. Physicke* 49/1 Those great Flyes which in the springe time of the yeare creepe out of inveterate walles. **1675** Evelyn *Terra* (1776) 54 Rotten wood,..especially that which is taken out of an Inveterate willow-tree. **1794** Gifford *Baviad* 217 There meagre shrubs inveterate mountains grace.

2. Firmly established by long continuance; long-established; deep-rooted; obstinate. (Now mostly of things evil.)

1563 *St. Andrews Kirk-sess. Reg.* (1889) 189 The delacionis gevyn in upon tham..for huyrmongyn inveterat. **1602** Fulbecke *Pandectes* 21 The king being the lawful owner then, because hee had inueterate possession in the same. **1616** R. C. *Times' Whistle* vi. 2508 This vice is so inveterate, Growne to so strong a custome. **1692** South *12 Serm.* (1697) I. 470 A Resistance, and an Extirpation of inveterate, sinfull Habits. **1877** J. D. Chambers *Div. Worship* 305 This abuse soon..became inveterate in the Ferial Office. **1883** Sir C. Bowen in *Law Rep.* 11 Q. Bench Div. 341 By inveterate practice among most of the commercial nations of Europe, bills of lading have long been drawn..in sets of three or more.

b. Of disease: Of long standing, chronic; hence, deep-seated and resisting treatment.

1541 R. Copland *Guydon's Quest. Chirurg.* 2 C iij b, The curacyon of inueterate vlceres. **1578** Lyte *Dodoens* v. lxxviii. 646 Medicines against an old inueterate cough. **1663** Cowley *Verses & Ess., Ode Harvey* (1669) 13 We now thy patient Physick see, From all inveterate diseases free. **1798** Malthus *Popul.* (1878) 226 The scurvy is in some places..inveterate. **1823** J. Badcock *Dom. Amusem.* 186 The blisters..become inveterate sores.

c. Of evil feelings, prejudices, and the like.

1593 Shaks. *Rich. II*, I. i. 14 [He appeals the Duke] On some apparant danger seene in him, Aym'd at your Highnesse, no inueterate malice. **1682** Wood *Life* 3 May (O.H.S.) III. 14 He became an inveterate enimy to the court and prerogative. **1789** Belsham *Ess.* I. ix. 183, I have an inveterate dislike to improvements merely speculative and theoretical. **1840** Alison *Hist. Europe* (1850) VIII. lii. §3. 292 His old and inveterate enemies. **1856** Froude *Hist. Eng.* (1858) I. v. 380 His relations with Francis..were those of inveterate hostility.

d. Persistent, lasting.

1777 Sheridan *Sch. Scand.* iv. i, The merit of these is the inveterate likeness—all stiff and awkward as the originals, and like nothing in human nature besides. **1864** D. G. Mitchell *Sev. Stories* 6 Is St. Peter's toe, of a truth, worn away with the inveterate kissings?

3. Full of obstinate prejudice or hatred; embittered, malignant; virulent. (Now *vulgar.*)

1528 Roy *Rede Me* (Arb.) 89 They were confederate, With antichrist so inveterate. **1563** Winȝet *Wks.* (1890) II. 54 Sa indurat, sa inueterat, and of sa schamelis a forret. **1648** *Hunting of Fox* 13 Which makes them so inveterate against him. **1674** *Essex Papers* (Camden) I. 222 There is also another party w[ch] I am sure is inveterate towards me. **1760–72** H. Brooke *Fool of Qual.* (1792) II. 84 He was informed, in terms the most aggravating and inveterate, of the whole course and history of Ned's misbehaviour. **1861** Dickens *Gt. Expect.* II. 264, I felt inveterate against him.

4. Settled or confirmed in habit, condition, or practice; habitual, hardened, obstinate.

1734 Fielding *Univ. Gallant* Advt., Authors, whose works have been rejected at the theatres, are of all persons, they say, the most inveterate. **1832** W. Irving *Alhambra* I. 6 Being a veteran and inveterate sportsman. **1859** W. Collins *Q. of Hearts* i, He was an inveterate smoker.

B. *sb.* One who is confirmed in some (evil) habit; a confirmed or hardened offender.

1828 P. Cunningham *N.S. Wales* (ed. 3) II. 286 You can make these inveterates work by no other plan.

inveterate (ɪn'vɛtəreɪt), *v. Obs.* or *arch.* [f. L. *inveterāt-*, ppl. stem of *inveterāre* to render old; or f. prec. adj.] *trans.* To render inveterate.

1. To make old; to establish or confirm by age or long continuance; to root or implant deeply; to render chronic; †also, to harden (the bowels); to render costive (*obs.*).

1574 Newton *Health Mag.* 2 Although they [electuaries] doo purge, yet do they inveterate. **1623** Cockeram II, To make Olde, *Antiquate, Inueterate.* *a* **1626** Bacon *Hist. Gt. Brit.*, An ancient tacit expectation which had by tradition been infused and inveterated into men's minds. **1749** Fielding *Grand Jury Charge* Wks. 1784 X. 149 There are evils..which have so inveterated themselves in the blood of the body politic. **1835** Emerson *Corr. w. Carlyle* I. v. 48 Love his catholicism that at his age can relish the *Sartor*, born and inveterated as he is in old books.

2. To render inveterate in enmity; to embitter.

1656 J. Harrington *Oceana* (1700) 193 It inveterated the Bosoms of the Senat and the People each against other.

in'veterated, *ppl. a. Obs.* or *arch.* [f. prec. + -ed[1].] Rendered or become inveterate; confirmed by age or long continuance.

1597 Lowe *Chirurg.* (1634) 124 Not inveterated, but recent. **1597** A. M. tr. *Guillemeau's Fr. Chirurg.* 29 b/1 Anye inveterated payn in the occipitalle partes of the heade. **1604** T. Wright *Passions* vi. 347 Mens soules, by inveterated customes vsed to sensuall and beastly delights. **1670** G. H. *Hist. Cardinals* I. II. 55 An old and inveterated Schism. **1692** Bentley *Boyle Lect.* i. 28 Temptations, which have all their force and prevalence from long custom and inveterated habit.

in'veterately, *adv.* [f. inveterate *a.* + -ly[2].] In an inveterate manner; in a manner confirmed by long existence or practice; to a degree firmly fixed or ingrained; virulently.

1645 Milton *Tetrach.* Wks. (1847) 188/2 How he could endure to let them slug and grow inveterately wicked. **1700** Congreve *Way of World* II. i, *Mrs. Marw.* You hate mankind? *Mrs. Fain.* Heartily, inveterately. **1705** Cibber *Careless Husb.* v. 64 Sir Charles has shewn himself so inveterately my Enemy. **1858** Froude *Hist. Eng.* IV. xviii. 4 But a slight check upon habits inveterately lawless.

in'veterateness. [f. as prec. + -ness.] The quality of being inveterate; inveteracy.

1646 Sir T. Browne *Pseud. Ep.* VII. xii. 363 As time hath rendred him more perfect in the Art, so hath the inveteratenesse of his malice more ready in the execution. **1660** Burney Κερδ. Δωρον (1661) 28 The swellings of hatred and inveterateness. *a* **1704** Locke (J.), Neither the inveterateness of the mischief, nor the prevalency of the fashion, shall be any excuse.

†**in'veteration.** *Obs. rare*[−1]. [ad. L. *inveterātiōn-em*, n. of action f. *inveterāre*: see inveterate and -ation.] The action of rendering, or process of becoming, inveterate.

a **1631** Donne *Serm.* lvii. 572 He confesses the reason from whence this Inveteration in his Bones, and this Incineration in his body proceeded. **1721** Bailey, *Inveteration*, a growing into Use by long Custom.

†**in'veteratist.** *Obs. rare*[−1]. [f. inveterate *a.* + -ist.] One who professes inveterate attachment to old ways; an opponent of reform.

1715 M. Davies *Athen. Brit.* I. Contents Yy iv b, Reform'd Catholicks persecuted by the Inveteratists, for reading and translating the Bible in the vulgar Tongues.

†**in'vetered,** *a. Obs. rare*[−1]. [f. F. *inveteré* (ad. L. *inveterāt-us* inveterate *a.*) + -ed[1].] Grown old; = inveterate *a.* 1.

1490 Caxton *Eneydos* xxii. 78 A grete oke tre antyque & in-uetered of many yeres among the grete stones harde strongely roted.

†**'invex.** *Obs. rare*[−1]. [f. L. *in-* (in-[2]) + stem of convex.] = concave.

1688 R. Holme *Armoury* III. 319/1 By means whereof any round body either with an Invex or Convex may be wrought.

Hence **invexed** (ɪn'vɛkst), *a. Her.*, concaved.

1828–40 Berry *Encycl. Herald.* I. Gloss. s.v., [Arched] only on one side, and bowed inward, it is called *invexed, concaved, champained,* or *champoined.*

†**in'vey,** *v. Obs. rare*[−1]. [var. of envay *v.*] *trans.* To invade.

1566 Painter *Pal. Pleas.* II. 249 Alexander de Medices..was hee that first..inveyed the seniory of Florence,..usurping the name, title, and prerogative of duke.

invey, -veye, -veygh, obs. forms of inveigh.

inviable (ɪn'vaɪəb(ə)l), *a. Biol.* [f. in-[3] + viable *a.*[1]] Unable to survive; unable to germinate, grow or develop; unable to perform its proper biological role.

1918 *Genetics* III. 476 The disadvantage of so many individuals being rendered sterile or inviable. **1946** *Nature* 12 Oct. 520/2 Among 986 seeds collected in 1941 from chimeral plants there were found six triploid ones, three of which proved inviable. **1948** *Mind* LVII. 297 He found that within one 'species' of frog..ranging from lat. 45° N. to 27° N. in the United States, representatives of the northern and southern ends of the range gave inviable hybrids, though parents not too far apart geographically gave normal development. **1955** *New Biol.* XIX. 21 More usually an unbalanced and inviable nucleus is formed [from an irregular mitosis] in which some chromosomes are represented twice, others once or not at all. **1956** *Nature* 31 Mar. 626/2 Damage arising from inviable recombinations of broken chromosome ends. **1962** *Lancet* 29 Dec. 1384/2 Since the O-sperm, if functional, leads to the Turner zygote which is in great deficit in the general population, it seems likely that O-sperm are inviable and that the Turners are due to a phenomenon other than fertilisation by O-sperm.

So **invia'bility,** the state or condition of being inviable.

1918 *Genetics* III. 614/2 (Index), Inviability. **1929** *Encycl. Brit.* XI. 495/1 The inviability of most gametic and zygotic combinations. **1972** [see inversion 2 h].

†**in'vict,** *a. Obs.* Also 5 invyct. [ad. L. *invict-us*, f. *in-* (in-[3]) + *victus*, pa. pple. of *vincĕre* to conquer. Cf. obs. F. *invicte* (Godef.).]

Unconquered; never vanquished or subdued.

1494 Fabyan *Chron.* VII. 488 He by Knyghthode due Was lyberde [= leopard] inuyct. **1545** Joye *Exp. Dan.* ii. D ij, With as invict a mind and manly an herte let us confesse thee worde of God. **1636** Brathwait *Lives Rom. Emp.* 123 The most famous and invict Commanders. **1678** Gale *Crt. Gentiles* III. 79 An indissoluble chain of invict Reason.

So †**in'victed,** *a. Obs.* = prec.

1600 W. Watson *Decacordon* (1602) 203 The stout, inuicted Macedonian Greeke. **1606** Ford *Fame's Memor.* B j b, A worthy whose sublime Inuicted spirit in most hard assayes, Still added reuerent statues to his daies.

†**invic'tissime,** *a. Obs. rare*[−1]. [a. obs. F. *invictissime* (Godef.), ad. L. *invictissimus*, superl. of *invictus*: see prec.] Most unconquered.

1549 *Compl. Scot.* Ep. Queen 4 The vailȝeant ande nobil rene inuictissime kyng of secilie.

†**in'victive,** *a. Obs. rare.* [f. L. *invict-us* (see invict) + -ive.] Invincible.

1631 *Trag. Hoffman* (N.), My invictive braine Hath cast a glorious prospect of revenge. **1639** G. Daniel *Ecclus.* xxiv. 32 My Invictive Power Was in Ierusalem.

†**invid,** *a. Obs. rare*[−0]. [ad. L. *invid-us* envious.] 'That hath envy, that spighteth or is malicious' (Blount *Glossogr.* 1656).

†**'invidency.** *Obs. rare*[−0]. [ad. L. *invidēntia* envy.] 'Enuie, repining' (Cockeram, 1623).

invidious (ɪn'vɪdɪəs), *a.* Also 8 *erron.* -uous. [ad. L. *invidiōs-us* (see -ous), f. *invidia* ill will, envy.]

1. Of a charge, complaint, report, etc.: Tending or fitted to excite odium, unpopularity, or ill feeling against some one. Now *rare.*

1606 HOLLAND *Sueton.* 58 Asinivs Pollio..made a grievous and invidious complaint in the Senate house, of the fall that Æserninvs his nephew tooke. **1697** DRYDEN *Æneid* XI. 518 He rose, and took th' advantage of the times, To load young Turnus with invidious crimes. **1755** (*title*) An answer to an invidious Pamphlet entituled, A Brief State of the Province of Pennsylvania. **1857** GLADSTONE *Glean.* (1879) VI. xvi. 56 The second is drawn from him by the invidious question of the Pharisees.

2. Of an action, duty, topic, etc.: Entailing odium or ill will upon the person performing, discharging, discussing, etc.; giving offence to others.

1701 ROWE *Amb. Step-Moth.* II. i, 'Twere an invidious Task to enter into The Insolence, and other Faults [etc.]. **1708** SWIFT *Sentim. Ch. Eng. Man* Wks. 1755 II. I. 78 A great deal hath been already said by other writers upon this invidious and beaten subject; therefore I shall let it fall. **1803** MACKINTOSH *Def. Peltier* Wks. 1846 III. 242 The charge which I have to defend is surrounded with the most invidious topics of discussion. **1846** HAWTHORNE *Mosses* II. viii. 148 (*Earth's Holocaust*) It would be invidious if not perilous to betray their awful secrets.

b. Of a comparison or distinction: Offensively discriminating.

1709 SACHEVERELL *Serm.* 5 *Nov.* 23 Those Inviduous Distinctions that..Distract..Us. **1868** ROGERS *Pol. Econ.* ix. (1876) 88 The laws against the combinations of labourers ..were seen to be unjust and invidious. **1875** JOWETT *Plato* (ed. 2) III. 105 They are all alike, and he will have no invidious distinctions between them.

3. Of a thing: Fitted to excite ill feeling or envy against the possessor.

a **1661** FULLER *Worthies* (1840) I. 556 Amounting to an invidious and almost incredible sum of one hundred thousand pounds. **1759** ROBERTSON *Hist. Scot.* II. Wks. 1813 I. 98 Without the invidious name of protector, he succeeded to all the power and influence of which Somerset was deprived. **1770** BURKE *Pres. Discont.* Wks. 1842 I. 128 His revenue..was ample without being invidious. **1849** MACAULAY *Hist. Eng.* vi. II. 71 Catharine saw all the peril of such a step, and declined the invidious honor.

4. That looks with an evil eye; envious, grudging, jealous. Now *rare.*

1668 WILKINS *Real Char.* II. ix. 232 Envy, Spite-full, invidious, grudge, repine, malign. **1711** PUCKLE *Club* 19 He [the Splenetic Detractor] had Ever an invidious eye upon the Clergy, and Men Eminent for virtue. **1734** tr. *Rollin's Anc. Hist.* (1827) II. 359 Some malignant invidious god, who looks upon men with a jealous eye. **1829** LANDOR *Imag. Conv.* Wks. 1846 I. 469/2 Thou, Plato, who hast cause to be invidious of not many, art of nearly all.

†**5.** Viewed with ill will or dislike; odious *to* a person. *Obs. rare.*

1710 STEELE *Tatler* No. 233 ¶2 Joseph, a beloved Child of Israel, became invidious to his elder Brethren. **1715–20** POPE *Iliad* I. 102, I must speak what wisdom would conceal, And truths, invidious to the great, reveal.

invidiously (ɪnˈvɪdɪəslɪ), *adv.* [f. prec. + -LY².] In an invidious manner (in various senses of the adj.).

1665 GLANVILL *Def. Vain Dogm.* 84 That [he] dealt so invidiously with the philosophers. **1779–81** JOHNSON *L.P.*, *Blackmore* Wks. III. 186 Blackmore..was in time neglected as a physician; his practice, which was once invidiously great, forsook him. **1789** P. SMYTH tr. *Aldrich's Archit.* (1818) 19 Vitruvius, of whom he appears to have been a little invidiously emulous. **1841** TRENCH *Parables, Prodigal Son* (1860) 415 Then he invidiously compares the father's conduct to his brother.

invidiousness (ɪnˈvɪdɪəsnɪs). [f. as prec. + -NESS.] The quality of being invidious; unpopularity, odium; offensiveness of discrimination.

1690 SOUTH *Serm.* (1737) II. vii. 243 Pythagoras was the first who abated of the invidiousness of the name, and from σοφὸς, brought it down to φιλόσοφος. **1775** JOHNSON *Journ. West. Isl.*, *Ulinish*, The offence has not the invidiousness of singularity. **1881** W. H. SMITH in *Daily Tel.* 19 Mar., If there had been a larger list to select from there would not have been that painful feeling of invidiousness.

inviduous, erron. form of INVIDIOUS *a.*

invie, var. of INVY, envy.

invi(e)orn, obs. form of ENVIRON *v.*

†**invier**, obs. Sc. var. ENVIER, one who envies.

1596 DALRYMPLE tr. *Leslie's Hist. Scot.* v. 299 Sum invieris of his vertue and honour. *Ibid.* VIII. 69 Noble men ..ar be invieris persewit.

in'vier, *v.*, var. of ENVIRE *Obs.*, to environ.

1596 *Edward III* D j b, Vnnaturall besecge, woe me vnhappie, To haue escapt the danger of my foes, And to be ten times worse inuier'd by friends.

invigilance (ɪnˈvɪdʒɪləns). *rare.* [f. L. type **invigilāntia*, f. *in-* (IN-³) + *vigilāntia* VIGILANCE: cf. obs. F. *invigilance* (Montaigne, 16th c.), It. *invigilanza* (Florio, 1611).] = next.

1828 in WEBSTER.

invigilancy (ɪnˈvɪdʒɪlənsɪ). *rare.* [f. as prec.: see -ANCY.] Absence of vigilance or watchfulness.

1611 COTGR., *Invigilance*, inuigilancie, sleepinesse..lacke of waking. **1626** W. SCLATER *Exp. 2 Thess.* (1629) 232 Blame thine owne inuigilancy. **1667** DUCHESS OF NEWCASTLE *Life Dk. of N.* (1886) I. 40 Which must necessarily be imputed to their invigilancy and carelessness. **1706** PHILLIPS, *Invigilancy*, want of Watchfulness, or Care.

†**in'vigilant**, *a.*¹ *Obs. rare*⁻⁰. [ad. L. *invigilānt-em*, pr. pple. of *invigilāre* to be on the watch: see INVIGILATE.] Watchful, alert, vigilant.

1570 LEVINS *Manip.* 26/7 Inuigilant, *inuigilans, solers.*

†**in'vigilant**, *a.*² *Obs. rare*⁻¹. [f. IN-³ + VIGILANT: cf. It. *invigilante* 'vnuigilant, vnwatchfull' (Florio).] Not vigilant, unwatchful.

1627–77 FELTHAM *Resolves* II. lxxi. 311 When we are invigilant, and careless of our selves.

invigilate (ɪnˈvɪdʒɪleɪt), *v.* [f. ppl. stem of L. *invigilāre* to watch over, f. *in-* (IN-²) + *vigilāre* to watch. Cf. It. *invigilare* 'watchfullie to studie or take paines' (Florio, 1598).]

1. *intr.* To keep watch; to watch carefully. Now *spec.* To watch over students at examination.

1553 T. WILSON *Rhet.* (1567) 83 b, I obtestate your clemencie, to inuigilate thus muche for me. **1651** tr. *Life Father Sarpi* (1676) 86 Princes ought to invigilate to the maintenance and conservation of Religion. **1668** H. MORE *Div. Dial.* II. x. (1713) 117 That invisible Power that invigilates over all things. **1721** BAILEY, *Invigilate*, to watch diligently. **1881** F. MADAN in *Letter*, I have myself invigilated within the last year.

†**2.** *trans.* To arouse; to make watchful (in quot. 1627 *absol.*). *Obs. rare.* [Cf. It. *invigilare*, to make vigilant (Florio, 1611).]

1627 FELTHAM *Resolves* II. [I.] xx. (1628) 65 If wee saw Diuinitie acted, the gesture and varietie would as much invigilate. But it is too high to bee personated by Humanitie. **16..** STAFFORD *Just Apol.* in *Fem. Glory* (1869) p. lxxxvii, Whatsoever invigilates the eye, leaves a stronger impression in the Soule, then that wᶜʰ onely pierceth the Eare.

Hence **in'vigilating** *vbl. sb.* and *ppl. a.*; also **in'vigilator**, one who watches over students at examination.

1882 *Oxf. Univ. Gaz.* XII. 239 The architect may see his way to fixing some of the Vicechancellor's and Proctors' seats at present in the Old Schools to serve as further invigilating stations in these three rooms. **1892** *Oxf. Mag.* 23 Mar. 273/1 In the Schools..Where's my table? alphabet all out of order here, apparently. Must ask invigilator. **1894** [A. D. GODLEY] *Aspects Mod. Oxf.* 72 A caricature of the 'invigilating' examiner.

invigilation (ɪnvɪdʒɪˈleɪʃən). [n. of action from INVIGILATE.] The action of keeping watch, *esp.* over students at examination.

1881 *Oxf. Univ. Gaz.* 17 May (*Calendar*), Voting on Statute respecting Invigilation in School of Natural Science. **1890** in *Ordin. Univ. Camb.* (1892) 18 One of the Pro-Proctors and two of the Examiners shall be present for the purpose of invigilation during every part of the Examinations. **1898** *Sat. Rev.* 24 Dec. 854 [Mary Stuart] transferred from the mild custody of Shrewsbury to the severe invigilation of Amyas Paulet.

invigorant (ɪnˈvɪɡərənt), *sb.* [f. as next: see -ANT¹: cf. obs. F. *invigorant* invigorating.] Something that invigorates; an invigorating drink or medicine, a tonic.

1822–34 *Good's Study Med.* (ed. 4) I. 333 The chalybeate springs..form the best mineral invigorant to which we can have recourse. **1895** *Columbus* (O.) *Disp.* 16 Nov. 11/4 A stimulant of nerves and brain and an invigorant of blood and muscles.

invigorate (ɪnˈvɪɡərət), *ppl. a. rare.* [f. L. type **invigorāt-us*, pa. pple. of **invigorāre*: see next.] Filled with vigour; invigorated.

1720 WELTON *Suffer. Son of God* II. xxiii. 625 In loving thee, I am Invigorate. **1795** SOUTHEY *Joan of Arc* VIII. 134 The soldiers from the earth Arise invigorate.

invigorate (ɪnˈvɪɡəreɪt), *v.* [f. L. type **invigorāre* (perh. in mod.L.) = F. *envigorer* (15–16th c.): see -ATE³ 7.]

1. *trans.* To impart vigour to; to render vigorous; to fill with life and energy; to strengthen, animate.

1646 SIR T. BROWNE *Pseud. Ep.* II. ii. 59 This polarity from refrigeration upon extremity and in defect of a Load-stone might serve to invigorate and touch a needle any where. **1670** G. H. *Hist. Cardinals* III. I. 242 To the end that this Decree might be invigorated, and in force. *a* **1691** SIR D. NORTH in North *Lives* (1826) II. 338 The spring is invigorated by clockwork underneath. **1788** GIBBON *Decl. & F.* lvi. (1869) III. 358 Their minds and bodies were invigorated by exercise. **1798** WASHINGTON *Lett.* Writ. 1893 XIV. 38 To countenance and invigorate opposition. **1884** W. S. LILLY in *Contemp. Rev.* Feb. 262 The Church poured into the nations crushed and degraded by imperialism, a new virility, freeing and invigorating the human faculties.

absol. **1847** A. BENNIE *Disc.* xi. 193 There is bread to invigorate and wine to revive.

2. *intr.* To become vigorous. *rare.*

1759 SARAH FIELDING *C'tess Dellwyn* I. 147 The Body, by being..properly exercised, grows and invigorates.

Hence **in'vigorated** *ppl. a.*

1646 SIR T. BROWNE *Pseud. Ep.* II. iii. 76 Needles..doe not attract, but avoyd each other..when their invigorated extreams approach unto one another. **1854** H. H. WILSON tr. *Rig-veda* II. 53 Every day..receive invigorated energy!

in'vigorating, *ppl. a.* [f. prec. vb. + -ING².] That invigorates; that imparts vigour or energy.

1694 F. BRAGGE *Disc. Parables* II. 38 The invigorating vertue of His precious Blood. **1705** STANHOPE *Paraphr.* II. 311 That enlivening and invigorating Principle. **1845** STOCQUELER *Handbk. Brit. India* (1854) 260 Their climate.. being quite as salubrious and invigorating.

Hence **in'vigoratingly** *adv.*, so as to invigorate.

1874 *Daily News* 13 Feb. 5/3 After its first plunge into a period of invigoratingly cold weather.

invigoration (ɪnvɪɡəˈreɪʃən). [n. of action from INVIGORATE *v.*] The action of invigorating or fact of being invigorated.

1662 GLANVILL *Lux Orient.* xiv. 150 That the inferiour life should have its turn of invigouration. **1678** NORRIS *Coll. Misc.* (1699) 235 In the very Height of Activity and Invigoration. **1857** H. H. WILSON tr. *Rig-veda* III. 19, I offer to thee..an oblation..for thy speed and invigoration.

invigorative (ɪnˈvɪɡərətɪv), *a.* [f. as INVIGORATE *v.* + -IVE.] That tends to invigorate; invigorating. Hence **in'vigoratively** *adv.*

1858 BUSHNELL *Serm. New Life* 374 God will co-work invigoratively, correctively and directively in all the good struggles of believing souls. **1860** I. TAYLOR *Ultimate Civiliz.* 25 This reciprocity, this invigorative interaction, is felt, and is recognized on all hands.

invigorator (ɪnˈvɪɡəreɪtə(r)). [agent-n. from INVIGORATE *v.*] One who or that which invigorates.

c **1842** LANCE *Cottage Farmer* 16 In China, so careful are they of all sorts of invigorators to vegetation. **1895** *Papers Ohio Ch. Hist. Soc.* V. 8 It was not considered possible to raise a house without this invigorator [whisky].

invigour (ɪnˈvɪɡə(r)), *v.* Also 7 en-. [In form *envigour*, a. OF. *envigorer*, *-ourer* (15–16th c. in Godef.), f. *en-* (IN-²) + *vigueur* vigour; subseq. conformed to a L. type **invigōrāre*.] *trans.* To inspire with vigour; to invigorate.

1611 FLORIO, *Vigoráre*,..to enuigor or giue vigor..vnto. **1613** M. RIDLEY *Magn. Bodies* 30 To comfort, and invigor all those goodly creatures. **1649** G. DANIEL *Trinarch.*, *Hen. IV*, cxciii, One Active Veine, t' envigour all yᵉ blood. **1791** COWPER *Iliad* x. 573 Then blue-eyed Pallas with fresh force Invigour'd Diomede. **1899** T. S. MOORE *Vinedresser* 7 Press on, and shoulder up thy lagging clouds! Invigour me!

†**in'vile**, *v. Obs. rare*⁻¹. [f. IN-² + VILE *a.*: cf. It. *invilire* 'to vilifie, to embase' (Florio, 1598).] *trans.* To render vile; to debase.

1599 DANIEL *Musoph.* cix, It did so much invile the estimate Of th' open'd and invulgar'd mysteries.

†**in'village**, *v. Obs. rare*⁻¹. [f. IN-² + VILLAGE.] *trans.* To make or reduce into a village.

1613–16 W. BROWNE *Brit. Past.* I. ii, There..Lies buried in his dust some ancient Towne; Who now invillaged, there's onely seene In his vaste ruines what his state had beene.

†**in'vilup**, *v. Obs. rare.* [ad. It. *inviluppare* 'to turne, enwrap, entangle', etc. (Florio, 1598): see ENVELOP.] *trans.* To wind, twine, coil.

1592 R. D. *Hypnerotomachia* 77 Their tresses..turned about their heads in an excellent manner, inuiluped [*printed* inuiluxed], and bound uppe together.

invinate (ɪnˈvaɪnət, ˈɪnvɪneɪt), *ppl. a.* [ad. med.L. *invīnāt-us*, pa. pple. of *invīnāre*: see next.] Embodied or included in wine.

1550 CRANMER *Defence* 33 b, The greate absurditie, whiche they speake vppon, that is to saye, that Christe shoulde be Impanate and Inuinate. **1855** PUSEY *Doctr. Real Presence* Note A. 3 Guitmundus..says..That Christ should be invinate,..no ground requireth, nor did Prophets foretel, nor Christ shew.

†**invinate**, *v. Obs. rare*⁻¹. [f. ppl. stem of L. *invīnāre*, f. *in-* (IN-²) + *vīnum* wine.] *trans.* To embody or enclose in wine: see next.

1579 FULKE *Heskins' Parl.* 257 He [Christ] is neither impanated, nor inuinated, nor inaccidentated, that is not ioyned to any of them in a personall union.

invination (ɪnvɪˈneɪʃən). [n. of action from med.L. *invīnāre*: see prec.] In Eucharistic theory: A local presence or inclusion of the blood of Christ in the wine after consecration; one of the modifications of the doctrine of the real presence.

1742 tr. *Bossuet's Variat. Prot. Ch.* (1829) I. 50 Osiander was left to defend alone his impanation and invination. **1855** PUSEY *Doctr. Real Presence* Note A. 5 What those to whom he imputes 'impanation' and 'invination' really held, was that the Body and Blood of Christ was present 'under the form of bread and wine', these 'remaining in their natural substances'.

†**in'vinced**, *ppl. a. Obs.* [f. IN-³ + L. *vinc-ĕre* to conquer + -ED¹, after L. *invictus*; cf. *convinced* = L. *convictus*, etc.] Unconquered.

1609 HEYWOOD *Brit. Troy* XIII. ciii, Where's the invinced Troylus to bestow His puissant stroakes before Prince Hector bleed? **1635** —— *Hierarch.* I. 18 For an inuinc'd shield Holinesse he hath.

invincibility (ɪnvɪnsɪˈbɪlɪtɪ). [f. next + -ITY.] The quality or condition of being invincible; incapability of being conquered or overcome; unconquerableness.

a **1677** BARROW *Wks.* (1687) I. Serm. vi. 76 Thus Omnipotence may be mastered, and a happy victory may be gained over Invincibility it self. **1728** MORGAN *Algiers* I. iii. 70 These Kabeyls value themselves excessively upon their

Antiquity, Purity of Blood, and Invincibility. **1812** L. Hunt in *Examiner* 7 Dec. 770/2 Your Lordship's invincibility to temptation. **1872** Liddon *Elem. Relig.* ii. 71 In a good man, belief in God results from belief in the invincibility of good.

invincible (ɪnˈvɪnsɪb(ə)l), *a.* (*sb.*) Also 6 invinceable, -sible, *Sc.* -sable, inwynciabill, 7 invintiable. [a. F. *invincible*, ad. L. *invincibilis*, f. *in-* (IN-³) + *vincibilis* conquerable, f. *vincĕre* to conquer.]

1. That cannot be vanquished, overcome, or subdued; unconquerable. **a.** Of combatants, fortresses, etc. ***Invincible Armada***: see ARMADA 2.

1412-20 Lydg. *Chron. Troy* (1555) iii. xxii. (MS. Digby 232) lf. 80 b/2 Of knyhthod ground of strengþe hardynesse þe verray stook, and þerto invyncyble. **1490** Caxton *Eneydos* viii. 36 As longe as cartage sholde abyde inuyncyble. **1500-20** Dunbar *Poems* lxxxvi. 22 Our wicht invinsable Sampson sprang the fra. **1563** in Strype *Ann. Ref.* I. xxxiv. 344 Taking up armes against the invinceable God and Christ. **1578** T. N. tr. *Conq. W. India* 45 Thinking the Christians to be invinsible. **1617** Moryson *Itin.* ii. 8 The Spanish..invincible Navy, sent to invade England, in the yeere 1588, being dispersed, and proving nothing lesse then invincible. **1679** *Season. Adv. Protest.* 6 She found out a way to batter these invincible Bulwarks. **1734** tr. *Rollin's Anc. Hist.* (1827) VI. xv. xvi. 263 Who was invincible by the rest of the world. **1781** Cowper *Expost.* 569 When presumptuous Spain Baptized her fleet invincible in vain. **1832** Macaulay *Armada* 3 When that great fleet invincible against her bore in vain The richest spoils of Mexico, the stoutest hearts of Spain. **1838** Prescott *Ferd. & Is.* (1846) I. x. 420 They deemed themselves invincible by any force which the Moslems could bring against them. **1894** J. K. Laughton *Span. Armada* Introd. 29 The name 'Invincible', so commonly given to this fleet, was not official ..By all the contemporary chroniclers the fleet is spoken of as the Grand Fleet.

b. *transf.* and *fig.* (*a*) of persons in spiritual or mental warfare, argument, etc.; (*b*) of material or immaterial things, obstacles, habits, conditions, attributes, arguments, etc.: That cannot be overcome, unsurmountable, insuperable.

1482 *Monk of Evesham* (Arb.) 72 Thys vyse was to her inuyncyble by cause of her imperfeccyon. **1526** *Pilgr. Perf.* (W. de W. 1531) 241 The inuincible charite, the vnsuperable loue and goodnes of god. **1548** Hall *Chron., Hen. VII* 33 An invincible reason and an argument infallible. **1560** Daus tr. *Sleidane's Comm.* 2 Whether Luther be so invincible that he can not be confuted or vanquished. **1577** tr. *Bullinger's Decades* (1592) 460 The iudgement of Paule in this matter remaineth firme and inuincible. **1615** G. Sandys *Trav.* 146 Jewes..subject to all wrongs and contumelies, which they support with an invincible patience. **1719** De Foe *Crusoe* i. xvi, I had an invincible Impression upon my Thoughts, that my Deliverance was at Hand. **1811** Pinkerton *Petral.* II. 72 A distance surely not invincible for sledges or other conveyances. **1871** L. Stephen *Playgr. Europe* x. (1894) 244, I have suffered from an invincible love of short cuts.

c. ***invincible ignorance*** [Schol.L. *ignorantia invincibilis* (Thomas Aquinas *Summa Theol.* lxxvi. §2)]: an ignorance the means of overcoming or removing which are not possessed by the ignorant person himself.

1612 J. Taylor *Comm. Titus* iii. 3 How farre better were it with vs, to haue been heathen or infidels, and neuer haue heard of Iesus Christ, that our ignorance had beene simple and invincible. **1655** Fuller *Ch. Hist.* i. iii. §2 Dark Corners ..where Prophaneness lives quietly with invincible Ignorance. **1699** Burnet *39 Art.* viii. (1700) 107 God only knows..how far our Ignorance is affected or invincible. **1721** *St. German's Doctor & Stud.* 603 Ignorance of the Law (though it be invincible) doth not excuse. **1885** *Cath. Dict.* (ed. 3) 424/2 With regard to the guilt of sins ignorantly committed, invincible ignorance altogether excuses from sin.

†**2.** That cannot be 'beaten' or excelled; unsurpassable. *Obs.*

1509 Hawes *Past. Pleas.* xliii. (Percy Soc.) 211 His most hie actes so moche invyncible. **1617** Moryson *Itin.* i. 73 Titus Livy of Paduva..by whose penne truely invincible, the Acts of the invincible Roman people should be written. *Ibid.* iii. 86 Germans..practising night and day the faculty of drinking, become strong and invincible professors therein.

3. Of or pertaining to the Invincibles: see B. b.

1885 in *Cassell's Encycl. Dict.*

¶ *Catachr.*, or error for *invisible*.

1597 Shaks. *2 Hen. IV*, iii. ii. 337 He was so forlorne, that his Dimensions (to any thicke sight) were inuincible [*altered by Rowe to* invisible].

B. *sb.* One who is invincible.

1640 tr. *Verdere's Romant of Rom.* iii. 183 Desiring to appeare invincibles, they made no shew of discontent. **1815** Southey in *Q. Rev.* XIII. 236 The reputation of his armies was wounded, the invincibles had been put to shame.

b. A member of an Irish assassination society so called, developed from the Fenians about 1881-82.

1883 *Illustr. Lond. News* 24 Feb. 186/3 The Irish Invincibles—the 'Assassination Circle'—organised by one Walsh from the North of England, was formed to 'make history' by the 'removal of tyrants'. *Ibid.* 193/2 Carey..says that he was one of the 'Directory' of an association called 'the Irish Invincibles' organized in November 1881. **1887** *Dict. Nat. Biog.* IX. 72/2 The object of the Invincibles was 'to remove all tyrants from the country', and several attempts, but without success, were made to assassinate Earl Cowper and Mr. W. E. Forster.

invincibleness (ɪnˈvɪnsɪb(ə)lnɪs). [f. prec. + -NESS.] The quality of being invincible; invincibility.

a **1617** Bayne *Lect.* (1634) 123 The invinciblenesse of our evils. **1624** Gee *Foot out of Snare* 18 More regarding the weaknes of men, than the invinciblenesse of Truth. *a* **1660** Hammond *Wks.* I. 303 (R.), I hope the invincibleness of their ignorance would [etc.]. **1668** Wilkins *Real Char.* i. v. 18 The invincibleness of general Custom, against which (for the most part) men strive in vain.

in'vincibleship. *nonce-wd.* [See -SHIP.] Used as a mock title for one said to be invincible.

1721 Cibber *Lady's last Stake* 1, So I e'en made her Invincibleship a low Bow.

invincibly (ɪnˈvɪnsɪblɪ), *adv.* [f. INVINCIBLE *a.* + -LY².] In an invincible manner; unconquerably.

invincibly ignorant: see INVINCIBLE 1 c.

1542-5 Brinklow *Lament.* 17 b, He..hath writen invyncibly in this matter. **1642** Fuller *Holy & Prof. St.* ii. xvi. 111 Those that are invincibly dull and negligent. **1654** Bramhall *Just Vind.* vi. (1661) 157 We grant..salvation to such Protestants as are invincibly ignorant of their errours. **1705** C. Purshall *Mech. Macrocosm* 16 Which proves invincibly that there is a God. **1813** Shelley *Q. Mab* iii. 153 He who leads Invincibly a life of resolute good. **1885** *Cath. Dict.* (ed. 3) 425/1 Censures are not incurred by those who are invincibly ignorant of their existence.

in vino veritas: see IN *Lat. prep.*

inviolability (ɪnˌvaɪələˈbɪlɪtɪ). [f. next + -ITY: corresp. to F. *inviolabilité* (Cotgr. 1611), late L. *inviolābilitās*.] The quality or fact of being inviolable.

1793 Bp. Horsley *Serm. 30 Jan.* 21 Our Constitution..unites the most perfect security of the Subject's Liberty, with the most absolute inviolability of the sacred person of the Sovereign. **1819** J. Marshall *Const. Opin.* (1839) 153 The principle was the inviolability of contracts. **1828** D'Israeli *Chas. I*, II. v. 106 The main point in the 'Petition of Right' was the inviolability of the personal freedom of the subject.

inviolable (ɪnˈvaɪələb(ə)l), *a.* [ad. L. *inviolābilis* (f. *in-* (IN-³) + *violābilis*, f. *violāre* to do violence to, VIOLATE), or a. F. *inviolable* (14th c.).]

1. Not to be violated; not liable or allowed to suffer violence; to be kept sacredly free from profanation, infraction, or assault.

a. Of laws, treaties, institutions, customs, principles, sacred or cherished feelings, etc.

1532 More *Confut. Tindale* Wks. 527/2 The churche is..the pyller of trouth for the inuiolable suretie of doctrine. **1555** W. Watreman *Fardle Facions* ii. iii. 131 Not at all adventures, and without rule, but by an inuiolable lawe of God. **1682** Norris *Hierocles* 41 So will our piety towards God, and the measures of Justice be kept inviolable. **1783** Watson *Philip III* (1839) 225 Maintaining the most inviolable secrecy. **1791** Cowper *Iliad* ii. 926 Styx is the inviolable oath. **1841** James *Brigand* xxix, My word is said, and it shall be inviolable. **1849** Macaulay *Hist. Eng.* vi. II. 135 He ought to have determined that the existing settlement of landed property should be inviolable.

b. Of persons, places, and things material.

1578 T. N. tr. *Conq. W. India* 159 You are persons inviolable, and messengers of a prince. **1674** Owen *Holy Spirit* (1693) 80 Things precious are sealed up, that they may be kept safe and inviolable. **1725** Pope *Odyss.* xxii. 372 Jove's inviolable altar. **1849** Grote *Greece* ii. lxxiii. (1862) VI. 396 The Spartan king was not legally inviolable. He might be, and occasionally was, arrested, tried, and punished for misbehaviour in the discharge of his functions. **1863** Mrs. Oliphant *Salem Ch.* I. xiii. 211 Safe..in a humble inviolable English home.

†**2.** That cannot be violated; that does not yield to force or violence; incapable of being broken, forced, or injured. *Obs.*

1530 Palsgr. 316/2 Invyolable nat able to be broken, *inuiolable*. **1561** T. Norton *Calvin's Inst.* i. 20 Those things that the Prophet hath ioined with an inuiolable knot. **1607** E. Grimstone tr. *Goulart's Mem. Hist.* 278 He never sturd one iot, but remained firme and inviolable, as if he had beene planted there. **1614** Lodge *Seneca* 95 Neither therefore can the fire burne lesse, if it light upon a matter inviolable by fire. **1667** Milton *P.L.* vi. 398 Th' inviolable Saints In Cubic Phalanx firm advanc't entire. **1719** Waterland *Vind. Christ's Div.* xxiii. (1720) 364 Tertullian intimates the strict and inviolable Harmony of the three Persons.

in'violableness. Now *rare.* [f. prec. + -NESS.] The quality of being inviolable; inviolability.

1611 Cotgr., *Inuiolableté*, inuiolablenesse. **1648** J. Goodwin *Right & Might* 31 That which gives a kinde of sacred inviolablenesse unto the rights and priviledges of Parliament. **1738** Warburton *Div. Legat.* I. 167 The Inviolableness of that Secrecy.

inviolably (ɪnˈvaɪələblɪ), *adv.* [f. as prec. + -LY².] In an inviolable manner; in a way reverently free from violation, profanation, or infringement; sacredly.

1535 *Act 27 Hen. VIII*, c. 26 §21 All suche Lawes..shalbe forever inviolably observed. **1617** Moryson *Itin.* ii. 48 He kept his word in publike affaires inviolably. **1675** Penn *Eng. Pres. Interest* 11 What I possess is inviolably mine own. **1788** Priestley *Lect. Hist.* v. liii. 414 The liberty of the whole people is inviolably established. **1874** Motley *Barneveld* I. iv. 201 Keep the secret inviolably.

inviolacy (ɪnˈvaɪələsɪ). [f. next: see -ACY.] The condition of being inviolate; inviolateness.

1846 Worcester cites Bulwer. **1852** *Fraser's Mag.* XLVI. 224 The inviolacy of that supreme consolation of our creed. **1861** G. Meredith *Evan Harrington* I. viii. 133 The old gentleman, whose inviolacy was thus rudely assailed, sat staring at the intruder. **1867** *Fortn. Rev.* July 118 The Treaty has done nothing to preserve the inviolacy of the Luxembourg territory.

inviolate (ɪnˈvaɪələt), *a.* [ad. L. *inviolāt-us* unhurt, f. *in-* (IN-³) + *violātus*, pa. pple. of *violāre* to VIOLATE. Cf. obs. F. *inviolé* (Godef. *Compl.*).] Not violated; free from violation; unhurt, uninjured, unbroken; unprofaned, unmarred; intact.

a. Of laws, compacts, principles, institutions, sacred or moral qualities.

1412-20 Lydg. *Chron. Troy* i. vi. (1555) D v b/2 With herte unfayned and fayth inuyolate. **1494** Fabyan *Chron.* vii. 540 That the amyte atwene yᵉ .ii. realmys..may be kepte inuyolet. *c* **1586** C'tess Pembroke *Ps.* lxxviii. v, They did not hold inviolate The league of God. **1646** P. Bulkeley *Gospel Covt.* v. 370 Though..man failed in his duty, yet the covenant on God's part remaines inviolate. **1734** Bolingbroke *Let. to Swift* 27 June, To see such a thing as sincere cordial friendship subsist inviolate. **1840** Mill *Diss. & Disc.* (1875) I. 431 The existing institutions..were to be preserved inviolate.

b. Of persons, places, sacred things, etc.

a **1420** Hoccleve *De Reg. Princ.* 3696 And in hir clene virginal estat Restored he þis mayde inuiolat. *c* **1450** *Mirour Saluacioun* 4882 To whame inviolat childid thi maydenes mylk was fedyng. **1615** Crooke *Body of Man* 376 The heat of the right must..be in time extinguished, the heat of the left remaining inviolate. **1744** Lady M. W. Montagu *Let. to Wortley Montagu* 6 May, Fearing that my letter will not come inviolate to your hands. **1848** Mrs. Jameson *Sacr. & Leg. Art* (1850) 347 Clement VIII ordered that the relics should remain untouched, inviolate.

†**c.** Of a person: Of unbroken faith. *Obs.*

1593 Drayton *Idea* 713 Though Heaven and Earth, prove both to me untrue, Yet still I am inviolate to You.

†**inviolate,** *v. Obs. rare.* [f. IN-² + VIOLATE.] *trans.* To violate.

1569 Sir J. Hawkins in *Hawkins' Voyages* (Hakluyt Soc.) 76 That none of either part should..inuiolate the peace vpon paine of death. **1603** Drayton *Bar. Wars* ii. xvi, Canst thou (vnkinde!) inuiolate that band? **1681** *Lond. Gaz.* No. 1638/6 Laws, Liberties, Properties..which had been..insolently inviolated, desperately invaded.

inviolated (ɪnˈvaɪəleɪtɪd), *a.* [f. IN-³ + VIOLATED.] Unviolated, inviolate.

1548 Hall *Chron., Hen. IV* 28 To kepe your promise sincerly inviolated and faithfully observed. **1610** Bp. Carleton *Jurisd.* 130 Bishops, who before..held their Allegeance inuiolated to their Soueraignes. **1749** Johnson *Irene* v. ii, When purity..Play'd fearless in th' inviolated shades. **1853** Trench *Proverbs* 87 The safety of this our beloved land, and..the inviolated honour of its shores.

inviolately (ɪnˈvaɪələtlɪ), *adv.* [f. INVIOLATE *a.* + -LY².] In an inviolate manner.

1494 Fabyan *Chron.* vii. 342 That theyr lybertyes shulde be hoolye and inuyolatlye preseruyd. **1548** Hall *Chron., Hen. VIII* 169 b, Whiche Articles he promised..inviolatly to observe and kepe. **1603** Knolles *Hist. Turks* (1621) 1183 That religion..should inviolately be kept. *a* **1716** South *Serm.* X. vi. (R.), All other things..remaining inviolately the same under both covenants. **1807** Coleridge in Cottle *Early Recoll.* (1837) II. 98 All the disciples of Christ..are inviolately united to him.

in'violateness. [f. as prec. + -NESS.] The quality of being inviolate.

1860 *Guardian* No. 772. 829/1 She proclaims the inviolateness of Rome. **1871** *Daily News* 11 Mar., To buy his withdrawal, and secure the inviolateness of the land.

†**'invious,** *a. Obs.* [f. L. *invi-us* (f. *in-*, IN-³ + *via* way) + -OUS.] Having no roads or ways; pathless, trackless.

1622 Peacham *Compl. Gent.* xvii. 180 Sertorius..could leap broken and unpasseable Rockes and like invious places. **1663** Butler *Hud.* i. iii. 386 If nothing can oppugn Love, And Virtue invious ways can prove. **1681** H. More *Exp. Dan.* i. 8 Invious and inaccessible Rocks.

Hence †**'inviousness.**

1710 R. Ward *Life H. More* 15 Ἀπορία, Inviousness and Emptiness.

†**'invious, -e, -vyous, -e,** obs. north. and Sc. var. of ENVIOUS. So †**'inviously** *adv.*

c **1440** *Promp. Parv.* 263/2 Invyouse, *invidus*. **1483** *Cath. Angl.* 197/1 Invyous, *emulus*. **1568** *Dunbar's Poems* xxiii. *heading*, Be mirry and glaid..For that suffisis to anger the invyous. **1570** Levins *Manip.* 227/17 Inuiouse, *inuidiosus*. **1596** Dalrymple tr. *Leslie's Hist. Scot.* xi. 462 The hæretikis, quha before Jnuiouslie..teached had [etc.].

†**in'viper,** *v. Obs. rare.* Also 6 en-. [ad. It. *inviperare*, f. *in-* (IN-²) + *vipera* VIPER.] *trans.* To make like a viper, to fill with a viper's nature.

1598 Florio, *Viperáre*, to enuenim, to enuiper. **1650** Howell *Giraffi's Rev. Naples* i. 27 Being inviper'd as it were with blood in their eyes.

So †**in'viperate** *v. Obs. rare*⁻¹. [-ATE³.]

1672-3 Marvell *Reh. Transp.* ii. Wks. 1776 II. 434 You ..infuriate and inviperate the nation against peaceable Dissenters.

in'virile, *a.* [IN-³.] Unmanly, effeminate.

1869 Lowell *Cathedral* 292 Ovid in Pontus, puling for his Rome Of men invirile and disnatured dames.

† **invi'rility.** *Obs.* [IN-^{3}.] Effeminacy.

1628 PRYNNE *Love-lockes* 48 It sauours of Effeminacie, and womanish inuirilitie. **1633** —— *1st Pt. Histrio-m.* v. iii. 171 The invirility of Nero, Heliogabalus, or Sardanapalus.

inviron(e, -oun, obs. forms of ENVIRON.

in'virtuate, *v. rare.* Also 7 **invertuate**. [f. as next + -ATE^{3}.] *trans.* **a.** To make virtuous. **b.** To endow with virtue or power.

1641 LD. DIGBY *Sp. Trienn. Parl.* in Rushw. *Hist. Coll.* III. (1692) I. 149 Where is the Legislative Authority?.. In the King circled in, and invertuated by his Parliament. **1650** J. JONES *Judges Judged* 112 Law it self..invirtuateth, dignifieth, and authorizeth her true servants to execute her precepts. **1821** COLERIDGE in *Blackw. Mag.* X. 257 They stir and invirtuate the sphere next below them.

† **in'virtue,** *v. Obs. rare*$^{-1}$. [IN-^{2}: cf. OF. *envertuer, -virtuer,* It. *invirtuare* (Florio).] Var. of ENVIRTUE, to endow with virtue. Hence † **in'virtued** *ppl. a.*

1609 HEYWOOD *Brit. Troy* IV. ix, The inuertued hearbes haue gainst such poison power.

in'viscant, *a. Med.* [ad. pr. pple. of L. *inviscāre*: see next.] 'Thickening; producing or promoting inviscation' (*Syd. Soc. Lex.* 1887).

inviscate (ɪn'vɪskeɪt), *v.* [f. L. *inviscāt-*, ppl. stem of *inviscāre* to smear with, or snare in, birdlime, f. *in-* (IN-^{2}) + *viscum* birdlime: see VISCID. The pa. pple. *inviscat*, first used, was ad. L. *inviscāt-us*.]

1. *trans.* To render viscid or sticky; to mix or cover with a sticky substance.

c **1400** *Lanfranc's Cirurg.* 136 (Add. MS.) Ne þilke blod ys noȝt inviscat in þe substaunce of dure matris as þe matere ys in apostemys. **1657** TOMLINSON *Renou's Disp.* 659 Myreol.. by its aromatical lentour, inviscates the fingers. **1684** tr. *Bonet's Merc. Compit.* VI. 220 When the matter of the Cough was inviscated and hardned. **1788** BLAGDEN in *Phil. Trans.* LXXVIII. 289 The deposited salt, in very minute crystals, ..inviscated and kept together with a little ice. **1822–34** *Good's Study Med.* III. 490 Caustic alkalies inviscated in oil or lard to render them less acid and corrosive.

2. To catch in some sticky substance. *rare.*

1646 SIR T. BROWNE *Pseud. Ep.* III. xxi. 158 It hath in the tongue a spongy and mucous extremity, whereby upon a sudden emission, it inviscates and tangleth those insects. **1776–96** WITHERING *Brit. Plants* (ed. 3) II. 433 A..clammy substance like tar, in which..insects are inviscated.

Hence **in'viscating** *ppl. a.*

1822–34 *Good's Study Med.* (ed. 4) I. 450 The difficulty of conceiving how a few drachms of bland oil or a few ounces of gum arabic, can be intermixed with many pounds of serosity, and still retain their sensible quality of inviscating sedatives. *Ibid.* II. 487 It would be our duty to..employ inviscating demulcents with oils and mucilages.

inviscation (ɪnvɪ'skeɪʃən). [n. of action f. prec.] The action of inviscating or making viscid.

1633 HART *Diet of Diseased* II. iii. 156 An agglutination, or inviscation of the haire of the head and beard. **1855** MAYNE *Expos. Lex., Inviscatio,* a thickening and making viscid or sticky: inviscation. **1887** *Syd. Soc. Lex., Inviscation,*.. the mixing up of the food with the saliva and mucous secretion of the mouth.

† **in'viscerate,** *ppl. a. Obs. rare*$^{-1}$. [ad. pa. pple. of L. *inviscerāre*: see next.] Deeply fixed in the 'bowels' or heart.

1648 W. MOUNTAGUE *Devout Ess.* I. xiv. §3. 190 When man sigheth..as burthened with inviscerate interests, longing to put on this pure spirituall vesture of Filiall love.

† **in'viscerate,** *v. Obs. rare.* [f. ppl. stem of late L. *inviscerāre*, f. *in-* (IN-^{2}) + *viscera* entrails.] *trans.* To put into the bowels. Also *fig.* To fix deeply in the heart or mind.

1626 AILESBURY *Passion Serm.* 11 The very divels inviscerated in men, at the sound of his imperiall word, yeeld up possession. **1648** W. MOUNTAGUE *Devout Ess.* I. xv. §1. 267 Our Savior seemeth to have affected so much, the inviscerating this disposition in our hearts [etc.].

† **invisce'ration.** *Obs. rare.* [n. of action f. prec.] The action of putting into the bowels; the fact of being deeply rooted in the inward parts.

1628 DONNE *Serm.* vi. 56 All these Inviscerations of Israel into his owne bosome. *a* **1631** *Ibid.* cii. (ed. Alford) IV. 380 Man is so enfeebled by the Inherence and Invisceration of original Sin as that thereby he is exposed to every emergent temptation to any actual Sin.

in'viscid, *a.* [IN-^{3}.] **1.** Not viscid or sticky.

In mod. Dicts.

2. Not possessing viscosity.

1913 *Phil. Mag.* XXVI. 1001 (*heading*) On the stability of the laminar motion of an inviscid fluid. **1930** *Flight* 3 Jan. 29/1 The practically useful theory of Prandtl comes from considering air as frictionless or inviscid. **1938** L. M. MILNE-THOMSON *Theoret. Hydrodynamics* 1 An inviscid fluid is a continuous substance which will yield instantly to any shearing stress however small. **1971** *Nature* 6 Aug. 427/1 The problem of the plane transonic flow of an inviscid gas.

† **invised,** *a. Obs. rare*$^{-1}$. [? f. L. *invīs-us* unseen + -ED^{1}.] ? Unseen, invisible.

1597 SHAKS. *Lover's Compl.* 212 The Diamond? why twas beautifull and hard, Whereto his inuis'd properties did tend.

invisibility (ɪnvɪzɪ'bɪlɪtɪ). [ad. late L. *invīsibilitās* (Tertull.): see next and -ITY. Cf. F. *invisibleté* (Palsgr., 1530), *invisibilité* (17th c. in Hatz.-Darm.).] The quality or condition of being invisible; incapacity of being seen.

1561 T. NORTON *Calvin's Inst.* IV. xvii. (1634) 689 *marg.*, Though the invisibilitie of the body of Christ were granted. **1577** DEE *Relat. Spir.* I. (1659) 22 She seemeth..to enter into a Cloud of invisibility, and so disappear. **1794** SULLIVAN *View Nat.* II. 137 Invisible by his essence, his invisibility was the primeval night which preceded time and light. **1876** MOZLEY *Univ. Serm.* iv, The invisibility of men's motive.

b. with *pl.*: An invisible entity.

a **1668** SIR W. WALLER *Div. Medit.* (1882) 28 Those invisibilities which mortal eye hath not seen. **1895** *Expositor* Feb. 148 The invisibilities which underlie the visibilities of the universe.

invisible (ɪn'vɪzɪb(ə)l), *a.* (*sb.*) [a. F. *invisible* (13th c. in Littré), ad. L. *invīsibilis*, f. *in-* (IN-^{3}) + *vīsibilis* VISIBLE.]

A. *adj.* **1. a.** That cannot be seen; that by its nature is not an object of sight.

1340 HAMPOLE *Pr. Consc.* 8231 How God invysible es, And unchaungeable, and endles. *c* **1415** LYDG. *Temple Glas* 128 Hou þat Mars was take Of Vulcanus,.. And wiþ þe Cheynes invisible bound. **1509** HAWES *Past. Pleas.* XXIII. (Percy Soc.) 106 Though that aungell[s] be invysyble, Inpalpable, and also celestiall. **1594** T. B. *La Primaud. Fr. Acad.* II. 137 There is yet in him another nature whose substance is inuisible, ouer and aboue this bodily nature which we see. **1638** F. JUNIUS *Paint. of Ancients* 19 Phidias ..had a singular abilitie to imagine things invisible. **1727** DE FOE *Syst. Magic* I. ii. (1840) 49 The Devil, or some of his invisible agents, which we call evil spirits. **1880** GEIKIE *Phys. Geog.* ii. 75 They collect in a visible form the ever-present invisible vapour of the air.

b. ***Invisible Church***: see CHURCH 4 c. ***invisible ink*** (called also *sympathetic ink*): see quot. 1823.

1682 BOYLE *Human Blood* App. IV. ix, This liquor may.. be employed as an invisible ink. **1704** J. HARRIS *Lex. Techn.* s.v. *Sympathetical*, The Writing..which was written with the Invisible Ink. **1823** J. BADCOCK *Dom. Amusem.* 35 An invisible ink, which requires heat, vapour, or some other liquid to be applied to it, to render visible what is so written. **1855** MACAULAY *Hist. Eng.* xv. III. 591 Their buttons contained letters written in invisible ink.

c. Applied to associations, etc. not having a visible, open organization, esp. as ***invisible college***.

1646–7 BOYLE *Let. to Tallents* 20 Feb., The corner-stones of the invisible, or (as they term themselves) the philosophical college, do now and then honour me with their company. **1647** —— *Let. to Hartlib* 8 May, You interest yourself so much in the Invisible College. **1743** BIRCH *Life Boyle* B.'s Wks. 1772 I. p. xlii, The Invisible College.. probably refer[s] to that assembly of learned and curious gentlemen, who..at length gave birth to the Royal Society. **1884** *Century Mag.* July 398/1 The secret history of the Invisible Empire, as the [Ku Klux] Klan was also called. **1962** D. J. DE S. PRICE *Science since Babylon* (new ed.) v. 99 Collaborative work now exceeds the single-author paper, and the device of prepublication duplicated sheets circulated to the new Invisible Colleges has begun to trespass upon the traditional functions of the printed paper in a published journal. *Ibid.*, The new Invisible Colleges, rapidly growing up in all the most hard-pressed sections of the scholarly research front, might well be the subject of an interesting sociological study. **1967** GARVEY & GRIFFITH in De Reuck & Knight *Communication in Sci.* 25 Once an author submits his manuscript the dissemination of this piece of work is small and usually only to members of his invisible college. **1971** HALSEY & TROW *Brit. Academics* xiii. 362 Here is evidence of the 'invisible college' having its greatest importance.

d. ***invisible exports, imports***: those items which do not appear in returns of exports and imports for which payment has to be accepted from or made to a foreign country, such as shipping services, insurance, profits on foreign investment, money spent by visitors from a country with a different currency, etc. Also ***invisible earnings, trader, transaction***, etc.

1911 C. G. ROBERTSON *Eng. under Hanoverians* II. iv. 344 Prior to the Industrial Revolution the seaborne and carrying trades, with their invisible exports, are an expanding source of wealth, but are not indispensable. **1919** J. A. TODD *Mech. Exchange* (ed. 2) xiv. 174 An invisible export is something which enables a country to import goods without paying for them directly by the export of other goods, and conversely, an invisible import is something which makes it necessary for a country to export goods without receiving payment directly in other goods. **1923** *Westm. Gaz.* 24 Feb., Depressed shipping means less insurance, less banking, and a smaller earning in freights—all the things we mean when we speak of our invisible exports. **1935** *Economist* 12 Oct. 712/2 Among 'invisible' traders with Italy, the shipping lines with Mediterranean routes would suffer some inconvenience. **1957** *Encycl. Brit.* VIII. 991/2 Invisible exports are of vital importance to countries whose limited resources..make them dependent on large imports. Italy's high percentage is due to foreign tourists' expenditure and to a steady flow of remittances from Italians living abroad. **1958** *Economist* 18 Oct. 256/1 The..government deficit on invisible account. **1963** *Ann. Reg. 1962* 479 Net earnings on invisible transactions improved somewhat. **1969** *Times* 27 Nov. 6/6 The rapid growth of invisible earnings. **1971** *Daily Tel.* 24 Apr. 2 The works of songwriters and composers are now one of Britain's major 'invisible' exports.

e. ***invisible man***: used esp. with direct or implied allusion to H. G. Wells's novel *The Invisible Man* (1897).

1911 CHESTERTON *Innocence of Father Brown* v. 120 (*title*) The invisible man. **1940** 'G. ORWELL' in *Horizon* Mar. 191 The one theme that is really new is the scientific one. Death-rays, Martians, invisible men, robots. **1959** N. POLSKY in N. Mailer *Advts. for Myself* (1961) 313 Even in the world of the hipster the Negro remains essentially what Ralph Ellison called him—an invisible man. **1963** D. B. HUGHES *Expendable Man* (1964) v. 139 He's safe only so long as he's the invisible man. I'm going to have to..find out who he is. **1966** J. WAINWRIGHT *Evil Intent* 123 He isn't The Invisible Man. Somebody must have seen him. **1973** E. BERCKMAN *Victorian Album* 144 Dancey'll work out how to be the invisible man, it's just up his street.

f. ***invisible mending***: repair of material, clothing, etc., so carefully executed that little or no sign of the repair can be seen. So ***invisible mender***, one who undertakes such repairs; ***invisibly-mend*** v. trans.

1921 *Dict. Occup. Terms* (1927) §419 *Invisible mender*,.. repairs tears, by hand, using stoating, finedrawing, or rentering process, according to kind of tear and material. **1931** W. HOLTBY *Poor Caroline* i. 33 She complained of the price of invisible mending. **1937** E. PRICE *Enter—Jane* i. 1 Until you have paid the invisible-mending bill..you shan't have your threepence a week pocket-money! **1959** G. FREEMAN *Jack would be Gent.* i. 16 Sitting in the shop window invisibly-mending nylons with a little hook. **1969** D. FRANCIS *Enquiry* xv. 201 My coat would cost a fortune at the invisible menders. **1970** —— *Rat Race* xv. 199 My coat was soaked... Have to get it cleaned, and the slit invisibly mended.

2. Not in sight; not to be seen at a particular place or time, or by a particular person.

1555 EDEN *Decades* 239 The starre of the pole Artike, is there inuisible. **1655** SIR E. NICHOLAS in *N. Papers* (Camden) II. 266 The letter is invisible, and hee keepes it as close as hee doth [etc.]. **1781** GIBBON *Decl. & F.* xvii. II. 52 The degenerate grandsons of Theodosius, who were invisible to their subjects. **1840** LADY C. BURY *Hist. of Flirt* vii, Langham called every day..but I was invisible.

3. a. Too small to be discerned; imperceptible.

1665 HOOKE *Microgr.* 97 Insinuating themselves into the invisible pores of the stone. **1794** BLAKE *Songs Exper., Sick Rose* 2 O rose,..The invisible worm..Has found out thy bed. **1834** E. E. PERKINS *Lady's Shopping Manual* 103 Invisible Wire for Lace and Nett Caps. **1873** MISS BROUGHTON *Nancy* I. i. 6 The thinnest legs,..the invisiblest nose, and over visiblest ears [etc.]. **1881** *Queen* 12 Mar. (Advt.), Invisible fringe nets made of hair. **1895** *Montgomery Ward Catal.* 87/1 Invisible Hairpins, about 50 in a box. **1897** *Sears, Roebuck Catal.* 322/2 Invisible Hair Pins made of Good Wire. **1901** Invisible stitch [see STOAT *v.*]. **1964** *McCall's Sewing* ii. 30/1 *Invisible stitch*, used for hems and attaching facings and interfacings in tailoring. **1966** J. S. COX *Illustr. Dict. Hairdressing* 83/2 *Invisible pins*, very fine hairpins which are difficult to see when placed in the hairdress. **1967** J. CAIRD *Murder Scholastic* xiv. 190 Mabel Glossop had worn her thick, beautiful white hair in a bun, over which she put a fine 'invisible' net. **1973** *Times* 19 Oct. 3/1 (Advt.), Without these foils such modern marvels as 'invisible' hearing aids or heart pacemakers simply could not exist.

b. ***invisible green***, 'a very dark shade of green, approaching to black, and not easily distinguished from it' (Webster, 1864). (Remembered in 1844.)

B. *sb.* **1. a.** An invisible thing, person, or being.

1646 SIR T. BROWNE *Pseud. Ep.* v. xxi. 268 The practise of those pencils, that will describe invisibles. **1742** H. BAKER *Microsc.* II. i. 68 There are as many, or even more kinds of these *Invisibles* (if I may use the Term) than of those whose Size is discernable by the naked Eye. **1781** COWPER *Conversat.* 738 Such a jest as filled with hellish glee Certain invisibles as shrewd as he. **1823** LAMB *Lett. to Southey* v. 39 You are as familiar with these antiquated monastics, as Swedenborg..with his invisibles.

b. ***the invisible***, the unseen world; the Deity.

1781 COWPER *Retirement* 61 The Invisible in things scarce seen reveal'd, To whom an atom is an ample field. **1868** FITZGERALD tr. *Omar* (ed. 2) lxxi, I sent my Soul through the Invisible Some letter of that After-life to spell. **1892** GLADSTONE in *Pall Mall G.* 13 Apr. 7/1 The maintenance of faith in the Invisible..And by that I mean a living faith in a personal God.

2. One who denies the visible character of the Church (Blunt *Dict. Sects* 1874); *spec.* in *pl.* certain German Protestants of the 16th c.

1852 HOOK *Ch. Dict.* (1871) 400 Invisibles is a distinguishing name given to the disciples of Osiander, Flacius Illyricus, Swenkfeld, &c.

3. Usu. in *pl.* Invisible exports and imports. Cf. sense 1 d of the adj.

1958 *Economist* 18 Oct. 256/1 Net earnings from commercial services ranked as invisibles also rose. **1962** H. O. BEECHENO *Introd. Business Stud.* xv. 143 These 'invisibles' arise mainly from services which we supply to other countries. **1964** *New Statesman* 3 Apr. 514/1 Angola and Mozambique provide one-third of all Portuguese exports, valued at £50 million, and this sum does not include invisibles from tourism, shipping and railways. **1973** *Daily Tel.* 13 July 19 The average deficit for the latest three months, excluding invisibles, is £22 million lower than in May at £133 million.

invisibleness (ɪn'vɪzɪb(ə)lnɪs). [f. prec. + -NESS.] The quality of being invisible.

1530 PALSGR. 234/2 Invysiblenesse, *inuisibleté*. **1601** CORNWALLIS *Ess.* II. xxxi. (1631) 55 The reason of Vertues difficulty is her invisiblenesse. **1842** MANNING *Serm.* (1848) I. 181 There has been..an inwardness and an invisibleness about all great movements of Christ's Church. **1866** *Sat. Rev.* 19 May 584/1 The comparative secrecy and invisibleness of the growth of intellectual habits.

invisibly (ɪn'vɪzɪblɪ), *adv.* [f. as prec. + -LY^{2}.] In an invisible manner; so that it cannot be seen; imperceptibly.

1382 WYCLIF *Sel. Wks.* III. 522 Þat same body and blood invisibly, and not þe same visibely. **1495** *Trevisa's Barth. De P.R.* VIII. xxviii. (W. de W.) X vij/2 Heuen byshynynth not in derknesse nother by nyght. Thenne alwaye lyght

shynyth Inuysibly. **1526** *Pilgr. Perf.* (W. de W. 1531) 219 b, Those thynges yͭ he wrought inuisybly in vs at our baptym. **1643** BURROUGHES *Exp. Hosea* vi. (1652) 262 God doth great things sometime so invisibly, as he cannot be seen. **1709** STEELE *Tatler* No. 138 ¶2 To be invisibly good, is as God-like, as to be invisibly ill, Diabolical. **1878** HUXLEY *Physiogr.* 84 The gaseous carbonic acid invisibly distributed through the surrounding atmosphere.

†in'vision. *Obs. rare*⁻¹. [IN-³.] Want of vision; inability to see; blindness of young animals.

1646 SIR T. BROWNE *Pseud. Ep.* III. xxv. 174 Aristotle.. computeth the time of their anopsie or invision by that of their gestation.

†in'visory. *Obs. rare*⁻¹. [Of obscure formation; app. based on VISOR.] (See quot.)

1583 STUBBES *Anat. Abus.* I. (1879) 80 When they use to ride abrod, they haue inuisories, or visors made of veluet.

invitable (ɪn'vaɪtəb(ə)l), *a.* [f. INVITE *v.* + -ABLE.] That may be invited; fit to be invited.

1879 GEO. ELIOT *Theo. Such* ix. 165 Without being proportionately amusing and invitable.

†in'vital, *a. Obs.* [ad. late L. *invītāl-is* (Boethius), f. *in-* (IN-³) + *vītālis* VITAL.] Not vital; having no vitality.

1650 BULWER *Anthropomet.* i. 12 Hofman agrees with Galen that such [square heads] are monstrous, rare, and invital.

invita Minerva (ɪn'vaɪtɑː mɪ'nɜːvɑː), *advb. phr.* [L., = 'Minerva (the goddess of wisdom) unwilling'.] When one is not in the vein or mood; without inspiration.

1584 R. SCOT *Discov. Witchcr.* XII. iii. 219 It should be vnto them (*Inuita Minerua*) to banket or danse with Minerua. **1626** BACON *Sylva* §292 That nothing bee done *Inuitâ Mineruâ*, but *Secundum Genium*. **1848** GEO. ELIOT *Let.* Feb. (1954) I. 250, I have tired myself with trying to write cleverly 'invita Minerva'. **1954** 'M. COST' *Invitation from Minerva* 126 It is always a mistake to do anything invita Minerva... Briefly, against the grain.

invitant ('ɪnvɪtənt). [a. F. *invitant*, pr. pple. of *inviter* to invite: see -ANT¹.]

1. One who invites: an inviter.

1608 T. ROGERS *Disp. Kneel. Sacram.* 2 The mutuall cariage of the invitant and his guests. **1631** DENISON *Heav. Banq.* 332 Could he..entertaine a thought of equality and fellow-like condition with the Inuitant? **1812** *Examiner* 24 Aug. 542/2 His congratulants and dinner invitants.

¶**2.** *erron.* An invited person.

1615 J. STEPHENS *Satyr. Ess.* A vij b, When many are invited to a Feast,.. Shall we condemne his liberall act.. If thanklesse invitants the same disprove? **1822** GALT *Sir A. Wylie* I. xvi. 134 He was chosen a regular invitant to all her parties.

invitation (ɪnvɪ'teɪʃən). [ad. L. *invītātiōn-em*, n. of action from *invītāre* to INVITE. Cf. F. *invitation* (1593 in Hatz.-Darm.).]

1. a. The action of inviting or requesting to come, attend, or take part in something.

1611 COTGR., *Invitation*, an inuitation, or inuiting. **1615** J. STEPHENS *Satyr. Ess.* 353 The invitation of guests, provision of meate,..and his nuptiall garments. **1657** R. LIGON *Barbadoes* (1673) 10 We saw him..at his own house, by his own invitation. **1711** SWIFT *Jrnl. to Stella* in *Lett.* (1767) III. 171 Dr. Gastrel and I dined, by invitation, with the dean of Carlisle. **1859** THACKERAY *Virgin.* vii, Those officers who came..on her son's invitation.

b. The spoken or written form in which a person is invited.

1615 J. STEPHENS *Satyr. Ess.* 368 She makes every new inhabitant pay the tribute of an invitation, before she speakes well of him. **1648** CROMWELL *Let.* 9 Oct. in *Carlyle*, I received an invitation from the Committee of Estates to come to Edinburgh. **1781** GIBBON *Decl. & F.* xvii. II. 19 The invitations of a master are scarcely to be distinguished from commands. **1864** J. WALKER *Faithf. Ministry* 200 The feast is waiting: the invitations are out.

c. In the Anglican Communion Office, the exhortation immediately preceding the Confession, beginning 'Ye that do truly and earnestly repent you of your sins'.

1883 F. E. WARREN in *Prayer-bk. Comm.* (S.P.C.K.) 106 The Invitation, Confession, Absolution, and Comfortable Words are a..distinguishing feature of the present Anglican Liturgy.

†d. An entertainment to which one is invited. *Obs. rare.*

1682 T. FLATMAN *Heraclitus Ridens* (1713) II. No. 57. 108 Two chief Magistrates..being merry at an Invitation, fell to Dancing.

2. *fig.* **a.** The presenting of attractions or inducements to come or advance; an instance of this; attraction; inducement.

1598 SHAKS. *Merry W.* I. iii. 50, I spie entertainment in her: shee discourses: shee carues: she giues the leere of inuitation. **1654** WHITLOCK *Zootomia* 561 This terrible of all terribles [death], as Aristotle calleth it, hath more of Invitation in it [than affrightment]. **1673** TEMPLE *Obs. Unit. Prov.* Wks. 1731 I. 62 The two first Invitations of People into this Country, were the Strength of their Towns, and Nature of their Government.

b. *Bridge.* (See quot. 1964.)

1928 A. E. M. FOSTER *Auction Bridge for All* I. i. 22 There still lurks amongst a number of players the notion that a bid of a minor suit by their partner is what they call 'an invitation to a No Trumper'. Again and again I have heard said: 'I responded to your invitation, partner.' **1958** *Listener* 23 Oct. 669/3 With his excellent controls it is easy for West to accept the slam invitation. **1964** *Official Encycl. Bridge* 265/1 *Invitation*, a bid which encourages the bidder's partner to continue to game or slam, but gives him the option of passing if he has no reserve values in terms of high-card strength or distribution.

3. *attrib.*, as *invitation-card*, *list*, etc.; **invitation-dinner, -performance,** one attended only by those who receive invitations.

1808 WOLCOTT (P. Pindar) *Ep. Mrs. Clarke* Wks. 1812 V. 398 For invitation-dinners soon grow slack. **1819** *Metropolis* I. 265 An invitation-card for a dinner party. *c* **1855** in M. Johnson *Amer. Advertising, 1800–1900* (1960), Invitation notices, and every arrangment for funerals personally attended to with correctness and dispatch. **1899** *Daily News* 25 May 9/1 The invitation performance was an immense success. **1902** A. BENNETT *Grand Babylon Hotel* vi. 71 The invitation-list..contained no reference to any such person. **1931** A. E. M. FOSTER *Auction Bridge made Clear* 124 An original bid of Two of a suit is by them reserved as a 'Demand' or 'Invitation' bid. That is, a demand or invitation to partner to show his quick tricks. *Ibid.* 125 Z has ..a hand of over seven tricks but under eleven—the 'Invitation Area'... Z bid 'Two Hearts' as an 'Invitation'. **1968** *Radio Times* 28 Nov. 27/1 Invitation concert... Recorded before an invited audience.

invitational (ɪnvɪ'teɪʃənəl), *a.* (and *sb.*) [f. INVITATION + -AL.] Characterized by invitation. Also as *sb.*, an invitational tournament (? only *N. Amer.*).

1922 *Chambers's Jrnl.* Aug. 543/1 Philip walked the room's length with invitational pauses. **1957** *Publ. Amer. Dial. Soc.* XXVIII. 58 Somebody like to help me?..*someone* in the context..would sound more factual..than invitational. **1958** *Listener* 23 Oct. 669/3 A cue bid of Five Hearts would be too strongly invitational. **1964** *Official Encycl. Bridge* 265/1 *Invitational bid*, bid indicating strong game prospects, which requests partner to continue if he has some reserve strength. **1964** N. SQUIRE *Bidding at Bridge* ii. 17 Your partner..will give an invitational raise to 2NT. **1968** *Globe & Mail* (Toronto) 3 Feb. 35/5 Yesterday Sinclair's mixed rink of his wife, Betty, Don Maclellan and Mildred Maclellan advanced to the quarter-finals of the Thornhill mixed invitational tournament. *Ibid.* (*headline*), 2 Thornhill rinks survive club's mixed invitational. **1972** *Evening Telegram* (St. John's, Newfoundland) 27 June 11/1 John Hamilton won the June Invitational on his first try Monday, despite a desperate charge by two Corner Brook golfers on the final day of the tournament.

†in'vitative, *a. Obs.* [f. L. *invītāt-*, ppl. stem of *invītāre* to invite + -IVE.] Inviting.

1634 M. PARKER *Hist. Arthur* A iij, The Saxons..having gotten an invitative entrance into this land (which pleased them so well).

†invi'tator. *Obs.* [a. L. *invītātor*, agent-n. from *invītāre* to INVITE.] = INVITER.

1603 HARSNET *Pop. Impost.* 2 The gentle invitator of us to come and see his wonders. **1642** *Declar. Lords & Comm. to Gen. Ass. Ch. Scot.* 13 When invitators shall be sent to any of them.

‖**invita'torium.** [med.L.; neuter sing. of L. *invītātōrius* inviting, used as sb.] = INVITATORY *sb.*

1853 ROCK *Ch. of Fathers* III. II. 213 The appropriate invitatorium, or strophe, repeated at intervals.

invitatory (ɪn'vaɪtətərɪ), *a.* and *sb.* [ad. L. *invītātōrius* inviting, f. *invītāre* to invite. Cf. F. *invitatoire*.]

A. *adj.* That invites or tends to invite; containing or conveying an invitation.

1646 R. BAILLIE *Lett. & Jrnls.* (1841) II. 363 A cold slight invitatorie letter. **1665** SIR T. HERBERT *Trav.* (1677) 304 Hippocrates to whom the great Artaxerxes wrote an invitatory Letter. **1761** WESLEY *Wks.* (1872) XII. 122, I wish you would give us two or three invitatory hymns. **1831** LAMB *Elia* Ser. II. *Newsp. 35 Years ago*, Other female whims followed, but none..so invitatory of shrewd conceits. **1834** *New Monthly Mag.* XLI. 456 The portal of a tavern..bore this invitatory inscription.

b. *Eccl.* **invitatory psalm**: the *Venite*, Psalm xcv (*Vulg.* xciv).

a **1340** HAMPOLE *Psalter* xciv. 1 Louynge fallis till deuocioun, sange til goed chere & delite, alswa it is cald inuytatory. **1657** SPARROW *Bk. Com. Prayer* (1664) 32 This is an Invitatory psalm; for herein we do mutually invite and call upon one another being come before His presence, to sing to the Lord. **1706** PHILLIPS s.v., *Invitatory Verse*, i.e. a Verse in the Roman Church-Service that stirs up to praise and glorifie God. **1760–5** [see B. 2].

B. *sb.* **1.** [= med.L. *invītātōrium*.] An invitation.

1666 LEIGHTON *Charge to Clergy* Wks. (1868) 340 How needful is that invitatory to be often rung in our ears. **1892** *Sat. Rev.* 30 July 139/1 'Apply Principal' is the grammatical invitatory of most of these advertising worthies.

2. A form of invitation used in religious worship.

spec. **a.** The invitatory psalm or *Venite*. **b.** An antiphon sung at matins before the *Venite*. In the Anglican Church, the versicle 'Praise ye the Lord', with its response 'The Lord's name be praised'. **c.** Any text of Scripture chosen for the day, and used before the *Venite*. **d.** 'An antiphon used in the course of the singing of the Psalms, and repeated several times in the course of a Psalm, as well as at the beginning and the end' (*Prayer Book Comment.* Gloss.). **e.** An early name of the Roman introit. **f.** Sometimes, the INVITATION in the Anglican Communion Office.

1450–1530 *Myrr. our Ladye* 220 On Thursday at mattyns, the Inuytatory *Ave maria*. **1483** *Festivall* (W. de W. 1515) 63 b, As he was abloute to saye our ladyes matyns, and as he was at the Invytatorye (yͭ is Ave Maria). **1548–9** (Mar.) *Bk. Com. Prayer, Morning P.* (Rubric), Then shalbe saied or song without any Inuitatori this Psalme, *Venite exultemus*, etc. in Englishe. **1641** R. BAILLIE *Parallel Liturgy w. Mass-Bk.* 10 All the Missals I have seen..have never *venite* for the *introitus*, only in the Breviarie, it is the invitatorie for the Matins. **1659** H. L'ESTRANGE *Alliance Div. Off.* 112 With the same congruity is 'praise ye the Lord' assigned as an impressive invitatory to a following hymn calling upon the people to join not only mentally but vocally. **1662** *Bk. Com. Prayer* Pref., For this cause be cut off Anthems, Responds, Invitatories, and such like things as did break the continual course of the reading of the Scripture. **1760–5** BURN *Eccl. Law* (1797) II. 347 Invitatory was a text of Scripture, adapted and chosen for the occasion of the day, and used before the Venite; which also itself was called the invitatory psalm. **1866** *Direct. Angl.* (ed. 3) 355 Our V. 'Praise ye the Lord' with the R. is our present unvarying Invitatory. In the Communion Service the second Exhortation is the Invitatory.

invite (ɪn'vaɪt), *v.* [f. F. *invite-r* (15–16th c. in Hatz.-Darm.), ad. L. *invītāre* to invite.]

1. *trans.* Of a person: To ask (a person) graciously, kindly, or courteously, **a.** to come *to* (*into*, etc.) a place or proceeding to which he is assumed to be pleased or willing to come. *to invite oneself*, to announce one's intention of coming, or say that one will have pleasure in being present. *to invite in*: to ask (a person) to come into one's house.

1553 S. CABOT *Ordinances* in Hakluyt *Voy.* (1589) 262 If you shall be invited into any Lords or Rulers house to dinner or other parliance. **1566** GRESHAM *Let.* 15 Dec. in Burgon *Life* (1839) II. 184 The Duke's Grace hath invited himself to Gresham-House upon Wedensdaye next at night, and wyll dyne with me upon Thursday. **1596** SPENSER *F.Q.* VI. ix. 16 But Melibœe..began Him to inuite vnto his simple home. **1611** BIBLE *Ecclus.* xiii. 9 If thou be inuited of a mightie man, withdraw thy selfe, and so much the more will he inuite thee. **1651** SIR E. NICHOLAS in *N. Papers* (Camden) 225 The ambassy of Titus to invite that Lord into Scotland. **1657** R. LIGON *Barbadoes* (1673) 8 He sent to us a very kind message, inviting himself aboard our ship. **1758** JOHNSON *Idler* No. 47 ¶3 My husband was often invited to dinner. **1838** LYTTON *Alice* I. vii, I was thinking, myself, that I should like to invite her. **1839** KEIGHTLEY *Hist. Eng.* II. 43 Aske was invited to court. **1875** *Harper's Mag.* Aug. 417 She found a house where she was invited in. **1888** MRS. H. WARD *R. Elsmere* II. III. xxii. 213 It was evidently the Squire's purpose to come in, so Robert invited him in. **1899** SKEEL & BREARLEY *King Washington* 37 Being occupied in a nice calculation whether or not her breakfast menu would stand the strain of an extra appetite should Mr. Ettrick.. invite the captain in. **1974** 'M. UNDERWOOD' *Pinch of Snuff* xi. 94 'I doubt whether we need a warrant,' Sergeant Ellis remarked. 'After all, he invited us in.'

b. *to do something* assumed to be agreeable.

1583 HOLLYBAND *Campo di Fior* 73 To daye a certeine cheese-seller invited them to eate Curdes. **1617** MORYSON *Itin.* II. 203 This gentleman was invited by the Lord Deputy to accompany him to Dublin. **1687** DRYDEN *Hind & P.* II. 670 She thought good manners bound her to invite The stranger dame to be her guest that night. **1797** MRS. RADCLIFFE *Italian* i. (1826) 5 She did not invite him to enter. **1823** MRS. MARKHAM *Hist. Eng.* vii. (1853) 39 They.. invited Edward..to ascend the throne. **1885** S. COX *Expos.* Ser. I. ii. 26, I was..inviting you to speculate too curiously.

c. To request graciously or courteously (something) to be done by a person.

1854 HAWTHORNE *Eng. Note-Bks.* (1879) II. 336 Nobody ..invited our entrance. **1856** KINGSLEY *Lett.* (1878) I. 474, I invite your attention to this side of the question. **1873** TRISTRAM *Moab* ii. 22 A return visit was invited. **1873** BLACK *Pr. Thule* xv, I never invite confidences. **1875** JOWETT *Plato* (ed. 2) I. 70, I was going to invite the opinion of some older person.

†d. To try to attract or induce. *Obs.*

a **1548** HALL *Chron., Rich. III* 38 By previe letters and cloked messengers, dyd sturre and invite to this newe conjuracion, al such which [etc.]. **1556** *Aurelio & Isab.* (1608) C v, She, that sholde have invitede me unto the lovinge faulte. **1617** MORYSON *Itin.* III. 115 They are not willingly invited to eate with other men.

e. *fig.* Unintentionally to bring on (something) or encourage (it) to come.

1650 FULLER *Pisgah* Ep. Ded. 49 b, Others degenerating by their vicious courses, invited neglect and contempt upon themselves. **1665** DRYDEN *Ind. Emperor* II. ii, You threaten Peace, and you invite a War. **1796** BURKE *Regic. Peace* iv. Wks. IX. 111 When we invite danger from a confidence in defensive measures. **1876** J. PARKER *Paracl.* I. xiii. 214 To be earnest in the cause of the Cross, is to invite the charge of fanaticism.

2. a. Of a thing: To present inducements to (a person) *to do* something or proceed *to* a place or action.

1533 MORE *Debell. Salem* Wks. 993/2 The law doth inuyte and hyre euery man to thaccusing of the breakers of the same by giuing them the tone half of the forfaiture. **1555** EDEN *Decades* 307 The exemples of owre fathers and predicessours doo inuite vs hereunto. **1615** G. SANDYS *Trav.* 11 The Merchants removing hither, invited by the immunities of the Temple, and conveniencie of the place. **1667** MILTON *P.L.* II. 278 All things invite To peaceful Counsels and the settl'd State Of order. **1761** HUME *Hist. Eng.* III. lx. 293 There were many circumstances which invited the natives of Ireland to embrace the king's party. **1821** BYRON *Sardan.* I. 553 Come, Myrrha, let us go on to the Euphrates: The hour invites, the galley is prepared.

b. To tend to bring on; to lie open to.

1599 H. BUTTES *Dyets drie Dinner* L iv b, [It] easily corrupteth in the stomack: inviteth the Ague. **1617** MORYSON *Itin.* III. 31 One looke invites another. **1790** BURKE *Corr.* (1844) III. 179 Though it was a far less dangerous measure..it still seemed to invite discussion. **1862** STANLEY *Jew. Ch.* (1877) I. xiii. 242 The characteristics of this period..invite our..inquiries.

†c. To draw to itself, attract physically. *Obs.*

1671 R. BOHUN *Wind* 50 If the..Vapors have gravity enough..to invite them Downward. *Ibid.* 72 An iron bullet,

heated, and drawn over the surface of water, that presently invites the ambient Air to follow the same course. **1800** tr. *Lagrange's Chem.* I. 315 Did not the presence of soda invite to it the acid, while the fluoric acid invites the metal.

invite (ˈɪnvaɪt, formerly ɪnˈvaɪt), *sb. colloq.* [f. INVITE *v.*: cf. *command*, *request*, etc.]

1. The act of inviting; an invitation.

1659 H. L'ESTRANGE *Alliance Div. Off.* 326 Bishop Cranmer..gives him an earnest invite to England. **1778** MAD. D'ARBLAY *Diary* (1842) I. 105 Everybody bowed and accepted the invite but me..for I have no intention of snapping at invites from the eminent. **1818** LADY MORGAN *Autobiog.* (1859) 39 We have refused two invites for to-day. *Ibid.* 292 For Monday we have had three dinner invites. **1825** T. HOOK *Man of Many Friends* in *Sayings & Doings* Ser. II. I. 279 Adepts in every little meanness or contrivance likely to bring about an invitation (or, as they call it with equal good taste, an 'invite'). **1883** C. R. SMITH *Retrospect.* I. 21 Mr. Isaacson readily accepted the invite. **1937** *Times* 28 Dec. 7/5 This little servant girl, who..believed that she would some day receive an 'invite' to a royal ball and marry the prince, [etc.]. **1968** *Listener* 13 June 770/1 Is it just an invite from the colonel for a working week-end? **1970** G. F. NEWMAN *Sir, You Bastard* v. 143 The four detectives didn't await an invite into the house.

†**2.** *pl.* (*nonce-use for rime.*) Attractions, baits.

1615 G. SANDYS *Trav.* 305 The Lamprey swims to his Lords invites [*natat ad magistrum delicata murena*], The Bedel the knowne Mullet cites.

†**invite**, *a.* (or *adv.*) *Obs. rare.* [ad. L. *invīt-us* unwilling (cf. It. *invito* 'against one's will', Florio); or perh. L. *invītē* adv., unwillingly, against one's will.] Unwilling(ly); against one's will.

c **1450** *Mirour Saluacioun* 2648 He soeffred it of free wille and invite [*gl.* maugre his] nevre the more.

invited (ɪnˈvaɪtɪd), *ppl. a.* [f. INVITE *v.* + -ED[1].] That has received an invitation.

1658 *Hist. Mem. K. James* 125 And all this once seene and having feasted the eyes of the Invited, was in a manner throwne away. **1821** BYRON *Sardan.* II. *ad fin.*, We must prepare To meet the invited guests, who grace our feast.

invitee (ɪnvaɪˈtiː). [f. INVITE *v.* + -EE.] **a.** One who is invited.

[**1803** S. PEGGE *Anecd. Eng. Lang.* 303 It rather appears to be the language of the Invité than of the inviter.] **1837** *Fraser's Mag.* XVI. 156 The list of invitees being at length resolved on. **1882** BERESF. HOPE *Brandreths* III. xlvii. 233 The other invitees had failed.

b. *spec.* (See quot. 1913.)

1913 *Law Rep. King's Bench* I. 410 The duty of the owner or occupier to use care..is..never very definitely measured... More care, though not much, is owed to a licensee—more again to an invitee. The latter term is reserved for those who are invited into the premises by the owner or occupier for some purpose of business or of material interest. Those who are invited as guests..are not in law invitees but licensees. **1953** *Times* 14 Nov. 2/7 Their Lordships now held that the plaintiff was himself to blame for the accident, and that he was not an 'invitee' because the business on which he was engaged was not one in which the defendant had a common interest. **1965** *Mod. Law Rev.* XXVIII. v. 519 A finding that a workman was *sciens* was sufficient to defeat his claim as an invitee, even if he was not *volens*. **1971** *N.Y. Law Jrnl.* 23 Nov. 19/3 In England the distinction between licensees and invitees have [*sic*] been abolished by statute.

invitement (ɪnˈvaɪtmənt). Now *rare.* [ad. L. *invītāment-um* an inviting, allurement, f. *invītāre* to invite; cf. F. *invitement* (Cotgr.), It. *invitamento* (Florio, 1598).]

†**1.** Inviting; an invitation. *Obs.*

1599 B. JONSON *Cynthia's Rev.* II. Wks. (Rtldg.) 76/2 Hee never makes generall invitement. **1608** GOLDING *Epit. Frossard* III. 162 Vppon often inuitements and embassages from the King of Portugall he was come into the kingdome. **1639** MASSINGER *Unnat. Combat* I. Wks. (Rtldg.) 27/2 But be his daily guest without invitement.

2. Inducement; allurement; encouragement to come.

1627 ABP. ABBOT *Narrative* in Rushw. *Hist. Coll.* (1659) I. 434 In the turbulency of some things I had no great invitements to draw me abroad. *a* **1680** CHARNOCK *Attrib. God* (1845) 665 What invitements could he have from lying, beastliness, gluttony? **1822** LAMB *Elia* Ser. I. *Praise Chimneysweepers*, Unable to resist the delicious invitement to repose.

inviter (ɪnˈvaɪtə(r)). Also 6–9 -or. [f. INVITE *v.* + -ER[1].] One who invites.

a **1586** SIDNEY *Arcadia* III. 1724 Wks. II. 410 The..pretty conversation of their inviters. **1598** FLORIO, *Inuitatore*, an inuitor, an intreator, a bidder of any feast. **1648** MILTON *Observ. Art. Peace* Wks. (1851) 561 The Subverter of true Religion, the Protecter and Inviter of Irreligion and Atheism. **1818** COBBETT *Pol. Reg.* XXXIII. 723 William began by rewarding with titles and grants all his principal invitors. **1885** *Law Reports* 15 Q. Bench Div. 318 The liability created by inviting a person into premises..in the occupation..of the inviter.

b. *spec.* (See quot.)

1837 WHITTOCK, etc. *Bk. Trades* (1842) 143 Either as salesmen, or 'inviters', a modern name for that class.. formerly known by the name of barkers..that stand in the street to persuade passers by to come into their shops to purchase clothes.

invitiate (ɪnˈvɪʃɪət), *a. rare.* [f. IN-[3] + VITIATE *ppl. a.*] Without blemish; unmarred.

1869 LOWELL *Cathedral* 169 Hers shall be The invitiate firstlings of experience.

†**inˈvitiate**, *v. Obs.* [f. med. or mod.L. *invitiāt-*, ppl. stem of *invitiāre* (cf. It. *invitiare*, Florio, 1598), f. *in-* (IN-[2]) + L. *vitiāre* to VITIATE.] *trans.* To render vicious; to corrupt, spoil.

1598 FLORIO, *Inuitiare*, to growe vitious or wicked; to corrupt, to inuitiate. **1656** BLOUNT *Glossogr.*, *Invitiate* (*invitio*), to mar, to spoil, to defile.

inviting (ɪnˈvaɪtɪŋ), *vbl. sb.* [f. INVITE *v.* + -ING[1].] The action of the vb. INVITE; invitation.

1586 A. DAY *Eng. Secretary* I. (1625) 12 A signe or inviting to good hap. **1603** HOLLAND *Plutarch's Mor.* 680 Courtesies and kindnesses of drinking one to another, and mutuall invitings. **1607** SHAKS. *Timon* III. vi. 11 He hath sent mee an earnest inuiting. **1618** J. WINTHROP *Let. to Marg. Tyndal* 4 Apr. in *Life & Lett.* (1864) I. vii. 136 Love was their ensigne; love was his invitinges. *Mod.* Not much inviting was needed.

inˈviting, *ppl. a.* [f. INVITE *v.* + -ING[2].]

1. That invites or gives an invitation.

c **1600** SHAKS. *Sonn.* cxxiv, Thralled discontent, Whereto the inviting time our fashion calls. **1684** BUNYAN *Pilgr.* II. 16 How the King of the Country..had sent her an inviting Letter to come thither. **1820** CHALMERS *Cong. Serm.* (1838) II. 204 The spectacle of an inviting God, plying His wandering prodigal with all the tenderness of entreaty.

2. Attractive; alluring; tempting.

1604 SHAKS. *Oth.* II. iii. 24 An inuiting eye: And yet me thinkes right modest. **1667** MILTON *P.L.* IX. 777 This Fruit Divine, Fair to the Eye, inviting to the Taste. **1703** MAUNDRELL *Journ. Jerus.* (1732) 43 So pleasant and inviting was its shade. **1863** MARY HOWITT *F. Bremer's Greece* I. iii. 80 The Greek saddles..do not look at all inviting. **1866** GEO. ELIOT *F. Holt* i, To let farms, a man must have the sense to see what will make them inviting to farmers.

inˈvitingly, *adv.* [f. prec. + -LY[2].] In a way that invites or allures; attractively.

1667 *Decay Chr. Piety* vi. 125 If he can but dress up a temptation to look invitingly, the business is done. **1724** RAMSAY '*O steer her up*' ii, See that shining glass of claret How invitingly it looks. **1876** BANCROFT *Hist. U.S.* III. vi. 373 America, with its new acquisitions..lay invitingly before him.

inˈvitingness. [f. as prec. + -NESS.] The quality of being alluring; attractiveness.

1656 *Artif. Handsom.* 165 Elegant flowers of speech, to which the nature and resemblances of things, as well as human fancies, have an aptitude and invitingness. **1892** *Chicago Advance* 28 Apr., Every satan's-chapel is kept.. open and invested with all possible invitingness.

invitor, -our, Sc. corrupt forms of INVENTAR, inventory. Cf. INVITORY *sb.*[2]

1545 *Aberdeen Reg.* V. 19 (Jam.) Ane inuitour. **1559** *Burgh Rec. Aberdeen* (1844) I. 320 Heir followis the inuitor of the said siluer wark and ornamentis. **1871** W. ALEXANDER *Johnny Gibb* xxxvii. (1873) 211 But the like o' 'im 'll never be able to pay the inveetor.

invitor, obs. variant of INVITER.

†**ˈinvitory**, *sb.*[1] *Obs.* Shortened form of INVITATORY B. 2.

1483 *Cath. Angl.* 197/1 Inuitory, *invitatorium*. **1509** BARCLAY *Shyp of Folys* (1874) II. 155 And in the mornynge when they come to the quere The one begynneth a Fable or a hystory..Taking it in stede of the Invitorie. **1563–87** FOXE *A. & M.* (1596) 513/2 Hauing a triple inuitorie, or a double, or els a single inuitorie.

invitory, *sb.*[2] Corrupt form of INVENTORY *sb.*

1483 *Cath. Angl.* 197/1 Inuitory, *inuentarium*. *c* **1530** H. RHODES in *Babees Bk.* 66 Take an Inuitory of such thinges as ye take charge of, and see how it is spente.

Hence †**invitory** *v.*, to inventory.

1526 in Dillon *Customs of Pale* (1892) 86 Wracke found by the sea coste muste be broughte to the Lagander's hous, and Invitoried.

†**inˈvitreate**, *v. Obs. rare*[−0]. In 6–7 -iate. [f. med.L. *invitreāre* (Du Cange), or It. *invetriare*, f. *vitreus* glassy: see -ATE[3].] *trans.* To glaze.

1598 FLORIO, *Inuetriare*, to glaze, to calcinat, or inuitriate. *Ibid.*, *Inuetriato*, glased..inuitriated.

So †**inˈvitreable (-iable)** *a.* = INVITRIFIABLE.

1794 SULLIVAN *View Nat.* I. 450 In fire, it is invitriable *per se*.

invitress (ɪnˈvaɪtrɪs). [f. INVITER + -ESS.] A female inviter.

1617 COLLINS *Def. Bp. Ely* II. ix. 364 Could Marcella, and her inuitresses, see these things without a figure? **1841** J. T. HEWLETT *Parish Clerk* III. 175 The disgusted looks of the husband of his invitress. **1852** SMEDLEY *L. Arundel* xxxvii. 281 'Dear me, how dreadfully provoking!' sighed the perplexed 'invitress'.

invitrifiable (ɪnˈvɪtrɪfaɪəb(ə)l), *a.* [IN-[3].] That cannot be vitrified or converted into glass.

1796 KIRWAN *Elem. Min.* (ed. 2) I. 120 Maquer found the purest gypsum invitrifiable by solar heat.

in vitro, in vivo: see IN *Lat. prep.*

†**inˈvivid**, *a. Obs. rare.* [IN-[3].] Not vivid.

1673 SIR P. WYCHE *Short Relat. Nile* 27 A pale invivid colour, nearer white than ash colour.

invocable (ˈɪnvəkəb(ə)l), *a. rare.* [ad. L. type **invocābil-is*, f. *invocā-re* to INVOKE: see -ABLE.] Capable of being invoked or called upon.

1839 BAILEY *Festus* vi. (1852) 78 The visible form of some obedient sprite Or invocable angel. **1857** H. H. WILSON tr. *Rig-veda* III. 463 Who hast been invocable of old.

ˈinvocant. [ad. L. *invocānt-em*, pr. pple. of *invocāre* to INVOKE.] One who invokes.

1751 J. BARTRAM *Observ. Trav. Pennsylv.* 33 He reveals to the invocant what he has taken so much pains to know. **1893** ATKINSON in Kath. Simpson *Jeanie o' Biggersdale* Pref. 8 The invocant took care not to wait for it.

invocate (ˈɪnvəkeɪt), *v.* Now *rare.* [f. L. *invocāt-*, ppl. stem of *invocāre* to INVOKE. The pa. pple. *invocate*, first used, was ad. L. *invocāt-us*.]

1. *trans.* = INVOKE.

1526 *Pilgr. Perf.* (W. de W. 1531) 219 b, Thy holy name is inuocate & named vpon vs. **1537** *Inst. Chr. Man, Creed* Art. vi. 45 Whensoever I do invocate and call upon him [Christ] in right faith and hope. *c* **1600** SHAKS. *Sonn.* xxxviii, Be thou the tenth Muse, ten times more in worth Then those old nine which rimers inuocate. **1738** WESLEY *Ps.* XVIII. ii, Still will I invocate his Name. **1848** KEBLE *Serm.* x. 272 That offering for sin..which the Holy Spirit, duly invocated, descends upon.

†**2.** *intr.* To make invocation; to call in prayer (*on* or *upon*). *Obs.*

1582 N. T. (Rhem.) *Acts* vii. 59 They stoned Stephen invocating, and saying: Lord Iesus, receive my spirit. **1593** DRAYTON *Idea* 535 Some call on Heaven, some invocate on Hell. **1601** HOLLAND *Pliny* II. 297 We obserue a peculiar adoration, and inuocat vpon the Greekish goddesse of vengeance Nemesis. **1638** SIR T. HERBERT *Trav.* (ed. 2) 256 After that houre to daybreak tis held an ungodly thing to invocate. **1802** H. MARTIN *Helen of Glenross* IV. 255 With the shriek of madness she invocated.

Hence **ˈinvocated** *ppl. a.*; **ˈinvocating** *vbl. sb.*

1585–7 T. ROGERS *39 Art.* (1607) 226 In these days protestant churches utterly condemn the invocating of, or praying unto, any creatures whatsoever. **1671** MILTON *Samson* 575 Till..oft-invocated death Hasten the welcome end of all my pains. **1746** SMOLLETT *Reproof* 200 Peace to that gentle soul that could deny His invocated voice to fill the cry.

invocation (ɪnvəʊˈkeɪʃən). Also 5 yn-. [a. OF. *invocation*, *-cion*, *-ciun* (12th c. in Hatz.-Darm.), ad. L. *invocātiōn-em*, n. of action from *invocāre* to INVOKE.]

1. The action or an act of invoking or calling upon (God, a deity, etc.) in prayer or attestation; supplication, or an act or form of supplication, for aid or protection.

c **1375** *Sc. Leg. Saints, Johannes* 306 Or he þe tempil suld ..Of dame diane gere Ryve done Of criste thru Invocacione. *c* **1384** CHAUCER *H. Fame* I. 67, I woll make invocation.. Unto the god of sleepe anone. **1433** LYDG. *S. Edmund* II. 901 The lord of lordys..Herde..ther Inuocacioun And gaff hem comfort of that they stood in dreed. **1537** *Inst. Chr. Man, 3rd Commandm.*, To pray to saints to be intercessors with us and for us to our Lord for our suits..so that we make no invocation of them [**1543** *Necess. Doct.* so that we esteem not or worship not them as givers of those gifts, but as intercessors for the same] is lawful and allowed by the Catholic Church. **1554** in Strype *Eccl. Mem.* (1721) III. App. xvii. 43 We disallow invocation or prayer to saints departed this life. **1607** E. GRIMSTONE tr. *Goulart's Mem. Hist.* 337 He..yeelded up the ghost in the invocation of the name of God. **1664** JER. TAYLOR *Dissuas. Popery* Wks. 1847–51 VI. 489 Invocation of Saints: which if it be no more than a mere desire for them to pray for us, why is it expressed in their public offices in words that differ not from our prayers to God? **1673** *True Worship God* 52 It is a piece of Religious worship, as every Vow made to God is, implying an Invocation of God to judge according to the Truth or Falshood of what we promise. **1782** PRIESTLEY *Corrupt. Chr.* I. IV. 350 This does not imply a direct invocation. **1863** MARY HOWITT *F. Bremer's Greece* II. xix. 211 The Greek new year's wishes for the present year contain a fervent invocation to Phœbus to protect their Majesties. **1899** *Ch. Q. Rev.* Jan. 274 We use the phrase 'invocation of saints' in the sense ordinarily attached to it at the present time: namely, to denote the practice of requesting departed saints for the help of their prayers to God.

b. *Eccl.* A form of invocatory prayer, as part of a public religious service. Also, The name or appellation used in invoking a divinity, etc.

spec. The petitions addressed to each person of the Godhead and to the Trinity, which form the opening part of the Anglican and Roman Catholic Litanies (including, in the latter case, petitions to saints also); also, the third part of the prayer of consecration in the Communion Office of the Nonjurors of 1718, and in the Office of the Scottish Episcopal Church of 1764, whence also in the American Book of Common Prayer.

1827 SOUTHEY *Penins. War* II. 682 The Valencians imputed their deliverance..to..the Virgin, under her invocation of Maria Santissima de los Desamparados. **1852** HOOK *Ch. Dict.* (1871) 400 The commencing part of the Litany, containing the invocation of each person of the Godhead, severally, of the Blessed Trinity in Unity. **1852** MRS. JAMESON *Leg. Madonna* Introd. 35 A new invocation was now added to her Litany, under the title of *Auxilium Christianorum*.

2. The action or an act of conjuring or summoning a devil or spirit by incantation; an incantation or magical formula used for this or a similar purpose; a charm, spell.

1390 GOWER *Conf.* III. 46 Babylla..With Cernes..He traceth ofte upon the grounde, Makend his invocation. **1483** CAXTON *Gold. Leg.* 130 b/2 He was taught in the arte of enchauntement and of thynuocacions of feendes. **1541** *Act 33 Hen. VIII*, c. 8 Sondrie persons..practised inuocacions and coniuracions of spirites. **1600** SHAKS. *A.Y.L.* II. v. 61 'Tis a Greeke inuocation, to call fools into a circle. **1613** PURCHAS *Pilgrimage* (1614) 444 Themselves renuing their former invocation, and the Divell entring into this man, causeth him to write. **1867** PARKMAN *Jesuits N. Amer.* vi.

(1875) 68 The sorcerers.. yelled incessant invocations to the spirits.

3. *Admiralty Prize Procedure.* The calling in of papers or evidence from another case: see INVOKE *v.* 5.

1806 SIR C. ROBINSON *Admiralty Rep.* VI. 355 In the practice of invoking evidence from other causes, it had been the rule not to permit invocation from any case till that cause had been heard. **1828** WEBSTER s.v., A judicial call, demand, or order; as the invocation of papers or evidence into a court.

invocative (ɪn'vɒkətɪv, 'ɪnvəkeɪtɪv), *a.* [f. L. *invocāt-*, ppl. stem of *invocāre* to INVOKE + -IVE.] Characterized by invocation; invocatory.

1821 *Examiner* 381/1 Two thousand lines of blank verse purely invocative. **1851** E. B. ELLIOTT *Horæ Apoc.* (1862) I. 481 The voice invocative of judgment.

'invocator. *rare.* [agent-n. in L. form f. *invocāre* to INVOKE: cf. F. *invocateur* (Godef. *Compl.*).] One who invokes, an invoker.

1604 J. DEE in *Lett. Lit. Men* (Camden) 47 That he is, or hath bin a Conjurer, or Caller, or Invocator of divels. *a* **1641** BP. MOUNTAGU *Acts & Mon.* (1642) 161 Conjurors, Witches, Necromantics, Invocators of Devils.

invocatory (ɪn'vɒkətərɪ, 'ɪnvəkeɪtərɪ), *a.* [f. L. *invocāre*, *invocāt-* (see above) + -ORY; cf. F. *invocatoire* (Littré).] Of the nature of, characterized by, or used in, invocation.

1691 HICKES *Apol. New Separ.* 11 In the invocatory part of any Collect in the Liturgy. **1845** J. H. NEWMAN *Ess. Developm.* 365 The Eastern Church seemed to consider the consecration of the elements.. to lie in the invocatory prayer. **1855** *Househ. Words* XII. 407 A volley of strange nasal sounds, imprecatory and invocatory. **1891** LOUNSBURY *Stud. Chaucer* II. iv. 101 The invocatory phrases which are among those oftenest occurring.. in the poet's works.

invoice ('ɪnvɔɪs), *sb.* Also 7 envoice, 7–8 invoyce. [app. orig. = *invoyes*, pl. of INVOY, corresp. to 16th c. F. *envoy* (now *envoi*), f. *envoyer* to send: cf. F. *lettre d'envoi* letter of consignment, invoice.

Inferentially, this derivation is satisfactory, both as to meaning and form. *In-* from F. and earlier Eng. *en-* is usual; and the writing of *-ce* for the plural *-s* is found in other words, as *dice*, *mice*, *pence*, in some of which also, as *accidence*, *bodice*, *dace*, *truce*, the resulting form is treated as a singular. But the historical record is not complete: the examples of *invoy*, *invoyes*, are scanty and not very early, and an earlier *envoy* in this sense is not exemplified.]

A list of the particular items of goods shipped or sent to a factor, consignee, or purchaser, with their value or prices, and charges.

1560 *Let.* in Hakluyt *Voy.* (1599) I. 308 We haue laden.. twenty seuen pipes of bastards and seckes, as by the Inuoices herewith inclosed may appeare. **1622** MALYNES *Anc. Law-Merch.* 114 If a Factor, by a Letter of aduice, or by an Inuoyce of commodities which the Merchant sendeth, doe make a short entrie into the Custome house. **1628** WOODALL *Viaticum* 10 The pills in the inuoyce of this Chest. **1670** BLOUNT *Law Dict.*, *Invoice*,.. a particular of the value, custom, and charges of any goods sent by a Merchant in another mans Ship, and consign'd to a Factor or correspondent in another Country. **1687** A. LOVELL tr. *Thevenot's Trav.* III. 111 The Dutch set the price, and wrote a List or Envoice of them, with the price on the Margin. **1809** R. LANGFORD *Introd. Trade* 60 Inland Invoices are sometimes distinguished as buying or selling Invoices. **1840** MACAULAY *Ess.*, *Clive* (1887) 531 When the ablest servants of the English Company were busied only about invoices and bills of lading.

b. *loosely.* A consignment of invoiced goods.

1881 P. S. ROBINSON *Under the Punkah* 39 Here and there, monster fungi clustered, like a condemned invoice of umbrellas and parasols.

c. *attrib.*, as ***invoice-book***, ***price***, ***weight***, etc.

1678 J. VERNON *Comptingho.* 14 Some take the Tare as it is marked upon the several Casks, and that is called *Invoice Tare*, or Tare according to Factory. **1706** PHILLIPS, *Invoice-Tare*, the Tare or Weight of the Cask, Bag, etc. in which Goods are put, mention'd in the Invoice, or Factor's Account. **1812** J. SMYTH *Pract. of Customs* (1821) 9 Mogadore Tare is commonly reduced to British pounds by adding 20 per cent... to the Invoice weight. **1849** FREESE *Comm. Class-bk.* 101 The *Invoice-Book*, in which are copied the Invoices received from, and sent abroad. It is.. not unusual to have separate books for the two—then called 'Inward Invoice-Book', and 'Outward Invoice-Book'. **1864** *Daily Tel.* 7 Sept., Did you buy these per invoice price or retail?

invoice ('ɪnvɔɪs), *v.* [f. prec. sb.] *trans.* To make an invoice of, to enter in an invoice. Also, to send or submit an invoice to (a person). Hence **'invoiced** *ppl. a.*, **'invoicing** *vbl. sb.*

Rarely occurs in written English, but common in speech. The contextual sense in quot. 1939 is not certain.

1698 FRYER *Acc. E. India & P.* 88 When they are publickly Invoiced, it will be at their own Wills to make their Bargains. **1800** MRQ. WELLESLEY in Owen *Desp.* (1877) 650 They should be invoiced at a reasonable and just price. **1855** BROWNING *Old Pict. in Florence* xxxii, No parcel that needs invoicing. **1883** *Stubbs' Mercantile Circular* 31 Oct. 980/1 You can recover the amount.. from your customer, presuming you invoiced to him. **1888** *Daily News* 6 June 3/1 To impose on bottled sparkling wines of the invoiced value of over 30*s.* a dozen an additional duty of 5*s.* **1939** JOYCE *Finnegans Wake* (1964) III. 623 You invoiced him last Eatster so he ought to give us hockockles and everything. **1956** *Invoicing Methods* (Brit. Inst. Managem.) xv. 124 An opaque signal is placed over the ledger folio on the customer record in order to prevent subsequent orders from the customer being inadvertently stamped with the ledger folio as a sign that they may be invoiced in the ordinary way. **1972** *Daily Tel.* 12 July 11 (Advt.), I enclose my remittance of £6 for the first ingot, and agree to pay for each subsequent ingot upon being invoiced on a monthly prepayment basis.

invoke (ɪn'vəʊk), *v.* Also 5 invoque, 6 envoke, 7 invoak. [a. F. *invoque-r* (12th c. in Hatz.-Darm.), ad. L. *invocāre* to call upon, esp. as a witness or for aid; to implore; to call by name, f. *in-* (IN-[2]) + *vocāre* to call.]

1. *trans.* To call on (God, a deity, etc.) in prayer or as a witness; to appeal to for aid or protection; to summon or invite in prayer.

1490 CAXTON *Eneydos* xxiv. 88 She inuoqued and called thre tymes by hidous wordes thre hundred goddes infernall. *c* **1586** C'TESS PEMBROKE *Ps.* cxix. T, Since I have envoked thee Lett me Lord thy succour see. *a* **1633** AUSTIN *Medit.* (1635) 256 As wee must not Invoke them [angels], so much lesse must we adore or worship them. **1697** DRYDEN *Virg. Georg.* I. 145 Ye Swains, invoke the Pow'rs who rule the Sky, For a moist Summer, and a Winter dry. **1777** WATSON *Philip II* (1839) 117 In witness of this our league, we invoke the holy name of the living God. **1885** *Athenæum* 21 Mar. 369/3 Apollo, then, is invoked in this passage as an avenging victor.

b. To appeal to, in confirmation of something.

1851 GLADSTONE *Glean.* (1879) VI. xxix. 19, I cannot here do better than invoke the authority of Hooker.

2. To summon (a spirit) by charms or incantation; to conjure; also *fig.* (Cf. CONJURE 9.)

1602 MARSTON *Antonio's Rev.* III. ii, Invoking all the spirits of the graves To tell me. **1838** LYTTON *Leila* I. ii, I can invoke and conjure up those whose eyes are more piercing, whose natures are more gifted. **1848** —— *Harold* VIII. iv, Thou shalt stand by my side while I invoke the phantom. **1862** HOOK *Lives Abps.* II. ii. 132 Thus was the science of architecture invoked.

b. To utter (a sacred *name*) in invocation.

1698 FRYER *Acc. E. India & P.* 262 His Name being invoked when any Commendable or Famous Action is performed; saying *Shaw Abas*, or *Shabas*, as we are wont to say, *Well done*. *a* **1704** T. BROWN *Sat. Quack* Wks. 1730 I. 65 Wrinkled witches, when they truck with hell, Invoke thy name, and use it for a spell.

3. To call upon, or call to (a person) to come or to do something.

1697 DRYDEN *Virg. Georg.* IV. 762 Ev'n then his trembling Tongue invok'd his Bride; With his last Voice, Eurydice, he cry'd. **1878** *Masque Poets* 213 All things In youth and loveliness to love invoke us.

4. To call for (a thing) with earnest entreaty; to make supplication for, to implore.

1617 MORYSON *Itin.* III. 156 Upon condition that my Inviter would be my protection from large drinking, which I was many times forced to invoke. **1773** HAN. MORE *Search Happ.* II. 136 Then let us, Power Supreme! thy will adore, Invoke thy mercies, and proclaim thy power. **1832** W. IRVING *Alhambra* I. 58 The spirits.. who nightly haunt the scene of their suffering, and invoke the vengeance of Heaven on their destroyer. **1865** GROTE *Plato* I. iii. 129 His advice was respectfully invoked.

5. *Admiralty Prize Procedure.* To call in evidence from a parallel case, or from the papers of a sister ship of the same owners, etc.

1802 SIR C. ROBINSON *Admiralty Rep.* IV. 167 Laurence .. objected that it was not admissible, according to the rules of evidence, to invoke depositions from other cases. **1817** WHEATON *Rep.* (U.S. Supreme Crt.) II. App. Note i. 23 Papers found on board another captured ship may be invoked into the cause.. but the authenticity of papers thus invoked must be verified by affidavit. **1828** WEBSTER s.v., To order, to call judicially; as to invoke depositions or evidence into a court.

Hence **in'voked** *ppl. a.*; **in'voking** *vbl. sb.* and *ppl. a.*

1611 FLORIO, *Inuocatione*, an inuoking or calling vpon for aide. **1631** MILTON *Epit. Marchioness Winchester* 19 The god that sits at marriage-feast; He at their invoking came. **1801** RANKEN *Hist. France* I. I. iii. 85 Afraid.. of the vengeance of these invoked tutelary saints. **1834** J. H. NEWMAN in *Lyra Apost.*, *Rest* (1849) 63 We may not stir the heaven of their repose By rude invoking voice.

invoker (ɪn'vəʊkə(r)). [-ER[1].] One who invokes.

a **1649** DRUMMOND OF HAWTH. *Skiamachia* Wks. (1711) 199 Ye are mass-mongers.. worshippers of images, invokers of the defunct saints. **1831** LYTTON *Godolphin* xxviii. (1877) 155 This image will be placed under the head of the invoker. **1865** M. ARNOLD *Ess. Crit.* v. (1875) 190 The invokers of reason against custom.

†**'involate**, *v. Obs. rare*$^{-0}$. [f. ppl. stem of L. *involāre* to fly into or upon, f. *in-* (IN-[2]) + *volāre* to fly.] *trans.* To fly into or upon.

1623 COCKERAM, *Inuolate*, to flie into some place.

involatile (ɪn'vɒlətaɪl), *a.* [IN-[3].]

†**1.** Not flying, wingless. *Obs.*

1659 D. PELL *Impr. Sea* 232 The Involatile creatures.. viz. Deer, Wolves, Beares, etc. which would, if winged.. bee gone.

2. Not volatile; incapable of being vaporized.

1869 TYNDALL in *Fortn. Rev.* 1 Feb. 231 One or more of the substances into which the waves of light break up compound molecules are comparatively involatile. **1962** SIMPSON & RICHARDS *Physical Princ. Junction Transistors* xii. 263 When wetted with an involatile (silicone) oil the mica may introduce a resistance of some 0·5°C/watt. **1965** PHILLIPS & WILLIAMS *Inorg. Chem.* I. xvii. 623 Many of the compounds of this section are very high-melting solids, while many others are relatively involatile solids or oils.

†**invo'lation.** *Obs. rare.* [n. of action from INVOLATE.] **a.** A flying into or upon. **b.** A seizing by or as by robbery, plunder.

1658 PHILLIPS, *Involation*, a flying into. *a* **1680** BUTLER *Rem.* (1759) I. 407 The Dr... adventured.. to invade it by Surreption and Involation.

†**in'voluble**, *a. Obs. rare.* [ad. late L. *involūbilis* (Ambrosius, *c* 375), f. *in-* (IN-[3]) + *volūbilis* able to be turned round, mutable, f. *volv-ĕre* to roll, turn round.]

1. That cannot turn or change; immutable.

1614 SYLVESTER *Lit. Bartas* I. 161 Even Thee, the Cause of Causes: Sourse of all,.. Infallible, involuble, insensible.

2. Incapable of being rolled up.

1654 HOBBES *Lib. & Nec.* Wks. 1840 IV. 234 Vast and involuble volumes concerning predestination [etc.].

involucel (ɪn'vɒljuːsɛl). *Bot.* Formerly **-ell**. [ad. mod.L. *involūcellum*, (also in Eng. use), dim. of INVOLUCRUM. Cf. F. *involucelle* (Littré).] A whorl of bracts surrounding one of the divisions in an inflorescence; a partial or secondary involucre.

α. in L. form **involucellum**.

1765 J. LEE *Introd. Bot.* Gloss., *Involucellum*, a partial Involucrum. **1776–96** WITHERING *Brit. Plants* (ed. 3) II. 449 Umbel with 5 spokes.. involucella egg-shaped. **1830** LINDLEY *Nat. Syst. Bot.* 76 Apetalous dicotyledons, with.. a calycine involucellum to the female or hermaphrodite flowers.

β. In Eng. form **involucel**.

1804 *Med. Jrnl.* XII. 368 Involucell, reaching half way round, three-leaved, bent downwards. **1806** GALPINE *Brit. Bot.* 145 Chærophyllum.. Involucells reflexed, concave. **1870** HOOKER *Stud. Flora* 183 Scabiosa.. calyx-tube contracted at the top, included in the tubular involucel.

involu'cellate, *a. Bot.* [ad. mod.L. *involūcellātus*: see INVOLUCEL and -ATE[2].] Furnished with involucels. So **involu'cellated** *a.*

1828 WEBSTER, *Involucellate*, surrounded with involucels. *Barton.* **1880** GRAY *Struct. Bot.* (ed. 6) 417/1.

involucral (ɪnvəʊ'l(j)uːkrəl), *a. Bot.* [f. L. *involūcr-um* INVOLUCRE + -AL[1]. So in mod.F.] Of or pertaining to an involucre.

1845 LINDLEY *Sch. Bot.* vi. (1858) 86 Outer involucral scales lanceolate. **1857** H. MILLER *Test. Rocks* xi. 480 The involucral appendages of the hazel-nut. **1872** OLIVER *Elem. Bot.* II. 187 The white involucral bracts of Dwarf Cornel.

involucrate (ɪnvəʊ'l(j)uːkrət), *a. Bot.* [ad. mod.L. *involūcrāt-us*, f. *involūcr-um*: see -ATE[2].] Furnished with an involucre. So **invo'lucrated** *a.*

1830 LINDLEY *Nat. Syst. Bot.* 35 Monadelphous stamens and involucrated flowers. **1847** CRAIG, *Involucrate*. **1870** HOOKER *Stud. Flora* 299 Flowers in involucrate umbels.

invo'lucrating, *ppl. a. Bot. rare.* [As if from a vb. *involucrate*: cf. *involucrated*.] Forming an involucre.

1830 LINDLEY *Nat. Syst. Bot.* 51 Flowers.. naked, or with large involucrating bracteæ.

involucre ('ɪnvəl(j)uːkə(r)). [a. F. *involucre* (1545 in Hatz.-Darm.), ad. L. *involūcrum*.]

1. That which envelops or enwraps; a case, covering, envelope; *spec.* in *Anat.*, a membranous envelope, as the pericardium.

1578 BANISTER *Hist. Man* I. 25 Pericardon (which is the Inuolucre of the hart). **1822–34** *Good's Study Med.* (ed. 4) I. 29 The involucres of the teeth are their gums, membranes, and sockets or alveoli.

fig. **1873** EARLE *Philol. Eng. Tongue* (ed. 2) §196 The verb is the central representative and focus of that predicative force.. which in the interjection is wrapped round and enfolded with an involucre of emotion. **1898** *Month* June 600 To distinguish the emotional substance of religion from its intellectual involucre.

2. *Bot.* A whorl or rosette of bracts surrounding an inflorescence, or at the base of an umbel.

Also **b.** In ferns, sometimes applied to the indusium. **c.** In liverworts, a sheath of tissue surrounding the female sexual organs. **d.** In fungi, the velum. ***partial involucre*** = INVOLUCEL. See also INVOLUCRUM 2.

1794 MARTYN *Rousseau's Bot.* v. 56 This set of small leaves or folioles is called the involucre. **1800** *Asiatic Ann. Reg.*, *Misc. Tr.* 165/1 Flowers.. in umbells.. Involucre many leaved, the leaves toothed. **1845** LINDLEY *Sch. Bot.* i. (1858) 11 When many bracts are collected in a whorl round several flowers they form an *involucre*. **1861** MISS PRATT *Flower. Pl.* VI. 146 The indusium.. in some few of our native species, as in the Filmy Ferns,.. is cup-shaped,.. it is then often called an *involucre*. **1875** BENNETT & DYER *Sachs' Bot.* 303 The surrounding tissue of the thallus divides repeatedly and grows into an involucre which is arched upwards and through which the elongating sporogonium afterwards pushes its way. *Ibid.* 306.

3. *Zool.* = INVOLUCRUM 3.

'involucred (-l(j)uːkəd), *a. rare.* [f. INVOLUCRE + -ED[2].] Furnished with an involucre; INVOLUCRATE.

1806 GALPINE *Brit. Bot.* 62 Cornus.. umb. axillary, peduncled, involucred. **1811** A. T. THOMSON *Lond. Disp.* (1818) 97 Cephaelis.. Flowers in an involucred head.

invo'lucret. *Bot. rare.* [-ET[1] diminutive.] = INVOLUCEL.

1796 MARTYN *Lang. Bot.* (ed. 2), *Involucellum*, an Involucret. A little or partial involucre. **1806** GALPINE *Brit. Bot.* 126 Involucrets as long as the flow[er] leafl[ets].

invo'lucriform, *a.* [ad. mod.L. *involūcriform-is*, f. *involūcr-um* INVOLUCRE: see -FORM.] Having the form of an involucre.

1851 T. MOORE *Brit. Ferns* (1864) 20 *Woodsia* = Dorsal-fruited Ferns, having the indusia involucriform, *i.e.*, attached beneath the sori, and divided at the margin into hair-like incurved segments. **1870** HOOKER *Stud. Flora* 10 Winter Aconite..Radical leaves palmate, cauline whorled and involucriform.

†**invo'lucrous,** *a. Obs. rare*$^{-1}$. [f. L. *involūcr-um* (see next) + -OUS.] Covered up, veiled.

1622 H. SYDENHAM *Serm. Sol. Occ.* II. (1637) 67 So involucrous and hidden are Gods eternall projects.

‖**involucrum** (ɪnvəʊ'l(j)uːkrəm). Pl. **-a**. [L., = wrapper, covering, envelope; f. *involvĕre* to enwrap, envelop, INVOLVE.]

1. Outer covering, envelope; covering membrane; = INVOLUCRE 1.

a **1677** HALE *Prim. Orig. Man.* IV. ii. 299 By this means the Earth was not at all conspicuous, but involved in an *involucrum* of Water. **1822–34** *Good's Study Med.* (ed. 4) IV. 186 Fragments of a fetus, which..have sometimes been surrounded by an adscititious involucrum. **1843** J. G. WILKINSON *Swedenborg's Anim. Kingd.* I. i. 18 The tongue is principally composed of small muscles, of nervous involucra or membranes, and of fat.

2. *Bot.* = INVOLUCRE 2.

1753 CHAMBERS *Cycl. Supp.* s.v., The Involucrum consists of a multitude of little leaves disposed in a radiated manner. **1776–96** WITHERING *Brit. Plants* (ed. 3) I. 11 When it surrounds the base of the Umbel, it is called the *general* Involucrum; but, when it surrounds the base of an Umbellule, or little Umbel, it is called the *partial* Involucrum, or Involucellum. **1859** DARWIN *Orig. Spec.* v. (1872) 116 These differences have sometimes been attributed to the pressure of the involucra on the florets.

3. *Zool.* A kind of sheath about the base of the thread-cells of acalephs.

1877 HUXLEY *Anat. Inv. Anim.* iii. 141 In this state it is invested by an *involucrum*, which surrounds its base.

involume, variant of ENVOLUME *v.*, *Obs.*

†**in'volument.** *Obs.* [ad. late L. *involūment-um* (Vulgate), wrapper, f. *involvĕre* to INVOLVE: see -MENT.] An envelope, covering.

1578 BANISTER *Hist. Man* VIII. 100 The hard Membran is both to the brayne an inuol[u]ment, as also an apt proppe. **1657** TOMLINSON *Renou's Disp.* 278 That same tenuious involument is Mace.

involuntarily (ɪn'vɒləntərɪlɪ), *adv.* [f. as next + -LY[2].] In an involuntary manner; without exercise or co-operation of the will.

1562 BULLEYN *Def. agst. Sickness, Bk. Sicke men* 81 a, If the paciente..wepe inuoluntarily without cause. **1665** T. MALL *Offer F. Help* 36 He that suffers involuntarily..shall neither have acceptance nor reward. **1852** G. WILSON *Life Reid* v. 93 We execute many movements involuntarily. **1860** MAURY *Phys. Geog. Sea* (Low) vi. §316, I was involuntarily led from one research to another.

in'voluntariness. [f. next + -NESS.] The quality of being involuntary.

1649 BP. HALL *Cases Consc.* vii. (1654) 56, I apprehend there is not an absolute involuntarinesse in this engagement but a mixt one. **1812** SHELLEY *Address* Pr. Wks. 1888 I. 260 The religious freedom which the involuntariness of faith ought to have taught all monopolists of Heaven long, long ago, that every one had a right to possess. **1875** JOWETT *Plato* (ed. 2) I. 344 The Socratic doctrine of the involuntariness of evil.

involuntary (ɪn'vɒləntərɪ), *a.* [ad. L. *involuntāri-us*, f. *in-* (IN-[3]) + *voluntārius* VOLUNTARY: cf. F. *involontaire* (14th c., Oresme).]

1. Not voluntary; done or happening without exercise or without co-operation of the will; not done willingly or by choice; independent of volition, unintentional.

1531 ELYOT *Gov.* III. i, Intermedlynge involuntary somtyme is priuely done, as stelynge, auoutry, poisonyng, false-hede..somtyme it is violent, as batry, open murdre and manslaughter. **1578** LYTE *Dodoens* IV. xlv. 505 Phoenix ..stoppeth..the inuoluntarie running of vrine. **1620** GRANGER *Div. Logike* 57 No pure involuntarie, or meere violent-compelled action is a sinne. **1751** JOHNSON *Rambler* No. 154. ⁋11 Sometimes unexpected flashes of instruction were struck out by..an involuntary concurrence of ideas. **1872** DARWIN *Emotions* i. 37 Another familiar instance of a reflex action is the involuntary closing of the eyelids when the surface of the eye is touched.

b. *Physiol.* Concerned in bodily actions or processes which are independent of the will.

1840 E. WILSON *Anat. Vade M.* (1842) 139 Muscles are divided into two great classes, voluntary and involuntary. **1887** *Syd. Soc. Lex.*, *I[nvoluntary] nerves*, the nerves which supply involuntary muscles.

2. Unwilling (†*to do* something).

1597 A. M. tr. *Guillemeau's Fr. Chirurg.* *iij, We shewe our selves involuntary to helpe the one the other. **1742** POPE *Dunc.* IV. 82 The gath'ring number, as it moves along, Involves a vast involuntary throng.

in-voluntary (*Music*): see VOLUNTARY *sb.*

in,volunto-'motory, *a. Physiol.* [f. INVOLUNTARY + MOTORY: cf. *volunto-motory*.] Pertaining to or characterized by involuntary motion; *spec.* applied, after Remak, to the inner division of the mesoblast, otherwise called the splanchnopleure.

1878 ALLEN THOMSON in *Encycl. Brit.* VIII. 167/2 The inner division, the involunto-motory, corresponding to the visceral wall or splanchno-pleure.

involup, obs. form of ENVELOPE *v.*

involutant (ɪnvə'l(j)uːtənt). *Math.* [f. L. *involūt-*, ppl. stem of *involvĕre* to INVOLVE + -ANT: see INVOLUTION 6 a, and cf. *determinant*, etc.] (See quot.)

1890 TABER in *Proc. Lond. Math. Soc.* XXII. 73 The involutant of m, n, two matrices of order ω, is the resultant of the ω^2 scalar equations obtained by equating to zero a linear function with scalar coefficients of the ω^2 matrices which result from multiplying $1, m, m^2, \ldots m^{\omega-1}$ into $1, n, n^2, \ldots n^{\omega-1}$.

involute ('ɪnvəl(j)uːt), *a.* and *sb.* [ad. L. *involūt-us, -um*, pa. pple. of *involvĕre* to roll in or up, INVOLVE.]

A. *adj.* **1.** Involved; entangled; intricate; †hidden, obscure (*obs.*).

1669 GALE *Crt. Gentiles* I. III. x. 101 They import an involute Speech or obscure question. **1690** NORRIS *Beatitudes* (1692) 10 Earthly-mindedness..was really forbidden according to the more retired and involute Sense of the Law. **1837** CARLYLE *Diam. Neckl.* xvi. in *Misc. Ess.* (1872) V. 190 This most involute of Lies is finally winded off. *a* **1849** POE *Murders in Rue Morgue* Wks. 1865 I. 179 ⁋2 The possible moves [in chess] being not only manifold, but involute, the chances of such oversight are multiplied. **1889** *Longm. Mag.* Oct. 590 We all know good novels which are complex, involute, tortuous.

2. Rolled or curled up spirally; spiral; *spec.* in *Conch.* Having the whorls wound closely round the axis, and nearly or wholly concealing it.

1661 LOVELL *Hist. Anim. & Min.* Introd., III. Fishes, which are, I. Marine..or testaceous, and are turbinate, which are either involute, as the Nautilus..or orbicular, as the Welke. **1828** STARK *Elem. Nat. Hist.* II. 62 Bulla..body behind covered by an external oval involute shell. **1851–6** WOODWARD *Mollusca* 77 Shell placed vertically in the posterior part of the body, with the involute spire towards the ventral side. **1856–8** W. CLARK *Van der Hoeven's Zool.* I. 389 Mouth with involute spiral tongue, composed of protracted maxillæ.

3. *Bot.* Rolled inwards at the edges.

1760 J. LEE *Introd. Bot.* III. xvi. (1765) 206 *Involute*, rowled in; when their lateral Margins are rowled spirally inwards on both sides. **1806** GALPINE *Brit. Bot.* 40 L[eaves] involute, pungent. **1830** LINDLEY *Nat. Syst. Bot.* 144 Entire petals involute in æstivation. **1880** GRAY *Struct. Bot.* iv. §2. 133 Leaves are as to the mode of packing..Involute, both margins rolled toward the midrib on the upper face.

4. *Geom.* †*involute figure* or *curve*: = B. 2. *Obs.* Of a tooth in a cog-wheel: Having its working face in the form of an involute.

1706 PHILLIPS, *Involute* and *Evolute Figures.* **1796** HUTTON *Math. Dict.* I. 642/2 *Involute Figure* or *Curve*, is that which is traced out by the outer extremity of a string as it is folded or wrapped upon another figure, or as it is unwound from off it. **1884** F. J. BRITTEN *Watch & Clockm.* 125 Wheels with involute teeth..are now rarely used.

B. *sb.* **1.** Something involved or entangled. *rare.*

1845 DE QUINCEY *Susp. de Prof.* I. Wks. 1863 XIV. 13 Far more of our deepest feelings..pass to us as *involutes* (if I may coin that word) in compound experiences incapable of being disentangled, than ever reach us directly. **1850** —— *Ibid.* 121 One of those many important cases which elsewhere I have called involutes of human sensibility.

2. *Geom.* A curve such as would be traced out by the end of a flexible inextensible string if unwrapped (being still kept stretched) from a given curve in the plane of that curve; the locus of a point in a straight line which rolls without sliding on a given curve. Correlative to EVOLUTE.

1796 HUTTON *Math. Dict.* I. 642/2 The Involute of a cycloid, is also a cycloid equal to the former. **1879** THOMSON & TAIT *Nat. Phil.* I. I. §17 If a flexible and inextensible string be fixed at one point of a plane curve, and stretched along the curve, and be then unwound in the plane of the curve, its extremity will describe an Involute of the curve. **1881** ROUTLEDGE *Science* ii. 44 Apollonius treated also of involutes and evolutes. *Ibid.* ix. 208 Huyghens..discovered another curious property of the cycloid, and introduced a new idea into geometry, namely, that of the involutes.

Hence **'involutely** *adv.*, in an involved manner.

1681 H. MORE *Exp. Dan.* VI. 226 The sense is very coherent with what follows..which contains though something involutely and contractedly both the first and second Resurrection.

involute ('ɪnvəl(j)uːt), *v.* [Back-formation from INVOLUTED *a.*] *intr.* **a.** 'To return to a normal condition' (*Cent. Dict.* Suppl.). **b.** To undergo involution (sense 4). Hence **'involuting** *ppl. a.*

1904 *Buck's Handbk. Med. Sci.* (rev. ed.) VII. 782/2 A circular scaly pink patch that spreads peripherally with a pinkish border, and clears up or involutes in the central portion. **1910** *Practitioner* July 106 The uterus had involuted normally. **1968** *Amer. Jrnl. Obstetr. & Gynecol.* CII. 33/1 Deeper arteries and veins contract and are compressed from without by the involuting muscle mass of the uterus. **1971** *Jrnl. Insect Physiol.* XVII. 857 These..glands reach the peak of their metabolic and synthetic activity shortly before rapidly involuting, leaving only a small remnant.

involuted ('ɪnvəl(j)uːtɪd), *a.* [f. INVOLUTE *a.* and *sb.* + -ED[1].]

1. a. = INVOLUTE *a.* 2, 3.

1816 KIRBY & SP. *Entomol.* (1818) II. 327 A Brazilian beetle in my cabinet..has curious involuted suckers on its feet. **1848** CARPENTER *Anim. Phys.* 37 Where it is to absorb as well as to secrete, it is usually involuted or folded upon itself. **1851–6** WOODWARD *Mollusca* 66 A symmetrical involuted shell. **1875** DARWIN *Insectiv. Pl.* xvi. 392 The leaves catch many small insects which are found chiefly beneath the involuted margins.

b. *fig.*

a **1910** 'MARK TWAIN' *Speeches* (1910) 290 Whatever moral..you put into a speech,..gets diffused among those involuted sentences. **1972** *Times Lit. Suppl.* 22 Dec. 1552/1 Clothed in orthodoxy, that could be no more than an involuted way of saying that God is love.

2. *Phys.* That has passed through the process of involution: see INVOLUTION 4.

1898 G. E. HERMAN *Dis. Wom.* ix. 94 A uterus which is imperfectly involuted receives more blood than it should.

Hence **invo'lutedly** *adv.*, in an involuted or entangled manner.

1879 G. MEREDITH *Egoist* I. ix. 163 Curls, half curls, root curls, vine ringlets, wedding rings..waved or fell, waved over or up or involutedly, or strayed loose and downward.

'involuting, *vbl. sb. rare*$^{-1}$. [as if from a vb. **involute* (f. ppl. stem of L. *involvĕre* to INVOLVE) + -ING[1]. Cf. CONVOLUTE *v.*] Involving.

1884 *Brit. & For. Evang. Rev.* Oct. 682 He has taken liberties with his native language in the involuting and coining of words.

involution (ɪnvə'l(j)uːʃən). [ad. L. *involūtiōn-em*, n. of action from *involvĕre* to INVOLVE: cf. F. *involution* (13–14th c. in Hatz.-Darm.).]

1. a. The action of involving or fact of being involved; implicit comprehension or inclusion; implication; also, quasi-*concr.*, that which is involved.

1611 COTGR., *Involution*, an inuolution, enwrapping, infoulding. **1642** JER. TAYLOR *Episc.* (1647) 136 Often..a Bishop nay an Apostle is called a Presbyter..by reason of the involution or comprehension of Presbyter within Episcopus. **1790** GIBBON *Misc. Wks.* (1814) III. 489 According to the philosophers, who can discern an endless involution of germs or organized bodies, the future animal exists in the female parent. **1798** COLERIDGE *Satyrane's Lett.* ii. 223 Aristotle has..required of the poet an involution of the universal in the individual. **1867** STUBBS *Lect. Hist.* (1886) 17 From his own involution in the matter of which he is to judge. **1892** NEWMAN SMYTH *Chr. Ethics* II. iii. 420 The instinct to discover the deeper moral involutions of current political questions is a power of great ethical value.

b. *concr.* Something that involves or enwraps; an envelope, covering, etc.

1646 SIR T. BROWNE *Pseud. Ep.* v. xxi. 269 The involution or membranous covering..called the silly how, that sometimes is found about the heads of children upon their birth.

2. An involved or entangled condition; entanglement, complication; intricacy of construction or style (as in a literary work or the arrangement of words in a sentence); also *concr.*, something complicated; an intricate movement, a tangle, etc.

1611 COTGR., *Anfractueux*, full of turnings, compasses, involutions. **1647** MAY *Hist. Parl.* I. i. 73 All their acts and actions are so full of mixtures, involutions, and complications. **1751** JOHNSON *Rambler* No. 168 ⁋7 Mackbeth proceeds to wish..that he may, in the involutions of infernal darkness, escape the eye of providence. *a* **1763** SHENSTONE *Economy* III. 33 Such the clue Of Cretan Ariadne ne'er explain'd! Hooks! angles! crooks! and involutions wild! **1820** HAZLITT *Lect. Dram. Lit.* 156 The style of the first act has..more involution, than the general style of Fletcher. **1837–9** HALLAM *Hist. Lit.* I. I. viii. §24. 433 He introduced..a sort of involution into his style, which gives an air of dignity and remoteness from common life. **1858** G. MACDONALD *Phantastes* xiv, The whole place..swam with the involutions of an intricate dance.

3. *Anat.* A rolling, curling, or turning inwards; *concr.* a part of a structure formed by this action.

1851 CARPENTER *Man. Phys.* (ed. 2) 494 A cavity..which is subsequently rendered more complex by the prolongation and involution of its walls in various parts. **1870** ROLLESTON *Anim. Life* Introd. 36 The peripheral apparatus retains its typical character as an involution of the integument in the olfactory..organs. **1873** MIVART *Elem. Anat.* ix. 392 The ear like the eye is formed by an involution of the skin. **1880** —— *Cat* 230 Glands..are..complex involutions of an epithelial surface.

4. *Phys.* 'The retrograde change which occurs in the body in old age, or in some organ when its permanent or temporary purpose has been fulfilled' (*Syd. Soc. Lex.*). Also *attrib.*

1860 TANNER *Pregnancy* ii. 93 The whole process of degeneration and reconstruction is spoken of as the involution of the uterus. **1878** GAMGEE tr. *Hermann's Hum. Phys.* 530 The close of the period of fecundity and the arrest of menstruation are associated with certain bodily changes, especially of the generative apparatus, which are comprehended in the term 'involution'. **1887** *Syd. Soc. Lex.*, *Senile Involution*, the shrinking of the whole body which accompanies old age. *Ibid.*, *Involution cysts*, the cysts found in the shrivelled mammary glands of old women, being dilated acini or ducts of the gland filled with a thick fluid. **1898** G. E. HERMAN *Dis. Wom.* ix. 87 During the last few days of pregnancy, and the first few days of involution, giant cells with many nuclei are to be seen.

5. *Biol.* A retrograde process of development; the opposite of evolution; degeneration. Chiefly in *Comb.*, as ***involution-form.***

1896 *Allbutt's Syst. Med.* I. 761 Involution forms [of bacilli] being pretty constantly developed. **1897** *Ibid.* II. 90 Evidence that the clubs are involution-forms.

6. *Math.* **a.** *Arith.* and *Alg.* The multiplication of a quantity into itself any number of times, so as to raise it to any assigned power. Hence, in extended sense, the raising of a quantity to any power, positive, negative, fractional, or imaginary.

1706 W. JONES *Syn. Palmar. Matheseos* 51 By the Involution of the Binomial Root. **1806** HUTTON *Course Math.* I. 197 Involution is the raising of powers from any proposed root; or the method of finding the square, cube, biquadrate, &c., of any given quantity.

b. *Geom.* A system of pairs of points on a right line, so situated that the product of the distances of the two points of each pair from a certain fixed point on the line (the ***centre of involution***) is equal to a constant quantity. Hence in various extended uses (see quot. 1847).

[**1837** CHASLES *Aperçu Hist.* 77 Desargues appelait la rélation qui constitue son beau théorème *involution de six points.*] **1847** CAYLEY in *Camb. & Dubl. Math. Jrnl.* II. 52 When three conics have the same points of intersection, any transversal intersects the system in six points, which are said to be in involution. It appears natural to apply the term to the conics themselves; and then it is easy to generalize the notion of involution so as to apply it to functions of any number of variables. **1879** SALMON *Conics* 311. **1885** LEUDESDORF tr. *Cremona's Proj. Geom.* 101 In an involution the elements are conjugate to one another in pairs.

c. A function or transformation that is equal to its inverse.

1916 E. KASNER in *Amer. Jrnl. Math.* XXXVIII. 177 It is easy to determine all regular transformations of period 2. In the direct type $Z = f(z)$ the functional equation is $f(f(z)) \equiv z$, that is, $f^2 = 1$; in the reverse type $Z = \bar{f}(z_0)$ the functional equation is $f(f_0(z)) \equiv z$, that is, $ff_0 = 1$, where f_0 denotes the series whose coefficients are the conjugates of the coefficients of series f. We shall call a transformation of the former type (excluding the identical transformation) a conformal involution, and one of the latter type a conformal symmetry. **1969** F. M. HALL *Introd. Abstr. Algebra* II. ii. 31 If θ is a 1-1 correspondence between elements of A and itself such that $\theta = \theta^{-1}$, then θ is said to be an involution.

involutional (ɪnvəˈl(j)uːʃənəl), *a. Psychol.* [f. INVOLUTION + -AL.] Of or pertaining to the bodily change of involution (sense 4), or to mental disturbances associated with this change.

1910 *Rev. Neurol. & Psychiatry* VIII. 8, I refer to the work of Dreyfus, who, after reviewing Kraepelin's own cases of involutional melancholia, concludes that the involutional depression is a mixed form of manic-depressive insanity. **1934** P. BOTTOME *Private Worlds* 111 It's not an ordinary melancholic case. She hasn't had any attacks before; and it is not involutional; she is only thirty. **1945** E. DAVIDOFF in O. J. Kaplan *Mental Disorders Later Life* viii. 189 There may be a qualitative as well as a quantitative difference between the nonpsychotic involutional syndrome and the involutional psychosis. **1950** J. ZINKIN tr. *Bleuler's Dementia Praecox* II. 242 Kraepelin was the first to draw attention to the high incidence of cases who develop an apparently common melancholia during the involutional period. **1965** FOULDS & CAINE *Personality & Personal Illness* II. iv. 67 We do not have much difficulty in understanding what is meant by an involutional melancholia with obsessional features. **1968** *Amer. Jrnl. Obstetr. & Gynecol.* CII. 29/1 Pronounced involutional atrophy occurred in the ..myometrium at 7 weeks post partum. **1969** *Biochem. Jrnl.* CXII. 641/1 Oestradiol might not have a differential effect on two separate involutionary processes, but might just decrease the water content of the treated uteri.

involutionary (ɪnvəˈl(j)uːʃənərɪ), *a.* [f. INVOLUTION + -ARY[1].] Characterized by involution; retrograde.

1920 *Discovery* Nov. 338/2 Our conceptions of psychical ..'regression'.., the backward or involutionary path of mental processes to more infantile conditions. **1942** *Mind* LI. 146 The infinite series of causes to which *Ethices I, xxviii* [of Spinoza] refers is not a temporal regress to an impossible 'first' cause, but the involutionary sequence of eternal causes to a necessary First Cause.

ˈinvolutive, *a. Bot.* [ad. mod.L. *involūtīv-us*, f. *involūt-*, ppl. stem of *involvĕre* to INVOLVE: see -IVE, and cf. F. *involutif* (1798 in Hatz.-Darm.).] Characterized by involution; see INVOLUTE *a.* 3.

1855 MAYNE *Expos. Lex, Involutivus*, applied by Candolle to estivation in which the floral organs are rolled inwards;.. to perfoliation where the two bodies of a leaf contained in the bud roll themselves from without inwards:..involutive.

involutorial (ɪnvɒl(j)uːˈtɔərɪəl), *a. Geom.* [f. It. *involutorio*, L. type **involūtōri-us* (f. *involvĕre*, *involūt-*: see -ORY) + -AL[1]. Cf. med.L. *involūtōrium* a wrapper, cover (Du Cange).] Of or pertaining to geometrical involution; connecting a system of objects in pairs.

involutorial homology, a homology whose parameter is −1.

1885 LEUDESDORF *Cremona's Proj. Geom.* 64 In this case the homology is called *harmonic* or *involutorial*, and two corresponding points (or lines) correspond to one another doubly; that is to say, every point (or line) has the same correspondent whether it be regarded as belonging to the first or the second figure.

involutory (ɪnvəˈl(j)uːtərɪ), *a. Math.* [f. L. type **involūtōri-us*: see INVOLUTORIAL *a.* and -ORY[2].] That is an involution (sense 6 c).

1941 BIRKHOFF & MACLANE *Survey Mod. Algebra* viii. 203 The correspondence $A \leftrightarrow A'$ therefore preserves sums and inverts the order of products, so is sometimes called an anti-automorphism. Since $(A')' = A$, this anti-automorphism is called 'involutory'. **1971** J. H. CONWAY in Powell & Higman *Finite Simple Groups* vii. 217 The p objects permuted by $L_2(p)$..can in each case be taken as p involutory permutations of the set Ω. **1972** F. J. BUDDEN *Fascination of Groups* viii. 81, 2-groups always arise as subgroups of larger groups whenever there is an 'involutory' element present, that is, an element whose square is equal to the identity.

involve (ɪnˈvɒlv), *v.* Also 4–8 **en-**. [ad. L. *involvĕre* to roll into or upon, to wrap up, envelop, surround, entangle, make obscure, f. *in-* (IN-[2]) + *volvĕre* to roll. Cf. OF. *involver* (1464 in Godef.).] To enfold, envelop, entangle, include: predicated either of an agent or of a surrounding or enveloping substance or material.

1. *trans.* To roll or enwrap in anything that is wound round, or surrounds as a case or covering; to enfold, to envelop. Const. *in*, †*with.*

1482 *Monk of Evesham* (Arb.) 37 Anone fro benethe..ther brake vppe a flame of fier that inuoluyd hem. **1526** *Pilgr. Perf.* (W. de W. 1531) 259 The corporas..wherin his blessed body was inuolued or wrapped. **1553** EDEN *Treat. Newe Ind.* (Arb.) 27 Inuoluinge with cereclothe, & pouderinge with spyces the body. **1650** BULWER *Anthropomet.* i. 1 The Heads of Infants..are involved in head-bands. *a* **1677** HALE *Prim. Orig. Man.* I. ii. 63 They lye more torpid, and inactive, and inevident,..like a spark involved in ashes. **1774** GOLDSM. *Nat. Hist.* (1862) I. 159 Within this the embryo is still farther involved, in two membranes called the *chorion* and *amnios*. **1856** MRS. BROWNING *Aur. Leigh* III. 179, I saw Fog only, the great tawny weltering fog, Involve the passive city.

fig. **1387–8** T. USK *Test. Love* I. ii. (Skeat) l. 56 Tho I was in prosperitie, and with forain goodes enuolued. *a* **1420** HOCCLEVE *De Reg. Princ.* 2657 A cursed caitif Inuolued and y-wrapped in þe vice Of couetise. **1651** C. CARTWRIGHT *Cert. Relig.* I. 205 What sentence we should all have, if God ..had not involved and wrapped us in his righteousnesse. **1896** SIR W. HARCOURT *Sp. Ho. Comm.* 29 July, The hon. member made a speech last night in which he proceeded to involve himself in his own virtue. [Cf. HORACE *Od.* III. xxix. 55 *Mea virtute me involvo.*]

2. To wind in a spiral form, or in a series of curves, coils, or folds; to wreathe, coil, entwine.

1555 EDEN *Decades* 26 Rouling them togyther on a cyrcle inuolued after the maner of a slepyng snake. **1597** A. M. tr. *Guillemeau's Fr. Chirurg.* xvi b/1 The threde which is involvde rounde about the Needle. **1602** MARSTON *Antonio's Rev.* IV. v, Let's thus our hands, our hearts, our armes involve. **1667** MILTON *P.L.* VII. 483 Some of Serpent kinde, ..involv'd Thir Snakie foulds. **1818** SHELLEY *Rev. Islam* III. xxiii, Like a choir of devils, Around me they involved a giddy dance.

b. *fig.* To join as by winding together or intertwining; to 'wrap up' *with.*

1651 BAXTER *Inf. Bapt.* 254 You will needs involve your own esteem with the credit of your ill cause. **1667** MILTON *P.L.* II. 806 He knows His end with mine involved. **1768** STERNE *Sent. Journ.* (1778) II. 146 (*Fragment*) Our misfortunes were involved together. **1852** H. ROGERS *Ecl. Faith* (1853) 108 Whether faith can ever exist independently of belief,—whether it is not always involved with it,..that is the point on which I want light.

3. *fig.* To envelop within the folds of some condition or circumstance; to environ, esp. so as to obscure or embarrass; to beset with difficulty or obscurity. Const. *in*, †*with.*

1382 WYCLIF *Pref. Ep. Jerome* vii. 71 The thrid hath bigynnyngis and ende with so feel derknessis enuolued. **1531** ELYOT *Gov.* I. xiv, That reuerende studie is inuolued in so barbarouse a langage,..no man understandyng it but they whiche haue studyed the lawes. **1598** MARSTON *Pygmal.* II. 142 That such Cymerian darknes should inuolue A quaint conceit. **1635** PAGITT *Christianogr.* I. iii. (1636) 92 This doctrine..is involved with absurdities, and inexplicable contradictions. **1790** PALEY *Horæ Paul.* Wks. 1825 III. 207 This passage is involved in great obscurity. **1875** JOWETT *Plato* (ed. 2) III. 391 The numerous difficulties in which this question is involved.

b. To entangle (a matter), to render intricate.

1533 MORE *Debell. Salem* Wks. 1004/2 As wililye as those shrewes that beguyle hym haue holpe hym to inuolue and intryke the matter. **1627** HAKEWILL *Apol.* (1635) 541 Rather ..to dispatch the busines with judgement, then to inuolue it with nice distinctions. *Mod.* We must not further involve the statement; it is intricate enough already.

4. To envelop or (in later use, more usually) entangle (a person) in trouble, difficulties, perplexity, etc.; to embarrass; to engage in circumstances from which it is difficult to withdraw. Const. *in*, †*with*, †*into.*

1387–8 T. USK *Test. Love* I. i. (Skeat) l. 111 These thynges ..haue me so enuolued with care, that wanhope of helpe is throughout me ronne. *c* **1440** *Gesta Rom.* (1838) II. i. 276 His conscience..involves hym in grete sorowes and diseases of hert, for his synne. **1665** SIR T. HERBERT *Trav.* (1677) 321 Involved with more perplexity now than ever, he was at his wits end. **1704** *Lond. Gaz.* No. 4058/5 The Differences wherein he finds himself..involved with the Emperor. **1716** ATTERBURY *Let. to Swift* 6 Apr., Involving me designedly into those squabbles. **1828** D'ISRAELI *Chas. I*, I. xi. 300 The war in which Charles was now involved..was of the most popular character. **1839** YEOWELL *Anc. Brit. Ch.* x. (1847) 104 Their misconduct soon involved both kings and people in one common ruin. **1875** JOWETT *Plato* (ed. 2) I. 282 You imagine that you will involve me in a contradiction. **1898** A. W. W. DALE *Life R.W. Dale* ii. 35 Mr. Müller had been involved in financial difficulties.

5. To implicate in a charge or crime; to cause or prove (a person) to be concerned in it.

1655 SIR E. NICHOLAS in *N. Papers* (Camden) II. 255 Hee [the King] passed fower arrests, which inuolued diuers to the great dissatisfaction of many Presidents. **1660** R. COKE *Justice Vind.* 16 That the King may be involved in the same crime with themselves, he [Strafford] must die by Act of Parliament. **1695** BLACKMORE *Pr. Arth.* I. 287 Let not my Crime involve the Innocent. **1838** THIRLWALL *Greece* III. 391 It was the interest of the enemies of Alcibiades..to involve as many persons as they could in the charge. **1885** *Dict. Nat. Biog.* III. 213/2 He was soon induced..to make confessions which seriously involved the duke.

6. *trans.* To include; to contain, imply. †**a.** Of a person, or with reference to personal action: To include covertly *in* or *under* something; to wrap up. Also in indirect passive. *Obs.*

1605 BACON *Adv. Learn.* II. iv. §4 When the secrets and mysteries of religion..are involved in fables or parables. **1646** SIR T. BROWNE *Pseud. Ep.* III. xii. 132 Some have written Mystically, as Paracelsus,..involving therein the secret of their Elixir, and enigmatically expressing the nature of their great worke. **1710** BERKELEY *Princ. Hum. Knowl.* §119 They have dreamed of mighty mysteries involved in numbers. **1724** A. COLLINS *Gr. Chr. Relig.* 85 The antient Greek Poets were reputed to involve divine, and natural..notions of their gods under mystical and parabolical expressions.

b. Of a thing: To include within its folds or ramifications; to contain, comprise, comprehend. Now chiefly *Math.*, or passing into c.

1651 C. CARTWRIGHT *Cert. Relig.* I. 15 The Church of England involves all the Brittains within her Communion. **1799** WILSON in *Phil. Trans.* LXXXIX. 298 It involves.. not a cube, but a truncate sixth power in a cubic shape. **1811** I. M. WILLIAMS (*title*) The Dramatic Censor..involving a correct register of every night's Performances at our Metropolitan Theatres. **1875** TODHUNTER *Algebra* (ed. 7) xix. §299 Any equation which involves rational quantities and quadratic surds.

c. *esp.* To contain implicitly; to include as a necessary (and therefore unexpressed) feature, circumstance, antecedent condition, or consequence; to imply, entail.

1646 SIR T. BROWNE *Pseud. Ep.* V. xxi. 267 Wherein (although most know not what they say) there are involved unknowne considerations. **1651** HOBBES *Leviath.* III. xl. 249 Their wills..were before the Contract involved in the will of Abraham. **1809–10** COLERIDGE *Friend* (1865) 23 In moral truth, we involve likewise the intention of the speaker, that his words should correspond to his thoughts in the sense in which he expects them to be understood. **1839** THIRLWALL *Greece* xlv. VI. 43 The submission of Byzantium would probably involve that of Perinthus. **1855** LYNCH *Rivulet* XC. i, Some new task Involving care and strife. **1892** WESTCOTT *Gospel of Life* p. xviii, Every argument involves some assumptions.

d. To include or affect in its operation.

1847 MRS. A. KERR *Hist. Servia* 4 To promote those general ideas which involve the destiny of the human race. **1857** RUSKIN *Pol. Econ. Art* 6 It will be held a worthy subject of consideration what are the political interests involved in such accumulation. *a* **1885** U. S. GRANT *Pers. Mem.* II. 531 Men who..could not be induced to serve as soldiers, except in an emergency, when the safety of the nation was involved.

7. To roll up within itself, to envelop and take in; to overwhelm and swallow up.

1605 BACON *Adv. Learn.* I. i. §3, I learned, that the same mortality involveth them both. **1649** JER. TAYLOR *Gt. Exemp.* Disc. xv. §27 They..were all involved and swallowed up into the body of the sun of righteousness. **1727–46** THOMSON *Summer* 1022 The stormy fates descend: one death involves Tyrants and slaves. **1742** POPE *Dunc.* IV. 82 The gathering number, as it moves along, Involves a vast involuntary throng. **1850** TENNYSON *In Mem.* cxxx, My love involves the love before; My love is vaster passion now.

8. *Math.* To multiply (a quantity) into itself any desired number of times; to raise to a power. Now *rare* or *Obs.*

1673 KERSEY *Algebra* 3 These numbers..are usually called the Indices, or Exponents of those Powers..because they shew..how many times the Root is involved or multiplyed in producing each Power respectively. **1706** W. JONES *Syn. Palmar. Matheseos* 46. **1811** HUTTON *Course Math.* (ed. 6) I. 191 Let $a + x$ be involved to the 5th power. **1875** TODHUNTER *Algebra* (ed. 7) xvi. §222 If the quantity which is to be involved be a fraction, both its numerator and its denominator must be raised to the proposed power.

†**9.** To turn over in the mind; to revolve. *rare.*

c **1470** HARDING *Chron.* LXXV. ii, The kyng..in his mynde ymagened and inuolued Howe sone and when..They might agayn bee consociate.

Hence **inˈvolving** *vbl. sb.* and *ppl. a.*; also **inˈvolver**, one who or that which involves.

1611 FLORIO, *Inuoglia*, an enuoluing. **1660** BOYLE *New Exp. Phys. Mech.* Digress. 374 The upper part of the involving Amnios. **1738** GLOVER *Leonidas* II. 172 Rapid torrents of involving flames. ?*c* **1860** L. OLIPHANT in *Athenæum* (1891) 23 May 659/3 The hand that has used a revolver..does not waver with a pen, though the lines he traces may be an involver of a revolver again. **1880** *Mem. John Legge* vii. 84 A seemingly needless involving of the truth.

involved (ɪnˈvɒlvd), *ppl. a.* [f. prec. + -ED[1].]

1. *lit.* **a.** Curved spirally. **b.** Enfolded, enwrapped.

c **1611** CHAPMAN *Iliad* II. 179 His sandie confines; whose sides, grone with his inuolued waue. **1665** G. HAVERS *P. della Valle's Trav. E. India* 52 Their Beards and Hair they wear long, untrim'd, rudely involv'd. **1897** *Allbutt's Syst. Med.* III. 809 An engorgement of the involved bowel.

†**2.** Of persons, their actions, etc. Not straightforward and open; underhand, covert, crooked, reserved. *Obs.*

1607–12 BACON *Ess.*, *Counsel* (Arb.) 322 There be men that are in nature faithfull, and sincere and plaine, and direct, not craftye, and involved. **1640** HABINGTON *Castara* III. (Arb.) 118 All th' involv'd designements of the wise. **1713** STEELE *Guardian* No. 44 ¶4 They are very sullen and involved.

3. Intricate, complicated. **b.** Contained by implication, implicit.

1643 SIR T. BROWNE *Relig. Med.* I. §9 To pose my apprehension with those involved Ænigmas and riddles of the Trinity. **1791** BOSWELL *Johnson* an. 1750, The style of this work [Rambler] has been censured by some shallow criticks as involved and turgid. **1839** YEOWELL *Anc. Brit. Ch.* ii. (1847) 21 The involved language of Gildas..has led to much misapprehension of his meaning. **1864** BOWEN *Logic* ii. 40 These Laws of Thought exist there in a latent or involved form.

Hence **in'volvedly** *adv.*, in a way that is involved implicitly; **in'volvedness**, the fact, state, or quality of being involved.

1624 F. WHITE *Repl. Fisher* 33 Doctrine neither expresly nor inuoluedly contained in holy Scripture. **1647** BOYLE *Disc. Swearing* i. §1 The involvedness of all men in the guilt of swearing. **1654** W. MOUNTAGUE *Devout Ess.* II. x. §1. 193 How shall the mind of man..extricate itself, out of this comprisure and involvedness in the bodies passions and infirmities? **1840** G. S. FABER *Regeneration* I. ii. 28 A moral change of disposition; and thence, subordinately and involvedly, a federal change of relative condition. **1867** *Pall Mall G.* 30 Jan. 4 The Indian Statute-book..bids fair to emulate our own in confusion, bulk, and involvedness.

involvement (ɪn'vɒlvmənt). [f. as prec. + -MENT.]

1. The action or process of involving; the fact of being involved; the condition of being implicated, entangled, or engaged; engagement, embarrassment; financial or pecuniary embarrassment.

1706 A. SHIELDS *Inq. Ch. Comm.* (1747) 46 There is no involvement either in personal guilt or accession to the guilt of others. **1776** T. HUTCHINSON *Diary* July II. 80 With frugality [it] would enable me to spend a few weeks abroad without involvement [i.e. in debt]. **1802** G. COLMAN *Poor Gentleman* v. ii. 74 He has left me in involvements, which, in a few hours, may inclose me in a prison. **1855** LYNCH *Lett. to Scattered* vii. 94 How the innocent suffer with the evil, by necessary involvement. **1875** H. C. WOOD *Therap.* (1879) 676 There are certain palsies..in which the muscular structure is..destroyed independently of any involvement of the nervous system.

b. An involved or entangled condition, manner, or style; complicated state of affairs, imbroglio.

1821 FOSTER in *Life & Corr.* (1846) II. 35 Further complaints of obscurity, involvement [etc.]. **1862** *Fraser's Mag.* July 63 The plot..depended..on the 'involvement' consequent on the fact that every one except her grandmother is in love with the gentle and lovely Celeste. **1883** *Gd. Words* Dec. 791/2 Evil and good..are interlaced together in seemingly hopeless involvement. **1884** WEDMORE in *Academy* 9 Feb. 100 He sets forth his discovery, not with style..but crabbedly, with involvement.

†**2.** An enveloping structure; a wrapping; an envelope, case, or covering. *Obs.*

1630 H. R. *Mythomystes* 30 Orpheus, within the foulds and inuoluements of fables, hid the misteries of his doctrine. *Ibid.* 80 Among such may they euer rest, safe wrapt up in their huskes and inuoluements.

3. That which is involved or implied in something; a necessary consequence or condition.

1879 'E. GARRETT' (Mrs. Mayo) *Ho. by Wks.* I. 110 She will presently see the curious involvements and necessities of English society. **1881** FRASER *Berkeley* 210 The issue of creative will, rather than necessary involvements of finite experience.

in'volvent, *a.* and *sb.* [ad. L. *involvent-em*, pr. pple. of *involvĕre* to INVOLVE.] **A.** *adj.* Involving. *rare*$^{-0}$. **B.** *sb.* That which involves.

1656 BLOUNT *Glossogr.*, *Involvent*, wrapping or folding in, covering or overwhelming. *a***1834** COLERIDGE *Lit. Rem.* (1839) IV. 227 The one substrative truth which is the form, manner, and involvent of all truths.

involver, involving: see under INVOLVE *v.*

†**'invoy.** *Obs.* [Variant of ENVOY, a. OF. *envoy*, now *envoi*, sending, dispatch of goods, f. *envoyer* to send. App. the word of which the plural remains as INVOICE; cf. F. *lettre d'envoi* letter of consignment, invoice.] An INVOICE.

1617 MORYSON *Itin.* II. III. i. 242 That doth alwaies appeare vnto vs vpon the certificates of the Inuoyes. *Ibid.* 243 If your Lordship will bee as strict to call for the certificates of the vnlading there, as wee do cause the Invoy to be perused there can be no abuse in that case.

†**in'vulgar,** *a. Obs.* [IN-³.] Not vulgar. **a.** Free from vulgarity; not of low rank; refined. **b.** Not common; unfamiliar, strange; unusual.

1604 DRAYTON *Moses* I, [She] Iudg'd the sad parents this lost infant ow'd, Were as invulgar as their fruit was faire. **1610** W. FOLKINGHAM *Art of Survey* I. x. 27 Neuer practising any new or invulgar inuention. **1627** SIR S. D'EWES *Autobiog.* (1845) II. 194 A collaterall covenant..to free them from invulgar taxes.

†**in'vulgar,** *v. Obs.* [IN-².] *trans.* To divulge or communicate to the common people; to render vulgar, vulgarize.

1599 DANIEL *Musophilus* Wks. (1717) 386 It did so much invile the Estimate Of th' open'd and invulgar'd Mysteries.

invulnerability (ɪn,vʌlnərə'bɪlɪtɪ). [f. next + -ITY.] The quality or state of being invulnerable; incapability of being wounded or injured.

1775 in ASH. **1831** CARLYLE *Misc.* (1857) II. 231 His Hornedness meant only an Invulnerability. **1881** *Times* 23 Apr. 6/5 The practical invulnerability of the armour. **1900** *Daily News* 4 Sept. 6/1 The superstition of their [*sc.* the Boxers'] invulnerability to cannon shot... The Empress-Dowager..is said to have been deceived by the invulnerability superstition. **1962** *Listener* 29 Mar. 540/1 'Invulnerability' suggests, first of all, protecting your missiles under concrete, or hiding missiles and bombers and submarines by having them moving about. But 'invulnerability' also includes having too many missile sites for your enemy to be able to knock out even with a perfectly executed first strike; it includes having a mixed deterrent of bombers and land-base missiles and sea-going missiles, and it includes the case where your enemy knows that you are sure to have enough warning to launch your missiles and get your bombers aloft. This business of warning introduces serious ambiguities in the idea of 'invulnerability'. **1972** *Sci. Amer.* July 14/2 As a result of this possibility each country will be concerned to maintain the invulnerability of its submarine-based strategic missiles, which are essentially immune to attack from land-based weapons.

invulnerable (ɪn'vʌlnərəb(ə)l), *a.* (*sb.*) [ad. L. *invulnerābil-is*, f. *in-* (IN-³) + *vulnerābilis* VULNERABLE: cf. F. *invulnerable* (15–16th c. in Hatz.).]

A. *adj.* **1.** Incapable of being wounded; not liable to be physically hurt or damaged.

1595 SHAKS. *John* II. i. 252 Our Cannons malice vainly shall be spent Against th'involnerable clouds of heauen. **1596** SPENSER *F.Q.* VI. iv. 4 From his mothers wombe, which him did beare, He was invulnerable made by Magicke leare. **1693** SHADWELL *Volunteers* I. i, As fearless as if he were invulnerable. *a***1704** T. BROWN *Observ. Homer* Wks. 1730 I. 72 Homer..makes Achilles invulnerable everywhere but in his heel. **1879** *Cassell's Techn. Educ.* I. 223/2 Ships..whose decks, even in iron-clads, are rarely invulnerable. **1962** *Listener* 29 Mar. 540/1 It is essential, isn't it, to have what are called 'invulnerable strategic forces'? *Ibid.* 554/1 The speediest possible development of 'invulnerable' nuclear retaliatory power. *Ibid.*, The 'increasingly invulnerable' missile.

2. *fig.* Incapable of being damaged or injuriously affected by attack; not effectively assailable.

1663 COWLEY *Verses & Ess.*, *Death Mrs. Philips* (1669) 34 Never did Spirit of the Manly make..A temper more invulnerable take. **1713** SWIFT *Cadenus & Vanessa* 489 Vanessa, though by Pallas taught, By Love invulnerable thought. **1814** D'ISRAELI *Quarrels Auth.* (1867) 470 The genius of Hobbes was invulnerable to mere human opposition. **1876** GLADSTONE *Homeric Synchr.* 44 A general proposition, not less important, and I think invulnerable.

B. *sb.* An invulnerable person.

1825 *Gentl. Mag.* XCV. I. 358 Some hundreds assume the title of Invulnerables.

Hence **in'vulnerableness** = INVULNERABILITY; **in'vulnerably** *adv.*, so as to be invulnerable.

1655 BP. PRIDEAUX *Euchol.* I. vi. (1656) 92 Powers..most dangerous..For their invulnerablenesse, they being Spirits. **1847** A. BENNIE *Disc.* iv. 67 Faith in Christ renders his life invulnerably secure. **1865** *Cornh. Mag.* XI. 476 The invulnerableness of their skin was yet more extraordinary.

†**in'vulnerate,** *a. Obs. rare.* [ad. L. *invulnerāt-us*, f. *in-* (IN-³) + *vulnerātus*, pa. pple. of *vulnerāre* to wound.] Unwounded.

*a***1680** BUTLER *Rem.* (1759) I. 121 Sculls..That are invulnerate, and free from Blows.

†**invulne'ration.** *Obs. rare.* [n. of action or condition from L. *invulnerāt-us* unwounded: see prec. and -ATION.] The action of making, or condition of being invulnerable.

1654 GAYTON *Pleas. Notes* III. i. 68 The daily sowsing of that valiant Greeks body in the inchanted Bath for Invulneration.

†**in'vulnered,** *a. Obs. rare.* [f. L. *invulnerātus* (see INVULNERATE), with substitution of -ED¹ for the L. ppl. ending.] = INVULNERATE.

1613 HEYWOOD *Brazen Age* v. Wks. 1874 III. 254 Lye there thou dread of Tyrants, and thou skin, Invulner'd still, burne with thy maisters bones. **1635** —— *Hierarch.* III. 131 Ashamed A Beast by him should be so long untam'd Although invulner'd.

invultuation (ɪnvʌltjuː'eɪʃən). *rare.* Also **invultation.** [n. of action from med.L. *invultuāre*, *invultāre* (in OF. *envouter*, 13th c. in Hatz.-Darm.), to make a likeness, f. *in-* (IN-²) + *vultus* countenance, visage, likeness.] The making of a likeness, esp. the waxen effigy of a person for purposes of witchcraft.

1856 S. R. MAITLAND *False Worship* xiii. 150 Words which belong to the subject of invultation and facillation. *Ibid.* Note G. 295 All this does not appear to me to contain a full explanation of invultuation. **1897** *N. & Q.* 8th ser. XI. 236, 314, 395, (*Heading*) Invultation.

in'vy(e, invie, inwi, inwy(e, obs. variants (chiefly Sc.) of ENVY *sb.*

14.. *Sc. Leg. Saints*, *Andrew* 876 þe fals fend..had invy he liffit sa. *Ibid.*, *Mathias* 390 For Inwy & gret ill-wyll. *c***1440** *Promp. Parv.* 263/1 Invye, or envye, *invidia*. **1488** HENRY *Wallace* XI. 141 He saw thai had him at inwye. **1533** GAU *Richt Vay* 43 The dewil throw quhais inwi deid com in the vardil. **1596** DALRYMPLE tr. *Leslie's Hist. Scot.* I. 63 To speik without al invie the verie truth. *a***1657** SIR W. MURE *Misc. Poems* ii. 41 Ye bow, ye schafts..now w^t^out invy I yeild to the.

So **in'vy(e,** etc., *v.*

1483 *Cath. Angl.* 197/1 To Invye.., *emulari*. **1500–20** DUNBAR *Poems* xx. 2 For gift of fortoun invy thow no degre. **1533** GAU *Richt Vay* 44 He inwiit that man vesz maid to the euerlestand blis quhilk he had tint. **1596** DALRYMPLE tr. *Leslie's Hist. Scot.* v. 271 *marg.*, He is..Jnuiet be his Nobilitie. *a***1605** MONTGOMERIE *Flyting w. Polwart* 268 Wanshapen woubet, of the weirds invyit.

invyful(l, variant of ENVYFUL, *Obs.*, envious.

invyous(e, variant of INVIOUS, ENVIOUS.

invyroun, obs. form of ENVIRON.

inw-, a frequent Sc. spelling, in 15–16th c. MSS., of INV-, e.g. *inwey*, INVEIGH, *inwi*, *inwy*, INVY, *inwiolat*, INVIOLATE.

in-wale ('ɪnweɪl). [IN *adv.* 12.] A wale or rib of wood on the inside of a boat.

In some boats it runs from stem to stern; in others only alongside the space occupied by the sculler (about 8 ft.). **1875** 'STONEHENGE' *Brit. Sports* II. VIII. ii. §1. 639 The in-wale is continued fore and aft on each side to the stem and stern.

inwall ('ɪnwɔːl), *sb.* [IN *adv.* 12.] An inner or inside wall.

*c***1611** CHAPMAN *Iliad* XII. 448 With his weight th'inwall his breast did knock, And in rush'd Hector, fierce and grim as any stormy night. **1881** RAYMOND *Mining Gloss.*, *Inwalls*, the interior walls or lining of a shaft-furnace.

inwall, *v.*, variant of ENWALL.

inwandering ('ɪn,wɒndərɪŋ). *vbl. sb. rare.* [IN *adv.* 11 c, after Ger. *einwanderung*.] The action of wandering or straying into some place.

*c***1880** A. HYATT (Cent.), This inwandering of differentiated cells.

inward ('ɪnwəd), *a.* and *sb.* Forms: see next. Comp. **inwarder** *obs.*, superl. **inwardest** now *rare*. [OE. *innanweard*, *inneweard*, *inweard*, f. *innan*, *inne*, *inn* adv. and prep. + *-weard* (see -WARD): cognate with ON. *innanverðr* adj. interior, inward, OHG. *inwart*, *inwarti*, MHG. *inwart*, *inwarte*, MDu. *inwaert* (*inwert*).]

A. *adj.* **I.** In reference to situation or condition.

1. Situated within; that is the inner or inmost part; that is in or on the inside; belonging to or connected with the inside (esp. of the body): = INNER *a.* 1 a, INTERIOR *a.* 1, INTERNAL *a.* 1.

In OE. chiefly used of the interior or inner part of anything, like L. *interior domus* the inner (part of the) house, *intimum pectus*, the inmost (part of the) breast.

Beowulf (Z.) 992 Ða wæs haten hreþe heort innanweard folmum ȝefrætwod. *c***888** K. ÆLFRED *Boeth.* xxxiv. §10 Ælc wuht cwices biþ innanweard hnescost. *a***1000** *Christ & Satan* (Gr.) 707 Hu heh and deop hell inneweard seo, grim græfhus. *a***1225** *Leg. Kath.* 1815 Ne schal him neauer teone ..trukien in inwarde helle. *c***1374** CHAUCER *Boeth.* v. met. ii. 119 (Camb. MS.) Natheles yit ne may it [the sun]..percen the inward entrailes of the erthe or elles of the see. **1398** TREVISA *Barth. De P.R.* VII. lxvii. (MS. Bodl.) lf. 72 b, þe Iuyes..swageþ inward brennyng in a wondre manere. *c***1400** *Apol. Loll.* 24 He dede on cursyng os a cloþ, & entred as water in to his inword þings. **1483** *Cath. Angl.* 197/1 Inwarde,..*jnterior*, *jntestinus*. **1576** NEWTON *Lemnie's Complex.* (1633) 73 Fevers hecticke, which taking once hold in the inwardest parts..bringeth the body into apparant consumption. **1584** COGAN *Haven Health* cxxxii. 132 The inward parts of a swine..be very like to the inward parts of a man. **1617** MORYSON *Itin.* I. 185 They tooke from me the inward doublet wherein I had quilted the gold. **1660** BARROW *Euclid* I. xvi, The outward angle will be greater than either of the inward and opposite angles. **1697** tr. *C'tess D'Aunoy's Trav.* (1706) 29 He found her alone in an inward Room. **1796** MORSE *Amer. Geog.* I. 542 The inward carpentry-work on private and public buildings. **1841** GLADSTONE *State & Church* (ed. 4) I. iv. §78. 252 The term activity applies much more to outward than to inward vitality. **1899** J. HUTCHINSON *Archives Surg.* X. No. 38. 123 Nurse said child had had 'inward convulsions'.

†**b.** Said of the heart as a material organ possessing an interior part; and so, figuratively, of the heart, mind, soul, spirit, regarded as seats of feeling and thought. *Obs.*

*c***888** K. ÆLFRED *Boeth.* xxii. §1 Swiþe lust bære hine to ȝehyranne mid innewEardum mode. *c***1000** ÆLFRIC *Deut.* iv. 29 ȝif ȝe hine mid inweardre heortan seceaþ and mid ealre mihte. *c***1200** ORMIN 5925 Itt tacneþþ uss þatt mann þatt doþ God werrc wiþþ innwarrd herrte. *a***1240** *Lofsong* in *Cott. Hom.* 209 Ich..bi-seche þe wið inwarde heorte.

†**c.** Of medicine: = INTERNAL *a.* 1 c. *Obs.*

1607 E. GRIMSTONE tr. *Goulart's Mem. Hist.* 289 Cured by diet, rest, and glisters, without any inward medicines. **1655** DIGGES *Compl. Ambass.* 387 To councel the application of inward medicines when outward will serve.

d. Of the voice or a sound: Uttered without due opening of the mouth, so as not to be clearly

heard; muffled, indistinct. (Cf. 'to speak *out*'.) Also *transf.* of the utterer (quot. 1774).

1774 G. WHITE *Selborne* lviii, The marten.. when it sings, is so inward as scarce to be heard. **1797** MRS. RADCLIFFE *Italian* xx, Her words were inward and indistinct. **1825** MRS. CAMERON *Proper Spirit* in *Houlston Tracts* I. ix. 5 He read in his turn, but with an inward voice.

Comb. **1876** LANIER *Clover* 17 in *Poems*, Eight lingering strokes.. That speak the hour so inward-voiced.

e. Situated in, or belonging to, the interior of a country or region; inland: = INTERIOR *a.* 1 c.

1635 PAGITT *Christianogr.* 46 The inward and wilder parts thereof remayne in their ancient Paganisme. **1732** LEDIARD *Sethos* II. VIII. 145 Some provinces in the inward parts of Africa.

†**f.** *Mus.* Applied to parts intermediate between the highest and lowest of the harmony: = INNER *a.* 1 d. *Obs.*

1674 PLAYFORD *Skill Mus.* I. iv. 14 In any Cliff whatsoever, be it Bass, Treble, or any Inward Part. *Ibid.* II. 99 The Tenor-Viol is an excellent inward part.

2. Applied to the mind, thoughts, and mental faculties as located within the body; hence to mental or spiritual conditions and actions, as distinguished from bodily or external phenomena, and so = mental or spiritual. Cf. INNER *a.* 2, INTERIOR *a.* 3, INTERNAL *a.* 3.

inward man (*arch.*) the spiritual part of man, the spirit: = *inner man* (INNER *a.* 3 a.).

a **1225** *Juliana* 44 Þer is riht bileaue ant inward bone [*MS. Bodl.* inwardliche bonen] ant swa icweme to godd. *c* **1485** *Digby Myst.* IV. 1134 Which with thyn inward Ee Seest the depest place of mannys conscience. **1526** TINDALE *2 Cor.* iv. 16 Though oure vttward man perisshe, yet the inwarde man is renewed daye by daye. **1532** MORE *Confut. Tindale* Wks. 521/1 By a secrete inward instincte of nature. **1587** *Mirr. Mag., Q. Cordila* v, To ease her inward smarte. **1611** BIBLE *Ps.* li. 6 Behold, thou desirest trueth in the inward parts. **1664** BUTLER *Hud.* II. ii. 77 The inward Man And Outward, like a Clan and Clan, Have always been at Daggers-drawing. **1736** BUTLER *Anal.* I. iii. Wks. 1874 I. 56 Inward security and peace.. are the natural attendants of innocence and virtue. **1807** CRABBE *Par. Reg.* III. 401 Then shall thy inward eye with joy survey, The angel Mercy tempering Death's delay. **1885** S. COX *Expos.* Ser. I. iii. 36 The most perplexing facts of our inward experience.

†**b.** Conceived in or coming from one's inmost heart; deeply felt, heartfelt; hence, earnest, fervent.

c **1402** LYDG. *Compl. Bl. Knt.* 218 The thought oppressed with inward sighes sore. *Ibid.* 580 The teares gonne fro mine eyen raine Full pitously, for very inward roth. **1508** DUNBAR *Poems* vii. 37 Is none of Scotland borne.. Bot he.. wald of inwart hie effectioun, Bot dreyd of danger, de in thi defence. *a* **1548** HALL *Chron., Edw. IV* 229 What inward affeccion, and fervent desire, the kyng my Master hath alwaies had, to have a perfecte peace. **1627** WOTTON *Let. to Chas. I* in *Reliq.* (1672) d vj b, With whom he did communicate the inwardest thoughts of his heart.

c. Spiritually minded, devout, pious: = INTERIOR *a.* 3 c. ? *Obs.*

c **1450** tr. *De Imitatione* II. i. 41 A very inwarde man, & fre from inordinat affeccions. *Ibid.* v. 45 Thou shalt neuer be inwarde & deuoute man, but yf þou kepe silence of oþir men, & specialy beholde þiself. **1690** PENN *Rise & Prog. Quakers* (1834) 49 Being more religious, inward, still, solid, and observing. **1694** —— *Trav. Holland & Germ.* Pref. A iij, Wherefore, Reader, be Serious, Inward and Inquisitive for thy souls Sake.

†**3.** Belonging to the inner circle of one's acquaintance or friends; closely associated or acquainted; intimate, familiar, confidential. *Obs.* (Common in 16th and 17th c.)

c **1475** *Rauf Coilȝear* 236 Ane Chyld of hir Chalmer, Schir, .. maist inwart of ane. **1535** STEWART *Cron. Scot.* I. 519 Ane Murra man maist inwart with the king. **1587** FLEMING *Contn. Holinshed* III. 1371/2 Men knowne.. to be.. verie inward with the duke of Guise. **1602** DANIEL *Hymen's Tri.* III. i, You two were wont to be most inward Friends. **1606** DAY *Ile of Guls* I. iv. (1881) 24 These Ladies are so inward with our tricks, theres no good to be done uppon them. **1609** HOLLAND *Amm. Marcell.* XV. v. 35 One that would seeme most inward unto him, and of his familiar acquaintance. **1621** QUARLES *Argalus & P.* (1678) 20 Friendly to all men, inward but with few. **1675** tr. *Camden's Hist. Eliz.* (1688) 13 She applied her first Care (howbeit with but a few of her inwardest Counsellours) to the restoring of the Protestant Religion.

†**b.** Of a relation or feeling between two persons: Close, intimate. *Obs.*

1525 LD. BERNERS *Froiss.* II. ci. [xcvii.] 295 All weren nat in his inwarde loue. **1617** MORYSON *Itin.* I. 174 For their inward conversation, love, affinitie. **1645** MILTON *Tetrach.* Wks. (1847) 209/1 (*1 Cor.* vii. 10) The most inward and dear alliance of marriage.

†**c.** Of a bird or beast: Domesticated, tame.

1575 TURBERV. *Faulconrie* 9 That Eagle.. is by al probabilitie and conjecture, no inwarde Eagle, but a fugitive and a rangler. **1611** COTGR., *Accoquiner*, to make tame, inward, familiar; to reclaim a wild thing. *a* **1643** W. CARTWRIGHT *Lady Errant* II. ii, Wee'l keep you As they doe Hawkes.. Watching untill you leave Your wildness, and prove inward.

†**4.** Secret, not disclosed; private; in quot. 1607–12, that is such secretly. *Obs.*

a **1548** HALL *Chron., Edw. IV* 225 b, All inward grudges and open discordes. **1588** SHAKS. *L.L.L.* v. i. 102 What is inward betweene vs, let it passe. **1607–12** BACON *Ess., Seeming Wise* (Arb.) 218 There is noe decaying Merchaunt, or inward Begger, hath so manie trickes to vphold the creditt of theire Wealth. **1609** HOLLAND *Amm. Marcell.* XVIII. iv. 109 In their neere attendance which they gave about privie and inward ministeries [*inter ministeria vitæ secretioris*]. **1611** CHAPMAN *May Day* Plays 1873 II. 337 Pray eene goe in againe for I haue some inward newes for you.

5. Existing in or pertaining to the country or place itself; domestic, intestine. *Obs.* or *arch.*

1513 MORE in Grafton *Chron.* (1568) II. 792 Inward war amongst our selves. *a* **1548** HALL *Chron., Hen. VI* 83 The inward affaires of the realme of Englande. *a* **1626** BACON *Max. & Uses Com. Law* Ep. Ded. (1636) 4 Your Majesties reigne having been blessed from the Highest with inward peace. **1675** tr. *Camden's Hist. Eliz.* I. (1688) 16 The Dangers inward they foresaw would be from the Noblemen removed from the Queen's Council. *a* **1825** FORBY *Voc. E. Anglia, Inward-maid*, the house-maid in a farm-house, who has no work in the dairy, etc.

†**6.** Pertaining to the thing in itself; intrinsic.

1587 GOLDING *De Mornay* 52 Forasmuch as the onely God is.. the highest degree of life, he hath his maner of conceiuing and begetting most inward of al. **1613** PURCHAS *Pilgrimage* (1614) 512 The neerest inward and most proper cause of marine movings. **1620** T. GRANGER *Div. Logike* 38 Necessitie Absolute, by supposition, proceding from causes Inward, which is necessitie of nature, and appetite.

II. In reference to direction or motion. [From the adverb.]

7. Directed or proceeding towards the inside.

1849 CLARIDGE *Cold Water-cure* 81 The eruption took an inward direction and inflammation of the lungs was the consequence. **1875** CLERY *Min. Tact.* x. (1877) 131 Charged the Russian left wing when it had nearly completed its inward wheel. **1898** *Daily News* 13 July 4/7 Each Government.. receives all the money on outward postages, and none on inward postages.

B. *sb.* [absol. use of the adj., already in OE.]

1. The inward or internal part, the inside; usually *spec.* the internal parts or organs of the body, the entrails. **a.** *sing.* (Now *rare.*)

c **1000** ÆLFRIC *Gloss.* in Wr.-Wülcker 159/35 *Intestina*, smælþearmas, uel inneweard. *c* **1000** ÆLFRIC *Exod.* xxix. 17 His innewerde and his fet þu leȝst uppan his heofod. *c* **1275** *XI Pains Hell* 151 in *O. Eng. Misc.* 151 Gripes freteþ heore Mawen.. And heore ineward vych del. **1297** R. GLOUC. (Rolls) 2864 Þat ich in is Ineward mid suerd make a sseþe. **1481** CAXTON *Reynard* (Arb.) 92 The moghettis Lyuer longes and the Inward shal be for your chyldren. **1584** COGAN *Haven Health* (1636) 146 The intraile or inward of beastes. *c* **1600** SHAKS. *Sonn.* cxxviii, To kisse the tender inward of thy hand. **1817** COLERIDGE *Biog. Lit.* 63 Matter has no inward. **1884** J. PAYNE *1001 Nights* VII. 80 He snatched up the man who had kicked him and carried him into the inward of the island.

b. *pl.* (Now only in *spec.* sense: = Entrails.)

a **1300** *E.E. Psalter* cviii[i.]. 18 Als watre, it in-yhede In his inwardes. *c* **1425** *Found. St. Bartholomew's* (E.E.T.S.) 30 His ynwardes were purgid from this dedly fylthe. **1531** TINDALE *Exp. 1 John* (1537) 82 [To] brynge a beaste and slay it and offre the bloude and the fat of the inwardes. **1570–6** LAMBARDE *Peramb. Kent* (1826) 475 Assured that the Inwardes of each place may best be knowen by such as reside therein. **1671** SALMON *Syn. Med.* I. xxxvii. 83 Obstruction is a Stoppage of the Inwards by thickned Flegm. **1725** POPE *Odyss.* xx. 325 The prince.. to his sire assigns The tasteful inwards, and nectareous wines. **1850** KINGSLEY *Alt. Locke* xii, Ups and downs o' hills.. enough to shake a body's victuals out of his inwards.

2. The inner nature or essence of a thing or person; that which is within; the interior, secret, or intrinsic character, qualities, thoughts, etc.

a. *sing. rare.*

1398 TREVISA *Barth. De P.R.* II. viii. (Add. MS. 27, 944) lf. 15/1 An aungel.. settith his entent in-to þe inwarde of god. **1832** TENNYSON *Eleanore* i, There is nothing here, Which, from the outward to the inward brought, Moulded thy baby thought. **1884** J. PAYNE *Tales fr. Arabic* I. 106 O vizier.. make thine inward like unto thine outward.

†**b.** *pl. Obs.*

c **975** *Rushw. Gosp.* Mark vii. 21 From ionnawordum.. of heorte monna sweaunga yfel oft cumað. *c* **1450** tr. *De Imitatione* II. i. 41 Yf þou haddist ones parfitly entrid in to þe inwardes of Ihesu, & haddist sauored a litel of his brennyng loue. **1548** UDALL, etc. *Erasm. Par. Matt.* xiii. 76 He printeth it not utterly in the inwardes of his minde. **1680** ALLEN *Peace & Unity* Pref. 36 How necessary it is to look into the inwards of things. **1721** R. KEITH tr. *à Kempis' Solil. Soul* x. 178 How disturbed my Conscience is; how confused all my Inwards.

†**3.** An intimate or familiar acquaintance: = INTIMATE *sb.* (Cf. A. 3.) *Obs.*

1603 SHAKS. *Meas. for M.* III. ii. 138 Sir, I was an inward of his and I beleeue I know the cause of his withdrawing. **1607** MIDDLETON *Michaelmas Term* II. iii, He's a kind gentleman, a very inward of mine.

4. *pl.* Articles coming in or imported, or dues on such articles. Also *attrib.*

1761 *Gentl. Mag.* 604 Mann, E. L. Collector of Inwards at Custom House. **1878** F. S. WILLIAMS *Midl. Railw.* 643 Upon the 'Inwards' platform we find cases of hard-ware from Birmingham, casks of shoes from Leicester, hampers of lace from Nottingham [etc.].

inward ('ɪnwəd), *adv.* (*prep.*) Forms: 1 inweard, (inneweard, ionnaword, 2–3 innewardd, ineward(e), 2– inward; (4 inwar, 4–7 inwarde, 5 inword, ynwarde, 5–6 *Sc.* inwart, inuart, 6 inwerd, *Sc.* inuert). [OE. *innan-, inne-, inweard* = OHG. *inwert*, MDu. *inne-, inwaert, -wert, -wart*: see prec.]

A. *adv.* **1.** Towards the inside or interior (of a place, space, or material body).

a. Of motion or direction.

c **1000** *Nicodemus* xxxi, in Thwaite *Heptat.* App. (1698) 18 Ða hiȝ inweard foron þa ȝemytton hiȝ tweȝen ealde weras. *a* **1225** *St. Marher.* 8 As me ledde hire inward. **1297** R. GLOUC. (Rolls) 11094 Arblastes sone & ginnes wiþoute me bende, & ssote inward vaste inou. **1375** BARBOUR *Bruce* x. 397 Als-soyn thai Held carpand Inward on thar way. **1413** *Pilgr. Sowle* (Caxton 1483) I. iv. 4 Beholdyng inward as fer as I myȝt, thenne saw I many syeges ryal and wonderful. **1590** SPENSER *F.Q.* I. i. 7 Pathes and alleies wide.. leading inward farr. **1658** A. FOX *Wurtz' Surg.* II. vii. 67 It happeneth sometimes, that the scull by a heavy blow is bowed inward. **1707** CHAMBERLAYNE *St. Eng.* 497 Comptroller of the Cloth and Petty-Custom inward and outward. *Ibid.* 501 Patent-Officers in the Out-Ports.. Southampton, one Customer inward, One Customer outward. *Passim.* **1799** *Med. Jrnl.* II. 230 When the eye rolls inward. **1871** ROSSETTI *Poems, Ave* 103 The cherubim, arrayed, conjoint, Float inward to a golden point.

b. Of position or situation: In or on the inside; in the interior, within; internally: = INWARDLY *adv.* 1. ? *Obs.*

c **1400** *Rom. Rose* 4411 Inward myn herte I fele blede. **1471** RIPLEY *Comp. Alch.* VI. ix. in Ashm. (1652) 163 The Mater ys alterate, Both inward and outward substancyally. **1515** BARCLAY *Egloges* iv. (1570) C vj b/1 A castell or toure moste curious, Dreadfull vnto sight but inwarde excellent. **1590** SPENSER *F.Q.* I. i. 9 The Maple seeldom inward sound. **1611** BIBLE *1 Kings* vii. 25 The Sea was set aboue vpon them, and all their hinder parts were inward. **1688** R. HOLME *Armoury* II. 16/2 Such Lines or Circles, as ly inward in the material Sphere.

†**c.** With an 'inward' tone, with muffled utterance, indistinctly: cf. INWARD *a.* 1 d. *Obs.*

1644 MILTON *Educ.* Wks. (1847) 99/2 Englishmen.. are observed by all other nations to speak exceeding close and inward.

2. *fig.* **a.** Towards that which is within; into the mind or soul; into one's own thoughts.

a **1225** *Ancr. R.* 272 So sone so me biginneð kunsenten to sunne, and let þene lust gon inward and delit waxen. **1526** *Pilgr. Perf.* (W. de W. 1531) 111 Loke inwarde on our owne conscyence, and remembre our synnes. *a* **1600** HOOKER (J.), Looking inward we are stricken dumb; looking upward we speak and prevail. **1766** FORDYCE *Serm. Yng. Wom.* (1767) II. viii. 36 Satiated with external pleasures, she turns inward.

b. Within, in, or in relation to, the mind or soul; mentally or spiritually; = INWARDLY *adv.* 3.

c **950** *Lindisf. Gosp.* Luke xi. 39 Þætte ðonne inweard [*Rushw.* ionnaword] is iuer [Vulg. *intus est vestrum*] full is mið nedniminicg and mið unrehtwisnise. *c* **1420** HOCCLEVE *De Reg. Princ.* 321 If he inward hadde any repentaunce. *c* **1450** HOLLAND *Howlat* 389 It synkis sone in all part Of a trewe Scottis hart, Reiosand ws inwart. **1526** TINDALE *2 Cor.* vii. 5 Outwarde was fightynge, in warde was feare. *c* **1600** SHAKS. *Sonn.* lxii, It is so grounded inward in my heart. **1659** DRYDEN *Stanzas Cromwell* xii, We inward bled, whilst they prolonged our pain.

3. *Comb.*

c **1425** *Found. St. Bartholomew's* (E.E.T.S.) 23 A-noone the Inward-borne blyndenesse fledde a-way. **1850** J. G. WHITTIER *Songs of Labor* 59 Still dreamed my inward-turning eye. **1866** R. M. BALLANTYNE *Shift. Winds* xiv. (1881) 136 The Captain hailed the first inward-bound vessel he met with. **1890** W. JAMES *Princ. Psychol.* I. x. 320 The more utterly 'selfish' I am in this primitive way, the more blindly absorbed my thought will be in the objects and impulses of my lusts, and the more devoid of any inward looking glance. **1910** KIPLING *Rewards & Fairies* p. x, These shall cleanse and purify Webbed and inward-turning eye. **1946** KOESTLER *Thieves in Night* 207 She sipped her dry Martini with an inward-turned look. **1961** A. MILLER *Misfits* xii. 131 His eyes are sightless, inward-looking. **1963** *Times* 28 Jan. 5/2 Yet Schumann's poetry has its feet on German earth, and it was possible to feel that Mr. Richter's presentation of it was just a little too disembodied and wraithlike, his interpretation a little too inward-looking. **1968** *Guardian* 15 Apr. 9/6 Pressure from inward-looking, anti-national groups.

†**B.** *prep.* In the interior of; within. *Obs. rare.*

14.. *Sir Beues* (MS. M) 1208 Right on the bryge, the Romans seys, They met Beues inwarde the paleys.

inward, *v. rare.* [f. prec. adv. or adj.]

†**1.** *intr.* and *refl.* To come inwards or in, to enter. *Obs. rare*⁻⁰.

1611 FLORIO, *Indentrarsi*, to inward himselfe. *Ibid.*, *Innentrare*, to inward or enter into.

2. *trans.* To make inward or subjective. *rare*⁻¹.

1868 *Contemp. Rev.* VIII. 618 The oriental mind.. subjectifies the individuality, or, to frame a word for the occasion, inwards it.

inwardly ('ɪnwədlɪ), *a. rare.* [OE. *inweardlíc*, f. *inweard* internal + *-líc*, -LY¹.] †**a.** = INWARD *a.* *Obs.*

c **1000** *Sax. Leechd.* I. 338 Wið wifa earfoðnyssum þe on heora inwerdlicum [*v.r.* inweardlicum] stowum earfeþu þrowiað. *c* **1200** *Trin. Coll. Hom.* 45 Rechelis, for his swetnesse, bitocneð inwardliche bede. *a* **1225** [see INWARD *a.* 2]. **1504** LADY MARGARET tr. *De Imitatione* IV. xvi. 280 Take a waye from my thought all the erthely and inwardelye thynges.

b. Relating to what is inward or spiritual.

1820 COLERIDGE *Lett., Convers.*, etc. I. Let. viii. 50 In moral, or if that be too high and inwardly a word, in mannerly manliness of taste the present age and its best writers have the decided advantage.

inwardly ('ɪnwədlɪ), *adv.* Forms: see INWARD *adv.* [OE. *inweardlíce*: see prec. and -LY².]

I. In reference to situation or condition.

1. In, on, or in reference to, the inside or inner part; within; = INTERNALLY 1.

1483 *Cath. Angl.* 197/2 Inwardly, .. *jntime.* **1495** *Trevisa's Barth. De P.R.* XVII. lxxix. (W. de W.) Q iv b, Clowes.. ben perfyte fruyte wyth sharpe sauoure.. also moyst inwardly. **1580** LD. GREY in Grosart *Spenser's Wks.* I. 473 Propped outwardlie like a hovel, and inwardlie slanting like a pentisse. **1599** SHAKS. *Much Ado* III. i. 78 Therefore let Benedicke like couered fire, Consume away in sighes, waste

inwardly. **1617** MORYSON *Itin.* III. 154 More inwardly where..Rosse, and Southerland are seated, the..Mertæ of old inhabited. **1631** JORDAN *Nat. Bathes* xvi. (1669) 154 Inwardly also Bath-waters are used, for Broths, Beer, Juleps, &c. although some do mislike it. **1660** BARROW *Euclid* III. vi, If two circles inwardly touch one the other. **1719** DE FOE *Crusoe* I. xiv, He had bled inwardly. **1770** THORPE in *Phil. Trans.* LXI. 158 The characteristick of the chesnut trees decaying inwardly.

b. With a voice that does not pass the lips; in low tones spoken to oneself; not aloud.

1530 PALSGR. Introd. 15 They make a maner of modulation inwardly. **18..** WORDSW. *White Doe* ii, He shrunk and muttered inwardly. **1859** TENNYSON *Geraint & Enid* 109 Half inwardly, half audibly she spoke.

2. Intimately, thoroughly; closely.

a **1225** *Ancr. R.* 52 Lo hu holi writ spekeð, & hu inwardliche hit telleð hu sunegunge bigon. *c* **1300** *Speculum Guy Warw.* 389 Hit greueþ euere mannes eiȝe, Inwardliche on hire [þe sunne] to se For hire grete clerte. *c* **1450** LONELICH *Grail* xxxv. 516 They behelden Abowtes ful Inwardly. **1579–80** NORTH *Plutarch* (1676) 946 The people not looking so inwardly into it. **1584** J. CARMICHAEL in *Wodrow Misc.* (1844) 422 Thai will deill moir invartly with hir Majestie nor with ony other foren prince. **1659** MILTON *Rupt. Commw.* ¶ 1 Acquainting me with the state of Affairs, more inwardly then I knew before. **1660** *Hist. Wars Scot. under Montrose* ix. 69 When he came to understand him more inwardly. **1703** PENN in *Pa. Hist. Soc. Mem.* IX. 210 For my government I refer thee to the deputy governor, and my son more inwardly.

b. Intrinsically, in its own nature.

1884 tr. *Lotze's Logic* 30 The line which divides what is inwardly coherent from casual accessions.

3. In heart; in mind or thought; in spirit. (Hence implying 'in reality, sincerely, at heart', or 'secretly'.)

c **1175** *Lamb. Hom.* 39 Bute we inwarliche imilcien and forȝeuen þan monne þe us wreðeð. *a* **1300** *Cursor M.* 20754 'I tru', he said, 'it inwardli'. *c* **1485** *Digby Myst.* IV. 1035 Yit must myn herte wepe Inwerdlye. **1513** MORE *Rich. III* Wks. 67/2 Men had it euer inwardely suspect, as many well counterfaited iewels make yᵉ true mistrusted. *a* **1548** HALL *Chron., Rich. III* 53 Diverse other noble personages whiche inwardely hated kyng Richard. **1611** BIBLE *Ps.* lxii. 4 They blesse with their mouth, but they curse inwardly. **1666** TEMPLE *Let. to Bp. of Munster* 19 Mar., I pretended to believe what I am told, tho' I am inwardly assured to the contrary. **1726** LAW *Serious C.* xviii. (1729) 343 It is highly reasonable, that you should..appear outwardly such as you are inwardly. **1845** M. PATTISON *Ess.* (1889) I. 26 The others laughing inwardly at the scene that was being acted before them.

†**b.** In or from the inmost heart; with deep emotion or feeling; heartily, fervently, earnestly.

a **1000** *Boeth. Metr.* xxii. 2 Se þe æfter rihte mid ȝerece wille inweardlice æfterspyrian. *c* **1000** ÆLFRIC *Hom.* I. 58 Iohannes..symle syððan Drihtne folgode, and weard ða him inweardlice ȝelufod. *c* **1200** ORMIN 697 Þeȝȝ alle bædenn innwarrdliȝ Wiþþ bedess & wiþþ dedess, þatt Drihhtin shollde lesenn hemm Ut off þe deofless walde. *a* **1225** *Ancr. R.* 282 Þet was þet lescun þet ure Louerd inwardlukest lerede alle his icorene. *c* **1440** *York Myst.* xxiv: 75 A! lorde, we loue þe inwardly. **1526** *Pilgr. Perf.* (W. de W. 1531) 7 b, They..can for his sake moost inwardly in herte despyse this worlde. **1632** J. HAYWARD tr. *Biondi's Eromena* 47 But I..am..disinabled herein (which at this present inwardly grieves me).

II. In reference to direction or motion.

4. a. Towards the inside or inner part; = INWARD *adv.* 1 a. **b.** *fig.* Towards that which is within; into the mind or soul; = INWARD *adv.* 2 a. Now *rare.*

1667 *Obs. Burn. Lond.* in *Select. fr. Harl. Misc.* (1793) 447 We shut them inwardly, as well as possibly we could. **1697** DAMPIER *Voy.* I. 391 Cutting the upper part of the body aslope inwardly downward. **1822–34** *Good's Study Med.* (ed. 4) I. 63 The ulceration stretched outwardly under the upper lip and nose, and inwardly to cheeks and throat.

¶ **5.** By some ME. writers, *inwardly* was used to render L. *in-* in composition, e.g. 'to seek inwardly' = L. *inquīrĕre*, 'to call or clepe inwardly' = L. *invocare*.

a **1340** HAMPOLE *Psalter* xix. 10 Here vs in þe light of trouth and luf, in þe whilke lyght we inwardly call þe [*in die qua invocaverimus te*]. **1382** WYCLIF *Ps.* cxiv. 4 The name of the Lord I inwardli clepede [*invocavi*]. —— *Isa.* ix. 13 The Lord of ostes thei inwardlyche soȝten not [*non inquisierunt*].

†**'inwardmost**, *a. Obs. rare.* [f. INWARD *a.* + -MOST.] Most inward; = INMOST, INNERMOST.

1651 *Raleigh's Ghost* 92 The inwardmost [teeth] are broad and blunt to grind and make small the meat.

inwardness ('ɪnwədnɪs). [f. INWARD *a.* + -NESS.]

†**1.** The inner part or region; *pl.* Inward parts, entrails (rendering L. *viscera*; in quots. only *fig.*: see BOWEL *sb.*¹ 3). *Obs.*

1388 WYCLIF *Luke* i. 78 Bi the inwardnesse of the merci of oure God. —— *2 Cor.* vi. 12 Ȝe ben not angwischid in vs, but ȝe ben anguischid in ȝoure inwardnessis [1382 entrailis]. —— *Phil.* ii. 1 If ony inwardnesse of merci. **1450–1530** *Myrr. our Ladye* 158 Not faynedly only with tongue, but of all the inwardenesse of sowle.

2. The inward or intrinsic character or quality of a thing; the inner nature, essence, or meaning.

1605 BACON *Adv. Learn.* II. iv. §4, I should without any difficulty pronounce that his fables had no such inwardnesse in his own meaning. **1647** H. MORE *Song of Soul* I. I. xxviii, Sense cannot arrive to th' inwardnesse Of things. **1830** COLERIDGE *Grk. Poets* (1834) 307 Perhaps Lord Bacon is right in thinking that there was but little of such inwardness in the poet's own meaning. **1869** LOWELL *Fam. Ep. to Friend* vii, Nor Nature fails my walks to bless With all her golden inwardness. **1877** *N. York Tribune* Apr. (Cent. Dict.), The true inwardness of the late Southern policy of the Republican party. **1887** *Pall Mall G.* 18 July 1/1 We have always contended that the true 'inwardness' of the Land Bill was not the wish to stop evictions, but the wish to stop the scandal of evictions. *Ibid.* 21 Nov. 5/1 How can we trust any book to show us the true inwardness of a man we never set eyes on? **1895** MASSINGHAM in *Contemp. Rev.* Aug. 301 In another sense we have taken too little account of the inwardness of the lives of the poor.

3. The quality or condition of being inward or internal to something else (*lit.* or *fig.*).

1611 FLORIO, *Interiorita*, inwardnesse. *a* **1680** CHARNOCK *Attrib. God* (1834) I. 459 The apostle doth not say, by him, but in him, to show the inwardness of his presence. **1858** GLADSTONE *Homer* II. 130 That inwardness and universality of function which belongs to Minerva. **1858** MISS MULOCK *Th. Wom.* 266 It must always be, from its very secretness and inwardness, the sharpest of all pangs.

†**4.** The fact of being intimately acquainted; intimacy, familiarity; close friendship. *Obs.*

1578 in Tytler *Hist. Scot.* (1864) IV. 19, I fear that no great inwardness shall be found in them, when they find her majesty's liberality coming slowly to them. **1599** SHAKS. *Much Ado* IV. i. 247 You know my inwardnesse and loue Is very much vnto the Prince and Claudio. **1652–62** HEYLIN *Cosmogr.* I. (1682) 41 Menas..by reason of his inwardness with his Master, knew most of his designs. **1668** PEPYS *Diary* 23 Aug., The Duke of York..did, with much inwardness, tell me what was doing. **1715** STEELE *Town-talk* No. 1 It probably dropt hastily in the..inwardness of conjugal confidence, from the pen of a fond husband writing to a young, gay, and beautiful wife.

5. a. Depth or intensity of feeling or thought; subjectivity.

1836 HARE *Guesses* (1859) 72 That depth and inwardness of thought, which seems to belong to the Germanic mind. **1845** *P. Parley's Ann.* VI. 106 The..blackcap..pours..his ..love-song—scarcely inferior, in a certain plaintive inwardness, to the autumn song of the robin. **1871** R. H. HUTTON *Ess.* (1877) I. Pref. 27 The new inwardness with which men are conceiving their relation to each other.

b. Relation to or occupation with what is inward or concerns man's inner nature, as opposed to occupation with externalities; spirituality.

1859 JOWETT *Ess. Interpr. Script.* in *Comm. Paul's Epist.* (1894) 28 This inwardness of the words of Christ is what few are able to receive. **1873** M. ARNOLD *Lit. & Dogma* (1876) 100 Trying to identify the Messiah of popular hope..with an ideal of meekness, inwardness, patience, and self-denial. **1876** C. D. WARNER *Wint. Nile* x. 132 They sleep the sleep of 'inwardness' and peace.

inwards ('ɪnwədz), *adv.* (*a.*). [ME. *inwardes*, f. *inward* adv., with advb. genitive *-es*, *-s*, as in *besides*, etc. Cf. the parallel MDu. *inwaerts*, Du. *inwaarts*, MHG. *inwertes*, Ger. *inwärts*, Da. *indvortes*, Sw. *invertes*.]

1. a. = INWARD *adv.* 1 a.

1597 A. M. tr. *Guillemeau's Fr. Chirurg.* 16 b/2 Drawinge the needle from inwardes, outwardes. **1613** PURCHAS *Pilgrimage* (1614) 418 A mile inwards is another wall. **1703** MOXON *Mech. Exerc.* 205 Do not direct the cutting Corner of the Chissel inwards, but rather outwards. **1796** *Instr. & Reg. Cavalry* (1813) 61 The advantages of making central changes, by breaking inwards, so as the whole stand faced to the given division or divisions in two columns. **1846** J. BAXTER *Libr. Pract. Agric.* (ed. 4) I. 70 Globe Artichoke, with..the scales turned inwards at the top.

b. *spec.* With respect to goods coming in or imported. (Cf. INWARD *sb.* 4.)

1583 *Rates of Custome-ho.* To Rdr., The..poundage for all maner of merchandise aswel outwards as inwards. **1679–88** *Secr. Serv. Money Chas. & Jas.* (Camden) 144 To Rowland Thrupp, collector inwards in the port of Bristoll. **1688** *N. Jersey Archives* (1880) I. 525 Paying noe Custom nor Excise inwards or outwards. **1722** *Act Encour. Silk Manuf.* in *Lond. Gaz.* No. 6040/3 The..Silk when exported unmanufactured do draw back great part of the Duties paid Inwards.

c. = INWARD *adv.* 1 b.

1597 [see a]. **1601** R. JOHNSON *Kingd. & Commw.* (1603) 159 A black sheep skinne with the wool-side outward in the day time, and inwards, in the night time. *a* **1626** BACON (J.), The medicines..are so strong, that if they were used inwards they would kill.

2. a. = INWARD *adv.* 2 a.

a **1225** *Ancr. R.* 92 Euer so þe wittes beoð more ispreinde utwardes, se heo lesse wendet inwardes. **1768–74** TUCKER *Lt. Nat.* (1834) I. I. xi. §36. 125 What else is reflecting besides turning the mental eye inwards? **1866** J. MARTINEAU *Ess.* I. 127 Conjecture will turn inwards.

b. = INWARD *adv.* 2 b.

a **1225** *Ancr. R.* 92 Euer se recluses toteð more utwardes, se heo habbeð lesse luue of vre Louerd inwardes.

†**B.** *adj.* = INWARD *a.* in various senses. *rare.*

1550 J. COKE *Eng. & Fr. Heralds* §97 (1877) 87 The names of them..casteth into theyr hartes an inwardes feare and tremour. **1575** TURBERV. *Faulconrie* 158 The high fleeing hawke should be made inwards and (as we tearme it) fond of the lewre.

in'warp, *v. rare.* [IN-¹.] *trans.* To inweave or work in, as the warp in the web.

1824 E. IRVING in Mrs. Oliphant *Life* (1862) I. 194 The interests of religion are too much inwarped..with my character and writing, that I should not do my best.

inwart, obs. Sc. form of INWARD.

inwave, variant of ENWAVE *v.*, *Obs.*

†**'inways**, *adv. Obs. rare*⁻¹. [f. IN *adv.* + *-ways*, as in *sideways*.] = INWARDS *adv.* 1 b.

1552 GRESHAM in Strype *Eccl. Mem.* (1721) III. II. App. C. 147 The formal bargains heretofore made in taking the *fourth peny* inways.

†**in'wealdy**, variant of UNWIELDY *a.*

1650 BULWER *Anthropomet.* 108 Inwealdy pourers out of speech.

inweaIthy, var. ENWEALTHY *v.*, *Obs.* to enrich.

†**in'weary**, *v. Obs. rare*⁻⁰. [IN-².] To weary.

1611 FLORIO, *Instancare*, to tire, to inweary.

inweave (ɪn'wiːv), **enweave**, *v.* Pa. t. -wove. Pa. pple. -woven (also 7 -weav'd, 8–9 -wove). [f. IN-¹ (or ²), EN-¹ + WEAVE *v.*; cf. Du. *inweven*, G. *einweben*, Da. *indvæve*, Sw. *inväfva*, and L. *intexĕre*. Chiefly used in pa. pple.]

1. *trans.* To weave in; to weave (threads or materials) in, so as to form a web or tissue; to weave (things) together, or one thing *with* another; to interweave. Also *fig.*

1578 BANISTER *Hist. Man* v. 70 This is with two kindes of Fibres intertexed, or enwouen. **1652** BENLOWES *Theoph.* XII. xv, When two enweav'd are in one high desire They feel like Angels, mutuall fire. **1831** CARLYLE *Sart. Res.* I. iii, A living link in that Tissue of History, which inweaves all Being. **1846** RUSKIN *Mod. Paint.* I. I. I. vi. §4. 26 All our moral feelings are so inwoven with our intellectual powers, that [etc.]. *a* **1859** J. A. JAMES in Spurgeon *Treas. Dav.* Ps. cxix. 126 Infidelity..has endeavoured to enweave itself with science. **1876** T. HARDY *Ethelberta* (1890) 259 The newly-lit lamps on the quay, and the evening glow shining over the river, inwove their harmonious rays as the warp and woof of one lustrous tissue.

2. To insert or introduce (a thread, pattern, or material) into a fabric which is being woven; to insert (one thing) in or into another by weaving in or entwining. Const. *in*, *into* (*among*, *through*).

1596 DALRYMPLE tr. *Leslie's Hist. Scot.* v. 266 Tua lynes ..Wouen in threid of golde, to quhilkes Jngeniouslie ar coupled the Lillies inwouen, inwounde, and drawin throuch, as it war. **1670** MILTON *Hist. Eng.* VI. Wks. (1847) 560/2 The royal standard, wherin the figure of a man fighting was inwoven with gold and precious stones. **1725** POPE *Odyss.* IX. 513 In his deep fleece my grasping hands I lock, And fast beneath, in woolly curls inwove, There cling implicit. **1797** T. PARK *Sonn.* 16 On every leaf enweave a druid-spell. **1876** ROCK *Text. Fabr.* i. 5 A vast number of figures and animals inwoven into its fabric.

b. *fig.* with ref. to immaterial things, words, incidents in a story, etc.

a **1628** F. GREVIL *Poems* II. (1633) 66 Closely to be inweau'd in euery heart. *a* **1656** USSHER *Power Princes* II. (1683) 160 Cæsar heretofore did so embosom and enweaue himselfe into the Commonwealth. **1817** COLERIDGE *Biog. Lit.* 219 To inweave in a poem of the loftiest style..such minute matters of fact. **1869** GOULBURN *Purs. Holiness* v. 43 A study which inweaves the Word into the daily life of the Christian.

3. To combine, furnish, decorate, etc. *with* something inserted or entwined.

1591 SPENSER *Muiopotmos* 299 A faire border wrought of sundrie flowres, Enwoven with an yvie-winding trayle. **1717** tr. *Ovid's Met., Arachne* 209 Festoons of flow'rs inwove with ivy shine. **1835** WILLIS *Pencillings* II. xlvii. 71 Gauze-like fabrics inwoven with flowers of silver.

4. To form by weaving or plaiting. *rare.*

1667 MILTON *P.L.* III. 352 Down they cast Thir Crowns inwove with Amarant and Gold. **1864** NEALE *Seaton. Poems* 21 The Crown inwove with twisted Thorn. **1887** BOWEN *Virg. Æneid* v. 308 Three winners receive Prizes beyond, and of olive pale their garlands inweave.

Hence **in-**, **en'weavement**. *rare.*

1842 *Tait's Mag.* IX. 606 Mind with mind it links in long Enweavement round the world.

inwedged ('ɪn,wɛdʒd), *ppl. a.* [IN *adv.* 11 b.] Wedged in, confined. Const. as *pple.* or as *adj.*

1875 KINGLAKE *Crimea* (1877) V. i. 126 Whenever the red-coated horseman thus found himself inwedged and surrounded. **1885** W. K. PARKER *Mammal. Desc.* VII. 179 Its walls are the inwedged outgrowth of the..ear ring.

†**in'weed**, *v. Obs. rare*⁻¹. [f. IN-¹ + WEED.] *trans.* To hide or shelter in weeds.

a **1586** SIDNEY *Arcadia* II. xi. (1590) Vv, [The dog] got out of the riuer, and shaking off the water..inweeded [*quoted in J. as* inwooded] himselfe so, as the Ladies lost the further marking his sportfulnesse.

in-went, pa. t. of IN-GO *v.*, *Obs.*

inwerd, **inwey**, obs. ff. INWARD, INVEIGH.

inweroun, **-wirone**, obs. ff. *inviron*, ENVIRON.

14.. *Sc. Leg. Saints, Matthew* 463 He gert Inwirone al hyre In with mekil fuel. **1489** *Barbour's Bruce* XI. 607 (Edin. MS.) Thai all about War inweround [*Camb. MS.* enveronyt].

†**in'wet**, *v. Obs. rare*⁻¹. [f. IN-¹ + WET *v.*, after L. *intingĕre*.] *trans.* To wet (*in* something).

1382 WYCLIF *Ps.* lxvii. 24 [lxviii. 23] That inwet be [Vulg. *intingatur*] thi foot in blood; the tunge of thin houndis fro hym of the enemys.

inwheel, variant of ENWHEEL *v.*, *Obs.*

inwick ('ɪn,wɪk), *sb. Sc. Curling.* [f. IN *adv.* + (?) WICK *v.*] A shot which strikes the inside of another stone and glances off it to the tee, as in a cannon in billiards; practised when an

adversary's stone is *in*, and strongly guarded from front attack; the same as an INRING (but see the vb.).

1820 *Blackw. Mag.* VI. 572 Bringing up by means of what is termed an in-wick his next stone. **1824** MACTAGGART *Gallovid. Encycl.* s.v., To take an inwick is considered by all curlers the finest trick in the game. **1831** in *Blackw. Mag.* XXX. 970 Then by a dexterous in-wick eject the winner. *Ibid.* 971 To make a succession of in-wicks up a port. **1857** *Chambers' Inform.* II. 683/2 The player..does his best to take the inwick or angle; and by a skilfully 'laid on' stone.. the inwick is taken; his stone glides off, angles towards the tee, knocks his adversary's stone out of shot—himself remaining in the while.

ˌin'wick, *v. Sc. Curling.* [f. prec. sb.] *intr.* To take or make an inwick; to 'cannon' off the inner side of another stone so as to reach the tee and knock out an opponent's stone when this is guarded in front. Usually in *vbl. sb.* **inwicking.**

(Mactaggart in quot. 1824 distinguishes *inwick* and *inring*, but this is not done by other authorities.)

1823 *Cal. Merc.* 4 Jan. (Jam.), The contest was keen at drawing, striking off, and inwicking. **1824** MACTAGGART *Gallovid. Encycl.* 280 This is somewhat different from *inring*; to *inwick a stone* is to come up a *port* or *wick*, and strike the inring of a stone seen through that wick; now this is different from a common open *inring*—the two are often confounded with each other, but they are quite different. **1898** *R. Caled. Curling Club Ann.* Const. 24 Every Competitor shall play 4 shots at each of the nine following points of the game, viz. Striking, Inwicking, Drawing, Guarding, Chap and Lie, Wick and Curl in, Raising, Chipping the Winner, and Drawing through a Port, according to the definitions and diagrams here given.

inwind, variant of ENWIND.

'inˌwinding, *ppl. a. rare.* [IN *adv.* 11 a.] Winding inwards.

1610 HOLLAND *Camden's Brit.* I. 319 A beacon is hollowed with an in-winding Bay. **1861** W. BARNES in *Macm. Mag.* June 130 The outswelling and inwinding lines from the head to the leg.

in-winter ('ɪnwɪntə(r)), *v.* [IN-*pref.*¹] *trans.* To protect (animals, particularly sheep) by keeping them indoors during severe weather and providing food for them. So **in-'wintered** *ppl. a.*, **in-'wintering** *sb.*

1961 *2nd Rep. Hill Farming Res. Organisation 1958–61* 25 Hoggs have been in-wintered experimentally in improvised cattle courts... In-wintered Blackface hoggs..thrived normally on diets of hay... Indoor wintering is quite satisfactory. **1962** *Times* 26 Nov. 17/6 The in-wintering of in-lamb ewes. **1965** COOPER & THOMAS *Profitable Sheep Farming* viii. 69 The main interest today..is the inwintering of breeding ewes on lowland farms. *Ibid.* 70 A hundred six and seven-crop Mule ewes..were inwintered in a Dutch barn. **1971** *Farmer & Stockbreeder* 16 Feb. 25/3 In-wintered ewes should also be dosed two weeks after being brought in.

†inwise, *a. Obs. rare*⁻¹. [IN-⁴. Cf. OE. *infród.*] Very wise.

1450–80 tr. *Secreta Secret.* 8 It nedith..to haue an Inwijs man and a discrete to counselle.

†inwit. *Obs.* Also 4–5 inwitt(e, -wyt(t(e, ynwitt, -wytt. [f. IN *adv.* 12 + WIT *sb.*

Formed in ME.; not related to OE. *inwit, inwid* deceit.]

1. Conscience; inward sense of right and wrong. Also ***clean inwit*** = 'a clean heart'.

a **1225** *Ancr. R.* 2 Of schir heorte & cleane inwit [L. *conscientia bona*], & trewe bileaue. *Ibid.* 306 Ure owune conscience, þet is ure inwit. **1340** HAMPOLE *Pr. Consc.* 5428 Conscience þat es called Ynwitt, And þair awen syns..there ogayne the synful sal be. **1340** *Ayenb.* 1 Þis boc is dan Michelis of Northgate, y-write an englis of his oȝene hand þet hatte: Ayenbyte of inwyt. *Ibid.* 202 Þe uerste stape is clene inwyt, þet is þe rote of þise trawe, uor wyþ-oute clene inwyt, no chastete ne lykeþ to god. **1393** LANGL. *P. Pl.* C. VII. 421 Hus wif and hys inwit edwited hym of hus synne. [**1605** CAMDEN *Rem.* (1636) 26 The certaine and inward knowledge of that which is in our minde, be it good or bad, which in the latine word we call conscience, they called *Inwit.*]

2. a. Reason, intellect, understanding; wisdom.

c **1305** *St. Katherine* 28 in *E.E.P.* (1862) 90 Biþench þe bet and turn þi þoȝt to som wysdom ic rede And whan þyn owene inwit þe saiþ þat no whar nis such a dede Almiȝtie god þu him holde þat such wonder can make. *c* **1330** R. BRUNNE *Chron. Wace* (Rolls) 16590 Hit was er a wel good þrowe, As mannes inwyt may þat wel knowe. **1387** TREVISA *Higden* (Rolls) III. 65 Anaxagorus seide þat Inwitte of god is makere of alle þinges. **1481** CAXTON *Reynard* (Arb.) 68 Suche be so woo lyke as they had loste theyr inwytte. **1587** GOLDING *De Mornay* xi. (1617) 160 Yet is there an In-wit in it which the Beast knoweth not of, which In-wit concocteth, disgesteth, and distributeth that which the Beast hath eaten.

b. *pl.* (See quot. 1380.)

[**1362** LANGL. *P. Pl.* A. x. 17 A wys kniht wiþ alle Sire Inwit he hette And haþ fyue feire sones.] *c* **1380** WYCLIF *Sel. Wks.* III. 117 Þese ben also þy fyve inwyttys; Wyl, Resoun, Mynd, Ymaginacioun, and Thogth. *c* **1440** *Gesta Rom.* I. viii. 18 (Harl. MS.) Þe Iuge, scil. Reson, owith to come don, when conscience mevith him to ȝeve dome bitwix þe v. Inwittis.

3. (Rendering L. *animus.*) Heart, soul, mind; cheer, courage.

1382 WYCLIF *Deut.* xxi. 14 If afterward she sittith not in thin inwit [1388 soule], thow shalt leeue hir free. —— *1 Sam.* i. 10 Whanne Anna was in bitter inwit [1388 soule], she preiede the Lord, wepynge largeli. —— *Acts* xxvii. 22, I counceile ȝou for to be of good ynwitt [*gloss* or herte; 1388 coumfort].

¶4. Now used as a conscious archaism in senses 1 and 2 by some modern writers.

In Joyce's *Ulysses* adopted from Dan Michel's title *Ayenbite of Inwyt* (1340); so also in quots. 1967 and 1968. Cf. AYENBITE.

1894 F. S. ELLIS *Reynard the Fox* 213 By what is truly but a bubble, Letting it master his inwit. **1922** R. BRIDGES *Coll. Ess.* (1928) III. 68 If..such good old English words as *inwit* and *wanhope* should be rehabilitated (and they have been pushing up their heads for thirty years), we should gain a great deal. **1922** JOYCE *Ulysses* 17 They wash and tub and scrub. Agenbite of inwit. Conscience. **1955** E. POUND *Classic Anthol.* III. 150 Designing in his heart felicity From inwit to his act moved ever so straight He got in sovereignty the whole Quadrate. *Ibid.* 174 There is no light in your conscience And your acts shed, therefore, no light In your inwit. **1967** *Punch* 12 July 72/1 There's this dedicated, totally frenetic fumble under the skin of the times' underbelly..for the agenbite of inwit. **1968** *Listener* 28 Mar. 411/3 Very probably Bond fans will be able to turn a blind eye to the bites and agenbites of new-Bond's *inwit.*

inwith ('ɪnwɪθ), *prep.* and *adv.* (*a.*, *sb.*) *Obs.* exc. *Sc.* Also 3 **inewið, iwið,** 5 **inweth;** 5–6 *Sc.* in(n)outh. [f. IN *adv.* + WITH *prep.* Cf. WITHIN.]

A. *prep.* Within, inside of.

†1. Of place. *Obs.*

a **1225** *Ancr. R.* 424 (MS.C.), Inwið þe wanes ha muhe werie scapeloris. *a* **1240** *Ureisun* in *Cott. Hom.* 187 Hwa is þenne unwaschen þe haueþ þis halwende wet inwið his heorte? **13..** *Gaw. & Gr. Knt.* 1055, I nolde..For alle þe londe inwyth Logres. *c* **1386** CHAUCER *Merch. T.* 700 This purs hath she inwith hir bosom hyd. *c* **1420** *Pallad. on Husb.* III. 1133 Summe ek hem sette inweth a bulbe of squille. **1489** *Barbour's Bruce* v. 348 (Edin. MS.) Till thaim that war off the castell, That war all innouth the chancell. **1513** DOUGLAS *Æneis* x. xi. 132 Turnus..spedis to this schip, Ran owr the brig, and inwith burd can skyp.

†b. On the inner side of. *Sc. Obs.*

1535 STEWART *Cron. Scot.* III. 271 Intumulat..Ben in the queir sum thing inwith his quene.

†2. Of time. *Obs.*

a **1225** *Leg. Kath.* 1941 Inwið þeos þre dahes. **13..** *Seuyn Sag.* (W.) 126 Inwith yeres thre, Sal he be so wise of lare, That ye sal thank me euermare. *c* **1386** CHAUCER *L.G.W.* Prol. 209, I fel on slepe, in with an houre or twoo. *a* **1400–50** *Alexander* 3900 Be þai had fyneschid þis fiȝt was ferre in with euyn, Foure houres full farne & þe fifte neghes.

†3. Of state or condition. *Obs.*

a **1300** *Cursor M.* 26604 In-wit [*Fairf. MS.* wiþ-in] mi soru al o mi lijf I sal fast wit mi-seluen strijf.

B. *adv.* **†1.** Denoting position: Within, on the inside, inwardly. *Obs.*

a **1225** *Juliana* 7 He..felde him iwundet in wið in his heorte. *a* **1225** *Ancr. R.* 38 Make me tellen lutel of euerich blisse vtewið, & froure me inewið. *c* **1230** *Hali Meid.* 29 Ha beoð riche & weolefule iwið iþe herte. *a* **1300** *Cursor M.* 8860 Þat sais þe men þat þar has ben And in-wit bath and vte-wit sene. *c* **1420** *Anturs of Arth.* 445 In-withe was a chapelle, a chambour, a halle. **1536** BELLENDEN *Cron. Scot., Cosmogr.* viii. (1541) B v b, Ane lang mand narow halsit and wyid mouthit, with mony stobis Inouth. **1565** *Privy Counc. Rec.* 19 May in Keith *Hist. Ch. Scot.* (1734) 279 *note*, It is appoynted that the saidis Lordis of Secret-Counsale schall convene inwith upon the 10. of June next.

2. Denoting direction: Inwards; = IN-BY. *Sc.*

1768 ROSS *Helenore* 82 Upo' a burn I fell, Wi' bony even rode an' in-with sett. *Mod. Sc. dial.* Come inwith; ye'll be cauld outbye there.

b. Hence attrib. as *adj. Sc.*

1768 ROSS *Helenore* 69 We Or e'en may chance some in-with place to see. **1789** *Ibid.* 47 He the west and she the east hand took, The inwith road by favour of the brook.

†C. as *sb.* (See quot.) *Obs.*

1607 MARKHAM *Caval.* VI. (1617) 9 If the fierce Horse haue in his skelping course, either vpwithes, inwithes, or downe-withes, which is that he may either runne within the side of hilles, vp hils, or downe hils [etc.].

inwlappen, early form of INLAP *v.*, *Obs.*

inwomb, obs. variant of ENWOMB *v.*

†in'wone, *v. Obs.* Also 4 **-won, -wun.** [f. IN-¹ + WONE *v.*, after L. *inhabitāre*: cf. MDu., MLG. *inwonen*, Ger. *einwohnen.*] *trans.* and *intr.* To inhabit.

a **1300** *E.E. Psalter* lxviii. 41 [lxix. 35] Inwone þare sal þai yhite. *a* **1340** HAMPOLE *Psalter* xxxvi. 3 Hope in lord & doe goednes & inwon þe erth. *c* **1400** *Destr. Troy* 13864 Ho.. enfourmet hym fully of þe fre rewme, Þat the worthy in-wonet.

†'inwoning, *vbl. sb. Obs. rare*⁻¹. [IN *adv.* 11 c. Cf. Du. *inwoning*, Ger. *einwohnung.*] Inhabiting, indwelling.

1647 H. MORE *Song of Soul* III. App. lxxvii, This was his guerdon, this his wicked wage, From the inwoning of that Stygian Crow.

[**inwood**, mistake for INWEED *v.*, q.v.]

inword, obs. form of INWARD.

in-word: see IN *a.* 2 b.

†'in-work, *sb. Obs. rare.* [IN *adv.* 12.]

a. Interior or inside work; work on the inner side. **b.** *pl.* Inner works or defences of a fortified place.

1601–2 in Willis & Clark *Cambridge* (1886) II. 486 Diuers bricklayers raising in-worke of the imbattlements. **1623** JAS. I *Repl. Parl.* in Rushw. *Hist. Coll.* (1659) I. 136 A Fortification, which must have Out-works and In-works. **1645** RUTHERFORD *Tryal & Tri. Faith* (1845) 30 Christ hath taken the castle, both in-works and out-works. **1658** EARL MONMOUTH tr. *Paruta's Wars of Cyprus* 56.

inwork (ˌɪn'wɜːk), *v. rare.* [IN-¹ or IN *adv.* 7. Cf. Du. *inwerken*, Ger. *einwirken*, Da. *indvirke*, Sw. *invirka.* See also INWROUGHT.]

1. *trans.* To work (something) into a tissue as by weaving or embroidering. See INWROUGHT.

1681–6 J. SCOTT *Chr. Life* I. iv. §5 (R.) From these dangers you will never be wholly free, till you have..in-wrought all the virtues of religion into your natures.

2. To work, operate, or produce (some effect) *in.*

1855 PUSEY *Doctr. Real Presence* Note S. 347 Inworking good in a good disposition which receives It, and implanting damnation in the evil. **1865** —— *Truth Eng. Ch.* 47 An actual mystical oneness, inwrought by Christ our Head. **1866** —— *Min. Proph.* 19/2 Where he inworketh in her that hope.

3. *intr.* To work within.

1874 PUSEY *Lent. Serm.* 185 Paul..by whose mouth Christ spake, he, in whom Christ inworked.

in-work: see also IN *prep.* 10 a.

'inˌworker. *rare.* [IN *adv.* 12.] **1.** A worker within.

1587 GOLDING *De Mornay* xiv. 203 A plaine proofe of that she [the soul] is not the body nor any part of the body, but the very life and inworker of the body.

2. One who works on the premises of a shop or factory.

1909 *Fabian News* XX. 75/1 A minimum wage for both inworkers and outworkers.

'inˌworking, *vbl. sb.* [IN-¹, or IN *adv.* 11 c. In 16th c. app. a rendering of Gr. ἐνέργεια ENERGY (f. ἐν in + ἔργον work).] **†a.** Operation, action, energy. *Obs.* **b.** Internal operation, working within.

1587 GOLDING *De Mornay* v. 50 Vnderstanding is an in-working which abideth..in the partie which hath it, and passeth not into any outward thing. *Ibid.* xv. 231 If the Minde haue any inworking of its owne without any helpe of the Sences. *a* **1800** MACKNIGHT cited by WEBSTER (1828). **1829** P. N. SHUTTLEWORTH *Paraphr. Apost. Ep.* 134 Yet all this variety of faculties is nothing more than the inworkings of one and the same Spirit. **1873** GOULBURN *Pers. Relig.* iii. 22 The result of His inworking in the heart.

'inˌworking, *ppl. a.* [IN *adv.* 11 a.] **†a.** Active, effective (= Gr. ἐνεργής). *Obs.* **b.** Working within; operating internally.

1587 GOLDING *De Mornay* v. 49–50 The actiue or inworking vertue, power and nature, which we marke in all things in this world. *Ibid.* 60 In which worke both our inworking power and also our wit and our will doe concurre all together. **1828** WEBSTER, *Inworking*, working or operating within. **1860** ELLICOTT *Life Our Lord* I. 35 By the grace of the inworking Spirit. **1893** in Barrows *Parl. Relig.* II. 1084 The Vedic sages beheld in every force and phenomenon of nature an inworking light of the divinity.

inworn, *ppl. a.* [IN *adv.* 11 b.] **a.** *pa. pple.* of *wear in*: Worn or pressed in. **b.** as *a.* Inveterate.

1641 MILTON *Ch. Govt.* II. i, That whatever faultines was but superficial to Prelaty at the beginning, is..long since branded and inworn into the very essence therof. **1864** PUSEY *Lect. Daniel* vii. 447 Following the old and inworn error of his race.

inwound ('ɪnwaʊnd), *ppl. a.* [f. IN *adv.* 11 b + *wound*, pa. pple. of WIND *v.*] Wound in.

18.. G. MEREDITH *Ball. Past Merid.* iii, Then memory.. And sightless hope..Joined notes of Death and Life till night's decline: Of Death, of Life, those inwound notes are mine.

inwoven (ɪn'wəʊv(ə)n), *ppl. a.* Also 9 **en-.** [pa. pple. of INWEAVE: see IN *adv.* 11 b.] Woven in; interwoven.

1667 MILTON *P.L.* IV. 693 The roofe Of thickest covert was inwoven shade. **1725** POPE *Odyss.* IV. 406 Rich tapestry, stiff with inwoven gold. *a* **1794** SIR W. JONES *Hymn to Lacshmi* Wks. 1799 VI. 363 He saw brisk fountains dance, crisp riv'lets wind O'er borders trim, and round inwoven bow'rs. **1816** SHELLEY *Alastor* 648 His last sight Was the great moon..With whose dun beams inwoven darkness seemed To mingle. *a* **1822** —— *Mann. Anc.* in *Ess. & Lett.* (Camelot) 47 Their eyes..could have entangled no heart in soul-enwoven labyrinths.

inwrap, -ment, variant of ENWRAP, -MENT.

†in'wrapper. *Obs.* [f. prec. + -ER¹.] That which enwraps; an enveloping structure.

1553 UDALL tr. *Geminus' Anat.* I vj b/2 In this figure we haue sette forth the inwrapper called *Plexus.*

inwreathe, variant of ENWREATHE *v.*

†in'writing, *vbl. sb. Obs. rare.* [IN-¹ or IN *adv.* 11 c: after L. *inscriptio.*] Inscription.

1382 WYCLIF *Mark* xii. 16 Whos is this ymage, and the in wrytinge? **1611** FLORIO, *Inscrittura*, an inwriting, an inscription.

†in'written, *pa. pple. Obs.* [IN-¹ or IN *adv.* 11 b; after L. *inscriptus.*] **a.** Inscribed, written (*in* a book or list). **b.** Inscribed, written on or in.

1382 WYCLIF *Prov.* Prol., The boc..that is inwriten the Wisdam of Salamon. —— *Ecclus.* xlviii. 10 Thou art inwrite in domes of tymes. **1598** FLORIO, *Inscritto*, inwritten, made an inscription or superscription. **1605** CAMDEN *Rem.* 168 With a scrole inwritten, *Mihi Vita Spica Virginis.*

ˈin-ˌwritten, *ppl. a. rare.* [IN *adv.* 11 b.] Written within, i.e. on the mind.

1684 Z. CAWDREY *Certainty Salvat.* 2 The In-written Law of his own Conscience.

inwrought (see below), *ppl. a.* Also 8–9 **en-.** [f. IN *adv.* 11 b + *wrought*, pa. pple. of *work* vb.: cf. INWORK *v.* The form in *en-* is due to the exchange of *en-*, *in-*, in other words: see IN-².]

I. as *pa. pple.* (ɪnˈrɔːt).

1. Of a fabric, etc.: Having something worked in by way of decoration. *lit.* and *fig.*

α. **1637** MILTON *Lycidas* 105 Next Camus,..His mantle hairy and his bonnet sedge, Inwrought with figures dim. **1725** POPE *Odyss.* I. 212 With purple robes inwrought, and stiff with gold. **1855** LONGF. *Hiaw.* XI. 76 Shirt of doe-skin, ..All inwrought with beads of wampum.

β. **1754** DODSLEY *Agric.* I. (R.), Massy plate, enwrought With curious costly workmanship. **1850** MRS. BROWNING *Poems* II. 386 Now God be thanked for years enwrought With love. **1870** MORRIS *Earthly Par.* III. IV. 181 The brazen gates enwrought With many a dreamer's steadfast thought.

2. Of a pattern, figure, etc.: Worked into, or embroidered on, a fabric. Also *transf.*

α. **1740** C. PITT *Virg. Æneid* V. 323 There royal Ganymede, inwrought with art, O'er hills and forests hunts the bounding hart. **1791** E. DARWIN *Bot. Gard.* I. 134 Raised o'er the woof, by Beauty's hand inwrought. **1892** A. E. LEE *Hist. Columbus* (O.) II. 225 A beautiful floral arch with the name U. S. Grant inwrought.

β. **1805** WORDSW. *Prelude* VIII. 243 The flowers Of lowly thyme, by Nature's skill enwrought In the wild turf. **1819** —— *Haunted Tree* 12 Flowers enwrought On silken tissue.

3. Worked into the same tissue, intimately combined or worked together *with* something.

α. **1824** CAMPBELL *Theodric* 216 With her graceful wit there was inwrought A wildly sweet unworldliness of thought. **1863** GEO. ELIOT *Romola* xxx, All that part of his life which was closely inwrought with his emotions.

β. **1844** MRS. BROWNING *Lost Bower* xxiv, And the ivy, veined and glossy, Was enwrought with eglantine.

b. Worked into anything as a constituent.

1734 WATTS *Reliq. Juv.* xlvi. (1789) 129 A good degree of courage inwrought into our very frame. **1864** BOWEN *Logic* x. 328 Native to the mind and inwrought into its very constitution. **1882** FARRAR *Early Chr.* I. 249 Even discords can be inwrought into the vast sequences of some mighty harmony.

II. 4. as *adj.* (ˈɪnrɔːt). (In senses as above.)

1830 TENNYSON *Arab. Nts.* xiv, Engarlanded and diaper'd With inwrought flowers, a cloth of gold. **1862** M. HOPKINS *Hawaii* 127 The inwrought sacerdotalism ruling over..all the systems. **1880** BIRDWOOD *Indian Arts* II. 68 Its marvellously woven tissues and sumptuously inwrought apparel. **1883** *Harper's Mag.* 904/2 Brocaded satin with inwrought daisies.

inwy(e, obs. Sc. form of ENVY: see INVY.

‖**inyala** (ɪˈnjɑːlə). [Native name: see quots.] An antelope of S. Africa, *Tragelaphus angasi*, ranging from Nyasaland to Zululand.

1848 G. F. ANGAS in *Proc. Zool. Soc.* 89 This new and brilliant Antelope, the Inyala of the Amazulu. **1850** PROUDFOOT *ibid.* 199 The Mahlengas (or Cutfaces) which people call this animal Inyala. **1863** W. BALDWIN *Afr. Hunting* 92 A moment after I beheld a noble buck inyala walking leisurely away. **1900** *Q. Rev.* Apr. 304 Buffalo, koodoo, inyala and other animals that need considerable supplies of water.

‖**inyanga** (ɪˈnjɑːŋə). *S. Afr.* Also **enyanga, inyanger.** [Zulu.] A medicine-man (see also quot. 1826).

1826 N. ISAACS *Jrnl.* 1 Apr. in *Trav. E. Afr.* (1936) I. vi. 82 The 'inyangers', or water doctors, arrived to take us across the river. *Ibid.* 83 The inyangers from their great muscular power, and experience in their occupation, kept us above the water. **1862** G. H. MASON *Zululand* xiv. 180 An 'Enyanga', as the said professor is called, is a formidable foe; merely as being master of the most deadly poisons in the world. **1946** *Archit. Rev.* C. 22/1 Before the first stick or stone is cleared the headman has the new site approved and then treated by an inyanga—a specialist in various types of native medicine, a man usually labelled by the ethnocentric European as 'magician'. **1954** H. GIBBS *Background to Bitterness* II. ii. 66 He [*sc.* Dingaan] decided to spare Owen and a few American missionaries in Natal—the next morning his inyangas told Owen they would be spared. **1970** *Golden City Post* 28 June, Millionaire inyanga Sethuntsa Khotso, who last year threw the bones and successfully tipped Naval Escort, says that Golden Jewel will win the Durban July next Saturday.

in-yede, -yhede, -yode, pa. t. of IN-GO *v. Obs.*

†**inˈyet,** *v. Obs.* In 4–6 **inȝet(t.** [f. IN-¹ + YET *v.* to pour.] *trans.* To pour in, infuse. Hence †**inˈyetting** *vbl. sb.*, infusion.

c **1340** HAMPOLE *Prose Tr.* 3 This name Ihesu..inȝettes savoure of heuenly thynges. *Ibid.* 4 Sothely þay sall joye now be in-ȝettynge of grace. *c* **1400** *Prymer* in Maskell *Mon. Rit.* II. 108 God, that..inȝettist ȝiftis of charite to the hertis of thi feithful seruauntis. **1513** DOUGLAS *Æneis* VII. vii. 30 Sone as the first infectioun..inȝet quietlie had sche.

†**inˈyoated,** *pa. pple. Obs. rare.* [Altered from *inyote(n*, pa. pple. of INYET *v.*] Poured in.

a **1618** SYLVESTER *Job Triumph.* II. 271 O that my words.. Were grav'n in Marble with an yron pen With Lead in-yoated (to fill up agen).

inyoite (ˈɪnjəʊaɪt). *Min.* [f. the name of *Inyo* County, California + -ITE¹.] A hydrated calcium borate, $Ca_2B_6O_{11}.13H_2O$, found as colourless rhombic crystals.

1914 W. T. SCHALLER in *Jrnl. Washington Acad. Sci.* IV. 355 Inyoite and Meyerhofferite, two new Calcium Borates from Death Valley, Inyo County, California, belong to the Colemanite series. **1921** *Bull. Geol. Survey Canada* XXXII. 2 The crystals of inyoite from Hillsborough are remarkably well developed and clear. **1959** *Acta Crystallogr.* XII. 162 Polyions of inyoite are connected to one another and to neighboring water molecules by bonding through calcium ions and by hydrogen bonds.

inˈyoke, *v. rare.* [IN-¹: cf. *enyoke* (EN-¹ 3).] *trans.* **a.** To yoke or unite *to* something. **b.** To yoke in a wagon, etc. Hence **inˈyoking** *vbl. sb.*

1595 MARKHAM *Sir R. Grinvile* cxxx, These all accord.. To end his liues date by their cruell strife, And him vnto a blessed state inyoke. *a* **1654** J. TAYLOR (Water-p.) *Unnat. Father*, A chaine consists of diuers links and every linke depends and is inyoak'd vpon one another. **1842** MOFFAT *Mission. Labours S. Afr.* 118 Daily inyoking and unyoking. *Ibid.* 391 All inyoked their oxen at the same time.

Io¹ (ˈaɪəʊ). [a. L. *īō*, Gr. *ἰώ*.] A Greek and Latin exclamation of joy or triumph; sometimes in Eng. as *sb.*, an utterance of 'Io!', an exultant shout or song. Also ***Io pæan***: see PÆAN.

1592 LYLY *Midas* v. iii, Io paeans let us sing, To physicke's, and to poesie's king. **1602** MARSTON *Antonio's Rev.* v. iv, Why then Io to Hymen. **1640** GLAPTHORNE *Wallenstein* I. i. Wks. 1874 II. 19 When their loud voyces sing, Ios to victory. **1678** DRYDEN & LEE *Œdipus* IV. i, Rocks, valleys, hills, with splitting Ios ring: Io, Jocasta, Io pæan sing! **1709** *Let. to Ld. M[ayor]* 4 Some of our false Brothers..had long before this been singing their Io-Pæans in St. Paul's.

io² (ˈaɪəʊ). [mod.L., the specific name of the insect, a. Gr. *Ἰώ*, daughter of the river god Inachus.] In full, ***io moth***. A large yellow North American moth, *Automeris io*, distinguished by prominent ocelli on the hind wings.

[**1869** *Canad. Entomologist* II. 20 These caterpillars.. proved to be the very familiar larvae of what is commonly known as the Io Emperor-moth.] **1870** *Canada Farmer* 15 Sept. 336/2 The beautiful, pale yellowish-green caterpillar ..is the larva of the handsome Io-moth. **1873** C. V. RILEY in *5th Ann. Rep. Missouri State Entom.* 133 The Io Moth.. is one of our most beautiful moths, receiving its name from two conspicuous eye-spots on the hind wings, in allusion to the ancient Greek heroine, Io. **1912** G. STRATTON-PORTER *Moths of Limberlost* viii. 207 Mr. Eisen presented me with a pair of *Hyperchiria Io*... Because the Io was yellow, I wanted it. **1954** BORROR & DELONG *Introd. Study Insects* i. 6 A few caterpillars, such as the saddleback and the larva of the io moth, have stinging hairs.

io-, earlier spelling of JO-: see I, J, the letters.

ioate, iobardy, obs. forms of JOT, JEOPARDY.

iod- (aɪəʊd), combining form of mod.L. *iodum* IODINE, used (chiefly before a vowel) in forming names of iodine compounds. (Before a cons. usu. IODO-, q.v.) Among these are **iodaˈcetic** *a.*, in ***iodacetic acid***: see *iodoacetic adj.* s.v. IODO-; its salts are **iodˈacetates**; **ˈiodamide, iodaˈmmonium,** compounds formed by the action of iodine on ammonia, mostly of an explosive character; **iodˈargyrite** *Min.* = IODYRITE; see quot. 1971; **iodarˈsenious** *a.*, containing iodine and arsenic; **iodˈembolite** *Min.* [EMBOLITE], the name now given to IODOBROMITE; **iodˈethane, iodˈethyl,** ethyl iodide; **iodhyˈdrargyrate**: see IODO-; **iodˈhydrate** = HYDRIODATE; **iodˈhydric** *a.*, = HYDRIODIC; **iodˈhydrin,** an iodine ether of glycerin; **iodˈiodide**: see IODO-; **iodˈozone** (see quot.); **iodruˈbidium,** iodide of rubidium, RbI.

1873 WATTS *Fownes' Chem.* (ed. 11) 681 *Iodacetic Acid and Di-iodacetic Acid have likewise been obtained. **1868** A. RAMSAY *Rudiments of Mineral.* v. 143 *Iodargyrite readily fuses, colours the flame red, and yields a globule of silver when reduced. **1950** *Thorpe's Dict. Appl. Chem.* (ed. 4) X. 766/1 Silver iodide, AgI, occurs in Chili, Peru, Mexico, and Spain as the mineral iodargyrite in citron-yellow hexagonal crystals. **1971** *Mineral. Mag.* XXXVIII. 104 Recommendations of the Commission [on New Minerals and Mineral Names of the International Mineralogical Association] on minerals for which more than one name is in common use... Iodargyrite, not iodyrite. **1902** PRIOR & SPENCER in *Mineral. Mag.* XIII. 176 Since the name [*sc.* iodobromite] is a particularly misleading one..we propose to refer to the varieties of the cerargyrite group which contain all three halogens as iodiferous embolites or briefly *iodembolites. **1944** *Mineral. Abstr.* IX. 59 At Maikan, near Pavlodar, iodembolite and embolite occur in native sulphur. **1873** WATTS *Fownes' Chem.* (ed. 11) 580 *Iodethane is a colourless liquid, of penetrating ethereal odour. **1866** ODLING *Anim. Chem.* 154 Tartaric acid, when heated with aqueous iodide of hydrogen or *iodhydric acid, is converted into malic acid with liberation of iodine. **1872** WATTS *Dict. Chem.* III. 284 Iodhydric or hydriodic acid. *Ibid.* 283 *Iodhydrins..only two have hitherto been obtained, both of which are glycidic ethers. **1877** —— *Fownes' Chem.* (ed. 12) II. 183 Iodhydrins..di-iodhydrin..tri-iodhydrin or glyceryl tri-iodide. **1872** C. B. FOX *Ozone* 188 A portion of the Iodine set free by the Ozone has been said to be converted by additional Ozone into *Iodozone. **1894** *Brit. Med. Jrnl.* 13 Jan., Epit. 8/1 *Iodrubidium, a substance resembling iodide of potassium in being odourless, somewhat bitter and saline in taste.

iodal (ˈaɪədəl). *Chem.* [f. IOD- + AL(COHOL), after CHLORAL.] A compound of iodine (CI_3COH) obtained as an oily liquid; analogous to chloral, and said to possess similar properties.

1863–72 WATTS *Dict. Chem.* I. 34 (s.v. *Acetyl*), Hydride of Tri-iodacetyl, $C_2I_3O.H$, Iodal.

iodate (ˈaɪədeɪt), *sb. Chem.* [f. IOD-IC + -ATE⁴.] A salt of iodic acid.

1826 HENRY *Elem. Chem.* II. 16 Iodate of zinc falls down in an insoluble state, when iodate of potassa is added to a solution of sulphate of zinc. **1871** ROSCOE *Elem. Chem.* 122 Iodine and caustic potash give potassium iodate, potassium iodide, and water.

ˈiodate, *v.* [f. prec.: cf. -ATE³ 7.] *trans.* To impregnate or treat with iodine. Chiefly in ppl. adj. **ˈiodated,** impregnated with or containing iodine. **ioˈdation,** the action of impregnating with iodine.

1836 J. M. GULLY *Magendie's Formul.*, I have long used the iodated and ioduretted waters. **1855** MAYNE *Expos. Lex.*, *Iodatus*, containing iodine; applied to a solid combination of iodine with olefiant gas, termed *iodated ether*, discovered by Faraday: iodated. **1875** *Ure's Dict. Arts* III. 567 Experiment has proved that the blackening of one variety of iodated paper, and the preservation of another, depends on the simple admixture of a very minute excess of the nitrate of silver.

†**iode.** *Chem. Obs.* [a. F. *iode* IODINE.]

1. = IODINE.

1830 HERSCHEL *Stud. Nat. Phil.* 94 The general family resemblance between certain groups of bodies, now regarded as elementary, (as..for instance, chlorine, iode, and brome).

2. = IODIDE.

1826 HENRY *Elem. Chem.* I. 500 All the metals unite with iodine, and form compounds which have been called *iodes*, *iodures*, or *iodides*. The last term is to be preferred, on account of the analogy of the compounds denoted by it with *oxides* and *chlorides*.

iodic (aɪˈɒdɪk), *a.* [f. IOD- + -IC: cf. F. *iodique* (Gay-Lussac, 1812).] Of or pertaining to iodine.

1. *Chem.* Containing iodine in union with oxygen; as in ***iodic acid*** (*hydrogen iodate*), an oxygen-acid of iodine (HIO_3), obtained in white semitransparent crystals; ***iodic anhydride*** (*iodine pentoxide*), I_2O_5. Also *Min.* in ***iodic silver*** = IODYRITE.

Compounds containing a smaller proportion of iodine are called *per-iodic*, as periodic acid, H_5IO_6.

1826 HENRY *Elem. Chem.* I. 225 Iodic acid enters into combination with all those fluid or solid acids, which it does not decompose. **1831** T. P. JONES *Convers. Chem.* xxiv. 252 With oxygen it [Iodine] produces iodic acid, and with chlorine chloriodic acid. **1845** DARWIN *Voy. Nat.* xvi. (1873) 365 The presence of iodic salts. **1868** DANA *Min.* (ed. 5) §143 Iodyrite..Iodic Silver.

2. *Path.* Caused by administration of iodine.

1887 *Syd. Soc. Lex.*, *Iodic intoxication*, same as Iodism. **1897** *Allbutt's Syst. Med.* IV. 792 The curious feature about the iodic œdema is, that it may come on after the administration of a few small doses.

iodidate (ˈaɪədɪdeɪt), *v. Photogr.* [f. IODIDE + -ATE³ 7.] *trans.* To convert (silver) into its iodide. Chiefly in ppl. adj. **ˈiodidated**: cf. *oxidated.*

1853 R. HUNT *Man. Photogr.* 255 The influence of all the rays, excepting the yellow, was to loosen the adhesion of the iodidated surface, and the under layer of unaffected silver. **1859** *Encycl. Brit.* XVII. 552/2 The most beautiful were upon 'the daguerrotype iodidated tablets'.

iodide (ˈaɪədaɪd). *Chem.* [f. IOD- + -IDE.] A binary compound of iodine with a more positive element, or an organic radical; analogous to one or more atoms of hydriodic acid (HI), itself called on this type ***hydrogen iodide***.

1822 IMISON *Sc. & Art* II. 20 The same syllables are prefixed to chlorides and iodides. **1826** HENRY *Elem. Chem.* II. 136 Iodide of silver is formed when hydriodic acid is added to nitrate of silver. **1842** *E. Turner's Elem. Chem.* II. xiii. (ed. 7) 299 Iodine..has a strong attraction for the pure metals, and for most of the simple non-metallic substances, producing substances which are termed *Iodides* or *Iodurets*. **1873** WATTS *Fownes' Chem.* (ed. 11) 227 Phosphorus forms also two iodides. **1898** J. HUTCHINSON *Archives Surg.* IX. No. 36. 326 He had..been taking iodides and mercury.

iodiferous (aɪəˈdɪfərəs), *a.* [f. IOD- + -(I)FEROUS.] Producing iodine.

iodimetry (aɪəˈdɪmɪtrɪ). *Chem.* [f. IODI(NE *sb.* + -METRY.] The titrimetric analysis of an oxidizing or reducing agent using the iodine/iodide redox system; *spec.* the quantitative analysis of a solution of a reducing agent by titration with a standard solution of iodine. Cf. IODOMETRY.

1897 *Jrnl. Chem. Soc.* LXXII. II. 342 (*heading*) Barium thiosulphate as basis for iodimetry. **1907** LINCOLN & WALTON *Exerc. Elem. Quantitative Chem. Analysis* 78 The methods of determination in iodimetry may be divided into three general classes: 1. The titration of..reducing agents. 2...oxidizing agents... 3. Free chlorine. **1939** A. I. VOGEL *Text-bk. Quantitative Inorg. Analysis* iii. 401 Iodimetry covers titrations *with* a standard solution of iodine. Iodometry deals with the titration *of* iodine liberated in chemical reactions. **1960** R. J. WINTERTON in C. L. & D. W.

Wilson *Comprehensive Analytical Chem.* IB. vii. 249 Iodine ..may be used as a standard solution and titrated into the reducing solution, or it may be liberated from potassium iodide or some other compound of iodine by an oxidising agent in solution, and titrated with thiosulphate solution... The use of standard iodine is called direct iodimetry, and the other method indirect iodimetry.

So **iodi'metric**, *a.*, of or pertaining to iodimetry; **iodi'metrically** *adv.*, by means of iodimetry.

1887 *Jrnl. Chem. Soc.* LII. 997 The iodimetric method serves well for the assay of commercial sodium sulphide. *Ibid.* 998 Ferrous and ferric oxides, in hydrochloric acid solution, can be determined iodimetrically. **1931** JENKINS & DUMEZ *Quantitative Pharmaceutical Chem.* viii. 123 Iodimetric methods include some of the most exact processes of volumetric analysis, because..the presence of one part of iodine in several million parts of solution can be recognised by means of starch indicator solution. **1963** SKOOG & WEST *Fund. Analytical Chem.* xx. 458 The first [category] is made up of procedures that use a standard solution of iodine to titrate easily oxidized substances. These are termed direct or iodimetric methods and have rather limited applicability since iodine is a relatively weak oxidizing agent. **1969** H. T. EVANS tr. *Hägg's Gen. & Inorg. Chem.* xxi. 534 Since many oxidizing agents oxidize iodide ion to iodine, such substances can also be determined iodimetrically.

iodinate ('aɪədɪneɪt), *v.* [f. IODIN(E *sb.* + -ATE *suffix*[3].] *trans.* **a.** To introduce an iodine atom into (a compound or molecule) in place of a hydrogen atom. **b.** To treat with iodine. Hence **'iodinated** *ppl. a.*, **'iodinating** *vbl. sb.*

1908 *Jrnl. Chem. Soc.* XCIV. 778, *m*-Nitroaniline is readily iodinated by adding iodine..to a solution of the base. **1917** *Jrnl. Amer. Chem. Soc.* XXXIX. 444 The xylenols are not so readily iodinated as the lower members. **1921** *Biochem. Jrnl.* XV. 320 The monochloride of iodine has been used before as an iodinating agent. **1926** *Chem. Abstr.* XX. 596 (*heading*) Iodinated pyrrole derivatives. **1948** *New Biol.* IV. 138 Similar improvements in the yields of cows can be obtained by injecting the thyroid hormone—thyroxine—or by feeding the closely related substances known as iodinated proteins. **1964** N. G. CLARK *Mod. Org. Chem.* xiv. 275 They are then all iodinated three times on the methyl group. **1968** *Canad. Jrnl. Physiol. & Pharmacol.* XLVI. 449 The effects of increasing or decreasing the endogenous secretion of thyroid-stimulating hormone on the iodinating activity of the rat thyroid gland were investigated. **1969** *Nature* 23 Aug. 778/2 Thomas [etc.].. have measured..the uptake of radioactive iodine in twenty-two adults before and after swimming in an iodinated pool.

iodination (aɪədɪ'neɪʃən). *Chem.* [f. IODIN(E *sb.* + -ATION.] **a.** The replacement of a hydrogen atom in a compound or molecule by an iodine atom.

1873 *Chem. News* 26 Sept. 167/2 (*heading*) On the chlorination and iodination of anthracen. **1919** *Jrnl. Chem. Soc.* XLI. 293 Iodobenzene on iodination with the required quantity of iodine and nitric acid gives *p*-diiodobenzene. **1971** *Jrnl. Chem. Educ.* XLVIII. 508/1 Iodination by molecular iodine occurs only with phenols and amines.

b. Addition of iodine (e.g. to a water supply).

1966 *Jrnl. Clin. Endocrinol. & Metabolism* XVI. 620/1 Prior to iodination of the water. **1969** *Arch. Environmental Health* XIX. 127/1 Iodination of a public water supply has proven to be technically and commercially feasible.

iodine ('aɪədɪn, -aɪn), *sb. Chem.* [Named by Sir H. Davy in 1814, from F. *iode*, the name given by Gay-Lussac (ad. Gr. ἰώδης violet-coloured, f. ἴον violet + -ειδης like, resembling) from the colour of its vapour, with termination -INE[3], as in *chlorine*.]

1. One of the non-metallic elements, belonging to the halogen group; at ordinary temperatures a greyish-black soft brittle solid with a metallic lustre, volatilizing into a dense vapour of a deep violet colour; in chemical properties resembling chlorine and bromine, but less energetic. Symbol I; atomic weight 127.

It exists in sea-water and mineral springs, and in sea-weed and many marine animals, and is extensively obtained from the mother-liquor of Chilian sodium nitrate.

1814 DAVY in *Phil. Trans.* 91 The name *ione* has been proposed in France for this new substance from its colour in the gaseous state, from ἴον viola... The name *ione*, in English, would lead to confusion. By terming it *iodine*, from ἰώδης violaceous, this confusion will be avoided, and the name will be more analogous to chlorine and fluorine. *Ibid.* 92 It is probable that *iodine* will be found in many combinations in nature. **1826** HENRY *Elem. Chem.* I. 222 Iodine was discovered accidentally, about the beginning of the year 1812, by M. Courtois, a manufacturer of saltpetre at Paris. **1853** W. GREGORY *Inorg. Chem.* (ed. 3) 114 In power of affinity iodine stands below bromine, as bromine does below chlorine. **1862** ANSTED *Channel Isl.* 512 The source of supply of iodine is the seaweed growing on the rocks round the Channel Islands.

2. *attrib.* **a.** Containing or impregnated with iodine, as ***iodine fluid, liniment, ointment, water***. **b.** Of iodine, as ***iodine injection, vapour***; esp. in names of compounds, as ***iodine monochloride***, ICl; ***iodine trichloride***, ICl_3; ***iodine pentoxide*** (iodic anhydride), I_2O_5. **c.** Caused by the action of iodine, as ***iodine fever, poisoning***.

1836 J. M. GULLY *Magendie's Formul.* 114 The iodine ointment applied to the nodes relieved the pain. **1860** *N. Syd. Soc. Year-bk. for 1859*. 317 The child..died two hours afterwards, from peritonitis and iodine-poisoning. **1877** WATTS *Fownes' Chem.* (ed. 12) I. 200 Hydriodic acid gas.. is composed..of equal volumes of iodine vapour and hydrogen. *Ibid.* 202 Iodine monochloride is a reddish-brown oily liquid. **1898** P. MANSON *Trop. Dis.* viii. 167 Indolent bubonic [plague] swellings should be treated with iodine liniment.

d. Other *attrib.* uses, as **iodine number, value** [tr. G. *jodzahl* (A. Hübl 1884, in *Dingler's polytechn. Jrnl.* CCLIII. 287)], the proportion of unsaturated matter present in a substance as measured by the number of grammes of iodine which can be taken up by 100 grammes of the substance; **iodine scarlet**, mercuric iodide, HgI_2, a brilliant red powder.

1885 *Analyst* X. 123 About everything on the list which might be used to adulterate or be substituted for butter, gave iodine numbers so far removed from that for genuine butter that no difficulty would occur. **1969** J. R. HOLUM *Introd. Org. & Biol. Chem.* ix. 302 Oleic acid has an iodine number of 90, linoleic acid 181, and linolenic acid 274. **1835** G. FIELD *Chromatography* x. 94 Iodine scarlet is a new pigment of a most vivid and beautiful scarlet colour, exceeding the brilliancy of vermilion. **1885** *Encycl. Brit.* XIX. 87/2 From mercury combined with iodine is prepared a pigment of unequalled vivacity and brilliance, Iodine Scarlet, but unfortunately as fugitive as it is bright. **1969** R. MAYER *Dict. Art Terms & Techniques* 198/1 *Iodine Scarlet*, mercuric iodide; a dangerously poisonous inorganic pigment of the most brilliant scarlet hue. It is useless as a paint pigment because it fades to a pale yellow. **1898** *Analyst* XXIII. 241 Purified allyl alcohol has a theoretical iodine value of 435. **1921** *Biochem. Jrnl.* XV. 319 Resins also show great variations in iodine values according to the conditions of the determination. **1953** J. DAVIDSOHN et al. *Soap Manuf.* I. xviii. 365 In order to produce a hard soap, a fat charge with low iodine value and low saponification value should be selected.

Hence **'iodine** *v. trans.*, to iodize.

1843 *Mech. Mag.* XXXVIII. 520 To iodine the plate, remove the lid and plate of glass, and place it, face downwards, on the ledge for that purpose, on the top of the box. **1929** C. C. MARTINDALE *Risen Sun* 173 His grooms..were iodining his abrasions. **1936** A. HUXLEY *Eyeless in Gaza* li. 571 How I regret those cretins one used to see in Switzerland when I was a child! They've iodined them out of existence now.

'iodinized, *ppl. a.* [f. IODINE *sb.*: see -IZE.] Of a material: treated or impregnated with iodine.

1919 *Chem. Abstr.* XIII. 2254 (*heading*) Iodinized emulsion. **1962** *Jrnl. Laboratory & Clin. Med.* LIX. 118 (*heading*) Effects of iodinized contrast media upon electrophoretic mobilities of blood proteins. **1963** *Neurology* XIII. 492/1 All the water-soluble iodinized contrast media currently used in diagnostic procedures..have been reported to cause side effects and complications.

iodipin (aɪ'əʊdɪpɪn). *Pharm.* [ad. G. *jodipin*, f. *jod* iodine + L. *adip-*, *adeps* fat: see -IN[1].] A liquid obtained by treating sesame oil with iodine, formerly used in treating syphilis and scrofula and as a contrast medium in radiography.

1899 *Brit. Med. Jrnl. Epitome* 18 Nov. 81/1 Iodipin, apart from its uses as a test is, as an iodine preparation, also therapeutically active. **1907** WOOD & BACHE *Dispensatory U.S.A.* (ed. 19) 1532/1 Iodipin.—A yellow, oily fluid, of a purely oleaginous taste. **1930** *Biol. Abstr.* IV. 2568/2 Injection of a medicinal iodine compound ('Iodipin') into the uterine cavity promises to yield clinical diagnostic results of some value by outlining the uterine cavity and the Fallopian tubes. **1940** H. A. MCGUIGAN *Appl. Pharmacol.* 190 Iodipin is iodized sesame oil. The dose of 10 per cent iodipin is 4 to 8 Gm.

iodism ('aɪədɪz(ə)m). *Path.* [f. IOD- + -ISM.] A morbid state induced by excessive or long-continued medicinal use of iodine (or its compounds).

1832 R. CHRISTISON *Treat. Poisons* iv. (ed. 2) 175 This affection, which in conformity with the name he [Dr. Jahn] has given it, may be termed Iodism [Iodkrankheit], he contrasts with mercurialism. **1861** BUMSTEAD *Ven. Dis.* (1879) 816 Iodide of potassium in large doses sometimes gives rise to a combination of symptoms known under the name of 'iodism', and consisting of a sensation of oppression in the head, *tinnitus aurium*, neuralgia, spasmodic action of the muscles [etc.]. **1876** HARLEY *Mat. Med.* (ed. 6) 77.

iodite ('aɪədaɪt). [f. IOD-INE + -ITE.]

1. *Chem.* A salt of (hypothetical) iodous acid. So ***hypo-iodite***, a salt of hypo-iodous acid (see IODOUS).

1842 *E. Turner's Elem. Chem.* xiii. (ed. 7) 303 Mitscherlich infers the crystals to be iodite of soda. **1865–72** WATTS *Dict. Chem.* III. 297 Hypo-iodite of potassium.

2. *Min.* = IODYRITE.

1854 DANA *Min.* 95 Iodyrite. Iodic Silver. Iodite. **1865–72** WATTS *Dict. Chem.* III. 310 *Iodite, Iodopyrite, Iodic Silver.* Native iodide of silver.

iodization (ˌaɪədaɪ'zeɪʃən). [f. IODIZ(E *v.* + -ATION.] The process or practice of iodizing; the addition of iodine or an iodine compound to a substance.

1909 *Jrnl. Chem. Soc.* XCVI. II. 919 The species specificity of a protein is considerably modified as regards its biological action by iodisation. **1956** *Nature* 24 Mar. 562/2 Iodine metabolism and the iodization of food will first be considered. **1971** *Sci. Amer.* June 97/1 This aspect of thyroid physiology, together with increasing reports of severe iodine toxicity..elicited strenuous opposition to the iodization of table salt.

iodize ('aɪədaɪz), *v.* [f. IOD- + -IZE.] *trans.* To treat or impregnate with iodine or an iodide. (Chiefly in *Photogr.* and *Med.*) Usually in *ppl. a.* **'iodized.** Hence also **'iodizing** *vbl. sb.* and *ppl. a.*

1841 *Athenæum* 17 July 541/1 The paper so..prepared the author [W. H. F. Talbot] calls *iodized paper*, because it has a uniform pale yellow coating of iodide of silver. **1842** GROVE *Corr. Phys. Forces* 56 A thin film of iodide of silver is thus formed on the surface of the metal, and when these iodized plates are exposed in the camera, a chemical alteration takes place. **1854** J. SCOFFERN in *Orr's Circ. Sc., Chem.* 90 A silver plate, which had..been iodized. *Ibid.* 91 The iodizing process. **1860** *N. Syd. Soc. Year-bk. for 1859*. 167 A case of inveterate and hereditary scrofula cured by the sole use of iodized bread. *c* **1865** J. WYLDE in *Circ. Sc.* I. 145/2 The iodising of the collodion is a question on which almost every operator differs. **1887** *Syd. Soc. Lex.*, *I[odized] serum*, a dark brown liquid obtained by keeping iodine in contact with the amniotic fluid of the cow..is used as a reagent in microscopy. **1933** *Radio Times* 14 Apr. 112/2 Finest iodised table salt.

iodizer ('aɪədaɪzə(r)). [f. prec. + -ER[1].] One who or that which iodizes; an iodizing agent.

1859 *Athenæum* 16 July 91 Negative Collodion with usual Iodizer. **1879** *Cassell's Techn. Educ.* III. 1 Certain salts called iodisers, such as the iodides of potassium, cadmium, or ammonium. **1883** *Hardwich's Photogr. Chem.* (ed. Taylor) 170 A rapid elimination of Iodine takes place on adding the iodizer.

iodo- (ˌaɪədəʊ, aɪˌəʊdəʊ), used as combining form of mod.L. *iodum* IODINE (chiefly before a consonant):

a. to form names of iodine compounds and substitution products resulting from the action of iodine on other bodies specified, e.g. **ˌiodo-'benzene**, $C_6H_5I_1$, formed from benzene by substitution of one or more iodine for hydrogen atoms; **ˌiodo-'brucine**, $C_{23}H_{26}N_2O_4{\cdot}I_3$, the iodide of brucine, $C_{23}H_{26}N_2O_4$. So ***iodobenzoic*** (acid), ***iodocinchonine, iodocodeine, iodomecone, iodomeconine, iodomorphine, iodonicotine, iodoquinine, iodosalycilic*** adj., ***iodostrychnine***, etc. Also **iodo-a'cetic** *a.*, in ***iodoacetic acid***: $CH_2I{\cdot}CO_2H$, obtained in thin, tough, colourless, rhombohedral plates, having a very sour taste; hence **iodo'acetate**, an ester or salt of iodoacetic acid; **iodo'carbon *paste***, a medical preparation containing iodoform, carbon, and glycerin; **iodo-'chloride**, **† -'chloruret**, a compound of iodine and chlorine in union with some base; **iodo-'ethane, -'ethyl**, etc.: see IOD-; **iodo'glycerin**, a medical solution of iodine and potassium iodide in glycerin; **iodohy'drargyrate**, a combination of mercuric iodide with the iodide of an electro-positive metal, e.g. ***potassium iodohydrargyrate***, $2(HgI_2{\cdot}KI) + 3H_2O$; **iodo-'hydric** = HYDRIODIC; **iodo-'iodide**, a combination of iodine with its own iodide of some base, as ***ammonium iodo-iodide***, also called *iodide of iodammonium* $(NH_3I){\cdot}I$; **iodo'mercurate**, a compound of mercuric iodide with a more basic iodide; **iodo'methane, iodo'methyl**, methyl iodide; **iodo'phenol**, a class of bodies, liquid and solid, obtained by treating phenol with iodine and iodic acid; **iodo'protein**, any protein containing iodine; **iodopyracet** (-'paɪərəsɛt) *U.S.* [f. di-*iodo-pyr*idone-*acet*ic], the diethanolamine salt $C_{11}H_{16}N_2O_5I_2$, of 3,5-di-iodo-4-pyridone-*N*-acetic acid, used in radiography as a contrast medium, principally for intravenous urography and for measuring renal plasma flow; called *diodone* in the U.K.; **iodo'pyrin(e** *Pharm.*, a crystalline iodinated derivative, $C_{11}H_{11}N_2OI$, of antipyrin, used as an antipyretic; **iodo'sulphate**, a salt of iodosulphuric acid; **iodo'sulphide**, a compound of iodine and sulphur with a base, as iodosulphide of antimony, SbSI; **iodosul'phuric *acid***, $H_2SO_3I_2$; ***iodosulphuric anhydride***, SO_2I_2; **iodo'tannin**, a solution of iodine in tannic acid; **iodo'terebene**, a liquid formed by the action of iodine on spirit of turpentine; **iodo'thyrin** = *thyro-iodine* (s.v. THYRO-).

b. also in other derivatives: as **iodog'nosis**, Dorvault's term for a knowledge of the properties of iodine. **'iodo-, i'odophil(e** [-PHIL, -PHILE], **iodo'philic** *adjs.*, readily stained by iodine. **iodo'phthisis** (*Path.*), wasting of flesh or of some organ, caused by excessive use of iodine. **iodo'plumbism**, a pathological term for the conjoined symptoms of iodism and plumbism or lead-colic. **iodo'therapy**, the treatment of disease by iodine and its compounds.

1902 *Jrnl. Chem. Soc.* LXXXII. I. 585 By the condensation of ethyl *iodoacetate with citraldehyde, a mixture of substances is apparently obtained. **1931** *Times Lit. Suppl.* 9 July 550/3 Sodium iodoacetate prevents a

similar breakdown of methylglyoxal by its inhibition of the enzyme glyoxalase. **1964** W. G. SMITH *Allergy & Tissue Metabolism* ii. 25 Inhibition of histamine and SRS-A release by antigen was noted with iodoacetate. **1888** *Syd. Soc. Lex.*, **Iodo-acetic acid*, see Iodacetic acid. **1948** *Jrnl. Biol. Chem.* CLXXVI. 88 The irreversible toxic action of the inhibitor toward yeast cells is proportional to the concentration of undissociated iodoacetic acid. **1962** *Lancet* 15 Dec. 1275/1 Although iodoacetic acid and acetoacetate might have a different action on the metabolism of the heart muscle, both seem to inhibit contractions. **1873** WATTS *Fownes' Chem.* (ed. 11) 760 *Iodobenzenes are likewise crystalline solids. **1880** *Athenæum* 27 Nov. 713/1 Aluminic *iodoethylate $(C_2H_5O)_3I_3Al_2$. **1899** J. CAGNEY tr. *Jaksch's Clin. Diagnosis* vi. (ed. 4) 201 The various micro-organisms above alluded to stain brown or brownish yellow in solution of iodine and iodide of potassium or of ammonium *iodo-iodide. **1873** WATTS *Fownes' Chem.* (ed. 11) 568 *Iodomethane is insoluble in water. **1888** REMSEN *Org. Chem.* 42 A mono-halogen derivative of a hydrocarbon, as, for example, iodo-methane, CH_3I. **1871** ROSCOE *Elem. Chem.* 412 By the action of potash on *iodophenol. **1873** WATTS *Fownes' Chem.* (ed. 11) 795 Iodophenols are produced by the action of iodine-chloride on phenol. **1902** *Encycl. Brit.* XXXII. 817/2 The Myxobolidæ.., which have an *iodophile vacuole. **1927** THAYSEN & BUNKER *Microbiol. Cellulose* viii. 218 Henneberg's statement that most of the cellulose-decomposing organisms found in the intestine are iodophil ..disagrees with all previous observations. **1942** *Nature* 23 May 582/1 Both the rumen in ruminant and the cæcum in non-ruminant Herbivora support an abundant iodophile microflora: that is, an association of taxonomically diverse species exhibiting, in consequence of the decomposition within them of bacterial starch or granulose, the common characteristic of giving a blue colour with iodine. **1948** *Jrnl. Bacteriol.* LV. 197 In the majority of instances *iodophilic colonies were frequent on the sucrose agar plates containing penicillin. **1971** HAWKER & LINTON *Micro-Organisms* xv. 543 Cellulose decomposition is associated with iodophilic bacteria (i.e. organisms which reveal starch-like substances when stained with iodine). **1881** *Nature* XXIII. 245 The amido-acids obtained from..*iodo-propionic acid by the action of ammonia. **1909** *Jrnl. Chem. Soc.* XCVI. II. 919 The behaviour of *iodoproteins as regards the formation of specific anti-substances was investigated. **1951** *Adv. Protein Chem.* VI. 253 (*heading*) Natural and artificial iodoproteins. **1963** *Lancet* 5 Jan. 12/1 Very rare examples of absent T_3 suppression in patients not having hyperthyroidism have been recorded when a thyroid nodule with autonomous iodine uptake synthesises abnormal iodoproteins. **1947** *Dispensatory U.S.A.* (ed. 24) 584/2 The *iodopyracet injection is warmed to body temperature and 20 cc..., containing 7 Gm..of the drug, is injected slowly intravenously. **1951** A. GROLLMAN *Pharmacol. & Therapeutics* xxxii. 751 Iodopyracet may be injected into the aorta in order to visualize the renal arteries; or into the brachial vein to visualize the chambers of the heart in the diagnosis of congenital cardiac lesions. **1971** *Amer. Jrnl. Obstetr. & Gynecol.* CX. 566/1 Following injection of radioactive iodopyracet into the fetal circulation radioactivity moved equally rapidly into amniotic fluid in preparations involving nephrectomized or normal fetuses. **1892** *Brit. Med. Jrnl.* 2 Jan. 22/1 *Iodopyrin. This product is a chemical compound of iodine with antipyrin, in which an atom of hydrogen is replaced by iodine. It occurs in colourless crystals. **1909** H. A. HARE et al. *National Stand. Dispensatory* (ed. 2) 201 Iodopyrine presents the combined physiological action of iodine and an antipyretic, and has been recommended in bronchial asthma and tertiary syphilis. **1961** L. MARTIN *Clinical Endocrinol.* (ed. 3) iii. 68 There are also certain other therapeutic substances which will produce a simple goitre... These include..iodopyrine (..found in Felsol powders which are used for asthma). **1882** *Athenæum* 11 Nov. 632/1 By heating salicylic acid and iodine in alcoholic solution, two *iodosalicylic acids were formed. **1865** *Ibid.* No. 1959. 656/2 The *iodo-strychnine of Pelletier. **1897** *Jrnl. Chem. Soc.* LXXII. II. 330 The animal was taking..diet to which was added either fresh thyroid or *iodothyrin. **1909** H. A. HARE et al. *National Stand. Dispensatory* (ed. 2) 855 Iodothyrine is a white or yellowish-white powder, having a sweet taste, and is prepared..by boiling fresh thyroid glands..with dilute sulphuric acid. **1932** *Discovery* Mar. 96/2 The flattened gilled water newt called the Axolotl [is] changed into a smaller differently shaped land newt in the course of a few weeks by feeding it with thyroid. In this case the active substance can be extracted from the gland and chemically analysed; it is termed iodothyrin.

iodobromite (ˌaɪədəʊˈbrəʊmaɪt). *Min.* [f. IODO- + BROM(IDE + -ITE: cf. Ger. *jodobromit* (Jahrb. Min. 1878. 619).] A mineral, the chloro-bromo-iodide of silver, found in sulphur-yellow or greenish octahedral crystals.

1890 in *Cent. Dict.* **1896** in CHESTER *Dict. Names Min.*

iodoform (aɪˈəʊdəʊfɔːm, ˈaɪədəʊfɔːm), *sb.* [f. IODO- + FORM(YL): cf. *chloroform.*] A compound of iodine (= tri-iodomethane, or methenyl tri-iodide, CHI_3), analogous to chloroform, obtained in light yellow scaly crystals, having an odour of saffron and a sweet taste; used medicinally, and as an antiseptic, esp. in surgical dressings.

1838 T. THOMSON *Chem. Org. Bodies* 315 Iodoform.. was first observed by Serullas in the year 1822. **1867** *N. Syd. Soc. Bien. Retrosp. for 1865–6.* 378 Dr. Eastlake advocates iodoform as a topical application. **1895** *Westm. Gaz.* 13 Dec. 8/1 Ladies had frequently complained of late of the too perceptible odour of iodoform in the theatres and concert-rooms [at Halle] which duelling students in a convalescent state were accustomed to grace with their presence.

attrib. **1878** *Braithwaite's Med. Retrosp.* LXXVII. 254 Iodoform pills have acted like a charm. **1885** *Ibid.* XC. 371, I painted the surface of the inflamed skin with the iodoform-collodion. **1897** W. ANDERSON *Surg. Treat. Lupus* 7 The wound may..be dressed with iodoform powder.

Hence **iˈodoform, iodoˈformize** *vbs. trans.*, to treat or impregnate with iodoform. **iodoˈformism**, 'poisoning by the medical use of iodoform' (*Syd. Soc. Lex.* 1887).

iodol (ˈaɪədɒl). *Chem.* [f. IOD- + -OL.] A brown inodorous powder, the tetra-iodide of pyrrol (C_4I_4NH), used as an antiseptic dressing instead of iodoform.

1887 in *Syd. Soc. Lex.*

iodometry (aɪəˈdɒmɪtrɪ). *Chem.* [f. IODO- + -METRY.] The titrimetric analysis of an oxidizing or reducing agent using the iodine/iodide redox system; *spec.* the quantitative analysis of a solution of an oxidizing agent by the addition of excess iodide followed by titration of the iodine so liberated with thiosulphate or arsenite solution. Cf. IODIMETRY.

1883 *Chem. News* 6 Apr. 166/1 (*heading*) Preparation of a durable starch solution for iodometry. **1916** *Chem. Abstr.* X. 730 (*heading*) Differential iodometry. I. Determination of periodates, iodates, bromates and chlorates in the presence of each other. **1928** *Ibid.* XXII. 2901 Reaction between iodic and hydriodic acids in very dilute solution and the titration of the liberated iodine with thiosulfate... An investigation of reactions involved in iodometry. **1939** [see IODIMETRY]. **1973** *Chem. Abstr.* LXXVIII. 23524 Iodometry can be employed for detn. of small amts. of Zn, Cu, Cd, Co and Hg.

So **iodoˈmetric** *a.*, of or pertaining to iodometry; **iodoˈmetrically** *adv.*, by means of iodometry.

1856 *Q. Jrnl. Chem. Soc.* VIII. 194 We have employed the much more accurate and convenient iodometric method, which..gives a degree of accuracy attainable by very few analytical processes. **1891** *Jrnl. Chem. Soc.* LX. 614 The facility with which pure potassium iodate is prepared renders it an admirable basis for iodometric analysis. **1928** A. W. WELLINGS *Volumetric Analysis* v. 102 Nitrites may also be estimated iodometrically. **1957** G. E. HUTCHINSON *Treat. Limnol.* I. xiii. 769 The excess chromate, equivalent to the original sulfate, is determined iodometrically. **1960** *Limnology & Oceanogr.* V. 343 (*heading*) A note on a stabilized starch indicator for use in iodometric and iodimetric determinations. **1971** G. D. CHRISTIAN *Analytical Chem.* xv. 238 Sodium thiosulfate solution is standardized iodometrically against a pure oxidizing agent such as $K_2Cr_2O_7$, KIO_3, $KBrO_3$, or metallic copper.

iodonium (aɪəˈdəʊnɪəm). *Chem.* [f. IOD- + -ONIUM.] The name of cations of the type $RR'I_2+$ where R and R′ are (different or the same) alkyl or aryl radicals, or part of a ring. Usu. *attrib.* or as a formative element.

1894 *Jrnl. Chem. Soc.* LXVI. I. 242 Diphenyliodonium iodide, I·IPh₂. *Ibid.* 243 Phenyl, which does not form ammonium and sulphonium bases, forms iodonium bases. **1922** J. MELLOR *Comprehensive Treat. Inorg. & Theoret. Chem.* II. 108 The iodonium bases and salts resemble those of lead and silver but particularly those of thallium. **1950** N. V. SIDGWICK *Chem. Elements* II. 1257 The free iodonium bases $Ar_2I{\cdot}OH$ are only known in solution, being made from the halides with silver oxide. **1962** P. J. & B. DURRANT *Introd. Adv. Inorg. Chem.* xxiii. 931 Diphenyliodonium hydroxide $[(C_6H_5)_2I]OH$. **1966** *Chem. Abstr.* LXV. 8872 (*heading*) Chemistry of heterocyclic iodonium compounds.

iodophor (aɪˈəʊdəʊf-, ˈaɪədəʊfɔː(r)). [f. IODO- + -PHOR.] Any substance in which iodine is combined with a surface-active agent to render it more soluble and chemically stable in aqueous solution, and so more suitable for use (in solution) as a disinfectant.

1952 TERRY & SHELANSKI in *Mod. Sanitation & Building Maintenance* IV. 62/2 This combination of iodine with a carrier is called a halophor (or more specifically it could be referred to as an iodophor). **1962** *Lancet* 22 Dec. 1330/2 A convenient way of using iodine would be to employ an iodophor, which, incidentally, would add a little cleaning power to the water. **1963** *Surg., Gynecol. & Obstetr.* CXVI. 363 The iodophor solutions were all pleasant to use. They did not irritate the skin, eyes, or nasal passages. **1967** *Biol. Abstr.* XLVIII. 10833/1 The percentage dissociation of the iodine complex in 16 commercial iodophors at use dilution was calculated from the partition coefficients. **1972** *Dairy Sci. Abstr.* XXXIV. 205/2 The development and use of foamless iodophors, particularly for cleaning milking equipment..and in combatting mastitis when used as a teat dip.

iodoso(-) (aɪəˈdəʊsəʊ), used in *Chem.* as comb. form of IODOUS *a.* to indicate the presence of an IO– group in a compound, as in **ioˌdosoˈbenzene**, C_6H_5IO, a yellow amorphous powder which disproportionates to iodobenzene and iodoxybenzene, and explodes when heated. Also as quasi-*adj*.

1892 *Jrnl. Chem. Soc.* LXII. 1460 On heating the solution for some seconds, cooling, and pouring into water, a precipitate of iodosobenzoic acid, $C_7H_5IO_3$, separates. **1893** Iodosobenzene [see next]. **1893** *Jrnl. Chem. Soc.* LXIV. I. 508 All attempts to obtain iodoso-derivatives from meta- and para-iodobenzoic acid have been without success. **1935** *Ibid.* 1671 Other reactions of iodoso-compounds point to the vulnerability of their I-O link to addition. **1936** *Chem. Abstr.* XXX. 6662 (*heading*) Use of iodosobenzene in developers and emulsions. **1950** N. V. SIDGWICK *Chem. Elements* II. 1249 The iodoso-compounds are greyish-white, amorphous substances, with a very characteristic penetrating 'iodoso smell'. **1968** Iodosobenzene [see next].

ˈiodous, *a.* [f. IOD- + -OUS: cf. F. *iodeux.*]

1. *Chem.* Applied to compounds containing iodine in greater proportion to oxygen than those called *iodic*; e.g. a hypothetical *iodous acid*, HIO_2.

Compounds with a still greater proportion of iodine are termed ***hypo-iodous***, as a supposed ***hypo-iodous acid***, HIO (Watts *Dict. Chem.* 1882, III. 297).

1826 HENRY *Elem. Chem.* I. 225 Iodous Acid. **1881** WATTS *Dict. Chem.* VIII. 1095 *Iodine trioxide* or *Iodous Oxide*, I_2O_3, is formed, together with the pentoxide, which is the ultimate product, by the action of ozone on iodine.

2. Having the quality of, or resembling, iodine.

iodoxy(-) (aɪəˈdɒksɪ), *prefix.* [f. IOD- + OXY- 2.] Used in chemical names to indicate the presence of the radical IO_2– (or, formerly, IO–), as in **ˌiodoxyˈbenzene**, a compound, $C_6H_5IO_2$, forming colourless needles and obtained by disproportionation of iodosobenzene. Also as quasi-*adj*.

1865 *Jrnl. Chem. Soc.* XVIII. 308 A combustion made of the pure acid gave numbers leading to the formula of iodoxybenzoic acid $C_7H_5IO_3$. **1889** *Ibid.* LVI. 1150 The authors are inclined to regard it as an iodoxydiiodobenzene, $C_6H_3I_2{\cdot}OI$. **1893** *Ibid.* LXIV. I. 506 Iodoxybenzene, $C_6H_5IO_2$, when treated with hydrochloric acid in aqueous solution, is converted into iodosobenzene hydrochloride. **1905** *Jrnl. Soc. Chem. Industry* 31 Jan. 104/1 (*heading*) Iodoxy compound (*p*-iodoxyphenol ester): and process of making same. **1935** *Jrnl. Chem. Soc.* 1669 The present summary of several of our investigations, dealing particularly with the iodoxy-group IO_2. **1950** N. V. SIDGWICK *Chem. Elements* II. 1251 The iodoxy-compounds hold their oxygen more firmly than the iodoso, and they are not such strong oxidizing agents. **1968** R. O. C. NORMAN *Princ. Org. Synthesis* xvi. 535 Iodoxybenzene may be obtained in over 90% yield by steam-distilling iodosobenzene to remove the iodobenzene formed by the disproportionation.

iodurated: see IODURETTED.

†**ˈiodure.** *Chem. Obs.* [a. F. *iodure.*] = next.

1826 [see IODE 2].

†**ioduret** (aɪˈɒdjʊərɛt). *Chem. Obs.* [f. IOD- + -URET: in F. *iodure*. Cf. CHLORURET.] An earlier synonym of IODIDE.

1816 ACCUM *Chem. Tests* (1818) 287 Ioduret of starch. **1822** IMISON *Sc. & Art* II. 67 Iodine..unites with all the metals, forming with them iodurets. **1826** HENRY *Elem. Chem.* II. 264 The colour of this ioduret, or iodide of starch, is reddish, if the starch be in excess; a beautiful blue, when the two bodies are in due proportion. **1853** R. HUNT *Man. Photogr.* 137 To decompose the film of ioduret of silver.

†**ioduretted** (aɪˈɒdjʊərɛtɪd), *ppl. a. Chem. Obs.* Also **-ated**. [f. prec. + -ED[1]: cf. F. *ioduré*, f. *iodure.*] Combined or impregnated with iodine.

1832 R. CHRISTISON *Treat. Poisons* (ed. 2) 173 The ioduretted solution of hydriodate of potass. **1836** J. M. GULLY *Magendie's Formul.* 107 *note*, A drop of the solution of the hydriodate of potass weighs more than a grain, or even two grains if the hydriodate be ioduretted. **1847–9** TODD *Cycl. Anat.* IV. 119/1 This [opacity] is rendered more obvious..by ioduretted solutions. **1887** *Syd. Soc. Lex.*, Iodurated..Ioduretted.

iodyrite (aɪˈɒdɪraɪt). *Min.* [f. IOD-INE, after *argyrite*; substituted by Dana for the earlier name IODITE.] Native iodide of silver, a sectile mineral, usually of a yellow colour, occurring in Mexico, Chili, etc.

1854 DANA *Min.* (ed. 4) 95. **1892** *Ibid.* 160 Iodyrite is homomorphous with greenockite.

i-offred, ME. pa. pple. of OFFER *v.*

iogelour, obs. form of JUGGLER.

ioissh, ioit, obs. forms of JUICE, JOT.

iolite (ˈaɪəlaɪt). *Min.* Also **yolite, iolithe.** [= Ger. *iolith* (Werner, 1808), f. Gr. ἴον violet + λίθος stone: see -LITE.] A silicate of aluminium, iron, and magnesium, occurring in short orthorhombic crystals, or granular; of various shades of blue or violet-blue, and commonly showing different colours in different directions; very subject to alteration by exposure, giving rise to many varieties. Also called CORDIERITE or DICHROITE.

[**1758** SIR J. HILL (*title*) An Account of a Stone [etc.].. with the History of the Iolithos, or Violet Stone, of the Germans.] **1810** *Nicholson's Jrnl.* XXVII. 235 The denomination of yolite (violet-stone). **1821** R. JAMESON *Man. Min.* 193 Prismato-Rhomboidal Quartz, or Iolite. **1831** BREWSTER *Optics* xxx. 249 M. Cordier observed the same change of colour in a mineral called *iolite*, to which Haüy gave the name of dichroite. **1868** DANA *Min.* (ed. 5) §287 Iolite..Lustre vitreous. Pleochroic, being often deep blue along the vertical axis, and brownish yellow or yellowish gray perpendicular to it.

ion (ˈaɪən). *Electr.* [a. Gr. ἰόν, neut. pr. pple. of ἰέναι to go.] **1.** Name given by Faraday to either of the constituents which pass to the 'poles' or electrodes in electrolysis: the general term including ANION and CATION. In modern use, any individual atom, molecule, or group having a net electric charge (either positive or negative), whether in an electrolytic solution or not.

1834 W. WHEWELL *Let. to Faraday* 5 May in I. Todhunter *William Whewell* (1876) II. 182 For the two together you

might use the term *ions*. **1834** FARADAY in *Phil. Trans. R. Soc.* CXXIV. 79 Finally, I require a term to express those bodies which can pass to the electrodes... I propose to distinguish these bodies by calling those anions which go to the anode of the decomposing body; and those passing to the cathode, cations; and when I have occasion to speak of these together, I shall call them ions. [*Note*] Since this paper was read, I have changed some of the terms which were first proposed. *Ibid.* 112 A body decomposable directly by the electric current, i.e. an electrolyte, must consist of two ions. *Ibid.*, Compound ions are not necessarily composed of electro-chemical equivalents of simple ions. For instance, sulphuric acid, boracic acid, phosphoric acid, are ions, but not electrolytes, i.e. not composed of electro-chemical equivalents of simple ions. **1856** W. A. MILLER *Elem. Chem.* II. xviii. 110 When a binary compound, such as a fused chloride,..is submitted to electrolysis, the ions or components of the compound are separated at the respective electrodes in equivalent proportions. **1870** R. M. FERGUSON *Electr.* 161 The constituents into which the electrolyte is decomposed are called *ions*. **1879** *Encycl. Brit.* VIII. 107/1 Sodium acetate and silver chloride are therefore electrolytes of which Ag, Cl, Na, $C_2H_3O_2$ are the respective ions. **1896** W. R. WHITNEY tr. *Le Blanc's Elem. Electrochem.* iii. 60 Only those substances conduct which are at least partly dissociated, and therefore the conductivity is due to the dissociated parts; to the latter, which were called by him the 'ions', Arrhenius ascribed electric charges. **1896** RUTHERFORD & THOMSON in *Phil. Mag.* XLII. 405 We have made..experiments with the view to seeing whether there is any polarization when a current of electricity passes through a gas; we have not, however, been able to satisfy ourselves of the existence of this effect. The absence of polarization implies, however, that the ions are able to give up their charges to the metal electrodes. **1899** RUTHERFORD in *Ibid.* XLVII. 112 The theory has been put forward that the rays in passing through the gas produce positively and negatively charged particles in the gas, and that the number produced per second depends on the intensity of the radiation and the pressure... The term ion was given to them from analogy with electrolytic conduction, but in using the term it is not assumed that the ion is necessarily of atomic dimensions; it may be a multiple or submultiple of the atom. **1927** N. V. SIDGWICK *Electronic Theory of Valency* vi. 91 In a crystal like calcium carbonate we find the same kind of relation between the calcium ion and the CO_3 ion, but a different one for the constituent atoms of the CO_3 group;..this may be taken as evidence that the calcium and the CO_3 are themselves ions, but that the atoms of the CO_3 group are covalently linked to one another. **1962** P. J. & B. DURRANT *Introd. Adv. Inorg. Chem.* xii. 346 An ionic crystal is one in which the units of crystal structure are the ions of a salt. **1967** *New Scientist* 30 Nov. 531/1 The normal electrode separation is less than 1 mm, so there is a very strong electric field which ionizes the gas atoms, giving ions and electrons.

2. Special Comb.: **ion beam**, a current of ions moving in a fixed direction; **ion bombardment**, the process of bombarding a surface with ions (usu. of an inert gas), so breaking up the surface, used to remove impurities; hence **ion-bombarded** *a.*; **ion burn**, the damaging of the phosphor of a cathode-ray tube by negatively ionized gas molecules produced by the electron beam and focused on to the screen; also, an ion spot so produced; **ion chamber**, an ionization chamber; **ion drive**, (*a*) = *ion propulsion*; (*b*) = *ion engine*; **ion engine**, a rocket engine that employs ion propulsion; **ion etching**, the controlled removal of extremely thin layers of material from the surface of an object by the use of an ion beam; **ion gun**, a device in which ions are produced (usu. by the ionization of a gas) and emitted in a beam; **ion implantation**, the implantation of ions in a crystalline material (see IMPLANTATION 7); **ion pair**, (*a*) a pair of oppositely charged ions held together in a solution by electrostatic attraction; (*b*) a negative ion (or an electron) and a positive ion formed from a neutral atom or molecule by the action of radiation; **ion propulsion**, a mode of rocket propulsion in which thrust is produced by the ejection of ions produced inside the engine and accelerated by an electric field; **ion rocket**, (*a*) = *ion engine*; (*b*) a rocket in which an ion engine is the means of propulsion; **ion source**, a device for producing ions, *spec.* an ion gun; **ion spot**, (*a*) a dark spot in the middle of the screen of a cathode-ray tube where the phosphor is damaged as a result of ion burn; (*b*) a white spot in a television picture produced as a spurious signal when ionized gas molecules strike the target of a television camera tube; **ion trap**, a device designed to catch ions; *spec.* one in a cathode-ray tube or television camera tube that prevents ionized molecules from reaching the screen or the target and causing an ion spot. Also ION EXCHANGE.

1932 *Physical Rev.* XL. 33 Intense high speed ion beams. **1951** *Jrnl. Brit. Interplanetary Soc.* X. 253 The acceleration of a space ship by an ion beem seems to offer no particular difficulties. **1970** *New Scientist* 5 Feb. 256/1 The ion beam, projected at a small area of the sample, consists of heavy, positively charged ions of inert gas, which remove atoms from the specimen's surface layers. **1959** *Jrnl. Chem. Physics* XXX. 926/2 The relative ease of removal of oxygen can therefore not be explained by the assumption that the ion-bombarded and annealed surface is partially oxygen contaminated. **1930** *Rev. Mod. Physics* II. 186 'Sputtering', or disintegration of an electrode subjected to positive ion bombardment is a well known and often troublesome phenomenon. **1952** *Trans. Faraday Soc.* XLVIII. 747 As a general procedure for cleaning surfaces, the inert gas ion-bombardment has some advantages: its main disadvantage is that there is sputtering of the metal on to the walls of the vessel. **1960** *Jrnl. Appl. Physics* XXXI. 1516 (*title*) Ion-bombardment etching of synthetic fibers. **1954** E. MOLLOY *Radio & Television Engineers' Ref. Bk.* xxiv. 27 The third technique of preventing ion burn is by protecting the screen with a layer of aluminium. **1956** [see *ion spot* below]. **1963** J. R. DAVIES *Understanding Television* ii. 62 Ion burns normally show up as brown circles an inch or so in diameter, the discoloration being greatest at the centre of the burn. In some cathode ray tubes, protection against ion burn is achieved by mounting part of the electron gun assembly at an angle, and..applying across the tube neck a fixed magnetic field which causes electrons only to be deflected across the screen. **1955** *Bull. Atomic Sci.* June 213/3 An ion chamber, however, is a device which directly measures the dose to the air volume it encloses. **1962** F. I. ORDWAY et al. *Basic Astronautics* iv. 121 Solar radiation intensities in the Lyman-alpha experiment were measured by a photo-sensitive ion chamber. **1958** C. C. ADAMS et al. *Space Flight* xiv. 346 Both rubidium and cesium have been considered as the propellant for the ion drive. **1960** *Aeroplane* XCVIII. 776/2 Ion-drive cannot be used in propelling space-vehicles from the Earth's surface because of their inherently low thrust. **1962** F. I. ORDWAY et al. *Basic Astronautics* x. 424 The three basic elements of the ion drive are the emitter, the accelerator, and the beam neutralizer. **1960** *Aeroplane* XCVIII. 776/2 (*heading*) Experimental ion engine. **1961** [see *ion rocket* below]. **1971** *Jrnl. Brit. Interplanetary Soc.* XXIV. 573 The use of pulsed plasma thrusters rather than ion engines for attitude control has..become a distinct possibility. **1965** *Chem. Abstr.* LXII. 3491 (*heading*) Ion etching: an effective method for the elimination of foreign layers in ultra vacuum. **1968** *Times* 13 Nov. 16/1 The inside appearance of a red blood cell has been revealed for the first time by the novel combination of two physical techniques, scanning electron microscopy and ion etching... Ion etching has so far been used chiefly to study the structure of metals. The specimen is bombarded with a stream of high energy ions and the inner structure of the material is revealed as successive layers are stripped off. **1970** *New Scientist* 5 Feb. 256/2 It has been possible to use ion etching to penetrate the cuticular layers of insects. **1952** *Jrnl. Brit. Interplanetary Society* XI. 179 Any rocket system requiring the conversion of electric to kinetic energy will require one or more ion guns. **1957** *Physical Rev.* CVII. 642/1 The performance of the spectrometers was tested with an electron gun and with an ion gun. **1967** *New Scientist* 30 Nov. 531/1 The apparatus..consists of two ion sources (ion guns) which direct beams of ions at shallow angles on to the centres of the faces of a disc-like sample of ceramic. **1965** *Nuclear Instruments & Methods* XXXVIII. 169 (*heading*) Doping of silicon by ion implantation. **1970** *Times* 23 Jan. 27/8 This makes a low-temperature method of doping the silicon, such as ion implantation, an attractive approach to.. flexible circuit fabrication. **1970** *New Scientist* 15 Oct. Suppl. 16/1 In ion implantation, the necessary impurities are accelerated by an electric field to an energy sufficient to embed them into the silicon to the depth required. **1972** *Physics Bull.* Oct. 612/3 Ion implantation can be helpful in understanding already known damage centres by careful choice of bombarding isotope. **1933** *Jrnl. Amer. Chem. Soc.* LV. 477 The changes in the properties of the solvent.. caused by the presence of undissociated (non-conducting) ion pairs will be neglected. **1941** *Proc. 7th Internat. Congr. Genetics* 246 At 0·01 r. per min. there is on the average only one ion pair produced in a sperm nucleus every 27 min. and since the ion pairs produced by γ-rays are rather far apart, it is now more difficult than ever to avoid the conclusion that individual mutations arise from individual ionizations and that there is no threshold intensity. **1963** B. FOZARD *Instrumentation Nucl. Reactors* ii. 13 When a charged particle of high energy is introduced into the sensitive volume of a gas ionisation detector it undergoes large numbers of ionising and exciting collisions... In suitable conditions the whole of this energy is expended within the sensitive volume. In such cases the total number of ion pairs produced is a direct measure of the particle energy. **1964** BLACK & WAGNER *Dynamic Path.* xi. 231 The different types of ionizing radiation produce the same fundamental change in matter, that is, the ejection of planetary electrons from atoms or molecules, leading to the formation of ion pairs. **1957** *Jrnl. Brit. Interplanetary Soc.* XVI. 233 A system which may ultimately utilize power from fusion is that of ion (or plasma) propulsion. *Ibid.*, Much serious attention is being given to the ion-propulsion problem in the U.S.A. **1966** *McGraw-Hill Encycl. Sci. & Technol.* VII. 245/2 The space charge represents one of the serious obstacles of any ion-propulsion system. **1949** *Jrnl. Brit. Interplanetary Soc.* VIII. 64 These techniques form the basis for what we shall here call the 'ion rocket', the jet of which might more correctly be termed an exhaust beam. **1951** *Ibid.* X. 248 The use of ion rockets as a means for propelling vehicles between satellite stations. **1953** *Ann. Reg. 1952* 406 The 'most feasible project' was described as consisting of space stations circling the most important planets with ion rockets plying between them. **1961** *Flight* LXXIX. 330/2 The earliest ion rockets to be considered for spaceflight will have a thrust of one-tenth of a pound and will be powered by 30kW SNAP-8 nuclear reactors after first-stage launch by Atlas-Centaur or Saturn C-1 boosters. Higher-powered ion engines (up to one megawatt) will also be considered. **1971** *Nature* 6 Aug. 357/1 What was called space technology—the design and operation of solar cells, ion rockets and the like. **1955** *Gloss. Terms Radiology* (*B.S.I.*) 43 *Ion source*, a device in which gas ions are produced, focused and accelerated, and emitted as a narrow beam. **1966** *McGraw-Hill Encycl. Sci. & Technol.* VII. 245/1 The ionizer or ion source converts the propellant from its original stored form to a system of charged corpuscles. **1967** Ion source [see *ion gun* above]. **1940** D. G. FINK *Princ. Television Engin.* viii. 341 If magneto-static focusing is used, the ion spot is spread over a much larger area (often the full area of the screen) and is much less troublesome, whether electric or magnetic deflection is used. **1953** AMOS & BIRKINSHAW *Television Engin.* I. v. 93 Spurious signals in the form of a white ion spot are eliminated by use of an ion-trap mesh situated close to the target. **1953** H. A. CHINN *Television Broadcasting* ii. 69 Occasionally, a white spot..may be observed in the center of the picture. Such a spot, especially if it is visible on the monitor with the camera lens capped, is probably an ion spot. **1956** M. SLURZBERG et al. *Essent. Television* x. 375 A concentrated bombardment of the fluorescent screen by the heavy ions produces a small brown circle in the centre of the picture screen, called an ion burn or ion spot. **1905** BRAGG & KLEEMAN in *Phil. Mag.* X. 321 An arrangement which we find to be of great importance is the ion-trap which is placed under the gauze of the ionization chamber. **1940** D. G. FINK *Princ. Television Engin.* viii. 342 The ion spot may..be eliminated by an ingenious construction in the electron gun known as an 'ion trap'. **1953** Ion-trap [see *ion spot* above]. **1954** E. MOLLOY *Radio & Television Engineers' Ref. Bk.* xxiv. 27 The successful operation of..ion traps depends upon the different paths followed by the electrons and negative ions under the action of magnetic fields. **1967** WHARTON & HOWORTH *Princ. Television Reception* iv. 59 A small permanent magnet known as the ion trap magnet was mounted on the neck of the tube to deflect the electrons so that they travelled axially and landed on the screen.

-ion, *suffix*[1], repr. F. *-ion*, L. *-io*, *-iōnem*, a suffix forming sbs. of condition or action, rarely formed from adjs. or sbs., as *commūniōn-em* sharing in common, *portiōn-em* share, *rebelliōn-em* rebellion, *tāliōn-em* retaliation; sometimes from the verb-stem, as *alluviōn-em* alluvion, *condiciōn-em* terms of agreement, *legiōn-em* a chosen body of soldiers, *obliviōn-em* forgetfulness, *opiniōn-em* opinion; but chiefly from the ppl. or supine stem in *t-*, *s-*, *x-*, where it was a permanent possibility, and, from most verbs, in actual use, e.g. *damnātiōn-em* condemning, *complētiōn-em* fulfilling, *monitiōn-em* warning, *mūnītiōn-em* fortification, *nōtiōn-em* a taking note, *solūtiōn-em* loosening, *actiōn-em* acting, *mansiōn-em* staying, abode, *missiōn-em* sending, *co(n)nexiōn-em* close union. Examples of all these classes occur in English, through Fr. or from L. directly, or formed analogically in Eng. itself, e.g. *union*, *portion*, *religion*, *oblivion*, but chiefly those in *-tion*, (*-sion*, *-xion*), as *damnation*, *completion*, *munition*, *notion*, *pollution*, *action*, *session*, *connexion*; the form in -ATION (q.v.) is by far the most frequent, and has become a living formative.

-ion, *suffix*[2], the ending of INION[1], proposed by P. Broca, 1875 (in *Bull. de la Soc. d'Anthrop. de Paris* X. 346), as a suffix for forming the names of other craniometric points (as GNATHION, GONION).

-ion, *suffix*[3], the word ION added to abbreviated forms of the names of elements and radicals to form the names of their ions, as ***chlorion***, HYDRION, ***nitrion***, ***sodion***.

-ion, *suffix*[4]. (See quot. and ALLIANCE *sb.* 6.)

1930 F. R. BHARUCHA tr. *Braun-Blanquet's Vocab. Plant Sociol.* 23 For designation of Alliances, the suffix '*-ion*' is added to the radical of the name of one of the principal associations of the alliance. Ex. *Ammophilion-Genisteto-Vaccinion.*

ionamine (aɪˈɒnəmiːn). *Dye Chem.* Also **Ionamine.** [f. ION + AMINE.] Any of various [(arylazo)arylamino] methane sulphonates, $X{\cdot}N_2{\cdot}Y{\cdot}NRCH_2SO_3Na$ (where X and Y are (substituted) benzene nuclei), formerly used as specific dyes for acetate silk.

1922 *Glasgow Herald* 24 Apr. 10 The 'ionamines' will have nothing to do with this homely fibre [*sc.* cotton]. They will only dye silk, either real or artificial. **1923** GREEN & SAUNDERS in *Jrnl. Soc. Dyers & Colourists* XXXIX. 12/1 Those Ionamines which are derived from primary amido compounds or contain free amido groups are capable of being diazotised upon the fibre, and in combination with various developers produce a wide range of shades from orange to scarlet, red, maroon, violet, blue and black. **1946** S. R. & E. R. TROTMAN *Bleaching, Dyeing & Chem. Technol. Textile Fibres* (ed. 2) 474 The chief advantages of the ionamines are (i) ready solubility, and (ii) miscibility with direct dyestuffs. **1971** R. L. M. ALLEN *Colour Chem.* i. 12 Systems in which the solubilising groups are eliminated by hydrolysis during or after dyeing have also been used in dyes such as the Ionamine (British Dyestuffs Corp.) and Neocotone..ranges, but these have now been superseded.

ionene (ˈaɪəniːn). *Chem.* [ad. G. *ionen* (Tiemann & Krüger 1893, in *Ber. d. Deut. Chem. Ges.* XXVI. 2693), f. Gr. ἴον violet: see -ENE.] 1,1,6-Trimethyltetralin, $C_{13}H_{18}$; a bicyclic oily liquid obtained on elimination of a water molecule from α- or β-ionone.

1894 *Jrnl. Chem. Soc.* LXVI. I. 82 When heated with hydriodic acid and phosphorus, it [*sc.* ionone] loses water, and yields ionene, $C_{13}H_{18}$, which boils at 106–107° (10 mm.)... It resembles irene very closely. **1933** *Jrnl. Amer. Chem. Soc.* LV. 4680 That ionene is a true 1,1,6-trimethyltetralin is evidenced by its smooth sulphonation and nitration, and by the oxidation products obtained from ionene. **1960** *Jrnl. Chem. Soc.* 3128 *Ionene.* —This hydrocarbon was prepared in 53% yield from β-ionone.

ion exchange. The interchange of ions of like charge between an insoluble solid and a solution in contact with it. Freq. *attrib.* (usu. hyphenated), as **ion-exchange resin**, any synthetic resin or polymer suitable for use as an

ion exchanger, characterized in general by a cross-linked molecular network which allows the penetration of solvent and ions (causing swelling) and has ionized or ionizable groups weakly attached to it.

1923 *Chem. Abstr.* XVII. 578 (*heading*) The ion exchange between the blood corpuscles and the serum. **1943** *Industr. & Engin. Chem.* Aug. 858 (*heading*) Ion exchange resins. New tools for process industries. **1946** *Jrnl. Amer. Leather Chemists' Assoc.* XLI. 555 The present work is an attempt to explore the possibilities of utilizing ion exchange resins in the analysis of some chromium liquors of various types. **1949** [see *ion exchanger* below]. **1950** *Sci. Amer.* Nov. 51/3 Ion exchange has provided a tool for fascinating studies of the constituents of cell nuclei—nucleic acids and nucleotides—which are so similar to one another that they are nearly impossible to separate by conventional means. **1951** J. E. Maudru in R. A. McGinnis *Beet-Sugar Technol.* x. 289 Ion exchange..is another type of juice purification which has recently been applied to the beet-sugar industry. This process consists of passing dilute juice..through beds of active synthetic resinous material, which removes ionized impurities. **1952** *Sci. News* XXVI. 83 Ion-exchange resins are usually marketed in the form of coarse or spherical granules, about 1–2 millimetres in diameter... The major use of these resins is in the complete removal of salts from water by ion-exchange. **1963** *Guardian* 28 Feb. 18/1 The Government had decided to establish an experimental pilot plant to examine the problems in the removal of strontium 90 from milk by an ion-exchange process. **1964** *Oceanogr. & Marine Biol.* II. 149 The amino acid compositions of phytoplankton and pure cultures of phytoplanktonic species have been determined by paper chromatography and by ion-exchange chromatography.

Also **ion exchanger**, a solid involved or used in ion exchange; also, an apparatus for effecting ion exchange.

1941 *Jrnl. Franklin Inst.* CCXXXII. 317 It is possible..that the characteristics of an ion exchanger are conditioned by the nature of the ion with which it was last saturated. **1949** H. F. Walton in F. C. Nachod *Ion Exchange* 4 In the materials which find practical use as ion exchangers, such as the synthetic aluminosilicates, synthetic resins, or sulfuric acid-treated coals, nearly all of the ion exchange takes place in the interior of the granules, which have a gel structure, something like a sponge on the molecular scale. **1950** *Sci. Amer.* Nov. 50/2 During the war compact little ion exchangers were used in life-raft emergency kits for making drinking water from sea water. **1960** R. Kunin *Elem. Ion Exchange* iii. 24 Only the zeolite minerals have a sufficiently satisfactory combination of the above-mentioned characteristics..to permit their use as ion exchangers on a commercial scale.

Ionian (aɪ'əʊnɪən), *a.* and *sb.* [f. L. *Iōni-us*, a. Gr. Ἰώνιος + -an. Cf. mod.F. *ionien*.]

A. *adj.* **1.** Of or pertaining to the district Ionia or to the Ionians (see B.); Ionic.

Ionian Sea, the part of the Mediterranean between Greece and Southern Italy; ***Ionian Islands***, the seven Greek islands which lie on the eastern coast of this sea.

1594 R. Ashley tr. *le Roy's Interch. Var. Things* 61 a, Thales..was the author of the Ionian sect. **1624** Wotton *Archit.* in *Reliq.* (1651) 231 The Capitall dressed on each side..in a spirall wreathing, which they call the Ionian Voluta. **1632** Lithgow *Trav.* ii. 66, I left the turmoyling dangers of the intricated Iles, of the Ionean and Adriaticall seas. **1669** Sturmy *Mariner's Mag.* 20 If Ovid in that straight Ionian Deep Was lost so hard, much more are we on Seas of larger Bounds. **1835** Thirlwall *Greece* I. 87 Xuthus..through his sons, Ion and Achæus..was considered as the forefather of the Achæan and the Ionian tribes. **1838** *Ibid.* II. 139 Less intimately connected with the Ionian schools. **1839** *Penny Cycl.* XIII. 14 *Ionian Islands* is the name given to the seven islands of Corfu, Cephalonia, Zante, Santa Maura, Ithaca, Paxo, and Cerigo, which are scattered along the coast of Epirus and of the Peloponnesus. **1900** *U.P. Magazine* Feb. 68/1 Some hundreds of hardy Ionian oarsmen from Phocee.

2. *Mus.* ***Ionian mode.*** **a.** One of the modes in ancient Greek music, characterized as soft and effeminate. **b.** The last of the 'authentic' ecclesiastical modes, having C for its 'final', and G for its 'dominant', and thus corresponding to the modern major diatonic scale.

1844 Beck & Felton tr. *Munk's Metres* 289 The Greeks had seven principal modes, the Dorian, Aeolian..and Ionian. *Ibid.* 290 The Ionian..Plato rejects as effeminate. **1867** Macfarren *Harmony* ii. 35 At last, under the name of the Ionian mode, our modern scale of C. **1893** H. E. Wooldridge in *Chappell's O.E. Pop. Mus.* I. p. xi, Popular Scale of C. Called in the 16th century the 13th or Ionian Mode.

B. *sb.* A member of that great division of the Hellenic race, which occupied Attica and the northern coast of the Peloponnesus, and established colonies in Sicily, Italy, Gaul, on the shores and islands of the Euxine, and especially in Asia Minor, where a large district was named from them Ionia. **b.** An Ionian Islander.

1563 Shute *Archit.* C iv b, Ionica..was deuised by the Ionians and set in the temple of Diana. **1807** Robinson *Archæol. Græca* v. xxi. 521 The Ionians delighted in wanton dances and songs more than the rest of the Greeks..and wanton gestures were proverbially termed Ionic motions. **1839** *Penny Cycl.* XIII. 13 Miletus seems to have fallen to the share of the Athenian Ionians..Another party of Ionians under Androclus took possession of Ephesus. **1898** J. McCarthy *Story Gladstone* xvii. 192 The Ionians had one uncompromising grievance.

Ionic (aɪ'ɒnɪk), *a.*[1] and *sb.* [ad. L. *Iōnic-us*, a. Gr. Ἰωνικός: cf. F. *ionique* (16th c.).]

A. *adj.* **1.** Of or pertaining to Ionia or the Ionians: = Ionian *a.* 1. ***Ionic dialect***, the most important of the three main branches of ancient Greek, of which also the Attic was a development. ***Ionic school*** or ***sect of philosophy***, that founded by Thales of Miletus in Asiatic Ionia.

1602 Carew *Eng. Tongue* in Camden *Rem.* (1614) 43 Will you haue Platoes veine? reade Sir Thomas Smith, the Ionicke? Sir Thomas Moore. **1613** Purchas *Pilgrimage* (1614) 94 He saw the Cadmean letters engraven in a Temple at Thebes, much like the Ionike letters. **1662** Stillingfl. *Orig. Sacr.* iii. ii. §4 The difference of the former Philosophers of the Ionick sect, after the time of Thales, as to the material principle of the world. **1702** tr. *Le Clerc's Prim. Fathers* 8 The Ionick Sect ended in Archelaus, Master of Socrates. **1731** Blackwall *Sacr. Class.* II. i. ii. 56 Frequent in the Ionic and poetical dialect. **1821** Byron *Sardan.* i. ii. 38, I know each glance of those Ionic eyes. *a* **1829** J. Young *Lect. Intell. Philos.* xl. (1835) 399 The system of the original Ionic school.

2. *Arch.* Name of one of the three orders of Grecian architecture (Doric, Ionic, Corinthian), characterized by the two lateral volutes of the capital.

[**1563** Shute *Archit.* E iv b, Tuscana, Dorica, Ionica, Corinthia, and Composita, increase their heightes by Diameters.] **1585** T. Washington tr. *Nicholay's Voy.* ii. iii. 33 Two high pillers Ionique without heads. **1614** Selden *Titles Hon.* Ded. A ij a, Architecture of olde Temples..was either Dorique, Jonique, or Corinthian. **1705** Elstob in Hearne *Collect.* 30 Nov. (O.H.S.) I. 107 Capitals of yᵉ Ionick size. **1841** W. Spalding *Italy & It. Isl.* I. 302 A large triangular space, approached by an Ionic vestibule, and enclosed by a Doric colonnade.

3. *Mus.* (See Ionian *a.* 2 a.) ? *Obs.*

1579 E. K. *Gloss. Spenser's Sheph. Cal.* Oct. 27 The Lydian and Ionique harmony. **1674** Playford *Skill Mus.* i. 61 The Ionick Mood was for more light and effeminate Musick. **1807** Robinson *Archæol. Græca* v. xxiii. 534 There were four principal νόμοι or modes; the Phrygian, the Lydian, the Doric, and the Ionic..The Phrygian mode was religious..the Ionic, gay and cheerful.

4. *Gr.* and *Lat. Pros.* Name of a foot consisting of two long syllables followed by two short ('ionic *a majore*'), or two short followed by two long ('ionic *a minore*'); pertaining to or consisting of such feet: see B. 3. ***Ionic metre***, a metre consisting of Ionic feet.

B. *sb.* †**1.** = Ionian *sb.*; a member of the Ionic School of philosophy. *Obs.*

1594 R. Ashley tr. *le Roy's Interch. Var. Things* 61 a, The Philosophers..diuided themselues into two sects, thone being called Ionicques, thother Italiques. **1613** Purchas *Pilgrimage* (1614) 93 These letters..being by the Ioniks principally learned.

2. The Ionic dialect of ancient Greek.

1668 Wilkins *Real Char.* i. i. §3.

3. *Gr.* and *Lat. Pros.* An Ionic foot or verse; Ionic metre: See A. 4.

1656 Blount *Glossogr.*, *Ionick*..a certain foot in a verse consisting of two long syllables and two short. **1885** R. C. Jebb *Œdipus Tyrannus* p. lxxxi, When the ionic ‒‒◡◡..is interchanged with the dichoree ‒◡‒◡.

4. *Typogr.* A type face distinguished by prominent serifs and a high degree of legibility.

1842 H. Caslon *Specimen of Printing Types* in *Two Centuries of Typefounding* (Caslon Letter Foundry) (1920) 71 (*caption*) Diamond two-line Ionic. **1934** A. F. Johnson *Type Designs* viii. 205 Ionic in some cases appears to be only another name for Egyptian. **1954** *Archit. Rev.* CXVI. 119/1 Ionic, or Clarendon, is familiar to all readers of *The Architectural Review* as a type face. It can also be pleasing and useful as an architectural letter. **1970** W. P. Jaspert et al. *Encycl. Type Faces* (ed. 4) 121 The first Ionic was a bold face cut by Caslon and shown 1842... It has been revived as a suitable newspaper type... Linotype Ionic was introduced in 1926 in the *Newark Evening News*.

i'onic, *a.*[2] *Physics.* [f. ion + -ic.] Of or pertaining to ions; composed of or containing ions; that is an ion.

1890 *Nature* 9 Oct. 576 In accordance with the laws of ionic migrations enunciated by Sir F. Bramwell..the ions collected at the tray..fell to pieces. **1898** Sir W. Crookes *Addr. Brit. Assoc.* 22 It becomes more and more clear that cathode rays consist of electrified atoms or ions in rapid progressive motion..Dr. Larmor's theory..likewise involves the idea of an ionic substratum of matter. **1913** *Q. Rev.* July 122 A knowledge of the total mass of water precipitated by the expansion enabled Mr. Wilson..to estimate the number of ionic nuclei required to form the cloud. **1914** J. J. Thomson in *Phil. Mag.* XXVII. 761 Molecules of this type, which I shall call ionic molecules. **1936** *Discovery* June 197/2 A description of ionic clouds formed in electrolytes is given. **1936** *Jrnl. R. Aeronaut. Soc.* XL. 594 Experiments on ionic crystals have determined the weakening effect of minute cracks. **1962** [see ion 1]. **1966** C. R. Tottle *Sci. Engin. Materials* ii. 33 Magnesium..will form an ionic compound with two chlorine atoms, $MgCl_2$, by donating its two 3*s* electrons, one to each of two chlorine atoms. The magnesium will be doubly charged (positive) and will therefore take up a position in the crystal lattice in which for each magnesium atom there are two chlorine atoms.

b. Brought about by, employing, or depending on ions; applied *spec.* to an electrovalent bond.

1907 *Brit. Med. Jrnl.* 14 Sept. 631/1 The study of ionic medication—the subject of Professor Leduc's paper—has been in many respects the most fruitful of modern times. **1910** E. R. Morton *Essent. Med. Electr. & Radiogr.* (ed. 2) v. 120 The advantages of the ionic method are very obvious. .. We can introduce a drug exactly where it is required. **1930** [see heteropolar *a.* 3]. **1938** R. W. Lawson tr. *Hevesy & Paneth's Man. Radioactivity* (ed. 2) xxiv. 261 The phenomenon of the 'ionic wind'... When the air between the plates of an ionization chamber is ionized, then on applying an electric field the air between the plates is set in motion. **1939** L. Pauling *Nature Chem. Bond* i. 4 We describe the interactions in this crystal by saying that each ion forms ionic bonds with its six neighbors, these bonds combining all of the ions in the crystal into one giant molecule. **1958** C. C. Adams et al. *Space Flight* ix. 236 When atomic energy, ionic drive, and light beams have been harnessed for propulsion, combined perhaps with anti-gravity, flight to the stars may be possible. **1966** C. R. Tottle *Sci. Engin. Materials* vi. 127 In solid materials ionic conduction is strongly structure-sensitive, particularly with respect to impurities and flaws or defects in the lattice. **1972** *Physics Bull.* Nov. 651/3 The atomic bonding within the network is partly covalent, partly ionic.

†**I'onical**, *a. Obs.* [f. as Ionic *a.*[1] + -al[1].] = Ionic *a.*[1] 2.

1624 Wotton *Archit.* in *Reliq.* (1651) 234 In an..Ionicall..Porch or Cloister.

ionically (aɪ'ɒnɪkəlɪ), *adv.* [f. ionic *a.*[2]: see -ically.] By means of ions or an ionic bond; as regards or in terms of ions.

1912 *Marconigraph* II. 340/1 The author's own observations on the influence of ordinary cloud on signals proved that the ionically turbulent belt was above the ordinary cloud level. **1925** H. H. U. Cross *Electro-Therapy & Ionic Medication* vi. 172 The efficacy of introducing drugs ionically depends..upon the fact that a drug introduced by ionic medication does not quickly pass out of the tissues which surround the point of introduction. **1965** Phillips & Williams *Inorg. Chem.* I. xv. 567 The electrical conductivity of liquid SO_2 has been commonly interpreted as due to the doubly-charged ions SO^{2+} and SO_3^{2-}, which would mean that a typical acid-base reaction would be written ionically as $SO^{2+} + SO_3^{2-} \rightarrow 2SO_2$. **1972** *Nature* 4 Feb. 262/1 The passage of dyes and small molecules between excitable cells which are ionically coupled has also been observed.

Ionicism (aɪ'ɒnɪsɪz(ə)m). [f. L. *Iōnic-us* Ionic *a.*[1] + -ism.] Ionic character, or an Ionic characteristic; the use of, or an idiom of, the Ionic dialect.

1827 I. Taylor *Transm. Anc. Bks.* (1859) 273 He..restores the ionicisms only when he has the authority of MSS. for so doing. **1892** *Knowledge* (N.Y.) 27 Aug., The fragments of his poems quoted by ancient writers are full of Ionicisms.

ionicity (aɪə'nɪsɪtɪ). *Chem.* [f. ionic *a.*[2]: see -icity.] Ionic character (in a chemical bond or a crystal).

1946 *Nature* 26 Oct. 592/2 The absence of a similar fall in the C–O bond-breaking energy passing from methyl to ethyl alcohol can be satisfactorily explained in terms of the increased ionicity of the C–O bond in ethyl alcohol relative to C–O in methyl alcohol. **1952** C. A. Coulson *Valence* v. 123 The asymmetry of charge, i.e. the polar character of the bond, sometimes called the degree of ionicity. **1960** *Nature* 13 Aug. 590/1 In discussions..regarding bonding in inorganic semiconducting (or insulating) crystals there seems to be some confusion between bond ionicity on one hand and charge separation effects due to electronegativity differences on the other. **1966** *Bull. Amer. Physical Soc.* XI. 187/1 The large hyperfine parameter for the NaCl structure is consistent with the expected greater ionicity.

Ionicize (aɪ'ɒnɪsaɪz), *v.* [f. as Ionicism + -ize.] **a.** *intr.* To use the Ionic dialect. **b.** *trans.* To render Ionic (in style or dialect). Hence **I,onici'zation.**

1842 De Quincey *Philos. Herodotus* Wks. 1862 VIII. 180 Herodotus, even whilst Ionicizing..had yet spelt a particular name with the *alpha* and not with the *eta*. **18..** *New Princeton Rev.* V. 412 (Cent.) A primitive Aeolic core, afterwards Ionicized. **1892** Agnes M. Clerke *Fam. Stud. Homer* i. 10 Fick's remarkable demonstration that the Iliad and the Odyssey underwent an early process of Ionicisation.

Ionism ('aɪənɪz(ə)m). [f. Ionize *v.*[1]: see -ism.] = Ionicism.

1795 *Brit. Crit.* Feb. 133 We lament that in any of the versions [of Gray's *Elegy*] a preference should have been shown to Ionisms. **1847** Grote *Greece* ii. xiii. III. 231 *note*, The test of Ionism, according to the statement of Herodotus, is, that a city should derive its origin from Athens, and that it should celebrate the solemnity of the Apaturia.

So **'Ionist**, one who uses Ionisms.

1886 F. G. Allinson in *Amer. Jrnl. Philol.* July 209 The Ionists of the second century A.D.

ionite ('aɪənaɪt). *Min.* [f. place-name *Iona* + -ite.] A brownish-yellow mineral resin found in the Iona valley, California.

1878 S. Purnell in *Amer. Jrnl. Sc. & Art* Ser. iii. XVI. 153.

ionium (aɪ'əʊnɪəm). *Chem.* [f. ion + -ium: see quot. 1907.] A radioactive isotope of thorium with mass number 230, produced by the α-decay of uranium 234. Symbols Io, ^{230}Th.

1907 B. B. Boltwood in *Amer. Jrnl. Sci.* XXIV. 372 The name 'Ionium' is proposed for this new substance... This name is believed to be appropriate because of the ionizing action which it possesses in common with the other elements which emit α-radiations. **1930** *Engineering* 4 Apr. 461/2 The elements ionium and thorium were actually found to have the same chemical properties, though differing in mass. **1954** K. Rankama *Isotope Geol.* lxxxiii. 410 The age of deep-sea sediments younger than approximately 0·5 × 10^6 years may be determined from their ^{230}Th (ionium) content. A plot of the ionium content against the depth in these sediments reveals the decay of the 80 000-year ^{230}Th, and from this graph the age of the sediment at a given depth may be calculated... This is the ionium method for dating deep-

ocean sediments. **1970** *Geochim. et Cosmochim. Acta* XXXIV. 389 (*heading*) A system for detection of ionium, thorium and protactinium to date deep-sea cores.

ionizable (ˈaɪənaɪzəb(ə)l), *a.* [f. IONIZ(E *v.*² + -ABLE.] Capable of being ionized.

1907 *Jrnl. Chem. Soc.* XCII. II. 560 In the haloid salts all the halogen is in an ionisable state. **1946** *Nature* 7 Sept. 325/2 One notable change in this edition is that the 1940 table of 'available' (ionizable) iron contents has been dropped. **1968** R. F. STEINER *Life Chem.* ii. 27 Each amino acid in the free state contains at least two ionizable sites. **1972** *Exper. Cell Res.* LXX. 122/1 The pI of the cells would ..give information about the nature of ionisable groups present on the surface.

ionization² (ˌaɪənaɪˈzeɪʃən). [f. ION + -IZATION.] **1.** The state of being ionized, or the process of ionizing.

1891 G. F. FITZGERALD in *Rep. Brit. Assoc. Adv. Sci. 1890* 327, I object to the term dissociation as applied to the ions in an electrolyte... I would..appeal to both sides to adopt some neutral term such as 'ionisation' to express the state of ions in electrolytes. **1898** *Nature* 8 Dec. 142/1 The measurements of the ionisation produced by Röntgen rays in fourteen gases showed that the ionisation was connected with the chemical composition in a very simple manner. **1908** *Westm. Gaz.* 13 Mar. 2/1 Paulsen urges that the aurora is due to an immense ionisation of the upper layers of the air. **1926** A. S. EDDINGTON *Internal Constitution of Stars* i. 10 In the actual conditions of a star the ionisation is not quite complete. **1938** R. W. LAWSON tr. *Hevesy & Paneth's Man. Radioactivity* (ed. 2) i. 12 This kind of ionization of a gas, in which the ions initially produced gain sufficient energy by their acceleration in the electric field to produce fresh ions by collision, is called 'ionization by collison'. **1947** GLASSTONE *Elem. Physical Chem.* xiii. 422 It is essential to distinguish between 'dissociation' and 'ionization'... The term 'ionization' applies to the total number of ions, irrespective of whether they are free or are held in ion-pairs. **1962** *Newnes Conc. Encycl. Electr. Engin.* 161/2 The ionization of an atom by the removal of an outermost electron (or electrons) requires a definite amount of energy.

2. *Med.* = CATAPHORESIS a.

1908 *Practitioner* June 785 The modern zinc mercury ionisation treatment is a very definite way of directly applying powerful drugs to a diseased area. **1909** [see IONTOPHORESIS]. **1934** E. P. CUMBERBATCH *Lect. Med. Electr.* iii. 32 Ionization is a form of treatment in which ions possessing therapeutic properties are made to migrate into the body by the agency of electro-motive force. **1944** E. B. CLAYTON *Electrotherapy* xi. 171 The patient should receive the ionisation reclining on a couch. **1960** B. SAVAGE *Pract. Electrotherapy* iv. 63 Histamine ionization is used whenever there is need for a marked increase in local circulation.

3. *Comb.*: **ionization chamber**, an instrument for measuring the intensity of ionizing radiation by collecting and measuring the charge on the ions which the radiation produces in a volume of gas; **ionization constant** *Physical Chem.* = *dissociation constant* (DISSOCIATION 2); **ionization current**, an electric current arising out of the movement, under the influence of an electric field, of ions and electrons produced in a gas; **ionization energy** = *ionization potential*; **ionization gauge**, an instrument for measuring the pressure in an evacuated vessel by ionizing the residual gas and measuring the resulting ionization current; **ionization potential**, the potential difference through which an electron must be accelerated in an electron impact experiment, or the energy required, to remove an electron in its lowest energy state from an atom or molecule of a gas.

1904 *Phil. Mag.* VIII. 721 In Rutherford's experiment.. the radioactive material was scattered over the floor of the ionization chamber. **1919** J. A. CROWTHER *Ions, Electrons & Ionizing Radiations* ii. 15 The gas under investigation is contained in a metal box which is connected to earth... The box and its electrodes forms what is known as an ionization chamber. **1945** *Electronic Engin.* XVII. 405 These experiments were carried out by means of ionisation chambers, like most of the early investigations on cosmic rays. **1966** *McGraw-Hill Encycl. Sci. & Technol.* VI. 92/1 If the voltage is too low, the electron avalanche never builds up, and the [Geiger] counter operates only as an ionization chamber (a device which gives the total ionization produced in the gas) or proportional counter, in which the output pulses are much smaller. **1904** T. S. MOORE in R. A. Lehfeldt *Electro-Chem.* I. ii. 101 For binary electrolytes, in comparing the ionisation-constants, we are comparing the concentration necessary to produce a given degree of dissociation. **1924** J. R. PARTINGTON in H. S. Taylor *Treat. Physical Chem.* I. xi. 538 The ionization constant of water.. increases very rapidly at lower temperatures, passing through a maximum about 218°. **1972** MOELLER & O'CONNOR *Ions in Aqueous Systems* iv. 74 Inasmuch as numerical values for ionization constants are available for many weak acids and bases, it is possible to calculate ion concentrations in solutions containing these substances under a variety of conditions. **1902** *Phil. Mag.* IV. 375 The time taken to pass over 100 divisions of the scale is taken by a stop-watch. The rate of movement is a measure of the ionization-current between the plates. **1956** HINE & BROWNELL *Radiation Dosimetry* i. 18 The determination of dose in roentgens requires the measurement of an ionization current under saturation conditions. **1928** F. J. FUCHS tr. *Gerlach's Matter, Electr., Energy* v. 69 On account of its large diameter and high ionization energy.., this singly charged helium atom appropriates to itself very rapidly a second electron. **1940** GLASSTONE *Text-bk. Physical Chem.* i. 52 The ionization energy is the work required to remove an electron from its lowest level to infinity. **1973** *Sci. Amer.* Feb. 91/1 Each kind of atom has a different ionization energy depending on the number of protons, neutrons and electrons it has. **1934** *Physical Rev.* XLV. 611/2 The pressure within the vacuum chamber as recorded by an ionization gauge..is often less than 10^{-6} mm Hg. **1966** *McGraw-Hill Encycl. Sci. & Technol.* VII. 253/2 In another type of ionization gage, the gas is ionized by high-energy alpha particles emitted by a radioactive source such as radium. **1914** *Phil. Mag.* XXVIII. 753 (*heading*) Note on the ionization potential of mercury vapour. **1927** *Physical Rev.* XXIX. 287 The second ionization potential of lithium, the amount of work required in order to remove one further electron from the singly ionized lithium atom, Li^+, in the normal state 1S, has not been directly determined by the method of electron impact. **1935** J. N. FRIEND *Text-bk. Physical Chem.* II. viii. 362 Upon raising the P.D. still more, gaseous ionisation occurs, the lowest potential producing this being known as the ionisation potential. **1950** W. J. MOORE *Physical Chem.* x. 262 The alkali metals have low ionization potentials; the inert gases, high ionization potentials. **1972** C. E. BRION in A. Maccoll *Mass Spectrometry* iii. 61 PES [*sc.* photoelectron spectroscopy] is a detector of direct photoionisation and as a result has proved to be the best and most prolific source of both inner and outer ionisation potentials.

Ionize (ˈaɪənaɪz), *v.*¹ [ad. Gr. ἰωνίζ-ειν to use the Ionic speech or fashions.] = IONICIZE.

1816 G. S. FABER *Orig. Pagan Idol.* III. 506 The wrathful excommunication of the Ionizing Brahmans. **1886** H. W. SMYTH in *Amer. Jrnl. Philol.* July 234 After such older portions as the Μῆνις had been Ionized.

Hence **Ioniˈzation**.

1899 B. L. GILDERSLEEVE in *Amer. Jrnl. Philol.* XX. 91 Fick's theory of the Ionization of Aeolic songs.

ˈionize, *v.*² *Physics.* [f. ION + -IZE.] **1.** *trans.* To convert into an ion or ions; to produce ions in (a substance or medium). Also *absol.*

1898 SIR W. CROOKES *Addr. Brit. Assoc.* 24 The thorium rays affect photographic plates through screens of paper or aluminium... They ionise the air, making it an electrical conductor. **1901** B. BLOUNT *Pract. Electro-Chem.* i. 16 Solutions of moderate strength..behave as if a portion of the molecules were ionised and a portion were present as ordinary molecules. **1915** *Proc. R. Soc.* XCI. 485 The minimum energy required to ionise an atom of mercury is that acquired by an electron in passing through a fall of potential of 4·9 volts. **1916** *Physical Rev.* VIII. 386 None of the electrons emitted by the cathode are able to ionize until they have moved a fraction V_0/V of the distance toward the anode. **1927** N. V. SIDGWICK *Electronic Theory of Valency* i. 10 Whenever an atom is ionized, whether by chemical combination, or by exposure under suitable conditions to the action of light, heat, or electricity, it gains or loses one or more electrons. **1947** *Sci. News* IV. 55 Through the action of various radiations the gas in this region is ionised, *i.e.*, split into electrically positive or negative particles. **1956** HINE & BROWNELL *Radiation Dosimetry* i. 2 Electromagnetic radiations, having energies above a few kev, ionize by virtue of the secondary electrons released when they are absorbed. **1963** C. A. MCDOWELL *Mass Spectrometry* xii. 507 Electrons with sufficient energy can ionize molecules by the following process.

2. *intr.* To dissociate into ions; to become converted (wholly or partly) into ions.

1904 T. S. MOORE in R. A. Lehfeldt *Electro-Chem.* ii. 130 Those di-acid bases which ionise in stages show the same relation between the first and second ionisation as the dibasic acids. **1930** FIELD & WEILL *Electro-Plating* vii. 92 Copper sulphate ionises as follows: $CuSO_4 \rightleftharpoons Cu^{\cdot\cdot} + SO_4^{-}$. **1966** *McGraw-Hill Encycl. Sci. & Technol.* VI. 60/1 At.. the breakdown voltage, the nearly conducting gas ionizes and becomes a good conductor, and a self-sustained discharge is established. **1968** R. O. C. NORMAN *Princ. Org. Synthesis* ii. 63 There is an increase in stabilization energy when acetic acid ionizes.

3. *Med.* (*trans.*) **a.** To introduce (a substance) *into* tissue by means of medical ionization. **b.** To treat by medical ionization.

1909 *Lancet* 13 Mar. 756/2 If a person ionises cocaine into himself..the skin becomes anæsthetic. *Ibid.*, I have placed under the microscope a piece of skin ionised with calcium. **1913** H. L. JONES *Ionic Medication* iii. 84 They [*sc.* corns] should have a thorough preliminary soaking.., and then may be ionized. **1936** J. N. DYSON *Pract. Ionization* iv. 51 For certain reasons the ulcer was ionized in two parts. **1949** *Brit. Jrnl. Physical Med.* XII. 144/2 Penicillin was 'ionized' into the skin covering the paronychia.

Hence **ˈionized** *ppl. a.*; **ˈionizing** *vbl. sb.* and *ppl. a.*; †*ionizing potential* = *ionization potential* (s.v. IONIZATION² 3); ***ionizing radiation***, radiation which produces ionization in matter through which it passes.

1899 *Nature* 30 Nov. 114/1 The only ionising inorganic solvents hitherto found in addition to water are nitric acid and liquefied ammonia. **1902** *Phil. Mag.* IV. 704 The ionization observed in gases may be due..to the emission of an ionizing radiation from the walls of the containing vessel. **1914** *Proc. R. Soc.* A. XC. 398 It appeared to be of interest to measure the ionising potential for negative corpuscles under experimental conditions somewhat different from those previously adopted. **1919** J. A. CROWTHER (*title*) Ions, electrons, and ionizing radiations. *Ibid.* v. 52 We have already seen..that the current through an ionized gas increases with increasing electric field up to a certain maximum value known as the saturation current. **1924** S. DUSHMAN in H. S. Taylor *Treat. Physical Chem.* II. xvi. 1110 This accounts for the production of arcs in gases at voltages below the ionizing potential. **1935** *Brit. Jrnl. Radiol.* VIII. 479 The Hospital Physicist is required to measure ionising radiations covering the vast range of intensities from many röntgens per second down to comparatively weak intensities. **1935** *Discovery* Mar. 76/2 It was clear that the sun is the ionising agent. **1937** *Ibid.* Jan. 5/2 (*caption*) The transmitter sends out 50 pulses per second, which after travelling to the ionised layers are reflected and received by the receiver. **1956** A. H. COMPTON *Atomic Quest* 42 He had perfected to a high degree the Geiger counters that have become so valuable for measuring ionizing radiations. **1969** R. & E. BRECHER *Rays* xxvi. 416 Of special interest during the 1960's were the studies of what happens when ionizing radiation is absorbed by human cells. **1970** D. W. TURNER et al. *Molecular Photoelectron Spectroscopy* i. 2 This instrument possessed the advantage of ..intimate juxtaposition of ionizing region and analyser entrance slit.

ionizer (ˈaɪənaɪzə(r)). [f. prec. + -ER¹.] That which produces ionization.

1901 *Smithsonian Contrib. Knowl.* No. 1309. 27 Instead of a single tube, two or more ionizers..are used simultaneously, each of them being charged with phosphorus. **1905** *Phil. Mag.* X. 207 An α particle is nearly twice as efficient an ionizer as the electron at its maximum efficiency. **1933** *Discovery* Apr. 107/2 This recoiling nucleus, on the other hand, is an efficient ionizer. **1967** S. W. TROMP et al. *Biometeorol.* II. II. 1025 Unavoidable by-production of chemical compounds, and poor knowledge of ion distribution around emitting electrodes, have largely hampered the design and practical use of electrical ionizers. *Ibid.*, Sufficient ion concentration can be achieved in the centre of a room by inconspicuous ionizers.

iono- (ˈaɪənəʊ-, aɪˈɒnəʊ-), used as comb. form of (*a*) ION, (*b*) IONOSPHERE.

ionogen (ˈaɪənəʊdʒɪn, aɪˈɒnəʊdʒɪn). *Physical Chem.* [f. IONO- + -GEN I.] Any compound which exists as ions when dissolved in a solvent.

1906 A. SMITH *Introd. Gen. Inorg. Chem.* xvii. 296 The substances of the three classes which alone are ionized may be designated ionogens... The electrolytic property of ions is only one amongst many special properties of electrolytes, and the majority of these properties are chemical and have nothing to do with electrolysis. Hence we have preferred the more general word 'ionogen'. **1922** *Chem. Abstr.* XVI. 1890 (*heading*) Nature of the ionogen linkage. **1935** J. N. FRIEND *Text-bk. Physical Chem.* II. vii. 217 The undissociated molecules and the ions of an ionogen in aqueous solution constitute a system in equilibrium. **1943** *Gloss. Terms Electr. Engin.* (*B.S.I.*) 91 The term 'ionogen' has been suggested as an alternative to the term 'electrolyte' when used with this meaning [*sc.* a substance which, when dissolved in a specified solvent, produces a conducting medium].

ionogenic (aɪˌɒnəʊˈdʒɛnɪk), *a. Chem.* [f. IONO- + -GENIC.] †**a.** [ad. G. *ionogen* (O. Hinsberg 1911, in *Jrnl. f. prakt. Chem.* LXXXIV. 179).] Of an atom or radical: promoting ionization elsewhere in the molecule of which it forms part. *Obs.*

1912 *Chem. Abstr.* VI. 351 (*heading*) Ionogenic atomic groups and atoms.

b. Capable of being ionized chemically.

1922 J. LOEB *Proteins & Theory Colloidal Behavior* ii. 34 If we wish to prepare gelatin or casein free from ionogenic impurities, we must bring these proteins..to the isoelectric point and then wash them. **1955** *Federation Proc.* XIV. 735/1 The electrophoretic mobility of a given protein is a function of the net electric charge and hence of the number of ionogenic groups. **1967** *Jrnl. Cell. Physiol.* LXIX. 287/1 It appears likely..that ionogenic groups of RNA, i.e. phosphate groups, are present at the electrokinetic surfaces of the two cell types. **1972** *Materials & Technol.* V. x. 275 Of the water-soluble surface-active agents.., some undergo ionization when dissolved in water whereas others do not ionize. On this basis, they are divided into two broad groups, namely ionogenic, or ion-forming, and non-ionogenic.

ionogram (aɪˈɒnəʊgræm). [f. IONO- + -GRAM.] **1.** A record of radio pulses received by an ionosonde following their reflection by the ionosphere.

1955 *Sci. Amer.* Sept. 128/2 To make an ionosonde record (ionogram) the transmitter and receiver are tuned rapidly through a range of frequencies. The echoes received are displayed on a cathode ray oscilloscope and photographed. **1963** *Times* 15 Feb. 7/7 Some 70,000 'ionograms'—graphs of frequency against depth of reflection below the satellite—have so far been obtained and are of good quality. **1967** *Encycl. Dict. Physics* Suppl. II. 240 The resulting 'ionogram', showing time delay as a function of frequency, can be interpreted as electron density as a function of 'virtual height' in the atmosphere.

2. *Chem.* The result of an ionographic separation, usually a series of spots or bands on the support medium.

1955 *Federation Proc.* XIV. 736/2 To determine the location of the various zones on an ionogram occupied by the individual components of a mixture, a number of procedures have been developed. **1963** *Proc. 17th World Veterinary Congr.* II. 1107 The ionogram of serum represents the electrolytic compounds of extracellular fluid in dogs. **1970** *Biol. Abstr.* LI. 354/1 Pre- and post-operational ionograms should be examined, in patients with a funnel-shaped deformation of the thorax.

ionography (aɪəˈnɒgrəfɪ). *Chem.* [f. IONO- + -GRAPHY.] The migration of ions or charged colloidal particles in a buffer solution held on a support (usu. filter paper) under the influence of an electric field, esp. as used to separate the components of a mixture; = *electrochromatography* (s.v. ELECTRO-).

1950 H. J. MCDONALD et al. in *Science* 25 Aug. 228/1 It is suggested that the term *ionography* be used to describe the technique. *Ibid.* 228/2 The isoelectric point of proteins can be determined, and..amino acids and proteins can be separated by ionography. **1955** *Federation Proc.* XIV. 736/2 Although paper has been used as the stabilizer in over 95% of the published articles on ionography, the use of starch has been found to have certain advantages in special cases. **1957** *Texas Rep. Biol. & Med.* XV. 235 An investigation into the

lipoprotein levels of serum from patients was undertaken, using the technique of ionography.

Hence **iono'graphic** *a.*, of or pertaining to ionography.

1955 *Federation Proc.* XIV. 733/1 The term 'ionographic apparatus' will refer to the instrument used in carrying out ionographic separations. **1968** *Compar. Biochem. & Physiol.* XXV. 727 The ionographic properties of the hemoglobins from ten species of *Peromyscus* have been compared.

ionomer (aɪ'ɒnəmə(r)). [f. IONO- + -MER.] Any of a class of thermoplastics in which there is ionic bonding between the polymer chains.

1964 *Mod. Plastics* Sept. 98/1 E. I. du Pont de Nemours & Co. Inc. has finally announced the introduction of an exciting new transparent thermoplastic it calls 'ionomer'. *Ibid.* 98/2 The tensile strength of many grades of ionomers is higher than that of any commercial polyolefin. **1967** H. F. MARK et al. *Encycl. Polymer Sci. & Technol.* VI. 395 Another class of copolymers with exceptional properties are the ionomers, which are essentially the metal salts of ethylene-acrylic acid copolymers. The resulting ionic bonding makes these materials a special class. **1967** *Times Rev. Industry* May 76/2 Among the newer plastics materials offered for use in packaging are ionomer and ethylene/vinyl acetate (EVA) films for meat and other retail produce.

ionone ('aɪənəʊn). *Chem.* [ad. G. *ionon* (Tiemann & Krüger 1893, in *Ber. d. Deut. Chem. Ges.* XXVI. 2693), f. Gr. ἴον violet + -ONE.] **a.** Either of two liquids (*α-ionone* and *β-ionone*) that are used in perfumery for their strong odour of violets and are isomeric cyclic ketones, $(CH_3)_3C_6H_6CH{:}CH{\cdot}CO{\cdot}CH_3$, differing only in the position of the double bond in the C_6H_6 ring.

Ionone is a proprietary name in the U.S.

1894 *Jrnl. Chem. Soc.* LXVI. I. 82 When pseudoionone is heated with dilute sulphuric acid and a little glycerol, it is converted into the isomeric ionone... This substance boils at 126–128° at 12 mm. **1900** *Ibid.* LXXVIII. II. 375 In order to separate and detect the α- and β-ionone, the crude ketones are boiled with a little alcohol and an aqueous solution of sodium sulphite. **1929** *Encycl. Brit.* VIII. 721/1 Ionone, derived from citral isolated from oil of lemongrass,..is the basis of all violet scents, and perhaps the most important of all synthetic perfumes. **1943** *Jrnl. Amer. Chem. Soc.* LXV. 2062/2 The resolution of *dl-α*-ionone was accomplished by means of *l*-menthydrazone. **1957** T. MOORE *Vitamin A* x. 100 The synthesis of vitamin A from β-ionone obviously requires the formation of a longer side chain to the trimethylcyclohexenyl ring. **1971** *New Scientist* 6 May 351/2 The pleasant-smelling ionones are breakdown products of carotenoids.

b. **ψ-ionone** (*pseudoionone*), $C_{13}H_{20}O$, a third isomer which can be cyclized to form α- and β-ionones.

1897 *Jrnl. Chem. Soc.* LXXII. I. 538 Ionone is..easily prepared by the action of sulphuric acid on ψ-ionone, the latter substance being produced from geranaldehyde by condensation with acetone. **1969** W. TEMPLETON *Introd. Chem. Terpenoids & Steroids* iii. 46 Similarly ψ-ionone.., obtained by condensation of citral with acetone, cyclizes under acidic conditions to α- and β-ionones, which are found in Nature.

ionophone (aɪ'ɒnəʊfəʊn). [f. IONO- + -PHONE.] A type of loudspeaker using the vibrations of a volume of ionized air in place of those of a diaphragm.

1955 *Sci. News Let.* 23 July 63/3 The vibrating pocket of air in the new loud speaker, called the Ionophone, will create the sound without this setback, the designers say. **1962** A. NISBETT *Technique Sound Studio* 257 *Ionophone*, a type of loudspeaker which has no moving parts.

ionophore (aɪ'ɒnəʊfɔə(r)). *Biol.* [f. IONO- + -PHORE.] An agent which is able to transport ions across a lipid membrane in a cell. So **iono'phorous** *a.*

1967 B. C. PRESSMAN et al. in *Proc. Nat. Acad. Sci.* LVIII. 1954 It is our conclusion that both the valinomycin and the nigericin classes of antibiotics induce alkali ion permeability in mitochondrial and other systems by carrying ions across lipid barriers as lipid-soluble complexes. Accordingly we propose to classify them generically as ionophores or ionophorous agents. **1970** *Jrnl. Biol. Chem.* CCXLV. 5606 (*heading*) Effect of nucleo-tides on the transport of alkali metal cations catalyzed by ionophorous antibiotics across mitochondrial membranes. **1971** *Nature* 5 Nov. 12/2 Cyclic peptides such as gramicidin-S or alamethecin which can act as ionophores..in membranes.

ionophoresis (aɪˌɒnəʊfə'riːsɪs). *Biochem.* [f. IONO- + -PHORESIS.] The migration of ions in solution under the influence of an electric field, esp. as used to separate the components of a mixture. Hence **iˌonopho'retic** *a.*

1945 *Adv. Protein Chem.* II. 31 We propose to use *ionophoresis* to describe processes concerned with the movement in an electric field of relatively small ions, *electrophoresis* for movement of large molecules and particles. *Ibid.* (*heading*), Ionophoretic methods. **1949** ABRAHAM & HEATLEY in H. W. Florey et al. *Antibiotics* I. II. 106 An apparatus in which ionophoretic separation takes place in a slab of silica jelly, the substances under investigation being inlaid in a gutter at right angles to the length of the slab. **1956** *Nature* 25 Feb. 393/2 A number of primary aliphatic amines can readily be separated..by ionophoresis on paper at *p*H 7 using collidine acetate buffer, and the spots revealed with ninhydrin. **1967** *Biol. Abstr.* XLVIII. 895/2 (*heading*) Detection of metal cations in soil by chromatographic and ionophoretic techniques. **1971** *European Jrnl. Biochem.* XIX. 125/1 Ionophoresis in the second dimension was carried out on an 85 × 45 cm sheet of DEAE-cellulose paper..in 7% formic acid.

ionosonde (aɪ'ɒnəʊsɒnd). [f. IONO- + SONDE.] An instrument for obtaining information about the ionosphere by transmitting a succession of radio pulses into it at different frequencies and recording their echoes.

1955 *Sci. Amer.* Sept. 128/2 The instrument used to explore the ionosphere is called an ionosonde. **1962** *Flight International* LXXXI. 681/2 The 95 (US) tons of water ballast was released by explosion of the vehicle at a height of about 65 miles 160 sec after lift-off, and a large white cloud of ice particles was formed... Observations were made by ground-based cameras, aircraft at various altitudes, ground radars and ionosondes. **1971** *New Scientist* 18 Mar. 598/2 Reflections of a swept-frequency pulse of radio waves by the ionosphere — the ionosonde technique — provide information about the distribution and density of its constituent electrons. **1972** *Science* 5 May 464/1 Lightweight ionosondes have been placed in satellites.

ionosphere (aɪ'ɒnəsfɪə(r)). [f. IONO- + -SPHERE.] A region of the outer atmosphere, beginning at a height of 50–80 km. (30–50 miles), which contains many ions and free electrons and is capable of reflecting radio waves; also, a corresponding region above other planets.

1926 R. A. WATSON-WATT *Let.* 8 Nov. in *Nature* (1969) 13 Dec. 1096/1 We have in quite recent years seen the universal adoption of the term 'stratosphere'..and..the companion term 'troposphere'... The term 'ionosphere', for the region in which the main characteristic is large scale ionisation with considerable mean free paths, appears appropriate as an addition to this series. **1929** —— in *Q. Jrnl. R. Meteorol. Soc.* LV. 278, I have suggested the name ionosphere to make the systematic group troposphere, stratosphere, ionosphere, but meanwhile the term 'upper conducting layers' seems to hold the field. **1932** E. V. APPLETON in *Jrnl. Inst. Electr. Engin.* LXXI. 642 (*heading*) Wireless studies of the ionosphere. [*Note*] This is a convenient term, suggested by Mr R. A. Watson Watt, connoting the ionized regions of the upper atmosphere. **1934** *Times* 23 Feb. 20/2 Beyond lies the ionosphere, and of the layers in this we learn from the paths of radio-waves. **1947** *Sci. News* IV. 55 Sir Edward Appleton, whom one might call the Master of the Ionosphere, distinguishes in it the following layers: the complex F-layer 250 kilometres (150 miles) above the earth (also called the Appleton layer), the E- or Heaviside layer at about 100 km., and further down the D layer which is little noticeable in normal times, but whose ionisation is considerably increased as long as a solar flare is visible. **1955** *Times* 15 June 5/5 The ionosphere, a belt of gases ionized.. by ultra violet rays from the sun and lying between 70km. and 300–400km. above the earth, makes medium and short wave radio propagation possible by reflecting signals back to earth. **1959** DAVIES & PALMER *Radio Stud. Universe* IV. 66 This is difficult to explain if Jupiter is surrounded by an ionosphere similar to the Earth's. **1973** *Physics Bull.* Feb. 93/3 Spacecraft observations of the ionospheres of Venus and Mars.

ionospheric (aɪˌɒnəʊ'sfɛrɪk), *a.* [f. prec. + -IC.] Of, pertaining to, or involving the ionosphere.

1933 *Proc. Physical Soc.* XLV. 673 (*heading*) On two methods of ionospheric investigation. **1937** *Discovery* Jan. 3/2 (*heading*) The base hut in Brandy Bay..with the wireless and ionospheric research masts behind. **1955** *Sci. News Let.* 28 May 339 Most of the radio frequency power in the new method is lost, but some is scattered by the lower part of the E region... This portion is received hundreds of miles away by high-gain antennas aimed at the exact spot. The system is called either forward scatter, or FPIS, for forward propagation by ionospheric scatter. **1958** *Times* 8 Nov. 4/7 Assurances that the ionospheric forward-scatter radio station..will not represent a radiation hazard to the public have now been given officially. **1966** *Electronics* 3 Oct. 181 Boelkow has designed a fixed-wing rocket—intended for ionospheric studies—that can be recovered from 48 miles.

Hence **iˌono'spherically** *adv.*, by the ionosphere.

1955 *Proc. IRE* XLIII. 1174 Ionospherically propagated waves. **1971** *Nature Physical Sci.* 5 Apr. 125/1 There is no fading such as occurs in ionospherically reflected sky waves.

ionospherist (aɪˌɒnəʊ'sfɛrɪst). *rare.* [f. as prec. + -IST 4 b.] One who studies the ionosphere. Also **iˌono'sphericist**, in the same sense.

1933 *Proc. R. Soc.* A. CXLI. 715, I should be most disappointed if time permitted only those whom I might call the professional ionospherists to take part in the discussion. **1955** *Jrnl. Brit. Interplanetary Soc.* XIV. 19 Moving concentrations of electrons account for the other main type of irregularity [in the ionosphere]; ionospherists seem never to grow tired of studying them. **1971** *Nature* 1 Jan. 15/3 The angle of arrival of radio waves is determined by ionosphericists using spaced receivers.

ionotropy (aɪə'nɒtrəpɪ). *Chem.* [f. IONO- + Gr. -τροπ-ία turning (f. τρέπειν to turn) + -Y[3].]

1. Tautomerism or tautomeric change, regarded as occurring through the detachment of an ion from the molecule concerned followed by a redistribution of the charge in the resulting molecular ion and reattachment of the ion to a different part of it. *rare.*

[**1926** T. M. LOWRY in *Inst. Internat. de Chimie Solvay: Deuxième Conseil de Chimie..1925..Rapports et Discussions* 151 Les transformations dans lesquelles des radicaux autres que l'hydrogène se déplacent peuvent..être formulées comme comportant une *migration d'ions* et peuvent être désignées sous le terme d'*ionotropie*.] **1928** *Ann. Rep. Progr. Chem. 1927* XXIV. 107 Lowry has also used the word 'ionotropy' (Report of the Second Solvay Conference 1925, p. 182). **1955** *Chem. Abstr.* XLIX. 40 Reactions of acids and bases can be described by assuming the fundamental reaction of 'ionotropy'.

2. [ad. G. *ionotropie* (H. Thiele 1947, in *Naturwiss.* XXXIV. 123/2.] The ordering of particles in a gel that results when an electrolyte is added to a colloidal suspension.

1949 *Chem. Abstr.* XLIII. 4539 Usually the sign of the ionotropy is the same as that of flow anisotropy. **1958** *Jrnl. Physical Chem.* LXII. 1277/1 The phenomenon of ionotropy can be simply demonstrated by placing a thin layer of 2% suspension of salt-free Wyoming bentonite on a glass slide and then placing a crystal of sodium chloride on the layer of suspension.

Hence **iono'tropic** *a.*, exhibiting ionotropy (sense 2).

1944 *Handbk. Descr.* in *Chem. & Chem. Engin.* (U.S. Manpower Comm.) Nov. 66 Polarity, ionotropic change and conjugation. **1954** H. THIELE in *Discussions Faraday Soc.* XVIII. 295 Since ionotropic gels are formed by chemical or electrical forces the degree of order decreases with decreasing dissociation of the ionic groups of the colloid particles. **1969** *Jrnl. Biomed. Materials Res.* III. 432 The ordered ionotropic structure of the fibers of the polyelectrolyte directs the mineralization and calcification in the same manner as in biological tissue.

iontophoresis (aɪˌɒntəʊfə'riːsɪs). *Med.* [f. Gr. ἰοντ-, ἰόν pr. pple. of ἰέναι to go + -O + -PHORESIS.] = CATAPHORESIS a.

1909 *Lancet* 13 Mar. 756/1 By medical ionisation, or, as it is called abroad..'iontophoresis', we mean the introduction of ions of different sorts into the tissues of the human body. **1937** *New Eng. Jrnl. Med.* 5 Aug. 202/2 Ionotophoresis is a term used for denoting the act of driving negatively or positively charged ions into the subcutaneous tissues by means of a galvanic or direct current of electricity. **1949** A. HUXLEY *Let.* 26 Feb. (1969) 591 Dr. Gustav Erlanger..has developed a method for treating the eyes by iontophoresis and gets remarkable results. **1971** *Jrnl. Physiol.* CCXV. 199 DNP and other metabolic inhibitors were tested on cortical neurones by iontophoresis from micropipettes.

Hence **iˌontopho'retic** *a.*, of, pertaining to, or employing iontophoresis; **iˌontopho'retically** *adv.*, by means of iontophoresis.

1937 *New Eng. Jrnl. Med.* 5 Aug. 204/1 The changes were not of sufficient degree to make us feel that the iontophoretic administration of acetyl β-methylcholine produced constant changes in the blood-sugar level. **1947** ABRAMOWITSCH & NEOUSSIKINE *Treatm. by Ion Transfer* iii. 68 Novocain was introduced iontophoretically. **1955** *Jrnl. Investigative Dermatol.* XXV. 223 It seemed logical to first find out whether or not the thorium X..could be introduced into a test material by the galvanic iontophoretic current. **1964** D. M. GORDON *Med. Managem. Ocular Dis.* iv. 20 Many of the systemic preparations can be..administered iontophoretically. **1971** *Jrnl. Cell. Physiol.* LXXVII. 339/2 Iontophoretic application of materials was accomplished by connecting a variable voltage source with a micropipette containing the material. **1972** *Science* 5 May 515/1 The ACh was applied iontophoretically by a micropipette containing a 4M solution of ACh chloride.

i-opened, -oponed, ME. pa. pple. of OPEN *v.*

iopterous (aɪ'ɒptərəs), *a.* *Entom.* [f. mod.L. *iopter-us* (f. Gr. ἴον violet + πτέρον wing) + -OUS.] Having violet-coloured wings.

1855 in MAYNE *Expos. Lex.*

-ior, *suffix*[1], later spelling of -IOUR, in which *i* represents an earlier *i*, *ei*, *e*, as *warrior*, formerly *warriour*, ME. *werriour*, *-eour*, *-eyour*, *-aiour*, ONF. *werreior*, *-ur*, OF. *guerroyeur*, *guerrieur*.

-ior, *suffix*[2], repr. L. *-ior* of comparatives, as *inferior*, *superior*, *ulterior*, *junior*, *senior*; formerly written *-iour* = F. *-ieur*.

i-ordeined, -ordeyned, ME. pa. pple. of ORDAIN *v.*

i-ordred, ME. pa. pple. of ORDER *v.*

i-orne, var. of *i-runne*, ME. pa. pple. of RUN *v.*

iot, obs. spelling of JOT.

iota (aɪ'əʊtə). Also 7 **jota**. [a. Gr. ἰῶτα.]

1. The name of the Greek letter *I*, *ι*, corresponding to the Roman I, i; the smallest letter of the Greek alphabet.

iota subscript (L. *iota subscriptum*), a small iota written beneath a long vowel, forming the second element of a diphthong, as in ᾳ, ῃ, ῳ.

1607 TOPSELL *Four-f. Beasts* 290 The Nisæan horses (written with *Iota* [**1658** Jota] and simple *Sigma*, as Eustathius writeth) are the most excellent. **1679** PENN *Addr. Prot.* II. ii. (1692) 65 All this Stir had been made about an *Iota*: For the whole Question was, Whether *homousia* or *homoiusia* should be received for Faith. **1893** E. M. THOMPSON *Grk. & Lat. Palæogr.* xii. 175 The frequent dotting of the *iota* in this MS. is peculiar.

2. *fig.* (after Matt. v. 18; see JOT): The least, or a very small, particle or quantity; an atom. (Mostly with negative expressed or implied.)

1636 FEATLY *Clavis Myst.* iv. 42 Shall we lose, or slightly pass by, any *iota* or tittle of the Booke of God? **1643** A. BURGES *Serm. bef. Ho. Comm.* 27 Sept. 19 You are accomptable to God for jotaes and tittles. **1696** BROOKHOUSE *Temple Open.* 28 This has been done in England to an *Iota*. **1771** BURKE *Corr.* (1844) I. 251 Not an iota should be yielded of the principle of the bill. **1786** J. ADAMS *Wks.* (1854) IX. 549, I would..demand, in a tone that could not be resisted, the punctual fulfilment of every iota of the treaty on the part of Britain. **1863** WHYTE

MELVILLE *Gladiators* III. 124 We will not part with one iota of our privileges.

iotacism (aɪˈəʊtəsɪz(ə)m). [ad. L. *iotacismus*, a. Gr. *ἰωτακισμός* a laying too much stress upon the *ι*, repetition of *ι*, f. *ἰῶτα* IOTA.] Excessive use or repetition of the letter *iota* or *I*; *spec.* the pronunciation of other Greek vowels like *iota* (i.e. as Latin *ī* or mod.Eng. *ee*), as in modern Greek: see ITACISM, and cf. ETACISM.

1656 BLOUNT *Glossogr.*, *Iotacism*..is when the letter (*I* or *Iota*) sounds much; as if we say, *Juno Jovi irascitur*. It is also sometimes taken for an error in pronouncing the letter *I*. **1834** *Fraser's Mag.* IX. 502 The letter *I* is a great letter. There was a prejudice against it among the Latins, and the Greeks were accused of Iotacism. *a* **1843** SOUTHEY *Comm. pl. Bk.* IV. 428 In the pronunciation of modern Greek Alfieri says the most melodious language in the world becomes a continual iotacism, like the neighing of a horse.

So **iˈotacist**, one who practises iotacism in the pronunciation of Greek; = ITACIST.

iotal (aɪˈəʊtəl), *a. nonce-wd.* [f. IOT-A + -AL[1].] Existing with respect to every iota; absolute in every detail.

1810 *Q. Rev.* III. 189 Mr. Smith's flaming profession as to the *iotal* accuracy of his creed.

iote, obs. form of JOT.

iotize (ˈaɪətaɪz), *v. rare.* [ad. Gr. *ἰωτίζειν* to write with an iota: see -IZE.] (See quot.)

1880 GRANT WHITE *Every-Day Eng.* 33 The introduction of it [the *i* sound] before another letter is called the iotizing of that letter.

I O U (ˌaɪˌəʊˈjuː). [= 'I owe you'.] A document bearing these three letters followed by a specified sum, and signed, constituting a formal acknowledgement of a debt.

[**1618** BRETON *Court. & Countryman* *C, Hee teacheth od fellowes play tricks with their Creditors, who in stead of payments, write *IOV*, and so scoffe many an honest man out of his goods.] **1795** ESPINASSE *Rep.* I. 426 *marg. note*, An I.O.U. is admissible evidence of a debt without a stamp. **1808** CAMPBELL *Rep.* I. 499 It had been held by Eyre C. J. that an I.O.U. was good without a stamp. **1817** MAR. EDGEWORTH *Harrington* xvi. 442 The fellow understands nothing, in short, but his IOUs. **1833** CHITTY *Bills of Exch.* 558. **1836** JAS. GRANT *Gt. Metrop.* I. iv. 190, I shall be able to pay it you in a couple of months', said his Lordship, handing the ex-fishmonger his IOU. **1840** MARRYAT *Olla Podr.* (Rtldg.) 300 Of course with *IOU's* upon his.. domains. *a* **1845** HOOD *Sniffing a Birthday* vii, I'm free to give my IOU, Sign, draw, accept, as majors do. **1893** BITHELL *Counting-Ho. Dict.*, *IOU*, a recognized contraction of the sentence, 'I owe you.' It is a simple acknowledgment of indebtedness to some particular person. As it is neither a promissory note nor a receipt, it requires no stamp. It is not a negotiable instrument, but as it is an acknowledgment of a debt, that debt can be sued for at any time, and is so far equal to a promissory note payable on demand.

-iour, a compound suffix, viz. -OUR (OF. *-ur*, *-or*, F. *-eur*), preceded by an *i* representing *i*, *ei*, *e*, of another element; as in *saviour*, ME. and AF. *sauveour*, OF. *sauve-ur*, *-e-or*, early OF. *salvedur*:—L. *salvātōrem*; later F. *sauveur*; in some cases a corruption of a different suffix, as in *haviour*, *behaviour*: see -OUR. Through the general later change of *-our* to *-or*, and the confusion of this with *-er*, several words formerly in *-iour* are now written *-ior* (as *warrior*), *-ier* (as *currier*, *soldier*).

-ious, a compound suffix, consisting of the suffix *-ous*, added to an *i* which is part of another suffix, repr. L. *-iōsus*, F. *-ieux*, with sense 'characterized by, full of'. Found in L. in adjs. formed from derivative sbs. in *-ia*, *-ies*, *-ius*, *-ium*, as *invidiōsus* invidious, *perniciōsus* pernicious, *ēbriōsus* drunken, ebrious, *odiōsus* odious; by false analogy in *cūriōsus* curious (from *cūra*): see -OUS. Also in adjs. belonging to sbs. in *-io*, *-iōn-em*, as *ambit-iōs-us* (from *ambit-iōn-em*) ambitious; so *captiōsus* captious, *factiōsus* factious, *obliviōsus* oblivious, *religiōsus* scrupulous, religious, *seditiōsus* seditious, *suspiciōsus* suspicious, etc. By analogical extension from these, there is a tendency in English to form an adj. in *-ious* beside any sb. in *-ion*, esp. those in *-tion*, *-cion*, *-sion*, e.g. *rebell-ion*, *-ious*, *caution*, *-ious*, *infection*, *-ious*, *contradictious*, *deceptious*, *disputatious*, *dissentious* (for *-sious*), *ignitious*. Adjs. in *-ious* are also formed in Eng. by adding *-ous* to the stem of L. adjs. in *-i-us*, e.g. L. *vari-us* various; also in *-itious* from L. *-īci-us*, as *adventitious*: see -ITIOUS, and -OUS.

iow, obs. f. JAW, JEW.

Iowan (ˈaɪəwən), *sb.* and *a.* Also formerly **Iowaian** (from the pronunciation *Ioway* of *Iowa*, which is still heard.) [f. *Iowa*, name of one of the United States of America, formerly of an Indian people inhabiting Iowa and Minnesota.]

A. *sb.* A native or inhabitant of Iowa.

c **1848** W. WHITMAN in *Amer. Speech* (1961) XXXVI. 297 Iowans *Gophers*. **1856** N. H. PARKER *Iowa as it Is* 56 Our ferry is busy all hours in passing over the large canvas-backed wagons, densely populated with becoming Iowaians. **1928** *Glasgow Herald* 6 Apr. 12 Iowans..used to console themselves by telling the world..that their largest city had the greatest consumption of ice-cream per head of population. **1964** MRS. L. B. JOHNSON *White House Diary* 21 Nov. (1970) 208 Just enough places for the Iowans and the kinfolks.

B. *adj.* Of, pertaining to, or designating what was formerly considered the fourth Pleistocene glaciation of North America, but which is now considered the earliest phase of the Wisconsin glaciation. Also *absol.*, the Iowan glaciation or the deposits it produced.

1894 in J. Geikie *Gt. Ice Age* (ed. 3) xlii. 756 It may..be the equivalent of the next later formation—the East-Iowan. *Ibid.* 760 The East-Iowan till-sheet..is not usually bordered by any definite terminal moraine. *Ibid.*, The designation 'East-Iowan formation' is chosen because it has been most carefully worked out by Mr. McGee in north-eastern Iowa. **1896**, etc. [see ILLINOIAN *a.*]. **1968** R. W. FAIRBRIDGE *Encycl. Geomorphol.* 292/2 In the Wisconsin phase, the Iowan Lobe was considerably smaller.

iowell, obs. f. JEWEL.

i-paid, i-paied, ME. pa. pple. of PAY *v.*

i-paised, ME. pa. pple. of PEASE *v.*, to pacify.

i-parceived, ME. pa. pple. of PERCEIVE *v.*

i-parroked, ME. pa. pple. of PARROCK *v.*, to confine or shut in.

i-passed, i-past, ME. pa. pple. of PASS *v.*

i-payde, ME. pa. pple. of PAY *v.*

ipecac, shortened form of IPECACUANHA.

1788 M. CUTLER in *Life, Jrnls. & Corr.* (1888) I. 409 Examined several vegetables, the Pawpaw, Ipecac, Red-bud, Spanish Oak, Honey-locust. **1855** O. W. HOLMES *Poems* 174 Ye healers of men, for a moment decline Your feats in the rhubarb and ipecac line. **1875** H. C. WOOD *Therap.* (1879) 433 Ipecac acts upon the digestive tract.

ipecacuanha (ɪpɪkækjuːˈænə). Forms: 7 **ipe-, hypepocoanha, hypopecovana, -couana, hypocochoana,** 8 **hypecacuana, ipecacuana, ipececuanha, ipecacoanha,** 8- **ipecacuanha;** *contracted* **ipecacuan,** IPECAC. [a. Pg. *ipecacuanha* (ipekaˈkwanja), ad. Tupi-Guarani *ipe-kaa-guéne*.

According to Cavalcanti, cited by Skeat *Trans. Philol. Soc.* 1885, 91, the meaning of *ipe-kaa-guene* is 'low or creeping plant causing vomit'. The word is said to be a descriptive appellation applied to several medicinal plants, the proper name of the *Cephaëlis*, which produces the ipecacuanha of commerce, being *poaya*.]

1. The root of *Cephaëlis Ipecacuanha*, N.O. *Cinchonaceæ*, a South American small shrubby plant, which possesses emetic, diaphoretic, and purgative properties; also popularly applied to various forms in which the drug is employed.

1682 J. PECHEY (*title*) Some Observations made upon the Brasilian Root, called Ipepocoanha. *Ibid.* 4 What wonderful Virtue I have found in the Root called Hypepocoanha. **1698** FROGER *Voy.* 114 As for the Hypopecovana it's a small Root, that in our Armies has sufficiently discovered the Vertues of it against the Bloody-flux. **1698** M. LISTER *Journ. Paris* (1699) 134 Tho' he took..Hypocochoana five times, it had no effect upon him. **1712** tr. *Pomet's Hist. Drugs* I. 24 The Ipecacuana..is a little Root; which the Dutch and Portuguese bring us from the coast of Brazil. **1717** tr. *Frezier's Voy.* 303 Oil of Copayoa, Hypecacuana. **1744** BERKELEY *Siris* §84 The violent operation of ipecacuanha lies in its resin. **1747** WESLEY *Prim. Physick* (1762) 113 Pour a Dish of tea on twenty Grains of Ipececuanha. **1764** GRAINGER *Sugar Cane* II. 114 *note*, Almost as useful in dysenteric complaints as ipecacuan. **1772** HEY in *Phil. Trans.* LXII. 260 Five grains of ipecacoanha. **1822-34** *Good's Study Med.* (ed. 4) IV. 130 Two or three grains of ipecacuan. **1829** SOUTHEY *O. Newman* v, Words..which from me or you Could not be forced by ipecacuanha, Drop from his oratoric lips like manna.

2. The plant *Cephaëlis Ipecacuanha.*

1788 M. CUTLER in *Life, Jrnls. & Corr.* (1888) I. 427 Found vast quantities of Ipecacuanha on a hill. **1870** *Pall Mall G.* 26 Aug. 4 In Calcutta some experiments have been made in the cultivation of ipecacuanha. **1885** LADY BRASSEY *The Trades* 175 Ipecacuanha, covered with bright red and yellow flowers grew in profusion.

3. Transferred to many other plants whose roots have emetic properties, e.g.

American ipecacuanha (*Euphorbia Ipecacuanha*, also *Gillenia trifoliata*); **bastard i.** (*Asclepias curassavica*); **Indian, Ceylon, Coromandel i.** (*Tylophora asthmatica*); **Peruvian, striated,** or **black i.** (*Psychotria emetica*); **wild i.** (*Asclepias curassavica, Triosteum perfoliatum*); **white, amylaceous,** or **undulated i.** (*Richardsonia scabra*). **false i.**, a term applied to nearly all these plants, but esp. to species of *Ionidium*.

1760 J. LEE *Introd. Bot.* App. 316 Bastard Ipecacuana, *Asclepias*. False Ipecacuana, *Triosteum*.

4. *fig.* Something that produces nausea.

a **1763** SHENSTONE *Ess.* (1765) 191 The foppery of love-verses, when a person is ill and indisposed, is perfect ipecacuanha. **1788** H. WALPOLE in *Walpoliana, Auth. & Artists* 11 An author, talking of his own works, or censuring those of others, is to me a dose of ipecacuanha.

5. *attrib.*, as ***ipecacuanha cuttings***, ***lozenge***, ***root***; **ipecacuanha wine**, the filtered infusion of the root in wine.

1761 ARMSTRONG *Day* 194 I've known a dame, sage else as a divine, For brandy whip off ipecacuan wine. **1789** W. BUCHAN *Dom. Med.* (1790) 707 Ipecacuanha Wine. **1847** F. A. KEMBLE *Let.* 7 Mar. in *Rec. Later Life* (1882) III. 173, I ..am swallowing ipecacuanha lozenges by the gross. **1870** SIR. R. CHRISTISON *Jrnl.* in *Life* II. 211 The ipecacuan cuttings for India. **1926-7** *Army & Navy Stores Catal.* p. xlix, Ipecacuanha lozenges.

ipecacuanhic (ɪpɪˌkækjuːˈænɪk), *a.* [f. prec. + -IC.] Of or pertaining to ipecacuanha; containing ipecacuanha in chemical combination, as ***ipecacuanhic acid***, $C_{14}H_{18}O_7$, a peculiar form of tannic acid found in ipecacuanha root.

1865-72 WATTS *Dict. Chem.* III. 314 Ipe[ca]cuanic acid.. is a reddish-brown, very bitter, amorphous mass, soluble in ..alcohol and water. **1876** HARLEY *Mat. Med.* (ed. 6) 548.

i-peȝt, ME. pa. pple. of PITCH *v.*

i-peint(ed, ME. pa. pple. of PAINT *v.*

†**i-peˈlured**, *ppl. a. Obs.* [f. I-[1] + F. *pelure* PELLURE, fur + -ED[1].] Lined with pellure; furred.

c **1460** *Launfal* 237 Har manteles wer of grene felwet,.. Ipelvred with grys and gro. *Ibid.* 417 Launfal yn purpure gan hym schrede Ipelvred with whyt ermyne.

†**i-ˈpend**, *v. Obs. rare.* [f. I- *pref.*[1] (here pseudo-archaic) + *pend*, extended form of PEN *v.*: cf. next.] *trans.* To pen or shut in.

1600 FAIRFAX *Tasso* X. xl. 2 The earnest zeal..From courage sprung, which seld we close ipend In swelling stomach without violent breach.

i-pent, obs. pa. pple. of PEN *v.*

1600 FAIRFAX *Tasso* XIII. xx. 1 These drawing near the Wood, where close ipent The wicked Sprites in sylvan Pinfolds were.

i-perced, ME. pa. pple. of PIERCE *v.*

i-perised, ME. pa. pple. of PERISH *v.*

i-pesed, ME. pa. pple. of PEASE *v.*, to appease.

i-peynt, ME. pa. pple. of PAINT *v.*

i-peyred, ME. pa. pple. of PAIR *v.*, to impair.

i-piched, i-picht, i-pight, i-piȝt, ME. pa. pple. of PITCH *v.*

ipid (ˈɪpɪd, ˈaɪpɪd), *sb.* and *a.* [a. mod.L. *Ipidæ*, f. Gr. *ἴπ-*, *ἴψ* woodworm.] **A.** *sb.* A bark-beetle of the family Ipidæ, which is now included in the Curculionidæ. **B.** *adj.* Of or pertaining to a beetle of this type. Cf. SCOLYTID.

1866 E. C. RYE *Brit. Beetles* xii. 100 The Ipides have a single lobe to the maxillæ. **1922** W. M. WHEELER *Soc. Life Insects* 40 The females of the Ipid ambrosia beetles carry the fungus in the fore part of the stomach.

i-piled, ME. pa. pple. of PILL *v.*, to plunder.

i-pilt, ME. pa. pple. of PELT *v.*

i-pined, ME. pa. pple. of PINE *v.*

ipiti (ˈɪpɪtɪ). *S. Afr.* Also **impiti, ipiete.** [Zulu *i-mpiti.*] The blue duiker, *Cephalophus monticola*, the smallest South African antelope.

1836 R. M. MARTIN *Hist. S. Afr.* I. iv. 138 They [*sc.* the 'Caffres'] display considerable taste in the arrangement of their dress, particularly for the head, which is covered by a turban made of the skin of the '*ipiete*', a species of antelope. **1878** T. J. LUCAS *Camp Life & Sport S. Afr.* viii. 101 Immediately around Pietermaritzberg the game is comparatively scarce, consisting principally of the small Ipite Bok, a graceful little antelope. **1879** R. J. ATCHERLEY *Trip to Boerland* 26, I shot a few small buck known as *impiti* ..not much larger than a hare. **1905** D. BLACKBURN *Richard Hartley* xiii. 244 The beautiful little ipiti, no bigger than a toy-terrier and quite as sprightly and alert. **1926** R. LYDEKKER *Game Animals Afr.* (ed. 2) 143 (*heading*) Blue Buck or Blue Duiker... Ipiti, Zulu. **1934** B. I. BUCHANAN *Pioneer Days Natal* ii. 33 Twice we saw some of the fairy bucks—the darling little ipiti—which immediately won our hearts.

i-plaied, ME. pa. pple. of PLAY *v.*

i-plesed, ME. pa. pple. of PLEASE *v.*

i-pleyned, ME. pa. pple. of PLAIN *v.*, to complain.

i-plight, i-pliȝt, i-pliht, i-pluht, ME. pa. pple. of PLIGHT *v.*

ipocras, obs. form of HIPPOCRAS.

ipocrisie, -crite, obs. ff. HYPOCRISY, -CRITE.

ipoh (ˈiːpəʊ). Also **Ipoh.** [Malay.] The upas tree, *Antiaris toxicaria*, or a creeping shrub, *Strychnos ignatii*, both of which are native to SE.

Asia and have a poisonous sap; also, the poison itself.

1779 T. FORREST *Voy. New Guinea* I. xviii. 369 They [*sc.* the Sooloos] are acquainted with a subtle poison called Ippoo, the juice of a tree, in which they dip small darts. **1820** J. CRAWFURD *Hist. Indian Archipelago* I. IV. 468 The Malays call this last [shrub] *Ipoh.* **1836** J. LOW *Diss. Soil & Agric. Penang* iv. 206 Many arrows tipped with Ipoh were given to me by the different tribes in Perak. **1839** T. J. NEWBOLD *Pol. & Statistical Acc. Straits of Malacca* I. vii. 444 The Upas tree of the Javanese, or the Ipoh of the Malays, is found though rarely in the forests. *Ibid.* II. xii. 211, I had the greatest difficulty to prevail on one of this wild race to part with.. a small quantity of the ipoh poison. **1907** *Q. Rev.* July 190 The poison for their arrows is obtained from the ipoh or upas tree. **1958** J. SLIMMING *Temiar Jungle* v. 78 The poison with which the darts are smeared is a mixture of the saps from the Ipoh tree and the Ipoh creeper. **1965** C. SHUTTLEWORTH *Malayan Safari* ii. 27 Perhaps the most dangerous poison is found in the sap of the ipoh tree from which the aborigines obtain poison for their blowpipe darts.

i-pointed, ME. pa. pple. of POINT *v.*

†**I'pokrephum**, ME. corrupt f. *apocryphum*, sing. of APOCRYPHA.

13.. *Childh. Jesus* in *Archiv Stud. neu. Spr.* LXXIV. 327 Here bigynnys the Romance of the childhode of Jhesu Criste þat clerkys callys Ipokrephum.

‖**Ipomœa** (aɪpəʊ'miːə). *Bot.* Also **ipomæa, ipomea.** [mod.L. (Linnæus), f. Gr. ἰπ-, stem of ἴψ a worm + ὅμοιος like.] A genus of twining or creeping plants, mostly tropical, N.O. *Convolvulaceæ*, with trumpet- or salver-shaped corolla; many of the species possess medicinal properties, many are cultivated as flowering plants, and one, *I. Batatas*, furnishes the sweet potato.

1794 MARTYN *Rousseau's Bot.* xvi. 185 Ipomœa has rather a funnel-shaped than a campanulate corolla. **1867** LADY HERBERT *Cradle L.* i. 5 Ipomæas of every shade.. climbing over the ruined wall. **1877** BLACKMORE *Erema* xiv. (1880) 82 Against the golden leaves of maple.. a special wreath of blue shone like a climbing ipomœa. **1878** H. M. STANLEY *Dark Cont.* II. xii. 351 The Ipomœa's purple buds gemmed with colour the tall stem of some sturdy tree.

Hence **ipo'mœic** *a.*, of Ipomœa, in *ipomœic acid*, named from *Ipomœa Jalapa*, jalap: see quot.

1865-72 WATTS *Dict. Chem.* III. 314 *Ipomæic acid.* **1868** *Ibid.* (1877) V. 214 Ipomæic acid.. isomeric with sebacic acid, produced by the action of moderately strong nitric acid on convolvulic acid, convolvulinolic acid, jalapin, jalapic acid, or jalapinolic acid.

†**i-'pone**, *v. Obs.* [OE. *ȝepunian*, f. *ȝe-* (I-[1]) + *punian* to beat.] *trans.* To pound.

c **1000** *Sax. Leechd.* I. 216 ȝepuna.. eall tosomne. *c* **1400** *Lanfranc's Cirurg.* 62 (Add. MS.) Ipone hem wel & make of hem smale ballys.

i-porchaced, ME. pa. pple. of PURCHASE *v.*

ipostacis, obs. form of HYPOSTASIS.

ipotame, ipotayne, obs. var. HIPPOPOTAMUS.

i-poysened, -oned, ME. pa. pple. of POISON *v.*

ippocras, obs. form of HIPPOCRAS.

i-praied, i-prayed(e, ME. pa. pple. of PRAY *v.*

i-preched, ME. pa. pple. of PREACH *v.*

i-preised, i-preysed, ME. pa. pple. of PRAISE *v.*

i-preoved, i-preved, ME. pa. pple. of PREVE *v.*, to prove.

i-priked, ME. pa. pple. of PRICK *v.*

i-prisoned, ME. pa. pple. of PRISON *v.*

i-prived, i-pryved, ME. pa. pple. of PRIVE *v.*, to deprive.

i-procured, ME. pa. pple. of PROCURE *v.*

i-profred, ME. pa. pple. of PROFFER *v.*

iproniazid (aɪprɒ'naɪəzɪd). *Pharm.* [f. *i(so)pro(pyl* (s.v. ISO- b) + ISO)NIAZID (iproniazid being the isopropyl derivative of isoniazid).] A derivative of isoniazid which was used for a time (usually as the phosphate, a white crystalline powder) in the treatment of tuberculosis and as an antidepressant; 1-isonicotinyl-2-isopropyl hydrazine, $(CH_3)_2CH{\cdot}NH{\cdot}NH{\cdot}CO{\cdot}C_5H_4N$.

1953 *Amer. Rev. Tuberculosis & Pulmonary Dis.* LXVII. 214 A definite pattern of withdrawal has been observed following discontinuance of isoniazid and iproniazid therapy. **1960** *Times* 4 Mar. 15/7 Yet another of the psychotropic drugs now being used, iproniazid, reverses the effect of reserpine. **1968** W. C. BOWMAN et al. *Textbk. Pharmacol.* xxiii. 623 The antitubercular drug iproniazid.. possesses marked antidepressant activity and inhibits MAO [*sc.* monoamine oxidase]... Iproniazid may cause a number of side-effects, the most serious being acute hepatic necrosis which is occasionally fatal. Because of this, the use of iproniazid as an antidepressant has been discontinued. **1971** *Brit. Med. Bull.* XXVII. 28/2 Hypertensive attacks were described in patients who were given iproniazid for tuberculosis.

i-prophecied, ME. pa. pple. of PROPHESY *v.*

i-proved, i-prowed, ME. pa. pple. of PROVE *v.*

†**ipse**, *pron.* and *sb.* [L. *ipse* he himself, very.]

‖**1.** *pron.* Himself; truly himself; in his right mind.

1579 LYLY *Euphues* (Arb.) 106 Though Curio be olde huddle and twang, *ipse*, he. **1787** 'G. GAMBADO' *Acad. Horsemen* (1809) 28 *note*, Our author could not be, ipse, he, when he wrote this!

2. *sb.* A slang name for a kind of ale, quasi 'the very thing'.

1719 D'URFEY *Pills* IV. 106 The strongest Wine.. Is nothing like t' our English Ale, That Liquor of Life, call'd *Ipse.*

†**,ipse'and.** Corruption of '*et per se*, and', an old way of naming the character & at the end of the alphabet; i.e. '& by itself = and'. Cf. AMPERSAND.

1847 MAR. EDGEWORTH *Orlandino* (1848) 86 As ugly as sin, and as crooked as an ipseand, as Sir Pertinax Macsycophant in the play says.

‖**ipse dixit** ('ɪpsiː 'dɪksɪt). Pl. **ipse dixits.** [L. *ipse dixit*, a translation of Gr. αὐτὸς ἔφα 'he himself (the master) said it', a phrase used by the Pythagoreans.] An unproved assertion resting on the bare authority of some speaker; a dogmatic statement; a dictum.

[**1477** *Paston Lett.* III. 214 He wold yeffe you his labore, be so ye payd for his costes. Ipse dixit.] **1572** WHITGIFT *Def. Aunsw. Admon.* Tract VIII. v. §13 Here is neither scripture, doctor, story, council, or anything else, but *ipse dixit.* **1601** A. C. *Answ. Let. Jesuited Gent.* 13 A bare *Ipse dixit*, and nothing else. **1672** MARVELL *Reh. Transp.* I. 57 His Dogmatical *Ipse Dixits* may rather be a reason why we should not believe him. **1800** W. TAYLOR in *Monthly Mag.* X. 423 Criticism deals too much in ipse-dixits. **1870** J. H. NEWMAN *Gram. Assent* II. viii. 255 To emancipate us from the capricious *ipse dixit* of authority.

attrib. **1802-12** BENTHAM *Ration. Judic. Evid.* (1827) I. 125 *note*, On other occasions the ipse dixit principle.. was.. seated.. on the same throne.

†**b.** *transf.* Applied to the speaker. *Obs.*

1641 TRAPP *Theol. Theol.* 126 Christ is the only Rabbin, the irrefragable Doctor, the *Ipse dixit*, all the words of whose mouth are right words.

Hence **ipse-dixitism** (ɪpsɪ'dɪksɪtɪz(ə)m), dogmatic assertion. So **ipse-'dixitish** *a.*, **ipse-'dixitist.**

1808 COLERIDGE in *Sir H. Davy's Rem.* (1858) 103, I.. myself think it shallow, flippant, and ipse dixitish. *a* **1832** BENTHAM *Deontology* (1834) I. xx. 321 Why the ipse-dixit root should not produce all the branches necessary to discourse,—as *ipse-dixitists*, and *ipse-dixitism.* **1885** J. MARTINEAU *Types Eth. The.* II. 93 Bentham denounces all appeals to a moral faculty as sheer 'ipse dixitism'. **1896** J. B. MAYOR *New Suppl. Guide Choice Classical Bks.* Pref. 11 In contrast to this *ipse-dixitism*, as Bentham would have called it.

ipseity (ɪp'siːɪtɪ). [f. L. *ipse* self + -ITY.] Personal identity and individuality; selfhood.

1659 H. MORE *Immort. Soul* III. xvi. (1662) 213 The Soul of the World will be every man's personal Ipseity as well as his. **1668** —— *Div. Dial.* II. xvii. 270 Those mysterious depths of Satan which the Theosophers so diligently discover, such as are *Ipseity, Egoity*, or *Selfishness.* **1827** COLERIDGE *Table-t.* 8 July, In the Trinity there is, 1. Ipseity. 2. Alterity. 3. Community. **1845** F. BARHAM *Odd Medley* 8 The designative preposition *ath*.. indicates the ipseity or objectivity of things.

ipsilateral (ɪpsɪ'lætərəl), *a.* Formerly also **ipse-, ipsolateral.** [*ipselateral* f. L. *ipse* self + LATERAL *a.*, after CONTRALATERAL *a.*; *ipsi-, ipsolateral* app. formed by alteration.] Belonging to or occurring on the same side of the body; connecting two parts on the same side.

1907 *Jrnl. Physiol.* XXXVI. 187 On then eliciting the ipselateral 'flexion-reflex' this latter will.. appear in the full diphasic form. **1910** *Ibid.* XL. 30 This reflex contraction is readily seen to be inhibited by stimulation of the ipsilateral musculo-cutaneous nerve. **1911** STEDMAN *Med. Dict.* 438/1 Ipsolateral. **1917** *Jrnl. Physiol.* LI. 405 The ipsilateral hind-foot is brought forward to scratch the stimulated part. **1962** J. W. PATTERSON et al. in A. Pirie *Lens Metabolism Rel. Cataract* 413 The initial cataract was contralateral in 9 animals, ipsilateral in 4 animals, and in 3 animals it developed simultaneously in both eyes. **1972** *Sci. Amer.* Aug. 84/3 The rabbit, with only a tiny binocular portion in its visual field, has a very small number of ipsilateral, or uncrossed, fibers in the optic chiasm.

Hence **ipsi'laterally** *adv.*, on the same or on one side of the body.

1950 *Merck's Man. Materia Med.* (ed. 8) 300 It [*sc.* the pain] may be referred ipsilaterally to the ear or to an adjacent tooth. **1962** J. W. PATTERSON et al. in A. Pirie *Lens Metabolism Rel. Cataract* 413, 14 developed cataracts contralaterally and 2 ipsilaterally. **1968** A. SOULAIRAC et al. *Pain* 39 A number of fibers which ascend ipsilaterally to their origin.

ipsissima verba (ɪp'sɪsɪmə 'vɜːbə). [L.] The precise words used by a writer or speaker.

1807 SOUTHEY *Lett.* (1856) II. 40 Last night I was in too much haste to look for the *ipsissima verba* of Fuller. **1834** *Edin. Rev.* Apr. 151 We.. shall, therefore,.. treat the reader to our author's *ipsissima verba.* **1886** *Athenæum* 13 Nov. 630/1 An assurance that the extracts contain the *ipsissima verba* of the poet would be.. valuable. **1888** W. JAMES *Let.* 2 Jan. in R. B. Perry *Tht. & Char. W. James* (1935) I. 403 Your *ipsissima verba* of latest date were what I required. **1931** *Times Lit. Suppl.* 28 May 416/2 An undergraduate named Brauer,.. who.. seems to have taken down the *ipsissima verba* of Kant with almost impeccable accuracy. **1937** *Mind* XLVI. 302 Mr. Paton's interpretations.. where they exceed Kant's *ipsissima verba*.. seem to be careful and reasonable. **1961** A. HUXLEY *Let.* 21 Feb. (1969) 904 D. H. L[awrence]'s *ipsissima verba* are: 'The hot stinging centrality of the goose on the cold shifting flux of mud and waters.' **1972** J. A. W. BENNETT *Piers Plowman* p. ix, Some of my notes may retain vestiges of his *ipsissima verba.*

‖**ipso facto** ('ɪpsəʊ 'fæktəʊ), *advb. phrase.* [L.] By that very fact; by the fact itself.

1548 *Act 2 & 3 Edw. VI*, c. 1 §1 The same person.. shall therefore be deprived ipso facto of all his spirituall promocions. **1647** SANDERSON *Serm.* II. 214 By taking Christendom upon us at our Baptism, we did *ipso facto* renounce the world. **1790** SIR P. FRANCIS *Let. Burke* in *B's Corr.* (1844) III. 129 The best possible critic of the Iliad would be, *ipso facto*, and by virtue of that very character, incapable of being the author of it. **1870** J. H. NEWMAN *Gram. Assent* II. x. 433 In rejecting their Divine King, they *ipso facto* lost the living principle and tie of their nationality.

ipsographic (ɪpsəʊ'græfɪk), *a.* [irreg. f. L. *ipso-* as stem of *ipse* self + Gr. γραφικ-ός pertaining to writing.] Self-recording.

1817 *Blackw. Mag.* II. 222/1 This complex machine Professor Bertoncelli calls an Ipsographic scale.

ipso jure ('ɪpsəʊ 'dʒʊəriː), *advb. phr.* [L.] By the operation of the law itself.

1909 in WEBSTER. **1913** *Act 3 & 4 Geo. V* c. 20 §97 The act and warrant of confirmation in favour of the trustee shall ipso jure transfer to and vest in him.. the whole property of the debtor.

i-publesched, ME. pa. pple. of PUBLISH *v.*

i-pudrid, ME. pa. pple. of POWDER *v.*

i-pulled, ME. pa. pple. of PULL *v.*

i-pult, ME. pa. pple. of PELT *v.*

i-pund, ME. pa. pple. of POUND *v.*, to poind.

i-punished, i-punsched, ME. pa. pple. of PUNISH *v.*, PUNCH *v.*

i-pursewed, ME. pa. pple. of PURSUE *v.*

i-put, i-putte, ME. pa. pple. of PUT *v.*

i-pyght, i-pyȝt, ME. pa. pple. of PITCH *v.*

i-pylled, ME. pa. pple. of PILL *v.*

i-pynched, ME. pa. pple. of PINCH *v.*

i-quartred, i-quasched, ME. pa. pples. of QUARTER, QUASH *vbs.*

†**i-queme**, *a. Obs.* Also **i-cweme.** [OE. *ȝecwǽme, ȝecwéme*: see I-[1], and QUEME *a.*] Pleasing, acceptable, agreeable.

c **950** *Lindisf. Gosp.* John viii. 29 Ðaðe ȝe-cuoemo [*Rushw.* ȝicwoeme] sint him, ic wyrco symble. *c* **1000** *Ags. Gosp.* Matt. xi. 26 Forþam hyt wæs swa ȝecweme beforan þe. *c* **1175** *Lamb. Hom.* 109 Ne bið naut his lare fremful ne icweme þan ileweden. *a* **1225** *Ancr. R.* 146 Hesteres bone.. was þe kinge Assuer licwurðe & icweme.

†**i-queme**, *v. Obs.* Also 2-3 **icweme**, 4 **yqueme.** [OE. *ȝecwǽman, -cwéman*: see I-[1], and QUEME *v.*] *trans.* To please, gratify.

c **893** K. ÆLFRED *Oros.* III. vii. §6 þæt he.. ne mehte þæm folce mid ȝifan ȝecweman. *c* **1000** ÆLFRIC *Hom.* II. 286 Sume ȝecwemdon englum.. þurh cumliðnysse. *c* **1175** *Lamb. Hom.* 63 We hit aȝen to ȝeme and god solf þer mid iqueme. *c* **1205** LAY. 13288 Ofte he hine biðohte.. hu he mihte mid læsinge iquemen þan kinge. *a* **1300** *K. Horn* 485 Horn me wel iquemeþ, God kniȝt him bisemeþ. **1340** *Ayenb.* 228 Non ne may y-queme god and to his yuo.

†**i-quethe**, *v. Obs.* [OE. *ȝecweðan* = OS. *giquethan*, OHG. *giquedan*, Goth. *gaqiþan*: see I-[1], Y-, and QUETHE *v.*] *intr.* To say, speak; to arrange, come to terms, agree.

c **900** tr. *Bæda's Hist.* V. ii. (1890) 388 Se næfre ænig word ȝecweðan meahte. *a* **1100** *O.E. Chron.* (Laud MS.) an. 1094 He & his broðer.. ȝecweðan þæt hi mid griðe to gædere cuman sceoldan. *c* **1205** LAY. 2267 He stod biforen Locrine .. & þas word him iqueð [*c* **1275** seide]. *a* **1250** *Owl & Night.* 501 Ne miȝtu leng a word iquethe.

i-queðen, i-queynt, i-quidded, i-quiked, i-quykned, i-quytt, ME. pa. pples. of QUETHE, QUENCH, QUID, QUICK, QUICKEN, QUIT *vbs.*

ir, obs. form of IRE.

†**ir**, obs. var. of *hir*, HER, pers. and poss. pron.

1297 R. GLOUC. (Rolls) 10119 He wende to is moder to deliuery ir þere. *Ibid.* 11803 Þo heo hadde al clene ir ioye al vorlore. Me flemde ir out of engelond.

ir-[1], assimilated form in L. of the prefix IN-[2] before initial *r*, used in the same way in Eng., as in *ir-radiate, ir-ruption.* In these derivatives only one *r* is pronounced.

ir-[2], assimilated form in L. of the prefix IN-[3] before initial *r*, used in the same way in Eng.

(and much more frequent than IR-[1]); as in *ir-rational*, *ir-reclaimable*, *ir-recoverable*, *ir-refragable*, *ir-religion*, *ir-revocable*. In these only one *r* is pronounced, the prefix being really reduced to *i-*.

-ir-. *Chem.* [See quot.] A formative element in the names of three-membered heterocyclic ring systems. A systematic nomenclature is generated by appending to *-ir-* a prefix (or prefixes) representing the hetero-atom(s), and one of the suffixes -ANE 2, -ENE, -IDINE c, or -INE[5], to indicate saturation or unsaturation and the presence or absence of a nitrogen atom in the ring. (Cf. -IRANE, -IRENE, -IRIDINE, -IRINE.)

1928 A. M. PATTERSON in *Jrnl. Amer. Chem. Soc.* L. 3079 With a precedent already set for *et* (four members, compare '*tetra*') and with *ol* (five members) and *in* (six members) already confirmed by usage, it would only be necessary to supply three syllables more to cover all but rare cases. These might be *ir* (from '*tri*', reversed) for three members. *Ibid.*, Examples of the resulting names and combining forms are: ox*ir*ene, ox*ir*ane (ethylene oxide).

iracund ('aɪrəkʌnd), *a.* [ad. L. *īrācund-us*, f. *īra* anger, IRE + *-cund-us*, suffix of verbal adjs. with sense 'inclining to': cf. obs. F. *iracond*, *-cund*.] Inclined to wrath; choleric, passionate, irascible.

1821 *New Monthly Mag.* I. 645 The iracund veins of church and schoolmen. **1851** CARLYLE *Sterling* I. iii. (1872) 13 A man..iracund, but cheerfully vigorous. **1853** DE QUINCEY *Wks.* (1882) XIV. 403 That particular chancellor ..was..the iracund Lord Thurlow.

†**ira'cundious**, *a. Obs.* [a. OF. *iracondieux* (15th c.), f. L. *īrācundi-a*, n. of quality f. *īrācund-us*: see -OUS.] Inclined to wrath; = prec.

1491 CAXTON *Vitas Patr.* (W. de W. 1495) II. 265/2 Yf a man yracundyous were so vertuous..yet it sholde not please god bycause of his yre. **15..** *Kalender of Sheph.* (1656) lii, He the which is born under Capricornus,..shall be iracundious a lyer. **1662** J. CHANDLER *Van Helmont's Oriat.* Proph. conc. Author, Th' scorching flame of iracundious Jove.

Hence **ira'cundiously** *adv.* [cf. 16th c. F. *iracundieusement*], wrathfully.

1599 NASHE *Lenten Stuffe* 41 He,..then drawing out his knife most iracundiously, at one whiske lopt off his head.

iracundity (aɪrə'kʌndɪtɪ). [f. L. *īrācund-us*: see -ITY.] Irefulness, wrathfulness.

1840 *New Monthly Mag.* LIX. 491 This indiscreet exhibition of my wife's iracundity. **1865** *Pall Mall G.* 8 Apr. 11 He..provides one with the following measure of his iracundity.

ira'cundulous, *a. nonce-wd.* [f. L. *īrācund-us* with dim. formative *-ul-us*, as in *albulus*, *lentulus*, etc.] Inclined to anger; irascible.

1765 STERNE *Tr. Shandy* VIII. xiii, Love is..one of the most..Iracundulous..of all human passions.

†**i-rad**, *a. Obs.* [OE. *ȝerád* = MHG. *gereit*, Goth. *garaids* appointed:—OTeut. **garaiđo-z*, f. **ga-* (I-[1], Y-) + *raid-* to prepare, make ready. Cf. I-REDE.] Prepared, made ready; instructed, learned, expert.

c **888** K. ÆLFRED *Boeth.* x, Sio is swiðe wel ȝerad & swiðe ȝemetfæst. *c* **1000** *Guthlac* Prol., Ic him rumne weȝ and ȝeradne tæhte. *c* **1205** LAY. 24990 To moni feohte ich habbe eou ilad, and æuere ȝet [*c* **1275** ȝe] weoren wel irad.

i-rad, -radde, -ræd, ME. pa. pple. of READ *v.*

‖**irade** (i'rɑːde). *Hist.* [Turkish, a. Ar. *irādah* will, desire.] A written decree issued by the Sultan of Turkey.

1883 *Standard* 23 Apr. 5 (Stanf.) The Irade summoning another meeting of the Ambassadors to discuss the question of the Governorship of the Lebanon. **1884** *Pall Mall G.* 10 May 4/1 Baron Hirsch..has..obtained an iradé for his great railway-junction scheme. **1891** *Blackw. Mag.* Oct. 472 The Sultan can issue iradés.

†**i-'radliche**, *adv. Obs.* Also -ræd-. [Early ME., f. I-RAD *a.* + *-liche*, -LY[2].] Promptly, readily, straightway.

c **1205** LAY. 11532 He iradliche lædde hine to ræde. *Ibid.* 29631 Þu scalt irædliche in to hefne-riche; heofne is þe al ȝaru. **1340** *Ayenb.* 1 To vynde yredliche..ine huyche leave of þe boc þet hy by.

†**i-raht**, ME. pa. pple. of RECCHE *v.*, to tell.

I-rail: see I, *the letter*, 2.

i-railed, ME. pa. pple. of RAIL *v.*, to cover.

irain, variant of ARAIN, spider. *Obs.*

†**iral(e**. *Obs. rare.* Also iraille. [Of uncertain origin: cf. IRIS 3.] Some precious stone.

c **1420** *Anturs of Arth.* 590 (Douce MS.) Þei betene downe beriles and bourdures bright..Stones of Iral þey strenkel and strewe [*Irel. MS.* That with stones iraille were strencult and strauen]. *c* **1425** *Thomas of Erceld.* 61 Hir payetrelle was of irale fyne, Hir cropoure was of orphare.

iran, variant of IRON *sb.*[2] = ERNE, eagle.

iran(e, variant of ARAIN, spider. *Obs.*

c **1440** *Jacob's Well* 74 An ypocryte, a popholy man, is lyche an irane; for an eran, whan he hath longe trauayled & myche, to makyn his web, þanne comyth a lytel wynd and blowyth awey all to-gedere.

-irane. *Chem.* [See -IR-.] A suffix used systematically to form the names of saturated heterocyclic monocyclic compounds having a three-membered ring containing no nitrogen atom. Cf. -IR-.

Iranian (ɪ'reɪnɪən, formerly aɪ'reɪnɪən), *a.* and *sb.* [f. Pers. *īrān* Persia + -IAN.]

A. *adj.* **1.** Of or pertaining to Iran or Persia; in *Compar. Philol.* applied to one of the two Asiatic families of the Indo-European languages, comprising Zend and Old Persian and their modern descendants or cognates.

1841 LATHAM *Eng. Lang.* 3 The Iranian stock, so called from the native name of Persia (Iran), containing the ancient, middle and modern Persian, with the allied tongues ..of Curdistan, Affgaunistan, Beloochistan, and Bocharia. **1873** FARRAR *Fam. Speech* 58 The Aryans proper..still lingering in or near their old Iranian home. **1883** *St. James's Gaz.* 7 Sept., The great depression to the north of the Iranian plateau.

†**2. a.** = ARYAN *a.* 1 a; Indo-European. **b.** = Indo-Iranian. *Obs.*

1847 PRICHARD in *Rep. Brit. Assoc.* 241 The Indo-European, sometimes termed Indo-German, and, by late writers, Arian or Iranian languages. **1850** LATHAM *Eng. Lang.* (ed. 3) 94 The Iranian stock of languages.—This contains the proper Persian languages of Persia (Iran)..the Kurd language, and all the languages of Asia..derived from the Zend or Sanskrit.

B. *sb.* **1.** A member of the Iranian race; a speaker of an Iranian language.

1873 FARRAR *Fam. Speech* 77 The Aryans proper, who subsequently divided into Iranians and Hindoos. **1877** G. RAWLINSON *Orig. Nations* vi. 102 For the ornamentation of their buildings..the Iranians..employed sculpture.

2. The Iranian language.

1885 *Encycl. Brit.* XVIII. 655/2 Afghan..is at bottom a pure Iranian language, not merely intermediate between Iranian and Indian. **1898** R. BROWN *Semitic Influence Hellenic Mythol.* III. iii. 89 Its truth does not depend upon the fact that Iranian and Greek are two dialects of an original common speech. **1952** G. SARTON *Hist. Sci.* I. xii. 312 Scythian was probably a form of Iranian, the northwestern branch of it. **1966** *Chambers's Encycl.* VII. 705/2 The nations speaking Iranian are divided linguistically into two main groups.

So **I'ranic** *a.*; **I'ranicize, I'ranize** *v. trans.*, to make Iranian in character, etc.

1873 FARRAR *Fam. Speech* 80* [Table of the Aryan Languages] Iranic Family. **1877** G. RAWLINSON *Orig. Nations* vi. (1883) 21 Iranic civilization, of that or the Medes, the Persians, and..the Bactrians. **1899** W. Z. RIPLEY *Races of Europe* xv. 420 The Azerbeidjians..have become much Iranized by contact with the dolichocephalic peoples of this region. **1945** *Jrnl. R. Anthrop. Inst.* LXXV. 74/1 There is some reason to believe that the Daylamites were of pre-Iranian origin, but by the tenth century they were iranicized, although not entirely assimilated to the dominant race. **1948** D. DIRINGER *Alphabet* 316 They [*sc.* Uighurs]..may conveniently be called Iranized Turks. **1961** L. F. BROSNAHAN *Sounds of Lang.* viii. 177 A palatalisation..occurs in most of the Turco-Tartar languages..but not in..the iranised Uzbek dialects.

i-ranne, var. *i-ronne*, ME. pa. pple. of RUN *v.*

irany, variant of ARAIN, spider. *Obs.*

Iraqi (ɪ'rɑːkɪ). Also **Iraki**. [Arab.: f. *'irāq* (see def.) + *-ī* adj. suffix.] A native or inhabitant of Iraq, a republic in the Persian Gulf, formerly (before 23 Aug. 1921) known as Mesopotamia: a kingdom from 1921 until the assassination of Faisal II in 1958 when it became a republic; the capital is Baghdad. Also as *adj.*, of or belonging to Iraq or its inhabitants. Also (now *rare*) **I'raq(u)ian** *sb.* and *a.*

1777 J. RICHARDSON *Dict. Persian, Arabic & Eng.* I. p. xliv/2 They [*sc.* Arabians] have three principal *perdes* or modes; called the *Isphahani*, which appears to be the original Persian melody; the *Iraki* or the Babylonish; and the *Hejazi* or the Arabian. **1824** J. MORIER *Adventures Hajji Baba* II. xi. 163 'Untie the string of your trowsers,' said an old Irâki. **1923** *Glasgow Herald* 9 Apr. 10 The Iraqians declare that it took the British all their time to win. **1924** *Blackw. Mag.* Mar. 345/1 The administration is now in the hands of Iraqis, assisted by a mere handful of British advisers. **1927** *Observer* 7 Aug. 13/5 An addition of Iraqi or Syrian territory to the Turkish Republic would constitute a danger to his State. *Ibid.*, The Iraqi movement towards Westernisation. **1939** L. H. GRAY *Foundations of Language* 364 [Arabic] was divided into several dialects, of which only that of Mekkah has survived, this being the parent of a large number of modern vernaculars, notably Arabian.., Irāqian (Baghdādh, Mōṣul, Mardīn), [etc.]. **1958** *Economist* 26 July 267 Among Iraqis in general there were..widespread desires to be Arab and to be neutral. *Ibid.* 268 No Iraqi statement has been made concerning withdrawal from the [Baghdad] pact. **1965** *Listener* 17 June 900/1 Zamal, an Iraki..was..expected to be the life and soul of a diplomatic party. **1973** *Times* 16 Apr. 14/1 Such a flexing of Iraqi muscles would (if taken too far) provide the Shah with ample pretext to cut the Iraqis down to size.

So **I'raqize** *v. trans.*, to make Iraqi in character, etc.; hence **Iraqi'zation**.

1959 *Economist* 23 May 751/1 'Iraqisation'..aims at a system in which 'no job is done by a foreigner if an Iraqi can do it as well'. *Ibid.* 752/1 The company is prepared to help in its exploitation on behalf of a fully 'Iraqised' industry. **1961** *Ann. Reg. 1960* 311 Prolonged conversations took place ..on..increased 'iraqization' of senior staff. **1964** *Ann. Reg. 1963* 312 Already 633 commercial agencies..had 'Iraqized' themselves by allocating 51 per cent of their shareholding to Iraqis.

irascent (aɪ'ræsənt), *a.* [ad. L. *īrāscent-em*, pr. pple. of *īrāscī* to grow or be angry, f. *īra* anger.] Becoming angry; leading to anger.

1794-6 E. DARWIN *Zoon.* IV. 292 Between the irascent ideas and irascent muscular actions.

irascibility (ɪræsɪ'bɪlɪtɪ, aɪræs-). [f. next: see -ITY. Cf. F. *irascibilité* (1550 in Hatz.-Darm.).] The quality of being irascible; proneness to anger, quickness of temper, irritability.

1750 JOHNSON *Rambler* No. 40 ¶1 They seldom fail of giving proofs of their irascibility upon the slightest attack of criticism. **1779-81** —— *L.P.*, *Pope* Wks. IV. 83 Pope's irascibility prevailed. **1814** D'ISRAELI *Quarrels Auth.* (1867) 301 The statements of Cibber..show sufficient motives to excite the poetic irascibility. **1861** READE *Cloister & H.* I. 117 The fallibility and irascibility of human nature.

irascible (ɪ'ræsɪb(ə)l, aɪ'ræs-), *a.* Also 7 **irasible**, 8 **irrascible**. [a. F. *irascible* (12th c. in Littré), ad. L. *īrāscibil-is*, f. *īrāscī* to grow angry.] Easily provoked to anger or resentment; prone to anger; irritable, choleric, hot-tempered, passionate.

1530 PALSGR. 316/2 Irascible, inclyned or disposed to anger, *irascible*. **1656** BLOUNT *Glossogr.*, *Irascible*, cholerick, soon angred, subject to anger. **1759** ROBERTSON *Hist. Scot.* (1817) I. II. 345 The Scots, naturally an irascible and high spirited people. **1831** SCOTT *Cast. Dang.* vii, The boar..was a much more irascible and courageous animal. **1873** BLACK *Pr. Thule* viii. (1874) 114 The only daughter of a solitary and irascible old gentleman.

b. Of emotions, actions, etc.: Characterized by, arising from, or exhibiting anger.

1659 D. PELL *Impr. Sea* 426 Irascible, and objurgatory speech. **1734** WATTS *Reliq. Juv.* lx. (1789) 200 Our irascible passions..indulged..are ready to defile the whole man. **1774** GOLDSM. *Nat. Hist.* (1776) VII. 296 No animal in the creation seems endued with such an irascible nature. **1824** W. IRVING *T. Trav.* I. 302 Dignity is always more irascible the more petty the potentate. **1882** A. W. WARD *Dickens* v. 119 His irascible nature failed to resent a rather doubtful compliment.

c. ***irascible appetite, affection, part of the soul***, in Plato's tripartite division of the soul, τὸ θυμοειδές, one of the two parts of the irrational nature, being that in which courage, spirit, passion, were held to reside; and which was superior to τὸ ἐπιθυμητικόν, the CONCUPISCIBLE part in which resided the appetites.

1398 TREVISA *Barth. De P.R.* III. vi. (Add. MS. 27944) lf. 20 b/2 Drede & sorwe comeþ of þe irascibel, for of þing þat we hatiþ, we haueþ sorowe. **1526** *Pilgr. Perf.* (W. de W. 1531) 112 b, It is called the appetyte irascyble, or the angry appetyte. **1606** BRYSKETT *Civ. Life* 48 The seates of the two principall appetites, the irascible and the concupiscible; of that the heart, of this the liuer. **1691** HARTCLIFFE *Virtues* 23 Pride, Contempt, Impatience, Anger, Fear, Boldness and the like generous and brave Passions, belong to what we say is the *irascible* part of the mind. **1863** DRAPER *Intell. Devel. Europe* v. (1865) 116 Now, the reason being seated in the head, the spirit or irascible soul has its seat in the breast.

†**d.** quasi-*sb.* = Irascible appetite, etc. *Obs.*

1594 [see CONCUPISCIBLE 2 b]. **1656** H. MORE *Enthus. Tri.* To Rdr. A iij a, These I spread before him..to provoke his Irascible.

Hence **i'rascibleness**, irascibility; **i'rascibly** *adv.*, in an irascible manner, angrily.

1727 BAILEY vol. II, *Irascibleness.* **1828** *Mirror* V. 264/1 Nothing irascibly said will..make way with an obstinate or wilful man.

irascid (aɪ'ræsɪd), *a. rare*[−1]. [f. L. *īrāscī* to grow angry + -ID[1].] Easily angered, irascible.

1823 *Blackw. Mag.* XIII. 278 The head of Julius..is a fine portrait of that arrogant and irascid priest.

irate (aɪ'reɪt, 'aɪərət), *a.* [ad. L. *īrāt-us* angered, enraged, pa. pple. of **īrārī*, inceptive *īrāscī* to be or become angry, f. *īra* anger, IRE.] Excited to ire; incensed, enraged, angry.

1838 J. GILMAN *Life Coleridge* 22 Not to heed his anger should he become irate. **1848** DICKENS *Dombey* viii, [He] seemed a little more irate when it was over. **1865** LIVINGSTONE *Zambesi* vi. 142 He was at once hauled up before the irate Commandant.

Hence **i'rately** *adv.*, in an irate manner, angrily.

1883 MISS BROUGHTON *Belinda* II. II. iii. 9 She looks at him full and irately. **1889** MRS. R. JOCELYN *Distracting Guest* II. ix. 153 'What nonsense!'..I continued irately.

i-raunsond, -ravissed, -rawt, ME. pa. pples. of RANSOM, RAVISH, REACH *vbs.*

†**'irchepil**. *Obs. rare.* [A corruption of ILESPIL (*ilspil*, *irspil*), hedgehog, influenced by IRCHIN.] A hedgehog or urchin.

c **1290** *S. Eng. Leg.* I. 298/49 Ase ful ase is an Irchepil of piles al-a-boute, So ful he stikede of Arewene.

†**'irchin, irchon**. *Obs.* Forms: 3 yrichon, 4 irchouon, 4–5 irchoun, yrchoun, 5 erchon, irchyn, yrchyn, 6 irchen, 6–7 irchin. [a. ONF. **ir(e)chon* (cf. Picard *irechon*, Walloon *ireson*, Hainaut

hirchon) = OF. *heriçun*, F. *hérisson*:—pop.L. **herīciōn-em*: see HURCHEON and URCHIN.]

1. A hedgehog.

c **1290** *S. Eng. Leg.* I. 179/50 Heo stikeden al-so þicke on him so yrichon deth of piles. **1382** WYCLIF *Zeph.* ii. 14 Onacratulus..and the yrchoun shuln dwelle in the threshefoldis therof. *c* **1430** *Pilgr. Lyf Manhode* II. cxlv. (1869) 133 With poyntes she was armed al aboute, as an irchoun. **1486** *Bk. St. Albans* C iv b, Fede yowre hawke with an Irchyn onys or twyes, & it shall helpe hir. **1530** PALSGR. 235/1 Irchen a lyttel beest full of prickes, *herisson*. **1609** BIBLE (Douay) *Ps.* ciii[i]. 18 The rocke a refuge for the Irchins.

b. A dish in cookery, so called from being made to bristle with almonds, etc. stuck over its surface.

c **1430** *Two Cookery-bks.* 38 *Yrchouns.* Take Piggis mawys ..Take a litel prycke, & prykke þe yrchons, An putte in þe holes þe Almaundys. *c* **1440** *Anc. Cookery* in *Househ. Ord.* (1790) 443.

2. An urchin; a brat.

1625 BP. MOUNTAGU *App. Cæsar* Ep. Ded. a ij b, Such Irchins it was necessary to disband, and send them away to shift for themselves, that our Mother the Church might no more be troubled with them.

ire (aɪə(r)), *sb.* Also 4–6 yre, ir, 5 yr, iere, 5–6 yer, 6 *Sc.* yire, iyre. [a. OF. *ire*, *yre* (11th c. in Littré), ad. L. *īra* anger, wrath, rage.] Anger; wrath. Now chiefly *poet.* and *rhet.*

a **1300** *E.E. Ps.* lxxvii. 25 [lxxviii. 21] Ire somdele Vpstegh þanne in Ireale. *a* **1325** *Sir Beues* (MS. A.) 2488 Þo was Beues in gret yre. *c* **1330** R. BRUNNE *Chron. Wace* (Rolls) 2336 Ne he ne saide namore til hire, Bot wente fro hure al in ire. **1388** WYCLIF *Prov.* xv. 1 A soft answere brekith ire. **1477** EARL RIVERS (Caxton) *Dictes* 22 b, It shulde appease hys Iere. **1556** LAUDER *Tractate* 456 Frome all Inuyne thay suld be fre, Frome Malyce, Yre, and Creueltie. **1583** *Leg. Bp. St. Androis* Pref. 57 in *Satir. Poems Reform.* xlv, Baals bischops, provocking God to yire. **1667** MILTON *P.L.* VI. 843 That wish'd the Mountains now might be again Thrown on them as a shelter from his ire. **1706** PRIOR *Ode to Queen* 141 While with fiercest ire Bellona glows. **1808** SCOTT *Marm.* VI. xiv, Burn'd Marmion's swarthy cheek like fire, And shook his very frame for ire. **1865** KINGSLEY *Herew.* xii, Hereward was flushed with ire and scorn.

†**b.** rarely in *plural*. *Obs.*

1388 WYCLIF *Prov.* xxx. 33 He that stirith iris [Vulg. *iras*], bringith forth discordis.

†**ire**, *v. Obs. rare*⁻¹. [f. IRE *sb.*] *trans.* To anger, irritate.

c **1420** *Pallad. on Husb.* II. 361 Her brethron & her owne kynde hit ireth [L. *irritat*].

ire, obs. form of AIR *sb.*[1] (in quot. in sense 7).

1494 FABYAN *Chron.* VI. clxv. 160 All myghte not stoppe the intollerable ire of his body.

ire, obs. or dial. f. IRON; obs. f. HER.

i-readed, -reaved, ME. pa. pples. of RED, REAVE *vbs.*

i-red, ME. pa. pple. of READ *v.*

†**i-rede**, *a. Obs.* [OE. *ȝerǽde* = MHG. *gereite*:—OTeut. **garaidjo-z*: cf. I-RAD *a.* and GRAITH *a.*] Prepared, ready.

c **1000** *Ags. Ps.* (Th.) xvii. 32 [xviii. 33] He ȝedyde mine fet swa ȝeræde [L. *perfecit pedes meos*] swa swa heorotum. *c* **1275** *Passion Our Lord* 119 in *O.E. Misc.* 40 If ich..bitraye ihesu hwat schal beon my mede. Þrytty panewes, hi seyden, hi beoþ alle irede.

†**i-redy**, *a. Obs.* Forms: 2 ȝeredi, 3 i-readi, -redy, 3–4 i-redi, y-redy. [ME.; see I-[1], Y-, and READY.] = READY.

a **1175** *Cott. Hom.* 239 Þer beoð anu ȝeredie þe wereȝede gastes þe hine uniredlice underfangeð. *a* **1225** *Juliana* 8 Wite þu hit wel ireadi..no lengre nulich hit heolen þe. **1297** R. GLOUC. (Rolls) 3094 Vter & is compaynie yredy aȝen hom were. *c* **1300** *Beket* 766 Iredi ich am the deth to afonge. **1340** *Ayenb.* 173 Þe dyað þet is yredy, ond oueral aspiþ þane zeneȝere. *c* **1380** *Sir Ferumb.* 354 Y am come her o semple knyȝt y-redy with þe to fiȝte.

i-refe, early ME.:—OE. *ȝeréfa*: see REEVE *sb.*

ireful (ˈaɪəfʊl), *a.* [f. IRE *sb.* + -FUL.]

1. Full of ire; angry, wrathful.

c **1300** *Cursor M.* 27798 (Cott. Galba) Heuy chere, irefull and ill. **13..** *Coer de L.* 366 In his stirope up he stode, And smote to hym with irefull mode. *c* **1475** *Partenay* 3258 A man chaufed with yerfull manace. **1562** J. HEYWOOD *Prov. & Epigr.* (1867) 155 Foule woordis make all folke, Irefull or ferefull. **1652** C. B. STAPYLTON *Herodian* 41 Electus, Lætus, Marcia too must looke, With many moe, to tast his Irefull spight. **1725** POPE *Odyss.* III. 179 With ire-full taunts each other they oppose. **1848** C. BRONTË *J. Eyre* xii, His eyes and gathered eyebrows looked ireful and thwarted just now.

2. Choleric, passionate, irascible.

c **1400** *Solomon's Bk. Wisdom* 20 Aȝein stronge men & ireful look þat þou ne fiȝth. **1574** HELLOWES *Gueuara's Fam. Ep.* (1577) 116 With the irefull we must not be importunate to entreate a pardon. **1613** PURCHAS *Pilgrimage* (1614) 638 The inhabitants of..Barbary are poore and proude, irefull, and writing all injuries in marble. **1819** L. HUNT *Indicator* No. 1 (1822) I. 6 The want of this sympathy from others made him ireful, revengeful, impious.

irefully (ˈaɪəfʊlɪ), *adv.* [f. prec. + -LY[2].] In an ireful manner; angrily, wrathfully.

c **1489** CAXTON *Sonnes of Aymon* ix. 230 They..cam to Reynawde for to sle hym yrefully. **1555** ABP. PARKER *Ps.* xxxiv. 81 God's face is seene, most irefully to wycked men of hand. **1607** TOPSELL *Four-f. Beasts* (1658) 543 The dams fight for their young ones most irefully. **1632** J. HAYWARD tr. *Biondi's Eromena* 4, I will not (answered irefully the Prince). **1865** E. C. CLAYTON *Cruel Fortune* I. 237 'She is a stupid.. discontented little fool', she irefully reflected.

irefulness (ˈaɪəfʊlnɪs). [f. as prec. + -NESS.] The condition of being ireful; wrathfulness.

1388 WYCLIF *1 Sam.* xix. 21 And Saul was wrooth with irefulnesse. **1526** *Pilgr. Perf.* (W. de W. 1531) 110 Obstynacy or frowardnesse, Hastynesse or Irefulnesse, Vngentylnesse. **1574** HYLL *Ord. Bees* ix, Although the fierce bees are very ill, yet is their yrefulnesse a note of better bees. **1647** H. MORE *Song of Soul* II. ii. III. iv, Not rage.. Nor eating irefulnesse, harsh cruelty.

i-regned, -reht, ME. pa. pples. of REIGN *v.*, RECCHE *v.*, to relate.

†**Ireis.** *Obs. rare*⁻¹. In 3 yreis. [a. OF. *ireis*, *irois* adj. and sb., Irish (Godef.), f. OE. *Ir-as* the Irish.] = IRISH B. 1 b.

1297 R. GLOUC. (Rolls) 5551 Þer were of deneys [*v.r.* denys] & of scottes aslawe & al so of yreis [*v.rr.* yreyns, yrenys] vif ȝonge kinges.

i-reke, -rekened, ME. pa. pples. of REKE, RECKON *vbs.*

Ireland (ˈaɪələnd). The name of a classical scholarship at Oxford University founded in 1825 by John *Ireland*, D.D. (1761–1842), of Oriel College, Dean of Westminster.

1861 J. A. SYMONDS *Let.* 13 Mar. (1967) I. 282 We hope to secure the Ireland too this Term. If we do not, we shall be in a poor way. **1877** O. WILDE *Let.* Mar. (1962) 32, I have been in for 'the Ireland' and of course lost it: on six weeks' reading I could not expect to get a prize for which men work two and three years. **1951** M. KENNEDY *Lucy Carmichael* II. 80 He really is clever; he got the Ireland or the Hertford, I forget which, at Oxford. **1953** E. BARKER *Age & Youth* II. iii. 317 A year later, when I tried my luck for the Ireland, the king of classical scholar-ships, I had less confidence. **1972** *Oxf. Univ. Cal. 1972–73* 216 Dean Ireland's Scholarship... Value: £120. Awarded annually in Michaelmas Term after an examination... The examination is the same as that for the Craven Scholarships and the person elected to the Ireland Scholarship is, if not already a Craven Scholar, elected to the first Craven Scholarship.

ireless (ˈaɪəlɪs), *a. rare.* [f. IRE *sb.* + -LESS.] Void of ire or anger.

1829 *Blackw. Mag.* XXVI. 239 Your ireless and soothing lucubrations.

i-remd, i-remewed, ME. pa. pples. of REME, REMOVE *vbs.*

ire-monger, iren, obs. ff. IRONMONGER, IRON.

irenarch (ˈaɪərɪnɑːk). *Hist.* [ad. late L. *īrēnarcha*, a. Gr. εἰρηνάρχης: see EIRENARCH. Cf. F. *irénarque* (Littré).] An Eastern provincial governor or keeper of the peace, under the Roman and Byzantine empires.

1702 ECHARD *Eccl. Hist.* (1710) 490 Upon the road he was met by Herod the Irenarch. **1745** A. BUTLER *Lives Saints* (1836) I. 114 Herod the Irenarch, or keeper of the peace.

i-rend, ME. pa. pple. of REND *v.*

irene (ˈaɪəriːn). *Chem.* [ad. G. *iren* (Tiemann & Krüger 1893, in *Ber. d. Deut. Chem. Ges.* XXVI. 2682), f. G. *ir-on* IRONE + *-en* -ENE.] A colourless, liquid, bicyclic hydrocarbon, $C_{14}H_{20}$, obtained by the dehydration of irone.

1894 *Jrnl. Chem. Soc.* LXVI. I. 81 When treated with hydriodic acid and phosphorus, irone loses a molecule of water, and forms irene, $C_{13}H_{18}$, which is a colourless oil boiling at 113–115° (9 mm.). **1938** *Jrnl. Amer. Chem. Soc.* LX. 933 The 1, 1, 2, 6-tetramethyltetralin structure for irene..has been supported by the synthesis of this tetralin from *m*-bromotoluene.

-irene. *Chem.* [See -IR-.] A suffix used systematically to form the names of unsaturated heterocyclic monocyclic compounds having a three-membered ring containing no nitrogen atom. Cf. -IR-.

†**ireness-bag**, obs. var. (of obscure formation) of *earning-bag*: see EARNING *vbl. sb.*[3]

1611 COTGR., *Mulette*,..the maw of a Calfe; which being dressed is called the Renet-bag, Jreness-bag, or Cheslop-bag.

irenic (aɪˈrɛnɪk, aɪˈriːnɪk), *a.* and *sb.* [ad. Gr. εἰρηνικ-ός, f. εἰρήνη peace. Cf. EIRENIC and F. *irénique* (Littré).

In this and the following word, the first pronunciation is that given by Smart, Ogilvie, and Cassell, and by Webster and the other American Dictionaries, and is in accordance with the general analogies of the language, as in *academic*, *clinical*, *energetic*, *euphonic*, *Platonic*, in which the long vowel of the Greek is uniformly shortened; but the modern use of the Greek Εἰρηνικόν, *Eirēnicon*, to which scholars naturally give the English academic pronunciation of Greek, affects the derivatives also, and makes the second pronunciation frequent among university men.]

A. *adj.* Pacific, non-polemic; = IRENICAL.

1864 in WEBSTER. **1878** *N. Amer. Rev.* 335 President Porter, in his admirable and irenic opening of this discussion, makes it very difficult, for one who follows him. **1882–3** SCHAFF *Encycl. Relig. Knowl.* I. 710 He was a man of irenic temperament. **1885** *Ch. Times* 343/1 No irenic propositions will do the least good till we have had those standards restored.

B. *sb. pl.* **irenics**: irenical theology.

1882–3 SCHAFF *Encycl. Relig. Knowl.* II. 1118 Irenical Theology, or Irenics..presents the points of agreement among Christians with a view to the ultimate unity..of Christendom. **1890** *Congreg. Rev.* Apr. 158 Our mission is not one of polemics but irenics.

irenical (aɪˈrɛnɪkəl, aɪˈriːnɪkəl), *a.* [f. as prec. + -AL[1]. As to pronunciation, see prec.] Peaceful; pacific; tending to promote peace, esp. in relation to theological or ecclesiastical differences.

1660 *Pref. Bp. Hall's Rem.* b, How meek his temper was, his many irenical tracts do shew. **1845** J. MACKIE *Life Leibnitz* 153 To these irenical negotiations an end was suddenly put..by the decease of the Duke of Hanover. **1876** FAIRBAIRN *Strauss* II. in *Contemp. Rev.* June 125 Ullmann, a theologian, modern, irenical, anxious to give to reason the things that are reason's, to faith the things that are faith's. **1882** FARRAR *Early Chr.* II. 357 The method which St. John adopts is not polemical but irenical.

Hence **i'renically** *adv.*, in the spirit of peace.

1895 *Chicago Advance* 31 Oct. 619/1 On the..conflicts between religion and science..Prof. N. S. Shaler..writes irenically and suggestively.

‖**irenicon** (aɪˈriːnɪkən, aɪˈrɛnɪkən). [a. Gr. εἰρηνικόν, neut. of εἰρηνικός: see IRENIC. Also spelt EIRENICON, q.v. The *e* is made short in Cassell, Ogilvie, and the American dictionaries, but in academic pronunciation the word is generally treated as Greek with *ē* long: cf. IRENIC.] A proposal designed to promote peace, esp. in a church or between churches; a message of peace.

1618 *Barnevelt's Apol.* Ded. A ij b, A Nationall Synod must be assembled: and happily by your aduice declared in your *Irenicon*. *a* **1716** SOUTH (Webster, 1864), They must in all likelihood (without any other irenicon) have restored peace to the Church. **1893** *Nation* (N.Y.) 12 Jan. 25/1 It was really an *irenicon*—a message of good-will at the Christmas season.

‖**i'renicum.** ? *Obs.* [L. form of prec.] = prec.

1647 TRAPP *Comm. Matt.* v. 9 Although it be, for the most part, a thankless office..to sound an *irenicum*; yet do it for God's sake. **1662** STILLINGFL. (*title*) Irenicum, a Weapon-Salve for the Church's Wounds;..whereby a foundation is laid for the Church's peace. *a* **1715** BURNET *Own Time* (1724) I. II. 189.

†**'ireos.** *Obs.* Also 5 yrios, 5–6 yreos, 6–7 irios. [a. med.L. *yreos*, **ireos*, an unexplained derivative or altered form of IRIS, arbitrarily applied to the white-flowered species in contrast to the purple ('Yris purpureum florem gerit, yreos album', *Sinon. Barthol.* 25/2).] The Florentine Iris (*Iris florentina*), a species with large white flowers. **b.** The root of this, used in pharmacy; orris-root.

[*a* **1387** *Sinon. Barthol.* (Anecd. Oxon.) 25/2 Yri, i. radicis quæ yreos appellatur.] *c* **1400** *Lanfranc's Cirurg.* 88 Þese medicyns ben sumwhat more driere: yrios [*v.r.* yreos], aristologie [etc.]. **1480** *Wardr. Acc. Edw. IV.* (1830) 131 Lytill bagges of fustian stuffed with ireos and anneys xxvj. **1533** ELYOT *Cast. Helthe* (1541) 11 a, Thinges good for a colde head: Cububes, Galingale..Spyke: Yreos. **1579** LANGHAM *Gard. Health* (1633) 255 The Irios of Florence is taken for the best. **1615** MARKHAM *Eng. Housew.* (1660) 92 Others to make sweet Water, take of Ireos two ounces [etc.]. *attrib.* **1578** LYTE *Dodoens* II. xxxv. 194 The Ireos rootes ..are hoate and dry in the thirde degree.

ireous, variant of IROUS *a. Obs.*

i-resed, ME. pa. pple. of RESE *v. Obs.*, to rush.

‖**iresine** (aɪərɪˈsaɪniː). *Bot.* [mod.L. (Linnæus), altered from Gr. εἰρησιώνη a branch of laurel or olive entwined with wool carried at certain festivals; the reference is to the woolly calyx.] A genus of plants (N.O. *Amarantaceæ*), natives of tropical and subtropical America and of Australia, of which several species are cultivated as ornamental foliage plants; a plant of this genus.

1866 in *Treas. Bot.* **1882** *Garden* 25 Mar. 205/2 Coleuses and Iresines may still be struck. **1883** *Pall Mall G.* 7 Sept. 4/1 Some bronze-leaved plant, such as one of the Iresines. **1892** *Daily News* 15 Aug. 3/2 Fenced in by lines of chocolate iresines with outer lines of lobelia.

iresipilis, obs. form of ERYSIPELAS.

i-reste, i-revayd, i-revested, ME. pa. pples. of REST, REVAY, REVEST *vbs.*

iretol (ˈaɪərɪtɒl). *Chem.* [a. G. *iretol* (De Laire & Tiemann 1893, in *Ber. d. Deut. Chem. Ges.* XXVI. 2015), f. G. *ir-igenin* IRIGENIN: see -ET and -OL.] 2,4,6-Trihydroxyanisole, $C_7H_8O_4$, a crystalline compound obtained by alkaline hydrolysis of irigenin.

1894 *Jrnl. Chem. Soc.* LXVI. I. 48 Iretol, $C_6H_2(OH)_3{\cdot}OMe$...is ultimately obtained in white needles melting at 186°. **1937** *Jrnl. Amer. Chem. Soc.* LIX. 933/1 Iretol is stable when pure and dry, but readily turns dark if exposed to moisture and oxygen. **1960** *Tetrahedron Let.* v. 8 Iridonitrile and iretol (Hoesch reaction) yielded the deoxybenzoin (I).

†**i-rew**, *v. Obs.* [OE. *ʒehréowan*, f. *ʒe-* (I-[1]) + *hréowan* RUE *v.*] To rue, repent: often *impers.*
a **900** CYNEWULF *Crist* 1493 þa mec þin wéa swiþast æt heortan ʒehreaw. *c* **1340** *Cursor M.* 20529 (Fairf.) Irewed hit me [*Gött.* & *Cott.* It reud me] & for-þuȝt hit sare.

ireyn(e, variants of ARAIN *Obs.*, spider.

Irgun (ɪə'gʊn). [mod.Heb., organization; in full *Irgun Zvai Leumi* national military organization (also used).] Name of a militant right-wing Zionist organization. Hence **Ir'gunist**, a member of this organization.
1946 KOESTLER *Thieves in Night* 243 The new organisation, 'Irgun', was numerically smaller and organised on the conspiratorial lines of a terrorist underground movement. **1947** *Ann. Reg. 1946* 299 The Irgun Zvai Leumi and the Stern Group had worked with the Hagana High Command in certain of these operations. **1949** KOESTLER *Promise & Fulfilment* II. v. 260 A woman of sixty-five, who escorted her grandson, an Irgunist wanted by the police, across Tel Aviv to a safe hiding place. **1959** *Chambers's Encycl.* XII. 398/1 The immediate post-war years saw such Jewish organizations as the *Irgun Zvai Leumi* and the Stern Gang undertake planned terrorist activities against the mandatory power. **1968** P. DURST *Badge of Infamy* iii. 26 Eichmann..was kidnapped in South America by the Irgun and brought to trial by the State of Israel. **1970** *Observer* 12 Sept. 9/6 Leila Khaled is inspired by the same fanatical devotion..as the Irgun Zvai Leumi and the Stern Group, who fought against the British and the Arabs to establish the State of Israel. **1972** *Guardian* 11 Jan. 11/1 The news agency's stringer was a secret member of the Irgun. **1972** *Times* 23 Sept. 5/1 The district Court here refused a police request to remand Mr. Amihai Paglin, the key strategist of the Irgun Zvai Leumi during British rule in Palestine.

iriach, var. *eriach*, ERIC, blood-fine (*Irish Hist.*).
1600 DYMMOK *Ireland* (1843) 9 The party offendinge..is alloted to paye to the wife or childe of the party murdered, or to the party agreeed, a kind of satisfaction, termed by them an *Iriach*.

irian ('aɪərɪən), *a.*[1] *Anat.* [f. IRI-S 4 + -AN. F. *irien.*] Belonging to the iris of the eye.
1857 DUNGLISON *Med. Lex.* 509 *Irian*,..belonging to the Iris. *Ibid.*, The iris receives the irian nerves.

Irian ('ɪrɪən), *a.*[2] [Native name.] Of or pertaining to Irian Barat or West Irian, formerly Dutch New Guinea or Netherlands New Guinea, since 1963 a province of Indonesia. Hence **Iria'nese**, a native or inhabitant of this province; also *collect.*
1950 tr. *Rep. Comm. New Guinea (Irian)* III. iv. 96 The Netherlands promise that it is prepared to listen to the voice of the original Irian people. **1958** *Times* 9 Sept. 9/3 'West Irian action', meaning the 'liberation' of west New Guinea from the Dutch. **1967** *Guardian* 17 Nov. 12/7 To talk of self-determination for West Irian by 1969 is, of course, unrealistic... To most of the Irianese..considerations of this sort are academic. **1969** *New Yorker* 31 May 44/2 Suharto..rose steadily... His outstanding military performance was as a co-ordinator of the West Irian campaign in 1961–62.

i-richet, ME. pa. pple. of RICH *v.*, to enrich.

Iricism, ('aɪərɪsɪz(ə)m). [irreg. f. IRISH, after *Scotticism*.] An Irish trait of character, expression, etc.: an Irishism, Hibernicism.
1743 H. WALPOLE *Lett. H. Mann* (1834) VII. 259 There is a great fracas in Ireland in a noble family or two, heightened by a pretty strong circumstance of Iricism. **1833** *New Monthly Mag.* XXXIX. 52 The first of September, this year, to use an Iricism, will not take place until the second. **1853** MISS YONGE *Heir of Redclyffe* xliii. (1861) 492 Charlotte wrote her brother very full and very droll accounts of the Iricisms around her.

Iricize ('aɪərɪsaɪz), *v. rare.* [f. as prec., after *Scotticize*, *Anglicize*, etc.] *trans.* and *intr.* To make or become Irish; to Hibernicize.
1863 MISS SEWELL *Chr. Names* I. 112 The Connaught branch of the great Norman family of De Burgh first Iricised themselves in McWilliam. *Ibid.* II. 481 Norman names.. iricized gradually with their owners.

irid ('aɪərɪd). *rare.* [f. L. *īrid-*, Gr. ἰριδ-, stem of *īris*, ἶρις, IRIS.] **1.** The iris of the eye.
1822–34 *Good's Study Med.* (ed. 4) IV. 544 Negro albino. Hair white and wooly: irids white. **1848** C. BRONTË *J. Eyre* v. (1857) 43 Brown eyes, with a benignant light in their irids. **1895** F. THOMPSON *Sister Songs*, [A joy that] Only lurks retired In the dim gloaming of thine irid.
2. *Bot.* A plant of the N.O. *Iridaceæ.*
1866 *Treas. Bot.* 626 Iridaceæ..Irids.

iridaceous (aɪərɪ'deɪʃəs), *a. Bot.* [f. L. *īrid-* (see prec.) + -ACEOUS.] Related to plants of the genus *Iris*; belonging to the natural order *Iridaceæ.*
1851 GLENNY *Handbk. Fl. Gard.* 264 A family of showy iridaceous bulbs, requiring a frame or greenhouse. **1855** in MAYNE *Expos. Lex.*

iridal ('aɪərɪdəl), *a. rare.* [f. as prec. + -AL[1].]
1. Of or belonging to the rainbow.
1837 WHEWELL *Hist. Induct. Sc.* (1857) II. 280 Descartes came far nearer the true philosophy of the iridal colours.
2. *Med.* Of or pertaining to the iris of the eye; = IRIDIC *a.*[2]
1830 W. MACKENZIE *Pract. Treat. Dis. Eye* xix. 770 One anatomist supposes that he has traced branches from the ciliary or iridal nerves, where they lie between the sclerotica and choroid. **1879** *Brain* I. 8 In addition to..absence of iridal susceptibility to influence from the other eye, we have ..failure of accommodation. **1965** *Ophthalmologica* CXLIX. 35 Although the iridal tumour revealed no sign of malignancy, it metastasized to the ipsilateral cervical lymph nodes prior to the enucleation of the eyeball.

iriddesis, erron. variant of IRIDODESIS.

iridectomize (aɪərɪ'dɛktəmaɪz, ɪrɪ-), *v. Surg.* [f. next + -IZE.] *trans.* To subject to the operation of iridectomy.
1879 *St. George's Hosp. Rep.* IX. 489 A cook..whose left eye had been iridectomised..for glaucoma. *Ibid.* 505 Five months ago R. was iridectomised for glaucoma.

iridectomy (aɪərɪ'dɛktəmɪ, ɪrɪ-). *Surg.* [f. Gr. ἰριδ-, stem of ἶρις IRIS + ἐκτομ-ή a cutting out (f. ἐκ out + τέμνειν to cut) + -Y (cf. ANATOMY). Mod.F. *iridectomie* (Littré).] Excision of a portion of the iris. Also *attrib.*
1855 MAYNE *Expos. Lex.*, *Iridectomus*, an instrument.. proper for the operation of iridectomy. **1874** LAWSON *Dis. Eye* 92 The point of the iridectomy knife. **1894** DOYLE *Round red Lamp* 296 He would sit up half the night performing iridectomies and extractions upon the sheep's eyes sent in by the village butcher.

irideous (aɪ'rɪdiːəs), *a. Bot.* [f. mod. Bot.L. *Iride-æ*, f. *Iris* + -OUS.] = IRIDACEOUS.
1855 in MAYNE *Expos. Lex.* **1887** in *Syd. Soc. Lex.*

‖**irideremia** (aɪərɪdə'riːmɪə, ɪrɪd-). *Path.* [f. Gr. ἰριδ-, ἶρις IRIS + ἐρημία want, absence.] Congenital absence of the iris.
1855 DIXON *Dis. Eye* (1860) 132 Children affected with *Irideremia* appear to be confused and dazzled by ordinary daylight. **1878** T. BRYANT *Pract. Surg.* I. 323 Irideremia, or congenital absence of the iris, is occasionally observed.

irides, pl. of IRIS.

iridesce (ɪrɪ'dɛs), *v. rare.* [Back-formation from IRIDESCENT *a.*] *intr.* To exhibit iridescence; to shine in an iridescent manner.
1884 E. COUES *Key to N. Amer. Birds* (ed. 2) III. i. 427 General plumage of metallic lustre, iridescing dark green on most parts. **1905** J. LONDON *Jacket* (1915) 48 Sun-flashed water where coral-growths iridesced from profounds of turquoise deeps.

iridescence (ɪrɪ'dɛsəns). [f. IRIDESCENT: see -ENCE.] The quality of being iridescent; the intermingling and interchange of brilliant colours as in the rainbow, soap-bubbles, and mother-of-pearl; a play of glittering and changing colours.
1804 *Phil. Trans.* XCIV. 386 The shells..which still possess the lustre and iridescence of their original nacre. **1811** PINKERTON *Petral.* I. 580 In the peacock coal of Wales or Somersetshire, this iridescence often assumes a strong resemblance of what are called the eyes in a peacock's tail. **1861** MISS BEAUFORT *Egypt. Sepulchres*, etc. II. xvi. 31 Bits of ancient pottery and glass..with the iridescence of time very strongly marked upon it. **1863** TYNDALL *Heat* i. 20 Nothing can exceed the splendour of the iridescences exhibited by many of these clouds. **1874** COUES *Birds N.W.* 291 The plumage..is peculiar..no other species of our country shows such a rich metallic iridescence.
b. *fig.* Brilliant flashing of genius or character.
1803 W. TAYLOR in *Ann. Rev.* I. 268 Occasional corruscations of wit, and frequent iridescences of fancy. **1876** GEO. ELIOT *Dan. Der.* iv, What may be called the iridescence of her character—the play of various, nay, contrary tendencies.

iri'descency. ? *Obs.* [f. as prec.: see -ENCY.] = prec. (*lit.* and *fig.*); also, an iridescent formation.
1799 HATCHETT in *Phil. Trans.* LXXXIX. 320 The wavy appearance and irridescency of mother of pearl. **1802** W. TAYLOR in Robberds *Mem.* I. 449, I have got a little blue book for the iridescencies of my imagination.

iridescent (ɪrɪ'dɛsənt), *a.* [f. L. *īrid-* IRIS + -ESCENT. Cf. F. *iridescent* (Littré).] Displaying colours like those of the rainbow, or those reflected from soap-bubbles and the like; glittering or flashing with colours which change according to the position from which they are viewed.
1796 KIRWAN *Elem. Min.* (ed. 2) I. 106 An iridescent or tarnished metallic appearance. **1834** MRS. SOMERVILLE *Connex. Phys. Sc.* xx. (1849) 191 The iridescent colours produced by heat on polished steel and copper. **1837** M. DONOVAN *Dom. Econ.* II. 183 The Mackerel is a handsome fish..The sides are iridescent like mother-of-pearl, but more silvery. **1879** G. ALLEN *Colour-Sense* i. 5 We do not owe to the colour-sense the existence in nature of the rainbow, the sunset, or the other effects of iridescent light. **1897** MARY KINGSLEY *W. Africa* 242 On the top of the water is a film of exquisite iridescent colours like those on a soap bubble, only darker and brighter.
b. *fig.* or in fig. context.
1864 *Realm* 18 May 6 This iridescent bubble-chaos of false sentiment. **1873** BLACKIE *Self-Cult.* (1874) 84 The best fictions, without a deep moral significance beneath, are only iridescent froth. **1897** MRS. J. R. GREEN in *19th Cent.* June 966 The iridescent activities of a sympathetic and gifted intellect.
Hence **iri'descently** *adv.*, in an iridescent manner.
1796 KIRWAN *Elem. Min.* (ed. 2) II. 247 Bluish grey or steel grey, when tarnished Iridescently variegated blue or purplish. **1865** STIRLING *Secr. Hegel* Proleg. i. 8 To see..the whole huge universe iridescently collapse into the crystal of the Idea.

iridesis, erron. variant of IRIDODESIS.

iridiagnosis (ˌaɪərɪdaɪəg'nəʊsɪs). [f. IRIS *sb.* 4 a + DIAGNOSIS.] Diagnosis of disease from observation of the iris of the eye; iris diagnosis.
1918 F. W. COLLINS in P. J. Thiel *Dis. diagnosed by Observations of Eye* xvi. 76 See our works under preparation: ..'Pathology, Iridiagnosis and Treatment', by F. W. Collins..and Charles F. Haverin. **1919** H. LINDLAHR (*title*) Iridiagnosis and other diagnostic methods. **1928** *Sunday Express* 8 Apr. 10/7, I had never come across iridiagnosis before.

iridial (aɪ'rɪdɪəl), *a. Med.* [Irreg. f. L. *īrid-* (see IRID) + -IAL.] = IRIDAL *a.* 2, IRIDIC *a.*[2]
1911 STEDMAN *Med. Dict.* 438/2 *Iridial*, *iridian*, iridal. **1920** I. F. & W. D. HENDERSON *Dict. Sci. Terms* 156/2 *Iridial angle*, the filtration angle of the eye; an angular recess at the anterior surface of the attached margin of the eye. **1960** *Anatomical Rec.* CXXXVI. 345/1 The iridial muscles of reptiles.

iridian (aɪ'rɪdɪən), *a.* [f. L. *īrid-* IRIS + -IAN.]
1. Pertaining to the iris of the eye.
1864 in WEBSTER.
2. Rainbow-like; brilliantly coloured.
1884 in *Cassell's Encycl. Dict.* **1888** UPWARD *Songs in Ziklag* 146 *Consistency* ii, Truth's iridian arch.

iridiate (aɪ'rɪdɪət). *Chem.* [f. IRIDI-UM + -ATE[1].] A salt of iridic acid.
1854 J. SCOFFERN in *Orr's Circ. Sc.*, *Chem.* 515 The fused mass..contains osmiate and iridiate of potash. [**1873** Chlor-iridiates: see IRIDIO-.]

iridic (aɪ'rɪdɪk), *a.*[1] *Chem.* [f. IRID-IUM + -IC. Cf. F. *iridique* (Littré).] Containing iridium; applied to compounds in which iridium is quadrivalent, as $IrCl_4$: cf. IRIDIOUS.
1845 PARNELL *Chem. Anal.* 78 Iridic oxide. **1865–72** WATTS *Dict. Chem.* III. 319 Iridic solutions..are of a dark brown-red colour; iridious solutions (containing the sesquioxide or trichloride)..have an olive-green colour. *Ibid.* 322 The dioxide, or Iridic oxide, IrO_2.

iridic (aɪ'rɪdɪk), *a.*[2] *Med.* [f. as IRIDAL *a.* + -IC.] Of or pertaining to the iris of the eye; = IRIDAL *a.* 2.
1891 M. FOSTER *Textbk. Physiol.* (ed. 5) IV. iii. 717 On the inside the curved circumferential portion of the cornea makes a blunt angle, 'iridic angle', with the outer edge of the more or less horizontal iris. **1907** *Ophthalmoscope* V. 378 A true fistulous passage lined by iridic pigmented epithelium. **1964** S. DUKE-ELDER *Parsons' Dis. Eye* (ed. 14) i. 6 The third portion of the muscle is composed of a few tenuous iridic fibres..finding insertion in the root of the iris.

iridical (aɪ'rɪdɪkəl), *a. rare*[−1]. [f. L. *irid-* IRIS + -ICAL.] Brilliant with rainbow colours.
1862 S. LUCAS *Secularia* 100 The iridical window and the flaming shrine.

i'ridico-, combining form of IRIDIC, entering into adjectives naming double salts of iridium and another element, e.g. ***iridico-ammonic***, ***iridico-potassic***, ***iridico-sodic***, as ***iridico-ammonic sulphate*** or ***iridammonium sulphate***, $N_2H_6Ir''SO_4$.

iridin ('aɪrɪdɪn). Also iridine. [f. as IRIDIC *a.*[2] + -IN[1].] **1.** *Pharm.* A substance obtained from the rhizome of the blue flag, *Iris versicolor*, and formerly used as a hepatic stimulant.
1879 *Pharmaceutical Jrnl. & Trans.* IX. 988/2 Iridin is obtained from the fresh rhizome of *Iris versicolor*. It is usually mixed with liquorice, or some other absorbent powder. **1907** *Yesterday's Shopping* (1969) 504/1 Iridin Compound. **1921** *Oxf. Index Therap.* 992 *Iridin*. Dose 1 to 5 grains..in pill... Cholagogue and diuretic in its action.
2. *Chem.* [a. G. *iridin* (De Laire & Tiemann 1893, in *Ber. d. Deut. Chem. Ges.* XXVI. 2011).] 5, 7, 3′-Trihydroxy-6, 4′, 5′-trimethoxy-isoflavone 7-glucoside, $C_{24}H_{26}O_{13}$, a crystalline compound occurring in the rhizome (orris-root) of the Florentine iris (*Iris florentina*).
1894 *Jrnl. Chem. Soc.* LXVI. I. 47 The dried roots of the violet (*Iris florentina*) on extraction with alcohol, yield a glucoside iridin, $C_{24}H_{26}O_{13}$; it forms slender, white needles. **1928** *Ibid.* 1027 An alcoholic solution of iridin develops with a trace of ferric chloride a somewhat intense, dull reddish-violet colour. **1966** *Chem. Abstr.* LXIV. 15826 (*heading*) Final structure elucidation and complete synthesis of iridine.
3. *Chem.* [a. G. *iridin* (K. Felix et al. 1951, in *Zeitschr. f. physiol. Chem.* CCLXXXVII. 226).] A protamine or mixture of protamines found in the heads of spermatozoa of the rainbow trout, *Salmo gairdneri* (= *S. irideus*).
1953 *Chem. Abstr.* XLVII. 10018 Fresh spermatozoa heads of *Salmo iridis* [*sic*] and..of herring were shown to consist of nucleoprotamine..[which] contained the protamines iridin and clupein. **1969** *Internat. Jrnl. Protein Res.* I. 221/1 Iridine from rainbow-trout..has been separated by column chromatography..into three main fractions.

iridine ('aɪrɪdɪn, -aɪn), *a. rare.* [f. L. *irid-* IRIS 2 + -INE.] Rainbow-like; iridescent.

1851 S. JUDD *Margaret* I. xiv. (Ward & Lock) 110 The horned-pout, with its pearly iridine breast and iron-brown back.

-iridine. *Chem.* [See -IR-.] A suffix used systematically to form the names of saturated monocyclic compounds having a three-membered ring which includes a nitrogen atom. Cf. -IR-.

iridio- (aɪ'rɪdɪəʊ), comb. form of IRIDIUM, forming names of alloys or chemical combinations of iridium with another element or substance, as ***iridio-platinum*** an alloy of iridium and platinum, ***iridio-cyanogen*** (see quot. 1858); also of compounds in which iridium and another element combine with a third, as ***iridio-chloride, -cyanide, irido-cyanic*** adj.

1858 *Penny Cycl.* 2nd Suppl. 133/1 *Iridiocyanogen*, C_2N + Ir, is a hypothetical compound radical. It forms with hydrogen Iridiocyanic acid, and with potassium an Iridio-cyanide of potassium. **1865–72** WATTS *Dict. Chem.* III. 316 Iridio-cyanides of barium. **1894** *Times* 29 Sept. 11/2 The force exerted by gravity..upon the iridio-platinum weight.

iridious (aɪ'rɪdɪəs), *a. Chem.* [f. IRIDI-UM + -OUS. Cf. F. *irideux* (Littré).] Containing iridium; applied to compounds in which iridium is trivalent, as $IrCl_3$: cf. IRIDIC.

1865–72 WATTS *Dict. Chem.* III. 322 The sesquioxide [of iridium] or Iridious oxide, Ir_2O_3. **1873** —— *Fownes' Chem.* (ed. 11) 434 The trichloride or Iridious Chloride, is prepared by strongly heating iridium with nitre.

iridite ('aɪərɪdaɪt). *Chem.* [f. IRID-IUM + -ITE.] A salt of iridious acid.

1873 WATTS *Fownes' Chem.* (ed. 11) 435 It unites with bases, forming salts which may be called iridites.

iri'ditis. *Path.* A rare synonym of IRITIS (*Syd. Soc. Lex.*).

iridium (aɪ'rɪdɪəm, ɪ-). [f. L. *īrid-* IRIS 2 + -IUM; named by Tennant in 1803 (see quot. 1804).] A white metal of the platinum group, resembling polished steel, and fusible with great difficulty, found (usually in conjunction with osmium) in native platinum, and in the native alloy IRIDOSMIUM. Chemical symbol Ir; atomic weight 193. *Comb.*, as ***iridium-pointed*** adj.

1804 TENNANT in *Phil. Trans.* XCIV. 414, I should incline to call this metal *Iridium*, from the striking variety of colours which it gives, while dissolving in marine acid. **1805** W. H. WOLLASTON *ibid.* XCV. 317 Metals that were found by Mr. Tennant..and which he has called Iridium and Osmium. **1849** D. CAMPBELL *Inorg. Chem.* 259 Iridium is not unlike platinum..though harder, and less easily acted upon by acids. **1871** TYNDALL *Fragm. Sc.* (1879) II. xvi. 442 When sent through a short bar of iridium, this refractory metal emits a light of extraordinary splendour.

attrib. and *Comb.* **1849** D. CAMPBELL *Inorg. Chem.* 249 To separate the iridium oxide from platinum. **1865–72** WATTS *Dict. Chem.* III. 316 The mother-liquor of the iridium-salt. **1897** *Sears, Roebuck Catal.* 433 Gold filled and ebony telescopic Holder, with best quality iridium pointed pens. **1908** *Daily Chron.* 27 Feb. 7/3 A gold-iridium-pointed nib. **1926–7** *Army & Navy Stores Catal.* 425 Fountain pens. Fitted with 14-ct. gold nib, iridium-pointed.

iridization (ˌɪrɪdaɪ'zeɪʃən). [f. next + -ATION.] **1.** The action or process of showing prismatic colours as in the rainbow; irisation.

1884 *Pop. Sci. Monthly* June 288 M. Cornu lately described to the French Academy of Sciences a white rainbow..This rainbow was wholly white, without even as much iridization as is noticeable in halos, and had a fleecy appearance.

2. *Path.* The coloured halo seen round a light by persons affected with glaucoma (*Cent. Dict.*).

iridize ('ɪr-, 'aɪrɪdaɪz), *v.* [f. L. *irid-* IRIS, or IRID-IUM + -IZE.] **1.** *trans.* To make iridescent.

1874 [see IRIS *sb.* 3].

2. To cover with iridium; to tip with iridium.

1864 in WEBSTER.

irido- ('aɪərɪdəʊ, 'ɪrɪdəʊ), also before a vowel irid-, a. Gr. *ἰριδο-, comb. form of ἶρις IRIS, employed in the formation of many pathological and surgical terms, chiefly denoting diseases of the iris and operations upon it; those in more common use are the following:

iridencleisis (-'klaɪsɪs) [Gr. ἐγκλείειν to shut up], the trapping of a portion of the iris in an incision of the cornea. **iridochoroiditis** (-kɔərɔɪ'daɪtɪs) [CHOROIDITIS], inflammation of the iris and the choroid coat of the eye. **iridocyclitis** (-sɪ'klaɪtɪs) [CYCLITIS], inflammation of the iris and the ciliary body. **ˌiridodi'alysis** [DIALYSIS], the artificial separation of the iris from the ciliary ring. **iridodonesis** (-dəʊ'niːsɪs) [Gr. δονέειν to shake], tremulousness of the iris. **iridomotor** (-'məʊtə(r)) [MOTOR], pertaining to movements of the iris. **irido'plegia** [-PLEGIA], paralysis of the iris. **'iridoscope** (aɪ'rɪdəʊskəʊp) [-SCOPE], an instrument for examining the iris. See also IRIDODESIS, IRIDOTOMY.

1855 R. G. MAYNE *Expos. Lex. Med. Sci.* (1860) 540/2 **Iridencleisis*, old term for strangulation of a prolapsed portion of the iris, between the lips of an incision in the cornea. **1879** *Arch. Ophthalm.* VIII. 497 (*heading*) A case of severe iritis and glaucoma, following iridencleisis. **1964** D. M. GORDON *Med. Managem. Ocular Dis.* xviii. 335 Chandler prefers peripheral iridectomy in acute cases in which the pressure is rapidly brought under control. If the pressure has been elevated for 36 or more hours.., he prefers an iridencleisis. **1874** LAWSON *Dis. Eye* 62 In the majority of cases it [ciliary staphyloma] is dependent on a chronic *irido-choroiditis. *Ibid.* 77 Primary iritis may..implicate secondarily the neighbouring structures; thus we have *irido-cyclitis, and irido-choroiditis. **1900** J. HUTCHINSON *Archives Surg.* XI. 17 A most threatening form of relapsing irido-cyclitis. [**1822–34** *Good's Study Med.* (ed. 4) II. 216 It is the more singular however that iritis should have ever been used by its inventor as the Germans have long employed the more correct relative compounds of iridotomia, iridectomia and *iridodialysis.] **1878** T. BRYANT *Pract. Surg.* I. 364 Tearing away the iris from its insertion (Iridodialysis). **1879** P. SMITH *Glaucoma* 109 The zonula became loose and the lens hung slack, causing a visible *irido-donesis. **1876** FERRIER *Functions of Brain* 72 Co-ordination of retinal impressions with *irido-motor action in the corpora quadrigemina. [**1854** W. MACKENZIE *Pract. Treat. Dis. Eye* (ed. 4) xxii. 882 (*heading*) Myosis... *Iridoplegia pupillam contrahens.] **1878** *Brain* I. 8 Iridoplegia is a term applicable wherever both circular and radiating fibres of the iris are paralysed, and the pupil fails wholly to respond to the stimulus of light. **1970** E. ZAGORA *Eye Injuries* i. 12/1 Occasionally traumatic iridoplegia and cycloplegia occur as a result of concussion of the eye. **1866** *Intell. Observ.* No. 52. 315 A new optical instrument..the *iridoscope.

iridocyte ('aɪərɪdəʊsaɪt). *Zool.* [a. Fr. *iridocyte* (G. Pouchet 1876, in *Jrnl. de l'Anat. & de la Physiol.* XII. 45), f. Gr. ἰριδ-, IRIS *sb.* + κύτος a hollow, cell.] A cell which refracts light to cause iridescence, found in the skin of fishes, cephalopods, and certain other animals.

1893 CUNNINGHAM & MACMUNN in *Phil. Trans. R. Soc.* B. CLXXXIV. 767 The chief features of the iridocytes are their regularity of outline, and their great reflecting power. **1923** *Glasgow Herald* 23 June 4 The silveriness [of plaice] is due to the reflection of light from minute spangles of a waste-product called guanin, which accumulates in certain skin-cells called iridocytes. **1940** *Proc. Zool. Soc.* A. CX. 19 Throughout the epithelial tissues of the animal [sc. *Sepia officinalis*], lying below the chromatophores, is a layer of immobile reflector cells, the iridocytes or iridophores. **1960** FOX & VEVERS *Nature of Animal Colours* x. 150 In scales the guanine crystals may cause iridescence by interference of light and the chromatophores are then called iridocytes.

iridodesis (aɪərɪ'dɒdɪsɪs). *Surg.* Also 9 *erron.* iriddesis, iridesis. [f. Gr. ἶρις, ἰριδ- (IRIDO-) + δέσις binding.] An operation in which the iris is secured in a certain position by a ligature.

1858 CRITCHETT in *Ophthal. Hosp. Rep.* I. 220 Iriddesis: or the formation of Artificial pupil by tying the iris. *Ibid.* 225, I feel satisfied that this twofold object could not have been attained in any other way than by *Iriddesis.* **1859** DIXON *Dis. Eye* (ed. 2) 370 Mr. Critchett has very recently proposed an operation, which he terms 'Iriddesis' (Iridodesis?). **1874** LAWSON *Dis. Eye* 94 By iridodesis of ligature of the iris. **1875** H. WALTON *Dis. Eye* (ed. 3) 587 Iriddesis..differs from the last described merely in the pupil not being entirely lost. **1878** T. BRYANT *Pract. Surg.* I. 364 By ligature, Iridodesis, or Iridesis.

iridoline (aɪ'rɪdəʊlaɪn). *Chem.* [f. L. *īrid-* IRIS + *ol-eum* oil + -INE.] A base ($C_{10}H_9N$) occurring in coal tar oil.

1892 MORLEY & MUIR *Dict. Chem.* III. 50.

iridosmine (aɪərɪ'dɒsmaɪn, ɪrɪ-). [f. IRID-IUM + OSM-IUM + -INE[5]; named by Breithaupt 1827.] A native alloy of the metals iridium and osmium, usually occurring in flattened grains with platinum. Also **iri'dosmium**, and *osmiridium.*

1827 *Edin. New Philos. Jrnl.* III. 273 Irid-osmin..is a compound of iridium and osmium. **1865–72** WATTS *Dict. Chem.* III. 314 The black scales which remain when native platinum is dissolved in nitromuriatic acid were found by Smithson Tennant to consist of an alloy of two metals, iridium and osmium, hence called iridosmine. **1880** *Libr. Univ. Knowl.* (N.Y.) VIII. 137 The chief use of iridosmine is in tipping the nibs of gold pens.

iridotomy (aɪərɪ'dɒtəmɪ, ɪrɪ-). [f. IRIDO- + Gr. -τομία cutting; cf. *lithotomy*. Cf. F. *iridotomie* (Littré).] Section of the iris.

1855 in MAYNE *Expos. Lex.* **1876** *Clin. Soc. Trans.* IX. 3 M. de Wecker of Paris..endeavoured to improve Mr. Bowman's operation by one which he called 'iridotomy'. **1878** T. BRYANT *Pract. Surg.* I. 363 Double iridotomy is applicable to cases of closed pupil after cataract extraction.

So **i'ridotome**, 'a knife devised by Sichel for excising the iris' (*Syd. Soc. Lex.*).

irigenin (aɪrɪ'dʒenɪn). *Chem.* [a. G. *irigenin* (De Laire & Tiemann 1893, in *Ber. d. Deut. Chem. Ges.* XXVI. 2011), f. G. *iri-din* IRIDIN 2: see GENIN.] A pale yellow crystalline flavonoid, $C_{18}H_{16}O_8$, obtained on acid hydrolysis of iridin, of which it is the aglycone.

1894 *Jrnl. Chem. Soc.* LXVI. I. 47 Iridin undergoes hydrolysis when heated with dilute sulphuric acid at 80–100°, yielding *d*-glucose and irigenin... This substance crystallises in rhombohedra, melting at 186°. **1928** *Ibid.* 1925 These results prove that irigenin..is consequently 5:7:3′-trihydroxy-6:4′:5′-trimethoxy*iso*flavone. **1960** *Tetrahedron Let.* v. 9 The synthetic irigenin..was identical with the natural product.

†**i-'riht.** *Obs.* [OE. *ȝerihto, -rihta* pl.; see I-[1], Y-, and RIGHT *sb.*] *pl.* Rights, dues; rightful possession.

c **1000** ÆLFRIC *Hom.* I. 74 Se apostol..Godes ȝerihta lærde. *a* **1100** *O.E. Chron.* (Laud MS.) an. 1074 He..nam swilce ȝerihta swa se cyng him ȝeuðe. *c* **1205** LAY. 7906 Rome is eowre irihte; nu hit halt Julius Cesar. *c* **1275** *Luue Ron* 130 in *O.E. Misc.* 97 Þer ne may no freond fleon oþer, ne non furleosen his iryhte.

i-riht, ME. pa. pple. of RIGHT *v.*

irin, obs. form of IRON.

-irine. *Chem.* [See -IR-.] A suffix used systematically to form the names of unsaturated monocyclic compounds having a three-membered ring which includes a nitrogen atom. Cf. -IR-.

i-rinen, ME. pa. pple. of RINE *v.*, to touch.

i'ringo, obs. variant of ERYNGO.

1620 VENNER *Via Recta* vii. 137 Iringo-roots are hot and dry in the second degree.

irinite ('ɪrɪnaɪt). *Min.* [ad. Russ. *irinit* (Borodin & Kazakova 1954, in *Doklady Akad. Nauk S.S.S.R.* XCVII. 725), f. the name of *Irin*-a Dmitrievna Borneman-Starynkevich, Russian geochemist: see -ITE[1].] An oxide-hydroxide of sodium, cerium, thorium, titanium, and niobium occurring as red-brown crystals in the Khibiny Massif, U.S.S.R., and belonging to the perovskite group of minerals.

1955 *Mineral. Abstr.* XII. 462 Irinite occurs as combination of cube and octahedron from 0·5 to 1 cm. in size... Formula ABX_3, namely (Na, Ce, Th)$_{1-x}$(Ti, Nb)(O_{3-x}, $(OH)_x$) with deficiency of A cations. **1962** W. A. DEER et al. *Rock-forming Min.* V. 51 Irinite, described as a new mineral of the perovskite group..has a high thorium and rare earth content.

irios, variant of IREOS, *Obs.*

iris ('aɪərɪs), *sb.* Pl. irides ('aɪərɪdiːz), irises. [a. Gr. ἶρις, stem ἰριδ-. The senses (except 3 and 6) correspond to those of the Gr. word; so also F. *iris.* The pl. *irides* is chiefly used in sense 4.]

1. *Gr. Myth.* The goddess who acted as the messenger of the gods, and was held to display as her sign, or appear as, the rainbow; hence, allusively, a messenger.

1593 SHAKS. *2 Hen. VI*, III. ii. 407 Wheresoere thou art in this worlds Globe, Ille haue an Iris that shall finde thee out.

2. a. A rainbow; a many-coloured refraction of light from drops of water.

1490 CAXTON *Eneydos* xxviii. 109 Yris..is the rayen bowe wyth hir fayr cote of dyuerse fygures. **1582** T. WATSON *Centurie of Loue* vii. (Arb.) 43 Each eybrowe hanges like Iris in the skies. **1606** SHAKS. *Tr. & Cr.* I. iii. 380 His Crest, that prouder then blew Iris bends. **1742** YOUNG *Nt. Th.* II. 21 The good Deed would..half-impress On my dark Cloud an Iris. **1782** TUNSTALL in *Phil. Trans.* LXXIII. 103 No lunar Iris, I ever heard or read of, lasted near so long as that on the 18th instant. **1831** BREWSTER *Optics* xiii. 110 Illuminating its perimeter like two mock suns in the opposite parts of an iris.

b. *transf.* A rainbow-like or iridescent appearance; a circle or halo of prismatic colours; a combination or alternation of brilliant colours.

1601 SHAKS. *All's Well* I. iii. 158 What's the matter, That this distempered messenger of wet, The manie colour'd Iris rounds thine eye [cf. *Lucrece* 1586]? **1665** *Phil. Trans.* I. 2 He useth three Eye-Glasses for his great Telescopes, without finding any Iris, or such Rain-bow colors as do usually appear in ordinary Glasses. **1670** LASSELS *Voy. Italy* II. 340 Pretious stones of seueral sorts and Lustures.. composeing a rich Iris of seueral colours. **1760–72** tr. *Juan & Ulloa's Voy.* (ed. 3) I. 442 We saw, as in a looking-glass, the image of each of us, the head being as it were the centre of three concentrick iris's. **1842** TENNYSON *Locksley Hall* 19 In the Spring a livelier iris changes on the burnish'd dove.

c. *fig.*

1821 SHELLEY *Hellas* 43 If Liberty Lent not life its soul of light, Hope its iris of delight. **1834** DISRAELI *Rev. Epick* II. xiii, Is Virtue but a shade? And Freedom but the iris of a storm? **1878** B. TAYLOR *Deukalion* I. ii. 26 Print thy soft iris on white wings of prayer.

3. a. A hexagonal prismatic crystal (mentioned by Pliny *Nat. Hist.* XXXVII. ix. 52). **b.** 'Applied by French jewellers to a variety of rock-crystal, possessing the property of reflecting the prismatic colours by means of natural flaws in the interior of the stone' (Westropp *Precious Stones*).

Opinions differ as to the identity of these, some taking the former as 'the prismatic crystals of limpid quartz, which decompose the rays of the sun' (Westropp).

1387 TREVISA *Higden* (Rolls) I. 337 Also þere [in Ireland] groweþ þat stoon Saxagonus, and is i-cleped Iris also, as it were þe reynebowe. *c* **1400** MAUNDEV. xxviii. (1839) 219 The white ben of cristalle and of berylle and of Iris. **1563** W. FULKE *Meteors* (1640) 36 The image of the Rayne-bow may bee seen on a wall, the Sunne striking thorow a six-pointed stone, called Iris, or any other Christall of the same fashion. **1601** HOLLAND *Pliny* II. 623 Next after the Ceraunia, there is a stone named Iris: digged out of the ground it is in a

certain Isle of the red sea... For the most part it resembleth Crystal... If the beams of the Sun strike vpon it directly within house, it sendeth from it against the wals that be near, the very resemblance of a rainbow both in form and colour. **1646** SIR T. BROWNE *Pseud. Ep.* II. iv. 78 Diamonds, Saphyres, Carbuncles, Iris, Opalls. **1748** SIR J. HILL *Hist. Fossils* 179 The Iris, or Rain-bow Crystal of authors. **1861** BRISTOW *Gloss. Min.* 191 Rock Crystal can be made into Iris. **1874** WESTROPP *Prec. Stones* 90 Hyaline quartz iridized internally (called at the present day iris).

4. a. *Anat.* A flat, circular, coloured membrane suspended vertically in the aqueous humour of the eye, and separating the anterior from the posterior chamber; in its centre is a circular opening, called the pupil, which may be enlarged or diminished so as to regulate the amount of light transmitted to the retina.

The colour of the iris, blue, brown, grey, etc., is what is known as the colour of the eye.

1525 tr. *Jerome of Brunswick's Surg.* Bjb/2 There be iij. materyall circles y[t] ronne about the iye, and because they be so different of colours they be callyd yride[s] or rain bowys. **1619** PURCHAS *Microcosmus* viii. 90 This Centre is enuironed with a Circle, called *Iris*, of many colours in Man onely. **1777** DARWIN in *Phil. Trans.* LXVIII. 87 There was no perceptible difference in the diameter of the irises. **1881** MIVART *Cat* 473 An iris capable of contracting its aperture to a vertical linear slit. **1881** E. COPE in *Knowledge* (1883) 136/2 The colour of the skin, hair, and irides.

b. (*transf.*) *Entom.* The inner ring of an ocellated spot on an insect's wing; usually lighter than the outer ring, and the central spot or pupil.

1826 KIRBY & SPENCE *Entomol.* III. 727 Caudate wing. Pupil. Iris. **1838** WESTWOOD *Entomol. Text Bk.* 278 Eyelets (*Ocelli*),..the centre..is termed the pupil, and is surrounded by the iris.

c. *Photogr.* = *iris-diaphragm*; also *attrib.* Also **iris-in** *sb.*, **iris-out** *sb.* (see quot. 1959): both used as vbs. Also *transf.* and *fig.*

1911 C. N. BENNETT et al. *Handbk. Kinematogr.* I. iv. 28 In the form of lens attached to kinematograph cameras, alteration of diaphragm is effected by the movement of a ring or pin on the lens mount which causes the 'iris' inside to open and close like the iris of a cat's eye, except that the hole in the middle always remains circular in shape. **1929** I. MONTAGU tr. *Pudovkin's On Film Technique* App. 191 The author gives..the iris-in and iris-out, mentioning what is called the fade only as a variant. **1934** WEBSTER, *Iris*, to operate the iris of a camera so as to fade (a picture). With *in* or *out*. **1958** *Spectator* 6 June 730/3 He can iris himself in and out of the scene at will. **1959** W. S. SHARPS *Dict. Cinematogr.* 104/2 *Iris-in*, the film wipe, in which the image viewed progressively disappears and at the same time is replaced by another, moving from the centre of the frame outwards in the form of a circle. *Ibid.*, *Iris-out*, the film wipe, in which the image viewed progressively disappears and is replaced by another from the outside of the frame, moving inwards in the form of a circle. **1961** K. REISZ *Technique Film Editing* (ed. 9) iii. 246 An iris may on occasion introduce or close a shot in a more telling way than a fade. **1962** *B.B.C. Handbook* 119 The control of the zooming, focusing, and iris setting, of a television camera. **1966** WODEHOUSE *Plum Pie* vii. 177 After a terrific struggle the hood called it a day and irised out. **1968** BLISH & KNIGHT *Torrent of Faces* II. vii. 137 Fongaváro glided silently through the Rest Stop door, which irised shut as silently behind him. **1969** GISH & PINCHOT *Lilian Gish* xi. 145 The scene of Sherman's march to the sea opened with an iris shot —a small area. *Ibid.*, Slowly the iris opened wider to reveal a great panorama. **1972** WODEHOUSE *Pearls, Girls, & Monty Bodkin* vii. 102 When a bunch of flatfeet burst in with their uncouth cry of 'Everybody keep their seats, please,' the thing to do is to iris out unobtrusively through the kitchen.

5. *Bot.* A genus of plants, the type of the natural order *Iridaceæ*, natives of Europe, N. Africa, and the temperate regions of Asia and America; most of the species have tuberous (less commonly bulbous or fibrous) roots, sword-shaped equitant leaves, and showy flowers; formerly often called Fleur-de-lis or Flower-de-luce. Also, a plant of this genus.

blue iris, *Iris germanica*, the German Flag, a common cultivated species; **fetid iris**, the Gladden, *Iris fœtidissima*; **Florentine iris** = *white iris*; **stinking iris** = *fetid iris*; **white iris**, *Iris florentina*, from which orrisroot is obtained; **yellow iris**, the Yellow Flag, *Iris Pseudacorus*, the common British species.

[**1562** TURNER *Herbal.* II. 23 a, Iris is knowen both of the Grecianes and Latines by that name; it is called..in Englishe flour de lyce.] **1578** LYTE *Dodoens* II. xxxv. 192 There be many kindes of Iris, or floure Deluce. *Ibid.*, The stincking Iris, and the yellow Iris. *Ibid.* 193 The Irides or flower Deluces do most commonly flower about May. **1667** MILTON *P.L.* IV. 698 Each beauteous flour, Iris all hues, Roses, and Gessamin. **1741** *Compl. Fam. Piece* II. iii. 383 Transplant your..Persian and bulbous Iris's. **1850** TENNYSON *In Mem.* ciii, We glided winding under ranks Of iris, and the golden reed. **1882** *Garden* 3 June 385/3 The drought of the past week has burnt up the Irises. **1886** *Pall Mall G.* 2 Oct. 4 The plains were ornamented with dwarfed blue irides.

6. *Astron.* Name of the seventh of the asteroids.

1858 *Penny Cycl.* 2nd Supp. 708/1 Minor planets..Iris ..[discoverer] Hind..[date of discovery] August 13, 1847.

7. *attrib.* and *Comb.*, as (sense 2) ***iris-colour***, ***-glow***, ***-gradation***, ***-ornament***, ***-ring***, ***-tint***; also ***iris-coloured***, ***-hued***, ***-like*** adjs.; (sense 4) ***iris-forceps***, ***-hook***, ***-knife***, ***-scissors*** (used in surgical operations on the iris); (sense 5) ***iris-blossom***, ***blue***, ***-family***, ***-flower***, ***green***, ***-root***; also **iris-camphor**, an ethereal oil obtained from iris-roots (*Syd. Soc. Lex.* 1887); **iris-coffee**, the seeds of *Iris pseudacorus*, used as a substitute for coffee (*ibid.*); **iris diagnosis** = IRIDIAGNOSIS; **iris-diaphragm**, a contractile diaphragm for lenses, contrived so as to imitate the action of the iris; **iris-disease**, a form of herpes, generally affecting the back of the hands; **iris-root**, the root of *Iris florentina*, orris-root; **iris-swallow**, a swallow of the sub-genus *Iridoprocne*, having iridescent plumage.

1899 *Edin. Rev.* Jan. 30 The tall grass, green herb and leaf, the *iris blossoms. **1908** F. TREVES *Cradle of Deep* x. 57 A West Indian island..rising aloft from an *iris-blue sea. **18..** DANA *Min.* (L.), The tarnish and *iris colours of minerals are owing to a thin surface film. **1869** TYNDALL *Notes Lect. Light* 58 With white light the circles display iris-colours. *Ibid.* 74 A series of *iris-coloured bands. **1921** *Glasgow Herald* 17 Feb. 9 *Iris diagnosis and its relation to true health. **1938** H. ORBELL (*title*) The science of iris-diagnosis. **1867** *Trans. R. Miscrosc. Soc.* XV. 74 (*heading*) *Iris diaphragm proving the circular form whether expanding or contracting. *a* **1877** KNIGHT *Dict. Mech.* II. 1195/2 *Iris-diaphragm*, a contractile diaphragm, simulating the action of the natural iris. **1889** *Anthony's Photogr. Bull.* II. 66 These lenses may be had with iris diaphragms. **1890** *Ibid.* III. 119 Iris diaphragms applied to photographic lenses are a recent reintroduction. **1836** MACGILLIVRAY tr. *Humboldt's Trav.* xxi. 304 Covered with rushes and plants of the *Iris family. **1818** SHELLEY *Marenghi* xxiv. 5 The coarse bulbs of *iris-flowers. **1874** LAWSON *Dis. Eye* 144 He draws out with a pair of *iris forceps the corresponding segment of the iris. **1823** MRS. HEMANS *Last Constantine* lxxiv, Such an *iris-glow as emulates the skies. **1862** THORNBURY *Turner* I. 357 Tender *iris-gradations of colour. **1875** E. SPON *Workshop Receipts* 95/1 **Iris green*, a pigment prepared by grinding the juice of the petals of the blue flag with quicklime. It is very fugitive. **1880** *Encycl. Brit.* XIII. 276/2 From the flowers of *Iris florentina* a pigment—the 'verdelis', 'vert d'iris', or iris-green, formerly used by miniature painters—was prepared by maceration. **1887** FENN *Master of Cerem.* i, Delivering its take of *iris-hued mackerel. **1839–47** TODD *Cycl. Anat.* III. 346/2 The *iris-knife is a convenient size and form for many purposes. **1849** H. MAYO *Truths Pop. Superst.* ii. 26 Returning hope shone, *Iris-like, amid her falling tears. **1863** TYNDALL *Heat* xv. (1870) 539 A series of most splendidly-coloured *iris-rings. **1673** GREW *Anat. Roots* I. i. §11 Some Parts of *Iris-root appear oftentimes above the ground. **1874** LAWSON *Dis. Eye* 158 Through the wound in the cornea the blades of a pair of fine *iris scissors may be introduced. **1864** SALA in *Daily Tel.* 5 Dec., The snow was all bathed in *iris tints.

iris ('aɪərɪs), *v.* [f. prec. Cf. F. *iriser*.] *trans.* To make iridescent; to form into, or place as, a rainbow. Only in *pa. pple.*

1816 CLEAVELAND *Min.* 558 Its color is a light lead gray, often tarnished with a tinge of yellow, and sometimes irised. **1856** RUSKIN *Mod. Paint.* IV. v. v. §21 The wreaths of fitful vapour..irised around the pillars of waterfalls. **1894** *Outing* (U.S.) Aug. 348/2 Watch the bubbles go and come Irised on the crystal stream.

irisate ('aɪərɪseɪt), *v.* [irreg. f. IRIS *sb.* + -ATE[3].] *trans.* To render iridescent. Hence '**irisated** *ppl. a.*, iridescent.

1828 WEBSTER cites PHILLIPS. **1887** *Science* Sept. 115 A variety of hooks were used for different kinds of fish and according to the time of day, irisated shells being applied at noon and in a bright sun.

irisation (aɪərɪ'seɪʃən). [f. prec.: see -ATION. Cf. F. *irisation* (Littré).] The process of making iridescent; iridescence.

1855 MAYNE *Expos. Lex.*, *Irisation*,..the effect of the decomposition of light by the prism. **1881** *Metal World* No. 9. 131 Certain metallic irisations are produced on the surface of the object. **1892** A. MICHEL in *Athenæum* 2 July 39/3 The coloured bubbles and the irisations formed in the thickness of the glass.

iriscope ('aɪərɪskəʊp), *sb.* [irreg. f. IRIS *sb.*[2] + -SCOPE.] A device for exhibiting the primary colours by the action of the breath on a specially prepared plate of highly polished black glass.

1841 BREWSTER in *Phil. Trans.* 43 Having received from Dr. Joseph Reade one of his beautiful instruments called the Iriscope,..I soon perceived that it might be advantageously employed in various investigations in physical optics. [Description follows.]

†**i-'rise**, *v.* *Obs.* [OE. *ȝeris-an.*] *trans.* To become, suit, be suitable to. (Orig. const. with *dat.*)

a **1000** *Guthlac* 1087 (Gr.) Swa þam þeodne ȝeras. *c* **1000** ÆLFRIC *Hom.* II. 318 Cyninge ȝerist rihtwisnys and wisdom. *c* **1200** *Trin. Coll. Hom.* 141 þe ȝeriseð wel here eiðer.

i-rise(n, ME. pa. pple. of RISE *v.*

irised ('aɪərɪst), *a.* [f. IRIS *sb.* and *v.* + -ED.]

1. Having the colours of the rainbow; coloured by a rainbow.

1816 CLEAVELAND *Min.* 558 In Hessia, it occurs in delicate, irised needles in a mine of sparry iron. **1837** DANA *Min.* 76 The tarnish is described as *irised*, when it exhibits the fixed prismatic colors. **1880** *Scribner's Mag.* July 347 Bathing from time to time in waftings of irised spray.

2. Having an iris or irises; usually with qualifying word, as ***large-irised*** (see IRIS *sb.* 4).

1879 *Scribner's Mag.* XIX. 514/2 Large-irised eyes. **1880** MRS. BURNETT *Louisiana* i, They were the loveliest eyes,.. large-irised, and with wonderful long lashes.

Irish ('aɪərɪʃ), *a.* and *sb.* Forms: 3 Irisc, Irreisc, Iriss, Yriss, 4 Irisch, (Yrisch, Hyrisch), Iris, 5 Yrissh, -yssh, Iressh, Hiressche, 5–6 Irysh, 6 Irishe, (*Sc.* -isch(e), -eshe, Yris(c)he, -esshe, 3– Irish. [f. *Ir-*, stem of OE. *I'ras* (ON. *I'rar*) the inhabitants of Ireland (OE. and ON. *I'rland*) + *-isc*, -ISH: cf. ON. *I'rskr.* The stem *ír-* is no doubt from OIr. *Ériu* Erin (see HIBERNIAN); but the phonological relation is not clear.]

A. *adj.*

1. Of persons: Of, belonging to, or native to Ireland; orig. and esp. used of the Celtic inhabitants.

c **1205** LAY. 18060 þa iseȝen Irisce men þat Brutten wes an eornest. *a* **1250** *Owl & Night.* 322 Thu chaterest so doth on Irish preost. *a* **1300** *K. Horn* 1290 Horn gan to schupe draȝe Wiþ his yrisse felaȝes. *c* **1330** R. BRUNNE *Chron. Wace* (Rolls) 8834 þe Irisch kyng gadered his host. **1422** tr. *Secreta Secret., Priv. Priv.* 166 Consydyr ye that youre yrysshe enemys ne hare auncestres..was trewe to you. **1596** SPENSER *State Irel.* Wks. (Globe) 637/2 Other greate howses there be of the old English in Ireland, which..are nowe growen as Irish as O-hanlans breeche. *Ibid.* 647/2 Benefices ..of soe small profitt in these Irish countreyes, through the ill husbandrye of the Irish people which inhabite them. **1672** PETTY *Pol. Anat.* xii. in *Tracts* (1769) 363 The priests are chosen for the most part out of old Irish gentry. **1763** HUME in *Rep. on Ossian* (1805) 7 A very ingenious Irish gentleman. **1855** MACAULAY *Hist. Eng.* xvii, Scattered over all Europe were to be found brave Irish generals, dexterous Irish diplomatists, Irish Counts, Irish Barons.

†**b.** Belonging to the Scottish Highlands or the Gaelic inhabitants of them. *Obs.*

1548 W. PATTEN *Exp. Scotl.* in Arb. *Garner* III. 63 Four thousand Irish archers brought by the Earl of Argyle. **1652** *Rec. Dingwall Presb.* (Sc. Hist. Soc.) 247 The contributione allotted to the Irishe boyes.

2. Of things: Of or pertaining to Ireland or its inhabitants (freq. denoting a particular variety or quality of the thing named, e.g. ***Irish butter***, ***car***, ***freize***, ***guipure***, ***linen***, ***mile***, ***poplin***, ***tweed***, ***penny***, ***whiskey***, etc.).

1398 TREVISA *Barth. De P.R.* xv. lxxxi. [lxxix.] (MS. Bodl.) lf. 157 b/2 Hiressche [**1495** yryssh] wolle and skynnes al venemous beestes fleeþ it. **1436** *Libel Eng. Policy* in *Pol. Songs* (Rolls) II. 186 Irish wollen, lynyn cloth. **1547** BOORDE *Introd. Knowl.* iii. (1870) 131, I can make good mantyls, and good Irysh fryce. **1645** BOATE *Irel. Nat. Hist.* (1652) 153 The load of an Irish-car, drawn by one Garron. **1741** RICHARDSON *Pamela* IV. xiii. 75 A Piece of Irish or Scotish Linen. **1751** [see POPLIN[2] *attrib.*]. **1780** A. YOUNG *Tour in Ireland* I. 276 The salt for the fish trade [comes] from Rochelle: for butter english and irish. **1785** J. WEDGWOOD *Let.* 3 Oct. (1965) 285 Irish linens in the British market. **1798** C. MORDAUNT *Let.* July in E. Hamilton *Mordaunts* (1965) x. 243, I hope our conduct may gain us credit for discipline, but am terribly afraid of the cheap Irish whiskey. **1805** *Times* 6 Nov. 1/2 (Advt.), The Public supplied, as usual, with pieces of Irish linen, at the wholesale prices, at the Irish Linen Company's, No. 4, Bloomsbury-square, near Hart-street. **1813** JANE AUSTEN *Let.* 15 Sept. (1932) II. 321 Very pretty English poplins at 4*s.* 3*d.*; Irish, ditto at 6*s.* **1828** M. R. MITFORD *Our Village* III. 178 Crockery ware was piled on one side of her door-way, Dutch cheese and Irish butter encumbered the other. **1839** *Penny Cycl.* XIII. 21/1 The Irish round towers are now generally ascribed to an ecclesiastical origin. **1851** *Illustr. Catal. Gt. Exhib.* III. 516/1 Dowlas is a strong kind of Irish linen, for shirting. *Ibid.* 561/1 Laces: Royal Irish guipure; Irish appliqué. **1855** [see SCOTCH *a.* 2 a]. **1861** MRS. BEETON *Bk. Househ. Managem.* 808 Irish butter sold in London is all salted, but is generally good. **1865** F. B. PALLISER *Hist. Lace* xxxv. 416 Irish Brussels is made at Clones,...Irish guipure at Carrickmacross, in the same Co. **1879** M. E. BRADDON *Vixen* III. 319 She wore Irish poplin, and Irish lace, Irish stockings, and Irish linen. **1892–3** *T. Eaton & Co. Catal.* Fall & Winter 33/1 Boys' Overcoats... In Scotch, English and Irish tweeds. **1895** *Army & Navy Co-op. Soc. Price List* 15 Sept. 1094 Irish poplin. *Ibid.* 1099 Irish lawn... Irish diapers. **1896** *Illustr. London News* 25 Feb. (jacket) 4/3 (Advt.), A three-garment suit for boys... In Scotch and Irish tweeds. **1907** *Yesterday's Shopping* (1969) 12/1 Butter ..Irish (finest Creamery)—lb. 1/2. **1909** Irish tweed [see DONEGAL]. **1966** MRS. L. B. JOHNSON *White House Diary* 17 Mar. (1970) 373 Irish whiskey for St. Patrick's Day, the first time it's been served in the White House, I'll bet, and not a soul wanted tea! **1968** J. IRONSIDE *Fashion Alphabet* 233 *Irish linen*, a very fine light-weight linen woven of Irish flax. *Ibid.*, The linen industry in Ireland now, however, produces all weights of linen and linen mixtures..which are collectively and erroneously referred to as 'Irish' linen. **1968** L. ROSTEN *Joys of Yiddish* p. xiii, Yiddish phrasing and overtones are found in, say, the way an Irish whiskey advertises itself. **1970** J. FLEMING *Young Man, I think you're Dying* viii. 106 There was an Irish tweed jacket for Joe and a toy leprechaun. **1973** P. GEDDES *Ottawa Allegation* viii. 102 In a department store on the Mall she stood and fingered Irish linens.

b. With names of animals and plants, usually denoting a species or variety peculiar to Ireland, as ***Irish greyhound***, ***hare***, ***hobby***, ***rat***, ***setter***, ***sheep***, ***wolf***, ***wolf-dog***; ***Irish broom***, ***heath***, ***ivy***, ***juniper***, ***potato***, ***yew***, etc.: see the sbs. Also **Irish daisy**, the dandelion; **Irish deer**, the extinct giant deer, *Megaceros giganteus*, whose remains have been found in Ireland and other parts of Europe; **Irish elk** = *Irish deer*; **Irish moss**, the edible seaweed *Chondrus crispus*, also called carrageen; **Irish terrier**, a large wire-haired terrier, with a sandy or reddish-coloured coat; **Irish wolfhound**, a large, rough-coated hound, often grey in colour.

1375–6 *Durham Acc. Rolls* (Surtees) 582 In 2 furur. de irislams, 5s. **1436** *Libel Eng. Policy* in *Pol. Songs* (Rolls) II. 186 Skynnes of otere, squerel, and Irysh [h]are. **1600** SHAKS. *A.Y.L.* v. ii. 119 'Tis like the howling of Irish Wolues against the Moone. **1670** EVELYN *Diary* 16 June, The Irish wolfe-dog..which was a tall greyhound, a stately creature indeede, who beate a cruel mastiff. **1697** T. MOLYNEUX in *Phil. Trans. R. Soc.* XIX. 505 We shall not have the least Reason to question but these vastly large Irish Deer and the American Moose, were certainly one and the same sort of Animal. **1824** BEWICK *Hist. Quadrup.* (ed. 8) 340 The Irish Greyhound..is the largest of the Dog Kind... It is only to be found in Ireland, where it was formerly of great use in clearing the country from Wolves. It is now extremely rare. **1825** S. HIBBERT in *Edin. Jrnl. Sci.* III. 15 The Irish Elk attracts no small share of attention. **1835** HOOKER *Brit. Flora* I. 321 It [*Ulex strictus*] was discovered in the Marquess of Londonderry's Park, county of Down..now well known..under the name of Irish Furze. **1844** *Rep. Brit. Assoc. Adv. Sci.* 237 The most remarkable of the unquestionably extinct species of the Cervine family is that which is commonly called the Irish Elk. *Ibid.* 238 Mr. Parkinson refers the beams of two antlers found in the till at Walton in Essex, on account of their large size, to the great Irish Deer. **1845** *Penny Cycl.* Suppl. I. 321/1 Many substitutes for Iceland moss have been proposed; one of the best of which is the Carrageen or Irish moss (*Fucus crispus*). **1857** C. KINGSLEY *Two Yrs. Ago* II. viii. 269 Round the burleaf-bed dances a rough, white Irish terrier. **1880** G. A. GRAHAM in H. Dalziel *Brit. Dogs* iii. 34 The Irish wolfhound, being used for both the capture and despatch of the wolf, it would necessarily have been of greyhound conformation, besides being of enormous power. **1892** H. N. HUTCHINSON *Extinct Monsters* xvi. 224 The 'Great Irish Elk', as it is generally called, deserves special notice. *Ibid.*, The term 'Elk' is misleading, for it is not an elk (*Alces*) at all, but a true *Cervus* (stag). It should be called 'the Great Irish Deer'. **1897** *Encycl. Sport* I. 323/1 It is just twenty years since the Irish terrier first obtained recognition in the Kennel Club Stud Book. **1908** A. J. DAWSON *Finn* vi. 59 Finn had won two special prizes; one, a medal offered by the Irish Wolfhound Club..and another..for the biggest Irish Wolfhound in the Show. **1933** A. S. ROMER *Vertebr. Paleontol.* xviii. 356 Among the more interesting forms was the gigantic 'Irish elk', *Megaceros*, with the largest antlers of any known deer. **1947** J. STEVENSON-HAMILTON *Wild Life S. Afr.* viii. 68 A plucky Irish terrier diverted the pig's attention by attacking it from behind. **1964** G. K. WHITEHEAD *Deer Gt. Brit. & Ireland* xxx. 435 The giant deer—variously called great fallow deer and, quite erroneously, the Irish elk—was undoubtedly the finest deer that has ever inhabited Great Britain. **1969** E. H. HART *Encycl. Dog Breeds* 313 The Irish Wolfhound is remarkable in combining power and swiftness with keen sight. *Ibid.* 521 Origin of the Irish Terrier is a subject likely to provide debate as long as interest in the breed continues.

c. In special phrases, as **Irish American**, an American of Irish origin; as *adj.* (with hyphen), of or pertaining to such a person, or to the Irish community, in the United States; **Irish apricot** *humorous*, a potato; **Irish articles**, articles of belief drawn up by Archbishop Ussher in 1615; **Irish-Australian** *a.*, of or pertaining to an Australian of Irish origin; (as two words) such a person; **Irish blackguard**, a kind of snuff (see BLACKGUARD 7); **Irish bridge**, an open stone drain carrying water across a road (see quots.); **Irish bull** (see BULL *sb.*[4] 2); **Irish coffee** = *Gaelic coffee*; **Irish confetti** *slang*, stones, bricks, etc., esp. when used as weapons; **Irish crochet** = *Irish lace* (*a*); *also attrib.*, as ***Irish crochet lace, point***; **Irish diamond**, rock crystal: see DIAMOND 2; **Irish Free State**, (from 1921) name of the independent democratic State of Southern Ireland (since 1937 called Eire, and since 1949 the Republic of Ireland); †**Irish game** (see B. 3); **Irish green**, Connemara marble; **Irish Guards** [GUARD *sb.* 8], an infantry regiment of the British Army formed to signalize the bravery of Irish troops in the Boer War of 1899–1902; **Irish harp** = CLAIRSCHACH; **Irish horse** *slang*, salted meat; **Irish hurricane** *Naut. slang*, see quots.; **Irish Ireland** *a.*, designating a movement to arouse the interest of all Irish people in their own country; **Irish lace**, (*a*) a type of lace that resembles crochet; (*b*) see quot. 1957; **Irish martingale** (see quot. 1958); **Irish pennant** *Naut. slang*, see quot. 1962; **Irish point**, a kind of lace made in Ireland; **Irish Society**, a society founded in the reign of James I to have jurisdiction over the new Protestant settlement in Ulster; **Irish stew**: see STEW; **Irish stitch** (see quot. 1753); **Irish Sweep** (or **Sweepstake**), a sweepstake organized by Irish hospitals on the results of English horse-races, esp. the Derby and the Grand National Steeplechase; †**Irish toyle**, a species of beggar (see quot. 1561); **Irish work**, embroidery done in white thread upon a white ground.

1832 *New-England Mag.* June 490 *Irish-American Literature. **1836** T. POWER *Impressions Amer.* I. 185 The accent of the Irish American..differs [little] from that of the settler of a year. **1891** KIPLING *Life's Handicap* 197 My Irish American-Jew boy. **1902** *Irish Rosary* Jan. 77/1 The Irish-American Press should urge upon the Irish in America a sense of their duty in this matter. **1957** P. KEMP *Mine were of Trouble* x. 197 The famous Irish-American plastic surgeon, Eastman Sheean. **1971** *Guardian* 27 Oct. 12/6 The Irish-Americans are interested in Ireland. **1972** T. P. MCMAHON *Issue of Bishop's Blood* (1973) xiii. 188 The nylon-curtain Irish Americans of the Seventies. **1785** GROSE *Dict. Vulgar T.*, **Irish apricots*, potatoes; it is a common joke against the Irish vessels to say they are loaded with fruit and timber, that is, potatoes and broomsticks. **1846** *Swell's Night Guide* 122/2 *Irish apricots*, potatoes. **1973** *Times* 15 Feb. 14/3 Like the Norfolk Capon (a red herring), the Irish Apricot (a potato)..the Welsh Rabbit is a time-honoured joke. **1877** P. SCHAFF *Hist. Creeds of Christendom* I. 664 The *Irish Articles are one hundred and four in number. **1967** D. T. KAUFFMAN *Dict. Relig. Terms* 253/2 *Irish articles*, the Calvinistic statement of faith, adopted in 1615 by the Irish Episcopal Church in the form of 104 articles, which became part of the basis of the Westminster Confession. **1907** *Westm. Gaz.* 17 Sept. 1/3 The..*Irish-Australian baronet. **1957** P. KEMP *Mine were of Trouble* vi. 106 Peter Lawler, a hard-bitten little Irish-Australian. **1837** MAJ. RICHARDSON *Brit. Leg.* i. (ed. 2) 34 His dress was a coarse *Irish-blackguard-snuff colored frock coat. *a* **1845** HOOD *Forlorn Sheph. Compl.* x, A Box Of Irish Blackguard. **1923** W. L. STRANGE *Indian Engin.* xlvi. 205 For lower-class roads.. stream crossings may be substituted... The cheapest form is a level crossing... The next higher type is a road dam, or '*Irish bridge', for which two parallel curtain walls are constructed across the stream bed and continued for a short distance as flanks up the approaches; between them is the roadway: the downstream wall should be securely founded. **1969** 'M. INNES' *Family Affair* xv. 167 You cross the river by an Irish bridge... It's just a bridge, but built under the water instead of over it... It's really a reliable sort of ford. **1950** *Social & Personal* Dec. 57/1, I am..drinking *Irish coffee, which..is a mixture of very, very good Power's whiskey and very, very bad coffee. I am deciding that my next drink will be an Irish coffee without the coffee. **1959** D. O'NEILL *Life has no Price* vii. 102 Donal ordered himself an Irish coffee. **1966** 'S. FORBES' *Terror touches Me* iv. 37 Everyone..had Irish coffee after dinner... He spooned brown sugar into glasses... Over the sugar he poured dollops of Irish whiskey... Next came steaming dark coffee ..and..cream..poured slowly over the back of a spoon. **1969** *Observer* (Colour Suppl.) 30 Nov. 10/1, 17/6 each... The Irish Coffee glass. **1935** A. J. POLLOCK *Underworld Speaks* 62/1 **Irish confetti*, bricks. **1939** G. KERSH *I got References* xii. 161, I learned the use of Irish Confetti, or Brickbats, at a tender age. **1966** *Observer* 19 June 40/1 An American friend in Amsterdam, describing last week's riots there, said: 'There's just a lot of Irish confetti around.' **1966** F. SHAW et al. *Lern Yerself Scouse* 57 *A cargo uv Irish confetti*, a cargo of stone chippings. **1881** C. C. HARRISON *Woman's Handiwork* III. 217 A deep fall of large-patterned *Irish crochet lace. **1900** Irish crochet point [see POINT *sb.*[1] A. 31]. **1932** D. C. MINTER *Mod. Needlecraft* 103/1 A fine linen thread is most suitable for Irish crochet. **1965** *Daily Express* 14 Apr. 8/3 Linen..covers her drawing room walls (held down by strips of Irish crochet). **1969** *New Yorker* 31 May 92/2 The attached vestees are done in oyster bolillo lace, which is rather like heavy Irish crochet. **1796** KIRWAN *Elem. Min.* (ed. 2) II. 257 The Marcasite found near Dublin, called *Irish Diamond. **1884** F. J. BRITTEN *Watch & Clockm.* 215 Rock crystal..also known as..'Irish' diamond, is also much used by watch jewellers. **1922** *Act 13 Geo. V* c. 2 An Act to make such provisions as are consequential on or incidental to the establishment of the *Irish Free State. **1929** *Encycl. Brit.* XII. 628/1 The Irish Free State, with the status of a British Dominion, came officially into being on January 15, 1922. **1937** V. BARTLETT *This is my Life* x. 144 When the Irish Free State was admitted [to the League of Nations]..President Cosgrave made his opening speech in Gaelic. **1959** *Chambers's Encycl.* V. 49/1 The constitution is considered by the *dáil* to apply to the whole of Ireland..but, 'pending the reintegration of the national territory' to have effect only in the area formerly known as the Irish Free State. **1509** BARCLAY *Shyp of Folys* 14 Thoughe one knowe but the *yresshe game Yet wolde he haue a gentyllmannys name. **1883** *Encycl. Brit.* XV. 529/1 The '*Irish green' of architects is a similar rock from Connemara in western Galway. **1886** Irish green [see CONNEMARA]. **1902** *Encycl. Brit.* XXXIII. 684/1 The Queen..issued an order..for a new regiment of *Irish Guards to be constituted. **1923** KIPLING (*title*) The Irish Guards in the Great War. **1967** A. FARRAR-HOCKLEY *Death of Army* v. 179 General Landon had sent him the 2nd Grenadier Guards and the Irish Guards. **1611** G. VADIANUS in *Coryat's Crudities* sig. I2 Torn is an *Irish Harpe, whose heart-strings tune As fancies wrest doth straine or slacke his cord. *a* **1700** EVELYN *Diary* an. 1654 (1955) III. 92 My old acquaintance & most incomparable player on the Irish-Harp, Mr. Clarke. **1797** *Encycl. Brit.* VIII. 326/1 There are among us two sorts of this instrument, *viz.* the Welch harp..and the Irish harp. **1879** GROVE *Dict. Mus.* I. 686/1 The beautiful form of the more modern Irish harp is well known from its representation in the royal coat of arms. **1969** *Guardian* 16 Sept. 11/3 They only need to play Irish harps..to complete the absurd romanticism of Free Belfast. **1973** *Country Life* 29 Mar. 861/3 A finished harp costs at least £1,300. Happily ..small Irish harps..made almost entirely of wood..can be bought for £130. They serve as a sort of apprenticeship for would be serious harp players. **1748** SMOLLETT *R. Random* I. xxxiii. 291 Our provision consisted of putrid salt beef, to which the sailors gave the name of *Irish horse. **1886** H. BAUMANN *Londinismen* 83/2 *Irish horse*, Pökelfleisch, s. salt horse. **1929** F. C. BOWEN *Sea Slang* 72 **Irish hurricane*, a flat calm with drizzling rain. **1962** *John o' London's* 14 June 571/2 An Irish hurricane is a flat calm. **1904** W. B. YEATS in *Daily Chron.* 18 Mar. 3/4, I went..to tell the Irish of America of what we call the *Irish Ireland movement. **1854** C. M. YONGE *Heartsease* I. xiv. 336 She was..prettily dressed with some *Irish lace. **1880** L. HIGGIN *Handbk. Embroidery* v. 51 Tambour work..is now almost confined to the manufacture of what is known as Irish or Limerick lace ..made as net..with a tambour or crochet hook. **1881** C. C. HARRISON *Woman's Handiwork* I. 94 Irish lace, made of flax-thread with a ground-work of crochet. **1895** *Army & Navy Co-op. Soc. Price List* 1126/1 (*heading*) Real Lace Sets.. Irish..per set 4/6 to 20/0. **1907** E. WHARTON *Fruit of Tree* II. ix. 139 Let me lend you my dress with the Irish lace. *a* **1929** L. TROUBRIDGE *Life amongst Troubridges* (1966) iii. 16 We all had new poplin dresses with Irish lace collars. **1957** M. B. PICKEN *Fashion Dict.* 201/2 *Irish lace*, variety of laces made in Ireland. Best known are crochet, net embroideries of Limerick, and Carrick-macross cut work or Irish guipure. **1937** P. RODZIANKO *Mod. Horsemanship* iii. 94 An ordinary *Irish martingale has two rings that are connected with a leather strap, of about three inches long. This..prevents the reins going over his [the horse's] head as it catches him under the jaws. **1946** M. C. SELF *Horseman's Encycl.* 272 *Irish martingale.* This is a short strap with a ring at each end. The reins of the snaffle bridle run through the rings and the strap slide up to about six inches from the bit. It gives additional control and prevents the snaffle being pulled too far through the animal's mouth. **1958** J. HISLOP *From Start to Finish* 172 *Irish martingale*, two rings joined by a leather strap, about six inches long, through which the reins are passed. It is the type of martingale most used on racecourses and is more usually called 'rings', sometimes 'spectacles'. **1883** W. C. RUSSELL *Sailors' Lang.* 73 **Irish pennants*, fag-ends of rope, rope-yarns, etc., flying about. **1910** D. W. BONE *Brassbounder* i. 14 'Irish pennants' fluttering wildly on spar and rigging tell of scamped work of those whose names are not on our 'Articles'. **1962** A. G. COURSE *Dict. Naut. Terms* 108 *Irish Pennants or Pendants*, untidy ends of ropes, rope yarns, etc., flying in the wind. It is said that it was originally the name given to a flag with a torn or frayed fly or end. **1865** F. B. PALLISER *Hist. Lace* xxxv. 416 The fabric flourishes, and is known by the name of '*Irish', or 'Curragh point'. **1882** CAULFEILD & SAWARD *Dict. Needlework* 272/1 Irish Point can be worked entirely as old Brussels needle point. **1613** in *Hist. Narr. Irish Soc.* (1916) 163 After all which done information was given by the Governor and Assistants of the *Irish Society, that all the monies formerly levied towards that charge is altogether issued. **1846** T. MACNEVIN *Confiscation of Ulster* vii. 214 The Irish Society is a type and symbolical representation of English rule in Ireland from the beginning. **1877** *Encycl. Brit.* VI. 224/2 The separate estates are still held to be under the paramount jurisdiction of the Irish Society. **1634** J. TAYLOR *Needles Excellency* (ed. 10) sig. A2 Fisher stitch, *Irish-stitch, and Queen stitch. **1738** C. FIENNES *Journeys* (1947) 364 A 'seatee of Irish stitch'... '8 Irish stitch coushons.' **1753** HOGARTH *Anal. Beauty* xii. 164 Retiring shades..gradate or go off by degrees... There is a sort of needle-work, called Irish-stitch, done in these shades only, which pleases still, though it has long been out of fashion. **1932** D. C. MINTER *Mod. Needlecraft* 10/1 Intergradating one stitch and colour with another, as is possible with Irish stitch. **1931** F. LENWOOD *Why all this Fuss about 'Sweeps'?* 10 How unsocial it all is may be seen from the excitement over the *Irish Sweep and the Derby of 1931. **1933** W. S. MAUGHAM *Sheppey* I. 12 Did you have a ticket for the Irish Sweep? **1937** G. GREENE *Coll. Ess.* (1969) IV. 425 The great muted chromium shadows wait ..the novelist's Irish sweep: money for no thought, for the banal situation and the inhuman romance. **1963** 'G. BAGBY' *Murder's Little Helper* (1964) vi. 52 When you people come around, it's never been to tell one of my roomers that he's won the Irish Sweepstakes. **1965** N. GULBENKIAN *Pantaraxia* viii. 152 Although I was not a gambler, I did buy a ticket in the first Irish Sweep... One afternoon..the.. commissionaire came in..and he said..'You've drawn a horse in the Irish Sweep.' **1974** A. ROSS *Bradford Business* 48 A wad of Irish Sweepstake tickets. **1561** AWDELAY *Frat. Vacab.* (1869) 5 An *Irishe toyle is he that carieth his ware in hys wallet, as laces, pins, poyntes, and such like.

3. The distinguishing epithet of the language of the Celtic inhabitants of Ireland. Hence applied to words, idioms, etc. belonging to that language, and to anything composed or written in it.

1547 BOORDE *Introd. Knowl.* iv. (1870) 137 In Scotlande they haue two sondry speches. In..the part ioynyng to Ierland, that speche is muche lyke the Iryshe speche. **1596** SPENSER *State Irel.* Wks. (Globe) 623/2, I knowe not whether the woordes be English or Irish. **1672** PETTY *Pol. Anat.* xiii. in *Tracts* (1769) 371 The Irish language..hath but few words. **1763** in *Rep. on Ossian* (1805) App. 18 The Irish manuscripts in the duke of Chandos's library. **1884** RHYS *Celt. Brit.* vii. (ed. 2) 242 The term..is hardly ever to be met with in Irish literature. *Ibid.* App. 283 The Irish word was *caill*, a wood.

b. Applied to the Scottish Gaelic (cf. B. 2 b).

In early examples a graphic variant of *er(i)sch*, ERSE.

1552 LYNDESAY *Monarche* I. 628 Had Sanct Ierome bene borne in tyll Argyle, In to Yrische toung his bukis had done compyle. **1596** DALRYMPLE tr. *Leslie's Hist. Scot.* I. 86 The rest of the scottis..vse thair alde Irishe toung. *a* **1639** SPOTTISWOOD *Hist. Ch. Scotl.* (1655) 9 We oft finde the Scots called Irishes, like as we yet term commonly our Highlandmen, in regard they speak the Irish language. *c* **1730** BURT *Lett. N. Scotl.* (1818) I. 158 The Irish tongue was..lately universal even in many parts of the Lowlands.

4. Irish in character or nature; having what are considered Irish characteristics. *spec.* Used of seemingly contradictory statements. (See also *Irish hurricane* s.v. sense A. 2 c.)

In quot. 1589 with allusion to B. 3.

1589 *Pappe w. Hatchet* B iij, We would show them an Irish tricke, that when they thinke to winne the game with one man [etc.]. **1725** SWIFT *Wood the Ironmonger* Wks. 1755 IV. I. 66 They laugh'd at such an irish blunder, To take the noise of brass for thunder. **1820** H. BROUGHAM *Let.* 5 Feb. in H. Maxwell *Creevey Papers* (1903) I. 297 Your advice has been followed by anticipation (to speak Irish). **1838** GEO. ELIOT *Let.* 18 Aug. (1954) I. 6 Isaac and I went alone (that seems rather Irish), and staid only a week. **1843** F. A. KEMBLE *Let.* 25 Aug. in *Rec. Later Life* (1882) III. 36 We are going out of town,..to-morrow at half-past six in the morning, and it is now past midnight, and I have every mortal and immortal thing to pack, with my own single pair of hands, which is Irish, Lord bless us! **1857** MRS. GASKELL *Let.* 7 Dec. (1966) 491 The lecture was not (to me) so very interesting, being a sort of recapitulation of what he was *going* to say (if that's not Irish). **1891** *Spectator* 3 Jan. 5/1 If we fail in anything, people say, How Irish! **1892** C. H. FRETWELL *Anc. Mariner* 94, I had what sailors call 'an Irish rise', becoming second officer after being for a time commanding officer. **1897** MARY KINGSLEY *W. Africa* 171 There is also no doubt that the Fan mile is a bit Irish, a matter of nine or so of those of ordinary mortals. **1903** H. C. ROWLAND *Sea Scamps* 4, I was promptly addressed as 'lieutenant', which struck me as being rather an Irish promotion, having once previously served as major. **1926** J. S. HUXLEY *Essays Pop. Sci.* 121 To be Irish, the longer it lives, the sooner it ought to die. **1937** A. UPFIELD *Mr. Jelly's Business* (1938) iii. 28 He doesn't seem to mind me courting his daughter, but he doesn't give me a chance to do any courting. That's Irish, but it's a fact.

1970 R. Hill *Clubbable Woman* vi. 192 'Marcus wouldn't dare to tell a lie like that unless it was true!' 'Irish,' said Pascoe.

5. *Comb.*, as ***Irish-born, -bred, -grown***.

1850 S. G. Osborne *Gleanings* 250 Irish-grown flax.

B. *sb.* (Elliptical uses of the adj.).

1. a. as *pl.* The inhabitants of Ireland, or their immediate descendants in other countries, esp. those of Celtic race. ***wild Irish***, the less civilized Irish; formerly, those not subject to English rule, also called †***mere Irish*** (*puri Hibernici*). ***black Irish***, Irish of Mediterranean appearance.

c 1205 Lay. 12855 Scottes..Galewaȝes & Irreisce [*c* 1275 Yrisse]. *Ibid.* 18069 þa Irisce weoren nakede. 1399 Langl. *Rich. Redeles* Prol. 10 Whyle he werrid be west on þe wilde yrisshe. [14.. *Eulogium Historiarum* (Rolls) III. Contn. Eulog. 371 Makamor et quidam alii principales purorum Hibernicorum capti fuerunt.] 1547 Boorde *Introd. Knowl.* iv. (1870) 136 The other parte of Scotlande is..lyke the lande of the wylde Ireshe. 1596 Dalrymple tr. *Leslie's Hist. Scot.* I. 73 The Irishe men and our Scottis Irishe acknawledge the same for thair first and mother toung. 1610 [see Irishry 1]. 1612 Davies *Why Ireland*, etc. (1787) 192 The mere Irish, whom they reputed as aliens or enemies of the crown. 1672 Petty *Pol. Anat.* xiii. in *Tracts* (1769) 375 English in Ireland, growing poor and discontented, degenerate into Irish. 1724 Swift *Drapier's Lett.* Wks. 1755 V. ii. 76 They look upon us as a sort of savage Irish. 1866 Bright *Sp. Irel.* 17 Feb. (1868) 179/2 If the Irish in America ..settled there with so strong a hostility to us, they have had their reasons. 1888 Kipling *Soldiers Three* (1890) 82 Those are the Black Oirish an' 'tis they that bring dishgrace upon the name av Oireland. 1953 K. Tennant *Joyful Condemned* v. 46 His fleshy hooked nose..suggested Jewish blood, but he claimed he was black Irish. 1961 J. B. Priestley *Saturn over Water* xiv. 201 He was a black Irish type, with centuries of rebelliousness behind him. 1962 *Guardian* 18 July 5/5 That haunted 'Black Irish' face [of Eugene O'Neill]. 1970 K. Giles *Death in Church* vii. 177 Have you ever seen the black Irish?

†b. In *sing.* (with pl. *Irishes*). An Irishman. (Chiefly *Sc.*) *Obs.*

[1596 Spenser *State Irel.* Wks. (Globe) 618/2 When the cause shall fall betwixt an Englishman and an Irish.] 1613 Wither *Abuses* ii. iv. in *Juvenilia* (1633) 220 If but by his Lords hand an Irish sweare, To violate that oath he stands in feare. *a* 1639 Spottiswood *Hist. Ch. Scot.* (1655) 8 He was taken prisoner by some Irishes. [See also A. 3 b.] 1719 *Wodrow Corr.* (1843) II. 426 It vexeth us to hear that the wild Irishes are coming down. 1828 Stonehouse *Crusade Fidelis* p. viii, To preach a sermon for the distressed Irishes.

2. The Irish language: see A. 3.

13.. *S.E. Leg.* (MS. Bodl. 779) in *Archiv Stud. neu. Spr.* LXXXII 375/309 'Certis', quaþ þe bysschop [Aidan] an yrischs, 'Ic wepe for þis king'. 1547 Boorde *Introd. Knowl.* iii. (1870) 133 If there be any man the which wyll lerne some Irysh, Englysh and Irysh dothe folow here together. 1672 Petty *Pol. Anat.* xiii. in *Tracts* (1769) 371 In Ireland the Fingallians speak neither English, Irish, nor Welch. 1772 Johnson in *Boswell* 22 Mar., If the Highlanders understood Irish, why translate the New Testament into Erse? 1884 Rhys *Celt. Brit.* vii. (ed. 2) 242 The term Scotti was made in Irish into Scuit.

†b. Scottish Gaelic; Erse. *Obs.*

In its written form, Scottish Gaelic was not clearly distinguished from Irish until *c* 1750.

1508 Kennedie *Flyting w. Dunbar* 345 Thow lufis nane Irische..Bot it suld be all trew Scottis mennis lede. *Ibid.* 350 Thy forefader maid Irisch and Irisch men thin. *c* 1645 Howell *Lett.* (1650) I. ii. lvi. 377 The antient langage of Scotland is Irish, which the mountaineers..retain to this day. 1702 in *Boyle's Wks.* (1772) I. p. cxcii, About one half of the ministers in the Highlands..preach only in Irish.

c. English as spoken by natives of Ireland, affected in varying degrees by the sounds and vocabulary of the Celtic language, and partly retaining older features of English pronunciation.

1834 *Westm. Rev.* XXI. 348 The Irish of the peasants (which is nothing but English Hibernicised).

†3. An old game resembling backgammon.

Fully described in Cotton's *Compleat Gamester* (1680) 109.

1590 Tarlton *News Purgat.* 74 Her husband that loved Irish well, thoughte it no ill tricke to beare a man too many. 1601 Sir W. Cornwallis *Ess.* ii. xlix. (1631) 314 Like an after-game at Irish, that is wonne and lost divers times in an instant. 1664 Etheredge *Love in Tub* v. ii, Here's a turn with all my heart like an after-game at Irish.

4. Often *elliptically* (the sb. being contextually known), e.g. for Irish linen, snuff, whisky, etc.

1784 Cowper *Let.* 21 Mar. in *Corr.* (1904) II. 181 Your mother wishes you to buy for her ten yards and a half of yard-wide Irish, from two shillings to two shillings and sixpence per yard. 1799 Jane Austen *Lett.* (1884) I. 203 Mrs. Davies frightened him into buying a piece of Irish when we were in Basingstoke. 1806–7 J. Beresford *Miseries Hum. Life* (1826) ii. xxix, Venturing upon a pinch of high dried Irish in the open air. 1834 E. E. Perkins *Lady's Shopping Manual* 63 The regard to time and other circumstances which has been recommended in choosing Irishes, should be observed in the purchase of all linens. 1889 J. K. Jerome *Three Men in Boat* ii. 29 Harris.. proposed that we should go out and have a smile, saying that he had found a place..where you could really get a drop of Irish worth drinking. 1893 H. Crackanthorpe *Wreckage* 125 Two bitters and a small Scotch..and a large Irish. 1914 [see Apollinaris]. 1972 P. Ruell *Red Christmas* vi. 58 Irish. I drink Irish. Not this muck.

5. Temper; passion. orig. *U.S.* and *dial.*

1834 D. Crockett *Narr. Life* iv. 30 Her Irish was up too high to do any thing with her. 1860 Bartlett *Dict. Amer.* (ed. 3) 217 My friends say that my Irish is getting up, meaning, I am getting angry. 1877 F. Ross et al. *Gloss. Words Holderness* 80/1 *Iry*; *Irish*, E. and N., passion; anger; rage; fury. 1933 Partridge *Words, Words, Words!* i. 9 Both *Irish* and the colloquial *Paddy* are used for anger. 1949 R. Harvey *Curtain Time* vii. 73 But George's Irish was up. 1972 *Evening Telegram* (St. John's, Newfoundland) 23 June 1/4 'I got my Irish up,' he said, 'and here's a man that's going to fight back.'

Irisher (ˈaɪərɪʃə(r)). *colloq.* [f. Irish *a.* + -er¹.] A person of Irish origin, an Irishman.

1807 C. Schultz *Let.* 15 July in *Trav. on Inland Voy.* (1810) I. 8 The inhabitants are mostly of German descent, and still, in a great measure, retain their national prejudices, and consider all who do not speak their own language either as Yankees or Irishers. 1832 J. Barrington *Personal Sk. Own Times* (ed. 2) III. 35 What would the poor Irishers have done in owld times? 1854 Mrs. Gaskell *North & South* (1855) II. iii. 35 This indignation was tempered..by contempt for 'them Irishers'. 1882 W. D. Hay *Brighter Britain!* II. 283 A big, red-headed Irisher. 1956 H. Gold *Man who was not with It* (1965) xi. 90 I'm a Wop Irisher from Boston. 1973 M. Mackintosh *King & Two Queens* xii. 180 I'm only a no-account Irisher, but I like to pay my debts.

Irishery: see Irishry.

ˈIrishian. *nonce-wd.* [f. Irish + -ian: cf. *Grecian*.] One skilled in the Irish language.

1834 H. O'Brien *Round Towers Irel.* 255 His perseverance had rendered him the best Irishian of his age.

Irishism (ˈaɪərɪʃɪz(ə)m). [f. Irish + -ism.] An Irish peculiarity, esp. of expression; a Hibernicism; an Irish bull.

1734 W. Pulteney in *Lett. C'tess Suffolk* (1824) II. 101 So I, supported by so great an authority, may venture on an Irishism, too. 1737 Ozell *Rabelais* III. 231 This is not a Scotch-ism but an Irish-ism. 1791 Gibbon *Misc. Wks.* (1814) I. 325, I was just going to exhort you to pass through Brussels..a fair Irishism, since if you read this you are already at Paris. 1825 *New Monthly Mag.* XIII. 13 There are many Irishisms in his works. 1879 G. Meredith *Egoist* II. xi. 243.

Irishize (ˈaɪərɪʃaɪz), *v.* [f. as prec. + -ize.] *trans.* To make Irish or Irish-like; to communicate an Irish character to. Hence **ˈIrishized** *ppl. a.*

1831 *Fraser's Mag.* III. 67 He..conceived the idea of Irishizing the fairies. 1865 *Reader* 26 Aug. 237/2 Irishized, however, they [the Danes] soon became. 1869 J. A. Robertson *Gaelic Topogr. Scotl.* xvii. 518 The only language that could have come from Argyleshire in the 9th century was a corrupt Irishised Gaelic.

ˈIrish-like, *a.* and *adv.* [See like *a.*] Like the Irish; in Irish fashion.

1596 Spenser *State Irel.* Wks. (Globe) 621/1 Those sayd gentellmens children..are..therby brought up lewdly, and Irish-like. 1610 Holland *Camden's Brit.* ii. 5 Highlandmen ..which are rude and unruly, speake Irish, and go apparailed Irish-like. *Mod.* [See def. of prec.]

Irishly (ˈaɪərɪʃlɪ), *adv.* [-ly².] In Irish fashion; with Irish leanings.

1571 *Act 13 Eliz.* in Bolton *Stat. Irel.* (1621) 369 A verie fewe of them both by nation, education, and custome Irish Irishly affectioned. 1825 Lockhart in *Scott's Fam. Lett.* (1894) II. 306 A fine lad..very Irishly gentlemanlike. 1907 *Daily Chron.* 23 May 6/4 That solitary English engineer—who is, to speak Irishly, of course, a Scotchman—holds the Nile in fee. 1915 W. Owen *Let.* 4 Apr. (1967) 329 She is.. badly off; and though spending irishly, spends every penny. 1929 E. Bowen *Joining Charles* 64 Grizelda and Doris were best in the Irish Jig; so saucy, quite Irishly saucy. 1959 R. Graves *Coll. Poems* 290 How Irishly you sacrifice Love to pity, pity to ill-humour.

Irishman (ˈaɪərɪʃmən). Pl. **-men**. [f. Irish *a.* + man. Originally two words.]

1. A native of Ireland; a man of Irish race.

c 1205 [see Irish *a.* 1]. *a* 1300 *K. Horn* 1004 He dude writes sende Into yrlonde After kniȝtes liȝte Irisse men to fiȝte. 1387 Trevisa *Higden* (Rolls) I. 347 Irische men reccheþ nouȝt of castelles. 1480 Caxton *Descr. Brit.* 32 They sailled in to Irlande and toke to theyr wyues Irisshmens doughtres. 1547 Boorde *Introd. Knowl.* iii. (1870) 131, I am an Iryshe man, in Irland I was borne. 1672 Petty *Pol. Anat.* xiii. in *Tracts* (1769) 375 An Englishman was not punishable for killing an Irishman. 1724 Swift *Drapier's Lett.* Wks. 1761 III. 111 The arrival of an Irish man to a country town. 1839 Carlyle *Chartism* iv. 18 Let no true Irishman, who believes and sees all this, despair by reason of it. 1848 Bright *Sp. Irel.* 25 Aug. (1868) 159/1 Driven forth by poverty, Irishmen emigrate in great numbers.

2. ***wild Irishman***. (*a*) *Hist.* One of the Wild Irish: see Irish B. 1. (*b*) *Hist.* The familiar name of the Irish mail train between London and Holyhead on the London and North Western Railway. (*c*) A thorny New Zealand shrub, *Discaria toumatou*; also called matagouri and tumatakuru. Also *ellipt.* as *Irishman*.

1857 C. W. Richmond in *Richmond-Atkinson Papers* (1960) I. vi. 317 Besides the grasses there is flax, *tutu* and wild Irishman. 1860 S. Butler in H. F. Jones *Samuel Butler* (1919) I. 80 There is a large quantity of Irishman (the name given to a thorny shrub which, in the back country, attains to a considerable size)... A glorious lurid flare marks the ignition of an Irishman. 1862 *Times* 27 Mar., To facilitate still further the rapid progress of the Irish express train (better known as the Wild Irishman) between Holyhead and London. 1883 *B'ham Weekly Post* 1 Sept. 1/5, I have just seen the 'Wild Irish-man' dash through the station. 1883 [see tumata-kuru]. 1896 *Australasian* 28 Aug. 407/5 It seems uncivil to a whole nation—another injustice to Ireland—to call a bramble a wild Irishman. 1941 O. Duff *N.Z. Now* i. 1 If a wild Irishman is grown in a hothouse it loses its spines and develops soft leaves. 1966 G. W. Turner *Eng. Lang. Austral. & N.Z.* viii. 168 The shrub matogowrie, called Irishman in early writings, is especially common in the South Island where Maori influence is least strong and anglicization is most likely.

3. **Irishman's hurricane** *Naut. slang*, a dead calm (see also quot. 1961); cf. *Irish hurricane* (Irish *a.* 2 c); **Irishman's promotion, rise**, reduced wages; cf. Irish *a.* 4 (quots. 1892, 1903).

1827 J. F. Cooper *Red Rover* III. v. 107 There was an Irishman's hurricane, right up and down, for a day. 1873 'Vanderdecken' *Yachts & Yachting* xxxi. 264 She is like a hurrah's nest, or a billyboy caught in an Irishman's hurricane! 1889 Barrère & Leland *Dict. Slang* I. 488/1 *Irishman's rise*,..wages reduced. 1902 C. J. C. Hyne *Mr. Horrocks, Purser* ii. 27 I've a sort of memory that you got Irishman's promotion for a bit of a mistake just recently. 1915 *Truth* 25 Aug. 295/2 The utmost the surveyor might expect from most corporations would be an Irishman's rise. 1957 A. MacNab *Bulls of Iberia* xiii. 140 He..asked for a job as a picador. His offer was accepted immediately—on condition that he would stand guarantee for any horses that might be killed under him! This would have been an Irishman's rise, even in those days when they used worn-out horses from the U.S.A. at five dollars a head. 1961 F. H. Burgess *Dict. Sailing* 121 *Irishman's hurricane*, a slight drizzle in a calm. 1972 *Times* 29 Sept. 15/4 For many low-paid workers with children, an extra £2 a week may be no more than an 'Irishman's rise'.

Irishness (ˈaɪərɪʃnɪs). [f. Irish *a.* + -ness.] Irish quality or character.

1804 Southey *Lett.* (1856) I. 279 The desk might pass safely through the Inquisition, but what is to be done about the Irishness of Bruce's Travels? 1902 *Daily Chron.* 12 Sept. 3/3 Mr. Cobb's 'man of sentiment' is an Irishman with a broad brogue, who out-Herods Herod in his Irishness. 1930 H. V. Morton *In Search of Ireland* vi. 119 At times this Irishness is a rather pleasant melancholy. 1972 'R. Crawford' *Whip Hand* i. iv. 18 What made Mullins' [a public house] special was its authentic uncompromising Irishness. 1973 *Times* 5 Dec. 18/1 The contemplation of a common Irishness between north and south.

Irishry (ˈaɪərɪʃrɪ). *Hist.* or *arch.* Also 5 **-ery**. [f. Irish *a.* + -ry. Cf. Sc. *ershry*, s.v. Erse.]

1. *collect.* The native Irish, as opposed to English settlers in Ireland.

1375 Barbour *Bruce* xvi. 317 (Camb. MS.) He had apon his party The eryschry [*Edin. MS.* Irschery; *ed.* 1616 Irishry]. *c* 1450 Holland *Howlat* 801 Thir ar his Irland kingis of the Irischerye. 1495 *Stat. Ireland* (1765) I. 51 [To] stirre Irishery or Englishry to make warre against our soverain lord the Kings authority. 1586 J. Hooker *Girald. Irel.* in *Holinshed* II. 44/1 As the manner and custome was among the Irishrie. 1610 Holland *Camden's Brit.* ii. 72 They that refuse to be under lawes,..are tearmed the Irishry, and commonly the Wilde Irish. 1792 Burke *Let. to Sir H. Langrishe* Wks. VI. 336 The spirit of the popery laws ..as applied between Englishry and Irishry. 1827 Hallam *Const. Hist.* (1876) III. xviii. 353 It is not to be imagined that the entire Irishry partook in this desire of renouncing their ancient customs.

2. Irish character or nationality; an instance of this; an Irish trait.

1834 H. O'Brien *Round Towers Irel.* 116 A country which piques itself on its Irishry. 1850 E. Warburton *R. Hastings* II. 247 One thing they used to vex me about..and that was about my Irishry as they used to call it. 1872 Lever *Ld. Kilgobbin* lxxi. (1875) 391 Awkwardnesses of manner—Walpole called them Irishries.

ˈIrish,woman. [f. Irish *a.* + woman; orig. two words.] A woman who is a native of Ireland or of Irish descent.

c 1400 *Rom. Rose* 3811 Hym an irish womman bare [Fr. *Qu'il fu filz d'une vielle irese*]. 1870 Emerson *Soc. & Solit.* iv. 60 A poor Irishwoman recounting some experience.

Irishy (ˈaɪərɪʃɪ), *a.* [f. Irish *a.* and *sb.* + -y¹.] Like the Irish, somewhat Irish.

1884 'Mark Twain' *Lett. to Publishers* (1967) 174 The boy's mouth is a trifle more Irishy than necessary. 1913 D. H. Lawrence *Let.* 1 Feb. (1962) I. 182 A reaction against Shaw and Galsworthy and Barker and Irishy (except Synge) people.

irisin (ˈaɪrɪsɪn). *Chem.* [a. G. *irisin* (O. Wallach 1886, in *Ann. d. Chem.* CCXXXIV. 374), f. G. *iris* iris *sb.* + *-in* -in¹.] A fructan present in the rhizome of the yellow iris, *Iris pseudacorus*.

1887 *Jrnl. Chem. Soc.* LII. i. 26 The rhizome of the water lily, *Iris pseudacorus*, contains a peculiar carbohydrate, called 'irisin' by the author. Irisin..closely resembles inulin. 1925 *Chem. Abstr.* XIX. 2813 Irisin..by the diffusion method shows a mol. wt. of 10,300. 1946 *Ibid.* XL. 550 Of the fructosans, irisin is the most stable to dry heat. 1953 *Q. Jrnl. Exper. Physiol.* XXXVIII. 9 Intravenous administration of low molecular weight grass levan and irisin is unaccompanied by vasomotor and respiratory disturbances.

iris-in, iris-out: see Iris *sb.* 4 c.

ˈirite. *Min.* [f. Ir-idium + -ite.] A supposed mineral, named by R. Hermann in 1841, now proved to be a mixture of iridosmine, chromite, etc.

iritic (aɪˈrɪtɪk), *a.* *Path.* [f. Irit-is + -ic.] Pertaining to or affected with iritis; affecting the iris.

1855 in Mayne *Expos. Lex.* 1879 *St. George's Hosp. Rep.* IX. 476 In addition to her iritic inflammation, there was considerable turbidity of the vitreous.

iritis (aɪ'raɪtɪs). *Path.* [mod. f. (1801 in German) IR-IS + -ITIS (see quot. 1855).] Inflammation of the iris.

1818 TRAVERS in A. Cooper & Travers *Surg. Ess.* I. (ed. 3) 65 By the term 'Iritis' I mean to express the deep-seated inflammation of the eye. **1855** DIXON *Dis. Eye* (1860) 137 We first meet with the word 'Iritis' in a treatise by Schmidt of Vienna, published in 1801. **1879** HARLAN *Eyesight* v. 58 Iritis..often destroys sight by closing the pupil, and shutting off the light from the interior of the eye.

irk (ɜːrk), *sb. rare.* [f. IRK *a.* or *v.*] Tedium, irksomeness, annoyance.

1570 LEVINS *Manip.* 142/14 Hirk, or irk, *tædium.* **1870** *Vera* xix. (1871) 179 [If] Princess Anna had felt any irk, privation, or strain.

†**irk,** *a. Obs.* Also 4-5 **yrk,** 4-6 **irke,** (5 **erke**), 5-6 **yrke.** [ME., orig. northern and north midl.; not known outside Eng.: see next.] Weary, tired; troubled; 'bored', disgusted; loath. Const. *of* (rarely *with*), or with *inf.*

a **1300** *Cursor M.* 6425 Sua lang he heild [his hend] vp ..þof he was irk it was na wonder. **1303** R. BRUNNE *Handl. Synne* 4542 Yn goddys seruyse are swyche men yrk. *c* **1400** *Rom. Rose* 4867 Men therynne shulde hem delite, And of that deede be not erke. *c* **1420** *Anturs of Arth.* 77 The daye woxe als dirke Als it were mydnyghte myrke, Ther of sir Gawane was irke. *c* **1440** *Gesta Rom.* I. xv. 51 (Add. MS.) His doughter was yrke of hym and of his meany. *c* **1460** *Play Sacram.* 917 To Calle to god for grace looke þou neuer be Irke. **1540** tr. *Pol. Verg. Eng. Hist.* (Camden No. 29) 100 So yrke were all men of domesticall discorde. **1576** LD. VAUX *Poems, Desyreth exchange of life* (Grosart) 18 The life is irke of joyes that be delayed. *a* **1650** *Heir of Sin* 54 in Furniv. *Percy Fol.* I. 177 That mery man is irke with mee.

irk (ɜːk), *v. arch.* Also 4-7 **irke, yrk(e,** (5 **erke,** 5-6 **hirk,** 6 **erk, irck, yirke, yerk, urke**). [ME. *irke-n, yrke-n,* orig. northern and north midl.; found with the cognate adj. IRK, from *c* 1300; the compound FORIRK *v.* occurs as early as *c* 1250; of uncertain origin.

It does not appear whether the vb. was formed from the adj. (which would *a priori* be the more likely) or *vice versa.* The affinities outside Eng. are also uncertain; there was a rare MHG. *erken* to be disagreeable, to disgust, nauseate, with freq. *erkeln,* and adj. *erklich* abhorrent, which suits the sense; but the rarity of this, with its non-appearance in LG., causes difficulties. On the other hand, the northern character of the word in Eng. has suggested its identity with ON. *yrkja* (= Goth. *waurkjan,* OE. *wyrcean*) to work, to take effect upon, Sw. *yrka* to urge, press, enforce; the theory being that the notion 'it works me' might have developed in Eng. that of 'it wearies, tires, or disgusts me'. But for this there is no actual evidence; ON. *yrkir* does not even appear impersonally used.]

†**1.** *intr.* To grow weary or tired; to feel vexed, 'bothered' or disgusted; to feel it burdensome, to be loath (to do something). Const. *of* (rarely *with, at*), or with *inf. Obs.*

c **1330** R. BRUNNE *Chron. Wace* (Rolls) 11122 So manye þer were in chaumbre & halle, Man schuld yrke to telle þem alle. *c* **1375** *Sc. Leg. Saints* xviii. (*Egipciane*) 786 Modir als of haly kyrk, to safe synful þat wil nocht Irk. *c* **1450** *Cov. Myst.* xviii. (Shaks. Soc.) 178 In Goddys servyse I xal nevyr irke. **1485** *Digby Myst.* IV. 111 The wounder was so grete, I yrkit to com nere. **1513** DOUGLAS *Æneis* XII. Prol. 302 For the dynnyng of hir wanton cry I irkyt of my bed, and mycht nocht ly. **1535** STEWART *Cron. Scot.* II. 719 My pen wald tyre and eik my self wald irk. **1549** LATIMER *4th Serm. bef. Edw. VI* (Arb.) 117 If I should haue sayed al that I knewe, youre eares woulde haue yrked, to haue hearde it. **1596** H. CLAPHAM *Briefe Bible* II. 148 The wretch yrking at his former fact, came and brought his 30 peeces of Silver to the Rulers. **1598** GRENEWEY *Tacitus' Ann.* IV. vi. (1622) 98 Euery souldier irked with the remembrance of his labours. **1619** SANDERSON *Serm.* (1637) 39, I irke to rake longer in this sinke. **1659** D. PELL *Impr. Sea* 72 An honest heart will irk ill, and fret, and grow discontented at it. **1797** T. WRIGHT *Autobiog.* (1864) 40 My poor old aunt evidently irked with the business.

†**2.** *trans.* To be weary of or disgusted with; to loathe. *Obs.*

c **1460** *Towneley Myst.* xxi. 210 All is out of har and that shall he yrk. **1523** LD. BERNERS *Froiss.* I. Pref. 2 Hystorie.. detesteth, erketh, and abhorreth vices. **1575** *Mirr. Mag., Collingbourne* vi, This ougly fault, no tyrant lyues but vrkes. **1628** GAULE *Pract. The.* (1629) 226 He..irkes the vntimely trouble, to haue sought witnesses elsewhere.

3. Of a thing: To affect with weariness, dislike, or disgust; to weary, tire; to trouble; to disgust, to 'bore'. Also *absol. arch.*

1513 MORE *Rich. III,* Wks. 38/1 This discencion beetwene hys frendes sommewhat yrked hym. **1595** SPENSER *Col. Clout* 906 He is repayd with scorne and foule despite, That yrkes each gentle heart which it doth heare. **1599** H. BUTTES *Dyets drie Dinner* D ij, Medlers..if you deale much with them, they wil extremely irck, and loath you. **1702** ROWE *Tamerl.* I. ii. 614 This After-game of Words is what most irks me. **1848** C. BRONTË *J. Eyre* xxxiv, The garrulous glee of reception irked him. **1864** BROWNING *Rabbi Ben Ezra* iv, Irks care the crop-full bird? **1886** *Manch. Exam.* 28 May 5/5 It was not thought well to irk them by an unpleasant policy of coercion.

b. impers. *it irks (me),* it wearies, annoys, troubles (me); = L. *piget.* Const. *inf.* or clause; formerly *of. arch.*

1483 *Cath. Angl.* 198/2 To irke, *fastidire, tedere, pigere.* *c* **1530** MORE *Answ. Poysoned Bk.* Wks. 1135/1 It yrketh me to looke vppon the place agayne nowe when it is to late to mend it. **1552** LATIMER *Serm. Lincoln* iv. 88 It irked them that they should pay tribute. **1600** J. PORY tr. *Leo's Africa* (Hakluyt Soc.) II. 414 This towne is so durtie, that it would irke a man to walke the streets. **1646** P. BULKELEY *Gospel Covt.* v. 372 Mony times it irks us that we had them, and now have them not. **1721** STRYPE *Eccl. Mem.* III. I. xxx. 236 Then it irked him of his theft. **1742** SHENSTONE *Schoolmistr.* 164 It irks me while I write. **1813** BYRON *Corsair* I. xiii, It irks not me to die. **1850** HAWTHORNE *Scarlet L.* iii. (1883) 84 It irks me..that the partner of her iniquity should not.. stand on the scaffold by her side.

c. *pass.* To be wearied, tired, grieved, or vexed. *arch.*

1514 BARCLAY *Cyt. & Uplondyshm.* (Percy Soc.) p. xlv, Sometime art thou yrked of them at the table. **1588** A. KING tr. *Canisius' Catech.* 72 My saule is irked to liue. **1647** TRAPP *Comm. 1 Thess.* ii. 14 Moab was irked, because of Israel, or vexed at them. **1883** E. C. STEDMAN in *Century Mag.* XXVI. 940 People are irked by his acceptance of life. **1898** T. HARDY *Wessex Poems* 31 You are irked that they have withered so.

Hence '**irked** *ppl. a.*; '**irking** *vbl. sb.* and *ppl. a.*

c **1400** in *Hampole's Wks.* (1895) I. 166 In þe begynnyng or it come to any hirkyng or hewenes of sclauth. *c* **1400** *Lay Folks Mass Bk.* App. iii. 123 Wiþ irkynge of herte. **1513** DOUGLAS *Æneis* III. viii. 11 Sone on our irkit lymmis, lethis, and banis The naturall rest of sleip slaid all at anis. **1602** *2nd Pt. Return fr. Parnass.* III. v. 1468 By his counsell we Will end our too much yrked misery. **1628** GAULE *Pract. The.* (1629) 319 They find this Serpent..somewhat cold and irkeing. **1650** W. BROUGH *Sacr. Princ.* (1659) 476 The irkings of a moment undo the ills of all thy ages. **1887** R. L. STEVENSON *Mem. & Portr.* x. 174 They have more or less solved the irking problem.

irk, var. ERK.

†'**irkful,** *a. Obs. rare*⁻⁰. [f. IRK *sb.* or *v.* + -FUL.] Tedious; irksome.

1570 LEVINS *Manip.* 187/6 Hirkful, *tædiosus.*

irksome ('ɜːksəm), *a.* Forms: see IRK *v.* [f. IRK *v.* + -SOME.]

†**1.** Affected with weariness or disgust; tired; disgusted; 'bored'. Const. *of. Obs.*

1435 [implied in IRKSOMENESS 1]. *c* **1440** *Promp. Parv.* 266/1 Irkesoum (*K.,P.* irksum), *fastidiosus.* **1483** *Cath. Angl.* 198/2 Irkesome *fastidiosus.* **1534** MORE *Treat. Passion* Wks. 1289/1 Vnto sufferaunce for our synne, how lothe and irkesom wold we be of our selfe. **1549** CHALONER *Erasm. on Folly* I iij a, He shall see straight all the audience, other slepe, or gaspe, or be urksome. **1590** SPENSER *F.Q.* I. ii. 6 Yrkesome of life, and too long lingring night.

2. Wearisome, tedious, tiresome; troublesome, burdensome, annoying. Formerly also, in wider sense, Distressing, painful; in early use, Disgusting, loathsome.

1513 DOUGLAS *Æneis* VI. viii. 90 Hevy curis lang Of irksum weir and sad. *a* **1530** *Prov. Howsolde-Kepyng* in *Pol. Rel. & L. Poems* 31 A sity garment is yrksome to neybors. **1576** FLEMING *Panopl. Epist.* 290 The putrified botches and irksome scabs of vice. **1590** GREENE *Mourn. Garm.* (1616) 7 Thou shalt pocket vp much disparagement of humor, which I know will be yerksome to thy patience. **1596** SHAKS. *Tam. Shr.* I. ii. 188, I know she is an irkesome brawling scold. **1667** MILTON *P.L.* IX. 242 Not to irksom toile, but to delight He made us. **1769** BURKE *Corr.* (1844) I. 168, I know and feel what an irksome task the writing of long letters is. **1808** SYD. SMITH *Wks.* (1867) I. 126 It is very galling and irksome to any..men to be compelled to disclose their private circumstances. **1835** MARRYAT *Jac. Faithf.* xv, The confinement to the desk was irksome.

irksomely ('ɜːksəmlɪ), *adv.* [f. prec. + -LY².] In an irksome manner; in a way that tires, annoys, or troubles.

1549 LATIMER *4th Serm. bef. Edw. VI* (Arb.) 117 He dyed verye daungerously, yrkesomelye, horryblye. **1643** MILTON *Divorce* I. xiii, If it [a vow] be found rash, if offensive..our doctrine forces not error and unwillingness irksomly to keep it. **1713** STEELE *Guard.* No. 143 ⁋1 A bar of cold iron so irksomly long, that it banged against his calf. **1860** *Med. Times* 15 Sept. 266/1 Everyone who has work to do should seek bodily strength to do it less irksomely.

irksomeness ('ɜːksəmnɪs). [f. as prec. + -NESS.]

†**1.** The state of being tired or disgusted; wearied or disgusted feeling; weariness, tedium, ennui.

1435 MISYN *Fire of Love* 22 þat godis lufar, þe warld, idylnes & irksumnes forsakis. *c* **1440** *Promp. Parv.* 266/1 Irkesumnesse, *fastidium.* **1530** PALSGR. 235/1 Irkesomnesse, ..*ennuÿ.* **1577** NORTHBROOKE *Dicing* (1843) 44 It driueth awaye irkesomnesse, gotten by serious toile. **1601** HOLLAND *Pliny* I. 186 L. Domitius,..for very irksomnesse of his tedious life, poisoned himselfe. **1721** R. KEITH tr. *à Kempis' Solil. Soul* Pref. 114 Subjects..proper to cherish and refresh the Mind when clouded with Irksomness or oppressed with Melancholy. **1822** LAMB *Elia* Ser. II. *Detached Th. Bks.,* I could never listen to even the better kind of modern novels without extreme irksomeness.

2. The quality of being irksome, tedious, annoying, or distasteful; tediousness; formerly, also, disagreeableness, painfulness, revolting quality.

1533 BELLENDEN *Livy* v. (1822) 401 Fra owre army be laid to ane toun, na irksumnes of remote and fer sege,..may remove the samin. **1599** B. JONSON *Cynthia's Rev.* I. i, Drunkards That buy the merry madness of one hour With the long irksomeness of following time. **1641** MILTON *Ch. Govt.* II. Introd., Wks. (1851) 139 The irksomnesse of that truth which they brought was so unpleasant to them, that every where they call it a burden. **1751** JOHNSON *Rambler* No. 184 ⁋2 He..finds the irksomeness of his task rather increased than lessened by every production. **1884** *Edin. Even. News* 19 Dec. 2/2 Grievances..that gall with a most aggravating irksomeness.

irn, irne, obs. variants of IRON.

irne, obs. form of RUN, YEARN.

†**irnen,** *a. Obs.* Also 4 **yrnen.** 5 **yirnen.** [Early ME. f. *iren* IRON + -EN. (The OE. adj. was *iren* like the sb. Mod. s.w. dialect has *ire* sb., *ire-n* adj. *Iron-en* also occurs in mod. dialect.] = IRON *a.* I.

c **1175** *Lamb. Hom.* 149 His fet and his honde if heo þurh irnene neile were þurh-stunge. **13..** *K. Alis.* 5831 (MS. Bodl.) Hy weren redy in þat stede..And piȝtten hym in wiþ yrnen hoke. **1306** in *Pol. Songs* (Camden) 222 With yrnene claspes longe to laste. **1447** BOKENHAM *Seyntys* (Roxb.) 205 Yche spook..Ful of yirnene sawys shul be set. [**1886** ELWORTHY *W. Somerset Word-bk., Ironen,* made of iron. This use is emphatic—*i.e.* of iron and of nothing else.]

irness, -e, obs. var. *irons,* pl. of IRON.

i-robbed, ME. pa. pple. of ROB *v.*

‖**iroha** (i'roha). Also **irofa, irova.** [Jap., named from the first three syllables *i, ro,* and *ha* or *fa.*] The Japanese kana or syllabary.

1845 *Encycl. Metrop.* XX. 482/2 They..formed a collection of 47 syllables, comprehending all the sounds which are found in their language... This syllabarium, or alphabet, is called *irofa,* from its three first elements. **1868** J. J. HOFFMAN *Japanese Gram.* 9 To facilitate the learning of the Japanese sounds or syllables, they have been so arranged as to compose a couple of sentences, and as these begin with the word *Irová,* that name has been given to the Japanese alphabet. **1890** B. H. CHAMBERLAIN *Things Japanese* 379 The order of the I-ro-ha bears witness to the Buddhist belief of the father of Japanese writing. **1903** C. NOSS tr. *Lange's Text-bk. Colloquial Japanese* Introd. p. xvi, There is another arrangement of the syllabary called *iroha*... This is in the form of a stanza of poetry giving expression to Buddhistic sentiment. **1937** I. NITOBÉ *Lect. Japan* xi. 177 Our language is polysyllabic and is expressed in forty-seven sounds... We call the whole collection a syllab[a]ry instead of an alphabet. In our own language it is called *i-ro-ha* from the first three syllables. **1967** R. A. MILLER *Japanese Lang.* iii. 127 The *kana* symbols have at various times been arranged into mnemonic word lists... One such is the *ame tsuchi* list... A somewhat later example..is the *iroha* list..thought today to have been the work of the priest Kūya (903-972) or of the priest Senkan (918-983).

iroko (ɪ'rəʊkəʊ). [Yoruba.] A hardwood tree of the genus *Chlorophora,* either *C. excelsa,* which is found across the central part of Africa, or *C. regia,* which grows in the western region; also, the timber from these trees, sometimes called West African or Nigerian teak.

1890 A. MILLSON in *Kew Bull.* 240 The only trees of unusual bulk [in Yorubaland] are the cotton trees and an occasional 'Iroko' tree. **1894** H. M. WARD *Laslett's Timber & Timber Trees* (ed. 2) xxv. 307 Mention may also be made of Iroko, a very valuable and handsome building and cabinet wood. **1939** EGGELING & HARRIS in L. Chalk et al. *Forest Trees & Timbers Brit. Empire* IV. 84 The harder, more durable 'Brown Iroko' is probably *C. excelsa;* the softer, less durable 'Yellow Iroko' *C. regia.* **1955** *Times* 18 July 9/7 The good stout hull, framed with English oak, planked with iroko—a type of teak from Africa—and copper fastened, shows not the slightest sign of movement or decay. **1964** R. W. J. KEAY et al. *Nigerian Trees* II. 188 This [sc. *Chlorophora excelsa*] is a very common large forest tree with dark green foliage and distinctive leaves. It is widely known by the Yoruba name Iroko. **1967** W. SOYINKA *Kongi's Harvest* 58 When a squirrel Seeks sanctuary up the *iroko* tree The hunter's chase is ended. **1974** *Habitat Catal.* 76/3 Work top; warm honey coloured Iroko, a West African hardwood similar to teak.

iron ('aɪən), *sb.*¹ Forms: α. 1 **îsern.** β. 1 **îsen,** 4 **yzen, ysen, yse.** γ. 1 **îren,** 2-6 **iren,** (3-5 **irin, -un, -yn(e),** 3-6 **yren,** (4-5 **yrin, -un(ne), -yn(e),** 4-7 **yron,** (5 **eiren, eyren, iyron, hyrone,** 6 **yrone**), 5- **iron.** δ. 3-7 (9 *dial.*) **ire, yre,** (3 **eire**), 6-7 **yer-(monger).** ε. (Chiefly *north.* and *Sc.*) 3-6 **yrn,** 4-6 **yrne,** 4-7 (9 *dial.*) **irn(e,** (5 **irnne, herne,** *pl.* **yrnyss,** 5-6 **irness(e,** 8-9 **airn, ern.** ζ. 5 **ierne, iyrne, yirn,** 5-6 **yern(e, yeron,** 6 **yeirne, hierne.** [OE. *îren,* used beside *îsern, îsen,* = OFris. *îsern,* OS. *îsarn* (MDu. *ijzen, ijzer,* Du. *ijzer*), OHG. *îsarn,* later *îsan* (MHG., MLG. *îsern, îsen,* Ger. *eisen*), ON. *ísarn* (also later *earn, jarn,* Sw. *järn,* Da. *jern*), Goth. *eisarn*:—OTeut. type **îsarno*ᵐ; cognate with OCelt. **īsarnom,* whence Gaulish compounds in *īsarno-,* OIr. *íarn* (Ir. *iaran, iarun,* Gael. *iarunn,* Manx *yiarn*), OWelsh *hearn* (:—*eharn, iharn*:—*isarn*), Corn. *hoern,* OBreton *hoiarn,* now *houarn,* pl. *hern.* The ulterior etymology of the Celto-Teut. *īsarno-* is uncertain; and the relationship of the various types in Eng. and the cognate languages involves many difficulties. The full Eng. type (= OHG., ON. *ísarn*) was *îsern,* found only in OE., though still in the 11th c. The form *îsen,* corresp. to later OHG. *îsan,* MHG. *îsen,* Ger. *eisen,* MDu. *ijzen,* extends from OE. to the 14th c. in Kentish and perh. other south. dial. (at length reduced to *yse,* also in the comb. *ysmonger*: see IRONMONGER). The Eng. type *îren* has no continental parallel; in OE., as a simple sb., it was app. chiefly poetic, but it became the standard form in ME.; the second syllable was from the 14th c. variously spelt *-en, -yn, -un,* and from early in the 16th c. always *-on,* the prevalent 16th c. form being *yron,* on which *iron*

gradually gained, and became universal about 1630. In early ME. southern dial., *iren* was reduced to *ire*, *yre*, found in literature in 15th c., and still the s.w. dialect form from Berkshire to Cornwall. In north. dial., on the other hand, *iren* was compressed to *irn*, *yrn*, still used as *irn*, *irne*, *ern*, *airn*, in Sc. and north. Eng. dial. (See *Eng. Dialect Dict.* s.v.) In the standard Eng. *īren*, *īron*, syncopation app. did not take place until after diphthongation of the *ī*, whence through a phonetic series ('iːrən), ('aɪrən), ('aɪərən), ('aɪər(ə)n), ('aɪə(r)n), came the existing ('aɪən); cf. the syncopated pa. pples. *born*, *borne*, *torn*, *worn*, *boln*, *swoln*, and Sc. *fal'n*, *fawn*, from earlier *boren*, *toren*, *woren*, *bollen*, *swollen*, *fallen*. The 15–16th c. dial. spellings *iern*, *yern*, *yirn*, are ambiguous: in some cases they may have meant ('iːərn, 'aɪərn), in others yern, (jərn), the latter prob. from Norse *jarn*, Da. *jern*. The plural *yrnes*, *irnes* (*-ys*, *-esse*, etc.) could arise alike from *yrn*, *irn*, or from *yren*, *iren* (as in *heven*, *hevnes*).

The form of the original *īsarn* has been much discussed; it has been viewed by some as a derivative, and perhaps adj. form, and suggestions made of its relation to *īs* ice (with the notion of 'glancing'), or to L. *æs*, *ær-*, Goth. *aiz*, OHG. *êr*, OE. *âr* brass; but in neither case with much probability. Some class it among the Inde-eur. neuter words with *r* in nom.-acc., and *-n* in oblique cases (e.g. Skt. *'ūdhar* gen. *'ūdhnas*, L. *femur*, *femin-is*), and suppose an orig. nom. **'īsar*, gen. **ī'sonos* (yielding by Verner's Law **izan-az*), whence the later forms in *-r* and *-n*, and (by contamination) *-rn*. The phonetic history of ON. *jarn* and its cognates is also doubtful. Grimm and others suggested a borrowing of OIr. *iarn*, giving ON. *íarn*, *iárn*, *járn*; others would derive it from *izan-* through *eran*, *earn*, *jarn-*. (See Möller in *P. & B. Beiträge* VII. 547; Noreen in *Arkiv for Nordisk Filologi* IV. 110 note, *Abriss der urgerm. Lautlehre* 195.) Uncertainty also attaches to the phonetic history of OE. *íren* whether it merely arose by rhotacism from *īsen*, or from *īsern* through an intermediate *irern*, shortened like *berern*, *beren*, *cweartern*, *cwearten*.]

1. a. A metal, the most abundant and useful of those used in the metallic state; very variously employed for tools, implements, machinery, constructions, and in many other applications.

Pure iron is soft and of a silver-white colour, but is scarcely known; the metal as commonly used has always an admixture of some other substance, usually carbon, and varies in colour from tin-white to dark grey. It is of three kinds, differing in the proportion of carbon present, and in properties: ***malleable iron***, or WROUGHT IRON, which is comparatively soft, very tenacious, fusible only at a very high temperature, and capable at a red heat of being hammered or rolled into any required shape; CAST IRON, which is hard and brittle, and fusible at a lower temperature; and STEEL, which partakes of the properties of both. Iron is very rarely found native (the known instances being mostly of meteoric origin), but is obtained from its ores, which are chiefly oxides or salts of the metal. Chemically, iron is a metallic element: symbol Fe (*ferrum*); atomic weight, 56. In alchemy it was represented by the sign for the planet Mars (♂).

α. **a 700** *Epinal Gloss.* 25 *Alchior*, isern [*Erfurt Gloss.*, *Alchior*, isærn; *Corpus Gloss.*, *Alcion*, isern]. **c 897** K. ÆLFRED *Gregory's Past* xxi. 163 Đurh ðæt isern [is ȝetacnod] ðæt mæȝen ðara ðreatunga. **c 900** tr. *Bæda's Hist.* I. Introd. (1890) 26 Hit is eac berende on wecga orum ares and isernes [*MS. B.* **c 1050** irenes] leades and seolfres. **a 1000** *Cædmon's Gen.* 1088 Siððan folca bearn æres cuðon and isernes.. brucan.

β. **c 940** *Laws of Æthelstan* II. c. 14 in Schmid *Gesetze*, Ðæt mon ga he to þam hatum isene. **c 1000** *Laws of Æthelred* III. c. 6 *ibid.*, Ælc tiond aȝe ȝeweald swa hwæðer he wille swa wæter swa isen. **c 1000** ÆLFRIC *Deut.* xxviii. 23 Si þe heofene swilce ar, and eorþe swilce isen. **c 1000** *Sax. Leechd.* III. 30 Ne delfe.. nan man þa moran mid isene. **1340** *Ayenb.* 139 Þat nele naȝt sette ine gold, ac ine poure metal ase yzen. *Ibid.* 167 Moche þoleþ þe coupe of gold of strokes of yzen. **13..** *K. Alis.* 5149 The kyng hete.. Armen hem in breny of yse.

γ. **a 1000** *Cædmon's Gen.* 383 Heardes irenes hate ȝeslæȝene grindlas greate. **a 1154** *O.E. Chron.* an. 1137 And diden an scærp iren. **c 1250** *Gen. & Ex.* 467 Of irin, of golde, siluer, and bras To sundren and mengen wis he was. **a 1300** *Cursor M.* 7545 (Cott.) Noiþer irin [*other MSS.* iren] ne yeitt ne stile. **1340** HAMPOLE *Pr. Consc.* 6572 Dyngyng of devels hand, With melles of yren hate glowand. **c 1386** CHAUCER *Prol.* 500 If gold ruste, what shal Iren doo? **1388** WYCLIF *Job* xxviii. 2 Irun is takun fro erthe. **a 1400** *Sir Perc.* 745 He was armede so wele In gude iryne and in stele. **c 1420** *Chron. Vilod.* 4396 Gret gyus of hyrone y-leyde hym vpone. **1450–1530** *Myrr. our Ladye* 58 In lyknesse of hotte brennynge yren. **c 1489** CAXTON *Sonnes of Aymon* vi. 136 Whan the yron is well hoote, hit werketh the better. **c 1511** *1st Eng. Bk. Amer.* (Arb.) Introd. 33/1 Nether harnayse, yrone, nor stele. **1530** PALSGR. 235/1 Iron, *fer*. **1581** STYWARD *Mart. Discipl.* I. 44 A good and sufficient peece, flaske, touch bore, pouder, shot, fier, yron. **1611** BIBLE *Deut.* iii. 11 His bedsted was a bedsted of yron. **1617** HIERON *Wks.* II 337 As yron by yron.. so one man by another might be sharpened. **1677** YARRANTON *Eng. Improv.* 147 The best Iron in the known World, is in the Forest of Dean, and in the Clay-Hill in Shropshire. **1776** GIBBON *Decl. & F.* ix. I. 236 It has been observed.. that the command of iron soon gives a nation the command of gold. **1884** W. H. GREENWOOD *Iron & Steel* 1 Chemically pure iron exists only as a curiosity and has no practical application in the arts.

δ. **c 1250** *Gen. & Ex.* 2451 Noȝt sone deluen it wið yre. **c 1290** *S. Eng. Leg.* I. 187/79 He let nime platus of Ire. **1297** R. GLOUC. (Rolls) 1171 Stakes of ire.. he piȝte in temese grounde. **1387** TREVISA *Higden* I. xli. (MS. Tib. D. vii.), Flaundres loueþ þe wolle of þis lond.. Gaskuyn þe yre & þe leed. **1393** LANGL. *P. Pl.* C. I. 97 Boxes ben broght forþ I-bounden with yre. **c 1440** *Gesta Rom.* I. lxix. 312 (Harl. MS.) And bond him in þe prison, with bondis of yre. **1474–5** in *Sarum Churchw. Acc.* (ed. Swayne, 1896) 19 For ij plates of ire, iiijd. **1825** BRITTON *Beauties Wiltsh.* III. Gloss., *Ire*, iron. **1886** ELWORTHY *W. Somerset Word-bk.*, *Ire*, iron.. *iron* is the adjective form. Compare *Iron-Bar* with *Bar-ire*. *Ibid.*, *Ire gear*, iron work generally.

ε. **a 1300** *Cursor M.* 22207 Wit irne, or fire, or atter beist. **1306** in *Pol. Songs* (Camden) 217 He wes y-fetered weel Both with yrn ant wyth steel. **1375** BARBOUR *Bruce* x. 364 A cruk.. Of Irn, that wes styth and square. **c 1400** *Apol. Loll.* 86 Festining it wiþ irne þat it fal not. **c 1420** *Liber Cocorum* (1862) 36 Rost hit on broche of irne. **c 1440** *York Myst.* xxxiv. 96 Bragges Of irnne and stele full strange. **a 1450** *Mankind* (Brandl 1898) 276 Lyke as þe smyth trieth erne in þe feere. **1549** *Compl. Scot.* vi. 59 Quhen.. marcus crassus, vas slane be the parthiens, the lyft did rane yrn. **1621** G. SANDYS *Ovid's Met.* xv. (1626) 311 To Brasse from Silver; and to Yr'ne from Brasse. **1816** SCOTT *Antiq.* xxiii, Bits o' capper and horn and airn. **1826** J. WILSON *Noct. Ambr.* Wks. 1855 I. 208 Like a great anvil.. made o' wood instead o' airn. **1868** ATKINSON *Cleveland Gloss.*, *Airn*, iron.

ζ. **c 1400** *Destr. Troy* 9133 As pure watur pouret vn polishet yerin. *Ibid.* 10463 Barrit hom full bigly with boltes of yerne. **1447** BOKENHAM *Seyntys* (Roxb.) 205 Wyth hookys of yirn. **1516** in *10th Rep. Hist. MSS. Comm.* App. v. 397 Canvas, rossen, ropis, bordes, yerne, or yeirne, or any thinge elles to them belonginge. **1535** in Weaver *Wells Wills* (1890) 51 A payre of wells bownd with yeron. **1545** JOYE *Exp. Dan.* iii. D vij, Golde, syluer, latyne, yerne. **1577** DEE *Relat. Spir.* I. (1659) 167 A black box of yern.

b. with *an* and *pl.* A variety or sort of iron.

1858 GREENER *Gunnery* 194 If you wish to have a heavy single barrel made from Damascus, or any of the best irons. **1887** D. A. LOW *Machine Draw.* (1892) 77 The grey varieties of cast iron are called foundry irons.. while the white varieties are called forge irons.. from the fact that they are used for conversion into wrought iron.

c. *Med.* A preparation of iron or of some compound of it, used in medicine as a tonic.

[**1753** CHAMBERS *Cycl. Supp.* s.v., Every preparation of Iron is both aperient and astringent in degree.] **1803** *Med. Jrnl.* X. 186 It is cured by iron which has undergone no preparation, but the minutest division of its particles. **1831** J. DAVIES *Manual Mat. Med.* 86 Iron and its different preparations are endowed with a very manifest tonic action. **1844–57** G. BIRD *Urin. Deposits* (ed. 5) 256 The headache occasionally following the use of iron is readily prevented. *Mod.* The girl is anæmic; she ought to take iron.

d. *Geol.* Any meteorite which contains a high proportion of iron.

1802 [see STONE *sb.* 1 c]. **1842** *Amer. Jrnl. Sci. & Arts* XLIII. 358 The imbedded grains of olivin in the Pallas iron of Siberia, and the Otampa iron of South America. **1868** *Geol. Mag.* V. 75 The bodies which are comprised under the general name of meteorites have long since been arranged under two great divisions, the irons and the stones. **1920** *Mineral. Mag.* XIX. 56 In this scheme [of the author], meteorites are divided into four classes, viz. Irons, Stony-irons, Chondritic Stones, and Non-chondritic Stones. **1962** B. MASON *Meteorites* ix. 130 In total mass the iron meteorites far outweigh the stones, since all large meteorites are irons, and the average mass of an iron is much greater than that of a stone. **1971** I. G. GASS et al. *Understanding Earth* viii. 116/1 The basic division [of meteorites] into irons, stony-irons, and stones is simple and straightforward.

2. a. With defining attribute: see also BAR- (*sb.*[1] 30), BOG- (*sb.*[1]), CAST-, PIG-, WROUGHT-IRON, etc.

white iron: see quot. 1881; also popularly applied to tinned iron.

1632 LITHGOW *Trav.* v. 205 Joynd in three parts, with Lead or white Iron. **1665** D. DUDLEY *Met. Martis* (1851) 32 The Author did sell pigg or Cast Iron made with Pit coal at four pounds per Tun. **1745** *De Foe's Eng. Tradesm.* xlv. (1841) II. 165 Tin plates, single and double, called White Iron, from Saxony. **1795** PEARSON in *Phil. Trans.* LXXXV. 343 Varieties.. differently named by artizans, namely.. pig, or sow iron; blue, gray, white cast iron;—soft iron; tough iron; brittle iron; hard iron. **1841** H. MILLER *O.R. Sandst.* viii. (1842) 184 Bog iron, and the clay ironstone, so abundant in the Coal Measures. **1881** RAYMOND *Mining Gloss.* s.v., *Wrought-iron*, also called *bar-iron* and *weld-iron*, is the product of the forge or the puddling furnace, *cast-iron* of the blast furnace... *Gray forge* or *mill-iron*.. *mottled* (spotted with *white iron*), and *white* (hard, brittle, radially crystalline, containing its carbon mostly in alloy with the iron, and showing no visible graphite)... So-called *silver-gray*, *glazy*, or *carbonized iron* is usually an iron rendered brittle by excess of silicon.

3. In figurative uses, as a type of extreme hardness or strength.

1612–15 BP. HALL *Contempl.*, *O.T.* XVIII. iv, This load-stone.. shall draw to us even hearts of iron. **1613** SHAKS. *Hen. VIII*, III. ii. 425 Beare witnesse, all that haue not hearts of Iron. **1695** TEMPLE *Hist. Eng.*, He had a Body of Iron, as well as a Heart of Steel. **1858** LONGF. *M. Standish* i, Short of stature he was,.. deep-chested, with muscles and sinews of iron. **1873** MISS BROUGHTON *Nancy* III. 238 Embraced in the icy iron of his [Death's] arms.

4. a. An instrument, appliance, tool, utensil, or particular part of one, made of the metal. (Often with defining word prefixed, as CURLING-IRON, GRAPPLING-IRON, etc.: see these words.)

a 700 *Epinal Gloss.* 883 *Scalbellum*, bredisern [*Erfurt Gloss.*, *Scabellum*, bred isærn]. **c 897** K. ÆLFRED *Gregory's Past.* xxvi. 185 Sua se læce hyd his isern wið ðone monn ðe he sniðan wile. **c 1000** *Sax. Leechd.* III. 4 Se man.. nime.. healswyrt and isenheardan butan ælcan isene ȝenumen. **1297** R. GLOUC. (Rolls) 6950 Heo stap vpe þis furi yre, euerich stape al clene. **13..** *S.E. Leg.* (MS. Bodl. 779) in *Herrig's Archiv* LXXXII. 311/197 Þe man nom his yrin & to þe brigge it drowȝ. **c 1400** MAUNDEV. (Roxb.) x. 39 Of ane of þase nayles gert.. Constantyne make him ane yrne till his brydill. **c 1400** *Lanfranc's Cirurg.* (MS. B.) 133 Þat he mowe noȝt here þe sonn of þe eyren þat trepanyth. **c 1420** *Pallad. on Husb.* I. 136 Thyn yrons.. For graffyng and for kittynge. **1463–4** *Durham Acc. Rolls* (Surtees) 153 Pro factura de le Milne Yrennys. **1523** FITZHERB. *Husb.* §3 It must be wel steeled, and that shall cause.. the yrens to laste moche lenger. **1563** *Edin. City Rec.* 26 Sept. in *Ann. Scott. Printing* xv. (1890) 156 The said Ihonne had na vtheris guddis saifing his prenting irnis and letteris. **1611** BIBLE *Job* xli. 7 Canst thou fill his skinne with barbed irons? **1703** MOXON *Mech. Exerc.* 66 When you set the Iron of the Fore-Plane. **1748** F. SMITH *Voy. Disc.* I. 41 *note*, With an Ice-Hook, which is an iron shaped like an S. **1824** LONGF. *Woods in Winter* iv, Shrilly the skater's iron rings. **1837** THACKERAY *Ravenswing* i, A little more of the iron to the left whisker. **c 1850** *Rudim. Navig.* (Weale) 126 *Irons*, the tools used by the caulkers for driving in the oakum. **1875** *Carpentry & Join.* 25 Under the supposition that the iron.. projects equally its entire breadth below the sole of the plane.

b. *esp.* An iron instrument used for branding or cauterizing; a brand-iron.

c 1380 WYCLIF *Wks.* (1880) 303 Brent wiþ hoot yren of coueytise. **c 1400** MAUNDEV. (Roxb.) xxi. 93 Þe folk of þis cuntree merk þam in þe visage with a hate yrne. **1541** *Act 33 Hen. VIII*, c. 12 §6 To.. make.. a fire of coles, and there to make redy searynge yrons. **1611** BIBLE *1 Tim.* iv. 2 Hauing their conscience seared with a hote iron. **1613** PURCHAS *Pilgrimage* (1614) 768 The women with an Iron pounce and race their bodies, legs.. and armes, in curious knots. **1856** MRS. BROWNING *Aur. Leigh* II. 699 As guiltless men may feel The felon's iron.. and scorn the mark Of what they are not.

†**c.** *pl.* Dies used in striking coins. *Obs.*

Clerk of the Irons, an officer of the Royal Mint who had charge of the manufacture and use of the dies; in 1815 merged in the Superintendent of machinery.

1483 in *Attorney-General's Rep. Mint Officers*, John Shaa, graver of the coining irons of gold and silver within England and Calais. **1540** *Sc. Acts Jas. V* (1814) II. 378/2 All personis þat.. counterfutis þe kingis Irnis of cunȝe. **1566** in *Harl. MS.* 698, lf. 120 Robert Hornby, Clerk of the Irons. **1656** CROMWELL in *Antiq. Rep.* (1808) II. 408 The office of Sole-chiefe Engraver of the irons of and for the moneyes of us and our successors. **1663** *Mint Records*, Puncheons, matrices, stamps and Dyes, or any Irons for Coyning. **1706** PHILLIPS, *Clerk of the Irons*, an Officer in the Mint, who is to take care that the Irons be clean and fit to work with. **1848** W. WYON *Evidence bef. Commission*, The Superintendent, as Clerk of the irons, keeps an account of all blank dies.

d. *Whaling*, etc. A harpoon. (= HARPING-IRON.)

1674 tr. *Martiniere's Voy. N. Countries* 115 One of our Shallops coming too near the other Fish before they threw out their Irons. **1697** DAMPIER *Voy.* I. 37 Striking Instruments, as Harpoons, Fish hooks, and Tortoise-Irons. **1853** *Househ. Words* 8 Jan. 400 The harpoon or 'iron' as we whalers call it. *Ibid.* 401 Both irons are buried in the whale.

e. *Golf.* A golf-club having an iron head which is more or less laid back in order to loft the ball: see quot. 1890.

1857 *Chambers's Inform.* II. 694/1 The sand-iron comes into play when the ball lies in a 'bunker', or sand-pit. *Ibid.*, When a ball lies in whins or other hazards of a similar nature.. the iron is the best club for freeing it from such impediments. *Ibid.* 696/1 Some few golfers put almost exclusively with a metal club, an iron or cleek, to wit. **1890** H. HUTCHINSON *Golf* (Badm. Libr.) 64 There are heavy irons and light irons, driving irons, lofting irons, and sand irons. **1894** *Times* 5 Mar. 7/5 His opponent used the iron well and played a very good short game.

f. *slang.* A portable fire-arm; a pistol.

1836 W. H. MAXWELL *Capt. Blake* III. xi, Take care and have the marking irons in your pocket. **1888** J. INGLIS *Tent Life Tigerland* 288 Once again.. our shooting irons spoke, adding still another quota to the bag. **1889** BOLDREWOOD *Robbery under Arms* xxxvii, Put down your irons.. or.. we'll drop ye where ye stand.

g. *slang.* Money. Cf. IRON-MAN 1 c and d.

1785 GROSE *Dict. Vulgar T.*, *Iron*, money in general. **1906** E. PUGH *Spoilers* i. 5 The iron you're goin' to give me. **1966** C. ROUGVIE *Gredos Reckoning* iii. 50 He was earning a bit of iron.

h. *pl.* Iron supports to correct bow-legs, etc.

1838 DICKENS *Nickleby* (1839) viii. 67 Children.. with irons upon their limbs, boys of stunted growth. **1884** W. PYE *Surg. Handicraft* xxv. 319 Wooden splints are.. preferable to 'irons'. **1927** W. E. COLLINSON *Contemp. Eng.* 56 We could see.. deformities due to rickets or injuries and the remedies e.g. irons to correct bow-legs.

i. (Usu. in *pl.*) A stirrup. Cf. STIRRUP-IRON 1.

1894 *Country Gentleman's Catal.* 173 Saddles.. with girths, stirrup leathers and irons, complete. **1907** *Yesterday's Shopping* (1969) 304 Gentleman's spring-side safety irons, with Prussian sides. **1955** *Times* 30 June 3/7 He bumped Gawthorpe badly, causing Nevett to stand up quickly in his irons. **1963** E. H. EDWARDS *Saddlery* xix. 145 There are two main variations of the basic iron which are the Bent Top iron.. and the Kournakoff. **1969** D. M. GOODALL tr. *Müller's Pocket Dict. Horseman's Terms* 70 *Stirrup/irons*, der Steigbügel.

j. *pl.* Eating utensils. *dial.* and *slang.*

1905 *Eng. Dial. Dict.* Suppl., *Irons*... Cum. Knife and fork, in phr. *to be a good fist with one's irons*, to have a good appetite. **1943** in HUNT & PRINGLE *Service Slang* 40. **1946** J. IRVING *Royal Navalese* 97 *Irons* (*eating irons*), the sailor's name for his knife, fork and spoon.

k. *slang.* An old motor vehicle.

1935 *Sun* (N.Y.) 19 Feb. 28/1 'Iron' is the dealer's name for an obsolete [automobile]. **1961** J. STROUD *Touch & Go* xi. 105 'This iron of yours ——' began Frank. **1963** *Amer. Speech* XXXVIII. 42 *Iron*, an old truck. **1967** M. REYNOLDS *After Some Tomorrow* 9 Well, it would mean being able to maintain a decent hovercar rather than the.. four wheel iron he was currently driving.

l. Used as a form of currency in Sierra Leone.

1936 G. GREENE *Journey without Maps* I. iii. 64 One could speculate in irons: the rate that day was twenty for fourpence.

m. *slang.* A jemmy used in housebreaking.

1941 'V. DAVIS' *Phenomena in Crime* xix. 251 The bishop, cane, iron, or stick. **1962** *John o' London's* 25 Jan. 82/1 Tools for breaking into other people's premises are *irons*.

5. *esp.* An implement of iron used when heated to smooth out linen, to press down the seams of cloth, etc.; defined according to shape and structure, as BOX-IRON, FLAT-IRON, ITALIAN-

IRON, etc. In recent use: an electric iron (see ELECTRIC *a.* 2 b).

1613 J. MAY *Declar. Est. Clothing* v. 27 With a wet cloth and a hotte Iron, they ouerrunne those lists. **1769** *Pub. Advertiser* 18 May 3/4 To be sold by Auction great variety of Box Irons and Flat Irons. **1833** J. HOLLAND *Manuf. Metal* II. 253 Dealers commonly distinguish these useful implements by the terms 'sad iron', 'box iron', and 'Italian iron'. **1840** DICKENS *Old C. Shop* x, [She] came to the fire-place for another iron.

6. †**a.** An iron weapon; a sword. *Obs.* **b.** Used (without *an* and *pl.*) in various allusive expressions referring to warfare or slaughter. Cf. F. *fer*.

Beowulf (Z.) 893 Ðæt swurd..dryhtlic iren. *c* **1000** *Sax. Leechd.* I. 132 Wið slege isernes oððe stenges þeos ylce wyrt ..wundurlice gehæleþ. *a* **1300** *Cursor M.* 23468 (Cott.) It mai nan iren o þam bite. *c* **1340** *Ibid.* 26924 Quilis þat irene is in wounde is plaster nane mai make hit sounde. **1387** TREVISA *Higden* (Rolls) V. 219 [Alaric] destroyed al..wiþ yre and wiþ fuyre [L. *ferro et igne*]. **1494** FABYAN *Chron.* v. cxiii. 87 Wastynge & destroyinge the countrey with fyre and irne. **1601** SHAKS. *Twel. N.* III. iv. 276 Meddle you must that's certain, or forsweare to weare iron about you. **1608** D. T. *Ess. Pol. & Mor.* 66 b, To make way..through fieldes of Iron, and streames of blood, to that imperiall dignitie. **1639** T. BRUGIS tr. *Camus' Moral Relat.* 211 Such biting replyes ..that..hee would have sought to redresse it with an iron. **1665** SIR T. HERBERT *Trav.* (1677) 131 Undertakes to make the Turk eat cold Iron. **1871** R. ELLIS *Catullus* lxiv. 355 Charge Troy's children afield and fell them grimly with iron. **1898** *Daily News* 1 Aug. 4/7 Bismarck..is known throughout the world as 'the man of blood and iron'. The phrase was his own. Great questions (he said) are decided, not by speeches and majorities, but by iron and blood (1862).

7. a. An iron shackle or fetter; usually in *pl.* Most freq. in phr. ***in irons***, said of a person having the feet or hands fettered. Formerly also, less definitely, ***in iron***, in bonds, in captivity. Cf. F. *fers*.

c **825** *Vesp. Psalter* cvi[i]. 10 gebundne in weðelnisse & irene. *a* **1000** *Ags. Ps.* (Th.) cvi. 9 gebundene bealuwe feterum..and on iserne [*ferro*]. **1340** *Ayenb.* 128 þe ilke þet is ine prisone in ysnes and ine ueteres. **1377** LANGL. *P. Pl.* B. IV. 85 þe kynge..comaunded a constable to casten hym in yrens. *c* **1400** *Destr. Troy* 3523 The kyng..ffor hir tales of truthe teghit her in yernes. *c* **1489** CAXTON *Sonnes of Aymon* xvi. 369 And thenne he made to be broughte a grete payre of yrens, and fetred hym wyth theym, bothe hys fete togyder. **1533** BELLENDEN *Livy* III. (1822) 225 Virginius commandit the serjand to apprehend Ceso, and put him in irnis. **1539** BIBLE (Great) *Ps.* cvii. 10 Soch as syt in darcknesse & in the shadow of death, beyng fast bound in mysery & yron. **1588** GREENE *Pandosto* (1607) 46 Pained with the burden of cold and heauie Irons. **1611** BIBLE *Ps.* cv. 18 Ioseph..Whose feete they hurt with fetters: he was layd in iron. **1653** H. COGAN tr. *Pinto's Trav.* xxxii. 126 The Jaylors clapt irons on our feet, and manacles on our hands. **1676** tr. *Guillatiere's Voy. Athens* 272 They clapt him in irons. **1726** SHELVOCKE *Voy. round World* 26 He would see the ring-leaders.. punish'd..carrying them home in irons. **1790** BURNS *Tam O' Shanter* 131 A murderer's banes in gibbet airns. **1849** MACAULAY *Hist. Eng.* v. I. 562 When the Earl reached the Castle his legs were put in irons, and he was informed that he had but a few days to live. **1884** PAE *Eustace* 124 Boatswain, if those fellows make any more noise, have them taken below and put in irons.

b. *Phr.* 'The iron entered into his soul', Lat. *ferrum pertransiit animam ejus*, Ps. civ. (cv.) 18, a mistranslation in the Vulgate of the Heb. (lit. 'his person entered into the iron', i.e. fetters, chains) followed by the earlier Eng. versions (but not in that of 1611—see above), which has passed into fig. use to express the impression made by captivity, affliction, or hard usage, upon the very 'soul' or inner being of the sufferer.

c **825** *Vesp. Psalter* civ. 18 Iren ðorhleorde sawle his. *a* **1340** HAMPOLE *Psalter* civ. 17 Yryn passid thorgh his saule. **1388** WYCLIF *Ps.* civ. [cv.] 18 Thei maden lowe hise [Joseph's] feet in stockis, irun passide by his soule. **1539** BIBLE (Great) *Ps.* cv. 18 Whose fete they hurt in the stockes: the yron entred in to hys soule. **1768** STERNE *Sent. Journ.* (1778) II. 32 (*Captive*), I saw the iron enter into his soul. **1843** MACAULAY *Ess., Mad. D'Arblay* (1865) II. 304/2 She was sinking into a slavery worse than that of the body. The iron was beginning to enter into the soul.

c. *fig.* (*Naut.*) A square-rigged vessel is said to be ***in irons*** when, the yards being so braced that some sails are laid aback in coming up into the wind, she will not 'cast' or turn either way.

1832 MARRYAT *N. Forster* xxii, The yards would not swing round;..and the ship was *in irons*. *Ibid.* xlix, The pirate..not having been expeditious in trimming his sails, *laid in irons*, as seamen term it, heeling over to the blast. **1846** RAIKES *Life Sir J. Brenton* 371 Neither helm or sails had any power over the ships, which were to use the common phrase..completely in *irons*. **1897** MARY KINGSLEY *W. Africa* 350, I was in a canoe that made such audaciously bad tacks, missed stays, got into irons, and in general behaved in a way that ought to have lost her captain his certificate.

8. = *iron-shrub*: see 15.

1756 P. BROWNE *Jamaica* 179 The slender reclining Iron. This beautiful little plant rises generally in an oblique direction.

9. = *corrugated iron. Austral.* and *N.Z.*

1924 'R. DALY' *Outpost* iii. 28 The Residency was a large iron-and-weatherboard bungalow. **1944** D. STEWART in D. M. Davin *N.Z. Short Stories* (1953) 270 We sat for hours.. listening to the rain hammering on the iron roof. **1948** V. PALMER *Golconda* x. 73 Her banter usually glanced off Neda like hail from an iron roof. **1956** G. BOWEN *Wool Away!* (ed. 2) x. 115 Building paper should be used under the iron above the shearing board.

10. Ellipt. form of *iron hoof*, rhyming slang for 'poof', a homosexual.

1936 J. CURTIS *Gilt Kid* viii. 79 You gets into bed and goes straight off to kip, never touched me you didn't, you great iron. **1938** J. PHELAN *Lifer* iv. 39 Harry had a young iron an' Painter butted in on him. **1961** PARTRIDGE *Adventuring among Words* xii. 58 Gorblimey, 'e's an *iron*, did'n yeh know?

11. *Theatr. slang.* Ellipt. form of IRON CURTAIN 1.

1951 R. SOUTHERN in *Oxf. Compan. Theatre* 171/2 Another curtain in the proscenium opening is the Safety or Fireproof Curtain, sometimes nicknamed the Iron. **1952** GRANVILLE *Dict. Theatr. Terms* 102 Iron's down. **1967** N. MARSH *Death at Dolphin* v. 112 'I'll take the Iron up and you can see Jeremy Jones's set for the first act.' He..sent up the elegantly painted fireproof curtain.

12. Phrases. **a.** ***to strike while*** (***when***) ***the iron is hot,*** or ***at its highest heat***: to act at the appropriate time. **b.** ***to have*** (or ***put***) ***many*** (***too many,*** etc.) ***irons in the fire***: (*a*) to have or be engaged in (too) many occupations or undertakings; (*b*) to have or use several expedients or alternatives to attain a purpose. ***to put*** (or ***lay***) ***every iron*** (or ***all irons***) ***in the fire***: to try every means. **c.** ***fresh*** (or ***new***) ***off the irons***: fresh from school or studies; newly made or prepared; brand-new.

a. *c* **1386** CHAUCER *Melib.* ¶70 Right so as whil that Iren is hoot men sholden smyte. **1523** *St. Papers Hen. VIII*, IV. 85 And now the iron is hote, it is tyme to stryke. **1612–15** BP. HALL *Contempl., O.T.* XVIII. vii, The iron was now hot with this heavenly fire; Elijah..strikes immediately. **1615** CHAPMAN *Odyss.* XII. 487 [He] their iron strook At highest heat. **1753** FOOTE *Eng. in Paris* I. (1763) 13 Then strike while the Iron's hot.

b. **1549** SIR W. PAGET *Let. to Somerset* 7 July (P.R.O.) St. Pap. Dom. Edw. VI, VIII. No. 4), Put no more so many yrons in the fyre at ones. **1579–80** NORTH *Plutarch* (1676) 602 Now Pompey..under-hand did lay all the irons in the fire he could to bring it to pass. **1621** BURTON *Anat. Mel.* III. iv. I. ii. (1651) 393/2 He [the Pope] hath more actors in his Tragædy, more irons in the fire. **1624** CAPT. SMITH *Virginia* IV. 159 They that have many Irons in the fire, some must burne. *c* **1645** HOWELL *Lett.* (1650) I. II. xv. 89 That King ..having too many irons in the fire at his own home. **1721** KELLY *Scot. Prov.* 255 Many Irons in the Fire, some must cool. **1728** VANBR. & CIB. *Prov. Husb.* II. i. 44 *Man.* Is it full as practicable as what you have told me? *Sir Fran.* Ay.. you'll find that I have more Irons i' th' Fire than one! **1751** R. PALTOCK *P. Wilkins* (1884) II. xv. 156, I had now several important irons in the fire, and all to be struck whilst hot. **1762** SMOLLETT *Sir L. Greaves* iii. (1793) I. 62 Anthony Darnel had begun to canvass, and was putting every iron in the fire. **1852** A. GRAY *Lett.* (1893) 391 College work is now over and I can get on with fewer irons in the fire. **1886** OVERTON *Evang. Revival 18th C.* vii. 118 [He] had far too many irons in the fire to find time for original research. **1887** *19th Cent.* Aug. 240 The State..cannot add to its other irons the supervision of all that is interesting in art and architecture.

c. **1683** A. D. *Art Converse* 25 Young and unexperienced ..as they say commonly, fresh off the Irons. **1808–80** JAMIESON, *New aff the irnes*, a phrase used with respect to one who has recently finished his studies.

13. *attrib.* Of or pertaining to iron: cf. IRON *a.*

1530 PALSGR. 235/1 Iron ruste, *ferrvge.* **1638** SIR T. HERBERT *Trav.* (ed. 2) 235 Few of them know how to read, Bellona trayning them up in iron dances. **1756** (*title*) The Case of the Importation of Bar Iron from our own Colonies of North America; humbly recommended to the consideration of the present Parliament, by the Iron Manufacturers of Great Britain. **1785** W. GIBBONS *Reply Sir L. O'Brien* title-p., The present state of the Iron Trade between England and Ireland. **1854** RONALDS & RICHARDSON *Chem. Technol.* (ed. 2) I. 235 The mode of applying the hot blast to lead and iron smelting. **1868–72** WATTS *Dict. Chem.* V. 386 In the green portion alone, there exist no fewer than 70 bright iron lines. **1873** DAWSON *Earth & Man* vi. 110 Peroxide of iron or iron rust. **1884** *Pall Mall G.* 23 Sept. 8/2 The Iron and Steel Institute met at Chester this morning. **1896** *Daily News* 21 Oct. 2/7 The Blackburn iron trade strike was settled..yesterday afternoon. **1897** MARY KINGSLEY *W. Africa* 64 The Bubi is not only unlearned in iron lore, but he was learned in stone.

14. General Combinations. **a.** *attrib.*, as ***iron-bond, -borings, -dross, -filings, -furnace, -gear, -hail, -vein***, etc. (sense 1 c) ***iron pill, tablet, tonic.*** **b.** *objective* and *obj. genitive*, as ***iron-containing, -digesting, -eating, -producing, -using***, etc., adjs.; ***iron-drawing, -forging, -mining, -puddling, -smelting*** sbs.; ***iron-heater, -holder, -moulder, -planer, -puddler, -turner***, etc., sbs. **c.** *instrumental*, as ***iron-braced, -branded, -burnt, -clenched, -fastened, -guarded, -marked, -sheathed, -stained, -strapped, -teeming***, etc., adjs.; ***iron-crust*** vb. See also IRON-BOUND, -CASED, -CLAD, etc. **d.** *similative*, esp. with adjs. of colour: = like iron, as ***iron-black***, IRON-BLUE, IRON-GREY; or = like iron-rust, as ***iron-brown, -red.*** Also ***iron-coloured, iron-like.*** (See also IRON *a.* 2, IRON-HARD, etc.)

1868 DANA *Min.* (ed. 5) 144 Paracolumbite is an *iron-black mineral. **1494–5** in Swayne *Churchw. Acc. Sarum* (1896) 43 Michaeli Smyth pro..emendacione de lez *Ironbondes iiijd. **1874** RAYMOND *Statist. Mines & Mining* 423 A pretty good price is paid for the *iron-borings. **1590** SPENSER *F.Q.* II. v. 7 Hurling high his *yron braced arme. *c* **1400** *Apol. Loll.* 103 Hauing þer consciens *iren brondit. **1610** HOLLAND *Camden's Brit.* I. 84 Those *yron-brent markes in Picts now seene all bloodlesse as they die. **1851** S. JUDD *Margaret* I. xiv. (Ward & Lock) 110 The horned-pout, with its pearly iridine breast and *iron-brown back. **1874** THEARLE *Naval Archit.* 135 The joint..in the bolt hole is *iron-caulked. **1823** SCOTT *Quentin D.* xxviii, A strong *iron-clenched door admitted them. **1693** *Lond. Gaz.* No. 2843/4 He wears a French *Iron coloured Drugget Coat. **1730** A. GORDON *Maffei's Amphith.* 351 The red Iron-coloured, and yellow Coverings of the Theatre. **1843** BETHUNE *Sc. Fireside Stor.* 5 His complexion had in it.. little of that dusky hue which, for want of a better name, has been called iron coloured. **1849** D. G. ROSSETTI *Let.* 27 Sept. (1965) I. 61 The iron-coloured sea. **1909** S. W. BUSHELL *Chinese Art* (ed. 2) II. viii. 26 Bowls and cups with iron-coloured feet and brown mouths. **1901** *Brit. Med. Jrnl.* 23 Nov. 1540/1 It also revealed a yellowish-brown *iron-containing substance within the primitive nuclei of red globules. **1926** *Jrnl. Biol. Chem.* LXX. 474 The amounts of iron-containing supplements to be fed. **1946** *Nature* 12 Oct. 516/2 The intensification due to the formation of the iron-containing complex would increase the slope of the density/concentration curves at the lower concentrations of molybdenum. **1599** NASHE *Lenten Stuffe* (1871) 60 It will embrawn and *iron-crust his flesh. *a* **1716** SOUTH *Serm.* II. x. (R.), Such an *iron-digesting faith have they. **1620** T. GRANGER *Div. Logike* 66 Heate is the essentiall propertie of fire, *yron-drawing, of the loadstone. **1796** H. HUNTER *St. Pierre's Stud. Nat.* (1799) I. 124 Look at the anfractuosities of a simple morsel of *iron-dross. *a* **1631** DRAYTON *Noah's Flood* Wks. (1748) 464/1 The *iron-eating ostrich. **1858** SIMMONDS *Dict. Trade* s.v., Vessels whose planks and timbers are rivetted with iron nails and bolts instead of copper, are said to be *iron-fastened. **1772** PRIESTLEY in *Franklin's Wks.* (1887) IV. 489 A mixture of *iron filings and brimstone. **1839** CARLYLE *Chartism* viii. 168 The Saxon kindred burst forth into cotton-spinning..*iron-forging. **1874** RAYMOND *Statist. Mines & Mining* 332 An ironmine in this region is not deemed of any value..not an *iron-furnace has been built. **1871** PALGRAVE *Lyr. Poems* 103 Across the *iron-furrow'd way. **1477–8** in Swayne *Churchw. Acc. Sarum* (1896) 22 Pro ferramento vocato le *yregere. **1886** ELWORTHY *W. Somerset Word-bk.* 372 *Ire gear*..would mean all kinds of ironmongery, and completed iron-work. *c* **1820** S. ROGERS *Italy* (1839) 187 No strangers to the *iron-hail of war. **1858** SIMMONDS *Dict. Trade*, **Iron-heater*, the piece of metal which is heated in the fire for a laundress's box-iron or Italian-iron. *Ibid.*, **Iron-holder*, a stand for a laundress's smoothing-iron. **1896** 'M. FIELD' *Attila* II. 49 He shall be scourged With the *iron-knotted lash they use for slaves. **1577** tr. *Bullinger's Decades* (1592) 301 We Christians haue nothing to do with the *yronlike philosophy since our Lorde..vtterly condemned it. **1908** *Daily Chron.* 17 Sept. 6/3 The discipline is as iron-like as ever. **1963** *Times* 25 Feb. 5/7 Shepherds with Byzantine, iron-like faces protect their flocks against the wolves. **1674** *Lond. Gaz.* No. 896/4 Run away..a Blackamoor Man..*Iron-marked in his Brest with the sign of a Greyhound. **1710** *Ibid.* No. 4680/4 A dark Bay Gelding..with a T Iron-mark'd on the near Buttock. **1877** HEWITT in RAYMOND *Statist. Mines & Mining* 365 The commencement of *iron-mining at Lake Superior, about the year 1856. **1879** *Family Physician* 809 This condition, known as *chlorosis* or *green sickness*, is readily controlled by the use of iron... The systematic use of the *iron pills is almost invariably attended with the most satisfactory results. **1912** *More Secret Remedies* (B.M.A.) 203 The pills were..a form of Blaud's pill, somewhat weaker than the official iron pill. **1863** P. BARRY *Dockyard Econ.* 127 England is an *iron-producing and iron-manufacturing country. **1871** *Athenæum* 15 July 85 There is not any labour so severe as that of the *iron-puddler. **1820** D. WORDSWORTH *Jrnl.* 11 Aug. (1941) II. 125 Its crags of grey and *iron-red hues. **1909** S. W. BUSHELL *Chinese Art* (ed. 2) II. viii. 29 Coral or iron-red (*fan hung*). **1974** *Country Life* 3/10 Jan. 10/1 Asil game cocks..head and breast enamelled with iron-red flecks over a wash of rouge-de-fer. **1695** WOODWARD *Nat. Hist. Earth* IV. (1723) 198 Crystallised Ores, and Minerals, e.g. the *Iron-Rhombs, the Tin Grains. **1884** J. PARKER *Apost. Life* III. 258 A gate iron-bound and *iron-riveted. **1645** BOATE *Ireland's Nat. Hist.* (1652) 127 The *Iron-rock being full of joints, is with pick-axes easily divided. **1820** SCOTT *Abbot* iii, She rushed to him, clasped his *iron-sheathed frame in her arms. **1876** MEREDITH in *Fortn. Rev.* 1 June 829 A shape in stone, Sword-hacked and *iron-stained. **1915** E. R. LANKESTER *Diversions of Naturalist* vii. 63 A few only iron-stained and yellow. **1957** *Brit. Nat. Formulary* (B.M.A.) (ed. 4) 147 *Ferrous Carbonate Tablets*, B.P.C. Synonyms: Blaud's tablets: *iron tablets. **1777–8** R. POTTER *Æschylus* (1779) I. 28 (Jod.) And land upon this *iron-teeming earth. **1861** J. G. SHEPPARD *Fall Rome* iii. 140 The *iron-tipped arrows flew in clouds. **1933** E. C. PEARCE *Short Encycl. for Nurses* 24 Good nourishing food,..combined with the use of *iron tonics, is all that is necessary. **1973** J. PORTER *It's Murder with Dover* ix. 88 Getting her daughter to take a dose of iron tonic. **1865** TYLOR *Early Hist. Man.* ix. 247 The *iron-using races of Southern Africa. **1879** SIR. G. CAMPBELL *White & Black* 243 The best *iron-veins are..a good deal worked-out.

15. a. Special Combinations: **iron bacterium,** any of various bacteria, found esp. in fresh water, which are capable of oxidizing ferrous salts to ferric hydroxide (perhaps obtaining energy thereby) and storing the end product in their structure; **iron-binding** *a.*, able to combine chemically with iron; *sb.*, combination with iron; also *attrib.*; **iron buff,** hydrated ferric oxide used as a dye for cotton by impregnating the cloth with a soluble iron salt, passing it through an alkali solution, and oxidizing; **iron-cement,** a kind of very hard cement; **iron-clay** *a.*, of mixed iron and clay; **iron-cloth,** chain-mail, *esp.* as made in modern times for cleaning greasy vessels; **iron deficiency,** insufficient iron in an organism or in its food; also *attrib.*, so ***iron-deficient*** adj.; **iron-fall,** a fall of meteoric iron; **iron-free** *a.*, free from or destitute of iron; †proof against the force of iron; **iron gang**

Austral., a gang of prisoners working in irons; **iron-grass**, a local name for knot-grass (*Polygonum aviculare*), also for *Aira cæspitosa* and species of *Carex* (Britten & H.); **iron-liquor**, 'a solution of acetate of iron, used as a mordant by calico-printers' (Simmonds *Dict. Trade* 1858); **iron loss** *Electr.* = *core-loss* (CORE *sb.*[1] 16); **iron maiden**, an instrument of torture consisting of a coffin-shaped box lined inside with iron spikes, inside which the victim is confined; also *transf.* and *fig.*; also ***iron maid***; **iron-maker**, a manufacturer of iron; so **iron-making** *vbl. sb.*; **iron mask**, a mask, supposedly made of iron, worn by a political prisoner in France at the time of Louis XIV who died in the Bastille in 1703 and whose identity is disputed; hence used as the name of the prisoner himself; also *fig.*; †**iron-mill**, a place where bar-iron is made; **iron mountain**, a mountain rich in iron ore; **iron period** *Archæol.* = IRON AGE 2; **iron play** *Golf*, a specified manner of playing with irons (sense 4 e); so **iron player**; **iron ration**, (*a*) (usu. *pl.*) an emergency ration of tinned food, esp. as provided in the armed services; (*b*) various extended and *fig.* uses; **iron-saw**, a circular saw for cutting hot iron; **iron-scale** = *hammer-scale* (see HAMMER *sb.*[1] 7); **iron shot** *Golf*, a shot made with an iron; **iron-shrub**, a name for *Sauvagesia erecta*, also called *herb of St. Martin*; **iron-sponge**, spongy iron, iron in a loose state with little cohesion: see SPONGE; **iron-stain**, a stain (on cloth, etc.) produced by iron-rust or tincture of iron, or a similar stain produced on a plant by a fungus; **iron-stand**, a stand on which to place a heated iron (see 5); **iron-strap** (*Whaling*) = FOREGANGER 2 a (see 4 d); **iron virgin** = *iron maiden*; **iron-yellow**, a bright yellow pigment prepared from oxide of iron; *Mars yellow*. See also IRON AGE (2), etc.

1888 *Jrnl. R. Miscrosc. Soc.* 786 Bacteria which assume a rust-coloured hue were denominated *iron-bacteria by Ehrenberg. *Ibid.*, The oxidizing power of the cells of iron-bacteria must be extremely great. **1919** D. ELLIS (*title*) Iron bacteria. **1945** *Science* 23 Nov. 533/1 It seems unreasonable.. to conclude that an organism is an iron bacterium or that it is developing as an iron bacterium unless there are far greater quantities of ferric hydrate than cell substance in the accumulated materials resulting from bacterial growth. **1955** K. V. THIMANN *Life of Bacteria* xxi. 598 The iron bacteria are of two types, unicellular and multicellular. **1946** *Science* 11 Oct. 340/1 (*heading*) An *iron-binding component in human blood plasma. **1949** *Arch. Biochem.* XX. 170 (*heading*) Carbon dioxide and oxygen in complex formation with iron and siderophilin, the iron-binding component of human plasma. *Ibid.* 172 (*heading*) On the mode of iron binding by siderophilin. **1970** *Clin. Chem.* XVI. 148/1 An automated method has been developed for determining serum iron-binding capacity. **1902** *Encycl. Brit.* XXVII. 564/1 *Iron Buff is produced by impregnating the cotton with a solution of ferrous sulphate, squeezing, passing into sodium hydrate or carbonate solution, and finally exposing to air. **1925** S. R. & E. R. TROTMAN *Bleaching, Dyeing & Chem. Technol. Textile Fibres* xxxiii. 517 Iron buffs are fast to light, washing, and alkalis, but are sensitive to acids. **1971** R. J. ADROSKO *Nat. Dyes & Home Dyeing* 49 While one might deduce correctly that iron buff would not necessarily produce a lively color, it was expected to last for the life of the textile. **1825** J. NICHOLSON *Operat. Mechanic* 617 Detached ornaments.. fixed upon the ceiling, &c. with white-lead, or with the composition known by the name of *iron-cement. **1772** FLETCHER *Logica Genev.* 103 Uncovering the two *iron-clay feet of your great image. **1855** HEWITT *Anc. Armour* I. 238 Beneath the.. chain-mail was worn a coif of softer material, to mitigate the roughness of the *iron-cloth. **1923** *Biochem. Jrnl.* XVII. 205 The result was that the symptoms and effects of *iron deficiency as described appeared in the pigs. **1929** *Trans. & Proc. N.Z. Inst.* Mar. 51 The theory.. that iron deficiency in the pasture was the cause of 'Bush Sickness', was finally adopted. **1956** *Nature* 18 Jan. 336/1 Metal-induced iron-deficiency in crop plants. **1971** *Brit. Med. Bull.* XXVII. 6/2 The detection of iron deficiency anaemia by measuring the haemoglobin content of the blood. *Ibid.* 32/1 Iron deficiency is believed to be common in Great Britain in adult women of all ages. **1932** *Biol. Abstr.* VI. 792/1 'Salt sick' of cattle on certain *iron-deficient sandy and residual soils has proved to be a nutritional anemia due to deficiency of Fe, or of Fe and Cu in the forage crops. **1956** *Nature* 14 Jan. 95/1 In iron-deficient plants there is observed an increase of the soluble forms of nitrogen, with a simultaneous decrease of its protein forms. **1846** *Amer. Jrnl. Sci. & Arts* II. 385 We find in the weight of the two *iron-falls (Croatia, 1752, and Tennessee, 1835) as set off against that of all the stones.., a ratio approximating that of one (for irons) to twenty (for stones). **1868** LOCKYER *Elem. Astron.* §315 Meteors commonly so called, bolides, stone-falls and ironfalls. **1669** DRYDEN *Tyrannic Love* v. i. Wks. 1883 III. 454, I'll try if she be wholly *iron-free If not by sword, then she shall die by fire. **1896** *Allbutt's Syst. Med.* I. 196 All these pigments are iron-free. **1840** *Sydney Gaz.* 8 Feb. in Stewart & Keesing *Old Bush Songs* (1957) 29 I'll tell the Mahers, MacNamaras and McCartys All about *iron gangs and road parties. **1848** H. W. HAYGARTH *Recoll. Bush Life Austral.* iv. 35 Had escaped with one or two others from his 'iron gang'. **1945** BAKER *Austral. Lang.* ii. 44 A bullock wagon taking supplies to men in an iron gang. **1894** *Electrician* 14 Dec. 190/2 In the case of certain transformers specially tested for the purpose no time increase in the *iron loss takes place. **1931** A. W. HIRST *Direct Current Machine Design* vi. 106 (*heading*) Armature iron losses. **1958** E. H. FROST-SMITH *Theory & Design Magnetic Amplifiers* xiii. 366 Excessive iron losses cause reduced gain. **1951** E. E. CUMMINGS *Let.* 10 Feb. (1969) 211 Later or sooner I always glimpse a miserably exhausted me—tortured in his '*iron maid'—waiting & waiting. **1895** *Brewer's Dict. Phr. & Fable* (new ed.) 662/2 **Iron Maiden of Nuremberg*,.. a box big enough to admit a man, with folding-doors, the whole studded with sharp iron spikes. When the doors were pressed-to these spikes were forced into the body of the victim... (German, *Eiserne Jungfrau*.) **1958** J. BALDWIN in W. King *Black Short Story Anthol.* (1972) 278 Then she hated herself; thinking into what an iron maiden of love and hatred he had placed her, she hated him even more. **1962** F. I. ORDWAY et al. *Basic Astronautics* xii. 465 Submerged in this water-filled 'iron maiden'.. a subject was able to withstand 31 *G* for a period of 5 sec. **1972** *Daily Tel.* 11 Oct. 19/7 The 'callous and inhuman' treatment of a Moscow Jewish scientist said to have been incarcerated in an 'iron maiden'... He had been held.. in a cell measuring 3 ft by 18 inches... The walls of the cell were covered with spikes which prevented him leaning or sitting down. **1826** W. E. ANDREWS *Exam. Fox's Cal. Prot. Saints* 262 Fox says, this Woodman was an *iron-maker. **1875** WHITNEY *Life Lang.* ix. 155 The iron-maker.. has occasion every day to say many things which would not be understood by a man of any of the other classes. **1890** *Daily News* 17 Feb. 2/6 If the miners strike, *ironmaking will be stopped. **1752** tr. *Voltaire's Age of Lewis XIV.* II. xxiv. 10 The marshal de Feuillade.. has told me, that when his father-in-law [*sc.* Chamillard] was dying, he conjured him.. to tell him who this person was, who had been known by no other name than that of the *man with the *iron mask.* Chamillard answered him, it was the secret of state, and he had sworn never to reveal it. **1826** G. A. ELLIS (*title*) The true history of the state prisoner commonly called the Iron Mask, extracted from documents in the French archives. **1841** C. FOX *Jrnl.* 20 Apr. (1972) 104 Sterling.. believes that Kasper Häuser was an imposter. The Iron Mask much more fascinating, but unluckily there was no prince in Europe missing at the time. **1858** GEO. ELIOT *Let.* 21 Jan. (1954) II. 424 The iron mask of my incognito seems quite painful in forbidding me to tell Dickens how thoroughly his generous impulse has been appreciated. **1869** 'MARK TWAIN' *Innoc. Abr.* (1870) xi. 75 They showed us the noisome cell where the celebrated 'Iron Mask'—that ill-starred brother of a hard-hearted king of France—was confined. **1893** H. L. WILLIAMS tr. *Dumas's Man in Iron Mask* xliii. 332 D'Artagnan.. asked himself.. why the Iron Mask had thrown the silver plate at the feet of Raoul? **1959** *Oxf. Compan. French Lit.* 460/2 So persistent was the rumour that Monmouth had survived his supposed execution in 1685 that Voltaire thought it necessary to deny.. that he was the Man in the Iron Mask. **1968** M. GUYBON tr. *Solzhenitsyn's First Circle* x. 52 At all times the privileged prisoner's cell was in semi-darkness... The other prisoners nicknamed him 'The Man in the Iron Mask'. No one knew his real name. **1559** in *Cecil Papers* (H.M.C.) I. 164 Now there are *iron-mills English iron is sold at 9*l.* **1581** *Act 23 Eliz.* c. 5 *Preamble*, The late Erection of sundry Iron-Mills in divers Places of this Realm. **1632** SHIRLEY *Ball* II. ii, How do the fens? Goes the draining forward, and your iron mills? **1838** *Boston* (Mass.) *Weekly Mag.* 24 Nov. 91/1 Having visited the *Iron Mountain in Missouri.. I am happy to add my testimony.. respecting the remarkable deposites of iron ores. **1846** *Sci. Amer.* 12 Dec. 90/1 The new blast furnace at the iron mountain is again in blast. **1887** *Encycl. Brit.* XXII. 638/2 [Sumatra]. Iron is not unfrequent, and magnetic iron is obtained at the 'Iron Mountain' near Fort van der Capellen. **1969** *Times* 21 Nov. 27/3 The most poignant part of the trip was a visit to Hamersley [in Western Australia] to see Mount Tom Price, the 'iron mountain'. **1851** D. WILSON *Preh. Ann.* (1863) II. III. iv. 116 During this era to which the name of *Iron-Period is applied. **1874** BOUTELL *Arms & Arm.* i. 3 The third or 'Iron Period', when bronze generally was superseded by iron. **1892** *Iron play [see PUTTING *vbl. sb.*[2] 1]. **1973** *Country Life* 21 June 1806/3 An historic exhibition of iron play by a master of the game [*sc.* golf]. **1909** *Westm. Gaz.* 22 Feb. 12/2 He was also a most accomplished *iron player. **1876** VOYLE & STEVENSON *Mil. Dict.* (ed. 3) 20/2 The ordinary *iron rations for two days should be 2 lbs. preserved meat and 2 lbs. biscuits, supplemented in such manner as circumstances admit. **1896** FARMER & HENLEY *Slang* IV. 16/1 *Iron-rations* (nautical), tinned meat; specifically boiled salt-beef. **1915** 'I. HAY' *First Hundred Thousand* xvi. 215 A haversack, occupied by his 'iron ration'— an emergency meal of the tinned variety, which must never on any account be opened except by order of the C.O. **1918** E. S. FARROW *Dict. Mil. Terms* 318 Fritz is getting his iron rations. **1925** FRASER & GIBBONS *Soldier & Sailor Words* 128 'Iron rations' was in the War also a colloquial expression in speaking of a hot shell-fire, *e.g.*, 'Jerry is letting them have it, lots of iron rations flying about!' **1951** L. MACNEICE tr. *Goethe's Faust* I. 61 O believe *me*, who have been chewing These iron rations many a thousand year. **1970** R. LOWELL *Notebk.* 235 The new painting has to live on iron rations. **1973** *Daily Tel.* 25 Apr. 36/6 When the boys left on their expedition they took with them only one day's supply of food, and intended to pick up more provisions during their journey. They.. included in their packs 'iron rations' of chocolate, raisins and Kendal mint cake. **1909** *Westm. Gaz.* 28 May 12/3 Maxwell.. had made a splendid *iron shot. **1877** RAYMOND *Statist. Mines & Mining* 4 Leaving *iron-sponge in the ore, which would greatly complicate the subsequent treatment. **1880** *Spon's Encycl. Manuf.* I. 700 (*Coffee*) A minute fungus named *Depazea maculosa*, which causes the so-called '*iron stain', circular or elliptical blotches of an ochreish-yellow colour. **1882** ROSA MULHOLLAND *4 Little Mischiefs* xiii. 158 Last of all came the hot iron, with a little *iron-stand to hold it. *c* **1895** B. STOKER *Squaw* in *B. Stoker Bedside Compan.* (1973) 123 When we got back to the chamber we found Hutcheson still opposite the *Iron Virgin. **1906** J. HUNEKER *Melomaniacs* 273 You remember the summer I spent at Nuremberg digging up the old legend, and the numberless times I visited the torture chamber where stands the real Iron Virgin, her interior studded with horrid spikes? **1973** C. OSBORNE in B. Stoker *B. Stoker Bedside Compan.* 11 'The Squaw'.. involves a torture device which Bram had examined in Nuremburg, a contraption known as the 'Iron Virgin'. **1860** WEALE *Dict. Terms*, **Iron yellow*, jaune de fer, or jaune de Mars, etc., is a bright iron ochre, prepared artificially, of the nature of sienna earth.

b. Esp. in names of chemical compounds and minerals; as ***iron carbide***, ***chloride***, ***iodide***, ***salts***, ***sulphate***, etc. (where FERRIC and FERROUS, q.v., or the forms *carbide of iron*, etc., are more usual); **iron-clay**, same as *clay ironstone* (see CLAY *sb.* 9); **iron-flint**, a name for ferruginous quartz; **iron-glance**, specular iron-ore (see GLANCE *sb.*[2]); **iron-monticellite** [tr. G. *eisenmonticellit* (C. Doelter *Handb. d. Mineralchem.* (1914) II. I. 499)], a silicate of calcium and iron, $CaFeSiO_4$, analogous to monticellite, found as a constituent of slag and more recently as a natural mineral (kirschsteinite); **iron pan** (see quot. and PAN *sb.*, and cf. HARD-PAN); **iron pyrites**, native bisulphuret of iron (see PYRITES). See also IRON ALUM, IRONSTONE, etc.

1890 SIR F. A. ABEL *Pres. Addr. Brit. Assoc.*, The elimination, within the mass, of carbon as an *iron-carbide perfectly stable at low temperatures. **1877** RAYMOND *Statist. Mines & Mining* 397 To repair unavoidable losses in the *iron-chloride of the bath. **1811** PINKERTON *Petral.* II. 49 The *eisenkiesel*, or *iron-flint of the Germans, is only found in veins. **1843** PORTLOCK *Geol.* 226 Silicate of Iron.. occurs associated with Iron-flint at Tullybrick, Ballynascreen. **1805–17** R. JAMESON *Char. Min.* (ed. 3) 256 Dissimilar streak, as in specular iron-ore, or *iron-glance. **1883** A. H. CHURCH *Precious Stones* vii. 88 Black hæmatite is an oxide of iron occurring under several common names, as specular iron ore, iron glance, and micaceous iron ore. **1843** PORTLOCK *Geol.* 225 Micaceous Iron Ore.. associated with *Iron Jasper, and slightly titaniferous. **1937** *Mineral. Mag.* XXIV. 613 *Iron-monticellite. **1950** *Jrnl. Amer. Ceramic Soc.* XXXIII. 164/2 Iron-monticellite ($CaFeSiO_4$) is a compound that forms an unbroken series of solid solutions with fayalite (Fe_2SiO_4). **1957** *Mineral. Mag.* XXXI. 698 (*heading*) Kirschsteinite, a natural analogue to synthetic iron monticellite, from the Belgian Congo. **1840** *Outl. Flemish Husbandry* in *Brit. Husbandry* III. II. ii. 12 Between the sand and the loam, an indurated crust of earth cemented by carbonate of iron, which is well known to all improvers of poor sands by the name of the *iron pan. **1847** *Nat. Cycl.* II. 913 A loose sandy surface soil, beneath which is an impervious stratum, called the *iron pan*, formed by the deposition of iron particles from the sand. **1949** *Antiquity* XXIII. 35 A thick layer of the same blue clay.. was incorporated in the body of the cairn between two layers of stones: it had been trampled down and iron-pan had formed on it. **1961** *Listener* 12 Oct. 559/1 The soil is a 'podsol', with its contrasting dark, humic, white-leached, and iron-pan layers. **1805–17** R. JAMESON *Char. Min.* (ed. 3) 110 The convexity is parallel with the sides, as in *iron-pyrites. **1853** W. GREGORY *Inorg. Chem.* (ed. 3) 216 *Iron Pyrites*,.. a very abundant mineral, of a yellow colour and metallic lustre, crystallising in cubes or octahedrons. **1879** *St. George's Hosp. Rep.* IX. 43 Zinc sulphate in progressive doses, with *iron sulphate.

†**iron**, *sb.*[2] *Obs.* Also 7 iran. [app. a var. of *eren*, ERNE, eagle. The spelling may be due to confusion with *ern*, dial. form of prec.] A variant of ERNE, eagle; explained in 17th c. dicts. as, A male eagle.

1623 COCKERAM III, *Hawks*, An *Eagle*, the male is called an *Iran*. *a* **1683** WALTON *Angler* i. (1886) 17 There is of short-winged hawks, The eagle and iron. **1688** R. HOLME *Armoury* II. 236/1 An *Iron* is the Male of an Eagle.

iron ('aɪən), *a.* Forms: see IRON *sb.* [OE. *ísern*, *ísen*, *íren*, for **ísern-en*, etc., corresp. to Goth. *eisarn-eins*, OHG. *îsarn-în*, *îsern-in*, MHG. *îser-in*, *îser-en*, *îser-n*, Ger. *eiser-n*, MDu. *iser-ijn*, *-in*, *-en*, Du. *ijzer-en*.

The OE. forms, though identical in the nom. with the sb. (app. through loss of the adj. ending *-en*, after *-n* of the sb.) were real adjs., so inflected and entering into concord with sbs., as seen in sense 1. During the ME. period the inflexions disappeared, first in the northern dialect, and last in the south (where the pl. in *-e* survived to *c* 1400). The adj. was thenceforth indistinguishable from the attributive use of the sb. (as in *gold*, *silver*, *brass*, for *golden*, *silvern*, *brazen*), which again is largely owing to resolution of OE. compounds such as *íren-bend*, *íren-byrne*, *ísern-scur*, etc.; but the feeling of its being an adj. often permits the use of *iron* in senses and constructions in which it is parallel to *golden*, *brazen*, rather than to *gold*, *brass*. But in most modern uses it is impossible to distinguish it from the sb. used attrib., from which it is here separated on historical grounds. An actual derivative adj. is found in IRNEN.]

1. Of iron; consisting or formed of iron. (L. *ferreus*.)

Beowulf (Z.) 2829 Ac him irenna ecȝa for-namon. *c* **825** *Vesp. Psalter* ii. 9 Ðu reces hie in ȝerde iserre. *Ibid.* cxlix. 8 To ȝebindenne.. eðele heara in bendum irnum. *c* **897** K. ÆLFRED *Gregory's Past.* xxi. 165 Sete iserne weall betuh ðe and ða burh. ? *a* **900** *O.E. Martyrol.* 142 Se casere hine het swingan mid irenum gyrdum. **971** *Blickl. Hom.* 43 Þonne bið he ȝeteald to þære fyrenan eá, and to þæm isenan hoce. *a* **1000** *Cædmon's Dan.* 520 Het eac ȝebindan beam.. ærenum clammum and isernum. *c* **1000** ÆLFRIC *Hom.* I. 424 Lecgað ða isenan clutas hate glowende to his sidan. *c* **1175** *Lamb. Hom.* 121 Mid irenen Neilen he wes on þere rode ifestned. **1297** R. GLOUC. (Rolls) 6890 Lat nime foure yrene ssares.. al a fure. *a* **1300** *Cursor M.* 23240 Þaa dintes ar ful fers and fell, herder þan es here irinn mell. **1387** TREVISA *Higden* (Rolls) VI. 427 Þe foure irene nayles þat Crist was i-nayled with to þe rode. *c* **1400** MAUNDEV. (Roxb.) viii. 30 Enclosed with hie walles and yrne ȝates. **1483** *Cath. Angl.* 198/1 Iren, *ferrum*, *ferreus*. **1532** *Inv.* in J. Noake *Worcester Mon.* (1866) 157 A brasen morter, with a yerne pestell. **1549** *Act 3 & 4 Edw. VI*, c. 2 §7 No Person shall.. occupy any Yeron Cards or Pickards, in rowing of any set Cloth. **1611** BIBLE *Deut.* xxvii. 5 Thou shalt not lift vp any yron toole vpon them. **1697** DRYDEN *Virg. Georg.* I. 220 First Ceres.. arm'd with Iron Shares the crooked Plough. **1764** GOLDSM. *Trav.* 436 Luke's iron crown, and Damien's

bed of steel. **1861** M. PATTISON *Ess.* (1889) I. 47 An iron helmet and harness.

2. Having the appearance of iron; of the colour of iron (or iron-rust).

1613 PURCHAS *Pilgrimage* (1614) 229 Hard stone of yron colour. **1632** J. HAYWARD tr. *Biondi's Eromena* 60 A Knight of a low stature, and iron hue. **1697** DRYDEN *Virg. Georg.* I. 630 The Sun.. In Iron Clouds conceal'd the Publick Light. *a* **1728** WOODWARD (J.), Some of them are of an iron red, and very bright. **1871** PALGRAVE *Lyr. Poems* 85 Earth all one tomb lies round me, Domed with an iron sky.

3. *fig.* Resembling, or figured as resembling, iron in some characteristic quality, esp. hardness.

a. Extremely hard or strong (physically).

1382 WYCLIF *Isa.* xlviii. 4, I kneȝ forsothe for thou art hard, and an irene senewe thin haterel, and thi frount brasene [**1611** thy necke is an yron Sinew]. **1772** HOLWEL in *Phil. Trans.* LXII. 128 Acorns, saved from a tree.. of the iron or wainscot species. **1798** WELLINGTON in Owen *Wellesley's Desp.* 764 We have now that iron frontier. **1834** MEDWIN *Angler in Wales* I. 195 The compact and iron nature of the ground.

b. Extremely hardy or robust; capable of great endurance.

1617 T. CAMPION *Elegy Pr. Henry* Wks. (Bullen) 137 How fit to stand in troops of iron heads. **1627** tr. *Bacon's Life & Death* (1651) 16 A Man of an Iron body and minde. **1816** BYRON *Siege Cor.* xxv, Though aged, he was so iron of limb, Few of our youth could cope with him. **1833** ALISON *Hist. Europe* i. §4 (1849–50) I. 51 The iron and disciplined bands of Cromwell. *a* **1864** J. D. BURNS *Mem. & Rem.* (1879) 338 The iron frame wasted by inward trouble.

c. Firm, inflexible; stubborn, obstinate, unyielding. ***iron hand***: in var. phrases with *velvet glove* indicative of firmness or inflexibility combined with apparent softness or gentleness; also, formerly in Australia, the closure (see quots. 1876, 1883).

1602–17 HIERON *Wks.* I. 8 Begge we of God therefore, that He would bend our yron necke. **1703** ROWE *Fair Penit.* v. i. 1790, I have held the Ballance with an Iron Hand. **1849** MACAULAY *Hist. Eng.* ix. II. 476 The iron stoicism of William never gave way. **1849** ROBERTSON *Serm.* Ser. I. iv. (1866) 76 No iron strength of mind. **1850** T. CARLYLE *Latter-Day Pamph.* ii. 8 Soft of speech and manner, yet with an inflexible rigour of command..'iron hand in a velvet glove', as Napoleon defined it. **1852** TENNYSON *Death Wellington* viii, Their ever-loyal iron leader's fame. **1854** J. S. C. ABBOTT *Napoleon* (1855) I. iii. 58 With the same exhaustless, iron, diligence. **1876** *Victorian Hansard* 20 Jan. 2002 They [*sc.* the Government] have dealt with the Opposition with a velvet glove; but the iron hand is beneath, and they shall feel it. **1883** G. W. RUSDEN *Hist. Austral.* III. 406 The *clôture*, or the 'iron hand', as McCulloch's resolution was called, was adopted in Victoria, for one session. **1899** G. MATHESON *Stud. Portrait Christ* xii. 168 There is no grasp so iron as the grasp with which an idea holds. **1925** WODEHOUSE *Carry on, Jeeves!* i. 14 You have to keep these fellows in their place, don't you know. You have to work the good old iron-hand-in-the-velvet-glove wheeze. **1941** S. WOOD *Murder of Novelist* (1946) xvi. 123 She.. runs the town.. with an iron hand. And no nonsense about a velvet glove. **1942** R. A. J. WALLING *Corpse with Eerie Eye* vi. 177 The velvet glove and the iron hand are outmoded. **1963** *Times* 2 Feb. 7/2 Mr. Winston Field, who has so far shown only the velvet glove since he was elected Prime Minister of Southern Rhodesia in December, today revealed the iron hand expected of Rhodesian Front Government when he announced a Bill to introduce the death penalty by hanging for various offences, including the throwing of petrol bombs.

†**d.** Unimpressionable, 'stony'. *Obs.*

1596 SPENSER *F.Q.* v. x. 28 Powring forth their bloud in brutishe wize, That any yron eyes to see it would agnize. **1607** HIERON *Wks.* I. 439 The iron deadnesse of mens hearts. **1651** *Raleigh's Ghost* 13 There is no country so barbarous, or of so iron and hard a disposition.

e. Harsh, cruel, merciless; stern, severe.

1591 SPENSER *M. Hubberd* 254 This yron world.. Brings downe the stowtest hearts to lowest state. **1665** SIR T. HERBERT *Trav.* (1677) 136 Abumansor one would think was born to an Iron destiny. **1796** BURKE *Let. Regic. Peace* iv. Wks. IX. 20 The first Republick in the World.. is under her iron yoke. **1871** R. ELLIS *Catullus* lxiv. 203 Words which on iron deeds did sue for deadly requital.

f. Of or pertaining to the IRON AGE (q.v.); 'of baser vein', debased; wicked. (Sometimes mixed with prec. sense.)

a **1592** H. SMITH *Serm.* (Tegg's ed.) I. 241 Look not for a golden life in an iron world. **1614** RALEIGH *Hist. World* I. (1634) 155 But they.. account the times injurious and yron. **1697** DRYDEN *Virg. Past.* IX. 16 In these hard Iron Times. **1805** SCOTT *Last Minstr.* I. Introd. 21 The bigots of the iron time.

g. Of metallic tone, harsh, unmusical.

1871 SWINBURNE *Songs bef. Sunrise* Prel. 105 Heard their songs' iron cadences.

h. In phr. ***iron sleep*** or ***slumber***, tr. L. *ferreus somnus* (Virg. *Æn.* x. 745). Chiefly *poet.*

1624 *Trag. Nero* III. ii. in Bullen *O. Pl.* (1882) I. 49 Well, he shall sleepe the Iron sleepe of death. **1685** DRYDEN *Thren. August.* ii. 70 An iron slumber sat on his majestic eyes. **1697** —— *Virg. Georg.* IV. 717 An Iron Slumber shuts my swimming Eyes. **1835** LYTTON *Rienzi* VI. v, His face was still locked, as in a vice, with that iron sleep.

4. Combinations and special collocations.

a. Parasynthetic combinations (in *lit.* and *fig.* senses): as ***iron-banded***, ***-barred***, ***-bowelled***, ***-coated***, ***-faced***, ***-fisted*** (close-fisted, niggardly), ***-grated***, ***-hooped***, ***-jawed***, ***-knobbed***, ***-mailed***, ***-minded***, ***-mooded***, ***-nerved***, ***-pated***, ***-railed***, ***-ribbed***, ***-sceptred***, ***-souled***, ***-studded***, ***-visaged***, ***-willed***, ***-winged***, ***-witted*** (dull-witted, stupid: see 3 d), ***-worded*** adjs.

1812 SCOTT *Rokeby* IV. xxv, Mortham's *iron-banded chests. **1600** ROWLANDS *Lett. Humours Blood* VII. 84 To fill old *Iron barred chests, he rakes. **1604** MIDDLETON *Father Hubburd's T.* Wks. (Bullen) VIII. 104 An usurer's great iron-barred chest. **1647** TRAPP *Comm. Matt.* vi. 24 An *iron-bowelled wretch. **1876** PREECE & SIVEWRIGHT *Telegraphy* 187 Upon no account should *iron-capped insulators be made use of upon such lines. **1590** SPENSER *F.Q.* I. vii. 2 Disarmed all of *yron-coted Plate. **1735** THOMSON *Liberty* III. 263 The deep phalanx.. Of iron-coated Macedon. **1677** W. HUGHES *Man of Sin* III. iii. 102 An *Iron-fac'd and Leaden-hearted.. Person. **1852** *Iron-fisted [see IRON-HEADED 2]. **1883** J. T. TROWBRIDGE in *Harper's Mag.* Jan. 213/1 An iron-fisted miser. **1876** OUIDA *Winter City* ii. 13 A giant murderer *iron-gloved to slay you. **1814** SCOTT *Wav.* xxxviii, A huge *iron-grated door.. formed the exterior defence of the gateway. **1887** G. MEREDITH *Ballads & P.* 74 Iron-capped and *iron-heeled. *a* **1744** POPE *Wks.* (1751) VII. 349 *Iron-hoop'd hogsheads of strong beer. **1883** 'MARK TWAIN' *Life on Mississippi* iii. 45 I'm the old original *iron-jawed, brass-mounted.. corpse-maker from the wilds of Arkansaw! **1926** E. HEMINGWAY *Torrents of Spring* (1933) i. 26 A short, iron-jawed man. **1842** TENNYSON *Locksley Hall* 169 *Iron-jointed, supple-sinew'd, they shall dive, and they shall run. **1895** B. M. CROKER *Village Tales* 196 Shut it out by merely closing to the street an *iron-knobbed wooden door. **1949** BLUNDEN *After Bombing* 41 At the iron-knobbed church door. **1828** CARLYLE *Miscel.*, *Burns* (1872) II. 12 Rose-coloured Novels and *iron-mailed Epics. **1897** J. L. ALLEN *Choir Invisible* xii. 168 Fighting it all over in his foolish, *iron-minded way. **1944** BLUNDEN *Shells by Stream* 9 Squadrons of gem-eyed hobby-horses Whirr round his iron-minded forces. **1968** *Punch* 28 Feb. 323/2 His blunt, iron-minded relatives in Yorkshire. **1877** TENNYSON *Harold* II. ii, This *iron-mooded Duke. *a* **1744** POPE *Wks.* (1751) VII. 345 Opening the *iron-nail'd door. **1828–40** TYTLER *Hist. Scot.* (1864) II. 63 The *iron-nerved and ferocious nobles. **1608** DAY *Hum. out of Br.* Ded. (1881) 3 The *Iron-pated Muse-mongers about the towne. **1883** 'MARK TWAIN' *Life on Mississippi* xliv. 442 Long, *iron-railed verandas running along the several stories. **1893** F. ADAMS *New Egypt* 130 Dusty iron-railed gardens. **1964** A. WYKES *Gambling* i. 10 He had set up an iron-railed podium. *a* **1667** COWLEY *Misc.*, *Chronicle* v, Under that *iron-sceptred queen. **1903** *Trawl* May 30 In the wall in front of him was an *iron-studded door. **1601** MUNDAY *Downf. Earl Huntingdon* IV. i. in Hazl. *Dodsley* VIII. 179 Opening (like hell) his *iron-toothed jaws. **1822** BYRON *Werner* IV. i. 44 Brave *iron-visaged fellows. **1804** J. GRAHAME *Sabbath* (1808) 21 With studded doors, And *iron-visor'd windows. **1848** J. R. LOWELL in *National Anti-Slavery Standard* 9 Nov. 96/1 In that far isle, whence, *iron-willed, The new-world's sires their bark unmoored. **1951** M. MCLUHAN *Mech. Bride* (1967) 67/1 Thurber's 'Mother' is a flint-eyed, iron-willed, Republican matriarch. **1600** FAIRFAX *Tasso* I. lxxxi. 1 The Brazen Trump of *iron-winged Fame. **1593** SHAKS. *Rich. III*, IV. ii. 28, I will conuerse with *Iron-witted Fooles, And vnrespectiue Boyes. **1830** TENNYSON *Sonnet to J.M.K.*, To embattail and to wall about thy cause With *iron-worded proof.

b. Combinations in which *iron* is in attributive relation to the second element: as **iron-face**, an impudent or obstinate person (cf. *brazen-face*).

1534 *Acc.* in J. Noake *Worcester Mon.* (1866) 192 A new cartt with yernband whelys. **1697** CIBBER *Woman's Wit* v. Wks. 1760 I. 194 Hark you Iron-face! Art not thou a perjur'd Rogue? **1847** SMEATON *Builder's Man.* 193 Brass iron-butt hinges. **1863** BATES *Nat. Amazon* I. 59 The entrance.. was by an iron-grille gateway.

c. Phrases with specialized sense: **iron cap** = IRON HAT 2; **iron chink** [CHINK *sb.*[5]] (see quot. 1942); **Iron Cross** [G. *das eiserne kreuz*], a German and Austrian decoration awarded for distinguished services in war (founded by Frederick William III of Prussia in 1813, to reward those who served in the wars against Napoleon, and later revived by William I in 1870); **iron crown**, the ancient crown of the kings of Lombardy, so called from having a circlet of iron inserted (reputed to have been made from one of the nails of the Cross); **Iron Duke**, a name for the first Duke of Wellington (1769–1852); **Iron Guard**, an anti-Semitic, Fascist, terrorist Romanian political party developed from the Legion of the Archangel Michael, found by C. Z. Codreanu (? 1899–1938) in 1927; **iron gum(-tree)** *Austral.*, one of several Queensland species of *Eucalyptus* which have particularly strong wood; **iron horse**, a locomotive steam-engine; also, a bicycle or tricycle; **iron jubilee**, the seventieth anniversary of an event; **iron law** (of wages), the law or idea that wages tend to sink to the level of mere subsistence; **iron mike** *slang*, a familiar name for the automatic steering device of a ship; **iron oak**, any of several oaks with particularly durable wood, as *Quercus cerris*, *Q. stellata*, etc.; **iron paper**, extremely thin sheet-iron; **iron walls**, the iron-clad ships of the British navy, regarded as a defence to the country (cf. *wooden walls*); **iron wedding** (see WEDDING). See also IRON AGE, IRON HAT.

1911 *Chambers's Jrnl.* Mar. 166/1 The indication of a deposit of pyrites is the appearance of an outcrop of oxide of iron more or less honeycombed. This is called the '*iron cap', or in Cornwall 'gossan'. **1913** *Heaton's Guide to Western Canada* 11 In the salmon canneries the introduction of a machine called the '*Iron Chink', for cleaning and cutting the fish has made a great economy in the cost of labor. **1914** *Star* 14 Nov. 4/4 The 'iron chink' cuts off the heads, tails, and fins, dresses the fish at the rate of 3,000 per hour. **1942** H. W. VON LOESECKE *Outl. Food Technol.* vi. 228 The fish.. go to the so-called 'iron chink', a machine which automatically severs the head and eviscerates the fish. In the early days of the [salmon] industry, this work was performed by Chinese labor, hence the name 'iron chink' for the machine. **1963** *Vancouver Sun* 5 Apr. 34/1 (Advt.), Fishing company requires qualified iron chink operator. **1871** *Monthly Packet* July 24 Two prints which appeared during the autumn of 1870 in the Illustrated London News, one.. of the Crown Prince distributing the *Iron Cross. **1902** *Encycl. Brit.* XXXI. 340/2 The Austrian Iron Cross, founded by Napoleon I. as king of Italy in 1805.. conferred for personal merit. **1914** *Punch* 11 Nov. 390/2 The Iron Cross. (For German looters.) **1944** V. G. GARVIN tr. *R. Gary's Forest of Anger* xxvi. 114 My Frieda would rather have me back with pox than dead with the Iron Cross! **1807** *Ann. Reg.* 1805 XLVII. 135/2 The *iron crown of Charlemagne was destined to circle the brows of Bonaparte. *Ibid.* 137/1 A new order of knighthood was instituted, that of 'the iron crown'. **1839** *Penny Cycl.* XIV. 104/2 At Pavia.. the successors of Charlemagne were crowned with the iron crown of Lombardy as kings of Italy. **1861** J. G. SHEPPARD *Fall Rome* i. 12 Yet the German still guards, though no longer in a Lombard fortress, the iron Crown. **1850** *Iron Duke [see DUKE *sb.* 3 a]. **1852** (*title*) The wisdom of Wellington; or maxims of the Iron Duke. **1882** [see CORSICAN *a.* and *sb.* 1]. **1928** O. BRETT *Wellington* xix. 278 (*heading*) The Iron Duke. **1957** *Encycl. Brit.* XXIII. 501 As a diplomatist the 'Iron Duke'.. was no match for the 'Iron Tsar'. **1965** W. R. BENÉT *Reader's Encycl.* (ed. 2) 1081/1 Wellington, 1st duke of. Arthur Wellesley. Known as the Iron Duke. **1933** *Times* 16 Nov. 13/2 It is reported that the new Government has decided to dissolve the *Iron Guard organization.. anti-Semitic and pro-Fascist and Hitlerist. **1934** *Ann. Reg. 1933* 210 M. Duca.. was assassinated.. by a student member of the Iron Guard. **1942** L. B. NAMIER *Conflicts* 46 The Iron Guard, which was indebted to Germany for much of its income and of its revolutionary *élan*, indulged in the extremest forms of anti-Semitism, demanded a complete dictatorship with a social revolutionary programme. **1971** W. LAQUEUR *Dict. Politics* 438 After mounting Iron Guard atrocities and massacres of Gentiles as well as Jews, Antonescu repressed the Iron Guards with German consent. **1879** F. VON MUELLER *Eucalyptographia* I, s.v. *Eucalyptus Raveretiana.* Vernacularly it passes in the districts of its growth as 'Grey Gum-tree' and '*Iron Gum-tree'. **1888** F. M. BAILEY *Queensland Woods* 63 *E[ucalyptus] Raveretiana*... Thozet's Box or Iron Gum-tree. A large tree with a scaly bark persistent on the trunk. **1919** R. T. BAKER *Hardwoods Austral.* 173 *Eucalyptus Raveretiana*, F. von M. 'Thozet's Box' or 'Iron Gum Tree'... close-grained, very hard, and tough; valuable for building purposes. **1957** *N.Z. Timber Jrnl.* Sept. 61/1 *Irongum*: Eucalyptus spp. Australia. The best known is E. maculata Hook, or spotted gum. Weight 64 lbs. **1970** N. HALL et al. *Forest Trees Austral.* 46 Spotted iron gum (Qld) *Eucalyptus maculata*. **1840** D. MARCH *Yankee Land* 23 There were noble steeds in the days of old... But the *iron horse, there were none like him! **1846** *Congress. Globe* 6 Feb. 323/3 The iron horse.. with the wings of the wind,.. vomiting fire and smoke. **1874** Iron horse [see HORSE *sb.* 6 a]. **1875** *Echo* 29 Oct. (Farmer), Mr. S. started on his third day's journey of the 650 miles ride on his iron-horse. **1887** T. A. TROLLOPE *What I remember* I. vii. 156 Before the iron horse had been trained to cross the Atlantic. **1958** C. ACHEBE *Things fall Apart* xvi. 129 Stories about these strange men [*sc.* missionaries] had grown since one of them had been killed in Abame and his iron horse tied to the sacred silk-cotton tree. **1967** C. O. SKINNER *Madame Sarah* viii. 171 The engineer returned to his iron horse and the train started. **1903** *Westm. Gaz.* 6 Feb. 10/1 Pope Leo XIII. will celebrate.. during the present year.. his '*Iron Jubilee' as a priest—he was ordained seventy years ago. **1896** R. H. I. PALGRAVE *Dict. Pol. Econ.* II. 568/1 He [*sc.* Lassalle] dwelt on what he called the *iron or 'brazen law' (*ehernes Gesetz*) of wages, already laid down by Turgot and Ricardo. **1907** J. S. NICHOLSON in *Cambr. Mod. Hist.* X. 774 Ricardo.. was credited with the 'iron law of wages' on the one side and the theories of the continuous growth of rent and the unearned increment on the other. **1913** *Pitman's Commercial Encycl.* IV. 1662/2 The 'iron law'.. of the mere subsistence wage taught that the general rate of wages constantly tends to starvation limit. **1966** A. GILPIN *Dict. Econ. Terms* 219 *Subsistence theory.* Of French origin, this 'iron law' of wages asserted that if wages rose above subsistence level an increase in population would inevitably follow, thus forcing wages down again to subsistence level. **1926** M. CRANE *Yarns from Windjammer* 27 He [*sc.* the quartermaster] will be jealous indeed of the praise bestowed on *Iron Mike, an eight-foot high iron box, with complicated electrical 'innards', for the Captain of the liner on which Gyro-pilot—Iron Mike's Sunday name—was tried, stated that the ship saved eight or ten miles a day by superior steering. **1937** *Jrnl. R. Aeronaut. Soc.* XLI. 415 The automatic helmsman or 'Iron Mike' for marine craft was a proved success. **1956** A. G. COURSE *Merchant Navy Today* ix. 130 Now we have a gyro-compass pilot or automatic helmsman—often known as an 'iron mike'—which steers the ship. **1742** W. ELLIS *Timber-Tree Improved* II. i. 15 The white *iron or ring Oak has its Name from the long Duration of its Timber. **1810** W. WADE tr. *Michaux's Quercus 1 Chêne gris.* Upland white oak, iron oak. **1832** D. J. BROWNE *Sylva Amer.* 275 In Maryland and a great part of Virginia.. it [sc. *Quercus stellata*] is called Box White Oak, and sometimes Iron Oak and Post Oak. **1838** J. C. LOUDON *Arboretum* III. 1846 *Q[uercus] Cerris* L. The bitter, or mossy-cupped, Oak... the Turkey Oak; the Iron, or Wainscot, Oak. **1908** N. L. BRITTON *N. Amer. Trees* 342 It [*sc. Quercus stellata*, post oak] is also known as Box white oak, Iron oak [etc.]. **1871** F. KILVERT *Diary* 27 Dec. (1969) II. 101 A new invention, *iron paper, as thin as the thinnest tissue paper. The sheets of iron are rolled so thin that 3000 sheets together are only an inch thick. **1897** *Westm. Gaz.* 26 June 1/3 Fortified by the sense of our *iron-walls.

iron ('aɪən), *v.* [f. IRON *sb.*[1]]

1. *trans.* To fit, furnish, cover, or arm with iron. (Chiefly in pa. pple.: see IRONED *a.* 2.)

c **1430** *Pilgr. Lyf Manhode* I. cvii. (1869) 57 It misliked me of my burdoun that it was not yrened. *c* **1489** CAXTON *Sonnes*

of Aymon xxii. 491 A palster well yrened for to bere in his hande. **1517** J. FITZHERB. in *Eng. Hist. Rev.* XII. 235, ij horse harrowes yroned. **1649** BLITHE *Eng. Improv. Impr.* (1653) 197 Let him not neglect a day, but iron his plough with slips or clouts in all the wearing places. **1793** *Trans. Soc. Arts* XI. 195 Made of ash..and ironed as the model. **1797** COLERIDGE *Christabel* I. 126 The gate that was ironed within and without. **1847** EMERSON *Poems* (1857) 26 What if Trade..thatch with towns the prairie broad With railways ironed o'er.

2. To shackle with irons; to put in irons.

1653 MIDDLETON & ROWLEY *Sp. Gypsy* IV. iii. H ij b, Iron him then, let the rest goe free. **1794** BURKE *Sp. agst. W. Hastings* Wks. XV. 457 The miserable victims were imprisoned, ironed, scourged. **1831** TYTLER *Lives Sc. Worthies* I. 276 Wallace was cast into a dungeon and heavily ironed. **1856** FROUDE *Hist. Eng.* II. 473 Mark Smeton, who had confessed his guilt, was ironed.

3. a. To smooth or press with a heated flat-iron, as cloth, and the like. Also *absol.* and *fig.* esp. with *out*.

a **1680** EARL ROCHESTER *Trial of the Poets* (R.), Little starch'd Johnny Crown at his elbow he found, His cravat-string new iron'd. **1708** MOTTEUX *Rabelais* IV. lii. (1737) 214 Their..Neck-Ruffs, new wash'd, starch'd, and iron'd. **1737** FIELDING *Tumble Down Dick* 1068/2 Draw the scene, and discover..her maid ironing her linen. **1789** *Loiterer* No. 44. 9 The servants are all ironing. **1840** DICKENS *Old C. Shop* x, Mrs. Nubbles ironed away in silence for a minute or two. **1870** RAMSAY *Remin.* ii. (ed. 18) 23 She..found the occupant busy..ironing out some linens. **1879** MRS. OLIPHANT *Within Precincts* v, Her white muslin frock..she ironed herself most carefully.

fig. **1863** W. PHILLIPS *Speeches* xiv. 312 He irons his face out to portentous length and sadness. **1892** OUIDA in *Fortn. Rev.* LII. 797 The whole tendency of Socialism..is to iron down humanity into one dreary level. **1905** *Springfield* (Mass.) *Weekly Republ.* 31 Mar. 8 The differences between Chairman Flaherty..and Col. William A. Gaston are in a fair way to be amicably ironed out. **1924** 'L. MALET' *Dogs of Want* v. 122 Mr. Harvey-Noakes plays a ripping game... He has flattened me out,..completely ironed me out. **1929** *Observer* 17 Nov. 3/4 The best practical method of ironing out ups and downs of the business cycle. **1930** *Time & Tide* 28 Mar. 389 The progress of negotiations to 'iron out' differences between Britain, Japan, and America. **1949** F. SWINNERTON *Doctor's Wife comes to Stay* vii. 80 Roly..had married a widow with children,..and been—in the cliché of the day—'ironed out'. **1971** *Daily Tel.* 28 Oct. 29/5 Like the great horseman he is, he patiently ironed out the kinks in plenty of time to catch Hush Money on the flat. **1971** *Guardian* 1 Nov. 6/4 The new computer was delivered..last week... Ironing out the bugs will probably take until the new year.

b. *intr.* Of a garment, material, etc.: to respond to ironing, to undergo smoothing or pressing with an iron.

1943 *Mod. Lang. Notes* Jan. 12 They claim that..'lingerie *tubs* quickly and *irons* easily'. **1946** *Ibid.* Nov. 444 The use, in advertising, of the 'potential intransitive', in such examples as..'this dress *washes* and *irons* and *packs* easily'.

¶ **4.** By ignorant or humorous perversion from IRONY *sb.*, sometimes with allusion to sense 3: **a.** *intr.* To use irony, speak ironically; **b.** *trans.* To treat with irony, speak ironically to.

1742 FIELDING *J. Andrews* I. vi, *Mrs. Slipslop.* You must treat me with ironing? Barbarous monster! **1813** *Sporting Mag.* XLI. 261 Others, who are blest with Mrs. Slipslop's second-hand knowledge and comprehension of words and rhetoric, will say, that I am ironing. **1823** BEE *Dict. Turf* s.v. *Ironing* (Farmer), Nay, my Coney, now you're ironing me.. all down the back. **1840** MARRYAT *Olla Podr.* (Rtldg.) 326 The fellow's *ironing* me.

i-ron, i-ronne, ME. pa. pple. of RUN *v.*

Iron Age. Also **iron age.** [See IRON *a.* 3 f]

1. The last and worst age of the world according to Greek and Roman mythology, succeeding the Golden, Silver, and Brazen Ages. Hence *allusively*, An age or period of wickedness, cruelty, oppression, debasement, etc.

a **1592** H. SMITH *Wks.* (1867) II. 41 In these days, and in this iron age, it is as hard a thing to persuade men to part with money, as to pull out their eyes, and cast them away. **1656** B. HARRIS tr. Parival (*title*) The Historie of this Iron Age. **1693** T. CREECH in *Dryden's Juvenal* (1697) 323 Worse than the Iron Age, and wretched Times Roul on. **1772** FLETCHER *Logica Genev.* 188 Does not this exceed Ovid's descripton of the iron-age? **1900** J. A. H. MURRAY *Romanes Lect.* 36 The golden age of Latinity had passed into a silvern, and that into a brazen and an iron age.

2. *Archæol.* That period in the history of mankind or of any race in which iron weapons and implements were or are used (subsequent to the *stone age* and *bronze age*). Hence *transf.*, a period characterized by the general use of iron.

1879 LUBBOCK *Sci. Lect.* v. 164 The Iron Age is the period when this metal was first used for weapons and cutting instruments. **1890** W. J. GORDON *Foundry* 107 The Iron Age has passed; this is the Age of Steel. We shall see immediately that even our 'tin' pots and kettles are now made of steel.

¶ In the following perh. = mass of irons.

1607 TOURNEUR *Rev. Trag.* IV. i. Wks. 1878 II. 101 Make thee a perpetuall prisoner And laye this yron-age upon thee.

iron alum. a. *Min.* A double sulphate of iron and aluminium (see ALUM *sb.* 2), occurring native as HALOTRICHITE. **b.** *Chem.* A double sulphate of iron and potassium (or ammonium), belonging to the series of alums in the extended sense: see ALUM *sb.* 3).

1868 DANA *Min.* 654 *Halotrichite*..Iron Alum. **1868–72** WATTS *Dict. Chem.* V. 596 Ammonio-ferric sulphate, or Ammonia-iron-alum..Potassio-ferric sulphate, or Potash-iron-alum. **1876** HARLEY *Mat. Med.* 192 Iron alum results when the alumina is replaced by peroxyde of iron.

'iron-bark. [Of Austral-Eng. formation, from IRON *a.* or *sb.* + BARK.] **a.** Any species of *Eucalyptus* having solid bark, as *E. resinifera, paniculata, Leucoxylon, Sideroxylon*, etc., trees valued in Australia for their timber and other purposes.

1802 G. BARRINGTON *Hist. N.S. Wales* viii. 263 The bark of which on the trunk is..the iron bark of Port Jackson. **1820** OXLEY *Jrnl. Exped. Australia* 170 Iron and stringy barks of small size were also common. **1833** C. STURT *S. Australia* I. i. 11 Iron-bark and cypresses generally prevailed along our line of route. **1868** CARLETON *Australian Nights* 29, I was swarthy grown and dark, Yes, as the rugged iron-bark. **1909** A. E. MACK *Bush Calendar* 4 The blue gums, iron-barks, and turpentines gave way to scribbly gums and banksias. **1911** E. M. CLOWES *On Wallaby* ix. 249 In the Victorian Grampians is to be found for the most part blue gum and messmate, stringy bark, and red and white iron bark. **1967** A. RULE *Forests Austral.* ii. 27 A list of the more valuable species would include the red and the grey ironbarks—those hard, heavy and tremendously tough timbers that make the name ironbark almost synonymous with durability.

b. The wood of any of these trees.

1894 *Westm. Gaz.* 20 Nov. 6/1 One thousand ironbark sleepers were recently shipped from Sydney for..the Great Eastern Railway Company... Ironbark has been proved to last on the ground for ninety years.

c. *attrib.*

1820 OXLEY *Jrnl. Exped. Australia* 170 Iron bark trees were..growing on the very summit. **1889** BOLDREWOOD *Robbery under Arms* xxxv, We made an ironbark coffer for it. **1890** —— *Miner's Right* xxvii. 249 The corrugated stems of the great ironbark trees stood black and columnar.

d. Passing into *adj.*: hard, unyielding. *Austral.*

1888 'R. BOLDREWOOD' *Robbery under Arms* I. vi. 85, I always thought he was ironbark outside and in. **1945** BAKER *Austral. Lang.* 90 From countrymen in general, *ironbark*, unyielding.

iron-'bind, *v. rare.* [f. IRON *sb.*[1] + BIND *v.*: a back-formation from IRON-BOUND.] *trans.* To bind with iron; to confine with iron bands.

1708 MOTTEUX *Rabelais* v. xvii, Why don't you Iron-bind him?

iron-blue, *a.* and *sb.* **a.** *adj.* Of a blue colour like some kinds of iron or steel. **b.** *sb.* A blue colour like that of some iron; steel-blue; also (for ***iron-blue fly***), a kind of fly used by anglers.

1697 DRYDEN *Virg. Past.* II. 67 The Daughters of the Flood have..set soft Hyacinths with Iron blue, To shade marsh Marigolds of shining Hue. **1787** BEST *Angling* (ed. 2) 113 The little Iron blue fly comes on about the seventh of May. **1897** *Daily News* 27 July 8/1 That was an Iron Blue changing into a Jenny Spinner.

c. *sb.* The pigment Prussian blue (PRUSSIAN *a.* 2).

1930 A. W. C. HARRISON *Manuf. Lakes & Precipitated Pigments* ix. 124 The term 'iron blue' covers a number of types and shades of 'Prussian blues'. **1948** S. F. DIMLICH in W. von Fischer *Paint & Varnish Technol.* vi. 93 Iron blue is probably the most important blue pigment used by the paint industry. **1967** KARCH & BUBER *Offset Processes* vii. 268 Iron blue (made in a number of shades, such as milori blue, bronze blue, prussian blue, etc.) is a chemical compound of iron.

iron-bound, *a.* Also 4–6 **-bounden.** [f. IRON *sb.*[1] + BOUND, pa. pple. of BIND *v.* (With shifting stress.)]

1. Bound with iron; confined with bands of iron; in quot. 1802, Confined with irons, fettered.

1377 LANGL. *P. Pl.* B. XIV. 246 þere auarice hath almaries and yren-bounde coffres. **1497** *Naval Acc. Hen. VII* (1896) 94, iiij wheles iren bounden. *Ibid.* 99 Iren bounden. **1523** FITZHERB. *Husb.* §5 If they be yren bounden, they are moche the better..for a payre of wheles yren bounde, wyl weare .vii. or .viii. payre of other wheles. **1561** in W. H. Turner *Select. Rec. Oxford* 285 No bruer..shall carry any bere..w[t] iernebond carts w[t]in the Citie. **1641** HINDE *J. Bruen* xlvi. 147 The wheele went over his legge, being iron bound. **1705** *Lond. Gaz.* No. 4163/3 A large Iron-bound Box. **1802** CAMPBELL *Lochiel's Warning* 65 But where is the iron-bound prisoner? Where? **1884** J. PARKER *Apost. Life* III. 258 A gate iron-bound and iron-riveted.

2. *transf.* Of a coast: Faced or enclosed with hard rocks; rock-bound. In quot. 1887, Hardened by frost, frost-bound.

1769 FALCONER *Dict. Marine* (1789), *Terres hautes*..a bold, or iron-bound coast. **1852** EARP *Gold Col. Australia* 30 Mr. Bass..and Lieutenant..Flinders started with him on a survey of the iron-bound coast of Australia, in a boat only eight feet long! **1867** J. MACGREGOR *Voy. Alone* (1868) 73 This part of the coast..besides being iron-bound has no port that is easy to enter. **1887** J. BALL *Nat. in S. Amer.* 267 The muddy streets were iron-bound with frost.

3. *fig.* Rigidly confined or restricted; hard, unimpressionable; rigorous, hard and fast.

1807–8 W. IRVING *Salmag.* (1824) 235 My ironbound physiognomy [would]..be as notorious as that of Noah Webster. **1847** EMERSON *Repr. Men, Napoleon* Wks. (Bohn) I. 374 The old iron-bound, feudal France was changed into a young Ohio or New York. *a* **1898** J. CAIRD *Fundam. Ideas Chr.* II. xiv. 145 If there be in the divine nature an iron-bound impassibility.

'iron-cased (-keɪst), *a.* [f. IRON *sb.*[1] + *cased*, pa. pple. of CASE *v.*] Cased in iron; having an iron casing: applied to ships of war, now called IRONCLAD. Also in other uses.

1859 *Engineer* VIII. 274/3 This new kind of iron-cased floating batteries. **1860** *Ann. Reg.* 202 The Warrior was ordered to be completed as an iron-cased frigate. **1861** *Ho. Comm. Return* 7 June, Return respecting Iron-cased Ships as to Date of Contract, Time for Completion, and Penalties. **1864** *Times* 17 Oct., To complete her as an iron-cased frigate. **1901** L. M. WATERHOUSE *Conduit Wiring* 50 The Simplex iron-cased distributing boards. **1906** *Westm. Gaz.* 29 Aug. 10/1 His tubular iron-cased telephone. **1921** *Wireless World* 25 June 200/1 T_4 and T_5 are fixed audio-frequency transformers, iron-cased and with iron cores.

So **'iron-casing.**

1863 P. BARRY *Dockyard Econ.* 14 Improvements in gunnery and the iron-casing of ships divest the strongest dockyards of more than half their once boasted power.

'ironclad, iron-clad, *a.* and *sb.*

A. *adj.* **1. a.** Clad in iron; protected or covered with iron; *esp.* of a vessel for naval warfare: Cased wholly or partly with thick plates of iron or steel, as a defence against shot, etc.

[*Note.* When the question of protecting ships of war, etc., by iron or steel armour first aroused general attention (*c* 1859), various terms were used to describe ships so protected, as *iron-cased, -clad, -clothed, -coated, -plated, -sided; steel-clad, -clothed; armour-clad, -plated*; of these, *iron-cased, -plated*, were at first preferred, and for several years were those usually employed in England, officially and otherwise; *iron-clad*, occasionally used in England before, appears to have come into common use at first in the United States, during the Civil War, and established itself as the preferred term *c* 1862–3, its adaptability as a substantive facilitating its general adoption. But its official use in England dates from *c* 1866.

1859 *Engineer* VIII. 157/3 (*heading*) Iron-sided Ships. *Ibid.*, At from 600 to 800 yards, iron-clothed ships would be in comparative safety from the effects of an enemy's broadside. *Ibid.*, That a steel-clothed ship could be far more easily destroyed than a wooden-sided one. **1859–64** [see IRON-CASED]. **1860** *Engineer* IX. 255/3 (*heading*) Iron Plated Ships. **1860** *Quart. Rev.* ibid. X. 268/1 Napoleon III..designed a class of iron-plated vessels known as the floating batteries of 1854. **1862** *Engineer* XIII. 93/1 (*heading*) The Iron-Plated Ship Question. *Ibid.* 232/2 (*heading*) Our Iron Plated Fleet. **1863** *Ibid.* XV. 37/2 It was discovered that iron-coated ships only were good for warlike purposes. **1863** *Admiralty Ret.* 4 May (*heading*), A return of Iron-plated or armour-clad ships built or building.]

1852 [see IRON-HEADED 2]. **1859** *Engineer* VIII. 157/3 The present experiments..would appear to prove that an iron or steel-clad ship, on receiving a concentrated broadside from a frigate..must sink then and there. **1861** *Ibid.* XI. 152/1 Iron-clad Ships..Of this supposed [French] fleet of fifteen iron-plated vessels only one was now ready, *La Gloire*. **1861** *Rep. to U.S. Navy Deptmt.* ibid. XII. 384/2 (heading 'Iron-plated Vessels in America') For river and harbour service we consider iron-clad vessels of light draught..as very important. **1861** *Ann. Reg.* 204 One of the smaller of these iron-clad ships. **1864** *Times* 17 Oct., Wooden liners.. acknowledged as useless to compete with ironclad frigates. **1866** *Stat. Abstr. Health Navy* 12 It is particularly satisfactory to find that..the iron-clad vessels are likely to prove at least as healthy as those not iron-clad. **1877** RAYMOND *Statist. Mines & Mining* 17 The foundation for a new ironclad furnace. **1878** *N. Amer. Rev.* CXXVII. 225 Two powerful iron-clad rams.

b. Applied to electrical apparatus.

1876 J. ERICSSON *Contributions to Centennial Exhib.* xxviii. 410 (*heading*) Iron-clad steam battery, with revolving cupola. **1902** *Encycl. Brit.* XXVII. 584/2 The two-poled iron-clad type [of field-magnet], so called from the exciting coil being more or less encased by the iron yoke. **1910** *Hawkins' Electr. Dict.*, *Iron-clad dynamo*, a dynamo having an iron-clad armature. **1927** W. WILSON *Electr. Control Gear* xvi. 226 There are..reasonably cheap ironclad types of starting equipment on the market. **1939** READ & CORCORAN *Electr. Engin. Exper.* 91 The iron-clad solenoid can be made more effective by providing it with a stationary iron core which occupies about 20 or 30 per cent of the axial length.

2. *fig.* In reference to the action of frost in covering water and land with a hard surface. (Cf. IRON-BOUND 2, quot. 1887.) *rare.* Also, of plants, able to withstand cold and frost. *U.S.*

1872 *Rep. Vermont Board Agric.* I. 54 Currants and gooseberries are iron clad as regards climate. **1882** *Rep. Maine Board Agric.* XXVI. 336 It is an early winter fruit, the tree not perfectly 'iron clad', notwithstanding its origin, yet hardy enough for most places. **1889** JEFFERIES *Field & Hedgerow* 103 Warm summer and iron-clad winter.

3. *fig.* (chiefly *U.S.*) Of an extremely strict or rigorous character; so framed as to be incapable of being evaded, as a regulation, agreement, etc.

ironclad oath: an oath characterized by the severity of its requirements and penalties; esp. applied to the rigorous oath required by the United States Government from certain official and other persons after the civil war of 1861–5. (*Cent. Dict.*)

1866 *Congress. Globe* 14 Feb. 835/1 Traitors never would be troubled with the 'iron-clad oath', for they never would have a chance to take it. **1868** *Harper's Mag.* Sept. 484/2 [He] was as well reconstructed as a man might be who could not take the iron-clad oath. **1873** J. MILLER *Life amongst Modocs* xxvi. 304 Some hard, iron-clad oaths and then shot after shot. **1884** *Boston* (Mass.) *Jrnl.* 25 Apr., The Governor signed the Oleomargarine bill to-day..the law..was drawn with care and is presumably ironclad. **1885** *Economist* in *Pall Mall G.* 6 June, The British parties..may try..to follow the American precedent, and make 'an ironclad oath' to preserve the union of the two countries [Great Britain and Ireland] a condition of election. **1887** *Contemp. Rev.* May 699 Bills..full of the most arbitrary and 'iron-clad' provisions. **1888** BRYCE *Amer. Commw.* II. III. lxix. 548 At the Republican national convention at Chicago in June 1880 an attempt was successfully made to impose the obligation

by the following resolution, commonly called the 'Iron clad Pledge'. **1891** *Pall Mall G.* 1 May 4/3 The contractors [in the Pittsburg district] have signed 'ironclad' articles refusing the demands of the men. **1911** H. S. HARRISON *Queed* x. 114 He insisted on doing it after an ironclad schedule. **1930** *Observer* 1 June 11 The rationing system.. is not so complete or ironclad as those which prevailed in various European countries during the war. **1951** E. KEFAUVER *Crime in America* (1952) xix. 223 The operations of Murder, Inc., finally came to light when.. police obtained ironclad evidence against a gangster known as Abe (Kid Twist) Reles.

B. *sb.* **1.** An ironclad ship: see A. 1.

1862 LONGF. in *Life* (1891) III. 18 Went..to see the Nahant,—an ironclad with revolving turret, like the Monitor. **1863** *Engineer* XV. 249/3 The presence before Charleston of three distinct types of iron-clads represented by the Monitors, the Keokuk, and the Ironsides. *Ibid.* 295/2 (*heading*) Launch of a Russian iron-clad. On Monday afternoon the first iron-cased frigate for the Russian navy was launched from the yard of the Thames Ironworks. *Ibid.*, There is not as yet one foreign iron-clad which in real efficiency is worth a tenth of one of ours. **1866** *Admiralty Ret.* 19 Mar. (*heading*), Return of all the Iron-clads built of wood [etc.]. *a* **1895** LD. C. E. PAGET *Autobiog.* vi. (1896) 193 Already [1859] the French had launched *La Gloire* ironclad ..I had given my evidence before the royal commission strongly urging the construction of ironclads.

2. *transf.* and *fig.*

1867 J. N. EDWARDS *Shelby* 483 The West Pointers were the iron-clads in our wooden navy. **1875** 'MARK TWAIN' *Sk. New & Old* (1900) 157 After the Tortoises came another long train of ironclads—stately and spacious Mud Turtles. **1889** —— *Connecticut Yankee* xxxix. 456 Things began to look serious to the iron-clads [*sc.* knights in armour]. **1892** O. F. WHITNEY *Hist. Utah* I. 547 The ravages of the 'iron-clads' [i.e. grasshoppers] were wide-spread and far-reaching. **1974** *Country Life* 28 Mar. 752/1 Those plants that are always a risk, climatewise, but which do offer rewards..such as the hardy ironclads can never quite match. **1974** *Oxford Times* 19 Apr. 3/3 'Iron clads' are the.. term for day-old Chelsea buns.

iron curtain. [f. IRON *sb.*[1] + CURTAIN *sb.*[1]]

1. In a theatre, a curtain of iron which can be lowered between the stage and the auditorium in order to prevent passage or communication, or for protection.

1794 *Times* 13 Mar. 3/2 Besides other precautions, an iron curtain has been contrived, which, on such occasion [of fire], would compleatly prevent all communication between the audience and stage. **1829** H. FOOTE *Compan. to Theatres* 30 As a precaution against fire, an iron curtain was constructed, so as to let down in a moment of danger and separate the audience from the stage. **1891** SCOTT & HOWARD *Life E. L. Blanchard* II. 557 And provision against fire is made [in the Prince of Wales' Theatre] by an iron curtain. **1908** WODEHOUSE & WESTBROOK *Globe by the Way Bk.* 51/2 'The iron curtain,' she gasped, and exerting her full strength, held the actor under the descending sheet of metal.

2. *fig.* Any impenetrable barrier.

After 1946 regarded as a transf. use of sense 2 b.

1819 EARL OF MUNSTER *Jrnl. Route across India 1817–18* iv. 58 On the 19th November we crossed the river Betwah, and as if an iron curtain had dropt between us and the avenging angel, the deaths diminished. **1904** H. G. WELLS *Food of Gods* III. iv. 274 It became evident that Redwood had still imperfectly apprehended the fact that an iron curtain had dropped between him and the outer world. **1915** G. W. CRILE *Mechanistic View War & Peace* iv. 69 Suppose that Mexico were a rich, cultured, and brave nation of forty million with a deep-rooted grievance, and an iron curtain at its frontier. [**1916** E. HOWARD *Potsdam Princes* 250 The war, of course, has made them bitter enemies, and when reminded of her German relations, Queen Elizabeth of Belgium is reported to have said that between her and her people in Bavaria a curtain of iron had fallen.] **1939** J. GLOAG *Word Warfare* xi. 113 In an international crisis Germany can be cut off from the world by an iron curtain of censorship. **1946** J. C. DAVIES *Episcopal Acts Welsh Dioceses 1066–1272* I. 43 Within this iron curtain in the south the princes of Deheubarth maintained a precarious independence until the middle of the thirteenth century. **1959** *Listener* 29 Jan. 198/1 By tact and determination she gradually broke down the iron curtain and mobilized the women into a united Conservative front. **1962** *Daily Tel.* 15 Aug. 13/2 There was no 'Iron Curtain' between them and the consumer. **1967** *Freedomways* VII. 119 Since I don't want the United States to appear like an 'Iron Curtain' to the Vietnamese, I think it would be good for several Vietnamese women to visit this country.

b. *spec.* (usually with initial capitals). A barrier to the passage of information, etc., at the limit of the sphere of influence of the Soviet Union. Cf. *bamboo curtain* (BAMBOO *sb.* 2), CURTAIN *sb.*[1] 3 c. Also in extended use (as quot. 1924).

The *locus classicus* is quot. 1946.

1920 MRS. P. SNOWDEN *Through Bolshevik Russia* ii. 32 We were behind the 'iron curtain' at last! **1924** LORD D'ABERNON *Diary* 14 Sept. in *Ambassador of Peace* (1930) III. iv. 101 Stresemann considered that it was essential for the Rhineland to be frankly part of Germany, also for Danzig to be reincorporated. Without this there could be no permanent peace. I put forward my view of the reciprocal iron curtain or strip of inviolable territory as a protection. [**1945** *Times* 23 Feb. 3/4 (tr. Paul Josef Goebbels, German Minister for Propaganda, from *Das Reich*) If the German people lay down their arms, the whole of eastern and south-eastern Europe, together with the Reich, would come under Russian occupation. Behind an iron screen [*ein eiserner Vorhang*] mass butcheries of peoples would begin.] **1945** *Times* 3 May 4/5 (speech by the German Foreign Minister, Schwerin von Krosigk) In the East the iron curtain behind which, unseen by the eyes of the world, the work of destruction goes on is moving steadily forward. **1945** SIR ST. V. TROUBRIDGE in *Sunday Empire News* 21 Oct. 2/2 A Curtain Across Europe... Yet at present an iron curtain of silence has descended, cutting off the Russian zone from the Western Allies. **1946** W. S. CHURCHILL in *Times* 6 Mar. 6/1 (Address at Westminster College, Fulton, U.S.A., 5 March) From Stettin, in the Baltic, to Trieste, in the Adriatic, an iron curtain has descended across the Continent. **1953** *Encounter* Oct. 58/1 If they live behind the Iron Curtain they can do none of these things—for, while the Communists agree that knowledge is power, they are persuaded that they are already in essential possession of both. **1953** W. S. CHURCHILL *Second World War* (1954) VI. xxxiv. 498 In these same days I also sent what may be called the 'Iron Curtain' telegram to President Truman..*Prime Minister to President Truman* 12 May 45..An iron curtain is drawn down upon their front. We do not know what is going on behind. **1971** *Times Lit. Suppl.* 31 Dec. 1621/5 The theory of convergence informs us that societies on both sides of the Iron Curtain are conditioned by similar forces in all essential respects, whatever the differences in kind or degree of individual liberty enjoyed by their members. **1972** *Guardian* 23 Aug. 7/5 The iron curtain that fell on Anglo-Soviet cultural deals when 105 Soviet diplomats were expelled from Britain last year has been lifted. **1973** J. M. WHITE *Gooden Game* 184 One of Harrison's local contacts, an experienced Iron Curtain operator.

irone ('aɪərəʊn). *Chem.* [ad. *G. iron* (Tiemann & Krüger 1893, in *Ber. d. Deut. Chem. Ges.* XXVI. 2679), f. G. *ir-is* IRIS *sb.* 5: see -ONE.] Orig., an essential oil obtained from orris-root; hence, any of the three isomers (*α*-, *β*-, and *γ*-*irone*) of which this is composed, which are cyclic ketones, $(CH_3)_4C_6H_5{\cdot}CH{:}CH{\cdot}CO{\cdot}CH_3$, that differ only in the position of the double bond in the C_6H_5 ring and are methyl derivatives of the ionones.

1894 *Jrnl. Chem. Soc.* LXVI. I. 80 The readily-volatile fraction [of iris root] contains the irone or fragrant oil. *Ibid.*, Irone..is an oil which is scarcely soluble in water. **1934** *Chem. Abstr.* XXVIII. 4053 Analyses of irone..establish the compn. $C_{14}H_{22}O$. **1948** *Ann. Rep. Progr. Chem.* XLIV. 148 While *α*- and *γ*-irone possess a fresh violet odour (the 'irone' odour), the *β*-isomer has an ionone smell. **1952** SIMONSEN & OWEN *Terpenes* (ed. 2) III. 497 It is now recognised that irone is 6-methylionone, and that it can exist in the *α*-, *β*-, and *γ*-forms..each of which has several stereoisomeric modifications. *Ibid.* 503 *γ*-Irone is transformed into a mixture of *α*- and *β*-irones when treated with dilute sulphuric acid. **1963** *Chem. Abstr.* LVIII. 1500 Irones are used in the manuf. of perfumes; and they can be synthesized from dextro-*α*-pinene.

ironed ('aɪənd), *a.* [f. IRON *sb.* or *v.* + -ED.]

†**1.** Made of iron: = IRON *a.* 1. *Obs.*

a **1300** *E.E. Psalter* ii. 9 In yherde irened [L. *in virga ferrea*, WYCLIF in an irene ȝerde] salt þou stere þa.

2. Fitted, furnished, covered, armed, or strengthened with iron: see IRON *v.* 1.

c **1430** *Pilgr. Lyf Manhode* II. cxliii. (1869) 132 Anoon with his yrened foot he shulde yiue me. **1833** *Fraser's Mag.* VII. 482 His ironed hoof had dashed the sod. **1884** *Ch. Times* 7 Mar. 194/1 One of those artistically ironed coffers. **1899** R. HAGGARD in *Longm. Mag.* Mar. 413 The arched and ironed timber axle.

3. Put in or bound with irons.

1849 MACAULAY *Hist. Eng.* v. I. 644 Ironed corpses clattering in the wind. **1852** TENNYSON in *Mem.* (1897) I. xii. 345 Heaven guard them From ironed limbs and tortured nails.

ironer ('aɪənə(r)). [f. IRON *v.* + -ER[1].]

1. One who irons; *spec.* one whose occupation it is to iron clothes, etc.: see IRON *v.* 3.

1773 *South Carolina Gaz.* 26 July, To be sold...a complete Washer and Ironer, and remarkable for doing up Ladies fine Cloaths. **1820** *Barbados Mercury & Bridge-Town Gaz.* 16 Sept. 4/3 (Advt.), Also for sale, a family of Negroes, consisting of a woman, a complete washer and ironer, [etc.]. **1857** R. TOMES *Amer. in Japan* viii. 179 Washers, ironers, and doers-up of fine linen. **1883** C. J. WILLS *Mod. Persia* 191 The ūtūkash, or ironer, is employed to ornamentally iron the dresses of the lower orders.

2. *nonce-use.* A man of iron: cf. IRON-MAN 1 a.

1880 G. MEREDITH *Tragic Com.* (1881) 121 The old Ironer! I love him for his love of common sense, his contempt of mean deceit.

'iron-,founder. [f. IRON *sb.*[1] + FOUNDER *sb.*[3]] One who founds or casts iron.

1817 COLERIDGE *Lay Serm.* 393 The ship-builder, the clothier, the iron-founder. **1897** *Daily News* 6 Dec. 11/5 Heavy ironfounders continue well employed.

So **'iron-,founding**; **'iron-,foundry**: see FOUNDRY 1, 2.

1784 MORGAN in *Phil. Trans.* LXXV. 198 The furnace of an iron foundery. **1828** P. CUNNINGHAM *N.S. Wales* (ed. 3) II. 106 Iron-founding on a small scale; manufacturing of axes, adzes, steel-mills, and sundry other strong iron tools and utensils. **1832** BABBAGE *Econ. Manuf.* xxiv. (ed. 3) 239 The gases issuing from the chimnies of iron-foundries. **1895** *Daily News* 21 Jan. 9/1 It has imparted a stimulus to business in plumbers' ironfoundry.

i-rong, -e(n, ME. pa. pple. of RING *v.*

iron-grey, -gray, *a.* and *sb.* [f. IRON *sb.* + GREY. OE. *īsen-grǣȝ*; in ON. *jarn-grár*, OHG. *īsen-grâ*, Ger. *eisen-grau*.]

A. *adj.* Of the grey colour of freshly broken iron, or of dark hair when 'turning grey'.

a **1000** *O.E. Gloss.* in Wr.-Wülcker 236/35 *Ferrugineo flore* ..isengræȝum blostme. *Ibid.* 408/33 *Ferrugineas*, þa isengrægan. **1483** *Cath. Angl.* 198/2 Irengray, *glaucus*. **1687** *Lond. Gaz.* No. 2248/4 An Iron grey Nag, about 14 hands high. **1711** ADDISON *Spect.* No. 64 ¶2 A fresh black Button upon his Iron-gray Suit. **1848** DICKENS *Dombey* v, An iron-grey autumnal day. **1865** TROLLOPE *Belton Est.* v. 49 A.. wiry man, about fifty, with iron-grey hair and beard.

B. *sb.* **1.** A dark grey colour resembling that of freshly broken iron.

[*a* **1000** *O.E. Gloss.* in Wr.-Wülcker 236/32 *Color purpuræ subnigræ*, isengræȝ.] **1552** *Act 5 & 6 Edw. VI*, c. 6 §46 Any other Colour..than..Motley or Iron-gray. **1766** PENNANT *Brit. Zool.* (1768) I. 98 A deep iron-grey, bordering on black.

2. An iron-grey horse, or (quot. 1856) dog; also *transf.* a person whose dark hair is grizzled.

1523 FITZHERB. *Husb.* §68 A sandy colte, lyke an yren grey, neyther lyke syre nor damme. **1822** *Hermit in Lond.* I. 269 Everywhere..do these disguised iron-greys still bear the belle by taper-light. **1852** SMEDLEY *L. Arundel* xviii. 129 A splendid pair of dark iron-grays, with silver manes and tails. **1856** KANE *Arct. Expl.* I. xix. 238 A span of thoroughly wolfish iron-grays.

Hence **iron-greyed** *ppl. a.*, turned iron-grey.

1826 DISRAELI *Viv. Grey* III. viii, His hair..was now silvered, or rather iron-greyed, not by age.

iron-handed, *a.* [f. *iron hand* (see IRON *a.* 3 c, e, and HAND *sb.*) + -ED[2].] Having a 'hand of iron'; acting or ruling with an 'iron hand'; inflexible; severe, rigorous, despotic.

1768–74 TUCKER *Lt. Nat.* (1834) I. 565 We are not obliged to Him, but to the iron-handed goddess, Necessity. **1845** HIRST *Poems* 142 We go iron-handed our fortune to woo. **1855** MOTLEY *Dutch Rep.* (1861) I. 36 This iron-handed, hot-headed, adventurous race, placed as sovereign upon its little sandy hook. **1875** W. E. GRIFFIS in *N. Amer. Rev.* CXX. 289 The iron-handed rule of the great commander.. was felt all over the empire.

'iron-,hard, *a.* and *sb.* [f. IRON *sb.*[1] + HARD: OE. *īrenheard*.]

A. *adj.* As hard as iron: extremely hard.

Beowulf (Z.) 1112 Eofer iren-heard. **1591** SYLVESTER *Du Bartas* I. iii. 1045 Men..Whose wits are Lead, whose bodies Iron-hard. **1889** A. T. PASK *Eyes Thames* 3 Small iron-hard bricks. **1899** *Westm. Gaz.* 3 Feb. 2/1 Montmorency..fell prone on to the iron-hard earth.

†**B.** *sb.* [OE. *īsenhearde*, MDu. *îserhart*, Du. *ijzerhard*, MHG. *îsenhart* vervain.] An old name for the herbs Vervain (*Verbena officinalis*) and Knapweed (*Centaurea nigra*), from the toughness of their stalks. *Obs.*

c **1000** *Sax. Leechd.* III. 4 Eofor þrotan and ȝarclifan and isenheardan. *c* **1265** *Voc. Names Plants* in Wr.-Wülcker 556/41 *Uerueua*, *i.* uerueine, *i.* irenharde. **14..** *MS. Laud* 553 lf. 13 *Iasia nigra*..yrnehard. ?**15..** in *Archæol.* XXX. 409 Hyrne hard, Bolleweed, *Jasia nigra.* **1597** GERARDE *Herbal* App., Yronhard is Knapweed.

iron hat. [IRON *a.* and HAT.]

1. An iron helmet shaped like a hat. (Cf. HAT *sb.* 1, quots. 1400, 1484.)

13.. *K. Alis.* 1629 Of sum weore the brayn out-spat, Al undur theo iren [*Bodl. MS.* yrnen] hat. **13..** *Coer de L.* 367 He sette hys stroke on hys yren hat.

2. *Mining.* = GOSSAN. *U.S.*

1881 in RAYMOND *Mining Gloss.*

'ironhead (-hɛd). A local name in North Carolina of a kind of duck, also called *goldeneye* or *whistlewing*.

1888 G. TRUMBULL cited in *Cent. Dict.*

'iron-headed (-,hɛdɪd), *a.*

1. Having an iron head; tipped with iron.

1588 SPENSER *Virg. Gnat* 653 His yron-headed spade tho making cleene, To dig up sods out of the flowrie grasse. **1697** DRYDEN *Virg. Georg.* II. 233 Volscians arm'd with Iron-headed Darts. **1820** SCOTT *Abbot* x, A door well clenched with iron-headed nails.

2. *fig.* Very hard-headed or determined.

1852 MUNDY *Our Antipodes* (1857) 126 The burly baron of feudal times..those iron-clad, iron-fisted, and iron-headed nobles despised all manner of clerk-craft.

'ironheads (-hɛdz). A local name of the Knapweed (*Centaurea nigra*), from its hard involucre.

1863 in PRIOR *Plant-n.* **1866** *Treas. Bot.* 627/2 Iron-weed or -heads, *Centaurea nigra*.

'ironheart (-hɑːt). A name for *Metrosidēros tomentosa*, a New Zealand tree having hard wood valuable for timber; also called *fire-tree*.

1872 DOMETT *Ranolf* XVIII. vi. 311 It was the 'downy ironheart' That from the cliffs o'erhanging grew.

'iron-hearted (-,hɑːtɪd), *a.* Extremely hard-hearted; unfeeling; cruel; insensible to pity.

a **1618** SYLVESTER *Hymn of Almes* 557 Such Gold-heaped Iron-hearted Wretches As to the Poor impart no part of Riches. **1652** WARREN *Unbelievers* (1654) 21 The most iron-hearted sinner. **1725** POPE *Odyss.* XXIV. 80 And iron-hearted heroes melt in tears. **1849** PRESCOTT *Peru* (1850) II. 286 Finding that no impression was to be made on his iron-hearted conqueror.

ironic (aɪ'rɒnɪk), *a.* [ad. late L. *īrōnic-us*, a. Gr. εἰρωνικός 'dissembling, putting on a feigned ignorance', f. εἰρωνεία dissimulation, IRONY. Cf. F. *ironique* (*yronicque*, 1521 in Hatz.-Darm.).] Pertaining to irony; uttering or given to irony; of the nature of or containing irony; = IRONICAL.

1630 B. JONSON *New Inn* III. ii, Most Socratick lady! Or if you will, ironick! **1638** SIR T. HERBERT *Trav.* (ed. 2) 12 That Ironic Satyre of Juvenal. **1788** H. WALPOLE *Lett.* XV. 118 If there was anything ironic in my meaning, it was levelled at your readers, not at you. **1831** CARLYLE *Sart. Res.* II. iv, An ironic man..more especially an ironic young man

. . may be viewed as a pest to society. **1879** G. Meredith *Egoist* xv. (1889) 140 She could have asked him in her fit of ironic iciness . . whether the romance might be his piece of religion. **1883** A. Dobson *Fielding* 29 How his ironic lightning plays Around a rogue and all his ways!

ironical (aɪˈrɒnɪkəl), *a.* [f. as prec. + -al[1].]
1. Of the nature of irony or covert sarcasm; meaning the opposite of what is expressed.
1576 Fleming *Panopl. Epist.* 237 *note,* He was (belike) some Pomilio or litle dwarfe, and that made him to use this eironical method. **1603** Holland *Plutarch's Mor.* 665 Another kinde there seemes to be of ironicall praise, opposite unto the former; namely, when semblant is made of blame and reproofe. **1621** Burton *Anat. Mel.* Democr. to Rdr. (1676) 14/1 Democritus . . was so far carried with this ironical passion, that the Citizens of Abdera took him to be mad. **1707** *Reflex. upon Ridicule* 222 They praise themselves . . and drink like Nectar, the ironical Encomiums that are made them. **1794** Mrs. Radcliffe *Myst. Udolpho* xii, 'Your reasons are indeed such as cannot be doubted', replied the lady with an ironical smile. **1853** Macaulay *Biog., Atterbury* (1867) 8 Boyle . . paid, in his preface, a bitterly ironical compliment to Bentley's courtesy.
2. That uses or is addicted to irony.
1589 Nashe *Pref. to Greene's Menaphon* (Arb.) 6 Some deepe read Grammarians, who . . take vpon them to be the ironicall censors of all. **1793** Beattie *Moral Sc.* iv. i. §1. II. 464 Socrates used it so happily . . that he got the name of ὁ εἴρων, or the ironical philosopher. **1848** W. H. Kelly tr. *L. Blanc's Hist. Ten Y.* I. 337 Ostrowski was dignified, Lelewel ironical and inflexible.
†**b.** *transf.* ? Mockingly imitative. *Obs.*
1607 Topsell *Four-f. Beasts* (1658) 2 [Apes] are held for a subtill, ironicall, ridiculous and unprofitable Beast . . of the Grecians termed *Gelotopoios,* made for laughter.
†**3.** Dissembling; feigned, pretended. *Obs. rare.*
1646 Sir T. Browne *Pseud. Ep.* i. iv. 14 The circle of this fallacie is very large, and herein may be comprised all Ironicall mistakes; for intended expressions receiving inverted significations, all deductions from metaphors, parables, allegories, unto reall and rigid interpretations. **1727** De Foe *Syst. Magic* i. iv. (1840) 115 So much force is ironical righteousness.
Hence **iˈronicalness**, ironical quality.
1775 in Ash. **1846** in Worcester.

ironically (aɪˈrɒnɪkəlɪ), *adv.* [f. prec. + -ly[2]. Cf. Gr. εἰρωνικῶς, L. *īrōnice,* F. *ironiquement.*]
1. In an ironical manner; by way of irony.
1576 Fleming *Panopl. Epist.* 211 *note,* It may be spoken eironically, for familiar friends use jeasting nowe and then, in their letters. **1649** Roberts *Clavis Bibl.* 109 Ironically bidding them cry to their idols for help. **1731** Swift *On his Death* 309 Although ironically grave, He sham'd the fool, and lash'd the knave. **1866** Geo. Eliot *F. Holt* Introd., Saying that there had been fine stories—meaning, ironically, stories not altogether creditable to the parties concerned.
†**2.** With dissimulation or personation. *Obs. rare.*
1682 Sir T. Browne *Chr. Mor.* iii. §20 Though the World be histrionical and most Men live ironically, yet be thou what thou singly art, and personate only thy self.

ironing (ˈaɪənɪŋ), *vbl. sb.* [f. iron *v.* + -ing[1].] The action of the verb iron.
1. a. The pressing and smoothing of clothes, cloth, etc., with a heated iron.
c **1710** Celia Fiennes *Diary* (1888) 7 Mr. Newbery . . would keep no women servants—had all washing, Ironing, dairy and all performed by men. **1838** Dickens *Nich. Nick.* xxiv, A strong smell of ironing pervaded the little passage. **1885** *Manch. Exam.* 9 Sept. 3/1 Equal to the task of instructing a laundress in the ironing of a table-cloth.
b. *attrib.,* as *ironing blanket, board, machine, room, stool, table.*
1810 E. Weeton *Let.* 25 Feb. in *Jrnl. of Governess* (1969) I. 232, I flew into the servants' hall for the ironing blanket. **1854** Mrs. Gaskell *North & South* (1855) I. iv. 44 Dixon had complained that the ironing-blanket had been burnt again. **1843** *New Mirror* 8 Apr. 4/2 Swapped away for a wash-bench or an ironing-board. **1876** H. E. Scudder *Dwellers in Five-Sisters Court* iii. 52 Nicholas will have to carry the ironing-board for her. **1928–9** *T. Eaton & Co. Catal.* Fall & Winter 391/4 Ironing Board Cover . . padded with wadding . . fits any regulation-sized board. **1969** E. H. Pinto *Treen* 151 Ironing boards . . are found in a variety of shapes and sizes, for skirts, . . trousers, . . and sleeves. **1972** *Guardian* 30 June 7/7 This superb new Milium Ironing Board Cover . . is scorch resistant. **1972** *Sci. Amer.* Dec. 48/3 The development of fine glass yarns . . has brought glass fibers into such products as bedspreads and covers for ironing boards. **1759** Colebrooke in *Phil. Trans.* LI. 44 An ironing box, charged with an hot heater. **1852** Mrs. Stowe *Uncle Tom's C.* ix. 79 The little table stood out before the fire, covered with an ironing-cloth. **1817** H. Lee (*title*) Poetic Impressions, . . including the Washing Day, Ironing Day, Brewing Day, Quarter Day, and Saturday. *a* **1877** Knight *Dict. Mech.* II. 1203/2 *Ironing-machine,* one for ironing clothes, etc. **1962** *Which?* June 170/1 We should like to hear from members who have bought a dishwashing machine or an ironing machine during 1960 or 1961. **1894** E. Banks *Campaigns of Curiosity* 195 The one large room . . should be divided into . . three apartments; wash-house, sorting-room, and ironing-room. **1906** *Westm. Gaz.* 5 July 2/1 The hooded fireplace of the ironing-room. **1962** *Guardian* 3 Dec. 4/7 Mothers come . . to enjoy working in the little ironing room. **1878** Mrs. Stowe *Poganuc People* xxv. 268 Will seized her off the ironing stool and, perching her on his shoulder, danced round the table. **1840** Dickens *Old C. Shop* x, The poor woman was still hard at work at an ironing-table. **1911** F. B. Jack *Woman's Bk.* 273/1 The Ironing Table.—This must be of a good size, strong, and steady, and of a convenient height for working at. *Ibid.* 273/2 In addition to the ironing table, a smaller one for placing the work on will be found a great convenience if space permits. **1959** *Sears, Roebuck Catal.* Spring & Summer 966/2 Ironing Table Designed for stand-up and sit-down ironing. **1974** *J. Frazer Catal.* 739/1 Ironing surface 36″ × 13″ All-metal ironing table . . £4.50.
2. The putting (*of* persons) in irons. *rare.*
1820 *Examiner* No. 650. 620/1 The dungeonings and ironings of Reformers.
3. The action of fitting or arming with iron.
¶**4.** As a perversion of *irony*: see iron *v.* 4.

†**iˈronious,** *a. Obs.*—[0] [f. L. *īrōnīa* irony *sb.* + -ous.] = ironical. Hence †**iˈroniously** *adv.,* ironically.
c **1530** L. Cox *Rhet.* (1899) 81 Whiche place Cato vseth ironiously in Salust. **1535** Joye *Apol. Tindale* (Arb.) 14 This saith Tindale yroniously. **1609** Bible (Douay) *Jer.* xlvi. *comm.,* Aegypt accounted itself invincible, and so the prophet ironiously calleth it the virgin daughter, as in this whole passage he speaketh by the same figure ironia.

ˈ**ironish,** *a.* Now *rare.* [f. iron *sb.*[1] + -ish.]
†**1.** Of iron: = iron *a.* 1. *Obs.*
c **1450** *Mirour Saluacioun* 1360 The leggis als thoght the king of yrnysshe matieres wasse.
2. Partaking of the qualities of iron; irony; ferruginous.
1641 French *Distill.* v. (1651) 165 That acidity and that ironish and vitriolated tast and odour. **1675** E. Wilson *Spadacr. Dunelm.* 66 A strong irritation of Nature to expel her Ironish Enemy [iron taken medicinally]. *a* **1691** Boyle *Hist. Air* (1692) 219 A kind of black taffety, which . . will, after . . a very few days, degenerate into an ironish colour.

ironism (ˈaɪərənɪz(ə)m). *rare.* [mod. f. Gr. εἴρων dissembler, user of irony + -ism.] The practice of using irony.
1899 *Speaker* 15 Apr. 426/2 The 'ironism' which Mr. Davidson has borrowed from Renan has the rare distinction of satisfying neither reason nor emotion.

ironist[1] (ˈaɪərənɪst). [f. as prec. + -ist: in F. *ironiste.*] One who uses irony; an ironical speaker or writer.
1727 Pope, etc. *Art Sinking* 115 A poet or orator would have no more to do but to send to . . the ironist for his sarcasms, to the apothegmatist for his sentences. **1832** W. Anderson in *Mem. R. Hall* H.'s Wks. VI. 134 Socrates was called the ironist from his constant assumption of a character that did not belong to him. **1836** *Blackw. Mag.* XL. 309 All this time you have been playing the Ironist.

†ˈ**ironist**[2]. *Obs.* [f. iron *sb.*[1] + -ist.] One who uses iron weapons.
1650 R. Stapylton *Strada's Low C. Warres* viii. 4 That kind of Raiters, which from their many pistols and other iron weapons are called *Ironists* [L. *Ferreolos*].

ˈ**ironize,** *v.*[1] [f. as *ironism* + ize.] **a.** *trans.* To make ironical, use ironically. **b.** *intr.* To use irony, speak ironically. Hence ˈ**ironized** *ppl. a.*[1], used or spoken ironically.
1602 Warner *Alb. Eng.* ix. liii. (1612) 239 If Hypocrites why Puritaines we terme be ask't, in breefe, T'is but an *Ironized* Tearme, good-fellow so spels Theefe. **1638** Sir T. Herbert *Trav.* (ed. 2) 240 To memorize their Cheese and Butter will make your mouths water at it; I ironize: in good earnest the cheese is the worst any ever tasted of. **1906** H. Bland *Lett. to Daughter* 116 Does one satirise, ironise, slate, bully-rag, and squirt verbal vitriol at the thing one loves? **1933** Partridge *Words, Words, Words!* iii. 184 The tendency either to ironize or to belittle one's fears, sufferings and discomforts. **1969** *Daily Tel.* 13 Feb. 22/4 There is also the ironist, ironising himself.

†ˈ**ironize,** *v.*[2] *Obs. nonce-wd.* [f. iron *sb.*[1] + -ize.] *trans.* To impregnate with iron. Hence ˈ**ironized** *ppl. a.*[2], impregnated with iron.
1780 J. T. Dillon *Trav. Spain* (1781) 250, I have seen . . a great part of ironized mineral serve as a matrice to cinnabar.

ˈ**ironless,** *a. rare.* [f. iron *sb.*[1] + -less.] Destitute of iron; not possessing iron. In quot. 1420 quasi-*adv.* 'without the aid of iron tools' (Lodge, *Gloss. to Palladius*).
c **1420** *Pallad. on Husb.* iii. 685 And rape seed in to their hedes gete Al yronles, wol make hem growe faste; And ofte ydoon the faster wyl they haste. **1865** Tylor *Early Hist. Man.* vii. 169 Their connection with the ironless Maoris and Tahitians.

iron lung. 1. A kind of respirator for giving prolonged artificial respiration mechanically, consisting of a metal case that fits over the patient's chest or trunk with an air-tight aperture for the neck (and limbs), so that air may be forced into and out of the lungs by producing rhythmic variations in the air pressure in the case. orig. *U.S.*
1932 *N.Y. Times* 3 Oct. 19/5 Surgeons revealed today that Birdsall Sweet, 14, of Beacon has just rounded out one year in the artificial respirator or 'iron lung' in Vassar Brothers hospital, Poughkeepsie. **1934** E. Podolsky *Medicine marches On* v. xvi. 140 Dr. Drinker's machine was called into service. The patient was placed in the machine that was to do his breathing for him. The iron lung forced air into his paralyzed chest and drew it out again. **1938** *Encycl. Brit. Bk. of Yr.* 406/2 The new type of respirator or iron lung . . covers only the upper half of the body and does not involve the insertion of the complete person into the apparatus. **1938** *Times* 12 Aug. 14/4 Eric Baker, aged 11, died at Braintree . . from infantile paralysis. He was taken ill on Monday and was placed in an iron lung. **1948** *Electronic Engin.* XX. 4/1 In the modern 'iron lung' bellows are used which take upon them the work usually done by the muscles of chest and diaphragm. *a* **1963** S. Plath *Ariel* (1965) 78 No fingers to grip, no tongue, My god the iron lung That loves me, pumps My two Dust bags in and out.
2. *slang.* A Nissen hut.
1943 Hunt & Pringle *Service Slang* 40 *Iron lung,* Barrage Balloon boys' phrase for Nissen hut.

ˈ**ironly,** *adv. rare.* [f. iron *a.* + -ly[2].] In an 'iron' manner; oppressively, rigorously.
1895 *Eclectic Mag.* Oct. 564 The one ironly tyrannical, no doubt.

iron-man. [f. iron *sb.*[1] or *a.* + man *sb.*]
1. (Properly two words, iron *a.* and man *sb.*)
a. A man of iron (in *fig.* sense).
1617 A. Newman *Pleas. Vis.* (1840) 31 They draw, like Loadstones, Iron-men.
b. Name of a coal-cutting machine. *local.*
1897 *Star* 17 Sept. 2/6 In some of the thin seams of that district [Yorkshire coalfield], the coal-cutting has for some time been done by machine—by the 'iron man'.
c. *U.S. slang.* A dollar.
1908 H. Green *Maison de Shine* 45 A feller who shells out his six iron men every week. **1926** *Flynn's* 16 Jan. 639/1 Still I can flash a toad-skin now and then, and have a few iron men planted where th' berries grow. **1932** J. Dos Passos *1919* 52 He still had more'n fifty iron men. **1945** *This Week Mag.* 21 Apr. 15/2 When I'd given the boys back their dough I had a nice little profit of two hundred iron men. **1970** E. R. Johnson *God Keepers* (1971) vi. 62 An ounce should bring a street pusher about two thousand iron men.
d. *slang* (orig. *Austral.*). A pound. Cf. iron *sb.*[1] 4 g.
1959 Baker *Drum* 119 *Iron man,* a £1 note. **1973** J. Leasor *Host of Extras* i. 16 A nut . . to whom I'd sold a Bean Tourer —not the most exciting car . . but what did he expect for five hundred iron men? **1974** J. Wainwright *Evidence I shall Give* xxviii. 141 Ten thousand iron men. . . We're talking bank-notes.
†**2.** A kind of iron-ore. *Obs. local.*
1683 Pettus *Fleta Min.* i. (1686) 101 There breaks a small grey spissy Oar . . called Iron-man.
3. A workman in ironworks. ? *nonce-wd.*
1875 M. Collins *Sweet & Twenty* I. i. iv. 59 He drew strong pictures of the ironmaster's unlimited champagne and the ironman's limited beer.

ironmaster (ˈaɪənˌmɑːstə(r), -æ-). The master of an iron-foundry or ironworks; a manufacturer of iron, esp. on a large scale.
1674 Ray *Words, Iron Work* 129 This account of the whole process of the Iron work I had from one of the chief Ironmasters in Sussex. **1731** *Gentl. Mag.* I. 268 Bilby Laycock of Tamworth Staffordshire, Ironmaster. **1825** J. Nicholson *Operat. Mechanic* 328 Iron-masters are so very inattentive to its quality . . we sometimes see them use lime-stone as a flux when the ore already abounds with calcareous ingredients. **1859** Lewin *Invas. Brit.* 116 *note,* A tablet . . bearing the name of Cogidubnus . . and indicating that under his auspices a temple, dedicated to Minerva and Neptune, had been erected in the reign of Claudius at the expense of the ironmasters of Sussex. **1861** Smiles *Engineers* II. 360 *note,* The bridge was cast in an admirable manner by the Coalbrookdale ironmasters in the year 1796.

iron-mine.
1. A mine from which iron-ore is obtained.
1601 R. Johnson *Kingd. & Commw.* (1603) 40 Nature hir-selfe . . giving them the iron mines of Biskay. **1762** Ld. Mansfield in Burrow *Rep.* III. 1344 Coal-mines are not lead-mines, tin-mines, copper-mines, iron-mines, or any other but coal-mines. **1872** Yeats *Techn. Hist. Comm.* 97 More conveniently placed in regard to iron-mines.
2. Iron-ore. (See mine *sb.*) Now *dial.*
1645 Boate *Irel. Nat. Hist.* (1652) 132 Where the Iron-mine is melted. *Ibid.* 137 A Tun of the Iron-mine or Oar. **1674** Ray *Collect. Words* 125 The Iron-mine lies sometimes deeper, sometimes shallower in the Earth. **1709** *Lond. Gaz.* No. 4527/3 In the Land is a great quantity of Iron-Mine.

ironmonger (ˈaɪənmʌŋgə(r)). Forms: 4 is-, ysmonger, irmongere, 5 yremongere, erne-, hermonger, ironmounger, 5–6 yren-, irenmonger, -yr, 5–7 irne-, 6 yer-, iernmonger, 6–7 iremonger, -munger, 6– ironmonger [f. iron *sb.*[1] + monger.] A dealer in ironware; a hardware merchant.
1343 *Merton Coll. Rec.* No. 2115 (MS.) Roger le Irmongere. **1347** *Ibid.* No. 2096 Roger le Ysmonger. **1393** *Close Roll 16 Rich. II* dorso (P.R.O.), Johannes Warner, ismonger. **1406** *Ibid., 8 Hen. IV* dorso, Petrus Feryby, ernemonger. **1409** *Ibid. 11 Hen. IV* dorso, Willielmus Baker, hermonger. **1415** *Nottingham Rec.* II. 100 Nicholaum Alastre, de Notyngham, irenmonger. **1415** *York Myst.* Introd. 22 Irenmangers. **1486** *Naval Acc. Hen. VII* (1896) 10 Payd vnto William Remyngton of London Ironmounger for diuers cabilles. *Ibid.* 12 Payd . . to John Halyngbury of London Irnemonger for vj cables. *c* **1515** *Cocke Lorell's B.* 9 Yermongers, py-bakers, and waferers. **1562** *Act 5 Eliz.* c. 4 §20 The Misteries or Craftes of a . . Draper Goldesmithe Ironmonger. **1591** in *Child Marriages* 151 Thomas Thornton . . Iremonger and Marchaunte. **1613** Beaum. & Fl. *Cupids Rev.* iv. iii, Come, let's call up the new Iremonger, he's as tough as Steel. **1620** in Swayne *Sarum Church-w. Acc.* (1896) 170 Rec. . . of the Ire mvngers . . 18*d.* **1646** *Ord. Lords & Com. Presb. Govt.* 11 John Arrowsmith of Martins Iremonger-lane. **1720** Strype *Stow's Surv.* (1754) II. v. x. 280/1 The Ironmongers were incorporated in the third Year of King Edward the Fourth, Anno Dom. 1462. **1876** Bancroft *Hist. U.S.* II. xli. 521 The English ironmongers asked for a total prohibition of forges.
Hence ˈ**ironmongering** *ppl. a.,* dealing in iron. (In quot. = having ironworks.)
1863 Hawthorne *Our Old Home* (1883) I. 169 These hillocks of waste and effete mineral always disfigure the neighborhood of iron-mongering towns.

ironmongery ('aɪən,mʌŋgərɪ). [f. prec.: see -ERY.]

1. a. The goods dealt in by an ironmonger; hardware; a general name for all articles made of iron.

1711 *Lond. Gaz.* No. 4831/4 Ironmongery, Cutlery, and other small Wares. **1796** MORSE *Amer. Geog.* I. 452 Ironmongery.. manufactured in this state. **1851** *Art Jrnl. Gt. Exhib. Catal.* 39/3 Manufacturers of what is termed 'saddlers' ironmongery', such as steel-bits, stirrups, whips and whip-mounts. **1876** JAS. GRANT *One of the '600'* xxiii. 181 The great Norman line.. who had ridden in all their ironmongery in Edward's ranks at Bannockburn.

b. An ironmonger's shop or place of business.

1841 ORDERSON *Creol.* vi. 60 Premises.. occupied as an ironmongery.. and a saddlery. **1896** DU MAURIER *Martian* (1898) 227 A well-to-do burgher with a prosperous ironmongery in the 'Petit Brul'.

c. *slang.* Firearms.

1902 KIPLING *Traffics & Discov.* (1904) 11 They'd all stand to their horses and pile on the ironmongery, and washers, and typewriters, and.. they'd sail out.. lying down and firing. **1905** A. H. LEWIS *Sunset Trail* (1914) x. 160 All men have their delicate side, and it was Mr. Allison's to regard the open wearing of one's iron-mongery as bad form. **1942** E. WAUGH *Put out More Flags* 275 Their '098 stores arrived; a vast profusion of ironmongery which.. included Alastair's mortar. **1960** 'W. HAGGARD' *Closed Circuit* xv. 177 He wasn't armed. He had never carried ironmongery. **1973** J. WAINWRIGHT *Devil you Don't* 112 Shove it. You are only here for the ride. If you hadn't been so damned handy with the ironmongery—.

d. Also in other applications (see quots.).

1892 *Century Mag.* Dec. 218/2 The broad veranda.. had the customary array of.. hanging lamps set with bosses of colored glass, and much ironmongery in spirals and curlicues. **1934** H. G. WELLS *Exper. Autobiogr.* II. viii. 568, I tried to make him [*sc.* Gissing] a cyclist... 'Get on to your ironmongery,' said I. **1955** *Times* 4 Aug. 8/7 A pike which was already the subject of legend.. had broken anglers' tackle seven times.. appeared to thrive on a diet of triangles, and snap-tackles, plug-baits, five-inch spoons, and other ironmongery. **1958** *Engineering* 4 Apr. 425/1 No good starting with ironmongery—computers—got to start with systems analysis. **1967** *Guardian* 5 May 6/7 With the 'attached ironmongery', there is a disturbing lack of coordination... The lighting standards are not inelegant, but there are too many of them... Guard-rails, crash barriers, gantries, and direction signs.. have the appearance of rushed afterthoughts. **1971** D. HASTON in C. Bonington *Annapurna South Face* xvii. 212, I started off on the chimney. At this time we were badly short of rope and ironmongery. I had about three hundred feet of rope, four pegs and about six karabiners.

2. The craft or business of the ironmonger; smith's work.

1871 *Athenæum* 16 Sept. 374 A point in ironmongery rather than architecture.

3. *attrib.*

1769 *Public Advertiser* 18 May 3/4 All other things in the Ironmongery Business. **1879** *Law Rep.* 14 Queen's Bench Div. 814 Their ironmongery stock.. having been seized and sold.

iron-mould, -mold ('aɪən'məʊld), *sb.* Also 7 **-mole.** [f. IRON *sb.*[1] + MOULD, MOLD, earlier *mole*, OE. *mál*, mole, spot, mark.]

1. A spot or discoloration on cloth, etc., caused by iron-rust or an ink-stain.

α. **1601** HOLLAND *Pliny* II. 47 The decoction will.. take out any stain in cloths, euen the very iron-mole. **1642** ROGERS *Naaman* 447 Some grosse sins.. which are as iron moles, and will hardly be worne out of the flesh. *a* **1659** OSBORN *Observ. Turks* Pref. (1673) 4 Book-worms, who, like Iron-moles, discolour the sense and obliterate the natural meaning of Authors.

β. **1639** JUNIUS *Sin Stigmat.* §98. 378 Fine linnen being once stained with black Inke.. will retaine an Iron-mould ever after. **1788** *Trans. Soc. Arts* VI. 169 In this [paper] there are no Iron Moulds. **1828** WEBSTER, *Ironmold.* **1833** J. RENNIE *Alph. Angling* 67 Yellowish spots very much like iron-moulds. **1872** J. G. MURPHY *Comm. Levit.* xiii. 49 Ironmould is a familiar example of a stain caused by a chemical process.

b. *fig.*

1644 MILTON *Areop.* (Arb.) 58 Such iron moulds as these shall have autority to knaw out the choicest periods of exquisitest books. **1660** J. SPENCER *Righteous Ruler* 37 Arms, the iron-mole that stained our religion, and eat out order and law.

2. (See quot.)

1706 PHILLIPS, *Iron-moulds*, certain yellow Lumps of Earth or Stone found in Chalk-pits about the Chiltern in Oxfordshire, which are really a kind of indigested Iron-Oar. **1778** *England's Gazetteer* (ed. 2), *Berrick-Priory*.. noted for chalk pits, in which is found a sort of iron-coloured *terra lapidosa*, in the very body of the chalk, which the diggers call iron-moulds.

'iron-,mould, -mold, *v.* [f. prec. sb.] *trans.* and *intr.* To stain or become stained with iron-mould. Hence **'iron-,moulded** *ppl. a.*

1727 BRADLEY *Fam. Dict.* s.v. *Clear Starching*, If your Muslins be Iron-moulded. **1873** DAWSON *Earth & Man* vi. 112 The superabundant oxide of iron.. so to speak 'iron-moulds' them. ?*c* **1890** W. H. CASNEY *Notes Ventilation* 8 Drops falling from the beams often caused the warps to iron-mould.

ironness ('aɪənnɪs). *rare.* Also 4 irinnes. [f. IRON *a.* + -NESS.] The quality of 'iron'; in quot. *a* 1300, ? the fact of being clad in iron; in quot. 1803, physical strength and hardiness.

a **1300** *Cursor M.* 7544 Qua-sa fightes in wrangwisnes, Him helpes noght his Irinnes. **1803** H. SWINBURNE in *Crts. Europe Close last Cent.* (1841) II. 375 An ironness of constitution hammered when red-hot by adversity.

'iron-'on, *a.* [f. IRON *v.* 3 + ON *adv.*] Such as can be affixed to the surface of a fabric by ironing.

1959 *Times* 12 Jan. 11/5 Woven cotton iron-on interlining. **1966** *Olney Amsden & Sons Ltd. Price List* 35 Iron-on Sheet Markers. **1967** E. SHORT *Embroidery & Fabric Collage* iv. 94 (*caption*) The fabric, previously backed with an iron-on interlining, is cut with a razor blade and pressed. **1970** *Guardian* 10 Sept. 13/3 Sewing on name tapes is a tedious job. Iron-on tapes can cut down the sewing.

'iron-'ore, iron ore. The ore of iron; any crude form in which iron is found in the earth.

1601 HOLLAND *Pliny* XXXIV. xiv. II. 514 Mines of yron ore. **1645** BOATE *Irel. Nat. Hist.* (1652) 138 The manner of melting the Iron-oar. **1799** *Med. Jrnl.* I. 202 As completely terrigenous and opaque as any argillaceous iron-ore. **1805–17** R. JAMESON *Char. Min.* (ed. 3) 256 Specular iron-ore, or iron-glance. **1881** RAYMOND *Mining Gloss., Iron-ores: Magnetic* (magnetite, protoperoxide), *specular* (hematite proper, red hematite, anhydrous peroxide), *brown iron ore* (hematite, brown hematite,limonite, etc., hydrated peroxides), *spathic* (siderite, carbonate), *clay-ironstone* (black band, argillaceous siderite).

attrib. **1892** *Labour Commission Gloss., Iron-ore Men*, men who discharge iron-ore cargoes. **1895** *Westm. Gaz.* 17 Dec. 3/2 Colliers, iron-ore miners, quarrymen.

'iron-plated, *a.* Protected by plates of iron; = IRONCLAD *a.*

1860–1863 [see IRONCLAD, A. 1 a *note*].

'iron-,sand.

1. *Geol.* Sand containing particles of iron-ore, usually either magnetite or titaniferous oxide.

1805 D. MCCLURE *Diary* (1899) 29 The soil abounds in iron sand Ore. **1862** W. K. HULKE *Let.* 9 Aug. in *Richmond-Atkinson Papers* (1960) I. 781 Yesterday the battle about the iron-sand leases came off. **1876** PAGE *Adv. Text-bk. Geol.* xvii. 329 The nodules and pisiform ironsands of the Wealden. **1894** *Harper's Mag.* Jan. 409 'Iron-sand' is a form of magnetite.. consisting of silicious particles mixed with grains of iron ore. **1963** *Times* 6 Feb. (N.Z. Suppl.) p. iv/5 New methods have been developed to process the ironsands of the North Island beaches.

2. 'The steel-filings used in fireworks' (*Cent. Dict.*).

'iron-shod, *a.* [f. IRON *sb.*[1] + SHOD, pa. pple. of SHOE *v.*] Shod, tipped, or armed with iron.

c **1330** R. BRUNNE *Chron. Wace* (Rolls) 4637 Iren-schod was ilka peel. **1774** GOLDSM. *Nat. Hist.* (1776) VI. 383 Like the nails of an iron shod wheel. **1850** W. IRVING *Mahomet* xi. (1853) 44 The soles of their iron shod boots were torn from the upper leathers. **1871–4** J. THOMSON *City Dreadf. Nt.* IX. i, The trampling clash of heavy iron-shod feet.

'iron-shot, *a. Min.* [f. as prec. + SHOT, pa. pple. of SHOOT *v.*] 'Shot' with iron; containing streaks or markings of iron.

1796 KIRWAN *Elem. Min.* (ed. 2) I. 293 Is it not rather an iron-shot quartz? *Ibid.* 390 Iron shot hornstones. **1821** R. JAMESON *Man. Min* 93 Slaggy Ironshot Copper-Green. **1847–8** H. MILLER *First Impr.* i. (1857) 15 They [potatoes] were freckled over with minute circular spots, that bore a ferruginous tinge, somewhat resembling the specks on iron-shot sandstone. **1858** G. P. SCROPE *Geol. Centr. France* (ed. 2) 171 Many varieties are much iron-shot.

'iron-,sick, *a. Naut.* Now *rare* or *Obs.* Said of a wooden ship when her bolts and nails are so corroded with rust that she has become leaky.

1626 CAPT. SMITH *Accid. Yng. Seamen* 13 A ship cranke sided, Iron sicke, spewes her okum. **1627** —— *Seaman's Gram.* xi. 54 *Iron sicke*, is when the Bolts, Spikes, or Nailes are so eaten with rust they stand hollow in the plankes, and so makes her leake. **1664** P. PETT *Let. to S. Pepys* in *Cal. St. Papers, Domestic* 113 The Unicorn is iron-sick under the water. **1691** T. H[ALE] *Acc. New Invent.* 79 Ships in ten or twelve years are generally Iron-sick. **1841** *Proc. Inst. Civ. Eng.* 132 What is technically termed 'ironsick', meaning that the bolt-holes became so widened by corrosion that the bolts were loosened.

Ironside ('aɪənsaɪd). Also (*sing.*) **Ironsides.**

1. *sing.* A name given to a man of great hardihood or bravery; *spec.* in *Eng. Hist.* (*Ironside*) to Edmund II king of England (A.D. 1016), and (also *Ironsides*) to Oliver Cromwell; also, independently or transf., to other persons.

In the case of Cromwell the appellation was a nickname of Royalist origin.

1297 R. GLOUC. (Rolls) 6084 Is eldoste sone, Edmond yrene syde, Vor he was hardi and god kniȝt, at hom he let abide. **1350–70** *Eulog. Histor.* (Rolls) III. v. xci. 24 Nomen primi est Edmundus, vocabulo Irenside [*v.r.* Yrensyde]. *a* **1635** CORBET *Poems, To Ld. Mordant* 154 One [of the guard at Windsor] I remember with a grisly beard,.. This Ironside tooke hold, and sodainly Hurled mee.. Some twelve foote by the square. **1644** *Mercurius Civicus* 19–26 Sept., Monday we had intelligence that Lieutenant General Cromwell *alias* Ironside, for that title was given him by Prince Rupert after his defeat neare York [etc.]. **1645** *Relation of Victory on Naseby Field* in *Eng. Hist. Rev.* (1899) 17 News being brought them.. that Iron-sides was comming to joyne with the Parliament's Army. **1647** TRAPP *Comm. Acts* xix. 9 So indefatigable a preacher was Paul, a very.. iron-sides. **1660** BURNEY *Κέρδ. Δῶρον* (1661) 97 Henrie the 8.. who appeared an ironsides against the Principalities of darknesse. **1663** *Flagellum or O. Cromwell* vi. in *Harl. Misc.* (1753) I. 275 Hence he [Cromwell] acquired that terrible Name of Ironsides. **1898** *Westm. Gaz.* 30 Mar. 1/3 Mrs. Parnell.. was her father's child, and he had won for himself the appellation of Iron-sides, as a testimony to the strength of his character and the resolution with which he pursued the British Fleet in those days of trouble between Great Britain and America.

2. *pl.* (*Ironsides.*) Applied to Cromwell's troopers in the Civil War; hence allusively in later uses. The sing. is sometimes used of one member of such a force: a Puritan warrior; a devout soldier of the Puritan type.

As applied to Cromwell's regiment it may have been orig. a possessive, *Ironside's men*: cf. the *Queen's*, *Prince of Wales's*, and similar modern titles of regiments. See also Lieut.-Col. Ross *Oliver Cromwell and his Ironsides* 19.

1648 *Resol. King's subj. Cornwall* 2 Aug. (in *Thomasson Tracts* CCCLXXX. No. 18. 3), The soldiers shouted saying 'that Cromwell and his Iron sides were now taken'. **1648** *Let.* 8 Aug. in *Moderate* (*ibid.* CCCLXXXII. No. 21 Eij), These Ironsides advancing make them search every corner for security. **1667** LILLY *Life & Times* (1774) 144 Sir Thomas Fairfax's brigade of horse, and Oliver Cromwell's ironsides; for Cromwell's horse in those times usually wore headpieces, back and breastplates of iron. **1859** MOWBRAY THOMSON *Story of Cawnpore* iii. 48, I was there also when Havelock's Ironsides gave their entertainment, shattering to powder all that was fragile. **1889** *Dict. Nat. Biog.* XVII. 111/1 With the dashing spirit of the cavalier the early Punjab officer united something of the earnestness of the Ironside. **1891** GARDINER *Hist. Civil War* III. lxiv. 432 It was at Pontefract (1648 August) that Cromwell's men were first called by the nickname of Ironsides, a term which had hitherto been appropriated to himself. It was not.. an epithet which came into general use for some time to come.

3. A ship plated with iron; an ironclad.

1861 *Times* 13 Mar. 9/3 Our own fleet of ironsides comprises two first-rates actually launched, and one on the stocks.

'iron-sided, *a.* [f. *iron side* + -ED[2].] Having sides made of or resembling iron; protected on the sides with iron; ironclad. **b.** *dial.* (See quot.)

a **1825** FORBY *Voc. E. Anglia, Iron-sided*, hardy, rough; unmanageable. A boy who fears nobody, and plays.. mischievous tricks, is called an iron-sided dog. **1859** [see IRONCLAD, A. 1 a *note*]. **1860** *Sat. Rev.* X. 450/1 These iron-sided ships.

ironsmith. Now *rare* or *Obs.* [f. IRON *sb.*[1] + SMITH.] An artificer in iron; a blacksmith.

1382 WYCLIF *Ecclus.* xxxviii. 29 [28] The iren smyth sittende biside the stithie. **1535** COVERDALE *ibid.*, The yronsmyth in like maner bydeth by his stythie. **1551** ROBINSON tr. *More's Utop.* II. ix. (1895) 301 Poore labourers, carters, yronsmythes, carpenters, and plowmen. **1609** BIBLE (Douay) 1 *Sam.* xiii. 19 There was not found an yron smith in al the Land of Israel. **1634** SIR T. HERBERT *Trav.* 202 An Iron-smith. **1844** LINGARD *Anglo-Sax. Ch.* (1858) I. 244 The ironsmith, the joiner, and the goldsmith.

b. As a rendering of the native name of a bird, a species of barbet (*Megalæma faber*).

1885 R. SWINHOE in *Stand. Nat. Hist.* (1888) IV. 420 From its loud, peculiar call, the Hainan species has earned among the natives of the island the appellation of 'ironsmith', whence I have derived its specific name [*faber*].

ironstone, iron-stone ('aɪənstəʊn, -stən). The name given to various hard iron-ores containing admixtures of silica, clay, etc.

1522 *Test. Ebor.* (Surtees) V. 160 As much yren stone to be deliverid in one word callid Freretaile. **1523** FITZHERB. *Surv.* 15 Leed ore tyn cole yrenston. **1677** YARRANTON *Eng. Improv.* 43 Having Iron Stone of his own for gathering up, and Wood of his own for nothing, he will have very cheap Guns and Iron. **1802** PLAYFAIR *Illustr. Hutton. The.* 30 On the structure of certain iron-stones, called septaria. **1816** W. SMITH *Strata Ident.* 1 The Muscles and Ammonites found in Ironstone. **1854** H. MILLER *Sch. & Schm.* (1858) 60 A shattered and ruined precipice, seamed with blood-red ironstone.

b. *attrib.* **ironstone china, i. ware,** a hard kind of white pottery (see quot. 1875).

1825 J. NICHOLSON *Operat. Mechanic* 479 Iron-stone china is not very transparent; but possesses great strength, compactness, density, and durability. **1875** *Ure's Dict. Arts* III. 616 Some of the English porcelain has been called ironstone-china. This is composed usually of 60 parts of Cornish stone, 40 of China-clay, and 2 of flint-glass; or 42 of felspar, the same quantity of clay, 10 parts of flints ground, and 8 of flint-glass. Slag from iron-smelting is sometimes introduced into the paste. **1897** OLIVE SCHREINER *P. Halkett* i. 14 He had wandered among long grasses and ironstone Koppjes.

iron-tree. A name (more or less local) for various trees and shrubs with very hard wood, as *Ixora ferrea* of the West Indies (also called *hardwood*), and *Mesua ferrea* of the East Indies (also called *ironwood*).

1719 DE FOE *Crusoe* I. v, A tree.. which in the Brazils they call the Iron Tree, for its exceeding hardness. **1836** MACGILLIVRAY tr. *Humboldt's Trav.* iii. 53 Two species of iron-tree, the arbutus callicarpa, and other evergreens, adorn this zone. **1859** TENNENT *Ceylon* I. I. iii. 94 Near every Buddhist temple the priests plant the Iron tree.. for the sake of its flowers.

ironware ('aɪənwɛə(r)). A general name for all light articles made of iron; hardware.

1447–8 in Willis & Clark *Cambridge* (1886) I. 399 Iren steel Nailles and iren ware. *Ibid.* 401 Iren Steel ferment neyles and Irenware. **1523** FITZHERB. *Surv.* 1 b, The yron ware as barres, bandes, hokes, boltes, staples or latches. **1675** COTTON *Scoffer Scoft* 112 To get him make their Iron-ware Sword, Trident, Sickles, Gieves.

'ironweed. [f. IRON *sb.* + WEED *sb.*; so called from the hard stem.] The Knapweed

(*Centaurea nigra*), and the N. American species of *Vernonia*.

1819 D. THOMAS *Trav. Western Country* 231 The iron-weed, which I first saw above Pittsburgh, extends on clayey lands all the way to the Wabash. **1827** CLARE *Sheph. Cal.* 47 And 'Iron-weed', content to share The meanest spot that spring can spare. **1860** BARTLETT *Dict. Amer.*, *Iron Weed* (Vernonia noveboracensis)..almost the only tall weed found in the beautiful 'woods pastures' of Kentucky and Tennessee. **1880** J. HAY *Pike Country Ball.* 97 And widely weaves the Iron-Weed A woof of purple dyes. **1963** GLEASON & CRONQUIST *Man. Vasc. Plants Northeastern U.S.* 746 *Vernonia* Schreb. Ironweed... Our spp. bloom in late summer and fall.

ironwood, iron-wood ('aɪənwʊd). Name given (more or less locally) to the extremely hard wood of various trees, of many different orders and countries; also to the trees themselves.

Among these are the genus *Sideroxylon* (chiefly tropical); several species of *Diospyros* or Ebony; *Ostrya virginica*, *Bumelia lycioides*, *Carpinus americana*, etc. of N. America; *Sloanea jamaicensis* and *Erythroxylon areolatum* of the W. Indies; *Xylia dolabriformis*, *Mesua ferrea*, *Metrosideros vera*, *Stadtmannia Sideroxylon*, etc. of the E. Indies; *Copaifera Mopane* of E. tropical Africa; *Olea capensis* and *O. undulata* of S. Africa; *Notelæa ligustrina* of Tasmania and N.S. Wales; etc. Also with defining epithet, as **bastard ironwood**, *Fagara lentiscifolia* and *Trichilia hirta*, of the W. Indies; **black ironwood**, *Condalia ferrea* of N. America, and *Olea undulata* of S. Africa; **red ironwood**, *Reynosia latifolia* of N. America; **white ironwood**, *Hypelate trifoliata* of N. America, and *Vepris (Toddalia) lanceolata* of S. Africa.

1657 R. LIGON *Barbadoes* (1673) 74 Iron wood is called so, for the extream hardness;..'Tis much used for Coggs to the Rollers. **1693** *Phil. Trans.* XVII. 621 An Ironwood from the Cape. **1719** DE FOE *Crusoe* I. ix, The wood called the iron-wood. **1731** MEDLEY *Kolben's Cape G. Hope* II. 248 African Iron wood..so call'd because, when dry, 'tis as hard as iron, and not to be clove by the most furious strokes with the hatchet. **1781** SMEATHMAN in *Phil. Trans.* LXXI. 183 Unless iron-wood posts have been made use of, not the least vestige of an house is to be discovered. **1802** BARRINGTON *Hist. N.S. Wales* xii. 479 A club of iron wood, which the cannibals had left in the boat. **1872** RAYMOND *Statist. Mines & Mining* 271 The ravines..are well stocked with a species of lignum-vitæ, known here as 'ironwood'.

ironwork, iron-work (-wɜːk). Forms: see IRON *sb.*[1]

1. Work in iron; usually *concr.* that part of anything that is made of iron, or articles made of iron collectively.

1451 *Yatton Church-w. Acc.* (Somerset Rec. Soc.) 92 For yreworke for ij wyndowys..iii *s.* ix *d.* **1475** in Willis & Clark *Cambridge* (1886) I. 597 All other Irnewerk redy wrought. **1497** *Naval Acc. Hen. VII* (1896) 83 Irenwerk nailes and other store. **1556–7** in Willis & Clark *Cambridge* (1886) I. 442 For Iron and Iron worke abowte the Roode. **1592–3** in Swayne *Sarum Church-w. Acc.* (1896) 141 Ire work abought the church. **1613** PURCHASE *Pilgrimage* (1614) 88 Inventers of Artes..building, yron-workes, tents, and such like. **1691** T. H[ALE] *Acc. New Invent.* 11 The ill condition of the Harwich's Iron-works discovered at her cleaning in 1682. **1722** DE FOE *Col. Jack* (1840) 167, I had more iron-work saved out of the ship. **1866** ROGERS *Agric. & Prices* I. xxi. 545 Wheels fitted with their iron-work.

2. An establishment where iron is smelted, or where heavy iron goods are made. Now always in *pl.* form **ironworks** (which is sometimes construed as a *sing.*).

1581 *Act 23 Eliz.* c. 5 Which woods..be by him preserued and coppised for the vse of his Iron workes. **1634–5** BRERETON *Trav.* (Chetham Soc.) I. 148 Here he shewed me a convenient seat for an iron-work. **1645** BOATE *Irel. Nat. Hist.* (1652) 132 Of the lesser Iron-works, called Bloomeries. **1685** PETTY *Last Will* in *Tracts* (1769) p. vi, I set up iron-works and pilchard-fishing in Kerry. **1855** MACAULAY *Hist. Eng.* xx. IV. 466 A man of great merit, who, having begun life with nothing, had created a noble estate by ironworks.

†**b.** A mine for digging iron-ore. *Obs.*

1713 *Phil. Trans.* XXVIII. 290 The Bath-Fabric had Ore and Fuel from the Silures..where Adrian sunk an Iron-work.

3. *attrib.*

1674 PETTY *Disc. Dupl. Proport.* 104 In Iron-work Furnaces are the greatest and most regular moving Bellows that are any where used. **1899** *Westm. Gaz.* 30 Dec. 8/3 Two ironwork contractors.

Hence '**ironworky** *a.* (*nonce-wd.*), abounding in or characterized by ironwork.

1886 RUSKIN *Præterita* I. vi. 189, I was already wise enough to feel the Cathedral stiff and iron-worky.

ironworker ('aɪən,wɜːkə(r)). One who works in iron; one engaged at ironworks.

14.. *Voc.* in Wr.-Wülcker 583/2 *Ferrarius*, an yreworchere or an yremongere, or a ferrour. **1882** OUIDA *Maremma* I. 151 The ironworkers of Follonica beating the ore of Elba into shape. **1889** *Boy's Own Paper* 7 Sept. 779/2 That picturesque town of ironworkers.

So 'iron-,**worked** *ppl. a.*, worked in iron, of wrought iron; '**iron-,working** *vbl. sb.* and *ppl. a.*

1730 in Willis & Clark *Cambridge* (1886) I. 231 An Iron-work'd Desk for ye Bible. **1846** C. G. PROWETT *Prometh. Bound* 33 On thy left hand the iron-working tribe. **1874** RAYMOND *Statist. Mines & Mining* 499 Apparatus for iron-working is not yet represented in the laboratories. **1895** *Daily News* 23 Sept. 7/4 Increased strength has been imparted to the iron-working branches by the further advance this week in unmarked iron. **1897** MARY KINGSLEY *W. Africa* 324 The other iron-working West Coast tribes.

'**ironwort** (-wɜːt). [f. IRON *sb.* + WORT, tr. L. *sidēritis* (Pliny), a. Gr. σιδηρῖτις, name of a herb having the reputed power of healing sword-wounds, f. σίδηρος iron.] Name for plants of the genus *Sideritis* (N.O. *Labiatæ*); also applied to some other labiates, as species of *Galeopsis*.

1562 TURNER *Herbal* II. 135 b, Thys kinde [of Sideritis] is called in Duche Glitkraut, it may be called in English Yronwurt or Rock sage. **1682** GREW *Anat. Flowers* App. § 11 The Top is..Poynted, or at least, Roundish, as in Lamium, Ironwort. **1866** *Treas. Bot.*, Ironwort, *Sideritis*; also *Galeopsis Ladanum*. Yellow I., *Galeopsis villosa*.

irony ('aɪərənɪ), *sb.* In early use often in Lat. form **ironia**. [ad. L. *īrōnia* (Cicero), a. Gr. εἰρωνεία 'dissimulation, ignorance purposely affected'. Cf. F. *ironie* (*yronie*, Oresme, 14th c.).]

1. A figure of speech in which the intended meaning is the opposite of that expressed by the words used; usually taking the form of sarcasm or ridicule in which laudatory expressions are used to imply condemnation or contempt.

1502 [see 3]. **1533** MORE *Debell. Salem* v. Wks. 939/1 When he calleth one self noughty lad, both a shreud boy & a good sonne, the tone in ye proper simple spech, the tother by the fygure of ironye or antiphrasis. **1540** COVERDALE *Confut. Standish* Wks. (Parker Soc.) II. 333 Now is *ironia* as much to say as a mockage, derision. **1589** PUTTENHAM *Eng. Poesie* III. xviii. (Arb.) 199 By the figure *Ironia*, which we call the *drye mock*. **1617** MORYSON *Itin.* I. 160 Your quip..that you were ashamed to write to mee for your rude stile. Very good, I finde the Irony. **1620** MIDDLETON & ROWLEY *World Tost at Tennis* 124 By his needle he understands ironia, That with one eye looks two ways at once. **1788** MAD. D'ARBLAY *Diary* 13 Feb., He believed Irony the ablest weapon of oratory. **1828** WHATELY *Rhet.* in *Encycl. Metrop.* (1845) I. 265/1 Aristotle mentions..*Eironeia*, which in his time was commonly employed to signify, not according to the modern use of 'Irony, saying the *contrary* to what is meant', but, what later writers usually express by *Litotes*, i.e. 'saying *less* than is meant'. **1837** MACAULAY *Ess.*, *Bacon* (1887) 428 A drayman, in a passion, calls out, 'You are a pretty fellow', without suspecting that he is uttering irony. **1876** J. WEISS *Wit, Hum, & Shaks.* ii. 44 It is irony when Lowell, speaking of Dante's intimacy with the Scriptures, adds, 'They do even a scholar no harm'.

b. with *an* and *pl.* An instance of this; an ironical utterance or expression.

1551 GARDINER *Sacram.* 22 He spake it by an Ironie or skorne. **1612–15** BP. HALL *Contempl.*, *O.T.* XIX. iii, Ironies deny strongest in affirming. **1656** E. REYNER *Rules Govt. Tongue* 227 An Irony is a nipping jeast, or a speech that hath the honey of pleasantnesse in its mouth, and a sting of rebuke in its taile. **1706–7** *Reflex. upon Ridicule* 221 Subtil and delicate Ironies. **1738** WARBURTON *Div. Legat.* I. Ded. 9 A thorough Irony addressed to some hot Bigots. **1894** W. J. DAWSON *Making of Manhood* 29 Smart sneers and barbed ironies at the expense of every movement which seeks to meliorate the common lot.

2. *fig.* A condition of affairs or events of a character opposite to what was, or might naturally be, expected; a contradictory outcome of events as if in mockery of the promise and fitness of things. (In F. *ironie du sort*.)

1649 G. DANIEL *Trinarch.*, *Hen. V*, cxcviii, Yet here: (and 'tis the Ironie of Warre Where Arrowes forme the Argument,) he best Acquitts himselfe, who doth a Horse præfer To his proud Rider. **1833** THIRLWALL in *Philol. Museum* II. 483 (*title*) On the Irony of Sophocles. *Ibid.* 493 The contrast between man with his hopes, fears, wishes, and undertakings, and a dark, inflexible fate, affords abundant room for the exhibition of tragic irony. **1860** W. COLLINS *Wom. White* III. xi. 413 The irony of circumstances holds no mortal catastrophe in respect. **1878** MORLEY *Carlyle* 194 With no eye for..the irony of their fate. **1884** *Nonconf. & Indep.* Lit. Suppl. 6 Nov. 1/1 The irony of time is wonderful. **1894** T. HARDY (*title*) Life's Little Ironies.

3. In etymological sense: Dissimulation, pretence; esp. in reference to the dissimulation of ignorance practised by Socrates as a means of confuting an adversary (*Socratic irony*).

1502 *Ord. Crysten Men* (W. de W. 1506) IV. xxii. 293 To say of hym selfe ony thynge of his feblenesses & necessytes, or of his synnes..to the end that a man be renowmed & reputed humble abiect & grete thynge in merytes & deuocyons before god..such synne is named yronye, not that the whiche is of grammare, by the whiche a man sayth one & gyueth to understande the contrarye. **1655** STANLEY *Hist. Philos.* III. (1701) 76/1 The whole confirmation of the Cause, even the whole Life seems to carry an Irony, such was the Life of Socrates, who was for that reason called εἴρων; that is, one that personates an unlearned Man, and is an admirer of others as Wise. **1848** H. ROGERS *Ess.* I. vi. 318 The irony of Socrates..may be not unfittingly expressed by saying, that it is a *logical masked battery*. **1860** EMERSON *Cond. Life*, *Considerat.* Wks. (Bohn) II. 416 Like Socrates, with his famous irony; like Bacon, with life-long dissimulation.

irony ('aɪənɪ, 'aɪərənɪ), *a.* Also 4–7 yrony, -ie, 6 yrnye. [f. IRON *sb.*[1] + -Y.] Consisting of iron; of the nature of iron; resembling iron in some quality, as hardness, taste, or colour; abounding in or containing iron.

1382 WYCLIF *Deut.* xxviii. 23 Be heuene that is aboue thee braasny [1388 brasun]; and the lond that thou tredist yrony [1388 yrun, 1611 of iron]. **1583** STANYHURST *Æneis*, etc. Ps. ii. (Arb.) 127 From oure persons pluck we there yrnye yokes. **1654** HAMMOND *Fundamentals* (J.), It is not strange if the irony chains have more solidity than the contemplative. **1764** *Nat. Hist.* in *Ann. Reg.* 82/2 It is a ponderous irony earth. **1843** PORTLOCK *Geol.* 541 Sulphate of barytes, associated with irony quartz. **1875** G. MACDONALD *Malcolm* II. xviii. 243 Crystals of a clear irony brown.

i-rooted, i-roted, ME. pa. pple. of ROOT *v.*

Iroquoian ('ɪrəkwɔɪən, -kɔɪ-), *a.* and *sb.* [f. IROQUOI(S *a.* and *sb.* + -AN.] **A.** *adj.* Of or pertaining to the Iroquois, or to the language family defined in sense B a below. **B.** *sb.* **a.** A language family which includes the Iroquois, Huron, Cherokee, and several lesser-known American Indian languages. **b.** A member of this linguistic group.

1697 L. LE COMPTE *Mem. Journey through China* I. v. 124 Iroquian Mathematicians, or Learned Alkonkins. **1888** J. C. PILLING (*title*) Bibliography of the Iroquoian languages. *Ibid.* Pref. p. v, To the Iroquoian perhaps belongs the honor of being the first of our American families of languages to be placed upon record. **1906** *Rep. Brit. Assoc. Adv. Sci.* 679 The Iroquoian tribes of North America possess a word which exactly expresses this potentiality. **1917** W. K. MOOREHEAD *Stone Ornaments Indians* 170 A surface find in the Iroquoian area in New York is no sure indication that the artifact is Iroquoian. **1933** L. BLOOMFIELD *Lang.* iv. 72 The Iroquoian family was spoken in a district surrounded by Algonquian; it includes..the Huron (or Wyandot) language, and the languages of the Iroquois type..; in a detached region to the south Cherokee was spoken. **1934** D. JENNESS *Indians of Canada* (ed. 2) xix. 288 When Jacques Cartier sailed up the St. Lawrence river in 1535 he found Iroquoians cultivating the land and controlling the country around the present site of Montreal. **1959** E. TUNIS *Indians* 19/2 Remnants of the temple-mound culture survived into historical times among the Muskhogean Indians of the Southeast and there are broad hints of a connection between the burial-mound people and the Iroquoians. **1968** F. G. LOUNSBURY in J. A. Fishman *Readings Sociol. of Lang.* (1968) 51 The writer has done intensive field work on a language—Cayuga, one of the languages of the Iroquoian family. **1969** *Observer* (Colour Suppl.) 25 May 53/1 Various groups that spoke dialects of the Iroquoian language.

Iroquois ('ɪrəkwɔɪ, -kɔɪ *U.S.*, 'ɪrəkwa *Canad.*), *a.* and *sb.* [Fr., from some Algonquian language, perh. Montagnais (G. Day in E. Tooker *Iroquois Culture* (1967), 57–61).] **A.** *adj.* Of or pertaining to an American Indian group of peoples (the 'Five Nations') encountered esp. in Ontario and central and northern New York State, or to the languages of this group; = IROQUOIAN *a.* **B.** *sb.* **a.** A member of this group (see *Five Nations* (FIVE *a.* and *sb.* C. 2)); also as collect. sing., this confederacy. **b.** More widely = IROQUOIAN *sb.* **c.** The languages of this group.

1666 in *Documents Colonial Hist. New-York* (1853) III. 134 The Irocquois Indians should not cômit any Act of hostilety. **1677** LOCKE tr. *Nicole's Ess.* (1828) 71 There needs not many other thoughts to make up the complete idea of an Iroquois. **1705** [see ALGONQUIN, -KIN *sb.* and *a.*]. **1710** SHAFTESBURY *Advice to Author* 179 Historys of Incas or Iroquois, written by Friars and Missionarys. **1756** [see HURON]. **1791** [see ESKIMO *a.* 1]. **1851** *Harper's Mag.* Aug. 390/2 He fancied he heard her mutter in Iroquois one word—'revenged'! **1852** [see *Five Nations* (FIVE *a.* and *sb.* C. 2)]. **1866** G. M. WALLACE tr. *Beethoven's Lett.* II. 91, I must also strive to make some future provision for him [his nephew]; being neither Indians nor Iroquois, who, as we know, leave everything to Providence, whereas we consider a pauper's existence to be a very sad one. **1881** [see GYNEOCRACY]. **1922** D. CANFIELD *Rough-Hewn* (1923) i, Neale was silent as an Iroquois. *Ibid.* xxv, His Iroquois mask of insensibility. **1933** [see CAYUGA]. **1959** [see *Five Nations* (FIVE *a.* and *sb.* C. 2)]. **1965** *Canad. Jrnl. Ling.* Spring 135 Iroquois speakers remain in New York State;..others remain in the Carolinas (Cherokee). **1969** *Listener* 12 June 834/1 It is curious to think of Winston Churchill having Red Indian blood, but his mother was one-eighth Iroquois.

i-rost, -ed, ME. pa. pple. of ROAST *v.*

i-roted, i-rotted, ME. pa. pple. of ROT *v.*

i-rouned, ME. pa. pple. of ROUN *v.*, to whisper.

†**i'rour.** *Obs.* Also 4 irrour. [a. AF. *irour*, OF. *iror*, *irur* (12th c.), later *ireur* anger = Pr. *iror*, f. L. *ira* IRE, with ending of *furor*, *horror*, *terror*, etc.] Ire, anger.

13.. *Seuyn Sag.* (W.) 954 With herte wroth, & gret irour. *a* **1380** *St. Ambrosius* 824 in Horstm. *Altengl. Leg.* 21 Þe biddyng of þe emperour þreteþ me wiþ gret irrour.

†'**irous**, *a.* *Obs.* Also 4 irwis, irose, 4–6 irus, yrous, -ows, 5 irows, -eous, irrous, 5–6 irouse. [a. AF. *irous*, OF. *iros*, *irus*, later *ireux*, = Pr. *iros*, It. *iroso*:—pop. L. type **īrōs-us*, f. *ira* IRE.]

1. Given to anger, hot-tempered, irascible.

1303 R. BRUNNE *Handl. Synne* 7152 Charyte ys nat irus, And charyte ys nat coveytous. *a* **1450** *Knt. de la Tour* (1868) 74 This Henana was yrous and felon, and of euyl lyf. **1530** ELYOT *Gov.* I. ix, By a cruell and irous maister the wittes of children be dulled. **1574** HELLOWES *Gueuara's Fam. Ep.* (1584) 114 Solon Solonio being demanded whom we call properly irous, answered, hee that little esteemeth to loose his friendes, and maketh no account to recover enimies.

2. Wrathful, angry, enraged.

13.. *K. Alis.* 330 (MS. Bodl.) His leue took Neptenabus, To his In wel yrous. *a* **1340** HAMPOLE *Psalter* xvii. 51 My delyuerere of myn enmys yrous. *c* **1386** CHAUCER *Pars. T.* ⁋545 Swich cursynge as comth of Irous herte. *c* **1425** WYNTOUN *Cron.* VII. vii. 206 Agayne hym thai ware all irows. **1474** CAXTON *Chesse* II. iii. C j b, An angry and yrous persone weneth that for to doo evyl is good counceyl. *c* **1500** *New Notbroune Mayd* 435 in Hazl. *E.P.P.* III. 18 His irous brayde Wyll not be layed For me nor yet for you.

†**ˈirously,** *adv. Obs.* [f. prec. + -LY².] In an angry manner, angrily, wrathfully.

1375 BARBOUR *Bruce* VIII. 144 Thairfor he ansueryt irusly. *c* **1450** LONELICH *Grail* xiv. 263 Ful Irowsly torned they Into that pres. *c* **1475** *Partenay* 4692 Gaffray..After sped Apace, yrously being.

†**irpe,** *sb. Obs. rare.* [Origin unknown; found with the following in Ben Jonson.] Some kind of gesture: ? a toss or jerk of the head, the act of perking. Gifford suggested 'a fantastic grimace, or contortion of the body'.

1599 B. JONSON *Cynthia's Rev.* v. iii. *Palinode,* From Spanish shrugs, French faces, smirks, irpes, and all affected humours, Good Mercury defend us.

So †**irpe** ? *a.*, ? perk, smart. *Obs.*

1599 B. JONSON *Cynthia's Rev.* III. v, Maintaine your station, brisk, and irpe, shew the supple motion of your pliant body.

irradiance (ɪˈreɪdɪəns). [f. IRRADIANT: see -ANCE.] **1.** The fact of irradiating; the emission of rays of light, emitted radiance. Also *fig.* in reference to spiritual or intellectual radiance.

1667 MILTON *P.L.* VIII. 617 Do they mix Irradiance, virtual or immediate touch? **1735–6** H. BROOKE *Univ. Beauty* VI. 339 Thou awful Depth of Wisdom unexplor'd! Thou Height, where never human fancy soar'd! Supreme Irradiance! *a* **1760** I. H. BROWNE *Poems, Design & Beauty* (1768) 106 They, from irradiance of thy genial beam Prolific, with immortal offspring teem. **1888** B. W. RICHARDSON *Son of a Star* III. xi. 176 A kingdom to which the world will come for irradiance.

2. The flux of radiant energy per unit area, esp. an area normal to the direction of travel through a medium.

1956 A. HOLLAENDER *Radiation Biol.* III. iii. 129 'Irradiance' is the intensity term applicable to the interception of radiant energy by objects and is power per unit area. Frequently 'intensity' is used loosely as a substitute for 'irradiance'. *Ibid.* 136 The U.S. Weather Bureau..still uses the calorie per minute per square centimeter for the specification of solar irradiance. **1966** *McGraw-Hill Encycl. Sci. & Technol.* XII. 105/2 At a depth of 64 m where the irradiance is 0·5 watt/m²..approximately 0·04 watt of radiant power is absorbed by every cubic meter of sea water. **1969** *Physics Bull.* Oct. 409/2 Outside the earth's atmosphere..the annual mean irradiance of the sun is about 270 W m⁻² on a plane parallel to the earth's surface at latitude 52° N. **1973** *Nature* 9 Feb. 402/1 The total irradiance of the unattenuated light..was approximately 4·5 × 10³ μW/cm².

irradiancy (ɪˈreɪdɪənsɪ). [f. as prec.: see -ANCY.] The quality or fact of being irradiant.

1646 SIR T. BROWNE *Pseud. Ep.* II. i. 55 As for irradiancy or sparkling which is found in many gems it is not discoverable in this. **1830** *Fraser's Mag.* I. 218 Mark..the benign irradiancy of his eyes. **1882–3** SCHAFF *Encycl. Relig. Knowl.* II. 1658 That luminous irradiancy which was supposed to emanate and surround a divine being.

irradiant (ɪˈreɪdɪənt), *a.* [ad. L. *irradiānt-em,* pr. pple. of *irradiāre* to IRRADIATE.] Emitting rays of light; shining brightly. Also *fig.* in reference to spiritual or intellectual radiance.

1526 *Pilgr. Perf.* (W. de W. 1531) 299 b, Moost clere beme & irradyant splendour of yᵉ glory eternall. **1592** R. D. *Hypnerotomachia* 1 He crysped up his irradient heyres. **1611** SPEED *Hist. Gt. Brit.* IX. xii. §109. 694 The just brightnesse of his irradiant vertues..adorning her with Garlands, conquered Spoyles, and Trophees. **1710** *Brit. Apollo* III. No. 15. 3/1 As Fire extinguish'd by th' Irradiant Sun. **1865** PUSEY *Truth Eng. Ch.* 27 Effulgent with the glory of His Godhead, irradiant with His Divine love. **1882** MYERS *Renewal Youth* 160 O Nature's darling, pure and fair, From light foot to irradiant hair!

irradiate (ɪˈreɪdɪət), *ppl. a.* [ad. L. *irradiātus,* pa. pple. of *irradiāre* (see next).] Illumined; made bright or brilliant. Const. as pple. or adj.

1526 *Pilgr. Perf.* (W. de W. 1531) 129 Our soule irradiate or made bryght with the lyght of the aungell. **1725** POPE *Odyss.* x. 583 The Theban Bard, depriv'd of sight, Within, irradiate with prophetic light. **1729** SAVAGE *Wanderer* II. 86 A phœnix, with irradiate crest. **1814** CARY *Dante* (Chandos) 277 The sky Erewhile irradiate only with his beam. **1874** SYMONDS *Sk. Italy & Greece* (1898) I. i. 24 Sailing through ..tracts of light irradiate heavens.

irradiate (ɪˈreɪdɪeɪt), *v.* Also 7 **inradiate.** [f. ppl. stem of L. *irradiāre* to shine forth, f. *ir-* (IR-¹) + *radiāre* to shine, f. *radius* ray: cf. prec.]

1. *trans.* **a.** To direct rays of light upon; to shine upon; to make bright by causing light to fall upon; to illumine.

1623 COCKERAM, *Irradiate,* to shine vpon. **1669** GALE *Crt. Gentiles* I. I. i. 7 As the greater light irradiates and enlightens the world. *a* **1794** SIR W. JONES *Hymn to Lacshmi* Wks. 1799 VI. 363 When thy smile irradiates yon blue fields, Observant Indra sheds the genial show'r. **1805** SOUTHEY *Madoc* II. xviii, The midnight lightnings..That with their awful blaze, irradiate heaven, Then leave a blacker night. **1873** L. FERGUSON *Disc.* 64 The face that was irradiated on the Mount was the very face his disciples knew so well.

b. *spec.* in *Astrol.* To cast beams upon. Also *absol.*

1603 SIR C. HEYDON *Jud. Astrol.* xxiii. 498 Originally they were friendly irradiated of Iupiter, the Sunne, Venus, and Mercurie. **1621** BURTON *Anat. Mel.* I. ii. I. iv. 75 In the Horoscope, irradiated by those quartile aspects of Saturne or Mars, the childe shall be mad or melancholy. **1686** GOAD *Celest. Bodies* III. i. 393 ♄ from the Opposite Sign irradiates between ♂ and ♀ so posited.

†**c.** To influence with or as with rays of heat or anything else of radiant character. *Obs.*

1668 CULPEPPER & COLE *Barthol. Anat.* I. xvii. 48 The neighbouring Spermatick Vessels are irradiated and virtuated by the Kidneys, even as the Brain irradiates the lower Parts, by an inbred property resembling light. *a* **1677** HALE *Prim. Orig. Man.* I. iii. 76 That Ethereal or Solar heat, that must digest, influence, irradiate, and put those more simple parts of Matter into motion and coalition.

d. To expose to the action of some kind of radiation (other than visible light, as X-rays, ultra-violet radiation, or neutrons).

1901 *N.Y. Med. Jrnl.* 16 Nov. 909/1 The inguinal tumor was removed..and now the inguinal area is also irradiated. **1927** *Jrnl. Biol. Chem.* LXXIII. 383 Cholesterol solutions were also irradiated by the γ-rays from radium emanation. **1952** COOK & DUNCAN *Mod. Radiochem. Pract.* v. 203 To obtain the maximum yield of a radio-element by use of a laboratory neutron source it is often of advantage to irradiate an aqueous solution of the absorbing element. **1957** *Technology* Mar. 14/2 Food can be preserved for long periods if irradiated. **1963** BOWEN & GIBBONS *Radioactivation Analysis* ii. 5 When a material is bombarded or irradiated by the nuclear particles produced in a nuclear reactor, particle accelerator, or other suitable source, some of the atoms present in the sample will interact with the bombarding particles. **1964** M. PYKE *Food Sci. & Technol.* viii. 153 By irradiating frozen whole egg with from 0·1 to 1·0 Mrad, it is possible to destroy certain pathological micro-organisms. **1971** *Nature* 4 June 317/1 When the spores were initially irradiated with γ-rays, the germination rate increased remarkably. **1973** *Sci. Amer.* Apr. 71/1 The diffusion constant can now be determined by irradiating the silicon with slow neutrons and measuring the energy of the alpha particles that emerge.

2. *fig.* and *transf.* **a.** To illumine with spiritual or intellectual light; to throw light upon anything intellectually obscure.

1627 FELTHAM *Resolves* II. [I.] xiv. (1628) 40 It.. inradiates the soul. **1638** ROUSE *Heav. Univ.* ii. (1702) 19 Universally to irradiate and teach them. *a* **1710** BP. BULL *Serm.* II. v. (R.), That his mind was irradiated with a divine illumination. **1838–9** HALLAM *Hist. Lit.* IV. IV. viii. §48. 368 He first irradiated the entire annals of antiquity..with flashes of light. **1864** BOWEN *Logic* 10 With their light they irradiate and make clearly intelligible everything to which they are referred.

b. To brighten as with light; to light up (the face) with beauty, gladness, animation, etc.

1651 SHERBURNE *Rape of Helen* Poems 55 Such Beauty did his Looks irradiate. **1805** WORDSW. *Prelude* II. 239 A virtue which irradiates and exalts Objects through widest intercourse of sense. **1843** LEVER *J. Hinton* xxxv. (1878) 241 The priest's jovial good humour irradiated his happy countenance. **1877** BLACK *Green Past.* xxix. 236 The sublime features of Madame Columbus, now irradiated with triumph.

c. *transf.* To adorn with splendour.

1717 POPE *Eloisa* 136 No weeping orphan saw his father's stores Our shrines irradiate, or emblaze the floors.

3. To radiate; to send forth in or as in rays.

a **1617** BAYNE *Lect.* (1634) 115 Light irradiated upon our mindes. **1794** J. HUTTON *Philos. Light,* etc. 63 Heat cannot be irradiated or move from bodies, as light does, either by reflection or transmission. **1893** *Chicago Advance* 21 Sept., Whose presence upon the platform had irradiated strength and cheer.

†**4.** *intr.* To radiate, to diverge in the form of rays. *Obs.*

1677 PLOT *Oxfordsh.* 84 Irradiating all manner of ways into the form of a Globe, the several Selenites, like so many radii, all pointing to the center. *a* **1704** LOCKE *Paraphr. 2 Cor.* iv. 6 *note,* A Communication of Glory or Light..which irradiated from his Face when he descended from the Mount. **1794** G. ADAMS *Nat. & Exp. Philos.* II. xxi. 414 Their powers decay according to their distances from the centres from which they irradiated.

5. *intr.* To emit rays, to shine (*on* or *upon*).

1642 W. PRICE *Serm.* 17 That not a beame of divine grace should..irradiate on his soule. **1656** S. WINTER *Serm.* 141 If the Lord irradiate upon the souls of children in heaven. **1784** BP. HORNE *Lett. Infidel.* x. 167 Day was the state of the hemisphere, on which light irradiated.

6. *intr.* To become radiant; to light up.

1800 COLERIDGE in C. K. Paul *W. Godwin* (1876) II. 3 Lamb every now and then irradiates. **1807–8** W. IRVING *Salmag.* xx. (1860) 462 The eye is taught to brighten, the lip to smile, and the whole countenance to irradiate.

Hence **iˈrradiating** *vbl. sb.* and *ppl. a.*; whence **iˈrradiatingly** *adv.*, in an irradiating manner.

1651 HOBBES *Govt. & Soc.* Ep. Ded., The light to be carried thither for the irradiating its doubts. **1659** D. PELL *Impr. Sea* 219 *note,* As the Sun does upon the Rainbow, by gilding of it with its golden, and irradiating beams. **1794** J. HUTTON *Philos. Light,* etc. 75 An irradiating body, such as a candle. **1857** DUNGLISON *Med. Lex.* 510 *Irradiation,*.. shooting or proceeding from a centre—as an *irradiating pain.* **1893** G. MEREDITH *Odes Fr. Hist.* 40 Amid the plumed and sceptred ones Irradiatingly Jovian.

irradiated (ɪˈreɪdɪeɪtɪd), *ppl. a.* [f. prec. + -ED¹.]

1. a. Emitted as rays from a centre. **b.** Made luminous; shone upon, lighted up by rays from some luminous source.

1794 J. HUTTON *Philos. Light,* etc. 61 The theory of irradiated heat. **1876** GEO. ELIOT *Dan. Der.* lxiii, With an irradiated face and opened eyes.

c. Exposed to the action of some kind of radiation (see prec., 1 d).

1915 COLWELL & RUSS *Radium, X-Rays & Living Cell* iii. 117 The nuclear changes observed in the development of such irradiated ova have been investigated. **1931** *Times* 13 May 17/4 A cheap and effective means of obtaining Vitamin D has been made available in the form of irradiated ergosterol. **1957** BENEDICT & PIGFORD *Nucl. Chem. Engin.* i. 17 The most important neutron-absorbing and long-lived fission products in irradiated uranium are listed in Table 1.2. **1958** *Observer* 11 May 8/3 Japanese doctors could draw upon a wealth of medical information gained by systematic examination of men, women and children who had survived the blast, heat and radiation at Hiroshima and Nagasaki. But..knowledge about the treatment of irradiated individuals was woefully inadequate. **1970** *New Scientist* 6 Aug. 284/1 Most countries have banned the sale of irradiated food.. However, in the UK the Minister of Health can exempt a particular food..if evidence is submitted to show that irradiation is harmless.

2. *Her.* Having a representation of rays.

1864 BOUTELL *Her. Hist. & Pop.* xx. §12 (ed. 3) 352 The Star..is also a mullet, on an irradiated field of gold.

irradiation (ɪreɪdɪˈeɪʃən). [a. F. *irradiation,* ad. L. **irradiātiōn-em,* n. of action from *irradiāre*: see IRRADIATE *v.*]

I. In reference to rays of light.

1. a. The action of irradiating, or emitting rays or beams of light; shining.

1599 SPARRY tr. *Cattan's Geomancie* 59 The beaming and irradiation of the saide Signes. **1615** E. HOWES *Stow's Ann.* 1030/2 The Irradiation of this Comets streame was sometime extended to a wonderfull length. **1621** BURTON *Anat. Mel.* II. ii. III. 323 The same verticall stars, the same irradiations of Planets, aspects alike. **1658** SOUTH *Serm.* (1744) VIII. xiii. 363 Sooner may a dark room enlighten itself, without the irradiation of a candle or the sun. **1800** HERSCHEL in *Phil. Trans.* XC. 257 Advanced far enough to receive the irradiation of the colour which passed through the opening. **1890** CLARK RUSSELL *Ocean Trag.* I. iii. 46 There was something positively phosphoric in the irradiation on her face and hair, as though in sober truth they were self-luminous.

b. A ray of light, a beam.

1643 HOWELL *Parables on Times* 6 The Sunne detained his beames and irradiations from them. **1698** FRYER *Acc. E. India & P.* 181 How he..dispenses his Irradiations as far as either Pole. **1790** UMFREVILLE *Hudson's Bay* 23 The Aurora Borealis..sometimes the irradiations are seen of a very bright red, at other times of a pale milky colour.

2. *fig.* **a.** A beaming forth of spiritual light.

1633 EARL MANCH. *Al Mondo* (1636) 28 If in this life holinesse maketh the face of a man to shine, by an irradiation from the heart. **1648** *Eikon Bas.* 76 God..from whom alone are all the irradiations of true Glory and Majesty. *a* **1711** KEN *Serm.* Wks. (1838) 114 His conversation had so many irradiations of divinity in it. **1747** HERVEY *Medit.* II. 100 Opening our Minds to the Irradiations of his Wisdom. **1807** G. CHALMERS *Caledonia* I. I. i. 5 The sun of truth shot forth the irradiations of a clearer light on the dark events of the most ancient times.

b. Intellectual enlightenment; illumination of the mind.

1589 PUTTENHAM *Eng. Poesie* I. viii. (Arb.) 35 Such persons as be illuminated with the brightest irradiations of knowledge and of the veritie and due proportion of things. **1608** T. JAMES *Apol. Wyclif* 11 Some are illuminated and enlightened from aboue,..which illumination and irradiation of theirs..is much confirmed and warranted vnto vs, by their holy liues and conuersations. **1661** K. W. *Conf. Charac., Pragm. Pulpit-filler* (1860) 83 Their poetical faculties devoid of all philosophick irradiations. **1754** JOHNSON *Adventurer* No. 137 ¶9 They are universally ignorant, yet with greater or less irradiations of knowledge. **1860** W. COLLINS *Wom. White* II. i. 158 She..brightened suddenly with the irradiation of a new idea.

3. a. *Optics.* The apparent enlargement or extension of the edges of an object strongly illuminated, when seen against a dark ground.

1834 *Nat. Philos.* III. *Astronomy* xii. 249 *note* (U.K.S.), The first of these corrections is attributed to an optical effect called irradiation. **1867–77** G. F. CHAMBERS *Astron.* I. vii. 78 To allow for exaggeration of its dimensions by irradiation. **1876** BERNSTEIN *Five Senses* 77 People look larger in light clothes than in dark, which may also be explained as the effect of irradiation. **1878** FOSTER *Phys.* III. ii. 433 *Irradiation,* a white patch on a dark ground appears larger, and a dark patch on a white ground smaller, than it really is.

b. *Photogr.* The scattering of light by silver halide crystals in a photographic emulsion causing diffuseness of the image obtained on development.

1924 L. P. CLERC *Ilford Man. Process Work* vi. 53 The effect of irradiation, evidently, is the more marked,..as the exposure is longer. **1940** 'C. I. JACOBSON' *Developing* ii. 43 If the exposure is longer, then the light is scattered so that it spreads beyond the area protected by the metal, and hence irradiation takes place. **1968** H. BAINES in C. E. Engel *Photogr. for Scientist* i. 20 This scatter from one crystal to others is known as 'irradiation'.

II. In reference to other rays.

4. The emission of heat-rays.

1794 J. HUTTON *Phil. Light,* etc. 67 Those philosophers, who have adopted the theory of irradiated heat,..suppose, that there is no irradiation when there is an equilibrium of heat among bodies.

5. Emanation from a common centre.

1879 tr. *De Quatrefages' Hum. Spec.* 179 Zoological geography is now met with everywhere, because it has spread by irradiation in every direction from this centre.

†**6. a.** In older Physiology: The emission or emanation of any fluid, influence, principle, or virtue, from an active centre. *Obs.*

1615 CROOKE *Body of Man* 57 If a nerue be deriued vnto the part, by whose illustration and irradiation, all the particles of that part haue sence. **1646** SIR T. BROWNE *Pseud. Ep.* III. ix. 124 The generation of bodies is not effected as some conceive, of soules, that is, by Irradiation. **1666** HARVEY *Morb. Angl.* iv. 38 The manner whereby the faculty of the brain effects a locomotive action in any muscul is by irradiation. **1706** PHILLIPS, *Irradiation,*..us'd by Van Helmont..to express the Operation of some Mineral Medicines, which they will have to impart their Virtue

without sending forth any thing material out of them, and without loss of their own Substance or Weight.

†**b.** The (fancied) emission of an immaterial fluid or influence from the eye. *Obs.*

1625 Bacon *Ess.*, *Envy* (Arb.) 511 There seemeth to be acknowledged, in the Act of Enuy, an Eiaculation, or Irradiation of the Eye. **1660** tr. *Amyraldus' Treat. conc. Relig.* I. iii. 38 As the irradiations of our Eyes are dissipated in the wide Aer. **1696** Aubrey *Misc.* (1721) 185 Infants are very sensible of these Iradiations of the Eyes; In.. Southern Countries, the Nurses and Parents are very shy to let People look upon their young Children for fear of Fascination.

7. *Physiol.* 'A movement which proceeds from the centre peripherically' (*Syd. Soc. Lex.*); the transmission of nerve-excitation from a nerve-centre outwards; also, the spreading of a stimulus from one nerve-centre to others.

1847 tr. *Feuchtersleben's Med. Psychol.* (Syd. Soc.) 88 The transition to the homogeneous is called irradiation (in motor nerves synergy—in sensitive, sympathy). **1855** Mayne *Expos. Lex.*, *Irradiatio*,.. term used in physics, for the movement from the centre to the circumference of a body: irradiation.

8. *Anat.* 'Applied to the disposition of fibres or other structures in the form of a star, with a centre and diverging rays' (*Syd. Soc. Lex.* 1887).

9. Exposure to the action of some kind of radiation (other than visible light, as X-rays, ultra-violet radiation, or neutrons); the (or an) action or process of irradiating something. Also, radiation allowed to be incident upon something.

1901 *N.Y. Med. Jrnl.* 16 Nov. 908/2 Up to today irradiation has been done seven times [on the same patient]. *Ibid.* 909/1 If a strong effect is desired, intense irradiation must naturally be employed. **1915** Colwell & Russ *Radium, X-Rays & Living Cell* iii. 116 Radium, like X rays, does not effect the immediate death of the cell; specimens subjected to three days' continuous irradiation still underwent division. **1935** *Practitioners Libr. Med. & Surg.* VII. v. 158 Ultraviolet irradiation of the skin is effective in preventing or curing rickets. *Ibid.* 159 Short exposures of thin films of milk to ultraviolet irradiation. **1936** B. J. M. Harrison *Textbk. Roentgenology* iii. 52 If he moves out of position the irradiation falls on the protected covers and not upon the patient. **1951** *Jrnl. Sci. Instruments* XXVIII. 191/1 The neutron irradiation of small quantities of material in the pile is often carried out in aluminium foil 'envelopes' or in silica capsules. **1953** Carter & Merritt in Smith & Wermer *Mod. Treatm.* xx. 433/1 Daily shortwave diathermy in combination with infra-red irradiation twice applied to the lumbar area may be of value. **1953** *Cold Spring Harbor Symp. Quant. Biol.* XVIII. 101/2 Irradiation of cultures of lysogenic *Bacillus megatherium* with ultraviolet light greatly increased the proportion of bacteria producing phage. **1957** *Times* 3 Sept. 9/2 Therapeutic irradiation of the pelvic region would certainly involve considerable risk to an embryo in the direct beam. **1972** *Physics Bull.* July 398 The damage produced during irradiations with 20 MeV C ions and 48 MeV Ni ions has been normalized to that produced by 4 MeV protons where we can make reasonably accurate estimates of the number of displaced atoms.

irradiative (ɪˈreɪdɪətɪv), *a.* [f. L. *irradiāt-*, ppl. stem of *irradiāre* to irradiate: see -ative.] Of which the property or tendency is to irradiate; illuminative.

a **1834** Coleridge *Lit. Rem.* (1839) IV. 433 The reason, as the irradiative power, and the representative of the infinite, judges the understanding as the faculty of the finite. **1858** Carlyle *Fredk. Gt.* x. ii. (1872) III. 233 Of another Correspondence, beautifully irradiative for the young heart, we must say almost nothing. **1864** *Ibid.* xiii. ix. V. 92 Radiant, and irradiative, like paths of the gods.

irradiator (ɪˈreɪdɪeɪtə(r)). [agent-n. in L. form from irradiate *v.*] One who or that which irradiates; an illuminator. (Cf. also irradiate *v.* 1 d.)

1750 W. Hodges *Elihu* (1755) 10 The word.. signifies the Irradiator, or he that irradiates and enlightens. **1812** H. & J. Smith *Rej. Addr.* x. 61 At such a distance from the oily irradiators which now dazzle the eyes of him who addresses you. **1971** *Nature* 12 Mar. 120/2 Corneas were first irradiated for 15 h in a γ-irradiator.. delivering $1{\cdot}2 \times 10^5$ rad/h.

irradicable (ɪˈrædɪkəb(ə)l), *a. rare.* [f. ir-² + L. *rādīcāre* to take root, to root (taken as if = 'to root out, uproot') + -able: cf. eradicable.] That cannot be rooted out; = ineradicable.

1728 Morgan *Algiers* I. Pref. 2 So deep is that irradicable Inveteracy ingrafted in my Mind. **1795** *Hist.* in *Ann. Reg.* 66 For which they would always be suspected to retain an irradicable predilection. **1846** Pusey *Serm.* in Mozley *Ess.* (1878) II. 160 Guilt is fastened on its feelings, as if it were irradicable and eternal.

†**irradical** (ɪˈrædɪkəl), *a. Math. Obs. rare*⁻¹. [ir-².] Of which the root cannot be extracted.

1674 Jeake *Arith.* (1696) 330 Among particular Compound Surdes, some are in a sort Irradical, and have their Roots extracted only by altering their characters.

†**i'rradicate,** *ppl. a. Obs. rare*⁻¹. In 5 iradicate. [f. ir-¹ + L. *rādīcāt-us*, pa. pple. of *rādīcāre* to take root.] Rooted, enrooted.

1436 *Pol. Poems* (Rolls) II. 204 He [Christ].. Mote gefe us pease so welle iradicate Here in this worlde, that after alle this feste Wee mowe have pease in the londe of byheste.

irradicate (ɪˈrædɪkeɪt), *v. rare.* [f. ir-¹ + L. *rādīcāre*, *-ārī* to take root, f. *rādīc-em* root: cf. *eradicate.*] *trans.* To fix by the root, to enroot.

1836 Sir W. Hamilton *Discuss.*, *Stud. Math.* (1852) 292 Irradicated in it by custom. **1838** — *Logic* xxviii. (1866) II. 86 To tear up what has become irradicated in his intellectual and moral being.

i'rrarefiable, *a. rare.* [ir-².] That cannot be rarefied.

1665 R. Hooke *Microgr.* 104 Many terrestrial, or indissoluble and irrarefiable parts, we find in Soot.

irrascible, erron. form of irascible.

†**i'rrased, -it,** *ppl. a. Her. Obs.* In 9 *erron.* inraced. [f. ir-¹ + rased, in med.L. *irrāsa* 'scraped in'.] = indented 2. (Cf. erased 2, 2 b.)

1486 *Bk. St. Albans, Her.* D ij b, Off armys qua[r]terit and irrasyt now I will speke.. called quarterit armys irrasit for the colouris be rasit owt as oon coloure in rasyng ware take away from an othir. *Ibid.* D iv a, D v b. **1828-40** Berry *Encycl. Herald.* I, *Inraced*, or *Racée*, are terms used by Upton [i.e. in *Bk. St. Albans*, as above] and others, meaning indented. **1830** in Robson *Brit. Herald* III. Gloss. **1889** in Elvin *Dict. Her.*

†**irrationa'bility.** *Obs.* or *arch.* [ad. L. *irratiōnābilitās*, f. *irratiōnābilis*: see next and -ity.] Unreasonableness, irrationality.

1627-77 Feltham *Resolves* ii. lxvii. 302 By the Irrationabilities arising from our selves or others. **1645** *City Alarum* 7, I hate irrationability in whom soever I find it. **1820** Coleridge *Lett.*, *to J. H. Green* 25 May (1895) 711 Easier to laugh.. at the question than to prove its irrationability.

†**irrationable** (ɪˈræʃənəb(ə)l), *a. Obs.* or *arch.* [ad. late L. *irratiōnābil-is* without reason, f. *ir-* (ir-²) + *ratiōnābilis* rationable.]

1. Not endowed with reason; = irrational *a.* 1.

1583 Stubbes *Anat. Abus.* i. (1877) 92 There is no creature.. how irrationable soeuer, that dooth degenerate as man dooth. **1651** *Raleigh's Ghost* 116 Irrationable Creatures do know such kinde of meats, as are hurtful and dangerous to them.

2. Not in accordance with reason; unreasonable; = irrational *a.* 2.

a **1650** May *Satyr. Puppy* (1657) 55, I had three reasons.. First, I was drunke, a strong one, extracted from my irrationable weaknesse. **1731** *Gentl. Mag.* I. 421 Amongst our popular Errors none are more inexcusable than those irrationable and reciprocal Dislikes of the great and small Vulgar of the City and Country. **1832** I. Taylor *Saturday Even.* (1833) 70 Enforcing from the people an irrationable homage to certain excrescences.

Hence †**i'rrationably** *adv.*, unreasonably.

a **1650** May *Satyr. Puppy* (1657) 95 Embassadors.. were almost fain to beg a life of them, who (irrationably) under-valewed it in themselves.

irrational (ɪˈræʃənəl), *a.* and *sb.* [ad. L. *irratiōnāl-is*, f. *ir-* (ir-²) + *ratiōnāl-is* rational.]

A. *adj.* **1.** Not endowed with reason.

c **1470** Henryson *Mor. Fab.* iii. (*Cock & Fox*) i, Thocht brutall beistis be irrationall, That is to say, wantand discretioun. **1635** J. Hayward tr. *Biondi's Banish'd Virg.* 128 Confirmed in such an opinion by the nature of irrationall animals. **1661** Lovell *Hist. Anim. & Min.* Introd., As for Animals, they are animate bodies, and sentient, having locall motion, and are either irrationall or rationall. **1752** Hume *Ess. & Treat.* (1777) I. 221 Nothing has a greater effect on all plants and irrational animals. **1826** Scott *Woodst.* iv, That may be true of the more irrational kinds of animals among each other.

2. Contrary to or not in accordance with reason; unreasonable, utterly illogical, absurd.

1641 Ld. Brooke *Eng. Episc.* 23 All my acts may be Irrationall, and yet not sinfull. **1664-94** South *Twelve Serm.* II. 15 This certainly is a Confidence of all others the most ungrounded and irrational. **1796** Burke *Regic. Peace* i. Wks. VIII. 84 Inconsiderate courage has given way to irrational fear. **1825** McCulloch *Pol. Econ.* ii. ii. 123 Nothing can be more irrational and absurd, than that dread of the progress of others in wealth and civilization that was once so prevalent. **1875** Jowett *Plato* (ed. 2) V. 186 If men cannot have a rational belief, they will have an irrational.

3. *Math.* Of a number, quantity, or magnitude: Not rational; not commensurable with ordinary quantities such as the natural numbers; not expressible by an ordinary (finite) fraction, proper or improper (but only by an infinite continued fraction, or an infinite series, *e.g.* an interminate decimal). Usually applied to roots (denoted by the radical sign √, or in *Alg.* by fractional indices) whose value cannot be exactly found in finite terms of the unit, or to expressions involving such roots; the same as *surd.*

In translations of Euclid (following his peculiar use of ἄλογος), applied to a quantity which is itself incommensurable with the unit and whose square is incommensurable with that of the unit.

1551 Recorde *Pathw. Knowl.* ii. Pref., Numbres and quantitees surde or irrationall. **1673** Wallis in Rigaud *Corr. Sci. Men* (1841) II. 567, I depress the irrational part $\sqrt{3200}$ by dividing 3200 by the greatest square number I can. **1743** Emerson *Fluxions* 45 The Fluent of an irrational Fluxion may sometimes.. be found by assuming an indetermin'd Series. **1827** Hutton *Course Math.* I. 82 The cube root of 8 is rational, being equal to 2; but the cube root of 9 is surd or irrational. **1879** Thomson & Tait *Nat. Phil.* I. i. §359 We may have.. three different values of one algebraic irrational expression.

4. *Gr. Pros.* Said of a syllable having a metrical value not corresponding to its actual time-value, or of a metrical foot containing such a syllable.

1844 Beck & Felton tr. *Munk's Metres* 17 There is also an irrational (ἄλογον) relation which cannot be measured by the unit. **1883** Jebb *Œdipus Tyrannus* p. lxxiii, The anacrusis.. is an irrational syllable, a long serving for a short.

B. *sb.* **1.** A being not endowed with reason; one not guided by reason.

1646 J. Hall *Horæ Vac.* 16 We live under the Colours of vertue; in other actions we are no more than Irrationals. **1713** Derham *Phys.-Theol.* iv. xiii. (1714) 236 The architectonick Faculty of Animals, especially the Irrationals. **1810** D. Savile *Disc. Revel.* 280 Infants and irrationals neither have nor can have clear, distinct, and explicit knowledge of Christ. **1858** Gen. P. Thompson *Audi Alt.* I. lxi. 239 There is that in progress, which will put down the reign of irrationals whether on four feet or on two.

2. *Math.* An irrational number or quantity; a surd. (In quot. 1875 applied to a number having no measure but unity, a prime number: cf. incommensurable 1 b.)

1674 Jeake *Arith.* (1696) 360 In pursuit of Species, I now come to Irrationals, which in their Operations.. follow Surds. **1875** Jowett *Plato* (ed. 2) III. 115 Two incommensurable diameters, i.e. the two first irrationals, 2 and 3.

irrationalism (ɪˈræʃənəlɪz(ə)m). [f. prec. + -ism.] A system of belief or action that disregards or contradicts rational principles; irrationality.

1811 Shelley in Dowden *Life* (1887) I. 151 He is nothing, no -ist, professes no -ism but superbism and irrationalism. **1846** Hare *Mission Comf.* (1850) 311 The reaction from the dry prosaic spirit of the last century having produced a craving for all manner of extravagant follies.. this shall be signalized as the Age of Irrationalism. **1853** (*title*) The Irrationalism of Infidelity.

So **i'rrationalist** [see -ist]. Also *attrib.* or as *adj.*

1836 Hor. Smith *Tin Trump.* (1876) 307 These irrationalists seem to think, that the intellectual faculties of man are like hemlock and henbane. **1839** Whately *Dangers Chr. Faith* (1857) I. ix. 38 We may.. call the one of these a 'Rationalist', and the other an 'Irrationalist'. **1897** H. M. Cecil (*title*) Pseudo-philosophy at the end of the nineteenth century: an irrationalist trio: Kidd, Drummond, Balfour. **1910** W. James *Mem. & Stud.* (1911) xv. 392 Listen for a moment to such irrationalist deliverances on his part as these.

irrationalistic (ɪræʃənəˈlɪstɪk), *a.* [f. irrational *a.* + -istic.] Characterized by irrationalism; contrary to reason; illogical.

1910 W. James *Mem. & Stud.* (1911) xv. 400, I spoke a while ago of its being an 'irrationalistic' philosophy in its latest phase. **1912** *Q. Rev.* Oct. 364 This brings us to the fundamental difference between the standpoints of history and science, which the theology called 'irrationalistic' appears to have overlooked. **1920** A. S. Pringle-Pattison *Idea of God* (ed. 2) 64, I have dwelt in the latter part of this lecture on the tendency to slip into an anti-intellectualistic, and even irrationalistic, mode of statement in expressing the principle of value. **1934** A. C. Ewing *Idealism* v. 250 The irrationalistic and excessively pluralistic tendencies of the present day. **1963** R. Wellek in N. Frye *Romanticism Reconsidered* 121 He singles out the most irrationalistic writers.

irrationality (ɪræʃəˈnælɪtɪ). [f. irrational + -ity.]

1. The quality of being devoid of reason.

1822-34 *Good's Study Med.* (ed. 4) III. 139 Species II. Mória Demens. Witlessness, Irrationality. **1874** Carpenter *Ment. Phys.* i. ii. §59 (1879) 60 The irrationality of the impulse which prompts the Bees to this action, is evidenced by its occasional performance under circumstances which, if they could reason, would have shown them that it must be ineffective.

2. The quality of not being guided by, or not being in accordance with, reason; absurdity of thought or action.

1647 Boyle *Let. J. Dury* 3 May in *Wks.* (1772) I. p. xl, Like Jonah's gourd, smitten at the root with the worm of their irrationality. **1662** Sir A. Mervyn *Sp. Irish Aff.* 37 It were to impose too much irrationality on our Law. **1717** Lady M. W. Montagu *Let. to Pope* 12 Feb., Nothing seems to me a plainer proof of the irrationality of mankind.. than the rage with which they contest for a small spot of ground. **1863** Cowden Clarke *Shaks. Char.* vii. 185 That strange mixture of cunning, and love of stratagem, with irrationality in the contrivance, so remarkable in insane people. **1866** Geo. Eliot *F. Holt* xxxiii, Some sharp-visaged men who loved the irrationality of riots.

b. An irrational thing, action, or thought; an absurdity.

a **1680** Charnock *Attrib. God* (1834) I. 26 To.. forge irrationalities for the support of his fancy. **1857** De Quincey *Iscariot* Wks. VII. 21 A dismal heap of irrationalities.

3. *Math.* The quality of being irrational: see irrational *a.* 3.

1570 Dee *Math. Pref.* in Rudd *Euclid* (1651) C b, Practise hath led Numbers farther.. to take upon them the shew of Magnitudes property: which is Incommensurability and Irrationality. **1838-9** Hallam *Hist. Lit.* II. ii. viii. §2. 320 Pelletier does not employ the signs + and −,.. but we find the sign √ of irrationality.

4. *Optics.* The inequality of the ratios of the dispersion of the various colours in spectra

produced by refraction through different substances.

1797 *Encycl. Brit.* s.v. *Telescope*, The effect of this irrationality (so to call it) of dispersion, will appear plainly. 1829 *Nat. Philos.* I. *Optics* ix. 26 (U.K.S.) Hence the coloured spaces have not the same ratio to each other as the lengths of the spectrum; and therefore this property is called the irrationality of dispersion, or of the coloured spaces in the spectrum. 1866 GROVE *Contrib. Sc.* in *Corr. Phys. Forces* 194 The irrationality of the spectrum or the incommensurate divisions of the spectra formed by flint and crown glass.

5. *Gr. Pros.* See IRRATIONAL *a.* 4.

1844 BECK & FELTON tr. *Munk's Metres* 17 Irrationality takes place in the double kind in the thesis, in the equal in the arsis.

irrationalize (ɪ'ræʃənəlaɪz), *v.* [f. IRRATIONAL + -IZE: cf. *rationalize.*] *trans.* To render irrational.

1895 A. J. BALFOUR *Foundat. Belief* IV. i 235 To pursue the opposite course would be gratuitously to irrationalise (to coin a convenient word) our scheme from the very start. 1896 SETH in *Contemp. Rev.* Aug. 177 The denial of the postulated reality..irrationalises the whole scheme of things presupposed by our ordinary experience.

irrationally (ɪ'ræʃənəlɪ), *adv.* [f. IRRATIONAL + -LY².] In an irrational manner; in a way devoid of or contrary to reason; absurdly.

1652 GAULE *Magastrom.* 295 An effect of his rationally perswading art, quite contrary to the other, irrationally prognosticating. 1668 WILKINS *Real Char.* IV. vi. 444 These Genders are irrationally applyed. 1753 N. TORRIANO *Gangr. Sore Throat* 76 Very odd in her Head, talking irrationally. 1841 W. SPALDING *Italy & It. Isl.* III. 42 The wrecks of this irrationally brave multitude next defended the city.

b. *Gr. Pros.* See IRRATIONAL *a.* 4.

1883 JEBB *Œdipus Tyrannus* p. lxxiii, The anacrusis..is a really short syllable serving 'irrationally' as a long one.

i'rrationalness. *rare.* [f. as prec. + -NESS.] The quality of being irrational or without reason; irrationality.

1727 in BAILEY vol. II.

†**i'rrazable**, *a. Obs. rare*⁻¹. [f. IR-² + RAZE + -ABLE. Cf. ERASABLE.] That cannot be razed or erased.

1622 H. SYDENHAM *Serm. Sol. Occ.* II. (1637) 74 That sinne then is irrazable which is so steeled with custom.

†**irre, erre**, *sb. Obs.* Forms: 1 ierre, irre, yrre, iorre, eorre, erre, 1–3 irre, eorre, 3 urre, (eire), 3–5 erre. [OE., WSax. *ierre, irre, yrre*, Angl. *iorre, eorre, erre*, neuter *jo*-stem, corresp. exc. in formative suffix to OHG. **irrî*, MHG. and Ger. *irre*, MG. *erre* error, Goth. *airzei* weak fem., from OTeut. root **erz*-: see next.] Anger, wrath.

c825 *Vesp. Psalter* ci. 11 [cii. 10] From onsiene eorres & ebylðu ðinre. c897 K. ÆLFRED *Gregory's Past.* xl. 289 Đonne ðæt ierre [h]æfð anwald ðæs monnes..he self nat huæt he on ðæt irre deð. 971 *Blickl. Hom.* 25 Nis þær eȝe, ne ȝeflit, ne yrre. *Ibid.* 47 Gif hi hi sylfe willon wiþ Godes erre ȝehealdan. a1000 *Elene* 401 (Gr.) Ne we ȝeare cunnun, þurh hwæt þu þus hearde, hlæfdiȝe, us eorre wurde. c1000 *Ags. Gosp.* Luke iii. 7 Đ æt ȝe fleon fram þam towerdan yrre [c1160 *Hatton G.*, fram þam towearde eorre]. c1050 *Byrhtferth's Handboc* in *Anglia* (1885) VIII. 337 Se þridda ys *ira* þæt byð yrre. c1175 *Lamb. Hom.* 83 Adam wes..forwunded..mid spere of prude, of ȝitcunge, of ȝifernesse, of eorre. c1200 ORMIN 9266 To fleon and to forrbuȝhenn þatt irre þatt to cumenn iss. a1250 *Prov. Ælfred* 205 in *O.E. Misc.* 114 Monymon for his gold haueþ godes vrre [*v.r.* eire]. c1450 MYRC 1225 Hast þow had enuye and erre To hym þat was þyn ouer herre?

†**irre**, *a. Obs.* Forms: 1 ierre, yrre, iorre, 1–3 irre, eorre, ire, yr(e. [OE., WSax. *ierre, irre*, later *yrre*, Angl. *iorre, eorre* = OS. *irri* angry, OHG. *irri* wandering, deranged, angry (MHG. and Ger. *irre*), Goth. *airzeis* astray, from OTeut. root **erz*-, pre-Teut. **ers*-, L. *err*- (from *ers*-), in *errāre* to stray, *error* wandering. The transition to the sense 'angry', seen in OS. and OHG., and completed in OE., arose from the consideration of anger as a wandering or aberration of the mind.]

1. Gone astray, confused, perverted, depraved. Only in OE.

a1000 *Sol. & Sat.* 498 Oððæt his saȝe bið..yrre ȝeworden. c1000 *Ags. Ps.* (Th.) lxxv. 4 Ealle synt yrre [= *turbati sunt omnes*]. *Ibid.* lxxvii. 10 þæt wæs earfoð cynn, yrre and reðe.

2. Enraged, angry.

c825 *Vesp. Psalter* lix. 3 [lx. 1] God ðu..tuwurpe usic, eorre earð. c855 *O.E. Chron.* an. 584 Ierre he hwearf þonan to his aȝnum. c897 K. ÆLFRED *Gregory's Past.* xl. 289 þa ierran [*v.r.* irran] nyton hwæt hie on him selfum habbað. 971 *Blickl. Hom.* 33 Gif us hwa abylȝþ, þonne beo we sona yrre. c1000 ÆLFRIC *Gen.* xli. 10 Se cyning wæs yrre wið me. c1000 *Ags. Gosp.* Matt. xviii. 34 Đa wæs se hlaford yrre [c1160 *Hatton* eorre]. c1205 LAY. 18597 Forð wende þe eorl, ire [c1275 yr] on his mode. a1225 *Ancr. R.* 304 Abuuen us, þe eorre Demare.

irre'ality. *rare.* [IR-².] Unreality.

1803 W. TAYLOR in *Monthly Mag.* XIV. 491 The irreality, which may be predicated of those hypothetical existencies, signified by general terms.

irrealizable (ɪ'ri:əlaɪzəb(ə)l), *a.* [IR-².] That cannot be realized; unrealizable.

1853 C. BRONTE *Villette* xxxvi, The just motion..of suns around that mighty, unseen centre incomprehensible, irrealizable, with strange mental effort only divined. 1866 *Fortn. Rev.* V. 138 His was no visionary, overstrained, irrealisable virtue.

irrebuttable (ɪrɪ'bʌtəb(ə)l), *a.* [IR-².] That cannot be rebutted.

a1834 COLERIDGE *Lit. Rem.* (1838) III. 218 Compare this sixth section with the manful, senseful, irrebuttable fourth section. 1892 *Daily News* 23 Mar. 5/2 Perhaps..the presumption might be made absolute and irrebuttable.

irreceptive (ɪrɪ'sɛptɪv), *a.* [IR-².] Not receptive; incapable of receiving; unreceptive.

1846 TRENCH *Mirac.* v. (1862) 178 The working..of the spiritual life on the bestial, which seems altogether irreceptive of it. 1868 GLADSTONE *Glean.* (1879) III. 46 The religious mind..has, from want of habitual cultivation, grown dry and irreceptive on that side of the Christian creed.

irreceptivity (ɪri:sɛp'tɪvɪtɪ). *rare.* [IR-².] The quality of being irreceptive; incapacity to receive; unreceptiveness.

1881 *Spectator* 17 Sept. 1191 On account of some irreceptivity of mind.

irreciprocal (ɪrɪ'sɪprəkəl), *a.* [IR-².] Not reciprocal.

irreciprocal conduction (*Electr.*): conduction through electrolytes in which the magnitude of the current changes when it is reversed; unipolar conduction.

1886 *Nature* 25 Feb. 407/2 The conduction power of the electrical organ of the torpedo was consequently irreciprocal. 1888 GEE & HOLDEN in *Philos. Mag.* Aug. 126 *Note*, Following Christiani's use of the term, irreciprocal conduction is said to occur if a reversal of the direction of a current causes any change in its magnitude.

irreciprocity (ɪrɛsɪ'prɒsɪtɪ). [IR-².] Absence of reciprocity.

irreciprocity of conduction (*Electr.*): alteration in the magnitude of a current when its direction is reversed.

1886 *Nature* 25 Feb. 407/2 This irreciprocity of conduction obtained only for strong currents and for those of short duration. *Ibid.* 408/1 This irreciprocity of conduction explained in a most highly interesting manner the powerful effect of the strokes directed outwards of electrical fish. 1888 GEE & HOLDEN in *Philos. Mag.* Aug. 133 Here it seems evident that the irreciprocity is due to the gradual formation of a badly-conducting film on the anode.

irreclaimable (ɪrɪ'kleɪməb(ə)l), *a.* Also 7–8 irreclamable. [IR-².]

†1. Uncontrollable, implacable. *Obs. rare.*

1609 HOLLAND *Amm. Marcell.* XIV. xi. 26 The Emperour when he understood this, falling into an irreclamable fit of anger and wrath, reposed all the assurance and confidence hee had..in making him away.

2. That cannot be reclaimed, reformed, or called back to right ways.

1662 GLANVILL *Lux Orient.* x. 97 Such impetuous, ungovernable, irreclaimable inclinations to what is vitious. 1681–6 J. SCOTT *Chr. Life* (1747) III. 556 The irreclaimable Enemies of God. 1690 NORRIS *Beatitudes* (1692) 125 The greatest object of Pity in the World is an irreclaimable Sinner. 1743 J. MORRIS *Serm.* vii. 199 Good governors may justly cut off irreclamable offenders. 1882 A. W. WARD *Dickens* iii. 69 He had not yet become the irreclaimable political sceptic of later days.

b. Of land: That cannot be reclaimed or brought into cultivation.

1812 BRACKENRIDGE *Views of Louisiana* (1814) 159 Of this portion, there is not more than a fourth which can be considered irreclaimable. 1885 *Spectator* 22 Aug. 1097/2, 56,000 square kilometres are either covered with snow or strewn with rocks, and utterly irreclaimable.

3. That cannot be called back or revoked; irrevocable.

1834 HT. MARTINEAU *Moral* IV. 132 The only irreclaimable human decree,—that of an enlightened multitude,—has gone forth against the abuses of the Church and the Law.

Hence **irre'claimableness, irreclaima'bility**, the quality of being irreclaimable.

1748 RICHARDSON *Clarissa* (1811) VIII. 407 (D.) Enormities..which are out of his power to atone for, by reason of the death of some of the injured parties, and the irreclaimableness of others. 1881 *Blackw. Mag.* July 29 The irreclaimability of the habitual drunkard.

irre'claimably, *adv.* [f. prec. + -LY².] Without the possibility of being reclaimed.

1662 GLANVILL *Lux Orient.* Aerial St. 154 Others irreclaimeably persisting in their Rebellion. 1837 WHEWELL *Hist. Induct. Sc.* (1857) I. 376 Being irreclaimably barbarous. 1875 LYELL *Princ. Geol.* II. III. xlix. 603 Each inch is irreclaimably gone.

irreclaimed (ɪrɪ'kleɪmd), *a. rare.* [IR-².] Not reclaimed; not brought under civilization or cultivation; unreclaimed.

1812 BRACKENRIDGE *Views Louisiana* (1814) 176 The soil of Louisiana is the most fertile in the world, the climate delightful during nine months of the year, and bad the remainder, only from being irreclaimed. 1814 SOUTHEY *Carmina Aul.* VII. ii, If the brute Multitude..Wild as their savage ancestors, Go irreclaim'd the while. 1871 *Times* 17 Feb. 4/1 This redistribution..bringing into convenient juxtaposition the irreclaimed and the reclaimed lands.

irrecognition (ɪrɛkəg'nɪʃən). [IR-².] Absence of recognition; non-recognition.

1820 LAMB *Elia* Ser. I. *Christ's Hosp. 35 Y. ago*, This exquisite irrecognition of any law antecedent to the oral and declaratory. 1872 LOWELL *Dante* Pr. Wks. 1890 IV. 162 In all literary history there is no such figure as Dante, no..such loyalty to ideas, such sublime irrecognition of the unessential.

irrecognizable (ɪ'rɛkəg,naɪzəb(ə)l), *a.* [IR-².] Incapable of being recognized; unrecognizable.

1837 CARLYLE *Fr. Rev.* II. III. vii, Mirabeau..is cast forth..and rests now, irrecognisable, reburied hastily at dead of night. a1849 POE *Longfellow*, etc. Wks. 1864 III. 357 That a lover may so disguise his voice from his mistress as even to render his person in full view irrecognisable. 1887 *Spectator* 10 Sept. 1209 Of the dead a large number are irrecognisable, so deeply have they been charred.

Hence **irrecognizability** (ɪ,rɛkəgnaɪzə'bɪlɪtɪ), the condition of being unrecognizable; **i'rrecog,nizably** *adv.*

1840 CARLYLE *Heroes* iii. (1872) 95 No thought, word or act of man but has sprung withal out of all men, and works sooner or later, recognisably or irrecognisably, on all men! 1847 —— in *Corr. w. Emerson* II. cvi. 131 May the Lord..teach us to look Facts honestly in the face and to beware..of smearing them over with our despicable and damnable palaver into irrecognizability.

irrecognizant (ɪrɪ'kɒgnɪzənt), *a. rare.* [IR-².] Not recognizant; not having recognition.

1845 CARLYLE *Cromwell* II. 158 Irrecognisant of the Perennial because not dressed in the fashionable Temporary.

irrecollection (ɪrɛkɒ'lɛkʃən). [IR-².] The absence of recollection; forgetfulness.

1737 WESLEY *Wks.* (1872) I. 72, I am convinced..of gross irrecollection. 1802 WOLCOTT (P. Pindar) *Gt. Cry & Lit. Wool* Wks. 1812 V. 199 Sad scene of sad irrecollection.

†**irrecom'pensable**, *a. Obs.* Also 6 -ible. [IR-².] That cannot be recompensed or requited; irreparable.

1557 *Primer, Godly prayers*, Geuinge to me mooste unworthy many greate and irrecompensable giftes. 1604 T. WRIGHT *Passions* v. §4. 246 The gifts of instructors in learning and manners are vnvaluable, and irrecompensable. 1615 SIR E. HOBY *Curry-combe* ii. 75 To haue taxed him with Reseruations..had beene an irrecompensable wrong.

Hence †**irrecom'pensably** *adv.*, irreparably.

1615 SIR E. HOBY *Curry-combe* iii. 143 You would thinke that blessed and holy Virgin irrecompensably disparaged.

irreconcilability (ɪ,rɛkənsaɪlə'bɪlɪtɪ). [f. next: see -ITY.] The quality of being irreconcilable; irreconcilableness.

1830 *Blackw. Mag.* XXVIII. 735 Notwithstanding the utter irreconcilability of the several statements. 1861 *Westm. Rev.* Oct. 490 Proof..of the irreconcilability of Northern and Southern domestic politics. 1897 *Century Mag.* 621/1 The irreconcilability of the squirrel to captivity.

irreconcilable (ɪ,rɛkən'saɪləb(ə)l, ɪ'rɛkənsaɪləb(ə)l), *a.* (*sb.*) Also -cileable. [IR-².]

1. Of persons, their feelings, etc.: That cannot be reconciled or brought into friendly relations; implacably hostile. Const. *to.*

1599 SANDYS *Europæ Spec.* (1632) 41 He may..have them for ever most firm and irreconcileable adversaries. 1614 RALEIGH *Hist. World* II. (1634) 412 That hee [Absalom] was irreconcilable to his Father. 1653 A. WILSON *Jas. I* 51 The irreconcileable malice of that party. 1693 DRYDEN *Juvenal* Ded. (1697) 1 There are no Factions, tho' irreconcileable to one another, that are not united in their Affection to you. 1709 STEELE *Tatler* No. 5 ¶8 A Dispute about a Matter of Love, which..grew to an irreconcileable Hatred. *Ibid.* No. 79 ¶1 The Quarrel between Sir Harry Willit and his Lady..is irreconcilable. 1801 RANKEN *Hist. Fr.* I. I. v. 157 Their minds were irreconcilable to the dominion of France. 1874 GREEN *Short Hist.* viii. §10. 573 In England Cromwell dealt with the Royalists as irreconcilable enemies.

2. Of statements, ideas, etc.: That cannot be brought into harmony or made consistent; incompatible. Const. *to, with.*

1646 SIR T. BROWNE *Pseud. Ep.* v. xi. 250 Many conclude an irreconcilable incertainty; some making more, others fewer. 1671 R. BOHUN *Wind* 4 Their..Aeriall impressions, how different and irreconcileable to Ours? 1709 BERKELEY *The. Vision* §71 Neither would it prove in the least irreconcilable with what we have said. 1761–2 HUME *Hist. Eng.* (1806) V. lxvii. 94 Bedloe's evidence and Prance's were in many circumstances totally irreconcilable. 1824 L. MURRAY *Eng. Gram.* (ed. 5) I. 277 'Expected to have found him', is irreconcilable to grammar and to sense. 1866 GEO. ELIOT *F. Holt* v, Creeds that were painfully wrong, and, indeed, irreconcilable with salvation. 1870 FREEMAN *Norm. Conq.* (ed. 2) I. App. 567 There is nothing irreconcileable in the two statements.

3. *Math.* Applied to paths between two fixed points in a surface, which paths cannot be made to coincide by gradual approximation without passing outside the surface.

Such are, e.g., two paths between opposite points in an anchor ring, which proceed in opposite directions; or two sea-routes between the N. and S. points of an island, which proceed along its E. and W. sides respectively.

1881 MAXWELL *Electr. & Magn.* I. 19 Curves for which this transformation cannot be effected are called Irreconcileable curves.

B. *sb.* a. A person who refuses to be reconciled; *esp.* One of a political party who refuses to come to any agreement or make any compromise, or remains implacably opposed to an arrangement.

1748 RICHARDSON *Clarissa* (1811) III. 178 Sleep and I have quarrelled; and although I court it, it will not be friends. I hope its fellow-irreconcilables at Harlowe-place enjoy its balmy comforts. **1878** BESANT & RICE *Celia's Arb.* xx. (1887) 146 No Red Irreconcilable ever preached a policy so sanguinary and thorough. **1884** H. SPENCER in *Pop. Sci. Monthly* XXIV. 731 From Oxford graduates down to Irish irreconcilables.

b. *pl.* Principles, ideas, etc. that cannot be harmonized with each other.

1895 *Westm. Gaz.* 26 Aug. 3/3 In her endeavour to harmonise two irreconcilables—to be at once conventional and insurgent.

irreconcilableness (see prec.). [f. prec. + -NESS.] The quality or fact of being irreconcilable.

1628 BP. HALL *Old Relig.* 195 That which long since I wrote, of the irreconcileablenesse of Rome. **1711** SHAFTESB. *Charac.* (1737) II. 171 This disagreement with every thing, this irreconcilableness and opposition to the order and government of the universe. **1841-4** EMERSON *Ess.* Ser. II. ii. (1876) 71 The conviction of the irreconcilableness of the two spheres. **1857** J. PULSFORD *Quiet Hours* Ser. I. (1897) 87 The irreconcilableness of sin with the Divine Nature.

irreconcilably (see above), *adv.* [f. as prec. + -LY².] In an irreconcilable manner.

1604 F. HERING *Modest Def.* 13 Poison is absolutely and irreconcilably opposed vnto nature. **1712** STEELE *Spect.* No. 398 ¶9 He had not much more to do to accomplish being irreconcileably banished. **1807** G. CHALMERS *Caledonia* I. III. vii. 390 Malcolm..had irreconcileably incensed the men of Moray, by killing their chief. **1855** MILMAN *Lat. Chr.* VII. vi. (1864) IV. 184 A war of religion is essentially irreconcileably oppugnant to the spirit of Christianity.

†**i'rreconcile,** *v. Obs.* [IR-².] *trans.* To render unreconciled; to make incompatible or antagonistic; to estrange.

1647 CLARENDON *Hist. Reb.* II. §73 Which expression, how necessary..soever to reconcile the affections of the House..very much irreconciled him at Court. **1649** JER. TAYLOR *Gt. Exemp.* III. Ad sect. xv. 161 As this object calls for our devotion..so it must needs irreconcile us to sin. **1670** CLARENDON *Ess.* Tracts (1727) 209 Nor can any aversion or malignity towards the object, irreconcile the eyes from looking upon it.

†**i'rreconciled,** *a. Obs.* [IR-².] Not reconciled; *spec.* in a state at variance with God.

1599 SHAKS. *Hen. V,* IV. i. 160 If a Seruant, vnder his Masters command..be assayled by Robbers, and dye in many irreconcil'd Iniquities. **1691** NORRIS *Pract. Disc.* 32 To sleep soundly and securely, in a Doubtful and sometimes in a Damnable and Irreconciled State. **1750** WARBURTON *Julian* Wks. 1811 VIII. 140 A concerted agreement or irreconciled contradiction.

irreconcilement (ɪ'rɛkənˌsaɪlmənt). [IR-².] The state or fact of being unreconciled.

a **1737** ABP. WAKE *Ration. Texts Script.* 85 (T.) Such an irreconcilement between God and Mammon. **1887** G. MACDONALD *Home Again* xxvi. 221 The two stared at each other in mortal irreconcilement.

irreconciliable (ɪrɛkən'sɪlɪəb(ə)l), *a.* Now *rare.* [a. F. *irréconciliable* (16th c. in Littré), ad. med.L. type **irreconciliābilis*, f. *ir-* (IR-²) + *reconciliāre* to RECONCILE.]

1. = IRRECONCILABLE I.

1601 in Bp. W. Barlow *Defence* 200 The irreconciliable iarres betwixt them and the Puritanes. **1603** HOLLAND *Plutarch's Mor.* 123 The very mother and work-mistresse of irreconciliable enmitie. *a* **1649** DRUMM. OF HAWTH. *Hist. Scot.* (1655) 176 He was an irreconciliable enemy to the whole Family of the Dowglasses. **1863** LD. LYTTON *Ring Amasis* I. 73 It involves them both in the anguish of an irreconciliable destiny.

2. = IRRECONCILABLE 2.

a **1615** DONNE *Ess.* (1651) 33 The Chineses vex us at this day with irreconciliable accounts. **1615** G. SANDYS *Trav.* 142 *note,* Irreconciliable are the computations of Chronologers.

Hence **irreconcilia'bility, -'ciliableness; irrecon'ciliably** *adv.*

1604 PARSONS *3rd Pt. Three Convers. Eng.* 130 Fallinge out with Luther irreconciliably. **1609** SIR E. HOBY *Let. to Mr. T. H.* 5 Then did I begin irreconciliable to detest all the Incendiaries of your Romish forge. *a* **1631** DONNE *Serm.* lxxii. 727 Illimited and boundlesse anger, a vindicative irreconciliablenesse is imputed to God. **1661** *Sir H. Vane's Politics* 13, I was naturally..irreconciliably passive in the burden of an injury. **1847** LEWES *Hist. Philos.* (1867) II. 561 His keen perception of the irreconciliability of his ideas with the ideas of St. Simon.

irreconcili'ation. [IR-².] The fact or condition of being unreconciled.

a **1650** J. PRIDEAUX *Euchol.* I. v. (1656) 71 How irreconciliation with our brethren, voids all our addresses to God. **1658** BP. REYNOLDS *Van. Creature* Wks. (1679) 9 God ..can..let in upon thy Soul..the evident presumptions of irreconciliation with him. **1678** BP. OF GLOUCESTER *Expos. Catech.* 120 Desire of revenge, irreconciliation, frowardness, contention. **1906** *Daily Chron.* 1 Oct. 5/6 Where..brotherly love and charity [have long been] enemies sworn to irreconciliation. **1927** *Brit. Weekly* 24 Mar. 639/1 Science has its confusions and irreconciliations no less than religion.

irrecordable (ɪrɪ'kɔːdəb(ə)l), *a.* [IR-².] That cannot be recorded.

1623 COCKERAM, *Irrecordable,* not to bee remembred. So in PHILLIPS, BAILEY, and mod. Dicts.

irrecoverable (ɪrɪ'kʌvərəb(ə)l), *a.* [f. IR-² + RECOVER *v.* + -ABLE: cf. RECOVERABLE and F. *irrécouvrable* (*c* 1586 in Littré).]

†**1.** That cannot be recalled or revoked; irrevocable. *Obs.*

1540 *Wills & Inv. N.C.* (Surtees 1835) 115, I Syr Rogr Gray..thoft I be seke in my body, maks my last Wyll irrecou'able & testament in manner & form folowyng. **1635** *Gram. Warre* D vij, There was giuen irrecouerable power to the deputed, to exile all corrupters of Grammar. **1768-74** TUCKER *Lt. Nat.* (1834) II. 377 Persons lying under an irrecoverable sentence of death. **1817** CHALMERS *Astron. Disc.* v. (1852) 128 Loaded with the fetters of irrecoverable bondage.

2. That cannot be recovered or got back: chiefly in reference to things lost.

1645 *City Alarum* 6 Occasions once lost are irrecoverable. **1665** SIR T. HERBERT *Trav.* (1677) 250 The greater part is lost and buried in the Sea, where it is irrecoverable. **1782** JEFFERSON *Notes Virginia* xvi. (1787) 259 Their lands were.. forfeited, and their debts irrecoverable. **1809** R. LANGFORD *Introd. Trade* 131 Which renders the assurance irrecoverable if the ship is lost. **1835** I. TAYLOR *Spir. Despot.* i. 10 Without losing a day of irrecoverable time.

3. Incapable of being restored to health; incurable; past recovery; incapable of being restored to life, as after drowning, suffocation, etc. *arch.*

1594 T. B. *La Primaud. Fr. Acad.* II. *Seneca,* By some irrecouerable disease. **1631** WEEVER *Anc. Fun. Mon.* 607 Being taken with an irrecouerable Palsie, he well knew his time to be short. **1708** O. BRIDGMAN in *Phil. Trans.* XXVI. 139 He fell..into a Violent Fever..and if not dead yet, is pronounced irrecoverable. **1772** PRIESTLEY ibid. LXII. 182 They..are sometimes affected so suddenly, that they are irrecoverable after a single inspiration. **1809** G. ROSE *Diaries* (1860) II. 369 Irrecoverable ill health. **1875** BEDFORD *Sailor's Pocket Bk.* viii. (ed. 2) 299 It is an erroneous opinion that persons are irrecoverable because life does not soon make its appearance.

b. *fig.* Not capable of being remedied or rectified; that cannot be made good; irretrievable; irremediable; irreclaimable.

1536 BELLENDEN *Cron. Scot.* (1821) I. 169 Corbreid.. brocht thaim to sic irrecoverabill afflictioun and slauchter, that thay micht nevir invade this realme during his liffe. **1586** *Let. Earle Leycester* 24 A person obdurate..and irrecouerable. **1632** J. HAYWARD tr. *Biondi's Eromena* 31 The losse that both you and the Kingdome have now sustained, is irrecoverable. **1679** C. NESSE *Antid. agst. Popery* Ded. 8 A final and irrecoverable fall. **1745** *De Foe's Eng. Tradesman* (1841) I. vii. 53 After he sees his circumstances irrecoverable. **1808** G. EDWARDS *Pract. Plan* iii. 22 Extensive and irrecoverable deteriorations. **1878** FR. A. KEMBLE *Record of a Girlhood* I. ii. 38 The loss of her favourite son affected her with irrecoverable sorrow.

†**4.** That cannot be recovered from. *Obs.*

1614 RALEIGH *Hist. World* II. v. iii. §15. 441 Giuing some deadly and irrecouerable poyson. **1674** R. GODFREY *Inj. & Ab. Physic* 190 Their pretended gentle Rest, to the shame of Medicine, is a horrid irrecoverable Sleep.

irre'coverableness. [f. prec. + -NESS.] The quality of being irrecoverable.

1607 HIERON *Wks.* I. 110 Afterwards is set downe both the easiness and the irrecouerablenesse of their destruction. **1681** KETTLEWELL *Chr. Obed.* (1715) 466 Therein it is, the irrecoverableness of those lost sinners consists. **1889** R. A. KING *Passion's Slave* III. xxix. 61 Clare..had not yet realised the bankruptcy of her influence, or rather, perhaps its irrecoverableness.

irrecoverably (ɪrɪ'kʌvərəblɪ), *adv.* [f. as prec. + -LY².] In an irrecoverable manner; without the possibility of recovery, restoration, or cure; irretrievably; incurably.

1589 J. WOLLEY *Let. to Burghley* in Ellis *Orig. Lett.* Ser. III. IV. 75 He should not hasten irrecoverably the sale of his land. **1599** SANDYS *Europæ Spec.* (1632) 20 What griefe..to see men fall irrecoverably from the loue and lawes of the Creatour? **1605** TIMME *Quersit.* II. iv. 118 Men which are irrecouerably diseased. **1683** DRYDEN *Life Plutarch* 74 Works of his which are irrecoverably lost. **1781** GIBBON *Decl. & F.* xxix. III. 131 While they delayed the necessary assistance, the unfortunate Mascezel was irrecoverably drowned. **1847** GROTE *Greece* II. xlv. (1862) IV. 74 The maritime power of Ægina was irrecoverably ruined.

†**irrecuperable** (ɪrɪ'kjuːpərəb(ə)l), *a. Obs.* Also 4-6 **-arable.** [a. OF. *irrecuperable* (1386 in Godef.), ad. late L. *irrecuperābilis* irreparable, f. *ir-* (IR-²) + *recuperāre* to recover: see -ABLE.]

1. That cannot be recovered or regained.

1387-8 T. USK *Test. Love* II. i. (Skeat) l. 34 Thus irrecuparable ioy is went, and anoy endlesse is entred. **1483** CAXTON *Gold. Leg.* 404 b/2 Thou art ryght sorouful for me whome thou haste loste whyche am Irrecuperable. **1538** LELAND *Itin.* VII. 117 The Ruine of the Fortelet..ys at thys day a Hold irrecuperable for the Fox. *c* **1575** HACKET *Treas. Amadis* 274 Teares be lost upon a thing irrecuperable. **1644** PRYNNE & WALKER *Fiennes' Trial* 86 A most certaine present losse..(perchance irrecuperable for the future too).

2. That cannot be recovered from or cured; incurable.

1430-40 LYDG. *Bochas* (ed. Wayland) 58 a, Syth that his dole was irrecuperable. *c* **1489** CAXTON *Blanchardyn* 215 The salue commeth to late, where the sore is irrecuperable. **1511-12** *Act 3 Hen. VIII,* c. 5 *Preamble,* Irrecuperable damages may ensue if remedy therfor be not seen and had. **1590** *Serpent of Devis.* ad fin., This makes vs consider the irrecuperable harmes of devision. **1626** in *3rd Rep. Hist. MSS. Comm.* 348/2 To the irrecuperable decay of my aged and benummed carkaise.

Hence †**irre'cuperably** *adv.*, incurably.

1535 in *Suppress. Monast.* (Camden) 106 Utterlye and irrecuperablye decayed and undone. **1683** E. HOOKER *Pref. Pordage's Mystic Div.* 21 Sin is..in public, countenanced, encouraged, taught, and..men are becom..irrevocably and irrecuperably and impudently impious.

†**irre'curable,** *a. Obs. rare.* [f. IR-² + RECURE *v.* + -ABLE.] Incapable of being remedied; incurable; irremediable.

a **1548** HALL *Chron., 1 Hen. IV* (1809) 22 They determined rather to abide in their old Subieccion..then for a Displeasure irrecurable to auenture themselfes on a new and a doubtfull parell. **1579** U. FULWELL *Arte Flatterie* F ij b (N.), Forced to sustayne a most grevous and irrecurable fall.

†**irre'cured,** *a. Obs. rare*⁻¹. [f. IR-² + *recured,* pa. pple. of RECURE *v.*] Incurable.

1598 ROUS *Thule* II. I. xxiv, Striking his soule with irrecured wound.

irrecusable (ɪrɪ'kjuːzəb(ə)l), *a.* [a. F. *irrécusable* (1782 in Hatz.-Darm.) or ad. late L. *irrecūsābilis*, f. *ir-* (IR-²) + *recūsābilis*, f. *recūsāre* to refuse: see RECUSANT and -ABLE.] Incapable of being refused acceptance.

1776 BENTHAM *Fragm. Govt.* Pref., Wks. 1843 I. 232/2 Merit in one department of letters affords a natural, and in a manner irrecusable presumption of merit in another. **1785** H. WALPOLE *Let. to C'tess Ossory* 29 Aug., I will give him an irrecusable proof. **1851** SIR F. PALGRAVE *Norm. & Eng.* I. 441 The silent but irrecusable testimonies of Regner's victory. **1882** J. B. STALLO *Concepts Mod. Physics* 67 The proposition here insisted upon is irrecusable by any consistent advocate of the mechanical theory.

Hence **irre'cusably** *adv.*, so as to preclude refusal of acceptance.

1862 F. HALL *Hindu Philos. Syst.* 71 The Acceptance of the Veda as having had no Conscious Author, and as being irrecusably authoritative.

irredeemable (ɪrɪ'diːməb(ə)l), *a.* (*sb.*) [IR-².]

A. *adj.* **1. a.** Incapable of being redeemed or bought back.

Of Government annuities: Not terminable by repayment of the sum originally paid by the annuitant. ***irredeemable debenture*** (see quot. 1965).

1609 SKENE *Reg. Mag.* Table 105 Gif ane pley is anent lands, quhither they be redemable, or irredemable, ane warrant may be called. **1732** *Gentl. Mag.* II. 709 There was 1,200,000*l.* due to the Bank, 2,000,000*l.* to the East India Company, and the irredeemable Annuities, being about as much as both. **1742** LD. HARDWICKE in *Mod. Rep.* IX. 278 If this had been land which had been mortgaged, the defendants could not have held it irredeemable without coming into this court for a foreclosure. **1818** CRUISE *Digest* (ed. 2) II. 125 If a mortgage becomes irredeemable by this statute, it will remain so in the hands of an assignee. **1820** G. G. CAREY *Funds* 17 The debt..for which annuities have been granted for a limited period is called the Irredeemable debt. **1855** J. D. MACLAREN in *Mem.* (1861) 245 Time is irredeemable. **1900** *Daily News* 3 July 2/5, £800,000 in Four-and-a Half per Cent. Irredeemable Mortgage Debenture stock at £108. **1965** PERRY & RYDER *Thomson's Dict. Banking* (ed. 11) 317/1 *Irredeemable debenture,* a debenture which does not contain any provision for repayment of the principal money. Even if irredeemable, it falls to be paid upon the company going into liquidation.

b. Of paper currency: For which the issuing authority does not undertake ever to pay coin; not convertible into cash.

1837 D. WEBSTER in *Niles' Weekly Reg.* 6 May 155/3, I abhor paper; that is to say irredeemable paper, paper that may not be converted into gold or silver at the will of the holder. *a* **1850** CALHOUN *Wks.* I. 362 It left the country nearly without any currency, except irredeemable bank notes. **1866** H. PHILLIPS *Amer. Paper Curr.* II. 82 All such bills not presented by a certain reasonable time..should be forever after irredeemable. **1879** LUBBOCK *Addr. Pol. & Educ.* ii. 28 Those who regard an unlimited and irredeemable paper currency as a panacea for all financial evils.

2. *fig.* That admits of no release or change of state; absolute, fixed, hopeless.

1839 POE *Fall House of Usher* Wks. 1864 I. 295 An air of stern, deep, and irredeemable gloom hung over and pervaded all. **1855** TENNYSON *Maud* II. i. 22 He..Wrought for his house an irredeemable woe.

3. Beyond redemption; irreclaimable; thoroughly depraved.

a **1834** COLERIDGE *Notes Lear* in *Lit. Rem.* (1836) II. 196 The Steward..the only character of utter irredeemable baseness in Shakspeare. **1892** *Columbus* (O.) *Disp.* 1 Sept., They are irredeemable in their thriftlessness.

B. *sb.* †**a.** An irredeemable annuity. *Obs.*

1720 *Lond. Gaz.* No. 5877/3 That for the Redeemables and Irredeemables subscribed..no Stock be allowed but in even 5*l.*

b. Anything that is irredeemable; *spec.* an irredeemable debenture.

1904 *Daily Chron.* 6 Feb. 3/2 The redemption of the irredeemable by woman's sweet and subtle influence the author has spared us. **1952** *Economist* 30 Aug. 514/1 Prices of most stocks at their lowest for twenty years, with irredeemables offering flat yields ranging up to..4¾ per cent. **1967** *Ibid.* 18 Nov. 785/2 The main effect..would eventually be felt by the long end of the market, especially by the irredeemables. **1973** *Daily Tel.* 24 Nov. 27/4 Most of the irredeemables return over 12 p.c. on income.

Hence **irredeema'bility, irre'deemableness,** 'the quality of being not redeemable' (Webster, 1828).

irredeemably (ɪrɪ'diːməblɪ), *adv.* [f. prec. + -LY².] In an irredeemable manner; to an

irredeemable extent; so as to be past redemption; hopelessly, absolutely, utterly.

1790 Blair *Serm.* III. iii. 48 But though past time be gone, we are not to consider it irredeemably lost. **1845** Ld. Campbell *Chancellors* (1857) III. lxxiii. 409 He considered that they were irredeemably doomed to destruction. **1868** *Act 31 & 32 Vict.* c. 101 Sched. B, C.D. sold..to the said A.B...heritably and irredeemably..all and the whole [etc.]. **1883** *Manch. Exam.* 22 Nov. 5/4 The government of Morocco is irredeemably bad.

irre'deemed, *a. rare.* [transl. It. *irredenta* unredeemed: see irredentist.] Not redeemed, not liberated from a foreign yoke.

1898 *Daily News* 22 Sept. 4/5 Against the renunciation of 'irredeemed' territory (to use the Italian term) must be set the implied guarantee of the remainder.

‖**irredenta** (ɪrɪˈdɛntə). [It. (see irredentist).] A region containing people who are ethnically related to the inhabitants of one state but are politically subject to another. Also, post-positively, as *adj.*

1914 *Everybody's Mag.* Sept. 333 These million Germans along the Baltic..constitute a Germania Irredenta which is one of the things that Kaiser Wilhelm is after. **1916** *Times Hist. War* 31 Oct. 407/2 Rumanian interests would..have become wholly identified with those of the Central European *bloc* but for the fact that between them loomed the question of Rumania irredenta. *Ibid.* 408/2 She [*sc.* Rumania] had no territorial irredenta to secure. **1934** A. Huxley *Beyond Mexique Bay* 73 British Honduras still is regarded by the Guatemalans as an *irredenta.* **1938** H. Nicolson *Diary* 22 Aug. (1966) 356 Even if Germany absorbed a portion of the Ukraine, how would it benefit her? It would create an *irredenta* and perpetuate Russo-German enmity. **1967** *Punch* 1 Feb. 141/2 They annexed Tibet, but they had argued themselves into the belief that this was ancient Chinese territory, China *irredenta.*

irredential (ɪrɪˈdɛnʃəl), *a.* [f. as next + -ial, after such words as *potential.*] Given to irredentism.

1891 *Review of Rev.* Jan. 87/2 Italian Radicals..are merely destructive and irredential.

irredentism (ɪrɪˈdɛntɪz(ə)m). [See next and -ism.] The policy or programme of the Irredentists. Also in extended use: any policy of seeking the recovery and reunion to one country of a region or regions for the time being subject to another country.

1883 *Standard* 30 Apr. 5/5 Irredentism is less powerful than the need felt by all the Central European States for mutual peace and safety. **1889** *Times* 25 Apr. 5/3 An estrangement between Austria and Italy would lead to a very swift revival of irredentism in the Italian kingdom. **1922** *Encycl. Brit.* XXX. 314/1 Up to the World War there was actually no articulate irredentism among the Austrian Poles. **1932** *Times Lit. Suppl.* 5 May 319/1 Never was 'irredentism' so rampant as it is today; and so far as Germans and Magyars are concerned there does not seem much prospect of their reshaping their minds. **1961** *Listener* 21 Dec. 1057/1 The young African states are..learning that they are no more immune than the wicked old nations from the evils of frontier disputes, irredentism, and even ideological differences. **1973** *Ibid.* 20 Dec. 845/3 The seeds of Japanese irredentism, already latent, will begin to sprout.

irredentist (ɪrɪˈdɛntɪst). [ad. It. *irredentista*, f. (*Italia*) *irredenta* unredeemed, unrecovered (Italy).] In Italian politics (after 1878), an adherent of the party which advocated the recovery and union to Italy of all Italian-speaking districts subject to other countries. Also in extended use (see prec.). Also *attrib.* as *adj.*

1882 *Standard* 4 Aug. 5/7 Irredentist outrage and riot at Trieste. **1883** *Times* 27 Sept. 3 The editor of the Irredentist journal Alba. **1887** *Edin. Rev.* Apr. 405 Capponi..was not an out-and-out Irredentist clamouring for Trieste and Istria, the Canton Ticino, Nice, Corsica, and Malta. **1919** G. B. Shaw *Peace Conf. Hints* vi. 75 The French and Italian Jingos have been..making no secret of their determination to annex parts of the Rhineland and the Austrian Tyrol.. without regard to the irredentist movements which must follow such annexations. **1920** [see crab *v.*² 2 b]. **1958** G. Mikes *East is East* 28 Naturally, I instinctively sympathised with Hungary and became a staunch irredentist at the age of six or so. Later..some subversive older friends assured me that irredentism was wrong. **1961** *Listener* 21 Sept. 411/1 The extremist parties [in the German Federal Republic] representing communist, neo-nazi, and irredentist tendencies. **1972** D. Dakin *Unification of Greece* v. 73 The bolder irredentists in Greece had taken the field.

†**irredimable**, *a. Sc. Obs. rare*⁻¹. [f. ir-² + L. *redim-ĕre* to redeem + -able. Cf. med.L. *redimibilis* (Du Cange).] = irredeemable 1. Hence †**irredimably** *adv.*

1609 Skene *Reg. Maj.* 64 It rests to speik of that recognition, quhither ane man deceissed vested and saised in lands, as of fie (irredimable) or as lands wadset (vnder reversion). *Ibid.*, Gif it be found..that the lands perteines heretablie, and irredimablie to the defender [etc.].

†**irredi'vivous**, *a. Obs. rare*⁻⁰. [f. L. *irredivīv-us* (Catullus) + -ous. See redivivous.] 'That cannot be revived or repaired' (Blount *Glossogr.* 1656).

irredressible, -able (ɪrɪˈdrɛsɪb(ə)l, -əb(ə)l), *a. rare.* [ir-². (The etymological spelling from F. *redresser* would be in *-able*; that in *-ible* is perh. due to false analogy with *irrepressible.*)] Incapable of being redressed or put right. Hence **irredressi'bility**; **irre'dressibly** *adv.*

1871 B. Taylor *Faust* (1875) I. iii. 53 Pierced irredressibly. **1892** *Spectator* 2 Apr. 455/1 A grievance.. safely ramparted behind a triple wall of irredressibility.

irreduci'bility. [f. next: see -ity.] The quality of being irreducible.

1799 Wilson in *Phil. Trans.* LXXXIX. 298 The irreducibility happening uniformly in cases where it has been supposed least to be expected, i.e. when the roots are real. **1886** *Athenæum* 20 Feb. 266/1 The irreducibility of differential equations. **1897** *Allbutt's Syst. Med.* III. 822 Obstruction, strangulation, and irreducibility.

irreducible (ɪrɪˈdjuːsɪb(ə)l), *a.* [ir-²: cf. F. *irréductible.*] That cannot be reduced.

1. That cannot be brought to a desired form, state, condition, etc. Const. †*into*, *to.*

1633 Prynne *Histriom.* I. ii. 41 They are irreducible, vnconuertible to any lawfull, good, or Christian purposes. **1669** W. Simpson *Hydrol. Chym.* 166 Irreducible to their pristine metalline form. **1818** Hallam *Mid. Ages* (1878) III. ix. ii. 346 The fashions of dress and amusements are generally capricious and irreducible to rule. **1881** Maxwell *Electr. & Magn.* I. 355 When chemical affinity was regarded as a quality *sui generis*, and irreducible to numerical measurement.

b. *spec.* That cannot be reduced to a simpler or more intelligible form; incapable of being resolved into elements, or of being brought under any recognized law or principle.

1835 Poe *Adv. Hans Pfaall* Wks. 1864 I. 8 A constituent of azote, so long considered irreducible. **1841** Myers *Cath. Th.* iv. §15. 259 The great primary Fact..irreducible and unintelligible by any faculty of ours. **1868** Lockyer *Guillemin's Heavens* (ed. 3) 396 Each new triumph of optical skill results in a resolution of some nebulæ, before irreducible. **1871** R. H. Hutton *Ess.* (1877) I. 42 To admit the..irreducible nature of mental phenomena—to admit that they cannot anyhow be analysed into physical.

c. *Algebra.* (See quots.)

1753 Chambers *Cycl. Supp.*, *Irreducible case*,..that case of cubic equations where the root, according to Cardan's rule, appears under an impossible or imaginary form, and yet is real. **1778** Maseres in *Phil. Trans.* LXVIII. 920 The remaining case of the cubick equation..which..cannot be resolved by the rules above mentioned, has..obtained amongst algebraists the name of the *irreducible case*: at least it is often called by the French writers of algebra *le cas irréductible.* **1838-9** Hallam *Hist. Lit.* II. viii. §7. 325 Bombelli saw better than Cardan the nature of what is called the irreducible case in cubic equations.

2. *Path.* That cannot be reduced by treatment to a desired form or condition.

1836-9 Todd *Cycl. Anat.* II. 740/1 Old ruptures that have become irreducible. **1859** *Ibid.* V. 684/1 An irreducible tumour in the right groin.

3. Incapable of being reduced to a smaller number or amount; the fewest or smallest possible.

1860 Farrar *Orig. Lang.* x. 205 The three families of language are irreducible, i.e. incapable of being derived from one another. **188.** *American* XIV. 134 (Cent.) What is it that we must hold fast as the irreducible minimum of churchmanship?

4. That cannot be reduced to submission; invincible, insuperable.

1858 *National Rev.* Oct. 500 Allowing the irreducible, uncontrollable nature of the prophetic impulse. **1859** Masson *Brit. Novelists* 100 At last, foiled by her irreducible virtue, he is compelled to call in the clergyman. **1885** Wingfield *Barbara Philpot* II. vi. 193 So 'twas irreducible dislike of his person that had caused the uproar.

Hence **irre'ducibleness**; **irre'ducibly** *adv.*

1828 Webster, *Irreducibleness.* **1841-4** Emerson *Ess.*, *Experience* Wks. (Bohn) I. 183 The ancients, struck with this irreducibleness of the elements of human life to calculation, exalted Chance into a divinity. **1847** Craig, *Irreducibly.* **1923** C. D. Broad *Sci. Thought* x. 368 The temporal relations..are really irreducibly triadic.

irreducti'bility. *rare.* [a. F. *irréductibilité* (1798 in *Dict. Acad.*): see next and -ity.] = irreducibility.

1865 Mill *Comte & Positivism* 196 M. Comte's puerile predilection for prime numbers almost passes belief. His reason is that they are the type of irreductibility: each of them is a kind of ultimate arithmetical fact.

irreductible (ɪrɪˈdʌktɪb(ə)l), *a. rare.* [a. F. *irréductible* (1752 in Hatz.-Darm.), f. *ir-* (ir-²) + *réductible* (f. *reduct-*, ppl. stem of L. *redūcĕre* to reduce + -ible).] = irreducible.

1753 Chambers *Cycl. Supp.*, *Irreductible Case*, in Algebra. **1922** Joyce *Ulysses* 673 What anthem did Bloom chant partially in anticipation of that multiple, ethnically irreducible consummation? **1964** *English Studies* XLV. 98 He described the scientist's labour as a hammering out of truth in the teeth of irreductible stubborn facts.

irreduction (ɪrɪˈdʌkʃən). *rare.* [ir-².] Non-reduction; the fact of not being reduced.

1888 *Med. News* (U.S.) LII. 442 This increase in volume was the only cause of irreduction [of the hernia].

irredundant (ɪrɪˈdʌndənt), *a. Math.* [f. ir-² + redundant *a.*] Containing no redundant elements.

1925 A. Church in *Trans. Amer. Math. Soc.* XXVII. 318 A set of postulates is irredundant if the postulates are independent and no one of them can be weakened with respect to the set. **1957** *IBM Jrnl. Res. & Devel.* I. 175/2 To be irredundant the statement has to involve the complete list of reasons which are necessary and sufficient to make this prime implicant dispensable. **1965** R. E. Miller *Switching Theory* I. 195 An 'irredundant cover' of a complex has the property that if any cube is eliminated from the cover, the resulting set of cubes is no longer a cover. **1966** *Math. Rev.* XXXI. 37/1 A factorization $a = a_1 a_2 \ldots a_m$ of a into simple factors is irredundant if no product $a_i a_{i+1} \ldots a_{i+p}$, $p > 0$, is simple.

Hence **irre'dundance**, **irre'dundancy** *sbs.*, the property of being irredundant.

1925 *Trans. Amer. Math. Soc.* XXVII. 320 (*heading*) A criterion for irredundance. **1952** *Proc. Amer. Catholic Philos. Assoc.* XXVI. 112, *f* fulfills the irredundancy requirement. **1960** *IRE Trans. Electronic Computers* IX. 248/2 Comparing all the resulting implications for irredundancy.

†**irre-'edifiable**, *a. Obs. rare*⁻¹. [f. ir-² + re-edify *v.* + -able.] Incapable of being rebuilt.

1647 Trapp *Comm. Matt.* vii. 27 And the fall thereof was great: Great and grievous, because irreparable, irre-edifiable.

i'rreferable, *a. rare.* [ir-².] Not referable; that cannot be referred (*to* something).

1810 Coleridge *Rem.* (1836) III. 312 Pure action, that is, the will, is a 'noumenon', and irreferable to time. **1827** Faraday *Chem. Manip.* ii. 38 Irreferable either to the weights or each other.

irreflection, -flexion (ɪrɪˈflɛkʃən). [ir-²: perh. after F. *irréflexion* (1835 in *Dict. Acad.*).] Want of reflection; unreflecting action or conduct.

1861 Maine *Anc. Law* ix. (1876) 328 So meagre a protection against haste and irreflection. **1891** H. Jones *Browning as Teacher* 46 They must reap the harvest of their irreflection. **1894** *Westm. Gaz.* 20 Dec. 2/2 He develops the principle that a masterly habit of 'irreflexion' is really the literary artist's highest virtue.

irreflective (ɪrɪˈflɛktɪv), *a.* [ir-²: cf. F. *irréfléchi.*] Unreflecting, unthinking.

1833 Whewell *Bridgewater Treat.* (1853) 230 The gratification of our irreflective impulses. **1853** De Quincey *Autobiog. Sk.* Wks. I. 357 The careless, irreflective mind of childhood.

Hence **irre'flectively** *adv.*; **irre'flectiveness.**

1842 De Quincey *Philos. Herodotus* Wks. 1858 IX. 166 The reason is palpable: it was the ignorance of irreflectiveness. **1858** —— *Wks.* (1862) VII. 186 *note*, Irreflectively he had allowed himself to anticipate..an impression. **1861** *Temple Bar Mag.* I. 341 Sometimes, when irreflectively irate, threatening to leave it away to strangers. **1899** *Atlantic Monthly* May 623 We read them a moral lecture on their irreflectiveness.

†**irre'flex**, *a. Obs. rare*⁻¹. [ad. late L. *irreflexus* (Boeth.), f. *ir-* (ir-²) + *reflexus* reflex.] Not turned back or aside. So **irre'flexed** *a.*

a **1711** Ken *Hymnarium* Poet. Wks. 1721 II. 121 Eagles the sun see Face to Face, To teach all human Race, With irreflexed Eyes, Towards Heav'n to rise. —— *Hymnotheo* ibid. III. 145 Praise with an irreflex and steddy view Strives only to give God his Glory due.

irre'flexive, *a.* [ir-².] Not reflexive. *spec.* in *Logic* and *Math.*, of a relation which no postulate can have to itself. Hence **irre'flexiveness**, **irrefle'xivity**, the quality or property of being irreflexive. See also non-reflexive *a.*, reflexive *a.*

1890 in *Cent. Dict.* **1933** *Mind* XLII. 36, $a < b. \supset. a \neq b$ ..gives..the property of irreflexiveness. **1937** A. Smeaton tr. *Carnap's Logical Syntax of Lang.* iv. §63. 234 A relation P is called irreflexive when no object has this relation to itself. **1942** J. C. Cooley *Primer of Formal Logic* 157 A relation, *f*, is said to be irreflexive when: $(x) \sim fxx$. **1952** S. C. Kleene *Introd. Metamath.* vii. 188 Connexity, irreflexiveness, asymmetry. **1954** I. M. Copi *Symbolic Logic* v. 143 An irreflexive relation is one which no individual has to itself. **1963** W. V. Quine *Set Theory* §21. 147 Or, better, stipulate the irreflexivity and derive the asymmetry. **1964** E. Bach *Introd. Transformational Gram.* vii. 156 No item precedes itself (irreflexivity). **1967** R. A. George tr. *Carnap's Logical Struct. of World* §11. 22 A relation is called a *sequence* if it is irreflexive and transitive (and hence asymmetrical) and connected.

irreformable (ɪrɪˈfɔːməb(ə)l), *a.* [f. ir-² + reformable: cf. late L. *irreformābilis* (Tertull.) and F. *irréformable* (1725 in Hatz.-Darm.).]

1. Incapable of being reformed.

1609 W. M. *Man in Moone* (1849) 13, I have heard of some, who through an irreformable conceit, have imagined their noses to be as bigge as pinnicles. **1647** Trapp *Comm. Matt.* vii. 6 Every good man is bound in conscience to pass by them [scoffers] as incorrigible, irreformable. **1856** Olmsted *Slave States* 251 The irreformable improvidence of the people. **1892** *Illustr. Lond. News* 24 Sept. 393/1 She was unteachable, irreformable.

2. Incapable of revision or alteration.

1812 C. Butler *Bossuet* Wks. 1817 III. 262 The fourth article [in the Declaration of the General Assembly of the Gallican Clergy in 1682] declares, that, in questions of faith, the pope has the principal authority, and that his decisions extend over the universal church..but that, unless they have the consent of the church, they are not irreformable. **1897** *Contemp. Rev.* Jan. 40 The Bull is irreformable.

Hence **irreforma'bility.**

1883 *Church Times* 31 Aug. 603 All the high-flying theories of Supremacy and irreformability on which Ultramontane writers rest their case.

†**irre'formed**, *a.* *Obs.* *rare.* [IR-².] Not reformed; unreformed.

1589 T. L. *Advt. Q. Eliz.* (1651) 49 Those foolish and irreformed reformers. **1690** LEYBOURN *Curs. Math.* 467 The 29th of August, according to the Old Account in the irreformed Calendar.

irrefragability (ɪˌrɛfrəgə'bɪlɪtɪ). [f. next: see -ITY.] The quality of being irrefragable. Rarely with *pl.* An irrefragable statement.

1609 BP. W. BARLOW *Answ. Nameless Cath.* 156 It not standing with the Popes irrefragabilitie to yeeld a reason. **1768** H. WALPOLE *Hist. Doubts* 73 The comparison and irrefragability of dates puts this matter out of all doubt. **1858** CARLYLE *Fredk. Gt.* IV. xii. (1872) II. 47 Such a burly *ne-plus-ultra* of a Squire, with his broad-based rectitudes and surly irrefragabilities.

irrefragable (ɪ'rɛfrəgəb(ə)l), *a.* In 6 *erron.* -ible. [ad. late L. *irrefragābil-is* (Pseudo-August.), f. *ir-* (IR-²) + *refragārī* to oppose, contest: see -ABLE. So F. *irréfragable* (15–16th c. in Hatz.-Darm.).]

1. That cannot be refuted or disproved; incontrovertible, incontestable, indisputable, irrefutable, undeniable. (Said of a statement, argument, etc., or of the person who advances it.) ***Irrefragable Doctor***: see DOCTOR *sb.* 3.

1533 MORE *Debell. Salem* Wks. 1031/1 What is hys owne irrefragable reson yᵗ he layeth against al thys? **1603** HOLLAND *Plutarch's Mor.* 65 A truth confessed, certeine, firme and irrefragable. **1605** CAMDEN *Rem.* 10 Alexander of Hales, the irrefragable Doctor. **1748** HARTLEY *Observ. Man* I. iv. 423 Irrefragable Evidences of the Truth of the Facts. **1795** SOUTHEY *Joan of Arc* III. 287 Doctors: teachers grave and with great names, Seraphic, Subtile, or Irrefragable, By their admiring scholars dignified. **1846** RUSKIN *Mod. Paint.* II. III. I. v. §9. 41, I look to them [early Italian masters] as in all points of principle..the most irrefragable authorities. **1875** STUBBS *Const. Hist.* III. xxi. 555 These are an irrefragable answer to the popular theories.

2. That cannot or must not be broken; indestructible; inviolable; irresistible. Now *rare.*

1562 *Latimer's Serm., 2nd Sunday Advent* 135 They shal bee condemned with the irrefragible [*ed.* 1552 irreuocable] and vnchangeable iudgemente of god. *c* **1640** *New Serm. of newest fashion* (1877) 20 The orall Pack-needle of zeale, and stubborn irrefragable thred of ignorance. **1711** SHAFTESB. *Charac.* (1737) II. II. II. i. 111 Intire Affection..is irrefragable, solid, and durable. **1847** MEDWIN *Life Shelley* II. 28 A vain attempt to snap the chain only renders it more irrefragable. **1848** BUCKLEY *Homer's Iliad* 229 Round their feet he threw golden fetters, irrefragable, indissoluble.

†**3.** Of persons: Obstinate, inflexible, stubborn.

1601 DENT *Pathw. Heaven* 332 For men are so obstinate and irrefragable, that they will be brought into no order. **1621** BURTON *Anat. Mel.* Democr. to Rdr. 38 He is irrefragable in his humour. *Ibid.* III. ii. VI. v. (1651) 575 Many yong men are..as irrefragable and peevish on the other side, Narcissus like.

Hence **i'rrefragableness** = IRREFRAGABILITY.

1682 H. MORE *Annot. Glanvill's Lux O.* 256 The plainness and irrefragableness of this truth.

irrefragably (ɪ'rɛfrəgəblɪ), *adv.* [f. prec. + -LY².] In an irrefragable manner.

1. So as not to admit of being refuted; incontrovertibly, indisputably.

1626 JACKSON *Creed* VIII. xxiv. §2 The argument or demonstration is..most irrefragably prest home to this purpose by our apostle. **1751** JOHNSON *Rambler* No. 176 ⁋6 Even when he can irrefragably refute all objections. **1850** CARLYLE *Latter-d. Pamph.* IV. 25 This demand is irrefragably just, is growing urgent too. **1885** *L'pool Daily Post* 27 Mar. 4/6 Words in which the Premier irrefragably lays down the principle by which the new Convention is justified.

2. So as not to admit of being broken; inviolably; irresistibly. Now *rare.*

1593 R. HARVEY *Philad.* 9, I cannot tell which historie may stand irrefragably by this determination. **1646** SIR J. TEMPLE *Irish Rebell.* 10 The malignant impressions of irreligion and barbarisme..had irrefragably stiffned their necks. **1647** *Case Kingd.* 15 All men must be irrefragably subject to their pleasure. **1875** STUBBS *Const. Hist.* II. xiv. 152 By custom irrefragably preserved at all times.

†**i'rrefragate**, *a.* *Obs.* *rare.* [f. IR-² + L. *refragātus*, pa. pple. of *refragārī*: see IRREFRAGABLE.] Uncontested, undisputed.

a **1592** H. SMITH *Wks.* (1867) II. 97 The palpable proofs they had by the cluster of grapes and other things which they brought from thence were irrefragate witness.

irrefrangible (ɪrɪ'frændʒɪb(ə)l), *a.* [f. IR-² + REFRANGIBLE (an irreg. formation for *refringible*, after *refraction*).]

1. That cannot or must not be broken or violated; inviolable.

c **1719** *Lett. fr. Mist's Jrnl.* (1722) I. 183 Nothing.. signalizes our Integrity so much as a strict and irrefrangible Adhesion to our Friend. **1853** MISS MULOCK *Agatha's Husb.* xx. II. 290 An irrefrangible law of country etiquette—of a bride's going to church for the first time, ceremoniously, in bridal dress.

2. *Optics.* Not refrangible; incapable of being refracted.

Mod. The Röntgen rays are irrefrangible.

Hence **irre'frangibly** *adv.*, so as not to be broken; fixedly, inviolably.

1885 H. CONWAY *Family Affair* iii, They knew..that the dragons were welded to their vases more irrefrangibly than Prometheus to his rock.

†**irrefrenable, -freynable**, *a.* *Obs.* *rare.* [a. obs. F. *irrefrénable* (15–16th c. in Godef.), f. *ir-* (IR-²) + *refréner*, ad. L. *refrēnāre* to curb: see next. (In spelling accommodated to *refreyne*, REFRAIN *v.*)] That cannot be 'refrained' or held in check.

1546 J. HEYWOOD *Prov.* (1867) 45 To know how they bothe were irrefreynable, Marke how they fell out, and how they fell in.

†**irre'frenary**, *a.* *Obs.* *rare.* [irreg. f. IR-² + L. *refrēnāre* to bridle, curb (f. *re-* back + *frēnāre* to bridle) + -ARY.] = prec.

1658 WILLSFORD *Secrets Nat.* 196 Angry Clouds, as if bestri'd by Furies hurried along by irrefrenary Tempests!

†**irre'fringible**, *a.* *Obs.* [f. IR-² + L. *refringĕre* to break up, check, etc., f. *re-* back + *frangĕre* to break.] That cannot or may not be broken down or demolished.

1596 BELL *Surv. Popery* I. I. ii. 3 My just and irrefringible probations.

irrefusable (ɪrɪ'fjuːzəb(ə)l), *a.* *rare.* [IR-².] That cannot be refused.

1880 RUSKIN *Fathers Have Told Us* I. i. 25 The barbarian enemy sends embassy with irrefusable offers of submission and peace.

irrefuta'bility. [f. next: see -ITY.] The quality of being irrefutable.

1864 *Daily Tel.* 7 June, The irrefutability of their conclusions. **1885** *Century Mag.* XXXI. 178 On the irrefutability of which he had privately prided himself.

irrefutable (ɪrɪ'fjuːtəb(ə)l, ɪ'rɛfjuːtəb(ə)l), *a.* [ad. L. *irrefutābil-is*, f. *ir-* (IR-²) + *refutābilis*, f. *refutāre* to REFUTE. So mod.F. *irréfutable*. The pronunciations *re'futable*, *irre'futable*, in most Dicts. from Bailey and Johnson, show that the words were referred to the Eng. *refute* rather than L. *refutāre.*] That cannot be refuted or disproved; incontrovertible, irrefragable.

1620 BP. HALL *Hon. Mar. Clergy* iii. 12 Heare that irrefutable discourse of Cardinall Caietan. **1655** H. MORE *App. Antid.* (1662) 190 Though our Argumentations for an Immaterial Soul in the Body of man be solid and irrefutable. **1826** SOUTHEY *Vind. Eccl. Angl.* 50 Our unrefuted and irrefutable apologist. **1886** J. E. C. WELLDON tr. *Aristotle's Rhet.* 18 When we suppose the statement we make to be irrefutable.

irrefutably (see prec.), *adv.* [f. prec. + -LY².] In an irrefutable manner; so as to be incapable of being refuted; incontrovertibly.

1681 H. MORE *Expos. Dan.* Pref. 81 It is irrefutably proved by able writers. *a* **1807** WALKER *Key to Classicks* 13 (Jod.) This opinion has been irrefutably maintained by Mr. Foster. **1883** *Standard* 31 Aug. 5/1 A statement so manifestly and irrefutably true.

irre'gardless, *a.* and *adv.* Chiefly *N. Amer.* [Prob. blend of *irrespective* and *regardless.*] In non-standard or humorous use: regardless.

1912 in WENTWORTH *Amer. Dial. Dict.* **1923** *Lit. Digest* 17 Feb. 76 Is there such a word as *irregardless* in the English language? **1934** in WEBSTER (*labelled* Erron. or Humorous, U.S.). **1938** I. KUHN *Assigned to Adventure* xxx. 310, I made a grand entrance and suffered immediate and complete obliteration, except on the pay-roll, which functioned automatically to present me with a three-figure cheque every week, 'irregardless', as Hollywood says. **1939** C. MORLEY *Kitty Foyle* xxvii. 267 But she can take things in her stride, irregardless what's happened. **1955** *Publ. Amer. Dial. Soc.* XXIV. 19, I don't think like other people do and irregardless of how much or how little dope would cost me [etc.]. **1970** *Current Trends in Linguistics* X. 590 She tells the pastor that he should please quit using the word 'irregardless' in his sermons as there is no such word. **1971** M. MCSHANE *Man who left Well Enough* iv. 96 The sun poured down on Purity irregardless of the fact that it received no welcome.

irregenerate (ɪrɪ'dʒɛnərət), *a.* *rare.* [IR-².] Not regenerate; unregenerate.

1657 W. MORICE *Coena quasi Κοινὴ* Def. v. 54 Irregenerate men admitted to the Sacraments enjoy no proper priviledges of the godly. **1675** O. WALKER, etc. *Paraphr. Paul* 69 Carnal absolutely none are called but the irregenerate. **1720** T. BOSTON *Fourf. State* title-p., Entire Depravation Subsisting in The Irregenerate. **1892** A. B. BRUCE *Moral Order of World* viii. 375 There is something of the kind even in irregenerate man.

Hence †**irre'generacy**, †**irregene'ration**, unregenerate state.

1641 J. JACKSON *True Evang. T.* I. 76 This taint and irregeneracy of our nature. *a* **1654** BINNING *Serm.* xvi. Wks. (1735) 434 Thinking it sufficient to have so much Honesty and Grace, as..may put you over the black Line of Irregeneration. **1657** F. ROUS in Z. Boyd *Zion's Flowers* (1855) App. 19/1 His free grace..took me up lying in the blood of irregeneration.

†**i'rregulacy**. *Obs.* *rare.* [f. IRREGULATE *a.*: see -ACY 3.] Irregularity, disorder.

1645 T. COLEMAN *Hopes Deferred* 13 He even inforced himselfe to pray, and that with some irregulacy, when the battels were to joyne.

irregular (ɪ'rɛgjʊlə(r)), *a.* and *sb.* Forms: 4–5 irregulere, (4 -eer, inreguler), 4–7 irreguler, (6 irriguler, 7 irregualler), 6– irregular. [ME. a. OF. *irreguler* (13th c. in Hatz.-Darm.), ad. med.L. *irrēgulār-is*, f. *ir-* (IR-²) + L. *rēgulāris*: see REGULAR.]

A. *adj.* Not regular. **I.** General senses.

1. a. Of things: Not in conformity with rule or principle; contrary to rule; disorderly in action or conduct; not in accordance with what is usual or normal; anomalous, abnormal.

1483 *Cath. Angl.* 198/2 Irregulere, *irregularis.* **1623** COCKERAM, *Irregular*, contrary to rule. **1674** PLAYFORD *Skill Mus.* III. 22 If the Bass and Treble do rise together in thirds, then the first Note of the Treble is regular with the other Part, but the second of it is irregular. **1781** GIBBON *Decl. & F.* xix. II. 148 He..repelled with skill and firmness the efforts of their irregular valour. **1800** *Med. Jrnl.* V. 27 What proportion the irregular cases may bear to the regular is not yet known. **1850** BAYNES *Analytic* 12 Unnatural, indirect, or irregular predication [with the old logicians] was..that..in which the species was predicated of the genus, the subject of its attribute, and, in general, the extensive part of its whole. **1894** *Law Times Rep.* LXXI. 9/2 The order is altogether irregular, and should be discharged.

b. Not in accordance with, or not subjected to, moral law or principle; unregulated; morally disorderly. ? *Obs.* (or merged in general sense).

1608 D. T. *Ess. Pol. & Mor.* 44 Subject to the commaunde of such irregular and confused Passions. **1617** MORYSON *Itin.* II. 63 He hoped shortly to give law to their irregular humours. **1746–7** HERVEY *Medit.* (1818) 263 May every sordid desire wear away, and every irregular appetite be gradually lost. **1794** S. WILLIAMS *Vermont* 159 His appetite the more inflamed by irregular enjoyment. **1804** W. TENNANT *Ind. Recreat.* (ed. 2) I. 97 With irreligious principles, irregular conduct is intimately connected.

2. Of persons: Not conforming or obedient to rule, law, or moral principle; lawless, disorderly.

1395 PURVEY *Remonstr.* (1851) 92 Thei [monks] moun not lawfulli werre..for thanne thei shulden been irreguler bi Goddis lawe and mannis. **1508** KENNEDIE *Flyting w. Dunbar* 36 Ignorant elf, aip, owll irregular. **1596** SHAKS. *1 Hen. IV*, I. i. 40 The irregular and wilde Glendower. **1606** WARNER *Alb. Eng.* XIV. lxxxv. (1612) 352 So much the more, though lesse secure, men liue irreguler. **1649** *Petit. City Oxford* in *Def. Rights Univ. Oxf.* (1690) 5 In case the City punisheth any irregular freeman for misdemeanour. **1752** YOUNG *Brothers* I. i, O, that's the jealous elder brother; Irregular in manners, as in form.

3. Not of regular or symmetrical form; unevenly shaped or placed; disorderly in form or arrangement.

1584 R. SCOT *Discov. Witchcr.* XIII. xix. (1886) 258 Diverse sorts of glasses;..the round, the cornerd,..the regular, the irregular, the coloured and cleare glasses. **1607** DEKKER *Knt.'s Conjur.* (1842) 15 The most perfect circles of it drawne so irregualler awrye. **1665** *Phil. Trans.* I. 105 If curve, whether regular or irregular. **1718** LADY M. W. MONTAGU *Let. to C'tess Bristol* 10 Apr., It is a..palace of prodigious extent, but very irregular. **1806** *Gazetteer Scotl.* (ed. 2) 57 A parish..of an irregular form. **1839** DICKENS *Nich. Nick.* xiv, Two irregular rows of tall meagre houses. **1843** JAMES *Forest Days* i, The surface was irregular.

4. In reference to time or motion: Unequal or uneven in continuance, occurrence, or succession; occurring at variously unequal rates or intervals. Hence of an agent: Doing something at irregular intervals or times; as an ***irregular attendant***, etc.

1608 D. T. *Ess. Pol. & Mor.* 125 Every thing is presently brought to a most irregular, and confused motion. **1609** CHAPMAN *Descr. Fever* in Farr *S.P. Jas. I* (1848) 252 Languor-chill trembling, fits irregulare. **1694** F. BRAGGE *Disc. Parables* ix. 311 When a child would catch a grass-hopper, its motions are so irregular, that he finds it very difficult at all to come near it. **1791** MRS. RADCLIFFE *Rom. Forest* i, Her breathing was short and irregular. **1867** LADY HERBERT *Cradle L.* iii. 93 The most curious thing about this fountain is the irregular flow of the water. **1869** PHILLIPS *Vesuv.* v. 145 At irregular intervals a different kind of cloud rises.

II. Technical senses.

5. *Eccl.* (chiefly *R.C. Ch.*) Not in conformity with the rule of the Church or of some ecclesiastical order; disqualified for ordination, or for exercise of clerical functions. (The earliest sense in Eng., repr. eccl. L. *irregularis*, Thomas Aquinas.)

c **1380** WYCLIF *Wks.* (1880) 242 þouȝ he be..a fals suerere, a man-quellere & inreguler. *c* **1386** CHAUCER *Pars. T.* ⁋708 Yet is it to hym a deedly synne, and if he be ordred, he is irreguleer [*v.rr.* -ler(e]. **1529** RASTELL *Pastyme, Hist. Pap.* (1811) 50 That who so ever were a morderar shuld be irriguler, and unable to receyve holy orders. **1655** SIR E. NICHOLAS in *N. Papers* (Camden) II. 164 The Cardinall of Rets..has gotten a declaration from the Pope, to make all those Priests irregular who have beene lately ordained here in his diocese without his consent. **1885** *Catholic Dict.* (ed. 3) 885 Lunatics, etc. are irregular, so are persons without sufficient knowledge.

6. *Gram.* Of a word or part of speech: Inflected not according to the normal or usual method. Also said of an inflexion so formed.

1611 COTGR. *Fr. Dict.* Brief Direct. 5 The Anomala or irregular Verbes of the first Coniugation. *Ibid.*, Martin Caucius..doth further obserue, that the word *doint* is an irregular third person from the Verbe *Donner*. **1669** MILTON *Accedence commenced Gram.* Wks. (1847) 463 Verbs of the third conjugation irregular in some Tenses of the Active Voice. **1762** LOWTH *Introd. Eng. Gram.* (1838) 77 The Irregular Verbs in English are all Monosyllables, unless

compounded. **1874** GRECE tr. *Mätzner's Eng. Gram.* I. 226 A few irregular plural forms are remnants of the strong declension of the Anglosaxon. **1899** MORFILL *Gram. Bohem. Lang.* 19 The following comparatives are altogether irregular.

7. *Math.* (see quots.).

1700 MOXON *Math. Dict.* s.v. *Regular*, Those [figures are] called Irregular, which have not the Equality of Sides and Angles, as are Prisms and Trapezia's. **1734** J. WARD *Introd. Math.* III. i. §4 (ed. 6) 290 An Irregular Polygon is that figure which hath many unequal Sides standing at unequal Angles.

8. *Bot.* and *Zool.* **a.** Varying from the form usual in the genus or other group; abnormal. **b.** Not having a definite, symmetrical, or uniform shape or arrangement; *spec.* of a flower, Having the members of the same cycle (esp. the petals) unlike in form or size.

1794 MARTYN *Rousseau's Bot.* iii. 34 One general division of flowers is into regular and irregular. **1826** KIRBY & SP. *Entomol.* IV. 322 Antennæ..Figure and Size..Irregular. **1828** STARK *Elem. Nat. Hist.* II. 87 Shell irregular, always inequivalve. **1857** HENFREY *Elem. Bot.* II. §435 Order XXXIX. Polygalaceæ..Herbs or shrubs with irregular hypogynous flowers.

9. *Mil.* Of troops: Not belonging to the regular or established army organization; not in regular service; not forming an organized military body.

1856 J. W. KAYE *Life Sir J. Malcolm* I. xiii. 362 The great work of reducing the irregular troops was to be accomplished. **1859** SIR G. WETHERALL in *Daily News* (1869) 12 June, In a country like England..there is no sort of irregular troops so formidable as mounted riflemen. **1867** FREEMAN *Norm. Conq.* I. v. 340 The Danes..put the irregular English levies to flight. **1896** T. F. TOUT *Edw. I*, iv. 74 His early defeats by the light-armed and nimble Welsh footmen taught him the value of a dexterous and daring irregular infantry.

10. *Astr.* **a.** Of a galaxy: having an irregular shape and lacking any axis of symmetry or central nucleus. Also *ellipt.* as *sb.*

1811 W. HERSCHEL in *Phil. Trans. R. Soc.* CI. 296 By calling the figure of a nebula irregular, it must be understood that I saw no particular dimension of it sufficiently marked to deserve the name of length. **1875** *Encycl. Brit.* II. 821/1 Among the varieties of form may be noted spiral, elliptic, and ring nebulæ, double nebulæ, and irregular nebulæ. **1928** J. H. JEANS *Astron. & Cosmogony* i. 28 The irregular nebulae shew the bright line spectrum which is characteristic of a transparent gas. **1936** E. HUBBLE *Realm of Nebulæ* ii. 47 About half of the irregulars form a homogeneous group, in which the Magellanic Clouds are typical examples. **1959** *Listener* 31 Dec. 1152/1 There are a few galaxies that do not fit conveniently into this classification of spirals, ellipticals, and irregulars. **1965** J. MUIRDEN *Handbk. Astron.* xxiv. 239 Irregular galaxies seem to be the adolescents; spirals are in the prime of life, while elliptical galaxies are bankrupt.

b. Of a variable star: fluctuating in brightness in a way that lacks any definite rhythm.

1903 A. M. CLERKE *Probl. Astrophysics* xxiii. 363 (*heading*) Peculiar and irregular variables. **1955** F. HOYLE *Frontiers Astron.* xi. 190 Certain irregular variables are among the brightest of all stars. **1970** D. H. MENZEL et al. *Survey Universe* xxvi. 551 Truly irregular variables, like R Coronae Borealis, suffer brightness changes in abrupt and unpredictable fashion.

11. *Comb.*, as ***irregular-shaped***.

1762 R. GUY *Pract. Obs. Cancers* 159 The Tumour was..a perfect, irregular-shaped Schirrus. **1877** RAYMOND *Statist. Mines & Mining* 424 The separation of irregular-shaped grains.

B. *sb.*

1. *Gram.* A word having irregular inflexion; an irregular noun, verb, etc. (see A. 6). *rare.*

1611 COTGR. *Fr. Dict.* Brief Direct. 3 Words ending in *l*, change *l* into *ux*;..except these irregulars..*œil*, *yeux* [etc.]. *Ibid.* 5 The irregulars of the second Coniugation.

2. **a.** One not belonging to the regular body; an agent of any kind who does something irregularly; one not of the 'regular' clergy; an irregular practitioner, attendant, etc.

1619 W. SCLATER *Exp. 2 Thess.* (1630) 545 The bare opinion of some Ministers, to whom our irregulars haue inclosed sincerity. **1620** BP. HALL *Hon. Mar. Clergy* xi. 314 The secular Prebendaries of Waltham, were first turned out, to give way to their Irregulars. **1809** *Med. Jrnl.* XXI. 99 The multitude of practitioners scattered over this country, are comprehended in two classes:—*regulars* and *irregulars*. **1893** *Chicago Advance* 13 Apr., To ask them [regular hearers] to abide at home that the irregulars may find sittings.

b. *Mil.* A soldier not of the regular army; almost always in *pl.* = irregular troops (see A. 9).

1747 *Gentl. Mag.* 315 Before six their irregulars..were skirmishing with our advanced Hussars and Lycanians. **1756** WASHINGTON *Lett.* Writ. 1889 I. 374 With this small company of irregulars..we set out. **1867** BAKER *Nile Tribut.* xi. (1872) 189 Large bodies of Egyptian irregulars threatened Mek Nimmur's country.

i'rregularist. *nonce-wd.* [f. prec. + -IST.] One who adheres to an irregular course or proceeding.

1846 WORCESTER cites BAXTER.

irregularity (ɪrɛgjuːˈlærɪtɪ). [a. F. *irregularité* (14th c. in Hatz.-Darm.), ad. med.L. *irrēgulāritās* (Aquinas *Summa Theol.* 1-2.20.5.4), f. *irrēgulāri-s*: see -ITY.] The quality or state of being irregular; something that is irregular. (First used in the ecclesiastical sense 1 c.)

1. Want of conformity to rule; deviation from or violation of a rule, law, or principle; disorderliness in action; deviation from what is usual or normal; abnormality, anomalousness.

1598 FLORIO, *Irregolarita*, irregularitie. **1616** BULLOKAR, *Irregularitie*, a going out of right rule, etc. **1651** HOBBES *Leviath.* II. xxix. 172 To what Disease..I may exactly compare this irregularity of a Common-wealth. **1654** WHITLOCK *Zootomia* 267 Such is the irregularity of Custome, it doth not extoll things because worthy, but thinks them worthy, because they are extolled. **1734** tr. *Rollin's Anc. Hist.* (1827) I. Pref. 8 A holiness that will not allow of the least irregularity. **1781** GIBBON *Decl. & F.* xxii. (1869) I. 622 He acknowledges the irregularity of his own election. **1829** BENTHAM *Justice & Codif. Petit.*, *Petit. Justice* 91 With the word irregularity sentiments of disapprobation have, from the earliest time of life, stood associated. **1870** MISS BRIDGMAN *R. Lynne* I. vii. 98 Selwyn was regular only in irregularity. **1882** *Med. Temp. Jrnl.* No. 52. 168 Great irregularity of living, during which he drank constantly large quantities of whisky.

b. (with *an* and *pl.*) An instance of this; a breach of rule or principle; an irregular, lawless, or disorderly act.

1483 *Cath. Angl.* 198/2 An irregularite, *irregularitas*. **1613** PURCHAS *Pilgrimage* (1614) 28 A deformitie, irregularitie, and unlawfulnesse in our naturall condition. **1688** LUTTRELL *Brief Rel.* (1857) I. 487 Some of them committed some irregularities at Gravesend. **1755** JOHNSON *Pref. Dict.* ¶6, I found it necessary to distinguish those irregularities that are inherent in our tongue, and perhaps coeval with it, from others which the ignorance or negligence of later writers has produced. **1804** W. TENNANT *Ind. Recreat.* (ed. 2) I. 150 In a rude age..crimes and irregularities are more frequent. **1840** MACAULAY *Ess.*, *Ranke* (1865) II. 137/2 An easy well-bred man of the world, who knew how to make allowance for the little irregularities of people of fashion. *a* **1862** BUCKLE *Civiliz.* (1869) III. v. 444 To generalize such irregularities, or in other words to show that they are not irregularities at all.

c. *Eccl.* (chiefly *R.C. Ch.*) Infraction of the rules as to entrance into or exercise of holy orders; an impediment or disqualification by which a person is debarred from ordination, discharge of clerical functions, or ecclesiastical advancement. (The earliest sense in Eng.)

a **1300** *Cursor M.* 27253 Enentes clergis seculers..if he in hali order be, In scrift þe preist agh spere of irregularite. *c* **1380** WYCLIF *Sel. Wks.* III. 87 Ofte tymes ben priistis irreguler, for þe multitude of soulis þat þei sleen þus; and þis irregularite is moore for to drede þan irregularite chargid of þe worlde. **1502** *Ord. Crysten Men* (W. de W. 1506) IV. vi. 181 Of symony, of irregularyte, of sacrylege, of the euyll dyspendynge of the patrymony of Ihesu cryst. **1590** SWINBURNE *Testaments* 56 Apostasie of irregularity is, when he that hath entred into the ministery and taken holy orders, forsaketh his spirituall profession. **1608** WILLET *Hexapla Exod.* 773 The Romanists obseruation..of irregularitie..that allow none to be admitted to orders which haue bin shedders of blood. **1658** PHILLIPS, *Irregularity*,..also an incapacity of taking holy orders, as being maimed, or very deformed, base-born, or guilty of any hainous crime, a Term in Canon-law. **1885** *Catholic Dict.* (ed. 3) 885 *Irregularity* is defined as a 'canonical impediment, which prevents a person from entering the ranks of the clergy, from rising to a higher order, or from exercising the order which he has received' (Gury)... The division of irregularities which still prevails among canonists and theologians, viz. into such as proceed from defect (ex defectu), and from crime (ex delicto)..is a convenient one, but it is not strictly scientific. In reality irregularity is always 'ex defectu'.

2. Want of regularity, symmetry, evenness, or uniformity, in shape, arrangement, succession, etc.; inequality of form, position, rate, etc.; occurring without any order; *spec.* in *Bot.* (see IRREGULAR A. 8 b).

1646 SIR T. BROWNE *Pseud. Ep.* VII. xiii. 365 Sometimes it observed not that certaine course. And this irregularity..together with its unruly and tumultuous motion might afford a beginning unto the common opinion. **1665** HOOKE *Microgr.* 3 The irregularity of the Type or Ingraving. **1774** GOLDSM. *Nat. Hist.* (1776) I. 273 The waves roll against land with great weight and irregularity. **1853** RUSKIN *Stones Ven.* II. vi, The tendency to the adoption of Gothic types being always first shown by greater irregularity and richer variation in the forms of the architecture it is about to supersede. **1853** SIR H. DOUGLAS *Milit. Bridges* (ed. 3) 141 The irregularity of the ground on the left bank would have occasioned many delays. **1879** *Cassell's Techn. Educ.* VII. 34/2 The irregularity in the thickness of some seams. **1880** GRAY *Struct. Bot.* vi. §4. 219 Irregularity is one of the commonest modifications of the flower: it is never conspicuous except in blossoms visited by insects and generally fertilized by their aid.

b. (with *an* and *pl.*) An instance of this; *esp.* a part not uniform or symmetrical with the rest, as an unevenness of surface, etc.

1665 HOOKE *Microgr.* 91 The bigger they were magnify'd, the more irregularities appear'd in them. **1703** MOXON *Mech. Exerc.* 21 File down all the Irregularities the Cold-Chissel made on the Edges of your Work. **1861** GEO. ELIOT *Silas M.* i, Marner, pausing to adjust an irregularity in his thread. **1879** *Cassell's Techn. Educ.* IV. 95/1 The physical irregularities of the terrain.

irregularly (ɪˈrɛgjʊləlɪ), *adv.* [f. IRREGULAR + -LY².] In an irregular manner.

1. In a way not according to rule; with deviation from or violation of rule; lawlessly; anomalously, abnormally.

1591 PERCIVALL *Sp. Dict.*, *Irregularmente*, irregularly, without rule. **1675** *Essex Papers* (Camden) I. 300 There were 8 Aldermen & yᵉ Recorder most violently & irregularly thrust out of their places. **1764** GOLDSM. *Trav.* 326 With daring aims irregularly great. **1885** *Law Rep.* 29 Chanc. Div. 827 He considered..that the order had been irregularly made.

2. Without regularity, symmetry, or uniformity; without order of arrangement, formation, motion, succession, etc.; unevenly; in disorder.

1595 DANIEL *Civ. Wars* I. lxxxiv, Like to a riuer that..breakes his owne bed, Destroies his bounds and ouer-runs by force The neighbour fields irregularly spread. **1665** HOOKE *Microgr.* 36 The contraction is performed very unequally and irregularly. **1769** ROBERTSON *Chas. V*, XI. (1796) III. 262 The soldiers in garrison being paid irregularly. **1776** PENNANT *Zool.* III. 296 (Jod.) Marked with large, distinct, irregularly shaped spots of black. **1776–96** WITHERING *Brit. Plants* (ed. 3) IV. 252 Irregularly serrated at the edges. **1878** JEVONS *Prim. Pol. Econ.* ii. 19 In some countries rain comes very irregularly and uncertainly. **1881** JOWETT *Thucyd.* I. 167 The islands..lying irregularly and not one behind the other.

†**i'rregularness.** *Obs.* [f. as prec. + -NESS.] = IRREGULARITY.

1609 DOULAND *Ornith. Microl.* 27 Now this irregularnesse of Songs..comes sometime by licence, sometime by the negligence of the Cantors. **1673** JANEWAY *Heaven on E.* (1847) 75 We cannot discern our own crookedness and irregularness.

†**i'rregularship.** *Obs. rare*⁻¹. [f. as prec. + -SHIP.] = IRREGULARITY.

1575 T. ROGERS *Sec. Coming Christ* 31/1 If they haue alreadye contracted Matrimonie, without any respect of irregularship they must be seperated.

†**i'rregulate,** *a.* (*sb.*) *Obs. rare.* [ad. med.L. *irrēgulāt-us*, It. *irregolato* unregulated: see IR-².] Unregulated; irregular, disorderly.

1579 FENTON *Guicciard.* VII. (1599) 280 So irregulate is a commonaltie or multitude once drawne into mutinie. **1600** W. WATSON *Decacordon* (1602) 129, I imagine thou art an irregulate Priest. **1650** EARL MONMOUTH tr. *Senault's Man become Guilty* 160 Though this irregulate love be both his fault and his punishment.

†**B.** *sb.* An irregular person: see IRREGULAR *a.* 5. *Obs.*

1600 W. WATSON *Decacordon* (1602) 115 [The] enabling of such irregulates and defectiues to aduancement in the Church and common wealth.

†**i'rregulate,** *v.* *Obs.* [f. prec., or f. IR-² + REGULATE *v.*, after *irregular.*] *trans.* To render irregular; to disorder.

1600 W. WATSON *Decacordon* (1602) 81 All these things..irregulate the partie that hath them, and makes him incapable of priesthood. **1628** EARLE *Microcosm.*, *Scepticke* (Arb.) 67 It do's only distract and irregulate him and the world by him. **1646** SIR T. BROWNE *Pseud. Ep.* VII. xvii. 377 Its fluctuations are but motions subservient, which winds, stormes, shoares, shelves, and every interjacency irregulates.

i'rregulated, *a. rare.* [f. IR-² + *regulated*, pa. pple. of REGULATE *v.*] Unregulated.

1660 N. INGELO *Bentivolio & Urania* (1682) II. 17 By reason of an irregulated heat, they venture upon such rash Actions. **1831** LYTTON *Godolph.* xxxiv, There was nothing unfeminine or sullen in Lucilla's irregulated moods.

irregu'lation. *rare.* [f. IR-² + REGULATION.] Want of regulation; irregular action or condition.

a **1897** H. DRUMMOND *Ideal Life* 79 It is..a disorderly succession of religious impulses, an irregulation of conduct, now on this principle, now on that.

†**i'rregulous,** *a.* *Obs. rare*⁻¹. [f. IR-² + L. *rēgula* rule + -OUS.] Characterized by absence or disregard of rule; unruly, disorderly, lawless.

1611 SHAKS. *Cymb.* IV. ii. 315 Thou Conspir'd with that Irregulous diuell Cloten, Hath heere cut off my Lord.

†**irre'iterable,** *a.* *Obs. rare*⁻¹. [f. IR-² + L. *reiterā-re* to REITERATE + -BLE.] That cannot be reiterated or repeated.

1582 N. T. (Rhem.) *Heb.* vii. 27 *note*, His death..the only oblation that is by the Apostle declared to bee irreiterable in it selfe.

†**irre'jectable,** *a.* *Obs. rare*⁻¹. [IR-².] That cannot be rejected.

1648 BOYLE *Seraph. Love* xvii. (1700) 105 The former [Calvinists] affirming grace to be irresistibly presented; the latter [Arminians], though they deny it to be irrejectable yet [etc.].

†**irre'lapsable,** *a.* *Obs. rare.* [IR-².] Not liable to relapse.

1660 H. MORE *Myst. Godl.* X. v. 503 When he has got to that irrelapsable condition of those whose Souls are..perfected in Faith and Holiness.

irrelate (ɪrɪˈleɪt), *a. rare.* [f. IR-² + RELATE *ppl. a.*, L. *relāt-us*, pa. pple. of *referre* to bring back, to refer.] Not related, unrelated.

1845 DE QUINCEY *Suspiria* Wks. 1890 XIII. 347 The fleeting accidents of a man's life, and its external shows, may indeed be irrelate and incongruous. **1845** —— *Wordsworth's Poetry* Wks. 1857 VI. 259 A connection between objects hitherto regarded as irrelate and independent. **1862** F. HALL *Refut. Hindu Philos. Syst.* 248 The faculty of concealment..is a power such that, by it, ignorance..as it were, covers Spirit, unlimited and irrelate to the world.

irre'lated, *a. rare.* [IR-².] = prec.
1886 *Mind* Jan. 3 The only reals for him [Hume] were certain irrelated sensations.

irrelation (ɪrɪ'leɪʃən). [IR-².] Absence of relation, want of connexion.
1848 DE QUINCEY *Goldsmith* Wks. 1890 IV. 310 The instinct of contempt..towards literature was supported by the irrelation of literature to the state. **1853** —— *Autobiog. Sk.* Wks. 1857 I. 187 The utter irrelation, in both cases, of the audience to the scene..threw upon each a ridicule not to be effaced. **1873** H. SPENCER *Study Sociol.* xv. (ed. 6) 363 The irrelation between such causes and such effects.

irrelative (ɪ'rɛlətɪv), *a.* (*sb.*) [f. IR-² + RELATIVE. Cf. F. *irrelatif* (Littré).] Not relative; without relations to each other, or *to* something else; unrelated, unconnected; hence, in *Metaph.*, having no relations, absolute.
1640 BP. REYNOLDS *Passions* xl. 526 Continuance is altogether Extrinsicall and Irrelative in respect of White. **1666** BOYLE *Orig. Formes & Qual.* (1667) 28 It seems evident, that they [colours, odours, etc.] have an absolute Being irrelative to Us. **1849–52** OWEN in *Todd's Cycl. Anat.* IV. 881/2 This endless succession and decadence of the Teeth..illustrate the law of Vegetative or Irrelative Repetition. **1862** F. HALL *Refut. Hindu Philos. Syst.* 230 The cognition which is given out as a constituent of Brahma, is irrelative to objects. **1862** H. SPENCER *First Princ.* I. iv. §26 (1875) 89 The Relative is itself conceivable as such, only by opposition to the Irrelative or Absolute.
b. Having no relation to or bearing on the matter in hand; irrelevant.
1649 G. DANIEL *Trinarch., Hen. V*, cxxxi, Lyllies Spin not! a strange Doctrine Irrelative; but lately vrg'd 'Gainst Harrie's Title. **1785** PALEY *Mor. Philos.* (ed. 21) I. 201 Questions may be asked which are irrelative to the cause. **1849** THACKERAY *Pendennis* xxi, The widow's answer was made up of a great number of incoherent ejaculations, embraces, and other irrelative matter.
c. *Mus.* (See quot.)
1811 BUSBY *Dict. Mus.* (ed. 3), *Irrelative*, a term applied to any two chords which do not contain some sound common to both.
B. *sb. Metaph.* Something that has no relation.
a **1856** SIR W. HAMILTON (Ogilvie), This same mental necessity is involved in the general inability we find of construing positively to thought any irrelative.

irrelatively (ɪ'rɛlətɪvlɪ), *adv.* [f. prec. + -LY².] In an irrelative manner; without relation to some other thing or things. Const. *to*, *of*.
1648 BOYLE *Seraph. Love* iv. (1700) 24 Consider'd abstractedly in itself and irrelatively to the rest. **1778** *Char.* in *Ann. Reg.* 157 *note*, Whenever the word *sex* is used absolutely and irrelatively, it is always to be understood of the *female*. **1823** DE QUINCEY *Language* Wks. IX. 93 Style has an absolute value..irrelatively to the subject. **1864** PUSEY *Lect. Daniel* viii. 483 If asked irrelatively of any context, 'what is the meaning of the words?'

irrelativeness (ɪ'rɛlətɪvnɪs). [f. as prec. + -NESS.] The quality of being irrelative; want of relativity.
a **1665** J. GOODWIN *Filled w. the Spirit* (1867) 29 A flat or dead irrelativeness, in point of merit, in him to whom grace is shewn or to be shewn, in reference unto him that is supposed to shew grace. **1871** *Athenæum* 4 Mar. 277 In this spirit too we are not concerned about vagueness or irrelativeness; we accept the volumes as a naturalist's miscellany.

†**irre'lenting**, *a. Obs. rare.* [IR-².] Not relenting, unrelenting.
1616 W. FORDE *Serm.* 40 O death, how irrelenting is thy heart! **1636** FITZ-GEFFRAY *Holy Transport.* Wks. (1881) 194 Behold the irrelenting slaier comes.

†**irre'lentlessly**, *adv. Obs.* Used erroneously for RELENTLESSLY.
1624 BP. MOUNTAGU *Immed. Addr.* 14 Hee that can diuert or preuent a mischiefe, will not..irrelentlesly see the desolation of those, who are indeed..the receiued ones of God.

irrelevance (ɪ'rɛlɪvəns). [f. IRRELEVANT: see -ANCE.] The fact or quality of being irrelevant, want of pertinence; with *an* and *pl.* an irrelevant remark, circumstance, etc.
1847 L. HUNT *Men, Women, & B.* III. xii. 357 All her wit is healthy; all its images entire and applicable throughout —not palsy-stricken with irrelevance. **1872** MINTO *Eng. Prose Lit.* I. i. 64 A second irrelevance foisted in upon the back of the first. **1873** 'F. TRAFFORD' (Mrs. Riddell) *Earl's Prom.* II. 123, 'I am going away', began Grace with apparent irrelevance.

irrelevancy (ɪ'rɛlɪvənsɪ). [f. as prec.: see -ANCY.] = prec.
1592 *Sc. Acts Jas. VI* (1597) §151 Seeing that diverse exceptiones and objectiones risis vpon criminall libelles..be alleged irrelevancie thereof. **1802–12** BENTHAM *Ration. Judic. Evid.* (1827) IV. 576 In the following modes of collection..the plague of irrelevancy is in a manner unknown. **1833** LAMB *Elia, Pop. Fallacies* ix, The utter and inextricable irrelevancy of the second [member of the question]. **1876** MOZLEY *Univ. Serm.* i. (1877) 7 To use the weapons of one of these societies against a sin or error in the other society, is a total irrelevancy and misapplication.

irrelevant (ɪ'rɛlɪvənt), *a.* [f. IR-² + RELEVANT: cf. OF. *irrelevant* legally inadmissible, not helping to an issue. (A frequent blunder is *irrevalent*.)] Not relevant or pertinent to the case; not to the purpose; that does not apply: said orig. of evidence or arguments.
fallacy of the irrelevant conclusion = *ignoratio elenchi*: see IGNORATION 3.
1786 BURKE *W. Hastings* Wks. XI. 455 All or most of which [depositions] were of an irregular and irrelevant nature, and not fit or decent to be taken by a British magistrate. **1789** BELSHAM *Ess.* II. xl. 505 They are manifestly irrevalent, and totally foreign to the..argument. **1799** MRS. J. WEST *Tale of Times* I. 152 The above observation..is..irrelevant to the case before us. **1823** LAMB *Elia* Ser. II. *Poor Relation*, A Poor Relation..is the most irrelevant thing in nature. **1838** THIRLWALL *Greece* xxxii. IV. 239 He enters into a history of his early life, which ..is wholly irrelevant to the proper question. **1877** E. R. CONDER *Bas. Faith* ii. 79 No accumulation of facts can establish an irrelevant conclusion. **1883** *Law Rep.* 11 Queen's Bench Div. 595 The words complained of..were irrelevant to the proceedings before the police court.
Hence **i'rrelevantly** *adv.*, in an irrelevant manner, not to the purpose.
1818 in TODD. **1821** LAMB *Elia* Ser. I. *All Fools' Day*, It will come in most irrelevantly and impertinently seasonable to the time of day. **1894** *Chicago Advance* 18 Jan., 'I suppose Mr. Morrison has returned', she remarked, rather irrelevantly, as it seemed to Maud.

irrelievable (ɪrɪ'liːvəb(ə)l), *a.* [IR-².] Not relievable, that cannot be relieved.
1670 H. STUBBE *Plus Ultra* 67 Violent impressions..upon the membranes of the Stomach, which may introduce an irrelievable distemper in..that part. **1797** F. HARGRAVE *Juridical Argts.* I. 16 Gross as we must confess the case to be, it is irrelievable. **1849** KINGSLEY *Misc., N. Devon* II. 266, I never think, on principle, of things so painful, and yet so irrelievable.

irreligion (ɪrɪ'lɪdʒən). [a. F. *irréligion* (16–17th c. in Hatz.-Darm.), or immed. ad. L. *irreligiōn-em* (Apuleius), f. *ir-* (IR-²) + *religiōn-em* RELIGION.]
1. Want of religion; hostility to or disregard of religious principles; irreligious conduct.
1598 FLORIO, *Irreligione*, irreligion. **1613** PURCHAS *Pilgrimage* (1614) 51 By Noahs Curse it may appeare,..that Cham was the first Author, after the Floud, of irreligion. **1659** *Gentl. Calling* (1696) 138 To a Christian 'tis certain the irreligion of fighting a Duel would be the most infamous thing. **1732** BERKELEY *Alciphr.* II. §24 Nothing leads to vice so surely as irreligion. **1875** JOWETT *Plato* (ed. 2) V. 183 If laws are based upon religion, the greatest offence against them must be irreligion.
†**2.** A false or perverted religion. *Obs.*
1592 WARNER *Alb. Eng.* VIII. xliii. (1612) 208 Henrie the Eight did happely Romes Irreligion cease. **1634** SIR T. HERBERT *Trav.* 78 Passing by his irreligion and Mahumetisme. **1655** E. TERRY *Voy. E. India* 345 Each [sect of Hindoos] differing from others very much in opinion about their irreligion.

irre'ligionism. [f. prec. + -ISM.] A system of irreligion; irreligious theory.
1843 *Blackw. Mag.* LIV. 411 The immoral schools of radicalism, irreligionism, and Anti-corn-Law Cobdenism.

irre'ligionist. [f. as prec. + -IST.] One who supports or practises irreligion; a professed opponent of religion.
a **1779** WARBURTON in Kilvert *Select.* (1841) 367 The irreligionist, with the malice to embarrass, and the religionist, with the vanity of doing what no one was able to do before, has been always forward in writing upon this subject. **1877** *Recoll. S. Buck* iii. 118 Those only who were confirmed irreligionists. **1880** *Sat. Rev.* 26 June 820/1 Any class of religionists, or irreligionists—if the term may be allowed—who had specially outraged the national sentiment and thus incurred popular odium.

irre'ligionize, *v. nonce-wd.* [f. as prec. + -IZE.] *trans.* To turn to irreligion, make irreligious.
1854 S. WILBERFORCE *Let.* in *Life* II. 261 Romanizing a few, irreligionizing a multitude.

†**irreligi'osity.** *Obs.* [ad. late L. *irreligiōsitās* (Tert.), n. of quality f. *irreligiōsus* IRRELIGIOUS. Cf. OF. *irreligieuseté* (Godef.), F. *irréligiosité*, It. *irreligiosità*.] The quality of being irreligious; irreligiousness; irreligious conduct.
1382 WYCLIF *1 Esdras* i. 52 The whiche [God] vnto wrathe is stirid vp on his folc, for their irreligiosite [Vulg. *propter irreligiositatem*]. **1588** ALLEN *Admonit.* 14 A thinge..that aboue all other kindes of irreligiosity most deservethe and sonest procurethe the Gods vengeance. **1612** T. JAMES *Jesuit's Downf.* 31 There is not a Iesuit in all England, but hath a smacke of impietie, irreligiositie..and Machiavillian Atheisme.

irreligious (ɪrɪ'lɪdʒəs), *a.* [ad. L. *irreligiōsus*, f. *ir-* (IR-²) + *religiōsus* RELIGIOUS. Cf. F. *irréligieux* (15–16th c. in Godef. *Compl.*).]
1. Not religious; hostile to or without regard for religion; ungodly; godless. **a.** Of persons, their actions, etc.
1561 T. NORTON *Calvin's Inst.* II. 112 In all ages that irreligious affectation of religion..hath shewed and yet doth shew forth itself. **1563** GOLDING *Cæsar* 158 It seldome or neuer chaunceth, that any man is so irreligious that he dareth..hide any thyng that is so taken. **1659** D. PELL *Impr. Sea* 90 Their vain, idle, irreligious, soul-damning, deboyst, and ungodly lives. **1671** MILTON *Samson* 860 An irreligious Dishonourer of Dagon. **1713** BERKELEY *Guardian* No. 70 ¶11 Irreligious men, whose short prospects are filled with earth, and sense, and mortal life. **1836** H. ROGERS *J. Howe* vii. (1863) 188 The irreligious monarch..slept during the greater part of the sermon. **1863** GEO. ELIOT *Romola* Proem, Learned personages..maintained that Aristotle..was a thoroughly irreligious philosopher. **1868** BROWNING *Ring & Bk.* x. 453 This is the man proves irreligiousest Of all mankind.
b. *transf.* Of things: Showing a want of religion; at variance with religious principles.
a **1704** T. BROWN *Pleas. Epistle* Wks. 1730 I. 109 Our posies for rings are either immodest or irreligious. **1856** OLMSTED *Slave States* 319 None of the irreligious falsities in stucco and paint that so generally disenchant all expression of worship in our city meeting-houses.
†**2.** Believing in, practising, or pertaining to a false religion. *Obs.*
1575–85 ABP. SANDYS *Serm.* (Parker Soc.) 378 That irreligious crew..which fight for antichrist, for heresy, for popery. **1588** SHAKS. *Tit. A.* v. iii. 121 The issue of an Irreligious Moore. **1613** W. BROWNE *Sheph. Pipe* iv, Cypresse may fade..A herse 'mongst irreligious rites be ranged. **1634** SIR T. HERBERT *Trav.* 193 Their Religion is austere (but irreligious)..some adore a Cow, others a Snake, other-some the Sunne.

irreligiously (ɪrɪ'lɪdʒəslɪ), *adv.* [f. prec. + -LY².] In an irreligious manner; in a way contrary to religion; †in accordance with a false religion (*obs.*).
1577 tr. *Bullinger's Decades* (1592) 117 Outward honour irreligiously exhibited to the true and verie God. *c* **1630** RISDON *Surv. Devon* §45 (1810) 51 There is a small market, in former times irreligiously kept on the sabbath day. **1769** BLACKSTONE *Comm.* (1830) IV. iv. 52 If they keep any inmate, thus irreligiously disposed, in their houses, they forfeit 10*l. per* month.

irreligiousness (ɪrɪ'lɪdʒəsnɪs). [f. as prec. + -NESS.] The quality of being irreligious; ungodliness; †adherence to a false religion (*obs.*).
1577 NORTHBROOKE *Dicing* (1843) 92 Will God suffer them nonpunished that..handle..God's diuine mysteries with such vnreuerentnesse and irreligiousnesse? **1643** LIGHTFOOT *Glean. Ex.* (1648) 14 Changing his Idolatry, and irreligiousnesse for the worship of the true God. **1692** LOCKE *3rd Let. Toleration* 391 (Seager) The ignorance or irreligiousness to be found amongst conformists—I lay not the blame of upon conformity. **1858** DORAN *Crt. Fools* 26 He illustrates the irreligiousness of men.

†**i'rrelishable,** *a. Obs. rare*⁻¹. [IR-².] Not relishable, unpalatable.
1608 DAY *Law Trickes* II. (1881) 33 More irrelishable Then ore-dride Stock-fish.

irre'luctant, *a. rare.* [IR-².] Not reluctant; willing.
1657–83 EVELYN *Hist. Relig.* (1850) I. 2 An irreluctant and free assent to such truths as are the continual objects of our senses. **1852** *Tait's Mag.* XIX. 664 The torrent-fountains.. Whose irreluctant streams supply A quick relief to lowlier woe.

†**irre'markable,** *a. Obs. rare*⁻¹. Also 7 inr-. [IR-². Cf. F. *irremarquable* (Cotgr.).] Not remarkable; having no mark by which it may be distinguished; unremarkable.
1635 CAPT. FOX *North West* 189, I was in Latitude 61 d. 57 m. and stood in close to this inremarkeable shore, and so all the land within this straight, may be called, for it is all shoring, or descending from the highest mountaine to the Sea. [In F. Smith *Voy. Disc.* (1748) I. 68, this Irremarkable Shore.]

irremeable (ɪ'rɛmiːəb(ə)l, ɪ'riːmiːəb(ə)l), *a.* [ad. L. *irremeābil-is*, f. *ir-* (IR-²) + *remeāre* to go back, return, f. *re-* back + *meāre* to go, pass: see -ABLE. In OF. *irremeable* (Godef.). Cf. *permeable*.] Admitting of no return; from, by, or through which there is no return. Now only *poet.*
1569 J. SANFORD tr. *Agrippa's Van. Artes* 145 The countrie of the dead is irremeable. **1611** CORYAT *Crudities* 464, I was for the time in a kinde of irremeable labyrinth. **1697** DRYDEN *Æneid* VI. 575 The chief without delay Pass'd on, and took th' irremeable way. **1715–20** POPE *Iliad* XIX. 312 My three brave brothers, in one mournful day, All trod the dark irremeable way. **1767** JOHNSON *Lett. to Mrs. Thrale* 3 Oct., I perhaps shall not be easily persuaded..to venture myself on the irremeable road. **1768** HAWKESWORTH tr. *Télémaque* VII. (1784) 73 The irremeable waters of Styx.. preclude for ever the return of hope. **1864** SWINBURNE *Atalanta* 600 We shot after and sped Clear through the irremeable Symplegades. **1974** *Encounter* Feb. 54/1 The subject of correctness in language is now tending to be lost in an irremeable labyrinth.
Hence **i'rremeably** *adv.*, without possibility of return.
1805 T. HARRAL *Scenes of Life* II. 94 The time of remedy, as well as of prevention, was now irremeably past.

irremediable (ɪrɪ'miːdɪəb(ə)l), *a.* [ad. L. *irremediābil-is*, f. *ir-* (IR-²) + *remediābilis* REMEDIABLE: cf. F. *irrémédiable* (1474 in Hatz.-Darm.).] Not remediable; that does not admit of remedy, cure, or correction; incurable; irreparable.
1547 J. HARRISON *Exhort. Scottes* Bivb, Vexed with intestine warres..to the irremediable ruine and desolacion therof. **1603** HOLLAND *Plutarch's Mor.* 99 Pure wine..if a man doe mingle it with the juice of the said hemlocke, doth mightily enforce the poison thereof, and make it irremediable. **1660** JER. TAYLOR *Duct. Dubit.* I. v, A person of a desperate fortune, irremediable and irrecoverable. **1712** LADY M. W. MONTAGU *Let. to W. Montagu* 9 Dec., I know and foresee all the irremediable mischiefs. **1735** JOHNSON tr. *Lobo's Voy. Abyssinia* Pref., The reader will here find no

regions cursed with irremediable barrenness or blest with spontaneous fecundity. **1801** A. RANKEN *Hist. France* I. II. i. 182 In irremediable diseases, says Cæsar,..men are sacrificed as victims by the Gauls. **1865** PUSEY *Truth Eng. Ch.* 62 The conquest of Constantinople..made the schism of the Greeks irremediable.

Hence **irre'mediableness**, the quality of being irremediable.

a **1614** DONNE *Βιαθανατος* (1644) 117 Such faults as are greatest, either in their owne nature, or in an irremediablenesse when they are done. **1798** MALTHUS *Popul.* III. ii. (1806) II. 105 The irremediableness of marriage, as it is at present constituted, undoubtedly deters many from entering into this state.

irremediably (ɪrɪ'miːdɪəblɪ), *adv.* [f. prec. + -LY^2.] In an irremediable manner or degree; so as not to admit of remedy, cure, or correction.

1624 DONNE *Devotions*, etc. 565 A relapse proceeds with a more violent dispatch, and more irremediably, because it finds the country weakned. **1755** YOUNG *Centaur* i. Wks. 1757 IV. 114 Thus they..are deplorably gay, till they are irremediably undone. **1841** EMERSON *Conservative* Wks. (Bohn) II. 272 Is it so irremediably bad?

†**i'rremediless**, *a. Obs.* Used erroneously for REMEDILESS.

1600 W. WATSON *Decacordon* (1602) 230 The most dangerous, infectious, and..irremedilesse poyson. *c* **1630** STRAFFORD in Browning *Life* (1891) 70 It is irremediless, and therefore must be yielden unto. **1665** EVELYN *Mem.* (1857) III. 150 Upon these irremediless assaults. **1675** BROOKS *Gold. Key* Wks. 1867 V. 108 This despair is..an effect occasioned by the sinner's view of his irremediless, woeful condition.

†**irre'medious**, *a. Obs. rare*$^{-0}$. [f. IR-^{2} + L. *remedium* REMEDY + -OUS.] Without remedy. Hence †**irre'mediously** *adv.*

1659 HEYLIN *Certamen Epist.* 268 Jeroboham..thereby plagued them irremediously..into the heavy anger and displeasure of the Lord their God.

irre'memberable, *a. rare.* [IR-^{2}.] That cannot be remembered.

1830 W. TAYLOR *Germ. Poetry* I. 179 The same hero is repeatedly..abandoned, and returned to, with confusing and irrememberable alternation.

irremissible (ɪrɪ'mɪsɪb(ə)l), *a.* Also 6 inre-, 7–9 *erron.* irremissable. [a. F. *irrémissible* (1234 in Hatz.-Darm.), ad. L. *irremissibil-is*, f. *ir-* (IR-^{2}) + *remissibilis* REMISSIBLE.] Not remissible; for or of which there is no remission.

a. That cannot be forgiven; unpardonable.

1413 *Pilgr. Sowle* (Caxton) II. li. (1859) 54 He is entatched with synne irremyssyble. **1502** *Ord. Crysten Men* (W. de W. 1506) II. v. 103 These .vi. maner of synnes beforesayd be sayd inremyssyble. **1543** BECON *New Year's Gift* in *Early Wks.* (Parker Soc.) 330 Only the sin against the Holy Ghost ..is irremissible and never forgiven. *a* **1656** HALES *Tracts* (1677) 21 Many would conclude there is a sin for which we may not pray; first, because it is irremissable. *a* **1797** H. WALPOLE *Mem. Geo. II* (1847) III. i. 19 Those, who, two years ago, lay under the irremissible crime of being Tories. **1831–3** E. BURTON *Eccl. Hist.* xix. (1845) 406 The heavier and more atrocious sins, such as apostasy, murder, and adultery, were considered..to be irremissible.

b. That cannot be remitted as an obligation or duty; unalterably obligatory or binding.

1631 R. BYFIELD *Doctr. Sabb.* 32 Sanctification.. indispensable, irremissable to any man. **1728** MORGAN *Algiers* II. iv. 286 The kings of Tunis shall pay to the kings of Spain an irremissible annual Tribute of six Horses and twelve Falcons. **1838** *New Monthly Mag.* LIV. 167 The Mufti reminded the young prince of this irremissible ceremony, which the Dey himself never presumed to violate. **1892** *Contemp. Rev.* Aug. 204 Their irremissible duties to their own countrymen.

Hence **irremissi'bility**, **irre'missibleness**, the quality or condition of being irremissible; unpardonableness.

1612–15 BP. HALL *Contempl., N.T.* III. iii, That dreadful sentence of the irremissiblenesse of that sinne unto death. **1710** *Brit. Apollo* II. Quarterly No. 2. 8/2 The Irremissibleness of Sins after Baptism. **1847** LD. LINDSAY *Chr. Art* I. 30 The frequent practice of postponing baptism to manhood, from belief in the plenary remission of sins at baptism, and the quasi irremissibility of sin after it. **1895** H. C. G. MOULE *Veni Creator* 21 Some further light is thrown on this irremissibility by the fact that the Gospel is seen in Scripture as the final message of divine mercy.

irre'missibly, *adv.* [f. prec. + -LY^2.] In an irremissible way; without possibility of remission or pardon.

1491 CAXTON *Vitas Patr.* (W. de W. 1495) II. 302 a/1 So many myserable soules; whiche ben..soo yrremyssybly loste and dampned. **1650** HOWELL *Giraffi's Rev. Naples* 98 Whoever was found upon the streets should die irremissibly without mercy. **1738** WARBURTON *Div. Legat.* I. 448 Punishment irremissibly pursued the Transgressor. **1824** SOUTHEY *Bk. of Ch.* (1841) 508 Eight heresies were made punishable with death upon the first offence, unless the offender abjured his errors, and irremissibly if he relapsed. **1892** *Blackw. Mag.* CLI. 432/2 That hour was known to have irremissably sounded.

†**irre'mission.** *Obs. rare*$^{-1}$. [IR-^{2}.] The fact of not being remitted; non-remission.

a **1631** DONNE *Serm.* xxxv. 347 'It shall not be forgiven'; It is not, it cannot be forgiven: It is an irremission, it is not an irremissiblenesse.

irre'missive, *a. rare.* [IR-^{2}.] Characterized by being without remission; unremitting.

1817 COLERIDGE *Biog. Lit.* 149 This power, first put in action by the will and understanding, and retained under their irremissive, though gentle and unnoticed, control.

†**irre'mittable**, *a. Obs. rare.* [IR-^{2}.] Not capable of being remitted; = IRREMISSIBLE.

1587 HOLINSHED *Chron. I. Hist. Scot.* 463/2 The first doth intreat of the sinne against the Holie-ghost, which they call irremittable or vnto death. **1635** HEYWOOD *Hierarch.* VI. 399 Against which irremittable sin, Seneca..thus counsels us.

irremovable (ɪrɪ'muːvəb(ə)l), *a.* (*sb.*) Also 6 -mooueable, 6–9 -moveable. [IR-^{2}.]

1. Not removable; incapable of being removed or displaced; not subject to removal.

1598 J. DICKENSON *Greene in Conc.* (1878) 149 Left on her bruised limmes for lasting monument the irremooueable characters of his barbarous crueltie. **1598** YONG *Diana* 125, I onely wish I may haue harbour and entertainment there, where my irremooueable and infinite loue is so firmely placed. **1665** HOOKE *Microgr.* 25 Finding in it several difficulties almost irremovable. **1768–74** TUCKER *Lt. Nat.* (1834) I. 359 Let us consider from whence they [perplexities] generally arise, and perhaps we shall find them not irremoveable. **1851** SIR F. PALGRAVE *Norm. & Eng.* I. 172 Faith failing through irremovable ignorance. **1876** GEO. ELIOT *Dan. Der.* I. 303 An ominous irremovable guest.

b. Incapable of being displaced from office or position; permanent.

1648 MILTON *Tenure Kings* Wks. (1847) 243/1 The right of birth or succession can be no privilege in nature, to let a tyrant sit irremovable over a nation freeborn. **1753** LD. COBHAM in H. Walpole *Mem. Geo. II* (1847) I. v. 135 The Parliament could not be dissolved, but by an irremovable Council. **1832** tr. *Sismondi's Ital. Rep.* v. 119 A body of judges, numerous, independent, and irremovable. **1872** E. W. ROBERTSON *Hist. Ess.* 253 As long as he performed the obligations required of him, the Emphyteuta was irremoveable.

†**2.** Incapable of being moved; immovable, inflexible. *lit.* and *fig. Obs.*

1597 A. M. tr. *Guillemeau's Fr. Chirurg.* 10/1 With the tonge tiede, and with irremoveable eyes. **1603** KNOLLES *Hist. Turks* (1621) 323 These are the irremovable stones and surest sement. **1611** SHAKS. *Wint. T.* IV. iv. 518 Hee's irremoueable, Resolu'd for flight. **1822** LAMB *Elia* Ser. I. *Chimney-Sweepers*, There he stood, as he stands in the picture, irremovable.

B. *sb.* One who cannot be removed; one whose position is permanent.

1848 LEWIS *Lett.* (1870) 183 A Bill making vagrants and irremovables a union charge. **1895** *Chicago Advance* 1 Aug. 151/1 The English Lords have been called the incapable irremovables.

Hence **irremova'bility**, **irre'movableness**, the quality of being irremovable.

1610 DONNE *Pseudo-martyr* x. 276 These Canons.. cannot preuaile so much vpon our consciences, as to imprint and worke such a[n]..irremoueablenesse from them. **1828** WEBSTER, *Irremovability*. **1858** *Times* 29 Nov. 4/1 He defended..the principle of judicial irremovability. **1893** DK. ARGYLL *Unseen Found. Society* ix. 267 Irremovability from the soil of some particular area.

irre'movably, *adv.* [f. prec. + -LY^2.] In an irremovable manner; immovably; without capability of, or liability to, removal.

1660 EVELYN *News fr. Brussels* Misc. Writ. (1825) 202 But above all, so firmly and irremoveably fixed to the profession of the true Protestant religion. **1851** *Fraser's Mag.* XLIII. 391 The dead jaws being irremoveably locked to the body of the conquerors. **1858** CARLYLE *Fredk. Gt.* VII. vi. (1872) II. 303 This Serene Lady stands like a fateful monument irremovably in the way.

irre'moval. *rare*$^{-0}$. [IR-^{2}.] 'Absence of removal.'

1847 in CRAIG. **1856** in WEBSTER.

†**irre'moved**, *a. Obs. rare.* [IR-^{2}.] Not removed, unmoved.

1622 PEACHAM *Compl. Gent.* x. (1634) 87 Some aged Oake ..stands firme, and irremoved cleaves Vnto the Rocke.

irre'munerable, *a. rare.* [IR-^{2}.] That cannot be remunerated, rewarded, or repaid.

1623 COCKERAM, *Irremunerable*, not to be rewarded. **1721** in BAILEY. **1822–34** *Good's Study Med.* (ed. 4) II. 372 Dr. Thompson, to whose indefatigable zeal the profession is under an irremunerable obligation.

†**irre'munerated**, *a. Obs. rare.* [IR-^{2}.] Not remunerated; unremunerated.

a **1648** LD. HERBERT *Hen. VIII* (1683) 358 Lest the Court of Rome should think themselves irremunerated for their pain. **1651** *Raleigh's Ghost* 323 No evil shall remain unrevenged, nor good irremunerated and unrewarded.

i'rrenderable, *a. rare.* [IR-^{2}.] Incapable of being rendered or expressed in another language.

1879 J. D. LONG *Æneid* p. v, And yet, because of its rare, though irrenderable, sweetness of versification,..the Æneid is an immortal poem.

irre'newable, *a. rare.* [IR-^{2}.] Not renewable; that cannot be renewed.

1888 *Harper's Mag.* Nov. 963/2 The hope of renewing an irrenewable experience.

†**irrenitible**, *a. Obs. rare.* [f. IR-^{2} + *renitible*, f. L. *renitī* to struggle against, resist: see -BLE.] Not to be struggled against or withstood.

Apparently the word intended here, though in both instances printed *irreuitable*.

1605 CHAPMAN *All Fools* v. K, To conclude for there force it is irrenitible [*printed* irreuitable], for were they not irrenitible, then might eyther propernesse of person secure a man, or wisedome preuent am [= them].

†**irre'nowned**, *a. Obs. rare.* [IR-^{2}.] Not renowned; without renown or fame; unrenowned.

1590 SPENSER *F.Q.* II. i. 23 To slug in slouth and sensuall delights, And end their daies with irrenowmed shame.

irrenunciable (ɪrɪ'nʌnsɪəb(ə)l), *a. rare*$^{-1}$. [IR-^{2}.] That cannot be renounced.

1890 *Sat. Rev.* 2 Aug. 128/1 The noble, the inspiring, the irrenunciable mission of commerce amongst African tribes.

irrepair (ɪrɪ'pɛə(r)). *rare.* [IR-^{2}.] Unrepaired state; = DISREPAIR.

1822 COBBETT *Rur. Rides* (1886) I. 201 The whole is falling into a state of irrepair. **1830** *Ibid.* (1885) II. 302 The cathedral is in a state of disgraceful irrepair and disfigurement. **1884** *Fortn. Rev.* Mar. 350 Leasehold tenure ..led to the supply of poor, mean, and rotten habitations, and it had almost of necessity permitted them to fall into irrepair in the latter years of the lease.

irre'pairable, *a.* Now *rare.* [IR-^{2}.] That cannot be repaired.

1. Too far decayed to be repaired; past repair.

1722 *Lond. Gaz.* No. 6118/3 The Houses..are irrepairable.

†**2.** Of loss, damage, etc. = next. *Obs.*

1594 R. ASHLEY tr. *le Roy's Interch. Var. Things* 126 b, Whose losse would be almost irrepairable. **1614** RALEIGH *Hist. World* III. (1634) 129 To the utter dishonour of Sparta, and the irrepairable losse of all her former greatness. **1679** PENN *Addr. Prot.* II. 188 That Deceit is irrepairable. **1755** *Man* No. 27. 7 To the irrepairable loss of these poor orphans.

irreparable (ɪ'rɛpərəb(ə)l), *a.* Also 5 irreper-, 7 inreparable. [a. F. *irréparable* (12th c. in Hatz.-Darm.; *inrep-* 15th c. in Littré), ad. L. *irreparābil-is*, f. *ir-* (IR-^{2}) + *reparābilis* REPARABLE.] Not reparable; that cannot be rectified, remedied, or made good.

a **1420** HOCCLEVE *De Reg. Princ.* 2082 Dethe by thy dethe hathe harme irreperable Unto us done. **1530** PALSGR. 316/2 Irreparable, nat able to be recovered, *irreparable*. **1610** SHAKS. *Temp.* v. i. 140 Irreparable is the losse, and patience Saies, it is past her cure. **1631** *Celestina* xv. 164 O incurable destruction! O inrreparable losse! **1647** CLARENDON *Hist. Reb.* II. §89 Before he could arrive with the Army, that infamous, irreparable Rout at Newburn was fall'n out. **1769** ROBERTSON *Chas. V*, x. III. 247 The breach, instead of being closed, was widened and made irreparable. **1811** LD. BYRON in *Four C. Eng. Lett.* 485, I pass through town to repair my irreparable affairs. **1888** A. K. GREEN *Behind Closed Doors* iv, It is an irreparable injury which I shall never forgive.

b. Incapable of being repaired; = IRREPAIRABLE 1. ? *Obs.*

1772 *Hist. Rochester* 99 [The building] being judged irreparable.

Hence **i,rrepara'bility**, **i'rreparableness**, the quality of being irreparable.

1727 BAILEY vol. II, *Irreparableness*. **1768** STERNE *Sent. Journ.* (1778) II. 145 (*Fragment*) The simple irreparability of the fragment. **1839** LADY LYTTON *Cheveley* (ed. 2) II. ii. 50 She felt the premeditation of the insult, the hopelessness, the irreparableness of the injury. **1851** GALLENGA *Italy in 1848* i. 10 Italy had been made aware of the enormity and irreparableness of her loss.

i'rreparably, *adv.* [f. prec. + -LY^2.] In an irreparable manner, so as to be beyond reparation or remedy.

1545 JOYE *Exp. Dan.* vii. (R.), Most cruelly to persecute Crystes chirche and to destroye vtterly and irreparably the Iewes policye for euer. *a* **1631** DONNE in *Select.* (1840) 109 We are weighed down, swallowed up, irreparably. **1769** ROBERTSON *Chas. V*, IX. (1796) III. 156 An event happened which widened the breach irreparably. **1839** MISS MITFORD in L'Estrange *Life* III. vii. 100 The beginning of this letter is irreparably defaced. **1884** CHURCH *Bacon* vi. 125 His sudden and unexpected fall, so astonishing and so irreparably complete.

irre'passable, *a. rare.* [IR-^{2}; cf. F. *irrépassable* (Cotgr.).] That cannot be passed again.

1584 HUDSON *Du Bartas' Judith* vi. 250 He had past already..Of Styx so black the flood irrepassable. **1860** BORROW *Sleeping Bard* 56 It is called the irrepassable wall, for when once you have come through you may abandon all hope of returning.

irrepealable (ɪrɪ'piːləb(ə)l), *a.* [IR-^{2}.] Incapable of being repealed or annulled; irrevocable.

1633 PRYNNE *Histriomastix* I. VI. Chorus 568 b, Let us henceforth passe an irrepealable sentence of condemnation against all popular Stage-playes. **1642** SIR E. DERING *Sp. on Relig.* vii. D iv, Let..this inhibitory Statute..stand.. irrepealable. **1710** *Managers' Pro & Con* 18 The irrepealable Act of Union. **1876** *Const. Colorado* in Bryce *Amer. Commw.* (1888) II. App. 628 An ordinance..shall be irrepealable until the indebtedness therein provided for shall have been fully paid.

Hence **irrepeala'bility**, **irre'pealableness**, the quality of being irrepealable; **irre'pealably** *adv.*, in an irrepealable manner.

1653 GAUDEN *Hierasp.* 120 All degrees of excommunication, and censures are irrepealably transacted by them. **1685** R. L'ESTRANGE *Observator Defended* 3 Written and enacted irrepealably in her Magna Charta. **1802** *Deb. Congress U.S.* 18 Feb. 592 The character of irrepealability was not exclusively attached to this law. **1828** WEBSTER, *Irrepealability,.. Irrepealableness.* **1829** H. MURRAY *N. Amer.* II. III. iii. 365 Some.. political terms, as Gubernatorial Irrepealability.

†**irre'pentable**, *a. Obs. rare.* [IR-^{2}.] That cannot be repented of.

1633 PRYNNE *Histriomastix* 380 Who then would ingage his soule upon such irrecoverable irrepentable [*mispr.* irrepenitable] sins as these?

irre'pentance. *rare.* [IR-^{2}.] Absence of repentance; non-repentance.

1607 *Schol. Disc. agst. Antichr.* II. ix. 114 With manifest shewe of vnbeliefe, or irrepentance. **1648** BP. HALL *Cent. Sel. Th.* §47 There are some dispositions blameworthy in men, which are yet, in a right sense, holily ascribed unto God; as unchangeableness and irrepentance. **1900** *Month* June 583 The young man both in his fall and his irrepentance sins necessarily because Adam sinned.

irre'pentant, *a. rare.* [IR-^{2}.] Not repentant; impenitent.

1583 STUBBES *Anat. Abus.* II. (1882) 99 He might.. haue died irrepentant or vtterly desperate to his euerlasting destruction. *a* **1625** BOYS *Wks.* (1630) 274 A sinner irrepentant is like the sow wallowing in dirt and mire. *Ibid.*, Every man irrepentant without faith and feeling of his sinnes is dead.

Hence **irre'pentantly** *adv.*, without repentance, impenitently.

a **1631** DONNE *Serm.* lv. 559 They shall.. sin as their neighbours sin and fall as they fall, irrepentantly.. irrecoverably. **1654** tr. *Scudery's Curia Pol.* 133 Having offended, (and that irrepentantly) the just authority of all divine and humane rights.

irreplaceable (ɪrɪ'pleɪsəb(ə)l), *a.* [IR-^{2}.] Not replaceable; that cannot be replaced. **a.** Not liable to be restored or paid back, irredeemable. **b.** Of which the loss cannot be supplied, or the place filled by an equivalent.

1807 W. TAYLOR in *Ann. Rev.* V. 193 Almost the whole mass of revenue is.. funded, and irreplaceable. **1842** MRS. CARLYLE *Lett.* I. 150 The desire to replace to me the irreplaceable. **1884** *Nonconf. & Indep.* 11 Dec. 1181/3 An invaluable and irreplaceable colleague. **1885** *Times* 13 June 9 A place where these invaluable and irreplaceable treasures will be safe.

†**irre'plegiable**, *a. Law. Obs.* [ad. med.L. *irreplegiābil-is*, f. *ir-* (IR-^{2}) + *replegiābilis*, f. *replegiā-re* to REPLEDGE.] = IRREPLEVISABLE.

[**1285** *Act 13 Edw. I*, c. 2 Et si iterato ille qui replegiaverit fecerit defaltam vel alia occasione adjudicetur returnum districcionis jam bis replegiate, remaneat districcio illa imperpetuum irreplegiabilis.] **1538** *Act Comm. Council* 28 Sept. in Stow *Surv.* (1754) I. I. xi. 48/1 It shall be lawful for the said Constable.. to distrain for the same Offence, and to retain the same irreplegiable. **1613** SIR H. FINCH *Law* (1636) 35 A man may milke a Cow that hee hath by returne irreplegiable. And that is for the necessity. **1696** PHILLIPS (ed. 5), *Irreplegiable*, that may not, or ought not by Law to be replevied, or set at large upon Sureties.

irrepleviable (ɪrɪ'plɛvɪəb(ə)l), *a. Law.* [ad. med.L. *irrepleviābil-is*, f. *ir-* (IR-^{2}) + *repleviābilis* REPLEVIABLE.] = next.

1543 transl. *Act 13 Edw. I*, c. 2 If he that repleuied make defaut agayne, or for an other cause retourne of the dystres beyng now twyse repleuied be awarded, the distres shal remaine irrepleuiable. **1670** BLOUNT *Law Dict.*, *Irrepleviable*, or *Irreplevisable*, that may not, or ought not by Law to be replevied, or set at large upon Sureties. **1883** *Wharton's Law Lex.* (ed. 7), *Irrepleviable*, or *Irreplevisable*.

irreplevisable (ɪrɪ'plɛvɪzəb(ə)l), *a. Law.* [f. IR-^{2} + REPLEVISABLE.] Not replevisable; that cannot be replevied or delivered on sureties.

1621 SIR R. BOYLE in *Lismore Papers* (1886) II. 10 To distreyn vppon any his own Lands, and to hold yt irreplevizable till I was paid. **1622** CALLIS *Stat. Sewers* (1647) 148 Although.. a return irreplevisable was awarded to the Lord or Avowant, yet he cannot sell this Distresse, nor work them. *a* **1676** HALE *Hist. Placit. Cor.* II. xv. (1736) II. 129 Those that were irreplevisable at common law. **1821** *New Monthly Mag.* I. 182 '*Anne averia carucæ capta in vetito namio sint irreplegibilia*', that is to say, 'whether beasts of the plough taken in *withernam* are irreplevisable'.

†**irre'pliable**, *a. Obs. rare*$^{-1}$. [f. IR-^{2} + REPLY *v.* + -ABLE.] Admitting of no reply.

1632 J. HAYWARD tr. *Biondi's Eromena* 6 Having heard his Lords irrepliable reasons, without any more adoe went.

irre'portable, *a. rare.* [IR-^{2}.] Not reportable; that cannot be reported.

1890 *Harper's Mag.* Jan. 321/1 The consequences flowing from this situation.. are simply irreportable.

†**irre'poscible**, *a. Obs. rare*$^{-0}$. [ad. L. *irreposcibil-is* that cannot be demanded back (Apul.), f. *ir-* (IR-^{2}) + *reposcĕre* to demand back: see -IBLE.]

1656 BLOUNT *Glossogr.*, *Irreposcible*, that cannot be required again.

†**irrepre'hendable**, *a. Obs. rare*$^{-1}$. [f. IR-^{2} + REPREHENDABLE.] = IRREPREHENSIBLE.

1597 A. M. tr. *Guillemeau's Fr. Chirurg.* 1 b/2 Hippocrates havinge published his knowledge, shalbe irreprehendable, and of all men admired. *Ibid.* 51 b/1 Certayne times of the yeare, which are irreprehendable.

irreprehensible (ɪrɛprɪ'hɛnsɪb(ə)l), *a.* Now *rare.* [ad. late L. *irreprehensibil-is*, f. *ir-* (IR-^{2}) + *reprehens-*, ppl. stem of *reprehendĕre* to REPREHEND: see -IBLE, and cf. F. *irrépréhensible* (14th c. in Hatz.-Darm.).] Not reprehensible or blameworthy; not liable to blame or reproof; irreproachable.

1382 WYCLIF *1 Tim.* iii. 2 It bihoueth a byschop for to be irreprehensyble [*gloss* or withoute reproue], and the hosebonde of oo wyf. **1561** T. NORTON *Calvin's Inst.* III. 305 Hys iugement which is in dede iust and irreprehensible but also incomprehensible. **1590** SWINBURNE *Testaments* 7 The definition remaineth irreprehensible. **1656** EARL MONM. *Advt. fr. Parnass.* 266 A man as excellent for Learning, as for his plain-dealing, and sincerity of an irreprehensible life. **1702** VANBRUGH *False Friend* I. i. 25, I profess.. a most perfect knowledge of men and manners. Yours, gracious sir, .. are not irreprehensible. **1848** R. TURNBULL *Pulpit Orators France* 87 You ought to have been strict and irreprehensible in your compliance with the dictates of reason.

Hence **irrepre'hensibleness, irrepre'hensibly** *adv.*

1611 COTGR., *Irreprehensiblement*, irreprehensibly, blamelesly, vnreprouably. **1656** HOBBES *6 Lessons* iii. Wks. 1845 VII. 241 He defined the same proportion irreprehensibly. **1727** BAILEY vol. II, *Irreprehensibleness.*

irrepresentable (ɪrɛprɪ'zɛntəb(ə)l), *a.* [IR-^{2}.] Not representable; incapable of representation.

1673 H. MORE *App. Antid. Idol.* 4 To set up such a Symbolical presence.. to represent God, who is irrepresentable, as being infinite in Majesty and Greatness. *a* **1699** STILLINGFLEET (J.), God's irrepresentable nature doth hold against making images of God. **1817** COLERIDGE *Biog. Lit.* I. xii. 278 They take.. the words irrepresentable and impossible in one and the same meaning. **1827** DE QUINCEY in *Blackw. Mag.* XXI. 17 Progressive actions, as such, are irrepresentable by painting. **1856** FERRIER *Inst. Metaph.* XIII. vi. 315 No model whatever of matter *per se* being presentable to us in knowledge, the material universe *per se* must for ever remain absolutely irrepresentable by us in thought.

Hence **irrepre'sentableness.**

1673 H. MORE *App. Antid. Idol.* 28 Whether the doing Divine worship towards the Image of Christ violates the irrepresentableness of the Godhead or no.

irrepressible (ɪrɪ'prɛsɪb(ə)l), *a.* (*sb.*) [f. IR-^{2} + REPRESS + -IBLE. Cf. F. *irrépressible* (adm. Acad. 1878).] **A.** *adj.* Not repressible; that cannot be repressed, restrained, or put down; irrestrainable. (Of persons, often more or less humorous.)

1811 JANE AUSTEN *Sense & Sens.* III. ix. 198 His was an involuntary confidence, an irrepressible effusion. **1818** in TODD. **1828** CARLYLE *Misc., Burns* (1872) II. 5 Impelled by the expansive movement of his own irrepressible soul. **1830** HERSCHEL *Stud. Nat. Phil.* 347 That irrepressible thirst after knowledge, which in minds of the highest order, supplies the absence both of external stimulus and opportunity. **1848** C. BRONTE *J. Eyre* vii. (1873) 57 Irrepressible yawns attested her weariness. **1878** BOSW. SMITH *Carthage* 4 Wherever a ship could penetrate.. there we find these ubiquitous, these irrepressible Phoenicians. **1879** *Daily Tel.* 17 June, The speeches were delivered amid the tumultuous and often unseemly uproar of the irrepressible undergraduates. **1894** H. GARDENER *Unoff. Patriot* 278 Shiloh had passed into history, and Grant was famous!.. One more milestone in the devious road was past. One more reef was taken in the irrepressible conflict.

B. *sb.* An irrepressible person.

1890 *Pall Mall G.* 15 July 3/2 Love is always the poet's test. Note the original way in which these irrepressibles essay it. **1895** *Amer. Missionary* (N.Y.) Sept. 304 The.. boy being one of those irrepressibles who find it difficult to sit still.

Hence **irrepressi'bility, irre'pressibleness,** the quality of being irrepressible.

1867 *Pall Mall G.* 1 Mar. 5 His irrepressibility rises to something like heroism. **1875** MRS. MACQUOID *My Story* II. xx. 308 Any irrepressibleness or impulsiveness.. had been smiled at as ignorance and rawness.

irrepressibly (ɪrɪ'prɛsɪblɪ), *adv.* [f. prec. + -LY^2.] In an irrepressible manner or degree.

1856 in WEBSTER. **1862** S. LUCAS *Secularia* 209 The Americans.. thrived irrepressibly through 'a salutary neglect'. **1876** BANCROFT *Hist. U.S.* II. xxiv. 118 The sentiment of cheerful humanity was irrepressibly strong in his bosom.

irre'pressive, *a. rare.* [f. IR-^{2} + REPRESSIVE: see -IVE.] = IRREPRESSIBLE.

1856 MRS. BROWNING *Aur. Leigh* III. 882 That pathetic vacillating roll Of the infant body.. At which most women's arms unclose at once With irrepressive instinct.

†**irre'prevable**, *a. Obs. rare*$^{-0}$. [f. IR-^{2} + REPREVABLE.] = IRREPROVABLE.

c **1440** *Promp. Parv.* 266/1 Irrepreuable, *irreprehensibilis.*

†**irre'proach.** *Obs. rare.* [IR-^{2}.] Absence of reproach.

1793 W. ROBERTS *Looker-on* No. 49 ¶2 The only place where I can have that with innocence and irreproach.

irreproachable (ɪrɪ'prəʊtʃəb(ə)l), *a.* [a. F. *irréprochable* (15th c. in Hatz.-Darm.), f. *ir-* (IR-^{2}) + *réprochable* REPROACHABLE.] Not reproachable; not open to reproach or blame; free from blame, faultless.

1634 W. TIRWHYT tr. *Balzac's Lett.* (vol. I.) 300 The disgrace of so irreproachable a Minister. **1664** EVELYN *Architects & Archit.* in *Freart's Archit.* 118 An exact and irreproachable Piece of Architecture. **1741** tr. *D'Argens' Chinese Lett.* xxxvi. 272 This Man, whose Behaviour was always irreproachable. **1897** MARY KINGSLEY *W. Africa* 305, I found an exceedingly neat, well-educated M'pongwe gentleman in irreproachable English garments, and with irreproachable, but slightly floreate, English language.

Hence **irreproacha'bility** [F. *irréprochabilité* (1791 in Hatz.-Darm.)]; **irre'proachableness,** the quality of being irreproachable.

1828 WEBSTER, *Irreproachableness*, the quality or state of being not reproachable. **1833** T. HOOK *Parson's Dau.* I. i. 2 A noble lady.. satisfied of the irreproachability of her conduct. **1879** FARRAR *St. Paul* II. 520 The qualifications on which St. Paul insists are irreproachableness, faithful domestic life. **1890** H. S. MERRIMAN *Suspense* II. i. 12 Bristling with the consciousness of her own wearisome irreproachability.

irreproachably (ɪrɪ'prəʊtʃəblɪ), *adv.* [f. prec. + -LY^2.] In an irreproachable manner; in a manner above reproach or blame.

1705 ADDISON *Italy, Switzerland* 496 From this time, says the Monk, the bear liv'd irreproachably. **1880** H. JAMES *Mme. de Mauves* II. 122 He had learned to be irreproachably polite. **1881** MISS BRADDON *Asph.* III. 5 Daphne.. behaved irreproachably all the afternoon.

irreproducible (ɪriːprəʊ'djuːsɪb(ə)l), *a.* [IR-^{2}.] Not reproducible; incapable of being reproduced.

1868 *Sat. Rev.* 26 Dec. 824/1 The deadness of his expression is irreproducible in words. **1883** *Fortn. Rev.* 1 Aug. 277 These phenomena [are] irreproducible.

irreproductive (ɪriːprəʊ'dʌktɪv), *a.* [IR-^{2}.] Not reproductive; not capable of reproducing.

irreproductive function (*Math.*), a reproductive function of order zero.

irreprovable (ɪrɪ'pruːvəb(ə)l), *a.* [IR-^{2}.]

1. Not reprovable or blameable; undeserving of reproof; blameless, irreproachable. Now *rare.*

1504 LADY MARGARET tr. *De Imitatione* IV. v. 268 Shewe thy selfe irreprouable and withoute defaute. **1601** R. JOHNSON *Kingd. & Commw.* (1603) 95 The Turk in all his attempts against Hungerland hath used irreprovable judgement. **1642** SIR E. DERING *Sp. on Relig.* 89 Divines of irreproveable life. **1755** YOUNG *Centaur* ii. Wks. 1757 IV. 144 An indulgent Providence has abundantly provided us with irreproveable pleasures. **1838** W. B. WHITMARSH *Fam. Prayers* 168 That all the.. actions.. may be pure, holy, and irreproveable in thy sight.

†**2.** That cannot be disproved or confuted; irrefutable. *Obs.*

1581 J. BELL *Haddon's Answ. Osor.* 453 b, Where be those irreproveable Testimonyes, and undeceivable examples, whereupon you crake so lustely? **1646** SIR T. BROWNE *Pseud. Ep.* I. iii. 11 In some Christian Churches, wherein is presumed an irreproveable truth.

Hence **irre'provableness.**

1775 in ASH. **1846** in WORCESTER; and in mod. Dicts.

irre'provably, *adv.* [f. prec. + -LY^2.] In an irreprovable manner.

1599 *Broughton's Let.* v. 16 He hath walked irreproueably before God and men. **1615** G. SANDYS *Trav.* 159 To live chastly, irreproveably, and in word and deed to shew themselves worthy of such a dignity.

i'rreption. [ad. late L. *irreptiōn-em*, n. of action from *irrepĕre* to creep in or on.] Creeping or stealing in, stealthy entrance.

1598 *Ord. for Prayer* in *Liturg. Serv. Q. Eliz.* (Parker Soc.) 680 The irreption of those undermining vermin the Priests and Jesuits covertly sent in. **1649** JER. TAYLOR *Gt. Exemp.* II. Disc. ix. 122 By continuall watchfulnesse, we shall lessen the inclination, and account fewer sudden irreptions. **1926** G. W. S. FRIEDRICHSEN *Gothic Version of Gospels* 190 Previous to this there had been casual but continued irreptions from the Old Latin. *Ibid.* 249 The Gothic reading could.. be explained as a corruption due to the irreption of some parallel or reminiscent passage. **1974** *Encounter* Feb. 54/1 A protection against casual and deplorable irreptions creeping into the language.

irreptitious (ɪrɛp'tɪʃəs), *a.* [f. L. *irrept-*, ppl. stem of *irrepĕre* (see prec.) + -ITIOUS.] Characterized by creeping in or having crept in, esp. into a text.

1673 CASTELL *Let.* in Nichols *Lit. Anecd. 18th C.* IV. 695 The first [text] he illustrates, Esa. ix. 1 where all condemn πιε as irreptitious. **1680** H. DODWELL *Two Lett.* (1691) 7 Where it [this design] is irreptitious and by way of surprize. **1868** *Contemp. Rev.* IX. 283 Omit οὐδαμῶς which contradicts Micah, and is irreptitious from preceding αἰδου.

†**irre'pugnable**, *a. Obs.* [f. IR-^{2} + REPUGNABLE, or a. OF. *irrepugnable* (15th c. in Godef.).] That cannot be fought against or resisted; irresistible.

1578 BANISTER *Hist. Man* I. 9 Sited in most eminent perilles, and as it were in the forefront of irrepugnable damages. **1632** LITHGOW *Trav.* IX. 398 *note*, A comparison of irrepugnable streames. **1683** TRYON *Way to Health* 475 An irrepugnable Tower against all Evil and Violence.

†**i'rreputable**, *a. Obs.* [IR-².] Not reputable, not of good repute; disreputable.

1709 T. BAKER *Female Tatler* No. 4 ¶1 'Tis very irreputable for a young Woman to gad about to Mens Lodgings. **1749** BP. LAW *Life Christ* (R.), Nor does he [Socrates] declare against their [the Athenians'] most predominant, and not irreputable vices.

†**i'rrequiate**, *v. Obs. rare*⁻¹. [erron. f. late L. *irrequiēs, -ētis* unquiet, restless + -ATE³.] *trans.* To render unquiet, to disturb.

1597 A. M. tr. *Guillemeau's Fr. Chirurg.* 46b/2 A hard situation might disturbe and irrequiate the vulnerated part.

†**i'rrequisite**, *a. Obs.* [f. IR-² + REQUISITE, or ad. late L. *irrequīsītus* (Sidonius).] Not requisite, unnecessary.

1599 R. LINCHE *Fount. Anc. Fict.* G iij, I thought it not irrequisite so to discover it. **1665** J. WEBB *Stone-Heng* (1725) 131 It will not be irrequisite..to say somewhat in this Place ..of the Rites introduced by them.

†**irre'quitable**, *a. Obs. rare*⁻¹. [IR-².] Not requitable; that cannot be requited or repaid.

1615 SIR E. HOBY *Curry-combe* iv. 159 He should haue bene very vngrateful for so irrequitable a benefit.

†**irre'semblance**. *Obs. rare*⁻¹. [IR-².] Want of resemblance, non-resemblance.

1628 BP. HALL *Old Relig.* 84 Neither doth he finde fault with the irresemblance but with the Image.

†**i'rresiant**, *a. Obs. rare.* [f. IR-² + RESIANT.] Non-resident, having no residence.

a **1653** G. DANIEL *Idyll* iii. 97 New Letters-pattents give Vs Libertie to wander with a Breife; Irresiant, now content.

†**irresig'nation**. *Obs. rare.* [IR-².] The opposite of resignation; unresignedness.

1657 *Divine Lover* 215 Pride, Ambition, and Irresignation in the point of Offices. **1752** LAW *Spirit of Love* II. (1816) 174 When your own impatience, wrath, pride, and irresignation attacks you.

irresilient (ɪrɪ'sɪlɪənt), *a.* [IR-².] Not resilient; that does not spring back or rebound.

1855 H. SPENCER *Princ. Psychol.* (1872) II. VI. xii. 156 Of bodies that resist in different modes..we have..the Resilient and Irresilient.

irresistance (ɪrɪ'zɪstəns). [IR-².] Absence of resistance; non-resistance.

1643 PRYNNE *Sov. Power Parl.* III. 106 The Apostle hath no where in this Text, nor God himselfe in any other Scripture, expressed such..irresistance..to be due unto them. **1794** PALEY *Evid.* II. ii. (1817) 28 Patience under affronts and injuries, humility, irresistance, placability. **1894** *Athenæum* 1 Sept. 284/3 The Frenchman, who.. reduced Trocadéro to stupefaction and irresistance, sufficient for shoeing purposes, by simply staring the horse in the face.

†**irre'sisted**, *a. Obs. rare*⁻¹. [IR-².] Unresisted; irresistible.

1596 R. L[INCHE] *Diella* (1877) 67 O irresisted force of purest Loue.

irresistibility (ɪrɪzɪstɪ'bɪlɪtɪ). Also 7 **-ability**. [f. next: see -ITY, and cf. F. *irrésistibilité* (Fénélon *a* 1715 in Littré).]

1. The quality of being irresistible or incapable of being withstood.

In early use chiefly with reference to the doctrine of 'irresistible grace', *irresistibleness* being otherwise the more common word.

1617 DONNE *Serm.* cxxxii. V. 365 Resistibility and Irresistibility of Grace..was..a language that pure Antiquity spake not. **1652** BENLOWES *Theoph.* VII. xcviii, For Peace, what passeth understandings Eye, Power, Irresistabilitie. **1676** R. DIXON *Two Testam.* 342 O Irresistibility, Irresistibility! thou takest away all Sin and all Goodness, because thou takest away all will to either. **1718** POPE *Iliad* XIII. 191 *note*, The..leaping of the Stone,..the Irresistibility, and..Augmentation of Force in its Progress. **1865** CARLYLE *Fredk. Gt.* XV. xii, Ferdinand..had the charge of attacking; and he did it with his usual impetus and irresistibility.

b. The quality of being irresistibly fascinating.

1763 MRS. BROOKE *Lady J. Mandeville* (1782) I. 70 He descended, like Adonis from the carr of Venus,—full of the idea of his own irresistibility. **1826** MISS MITFORD *Village* Ser. II. (1863) 225, I was fairly coaxed into some articles by the irresistibility of the sellers.

†**2.** The quality or fact of not being lawfully resistible. *Obs.*

1643 PRYNNE *Sov. Power Parl.* III. 128 There is then no speciall Prerogative or irresistability given to Kings by this Text in injurious violent Courses. *Ibid.* 131 The Argument ..for the absolute Soveraigntie and irresistibility of Kings. **1775** J. BOUCHER *Causes Amer. Rev.* xii. (1797) 547 The injudicious defenders of this doctrine, who..have argued for the exclusive irresistibility of kings.

irresistible (ɪrɪ'zɪstɪb(ə)l), *a.* (*sb.*) Also 7-8 **-able**, 7 **inresistable**. [ad. late L. *irresistibil-is* (see Quicherat), f. *ir-* (IR-²) + *resistĕre* to RESIST: see -IBLE, and cf. F. *irrésistible* (adm. Acad. 1762). The forms *resistable, irresistable* were Eng. formations on *resist* vb.]

1. Not resistible; that cannot be withstood; too strong, weighty, or fascinating to be resisted.

α. **1597** HOOKER *Eccl. Pol.* v. iii. §1 Fear in this kind doth grow from an apprehension of deitie, indued with irresistible power to hurt. *a* **1631** DONNE in *Select.* (1840) 109 Mine enemy is a real, and an irresistible..enemy. **1692** SOUTH *12 Serm.* (1697) I. 469 Possibly the grace of God may, in some cases, be irresistible. **1776** GIBBON *Decl. & F.* xii. I. 347 The power of opinion is irresistible. **1838** LYTTON *Alice* II. i, There was so charming and irresistible a grace about her.

β. **1601** R. JOHNSON *Kingd. & Commw.* (1603) 95 The irresistable power of the Turk. **1650** HOBBES *De Corp. Pol.* 7 Inresistable Might in the state of Nature, is Right. **1671** MILTON *Samson* 126 Can this be Hee, That Heroic, that Renown'd, Irresistable Samson? **1755** YOUNG *Centaur* vi. Wks. 1757 IV. 270 That call irresistable, which every moment should expect; which every fool forgets.

†**2.** Not to be resisted lawfully: cf. IRRESISTIBILITY 2. *Obs.*

1643 PRYNNE *Sov. Power Parl.* III. 121 Our Opposites must grant..all other Magistrates whatsoever, as irresistible ..as they say kings are.

B. *sb.* An irresistible person.

1774 *Trinket* 36 A sprightly widow, a fine girl, or a society of *beaux esprits*, are three irresistibles. **1796** CHARLOTTE SMITH *Marchmont* I. 139 One of those irresistibles who are always seen..riding in Hyde-park.

irresistibleness (ɪrɪ'zɪstɪb(ə)lnɪs). Also 7 **-ableness**. [f. prec. + -NESS.] The quality of being irresistible.

1627 DONNE *Serm.* v. 49 The spirit of eloquence, and the irresistiblenesse of perswasion. **1639** FULLER *Holy War* v. vii. (1647) 239 Such was the irresistibleness of the Kings spirit. **1675** STERRY *Freed. Will* 222 With a necessity and irresistablenesse most rational. **1880** A. RALEIGH *Way to City* (1881) 294 Unchangeableness, unsearchableness, irresistibleness, invisibility are all negative attributes of God.

irresistibly (ɪrɪ'zɪstɪblɪ), *adv.* Also 7-9 **-ably**. [f. prec. + -LY².] In an irresistible manner; so as to be irresistible.

a **1641** BP. MOUNTAGU *Acts & Mon.* (1642) 410 Being so ordered and disposed irreversibly and irresistibly. **1643** PRYNNE *Sov. Power Parl.* III. 129 That any man or Nation should so absolutely, irresistably inslave themselves. **1709** STEELE *Tatler* No. 30 ¶4, I shall come Home this Winter irresistibly dress'd, and with quite a new Foreign Air. **1871** TYNDALL *Fragm. Sc.* (1879) I. ii. 72 We are led irresistably to enquire, 'What is light and what is heat?' **1874** L. STEPHEN *Hours in Library* (1892) I. vi. 217 We are irresistibly carried away by his enthusiasm.

†**irre'sistless**, *a. Obs.* [An erroneous blending of *irresistible* and *resistless*. Cf. *irrelentlessly, irremediless*.] Resistless, irresistible.

1669 COKAINE *Poems, Of Fletcher's Plays* 102 The Seas vast rore, and Irresistless shake Of horrid winds a Sympathie compose. *a* **1773** CUNNINGHAM *Sappho's Hymn to Venus* vi, Again I've felt the furious stroke Of irresistless love. **1774** PENNANT *Tour Scotl. in 1772*, 125 Irresistless beauty brings up the rear. **1796** P. COURTIER *Poems, Elegy Westm. Abb.*, Then comes oblivion's irresistless stream.

irresoluble (ɪ'rɛzəl(j)uːb(ə)l), *a.* [ad. L. *irresolūbil-is* (Apul.), f. *ir-* (IR-²) + *resolūbilis* RESOLUBLE: cf. F. *irrésoluble* (Littré).] Not resoluble.

1. Incapable of being resolved into elements, or dissolved in water, or liquefied; indissoluble; insoluble.

1666 BOYLE *Orig. Formes & Qual.* Wks. 1772 III. 105 Induring the fire, and, which is the main, irresoluble by water. **1674** —— *Grounds Corpusc. Philos.* 25 The productions of Chymical analyses are simple bodies, and upon that account irresoluble. **1744** ARMSTRONG *Preserv. Health* II. 83 The irresoluble oil..in floods Of rancid bile o'erflows.

fig. *a* **1849** POE *F.S. Osgood* Wks. 1864 III. 93 It is in this irresoluble effect that Mrs. Osgood excels any poetess of her country.

2. Incapable of being loosened and dispelled or relieved.

1646 GAULE *Cases Consc.* 107 With many moe almost irresoluble scruples. **1649** BP. HALL *Cases Consc.* III. ix. (1654) 253 The second is in the irresoluble condition of our souls after a known sin. **1684** tr. *Bonet's Merc. Compit.* I. 10 A Maid laboured of irresoluble Obstructions. **1862** *Athenæum* 30 Aug. 265 The progress of disease is slow,—phthisis scarcely making itself felt till it has stealthily got an irresoluble hold on life.

3. Incapable of being solved or explained; insoluble.

1868 SYMONDS *Clough* in *Fortn. Rev.* Dec. 589 Problems by their very nature irresoluble in one lifetime.

Hence **i'rresolubleness**, the quality of being irresoluble or undissolvable.

1680 BOYLE *Scept. Chem.* III. 179 Quercetanus himself.. has this Confession of the Irresolubleness of Diamonds.

irresolute (ɪ'rɛzəl(j)uːt), *a.* [ad. L. *irresolūt-us*, f. *ir-* (IR-²) + *resolūtus* RESOLUTE.]

†**1.** Not resolved or explained; left ambiguous or obscure. *Obs.*

1573 MURRAY *Let.* in *Wodrow Soc. Misc.* 289 Thingis ambiguouss and irresolute. **1603** FLORIO *Montaigne* I. lvi. (1632) 172, I propose certaine formelesse and irresolute fantasies.

2. Unresolved or undecided as to a course of action. Also *fig.*

1579 FENTON *Guicciard.* I. (1599) 15 Some times inclining to his ambition and glory, and sometimes restrained with feares and dangers, he would often be irresolute. **1608** D. T. *Ess. Pol. & Mor.* 20 After many long suspensions, and irresolute determinations,..affection..commanded him to [etc.]. **1700** DRYDEN *Cinyras & Myrrha* 105 Irresolute to grant or to refuse. **1747** FRANKLIN *Ess.* Wks. 1840 III. 8 The rest appear irresolute what part to take. **1828** D'ISRAELI *Chas. I*, II. ii. 60 At this moment Buckingham was irresolute, and scarcely knew what to decide on. **1867** BAILEY *Univ. Hymn* 8 The nebulous star, Of pale, irresolute sheen.

3. Wanting in resolution or decision of character; infirm of purpose; vacillating; characterized by irresolution.

1600 E. BLOUNT tr. *Conestaggio* 181 They cursed the Governors..concluding that rashnes had raigned with S.., irresolute arrogancie with H... **1698** FRYER *Acc. E. India & P.* 417 This shews..an irresolute Temper in the Ranna. **1853** J. H. NEWMAN *Hist. Sk.* (1873) II. II. ii. 251 Cicero.. was irresolute, timid, and inconsistent.

irresolutely (ɪ'rɛzəl(j)uːtlɪ), *adv.* [f. prec. + -LY².] In an irresolute manner.

1617 MORYSON *Itin.* II. 214 The continuall rumours wee heard of preparations in Spaine, made us proceede more irresolutely. **1658** EARL MONMOUTH tr. *Paruta's Wars Cyprus* 196 The Venetians proceeded doubtfully and irresolutely in the businesse of the Peace. **1838** DICKENS *Nich. Nick.* xvi, Pausing irresolutely several times before the door.

irresoluteness (ɪ'rɛzəl(j)uːtnɪs). [f. as prec. + -NESS.] The quality of being irresolute; irresolution.

1686 HORNECK *Crucif. Jesus* xvii. 472 Where men..with this irresoluteness come. **1837-9** HALLAM *Hist. Lit.* III. iv. §36 An appearance of vacillation and irresoluteness which probably represents the real state of his mind. **1851** GALLENGA *Italy* 377 The lukewarmness, irresoluteness, and bad faith of the princes.

irresolution (ɪrɛzə'l(j)uːʃən). [prob. a. F. *irrésolution* (Montaigne, 16th c.), f. *ir-* (IR-²) + *résolution*: cf. It. *irresoluzione, -solutione* (Florio, 1598).] Want of resolution.

†**1.** The condition of not having arrived at a settled opinion on some subject; undecided opinion, uncertainty, doubt. With *pl.*, An instance of this.

1592 UNTON *Corr.* (Roxb.) 291 The vnhappie accident of the Kinges late hurte dothe..nourishe strange conceipts and irresolutions. **1603** FLORIO *Montaigne* (1632) 431 Their irresolution, the weakenesse of their arguments..being apparent to all men. *a* **1648** LD. HERBERT *Hen. VIII* (1683) 351 Bringing Religion thus into much irresolution and Controversie. **1652** KIRKMAN *Clerio & Lozia* 89 The Souls of these amorous Lovers floated all this night among an hundred different irresolutions. **1704** NORRIS *Ideal World* II. Pref. 1, I expressed myself with some suspense and irresolution. **1813** W. TAYLOR *Eng. Synon.* 23 Doubt is the hesitation of ignorance; uncertainty, of irresolution; and suspense, of indecision.

2. The condition of being irresolute or undecided; indecision as to a course of action; indecision of character; vacillation. With *an* and *plural*, An instance of this.

1601 R. JOHNSON *Kingd. & Commw.* (1603) 140 For the conquest of any forren place, I beleeve they would proceede with like slownesse and irresolution. **1635** J. HAYWARD tr. *Biondi's Banish'd Virg.* 149, I being for my owne part in such affaires a mortall enemy of irresolutions. **1701** ROWE *Amb. Step-Moth.* I. i, Be fix'd, my Soul,..nor know the Weakness, The poor Irresolution of my Sex. **1810** *House of Lancaster* I. 44 [This] cast him into an irresolution much easier to be imagined than described. **1823** LINGARD *Hist. Eng.* VI. 260 His irresolution of mind..induced him to listen to the suggestions of the French ambassadors. **1863** GEO. ELIOT *Romola* xi, When Fra Luca had ceased to speak, Tito still stood by him in irresolution.

irresolvable (ɪrɪ'zɒlvəb(ə)l), *a.* [IR-².] Not resolvable.

1. Incapable of being resolved or solved; insoluble.

1660 tr. *Amyraldus' Treat. conc. Relig.* III. xi. 535 A thing full of spinous questions and irresolvable difficulties. **1708** *Brit. Apollo* No. 8. 1/2 Your Question is irresolvable. **1883** A. BARRATT *Phys. Metempiric* 180 This suggests a question which..is irresolvable by Metaphysic.

2. That cannot be resolved into elements or parts; that cannot be analysed.

irresolvable nebulæ, nebulæ that cannot be resolved into stars by telescopic examination.

1785 HERSCHEL in *Phil. Trans.* LXXV. 262 The three nebulosities: *viz.* the resolvable, the coloured but irresolvable, and a tincture of the milky kind. **1869** *Contemp. Rev.* XI. 332 Is not he a spiritualist, who..believes consciousness to be a primary irresolvable fact? **1881** PROCTOR *Poetry Astron.* xii. 432 Irresolvable nebulae really consisting of stars, but too remote for telescopic mastery. **1899** *Westm. Gaz.* 8 Aug. 3/3 That the Reality of the Ego is a datum of the individual consciousness, irresolvable into more primitive elements.

3. That cannot be disentangled; inextricable.

1886 *Athenæum* 13 Feb. 238/3 The countless leaves and the irresolvable intricacy of the willow-boughs overhanging the water.

Hence **irresolva'bility**, **irre'solvableness**.

1838 NICHOL *Archit. Heav.* (1851) 122 Such a fluid.. could not..be distinguished from unresolved clusters of stars, either by the nature of its light, or the simple fact of its irresolvability. **1847** CRAIG, *Irresolvableness*.

†**irre'solve**. *Obs. rare.* [IR-².] An incompleted resolve.

1769 R. GRIFFITH *Gordian Knot* II. 115 After forming many irresolves, I, at last, thought it most prudent to acquiesce in my misfortune.

†**irre'solved**, *a. Obs.* [IR-^{2}.] Not resolved; not settled in opinion; undecided, uncertain; wavering, irresolute.
1621 BP. MOUNTAGU *Diatribae* I. 163, I am as irresolued as I was before. **1623** BINGHAM *Xenophon* 85 Fighting in this sort, and irresolued what to doe, some God gaue a meanes of safetie. *a* **1631** DONNE in *Select.* (1840) 223 A divided, a distracted, a perplexed, an irresolved heart. **1666** BOYLE *Orig. Formes & Qual.* Wks. 1772 III. 38 He seems to me.. to have been irresolved, whether there were any such substances or no. **1864** JANE CAMERON *Mem. Convict* I. 179 Down the dark stairs..she went again, irresolved what to do, whether to give him up or not.
Hence **irre'solvedly** *adv.*
1680 BOYLE *Scept. Chem.* Introd. 1 Friends have thought it very strange to hear me speak so irresolvedly, as I have been wont to do, concerning those things.

irresonance (ɪ'rɛzənəns). [IR-^{2}.] Absence of resonance.
1880 BARWELL *Aneurism* 40 Downward the irresonance usually mingles with the normal aortic; further downward and to the left, with the cardiac dulness.

i'rresonant, *a.* [IR-^{2}.] Not resonant; devoid of resonance.
1899 HOWELLS *Ragged Lady* 303 A flat irresonant voice.

irre'spectable, *rare.* [IR-^{2}.] Not respectable. So **irrespecta'bility**, want of respectability.
1858 *Sat. Rev.* V. 4/1 They have been trying to enclose for their own behest the common of irrespectability. **1890** *Blackw. Mag.* CXLVIII. 76/1 His very existence as a dramatist denied point-blank by some irrespectable persons.

irre'spectful, *a. rare.* [IR-^{2}.] Not respectful, disrespectful.
1678 *Trans. Crt. Spain* 46 The refusal..and the letter.. are criminal and irrespectful proceedings. **1897** *Sat. Rev.* LXXXIII. 183/2 The most outrageous and irrespectful democrats in modern Europe.

†**irre'specting**, *a. Obs. rare*$^{-1}$. [IR-^{2}.] = IRRESPECTIVE 2.
1625 BP. MOUNTAGU *App. Caesar* 64 His meer irrespecting will.

irrespective (ɪrɪ'spɛktɪv), *a.* and *adv.* [IR-^{2}.] Not respective; without respect or regard.
†**1.** Not respectful, disrespectful. *Obs.*
1640 R. BAILLIE *Canterb. Self-convict.* 25 His followers are become so wicked and irrespective, as to..cast their owne misdeeds upon the broad back of the Prince. **1654** in *Cabbala* Suppl. 101 Irreverend and Irrespective behaviour towards my self and some of mine.
2. Characterized by disregard of particular persons, circumstances, or conditions. Now *rare*.
1650 A. A. *Repl. Sanderson* 10 Our Author hath shewn how impossible it is that any Promissory Oath can be absolute and irrespective. **1658** SOUTH *Serm.* (1744) VIII. xiii. 354 The execution of that decree in conferring grace upon one, and withholding it from the other, is equally free and irrespective. *a* **1660** HAMMOND *Wks.* I. 462 (R.) These two doctrines, 1. of Christ's dying for none but the elect, 2. of God's absolute irrespective decrees of election and reprobation, are inconvenient interpositions. *a* **1672** WREN in Gutch *Coll. Cur.* I. 229 In the matter of irrespective decrees, Election, and Reprobation. **1833** COLERIDGE *Table-t.* 14 Aug., He..oversteps, in his irrespective zeal, every decency and every right opposed to his course. **1857** BADEN POWELL *Christianity without Judaism* 44 The grand dogma of the eternal, arbitrary, irrespective, irreversible decrees.
3. Existing or considered without respect or regard to something else; without taking account *of*, independent *of*.
1694 COLLIER *Ess. Mor. Subj.* I. (1703) 7 A man does not delight in an Advantage..so much for it's own irrespective Goodness, as because others want it. *a* **1862** BUCKLE *Civiliz.* (1873) III. v. 416 The science has a speculative interest, which is irrespective of all practical considerations.
b. Now chiefly in adverbial construction, qualifying a verb expressed or understood; = IRRESPECTIVELY. Const. *of*.
1839 *Times* 15 July in *Spirit Metropol. Conserv. Press* (1840) II. 171 Their announced determination to empower Scotch Dissenters to print the bible *jure coronae*, irrespective of parliamentary sanction. **1849** R. I. WILBERFORCE *Holy Bapt.* (1850) 129 Whether..anything is ..done by God, irrespective of the instrumentality of mortals. **1860** TYNDALL *Glac.* II. xxvi. 373 Irrespective of the snow, the mere tendency of the dirt to accumulate [etc.]. **1883** C. J. WILLS *Mod. Persia* 253 The application of the funds was carried out irrespective of the religion of the applicants.

irrespectively (ɪrɪ'spɛktɪvlɪ), *adv.* [f. prec. + -LY^2.] In an irrespective manner.
†**1.** Without showing respect; disrespectfully. *Obs.*
1636 FEATLY in Spurgeon *Treas. Dav.* Ps. lxiii. 10 To see the vilest of all creatures..irrespectively hale and tear in pieces the casket which whilome enclosed the richest jewel in the world.
†**2.** In a manner showing disregard of particular persons or circumstances. *Obs.*
1624 BP. MOUNTAGU *Gagg* 178 That God, by his sole will and absolute decree, hath irrespectiuely resolued, and ineuitably decreed, some to be saued, some to be damned, from all Eternity. *a* **1660** HAMMOND *Wks.* I. 485 (R.) He is all the while convinced that all the promises..belong to him absolutely and irrespectively. *a* **1711** KEN *Hymnarium* Poet. Wks. 1721 II. 104 None doom'd to endless Flame can plead Hell irrespectively decreed. *a* **1716** SOUTH *Serm.* (1744) VII. xi. 218 Mere undeserved mercy, that places the marks of its favour absolutely and irrespectively upon whom it pleases.
3. Without regard to or consideration of other things or *of* (†*to*) something specified; independently.
1648 W. MOUNTAGUE *Devout Ess.* I. x. §4. 111 The solid meat of vertue, which is the discharge of our duty to God and man, irrespectively to humane praise. *a* **1716** SOUTH *Serm.* (1744) X. v. 138 Prosperity, considered absolutely and irrespectively, is better and more desirable than adversity. **1842** MIALL in *Nonconf.* II. 1 A conscientious and uncompromising advocacy of truth, quite irrespectively of party convenience. **1865** M. ARNOLD *Ess. Crit.* v. (1875) 192 He values them, irrespectively of the practical conveniences which their triumph may obtain for him. **1884** LD. COLERIDGE in *Law Rep.* 13 Queen's Bench Div. 691 The Court could enlarge the time irrespectively of the contract of the parties.

†**irrespectu'ose**, *a. Obs. rare*$^{-1}$. [f. IR-^{2} + **respectuose*, var. of RESPECTUOUS: cf. F. *irrespectueux* (Cotgr. 1611), It. *irrispettoso* (Florio 1611).] Not respectuous or respectful; disrespectful.
1677 GALE *Crt. Gentiles* IV. Pref., The Imputation of being contentiose, disaffected, or irrespectuose towards persons of so great estime.

irrespirable (ɪrɪ'spaɪərəb(ə)l, ɪ'rɛspɪrəb(ə)l), *a.* [f. IR-^{2} + RESPIRABLE, or a. F. *irrespirable* (1779 in Hatz.-Darm.), ad. late L. *irrespīrābil-is* (Tert.), f. *ir-* (IR-^{2}) + *respīrā-re* to RESPIRE: see -ABLE.] Not respirable; unfit for respiration.
1822–34 *Good's Study Med.* (ed. 4) III. 421 Produced by inhaling carbonic-acid or some other irrespirable exhalation. **1836** MACGILLIVRAY tr. *Humboldt's Trav.* xxviii. 410 The mud-volcanoes of South America, Italy, and the Caspian Sea, which..vomit muddy clay, naphtha, and irrespirable gases. **1876** FOSTER *Phys.* II. ii. (1879) 355 Some gases are irrespirable, on account of their causing spasm of the glottis.

irre'spondence. *rare.* [IR-^{2}.] Want of respondence; the fact of not responding (*to* something else).
1822–34 *Good's Study Med.* (ed. 4) III. 47 A morbid condition of one or more of the mental faculties or feelings, or an irrespondence of them to others. *Ibid.* IV. 107 An irrespondence in the feelings of the female to those of the male.

†**irre'sponsal**, *a. Sc. Obs.* [f. IR-^{2} + RESPONSAL *a.*] = IRRESPONSIBLE.
1637 RUTHERFORD *Let. Lady Kenmure* 7 Mar., Away, away with irresponsall Tutours, that would play me a slip. —— *Let. Marg. Fullerton* Lett. (1671) 308 They shall prove irresponsall debters: And therefore best here look ere we leap.

irresponsibility (ɪrɪspɒnsɪ'bɪlɪtɪ). [f. next: see -ITY.]
1. The quality or fact of being irresponsible.
1818 in TODD. **1850** HAWTHORNE *Scarlet L.* xx, A remarkable irresponsibility of character. **1856** SIR B. BRODIE *Psychol. Inq.* I. iii. 96 It is dangerous to admit the plea of irresponsibility for those who labour under..Moral Insanity. **1884** BRYCE in *Contemp. Rev.* Nov. 720 Irresponsibility breeds, and must always breed, laziness and selfishness.
2. Incapability of responding physically. *rare.*
1822–34 *Good's Study Med.* (ed. 4) II. 482 While ordinary purgatives are incapable of exciting evacuations from the torpitude and irresponsibility of the palsied parts, they are sufficient to occasion inflammation.

irresponsible (ɪrɪ'spɒnsɪb(ə)l), *a.* (*sb.*) Also 7 -able. [f. IR-^{2} + RESPONSIBLE. The variant in *-able* corresponds to F. *irresponsable*.]
1. Not responsible; not answerable for conduct or actions; not liable to be called to account; exempt from or incapable of legal responsibility. Also (by extension), Acting or done without a sense of responsibility.
1648 MILTON *Tenure Kings* Wks. (1847) 241/2 That no.. tyrant..may presume such high and irresponsible licence over mankind, to havoc and turn upside down whole kingdoms of men. **1681–6** J. SCOTT *Chr. Life* I. iv. (R.), What a dangerous thing..is it for men to intrust..their innocence and religion in such irresponsible hands. **1790** BURKE *Fr. Rev.* 39 They left the crown..perfectly irresponsible. **1860** MOTLEY *Netherl.* (1868) I. i. 2 Epistles which contained the irresponsible commands of this one individual. **1890** T. DE W. TALMAGE *Fr. Manger to Throne* 643 The prisoner was idiotic and irresponsible.
fig. **1871–3** EARLE *Philol. Eng. Tongue* (ed. 2) §374 Our public-school and university life is a great wellhead of new and irresponsible words.
2. Unable to respond to a legal obligation; insolvent.
1890 in *Cent. Dict.*
B. *sb.* An irresponsible person.
1894 *Voice* (N.Y.) 22 Feb., 8,000,000 workmen..would be frustrated by a body of legislative irresponsibles. **1897** *Daily News* 14 Apr. 5/4 The Greek Irresponsibles: still raiding... The Turkish Irresponsibles: becoming restive.
Hence **irre'sponsibleness**, the quality of being irresponsible, irresponsibility.
1655 in Z. Boyd *Zion's Flowers* (1855) App. 38/2 Haisard in the security of moneyes throw the irresponsablnes of debitors. **1887** G. R. LEAVITT in W. Gladden *Parish Probl.* 205 It develops self-will and self-sufficiency in the pastor, and in the people criticism and irresponsibleness.

irresponsibly (ɪrɪ'spɒnsɪblɪ), *adv.* [f. prec. + -LY^2.] In an irresponsible manner.
1847 BUSHNELL *Chr. Nurt.* II. ii. (1861) 255 They discharge the holiest responsibilities irresponsibly. **1870** EMERSON *Soc. & Solit.* vii. 147 Poems have been written between sleeping and waking, irresponsibly. **1894** CROCKETT *Lilac Sunbonnet* 16 The lambs..frisked irresponsibly about.

irresponsive (ˌɪrɪ'spɒnsɪv), *a.* [IR-^{2}.]
1. Not responsive or answering; not responding to a force or stimulus, or to something which appeals to the emotions; giving no answer to a question or inquiry.
1846 in WORCESTER, who cites *Edin. Rev.* **1866** J. H. NEWMAN *Let. Pusey* 11, I trust I am not ungrateful or irresponsive to you in this respect. **1874** CARPENTER *Ment. Phys.* (1879) App. 714 The whole of the posterior lobe is similarly irresponsive. **1886** SYMONDS *Renaiss. It., Cath. React.* (1898) VII. xiii. 226 Works to which our forefathers were unintelligibly irresponsive.
2. = IRRESPONSIBLE 1. *rare.*
1884 GLADSTONE in *Mem. Tennyson* II. xvi. 306 Irresponsive power is a dangerous thing unless curbed by wisdom.
Hence **irre'sponsiveness**, the quality or state of being irresponsive.
1864 LOWELL *Fireside Trav.* 282 A long period of sullen irresponsiveness. **1872** *Spectator* 5 Oct. 1263 Nothing can be more marvellously painted than the picture of her irresponsiveness to her husband's anxieties, fears, and hopes.

irrestrainable (ɪrɪ'streɪnəb(ə)l), *a.* [IR-^{2}.] Not restrainable; that cannot be restrained or held in check.
1643 PRYNNE *Sov. Power Parl.* I. (ed. 2) 91 An absolute, irrevocable, uncontroulable Supremacy over them, superiour to, irrestrainable, irresistable, or unalterable by their owne primitive inherent Nationall Soveraignety. **1854** *Blackw. Mag.* LXXVI. 373 The intense enthusiasm.. became almost irrestrainable. **1886** *Greatheart* II. 174 'Here's Arthur', cried the children; and irrestrainable Johnny let himself down out of the carriage to meet him.
Hence **irre'strainably** *adv.*, in a way that cannot be restrained.
1685 R. L'ESTRANGE *Observator Defended* 8 Which facultie he vindicates to himself irrestrainably. **1873** RUSKIN *Fors Clav.* xxxviii. 26 Liars and traitors..soak their way down, irrestrainably, to the gutter grating.

irrestrictive (ɪrɪ'strɪktɪv), *a.* [IR-^{2}.] Not restrictive; without restriction.
1708 *Brit. Apollo* No. 102. 1/2 If we canvass the matter in an Absolute, in an Irrestrictive Sense. **1854** J. CAIRNS *Let.* in *Life* xiv. (1895) 377 The statements regarding space and time as irrestrictive conditions.

irre'sultive, *a. rare.* [IR-^{2}.] Having no result.
1833 MRS. BROWNING *Prometh. Bound* Poems 1850 I. 157 An empty wish,—and irresultive work.

irre'suscitable, *a. rare.* [IR-^{2}.] Not resuscitable; that cannot be resuscitated or restored to life. Hence **irre'suscitably** *adv.*
1831 CARLYLE *Sart. Res.* II. ii, The inner man..sleeps now irresuscitably stagnant at the bottom of his stomach. **1843** —— *Past & Pr.* I. vi, If it prove irresuscitable. **1865** —— *Fredk. Gt.* XVII. i. (1872) VII. 6 Clamorous rage and logic, which has now sunk irresuscitably dead.

irretention (ɪrɪ'tɛnʃən). [IR-^{2}.] Lack of retention; want of the power of retaining; irretentiveness.
1827 DE QUINCEY *Last days Kant* Wks. 1854 III. 154 From irretention of memory, he could not recollect the letters which composed his name. **1963** V. NABOKOV *Gift* ii. 85 All this sick irretention of electric light.

irretentive (ɪrɪ'tɛntɪv), *a.* [IR-^{2}.] Not retentive; lacking the power of retention.
1749 SKELTON *Deism Revealed* iv. (T.), His imagination irregular and wild, his memory weak and irretentive. **1879** A. W. WARD *Chaucer* iii. 147 A manliness of tone, the direct opposite of the irretentive querulousness found in so great a number of poets. **1897** F. HALL in *Nation* (N.Y.) LXIV. 163/1 A narrow range of reading, or an irretentive memory.
Hence **irre'tentiveness**, the quality of being irretentive; want of the power of retention.
1849 *Chambers' Hist. Scot.* ix. 114 All the rest..made their escape from Newgate, which on this occasion manifested a peculiar irretentiveness. **1867** LOWELL *Rousseau* Pr. Wks. 1890 II. 261 Montaigne..reports of himself with the impartiality of a naturalist, and Boswell, in his letters to Temple, shows a maudlin irretentiveness.

†**i'rretiate**, *v. Obs.* [f. ppl. stem of L. *irrētiāre* to ensnare, f. *ir-* (IR-^{1}) + *rēte* net.] *trans.* To catch as in a net; to ensnare, entrap.
1660 *Charac. Italy* 3 You are in continual fear..by reason of those hellish snares they usually lay to irretiate and massacre strangers. **1705** *Phil. Trans.* XXV. 1914 While the said Crystal was growing or coagulating, several small Insects..were irretiated or imprisoned therein.

i'rreticence. [IR-^{2}.] The condition of being irreticent. With *an* and *plural*: an instance of this.
1919 V. WOOLF *Night & Day* xvi. 211 Rodney might begin to talk about his feelings, and irreticence is apt to be extremely painful. *a* **1941** —— *Captain's Death Bed* (1950) 112 Those irreticences and hyperboles which the voice of the speaker corrects in talk.

irreticent (ɪ'rɛtɪsənt), *a.* [IR-².] Not reticent; wanting in reticence.

1864 *Realm* 11 May 7 We English have an ineradicable distaste to coarse, irreticent, rampant vulgarity, whether in action, writing, or speech. **1932** V. WOOLF *Let. to Young Poet* 6 Therefore you could afford to be intimate, irreticent, indiscreet in the extreme.

irretraceable (ɪrɪ'treɪsəb(ə)l), *a.* [IR-².] That cannot be retraced.

1847 in CRAIG. *a* **1859** DE QUINCEY *Posth. Wks.* (1891) I. 23 An error..travels off into..spaces incalculable and irretraceable. **1876** HOLLAND *Sev. Oaks* xii. 168 He had taken a step upward and forward, a step irretraceable.

irretractable (ɪrɪ'træktəb(ə)l), *a.* [ad. late L. *irretractābil-is* (Augustine), f. *ir-* (IR-²) + *retractāre* to retract: see -BLE. Cf. F. *irretractable* (14th c. in Hatz.-Darm.).] That cannot be retracted or taken back.

1880 CHEYNE *Isaiah* (1884) I. 256 The gifts and calling of God are irretractable.

irretractile (ɪrɪ'træktɪl, -taɪl), *a.* [IR-².] Not retractile; incapable of being retracted or drawn back.

1855 H. SPENCER *Princ. Psychol.* (1872) II. VI. xii. 156 Of bodies that resist in different modes..we have..the Retractile and Irretractile.

irretrievable (ɪrɪ'triːvəb(ə)l), *a.* [IR-².] That cannot be retrieved; irrecoverable; irreparable.

1695 [implied in IRRETRIEVABLY]. **1702** DE FOE *Shortest Way w. Dissenters* Misc. (1703) 423 With an absolute, and, as they suppose, irretrievable Victory. **1712** STEELE *Spect.* No. 423 ¶5 The Condition of Gloriana, I am afraid, is irretrievable. **1788** GIBBON *Decl. & F.* xlviii. (1869) III. 49 He perceived the irretrievable decline of his brother's health. **1821** WELLINGTON *Disp.*, etc. Oct. (1867) I. 195 Whether we shall.. give up the government to the Whigs and Radicals, or, in other words, the country in all its relations, to irretrievable ruin? **1871** H. AINSWORTH *Tower Hill* II. vii, The time approached when the irretrievable step must be taken.

Hence **irretrieva'bility**, **irre'trievableness**, the quality of being irretrievable.

1727 BAILEY vol. II, *Irretrievableness.* **1847** DE QUINCEY *Secr. Soc.* Wks. 1857 VII. 269 The fatal irretrievability of errors in early life. **1882** ANNIE THOMAS *Allerton Towers* I. viii. 137 The boldness and irretrievability of the step he has taken.

irretrievably (ɪrɪ'triːvəblɪ), *adv.* [f. prec. + -LY².] In an irretrievable manner; so as to be irretrievable; beyond recovery or repair; irreparably.

1695 WOODWARD *Nat. Hist. Earth* IV. ix. (1723) 215 It must needs have been all irretrievably lost and useless to Mankind. **1766** GOLDSM. *Vic. W.* xxxi, Miss Wilmot.. perceiving that her fortune was irretrievably lost. **1869** M. PATTISON *Serm.* (1885) 190 The Church of Rome has irretrievably broken with knowledge.

†**irre'turnable**, *a. Obs.* [f. IR-² + RETURN *v.* + -ABLE.] **a.** That cannot be returned or turned back. **b.** Admitting of no return; from which it is impossible to return.

1563 *Mirr. Mag.*, *Hastings* lxxxii, Forth irreturnable flyeth the spoken word, Be it in scoffe, in earnest, or in bourd. **1579** J. STUBBES *Gaping Gulf* B j, His kingdom cam to naught, and the whole people suffered a transmigration irretornable in Assiria. **1600** E. BLOUNT tr. *Garzoni's Hosp. Incur. Fooles* 36 To enter the irreturnable shadowes of god Ditis his house.

[**irrevalent**, a frequent perversion of IRRELEVANT.]

irrevealable (ɪrɪ'viːləb(ə)l), *a. rare*⁻⁰. [IR-².] That cannot be revealed. So **irre'vealably** *adv.*

1847 in CRAIG.

†**irrevealed**, *a. Obs.* [IR-².] Not revealed or disclosed; unrevealed.

1610 DONNE *Pseudo Martyr* v. 12 Obscure and irrevealed things. **1628** GAULE *Pract. The.* (1629) 107 The irreuealed Will of God. *a* **1631** DONNE *Paradoxes* (1652) 63 So deep and so irreveald.

irreverence (ɪ'rɛvərəns). [ad. L. *irreverentia*, f. *irreverent-em* IRREVERENT: see -ENCE. Cf. F. *inrévérence* 13th c., *irrévérence* 14th c. (Hatz.-Darm. and Littré).]

1. The fact or quality of being irreverent; absence or violation of reverence; disrespect to a person or thing held sacred or worthy of honour.

c **1340** HAMPOLE *Prose Tr.* 10 If he swere be Cryste wondes or blude..it sounes in irreu[er]ence of Ihesu Cryste. **1382** WYCLIF *Ecclus.* xxvi. 14 Fro alle irreuerence of the eȝen of hir waar [**1388** Be thou war of al vnreuerence of hir iȝen]. *c* **1386** CHAUCER *Pars. T.* ¶329 Irreuerence is whan men do nat honour there as hem oghte to doon. *c* **1440** *Jacob's Well* 94 Whanne þou iapyst, & scornyst, & dost irreuerence to god & to his sayntes. **1651** DAVENANT *Gondibert* Pref. 3 If it be not irreverence to record their opinion. **1684** *Contempl. St. Man* II. x. (1699) 236 The irreverence and great incivility towards God in a Mortal Sin. *a* **1779** WARBURTON *Serm.* IX. ii. (R.), Turnus..is, on the very first appearance, marked out by his irreverence to the priestess of Juno. **1861** WRIGHT *Ess. Archæol.* II. xxi. 176 A feeling of irreverence for things sacred. **1871** TYNDALL *Fragm. Sc.* (1879) I. xi. 353 Lowering the moral tone, and exciting irreverence and cunning.

b. With *an* and *pl.* An instance of this; an irreverent act or utterance.

a **1744** POPE (J.), Attributes..which it was an irreverence to omit. **1873** LD. HOUGHTON *Monogr.* 20 Make yourself quite easy in the possession of my irreverences. **1899** A. E. GARVIE *Ritschlian Theol.* VI. ii. 344 The spiritual dissection of some theologians is..an impertinence, one could even say an irreverence.

2. The condition of not being reverenced; state of dishonour.

1647 CLARENDON *Hist. Reb.* I. §151 The irreverence and scorn the Judges were justly in. *Mod.* To be held in irreverence.

irreverend (ɪ'rɛvərənd), *a.* [IR-².]

1. Not reverend; unworthy of veneration.

[**1494**: see IRREVERENT 1.] **1748** RICHARDSON *Clarissa* (1811) VIII. xli. 158 Her matted, griesly hair, made irreverend by her wickedness. **1879** SWINBURNE *Stud. Shaks.* ii. (1880) 110 That most irreverend father in God, Friar John, belongs to a higher class in the moral order of being.

¶**2.** Formerly often misused for, or confused with, IRREVERENT.

[Arising from the earlier use of IRREVERENT in both senses.]

1576 GRINDAL *Let. to Queen* 20 Dec. in Strype *Life* (1710) II. App. 80 If eny Man use immodest Speech, or irreverend Gesture or Behaviour. **1597** HOOKER *Eccl. Pol.* v. xlvii. §4 That irreverend confidence wherewith true humilitie can neuer stand. **1721** STRYPE *Eccl. Mem.* an. 1556 (R.) A certain learned person..impugned some part of what he had spoken, urging that he had used irreverend speech. **1796** W. TAYLOR in *Monthly Mag.* II. 465 To preserve their monumental altars within precincts where they will be guarded from irreverend mutilation. **1849** ROCK *Ch. of Fathers* I. ii. 79 Handled with a rough, irreverend touch.

Hence **i'rreverendly** *adv.* (in quots. misused for *irreverently*).

1655 H. VAUGHAN *Silex Scint.* Pref. (1858) 7 So irreverendly bold, as to dash Scripture with their impious conceits. **1738** WARBURTON *Div. Legat.* App. 58 He irreverendly aims at wit with the face of an Irish inquisitor.

irreverent (ɪ'rɛvərənt), *a.* Also 5 inr-. [ad. L. *in-*, *irreverent-em*, f. *in-*, *ir-* (IR-²) + *reverēns*, *-ēntem*, pr. pple. of *reverērī* to REVERE. Cf. F. *irrévérent* (15th c.).]

In OF. *reverent* represented L. *reverendus*; hence, in English also, *reverent* and *irreverent* were orig. used in the sense of *reverend*, *irreverend*, which were of later introduction: see REVERENT.]

†**1.** = IRREVEREND. *Obs.*

1494 FABYAN *Chron.* VII. 644 To company wᵗ symple & inreuerent persones.

2. Not reverent; wanting in reverence or veneration; showing disrespect to a sacred or venerable person or thing.

1550 VERON *Godly Sayings* (1846) 13 That no man shuld ..loke in the Arke..wyth prophane & irreverente eies. **1667** MILTON *P.L.* XII. 101 Th' irreverent Son Of him who built the Ark, who for the shame Don to his Father, heard this heavie curse, Servant of Servants, on his vitious Race. **1746** AKENSIDE *Hymn Naiads* 288 Of highest Jove, Irreverent. **1864** *Dublin Univ. Mag.* 612 'Parker is an old hunks', was the irreverent reply. **1871** B. TAYLOR *Faust* (1875) I. Notes 281 The irreverent irony of Mephistopheles.

irreverential (ɪrɛvə'rɛnʃəl), *a.* [f. L. *irreverentia* IRREVERENCE + -AL¹.] Not reverential; characterized by irreverence; irreverent.

1652 *Rec. Dingwall Presb.* (Sc. Hist. Soc.) 242 Sentenced for his irreverentiall words against his Minister. **1675** *Case Quakers conc. Oaths defended* 15 Irreverential and common Swearing. **1848** LONGF. in *Life* (1891) II. 137 The old General Washington *dodge*—pardon the irreverential word—of thanking the donor before reading the book. **1861** WILSON & GEIKIE *Mem. E. Forbes* vi. 181 The irreverential portraits of academic dignitaries which were weekly displayed at the College gate.

Hence **irreve'rentialism**, irreverential practice. **irreve'rentially** *adv.*, irreverently.

1675 *Case Quakers conc. Oaths defended* 15 Swearing rashly, prophanely, irreverentially. **1850** DE QUINCEY *Wks.* (1871) XVI. 54 To complain of irreverentialism through an irreverential word. **1855** F. M. BROWN in W. M. Rossetti *Ruskin, Rossetti*, etc. (1899) 44 Stephens speaking irreverentially on the subject of Guggum.

irreverently (ɪ'rɛvərəntlɪ), *adv.* [f. IRREVERENT + -LY².] In an irreverent manner; without reverence; disrespectfully.

1494 FABYAN *Chron.* VII. 516 They .vi. Corpsys..were than put in a carte & drawen vnto a house of Seynt Katheryne, & there buryed inreuerently. **1550** VERON *Godly Sayings* (1846) 12 The people which loked in it irreverently were slayne. **1658** *Hist. Mem. K. James* 25 Surprised that he spake irreverently of King Henry the eighth. **1716** ADDISON *Freeholder* No. 6 ¶8 Those who speak irreverently of the Person to whom they have sworn Allegiance. **1828** D'ISRAELI *Chas. I*, I. iv. 71 A land where the haughtiest Don trembled to touch irreverently the meanest friar. **1859** GEO. ELIOT *A. Bede* ii, Nor was it a 'spotty globe', as Milton has irreverently called the moon.

irreversible (ɪrɪ'vɜːsɪb(ə)l), *a.* Also 7-8 -able. [IR-².] That cannot be reversed.

1. That cannot be undone, repealed, or annulled; unalterable, irrevocable.

1630 PRYNNE *Anti-Armin.* 114 The euerlasting, the irreuersible Decrees of Election. **1649** BP. HALL *Cases Consc.* IV. vi. 457 That since marriage once passed, is irreversible, we may have some breathing-time betwixt our promise and accomplishment. **1677** W. SHERLOCK *Answ. T. Dawson* 23 He is under an irreversible Decree. **1728** R. MORRIS *Ess. Anc. Archit.* 7 The irreversable Decree of Fate. **1867** BRIGHT *Sp.*, *Amer.* 29 June (1876) 144 A triumph which has pronounced the irreversible doom of slavery. **1885** *Law Times* LXXVIII. 183/2 It was so taken [to the House of Lords] and the previously irreversible decisions of the Queen's Bench were reversed.

2. That cannot be turned backwards, upside down, or in the opposite direction. (In quot. 1821, That cannot be upset or overturned.)

1821 LAMB *Elia* Ser. I. *Valentine's Day*, Delightful eternal commonplaces..having your irreversible throne in the fancy and affections. **1864** BOWEN *Logic* xii. 398 It is Causal relation, and, as such, is absolute and unchangeable, for it is irreversible even in thought. **1870** YEATS *Nat. Hist. Comm.* 28 The irreversible order of deposits.

3. *Physical Chem.* Of a colloid or colloidal system: incapable of being changed from a gelatinous state into a sol by a reversal of the treatment which turns the sol into a gel or gelatinous precipitate. Of a change of state: characterized by this property.

[**1899** *Jrnl. Physiol.* XXIV. 180 *(heading)* Colloidal mixtures which form irreversible molecular aggregates when they pass into the gel state.] **1900** *Proc. R. Soc.* LXVI. 110 A large number of colloidal solutions..belong to the class of irreversible colloidal mixtures. **1915** M. H. FISCHER tr. *Ostwald's Handbk. Colloid-Chem.* 40 When a change in the state of a colloid may be reversed by reversing the conditions which brought that change about, it is said to be 'reversible'. Thus when a colloid which has been precipitated by a salt goes back into solution on removal of the salt, the colloid change is said to be 'reversible'. On the other hand, if this does not occur it is 'irreversible'. **1930** J. C. WARE *Chem. Colloidal State* ix. 204 When a reversible colloid is evaporated to dryness and later stirred into the fluid which constituted the external phase, a very complete dispersion will again result. With an irreversible colloid, a suspension will not result by mixing with the solvent but one of the regular methods for the preparation of the colloidal state must be applied. **1930** *Engineering* 18 July 61/1 Gels which cannot be converted into sols are 'irreversible'. **1959** K. J. MYSELS *Introd. Colloid Chem.* iv. 82 These different behaviors are quite generally called reversible and irreversible flocculations.

Hence **irreversi'bility**, **irre'versibleness**, the quality or character of being irreversible.

1625 DONNE *Serm.* lxvi. 673 In the anguish of that dissolution, in the sorrows of that valediction, in the irreversiblenesse of that transmigration. **1678** J. J[ONES] *Brit. Ch.* 441 The perpetuity and irreversibleness of this decree. **1732** STACKHOUSE *Hist. Bible* v. ii. (T. Suppl.), A precedent of the irreversibleness of oaths. **1824** *Blackw. Mag.* XV. 520 The irreversibility of the judgments. **1873** B. STEWART *Conserv. Energy* v. 142 The irreversibility of the process puts a stop to all this.

irreversibly (ɪrɪ'vɜːsɪblɪ), *adv.* [f. prec. + -LY².] In an irreversible manner; so as not to admit of being reversed; unalterably, irrevocably.

1626 JACKSON *Creed* VIII. iv. §3 Whether they were irreversibly cast out of God's gratious presence before their accomplishment of..their project against man, is not so certaine. **1750** JOHNSON *Rambler* No. 16 ¶5, I am now.. known to be an Author and..irreversibly condemned to all the miseries of high reputation. *a* **1842** ARNOLD *Lect. Mod. Hist.* ii. (1878) 140 Taking their shape for good or for evil, and sometimes irreversibly.

irrevertible (ɪrɪ'vɜːtɪb(ə)l), *a. rare.* [f. IR-² + L. *revertī* to return + -IBLE.] **a.** Incapable of reverting (to the former owner). **b.** Irreversible, unalterable.

1725 KIRKPATRICK *Relig. Ord. Norwich* 129 Unexpirable, or at least irrevertible, leases. **1822** *Blackw. Mag.* XI. 165 The irrevertible tendency to monarchy of a great, a chivalrous, and a territorial people.

†**irre'vincible**, *a. Obs. rare.* [f. IR-² + REVINCIBLE, ad. late L. *revincibilis* (Tertull.).] That cannot be overcome or refuted; invincible, incontrovertible.

a **1746** J. LEWIS *Life Fisher* (1855) I. xvi. 269 Bede.. proves by irrevincible arguments, that those fourteen years are to be counted from the conversion of Paul.

irrevisable (ɪrɪ'vaɪzəb(ə)l), *a. rare.* [IR-².] That cannot or must not be revised.

1884 *Leeds Mercury* 15 Aug. 5/1 The Republic has been declared inviolable, irrevisable.

[**i'rrevitable**: see IRRENITIBLE.]

irrevocability (ɪˌrɛvəkə'bɪlɪtɪ). [f. next + -ITY: cf. F. *irrévocabilité* (1534 in Hatz.-Darm.).] The quality, character, or condition of being irrevocable; incapability of being recalled or revoked.

1613 F. ROBARTS *Reven. Gosp.* 1 He enacteth it..in more then Mede and Persian irrevocabilitie. **1837** DICKENS *Pickw.* xxxi, Confirmation of the irrevocability of his intention. **1884** *Pall Mall G.* 25 Sept. 5/2 The new agreement..If it is to share the fate of other 'irrevocabilities'..will not be worth much.

irrevocable (ɪ'rɛvəkəb(ə)l), *a.* Also 5 inrevocable, 7-8 irre'vokable. [ad. L. *irrevocābil-is*, f. *ir-* (IR-²) + *revocābilis*, f. *revocāre* to recall: perh. in part through F. *irrévocable* (1357 in Godef. *Compl.*). *Irrevokable* follows Eng. *revoke*.

1589 PUTTENHAM *Eng. Poesie* II. xii[i]. (Arb.) 130 Not content with the vsual Normane or Saxon word, would conuert the very Latine and Greeke word into vulgar French, as to say innumerable for innombrable, reuocable,

irreuocable, .. and such like, which are not naturall Normans nor yet French, but altered Latines.]

That cannot be recalled.

1. That cannot be called, brought, fetched, or taken back; that is beyond recall or recovery. (In reference to past time or events often with admixture of sense 2.)

1382 Wyclif *Ezek.* xxi. 5 For I the Lord ledde out my swerd of his sheethe irreuocable [*gloss* or that may not be clepid aȝen]. **1490** Caxton *Eneydos* xi. 42 Alas he .. hath my loue entierly wyth hym, wherof inreuocable a yefte I doo make to hym. **1596** Spenser *F.Q.* vi. ii. 15 Sith that he is gone irrevocable. **1607** Rowlands *Guy Warw.* 74 Irrevocable time is posting gone. **1706** Rowe *Ulysses* iv. i. 1768 She is lost—most certain—gone irrevocable. **1865** Kingsley *Herew.* xii, She sat .. half wishing that the irrevocable yesterday had never come. **1866** Liddon *Bampt. Lect.* vi. (1875) 345 Regarded historically these events belong to the irrevocable past.

2. That cannot be revoked, repealed, annulled, or undone; unalterable, irreversible. (The prevailing sense.)

1490 Caxton *Eneydos* iv. 20 Bi the sentence irreuocable of theym [the gods]. **1575–85** Abp. Sandys *Serm.* (Parker Soc.) 303 As a seal and sure pledge of his irrevocable promise. **1600** Shaks. *A.Y.L.* i. iii. 85 Firme, and irreuocable is my doombe, Which I haue past vpon her, she is banish'd. **1692** Washington tr. *Milton's Def. Pop.* v. Wks. (1851) 141 The Laws of the Medes and Persians; which Laws were irrevocable. **1791** Paine *Rights of Man* (ed. 4) 145 An hereditary aristocracy, assuming and asserting indefeasible, irrevokable rights and authority, wholly independent of the Nation. **1862** Merivale *Rom. Emp.* xxii. (1865) III. 33 This tenant-right was equivalent to actual possession; it was perpetual and irrevocable. **1880** Mrs. Forrester *Roy & V.* I. 81 You need feel certain that her decision of to-night is irrevocable.

irrevocableness (ɪˈrɛvəkəb(ə)lnɪs). [f. prec. + -ness.] The quality or character of being irrevocable.

1649 Roberts *Clavis Bibl.* 493 The incurablenesse of their sins, and irrevocablenesse of their judgements. **1753** Richardson *Grandison* (1781) VI. xxxii. 226 The irrevocableness of the event. **1859** Geo. Eliot *A. Bede* xlviii, Adam was forcing Arthur to feel more intensely the irrevocableness of his own wrong-doing.

irrevocably (ɪˈrɛvəkəblɪ), *adv.* [f. as prec. + -ly².] In an irrevocable manner; so as to be irrevocable.

1. So as not to admit of being called or brought back; beyond recall or recovery.

1611 Cotgr., *Irrevocablement*, irreuocably, vnrecallably. **1627** May *Lucan* i. (1631) 16 Irrevocably doe the people flye. **1742** Young *Nt. Th.* v. 402 Nor mark the *much* irrevocably laps'd, And mingled with the sea. **1855** Thackeray *Newcomes* Concl., Tho' he has disappeared as irrevocably as Eurydice.

2. So as not to admit of being revoked or annulled; unalterably, irreversibly.

1608 D. T. *Ess. Pol. & Mor.* 26b, Ligarius .. is by me already irrevocably condemn'd. **1644** Bp. Maxwell *Prerog. Chr. Kings* ix. 100 They were totally and irrevocably invested with all power. **1765** Blackstone *Comm.* I. vii. 252 The king may make a treaty with a foreign state, which shall irrevocably bind the nation. **1810** *House of Lancaster* I. 103, I remained firmly and irrevocably fixed in my first resolution. **1841** Macaulay *Ess., Hastings* (1887) 678 The whole party was irrevocably pledged to a prosecution.

irrevoluble (ɪˈrɛvəljuːb(ə)l), *a. rare.* [f. ir-² + revoluble, ad. L. *revolūbilis* that may be rolled back.] That has no finite period of revolution, whose revolution is never completed; of infinite circuit.

1641 Milton *Reform.* ii. (1851) 71 In supereminence of beatifick Vision progressing the datelesse and irrevoluble Circle of Eternity. **1876** Farrar *Marlb. Serm.* xxviii. 284 The exceeding immortality—'the dateless and irrevoluble circle of eternity'—is for all who can say, 'I have finished my race'.

irrheˈtorical, *a. rare*—⁰. [ir-².] 'Not rhetorical; inelegant in phrase; unpersuasive' (Smart, 1836).

†**iˈrride**, *v. Obs.* [ad. L. *irrīdē-re* to laugh at, f. *ir-* (ir-¹) + *rīdēre* to laugh.] *trans.* To laugh at; to deride.

1637 Mede *Ep., to Twisse* Wks. (1672) iv. lxxi. 850 Did I merit to be irrided for having found out I know not what Mystery? *a* **1648** Ld. Herbert *Hen. VIII* (1683) 489 Luther, Stermius, and others .. irrided it publickly.

irrigable (ˈɪrɪgəb(ə)l), *a.* [f. L. *irrigā-re* to irrigate: see -ble: so mod.F. *irrigable* (*Dict. Acad.* 1878).] Capable of being irrigated; susceptible of irrigation.

1844 *Blackw. Mag.* LVI. 193 To employ the irrigable land on the banks of the canal for agricultural purposes. **1895** *Athenæum* 14 Sept. 354/1 There is a considerable amount of irrigated country paying well, and an enormous amount of country easily irrigable.

Hence **ˈirrigably** *adv.*, so as to be irrigable.

1893 *Scribner's Mag.* XIII. 94/1 A ribbon of irrigably level land.

†**ˈirrigate**, *ppl. a. Obs.* In 5 irrigat. [ad. L. *irrigāt-us*, pa. pple. of *irrigāre* to irrigate.] Irrigated, watered.

? *a* **1412** Lydg. *Two Merchants* 24 But yeer by yeer the soil is irrigat, And ouyrflowyd with the flood of Nyle.

irrigate (ˈɪrɪgeɪt), *v.* [f. L. *irrigāt-*, ppl. stem of *irrigāre* to lead water to, to water, f. *ir-* (ir-¹) + *rigāre* to wet, moisten, water.]

1. *trans.* To supply with moisture; to moisten, wet. (Now *rare* in the general sense, and regarded as *transf.* from 2a.)

1615 Crooke *Body of Man* 285 The thirde vse is to irrigate or moysten the sides of the wombe. **1688** Boyle *Final Causes Nat. Things* iv. 158 Not that they think the blood .. unfit to irrigate the parts with that vital liquor. **1708** J. Philips *Cyder* ii. 65 With which .. to irrigate Their dry-furr'd Tongues. **1898** *Allbutt's Syst. Med.* V. 3 Only the larger bronchi are irrigated by the bronchial arteries.

2. *spec.* **a.** To supply (land) with water by means of channels or streams passing through it; also said of such channels or streams (natural or artificial); to water. (The prevailing sense.)

1623 Cockeram, *Irrigate*, to water ground, or so. **1706** Phillips s.v., A Country irrigated by several fine Rivers. **1834** Pringle *Afr. Sk.* iv. 180 The orchard .. and garden ground .. were irrigated by the waters of a small mountain-rill which were collected and led down in front of the house by an artificial canal. **1852** Conybeare & Howson *St. Paul* (1862) I. x. 332 Its waters still irrigate the suburban gardens of the Athenians. **1872** Yeats *Growth Comm.* 37 The country was .. artificially irrigated by a network of canals.

b. *Med.* To supply (a part, a wound, etc.) with a constant flow or sprinkling of some liquid, for the purpose of cooling, cleansing, or disinfecting.

1876 *Clin. Soc. Trans.* IX. 123 Stuffed with sponges, and sutures left unfastened for three hours, during which time it was irrigated with carbolic acid.

3. *fig.* To refresh or make fruitful as with a supply of moisture.

1686 Horneck *Crucif. Jesus* xiii. 276 The wine of angels .. inebriates their understandings, irrigates the spirits of men made perfect. **1823** Byron *Juan* xiii. v, But then they have their claret and Madeira To irrigate the dryness of decline. **1873** Hamerton *Intell. Life* x. iii. (1875) 352 Her mind irrigated their minds, which would have remained permanently barren without that help and refreshment.

4. *intr.* To drink; to take a drink. *slang* (chiefly *U.S.*).

1856 'J. Phoenix' *Phœnixiana* 104 [He] was invited by the urbane proprietor to irrigate. *c* **1880** in Thornton *Amer. Gloss.* (1912) II. App. 975 'Stranger, do you irrigate?' 'If you mean drink, sir, I do not.' **1905** A. Adams *Outlet* xxi. 298 Sponsilier .. called every one to the bar to irrigate. **1911** E. M. Clowes *On Wallaby* viii. 202 There was even a further decrease in drunkenness, people having no money, I suppose, for what out here [*sc.* Victoria] they call 'irrigating'.

Hence **ˈirrigated, ˈirrigating** *ppl. adjs.*

1669 W. Simpson *Hydrol. Chym.* 287 The earth becomes again satiated by irrigating showers. **1846** J. Baxter *Libr. Pract. Agric.* (ed. 4) I. 353 Irrigated pasture, or best water meadow. **1892** *Athenæum* 30 July 153/3 He .. set them to work digging an irrigating canal. **1895** *Westm. Gaz.* 1 July 1/3 The fertilising and irrigating effect which the Darwinian hypothesis has exercised in all departments of contemporary thought.

irrigation (ɪrɪˈgeɪʃən). [ad. L. *irrigātiōn-em* watering, n. of action from *irrigāre* to irrigate: cf. F. *irrigation* (15th c. in Godef. *Compl.*).] The action or process of irrigating.

1. The action of supplying or fact of being supplied with moisture; a moistening or wetting. (Now *rare* in *gen.* sense, and regarded as *transf.* from 2a.)

a **1618** Sylvester *Tobacco Battered* 503 It dries the Body, robs of irrigation The thirsty parts. **1641** French *Distill.* i. (1651) 11 Humectation or Irrigation, is a sprinkling of moisture upon any thing. *a* **1693** Aubrey *Lives, Bacon* (1898) I. 84 His lordship would, when it rayned, take his coach (open) to receive the benefit of irrigation. **1809** *Europ. Mag.* LV. 20 The streets and lanes .. were in a complete state of irrigation.

2. *spec.* **a.** The action of supplying land with water by means of channels or streams; the distribution of water over the surface of the ground, in order to promote the growth and productiveness of plants.

1626 Bacon *Sylva* §600 The Sixth Helpe of Ground is by Watering and Irrigation. **1664** Evelyn *Sylva* Advt., I did not altogether compile this Work for the sake of our Ordinary Rustics, but for the more Ingenious.. . That this may yet be no prejudice to the meaner capacities let them read for .. irrigation, watering. **1807** Vancouver *Agric. Devon* (1813) 18 This valley .. is supplied by a constant stream for the purposes of irrigation. **1825** J. Nicholson *Operat. Mechanic* 232 A machine designed to raise water to a great height for the irrigation of land. **1862** Stanley *Jew. Ch.* (1877) I. iv. 72 Peasants .. drawing up the buckets of water from the river for the irrigation of the fields above.

b. *Med.* The application of a constant stream or shower of some liquid to a part of the body, *e.g.* to allay inflammation, or to cleanse and disinfect an ulcer, etc. (In quot. 1632 *concr.* A liquid for this purpose; an embrocation, lotion.)

1612 Woodall *Surg. Mate* Wks. (1653) 272 Irrigation .. is an aspersion of humidity upon things that are to be dissolved, that so they may the more easily deliquate. **1621** Burton *Anat. Mel.* ii. iv. i. v, Irrigations of the head, with water lillies, lettice, violets, camomile, &c. **1632** tr. *Bruel's Praxis Med.* 39 Make an irrhigation for the head with sweete waters. **1842** Abdy *Water Cure* (1843) 68 Cold half baths, and irrigation afterwards. **1887** *Syd. Soc. Lex., Irrigation*, .. the continuous application of a stream of simple or antiseptic fluid to a part so as to keep it wet with a constant change of the moisture.

3. *fig.* Cf. irrigate *v.* 3.

a **1660** Hammond *Wks.* IV. 574 (T.) That every of us fructify in some proportion answerable to our irrigation. **1884** J. Hall *Chr. Home* 69 Such spiritual irrigation we must use in the home for the good of one another.

4. *attrib.* **irrigation canal, ditch**; **irrigation-wheel**, a wheel by means of which land is irrigated.

1910 *Encycl. Brit.* XIV. 841/2 When a river partakes of the nature of a torrent, .. it is impossible to construct a system of *irrigation canals without very costly engineering works. **1923** R. Fry *Let.* 21 May (1972) II. 536 A vast flat plain perfectly green with corn, .. and all run by irrigation canals from the Ebro. **1880** C. R. Markham *Peruv. Bark* 479 In June the people were occupied with the *irrigation channels. **1870** Gov. Hunt *Own Story* (MS.) 1 *Irrigation ditches were dug for as much of the land as could be covered with water. **1902** O. Wister *Virginian* vi. 77 One of the irrigation ditches ran under the fence from the hay-field to supply the house with water. **1958** [see acequia]. **1974** J. Thomson *Long Revenge* vi. 67 The only possible cover was that provided by the tall reeds that grew in the deeper irrigation ditches. **1877** *Daily News* 5 Oct. 4/4 Having erected new *irrigation tanks in India. **1883** F. Day *Indian Fish* 50 (Fish. Exh. Publ.) To watch these enormous reptiles feeding in the river below the *irrigation weir which impedes the upward ascent of breeding fish. **1864** J. A. Grant *Walk Across Afr.* 410 Mr. Aipperly had .. made friends with the natives by assisting to put up their *irrigation-wheels. **1858** J. B. Norton *Topics* 184 The whole revenue being immediately dependent on the *irrigation works.

Hence **irriˈgational** *a.*, belonging to irrigation; **irriˈgationist**, a person interested in irrigation.

1877 *Athenæum* 1 Dec. 695/3 Public works .. both roads and irrigational. **1887** *Detroit Free Press* 21 May 2/4 Of interest to irrigationists. **1894** *Naturalist* 58 A product of the sewage farm irrigational proceedings. **1894** *Voice* (N.Y.) 18 Oct. 3/4 The Denver congress of irrigationists.

irrigative (ˈɪrɪgeɪtɪv), *a.* [f. as irrigate *v.* + -ive.] Serving to irrigate; of or pertaining to irrigation.

1861 *Jrnl. R. Agric. Soc.* XXII. ii. 443 Many irrigative canals. **1887** W. G. Palgrave *Ulysses* 158 Mr. Fergusson does not err in assigning the palm of irrigative skill to the Turanian races.

irrigator (ˈɪrɪgeɪtə(r)). [a. late L. *irrigātor* (Augustine), agent-n. from *irrigāre* to irrigate.]

1. One who or that which irrigates.

1829 G. Stephens (*title*) Practical Irrigator and Drainer. **1846** J. Baxter *Libr. Pract. Agric.* (ed. 4) II. 13 The irrigator should admit the water at the time and for the periods which experience points out as the best. **1885–6** Spurgeon *Treas. Dav.* Ps. cxlvii. 8 God makes the .. clouds the irrigators of the mountain meadows.

2. *Med.* A contrivance for irrigation (sense 2b).

1887 in *Syd. Soc. Lex.* **1894** *Lancet* 3 Nov. 1032 Efficient washing out of all the peritoneum .. with an aseptic solution by means of an irrigator or similar instrument. **1896** *Allbutt's Syst. Med.* I. 451 Hypodermic syringe, irrigator .. should be at hand.

irrigatorial (ˌɪrɪgəˈtɔərɪəl), *a.* [f. L. stem *irrigāt-* + -ory + -al¹.] Relating to irrigation. So **irrigatory** (ˈɪrɪgətərɪ) *a.* in same sense.

1867 Ld. Napier in Sir S. Northcote *Life* (1890) I. ix. 291 The localities fit for irrigatorial purposes. **1884** *Chamb. Jrnl.* 13 Dec. 796 All Sicilian agricultural and irrigatory terms recall them.

†**irriguate** (ɪˈrɪgjuːeɪt), *v. Obs.* [f. L. *irrigu-us* (see next) + -ate³.] *trans.* = irrigate *v.* So †**iˈrriguate** *ppl. a.*, irrigated, well-watered (cf. irrigate *a.*).

1632 Lithgow *Trav.* v. 176 Not farre from the irriguate plaine of Darmille. *Ibid.* vii. 316 Now to discourse of Nylus, this flood irriguateth all the low playnes. *Ibid.* x. 499 Even so is melting Tweed and weeping Tiviot .. that irriguat the fertile fields. **1670** *Lex Talionis* 26 The Circulation of the Blood, whereby every part is irriguated and nourished.

irriguous (ɪˈrɪgjuːəs), *a.* Now *rare.* [f. L. *irrigu-us* supplied with water, f. *in-*, *ir-* (ir-¹) + *rigu-us* watered, from stem of *rigāre* to wet, water.]

1. Irrigated; moistened, bedewed, wet; *esp.* of a region or tract of land: Well-watered, moist, watery. Also *fig.*

1651–3 Jer. Taylor *Serm. for Year* Ded., Like Gideon's Fleece, irriguous with a dew from Heaven, when much of the vicinage is dry. **1667** Milton *P.L.* iv. 255 The flourie lap Of som irriguous Valley. **1735** Somerville *Chase* iv. 349 Skim with wanton Wing th' irriguous Vale. **1749** Bp. Lavington *Enthus. Meth. & Papists* (1754) I. ii. 63 Opposite Vicissitudes of Soul, the irriguous and dry, the anxious and secure. **1802** *Brookes' Gazetteer* (ed. 12) s.v. *Lomond*, Herds of cattle feed in the irriguous vallies at its base.

2. Having the quality of irrigating; affording a supply of water or moisture; watering, bedewing. Also *fig.*

1684 tr. *Bonet's Merc. Compit.* xvi. 560 If .. the Scorbutick Infection break into the Brain .. and very much infect the irriguous Liquor of either Province. **1762–71** H. Walpole *Vertue's Anecd. Paint.* (1786) IV. 254 The refreshing hollows of mountains, near irriguous and shady founts. **1801** *Trans. Soc. Arts* XIX. 176 The Grubs were seen lying in irriguous channels. **1861** Clough *Ess. Class. Metres, Elegiacs* i. 6 A lordly river .. Through the meadows sinuous, wandered irriguous.

Hence **iˈrriguousness** (Bailey vol. II, 1727).

†**irrisible** (ɪˈrɪzɪb(ə)l), *a. Obs. rare.* [ad. late L. *irrīsibil-is* (Augustine), f. *irrīdēre* to laugh at, IRRIDE.] Ridiculous; worthy of derision.

1767 A. CAMPBELL *Lexiph.* 37 *note*, That the natives of one of our three kingdoms are really no better than irrational, irrisible, four-legged animals, and considered by their fellow-subjects, and the legislature in no other capacity.

irrision (ɪˈrɪʒən). Now *rare* or *arch.* [ad. L. *irrīsiōn-em*, n. of action from *irrīdēre* to laugh at, IRRIDE. Cf. F. *irrision* (Cotgr. 1611).] The action of laughing at a person or thing in scorn or contempt; derision, mockery.

1526 *Pilgr. Perf.* (W. de W. 1531) 97 b, He was illuded and scorned with garmentes of irrisyon. **1579** TWYNE *Phisicke agst. Fort.* I. lxix. 95 b, They seeke to auoyde infamie and irrision. **1649** JER. TAYLOR *Gt. Exemp.* II. Ad Sect. xii. 100 To abstain from all mockings of our neighbour, not giving him appellatives of scorne, or irrision. **1696** BP. PATRICK *Comm. Exod.* x. (1697) 168 Some look upon it as an Irrision or a jeer. **1833** H. J. ROSE *Prelim. Obs. Middleton's Grk. Article* (1858) p. xxiv, Stallbaum also says that the omission of the article denotes irrision. **1858** HOGG *Life Shelley* II. xi. 385 An indecent irrision of the sacred character of the loverpoet.

irrisor (ɪˈraɪsə(r)). *rare.* [a. L. *irrīsor*, agent-n. from *irrīdēre*: see prec.]

1. One who laughs at another; a mocker, a derider.

1739 J. HILDROP *Regul. Free-thinking* 23 They shall then be admitted into the highest Rank or Degree of Risors, called the Irrisors, answering to the Degree of Senior Sophs; and shall be allowed not only to laugh and be witty, but to insult upon proper Occasions.

2. *Zool.* A bird of the genus *Irrisor* or family *Irrisoridæ*, natives of Africa, so called from their noisy cry; a wood-hoopoe.

irrisory (ɪˈraɪsərɪ), *a. rare.* [f. L. type **irrīsōri-us*, f. *irrīsor*, *irrīsōr-em*: see prec. and -ORY.] Having the character of deriding or mocking.

1824 LANDOR *Imag. Conv.* Wks. 1846 I. xxxviii. 244/2, I wish that, even there, you had been less irrisory, less of a pleader. **1829** *Ibid.* II. 146/1 The young men continued in their irrisory mood.

irrit, variant of IRRITE *a. Obs.*, void.

irritability (ˌɪrɪtəˈbɪlɪtɪ). [ad. L. *irrītābilitās*, f. *irrītābilis*: see next and -ITY. Cf. F. *irritabilité* (Haller, 1756).] The quality or state of being irritable.

1. The quality or state of being easily annoyed or excited to anger or impatience; proneness to vexation or annoyance; petulance.

1791 BOSWELL *Johnson* Mar. an. 1753, The gloomy irritability of his existence was more painful to him than ever. **1828** SCOTT *F.M. Perth* xvi, His second subject of conversation..seemed rather delicate for the smith's present state of irritability. **1837** HT. MARTINEAU *Soc. Amer.* III. 26 The irritability of their vanity has been much exaggerated. **1847** EMERSON *Repr. Men, Shakespeare* Wks. (Bohn) I. 354 The perilous irritability of poetic talent. **1881** W. COLLINS *Bl. Robe* I. vi. 205 There was not only irritability, there was contempt..in her tone.

2. *Path.* Of a bodily organ or part: The condition of being excessively or morbidly excitable or sensitive to the contact or action of anything.

1785 ALEX. GRANT (*title*) Observations on the Use of Opium, in Diseases supposed to be owing to morbid irritability. **1789** W. BUCHAN *Dom. Med.* (1790) 315 From a peculiar weakness, or too great an irritability of the bowels. **1875** B. MEADOWS *Clin. Observ.* 51 He is all right, save slight irritability and scurf in the scalp.

3. *Physiol.* and *Biol.* The capacity of being excited to vital action (*e.g.* motion, contraction, nervous impulse, etc.) by the application of an external stimulus: a property of living matter or protoplasm in general, and characteristic in a special degree of certain organs or tissues of animals and plants, esp. muscles and nerves: see IRRITABLE 3.

[**1751** J. G. ZIMMERMAN (*title*) Dissertatio Physiologica de Irritabilitate, quam publice defendet.] **1755** R. WHYTT (*title*) Physiological Essays..On the Sensibility and Irritability of the Parts of Men and other Animals; occasioned by Dr. Haller's Treatise on these Subjects. **1788** SIR J. E. SMITH in *Phil. Trans.* Abr. XVI. 421 (*heading*) On the Irritability of Vegetables. **1794** G. ADAMS *Nat. & Exp. Philos.* IV. xlix. 349 Physicians talk of the irritability of our nervous system. **1805** A. CARLISLE in *Phil. Trans.* XCV. 3 When muscles are capable of reiterated contractions and relaxations, they are said to be alive, or to possess irritability. **1846** J. BAXTER *Libr. Pract. Agric.* (ed. 4) I. 115 Some leaves possess the property, when acted upon by certain bodies, of moving. This is called, in reference to leaves, *Irritability*. **1862** DARWIN *Fertil. Orchids* v. 172 The irritability of the labellum in several distantly-allied forms is highly remarkable. **1898** *Allbutt's Syst. Med.* V. 401 Instances of that response of living matter, as a manifestation of 'irritability', to chemical changes in its surroundings which is denoted by the term 'chemiotaxis'.

irritable (ˈɪrɪtəb(ə)l), *a.* [ad. L. *irrītābilis*, f. *irrītāre* IRRITATE *v.*[1]: see -BLE. Cf. F. *irritable* (1547 in Hatz.-Darm.).] Capable of being irritated; susceptible of irritation.

1. Readily excited to anger or impatience; easily ruffled or annoyed.

1662 H. MORE *Philos. Writ.* Pref. Gen. 10 It could never enter into my minde that he was either irritable or propitiable by the omitting or performing of any mean and insignificant services. **1779–81** JOHNSON *L.P., Pope* Wks. IV. 101 He was irritable and resentful. **1841** ELPHINSTONE *Hist. Ind.* II. 47 His ill health made him more suspicious and irritable than ever. **1877** ERICHSEN *Surg.* I. 5 Persons of an irritable and anxious mind do not bear operations so well as those of a more tranquil mental constitution. **1879** F. W. ROBINSON *Coward Consc.* I. xi, I have lived in..the irritablest of families.

2. **a.** Readily excited to action; highly responsive to stimulus; (of a bodily organ or part), Excessively or morbidly excitable or sensitive (see IRRITATE *v.*[1] 3).

1791 BURKE *App. Whigs* Wks. VI. 8 Accused of provoking irritable power to new excesses. **1800** *Med. Jrnl.* IV. 78 When its excretion is by any means obstructed, it produces insensible and irritable constitutions. **1804** ABERNETHY *Surg. Obs.* 59 The destruction of the irritable decayed surface [of a tooth]. **1875** B. MEADOWS *Clin. Observ.* 27 He had an irritable stomach and was..much annoyed with acidity. **1885** H. JAMES *Lit. Tour France* xxxiv. 220 Our modern nerves, our irritable sympathies, our easy discomforts and fears, make one think (in some relations) less respectfully of human nature. **1887** MRS. EWING *Dandel. Clocks* 13 One cannot help having an irritable brain, which rides an idea to the moon and home again..whilst some folks are getting the harness of words on to its back. **1897** *Allbutt's Syst. Med.* III. 751 The tongue is slightly furred or is red and irritable looking.

b. ***irritable heart***, a syndrome characterized by shortness of breath on exertion, palpitation, fatigue, chest pain, and dizziness, and believed to be psychosomatic; 'soldier's heart'.

1864 J. M. DA COSTA *Med. Diagn.* iv. 280 These statements are not intended to be final. They are but a very short summary of the results of a large number of observations which I have had an opportunity of making on these cases of 'irritable heart', and which elsewhere..will be laid before the profession. **1922** [see *cardiological* adj. s.v. CARDIO-]. **1971** CONN & HORWITZ *Cardiac & Vascular Dis.* I. xxiv. 600/1 This condition has been known by many names, such as irritable heart, soldier's heart, disordered action of the heart, functional heart disease, effort syndrome, and neurocirculatory asthenia.

3. *Physiol.* and *Biol.* Of an organ, tissue, etc. of an animal or plant: Capable of being excited to vital action by the application of some physical stimulus; said *esp.* of muscles and nerves, as subject respectively to contraction and to motor or sensory impulse under the influence of the proper external forces.

1793 BEDDOES *Calculus*, etc. 181 The irritable fibres in the same system have not all the same degree of irritability. They have different degrees of capacity for the irritable principle. **1875** BENNETT & DYER *Sachs' Bot.* 784 In a smaller number of instances periodically motile foliage-leaves..are irritable to touch or concussion. **1878** FOSTER *Phys.* III. i. 394 A sensory nerve in its simplest form may be regarded as a strand of eminently irritable protoplasm.

ˈ**irritableness.** *rare.* [f. prec. + -NESS.] = IRRITABILITY.

1805 in W. PERRY *Eng. Dict.* **1825** E. IRVING *Last Days* 255 No irritableness of an afflicted body, nor weariness of bed-ridden age. **1857–8** SEARS *Athan.* xi. 92 This excessive irritableness of the body.

irritably (ˈɪrɪtəblɪ), *adv.* [f. as prec. + -LY[2].] In an irritable manner; with irritation; petulantly.

1855 in HYDE CLARKE *Eng. Dict.* **1880** OUIDA *Moths* I. ix. 249 'Oh! you don't believe me', she said irritably, 'ask anybody'. **1896** MRS. CAFFYN *Quaker Grandmother* 204 All this made her feel generally cross, and irritably resentful.

ˈ**irritament.** Now *rare* or *Obs.* [ad. L. *irrītāment-um* a provocative, f. *irrītāre* IRRITATE *v.*[1]: see -MENT.] Something that excites or provokes an action, feeling, or state; an exciting cause; a provocative, an incentive; an irritant.

1634 W. TIRWHYT tr. *Balzac's Lett.* (vol. I.) 91 The Irritaments of Despaire. **1647** WARD *Simp. Cobler* 5 Perillous irritaments of carnall and spirituall enmity. **1800** *Med. Jrnl.* IV. 274 There is no specific irritament, which does not prove for the whole constitution either asthenic or sthenic. **1844** GLADSTONE *Glean.* (1879) III. 27 He was wrong; for the bearing of his argument would have been this; Sacraments are irritaments of faith, therefore baptise those who have it not, in order that they may be aroused to conceive it.

irritancy[1] (ˈɪrɪtənsɪ). [f. IRRITANT *a.*[1]: see -ANCY.] Irritating quality or character; irritation, annoyance.

1831 CARLYLE *Sart. Res.* III. xii, Not without a certain irritancy and even spoken invective. **1849** *Tait's Mag.* XVI. 754 The source of great irritancy and vexation to the Colonists. **1900** *Westm. Gaz.* 6 Apr. 8/2 A superior altitude ..adds an irritancy to the monition tendered.

ˈ**irritancy**[2]. *Rom., Civil,* and *Sc. Law.* [f. IRRITANT *a.*[2]: see -ANCY.] The fact of rendering, or condition of being rendered, null and void.

1681 STAIR *Inst. Law Scot.* (1693) I. xiii. §14. 122 By payment at the Barr, it was allowed to be purged, even though the Party after the Irritancy got Possession. **1773** ERSKINE *Inst. Law Scot.* II. v. §27 Where the irritant clause was conceived in these words, 'That the feu-right should fall, if two years duty happened to run into a third', which was long the usual style, the irritancy was not incurred by our older practice till the whole of the third year's duty was due. **1861** W. BELL *Dict. Law Scot.* s.v., The irritancy of a right is its forfeiture in consequence of some neglect or contravention... A lease may be dissolved during its currency by the operation of a legal as well as of a conventional irritancy. **1880** MUIRHEAD *Gaius* Dig. 613 *Irritancy of a testament.* A testament was irritated when the testator suffered *capitis deminutio.* **1886** *Pall Mall G.* 9 Oct. 11/1 Guilty of that heinous Scotch crime known as 'irritancy of the lease'.

irritant (ˈɪrɪtənt), *a.*[1] and *sb.* [ad. L. *irrītānt-em*, pr. pple. of *irrītāre* IRRITATE *v.*[1]: cf. F. *irritant* (17th c. in Hatz.-Darm.).]

A. *adj.*

†1. That 'irritates' or stirs up (see IRRITATE *v.*[1] 1 b); exciting, provocative. *Obs.*

1636 W. SCOT *Apol. Narr.* (1846) 65 The occasion or irritant cause of the alteration of the Church Government.

2. Causing irritation, physical or (rarely) mental; irritating. Chiefly in *Path.*, of poisons, etc.

1828 WEBSTER, *Irritant*, irritating. **1834** *Penny Cycl.* II. 100/1 Irritant poisons, such as arsenic. **1875** H. C. WOOD *Therap.* (1879) 493 The symptoms.., as in other irritant poisoning, vary within certain limits. **1885** *Manch. Exam.* 21 Jan. 4/7 They..have had no irritant or factious opposition to encounter.

B. *sb.* An irritant substance, body, or agency; in *Path.* a poison, etc. which produces irritation; in *Physiol.* and *Biol.* anything that stimulates an organ to its characteristic vital action. Also *fig.* in reference to mental irritation.

1802 *Med. Jrnl.* VIII. 11 A glass of mustard whey, at times, is a good nutritive irritant. **1842** A. COMBE *Physiol. Digestion* (ed. 4) 148 It..is always excited to discharge itself by the introduction of food or other irritants. **1863** *Cornh. Mag.* VII. 345 Any poison, even those which, like the metallic irritants, are with the greatest difficulty dislodged. **1877** ROSENTHAL *Muscles & Nerves* 30 The influences which cause the contraction of the muscle..are called irritants. *fig.* **1862** HELPS *Organ. Daily Life* 73 A persecution which pinches, but does not suppress, is merely an irritant, and not an absorbent.

ˈ**irritant**, *a.*[2] *Rom., Civil,* and *Sc. Law.* [ad. L. *irrītānt-em*, pr. pple. of *irrītāre* to make void, IRRITATE *v.*[2]: cf. F. *irritant* (1762 in Dict. Acad.).] Rendering null and void.

irritant clause: 'a clause by which certain prohibited acts specified in a deed, if committed by the person holding under the deed, are declared to be void and null' (W. Bell *Dict. Law Scot.* 1861).

1592 *Acts Sederunt* 27 Nov. (1790) 19 In all tyme cuming, thay will juge and decide upon clausis irritant, conteinit in contractis, takis, infeftments, bandis, and obligationis. **1603** HAYWARD *Answ. Doleman* v. M iv, The States elected Henry Duke of Anjowe for their king, with this clause irritant; That if hee did violate any point of his oath, the people should owe him no allegeance. **1773** [see IRRITANCY[2]]. **1799** J. ROBERTSON *Agric. Perth* 82 The leases..are clogged with so many arbitrary covenants, capricious articles and irritant clauses, that they may be broke, whenever the landlord pleases. **1868** *Act 31 & 32 Vict.* c. 101 §9 It shall not be necessary..to insert..prohibitory, irritant, and resolutive clauses.

irritate (ˈɪrɪteɪt), *v.*[1] [f. L. *irrītāt-*, ppl. stem of *irrītā-re* to incite, excite, provoke, irritate. Cf. IRRITE *v.*]

†1. *trans.* To stir up, excite, provoke, incite, rouse (a person, etc.) to some action. Const. *to*, *into*, or *inf. Obs.* (or merged in 2.)

1531 ELYOT *Gov.* I. xix, Suche daunsis, whiche..dyd with vnclene motions or countinances irritate the myndes of the dauncers to venereall lustes. **1626** BACON *Sylva* §315 Cold maketh the Spirits vigorous, and irritateth them. **1651** BAXTER *Inf. Bapt.* Apol. 8 Least my touching that Controversie..might irritate him to fall upon it. **1795** BURKE *Let. Sir H. Langrishe* 26 May, Whatever tends to irritate the talents of a country..is of infinite service to that formidable cause. **1841** W. SPALDING *Italy & It. Isl.* III. 43 His successor soon contrived to irritate into open resistance the new prince.

†**b.** To stir up, excite, provoke, give rise to (an action, feeling, etc.); to excite to greater intensity, heighten, aggravate. *Obs.*

1607–12 BACON *Ess., Praise* (Arb.) 354 To much magnifying of Man..doth irritate Contradiccion, and procure Envye and skorne. **1634** SIR T. HERBERT *Trav.* 149 With us drink irritates quarrels. **1732** ARBUTHNOT *Rules of Diet* 318 Oily Substances in themselves do not irritate or provoke Diarrhœas. **1738** G. LILLO *Marina* III. ii. 45 Yet trouble, in her, irritates devotion. **1776** GIBBON *Decl. & F.* vi. (1869) I. 110 The disorder of his mind irritated the pains of his body. **1824** R. HALL *Let.* Wks. 1841 V. 539 Premature attempts to console only irritate the sorrows they are meant to heal.

2. To excite to impatient or angry feeling; to exasperate, provoke; to vex, fret, annoy, ruffle the feelings of.

1598 FLORIO, *Iritare*, to irritate, or prouoke to ire. **1604** R. CAWDREY *Table Alph.*, *Irritate*, to make angry. *a* **1649** DRUMM. OF HAWTH. *Hist. Scot.* (1655) 1 Irritated by the misedemeanour of his children. **1725** POPE *Odyss.* v. 186 Dismiss the man, nor irritate the god. **1749** FIELDING *Tom Jones* XVI. iv, Let me beg you, Madam,..not to irritate his Worship. **1847** MRS. A. KERR *Hist. Servia* 319 He did not wish to irritate the enemy with insults.

3. *Path.* To excite (a bodily organ or part) to morbid action, or to abnormal condition; to bring into a morbidly excited condition, or produce an uneasy sensation in.

1674 tr. *Martiniere's Voy. N. Countries* 111 From a great cold I had upon me,..which had irritated my pituitary glandule. **1732** ARBUTHNOT *Rules of Diet* 260 By their Salts they irritate the Solids. **1836** J. M. GULLY *Magendie's*

Formul. (ed. 2) 27 The physicians..assert that it does not irritate the stomach, causes no headache, vertigo, nausea. **1845** BUDD *Dis. Liver* 256 It may inflame or irritate..the parts of the intestine with which it is brought into contact.

4. *Physiol.* and *Biol.* To excite (an organ of an animal or plant) to some characteristic action or condition, as motion, contraction, or nervous impulse, by the application of a stimulus; to stimulate to vital action. (See IRRITABLE 3, IRRITABILITY 3.)

1803 *Med. Jrnl.* IX. 131, I endeavour to irritate the three branches of the fifth pair, by means of Galvanism. **1874** CARPENTER *Ment. Phys.* I. ii. §68 (1879) 71 Irritating the soles, by tickling or otherwise. **1875** DARWIN *Insectiv. Pl.* ii. 20 The central glands of a leaf were irritated with a small camel hair brush.

'irritate, *v.*[2] *Rom.*, *Civil*, and *Sc. Law.* [f. L. *irritāt-*, ppl. stem of *irritā-re* to make void, f. *irrit-us* invalid: see IRRITE *a.*] *trans.* To make void, render of no effect, nullify; = DEFEAT *v.* 6 (the corresponding term in Eng. Law).

1605 *Answ. Supposed Discov. Rom. Doctr.* 42 Superiors.. may irritate the oaths and vows also of their subiects. **1660** R. COKE *Justice Vind.* Pref. 4 Nor is there any thing more abominable, then to conceive that the Acts of mens Wills should irritate the Law of Nature. **1726** AYLIFFE *Parergon* 308 Such Will is irritated and made void. **1874** *Act 37 & 38 Vict.* c. 94 §4 All rights and remedies..for irritating the feu *ob non solutum canonem.* **1880** MUIRHEAD *Gaius* II. §148 A testament that..has..been broken or irritated.

† **'irritate,** *ppl. a.*[1] *Obs.* [ad. L. *irrītāt-us*, pa. pple. of *irrītāre* (see IRRITATE *v.*[1]); but also capable of being viewed as a shortening of *irritated.*] = IRRITATED.

1626 BACON *Sylva* §709 The Heat becommeth more Violent, and Irritate; And thereby expelleth Sweat. **1712** A. MONCRIEFF in Young *Life* (1849) 26 Man being in this fallen, undone, and miserable condition, God's justice was irritate.

† **'irritate,** *ppl. a.*[2] *Obs.* [ad. L. *irritāt-us*, pa. pple. of *irritāre*: see IRRITATE *v.*[2]] Rendered void or of no effect.

1600 F. CLARK in *Archpriest Controv.* (Camden) I. 164 All confessions heard by vs [would be] voyd and irritat.

irritated ('ɪrɪteɪtɪd), *ppl. a.* [f. IRRITATE *v.*[1] + -ED[1].] Stirred up, excited (*obs.*); exasperated, provoked, annoyed; stimulated to vital action, etc.: see the verb.

1595 DANIEL *Civ. Wars* IV. xxxxix, Then when proud-growne the irritated bloud Enduring not it selfe, it selfe assaild. **1678** *Trans. Crt. Spain* 47 Your Majesty should labour to appease these two irritated spirits. **1776** GIBBON *Decl. & F.* xiv. I. 410 Not to expose himself to the discretion of an irritated conqueror. **1875** BENNETT & DYER tr. *Sachs' Bot.* 797 The contraction of the irritated filament begins at the moment of contact.

Hence **'irritatedly** *adv.*, in an irritated manner; with an expression of irritation or annoyance.

1873 MRS. WHITNEY *Other Girls* xxiii. (1876) 316 'Don't tell me what!' cried Bel irritatedly. **1883** MISS BROUGHTON *Belinda* III. IV. ii. 177 He looks up irritatedly at her.

irritating ('ɪrɪteɪtɪŋ), *ppl. a.* [f. IRRITATE *v.*[1] + -ING[2].] That irritates, in various senses: see the verb.

1707 FLOYER *Physic. Pulse-Watch* 58 These particular Secretions supply both quantity of Humours and irritating Qualities. **1727-46** THOMSON *Summer* 1114 The dash of clouds, or irritating war Of fighting winds. **1789** W. BUCHAN *Dom. Med.* (1790) 307 Medicines of an acrid or irritating nature. **1859** GEO. ELIOT *A. Bede* iv, A sort of wail, the most irritating of all sounds where real sorrows are to be borne, and real work to be done.

Hence **'irritatingly** *adv.*, in an irritating way.

1865 E. C. CLAYTON *Cruel Fortune* II. 71 Lady Charrington slightly raised her shoulders, and smiled irritatingly. **1882** *Athenæum* 1 July 10 Such a passage as the following is irritatingly dogmatic.

irritation (ɪrɪ'teɪʃən). [ad. L. *irrītātiōn-em*, n. of action from *irrītāre* IRRITATE *v.*[1]: cf. F. *irritation* (14-15th c. in Godef. *Compl.*).] The action of irritating, or condition of being irritated.

† **1.** The action of stirring up or provoking to activity; incitement. *Obs.* exc. as *transf.* from other senses.

1589 PUTTENHAM *Eng. Poesie* I. xix. (Arb.) 56 Therefore was nothing committed to historie, but matters of great and excellent persons and things that the same by irritation of good courages..might worke more effectually. **1612-15** BP. HALL *Contempl., O.T.* XIV. vii, If it had not beene for his proud irritation, the people had in the morning before ceased from that bloudy pursuit of their brethren. *a* **1859** DE QUINCEY (Webster 1864), The whole body of the arts and sciences composes one vast machinery for the irritation and development of the human intellect.

2. Excitement of anger or impatience; exasperation, provocation, vexation, annoyance.

1703 DK. QUEENSBERRY in Ellis *Orig. Lett.* Ser. II. IV. 238 One sort of people are pleased, and the other have got no irritation. **1796** BURKE *Corr.* (1844) IV. 380 Jacobinism which arises from penury and irritation, from scorned loyalty and rejected allegiance. **1818** A. RANKEN *Hist. France* VI. I. 58 Any new taxation..might excite general irritation. **1875** JOWETT *Plato* (ed. 2) V. 6 The Lacedaemonian expresses a momentary irritation at the accusation.

3. *Path.* (and *Med.*) Excitement of a bodily part or organ to excessive sensitiveness or morbid action; the resulting condition.

1685 BOYLE *Enq. Notion Nat.* vi. Wks. V. 212 The fibres ..being distended or vellicated by the plenty or acrimony of the peccant matter, will, by that irritation, be brought to contract themselves vigorously. **1702** J. PURCELL *Cholick* (1714) 113 Subject to the greatest Irritations, Heart-burnings, and Vomiting. **1799** *Med. Jrnl.* II. 126 If it allay ..the cough and irritation of the lungs. **1842** A. COMBE *Physiol. Digestion* (ed. 4) 119 In some states of the stomach ..even farinaceous food excites acrimony and irritation. **1876** BARTHOLOW *Mat. Med.* (1879) 536 External irritation, utilized for the relief or cure of internal maladies, is entitled *counter-irritation.*

4. *Physiol.* and *Biol.* The inducement of some vital action or condition (as motion, contraction, nervous impulse) in an organ, tissue, etc. of an animal or plant by the application of a stimulus.

1794 E. DARWIN *Zoon.* I. xviii. §15. 209 We come now to those motions which depend on irritation. *Ibid.* 210 Not only those parts of the system, which are always excited by internal stimuli,..but the organs of sense also may be more violently excited into action by the irritation from internal stimuli, or by sensation, during our sleep than in our waking hours. **1855** BAIN *Senses & Int.* I. ii. §20 (1864) 57 When irritation is applied to the hemispheres, as by pricking or cutting. **1875** BENNETT & DYER tr. *Sachs' Bot.* 782 Periodic movements of the mature parts of plants and movements dependent on irritation. *Ibid.* 784 In the case of irritable stamens..the insects that visit the flowers cause the irritation. *a* **1899** J. CAIRD *Fundamental Ideas Chr.* II. xxi. 276 Irritations and molecular changes of tissue are transformed into the feeling of shimmering light or ringing sound.

irritative ('ɪrɪteɪtɪv), *a.* [f. as IRRITATE *v.*[1] + -IVE.]

1. Having the quality of stirring up or exciting to action; now in *Physiol.* or *Biol.* Having the property of stimulating to vital action, *e.g.* to sensuous perception, muscular contraction, etc.

1686 GOAD *Celest. Bodies* I. xiii. 65 Invested with Power, not Illuminative..but Irritative also. **1794** E. DARWIN *Zoon.* I. xx. §7. 234 The irritative ideas of objects..are perpetually present to our sense of Sight. **1796** *Ibid.* II. 678 Those things, which increase the exertions of all the irritative motions, are termed incitantia. **1822** GOOD *Study Med.* (1834) III. 401 Hysteria is a disease of the irritative fibres, hypochondrias of the sentient.

2. Having the quality of causing mental irritation; tending to irritate; annoying, irritating.

1878 *Fraser's Mag.* XVIII. 168 Let us put away utterly all irritative thoughts. **1881** MRS. C. PRAED *Policy & P.* II. 208 Tones which were specially irritative to Mr. Longleat's temper.

3. *Path.* Characterized by or accompanied with irritation of the system or of some organ.

1807 *Med. Jrnl.* XVII. 7 He laboured under a considerable degree of irritative fever. **1873** T. H. GREEN *Introd. Pathol.* (ed. 2) 139 Irritative conditions of the bone and periosteum are often attended by a large formation of new bone. **1888** FAGGE & PYE-SMITH *Princ. Med.* (ed. 2) I. 70 The immediate effect of wounds in producing what was called irritative fever was confounded with the later appearance of pyæmia.

irritator ('ɪrɪteɪtə(r)). *rare.* [a. L. *irrītātor*, agent-n. from *irrītāre* IRRITATE *v.*[1]] One who or that which irritates.

1855 in HYDE CLARKE *Eng. Dict.* **1889** *Chamb. Jrnl.* Jan. 36/2 'You didn't think I was going to sit here..?' the irritator asked.

irritatory ('ɪrɪteɪtərɪ, -ətərɪ), *a. rare.* [f. as IRRITATE *v.*[1] + -ORY.] Causing irritation; irritative.

a **1656** HALES *Gold. Rem.* (1688) 59 Some irritatory and troublesome Humour. *Ibid.* (1673) 285 Nothing hinders wounds from cicatrising, more then..keeping things irritatory about the orifice of the wound.

† **irrite,** *a. Obs.* Also irrit. [ad. L. *irrit-us* invalid, f. *ir-*, *in-* (IR-[2]) + *ratus* established, valid. Prob. through AF. *irrit* (Stat. 5 Edw. II), obs. F. *irrite* (1365 in Godef.).] Void, of no effect.

1482 in *Eng. Gilds* (1870) 311 To ordeyn..that the seid letters patentes..and all thyng perteynyng to the same Gilde and fraternyte, be irrite, cassed, adnulled, voide, and of noo force nor effect. **1600** J. MELVILL *Diary* (1842) 356 It sould nocht be forgot and maid irrit. **1623** T. ADAMS *Barren Tree* Wks. 1861 II. 180 These irrite, forceless, bug-bear excommunications. **1657** HAWKE *Killing is M.* 12 To make void and irrite all their former and glorious victories. **1741** W. WILSON *Contn. Def. Reform. Princ. Ch. Scot.* (1769) 469 They have made thy word and law irrit and of no avail.

† **irrite,** *v. Obs.* Also 6 yrryte. [a. F. *irrite-r* (14th c. in Littré), ad. L. *irrītāre* to irritate.] = IRRITATE *v.*[1] (in various senses).

c **1450** *Mirour Saluacioun* 1627 Irrited haue I thyne ire o swete godde of clemence. **1522** MORE *De Quat. Noviss.* Wks. 76/1 Rather..than blunt forth rudely, and yrryte them to anger. **1574** NEWTON *Health Mag.* 16 We must beware.. that we doo not irrite our Stomack and provoke an appetite with fine Junkets and delicious Sauces. **1661** LOVELL *Hist. Anim. & Min.* 336 Vellicating the beginning of the nerves, contracting them, and irriting to expulsion.

† **i'rroborate,** *v. Obs. rare*-[0]. [f. (doubtful) L. *irrōborāre*, f. *ir-* (IR-[1]) + *rōborāre* to strengthen.]

1623 COCKERAM, *Irroborate*, to make strong. **1656** in BLOUNT *Glossogr.*

† **'irrogate,** *v. Sc. Law. Obs.* [f. ppl. stem of L. *irrogāre* to propose against, impose, inflict, f. *ir-* (IR-[1]) + *rogāre* to ask, demand.] *trans.* To impose (a penalty). So † **'irrogate** *ppl. a.* (used as *pa. pple.*); † **irro'gation.**

1592 *Sc. Acts Jas. VI* (1597) §152 Quhilkis haue not bene, nor yit ar observed be reason that there is na penaltie irrogat to the persones contraveeners thereof. **1623** COCKERAM, *Irrogate*, to impose. *Irrogation*, an imposition. **1666** LD. FOUNTAINHALL in M. P. Brown *Suppl. Decis.* II. 426 It came to be debated..if a judge might mitigate the punishment which is imposed by law, *vid.* hanging, and confiscate his moveables, or irrogat a mulct, in lieu thereof.

irrorate ('ɪrərət), *a. Zool.*, esp. *Entom.* [ad. L. *irrōrāt-us* bedewed, pa. pple. of *irrōrāre*: see next.] = Irrorated: see next 2.

1826 KIRBY & SP. *Entomol.* IV. 285 *Atom*, a very minute dot. *Irrorate*, sprinkled with atoms, as the earth with dew.

irrorate ('ɪrəreɪt), *v.* [f. ppl. stem of L. *irrōrā-re* to bedew, f. *ir-* (IR-[1]) + *rōrāre* to drop dew, from *rōs*, *rōrem* dew.]

† **1.** *trans.* To wet or sprinkle as with dew; to bedew, besprinkle; to moisten. *Obs.*

1623 COCKERAM, *Irrorate*, to sprinckle, to moysten. **1629** PARKINSON *Gard. Pleas.* viii. 20 Doe not give them too much water to over-glut them, but temperately to ir[r]orate, bedew or sprinkle them. **1661** LOVELL *Hist. Anim. & Min.* 237 They are to be fryed and irrorated with the juyce of Oranges. **1676** tr. *Garencieres' Coral* 44 A plant..irrorated or steeped in common water.

2. *Zool.*, esp. *Entom.* In *pa. pple.* **'irrorated**: sprinkled minutely (*with* dots).

1843 HUMPHREYS *Brit. Moths* I. 85 The caterpillar is dusky, irrorated with black spots. **1882** *Entomol. Mag.* Mar. 220 The mature larva is of a dark pea-green colour, thickly irrorated with slightly raised black dots.

irroration (ɪrɒ'reɪʃən). [n. of action from IRRORATE *v.*: cf. F. *irroration* (1762 in *Dict. Acad.*).]

† **1.** A sprinkling or wetting as with dew; a bedewing, besprinkling, moistening. *Obs.*

1623 COCKERAM, *Irroration*, a sprinckling, a moystning. **1638** RAWLEY tr. *Bacon's Life & Death* (1651) 41 To the Irroration of the Body, much use of sweet things is profitable. **1672** *Phil. Trans.* VII. 5033 A confused irroration of the external surface, without any ebullition. **1784** tr. *Spallanzani's Dissert.* (L.), If..the irroration should be interrupted, the portion of eggs then excluded will be barren.

2. *Zool.*, esp. *Entom.* A sprinkling of minute dots or spots of colour.

1843 HUMPHREYS *Brit. Moths* I. 124 Of a nearly uniform pale brownish buff, without irrorations.

irrotational (ɪrəʊ'teɪʃənəl), *a. Dynamics.* [IR-[2].] Not rotational; characterized by absence of rotation: said of fluid motion in which each elementary or infinitesimal part of the fluid has no rotation about its own axis.

1875 CLERK MAXWELL in *Encycl. Brit.* III. 44/1 The motion of a fluid is said to be irrotational when it is such that if a spherical portion of the fluid were suddenly solidified, the solid sphere so formed would not be rotating about any axis. **1880** G. H. DARWIN in *Nature* XXII. 95/2 Two vortices exercise very remarkable influences on one another, which are due to the irrotational motion of the parts of the fluid outside the vortices. **1883** O. LODGE *ibid.* XXVII. 330/1 Portions [of ether] either at rest or in simple irrotational motion.

Hence **irro'tationally** *adv.*

1881 MAXWELL *Electr. & Magn.* I. 117 A vector which is distributed irrotationally in all cases of electric equilibrium. **1881** *Nature* XXIII. 475/2 A mass of fluid revolving irrotationally inside an imperfectly elastic cylindrical case.

irrotationality (ˌɪrəʊteɪʃə'nælɪtɪ). *Physics.* [f. IRROTATIONAL *a.* + -ITY.] The property or state of being irrotational.

1960 *McGraw-Hill Encycl. Sci. & Technol.* VII. 402/1 For an incompressible fluid, the continuity equation..is div v = 0; hence, combining this relation with irrotationality gives Laplace's equation, div (grad ϕ) = 0. **1967** *Progress Aeronaut. Sci.* VIII. 6 The velocity field is determined by the equation of continuity and the condition of irrotationality.

† **i'rrotulate,** *ppl. a. Obs.* [f. ppl. stem of med.L. *ir-*, *inrotulāre* (Du Cange), f. *ir-*, *in-* (IR-[1]) + *rotul-us* ROLL.] Entered upon a roll or list; enrolled.

1594 *Zepheria* xxxviii, Yet, 'mongst acquaintance who their faith haue crackt, My name thou findest not irrotulat!

irrour, irrous, variants of IROUR, -OUS, *Obs.*

† **i'rroyal,** *a. Obs.* [IR-[2]. Cf. *illoyal.*] Not royal; not befitting a king.

1648 *Pet. East. Assoc.* 18 Was the pawning of the Jewels of the Crown so Irroyall?

irrubrical (ɪ'ruːbrɪkəl), *a.* [IR-[2].] Not rubrical; contrary to the rubric.

1846 WORCESTER cites *Ch. Ob.*

† **'irruent**, *a. Obs. rare*$^{-0}$. [ad. L. *irruent-em*, pr. pple. of *irruĕre* to rush in or upon.]
1656 BLOUNT *Glossogr.*, *Irruent*, running hastily, or rushing in violently.

† **'irrugate**, *v. Obs.* [f. ppl. stem of L. *irrūgāre* to wrinkle, f. *ir-*, *in-* (IR-^{1}) + *rūgāre* to wrinkle, from *rūga* a wrinkle, a crease.] *trans.* To wrinkle. So † **'irrugation** (*obs. rare*$^{-0}$.)
1566 PAINTER *Pal. Pleas.* (1569) I. F iv, That the swelling of their body, might not irrugate and wrinckle their faces. **1656** BLOUNT *Glossogr.*, *Irrugation*, a wrinkling, or making wrinkles.

† **'irrumate**, *v. Obs. rare*$^{-0}$. [f. L. *irrumāre* to give suck, f. *ruma* teat, dug.]
1623 COCKERAM, *Irrumate*, to sucke in.

irrumation (ɪrʊ'meɪʃən). [f. ppl. stem of L. *irrumāre* to practise fellatio on or L. *irrumātiō*, *-ōnis* the action of the verb.] (See quot. 1901.) Also **'irrumate** *v. trans.*, to practise irrumation on (a person); **'irrumator**, one who practises irrumation.
1887 L. C. SMITHERS tr. *Forberg's Man. Classical Erotology* iii. 72 To put the member in erection into some one's mouth is called to irrumate, a word, which in its proper sense means to give the breast. *Ibid.* 90 Irrumators are less feared by married men. *Ibid.* 97 Erasmus, in his *Sayings*,.. does not deny that in his time the obscene practice of irrumation was still known. **1888** tr. *Priapeia* 39 If thou shalt attempt a third theft,.. I will sodomise and irrumate thee. **1901** A. ALLINSON tr. *Rosenbaum's Plague of Lust* II. xxi. 3 Very much more abominable and repulsive still is the habit of Irrumation (..to erect the *penis* and insert it into the mouth of another person). *Ibid.* 20 The *irrumator*..takes the *fellator* between his opened thighs. **1947** P. L. HARRIMAN *Dict. Psychol.* 187 *Irrumation*, the act of obtaining an orgasm by the mouth; fellatio or penilingus.

† **i'rruminating**, *a. Obs.* [IR-^{2}.] Not ruminating; that does not chew the cud.
1631 BRATHWAIT *Whimzies*, *Zealous Bro.* 117 That uncleane and irruminating beast, a pig.

i'rrumpent, *a. rare*$^{-0}$. [ad. L. *irrumpent-em*, pr. pple. of *irrumpĕre* to break in, f. *ir-* (IR-^{1}) + *rumpĕre* to break.] Bursting or breaking in; making an irruption.
1656 BLOUNT *Glossogr.*, *Irrumpent*, entring in by force, rushing in violently.

irrupt (ɪ'rʌpt), *v. rare.* [f. L. *irrupt-*, ppl. stem of *irrump-ĕre*: see prec.]
1. *trans.* To break into. Hence **i'rrupted** *ppl. a.*
1855 HYDE CLARKE *Eng. Dict.*, *Irrupted*, forced through. **1856** WEBSTER, *Irrupted*, broken with violence. Hence in later Dicts.
2. *intr.* To burst in, break in, enter forcibly, make an irruption.
1886 F. H. H. GUILLEMARD *Cruise Marchesa* II. 9 We were in the crater of an extinct volcano into which the sea had at some later period irrupted. **1893** *Temple Bar* XCVIII. 154 She 'irrupted' recklessly into the bedroom.

irruptible (ɪ'rʌptɪb(ə)l), *a. rare.* (erron. -able.) [f. IR-^{2} + L. *rupt-*, ppl. stem of *rumpĕre* to break + -IBLE.] That cannot be broken; unbreakable.
1835 SIR J. ROSS *Arct. Exp.* xlvii. 611 We were locked up by irruptable chains.

irruption (ɪ'rʌpʃən). [ad. L. *irruptiōn-em*, n. of action from *irrump-ĕre*: see IRRUMPENT. Cf. F. *irruption* (14th c. in Hatz.-Darm.).] The action of bursting or breaking in; a violent entry, inroad, incursion, or invasion, esp. of a hostile force or tribe. *spec.* An abrupt local increase in the numbers of a species of animals.
1577 tr. *Bullinger's Decades* (1592) 297 In that hurlie burlie and irruption made by the barbarous people. **1601** HOLLAND *Pliny* I. 75 As if Nature made recompence for the irruptions of the seas. **1637** R. HUMPHREY tr. *St. Ambrose* Pref., The Goths..making irruptions into Gaule. **1707** *Lond. Gaz.* No. 4375/3 That the whole Body of the Troops ..lie in a readiness to oppose any new Irruption of the Enemy. **1803** WELLINGTON *Let. to Lieut.-Gen. Stuart* in Gurw. *Desp.* (1837) II. 8 Not a word is said of the supposed irruption of Holkar. **1874** HELPS *Soc. Press.* ii. 26 You do not seem to perceive the irruption of vulgarity. **1912** W. E. CLARKE *Stud. Bird Migration* II. xxi. 112 During the remarkable irruption of Crossbills from the Continent in the summer of 1909, Fair Isle received many of the visitors. **1936** A. L. THOMSON *Bird Migration* ii. 42 Apart from all the categories of annual movements, there are movements which occur at irregular intervals in the form of invasions or irruptions... In the spring of certain years the birds have 'irrupted' in large numbers. **1968** *New Scientist* 21 Nov. 425/2 The majority of migrants [*sc.* butterflies] reaching Britain are regularly seen within a few days of an irruption in their home territory.
¶ Confused with ERUPTION.
1613 PURCHAS *Pilgrimage* (1614) 814 In the yeare 1581 there issued from another Vulcan..such an irruption of fire. **1691** LUTTRELL *Brief Rel.* (1857) II. 216 Those from Italy say, that mount Vesuvius had lately made a terrible irruption. **1732** ARBUTHNOT *Rules of Diet* iv. in *Aliments*, etc. (1736) 418 In the Article of Feverish Irruptions. **1811** *Ora & Juliet* III. 195 The irruption was coming out in a most favourable way. **1883** 'MARK TWAIN' *Life on Mississippi* 244 A filament-obliterating irruption of profanity. **1892** —— *Amer. Claimant* 62 A volcanic irruption.

irruptive (ɪ'rʌptɪv), *a.* [f. as IRRUPT + -IVE.] Having the quality or character of bursting in; making, or tending to, irruption.
1593 NASHE *Christ's T.* (1613) 58 Trodden out of sent, by the irruptiue ouer-trampling of the Romanes. **1794** WHITEHOUSE *Ode to Justice* (T.), Ready to displode irruptive on his head. **1816** T. BUSBY *Lucretius* VI. Comment. xiii, By Thales and Democritus they [earthquakes] were attributed to the irruptive force of subterraneous winds. **1873** BURTON *Hist. Scot.* I. i. 24 Masses of irruptive rock.

Irsche, obs. Sc. form of ERSE.
1508 DUNBAR *Flyting* 49 Irsche [*v.r.* Iersche] brybour baird, wyle beggar with thy brattis.

irspile, a variant of *ilespile*, *ilspile*, hedgehog (see IL): cf. also IRCHEPIL.

i-rudded, i-ruded, ME. pa. pple. of RED *v.*, to redden.

i-ruled, of RULE *v.*

irun, obs. form of IRON.

i-rung(en, ME. pa. pple. of RING *v.*

irus, obs. variant of IROUS.

Irvingite ('ɜːvɪŋaɪt). [f. surname *Irving* (see below) + -ITE.] A member of a religious body founded about 1835 on the basis of principles promulgated by Edward Irving (1792–1834), a minister of the Church of Scotland, settled in London, and excommunicated in 1833.
The name is not accepted by the body itself, which assumes the title of *Catholic Apostolic Church*: see CATHOLIC A 10.
1836 R. BAXTER *Irvingism* 36 The idol of the Irvingites is the power of utterance. **1872** tr. *Lange's Comm.*, *1 Thess.* iv. 79/2 The other name of Irvingites they expressly disclaim. **1883** *American* VII. 22 None of our churches, except, perhaps, the little body called Irvingites, are doing their full duty by the public in this regard.
b. *attrib.* or *adj.*
1872 tr. *Lange's Comm.*, *1 Thess.* iv. 79/2 The Irvingite interpretation erroneously explained. **1882–3** SCHAFF *Encycl. Relig. Knowl.* II. 1119 Henry Drummond..took a prominent part in the Irvingite movement.
So **'Irvingism**, the doctrine and principles of the Irvingites.
1836 R. BAXTER (*title*) Irvingism. **1876** C. M. DAVIES *Unorth. Lond.* (ed. 2) 86 'Irvingism' as it is still called by outsiders, or the 'Catholic Apostolic Church' as..it is designated by its own adherents.

irwis, obs. variant of IROUS.

† **iry**, *a. Obs.* [f. IRE *sb.* + -Y.] = IRASCIBLE c.
1603 J. DAVIES *Microcosmos* (1878) 74/2 For in our Soules the iry pow'r it is That makes vs at vnhallowed thoughts repine.

iry, obs. variant of EERIE *a.*
1728 RAMSAY *Cordial* iv, My dear, I'm faint and iry.

iryn(e, obs. form of IRON.

is (ɪz), *v.* 3 sing. pres. indic. of vb. BE, q.v. Also used (cf. BE *v.* 10) in variants of the expression (*a*) — *is a* — *is a* —, on the model of Gertrude Stein's line (see quot. 1922).
1922 G. STEIN *Geogr. & Plays* 187 Rose is a rose is a rose. Loveliness extreme. **1968** *Listener* 5 Sept. 292/1 Trevelyan is Trevelyan is Trevelyan, and film censorship will endure for as long as he keeps on fighting. **1970** *Guardian* 2 Apr. 10/1 There is only one art form common to all sorts and conditions of people: the poster..a hoarding is a hoarding is a hoarding. **1971** 'L. BLACK' *Death has Green Fingers* xiv. 158 Let me adapt the quotation. 'A crook is a crook is a crook.' **1974** *Times* 4 Jan. 12/5 As Miss Gertrude Stein would have said: 'A union is a union is a union.'

is (ɪz), *sb.* [f. *is*: see prec. and BE *v.* A 1 c.] That which exists, that which is; the fact or quality of existence.
1897 F. THOMPSON *New Poems* 164 Could I face firm the Is, and with To-be Trust Heaven. **1903** *North Amer. Rev.* Apr. 507 She is not a Has Been, she is an Is. **1951** S. F. NADEL *Found. Social Anthropol.* iii. 37 The blueprint of his culture and society, the 'should-be' rather than the 'is'. **1958** C. PEPLER *Eng. Relig. Heritage* IV. viii. 300 The man is conscious that he *is*, and in comparison to the Is of God, this realisation is itself the greatest sorrow.

is, obs. form of HIS, ICE, YES.

is-: see ISO-.

-is^{1} **(-ys)**, a frequent ME. and esp. Sc. variant of the grammatical inflexion *-es*, *-s*, of the genitive sing., and the pl. of sbs., and of the 3rd pers. sing. of verbs. In MSS. sometimes treated as a separate word or element, esp. in genitive sing., where prob. it was often confounded with the poss. pron. *his* (*is*).
1297 R. GLOUC. (Rolls) 290 þe king tok brut is oue bodi, in ostage as it were. *Ibid.* 656 Salomon..þat king dauid is sone was. *c* **1440** *Partonope* 271, I loue Jhesu ys name. *a* **1450** *Knt. de la Tour* (1868) 10 A cristen man ys hede was smiten of. **1456** *Paston Lett.* I. 373 My Lord of Caunterbury is avis and agreement. *c* **1465** G. ASHBY *Active Policy* 464 Prouide you sadly for youre sowles is helthe. **1527** in Strype *Eccl. Mem.* (1824) I. App. xiv. 45 We receyvyd your Grace is lettres. *Ibid.* 47 We went unto the Chancellor who is answer was, that it shold be done. **1530** PALSGR. *Lesclaircissement* Introd. p. xl, By adding of is to our substantyve, we signifye possessyon, as, my maisteris gowne, my ladyis boke. **1577** HOLINSHED *Chron. I. Hist. Scot.* 507/2 Giftis of wairdis, nonentressis, and releues of landis, and mariageis of airis falland.

-is^{2}, northern and esp. Sc. f. -ISH^{1}, q.v.

I's: see ISE, I'SE b.

Isaac, Izaac, dial. perversions (after the proper name *Isaac*) of *haysuck*, HAYSUGGE, hedge-sparrow.
1834 MEDWIN *Angler in Wales* I. 219 Then arose..the screams of the young Izaacs for help. **1885** SWAINSON *Prov. Names Birds* 29 Hedge sparrow..Isaac, or Hazock (Worcestershire).

Isabel ('ɪzəbɛl). [a. F. *isabelle* = ISABELLA.]
1. Name of a colour; = ISABELLA 1.
1828 WEBSTER s.v., Isabel yellow is a brownish yellow, with a shade of brownish red. **1838** JAMES *Richelieu* i, His dress was a rich livery suit of Isabel and silver.
2. A kind of fancy pigeon, a small variety of the Pouter: so called in reference to its colour.
1867 W. B. TEGETMEIER *Pigeons* vi. 71 Among the best known..are the birds known at the pigeon-shows as *Isabels*, and so named, we may presume, in consequence of their colour.
3. A variety of North American grape: see ISABELLA 2 b.
1854 LONGF. *Catawba Wine* ii, Nor the Isabel And the Muscadel That bask in our garden alleys.

isabelite (ɪzə'bɛlaɪt). [? ad. Sp. *Isabellita*, dim. of female name *Isabella*.] A name given in the West Indies to the angel-fish (*Pomacanthus ciliaris*).
1890 in *Cent. Dict.*

Isabella (ɪzə'bɛlə), *a.* (*sb.*) Also 7 iz-. [From the female name *Isabella*, F. *Isabelle*.]
1. Greyish yellow; light buff. Like other colour names, also used as *sb.*
(Various stories have been put forth to account for the name. That given in D'Israeli *Cur. Lit.* (Article *Anecdotes of Fashion*), and also in Littré, associating it with the archduchess Isabella and the siege of Ostend 1601–1604, is shown by our first quotation to be chronologically impossible.)
1600 (July) *Inv. Queen's Garderobe* in Nichols *Progr. Q. Eliz.* (1823) III. 505 Item, one rounde gowne of Isabella-colour satten,..set with silver spangles. **1622** PEACHAM *Compl. Gent.* (1661) 156 Isabella colour signifieth Beauty. **1689** *Lond. Gaz.* No. 2459/4 A new red Coat with an Izabella colour Lining. **1719** LONDON & WISE *Compl. Gard.* 71 Is in Shape like the Rousselet, of a very light Isabella Colour, like the Martin Sec. **1805–17** R. JAMESON *Char. Min.* (ed. 3) 59 From the names of persons, as Isabella-yellow, now called Cream-yellow. **1811** PINKERTON *Petral.* I. 329 Of a yellowish grey, verging on Isabella colour. **1870** A. L. ADAMS *Nile Valley*, etc. 38 The desert lark..is..of a light Isabella colour above, and white below.
2. Applied to varieties of fruits: **a.** A kind of peach. **b.** A species of North American grape (*Vitis Labrusca*) with large fruit, sometimes purple, often green and red.
1664 EVELYN *Kal. Hort.* (1729) 210 *Peaches.* Nutmeg, Isabella, Persian [etc.]. **1835–40** HALIBURTON *Clockm.* (1862) 197 In an arbor, surrounded with honeysuckle, and Isabella grape. **1846** *Knickerbocker* XXVII. 419 A snaky looking vine..from which glorious bunches of Catawbas and Isabellas may be gathered. **1863** *Handbk. Bot.* 292 The Isabella..varieties of this species. **1864** [see CONCORD *sb.*^{2} 2]. **1949** *Amer. Photography* Apr. 244/1 *Vitis labrusca*..has furnished the catawba,..the Concord,..and the Isabella.
3. *Comb.*, as ***Isabella-coloured*** adj.
1681 CHETHAM *Angler's Vade-m.* iv. §31 (1689) 59 Isabella coloured mohair. **1686** tr. *Chardin's Trav.* 371 All the Nysain horses were Isabella coloured. **1835** *Penny Cycl.* IV. 89/2 Isabella-coloured Bear, *Ursus Isabellinus.* **1858** PLANCHÉ tr. *C'tess D'Aulnoy's Fairy Tales*, *P'cess Belle-Etoile & Pr. Cheri* 573 She mounted an Isabella-coloured horse; the black mane of which was dressed with rows of diamonds.

isabelline (ɪzə'bɛlɪn, -aɪn), *a.* [f. prec. + -INE.] Of an Isabella colour, greyish yellow.
isabelline bear: a variety of the Syrian bear, found in the Himalaya Mountains, of a yellowish-brown colour; the Indian white bear; cf. ISABELLA 3, quot. 1835.
1859 TRISTRAM in *Ibis* I. 430 The upper plumage of every bird, whether Lark, Chat, Sylvian, or Sand-grouse..is of one uniform isabelline or sand colour. **1889** *Cornh. Mag.* Mar. 307 The smaller denizens of the desert..must be quite uniformly isabelline or sand-coloured. **1893** LYDEKKER *Horns & Hoofs* 198 The face is of the same isabelline tint as the body.
b. *Comb.*, as ***isabelline-hued***.
1883 *Athenæum* 15 Sept. 336/3 We turn with a sigh of relief to the old leather-covered, isabelline-hued copies of the angling patriarch.

isabnormal, isacoustic: see ISO-.

i-sacred, ME. pa. pple. of SACRE *v.*

isadelphous: see ISO-.

i-sæid, ME. pa. pple. of SAY *v.*

isagoge (aɪsə'gəʊdʒiː, -'gəʊgiː). Also 7 -gogue. [a. L. *isagōgē*, a. Gr. εἰσαγωγή introduction, f. εἰς

into + ἀγωγή leading, bringing. With Blount's form *isagogue*, cf. *synagogue*.] An introduction.

1652 BOYLE *Let. to Mallet* Jan. in *Wks.* (1772) I. *Life* p. li, No bad isagoge to the Eastern languages. **1656** BLOUNT *Glossogr.*, *Isagogue*, an introduction. **1661** LOVELL *Hist. Anim. & Min.* Isagoge. **1751** HARRIS *Hermes* I. iv. 39 *note*, See the Isagoge or Introduction of Porphyry to Aristotle's Logick. **1855** MAYNE *Expos. Lex.*, *Isagoge*,..term for an introduction.

isagogic (aɪsəˈgɒdʒɪk), *a.* (*sb.*) [ad. L. *īsagōgic-us*, a. Gr. εἰσαγωγικός introductory, f. εἰσαγωγή: see prec.] Of or pertaining to isagoge; introductory to any branch of study.

1828 in WEBSTER. **1887** FAIRBAIRN in *Contemp. Rev.* Feb. 208 The formal, introductory or isagogic, studies have a wide range, requiring, perhaps more than any other, educated faculty and the scientific mind.

B. *sb.* (generally in plural *isagogics*). Introductory studies; *esp.* that department of theology which is introductory to exegesis, and is concerned with the literary and external history of the books of the Bible.

1864 in WEBSTER. **1882–3** SCHAFF *Encycl. Relig. Knowl.* III. 2185 Richard Simon, the founder of biblical isagogics. **1898** J. ROBERTSON *Poetry Ps.* ii. 24 In the Compendium of Isagogic of Junilius Africanus..the Psalms are reckoned among the prophetical writings.

†**isaˈgogical**, *a. Obs.* [f. as prec. + -AL[1].] Introductory, isagogic.

a **1529** SKELTON *Why nat to Court* 714, I wyll make further relacion Of this isagogicall colation. *a* **1646** J. GREGORY *Assyr. Monarchie* in *Posthuma* (1650) 239 So Ioseph Scaliger in his Isagogical Canons. **1721** BAILEY, *Isagogical*,.. introductory.

Hence **isaˈgogically** *adv.* (Bailey vol. II, 1727).

isagon, -ic, erron. forms of ISOGON, -IC.

Isaian (aɪˈzaɪən, -ˈeɪən), *a.* Also **Isaiahan**. [f. proper name *Isaiah* + -AN.] Of or belonging to the prophet Isaiah, or the book of the Old Testament that bears his name.

1883 M. ARNOLD *Isaiah of Jerus.* in *19th Cent.*, The Isaian eloquence, the Isaian spirit and power. **1896** R. G. MOULTON *Lit. Study Bible* xvii. 434 Spoken before by the Servant of Jehovah in the Isaiahan Rhapsody.

Isaianic (aɪzaɪ-, aɪzeɪˈænɪk), *a.* [f. as prec. + -IC.] = prec.

1882 CHEYNE *Isaiah* vii. 14 *note*, The two Isaianic prophecies of God-with-us and Wonder-Counsellor. **1898** *Expositor* Nov. 367 A passage confessedly Isaianic.

i-said, i-sait, ME. pa. pples. of SAY *v.*

i-sald, ME. pa. pple. of SELL *v.*

is all. [Cf. ALL *a.* 8 g.] *U.S.* and *Canad. colloq. phr.*, a shortened form of *that is all*.

1954 G. BREWER *Killer is Loose* iii. 27 You didn't see the bus, is all. **1967** 'W. WRIGHT' *Shadows don't Bleed* vii. 126 I'm not married. Paula looks after the house for me, is all. **1969** C. HIMES *Blind Man with Pistol* xiv. 152, I help you look, just don't call me nigger is all.

isallobar (aɪsˈæləʊbɑː(r)). *Meteorol.* [f. Gr. ἴσ-ος equal (ISO-) + ἄλλο-ς other (ALLO-) + βάρ-ος weight, after *isobar*.] A line (imaginary or on a map) connecting points at which the barometric pressure has changed by an equal amount during a specified time. Hence **isalloˈbaric** *a.*

1911 N. SHAW *Forecasting Weather* xv. 337 Dr. Nils Ekholm, of Stockholm,..uses charts of isallobars. *Ibid.*, Similar groups of isallobars appear on both maps, so that the isallobaric groups may be regarded as travelling as well as the isobaric groups. **1934** D. BRUNT *Physical & Dynamical Meteorol.* ix. 189 Brunt and Douglas found that the isallobaric component of wind frequently amounted to as much as 5 metres/sec. **1959** S. L. HESS *Introd. Theoret. Meteorol.* xiv. 226 This solution is for the case of isobars and isallobars (lines of constant pressure tendency) which are oriented east-west. **1962** *Course Elem. Meteorol.* (Meteorol. Office) ii. 25 By analogy with isobars we have isallobaric highs and lows, showing centres of rising and falling pressure respectively.

i-salued, ME. pa. pple. of SALUE *v.*, to salute.

†**i-same**, *adv. Obs.* Also 4 **i-some, y-same**. [Another form of INSAME; app. f. *i-*, IN + SAME(N *adv.* together: cf. MHG. *ensamen, -ent*. As the *in* of *in-same(n* was pleonastic, and *i* was not used in southern dial. for *in* in 14th c., the *i-* was prob. associated with I- *pref.*[1], and was hence sometimes written *y*. *I-some* in *Castel of Love* has *ǫ* from *a*, and is to be distinguished from the adj. I-SOME, in which *i-* is I-[1].] Together; in company.

c **1320** *Sir Beues* (MS. A) 705 Forþ þai wente al isame, To Beues chaumber þat he came. *Ibid.* 3449 And to þe castel þai wente isame Wiþ gret solas, gle and game. *c* **1320** *Cast. Love* 1418 Vppon holy þoresday þer on his nome Heo weren i-gedered alle i-some. *c* **1330** *Amis. & Amil.* 1089 Hou he and that maiden was Bothe togider y-same. *c* **1380** *Sir Ferumb.* 1188 Goþ now alle y-same & helpeþ him. *c* **1400** *Sowdone Bab.* 3201 And so thay livede in ioye and game, And brethern both thay wer, In pees and werr both I-same.

isamic (aɪˈsæmɪk), *a. Chem.* [f. IS(AT- + AMIC.] Related to isatin and to ammonia; in *isamic acid*, $C_{16}H_{13}N_3O_4$, produced by the action of warm ammonia on isatin. Its salts are **ˈisamates**.

1865–72 WATTS *Dict. Chem.* III. 404 Isamic acid crystallises in splendid, shining, rhombic laminæ, of the colour of red iodide of mercury. *Ibid.*, Isamate of ammonium..crystallises in small needles or very acute microscopic rhombs.

So **ˈisamide**, the amide, $C_{16}H_{14}N_2O_3$, related to isamic acid; 'pulverulent, of a fine yellow colour, tasteless, inodorous, insoluble in water' (Watts).

isandrous: see ISO-.

†**isanˈgelical**, *a. Obs. rare*[−1]. [f. Gr. ἰσάγγελ-ος (see next): cf. ANGELICAL.] = next.

1678 CUDWORTH *Intell. Syst.* I. v. 797 We may venture to call this Resurrection-Body..an Angelical, or Isangelical Body.

†**iˈsangelous**, *a. Obs. rare*[−1]. [f. Gr. ἰσάγγελ-ος equal to or like an angel (see ISO-) + -OUS.] Equal to the angels.

1768–74 TUCKER *Lt. Nat.* (1834) II. 291 Let us look back upon ourselves, who we expect shall one day be made isangelous, equal to the angels.

isanomal (-ous, -y), -antherous, -anthous: see ISO-.

isapostolic (aɪsæpɒˈstɒlɪk), *a.* [f. eccl. Gr. ἰσαπόστολ-ος equal to an apostle + -IC: cf. *apostolic*.] Equal to, or contemporary with, the apostles; a name given in the Greek Church to bishops consecrated by the apostles, and to other persons eminent in the primitive church.

1860 NEALE in *Lit. Churchman* VI. 168/1 The Isapostolic writers of the first century. **1862** *Chr. Remembrancer* XLIV. 407 With reference to the Isapostolic fathers. **1881** *Ch. Times* 11 Mar. 164 The representative of the apostolic or isapostolic succession of the Britons.

isard, variant of IZARD.

‖**Isaria** (aɪˈsɛərɪə). *Bot.* [f. Gr. ἴσ-ος equal + *-aria* = -ARY[1] B 3.] A genus of filamentous moulds, some species of which attack and destroy insects, especially Hymenoptera. It is now believed that many of the species are merely sporiferous forms of other fungi.

1874 COOKE *Fungi* 7 Wasps, spiders, moths, and butterflies become enveloped in a kind of mould named Isaria, which constitutes the conidia of Torrubia.

Hence **isarioid** (ɪˈsɛərɪɔɪd) *a.* [see -OID], belonging to or resembling the genus *Isaria*.

1890 in *Cent. Dict.*

isat-, an element derived from L. *isat-is* (Gr. ἰσάτις) woad, used in *Chem.* to form the name of ISATIN (see below), and of other bodies related to it and to indigo. Among these are:

isatic (aɪˈsætɪk) *acid*, $C_8H_7NO_3$ (= isatin + H_2O), substitution products of which are ***bromisatic*** ($C_8H_6BrNO_3$), ***chlorisatic***, etc., ***acids***; the salts are **isatates** (ˈaɪsəteɪts), ***broˈmisatates***, ***chloˈrisatates***, etc. **isatimide** (aɪˈsætɪmaɪd), the imide of isatin, $C_{24}H_{17}N_5O_4$. **isatite**: see ISATIN. **iˈsatogen**, any compound containing the bicyclic group $C_8H_4NO_2$ found in isatin; hence **isatoˈgenic** *a.* **ˌisato-sulˈphuric** *acid*, an acid containing the elements of isatin and sulphuric acid or sulphuric anhydride; the salts of which are **isato-sulphates**. **ˈisatyde** (†**isathyd**), a substance bearing the same relation to isatin that indigo-white bears to indigo-blue, being formed from it by the addition of one atom of hydrogen.

1845 *Penny Cycl.* 1st Suppl. 346/1 Isatic acid..is perfectly insoluble in cold water, but when heated in water it is decomposed into isatin and water. **1865–72** WATTS *Dict. Chem.* III. 404 The solution..deposits..crystals of isatin, which in fact differs from isatic acid, only by the elements of water. *Ibid.* 405 Chlorisatate of potassium..crystallizes in shining flattened quadrilateral needles of a light yellow colour. *Ibid.*, The other salts of chlorisatic acid are obtained by double decomposition. *Ibid.* 409 Isatosulphuric acid is a strong acid, separating even the stronger mineral acids from their salts. *Ibid.* 410 Isatosulphite of Ammonium,..of Potassium. *Ibid.* 411 Isatyde is white, with a slightly greyish tint, tasteless, and inodorous. It..separates on cooling in microscopic scales. **1882** *Jrnl. Chem. Soc.* XLII. 198 Isatogenic acid is very unstable, and cannot be obtained either from the above salt, or from free orthonitropropiolic acid, as it is immediately converted into isatin. *Ibid.* 620 To ascertain the nature of the isatogen-group, experiments were made on its derivatives. **1889** ROSCOE & SCHORLEMMER *Treat. Chem.* III. v. 262 When the solution is poured into water, the isatogenic acid decomposes instantaneously into carbon dioxide and isatin. **1916** *Chem. Abstr.* X. 1334 The isatogens are typical quinones, forming a new class of *m*-quinoid compds., in which the group N:O plays the role of a CO group. **1948** WENGRAF & BAUMANN tr. *Diseren's Chem. Technol. Dyeing & Printing* I. i. 26 The formation of indigo can be explained by an intermediate rearrangement of the *o*-nitrophenyl propiolic acid into isatogenic acid... The latter product is reduced to indigo by splitting off CO_2. **1965** *Jrnl. Pharmacy & Pharmacol.* XVII. 736 The isatogens..were all effective against Gram-positive organisms. **1972** W. A. REMERS in W. J. Houlihan *Chem. Heterocyclic Compounds* XXV. i. 193 Isatogens..also undergo addition to the 1,2-double bond.

isatin (ˈaɪsətɪn). *Chem.* Also **-ine**. [f. L. *isat-is*, a. Gr. ἰσάτις the plant woad, whence a blue dye is obtained + -IN[1].] A crystalline, reddish-orange substance ($C_8H_5NO_2$), of brilliant lustre, obtained from indigo by oxidation.

Isatin in combination plays the part of an acid, forming **ˈisatites**, e.g. potassium isatite, $C_8H_4KNO_2$. With bromine and chlorine it forms ***broˈmisatin*** ($C_8H_4BrNO_2$), ***chloˈrisatin***, in which one or two atoms of hydrogen are replaced by equivalent quantities of bromine or chlorine. The salts of these are ***bromisatites, chlorisatites***.

1845 *Penny Cycl.* 1st Suppl. 346/1 *Isatin*, a substance obtained from indigo by the addition of two equivalents of oxygen..It crystallizes in prisms, which are of a yellowish red or deep aurora-red colour. **1850** DAUBENY *Atom. The.* viii. (ed. 2) 237 When indigo is oxidized by means of nitric acid, it becomes converted into a bright red crystalline body termed isatine. **1875** H. C. WOOD *Therap.* (1879) 67 A green color begins at once to develop, and in a little while passes into the clear yellow of isatin.

-isation, frequent variant of -IZATION.

isatis (ˈaɪsətɪs). *Zool.* [Said to be from the native name in a northern language.] The white or Arctic fox, *Canis lagopus*.

Named by J. G. Gmelin, 1760, *Canis isatis*; his specific name, though abandoned for *lagopus*, has been sometimes used as the English name.

1774 GOLDSM. *Nat. Hist.* III. viii. 339 As the jackall is a sort of intermediate species between the dog and the wolf, so the isatis may be considered as placed between the dog and the fox. **1854** *Hand-bk. Nat. Philos.* III. *Phys. Geog.* 55/1 The *lagopus* or *isatis* (arctic fox) is found at Spitzbergen.

isatoic (aɪsəˈtəʊɪk), *a. Chem.* [See below.]

1. *isatoic acid* [tr. G. *isatosäure* (H. Kolbe 1884, in *Jrnl. f. prakt. Chem.* XXX. 85): see ISAT-]. †**a.** = *isatoic anhydride* (below). *Obs.* **b.** *N*-Carboxyanthranilic acid, $C_6H_4(COOH)(NHCOOH)$, known only as its derivatives.

1885 *Jrnl. Chem. Soc.* XLVIII. I. 58 Isatin is converted by chromic acid, dissolved in glacial acetic acid, into an acid which the author styles isatoic acid... It is sparingly soluble in cold water and alcohol. *Ibid.* 666 Anthranil-carboxylic acid..has the same composition as isatoic acid. **1899** [see sense 2]. **1930** *Chem. Abstr.* XXIV. 4793 Isatoic acid and its derivs. are obtained by treating congo acid solns. of aromatic *o*-aminocarboxylic acids with $COCl_2$.

2. *isatoic anhydride* [after G. *isatosäure-anhydrid* (E. Erdmann 1889, in *Ber. d. Deut. Chem. Ges.* XXXII. 2163)]. The anhydride,

$$\underbrace{C_6H_4\cdot CO\cdot O\cdot CO\cdot NH}$$

of isatoic acid, obtained by oxidation of isatin.

1899 *Jrnl. Chem. Soc.* LXXVI. I. 939 'Isatoic acid' is thus not an acid, but the anhydride of a dicarboxylic acid, $COOH\cdot C_6H_4\cdot NH\cdot COOH$. The author calls this dibasic acid isatoic acid, and the anhydride, previously known as isatoic acid he terms isatoic anhydride. **1944** *Jrnl. Org. Chem.* IX. 55 Isatoic anhydride is a convenient reagent for certain anthranoylations. **1971** *Jrnl. Pharmaceutical Sci.* LX. 1252/1 The condensation of isatoic anhydride with primary amines was found to yield the corresponding substituted anthranilamides.

i-saught, ME. pa. pple. of SAUGHT *v.*, to reconcile.

Isaurian (aɪˈsɔːrɪən), *sb.* and *a.* [f. *Isauria* (see below) + -AN.] **A.** *sb.* A native or inhabitant of Isauria, an ancient country in Asia Minor, between Cilicia and Phrygia; *spec.* applied to a line of emperors of the Eastern Roman Empire. **B.** *adj.* Of or belonging to Isauria, or to the emperors thus called.

1776 GIBBON *Decl. & F.* I. x. 285 In the heart of the Roman monarchy, the Isaurians ever continued a nation of wild barbarians. **1843** *Penny Cycl.* XXVII. 770/2 The increasing power of the brothers and other Isaurian friends of Zeno. **1880** *Encycl. Brit.* XI. 114/2 The emperors of this time were those of the Isaurian, Armenian, and Amorian dynasties. **1904** W. M. RAMSAY *Lett. Seven Churches* xxvii. 399 The Empire of Rome has been..transformed into a Roman-Asiatic Empire, on whose throne sat successively Phrygians, Isaurians, Cappadocians, and Armenians. **1957** J. M. HUSSEY *Byzantine World* I. ii. 29 The Isaurians were administrators as well as soldiers.

i-sauved, i-saved, ME. pa. pple. of SAVE *v.*

i-savered, ME. pa. pple. of SAVOUR *v.*

i-sawed, ME. pa. pple. of SAW *v.*

†**i-sayed**, ME. pa. pple. of SAY *v.*, aphetized form of ASSAY.

1387 TREVISA *Higden* (Rolls) VI. 191 þat we haveþ i-sayed and i-preved by an orlege.

I-say-so, *phrase* used as *sb.* An assertion, an *ipse dixit*: cf. SAY-SO.

1800 W. TAYLOR in *Monthly Mag.* X. 424 Heeds the I-say-so's even of authority.

‖**isba** (izˈba). Also **isbah, izba**. [ad. Russ. *izbá* (related to STOVE *sb.*[1]).] A Russian hut or log-house.

1784 J. KING in Cook *Voy. Pacific Ocean* III. 374 These houses consist of three distinct sorts, jourts, balagans, and loghouses, called here isbas. **1833** R. PINKERTON *Russia* 24 These simple articles compose the whole..furniture of a Russian izba. **1883** *Harper's Mag.* Jan. 251/1 Her serfs, if they wanted new isbahs—alias log huts—..would get the

priests .. to versify their petition. **1892** *Daily News* 22 Jan. 6/7 The meanest Kirghis yourt was more artistically decorated than his grimy, unventilated isba. **1943** E. M. ALMEDINGEN *Frossia* ii. 89, I was twenty-one, married, had my own *izba*, owned my own livestock. **1962** *Observer* 20 May 21/1 We lived in a tiny *isba*, or log cabin, together with three other families.

‖**isblink** (ˈiːsblɪŋk). Also 8-9 eis-blink, iisblink. [Sw. (and mod. Dan.) *isblink*, etc.: see ICEBLINK.] = ICEBLINK 2.

1796 Eis-blink [see ICEBLINK 2]. **1870** *Q. Jrnl. Geol. Soc.* XXVI. 679 Here the 'Iisblink', or the 'ice glance', of the Danes (*i.e.* the projecting glacier—though English seamen use the word iceblink in a totally different sense, meaning thereby the 'loom' of ice at a distance), projects bodily out to sea for more than a mile. **1880** *Encycl. Brit.* XI. 167/2 If.. the sea is shallow, the glacier will protrude for a considerable distance, as in the case of the Isblink. **1957** J. K. CHARLESWORTH *Quaternary Era* I. iv. 72 For this type [*sc.* continental ice-sheet] there is almost universal assent: it constitutes O. Nordenskiöld's 'continental glaciers', Hobbs' 'ice-cap type', and the 'inland ice' of Drygalski, Ferrar and Gourdon. Early writers, following H. Rink (1851), named it *Isblink* from the peculiar light seen over the inland ice when approached from the sea.

i-scalded, ME. pa. pple. of SCALD *v.*

Iscariot (ɪˈskærɪət). [ad. L. *Iscariōta*, a. Gr. Ἰσκαριώτης, understood to be ad. Heb. *īsh-q'rīyōth* man of Kerioth (a place in Palestine).] The surname of Judas, the disciple who betrayed Jesus Christ. Hence, an appellation for an accursed traitor. Also *attrib.*

1647 WARD *Simp. Cobler* 43 He may be a zelot.., and yet an Iscariot. **1795-7** SOUTHEY *Juvenile & Minor Poems* Poet. Wks. II. 116 An Iscariot curse will lie Upon the name. **1878** E. JENKINS *Haverholme* 63 Those.. he deemed Iscariots to a Divine cause.

Hence **Iscariotic** (ɪskærɪˈɒtɪk) *a.*, of or relating to Judas Iscariot; **Iscariˈotical** *a.*, characteristic of or resembling Judas Iscariot; wickedly treacherous; **Iˈscariotism**, a practice characteristic of Judas Iscariot, esp. in reference to parsimonious employment of church funds (cf. John xii. 5).

1879 FARRAR *St. Paul* (1883) 63 The 109th has been called the *Iscariotic Psalm. *a* **1625** BOYS *Wks.* (1630) 282 This *Iscarioticall feat. *Ibid.* 285 To whet.. tongue and pen against that Iscariotticall legerdemaine. **1641** MILTON *Reform.* II. (1851) 64 No such prostitution, no such Iscariotical drifts are to be doubted. **1883** *Ch. Times* 18 May 357 The Congregation.. will also reject the principle of *Iscariotism, or the cheap-and-nasty in religion. **1885** *Ibid.* 16 Jan. 37 Far be it from me to advocate Iscariotism.

i-sceawed, ME. pa. pple. of SHOW *v.*

i-scend, ME. pa. pple. of SHEND *v.*

i-schad, ME. pa. pple. of SHED *v.*

i-schadewed, ME. pa. pple. of SHADOW *v.*

‖**ischæmia, -emia** (ɪˈskiːmɪə). *Path.* [mod.L., f. Gr. ἴσχαιμ-ος stanching or stopping blood, f. ἴσχ-ειν to hold + αἷμα blood.] Repression of a habitual bleeding; local anæmia caused by obstruction of the blood.

1866 A. FLINT *Princ. Med.* (1880) 26 Local anaemia or ischaemia signifies a deficiency of blood in a part. **1878** A. M. HAMILTON *Nerv. Dis.* 134 The formation of an extended clot which blocks up the vessel more fully, and consequent ischæmia.

So **ischæmic** (ɪˈskiːmɪk), †**iˈschæmous** (iˈskiːməs) *adjs.*, pertaining to or characterized by ischæmia; hence **iˈschæmically** *adv.*, by, or as a result of, ischæmia; †**iˈschaime**, a styptic medicine (*obs.*); †**iˈschemy**, anglicized form of *ischæmia.*

1661 LOVELL *Hist. Anim. & Min.* 331 Cured by ischaimes, anodynes. **1684** tr. *Bonet's Merc. Compit.* VIII. 270 We say, that all Ischaimous Medicines respect the Bloud it self. **1855** MAYNE *Expos. Lex.*, *Ischæmia*, term for the restraining or stopping of hemorrhage; ischemy. **1876** *Clin. Soc. Trans.* IX. 134 The ischæmic state, which.. may exist in a stationary condition for months, and then disappear, leaving vision unaffected. **1967** *Urologia Internat.* XXII. 381 (*heading*) Electron-microscopic investigation of the action of mannitol in ischemically-damaged rat kidneys. **1970** *Nature* 27 June 1272/1 In 1963 and 1964.. a high attrition rate resulted from the use of ischaemically damaged grafts.. and absence of tissue typing facilities. **1972** *Ibid.* 21 Jan. 171/2 We have tried to develop a simple perfusing system with better protection of the organ.. and eventually to test this system with ischaemically damaged kidneys.

i-schake, ME. pa. pple. of SHAKE *v.*

†**i-ˈschape**, *v. Obs.* [OE. *ȝescęppan*, f. *ȝe-*, I-¹ + *scęppan* to create, SHAPE; = Goth. *gaskapjan*, OS. *giscapan*, OHG. *gascaffan*, MHG. *geschaffen.*] *trans.* To create, form, shape.

a **1000** *Cædmon's Gen.* 112 Her ærest ȝesceop ece Drihten heofon and eorþan. *a* **1175** *Cott. Hom.* 219 God ȝesceop alle gode. *c* **1175** *Lamb. Hom.* 129 Vre drihten þe hine iscop. *c* **1275** *Passion our Lord* 703 in *O.E. Misc.* 57 He þet alle þing ischop þis vs graunty.

i-schape(n, ME. pa. pple. of SHAPE *v.*

ischar, ischear, obs. Sc. forms of USHER.

i-schave, i-schaven, ME. pa. pple. of SHAVE *v.*

i-schawed, ME. pa. pple. of SHOW *v.*

ischay, obs. Sc. form of ISSUE *sb.*

ische, isch, variants of ISH *sb.* and *v.*, issue.

ische, obs. Sc. form of ICE.

i-scheaued, i-scheawed, ME. pa. pple. of SHOW *v.*

i-sched, ME. pa. pple. of SHED *v.*

i-schelde, var. I-SCHIELD *v.*

i-schend, i-schent, ME. pa. pple. of SHEND *v.*

i-schet(te, ME. pa. pple. of SHUT *v.*

i-schete, ME. pa. pple. of SHIT *v.*

ischewe, obs. form of ISSUE.

i-schewed, i-schewen, ME. pa. pple. of SHOW *v.*

ischiadic (ɪskɪˈædɪk), *a.* [ad. L. *ischiadic-us*, a. Gr. ἰσχιαδικ-ός, f. ἰσχιάς, ἰσχιάδ- pain in the hip, f. ἰσχί-ον hip-joint.] Of or pertaining to the ischium; ischiatic.

1727-41 CHAMBERS *Cycl.*, *Ischiadic*, an epithet given by physicians to two veins of the foot, which terminate in the crural. **1827** ABERNETHY *Surg. Wks.* II. 217 Do not the sacral nerves form a plexus, in order to form the ischiadic or posterior crural nerve? **1835-6** TODD *Cycl. Anat.* I. 287/1 The ilium.. becomes anchylosed with the ischium posterior to the ischiadic notch. **1870** ROLLESTON *Anim. Life* 16 The ischiadic artery.

ischial (ˈɪskɪəl), *a.* [f. ISCHI-UM + -AL¹.] Of or pertaining to the ischium; = prec.

1855 in MAYNE *Expos. Lex.* **1864** HUXLEY in *Reader* 27 Feb. The width between the ischial bones. **1875** BLAKE *Zool.* 17 The latter section.. possessing ischial callosities, which are absent in the members of the order nearest to Man.

‖**ischialgia** (ɪskɪˈældʒɪə). Also anglicized ˈischialgy. [f. Gr. ἰσχι-ον ischium + ἄλγος, -αλγία pain.] Pain in the ischium or hip-joint; sciatica. Hence **ischiˈalgic** *a.*

1847 CRAIG, *Ischialgia*, pain about the haunch, or coxo-femoral articulation, or in the course of the ischiatic nerve. **1855** MAYNE *Expos. Lex.*, *Ischialgia*,.. ischialgy. *Ischialgicus*, of or belonging to Ischialgia: ischialgic.

ischiatic (ɪskɪˈætɪk), *a.* [ad. med.L. *ischiatic-us*, altered from *ischiadic-us* ISCHIADIC, after adjs. in *-aticus*: cf. mod.F. *ischiatique.*]

1. Of or pertaining to the ischium or hip; sciatic.

1741 MONRO *Anat. Nerves* (ed. 3) 69 Known by the Name of Sciatic or Ischiatic Nerve. **1774** *Westm. Mag.* II. 255 In ischiatick and rheumatick pains. **1863** HUXLEY *Man's Place Nat.* II. 76 The coarse, outwardly curved ischiatic prominences on which the gibbon habitually rests. **1881** MIVART *Cat* 107 The concavity.. between the posterior spinous process of the ilium and the spine of the ischium, is called the greater ischiatic notch.

2. Troubled or affected with sciatica.

1656 BLOUNT *Glossogr.*, *Ischiatick*, that hath the ache in the hip, or the hip-gout, or Sciatica. **1708** MOTTEUX *Rabelais* v. x, You.. feel.. every change of Weather at your Ischiatic Legs.

‖**ischiˈatica**. *Obs.* Also 7 -adica. [med. or mod.L. fem. of *ischiadic-us*, *ischiatic-us*: see prec.] = SCIATICA.

1581 MULCASTER *Positions* xxiv. 98 Quick riding is naught for.. the *Ischiatica*, bycause the hippes are to much heated and weakned, by the vehementnesse of the motion. **1664** EVELYN *Sylva* (1776) 135 A most admirable remedy for the ischiadica or hip-pain. **1693** J. EDWARDS *Bks. O. & N. Test.* 427 Sciatica for Ischiatica, ab ἰσχίας, the hip or huckle-bone.

†**i-schield**, *v. Obs.* Also 2 iscilden, 3 ischulden, 4 ischelde. [OE. *ȝescieldan*, *-sceld-*, *-scild-*, *-scyld-*, f. *ȝe-*, I-¹ + OE. *scieldan* to SHIELD.] *trans.* To shield, protect.

971 *Blickl. Hom.* 51 He us eac ȝesceldeþ wið eallum feondum. *c* **1000** ÆLFRIC *Exod.* xxxiii. 22 Ic ȝescilde þe mid minre swyðran handan. *c* **1000** *Ags. Ps.* (Th.) lxiii[i]. 1 Wið eȝesan yfeles feondes mine sawle ȝescyld. *c* **1175** *Lamb. Hom.* 111 Þe clenesse iscilt heo wið unþeawes. **12..** *Prayer to our Lady* in *O.E. Misc.* 193 Þat us ischulde he eure fram alle helle pine. *c* **1315** SHOREHAM 85 I-schelde ous, wanne we dede beth, Fram alle fendene jewyse.

ischio- (ˌɪskɪəʊ), ad. Gr. ἰσχιο-, combining form of ἰσχίον ISCHIUM, used in anatomical terms, in comb. with adjs. relating to other parts of the body, with the sense 'pertaining to or connecting the ischium and . . . ', as **ischio-ˈanal**, **-ˈcaudal**, **-ˈcavernous**, **-cocˈcygeal**, **-ˈfemoral**, **-ˈfibular**, **-ˈiliac**, **-ˈpubal**, **-ˈpubic**, **-ˈrectal**, **-ˈsacral**, **-ˈtibial**, **-uˈrethral**, **-ˈvertebral**.

Hence also **ischio-ˈcapsular** *a.*, relating to or connected with the ischium and the capsular ligament of the hip-joint. **ischiocaverˈnosus** *Anat.* [mod.L. (ad. F. *ischio-caverneux* (J.-B. Winslow *Expos. anat. de la Struct. du Corps Humain* (1732) 571/1)), f. L. *cavernōsus* full of hollows, in *corpus cavernosum* (see CORPUS 2)], either of a pair of small perineal muscles, each of which arises partly from the ischial tuberosity and partly from the ramus of the ischium and is inserted into the crus of the penis (or clitoris) and perhaps helps to maintain erection. **ischiˈocerite** *Zool.* [Gr. κέρας horn], the third joint of a fully developed antenna of a crustacean. **ischiˈopodite** *sb. Zool.* [Gr. πούς, ποδ- foot], the third joint of a fully developed limb of a crustacean.

1855 MAYNE *Expos. Lex.*, *Ischio-Analis*,.. applied to the *Levator ani* muscle: *ischio-anal. **1733** G. DOUGLAS tr. *Winslow's Anat. Expos. Struct. Human Body* II. viii. 198 The first two muscles are commonly termed erectores, but might be more properly named *ischio-cavernosi. **1867** *Quain's Elem. Anat.* (ed. 7) I. 264 The ischio-cavernosus, or erector penis muscle, embracing the crus penis, arises from the inner part of the tuber ischii, behind the extremity of the crus penis, and from the pubic arch along the inner and outer sides of the crus. **1967** G. M. WYBURN et al. *Conc. Anat.* i. 17/2 Each crus is covered by the ischiocavernosus muscle. **1877** HUXLEY *Anat. Inv. Anim.* vi. 314 While to its inner portion an *ischiocerite is connected, bearing a merocerite. **1857** BULLOCK *Cazeaux' Midwif.* 20 The attachments of the anterior sacro-sciatic ligaments, and the *ischio-coccygeal muscles. **1872** HUMPHRY *Myology* 20 A hinder—*ischio-femoral—part arising from the hinder edge of the ischium is inserted rather above and behind the preceding. **1870** ROLLESTON *Anim. Life* 94 The third [joint], or '*ischiopodite', is marked by an annular constriction a little way distally to its articulation with.. the basipodite. **1857** BULLOCK *Cazeaux' Midwif.* 22 The *ischio-pubic ramus. **1835-6** TODD *Cycl. Anat.* I. 177/1 Each *Ischio-rectal space is a deep triangular hollow.

ischiocele (ˈɪskɪəʊsiːl). [f. ISCHIO- + Gr. κήλη tumour.] A hernia in the ischiatic notch. Hence **ischioˈcelic** *a.*, of or pertaining to ischiocele.

1847 CRAIG, *Ischiocele*, *Ischiatocele*, hernia formed by protrusion of the viscera through the great foramen. **1855** in MAYNE *Expos. Lex.*

ischiorrhogic (-ˈrɒdʒɪk), *a.* *Pros.* [ad. Gr. ἰσχιορρωγικός having broken hips, limping: used only as a term of prosody; f. ἰσχίο-ν hip-joint + ῥώξ, ῥωγ- cleft.] Applied to an iambic line with spondees in the second, fourth, or sixth place.

1832 LEWIS in *Philol. Mus.* I. 289 Babrius seems to have occasionally admitted a spondee into the fifth foot; a variety of iambic metre called ischiorrhogic, or disjointed, by the ancient grammarians.

i-schipped, ME. pa. pple. of SHIP *v.*

†**i-ˈschire**, *v. Obs.* Also 3 iscire. [OE. type **ȝescíran*, corresp. to Goth. *gaskeirjan* to interpret: cf. OE. *scíran* to make clear, declare, make known, tell.] *trans.* To tell, say, speak.

c **1205** LAY. 17129 Loke þat þu na mare swulc þing ne iscire. *a* **1250** *Owl & Night.* 1530 Ne dar heo noȝt a word ischire.

i-schitte, ME. pa. pple. of SHUT *v.*

‖**ischium** (ˈɪskɪəm). Pl. ischia (in 7 erron. -ias). [L. *ischium*, a. Gr. ἰσχίον hip-joint; later as now used.] The lowest of the three parts of the *os innominatum*, the bone on which the body rests when sitting.

1646 SIR T. BROWNE *Pseud. Ep.* IV. i. 179 If we define sitting to be a firmation of the body upon the Ischias. **1727-41** CHAMBERS *Cycl.* s.v., In the ischium is a deep cavity .. which receives the head of the thigh-bone. **1825** J. NICHOLSON *Operat. Mechanic* 61 Those parts of this bony circumference, which receive the heads of the thigh-bone above,.. called the ischium or coxendix, are the strongest of all. **1854** OWEN *Skel. & Teeth* in *Circ. Sc.*, *Organ. Nat.* I. 183 The hæmapophyses of, probably, the last abdominal vertebra, called 'ischia',.. are detached from the rest of their segment. **1883** MARTIN & MOALE *Vertebr. Dissect.* 123 The *ischium* is nearly vertically placed beneath the hinder portion of the ilium.

i-schod, ME. pa. pple. of SHED *v.*, SHOE *v.*

i-schore, i-schorn, ME. pa. pple. of SHEAR *v.*

i-schorted, ME. pa. pple. of SHORT *v.*

i-schote, ME. pa. pple. of SHOOT *v.*

i-schreve, i-schriven, ME. pa. pple. of SHRIVE *v.*

i-schrowdit, i-schrud, ME. pa. pple. of SHROUD *v.*

i-schryned, ME. pa. pple. of SHRINE *v.*

i-schryve, ME. pa. pple. of SHRIVE *v.*

i-schud, ME. pa. pple. of SHOE *v.*

i-schulde, var. of I-SCHIELD *v.*

ischuretic (ɪskjʊˈrɛtɪk), *a.* and *sb.* [f. Gr. ἰσχουρέ-ειν to suffer from retention of urine: cf. next, and *diuretic.*]

A. *adj.* Having the property of curing ischuria. **B.** *sb.* A medicine that cures ischuria.

1706 PHILLIPS, *Ischureticks*, Medicines that force Urine, when there is a Stoppage of it. **1855** MAYNE *Expos. Lex.*, *Ischureticus*, old term applied to medicines..: ischuretic.

So †**ischu'retical** *a.*, troubled with ischuria.
1681 tr. *Willis' Rem. Med. Wks.* Vocab., *Ischuretical*, one so troubled with that distemper.

‖**ischuria** (ɪ'skjʊərɪə). Also in English form **ischury** ('ɪskjʊərɪ). [L. *ischūria*, a. Gr. ἰσχουρία retention of urine, f. ἴσχ-ειν to hold + οὖρον urine, οὔριος of urine.] Difficulty in passing urine, due either to suppression or retention.
1675 BAXTER *Cath. Theol.* II. v. 82 Like the consulting Physicians who could not agree, whether their Patients Ischury should be cured by Succinum, or by Electrum,.. and the poor man died because they could not consent. **1678** PHILLIPS (ed. 4), *Ischuria*, a stoppage, or difficulty of the Urine. **1684** tr. *Bonet's Merc. Compit.* IX. 343 The Ischury proceeded from no fault in the Kidneys, or Bladder. **1748** tr. *Renatus' Distemp. Horses* 266 When he cannot piss at all, it is called an Ischury. **1790** J. C. SMYTH in *Med. Commun.* II. 514 It has been the.. practice in ischurias, to have recourse to purgatives. **1876** tr. *Wagner's Gen. Pathol.* 573 After ischuria of several days' duration.

Hence **i'schuric** *a.*, belonging to ischuria (Mayne, 1855).

i-schuven, ME. pa. pple. of SHOVE *v.*

i-scild, var. of I-SCHIELD *v. Obs.*

i-sclaundred, ME. pa. pple. of SLANDER *v.*

i-scod, ME. pa. pple. of SHOE *v.*

†**i-'scole.** *Obs.* [A deriv. in ʒe-, I-[1], of OE. *scolu*, *scól*, school, troop, shoal, OS. *skola* band, troop.] A troop, host.
a **1175** *Cott. Hom.* 243 In þes deofles heriscole.. In þes middeneardes iscole.. In þes flesces iscole [fihteð aȝen us] euel ȝeþanc and fule lustes.

i-score, ME. pa. pple. of SHEAR *v.*

i-scorned, ME. pa. pple. of SCORN *v.*

i-scoten, ME. pa. pple. of SHOOT *v.*

i-scourged, ME. pa. pple. of SCOURGE *v.*

i-scoven, ME. pa. pple. of SHOVE *v.*

i-scrape, ME. pa. pple. of SCRAPE *v.*

i-scrifen, ME. pa. pple. of SHRIVE *v.*

i-scrud, ME. pa. pple. of SHROUD *v.*

Ise, I'se. a. Dial. or archaic abbreviation of *I shall*; also = *I's*, *I is*, dial. for *I am*.
1796 *Ned Evans* I. 136 I'se warrant you've been at Mr. Muckworm's. **1814** SCOTT *Wav.* xxx, I'se warrant him nane of your whingeing King George folk. *Ibid.* xlii, Troth I'se ensure him, an he'll bide us. **1828** *Craven Dial.*, *Ise*, I am or I will. *c* **1863** T. TAYLOR in M. R. Booth *Eng. Plays of 19th Cent.* (1969) II. 91 *Waiter.* Beg pardon sir, it's for No. 1. *Brierly.* I'se No. 1.

b. *spec.* in the United States. Also **I's.**
Freq. in Black English writings.
1852 W. L. G. SMITH *Life at South* iii. 51 I'se tinking wha' jolly time we will hab on Saturday arternoon, down under ole elm trees, on bank ob de riber. **1875** S. & C. LANIER in *Scribner's Monthly* June 240 I'se pow'ful skeered; but neversomeless I ain't gwine run away. *Ibid.*, I's like a word dat somebody done said, and den forgotten. **1898** P. L. DUNBAR *Folks from Dixie* 32 No, suh, I's a Babtist myse'f. *Ibid.* 49 I's mighty fond o' fishin', myse'f. **1902** J. D. CORROTHERS *Black Cat Club: Negro Humor & Folklore* i. 14 I'se a genamum, mase'f. *Ibid.* iii. 43, I writes a good han' and I's done read de dictionary. *Ibid.* iv. 56 De kine o' dahkey I'se talkin' 'bout am de feller whut's done bumped his head up ag'inst some college 'tel he cain't talk nothin' but Greek an' Latin, an' cuss you in Trinogometry. **1922** T. W. TALLEY *Negro Folk Rhymes* 135 I'se a bird o' one fedder, w'en it comes to you. **1927** A. P. RANDOLPH in A. Dundes *Mother Wit* (1973) 201/2 Wait a minute, son. I's wid you. *Ibid.*, Suppose des white folks find out I'se jined dis Brotherhood? *Ibid.*, Suppose des white folks ask me whether I'se a member? **1940** J. STREET in *Sat. Even. Post* 6 Jan. 32/2 I knows Ise out-figger'd. I knows Ise whupped. **1967** C. HIMES *Black on Black* (1973) 133 'I'se tired as you are,' she said evilly. *Ibid.* 136 Ise already free.

-ise[1], a frequent spelling of -IZE, suffix forming vbs., which see.

-ise[2], suffix of sbs., repr. OF. *-ise*, properly:—L. *-ītia*, but also, in words of learned formation, put for L. *-icia*, *-itia*, *-icium*, *-itium*, as in L. *justitia*, *judicium*, *servitium*, OF. *justise*, *juise*, *servise*. Hence it became a living suffix, forming abstract sbs. of quality, state, or function, as in *couard-ise*, *friand-ise*, *gaillard-ise*, *marchand-ise*. In the words from L., *-ise* was subsequently changed in F. to *-ice*, as in *justice*, *service*, in which form the suffix mostly appears in Eng., as in *justice*, *service*, *cowardice*; but *-ise* is found in *franchise*, *merchandise*, the obsolete or archaic *niggardise*, *quaintise*, *riotise*, *truandise*, *valiantise*, *warrantise*, and in such barely-naturalized words as *galliardise*, *gourmandise*, *paliardise*; also, in *exercise*, F. *exercice*, L. *exercitium*. Native formations on the same type are *inconvenientise*, *sluggardise*.

i-seaid, ME. pa. pple. of SAY *v.*

i-seald, ME. pa. pple. of SELL *v.*

i-sealed, ME. pa. pple. of SEAL *v.*

†**i-seche**, *v. Obs.* [OE. *ʒesécan*, *-sécean*, f. *ʒe-*, I-[1] + *séc(e)an* to SEEK.] *trans.* To seek, seek for.
Beowulf (Z.) 684 ʒif he ʒesecean dear wiʒ. *a* **1000** *Cædmon's Gen.* 1668 (Gr.) þæs þe hie ʒesohton Sennera feld. *c* **1000** *Satan* 213 He oðer lif eft ʒeseceð. *c* **1175** *Lamb. Hom.* 31 þene preost he mot isechen þe hine acursede. *c* **1200** *Trin. Coll. Hom.* 145 þa þohte hie þat hie hine ȝeseche wolde. *c* **1205** LAY. 9223 He hætte.. alle his hæȝe men his husti[n]gge isechen. *Ibid.* 25029 Cesar isohte Bruttene mid baldere strengðe. *a* **1250** *Owl & Night.* 741 Ich.. bidde þat hi moten iseche þan ilke song that ever is eche.

isechele, isechokil, isecle, obs. ff. ICICLE.

†**i-'see**, *v. Obs.* Forms: see SEE *v.* [OE. *ʒeséon*, f. *ʒe-*, I-[1] + *séon* to SEE; = Goth. *gasaihwan*, OHG. *gasehan*, MHG. *gesehen*.] *trans.* To see, behold.
Beowulf (Z.) 221 Ða liðende land ʒesawon. *a* **1000** *Cædmon's Gen.* 666 (Gr.) Ic mæʒ heonon ʒeseon hwær he sylf siteð. *c* **1000** *Ags. Gosp.* Matt. xiii. 17 Maneʒa.. rihtwise ʒewilnudon þa þing to ʒe-seonne [*Lindisf.* ʒesea] þe ʒe ʒeseoþ and hiʒ ne ʒe-sawon [*Hatt. G.* ʒe-seaʒen]. *Ibid.* Mark viii. 24 Ic ʒe-seo [*Lindisf.* ʒeseom, *Rushw.* ʒisiom] men swylce treow gangende. *c* **1175** *Lamb. Hom.* 123 Alswa deð mahȝe fisce þe isið þet es, and ne isihȝ na þene hoc þe sticað on þan ese. *a* **1240** *Ureisun* in *Cott. Hom.* 197 Ful wel þu me iseie þauh þu stille were. *c* **1305** *St. Dunstan* 86 in *E.E. Poems* (1862) 36 He ne miȝte iseo nomore. *c* **1315** SHOREHAM 107 Thys may ech man ysy. *c* **1320** *Cast. Love* 1247 Me may.. I-syn that he is God by his dede. **1340** *Ayenb.* 81 Uayrhede þet þe eȝe of þe bodye yzyȝþ. *Ibid.* 185 Yziȝ and þench huo yefþ þane red. *c* **1369** CHAUCER *Dethe Blaunche* 205 Ye shul me neuer on lyve y-se. **1387** TREVISA *Higden* (Rolls) III. 345 [Plato] miȝt nouȝt i-see Ieremyas. ? *a* **1400** *S.E. Leg.* (MS. Bodl. 779) in *Archiv Stud. neu. Spr.* LXXXII. 314/91 So þou I-syxt I-wis.

i-seeled, -et, ME. pa. pple. of SEAL *v.*

i-seen, ME. pa. pple. of SEE *v.*

†**i-'seggen**, *v. Obs.* Forms: see SAY *v.* [OE. *ʒesęcgan*, f. *ʒe-*, I-[1] + *sęcgan* to say: cognate with OS. *giseggian*, OHG. *gasagên*, MHG. *gesagen*.] *trans.* To say, tell, declare, relate, confess.
c **900** tr. *Bæda's Hist.* II. xi[iii]. (1890) 190 Ic will mine leathorfulle þeawas ʒesecgan. *a* **1000** *Cædmon's Daniel* 165 He ʒesæde swefen cyninge. *c* **1000** *Guthlac* 676 Mec dryhten heht snude ʒesecgan þæt ʒe.. him hearsume.. wæron. *c* **1175** *Lamb. Hom.* 15 Hit is riht þet me us nede and isegge þet sceamie. *c* **1205** LAY. 21885 Heo.. þus iseiden.

ise-ȝekille, -yokel, obs. var. ICICLE.

Isegrim ('aɪzəgrɪm). Also 7 **Isgrin.** [a. MHG., Ger. *Isegrimm*, *Isengrimm*, also *Isengrîn*, *Eisengrein*, MDu. *Isengryn*, *Isegrijn*, *-grijm*, Du. *Ijzegrim*, the name of the wolf in *Reynard the Fox*, and other beast-fables; in OHG. *Isangrîm* as a man's name, f. *îsan*, *îsen*, etc. 'iron' + *-grîm*, cf. *grîma*, mask, hood, helmet; but in later use often associated with *grime*, grim, wrathful, fierce.] An appellation applied, after the manner of a proper name, to the wolf. *rare* in Eng. use.
1481 CAXTON *Reynard* ii, Isegrym the wulf wyth his lynage and frendes cam and stode to fore the kynge. *Passim.* **1622** FLETCHER *Beggar's Bush* III. iii, I know to chase the Roe, The winde out-stripping, Isgrin [*mod. ed.* Isgrim] himself.

†**i-'sehtne**, *v. Obs.* [f. *ȝe-*, I-[1] + *sehtnien*, *sahtnien*, to reconcile.] *trans.* To reconcile.
c **1175** *Lamb. Hom.* 83 He isehtnede god and man.

i-seid, ME. pa. pple. of SAY *v.*

iseidomal: see ISO-.

i-seie, i-seiȝe, ME. pa. pple. of SEE *v.*

i-seilet, ME. pa. pple. of SEAL *v.*

i-seilled, ME. pa. pple. of SAIL *v.*

i-seined, ME. pa. pple. of *sein*, SIGN *v.*

isel, izle ('aɪz(ə)l). Now only *dial.* Forms: 1 **ysel, ysle,** 3 **isel,** 4 **usle, usel,** 5 **iselle, isyl(le, ysel,** 6 **isille, ysyle,** 6–7 (9 *Sc. dial.*) **isle,** 7 **issle,** 8 *Sc.* **aizle,** 9 *Sc.* **eizel.** [OE. *ysel*, *ysle*, cogn. with MHG. *usele*, *usel*, *üsele*, mod.Ger. dial. *üsel*, *isel*, *üssel*, *issel*, spark, LG. *ösel*, ON. *usli* fire, conflagration; f. root *us-* (L. *ur-ĕre*, *us-tum* to burn).] A spark; an ember; chiefly in *pl.*, Sparks, embers; ashes; in *mod. dial.*, Floating sparks from a conflagration; extinct sparks, particles of soot, smuts.
c **1000** ÆLFRIC *Gen.* xix. 28 þa beheolde Abraham.. and ʒeseah hu þa ysla upfluʒon mid þam smice. *c* **1200** *Trin. Coll. Hom.* 65 Ich.. pine me seluen on asshen and on iselen. **13..** *E.E. Allit. P.* B. 747, I am bot erþe ful euel and vsle so blake. **1387** TREVISA *Higden* (Rolls) IV. 431 Iosephus was i-founde y-hid among useles. *c* **1420** *Pallad. on Husb.* IX. 184 Ysels myxt with litel water. *c* **1440** *Promp. Parv.* 266/1 Isyl of fyre, *favilla.* **1513** DOUGLAS *Æneis* X. i. 135 Amang the assys cauld And lattyr isillys of thar kynd cuntre. **1547** SALESBURY *Welsh Dict.*, *Elw tan*, ysyle. **1609** BIBLE (Douay) *Isa.* xxix. 5 As smal dust: and as issles passing away. **1785** BURNS *Halloween* 115 An aizle brunt Her braw new worset apron. **1866** *Reader* 15 Dec. 1001 Killmoulis.. often torments the goodman sorely by throwing 'isles' or ashes out when sheelin or shelled oats are spread out to dry. **1877** *N.W. Linc. Gloss.*, *Izles*, floating particles of soot, smuts.
Comb. *c* **1440** *Promp. Parv.* 266/1 Isylkake.. bakyne vndyr askys, *flamicia.*

Iseland, obs. form of ICELAND.

i-seld, ME. pa. pple. of SELL *v.*

†**i-sele**, *a. Obs.* Also 3 **i-sæle.** [Cf. OE. *ʒesǽl* in *ʒesǽllíc* happy, and next.] = next.
c **1205** LAY. 7666 Ne wurðe he nauere isæle. *Ibid.* 29480 þe pape was isele.

†**i-'seli**, *a. Obs.* [OE. *ʒesǽliʒ*, f. *ʒe-*, I-[1] + *sǽliʒ* happy: see SILLY.] Happy, fortunate, prosperous.
c **888** K. ÆLFRED *Boeth.* xxvi. §1 Hweðer micel feoh mæʒe ænigne mon don swa ʒesæline, ðæt he nanes þinges maran ne þyrfe. *c* **893** —— *Oros.* v. ii. §9 Hi fram ʒesælʒum tidum ʒilpað. *a* **1000** *Cædmon's Gen.* 1138 Seth wæs ʒesæliʒ. *c* **1175** *Lamb. Hom.* 15 ȝef we weren iseli. *Ibid.* 109 Iselie beoð efre þa mildheortan. *c* **1205** LAY. 28861 Snel cniht wes Carriz, ah he nes noht iseli. *a* **1225** *Ancr. R.* 308 Eadi is he and iseli.

†**i-selth.** *Obs.* Forms: 1 **ʒesǽlð,** 2 **iselhðe,** 2–3 **iselðe, iseluhðe.** [OE. *ʒesǽlþ*, f. *ʒesǽl-* happy; in early ME., in part from *ʒesǽliʒ*: see prec.] Happiness, felicity, fortune.
c **888** K. ÆLFRED *Boeth.* xxiii, Sio soðe ʒesælð. *c* **1175** *Lamb. Hom.* 105 Swa þet we.. on iselhðan to swiðe ne blissian. *a* **1200** *Moral Ode* 13 Ich mihte habbe bet idon, hefde ich þe iselþe. *a* **1225** *Ancr. R.* 382 þet is ure iseluhðe þet we beoren in ure bodie Jesu Cristes deadlicnesse.

†**i-seme**, *v. Obs.* [OE. *ʒeséman*, f. *ʒe-*, I-[1] + *séman* to bring to agreement, settle, f. *sóm* agreement.]
1. *trans.* To reconcile, to settle.
c **893** K. ÆLFRED *Oros.* III. vii. §5 Ðæt he hie ʒeseman wolde. *c* **1100** *O.E. Chron.* an. 1094 Hi ʒesemede beon ne mihtan.
2. To suit, to beseem.
c **1205** LAY. 9587 He hæhte setten hire on nome þe hire [þe burh] mihte isemen [*c* **1275** semi].

†**i-semeliche**, *adv. Obs.* [f. I-[1] + *sémeliche* SEEMLY.] In a seemly or becoming manner; quietly.
c **1205** LAY. 21785 An imetliche broc, þe.. swiðe isemeliche into sæ wendeð.

isen, obs. variant of IRON.

i-sen(e, ME. pa. pple. of SEE *v.*

†**i-'send**, *v. Obs.* [OE. *ʒesendan*, f. *ʒe-*, I-[1] + *sendan* to SEND; = Goth. *gasandjan*, OHG. *gisenten*, MHG. *gesenden*.] *trans.* To send.
971 *Blickl. Hom.* 9 þa wæs ʒesended þæt goldhord. *c* **1325** in *O.E. Misc.* 196 þat he me isende. **13..** *K. Alis.* 1487 They ..four thousand mark ysende.

i-send, i-sent, ME. pa. pple. of SEND *v.*

isenergic, isenthalpic, isentropic, -ally: see ISO-.

i-seowed, ME. pa. pple. of SEW *v.*

isepiptesis, isopiptesis (aɪ,sɛpɪ'(p)tiːsɪs, aɪsəʊpɪ'(p)tiːsɪs). *rare.* [a. G. *isepiptese* (A. T. von Middendorff 1855, in *Mém. Acad. Imp. Sci. St. Pétersbourg, 6e série, Sci. nat.* VIII. 8), f. Gr. ἐπίπτησις flying down upon.] A line (either imaginary or on a map) connecting points which migrating birds reach at the same time. Hence **isepi'ptesial** *a.*
1875 A. NEWTON in *Encycl. Brit.* III. 768/1 His [*sc.* Middendorff's] chief object has been to trace what he has termed the isepipteses... Assuming that the advance is directly across the isepiptesial lines.. the whole course of the migration is thus most accurately made known. **1926** A. L. THOMSON *Probl. Bird-Migration* viii. 132 His [*sc.* Middendorff's] method was to plot out 'isepipteses', or isochronal lines, joining up all localities corresponding with each other as to their average dates for the arrival of particular summer visitors. [**1962** C. D. SHERMAN tr. *Dorst's Migrations of Birds* viii. 233 He [*sc.* Middendorff] plotted these data on a map, linked the localities which migrants reach on the same date and thus obtained a line he called the isopiptes.. (this line was later named the isochronal line).]

i-serched, ME. pa. pple. of SEARCH *v.*

iserine ('aɪzərɪn). *Min.* [ad. Ger. *iserin* (Werner, 1797); named from *Iserwiese* in Bohemia, one of the localities for the mineral.] = next.
1805 R. JAMESON *Min.* II. 502 Fifth Species, Iserine. **1868** DANA *Min.* (ed. 5) §181 The loose Iron-sand of Iserwiese, called *iserine*, is in part, at least, in isometric octahedrons.

iserite ('aɪzəraɪt). *Min.* [Altered by Dana from prec.: see -ITE.] A variety of ILMENITE, found as a black crystalline sand.
1868 DANA *Min.* (ed. 5) §181 Iserite is supposed to be isometric titanic iron.

i-served, ME. pa. pple. of SERVE *v.*

i-sesed, ME. pa. pple. of CEASE, SEIZE *v.*

i-set, i-sette, ME. pa. pple. of SET *v.*

†**i-set,** *v. Obs.* [OE. *ȝesętt-an*, f. *ȝe-*, I-¹ + *sęttan* to SET. Cognate with OS. *gisettian*, OHG. *gasezzan*, Goth. *gasatjan*.] *trans.* To set; to set up, establish.

971 *Blickl. Hom.* 143 Þa apostolas . . hie ȝesetton on þæm fæȝran neorxna wange. *a* **1000** *O.E. Chron.* an. 604 Sæberht . . þone Æðelberht ȝesette þær to cininga. *a* **1175** *Cott. Hom.* 227 Þes cenne god sælde and ȝesette ǽ *vel* laga. *c* **1175** *Lamb. Hom.* 93 Ða apostoli siððan . . isetten iacob þet wes ihaten rihtwis on cristes selt [= setl]. *c* **1205** LAY. 22053 Seollic is þe lauerd þat al hit isette.

isethionic (aɪsiːθɪˈɒnɪk), *a. Chem.* [f. ISO- b + ETHIONIC.] In ***isethionic acid***, a monobasic acid, $C_2H_6SO_4$, formed together with sulphuric acid, by boiling ethionic acid with water. Its salts are **i'sethionates**.

1838 T. THOMSON *Chem. Org. Bodies* 190 In 1833, M. Magnus . . discovered three acids. . . He distinguished them by the names of althionic, ethionic, and isethionic acids. **1859** *Fownes' Man. Chem.* 383 When a solution of ethionic acid is boiled, it is decomposed into sulphuric acid, and a second new acid, the isethionic, isomeric with sulphovinic acid. *Ibid.*, The isethionates of baryta, lead, copper, potassa, soda, and ammonia crystallize with facility . . into taurin. **1878** KINGZETT *Anim. Chem.* 95 Taurin appears to be dehydrated isæthionate of ammonium. **1888** REMSEN *Org. Chem.* 357 Isethionic acid, . . also known as hydroxyethyl-sulphonic acid.

†**i-'setnesse.** *Obs.* [OE. *ȝesętnes*, f. *ȝesęttan*, I-SET *v.*: see -NESS.] Institution, ordinance, statute, law.

c **900** tr. *Bæda's Hist.* IV. v. (1890) 274 In swa micle lufan þære Romaniscan cirican ȝesetenisse. *c* **1000** ÆLFRIC *Hom.* I. 358 Seo ealde æ wæs eaðelicre þonne Cristes ȝesetnys sy. *c* **1000** *Ags. Gosp.* Mark vii. 3 Healdende hyra yldrena ȝesetnessa. *c* **1175** *Lamb. Hom.* 87 Þe dei pentecostes ihaten on þere alde isetnesse. *Ibid.* 119 Butan godes laȝe and godes isetnesse. **1258** *Proclam. Hen. III* (Rot. Pat. 43 Hen. III, M. 15. No. 40. l. 4), To healden and to werien þo itsetnesses þæt beon imakede & beon to makien.

i-seyd, ME. pa. pple. of SAY *v.*

i-seye, i-seyn, ME. pa. pple. of SEE *v.*

Isfahan: see ISPAHAN.

ish (ɪʃ), *sb. Sc.* Forms: 4 ysche, 5-6 ische, 7- ish. [f. ISH *v.*¹]

1. Issue, egress, exit; right of exit; †place of egress. Now only in *Sc. Law*, in phr. ***ish and entry*** (see quot. 1861).

1375 BARBOUR *Bruce* VI. 363 The strat entre Of the furde, and the ysche alsua. **14..** *Burgh Lawis* (Rec. Soc.) No. 52 The tane sall geyff to the aldyrman a penny for the ische and the tothir sall geyff a penny for the entre. **1513** DOUGLAS *Æneis* VII. xiv. 51 Quhair as the chill river hait Vfens Seikis . . Amyd how valeis his renk and ische. *a* **1651** CALDERWOOD *Hist. Kirk*, Souldiours placed to stop all ish and entrie. **1861** W. BELL *Dict. Law Scot.* 476/1 The clause, *cum libero exitu et introitu* ('with free ish and entry'), in the *tenendas* of a charter, imports a right to all ways and passages, in so far as they may be necessary, to kirk and market, through the adjacent grounds of the granter.

2. The conclusion of a period of time; the expiry of a legal term, a lease, etc. Now only in *Sc. Law*.

1502 in Pitcairn *Anc. Crim. Trials* I. *30 For þe space of fourty days; at the ische of þe quhilk terme ande ende of xl dais [etc.]. **1533** BELLENDEN *Livy* II. (1822) 159 At the ische of this yere, Marcus Minucius and Aulus Sempronius war maid consullis. *c* **1575** *Balfour's Practicks* (1754) 209 Gif ane man, efter the ische of his takkis . . ressavis foir-maill for the samin landis. **1754** ERSKINE *Princ. Sc. Law* (1809) 196 Seldom reduced into writing, when they are not to have effect before the ish. **1886** *Act 49 & 50 Vict.* c. 50 §5 Notice of removal . . shall . . be given as many days before the date of ish as shall be equivalent to at least one third of the full period of duration of the lease.

†**ish, iss,** *v.*¹ *Obs.* Forms: α. 4 ice, 4-5 isse. β. *Sc.* 4-5 ysche, 4-6 isch(e, 5 issh, yssh, yss(e, (ussh), 6 ish(e. [ME. a. OF. *issir*, (*yssir*, *ussir*), (cf. ISSANT), earlier *eissir* = It. *escire*, *uscire*:—L. *exīre* to go out, f. *ex* out + *īre* to go.]

1. *intr.* = ISSUE *v.* 1-3.

α. [**1292** BRITTON III. xvii. §3 Qe de soen gre . . s'en issi et se demist. *transl.* That of his own accord he . . went out and dispossessed himself.] *c* **1330** R. BRUNNE *Chron. Wace* (Rolls) 3466 Þey armede hem, and isseden out. *c* **1350** *Will. Palerne* 3789 William & his wiȝes . . softly Iced out of þe cite whan þei seie time. **1426** LYDG. *De Guil. Pilgr.* 14407 Wynd and wordys rud and dul Yssen out fful gret plente.

β. **1375** BARBOUR *Bruce* II. 278 Ȝe sall Isch furth to the bataill, And fecht with thaim. *c* **1400** *Destr. Troy* 5784 Arowes vp in the aire ysshit full þicke. *c* **1420** *Avow. Arth.* lxiv, On a day we vsshet oute. **1558** *Sc. Acts Mary* (1814) II. 508 Gife It sal happin . . oure sade souerane departe of þis mortale life wᵗout airis Ischeit of hir body. *a* **1578** LINDESAY (Pitscottie) *Chron. Scot.* (S.T.S.) II. 11 Certaine of the castell men wschit [*ed.* 1728 ishing] out and skirmischit thame.

fig. *c* **1374** CHAUCER *Boeth.* III. pr. xii. 82 (Camb. MS.) Þat hast so wouen me with thy resouns . . thow þat ooþer while entrist ther þou issest and oother while issest ther thow entrist.

2. *trans.* To go out of, depart from. *rare.*

c **1450** *Mirour Saluacioun* 5031 With joye isshed thow the Citee of his swete birth Bethelem.

3. *trans.* To clear (a place) by driving out those within.

1537 *Sc. Acts. Jas. V*, c. 50 That an Maisser ische the Councel-house, and himselfe sall stande at the dure, and let na man enter.

Hence †**ishing** *vbl. sb.* = ISSUING *vbl. sb.*

1375 BARBOUR *Bruce* XV. 158 Till warn hym of thair ysching. *c* **1422** HOCCLEVE *Learn to Die* 629 Of his spirit shal be the issynge, In-to eternal blisse the entrynge. **1549** *Compl. Scot.* xi. 98 The . . place had ane narrou entres & narrou isching.

ish, *v.*² *nonce-wd.* [Echoic.] *intr.* To make the sound *ish!* or *sh!* as in striking the air forcibly.

1898 SIR G. ROBERTSON *Chitral* xxi. 201 Bullets went 'ishing' just over it with curious monotony.

-ish¹, a suffix forming adjs., of Com. Teut. origin; Goth. *-isks*, ON. *-iskr*, OHG., OS., OFris., OE. *-isc*, Ger., Du. *-isch*: cognate with Gr. *-ισκ-ος* dim. suffix of sbs. Sometimes syncopated to *-sh* (spelt also *-ch*). In Scottish usually *-is*, syncopated *-s*, *-ce*. In words of old formation, the prec. vowel had umlaut (which was often present in the sb. whence the adj. in *-isc* was formed); in later use the vowel has usually been altered back to that of the sb. when this is in use; e.g. *Scottish*, *Danish*, after *Scot*, *Dane*; the modified vowel being retained in other cases, as in *English*, *French*, *Welsh*.

1. In OE. and the cognate langs., chiefly forming gentile adjs. from national names: e.g. *British* (OE. *Brittisc*), *English* (OE. *Englisc*, †Sc. *Inglis*), *Scottish*, *Scotch* (OE. *Scyttisc*, Sc. †*Scottis*, *Scots*), *Irish* (OE. *Irisc*), *Welsh* (OE. *Wielisc*, †Sc. *Walys*, *Wallis*); *Danish* (OE. *Dęnisc*, †Sc. *Dense*, *Dence*); *Frankish*, *French* (OE. *Fręncisc*); so in many adjs. of various ages, as *Alemannish*, *Finnish*, *Flemish*, *Gaulish*, †*Greekish* (OE. *Grécisc*), *Icelandish*, *Jewish*, *Jutish*, *Netherlandish*, *Pictish*, *Polish*, *Romish*, *Spanish*, *Swedish*, *Turkish*, *Wendish*.

2. Added to other sbs., with the sense 'Of or belonging to a person or thing, of the nature or character of'. These were not numerous in OE., whence only a few have come down to later times. Examples are *folcisc* popular, *hǽðenisc* heathenish, *þéodisc* national, *inlęndisc* inlandish, *utlęndisc* outlandish (which come close to the gentile group in 1); also *męnnisc* human, *cildisc* childish, *cierlisc* churlish. In later times this ending has become exceedingly common, sometimes in the earlier colourless sense as *boyish*, *girlish*, *waggish*, but chiefly in a derogatory sense, 'Having the (bad or objectionable) qualities of': as in *apish*, *babyish*, *boarish*, *boorish*, *brutish*, *clownish*, *currish*, *devilish*, *doggish*, *doltish*, *dronish*, *foolish*, *foppish*, *goatish*, *ghoulish*, *hoggish*, *impish*, *knavish*, *mannish*, *monkish*, *mulish*, *owlish*, *prudish*, *roguish*, *selfish*, *shrewish*, *sluggish*, *sluttish*, *sottish*, *swinish*, *thievish*, *waspish*, *whorish*, *wolvish*, *womanish*. (These have usually corresponding Ger. forms in *-isch*.) Also from names of things, with sense 'of the nature of, tending to', as in *aguish*, *blockish*, *bookish*, *brinish*, *feverish*, *freakish*, *hellish*, *moorish*; or from other parts of speech, as *snappish*, *stand-offish*, *uppish*.

In recent colloquial and journalistic use, *-ish* has become the favourite ending for forming adjs. for the nonce (esp. of a slighting or depreciatory nature) on proper names of persons, places, or things, and even on phrases, e.g. *Disraelitish*, *Heine-ish*, *Mark Twainish*, *Micawberish*, *Miss Martineauish*, *Queen Annish*, *Spectator-ish*, *Tupperish*, *West Endish*; *all-over-ish*, *at-homeish*, *devil-may-care-ish*, *how-d'ye-doish*, *jolly-good-fellowish*, *merry-go-roundish*, *out-of-townish*, and the like.

1815 *Hist. Mr. J. Decastro* II. 243 She might have an I-dont-know-howishness about her which no lady can run away from unless she runs one way. **1836** DICKENS *Sk. Boz* (1837) II. 2 A clean-cravatish formality of manner. **1845** TENNYSON in Ld. Tennyson *Mem.* (1897) I. 227, I feel the least bit possible Miss Martineauish about it. **1883** 'ANNIE THOMAS' *Mod. Housewife* 150 The Micawberish prospect of anything turning up. **1887** *Pall Mall G.* 17 Oct. 3/1 A Heine-ish sneer at the tendency of the Eternal-Feminine to relax the tension of our ideals. **1894** *Daily News* 4 Jan. 4/7 Some huge pile of building, generally much more Queen Anne-ish than the houses of Queen Anne's own time.

3. Added to adjs. with the sense 'Of the nature of, approaching the quality of, somewhat', apparently first with words of colour (which may have been treated as sbs., and so have originally come under 2): e.g. *bluish* (*a* 1400), *blackish* (*a* 1500), *brownish*, *reddish*, *whitish*, *yellowish*, etc. In later use also with other adjs., and now, in colloquial use, possible with nearly all monosyllabic adjs., and some others, e.g. *brightish*, *broadish*, *coldish*, *darkish*, *dimmish*, *dryish*, *dullish*, *duskish*, *feeblish*, *goodish*, *hardish*, *loudish*, *narrowish*, *oldish*, *palish*, *poorish*, *queerish*, *smallish*, *smartish*, *softish*, *tallish*, *thickish*, *thinnish*, *warmish*, *weakish*, *wettish*, *youngish*. Derivatives of this type are peculiar to English among the cognate languages: those formed on adjs. of colour answer to F. adjs. in *-âtre*, as *bleuâtre*, *noirâtre*, and to Ger. adjs. in *-lich*, as *bläulich*, *schwärtzlich*. Of other adjectives, only a few have equivalent Ger. forms in *-lich*; the force of *-ish* is ordinarily given in Ger. by the qualifying *etwas* or *ein wenig*.

4. Added to names of hours of the day or numbers of years to denote: round about, somewhere near (the time or period of) (prob. after *earlyish*, *latish*).

1916 'PETER' *Trench Yarns* ix. 110 'What time shall I come?' 'Elevenish,' Sam replied. **1925** B. TRAVERS *Mischief* xiv. 209, I shall be going to Shady Nook at about tenish. **1930** J. B. PRIESTLEY *Angel Pavement* iii. 106 Eightish then, next Tuesday, eh? **1941** *Britannia & Eve* Sept. 15/3 Lady Regan was probably thirty. Sir Gerald looked fifty-five-ish. **1950** *Sat. Rev. Lit.* 28 Jan., The ninetyish, gentle Chandler at the reception desk. **1955** E. HYAMS *Slaughterhouse Informer* xiv. 220 'We'll make a party of it.' 'Sixish?' **1967** B. NORMAN *Matter of Mandrake* xx. 174 Will you be in your room about sevenish? **1971** P. PURSER *Holy Father's Navy* iii. 19 Thirtyish furniture in pale, shabby wood. **1972** C. FREMLIN *Appointment with Yesterday* iv. 24 This anxious thirty-five-ish person.

From adjs. in *-ish*, advbs. in **-ishly** and sbs. of quality in **-ishness**, are formed *ad libitum*: e.g. *girlishly*, *girlishness*, *feverishly*, *feverishness*.

-ish², a suffix of verbs, repr. F. *-iss-*, extended stem of verbs in *-ir*, e.g. *périr* to perish, *periss-ant*, *ils periss-ent*. The F. *-iss-* originated in the L. *-isc-* of inceptive verbs, which in It., Pr., and Fr. was extended to form a class of simple verbs, corresp. to L. verbs in *-īre* and *-ēre*, and including others which were assimilated to these. At their first adoption, these verbs ended in Eng. in *-is*, *-ise*, *-iss(e*, which before 1400 changed to *-isshe*. In Sc. the original *-is*, *-isse*, was retained longer, and appeared in 16th c. as *-eis(e*: *pereis*, *fleureis*. Among the chief examples of this ending are *abolish*, *accomplish*, *banish*, *blandish*, *blemish*, *brandish*, *burnish*, *cherish*, *demolish*, *embellish*, *establish*, *finish*, *flourish*, *furbish*, *furnish*, *garnish*, *impoverish*, *languish*, *nourish*, *perish*, *polish*, *punish*, *ravish*, *relinquish*, *replenish*, *tarnish*, *vanish*, *varnish*.

In some cases, other Fr. endings have been levelled under this suffix in AFr. or English: such are *admonish*, *astonish*, *diminish*, *distinguish*, *eternish*, *famish*, *lavish*, *minish*, *monish*, *publish*, *relish*, etc., for the history of which see the individual words.

In a few words the F. *-iss-* is represented in Eng. by *-ise*, or even *-ize*: e.g. *avertir*, *-iss-* ADVERTISE, *châstir*, *-iss-* CHASTISE; *amortir*, *-iss-* AMORTIZE; *réjouir*, *rejouiss-* has given REJOICE.

ishan (ˈiːʃɑːn). [Pers., = hill, landmark.] A prehistoric mound in Iraq.

1921 *Blackw. Mag.* June 708/1 They had just moved their home to an ishan or mound only some ten or fifteen minutes from the river. **1927** 'FULANAIN' *Haji Rikkan* i. 8 Facing us was a group of the strange mounds or *ishans* which here and there, in the marshes of Southern 'Iraq, stand out high, or seeming high in that vast watery expanse. **1964** W. THESIGER *Marsh Arabs* xix. 173 We passed a bare black mound . . known to the Madan as Ishan Waqif, or Standing Island.

i-shape(n, ME. pa. pple. of SHAPE *v.*

isher, -erie, obs. Sc. forms of USHER, -ERY.

ishew, -u, -we, obs. forms of ISSUE *sb.* and *v.*

†**'ishies,** *sb. pl. Obs. rare.* [ad. L. *ischia*, Gr. *ἰσχία*: see ISCHIUM.] Hip-joints.

1653 URQUHART *Rabelais* I. xxvii, He spoiled the frame of their kidneys . . heaved off of the hinges their ishies.

Ishihara (ɪʃɪˈhɑːrə). *Ophthalm.* The name of Shinobu *Ishihara* (1879-1963), Japanese ophthalmologist, used *attrib.* with reference to a test for colour-blindness (the ***Ishihara test***) devised by him in 1917, in which the subject is asked to name the numbers in (or, for illiterates, to distinguish pathways through) a series of printed plates (***Ishihara plates***), in each of which the numbers or pathways are formed of coloured spots in a background of spots of a different colour or colours; so ***Ishihara-blind*** adj., ***method***, etc.

1924 *Amer. Jrnl. Physiol. Optics* V. 269 (*heading*) The Ishihara test for color blindness. **1944** *Amer. Jrnl. Physiol.* CXL. 578 The color vision was tested by the Ishihara method. *Ibid.* 579 Twelve of the 'Ishihara blind' students were trichromats. *Ibid.*, The Ishihara test gave a correct diagnosis. **1968** C. BEARD et al. *Symposium Surg. & Med. Managem. Congenital Anomalies Eye* xvi. 423 In the Ishihara plates the colors of the test symbols and of the background are of such saturation, hue, and brightness that they are regularly confused by either the deutan or protan or both.

Ibid. 425 The tracing plates in the Ishihara test.. are useful for young children and illiterates.

ishikawaite (ɪʃɪˈkɑːwəaɪt). *Min.* Also †ishikawite. [ad. Jap. *ishikawaishi* (K. Kimura 1922, in *Jrnl. Geol. Soc. Tokyo* XXIX. 320), f. *Ishikawa*, the name of a district in Honshu, Japan + *ishi* stone, mineral: see -ITE[1].] A black oxide of various metals, perhaps (U, Fe, Yt, Ce) (Nb, Ta)O_4.

1922 *Jrnl. Geol. Soc. Tokyo* XXIX. No. 347 (contents list), On ishikawite, a new mineral from Ishikawa District. **1923** *Mineral. Abstr.* II. 380 For ishikawaite.. new axes are suggested. **1944** C. PALACHE et al. *Dana's Syst. Min.* (ed. 7) I. 766 *Ishikawaite*... The tabular crystals {100} are supposedly orthorhombic.

ishilde, variant of I-SCHIELD *v.*

Ishmael (ˈɪʃmeɪəl). [A Heb. proper name *Yishmāʿēʾl* 'God will hear'. See also ISMAELIAN.] Proper name of the son of Abraham by Hagar; hence, allusively: An outcast; one 'whose hand is against every man, and every man's hand against him' (Gen. xvi. 12), one at war with society.

[**1835** W. IRVING *Tour Prairies* 100 Like.. the sons of Ishmael, their hand is against every one, and every one's hand against them.] **1899** *Westm. Gaz.* 16 Jan. 4/3 Men who were the very Ishmaels of the labour world.

Hence **ˈIshmaelite** (a descendant of Ishmael, as the Arabs claim to be): *fig.* = ISHMAEL; **Ishmaelitic** (-ˈɪtɪk), **ˈIshmaelitish** (-ˌaɪtɪʃ), of, pertaining to, of the nature of an Ishmaelite; **Ishmaelitism** (ˈɪʃmeɪəˌlaɪtɪz(ə)m), the character and action of an Ishmaelite.

1577 VAUTROUILLIER *Luther on Ep. Gal.* iv. 29 (1588) 227 a, It greeueth vs that these Ishmaelites hate and persecute vs so grievously. **1687** A. LOVELL tr. *Thevenot's Trav.* e, The name of *Sarazins* was given to the Ishmaelitish Arabians, or.. the Arabs of the Desart. **1848** THACKERAY *Van. Fair* lxvii, Jos's tents and pilau were pleasant to this little Ishmaelite. **1855** HYDE CLARKE *Eng. Dict.*, *Ishmaelitish*, like Ishmael; thievish. **1876** FAIRBAIRN *Strauss* II. in *Contemp. Rev.* June 125 Menzel was a literary Ishmaelite. **1880** M. D. CONWAY in *Academy* 24 July 55 An Ishmaelitish style of criticising his literary contemporaries. **1896** D. L. LEONARD *Cent. Congreg. Ohio* 71 Lonesome and in peril were they.. and fell into a wretched Ishmaelitish frame. **1897** O. SMEATON *Smollett* ii. 26 The same evil spirit of Social Ishmaelitism.. was present with him until a year or two of his death.

i-shote, ME. pa. pple. of SHOOT *v.*

Isiac (ˈaɪsɪæk, ˈɪsɪæk), *a.* and *sb.* [ad. L. *īsiac-us*, a. Gr. Ἰσιακός, f. *Isis*: see below.]

A. *adj.* Of or relating to Isis, the principal goddess of ancient Egyptian mythology.

Isiac table, a copper tablet of unknown origin, now in the royal gallery of Turin, containing figures of Egyptian deities with Isis in the middle.

1740 WARBURTON *Div. Legat.* IV. vi. Wks. 1811 IV. 296 There is a famous antique monument.. well known to the curious by the name of the Isiac or Bembine Table. **1796** J. OWEN *Trav. Europe* I. 320 The second, or Isiac table, is considered as one of the most precious monuments of ancient times, which Italy preserves. **1876** GLADSTONE *Homeric Synchr.* 234 This head, with the snakes, was apparently an Isiac symbol.

B. *sb.* A priest or worshipper of Isis.

1708 MOTTEUX *Rabelais* v. iv. (1737) 13 The Egyptian Heathens.. us'd to constitute their Isiacs, by shaving them.

Hence **Isiacal** (aɪˈsaɪəkəl) *a.* = ISIAC *a.*

1613 PURCHAS *Pilgrimage* (1614) 570 The Isiacall rites. **1889** FARRAR *Lives Fathers* I. III. 115 The Isiacal traditions of Egypt.

†**i-sib, i-sibbe**, *a. Obs.* [OE. *ȝesib(b* related, akin, f. *ȝe-*, I-[1] + *sibb* related, SIB. Cogn. with OHG. *gisibbo*.] Related, akin.

c **1000** *Job* in Thwaites *Heptat.* (1698) 167 Þry cyningas þe him ȝesibbe wæron. **1014** WULFSTAN *Sermo ad Anglos* (Napier xxxiii. 159), Ne bearh nu for oft ȝesib ȝesibban ðe ma þe fremdan. *c* **1175** *Lamb. Hom.* 137 Feader oðer moder broðer oðer suster oðer oðre swa isibbe. *c* **1205** LAY. 30533 Heo weoren isibbe. *c* **1275** *Duty Christians* 102 in *O.E. Misc.* 144 We beoþ alle isybbe. **1297** R. GLOUC. (Rolls) 6438 Alle þat were oȝt ysyb Edmond þe kynge. *c* **1305** 11000 *Virgins* 85 Meniee of hem him were isibbe.

Hence †**iˈsibsum**, OE. **ȝesib(b)sum**, peaceful.

c **897** K. ÆLFRED *Gregory's Past.* xlvi. 349 Se ðe of Gode cymð he bið godes willan and ȝesibsum. *c* **1175** *Lamb. Hom.* 95 Witutan laðe and isibsum. *Ibid.* 113 Þa beoð godes bern þe beoð isibsumme.

isicle, isi(c)kle, obs. forms of ICICLE.

‖**isidium** (aɪˈsɪdɪəm). *Bot.* Pl. isidia. [ad. mod.L. generic name *Isidium* (E. Acharius *Lichenographiae Suecicae Prodromus* (1798) 87), formerly used to include all lichens bearing isidia, f. *Isis*, *Isid-em*, Isis (in reference to her disc and horns).] One of a number of coral-like or wart-like elevations or excrescences of the thallus in certain lichens, having the function of soredia.

1866 *Treas. Bot.* 629/2 *Isidium*, a coral-like elevation of the thallus of a lichen, bearing a globule at its end. **1882** J. M. CROMBIE in *Encycl. Brit.* XIV. 557/2 Nylander observes.. that the isidia in the *Collemacei*.. 'show very clearly under the microscope the entire history of the evolution of the thallus'.

Hence **iˈsidial** *a.*, of or pertaining to an isidium; **iˈsidiate**, **isidiiferous** (aɪˌsɪdɪˈɪfərəs), **isidiophorous** (-ˈɒfərəs) *adjs.* [see -FEROUS, -PHOROUS], bearing isidia; **isidioid** (aɪˈsɪdɪɔɪd), **isidiˈose** *adjs.*, resembling or of the nature of an isidium; characterized by or provided with isidia.

1856 W. L. LINDSAY *Brit. Lichens* 43 The isidioid thallus resembles the tartareous in being usually pale or whitish. **1857** BERKELEY *Cryptog. Botany* 418 Many other forms are assumed by the crusts of Lichens;.. the isidioid, in which the thallus is broken up into short erect cylindrical projections. **1882** J. M. CROMBIE in *Encycl. Brit.* XIV. 554/1 This isidioid condition in crustaceous thalli is the basis of the old pseudo-genus *Isidium*. *Ibid.* 556/1 On the margin of the thallus of isidiiferous states of *Peltigera canina*. **1887** *Syd. Soc. Lex.*, *Isidioid*,.. applied to those lichens which are covered with a dense mass of conical soredia. **1921** A. L. SMITH *Lichens* iii. 149 In the genus [sc. *Isidium*] were included the more densely isidioid states of various crustaceous species. *Ibid.* 150 The centre of the isidial tuft [of *Umbilicaria pustulata*] may fall out. **1959** U. K. DUNCAN *Guide to Study of Lichens* 7 *P[armelia] crinita*... Resembles an isidiate form of *P. trichotera*. **1962** *Lichenologist* II. 3 *P[armelia] reddenda* is a pseudo-cyphellate species with peculiar granular or granular-isidiate outgrowths on the upper surface. **1967** M. E. HALE *Biol. Lichens* i. 22 It is not apparent that isidiate species hold any advantage over non-isidiate species. **1970** *Lichenologist* IV. 216 Further development of the isidial initials leads to a definite dorsi-ventral organization.

Isidorian (ɪsɪˈdɔərɪən), *a.* [f. *Isidor-us* pr. name: see -IAN.] Of or pertaining to Isidorus or Isidore; spec. to St. Isidore, archbishop of Seville 600–636, author of several historical and ecclesiastical works, and of Twenty Books of *Origines* or Etymologies, of value for the history of late Latin.

On account of his reputation for learning, his name was in the Middle Ages attached to various other works, particularly to a collection of canons and decretals, a later interpolated collection of which is known as the *pseudo-Isidorian* or *false decretals*.

1882–3 SCHAFF *Encycl. Relig. Knowl.* I. 393 The Spanish or Isidorian translation [of Greek Canons] ascribed to Isidore of Seville. **1883** *Pall Mall G.* 1 Sept. 1/2 The forgery of the Isidorian Decretals, which did so much to augment the power of the Popes. **1900** *United Presb. Mag.* May 238/1 Mediaeval history has a parallel in the famous 'Isidorian Decretals'.

isie, obs. form of ICY.

†**i-sight, i-siht.** *Obs.* Also **ȝesichðe, ȝesec(h)ðe, isihðe, isehðe.** [OE. *ȝesihþ*, *-siht*, f. *séon* to see: cf. SIGHT. Cogn. with OS. *gisiht*, OHG. *gasiht*, MHG. *gesiht*, Ger. *gesicht*.] Sight, vision.

c **888** K. ÆLFRED *Boeth.* v. § 3 Þa mistas ðe.. fordwilmað ða soðan ȝesihðe. *c* **1000** ÆLFRIC *Hom.* I. 60 On ealles þæs folces ȝesihðe. *c* **1000** *Ags. Gosp.* Mark vii. 22 Yfel ȝesihð [*c* **1160** *Hatton G.* ȝe-sihðe]. *a* **1175** *Cott. Hom.* 223 Naðor ne an isehðe, ne on sprece. *Ibid.* 229 Etfor har alra ȝesychðe. *Ibid.* 241 Abroden of his ȝesecþe. *c* **1205** LAY. 13990 Bruttes weoren særi for swulchere isihðe.

i-sihen, i-siȝhe(n, ME. pa. pple. of SIE *v.*, to sink, fall.

isille, var. of ISEL *Obs.*, ember, spark.

†**ising.** *Obs.* [Origin obscure: perh. a corrupted deriv. of L. *insicia*, *insicium*, in 16th c. L. dicts. *insitium* 'stuffing, force-meat'.] A kind of 'pudding'; a sausage: see quots.

c **1550** *Wyll Burke's Test.* in Halliwell *Lit. 16 & 17 Cent.* (1851) 54 Chitterlinges broyled and therbur and isinge. *Ibid.* 55 For to make Isinge Poding.. fair broile him on a grediron and cast salte on him, and serve him forthe for an isinge. **1573–80** BARET *Alv.* P 825 A pudding called an Ising, *isitium*. **1597** *Bk. Cookerie* 50 To make Ising puddings. **1599** MINSHEU *Sp. Dict.*, A Sausage or ising made of porke, vide Salchicha (a Sawsidge). **1706** PHILLIPS, *Isicium*, a kind of Pudding call'd an Ising or Sausage.

isinglass (ˈaɪzɪŋglɑːs, -æ-). Forms: 6 isonglas, 7 ison glass, 7–8 isonglass, ising-glass, 8 icinglass, icing-glass, 7– isinglass. [Supposed to be a corruption or imperfect imitation of an obs. Du. *huisenblas* (Kilian *huysenblase*, *huysblas*), Ger. *hausenblase* isinglass, lit. 'sturgeon's bladder': see HAUSEN and HUSO.

No English forms approaching the Du. more closely have been found, so that, if this was the source, the perversion of the name would seem to have been made at its first adoption.]

1. A firm whitish semitransparent substance (being a comparatively pure form of gelatin) obtained from the sounds or air-bladders of some fresh-water fishes, esp. the sturgeon; used in cookery for making jellies, etc., also for clarifying liquors, in the manufacture of glue, and for other purposes. Also extended to similar substances made from hides, hoofs, etc.

(Cited in Rogers *Agric. & Prices* IV and VI for the years 1527, 1585, 1601, 1623, etc., but without any information as to the name under which it is mentioned.)

1545 *Rates of Custome-ho.* b v b, Ison [*printed* m] glas the C. li. xxxiiis. iiiid. **1660** *Act 12 Chas II*, c. 25 § 11 That noe Merchant Vintner.. retailing any Wine shall.. put in any Isinglasse Brimstone Lime Raisons Juice of Raisons [etc.]. **1662** *Stat. Irel.* (1765) II. 401 Ison glass the hundred pound 10l. **1663** BOYLE *Usef. Exp. Nat. Philos.* II. i. 24 Ising-glass steeped two days in water, and then boiled up. **1678** PHILLIPS (ed. 4), *Ichthyocolla*, a kind of Glew made of the skin of Fishes, commonly called Isonglass. **1723** *Pres. St. Russia* I. 76 Icing-glass, (of that sort which is a Glue made of a Fish). **1727** W. MATHER *Yng. Man's Comp.* 439 A Beer-Glass full of White-Wine, wherein an Ounce of Isonglass is dissolved. **1802** BINGLEY *Anim. Biog.* (1813) III. 91 The isinglass most common in our shops, is made from a species of dolphin, called the beluga. **1842** BARHAM *Ingol. Leg.*, *Blasphemer's Warn.*, Jellies composed of punch, calves' feet and isinglass. **1879** *Cassell's Techn. Educ.* IV. 192/1 A little isinglass or white of egg is first spread over the surface.

2. A name given to mica, from its resembling in appearance some kinds of isinglass.

1747 DR. COOKE in Hanway *Trav.* (1762) I. IV. lviii. 266 We observed a great quantity of sea-glass [*note*] Commonly called isinglass, of which lanthorns are made. **1750** G. HUGHES *Barbados* II. 55 The Soil.. is often mixed with small Flakes of Icinglass, as well as pieces of transparent Talc. **1751** SIR J. HILL *Mat. Med.* 247 Muscovy Talk or Isinglass. **1796** MORSE *Amer. Geog.* II. 75 Isinglass (*mica membranacea*).. is a famous mineral production of Russia. **1868** ISAB. SAXON *5 Yrs. within the Golden Gate* 84 Those gleaming particles in the rich-looking red earth being nothing more than a substance called by miners 'isinglass'.

†**3.** A kind of moth. *Obs.*

1759 PULLEIN in *Phil. Trans.* LI. 56 The moth of this pod is called the Isinglass by Marian.

4. *attrib.* and *Comb.*, as **isinglass glue**, **size**; **isinglass-fish**, a sturgeon or other fish from which isinglass is obtained; **isinglass-stone**, mica.

1688 G. PARKER & J. STALKER *Treat. Japanning* v. 22 To make Isinglass-Size. **1740** R. BROOKES *Art of Angling* II. xli. 159 The Ising-Glass-Fish.. is usually met with in the Seas about Muscovy. **1751** SIR J. HILL *Mat. Med.* Index, Isinglass Stone. **1772** *Ann. Reg.* 126/1 If this tin-foil be gilt with gold leaf, by means of thin isinglass glue, the medal will resemble gold. **1825** J. NICHOLSON *Operat. Mechanic* 716 The colours may be.. laid on with isinglass size. **1828** WEBSTER, *Isinglass-stone*, see *Mica*.

ising-star. *nonce-wd.* [irreg. f. ISING(LASS) + STAR.] A shining piece of 'isinglass' or mica.

a **1820** J. R. DRAKE *Culprit Fay*, iv, Some had lain in the scoop of the rock, With glittering ising-stars inlaid.

iskie-bae, obs. Sc. f. USQUEBAUGH, whisky.

i-slain, ME. pa. pple. of SLAY *v.*

i-slaked, ME. pa. pple. of SLAKE *v.*

Islam (ˈɪsləm, ˈɪz-, ɪsˈlɑːm, ɪzˈlɑːm). [a. Arab. *islām* lit. 'resignation, surrendering', inf. noun of *aslama* 'he resigned or surrendered (himself)', spec. 'he became or was resigned or submissive (to God)', hence 'he became or was sincere in his religion', 4th conjug. of *salama* 'he was or became safe, secure, or free'; whence also the words *salaam*, *Muslim*, *Mussulman*.]

a. The religious system of Muhammad, Muhammadanism; the body of Muslims, the Muslim world.

As the proper name of orthodox Muhammadanism, *islām* is understood as 'the manifesting of humility or submission and outward conformity with the law of God' (Lane).

1818 SHELLEY (*title*) The Revolt of Islam. **1821** —— *Hellas* 916 Poor faint smile Of dying Islam! **1845** FORD *Handbk. Spain* I. Pref. 9 His creed and practice are 'Resignation', the *Islam* of the Oriental. **1855** MILMAN *Lat. Chr.* IV. i. (1864) II. 169 To subdue to the faith of Islam. *Ibid.* 213 The potentates summoned by Mohammed himself to receive the doctrine of Islam. **1877** J. E. CARPENTER tr. *Tiele's Hist. Relig.* 99 With this gloomy conception of deity corresponds the view taken by Islâm of the world.

†**b.** An orthodox Muslim. *Obs.*

1613 PURCHAS *Pilgrimage* (1614) 311 These (they say) are friends to the Islams, that is, Catholike, or right-beleeving Musulmans. **1814** *Spaniards* I. iii, Thou art my country's foe, an Islam in thy creed. *Ibid.*, No Islam born.

Islamic (ɪsˈlæmɪk, ɪsˈlɑːmɪk, ɪz-), *a.* [f. prec. + -IC. Cf. F. *Islamique* (in Littré).] Of or pertaining to Islam; Muhammadan, Muslim.

1791 W. ENFIELD *Hist. Philos.* II. 244 Avenpace.. applied it to the illustration of the Islamic system of theology. **1882** *Athenæum* 5 Aug. 179/1 To show how little the sacred book of the Mohammedans is responsible for the present shape of Islamic dogma and ritual. **1895** *Q. Rev.* July 244 The character of the Prophet of Islâm follows naturally from the Islâmic conception of God.

Islamism (ˈɪsləmɪz(ə)m, ɪz-). [f. as prec. + -ISM. Cf. F. *Islamisme* (Voltaire in Littré).] The religious system of the Muslims; Muhammadanism.

1747 *Gentl. Mag.* 373 Never since the rise of Islamism [*note* So the Mahometans call their own religion] has our worship once varied. **1754** *Phil. Trans.* XLVIII. 755 Before the introduction of Islamism into Arabia. **1827** SCOTT *Napoleon* IV. 85 'There is no god but God, and Mahommed is his prophet'—a confession of faith which is in itself a declaration of Islamism. **1855** MILMAN *Lat. Chr.* IV. ii. (1864) II. 212 Syria.. became a province of Islamism.

So **ˈIslamist**, an orthodox Muslim; **Islaˈmistic** *a.*, Islamic; **ˈIslamize** *v.*, to convert or conform to Islam; also *intr.*

1846 WORCESTER citing E. E. SALISBURY, *Islamize*. **1851** F. HALL in *Benares Mag.* V. 28 Our author's conversion of several unfortunate Musalmáns into mere Islamized Hindús. **1855** MILMAN *Lat. Chr.* XIV. iii. (1864) IX. 108 Caliphs who were, at least no longer, rigid Islamists. **1893**

Miss. Herald (Boston) Feb. 50 Saying that 'the Western World is waiting to be Islamized'. **1893** in Barrows *Parlt. Relig.* II. 995 The decadence of the Islâmitic power in Spain. **1895** *19th Cent.* Nov. 785 Judgment should not be pronounced against Islâm and Islâmists on rancorous and partizan statements.

Islamite ('ɪsləmaɪt, ɪz-), *sb.* (*a.*) [f. ISLAM + -ITE. Cf. F. *Islamite.*] A Muslim.

1799 [implied in ISLAMITISH]. **1821** SHELLEY *Hellas* 549 Every Islamite who made his dogs Fat with the flesh of Galilean slaves. **1832** TENNYSON *Palace of Art* xxvi, Thronging all one porch of Paradise, A group of Houris bow'd to see The dying Islamite. **1855** MILMAN *Lat. Chr.* IV. 168 The erring believer was as declared an enemy of God as the Pagan or the Islamite.

B. *attrib.* and *adj.* Islamic, Islamitic.

1847 MRS. A. KERR *Hist. Servia* 461 The Porte.. has her Islamite subjects too little under control. **1871** FARRAR *Witn. Hist.* iii. 114 All the places which are purely Islamite look as though they had been smitten.. by some withering and irreparable curse.

Isla'mitic, *a.* [f. prec. + -IC.] Muslim.

1791 W. ENFIELD *Hist. Philos.* II. 240 Al-Ashari.. applied an extensive knowledge of the Peripatetic philosophy to the explanation of the Islamitic law. **1846** WORCESTER citing E. E. SALISBURY. **1865** *Intell. Observ.* No. 40. 250 Islamitic Asia. **1884** *Q. Rev.* Apr. 331 [The Malay is] when not overweighted by the Islamitic incubus, reasonably progressive.

†**Isla'mitish**, *a. Obs.* In 8 Islaumitish. [f. as prec. + -ISH[1].] = prec.

1799 *Ann. Reg.* 67 His doctrine, a kind of Islaumitish Socinianism, did not extend to a denial of the prophet's mission.

i-slan, ME. pa. pple. of SLAY *v.*

island ('aɪlənd), *sb.* Forms: *α.* 1 **íȝland, iland, eȝland, -lond;** 3 **illond, yllond,** (4–5 **eland**), 4–6 **yland, ylond,** 5–6 **ilond,** (5 **hylyn**), 5–7 **iland.** *β.* 5 **ile-land, yle-,** 6 **ysle-, isle-land.** *γ.* 6– **island.** [OE. *íȝland* (*íeȝland*), *íland*, Anglian *éȝland* = ON. *eyland*, OFris. *eiland* (MDu., MLG. *eilant*, Du., EFris. *eiland*), a compound of OE. *íeȝ*, *íȝ*, ON. *ey* (Norw. *öy*), OFris. *ey* 'isle' + LAND. The simple *íeȝ* = OHG. *auwa*, *ouwa*, MHG. *ouwe*, Ger. *aue*, *au*, corresponded to Gothic type **ahwiô*, *aujô*, a substantivized fem. of an adj. derived from *ahwa* 'water' (OS. and OHG. *aha*, OFris. and ON. *á*, OE. *éa*), with sense 'of or pertaining to water', 'watery', 'watered', and hence 'watered place, meadow, island'. A cognate compound frequent in OE. was *éaland*, lit. 'water-land', 'river-land'; and a deriv. of the simple *íeȝ*, *éȝ*, exists in *eyot*, *ait*. The ordinary ME. and early mod.Eng. form was *iland*, *yland*. (*Eland* in 14–15th c. may repr. OE. *éaland* or *eȝland.*) In 15th c. the first part of the word began to be associated with the synonymous *ile*, *yle* (of Fr. origin), and sometimes analytically written *ile-land*; and when *ile* was spelt *isle*, *iland* erroneously followed it as *isle-land*, *island*; the latter spelling became established as the current form before 1700.]

1. a. A piece of land completely surrounded by water.

Formerly used less definitely, including a peninsula, or a place insulated at high water or during floods, or begirt by marshes, a usage which survives in particular instances, as Portland Island, Hayling Island, Mochras or Shell Island, etc.

α. *c* **888** K. ÆLFRED *Boeth.* xxix. §3 Ðæt iland þe we hatað Tyle. *a* **900** *O.E. Chron.* an. 895 Hie comon.. on an iȝland ..þæt is Meres iȝ haten. *c* **900** tr. *Bæda's Hist.* I. Introd. (1890) 24 Breoton ist garsecges ealond [*MS. B.* iȝland], ðæt wæs iu ȝeara Albion haten. *a* **1000** *Whale* 16 in *Cod. Exon.* (Th.) 360 And þonne in þæt eȝlond up ȝewitað collenferðe. **11..** *Charter* (dated 1023) *of Cnut* in Kemble *Cod. Dipl.* IV. 23 Ic Cnut.. Ænglelandes kining and ealre ðare eȝlande ðe ðærto licgeð. *c* **1275** LAY. 7340 We beoþ in on illond [*c* 1205 æit-londe]. *Ibid.* 14741 And a-non wende to þan yllonde [*c* 1205 æit-londe]. *c* **1320** *Sir Tristr.* 1024 Þe yland was ful brade þat þai gun in fiȝt. *c* **1330** R. BRUNNE *Chron.* (1810) 77 Þe ferth was holy Eland, þer þe se it withdrouh, þei ȝede on þe sand, to þat Ilde wele inouh. *a* **1400** *Octouian* 539 A wast ylond they dryuen tylle, Fer yn the est. *c* **1450** *St. Cuthbert* (Surt.) 1241 Þat bischop of haly eland was. *c* **1475** *Voc.* in Wr.-Wülcker 798/14 *Hec insula*, a hylyn of the see. **1509** HAWES *Past. Pleas.* XXXVI. (Percy Soc.) 186 The fyre was great, it made the ylande lyght. **1547** BOORDE *Introd. Knowl.* vi. (1870) 141 Norway is a great Ilond compassed abowt almost wyth the See. *a* **1586** SIDNEY *Arcadia* III. (1590) 267 The iland within the lake. **1611** BIBLE *Acts* xxviii. 1 The Iland was called Melita. **1667** MILTON *P.L.* XI. 834 Down the great River to the op'ning Gulf, And there take root an Iland salt and bare.

β. **1494** FABYAN *Chron.* VII. 293 Sene the fyrste wynnynge Of this ile land by Brute. **1506** GUYLFORDE *Pilgr.* (Camden) 58 We sayled by Alango, Nio, with many mo yle londes. **1546** LANGLEY *Pol. Verg. de Invent.* II. xii. 56 Midacritus fet lead out of the islelandes against spayne called Cassitrides. **1566** ADLINGTON *Apuleius* 44 And now is her flying fame dispersed into the next yslelonde.

γ. [*c* **1550** *islander*, **1577** *islandman.*] **1598** HAKLUYT *Voy.* I. 10 Godred.. tooke possession of the South part of the Island. **1695** TEMPLE *Hist. Eng.* 1 Britain was by the Ancients accounted the greatest Island of the known World. **1774** M. MACKENZIE *Maritime Surv.* 80 How to survey small Islands that extend East or West in a long narrow Train. **1856** EMERSON *Eng. Traits, Ability* Wks. (Bohn) II. 45 The island [Britain] has produced two or three of the greatest men that ever existed.

b. In Biblical lang., after the corresp. Heb. word, applied to the lands across the sea, the coasts of the Mediterranean: cf. ISLE *sb.* 1 b.

1535 COVERDALE *Isa.* li. 5 The Ilondes (that is yᵉ Gentiles) shal hope in me. **1839** YEOWELL *Anc. Brit. Ch.* App. ii. (1847) 170 The Jews call all those places *islands* that lie on the sea coast: thus the posterity of Japheth is said to have peopled 'the islands of the Gentiles' (Gen. x. 5); that is, the sea-coasts of Asia and Greece.

†**c.** *island of ice*: an iceberg, or a large mass of floating ice. *Obs.*

1613 PURCHAS *Pilgrimage* (1614) 744 They plied Northwest among Ilands of Ice,.. some of them aground. *Ibid.* 748 The Ilands of Ice which the current bringeth at that time from the North. **1760–72** tr. *Juan & Ulloa's Voy.* (ed. 3) II. 318 The Hector.. was lost on one of these islands of ice. **1769** FALCONER *Dict. Marine* (1789), *Island of Ice*, a name given by sailors to a great quantity of ice collected.. and floating about.. near.. the arctic circle.

d. In specific elliptical uses for some particular island or islands, as the Isle of Wight, the Hebrides, some islands in the western Pacific. Also, by further extension, for a specific prison on an island.

1814 JANE AUSTEN *Mansf. Park* I. ii. 34 She thinks of nothing but the Isle of Wight, and she calls it *the Island*, as if there were no other island in the world. **1817** KEATS *Let.* 17 Apr. (1931) I. 19, I intend to walk over the Island east —West—North South. **1852** C. M. YONGE *Two Guardians* xiii. 239 Suppose I was to take him to Marchmont's grouse shooting place in Scotland, and about among the Highlands and Islands. **1896** CONRAD *Outcast of Islands* I. ii. 15 There was not a white man in the islands, from Palembang to Ternate, from Ombawa to Palawan, that did not know Captain Tom and his lucky craft. **1901** *N.E.D.* s.v. *Isle*, The Isle of Wight is commonly referred to as 'the island'. **1902** *Captain* VII. 141 We used to gather the niggers in from all round the islands [*sc.* Pacific Islands]. *a* **1911** D. G. PHILLIPS *Susan Lenox* (1917) II. vii. 185 He was caught, did a year on the Island before his 'pull' could get him out. **1930** V. PALMER *Men are Human* xxiii. 205 He was tormented by sporadic impulses to scrap his responsibilities and go off to the [Pacific] Islands. **1935** A. J. POLLOCK *Underworld Speaks* 62/2 *Island*, Portland prison, England; Blackwell's Island, N.Y. **1939** J. PHELAN *In Can* iii. 28 He's bin on the Moor and the Island an' in the Ville, but I ain't never heard as he was in *Eton*. **1968** R. C. GALWAY *Assignment Gaolbreak* viii. 71 You're going straight to the island, via the cells at the Old Bailey. **1974** *Times* 9 Mar. 3/1 It was here in the Isle of Wight that the Conservatives last week suffered their biggest electoral disaster... For the past 50 years the island.. had been considered a Tory fortress.

2. *transf.* **a.** An elevated piece of land surrounded by marsh or 'intervale' land; a piece of woodland surrounded by prairie or flat open country; a block of buildings [= L. *insula*]; also an individual or a race, detached or standing out by itself; † *to stand in island*, to be detached or isolated (*obs.*).

1620–55 I. JONES *Stone-Heng* (1725) 53 The Pillars standing in Island (as we say) the Work could not securely bear a Roof. **1638** *Dedham* (U.S.) *Rec.* (1892) III. 51 Abraham Shawe selleth vnto Ferdinando Adam one portion of Grownd called an hill or Iland as it lyeth to his home lott. **1641** *Plymouth Col. Rec.* (1855) I. 169 The Court hath graunted vnto Willm Thomas.. all that whole neck of vpland.. as also those hammocks of vpland called ilands in the marshes before the same. **1650** *Mass. Col. Rec.* (1854) III. 188 A small hill, or iland, in the meddow on the west side of Charles Riuer. **1652** L. S. *People's Liberty* x. 22 Every man is an Iland, or a little world. **1715** LEONI *Palladio's Archit.* I. (1742) 47 This House.. stands in an Island, being surrounded by four Streets. **1776** A. HENRY *Trav. & Adv. Canada* (1901) xi. 282 The country was one uninterrupted plain,.. a frozen sea, of which the little coppices were the islands. **1784** COWPER *Task* III. 630 The shapely knoll, That, softly swelled and gaily dressed, appears A flowery island, from the dark green lawn Emerging. **1794** S. WILLIAMS *Vermont* 35 The small islands in these intervales, are of a different soil, and.. are evidently the tops of small hills, which have not been covered by the inundations of the rivers. **1805** T. M. HARRIS *Jrnl. Tour*, etc. 178 (Bartlett) In some [prairies] are little clumps of trees on higher ground, which are called islands. **1809** A. HENRY *Trav.* 281 We were in sight of a wood, or island, as the term not unnaturally is, as well with the Indians as others. **1834** *Visit to Texas* iv. 41 These groves are called islands, from the striking resemblance they present to small tracts of land surrounded by water. **1838** DICKENS *Nich. Nick.* vii, A man may call his house an island if he likes. **1843** *Amer. Pioneer* II. 283 An island of timber. **1853** F. W. THOMAS *John Randolph* 61 Islands—that is, great clumps of trees, covering some-times many acres, appearing just like many islands in an outstretched ocean. **1856** STANLEY *Sinai & Pal.* i. (1858) 66 It is a strange spot—this plot of tamarisks with its seventeen wells,—literally an island in the Desert. **1880** DAWKINS *Early Man* ix. 330 The Silures no longer form a compact ethnological island, but are.. mingled with other races. **1897** *Daily News* 11 May 4/6 The island of houses between the Churches of St. Mary-le-Strand and St. Clement Danes. **1902** S. E. WHITE *Blazed Trail* ix. 63 The pine there grew thick on isolated 'islands' of not more than an acre or so in extent,—little knolls rising from the level of a marsh. **1930** *19th Cent.* Dec. 713 Now, the drawback of this plan, from the Zionist point of view, is that it will prevent land purchase for the meantime and the growth of the Jewish 'islands' in the country. **1962** A. FRY *Ranch on Cariboo* iv. 42 The islands were small patches of pine and spruce timber on little rises of high ground that occurred here and there in the several hundred acres of the meadow. **1974** *Country Life* 21 Feb. 350/1 A churchyard.. is.. perhaps a well-wooded 'island' in an agricultural countryside.

b. *Physiol.* A detached or insulated portion of tissue or group of cells, entirely surrounded by parts of a different structure; *island of Reil*, the central lobe of the cerebrum, insula; *island* (or *Island*) *of Langerhans* = *islet of Langerhans* (ISLET 2 b); also *ellipt.*

1879 *St. George's Hosp. Rep.* IX. 339 Microscopically the diseased tissue consisted of vascular meshes, containing numerous small cellular islands. **1879** CALDERWOOD *Mind & Br.* 25 The concealed central lobe (island of Reil) shows the grey matter always deep. **1898** P. MANSON *Trop. Dis.* ix. 173 The islands of sound skin [in the eruption of dengue] give rise at first sight to the impression that they constitute the eruption. **1899** *Jrnl. Exper. Med.* IV. 285 Pigment is frequently abundant in the cells composing the intertubular cell-groups or islands of Langerhans. **1900** *Bull. Johns Hopkins Hosp.* XI. 205 (*heading*) On the histology of the islands of Langerhans of the pancreas. *Ibid.* 207 When the fœtal pancreas is affected by congenital syphillis, the islands .. retain their continuity with the secreting structures. **1951** A. GROLLMAN *Pharmacol. & Therapeutics* xxvi. 571 Banting and Best.. obtained a preparation which was named insulin, since it is derived from the Islands of Langerhans in the pancreas, and not from the general parenchyma of the gland. **1962** W. H. HOLLINSHEAD *Textbk. Anat.* ix. 140/2 The endocrine tissue of the pancreas, the pancreatic islands (islets) or islands of Langerhans, consists of small groups of cells scattered among the more numerous acini.

c. = REFUGE *sb.* 3 c.

1869 *Spectator* 12 June 695/1 We have already 'refuges', or 'islands', or whatever they are, in most crossings. **1878** *Social Notes* 10 Aug. 358/1 It is only very lately that 'islands' —those necessary havens of refuge—have been placed at the most dangerous portions of the boulevards. **1899** *Daily Tel.* 31 Jan. 6/6 The statue being situated on an 'island', a certain amount of skirmishing was necessary in order to reach it. **1926** C. SIDGWICK *Sack & Sugar* xi. 131, I took Gerda's arm, and was nearly at the island, when the bus swept round a corner and was on us. **1930** L. COOPER *Ship of Truth* ii. 178 He stood on an island in the middle and saw the traffic sweep past him. **1956** D. GASCOYNE *Night Thoughts* 26 Street-crossing islands stand becalmed. **1970** P. LAURIE *Scotland Yard* iii. 72 The cart collided with a concrete bollard and finished up on an island. **1972** *Daily Tel.* 20 Jan. 17/7 The gang lifted a grill on a Shaftesbury Avenue island to gain access to the inspection tunnel.

d. A small isolated ridge or structure between the lines in finger-prints.

1891 *Proc. R. Soc.* XLIX. 545 Any one well-marked characteristic of a minute kind, such as an island, or enclosure, or a couple of adjacent bifurcations. **1930** E. WALLACE *White Face* xii. 183 Before we start discussing whorls, islands and circles.. what is this? **1950** *Gross's Criminal Investigation* (ed. 4) v. 127 On Fig. 4 are marked some of the common types of ridge characteristics:—'A' is an enclosure or lake... 'F' is a short independent ridge or island.

e. = *speech island.*

1882 A. J. ELLIS in *Trans. Philol. Soc.* 30 The maps being thus arranged, coloured lines are drawn on them marking boundaries, which sometimes unite and form islands. **1892** *Dialect Notes* I. iv. 225 One of his own students was thinking of a linguistic island in the Tennessee mountains as a field for future work. **1923** A. L. KROEBER *Anthropol.* v. 105 This explains the numerous survivals and 'islands' of speech. **1934** H. KURATH in *Proc. Amer. Philos. Soc.* LXXIV. 239 R-islands still exist in eastern New England.

f. A piece of furniture, in a private house or in a museum, library, etc., surrounded by unoccupied floor space. Freq. *attrib.*

1932 *Museums Jrnl.* June 127 In the vertical island-cases with different displays on opposite sides. **1960** *Guardian* 1 Mar. 3/5 Living and dining space planned round a large island range and barbecue grill. *Ibid.*, Peter Jones and Heal's both show island fireplaces. **1960** *Oxf. Univ. Gaz.* 4 Mar. 806/2 A new island bookcase has been acquired for the library. **1960** *House & Garden* Aug. 65/2 The cooking island screens a small corner used for informal meals. **1968** *Globe & Mail* (Toronto) 13 Feb. 30/1 (Advt.), Huge kitchen with built-ins and double sink plus island sink for children. **1972** *House & Garden* Dec.–Jan. 77 Country-style kitchen.. has a central butcher-block island with built-in hot-plates.

g. The superstructure of a ship, esp. an aircraft carrier.

1937 *Jane's Fighting Ships* 497 Adding 2½ feet to the beam .. to balance the island superstructure. **1964** *New Scientist* 2 July 22 (*caption*) The 'island' which supports a giant radar scanner on HMS *Hermes*.

3. *attrib.* and *Comb.* **a.** *simple attrib.* Of an island or islands; pertaining or belonging to an island. *island fortress*, *race* (i.e. the British).

1621 FLETCHER (*title*) The Island Princess. **1725** POPE *Odyss.* v. 385 The island goddess knew, On the black sea what perils should ensue. **1790** BEATSON *Nav. & Mil. Mem.* II. 154 Some shot were fired at his headmost ships from the Island-battery. **1832** TENNYSON *Sonn. Buonaparte*, That island queen who sways the floods and lands From Ind to Ind. **1841** W. SPALDING *Italy & It. Isl.* I. 35 Their highest cluster of peaks.. is in the island-chain which shoots off from Tuscany. **1844** MONCKTON MILNES *Palm Leaves* 10 St. John's proud island-chevaliers. **1852** TENNYSON *Ode Death Wellington* viii, Not once or twice in our rough island-story, The path of duty was the way to glory. **1897** MARY KINGSLEY *W. Africa* 129 A good deal of the bank we have passed by.. has been island shore, with a channel between the islands and the true south bank. **1898** H. NEWBOLT (*title*) The island race. **1902** BELLOC *Path to Rome* 51 Some kinds of men begin talking of Dogged Determination, Bull-dog pluck, the stubborn spirit of the Island race, and so forth. **1942** *R.A.F. Jrnl.* 18 Apr. 28 In the strongly defended island fortress of Corregidor. **1958** *Spectator* 14 Feb. 199/2, I could wish that the Island Race as a whole were a little more discriminating in its drooling. **1966** *Listener* 26 May 771/1 Aware of Mr Menuhin's devotion to his adopted country, one felt it matched by the island-race stateliness of Sir Adrian.

b. That is, or consists of an island; insular.

1859 TENNYSON *Morte D'Arthur* 259, I am going a long way With these.. To the island-valley of Avilion. **1879** GEO. ELIOT *Theo. Such* xviii. 318 To keep the island-home they won for us. **1899** *Daily News* 27 Oct. 5/1 The 'House of

Keys', the legislative chamber of the little island-kingdom [Isle of Man].

c. objective and obj. genitive, as ***island-making***, ***-taking***, etc.; locative, as ***island-fishing***, ***-voyage***; ***island-born***, ***-contained*** adjs.; instrumental, as ***island belted***, ***-dotted***, ***-strewn***, ***-studded*** adjs.; also ***island-like*** adj.

1884 *Leisure Hour* June 342/1 The *island-belted shores or North-Western Norway. **1803** *Edin. Rev.* I. 413 Crisna, the *island-born. **1894** *Outing* (U.S.) XXIV. 152/1 Loch Awe is a long, narrow *island-dotted ribbon of water. *a* **1649** DRUMM. OF HAWTH. *Jas. V*, Wks. (1711) 102 A complaint against the Londoners, who, in their passage to the *island-fishing, spoiled the coasts of Orkney and the adjacent islands. **1859** CORNWALLIS *New World* I. 280 A series of isolated volcanic hills rise *island-like out of the western plains. **1880** A. R. WALLACE *Isl. Life* 73 They [birds] generally require..an *island-strewn sea as a means of dispersal to new homes. **1898** *Nat. Rev.* Aug. 856 The vast area of *island-studded ocean east of Java. **1613** PURCHAS *Pilgrimage* (1614) 542, I was pressed for this *Iland-voyage, and ready to set saile for Samatra.

4. Special Comb.: **island arc**, any arcuate chain of islands located and aligned in relation to an orogenic belt and characteristically having a deep trench on the convex side; **Island Carib**, (*a*) the Carib people of the Lesser Antilles; (*b*) the language of this people; **island-cedar**, a species of cedar; **island-continent**, a large island, approaching the size of the continents, or large enough to contain several states, as Australia or Greenland; **island-harbour**, 'that which is protected from the violence of the sea by one or more islands or islets screening its mouth' (Smyth *Sailor's Word-bk.* 1867); **island-hill**, a hill or mountain rising out of a plain; **island-hop** *v. intr.* (of the U.S. army in the Pacific during the war of 1941–45), to recapture Japanese-occupied islands one after another; also *transf.*; chiefly in *vbl. sb.*; **island-mountain** = *island-hill* above; **island platform**, a platform at a railway station, with lines on each side of it; **island plot**, a plot of land on a building site surrounded by streets or open spaces; **island-refuge** = 2 c; **island site** = *island plot* above; **island-universe** [app. tr. G. *weltinsel* (von Humboldt), though the term has been attributed to Sir William Herschel], a distinct stellar system, such as that to which our sun belongs, occupying a detached position in space.

1906 H. B. C. & W. J. SOLLAS tr. *Suess's Face of Earth* II. iv. 207 It would be sound geology to draw the western boundary of the Pacific Ocean outside the *island arcs from Kamchatka through Japan. **1971** I. G. GASS et al. *Understanding Earth* xix. 271/1 The zone meets the surface close to the line of the deep ocean trench and dips away beneath the island-arc. **1938** D. TAYLOR in *U.S. Bureau Amer. Ethnol. Bull.* No. 119. 140 The most typical product of the *Island Carib is..the dugout canoe. **1951** —— *Black Carib of Brit. Honduras* 41 The Black Carib of Central America speak a dialect of Island Carib—of the language, that is to say, spoken by the native Indian inhabitants of the 'Caribee' islands at the time of Breton's stay among them (1635–1653). **1968** *Encycl. Brit.* XXIII. 433/1 These island Carib [of Dominica] have not retained as much of their aboriginal language and culture [as the Black Carib]. **1969** *Word* XXV. 276 In Island-Carib, the plural is employed only with reference to animate..beings. **1885** LADY BRASSEY *The Trades* 396 Little islets covered with firs of various sorts, principally the *island-cedar. **1872** R. B. SMYTH *Mining Statist.* 5 The colony of Victoria embraces the southern extremity of the *island-continent of Australia. **1898** *Westm. Gaz.* 12 Sept. 3/2 The labours..of the plucky lieutenant and his party in the inhospitable and cheerless island-continent of the Far Northern seas. **1839** H. T. DE LA BECHE *Rep. Geol. Cornwall, Devon & W. Somerset* i. 26 The lower *island-hills of Pawlet and Chedzoy..rise out of the plain near Bridgewater. **1907** Island-hill [see INSELBERG]. **1944** *Sat. Even. Post* 28 Oct. 98/3 American air power won the battles for Attu, Kwajalein and Tarawa, and has made possible *island hopping. **1946** *Sat. Rev. Lit.* 23 Feb. 33/1 Cant takes us along on the island-hopping campaigns. **1955** in *Amer. Speech* (1956) XXXI. 85 Did you island-hop or did you take the plane directly? **1971** P. DRISCOLL *White Lie Assignment* vii. 61 The caiques are built for coasting and island-hopping. They can't take much rough weather. **1972** *Guardian* 11 Aug. 1/1 The airlift by small, island-hopping aircraft. **1906** *Daily Chron.* 31 Aug. 4/4 They [*sc.* the Malvern Hills] lie precisely north by south, moored like some great *island-mountain to the westward of the central plain of England. **1913** *Geogr. Jrnl.* XLII. 149 The fantastic peaks and domes of the rocky island-mountains. **1941** F. H. LAHEE *Field Geol.* (ed. 4) xi. 360 A similar residual type in arid regions is the island mountain, or island mount (German, Inselberg). **1885** *Standard* 6 Mar. 3/2 There was ..a refreshment bar on the up platform, but no such accommodation on the *island platform. **1898** *Daily News* 23 Nov. 5/1 The new station..will consist of an island platform placed between the up and down relief lines. **1908** *Daily Chron.* 20 Apr. 3/5 On this '*island' plot of land has been erected a building which is certainly an adornment to Great Portland-street. **1922** F. MUIRHEAD *London & Environs* (ed. 2) 8 A busy street should be crossed only at a point where an '*island-refuge' is provided in the middle. **1907** *Westm. Gaz.* 20 Sept. 10/1 Australia and the Strand '*Island Site'. **1936** C. ROUSE *Old Towns* i. 17 The market house or town hall was often built on an island site in those wide streets. **1972** *Accountant* 17 Aug. 206/1 Two important island sites with main frontages to Great Portland Street have been assembled over the course of many years. [**1845** A. VON HUMBOLDT *Kosmos* I. 93 Unter den vielen selbstleuchtenden ihren Ort verändernden Sonnen.. welche unsre Weltinsel bilden.] **1867** A. J. DAVIS *Stellar Key to Summer Land* vi. 32 The expression '*Island Universe' was suggested by the immense distance of the fixed stars from our Sun and Planets; giving the impression that our Solar System occupies an isolated position in the boundless ocean of space. **1887** R. A. PROCTOR *Other Suns than Ours* i. 1 Our 'island universe', as Humboldt poetically called the stellar system. *Ibid.* 11 The results which Sir W. Herschel published in 1817 and 1818 justify the belief that ..large numbers of the nebulæ must be regarded as external galaxies. This grand conception fascinated..some who, like Humboldt,..had understood and appreciated the work of the great observer. The idea of 'island universes' strewn throughout the ocean of space impressed the world. **1898** *Daily News* 7 May 8/1 The distance between these separate systems—or 'island universes' as they have been called—may be very great compared with the diameter of each system. **1928** J. H. JEANS *Astron. & Cosmogony* i. 19 These figures amply show that these nebulae and star-clouds are quite outside our system of stars; they constitute what Herschel described as 'island-universes' distinct from the universe which contains our sun. **1959** DAVIES & PALMER *Radio Stud. Universe* i. 2 Many..nebulae were discovered. However, it was not until the 1920's that the problem of their distance and spacing was unravelled by Hubble, who showed that they were very distant island universes (galaxies) of stars many of which were similar to our Milky Way system.

Hence **'islandhood** *nonce-wd.*, the condition of being an island; insularity; **'islandless** *a.*, devoid of islands.

1842 LD. COCKBURN *Circuit Journeys* (1883) 170 There was too much islandless sea. **1862** ANSTED *Channel Isl.* II. xii. (ed. 2) 300 It is the insularity (the islandhood, so to say), of the islands, which determines these.

island ('aɪlənd), *v.* [f. prec. sb.]

1. *trans.* To make into or as into an island; to place as an island; to place, settle, or enclose on, or as on, an island; to insulate, isolate.

1661 FELTHAM *Resolves* II. lxvi. 328 Those shallows which Islanded that Countrey of felicity. **1820** SHELLEY *Let.* 26 May in *Essays*, etc. (1852) II. 224 The Apennines..islanded in the misty distance of the air. **1821** —— *Prometh. Unb.* II. iii, Billowy mist.. Behold it, rolling on Under the curdling winds, and islanding The peak whereon we stand. **1822** T. L. PEACOCK *Maid Marian* 263 Upon a little rock she stood ..She marked not that the rain-swoln flood Was islanding her station. **1860** RUSKIN *Mod. Paint.* V. IX. ii. §11. 210 A clear brown stream,..islanding a purple and white rock with an amber pool. **1849** THOREAU *Week Concord* Wedn. 276 The smothered streams of love.. Island us ever.

2. To set or dot with or as with islands.

1805 SOUTHEY *Madoc* I. v, Not a cloud by day With purple islanded the dark-blue deep. **1818** SHELLEY *Lines Eugan. Hills* 93 The waveless plain of Lombardy,..Islanded by cities fair. **1837** *Tait's Mag.* IV. 183 The hill-tops islanded the night Of billowy shade around us. **1886** MRS. F. CADDY *Footst. Jeanne D'Arc* 142 The united river..now becomes wonderfully islanded in its widened course.

Island, obs. form of ICELAND. ***Island crystal***, Iceland spar.

1676 WORLIDGE *Bees* i. 3 That fossile Glass we call Island glass, wherewith Ships are glaz'd. **1727–41** CHAMBERS *Cycl.* s.v. *Crystal*, Island Crystal, is a transparent fissile stone, brought from Iceland, soft as talc, clear as rock-crystal.., famous among optic writers for its unusual refractions.. Whereas in other pellucid bodies there is only one refraction, in this there are two; so that objects received thro' it appear double. **1812** SIR H. DAVY *Chem. Philos.* 197 A plain surface of island crystal, or rhomboidal carbonate of lime.

islanded ('aɪləndɪd), *ppl. a.* [f. ISLAND *v.* and *sb.* + -ED.]

1. Made into or like an island; insulated, isolated.

1801 SOUTHEY *Thalaba* I. ii, Palm-grove, islanded amid the waste. **1843** RUSKIN *Mod. Paint.* I. II. III. iv. (1846) 259 The islanded summits of the lower hills. **1850** BLACKIE *Æschylus* II. 275 The islanded cities of Strymon.

2. Furnished or studded with islands.

1815 SHELLEY *Alastor* 555 Wide expand, Beneath the wan stars and descending moon, Islanded seas, blue mountains, mighty streams. **1883** W. C. SMITH *North Country Folk* 220 Meet home for a sage and a poet, With..the islanded sea below it.

islander ('aɪləndə(r)). [f. ISLAND *sb.* + -ER¹.] A native or inhabitant of an island. Also in *comb.*, as ***Channel Islander***, ***South Sea Islander***.

c **1550** *Life Fisher* in *F.'s Wks.* (E.E.T.S.) II. p. xxxvi, Lyke the nature of Islanders that commonly be changeable and desirous of novelties. **1613** PURCHAS *Pilgrimage* (1614) 709 In S. Marie..they buried one of their dead men, the Ilanders being present. **1658–9** *Burton's Diary* (1828) III. 392 We are islanders, and our life and soul is traffic. **1714** STANHOPE (*title*) The Early Conversion of Islanders, a wise expedient for propagating Christianity; on Isa. lx. 9. **1725** POPE *Odyss.* XXIV. 307 Some surly islander, of manners rude. **1897** GLADSTONE *E. Crisis* 10 Into one more of these struggles the gallant islanders have now entered.

attrib. **1652** NEEDHAM tr. *Selden's Mare Cl.* 470 His Majestie being an Islander-Prince is not ignorant of the Laws and Rights of his own Kingdom.

Hence **'islandress**, a female islander. **'islandry**, a body of islanders.

1875 R. F. BURTON *Ultima Thule* I. 89 The roving islandry throve by piracy and discovery. **1892** STEVENSON *Vailima Lett.* (1895) 156, I go to the club to dance with the islandresses.

Is'landian, -ic, -ish, variants, mostly obs., of ICELANDIAN, -IC, -ISH. [Cf. mod.L. *Islandicus*.]

1695 BLACKMORE *Pr. Arth.* VIII. 105 As when by Night th' Islandian Ocean roars. **1881** ROSCOE in *Nature* XXIII. 598/1 The several memoirs..are the result of a visit to Iceland in 1847. All the Islandic rocks, of whatever age, may be considered as mixtures..of two normal silicates.

islandic ('aɪləndɪk), *a. rare.* [f. ISLAND *sb.* + -IC.] Of or pertaining to an island.

1846 J. MACLEOD *Let. to Wightman* 29 Apr. in Hogg *Life Wightman* (1873) 374 There is no fine scenery—none of our own bold peaks and islandic glens.

islandish ('aɪləndɪʃ), *a. rare.* [f. ISLAND *sb.* + -ISH¹.] Of, pertaining to, or characteristic of an island; insular.

1577 DEE *Gen. & rare Mem.* in Arb. *Garner* II. 65 Our peculiar commodity (to our Islandish Monarchy, by God and Nature assigned). **1598** HAKLUYT *Voy.* I. 8 Purposing first inuincibly to fortifie the chiefe and vttermost walles of his Islandish Monarchie, against all forreine encombrance possible. **1615** E. S. *Brit. Buss* in Arb. *Garner* III. 648 This Islandish Monarchy. **1852** *Fraser's Mag.* XLV. 246 To a moderate infusion of these prejudices..we do not object, but the misfortune is that we often find them put forth with too Islandish an intensity.

'islandman. Now *rare* or *local.* = ISLANDER.

At Belfast, applied to the ship-builders on Queen's Island, more fully ***Queen's Islandmen***.

1577 FENTON *Gold. Epist.* 137 Eschines..in an oration he made to the Rhodians, commended the gouernement of the Islandmen. **1590** NASHE *Pasquil's Apol.* I. B iij, He speakes like an Iland man. **1596** DALRYMPLE tr. *Leslie's Hist. Scot.* II. 138 To commend lyfe and gudes vnto the credence and custodie of the ylandmen thay war forced. **1886** *Pall Mall G.* 10 Aug. 1/1 A great contingent of the iron shipbuilders employed by the Mayor of Belfast—a powerful body of men and lads known as the 'Islandmen'. **1893** *Westm. Gaz.* 29 Apr. 7/2 The Islandmen proceeded to and returned from their work yesterday as if nothing unusual had recently occurred... The movement which is on foot among the Queen's Islandmen for the reinstatement of evicted Catholics is making progress.

'Islandshire. *Hist.* Short for Holy Island-shire, name of that division of the county palatine of Durham to which Holy Island belonged. Along with Norham-shire, it formed a detached portion of the county lying north of Northumberland.

c **1100** *Charter* in Murray *Dial. S.C. Scot.* 22 *note*, R[anulf] bisceop greteð wel alle his þeines & drenges of Ealondscire & of Norhamscire. **1705** *Lond. Gaz.* No. 4089/4 Islandshire in the County of Durham. **1707** *Ibid.* No. 4307/3 Tenements,..situate in Beale in Islandshire in the County of Durham.

† **'islandy**, *a. Obs. rare.* [f. ISLAND *sb.* + -Y¹.]

1611 COTGR., *Isleux*, islandie; full of, or belonging to, Islands.

islare, obs. Sc. form of ASHLAR *sb.*

i-slawe(n, -slayen, -slayn(e, -slaȝe(n, ME. pa. pple. of SLAY *v.*

isle (aɪl), *sb.* Forms: α. 3–7 ile, yle, (4 ille, hil(l), 4–5 ylle, 6 ill). β. 5 ysle, 5– isle. γ. 4 idle, ydle. δ. 4–5 ilde, ylde. [ME. *ile* (*ille*), a. OF. *ile* (*ille*), earlier *isle*, mod.F. *île* = Pr. *isla*, It. *isola*:—L. *insula* island. In 15th c. Fr. again often spelt *isle* (a Latinized artificial spelling of the Renascence), whence occas. in Eng. in Caxton, and again persistently from Spenser onward, although the historical *ile* survived to *c* 1700. The form *idle* was AF., from **isdle*, with *d* developed between *s* and *l*, and loss of *s*, as in *meddle* (from *mesdler*, *mesler*), *medlar* (from **mesdler*, *meslier*); cf. also CIDER, and F. *coudre* from **cosdre*, *cosre*, L. *consuere*. The form *ilde* contains a parasitic *d*, as in *vilde* (VILE), *tyld* (TILE), MOULD (*mole*), which was probably developed quite independently of *idle*, though formation from that by transposition was also possible: cf. *neld*, *neelde*, NEEDLE.]

1. A portion of land entirely surrounded by water; an island. Now more usually applied to an island of smaller size, except in established appellations, as 'the British Isles'.

In proper names *isle* is often prefixed, as Isle of Wight, Isle of Man, Isle of Dogs, Isle of Ely, Isle of Thanet; but it also follows, as in Coquet Isle, Scilly Isles, Orkney Isles: *island* usually follows, as in Lundy Island, Hayling Island, the Channel Islands, Canary Islands, West India Islands. As a common noun, *island* is the ordinary prose word; thus the Isle of Wight is commonly referred to as 'the island'.

α. *c* **1290** *S. Eng. Leg.* I. 25/36 Þe kyng toward þulke Ile; sone þerafter he him drouh. **1297** R. GLOUC. (Rolls) 29 Yles þer beþ manion aboute engelonde. *a* **1300** *K. Horn* 1318 Þo icom to þis ille Sarazins blake þat dude me forsake. *c* **1305** *St. Kenelm* 65 in *E.E.P.* (1862) 49 Þe ylle of Ely. *c* **1375** *Sc. Leg. Saints, Magdalena* 513 þai..rowit away, To þai var cumyne to þat hil. **1483** *Cath. Angl.* 194/2 An Ile, *jnsula.* **1517** TORKINGTON *Pilgr.* (1884) 20 The seyd Ill [Candy] ys v C myle a bowte... Thys Ile ys a grett Ile. **1526** TINDALE *Acts* XXVII. 15 An yle named Clauda. **1595** SHAKS. *John* IV. ii. 99 That blood which ow'd the bredth of all this Ile, Three foot of it doth hold. **1670–98** LASSELS *Voy. Italy* II. 50 Going out of the Ile by the bridge of four heads, which joins this Ile with the City.

β. *c* **1470** HARDING *Chron., Arthure*, The Scottes and the Peightes he drove into oute ysles of Scotland. *c* **1489** CAXTON *Blanchardyn* XXX. 112 The ysle was bylongyng vnto the kynge of ffryse. **1490** —— *Eneydos* XV. 54 He wylle retourne in to the Isle of Delon. **1590** SPENSER *F.Q.* I. Introd. 4 Great Ladie of the greatest Isle. **1610** SHAKS. *Temp.* V. i. 212

Prospero [found] his Dukedome In a poore Isle. **1719** DE FOE *Crusoe* II. vi, Resolved..to load salt at the Isle of May. **1885** TENNYSON *Fleet* ii, His isle, the mightiest Ocean-power on earth, Our own fair isle, the lord of every sea.

γ. [**1292** BRITTON II. ii. §8 Si acune idle crest de novel en l'ewe, a celi iert le idle a qi soil ele soit joynte plus pres. *transl.* If a new island is formed in the water, the island shall belong to him whose soil is nearest adjoining to it.] **13..** *K. Alis.* 4856 In that water an ydle is And in that ydle tounes of pris. *Ibid.* 5040, 5908, etc.

δ. *c* **1320** *Sir Beues* (MS. A.) 1335 Terri wente hom and telde His fader Saber in þe ilde of Wiȝt. *c* **1330** R. BRUNNE *Chron. Wace* (Rolls) 3690 Al þey founde wast and wylde. þey spredde hem aboute in ilkan ylde. *c* **1385** CHAUCER *L.G.W.* 1425 (*Hypsip.*) In an ylde that called was colcos. *c* **1440** *Promp. Parv.* 259/1 *Ilde*, londe in the see (*K.* iylde). **1473** SIR J. PASTON in *P. Lett.* III. 93 Men seye that the Erle off Oxenfford is abowt the Ilde off Tenett hoveryng.

b. In O.T., after the equivalent Heb., applied to the lands beyond the sea, esp. in phr. ***isles of the Gentiles***: cf. ISLAND *sb.* 1 b.

1382 WYCLIF *Isa.* xlii. 4 His lawe iles shul abiden [1611 BIBLE *ibid.*, The yles shall waite for his lawe].

c. *fig.*

1781 COWPER *Retirement* 148 Opening the map of God's extensive plan, We find a little isle, this life of man.

2. A building or block of buildings, surrounded by streets. [L. *insula*.]

1670 LASSELS *Voy. Italy* II. 218 The Pallace..makes an Ile, that is, it hath no houses joyning to it.

3. *Comb.*, as ***isle-altar***; ***isle-ruling***, ***-surrounding*** adjs.

1632 LITHGOW *Trav.* I. 35 The clementious Ile-ruling Lady of Trapundy in Sicilia. **1821** SHELLEY *Prometh. Unb.* I. i. 252 Prophetic caves, and isle-surrounding streams. **1832** TENNYSON *Of old sat Freedom on the heights* iv, Grave mother of majestic works, From her isle-altar gazing down.

Hence **ˈisleless** *a.*, devoid of or without islands; **ˈisleward** (*to the*) *adv.*, in the direction of the isle.

a **1586** SIDNEY *Arcadia* (1622) 1 The hopelesse Shepheard Strephon was come to the sands, which lye against the Island of Cithera, where..sometimes casting his eyes to the Isleward, he called his friendly riuall. **1832** J. WILSON in *Blackw. Mag.* XXXI. 861/2 The almost immaterial being of an isleless Lake! **1847** MARY HOWITT *Ballads* 77 The creatures God hath made To people the isleless main.

isle (aɪl), *v.* [f. ISLE *sb.*]

1. *trans.* To make an isle of; to place or set as an isle; to place or set in an isle; to insulate; = ISLAND *v.* 1.

1570-6 LAMBARDE *Peramb. Kent* (1826) 89 Tanet being peninsula and watered or iled (in manner) round about. **1833** TENNYSON *Fatima* 33 And, isled in sudden seas of light, My heart, pierced thro' with fierce delight, Bursts into blossom in his sight. **1852** —— *Ode Death Wellington* vii, Thank Him who isled us here, and roughly set His Briton in blown seas and storming showers. **1864** —— *En. Ard.* 131 That shadow of mischance appear'd No graver than as when some little cloud Cuts off the fiery highway of the Sun, And isles a light in the offing. **1871** G. MACDONALD *Wks. Fancy & Imag., Sonn. Jesus* vi, To see a purpose rise, like mountain isled.

2. *intr.* To remain or lodge on an isle.

1872 TENNYSON *Gareth & Lynette* 870 Lion and stoat have isled together, knave, In time of flood.

isle, obs. form of AISLE *sb.*

1598 STOW *Surv.* 198 Thomas Hinde..gave 10 feodar of lead to the couering of the middle Isle of this Aldermary Church.

i-sleien, -sleyn(e, ME. pa. pple. of SLAY *v.*

ˈIsleman. *rare.* [f. ISLE *sb.* + MAN.] = ISLESMAN, ISLANDER.

1814 SCOTT *Ld. of Isles* III. iii, The faith of Islemen ebbs and flows. **1817** CAMPBELL *Reullura* 98 Our islemen arose from slumbers, And buckled on their arms. **1882** *Standard* 23 Jan. 5 These islemen, the Shetlanders,..constitute one of the finest races in the British empire. *Ibid.*, The more Northern islemen very justly talk of 'the Scotch' as another race.

i-slend, i-slent, ME. pa. pple. of SLEND *v.*

Isle of Wight (aɪl əv ˈwaɪt). The name of an island off the coast of Hampshire, used *attrib.* to designate a disease of bees first found there in 1904, caused by the parasitic mite *Acarapis woodsi*; also called *acarine disease*.

[**1907** A. D. IMMS in *Jrnl. Board Agric.* XIV. 129 (*title*) Report on a disease of bees in the Isle of Wight.] **1909** W. MALDEN in *Jrnl. Board Agric.* XV. 815 In commencing my observations on the Isle of Wight disease, I first endeavoured to ascertain whether, by careful dissections, any characteristic lesions could be discovered in the internal anatomy of the diseased bees. **1932** E. B. WEDMORE *Man. Beekeeping* xvii. 401 In 1920 Miss E. J. Harvey observed a mite in the tracheæ of bees suffering from 'Isle of Wight' disease. **1965** M. HOYT *World of Bees* x. 171 Acarapis is sometimes called Isle of Wight disease.

i-slepe(n, ME. pa. pple. of SLEEP *v.*

islesman (ˈaɪlzmən). An inhabitant or native of any group of islands, esp. of the Hebrides, Orkneys, or Shetland Isles.

1808 SCOTT *Marm.* V. v, The Isles-men carried at their backs The ancient Danish battle-axe. *a* **1851** MOIR *Poet. Wks., Eric's Dirge* iii, Fear thine Islesmen never knew. **1887** *Pall Mall G.* 29 Nov. 2/1 Finer men there are not in the United Kingdom than these Islesmen, of mixed Celtic and Norse descent.

islet (ˈaɪlɪt). Also 6 islette. [a. F. *islette*, mod.F. *îlette*, dim. of ISLE *sb.*: see -ET[1]. See also ISLOT, ISOLET.]

1. A little island, an eyot or ait.

1538 LELAND *Itin.* II. 58, I passid over Frome Water,.. where the water brekith into Armelettes and makith Islettes. **1610** HOLLAND *Camden's Brit.* II. 219 Shetland is an Isle.. environed with other Islets. **1774** GOLDSM. *Nat. Hist.* (1776) VI. 118 Where there is an islet in the stream. **1859** JEPHSON *Brittany* vii. 89 A little islet on the coast still bears the name of Avalon.

fig. **1883** STEVENSON *Silverado Squatters* 228 Mere islets of business in a sea of sunny day-time.

2. *transf.* **a.** Something resembling an island in position; a small piece of land markedly differing in character from that by which it is surrounded, as a wooded eminence in a marsh or plain; any isolated tract or spot; = ISLAND *sb.* 2 a. Also = ISLAND *sb.* 2 d.

1645 BOATE *Irel. Nat. Hist.* (1652) 111 Little Tufts or Ilets ..consisting of Reeds, Rushes, high sower Grass,..a few feet in compass;..These little Ilets of Tufts being..spread over all the Bog. **1791** W. BARTRAM *Carolina* 140 Expansive green meadows or savannas, in which are to be seen..islets of Oak and Bays. **1826** KIRBY & SP. *Entomol.* IV. 286 Islet .., a spot of a different colour, included in a plaga or macula. Ex. The *Ocelli* in the Primary Wings of *Hipparchia Semele.* **1860** TYNDALL *Glac.* I. iii. 27 An islet of stones and débris, where we paused to rest ourselves. **1864** TENNYSON *Aylmer's Field* 65 A but less vivid hue Than of that islet in the chestnut-bloom Flamed in his cheek. **1871** E. F. BURR *Ad Fidem* xv. 308 Those islets of light which roam so mazily in the dark deeps. **1921** *Discovery* Oct. 257/2 A dozen guiding marks, consisting of the beginnings of lines, bifurcations and islets.

b. An isolated piece of animal or vegetable tissue. ***islet*** (or ***Islet***) ***of Langerhans*** [tr. F. *îlot de Langerhans* (E. Laguesse 1893, in *Compt. rend. hebdom. d. Séances et Mém. de la Soc. de Biol.* XLV. 819): named after Paul *Langerhans* (1847–1888), German anatomist, who, in 1869, first described such islets], any of numerous highly vascular islets of tissue in the pancreas, composed of light-staining cells of two principal types, one of which secretes insulin and the other glucagon; also *ellipt.*

1851 CARPENTER *Man. Phys.* 164 The temporary Cartilages..are equally destitute of vessels when their mass is small; but if their thickness exceed an eighth of an inch, they are permeated by canals for the transmission of vessels. Still these vessels do not ramify with any minuteness in the tissue; and they leave large *islets*, in which the nutritive process must take place on the plan just described. **1884** BOWER & SCOTT *De Bary's Phaner.* 499 Especially in their [the *Caryophylleæ*] rhizomes, thin-walled, long-celled parenchyma, often forming large irregular islets or annular segments, is inserted between fibrous masses of similar form. **1896** *Jrnl. R. Microsc. Soc.* 35 Besides the solid buds which form the first 'islets of Langerhans', they give rise to numerous hollow buds. **1897** *Allbutt's Syst. Med.* III. 955 The ulceration is so extensive that only islets of mucous membrane are left here and there. **1898** *Ibid.* V. 204 Islets of spongy tissue separate the individual nodules [of tubercle]. **1904** *Proc. R. Soc.* LXXIII. 84 The degeneration or absence of the islets in diabetes. **1910** *Practitioner* Jan. 32 Many other pathological conditions..have been ascribed to abnormalities of other ductless glands; e.g...glycosuria to the loss of the internal secretion formed by the islets of Langerhans in the pancreas. **1968** *Times* 27 Nov. 9/3 Those parts of the organ [*sc.* the pancreas] concerned with carbohydrate metabolism—known as the islets of Langerhans. **1973** *Nature* 23 Mar. 259 Yields of up to 350 Islets per rat pancreas have been achieved using this method.

3. *attrib.*

1810 SCOTT *Lady of L.* III. iii, Abrupt he paced the islet strand. **1861** *Sat. Rev.* XII. 388/1 St. Helier, too, has its islet-castle, built by Queen Elizabeth. *Ibid.* 388/2 An islet-breakwater. *Ibid.* 389/1 An islet-rock. **1871** R. ELLIS *Catullus* xxviii. 12 Was only this the plea Detain'd you in that islet angle of the west? **1879** C. GEIKIE *Christ* xxix. 335 Constellations anchored on the vast expanse like tiny islet clusters on the boundless ocean. **1899** *Westm. Gaz.* 2 Oct. 10/1 Signalling from lightships and islet lighthouses to the mainland. **1914**, etc. Islet-tissue [see INSULIN 1]. **1927** HALDANE & HUXLEY *Animal Biol.* xii. 279 Islet cell of human pancreas. **1962** *Lancet* 12 May 1003/2 The characteristics of the Zollinger-Ellison syndrome are extreme gastric hyper-secretion, intractable peptic ulceration..and either hyperplasia or tumour of the islet-cells of the pancreas. **1963** E. J. W. BARRINGTON *Introd. Gen. & Compar. Endocrinol.* iii. 43 We have evidence that islet tissue arose very early in vertebrate evolution. **1965** LEE & KNOWLES *Animal Hormones* vii. 113 Occasionally in man a tumour of the islet cell occurs and there is excessive secretion of insulin.

isleted (ˈaɪlɪtɪd), *ppl. a.* [f. prec. + -ED[2].]

a. Placed like an islet. **b.** Studded with islets.

1873 BROWNING *Red Cott. Nt.-cap* 899 And thus accompanied, the paled-off space, Isleted shrubs and verdure, gained the group. **1888** A. DOBSON *Goldsmith* 27 Fishing and otter-hunting in the isleted River Inny. **1890** H. M. STANLEY *Darkest Africa* I. xii. 317 Behind was a background of green groves isleted amid greenest sward.

i-sliden, i-sliken, ME. pa. pples. of SLIDE, SLIKE *vbs.*

†**i-sling**, *v. Obs.* [f. I-[1] + SLING *v.*] *trans.* To sling.

13.. *Coer de L.* 4148 Thomas off Multon..an other stone i-slong To ser Mahouns habitacle.

i-slitte, ME. pa. pple. of SLIT *v.*

islomania (ˌaɪləʊˈmeɪnɪə). [f. ISL(AND *sb.* + -O + -MANIA.] A passion or craze for islands.

1962 *Listener* 25 Oct. 693/1, I suffer from acute islomania, and was therefore specially interested in 'Let's Imagine'.. which investigated the Channel Island of Herm. **1971** D. CONOVER *One Man's Island* 110 Islomania runs in my blood. I would rather talk about islands than eat, would rather—and often do—think about islands than sleep. **1972** *Times* 4 May 11/6 Psychologists have a word for it—islomania—an insatiable attraction to islands.

islot, ilot (ˈaɪlət). [a. OF. *islot*, now *îlot*, dim. of *isle, île*, ISLE *sb.*] An islet.

1772-84 COOK *Voy.* (1790) IV. 1387 The islot itself is scarcely a mile in circuit. **1802** PLAYFAIR *Illustr. Hutton. The.* 455 The islots..which are thus formed, must have their bases laid on a solid rock. **1868** HOLME LEE *B. Godfrey* xxvi, A river..with many a curve and woody ilot in its course.

i-slou, i-slowe, ME. pa. pple. of SLAY *v.*

ism (ˈɪz(ə)m), *quasi-sb.* [The suffix *-ism* used generically as an independent word.] A form of doctrine, theory, or practice having, or claiming to have, a distinctive character or relation: chiefly used disparagingly, and sometimes with implied reference to *schism*.

1680 'HERACLIO DEMOCRITUS' *Vision of Purgatory* 46 He was the great Hieroglyphick of Jesuitism, Puritanism, Quaquerism, and of all Isms from Schism. **1756** *Monthly Rev.* XIV. 359 Arianism, Socinianism, Arminianism, or any other *ism*. *a* **1773** [see GERMANISM 1]. **1789** H. WALPOLE *Lett.* 4 Nov., Alas! you would soon squabble about Socianism, or some of those isms. **1809** SOUTHEY *Lett.* (1856) II. 182 It has nothing to do with Calvinism nor Arminianism, nor any of the other *isms*. **1811** SHELLEY in Hogg *Life* (1858) I. 373 He is nothing,—no 'ist', professes no '-ism' but superbism and irrationalism. **1820** R. POLWHELE *Introd. Lavington's Enthus. Method. & Papists* 118 It has no connection with Methodism, or Puritanism, or any ism or schism. **1820** CARLYLE *Let. to M. Allen* Oct., I expect much pleasure from talking over old bygone things, from discussing Spürzheimism, Whiggism, Church of Englandism, and all other imaginable 'isms'. **1840** *Fraser's Mag.* XXI. 702 All the untidy *isms* of the day shall be dissipated. **1843** CARLYLE *Past & Pr.* II. xv, This is Abbot Samson's Catholicism of the twelfth century—something like the *Ism* of all true men in all true centuries, I fancy. **1864** LOWELL *Rebellion* Pr. Wks. 1890 V. 138 That class of untried social theories which are known by the name of *isms*. **1884** *Kendal Mercury* 3 Oct. 4/7 The principles on which Education Acts are based, irrespective of isms and creeds. **1928** G. B. SHAW *Intelligent Woman's Guide Socialism* lxxxiii. 447 The proletarian Isms are very much alike. **1944** J. S. HUXLEY *On Living in Revolution* iii. 29 Democracy could become more dynamic than Fascism or Communism or any other ism or ideology. **1963** F. W. FREY in L. W. Pye *Communications & Political Devel.* xvii. 299 Movement towards..'Communism', or 'totalitarianism', or..whatever one's preferred 'ism'..happens to be. **1968** S. C. HUTCHISON *Hist. R. Acad.* xvii. 183 He saw no place in art for abstractions and 'isms' and had a very low opinion of their adherents. **1974** *Listener* 14 Feb. 220/1 Impressionism became the most successful 'ism' in the history of art.

Hence various nonce derivatives **ˈismal** *a.*, of or pertaining to an *ism*. **ˈismate** *v. trans.*, to furnish with the suffix *-ism*. **isˈmatic** *a.* [after *schismatic*], pertaining to *isms* or an *ism*; *sb.* an adherent of an *ism*. **isˈmatical** *a.* = *ismatic*; hence **isˈmaticalness**. **ˈismatize** *v.*, to designate as or with an *ism*. **ˈismdom**, the domain or world of *isms*.

1840 *Fraser's Mag.* XXII. 751 That my scheme..should have *ism*-atised my humble name, is an honour which I dreamt not of. **1841** *Ibid.* XXIII. 329 His name deserves also to be *ism*-ated, and this present article be headed Whittockism. **1851** S. JUDD *Margaret* III. (1871) 369 Their *Ismaticalness* conceals and extrudes the Christian—We meet them as Christians, they meet us as *Ismatics*—It is Christ versus *Isms*. **1859** SALA *Gas-light & D.* xv. 168 All the 'isms' in ismdom. **1884** J. ROBERTSON *Univ. Serm.* in *Cambr. Rev.* 5 Nov. Suppl. p. xxvi/1 To him..shall the breezes of all the influences, ismal or dismal, bring but bracing and the full shock of each new 'ology' bring new strength. **1888** *Voice* (N.Y.) 6 Dec., Ultramontanists, Communists, Socialists and every *ismatic* who wants something without knowing just what it is.

-ism, *suffix*, repr. F. *-isme*, L. *-ismus*, a. Gr. -ισμός, forming nouns of action from verbs in -ίζειν, e.g. βαπτίζειν to dip, baptize, βαπτισμός the action of dipping, baptism. An allied suffix was -ισμα(τ-), which more strictly expressed the finished act or thing done, and which in some cases is the source of modern *-ism*.

Besides its free use as a suffix forming vbs. on ordinary sbs. and adjs., -ίζειν was (as mentioned under -IZE) affixed to national names, with the sense to act or 'play' the people in question, and hence to act like, do after the manner of, practise the habits, customs, or language of, side with or adhere to the party of, those people. Hence the sb. in -ισμός had the sense of acting or doing like, siding with, adhesion to, or speaking like the people in question; e.g. Ἀττικίζειν to Atticize, to side with the Athenians, to use the Attic dialect; hence Ἀττικισμός, Atticism, a siding with Athens, Attic style of language, etc. The LXX (Esther viii. 17) and N.T. have Ἰουδαΐζειν to Judaize, to live like the Jews. The derivative Ἰουδαϊσμός Judaism, the manner of the Jews, occurs in the LXX (2 Macc. ii. 21). The Latin *Jūdaismus* occurs in Tertullian (*c* 200); *Jūdaizāre* in the Vulgate. Origen (*a* 250) has Χριστιανίζειν to play the Christian, act the part of a Christian, practise Christian principles, and Justin Martyr (*a* 150) has Χριστιανισμός the practice of Christians, Christianity. Hence late L. *christiānizāre* in Tertullian, *christiānismus* in Tertullian, Augustine and Jerome. On the

type of these, -ισμός, *-ismus*, became the ordinary ending to form names of religious, ecclesiastical, or philosophical systems; thus *pāgānismus* is cited by Du Cange from a council of 744. The OF. repr. of this, *paienisme, paienime, painime* (12th c.) is prob. the earliest Fr. example, and appears in Eng. as *painime, painim* in the 13th c. But, in the modern form and sense, *Judaisme* is found *a* 1500, and *christianisme* (*a* 1500 in Fr.) *c* 1525 in Eng. From the 16th c. such formations are numerous.

The following are the chief uses of the suffix:

1. Forming a simple noun of action (usually accompanying a vb. in -IZE), naming the process, or the completed action, or its result (rarely concrete); as in *agonism, aphorism, baptism, criticism, embolism, exorcism, magnetism, mechanism, nepotism, organism, plagiarism, ostracism, syllogism, synchronism, volcanism*. To this group in Gr. belonged *asterism*.

b. Applied to these, but with affinities to 2, are words in which *-ism* expresses the action or conduct of a class of persons, as *heroism, patriotism, despotism*, and the more colloquial *blackguardism, busybodyism, desperadoism, priggism, scoundrelism*; also the condition of a person or thing, as *barbarism, deaf-mutism, orphanism, anomalism, mediævalism, parallelism*; also *Daltonism*; with such nonce-words as *barmaidism, old maidism*; *all-roundism, cleverism, devil-may-care-ism, well-to-do-ism*.

2. Forming the name of a system of theory or practice, religious, ecclesiastical, philosophical, political, social, etc., sometimes founded on the name of its subject or object, sometimes on that of its founder. Such are *Alexandrianism, Arianism, Arminianism, Brahmanism, Buddhism, Calvinism, Catholicism, Chartism, Christianism, Congregationalism, Conservatism, Epicureanism, Judaism* (*a* 1500), *Latitudinarianism, Liberalism, Machiavellism, Muhammadanism, Platonism, Positivism, Presbyterianism, Protestantism, Puritanism, Puseyism, Quakerism, Quietism, Radicalism, Ritualism, Romanism, Socinianism, Taoism, Toryism, Wesleyanism, Whiggism*.

These pass into terms of more or less temporary currency, as *Berkeleyism, Fourierism, Jeremy Benthamism, Layardism, Owenism, St. Simonism*; with nonce-words formed *ad libitum*, as *John Bullism, Robert Elsmerism, Mahdiism*; and others designating the cult of a person or family, as *Bonapartism, Boulangism, Bronteism, Gladstonism, -onianism, Salisburyism, Stuartism*, etc.

b. More of the nature of class-names or descriptive terms, for doctrines or principles, are *agnosticism, altruism, animism, atheism, bimetallism, deism, egoism, egotism, empiricism, evangelism, fanaticism, feminism, heathenism, hedonism, idealism, imperialism, jingoism, libertinism, monachism, naturalism, opportunism, pædobaptism, paganism, polytheism, realism, romanticism, sansculottism, scepticism, stoicism, theism, universalism*.

These lead the way to nonce-formations of many kinds, often humorous, of which the following are specimens, chiefly from newspapers: *anti-slaveryism, anti-state-churchism, anti-whole-hogism, can't-help-myself-ism, know-nothingism, Little-Peddlingtonism, L.S. Deism* (after *deism*), *nothing-arianism, 19th-century-ism, other-ism, P.R. B-ism, Primrose-leaguism, red-tapeism, Rule-Britanniaism, self-ism*.

3. Forming a term denoting a peculiarity or characteristic, esp. of language, e.g. *Æolism, Americanism, Anglicism, Atticism, Devonshirism, Gallicism, Græcism, Hebraism, Hellenism, Latinism, Orientalism, Scotticism, Southernism, Westernism*, etc. To these add such as *archaism, classicism, colloquialism, modernism, newspaperism, solecism, sophism, witticism*.

Also denoting a peculiarity or characteristic of the language, style, or phraseology of a writer, speaker, character in fiction, etc., as *Browningism, Carlylism, De Quinceyism, Gibbonism, Montesquieuism, Micawberism*, and similar nonce-words without number.

Adjectives pertaining in sense to sbs. in *-ism* are formed in -ISTIC; e.g. *atheism, atheistic; naturalism, naturalistic*.

Ismaelian, Ismaïlian (ɪsmeɪˈiːlɪən, -ˈɪlɪən), *sb.* and *a.* [f. pr. name *Ismael* or *Ismaïl*, the former being the Gr., L., and F. spelling of *Ishmael*, sometimes also used, in place of the more correct *Ismaïl*, to represent the Arabic *ismaʿīl*. The Arabic adjective is *ismaʿīliy*.] A member of a sect of the Shiite (Shīʿite) branch of Islam which held that, at the death of Djafar Madeck, the sixth Imam from Ali, in the second century of the Hijrah, the Imamship ought to have descended to the posterity of his deceased elder son Ismail, and not to the surviving younger son Mousa, to whom his father left it. **b.** as *adj.*

To them belonged the powerful Fatimite dynasty in Egypt, and the fanatical sect of the Assassins.

1839 *Penny Cycl.* XIII. 47 The Druses..are a distinct people..from the present Ismaelians. In 1809 the Nosaïris ..murdered the Emir, with most of the Ismaelian inhabitants. **1883** *Encycl. Brit.* XVI. 587/1 ʿObaid Alláh was really descended from a certain ʿAbdalláh b. Maimún el-Kaddáh, the founder of the Ismailian sect;..This ʿObaid Alláh had himself become pontiff of the Ismailians. *Ibid.* 593 The Ismailians, like all the other Shiites, believed in the coming of a Messiah, whom they call the Mahdi. **1884** *Ibid.* XVII. 771/1 Hasan ibn Ṣabbáḥ who founded afterwards the terrible sect of the Ismaʿilis or Assassins.

ˈIsmaelite, *sb.* (*a.*) Also (in sense c) **ˈIsmailite**. [f. as prec. + -ITE.] **a.** Another form of ISHMAELITE. **b.** A name formerly sometimes given (esp. by Jews) to the Arabs as descendants of Ishmael, and so to Muslims generally. **c.** *spec.* = ISMAELIAN.

1571 GOLDING *Calvin on Ps.* lxxiii. 1 Many yᵗ proudly pretend yᵉ name of (Israel) as though they were the cheef members of yᵉ Church, are but Ismaelites. **1613** PURCHAS *Pilgrimage* (1614) 163 Of the Kingdome of the Calipha,.. the chiefe of the Ismaelite-Sect. *Ibid.* 164 The Jewes in Persia and Media make Vowes..in this place, to which also the Ismaelites resort to pray. **1625-6** —— *Pilgrims* II. 1449 Ghamar-Ben-Alehetah hauing taken that Arke from the ridge of the mountain, fitted it for the vse of the Ismaelites Mosche. **1632** LITHGOW *Trav.* IV. 145 Mahomet..whose father was Abdillas, an Ismaelite. **1839** *Penny Cycl.* XIII. 46/2 The Assassins of Persia and Syria were a fanatical sect of Ismaelites. **1875** *Encycl. Brit.* II. 722/2 Abdallah..was a free-thinker, and he succeeded in establishing among the Ismaelites a faith, or, rather a philosophy, wholly opposed to the doctrines of Islam.

Hence **Ismaeˈlitic, Ismaeˈlitical, ˈIsmaelitish** adjs.; also **ˈIsmaelism**, the doctrinal system of the Ismaelians (formerly, sometimes used as = Islamism, Muhammadanism).

1604 HIERON *Wks.* I. 502 Little to esteeme the schoffes of Ismalitish papists. **1613** PURCHAS *Pilgrimage* (1614) 338 Benjamen Tudelensis telleth that one..had taken..the remainder of the Arke, and therewith built an Ismaeliticall Meschit. **1750** WARBURTON *Doctr. Grace* III. iii. Wks. 1811 VIII. 451 What now has..[he] to oppose to this modest Apology for Ismaelism? **1799** *Ann. Reg., Hist. Europe* i. (1813) 10/2 He [Buonaparte] was careful to pay homage, on every occasion, to the prophet... The whole army took the tone of outward respect for Ismaulism. **1852** TH. ROSS *Humboldt's Trav.* II. xx. 249 Polygamy..sanctioned by Ismaelism, does not prevent the people of the east from loving their children with tenderness. **1875** *Encycl. Brit.* II. 722/2 Ismaelism thus secured a firm footing in the west, and its doctrines were propagated there with great success. **1883** *Ibid.* XVI. 594/1 Under the Fāṭimite Caliph Ḥākim, a new religion sprang out of Ismailism, that of the Druses. **1884** *Ibid.* XVII. 238/1 The eminent men who revealed to the poet in Cairo the secrets of the Ismaʿilitic faith.

i-smaht, i-smecched, i-smeiht, ME. pa. pple. of SMATCH *v.*, to smack.

i-smelled, ME. pa. pple. of SMELL *v.*

i-smered, ME. pa. pple. of SMEAR *v.*

i-smete, i-smite, i-smitte(n, i-smyte, ME. pa. pple. of SMITE *v.*

i-smeðed, ME. pa. pple. of *smeeth*, SMOOTH *v.*

i-smitted, ME. pa. pple. of SMIT *v.*, to infect.

i-smoothed, i-smothed, ME. pa. pple. of SMOOTH *v.*

ismus, obs. spelling of ISTHMUS.

-ismus, *suffix*, repr. G. *-ismus* or L. *-ismus* (see -ISM), used similarly to -ISM, indicating a typical condition or typical conduct, in nouns formed from proper names, or indicating a system or principle, as in ***historismus, mysticismus, Sherlockismus, snobismus***. Freq. with ironical or pejorative overtones.

1912 R. A. KNOX in *Blue Bk.* (Oxf.) July 132 There is a special kind of epigram, known as the Sherlockismus, of which the indefatigable Ratzegger has collected no less than 173 instances. The following may serve as examples: 'Let me call your attention to the curious incident of the dog in the night-time.' 'The dog did nothing at all in the night-time.' 'That was the curious incident,' said Sherlock Holmes. And again: 'I was following you, of course.' 'Following me? I saw nobody.' 'That is what you must expect to see when I am following you,' said Sherlock Holmes. **1948** *Scottish Jrnl. Theol.* I. 142 This kind of unhistorical thinking is neither Biblical nor Christian and..is allied to the speculations of Philo... *This* is certainly not the way to escape from the errors of *Historismus*. **1952** *Spectator* 14 Mar. 334/2 A sincere and compelling protest against *mysticismus* in power politics. **1959** H. KENNER *Invisible Poet: T. S. Eliot* (1960) v. 241 His exchange with the Third Tempter opens with the figure of rhetoric the late Rev. Ronald Knox christened the Sherlockismus: *Third Tempter*: I am an unexpected visitor. *Thomas*: I expected you. **1961** *Daily Tel.* 23 June 18/5 Of all the practitioners of this new cult of 'Sherlockismus', Mr Starrett is..far the most interesting. **1971** A. QUINTON in A. Bullock *20th Cent.* 260/2 Massive studies of *Historismus* by the historians Troeltsch and Meinecke. **1974** *Times Lit. Suppl.* 1 Feb. 113/2 Perhaps he has also done more than he reckoned to put an end to the tiresome excesses of Sherlockismus. **1974** V. GIELGUD *In Such a Night* xx. 172 His acquaintances accused him of Victorian *snobismus*.

isness (ɪznɪs). [f. *is*, 3rd pers. sing. pres. of BE *v.*] **a.** The fact that a thing *is*. **b.** That which a thing *is* in itself; essence.

1865 J. H. STIRLING *Secret of Hegel* II. III. i. 4 *Seyn*, in Germany, often in Hegel himself, means the abstraction of sensuous Isness. **1884** 'SCOTUS NOVANTICUS' *Metaphysica Nova et Vetusta* VI. 146 The moment of being or is-ness yields identity (A = A); and as this is-ness is given *in concreto* as a determined somewhat which *is*, we have the category of Essence as derivative category from Being. **1888** J. MARTINEAU *Stud. Relig.* I. II. i. 183 Both the fact of Being or 'is-ness' of each thing and the real nature of Cause are guaranteed to us by the free act of percipience. **1893** *Dublin Rev.* Jan. 217 That which the intellect first perceived is the transcendental essence or 'isness' of the thing. **1918** [see GOOD A. *adj.* 14c]. **1942** *Mind* LI. 257 Any one..who sets out along the *via negativa* in this spirit is confessing in the very act that 'is' can never be tortured into 'isness'. **1955** A. HUXLEY *Genius & Goddess* 46 The girl is who she is. Some of her isness spills over and impregnates the entire universe. **1965** L. R. HUBBARD *Scientology Abridged Dict., Is-ness*, one of the four conditions of existence. It is an apparency of existence brought about by the continuous alteration of an As-is-ness. This is called, when agreed upon, reality.

Isnik (ɪzˈnɪk). The name of a town in Asian Turkey, the classical Nicæa (see NICENE *a.* (and *sb.*)), used *attrib.* to denote pottery or tiles made there, or imitations thereof, from the fifteenth to the seventeenth centuries, characterized by the use of brilliant pigments.

[**1909** F. R. MARTIN in *Burlington Mag.* Aug. 270/2 The splendid blue and white bowls, commonly ascribed to Kutaya, which I am convinced come from Isnik.] **1932** R. L. HOBSON *Guide Islamic Pott. Near East* III. 87 There were doubtless potters at work in other towns in the sixteenth century,..and it is highly probable that they would adapt their wares to the prevailing Turkish taste as expressed by the Isnik pottery. **1939** A. LANE *Guide Coll. Tiles* (V. & A. Mus.) ii. 16 The pure white ground and tense drawing so characteristic of the later Isnik tiles. **1957** —— *Later Islamic Pott.* iii. 60 It will probably never be possible to stop dealers and collectors calling the later Isnik wares 'Rhodian', and the nickname is at any rate a convenient label for the whole class in which the 'sealing-wax red' appears. **1966** J. FOWLES *Magus* xv. 88 A triangular cabinet full of pale-blue and green Isnik ware. **1972** *Daily Tel.* 5 Dec. 12/5 A large Isnik pottery dish of the late 16th century was bought by Eskenazi for ..£8,000 at Sotheby's yesterday.

isn't, colloq. form of *is not*.

iso- (aɪsəʊ), before a vowel sometimes **is-**, combining form of Gr. ἴσος equal, used in numerous terms, nearly all scientific, the second element being properly and usually of Greek origin, rarely of Latin (the proper prefix in the latter case being EQUI-). The more important of these words are treated in their alphabetical places; others, of less importance or frequency, follow here.

Many recent words of this class are terms of Physical Geography, Meteorology, etc. formed on the analogy of *isotherm, isothere, isochimenal*, the Fr. originals of which were introduced by A. von Humboldt in 1817.

a. isabˈnormal *a.* and *sb.*, (a line on a map, etc.) connecting places having equal deviation of the mean temperature (for some particular period) from the normal temperature due to the latitude; also *iso-abnormal*. **isaˈcoustic** *a.*, (*a*) applied to a curve passing through those points (in a theatre, concert-room, etc.) at which a speaker or performer may be heard equally well; (*b*) *Seismology*, applied to a line (imaginary or on a map) connecting places where an equal percentage of observers heard the sound of an earthquake. **isadelphous** (aɪsəˈdɛlfəs) *a. Bot.* [cf. ADELPHOUS], having diadelphous stamens with the same number in each bundle. **iˈsandrous** *a. Bot.* [see -ANDROUS], having stamens equal in number to the parts of the perianth. **iˈsanomal** *a.* and *sb.* = *isabnormal*; hence **isaˈnomaly** *sb.* (also **isonomaly**); also used with reference to other kinds of anomaly (see quots.). **isaˈnomalous** *a.*, (of a line) isabnormal; (of a map) depicting such lines. **iˈsantherous** *a. Bot.*, having the anthers equal or alike. **isanˈthesical** *a.* (see quot.). **iˈsanthous** *a. Bot.* [Gr. ἄνθος flower], having the parts of the flower equal or alike; having regular flowers. **iseidomal** (-ˈaɪdəməl) *a.* [badly f. Gr. εἴδομαι I am seen, I appear], applied to a curve passing through points (in a theatre, etc.) from which a spectacle may be seen equally well. **iseˈnergic** *a. Physics*, indicating equal energy, as a line on a diagram. **isenˈthalpic** *a.*, of or denoting equal enthalpy. **isenˈtropic** *a.* and *sb. Physics*, of equal entropy; (a line on a diagram) indicating successive states of a body in which the entropy remains constant; also, taking place at constant entropy, involving no change in entropy; hence **isenˈtropically** *adv.*, without a change in entropy. **iso-abˈnormal**: see *isabnormal* above. **ˌisoacˈcentual** *a.*, of verse in which the syllables are of equal length and accent. **isoaˈgglutinate** *v. trans.* (also *absol.*), to cause isoagglutination (of); chiefly in **isoaˈgglutinating** *vbl. sb.* and *ppl. a.* **ˌisoaggluˈtiˈnation** *Immunol.* [a. G. *isoagglutination* (A. Klein 1902, in *Wiener klin. Wochenschr.* XV. 415/1)], agglutination of cells of an individual by a substance obtained from

another individual of the same species; so ˌ**isoa'gglutinative** *a.*, pertaining to or causing isoagglutination. ˌ**isoa'gglutinin** *Immunol.*, an agglutinin that agglutinates cells of other individuals of the same species as that in which it is found. ˌ**isoa'gglutinogen** *Immunol.*, a substance that elicits or reacts with an isoagglutinin. **isoallele** (aɪsəʊ'æliːl) *Genetics*, an allele indistinguishable from another allele in its effect on the phenotype except when special techniques are employed; hence **isoa'llelic** *a.* **iso'antibody** *Immunol.*, an antibody elicited by an isoantigen. **iso'antigen** *Immunol.*, an antigen in one individual which is capable of eliciting antibody formation only in other, genetically different, individuals of the same species; so **isoanti'genic** *a.* **iso-au'rore** = *isochasm.* **'isobase** *Geol.* [ad. Sw. *isobas* (G. De Geer 1890, in *Geol. Fören. i Stockholm Forhandl.* XII. 72), f. Gr. βάσις stepping, step], a line (either imaginary or on a map) connecting points on the earth which have undergone equal amounts of uplift (or more rarely depression) over a period of geological time; hence **iso'basic** *a.* **'isobath** (-bæθ) [Gr. βάθος depth], *a.*, trade-name for an inkstand with a float so contrived as to keep the ink in the dipping-well at a constant level; *sb.*, a line (either imaginary or on a map) joining places where water has equal depth; an underwater contour; **iso'bathic** *a.* **isobathytherm** (-'bæθɪθɜːm) [Gr. βαθύς deep + θέρμη heat], a line connecting points having the same temperature in a vertical section of any part of the sea (also ISOTHERMOBATH); so **isobathy'thermal, -'thermic** *adjs.* **isobi'lateral** *a.*, having the two sides equal and alike; applied to bilaterally symmetrical leaves in which there is no evident distinction of upper and under surface, as in some species of Iris. **isobryous, -brious** (aɪ'sɒbrɪəs) *a. Bot.* [Gr. βρύειν to swell, or βριάειν to be strong], growing with equal vigour on both sides; applied to a dicotyledonous embryo. **'isobront** [Gr. βροντή thunder] (see quot.). **iso'caloric** *a.*, of equal calorific value; hence **isoca'lorically** *adv.*, in a way that leaves the calorific value unchanged. **iso'carpous** *a.* [Gr. καρπός fruit] (see quot.). **iso'cellular** *a. Biol.*, consisting of equal cells: better *equicellular.* **isocephaly** (-'sɛfəlɪ), **-kephaly** (-'kɛfəlɪ) [Gr. κεφαλή head], the principle observed in some ancient Greek reliefs, esp. in friezes, of representing the heads of all the figures at nearly the same level. **isocercal** (-'sɜːkəl) *a. Ichthyol.* [Gr. κέρκος tail], having the tail part of the vertebral column straight, and not bent up; so **isocercy** ('aɪsəʊsɜːsɪ), the condition of being isocercal. **'isochasm** (-kæz(ə)m) [Gr. χάσμα gap, CHASM], a line on a map, etc. connecting places having equal frequency of auroral displays; so **iso'chasmic** *a.* (lines or curves) bounding zones of equal auroral frequency. **iso'chemical** *a. Geol.*, taking place with or characterized by constant chemical composition; hence **iso'chemically** *adv.*, without a change in chemical composition. **'isochlor** (-klɔː(r)) [CHLOR(INE *sb.*], a line (imaginary or on a map) connecting points where the concentration of chlorine in the surface water is the same; **'isochor** (-kɔː(r)) [Gr. χώρα space], a curve connecting points corresponding to equal volumes, on a diagram denoting relations between pressure and temperature; so **isochoric** (-'kɒrɪk) *a.* **iso'chromosome** *Cytology*, an abnormal chromosome having a pair of identical arms. **isochroous** (aɪ'sɒkrəʊəs) *a.* [Gr. χρόα colour], of the same colour throughout (Webster, 1864). **iso'colloid** *Chem.* [ad. G. *isokolloid* (W. Ostwald *Grundriss der Kolloidchemie* (ed. 2, 1911) I. iv. 128)], a colloidal solution in which the disperse phase and the dispersion medium are chemically identical (as ice dispersed in water) or chemically related (as a polymer dispersed in its monomer). **iso'cortex** *Anat.* [mod.L. (C. & O. Vogt 1919, in *Jrnl. f. Psychol. u. Neurol.* XXV. 293)] = NEOPALLIUM. **iso'cyclic** *a. Chem.* = *homocyclic* adj. s.v. HOMO-. **isocyclous** (aɪ'sɒsɪkləs) *a. Zool.* [Gr. ἰσόκυκλος 'equally round', f. κύκλος circle], consisting (as the bodies of some arthropoda) of a succession of equal rings. **iso'dactylous** *a. Zool.* [Gr. δάκτυλος digit], having the fore and hind toes or digits equal or alike. **isodimorphism** (ˌaɪsəʊdaɪ'mɔːfɪz(ə)m), *Cryst.* [see DIMORPHISM], 'isomorphism between the forms severally of two dimorphous substances' (Webster, 1864); so ˌ**isodi'morphous** *a.*, exhibiting isodimorphism. **isodont** ('aɪsəʊdɒnt), **iso'dontous** *adjs. Zool.* [Gr. ὀδούς tooth], having the teeth all alike, as some cetaceans. **iso-'echo** *a.*, applied to a line on a radar display along which the echo signal (from clouds and the like) has the same strength, and to devices and techniques relating to such lines (as in the detection of rain and atmospheric turbulence). **isoener'getic** *a.*, having, denoting, or giving rise to equal amounts of energy; taking place at constant energy. **'isogel** *Chem.*, an isocolloid in the form of a gel. **isognathous** (aɪ'sɒgnəθəs) *a. Zool.* [Gr. γνάθος jaw], having the molar teeth alike in both jaws. **'isograd** *Petrol.* [GRAD(E *sb.*], a line or surface (either imaginary or in a diagram) joining points where the rock originated under the same conditions of pressure and temperature, as indicated by similarity of facies or metamorphic grade; hence **'isograde, iso'gradic** *adjs.*, that is an isograd; of the same facies or metamorphic grade. **isogynous** (aɪ'sɒdʒɪnəs) *a. Bot.* [see -GYNOUS], having pistils or carpels equal in number to the parts of the perianth. **'isogyre**, a thick band or bow of darkness seen crossing the coloured fringes in an interference pattern. **isogyrous** (-'dʒaɪərəs) *a. Bot. rare*⁻⁰ [Gr. γῦρος circle], forming a complete spiral. ˌ**isohæmaggluti'nation** (also **-hem-**) *Immunol.*, isoagglutination of red blood cells. ˌ**isohæma'gglutinin** (also **-hem-**) *Immunol.*, an isoagglutinin which agglutinates red blood cells. ˌ**isohæmo'lysin** (also **-hem-**) *Immunol.*, a hæmolysin that lyses red blood cells of other individuals of the same species as that in which it is found. **isohaline** (-'heɪlaɪn) *sb. Oceanogr.* [Gr. ἅλινος of salt], a line (imaginary or on a chart), or an imaginary surface, connecting points which have the same salinity; *a.*, connecting such points; also, of a constant salinity throughout. **iso'halsine** [irreg. f. Gr. ἅλς, ἁλ- salt], a line on a map or chart connecting points at which the waters of the sea have an equal degree of saltness. **'isohel** [Gr. ἥλιος sun], a line (imaginary or on a map) connecting points having the same amount or duration of sunshine; so **isohelic** (-'hiːlɪk), *a.* **'isohyet** (-haɪɪt) [Gr. ὑετ-ός rain], = *isohyetal* sb. **isohyetal** (-'haɪɪtəl), **-'hyetose** *adjs.* (*sbs.*) [Gr. ὑετός rain], (a line on a map, etc.) connecting places having equal annual or seasonal rainfall. **isoi'mmune** *a.*, of, producing, or exhibiting isoimmunization. ˌ**isoimmuni'zation** (an instance of) the development of an isoantibody in an individual against an antigen derived from another individual of the same species. **isokephaly**: see *isocephaly.* **isoki'netic** *a.*, characterized by no disturbance to the speed and direction of a fluid when it is withdrawn as a sample from a flow; hence **isoki'netically** *adv.*, in an isokinetic manner, i.e. without causing such a disturbance. **iso'lecithal** *a.* = *homolecithal* adj. (s.v. HOMO-). **'isolex** *Linguistics*, a line connecting places in which there is uniformity of vocabulary; hence **iso'lexic** *a.*; also **iso'lectic** *a.* **'isoline** = ISOPLETH 1. **iso'lysin** *Immunol.* [a. G. *isolysin* (Ehrlich & Morgenroth 1900, in *Berliner klin. Wochenschr.* XXXVII. 455/1)] = *isohæmolysin* above. **isomag'netic** *a.*, denoting a line (either imaginary or on a map) connecting places which have the same value of a particular parameter of the earth's magnetic field, and a map or chart showing such lines; also as *sb.*, an isomagnetic line. **iso'mastigate** *a. Zool.* [Gr. μάστιξ whip], (of Infusoria) having the flagella alike; opp. to *heteromastigate.* **isomyarian** (-maɪ'ɛərɪən) *a. Zool.* [Gr. μῦς muscle], having two equal or nearly equal adductor muscles, as most bivalve molluscs. **isoneph** ('aɪsəʊnɛf) [Gr. νέφος cloud], a line on a map, etc. connecting places at which the amount of cloud for a given period (e.g. a year) is the same; so **isonephelic** (-nɪ'fɛlɪk) *a.* [Gr. νεφέλη cloud], indicating equality in respect of cloudiness. **isonomaly**, var. *isanomaly.* **iso'nuclear** *a. Chem.* = HOMONUCLEAR *a.* b. **iso-os'motic** *a. Physiol.* = *isosmotic* adj. (below). **iso'petalous** *a. Bot.*, having petals equal in size. **isophæ'nomenal** *a.*, (of a line on a map) connecting places at which phenomena of any kind are equal. **i'sophytoid** *Biol.* [Gr. φυτόν plant: see -OID], a 'phytoid', or individual plant of a compound plant-organism, not differentiated from the rest: opp. to *allophytoid* (cf. *isozooid*). **isopiestic** (-paɪ'ɛstɪk) *a.* [Gr. πιέζειν to press, squeeze], representing, having, or characterized by equal or constant pressure; also as *sb.*, a line in a diagram representing states of equal pressure. **isopogonous** (-'pɒgəʊnəs) *a.* [Gr. πώγων beard]: see quot. **'isopor** [Gr. πόρ-ος passage, way], a line (either imaginary or on a map) connecting points at which equal annual changes in some parameter of the earth's magnetic field are observed; hence **iso'poric** *a.* **'isoscope** [see -SCOPE], an instrument devised by Donders to determine the actual angle between directions which to the eye appear both vertical or both horizontal. **isoseismal** (-'saɪsməl) *a.* and *sb.* [Gr. σεισμός earthquake], (a line on a map, etc.) connecting points at which the intensity of an earthquake-shock is the same; so **iso'seismic** *a.* **isosmotic** (aɪsɒz'mɒtɪk) *a. Physiol.*, of or having the same osmotic pressure; const. *with.* **isosporous** (aɪ'sɒspərəs) *a. Bot.* [Gr. σπόρος seed], producing spores all of the same size or kind (opp. to *heterosporous*); so **isospore** ('aɪsəʊspɔə(r)), one of such spores. **isostemonous** (-'stiːmənəs) *a. Bot.* [Gr. στήμων warp, thread, taken in sense 'stamen'], having the stamens equal in number to the parts of the perianth (= *isandrous*); also said of the stamens; so **isostemony** (-'stiːmənɪ), the condition of being isostemonous. **'isostich** (-stɪk) *Biochem.* [Gr. στίχ-ος line (of poetry)], each of two or more fractions of a polynucleotide that contain the same number of nucleotides. **iso'structural** *a. Min.*, having the same or similar crystal structure; const. *with.* **isosy'llabic** *a. Linguistics*, of a metrical structure in which the syllables are of the same length. **isosyn'tactic** *a.* (see quot.). **isosyn'tagmic** *a. Linguistics* (see quot. 1954). **'isotach** [Gr. ταχ-ύς swift], a line on a chart or diagram connecting points where the speed of something, esp. the wind, is the same. **iso'teniscope** [irreg. f. TEN(SION *sb.* + -I- + -SCOPE], an instrument for measuring the vapour pressure of a liquid over a range of temperatures, consisting of a bulb for containing the liquid attached to one arm of a U-tube, which is used as a manometer to show when the pressure applied to the other arm is equal to the vapour pressure. **isotrimorphism** (ˌaɪsəʊtraɪ'mɔːfɪz(ə)m), *Cryst.* [see TRIMORPHISM], 'isomorphism between the forms, severally, of two trimorphous substances' (Webster, 1864); so ˌ**isotri'morphous** *a.*, exhibiting isotrimorphism. **'isovol** [VOL(ATILE *sb.* and *a.*], a line (either imaginary or on a map) joining places at which the coal has the same ratio of fixed to volatile carbon. **iso'zoic** *a.* [Gr. ζωή life], characterized by or indicating the same forms of animal or plant life. **iso'zooid** *Biol.*, a 'zooid', or individual of a compound or 'colonial' animal organism, not differentiated from the rest: opp. to *allozooid.*

1853 H. W. DOVE (*title*) Distribution of Heat over the surface of the Globe, illustrated by isothermal, thermic, *isabnormal and other curves of temperature. **1888** R. ABERCROMBY *Weather* i. 7 These lines were called *isabnormals*, that is, equal from the mean. **1842–76** GWILT *Archit.* (ed. 7) §2961 The points which indicate the places of the spectators will lie in . . a . . curve, which may be termed the iseidomal or the *isacoustic curve, that is, one of equal seeing or hearing. **1900** C. DAVISON in *Phil. Mag.* XLIX. 43 An isacoustic line may be defined as a line which passes through all places in which the percentage of persons who hear the sound is the same. **1938** L. D. LEET *Pract. Seismol.* viii. 282 Curves passing through the places at which equal percentages of the observers heard the earthquake sound were drawn in 1899, and Davison, followed by Knott and de Montessus, called them isacoustic lines. **1855** MAYNE *Expos. Lex.*, *Isadelphous. **1880** GRAY *Struct. Bot.* (ed. 6) 417/1 *Isadelphous*, . . when the number of stamens in two phalanges is equal. **1881** *Nature* XXIV. 266 Elucidated by **isanomals* (or lines of equal temperature-anomalies). **1887** *Syd. Soc. Lex.*, *I[sanomal] line.* **1900** *Geogr. Jrnl.* XV. 662 Maps of isotherms and *isanomalous lines for January and July. **1943** G. T. TREWARTHA *Introd. Climate* (ed. 2) i. 56/2 If lines, called isanomals, are drawn on a world map, joining places of equal thermal anomaly, an isanomalous map is the result. **1967** R. W. FAIRBRIDGE *Encycl. Atmospheric Sci.* 985/1 Isanomalous lines drawn on a map . . reflect regional distortions of the world patterns. **1881** *Nature* XXIV. 94 Relations between isobars and *isanomalies of temperature. **1930** *Meteorol. Gloss.* (Meteorol. Office) (ed. 2) 109 *Isanomaly.* This word . . is used of lines joining all points on a map or chart having equal anomalies, or differences from normal, of a particular meteorological element. **1931** F. H. LAHEE *Field Geol.* (ed. 3) xxiii. 674 Equal anomalies may be connected by flowing lines called isonomalies, or isanomalies, which express in gammas the local variations from the average total magnetic intensities in the area. **1962** F. I. ORDWAY et al. *Basic Astronautics* v. 199 Lines of regional vertical intensity are constructed, as are isonomaly charts expressing in gammas the local variations in the average total magnetic intensity of a given region. **1967** R. W. FAIRBRIDGE *Encycl. Atmospheric Sci.* 507/2 *Isanomaly*,

lines or contours of equal anomalies or departures from normal (often used with gravity anomalies, cf. *Isogal*). 1855 MAYNE *Expos. Lex.*, *Isantherous. 1848 *Jrnl. R. Agric. Soc.* IX. II. 323 Quêtelet proposes *isanthesical lines (lines of simultaneous flowering). 1855 MAYNE *Expos. Lex.*, *Isanthus*, applied by G. Allman to those plants which have the perigones or teguments of all their flowers alike: *isanthous. 1842–76 *Iseidomal [see *Isacoustic*]. 1925 *Proc. Amer. Acad. Arts & Sci.* LX. 581 The *isenthalpic curves themselves contain valuable information. 1937 M. W. ZEMANSKY *Heat & Thermodynamics* xiv. 245 (*caption*) Isenthalpic states of a gas. *Ibid.* 246 The numerical value of the slope of an isenthalpic curve on a *t-P* diagram at any point is called the Joule-Kelvin coefficient. 1973 J. S. TURTON *Macroscopic Thermodynamics* iv. 81 The process undergone by the gas or vapour in passing through the constriction cannot be represented by an isenthalpic curve. 1873 J. W. GIBBS in *Trans. Connecticut Acad. Arts & Sci.* II. 311 If, however, we.. call that quantity entropy.. it seems natural to.. call the lines in which this quantity has a constant value *isentropic. *Ibid.* 327 Although the inclination of the isentropics is independent of the quantity of gas under consideration, the rate of increase of η will vary with this quantity. 1885 WILLIAMSON & TARLETON *Dynamics* (1889) §326 In a reversible transformation, if no heat be lost or gained by the body.., this curve is called an adiabatic or isentropic curve. 1923 LEWIS & RANDALL *Thermodynamics* xii. 137 In such an isentropic compression there will ordinarily be a change in temperature. 1951 C. L. BROWN *Basic Thermodynamics* vi. 88 Two additional relations.. relate temperature and volume and pressure and volume for an isentropic. 1956 G. C. MCVITTIE *Gen. Relativity & Cosmol.* vii. 123 An equation determining the function *F* in isentropic flow. 1951 C. L. BROWN *Basic Thermodynamics* vi. 89 The gas expands *isentropically and is exhausted at 15 psia. 1972 *Nature* 15 Sept. 139/2 The pressure applied to an implosion system does *PdV* work generating kinetic energy which is converted near isentropically to internal energy concentrated in the compressed volume. 1956 H. WHITEHALL in *Kenyon Rev.* 420 There is.. in much of Milton, isochronic counterpointed with *isoaccentual rhythm. In some poems of Dylan Thomas, we find a most elaborate counterpoint of isoaccentual.. and, apparently, isotonic rhythms. 1957 N. FRYE *Sound & Poetry* 143 Isoaccentual, or, as it is often called, isosyllabic rhythm weights with stress. 1904 *Alienist & Neurologist* XXV. 386 The serum from such blood was also *isoagglutinating. 1910 *Johns Hopkins Hosp. Bull.* XXI. 70/1 Human beings can be divided into four groups according to the ability of their serum to cause isoagglutination and of their corpuscles to be isoagglutinated. 1921 *Biol. Bull.* XL. 18 The iso-agglutinating power of the egg-water. 1967 D. M. WEIR *Handbk. Exper. Immunol.* iv. 87 The isoagglutinating activity found in this sedimentation region of human serum. 1907 *Jrnl. Med. Res.* XVII. 338 Human bloods may be separated into three rather definite groups as regards *iso-agglutination. 1921 *Biol. Bull.* XL. 17 In iso-agglutination round solid masses of agglutinated spermatozoa form in a few seconds. 1927 Iso-agglutination [see A 7]. 1970 *Exper. Cell Res.* LIX. 37 (*heading*) Jelly coat substances of sea urchin eggs. I. Sperm isoagglutination and sialo-polysaccharide in the jelly. 1902 *Science* 28 Nov. 858/1 The *isoagglutinative and isolytic properties of human serums in health and in disease. 1911 *Jrnl. Exper. Med.* XIII. 537 Isoagglutinative serum is active at a considerable dilution. 1903 DORLAND *Med. Dict.* (ed. 3) 350/1 *iso-agglutinin. 1907 [see *isohæmagglutination* below]. 1971 J. A. BELLANTI *Immunol.* iii. 78 All mature individuals possess antibody in their serum, the so-called 'naturally occurring' isoantibodies (isoagglutinins) directed against the antigenic determinant absent from their own erythrocytes. 1926 *Jrnl. Immunol.* XI. 240 The main human *iso-agglutinogens A and B are to be detected not only by human serum but also by the sera of animals. 1972 W. E. HAESLER *Immunohematol.* i. 2 Immunohematology deals with hemagglutinogens (isoagglutinogens, immunogens, antigens) that are a natural phenomenon in human beings. 1943 STERN & SCHAEFFER in *Proc. Nat. Acad. Sci.* XXIX. 361 Different alleles indistinguishable except by special tests will be called *isoalleles. 1970 *Sci. Amer.* Mar. 104 These slightly different forms of the same gene that perform the same function are called isoalleles. 1944 *Genetics* XXIX. 485 These crosses established the *iso-allelic if not identical nature of all seven *pyd* mutants. 1961 *Lancet* 29 July 262/2 An isochromosome carries, on its two symmetrical arms, duplicate gene loci each influencing the same character. These arms can be both isologous and isoallelic. 1919 L. & H. HIRSCHFELD in *Lancet* 18 Oct. 676/1 The antibodies produced within the species which we call *isoantibodies.. act.. only against the differences between the blood of the animal which provides the blood for injection and that of the recipient. 1971 Isoantibody [see *isoagglutinin* above]. 1936 *Jrnl. Immunol.* XXX. 445 (*heading*) Procedure for the determination of *isoantigens in saliva. 1971 J. A. BELLANTI *Immunol.* iii. 76 Homologous antigens or isoantigens (alloantigens) are those genetically controlled antigenic determinants which distinguish one individual of a given species from another. 1938 *Jrnl. Path. & Bacteriol.* XLVI. 249 *Iso-antigenic factors present in the grafted tissue and absent in the host are capable of eliciting a response which results in the destruction of the graft. 1971 J. A. BELLANTI *Immunol.* iii. 80 New human iso-antigenic specificities. 1885 S. TROMHOLT *Aurora Bor.* I. 248, I have called these lines *iso-aurores. 1892 G. DE GEER in *Proc. Boston Soc. Nat. Hist.* XXV. 457 To get a general view of the warping of land .. I have used the graphic method of Mr. G. K. Gilbert.. and have connected with lines of equal deformation, or as I have called them *isobases, such points of the limit as were uplifted to the same height. 1957 J. K. CHARLESWORTH *Quaternary Era* II. xlv. 1289 (*caption*) Map of the sea's greatest area in Baltoscandia (black), with areas of most important glacier-lakes (shaded) and isobases of uplift in metres. 1969 BENNISON & WRIGHT *Geol. Hist. Brit. Isles* xvi. 366 It is still not possible to construct accurate isobases (lines joining points of equal uplift) for Britain, as has been done in the case of Scandinavia. 1932 E. G. WOODS *Baltic Region* x. 121 A glance at such a map with the *isobasic lines indicated, shows the late-glacial sea at about its maximum development. 1889 *Advt.*, New patent '*Isobath' Constant-level inkstand. 1895 *Rep. Sci. Results Voy. H.M.S. Challenger, Summary* I. 55 Bauche.. is.. considered as the first to make use of isobaths for the sea. 1938 *Jrnl. Marine Res.* I. 138 (*caption*) Isobaths (light broken lines) for every ten meters depth. 1956 *Trans. Amer. Microsc. Soc.* LXXV. 335 Miner's map is our primary source of that shore line.. just as it is for the contained isobaths. The Commission.. has in no way modified the lakes except to build a bathing beach and boat docks. 1972 *Nature* 4 Feb. 253/2 Thus Corsica makes a good fit with France along the 1,000-metre isobath. 1895 *Rep. Sci. Results Voy. H.M.S. Challenger, Summary* I. 50 These *isobathic curves are intended to show that certain elevations of the sea-bottom correspond with the orography of the neighbouring land. 1957 *Encycl. Brit.* VIII. 743/2 The isobathic chart of the Severn estuary.. shows a progressive deepening seaward by means of V-shaped lines which become blunter westward. 1876 SIR C. W. THOMSON cited in *Cent. Dict.* for *Isobathytherm*. 1887 *Syd. Soc. Lex.*, **Isobilateral*, equal and alike on both sides. 1835 *Isobrious [see ISODYNAMOUS]. 1886 *Sci. Amer.* Suppl. XXII. 9154/2 For 24 separate thunderstorms, drawings were made of the '*isobronts', isobars, and isothermals... The 'isobronts', or the lines uniting the places where the first peal of thunder was simultaneously heard, had in general a north-south direction. 1922 *Experiment Station Rec.* Sept. 370 The sugar tolerance of the diabetic patient was.. more markedly lowered by protein than by *isocaloric amounts of fat. 1956 *Biol. Abstr.* XXX. 2208/1 Male Wistar rats were divided into 3 groups receiving an isocaloric diet. 1971 *Jrnl. Gen. Psychol.* LXXXV. 155 Decreasing the amount of protein in the diet, while holding it isocaloric through addition of carbohydrate, resulted in an increase in the 'excitatory process' of rats. 1973 *Lancet* 2 June 1201/2 A programme of work on an isolated group of healthy young men, using isocaloric substitution of glucose syrup.. for dietary sucrose. 1971 *Jrnl. Gen. Psychol.* LXXXV. 156 Diets in which carbohydrate and protein were interchanged *isocalorically. 1972 *Science* 19 May 795/1 The animals fed alcohol received the identical diet except that ethanol.. isocalorically replaced carbohydrate. 1887 *Syd. Soc. Lex.*, **Isocarpous*, equal-fruited. Applied to those phanerogamous plants which have the divisions of the fruit equal in number to the divisions of the perianth. 1885 *Stand. Nat. Hist.* (1888) III. 121 The.. Gymnarchidæ, with the lower fins all wanting, and the *isocercal tail without a caudal fin. 1885 S. TROMHOLT *Aurora Bor.* I. 240 This interesting chart, which he has called an '*isochasm' chart, and the lines denoted 'isochasmes'. 1886 *Edin. Rev.* Oct. 425 Isochasms or lines of equal auroral frequency. 1875 H. R. PROCTER in *Encycl. Brit.* III. 97/2 Eastward from England, the *isochasmic curves tend rapidly northward, Archangel being in the same auroral parallel as Newcastle. 1937 *Trans. R. Soc. Edin.* LIX. 218 Correlation between rocks of the same bulk-composition metamorphosed under different physical controls—i.e. *isochemical correlation. 1951 TURNER & VERHOOGEN *Ign. & Metamorphic Petrol.* xv. 369 Metamorphism may be considered as commonly approaching, though seldom attaining, the nature of an isochemical change. 1952 T. F. W. BARTH *Theoret. Petrol.* IV. xii. 356 In geological discussions the fact that sediments at the very incipience of metamorphism regularly change their chemical composition has often been neglected. However, these changes are not to be neglected... Isochemical regional metamorphism *senso strictu* [sic].. does not exist. 1969 W. D. JOHNS tr. *Correns's Introd. Mineral.* ix. 298 Transformations in an isochemical system depend on the temperature and pressure to which the system has been subjected. 1964 J. CHALLINOR *Dict. Geol.* (ed. 2) 133/2 A rock changing its mineral composition *iso-chemically remains a closed 'system'. 1973 *Nature* 23 Mar. 243/2 The thickness of halite salt that could be precipitated isochemically from one basinful of Mediterranean waters.. is.. only about 20 m. 1890 *Rep. on Water Supply & Sewerage Pt. 1: Examinations of Water Supplies & Inland Waters* (Massachusetts State Board of Health) 679 In the accompanying map of normal chlorine of Massachusetts, the points of like normal chlorine have been connected by lines which we will call *isochlors. 1943 *Proc. R. Irish Acad.* XLVIII. B. 157 The geochemical data of chlorine are considered with respect to river and surface waters, and equations developed relating the distance of any particular isochlor from the sea coast. 1957 G. E. HUTCHINSON *Treat. Limnol.* I. viii. 545 In Europe a greater proportion of rain is derived from air which has moved in perpendicular to the isochlors than is likely to be the case in North America. 1939 C. D. DARLINGTON in *Jrnl. Genetics* XXXVII. 357 The attached-*X* chromosome has two exactly similar arms united at the centromere. It is what we may call an *iso-chromosome. 1972 W. V. BROWN *Textbk. Cytogenetics* xix. 268 The only likely iso-chromosomes found in human beings are of the long arm of a G-group chromosome, probably No. 21, and of the X chromosome. 1915 M. H. FISCHER tr. *W. Ostwald's Handbk. Colloid-Chem.* iv. 103 We shall term these structures in which disperse phase and dispersion means are chemically isomeric, *isocolloids. 1946 J. ALEXANDER *Colloid Chem., Theoret. & Appl.* VI. xxiii. 531 Wolfgang Ostwald considers high-boiling petroleum fractions as iso-colloids, in which the dispersed phase and the dispersion medium possess the same or similar chemical constitution. 1934 *Biol. Abstr.* VIII. 1476/1 Myelin reduction, at least in the *iso-cortex, is discontinuous. 1937 BEST & TAYLOR *Physiol. Basis Med. Pract.* lxiii. 1418 The laminated cortex, which in man constitutes the remaining eleven-twelfths [of the cortical area] and in animals is a much smaller fraction of the whole, is called the isocortex. 1951 K. S. LASHLEY in L. A. Jeffress *Cerebral Mechanisms in Behaviour* 132 In the rat, I have removed.. practically every other part of the isocortex without disturbing visual perception or memory. 1970 *Developmental Biol.* XXII. 575 Fetal mouse cerebral isocortex from normal animals.. was dissociated and aggregated. 1900 E. F. SMITH tr. *V. von Richer's Org. Chem.* (ed. 3) II. 435 The carbocyclic substances.. belong to the class of *isocyclic compounds which consist of rings of atoms of one and the same element. 1932 [see *homocyclic* adj. s.v. HOMO-]. 1951 I. L. FINAR *Org. Chem.* I. 667 The subject matter is divided into four main divisions: (i) Alicyclic compounds. (ii) Isocyclic compounds. (iii) Heterocyclic compounds. (iv) Natural products. 1887 *Syd. Soc. Lex.*, **Isocyclous*, consisting of equal rings. 1855 MAYNE *Expos. Lex.*, *Isodactylus*,.. birds.. which have four toes, two in front and two behind: *isodactylous. 1869 ROSCOE *Elem. Chem.* 238 These two oxides [Sb_2O_3, As_2O_3] are said to be *iso-dimorphous. 1887 *Syd. Soc. Lex.*, **Isodontous*, having equal teeth. 1951 *Jrnl. Meteorol.* VIII. 274/1 The distribution of echo intensity from all points in the two-dimensional cut through a storm may be plotted by use of the contour-mapping techniques suggested by Langille and Gunn or Atlas. The latter techniques produce a contour chart showing isopleths of reflected power throughout the area of the storm. (These isopleths will be referred to as '*isoecho lines' or 'power contours'.) 1959 L. J. BATTAN *Radar Meteorol.* xv. 141 (*heading*) Isoecho contouring. *Ibid.*, If range differences are negligible, the isoecho contour corresponds to a line of equal cloud reflectivity and equal rain intensity. 1961 *Aeroplane* CI. 573/2 For general weather observation the C.R. 353 has a 12-in. PPI unit incorporating iso-echo circuits which enable the operator to make cloud density determinations. 1969 *New Scientist* 4 Dec. 509/1 A.. height-finding radar system has been modified to observe cloud and rain up to 160 miles out to sea.. and to plot contours of constant rain intensity (iso-echo contours). 1899 *Ann. Rep. Board of Regents Smithsonian Inst.*, *1897–8* 543 Two weights of different aliments for which these numerical values are the same are said to be.. *isoenergetic weights. 1937 *Proc. R. Soc.* A. CLXI. 259 The mean free path in paraffin wax of the iso-energetic neutrons obtained by bombarding heavy hydrogen with deuterium ions has been measured. 1937 M. W. ZEMANSKY *Heat & Thermodynamics* xiv. 281 Show that the slope of an isoenergetic curve on a T-V diagram is equal to [etc.]. 1962 *Jrnl. Aerospace Sci.* XXIX. 400/2 During the first phase of re-entry, the motion is iso-energetic and no significant heating or deceleration problem will exist. 1936 *Trans. Faraday Soc.* XXXII. 124 As a consequence of the.. growth of the micelles the resin passes from its (assumed) *isogel state.. into the infusible *C* stage. 1937 *Jrnl. R. Aeronaut. Soc.* XLI. 531 Phenol-formaldehyde resins (at least in their initial stages of condensation) are 'isogels'. 1950 ROBITSCHEK & LEWIN *Phenolic Resins* iv. 56 As condensation proceeds, cross-linking takes place between some of the largely spherical bigger molecules (micelles) leading to a structure which.. can be likened to a sponge and is termed an isogel. 1924 C. E. TILLEY in *Geol. Mag.* LXI. 169 In the terminology suggested above, this line may be said to be an *Isograd... In reality an isograd is the intersection of an inclined isograd surface with the earth's surface. 1956 E. W. HEINRICH *Microscopic Petrogr.* vi. 173 By joining points on a map that mark the initial appearance of each of the diagnostic minerals, mineral isograds (biotite isograd, sillimanite isograd, etc.) may be defined. 1971 I. G. GASS et al. *Understanding Earth* i. 36/2 The garnet isograd for example is the surface (line on the map) separating the garnet-bearing rocks of the garnet zone (high-grade) from the garnet-free rocks of the biotite zone (low grade). 1924 C. E. TILLEY in *Geol. Mag.* LXI. 168 *Isograde rocks are those which have originated under closely similar physical conditions of temperature and pressure. 1966 *McGraw-Hill Encycl. Sci. & Technol.* VIII. 298/1 Rocks within the same zone [of metamorphism] may be called.. isograde. 1924 C. E. TILLEY in *Geol. Mag.* LXI. 168 Rocks which belong to the same facies can be said to be in the same metamorphic grade, and can be referred to by the terms which I now suggest as isofacial or *isogradic. 1926 G. W. TYRRELL *Princ. Petrol.* xv. 259 In the green-schist facies, a chlorite-quartz-muscovite-schist is isogradic with a green schist composed of chlorite, epidote, and albite. 1968 F. J. TURNER *Metamorphic Petrol.* viii. 376 On this model the isogradic surfaces near the heat source have a reversed dip. 1887 *Syd. Soc. Lex.*, **Isogynous*, a term applied to a flower of which the carpels are equal in number to the petals. 1902 MANN & MILLIKAN tr. *Drude's Theory of Optics* II. II. iii. 354 The whole field of view is now.. traversed by a black curve, the so-called principal *isogyre. 1922 N. H. & A. N. WINCHELL *Elem. Optical Mineral.* (ed. 2) I. xviii. 168 The biaxial optic axis interference figure differs from the uniaxial optic axis interference figure most clearly in the fact that it has only one isogyre instead of two. It also differs.. in the fact that the single isogyre is not fixed in position, nor constantly straight, when the crystal is rotated. *Ibid.* 172 As in uniaxial crystals, the isogyres are the locus of all points at which the light emerges with its vibration planes parallel with the planes of the nicols. 1964 HARTSHORNE & STUART *Pract. Optical Crystallogr.* v. 203 These interference bands are symmetrically arranged around the optic axis (or axes)... In addition to these bands there are dark 'brushes' or isogyres. 1907 *Jrnl. Med. Res.* XVII. 321 Earlier observers of human *isohemagglutination asserted that isoagglutinins occurred only in the sera of pathological states. 1940 *Amer. Jrnl. Physiol.* CXXXI. 205 Breed, sex and age of animals seemed to have no influence on the occurrence of natural isohemagglutination. 1907 *Jrnl. Med. Res.* XVII. 334 Such an experiment, in the case of human *isohemagglutinins, does more to prove the strict specificity of each 'bound agglutinin'. 1971 J. A. BELLANTI *Immunol.* ii. 44 It is known that isohemagglutinins—the antibody to blood groups—.. may develop as a result of exposure to enteric bacilli, containing blood grouplike substances in their structure. 1905 GOULD *Dict. New Med. Terms* 318/2 *Isohemolysin. 1916 Isohemolysin [see *blood group* s.v. BLOOD *sb.* 21]. 1972 W. E. HAESLER *Immunohematol.* i. 2 Hemolysis is most frequently observed in the detection of the group A and B isohemolysins and the Le^a antibodies. 1902 *Encycl. Brit.* XXXI. 404/2 South of the Tropic of Capricorn the *isohalines run nearly east and west. 1964 *Oceanogr. & Marine Biol.* II. 71 In winter the fiord water becomes isothermal and isohaline with average temperature and salinity of −1·76°C and 32·75‰. *Ibid.* 375 (*caption*) The increase in salinity in recent decades has altered.. the course of the isohalines given in the chart. 1968 G. NEUMANN *Ocean Currents* iv. 129 The slope of isobaric surfaces.. is small when compared to the slope of isothermal, isohaline (surfaces of equal salinity) and iso-pycnal surfaces. 1904 GOODCHILD & TWENEY *Technol. & Sci. Dict.* 323/1 **Isohels*, lines connecting places having the same amount of sunshine. 1931 A. A. MILLER *Climatol.* 22 The deviation of sunshine (shown on maps by lines of equal duration known as isohels). 1968 J. GENTILLI *Sun, Climate & Life* (1971) xiii. 141/2 These lines are called iso-pleths as a general term, but .. more specifically.. isobars (equal pressure), isotherms (equal temperature),.. isohels (equal sunshine),.. etc. 1897 *Geogr. Jrnl.* X. 306 König.. has found sufficient material for a first attempt to draw '*isohelic' lines for Western Europe. 1899 *Nature* 21 Dec. 172/2 Isobars and *isohyets indicating monthly and annual distribution of barometric pressure and rainfall. 1911 C. E. W. BEAN '*Dreadnought' of Darling* xv. 144 The carpet which covers a country within the ten-inch isohyet (rainfall line) is a pretty ticklish thing to play with. 1967 M. J. COE *Ecol. Alpine Zone Mt. Kenya* 63 The main peak area has a rainfall of between 30″ and 40″ per annum,

the 30″ Isohyet being displaced slightly to the South-west of the peaks. **1889** *Cent. Dict.*, **Isohyetal*, *a.* and *n.* **1895** T. Russell *Meteorol.* vii. 141 A graphic representation of quantity of rainfall by lines through places having equal depths of rainfall are 'isohyetals'. **1909** *British Rainfall 1908* 140 The isohyetal lines are drawn about the 18th of the following month. **1923** *Glasgow Herald* 1 Feb. 6 Most of these features are..illustrated by maps exhibiting them..by isohyetal lines. **1962** W. Stegner *Wolf Willow* iv. iv. 281 She knew nothing about minimal annual rainfall, distribution of precipitation, isohyetal lines. **1864** Webster cites A. K. Johnston for **Isohyetose*. **1938** *Jrnl. Path. & Bacteriol.* XLVII. 234 Fleisher found evidence of *iso-immune reactions working with grafts of renal tissue in the guinea-pig. **1967** D. M. Weir *Handbk. Exper. Immunol.* xxx. 991 Isoantigenic differences, though usually detected by isoimmune sera, may in some cases also be picked up with antisera produced by immunization across a species gap. **1969** B. Pirofsky *Autoimmunization* xxi. 479/1 The bulk of knowledge concerning the nature and effect of immune interactions on the erythrocytes has been derived from heteroimmune and isoimmune studies. **1939** *Jrnl. Amer. Med. Assoc.* 8 July 126/1 It would seem to resemble agglutinins resulting from *iso-immunization following repeated transfusions. **1971** J. A. Bellanti *Immunol.* iii. 77 Alternatively, isoimmunization can occur during the course of pregnancy when fetal cells..or proteins gain access to the maternal circulation. **1971** *Nature* 29 Oct. 608/1 The human foetus is at greater risk from maternal iso-immunizations than the bovid foetus. **1958** *Engineering* 22 Aug. 230/1 Regular production has..commenced..of the *isokinetic sampling apparatus developed by the British Iron and Steel Research Association. **1959** *Brit. Jrnl. Appl. Physics* X. 26/1 The dust concentration calculated from the sample will be correct provided the gas sample is drawn into the nozzle at the same velocity as that of the gas stream. This is known as isokinetic sampling. *Ibid.* 27/2 In the extreme case of isokinetic sampling the nozzle becomes effectively non-existent. **1967** *Ann. Occupational Hygiene* X. 77 Brass nozzles were fitted around the filter retaining ring in order to obtain iso-kinetic samples at windspeeds from 5·4 m.p.h. to 30 m.p.h. *Ibid.*, 3-in.-long nozzles were attached to the filter holder to allow isokinetic flow into the inlet. **1958** *Engineering* 22 Aug. 230/1 The stainless steel probe faces directly into the stream of dusty gas and a sample is withdrawn *iso-kinetically, that is, it flows into the nozzle in the same direction and with the same velocity as the local undisturbed gas stream. **1972** *Science* 16 June 1232/3 We sampled the suspended fly ash isokinetically at several locations across the outlet duct of the electrostatic precipitator. **1926** Jordan & Kindred *Textbk. Embryol.* v. 31 Since the small amount of yolk is evenly distributed throughout the cytoplasm, it [*sc.* the human egg] may also properly be called an *isolecithal egg. **1940** L. H. Hyman *Invertebrates* I. v. 256 When the yolk is slight in amount, it is also more or less evenly dispersed; such eggs are variously termed isolecithal, alecithal, or homolecithal. **1972** P. A. Meglitsch *Invertebr. Zool.* (ed. 2) iv. 81/2 Isolecithal ova usually cleave in a characteristic manner. **1921** *Jrnl. Eng. & Gmc. Philol.* XX. 183 The finding and fixing of the *isolectic lines is a task of word geography. **1921** *Jrnl. Eng. & Gmc. Philol.* XX. 182 There is danger in delay if certain phases of dialect life are to be recorded at all, and an accelerated pace in registering them would be advisable, especially in establishing the boundary lines of present dialects, with their maze of isophones, isomorphs, *isolexes, and isotaxes, i.e., lines connecting places of identical or nearly identical sounds, forms, words, and syntactical peculiarities. **1963** *Amer. Speech* XXXVIII. 127 The regional diversity and the complicated grid of isolexes in the Northern counties. *Ibid.* 128 Any attempt to correlate the isolexes with demographic factors. **1926** *Germanic Rev.* I. iv. 285 The *isolexic lines of this word..present a hopeless tangle. **1939** L. H. Gray *Foundations of Lang.* ii. 26 These lines will be iso-phonic, isotonic, isomorphic, isosyntagmic, or isolexic according as they indicate identical sounds, tones, inflexions, syntax, or vocabulary. **1954** Pei & Gaynor *Dict. Ling.* 107 *Isolexic lines*, lines on a linguistic map, indicating the approximate boundaries of the speech-areas in which a uniformity in the vocabulary of the speakers and in their use of words can be observed. **1944** V. Conrad *Methods in Climatol.* xiii. 167 *Isolines..are fully analogous to contour lines, or to the equipotential lines used in physics... Closed isolines surrounding a region indicate that this is either depressed or elevated. **1961** G. T. Trewartha *Earth's Problem Climates* xvi. 237/2 In summer..the isolines of rainfall frequency show a strong zonal arrangement. **1969** *Nature* 29 Nov. 903/1 Vertical sections show that isolines slope steeply to the surface [of the sea] during upwelling, but the slope of the isoline varies with the parameter chosen. **1970** *Biol. Abstr.* LI. 11534/1 The resulting pattern of the isolines can be readily related to the distribution of a particular organism. **1901** Dorland *Med. Dict.* (ed. 2) 333/2 *Iso-lysin. **1910** *Jrnl. Hygiene* X. 186 The injection of goats' blood into other goats resulted as a rule in the formation of isolysins. **1969** L. H. Crisp *Clin. Immunol. & Allergy* (ed. 2) xliv. 433/1 Isohemolysins, isolysins, or antibodies capable of lysis of erythrocytes may be found in the serum in paroxysmal hemoglobinuria. **1898** J. Milne *Seismol.* xii. 225 Slight changes in the *isomagnetics of a district. **1899** *Nature* 6 July 236/2 An opportunity will thus be afforded..to obtain some idea of the accuracy with which the isomagnetic lines can be determined. **1940** Chapman & Bartels *Geomagnetism* I. iii. 96 The lines are called isomagnetic lines, and a chart in which the distribution of a magnetic element is thus indicated..is called an isomagnetic chart. **1967** E. H. Vestine in Matsushita & Campbell *Physics of Geomagnetic Phenomena* I. ii. ii. 185 The isomagnetic lines for declination *D* or variation of the compass are also called 'isogonic' lines. **18..** *Eng. Mechanic* No. 509. 51 By tracing on the surface of the globe lines of equal nebulosity, M. Renou gets what he calls **isonephs*. **1881** *Smithsonian Rep.* 290 A chart of the world, showing lines of equal annual cloudiness (*isonephelic) is given by Rénan. **1900** E. F. Smith tr. *V. von Richter's Org. Chem.* (ed. 3) II. 390 *Isonuclear substitution products with adjacent substituents show in general the same deportment as the ortho-substitution products of benzene. **1951** I. L. Finar *Org. Chem.* I. xxix. 586 Introduction of a second substituent can give rise to homonuclear (isonuclear) substitution..or to heteronuclear substitution. **1908** *Jrnl. Exper. Med.* X. 137 An *iso-osmotic physiologically balanced solution. **1971** *Biochem. Jrnl.* CXXI. 261 Protein-polysaccharides of knee-joint cartilage of 9-month-old pigs were extracted sequentially with neutral iso-osmotic sodium acetate. **1855** Mayne *Expos. Lex.*, *Isopetalus*,..*isopetalous. **1851–9** Sabine in *Man. Sci. Enq.* 97 The *isophænomenal lines are drawn for that portion of the globe in correspondence with the observations. **1858** Carpenter *Veg. Phys.* §397 When the phytoids are of the usual form they are called **isophytoids*. **1873** J. W. Gibbs in *Trans. Connecticut Acad. Arts & Sci.* II. 311 In the same way we may conceive of lines of equal pressure... These lines we may also call ..*isopiestic. *Ibid.* 313 To prove that the ratio is independent of the shape of the circuit, let us suppose the area..divided up by an infinite number of isometrics..with equal differences of volume *dv*, and an infinite number of isopiestics..with equal differences of pressure *dp*. **1902** *Encycl. Brit.* XXXIII. 283/2 The isothermals..coincide with the iso-piestics for a saturated vapour in presence of its liquid. **1940** Glasstone *Text-bk. Physical Chem.* ix. 622 If two vessels containing different solutes in the same solvent are placed side by side in a closed space, vapor will distil from the solution of higher vapor pressure and condense in the one having the lower pressure until, when equilibrium is attained, both solutions are exerting the same pressure, that is to say they are isopiestic. **1966** R. Joel *Basic Engin. Thermodynamics* i. 80 The pressure remains constant throughout the process. It is often referred to as an isobaric or isopiestic process. **1855** Mayne *Expos. Lex.*, *Isopogonus*, *Ornithol.* Applied to a feather, of which the two sides are of equal size: *isopogonous. **1931** *Compt. Rend. de l'Assemb. de Stockholm 1930* (Union Géod. et Géophys. Internat., Sect. de Magn. et Électr. Terr.) 284 In that year the zero-*isopor (the line dividing easterly and westerly change) crossed central Siberia. **1963** J. A. Jacobs *Earth's Core* v. 53 Considerable changes take place in the general distribution of isopors even within 20 years. **1931** *Compt. Rend. de l'Assemb. de Stockholm 1930* (Union Géod. et Géophys. Internat., Sect. de Magn. et Électr. Terr.) 280 A consideration of the most recent published results of secular-variation observations..has revealed some very interesting and important conditions governing *isoporic movements. **1940** Chapman & Bartels *Geomagnetism* I. iii. 114 The rate of the secular variation in each element at any epoch..can..be represented by..isoporic charts, a term proposed by Harradon. **1973** M. W. McElhinny *Palaeomagnetism & Plate Tectonics* i. 6 Isoporic foci are not permanent, but grow and decay, their lifetime being of the order of 100 years, during which they move on the earth's surface in a somewhat irregular fashion. **1876** *S. Kens. Mus. Catal.* No. 3989 **Isoscope*. **1883** *Nature* XXVIII. 437 *Isoseismal lines over the injured districts..assume the form of elongated ellipsoids. **1887** *Science* (U.S.) 20 May 493/1 The relations of these isoseismals to each other. **1887** *Syd. Soc. Lex.*, **Isospore*. **1895** C. S. Palmer tr. *Nernst's Theoret. Chem.* i. v. 121 The investigation of solutions having the same osmotic pressure, viz. the so-called *is-osmotic solutions. **1905** W. H. Howell *Text-bk. Physiol.* 884 A 0·95 per cent. solution of NaCl is isotonic or isosmotic with mammalian serum. **1967** *Oceanogr. & Marine Biol.* V. 383 In life the muscle cells are probably isosmotic with the interstitial fluid and the plasma. **1875** Bennett & Dyer tr. *Sachs' Bot.* 338 *Isosporous Vascular Cryptogams. Only one kind of spore is produced. **1881** *Nature* XXIV. 474 Professor Williamson divides coals into 'Isosporous' and 'Heterosporous' coals. **1835** Lindley *Introd. Bot.* (1848) II. 367 *Isostemonous is said of plants the stamens of which are equal in number to the petals. **1882** Vines tr. *Sachs' Bot.* 659 In the isostemonous flowers the stamens are sometimes superposed on the petals. **1880** Gray *Struct. Bot.* (ed. 6) 196 With *Isostemony. **1964** Shapiro & Chargaff in *Biochim. & Biophys. Acta* XCI. 263 There exist procedures permitting the separation of the hydrolysates [of DNA] into a series of fractions, each comprising the equinumerant oligonucleotide runs of a given length... It may be convenient to refer to such a size group as an *isostich. **1970** *Nature* 26 Sept. 1296/1 The tracts were fractionated into isostichs by chromatography on DEAE-cellulose. **1971** F. von der Harr et al. in Cantoni & Davies *Procedures Nucleic Acid Res.* II. 682 The isostichs can be further separated into their components, differing in base composition, by paper chromatography. **1906** *Jrnl. Chem. Soc.* LXXXIX. ii. 1129 It is conceivable that in the case of two '*isostructural' substances the actual size of the structural unit may be of the greatest importance. **1965** Phillips & Williams *Inorg. Chem.* I. xvi. 576 Tellurium is only known in one form, isostructural with grey Se. **1922** Joyce *Ulysses* 307 The intricate alliterative and *iso-syllabic rules of the Welsh englyn. **1943** *Jrnl. Theol. Stud.* XLIV. 51 The isosyllabic metre of the Greek homilies of Ephraem, typical of Syriac poetry. **1957** Isosyllabic [see *isoaccentual* adj. above]. **1956** H. Whitehall in *Kenyon Rev.* XVIII. iii. 420 Of the non-syllabic rhythms, the first, found typically in Old Testament Hebrew verse and in some, though not all, 'free verse' is **isosyntactic*—the recurrent factor is repetition of the same syntactic construction, usually a phrase or clause, in strictly parallel sequences. **1939** *Isosyntagmic [see *isolexic* adj. above]. **1954** Pei & Gaynor *Dict. Ling.* 107 *Isosyntagmic lines*, lines on a linguistic map, indicating the approximate boundaries of the speech-areas in which a uniformity of syntax can be observed. **1957** Isosyntagmic [see isomorphic *a.* 5]. **1947** *Mineral. Abstr.* X. 159 Isogyres and *iso-taches (curves of equal velocity) are plotted on a stereographic net. **1955** W. J. Saucier *Princ. Meteorol. Analysis* x. 304/1 The wind field is analyzed by drawing streamlines and isotachs, which give, respectively, the course of flow and its speed. **1970** *Nature* 11 Apr. 133/2 (*caption*) Geostrophic isotachs (in knots) at 500 mbar for 00 GMT November 14, 1968. **1910** Smith & Menzies in *Jrnl. Amer. Chem. Soc.* XXXII. 1420 The purpose of the apparatus being to show when two pressures have become equal, the arrangement may be called an *isoteniscope. **1960** *Jrnl. Chem. Education* XXXVII. 533/1 Livingstone suggests the inclusion of a thermometer well in the iso-teniscope bulb so that temperature equilibrium can be ascertained at the time of the pressure measurements. **1864** Webster cites Dana for **Isotrimorphism*. **1864** Webster, **Isotrimorphous*. **1915** D. White in *Jrnl. Washington Acad. Sci.* V. 198 Lines were then drawn through the points of equal fixed carbon (or volatile matter). Such lines,..which I have termed '*isovols', are drawn to mark each 5 per cent increase in the fixed carbon in the pure coal. **1923** *Glasgow Herald* 11 June 7 The isovols for the Hutton seam take the form of a number of rings with a common centre to the north-west of Durham. **1928** E. R. Lilley *Geol. Petroleum & Nat. Gas* v. 113 The greater part of the oil of Pennsylvania is produced from pools lying between the isovols..of 55 and 60%. **1968** Murchison & Westoll *Coal* xv. 370 Fig. 15 shows lines of equal magnetic vertical intensity and the isovols of the Wealden coals. **1851** E. Forbes *Let. to Ramsay* in Wilson & Geikie *Life* xiv. 488 My new map of marine distribution, with my proposed *Isozoic belts on it. **1858** Carpenter *Veg. Phys.* §397 *Isozooids and allozooids.

b. In *Chemistry* sometimes prefixed to the name of a compound substance to denote another substance isomeric with it.

The simple name having originally been given to one such substance, an isomer of it, when found to exist, is distinguished by the prefix *iso-*; but in some cases the first-discovered substance is not the simplest or normal form, and is itself properly designated the *iso*-type, when the normal type is subsequently discovered; thus the first-known *butyl alcohol* is now known as *iso-butyl* alcohol, a *normal* butyl alcohol having been subsequently obtained. *Iso-* was formerly regarded as a separable prefix and printed in italics (often with a hyphen). The International Union of Pure and Applied Chemistry recommendation is that *iso-* should always be directly attached to the remainder of the parent name (and be printed in ordinary type).

Where the isomerism occurs within an alkane or alkyl radical, the prefix *iso-* is used to form the name of the isomer having a $(CH_3)_2CH-$group at the end of an otherwise straight chain: so $CH_3(CH_2)_3CH_3$ (normal or *n*-) pentane, $(CH_3)_2CHCH_2CH_3$ isopentane, $(CH_3)_3CCH_3$ neopentane.

The number of such names is unlimited, and liable to constant increase, as new isomeric forms of known compound bodies are discovered. Examples are **iso-amyl** (amyl), **iso-butyl** or **iso-tetryl** (see butyl), **iso-butylate**, **iso-butylic**, **iso-butyric** (see butyric), **iso-cajuputene** (cajuputene), **iso-caproic** (caproic), **iso-cholesterin**, **iso-cyanate** (= carbimide), **iso-cyanide** (= carbamine), **iso-heptane**, **iso-hexane**, **iso-hydrobenzoin**, **iso-propyl** (propyl) or **iso-trityl**, etc.

Also ˌ**isoa'lloxazine** [allox(an + azine], the hypothetical tricyclic parent compound, $C_{10}H_6N_4O_2$, of the flavins, which has a structure formed of fused benzene, pyrazine, and pyrimidine nuclei and is known only as substituted derivatives; **iso'amyl alcohol** = *isopentyl alcohol*; **iso'borneol** [a. G. *isoborneol* (Bertram & Walbaum 1894, in *Jrnl. f. prakt. Chem.* XLIX. 1)], a crystalline bicyclic alcohol, $C_{10}H_{18}O$, which is a stereoisomer of borneol and like it yields camphor on oxidation; **iso'butane**, 2-methylpropane, $(CH_3)_2CH{\cdot}CH_3$, a gaseous hydrocarbon used as a fuel; **iso'butene** = *isobutylene*; **iso'butyl**, the radical $(CH_3)_2CH{\cdot}CH_2-$, 2-methylpropyl, as in **isobutyl alcohol**, $(CH_3)_2CH{\cdot}CH_2OH$, a primary alcohol which is a colourless liquid and occurs in fusel oils; **iso'butylene** (†**-en**), 2-methylpropylene, $(CH_3)_2C{:}CH_2$, an easily liquefied gas used in the manufacture of butyl rubber; **iso'butyrate**, any of the esters of isobutyric acid, several of which are used as flavourings and in perfumery; **isobu'tyric acid** [tr. G. *isobuttersäure* (H. Kolbe 1864, in *Zeitschr. f. Chem. und Pharm.* VII. 33)], a liquid carboxylic acid, $(CH_3)_2CH{\cdot}COOH$, found in many plants and also obtained by oxidation of isobutyl alcohol; **iso'citrate**, the anion, or an ester or salt, of isocitric acid; **iso'citric acid** [tr. G. *isocitronsäure* (F. Rochleder 1869, in *Jrnl. f. prakt. Chem.* CVI. 320)], 1-hydroxypropane-1,2,3-tricarboxylic acid, $HOOC{\cdot}CH(OH)CH(COOH)CH_2COOH$, which occurs in blackberry juice and is formed in the Krebs cycle by dehydration of citric acid to *cis*-aconitic acid followed by rehydration; **iso'cyanate** [a. F. *isocyanate* (F.-S. Cloëz *Rech. sur Éthers Cyaniques* (Thesis, 1866) 18)], any of the class of compounds containing the group $-N{:}C{:}O$, some of which are used in making polyurethane resins; **isocy'anic acid**, the acid $HN{:}C{:}O$, which exists in equilibrium with cyanic acid $(HO{\cdot}CN)$; **iso'cyanide**, any member of the class of compounds having the formula $R-NC$ (where R is an alkyl, aryl, etc., radical), which in general are poisonous liquids with a strong unpleasant odour; also called carbylamines, isonitriles; **isoeugenol** (aɪsəʊ'juːdʒənɒl) [a. G. *isoeugenol* (Tiemann & Kraaz 1882, in *Ber. d. Deut. Chem. Ges.* XV. 2067)], an aromatic liquid that occurs in ylang-ylang and other essential oils, is produced commercially from eugenol, and has been used in the manufacture of vanillin and in perfumery; 2-methoxy-4-propenylphenol, $CH_3CH{:}CH{\cdot}C_6H_3(OCH_3)OH$; **iso'flavone**, (*a*) the crystalline tricyclic ketone 3-phenylbenzo-4-pyrone, $C_{15}H_{10}O_2$; (*b*) any of the derivatives of this compound, which occur (often as glycosides) in many plants; **iso'lichenin** [a. G. *isolichenin* (F. Beilstein *Handbuch d. Org. Chem.* (1881) i. xxxix. 602)], a

water-soluble starch occurring in lichens which yields glucose on hydrolysis; **iso'maltose** [a. G. *isomaltose* (E. Fischer 1890, in *Ber. d. Deut. Chem. Ges.* XXII. 3688)], 6-*O*-α-D-gluco pyranosyl-D-glucose, $C_6H_{11}O_5{\cdot}O{\cdot}C_6H_{11}O_5$, a syrupy disaccharide formed by the action of acid on glucose; **ˌisonico'tinic acid** [tr. G. *isonicotinsäure* (Weidel & Russo 1883, in *Sitzungsber. d. K. Akad. d. Wissen.* (Math.-Nat. Classe) LXXXVI. II. 1172)], pyridine-4-carboxylic acid, $(C_5H_4N)COOH$, a crystalline compound used in the synthesis of isoniazid; **isonicotinic (acid) hydrazide** = ISONIAZID; **iso'nitrile** = *isocyanide*; **iso'paraffin**, any branched-chain paraffin, *spec.* one containing the isopropyl group, $(CH_3)_2CH-$, attached to an otherwise straight chain; **iso'pentane**, 2-methylbutane, $(CH_3)_2CHCH_2CH_3$, a volatile liquid hydrocarbon present in petroleum; **iso'pentyl**, the radical $(CH_3)_2CHCH_2CH_2-$, as in **isopentyl alcohol**, a liquid primary alcohol, $(CH_3)_2CH_2CH_2OH$, which has a disagreeable odour and is obtained from fusel oil; **iso'phthalate**, a salt or ester of isophthalic acid; **iso'phthalic acid**, benzene-*m*-dicarboxylic acid, $C_6H_4(COOH)_2$, a crystalline compound made by the oxidation of *m*-xylene and used in the manufacture of polyester and alkyd resins; **iso'propanol** = *isopropyl alcohol*; **iso'propenyl**, the radical $CH_2{:}C(CH_3)-$; **iso'propyl**, the radical $(CH_3)_2CH-$, as in **isopropyl alcohol**, a liquid secondary alcohol, $CH_3CHOH{\cdot}CH_3$, made by the hydration of propylene and widely used as a solvent and in the production of acetone; **isopro'pylidene**, the bivalent radical $(CH_3)_2C=$, frequently introduced into compounds by reaction with acetone; **iso'quinoline** [ad. F. *isoquinoléine* (Hoogewerff & Van Dorp 1885, in *Rec. des Trav. chim. des Pays-Bas* IV. 128)], a low-melting, crystalline, bicyclic compound, C_9H_7N, found in coal tar and forming the nucleus of many alkaloids; **isovale'raldehyde**, 2-methylbutyraldehyde, $(CH_3)_2CH{\cdot}CH_2{\cdot}CHO$, a liquid which occurs in peppermint, sandalwood, eucalyptus, and other oils; **iso'valerate**, a salt or ester of isovaleric acid; **isovaleri'anic (acid)** = *isovaleric acid*; **isova'leric acid**, 2-methylbutyric acid, $(CH_3)_2CHCH_2COOH$, a liquid with a disagreeable odour found free in valerian root and as esters in porpoise and dolphin oils; **i'soxazole** [ad. G. *isoxazol* (A. Hantzsch 1888, in *Ann. d. Chem.* CCXLIX. 3)], (*a*) a liquid heterocyclic compound,

$$\underbrace{CH{:}CH{\cdot}O{\cdot}N{:}CH}$$

with a penetrating odour; (*b*) a derivative of this compound.

1866 ROSCOE *Elem. Chem.* xxxvi. 321 These so-called iso-alcohols readily yield the olefines from which they are derived, and on oxidation do not produce the corresponding acid, but form an acetone by loss of hydrogen. **1936** *Chem. Abstr.* XXX. 4512 Isoalloxazines with a substituent, e.g., alkyl, cycloalkyl or aryl, in the 9-position are prepd. by condensing *N*-monosubstituted aromatic *o*-diamines with alloxan. **1953** FRUTON & SIMMONDS *Gen. Biochem.* xiii. 320 In riboflavin, a sugar residue D-ribitol, is attached to a nitrogen atom of a heterocyclic nucleus, termed an isoalloxazine ring. **1968** I. L. FINAR *Org. Chem.* (ed. 4) II. 556 It appears that *iso*alloxazine, the tautomer of alloxazine, does not exist as such; only when the hydrogen atom is substituted is the *iso*alloxazine form retained. **1886** *Jrnl. Chem. Soc.* XLIX. 770 The value of the ratio [of vapour pressures] of isobutyl and isoamyl alcohol is practically a constant. **1927** *Chem. Abstr.* XXI. 985 Isoamyl alc. is considered as the mother substance of most of the compds. constituting oil of lavender. **1970** *New Phytologist* LXIX. 557 Iso-valeric acid and isoamyl alcohol have been identified as metabolites of *Agaricus bisporus*. **1894** *Chem. News* 30 Mar. 156/2 Isoborneol.. crystallises out of petroleum ether in thin, feathery leaflets. **1951** P. Z. BEDOUKIAN *Perfumery Synthetics & Isolates* 93 Iso-borneol and its esters, particularly the acetate, are employed in many types of industrial perfumes—for example, in sprays. **1972** G. D. SARGENT in Olah & Schleyer *Carbonium Ions* III. xxiv. 1122 On reduction with lithium aluminium hydride, camphor (34) gives isoborneol (35) in high yield. **1876** *Jrnl. Chem. Soc.* XXIX. 540 When isobutane is heated to 250° with iodine trichloride it gives the same products as propane. **1936** [see CALOR]. **1959** *Times Rev. Industry* Aug. 98/2 Other processes.. include alkylation, in which iso-butane is reacted with olefins to produce high octane material for aviation gasoline and high quality motor spirit. **1876** *Jrnl. Chem. Soc.* XXX. 397 Isobutene combines readily with hypochlorous acid. **1964** N. G. CLARK *Mod. Org. Chem.* viii. 141 t-Butyl alcohol.. is obtained from a 2-methylpropene [isobutene] using 65 per cent sulphuric acid. **1866** ROSCOE *Elem. Chem.* xxxvi. 320 Treated with hydriodic acid, erythrite forms isobutyl iodide. **1870** *Chem. News* 21 Jan. 34/2 (*heading*) Conversion of isobutyl-alcohol into tertiary pseudobutyl-alcohol. **1873** WATTS *Fownes' Chem.* (ed. 11) 597 The [isobutyl] iodide is decomposed by potassium or sodium, yielding isodibutyl, a limpid liquid, lighter than water. **1873** WATTS *Fownes' Chem.* (ed. 11) 597 Iso-propyl Carbinol or Isobutyl Alcohol.. By oxidation it is converted into isobutyric acid. **1964** D. A. SHIRLEY *Org. Chem.* x. 251 Isobutyl alcohol.. is manufactured by a modification of the carbon monoxide and hydrogen method for synthesis of methanol. **1966** *Nomencl. Org. Chem.* (I.U.P.A.C.) (ed. 2) A. 8 The following names are retained for the unsubstituted radicals only: Isopropyl.. Isobutyl.. Isopentyl [etc.]. **1872** *Chem. News* 29 Nov. 265/2 Chlorhydric acid behaves with isobutylen in the same manner as iodhydric acid, the result being the formation of a tertiary chloride of butyl. **1913** J. B. COHEN *Org. Chem. Adv. Students* II. ii. 119 Isobutylene when heated with strong sulphuric acid yields a mixture of isomeric diisobutylenes. **1951** *Economist* 29 Dec. 1599/2 It should produce butyl rubber based almost entirely on isobutylene. **1969** R. F. LANG tr. *Henglein's Chem. Technol.* 576 Cracking gases consist of ethylene, propylene and isobutylene... Isobutylene yields on polymerization a dimer which can be hydrogenated to iso-octane. **1873** *Jrnl. Chem. Soc.* XXVI. 55 Ethylic iso-butyrate boils at 113°. **1928** *Chem. Abstr.* XXII. 2809 A table of 23 butyrates and isobutyrates, giving their name, odor and specific use in perfume. **1973** *Proc. Soc. Exper. Biol. & Med.* CXLII. 595/1 Sucrose acetate isobutyrate.. is employed as a flavor-suspending agent in the manufacture of soft drinks. **1871** *Jrnl. Chem. Soc.* XXIV. 126 Iso-butyric acid.. is scarcely attacked by a mixture of potassium dichromate and dilute sulphuric acid. **1881** ROSCOE & SCHORLEMMER *Treat. Chem.* III. I. 599 Isobutyric acid is found in the free state in the flowers of the *Arnica montana*, as well as in the carob bean, and amongst the acids of croton oil. **1970** *Exper. Parasitol.* XXVII. 408 The branched chain acids, isobutyric and isovaleric, are also excreted by *A. caninum*. **1925** *Jrnl. Amer. Chem. Soc.* XLVII. 572 The ethyl isocitrate obtained from the first lot of blackberries was levorotatory. **1952** *Biochem. Jrnl.* LII. 528/2 The observations are in agreement with Martius's earlier assumption.. that *cis*-aconitate is an intermediate in the conversion of citrate into *iso*citrate. **1971** *Jrnl. Biol. Chem.* CCXLV. 4807/1 Studies are reported.. which indicate that there is a specific carrier system for the transport of citrate and isocitrate in mitochondria. **1869** *Chem. News* 11 June 287/1 The isocitric acid may be obtained pure.. and then exhibits a crystalline mass. **1930** *Jrnl. Amer. Chem. Soc.* LII. 2928 As there are two asymmetric carbon atoms in isocitric acid, and no meso form is possible, four optically active forms and two racemic forms of the acid may exist. **1968** R. F. STEINER *Life Chem.* xii. 219 The reversible transformation of citric acid to *cis*-aconitic acid, and of the latter to isocitric acid, is catalyzed by a single enzyme, aconitase. **1872** *Jrnl. Chem. Soc.* XXV. 446 The first members of the group of compounds, now generally described as the isocyanates and isocyanurates, were discovered by Wurtz in the ethyl and methyl series. **1877** WATTS *Fownes' Chem.* (ed. 12) II. 96 Potassium Cyanate, CNKO.. two modifications, viz. $N{\equiv}C-OK$ Normal cyanate, and $CO = NK$ Isocyanate. The normal cyanate.. crystallises in long needles, and is converted by fusion into the isocyanate. **1880** CLEMINSHAW *Wurtz' Atom. The.* 238 The isomer of urea, isocyanate of ammonium, contains nitrogen in two conditions. **1944** S. J. SMITH *Princ. Org. Chem.* xiv. 312 The alkyl isocyanates are liquids with a powerful stifling odour. **1961** *Times* 30 May (I.C.I. Suppl.) p. xxii (Advt.), Italians need isocyanates for lightweight rigid and flexible polyurethane foams. **1963** in *Amer. Speech* (1964) XXXIX. 146 A dummy man made of material resembling human flesh which has a base of isocyanate rubber. **1891** *Jrnl. Chem. Soc.* LX. I. 282 Hydrocyanic acid and a small quantity of isocyanic acid are evolved. **1919** *Jrnl. Amer. Chem. Soc.* XLI. 381 The reaction between isocyanic acid and benzylidenaniline leads directly to a four-membered cyclic-urea. **1973** J. J. LAGOWSKI *Mod. Inorg. Chem.* xi. 349 Isocyanic acid (mp −86·8°, bp 23·5°) is formed when cyanuric acid is passed through a hot tube; the product reverts to cyanuric acid spontaneously. **1877** WATTS *Fownes' Chem.* (ed. 12) II. 94 In the isocyanide the carbon belonging to the alcohol-radicle is united directly with the nitrogen; in the [normal] cyanide, only through the medium of the carbon belonging to the cyanogen. **1881** ROSCOE & SCHORLEMMER *Treat. Chem.* III. I. 162 Cyanides of the alcohol radicals. These bodies are formed when an alcoholic iodide is heated with silver cyanide... The compounds obtained in this way are usually termed isocyanides or carbamines. **1907** *Daily Chron.* 12 Dec. 5/5 Someone noiselessly discharged several squibs of iso-cyanide, and two ladies in the audience fled. **1928** *Sunday Dispatch* 16 Dec. 13/5 The new gas, cacodyl isocyanide, which.. was.. so terrible and destructive.. in its effect on life. **1964** N. G. CLARK *Mod. Org. Chem.* xiii. 265 The isocyanides are of no practical value, with the possible exception of the Carbylamine Reaction. However, the elucidation of their structure.. has provided an interesting chapter in the development of organic chemistry. **1883** *Jrnl. Chem. Soc.* XLIV. 201 By distilling it [*sc.* homoferulic acid] with lime a body is obtained which is isomeric with eugenol, and termed isoeugenol. **1891** *Jrnl. Soc. Chem. Industry* 31 Oct. 854/1 Iso-eugenol.. is prepared from eugenol, or the Essence of Cloves, by heating it with caustic potash in amyl alcohol for 16–24 hours. **1936** A. HUXLEY *Eyeless in Gaza* xviii. 243 That's one of the reasons why your scent costs you so much. The poor.. have to be content with plain iso-eugenol. **1965** *Chem. Abstr.* LXII. 6815 Eugenol and isoeugenol were estd. in the smoke at 4 and 14·7 mg./1000 Turkish tobacco cigarets, resp. **1925** *Jrnl. Chem. Soc.* CXXVII. 1981 The occurrence of derivatives of 3-phenylchromone (*iso*-flavone) has not yet been definitely proved. **1948** *Proc. Indian Acad. Sci.* A. XXVII. 36 Hydroxy isoflavones are more toxic than the corresponding flavones. **1951** *Ann. Rev. Biochem.* XX. 508 The.. occurrence of the iso-flavone (prunetin) along with its isomeric flavone (genkwanin) is a rare example of such association. **1965** T. SWAIN in Pridham & Swain *Biosynthetic Pathways Higher Plants* 33 Isoflavones.. are common in other members of the Leguminosae. **1898** *Amer. Jrnl. Physiol.* I. 455 The unusual behavior of isolichenin towards amylolytic enzymes—the formation of dextrins without sugars—recalls the formation (from glycogen) of dystropo-dextrin. **1934** *Chem. Abstr.* XXVIII. 2375 Isolichenin was proved in some varieties of the lichens produced in Japan, such as *Alectoria ochrolenca*... Isolichenin closely resembles amylose. **1967** M. E. HALE *Biol. Lichens* viii. 103 Iso-lichenin, the rarer of the two major lichen starches, is distinguished by a positive iodine test and consists of D-glucose residues with α-1,3 and α-1,4 glucosidic linkages. **1891** *Jrnl. Chem. Soc.* LX. I. 413 The author has obtained from glucose a new glucobiose, which from its properties is doubtless constituted like maltose, and is hence called isomaltose. **1892** *Jrnl. Soc. Chem. Industry* 30 July 627/2 Iso-maltose is an important constituent of beer and forms 25–30 per cent of beer extract. **1956** *New Biol.* XXI. 12 Maltose appears after two days [during malting], and then maltatriose and isomaltose, as a result of the degradation of starch. **1883** *Jrnl. Chem. Soc.* XLIV. 484 In the form of sulphate it [*sc.* γ-dipyridyl] is easily oxidised by potassium permanganate, yielding pyridine-monocarboxylic or isonicotinic acid... This acid.. forms a white crystalline mass melting at 307°. **1952** *Biol. Abstr.* XXVI. 35208 Isonicotinic acid hydrazide.. is effective against tuberculosis in the mouse. **1956** *Nature* 25 Feb. 367/2 An active programme of leprosy work at Singapore included a chemotherapeutic trial of isonicotinic hydrazide. **1961** *Biol. Abstr.* XXXVI. 2299/1 (*heading*) Antituberculous activity of isonicotinic acid derivatives in vitro. **1972** *Biochem. & Biophys. Res. Communications* XLVIII. 58 (*heading*) In vitro inhibition of tRNA and protein methylation by nicotinamide and isonicotinic acid hydrazide. **1871** *Jrnl. Chem. Soc.* XXIV. 137 This body [*sc.* a urea], when heated, is resolved into triethylphosphine sulphide and the isonitrile of the allyl series. **1915** R. H. A. PLIMMER *Pract. Org. & Biochem.* 61 To the dilute solution of chloroform in water is added some alcoholic sodium hydroxide and a drop of aniline and the mixture heated. Phenyl isonitrile or carbylamine is formed. **1965** *Chem. Communications* May 181/1 The ability of isonitriles to act as bridging groups has now been demonstrated by the preparation of the iron complex (I). **1971** GREEN & HOFFMANN in I. Ugi *Isonitrile Chem.* i. 1 The term isonitriles is used for the general class of compounds, whereas the term isocyanide is used for specific designations (e.g., ethyl isocyanide). **1876** *Phil. Mag.* I. 206 The dimethylated and trimethylated paraffins have been distinguished for some time past as normal and isoparaffins respectively. **1889** G. M'GOWAN tr. *Bernthsen's Text-bk. Org. Chem.* i. 43 Iso-paraffins, in which one assumes a single branching in the molecule. **1939** GRUENER & LANKELMA *Introd. Org. Chem.* vi. 85 A tertiary alcohol is obtained only in the case of branching carbon chains, or 'isoparaffins'. **1969** R. F. LANG tr. *Henglein's Chem. Technol.* xxi. 576 The synthesis of anti-knock isoparaffins for aviation gasoline is achieved also by chemical means. **1876** *Encycl. Brit.* V. 558/2 Iso-pentane.. is formed by the dehydration of amyl alcohol by means of zinc chloride. **1943** V. A. KALICHEVSKY *Amazing Petroleum Industry* iv. 55 Natural gasoline contains certain quantities of a hydrocarbon known as isopentane which is a valuable component of high-grade gasolines. **1964** ROBERTS & CASERIO *Basic Princ. Org. Chem.* iii. 92 The chlorination of isopentane at 300° gives all four possible monosubstitution products. **1876** *Phil. Mag.* I. 217 One of the two conceivable isopentyl alcohols would be derivable in this way from pseudobutyl alcohol. **1970** H. E. NURSTEN in A. C. Hulme *Biochem. Fruits* I. x. 247 Hultin and Proctor.. had already found.. isopentyl alcohol to be significant as regards the rank odour of over-ripe fruit. **1886** E. F. SMITH tr. *V. von Richter's Chem. Carbon Compounds* 566 It [*sc.* the barium salt] is not precipitated by barium chloride from a solution of ammonium isophthalate. **1968** A. L. WADDAMS *Chemicals from Petrol.* (ed. 2) xii. 182 Isophthalates have many properties in common with the phthalate esters so that the two are in competition to some extent. As the isophthalates are the more expensive their use is limited to more specialized applications. **1870** *Chem. News* 22 Apr. 191/2 (*heading*) On isophthalic acid and some of its derivatives. **1914** H. T. CLARKE *Introd. Study Org. Chem.* xxxiii. 399 Isophthalic acid.. differs from phthalic acid in being incapable of forming an anhydride or an imide. **1968** A. L. WADDAMS *Chemicals from Petrol.* (ed. 2) xii. 182 The production of isophthalic acid in the U.S.A. is about 30,000 long tons a year. Its major use is in unsaturated polyester resins (38 per cent of the total). 31 per cent of consumption is for alkyd resins. **1945** *Chem. Abstr.* XXXIX. 349 Isopropanol.. in blood and body fluids can be detd. iodometrically. **1956** *Nature* 11 Feb. 271/1 Fractions of ribonucleic acid were hydrolysed.. to mononucleotides, which were separated by paper chromatography in *iso*propanol-water-ammonia. **1972** P. WISEMAN *Introd. Industr. Org. Chem.* vi. 218 Acetone is made by the dehydrogenation of iso-propanol. **1885** *Jrnl. Chem. Soc.* XLVIII. 645 On heating isopropenyl carbinol with a small quantity of acid, iso-butaldehyde is formed. **1950** R. C. FUSON *Adv. Org. Chem.* xv. 347 The conversion of isopropenyl acetate to acetyl-acetone. **1965** *Nomencl. Org. Chem.* (I.U.P.A.C.) C. 239 Isopropenyl (replacing 1-methylvinyl) (unsubstituted only). **1866** *Jrnl. Chem. Soc.* XIX. 487 We know that isopropyl compounds do not yield propionic acid by oxidation. **1872** *Ibid.* XXV. 237 The production of iso-propyl alcohol, instead of the normal alcohol, by the decomposition of normal propylamine nitrite. **1888** REMSEN *Org. Chem.* 120 Secondary propyl or isopropyl alcohol. **1934** H. HILER *Notes Technique Painting* v. 288 Isopropyl alcohol or petrohol is one of the latest solvents used. It will dissolve most varnishes. **1948** *Economist* 31 July 193/1 American production of isopropyl alcohol (now the principal source of acetone) began in small quantities about fifteen years ago. **1955** H. R. DOWNS *Chem. Living Cells* xii. 410 Administration of doubly labeled isovaleric acid gives rise to cholesterol in which it appears that the carbons of the isopropyl group of that acid have been incorporated as a unit. **1966** [see *isobutyl* above]. **1970** PASSMORE & ROBSON *Compan. Med. Stud.* II. xviii. 40/2 Ethyl alcohol, or better isopropyl alcohol, are used for rapid skin disinfection and are probably the best substances for this purpose. **1880** *Athenæum* 27 Nov. 713/1 The authors.. have thus prepared aluminic methylate, ethylate, propylate (isopropylate could not be obtained). **1900** E. F. SMITH tr. *V. von Richter's Org. Chem.* (ed. 3) II. 495 The condensation of the same oxime in the presence of ketones or aldehydes gives rise to isopropylidene and benzylidene methyl isoxazolons, $(C_4H_3NO_2){:}C(CH_3)_2$ [etc.]. **1932** H. PRINGSHEIM *Chem. Monosaccharides & Polysaccharides* ii. 31 Into the hexoses and pentoses there can be introduced two isopropylidene remainders. **1967** R. J. MCILROY *Introd. Carbohydrate Chem.* v. 52 This displacement of the ring has led to the employment of isopropylidene derivatives in the synthesis of reference compounds of the furanose type. **1886** *Jrnl. Chem. Soc.* L. 78 By adding concentrated sulphuric acid to an alcoholic solution of crude quinoline from coal-tar, the sulphates of quinoline and isoquinoline, C_9H_7N, are precipitated. **1932** I. D. GARRARD *Introd. Org. Chem.* xii.

180 Morphine is one of the alkaloids obtained from opium. It is a derivative of isoquinoline. **1960** R. M. ACHESON *Introd. Chem. Heterocyclic Compounds* vi. 231 Many alkaloids (*e.g.* papaverine) contain either the aromatic, or the reduced, isoquinoline system. **1972** N. L. ALLINGER et al. *Org. Chem.* xxviii. 746 Isoquinoline may be synthesized from benzaldehyde by a cyclization reaction known as the Pomeranz–Fritsch synthesis. **1883** *Jrnl. Chem. Soc.* XLIII. 86 The same remark applies to the polymeride obtained.. from isovaleraldehyde. **1946** *Chem. Abstr.* XL. 6757 The oil examd., obtained in 1·2% yield by direct steam distn...of *Lavandula delphinensis* plants..had...isovaleraldehyde 0·02[%]. **1970** *Jrnl. Econ. Ent.* LXIII. 1819/1 Bioassay results with 37 terpenoids and related plant constituents indicate that..menthone, isovaleraldehyde, and linalool were among the most attractive to *Anthomus grandis* Boheman. **1882** *Jrnl. Chem. Soc.* XLII. 30 Fraction 3.. yielded impure isopentyl isovalerate. **1888** *Ibid.* LIV. 251 Silver isovalerate. **1963** *Chem. Abstr.* LVIII. 4974 Other compds. identified [in nutmeg oil] were..isoeugenol..and menthyl isovalerate. **1894** *Chem. News* 9 Feb. 66/1 (*heading*) Condensation of isovalerianic aldehyd with ordinary acetone. **1927** *Chem. Abstr.* XXI. 985 By oxidation iso-AmOH gives the aldehyde and isovalerianic acid, all 3 of which have been found in oil of lavender. **1971** *Angewandte Parasitol.* XII. 107 The pure attractants..valerianic acid and iso-valerianic acid had only a little attraction [for synanthropic flies]. **1882** *Jrnl. Chem. Soc.* XLII. 162 Of the lower homologues of isocaproic acid which contain the isopropyl group, isovaleric acid alone yields an acid similar to the above on oxidation. **1934** *Biochem. Jrnl.* XXXVIII. 401 The porpoise and dolphin depôt fats are unique in containing large amounts of *isovaleric* acid. **1950** J. BONNER *Plant Biochem.* xxv. 393 Fig. 25-3 gives an example of a fractionation conducted on oil of peppermint... Acetaldehyde, acetone, isovaleric acid, and isoamyl alcohol first distil over. **1960** K. S. MARKLEY *Fatty Acids* (ed. 2) II. ii. 55 Isovaleric acid has been reported to occur in the free state in large amounts in valerian root; in lesser amounts in the oils of pineapple and lavender, and among the volatile acids of mutton tallow.., and in the rumen of the sheep. **1891** *Jrnl. Chem. Soc.* LIX. 410 (*heading*) Formation of isoxazoles. **1946** A. A. MORTON *Chem. Heterocyclic Compounds* xiv. 421 No naturally occurring isoxazole compounds are known. They are often obtained in the course of laboratory work with nitroso and isonitroso compounds. **1960** R. M. ACHESON *Introd. Chem. Heterocyclic Compounds* vii. 272 Isoxazole itself is obtainable from propargyl aldehyde and hydroxylamine; 1,3-dicarbonyl compounds also give isoxazoles with hydroxylamine in a very general synthesis.

isoaccentual to **isoantigenic**: see ISO-.

isobar (ˈaɪsəʊbɑː(r)). *Phys. Geog.* and *Meteorol.* Also isobare. [f. Gr. ἰσοβαρή-ς of equal weight, f. ἰσο-, ISO- + βαρε-, βάρος weight, βαρύς heavy.]

1. a. A line (drawn on a map or chart, or imaginary) connecting places on the earth's surface at which the barometric pressure is the same (at a given time, or on the average for a given period); an isobaric line.

1864 in WEBSTER. **1878** HUXLEY *Physiogr.* 94 Another isobar [in the *Times* weather-chart] stretches across Scotland, and indicates a pressure of 29·9 inches. **1880** *Times* 16 Aug. 11/4 In the above chart the dotted lines are 'isobars' or lines of equal barometrical pressure. **1880** GEIKIE *Phys. Geog.* ii. 55 Charts showing, by means of lines of equal pressure called *Isobars*, the general distribution of atmospheric pressure.

b. A line in a diagram that represents states or conditions of equal pressure.

1892 P. ALEXANDER *Treat. Thermodynamics* v. 39 An isobar is a constant pressure thermogram. **1924** A. E. HILL in H. S. Taylor *Treat. Physical Chem.* I. ix. 383 The isobar *ab* drawn at 1 atmosphere pressure intersects the curve *BO* at −78·3°. **1969** S. M. BLINDER *Adv. Physical Chem.* viii. 144 In Fig. 8.2, the same data are represented as a series of isobars, plots of *V* versus *t* for fixed *P*.

2. *Physics.* Each of two or more nuclides which have the same mass number but different atomic numbers (and so are different elements). Orig. †**isobare** (*obs.*).

1918 A. W. STEWART in *Phil. Mag.* XXVI. 331 These elements [*sc.* mesothorium and radiothorium] differ completely from one another in chemical character; but they all possess the same atomic weight. For this reason the name isobares..is here suggested for them. **1928** M. STEEL *Physical Chem. & Biophysics* ii. 37 Any product of radioactive change due to the loss of a beta particle..is an isobar of the parent element. **1946** *Electronic Engin.* XVIII. 88/2 Neptunium and plutonium are isobares (same atomic mass but different atomic number). **1952** *Sci. News* XXIII. 37 These nuclei are called isobares. **1954** K. RANKAMA *Isotope Geol.* xxv. 302 The isotope ^{40}K is the active nuclide in the series of the three neighbouring isobars, ^{40}A–^{40}K–^{40}Ca. **1955** R. D. EVANS *Atomic Nucleus* iii. 99 The chemical properties of isobars are generally dissimilar, but their nuclear properties tend to present many parallel features. **1966** PHILLIPS & WILLIAMS *Inorg. Chem.* II. xxxv. 621 We shall use the symbol *Z* for the number of protons in a nucleus (i.e. the atomic number) and *N* for the number of neutrons, so that $A = Z + N$, where *A* is the mass number or 'rounded' atomic weight. All nuclei of the same *Z* are called isotopes, of the same *N* isotones, and of the same *A* isobars.

isobare, obs. var. ISOBAR 2.

isobaric (aɪsəʊˈbærɪk), *a.* and *sb.* [f. ISOBAR + -IC. (Not formed on Greek analogies.)]

A. *adj.* **1. a.** Indicating equal barometric pressure; containing or relating to isobars.

1878 HUXLEY *Physiogr.* 95 Much may be learned about winds by studying the isobaric lines. **1882** *Standard* 26 Dec. 7/4 The daily isobaric charts will receive greatly increased attention. **1883** A. BUCHAN in *Encycl. Brit.* XVI. 139 Isobaric maps may be considered as furnishing the key to the more important questions of meteorological inquiry.

b. Occurring at or pertaining to a constant pressure.

1903 A. OGG tr. *Planck's Treat. Thermodynamics* I. i. 7 (*heading*) Behaviour under constant pressure (isopiestic or isobaric changes). **1933** D. J. MARTIN *Introd. Thermodynamics for Chemists* xiii. 315 The isobaric heat of adsorption corresponds to the heat of a reaction in a condensed system, the amount adsorbed changes while the pressure remains practically constant. **1937** P. S. EPSTEIN *Textbk. Thermodynamics* iii. 46 The heat function acquires a particular importance in the so-called isobaric process, i.e. a process which takes place without change of pressure. **1966** [see *isopiestic* adj. s.v. ISO-].

2. *Physics.* Of, pertaining to, or being isobars (sense 2); *isobaric spin* = ISOSPIN. Const. *with.*

1919 *Nature* 18 Sept. 61/2 Elements can be regarded as divisible into three classes:—(1) Isotopic elements, each set of which have different atomic weights but identical chemical properties; (2) isobaric elements which have identical atomic weights but different chemical properties; and (3) normal elements which differ..both in atomic weights and chemical properties. **1933** F. W. ASTON *Mass-Spectra & Isotopes* xii. 158 Spectra were obtained which showed four strong isotopes and two very weak ones, one of which is isobaric with W^{186}. **1948** GLASSTONE *Textbk. Physical Chem.* (ed. 2) ii. 171 With the development of the study of artificial radioactivity it has become apparent that there are more than seventy pairs of such isobaric isotopes, now known as isomeric nuclei. **1953** D. R. INGLIS in *Rev. Mod. Physics* XXV. 395/2 One finds the states listed according to the usual quantum numbers *L* and *S* of the (*LS*)-coupling scheme and also according to the isobaric spin quantum number *T* (or isotopic spin as it has been less aptly called since it was named long ago by Wigner, who agrees to this renaming of his child). **1971** *Physics Bull.* Mar. 137/1 Isobaric spin was first introduced into nuclear interactions by Heisenberg purely as a mathematical convenience.

3. *Med.* Of, pertaining to, or designating a solution for spinal anæsthesia having the same density as the cerebro-spinal fluid.

1930, 1946 [see HYPERBARIC *a.* a]. **1947** J. ADRIANI *Techniques & Procedures Anesthesia* v. 222 A 2½% solution of procaine in distilled water is nearly isobaric. **1962** —— *Chem. & Phys. Anaesthesia* (ed. 2) xxxi. 653/1 The results obtained with isobaric techniques are unpredictable and variable. **1971** P. C. LUND *Princ. & Pract. Spinal Anesthesia* vii. 371 Isobaric solutions have not been popular..because of the difficulty of achieving predictable levels of anesthesia. *Ibid.*, An adaptation of isobaric spinal anesthesia for anorectal surgery was introduced by Jacoby et al. in 1965.

B. *sb.* = ISOBAR 1 b.

1903 *Engineer* 24 July 83/3 The isobarics of evaporation happen to be isothermals. **1937** M. W. ZEMANSKY *Heat & Thermodynamics* iv. 56 The series of short isobarics and isovolumics from *i* to *f* and the continuous curve from *i* to *f* represent other possibilities.

isobarically (aɪsəʊˈbærɪkəlɪ), *adv.* [f. prec. + -LY².] At constant pressure, without a change in pressure.

1951 R. B. MONTGOMERY in D. E. Kerr *Propagation Short Radio Waves* iii. 186 Wet-bulb Temperature.—This may be defined as the temperature at which saturation would occur if the air were cooled isobarically and adiabatically by means of contact with a water surface.

isobarism (aɪˈsɒbərɪz(ə)m). *rare*⁻⁰. [f. as ISOBARIC *a.* + -ISM.] Equality of weight.

1882 in OGILVIE.

isobarometric (ˌaɪsəʊbærəʊˈmɛtrɪk), *a. rare.* [f. ISO- + BAROMETRIC. (In mod.F. *isobarométrique*.)] = ISOBARIC.

1864 in WEBSTER. **1869** E. A. PARKES *Pract. Hygiene* (ed. 3) 445 The isobarometric lines..connecting places with the same mean annual height of barometer.

isobase to **isobathythermic**: see ISO-.

isobestic, var. ISOSBESTIC *a.*

isobilateral to **isocalorically**: see ISO-.

isocarboxazid (ˌaɪsəʊkɑːˈbɒksəzɪd). *Pharm.* [f. *isocarbox-* (by rearrangement of part of the chemical name: see quot. 1959) + HYDR)AZID(E.] A whitish powder that is a hydrazine derivative, $C_6H_5CH_2NH{\cdot}N$ $HCO{\cdot}C_3HNO{\cdot}CH_3$, and is used as an antidepressant.

1959 *Diseases Nervous Syst.* XX. 269/1 An analog of iproniazid, isocarboxazid.., has been used in pharmacological studies which show it to be a more potent amine oxidase inhibitor than its progenitor. Its chemical formula is 1-benzyl-2-(5-methyl-3-isoxazolylcarbonyl)-hydrazine. **1963** *Jrnl. Amer. Med. Assoc.* 16 Mar. 952/1 It is the opinion of the Council that isocarboxazid seems to be effective in the depressed phases of anxiety and manic-depressive states as well as in certain involutional, obsessive, and disassociative reactions. **1965** J. POLLITT *Depression & its Treatment* iv. 56 The monoamine oxidase inhibitors include several members, among which are phenelzine (Nardil), iproniazid (Marsilid), isocarboxazid (Marplan).

isocarpous: see ISO-.

isocel, obs. variant of ISOSCEL.

isocellular: see ISO-.

isocentre (ˈaɪsəʊsɛntə(r)). Also (*U.S.*) -center. [f. ISO- + CENTRE *sb.*] In aerial photography, the point at which the bisector of the angle between the optical axis of the camera and the vertical at the inner nodal point of the lens meets the plane of the camera plate or film (or the corresponding object point where the bisector meets the ground).

1931 C. M. HOTINE *Surveying from Air Photogr.* v. 63 We may, therefore, consider the plate isocentre as the centre of tilt distortions, in that images are displaced radially from the isocentre from the positions they would occupy if the photograph had not been tilted. **1950** L. G. TROREY *Handbk. Aerial Mapping* i. 3 Any photograph is angle true with respect to the isocentre for all points in the plane of the isocentre. **1970** J. A. HOWARD *Aerial Photo-Ecology* ix. 102 The isocentre and nadir are very important due to their relation to tilt and radial displacement.

isocephaly to **isocercy**: see ISO-.

isochar (ˈaɪsəʊkɑː(r)). [f. ISO- + CHAR(ACTER *sb.* rendering G. *isopsepher* (W. Rothmaler 1938, in *Beih. Rep. Spec. Nov. Reg. Veg.* C. 90), f. Gr. ψῆφος number + ἦρος sign.] A line (imaginary or on a map) linking areas containing plants showing similar numbers of distinguishing characteristics.

1963 DAVIS & HEYWOOD *Princ. Angiosperm Taxon.* ix. 317 The second procedure involves the drawing of *Isopsepheren*, a term which we can anglicise to *isochars*. These are based on the largest possible number of contrasting character expressions found in the taxa being studied... We are grateful to Dr. W. T. Stearn for suggesting this term.

isochasm, -chasmic: see ISO-.

isocheim (ˈaɪsəʊkaɪm). *Phys. Geog.* Also **isochime.** [f. Gr. ἰσο-, ISO- + stem of χεῖμα, χείματ- winter-weather.] A line (on a map, etc.) connecting places at which the mean winter temperature is the same; an isotherm of mean winter temperature; an isochimenal line.

1864 in WEBSTER. **1878** *N. Amer. Rev.* CXXVI. 160 The farmer who gets his crop under cover before a predicted heavy rainfall need know nothing of isobares and isocheims.

isocheimal (aɪsəʊˈkaɪməl), *a.* and *sb.* Also **isochimal.** [f. prec. + -AL¹. (Not on Gr. or L. analogies.)] = ISOCHIMENAL.

1839 *Penny Cycl.* XV. 139/2 The names of Isotheral, Isocheimal, and Isothermal lines have been given to lines passing through places which have equal mean summer, winter, or annual temperatures. **1846** WORCESTER, *Isochimal.* **1852** [see ISOCRYMAL]. **1880** W. B. CARPENTER in *19th Cent.* Apr. 610 The 'isocheimals', or lines of mean winter temperature, instead of corresponding to the parallels of latitude, lie parallel to the coast-line.

isocheimonal (-ˈkaɪmənəl), *a.* Also **-chimonal.** [Alteration of ISOCHIMENAL *a.*, after Gr. χειμών winter.]

1869 E. A. PARKES *Pract. Hygiene* (ed. 3) 437 The lines.. of mean winter temperature are called isocheimonal.

isochemical, -chemically: see ISO-.

isochimenal (-ˈkaɪmɪnəl), *a.* and *sb.* Also **isocheimenal.** [f. F. *isochimène* (introd. 1817 by Humboldt), f. Gr. ἰσο-, ISO- + χειμαίν-ειν to be stormy or wintry, f. χεῖμα winter-weather, storm.] **A.** *adj.* Indicating equal mean winter temperatures: said of lines on a map, etc. (see ISOCHEIM). **B.** *sb.* An isochimenal line, an isocheim.

1846 WORCESTER cites FRANCIS. **1863** LYELL *Antiq. Man* xviii. 365 In the actual state of the globe, the isochimenal lines, or lines of equal winter temperature, when traced westward from Europe to North America, bend 10° south. **1867** PROCTOR in *Intell. Observ.* No. 62. 117 The isochimenals of greatest cold.

isochlor, isochor, -choric: see ISO-.

isochromatic (ˌaɪsəʊkrəʊˈmætɪk), *a.* and *sb.* [f. ISO- + CHROMATIC; in mod.F. *isochromatique* (Littré).]

A. *adj.* **1.** *Optics.* Of a single colour or tint: applied to a fringe in an interference pattern obtained with birefringent material, such as a biaxial crystal or material used in photoelastic experiments (when such a fringe corresponds to points where the difference between the principal stresses is the same). Also, representing or depicting such fringes.

1829 *Hand-bk. Nat. Philos.* I. *Polaris. Light* vii. 24 (U.K.S.) A more accurate description of the form of these isochromatic curves, or lines of equal tint. **1831** BREWSTER *Newton* (1855) I. vii. 174 Owing to the curvature of the surfaces..the forms of the isochromatic lines, or the lines of equal tint, are various and beautiful. **1837** WHEWELL *Hist. Induct. Sc.* (1857) II. 309 They give oval and knotted isochromatic lines. **1931** COKER & FILON *Treat. Photo-Elasticity* iii. 248 The integrated tint remains the same over the whole of this locus, and it is for this reason that such lines are called lines of equal tint or isochromatic lines. **1932** HARDY & PERRIN *Princ. Optics* xxix. 617 Although the values of *p* and *q* themselves can be computed from the isoclinic and isochromatic patterns, the operations are extremely tedious. **1966** *McGraw-Hill Encycl. Sci. & Technol.* X. 150/1 Utilizing equations for the difference of the principal stresses from the isochromatic fringe orders, the stresses may be found by solving the two equations for the two principal stresses.

2. *Photog.* = ORTHOCHROMATIC.

1884 *Philadelphia Photographer* Oct. 315/1 (*heading*) Isochromatic gelatin plates. **1885** *Jrnl. Franklin Inst.* CXIX. 368 It was..the only truly isochromatic process ever discovered. Dr. Vogel's new process was not only no better in any respect, but the plates were insensitive to scarlet and ruby-red. *Ibid.* 371 Truly isochromatic photography. **1903** A. M. CLERKE *Probl. Astrophysics* II. iii. 191, D appeared conspicuously on Professor Campbell's isochromatic plates. **1904** *Westm. Gaz.* 19 Nov. 16/2 Not much has been heard of late about isochromatic plates, and it is to be feared that among amateurs their use is not on the increase. Generally speaking, the more recent advances in orthochromatic photography have been in the direction of increasing rather than lessening the difficulties. **1932** *Discovery* Sept. 292/1 The extension of the sensitivity of photographic emulsions ..has given rise to three..types of colour sensitive material. The first type includes materials in which the sensitivity has been extended to cover the green; such materials are generally known as 'orthochromatic' or 'isochromatic'. **1955** H. & A. GERNSHEIM *Hist. Photogr.* xxiii. 268 Vogel and others had transformed the hitherto colour-blind emulsion into one which was more accurately sensitive for most colours—i.e. the so-called iso- or orthochromatic plates.

B. *sb.* An isochromatic fringe or line.

1924 *Rep. Brit. Assoc. Adv. Sci. 1923* 354 The disc carried a network of reference lines and the appearances were projected on a screen, upon which the isoclinics and isochromatics were traced with a pencil. **1948** M. M. FROCHT *Photoelasticity* II. iv. 139 The fringes or isochromatics..all pass through the points of application of the loads. **1958** CONDON & ODISHAW *Handbk. Physics* III. vi. 86/2 With a white light source the stress patterns consists of colored bands, called isochromatics, which form in the order of yellow, red, and green followed by similar cycles.

isochromosome: see ISO-.

isochron ('aɪsəʊkrɒn), *a.* and *sb.* Also **isochrone** (-krəʊn), 8 *erron.* -crone. [f. Gr. ἰσόχρον-ος (see ISOCHRONAL *a.*).] **A.** *adj.* (In form *isochrone*) = ISOCHRONOUS *a.* 1

1697 EVELYN *Numism.* viii. 281 The Equated Isocrone Motion. **1762** tr. *Busching's Syst. Geog.* I. Pref. 35 The degrees of the meridian, and the lengths of an isochrone pendulum, will always increase together. **1859** L. F. SIMPSON *Handbk. Dining* vi. (1865) 57 The jaws did not display that isochrone movement which announces good work.

B. *sb.* †**1.** An isochronal line. *Obs.*

a **1774** GOLDSM. *Surv. Exp. Philos.* (1776) I. 292 Geometricians might make their calculations on several mathematical problems with greater precision, as in Brachystochrones, Isochrones, and such like.

2. A line (imaginary or on a map) connecting points at which a particular event occurs or occurred at the same time.

1881 F. GALTON in *Proc. R. Geogr. Soc.* III. 658 Along the coast of West Africa..the ports are regularly served by steamers that touch at every one of them..and which consequently occupy more than forty days to reach even the mouth of the Congo, whereas steamers occasionally sail direct to one or other of those ports in considerably shorter time than these mail steamers. This particular difficulty is met and explained by the sea isochrones, which in this case do not conform to those of the land. **1909** *Cent. Dict.* Suppl., *Isochrone*, n., a line connecting points at which the same events occur simultaneously. Thus the isochrone of travel is the line connecting points attainable by a person riding or an army marching from a given center forward during a given interval of time; the phenological isochrone, the line connecting points at which plants of any species attain simultaneously the same stage of development. **1948** *Antiquity* XXII. 114 While all competent authorities will agree that the practice of producing food..must have spread in some such way as this map shows, there will be differences of opinion... We expect for instance that the bulge made by the isochrones to include Anau and no more is largely artificial. **1955** W. J. SAUCIER *Princ. Meteorol. Analysis* xii. 389/1 If the weather occurs along a line, successive positions (isochrones) will be curves on the map. **1956** *Nature* 24 Mar. 571/1 The plots of radio blackout distribution in the North American and North Atlantic region..agree with the isochrons of the 'morning' maximum of magnetic disturbance in the Arctic region. **1970** *Ibid.* 17 Jan. 224 The map depicts..the course of withdrawal of the ice sheet from its greatest extent some 18,000 years ago... The detailed isochrons, separated in places by as little as 100 years, graphically depict the north-south corridor that had opened up to the east of the Rocky Mountains about 7,000 years ago.

3. A line (imaginary or on a map) connecting points at which some chosen time interval has the same value.

1940 C. A. HEILAND *Geophysical Explor.* ix. 548 Adjusted times are plotted against the location of depth points; points with equal time differences are connected by isochrons which, barring velocity variations and steep dips, give a true picture of the depth contours of the structure. **1945** *Electronic Engin.* XVII. 713/2 Sets of lines can be drawn, joining all the points having the same time-differences; and it has been agreed to call these lines 'isochrones', analogous to the 'isobars' of a weather-map. In general, these 'isochrone' lines are hyperbolae. **1952** F. H. LAHEE *Field Geol.* (ed. 5) xxiii. 779 On the assumption that velocity values [of seismic waves] are essentially constant and that reflecting horizons are continuous over a given area, the differences in arrival time from two such horizons can be plotted at each station and then lines of equal time difference (isochrons) can be drawn to produce an isochron map. **1958** *Jrnl. Brit. Interplanetary Soc.* XVI. 340 We have expresed the duration of the voyage in terms of *q*, ε and *n* only. In our diagram we can now draw lines of equal duration, which we call isochrones. In Fig. 9 are shown the isochrones for voyages from the Earth to Venus in days.

4. In the isotopic dating of rock, a straight line whose gradient is taken to represent the time since the isotopic content of a sample was fixed (e.g. by crystallization), and obtained by plotting the ratio of the amount of a radiogenic isotope to that of a non-radiogenic isotope against a corresponding ratio for a second radiogenic isotope and the same non-radiogenic one in two or more samples having the same history but different ratios.

1953 F. G. HOUTERMANS in *Nuovo Cimento* X. 1624 By dividing (3b) by (3a) the equations of 'isochrones' are obtained... These are a number of straight lines, intersecting at the point α_ω, β_ω corresponding to the isotopic constitution of 'primeval lead' at the time ω. **1963** K. RANKAMA *Progr. Isotope Geol.* lxxxvii. 543 When the ^{207}Pb/^{204}Pb ratio was plotted against the ^{206}Pb/^{204}Pb ratio, the slope of the ^{207}Pb = *f*(^{206}Pb) isochron yielded the age 4·55 Gy for meteoritic matter, and the isotopic constitution of rock lead fell close to the isochron. **1969** BENNISON & WRIGHT *Geol. Hist. Brit. Isles* iii. 41 This data can also be presented as isochrons.., the slope of a whole-rock isochron being proportional to the age of initial crystallization and the slope of the mineral isochron to that of the metamorphism. **1971** *Nature* 25 June 500/1 Bofinger..has carried out extensive radiometric dating on illitic sedimentary rocks..; he produced eight separate total-rock Rb-Sr isochrons from seventy-two samples.

5. A line (imaginary or on a map) connecting points on the sea-floor formed at the same time.

1968 *New Scientist* 30 May 452/2 American workers hope eventually to produce a complete 'isochron' (lines of equal age) map of the world's oceans. **1972** *Nature* 8 Dec. 339/2 The discharge curve for Iceland was constructed..by extrapolating seafloor spreading isochrons from the ocean floor immediately southwest of the aseismic ridge.

isochronal (aɪ'sɒkrənəl), *a.* Also 8 *erron.* -cronal. [f. mod.L. *isochron-us* (Leibnitz), a. Gr. ἰσόχρον-ος equal in time (f. ἰσο-, ISO- + χρόνος time) + -AL[1]. Cf. F. *isochrone* (1703 in Hatz.-Darm.).] **1.** = ISOCHRONOUS *a.* 1.

† *isochronal line* [tr. L. *linea isochrona* (Leibnitz, 1689)], a curve in which a heavy body descends with uniform velocity, i.e. moving through equal spaces in equal times. *Obs.*

1680 H. MORE *Apocal. Apoc.* 264 The Entireness of his Kingdom is Synchronal to the two Witnesses Prophesying in Sackcloth, they being both Isochronal, or of equal time. **1706** W. JONES *Syn. Palmar. Matheseos* 290 In a Medium that does not resist, the shorter Oscillations in a Cycloid are nearly Isocronal. **1794** ATWOOD in *Phil. Trans.* LXXXIV. 136 The isochronal property of spiral springs. **1838** *Penny Cycl.* XII. 298/2 The isochronal property which Galilei ascribed to the pendulum. **1866** BRANDE & COX *Dict. Sci.*, etc., *Isochronal axes*, in Mechanics, axes around which if a body be made to oscillate, the oscillations will be performed in equal times.

2. Of a line: connecting points at which a particular event occurs or occurred at the same time. Of a diagram: depicting such lines. Also as *sb.*, = ISOCHRON 2.

1926 [see ISEPIPTESIS, ISOPIPTESIS]. **1937** D. KENNEDY tr. *Imamura's Theoret. & Appl. Seismol.* iv. 42 If a line is passed through places where a certain phase of the earthquake motion..appears simultaneously..a line resembling an isoseismal is obtained. It is the coseismal, or the isochronal of some recent writers. **1948** R. B. HOUNSFIELD *Traffic Surveys* vi. 39 Another type of diagram used in planning is the 'isochronal' diagram. *Ibid.* 40 (*caption*) Isochronal diagram showing accessibility of different areas. **1962** C. D. SHERMAN tr. *Dorst's Migrations of Birds* vii. 236 The influence of temperature, revealed in this parallelism between isochronal lines and isotherms, may be less apparent because of other factors which also govern migration.

Hence **i'sochronally** *adv.* = I'SOCHRONOUSLY.

1882 OGILVIE, *Isochronally*, so as to be isochronal.

isochronic (aɪsəʊ'krɒnɪk), *a.* [f. as ISOCHRON-AL + -IC.] **1.** Also **iso'chronical**. = ISOCHRONOUS *a.* 1.

1779 MANN in *Phil. Trans.* LXIX. 583 This curve is what is called the Horizontal Isochronic. **1794** G. ADAMS *Nat. & Exp. Philos.* I. iii. 65 The isochronical vibrations of the pendulum. **1827** *Westm. Rev.* VIII. 382 He [Anacreon] mixed up Iambic catalectic dimeters..with Trochaic acatalectic dimeters..as if they were isochronical.

2. = ISOCHRONAL *a.* 2; *spec.* (see quots. 1881, 1959).

1881 F. GALTON in *Proc. R. Geogr. Soc.* III. 657 By 'isochronic' passage-charts, I mean charts constructed to show the extreme distances that can be traversed in 'equal times' from a common starting point. *Ibid.* 658 Isochronic maps might be..constructed for Continental travel or for home excursions. **1948** *Antiquity* XXII. 114 The second [map]..covers the Old World and shows the spread of the food-producing economy from five possible independent centres. The date at which food-production first appeared is shown by isochronic lines. These are an ingenious invention which show 'equal dates' exactly as contours show equal heights and isobars equal pressure. **1959** L. M. HARROD *Librarians' Gloss.* (ed. 2) 155 *Isochronic map*, one which shows possible progress of travel in all directions from a given centre in certain specified time intervals.

3. *Prosody.* Equal in metrical length.

1956 H. WHITEHALL in *Kenyon Rev.* XVIII. 111. 418 Unlike such 'syllable-timed' languages as Spanish, English is 'stress-timed' or *isochronic*. **1959** *PMLA* LXXIV. 587/1 Mr. Whitehall distinguishes a type of 'rhythm' which he calls the isochronic: it 'depends on equal time lapses between primary stresses'.

isochronism (aɪ'sɒkrənɪz(ə)m). [f. as ISOCHRONAL *a.* + -ISM: cf. Gr. χρονίζ-ειν to spend time, continue in time. Cf. F. *isochronisme* (1735 in Hatz.).] **1.** The character or property of being isochronous, or of oscillating or taking place in equal spaces of time.

1770 *Gentl. Mag.* XL. 416 Nothing seemed to stop its isochronism. **1786** BONNYCASTLE *Astron.* vi. 97 Galileo..is said to have discovered the isochronism of the pendulum. **1812–16** PLAYFAIR *Nat. Phil.* (1819) I. 285 Noise and discordant sounds arise from a want of isochronism of vibration. **1834** *Hand-bk. Nat. Philos.* III. *Hist. Astron.* xx. 104/1 (U.K.S.) The isochronism of spiral steel springs, when used as a balance in watches. **1857** DENISON *Clocks & Locks* 5 That peculiarly valuable quality of the pendulum called isochronism, or the disposition to vibrate different arcs in very nearly the same time (provided the arcs are none of them large).

2. *Prosody.* The character or property of being isochronous.

1942 WELLEK & WARREN *Theory of Lit.* 166 The artistic rhythm of prose..must not reach an apparent isochronism (that is, a regularity of time intervals between rhythmical accents). **1956** H. WHITEHALL in *Kenyon Rev.* XVIII. 111. 418 Isochronism is produced not only by accelerating and crushing together the syllables between primary stresses but also by increasing or decreasing the pauses. **1959** *PMLA* LXXIV. 587/1 If isochronism *were* a general principle, or even an approximate principle, of all English speech, it would clearly be a different thing from meter. **1966** M. PEI *Gloss. Ling. Terminol.* 133 *Isochronism*, a term applied to verse in which the amount of time between two primary stresses tends to be the same, irrespective of the amount of material between them. **1973** *Studies in Eng. Lit.: Eng. Number* (Tokyo) 31 Hopkins has nowhere upheld a principle of absolute isochronism.

isochronous (aɪ'sɒkrənəs), *a.* [f. as ISOCHRON-AL + -OUS.] **1. a.** Taking place in or occupying equal times; equal in metrical length; equal in duration, or in intervals of occurrence, as the vibrations of a pendulum; characterized by or relating to vibrations or motions of equal duration; vibrating uniformly, as a pendulum. *spec.* in *Prosody*, equal in metrical length.

1706 PHILLIPS s.v. *Isochrone*, The Vibrations or Swings of a Pendulum, or hanging Weight, that are made in the same Space of Time, are said to be Isochronous. **1748** HARTLEY *Observ. Man* I. ii. 119 Vibratory Motions of different Lengths can be isochronous only according to one Law. **1784** SEALE *Grk. Metres* (L.), The tribrach and iambic are isochronous. **1789** BURNEY *Hist. Mus.* III. i. 31 The poetical measures..when sung in the drawling and isochronous manner afford the ear no pleasure. **1822** SOUTHEY *Poet. Wks.* (1853) Pref. 23/2 If the English verse is not isochronous with the Latin, it must be shorter. **1825** J. NICHOLSON *Operat. Mechanic* 516 The great object of the escapement is to preserve this isochronous motion of the pendulum. **1857** C. PATMORE in *North Brit. Rev.* XXVII. 149 A metre which, totally abandoning the element of natural syllabic quantity, takes the isochronous bar for the metrical integer. **1884** F. J. BRITTEN *Watch & Clockm.* 126 A balance spring is said to be isochronous when it causes both the long and short arcs of the balance to be performed in the same time. **1942** J. C. POPE *Rhythm of Beowulf* 9 Isochronous measures are the rule..and it is easy to produce them in *Beowulf* by means of limited quantitative variation. **1948** *Mod. Philology* XLVI. 75 There is..no reason to suppose that, *if* the *Beowulf* was chanted to a real musical accompaniment, the lines were therefore delivered in isochronous groups. **1971** *Times Lit. Suppl.* 1 Oct. 1179/3 Its technique of isochronous rhythm—a metrical sequence which remains constant for a given part, though the pitch relationships change—is comparable with the Oriental tala.

b. Taking place (vibrating, etc.) in the same time, or at the same intervals of time, as something else; equal in duration (vibration-period, etc.) *to* or *with* something.

1776 CAVALLO in *Phil. Trans.* LXVI. 410 The snappings ..seemed at first isochronous with the shocks I had received. **1854** JONES & SIEV. *Pathol. Anat.* (1874) 415 The tumour..offers a pulsation to the touch isochronous with the arterial pulse. **1879** G. PRESCOTT *Sp. Telephone* 129 There follows..a series of oscillations, which are isochronous with the intermittence of the current.

2. *Palæont.* [ad. G. *isochron* (E. Mojsisovics *Die Cephalopoden der Hallstätter Kalke* (1893) II. 5).] Originating or formed at the same period.

1895 [see HOMŒOMORPHY]. **1913** [see HETEROCHRONOUS *a.* b]. **1952** R. C. MOORE et al. *Invertebr. Fossils* vi. 218/1 Such contemporaneous or near-contemporaneous forms he [*sc.* Buckman] designated as isochronous homeomorphs.

Hence **i'sochronously** *adv.*, in an isochronous manner; in equal times.

1748 HARTLEY *Observ. Man.* I. ii. 238 The Membrane will be fitted to vibrate isochronously with the several Tones. **1833** WHEATSTONE in *Phil. Trans.* 596 The resultants of very simple modes of vibration oscillating isochronously.

isochrony (aɪ'sɒkrənɪ). [f. as ISOCHRONISM, after *synchrony*, etc.] Isochronism; the character or property of being isochronous.

1953 *Word* Apr. 3 [The] tendency toward word isochrony whereby every simple word gets two moras either in one long syllable or in two short ones. **1961** *Brno Studies in English* III. 48 In his [*sc.* A. Martinet's] opinion, 12th century English achieves what he calls isochrony, i.e. the state of things resulting from the elimination of vocalic quantity as a phonematic feature. **1961** *Rev. Eng. Stud.* XII. 342 There exist all sorts of musical rhythms very different from the isochrony which has dominated European music for so long a time. **1966** J. C. POPE *Rhythm of Beowulf* (rev. ed.) p. x, Isochrony and initial rests are..vital, in my opinion, for the achievement of an adequate sense of order in opposition to the extraordinary variety of syllabic patterns in the verses. **1973** *Word 1966* XXII. 5 It is a whole chapter of the history of isochrony, the process through which the quantitative pattern of Proto-Indo-European was reorganized in most of the languages of that family.

i-socied, ME. pa. pple. of SOCIE *v.*, to associate.

isocitrate, isocitric: see ISO-.

isoclasite (aɪsəʊ'kleɪsaɪt, -zaɪt). *Min.* [f. G. *isoklas* (F. Sandberger 1870, in *Jrnl. f. prakt. Chem.* II. 125, f. Gr. κλάσ-ις fracture) + -ITE¹.] A colourless or white hydrated phosphate and hydroxide of calcium, $Ca_2(PO_4)(OH).2H_2O$, known from a single locality in Bohemia.

1872 G. J. BRUSH in J. D. Dana *Syst. Min.* (ed. 5) App. I. 7 Isoclasite. **1955** M. H. HEY *Index Min. Species* (ed. 2) 231 Isoclasite.

isoclinal (aɪsəʊ'klaɪnəl), *a.* and *sb.* [f. ISO- + Gr. κλῑν-ειν to bend, slope, slant: cf. ἰσοκλινή-ς equally balanced. In mod.F. *isocline.*]

A. *adj.* **1.** *Phys. Geog.* Indicating equal magnetic inclination: applied to lines connecting points on the earth's surface at which the magnetic inclination or dip is the same; relating to or containing such lines.

1839 SABINE (*title*) Report on the Magnetic Isoclinal and Isodynamic Lines in the British Islands. **1851-9** —— in *Man. Sci. Enq.* 97 In theoretical respects the Isodynamic and Isoclinal lines are not less essential. **1887** GUMMING *Electr. treated Experimentally* 52 The lines on the isoclinal map.

2. *Geol.* (See quot.)

Cf. the analogous *anticlinal*, *synclinal*, applied to less acute bends or folds of strata.

1882 GEIKIE *Text-bk. Geol.* 503 Where a series of strata has been so folded and inverted that its reduplicated members appear to dip regularly in one direction, the structure is termed *isoclinal*. *Ibid.* 930 The flexures are often so rapid that after denudation of the tops of the arches the strata are isoclinal, or appear to be dipping all in the same direction.

B. *sb. Phys. Geog.* An isoclinal line: see A. 1.

1889 *Nature* 11 Apr. 565/1 The directions of the isogonals, isoclinals, and lines of equal horizontal force have been found.

iso'clinally, *adv. Geol.* [f. ISOCLINAL a. + -LY².] In the manner of isoclinal strata (see ISOCLINAL *a.* 2.)

1936 *Bull. Geol. Soc. Amer.* XLVII. 720 Straight, seemingly undeformed layers of marble enclose isoclinally folded and dismembered fragments of stronger rocks. **1970** *Nature* 23 May 691/2 Greenstones..and associated serpentinites and stratiform basic complexes have been isoclinally folded on NNW-trending axes.

isocline ('aɪsəʊklaɪn). *Geol.* [f. Gr. ἰσοκλινή-ς: see ISOCLINAL *a.* and *sb.* Cf. F. *isocline* adj., isoclinal: cf. *anticline, syncline.*] An isoclinal fold of a stratum or series of strata.

1890 in *Cent. Dict.*

isoclinic (aɪsəʊ'klɪnɪk), *a.* and *sb.* [f. as prec. + -IC.] A. *adj.* **1.** = ISOCLINAL A. 1.

1855 MAYNE *Expos. Lex.*, Isoclinic. **1892** J. THORNTON *Adv. Physiogr.* xvi. §257 These two sets of magnetic lines, isogonics and isoclinics.

2. Corresponding to or depicting the locus of points in a body where each of the principal stresses is in some fixed direction.

1915 FILON & COKER in *Rep. Brit. Assoc. Adv. Sci. 1914* 203 The lines of principal stress are parallel to the axes of the Nicols... These may be called the lines of equal inclination or isoclinic lines. **1939** *Jrnl. Appl. Physics* X. 254/1 The direction of the stresses are taken from the isoclinic sketch. **1966** *McGraw-Hill Encycl. Sci. & Technol.* X. 150/1 Isoclinic fringes are a different set of interference patterns made by using white light, removing the quarter wave plates and rotating the polarizer and analyzer a fixed number of degrees. These fringes represent lines making known angles with the principal planes of stress.

B. *sb.* **1.** = ISOCLINAL B.

1892 J. THORNTON *Adv. Physiogr.* xvi. §257 Isoclinic Lines are lines drawn through places which have the same [magnetic] inclination or dip.

2. An isoclinic line or curve.

1924 L. N. G. FILON in *Rep. Brit. Assoc. Adv. Sci. 1923* 352 Consider a point A..through which passes the isoclinic of parameter ϕ. *Ibid.* 353 The isoclinics are usually well-defined brushes, of which the direction, at any point, can be observed with considerable accuracy. **1948** M. M. FROCHT *Photoelasticity* II. iv. 147 All isoclinics above the X axis pass through the point of application of the down-ward load and those below the X axis pass through the point of application of the upward load. *Ibid.* 150 The isoclinics are all horizontal where they intersect the boundary of the disk. **1958** CONDON & ODISHAW *Handbk. Physics* III. vi. 86/2 Isoclinics stand out more sharply against colored backgrounds.

isocolic (aɪsəʊ'kɒlɪk), *a. Gr. Rhet.* and *Pros.* [f. as ISOCOLON + IC. Cf. mod.F. *isocole* (Littré).] Consisting, as a sentence or period, of 'cola', members, or clauses, of equal length. Also (irreg.) †**isoco'letic** *a. Obs.* (in quot. loosely applied to the members themselves).

1652 URQUHART *Jewel* Wks. (1834) 293 The harmony of a well-concerted period, in its isocoletick and parisonal members.

isocolloid: see ISO-.

‖**isocolon** (aɪsəʊ'kəʊlən). *Gr. Rhet.* and *Pros.* [f. Gr. ἰσόκωλ-ος, -ον of equal members or clauses, f. ἰσο-, ISO- + κῶλον limb, member, COLON. Also in mod.F. (Littré).] **a.** The use of equal 'cola' or members of a period in immediate succession. **b.** An isocolic period.

1550 R. SHERRY *Treat. Schemes & Tropes* sig. D5 Isocolon. Compar, euen or equall, is when the oracion hath in it the partes of the whyche we spake before (Articulus, Dialyton), and that they be made of euen number of sillables: but thys equalitie must not stand by numbryng of them, but by perceyuyng of it in the mynd. **1706** PHILLIPS, *Isocolon*, a Term us'd when two Sentences are alike in length. **1941** *English Studies* XXIII. 16 When we start looking for Pettie's isocolon we do find an average of 8·5 words, but there is much more irregularity than in Lyly. **1962** [see AGNOMINATION 2].

isocortex: see ISO-.

i-socoured, ME. pa. pple. of SUCCOUR *v.*

isocracy (aɪ'sɒkrəsɪ). [ad. Gr. ἰσοκρατία equality of power or political rights, f. ἰσο-, ISO- + κράτος, κρατε- strength, power: see -CRACY.] Equality of power or rule; a system of government in which all the people possess equal political power.

1652 L. S. *People's Liberty* vii. 12 It remaineth doubtfull, whether people who live together, may lawfully retain an Isocracie among them. **1796** SOUTHEY in *Life* I. 265 There is a very seditious Spaniard there now, preaching Atheism and Isocracy. **1879** F. HALL in *Nation* (N.Y.) XXVIII. 155/1 Aspirations after social isocracy, and socialism in all its protean aspects. **1895** *Q. Rev.* Apr. 456 A debasing isocracy, which already views with suspicion the cultivation of the highest literature as savouring of patrician insolence.

So **isocrat** ('aɪsəʊkræt) [see -CRAT], an advocate of isocracy; **iso'cratic** *a.*, of or pertaining to or advocating isocracy; **i'socratize** *v.* ? *intr.* to practise isocracy.

1801 SOUTHEY *Comm.-pl. Bk.* Ser. IV. (1851) 3/2 The young hopes and heat of Japhet may force him into a livelier interest; he should be for isocratizing. **1894** *Daily News* 22 June 6/3 The new name which Mr. Allen suggests and Mr. Reid adopts is 'The Isocratic Party. Isocrats we are, Isocrats let us call ourselves'.

isocrymal (aɪsəʊ'kraɪməl), *a.* and *sb. Phys. Geog.* [f. ISO- + Gr. κρυμός cold + -AL¹.] A. *adj.* Applied to lines on a map, etc. connecting places at which the temperature is the same during a specified coldest part (*e.g.* the coldest 30 consecutive days) of the year. **B.** *sb.* An isocrymal line; also **isocryme** ('aɪsəʊkraɪm).

1852 DANA *Crust.* II. 1451 The lines are isocheimal lines, or, more properly, *isocrymal* lines. *Ibid.* 1453 It is..an objection to using the isotheres, that those towards the equator are much more irregular in course than the isocrymes. *Ibid.* 1456 The fitness of the other isocrymals for the purposes of illustrating the geographical distribution of marine species.

isocyanate to **isodactylous**: see ISO-.

i-sodden, i-sode(n, ME. pa. pple. of SEETHE *v.*

isodiabatic (,aɪsəʊdaɪə'bætɪk), *a. Physics.* [f. ISO- + Gr. διαβατικός able to pass through; cf. ADIABATIC.] Relating to or indicating the transmission of equal amounts of heat to and from a body or substance.

[**1854** RANKINE in *Phil. Trans.* CXLIV. I. 128 It is required to find, by the determination of points, a corresponding curve passing through a given point *B*, such, that the quantity of heat absorbed or emitted by the substance in passing from any given isothermal curve to another, shall be the same, whether the pressures and volumes be regulated according to the original curve, or according to the curve passing through the point *B*... This curve, and the curve *EF*, in their relation to each other, may be called *Curves of Equal Transmission*.] **1859** —— *Steam Eng.* (1861) 345 The lines *EF* and *GH* have the required property, and are said to be isodiabatic with respect to each other.

isodiametric (aɪsəʊdaɪə'mɛtrɪk), *a.* [f. ISO- + DIAMETRIC.] Having equal diameters; *spec.* applied in *Bot.* to cells of rounded or polyhedral form; in *Cryst.* to crystals having equal lateral axes.

1884 BOWER & SCOTT *De Bary's Phaner.* 117 The forms of thin-walled parenchymatous cells are in the main nearly iso-diametric; but there often occur also elongated-prismatic, spindle-shaped cells, and the like. **1885** GOODALE *Phys. Bot.* (1892) 60 Three principal shapes [of cells] may be.. distinguished..short or isodiametric, elongated, and flattened.

So **isodia'metrical** *a.* = prec.

1886 *Jrnl. R. Microsc. Soc.* Ser. II. VI. I. 109 Cells..which may be either iso-diametrical or elongated in a direction either parallel to or at right-angles with the axis.

isodimorphous, -ism: see ISO-.

‖**isodomon, -mum** (aɪ'sɒdəʊmən, -məm). *Anc. Gr. Arch.* [Gr. ἰσόδομον (L. *isodomum*), neuter adj., f. ἰσο-, ISO- + δόμος layer or course in a building.] A method of building in which blocks of equal length were laid in courses of uniform thickness, each vertical joint of a course being above the middle of a block in the course next below.

1601 HOLLAND *Pliny* II. 593 The Greekes haue a kinde of wall which they make of hard pebbles or flint couched euen and laid in order by line and leuell, like as we do in bricke wals: and this kind of building they call in Masonrie Isodomon. **1842-76** GWILT *Archit.* (ed. 7) Gloss., *Isodomum*, one of the methods of building walls practised by the Greeks.

isodomous (aɪ'sɒdəməs), *a.* [f. as prec. + -OUS.] Of the nature of, or belonging to, isodomon.

1850 LEITCH tr. *C. O. Müller's Anc. Art* (ed. 2) 219 The walls are isodomous or pseudisodomous, often also with oblique joints. **1865** C. T. NEWTON *Trav. Levant* viii. 95 At the foot..is a piece of ancient wall, composed partly of polygonal, partly of isodomous blocks.

isodose ('aɪsəʊdəʊs). [f. ISO- + DOSE *sb.*] An imaginary line or surface, or a graphical representation of one, connecting points, esp. points in the body, that receive equal doses of radiation; now always used *attrib.*, esp. of such lines and surfaces and of diagrams depicting them.

1922 H. SCHMITZ tr. *Kroenig & Friedrich's Princ. Physics & Biol. Radiation Therapy* 249 To render a graphical presentation of the distribution of the dose in radiated tissue one proceeded with the conception that the equal intensity curves of like doses in a body, which we may term 'isodoses', are spheres which surround the center of the preparation concentrically. *Ibid.*, The isodoses of such strong capsules as are used in deep therapy must deviate from the circular or cylindrical forms. **1923** O. GLASSER in *Amer. Jrnl. Roentgenology* X. 405 (*heading*) Isodose charts. *Ibid.* 405/2 The curves are called 'isodoses' a name I gave first to these curves in connection with radium five years ago. **1939** *Brit. Jrnl. Radiol.* XII. 263/1 The isodose curves or dose contours cut out in space complex solids whose surfaces are 'isodose surfaces'. **1950** *Rev. Sci. Instruments* XXI. 363/1 The automatic isodose recorder..satisfies the demand for tracing radiation fields with a good accuracy in a short length of time. *Ibid.* 365/1 Both the speed of the isodose tracing and the accuracy..are quite adequate. **1956** HINE & BROWNELL *Radiation Dosimetry* xii. 573 (*caption*) Isodose contours for cancer of the esophagus obtained by combining six 6 × 15-cm fields using Co^{60}. **1966** R. D. CADLE *Particles in Atmosphere & Space* iv. 104 Fallout patterns are maps consisting of families of isodose rate lines or contours. **1968** *Brit. Med. Bull.* XXIV. 242/1 The computer produced a mass of figures..which were easily converted with an x-y plotter to an isodose distribution form, with which all radio-therapists are familiar.

isodrin ('aɪsəʊdrɪn). [f. ISO- b + AL)DRIN.] An insecticide that is a stereoisomer of aldrin, $C_{12}H_8Cl_6$.

1953 *Rev. Appl. Entomol.* XLI. 144 Isodrin is defined by the Committee as 1,2,3,4,10,10-hexachloro-1,4,4a,5,8,8a-hexahydro-1,4,5,8-endo-endo-dimethanonaphthalene. **1955** *Jrnl. Hort. Sci.* XXX. 181 Isodrin and endrin are newer insecticides, but show great promise in their versatility of action; control of such completely different insects as aphids and cut-worms has been obtained by their use. **1971** *Jrnl. Agric. & Food Chem.* XIX. 5/1 Homogenates prepared from the excised roots of bean seedlings..oxidized isodrin, producing a compound corresponding chromatographically to endrin ketone.

isodynamic (,aɪsəʊdɪ'næmɪk), *a.* (*sb.*) [f. Gr. ἰσοδύναμ-ος equal in power + -IC: after *dynamic.*] Of or pertaining to equal force.

1. *Phys. Geog.*, etc. Indicating equal (magnetic) force; applied to lines connecting points (of the earth's surface, etc.) at which the intensity of the magnetic force is the same; or to a map or chart on which such lines are marked. Also as *sb.* An isodynamic line.

1837 BREWSTER *Magnet.* 254 M. Hansteen has projected on a map of the globe the lines passing through the places in which the [magnetic] intensity has the same value. These lines he calls isodynamic lines or those of equal force, and they are, generally speaking, nearly parallel to each other, and to the lines of equal dip. **1839** SABINE (*title*) Report on the Magnetic Isoclinal and Isodynamic Lines in the British Islands. **1857** WHEWELL *Hist. Induct. Sc.* (ed. 3) III. 52 The intensity of the magnetic force is expressed by charts..on which are drawn the isodynamic..curves.

2. Of equal force, value, or efficacy.

1842 *Blackw. Mag.* LII. 729 Forty gallons of water..in the 'Black Hole' of Calcutta, would have been rated..as isodynamic with gold.

isody'namical, *a.* [f. as prec. + -AL¹.] = prec. 1.

1837 BREWSTER *Magnet.* 31 Professor Hansteen resolved ..to determine the form of the lines of equal intensity, or, as he calls them, the *isodynamical* magnetic lines. **1870** R. M. FERGUSON *Electr.* 44 In 1837, Colonel Sabine published an isodynamical chart of the whole globe.

isodynamous (aɪsəʊ'dɪnəməs), *a. Bot.* [f. as prec. + -OUS.] Growing with equal vigour on both sides: = *isobryous* (see ISO-).

1835 LINDLEY *Introd. Bot.* (1848) II. 67 Cassini suggests isodynamous or isobrious for dicotyledons. **1855** in MAYNE.

isoelectric (aɪsəʊɪ'lɛktrɪk), *a.* [f. ISO- + ELECTRIC *a.*] **1.** Equal in electrical potential; containing or indicating no potential difference.

1877 ROSENTHAL *Muscles & Nerves* 179 On the outside of the cylinder these iso-electric surfaces are exposed. **1901** J. H. RAYMOND *Human Physiol.* (ed. 2) 445 A normal muscle in a condition of rest is iso-electric—*i.e.*, it is 'equally electric throughout, and hence has no electric current'; the same is true of dead muscle. **1940** SCHERF & BOYD *Clin. Electrocardiogr.* 2 The two waves are separated from each other by a short isoelectric line. **1972** T. P. FORDE in R. G. Sanderson *Cardiac Patient* iv. 149 The electrocardiographic tracing is flat or isoelectric during this event.

2. (Composed of particles) having no net electric charge; equal as regards electric charge;

chiefly in ***isoelectric point***, the point (usually *p*H value) at which an amphoteric molecule or a colloidal particle is electrically neutral in a solution.

1900 W. B. HARDY in *Proc. R. Soc.* LXVI. 112 It is clear that there exists some point at which the particles and the fluid in which they are immersed are iso-electric. This iso-electric point is found to be one of great importance. As it is neared, the stability of the hydrosol diminishes until, at the iso-electric point, it vanishes, and coagulation or precipitation occurs. **1922** J. LOEB *Proteins & Theory Colloidal Behavior* i. 6 The conception of the 'isoelectric point' of proteins was introduced before its chemical meaning was recognized and it attracted attention because it was connected with the precipitation of colloids. *Ibid.* iv. 42 When an acid, *e.g.*, HCl, is added to isoelectric gelatin (or any other isoelectric protein), an equilibrium is established between free HCl, protein chloride, and non-ionogenic (or isoelectric) protein. **1946** P. H. MITCHELL *Textbk. Biochem.* iv. 107 Crystallization of a protein is usually carried out at its isoelectric point. **1958** PACKER & VAUGHAN *Mod. Approach Org. Chem.* xiii. 433 In a solution at the isoelectric point, amino acid molecules will not migrate in the electric field created by the introduction of a cathode and an anode. **1966** *Acta Chem. Scand.* XX. 821 The peptides isoelectric between pH 5·0 and 6·5 proved to possess poor carrier ampholyte properties.

b. Carried out or occurring at the isoelectric point.

1961 *Acta Chem. Scand.* XV. 326 Isoelectric analysis and fractionation by electric transport is based on sending a direct current through a system of electrolytes such that the pH increases gradually from anode to cathode... Proteins and other ampholytes will..collect in a region where the local pH is identical with the isoelectric point of the ampholyte. **1971** *European Jrnl. Biochem.* XXI. 110/1 One might expect the 'isoelectric coagulation'..to represent a polymerization reaction based on unaltered native molecules.

Hence **isoe'lectrically** *adv. Biochem.*, by making use of the different isoelectric points of the components of a mixture (in order to separate them).

1966 *Acta Chem. Scand.* XX. 834 Viruses with an average molecular weight of 20 × 10^6 can be expected to be isoelectrically resolvable only about three times more effectively than myoglobins. **1970** *Zeitschr. Klin. Chem. Klin. Biochem.* VIII. 383 Iron-free transferrin was separated isoelectrically into 2 components with isoelectric points at pH 5·8 and 5·4.

isoelectronic (ˌaɪsəʊɪlɛk'trɒnɪk), *a. Chem.* and *Physics.* [f. ISO- + ELECTRON[2] + -IC.] (Composed of atoms or molecules) having the same number of electrons. Const. *with.*

1928 *Chem. Rev.* V. 155 Vertical lines represent atoms having the same number of external electrons ('iso-electronic systems'). **1929** *Physical Rev.* XXXIII. 538 The succeeding elements calcium, scandium, titanium, vanadium, etc., are made iso-electronic (that is, having the same number of electrons) with potassium by removing one electron from calcium, two electrons from scandium,..etc. **1946** *Nature* 5 Oct. 480/2 In particular, they have assigned the line at 1,400 $cm.^{-1}$ to NO_2^+, comparison with the isoelectronic molecule CO_2 having shown that a polarized Raman frequency would be expected to appear in this region. **1964** C. CHANDLER *Atomic Spectra* (ed. 2) ix. 138 Ions which have only one electron outside an inert gas shell and are therefore isoelectronic with the alkalis. **1971** *Internat. Jrnl. Quantum Chem.* V. 335 Wave functions of the ^1S (ground state), ^3P and ^1P states for the beryllium isoelectronic sequence have been obtained.

isoenergetic: see ISO-.

isoenzyme ('aɪsəʊˌɛnzaɪm). *Biochem.* Also **iso-enzyme.** [f. ISO- + ENZYME.] One of two or more chemically different forms of an enzyme (see quot. 1968). Cf. ISOZYME.

1960 *New England Jrnl. Med.* 15 Sept. 531 (*heading*) Isoenzymes and myocardial infarction. **1964** *Oceanogr. & Marine Biol.* II. 220 Species- and tissue-specific forms of enzymes (iso-enzymes) have been reported in animal material. **1968** LATNER & SKILLEN *Isoenzymes in Biol. & Med.* i. 1 It is now well recognized that a large number of enzymes exist in multiple forms. This applies not only to tissues and tissue extracts but also to enzyme proteins which have been isolated in the crystalline state and are really mixtures. Isoenzymes are examples of these multiple forms. Precise definition of the word 'isoenzyme' is, however, rather difficult. Different tissues of the same individual or even of different species may possess closely similar enzymes, which are not really isoenzymes. For the time being, most authorities believe that a broad definition such as 'different proteins with similar enzymatic activity' best suits the current state of our knowledge. It is customary, for the most part, to limit this definition to multiple enzymes obtained from one tissue of one individual animal or plant or possibly a small organ, or a culture of a unicellular organism. An exception would be the major multiple forms of human alkaline phosphatase. They are nevertheless referred to as isoenzymes. **1970** *Nature* 30 May 862/1 The enzyme glucose-6-phosphate dehydrogenase..exists in several different forms (isoenzymes) in the human erythrocyte... The structural differences between the isoenzymes lead to different enzymatic activities.

Hence **isoen'zymic** *a.*

1968 *Brit. Med. Bull.* XXIV. 222/2 Chemical differences between individuals have been much studied..for example ..the occurrence of isoenzymic variants of a number of well-known enzymes.

isoetes (aɪ'səʊɪtiːz, aɪsəʊ'iːtiːz). [mod.L. (Linnæus *Skånska Resa* (1751) 417), f. Gr. ἰσοετής, f. ἴσος equal + ἔτος year: the plants are evergreen.] An aquatic plant of the genus so called; = *quill-wort* (s.v. QUILL *sb.*[1] 8 b).

1886 *Encycl. Brit.* XX. 431/2 An Isoetes plant was produced on the leaf instead of a sporangium. **1910** *Rep. Brit. Assoc. Adv. Sci.* 784 The whole axis of the *Isoëtes* plant can be compared with that of *Lepidodendron.* **1965** R. F. SCAGEL et al. *Evolutionary Survey Plant Kingdom* xix. 375/1 One of the most distinctive vascular plants, *Isoetes*, consists of a thick mass of tubular to strap-shaped leaves borne in a rosette on a very short stem.

isoeugenol: see ISO-.

isofagus, obs. erron. f. ŒSOPHAGUS.

isoflavone: see ISO-.

isoflor ('aɪsəʊflɔə(r)). [f. ISO- + FLOR(A rendering G. *isoporie* (W. Rothmaler 1938, in *Beih. Rep. Spec. Nov. Reg. Veg.* C. 89), perh. f. Gr. πορεία load.] A line (imaginary or on a map) linking areas containing equal numbers of plant species.

1944 S. A. CAIN *Found. Plant Geogr.* xii. 163 Isoflors, lines delimiting regions with equal numbers of species (within the circle of affinity), can be drawn for the generic area as a whole. **1960** N. POLUNIN *Introd. Plant Geogr.* vii. 208 Sometimes a fair one [*sc.* indication of a centre of origin] may be given by isoflors, which are lines delimiting regions supporting equal numbers of species. **1963** DAVIS & HEYWOOD *Princ. Angiosperm Taxon.* ix. 317 In the construction of isoflors, it is not the distribution of the individual species that is important, but only the number of species occurring together at any one point. In order to produce the isoflor map, a grid is drawn on the map and the number of taxa noted which occur in each quadrat.

isogam ('aɪsəʊgæm). [app. f. ISO- + GAM(MA.] **1.** A line (imaginary or on a map) connecting points where the acceleration due to gravity has the same value. Freq. *attrib.*

1928 *Science* 13 July 37 *Isogam*, surface or line of equal gravitative attraction. **1931** F. H. LAHEE *Field Geol.* (ed. 3) xxiii. 661 *Isogam* is the name applied to lines of equal value of relative or absolute gravity. Isogam maps.. are used to picture the variation of gravity. **1940** *Geogr. Jrnl.* XCV. 135 The gravity pendulum..cannot produce a survey of gravity in which isogams at 2 milligal intervals can be drawn with confidence. **1954** *Geophysical Suppl. Monthly Notices R. Astron. Soc.* VI. 180 The easiest approach to the problem.. is to prepare a chart of density anomalies..and next an isogam chart of the gravity effect of these density anomalies.

2. [cf. GAMMA 1 c (iv).] An isodynamic line.

1940 L. L. NETTLETON *Geophysical Prospecting for Oil* viii. 163 Contours, or lines of equal magnetic intensity, are commonly called 'isogams'. **1965** G. J. WILLIAMS *Econ. Geol. N.Z.* xix. 354/2 A recent magnetic survey revealed a group of high values corresponding fairly well with the inferred position of the anticline; the trend of the isogams and of the high axis is almost parallel to that of the axis.

isogamy (aɪ'sɒgəmɪ). *Biol.* [f. ISO- + Gr. γάμος, -γαμια marriage.] The union of two equal and similar 'gametes' or cells in reproduction, as in conjugation. So **isogamete** (aɪ'sɒgəmiːt) [Gr. γαμέτης, γαμετή spouse], each of the two uniting cells, in isogamy. **isogamous** (aɪ'sɒgəməs) *a.*, characterized by isogamy.

1889 BENNETT & MURRAY *Handbk. Cryptogamic Bot.* 272 The only known sexual mode of reproduction [in the Confervoideae] is an isogamous one between two masses of protoplasm. **1891** HARTOG in *Nature* 17 Sept. 484 *Isogamy*, the union of gametes undistinguishable in size, form, and behaviour. *Ibid.*, The union may be isogamous or anisogamous. *Ibid.*, True Parthenogenesis..may occur in the case of (1) Isogametes (2) Anisogametes (male and female); (3) Oogametes. **1935** F. E. FRITSCH *Struct. & Reprod. Algae* I. 43 Isogamy (i.e. the fusion of morphologically identical gametes) is very usually.. combined with an absence of differentiated organs for the production of the sexual cells or gametes. *Ibid.* 46 Isogametes are commonly positively phototactic. **1938** G. M. SMITH *Cryptogamic Bot.* I. ii. 21 All green algae in which both gametes are nonflagellated..are isogamous. **1952** C. J. ALEXOPOULOS *Introd. Mycol.* i. 17 We use the terms isogametangia and isogametes..to designate gametangia and gametes which are morphologically indistinguishable. **1964** E. J. H. CORNER *Life of Plants* vi. 85 The process is called isogamy or the union of outwardly similar gametes. **1968** BELL & WOODCOCK *Diversity of Green Plants* ii. 39 The gametes [of *Stigeoclonium*] are noticeably smaller than the zoospores, and copulation is isogamous.

isogel: see ISO-.

isogen ('aɪsədʒɛn). [f. ISO- + Gr. γένος offspring.] A line or curve in a diagram showing the various combination of the ages of the parents which are associated with the same average birthrate.

1894 F. GALTON in *Proc. Royal Soc.* 12 Jan., In natality tables, the ages of the father and mother take the place of the latitudes and longitudes in weather charts, and lines of similar birth-rates, or, as I would call them, 'isogens', take the place of isobars.

isogeneic (aɪsəʊdʒɛ'niːɪk, -'eɪɪk), *a. Immunol.* [f. ISO- + Gr. γενε-ά race, stock + -IC.] = SYNGENEIC *a.*

1963 HUMPHREY & WHITE *Immunol. for Students of Med.* xi. 359 When grafts are made..from one animal to another isogeneic animal they are 'isografts'. *Ibid.* 365 Since surgeons rarely have the opportunity of working with isogeneic patients, successful grafting has been largely limited to autografts. **1973** *Nature* 23 Mar. 259/2 An animal strain in which inbred immunologically isogeneic lines are available, making possible transplantation studies uncomplicated by rejection problems.

isogenic (aɪsəʊ'dʒɛnɪk, aɪsəʊ'dʒiːnɪk), *a. Biol.* [ad. G. *isogen* (W. Johannsen *Elem. d. exakten Erblichkeitslehre* (ed. 2, 1913) xii. 208), f. ISO- + GEN(E + -IC.] Having the same genotype (GENOTYPE *sb.*[2]).

1933 *Biochem. Jrnl.* XXVII. 6 In all the work discussed in this paper we have, unless otherwise stated, compared only isogenic animals (animals of the same sex and from the same litter). **1943** *Proc. Nat. Acad. Sci.* XXIX. 361 Three homozygous stocks were obtained, which were isogenic except for the fourth chromosome. **1950** *Jrnl. Exper. Zool.* CXIII. 123 To obtain a culture isogenic with the recessive parent, employ the usual backcross procedure. **1956** *Nature* 7 Jan. 42/2 Males of a wild-type ('Canton-S') stock of *Drosophila melanogaster*, which had been made isogenic some time before the experiments, were crossed to homozygous *ci ey*[R] females. **1970** *Ibid.* 7 Feb. 557/1 This method..is especially suitable for characters in which the distributions of the isogenic parental strains are not clearly dichotomous. **1973** *Ibid.* 9 Feb. 383/2 The relatively uniform appearance and behaviour of the aggressive isolates suggest that these are highly isogenic, possibly with a recent origin from a single clone.

isogenous (aɪ'sɒdʒɪnəs), *a. Biol.* [f. eccl. Gr. ἰσογενή-ς equal in kind or nature (f. ἰσο-, ISO- + γένος race, descent, kind) + -OUS.] Having the same or a similar origin: said of organs or parts, in different groups of animals, derived from the same or corresponding tissue of the embryo. So **i'sogeny**, the condition of being isogenous.

1884 *Stand. Nat. Hist.* (1888) I. Introd. 17 A general homology may be indicated by the word isogeny, indicating a general similarity of origin; thus, the nervous systems of worms, arthropods, molluscs, and vertebrates are isogenous, all being derivations of the epiblast.

isogeotherm (aɪsəʊ'dʒiːəʊθɜːm). *Phys. Geog.* [f. ISO- + Gr. γεω- earth + θέρμη heat, θερμός hot: cf. *geothermic*, etc.] A line or surface (usually imaginary) connecting points in the interior of the earth having the same temperature; an isogeothermal line.

1864 in WEBSTER. **1877** LE CONTE *Elem. Geol.* II. (1879) 78 If the rate of increase were everywhere the same, the isogeotherms would be everywhere concentric. **1881** JUDD *Volcanoes* xii. 359 The isogeotherms, or lines indicating the depths at which the same mean temperature is found within the earth's crust.

Hence **isogeo'thermal, isogeo'thermic** *adjs.*, of the nature of an isogeotherm; indicating equal temperatures in the interior of the earth.

1832 DE LA BECHE *Geol. Man.* (ed. 2) 15 If we draw lines through all the points which have the same terrestrial temperature, these *isogeothermal lines* resemble the isothermal, as they are parallel to the equator, but diverge from it in several points. **1834** MRS. SOMERVILLE *Connex. Phys. Sc.* xxvi. (1849) 289 Lines drawn through all those points in the upper strata of the globe which have the same mean annual temperature..are isogeothermal lines.

isogloss ('aɪsəʊglɒs). [a. G. *isogloss* (A. Bielenstein *Die Grenzen des Lettischen Volksstammes* (1892) 397, f. ISO- + GLOSS *sb.*[1]] In Linguistic Geography, the boundary of an area of local concentration or dominance of a significant feature (as of vocabulary or pronunciation). Also, a line plotted on a map indicating the area in which such a feature is concentrated or is dominant. Hence **iso'glossic** *a.*

1925 O. JESPERSEN *Mankind, Nation & Individual* iii. 41 As a rule we find that the frontiers for one phenomenon do not exactly coincide with the frontiers for another, so that the 'isoglosses' (as such frontiers of single phenomena are called) sometimes agree, sometimes run somewhat parallel with one another, but fairly often cross one another in the most distracting manner. **1927** L. BLOOMFIELD in *Mod. Philology* Nov. 220 The boundaries of successive linguistic changes (isogloss lines) do not coincide... Isoglosses may be bundled along barriers to communication; if the barrier (e.g., a political boundary) is removed, the isoglossic bundle may be overlaid by later linguistic development. **1933** —— *Lang.* iii. 51 Within a dialect area, we can draw lines between places which differ as to any feature of language. Such lines are called isoglosses. **1949** H. KURATH *Word Geogr. Eastern U.S.* 11 In figure 2 the focus of each of the more distinctive sub-areas of the Eastern States is set off by a single word line or isogloss. **1953** J. B. CARROLL *Study of Lang.* ii. 59 The purpose of linguistic geography is to make a detailed analysis of local linguistic variations... Efforts are made to establish isoglosses, which may be described as cartographic lines separating the geographical localities which show a difference with respect to a specific linguistic item. **1955** *Publ. Amer. Dialect Soc.* XXIII. 40 When it [*sc.* a form] is found within a sharply defined area, one may draw a line called an isogloss, to indicate the boundaries of the area in which this form occurs. **1958** *Ibid.* XXX. 3 But a number of lexical terms do not occur in geographical patterns corresponding to the isogloss divisions for known Northern and Midland features. **1964** H. B. ALLEN in A. A. Marckwardt *Stud. Lang. & Ling. in Honor C.C. Fries* 305 The major isogloss bundle is shown on the map by the 1-1 line. **1968** *Amer. Speech* XLIII. 185 It is separated from other dialects of Yiddish by a bundle of grammatical, phonological, and lexical isoglosses. **1968** W. S. ALLEN *Vox Graeca* i. 12 The ττ of pure Attic is part of an isogloss having its probable point of origin in Boeotian. **1972** H. KURATH *Stud. Area Ling.* 60 The location of some representative isoglossic lines..is shown in Figure 21.

Hence also **iso'glottal, -glottic** *adjs.*

1932 *Missouri Alumnus* Apr. 232/1 The American Council of Learned Societies is financing a 'Dialect Atlas of the United States and Canada', and already the workers are making a survey of New England. They have a 'work-sheet' of 800 questions which bring to light the notable speech variations, and from the information so gathered they construct maps with 'iso-glottal' lines like those on a topographic map. **1939** L. H. GRAY *Foundations of Lang.* ii. 26 Such lines are termed isoglottic lines or isographs. **1954** *Word* X. 375 The location of different isoglottic lines did not coincide in one linguistic area.

isogon (ˈaɪsəgɒn). *Geom. rare*$^{-0}$. In 7–8 *erron.* isagon. [f. Gr. ἰσογώνι-ος equi-angular.] A figure having equal angles.
1696 PHILLIPS (ed. 5), *Isagon.* So **1700** in MOXON *Math. Dict.*; **1721** in BAILEY.

isogonal (aɪˈsɒgənəl), *a.* (*sb.*) [f. as prec. + -AL[1]: cf. *hexagonal*, etc.]
1. = ISOGONIC *a.*[1] and *sb.*
1857 WHEWELL *Hist. Induct. Sc.* (ed. 3) III. 52 The values of these elements at any given time..can be expressed by charts of the earth's surface, on which are drawn the isodynamic, isogonal, and isoclinal curves. *Ibid.* 54 The isogonal curves may be looked upon as deformations of the curves deduced by Euler from the supposition of two poles.
2. Having equal angles, equiangular.
1878 GURNEY *Crystallogr.* 21 When the angles between every two adjacent planes lying in one zone are equal to each other they constitute an isogonal (or equal-angled) zone.

isogonic (aɪsəʊˈgɒnɪk), *a.*[1] (*sb.*) *Phys. Geog.* [f. as prec. + -IC.] Indicating equal angles (of magnetic variation); applied to lines on a map, etc. connecting points of the earth's surface where the magnetic declination, or variation from the true north, is the same; or to a map, etc. exhibiting such lines. Also as *sb.* An isogonic line.
1851–9 SABINE in *Man. Sci. Enq.* 97 The Isogonic lines.. have a direct practical importance and value in navigation. **1870** R. M. FERGUSON *Electr.* 27 The lines of equal declination are called *isogonic* lines; those of equal dip, *isoclinic*; and those of equal intensity, *isodynamic* lines. **1876** DAVIS *Polaris Exp.* App. 642 With regard to the variations of the compass, as derived from an isogonic chart. **1892** J. THORNTON *Adv. Physiogr.* xvi. §257 These two sets of magnetic lines, isogonics and isoclinics.

iso'gonic, *a.*[2] *Biol.* [ad. Fr. *isogonique* (A. Pézard 1918, in *Bull. Biol. de la France et de la Belgique* LII. 24).] Characterized by isogonism. Of an organ, growing at the same rate as its parent body. So **i'sogony**, growth of this kind.
1901 In mod. Dicts. **1924** J. S. HUXLEY in *Nature* 20 Dec. 895/1 Pézard..has styled the growth of such an organ heterogonic..as opposed to isogonic. **1932** —— *Probl. Relative Growth* 1. ii. 8 An organ which..is growing at the same rate as the body..must be styled isogonic. *Ibid.* iii. 38 It is justifiable to regard isogony as a special case of heterogony, with growth-coefficiency unity. **1945** RICHARDS & KAVANAGH in Clark & Medawar *Ess. Growth & Form* 219 Isogonic growth is a special case of isotropic growth in which the specific growth-rate in length is the same at every point throughout the organism.

isogonism (aɪˈsɒgənɪz(ə)m). *Biol.* [f. ISO- + Gr. γόνος, γον-ή offspring + -ISM. Cf. Gr. ἰσογονία equality of kind.] The production of sexual individuals of the same structure from different stocks, occurring in some *Hydrozoa*.
1884 SEDGWICK & HEATHCOTE tr. *Claus' Zool.* I. vii. 240 Medusæ of identical structure also, which one would place in the same genus, may form the sexual generations of hydroid stocks belonging to different families (*isogonism*).

isograd, isograde, isogradic: see ISO-.

isograft (ˈaɪsəʊgrɑːft, -æ-), *sb. Med.* and *Biol.* [f. ISO- + GRAFT *sb.*[1]] **a.** = HOMOGRAFT. Now *rare* or *Obs.*
1909 *Jrnl. Exper. Med.* XI. 194 Three isografts were placed. **1919** J. S. DAVIS *Plastic Surg.* iv. 50, I have thought for some time that the success or failure of isografts may be dependent on the similarity or dissimilarity of blood groups of the host and donor. **1942** J. P. WEBSTER in F. Christopher *Textbk. Surg.* (ed. 3) xxxv. 1587 Successful free corneal isografts have been reported with maintenance of transparency. **1950** F. SMITH *Plastic & Reconstruction Surg.* i. 27 Homograft, homologous graft and isograft are synonymous terms indicating tissue transplanted from one to another person of the same species.
b. A graft taken from an identical twin of the recipient or from an animal of the same inbred strain.
1958 *Immunology* I. 1 Adrenal cortical grafts transplanted between members of an inbred strain of mice ('isografts') are held to be successful when they empower adrenalectomised mice to subsist on a diet low in NaCl. *Ibid.* 6 Homografts transplanted to the brain and testis were significantly inferior to isografts. **1963** HUMPHREY & WHITE *Immunol. for Students of Med.* xi. 359 Isografts usually also take permanently, although even within a pure line of mice male skin may be rejected by a female recipient, by virtue of the fact that the Y chromosome can carry sex-linked genetic differences. **1970** *Microvascular Res.* II. 91 The vascular dilation and petechiae, which were observed in the skin isografts in animals treated with cortisol, were similar in the allograft group.

isograft (ˈaɪsəʊgrɑːft, -æ-), *v. Med.* and *Biol.* [f. ISO- + GRAFT *v.*[1] or f. prec.] *trans.* **a.** To transplant from one individual to another of the same species; = HOMOTRANSPLANT *v.* **b.** To transplant between identical twins or animals of the same inbred strain. So **'isografted** *ppl. a.*, **'isografting** *vbl. sb.*
1909 *Jrnl. Exper. Med.* XI. 194 The following day the isografting was made. **1919** J. S. DAVIS *Plastic Surg.* iv. 50 Care must be taken when isografting is contemplated, not to transmit disease to a healthy person. **1959** *Proc. Soc. Exper. Biol. & Med.* CII. 651/1 (*caption*) Light-dark synchronized activity rhythm whether or not pituitaries were isografted. **1962** *Dissertation Abstr.* XXII. 2829/1 The sex of the recipient animal had no effect on the survival of isografted fetal tissue. **1970** *Zeitschr. für Anat. & Entwickl.-Gesch.* CXXXII. 318, 92 mammary duct-segments..were excised ..and microdissected for isografting into the fourth mammary gland-free fat pads of the 46 female hosts.

isogram (ˈaɪsəgræm). [f. ISO- + -GRAM.] A proposed general term for lines on a diagram, etc. indicating equality of some physical condition or quantity, as isotherms, isobars, etc.
1889 F. GALTON in *Nature* 31 Oct. 651 Isobars, isotherms, and other contour lines..(to which the general name *isograms* might well be given).

isograph (ˈaɪsəʊgrɑːf, -æ-). [f. ISO- + -GRAPH.]
1. A drawing instrument (see quots.).
1838 *Civil Engin. & Arch. Jrnl.* I. 349/1 These are a set of triangular rulers, drawing paper, with the lines and ellipses described upon it, and the isograph which consists of a number of rulers, made of brass or ivory, the fiducial edge of each being an inch apart, and parallel to each other. **1909** WEBSTER, *Isograph*, an instrument consisting of two short straightedges connected by a large circular joint marked with angular degrees, used with a T square on a drawing board and combining the functions of a protractor and a set square. **1926–7** *Army & Navy Stores Catal.* 456/1 Isograph. 12 in. boxwood, brass joint.
2. *Linguistics.* (See quots.)
1939 L. H. GRAY *Foundations of Lang.* ii. 26 Certain features of any one of the dialects will be common to some of the rest..so that it will be possible to draw upon a map lines indicating at least the approximate boundaries of these features... Such lines are termed isoglottic lines or isographs. **1954** PEI & GAYNOR *Dict. Ling.* 106 *Isograph*, any line on a linguistic map, indicating a uniformity in the use of sounds, vocabulary, syntax, inflexion, etc.

isographic (aɪsəʊˈgræfɪk), *a.* [f. ISO- + -GRAPHIC. Cf. Gr. ἰσόγραφος writing like.] = HOMALOGRAPHIC I.
1872 PROCTOR *Ess. Astron.* xxiii. 283 M. Babinet..called it the *homolographic* projection of the globe; the term *isographic* seems preferable, however.
Hence **iso'graphically** *adv.*, in the way of isographic projection.
1872 PROCTOR *Ess. Astron.* xxiii. 284 There is no single point for which any finite area of the globe can be isographically projected. **1885** A. M. CLERKE *Astron. 19th Cent.* xii. 437 The laborious process of isographically charting the whole of Argelander's 324,000 stars.

isography (aɪˈsɒgrəfɪ). *rare*$^{-0}$. [f. ISO- + -GRAPHY.] (See quot.)
1846 WORCESTER, *Isography*, imitation of handwriting. *Ency.*

isogynous to **isohelic:** see ISO-.

isohydric (aɪsəʊˈhaɪdrɪk), *a.* [ad. G. *isohydrisch* (S. Arrhenius 1887, in *Ann. d. Physik u. Chem.* XXX. 54): see ISO- and HYDRIC *a.*] **a.** *Physical Chem.* Having the same hydrogen ion concentration; maintaining the same hydrogen ion concentration after mixing; also used with reference to other ions.
1887 *Jrnl. Chem. Soc.* LII. I. 415 The molecular conductivity of a mixture of butyric and acetic acid solutions in any proportions is always the sum of the molecular conductivities of the constituent solutions. Each electrolyte behaves as if the other were absent. Such solutions are termed by the author [*sc.* S. Arrhenius] 'isohydric'. **1899** J. WALKER *Introd. Physical Chem.* xxv. 288 Let there be prepared isohydric solutions of the different salts, NaCl being made isohydric with NaBr, by getting the sodium ions of the same concentration in both solutions. **1930** GLASSTONE *Electrochem. Solutions* viii. 151 Solutions of acids which do not change their ionization on mixing are said to be isohydric with one another. **1952** J. E. RICCI *Hydrogen Ion Concentration* ii. 26 We shall here examine the conditions for the validity of the theorem of isohydric solutions, that isohydric solutions (solutions of the same *H*) mix without change of *H*.
b. *Physiol.* Occurring without causing any change in the *p*H of the blood: applied to the reactions by which carbon dioxide is removed from the tissues and taken up by the blood.
1920 *Proc. Soc. Exper. Biol. & Med.* XVII. 181 Curves.. have been obtained, showing an isohydric shift of base between hemoglobin and the other constituents of the blood. **1946** J. F. FULTON *Howell's Textbk. Physiol.* (ed. 15) xxxix. 887 This series of chemical reactions in the erythrocyte has been designated as the isohydric cycle because the uptake of CO_2 and the release of O_2 is accomplished without the production of an excess of H^+. **1954** A. WHITE et al. *Princ. Biochem.* xxvi. 691 The isohydric shift entails formation of about 0·7 meq. of bicarbonate for each millimole of oxygen which dissociates from oxyhemoglobin. **1970** R. W. MCGILVERY *Biochem.* xxv. 612 This action of the Bohr effect to permit the blood to take up CO_2 without a change in pH is known as the isohydric carriage of CO_2.

isohyet to **isohyetose:** see ISO-.

i-soilled, ME. pa. pple. of SOIL *v.*

isoimmune, -immunization: see ISO-.

isoionic (aɪsəʊaɪˈɒnɪk), *a. Physical Chem.* and *Biochem.* [f. ISO- + IONIC *a.*[2]] Of a solute or solution: giving rise to or containing no noncolloidal ions other than those formed by dissociation of the solvent; ***isoionic point***, †***reaction***, the point (usually *p*H value) at which the average number of hydrogen ions attached to the basic groups of solute molecules is equal to the average number dissociated from the acidic groups.
This is the 'theoretical' definition of *isoionic point*; for the 'practical' definitions, see quot. 1959.
1926 LINDERSTRØM-LANG & LUND in *Compt. Rend. Lab. Carlsberg* XVI. v. 22 We will therefore define isoionic reaction as the value of pa_H, $pa_H{}^0$ at which h [*sc.* the specific hydrogen ionisation of the ampholyte] is 0. **1934** *Biochem. Jrnl.* XXVIII. 1257 At 0°, the isoionic point of crystallised haemoglobin was at p_H 7·6. **1943** J. D. EDSALL in Cohn & Edsall *Proteins* xx. 446 If the protein binds no other ions than protons, the isoionic point may correspond to the isoelectric point of the protein... If the protein combines with other ions also, the isoelectric and isoionic points are different. **1949** *Jrnl. Physical & Colloid Chem.* LIII. 88 Operationally we may define the isoionic material as the limit approached by successful electro-dialysis. *Ibid.* 95 We may..calculate the change in pH of a solution which is not isoionic. **1959** LINDERSTRØM-LANG & NIELSEN in M. Bier *Electrophoresis* I. ii. 63 According to the first definition the isoionic point is the pH of the protein solution which does not change on the addition of more isoionic protein. According to the second definition the isoionic point is the pH of a solution of the isoionic protein in water, or in a solution which does not produce H^+ or OH^- ions when dissolved in water alone. Thus a mixture of proteins may be isoionic. **1969** OTTAWAY & IRVINE tr. *Netter's Theoret. Biochem.* vi. 192 Amino acids and proteins are usually characterised by their isoelectric or isoionic point.

i-soke(n, ME. pa. pple. of SUCK *v.*

isokinetic, -kinetically: see ISO-.

isokite (ɪˈsəʊkaɪt). *Min.* [f. *Isok-a*, name of a small town in Zambia: see -ITE[1].] A white, buff, or pinkish phosphate and fluoride of calcium and magnesium, $CaMgPO_4F$.
1955 DEANS & MCCONNELL in *Mineral. Mag.* XXX. 681 The mineral, for which the name isokite is now proposed, occurs in the carbonatite plug which forms Nkumbwa Hill (lat. 10° 10′ S. long. 32° 51′ E), 15 miles east of Isoka (pronounced Isōka) in Northern Rhodesia. *Ibid.* 686 The analysis leaves no doubt that isokite is essentially $CaMgPO_4F$. **1968** I. KOSTOV *Mineral.* II. 463 Tilasite and isokite are monoclinic (*C*2/*c*), isostructural with sphene.

isolable (ˈaɪsələb(ə)l, ˈɪs-), *a.* [f. ISOL-ATE + -ABLE.] Capable of being isolated.
a **1855** MANSFIELD *Salts* (1865) 441 The notion that the complex base H_3NH is a self-existent, probably isolable body. *a* **1856** SIR W. HAMILTON in *Daily News* (1883) 20 Sept. 5/6 Algebra and geometry are..isolated or at least isolable from all outward and accidental phenomena. **1926** A. R. LORD *Princ. Pol.* v. 147 Democracy is no isolable, dead element in the composition of social and political humanity. **1965** W. LAMB *Posture & Gesture* vii. 97 We can demonstrate, however, that there is a distinctly isolable quality of children's physical behaviour.

isolatable (aɪsəʊˈleɪtəb(ə)l), *a.* [f. ISOLAT(E + -ABLE.] = ISOLABLE *a.*
1936 *Chem. Abstr.* XXX. 6354 G[rundmann] has attempted to apply the reaction to certain substituted phenols in order to obtain aliphatic polyene polycarboxylic acids, *o*-Coumaric acid gave, as the only isolatable product, *I* in very small amt. **1949** E. A. NIDA *Morphol.* (ed. 2) ii. 60 The morphemes *cran-*, *rasp-*, and *cray-* are isolatable because the elements *berry* and *fish* occur in isolation or in other combinations. **1957** N. FRYE *Anat. Criticism* 198 Romance, like Comedy, has six isolatable phases. **1964** R. H. ROBINS *Gen. Ling.* vii. 277 The bound morpheme..is likely to be a much less semantically isolatable unit. **1971** *Jrnl. Gen. Psychol.* LXXXIV. 169 Personality is the name for something that is not 'time-bound': that is, it is not an event that occurs in a limited period of time and is not isolatable in the way other categories are.
Hence ˌ**isolata'bility**.
1949 E. A. NIDA *Morphol.* (ed. 2) 59 On the basis of the first condition of isolatability we may identify as morphemes such forms as *boy*, *cow*..since it is possible to utter..these forms in isolation.

isolate (ˈaɪsələt, ˈɪs-), *a.* (*sb.*) [ad. It. *isolato* (F. *isolé*):—L. *insulāt-us* insulated, f. *insula* island: see -ATE[2] 2.] **A.** *adj.* = ISOLATED.
1819 WIFFEN *Aonian Hours* (1820) 30 There isolate it stands. **1840** *Fraser's Mag.* XXII. 616 A thing isolate and apart amongst apparitions. **1854** R. G. LATHAM *Native Races Russian Emp.* 71 The isolate and sporadic Tshud..are called..Karelian. **1890** *Cornh. Mag.* Jan. 78 There is no life so isolate that beauty knows it not. **1923** D. H. LAWRENCE *Kangaroo* vii. 151 In the visible world I am alone, an isolate instance. **1956** R. REDFIELD *Peasant Soc. & Cult.* 8 Little isolate societies. *a* **1963** S. PLATH *Ariel* (1965) 26 These are the isolate, slow faults That kill, that kill, that kill. **1967** T. GUNN *Touch* 33 Drops are isolate on leaves. **1973** *Archivum Linguisticum* IV. 14 'Am' is a bound form, a pronoun which only occurs as an object and never as an isolate form.
B. *sb.* **a.** Something isolated; esp. something abstracted from its normal context for study.
1890 C. L. MORGAN *Anim. Life* 322 We may call the process..isolation, and the products of the process we may term isolates. **1934** *Nature* 8 Dec. 889/2 The method of science to search for useful isolates may easily lead the scientific worker to overlook the reactions of his social environment on his own scientific work. **1937** D. J. B.

Hawkins *Causality & Implication* iii. 57 Perhaps it will be best to use the term *isolate*, meaning what is *isolated* in thought but referring specifically to the factual element which is thus isolated. *Isolate* is an appropriate name for any conceptual object in itself, whether it be a simple character or a complex of characters. **1950** J. E. L. Farradane in *Jrnl. Documentation* June 87 An item of knowledge will thus be an object.. or an abstract.. which is clearly and, at its own level of complexity, uniquely definable, as far as may be possible. Any other item would in reality be composed of two or more concepts, leading to logical confusions. Let us call these items, as defined, isolates. **1951** S. F. Nadel *Found. Social Anthropol.* v. 75 In this sense no legitimate isolate can be discovered more basic than that of a standardized pattern of behaviour rendered unitary and relatively self-contained. **1956** R. Redfield *Peasant Society & Culture* 7 The primitive isolate, the community that is a whole all by itself, ..became the model of research. **1958** *Antiquity* XXXII. 148 Cultural isolates from archaeological material. **1961** *Encounter* May 74 'Homosexuality' is a false isolate, a term covering a number of conditions. **1964** C. D. Needham *Organizing Knowl. in Libraries* vii. 71 The isolates now need grouping so that those which are related are proximate. **1969** A. C. Foskett *Subject Approach to Information* I. v. 56 Copper as a topic taken out of context is an isolate, but if we place it in a facet in a particular basic class we can refer to it as a focus. **1972** *Jrnl. Social Psychol.* LXXXVI. 109 Ss reported that the isolate reduced the homogeneity.

b. *Perfumery.* A compound which is isolated in a more or less pure condition from a natural essential oil for use in perfumery.

1923 W. A. Poucher *Perfumes & Cosmetics* iii. 214 It is usual to combine both with a natural isolate of rose odour such as geraniol. **1949** R. W. Moncrieff *Chem. Perfumery Materials* I. ii. 29 Most of the alcohols used in the perfume industry are isolates rather than synthetics. **1957** E. Sagarin *Cosmetics* xxxiii. 743 Of the chemical bodies used in perfumery, the isolates from plant oils bear the strongest resemblance to the plant materials themselves.

c. *Biol.* A group of like micro-organisms obtained by isolation or culturing for study or experiment; *esp.* a pure culture.

1931 W. B. Brierley in *Ann. Appl. Biol.* XVIII. 421 The procedure I adopt in my *Botrytis* work is as follows. Each separate pure culture made by direct isolation from fresh material, whether a number of cultures are made from a single lesion or from one or more host plants, I term an Isolate. If the first culture direct from the diseased tissue contains, as is very often the case, two or more types, the pure or single-spore isolations from this mixture and not the first impure culture are the isolates. Each isolate is an individual line and sub-cultures are merely duplicates or replicates of that isolate or line. The isolate is the nearest equivalent to Lotsy's 'species'. **1949** H. W. Florey et al. *Antibiotics* I. i. 66 Many surveys for antibiotic activity have been performed on type-culture collections of fungi and on new isolates. **1958** *New Biol.* XXVII. 63 It seems to be no easier to establish experimental infections with isolates of *Candida albicans* derived from epidemic outbreaks than with isolates from any other source. **1971** *E. Afr. Standard* (Nairobi) 13 Apr. 9/8 Identification of isolates and antisera received from associate laboratories in Senegal..continued. **1972** *Nature* 17 Mar. 122/1 In an investigation of this increased severity, isolates of *Ceratocystis ulmi* were made from infected trees in the outbreak regions.

d. *Soc. Psychol.* A person who, either from choice or through separation or rejection, is isolated from normal social interaction; also occas. an animal separated from its kind.

1942 *Psychol. Bull.* XXXIX. 458 Differences in interpersonal capacity for participation with others, differences which are revealed when the personalities of isolates and leaders are studied. **1953** J. L. Moreno *Who shall Survive?* I. 100 A rough classification of the position of the individual in the groups was possible—the isolates, the pairs, and the bunch that clung to the leader. **1963** T. & P. Morris *Pentonville* vii. 174 The retreatist is difficult to detect because he *is* an isolate. **1966** T. Pynchon *Crying of Lot 49* v. 113 Nobody knows anybody else's name... We're isolates, Arnold. Meetings would destroy the whole point of it. **1968** *Observer* (Colour Suppl.) 14 Apr. 36/1 Woolly monkeys..who..live on as 'pets' become desocialised, isolates. **1969** *Sunday Times* (Colour Suppl.) 16 Mar. 23/4 Social isolates..often become so careless of their own welfare that they become undernourished. **1970** *New Scientist* 14 May 319/1 In previous attempts at social rehabilitation, normal monkeys of the same age as the isolates were placed in the cage with them. But the isolate ignored its visitor.

e. *Biol.* A group of plants or animals which has developed characteristics distinct from those of the parent species through the operation of an *isolating mechanism*.

1948 G. Dahlberg in *Adv. Genetics* II. 92 Recessive mutations will come to the fore more quickly in a population built up of small isolates than in one composed of large ones. **1967** M. E. Hale *Biol. Lichens* iv. 62 The form and appearance of colonies of different mycobionts and even different isolates of the same mycobiont vary considerably. **1969** E. Mayr *Princ. Systematic Zoology* iii. 49 Isolates are frequently of sufficient difference to merit subspecies rank.

f. *Linguistics.* A word, or words, or other linguistic feature(s) abstracted from context for special study. Also, a word or short phrase that functions as a clause.

1949 *Trans. Philol. Soc. 1948* 128 For the purpose of distinguishing prosodic systems from phonematic systems, words will be my principal isolates. **1961** R. B. Long *Sentence & its Parts* i. 20 Isolates sometimes take adjunct modifiers, much as nucleuses do. Adjuncts are italicized in the following sentences. Thanks *very much*. Good night, *Marian*. **1965** W. S. Allen *Vox Latina* 7 In French, stress is a feature of the word only as an isolate (in which case it falls on the final syllable). **1972** Hartmann & Stork *Dict. Lang. & Ling.* 119/2 *Isolate*, (*a*) a single word functioning as a clause.., (*b*) a term used occasionally as an alternative to segment.

isolate ('aɪsəleɪt, 'ɪs-), *v.* [A back-formation from ISOLATED; or f. F. *isoler* (1690 in Hatz.-Darm.), ad. It. *isolare* (:—L. *insulāre*) + -ATE[3].]

1. *trans.* To place or set apart or alone; to cause to stand alone, detached, separate, or unconnected with other things or persons; to insulate.

1807 Coxe *Austria* II. 517 The means of..isolating England from the states of the continent. **1845** R. W. Hamilton *Pop. Educ.* ix. (ed. 2) 257 Whatever isolates people from people is a mischievous partition wall. **1851** Willmott *Pleas. Lit.* xxi. (1857) 123 The historian cannot isolate a hero, or a saint. **1871** Tyndall *Fragm. Sc.* (1879) I. v. 164 He found germs in the mercury used to isolate his air. **1873** Hamerton *Intell. Life* IX. vi. (1896) 328 High culture always isolates.

2. *Chem.* To obtain (a substance) free from all its combinations; to obtain as a separate substance.

1836 J. M. Gully *Magendie's Formul.* (ed. 2) 152 Vauquelin and Pelletier have made some attempts to isolate the active principle of croton oil. **1853** W. Gregory *Inorg. Chem.* (ed. 3) 96 Ammonium, if it exists, is resolved into ammonia..and hydrogen, whenever we attempt to isolate it. **1854** J. Scoffern in *Orr's Circ. Sc., Chem.* 345 The natural form of carbon when isolated is a black solid. *Ibid.* 514 Osmious acid has never been isolated.

3. *Electr.* = INSULATE *v.* 3.

1855 [see ISOLATOR]. **1859** *All Year Round* No. 30. 80 A..fragment of the Atlantic cable, wire incased and isolated by gutta-percha. **1876** *S. Kens. Mus. Catal.* No. 1371 Mica-plates for isolating electrical apparatus.

4. To cut off (an infected person or place) from all contact with others; to subject to strict quarantine. Also *absol.*

1888 Mrs. H. Ward *R. Elsmere* II. III. xxi. 178 Three cases of diphtheria..I must go for..a nurse, and we must isolate and make a fight for it. **1890** *Spectator* 21 June, Both in Italy and Spain they do not scruple to 'isolate' any infected house in such a way that the inmates are imprisoned and cannot get food.

isolated ('aɪsəleɪtɪd, 'ɪs-), *ppl. a.* [f. F. *isolé* (1642 in Hatz.-Darm.), ad. It. *isolato* (see ISOLATE *a.*) + -ED. (The French *isolé* was at first used unchanged or with *-d*, *isolé'd*.) Since the formation of ISOLATE *v.*, *isolated* has ranked as its pa. pple.] **a.** Placed or standing apart or alone; detached or separate from other things or persons; unconnected with anything else; solitary.

[*a* **1751** Bolingbroke (*N. & Q.* 25 Feb. 1854), The events ..appear to us very often original, unprepared, single, and unrelative, if I may use such a word for want of a better. In French, I would say, *Isolés*. **1755** Chesterf. *Lett.* III. xxvii. Misc. Wks. 1777 II. 491 As for hearing I have none left; so that I am *isolé* in the midst of my friends. **1779** in J. H. Jesse *Selwyn & Contemp.* (1843–4) IV. 214 What must such a little *isolé* mortal as I do? **1779** G. Keate *Sk. fr. Nat.* (ed. 2) I. 40 You see me the same isolé'd, un-connected creature I was then. **1783** Johnson 21 Mar. in *Boswell*, Sir..this Hanoverian family is *isolée* here. They have no friends.]

1763 Warburton *Doctr. Grace* Pref. 4 Short, isolated Sentences were the mode in which Ancient wisdom delighted to convey its precepts for the regulation of human conduct. **1800** *Brit. Critic* Oct., The affected, frenchified, and unnecessary word *isolated* is not English, and we trust never will be. [Todd 1818 adds: 'I fully agree with the writer in considering it a most affected word'.] **1811** *Sporting Mag.* XXXVIII. 83 He appeared as an isolated inhabitant of this great globe. **1813** Shelley *Q. Mab* II. 253 High on an isolated pinnacle. **1824** W. Irving *T. Trav.* II. 102 Many an isolated inn among the lonely parts of the Roman territories. **1840** Carlyle *Heroes* v. (1872) 165 Johnson's youth was poor, isolated, hopeless, very miserable. **1865** Lubbock *Preh. Times* viii. (1869) 254 Occasionally we find them isolated, but more frequently in groups. **1875** Tylor in *Encycl. Brit.* II. 119/1 What philologists describe as *isolated languages*, such as the Basque appears to be, are rather isolated groups of dialects. **1879** M. Arnold *Ess. Democr.* 45 Collective action is more efficacious than isolated individual effort. **1881** Flower in *Nature* No. 619. 437 When groups of animals become so far differentiated from each other as to represent separate species, they remain isolated.

b. *Chess.* ***isolated pawn***: see quots.

1842 C. Pearson *Chess Exemplified* 27 An isolated pawn is one that has no comrade on the same or either adjoining file, so that he requires the support of a Piece. **1847** H. Staunton *Chess-Player's Handbk.* 23 A Pawn which stands alone, without the support or protection of other Pawns, is termed an isolated pawn. **1950** S. Tartakover in R. N. Coles *Chess-Player's Week-End Bk.* 153 An isolated pawn spreads gloom all over the chess-board. **1957** Cunnington & Du Mont *Chess Traps & Stratagems* II. 75 An isolated pawn is normally weak, a pawn supported by its neighbours is a strong asset.

Hence **'isolatedly** *adv.*

1843 Mozley *Ess., Strafford* (1878) I. 82 All the knots and rough spots..were brought up, singly and isolatedly enlarged upon. **1865** Stirling *Secr. Hegel* I. ii. 50 Being, looked at isolatedly, vanishes of its own accord, and disappears in its own opposite. **1877** Huxley *Anat. Inv. Anim.* xii. 685 The appearance, between the epiblast and the hypoblast, of cytodes, either isolatedly or in a continuous layer.

isolating ('aɪsəleɪtɪŋ), *ppl. a.* [f. ISOLATE *v.* + -ING[2].] **1.** *Linguistics.* Designating languages (e.g. Vietnamese) in which (for the most part) words do not vary in form according to their grammatical functions in sentences, as contrasted with agglutinating and inflecting languages.

1860 [see INFLEXIONAL, INFLECTIONAL *a.* 1]. **1861** Max Müller *Lect. Sci. Lang.* 1st Ser. viii. 274 Languages belonging to this first or Radical Stage, have sometimes been called Monosyllabic or Isolating. **1868** —— *Sel. Ess. Lang.* (1881) I. 44 We find it repeated again and again in most works on Comparative Philology, that Chinese belongs to the isolating class, the Turanian languages to the combinatory, the Aryan and Semitic to the inflectional. **1885** *Encycl. Brit.* XVIII. 774/2 Such languages, constituting the small minority of human tongues, are wont to be called 'isolating', i.e., using each element by itself, in its integral form. **1921** E. Sapir *Lang.* vi. 133 More justifiable [than the traditional classification of linguistic types as i) isolating, ii) agglutinative, iii) inflective] would be a classification according to the formal processes most typically developed in the language. Those languages that always identify the word with the radical element would be set off as an 'isolating' group against such as either affix modifying elements..or possess the power to change the significance of the radical element by internal changes. **1953** C. E. Bazell *Ling. Form* i. 2 In languages of so-called 'isolating' structure the syllable may often be regarded as the minimal unit having independent morphological relevance.

2. *Biol.* **isolating barrier, mechanism,** a geographical, ecological, seasonal, physiological, or other factor which limits or prevents interbreeding between groups of plants or animals.

1913 W. Bateson *Probl. Genetics* vi. 119 In one remarkable case the season of appearance plainly acts as the isolating barrier. **1937** T. Dobzhansky in *Amer. Naturalist* LXXI. 405 The expression 'isolating mechanisms' seems to be a convenient general name for all the mechanisms hindering or preventing the interbreeding of racial complexes or species. **1973** I. H. Herskowitz *Princ. Genetics* xxxvi. 564 It is expected..that natural selection would favor isolating mechanisms that operate prior to mating.

isolation (aɪsəʊ'leɪʃən, ɪs-). [a. F. *isolation* (1791 in Hatz.-Darm.), n. of action from *isoler* to ISOLATE.]

1. a. The action of isolating; the fact or condition of being isolated or standing alone; separation from other things or persons; solitariness.

1833 Ht. Martineau *Charmed Sea* ii. 14 The exiles condemned to the mines run a risk of isolation proportioned to the smallness of their numbers. **1843** Carlyle *Past & Pr.* IV. iv, Isolation is the sum-total of wretchedness to man. **1844** Stanley *Arnold* II. viii. 13 How complete was the isolation in which he found himself, when he was almost equally condemned, in London as a bigot, and in Oxford as a latitudinarian. **1856** —— *Sinai & Pal.* viii. (1858) 323 We naturally pass to its isolation from the rest of Palestine. **1860** Tyndall *Glac.* I. ii. 21 In savage isolation, stood the obelisk of the Matterhorn. **1876** Mozley *Univ. Serm.* v. 115 To meditate in solitude and isolation on the use of being wise. **1896** Sir W. Laurier in *Canadian Ho. Assembly* 5 Feb., Whether splendidly isolated or dangerously isolated, I will not now debate; but for my part, I think splendidly isolated, because this isolation of England comes from her superiority. **1896** Goschen *Sp. at Lewes* 26 Feb., We have stood alone in that which is called isolation—our splendid isolation, as one of our colonial friends was good enough to call it.

b. The obtaining of a chemical element or compound as a separate substance.

1854 J. Scoffern in *Orr's Circ. Sc., Chem.* 335 Whether the hypothetical compound ammonium can exist except in combination is unknown. Chemists have failed to accomplish its isolation. **1898** G. S. Newth *Inorg. Chem.* (ed. 6) 471 The method by which Davy first [in 1807] effected the isolation of potassium was by the electrolysis of potassium hydroxide.

c. *spec.* The complete separation of patients suffering from a contagious or infectious disease, or of a place so infected, from contact with other persons. Also *attrib.* in ***isolation hospital, camp***, etc., that by which isolation is effected.

1891 *Daily News* 8 Oct. 3/1 A much needed institution in the shape of an Isolation Hospital. **1894** *Lancet* 3 Nov. 1046 Since the new isolation hospital was erected. **1897** *Daily News* 5 Feb. 10/5 Owing to the breakdown of the medical examinations at Bombay numerous pilgrims had already reached Calcutta. He heartily supported the idea of isolation camps.

2. a. *Psychol.* and *Sociol.* The separation of a person or thing from its normal environment or context, either for purposes of experiment and study or as a result of its being, for some reason, set apart. Also *attrib.* or as *adj.*

1890 C. L. Morgan *Animal Life & Intelligence* viii. 322 We may call the process by which we select a certain quality, and consider it by itself to the neglect of other qualities, *isolation*. **1902** *Amer. Jrnl. Sociol.* VIII. 37 Thus isolation, apparently confined to a single person, consisting in the negation of sociality, is really a phenomenon of very positive sociological significance. **1934** *Ibid.* XL. 157 The hypothesis is that the cause of schizophrenia is isolation of the person. **1950** K. H. Wolff tr. *Simmel's Sociol.* iii. 119 Isolation thus is a relation which is lodged within an individual but which exists between him and a certain group or group life in general. **1961** D. O. Hebb in P. Solomon et al. *Sensory Deprivation* ii. 7 The isolation procedure seems to be contributing to more effective interrelations between psychiatry and psychology. **1964** Gould & Kolb *Dict. Social Sci.* 355/2 Isolation is regarded as one of the dynamic variables in the failure to acquire personality. **1969** Zigler & Child in Lindzey & Aronson *Handbk. Social Psychol.* (ed. 2) III. xxiv. 523 That early isolation increases later aggression is an especially interesting phenomenon which

has also been found in mice . . and monkeys. **1970** G. A. & A. G. THEODORSON *Mod. Dict. Sociol.* 216 The prolonged isolation of an individual from satisfying social . . involvement with others usually leads to or is a result of a mental disorder. **1971** *Jrnl. Gen. Psychol.* LXXXV. 107 Isolation fails to enhance total list acquisition. *Ibid.* 157 Operant tasks were performed in an isolation chamber. **1972** *Jrnl. Social Psychol.* LXXXVI. 106 The results of the experiment showed an isolation effect to the name 'Cecil'.

b. *Psychoanal.* A defence mechanism whereby a particular wish or thought loses emotional significance by being isolated from its normal context.

1926 *Brit. Jrnl. Med. Psychol.* VI. 125 In obsessional neurosis the isolation is given magical motor reinforcement —motor isolation is a guarantee for rupture of thought connections. **1937** tr. *Freud's Gen. Sel. Works* 280 Our attention has . . been drawn to a process of 'isolation' (whose technique cannot as yet be elucidated) which has direct symptomatic manifestations of its own. **1946** O. FENICHEL *Psychoanal. Theory of Neurosis* II. ix. 155 Another mechanism of defense prevalent in compulsion neuroses and of very general significance for psychopathology is isolation. **1951** P. M. SYMONDS *Ego & Self* xii. 181 The compulsive neurotic may use the mechanism of isolation in which a portion of his personality is walled off through lack of feeling. **1964** H. HARTMANN *Ess. Ego Psychol.* I. iii. 48 A tendency toward isolation ('good' things must not be contaminated with 'bad' things [etc.]). **1970** P. CHODOFF in H. S. Abram *Psychol. Aspects Stress* 54 Isolation of affect [among concentration camp inmates], which could be so extreme as to involve a kind of emotional anesthesia, seemed to have functioned particularly to protect the ego.

3. *Biol.* The limitation or prevention of interbreeding between groups of plants or animals by geographical, ecological, seasonal, or other factors, leading to the development of new species or varieties.

[**1859** DARWIN *Origin of Species* iv. 105 Isolation, by checking immigration and consequently competition, will give time for a new variety to be improved at a slow rate.] **1913** W. BATESON *Probl. Genetics* vi. 119 The distinctness of the two forms [of the moth *Tephrosia bistortata*] in the places where they co-exist is maintained by the seasonal isolation. **1929** *Biol. Abstr.* III. 1621/1 If foreign hereditary elements are mixed in a population, correlations will be established, partly through polymery, partly through isolation. **1937** T. DOBZHANSKY *Genetics & Origin of Species* viii. 230 The mechanisms that prevent the interbreeding of groups of individuals, and consequently engender isolation, are remarkably diversified. **1973** I. H. HERSKOWITZ *Princ. Genetics* xxxvi. 563 Although cross breeding may occur naturally or experimentally between closely related species, each maintains its unique gene pool via reproductive isolation.

isolationism (aɪsəˈleɪʃənɪz(ə)m). [f. ISOLATION + -ISM.] The policy of seeking (political or national) isolation: with special reference to the U.S.A. Also *transf.*

1922 *19th Cent.* Nov. 731 Her isolationism . . discovered that the strain of a formidable advance against freedom was more than it could bear. **1930** *Headway* June 112/2 Add to this the fact that half the people . . who have emigrated to America in the last generation or so are Europeans who have left Europe because they wanted to get away from Europe, and the secret of America's 'isolationism' is very largely explained. **1931** *Time & Tide* Suppl. 4 July, However much an instructed minority in America might be in favour of the abandonment of isolationism and a larger co-operation with Europe. **1934** [see AUTARKY b]. **1953** *Manch. Guardian Weekly* 27 Aug. 1 He was now ready to say that 'unilateralism is the new face of isolationism'. **1955** *Bull. Atomic Sci.* Oct. 274 Apparently, the period of enforced scientific isolationism imposed on them for several years has not destroyed this tradition. **1956** K. CLARK *Nude* v. 167 The rigid isolationism of the Parthenon metopes. **1969** *Nature* 8 Feb. 524/2 One of the lamentable consequences of intellectual isolation is isolationism—the unconscious fear of exposing the inadequacy of one's achievement to one's fellow scientists. **1973** *Guardian* 25 Apr. 11/1 The difference . . between the old isolationism and the new was that whereas the United States felt itself too good for the world in the 1930s, it now felt it was not good enough.

isolationist (aɪsəˈleɪʃənɪst). [f. ISOLATION + -IST.] One who favours or advocates isolation. In U.S. politics, one who thinks the Republic ought to pursue a policy of political isolation. Also *transf.*

1899 *Press* (Philadelphia) 25 Mar. 8 Their consent ought to have been obtained first, according to the creed of the isolationists. **1901** *Rep. Brit. Assoc. Adv. Sci.* 676 This way of accounting for progress in one or more directions may prove as inadequate as the one suggested by isolationists. **1929** *Times* 31 Oct. 16/1 If a grave crisis were ever to arise on the western borders of Russia, the isolationists might be swept off their feet. **1962** [see COMPARATIST]. **1969** *Guardian* 6 Feb. 10 A teacher cannot be an isolationist. He has to go out and meet the people whose opinions matter in education.

b. *attrib.* or as *adj.*

1921 *Glasgow Herald* 21 Apr. 8 Regarding the future policy of the United States... The isolationist attitude . . is . . much less obvious. **1922** *Ibid.* 30 Dec. 7 Senator Borah has been regarded as the foremost advocate . . of the isolationist policy. **1930** *New Statesman* 26 Apr. 69/2 When Mr. Hoover signed last year the prospect was good, but the prolonged bickerings in London have stiffened the isolationist sentiment of the interior. **1958** *Punch* 1 Jan. 75/1 They go further and speculate about the future of an isolationist Britain. **1958** M. WEST *Second Victory* iii. 56 You know what these mountain people are—irredentist, isolationist, intolerant of foreigners and officials alike.

Hence **isolatioˈnistic** *a.*; **isolatioˈnistically** *adv.*

1943 E. W. HALL in *Mind* LII. 232, I shall speak of them as the 'primitivistic', the 'isolationistic', and the 'semantical' usages, respectively. **1964** *Economist* 7 Nov. 567 To be . . isolationistically independent and . . internationally dominant.

isolative (ˈaɪsəleɪtɪv), *a.* [f. ISOLATE *v.* + -IVE.]

a. *Phonology.* Of a sound-change: taking place without reference to neighbouring sounds: opp. COMBINATIVE *a.* 3.

1888 H. SWEET *Hist. Eng. Sounds* 17 Isolative changes are those which affect a sound without any reference to its surroundings. *Ibid.* 26 Isolative change of s into ʃ is regular in Gm initial *s* followed by a cons., as in *schwan, stein.* **1906** H. C. WYLD *Hist. Study Mother Tongue* iv. 73 Sound changes are conveniently divided into two main classes: *Isolative Changes*, which take place independent of other neighbouring sounds in the word or sentence, and uninfluenced by them; and *Combinative Changes.* **1972** HARTMANN & STORK *Dict. Lang. & Ling.* 212/2 A sound change is said to be . . isolative, autonomous, spontaneous, sporadic when it is in no way dependent on its environment but occurs in all positions in which the sound in question occurs.

b. *gen.* Tending to isolate.

1957 *Antiquity* XXXI. 189 Natural selection and isolative mechanisms. **1968** G. JONES *Hist. Vikings* II. i. 69 The axe-resisting, isolative forests of central Sweden.

‖**isolato** (izoˈlato). [It.] An isolated person, an outcast.

The spelling in quot. 1950 is *erron.*

1851 H. MELVILLE *Moby Dick* I. xxvi. 191 They were nearly all Islanders in the *Pequod*, *Isolatos* too, I call such, not acknowledging the common continent of men, . . yet . . what a set these Isolatos were! **1950** AUDEN *Enchafèd Flood* i. 35 What it feels like to be such an isolatoe, who . . is left standing there alone in the wide waste. **1958** *New Statesman* 6 Sept. 322/2 What most of them failed to see . . was that the Negro was also, primarily, an American and faced many of the same problems as the displaced isolato, the white American.

ˈ**isolator.** [agent-n. from ISOLATE *v.*: see -OR.] One who or that which isolates; a contrivance for isolating, an insulator.

1855 MAYNE *Expos. Lex.*, *Isolator*, the apparatus used in electrical experiments for isolating bodies. **1884** F. J. BRITTEN *Watch & Clockm.* 126 [An] Isolator . . in a minute repeater [is] a device for keeping the click from contact with the surprise piece on the minute snail till the slide in the band of the case is pushed round. **1900** *Pilot* 4 Aug. 138/2 The piano must be . . placed on glass salt cellars, if the old fashioned isolators are not at hand.

i-sold, ME. pa. pple. of SELL *v.*

isolecithal, isolectic: see ISO-.

†ˈ**isolet.** *Obs. rare.* [ad. It. *isoletta*, dim. of *isola* island.] A small island, an islet.

1613 PURCHAS *Pilgrimage* (1614) 520 Babelmandel, Camaran, and Mazua are accounted amongst the chiefe of these Isolets. **1632** J. HAYWARD tr. *Biondi's Eromena* 181 Northward from that Cape stood a little disinhabited Isolet.

Isolette (aɪsəʊˈlɛt). *N. Amer.* Also **isolette.** [f. ISOL(ATION + -ETTE.] The proprietary name of a type of infants' incubator.

1949 *Official Gaz.* (U.S. Patent Office) 7 June 45/2 [Trademark] No. 542,499 Air Shields, Inc., Hatboro, Pa... Isolette. For Infant Incubators. **1950** *Collier's* 1 Apr. 71/2 Through the isolettes the baby can be seen at all times, yet need never be moved or exposed. **1951** *Trade Marks Jrnl.* 21 Feb. 182/1 Isolette... Incubators for the care of infants. Airshields, Inc., Hatboro, . . Pennsylvania, United States of America; Manufacturers. **1962** *Jrnl. Pediatrics* Aug. 306/1 Four model C 77 Isolette incubators were used. Two of these were equipped with an Infant Servo-Controller. **1970** *Daily Colonist* (Victoria, B.C.) 27 Feb. 23/2 Mrs. Margaret Kienast . . got her first look at her brood [*sc.* quintuplets] last Wednesday when she was brought from her room to the isolette in the centre's babies hospital.

isoleucine (aɪsəʊˈl(j)uːsiːn). *Biochem.* [ad. G. *isoleucin* (F. Ehrlich 1903, in *Zeitschr. Ver. d. Deut. Zucker-Ind.* LIII. 821), f. *iso-* ISO- b + *leucin* LEUCIN.] An amino-acid of which the dextrorotatory or L- form is an essential nutrient and a general constituent of proteins; 1-amino-2-methylvaleric acid, $CH_3CH_2CH(CH_3)CH(NH_2)COOH$.

1903 *Jrnl. Chem. Soc.* LXXXIV. I. 796 The author has isolated leucine and a new compound, *d-iso*leucine, isomeric with it. *d-iso*Leucine crystallises in shining rods or leaflets. **1936** *Jrnl. Biol. Chem.* CXIV. 89 Leucine and isoleucine have been isolated in considerable quantities by extracting the dried, defatted mycelium of *Aspergillus syndowi* with acetone. **1962** *Lancet* 6 Jan. 26/1 They demonstrated a marked elevation of four aminoacids in the blood and urine —namely, the three branched-chain aminoacids (leucine, isoleucine, and valine) and also methionine.

isolex to **isoline:** see ISO-.

isolichenin: see ISO- b.

isologous (aɪˈsɒləgəs), *a. Chem.* [f. ISO- + Gr. λόγος word, reason, ratio, relation + -OUS. First formed as F. *isologue* (C. Gerhardt *Traité de Chim. Org.* (1853) I. II. 127).]

1. a. Having equality or parallelism of relations: applied to two or more hydrocarbon series, of each of which the members are related to each other in the same way: see quots.

1857 W. A. MILLER *Elem. Chem.* §1184 III. 429 The groups of which we are now speaking are *isologous* with the alcohols—that is to say, that the compounds which constitute each of these groups are related to each other in a manner similar to that of the components of the alcohol group with which they are compared... The allylic, the benzoic, and the cinnamic series, are *isologous* with that of alcohol. **1899** DOBBIN tr. *Ladenbury's Hist. Chem.* xi. 217 The homologous and isologous series constitute the one part of Gerhardt's classification; the other part is represented by the heterologous series.

b. Applied to each of two or more chemically similar compounds having some difference in composition other than a multiple of CH_2; now usu. applied *spec.* to compounds which have different atoms of the same valency at some position(s) in the molecule but are otherwise of identical molecular structure.

1884 *Jrnl. Chem. Soc.* XLVI. 12 In the author's results differences of Br_2 in isologous compounds, as allyl and dibromopropyl alcohols, correspond with differences of specific volume varying from 49·96 to 59·14. **1931** F. J. MOORE *Hist. Chem.* (ed. 2) xiv. 163 By isologous compounds Gerhardt understood substances of analogous function like acetic and benzoic acids whose formulæ showed some other difference than CH_2. **1959** *Jrnl. Amer. Chem. Soc.* LXXXI. 6272/1 (*heading*) Partition of isologous oxygen, sulfur and selenium compounds between buffers and organic solvents. **1964** *Jrnl. Med. Chem.* VII. 229/1 Selenoacyl compounds undergo aminolysis much more readily than isologous thioacyl compounds.

2. *Med.* and *Biol.* Genetically identical, esp. with respect to immunological factors; derived from another individual that is genetically identical or belongs to the same inbred strain; carried out between such individuals.

1955 *Jrnl. Nat. Cancer Inst.* XV. 1023 Lorenz, Congdon and Uphoff have increased the 30-day survival time of mice . . by the injection of isologous, homologous and, in some cases, heterologous bone marrow. **1959** *Folia Biologica* V. 24/1 An isologous combination . . fulfils the conditions for reciprocal tolerance between the host and the haematopoietic tissue graft. **1961** [see *isoallelic* adj. s.v. ISO-]. **1962** *Cancer Res.* XXII. 947 Sera from mice which had been rendered resistant against the isologous transplantation of Gross virus-induced lymphomas . . were found to be cytotoxic. *Ibid.*, Admixture of lymph node cells from isologous mice . . inhibited the outgrowth. **1971** *Nature* 1 Oct. 310/2 Human antibodies . . against diphtheria toxoid likewise disappear rapidly when injected into isologous human skin.

isologue (ˈaɪsəʊlɒg). *Org. Chem.* Also (*U.S.*) **isolog.** [a. F. *isologue* (C. Gerhardt *Traité de Chim. Org.* (1853) I. II. 127): see ISO- and -LOGUE.] Each of two or more isologous compounds.

1889 in *Cent. Dict.* **1924** *Chem. Abstr.* XVIII. 2158 Preparation of the thiopene isolog of cocaine. **1949** G. B. BACHMAN *Org. Chem.* xi. 110 Propanoic, propenoic, and propynoic acids are isologs of each other. **1965** *Jrnl. Med. Chem.* VIII. 846/1 While the former compound has a pK_a of 7·7, that of its selenium isolog was found to be 4·68 ± 0·05. **1970** *Tetrahedron* XXVI. 2151 (*heading*) NMR studies on the conformation of acetylcholine isologues.

isolux (ˈaɪsəʊlʌks), *a.* Also **iso-lux.** [f. ISO- + L. *lux* light.] = ISOPHOTAL *a.*

1911 A. P. TROTTER *Illumination* iv. 47 (*heading*) Contour lines of equal illumination or iso-lux curves, due to two lights at a distance apart equal to four times their height. **1926** J. W. T. WALSH *Photometry* iv. 99 An iso-lux diagram may be used to obtain a mental conception of the effect of a given system of light sources of known distribution. **1934** *Archit. Rev.* LXXV. 66 (*caption*) Isolux diagram. This should be read similar to a contour map, the rings representing foot candle intensities on a plane 2 ft. 6 in. above the floor. **1967** E. CHAMBERS *Photolitho-Offset* xi. 164 With the glass screen the unit dots grow by exposure to a graded pattern formed by diffraction effects and . . their contour shapes follow the isolux lines of equal intensity.

isolysin, isomagnetic: see ISO-.

†**i-som, i-some,** *a. Obs.* [OE. *ȝesóm*, pl. *-e*, f. *sóm* agreement, concord, ablaut grade of *sam-*, in OE. *samen*, SAME, etc.] Unanimous, agreed, reconciled, at peace.

a **1000** *Riddles* lxxxv. 21 (Exon.) Wit wæron ȝesome. *c* **1000** ÆLFRIC *Gen.* xlv. 24 Beoþ swyþe ȝesome. *c* **1175** *Lamb. Hom.* 93 Nu eft . . weren alle ispechen aȝein inumen and isome. *c* **1205** LAY. 30613 Wind and þa wide se ba eke isome. *a* **1250** *Relig. Songs* in *Owl & Night.* (Percy Soc.) 79 And wið hali chirche maken us i-som Thenne mohe we cwemen Crist at the dom. **1297** R. GLOUC. (Rolls) 52 Suþþe haþ engelond ibe iwerred ilome Of þe folc in denemarch þat ne beþ noȝt ȝot isome. *Ibid.* 1858 Constaunce . . granted him þat Kinedom & þat pes of rome & bileuede in þis lond to gadere boþe isome. **13..** *Song of Joy* 20, 21 (in *Adam Davy*, etc. E.E.T.S. 1878, 94), Er he oure flesch nome . . to maken vs ysome; Ysome nere we nouȝth before.

isomaltose: see ISO- b.

isomer (ˈaɪsəmə(r)). [mod. (Berzelius, 1830) f. Gr. ἰσομερ-ής sharing equally, f. ἰσο- ISO- + μέρος part, share: in mod.F. *isomère.*]

1. *Chem.* A substance isomeric with another; any one of a number of isomeric compounds.

1866 ROSCOE *Elem. Chem.* 296 It [Ethylene Oxide] does not form like its isomer aldehyde a crystalline compound with ammonia. **1880** CLEMINSHAW *Wurtz' Atom. The.* 295 The notion of atomicity has furnished sure data for the interpretation of isomers. **1885** GOODALE *Physiol. Bot.* (1892) 51 The isomers of cellulose are mucilage, gums, and dextrin. **1893** PR. KRAPOTKIN in *19th Cent.* Aug. 251 Very

often such isomeres differ from each other by having different boiling-points.

2. *Physics.* A nucleus having the same atomic number and mass number but different radioactive properties, as a result of being in a different, long-lived, energy state from which a transition is inhibited; *esp.* one in a metastable excited state rather than the ground state. Also called ***nuclear isomer***.

1934 *Physical Rev.* XLV. 729/2 The introduction of isomers may be of help for the removal of existing contradictions in the estimation of neutronic mass from different nuclear reactions. **1950** GLASSTONE *Sourcebk. Atomic Energy* x. 278/1 The second class consists of genetically related isomers,..in which the metastable state decays to the ground state with a definite half life. **1955** R. D. EVANS *Atomic Nucleus* iii. 97 Isobaric isotopes with distinguishable nuclear properties are called isomers. **1968** F. B. MORINIGO tr. *H. von Buttlar's Nucl. Physics* xiv. 478 If the half-life is larger than 1 msec, the state is called a nuclear isomer (the choice of 1 msec for this definition is arbitrary).

isomerase (aɪˈsɒməreɪz, -s). *Biochem.* [f. ISOMER + -ASE.] Any enzyme which brings about an isomerization reaction; orig. applied to two particular enzymes (see quots. 1943, 1944).

1943 I. BANGA in *Stud. Inst. Med. Chem. Univ. Szeged* III. 67 When ADP had been incubated with isomerase, the product was split by actomyosin which suggested that isomerase had changed the molecular structure of ADP. It was for this reason that the name isomerase was given to the new protein. **1944** *Jrnl. Biol. Chem.* CLVI. 109 Triose phosphate isomerase (or more briefly isomerase) is an enzyme..which catalyzes the reaction glyceraldehyde phosphate ⇌ dihydroxyacetone phosphate. **1953** *Ibid.* CCI. 83 *Escherichia coli* contains an adaptive isomerase catalyzing the equilibrium, D-arabinose ⇌ D-ribulose. **1963** C. H. DOERING tr. *Karlson's Introd. Mod. Biochem.* ix. 173 Two enzyme systems are involved in the biosynthesis of uroporphyrin III from porphobilinogen: a deaminase and an isomerase. **1972** J. R. WHITAKER *Princ. Enzymol. for Food Scientists* xiv. 417 The 'isomerases' are enzymes which bring about an isomerization of the substrate. The name is formed on the order 'substrate prefix-isomerase'. The prefix indicates the type of isomerization involved, e.g., 'maleate *cis-trans*-isomerase'.

isomere (ˈaɪsəmɪə(r)). *Comp. Anat.* [Of same deriv. as ISOMER.] A part or segment of a limb in one species of animal homologous or corresponding to a part in another species.

1884 COUES *Key N.A. Birds* (ed. 2) 229 The lines 1–11 are *isotomes*, cutting the limbs into morphologically equal parts, or *isomeres*.

isomeric (aɪsəʊˈmɛrɪk), *a.* [f. as ISOMER + -IC; in mod.F. *isomérique*: after Ger. *isomerisch* (Berzelius, *Jahresbericht* of Swed. Acad. Sciences, 31 March 1831).]

1. a. *Chem.* Composed of the same elements in the same proportions, and having the same molecular weight, but forming different substances, with different properties (owing to the different grouping or arrangement of the constituent atoms). Said of two or more compounds, or of one compound in relation to another (const. *with*).

This was the sense in which the term was introduced by Berzelius; but many later chemists (e.g. Wanklyn in Watts *Dict. Chem.* 1865) have applied it in a wider sense, so as to include also the *polymeric* compounds of Berzelius, i.e. those which have their elements in the same *proportions*, but the number of atoms in one a multiple of those in the other, e.g. butyric acid $C_4H_8O_2$, and aldehyde C_2H_4O; by these the isomeric compounds of Berzelius have been distinguished as *metameric*. More recent authors again (e.g. Tilden in *Fownes' Chem.* 1886) have used these terms more narrowly, subdividing the *isomeric* of Berzelius into *isomeric strictly so called*, and *metameric*; the former being compounds of the same molecular composition, which exhibit the same or closely similar decompositions and transformations, when subjected to the action of the same re-agents, such as the $C_{10}H_8$ hydrocarbons, the glucoses, the tartaric acids, etc.; the latter, those which exhibit dissimilar transformations under similar circumstances, as propionic acid, methyl acetate, and ethyl formate $C_3H_6O_2$.

1838 T. THOMSON *Chem. Org. Bodies* 605 From the analysis of this substance [benzoin] it appears to be isomeric with the hydret of benzoyl. **1842-3** GROVE *Corr. Phys. Forces* (1874) 117 These solutions are what is termed isomeric, that is, have as far as can be discovered, the same chemical constitution. *c* **1865** J. WYLDE in *Circ. Sc.* I. 311/2 Isomeric bodies have similar chemical constituents in the same proportions, and yet their external form may differ, as in sugar and starch. **1865-72** WATTS *Dict. Chem.* III. 415 Two or more different bodies which are composed of the same elements, and of the same proportions of those elements (i.e. which have the same percentage composition) are said to be *isomeric*. **1880** CLEMINSHAW *Wurtz' Atom. The.* 294 We may..imagine isomeric compounds to be produced, according to the place occupied by the atoms fixed in the molecule. **1882** GILBURT in *Jrnl. Quekett Club* Ser. II. i. 27 We have already seen that cellulose, sugar, starch, and inulin, are isomeric with each other. **1892** MORLEY & MUIR *Watts' Dict. Chem.* III. 88/2 According to our modern conceptions, truly isomeric substances..are equi-molecular compounds containing identical radicles arranged in relatively different modes; and..bearing in mind that it was obviously the intention of Berzelius to limit the scope of the expression, the term isomeric should be used only with reference to such compounds.

b. *Physics.* Of, pertaining to, or designating nuclear isomers; *isomeric transition*, a radioactive transition from a metastable state to a lower energy state of the same nuclide.

1934 *Physical Rev.* XLV. 729/1 Another consequence of the introduction of negative protons is the possibility of the existence of isomeric nuclei, that is, nuclei with the same charge and mass but different internal structure. **1937** *Ibid.* LI. 1011 The 18 minute, 4·2 hour, and 35 hour activities must all belong to Br^{80} and Br^{82}, i.e. one of these isotopes appears to exist in two isomeric forms, from which it decays with different periods. **1950** GLASSTONE *Sourcebk. Atomic Energy* x. 276/1 Over seventy examples of nuclear isomerism have been discovered, and the phenomenon of decay by isomeric transition, that is, by the spontaneous conversion of one nuclear isomer into another, has been elucidated. In most instances there are isomeric pairs only, but triple isomerism has been observed in a few cases. **1955** R. D. EVANS *Atomic Nucleus* vi. 231 By the usual definition, an isomeric level is one whose half-period is 'measurably' long. **1970** MARMIER & SHELDON *Physics of Nuclei & Particles* II. xv. 1276 Those nuclei whose ground-state configuration is modified by the preferential-filling rule would be expected to display low-lying excited states whose configuration corresponds to that of an unmodified ground state; because of the large spin change occasioned by this effect, the excited state is usually an isomeric state.

2. *Comp. Anat.* Pertaining to or of the nature of an isomere; homologous.

1890 *Cent. Dict.* s.v., Isomeric segments of the limbs.

So **isoˈmerical** *a.* = ISOMERIC; **isoˈmerically** *adv.*

In recent Dicts.

isomeride (aɪˈsɒməraɪd). *Chem.* [f. as ISOMER + -IDE.] = ISOMER.

1857 W. A. MILLER *Elem. Chem.* III. i. 5 The formation of *isomerides, metamerides*, and *polymerides*, as bodies which possess the same percentage composition may be termed, can only be accounted for by supposing that differences of chemical arrangement occur in these different cases. **1892** MORLEY & MUIR *Watts' Dict. Chem.* III. 85/2 The hypothesis serves therefore at once to explain..the existence of isomerides which cannot be represented by formulae written in a single plane.

isomerism (aɪˈsɒmərɪz(ə)m). *Chem.* [f. ISOMER + -ISM: in mod.F. *isomérisme.*] **a.** The fact or condition of being isomeric; identity of percentage composition in compounds differing in properties. ***physical isomerism***: see quot. 1896.

1838 T. THOMSON *Chem. Org. Bodies* 58 This is one of the most extraordinary examples of isomerism at present known. **1851** RICHARDSON *Geol.* v. 78 Isomerism, discovered by Berzelius, is a principle which is somewhat vague and doubtful in its application. **1880** CLEMINSHAW *Wurtz' Atom. The.* 291 Isomerism is due to the difference in molecular grouping. **1884** FRANKLAND & JAPP *Inorg. Chem.* 111 Allotropy stands in the same relation to elements that isomerism does to compounds. **1892** MORLEY & MUIR *Watts' Dict. Chem.* III. 81/1 Berzelius never intended that polymerism should be regarded as a form of isomerism. **1896** REMSEN *Comp. Carbon* 163 Bodies may conduct themselves chemically in exactly the same way, and yet differ in some of their physical properties, as in their action towards polarized light. To distinguish this kind of isomerism..it is called *physical isomerism*... The branch of chemistry which has to deal with the kind of isomerism just referred to, is called *stereo-chemistry*.

b. *Physics.* The fact or condition of being nuclear isomers.

1938 R. W. LAWSON tr. *Hevesy & Paneth's Man. Radioactivity* (ed. 2) x. 124 This isotope of silver..has two half-value periods, 24·5 m. and 8·2 d., the former being associated with positron emission, and the latter with the emission of β- and γ-rays... Here we are confronted with the phenomenon of nuclear isomerism. **1950** [see ISOMERIC *a.* 1 b].

isomerization (aɪˌsɒməraɪˈzeɪʃən). *Chem.* [f. ISOMERIZ(E *v.* + -ATION.] The conversion of a compound into an isomer of itself.

1891 *Chem. News* 27 Nov. 274/1 The isomerisation is complete at 140°–170°. **1946** *Industr. Chemist* XXII. 45/1 Since 1944 Tide Water Associated Oil Company, California, has operated a liquid-phase pentane isomerisation plant of the Shell type. **1971** *Sci. Amer.* Dec. 48/3 Isomerization increases the compactness of gasoline molecules, thereby improving the fuel's antiknock quality.

isomerize (aɪˈsɒməraɪz), *v. Chem.* [f. ISOMER + -IZE 1.] *trans.* and *intr.* To change *into* or *to* an isomer (of the original substance).

1891 *Chem. News* 27 Nov. 274/1 Monosubstituted acetylenes with primary alkyl radicles are isomerised to bisubstituted acetylenes. **1903** *Notices Proc. R. Inst.* (1906) XVII. 100 It is isomerised into the quinonoid form by the addition of water. **1920** *Biochem. Jrnl.* XIV. 185 The free oxonium base (III) which more or less easily isomerises into the colourless pseudo-base (II). **1924** *Jrnl. Chem. Soc.* CXXV. II. 2545 These cycloids isomerise to hydroxyamidines at the moment of their formation. **1955** PINES & MAVITY in B. T. Brooks et al. *Chem. Petroleum Hydrocarbons* III. xxxix. 44 Incapable of isomerizing to a six membered ring compound, cyclopentane showed quite low reactivity in the presence of aluminium chloride. **1971** *Sci. Amer.* Dec. 48/3 The straight-chain saturated hydrocarbons can be catalytically isomerized to more compact structures.

Hence **iˈsomerized** *ppl. a.*, having undergone isomerization; **iˈsomerizing** *ppl. a.* and *vbl. sb.*

1908 *Chem. Abstr.* II. 1970 The velocity and the limits of the isomerizing power of a solvent are independent of each other. **1941** *Jrnl. Amer. Chem. Soc.* LXIII. 519 The question arises whether these catalysts have any isomerizing properties. **1942** *Canad. Chem. & Process Industries* XXVI. 637/2 The most outstanding recent development allied with fatty acids lies in the field of synthetic drying oils. Of these, two are outstanding—dehydrated castor oil, and the isomerized oils with conjugated double bond structure. **1954** Isomerized [see CYCLIZE *v.*]. **1963** *Agric. & Biol. Chem.* XXVII. A4/1 (*heading*) Identification and cultural conditions of glucose isomerizing bacteria. **1965** NYLÉN & SUNDERLAND *Mod. Surface Coatings* iii. 99 Isomerized linseed oil dries more rapidly than the normal oil.

isomeromorphism (aɪˌsəʊmərəʊˈmɔːfɪz(ə)m). *Cryst.* [f. *isomero-*, comb. form of next + Gr. μορφ-ή form + -ISM.] Isomorphism between isomeric substances.

1864 WEBSTER cites DANA.

isomerous (aɪˈsɒmərəs), *a.* [f. as ISOMER + -OUS.]

1. *Bot.* Of a flower: Having the same number of parts in each whorl. (Said also of the whorls.) Opp. to HETEROMEROUS 2 b.

1857 HENFREY *Bot.* §153 When the organs are equal in all the circles, the flowers are isomerous. *Ibid.*, The stamens are mostly isomerous, with either one, two, or more whorls, when the floral envelopes are regular. **1882** VINES tr. *Sachs' Bot.* 601 When the number of members is the same in each whorl [of a flower] they are said to be *isomerous*, when this is not the case *heteromerous*.

2. *Anat.* and *Zool.* Having the same number of parts or segments, as in the limbs; *spec.* belonging to the division *Isomera* of coleopterous insects, in which the number of tarsal joints is the same in all the legs: opp. to HETEROMEROUS 1. Applied also to molar teeth having the same number of ridges, as in existent elephants.

1878 BARTLEY tr. *Topinard's Anthrop.* ii. 74 In reptiles the two extremities are..symmetrical; and..isomerous, flexion being exerted in the same direction.

3. *Chem.* = ISOMERIC.

1864 WEBSTER, *Isomorphism*, A similarity of crystalline form; as, (*a*) Between substances of like composition or atomic proportions...(*b*) Between compounds of unlike composition or atomic proportions... The first of these is sometimes distinguished as *isomerous* or *isonomic* isomorphism; the second as *heteromerous* or *heteronomic* isomorphism. *Dana.* **1887** *Syd. Soc. Lex.*, *Isomerous*, same as *Isomeric*.

isomery (aɪˈsɒmərɪ). *Chem.* [= Ger. *isomerie* (Berzelius, 1832), f. Gr. type *ἰσομέρεια; in mod.F. *isomérie.*] = ISOMERISM.

isometric (aɪsəʊˈmɛtrɪk), *a.* and *sb.* [f. Gr. ἰσομετρία equality of measure (f. ἴσο-ς + μέτρος) + -IC: in mod.F. *isométrique.*]

A. *adj.* **1.** Of equal measure or dimensions.

1855 MAYNE *Expos. Lex.*, *Isometric*,..of equal measure, or extent. **1879** G. PRESCOTT *Sp. Telephone* 547 If an isometric block of metal be drawn out into a wire, its resistance may be indefinitely increased.

2. Applied to a method of projection or perspective, in which the plane of projection is equally inclined to the three principal axes of the object, so that all dimensions parallel to these axes are represented in their actual proportions; used in drawing figures of machines, etc.

1840 *Penny Cycl.* XVII. 492/1 This specific application of projection was termed *isometric* by the late Professor Farish, who pointed out its practical utility, and the facility of its application to the delineation of engines, etc. *Ibid.*, A scale for determining the lengths of the axes of the isometric projection of a circle.

3. *Cryst.* Applied to that system of crystalline forms characterized by three equal axes mutually at right angles (also called *cubic, tesseral*, etc.); belonging to this system.

1868 DANA *Min.* (ed. 5) Introd. 21 The systems of crystallization are..1. Having the axes equal. The Isometric system. *Ibid.* 22 Some of the simpler isometric forms are represented in figures 1 to 50.

4. *Physiol.* [ad. G. *isometrisch* (A. Fick *Mech. Arbeit u. Wärmeentwickelung bei d. Muskelthätigkeit* (1882) vii. 112).] Of, pertaining to, or designating muscular action in which tension is developed but appreciable shortening of the muscle is prevented.

1891 A. D. WALLER *Introd. Human Physiol.* ix. 330 If a muscle contracts against a large resistance..so that it can shorten very little, the curve described by a lever attached to it is termed 'isometric'. **1895** *Proc. R. Soc.* LVII. 423 The shortening of the muscle is prevented by resistance (isometric contraction of Fick). **1900** [see ISOTONIC *a.* 2]. **1920** *Jrnl. Physiol.* LIV. 85 During the development of tension in an isometric contraction both heat and potential energy are being produced by the muscle. **1951** [see ISOTONIC *a.* 3]. **1969** *New Yorker* 20 Dec. 43/2 He neither drinks nor smokes, and he devotes an hour a day to yoga and isometric exercises. **1971** [see ISOTONIC *a.* 3]. **1973** *Sci. Amer.* Mar. 83 Whereas a machine only performs mechanical work when a force moves through a distance, muscles consume energy when they are in tension but not moving (doing what is sometimes called 'isometric' work).

5. *Physics.* Indicating, or taking place under, conditions of constant volume.

1873 J. W. GIBBS in *Trans. Connecticut Acad. Arts & Sci.* II. 311 The points associated with states of equal volume will form lines, which..we may also call isometric. **1912** G. A. GOODENOUGH *Princ. Thermodynamics* (ed. 2) ii. 22 Lines of constant volume [are called] isometric lines. **1957** V. M. FAIRES *Thermodynamics* (ed. 3) v. 69 For a reversible steady flow isometric process..we have the energy equation from equation (7 A).

6. *Biol.* = ISOGONIC *a.*[2]

1950 J. S. HUXLEY in *Proc. R. Soc.* B. CXXXVII. 467 In an isometric organ we find no change in the proportions of its parts with increase in its absolute size.

7. *Math.* That is an isometry; related by an isometry. Const. *to*.

1952 C. C. KRIEGER tr. *Sierpinski's Gen. Topology* vi. 100 Two metric spaces consisting of the same elements but with different metrics may be isometric. **1959** L. F. BORON tr. *M.A. Naimark's Normed Rings* i. 38 Two metric spaces X, X' are said to be isometric if there exists an isometric mapping of X onto X'. **1966** J. H. CADWELL *Topics in Recreational Math.* xi. 117 A pattern is characterised by the set of isometric motions that bring it into self-coincidence, and this set forms a discrete group. **1968** E. T. COPSON *Metric Spaces* iv. 53 If the points **a**, **b** of A^* correspond to the points a and b of M, we have proved that $\rho^*(\mathbf{a}, \mathbf{b}) = \rho(a, b)$, so that A^* is isometric to M.

B. *sb.* **1.** *Physics.* A line in a diagram that corresponds to or represents states of equal volume.

1873 [see *isopiestic* adj. s.v. ISO-]. **1936** *Industr. & Engin. Chem.* Feb. 261/2 Not only are the isometrics of the pure substances themselves substantially straight, but the same is also true for mixtures. **1963** OBERT & GAGGIOLI *Thermodynamics* (ed. 2) x. 215 For the real gas, the isometrics are displaced from the origin and are either straight or slightly curved.

2. *pl.* A system of stationary physical exercises in which muscles are exercised isometrically by pitting one against another or against an unyielding object. orig. *U.S.*

1962 *Scholastic Coach* Nov. 31/1 This concludes a series of three comprehensive articles on isometrics. **1964** *Life* 17 Apr. 47/1 In 1921 Atlas began preaching the muscle-building system he called Dynamic Tension, which pits one muscle against another. Now variations of his system, in which muscles struggle against immobile objects, are the latest U.S. exercise fad. Scientists lump the systems under one fancy word, isometrics. **1970** *New Scientist* 20 Aug. 365/1 Isometrics, but recently hailed as the key to the good life, have also now been condemned for dangerously rocketing the blood pressure.

iso'metrical, *a.* [f. as prec. + -AL[1].]

1. = prec. 2.

1838 T. SOPWITH (*title*) Treatise on Isometrical Drawing. **1840** *Penny Cycl.* XVII. 492/1 The major axis of the isometrical projection of a circle is equal to the side of the circumscribing square. **1854** RONALDS & RICHARDSON *Chem. Technol.* (ed. 2) I. 265 An isometrical projection of the boiler and furnace.

2. = prec. 3.

1855 MAYNE *Expos. Lex.*, *Isometricus*, applied by Hausmann and Naumann to a system comprehending the crystalline forms in which the coördinate planes are perpendicular between them, and which relates to a system of axes three in number that are equal: isometrical.

iso'metrically, *adv.* [f. prec. + -LY[2].]

1. In the way of isometric projection.

1840 *Penny Cycl.* XVII. 492/1 The rhombus representing the inscribed or circumscribing square isometrically projected... The axes of the ellipse and the side of the circumscribing square, when isometrically projected, are as $\sqrt{3}$: $\sqrt{1}$: $\sqrt{2}$.

2. *Physiol.* Under isometric conditions (see ISOMETRIC *a.* 4).

1920 *Jrnl. Physiol.* LIV. 84 When a muscle is stimulated isometrically it passes gradually into a new elastic condition. **1945** *Amer. Jrnl. Physiol.* CXLIV. 477 Strings were tied to the tendons and the contractions were recorded isometrically under an initial tension of 50 grams. **1973** *Nature* 23 Feb. 537/2 The muscle twitch was measured isometrically.

3. *Math.* By means of or in the manner of an isometry.

1959 L. F. BORON tr. *Naimark's Normed Rings* ii. 181 Two normed rings R and R' are said to be isometrically isomorphic if there exists an isometric isomorphism of R onto R'. **1971** E. C. DADE in Powell & Higman *Finite Simple Groups* viii. 318 The map $\phi \to \phi^*$ sends x_+ isometrically into x_-.

isometrograph (aɪsəʊ'mɛtrəʊgrɑːf, -æ-). [f. Gr. ἰσό-μετρος of equal measure + -GRAPH.] An instrument for tracing parallel lines at exactly equal distances.

isometry (aɪ'sɒmɪtrɪ). [ad. Gr. ἰσομετρία equality of measure (f. μέτρος measure): see -Y[3].]

1. *Math.* A one-to-one transformation of one metric space into another that preserves the distances or metrics between each pair of points.

1941 BIRKHOFF & MACLANE *Survey Mod. Algebra* vi. 128 An obvious example is furnished by the symmetries of the cube. Geometrically speaking, these are the one-one transformations which preserve distances on the cube. They are known as 'isometries', and are 48 in number. **1965** S. LANG *Algebra* xiv. 356 If σ is a linear isomorphism, and is metric, then we say that σ is an isometry. **1966** J. H. CADWELL *Topics in Recreational Math.* xi. 113 A fundamental property of isometries is that any two carried out in succession define a third. Thus if isometry U takes figure F into figure F', while V takes F' into F'', their combined effect, taken in this order, is an isometry carrying F into F''.

2. *Biol.* = ISOGONY (s.v. ISOGONIC *a.*[2]).

1950 J. S. HUXLEY in *Proc. R. Soc.* B. CXXXVII. 465 Isometry is used of the special case when the organ grows at the same rate as the body.

i-sommed, ME. pa. pple. of SUM *v.*

i-somned, i-sompned, ME. pa. pple. of SUMMON *v.*

isomorph ('aɪsəʊmɔːf). [mod. f. Gr. type *ἰσόμορφ-ος of equal form, f. ἰσό-, ISO- + μορφή form: in mod.F. *isomorphe*.]

1. *Chem.* and *Min.* A substance or organism isomorphous with another.

1864 WEBSTER, *Isomorph*, a substance which has the same crystalline form with another. **1885** E. R. LANKESTER in *Encycl. Brit.* XIX. 849/1 Sandy isomorphs of Lagena, Nodosaria, Globigerina, and Rotalia.

2. *Linguistics.* A line in a linguistic atlas connecting places exhibiting identical or nearly identical morphological forms; a morphological isogloss.

1921 E. C. ROEDDER in *Jrnl. Eng. & Germ. Philol.* XX. 182 The boundary lines of present dialects, with their maze of.. isomorphs,..and isotaxes, i.e., lines connecting places of identical or nearly identical..forms,..and syntactical peculiarities. **1926** *Germanic Rev.* I. iv. 303 Like the larger dialects, they would have to be portioned off against each other by isophones, isomorphs, isolexes, and isotaxes, i.e., lines of agreement in sound, form, word (meaning), and syntax. **1937** J. ORR tr. *Iordan's Introd. Romance Ling.* iii. 215 Val d'Ajol alone offers certain well-marked individual features... A group of 'isophones' and 'isomorphs' passes exactly through the point where the two valleys.. investigated join each other.

isomorphic (aɪsəʊ'mɔːfɪk), *a.* [f. as prec. + -IC: in mod.F. *isomorphique*.]

1. *Chem.* and *Min.* Exhibiting isomorphism, isomorphous; pertaining to or involving isomorphism.

1862 SIR H. HOLLAND *Ess., Mod. Chem.* 444 This peculiar isomorphic relation between various chemical substances, having in themselves other singular resemblances. **1894** *Thinker* V. 435 This statement is not vitiated by the existence of such phenomena as those of pleomorphism and of isomorphic replacement.

2. *Math.* (Also *Logic* and *Linguistics.*) Said of groups or other sets corresponding to each other in form, and in the nature and product of their operations; related by an isomorphism; that is an isomorphism. Const. *to*, *with*.

1892 F. N. COLE tr. *Netto's Theory of Substitutions* iv. 83 If to every substitution of G correspond q substitutions of 𝔊, and to every substitution of 𝔊 p substitutions of G, then G and 𝔊 are said to be $(p\text{-}q)$-fold isomorphic, or if p and q are not specified, manifold isomorphic. If $p = q = 1$, the groups are said to be simply isomorphic. **1897** BURNSIDE *Theory of Groups* 21 If a correspondence can be established between the operations of G and G′, so that to every operation of G there corresponds a single operation of G′,.. while to the product AB of any two operations of G there corresponds the product A′B′ of the two corresponding operations of G′, the groups G and G′ are said to be ***simply isomorphic.*** **1900** *Ann. Math.* II. 48 Two abstract groups G, H which are 1-1 isomorphic are evidently, as far as structure goes, not distinct. **1934** J. A. ELDRIDGE *Physical Basis of Things* xxviii. 372 The scientist studies the infinite variety of nature's processes, acquaints himself with nature's group of operations, and then attempts to find a representation, in models or symbols, which is isomorphic therewith. **1937** A. SMEATON tr. *Carnap's Logical Syntax of Lang.* IV. 224 If S_1 is reversibly transformable in S_2 in respect of symbols, then S_1 and S_2 are called isomorphic. **1952** H. B. VEATCH *Intentional Logic* I. iii. 36 Whether it is necessary and proper that the structure of logical entities should correspond to, or be isomorphic with, or be similar to the structure of the facts which they are supposed to signify or represent. **1962** C. O. FRAKE in J. A. Fishman *Readings Sociol. of Lang.* (1968) 437 The items and arrangements of a structural description of the language code need not be isomorphic with the categories and propositions of the message. **1965** PATTERSON & RUTHERFORD *Elem. Abstr. Algebra* ii. 51 In other words, G_2 is isomorphic to G_1 if G_1 is isomorphic to G_2. **1968** J. LYONS *Introd. Theoret. Ling.* ii. 55 To the degree that the meanings of one language can be brought into one-to-one correspondence with those of another we will say that the two languages are semantically isomorphic (have the same semantic structure). **1971** *Nature* 22 Jan. 233/2 We can imagine the state of the whole system described by the states S_1, S_2,.. S_n of its S_n components. These values will determine a unique point in the n dimensional phase-space S such that there is an isomorphic correspondence between points in the space and the states of the system. **1973** J. HINTIKKA *Logic, Lang.-Games & Information* ii. 28 In order for anything to be an isomorphic representation of anything else, they must both have a certain structure.

3. *Biol.* Of the same or an analogous form.

1888 *Nature* 20 Dec. 180/1 Dicholophus.. has assumed peculiar Raptorial characters isomorphic with those of Gypogeranus, which is a true bird of prey.

4. *Bot.* In algæ and certain fungi, designating a type of alternation of generations in which the two forms are morphologically similar.

1935 F. E. FRITSCH *Struct. & Reprod. Algae* I. 52 Isomorphic (homologous) alternation occurs in each of the three largest classes of the Algae. **1951** M. O. P. IVENGAR in G. M. Smith *Man. Phycology* iii. 59 In the third type of life-cycle [of Chlorophyta], there is an alternation of two generations both externally similar... This kind of alternation has been called by Fritsch isomorphic alternation. *Ibid.* 60 Isomorphic types very probably originated from haploid types. **1964** E. J. H. CORNER *Life of Plants* vi. 93 Their [*sc.* slender brown seaweeds'] life-cycle is an isomorphic alternation of diploid sporophyte with haploid gametophyte. **1964** J. S. KARLING *Synchytrium* iii. 51 In 1905 Lowenthal described fusion of two motile isomorphic cells in *S*[*ynchytrium*] *taraxaci* and illustrated what appears to be a binucleate zygote. **1970** RAVEN & CURTIS *Biol. Plants* vi. 438/2 In *Ulva*, the alternation is isomorphic—that is, the mature sporophytes are morphologically identical to mature gametophytes.

5. *Linguistics.* Similar in morphological structure, having similar morphological forms.

1950 *Language Learning* III. iii. 93 The presentation of such items seems to be indicated in terms of lists the members of which are isomorphic (i.e. show similar differences between morpheme alternants). **1954** PEI & GAYNOR *Dict. Ling.* 107 *Isomorphic lines*, lines on a linguistic map, indicating the approximate boundaries of the speech-areas in which a uniformity in grammatical forms, inflections, etc. can be observed. **1957** S. POTTER *Mod. Ling.* vi. 134 On more detailed [linguistic] maps we might construct different kinds of lines called isophonic, isotonic, isomorphic, or isosyntagmic, which would record differentiating features of sound, tone, word-form and clause-structure respectively.

Hence **iso'morphically** *adv.*, by an isomorphism (sense 2); in an isomorphic manner.

1935 *Amer. Jrnl. Math.* LVII. 434 By means of $P_i \to P^*_i$ we thus map the algebra 11 reduced modulo $(1 - u)$ isomorphically upon itself. **1960** BROWN & GILMAN in J. A. Fishman *Readings Sociol. of Lang.* (1968) 266 There are a large number of expressions of subordination which are patterned isomorphically with T [*sc.* a familiar pronoun such as *tu*] and V [*sc.* a polite pronoun such as *vous*]. **1971** E. C. DADE in Powell & Higman *Finite Simple Groups* viii. 258 R_i sends the algebra A_i isomorphically onto $\mathrm{Hom}_F(I_i, I_i)$ for all $i = 1, \ldots, k$.

isomorphism (aɪsəʊ'mɔːfɪz(ə)m). [mod. (Mitscherlich, 1819) f. as prec. + -ISM: in mod.F. *isomorphisme*.] The character of being isomorphous.

1. *Chem.* and *Min.* The property of crystallizing in the same or closely related forms, esp. as exhibited by substances of analogous composition.

The general law of isomorphism affirms that bodies having a similar chemical composition have also the same form; or, in other words, that analogous elements and groups of elements may replace one another in composition without essential alteration of crystalline form. (Watts.)

1828 in WEBSTER. **1830** HERSCHEL *Stud. Nat. Phil.* 295 The isomorphism of certain groups of chemical elements. **1841** TRIMMER *Pract. Geol.* 83 The discovery by Professor Mitscherlich, of what is called the *isomorphism* of crystals, diminishes in some degree the value of crystalline form as a distinctive character. **1851** RICHARDSON *Geol.* (1855) 78 Isomorphism is the law by which an equal number of atoms, combining in the same manner, may give birth to similar crystalline forms, although the constituent elements are of a different nature. **1865–72** WATTS *Dict. Chem.* III. 423 Mitscherlich's first observation, presented to the Berlin Academy of Science in 1819, related to the isomorphism of the phosphates and arsenates. **1879** RUTLEY *Stud. Rocks* x. 97 Completely establishing the isomorphism of orthoclase and albite.

2. *Math.* (Also *Logic* and *Linguistics.*) Identity of form and of operations between two or more groups or other sets; an exact correspondence as regards the number of constituent elements and the relations between them; *spec.* a one-to-one homomorphism.

1892 F. N. COLE tr. *Netto's Theory of Substitutions* iv. 83 The correspondence of two groups as just defined is called isomorphism. **1897** W. BURNSIDE *Theory of Groups of Finite Order* xi. 222 A correspondence between the operations of a group, such that to every operation S there corresponds a single operation S', while to the product ST of two operations there corresponds the product $S'T'$ of the corresponding operations, is said to define an isomorphism of the group itself. **1941** W. V. QUINE in P. A. Schilpp *Philos. A. N. Whitehead* 160 The theory of relation numbers is the general theory of isomorphism, i.e., of structural identity among relations. **1949** HUTTEN & REICHENBACH tr. *H. Reichenbach's Theory of Probability* vi. §41. 207 By showing that both the frequency interpretation and the geometrical interpretation satisfy the axioms of the formal system of probability..we have demonstrated the isomorphism, or structural identity, of the two interpretations. **1956** E. M. PATTERSON *Topology* iv. 81 An isomorphism ϕ between two groups G_1, G_2 is a one—one transformation ϕ: $G_1 \to G_2$ of G_1 onto G_2 which preserves the group operation. **1962** *Anthropol. Ling.* June 26 An analysis of the special uses that an individual may make of other dialects..may tell us something about the range of prestige variants and the relative isomorphism of prestige scales that are involved in inter-dialect interchange. **1963** J. LYONS *Structural Semantics* ii. 17 In so far as semantic and distributional criteria converge on the establishment of the same [grammatical] units, this is due to the admitted partial isomorphism between the 'expression-plane' and the 'content-plane' of language. **1965** PATTERSON & RUTHERFORD *Elem. Abstr. Algebra* iii. 77 An isomorphism of a ring R_1 onto a ring R_2 is a one—one mapping f of R_1 onto R_2 such that, for all $x_1, x_2 \in R_1$, we have $f(x_1 + x_2) = f(x_1) + f(x_2)$, $f(x_1x_2) = f(x_1)\,f(x_2)$... In a similar manner, we define isomorphisms between integral domains and fields. **1971** *Sci. Amer.* Aug. 96/3 Boole..noticed that there was a considerable similarity (in fact a mathematical isomorphism) between the rules that govern the use in logic of the connectives 'and', 'or' and 'not', and the operations on sets of, respectively, intersection, union and complementation. **1973** J. HINTIKKA *Logic, Lang.-Games & Information* ii. 42 The basic idea of Wittgenstein's picture theory is the idea of an isomorphism obtaining between language and reality.., an isomorphism which can be established by any correlation or mapping.

3. *Biol.* A similarity of appearance displayed by organisms having different genotypes.

1902 *Encycl. Brit.* XXVI. 255/2 A few fundamental characters are better indications of the affinities of given groups of birds than a great number of agreements if these can be shown to be cases of isomorphism or heterophyletic, convergent analogy. **1920** I. F. & W. D. HENDERSON *Dict. Sci. Terms* 158/1 *Isomorphism*, apparent similarity of individuals of different race or species.

4. *Psychol.* The correspondence assumed to exist between mental perception and physiological processes.

1930 W. KÖHLER *Gestalt Psychol.* ii. 46 But I should have ever so much difficulty in trying to relate definite experiences to definite processes so long as I failed to assume one specific relationship between the two orders, viz., that of *congruence or isomorphism in their systematic properties.* This principle is sometimes formulated more explicitly in a number of 'psycho-physical axioms'. **1937** R. H. THOULESS *Gen. & Social Psychol.* (ed. 2) xii. 241 One of the boldest of the Gestalt speculations has been that of the 'isomorphism' of brain processes and mental processes. **1951** R. B. MACLEOD in Rohrer & Sherif *Social Psychol. at Crossroads* 223 In the doctrine of isomorphism, however, it is asserted that the all-important parallel to perceptual organization is to be found not in the patterning of stimulus processes but rather in the immediately underlying organization of brain activities. **1970** H. C. SHANDS *Semiotic Approaches to Psychiatry* xviii. 290 The evidence suggests strongly that at every level there is an isomorphism between physiological and psychological mechanisms [in cancer patients] when both are abstractly considered.

isomorphous (aɪsəʊˈmɔːfəs), *a.* [f. as ISOMORPH + -OUS.]

1. *Chem.* and *Min.* Having the property of crystallizing in the same or closely related geometric forms: said esp. of two compounds or groups of compounds of different elements, but of analogous composition (cf. HOMŒOMORPHOUS).

1828 in WEBSTER citing *Edin. Rev.* **1837** WHEWELL *Hist. Induct. Sc.* (1857) III. 189 Various elements which are isomorphous to each other. **1841** TRIMMER *Pract. Geol.* 83 The salts of arsenious acid are isomorphous with those of phosphoric acid. **1853** W. GREGORY *Inorg. Chem.* (ed. 3) 41 We observe next, that chromic acid may be substituted for sulphuric acid, without change of form; in other words, these acids are isomorphous. **1871** ROSCOE *Elem. Chem.* 197 Certain substances exhibiting a similarity in their chemical constitution are found to crystallize in the same forms,—these are said to be isomorphous. *Ibid.* 212 The salts of cæsium and rubidium are isomorphous with the corresponding potassium compounds. **1880** CLEMINSHAW *Wurtz' Atom. The.* 59 For the form to remain unchanged in analogous compounds, the elements which replace each other must be mutually isomorphous.

2. *Math.* = ISOMORPHIC 2.

isomorphously (aɪsəʊˈmɔːfəslɪ), *adv. Min.* [f. ISOMORPHOUS *a.* + -LY[2].] In such a way as to produce isomorphous substances.

1901 *Mineral. Mag.* XIII. 45 Miersite..mixes isomorphously with marshite (CuI) on the one hand, and on the other forms intimate intergrowths with iodyrite. **1906** *Jrnl. Chem. Soc.* LXXXIX. II. 1148 Chlorine and fluorine sometimes replace each other isomorphously. **1928** *Amer. Mineralogist* XIII. 52 $AlAlO_3$ may enter $CaMgSi_2O_6$.. isomorphously to as much as 25 per cent. **1947** *Q. Rev.* I. 254 When it is found that F′ can replace OH′ isomorphously, as in the apatites..this can be taken as strong presumptive evidence that the OH..is ionic. **1963** *Geochemistry* 1173 Manganese..is associated with the bivalent iron and calcium which it replaces isomorphously in the rock-forming minerals.

-ison, suffix of sbs., repr. OF. *-aison, -eison, -eson, -ison:*—L. *-ātiōn-em* (at a later date adopted in the learned form *-ation*, which is thus a doublet of *-ison*), *-etiōnem, -itiōnem.* Examples *comparison, fermison, garrison, jettison, orison, venison, warnison.*

Benison and *malison* represent OF. *beneiçon* (later *benisson*) and *maleïçon*, from L. *bene-, maledictionem.* *Caparison* is only attracted into this class. In *reason* and *season*, the suffix has, under the stress, retained a different form; so in *treason:*—OF. *traïsun:*—L. *tradition-em.* See also *inheriteson.* All these, with *poison* (:—L. *pōtiōnem*), etc., are really particular cases of a suffix -SON for L. *-tiōnem.*

i-sondred, ME. pa. pple. of SUNDER *v.*

isoneph, -nephelic: see ISO-.

i-songe(n, ME. pa. pple. of SING *v.*

isoniazid (aɪsəʊˈnaɪəzɪd). *Pharm.* [f. *isoni(cotinic acid* (s.v. ISO- b) + HYDR)AZID(E.] A white or colourless crystalline compound, $C_5H_5N{\cdot}CO{\cdot}NH{\cdot}NH_2$, which has bacteriostatic properties against mycobacteria and is used esp. in the treatment of tuberculosis.

1953 *Jrnl. Pharmacol. & Exper. Therap.* CVII. 219 Isonicotinic acid hydrazide (Nydrazid), generically designated as isoniazid, has been shown to be an effective chemotherapeutic agent against experimental..and human tuberculosis. **1962** *Lancet* 29 Dec. 1364/2 In the second phase, since the bacilli are no longer multiplying rapidly and resistant mutants are therefore unlikely to appear, a single drug only—isoniazid—need be continued to kill off those remaining. **1970** PASSMORE & ROBSON *Compan. Med. Stud.* II. xx. 32/2 Isoniazid (isonicotinic acid hydrazine INH) is the most powerful and effective antituberculous drug. **1973** TURNER & RICHENS *Clin. Pharmacol.* xiv. 186 Isoniazid can interfere with the metabolism of pyridoxine and can cause peripheral neuritis when prolonged courses are given.

isonicotinic, isonitrile: see ISO- b.

isonomaly: see ISO-.

isonomia (aɪsəʊˈnəʊmɪə). = ISONOMY.

1853 E. CREASY *Rise & Progress Eng. Constitution* xiii. 198 There is no part of our constitution so admirable as this equality of civil rights, this *isonomia*, which the philosophers of ancient Greece only hoped to find in democratical government. **1926** *Contemp. Rev.* Oct. 485 It was the *name* 'isonomia' that so commended a democracy.

isonomic (aɪsəʊˈnɒmɪk), *a.* [ad. Gr. ἰσονομικ-ός 'devoted to equality', f. ἰσονομία: see ISONOMY.]

1. Characterized by isonomy; having equal laws or rights. *rare*$^{-0}$.

1864 WEBSTER, *Isonomic*, the same, or equal, in law or right.

2. *Chem.* Having the same or a similar arrangement of elements; involving analogy of composition, as *isomorphism* in the stricter sense.

1864 [see ISOMEROUS 3].

3. Of the same or like polarity: applied to contact of parts of the body in experiments on animal magnetism: opp. to HETERONOMIC 1, q.v.

†**i'sonomous**, *a. Cryst. Obs.* [f. Gr. ἰσόνομ-ος (see next) + -OUS: in F. *isonome.*] See quot.

1805–17 R. JAMESON *Char. Min.* (ed. 3) 219 When the exponents which indicate the decrements on the edges are equal to each other, and also those which indicate the decrements in the angles. Example, Isonomous artificial blue vitriol.

isonomy (aɪˈsɒnəmɪ). [ad. It. *isonomia* 'equalitie of laws to all manner of persons' (Florio, 1598), perh. also in 16th c. L., a. Gr. ἰσονομία, n. of quality from ἰσόνομος having equal political rights, f. ἰσο-, ISO- + νόμος law. Frequent in 17th c.; obs. in 18th; used again in 19th.] Equality of laws, or of people before the law; equality of political rights among the citizens of a state.

1600 HOLLAND *Livy* III. xxxix. 114 The successive change and course of bearing rule, the only thing that maketh Isonomie, and equalitie of freedome. *Ibid.* lxvii. 134 Under the pretence and colour of Isonomie, or equall and indifferent lawes. *Ibid.* XXXVIII. l. 1016 Nothing preserveth isonomie in a citie, & mainteineth equall libertie more. **1659** *Quaeries on Proposalls Officers Armie to Parlt.* 8 Every one pretending to equality and Isonomy, lifteth up and advanceth himself whilst he shoveth at, and thrusteth down others. **1684** tr. *Agrippa's Van. Arts* lv. 155 They who prefer a Popular State have dignifi'd it with the most agreeable and specious Title of Isonomie. **1856** J. H. NEWMAN *Office & Work Universities* vii. 123 The Athenians felt that a democracy was but the political expression of an intellectual isonomy. **1882** W. CARY *Mod. Eng. Hist.* II. 272 To regulate the many varieties of man..in..Eastern Europe on the principle of isonomy.

isonuclear: see ISO-.

isooctane (aɪsəʊˈɒkteɪn). Also **iso-octane.** [f. ISO- + OCTANE.] †**a.** 2-Methylheptane, $CH_3{\cdot}(CH_2)_4{\cdot}CH(CH_3){\cdot}CH_3$, a liquid hydrocarbon that occurs in petroleum. *Obs.*

1909 L. CLARKE in *Jrnl. Amer. Chem. Soc.* XXXI. 107 In this paper are described the preparation and properties of iso-octane or 2-methyl heptane... Iso-octane is the ninth hydrocarbon to be prepared in the series C_8H_{18}. **1911** *Ibid.* XXXIII. 524 2-Methylheptane (or iso-octane) has the boiling point 116°. [**1966** *McGraw-Hill Encycl. Sci. & Technol.* I. 249/1 Although the name isooctane correctly designates 2-methylheptane, it should be avoided because of the unfortunate use of the misnomer 'isooctane' in the petroleum industry to represent 2, 2, 4-trimethylpentane.]

b. 2,2,4-Trimethylpentane, $(CH_3)_3C{\cdot}CH_2{\cdot}CH(CH_3){\cdot}CH_3$, a colourless liquid hydrocarbon which is used in aviation fuels and as a solvent and which, because of its good antiknock properties, is taken as a standard in the determination of octane numbers (being assigned the number 100).

This use of the name does not conform to the convention for using *iso-* described s.v. ISO- b.

1932 *Bureau of Standards Jrnl. Res.* (U.S.) IX. 269 As a criterion for the purity of commercial 'iso-octane', it is desirable to have a reliable value for the freezing point. **1938** *Jrnl. Chem. Soc.* 239 *iso*Octane..is now produced commercially for blending purposes from *iso*butylene via diisobutylene. **1946** *Industr. Chemist* XXII. 519/1 This small yield of isooctane was the backbone of the 87 octane no. finished aviation grade produced commercially before the war. **1954** D. M. DESOUTTER *All about Aircraft* vii. 120/2 A fuel of 130 octane is one which allows a standard test engine to give 30 per cent more power than it would when using pure iso-octane. **1962** *Biochim. & Biophys. Acta* LXI. 467 It occurred to us that the use of an organic solvent to detach lipid and lipoprotein from rat-liver microsomes might be possible, and this note presents results of the successful use of isooctane. **1971** R. J. & J. S. FESSENDEN *Basis Org. Chem.* ii. 36 At one time, the branched-chain alkane erroneously named isooctane was the best antiknock fuel known. It was given an octane number of 100.

iso-osmotic: see ISO-.

isop, isop(p)e, obs. forms of HYSSOP.

isopach (ˈaɪsəʊpæk). [f. ISO- + Gr. παχ-ύς thick.] **1.** *Geol.* = ISOPACHYTE.

1918 *Private Let. U.S. Geol. Survey* (G. & C. Merriam Co. files) 10 May, *Isopach, isopachous*—noun and adjective, referring to lines on a map that shows equal thicknesses of beds, e.g. coal beds. **1925** *Bull. Amer. Assoc. Petroleum Geologists* IX. 890 The term 'isopach' is used to designate lines through points of equal thickness. *Ibid.*, The isopachs swing from a general east-and-west direction to the north. **1957** *Bull. Geol. Survey Gt. Brit.* XII. 55 The total stratigraphical thickness in feet at each locality was plotted and isopachs drawn through points of equal thickness. **1969** *Nature* 8 Nov. 536/2 The measured thickness of the pyroclastic deposits at various localities and the proposed isopachs are shown in Fig. 2. The isopachs generally extend south-eastwards from the eruptive centres, indicating distribution under the influence of a prevailing north-westerly wind.

2. = ISOPACHIC *sb.*

1936 *Jrnl. R. Aeronaut. Soc.* XL. 55 An isopach is defined ..as lines along which the sum of the principal stresses is constant. **1962** J. C. JAEGER *Elasticity, Fracture & Flow* (ed. 2) iv. 182 Isopachs are curves of constant mean stress $\sigma_1 + \sigma_2$.

isopachic (aɪsəʊˈpækɪk), *a.* and *sb.* [f. as prec. + -IC.] **A.** *adj.* Corresponding to or depicting the locus of points in a body where the sum of the principal stresses has the same value.

1931 COKER & FILON *Treat. Photo-Elasticity* ii. 178 By observations with the lateral extensometer we can..obtain ..the curves for which $P + Q$ has an equal value. These may be briefly referred to as Isopachic curves, or curves of equal thickness. **1950** M. HETÉNYI *Handbk. Exper. Stress Analysis* xvii. 910 If the isochromatic and isopachic lines for a given model and loading are known, it becomes..simple.. to evaluate the two principal stresses at any point by direct addition and subtraction of the equivalent values. **1972** *Phys. Bull.* May 276/3 The use of double exposure holography to obtain isopachic-isochromatic fringe patterns in the reconstructed image has also been reported.

B. *sb.* An isopachic line or curve.

1931 COKER & FILON *Treat. Photo-Elasticity* ii. 179 The lines of equal P are..obtained by taking successive intersections of isochromatics and isopachics, the parameters of the isochromatics going up one at a time, those of the isopachics going down one at a time; or conversely. **1958** CONDON & ODISHAW *Handbk. Physics* III. vi. 88/1 Curves of constant $p + q$ are called isopachics.

isopachous (aɪsəʊˈpækəs, aɪˈsɒpəkəs), *a. Geol.* [f. as prec. + -OUS.] Depicting or pertaining to isopachs (sense 1); that is an isopach.

1913 *Bull. U.S. Geol. Survey* No. 537. 89 (*caption*) Sketch map showing lines along which a coal bed is of equal thickness (isopachous lines), drawn for use in valuation of coal land. **1938** *Bull. Amer. Assoc. Petroleum Geologists* XXII. 425 (*heading*) Thinning of Devonian shown by isopachous lines. **1940** *Ibid.* XXIV. 2151 (*heading*) Isopachous studies in Michigan. **1968** HARBAUGH & MERRIAM *Computer Applications in Stratigr. Analysis* v. 87/1 A thickness map (also termed an isopachous map).. portrays the interval between two stratigraphic horizons.

isopachyte (aɪsəʊˈpækaɪt). *Geol.* [f. ISO- + Gr. παχύτ-ης thickness.] A line on a map or diagram joining points below which a particular stratum or group of strata has the same thickness.

1912 *Compt. Rend. XI Congrès Géol. Internat.* I. 250 A series of maps was prepared..and on them were drawn isopachytes, or lines marking points of equal thickness. **1946** *Nature* 13 July 49/2 The detailed stratigraphy of the Coal Measures, shown by isopachyte maps and many other data, gives an insight into the development of this sedimentary series. **1969** BENNISON & WRIGHT *Geol. Hist. Brit. Isles* iv. 77 Isopachytes for the Cambrian as a whole..must be interpreted with caution.., but they provide some indication of the form of the Cambrian geosyncline in Wales.

isoparaffin to **isopentyl:** see ISO-.

isopathy (aɪˈsɒpəθɪ). *Med. rare*$^{-0}$. [f. ISO- + -PATHY.]

a. The theory that disease may be cured by a product of the disease, as small-pox by application of the variolous matter. **b.** The popular notion that disease in a particular organ may be cured by eating the same organ of a healthy animal.

1855 in MAYNE *Expos. Lex.*

isoperimeter (ˌaɪsəʊpəˈrɪmɪtə(r)). *Geom.* [ad. Gr. ἰσοπερίμετρος: see ISO- and PERIMETER: in F. *isopérimètre* (Rousseau in Littré).] A figure having a perimeter equal to that of another; usually in *pl.* Figures of equal perimeter.

1674 JEAKE *Arith.* (1696) 525 Plain Figures, called Isoperimeters, and also Bodies of Equal Surface, may be vastly different in their Area's and Solid Contents. **1715** TAYLOR in *Phil. Trans.* XXIX. 345 Where I give the Solution of the Problems concerning the Isoperimeter. **1870** CHAUVENET *Geom.* v. 162 Second method, called the method of isoperimeters.

†**isope'rimetral**, *a. Obs.* [f. as prec. + -AL[1].] = next, 1.

1625 N. CARPENTER *Geog. Del.* II. ii. (1635) 19 Those Figures called Isoperimetrall, or of equall Perimeter.

isoperimetrical (ˌaɪsəʊperɪˈmetrɪkəl), *a. Geom.* [f. Gr. ἰσοπερίμετρος (see ISOPERIMETER) + -ICAL.]

1. Of figures: Having equal perimeters.

1706 PHILLIPS, *Isoperimeters* or *Isoperimetrical Figures*, such Figures as have equal Perimeters, or Circumferences. **1796** HUTTON *Math. Dict.* I. 647 M. Cramer too, in the Berlin Memoirs for 1752..proposes to demonstrate..that the circle is the greatest of all isoperimetrical figures, regular or irregular. **1812** CRESSWELL *Max. & Min.* I. 49 The greatest of all isoperimetrical polygons, of the same number of sides, is necessarily equilateral. **1828** HUTTON *Course Math.* II. 328 Of all isoperimetrical triangles, the one which has the greatest surface is equilateral. **1828** LARDNER *Euclid* 72 The area of the square exceeds the area of any other isoperimetrical rectangle by the square of half the difference of the sides of the rectangle.

2. Relating to or connected with isoperimetry. *isoperimetrical problems*: see quot. 1865.

1743 *Phil. Trans.* XLII. 358 Isoperimetrical Problems are resolved..with like Facility by the same Method. **1816** tr. *Lacroix's Diff. & Int. Calculus* 463 Such is the simplest case of the *Isoperimetrical Problems* so called, because at first only curves of the same length were considered. **1821** *Blackw. Mag.* X. 557 From Cookery up to the Law of Contingent Remainders, Isoperimetrical Problems, or the world-wide difference between Objectivity and Subjectivity. **1865** B. PRICE *Infinites. Calc.* (ed. 2) II. 465 Problems of *relative* maxima and minima..wherein the variables are not independent of each other, but are connected by some given relation, which may be integral or differential, or in the form of a definite integral..are often called *isoperimetrical*, because the given condition when interpreted geometrically, is frequently equivalent to the length of the curve being given between certain fixed points or limiting lines.

isoperimetry (aɪsəʊpəˈrɪmɪtrɪ). *Geom.* [f. as ISOPERIMETER + -Y.] That branch of geometry which deals with isoperimetrical figures, and the problems connected with them.

1811 HUTTON *Course Math.* III. ii. 31 *heading*, Elements of Isoperimetry. *Ibid.* 32 The most abstruse inquiries concerning isoperimetry.

isopetalous to **isopiestic**: see ISO-.

isophane (ˈaɪsəʊfeɪn), **isophene** (-fiːn). [f. as next; cf. PHEN-, PHENO-.] A line (imaginary or on a map) linking places in which seasonal biological phenomena (the flowering of plants, etc.) occur at the same time. Hence **iso'phanal**, **iso'phenal** *adjs.*

1918 A. D. HOPKINS in *U.S. Dept. Agric. Monthly Weather Rev. Suppl.* IX. 8 (*caption*) Isophenal map of North America. *Ibid.* 9/1 Taking base maps of North America and of the major and minor political divisions, parallel lines (designated as isophanes) are drawn on them to define, according to the bioclimatic law, theoretical lines and zones of equal phenomena as to time of occurrence and equal bioclimatic conditions, at the same level. **1929** V. E. SHELFORD *Lab. & Field Ecol.* i. 15 An isophenal map was prepared with isophenes drawn through equal-event dates at the same altitude. **1931** *Trans. Entomol. Soc. Lond.* LXXIX. 183 Local conditions..cause considerable departures in the actual dates of seasonal events from those indicated by isophanes. *Ibid.*, Instead of basing the isophanal map on degrees of latitude and longitude, he [*sc.* Znamenskiĭ] made use of the mean annual isotherms. **1947** R. F. DAUBENMIRE *Plants & Environment* iv. 219 From phenologic data maps can be drawn with lines (isophenes) connecting locations where plants are in the same stage of development at the same time. **1963** E. MAYR *Animal Species & Evolution* xiii. 362 This north-south cline is crossed by the isophenes, lines connecting all populations with the same phenotype.

isophane (ˈaɪsəʊfeɪn), *a. Pharm.* [f. ISO- + Gr. -φανης showing, appearing (f. φαίνειν to show, cause to appear).] **a.** Designating that ratio of protamine to insulin which, in a solution made by mixing solutions of the individual substances, gives rise to equal turbidity in two equal samples taken after a precipitate has been allowed to form when one sample has sufficient insulin added to it to precipitate all the protamine in it and the other a sufficient amount of protamine to precipitate all the insulin.

1946 KRAYENBÜHL & ROSENBERG in *Rep. Steno Memorial Hosp.* I. 65 The proportion of protamine to insulin must be nearly isophane. At isophane proportions the formation of crystals is rapid. **1950** *Federal Register* (U.S.) 2 Nov. 7363/2 The isophane ratio shall be expressed as milligrams of protamine per 100 U.S.P. Units of insulin. **1955** *Dispensatory U.S.A.* (ed. 25) 686/2 The most useful of these mixtures, for many patients, proved to be the 2:1 mixture of regular insulin and protamine zinc insulin. In this mixture protamine is present to the extent of about 0·5 mg. per 100 units of insulin, which is the combining proportion, or so-called isophane ratio, of protamine and insulin.

b. Applied to a crystalline mixture of insulin and protamine in the isophane ratio with zinc, which has longer-lasting effects than pure insulin. Also *ellipt.* as *sb.*

1954 A. GROLLMAN *Pharmacol. & Therapeutics* (ed. 2) xxvi. 606 (*table*) NPH Insulin (Isophane). **1955** *Dispensatory U.S.A.* (ed. 25) 686/2 In preparing Isophane Insulin Injection, sufficient insulin is used to provide either 40 or 80 U.S.P. Insulin Units for each ml. of the Injection. **1955** *Brit. Med. Jrnl.* 19 Feb. 478/2 Having used isophane.. since November, 1953, and in more than 60 diabetics, I find it easily the most satisfactory one-shot-a-day insulin available. **1966** *Lancet* 24 Dec. 1389/2 A 20-year-old diabetic patient, who was poorly controlled on 45 units isophane insulin in the morning and 35 units isophane insulin in the evening, was admitted in diabetic ketoacidosis. **1968** POND & OAKLEY in W. G. Oakley et al. *Clin. Diabetes* xxiii. 602 A comparable method of control by a single morning injection is the use of a mixture of isophane (NPH) and SI.

isophone (ˈaɪsəʊfəʊn). *Linguistics.* [f. ISO- + PHONE *sb.*[1]] A phonetic isogloss; also, a phonetic feature shared by speakers in contiguous areas. Hence **iso'phonic** *a.*

1921 E. C. ROEDDER in *Jrnl. Eng. & Germ. Philol.* XX. 182 The boundary lines of present dialects, with their maze of isophones,..and isotaxes, i.e., lines connecting places of identical or nearly identical sounds,..and syntactical peculiarities. **1926** *Germanic Rev.* I. iv. 286 A map of France with all isophonic lines would show the wildest maze and confusion. **1926** [see ISOMORPH 2]. **1932** W. L. GRAFF *Lang.* 364 There were isoglosses and isophones which contained the germs of later developments. **1935** *Univ. Mich. Publ. Lang. & Lit.* XIII. 23 We believe..that these isophonic lines do reflect roughly at least approximate boundaries for eleven of the most important characteristics of the regional dialects of Middle English as they existed about the middle of the fourteenth century. *Ibid.* 32 The physiographical boundaries are an interpretation of the isophones and are therefore subject to the modifications that additional documentary evidence may bring. In some cases these modifications will result in a closer approximation of the isophones to the corresponding physiographical boundaries. **1936** *Trans. Philol. Soc. 1936* 79 It certainly raises the question as to how far the delimitation of dialects and dialect features in Middle English by means of 'isophones' can really be reliable. **1937** *Year's Work Eng. Stud. 1935* 42 The country marked out by 'isophonic' lines into ten areas, each of which presents a more or less distinct complex of dialect-characteristics. **1955** W. S. AVIS in *Amer. Speech* XXX. 7 In a very loose way this boundary approximates an *r*-isophone. **1970** *English Studies* LI. 445 The new and very clear ā/ǭ isophone there [*sc.* in Lincolnshire] is an important result of the investigation.

isophorous (aɪˈsɒfərəs), *a. Bot.* [f. Gr. ἰσοφόρος bearing equal weight, equal in strength, f. ἰσο-, ISO- + -φόρος bearing.] Term used by Lindley to express the relation of certain supposed genera (*e.g.* of orchids) to those of which they are held to be abnormal forms.

1866 *Treas. Bot.*, *Isophorous*, transformable into something else. Thus, *Aclinia* [printed *Actinia*] is an isophorous form of *Dendrobium*, *Paxtonia* of *Spathoglottis*, and, according to Morren, *Anguloa* and *Lycaste* of *Maxillaria*.

isophot, var. ISOPHOTE.

isophotal (aɪsəʊˈfəʊtəl), *a.* [f. as next + -AL.] Applied to an isophote and to a diagram depicting isophotes. Also as *sb.*, = ISOPHOTE.

1904 D. BURNETT in *Trans. Amer. Inst. Electr. Engin.* XX. 74 The impression they convey would much more nearly accord with what actually occurs if the curves showed not the intensity of light in the various directions, but the lines along which the lighting is equal at any point. Such curves may be called 'isophotals', and while they are of the same general shape as intensity curves, their dimensions are as the square root of the radii. *Ibid.*, The tendency of enclosing an arc.., either in the interior gas globe or more particularly in the outer diffusing globe, is to make such an isophotal curve approach more nearly a circle. **1930** *Astrophysical Jrnl.* LXXI. 365 The total luminosity of the entire nebula out to the distance *r/a* is found by integrating successive elliptical rings on the assumption that the isophotal contours are all similar ellipses. **1964** *Jrnl. Geophysical Res.* LXIX. 487/1 These regions were characterized by systems of isophotal contour lines, sometimes occupying virtually the whole observed area. *Ibid.* 487/2 Isophotal sky maps. **1964** A. COX *Syst. Optical Design* ix. 367 The contour lines are 'isophotals' mapping areas of equal intensity.

isophote (ˈaɪsəʊfəʊt). Also **-phot** (-fɒt). [f. ISO- + Gr. φῶς, φωτ- light.] A line (imaginary or in a diagram) connecting points where the brightness or the illumination is the same. Also *transf.* (of radiation other than light).

1909 *Cent. Dict.* Suppl., Isophote. **1937** *Nature* 2 Oct. 577/1 The successive isophotes of the corona round the sun are nearly circular. **1957** G. E. HUTCHINSON *Treat. Limnol.* I. vi. 373 (*caption*) Isophots in 1000 cal. cm.$^{-2}$ received during April, May, June, and July on the Scandinavian Peninsula. **1959** DAVIES & PALMER *Radio Stud. Universe* iv. 47 In some cases the radio isophotes are far more extensive than their optical counterparts. **1966** E. HARRISON-JONES in Hewitt & Vause *Lamps & Lighting* xxix. 466 In planning general window lighting of this kind..isophot diagrams are used to determine direct illumination. **1973** *Physics Bull.* July 417 (*caption*) Intensity map of elliptical galaxies NGC 4278 and 4283, showing the outermost faint isophotes.

isophotic (aɪsəʊˈfəʊtɪk), *a.* [f. as prec. + -IC.] = ISOPHOTAL *a.*

1931 *Nature* 14 Mar. 418/2 Diagrams are given, showing the isophotic lines in the two [Magellanic] clouds. **1935** E. A. MILNE *Relativity, Gravitation & World-Struct.* xiv. 279 The circular shape of the observed isophotic contours near a nebular nucleus. **1971** *Jrnl. Astron. Soc. Canada* LXV. 251 (*heading*) Monochromatic photographs and isophotic contours of planetary nebulae.

isophthalate, isophthalic: see ISO- b.

isopiestic: see ISO-.

isoplasty (ˈaɪsəʊplæstɪ). *Med.* and *Biol.* [f. ISO- + -PLASTY.]
= HOMOPLASTY, HOMOTRANSPLANTATION. Hence **iso'plastic** *a.* = HOMOPLASTIC *a.* 2.

1923 Isoplasty, -plastic [see HOMOGRAFTING *vbl. sb.*]. **1929** *Ann. Surg.* XC. 926 Homoplasty, homeoplasty and isoplasty mean tissue transplantation from one individual to another of the same species.

isopleth (ˈaɪsəʊplɛθ). [ad. Gr. ἰσοπληθ-ής equal in quantity, f. πλῆθος multitude, quantity.]

1. [ad. G. *isoplethe* (C. A. Vogler *Anleitung zum Entwerfen graph. Tafeln* (1877) i. 7).] A line (either imaginary or on a map or diagram) connecting points for which some chosen quantity has the same value, the points (if on a diagram) being defined by two variables of which one is usually distance and the other either distance or time.

1909 in *Cent. Dict.* Suppl. **1911** N. SHAW *Forecasting Weather* 4 Isobars are isopleths of pressure, isotherms are isopleths of temperature, and so on. **1935** *Geogr. Jrnl.* LXXXV. 145 Isopleths of population density are drawn. **1950** CONRAD & POLLAK *Methods in Climatol.* (ed. 2) iii. 69 The curves z = const., called isopleths, thus show the relationship of the two variables x and y only for selected values of the third variable z, which is constant for each curve. **1957** G. E. HUTCHINSON *Treat. Limnol.* I. ix. 630 Three days later a still more striking deflection of the oxygen isopleths downward at the upper end of the basin was noted. **1971** *Sci. Amer.* Sept. 92 (*caption*) Mean radiation of the earth is portrayed by isopleths..that give the net radiation in terms of calories per square centimeter per minute.

2. *Physical Chem.* A line or surface (in a diagram) joining points that represent mixtures of the same composition.

1924 G. EDGAR in H. S. Taylor *Treat. Physical Chem.* I. ix. 400 Assume a complex containing 60 per cent phenol to be warmed from 10° to 70°; the process can be followed by drawing a line of equal concentrations, *ab*, called an isopleth. **1950** W. J. MOORE *Physical Chem.* vi. 136 Let us follow the sequence of events as the pressure is gradually reduced along the line of constant composition, or isopleth, *xx'*. **1951** J. E. RICCI *Phase Rule* iii. 59 The representation of the melting point region may be completed by a constant composition section, the isopleth shown in Fig. 3-12.

Hence **'isoplethal** (-pliːθəl) *a.*, carried out or occurring at constant composition.

1924 G. EDGAR in H. S. Taylor *Treat. Physical Chem.* I. ix. 411 The general diagram..may be used to illustrate the effect of isothermal and isoplethal changes. **1951** J. E. RICCI *Phase Rule* ix. 189 Isoplethal or Synthetic Methods. These involve the measurement of the temperature of phase transition or of the curve of a miscibility gap, upon complexes of known composition.

isopleural (aɪsəʊˈpl(j)ʊərəl), *a.* [f. as next + -AL[1].] Having equal sides, equilateral; *spec.* in *Zool.* belonging to the sub-class *Isopleura* of gastropods, which have the body bilaterally symmetrical, as in the chitons. Also **iso'pleurous** *a.*

† **'isopleure.** *Obs.* Also in Gr. form **isopleuron**. [ad. Gr. ἰσόπλευρ-ος equilateral, f. ἰσο-, ISO- + πλευρά rib, side.] A figure with equal sides; an equilateral figure.

1592 R. D. *Hypnerotomachia* 18 Then in the voide ouer the Isopleures make foure Mediane prickes, drawing lines from one to another and they will make the Rhombus. **1647** H. MORE *Philos. Poems* 377 An *Isopleuron* or equilaterall Triangle. **1674** N. FAIRFAX *Bulk & Selv.* 116 The same Answer undoes the knot, that every triangle would be an *Isopleuron*, that the diagonial lines of a Rhomboides would be equal.

isopod (ˈaɪsəpɒd), *sb.* (*a.*) *Zool.* Also **isopode**. Pl. **isopods**; also freq. in L. form **isopoda** (aɪˈsɒpɒdə). [a. mod.F. *isopode*, f. mod.L. *Isopod-a* neuter pl., f. Gr. type *ἰσοποδ-, f. ISO- + πούς, ποδ- foot.] An animal of the order *Isopoda* of sessile-eyed Crustaceans, characterized by seven pairs of equal and similarly placed thoracic legs; comprising marine, fresh-water, and terrestrial species, some being parasitic.

1835 KIRBY *Hab. & Inst. Anim.* II. xv. 41 *Isopods. Head* distinct. *Eyes* sessile. *Legs* simple, equal. **1852** DANA *Crust.* I. 11 There are, however, true intermediate species between the Amphipods and Isopods. **1885** C. F. HOLDER *Marvels Anim. Life* 144 The little isopods, so common on our rocky shores.

b. *attrib.* or *adj.* = ISOPODOUS.

1864 in WEBSTER. **1875** BLAKE *Zool.* 308 The isopod Crustacea have the head distinct from the segment bearing the first pair of feet.

So **isopodan** (aɪˈsɒpəʊdən) *a.* and *sb.* = prec.; **isopodiform** (aɪsəʊˈpɒdɪfɔːm) *a.* [ad. mod.L. *isopodiformis*: see -FORM], having the form of or resembling an isopod, as certain insect larvæ; **isopodimorphous** (-ˈmɔːfəs) *a.* [Gr. μορφή form] = *isopodiform*.

1855 MAYNE *Expos. Lex.*, *Isopodiformis*, applied by Kirby to the hexapodous, antenniferous and saprophagous *larvæ* which have an oblong body, a distinct thoracic *clypeus* or buckler, and the anus furnished with filaments or plates: isopodiform. **1856** DANA in *Amer. Jrnl. Sc.* July 11 The size of the body far transcends the ordinary Isopodan limit.

isopodous (aɪˈsɒpədəs), *a. Zool.* [f. as ISOPOD + -OUS.] Belonging to, or having the characters of, the *Isopoda*: see prec.

1826 KIRBY & SP. *Entomol.* III. xxx. 168, I possess two specimens of larvæ of *Silphidæ* which seem to exhibit considerable analogy with the *Isopodous Crustacea.* **1862** ANSTED *Channel Isl.* II. ix. (ed. 2) 234 The isopodous and amphipodous species are also supplied by the same naturalist.

isopolity (aɪsəʊˈpɒlɪtɪ). Chiefly *Anc. Hist.* [ad. Gr. ἰσοπολιτεία, f. ἰσοπολίτης a citizen with equal or reciprocal right, f. ἰσο- + πολίτης citizen.] Equality of rights of citizenship between different communities or states; reciprocity of civic rights.

1836 C. F. HERMANN *Pol. Antiq. Gr.* 229 It is not known that Athens was ever on terms of perfect Isopolity with any other State. **1849** KEMBLE *Saxons Eng.* II. vii. II. 270 The period of the Social, Marsic or Italian war, when the cities of Italy wrested isopolity, or at least isotely, from Rome. **1853** CLOUGH *Let. to C. E. Norton* 21 Sept., Between America and England..one would be glad if there could exist some isopolity. **1897** A. V. DICEY in *Contemp. Rev.* Apr. 461 Community of citizenship would affect not civil, but political rights. If the Acts creating isopolity were

passed, a citizen of the United States would stand, when in England, in the same position as an English colonist.

b. *transf.* Equality of rights or privileges (of any kind).

1862 S. LUCAS *Secularia* 26 The Church..exemplifying in her own 'dignified isopolity' the equality of all men in the sight of God. **1879** FARRAR *St. Paul* viii. (1893) 80 The Crucifixion had, in fact, been the protest of the Jew against an isopolity of faith.

So **isopolite** (aɪ'sɒpəlaɪt) [Gr. ἰσοπολίτης (see above)] *sb.* and *a.*; **isopolitical** (aɪsəʊpəʊ'lɪtɪkəl), *a.*, of or relating to isopolity; involving mutual rights of citizenship.

1842–5 *W. Smith's Dict. Gr. & Rom. Antiq.* s.v. *Civitas*, The isopolite relation. **1871** *W. Smith's Smaller Dict. of Antiq.* (ed. 8) 173/1 If he withdrew to a state between which and Rome isopolitical relations existed, he would become a citizen of that state.

isopor, isoporic: see ISO-.

isoprenaline (aɪsəʊ'prɛnəliːn). *Pharm.* [f. the chemical name N-*isopro*pylnoradr*enaline*.] A sympathomimetic amine, $C_6H_3(OH)_2CH(OH)$-$CH_2NHCH(CH_3)_2$, that is a derivative of adrenaline and is used (usu. as the hydrochloride or sulphate, both whitish, bitter-tasting powders) either sublingually or in an aerosol for the relief of bronchial asthma and pulmonary emphysema.

This is the name in the *British Pharmacopœia*: cf. ISOPROTERENOL.

1951 *Brit. Jrnl. Pharmacol.* VI. 295 The amines used were *l*-adrenaline..and *dl*-isopropyl-*nor*adrenaline hydrochloride (isoprenaline). **1965** *Lancet* 19 June 1301/2, 75 patients with symptoms due to heart-block were treated with a long-acting formulation of isoprenaline. **1966** DUNLOP & ALSTEAD *Textbk. Med. Treatm.* (ed. 10) 716 Isoprenaline given by inhalation is effective within a few minutes and, although the relief is relatively short-lived, this form of treatment has a useful place in the treatment of episodic asthma. **1971** *Brit. Med. Bull.* XXVII. 27/1 Death might be caused by the excessive use of aerosol inhalers containing..isoprenaline.

isoprene ('aɪsəʊpriːn). [f. ISO-, perh. + PR(OPYL)ENE.] **a.** 2-Methyl-1, 3-butadiene, $CH_2{:}C(CH_3)CH{:}CH_2$, a colourless liquid obtained by the destructive distillation of rubber and from petroleum and used in the manufacture of certain synthetic rubbers.

1860 C. G. WILLIAMS in *Phil. Trans. R. Soc.* CL. 244, I have given the substance thus examined the name of isoprene. *Ibid.* 249 Isoprene combines explosively with bromine. *Ibid.* 255 The isolation of isoprene, $C^{10}H^8$. **1867** BLOXAM *Chem.* 481 Heated in a retort, caoutchouc is decomposed into several hydrocarbons, one of which, called isoprene, boils at about 100°F. **1906** *Westm. Gaz.* 8 Sept. 10/2 In forming caoutchouc from isoprene, the great problem is already practically solved. **1957** *Technology* July 176/3 By the use of Ziegler catalysts..Goodrich-Gulf were able to synthesize from isoprene a polymer almost identical with natural rubber. **1972** P. WISEMAN *Introd. Industr. Org. Chem.* vii. 253 More important than high molecular weight homopolymers of isobutene are copolymers with 1·5 to 4·5% of isoprene, known as butyl rubber.

b. *attrib.*, as **isoprene rule**, the rule that the carbon skeleton of a terpene is made up of isoprene units linked together; **isoprene unit**, the arrangement of five carbon atoms found in the isoprene molecule (the single or double nature of the bonds between them being disregarded).

1926 C. K. INGOLD in *Proc. Leeds Philos. & Lit. Soc.* (*Sci. Sect.*) I. 11 It is known..that the carbon skeletons of all terpenes of established constitution can empirically be built up from the skeleton of isoprene, the common product of thermal degradation of almost all terpenes. Divisibility into isoprene units may therefore be regarded as a *necessary* condition to be satisfied by the structure of any plant-synthesised terpene product. **1931** J. L. SIMONSEN *Terpenes* I. p. xii, An apparent exception to the 'isoprene rule', the hydrocarbon, sylvestrene, has been shown not to be a plant product. **1942** FUSON & SNYDER *Org. Chem.* xxvii. 358 Caoutchouc is composed of the isoprene unit repeated over and over. *Ibid.*, The occurrence of isoprene units is so general that investigators of the structures of natural products generally consider the most probable formula of an unknown compound to be that which contains the maximum number of isoprene units. **1959** L. RUZICKA in *Proc. Chem. Soc.* 343/2 Up to 1921, the idea that the higher terpenes are structurally composed of isoprene units was not used as an accepted working hypothesis. **1967** *Nature* 18 Nov. 642/2 The occurrence of a series of hydrocarbons, with structures based on the C_5H_8 isoprene unit, has been invoked as evidence for life-forms in Pre-Cambrian times. **1971** J. D. ROBERTS et. al. *Org. Chem.* xxix. 779 The empirical isoprene rule resulted from Ruzicka's observation that the majority of the terpene families could be considered as arising from head-to-tail combinations of isoprene units.

isoprenoid ('aɪsəprɪnɔɪd, aɪsəʊ'priːnɔɪd), *a.* and *sb. Chem.* [f. prec. + -OID.] **A.** *adj.* Containing or designating the isoprene unit; having a molecular structure composed of such units. **B.** *sb.* An isoprenoid compound.

1945 *Chem. Abstr.* XXXIX. 5887/1 Other isoprenoid hydrocarbons, as isoprene, diterpenes, triterpenes, sesquiterpenes, are either entered at their trivial names or named systematically. **1958** *Proc. Nat. Acad. Sci.* XLIV. 167 Squalene synthesis from branched-chain subunits will be treated as a two stage process, namely (a) the condensation of three 'isoprenoid' units to a sesquiterpene (C_{15}) [etc.]. **1965** *New Scientist* 24 June 867/2 The branched-chain compounds called isoprenoids, which have a branch every fourth carbon atom. **1971** *Nature* 24 Dec. 449/1 Pristane (2,6,10,14-tetramethylpentadecane) and phytane (2,6,10,14-tetramethylhexadecane), isoprenoid hydrocarbons, which probably arise from diagenetic degradation of algal chlorophylls, were present [in the sediment] in trace amounts. **1972** *Science* 9 June 1121/2 After 2 years, isoprenoids..and alicyclic and aromatic hydrocarbons remained prominent in the polluted sediments.

isopropanol to **isopropylidene:** see ISO-.

isoproterenol (ˌaɪsəʊprəʊtə'riːnɒl). *Pharm.* [f. the chemical name N-*isopro*pylar*terenol*.] The name in the *United States Pharmacopeia* for ISOPRENALINE.

1957 *Jrnl. Pharmacol. & Exper. Therap.* CXIX. 253 Isoproterenol..produces vasodilation and a marked increase in heart contractile force. **1961** *Lancet* 9 Sept. 574/1 Isoproterenol hydrochloride..was administered intravenously, and the nodal pacemaker gradually increased in rate with sudden re-emergence of ventricular fibrillation. **1972** R. HAIAT et al. in J. Han *Cardiac Arrhythmias* v. 91 Although some authors reported satisfactory medical management of chronic heart block, long-term drug therapy with isoproterenol is often unreliable and even hazardous.

isopsephic (aɪsəʊ'psɛfɪk, -'siːfɪk), *a.* (*sb.*) [f. Gr. ἰσοψηφία, f. ἰσόψηφ-ος (f. ἴσος equal + ψῆφος pebble, counter) + -IC.] Of equal numerical value; said of words in which the numerical values of the letters (according to the ancient Greek notation) made up the same amount. Also as *sb.* (in *pl.*) Isopsephic verses. So **isopsephism** (aɪsəʊ'psiːfɪz(ə)m), isopsephic relation.

1882 FARRAR *Early Chr.* II. 291 *note*, They [the Greeks] called verses isopsephics when their letters made up numerically the same sum... On the Gnostic gems the word Abraxas is used as isopsephic to Meithras (the Sun) because the letters of both names = 325. **1886** —— *Hist. Interpr.* ii. 98 This method resembled the Greek isopsephism and consisted in establishing mystic relations between different conceptions, based on the numerical equivalence of value in the letters by which they are expressed.

isopterous (aɪ'sɒptərəs), *a.* [f. ISO- + πτερ-όν wing, -πτερ-ος -winged + -OUS. Cf. late Gr. ἰσόπτερος swift as flight.] Having equal wings; *spec.* in *Entom.* Belonging to, or having the characters of, the *Isoptera* (reckoned by some as a sub-order of *Neuroptera*), comprising the termites or white ants, having four large equal wings.

isopycnal (aɪsəʊ'pɪknəl). *Oceanogr.* [f. ISO- + Gr. πυκν-ός dense + -AL.] A line (imaginary or on a chart) or an imaginary surface connecting points which have the same density. Also *attrib.* or as *adj.*

1927 *Geofysiske Publikasjoner* IV. II. 18 We may therefore assume the chief cause of the variations in the depth of the isopycnals to have been oscillations of the water-masses. **1962** C. A. M. KING *Oceanogr. for Geographers* iv. 119 A line joining points of equal density is called an 'isopycnal'. **1968** G. NEUMANN *Ocean Currents* iv. 129 The slope of isobaric surfaces..is small when compared to the slope of isothermal, isohaline (surfaces of equal salinity) and isopycnal surfaces. *Ibid.* 168 In the case of frictionless ocean currents and without mixing a non-accelerated current must always be parallel to the isobars and to the isopycnals.

isopycnic (aɪsəʊ'pɪknɪk), *a.* and *sb.* [f. as prec. + -AL.] **A.** *adj.* (Connecting points) of the same density or of constant density; also, in *Biochem.*, used with reference to ultracentrifugal separative techniques which rely on differences in density between the components of a mixture.

1890 WEBSTER *s.v.*, An isopycnic line or surface. **1910** V. BJERKNES et al. *Dynamic Meteorol. & Hydrogr.* I. iii. 39 We may represent the distribution of mass by drawing surfaces of constant value of the density, or isopycnic surfaces. **1930** N. SHAW *Man. Meteorol.* III. vi. 262 (*caption*) The isothermic, isobaric, isopycnic lines. **1955** *Exper. Cell Res.* IX. 457 Isopycnic gradient centrifugation for the stratification and separation of marine egg halves and quarters was first described by the Harveys. **1962** *Aeroplane* CII. 179/1 The isopycnic level at about 25,000 ft., known to meteorologists for its relative constancy, is being suggested as an accurate reference level for shifting safely from pressure instrument to density altimeter set according to the standard atmosphere. **1964** *Jrnl. Appl. Meteorol.* III. 292/2 A thick isopycnic zone might reasonably be said to exist there [in the equatorial region] from about 5–14 km. **1964** C. J. O. R. & P. MORRIS *Separation Methods in Biochem.* xxi. 807 On the application of the centrifugal field each particle migrates to a position in the gradient corresponding to its own density (the isopycnic point). Particles initially situated below their isopycnic level float upwards to it. *Ibid.* 809 The apparent density..found from isopycnic measurements. **1971** *Nature* 29 Jan. 299/3 Preparing material entirely uncontaminated by cytoplasmic ribosomes, by isolating the mitochondria by isopycnic centrifugation through sucrose gradients.

B. *sb. Meteorol.* A line (imaginary or on a map) or an imaginary surface connecting points at which the density is the same.

1890 WEBSTER, *Isopycnic* n., a line or surface passing through those points in a medium, at which the density is the same. **1924** *Q. Jrnl. R. Meteorol. Soc.* L. 32 In all probability the concentration of the isopycnics takes place over the antarctic continent. **1930** N. SHAW *Man. Meteorol.* III. vi. 260 (*table*) Isobars..Isotherms..Isopycnics.

isopycnosis (ˌaɪsəʊpɪk'nəʊsɪs). *Cytology.* Also **-pyknosis.** [f. ISO + HETERO)PYCNOSIS.] The character or condition of having such a degree of condensation and staining as is typical of the majority of chromosomes or chromosomal regions within a particular nucleus. Hence ˌ**isopyc'notic** *a.*

1950 G. ÖSTERGREN in *Hereditas* XXXVI. 511 Heteropycnosis is a term in current use in chromosome studies... It might be useful to have a term for the opposite effect to that called heteropycnosis. Since such a term might actually have a function to fulfil, I suggest that the term isopycnosis be introduced. *Ibid.* 512 That a chromosome region is isopycnotic should then mean simply that it does not differ from the majority of the chromosome regions of the cell in its appearance. **1962** *Lancet* 29 Dec. 1384/1 In female meiosis the two X chromosomes may show complete or partial isopyknosis according to the type of pairing. **1967** U. MITTWOCH *Sex Chromosomes* xii. 242 Both X-chromosomes of the female become isopycnotic [during gametogenesis].

isopyre ('aɪsəʊpaɪə(r)). *Min.* [Named 1827; f. ISO- + Gr. πῦρ fire.] An impure variety of opal, containing admixtures of alumina, sesquioxide of iron, and lime.

1827 *Edin. New Philos. Jrnl.* III. 264 The lustre of isopyre is less bright and glassy than that of obsidian. **1883** KUNZ *Amer. Gems* in *Min. Resources U.S.* 493 Isopyre is found in small veins from one to three inches in width.

isoquinoline: see ISO- b.

isorhythm ('aɪsəʊrɪð(ə)m). Also **isorr-**. [f. ISO- + Gr. ῥυθμ-ός measured motion.] The rhythmic structure of isorhythmic music.

1954 *Grove's Dict. Mus.* IV. 551/1 *Isorhythm*, the main feature of the French motet in the 14th and early 15th centuries. **1959** *Times* 13 Feb. 13/5 The hockets and isorrhythms of the Middle Ages. **1963** *Listener* 17 Jan. 141/1 A set of variations using the medieval technique of isorhythm (the repetition throughout of a certain rhythmic pattern, in the manner of a passacaglia).

isorhythmic (aɪsəʊ'rɪθmɪk), *a.* Also **isorrhythmic.** [f. ISO- + Gr. ῥυθμ-ός measured motion, ῥυθμικ-ός set to time, RHYTHMIC.]

1. *Anc. Pros.* Having the same number of moræ or units of time in thesis and arsis; characterized by feet of this kind (such as the dactyl, spondee, and anapæst).

2. Constructed in the same rhythm or metre (as something else).

1870 *Graphic* 20 Aug. 183/1 We should like to see an isorhythmic English version of Victor Hugo's 'Chasse du Burgrave' or 'Pas d'armes du Roi Jean'.

3. *Mus.* 'A modern musicological term applied to fourteenth-century choral works in which the tenor *canto fermo* (or sometimes an upper part) is many times repeated as to its rhythmic features, the pitch of the notes, however, being varied each time it appears' (*Oxf. Compan. Mus.* ed. 9). Also in more general use.

1954 *Grove's Dict. Mus.* IV. 551/1 The isorhythmic motet came to life shortly before 1316. **1957** *Listener* 26 Dec. 1086/1 An aria..on an isorrhythmic bass, that is to say, a 'ground' whose recurrencies begin on different beats in the bar. **1962** *Ibid.* 20 Sept. 453/1 Whether the demonstration is of isorhythmic patterns, classical thematic structures or rotations of a twelve-note succession, it rarely does more than rationalize a unity already intuitively experienced. **1963** *Medium Ævum* XXXII. 151 The elaborate isorhythmic setting of *O potores exquisiti* from the Carmina Burana. **1972** *Daily Tel.* 23 Feb. 11/7 To pinpoint some isorhythmic features when a given sequence of durations, though not of pitches, is reiterated in one or more parts. **1972** *Composer & Conductor* Aug. 6/1 Friedrich Ludwig proposed the term Isorhythmic to designate identical rhythmic patterns of different melodies in medieval motets.

isosbestic (aɪsəʊs'bɛstɪk), *a.* *Physical Chem.* Also erron. **isobestic.** [ad. G. *isosbestisch* (A. Thiel et al. 1924, in *Fortschr. d. Chem.* XVIII. 116), f. Gr. ἴσος equal + σβεστ-ός extinguished (f. σβεννύναι to quench, extinguish): see -IC.] ***isosbestic point***: a wave-length at which the absorption of light by a liquid remains constant as the acidity varies or, more generally, as the state of equilibrium between two interconvertible substances or states shifts.

1925 *Chem. Abstr.* XIX. 2180 Photometric measurements of the absorption spectra were plotted for equal degrees of acidity and these curves intersected in general in the 'isobetic' point [*sic*: rendering G. *isosbestischer Punkt.*]. **1943** W. R. BRODE *Chem. Spectroscopy* (ed. 2) ix. 249 (*caption*) Spectrophotometric determination of hydrogen-ion concentration; mixed indicator (methyl red + bromothymol blue). (Note isosbestic points at 467 and 500 mμ.) **1954** *Trans. Faraday Soc.* L. 802 The ionized form exhibits absorption at a longer wave-length (251 mμ) than the non-ionized (239 mμ) and there is an isobestic point at 245 mμ. **1958** MEITES & THOMAS *Adv. Analytical Chem.* viii. 277 The spectra of a number of solutions having equal formal concentrations of bromthymol blue but different pH values will all intersect at 501 mμ. Such a point is known as an isosbestic point, and the appearance of such a point on a family of spectra is a necessary (but not quite sufficient) criterion of the presence of two and only two forms of the absorbing substance in equilibrium with each other. **1960**

Jrnl. Biol. Chem. CCXXXV. 1026/2 Each of the absorption maxima and isosbestic points is essentially the same for normal as well as for sickle cells and homozygous C hemoglobins. **1962** R. E. DODD *Chem. Spectroscopy* v. 299 The absence of an isobestic point indicates a more complex system. **1971** F. A. BETTELHEIM *Exper. Physical Chem.* xiii. 144 The absence of an isosbestic point is definite proof of the presence of more than two absorbing species. **1972** *Nature* 24 Mar. 140/2 Control measurements are made at an isosbestic point for the rhodopsin and the product.

¶ Other anomalous forms (with quot. 1939 cf. quot. 1943 above).

1939 W. R. BRODE *Chem. Spectroscopy* ix. 206 There will be a point..where the extinction curves should have a common value at any *p*H concentration. Such a point is known as an isobastique point. **1949** A. C. CANDLER *Pract. Spectroscopy* iv. 90 As one absorption curve fades, another develops, while the absorption at an intermediate wavelength, called by Brode the isobastic point, remains unaltered. *Ibid.* 91 The indicator should be of standard strength, but slight variations may be corrected if the absorption at both the centre of the absorption band and at the isobastic point are measured.

†**i'soscel**, *a. Obs. rare.* (In 8 isocel.) [a. F. *isocèle, isoscèle* (1542 in Hatz.-Darm.), ad. L. *īsoscelēs*: see below.] = ISOSCELES.

1715 LEONI *Palladio's Archit.* (1742) I. 31 A Triangle Isocel, that is of two equal sides.

†**i'soscelar**, *a. Obs.* [f. as prec. + -AR.] = next.

1711 *Brit. Apollo* IV. No. 8. 1/2 An Isoscelar Triangle.

isosceles (aɪ'sɒsɪliːz), *a.* (*sb.*) *Geom.* Also 6–7 isosceles. [a. late L. *īsoscelēs*, a. Gr. ἰσοσκελής equal-legged, f. ἰσο- + σκέλος, σκελε- leg.] Of a triangle: Having two of its sides equal. (Formerly sometimes as *sb.*: An isosceles triangle.)

1551 RECORDE *Pathw. Knowl.* B iij, There is also an other distinction of the names of triangles, according to their sides, whiche other be all equal..other els two sydes bee equall and the thyrd vnequall, which the Greekes call *Isosceles*, the Latine men *æquicurio*, and in english tweyleke may they be called. **1570** BILLINGSLEY *Euclid* I. Def. xxv. 5 Isosceles, is a triangle, which hath onely two sides equall. **1571** DIGGES *Pantom.* I. B iij a, Isoscheles is such a Triangle as hath onely two sides like, the thirde being vnequall, and that is the Base. **1656** STANLEY *Hist. Philos.* v. (1701) 186/2 The Element of a Cube is an Isosceles Triangle, for four such Triangles concurring make a Square, and six Squares a Cube. **1674** N. FAIRFAX *Bulk & Selv.* 115 We are born in hand with this, That then a *Scalenum* and *Isosceles* would be all one. **1798** CANNING, etc. *Loves Triangles* in *Anti-Jacobin* 7 May, 'Twas thine alone, O youth of giant frame, Isosceles! that rebel heart to tame. **1802** BOURNON in *Phil. Trans.* XCII. 307 With isosceles triangular planes. **1812–16** PLAYFAIR *Nat. Phil.* (1819) I. 87 The resistance to the motion of an isosceles wedge.

Hence **i'soscelesism** (better **i'soscelism**) *nonce-wd.*, the character of being isosceles.

1851 RUSKIN *Stones Ven.* I. xxi. §32 But the spirit of the triangle must be put into the hawthorn. It must suck in isoscelesism with its sap.

isoscope, -seismal, etc.: see ISO-.

isosmotic: see ISO-.

isospin ('aɪsəʊspɪn). *Physics.* [Contraction of *isotopic spin, isobaric spin.*] A vector quantity associated with elementary particles and atomic nuclei which is used to give mathematical expression to the fact that the strong interaction is independent of electric charge; its quantum number (symbol *T* or *I*, $T = 0, \pm\frac{1}{2}, \pm 1, \pm\frac{3}{2}$, etc.) is assigned on the basis of there being $2T + 1$ particles in a charge multiplet, each with the same value of the quantum number *T* but differing in the value of the third component of isospin T_3 (or T_z) according to the charge of each particle, with the result that these can be treated as different states of a single particle.

1963 S. TOLANSKY *Introd. Atomic Physics* (ed. 5) xxiii. 395 The decay of a particle is controlled by a quantity T which has been called the isotopic spin vector or more simply, the isospin. **1965** H. MUIRHEAD *Physics Elem. Particles* i. 14 The isospin of a system is formally similar to angular momentum but is linked to the charge states of the system. **1970** *Physics Bull.* Jan. 22/1 These hadrons and their compounds (the atomic nuclei) appeared as charge multiplets, the members of which had essentially the same mass and the same strong interactions, but different charge values, these being the $(2I + 1)$ values $(\frac{1}{2}B - I)e, (\frac{1}{2}B - I + 1)e, ..(\frac{1}{2}B + I)e$ where *B* is the baryon number..and *I* (called the isospin) is characteristic of the multiplet. **1971** P. E. HODGSON *Nucl. Reactions* xix. 575 The isospin T of a nucleus is the sum of the isospins t_i of its constituent nucleons... The isospins t of the nucleons have the same mathematical properties as the spin vectors σ, that is $t^2x = t(t + 1)x$, $t_zx = \pm\frac{1}{2}x$, where $t_z = +\frac{1}{2}$ refers to neutrons and $t_z = -\frac{1}{2}$ to protons. Here the *z* component refers to isospin space and not to ordinary space.

isospondylous (aɪsəʊ'spɒndɪləs), *a. Ichthyol.* [f. mod.L. *Isospondyl-us* (in pl. *-yli*) (f. ISO- + Gr. σπόνδυλος, σφόν- vertebra, joint) + -OUS.] Belonging to, or having the characters of, the *Isospondyli*, an order of physostomous fishes, including most of the malacopterygians.

isostasy (aɪ'sɒstəsɪ). Also isostacy (*rare*). [f. Gr. ἰσο- ISO- + στάσις setting, weighing, standing, station; cf. Gr. ἰσοστάσι-ος in equipoise, equivalent.] Equilibrium or stability due to equality of pressure; the condition thought to exist within the earth's crust of approximate hydrostatic equilibrium between portions of different density, the land masses being supported by underlying denser material that yields or flows under their weight and those parts of them that reach to a greater height also extending to a greater depth, any (large) part slowly rising (or falling) if matter is removed from (or added to) its surface.

1889 C. E. DUTTON in *Bull. Philos. Soc. Washington* XI. 53 For this condition of equilibrium of figure, to which gravitation tends to reduce a planetary body, irrespective of whether it is homogeneous or not, I propose the name isostasy... We may also use the corresponding adjective isostatic. **1893** *Ann. Rep. U.S. Geol. Survey 1891–2* II. 280 The condition of isostasy prevailing in the earth's mass demanded that compensation should be made to the continental area for the load taken from it. **1896** *Pop. Sci. Monthly* L. 243 The general problems of isostasy. **1900** *Ibid.* LVI. 443 Now, so sensitive is the earth to changes of gravity that, given time enough, it responds to increase or decrease of pressure over large areas by corresponding subsidence or elevation...This principle of isostasy is undoubtedly a valuable one, which must be borne in mind in all our reasonings on crust movements. **1914** [see ASTHENOSPHERE]. **1923** *Discovery* Dec. 315/2 The suggestion which has gained most favour, and seems to fit in with many observations, is the theory of Isostacy, which contends that all visible land is composed of the lighter parts of the Earth's crust and is floating upon the components of greater density. **1944** A. HOLMES *Princ. Physical Geol.* iii. 34 It must..be clearly realized that isostasy is only a state of balance; it is not a force or a geological agent. It is the disturbance of isostasy by denudation and deposition, earth movements and igneous activity, that brings into play the gravitational forces that restore isostasy. **1950** *Antiquity* XXIV. 43 The dating of these sites involves the post-Algonquin changes in Great Lakes water-levels through isostasy and drainage. **1960** *New Scientist* 19 May 1278/2 The gravity variations are generally consistent with the theory of isostasy, according to which mountains 'float' in hydrostatic equilibrium in the dense mantle as do icebergs in the sea.

isostatic (aɪsəʊ'stætɪk), *a.* [f. as prec. + Gr. στατικός: see STATIC.] **1.** Pertaining to, produced by, or characterized by isostasy.

1889 [see ISOSTASY]. **1890** in *Cent. Dict.* **1893** *Ann. Rep. U.S. Geol. Survey 1891–2* II. 280 During the period of sedimentation, which ultimately set up isostatic adjustment, there had been continuous shrinkage of a nucleus cooling beneath the accumulating strata. **1927** PEAKE & FLEURE *Apes & Men* v. 80 There may have been a slight compensating, or as it is called isostatic, uprise in Denmark and other regions around the margin of the ice sheet. **1937** *Proc. Prehist. Soc.* III. 181 The isostatic emergence of the land from the sea since the last glacial maximum. **1944** A. HOLMES *Princ. Physical Geol.* xi. 189 While the crust was being thus unloaded by denudation, slow isostatic uplift must have been continuously in progress. **1955** *Antiquity* XXIX. 181 The complex eustatic and isostatic movements which determine the part played by land movements on one hand and changes of sea-level on the other. **1960** [see ISOSTATICALLY *adv.* a]. **1960** B. W. SPARKS *Geomorphol.* xiv. 311 Large ice sheets caused an isostatic depression of the areas they occupied and a subsequent rise as the ice melted away.

2. Performed under or involving conditions in which equal pressure is applied from all directions.

1957 *Ceramic News* Apr. 20 (*heading*) Unique 'isostatic process' marks manufacture of Coors famous high density grinding media. **1965** HOVE & RILEY *Ceramics for Adv. Technologies* iii. 79 In isostatic pressing, the powder material is compacted under uniform pressure. **1967** M. CHANDLER *Ceramics in Mod. World* vi. 163 (*caption*) New ceramic materials demand new forming techniques, such as this isostatic press for making ceramic spark plug insulators.

isostatically (aɪsəʊ'stætɪkəlɪ), *adv.* [f. prec.: see -ICALLY.] **a.** *Geol.* As regards isostasy; by, or as a result of, isostatic forces.

1901 *Geogr. Jrnl.* XVIII. 517 The elevation of the land caused an ice-sheet to form gradually over it until the surface was depressed, isostatically, by the weight of accumulated ice. **1924** J. G. A. SKERL tr. *Wegener's Orig. Continents & Oceans* xi. 160 It [*sc.* the map] shows us immediately the mass-defect under mountain chains through which the latter are isostatically compensated. **1957** G. E. HUTCHINSON *Treat. Limnol.* I. i. 8 The rebound of the southern part of the recently deglaciated Scandinavia, which rose isostatically more rapidly than the post-glacial eustatic rise in sea level. **1960** *New Scientist* 19 May 1278/3 Considerable local departures from isostatic equilibrium are known, but an area forming a considerable fraction of a continent is in general found to be isostatically compensated. **1969** *Nature* 21 June 1120/1 Continents and continental margins respond isostatically to pressure variations of ten bars or less.

b. By (means of) pressure applied equally from all directions.

1960 *Times Rev. Industry* Feb. 24/2 Silicon nitride.. powder may be formed to the required shape by..slip casting, or pressing either in steel dies, or isostatically in a thin walled rubber sac. **1972** *McGraw-Hill Yearbk. Sci. & Technol.* 332/2 The table shows a comparison of some of the properties achieved by hot isostatically pressed alloys compared to those of cast products of the same composition.

isostemonous, -steric, etc.: see ISO-.

isoster: see ISOSTERE 2.

isostere ('aɪsəʊstɪə(r)). [f. ISO- + Gr. στερε-ός solid.] **1. a.** [ad. G. *isoster* (A. R. v. Miller-Hauenfels *Theoret. Meteorol.* (1883) i. 2).] A line or surface (either imaginary or on a map or diagram) connecting points where some substance has an equal specific volume.

1900 V. BJERKNES in *U.S. Dept. Agric. Monthly Weather Rev.* XXVIII. 436/2 The upper isosteres surround the whole earth, whereas the lower ones intersect the earth's surface along the isosteric curves. **1944** H. R. BYERS *Gen. Meteorol.* ix. 217 The lines of constant specific volume, called isosteres, slope upward toward the pole. **1957** G. E. HUTCHINSON *Treat. Limnol.* I. v. 287 It is probable that in all cases in stratified lakes the deep water currents do not represent steady-state circulation systems maintained by a more or less constant wind stress, but rather continually changing readjustments to the changing position of the isosteres.

b. *Physical Chem.* [ad. G. *isoster* (H. Freundlich *Kapillarchemie* (1909) A. ii. 102).] A line on a graph showing the pressure of a gas required to produce a given amount of adsorption at different temperatures.

1919 *Proc. R. Soc.* XCVI. 289 It is..difficult to obtain observations of an adsorption isostere over a very wide stretch of temperature. **1940** GLASSTONE *Text-bk. Physical Chem.* xiv. 1173 The isostere for log *p* against 1/*T* is linear, as it should be if the van't Hoff equation is applicable. **1970** A. J. B. ROBERTSON *Catalysis Gas Reactions by Metals* ii. 22 Such isosteres can be derived from isotherms at different temperatures.

2. Also **isoster**. *Chem.* Each of two or more isosteric molecules or ions (see ISOSTERIC *a.* 4).

1919 I. LANGMUIR in *Jrnl. Amer. Chem. Soc.* XLI. 1544 Compounds showing a relationship to one another like that between carbon dioxide and nitrous oxide will be called isosteric compounds or isosteres. **1924** J. A. CRANSTON *Struct. Matter* viii. 160 The tabulation of isosteres is of special value in the study of the crystalline forms of compounds. **1958** A. ALBERT in *Current Trends in Heterocyclic Chem.* (Chem. Soc.) viii. 64 Thiazole and pyridine are another pair of isosteres said to resemble one another closely in properties. **1968** *European Jrnl. Cancer* IV. 222 The carcinogenic activity of 10 heteropolycyclic substances, of which 7 were sulfur-containing isosters, and 3 were isomers.

isosteric (aɪsəʊ'stɛrɪk), *a.* [f. as prec. + -IC.] **1.** Having equal atomic volumes.

1865–72 WATTS *Dict. Chem.* III. 432 If bodies of equal atomic volume be denominated *isosteric*.

2. Indicating equal specific volume.

1900 V. BJERKNES in *U.S. Dept. Agric. Monthly Weather Rev.* XXVIII. 436/1 This distribution can be expressed with the help of surfaces of equal specific volume, or isosteric surfaces. **1934** D. BRUNT *Physical & Dynamical Meteorol.* viii. 166 Any isosteric surface is also isopycnic. **1957** G. E. HUTCHINSON *Treat. Limnol.* I. v. 263 When isosteric surfaces or surfaces of equal density or specific volume do not correspond to the equigeopotential or level surfaces, a current must be flowing.

3. *Physical Chem.* Of a heat of adsorption: corresponding to a constant amount of adsorbed material as the pressure and temperature vary (equilibrium being maintained).

1918 *Proc. R. Soc. Edin.* XXXVIII. 31 Freundlich.. considers an 'isosteric' heat of adsorption where *a* [= number of mols. of gas adsorbed per grm. adsorbent, adsorbing at *p*, T] is constant, *p* and T variables... But it is difficult to see how we can have an isosteric heat of adsorption per mol. adsorbed, for under the defined conditions nothing is adsorbed. We have merely a readjustment of *p* and T. **1933** D. J. MARTIN *Introd. Thermodynamics for Chemists* xiii. 314 The isosteric heat of adsorption is such that the amount adsorbed is kept constant while the pressure and temperature are varied. **1970** *Biopolymers* IX. 1531 A comparison between calorimetric and isosteric heats of sorption..will indicate the degree of irreversibility of the sorption process.

4. *Chem.* Having the same number of valence electrons arranged in a similar manner.

1919 [see ISOSTERE 2]. **1921** F. H. LORING *Atomic Theories* xv. 134 Methane is isosteric with the ammonium ion. **1938** *Jrnl. Amer. Chem. Soc.* LX. 2628/1 In a few cases, isosteric compounds are interchangeable in serological reactions. **1971** *Arch. Biochem. & Biophysics* CXLIII. 252 These overall studies support the concept that the 1,4-cyclohexadienyl group is an effective isosteric replacement for a phenyl group.

isosterism (aɪsəʊ'stɪərɪz(ə)m). *Chem.* [f. as prec. + -ISM.] The condition of being isosteric (sense 4).

1865–72 WATTS *Dict. Chem.* III. 433 With regard to the elements, Schröder finds that isosterism is accompanied quite as frequently..by heteromorphism as by isomorphism. **1919** I. LANGMUIR in *Jrnl. Amer. Chem. Soc.* XLI. 1545 The isosterism of the cyanate and trinitride ions applies of course also to compounds derived from them. **1935** J. N. FRIEND *Text-bk. Physical Chem.* II. ix. 384 (*caption*) Isosterism of CO_2 and N_2O. **1963** *Pharmaceutica Acta Helv.* XXXVIII. 706 The two most important postulates for isosterism were there: similarity in shape and polarity.

isostich to **isotach**: see ISO-.

isotactic (aɪsəʊ'tæktɪk), *a. Chem.* [f. ISO- + Gr. τακτ-ός arranged, ordered + -IC, as ad. It. *isotattico* (G. Natta 1955, in *Atti d. Accad. Naz. d. Lincei, Mem.* (*Classe d. Sci. fis.*) 8th Ser. IV. II. 69), f. Attic τάττ-ειν (= Gr. τάσσειν) to arrange.] Having or designating a polymeric

structure in which all the repeating units have the same stereochemical configuration.

1955 *Chem. Abstr.* XLIX. 12912 The designation 'isotactic' is applied to chain polymers contg. alternating CH_2 and asym. C groups of identical configuration. **1963** *Times* 11 June 19/1 The entry into production of the Brindisi plant..considerably increased output of the isotactic polypropylene plastic ('Moplen'), now becoming popular in many countries throughout the world. **1964** *New Scientist* 23 Jan. 225 These arrangements, known as 'isotactic' and 'syndiotactic' configurations.., have now been realised with most of the common vinyl monomers. **1972** *Physics Bull.* Nov. 666/1 Isotactic polypropylene is a useful commercial plastic noted for its high strength/weight ratio.

Hence **isotac'ticity**, the quality of being isotactic.

1959 NATTA & DANUSSO in *Jrnl. Polymer Sci.* XXXIV. 7 All the arrangements which may compose the isotacticity must be only repetitive arrangements. **1968** *Ibid.* A-2. VI. 1495 The isotacticity and the crystallizability of the original sample remain unchanged after degradation.

‖**isoteles** (aɪ'sɒtɪliːz). *Anc. Gr. Hist.* [Gr. ἰσοτελής paying equal taxes, f. ἴσος equal + τέλος, τελε- tax, etc.] One of a favoured class of *metœci* or resident aliens at Athens, 'who enjoyed all civic rights except those of a political nature' (Liddell & Scott). So **isotely** (aɪ'sɒtɪlɪ) [ad. Gr. ἰσοτέλεια], the condition of an *isoteles*.

1849 GROTE *Greece* II. lxv. (1862) V. 592 That all metics who would lend aid should be put on the footing of isotely or equal payment of taxes with citizens. **1850** *Ibid.* lxvi. VI. 17 Lysias..passed the remainder of his life as an Isoteles, or non-freeman on the best condition. **1849** KEMBLE: see ISOPOLITY.

isoteniscope: see ISO-.

†**i-sothe**, *v. Obs.* In 3 i-soðien. [OE. *ȝesóþian* to prove the truth of, verify, f. *ȝe-*, I-[1] + *sóþ* true, SOOTH, *sóþian* to prove true.] *trans.* To prove true; to verify, confirm.

a **925** *Laws of Edw. & Guth.* c. 6 §7 Gif man þæt ȝesoðiȝe, licge ægylde. *c* **1205** LAY. 29011 Þis heo him to-ȝeornden mid ȝislen to isoðien. *c* **1240** *Sawles Warde* in *Cott. Hom.* 261 Ha..seoð nu al þat isoðet, þat ha hefden longe ear icwiddet of ure lauerd.

i-sothe, ME. pa. pple. of SEETHE *v.*

isotheral (aɪ'sɒθərəl, 'aɪsəʊθɪərəl), *a.* and *sb.* [f. next or its F. original *isothère* + -AL[1]. (The etymological form from Gr. would be *isothereal*.)]

A. *adj.* Applied to lines on a map, etc. connecting places having the same mean summer temperature. **B.** *sb.* An isotheral line, an isotherm of mean summer temperature.

1839 [see ISOCHEIMAL]. **1852** DANA *Crust.* II. 1452 There are several reasons why isocrymal are preferable to isotheral lines. **1867** PROCTOR in *Intell. Observ.* No. 62. 118 The isotheral of London. **1873** J. GEIKIE *Gt. Ice Age* xxx. 427 The charts of isotheral and isochimenal lines.

isothere ('aɪsəʊθɪə(r)). *Phys. Geog.* [a. F. *isothère* sb. (= *ligne isothère*), introd. by Humboldt, 1817, a. Gr. ἰσο- ISO- + θέρος, θερε- summer.] An imaginary line passing through points on the earth's surface that have the same mean summer temperature.

1852 DANA *Crust.* II. 1453 It is..an objection to using the isotheres, that those towards the equator are much more irregular in course than the isocrymes.

isotherm ('aɪsəʊθɜːm). [f. F. *isotherme*, introd. by Humboldt, 1817, f. Gr. ἰσο- ISO- + θέρμη heat, θερμ-ός hot.] **a.** *Phys. Geog.* An imaginary line passing through points on the earth's surface having the same mean temperature; an isothermal line: see next. Also, a similar line (either imaginary or in a diagram) connecting points other than on the earth's surface.

1860 MAURY *Phys. Geog. Sea* (Low) vii. 171 The isotherm of 65° skirts the northern limits of the sugar-cane. **1880** *Times* 16 Aug. 11/4 The isotherms are still distinctly of the summer type, but the difference between the temperatures at the inland and the coast stations is smaller. **1973** *Nature* 16 Feb. 446/2 A pressure-sensing float and a barrier driven by a motor, each fencing the film and connected to a recorder.., made it possible..to obtain isotherms of films.

b. = ISOTHERMAL *sb.* b.

1895 C. S. PALMER tr. *Nernst's Theoret. Chem.* II. ii. 192 The behaviour of gaseous and liquid carbon dioxide was studied very exactly by Andrews for those temperatures the isotherms of which are plotted. **1924** A. E. HILL in H.S. Taylor *Treat. Physical Chem.* I. ix. 383 The result of changing the pressure at constant temperature can be deduced by following a line drawn parallel to the pressure axis, and called an isotherm, or isothermal line. **1961** M. TRIBUS *Thermostatics & Thermodynamics* viii. 205 There is shown a line of constant temperature which is tangent to the top of the vapor-liquid region. This line represents the critical isotherm, since it represents the temperature above which only one phase exists. **1971** F. A. BETTELHEIM *Exper. Physical Chem.* xli. 378 In the graphic representation of the adsorption isotherm, one usually plots the amount of component 1 adsorbed on the surface of the solid per gram (or per unit surface area) of the solid against the equilibrium composition of the solution.

isothermal (aɪsəʊ'θɜːməl), *a.* and *sb.* [f. F. *isotherme* (see prec.) + -AL[1].]

A. *adj.* **1.** Of, pertaining to, indicating, or corresponding to equal temperatures; **a.** *esp.* in *Phys. Geog.* applied to a line (imaginary or on a map, etc.) connecting places on the earth's surface at which the temperature for a particular period, or (usually) the mean annual temperature, is the same; also to a map or chart exhibiting such lines.

1826 KIRBY & SP. *Entomol.* IV. xlix. 484 Fixed by the will of the Creator, rather than..regulated by any isothermal lines. **1830** LYELL *Princ. Geol.* I. 106 The lines of equal winter temperature do not coincide with the lines of equal annual heat, or the isothermal lines. **1880** HAUGHTON *Phys. Geol.* vi. 278 In Europe..51° N. Lat., which corresponds to the same isothermal line as 39° N. Lat. in America.

b. Applied to (imaginary) lines or surfaces of equal heat in a crystal or other body when heated.

1854 J. SCOFFERN in *Orr's Circ. Sc., Chem.* 137 In crystals having two optic axes..if a centre of heat be assumed to exist within, and the crystal to be indefinitely extended in all directions, the isothermal surfaces will be ellipsoids with three unequal axes. **1871** B. STEWART *Heat* §281. **1895** STORY-MASKELYNE *Crystallogr.* i. §11 As the form is invariably found to be either circular or elliptical, the continuous isothermal surface which would result from the maintenance of a given temperature at a point inside a crystal must be either a sphere, a spheroid, or an ellipsoid.

c. Applied to a line in a diagram that represents states or conditions of equal temperature.

1873 J. W. GIBBS in *Trans. Connecticut Acad. Arts & Sci.* II. 311 In the same way we may conceive of lines..of equal temperature... These lines we may also call..isothermal. **1922** GLAZEBROOK *Dict. Appl. Physics* I. 930/1 When a perfect gas expands isothermally PV is constant, and hence its isothermal line on the pressure-volume diagram, for any assigned temperature, is a rectangular hyperbola. **1949** F. TYLER *Intermediate Heat* vii. 146 The relative slopes of the isothermal and adiabatic curves passing through the point P_1..may be obtained as follows.

2. Occurring at a constant temperature; pertaining to or involving a constancy of temperature with time.

1887 *Encycl. Brit.* XXII. 481/1 During isothermal expansion a gas must take in an amount of heat just equal to the work it does. **1937** M. W. ZEMANSKY *Heat & Thermodynamics* xiii. 231 The isothermal compressibility of a gas may be calculated from an empiric equation expressing the dependence of *V* upon *P* at constant temperature. **1957** *Encycl. Brit.* VIII. 123/2 Under ordinary conditions the adiabatic constants for a solid substance are practically the same as the corresponding isothermal constants. **1967** A. H. COTTRELL *Introd. Metall.* xx. 373 Decisive progress [in the heat-treatment of steel] came only after the development of the technique of isothermal transformation..in which specimens are quenched into a bath of molten lead or salt at some pre-determined temperature and the course of their transformation at this fixed temperature is then determined.

3. Of the same temperature throughout.

1909 *Rep. Brit. Assoc. Adv. Sci. 1908* 591 Permit me to open the discussion on the Isothermal Layer, and the inversions of temperature which are found there. **1912** H. N. DICKSON *Climate & Weather* iii. 77 At heights greater than about nine miles the temperature..remains nearly constant at about −70°F at all levels... In this 'isothermal layer'..there would seem to be..little movement. **1951** J. A. HYNEK *Astrophysics* xiv. 662 It is possible that at this stage..the star develops a small isothermal core at the center. **1964** *Oceanogr. & Marine Biol.* II. 71 In winter the fiord water becomes isothermal and isohaline with average temperature and salinity of −1·76°C and 32·75‰.

B. *sb.* **a.** An isothermal line or surface; an isotherm.

1852 DANA *Crust.* II. 1453 The difficulty of dividing this space by convenient isothermals. **1872** NICHOLSON *Palæont.* 503 The present limit of trees is the isothermal which gives the mean temperature of 50° Fahr. in July, or about the parallel of 67° N. latitude. **1875** LYELL *Princ. Geol.* II. II. xxxiii. 231 The planes of the subterranean isothermals or surfaces of equal temperature being thus made to vary. **1875** *Academy* 21 Aug. 201/1 Professor Mayer describes the method invented by him for obtaining registers of the isothermals on the sun's disc.

b. A line in a diagram that is isothermal (sense A. 1 c).

1873 J. W. GIBBS in *Trans. Connecticut Acad. Arts & Sci.* II. 323 In that part of any diagram which represents a mixture of vapor and liquid, the isopiestics and isothermals will be identical, as the pressure is determined by the temperature alone. **1879** *Amer. Jrnl. Sci.* XVIII. 463 In Diagram A, are drawn Isothermals, curves of equal temperature, in which the abscissæ are wave lengths, the ordinates intensities. **1937** P. S. EPSTEIN *Textbk. Thermodynamics* iii. 49 The slope of the adiabatic ($dp/dv = -\gamma p/v$) is always steeper than the slope of the isothermal ($dp/dv = -p/v$) passing through the same point. **1968** WALLACE & LINNING *Basic Engin. Thermodynamics* 458 At very low pressures all isothermals tend towards a value of the compressibility function equal to unity, i.e. towards perfect gas behaviour.

So also **isothermobath** (aɪsəʊ'θɜːməʊbæθ) [Gr. βάθος depth], a line connecting points of equal temperature at various depths in a vertical section of the sea; **iso'thermous** *a.* = ISOTHERMAL *a.*

1876 SIR C. W. THOMSON, Isothermobath. **1855** MAYNE *Expos. Lex.* s.v. *Isothermus*, Isothermous lines do not follow the parallels at the equator.

isothermally (aɪsəʊ'θɜːməlɪ), *adv.* [f. prec. + -LY[2].] At a constant temperature, without a change in temperature.

1886 *Proc. R. Soc. Edin.* XIII. 79 Steam might be condensed isothermally to supersaturation without condensing. **1897** *Daily News* 15 June 5/5 The compression [of the air] takes place isothermally. **1922** [see ISOTHERMAL *a.* 1 c]. **1952** *New Biol.* XII. 75 In a system such as this the simultaneous dismantling and assembly can be described as 'energy-linked'; and since no heat is lost or gained the changes occur isothermally, that is, at constant temperature. **1967** A. H. COTTRELL *Introd. Metall.* xx. 374 Over the range in which the austenite decomposes isothermally the time of transformation follows a *C*-curve like that of Fig. 20.2.

isothermic (aɪsəʊ'θɜːmɪk), *a.* [f. ISO- + Gr. θέρμ-η heat, θερμ-ός hot + -IC.]

a. = ISOTHERMAL *a.* 1.

1879 *Amer. Jrnl. Sci.* CXVIII. 466 Such an error, in order to produce such an effect in *all* the isothermic curves, must be looked for either in my comparison of the sun's spectrum with that of the platinum wire, or in Lamansky's measurements of the sun's heat. **1881** *Proc. R. Geogr. Soc.* III. 657 Fall of temperature as we proceed in different directions is shown by means of isothermic lines. **1930** [see ISOPYCNIC *a.*].

b. = ISOTHERMAL *a.* 2.

1936 *Jrnl. Iron & Steel Inst.* CXXXIV. 265 A, A certain lowering of the tensile strength and limit of proportionality is revealed between certain temperature limits after isothermic treatment. **1951** R. A. DUTCHER et al. *Introd. Agric. Biochem.* xix. 383 Hydrolyses are characterized by no perceptible heat changes and..are known as isothermic reactions. **1965** B. E. FREEMAN tr. *Vandel's Biospeleol.* xxx. 474 The humus of these mountains possesses an isothermic climate.

c. = ISOTHERMAL *a.* 3.

1963 S. W. TROMP *Med. Biometeorol.* I. 22 Above the troposphere lies a region known as stratosphere..divided into three layers: a lower cold isothermic layer 12–35 km above sea level with fairly constant temperatures..a warm layer..and a very cold upper layer.

isotherombrose (ˌaɪsəʊθə'rɒmbrəʊs), *a. Phys. Geog.* [f. as ISOTHERE + Gr. ὄμβρος rain + -OSE.] Applied to a line (on a map, etc.) connecting places at which the ratio of the summer rainfall to the annual rainfall is the same.

1864 WEBSTER cites A. K. JOHNSTON.

isotome ('aɪsəʊtəʊm). *Zool.* [f. ISO- + Gr. τομή cutting, section.] An imaginary line conceived to pass through corresponding (homologous) joints or parts in a series of different animals, indicating homology.

Hence **isotomous** (aɪ'sɒtəməs) *a.*, of or pertaining to an isotome.

1884 [see ISOMERE].

isotone ('aɪsəʊtəʊn). *Physics.* [a. F. *isotone* (K. Guggenheimer 1934, in *Jrnl. de Physique et le Radium* V. 253), coined by replacing the *p* of *isotope* (the initial letter of *proton*) by *n* for *neutron*.] Each of two or more nuclides having the same number of neutrons (but usually different numbers of protons).

1934 *Sci. Abstr.* A. XXXVII. 734 It is proposed that elements having the same number of neutrons, but different atomic numbers shall be termed 'isotones'. **1952** *Sci. News* XXIII. 39 There is an exceptionally large number of nuclei all containing 20 protons (isotopes of calcium)... Nuclei containing 20, 50 or 82 neutrons also have a large number of isotones. **1966** [see ISOBAR 2]. **1972** *Physics Bull.* Mar. 148/3 The isotone shift differs from the isotope shifts in that the former measures the energy difference of atoms when protons are added to the nucleus with the number of neutrons remaining the same, whereas for the latter the role of protons and neutrons are reversed. The study of isotope as well as isotone shifts reveal the nuclear shell structure.

isotonic (aɪsəʊ'tɒnɪk), *a.* [f. Gr. ἰσότονος equally stretched, of equal tension or tone (f. ἰσο- ISO- + τόνος TONE) + -IC.]

1. *Mus.* Characterized by equal tones, as the system of tuning usually called *equal temperament*.

1828 WEBSTER *s.v.*, The isotonic system, in music, consists of intervals, in which each concord is alike tempered, and in which there are twelve equal semitones.

2. *Physiol.* [ad. G. *isotonisch* (H. de Vries 1884, in *Jahrb. f. wiss. Bot.* XIV. 427).] Of, pertaining to, or (of a solution) having the same osmotic pressure as some particular solution (usually that in a cell, or a body fluid). Const. *with*.

1895 [see HYPERTONIC *a.* 2]. **1898** *Allbutt's Syst. Med.* V. 461 Determination of the isotonic coefficient of the red corpuscles is another method of blood examination. **1899** CAGNEY tr. *Jaksch's Clin. Diagnosis* i. (ed. 4) 16 Mention must be made of von Limbeck's researches on the subject of the resistence of the red corpuscles and the isotonic property of blood-serum. **1902** POYNTING & THOMSON *Text-bk. Physics: Properties of Matter* xvi. 190 A series of solutions can be prepared which are isotonic with each other. **1936** A. P. MATHEWS *Princ. Biochem.* xxxiv. 364 Practically all the secretions of the body, except the urine, as for example the bile, the pancreatic juice, the saliva and so on, have the same osmotic pressure as the blood. They are isotonic with the blood. **1951** H. DAVSON *Textbk. Gen. Physiol.* vii. 159 For marine eggs the isotonic concentration will generally be approximately 0·5 M salts or 1 M non-electrolyte. *Ibid.* 158 In isotonic glycerol solution the cell is unstable because no osmotic equilibrium is possible. **1969** J. H. GREEN *Basic Clin. Physiol.* vi. 37/1 The sodium chloride is present in

plasma to the extent of 0·9 g. per 100 ml. A solution containing this amount of sodium chloride in water is termed normal, isotonic, or physiological saline, and it has the same electrolyte strength as blood. Such a solution.. could be run into the veins of a patient, whereas pure distilled water would destroy the red blood cells by the process of haemolysis. **1972** *Nature* 17 Mar. 117/2 Each animal received an intraperitoneal injection of ethanol (4 g kg^{-1}, 25% v/v solution in isotonic saline).

3. *Physiol.* [ad. G. *isotonisch* (A. Fick *Mech. Arbeit u. Wärmeentwickelung bei d. Muskelthätigkeit* (1882) vii. 112).] Of, pertaining to, or designating muscular action in which the muscle contracts more or less freely against a small, constant resistance.

1891 A. D. WALLER *Introd. Human Physiol.* ix. 330 If a muscle contracts against a small and constant resistance, so as to be extended by a constant force during its contraction, the curve described by a light lever attached to it is termed 'isotonic'. **1900** SIR J. BURDON-SANDERSON *Schäfer's Text-bk. Physiol.* II. 353 If, before and during excitation, its opposite attachments are so fixed that they cannot be brought nearer together by the effort of the muscle to contract, the excitation of the muscle is said to occur under isometric conditions. If, on the other hand, one end of the muscle is left free, so that it can shorten on excitation, and in so doing lift a weight which is attached to it, the excitation is said to take place under isotonic conditions. **1939** *Jrnl. Physiol.* XCVI. 63 The relation between applied force and speed of isotonic shortening was studied in frog and tortoise muscle. **1951** H. DAVSON *Textbk. Gen. Physiol.* xvii. 481 A record of an isometric twitch is thus a record of changes in tension of the muscle, whilst that for an isotonic twitch is a record of changes in length. **1971** A. C. GUYTON *Basic Human Physiol.* vii. 77/1 In comparing the rapidity of contraction of different types of muscles, isometric recordings..are usually used instead of isotonic recordings, because the duration of an isotonic recording is almost as dependent on the inertia of the recording system as upon the contraction itself.

isotonically (aɪsəʊˈtɒnɪkəlɪ), *adv.* *Physiol.* [f. prec.: see -ICALLY.] Under isotonic conditions (see ISOTONIC *a.* 3).

1953 A. SZENT-GYÖRGYI *Chem. Physiol. Contraction in Body & Heart Muscle* ix. 52 Fig. 8..sums up the experience ..on a widely varied material, registered both isotonically and isometrically, excited in different ways. **1970** *Nature* 16 May 656/1 The muscular activity was recorded isotonically on a kymograph. **1971** A. C. GUYTON *Basic Human Physiol.* vii. 77/2 Muscles can contract both isometrically and isotonically in the body, but most contractions are actually a mixture of the two.

isotonicity (ˌaɪsəʊtəˈnɪsɪtɪ). *Physiol.* [f. as prec. + -ITY.] The property or state of being isotonic (sense 2); equality of osmotic pressure; also, degree of osmotic pressure (of the blood).

1896 T. L. STEDMAN *20th Cent. Pract.* VII. 284 After twelve or twenty-four hours the solution which is exactly isotonic is determined..and the isotonicity of the blood corpuscles..determined at the same time. *Ibid.*, The isotonicity of the corpuscles is 0·45. **1906** *Amer. Jrnl. Physiol.* XV. 366 Every degree of dilution from isotonicity down to distilled water acts as a stimulus to the heart ganglion of Limulus. **1909** R. J. M. BUCHANAN *Blood in Health & Dis.* ix. 182 The isotonicity of the plasma is rather below normal. **1939** A. KROGH *Osmotic Regulation Aquatic Animals* 196 The isotonicity normally present between tissue cells and the surrounding medium need not mean, however, that the sum of free ions on both sides of the cellular membrane is the same. *Ibid.* 66 Schwabe (1933).. observed a definite hypotonicity for [the crab] *Pachygrapsus marmoratus* amounting to 57mM., while he confirmed the absolute isotonicity for *Portunus corrugatus*. **1951** [see HYPERTONIC *a.* 2]. **1974** *Nature* 4 Jan. 50/1 The concentration of calcium was varied from 0 to 2·5 mM (isotonicity was kept constant by appropriate adjustments in the concentration of NaCl).

isotope (ˈaɪsətəʊp). [f. ISO- + Gr. τόπ-ος place.] **1.** A variety of a chemical element (strictly, of one particular element) which is distinguished from the other varieties of the element by a different mass number but shares the same atomic number and chemical properties (and so occupies the same position in the periodic table); freq. used to denote any individual variety without reference to identity of atomic numbers (see quot. 1947 and cf. NUCLIDE).

1913 F. SODDY in *Nature* 4 Dec. 400/1 The same algebraic sum of the positive and negative charges in the nucleus, when the arithmetical sum is different, gives what I call 'isotopes' or 'isotopic elements', because they occupy the same place in the periodic table. They are chemically identical, and save only as regards the relatively few physical properties which depend upon atomic mass directly, physically identical also. **1915** *Rep. Brit. Assoc. Adv. Sci. 1914* 301 Sir E. Rutherford (replying) said that the chemical inseparability of certain isotopes was, indeed, derived from experiments with small quantities, but the methods used were very delicate. **1923** *Glasgow Herald* 7 Apr. 7 Another entirely revolutionary factor in chemical theory has been the discovery that the majority of the chemical elements are mixtures of isotopes. **1927** N. V. SIDGWICK *Electronic Theory of Valency* i. 11 What Soddy has called an isotope —an element of the same atomic number but a different atomic weight. *Ibid.*, The one element of which the isotopes can be obtained in any quantity in a state of approximate purity..is lead. **1942** J. D. STRANATHAN *'Particles' of Mod. Physics* v. 205 Hertz, employing gaseous diffusion at low pressure through a special porous material, succeeded in producing a real separation for the isotopes of Ne. *Ibid.* 207 By this method the isotopes H^2, Li^7, C^{13} and N^{15} have been produced in significant concentration. **1947** *Amer. Jrnl. Physics* XV. 356/2 There is at present no word in the English language to express the concept of a particular species of atom, differing from all others in the constitution of its nucleus... In recent years the word *isotope* has come into use for this purpose, less by design than by default. According to its definition [by Soddy], this general usage is incorrect, since *isotope* properly refers to a species of a particular and designated element, and emphasizes its relationship to other isotopes of that element. It is analogous to such words as *brother* and *colleague*. **1959** *New Biol.* XXX. 96 Radioactive isotopes behave chemically in identical fashion with the normal isotopes, but can be distinguished by means of their radioactivity. **1962** *Nature* 19 May 621/2 There are about 300 naturally occurring isotopes, and several hundred additional isotopes can be prepared artificially. **1963** D. W. & E. E. HUMPHRIES tr. *Termier's Erosion & Sedimentation* i. 4 The isotopes O^{16}, O^{17}, and O^{18} of oxygen are in different proportions in atmospheric and sea water, the latter being rich in heavy isotopes as a result of differential evaporation. **1966** *McGraw-Hill Encycl. Sci. & Technol.* VII. 291/2, 20 elements possess no isotopes; each of these consists of one type of atom only. **1966** C. R. TOTTLE *Sci. Engin. Materials* i. 23 Hydrogen has three isotopes, the two heavier ones being known as deuterium (originally called heavy hydrogen), with one neutron per atom, and tritium, with two neutrons per atom.

b. In the usage of biologists and biochemists: a less common, usually radioactive, isotope of an element as used in tracer or other studies, in contradistinction to the common, naturally occurring isotope of the element; freq. without *the*.

1945 *Jrnl. Biol. Chem.* CLIX. 697 Isotopic analyses were usually made on these inorganic salts, thus avoiding the dilution of the isotope [*sc.* C^{13}] by non-isotopic carbon. **1954** A. WHITE et al. *Princ. Biochem.* xiv. 307 By degradation of the product and determination of the distribution of isotope among its atoms, one may often procure information as to the mechanism of the transformation. **1954** CANTAROW & SCHEPARTZ *Biochem.* xiv. 352 The assay of stable isotopes is based upon the difference in atomic weight between the normal element and the isotope used. **1971** MAZUR & HARROW *Textbk. Biochem.* (ed. 10) iv. 99 Synthesis of physiologically important compounds, containing isotopes in place of the normally occurring elements, furnishes the worker with a 'tag' that can easily be followed. **1972** *Science* 2 June 1032/1 Swiss albino mice were labeled with ^{45}Ca by injection with 10 μc of isotope 1 day after birth.

2. Special combs.: **isotope dilution**, a diminution of the concentration of one isotope (or isotopically labelled compound) by the addition or presence of another isotope of the same element (or of the unlabelled compound); *esp.* as a technique for measuring the amount of an element or compound in a system by introducing a known amount of a different isotope (or a labelled compound) and then measuring its concentration in a sample withdrawn from the system after mixing; **isotope effect**, a variation in some physical or chemical characteristic between one isotope of an element and another; **isotope shift**, a small difference in the wavelength of corresponding spectral lines of different isotopes of an element owing to the different masses and charge distributions of their nuclei.

1940 RITTENBERG & FOSTER in *Jrnl. Biol. Chem.* CXXXIII. 737 (*heading*) A new procedure for quantitative analysis by isotope dilution. *Ibid.* 744 A new method (isotope dilution procedure) for the analysis of complex mixtures is described. **1956** *Nature* 28 Jan. 159/1 Isotope-dilution analysis, a technique which is now being increasingly applied in geology, agriculture, metallurgy and biology. **1971** *Metabolism* XX. 1099 (*heading*) Kinetics of potassium distribution in man using isotope dilution and whole-body counting. **1972** *Chemico-Biol. Interactions* IV. 103 This finding suggested that the decreases in specific activity were a result of isotope dilution rather than inhibition of protein synthesis. **1923** *Science* 31 Aug. 164/2 (*heading*) The vibrational isotope effect in the band spectrum of boron nitride. **1956** *Nature* 28 Jan. 159/2 Most properties of solids depend on the atomic masses, and the study of isotope effects can be a powerful means of testing the validity of theories. **1967** A. H. COTTRELL *Introd. Metall.* xxiv. 503 The importance of the lattice ions in superconductivity is shown by the isotope effect. Different isotopes of mercury (also tin) are found to have different critical temperatures, proportional to $M^{-\frac{1}{2}}$, where *M* is the atomic mass of the isotope concerned. **1968** A. WHITE et al. *Princ. Biochem.* (ed. 4) xiii. 288 Distinct isotope effects, *e.g.* differential rates of reaction between normal and tritiated compounds, have been observed. **1932** *Physical Rev.* XLII. 350 It appears that this determination fits in with the magnitude of the isotope shift. **1958** *Oxf. Mag.* 8 May 418/1 Work on high resolution optical spectroscopy is now mainly directed towards the study of 'isotope shifts'. **1971** *Physics Bull.* Oct. 583/2 Isotope shifts occur when the energy levels of different isotopes are slightly shifted with respect to one another, resulting in an apparent splitting of the 'line' if two or more isotopes are present in the source.

isotopic (aɪsəˈtɒpɪk), *a.* [f. prec. + -IC.] **a.** Of, pertaining to, or being an isotope or isotopes of an element; ***isotopic number***, the number of neutrons in a nucleus minus the number of protons.

Before Soddy coined the word in 1913, *isotopic* had previously (unknown to him) been used in a different sense (see quot. 1904), but this use did not gain currency.

[**1904** COHEN & MILLER in *Jrnl. Chem. Soc.* LXXXV. 1624 Supposing the bromine in the ortho- and meta-positions to retard oxidation more than the chlorine in these positions, the effect should become apparent when the isotopic dichloro-, chlorobromo-, and dibromo-toluenes are oxidised together. [*Note*] We propose..to employ the word 'isotopic'..in place of the rather awkward expression 'similarly substituted'.] **1913** [see ISOTOPE 1]. **1919** F. SODDY in *Jrnl. Chem. Soc.* CXV. 18 The chemistry of actinium has been enormously simplified by the discovery that mesothorium-2 is isotopic with it, for the latter may be used as an indicator to show in what way the actinium distributes itself after any chemical treatment. **1920** *Glasgow Herald* 7 Oct. 8 It had now been found that certain elements which hitherto had been stated to have atomic weights fractional were mixtures of isotopes, and such isotopic elements had atomic weights as whole numbers on the oxygen scale. **1921** W. D. HARKINS in *Nature* 14 Apr. 202/2 Let us specify the atoms of this important class as those of isotopic number 0. Then the isotopes of magnesium of atomic weights 24, 25, and 26 will have isotopic numbers 0, 1, and 2. *Ibid.*, The isotopic number *n* is the number which, when added to twice the atomic number, gives the atomic weight. **1933** F. W. ASTON *Mass-Spectra & Isotopes* xiv. 176 Atoms of isotopic number 0, such as C^{12}, O^{16}, Mg^{24}, etc., predominate in a marked degree. Abundance is much less for isotopic number 1 such as F^{19}, Na^{23}, Al^{27}, decreases again for 2:—N^{14}, Ne^{22}, and becomes practically zero for 3: —Cl^{37}. **1942** J. D. STRANATHAN *'Particles' of Mod. Physics* v. 200 Considerable isotopic data has been obtained from studies of hyperfine structure. **1954** *Sci. News* XXXIV. 51 The next simplest use of the mass spectrometer is to measure the quantity of one isotope of an element compared with another—the isotopic ratio as it is called. **1956** A. H. COMPTON *Atomic Quest* i. 52 The isotopic separation of U-235 from U-238. **1957** G. E. HUTCHINSON *Treat. Limnol.* I. viii. 549 A study of the isotopic constitution of the sulfur in the sulfate of rain. **1971** J. Z. YOUNG *Introd. Study Man* v. 82 Many of the elements exist in isotopic forms, which break down spontaneously.

b. Of, pertaining to, or designating isospin; orig. and chiefly in ***isotopic spin*** = ISOSPIN.

1937 E. WIGNER in *Physical Rev.* LI. 106/2 W. Heisenberg..considered protons and neutrons as different states of the same particle. Heisenberg introduced a variable τ which we shall call the isotopic spin, the value −1 of this variable can be assigned to the proton state of the particle, the value +1 to the neutron state. *Ibid.* 107/1 The Pauli principle requires that the wave function $\Psi(r_1 s_1 \tau_1, r_2 s_2 \tau_2, \ldots, r_n s_n \tau_n)$ be antisymmetric with respect to the simultaneous interchange of Cartesian, spin and isotopic spin variables of any pair of heavy particles. This fact is quite analogous to the similar statement for ordinary spin. *Ibid.* 117/1 Terms with different ζ components of the isotopic spin have the same energy in approximation 2. These are, of course, terms of different isobaric nuclei, and a total isotopic spin *T* will be a term with the same binding energy for all nuclei with isotopic numbers from −*T* to *T*. **1953** M. GELL-MANN in *Physical Rev.* XCII. 833/2 Let us suppose that the new unstable particles are fermions with integral isotopic spin and bosons with half-integral isotopic spin. For example, the V_1 particles may form an isotopic triplet, consisting of V_1^+, V_1^0, and V_1^-. The τ^+ and V_4^0 may form an isotopic doublet, which we may call τ^+ and τ^0. **1963** K. W. FORD *World of Elem. Particles* viii. 235 For a group of nucleons, a rotation of the total isotopic-spin vector in *I* space corresponds to changing from one nucleus to another without changing the total number of nucleons. *Ibid.*, New particles..were found to come in closely linked groups, like proton and neutron. There were three pions which formed a triplet and could be described as three states of a single pion with one unit of isotopic spin. **1965** *Listener* 2 Sept. 332/1 Abstract quantities known as 'isotopic spin' and 'hyper-charge'. **1969** D. H. WILKINSON *Isospin* i. 3 It is clear that Wigner gave the isotopic spin that name because it is a vector whose *z*-projection, $\frac{1}{2}(N-Z)$, distinguished one isotope from another along an isobaric multiplet. In fact Wigner often called T_z itself the isotopic spin and *T* 'the total isotopic spin quantum number'. Others felt that a stronger case could be made to call the new quantum number the isobaric spin because its magnitude was constant along an isobaric multiplet.

c. Containing or being a less common or special isotope, e.g. as a label. Cf. ISOTOPE 1 b.

1942 J. D. STRANATHAN *'Particles' of Mod. Physics* v. 209 Heavy water..is one of the few compounds which can be produced in practically pure isotopic form. **1953** FRUTON & SIMMONDS *Gen. Biochem.* xxviii. 641 The administered isotopic glycine had 'mixed' with nonisotopic glycine already present in the body of the animal. **1954** A. WHITE et al. *Princ. Biochem.* xiv. 306 The isotopic material may be administered and, from the subsequent analyses for the appropriate isotope in the various tissues.., the distribution of the isotopic atom may be ascertained. **1958** *Oxf. Univ. Gaz.* 5 June 1127/1 Studies on intermediary metabolism in whole animals using isotopic carbon.

d. Employing or depending on isotopes; obtained by such methods.

1956 A. H. COMPTON *Atomic Quest* v. 326 As of 1956, three hundred American companies are using isotopic thickness gauges. **1962** *Newnes Conc. Encycl. Nucl. Energy* 365/2 Another example of the application of the isotopic tracer technique..is furnished by the use of radio-active iron to investigate the economy of haemoglobin iron. **1969** BENNISON & WRIGHT *Geol. Hist. Brit. Isles* ii. 26 While isotopic dating does provide a system of dating of this kind, giving dates in millions of years, it is too imprecise to be relevant to this problem. **1971** I. G. GASS et al. *Understanding the Earth* ii. 42/1 Laboratory techniques for determining so-called radioisotopic, isotopic or radiometric ages of rocks (which used to be erroneously called absolute ages) are extremely complex.

isotopically (aɪsəˈtɒpɪkəlɪ), *adv.* [f. prec.: see -ICALLY.] **a.** As regards isotopes or isotopic constitution.

1933 in *O.E.D.* Suppl. **1940** *Jrnl. Biol. Chem.* CXXXIII. 737 A deuteropalmitic acid is added to a mixture of isotopically normal fatty acids. **1960** *New Scientist* 14 July 136/3 For an age determination it is not sufficient only to analyse the mineral for uranium, thorium and total lead, but the lead must also be analysed isotopically. **1963** G. TROUP *Masers & Lasers* (ed. 2) viii. 136 The electrons were localized on donor (Phosphorus) atoms in isotopically pure silicon of atomic weight 28 which has no nuclear magnetic moment. **1970** *Nature* 23 May 738/2 The solar wind may

actually deposit isotopically heavier carbon on the lunar surface. **1970** D. W. Tenquist et al. *University Optics* II. v. 190 Isotopically pure elements must therefore be used.

b. By means of isotopes or isotopic methods.

1954 *New Biol.* XVI. 74 The behaviour of isotopically labelled molecules. **1959** *Times* 15 May 3/3 (Advt.), Vacancies for Chemists to work on the following projects:.. c) the synthesis of isotopically labelled compounds. **1964** G. H. Haggis et al. *Introd. Molecular Biol.* ii. 33 Many steps in the metabolic pathways of cells have been discovered or confirmed using isotopically labelled compounds. **1969** Bennison & Wright *Geol. Hist. Brit. Isles* xii. 272 The rarity of isotopically datable rocks in the Triassic System of Britain and north-western Europe presents a further problem.

isotopy (aɪˈsɒtəpɪ). [f. isotop(ic *a.* + -y³.] The fact or condition of being isotopic.

1914 *Phil. Mag.* XXVIII. 839 The stability of RaG and its isotopy with lead. **1919** F. Soddy in *Jrnl. Chem. Soc.* CXV. 18 Its [*sc.* actinium's] definite location in the periodic table, by virtue of its isotopy with mesothorium-2. **1925** J. Joly *Surface-Hist. Earth* ix. 150 Isotopy is not peculiar to the uranium and thorium groups of elements. **1926** R. W. Lawson tr. *Hevesy & Paneth's Man. Radioactivity* xvi. 125 (*heading*) Isotopy and the displacement laws in the light of atomic constitution. **1966** *McGraw-Hill Encycl. Sci. & Technol.* VII. 291/2 The occurrence and degree of isotopy among the 83 elements that are found in nature in significant amounts have been ascertained by means of mass spectrometer studies.

Also **ˈisotopism** (in the same sense).

1914 F. Soddy *Chem. Radio-Elements* ii. 17 The new data are the isotopism of mesothorium ii and actinium, and of radio-actinium and thorium. **1938** *Chem. Abstr.* XXXII. 8925 Evidence is offered that the discovery of the existence of isotopism in nonradioactive elements is another confirmation of O.'s nuclear law of 4.

isotransplant (aɪsəʊˈtrɑːnsplɑːnt, -træns-, -plænt). *Med.* and *Biol.* [f. iso- + transplant *sb.*] A piece of tissue transplanted from one individual to another of the same inbred strain.

1953 G. D. Snell in Homburger & Fishman *Physiopath. Cancer* xiv. 358 There exists in the case of isotransplants a possibility for genetic difference between tumor and host that is not found in autotransplants. **1966** *Nature* 23 Apr. 429/2 There was a significantly higher number of acceptances of tumour isotransplants in mice which were pre-treated with 'Cytoxan'. **1971** *Radiology* XCIX. 187/1 The autotransplants were irradiated when they reached an average of approximately 1 cm diameter, significantly larger than the isotransplants.

Hence **isotransˈplanted** *ppl. a.*

1967 *Jrnl. Nat. Cancer Inst.* XXXIX. 1 (*heading*) Morphologic studies of lymphoid tissues during the growth of an isotransplanted mouse tumor. **1970** *Biol. Abstr.* LI. 3130/2 (*heading*) Role of the immune system in the growth of an isotransplanted urethan-induced lymphosarcoma.

isotransplantation (ˌaɪsəʊtrɑːnsplɑːnˈteɪʃən, -træns-, -plænt). *Med.* and *Biol.* [f. iso- + transplantation.]

†**1.** = homotransplantation. *Obs.*

1909 *Jrnl. Exper. Med.* XI. 194 Of 35 isotransplantations in 17 dogs.., thirty-two parathyroids were either absorbed or necrotic.

2. The operation of transplanting tissue from one individual to another of the same inbred strain.

1962 *Cancer Res.* XXII. 955 A state of relative resistance can be built up in highly inbred skin-compatible C_3H mice against the isotransplantation of lymphomas recently induced in the same strain. **1963** *Exper. Cell Res.* XXXII. 618 (*heading*) Resistance against isotransplantation of mouse tumors induced by Rous sarcoma virus. **1966** *Cancer Res.* XXVI. 127/2 Spontaneous loss.., induced loss.., and even gain of antigens..can occur on isotransplantation.

isotrimorphism, etc.: see iso-.

isotron (ˈaɪsəʊtrɒn). [f. iso- (repr. *isotope*) + -tron.] A machine for separating isotopes emitted as ions from an extended source by accelerating them by means of a varying electric field, which causes ions of like mass to bunch together, and applying a transverse radio-frequency field synchronized with the arrival of the bunches, so that the ions are deflected by an amount dependent on their mass.

1945 H. D. Smyth *Gen. Acct. Devel. Atomic Energy Mil. Purposes* xi. 112 The objective..shifted to the effecting of large-scale separation of uranium isotopes by electromagnetic methods... Of the many electromagnetic schemes suggested, three soon were recognized as being the most promising: the 'calutron' mass separator, the magnetron-type separator.., and the 'isotron' method of 'bunching' a beam of ions. *Ibid.* 118 The device which resulted from Wilson's idea was given the deliberately meaningless name 'isotron'. **1946** *Electronic Engin.* XVIII. 153/3 Another method, dispensing altogether with a magnetic field, makes use of the klystron bunching principle and the device has been called the isotron. *Ibid.*, It is understood from publications on the subject that the isotron method has not yet been fully developed.

isotropic (aɪsəʊˈtrɒpɪk), *a. Physics.* [f. iso- + Gr. τρόπ-ος turn, way, manner, disposition + -ic. Cf. Gr. ἰσότροπος of like character.] Exhibiting equal physical properties or actions (*e.g.* refraction of light, elasticity, conduction of heat or electricity) in all directions: opp. to *æolotropic* or *anisotropic*. Also **isoˈtropically** *adv.*, equally in all directions.

1864 in Webster citing Nichol. **1867** Thomson & Tait *Nat. Phil.* I. 518 The substance of a homogeneous solid is called isotropic when a spherical portion of it, tested by any physical agency, exhibits no difference in quality, however it is turned. **1879** Rutley *Stud. Rocks* ix. 79 To distinguish singly-refracting or isotropic from doubly-refracting or anisotropic minerals. **1885** *Electrician* 24 Jan. 220/1 If μ = constant, all space equally magnetisable isotropically, then B is the same multiple of H everywhere. **1894** *Naturalist* 68 The rock further resembles certain of the Leinster granites in containing grains of isotropic garnet. **1896** *Yale Univ. Grad. Course Instruct.* 71 Propagation of light in isotropic and aeolotropic media. **1946** *Nature* 5 Oct. 483/1 The crystal structure of silver is cubic and it expands isotropically. **1970** G. K. Woodgate *Elem. Atomic Struct.* vi. 98 The electrons are moving freely, with no forces acting on them, and their translational momenta can be taken to be directed isotropically in momentum space.

So **isotrope** (ˈaɪsəʊtrəʊp), *a.* **isotropous** (ˈaɪsəʊtrəʊpəs), *a.* = prec. **isotropy** (aɪˈsɒtrəpɪ), the condition or quality of being isotropous.

1885 Landois & Stirling *Hum. Physiol.* II. 624 The contractile substance [of muscle fibres] doubly refracts light and is said to be *anisotropous*, while the ground-substance causes single refraction, and is *isotropous*. **1888** Ld. Rayleigh in *Philos. Mag.* Sept. 242 There is involved no assumption as to the homogeneity or isotropy of the dielectric medium.

isotype (ˈaɪsəʊtaɪp). [f. iso- + Gr. τύπ-ος type *sb.*¹; cf. Gr. ἰσότυπος shaped alike.]

†**1.** *Biol.* A type or form of animal or plant common to different countries or regions.

1881 T. Gill in *Smithsonian Rep.* 460 The Shrews are isotypes in Europe and North America. **1905** *Bull. U.S. Nat. Museum* No. 53. 16 Isotypes (*equal* or *like* and *form*): Forms common to different countries; *e.g.* the Shrews are isotypes in Europe and North America.

2. *Min.* Any mineral which is isotypic with another; an assemblage of minerals of which all the members are isotypic with one another.

1901 *Mineral. Mag.* XIII. 52 These minerals are placed by F. Rinne in the 'magnesium type' of his isotypes. **1943** *Science* 22 Jan. 99/1 A more complex type formula is necessary to cover the phosphates, arsenates and hydrates which are now recognized as isotypes. **1947** *Mineral. Abstr.* X. 52 With substitution of Si by other elements various isotypes are illustrated.

3. *Bot.* A duplicate of the holotype.

1919 F. W. Pennell in *Torreya* XIX. 13 To meet this need [for a term for a duplicate type] I suggest the term isotype. **1943** *Rhodora* XLV. 485 If a type specimen is lost or unavailable an isotype is in general much more important than a paratype for the interpretation of a name. **1966** *Internat. Code Bot. Nomencl.* ii. 19 An isotype is any duplicate (part of a single gathering made by a collector at one time) of the holotype.

4. Also **Isotype**. [f. *I*nternational *s*ystem *o*f *ty*pographic *p*icture *e*ducation.] The name of an international picture language devised by O. Neurath (1882–1945): used esp. to display statistical information in a convenient visual form.

1936 O. Neurath *Internat. Picture Lang.* 17 We have made *one* international picture language..into which statements may be put from all the normal languages of the earth. We have given it the name 'isotype'. **1945** G. Williams *Women & Work* 10 Isotype charts..illustrate and elaborate the argument. **1948** *Sunday Times* 15 Feb. 2/6 A record in powerful and sometimes horrifying images of misery, interrupted by only a few isotypes. **1950** Neurath & Lauwerys *Living in Early Times* 1 These Isotype symbols ..are always kept as simple and clear as possible. **1966** *Chambers's Encycl.* IX. 792/2 He [*sc.* O. Neurath] developed the 'isotype', a system of visual linguistics... His isotype films, e.g. *World of Plenty*, attracted wide attention. **1966** M. Pei *Gloss. Ling. Terminology* 135 *Isotype*, a system of writing that uses non-phonetic symbols of universal significance, designed as a medium of education, but also to convey information in ready visual form (the picture of one soldier to indicate an army division).

isotypic (aɪsəʊˈtɪpɪk), *a.*

1. *Biol.* [f. prec. + -ic.] That is an isotype (sense 1).

2. *Min.* [ad. G. *isotyp* (F. Rinne 1894, in *Neues Jahrb. f. Mineral., Geol. u. Palaeontol.* I. 55).] Having the same or similar crystal structure (i.e. isostructural) and, with some authors, having in addition analogous chemical formulæ; exhibiting such similarity. Const. *with*.

1929 H. L. Bowman *Miers's Mineral.* (ed. 2) 251 Substances which thus have the same type of composition and resemble one another in their angles and structure have been described by F. Rinne as 'isotypic'. **1942** *Mineral. Abstr.* VIII. 220 It [*sc.* berlinite] is therefore identical with artificial $AlPO_4$..and isomorphous with $AlAsO_4$.., which are isotypic with quartz. **1943** *Amer. Mineralogist* XXVIII. 598 Na_2BeF_4 was shown by them to be isotypic with γ-Ca_2SiO_4. **1943** *Science* 22 Jan. 98/2 Investigations..have revealed new isomorphic and isotypic relationships among silicates and phosphates. **1959** W. H. Dennen *Princ. Mineral.* iii. 104 Isotypic minerals are those with both isostructural characteristics and chemical similarity. *Ibid.*, The members of an isomorphous series are isotypic, but.. isotypic minerals are not necessarily isomorphous. **1959** W. F. de Jong *Gen. Crystallogr.* 182 If the structures of two compounds are entirely or nearly equal, and if the ratios of the dimensions do not differ much, the structures are called isotypic. NaCl and PbS form isotypic structures. **1968** Mason & Berry *Elem. Mineral.* (new ed.) iii. 83 Sometimes the terms isostructural or isotypic are used instead of isomorphous.

isotypy (ˈaɪsəʊtaɪpɪ). *Min.* [ad. G. *isotypie* (F. Rinne 1894, in *Neues Jahrb. f. Mineral., Geol. u. Palaeontol.* I. 55): see isotype and -y³.] The character or state of being isotypic (sense 2); isotypic relationship. Also **isoˈtypism** (in the same sense).

1938 *Mineral. Abstr.* VII. 92 A list of similar isotypism between other silicates and phosphates (or arsenates) is given. **1942** *Chem. Abstr.* XXXVI. 694 (*heading*) Isotypy between phosphates of general composition $MLiPO_4$ and silicates of the olivine-monticellite series. **1943** *Science* 22 Jan. 98/2 The isotypism of $AlPO_4$ and SiO_2. **1943** *Amer. Mineralogist* XXVIII. 598 O'Daniel and Tscheischwili consider the isotypy of Ca_2SiO_4 and Na_2BeF_4 as limited to the low-temperature modifications. **1959** W. F. de Jong *Gen. Crystallogr.* 182 (*heading*) Isotypism. **1967** Isotypy [see flinkite].

i-sought, ME. pa. pple. of seek *v.*

i-soukoured, ME. pa. pple. of succour *v.*

†**iˈsound**, *a. Obs.* Forms 1 ȝesund, 2–4 i-sund, 4 ysound. [OE. *ȝesund* = OS. *gisund*, OHG. *gisunt*, Ger. *gesund*, Du. *gezond*. The prefix *ge-*, *ȝe-* of the old langs. has fallen off in later Eng. and Fris.: see sound *a.* The ulterior etymology is uncertain.] Sound, in health, well, safe.

Beowulf (Z.) 1628 þæs þe hi hyne ȝesundne ȝeseon moston. *c* **1000** Ælfric *Gram.* xxxiii. (Z.) 209 *Aue* oððe *salue* beo ȝesund,.. *Auete, saluete*, beoþ ȝesunde. *c* **1205** Lay. 295 þe child wes iboren isund. *c* **1275** *Passion our Lord* 186 in *O.E. Misc.* 42 Leteþ þeos bileuen hol and isunde. *c* **1380** *Sir Ferumb.* 1993 þat no lym be laft ysounde.

i-sounded, ME. pa. pple. of sound *v.*

isovaleraldehyde to **isovol**: see iso-.

i-sowe(n, ME. pa. pple. of sow *v.*

isoxazole: see iso-.

isozoic, etc.: see iso-.

isozyme (ˈaɪsəʊzaɪm). *Biochem.* [f. iso- + en)zyme.] = isoenzyme.

1959 Markert & Møller in *Proc. Nat. Acad. Sci.* XLV. 753 We propose, therefore, to use the term *isozyme* to describe the different molecular forms in which proteins may exist with the same enzymatic activity. **1968** T. Wieland in Thoai & Roche *Homologous Enzymes & Biochem. Evolution* iii. 3 The second group of multiple forms consists of the so called 'isozymes'. They may be defined as the multiple molecular forms of an enzyme existing within a single organism. *Ibid.* 9 Isozymes are multiple forms of enzymes, which occur in one cell or—less strictly defined —in one organ of an organism. **1968** *New Scientist* 21 Mar. 649/2 LDH exists in five very slightly different forms... Each version is known as an isozyme of LDH, and each will catalyze the final glycolysis step.

Hence **isoˈzymic** *a.*

1959 Markert & Møller in *Proc. Nat. Acad. Sci.* XLV. 756 The relative enzymatic activity disposed in each isozymic band. **1973** *Nature* 3 Aug. 261/2 The genes for isozymic forms of various enzymes are often not linked to each other.

ispaghul (ˈɪspaguːl). Also **ishabgul**, **ispagool**, **ispughool**, **isubgol**. [Hind., a. Pers. *asp* horse + *gol* ear, in allusion to the shape of the leaves or seeds.] A plantain, esp. *Plantago ovata*, native to India and Persia, the dried seeds of which are used medicinally.

1810 J. Fleming in *Asiatick Researches* XI. 174 *Plantago Ispaghul* (Roxb. MS.) *Ispaghul*, H[industani]... *Ispughool* [Sanskrit]. **1820** W. Roxburgh et al. *Flora Indica* I. 404 *Ispagool*, the Hindee and Persian name, and that by which it is most generally known in Bengal and on the coast of Coromandel. **1880** Bentley & Trimen *Medicinal Plants* III. §211 Ispaghŭl seeds have long been highly valued in India and other parts of the East for their cooling and demulcent properties. **1889** G. S. Boulger *Uses of Plants* ii. 111 The mucilaginous seeds of *Plantago decumbens*, Forsk., Ispaghúl, or Spogel, are used in India as a demulcent drink, especially in dysentery. **1931** M. Grieve *Mod. Herbal* II. 643/1 Plantain, Ispaghul. *Ibid.* 643/2 The seeds of the Indian species, *Plantago Amplexicaulis*, are sold in the bazaars as Ispaghula. **1953** B. Mukerji *Indian Pharmaceutical Codex* I. 124 Commercial samples of ishabgul consist of the seeds of *P. arenaria* Waldst., *P. lanceolata* Linn., *P. major* Linn. besides *P. ovata* Forsk. and *P. psyllium* Linn. **1969** *Wealth of India* (Council Sci. & Industr. Res. India) VIII. 151/1 The efficacy of isubgol is due entirely to the large quantity of mucilage present in the husk.

Ispahan (ˈɪspəhɑːn). Also **Isfahan**. The name of a province and town in West Central Persia, used *attrib.* and *ellipt.* to designate a type of hand-woven rug, the most distinguished of which were produced there in the 16th century.

1931 A. U. Dilley *Oriental Rugs & Carpets* ii. 32 From the succeeding court came, during the sixteenth century, the 'Ispahan' rugs so greatly esteemed by collectors. *Ibid.* iii. 61 A fourth group of superior rugs, distinguished by pattern of palmette and now called Ispahan. **1960** H. Hayward *Antique Coll.* 149/2 *Ispahan carpets*, Persian carpets or rugs, often employing medallion or vase designs..in a wide range of colours, the composition being very well balanced. **1969** 'W. Haggard' *Doubtful Disciple* xv. 166 The dealers call them Isfahans and..know they're Heratis. **1969** B. Weil *Dossier IX* v. 38 A carpet that..Asher could see was an Isfahan. **1970** V. Canning *Great Affair* iv. 50 He took the heavy Passavant carpet from the floor..added a smaller Ispahan rug.

i-spared, ME. pa. pple. of SPARE *v.*

i-sped, ME. pa. pple. of SPEED *v.*

i-speke(n, ME. pa. pple. of SPEAK *v.*

i-speled, ME. pa. pple. of SPELE *v.*, to spare.

i-spend, -ed, i-spent, ME. pa. pple. of SPEND *v.*

i-sperred, ME. pa. pple. of SPAR *v.*, to bar.

i-spild, -spilled, -spilt, ME. pa. pple. of SPILL *v.*

†**i-spile, isepile**, var. of *ilspile, ilespil* obs., hedgehog: see IL.

1398 TREVISA *Barth. De P.R.* XVIII. i. (MS. Bodl.) lf. 239/2 Som bestes gadreth store of mete and fedinge: as Isepiles and þe ampte. **1495** *Ibid.* lxii. 818 An ispile [*MS. Bodl.* vrchon] hath a lytyll body and many pykes that occupyeth more place than the body.

i-spited, ME. pa. pple. of SPIT *v.*, to transfix.

i-spoiled, ME. pa. pple. of SPOIL *v.*

i-spoke(n, ME. pa. pple. of SPEAK *v.*

i-sponne(n, -spun, ME. pa. pple. of SPIN *v.*

i-spoused, ME. pa. pple. of SPOUSE *v.*

i-spoyled, ME. pa. pple. of SPOIL *v.*

i-sprad, i-spred, ME. pa. pple. of SPREAD *v.*

‖**ispravnik** (is'pravɲik). *Hist.* Pl. ispravniki, ispravniks. [Russ., lit. 'executor'.] A chief of police in a rural district in Tsarist Russia.

1886 *Encycl. Brit.* XXI. 70/2 The organs of the central government..are..the *stanovoys* and *ispravniks* (chiefs of the police) in the districts. **1898** J. Y. SIMPSON *Side-Lights on Siberia* 90 The *ispravnik* of the district happened to be in the village. **1906** *Daily Chron.* 24 Aug. 5/6 The police informed the ispravnik (chief of rural police). **1911** *Encycl. Brit.* XXIII. 876/1 As organs of the central government there are further, the *ispravniki*, chiefs of police in the districts into which the governments are divided. **1952** H. ALTSCHULER tr. *Gorky's Artamonovs* i. 156 The ispravnik shook a threatening finger, and shouted: 'Hush, fool!' **1967** H. SETON-WATSON *Russ. Empire* I. i. 20 The chief executive officer at the *uezd* level was the *ispravnik*, who was elected by the nobility, and presided over the local court which was an administrative rather than a judicial body.

i-spreind, i-sprengd, ME. pa. pple. of SPRENGE *v.*

i-sprong(e, i-sprung(en, ME. pa. pple. of SPRING *v.*

I spy: see HY-SPY.

i-spyld, ME. pa. pple. of SPILL *v.*

Israel ('ɪzreɪəl). Also 4 (Wyclif) Yrael. [a. L. *Isrāēl*, Gr. Ἰσραήλ, a. Heb. *yisrāēl*, lit. 'he that striveth with God', symbolic proper name conferred upon Jacob, Gen. xxxii. 28.]

1. The people descended from Israel or Jacob, the 'children of Israel' collectively; the Jewish or Hebrew nation or people.

c **1000** ÆLFRIC *Exod.* v. 2 Ne can ic Drihten, ne ic nelle forlætan Israela folc. *c* **1250** *Gen. & Ex.* 3268 Wende we a-gen An[d] israel folc lete we ben. *Ibid.* 3449 Moyses tolde ðis israel. **1382** WYCLIF *Judg.* xxi. 25 In tho days was no kyng in Yrael [**1388** Israel]. **1535** COVERDALE *Exod.* xi. 7 The Lorde hath put a difference betwixte Egipte and Israel. **1613** PURCHAS *Pilgrimage* (1614) 162 At Tripoli many Jewes and Gentiles had..perished with an Earthquake, whereof died in all Israel twentie thousand. **1878** SCHILLER-SZINESSY in *Academy* 606/2 The German Jews, now the most accomplished in all Israel.

2. In *fig.* and allusive uses; *esp.* the chosen people of God, the elect: applied to the Christian church, or to true Christians collectively.

Often in phrases applied originally in O.T. to the Jewish people; e.g. *Israel of God, mother in Israel*, etc.

1382 WYCLIF *Gal.* vi. 16 Pees vpon hem, and mercy, and vpon Israel of God [*Rheims* & **1611** the Israel of God]. **1611** BIBLE *Rom.* ix. 6 For they are not all Israel [*earlier vv.* Israelites] which are of Israel. **1692** H. PRIDEAUX *Direct. Ch.-wardens* (ed. 4) 117 The greatest Troublers of our *Israel*. **1713** WARDER *True Amazons* Ded. 7 Though all the Thousands of your Britannick *Israel* esteem Your Majesty's Person as Sacred. **1856** OLMSTED *Slave States* 117 Old Aunt Ann was a sort of mother in the colored Israel of the town. **1882** FARRAR *Early Chr.* I. 152 The truth..that the converted Gentiles constituted the ideal Israel.

3. An independent Jewish State established in 1948 in the country formerly called Palestine. Also *attrib.*

1948 *Manch. Guardian* 15 May 5/1 The Jews yesterday proclaimed in Tel Aviv the new State of Israel. **1957** L. F. R. WILLIAMS *State of Israel* 13 The Israel Government has been kindness personified in helping me with my researches. *Ibid.* 17 The modern state of Israel occupies part of territory which in ancient times formed a link between the civilizations of Egypt, Asia Minor and Mesopotamia. **1958** *Economist* 26 July 300/2 The western armies cannot stay in the Middle East indefinitely, while Israel must live in the region forever. **1972** *Encycl. Judaica* I. 12 According to official government usage, Israel (and not Israeli) is the adjective relating to Israel: Israeli is a citizen (or permanent resident) of the State of Israel. **1972** *Times* 24 Mar. 10/4 Israel has decided to recall its military experts from Uganda. **1974** *Times* 17 Apr. 14/7 Israel newspaper correspondents were given preferential treatment. *Ibid.* 14/8 The ban remained for Israel-based reporters... The Israel government has followed a curious policy.

Hence **Is'raeli** *a.*, relating to the State of Israel, its inhabitants, etc.; *sb.*, (*a*) a native or inhabitant of the State of Israel; (*b*) the language spoken by the inhabitants of the State of Israel (more usually called *Modern Hebrew*); **'Israelism**, reference to God's Church under the name or figure of Israel; **Israe'listic** *a.*, using the name or guise of Israel.

1684 H. MORE *Answer* 185 That Israelism which runs through the whole Prophecy. *Ibid.* 241 He in this Hylastick and Israelistick way prophesies of the state of the New Jerusalem. **1948** *Daily Tel.* 23 June 1/1 A coastal vessel of the Israeli Navy stood by. **1948** *N.Y. Times Mag.* 5 Dec. 4/3 Shortly after the proclamation of the new State of Israel.. Moshe Shertok announced that its citizens would be called Israelis. **1949** KOESTLER *Promise & Fulfilment* II. ii. 222 His English is good with a specific Israeli-*sabra* accent. **1949** H. NICOLSON *Diary* 25 July (1968) 173 George Weidenfeld.. has been asked by [Chaim] Weizmann to become his personal assistant. The problem is whether he should become an Israeli and get a definite job in the Israeli civil service. **1958** *Economist* 26 July 300/1 The Israeli government has asked Britain to order another course for the airflight to Jordan. **1964** R. MACGREGOR-HASTIE *Pope Paul VI* x. 215 The Pope greeted Dr. Shazar in Israeli—'Shalom, Shalom!' **1967** *Listener* 8 June 741/1 The Israelis, with their small country and just over two million population, can never conquer the Arab States. **1972** [see 3 above].

Israelite ('ɪzreɪəlaɪt), *sb.* and *a.* [ad. L. *Isrāēlīta*, ad. Gr. Ἰσραηλίτης; in Heb. *yisrĕēlī*; see prec. and -ITE.]

A. *sb.* **1.** One of the people of Israel; one of the Hebrew people; a Jew.

1382 WYCLIF *2 Cor.* xi. 22 Thei ben Ysraelitis, and I. **1535** COVERDALE *ibid.*, They are Israelites, euen so am I. **1611** BIBLE *John* i. 47 Behold an Israelite indeed in whom is no guile. **1796** H. HUNTER tr. *St.-Pierre's Stud. Nat.* (1799) III. 704 Tears started to the Israelite's eyes. **1865** tr. *Renan's Life Jesus* 7 The assistance..given me for this part of my task by a learned Israelite, M. Neubauer, well versed in Talmudic literature.

2. *fig.* One of God's chosen people; a member of the spiritual Israel.

1382 WYCLIF *Rom.* ix. 6 Sothli not alle that ben of Israel, thes ben Israelitis. **1555** EDEN *Decades* To Rdr. 56 Howe muche more then ought the spirituall Israelites to vse all possible meanes. **1607** HIERON *Wks.* I. 102 The elect are called the Israel of God, and the true seruants of God Israelites indeede. **1699** S. SEWALL *Diary* 4 Nov. (1878) I. 504 Capt. Appleton of Ipswich..an Israelite indeed, a great Ornament of that Church and Town.

B. *adj.* Pertaining to Israel; Jewish, Israelitish.

1851 D. PITCAIRN in Spurgeon *Treas. Dav.* Ps. xi. 4 By drowning the Israelite males. **1899** SAYCE *Early Israel* I. 54 The peasantry was Israelite.

Hence **'Israeliteship** *nonce-wd.*, the position or standing of an Israelite.

1680 H. DODWELL *Two Lett.* (1691) 25 The opening of the ears..the true Israeliteship,..every where assigned as the reasons of the conversion of many of them.

Israelitic (,ɪzreɪə'lɪtɪk), *a.* *rare.* [ad. L. *Isrāēlītic-us*, f. *Isrāēlīta*: see prec. and -IC.] = ISRAELITISH. So †**Israelitical** *a. Obs.*

1609 BIBLE (Douay) *Exod.* xii. Comm., Did the Israelitical people in Ægypt use to eate a lambe raw? **1668** H. MORE *Div. Dial.* IV. xxiii. (1713) 346 These Congruities of the Israelitical Types. **1836** G. S. FABER *Prim. Doctr. Election* II. x. 423 The subject of the israelitic phraseology. **1882–3** SCHAFF *Encycl. Relig. Knowl.* I. 706 The next noticeable contact between Egyptian and Israelitic history.

Israelitish ('ɪzreɪə,laɪtɪʃ), *a.* [f. ISRAELITE + -ISH.] Belonging to the Israelites, or to the nation of Israel; Jewish.

1535 COVERDALE *Lev.* xxiv. 10 An Israelitish womans sonne. **1597** J. PAYNE *Royal Exch.* 26 The Isralitische church. **1656** BEN ISRAEL *Vind. Judæorum* in *Phenix* (1708) II. 401 In the Israelitish Senate no Torture was ever inflicted. **1884** *Brit. & For. Evang. Rev.* July 403 Secretary and archivist of the Israelitish community in Pesth.

b. *fig.* (cf. ISRAELITE A. 2).

1739 G. WHITEFIELD in *Life & Jrnls.* (1756) 269 An honest open hearted true Israelitish Quaker.

'Israelitism. *rare.* [f. as prec. + -ISM.] The religion of the Israelites; Judaism.

1626 W. SCLATER *Exp. 2 Thess.* (1629) 76 This only amazeth me; That in men pretending Israelitisme, as sincere as Nathaniels, the sentence should seeme plausible.

†**'Israelitize,** *v.* *nonce-wd.* [See -IZE.] In phr. *to Israelitize it*: to play the Israelite.

1652 URQUHART *Jewel* Wks. (1834) 211 Most rigidly Israelitizing it in their Synagogical Sanhedrins.

†**'Israelize,** *v.* *nonce-wd.* [f. ISRAEL + -IZE.] *trans.* To make like Israel; to cause to prevail (see Gen. xxxii. 28).

1600 TOURNEUR *Transf. Met.* xiii, Ioue, Israellize my tongue, and let my voyce Preuayle with thee.

iss (ɪs), *adv.* Dial. var. YES *adv.* (*sb.*²); also used to represent an inaccurate pronunciation of 'yes' by a speaker whose native language is not English.

1795 'P. PINDAR' *Royal Visit to Exeter* II. 17 Iss, iss, he'll do the feat. **1829** G. GRIFFIN *Collegians* (ed. 2) I. xii. 259 'Erra, no!' 'Iss, dear knows.' **1853** MRS. GASKELL *Ruth* I. vi. 154 One servant-girl..was wearied out of what little English she had knowledge of..and could only answer, 'Iss, indeed, ma'am,' to any question. **1890** A. GISSING *Village Hampden* I. i. 19 Iss, Miss—but 'ere her be. *a* **1966** C. S. FORESTER *Hornblower & Crisis* (1967) vii. 71 'You boy!..D'you want to earn a shilling?' 'Iss, that do I.'

†**'issant,** *a.* *Her. Obs. rare.* [a. F. *issant*, also *yessant*, pr. pple. of OF. *issir, eissir*, to go out; see ISH *v.*] = ISSUANT 2.

1513 in *Glover's Hist. Derby* (1829) I. App. 61 Robert Darley bayryth goulls halff a Buk gold and sylver per pale.. issant owt of a wrayth goulls and sylver. **1562** LEIGH *Armorie* 84 b, He beareth Argent, a Lion iesaunte & iesaunte Sable. *L.* This I take to be two halfe Lions. *G.*: Not so it is but one Lion. For if you marke it well, you shal perceaue yᵗ as he goweth out at the cheife, so cometh he in, at yᵉ baste of the Escocheon.

isschewe, obs. form of ESCHEW *v.*

i-sschilde, var. of I-SHIELD *v. Obs.*

†**isse,** *int. Obs.* [A natural utterance: cf. *hush, st, whisht.*] An ejaculation enjoining silence.

1598 FLORIO, *Zita*, an aduerbe to commaund or perswade silence, as we say isse, whisht or st.

isse, obs. form of ICE.

isse, issh, var. of ISH *v. Obs.*

i-ssed, ME. pa. pple. of SHED *v.*

issle, var. of ISEL, *Obs.*

i-ssryned, ME. pa. pple. of SHRINE *v.*

i-ssryue(n, ME. pa. pple. of SHRIVE *v.*

issuable ('ɪʃ(j)uːəb(ə)l, 'ɪsjuː-), *a.* [f. ISSUE *sb.* and *v.* + -ABLE.]

1. *Law.* That admits of an issue being taken; in regard to which or during which issue may be joined. Also *transf.*

c **1570** *Pride & Lowl.* (1841) 17 Until ye come to matter issuable. *a* **1577** SIR T. SMITH *Commw. Eng.* (1609) 66 If the aunswere be issuable they proceede to triall. **1598** KITCHIN *Courts Leet* (1675) 444 It is a matter in deed issuable. **1768** BLACKSTONE *Comm.* III. 353 Hilary or trinity terms, which from the making up of the issues therein are usually called issuable terms. **1890** *Scot. Leader* 28 Jan. 4 His Lordship held that there was no issueable matter in the paragraphs complained of.

2. That may be issued, as a writ or summons; liable or authorized to be issued.

1642 CHAS. I *Answ. Decl. Both Houses* 1 July 41 This Statute..doth onely enact a Commission issuable, without commanding that it shall issue. **1740** *Propos. Prov. Poor* 6 Cattle issuable for Naval Services. **1865** *Pall Mall G.* 18 July 10/1 He will be without a seat until February, no new writ being issuable until the election of a Speaker. **1886** GLADSTONE *Irish Quest.* iii. 25 Fifty million of Consols issuable under the act.

3. Liable to issue as the proceeds of any property, investment, or source of revenue.

1674 T. TURNOR *Case Bankers* vii. 30 [He] forthwith stops their Pensions issuable out of the said Tributes. **1737** L. CLARKE *Hist. Bible* (1740) II. XII. 706 An account of all the persons, possessions, and estates therein, and the taxes issuable from them. **1814** *Hist. Univ. Oxford* II. 127 To purchase lands, the issuable profits of which he ordered to be equally distributed between the Fellows and Scholars.

Hence **'issuably** *adv.*, in an issuable manner; so as to raise an issue.

1783 R. BURKE in *E. Burke's Corr.* (1844) III. 18, I expressed a wish that a certain person should be driven to plead issuably. **1825** KNAPP & BALDW. *Newgate Cal.* IV. 288/1 Obliged them to plead issuably.

issuance ('ɪʃ(j)uːəns, 'ɪsjuː-). *U.S.* [f. next: see -ANCE.] The action of issuing, putting forth, or giving out; = ISSUE *sb.*

1863 *National Almanac & Ann. Rec.* 545/2 A proclamation of neutrality..was issued by Victoria, Queen of England... A brigade of British Volunteers..enlisted in the North..disbanded after its issuance. **1865** *Proclam. President U.S.* 29 May, Whereas many persons who had so engaged in said rebellion have, since the issuance of said proclamation, failed or neglected to take the benefits offered thereby. **1885** *Century Mag.* XXX. 605 Such allotment and issuance of individual patents. **1892** LOUNSBURY *Stud. Chaucer* I. 88 The issuance of the letters of protection. **1895** *Voice* (N.Y.) 7 Feb. 3/2 The flexibility of issuance would be real, but the flexibility of circulation or distribution would be only nominal in respect to the more distant commercial centers. **1905** *Westm. Gaz.* 11 Jan. 1/3 The new canon insists on at least a year's delay after the issuance of a decree of divorce before any marriage can take place. **1931** G. T. CLARK *Leland Stanford* vii. 214 The Supreme Court rendered another decision..to compel the issuance of the bonds voted by the people of San Francisco. **1967** *Boston Sunday Herald* VI. 5/1 (Advt.), You save 25% on the issuance charge. **1972** *Science* 12 May 640/2 Overzealous concern with style and format of writing imposed by the issuance, first in 1909, of the Survey's style manual. **1972** *N.Y. Law Jrnl.* 22 Aug. 12/1 A brother..filed objections and cross-moved for issuance of letters to him.

issuant ('ɪʃ(j)u:ənt, 'ɪsju:-), *a.* (*sb.*) [f. ISSUE *v.* + -ANT[1], after F. pr. pples. in *-ant*.]

1. Issuing or proceeding from a place or source. Now *rare*.

1634 SIR T. HERBERT *Trav.* 7 Out of that Cloud is issuant so forcible a whirle-wind, as breeds feare and admiration. **1642** tr. *Perkins' Prof. Bk.* i. §13. 7 A rent charge to be issuant out of the same Carue. **1660** WATERHOUSE *Arms & Arm.* 81 Commensurate to the Knowledge we have of that thing or person, and issuant from it as the tribute we give to that Excellency of worth we apprehend. **1839** BAILEY *Festus* xxxi. (1852) 528 Issuant from the eternal throne, Came like a cloud of light, the bright response.

2. *Her.* Emerging from the bottom of a chief, or (less usually) rising from another bearing or from the bottom of an escutcheon. Said esp. of a beast of which the upper half alone is visible. Cf. ISSANT.

issuant and revertant, 'emerging and disappearing'; said of two beasts on a shield when only the lower part of one and the upper part of the other are seen.

1610 GUILLIM *Heraldry* III. ix. (1611) 111 He beareth Azure, Issuant out of a Mount, in Base, three Wheate stalkes, Bladed and Eared, all Proper... A Venetian Coatearmour. *Ibid.* xv. 142 This Lion is said to be issuant because he doth issue from out of the bottome of the Chiefe. **1687** A. LOVELL tr. *Thevenot's Trav.* I. 113 There are also three demy Lions issuant out of the Wall, from the Head to half the Body. **1823** RUTTER *Fonthill* p. xxiii, Issuant out of a ducal coronet, *Or*, an oak-tree fructed.

†**B.** *sb.* Something that issues or juts out. *Obs.*

1674 JEAKE *Arith.* (1696) 202 The little Issuants at Top denote the Table may be increased as occasion requires.

issue ('ɪʃ(j)u:, 'ɪsju:), *sb.* Forms: 4-6 issu, issew(e, isshue, (4 ysue, 4-5 yssu, *Sc.* ischow), 4-7 yssue, 5 yssew(e, isswe, ischewe, (isue, usshew, uschu), 6 essew(e, isshewe, ishew, ishu, ishwe, (isew, *Sc.* yschew, ischue, ischay), (7 essue), 4- issue. [ME. a. OF. *issue, eissue, isue, essue, uxuwe*, etc. (mod.F. *issue*):—pop.L. **exūta* sb. (analogous to those in *-ata*, -ADE) from fem. of **exūtus* pa. pple., for cl.L. *exitus* (cf. It. *escito, uscita* from **exitus*), from L. *exīre* to go out: see ISH *v.*]

I. 1. a. The action of going, passing, or flowing out; egress, exit; power of egress or exit; outgoing, outflow.

1382 WYCLIF *Ps.* cxx[i]. 8 The Lord kepe thin entre and thi issu. **1419** *Surtees Misc.* (1888) 14 The kynges dyke betwix Bouthumbarr and Munkbarr was so stopped, that the water myght noght hafe issue. *c* **1460** SIR R. ROS *La Belle Dame* 52 The wepyng teres haue so large yssewe. **1593** *Sc. Acts Jas. VI* (1597) §161 With freedome of foggage, pastourage.. free ischue and entrie. **1601** HOLLAND *Pliny* I. 39 The said winde within the earth.. was not powerfull enough to breake forth and make issue. **1673** TEMPLE *Obs. United Prov.* Wks. 1731 I. 44 The Maes.. fell.. into the Sea at the Briel, with mighty Issues of Waters. **1860** TYNDALL *Glac.* I. v. 38 The whole volume.. escaped from beneath the ice at the end of the glacier, forming a fine arch at its place of issue.

†**b.** A sally, sortie. *Obs.*

c **1489** CAXTON *Sonnes of Aymon* xx. 443 His bredren made an yssue vpon hym and hys folke, and slewe many of theym. **1577** HOLINSHED *Chron.* II. 1195/1 Dayly were issues made out of the Citie at dyuerse gates. **1685** TRAVESTIN *Siege Newheusel* 38 The besieged.. made an issue on the East side, with a strong Body of men.

c. *fig.* in reference to things immaterial, or to coming out of a condition.

c **1374** CHAUCER *Troylus* v. 205 His sorwes þat he spared hadde, He yaf an yssue large, and deth he cride. **1483** CAXTON *Gold. Leg.* 259/1 She.. ordeyned her body to abyde in her bedde unto her yssue and departyng. **1576** FLEMING *Panopl. Epist.* 33 That wherein I have given you advertisement,.. had issue from a heartie good will. **1611** BIBLE *Ps.* lxviii. 20 Vnto God the Lord belong the issues from death. —— *Prov.* iv. 23 Keepe thy heart with all diligence: for out of it are the issues of life. **1662** *Bk. Com. Prayer* Prayer all Condit. Men, Giving them.. a happy issue out of all their afflictions. **1865** M. ARNOLD *Ess. Crit.* iii. 83 He [Gray] is a poetical nature repressed and without free issue.

2. Outgoing; termination, end; close.

†**a.** of a period of time. *Obs.*

1483 CAXTON *G. de la Tour* A j, As I was in a garden.. as it were in thyssue of Aprylle.

b. of an action or proceeding.

1605 BACON *Adv. Learn.* II. xxiii. §6 Formal speakers, that study more about prefaces and inducements, than upon the conclusions and issues of speech. **1638** SIR T. HERBERT *Trav.* (ed. 2) 190 [He] gave a like issue to his life and Kingdome. **1769** ROBERTSON *Chas. V*, VII. Wks. 1813 III. 43 Before the negotiations at Crespy were brought to an issue.

c. of anything extended in space.

1871 R. ELLIS *Catullus* lxiv. 308 A folding robe.. Fell bright-white to the feet, with a purple border of issue.

†**3.** *Feudal Law.* ***issues of homage***, fines paid by vassals when released from the obligation of homage. *Obs.*

1648 *Art. Peace* c. 7 Such Composition and Agreement which shall be made with his most Excellent Majesty for the Court of Wards, Tenures, Respits and Issues of Homage.

4. *Med.* **a.** A discharge of blood or other matter from the body, either due to disease or produced surgically by counter-irritation.

1526 TINDALE *Matt.* ix. 20 A woman which was diseased with an issue of bloud [WYCLIF, the flix or rennynge of blood] xij yeres. **1535** COVERDALE *Lev.* xv. 2 Whan a man hath a runnynge yssue from out of his flesh, yᵉ same is vncleane. **1579** LYLY *Euphues* (Arb.) 43 Would you haue.. One playster to an olde issue and a fresh wound? **1726** LAW *Serious C.* xix, If physic or issues will keep the complexion from inclining to coarse or ruddy, she thinks them well employed. **1875** H. C. WOOD *Therap.* (1879) 570 Escharotics are employed to produce ulcerations which shall be the bases of issues.

fig. **1625** SANDERSON *12 Serm.* (1637) 229 It may be they had found some ease.. by an issue at the tongue or eye, in an humble confession of their sinnes, and in weeping and mourning for them with tears of repentance.

b. An incision or artificial ulcer made for the purpose of causing such a discharge.

1607 TOPSELL *Four-f. Beasts* (1658) 191 If at any time she be troubled with the Dropsie, an issue must be made under her shoulder. **1662** PEPYS *Diary* 14 June, He had a blister, or issue, upon his neck. **1800** *Med. Jrnl.* IV. 33 Two large issues were now cut, one below each knee, the discharge from which being copious, afforded considerable relief. **1861** MRS. CARLYLE *Lett.* III. 78 Lying there, with two issues in her back.

II. 5. a. A place or means of egress; way out; outlet.

13.. *K. Alis.* 816 (MS. Bodl.) At þe yssue of þe doren, Tholomeus dude on his sporen. *c* **1400** *Apol. Loll.* 34 In þe weyes of þe temple, bi al þe issewis of þe sanctuari. *c* **1450** *Merlin* xx. 357 Thei com to the issu of the foreste. **1597** A. M. tr. *Guillemeau's Fr. Chirurg.* 7/1 The wounde having two issues, the one vnder, and the other above. **1607** E. GRIMSTONE tr. *Goulart's Mem. Hist.* 570 At the mouth and issue of this straite. **1726** LEONI *Alberti's Archit.* I. 18/1 The Issues for Smoke and Water ought to be as direct as possible. **1750** JOHNSON *Rambler* No. 65 ¶4 He now resolved to.. try to find some issue where the wood might open into the plain. **1859** THACKERAY *Virgin.* xviii, As my Lady Castlewood.. passed through one door of the saloon.. my Lord Castlewood departed by another issue. **1885** STEVENSON *Dynamiter* 181 A spot whence his eye commanded the three issues of the square.

b. The point where a body of water flows out; the mouth of a river, outlet of an inland sea, etc. Also, the outflowing stream.

1375 BARBOUR *Bruce* XIV. 354 This fals tratour his men had maid.. The ischow [*v.r.* ysche] of a louch to den. **1513** DOUGLAS *Æneis* III. x. 80 Now eik, as thai say, Arethusa, at thi mouth or ischay It [Alpheus] enteris rynning in the Cicell se. **1601** HOLLAND *Pliny* I. 82 The vast and wide Ocean lying before Asia.. breaketh into the maine with a small and narrow issue. **1612** BREREWOOD *Lang. & Relig.* xiii. 131, I find the city of Arsaratha.. placed near the issue of the river Araxes into the Caspian sea. **1613** PURCHAS *Pilgrimage* (1614) 513 This Sea [the Caspian] is.. without any issue to other Seas. **1844** *Mem. Babylonian P'cess* II. 66 Neither its source nor its issue is known.

†**c.** A sewer or sink; a privy. *Obs.*

1588 *Nottingham Rec.* IV. 223 A great anoyinge to the whole stritte for lacke of an essewe. **1616** SURFL. & MARKH. *Country Farme* viii. 25 It is also a signe of Raine.. if the common Issues or Priuies doe stinke more than usually.

III. 6. a. Offspring, progeny; a child or children; a descendant or descendants. Now chiefly in legal use or with reference to legal succession. †Formerly sometimes with pl. *issues*. (Rarely used of the young of beasts.)

1377 LANGL. *P. Pl.* B. XVI. 239 Hym-self bihiȝte to me and to myne issue bothe Londe and lordship. *c* **1450** LONELICH *Grail* lv. 397 Of that damysele Cam forth Isswe kyng Carcelois bothe good and trewe. **1486** *Bk. St. Albans, Her.* B ij a, If he had vshew forth vnto the fifth degree from him by right lyne of vsshew he is a gentylman of blode. **1504** *Plumpton Corr.* 193 As for such essew as God sendeth them, it is noe doubt but he wyll.. provyd for them. **1560** DAUS tr. *Sleidane's Comm.* 101 b, The laste kynge of Fraunce of the heyre males of Charlemayne, was Lewys the fifte, who died without isshewe. **1614** RALEIGH *Hist. World* I. (1634) 92 There were founded by his [Noah's] Issues many great Cities. **1767** BLACKSTONE *Comm.* II. vii. 111 By the birth of issue, the possibility of the donor's reversion was rendered more distant and precarious. **1781** W. BLANE *Ess. Hunting* (1788) 70 How the impression of the Dog.. could occasion similitude in the issue of the Bitch, and for a continuance of years, after the Dog's death, nobody but the Doctor is capable of defending. **1850** HT. MARTINEAU *Hist. Peace* II. v. ix. 344 No issue from this marriage survived. **1871** R. ELLIS *Catullus* lxiv. 324 Rich Aemathia's arm, great sire of a goodlier issue.

fig. *c* **1420** ? HOCCLEVE *Piteous Compl. Soul* 50, I am adred that charite is deed,.. Withowt[en] eyre or issue of hire seed. **1581** J. BELL *Haddon's Answ. Osor.* 222 b, Issues and sproughts of Religiones never planted by god. **1679** DRYDEN *Tr. & Cr.* Prol. 19 Weak, short-liv'd issues of a feeble Age; Scarce living to be christened on the Stage! **1704** SWIFT *Batt. Bks.* Misc. (1711) 222 Lust and Avarice; which, tho'.. Brethren or collateral Branches of Pride, are certainly the Issues of Want.

†**b.** A race, stock, breed, brood; also *fig. Obs.*

1620 T. GRANGER *Div. Logike* 40 Deucalion cast stones over his shoulders, from whence we are sprung, an hard issue. **1634** SIR T. HERBERT *Trav.* 221 Though the Cambrian issue in the new found world may seeme extinct, the Language.. points at our Madocs former being there. **1680** ALLEN *Peace & Unity* Pref. 79 The numerous Issue and Company of Atheists, Infidels, Scepticks, Papists, and Quakers in this Nation.

7. a. Produce, proceeds; profits arising from lands or tenements, amerciaments, or fines. Now only in legal use.

c **1330** R. BRUNNE *Chron.* (1810) 19 He was first of Inglond, þat gaf God his tiþe, Of Isshue of bestes, of londes, or of liþe [*De l'yssue de ses bestes, de terre et tenement*]. **1399** LANGL. *Rich. Redeles* IV. 8 Alle þe issues of court þat to þe kyng longid. **1439** *E.E. Wills* (1882) 122 All profytes and issues of the maners. **1537** in W. H. Turner *Select. Rec. Oxford* 146, 5ˢ by the year to their clothing, of the issues of the said Hospital. **1574** tr. *Littleton's Tenures* 27 a, Such wardeine in socage shal take no issues or profites of suche landes. **1765** *Act 5 Geo. III*, c. 26 *Preamble*, All manner of issues, revenues, and profits of the said island. **1883** in WHARTON.

†**b.** A fine, an amerciament; an order for levying such. *Obs.*

1467 in *Eng. Gilds* (1870) 378 That euery Bailly.. yelde accomptes of the yssues, fines, amerciaments of Grenewax, in the kynges courte forfet by eny citezen dwellynge wᵗyn the cyte. **1562** J. HEYWOOD *Prov. & Epigr.* (1867) 205 Thou lostst a marke in issews, criers say. **1620** J. WILKINSON *Coroners & Sherifes* 57 Sherifes must levy their issues and amerciaments by their extracts under the seale of the Exchequer. **1640-4** in Rushw. *Hist. Coll.* III. (1692) I. 344 Appear while you will, plead what you will, submit to the Mercy of the Court, Issues shall go on still, as if you did neither, till you have done somewhat that the Court will not order you to do, nor is bound to take notice of when you have done. **1752** J. LOUTHIAN *Form of Process* (ed. 2) 184 A. B. come forth, or you lose 100*s.* in Issues.

8. a. That which proceeds from any source; the outcome or product *of* any practice or condition.

1601 SHAKS. *All's Well* II. i. 109 The dearest issue of his practice And of his olde experience, th' onlie darling. **1658** W. SANDERSON *Graphice* 22 From an Artizan's excellencies, proceed those extravagant varieties.. which are not the issues of an idle brain. **1672** CAVE *Prim. Chr.* I. v. (1673) 120 The issue of the most foolish spite. **1871** BLACKIE *Four Phases* i. 52 The product of my labour and the issues of my activity are mine.

†**b.** An action, a deed (in relation to the doer). *Obs. rare.*

1601 SHAKS. *Jul. C.* III. i. 294 There shall I try In my Oration, how the People take The cruell issue of these bloody men. **1611** —— *Cymb.* II. i. 51 You are a fool granted therefore your issues, being foolish, do not derogate.

†**c.** An emanation. *Obs.*

1659 D. PELL *Impr. Sea* Prœm. B viij *note*, There be certain incorporeal and spiritual evaporations and issues which proceed out of the Loadstone.

†**9.** The entrails of a butchered animal. *Obs.*

c **1420** *Liber Cocorum* (1862) 9 Take, wasshe þo isues of swannes anon, And skoure þo guttus with salt ichon. *c* **1440** *Promp. Parv.* 266/1 Issu (of) a slayne beeste,.. *intrale, vel in plur, intralia,.. extum.*

IV. 10. a. The outcome of an action or course of proceedings or the operation of something; event, result, consequence. Also in pl. ***in the issue*** (†***in issue***), in the event.

1382 WYCLIF *Ruth* iii. 18 Abide douȝter, to the tyme that we seen what yssu the thing wol han. *c* **1400** *Destr. Troy* 2708 Fortune.. Ordans an yssew, euyn as hym lyst. *a* **1568** ASCHAM *Scholem.* I. (Arb.) 62 Experience of all facions.. beinge, in profe, alwaise daungerous, in isshue, seldom lucklie. *a* **1572** KNOX *Hist. Ref.* Wks. 1846 I. 103 Diverse presonaris tackin.. war send home ransome free, upoun promesse of thair fidelitie, which, as it was keapt, the ishew will witnesse. **1631** GOUGE *God's Arrows* III. §47. 271 The issue of the combat can not be ill where the cause of the combatant is good. **1692** BENTLEY *Boyle Lect.* i. 6 All such Principles are.. all one in the issue with the rankest Atheism. **1777** WATSON *Philip II* (1793) III. xx. 45 The prosperity of the United Provinces was, in the issue, greatly augmented. **1853** J. H. NEWMAN *Hist. Sk.* (1873) II. I. iii. 108 If perseverance merited a favourable issue, at least he has had a right to expect it. **1860** MOTLEY *Netherl.* (1868) II. ix. 27 The issue was to show whether the sarcasm were just or not.

†**b.** The event or fortune befalling a person; luck in an undertaking. *Obs.*

1390 GOWER *Conf.* I. 360 To see to what issue The king befalleth at the laste. **1606** SHAKS. *Ant. & Cl.* I. ii. 97 Ioynting their force 'gainst Cæsar, Whose better issue in the warre from Italy Vpon the first encounter draue them. **1639** T. BRUGIS tr. *Camus' Moral Relat.* 309 [He] had done well in the Armies,.. and had had good issue on many good occasions.

†**c.** The result of a discussion or examination of a question; decision, conclusion. *Obs.*

1390 GOWER *Conf.* II. 206 Ate laste they accorde.. her tale to recorde To what issue they be falle A knight shall speke for hem alle. **1563-87** FOXE *A. & M.* (1684) III. 242 They came to this issue, that Willerton should draw out of the Scriptures and Docters his Reasons, and Bradford would peruse them. **1719** DE FOE *Crusoe* I. xviii, They.. said they would much rather venture to stay there than to be carried to England to be hanged: so I left it on that issue.

d. The outcome or upshot of an argument, evidence, etc.

1604 SHAKS. *Oth.* III. iii. 219, I am to pray you, not to straine my speech To grosser issues, nor to larger reach, Then to Suspition. **1699** BENTLEY *Phal.* 145 The Issue of this present Section. **1898** W. M. RAMSAY *Was Christ born in Bethlehem?* v. 110 All our positions are the most probable issue of the scanty evidence.

V. 11. a. *Law.* The point in question, at the conclusion of the pleadings between contending parties in an action, when one side affirms and the other denies.

issue of fact, an issue raised by denying something averred as a fact. ***issue of law***, an issue raised by a demurrer or analogous proceedings, conceding the fact alleged, but denying the application of the law as claimed. ***general issue***, an issue raised by simply traversing the allegations in the declaration, as in the pleas 'not guilty', 'not indebted'. ***special issue***, an issue raised by denying part of the allegations.

[**1308** *Year-bk. 1 Edw. II, Easter* (1678) 4 Naverrez james bone issue de plee. **1309** *Year-bk. 3 Edw. II, Mich.* (1678) 59 Si vous voielletz conustre et estre a un de la tenaunce douncz purra vostre plee avoir issue en ley scil. en jugement le quel vous poietz avowere faire ou ne mye ou dites que nyent severe & issint avoir issue en fet.] **1511-12** *Act 3 Hen. VIII*, c. 23 §7 If any issue or mater in lawe ryse or growe upon any mater. **1559** in Strype *Ann. Ref.* (1824) I. App. viii. 428 Triall in the king's temporall courts of issues. **1669-70** MARVELL *Corr.* Wks. 1872-5 II. 309 If any one be sued for executing this Act, he may plead generall issue. **1681** *Trial S. Colledge* 4 When you have pleaded to Issue, then we must award the Sheriff to impannel a Jury to try that Issue. **1768**

BLACKSTONE *Comm.* III. xxi. 314 Issue, *exitus*, being the end of all the pleadings, is the fourth part or stage of an action, and is either upon matter of *law*, or matter of *fact*. **1774** S. HALLIFAX *Anal. Rom. Civ. Law* (1795) 100 Pleas to the Action are 1. General, denying at once the whole Declaration; and called the General Issue. 2. Special, advancing some new fact, not mentioned in the Declaration, in bar of the Plaintiff's demand. **1891** *Law Times* XCII. 107/1 Other points were raised, and finally the master directed an issue to be tried.

b. *transf.* A point on the decision of which something depends or is made to rest; a point or matter in contention between two parties; the point at which a matter becomes ripe for decision. Esp. in ***to put to* (†*on, upon, an, the*) *issue*** and similar phrases: to bring to a point admitting of decision.

c **1566** J. ALDAY tr. *Boaystuau's Theat. World* B iij b, The battel of this world is so perillous, the yssue so terrible and fearfull. **1613** SHAKS. *Hen. VIII*, v. i. 178 Now, While 'tis hot, Ile put it to the issue. **1656** BRAMHALL *Replic.* vi. 279 If he stand to this ground, there are no more controversies between him and me for the future but this one, what is the true Catholick Church, whether the Church of Rome..or the Church of the whole World, Roman, Grecian, Armenian, Abyssene, Russian, Protestant,..I desire no fairer issue between him and me. **1665** GLANVILL *Def. Vain Dogm.* 20, I am willing to put it upon the issue, whether it be so to any body else but this philosopher. **1748** RICHARDSON *Clarissa* I. iv. 25, I saw plainly that to have denied myself to his visits..was to bring forward some desperate issue between the two. **1863** TYNDALL *Heat* vi. 193 The problem I think is thus narrowed to the precise issue on which its solution depends. **1873** BURTON *Hist. Scot.* VI. lxxii. 290 Look at the issue between England and Scotland as it stood at the moment.

c. A matter or point which remains to be decided; a matter the decision of which involves important consequences.

1836 J. GILBERT *Chr. Atonem.* v. (1852) 145 Conferring the power of choice, and connecting that choice with most important issues. **1875** JOWETT *Plato* (ed. 2) III. 133 There is a mighty issue at stake..the good or evil of the human soul. **1898** *Westm. Gaz.* 22 July 3/2 'We want issues'. In the absence of issues politics become a question of self-interest ..to manipulate the tariff for the benefit of trusts and manufacturers.

d. A choice between alternatives, a dilemma.

1850 McCOSH *Div. Govt.* III. ii. (1874) 357 Such is the issue in which conscience lands us—it drives us to thoughtlessness, or it goads us to madness.

12. at issue. a. In *Law*: see quot. 1768. Hence *gen.* of persons or parties: In controversy; taking opposite sides of a case or contrary views of a matter; at variance.

[*a* **1530** SIR E. HOWARD *Let to Wolsey* in Ellis *Orig. Lett.* Ser. III. I. 149 For all this we be att issew that I shewed you befor.] **1768** BLACKSTONE *Comm.* (1830) III. xx. 313 When in the course of pleading, they come to a point which is affirmed on one side, and denied on the other, they are then said to be at issue; all their debates being at last contracted into a single point, which must now be determined either in favour of the plaintiff or of the defendant. **1788** JEFFERSON *Writ.* (1859) II. 456 The authority of the crown on one part, and that of the parliaments on the other, are fairly at issue. **1790** BURKE *Fr. Rev.* 86 They are always at issue with governments..on..a question of title. **1812** W. GODWIN in *Four C. Eng. Lett.* 356 Your views and mine as to the improvement of mankind are decisively at issue. **1855** PRESCOTT *Philip II*, II. (1857) 291 On this the king and the country were at issue as much as ever. **1893** LYDEKKER *Horns & Hoofs* 353 Zoologists themselves are at issue as to the number of species that ought to be recognised.

b. Of a matter or question: In dispute; under discussion; in question. Also, rarely, ***in issue***.

1817 SHELLEY *Proposal* in D. F. MacCarthy *Early Life* 372 The question now at issue is, whether the majority.. desire or no a complete representation in the Legislative Assembly. **1840** MACAULAY *Ess., Clive* (1887) 539 The matter really at issue was..whether Newcastle or Fox was to be master of the new House of Commons. **1855** —— *Hist. Eng.* xii. III. 182 The point really in issue was whether the King should be in Irish or in British hands. **1871** R. ELLIS *Catullus* xvii. 20 As alive to the world, as if world nor wife were at issue. **1885** *Law Rep.* 29 Chanc. Div. 453 The question..was not in issue in that action.

13. to join issue. †Formerly also ***to join in issue***. (Also, in transf. senses, ***to take issue***: see b, c.)

a. *Law.* Of the parties: To submit an issue (sense 11) jointly for decision; also, of one party, To accept the issue tendered by the opposite party.

1430–1 *Rolls Parl.* IV. 376 Any ple..in which..bastardie is or shal be aleged ayens ony persone partie to the same ple, and yeruppon issue joyned or to be joyned. **1540** *Act 32 Hen. VIII*, c. 30 §1 Replycacyons, reioynders, rebutters, ioynyng of issues, and other pleadynges. **1628** COKE *On Littleton* I. §193 *note*, Where the issue is ioyned of the part of the Defendant the entrie is *et de hoc ponit se super patriam*: but if it be of the part of the Plaintife, the entrie is *et hoc petit quod inquiratur per patriam*. **1672** R. WILD *Poet. Licent.* 27 Let's joyn issue, and go fairly to't, And to a Kings-Bench-Trial put the Suit. **1768** BLACKSTONE *Comm.* III. xxi. 315 When he that denies or traverses the fact pleaded by his antagonist, has tendered the issue thus, 'and this he prays may be enquired of by the country':—it may immediately be subjoined by the other party, 'and the said A B doth the like'. Which done, the issue is said to be joined, both parties having agreed to rest the fate of the cause upon the truth of the fact in question. **1774** S. HALLIFAX *Anal. Rom. Civ. Law* (1795) 111 *Contestatio Litis* answers to what, in the law of England, is called Joining Issue. **1883** *Wharton's Law Lex.* (ed. 7) 630/2 Subject to the last preceding Rule, the plaintiff by his reply may join issue upon the defence.

b. *transf.* To accept or adopt a disputed point as the basis of argument in a controversy; to proceed to argument *with* a person *on* a particular point, offered or selected.

1551 BP. GARDINER *Explic.* 145 That issue will I ioine with him, which shall suffice for confutacion of this booke. *a* **1556** CRANMER *Answ. Gardiner* 6, I wil ioyne with you this issue, that neither scripture nor ancient author writeth in expresse wordes the doctrine of your faith. **1577** HANMER *Anc. Eccl. Hist.* v. xvi[ii], If they pleade innocencie, let them staie and ioyne with vs in ishwe, in the same matter. **1662** STILLINGFL. *Orig. Sacr.* II. vii. §6 He is no true Christian who dare not readily joyn issue with them. **1720** WATERLAND *Eight Serm.* 284 We shall be very ready to join issue with them upon this very Point. **1825** MACAULAY *Ess., Milton* (1887) 19 The enemies of parliament..rarely choose to take issue on the great points of the question.

c. To take up the opposite side of a case, or a contrary view *on* a question.

1697 C. LESLIE *Snake in Grass* (ed. 2) 84, I will joyn Issue with George Whitehead upon it, that there never were such Priests. **1771** *Junius Lett.* xliv. 236, I join issue with the advocates for privilege, and affirm [etc.]. **1876** C. M. DAVIES *Unorth. Lond.* (ed. 2) 296 A point on which I should take decided issue with a portion of Professor Tyndall's late address. **1899** J. MORRIS in *Amer. Jrnl. Philol.* XX. 438, I feel impelled to take issue with his conclusions.

¶ **d.** *erron.* To come to an agreement; to agree; to unite.

a **1778** TOPLADY in Spurgeon *Treas. Dav.* Ps. lxxxix. 2 Every true believer will here join issue with David that it is God, and God alone, who builds up the temple of his Church. **1839** MURCHISON *Silur. Syst.* I. v. 74 Being convinced of the igneous origin of trap, he joined issue with his former opponents, and has now become one of the most efficient expounders of that theory. **1863** COWDEN CLARKE *Shaks. Char.* xix. 491 His banishment, and willingness to join issue with his old enemy to lay waste his native country.

14. *the* (*whole*) *issue*: everything, the lot. *colloq.*

1919 W. H. DOWNING *Digger Dial.* 29 *Issue*, 1. A portion; 2. 'to get one's issue'—to be killed; 3. 'to get the whole issue of a shell'—to be struck bodily by a shell. **1925** FRASER & GIBBONS *Soldier & Sailor Words* 129 Not a soul got back; the whole issue were done in last night. **1930** BROPHY & PARTRIDGE *Songs & Slang 1914–18* 131 *The issue* was also used for 'the whole lot', e.g. 'There's no rum tonight. The sergeant's snaffled the issue.' **1941** BAKER *Dict. Austral. Slang* 38 *Issue*, all, everything, the lot. **1960** K. AMIS *Take Girl like You* I. 10 He put a metal flint-scratcher into the mouth of the geyser and went clicking away... 'Now the water... Funny. The whole issue should light up now.' **1966** 'L. LANE' *ABZ of Scouse* 53 Yer've buggered up ther 'ole issue.

VI. From ISSUE *v.*

15. a. The action of sending or giving out officially or publicly; an emission of bills of exchange, notes, bonds, shares, postage-stamps, etc. Also, **b.** The set number or amount (of coins, notes, stamps, copies of a newspaper, books and periodicals, etc.) issued at one time, or distinguished in pattern, design, colour, or numbers, from those issued at another time.

bank of issue: see BANK *sb.* 7 b.

1833 *Penny Mag.* Monthly Suppl. Nov.–Dec. 511/1, 12,000 copies of each number (the quantity required for the first issue of the volume [*sc.* of the *Penny Magazine*]) will have been delivered to two book-binders. **1835** *Penny Cycl.* III. 381/1 The necessity for the issue of notes for so small an amount as 1*l.* arose [etc.]. *Ibid.* 384/1 If more than one bank of issue were in operation in London. *Ibid.* 386/1 To lessen ..the issues of country bankers. **1845** McCULLOCH *Taxation* III. ii. (1852) 438 An additional issue of 33,289,300*l.* of Exchequer Bills. **1862** MOUNT BROWN *Catalogue Post. Stamps* (ed. 3) Pref., Take the stamps of Naples. The first issue was in circulation from 1857 till 1859. **1863** *Ibid.* (ed. 4) Pref. 5 Early notice of any new issue of stamps. *Ibid.* 12 The word *Essay* comprehends stamps designed for issue but never circulated. **1875** JEVONS *Money* (1878) 246 The first small issue of the French assignats. **1876** HUMPHREYS *Coin-Coll. Man.* vii. 83 Coins exist of this issue. **1878** BOSW. SMITH *Carthage* 27 In the issue..of a leather money of representative value which would circulate throughout her dependencies Carthage seems..to have anticipated the convenient invention..of paper money. **1885** E. B. EVANS *Philatelic Handbk.* 118 With the exception of the most recent issue..nothing that can be termed a *set* of stamps has been brought out. **1891** *Leeds Merc.* 27 Apr. 4/7 Larger powers of control should be given to the local authorities over the issue of the licenses and the hours of opening. **1895** B. WOOD in *Brontë Soc. Trans.* I. I. 4 Many of the editions of the Brontë Works are merely reprints of previous issues. **1910** C. SHORTER in E. Brontë *Compl. Poems* p. vi, It is a curious irony of circumstance that this little volume [*sc.* the Brontë *Poems*]..now sells..for more money than the whole issue cost Charlotte Brontë and her sisters when they had it published at their own expense. **1929** J. L. YOUNG *Bks. from MS. to Bookseller* viii. 93 Quite a considerable proportion of the issue of every book is given away for one purpose or another. **1954** *Willing's Press Guide* p. vii, With this issue.. we announce important policy developments... As from this edition special supplements will be issued. **1962** M. TOASE *Guide Current Brit. Periodicals* p. viii, Information given in the entries... Date of first issue. **1974** *Leisure Painter & Craftsman* Aug. (verso front cover), We have invited Mr. Harry Richardson to outline, in this issue, his.. approach to the problem.

(ii) *Bibliogr.* In bibliogr. classification and description, a subdivision of an edition (or of an impression [see IMPRESSION *sb.* 3 d] of an edition), denoting a distinct form, planned and put on sale by the publishers, of the edition (or impression) sheets; a new issue is normally indicated by the provision of a new title-leaf, with or without other changes.

In some cases the precise application of *issue* in this sense remains subject to discussion.

1928 M. SADLEIR *Trollope: a Bibliogr.* p. xiii, It would be well to distinguish clearly between an 'issue' and a 'binding-up'. An 'issue' represents an order from the publishers for a definite effort in publication... It is a *piece of publishing*, and reflects some definite intention in the publishers' mind. A 'binding-up', on the other hand, is a mere replenishment of the stock in a publisher's ware-house. **1949** F. BOWERS *Princ. Bibliogr. Descr.* ii. 41 *Issue* is included within *edition* and itself includes only *state*. *Ibid.* 78 Removed from consideration [*sc.* of issue] are all alterations made during continuous printing of the original sheets, as well as alterations made after public sale had begun which are largely for the purpose of constructing an 'ideal copy'. We must take it as a fundamental assumption that, except in the most uncommon circumstances, sheets will not be re-issued without a change of title-page... It is impossible to set up any standards for issue [*sc.* for hand-printed books] which have any likelihood of uniform and logical application unless the title-page is taken as the prime evidence. *Ibid.* xi. 403 Sadleir's correct refusal to admit as issues those bindings-up exhibiting small variants in the binding not the result of a publisher's order helps sweep away the majority of the ridiculously conceived modern 'issues' but still leaves various ambiguities. *Ibid.* 419 Alterations to the text [*sc.* of 19th- and 20th-century books] are a cause of re-issue even if the title-page is unaffected, providing they go beyond the standards of *ideal copy* and were not made during the course of printing the impression affected... At the publisher's request, the text of D. H. Lawrence's..*White Peacock* (1911) was altered in certain respects by the substitution of two cancellans leaves..causing re-issue... In *The White Peacock*..the second issue is found in a second state. **1952** J. CARTER *ABC for Bk.-Collectors* 108 Since differences of issue are bibliographically tidier and more straightforward than differences of state, and since the term falls much more pleasingly on the priority-conscious ear, a good many undeterminable cases have been, and no doubt will continue to be, given the benefit of the doubt. **1960** G. A. GLAISTER *Gloss. Bk.* 200/1 Before the term 'issue' can first be applied, copies of the work without any of the changes now involved must have already been published. Bibliographers then speak of a 'first issue' and a 'second issue' of the 'first edition'. The term is less precisely used in the book trade. **1969** E. W. PADWICK *Bibliogr. Method* xvi. 206 Both *issue* and *state* are included within *impression*... Basically, *issue* should be regarded as an act of intent by the publisher to effect some change in the yet unbound copies of an impression after the publication of some copies has taken place. **1972** P. GASKELL *New Introd. Bibliogr.* 317 The term 'edition' has always been used in the trade for 'impression' or 'issue' as well as for edition in the bibliographical sense; a book that is advertised as a 'new edition'..may be..simply a reissue of the original sheets with a new title-page.

c. An item or amount of something given out or distributed. orig. *U.S.*

1861 *Regulations Army U.S.* 283 His descriptive list..on which the surgeon shall enter all payments, stoppages, and issues of clothing to him in hospital. **1881** *Rep. Indian Affairs* (U.S.) 10 They agreed to go as soon as the issue of beef..had been made. **1882** *Cassell's Family Mag.* June 399/1 He is also responsible that the proper issues of bread and meat are made to the men. **1899** T. W. HALL *Tales* 109 Then our..aching bodies are loaded down with a further issue of ammunition. **1911** H. QUICK *Yellowstone Nights* xii. 305 'You represent the Elkins interests in the matter of supplying for the issue do you not?' says he. *Ibid.* 321 She hove in sight of the issue. **1919** *Athenæum* 8 Aug. 727/2 Anything supplied by the Army was an 'issue'. **1940** 'GUN BUSTER' *Return via Dunkirk* I. ii. 20 His beard..had all the luxuriance of a ten-days unhampered growth... Some of our gunners began to give themselves a morning shave... His face..said..'Do as you please. I'm sticking to mine. I'm not likely to get a better issue.' **1942** E. E. DALE *Cow Country* 163 They [*sc.* Amerindians] could not subsist upon the present issue of eighty thousand pounds a week.

VII. 16. *attrib.* and *Comb.*, as ***issue book, day, department, risk, room***; (sense 11) ***issue roll***; (sense 15 c) ***issue boot, cigarette, day, house, mess tin, shoe; issue-blest*** adj.; **issue-paper** (see quots.); **issue pea**, a pea or other small globular body placed in a surgical issue (4 b) to keep up irritation.

1598 SYLVESTER *Du Bartas* II. ii. III. *Colonies* 539 A certain Father..*issue-blest..In his own life-time, his own off-spring saw To wed each other without breach of Law. **1867** SMYTH *Sailor's Word-bk*, **Issue-book*, that which contains the record of issues to the crew, and the charges made against them. **1927** *Daily Express* 4 Oct. 3 Men..running up and down perpendicular 4-inch steel stairs in *issue boots without arriving in hospital. **1925** FRASER & GIBBONS *Soldier & Sailor Words* 129 An '*Issue' cigarette..was a ration cigarette, in contradistinction to one bought at the Canteen. **1874** R. GLISAN *Jrnl. Army Life* xxxi. 447 They gave the white physicians much annoyance by coming for medicine only on *issue or ration day. **1894** *Outing* (U.S.) XXIV. 89/1 We bought our live stock on the next issue-day. **1890** *Daily News* 14 Feb. 5/2 The transfer of 250,000*l.* cash from the *issue department to the banking department of the Bank of England. **1878** *Rep. Indian Affairs* (U.S.) 39 Other mechanics are putting up new store and *issue-houses. **1911** H. QUICK *Yellowstone Nights* xii. 316 The way we..hit the trail f'r the Issue House was a high-class piece o' teamin'. **1944** *Living off Land* vii. 145 The Australian *issue mess tin is light, durable and well-suited to bush cooking. **1657** W. COLES *Adam in Eden* xxvii. 56 A little piece of the Root [of ivy], made round like a pease, and put into the Orifice, keepeth it [an issue] running without Leaf or Plaster, if you lay upon it half a sheet of *issue-Paper, eight times double. **1710** T. FULLER *Farm. Extemp.* 203 Anoint an Issue-Paper with it [the liniment], lay it warm on the Place. **1664** WOOD *Life* 17 Sept. (O.H.S.) II. 20 [Spent for] *issue peas, 1*d.* **1896** *Allbutt's Syst. Med.* I. 477 *Issue risks [in insurance] are often affected when the 'heir presumptive' wishes to raise money on his expectations, there being no 'heir apparent'..Sometimes the issue risk to be covered is not only the birth of an heir, but his attaining 21. **1886** *Encycl. Brit.* XX. 312/1 The judgment rolls pass through three stages—first, they are plea rolls; then, when

the parties join issue, *issue rolls; and lastly,..judgment rolls. **1882** NARES *Seamanship* (ed. 6) 96 Where is the *issue-room? Aft. What is stowed there? The present issue provisions. **1946** *R.A.F. Jrnl.* May 155, I put on a pair of R.A.F. *issue shoes which I had grabbed.

issue ('ɪʃ(j)uː, 'ɪsjuː), *v.* Forms: 4–7 isshew(e, (4 isu(e), 5 isshu(e, isschu(e, isswe, yssew, yschew(e, 5–7 yssu(e, 6 issew, (7 ishu), 4– issue. [f. prec. sb., or f. F. *issu* pa. pple. of *issir*: see ISH *v.*[1]]

I. Intransitive senses.

1. a. To go or come out; to flow out; to come forth, sally out. Often with *out* or *forth*.

13.. *Coer de L.* 4432 At the foure gates they isuyd oute. *c* **1330** R. BRUNNE *Chron.* (1810) 276 Whan þei of þe castelle ..þat ere of wille fulle fre, to issue on þam oute. *c* **1440** *Bone Flor.* 458 Fyfty of them yssewed owte, For to juste in werre. **1495** *Trevisa's Barth. De P.R.* XVII. cxxxix. (W. de W.) 695 Resyne is droppynge whyche comyth and ysseweth oute by swetyng of trees. *a* **1533** LD. BERNERS *Huon* lxii. 214 They issuyd out of theyr shyp. **1593** SHAKS. *3 Hen. VI*, I. ii. 71 Let's set our men in order, And issue forth, and bid them Battaile straight. **1599** —— *Hen. V*, IV. iv. 72, I did neuer know so full a voyce issue from so emptie a heart. **1613** PURCHAS *Pilgrimage* (1614) 786 Planted by a Rivers side, which issued into the South-sea. **1684** *Scanderbeg Rediv.* iii. 34 He issued out upon them with a great slaughter of the Enemy, and little loss on his side. **1715–20** POPE *Iliad* III. 366 The vital spirit issued at the wound. **1796** H. HUNTER tr. *St.-Pierre's Stud. Nat.* (1799) I. p. xl, The other branch of the Current..issues through the passage called the North-Strait. **1860** TYNDALL *Glac.* I. ii. 13 From its clefts and fissures issued a delicate blue light. **1864** SKEAT *Uhland's Poems* 245 Pascal Vivas..Issues from Saint George's chapel.

†**b.** To go out so as to depart *from* or leave.

1484 CAXTON *Chivalry* i. 5 His palfroye yssued oute of the ryght waye. *a* **1562** G. CAVENDISH *Wolsey* (1893) 76 The kyng caused Monsieur Vademount to issue frome hyme, and to ride unto my lord.

c. To come out as a branch, to start forth, branch out; †to stand or stick out, to protrude.

a **1533** LD. BERNERS *Huon* xlii. 140 He had two teth yssuyng out of his mouth more then a fote longe. **1541** R. COPLAND *Guydon's Quest. Chirurg.*, Howe many payres of synewes yssue of the noddle and in summe of all yᵉ brayne. **1634** SIR T. HERBERT *Trav.* 188 From his head issue foure great hornes. **1638** *Ibid.* (ed. 2) 241 By long canes or pipes issuing from a round vessell. **1653** R. SANDERS *Physiogn.* 151 The forepart of his head big, the nostrils issuing out. **1831** R. KNOX *Cloquet's Anat.* 749 They [sacro-lateral veins].. issue by the anterior sacral foramina.

†**d.** To go out by way of expenditure; to be laid out or spent. *Obs.*

1657 R. LIGON *Barbadoes* (1673) Contents, An Estimate of the expence, that will issue out yearly to keep this Plantation in good order. *Ibid.* 115 An account of Expences issuing out yearly for Cloathing.

e. *transf.* and *fig.* To go or come out of a state or condition, to emerge.

1481 CAXTON *Myrr.* II. xxiv. 117 The euyl esperites..may appere..to make them to yssue out of their mynde. **1483** —— *Gold. Leg.* 430 b/1 He..that of late convalesshed and yssued out of a greuous seeknesse. **1638** F. JUNIUS *Paint. of Ancients* 48 The livelinesse of great spirits cannot containe it selfe within the compasse of an ordinary practice, but it will alwayes issue forth. **1639** T. BRUGIS tr. *Camus' Moral Relat.* 211 He had had many quarrels, and had issued out of them advantagiously. **1774** J. BRYANT *Mythol.* II. 318 By thy power of old The various tribes, that rove the realms below, Issued to life. **1878** BROWNING *La Saisiaz* 250 Truce to such old sad contention whence..we issue in a half-escape.

2. To proceed as offspring; to be born, or descended. Now only in legal use. Cf. sense 8.

c **1450** LONELICH *Grail* lv. 401 Of Carcelois Isewede kyng Mangel..and Of Mangel Isswede kyng lambor. **1568** GRAFTON *Chron.* I. 14 Among all the other that issued out of Noe. **1611** BIBLE *2 Kings* xx. 18 Of thy sonnes that shall issue from thee, which thou shalt beget, shall they take away. **1818** CRUISE *Digest* (ed. 2) VI. 343 The heirs of the body of such first, second, third, and every son and sons successively, lawfully issuing.

3. To come as proceeds or revenue; to accrue. Chiefly in phr. *issuing out of* (lands, etc.).

1443 *Test. Ebor.* (Surtees, 1855) 89 A rent charge of xxvjˢ. viijᵈ. issuand owte of my landes and tenementes in Stitnam. **1540** *Act 32 Hen. VIII*, c. 37 §4 Lands and tenementes out of the which the sayd rentes or fe fermes were issuyng and paiable. *a* **1626** BACON *Max. & Uses Com. Law* iii. (1636) 16 A fee farme rent issuing out of white acre of ten shillings. **1726** AYLIFFE *Parergon* 61 These Altarages issued out of the Offerings made to the Altar. **1818** CRUISE *Digest* (ed. 2) I. 211 A person devised to his wife an annuity of 200*l.* a year, to be issuing out of his lands.

4. a. To proceed as an outcome; to come forth as from a source; to take origin, be derived, spring.

1481 CAXTON *Myrr.* I. ii. 8 Thus wold god establisshe this world that suche thinge shold yssue that myght vnderstande and knowe the noblesse of his power. **1538** STARKEY *England* I. i. 16 Al gud cyuyle lawys spryng and yssue out of the law of nature. **1593** SHAKS. *Rich. II*, I. i. 143 As for the rest apeal'd, It issues from the rancour of a Villaine. **1601** ? MARSTON *Pasquil & Kath.* IV. 302 Women whose merit issues from their worth Of inward graces. **1746** JORTIN *Chr. Relig.* i. (R.), From this Supreme Being, from this eternal fountain of all truth and of all good gifts, there issues light, which lighteth every one that cometh into the world. **1820** R. HALL *Wks.* (1832) VI. 275 Can malevolence and misery issue from the bosom of infinite goodness?

b. To proceed or arise as a result or consequence; to result.

1576 FLEMING *Panopl. Epist.* To Rdr. ¶v, I will touche in brevitie, and the benefites that issue from this booke. **1600** E. BLOUNT tr. *Conestaggio* 15 Mishaps..issuing from their ill measured Counsell. **1654** BRAMHALL *Just Vind.* ix. 248 They do not oppose it, but acquiesce, to avoid such disadvantages as must issue thereupon. **1884** tr. *Lotze's Metaph.* 488 The extra-excitation which accompanies the main movement issuing from the stimulus.

5. a. To turn out (in a specified way); to have a certain issue or result; to end or result *in*.

1665 J. SPENCER *Vulg. Proph.* 91 When men shall see their Prophecies or Dreams, of future contingencies..thus strangely issued, they will..make no doubt of their near approaches to the prophetick grace. **1715** DE FOE *Fam. Instruct.* I. viii. (1841) I. 161 We have had a hard day's work, but I hope it will issue well. **1745** WESLEY *Answ. Ch.* 28 Such [doubts and fears] as actually issued in Repentance toward God. **1833** HT. MARTINEAU *Loom & Lugger* I. iii. 33 There is no saying how quarrels might otherwise issue. **1854** FROUDE *Short Stud.*, *Spinoza* (1867) 238 A philosophy which issues in such conclusions.

b. To turn out to be. *rare.*

1884 TENNYSON *Becket* I. iii, Snake—ay, but he that lookt a fangless one, Issues a venomous adder.

6. To 'come out' or be sent forth officially or publicly; to be published or emitted. Cf. 9.

1640–4 LD. FINCH in Rushw. *Hist. Coll.* III. (1692) I. 13 His Majesty..did resolve..to Summon a great Council of all the Peers,..and commanded Writs to issue out accordingly. **1665** SIR T. HERBERT *Trav.* (1677) 257 Summons issued for the holding a Parliament of no less than the whole World. **1793** JEFFERSON *Writ.* (1859) IV. 63 A minister from France was hourly expected when the proclamation issued. **1795** A. HAMILTON *Wks.* (1886) VII. 86 Before money can legally issue from the Treasury for any purpose, there must be a law authorizing an expenditure. **1863** H. COX *Instit.* III. viii. 721 The Commission is revoked, and a new Commission issues. **1866** CRUMP *Banking* x. 227 The number of coins issuing from the mint each year varies considerably.

II. Transitive senses.

7. a. To give exit to; to send forth, or allow to pass out; to let out; to emit; to discharge. Predicated of the containing thing; †formerly also of the means of exit, or of an operative force.

1442 *Searchers' Verdicts* in *Surtees Misc.* (1888) 18 To save and isshewe yᵉ wattere fro yᵉ said place of John of Bolton. **1596** SHAKS. *Merch. V.* III. ii. 269 Euerie word in it a gaping wound Issuing life blood. **1604** T. WRIGHT *Passions* VI. 343 Marke..the seede..how it fixeth its rootes ..erecteth the stem, springs the huskes, issues the eare. **1635** HAKEWILL *Apol.* 495 His loathsome legs, every where issueing forth corrupt matter. **1799** W. TOOKE *View Russian Emp.* I. 196 A mountain near upon the strand is continually issuing smoke. **1862** BEVERIDGE *Hist. India* III. VII. ii. 47 Expeditions annually issued by his orders. **1893** SIR R. BALL *Story of Sun* 315 Agents which stored up heat in summer and issued it in winter.

b. *absol.* To shed tears; to discharge.

1599 SHAKS. *Hen. V*, IV. vi. 34, I must perforce compound With mixtfull eyes, or they will issue to. **1680** *Lond. Gaz.* No. 1527/4 Lost..a Chesnut Sorrel Gelding,..with..a little hole on the near side of his Face, that doth sometimes issue.

†**8.** To give birth to; to bear (offspring), have issue. *Obs. rare* in active; frequent in pass. in sense: To be born, to spring; = sense 2.

1447 BOKENHAM *Seyntys* (Roxb.) 145 The fyrste sustyr yssud noht, But deyid baren. *a* **1533** LD. BERNERS *Huon* lxxxi. 251 He was yssued of yᵉ lygnage of Ganelon. *a* **1586** SIDNEY *Arcadia* I. Wks. 1725 I. 19 Between these two personages..it issued forth mistress Mopsa, a fit woman to participate of both their perfections. **1610** SHAKS. *Temp.* I. ii. 59. **1623** tr. *Favine's Theat. Hon.* v. i. 39 Of that marriage was issued the said King Edward. **1672** TEMPLE *Ess.*, *Orig. Govt.* Misc. (1681) 57 Heroes, that is, persons issued from the mixture of divine and humane race.

9. To give or send out authoritatively or officially; to send forth or deal out in a formal or public manner; to publish; to emit, put into circulation (coins, bank notes, stamps, and the like). Formerly often with *out* or *forth*.

1601 in Moryson *Itin.* II. (1617) 206 Gave direction to the Commissary of the victuals, to issue Oates..at sixe shillings. **1651** HOBBES *Leviath.* II. xxiv. 130 That Issueth the same [coin] out againe for publique payments. **1667–8** MARVELL *Corr.* Wks. 1872–5 II. 239 His Majesty answered, 'He would issue forth his Proclamation'. **1758** *Herald* I. v. 73 Every trader who issues notes beyond his abilities to answer.. must in the end be ruined. **1769** BLACKSTONE *Comm.* IV. xxiv. 318 We are next..to enquire into the manner of issuing process, after indictment found, to bring in the accused to answer it. **1769** BURKE *Late St. Nation* Wks. II. 139 The writs are issued for electing members for America and the West Indies. **1818** A. RANKEN *Hist. France* V. v. 402 A new coin was issued. **1833** *Penny Mag.* Monthly Suppl. Oct.–Nov. 472/1 Twenty million 'Penny Magazines' have been issued from the commencement. **1862** MOUNT BROWN *Cat. Post. Stamps* (ed. 3) Pref., So many new foreign postage-stamps have been issued. **1868** DICKENS *Uncomm. Trav.* xxiii, Within this little window,..a neat and brisk young woman presided to take money and issue tickets. **1871** MORLEY *Voltaire* (1886) 230 The bishop of the diocese had issued monitory proclamations. **1876** 'MARK TWAIN' *Lett. to Publishers* (1967) 95 It is going to rush you too tight to do your canvassing and issue 'Tom' [sc. *Tom Sawyer*] in the middle of April isn't it? **1877** MRS. FORRESTER *Mignon* I. 3 She did not issue cards for a series of days. **1892** *Speaker* 3 Sept. 278/1 The Government during the past twelve months has issued large amounts of inconvertible paper. **1897** *Times* 15 Jan. 7/4 Dr. Murray..has just issued Part IX of Series I of the New English Dictionary. **1954** [see ISSUE *sb.* 15 b]. **1966** (*title*) The English catalogue of books.. 1963–1965, giving..the size, price, date of publication, and publisher of books issued in the United Kingdom.

†**10. a.** To bring to an issue or settlement; to settle (a dispute, etc.); to terminate. Chiefly *American.*

1650 *Rec. Dedham, Mass.* (1892) III. 131 Being deputed and Authorised to issue a case as yet vnperfect..we settle and determine the bounds to be [etc.]. **1681** *No Protestant Plot* 13 [To] influence the next Parliament to issue differences by an Act of Oblivion. **1698** S. SEWALL *Diary* 13 Apr. (1878) I. 477 Capt. Frary and Bror. Perry desire Mʳ Sergeant and me to issue their difference. **1706** J. LOGAN in *Pa. Hist. Soc. Mem.* X. 120 Pray be prevailed on to issue that business, or drive it least toward a period.

b. To give a certain issue or result to; to cause to end *in* something. Now *rare.*

a **1676** R. CROMWELL *Let.* in *Eng. Hist. Rev.* (1898) XIII. 93 God can isshew all for good, and turne our feare and sorrowings into joy. **1690** PENN *Rise & Progr. Quakers* (1834) 69 To issue those things in the wisdom and power of God. **1847** BUSHNELL *Chr. Nurt.* II. iv. (1861) 304 The child is sure to be issued finally in a feeling of confirmed disrespect, which is the end of all good influence or advice. **1858** —— *Serm. New Life* 91 We complete sensation itself or issue it in perception, by assigning reality ourselves to the distant object.

c. To bring forth (as a result). *rare.*

1865 BUSHNELL *Vicar. Sacr.* III. iii. (1868) 284 When the mercy of sacrifice, working in and with the retributive causes of justice, issues a result which neither she nor they could issue alone. *Ibid.* (1865) 241 The specific variations to be issued by the interactions of mercy.

11. To give things out to (a person); to supply (a person) *with*. (Cf. ISSUE *sb.* 15 c.)

1925 T. G. BRUCE in E. F. Norton *Fight for Everest, 1924* 344 Every man in the Expedition should be issued with one blanket either in Kalimpong or Phari. **1927** *Daily Tel.* 27 Sept. 8/6 Infantry battalions were issued with two weighted dummies apiece. **1928** *Sunday Express* 18 Mar. 3/2 The extraordinary experience of being twice in a year issued by the same bank with a faulty £1 Treasury note. **1929** F. A. POTTLE *Stretchers* (1930) 37 Before we were issued our heavy trench shoes. **1953** *Listener* 6 Aug. 224/2 Then, the idiom 'issued with': 'He was issued with' a rifle, and a packet of cigarettes, or what not. I suppose this horror has come to stay. It is undeniably convenient. **1961** *Oxford Times* 15 Dec. 14/9 He stated that he had not been issued with a licence previously when, in fact, one had been issued by Surrey County Council earlier that year.

Hence '**issued**, '**issuing** *ppl. adjs.*; '**issuingly** *adv.*, in the course of issuing.

1588 SHAKS. *Tit. A.* II. iv. 30 This losse of blood, As from a Conduit with their issuing Spouts. **1593** —— *3 Hen. VI*, II. vi. 82 And with the issuing Blood Stifle the Villaine. **1662** J. CHANDLER *Van Helmont's Oriat.* 144 Whatsoever the immortall Soul..doth issuingly think of, it also reacheth to that very thing. **1878** HUXLEY *Physiogr.* 39 In the path of the issuing vapour. **1889** *Daily News* 27 Feb. 2/2 When the issuing company pays no dividend on the share capital. **1899** *Westm. Gaz.* 3 July 6/1 A company already possessing an issued capital and debenture stock of £2,398,000.

issueless ('ɪʃ(j)uːlɪs, 'ɪsjuːlɪs), *a.* [f. ISSUE *sb.* + -LESS.] Without issue.

a. Without offspring, having no child.

1447 BOKENHAM *Seyntys* (Roxb.) 45 Whan Ely issules his lyf dede fyne. **1605** HEYWOOD *If you know not me* Wks. 1874 I. 197 Shes next successive, should your maiesty Die issulesse, which heauen defend. **1791** *Gentl. Mag.* LXI. II. 924 Both had two sons and one daughter, and both their daughters issueless. **1825** *Ibid.* XCV. I. 305 Babington Whatton had a son William, who had several children: William, and Babington, who died issueless [etc.]. **1885** JEAFFRESON *Real Shelley* I. 20 His father..surviving his eldest and issueless son by some six years.

b. Without result.

1611 SPEED *Hist. Gt. Brit.* IX. viii. (1623) 563 This Ambassage was not onely thus issueless, but produced also effects tending to further irritation. **1645** T. COLEMAN *Hopes Deferred* 15 These purposes of mischiefe are either issulesse, or damagefull. **1862** S. LUCAS *Secularia* 89 The invention of printing was as yet issueless.

c. Having no issue at stake. (See ISSUE *sb.* 11 c.)

1897 *Voice* (N.Y.) 11 Nov. 4/5 Issueless great parties is the condition that confronts us to-day in the political world.

issuer ('ɪʃ(j)uːə(r), 'ɪsjuːə(r)). [f. ISSUE *v.* + -ER[1].] One who issues: see the verb.

1757 JOS. HARRIS *Money & Coins*, The issuer of a bill.. hath..to make it good in standard or lawful money. **1765** *Act 5 Geo. III*, c. 49 *Preamble*, Bank notes..in the option of the issuer or granter payable at the end of six months. **1848** MILL *Pol. Econ.* II. 74 Coin may..be obtained from the issuers, in exchange for notes. **1853–4** DICKENS *Child's Hist. Eng.* xxxvi. 364 The issuer of the Lyme proclamation [Monmouth]. **1880** BON. PRICE in *Fraser's Mag.* May 672 It is obvious..how the issuers of paper money reap a profit from their issues. **1882** *Pall Mall G.* 14 Nov. 2/1 'This is not a new loan', the issuers tell us. **1890** BALDOCK in *19th Cent.* Nov. 832 The issue of liquor, &c., is made by a sergeant called the canteen issuer, who is changed every month.

'**issuing**, *vbl. sb.* [f. as prec. + -ING[1].]

1. The action of the verb ISSUE in various senses.

a. in intr. senses.

1481 CAXTON *Godfrey* 164 By cause of this fortresse the yssuyng and goyng out of them of the toun was deffended. **1483** *Presentm. Juries* in *Surtees Misc.* (1888) 29 Evere mane clens his gutters againe the payment for uschuynge of the water. **1580** HOLLYBAND *Treas. Fr. Tong*, *Saillie avec impetuosité*.., an issuing out, as footemen doe on their enemies. **1597** A. M. tr. *Guillemeau's Fr. Chirurg.* 28 b/2 A hinderance vnto the issuinge or runninge out of the bloode.

b. in trans. senses.

1642 C. VERNON *Consid. Exch.* 42 Another Pell, called *Pellis Exitus*, wherein every dayes issuing of any of the moneyes..was to be entred. **1660–1** MARVELL *Corr.* Wks. 1872–5 II. 44 The insurrection..occasioned the issuing out of this Proclamation. **1831** in Picton *L'pool Munic. Rec.* (1886) II. 330 The issuing of the Election Writ has been suspended. **1891** *Law Rep.* Weekly Notes 78/2 The issuing of the possession warrant.

†**2.** *concr.* A place or point of issue; an outlet.

1523 LD. BERNERS *Froiss.* I. xlvii. 65 He rode forthe fro the sonne settyng, tyll he came to a forest in the yssuing out of Heynalt. *Ibid.* cxxvii. 153 The frenchemen defended so well the passage at the yssuing out of the water. **1590** MARLOWE *2nd Pt. Tamburl.* III. ii, It must have privy ditches, countermines, And secret issuings to defend the ditch. **1632** LITHGOW *Trav.* VI. 254 The Lake it selfe, never diminisheth, nor increaseth..: neyther hath it any issuing forth. **1712** J. JAMES tr. *Le Blond's Gardening* 198 The Pipe ..ought always to go diminishing to the very issuing out of the Water.

3. issuing house: see quot. 1965.

1929 *Issuing House Year Bk.* 3 The requirements of an Issuing House in the production of a Prospectus are more exacting than for almost any other work the printer is called upon to undertake. **1932** *Daily Tel.* 8 Oct. 2/3 Regarding the continued default on City of Riga 4½ p.c. Bonds,..what is inexplicable is that the bondholders have shown such apathy and negligence in this matter respecting the negotiations between the issuing house and the City of Riga. **1965** PERRY & RYDER *Thomson's Dict. Banking* (ed. 11) 317/2 The main function of an issuing house is to obtain from the public capital for the expansion of existing companies, for new public companies, or for private companies being converted into public concerns.

ist, quasi-*sb.* [The suffix *-ist* used generically as a nonce-word.] A professor of some *ism*; a holder of some special doctrine, or adherent of some system; a votary of, or expert in, a particular science, art, or pursuit. Chiefly used in a context suggesting some group of words in *-ist*, and often disparagingly or humorously.

1811 [see ISM]. **1835** CARLYLE in Froude *Life in Lond.* (1884) I. 44, I am neither Pagan nor Turk, nor circumcised Jew; but an unfortunate Christian individual resident at Chelsea,..neither Pantheist nor Pot-theist, nor any Theist or Ist whatsoever, having a decided contempt for all such manner of system-builders or sect-founders. **1841** —— *Pref. Emerson's Ess.* p. x, Ists and Isms are rather growing a weariness. **1875** GEO. ELIOT in Cross *Life* III. 253 We must not take every great physicist—or other 'ist'—for an apostle. **1887** T. HARDY *Woodlanders* I. xiv. 257 A dreamy 'ist of some sort, or too deeply steeped in some false kind of 'ism. **1897** *Literature* 27 Nov. 186 We are at a loss in what 'ist' his name shall terminate.

†**ist**, *int. Obs.* [A natural utterance.] An exclamation used to call attention, or to enjoin silence: cf. HIST. (In quot. 1540 as *sb.*)

1540 MORYSINE *Vives' Introd. Wysd.* D vj, If it go a stray, ..calle it ageyne, as it were with a lyttel ist. **1611** COTGR., *Houische*,..husht, whist, ist, not a word for your life.

is't (ɪst), archaic, poetic, colloq., or dial. abbreviation of *is it*.

1610 SHAKS. *Temp.* I. ii. 245 What is't thou canst demand? **1631** MABBE tr. *De Rojas' Celestina* xvii. (1894) 250 Who is't that knocks there? **1706** E. WARD *Hud. Rediv.* I. IV. 2 Nor is't but Justice that each Toe Should the same Pennance undergo. **1798** WORDSW. *Goody Blake & Harry Gill* i, What is't that ails young Harry Gill? **1876** BROWNING *Pacchiarotto* xxvi, That chord now—a groan or a grunt is't? Schumann's self was no worse contrapuntist.

-ist, *suffix*, corresponding to F. *-iste*, L. *-ista*, Gr. *-ιστής*, forming agent-nouns from verbs in *-ίζειν* (see -IZE), consisting of the agential suffix *-της* added to the verb-stem, as in *βαπτίζ-ειν* to dip, *βαπτισ-τής* dipper, L. *baptista*, F. *baptiste* baptist. Cognate to the suffix *-ισμός*, -ISM.

Examples of the Greek use are *ἀγωνιστής* combatant, competitor, *λογιστής* calculator, *πολεμιστής* warrior, *σοφιστής* clever man, sophist; *κιθαριστής* player on the cithara, *λυριστής* player on the lyre, *τυμπανιστής* drummer; *Ἀττικιστής* a partisan of Athens, one who Atticizes, *'Ελληνιστής* a Hellenizer, one who speaks Greek; *Λακωνιστής* one who sides with or imitates Lacedaemon, or uses laconism. A few words of this form were taken into Latin during or soon after the classical period, e.g. *citharista, cymbalista, danīsta* (usurer), *grammatista, logista, lyrista, petaurista* (rope-dancer), *sophista, tympanista*; the number of these was greatly increased by Christian writers, in the latinizing of scriptural and ecclesiastical terms, such as *agōnista, baptista, catēchista, collybista, euangelista, exorcista, psalmista, tocista.* In later use, *-ista* became a favourite formative of names denoting the observers of a particular rite, the holders of special religious or philosophical tenets, or the adherents of particular teachers or heresiarchs; hence such names as *Catharista, Origenista, Platōnista*, and in scholastic use *Scotista, Thōmista, nōminālista, reālista*, etc. Hence the suffix (with the needed adaptations, F. *-iste*, Eng. and Ger. *-ist*, etc.) has passed into the modern languages. In English, its use has received a wide extension, it being now used not merely as the agent-noun of verbs in *-ize* (beside -IZER), as in *plagiarize, plagiarist*, and in association with nouns of action or function in *-ism*, as in *altruism, altruist*, but also, on the analogy of these, in a multitude of terms, having no corresponding words in *-ize* or *-ism*, which denominate the professed followers of some leader or school, the professional devotees of some principle, or the practisers of some art. In some cases, the form in *-ist* approaches closely to the native agent-noun in *-er*, being distinguished only by the more professional or systematic sense which it implies: cf. *conformer, conformist; copier, copyist; cycler, cyclist; philologer, philologist.* Many of the sbs. in *-ist* give rise to adjs. in -ISTIC, -ISTICAL; but words of modern formation are to a great extent used adjectively unchanged, as in the *royalist* party, a *Bonapartist* plot, *nonconformist* principles.

The following are the chief modern English uses of the suffix:

1. Forming a simple agent-noun derived from a Gr. verb in *-ίζειν*, and often accompanying an Eng. verb in *-ize*. Such are *agonist, antagonist, baptist, catechist, epitomist, evangelist, exorcist; apologist, plagiarist, ostracist, syllogist.*

2. Designating a person who practises some art or method, or who prosecutes, studies, or devotes himself to some science, art, or branch of knowledge, originally expressed by a word of Greek formation in *-ια* (Eng. *-y*), *-μα(τ)* (*-ma, -m*), *-η* (*-e*), etc., but in later examples, also by words of Latin or other origin. Such are *archæologist, chronologist, economist, etymologist, genealogist, geologist, meteorologist, mineralogist, mythologist, philologist, physiologist, zoologist; alchemist, algebr(a)ist, anatomist, botanist, chemist, metallurgist, microscopist, phlebotomist, physicist, physiognomist, theorist; academist, chirographist, monopolist, rhapsodist, symmetrist; bigamist, monogamist, polygamist; dogmatist, dramatist, epigrammatist, schematist*, etc. To these may be added (from L. sources) *annalist, capitalist, journalist, memorialist, mineralist, moralist, satirist, scientist* (L. *scientia*), etc.

These have a possible verb in *-ize*, often in use, e.g. *anatomize, botanize, dogmatize, dramatize, economize, geologize, journalize, monopolize, moralize, theorize*, etc.

3. Designating an adherent or professor of some creed, doctrine, system, or art, which is usually denominated by a cognate *-ism*: e.g. *altruist* (a professor of *altruism*), *animist, atheist, Chartist, deist, egoist, egotist, hedonist, monotheist, pædobaptist, polytheist, ritualist, ventriloquist*, etc.; with a large number derived from personal names, as *Bonapartist, Brownist, Buddhist, Calvinist, Darwinist, Hattemist, Scotist, Spinozist, Thomist, Wycliffist*, and nonce-words without limit, as *Lambist, Lockeist, Stuartist, Weismannist*, etc.

b. Formed on an adjective (usually also with a cognate sb. in *-ism* and often an adj. in *-istic*), as *devotionalist, externalist, fatalist, formalist, humanist, idealist, imperialist, loyalist, materialist, naturalist, nominalist, opportunist, pluralist, positivist, purist, rationalist, realist, royalist, socialist, universalist.*

4. Formed from other sbs. (chiefly Latin) without accompanying words in *-ize* or *-ism*, and denoting one whose profession or business it is to have to do with the thing or subject in question, as *amorist, artist, canonist, casuist, colourist, decretist, dentist, duellist, fashionist, florist, humorist, jurist, linguist, medallist, novelist, numerist, oculist, opinionist, organist, querist, statist, tobacco(n)ist.* Also from names of languages, as *Americanist, Anglist, Germanist, Hebraist, Hellenist, Latinist, Orientalist.* Sometimes, from vbs., as *conformist, computist, controvertist, favourist, impartist, separatist, speculatist.*

b. These lead the way to modern formations from current words of all kinds and even from phrases; as *balloonist, billiardist, bimetallist, 'celloist, cocainist, cyclist, fetishist, footballist*; with such nonce-formations as *hammerist, selfist, semi-finalist, truthist; great aukist, physical forcist, red tapist, second adventist*, etc.

Words in *-ist* are treated, according to their importance, in their alphabetical places, or under the Main words on which they are formed; the following are illustrations of some of those of more trivial or ephemeral character, nonce-words, and the like.

1884 *Pall Mall G.* 17 Sept. 11/1 Associations of amateur *balloonists. **1897** *Pall Mall Mag.* Feb. 196 Chalmers the *'celloist and orientalist. **1897** *Westm. Gaz.* 22 Jan. 8/1 A considerable proportion of chronic *cocainists have fallen under the dominion of the drug from a desire to stimulate their powers of imagination. **1862** *Literary Churchman* VIII. 207/2 If by any chance the Benedicite should be used, the *Consecutivist would be completely bewildered. **1869** *Contemp. Rev.* XII. 278 The obstructive Conservative in art may just as naturally be a classicist as a mediævalist or *dark-ageist. **1868** FREEMAN *Norm. Conq.* (1876) II. App. 558 This time we for once get the *Godwinist version. **1900** *Daily Express* 20 June 5/2 The gem of the collection is a great auk's egg,..and is regarded by *great aukists as the finest specimen of its special type of marking in the world. **1857** READE *Course of True Love* 48 The *hammerist [*i.e.* field geologist] can jump out of his gig at any turn of the road. **1850** tr. *Mosheim's Eccl. Hist.* (1863) III. IV. ii. II. §36. 390 The Dutch sects of Verschorists and *Hattemists having been better known among us. **1876** JOHNSON *Univ. Cycl.*, *Hattemists*, the followers of one Pontianus van Hattem, a Dutch minister of the eighteenth century who was excommunicated for Spinozism. **1892** *Pall Mall G.* 19 May 6/1 Philosopher—artist—and general *impartist Of cynical views on society. **1898** *Daily News* 3 Jan. 6/4 The Prince was not disposed to reject contemptuously those *Lamaist miracles of which he heard. **1868** SALA *Lamb's Wks.* I. p. xiv, There have not been any *Lambists; on no particular shoulders did the mantle of his idiosyncrasies descend. **1856** EMERSON *Eng. Traits, Literature* Wks. (Bohn) II. 106 'Tis quite certain, that Spenser, Burns, Byron, and Wordsworth will be Platonists; and that the dull men will be *Lockeists. **1848** W. E. FORSTER 26 May in Wemyss Reid *Life* (1888) I. vii. 247 The *physical forcists have gained a strength in my absence which [etc.]. **1890** J. W. BROWN *Ital. Campaign* I. iv. 103 The Protestant movement..was prejudiced by *Plymouthists and their sectarian spirit. **1842** R. FORD *Let.* in Smiles *Mem. J. Murray* (1891) II. xxxvi. 491 [They] yield not in..insolence to any kind of *red-tapists. **1897** *Westm. Gaz.* 29 Dec. 2/1 The colony of German '*Second Adventists', just outside the Jaffa Gate, has done far more than anything else to spoil the approach to the Holy City. **1898** *Daily News* 10 Oct. 7/4 There were six heats, and the *semi-finalists were Gandin, Deltour, Ashe, and Machenry. **1889** *Daily News* 4 Oct. 5/1 The true *Stuartists..were all for the propagation of the faith, according to the profession of the Order of the White Rose. **1897** *Westm. Gaz.* 5 Feb. 10/1 Our Stuartist and 'White Rose' ladies and gentlemen. **1896** *Life A. J. Gordon* 315 Not that one should be a pessimist..he should, above all else, be a *truthist. **1890** *Times* (weekly ed.) 10 Jan. 7/3 There are [in biology] pure Darwinists, Wallaceists, *Weismannists, Lamarckites, and Romanesists.

i-stabled, ME. pa. pple. of STABLE *v.*

i-stad, ME. pa. pple. of STEAD *v.*, to place.

i-stald, i-stalled, ME. pa. pple. of STALL *v.*

‖**istana** (ɪ'staːnə). Also **astana, astanah.** [Mal. *istana*, ad. Skr. *ā-sthāna* place, site, assembly.] In Malay kingdoms, a ruler's palace.

1839 T. J. NEWBOLD *Pol. & Statistical Acct. Straits of Malacca* II. viii. 90 He married Tuanku Itam..and proceeded to his astánah in Srimenanti. **1907** F. A. SWETTENHAM *Brit. Malaya* xiii. 315 The Sultan's *astâna* or palace.. surrounds on three sides a court of sand. **1927** R. J. H. SIDNEY *In Brit. Malaya Today* xxiii. 271 His [*sc.* the Sultan's] *Istana* at Klang is filled with work done by his own hand. **1965** *Festival Malaysia 1965: Calendar of Events* 6/1 The Investiture Ceremony held in the afternoon at the Istana in Sri-Menanti is followed by a Garden Party in the evening. **1972** *Sunday Times* (Kuala Lumpur) 30 Apr. 5/2 The Yang di-Pertuan Agong today presented awards to 76 people at an investiture ceremony at the Istana Negara. **1972** *Straits Times* (Malaysia ed.) 24 Nov. 20/6 This Istana in the village of Bandar was the residence of Sultan Abdul Samad in the middle of the nineteenth century.

†**i-stand**, *v. Obs.* Also 2–3 **istond.** [OE. *ȝestandan* (f. *ȝe-*, I-[1] + *standan* to stand) = Goth. *gastandan*, OS. *gistandan*, OHG. *gistantan.*] *intr.* To stand, stand firm.

Beowulf (Z.) 2598 Æðelinga bearn ymbe ȝestodon. **971** *Blickl. Hom.* 173 Hie mon..to his andweardnesse heht ȝestandan. *c* **1205** LAY. 15505 Þat þe wal þe wes swa strong ne moste niht longes nauere istonden.

i-standen, i-stonden, ME. pa. pple. of STAND *v.*

i-statheled, i-staðeled, ME. pa. pple. of STATHEL *v.*, to establish.

i-stefned, ME. pa. pple. of STEVEN *v.*, to appoint.

i-steie(n, ME. pa. pple. of STY *v.*, to climb, mount.

i-steke(n, ME. pa. pple. of STEEK *v.*, to shut, etc.

i-stekyd, ME. pa. pple. of STICK *v.*

i-steled, ME. pa. pple. of STEEL *v.*

i-stellified, ME. pa. pple. of STELLIFY *v.*

i-stened, ME. pa. pple. of STENE *v.*, to stone.

-ister, †**-istre**, suffix repr. OF. *-istre*, a by-form of *-iste*, -IST, considered by French etymologists to have arisen through false analogy with words like *ministre*. Found in OF. at an early date, as in *evangelistre* (12–13th c. in Godef. *Compl.*), beside *evangeliste*; so *choristre, decretistre, legistre, listre* or *litre* (reader), etc. From OF., these forms passed into English, where they were spelt first *-istre*, as in *alkamystre, decretistre, divinistre, legistre, listre, queristre*; afterwards *-ister*, as in *alchimister, chorister, palmister, sophister.* In this latter form, the *-er* was app. associated with the native suffix *-er*, which appears as an addition in many nouns denoting office or occupation, derived from or through Fr., as *astrologer, astronomer, geographer, parishioner, practitioner,* †*musicianer*, etc.

†**isthm(e.** *Obs.* Also **isthim.** [a. F. *isthme* (Rabelais, 16th c.), ad. L. *isthmus.*] = ISTHMUS.

1609 HOLLAND *Amm. Marcell.* XXIII. vi. 228 A necke or Isthm of land. **1610** —— *Camden's Brit.* II. 110 Which, by a very narrow Isthim or necke of land groweth to the rest of the Iland. **1612** BREREWOOD *Lang. & Relig.* xiii. 127 That isthme between the Euxine and the Caspian seas. **1646** SIR T. BROWNE *Pseud. Ep.* VI. viii. 319 Some Isthmes have been eat through by the Sea, and others cut by the spade.

'**Isthmiad** (see ISTHMUS). [f. as next + -AD.] The space of time between two celebrations of the Isthmian games.

1831 KEIGHTLEY *Anc. Grk. & It. Mythol.* II. iv. 328 In the third Isthmiad afterwards, when the Eleans sent the Molionides to Cleonæ to offer sacrifice, he waylaid and killed them.

ˈisthmian (see ISTHMUS), *a.* (*sb.*) Isthmian in specific uses. [f. L. *isthmi-us*, a. Gr. *ἰσθμι-ος* of or pertaining to the (or an) ISTHMUS + -AN.]

1. Belonging to, situated upon, or forming, an isthmus or neck of land.

1654 VILVAIN *Epit. Ess.* IV. i, Isthmian neck of land. **1801** G. S. FABER *Horae Mosaicae* (1818) I. 241 The isthmian region. **1895** *N. Amer. Rev.* Mar. 375 These with Belize would control any isthmian canal on the Atlantic side. **1899** *Westm. Gaz.* 4 Mar. 5/1 An investigation by 'a competent board of engineers' of all the isthmian routes is to be made.

2. *spec.* Belonging to the Isthmus of Corinth; esp. in ***Isthmian games***, one of the national festivals of ancient Greece, celebrated in the Isthmian sanctuary in the first and third years of each Olympiad.

1603 HOLLAND *Plutarch's Mor.* 431 In the solemnitie of the Isthmian games. **1807** ROBINSON *Archæol. Græca* III. xxiv. 329 The Isthmian Games derived their name from the place where they were celebrated, which was the Corinthian Isthmus.. They were instituted in honor of Palæmon or Melicertes. **1816** BYRON *Siege Cor.* ii, And downward to the Isthmian plain.

transf. **18..** in *Harper's Mag.* (1883) Aug. 340/1 That the House do adjourn over Wednesday to allow honorable members to be present at our Isthmian games.

B. *sb.* An inhabitant of an isthmus (in quot., of the Isthmus of Corinth).

1601 HOLLAND *Pliny* II. 547 After Pausias, there arose one Euphranor the Isthmian.

ˈisthmiate (-ɪət: see ISTHMUS), *a.* *Entom.* [f. as prec. + -ATE² 2.] Having an isthmus, or narrow part connecting two broader parts.

1855 MAYNE *Expos. Lex.*, *Isthmiatus*, applied by Kirby to the trunk of insects when there exists an isthmus, or contraction between the prothorax and the elytra, as in the *Passalus*: isthmiate.

ˈisthmic (see ISTHMUS), *a.* [ad. Gr. *ἰσθμικ-ός*, f. *ἰσθμός* ISTHMUS: see -IC.] = ISTHMIAN *a.*

1585 T. WASHINGTON tr. *Nicholay's Voy.* IV. xxxiii. 156 To those yᵉ won the prise at yᵉ Istmick games. **1884** tr. *Reville's Native Relig. Mexico & Peru* (Hibb. Lect.) 18 Civilization was affiliated to that of the isthmic region.

isthmitis (-ˈaɪtɪs: see ISTHMUS). *Path.* [medical L., f. ISTHM-US + -ITIS.] Inflammation of the isthmus of the fauces.

1855 in MAYNE *Expos. Lex.* **1887** in *Syd. Soc. Lex.*

ˈisthmoid (see ISTHMUS), *a.* [ad. Gr. *ἰσθμοειδ-ής* like an isthmus: see -OID.] Resembling an isthmus.

1855 in MAYNE *Expos. Lex.* **1887** *Syd. Soc. Lex.*, *Isthmoid*, resembling the isthmus of the fauces.

isthmus (ˈɪsθməs, ˈɪstməs, ˈɪsməs). Pl. **isthmuses** (-əsɪz), rarely **isthmi** (-aɪ). Forms: 6–7 **isthmos, istmus, 7 istmos, 6– isthmus.** [a. L. *isthmus*, a. Gr. *ἰσθμός* neck, narrow passage, a neck of land between two seas, spec. the Isthmus of Corinth connecting the Peloponnesus with northern Greece.]

1. *Geog.* A narrow portion of land, enclosed on each side by water, and connecting two larger bodies of land; a neck of land.

1555 EDEN *Decades* To Rdr. (Arb.) 59 Certeyne places cauled Isthmi (beinge narrowe portions of lande so diuidynge twoo sees, that there is no passage from the one to the other). **1579–80** NORTH *Plutarch* (1676) 741 A generall assembly..kept in the straight of Peloponnesus, called Isthmos. **1591** G. FLETCHER *Russe Commw.* (Hakluyt Soc.) 7 By this riuer..you may passe..by water, drawing your boate..ouer a little isthmus or narrow slippe of lande, a fewe versts ouerthwart. **1613** PURCHAS *Pilgrimage* VIII. iii. 617 America is..divided by that Isthmus, or necke and narrow passage of Land at Darien, into two parts. *c* **1645** HOWELL *Lett.* (1650) II. lx. 90 Som do hold that this Island was tied to France..by an Istmos or neck of land 'twixt Dover and Bullen. **1646** SIR T. BROWNE *Pseud. Ep.* VI. viii. 319 Divers Princes have attempted to cut the Isthmus or tract of land which parteth the Arabian, and Mediterranean Sea. **1677** W. HUBBARD *Narrative* 120 They espyed a Company of Indians making towards the said Istmus. **1796** MORSE *Amer. Geog.* I. 84 The beasts of cold climes passed over the northern isthmusses, which probably connected Europe, America, and Asia. **1850** tr. *Goethe's Convers. w. Eckermann* 21 Feb. 1827, Lastly, I [Goethe] should wish to see England in possession of a canal through the Isthmus of Suez. **1882** FARRAR *Early Chr.* II. 159 *note*, It [Patmos] consists of three masses of rock united by narrow isthmuses.

transf. **1856** STANLEY *Sinai & Pal.* i. (1858) 96 A solitary cell hewn in an isolated cliff, and joined to this platform by a narrow isthmus of rock.

b. *fig.*

1601 DANIEL *Ep.*, *To Sir T. Egerton* i, Set thee in th' aidfulst roome of dignitie, As th' Isthmus these two Oceans to diuide Of Rigor and confus'd Vncertaintie. **1663** COWLEY *Pindar. Odes*, *Life* i, Vain weak-built Isthmus, which dost proudly rise Up betwixt two Eternities. **1755** YOUNG *Centaur* iii. Wks. 1757 IV. 176 He lies a sad deserted, outcast on a narrow isthmus between time and eternity. *a* **1864** J. D. BURNS *Mem. & Rem.* (1879) 416 They stood on a narrow isthmus between two great periods of their history.

2. *Anat.*, *Zool.*, and *Bot.* A narrow part or organ connecting two larger parts; *esp.* the narrow passage connecting the cavity of the mouth with that of the pharynx (more fully *isthmus of the fauces* or *throat*).

[*c* **1400** *Lanfranc's Cirurg.* 217 Bi þe place þat a mannes mete goiþ doun, or bi þe þrote, or..bitwixe þe .ij. placis in a place þat is clepid ismon.] **1706** PHILLIPS, *Isthmus*,..in Anatomy it is taken by some for that part which is between the Mouth and the Gullet; also the Ridge that separates the Nostrils. **1851** E. WILSON *Anat. Vade M.* 571 The space included between the soft palate and the root of the tongue is the isthmus of the fauces. .. It is the opening between the mouth and pharynx. **1859** SEMPLE *Diphtheria* 12 A sponge soaked in concentrated hydrochloric acid was applied to the isthmus of the throat. **1877** HUXLEY *Anat. Inv. Anim.* viii. 533 These two lobes are united behind by a thick isthmus. **1880** M. MACKENZIE *Dis. Throat & Nose* I. 501 Over the second, third, and fourth rings (of the trachea) we see the isthmus of the thyroid gland. **1880** GÜNTHER *Fishes* 39 The space on the chest between the two rami of the lower jaw and between the gill-openings is called the isthmus.

-istic, double suffix of adjs. and sbs., corresp. to F. *-istique*, L. *-isticus*, Gr. *-ιστικός*, viz. the suffix *-ικ-ός*, -IC, added to sbs. in *-ιστ-ής*, -IST; e.g. *σοφιστικ-ός* of, pertaining to, or like a sophist, sophistic; but also used where there is a vb. in *-ίζειν* (-IZE), or sb. in *-ισμός* (-ISM), and no sb. in *-ιστής*, as in *χαρακτηριστικός* characteristic. Not frequent in Gr.; but more numerous in med.L. and mod. langs.; and, in Eng., supplying a derivative adj. to many sbs. in *-ist*: e.g. *altruistic, antagonistic, atheistic, Calvinistic, deistic, egotistic, evangelistic, Hellenistic, idealistic, realistic, socialistic*, etc. In many cases the adj. serves also to express the quality of the sb. in *-ism*, e.g. *atheistic*, of or pertaining to an atheist, or to atheism; hence it may be found in cases where a sb. in *-ism*, but none in *-ist*, is in use. It is rarely found with the sbs. in -IST in groups 2, 4, 4 b, or with those formed from proper names in 3.

Words in *-istic* are essentially adj., but like other adjs. in -IC, they are sometimes used as sbs. Like other adjs. in *-ic* also, they sometimes have a secondary form in **-istical**, e.g. *casuistical, deistical, egotistical, sophistical*, etc., and on this type their adverbs are formed in **-istically**, as *Calvinistically, characteristically, Hellenistically, sophistically*. Some words in *-istic* originate verbs in **-isticate**, e.g. *sophisticate*.

i-stien, i-stihen, ME. pa. pple. of STY *v.*, to mount.

i-stikit, i-styked, ME. pa. pple. of STICK *v.*

†i-ˈstill, *v.* *Obs.* [OE. *ȝestillan*, f. *ȝe-*, I-¹ + *stillan* to STILL; = OS. *gistillian*, OHG. *gastillan*.] *trans.* To restrain, stay, still, calm.

c **900** tr. *Bæda's Hist.* III. xiii. [xv.] (1890) 200 Se Godes wer..þone storm..ȝestilde. *a* **1000** *Cædmon's Gen.* 1416 (Gr.) Hæfde..metod..reȝn ȝestilled. *a* **1175** *Cott. Hom.* 229 He ȝestilde windes mid his hesne. *c* **1315** SHOREHAM 133 That unecorn..Thou hast ytamed and istyld.

†i-ˈstink, *v.* *Obs.* [OE. *ȝestincan*, f. *ȝe-*, I-¹ + *stincan* to STINK; = OHG. *gestincan*, MHG. *gestinchen*.] *trans.* To smell, perceive by smell.

c **1000** *Ags. Ps.* (Th.) cxxxiv. 17 Hi..nose habbað, nawiht ȝestincað. *a* **1225** *Ancr. R.* 84 He heleð it & wrihð so þet he hit nout ne istinckeð.

istle (ˈɪstliː, *improp.* ˈɪst(ə)l). Also **ixtle, ixtli.** [Commercial corruption of the Mexican name *ixtli*.] A valuable fibre obtained (in Mexico and Central America) from *Bromelia sylvestris* and species of *Agave*, as *A. Ixtli*, and used for cordage, nets, carpets, etc. Also *attrib.*, as *istle fibre, plant*; **istle-grass**, a name for *Bromelia sylvestris*.

1883 *Cassell's Fam. Mag.* Dec. 61/1 Ixtli obtained from the henequen species of maguey is at present exported to London and New York as body material for carpets. **1884** *Harper's Mag.* Oct. 750/2 Baled in the coarse sacking of the ixtle plant. **1894** *U.S. Customs Tariff* §268 in *Times* 17 Aug. 9/2 Cables, cordage, and twine..composed in whole or in part of New Zealand hemp, istle or Tampico fibre.

i-stoken, ME. pa. pple. of STEEK *v.*

i-stolen, ME. pa. pple. of STEAL *v.*

i-stonde, ME. pa. pple. of STAND *v.*

i-stongen, ME. pa. pple. of STING *v.*

i-stopped, ME. pa. pple. of STOP *v.*

i-stored, ME. pa. pple. of STORE *v.*

i-straht, etc., ME. pa. pple. of STRETCH *v.*

i-strangled, ME. pa. pple. of STRANGLE *v.*

i-strawed, ME. pa. pple. of STREW *v.*

-istre: see -ISTER.

i-streiȝt, i-streiht, ME. pa. pple. of STRETCH *v.*

i-streined, ME. pa. pple. of STRAIN *v.*

i-strenget, ME. pa. pple. of STRENG *v.*

i-strengþed, ME. pa. pple. of STRENGTH *v.*

†i-streon. *Obs.* [OE. *ȝestreón* = OS. *gistriuni*, OHG. *gastriuni*. Cf. STRAIN.]

1. Gain, acquisition; wealth.

c **893** K. ÆLFRED *Oros.* V. xiii. §1 þæt he æfter him to eallum his ȝestreonum fenge. *c* **1000** ÆLFRIC *Gloss.* in Wr.-Wülcker 190/3 *Quæstus uel lucrum*, ȝestreon. *c* **1175** *Lamb. Hom.* 19 Oðer monnes istreon. *c* **1205** LAY. 18609 þæ castles aðele weore of his eoldrene istreon. *a* **1250** *Prov. Ælfred* 185 in *O.E. Misc.* 114 Ayhte nys non ildre istreon.

2. Begetting, procreation. [OE. *stréon*.]

c **1175** *Lamb. Hom.* 133 Nis na stude to istreone bicumelic, butan ða þe istreonieð beon bispused rihtliche to gedere.

b. Offspring, progeny. [OE. *stréon*.]

c **1175** *Lamb. Hom.* 133 He spec wið ðene halie mon abraham of his istreone. *c* **1205** LAY. 22597 Heore moder is kinges istreon. *c* **1275** *XI Pains Hell* 141 in *O.E. Misc.* 151 Heo..furduden heore istreon.

i-streoned, ME. pa. pple. of STRENE *v.* to get.

†i-stretche, *v.* *Obs.* In 3 i-strecche. [OE. *ȝestrecc(e)an* to lay flat, spread, stretch, f. *ȝe-*, I-¹ + *strecc(e)an* to STRETCH.] *trans.* To stretch, spread.

c **1000** *Sax. Leechd.* III. 208 Bet him ȝestreht & wel ȝestreht ȝesihð beorhtnysse ȝetacnað. *c* **1205** LAY. 26778 Beof..bræid hine of his stede & to eorðe hine istræhte.

i-strewed, ME. pa. pple. of STREW *v.*

i-streynd, ME. pa. pple. of STRAIN *v.*

Istrian (ˈɪstrɪən), *a.* and *sb.* [f. *Istria*, a peninsula near the head of the Adriatic sea; see -AN.]

A. *adj.* **1.** Of or belonging to Istria.

1607 TOPSELL *Four-f. Beasts* 288 The Istrian Horsses are of good able feete. **1881** E. A. FREEMAN *Sk. Subject Lands Venice* 98 The Istrian shore has lost its beauty. **1920** *Glasgow Herald* 16 Apr. 8 The 'conversation' broke down solely on the question of the Istrian frontier. **1967** C. SETON-WATSON *Italy from Liberalism to Fascism* xi. 426 A new and energetic Minister of War, General Vittorio Zupelli, of Istrian origin, took the job of military preparation systematically in hand.

2. Special Comb.: **Istrian marble, stone**, a fine limestone resembling marble; also *ellipt.*; **Istrian pointer**, a hunting dog (in Yugoslavia).

1611 CORYAT *Crudities* 163 Stately pillers made partly of white stone, and partly of Istrian marble. **1947** J. C. RICH *Materials & Methods Sculpture* viii. 228 Istrian marble, which is found on the Istrian peninsula and on some of the Dalmatian islands, is a large-grained, buff marble that compares favorably with the Greek marbles. **1971** *Country Life* 18 Feb. 16F Suppl., A most important 17th century Italian Istrian marble wall fountain. **1948** A. LOKAR in B. Vesey-Fitzgerald *Bk. Dog* II. 536 The Istrski Brak (Istrian Pointer) has a wide range in Yugoslavia. **1888** *Encycl. Brit.* XXIV. 149/2 This Istrian stone has for most architectural purposes all the beauty of the finest white marble. **1962** *Listener* 27 Dec. 1105/3 The sculptor is not above counterpointing the folds of a drapery or the positioning of a hand with the natural pressure lines in a fine piece of green Istrian. **1972** *Country Life* 6 Jan. 16/1 This colonnade.. culminates in an early baroque Italian fountain of Istrian stone.

B. *sb.* A native or inhabitant of Istria.

1880 *Encycl. Brit.* XIII. 433/2 The Istrians..were only subdued by the Romans in 177 B.C. after two wars. **1974** *She* Jan. 28/2 The Istrians are hospitable and friendly.

i-stript, ME. pa. pple. of STRIP *v.*

i-strived, ME. pa. pple. of STRIVE *v.*

i-stronged, ME. pa. pple. of STRONG *v.* to strengthen.

i-stuffed, ME. pa. pple. of STUFF *v.*

i-stufled, ME. pa. pple. of STIFLE *v.*

i-stunge(n, ME. pa. pple. of STING *v.*

i-stured, i-styrryd, ME. pa. pple. of STIR *v.*

i-sublymate, early form of SUBLIMATE *ppl. a.*

c **1425** *Found. St. Bartholomew's* (E.E.T.S.) 17 This holy chirche..ffowndyd and endewid with heuenly Answer, I-sublymate with many priuylegies of notable men.

i-suffred, ME. pa. pple. of SUFFER *v.*

i-sumned, ME. pa. pple. of SUMMON *v.*

†i-ˈsunde, *sb.* *Obs.* [OE. type **ȝesund* = OHG. *gisunte*, MHG. *gesunde*; f. I-SOUND *a.*] Soundness, wholeness, safety.

c **1205** LAY. 3983 Al mid isunde come to þisse londe. *Ibid.* 8603 Nime hine mid isunde. *c* **1275** *Orison our Lord* 48 in *O.E. Misc.* 140 Of seorewe and sunne wite vs myd isunde.

So **†i-ˈsundful** *a.*, quite sound or well, prosperous, happy; **†i-sundien** *v. trans.*, to heal, save; **†i-ˈsundung**, healing, salvation.

c **1000** ÆLFRIC *Saints' Lives* xxvi. 103 His swiðre hand is ȝesundful oð þis. *c* **1000** *Ags. Ps.* (Spelm.) lxvii. 21 (Bosw.) Gesundfull siþfæt do us. *c* **1175** *Lamb. Hom.* 115 þenne bið his riche isundful on liue. *Ibid.* 97 þet he walde monna cun on þisse deie isundian. *Ibid.* 99 Men under-fengen god þurh þes halȝan gastes isundunge.

i-sundred, ME. pa. pple. of SUNDER *v.*

i-suneȝed, -et, i-sunehed, i-sunged, ME. pa. pple. of SIN *v.*

i-sunge(n, ME. pa. pple. of SING *v.*

i-sunken, ME. pa. pple. of SINK *v.*

i-suore(n, ME. pa. pple. of SWEAR *v.*

i-sustained, ME. pa. pple. of SUSTAIN *v.*

i-suteled, ME. pa. pple. of SUTEL *v.* to manifest.

i-sweled, ME. pa. pple. of SWEAL *v.*

i-swelowed, ME. pa. pple. of SWALLOW *v.*

i-swenched, ME. pa. pple. of SWENCH *v.* to afflict.

i-sweued, ME. pa. pple. of SWEVE *v.*

†**i-'swike,** *v. Obs.* [OE. *ȝeswícan*, f. *ȝe-*, I-¹ + *swícan* to cease; = OS. *giswîcan*.] **a.** *intr.* To fail, cease. (In OE. with gen. or dat.) **b.** *trans.* To cease from (an action, etc.).

*c***893** K. ÆLFRED *Oros.* III. i. §6 Hie ðæs ȝefeohtes ȝeswicen. *Ibid.* v. x. §2 þæt hie wolden Romanum ȝeswican. *c***1000** *O.E. Chron.* an. 994 (MS. C.) Hi þære hereȝunge ȝeswicon. *c***1100** *Ibid.* an. 1001 (MS. E.) Hi næfre heora yfeles ȝeswicon. *c***1175** *Cott. Hom.* 227 Hi þa iswicon hare timbringe. *c***1175** *Lamb. Hom.* 17 ȝif heo nulluð nefre iswiken. *Ibid.* 101 He bið þes deofles bern buten he hit iswike. *a***1250** *Owl & Night.* 927, I bidde hom þat heo iswike.

†**i-'swinch, i-swink.** *Obs.* [OE. *ȝeswinc*, f. *ȝe-*, I-¹ + *swincan* to toil: see SWINK.] Toil, labour.

*a***1000** *Cædmon's Gen.* 317 (Gr.) Sum heard ȝeswinc habban sceoldon. *c***1000** ÆLFRIC *Gram.* ix. (Z.) 47 *Labor*, ȝeswinc. *a***1175** *Cott. Hom.* 225 Adam þa wes wniende on þeses life mid ȝeswince. *c***1175** *Lamb. Hom.* 129 Her heo leueden . . on pine and on unimete iswinche. *a***1200** *Moral Ode* 36 in *Lamb. Hom.*, Monies monnes sare iswinc habbeð oft unholde. *Ibid.* 316 We . . leggeð al ure iswinch on þinge un-stede-faste.

i-swolle(n, ME. pa. pple. of SWELL *v.*

i-swolwed, ME. pa. pple. of SWALLOW *v.*

i-swonge(n, -swounge, -swunge(n, ME. pa. pple. of SWING *v.*

i-swonke(n, i-swunke(n, ME. pa. pple. of SWINK *v.* to toil.

i-swowe(n, i-swoȝen, ME. pa. pple. of SWOUGH *v.* to swoon.

isy, isykle, obs. forms of ICY, ICICLE.

isyl(le, variant of ISEL *Obs.*, spark, ember.

i-synned, ME. pa. pple. of SIN *v.*

it (ɪt), *pron.* [The neuter nom. and acc. of the (orig. demonstr.) stem *hi-*, the nom. masc. of which is HE, q.v. OE. *hit* was identical in form and sense with OFris. *hit* (*het*), OLFrankish *hit*, MDu. *het* (*hit*), Du. *het*, and in form identical with Goth. *hita*, which remained a demonstr., 'this'. The pronoun was in Goth. *ita*, corresp. to OLG. (OS., OMFrank.) *it*, MLG. *it* (*et*), LG. *et*, OHG. *iz* (*ez*), MHG. *ez*, Ger. *es*, from the parallel stem *i-*. OE. *hit* was nominative and accusative; the dative and genitive were *him*, *his*, identical with the same cases of the masc. HE. During the ME. period, *hit* lost its initial *h*, first when unemphatic, and at length in all positions, in Standard Eng.; dialectally, the *h* was preserved to a much later period, esp. in the north; and in Sc. *hit* is still the emphatic, and *it* (*'t*, *'d*) the unemphatic form. Dialectally or colloquially, and to some extent in the literary language (though less now than formerly), *it* is further reduced in certain positions to *'t* (e.g. *'t is*, *'t was*, *'t were*, *is't*, *was't*, *do't*, *to't*, *in't*, *on't*), which in some dialects becomes, esp. after a long vowel, *'d*. While in the masc. the original acc. *hine* was supplanted by the dative *him*, in the neuter, on the contrary, the dative *him* gradually yielded to the acc. form *hit*, *it*. This was not yet complete in the beginning of the 17th c. In the 16th c. the tendency arose to restrict the genitive *his* to the masculine gender, or rather to the male sex. For the neuter was substituted the periphrasis *thereof* or *of it* (mod. dial. *o't*, *o'd*), also the uninflected nom.-acc. form *it* (used in n.w. dial. from 14th c., and still common in Lancash. and parts of Yorksh.), and finally *c* 1600 a new factitious genitive (possessive) *it's*, ITS. The plural neuter has always been in Eng. the same as the pl. masc. The historical inflection is therefore as follows:

	Goth.	OE.	ME.	16th c.	mod.E.	dial.
N.A.	hita	hit	hit, it	(hit) it	it, 't	(h)it, 't, 'd.
D.	himma	him	him	him, it	it, 't	,, ,, ,,
G.	*his	his	his (hit)	his, thereof, it	its	(h)its, it.

The following explanations and illustrations refer only to the nominative and accusative *hit, it*, and to the use of the same form as dative and genitive; for the inflexional HIM, HIS, and ITS, see the separate articles in their alphabetical places.]

A. Forms. **1. a.** α. 1-6 (*dial.* -9) **hit,** 1-6 **hyt,** (3 **hitt,** 5 **hitte**).

878 *O.E. Chron.*, Hit ȝedældon sum, ond sum Ceolwulfe saldon. *c***1000** *Ags. Gosp.* Matt. xiv. 27 Habbað ȝeleafan ic hyt eom. **1070** *O.E. Chron.*, He hit forsoc. *a***1225** *Ancr. R.* 88 Vuel me seið þæt hit is; and ȝet hit is wurse. *a***1300** *Cursor M.* 2961 (Cott.) Til a contre cades he flitt, Abimalech was lauerd of hitt [*Fairf.*, *Trin.* hit; *Gött.* itt]. **1303** R. BRUNNE *Handl. Synne* 1996 God wulde hyt were now so here. **13..** *Cursor M.* 14463 (Fairf.) ȝet walde þai noȝt traw on hitte. *c***1380** WYCLIF *Sel. Wks.* III. 426 Nouþer wolde I graunte hit, ne doute hit, ne denye hit. *c***1440** *Anc. Cookery* in *Househ. Ord.* (1790) 447 Do hit in a pot, and let hitte sethe. *c***1450** MYRC 74 Be hyt husbande, be hyt wyue. **1524** PACE *Let. to Hen. VIII* in Strype *Eccl. Mem.* I. App. xi. 20 Pleasith hyt your highnes. *Ibid.* 21 Hyt were able . . to discomfit the Turque. **1525** TINDALE *N.T.* Prol., Howe that hit is good . . , and that god is rightewes whych made it. **1555** EDEN *Decades* 92 Hit scarsely riseth . . a cubet aboue the bankes. **1586-7** Q. ELIZ. in *Four C. Eng. Lett.* 30 To truste my life in anothers hand and send hit out of my owne. *Ibid.*, Might fortune say hit. *Mod. Sc.*, Whulk'll be hit?

β. 3- **it,** (3 **-et,** 3-4 **itt,** 4-5 **itte**), 5-6 **yt.**

*c***1200** ORMIN Ded. 27 Unnc birrþ baþe þannkenn Crist þatt itt iss brohht till ende. *c***1250** *Gen. & Ex.* 590 Oðer fowerti . . Dais and niȝtes stodet [the water] so. *Ibid.* 1411 Quan god haueð it so bi-sen Alse he sendet, als it sal ben. *c***1375** *Cursor M.* 9960 (Laud) God hym-self devysid yt. *c***1400** *Rom. Rose* 2522 Feyne thee other cause than itte. *c***1450** LONELICH *Grail* lvi. 72 It Nys non nede. *c***1500** *Two Dandies Hen. VII* in Furniv. *Ballads fr. MSS.* I. 456 He that had yt in his hart. **1500** —— [see B. *passim*].

γ. 2-3 **-t,** 6- **'t.**

*c***1200** ORMIN 2343 Acc to Drihhtin ȝhot haffde seȝȝd. *Ibid.* 2858 ȝhot unnderrstod & wisste. *c***1250** *Gen. & Ex.* 749 Nov ist a water of loðlic ble Men callið it ðe dede se. *Ibid.* 3472 Ne ist noȝt moyses, amrame sune. **1598** R. HAYDOCKE tr. *Lomazzo* II. 47 T'is onely thou that can'st dis-arme this hande. **1605** SHAKS. *Macb.* I. vii. 1 If it were done, when 'tis done, then 'twer well, It were done quickly. **1606** —— *Ant. & Cl.* II. ii. 179 You staid well by 't in Egypt. **1610** —— *Temp.* I. ii. 61 What fowle play had we, that we came from thence? Or blessed was't we did? *Ibid.* 87 The Iuy which had hid my princely Trunck, And suckt my verdure out on't. *Ibid.* II. i. 176 'Twas you we laugh'd at. *Ibid.* III. i. 19 'Twill weepe for hauing wearied you. **1611** —— *Wint. T.* v. iii. 73 Let 't alone. **1610-1842** [see IN'T]. **1610-1876** [see IS'T]. **1674** BREVINT *Saul at Endor* 158 Tis she that takes care of us when we decay. **1684** BUNYAN *Pilgr.* II. 67 'Tis a Good Boy, said his Master. **1741** RICHARDSON *Pamela* I. 96 'Twill be rather too good for me. **1808** SCOTT *Marm.* v. xii, And the bride-maidens whispered, "Twere better by far To have matched our fair cousin with young Lochinvar'. **1844** MRS. BROWNING *Lady Geraldine's Courtship* xxxvi, 'T is a picture for remembrance.

(Beside *'t is* there is also the contraction *it's*, which is now the common colloquial form.)

1625 SKYNNER in *Ussher's Lett.* (1686) 367 It's likely my Lord Keeper would remember me the sooner. **1627** W. SCLATER *Exp. 2 Thess.* (1629) 283 They say its made for fees. **1651** CULPEPPER *Astrol. Judgem.* Dis. Epist., Speculation brings only pleasure to a mans self; its practice which benefits others. **1677** YARRANTON *Eng. Improv.* 69 It's impossible but upon the breaking out of Fire the greatest part of the Cities would be destroyed. **1710** PRIDEAUX *Orig. Tithes* ii. 65 Its true the Scripture saith [etc.]. **1789** BURNS *Capt. Grose's Peregrin.* v, Its tauld he was a sodger bred. **1859** GEO. ELIOT *A. Bede* ii, 'It's a pretty spot, whoever may own it', said the traveller. *Mod.* It's a fine day. *Mod. Sc.* 'Where's the ball, boy?' *Cadie.* 'Thair it 's.'

δ. *Sc.* 5-6 **-d,** 6- **'d.**

*c***1470** HENRY *Wallace* IV. 482 To tak him in thai maid thaim redy ford [= for it]. *a***1500** RATE *Thewis off Gud women* 201 Quhilk war nocht forss þai wald nocht dud [= do it] And ȝit it cummys thaim al for gud. **1535** LYNDESAY *Satyre* 2095 Gude, halie peopill, I stand for'd. **1560** ROLLAND *Crt. Venus* I. 122 Of biggest bind as he thocht best to haid [= hae it]. **1597** MONTGOMERIE *Cherrie & Slae* 1022, I marveld mekill ond. *Ibid.* 1064 Affection dois affermd. *a***1901** *Mod. Sc.* If you say'd I'll believe'd, for ye wadna tell'd if ye didna ken'd to be true.

B. Senses and constructions.

I. As nominative.

1. a. As the proper neuter pronoun of the third person sing. Used orig. instead of any neuter sb.; now only of things without life, and of animals when sex is not particularized; hence usually of all the lower animals, and sometimes of infants.

*c***1000** *Ags. Gosp.* Luke vi. 48 Hyt ne mihte þæt hus astyrian, hit wæs ofer þæne stan ȝetrymed. *c***1000** ÆLFRIC *Hom.* II. 266 Etað þisne hlaf, hit is min lichama. *a***1250** *Owl & Night.* 772 An hors is strengur than a mon, Ac for hit non iwit ne kon, Hit berth on rugge grete semes. *c***1300** *Harrow. Hell* 86 Whose buyth any thyng Hit ys hys ant hys ofspryng. *c***1315** SHOREHAM 9 Water is kendeliche cheld, Thaȝ hit be warmd of fere. *c***1330** R. BRUNNE *Chron.* (1810) 7 Þe folk þat is þerin, it is of diuers kynd. **1477** EARL RIVERS (Caxton) *Dictes* A ij b, Whyche book . . as I vnderstande it was translated out of latyn in to frenshe. **1611** BIBLE *Luke* xi. 14 And he was casting out a deuil, and it was dumbe. **1623** COCKERAM III. G vj b, *Hiena*, a subtill beast . . counterfeiting the voyce of a man; in the night it will call shepherds out of their houses, and kill them. *Ibid.* K vj, Being burnt, it [Ebone] yeelds a sweet smell. **1766** PENNANT *Zool.* (1768) II. 341 It [the heron] perches and builds in trees. **1847** CARPENTER *Zool.* §394 The Raven . . in its general habits it is not unlike the Eagle; for it resorts to the inaccessible ledges of rocks, tall trees, &c., to construct its nest. *Ibid.* §647 This species [of beetle] is remarkable for the pertinacity with which it feigns death when alarmed. **1879** BAIN *Higher Eng. Gram.* 27 It is a hearty child. *Mod.* The house was humble; but it was our own home. It is a promise, and it must be kept.

b. Used in childish language, and hence contemptuously or humorously, of a person.

*c***1300** *Beket* 1003 Wel we witeth hit is a wrecche. **1588** SHAKS. *L.L.L.* v. ii. 337 See where it comes. **1654** WHITLOCK *Zootomia* 91 Slip but from any Profession some little while, and say it hath travelled, and it may passe for an able Physitian.

c. *It* may refer, not to any thing or person mentioned, but to a matter expressed or implied in a statement, or occupying the attention of the speaker.

*c***1000** *Ags. Ps.* (Th.) l. 6 Nis hit nan wundor þeah þu sy god and ic yfel. *c***1175** *Lamb. Hom.* 69 We ne maȝen þe f[e]ond from us driue . . bute hit beo þurh godes ȝifte. *a***1225** *Juliana* 7 Ha wes him sone ihondsald, þah hit hire unwil were. **1307-27** *Maximon* in *Rel. Ant.* I. 125 Amen, par charite! Ant so mote hit be! *c***1420** *Avow. Arth.* xxxiii, I conne notte say the ther-tille Hit is atte the quene wille. *c***1460** *Towneley Myst.* v. 41 Isaac, it were my deth, If Iacob weddeth in kynd of Hethe. **1526** TINDALE *Mark* viii. 36 What shal it profet a man yf he shulde wyn all the worlde, and loose his awne soule? **1606** SHAKS. *Ant. & Cl.* I. iii. 87 Sir, you and I must part, but that's not it. *a***1901** *Mod.* Of course I must go, but it is a great nuisance. He has come out at the top of the list; is it not splendid?

d. Sexual intercourse. Now *slang* or *colloq.* Cf. DO *v.* 16 b.

1611 COTGRAVE *Dict.*, *Fretiller* . . to . . lust to be at it. **1896** FARMER *Vocab. Amatoria* 118/1 *Faire*, to copulate; 'to do it'. **1922** JOYCE *Ulysses* 747 Gardner said no man could look at my mouth and teeth smiling like that and not think of it. **1923** T. WOLFE *Lett.* (1956) 45, I have been reading the *Amores* of Ovid this morning. It is beautiful Latin and beautiful poetry—although it is altogether concerned with two topics: How am I going to get it and How fine it was when you let me have it. **1941** H. G. WELLS *You can't be too Careful* III. xi. 161 Edward Albert knew . . of venereal disease, clumsy 'precautions' and the repulsive aspects of the overwhelming desire for 'It'. **1949** N. MITFORD *Love in Cold Climate* I. xi. 119, I was lugged off to their secret meeting-place . . to be asked what IT was like. **1972** F. WARNER *Maquettes* 16 He doesn't even know I'm overdue. And he hasn't had it for a week.

e. In emphatic predicative use: the actual or very thing required or expected; that beyond which one cannot go; the *ne plus ultra*; the acme. (In 20th-c. use from U.S.)

*a***1834** C. LAMB *Dramatic Ess.* (1891) 52 Lovegrove . . revived the character . . and made it sufficiently grotesque; but Dodd was *it*, as it came out of Nature's hands. **1896** ADE *Artie* i. 4, I didn't do a thing but push my face in there about eight o'clock last night, and I was 'it' from the start. **1900** *Dialect Notes* II. I. 42 Did he know his Greek? I should say so. He was *it*. **1904** F. LYNDE *Grafters* xxx. 397 Mrs. Hepzibah . . thinks you are It. **1906** *Daily Chron.* 5 Mar. 6/6 There is in America a curious use of the word 'it' conveyed by emphasis. Pre-eminently Roosevelt is 'it'. Next after Roosevelt an American would say 'Shaw is it'. **1915** 'I. HAY' *First Hundred Thousand* xx. 307 You can't go anywhere in London without running up against him. He is It. **1916** 'TAFFRAIL' *Pincher Martin* vii. 111 On board his ship he had a very poor time; but ashore he was absolutely *it*, so far as the ladies were concerned. **1923** D. H. LAWRENCE *Birds, Beasts & Flowers* 206 Red Men still stick themselves over with bits of his fluff, And feel absolutely *it*. **1930** H. M. SMITH *Inspector Frost in City* III. v. 103, I have some new plus-fours which are 'it'. **1963** P. WILLMOTT *Evolution of Community* i. 8 People were making themselves out to be something they weren't. . . They thought they were it.

f. In children's games, the player who has the task of catching or touching the others. Also *transf.* and *fig.*

1842 R. CHAMBERS *Pop. Rhymes Scotl.* 62/2 The tig usually catches and touches some one upon the crown before all are *in*—otherwise he has to be *it* for another game. **1888** [see COUNT *v.* 15 b]. **1923** KIPLING *Land & Sea Tales* 279 As the sides are chosen and all submit To the chance of the lot that shall make them 'It'. **1949** J. B. PRIESTLEY *Delight* 137 The boy who was 'it' retrieved the can and replaced it in the circle. **1950** C. S. LEWIS *Lion, Witch & Wardrobe* iii. 30 They decided to play hide-and-seek. Susan was 'It' and . . the others scattered to hide. **1969** I. & P. OPIE *Children's Games* i. 18 They do whatever they can to avoid being . . the one who, as they express it, is . . 'it'. **1970** G. JACKSON *Let.* 23 Mar. in *Soledad Brother* (1971) 188 It's us against them, hide and seek. They're always it and getting caught means getting dusted. **1974** S. GULLIVER *Vulcan Bulletins* 111 'I'm not helping to get him knocked off to suit . . the CIA.' 'That's too bad, Lee,' said Selby quietly, 'because you're it.'

g. 'Sex appeal.'

1904 KIPLING *Traffics & Discoveries* 352 'Tisn't beauty, so to speak, nor good talk necessarily. It's just It. Some women'll stay in a man's memory if they once walk down a street. **1927** E. GLYN *'It'* i. 10 He had that nameless charm, with a strong magnetism which can only be called 'It'. **1930** G. B. STERN *Mosaic* III. i. 205 The Viennese composer made his first awed acquaintance with the words pep, kick, body-urge, sex-appeal, a hundred-per-cent. stuff, spin it along, put it over, and It. **1932** *Bystander* 23 Mar. 546 A film star who has proved to producers and film public alike that she is blessed with that undefinable quality called 'It'. **1972** L. P. BACHMANN *Ultimate Act* i. 16 She really had 'It', as it was called.

2. a. As nominative of the verb *to be*, *it* refers to the subject of thought, attention, or inquiry, whether impersonal or personal, in a sentence asking or stating what or who this is; as *What is it? Who was it? It is a diamond, a rare fern, a wild*

boar; *It is I*, *It was John*. Often with a relative clause implied when not actually expressed, as *Who is it* (that knocks)? *What is it* (that is wanted)? *What was it* (that excited your attention, that did this, etc.)? *It was the king* (who appeared, who so acted, etc.). So Fr. *ce*, Ger. *es*.

Formerly the verb agreed (as in German) with the following sb. or pron., thus *It am I* (= It is I), *it are ye* (= it is you), *it were two dragons*. When a relative clause is appended, the relative being the subject, its verb still agrees in number and person with the pronoun: *It is I who am to blame*; *It was they who were wrong, not we*.

c **1000** *Ags. Gosp.* Matt. XIV. 26 Hi..cwædon þus: Soþlice hyt ys scinlac. Ða spræc se hælend..ic hyt eom. *a* **1225** *Juliana* 39 Ich hit am þe deouel belial. *c* **1290** *Beket* 1209 in *S. Eng. Leg.* I. 141 'Sire', quad þe oste, 'þov it art'. *c* **1305** *St. Christopher* 41 in *E.E.P.* (1862) 60 Beau frere, quaþ þis oþer, ic hit am. **1377** LANGL. *P. Pl.* B. xv. 321 If any peple perfourme þat texte it ar þis pore freres. *c* **1380** *Sir Ferumb.* 3183 Hit ne buþ..none Vauasers, þat buþ þer on þe tour. *c* **1384** CHAUCER *H. Fame* 1323 Thoo atte last aspyed y That pursevantes and heraudes..Hyt weren alle. *c* **1386** —— *Shipman's T.* 214 Peter, it am I, Quod she. **1401** *Pol. Poems* (Rolls) II. 57 It ar ȝe that stonden bifore, in Anticristis vauwarde. **1413** *Pilgr. Sowle* (Caxton) II. xlv. (1859) 51 What is hit thenne that thou beryst soo trussed in thy fardel? *c* **1450** *Cov. Myst.* (Shaks. Soc.) 293 It is I that am here in ȝour syth. *c* **1460** *Towneley Myst.* xx. 372 Wene ye that I it am? **1593** SHAKS. *2 Hen VI*, IV. i. 117 It is thee I feare. **1611** BIBLE *Mark* vi. 50 It is I, be not afraid. **1852** MRS. STOWE *Uncle Tom's C.* xxiv. 232 Is it the secret instinct of decaying nature?

†**b.** *It* was formerly used where *there* is now substituted. (Cf. Ger. *es ist*, *es sind*.)

a **1300** *Cursor M.* 22169 It es na land þat man kan neuen ..þat he ne sal do þam to be soght. *c* **1330** R. BRUNNE *Chron.* Pref. 80 Many it ere þat strange Inglis In ryme wate neuer what it is. **13..** *Gaw. & Gr. Knt.* 280 Hit arn aboute on þis bench bot berdlez chylder. *c* **1380** WYCLIF *Wks.* III. 345 It is no nede to argue here for to disprove þis foli. *c* **1435** *Torr. Portugal* 1494 It were two dragons stiff and strong, Uppon theyre lay they sat and song, Beside a depe welle. **1577** tr. *Bullinger's Decades* Introd., It was sometime when he was not. **1577–87** HOLINSHED *Scot. Chron.* (1805) II. 256 It was no need to bid them pack away. **1590** MARLOWE *Edw. II*, II. ii, Cousin, it is no dealing with him now. *a* **1617** BAYNE *On Coloss.* 211 [They] are so proud, so censorious, that it is no living with them.

c. In archaic ballad style, the introductory *it* (*it was*, *it is*) is sometimes = *there* (as in mod.Ger. *es war*, *es ist*); but in other cases, it appears to mean 'the subject of my song' or 'tale'.

? *a* **1603** *Beggar's Dau. Bednall Gr.* I. 1 in Percy *Reliques* (1883) I. 361 Itt was a blind beggar, had long lost his sight, He had a faire daughter of bewty most bright. **1798** COLERIDGE *Anc. Mar.* 1 It is an ancient mariner, And he stoppeth one of three. **1805** SCOTT *Last Minstr.* VI. xi, It was an English Ladye bright..And she would marry a Scottish knight. **1832** TENNYSON *Miller's Daughter* 169 It is the miller's daughter, And she is grown so dear.

†**d.** *It* also occurs where *he*, *she*, or *that* would now be preferred. Cf. F. *c'est*, Ger. *es ist*.

1596 SHAKS. *Merch. V.* III. iii. 18 It is the most impenetrable curre That euer kept with men. **1605** —— *Macb.* I. iv. 58 It is a peerelesse Kinsman. **1684** [see A. γ.]

e. ***this is it*** colloq. phr.: used when something previously spoken about or foreboded has come to pass or is about to happen.

[**1908** G. MURRAY tr. *Aristophanes' Frogs* I. iii. 34 That's it, sir. These are the Initiated Rejoicing somewhere, just as he told us.] **1942** *Newsweek* 27 July 23/3 Finucane tried to settle the rocking plane onto the water. It hit the waves, then sank like a rock. Just before, Paddy spoke into the two-way radio: 'This is it, chaps.' **1959** *Sunday Times* 5 Apr. 15/7 He heard the sound of countless aircraft overhead. This is it, he thought.

f. ***that's it*** (and similar colloq. phrases): there is no more to it than that.

1966 P. WILLMOTT *Adolescent Boys E. London* v. 88 You got no encouragement. They'd look at the report at the end of term and that was about it. *Ibid.* 92 We just sat about.. doing half-witted things. You only had to find a weak teacher and that was it. **1968** *Listener* 31 Oct. 574/3 Really I think the Brummie likes to stay at home. And work. And shop in Birmingham. Holiday in Majorca—and that's it. **1968** *New Yorker* 2 Nov. 163 They are excellent musicians (except for one of the girls, whose function is obscure; she shakes a tambourine now and then, but that's about it). **1972** *Observer* (Colour Suppl.) 13 Feb. 18/1 Adoption agencies are wary..of any people who want to adopt for any reason other than that they love children, that they have homes and that there are children who need homes. To put it briefly, parents are parents and that's it.

3. As the subject of an impersonal verb or impersonal statement, expressing action or a condition of things simply, without reference to any agent. **a.** In statements of weather, as *it rains*, *it blows hard*, *it is cold*.

c **888** K. ÆLFRED *Boeth.* xxi, On sumera hit bið wearm and on wintra ceald. *c* **900** tr. *Bæda's Hist.* II. x. [xiii.] (1890) 134 Swa..hit rine and sniwe and styrme ute. *c* **1000** *Ags. Gosp.* Matt. vii. 27 þa rinde hit. *c* **1205** LAY. 3895 þre dæȝes hit rinde blod. *a* **1300** *Fragm. Pop. Sc.* (Wright) 223 Horfrost cometh whan hit is cold. *c* **1300** *St. Brandan* 683 Hit bigan to haweli faste. *c* **1305** *St. Edm. Conf.* 356 in *E.E.P.* (1862) 80 So durk hit was ek þerto, þat vneþe me miȝte iseo. **13..** *Seuyn Sag.* (W.) 2271 Sche saith hit hath ben thonder. *c* **1425** *Seven Sag.* (P.) 2213 Hyt raynyd and lygnyd and thonryd fast. **1526** TINDALE *John* xii. 29 Then sayde the people that stode by and herde: it thoundreth [**1611** said that it thundered]. **1719** DE FOE *Crusoe* I. i, By this time it blew a terrible storm indeed. **1766**, **1848** [see DOG *sb.*[1] 17 c]. **1820** KEATS *St. Agnes* i, St. Agnes' Eve—Ah, bitter chill it was! **1846** DICKENS *Italy, A Rapid Diorama*, It is now intensely cold. *a* **1901** *Mod.* Evidently it has thawed during the night. Is it freezing or thawing at present? I fear it is going to rain.

b. In statements as to the time of day, season of the year, and the like; as *It is midnight*, *it is very late*, *it is still winter*, *it is Christmas day*, *it draws towards evening*.

These are connected with the prec. by such as *it is dark*, *it is day-light*, *it dawns*.

c **1000** *Ags. Gosp.* Luke xxiv. 29 Hit æfenlæcð. *Ibid.* John i. 39 Hit wæs þa seo teoðe tid. *c* **1000** ÆLFRIC *Exod.* x. 9 Hit ys haliȝ tid. *c* **1000** *O.E. Chron.* (MS. C.) an. 979 þonne hit daȝian wolde. *a* **1100** *Ibid.* (MS. E.) an. 1006 þa hit winter læhte. *c* **1200** ORMIN 8917 Till þatt itt comm till efenn. *a* **1250** *Owl & Night.* 332 From eve fort hit is dailiȝt. **13..** *Seuyn Sag.* (W.) 1629 Sire, vp! vp! hit is dai! **13..** *Gaw. & Gr. Knt.* 284 Hit is ȝol & nwe ȝer. *c* **1400** *Ywaine & Gaw.* 596 It neghed nere the nyght. *c* **1450** *Erle Tolous* 457 When hyt dawed he rose up soone. **1526** TINDALE *John* x. 22 Hit was at Ierusalem the feaste of the dedicacion, and itt was wynter. **1599** SHAKS. *Hen. V*, III. vii. 2 Would it were day. *Ibid.* 6 Will it neuer be Morning? **1678** BUNYAN *Pilgr.* I. 44 It was almost night. **1727–46** THOMSON *Summer* 432 'Tis raging noon. **1800** COLERIDGE *Wallenst.* II. IV. ii. 137 It strikes eleven. **1832** TENNYSON *Miller's Daughter* 59 'T was April then. **1849** MACAULAY *Hist. Eng.* II. 175 It was ten o'clock. *Ibid.* 191 It was Monday night.

c. In statements as to space, distance, or length of time.

1593 SHAKS. *Rich. II*, II. iii. 1 How farre is it, my Lord, to Berkley now? **1594** —— *Rich. III*, v. iii. 234 How farre into the Morning is it? **1749** FIELDING *Tom Jones* v. ii, Nor was it indeed long before Jones was able to attend her to the harpsichord. **1819** SCOTT *Leg. Montrose* xii, 'It is a far cry to Lochow'..'It is not for me to say how far it may be to Lochow'. **1850–85** [see CRY *sb.* 18]. *Mod.* How far is it to London? It is only 6 miles to Oxford. It is a long way to the sea. It wants five minutes to the half-hour.

d. In statements of condition, welfare, course of life, and the like; as *It has fared badly with the soldiers*; *How is it in the city?* *It will soon come to a rupture between them*; *It is all over with poor Jack*; *It is very pleasant here*.

c **1000** ÆLFRIC *Gen.* xxxvii. 14 Loca hwæþer hit wel si mid him..and cyþ me hu hit si. *c* **1000** *Gosp. Nicod.* xxvi. in Thwaite *Hept.* (1698) 13 Hyt wæs ðа swyþe angreslic. *c* **1230** *Hali Meid.* 7 Sekerliche swa hit fareð. *a* **1310** in Wright *Lyric P.* 103 Thus hit geth bitwene hem tuo. *c* **1325** *Metr. Hom.* 31 Hou sal it far of us kaytefes? *c* **1481** CAXTON *Dialogues* 4/37 What do ye? How is it with you? **1535** COVERDALE *2 Kings* iv. 26 Axe her yf it go well with her. **1611** BIBLE *ibid.*, Is it well with thee? Is it well with thy husband? Is it well with the child? **1681** NEVILE *Plato Rediv.* 15 Well, Sir, How is it? Have you rested well to Night? **1810** SCOTT *Lady of L.* v. xv, Ill fared it then with Roderick Dhu, That on the ground his targe he threw. **1850** TENNYSON *In Mem.* iv, O heart, how fares it with thee now? **1881** F. HALL *Lett. to Editor N.Y. Nation* 21 As it has fared with all others..so, simply, it fares with me.

e. In statements of physical or mental affection, pleasurable, painful, etc.

These often have a clause expressing the affecting cause, and then pass into 4.

c **1000** *Ags. Gosp.* Matt. xiv. 6 Hit licode herode. *c* **1175** *Lamb. Hom.* 55 ȝif we leornið godes lare, þenne of-þuncheð hit him sare. *a* **1310** in Wright *Lyric P.* 83 In myn herte hit doth me god, when y thenke on Jesu blod. *c* **1420** *Avow. Arth.* xxiv, Hit schalle the noȝte greue. **1844** MRS. BROWNING *Fourfold Aspect* ii, How that true wife said to Pœtus..'Sweet, it hurts not!' *Mod.* Where does it feel painful? It pleases me when he does well.

f. In quoting from books, in the phrases *it says*, *it tells*, etc. Now *arch.* or *colloq.*; usually expressed by the passive ***it is said***, ***written***, etc.: see 4 b.

c **1175** *Lamb. Hom.* 15 Fulsoð hit seið, moni hit forlet for drihtenes eye. *a* **1225** *Ancr. R.* 356 Elies hweoles þet weren furene, ase hit telleð. *c* **1305** *Pilate* 169 in *E.E.P.* (1862) 115 As hit saiþ in þe godspel. *c* **1330** R. BRUNNE *Chron.* (1810) 55 In Saynt Edwardes life it sais, he was forsuorn. **1390** GOWER *Conf.* III. 224 In a cronique it telleth thus. **1482** *Monk of Evesham* (Arb.) 15 Founde hem as hit folowth wele aftir in this boke. **1840** K. H. DIGBY *Mores Catholici* x. vii. 171 In Saxon histories... Thus it says. **1894** G. F. X. GRIFFITH tr. *C. Fouard's St. Paul* xv. 352 From the sequel, as it reads in the Acts, it would seem [etc.]. **1902** H. K. MANN *Lives of Popes* I. II. 234 'In mense Junius Indictione ii,' or x., as by mistake it reads in the *Chronicle*. **1932** CHESTERTON *Chaucer* iii. 108 Chaucer was a man for whom the world teemed with quiet fun, as it says in the comic opera. **1955** tr. *William of Rubruck's Journey* in C. Dawson *Mongol Mission* xxxvii. 212 In Isaias it says that they fled into the land of Ararat.

g. In other expressions in which the subject is undefined.

1551 T. WILSON *Logike* (1580) 6 b, No one man could bee knowne from an other..if it were not for the accidentes. **1710** SWIFT *Jrnl. to Stella* 30 Sept. (1948) I. 47 They may talk of the *you know what*; but, gad, if it had not been for that I should never have been able to get the access I have had. *a* **1732** J. GAY *Fables* (1738) II. xiii. 118 Were it not for this cursed show'r, The park had whil'd away an hour. **1736** J. BUTLER *Analogy of Relig.* II. v. 200 Assistance which they would have had no Occasion for, had it not been for their Misconduct. **1780** *Mirror* No. 102 The misapplication of the term is so completely ridiculous, as to be beneath contempt, were it not for the mischief that I am convinced has been occasioned by it. **1864** G. MEREDITH *Emilia in England* II. v. 69, I feel better already, if it weren't for my legs. **1974** *Times Lit. Suppl.* 5 Apr. 375/2 Disaster that would have been total had it not been for the conventional crime-writer's beginning and end.

4. When the logical subject of a verb is an infinitive phrase, a clause, or sentence, this is usually placed after the verb, and its place before the verb is taken by *it* as 'provisional' or 'anticipatory subject'.

When the order of the clauses is reversed, *it* is omitted; but sometimes rhetorically retained.

a. with an infinitive phrase.

In OE. the infinitive was in the dative governed by *tó*, and its construction was rather that of the L. supine in *-u* after an adj., but this has passed without break into the present use.

c **900** tr. *Bæda's Hist.* Pref. (1890) 2 Forþon hit is god godne to herianne and yfelne to leanne. *c* **1205** LAY. 31106 Hit is on mine rede to don þat þu bede. *c* **1250** *Hymn Virg.* in *Trin. Coll. Hom.* App. ii. 257 On þe hit is best to calle. **1340** *Ayenb.* 53 Hit is grat wyt to loki mesure ine mete and ine drinke. *c* **1385** CHAUCER *L.G.W.* 634 *Cleopatras*, In the see hit happed hem to mete. *c* **1420** *Anturs of Arth.* xv, Hit were fulle tere for a tung my tourmentes to telle. **1548** UDALL, etc. *Erasm. Par. Matt.* 58 a, To lothe and dyspyse them, it is no holynes, but pryde. **1604** SHAKS. *Oth.* II. iii. 203 Vnlesse..to defend our selues it be a sinne. **1611** —— *Cymb.* III. iii. 79 How hard it is to hide the sparkes of Nature. **1635** J. HAYWARD tr. *Biondi's Banish'd Virg.* 98 Depends it on mee..to know either your being..or your stay here? **1667** MILTON *P.L.* VIII. 641 To stand or fall Free in thine own Arbitrement it lies. *a* **1717** BLACKALL *Wks.* (1723) I. 25 It has been commonly their Fate to fare hardlier. **1742** YOUNG *Nt. Th.* VI. 227 Is it in Time to hide Eternity? **1849** MACAULAY *Hist. Eng.* I. 49 It was necessary to make a choice.

b. with a clause introduced by *that* expressed or understood. Now esp. frequent with the passive voice, in *it is said*, *written*, *stated*, *thought*, *believed*, *known*, *seen*, etc., instead of the active *people say*, *one has written*, etc.

c **897** K. ÆLFRED *Gregory's Past.* xlvi. 355 Ðonne hit tocymð ðæt hie hit sprecan sculon. *c* **1000** ÆLFRIC *Hom.* II. 340 Hit is awriten, Lufa ðinne nextan. *a* **1250** *Owl & Night.* 1337 Soth hit is, of luve ich singe. **13..** *K. Alis.* 3720 Schame hit is we weore so faynt. *c* **1305** *St. Dunstan* 117 in *E.E.P.* (1862) 37 Hit biful þat þe bischop of wircetre was ded. *a* **1350** *Childh. Jesu* 99 (Mätz.) It es þe beste, vnder þis treo þat ich me reste. *c* **1369** CHAUCER *Dethe Blaunche* 805 Hit happed that I came on a day In-to a place. **1387** TREVISA *Higden* (Rolls) I. 7 Hyt is redde in storyes that Ytaly somme tyme..was callede the grete londe off Grece. *c* **1400** *Apol. Loll.* p. xvi, Hit is writen in the first book of holy writ, that ther weren thre patriarkes in the peple of God. **1611** BIBLE *1 Kings* xviii. 1 It came to passe after many daies, that the word of the Lord came to Elijah. *Ibid.* 4 It was so, when Iezebel cut off the Prophets of the Lord, that Obadiah tooke an hundred Prophets and hid them. **1650** WELDON *Crt. Jas. I*, 122 Its verily beleeved..it was intended the Law should run in its proper channell. **1749** FIELDING *Tom Jones* VI. iii, It may be objected, that very wise men have been notoriously avaricious. **1805** SCOTT *Last Minstr.* II. xxxii, Use lessens marvel, it is said. *Mod.* It appears that you were present.

c. The same construction is sometimes employed when the logical subject is a sb., esp. with attributes.

In mod. use, this is poetical or rhetorical; also dialectal or colloquial; in the latter use the verb is sometimes repeated, e.g. *It is a country of vast extent, is China*.

c **900** tr. *Bæda's Hist.* I. Introd. (1890) 26 Hit is weliȝ þis ealond on wæstmum. *a* **1225** *Juliana* 12 Hit nis nan eðelich þing þe refschipe of reme. **13..** *K. Alis.* 4154 Hit schal beo ful deore abought, Theo tole that was in Grece y-sought. **1432–50** tr. *Higden* (Rolls) I. 109 The cyte..where hit is schewede the palice of Melchisedech. *c* **1460** *Towneley Myst.* xiv. 463 Lord, it is sothe all, that we say. **1523** LD. BERNERS *Froiss.* I. clxix. 207 It canne nat be recorded the gret feest and chere that they of the Cytie..made to the prince. *c* **1530** LD. BERNERS *Arth. Lyt. Bryt.* 524 It greved her hert right sore, thassurance of her and of Arthur. **1805** SCOTT *Last Minstr.* I. xii, What may it be, the heavy sound? **1841** LONGF. *Goblet of Life* v, Above the lowly plants it towers, The fennel with its yellow flowers.

d. Also in a periphrastic construction (to bring into prominence an adverbial adjunct); as *it was on a Monday that I met him* = the day on which I met him was a Monday = I met him on a Monday.

Always with the verb *to be*, as in 2.
(In OE. *hit* is omitted, or its place taken by *þæt*.)

[*c* **888** K. ÆLFRED *Boeth.* xxvii. § 1 For þam þingum wæs ȝio þæt se wisa Catulus hine ȝebealȝ. *a* **1070** *O.E. Chron.* (MS. C.) an. 1052 Ðæt wæs on þone Monandæȝ æfter sca Marian mæsse þæt Godwine mid his scipum to Suðȝeweorce becom.] *a* **1250** *Owl & Night.* 1163 Hervore hit is that me the shuneth. **1297** R. GLOUC. 204 (MS. B.) In þe tyme bi twene Abraham & Moyses it was, þat men come to Engolond. *c* **1420** *Sir Amadas* (Weber) 284 Hyt is in the deyd name that Y speyke. *c* **1450** *Cov. Myst.* (Shaks. Soc.) 126 How is it that the modyr of God me xulde come to? **1593** SHAKS. *2 Hen. VI*, IV. ii. 137 It is to you good people, that I speake. **1776** GIBBON *Decl. & F.* x, It was not till the eighteenth year of his reign, that Diocletian could be persuaded by Galerius to begin a general persecution. **1849** MACAULAY *Hist. Eng.* I. 28 It was by him that money was coined. *a* **1901** *Mod.* It was there that Columbus was born. It is but seldom that he comes our way.

5. The pronoun is also used pleonastically after the noun subject: now esp. in ballad poetry, or, in an interrogative sentence, in rhetorical prose, for the sake of emphasis. Cf. HE 3 a.

c **1430** *Freemasonry* (1844) 36 Hys name hyt spradde ful wondur wyde. **1534** TINDALE *Mark* xi. 30 The baptyme of John, was it from heuen, or of men? Answer me. **1578** TIMME *Caluine on Gen.* 236 What grievous torments of mind, this horrible Confusion brought..it cannot by words be sufficiently expressed. **1601** SHAKS. *Twel. N.* v. i. 401 The raine it raineth euery day. **1742** YOUNG *Nt. Th.* v. 171 The sacred Shade, and Solitude, what is it? **1798** WORDSW. *Idiot Boy* lv, This piteous news so much it shocked her. *Ibid.* lxxxiii, And as her mind grew worse and worse, Her body —it grew better. **1801** CAMPBELL *Mariners of England* 13 The deck it was their field of fame, And Ocean was their grave. **1801** SCOTT *Fire King* vii, The tree green it grows..

The stream pure it flows. *a* **1806** KIRKE WHITE *Gondoline*, The night it was still, and the moon it shone. *a* **1849** POE *Annabel Lee* 27 Our love it was stronger by far than the love Of those who were older than we.

II. As objective case (accusative and dative).

6. a. The neuter accusative or direct object after a vb.: having the same range of reference as the nominative: see 1, 1 b, 1 c.

885 *O.E. Chron.*, þy ilcan ȝeare feng Carl to þam west rice ..swa hit his þridda fæder hæfde. *c* **893** K. ÆLFRED *Oros.* I. i. §7 On þam lande is twa and twentiȝ þeoda . nu hæt hit man eall Parthia. **971** *Blickl. Hom.* 231 Hu mæȝ ic hit on þrim daȝum ȝefaran? *c* **1000** ÆLFRIC *Exod.* ii. 9 Underfoh þis cild and fed hit me. *c* **1075** *O.E. Chron.* an. 1070 Se arcebiscop axode hyrsumnesse mid aþswerunge at him, and he hit forsoc. *c* **1200** *Moral Ode* 252 (Trin. MS.) þar is fur . . Ne mai hit quenche salt water. *c* **1200** ORMIN Ded. 125, & forrþi whase lerneþþ itt & follȝheþþ itt wiþþ dede. *a* **1250** *Owl & Night.* 235 Alvred king hit seide and wrot 'He schuntet that hi ne wl wot'. *c* **1305** *Judas* 142 in *E.E.P.* (1862) 111 His gvttes fulle to the grounde, menie men hit iseye. **1362** LANGL. *P. Pl.* A. I. 90 Clerkes þat knowen hit scholde techen hit aboute. *c* **1440** *Anc. Cookery* in *Househ. Ord.* (1790) 428 Set hit on the fyre, and let hit boyle. *c* **1440** LONELICH *Grail* l. 728 Certein me Semeth In My wyt that they han wel deservit It. **1532** MORE *Confut. Tindale* Wks. 600/1 Adam eate hit also through temptacion. **1535** COVERDALE *Exod.* ii. 9 Take this childe, and nurse it for me, I wyll geue yᵉ thy rewarde. **1606** SHAKS. *Tr. & Cr.* IV. ii. 34 Would he not (a naughty man) let it sleepe. **1611** BIBLE *Ps.* cxix. 140 Thy word is very pure: therefore thy seruant loueth it. —— *1 Kings* iii. 26 Let it be neither mine nor thine, but diuide it. **1635** J. HAYWARD tr. *Biondi's Banish'd Virg.* 98 Taking mee by the hand and gently wringing it. **1733** POPE *Ess. Man* III. 73 Heaven . . To Man imparts it [knowledge of his end]; but with such a view, As, while he dreads it, makes him hope it too. **1749** FIELDING *Tom Jones* v. vi, Pardon me if I have said anything to offend you. I did not mean it. **1808** SCOTT *Marm.* v. xii, The bride kissed the goblet, the knight took it up. **1859** GEO. ELIOT *A. Bede* xxii, She must keep it under her clothes, and no one would see it. **1879** BAIN *Higher Eng. Gram.* 27 The day will be fine; no one doubts it. *a* **1901** *Mod.* They say he has left the country, but I do not believe it.

b. Also used as anticipatory object when the logical object is a clause. Cf. 4.

1596 SHAKS. *Merch. V.* I. i. 63, I take it your owne business calls on you. **1599** —— *Much Ado* IV. i. 206 Publish it that she is dead. **1850** TENNYSON *In Mem.* i, I held it truth . . That men may rise on stepping-stones Of their dead selves to higher things. **1881** MASON *Engl. Gram.* §405 He made it clear that the plan was impossible. *Mod.* May I take it that you will sign the document?

7. After a preposition. (In OE. *hit* or *him*, according to the regimen of the prep. Cf. HIM 2 a.)

The usual ME. construction was *there-* (*þar-*) + *prep.*: e.g. *thereat, thereby, thereafter, therein, thereon, therewith.*

1340 HAMPOLE *Pr. Consc.* 674 þe rotes þat of it springes. *Ibid.* 1649 Afterward I sal speke of it. *Ibid.* 2795 þat place is neghest aboven hel pitte Bytwen purgatory and itte. **1382** WYCLIF *Rev.* xxi. 24 The kinges of erthe shulen bringe to her glory and honour in to it [**1526** TINDALE vnto hit]. **1485** CAXTON *Paris & V.* 3 Nor say nothynge to hyr of hyt. **1582** N. T. (Rhem.) *Matt.* xxviii. 4 What is that to vs? looke thou to it. *Ibid.* 24 Looke you to it [**1611** See ye to it]. **1590** TARLTON *Newes Purgat.* (1844) 82 He hyed him thither, and found them all hard at it by the teeth. **1590** SHAKS. *Mids. N.* III. i. 34 Wee ought to looke to it. **1608** —— *Per.* III. i. 21 A little daughter; for the sake of it be manly. **1611** —— *Cymb.* II. iv. 141 Another staine, as bigge as Hell can hold, Were there no more but it. **1635** J. HAYWARD tr. *Biondi's Banish'd Virg.* 99 Shee would oft-times sigh to thinke of it. **1663** PEPYS *Diary* 15 Apr., I to my office, and there hard at it till almost noon. **1749** FIELDING *Tom Jones* VI. vi, Unless you consent to it, I will not give you a groat. **1858** LYTTON (*title*) What will he do with it? *a* **1901** *Mod.* There is nothing for it but to run.

8. As simple dative = 'to it'. (In OE. *him*: see HIM 2 a.)

c **1400** MAUNDEV. (1839) xv. 165 To don it worschipe and reuerence. **1595** SHAKS. *John* II. i. 162 It grandame will Giue yt a plum. **1610** —— *Temp.* I. ii. 186 'Tis a good dulnesse, And giue it way. *a* **1822** SHELLEY *Superstition* 31 Converging thou didst give it name, and form. *a* **1901** *Mod.* Bring the calf and give it a drink. She took the child and gave it suck.

9. *It* is often used as an indefinite object of a transitive verb, e.g. *to carry it, fight it, face it, brave it*; so in imprecations, as *confound it! hang it!* Also of an intransitive verb, e.g. *to go it, run it, trip it, ride it, flaunt it.* And in this way verbs are formed for the nonce upon nouns, with the sense to do, act, or play the person or character, to use the thing; e.g. *to king it, queen it, lord it, foot it, boat it, cab it, coach it, train it*, etc. The use now is colloquial.

App. first used with transitive vbs., and with adv. *out*, as *to fight it* (i.e. the matter, affair) *out.* Afterwards *out* was omitted, and the usage extended through amphibolous to intransitive vbs., as *to flaunt it out, to flaunt it.* Through vbs. having sbs. of the same form, as *to lord*, it was extended to other sbs. as *king, queen*, etc. There may have been some influence from *do it* as a substitute, not only for any transitive vb. and its object, but for an intransitive vb. of action, as in 'he tried to *swim*, but could not *do it*', where *it* is the action in question.

1548 PATTEN *Exp. Scotl.* in Arb. *Garner* III. 109 If they had meant to fight it out. **1579** G. HARVEY *Letter-bk.* (Camden) 73 To face it oute lustelye. **1583** STUBBS *Anat. Abus.* II. (1882) 108 That flaunt it out in their saten doblets. **1588** SHAKS. *Tit. A.* IV. i. 121 Ile goe braue it at the Court. **1590** H. SMITH *Wedding Garm.* (1592) 335 When our backs flant it like courtiers. **1593** SHAKS. *2 Hen. VI*, I. iii. 80 She sweepes it through the Court with troups of Ladies. *Ibid.* IV. viii. 47, I see them Lording it in London streets. **1605** —— *Macb.* II. iii. 19 Ile Deuill-Porter it no further. **1610** —— *Temp.* I. ii. 380 Foote it featly heere, and there. **1611** —— *Wint. T.* IV. iv. 460 Ile Queene it no inch farther. **1632** MILTON *L'Allegro* 33 Come, and trip it, as you go, On the light fantastick toe. **1647** WARD *Simp. Cobler* (1843) 71 Taught many Successors to King it right for many Ages. *Ibid.* 91 Poore Coblers well may fault it now and then. **1650** FULLER *Pisgah* 194 Hissop doth tree it [*arborescit*] in Judæa. **1787** JEFFERSON *Writ.* (1859) II. 334 She is coqueting it with England. **1850** MRS. BROWNING *Calls on the Heart* ii, The world goes riding it fair and grand. **1856** R. EG.-WARBURTON *Hunt. Songs* (1883) xxxvi. 104 Dyspepsy and gout the amusement may share, So go it, ye cripples! and take a Bath chair. **1889** JEROME *Three Men in a Boat* ii, We decided that we would . . hotel it, and inn it, and pub. it when it was wet. *a* **1901** *Mod.* She is inclined to lord it over her brothers. (*colloq.*) Go it, old man! We will walk as far as we can, and then train it.

III. 10. As possessive case or possessive pronoun; = ITS. Now *dial.*

13.. *E.E. Allit. P.* B. 264 Kepe to hit, & alle hit cors clanly ful fylle. *Ibid.* 956 Aboute Sodamas & hit sydez alle. *c* **1420** *Anturs of Arth.* viii, Of hit woe wille I wete, Gif that I may hit bales And the body bare. **1541** R. COPLAND *Guydon's Quest. Chirurg.*, It sendeth the humour melencolyke to the stomacke for to prouoke it appetyte. **1548** UDALL *Erasm. Par. Luke* vii. 81 b, Loue . . also hath it infancie & it hath it commyng forewarde in growthe of age. **1563** DAVIDSON *Confut. Kennedy* in *Wodrow Misc.* (1844) 206 The Romane Kirk hes receavit be it awin judgement, the commune translatione. **1587** GOLDING *De Mornay* ii. 19 It hath no forme of it owne; for had it any of it owne, it could not breede them, because it owne would occupie it to the full. **1605** SHAKS. *Lear* I. iv. 236 It's had it head bit off by it young. **1608-27** BP. HALL *Medit. & Vowes* II. 86 That which with it owne glory can make them happy. **1611** BIBLE *Lev.* xxv. 5 That which groweth of it [*ed.* 1660 its] owne accord . . thou shalt not reape. **1616** SURFL. & MARKH. *Country Farme* 150 He shall suffer the young Asse to sucke it damme vntill it be two yeares old. **1622** WITHER *Mistr. Philar.* Wks. (1633) 653 Each part as faire doth show In it kind, as white in Snow.

Mod. dial. **1869** E. WAUGH *Lanc. Sketches* 89 Look at it een; they're as breet as th' north-star ov a frosty neet. **1881** *Lancash. Gloss.* s.v., If he can catch houd o' that dog he'll have it life. **1884** *Cheshire Gloss.* s.v., Come to it mammy. **1892** J. WRIGHT *Windhill Dial.* 121 Possessive it its. **1899** *N.E. Scotch* (Dundee, *arch.*), 'See at the cat pittin' up it paw an' clawin' it head'.

IV. As reflexive pronoun.

11. In accus. and dative = ITSELF (which is the ordinary equivalent).

The reflexive use of *it* is rarer than that of *him, her*, because of the less frequency of neuter agents.

1595 SHAKS. *John* v. vii. 55 My heart hath one poore string to stay it by. *a* **1901** *Mod.* The tree draws to it all the moisture from the adjacent ground. The horse sprang over the precipice carrying its rider with it.

12. As possessive = ITS (L. *suus*).

1548-1622 [see 10].

V. 13. As antecedent pronoun followed by relative expressed or understood. (Rare; more frequently expressed by *that which, the one that, what.*)

c **1200** *Vices & Virtues* 117 Hit is soð ðat tu seiest. *c* **1305** *St. Edm. Conf.* 562 in *E.E.P.* (1862) 86 Louerd . . þu hit ert þat ich habbe iloued. **1382** WYCLIF *Eccl.* i. 9 What is that was? it that is to come. What is that is mad? it that is to be maad. *a* **1533** LD. BERNERS *Gold. Bk. M. Aurel.* (1546) Q vj b, Idelnesse, whereby our envy entreth, is it whiche openeth the gate to all vyces. **1535** COVERDALE *1 Chron.* iv. 10 God caused it for to come that he axed. **1535** STEWART *Cron. Scot.* II. 541 It that tha wyn at our plesour to spend. **1562** J. HEYWOOD *Prov. & Epig.* (1867) 133 It hapth in an houre that hapth not in vii yeare. **1588** SHAKS. *Tit. A.* v. i. 59 An if it please me which thou speak'st. **1596** —— *1 Hen. IV*, II. i. 58 It holds currant that I told you yesternight. **1601** —— *Twel. N.* II. iv. 80 That's it, that alwayes makes a good voyage of nothing. **1611** BIBLE *Isa.* li. 9 Art thou not it that hath cut Rahab? **1651** HOBBES *Leviath.* II. xxvi. 137 But that is not it I intend to speak of here.

14. When the antecedent is the subject of a clause which precedes the relative, it may be used of persons as well as things.

1596 SHAKS. *Merch. V.* I. ii. 15 It is a good Diuine that followes his owne instructions. *Ibid.* II. ii. 80 It is a wise Father that knowes his owne childe. **1768** STERNE *Sent. Journ.* (1775) II. 124 (Fragment ii.) 'It is an ill wind', said a boatman . . 'which blows no body any good'. *a* **1901** *Mod.* It is not everybody who can afford to take a holiday.

It, it (it), *sb.* See *gin and it* s.v. GIN *sb.*² 2 b.

ita ('ɪtə). Also **eta, ite.** [f. Arawak *ite.*] In full, ***ita palm.*** The tropical South American fan-palm, *Mauritia flexuosa*, or the drink made from its fermented sap; cf. ETA².

1845 *Encycl. Metrop.* XX. 6/2 The Eta, a smaller kind of this [cabbage] palm, furnishes nuts. **1860** MAYNE REID *Odd People* 360 The *itá* is a true palm-tree. **1866** *Treas. Bot.* 725/2 *Mauritia flexuosa*, the Moriche or Ita Palm, is very abundant on the banks of the Amazon, Rio Negro, and Orinoco rivers. **1904** W. H. HUDSON *Green Mansions* xxii. 292 Even the Ita palm and mountain glory . . had lost all grace and beauty. **1922** W. E. ROTH tr. *Schomburgk's Trav. Brit. Guiana* I. 150 There was . . a considerable supply of a rarer drink, the Ite, manufactured by the Indians from the juice of *Mauritia flexuosa.* **1957** M. SWAN *Brit. Guiana* x. 152 An outcrop of sandy soil has produced a cluster of ite palms, those 'trees of life' found all over the coastal areas.

itabirite (ɪ'tæbɪraɪt). *Min.* Also **-yte.** [f. *Itabira*, name of a place in Minas Geraes, Brazil + -ITE.] A quartzose iron-slate or iron-mica slate, consisting chiefly of alternate layers of quartz and specular iron ore.

1868 DANA *Min.* (ed. 5) 141 Itabiryte is a schist resembling mica-schist, but containing much specular ore in grains or scales or in the micaceous form. **1880** *Nature* XXI. 412 The disappearance of iron pyrites in auriferous itabirites.

i-tached, ME. pa. pple. of TACH *v.*

itacism ('iːtəsɪz(ə)m). [f. Gr. ἦτα, the name of the letter η, pronounced ('iːtə) in later and modern Gr. (and English pronunciation of ancient Greek) as if spelt ἶτα; the suffix as in *iotacism, rhotacism.*] The giving to the Greek vowel η the sound-value (iː), like Eng. *ee* (opposed to ETACISM, in which it has the original value (eː)); also the reduction in pronunciation of different Greek vowels and diphthongs (as ει, η, οι, υ, υι) to the sound (iː) (represented in ancient Greek by the letter ι, iota); cf. IOTACISM; hence the erroneous substitution in MSS. of ι for any of these vowels or diphthongs. So **'itacist,** one who practises or favours itacism; **ita'cistic** *a.*, characterized by itacism.

1837 HALLAM *Hist. Lit.* v. I. §25 Reuchlin's school, of which Melanchthon was one . . were called Itacists, from the continual recurrence of the sound of Iota in modern Greek, being thus distinguished from the Etists of Erasmus's party. **1854** ELLICOTT *1 Ep. Gal.* Pref. (1859) 18 The apparent probabilities of erroneous transcription, permutation of letters, itacism, and so forth. **1861** SCRIVENER *Introd. Crit. N.T.* i. 10 It seems more simple to account for the itacisms . . by assuming that a vicious pronunciation gradually led to a loose mode of orthography adapted to it. **1881** WESTCOTT & HORT *Grk. N.T.* Introd. §303 Changes of an itacistic kind, as the confusion between imperatives . . and infinitives. **1882** FARRAR *Early Chr.* I. 158 *note*, Some have supposed a pleasant play of words founded on itacism between *chrestos* (sweet) and *Christos* (Christ).

i-tacned, -takned, ME. pa. pple. of TOKEN *v.*

itacolumite (ɪtə'kɒljuːmaɪt). *Min.* [f. *Itacolumi*, name of a mountain in Minas Geraes, Brazil + -ITE.] A granular, quartzose, talcomicaceous slate, sometimes flexible in thin slabs.

1862 DANA *Man. Geol.* §88. 83 *Itacolumite*, a schistose quartz rock, consisting of quartz grains with talc or mica. **1868** —— *Min.* (ed. 5) 22 The diamond appears generally to occur in regions that afford a laminated granular quartz rock, called itacolumite, which pertains to the talcose series, and which in thin slabs is more or less flexible. **1878** LAWRENCE tr. *Cotta's Rocks Class.* 240 In the Brazils itacolumite forms whole systems of strata of great thickness.

itaconic (ɪtə'kɒnɪk), *a. Chem.* [Formed by arbitrary transposition of letters from ACONITIC.] Of, pertaining to, or derived from aconitin. ***itaconic acid***, $C_5H_6O_4$, an acid isomeric with citraconic and mesaconic acids, obtained in the dry distillation of citric acid. Its salts are **i'taconates.**

1865-72 WATTS *Dict. Chem.* III. 435 Itaconic acid is dibasic, forming acid salts, $C_5H_5MO_4$, and neutral salts, $C_5H_4M_2O_4$. The neutral itaconates of the alkali-metals do not crystallise.

†**i-tæche,** *v. Obs.* Also 3 **i-tachen.** [OE. *ȝetǽc(e)an* to show, to assign, to teach, f. *ȝe-*, I-¹ + *tǽc(e)an* to TEACH.] *trans.* To show; to hand over, deliver; to teach.

c **888** K. ÆLFRED *Boeth.* xxxiv. §9 Ða cwæð he: Ic hit þe þonne wille ȝetæcan. *a* **1000** *Cædmon's Gen.* 2837 (Gr.) Him frea engla wic ȝetæhte. *c* **1205** LAY. 10395 He heom wolden mucle wele & wurðscipe itæchen. *Ibid.* 11169 þeo Judeus heo sohten & þere quene heo itæhten. *a* **1250** *Owl & Night.* 1345 Swiche luve ich itache and lere.

i-tæht, -taht, -taiht, -taȝt, ME. pa. pple. of TEACH *v.*

‖**itai-itai** ('ɪtaɪ'ɪtaɪ). [Jap., lit. 'ouch-ouch'.] A disease, first reported in Japan in 1955, caused by the ingestion of cadmium and characterized by severe pain particularly in the back.

1969 *Keio Jrnl. Med.* (Tokyo) XVIII. 181 (*title*) Causation of ouch-ouch disease (Itai-Itai byō). **1970** *Biol. Abstr.* LI. 4256/1 Rice straw samples used were 2 kinds of stubble grown in the 'Itai-itai' disease epidemic district. **1973** *Biol. Conservation* V. 143 *Itai-itai* originated in the prefectures of Toyama and Gumma, in north-western Japan. The cause of the affliction, however, is world-wide: rivers poisoned by effluence from smelters.

†**Itaile,** *sb.* and *a. Obs. rare.* In 5 **Ytaile,** 6 **Itale, -aill.** [ad. L. *Italus* (pl. *Itali*) ITALIAN.] = ITALIAN.

c **1400** tr. *Secreta Secret., Gov. Lordsh.* 51 þe ytailes sayen it ys no vice to a kynge if he be auers to hym seluen, so þat he be large to his subgitz. **1513** DOUGLAS *Æneis* VI. xiii. 6 And quhat successioun or posteritie Of Itale freyndschip sall discend of the. *Ibid.* VII. iii. (*heading*) Efter Eneas come to Itaill land.

itaka-wood ('ɪtəkə,wʊd). [f. *Itaka*, the native name + WOOD *sb.*] A cabinet-wood beautifully streaked with black and brown, obtained from the *Machærium Schomburgkii*, a leguminous tree of Guyana.

1866 *Treas. Bot.* 706/1 *Machærium Schomburgkii*, a British Guiana species, produces the beautifully mottled wood called Itaka, Itiki, or Tiger-wood, used for furniture in that country.

i-take(n, i-tald, ME. pa. pples. of TAKE, TELL *vbs.*

Italian (ɪ'tæljən), *a.* and *sb.* Forms: 5 Ytalian, Itallian, -aillian, -aylion, 5–6 Ytalyen, 6 Italyan(e, -ion, -yon, -ien, 6– Italian. [ad. L. *Italiān-us*, f. *Italia* Italy: cf. F. *Italien*.]

A. *adj.*

1. a. Of or pertaining to Italy or its people; native to or produced in Italy.

1547 BOORDE *Introd. Knowl.* xxi. (1870) 176 Calabre is a prouince ioyned to Italy; and they do vse the Italion fashion. **1576** A. HALL *Acc. Quarrel* (1815) 11 M. Mallerie hadde affirmed, that he would shew him an Italian tricke, intending therby to do him some secret and unlooked-for mischiefe. **1595** SHAKS. *John* III. i. 153 Adde thus much more, that no Italian Priest Shall tythe or toll in our dominions. **1655** FULLER *Ch. Hist.* VII. i. §21 Soon after the Lord Gray of Wilton..came with a company of Horsmen, and 300 Italian Shot, under Baptist Spinola their Leader, to recruit the Lord Russell. **1753** HANWAY *Trav.* (1762) II. I. x. 53 *note*, Italian operas are countenanced and even promoted by some of the burgomasters. **1834** MEDWIN *Angler in Wales* II. 166 The sky was of a deep, almost an Italian blue.

b. Of or pertaining to ancient Italy; = ITALIC *a.* 1, 1 b.

1513 DOUGLAS *Æneis* VI. xiii. 16 Commixit with the blude Italiane. **1783** H. SWINBURNE *Trav. Two Sicilies* I. 323 Hannibal..assembled all his Italian allies in this temple. **1841** *Penny Cycl.* XIX. 172/2 The philosophic school of which Pythagoras was the founder, is sometimes called the Italian or the Doric school. **1863** W. Y. SELLAR *Rom. Poets Rep.* ii. (1881) 45 It was from men of the Italian provinces, and not from her own sons, that Rome received her poetry.

†**c.** *Arch.* = ITALIC *a.* 1 c. *Obs.*

1624 WOTTON *Archit.* in *Reliq.* (1651) 225 The Compound Order, or as some call it, the Roman; others more generally the Italian.

†**d.** *Printing.* = ROMAN (type). *Obs.*

1711 STRYPE *Life Parker* IV. ch. xvi. 382 (an. 1572) The Archbishop had..spoken to Day the Printer, to cast a new Italian Letter. *Ibid.* IV. sect. iv. 541 To cast a new Sett of Italian Letters..For our black English Letter was not proper for the Printing of a Latin Book.

†**e.** = ITALIC *a.* 3. *Obs.*

1700 TYRRELL *Hist. Eng.* II. 809 Whatsoever is printed in an *Italian* Character. **1723** *True Briton* I. 66 Every Word.. that I lay any Stress upon, is printed in an Italian Character.

2. As the designation of the modern language of Italy (see B. 2). Hence of words, etc.: Belonging to this language. Of books, etc.: Composed or written in this language.

1530 PALSGR. 3, *e* shall be sounded lyke an italian *a* and some thynge in the noose. **1598** FLORIO *Ital. Dict.* Ep. Ded., So manie and so strange bookes..as be written in the Italian toong. *a* **1639** WOTTON *Let. to Dr. C.* in *Reliq.* (1651) 476, I cannot (according to the Italian Phrase..) accuse the receipt of any Letter from you. **1750** CHESTERF. *Lett.* (1774) II. 351 What Italian books have you read? **1820** SHELLEY *Lett. M. Gisborne* 298 We will have books, Spanish, Italian, Greek.

3. Applied to the form of handwriting developed in Italy, and now used in Great Britain, America, the Latin countries, and other countries of Western Europe, which approaches in form to italic printing: opposed to the Gothic hand, formerly used in England and still in Germany, etc.

1571 BEAUCHESNE & BAILDON (*title*) A Booke Containing Divers Sortes of hands, with the Italian, Roman, Chancelry & court hands. **1643** WOOD in *Life* (O.H.S.) I. 98 There was a paper found pasted, in a fayre Italian hand, thus inscribed: *Quaestiones* [etc.]. **1789** MRS. PIOZZI *France & Italy* I. 195 Italian hand was the first to become elegant. **1870** J. A. H. MURRAY in *Leisure Hour* 60 A specimen of the closing period of that Old English or Gothic hand-writing, which was so rapidly disappearing before the Italian or current hand of the present day.

4. In specific names of things produced in or originally from Italy, as ***Italian ferret, greyhound, lettuce, melilot, millet, oak***, etc.: see the sbs. Also ***Italian clover, paper, vermouth***.

Italian cloth, a kind of linen jean with satin face, largely employed for linings (in F. *satin de Chine*, It. *zanella*); **Italian cypress**, *Cupressus sempervirens* var. *stricta*; **Italian earth**, the colour sienna; **Italian garden**, a formal garden, characterized by clipped trees, box-edged beds of flowers, paved paths, statues, fountains, etc.; often arranged in terraces linked by steps and balustrades; **Italian Gothic**, the Gothic or pointed architecture of Italy in the 13th and 14th c.; **Italian juice**, the extract of liquorice; **Italian May**, the Dropwort, *Spiræa Filipendula*; **Italian paste**, the paste from which macaroni and vermicelli are made; **Italian pink** = *Dutch pink*; **Italian plaster**: see quot. 1887; **Italian quilting** (see quots.); **Italian roof**, a hip-roof; **Italian sixth** (*Mus.*), a chord consisting of a note with its major third and augmented sixth; **Italian stitch**, a form of CROSS-STITCH *sb.*; **Italian string**, a superior kind of violin-string of Italian manufacture; **Italian warehouse**, a shop where Italian groceries, fruits, olive oil, etc. are sold; hence **Italian warehouseman**.

1840 C. DEWEY in Dewey & Emerson *Rep. Herbaceous Plants & Quadrupeds Mass.* 66 *Trifolium incarnatum*, Italian clover. **1908** *Animal Managem.* 109 'Valerian', 'Italian' or 'Crimson clover', commonly called 'Trifolium'. **1838** J. C. LOUDON *Arboretum* IV. 2464 The common, or evergreen, Cypress... Synonymes...the Italian Cypress. **1923** L. H. BAILEY *Cultivated Evergreens* II. 208 Italian Cypress... Much planted since ancient times in southern Europe particularly in its columnar form. *Ibid.*, Columnar Italian C[ypress]... With erect branches, forming a narrow, columnar head. The classical cypress of the Greek and Roman writers. **1969** T. H. EVERETT *Living Trees of World* 35/1 The Italian cypress is really a horticultural form of venerable ancestry, its exact origin unknown. **1854** F. W. FAIRHOLT *Dict. Terms Art* 260/1 *Italian earth*, a pigment known as burnt Italian earth. **1897** *Sears, Roebuck Catal.* 361/2 Pastel Crayons..Burnt Sienna..Italian Earth.. Purple Brown. **1969** R. MAYER *Dict. Art Terms & Techniques* 200 *Italian earth*, an old name for sienna. [**1822** J. C. LOUDON *Encycl. Gardening* I. 16 He [*sc.* Volkman] considers the Italian gardens as inferior to those of France in point of superb alleys, lofty clipt hedges, and cabinets of verdure.] **1883** W. ROBINSON *Eng. Flower Garden* p. vi/2 It has been affirmed that none but an Italian garden would have suited South Kensington. **1928** L. ARCHER-HIND tr. *Gothein's Hist. Garden Art* II. xvi. 329 We feel the resemblance to the parterre of the Doria Pamfili when we walk through an 'Italian garden' at an English country seat. **1942** A. E. W. MASON *Musk & Amber* i. 10 The Italian garden.., an oblong of grass paths and glowing flower beds, of box trees and hedges, of stone seats..and..a ridiculous charming little temple with open pillars. **1961** G. MASSON *Italian Gardens* 274 Within the space of two hundred and fifty years, Italian gardens had been introduced into France, developed and expanded until they represented a national style that became the model for Europe, and then via Spain returned to their point of departure, the Neapolitan Realm, as a foreign innovation. **1866** *Treas. Bot.* 726/1 Italian May, *Spiræa Filipendula*. **1924** A. HUXLEY *Let.* 25 Feb. (1969) 228 The best form, I think, would be something small, cheap and pretty. Covers of Italian paper or something of the kind. **1930** *Times Lit. Suppl.* 6 Feb. 108/4 A large variety of Italian papers. **1845** E. ACTON *Mod. Cookery* i. 4 All the ingredients used for soups should be fresh,..particularly Italian pastes of every kind (maccaroni, vermicelli, &c.). **1907** *Army & Navy Stores Catal.* 1246/2 Italian paste, for soups. **1957** *Encycl. Brit.* XIV. 544/2 *Macaroni*... The same substance in different forms is also known as *vermicelli, pasta* or Italian pastes, *spaghetti, taglioni, fanti*, etc. **1835** Italian pink [see *English pink*]. **1934** H. HILER *Notes Technique Painting* ii. 111 *Italian pink, quercitron lake*, etc., organic pigments prepared from Turkish or Avignon berries, quercitron bark, etc. **1971** *Country Life* 10 June 1428/3 This leads into the north-facing hall, which has been painted an Italian pink as a background to full-length portraits. **1887** *Syd. Soc. Lex.*, *Italian plaster*, an old name for a plaster used for purging sordid ulcers and promoting granulation. **1937** E. HAKE *Eng. Quilting* iii. 16 Italian quilting..was as prevalent in England as in any other European country during the seventeenth and eighteenth centuries. **1955** *Oxf. Jun. Encycl.* XI. 323/1 Italian quilting consists of two layers of cloth sewn together in a design built up entirely of parallel lines. A padding of soft wool or piping cord is then threaded between the narrow channels. **1967** E. SHORT *Embroidery & Fabric Collage* ii. 47 In Italian quilting the design is worked entirely in parallel lines of running or back stitch, which are then padded by inserting a thick wool from the back. **1875** OUSELEY *Harmony* xi. 126 A discord which has been called an 'Italian Sixth'. **1882** Italian stitch [see HOLBEIN]. **1913** M. K. GIFFORD *Needlework* xvii. 262 *Italian stitch* can be worked either open or close. The latter makes a very solid filling. **1957** M. B. PICKEN *Fashion Dict.* 185/2 *Italian-stitch*, running stitch done twice on the same line. **1896** *T. W. Stapleton & Co. Wine List* Dec., Vermouth, Italian—36/-. **1925** TOYE & ADAIR *Drinks Long & Short* 12 Three and a half glasses of gin, one and a half of Italian Vermouth. **1967** A. LICHINE *Encycl. Wines* 541/1 Vermouth was certainly being made in Italy in the seventeenth century, and now it is produced all over the world, and the two main types are 'French' and 'Italian'. **1837** WHITTOCK, etc. *Bk. Trades*, Table, Italian Warehouse. **1863** *Good Words* 870/1 You are mistaken as to the Italian warehouse.

B. *sb.* **1.** A native of Italy.

1422 tr. *Secreta Secret., Priv. Priv.* 130 The ytaliance sayth, that in a kynge hit is noght reproue yf he be scarse to hym-Selfe. **1439** *Rolls Parlt.* V. 32/1 Lumbardes, Itaylions, and..other Merchauntes Aliens. **1573** *Nottingham Rec.* IV. 149 Geven to the Italyans for serteyne pastymes that they shewed before Master Meare. **1611** FLORIO *Ital. Dict.* 618 The Italians haue two very different sounds for the two vowels E and O. **1783** H. SWINBURNE *Trav. Two Sicilies* I. 398 Another monument..commemorating a victory gained ..by thirteen Italians over an equal number of French. **1818** A. RANKEN *Hist. France* V. v. 401 The great merchants of Europe were the Italians.

2. The Italian language.

1485 CAXTON *Pref. Malory's Arthur*, Moo bookes [are] made of his noble actes..as wel in duche ytalyen spaynysshe and grekysshe as in frensshe. **1547** BOORDE *Introd. Knowl.* xxiii. (1870) 179 Who that wyl learne some Italien. **1602** SHAKS. *Ham.* III. ii. 274 The Story is extant and writ in choyce Italian. **1756–7** tr. *Keysler's Trav.* (1760) II. 312 This distich was ingeniously translated into Italian by Bellori.

†**3.** One versed in the Italian language; an Italian scholar. *Obs.*

1598 FLORIO *Ital. Dict.* Ep. Ded., What and whosoeuer he be that thinkes himselfe a very good Italian.

4. *pl.* (*ellipt.*) Articles (defined by context) imported from Italy.

1883 *Daily News* 12 Sept. 2/5 Tows and hemps... Italians have advanced £1 per ton. **1891** *Ibid.* 20 Oct. 2/7 Eggs.. There has been a rise of 6d. on second Italians.

5. Ellipt. for *Italian cloth*. Also *attrib.*

1897 *Sears, Roebuck Catal.* 177/1 Fine Italian lining in fancy figured effects. **1900** *T. Eaton & Co. Catal.* Midwinter Sale 13/2 Ladies' black boucle curl cloth jackets.., lined throughout with mercerized Italian. **1907** *Yesterday's Shopping* (1969) 743/1 Jackets..in serges and cloths, lined Italian. **1960** *Textile Terms & Definitions* (Textile Inst.) (ed. 4) 82 *Italian*,..a cloth of 5-end sateen weave with a lustrous finish, used chiefly as a lining material.

6. = *Italian vermouth.* Chiefly in phr. ***gin and Italian***. Cf. GIN *sb.*² 2 b.

1929 J. B. PRIESTLEY *Good Companions* II. i. 264 Couldn't you take some cocktails—gin and Italian or sherry and bitters or something—upstairs to those people. **1957** G. BELLAIRS *Death in High Provence* vii. 80 Two long Italians with some ice and perrier, please.

C. *Comb.*, as ***Italian-like*** adj. and adv., ***Italian-minded*** adj.; also prefixed to other adjs., as ***Italian-English***, etc.

1598 FLORIO *Ital. Dict.* Ep. Ded., I may consecrate this lesser-volume..to all Italian-English, or English-Italian students. **1651** WALTON *Life Wotton* in *Reliq. Wott.* b x, His long Rapier, which Italian-like he then wore. **1658** W. SANDERSON *Graphice* 27 Lest..an Italian minded Guest gaze too long on them, and commend the worke for your wive's sake.

Italianate (ɪ'tæljənət), *a.* (*sb.*) Forms: see next; also 7 -at. [ad. It. *Italianato*: see -ATE².]

1. Rendered Italian; that has become or been made Italian in character: see ITALIANATE *v.*

Often with allusion to the Italian proverb *Inglese Italianato è un diavolo incarnato*, 'Englishman Italianate is a devil incarnate' (see quots. 1591, 1659, and quots. 1598, 1660 in ITALIANATED 1).

1572 GRINDAL *Let. Burleigh* Wks. (Parker Soc.) 332 The number of obdurate papists and Italianate atheists is great at this time. **1591** GREENE *Disc. Coosnage* (N.), I am Englishe borne, and I have English thoughts; not a devill incarnate because I am Italianate. **1659** HOWELL *Lex. Tetragl.* Ital. Prov., An Englishman Italionat is a Devill Incarnat. **1880** *Sat. Rev.* 30 Oct. 552/2 An English girl that is Italianate must expect..to live among ideas and manners so strange to her that her existence can scarcely be made harmonious.

2. Of Italian character, form, or aspect.

1592 NASHE *P. Penilesse* (Shaks. Soc.) 68, I comprehend.. vnder hypocrisie, al Machivalisme, Puritanisme..and finally, all Italionate conveyances. **1631** BRATHWAIT *Eng. Gentlew.* (1641) 324 A scru'd face, an artful cringe, or an Italionate ducke. **1894** MRS. H. WARD *Marcella* I. 98 The small Italianate physique of his son.

†**B.** *sb.* An Italianate person. *Obs. rare.*

1587 HARRISON *England* II. v. (1877) I. 130, I passe ouer to saie anie more of these Italionates.

Italianate (ɪ'tæljəneɪt), *v.* Also 6 ytal-, 6–7 italion-, -in-, -ien-, (7 -iannate). [Found first in pa. pple. *Italianated* (see next), f. It. *Italianato*, whence the simple vb. was deduced.] *trans.* To render Italian; to give an Italian character to; to Italianize.

Usually in a depreciatory sense, esp. with reference to the imitation of Italian fashions and morals by English courtiers in the 16th and 17th cents.; cf. ITALIANATE *ppl. a.* 1.

1567 FENTON *Trag. Disc.* 213 Ytalianated in legerdemaines of subteltye. **1599** H. HOLLAND *Wks. Greenham* To Rdr., The world was neuer more full of Italian conceits, nor men more in danger..to be Italianated. **1615** *Val. Welshm.* (1663) C j b, My brain Italinates my barren faculties To Machivilian blackness. **1655** FULLER *Ch. Hist.* VIII. iii. §49 The longer He lived in England, the less He had of an English-man, daily more and more Italianating Himself. **1704** S. BRISCOE *Key Rehearsal* Pref. 9 The Decorum of Foreign-Theatres, especially the French.. before it was so far Italianated. **1899** E. W. GOSSE *Donne* i. 36 Soft and voluptuous measures Italianating the rude tongues of the preceding generation.

Hence **I'talianating** *ppl. a.*

1879 E. W. GOSSE *Lit. N. Europe* 242 This Italianating spirit was not lessened..by the next step taken.

Italianated (ɪ'tæljəneɪtɪd), *ppl. a.* [f. It. *Italianato* (see prec.) + -ED¹.]

1. = ITALIANATE *a.* 1.

1553 T. WILSON *Rhet.* (1567) 82 b, An other choppes in with Englishe Italinated. **1581** ANDRESON *Serm. Paules Crosse* 80 Oure Italienated Papistes. **1598** BARCKLEY *Felic. Man* IV. (1603) 317 An English man italianated is a Devil incarnated. **1660** *Charac. Italy* 55 Nay, 'tis a Proverb of their own, *Tudesco Italianato è un Diavolo incarnato*: an Italianated German is a Devil incarnate. **1841** D'ISRAELI *Amen. Lit.* (1867) 425 This Italianated Englishman..raged against Elizabeth more furiously than had the Mar-prelate Knox. **1891** *Athenæum* 5 Sept. 315/3 His preference for the italianated suburb of Cairo.

†**2.** = ITALIANATE *a.* 2. *Obs.*

1616 SIR R. BOYLE in *Lismore Papers* (1887) Ser. II. II. 50 The Petitioner..seeketh to deteyne yt by his Italionated pollecie. **1658** W. SANDERSON *Graphice* 37 How she leers out of her inticeing Italianated eyes, able to confound a Saint.

Italianesque (ɪˌtæljə'nɛsk), *a.* [f. ITALIAN + -ESQUE.] Italian in style or character.

1850 *Ecclesiologist* X. 45 To replace the present Italianesque altar. **1884** H. R. REYNOLDS in *Life* xiv. (1898) 349 The picturesque undulations and Italianesque dotting of houses in impossible places.

Hence **I,talia'nesquery** *nonce-wd.* [cf. *grotesquerie, -ery*], work executed in Italian style.

1850 *Fraser's Mag.* XLI. 652 The 'White Angel', a close imitation of Browning's *Italianesquery*.

I'talian 'iron, *sb.* A cylindrical 'iron' with rounded end, made hollow for the reception of the cylindrical heater, used for fluting or crimping lace, frills, etc. Hence **I'talian-'iron** *v. trans.* to flute or crimp with an Italian iron, to goffer; **I'talian-'ironed** *ppl. a.*

1833 J. HOLLAND *Manuf. Metal* II. 253 'Sad iron', 'box iron', and 'Italian iron'. **1849** C. BRONTE *Shirley* i, The Italian-ironed double frills or its net-cap. **1861** E. WAUGH *Birtle Carter's T.* 5 A clean cap..thickly bordered with great, stiff, old-fashioned puffs, such as I used to watch my mother make on the end of the 'Italian iron' when I was a lad at home.

†**Italianish**, *a. Obs. rare.* [f. ITALIAN + -ISH¹: cf. Ger. *Italiänisch*.] Italian, Italic.

1535 COVERDALE *Acts* x. 1 Cornelius a captayne of yᵉ company which is called yᵉ Italianysh. **1540** —— *Confut. Standish* Wks. (Parker Soc.) II. 379 Cornelius, a captain of the Italianish company.

Italianism (ɪ'tæljənɪz(ə)m). [f. ITALIAN + -ISM; or a. F. *Italianisme* (16th c. in Godef. *Compl.*).]

1. An Italian practice, feature, or trait; *esp.* an Italian expression or idiom of language.

1594 NASHE *Unfort. Trav.* 91 Some notable newe Italionisme. **1611** COTGR., *Signale*,..notable,..(An Italianisme; and deriued from the custome of marking souldiors in auncient Garrisons). **1840** *Fraser's Mag.* XXI. 667 The introduction of Italianisms into the language. **1900** F. HALL in *Nation* (N.Y.) LXXI. 113/2 Of Italianisms and other foreignisms..I have amassed a large collection.

2. Italian quality, spirit, or taste; attachment to Italian ideas or principles; sympathy with Italy.

1824 *Blackw. Mag.* XVI. 163 An absurd pretension to Italianism, which caricatured refinement, and surpassed Keats in folly. **1851** GALLENGA *Italy in 1848*, 202 The very character of that ministry was, however, its Italianism. **1892** *Nation* (N.Y.) 1 Sept. 163/3 Such public expressions of sentiments by public functionaries in Trieste itself are proofs beyond all doubt of the Italianism of the citizens.

I'talianist. *rare.* [f. as prec. + -IST.] One who Italianizes.

1855 KINGSLEY *Westw. Ho!* viii, The bargain is hardly fair between such a gay Italianist and us country swains.

Itali'anity. *rare.* [f. ITALIAN + -ITY.] Italian quality or character.

1881 *Encycl. Brit.* XIII. 494/2 If the 'Venetian', in spite of its peculiar 'Italianity', has naturally special points of contact with the other dialects of Upper Italy [etc.].

Italianize (ɪ'tælɪənaɪz), *v.* [a. F. *Italianiser* (16th c. in Littré): cf. ITALIAN and -IZE.]

1. *intr.* (also in phr. *to Italianize it*): To practise Italian fashions or habits; to become Italian (in character, tastes, etc.).

1611 COTGR., *Italianizer*, to Italianize it; to speake Italian, play the Italian, doe like an Italian. **1656** BLOUNT, *Italianize.* **1658** in PHILLIPS.

2. *trans.* To make Italian in character or style.

1673 [R. LEIGH] *Transp. Reh.* 136 Nol's Latin clerks were somewhat Italianiz'd. **1729** MIDDLETON *Let. fr. Rome* (1741) 170 The adding of a modern termination, or Italianizing the old name of a Deity, has given existence to some of their present Saints. **1832** *Fraser's Mag.* V. 729 She Italianised her Christian name. **1886** WILLIS & CLARK *Cambridge* II. 46 The Hall was new wainscoted and thoroughly Italianized.

Hence **I'talianized** *ppl. a.*, **I'talianizing** *vbl. sb.* and *ppl. a.* Also **I,taliani'zation**, the action or process of Italianizing, an Italianized formation; **I'talianizer**, one who Italianizes.

a **1693** URQUHART *Rabelais* III. xix. 159 A Chironomatick Italianising of his Demand, with various Jectigation of his Fingers. **1771** MRS. HARRIS in *Priv. Lett. Ld. Malmesbury* I. 217 Louisa is gone to the oratorio, a great condescension for so Italianised a lady. **1847** LD. LINDSAY *Chr. Art* I. p. ccxvi, Mabuse, Van Orley, and the Italianisers of Antwerp—imitators chiefly of Raphael. **1855** MILMAN *Lat. Chr.* VI. iii. (1864) III. 430 This absolute Italianisation of the Pope. **1880** H. NICOL in *Academy* 24 July 57 We have Old French, Modern French, Italianisations, Latin expansions, and English abbreviations used indiscriminately. **1881** WESTCOTT & HORT *Grk. N.T.* II. App. 46 European of a comparatively late and Italianising type. **1900** *Pilot* 4 Aug. 140/2 There is only one example of the Italianising masters of Fontainebleau.

Italianly (ɪ'tælɪənlɪ), *adv. rare.* [f. ITALIAN + -LY².] In an Italian manner.

1599 H. BUTTES *Dyets drie Dinner* P iv, On English foole: wanton Italianly; Go Frenchly: Duchly drink: breath Indianly. **1884** *Harper's Mag.* Feb. 387/1 Sant' Agnese, pronounced..Italianly to rhyme with lazy.

Italic (ɪ'tælɪk), *a.* and *sb.* [ad. L. *Italicus*, a. Gr. Ἰταλικός, f. Ἰταλία, L. *Italia* Italy. Cf. F. *Italique* (15–16th c. in Godef. *Compl.*).]

A. *adj.*

1. Of or pertaining to ancient Italy or its tribes; *spec.*, in *Rom. Hist.* and *Law*, pertaining to parts of Italy other than Rome.

Italic version: see quot. 1852.

1685 STILLINGFL. *Orig. Brit.* iii. 113 St Ambrose at Milan, had as great authority as Damasus at Rome; And the Italick Diocese was as considerable as the Roman. **1724** WATERLAND *Athan. Creed* iv. 62 Neither are we to expect to meet with it in the Italick psalters. **1852** HOOK *Ch. Dict.* (1871) 403 The old Italic Version, or *Vetus Itala*, is the name usually given to that translation of the sacred Scriptures into the Latin language which was generally used till the time of St. Jerome. **1875** POSTE *Gaius* I. Comm. (ed. 2) 108 Italic soil was subject to Quiritary ownership. **1880** MUIRHEAD *Gaius* II. §31 A usufruct of lands that have italic privilege. **1900** *Contemp. Rev.* Feb. 272 The Italic groups, that is, the early languages of Italy.

b. Pertaining to the Greek colonies in southern Italy: said of the school of philosophy founded in Magna Græcia by Pythagoras in the 6th cent. B.C. (Sometimes used to include the Eleatic school.)

1662 H. MORE *Philos. Writ.* Pref. Gen. (1712) 17 This School was called the Italick School. **1728** T. SHERIDAN *Persius* iii. (1739) 45 He travelled to Magna Græcia where he was the Founder of the Italick Sect. **1836–7** SIR W. HAMILTON *Metaph.* vi. (1859) I. 105 Pythagoras, the founder of the Italic school.

c. *Arch.* A name of the fifth of the classical orders, the COMPOSITE. Formerly *Italica.*

1563 SHUTE *Archit.* A j b, The fifth piller named *Composita* or *Italica.* **1656** S. H. *Gold. Law* To Rdr. 1, If some Capitals should want their Italica distinctions and ornaments. **1706** PHILLIPS, *Italick Order of Architecture*, see *Composite Order.*

†2. = ITALIAN *a.* 1. *Obs.*

1638 SIR T. HERBERT *Trav.* (ed. 2) 159 A spatious Tanck, ..round set with pipes of lead which (after the Italick sort) spouts out the liquid element in variety of conceits. **1711** MADOX *Excheq.* Pref. 16 Persons that were by birth or education French or Italick. *a* **1734** NORTH *Lives* (1826) III. 39 The Italic caution of the ambassador.

3. (with small *i*) Applied to the species of printing type introduced by Aldus Manutius of Venice, in which the letters, instead of being erect as in Roman, slope towards the right; first used in an edition of Virgil, published in 1501 and dedicated to Italy. In early use also *Italica* (sc. *littera*).

1612 BRINSLEY *Pos. Parts* (1669) p. v, Beginning ther question ever at an Italike Capital Q. **1615** BEDWELL *Moham. Imp.* Pref. B, If I haue added any thing..that we haue caused to be imprinted in an Italica letter. **1733** SWIFT *Misc., On Poetry* 95 To Statesman wou'd you give a Wipe, You print it in *Italick Type.* When Letters are in vulgar Shapes, 'Tis ten to one the Wit escapes. **1789** FRANKLIN *Wks.* (1888) X. 180 The printers have of late banished also the italic types. **1818** A. RANKEN *Hist. France* V. IV. 391 Their printing was in Italic characters. **1855** THACKERAY *Newcomes* I. xxvi. 247 Documents..profusely underlined.. in which the *machinations of villains* are laid bare with italic fervour. **1861** N. A. WOODS *Pr. Wales in Canada & U.S.* 390 The reiterated headings, *italic* emphasis, and minute details, so peculiar to the American journals.

†b. Of handwriting: = ITALIAN *a.* 3. *Obs.*

1571 BEAUCHESNE & BAILDON *Booke contg. divers sortes of hands* (1602) D. (*heading*) Italique hande. *Ibid.* E iv. (*heading*) Italique Letter.

4. Pertaining to the older Latin version of the Bible known as *Vetus Itala.*

1861 C. D. GINSBURG tr. *Coheleth* App. I. 501 The Old Italic Version forms the basis of the one on which St. Jerome wrote the *Commentarium ad Paulam et Eustochium.* **1957** *Oxf. Dict. Chr. Ch.* 981/1 It has been generally supposed that there are two main types—the 'Italic' (represented by the MSS. *f*..and *q*..) and the 'European'.

B. *sb.*

1. A member of the Italic school of philosophy: see A. 1 b.

1594 R. ASHLEY tr. *le Roy's Interch. Var. Things* 61 a, The Philosophers..diuided themselues into two sects, thone being called Ionicques, thother Italiques. **1678** CUDWORTH *Intell. Syst.* Pref., Divers of the Italicks, and particularly Empedocles, before Democritus, Physiologized Atomically.

2. (with small *i*) *pl.* (rarely *sing.*) Italic letters; letters sloping to the right: now usually employed to emphasize a word or series of words, or to distinguish a word or phrase (e.g. one in a foreign language) from others in the same context (see A. 3); also, a modern adaptation of the old Italic hand. Hence **i'talicist**, one who favours or practises this style.

1676 MOXON *Print Lett.* 8 From the Bottom to the Foot is 12 of them in Romans and Italicks. **1712** STEELE *Spect.* No. 455 ¶6, I Desire you would print this in *Italick*, so it may be generally taken notice of. *c* **1823** T. HOWES in *S. Parr's Wks.* (1828) VIII. 194 The names in italic are those supplied by the editors. **1824** J. JOHNSON *Typogr.* II. i. 8 It would be a desirable object, if the use of *Italic* could be governed by some rules. **1898** A. W. W. DALE *Life R. W. Dale* ix. 217 In the book, the sentence in italics is developed into an entire lecture. **1955** W. BLUNT *Handwriting* 9 Many firms.. produce fountain-pens designed for Italic. **1956** *Jrnl. Educ.* July 304/1 Having myself been lambasted more than once by the Italicists because I dared to qualify my praise of their handwriting. *Ibid.* 304/2, I know of *no* school where italic is given a disproportionate share of the timetable. **1963** A. FAIRBANK *How to teach Italic Hand* 14 The following remarks relate to pen-and-ink italic.

†**I'talical**, *a. Obs. rare*⁻¹. [f. as ITALIC *a.* and *sb.* + -AL¹.] Italian. Hence †**I'talically** *adv.*, Italianly.

1609 BP. W. BARLOW *Answ. Nameless Cath.* 74 That frapling discourse of his Italicall progresse. **1821** BYRON *Wks.* (1837–40) V. 179 By the papers..I perceive that the Italian gazette had lied most *Italically*, and that the drama had *not* been hssed.

I'talican, *a. rare.* [f. L. *Italic-us* + -AN.] Of or pertaining to the ancient Italian group of languages.

1875 WHITNEY *Life Lang.* x. 188 Declared Indo-European and Italican by scholars.

†**i'talicate**, *v. Obs. rare.* [f. ITALIC *a.* and *sb.* + -ATE³.] *trans.* To italicize. Hence **i'talicated** *ppl. a.*

1839 J. R. DARLEY *Introd. Beaum. & Fl.'s Wks.* I. p. xxxiv, These five italicated syllables pass but for two.

Italicism (ɪ'tælɪsɪz(ə)m). *rare.* [f. ITALIC *a.* + -ISM.] An Italian expression or idiom; an Italianism.

1773 *Westm. Mag.* I. 15 (Jod.) Our language abounds with Italicisms. **1837–9** HALLAM *Hist. Lit.* I. I. ii. 140 *note*, The Gallicisms or Italicisms are very numerous [in Thomas à Kempis]. **1838** BRITTON *Dict. Archit.* 375 *Portico*, an Italicism of the Lat. *porticus.*

italicize (ɪ'tælɪsaɪz), *v.* [f. ITALIC + -IZE.] *trans.* To print in italics, or (in writing) underscore with a single line as a sign that the word or words thus marked are to be so printed, or in order to emphasize or otherwise distinguish them.

1795 PARR *Rem. Statem. Combe* 78 In p. 17 of his pamphlet the Dr. has printed, but not italicised another inaccuracy. **1858** RUSKIN *Arrows of Chace* (1880) I. 139 The words which I have italicized in the above extract are those which were surprising to me. **1865** *Spectator* 28 Jan. 100 The lines we have italicized are lines of very great beauty. **1871–3** EARLE *Philol. Eng. Tongue* (ed. 2) §30 There are no words in the Latin answering to the words which are italicised in the English version.

fig. **1870** H. SMART *Race for Wife* i, A slight inflection of voice just italicised the epithet.

Hence **i'talicized** *ppl. a.*, **i'talicizing** *vbl. sb.* Also **i,talici'zation**, the action of italicizing.

1888 W. SHARP in *Academy* 17 Mar. 184/3 The italicisation is mine; but comment I have none. **1894** *Westm. Gaz.* 20 Oct. 2/2 Carlyle, however, gave positive injunctions on the point,..running as follows, with the characteristic italicising here reproduced. **1898** E. S. WALLACE *Jerusalem the Holy* viii. 131 The italicized words briefly but accurately describe the land.

I,talico-, used as combining form of *Italic*, adverbially qualifying the following adj., as in **I,talico-'Gallic**, Gallic or French of an Italian sort.

1804 LARWOOD *No Gun Boats* 21 A certain Italico-Gallic Gentleman.

Italiot, -ote (ɪ'tælɪɒt, -əʊt), *sb.* and *a.* [ad. Gr. Ἰταλιώτης, f. Ἰταλία Italy.]

A. *sb.* A person of Greek descent dwelling in ancient Italy; an inhabitant of Magna Græcia.

B. *adj.* Of or pertaining to the Greek colonies in southern Italy or Magna Græcia.

1660 STANLEY *Hist. Philos.* IX. (1701) 359/1 A Councel being called, and it being put to the question, Whether they should deliver up the Italiotes to the Sybarites, or undergo a War with an enemy more powerful than themselves? **1841** W. SPALDING *Italy & It. Isl.* I. 117 Several illustrious names in Grecian poetry and science belong by birth to the Italiot settlements. **1892** *Athenæum* 6 Aug. 187/1 The concluding chapters..give a pretty full account of the literary side of Sicilian and Italiot history.

†**'Italish**, *a. Obs. rare.* [f. L. *Ital-us* Italian + -ISH¹.] Italian.

1544 BALE *Sel. Wks.* (Parker Soc.) 8 Polydorus Vergilius ..polluting our English Chronicles most shamefully with his Romish lies and other Italish beggarys. **1550** —— *Eng. Votaries* II. 69 Thys story is tenderly towched of the Italysh writers. **1587** FLEMING *Contn. Holinshed* III. 1575/2 The Italish preest and Spanish prince.

,Italo- used as the combining form of *Italian* in various formations, as **,Italo-By'zantine** *a.*, pertaining to Byzantine art as developed in Italy; **Italo-Celtic, Italo-Keltic**, a postulated common parent language of Italian and Celtic; also as *adj.*, of, pertaining to, or characteristic of this language; **,Italo-'Grecian, -'Greek** *a.*, pertaining to Greek settlers or Greek civilization in Italy; **,Italo-'mania**, a mania for things Italian; **'Italo,phil, -,phile** *a.*, friendly to Italy or to what is Italian; *sb.*, one who is Italophile; **'Italo,phobe**, one affected with **,Italo'phobia**, intense dislike or fear of Italy.

1783 H. SWINBURNE *Trav. Two Sicilies* I. 353 Sent to lay the first stone of this Italo-Græco-Corsinian seminary. **1841** W. SPALDING *Italy & It. Isl.* I. 325 The second period, which may be called the Italo-Grecian, continued till about the extinction of the Antonines. **1841–4** EMERSON *Ess.* Ser. I. i. (1876) 25 The..Italomania of Boston Bay. **1877** W. JONES *Finger-ring* 458 A splendid specimen of a large gold ring of the best Italo-Greek work. **1877** J. RHYS *Lect. Welsh Philol.* i. 5 Some subdivide the Southern division into an Italo-Celtic and a Hellenic group, while others prefer to suppose a Celtic and a Greco-Italic group. **1883** C. C. PERKINS *Ital. Sculpt.* Introd. 12 Ornaments and animals in the same Italo-Byzantine style. **1888** J. WRIGHT tr. *Brugmann's Elem. Compar. Gram. Indo-Gmc. Lang.* I. 3 The Italo-Keltic hypothesis has perhaps the best prospect of attaining a greater degree of probability in the future. **1906** *Daily Chron.* 28 Mar. 5/4 The appointment of the Italophile reactionary Miushkovitch Ministry. **1920** G. E. BUCKLE *Life Disraeli* V. iii. 130 Protestant and Italophil England rejoiced. **1921** *Contemp. Rev.* Oct. 494 Some Italophobe Germans. **1922** *Ibid.* Sept. 302 The official state of hostility between the Vatican and Italy and the periodical protests against it..maintain in the Catholic masses a feeling of Italophobia. **1927** *Scots Observer* 26 Mar. 12/5 Italy found it easier to buy Ahmed Zogu, turn him into an Italophil. **1932** W. L. GRAFF *Lang.* 375 Italo-Celtic was probably once a common group of closely related dialects. **1933** L. BLOOMFIELD *Lang.* iv. 62 Some scholars believe that Italic and Celtic are connected.., so as to form an Italo-Celtic sub-group within the Indo-European family. **1958** N. GORDIMER *World of Strangers* 20 She..was a passionate Italophile, scattering her speech with *cara mia's*. **1966** E. P. HAMP in Birnbaum & Puhvel *Anc. Indo-European Dial.* 116 Germanic and..Italo-Keltic have *-yo/ī*, almost leveled out for both verb types. **1967** C. SETON-WATSON *Italy from Liberalism to Fascism* x. 378 The Italophil Prime Minister of Bulgaria, Gueshov, offered an alliance. **1973** *Times Lit. Suppl.* 5 Oct. 1151/1 Such an experienced Italophile.

i-tan, i-taried, ME. pa. pples. of TAKE, TARRY.

ita-palm: see ITA.

†**i-'tase**, *a. Obs.* [OE. *ȝetǽse.*] Convenient, suitable, handy.

Beowulf (Z.) 1320 Frægn ȝif him wære æfter neod-laðu niht ȝe-tæse. *a* **1000** *Boeth. Metr.* xx. 11 þu þysne middan-ȝeard..tidum totældes, swa hit ȝetæsost wæs. *c* **1205** LAY. 6502 þe king droh his sweord þe him wes itase.

i-tasted, i-tauwed, i-tauȝt, i-taxed, ME. pa. pples. of TASTE, TAW, TEACH, TAX *vbs.*

itatartaric (ɪtətɑː'tærɪk), *a. Chem.* [tr. G. *itaweinsäure* itatartaric acid (T. Wilm 1867, in *Ann. d. Chem. u. Pharm.* CXLI. 33), f. *ita-* (in

itaconsäure itaconic acid (see ITACONIC *a.*)) + *weinsäure* tartaric acid.] **itatartaric** *acid*: dihydroxyitaconic acid, $CH_2OH{\cdot}C(OH)(COOH){\cdot}CH_2COOH$. Hence **ita'tartrate**, a salt of this acid.

1872 WATTS *Dict. Chem.* Suppl. 762 Pure itatartaric acid is amorphous, vitreous, smells like honey when gently heated, deliquesces in the air, dissolves easily in alcohol, and does not volatilise perceptibly at 100° with aqueous vapour. *Ibid.*, Calcium itatartrate..forms crystalline masses sparingly soluble in water. **1945** *Jrnl. Biol. Chem.* CLXI. 739 (*heading*) Itatartaric acid, a metabolic product of an ultraviolet-induced mutant of *Aspergillus terreus.*

itch (ɪtʃ), *sb.* Forms: α. 1 **ȝyccæ**, 4 **ȝicche**, 5 **ȝiche**, **ȝykche**, **ikche**, **icche**, 6 **ycch(e**, **ytch(e**, **itche**, **ych(e**, **iche**, 7 **ich**, 6– **itch**. β. 5 **ȝeke**. See also *Sc.* YUKE. [OE. *ȝicce*, sb. from stem of *ȝiccan*: see ITCH *v.*[1]]

1. An uneasy sensation of irritation in the skin, which is relieved by scratching or rubbing; *spec.* a contagious disease, in which the skin is covered with vesicles and pustules, accompanied by extreme irritation, now known to be produced by the itch-mite; scabies.

α. *a* **800** *Leiden Gloss.* 82 *Prorigo, urigo cutis*, ȝyccae. *c* **1340** *Cursor M.* 11823 (Trin.) þe ȝicche toke him sikerly þe fester smoot þourȝe his body. *c* **1380** WYCLIF *Sel. Wks.* III. 91 þe Lord schal smyte þe wiþ..scabbe..and ȝicche. *c* **1400** *Lanfranc's Cirurg.* 91 If it be drie, it schal propirlie by clepid icche, And if it be moist, it schal be clepid scabbe. *c* **1440** *Promp. Parv.* 259/1 Icche, orȝiche (*S.* ikche, orȝykche), *pruritus.* **1522** MORE *De quat. Noviss.* Wks. 99 If thou shouldest for a litle ytche claw thy self sodeinly depe into yᵉ flesh. **1563** T. GALE *Antidot.* II. 20 This vnguent is for iche of the leggs. **1617** MORYSON *Itin.* III. 117 The Italians..for the most part are troubled with an itch, witnesse the frequent cry in their streets..Ointment for the Itch. **1711** SHAFTESB. *Charac.* (1737) II. 152 In the case of that particular kind of itch, which belongs to a distemper nam'd from that effect, there are some who, far from disliking the sensation, find it highly acceptable and delightful. **1861** HULME tr. *Moquin-Tandon* II. VI. i. 308 There really is a special parasite which gives rise to the Itch. **1883** GILMOUR *Mongols* (1884) 184 One of the most prevalent diseases in Mongolia is itch. **1900** *N. & Q.* 9th Ser. V. 7 Stablemen refer to the itch in horses as 'the dukes' [YUKES]. A 'dukey horse' means a horse suffering from itch.

β. **1483** *Cath. Angl.* 426/1 A ȝeke, *prurigo.*

b. Applied, with qualification, to various forms of eczema and other skin diseases, as ***bakers'***, ***bricklayers'***, ***grocers' itch*** (see these words). ***Norwegian itch***, a form of leprosy occurring in Norway.

2. *fig.* An uneasy or restless desire or hankering after something; a restless propensity to do something: usually spoken contemptuously. Const. *of*, *for*, *after*, (†*at*), or *inf.*

1532 MORE *Confut. Tindale* Wks. 371/2 For no desyre of mans prayse or ytch of vain glory, but of mere humilitie. **1599** *Life More* in Wordsw. *Eccl. Biog.* (1853) II. 119 Some of this new sect had taken such an itch of preaching, that they could hardly charm their tongues. **1624** BP. HALL *Serm. Hampton Crt.* Sept., Rem. Wks. (1660) 4 There is an itch of the ear..that now is grown epidemical. **1638** RANDOLPH *Muse's Looking-Gl.* III. iv, One that, out of an itch to be thought modest, dissembles his qualities. **1665** SIR T. HERBERT *Trav.* (1677) 123 Their itch after Idol-worship is over. **1708** *Wooden World Dissected* 32 He has as great an Itch at breaking of Heads on Board, as he has ashore at breaking of Windows. **1726** AMHERST *Terræ Fil.* xlvii. 253 Nothing can restrain a thorough-bred gamester; all ties and obligations give way to this agreeable itch of the elbow. **1753** JOHNSON *Adventurer* No. 115 ¶3 The itch of literary praise. **1795** WOLCOTT (P. Pindar) *Pindariana* Wks. 1812 IV. 237 The virtuoso itch For making a rare Butterfly-collection. **1863** GEO. ELIOT *Romola* vii, He had an itch for authorship. **1870** LOWELL *Study Wind.* 201 The itch of originality infects his thought and style. **1876** BROWNING *Filippo Baldinucci* liv, We fret and fume and have an itch To strangle folk.

3. *attrib.* and *Comb.*, as ***itch-allaying*** adj.; **itch-acarus**, **-insect**, **-mite**, **-tick**, a small parasitic arachnid (*Sarcoptes scabiei*) of the family *Acaridæ*, which burrows in the human skin, and gives rise to the disease called itch or scabies; **itch-reed**, **itch-weed**, popular names of White and Swamp Hellebore (*Veratrum album* and *viride*) respectively.

1826 KIRBY & SP. *Entomol.* II. xxiii. 332 The *itch acarus (*A. Scabiei*, L.) is similarly circumstanced. **1599** MARSTON *Sco. Villanie* III. viii. 213 But if he get her *itch-alaying pinne, O sacred relique, straight he must beginne To raue out-right. **1846** GREGORY *The. & Pract. Med.* v. vi. (L.) The *itch insect was first accurately described by Bonomo in 1683. **1833** *Penny Cycl.* I. 70/1 The *itch mite is a microscopic animal, found under the human skin in the pustules of a well-known cutaneous disease. **1770** J. R. FORSTER tr. *Kalm's Trav. N. Amer.* (1772) I. 382 The English call it *Itch-reed. **1822–34** *Good's Study Med.* (ed. 4) IV. 509 Infestment of the *itch-tick. **1884** MILLER *Plant-n.*, *Itch-weed, *Veratrum viride.*

itch (ɪtʃ), *v.*[1] Forms: α. 1 **ȝicc(e)an**, 3 **ȝichen**, 3–4 **ȝicchen**, 4 **ȝitchen** (*pr. pple.* (Ayenb.) icinge), 5 **ȝichyn**, **ȝechin**, **icchen**, **ycchen**, **iȝcchen**, **ichen**, **ychen**, **ychyn**, 5–6 **ytche**, **itche**, 6–7 **ytch**, 6– **itch**. β. 5 **ȝykyn**, **ȝekyn**, **ykyn**, **ekyn**, **ȝeke**, 7 **yeck**. [OE. *ȝicc(e)an* (:—*ȝiecc(e)an*, with umlaut from *ȝeocc- :—ȝucc-):—WGer. *jukkjan (OHG. *jucchen*, MHG. *jucken*, *jücken*, Ger. *jucken*, OLG. *jukid* it itches, MDu. *joken*, *jeuken*, Du. *jeuken*), Goth. *jukjan*, from stem *juk-* whence OHG. *jukido*, OE. *ȝiecða*, later *ȝicða*, ME. *ȝykthe*, YEKTH, itch. In the 14–15th c. the form *ȝicch-*, *ȝitch-*, lost its initial *ȝ* before *i*, whence the later *itch*. In some northern dialects the word came down with hard *c* or *k*, as *ȝyk-*, *ȝik-*, in 15th c. *ȝeke*, *yeke*. See also the Sc. form *youk*, *yuck*, YUKE.]

1. *intr.* To have or feel irritation of the skin, such as causes an inclination to scratch the part affected: said of the part; also of the person affected. Also *impers.*, *it itches*, there is an itching.

α. *c* **1000** *Sax. Leechd.* III. 50 Wið ȝiccendre wombe. *Ibid.* 70 Wið oþrum ȝiccendum blece. *a* **1225** [see ITCHING *vbl. sb.* 1]. *c* **1386** CHAUCER *Miller's T.* 496 My mouth hath icched [*v. rr.* ȝechid, yched] al this longe day. *c* **1430** *Hymns Virg.* 80 Oure body wole icche, oure bonis wole ake. **1530** PALSGR. 595/1 Whan thy wounde begynneth to heale it wyll ytche. **1606** SHAKS. *Tr. & Cr.* II. i. 29, I would thou didst itch from head to foot, and I had the scratching of thee. **1768–74** TUCKER *Lt. Nat.* (1834) II. 558 After all, perhaps, we have no greater enjoyments among us than those of eating when we are hungry,..laying down when sleepy, or, as the second Solomon has pronounced, than scratching where it itches. **1875** JOWETT *Plato* (ed. 2) IV. 17 Socrates dilates on the pleasures of itching and scratching. **1897** *Allbutt's Syst. Med.* III. 343 The cracks often itch in a most troublesome way.

β. *c* **1440** *Promp. Parv.* 258/1 Ichyn, or ykyn, or ȝykyn (*K.* yekyn, *S.* ȝichyn, *H.*, *P.* ekyn), *prurio.* **1468** *Medulla Gram.* (Promp. Parv. 538 *note*), *Prurio*, to ȝeke. **1483** *Cath. Angl.* 426/1 To ȝeke, *prurire.* **1703** THORESBY *Let. to Ray* (E.D.S.), Yeeke, [*v.* to] itch.

2. *fig.* To have an irritating desire or uneasy craving provoking to action. Often in phr. ***one's fingers itch*** (to do something, orig. to give a person a thrashing). Const. with *inf.*; also *for*, (†*at*).

a **1225** *Ancr. R.* 80 Lokeð, seið sein Jerome, þæt ȝe nabben ȝicchinde nouðer tunge ne earen. **1382** WYCLIF *2 Tim.* iv. 3 Thei schulen gadere to gidere maistris ȝitchinge [*gloss.* or plesynge] to the eeris. **1579** J. STUBBES *Gaping Gulf* E viij b, [Our] fingers wyll itch at hym. **1592** *No-body and Some-body* (1878) 326 My Kinglie browes itch for a stately Crowne. **1598** SHAKS. *Merry W.* II. iii. 48 If I see a sword out, my finger itches to make one. **1622** MABBE tr. *Aleman's Guzman d'Alf.* I. 57 His tongue itch't to be let loose. **1712** ARBUTHNOT *John Bull* IV. i, His fingers itched to give Nic. a good slap on the chops. **1821** CLARE *Vill. Minstr.* I. 163 Keep thee from my failings free,—Nor itch at rhymes. **1853** KINGSLEY *Hypatia* xviii. 205 The men's fingers are itching for a fight. **1860** READE *Cloister & H.* xxxviii. (1896) 111 No wonder men itch to be soldiers.

3. *trans.* To cause to itch. Also *refl.* and *fig.*

1586 J. HOOKER *Girald. Irel.* in *Holinshed* II. 91/1 It may be, that..I shall be able like a fleshworme to itch the bodie of his kingdome, and force him to scratch deepelie. **1665**, **1756** [see ITCHING *ppl. a.* 3]. **1900** J. LONDON *Let.* 16 June (1966) 107 It is a fascinating subject. It has itched me for long, and it is often all I can do to keep away from writing on it. **1922** JOYCE *Ulysses* 748 My hole is itching me always when I think of him. **1947** *Penguin New Writing* XXIX. 12 With long sensuous strokes he smoothed a patina of paint down the chairlegs, then itched with fussing dabs the corners and underneath. **1951** R. CAMPBELL *Light on Dark Horse* vi. 99 The thick super-salty water of the Mediterranean, which tires and itches the naked eye. **1951** L. MACNEICE tr. *Goethe's Faust* II. i. 171 The dice already itch me in my pocket. **1954** S. BECKETT *Waiting for Godot* II. 46 Then I can keep it [*sc.* a hat]. Mine irked me... How shall I say?..It itched me. **1973** *Welcomat* (Philadelphia) 10 Oct. 4/2 The sticker that itches her most is the one that says: 'School's Open. Drive Carefully.'

†**itch**, *v.*[2] *Obs.* [app. identical with HITCH *v.* and early ME. ICCHE-N; but the history is not clear.] *intr.* To shift one's position a little; to move with a jerk or succession of jerks; = HITCH *v.* 3.

1579 GOSSON *Sch. Abuse* (Arb.) 35 You shall see suche heauing and shooving, suche ytching and shouldring, to sitte by women. **1589** *Pappe w. Hatchet* 1 Itch a little further for a good fellowe. **1621** LADY M. WROTH *Urania* 377 Shee still itcht neerer her husband.

Here perhaps belong the following:

1640 A. HARSNET *God's Summ.* 413 Riches cannot..each us one haires breadth neerer heaven. **1691** RAY *Creation* II. (1701) 245 Without shifting of sides or at least etching this way and that way more or less.

itch, *v.*[3], variant of ECHE *v. Obs.*, to augment, increase, eke *out.*

1614 B. JONSON *Barth. Fair* II. ii, Halfe pound of tobacco, and a quarter of a pound of Coltsfoot, mixt with it too, to itch it out. *a* **1624** BP. M. SMYTH *Serm.* (1632) 104 Where the lyon's skin will not reach, there they itch it with the fox skin. **1651** BEDELL in *Fuller's Abel Rediv.*, *Erasmus* 63 To itch out his travelling charges he agreed with Baptista Boeria ..to accompany his two sonnes to Bononia.

itch, obs. variant of ECHE *sb.*[1], EKE *sb.*[1] 2.

1595 in *Antiquary* (1888) May 211 For itches for the bell roapes vjᵈ.

†**'itchful**, *a. Obs. rare*⁻⁰. [f. ITCH *sb.* + -FUL.] Full of itching, itchy.

1530 PALSGR. 316/2 Itche or ytchefull, *grateux.*

itchiness ('ɪtʃɪnɪs). [f. ITCHY + -NESS.] The quality or state of being itchy; itchy sensation.

1822–34 *Good's Study Med.* (ed. 4) II. 383 He adds another character, not always present however, namely, itchiness of the skin. **1847** JOHNSTON in *Proc. Berw. Nat. Club* II. No. 5. 222 The place in which they had burrowed was indicated by itchiness.

itching ('ɪtʃɪŋ), *vbl. sb.* [f. ITCH *v.*[1] + -ING[1].]

1. A feeling of uneasiness or irritation in the skin, which leads to scratching: see ITCH *v.*[1] 1.

a **1225** *Ancr. R.* 238 þeo hwule þet ȝichinge ilest, hit þuncheð god for to gniden. **1382** WYCLIF *Deut.* xxviii. 27 Smyit thee the Lord with..scab forsothe and itchynge [**1388** ȝicchyng, ichynge, iȝcching]. **14..** *Nom.* in Wr.-Wülcker 708/21 *Hic pruritus*, a ȝekynge. *c* **1440** *Promp. Parv.* 538/2 ȝykynge, or ȝykthe, *pruritus.* **1662–3** PEPYS *Diary* 10 Feb., In the morning, most of my disease, that is, itching and pimples, were gone. **1797** M. BAILLIE *Morb. Anat.* (1807) 205 They have commonly an itching at the nose. **1845** BUDD *Dis. Liver* 159 She became affected with excessive itching of the skin, which prevented sleep.

attrib. **1608** ARMIN *Nest Ninn.* (1880) 48 The World.. scratching her braine with her itching pin,..answeres, What then? **1611** COTGR. s.v. *Alum*, We call it, stone Allum, or itching pouder.

2. *fig.* An uneasy desire or hankering: = ITCH *sb.* 2.

1340 *Ayenb.* 16 þet uerste heaued of þe beste of helle ys prede..þe uifte icinge, in cle[r]gie avarice oþer couaytise. **1676** tr. *Guillatiere's Voy. Athens* 33 A rich Turk in that City ..had an itching after the young Mans Estate. **1709** POPE *Ess. Crit.* 32 All fools have still an itching to deride. **1884** *St. James's Gaz.* 22 Aug. 3/1 An irrepressible itching for a little more military glory.

itching ('ɪtʃɪŋ), *ppl. a.* [f. ITCH *v.*[1] + -ING[2].] That itches.

1. That has or is characterized by a feeling of irritation in the skin; itchy.

c **1000** [see ITCH *v.*[1] 1]. **1665** HOOKE *Microgr.* xxvi. 146 The itching tickling pain quickly grew languid. **1746** BERKELEY *2nd. Let. Tar-water* §15 A very useful wash for weak, dry, or itching eyes. **1898** P. MANSON *Trop. Dis.* xxxiii. 523 With a papulo-vesicular itching eruption resembling scabies.

2. *fig.* That has an irritating desire or uneasy craving.

Often qualifying sbs. denoting bodily organs in metaphorical phrases, as ***itching ears***, a craving to hear something new, persons who crave to hear novelties (hence ***itching-eared***); ***an itching palm***, a hankering after gain, an avaricious disposition; †***an itching elbow***, a passion for gambling (cf. quot. 1726 in ITCH *sb.* 2).

a **1225** [see ITCH *v.*[1] 2]. **1581** SIDNEY *Apol. Poetrie* (Arb.) 49 There is nothing of so sacred a maiestie, but that an itching tongue may rubbe it selfe vpon it. **1582** N. T. (Rhem.) *2 Tim.* iv. 3 According to their owne desires they wil heape to them selues maisters, hauing itching eares. **1601** SHAKS. *Jul. C.* IV. iii. 10 Cassius, you your selfe Are much condemn'd to haue an itching Palme. **1607** HIERON *Wks.* I. 196 A few blotted leaues; such perhaps, as in this itching-generation..few will take notice of. **1617** MORYSON *Itin.* I. 198, I had an itching desire to see Jerusalem. **1693** in *Dryden's Juvenal* xiv. (1697) 342 If the Father, says Juvenal, love the Box and Dice, the Boy will be given to an itching Elbow. **1847** A. BENNIE *Disc.* xxii. 393 This is no idle crowd come to gaze or to fill an itching ear. **1871** DIXON *Tower* IV. vii. 63 Fees were always welcome to his itching palm. **1876** *World* No. 108. 11 The *causes célèbres*, which have supplied such piquant reading to an itching public.

†**3.** That causes itching. *Obs.*

1665 HOOKE *Microgr.* xxvi. 145 Of Cowage, and the itching operation of some bodies. **1756** P. BROWNE *Jamaica* 336 The plant is well known on account of its sharp itching hairs. **1879** BRITTEN & HOLLAND *Plant-n.*, *Itching Berries.* Fruit of *Rosa canina. Lanc.*

Hence **itchingly** *adv.*

1657 J. BENTHAM *Two Treat.* 19 Itchingly desiring Novelties.

†**'itchless**, *a. Obs.* [f. ITCH *sb.* + -LESS.] Free from itching or the itch; free from an itching palm, incorruptible.

1635 QUARLES *Embl.* I. x. (1718) 41 One rubs his itchless elbow. **1648** HERRICK *Hesper.*, *To Sir J. Berkley*, Thou art just and itchlesse, and dost please Thy genius with two strength'ning buttresses.

itchy ('ɪtʃɪ), *a.* Now *colloq.* [f. ITCH *sb.* + -Y. The form appears in OE. as *ȝicciȝ* glossing 'putridus, purulentus' Hpt. *Gl.* 453.] Affected with itching or the itch; of the nature of the itch.

1530 PALSGR. 316/2 Itche [*mispr. for* itchie *or* itchye] or ytchefull, *grateux.* **1580** HOLLYBAND *Treas. Fr. Tong*, *Galleux*, scabbed, itchie. **1599** A. M. tr. *Gabelhouer's Bk. Physicke* 253/2 When any yonge Personne is Itchye, let him laye of this pouldre in water, and the water wilbe like oyle. **1616** SURFL. & MARKH. *Country Farme* 201 His leaues or rootes applyed to itchie places..doe great good vnto the same. **1725** BRADLEY *Fam. Dict.* s.v. *Itch*, All Itchy humour will come out and be dry'd up entirely. *a* **1829** J. YOUNG *Intell. Philos.* xxxv. (1835) 350 Your elbow is itchy and your toe is sore.

fig. **1599** B. JONSON *Cynthia's Rev.* III. ii, A third..takes the coming gold..That hourly rubs his dry and itchy palms. **1784** COWPER *Task* IV. 582 Excess, the scrofulous and itchy plague.

ite (aɪt). [The suffix -ITE[1] used as an independent word: cf. ISM *quasi-sb.*] A person or thing that is or may be designated by a sb. in *-ite.*

1852 *Blackw. Mag.* Aug. 260/1 The right honourable gentleman has shown that he is neither a Derby-*ite* nor a Russell-*ite*. Then what *ite* are you? **1906** *Westm. Gaz.* 1 Dec. 9/2 A big factory for explosives, holding dynamite, ballistite, cordite..Heaven knows what 'ites'—sufficient to wreck half the world. **1926** R. W. HUTCHINSON *First Course Wireless* viii. 138 Most of the 'ites' on the market..are galena subjected to various treatments.

ite: see ITA.

-ite, *suffix*[1], corresponding to F. *-ite*, L. *-īta* (*-ītēs*), ad. Gr. *-ῖτης*, forming adjs. and sbs. (of adj. origin) with the sense '(one) connected with or belonging to', 'a member of', as in *ὁπλίτης adj.* heavy armed, *sb.* a heavy-armed soldier (f. *ὅπλα* armour), *πολίτης* citizen (f. *πόλις* city). Its fem. form is *-ῖτις* (-ITIS). Both the masc. and fem. forms were extensively used in forming technical names of natural products, diseases, etc.

A frequent use in Gr. was to form ethnic and local designations, as *Ἀβδηρίτης* Abderite, *Σταγιρίτης* Stagirite, *Συβαρίτης* Sybarite, *Ταρταρίτης* denizen of Tartarus. Hence, often used by the LXX to render Heb. names in *-ī*, as in *'Ισραηλίτης* Israelite, *Λευίτης* Levite, *Ἀμαληκίτης* Amalekite, *'Ισμαηλίτης* Ishmaelite, *Μωαβίτης* Moabite, *Σοδομῖται* Sodomites, etc. Later, in Christian use, in the names of sects, styled either after their locality, their founder, or some tenet, rite, or other characteristic, as *ἐρημίτης* a desert-dweller, eremite, hermit, *Νικολαῖται* Nicolaitans (pl.), *'Ιακωβῖται* Jacobites, *Μονοφυσῖται* Monophysites, etc. Some of the Greek terms (esp. those in Christian use) were adopted in Latin, either unchanged in *-ītēs* or often in *-īta*, the plural (which was more frequent in use) being in *-ītæ*: thus *Stagirītēs*, *Sybarīta*, and, in the Vulgate, etc., *Levītēs* or *Levīta*, *Israēlitæ*, *Ismaēlītæ*, *Ammonītæ*, *Mōabītæ*, *Nicolaītæ*, *Sodomītæ* (also *Gadītæ*, *Reubēnītæ*, etc., where the LXX have *Γάδ*, *'Ρουβήν*); and in later and mediæval writers *Marcionītæ*, *Ebiōnītæ*, *Azȳmītæ*, *Marōnītæ*, *Monophysītæ*, *etc*. Hence the suffix has passed into Fr. and Eng. in the form *-ite*, pl. *-ites*. Already in the metrical *Genesis & Exodus* *c* 1250 we find *Amonit*, *Arabit*; by Wyclif the Vulgate words in *-ītæ* are duly rendered by forms in *-ites*, *-ytis*. In later Biblical versions the ending is extended to other tribal names, e.g. *'Αμοῤῥαῖοι*, *Χαναναῖοι*, Vulg. *Amorræi*, *Chananæi*, Wyclif *Amorrei*, *Chananei*(*-ey*), 16th c. versions *Amorites*, *Canaanites*.

Another frequent use of the termination was to form names of minerals and gems (adjectively with *λίθος* 'stone' understood), e.g. *ἀνθρακίτης* anthracite, *αἱματίτης* blood-stone, hæmatite, *ὀφίτης* snake-stone, serpentine, *σεληνίτης* moon-stone, selenite, etc. Nearly all these occur also in L. in Pliny, who moreover adds several not recorded in Greek. These have been handed down and increased by mediæval and early modern Latin writers *de proprietatibus rerum*, and have given origin to our modern use of *-ite* in names of fossils and minerals.

The following are the chief English uses of the suffix:

1. Forming names of persons. (Often also used adjectively.)

a. In words already formed in Gr. or L., of the classes above mentioned, and in analogous terms; e.g. *Stagirite*, *Sybarite*; *Israelite*, *Levite*, *Ammonite*, *Amorite*, *Benjamite*, *Canaanite*, *Gadite*, *Gileadite*, *Hamite*, *Ishmaelite*, *Rechabite*, *Reubenite*, *Semite*, *Sodomite*, etc.; *eremite*, *Ebionite*, *Adamite*, *Jacobite*, *Marcionite*, *Maronite*, *Azymite*, *Monophysite*, *Anthropomorphite*, *Fatimite*, etc.

b. In words of modern formation: (*a*) Denoting an inhabitant of a place; as *Sydneyite*, *Claphamite*, *Durhamite*, *Ludlowite*: now rare, and mostly somewhat contemptuous. (*b*) Denoting a disciple, follower, or adherent of a person or doctrine; as *Wycliffite*, *Campbellite*, *Daleite*, *Glassite*, *Irvingite*, *Puseyite*, *Simeonite*; *Brontëite*, *Darwinite*, *Hugoite*, *Ruskinite*, *Shelleyite*, *Spencerite*, *Zolaite*; *Bryanite*, *Canningite*, *Healyite*, *Jacobite*, *Luddite*, *Mackinleyite*, *Parnellite*, *Peelite*, †*Williamite* (adherent of William III). So *Pre-raphaelite*, *Silverite*, *Independent Labourite*, etc.

These have a tendency to be depreciatory, being mostly given by opponents, and seldom acknowledged by those to whom they are applied. The following are illustrations of some of these formations:

1818 SCOTT *Hrt. of Midl.* xviii, I am not a MacMillanite or a Russelite, or a Hamiltonian, or a Harleyite, or a Howdenite. (*Note*, All various species of the great genus Cameronian.) **1820** *Lonsdale Mag.* Aug. 350/1 In 1814, the Inghamite churches formed a union with the Daleite churches in Scotland. **1883** *Athenæum* 27 Jan. 116/3 Of Musset, as becomes a good Hugoite, he has nothing to say. **1886** *Manch. Exam.* 13 Jan. 3/2 Legislation which is regarded as a violation of that principle by all thorough-going Herbert Spencerites. **1888** RIDER HAGGARD *Col. Quaritch* i, Other folk, yet more learned, declared it to be an ancient British dwelling..Mrs. Massey..was a British dwellingite. **1891** *Daily News* 5 Mar. 5/2 Swift was a Tolstoite before his day. **1892** *Athenæum* 1 Oct. 449/2 These short stories have not the attractions which the true Zolaite loveth. **1895** *Times* 8 Jan. 9/5 Ireland will see Healyites and Redmondites battling with Dillonites for the honour of representing the united will of the Irish nation. **1897** *Westm. Gaz.* 12 July 3/3 'The Shirley country'—as the Spen Valley is now called by Brontëites. **1898** *Daily News* 12 Jan. 6/6 The fine mass meeting of the Independent Labourites.

2. a. *Palæont.* Used to form the names of fossil organisms, animal or vegetable; as *ammonite*, *belemnite*, *calamite*, *dendrite*, *echinite*, *encrinite*, *lignite*, *trilobite*, etc.

These follow the type of Gr. *βατραχίτης* toadstone, etc., and were at first used in their Latin form in *-ītes*: see the individual words.

b. *Mineral.* The systematic ending of the names of mineral species, comprising names of ancient origin in *-ίτης*, as *anthracite*, *hæmatite*, *ophite*, *selenite*, or in *-ῖτις*, as *chlorite*, *hepatite*, *hyalite*, and a vast number of modern names in which *-ite* is added to an element expressing colour, structure, physical characters or affinities, or to the name of a locality, discoverer, mineralogist, distinguished scientist, or other person whom the discoverer may have desired to commemorate. Examples are *albite*, *azurite*, *melanite*, *dichroite*, *graphite*, *apatite*, *calcite*, *syenite*, *labradorite*, *leadhillite*, *humboldtite*, *wernerite*, *brewsterite*, *danaite*, *darwinite*. Earlier names of minerals have in some cases been displaced by names in *-ite*, and some names with other endings as *-ane*, *-in*, etc. have been conformed to the *-ite* type. For names of rocks, Dana has suggested the differentiated ending *-yte*, founded on *trachyte*, as in *aphanyte*, *dioryte*, *epidosyte*, and the like; but this has not found universal acceptance. It is also used more widely in *tektite*, and hence in the names of tektites from different regions (as *australite*, *indochinite*).

3. *Anat.* and *Zool.* Used to form terms denoting one of the constituent parts, segments, or joints of a body or organ; as in *somite* a segment of the body; so *cerite*, *pleurite*, *podite*, *tergite*, a segment of the horn or antenna, side, foot, back, etc. Cf. *cephalostegite*, *coxopodite*, *ischiocerite*, *ischiopodite*.

[These forms were introduced (in French) in 1851 by H. Milne Edwards (*Observations sur la squelette tégumentaire des Crustacées Décapodes*, in *Ann. Sci. Nat.* (Zool.) 3, XVI. 221). They were app. first used in Eng. in 1855, by C. Spence Bate (*Report Brit. Assoc.* 1855, 38); but they owe their general use esp. to Huxley (*Lect. on General Nat. Hist.* 1857, *Anat. Inverteb. Anim.* 1877, etc.). (F. A. Bather, M.A., Nat. Hist. Museum, South Kensington.)]

4. *Chem.* **a.** Used to form the names of some saccharine substances, glucoses, and other organic compounds, as *dambonite*, *dulcite*, *erythrite*, *inosite*, *isodulcite*, *mannite*, *melampyrite*, *pinite*, *quercite*, *sorbite*, chiefly f. the names of plants; also of explosives, as *cordite*, *dynamite*, *herculite*, *melinite*; and of commercial products, as *ebonite*, *vulcanite*, etc.

[In the earlier of these the suffix was in origin apparently the same as in the preceding groups, *mannite* being, as it were, the distinctive constituent of *manna*; but in the names of explosives and other products this sense disappears, and *-ite* is merely a derivative.]

b. In Inorganic Chemistry, *-ite* is the systematic termination of the names of the salts of acids denominated by adjectives in *-ous*; e.g. *nitrite* a salt of *nitrous* acid, *sulphite* a salt of *sulphurous* acid. This was part of the systematic nomenclature introduced by Guyton de Morveau and Lavoisier in their *Nomenclature Chimique* of 1787.

[In this use, the suffix has no direct connexion with the Gr. *-ίτης*, but was suggested by, and differentiated from, the suffix *-ate* (-ATE[1] 3), appropriated to salts of acids in *-ic*. In the words of the authors cited (*Nomencl. Chimique*, p. 40), these are 'terminaisons différentes adaptées à la même racine, de la manière qui a paru le plus convenable au jugement de l'oreille....

Sulph*ate* sera le nom générique de tous les sels formés de l'acide sulphurique.

Sulph*ite* sera le nom des sels formés de l'acide sulphureux.

(p. 49) Cette distinction une fois établie nous a donné les *nitrates* et les *nitrites*, les *phosphates* et les *phosphites*, les *acétates* et les *acétites*'.]

A few of the words in *-ite* have derivative adjs. in **-itic**, as *Hamitic*, *Semitic*, *dendritic*, *encrinitic*, *anthracitic*, *hæmatitic*; many of those in group 1 have adjs. in **-itish**, as *Israelitish*, *Moabitish*.

-ite, *suffix*[2], an ending of adjs., adapted from L. pa. pples. in *-ītus*, *-itus*, of vbs. in *-īre*, *-ĕre*, *-ēre*, as in *ērudītus* erudite, *exquīsītus* exquisite, *compositus* composite, or from the corresponding Romanic *-ito*, as *favourite*; also of sbs. derived from the same or from the cognate L. sbs. in *-us*, as *appetītus* appetite. Also, of verbs formed from the same ppl. stems, as *expedite*, *unite*; but from stems in *-ĭt*, the verbs usually end in *-it*, as *posit*, *exhibit*, *merit*; this was formerly also usual with adjs., as *opposit*, *recondit*.

i-teid, -teied, -et, ME. pa. pple. of TIE *v*.

i-teiht, -teiȝht, ME. pa. pple. of TEACH *v*.

†**i-teiled**, *a*. *Obs*. [f. I-[1] + TAIL *sb*. + -ED[2].] Tailed, having a tail.

a **1240** *Sawles Warde* in *Cott. Hom.* 251 Iteilede draken grisliche ase deoflen.

†**i-tel.** *Obs*. [OE. *ȝetæl*, *-tel* (= OS. *gital*, Du. *getal*), f. *ȝe-*, I-[1] + *tellan* to count, TELL.] Number.

c **1000** *Ags. Gosp.* Matt. xiv. 21 þæra etendra ȝetæl wæs fif þusenda wera butan wifum & cildum. *c* **1205** LAY. 7805 Nuste na mon þat itel Of þan scipen þat seileden after.

i-teld, i-telded, i-tield, ME. pa. pple. of TELD *v*. to erect.

i-teled, ME. pa. pple. of TILL *v*.

†**i-telle**, *v*. *Obs*. [OE. *ȝetellan* (= OS. *gitellian*, OHG. *ge-*, *gizellen*, MHG. *gezeln*), f. *ȝe-*, I-*pref.*[1] + *tellan*, TELL *v*.]

1. *trans*. To number, reckon, tell.

971 *Blickl. Hom.* 203 Hie..ȝetealdon þæt þær wæs eac syx hund manna..acweald. *c* **1175** *Lamb. Hom.* 133 Na man ne mihte itellen a mare þe me mei ðeo steorren of heuene.

2. To recount, narrate, tell.

c **1205** LAY. 24627 Nes he næuere iboren..þe cuðe him itelle..of halue þan richedome.

item ('aɪtəm), *adv*. and *sb*. [a. L. *item* adv., just so, in like manner, moreover, f. *i-s*, *i-d* he, it + advb. ending *-tem*. Used also in F. as adv. (1290 in Godef. *Compl.*) and as sb. from the 16th cent.]

‖**A.** *adv*. Likewise, also. Used to introduce a new fact or statement, or, more frequently, each new article or particular in an enumeration, esp. in a formal list or document, as an inventory, household-book, will, etc.

1398 in Rymer *Fœdera* (1709) VIII. 55 Item, it is Accordit and Ordaint that [etc.]. *Ibid.*, Item, for als mykil as [etc.]. *c* **1400** MAUNDEV. (1839) xxviii. 288 Item, in this Yle..there is a manner of Wode, hard and strong. **1418** in *E.E. Wills* (1882) 31 Item I be-quethe to the freres Menours of Bryggenorth..xl s. Item I bequethe..to the ffreres of Wodehouse xl s. **1484** CAXTON *Fables of Alfonce* i, Item my sone suppose it not a lytyll thynge to haue a good Frend. **1556** *Chron. Gr. Friars* (Camden) 56 Item this yere was alle the chaunterys put downe. Item also the wacche at mydsomer was begonne agayne... Item also the byshoppe of Wenchester..preched before the kyng. **1601** SHAKS. *Twel. N.* I. v. 265 It shalbe Inuentoried..As, Item two lippes indifferent redde, Item two grey eyes, with lids to them. **1732** FIELDING *Miser* II. i. Wks. 1882 IX. 308 *Item*, Two muskets, one of which only wants the lock. **1781** COWPER *Truth* 152 Not a grace appears on strictest search, But that she fasts, and, *item*, goes to church. *a* **1818** in Cruise *Digest* (ed. 2) VI. 337 He..added this clause: '*Item*, all the houses and lands which I have given between my sons, is to this purpose, that [etc.]'.

B. *sb*.

1. A statement, maxim, or admonition such as was commonly introduced by the word *item*; a saying with a particular bearing. Hence, generally, an intimation, a hint. Esp. in vbl. phrases, as ***to give*** (***take,*** etc.) ***an item***, also ***to give*** (***take,*** etc.) ***item***. Now *U.S. local*.

1561 T. NORTON *Calvin's Inst.* IV. xii. (1634) 616 *marg.*, Two Items to the Church of Rome concerning the single life which they require in the order of Priests. **1600** HOLLAND *Livy* XXV. xvi. 559 The Soothsayers aforesaid, had given an Item, and foretold, that this prodigious sight perteined properly unto the chiefe captaine. **1607** HIERON *Wks.* I. 171 'That nothing be lost', it was one of our Sauiours items. **1684** BUNYAN *Pilgr.* II. 150 He..has Need of an Itum, to caution him to take heed, every Moment of the Day. **1704** HEARNE *Duct. Hist.* II. 14 Getting item thereof, he departed to the sea. **1786** MRS. INCHBALD *Such things are* 51 (in *Br. Theat.*) If my friend had not given me an item of this I should think her downright angry. *a* **1860** *Spirit of Times* (N.Y.) (Bartlett), The minit yer get item that I'm back, set off for the cross-roads.

2. a. An article or unit of any kind included in an enumeration, computation, or sum total; an entry or thing entered in an account or register, a clause of a document, a detail of expenditure or income, etc.

1578 T. WILCOCKS *Serm. Paules* 50 The lawe layeth no Item to youre charge. **1588** *Marprel. Epist.* (Arb.) 39 His grace had need to prouide a bag ful of Items for you if you be so liberal. **1601** CORNWALLIS *Ess.* ix, That makes not the purse emptie, and the household-booke rich in Items. **1607** DEKKER *Knt.'s Conjur.* (1842) 34 Our vaunt' currer..offred to pay some of the tauern items. **1765** COWPER *Let. to J. Hill.* 3 Dec., Wks. 1837 XV. 7 That I may return as particular an answer to your letter as possible, I will take it item by item. **1870** J. YEATS *Nat. Hist. Comm.* 87 Timber is an important item in the national revenue. **1876** GEO. ELIOT *Dan. Der.* iii, I have to spend a good deal in that way; it is a large item. **1961** *Lancet* 12 Aug. 358/2 Questions [set]..included items that the undergraduate who had read something more.. than an introductory text could be expected to answer. **1970** *Jrnl. Gen. Psychol.* LXXXII. 63 A person may agree with an item and its opposite because he believes statements worded in the dogmatic (authoritarian) direction but agrees with a reversed item because of the high social desirability of this item.

b. A detail of information or news, esp. one in a newspaper.

1819 B. E. O'MEARA *Exp. Trans. St. Helena* 11 The general accuracy of these items may be inferred. **1865** LOWELL *Scotch the Snake* Pr. Wks. 1890 V. 241 We cannot estimate the value of the items in our daily newspapers. **1876** —— *Among my Bks.* Ser. II. 130 This item kind of description. **1888** J. INGLIS *Tent Life Tigerland* 2 Filling my sporting journal with many items of more than ordinary interest.

c. *Computers*. Any quantity of data treated as a unit, such as a field, a group of fields, or a record.

1954 *Computers & Automation* May 17/2 *Item*, a set of one or more fields containing related information. **1958** *Computer Jrnl.* I. 71/1 Let us call the units which are to be sorted items. *Ibid.* 71/2 If every item of data has a unique key, complete sorting will result in each place holding no more than one item. *Ibid.* 72/2 A typical item in commercial

data is an 80-column punched card. **1964** A. LYTEL *Fund. Data Processing* (1965) iv. 108 Information is stored in variable-length memory areas called fields... Consecutive fields can be combined to form a larger unit of information called an item. Grouping fields to form an item simplifies the manipulation of related-data fields, and minimizes the number of instruction executions required to move consecutive fields within the main memory. **1967** B. S. WALKER *Introd. Computer Engin.* vi. 157 The field or item is typically a group of letters or numbers, in association, to mean a name, or reference number, or a heading of some kind. **1971** *Computers & Humanities* VI. 67 Each item file is composed of an open-ended sequence of variable length records called 'items', every item being the description of one entity.

d. A member of a set of linguistic units.

1954 *Word* X. 230 'Items'..are either morphemes or sequences of morphemes, but still one has to contend with the independent status of order, constructions, and hierarchical structure. Even so, there is a clear difference between taking some phonemic material as 'root' (= item) and some as 'marker' of processes. **1964** R. A. HALL *Introd. Ling.* vi. 34 The first group [of linguistic analysts] wish to limit their description strictly to an enumeration of items and the arrangements or sequences in which they are found. .. The other group..take into account the passage of time when the observer moves from one part of his material to another... This approach is based on a listing of items involved and of 'processes' which the items 'undergo'. *Ibid.* 35 In some respects, the item-and-process (IP) approach is closer to our traditional type of grammatical description than is the item-and-arrangement (IA) approach. **1964** M. A. K. HALLIDAY et al. *Ling. Sci.* ii. 24 In English..'chair' is a lexical item: it operates as an item in open set choices. 'the', 'chair', the '-s' in 'chairs', 'in case'..are grammatical items. **1970** *Canad. Jrnl. Linguistics* XV. 95 This system grew out of a union of the item-and-process approach to linguistics with automata theory. **1971** T. F. MITCHELL in *Archivum Linguisticum* II. 64 In the English-speaking world of linguists little more than ten short years ago, the talk was of grammatical models labelled 'Item and Arrangement', 'Item and Process', and 'Word and Paradigm'.

C. *attrib.* and *Comb.*

1859 E. H. N. PATTERSON in L. Hafen *Overland Routes to Gold Fields* (1942) 68 This..is one of those cases, probably, that will remain a mystery only to be solved when the great item book of the recording angel shall be opened to justify the final sentence. **1961** *Lancet* 12 Aug. 359/2 Item analysis showed that there were fairly large differences between the groups on a few questions, and these were seen to be due to specific differences in teaching. **1970** *Jrnl. Gen. Psychol.* LXXXII. 166 Item-item and item-test correlations were computed. **1972** *Jrnl. Social Psychol.* LXXXVI. 221 An item analysis technique was used to select those items that discriminated between the high and low scores by 20 percentage points.

item ('aɪtəm), *v.* [f. prec.] *trans.* To set down or reckon up item by item; to enter as an item.

1601 ? MARSTON *Pasquil & Kath.* IV. 157 Here I haue item'd forth what I am worth. **1615** SIR E. HOBY *Curry-Combe* i. 14 Had he Itemd the lampe oyle, as well as hee summed the Spanish wine, his intruding curiosity would haue passed with lesse blame. **1716** ADDISON *Drummer* III. i, I have Item'd it in my memory. **1788** COWPER *Stanzas for Year*, I..item down the victims of the past. **1855** LEWES *Goethe* I. III. ix. 303 A process which looked less heroic when item'd in the bill next day.

i-temed, ME. pa. pple. of TAME *v.*[2]

itemize ('aɪtəmaɪz), *v.* Chiefly *U.S.* [f. ITEM *sb.* + -IZE.] *trans.* To set down by items or enter as an item; to specify the items of (an account, etc.). Hence **'itemized** *ppl. a.*; also **itemi'zation**, the action of itemizing.

1864 WEBSTER s.v., To itemize the cost of a railroad. *a* **1881** S. LANIER *Eng. Novel* v. (1883) 98 Æschylus paints these conclusions with a big brush..Shelley itemizes them. **1883** *Harper's Mag.* July 850/2 A kindness that can never be itemized in the bill. **1890** *Pall Mall G.* 20 June 7/2 The hostess reads an itemized list of her expenditures. **1894** *Columbus* (O.) *Disp.* 10 Nov. 6/4 Demanding from each, a separation and itemization of any and all bills paid during their official terms.

'itemizer. [f. prec. + -ER[1].] One who itemizes; also (*U.S.*), One who furnishes items to a newspaper.

1860 *Congregationalist* 21 Sept. (Cent. Dict.), An itemizer of the 'Adams Transcript'. **1887** in *Bible Soc. Rec.* (U.S.) Feb. 27/2 The itemizers have often been huge misinterpreters of the gospel.

'itempred, ME. pa. pple. of TEMPER *v.*

i-tempted, i-tented, ME. pa. pple. of TEMPT, TENT.

i-tend, ME. pa. pple. of TINE *v.* to shut.

i-tend(e, i-tent, ME. pa. pple. of TEND *v.* to kindle.

i-tened, ME. pa. pple. of TEEN *v.*

†**i-teon**, *v. Obs.* [OE. *ȝetéon* (cognate with Goth. *gatiuhan*, OHG. *giziahan*, *geziehen*), f. *téon* to draw, TEE.]

1. *trans.* To draw, draw on, attract. (Only OE.)

a **1000** *Guthlac* 546 Woldun hy ȝeteon..in orwennysse meotudes cempan.

2. To bring up, educate, instruct.

975 *O.E. Chron.*, þa þe ær wæran on rimcræfte rihte ȝetoȝene. *c* **1205** LAY. 2418 þe king..to Corinee hine sende in to his londe, þat he hine sculde wel iteon.

3. *intr.* To come or grow *to* (an end or result).

c **1250** LAY. 32114 Strongliche he wes auæred..to wulche þinge hit iteon wolde þat him wes itacned þere.

i-teoðeȝed, ME. pa. pple. of TITHE *v.*

iter ('ɪtə(r), 'aɪtə(r)), *sb.* Pl. **iters**, ‖**i'tinera**. [a. L. *iter* journey, way, road; in sense 1, med.L.]

1. *Hist.* A circuit of the Justices in Eyre or the Justices of Assize or the Forest; = EYRE 1. Also *transf.* Any similar circuit.

1647 N. BACON *Disc. Govt. Eng.* I. lxi. 192 These Iters were little other than visitations of the Country by the grand Council of Lords. **1682** *Enq. Elect. Sheriffs* 45 A Sentence or Verdict of the Judges of the Iter's, or of the Courts at Law. *a* **1734** NORTH *Lives* (1826) I. 79 The court of the forest is in the nature of an iter. **1876** W. C. SMITH in *Encycl. Brit.* IV. 64/1 The Lord Chamberlain, by his *Iter*, or circuit of visitation, maintained a common standard of right and duties in all burghs.

b. The record of proceedings during a circuit.

1598 MANWOOD *Lawes Forest* iii. §2 (1615) 34 The Assises or Iters of Pickring and Lancaster are, as it were, the bookes of yeeres and Termes, unto the Forest Lawes. **1668** *Ant. Kal. & Inv.* (1836) III. 441 Search such iters and other records..as..Chislett shall desire.

2. A Roman road or line of travel.

1751 *Phil. Trans.* XLVII. 216 In the second iter of Antonine's Itinerary, we find..Eboracum. **1771** *Antiq. Sarisb.* 8, A.D. 140, in the reign of Antoninus, Britain was divided into Itinera or public Roads from one end of the Kingdom to the other. **1851** D. WILSON *Preh. Ann.* (1863) I. 52 This singular structure..so unlike anything usually found on the line of the legionary iters. **1873** BURTON *Hist. Scot.* I. i. 14 In the route of the ninth iter.

3. *Anat.* A way or passage; *spec.* the tubular cavity leading from the third to the fourth ventricle of the brain.

1897 *Allbutt's Syst. Med.* III. 206 The lateral ventricles and the iter have been found dilated without any obvious mechanical cause.

†**'iter**, *v. Obs. rare.* [a. F. *itérer* (1488 in Godef.), ad. L. *iterā-re* to ITERATE.] *trans.* To iterate, repeat, renew. Hence †**'itering** *vbl. sb.*

1530 PALSGR. 145 Some betoken ittering or renewing of a dede. *Ibid.* 594/2, I iter, or renewe, or do a thyng agayne, or do a thyng ofte tymes, *je itere.*

†**iterable** ('ɪtərəb(ə)l), *a. Obs. rare.* [ad. late L. *iterābil-is* (Tert.), f. *iterā-re* to ITERATE: see -ABLE.] Capable of being iterated or repeated.

1561 T. NORTON *Calvin's Inst.* IV. i. (1634) 510 *marg.*, That repentance is no more iterable than baptisme. **1590** SWINBURNE *Testaments* 51 When licence is graunted to anie to doe an iterable acte, otherwise against lawe, it ought to be restrained to the first acte onely. *a* **1682** SIR T. BROWNE *Tracts* (1684) 178 They had made their Acts iterable by sober hands.

'iteral, *a. Anat.* [irreg. f. ITER *sb.* + -AL[1].] Pertaining to the iter of the brain.

iterance ('ɪtərəns). [f. ITERANT: see -ANCE.] Repetition, iteration.

1604 SHAKS. *Oth.* v. ii. 150 *Æmil.* My Husband? *Oth.* What needs this itterance, Woman? I say, thy Husband. **1850** MRS. BROWNING *Sonnets from the Portuguese* xxi, Say thou dost love me, love me, love me; toll The silver iterance. **1876** DOWDEN *Poems* 80 What voice is this the sea sends forth, Disconsolate iterance, a passionless moan? **1883** D. C. MURRAY *Hearts* III. xxvi. 40 The persistent iterance of this phrase alarmed the surgeon.

iterancy ('ɪtərənsɪ). [f. next: cf. prec., and see -ANCY.] The quality of being iterant; iterance.

1889 F. PIGOT *Strangest Journey my Life* 131 'But he comes home', I repeated, with the iterancy of despair. **1896** in *Daily News* 25 July 8/1 We had been told with a wearying iterancy that we would never return alive.

iterant ('ɪtərənt), *a.* [ad. L. *iterānt-em*, pr. pple. of *iterā-re* to ITERATE.] That iterates or repeats; repeating, echoing.

1626 BACON *Sylva* §241 A Reflexion Iterant, which we call Eccho. *Ibid.* §243 There is no difference betweene the Concurrent Eccho, and the Iterant, but the Quicknesse or Slownesse of the Returne. **1708** *Brit. Apollo* No. 9. 1/1. **1863** HOWELLS *Louis Lebeau's Convers.*, A flight of clamorous killdees Rose from their timorous sleep with piercing and iterant challenge. **1868** GEO. ELIOT *Sp. Gipsy* 289 The iterant voice Of heartless Echo, whom no pain can move To say aught else than we have said to her.

†**'iterate**, *ppl. a. Obs.* Forms: 5 iterat, 6–7 iterate. [ad. L. *iterāt-us*, pa. pple. of *iterāre*: see next.] = ITERATED.

a. as *adj.*

1471 RIPLEY *Comp. Alch.* XI. iv. in Ashm. (1652) 182 Hyt Multyplyeth by Iterat Fermentacion. **1657** W. MORICE *Coena quasi Κοινὴ* Def. xxxii. 298 When our faith is otherwise well enough known, there needs no iterate confession.

b. as *pa. pple.*: see ITERATE *v.*

1532 MORE *Confut. Tindale* Wks. 351/2 Hys open proclamacions diuers times iterate and renewed. **1558** BP. WATSON *Sev. Sacram.* II. 12 The baptisme is good and may not be iterate and geuen agayne. *a* **1626** BP. ANDREWES *Serm.* (1856) I. 374 These and these sins I have committed, so many so heinous, so oft iterate.

Hence †**'iterately** *adv.*, repeatedly.

1658 SIR T. BROWNE *Hydriot.* iii. 40 The cemeterial cells ..were filled with draughts of Scripture stories..iterately affecting the pourtraits of Enoch, Lazarus, Jonas, and the vision of Ezechiel.

iterate ('ɪtəreɪt), *v.* Also 6 **yterate**, 7 **iterat, itterate.** [f. L. *iterāt-*, ppl. stem of *iterā-re* to do again, repeat, rehearse, f. *iterum* again. Preceded in use by ITERATE *ppl. a.*; see prec.]

1. *trans.* To do (something) over again; to perform (an action) a second time, or reproduce (an effect); to repeat; to renew. Now *rare.*

1533 COVERDALE *Treat. Lord's Supper* Wks. (Parker Soc.) I. 448 Neither do they think that it ought to be so often iterated and repeated, after that we have once received Christ. **1594** WEST *2nd Pt. Symbol.* §175 Amongst heretikes are numbered Anabaptists, which wickedly yterate holy baptisme. **1650** ASHMOLE *Chym. Collect.* 78 The dregs being cast away, iterate the Sublimation of the most white Dust by it self. **1682** tr. *Boyle's 2nd Contn. Exp. Phys.-mech.* VII. iv, Having wiped and cleansed away the soot, I iterated the experiment. *a* **1734** NORTH *Lives* (1826) III. 341 He found that by often iterating, his thoughts lost of their force. **1862** HOOK *Lives Abps.* II. 642 That cannot be said to be iterated, which is not known to have been done before.

2. To say, mention, or assert again or repeatedly; to repeat.

1533 TINDALE *Supper of Lord* Wks. (Parker Soc.) III. 245, I am here compelled to inculk and iterate it with so many words. **1597** HOOKER *Eccl. Pol.* v. xxxvii. §2 This is the very cause why we iterate the Psalms oftener then any other part of Scripture. **1611** BIBLE *Ecclus.* xli. 23 Iterating and speaking againe that which thou hast heard. **1661** MORGAN *Sph. Gentry* II. i. 5 You must not itterate or name one Colour twice in the blazon of one Coat. **1858** *Sat. Rev.* 20 Nov. 500/2 Scientific research iterates and reiterates one moral.. the greatness of little things. **1863** COWDEN CLARKE *Shaks. Char.* v. 134 She iterates..to all the charges crowding in against him, 'My husband!'

†**3.** To make double or twofold; to duplicate. *Obs. rare.*

1660 J. LLOYD *Prim. Episc.* 70 Our Saviour iterated their ordinary into the pastoral extraordinary and ordinary offices.

4. *intr. Math.* To employ iteration; to make repeated use of a formula by substituting in it each time the result of the previous application.

1953 A. S. HOUSEHOLDER *Princ. Numerical Analysis* ii. 45 Since the 'approximation' x_0 with which one may start an iteration does not necessarily need to be close, it is sometimes advantageous to..start with an arbitrary x_0, perhaps $x_0 = 0$, and iterate until the approach is sufficiently close. **1957** L. FOX *Numerical Solution Two-Point Boundary Probl.* iv. 81 As an example..of an uncommon but convenient iterative procedure consider the solution of the differential equation $y'' - (1/x^4 - 2/x^3)y + 1/x^2 = 0$... We iterate according to the scheme $y_{n+1} = x^2(1 + x^2y_n'')/(1 - 2x)$, with $y_0 = 0$.

Hence **'iterating** *vbl. sb.*

c **1590** MARLOWE *Faust.* v. 157 The iterating of these lines brings gold. *a* **1626** BACON *Max. & Uses Com. Law* xxi. (1636) 74 The doubling or iterating of that and no more.. is reputed nugation. **1644** DIGBY *Mans Soul* (1645) 127 The iterating of those acts, which brought it from ignorance to knowledge.

iterate ('ɪtərət), *sb. Math.* [f. the vb., or ad. L. *iterāt-us*, pa. pple. of *iterāre* (see ITERATE *v.*): see -ATE[1].] A quantity arrived at by iteration.

1941 R. J. SCHMIDT in *Phil. Mag.* XXXII. 370 Denote the *n*th approximation to the value of any unknown *x*, by $x_r^{(n)}$. To solve these [simultaneous] equations by the method of successive approximations, we assume approximations $x_2^{(0)}$, $x_3^{(0)}, \ldots x_m^{(0)}$ to the unknowns $x_2, x_3, \ldots x_m$. Making use of these values we then use the first equation to find $x_1^{(1)}$, the first approximation to x_1. As the approximations will not always converge to the value of the unknowns, we shall, in future, call the numbers $x_r^{(r)}$ iterates. **1956** F. B. HILDEBRAND *Introd. Numerical Analysis* x. 449 The error ϵ_k in the *k*th iterate will be approximately the *square* of that in the preceding iterate, and will be of opposite sign. **1968** FOX & MAYERS *Computing Methods for Scientists & Engineers* i. 10 In the days of machine saturation it is tempting to take 25 iterates even though 250 are really necessary. **1968** N. BOURBAKI *Theory of Sets* iii. 186 The mapping f^n is called the *n*th iterate of the mapping *f*.

iterated ('ɪtəreɪtɪd), *ppl. a.* [f. ITERATE *v.* + -ED[1].] Done or said again; repeated; renewed.

1605 TIMME *Quersit.* II. v. 125–6 Which itterated circulations and distillations can also passe by the necke of the allembic. **1703** ROWE *Ulyss.* II. i. 683 To me it brings more Pain and iterated Woes. **1823** DE QUINCEY *Language* Wks. 1862 VIII. 83 The Greeks used the iterated syllables *barbar* to denote that a man was unintelligible in his talk. **1846** MASKELL *Mon. Rit.* I. p. ccxv, The after-taking of Holy Orders..in case of iterated confirmation, was not permitted, without a dispensation.

iteration (ɪtə'reɪʃən). Also 6 yt-, itt-. [ad. L. *iterātiōn-em*, n. of action from *iterāre* to ITERATE. Cf. F. *itération* (1488 in Godef.).] The action of iterating or repeating, or process of being iterated.

1. a. Repetition of an action or process (now usually implying frequency or long continuance); repeated performance; an

instance of this. Formerly said esp. of readministering a sacrament.

1477 NORTON *Ord. Alch.* vi. in Ashm. (1652) 100 The multitude of their Iteration. **1550** BALE *Apol.* 18 Than grewe it into a name and use amonge that sort (as amonge the sectes of owr tyme the iteracyon of baptysme). **1694** SALMON *Bate's Dispens.* (1713) 431/2 For three or four Iterations, the *Regulus* becomes apparently more bright and pure. **1790** PALEY *Horæ Paul.* (1825) 159 The rules of good writing taught the ear to be offended with the iteration of the same sound. **1845** S. AUSTIN *Ranke's Hist. Ref.* I. 3 The lifeless iteration of misunderstood doctrines and rites, which kill the soul. **1872** MINTO *Eng. Prose Lit.* Introd. 30 A person of strong tender feeling is not easily offended by the iteration of pathetic images.

b. *Math.* The repetition of an operation upon its product, as in finding the cube of a cube; *esp.* the repeated application of a formula devised to provide a closer approximation to the solution of a given equation when an approximate solution is substituted in the formula, so that a series of successively closer approximations may be obtained; a single application of such a formula; also, the formula itself.

1901 in N. E. D. **1924** WHITTAKER & ROBINSON *Calculus of Observations* vi. 79 In 1674 a method depending on a new principle, the principle of iteration, was communicated in a letter from Gregory to Collins. **1941** *Phil. Mag.* XXXII. 374 After a few iterations the values of e_r much less than unity will hardly affect the results. **1960** G. N. LANCE *Numerical Methods for High Speed Computers* i. 8 Whichever criterion is used to determine the end of the iteration, it is clear that the orders to evaluate $f(x_r)$ and $f(x_{r+1})$ are identical except that x_{r+1} is used instead of x_r. This kind of modification is made extremely simple on high-speed computers. **1968** E. T. COPSON *Metric Spaces* viii. 115 The Newton-Raphson iteration $x_{n+1} = x_n - f(x_n)/f'(x_n)$ for solving the equation $f(x) = 0$.

c. *Roman Law.* (See quot.)

1880 MUIRHEAD *Ulpian* iii. §4 By iteration he becomes a Roman citizen who, having been made a latin after he had passed the age of thirty, is anew formally manumitted by the person who had the quiritarian right in him when a slave.

2. The repetition of something said; repeated utterance or assertion.

1530 PALSGR. 333 After yteracyons of the pronowne they use ever *moij*. **1556** J. HEYWOOD *Spider & F.* Concl. 50 Tedius Iteration therof I let passe. **1634** HEYWOOD & BROME *Witches Lanc.* IV. H.'s Wks. 1874 IV. 228, I will not aggravate thy griefe too much, By needles iteration. **1759** JOHNSON *Idler* No. 77 ¶2 Any curious iteration of the same word. **1886** *Manch. Exam.* 29 Jan. 5/2 The House was told with suspicious iteration that the Government had nailed their colours to the mast.

iterative (ˈɪtərətɪv), *a.* and *sb.* Also 5 **yteratyve.** [a. F. *itératif, -ive* (1403 in Godef. *Compl.*), ad. late L. *iterātīv-us* (only as sb. *iterātīvum*, sc. *verbum*), f. ppl. stem of *iterāre* to ITERATE: see -IVE.]

A. *adj.* **1. a.** Characterized by repeating or being repeated.

1490 CAXTON *Eneydos* viii. 35 In payenge the extreme tribute of remembraunce yteratyue..[she] toke the swerde in hir honde, and mounted vp alle on hie vpon the woode. **1624** *Brief Inform. Aff. Palatinate* 18 The Estates redoubled their most humble instances, by their often and iteratiue Letters. **1807** W. TAYLOR in *Ann. Rev.* V. 232 The voice of gratitude is not..still and small, but iterative and sonorous. **1863** COWDEN CLARKE *Shaks. Char.* viii. 204 Shallow is iterative; he repeats and repeats. **1889** J. M. ROBERTSON *Essays towards Crit. Method* 119 One of Mr. Swinburne's iterative disquisitions. **1899** *Speaker* 30 Dec. 339/2 His manner hesitating, iterative, involved.

b. *iterative function* (*Math.*), a function resulting from successive operations with the same operator.

c. *Math.* Of the nature of or employing iteration.

1924 WHITTAKER & ROBINSON *Calculus of Observations* vi. 81 A pleasing characteristic of iterative processes may be observed..that a mistake in the performance of the numerical work does not invalidate the whole calculation. **1943** *Phil. Mag.* XXXIV. 409 Iterative methods have found favour with computers, despite an outward semblance of clumsiness which masks their solid advantages from the casual critic. **1949** *Proc. Cambr. Philos. Soc.* XLV. 230 Iterative methods seem very suitable, in principle, for application in large automatic calculating machines. **1953** A. S. HOUSEHOLDER *Princ. Numerical Analysis* ii. 44 Generally speaking, an iterative method for solving an equation or set of equations is a rule for operating upon an approximate solution x_p in order to obtain an improved solution x_{p+1}, and such that the sequence $\{x_q\}$ so defined has the solution x as its limit. **1968** E. T. COPSON *Metric Spaces* viii. 115 The iterative process $x_{n+1} = f(x_n)$ leads to a solution of the equation $x = f(x)$ when the mapping of the real line into itself is a contraction mapping.

2. *Gram.* Denoting repetition of action; frequentative. Applied to one of the aspects of the verb in Slavonic.

1827 J. HEARD *Gram. Russ. Lang.* v. §1. 142 The iterative [aspect of the verb] marks the frequent repetition of the action; as [*strelivat'*], to fire away, or to fire repeatedly. **1889** MORFILL *Gram. Russian* 36 Many verbs have no iterative aspect, and when a verb already ends in [*-ivat'*] or [*-ȳvat'*], it cannot take one.

B. *sb. Philol.* **a.** An iterative verb or aspect. **b.** A word expressing repetition of an action, sound, etc.

1853, 1884 [see ASPECT *sb.* 9b]. **1934** PRIEBSCH & COLLINSON *German Lang.* I. i. 13 Formation of distributive numerals in Latin by adding *-no* to the iteratives. *Ibid.* II. iii. 225 Verbs in *-ern.* Some are..iteratives..e.g. *flattern.* **1961** F. G. CASSIDY *Jamaica Talk* iv. 69 In Standard English one finds three kinds of iteratives: the simple ones like *hush-hush* ..; those with vowel gradation like *ding-dong*..; and the rhyming ones like *handy-dandy.*

Hence **ˈiteratively** *adv.*, in an iterative manner, with iteration; **ˈiterativeness.**

1844 *Fraser's Mag.* XXX. 716/1 The complaints..are iteratively urged. **1868** E. EDWARDS *Ralegh* I. vi. 104 The enormous proportion..of Irish matters, and their.. characteristic iterativeness. *Ibid.* xx. 444 How conspicuously and iteratively the offer of money from Spain figured in the trials.

i-teyed, ME. pa. t. of TIE *v.*

i'th' (ɪð). A contraction of *i'the, in the*: see IN *prep.* Formerly variously written *ith', i'th, ith, yth*, etc. Now only *dial.* or *arch.* in verse.

a **1500** *Chevy Chase* 50 Yth bowndes of Tividale. **1610** SHAKS. [see IN *prep.* etym.] i'th, ith', i'th'. **1677** PLOT *Oxfordsh.* 150 Not altering in the Autumn from what they were ith' Spring. **1711** E. WARD *Vulgus Brit.* XII. 142 Has left it still i'th' Bakers Pow'r, To Cheat their Customers much more. **1790** MRS. WHEELER *Westmld. Dial.* Pref. (1821) 8 Ith time of Oliver Crumel.

†**ithand,** *a. Sc.* and *north. dial. Obs.* Forms: 4 **iþen, iþin,** 4–5 **ithen, ythan, -en,** (6 **ithan**), 4–7 **ithand, ythand.** [ad. ON. *iðinn* assiduous, diligent. Cf. EIDENT and IDENT.]

1. Assiduous, diligent, busy.

a **1300** *Cursor M.* 25994 Þis reuth agh [hal] and i-þen [*Fairf.* iþin] be Wit will to scrife and mend ai þe. **1375** BARBOUR *Bruce* III. 285 Men may se be his ythen [*Hart's ed.* ithand] will. *c* **1375** *Sc. Leg. Saints, Ninian* 240 Deuote als in oracione, & ful ithand in lessone. *a* **1510** DOUGLAS *K. Hart* I. 33 Thir war the inwarde ythand seruitouris. **1570** *Satir. Poems Reform.* xix. 90 With Ithand trystis contractand vp new bandis To bring ȝow to schame and confusioun.

2. Constant, uninterrupted, continual.

a **1300** *Cursor M.* 23287 For þai her war won to li In þair stincand licheri..Þai sal haf iþen stinc i-wiss. *c* **1425** WYNTOUN *Cron.* I. xiii. 73 Wytht-in þat Yle is ythand nycht. *c* **1475** *Rauf Coilȝear* 27 Ithand wedderis of the eist draif on sa fast. **1536** BELLENDEN *Cron. Scot., Descr. Alb.* v. (1543) B iij b, Thay can nocht desist, but inuadis the cuntre..with Ithand heirshippis.

†**ithandly,** *adv. Sc.* and *north. dial. Obs.* Forms: see prec.; also 6 **ithinglie.** [f. prec. + -LY².] Assiduously, diligently; constantly, continually.

a **1300** *Cursor M.* 19664 (Edin.) Liggande lai his heuid dune ai iþinlic in orisune. *Ibid.* 12684 (Cott.) Sua haunted he on knes to lij, And for to prai sua Iþenli. **1375** BARBOUR *Bruce* II. 57 He..Duelt in his chambyr ythanly [*Hart's ed.* ithandly]. *c* **1570** *Satir. Poems Reform.* xx. 118 Tratours kene That Ithandly hes streuin For to deface the Nobill race Of Stewarts. *a* **1586** in Pinkerton *Anc. Scot. Poems* (1786) 246 Trimbling teires, distilling ithinglie Out from hir eis.

†**i-ˈthank.** *Obs.* Forms: 1 **ȝeþanc, -þonc,** 2 **ȝeþanc, i-þanc, -þonc.** [OE. *ȝeþanc, -þonc,* (= OHG. *gi-, gedanc, -danch,* MHG. *gedank*) f. *ȝe-,* I-¹ + *þanc, þonc*: see THANK *sb.*] Thinking, thought.

c **1000** *Ags. Gosp.* Luke ix. 46 Soðlice þæt ȝeþanc eode on hiȝ hwylc hyra yldest wære. *a* **1175** *Cott. Hom.* 243 In þes flesces iscole [fihteð aȝen us] euel ȝeþanc and fule lustes. *c* **1175** *Lamb. Hom.* 201 Þe ȝitsere þe biset his iþonc on his ehte he bið þes deofles bern. *a* **1200** *Moral Ode* 108 (Egerton MS.) His aȝe werc & his iþanc to witnesce he scal temen.

Hence †**i-ˈthanked** *a.*, -thoughted, -minded.

a **1225** *Ancr. R.* 210 Alle þeo luðere iðoncked. *Ibid.* 222 Oðre þe he ne mei nones weis makien vuele iðoncked.

i-thanked, ME. pa. pple. of THANK.

†**i-thave,** *v. Obs.* Forms: 1 **ȝeþafian,** 2–3 **iþauie(n,** 3 **i-theuen.** [f. *ȝe-,* I-¹ + *þafian*: see THAVE.] *trans.* To permit, allow. (In OE. also *absol.* or *intr.*)

c **900** tr. *Bæda's Hist.* III. xvii. [xxiii.] (1890) 232 He him þa lustlice ȝeþafode &..ȝetimbrede þær mynster. *c* **900** *Laws of Ælfred* c. 6 ȝif he þa hand lesan wille, and him mon þæt ȝeþafian wille, ȝelde swa to his were belimpe. *c* **1175** *Lamb. Hom.* 115 He scal..his of[s]pringe ne iþauie þet hi beon unrihtwise. *c* **1205** LAY. 15279 Hengest hine gon werien & nalde hit noht iþeuen. *a* **1240** *Ureisun* 142 in *Cott. Hom.* 199 ȝif þu wult hit iðauien iwis he wule ðurchut fawe.

ithe, variant of YTHE *Obs.*, a wave.

†**i-thee,** *v. Obs.* Forms: 1 **ȝeþeon,** 3–4 **i-þeo(n,** 3–4 **i-þe,** 4 **i-þy, yþe,** 5–6 **i-the.** *Pa. t.* 1 **ȝeþeah,** 3 **i-þæh, -þaih, -þei, -þeh;** *pl.* **i-þoȝen.** [OE. *ȝeþéon* (*ȝeþéah, ȝeþuȝon, ȝeþoȝen*) = OS. *githîhan,* OHG. *gadihan* (MHG. *gedihen,* mod.G. *gedeihen*), Goth. *gaþeihan*: see I-¹ and THEE *v.*] *intr.* To thrive, prosper.

971 *Blickl. Hom.* 211 His fæder..ȝeðeah þæt he wæs cininges þeȝna aldorman. *c* **1000** ÆLFRIC *Hom.* I. 130 Fela riccra manna ȝeðeoð Gode. *c* **1205** LAY. 9116 Swa ich mote gode iþeon al þu hit sælt wel biteon. *Ibid.* 24272 þa burh seoððe no iþæh. *Ibid.* 30074 þa children wuxen and wel iðoȝen. **1297** R. GLOUC. (Rolls) 8817 ȝif he iseþ godes grace he ne ssal neuere iþe. *c* **1315** SHOREHAM 102 Senne maketh many fal, That he ne mote i-thy. *c* **1330** *Arth. & Merl.* 377 So ich euer mot ythe, So ne schul ye nought serue me. *c* **1470** in *Archæologia* XXIX. 325 He is riche þat shalle neuer i-the. *c* **1530** *Hickscorner* in Hazl. *Dodsley* I. 155, I trow I shall never i-the.

i-theinet, ME. pa. pple. of THEINE *v.*, to minister.

ithel (ˈɪθɛl). Also **athel, athleh, atl, ithil.** [Local Arab.] A tamarisk, *Tamarix aphylla*, bearing panicles of pink flowers and minute leaves, native to western Asia and north-east Africa.

1838 W. AINSWORTH *Res. Assyria* 125 The common tamarisk of the country, the Athleh or Atle of Sonnini, is the Tamarix orientalis of Forskahl. **1875** *Encycl. Brit.* II. 236/2 Of plants there is an endless variety [in Arabia]... The tamarisk or 'Talh', the southern larch or 'Ithel', the chestnut, the sycamore, and several other trees. **1881** A. BLUNT *Pilgrimage to Nejd* I. 84 The Ithel, a tree grown in every village of Central Arabia. *Ibid.* 85 The roof was of ithel beams. **1924** *Blackw. Mag.* Mar. 351/1 Mackintosh..was watching them from the shelter of a clump of *ithil* bushes. **1949** L. H. BAILEY *Man. Cultivated Plants* (rev. ed.) 678 *T*[*amarix*] *aphylla*... Athel Tamarisk. Shrub or small tree. .. Useful as a windbreak in desert regions. **1963** F. VON BREITENBACH *Indigenous Trees Ethiopia* (ed. 2) 150 *Tamarix aphylla*... Atl (Arabic)... Leaves reduced to a minute triangular tooth on a sheathing base.

†**i-thenche,** *v. Obs.* [OE. *ȝeþencan, -þencean* (= OS. *githenkean,* OHG. *gadenchan, gidenchen, githenken,* MHG., mod.G., and Du. *gedenken*): see I-¹ and THINK *v.*] *trans.* To think of; to consider; to remember.

c **897** K. ÆLFRED *Gregory's Past.* Pref. 3 Swæ feawa hiora wæron ðæt ic furðum anne anlepne ne mæȝ ȝeðencean besuðan Temese. *c* **1175** *Lamb. Hom.* 21 Wei þet he eure hit wule iþenche in his þonke. *a* **1200** *Moral Ode* 203 (Egerton MS.) Lutel iþenchð mani man hu muchel wes þe synne. *Ibid.* 329 in *Lamb. Hom.*, ȝif we were wise men þis we scolden iþenche. *a* **1250** *Owl & Night.* 723 Vor-thi me singth in holi chirche..That man i-thenche bi the songe Wider he shal.

ither, Sc. form of OTHER.

i-theuwed, i-thewed, ME. pa. pple. of THEW *v.*

i-þeve: see I-THAVE.

i-þoht(e, i-þouht, i-þouȝt, i-þoȝt, ME. pa. pple. of THINK *v.*

†**i-thole,** *v. Obs.* In 2–3 **i-þolien.** [OE. *ȝeþolian* = OS. *githolôn,* OHG. **gadolôn,* MHG. *gedoln,* Goth. *gaþulan*: see I-¹ and THOLE *v.*] *trans.* and *intr.* To bear, suffer, endure.

a **1000** *Andreas* 1492 (Gr.) He..feala wita ȝeþolode. *c* **1175** *Lamb. Hom.* 43 þa pinen of helle, we ham ne maȝen iþolien. *c* **1205** LAY. 491 Leouere heom his to libben bi þan woderoten..þan heo þine þeowedomes lengre iþolien. *a* **1225** *Ancr. R.* 122 Seint Lorens also iðolede þet te gredil hef him upwardes mid berninde gleden. *Ibid.* 230 Ure Louerd, hwon he iðoleð þet we beoð itented, he plaieð mid us.

i-tholed, ME. pa. pple. of THOLE *v.*

ithomiid, ithomiine, *sb.* and *a.* (ɪˈθəʊmɪɪd, -iːn). [f. mod.L. family and subfamily names *Ithomiidæ, Ithomiinæ*, f. the generic name *Ithomia* (J. Hübner *Verzeichniss bekannter Schmetterlinge* (1816) 9), f. Gk. ἰθύς straight + ὦμος shoulder.] A tropical Central or South American butterfly belonging to the family Ithomiidæ, or this group treated as the subfamily Ithomiinæ of the family Nymphalidæ; of or pertaining to an insect of this kind.

1899 D. SHARP in *Cambr. Nat. Hist.* VI. vi. 346 The Ithomiides are peculiar to tropical America. **1912** G. B. LONGSTAFF *Butterfly-Hunting* vi. 312 The hour was earlier and the Ithomiines were not so closely packed. **1930** *Proc. Entomol. Soc. London* V. 91 An Ithomiine butterfly and its Heliconine mimic taken flying together in NW. Peru. **1972** BROWN & HEINEMAN *Jamaica & its Butterflies* 97 The number of ithomiids found in Central America is limited. *Ibid.* 99 *Greta* is among the most advanced in structure of all ithomiid genera.

i-thoncked: see I-THANKED *a.*

i-thorschen, ME. pa. pple. of THRESH *v.*

I-thou (ˈaɪðaʊ). [tr. G. *ich-du* (M. Buber (1923) *Ich und Du* 9), f. I *pers. pron., 1st sing. nom.* + THOU *pers. pron., 2nd sing. nom.*] Used *attrib.* of a personal relationship between man and God. Also *transf.*

1937 R. G. SMITH tr. *Buber's I and Thou* I. 3 The primary words are not isolated words, but combined words. The one primary word is the combination *I-Thou*. The other primary word is the combination *I-It*. *Ibid.*, If *Thou* is said, the *I* of the combination *I-Thou* is said along with it. **1958** *Church Times* 14 Feb. 10/3 Am I really prepared to obey God, in the utter loneliness of the 'I-Thou' relationship, even if it means the actual hatred of other people? **1961** *English Studies* Oct. 323 But Dr Esch also stresses the differences: while the other of the love-poetry is an equal partner, his God is *totaliter aliter*, which makes for a completely different I-Thou relation. **1967** C. DAVIS *Question of Conscience* 223 We may first take the I-Thou relationship of deep personal commitment. **1967** *Guardian* 19 May 9/1 When any chorus stands up to sing..it is so much more an I-Thou affair than opera.

i-thowen, i-þoȝen, ME. pa. pple. of THEE *v.* to thrive.

†**i-thrast**, *v. Obs.* [OE. *ʒeþrǽstan*, f. *ʒe-*, I-¹ + *þrǽstan* to twist, press, force, THRAST.] *trans.* To press, force.
c **900** tr. *Bæda's Hist.* III. i[i.] (1890) 156 Gefeoll he..on his earm ufan, and þone swyðe ʒeðræste and ʒebræc. *c* **1205** LAY. 28581 Mon mihte i þare lasten twa glouen iþraste.

i-thrat, ME. pa. pple. of THREAT *v.*

i-thrawe(n, i-throwe(n, i-throw, ME. pa. pple. of THROW *v.*

i-thretned, ME. pa. pple. of THREATEN *v.*

i-throsschen, ME. pa. pple. of THRESH *v.*

i-þrulled, ME. pa. pple. of THRILL *v.*

i-thrunge(n, ME. pa. pple. of THRING *v.*

i-thud, ME. pa. pple. of THUD *v.*

i-thungen, ME. pa. pple. of THEE *v.*

i-thurled, ME. pa. pple. of THIRL *v.*

†**ithy'phallian**, *a. Obs.* [f. L. *ithyphall-us*, a. Gr. *ἰθύφαλλ-ος* (see next) + -IAN.] = next, A.
a **1693** URQUHART *Rabelais* III. xxvii. 225 The sacred Ithyphallian Champion.

ithyphallic (ɪθɪ'fælɪk), *a.* and *sb.* Also 7 -ique. [ad. L. *ithyphallic-us*, ad. Gr. *ἰθυφαλλικός*, f. *ἰθύφαλλος* the phallus carried in procession at the festivals of Bacchus, f. *ἰθύς* straight + *φαλλός* PHALLUS; in neut. as sb., *ithyphallicum* sc. *carmen*, a poem in the measure of the hymns to Priapus.]

A. *adj.* **a.** Pertaining to or associated with the phallus carried in procession at the Bacchic festivals; *spec.* composed in the metre of the Bacchic hymns (the trochaic dimeter brachycatalectic).

By ancient writers applied also to several other metres, e.g. the Phalæcian, ending with three trochees; Selden applies it to the *Versus Priapeius.*
1795 S. PARR in E. H. Barker *Parriana* (1829) II. 595 Ithyphallic verse. **1818** R. P. KNIGHT *Symbolic Lang.* (1876) 98 Ithyphallic ceremonies. **1830** tr. *Aristophanes, Wasps* 122 *note*, The metre..is an asynartete of Iamb. and Troch. Dim. Brach., or Ithyphallic. **1854** BADHAM *Halieut.* 510 The Athenians received Demetrius..went out to meet him with ithyphallic hymns. **1898** *Edin. Rev.* July 62 Allying themselves with music in the dithyramb and with the ithyphallic procession.

b. Grossly indecent, obscene.
a **1864** *Chr. Examiner* (Webster), An ithyphallic audacity that insults what is most sacred and decent among men.

B. *sb.* A poem in ithyphallic metre; also, a poem of licentious or indecent character.
1614 SELDEN *Titles Hon.* 117 Wanton Catullus, comparing a heauie fellow..to a log, hath this Ithyphallique: *Talis iste meus Stupor nil videt, nihil audit.* **1778** APTHORPE *Preval. Chr.* 383 The pæon was peculiar to Apollo, the ithyphallic to Bacchus. **1822** BYRON *Vis. Judg.* Pref., I omit noticing some..Ithyphallics. *a* **1876** M. COLLINS *Pen Sketches* (1879) II. 130 Talk of ithyphallics! Byron might well blush at the *noyades* and lepers of this later time.

So **ithy'phallus**, an erect phallus.
1889 in *Cent. Dict.* **1967** *Listener* 28 Sept. 401/2 The fathers..exhibit their ithyphalluses. **1968** *Punch* 27 Mar. 469/3 The spike (Laius's sword) Jocasta steadily presses through her womb is replaced by a golden ithyphallus ten foot tall.

Iti ('aɪtaɪ), *sb.* and *a.* Also **Itie, Ity.** [Dim. of ITALIAN *a.* and *sb.*] Used with disparaging overtones: **A.** *sb.* An Italian. **B.** *adj.* Italian. Cf. EYETIE *sb.* and *a.*
1941 R. MOORE in Michie & Graebner *Lights of Freedom* x. 130 Ity planes were circling overhead. *Ibid.* 131 How surprised the Ities would be to see us. **1942** *E. Afr. Ann.* *1941–2* 109/1 The Itis ran away with it all, fancy even taking the macaroni, poor devils. **1944** A. JACOB *Traveller's War* xiv. 246 We thought you were Iti. *Ibid.* xviii. 278 The petulant Itie or the solid Boche. **1947** [see BRUSH *sb.*⁵]. **1959** G. JENKINS *Twist of Sand* iv. 68 Those Itie destroyers will have to come mighty close. **1965** *Economist* 4 Dec. 1100/3 With all these Ities and squareheads and Greeks around, it might be worth remembering. **1973** *Times* 1 Jan. 14/4 I'm going to be a German, an Iti, a Dutchman.

†**i-tide**, *v. Obs.* [OE. *ʒetídan*, f. *ʒe-*, I-¹ + *tídan* to TIDE.] *intr.* To happen, befall, betide.
c **888** K. ÆLFRED *Boeth.* xvi. §2 Ða ʒetydde [*v.r.* ʒeberede] hit ðæt Erculus Iobes sunu com to him. *Ibid.* xxxiii. §3 þonne ʒetideð oft..þæt he nætð nauðer ne þone anwald ne eac þæt he wið sealde. *c* **1175** *Lamb. Hom.* 21 ʒif itit itit þet þu brekest godes heste unþonkes. *a* **1200** MORAL ODE 125 He mei him sare adreden þet he ne muʒe þenne biden are for þet itit ilome. *c* **1205** LAY. 27898 For eoðer weis hit eode al oðer hit itidde. *a* **1225** *Ancr. R.* 152 Vreineð hwat itidde of Ezechie, þe gode king. *Ibid.* 186 Boðe ham itit o dom. *a* **1250** *Owl & Night.* 1731 Hunke schal itide harm and schonde. *c* **1300** *Beket* 1814 To Engelond ich wole nou drawe, itide what bitide.

i-tiʒed, ME. pa. pple. of TIE *v.*

i-tiled, ME. pa. pple. of TILL *v.*

i-timbred, ME. pa. pple. of TIMBER *v.*

i-timed, ME. pa. pple. of TIME *v.*

itineracy (aɪ'tɪnərəsɪ, ɪt-). [f. ITINERATE *a.*: see -ACY 3.] = ITINERANCY in its various senses.
1827 LAMB *Sir J. Dunstan*, Returning in an evening, after his long day's itineracy, to his domicile. **1870** ANDERSON *Missions Amer. Bd.* I. iv. 89 The year 1833 was distinguished for itineracies. **1875** WARBURTON *Edw. III* 229 These poor priests, with..their friendly intercourse with the people in their perpetual itineracy.

†**i'tineral**, *a. Obs. rare*⁻¹. [f. L. *iter, itiner-* (see ITER) + -AL¹.] = ITINERANT *a.*
1627 SPEED *England* xxviii. §2 The Itinerall Iustice of the Forrest.
Hence †**i'tinerally** *adv.*, = ITINERANTLY.
1657–83 EVELYN *Hist. Relig.* (1850) II. 261 To preach and constitute Churches from place to place itinerally.

itinerancy (aɪ'tɪnərənsɪ, ɪt-). [f. next: see -ANCY.]
1. The state or condition of being itinerant; the action of itinerating or travelling about, esp. for a specific purpose, as preaching or public speaking; a journey from place to place.
1802–12 BENTHAM *Ration. Judic. Evid.* (1827) IV. 197 Has he a fixed abode, or is he in a state of itinerancy? **1825** E. TAYLOR *Minnesingers* 198 When we contemplate the great extent of this itinerancy, we need not be surprised that the poetry and romance of these countries were so widely diffused. **1838** *Blackw. Mag.* XLIV. 801 We recommend Lord Headfort to Mr. O'Connell as his attendant..on his next sacred itinerancy through Ireland. **1878** GLADSTONE *Prim. Homer* i. 9 We thus hear of the itinerancy of a stationary bard.

b. A body of itinerants.
1836 *Blackw. Mag.* XL. 458 The itinerancy of rebellion is even now haranguing throughout the land.

2. Itinerant preaching; *spec.* the system in practice in various Methodist churches, esp. the Wesleyan, according to which the regular ministers or 'itinerant preachers' are appointed not to a single congregation, but to a group of these called a 'circuit', to 'itinerate' among the congregations within its limits, and are periodically (usually every three or five years) removed to another circuit.
1789 WESLEY *Wks.* (1872) XIII. 278 If the trustees of houses are to displace Preachers, their itinerancy is at an end. **1791** HAMPSON *Mem. Wesley* III. 72 A distinguishing feature in this œconomy is itinerancy. **1811** SYD. SMITH *Wks.* (1867) I. 201 The interchange or itinerancy of preachers. **1892** *Daily News* 24 May 6/6 The Rev. Hugh Price Hughes moved the following resolution: That this Council adheres strongly to the principle of the Itinerancy, ..and has no wish to disturb the three years' system wherever it is working well.

b. Itinerant ministry; *spec.* ministry in the Methodist churches.
1809 *Minutes Wesleyan Confer.* III. Obit., He fell asleep in Jesus Jan. 16 1809 in the seventh year of his Itinerancy..and the thirty third of his age. **1827** *Ibid.* VI. 280 When any offer themselves for our Itinerancy. **1840** *Ibid.* IX. 7 Thomas Hutton entered upon our itinerancy in the year 1789..In the year 1827 he retired from the regular ministry. **1885** *Ibid.* 37 He was thirty years in the itinerancy.

itinerant (aɪ'tɪnərənt, ɪt-), *a.* and *sb.* [ad. late and med.L. *itinerānt-em*, pr. pple. of late L. *itinerā-rī*, med.L. *itinerā-re* to travel, ITINERATE.]
A. *adj.* Journeying; travelling from place to place: not fixed or stationary.
a. Said of the Justices in Eyre, the Justices of Assize and the Forest, their courts, etc.: Travelling on circuit.
[**1292** *Rolls Parlt.* 86/1 Vos, & ceteri Justic' Itinerantes ad communia placita. **1293** *Ibid.* 99/1 Tam Justiciarii de utroque Banco, quam Justiciarii itinerantes.] **1570–6** LAMBARDE *Peramb. Kent* (1826) 105 Justices in Eire (or Itinerant as wee called them). **1591** in *Child Marriages* 150 John Milner, Bailiff Itinerant of this Countie Palantine of Chester. *a* **1661** FULLER *Worthies* (1840) II. 431 Such itinerant judges as go Oxford Circuit. **1670** MILTON *Hist. Eng.* v. Wks. (1851) 232 In the Winter and Spring time he usually rode the Circuit as a Judge Itinerant. **1746–7** *Act 20 Geo. II*, c. 43 §29 To hold itinerant courts at such times and places..as they shall judge to be expedient. **1843** CARLYLE *Past & Pr.* II. xi, One of the new Itinerant Judges.

b. Journeying, travelling, or pertaining to travel in connexion with some employment or vocation; preaching in a circuit; of or pertaining to the regular Wesleyan ministry.
1661 COWLEY *Advancem. Exp. Philos., College* 29 That the four Professors Itinerant be assigned to the four parts of the World, Europe, Asia, Africa, and America, there to reside three years at least. **1673** [R. LEIGH] *Transp. Reh.* 102 Itinerant gospellers that travel up and down. **1710** PALMER *Proverbs* 231 Old shoes and hats, and a few other things that our itinerant merchants deal in. **1755** *Connoisseur* No. 86 ¶3, I confess myself highly obliged to the itinerant missionaries of Whitefield, Wesley, and Zinzendorf. **1792** BELKNAP *Hist. New Hampsh.* III. 325 It has been usual for the clergymen of the elder towns to make itinerant excursions, of several weeks, to preach and baptize. **1829** *Minutes Wesleyan Confer.* VI. 447 Mr. Wesley appointed him to a Circuit as an Itinerant Preacher: in which office he continued. **1840** *Ibid.* IX. 10 After having been usefully employed as a Class-Leader and Local Preacher for several years [he] was taken into the itinerant work at the Conference in 1803. **1834** MEDWIN *Angler in Wales* I. 14 Some hanks of gut lately bought from an itinerant Italian. **1889** JESSOPP *Coming of Friars* ii. 85 The Friars..acting the part of itinerant preachers.

c. *fig.*
1634 SIR T. HERBERT *Trav.* 2 If my thoughts have wandred, I must intreat the wel-bred Reader..to afforde mee his helpe to call home my Itenerant Notions. **1660** H. MORE *Myst. Godl.* VII. ix. 315 The insupportable Wickedness of the Christians..may make this Kingdome of Christ very itinerant and to pass from one Nation to another People. **1850** BLACKIE *Æschylus* I. Pref. 22 The word, transmitted from age to age, and itinerant from East to West, remains.

d. *transf.* Movable from place to place.
1690 LUTTRELL *Brief Rel.* (1857) II. 12 Sir Christopher Wren has compleated the itinerant house for his majestie to carry into Ireland. **1796** MORSE *Amer. Geog.* I. 647 It was equally clear to all parties that the government should not be itinerant.

B. *sb.* One who itinerates or travels from place to place, esp. in the pursuit of a trade or calling; a travelling preacher, strolling player, etc.
1641 J. JACKSON *True Evang. T.* II. 112 S. Luke..had also been a plain itinerant in Preaching the Gospel. **1678** BUTLER *Hud.* III. ii. 92 Glad to turn itinerant, To stroll and teach from town to town. **1753** A. MURPHY *Gray's-Inn Jrnl.* No. 43 ¶7 Search was made after this mercantile Itinerant. **1774** WARTON *Hist. Eng. Poetry* I. Diss. i. 34 They [Scandinavian Scalds] were itinerants by their institution and made voyages. **1822** J. FLINT *Lett. Amer.* 268 In the evening two itinerants, a presbyterian preacher and his wife, arrived with an introduction from an acquaintance. **1833** HT. MARTINEAU *Charmed Sea* iv. 59 They were Siberian merchants,—that is, itinerants.
Hence **i'tinerantly** *adv.*
1855 in HYDE CLARKE. **1856** in WEBSTER; and in mod. Dicts.

itine'rarian, *a.* and *sb. rare.* [f. late L. *itinerāri-us* (see ITINERARY) + -AN.] **A.** *adj.* = ITINERARY *a.* 1.
1800 *Asiat. Ann. Reg.* p. xxiv, A Polymetrical Table, Shewing the Itinerarian Distances, in British Miles, between some of the most remarkable Places of Hindustan.
B. *sb.* One who itinerates; a traveller; = ITINERARY *sb.* 4.
1822 *New Monthly Mag.* IV. 14 Chateaubriand, the epic itinerarian, found..traces of them in Peloponnesus.

i'tinerarily, *adv. rare.* Also 7 *Sc.* -arly. [f. ITINERARY + -LY².] In an itinerary way; in the course of itinerancy.
1670 LD. FOUNTAINHALL in M. P. Brown *Suppl. Decis.* (1826) II. 470 Though he was Bishop of the Isles, and died there, yet..when he went there it was only itinerarly.

‖**itine'rario.** *Obs. rare.* [Sp., It., ad. late L. *itinerārium*: see next.] = ITINERARY *sb.* 2, 3.
1588 PARKE tr. *Mendoza's Hist. China* 319 This my discourse may more properly be called an Epitome or Itinerario then a historie. *Ibid.* 387 Whom, as I haue said, I do follow in many things of this Itinerario.

‖**itinerarium** (ɪtɪnə'rɛərɪəm). [late L., = an account of roads or of a route, with notices of stations, distances, etc., sb. use of neuter of *itinerārius*: see ITINERARY *a.*]
1. = ITINERARY *sb.* 2, 3.
1747 CHESTERF. *Lett. to Son* 30 Oct., I am very well pleased with your *Itinerarium*, which you sent me from Ratisbon. **1812** J. JEBB *Corr.* (1834) II. 97 The journey.. might be made in two days. An itinerarium I annex. **1869** I. BURNS *Life W. C. Burns* ix. (1870) 213 We must reluctantly break off this remarkable and deeply interesting itinerarium.
2. *Surg.* 'An old name for the staff used in lithotomy' (*Syd. Soc. Lex.*).
1706 PHILLIPS, *Itinerarium*,..also a Surgeon's Instrument, which being fix'd in the Urinary Passage shews the Sphincter, or Neck of the Bladder, in order to the more sure making of an Incision to find out the Stone. **1855** MAYNE *Expos. Lex.*, *Itinerarium.*

itinerarly, *adv.*: see ITINERARILY.

itinerary (aɪ'tɪnərərɪ, ɪt-), *sb.* [ad. L. *itinerārium*, sb. use of neuter of *itinerāri-us*: see next. Cf. OF. *itineraire* a journey, an account of a journey or travel (14th c. in Godef.).]
1. A line or course of travel; a route.
1432–50 tr. *Higden* (Rolls) I. 43 Messangers were sende.. to presidentes, dukes, and iuges of prouinces, that thei scholde describe and measure londes, waters,..and the itinerary of the see [*itinerarium maritimum*] to whiche places thei scholde sayle. **1651** BIGGS *New Disp.* ¶196 It is a dangerous itinerary [*printed* itinery] to go from one extreame to another. **1790** J. BRUCE *Source Nile* II. 474 It was the first intelligible itinerary made through these deserts. **1889** HISSEY *Tour in Phaeton* 14 Rambling leisurely fashion..careless of performing any definite itinerary.
2. A record or journal of travel; an account of a journey.
1483 CAXTON *Gold. Leg.* 379 b/1 Hys lyf he hym self sette in his book named Itynerarye. **1526** *Pilgr. Perf.* (W. de W. 1531) 24 Many may rede the itineraryes of them that hath ben at Jerusalem. **1617** (*title*) An Itinerary written by Fynes Moryson..containing his ten yeeres travell throvgh.. Germany [etc.]. **1760** JOHNSON *Idler* No. 97 ¶5 Of those who crowd the world with their itineraries, some have no other purpose than to describe the face of the country. **1866** LIVINGSTONE *Last Jrnls.* (1873) I. Introd. 4 The itinerary grows day by day.
3. A book describing a route by land or sea, or tracing the course of the roads in a region or district, with measurements of distance, accounts of places and objects of interest, and other information for travellers; a road-book, guide-book.

(In the earliest quotations identical with preceding, being records of actual journeys.)
1538 LELAND *Itin.* III. 83, I have the description of Wareham in an other Itinerarie of myne. **1634-5** BRERETON *Trav.* (Chetham Soc.) 41 An anatomy school, wherein, besides the rarities mentioned in the Itinerary, are many more. **1711** WALLIS *Pref. J. Greenwood's Eng. Gram.* 3 Those that would be farther inform'd, I refer..to the Itinerary and Description of Wales. **1871** LADY HERBERT tr. *Hübner's Ramble* (1878) II. iv. 277 In the official itineraries it is from thence that all the distances are counted.

b. *transf.* A sketch of a proposed route; a plan or scheme of travel.
1856 KANE *Arct. Expl.* II. xxvi. 260 Our friends of Etah had given me..a complete itinerary of this region. **1859** WRAXALL tr. *R. Houdin* xix. 276, I drew up an itinerary in which the first station would be Cambridge.

4. One who itinerates, an itinerant. *rare.*
1709 STRYPE *Ann. Ref.* I. xiii. 178 Some were commissionated to preach therefore, who went about as itineraries. **1721** —— *Eccl. Mem.* II. II. vii. 297 It was thought fit the King should retain six chaplains in ordinary: who should not only wait upon him, but be itineraries, and preach the Gospel all the nation over. **1853** D. KING *Presb. Ch. Govt.* 226 He was, therefore, when requested, an itinerary.

†**5.** A portable altar. *Obs.*
1631 WEEVER *Anc. Fun. Mon.* 340 An itinerarie or portable Aulter.

6. *R. C. Ch.* A form of prayer for the use of clerics when setting out on a journey.
1885 *Catholic Dict.* (ed. 3) 463/2 Gavantus refers to an ancient Pontifical which contains an itinerary for prelates, rather longer than ours but very similar.

†**7.** *Surg.* = ITINERARIUM 2. *Obs.*
1689 HARVEY *Curing Dis. by Expect.* viii. 58 The rash and too frequent sounding by Catheter and Itinerary.

itinerary (aɪˈtɪnərərɪ, ɪt-), *a.* [ad. late L. *itinerārius* of or pertaining to a journey, f. L. *iter, itiner-* a journey, way, road: cf. F. *itinéraire* adj.]
1. Of or pertaining to a journey, travelling, or a route. **b.** Pertaining to roads (esp. Roman roads) or the description of roads.
itinerary column, a column at a crossway, having several faces, bearing inscriptions, showing the different routes.
1552 HULOET, Itenerary booke wherein is wrytten the dystaunce from place to place, or wherin thexpenses in iourney be written. **1632** LITHGOW *Trav.* I. 26, I revert to mine itinerary relation. **1796** MORSE *Amer. Geog.* I. 20 Such itinerary maps of the places of encampment were of great importance to armies. **1797** W. TAYLOR in *Monthly Rev.* XXIV. 514 Dissertations on the antient measures of length ..on various itinerary columns. **1862** MERIVALE *Rom. Emp.* (1865) IV. xxxiv. 134 The itinerary system of the Romans was..an effective instrument of centralization. **1871** C. DAVIES *Metr. Syst.* II. 29 The pace..is the natural unit for all itinerary distances.
2. = ITINERANT *a.*
1617 MORYSON *Itin.* II. 300 English Lawyers..vaunted Ireland to be reduced to ful obedience by their Itinerary circuits. **1711** STRYPE *Parker* IV. xii. 366 At last he was appointed one of the King's Itinerary Preachers. **1785** PALEY *Mor. Philos.* VI. viii. (1830) 409 The law of England, by its circuit, or itinerary courts, contains a provision for the distribution of private justice.

itinerate (aɪˈtɪnəreɪt, ɪt-), *v.* [f. late L. *itinerāt-*, ppl. stem of *itinerārī* to travel, f. *iter, itiner-* a journey, way, road.]
1. *intr.* To journey or travel from place to place.
1600-9 ROWLANDS *Knave of Clubs* 37 As on the way I Itinerated, A Rurall person I Obuiated. **1676** MARVELL *Mr. Smirke* 4 They itinerated like Excise-spyes from one house to another. **1843** *Blackw. Mag.* LIV. 635 There are three separate modes of itinerating through the island. **1875** JOWETT *Plato* (ed. 2) I. 83 He who fancies that he can write a tragedy does not go about itinerating in the neighbouring states.
b. To travel from place to place preaching; *spec.* of a Methodist minister, To preach to the various congregations within the circuit to which he is appointed, and to go periodically from circuit to circuit as appointed, (usually) every three years: cf. ITINERANCY 2.
1775 E. WHEELOCK in *Mem.* (1811) 328, I have sent Mr. Dean to itinerate as a missionary this spring, among their tribes. **1824** SOUTHEY *Bk. of Ch.* (1841) 47 The clergy resided with the Bishop, and itinerated through the diocese. **1831** *Fraser's Mag.* III. 64 Bunyan received a roving commission..to itinerate in the villages round about. **1878** LECKY *Eng. in 18th C.* (1883) II. 603 He preached in the open air, itinerated, denounced fairs and wakes.
2. *trans.* To journey through, traverse. *rare.*
1830 CROLY *Geo. IV*, 493 The home secretary itinerated the country. **1839** *Britannia* 25 May in *Spirit Metropol. Conserv. Press* (1840) I. 433 They itinerate the empire, inflaming the popular passions,..and deluding the popular weakness. **1863** G. F. TOWNSEND *Leominster* 257 It was.. the custom for..Collectors to itinerate the country, and to collect the sums resulting from these Briefs.
Hence **i'tinerating** *vbl. sb.*, travelling, itineration. **i'tinerating** *ppl. a.*, that journeys from place to place; itinerant.
1611 CORYAT *Crudities* To Rdr., Thy benevolent itinerating friend T. C. the Odcombian Legge-stretcher. **1770** BP. FORBES *Jrnls.* (1886) 289 One of the seasons of his itinerating into Lochaber. **1845** J. SAUNDERS *Cab. Pict. Eng. Life, Chaucer* 168 The appointment of itinerating judges, the justices in Eyre, as they were afterwards called. **1860** C. DURFEE *Hist. Williams Coll.* 359 Mr. Eaton..had now resolved to become an itinerating lecturer.

†**i'tinerate,** *ppl. a. Obs.* [ad. late L. *itinerāt-us*, pa. pple. of *itinerārī*: see prec.] = ITINERANT *a.*
a **1628** DODERIDGE *Eng. Lawyer* (1631) 33 As well the Judges itinerate through the counties, as those that were sedentarie in the King's High Courts of Justice. **1755** SHEBBEARE *Lydia* (1769) I. 275 Mr. Cook..suggested the change was made by that itinerate trader.

itineration (aɪtɪnəˈreɪʃən, ɪt-). [n. of action from ITINERATE *v.*] The action of itinerating or journeying from place to place; a preaching or lecturing tour.
1623 COCKERAM II, A Iourneying, *Itineration.* **1755** SHEBBEARE *Lydia* (1769) II. 132 The jew..proceeding in his itineration, strolled to the house of lord Beef. **1884** *Bible Soc. Rec.* Feb., The missionaries..are obliged in large degree to suspend their itinerations. **1896** YOUNGSON *Punjab Mission* xxxi. 281 Miss Plumb took charge of the outlying schools, with village itineration.

i-tint, ME. pa. pple. of TINE *v.*, to lose.

†**ition.** *Obs. rare.* [ad. L. *itiōn-em.*] The action of going.
1668 WILKINS *Real Char.* II. i. 43 The General name denoting Transcendental Motion or rest, is *ition. Ibid.* IV. ii. 409 The sixth Difference, which is *Ition*, or the passing of things from one place or state to another.

-ition, *suffix*, repr. F. *-ition*, L. *-itiōnem*, *-ītiōnem*, forming nouns of action from verbs with ppl. stem in *-it-* or *īt-*, as in *position* from *posit-us*, *audition* from *audīt-us*. It is really a case of the suffix -ION[1], q.v. Instances occur of its non-etymological employment, as in *acuition*, *acutition*.

-itious[1], compound suffix of adjs., f. L. *-ici-us* or *-īci-us* + -OUS. These L. endings, from the confusion of *c* and *t* in late and med.L. MSS., were formerly written *-itius*, whence the current Eng. spelling for the etymologically correct *-icious*. The L. adjs. were of two classes: **a.** those in *-icius* from nouns, as *ciner-icius* of the nature of ashes, *gentīl-icius* of the clansmen, *tribūn-icius* of a tribune; **b.** those in *-īcius* from pa. pples., as *advent-īcius* characterized by having come in from without, *adscript-īcius* of the class of the *adscripti*, *comment-īcius* of an invented sort, *conduct-īcius* of a hired sort, *fact-īcius* of a made sort, *fict-īcius* of a feigned sort, *supposit-īcius* of a substituted nature. These are anglicized with the suffix *-ous*, as in *ascript-itious*, *comment-itious*, *conduct-itious*, *fact-itious*, *fict-itious*, *supposit-itious*; and the formation is freely extended when required, as in *abstractitious*, *adscititious*, *excrementitious*, etc.

-itious[2], a combination of the suffix -OUS, repr. L. *-ōsus*, with derivatives containing *iti-*, or *īti-*, of various kinds, chiefly sbs. in *-itiōn-em*; e.g. *ambition*, *ambitious*, L *ambitiōsus*, *superstition*, *superstitious*, L. *superstitiōsus*; so *nutritious*, *seditious*, etc.: see -IOUS, -OUS.

itis (ˈaɪtɪs), *sb.* [The suffix -ITIS used as an independent word.] A bodily condition, affection, or disease that is or may be described or designated by a word ending in *-itis*.
[**1896** *Allbutt's Syst. Med.* I. 120 To regard every condition of generalised or localised fibroid change of the organs of the body as a chronic '-itis' is equally erroneous.] **1909** *Practitioner* Nov. 706 It must be remembered that the complaint referred to [*sc.* mucous colitis] is not, strictly speaking, an *itis* at all.

-itis, *suffix*, a. Gr. -ῖτις, properly forming the fem. of adjs. in -ίτης, but often used absolutely with a fem. sb. understood, as in ἀσφαλτῖτις (λίμνη) Lake Asphaltitis, the Dead Sea; already in Greek used to qualify νόσος disease, expressed or understood, e.g. ἀρθρῖτις (disease) of the joints, gout, *arthritis*, νεφρῖτις (disease) of the kidneys, *nephritis*, πλευρῖτις pleurisy, ῥαχῖτις spinal (disease), *rhachitis*. On the analogy of these, *-itis* has become in mod. medical L., and hence in Eng., the regular name for affections of particular parts, and *spec.* (though this is not etymological) of inflammatory disease or inflammation of a part. Examples are *appendicitis* (inflammation of the vermiform appendix of the cæcum), *bronchitis*, *gastritis*, *peritonitis*, *pneumonitis*, *tonsilitis*, etc. The Fr. form is in *-ite*. In irregular trivial use applied to a state of mind or tendency fancifully regarded as a disease.
1903 ASQUITH in *Westm. Gaz.* 19 Oct. 5/1 All the people were suffering from a new disease—the disease of fiscalitis. **1906** *Ibid.* 27 Apr. 4/2 Several members of Parliament are suffering from a slight attack of Suffragitis. **1912** *Q. Rev.* Oct. 504 Cricket has just suffered from so severe an attack of 'testitis' as to render it highly improbable [etc.]. **1944** F. CLUNE *Red Heart* 68 Those were the days when the nor'-west of New South Wales was agog with bushrangeritis. **1945** W. S. CHURCHILL *Victory* (1946) 186 It was impossible to go on in a state of 'electionitis' all through the summer and autumn. **1969** *Sunday Express* 28 Dec. 24/3 As the year wears on, politicians' electionitis will have more influence on events than central bankers' views.

itisket, itasket (ɪˈtɪskɪt, ɪˈtɑːskɪt). A vocal utterance in verses accompanying any of several children's games, esp. 'Drop the handkerchief'.
1926 D. LA SALLE *Play Activities Elem. Sch.* II. 71 Itisket, itasket, a green and yellow basket. I lost a letter to my love and on the way I found it... (Drop and pick up the handkerchief.) **1969** R. D. ABRAHAMS *Jump-Rope Rhymes* p. xviii, This game [*sc.* drop the handkerchief] is found with a number of accompanying chants, including 'Itisket, Itasket'.

i-tohȝen, i-toȝen(e, i-towe(n, ME. pa. pple. of *teon* to draw: see TEE *v.*

-itol (ɪtɒl), *suffix. Chem.* [f. -IT(E[1] 4 + -OL I.]. Used to form the names of polyhydric alcohols other than di- or trihydric alcohols.
Such compounds were formerly given names terminated by *-ite*, as in *dulcite*, *inosite*, *mannite*. These names were later modified by the addition of *-ol* to express their alcoholic nature, giving e.g. *dulcitol*, *inositol*, *mannitol*. Hence in mod. use *-itol* has become an independent suffix, as in *hexitol*.

i-told, ME. pa. pple. of TELL *v.*

i-tore(n, i-torn, ME. pa. pple. of TEAR *v.*

i-tormented, ME. pa. pple. of TORMENT *v.*

i-torned, ME. pa. pple. of TURN *v.*

†**i-tost,** archaic pa. pple. of TOSS *v.*
1600 FAIRFAX *Tasso* VIII. xlv, But thou who part hast of thy race to run, With haps and hazards of this world itost.

†**i-tothed,** ME. form of TOOTHED *a.*

i-tourned, ME. pa. pple. of TURN *v.*

-itous, compound suffix, containing the *-it-* of sbs. in -ITY, and the adj. ending -OUS; corresp. to Fr. *-iteux*, L. *-itōsus*, contracted for *-itātōsus*, as in *calamitōsus* for *calamitātōsus*, *calamitous*; so *felicitous*, *gratuitous*, *iniquitous*, *necessitous*.

i-traid, ME. pa. pple. of TRAY *v.*, to betray.

i-translated, ME. pa. pple. of TRANSLATE *v.*

i-travailled, ME. pa. pple. of TRAVAIL *v.*

i-trent, ME. pa. pple. of TREND *v.*

†**i-treowe,** *a. Obs.* [OE. *ȝetréowe*, *-triewe* (= OHG. *gitriuwi*, MHG. *getriuwe*, G. *getreu*), f. *ȝe-*, I-[1] + *triewe*, *treowe*, TRUE.] True, faithful.
c **1000** ÆLFRIC *Gen.* xlii. 33 Ic wylle fandian hwæðer ȝe ȝetreowe synd. *a* **1100** *O.E. Chron.* anno 1086 Eallra folca ȝetreowast. *a* **1100** *Ags. Voc.* in Wr.-Wülcker 312/28 *Fidelis*, ȝetreowe oððe ȝeleafful. *c* **1205** LAY. 4451 þe sæg wes itreouwe. *Ibid.* 7395 þeos [scipen] weoren al neowe Stronge & wel itreowe.

i-treted, ME. pa. pple. of TREAT *v.*

i-tricchet, ME. pa. pple. of *tri(c)chen*: see TRICK *v.*

i-tried, ME. pa. pple. of TRY *v.*

i-trised, ME. pa. pple. of TRICE *v.*

i-trode(n, ME. pa. pple. of TREAD *v.*

i-truked, ME. pa. pple. of TRUKE *v. Obs.*, to fail.

its (ɪts), *poss. pron.* [Formed in end of 16th c. from IT + *'s* of the possessive or genitive case, and at first commonly written *it's*, a spelling retained by some to the beginning of the 19th c.
The original genitive or possessive neuter was HIS, as in the masc., which continued in literary use till the 17th c. But with the gradual substitution of sex for grammatical gender in the concord of the pronouns, the indiscriminate use of *his* for male beings and for inferior animals and things without life began to be felt inappropriate, and already in the ME. period its neuter use was often avoided, substitutes being found in *thereof*, *of it*, *the*, and in N.W. dialect, the genitive use of *hit*, *it*, which became very common about 1600, and is still retained in Westmorland, Lancashire, S.W. Yorkshire, Cheshire, Lincolnshire, and adjacent counties. Finally, *it's* arose, apparently in the south of England (London, Oxford), and appears in books just before 1600. It had no doubt been colloquial for some time previous, and only gradually attained to literary recognition. *Its* was not admitted in the Bible of 1611 (which has *thereof*, besides the *his*, *her*, of old grammatical gender); the possessive *it* occurs once (Lev. xxv. 5), but was altered (in an edition of 1660) to *its*, which appears in all current editions. *Its* does not appear in any of the works of Shakspere published during his life-time (in which and the first folio the possessive *it* occurs 15 times), but there are 9 examples of *it's*, and 1 of *its*, in the plays first printed in the folio of 1623. In one of these at least (Hen. VIII, I. i. 18; see B. below), the word is prob. Shakspere's own (unless he wrote *his*). By this time *it's* had become common in literature, from which the possessive use of *it* soon disappeared; the neuter *his* is found as late as 1675 (see HIS *poss. pron.* 3 c); the use of *the* = *its* continued almost as late in literature, and is still dialectal, as is also the periphrastic *the..of it* (*o't*), as in Sc. 'the heid o't' = its head. As *its* arose after the *h* of *hit* had been dropped, the form *hits* is not found in literary use, but it is the emphatic form of *its* in Scotch, '*his* heid strak *hits* heid'.]

A. As *adj. possess. pron.* Of or belonging to it, or that thing (L. *ejus*); also *refl.*, Of or belonging to itself, its own (L. *suus*).

The reflexive is often more fully *its own*, for which in earlier times *the own*, *it own*, were used: see OWN.

1598 FLORIO, *Spontaneamente*, willingly,..of himselfe, of his free will, for its owne sake [**1611** of free will or of it's owne sake]. **1603** —— *Montaigne* A v, From translation all Science had it's of-spring. *Ibid.* Ep. Ded., My weaknesse you might bidde doe it's best. *Ibid.* 3. *Ibid.* 612 Nothing remooveth from it's owne place. **1605** SYLVESTER *Du Bartas* I. ii. 1191 And tempers with it's moist-full coldnes so Th' excessiue heate. **1620** SHELTON *Quix.* III. xvi. 99 In its Perfection and natural Conformity. **1623** *Shaks.'s 2 Hen. VI*, III. ii. 393 (written *c* 1593) The Cradle-babe, Dying with mothers dugge betweene it's lips. —— So *Temp.* I. ii. 95, 393; *Wint. T.* I. ii. 151, 152, 157, 266; III. iii. 46. —— *Meas. for M.* I. ii. 4 (*c* 1603) Heauen grant vs its peace. **1634** A. WARWICK *Spare Min.* (1636) 15 There is nothing..to be lost (but its love) by its hate. **1647** LILLY *Chr. Astrol.* civ. 527 Being directed by his or its Digression. **1655** FULLER *Ch. Hist.* I. iv. §23 The Load-stone..forgetteth it's Property to draw Iron any longer. **1683** BURNET tr. *More's Utopia* Author's Epist. (1685) 24 If he consents to it's being published. **1728** T. SHERIDAN *Persius* Prol. (1739) 5 Who taught the Parrot it's usual Compliment? **1750** tr. *Leonardus' Mirr. Stones* 132 [212] It's notorious how great its virtue is. **1802** MAR. EDGEWORTH *Moral T.* (1816) I. vii. 47 Her warning only accelerated it's fate. **1834** J. H. NEWMAN *Par. Serm.* (1837) I. xvi. 234 The Gospel has its mysteries. **1879** McCARTHY *Own Times* II. xviii. 2 Its foreign policy was treacherous.

B. As *absolute possessive.* [Cf. HIS *abs. poss.*] The absolute form of prec., used when no sb. follows: Its one, its ones. *rare.*

1613-23 SHAKS. *Hen. VIII*, I. i. 18 (First Folio) Each following day Became the next dayes master, till the last Made former Wonders, it's.

it's, its, contraction of *it is*: see IT A. γ note.

itself (ɪt'sɛlf), *pron.* Also 7-8 its (it's) self, 8-9 *dial.* itsel'. [orig. two words, IT *pron.* and SELF: see HERSELF, HIMSELF. In 17-18th c. often treated as ITS + SELF; *its* is still used when an adj. intervenes, as in *its very self*, *its own self*; cf. HIMSELF IV.]

I. 1. Emphatic or limiting use. Usually in apposition with a sb. in nom. or obj.: Very, the very, that very; alone (L. *ipsum*). Rarely alone as subject.

c **1000** *Laws of Ælfred* Introd. c. 28 Gif hit þonne cucu feoh wære and he secgge þæt..hit self acwæle. **1382** WYCLIF *Isa.* lxiii. 5 Myn indignacioun itself halp to me. **1508** FISHER *Seven Penit. Ps.* cii. Wks. (1876) 197 It selfe erth sholde alway be bareyne & without fruyte yf it receyued no moysture & hete from heuen. **1513** MORE in Grafton *Chron.* (1568) II. 777 The dealing it selfe made men to muse. **1560** DAUS tr. *Sleidane's Comm.* 118 b, Unto their luste serveth heaven and hell, the earth and tyme it selfe. **1593** SHAKS. *Lucr.* 29 Beauty itself doth of itself persuade. **1610** —— *Temp.* IV. i. 153 The solemne Temples, the great Globe it selfe, Yea, all which it inherit, shall dissolue. **1611** —— *Cymb.* III. iv. 160 Feare and Nicenesse, The Handmaides of all Women, or more truely, Woman it pretty selfe. **1621** BURTON *Anat. Mel.* Democr. to Rdr. 19 As of Aristotle [we read] that he was wisdom itself in the abstract. **1665** BOYLE *Occas. Refl.* Disc. Occas. Med. III. v, Particulars, which are not necessary to the Meditation it self. **1728** T. SHERIDAN *Persius* (1739) 19 Tho' the Poem it self be not well digested. **1793** BURNS *Ld. Gregory* iv, And my fond heart, itsel sae true, It ne'er mistrusted thine. *a* **1822** SHELLEY *Chas. I*, I. 177 Or joy itself Without the touch of sorrow. **1837-9** HALLAM *Hist. Lit.* (1855) IV. IV. vii. §1. 316 Slang; a word which, I use with some unwillingness, as itself belongs to the vocabulary it denotes. **1882** S. COX in *Expositor* IV. 197 The story of the creation told by Moses is simplicity and sobriety itself when compared with them.

b. Used alone in predicate, emphatically, as opposed to something else: cf. HIMSELF 3, 3 b.

c **1600** SHAKS. *Sonn.* lxviii. 10 Without all ornament, itself and true. **1821** KEATS *Isabella* xxxiii, An eye all pale Striving to be itself. *Mod.* The dear old place looked just itself.

II. Reflexive use. = L. *sibi*, *se*; Ger. *sich*.

2. Accusative or direct object.

971 *Blickl. Hom.* 187 Nu mæᵹ soþ hit sylf ᵹecyðan. *a* **1300** *Cursor M.* 19231 (Edin.) Ilke suike it selue bisuikis. **1388** WYCLIF *2 Cor.* x. 5 And we distrien counsels, and alle hiᵹnesse that hiᵹeth it silf aᵹens the science of God. **1594** T. B. *La Primaud. Fr. Acad.* II. 298 As the heart doeth enlarge it selfe..so doeth it restraine and close vp it selfe. **1603** SHAKS. *Meas. for M.* v. i. 540 Th' offence pardons it selfe. **1610** —— *Temp.* III. i. 80 All the more it seekes to hide it selfe The bigger bulke it shewes. **1638-1843** [see INSINUATE *v.* 3]. **1665** HOOKE *Microgr.* 16[It] does immediately..disperse it self all over them. **1673** RAY *Journ. Low C.* 379 S. Marino hath maintained it self in the condition of a free State..for above 1000 years. **1793-1879** [see DEVELOP 8]. *Mod.* It is a fault that will cure itself in time.

3. Dative, and object of a preposition. (The latter was orig. acc. or dat. according to the prep.)

c **1000** *Ags. Gosp.* Luke xi. 17 Ælc rice on hyt sylf to-dæled byð toworpen. *c* **1380** WYCLIF *Wks.* (1880) 384 þe þinge in it sylfe beriþ witnesse. [**1382** —— *Gen.* i. 11 Appletre makynge fruyt after his kynd, whos seed ben in hym silf [**1611** it selfe] vpon the erthe.] *c* **1420** *Pallad. on Husb.* II. 148 Lond argillose, & not cley bi hit selue Is commodose. [**1513** MORE in Grafton *Chron.* (1568) II. 777 The sea..somtime swelleth of himselfe before a tempest.] *Ibid.* 782 Of it selfe so long a processe. **1532** HERVET *Xenophon's Househ.* (1768) 20 Somme it bryngethe by hit selfe, and some it nourisheth. **1611** BIBLE *Ps.* xli. 6 His heart gathereth iniquitie to it selfe. **1628** BP. HALL *Old Relig.* (1686) 46 That which is perfect in its self. **1655** E. TERRY *Voy. E. India* 13 Fragrant herbs (which the soyl produceth of its self). **1665** SIR T. HERBERT *Trav.* (1677) 17 No creature that dies of it self is good to eat. **1665** BOYLE *Occas. Refl.* IV. xii, The Sun has..elevated this Water in the form of Vapours, and drawn it near it self. **1710** STEELE *Tatler* No. 164 ¶6 This Letter..I intend to print..by it self very suddenly. **1870** FREEMAN *Norm. Conq.* (ed. 2) I. App. 739 This story may be true in itself. *Mod.* The horse gave itself a knock on the head. That child will do itself a mischief.

†**4.** In genitive or possessive case: = *its own.*

a **1300** *Cursor M.* 9466 (Gött.) So hy na thing was neuer wroght, þat thoru it seluen miss ne moght Fall dun into lauer state.

itsiboo: see ITZEBU.

itsy-bitsy ('ɪtsɪ'bɪtsɪ), *a. colloq.* [Baby-form of LITTLE *a.* + BITSY *a.*: see -SY.] Small, (charmingly) insubstantial, tiny; also, used disparagingly: arty-crafty, twee. So **'itsy-'bitsiness.** Cf. ITTY-BITTY *a.*

1938 I. GOLDBERG *Wonder of Words* viii. 162 Itsy-bitsy (little bit). **1939** R. CHANDLER *Trouble is my Business* (1950) 23 The same clerk was nuzzling at the same itsy-bitsy moustache. **1953** P. JONES in *Plays of Year* IX. 567 You should be allowed to revolve radiantly at some cocktail party ..a dry martini in one hand and an itsy-bitsy little thing on a stick in the other. **1957** P. WILDEBLOOD *Main Chance* 197 An itsy-bitsy tot of vodka and a teeny-weeny tranquilliser. **1958** *Observer* 15 June 11/2 The rather sentimental and itsy-bitsy patterns that used to be considered suitable for wear by the young. **1967** *House & Garden* Mar. 74/1 The Peter Pan statue..is the embodiment of all sentimental itsy-bitsiness. **1972** 'H. HOWARD' *Nice day for Funeral* iii. 45 If Frankie was here he'd break you into itsy-bitsy pieces. **1972** *Lady* 29 June 1052/1 Country accessories are also bold, far less itsy-bitsy than many town-worn ones.

itterance, -ate, etc., obs. ff. ITERANCE, -ATE, etc.

ittria, ittrium, ittro-, *Chem.*: see YTTRIA, etc.

itty ('ɪtɪ), *a. colloq.* Also ittie. [Baby-form of LITTLE *a.* + -Y *suffix*[6].] Used hypocoristically for 'little' (chiefly in reference to babies or small domestic animals).

1798 JANE AUSTEN *Let.* 27 Oct. (1932) I. 10 My dear itty Dordy's remembrance of me is very pleasing to me. **1853** MRS. GASKELL *Cranford* vii. 132 Come down stairs with me, poor ittie doggie, and it shall have its tea. **1938** D. RUNYON *Furthermore* viii. 159 He..starts whispering, 'There, there, there, my itty oddleums.' **1964** *Guardian* 30 Oct. 13/3 Now, ah reckon Lady Bird an' ah will git ahselves an itty bit o' sleep.

'itty-'bitty, *a.* = ITSY-BITSY *a.*

[**1938** *Amer. Speech* XIII. 314/1 Itty bitty kitty from the city, a country yokel who tries to be a cat.] **1940** R. CHANDLER *Farewell, my Lovely* xxxiii. 253 Itty-bitty frame houses on the wrong side of town. **1959** H. HOBSON *Mission House Murder* xiii. 89 No big swallows now. Itty-bitty sips —and take your time. **1968** W. GARNER *Deep, Deep Freeze* v. 62 I'll move every ittybitty piece on that goddammed fancy board. **1969** L. KENNEDY *Very Lovely People* i. 35, I felt, here I am in this itty-bitty tropical village, a tremendous long ways from anywhere.

-itude: see -TUDE *suffix.*

i-tuht, ME. pa. pple. of TIGHT *v.*

i-tuked, ME. pa. pple. of TUKE *v.*, to afflict, etc.

itum, obs. variant of ITEM.

i-turmented, ME. pa. pple. of TORMENT *v.*

i-turnd, -ed, ME. pa. pple. of TURN *v.*

i-turpled, ME. pa. pple. of TORPLE *v.*, to fall headlong.

i-tuðed, -et, ME. pa. pple. of TITHE *v.*, to grant.

itwin, itwyn: see TWIN.

i-twinned, ME. pa. pple. of TWIN *v.*, to divide.

†**i'twix**, *prep.* (*adv.*) *north. dial. Obs.* Also **itwyx, ituyx.** [f. *i*, IN *prep.* + TWIX(T: cf. ATWIX(T, BETWIXEN, BETWIXT.] = BETWIXT, between.

a **1340** HAMPOLE *Psalter* Prol., It..makes pees itwix body & saule. *Ibid.* ii. 13 Na tyme sall be ituyx will of demynge and of vengaunce. *Ibid.* v. 8 And i. twix [*v.r.* & betwix & þonne] .i. sall lout til þi haly tempill. *Ibid.* cii. 12 Als mykil as it is itwyx myrk and light.

Ity, var. ITI *sb.* and *a.*

-ity [ME. *-ite*, a. F. *-ité*, L. *-itāt-em*], the usual form in which the suffix (L. *-tās*, *-tātem*, expressing state or condition) appears, the *i*- being orig. either the stem vowel of the radical (e.g. L. *suāvi-tās* suavity), or its weakened repr. (e.g. L. *puro-*, *pūri-tās* purity), rarely a mere connective (e.g. L. *auctōr-i-tās* authority; so ME. *emperorite*, in Vernon MS., *St. Ambrose* 886). The last became more frequent in med. and mod.L., and the mod. langs., in abstracts from comparatives, as *majority*, *minority*, *superiority*, *inferiority*, *interiority*. Hence such formations as *egoity*, with playful or pedantic nonce-words of Eng. formation, as *between-ity*, *coxcomb-ity*, *cuppe-ity*, *table-ity*, *threadbar-ity*, *woman-ity* (after *humani-ty*), *youthfull-ity*.

After *i*, *-ity* becomes *-ety*, as in *pie-ty*, *varie-ty* (L. *pietātem*, *varie-tātem*). The termination was in L. often added to another adj. suffix, e.g. *-āci-*, *-āli-*, *-āno-*, *-āri-*, *-ārio-*, *-bili-*, *-eo-*, *-idi-*, *-ido-*, *-ili-*, *-īli-*, *-ino-*, *-īno-*, *-io-*, *-īvo-*, *-ōci-*, *-ōso-*, *-ui-*, *-uo-*, etc., whence the Eng. endings *-acity*, *-ality*, *-anity*, *-arity*, *-ariety*, *-bility*, *-eity*, *-idity*, *-ility*, *-inity*, *-iety*, *-ivity*, *-ocity*, *-osity*, *-uity*, some of which, as *-bility* (*-ability*, *-ibility*) attain almost to the rank of independent suffixes. The earlier popular Fr. form was *-eté*, in Eng. *-ety* and *-ty*, as in *safety*, *bounty*, *plenty*: see -TY.

‖**itzebu, -boo** (ɪtsɪ'buː). Also 7 ichebo, ichibo, 9 itsi-, itzi-, -bu, -bou, -bue, -boo. [Japanese: two words, *itse*, *itche* one, *bû* division, part, quarter. (Of Chinese origin.)] A Japanese phrase meaning 'one quarter', commonly applied to a silver coin in the form of a thin rectangular plate (with rounded corners), in use before 1871; it was the quarter of a *riô* or *tael*, and worth about 1*s.* 4*d.* sterling: see also quot. 1900.

The name is still sometimes applied to the quarter of the dollar or *yen*. As the meaning is 'one *bû* or quarter', its use in the plural in reference to a number of *bû* is an error.

1616 R. COCKS *Diary* (Hakl. Soc.) I. 176. **1618** *Ibid.* II. 77. **1868** E. SEYD *Bullion & For. Exchanges* 265. **1900** SATOW *Voy. Capt. Saris* 97 *note*, The Japanese coin called *ichibu*.. mentioned in Cocks's *Diary*..was the gold coin..not the silver *ichibu*, which was first issued in 1837.

iu-, earlier spelling of IV-, and of JU-, q.v.

iuanna, iwana, obs. forms of IGUANA.

iubard, iuce, obs. ff. JEOPARD, JUICE.

iue, obs. f. IVY, JEW.

iuel, obs. f. EVIL, JEWEL.

iuge, iuglour, obs. ff. JUDGE, JUGGLER.

iukinge, obs. f. YUKING, itching.

†**iulan** (aɪ'juːlən), *a. nonce-wd. Obs.* [f. Gr. ἴουλος down, the first growth of the beard + -AN.] Of the first growth of the beard.

1621-3 MIDDLETON & ROWLEY *Changeling* I. i. 178 Before our chins were worth iulan down.

Iule: see JULE.

iulidan (aɪ'juːlɪdən). *Zool.* [f. mod.L. *Iūlida*, *-idæ*, f. *Iūlus*: see below.] A myriapod of the family *Iulidæ*: see next 2.

[**1847** CARPENTER *Zool.* §824 The mouth of the *Iulidæ* strongly resembles that of the larvæ of many insects.] **1885** *Cassell's Encycl. Dict.*, Iulidan.

‖**iulus** (aɪ'juːləs). *Zool.* Formerly (and still with some) julus. [L. *iūlus*, a. Gr. ἴουλος down, a catkin, the animal described in 2.]

†**1.** A catkin. *Obs.*

1668 WILKINS *Real Char.* II. iv. 73 Having a leaf like a flag, bearing a *Julus* hard and close. **1757** A. COOPER *Distiller* III. lv. (1760) 248 The Male Shrubs produce in April or May a small kind of *Juli* with Apices on them.

2. A genus of animals of the class Myriapoda, order *Chilognatha* (*Diplopoda*); a millepede.

1658 ROWLAND *Moufet's Theat. Ins.* 1047 Unless they have many feet, they cannot be numbred or named amongst the Juli. Juli are as I said, short Scolopenders, that for the number of their feet, exceed..all other Insects. **1752** SIR J. HILL *Hist. Anim.* 17 Gallyworm, the brown Julus, with a hundred legs on each side. **1835** KIRBY *Hab. & Inst. Anim.* II. xvi. 75 The six original or natural legs of the Iulus are its first organs of locomotion. **1841-71** T. R. JONES *Anim. Kingd.* (ed. 4) 293 The eggs..are deposited in the earth or vegetable mould, in which the *Julus* is usually met with. **1847** CARPENTER *Zool.* §824 The body of the *Iulus* (of which one of the commonest species is known as the Gally-worm) is long and cylindrical; its number of segments is between 40 and 50; and many of these bear two pairs of..legs.

-ium, *suffix. Chem.* **a.** Used to form the names of metallic elements.

The L. names of metals were in *-um*, e.g. *aurum*, *argentum*, *ferrum*; the names of *sodium*, *potassium*, and *magnesium*, derived from *soda*, *potassa* or *potash*, and *magnesia*, were given by Davy in 1807, with the derivative form *-ium*; and although some of the later metals have received names in *-um*, the general form is in *-ium*, as in *cadmium*, *iridium*, *lithium*, *osmium*, *palladium*, *rhodium*, *titanium*, *uranium*; in conformity with which *aluminum* has been altered to *aluminium*. So *hydrogen*, when theoretically regarded as a metal, has been called *hydrogenium*; cf. also AMMONIUM.

b. Used to form the names of various protonated, mostly organic, bases, as *anilinium*, *benzenium*, *ethenium*, *flavylium*, *guanidinium*, *hydrazinium*, *imidazolium*, *pyrylium*. Cf. -ONIUM.

This usage of the suffix derives from AMMONIUM. For rules governing the application of the suffix see *Nomenclature of Organic Chemistry* and *Nomenclature of Inorganic Chemistry*, published by the International Union of Pure and Applied Chemistry.

i-umlaut: see I I. 2 b.

†**i-unne**, *v. Obs.* [OE. *ᵹe-unnan* (pres. *ᵹe-ann*, pa. t. *ᵹe-úðe*, pa. pple. *ᵹe-unnen*), f. *ᵹe-*, I-[1] +

unnan to grant; = OS., OHG. *giunnan*, MHG. *gunnen*, Ger. *gönnen*.] *trans.* To grant.

c **888** K. ÆLFRED *Boeth.* xxix. §2 þa nolde se cyning.. him his feores ȝeunnan. *a* **1000** *O.E. Chron.* an. 959 (Laud MS.) God him ȝeunne, þæt his gode dæda swyðran wearðan, þonne misdæda. *c* **1175** *Lamb. Hom.* 125 Ure drihten and ure alesend iunne us allen þet we swa.. maȝen his hest.. halden. *c* **1205** LAY. 16549 Godd hit me iuðe þat ich hine igripen habben. *a* **1225** *Ancr. R.* 30 Uor alle þeo þet habbeð eni god ido me, iseid me, oþer iunned me. **12..** *Prayer to Our Lady* in *O.E. Misc.* 193 [Ich] Swo me hadde ifurn do, ȝif hit me crist i-ȝuðe.

i-unnen, ME. pa. pple. of UNNE(N *v.*

iunte, obs. form of JOINT.

iuray(e, obs. spelling of IVRAY, darnel.

i-used, ME. pa. pple. of USE *v.*

iuyshe, obs. form of JUICE.

†**i'vads**, *int. Obs.* Also 7–8 **ivads, evads.** [var. I'FADS.] In faith.

1675 T. DUFFETT *Mock Tempest* II. i. 13 So we all think i'vads. **1675** WYCHERLEY *Country Wife* IV. ii, Evads! I'll try, so I will. **1719** D'URFEY *Pills* II. 342 Ivads no—I an't such a Baby neither.

Ivan (ˈaɪvən, ‖iˈvan). [Russ., = John.] Used for: a Russian, esp. a Russian soldier (as typical of the Russian army).

[**1870** *Brewer's Dict. Phr. & Fable* 448/1 *Ivanovitch*, a lazy, good-natured person, the national impersonation of the Russians as a people, as *John Bull* is of the English. **1890** WEBSTER, *Ivan Ivanovitch*, an ideal personification of the typical Russian or of the Russian people;—used as 'John Bull' is used for the typical Englishman.] **1925** FRASER & GIBBONS *Soldier & Sailor Words* 129 *Ivan*, the everyday name in the Russian Army, at any rate down to 1916, for a private soldier, equivalent to our 'Tommy Atkins'. **1959** M. CROSLAND tr. *Rovan's Germany* 51 The Russian 'Ivan' is the brutal sub-man and the giant with the kind, noble and spontaneous heart.. [to] the German spectator. **1968** 'B. MATHER' *Springers* xii. 128 We'd knocked off quite a few of their side so far, and even dedicated Ivans could be expected to show a little exacerbation under the circumstances. **1971** C. EGLETON *Last Post for Partisan* xvii. 174 So long as the Ivan kept on coming he wasn't worried. **1972** *Guardian* 8 Sept. 12/4 A situation in which Ivan continues to come a lot cheaper than GI Joe.

†**Ive**: see HERB IVE.

ive, obs. or dial. form of IVY.

Ive, obs. f. JEW.

I've, colloquial contraction of *I have*: see HAVE *v.*

1742 RICHARDSON *Pamela* III. 316 A queer sort of Name! I've heard of it somewhere! **1882** 'L. KEITH' *Alasnam's Lady* III. 223 I've ruffled her temper, too.

-ive, *suffix*, forming adjs. (and sbs.) Formerly also *-if*, *-ife*; a. Fr. *-if*, fem. *-ive* (= It., Sp. *-ivo*):—L. *īv-us*, a suffix added to the ppl. stem of verbs, as in *act-īvus* active, *pass-īvus* passive, *nātīv-us* of inborn kind; sometimes to the pres. stem, as *cad-īvus* falling, and to sbs. as *tempest-īvus* seasonable. Few of these words came down in OF., e.g. *naïf*, *naïve*:—L. *nātīv-um*; but the suffix is largely used in the modern Romanic langs., and in Eng., to adapt L. words in *-īvus*, or form words on L. analogies, with the sense 'having a tendency to, having the nature, character, or quality of, given to (some action)'. The meaning differs from that of ppl. adjs. in *-ing*, *-ant*, *-ent*, in implying a permanent or habitual quality or tendency: cf. *acting*, *active*, *attracting*, *attractive*, *coherent*, *cohesive*, *consequent*, *consecutive*. From their derivation, the great majority of these end in *-sive* and *-tive*, and of these about one half in -ATIVE, which tends consequently to become a living suffix, as in *talk-ative*, etc. A few are formed immediately on the vb. stem, esp. where this ends in *s* (*c*) or *t*, thus easily passing muster among those formed on the ppl. stem; such are *amusive*, *coercive*, *conducive*, *crescive*, *forcive*, *piercive*, *adaptive*, *adoptive*, *denotive*, *humective*; a few are from sbs., as *massive*. In *costive*, the *-ive* is not a suffix.

Already in L. many of these adjs. were used subst.; this precedent is freely followed in the mod. langs. and in English: e.g. *adjective*, *captive*, *derivative*, *expletive*, *explosive*, *fugitive*, *indicative*, *incentive*, *invective*, *locomotive*, *missive*, *native*, *nominative*, *prerogative*, *sedative*, *subjunctive*.

In some words the final consonant of OF. *-if*, from *-īvus*, was lost in ME., leaving in mod.Eng. -Y: e.g. *hasty*, *jolly*, *tardy*.

Adverbs from adjs. in *-ive* are formed in -ively; abstract sbs. in -iveness and -ivity (F. *-iveté*, *-ivité*, L. *-īvitāt-em*), as in *activity*, *conductivity*, *resistivity*, and similar terms; also *spec.* (see quot. 1895).

1885 O. HEAVISIDE in *Electrician* 4 Sept. 311/1 Thus, 'specific resistance' may well be called 'resistivity', and specific conductance 'conductivity', referring to the unit volume. Resistivity is the reciprocal of conductivity, and resistance of conductance. **1895** *Rep. Brit. Assoc. Adv. Sci.* 197 That the termination *-ance* be used in general for words expressing the properties of a definite body or piece of matter; *e.g.*, resistance, conductance, inductance, permeance, reluctance, &c.; and that the termination *-ivity* or *-ility* or the like be used for words expressing the specific properties of a material; *e.g.*, conductivity, resistivity, inductivity, refractivity, permeability, &c.

†**i-vee, i-fee**, *v. Obs.* Forms 1 *ȝefécȝan, (*north.* ȝefiaȝa, ȝefia), 3 iueie(n, iuee(n, ifæie(n, iuæie(n, iuaie, ifea(n, iue(n, ive(n. [f. OE. *ȝe-*, I-[1] + *féoȝan*, *féon* to hate = OHG. *fiên*, ON. *fjá*, Goth. *fijan*, *fian*, whence the pr. pple. *fijands*, OHG. *fijant*, ON. *fjándi*, OE. *féond*, FIEND, enemy.] *trans.* To hate; to make an enemy, put at enmity, render hateful or hostile.

c **975** *Lindisf. Gosp.* Luke xvi. 13 Enne ȝefiweð & oðerne lufæð. *Ibid.* xix. 14 Burȝwaras his ȝefiadon hine. *Ibid.* John iii. 20 Se ðe misdoeð ȝefieð þæt leht. *c* **1205** LAY. 964 We beoð ifead wið heom. *Ibid.* 7716 þæh heo weoren iuæiede. *Ibid.* 9843 þeonne beo ich wið mine sune iued. *Ibid.* 21214 Heo wusten heom ifæied. *a* **1240** *Ureisun* in *Cott. Hom.* 187 Mine sunnen habbeþ grimliche iwreþed me and iueed me towart te lueliche louerd. *c* **1320** *Cast. Love* 310 A þral þat dude amis.. Wiþ his lord was so i-vet.

ivel, -il, obs. forms of EVIL.

i-vele: see YFELE *v.*, to feel.

i-vencussed, i-venkessid, ME. pa. pple. of VANQUISH *v.*

i-venymed, ME. pa. pple. of *venym*, VENOM *v.*

iver, ivery(e, obs. forms of IVORY.

ivi (ˈiːviː). Also **eevie, ifi, ihi.** [Fijian *ivi*, Samoan *ifi*.] The Tahitian chestnut, *Inocarpus fagiferus* (*I. edulis*), a leguminous evergreen tree bearing spikes of white or yellow flowers and dark red, edible fruit.

1862 B. SEEMANN *Viti* xvi. 318 The Ivi, or Tahitian chestnut,.. is one of the common trees [in Fiji]. **1874** LINDLEY & MOORE *Treas. Bot.* II. Suppl. 1308/1 Ivi (Feejee). *Inocarpus edulis.* **1881** C. F. CUMMING *At Home in Fiji* I. 275 A group of eevie trees appears like one gigantic mass of lovely trailing foliage. **1888** W. HILLEBRAND *Flora Hawaiian Islands* 109 Here [*sc.* among the Caesalpinieae] also must be given a place to the anomalous *Inocarpus edulis*, Forst., or Tahitian Chestnut, the Ivi or Mapé. **1894** B. THOMSON *S. Sea Yarns* 7 He repaired to the mainland to consult a rival oracle named *Na-ivi* (the ivi-tree). **1935** *B. P. Bishop Mus. Bull.* (Honolulu) CXXX. 119 The native names [of *Inocarpus edulis*] are *ihi* or *mape* in Nukuhiva and Hivaoa of the Marquesas. **1964** C. S. BELSHAW (*title*) Under the ivi tree. Society and economic growth in rural Fiji. **1970** W. R. SYKES *Contrib. Flora Niue* 156 No ifi trees were seen growing in places other than those connected with man's activities.

ivi(e, ivin, obs. and dial. forms of IVY.

Ivicene (ˈɪvɪsiːn), *sb.* and *a.* [f. *Ibiza*, *Iviça*, one of the Balearic Islands + Sp. *-eño*, -ENE.] A type of hound, said to be descended from ancient Egyptian hunting dogs, native to the island of Ibiza and characterized by large, pointed, pricked ears and white, fawn, or reddish-brown colouring; also as *adj.*; also called *Ibizan* or *Balearic hound*.

1929 *Morning Post* 5 Feb. 15/3 The Ivicene Described. *Ibid.*, The Ivicene dog, a breed which has never before been seen in this country. **1929** *Dog World* 8 Feb. 912/1 Pedro of Chardia, Ivecine [*sic*], Greyhound type, wants time and should do well, rare and undeveloped at the moment. **1948** C. L. B. HUBBARD *Dogs in Brit.* III. xv. 124 The correct name of Cà Eivissenne is loosely pronounced as 'Ivicene', which led to considerable publicity in Britain about 1930, giving the dog the breed name of Ivicene. **1964** E. F. DAGLISH tr. *Schneider-Leyer's Dogs of World* 165 (*heading*) Balearic Hound or Ivicene.

ivied, ivyed (ˈaɪvɪd), *a.* Also 8 **ivy'd.** [f. IVY + -ED[2].] Overgrown or clothed with ivy.

a **1771** SMOLLETT *Love Elegy* iv, I'll seek some lonely church.. Where lamps hang mouldering on the ivy'd wall. **1777** WARTON *Ode Suicide* xiii, This votive dirge sad duty paid Within an ivy'd nook. **1877** BLACK *Green Past.* iv. (1878) 29 Its beautiful green foliage inclosed on one side by the ivied wall of the Bodleian.

i-viled, ME. pa. pple. of FILE *v.*[1]

i-visited, ME. pa. pple. of VISIT *v.*

-ivity: see under -IVE.

i-vlaȝen, ME. pa. pple. of FLAY *v.*

i-vo, ME. form of FOE *sb.*

†**i-voide**, *a. Obs.* [f. I-[1] + VOID *a.*] Void.

c **1415** LYDG. *Temp. Glas* 413 The end of sorow is ioi I-voide of drede.

ivoire, -ed, obs. ff. IVORY, IVORIED.

ivor(e, ivorey, ivorie, etc.: see IVORY.

-ivore, usual comb. form of the suffix -VORE.

ˈivoride (-aɪd). [f. IVORY + -IDE.] Tradename of an imitation of ivory.

1875 KNIGHT *Dict. Mech.*, *Ivoride*, an artificial ivory, a vulcanite whitened by abundant quantity of some white material. *Mod.* Table-knives with ivoride handles.

ivoried (ˈaɪvərɪd), *a.* Also 4 **ivoyred.** [f. IVORY + -ED[2].] †**a.** Made of ivory. *Obs.* **b.** Coloured and smoothed to resemble ivory. **c.** Furnished with ivory, or (*humorous*) with teeth.

a **1300** *E.E. Psalter* xliv. 9 [xlv. 8] Mir, and drope, and bike of schroudes þine, Of houses ivoyred bright þat shine. **1890** in *Cent. Dict.* **1893** *19th Cent.* Nov. 843 On thy bare and ivoried shoulder. **1928** HARDY *Coll. Poems* 156, I borrowed deep to carve the screen And raise the ivoried Rood. **1945** W. DE LA MARE *Burning-Glass* 76 Tipped arrow, ivoried bow, and rain-soaked quiver.

ˈivorine, *a.* Also 4 **yuerene**, 5 **yvoriene.** [In ME. a. OF. *ivorin*, *ivoirin*, f. *ivoire* ivory + *-in* (see -INE[1]); in mod. use app. a new formation.]

†**1.** Consisting or made of ivory. *Obs.*

1382 WYCLIF *Song Sol.* vii. 4 Thi necke as an yuerene tour [**1388** a tour of yuer]. *c* **1450** *Mirour Saluacioun* 5017 Thilk throne figurede yvoriene On whilk the kyng wysest Salomon to sitte was sene.

2. White and smooth like ivory.

1888 *Harper's Mag.* Apr. 740 The ivorine loveliness of glossy shoulders.

ˈivorine, *sb.* [f. IVORY + -INE[4].] A tradename for various productions: either such as imitate ivory or (as cosmetics, dentifrices, etc.) produce an ivory-like colour or smoothness. Also *attrib.*

1897 *Daily News* 23 Mar. 7/1 Picture books, ivorine plaques. *a* **1900** *Price List.* Cosmetics.. 'Ivorine' (emollient cream for the skin). Dentifrices, Tooth Pastes, etc... Ivorine.

ˈivoriness. *rare.* [f. IVORY *attrib.* or *adj.* + -NESS.] The quality of resembling ivory in appearance or colour.

1824 GALT *Rothelan* II. v. ii. 195 Her delicate hands also began to lose their ivoriness, and become ashy pale.

ivorist (ˈaɪvərɪst). [f. IVORY + -IST.] A professional worker or carver in ivory.

1888 *Harper's Mag.* Apr. 710 The names of famous Japanese ivorists.. are household words among native connoisseurs.

-ivorous, usual comb. form of the suffix -VOROUS.

ivory (ˈaɪvərɪ). Forms: *α.* 4 **iuor, yuor(e, -ere, iueer, iuoere, euor,** 4–5 **yvoyre, yuer, euour,** 5 **iv-, yvor(e, iuyr, iwr,** 5–6 **yvoire, evour(e,** 6 **evor(e, euir, euoir;** 6 **ebure.** *β.* 4– **ivory;** also 4 **ywori, yuory, -rie, iuory,** 4–5 **yuorye,** 4–6 **evorye, euery,** 4–7 **yvory,** 5 **yuori, -rye, yvere, iwery, evury, -erey,** 5–6 **ivery, yvery,** 6 **iuorey, iu-, yuery(e, yvorie, everye,** 6–7 **iu-, ivorie,** 7 **yv'ry,** 8–9 **iv'ry.** *γ. erron.* 5–6 **veveri,** 6 **vyveri.** [a. OF. *yvoire* (13th c.), Norm. Fr. *ivurie* (12th c.), *iviere*, *yvyere* (15th c.), mod.F. *ivoire* = Pr. *evori*, *avori*, It. *avorio*:—L. *eboreus* adj., from *ebur*, *ebor-* ivory: cf. Coptic *ebu* ivory, Skt. *ibhas* elephant. The form *ebure* in Lyndesay is refashioned after the Latin.]

I. 1. a. The hard, white, elastic, and fine-grained substance (being dentine of exceptional hardness) composing the main part of the tusks of the elephant, mammoth (*fossil ivory*), hippopotamus, walrus, and narwhal; it forms a very valuable article of commerce, being extensively employed as a material for many articles of use or ornament.

α. a **1300** *Cursor M.* 9944 (Cott.) A tron of iuor [*Gött.* yuor] graid. *c* **1320** *Sir Tristr.* 1888 Mirie notes he fand Opon his rote of yuere. *a* **1340** HAMPOLE *Psalter* xliv. 7 Howsis of euor. **13..** *E.E. Allit. P.* A. 178 Hyr vysage whyt as playn yuore. *c* **1369** CHAUCER *Dethe Blaunche* 946 Hyr throte.. Semed a rounde toure of yvoyre. **1388** WYCLIF *Song Sol.* vii. 4 Thi necke is as a tour of yuer. **1390** GOWER *Conf.* II. 17 Of yvor white He hath hire wroght. *c* **1400** MAUNDEV. (Roxb.) xxv. 115 Ilkane.. beres before him a table of iaspre, or of euour. **14..** LYDG. in *MS. Soc. Antiq.* 134 lf. 14 (Halliwell) Like yvor that cometh fro so ferre, His teeth schalle be even, smothe and white. *c* **1440** *Promp. Parv.* 267/1 Ivor, or ivery (*H.* iwr, or iwery, *S.* yvory, *P.* iuyr), *ebur.* *c* **1450** *Mirour Saluacioun* 1148 Of fynest gold and aldere whittest yvore. **1530** LYNDESAY *Test. Papyngo* 1107 Syne, close thame in one cais of Ebure fyne. *a* **1586** [see 8 b].

β. a **1300** *Cursor M.* 9360 (Cott.) Fair es þe muth o þat leuedi, And ilk toth es als ywori [*Gött.* yuory, *Trin.* Iuory]. **13..** *K. Alis.* 7666 (MS. Bodl.) þe pynnes weron of yuory. *c* **1386** CHAUCER *Sompn. T.* 33 A peyre of tables al of yuory. **1387** TREVISA *Higden* (Rolls) I. 79 Euery and precious stones. **1463** *Bury Wills* (Camden) 15 My tablees of ivory. ?*c* **1475** *Sqr. lowe Degre* 100 Anone that lady, fayre and fre Undyd a pynne of yverè. **1481** CAXTON *Myrr.* II. vi. 76 The tooth of an olyfaunt is yuorye. **1552** *Invent. Ch. Goods* (Surtees) 43 One pix of everye, bounde with silver. **1590** SPENSER *F.Q.* I. i. 40 Double gates.. The one faire fram'd of burnisht Yvory. **1596** SHAKS. *Merch. V.* III. i. 42 There is more difference betweene thy flesh and hers, then betweene Iet and Iuorie. **1610** HOLLAND *Camden's Brit.* I. 368 To the feate Of Artisan, give place the gould, stones Yv'ry, and Geat. **1611** BIBLE *Ezek.* xxvii. 15 Hornes of Iuorie, and Ebenie. *a* **1732** GAY *Poems* (1745) I. 56 For this, shall

Elephants their ivory shed. **1812** J. SMYTH *Pract. of Customs* (1821) 84 The Ceylon Ivory, and that of the Island of Achem, do not become yellow in the wearing, as all other Ivory does. **1875** *Ure's Dict. Arts* II. 1038 The hardest, toughest, whitest, and most translucent ivory has the preference in the market; for many purposes the horn of the narwhal being considered the best... The ivory of the hippopotamus is preferred by dentists. **1881** C. S. TOMES in *Encycl. Brit.* XIII. 522/2 When first cut it [African ivory] is semi-transparent and of a warm colour; in this state it is called 'green' ivory, and as it dries it becomes much lighter in colour and more opaque.

γ. ? *a* **1500** *Inventory* in *Paston Lett.* III. 408 A combe of veveri. **1560** *Reg. Gild Corpus Chr. York* (Surtees) 307 A pyx of vyvery with a lytle white canaby.

b. = DENTINE.

1831 R. KNOX *Cloquet's Anat.* 79 The bony portion of the teeth, or the Ivory, forms a very dense mass.

2. A substance resembling ivory, or made in imitation of it. ***vegetable ivory***, the hard albumen of the nut or seed of a South American palm, *Phytelephas macrocarpa*, which resembles ivory in hardness, colour, and texture, and is used for ornamental work, buttons, etc.

1842 D. COOPER in *Microsc. Jrnl.* No. 16 (*heading*) On Vegetable Ivory. **1857** HENFREY *Bot.* 394 Nuts suitable for turning are afforded by the seeds of *Attalea funifera* (Coquilla-nuts), *Phytelephas macrocarpa* (Vegetable Ivory). **1866** *Treas. Bot.* 884/2 The fruit consists of a collection of six or seven drupes... Each drupe contains from six to nine seeds, the Vegetable Ivory of commerce... The seed at first contains a clear insipid fluid.. afterwards this same liquor becomes milky and sweet, and it changes by degrees until it becomes as hard as ivory. **1875** KNIGHT *Dict. Mech.* 1207/1 *Ivory, Artificial*, a compound of caoutchouc, sulphur, and some white ingredients, such as gypsum.. or pipeclay. **1887** *Whitaker's Alm.* Advt. 12 Burmese Ivory.. Exact imitation of Real Ivory, in colour, grain, and finish.

3. ***black ivory***: African Negro slaves as an object of commerce. *slang.* [From the trade in these at the time being chiefly located in the same districts as that in ivory.]

1873 R. M. BALLANTYNE (*title*) Black Ivory: Adventures among Slavers. *Ibid.* 27 The price of black ivory was up in the market. **1884** *Sword & Trowel* June 258 The trade, which began with ivory, had now turned to slave-dealing —black ivory, as these, our fellow-men, are called in the market. **1885** *Pall Mall G.* 14 Mar. 11/2 Help them to make money otherwise than by dealing in black ivory, and we shall see the slave trade extirpated.

4. The colour of ivory; ivory-white; *esp.* whiteness of the human skin.

1590 SPENSER *F.Q.* III. iii. 20 The doubtfull Mayd.. Was all abasht, and her pure yvory Into a cleare Carnation suddeine dyde. *c* **1632** *Poem* in *Athenæum* No. 2883. 121/2 How well the Paynter to the life exprest The soft and swelling yvory of her Breast. **1725** POPE *Odyss.* XVIII. 228 The pure ivory o'er her bosom spreads. **1888** *Daily News* 1 May 5/7 Ivory-white is generally preferred to dead-white for the dress, as being less trying to the complexion. Nearly all recent brides have worn ivory.

5. a. An article made of ivory, esp. a carving in that material. **b.** A season ticket, etc. as consisting of a tablet of ivory. **c.** *slang* (usu. *pl.*) (*a*) Dice; ***to touch ivory***, to play at dice. (*b*) Billiard balls.

1830 LYTTON *P. Clifford* iv, Suppose we adjourn to Fish Lane, and rattle the ivories! **1858** SIMMONDS *Dict. Trade* 207/1 Ivory is also the name for a pass-ticket on a railway, or subscriber's admission to a theatre, public gardens, etc. **1864** SALA *Quite Alone* vii, Yes, I will promise you I will keep my head cool, and won't touch ivory tonight. **1875** MASKELL *Ivories* 15 The famous Assyrian ivories.. which are.. preserved in the British Museum. *Ibid.* 119, I advised that the ivories should be taken out of the wooden frames. **1888** *Sporting Life* 28 Nov. (Farmer), On new premises.. where erstwhile the click of ivories was heard. **1899** SIR A. WEST *Recoll.* I. iii. 95, I was given what was known as an 'ivory' for Lord Dudley's double box on the grand tier.

d. *collect. sing.* and *pl.* The keys of a piano or similar instrument. *colloq.*

1818 KEATS *Let.* 18 Dec. (1958) II. 13 She plays the Music without one sensation but the feel of the ivory at her fingers. **1854** THACKERAY *Newcomes* I. xi. 114 It is a wonder how any fingers can move over the jingling ivory so quickly as Miss Cann's. **1918** [see JAZZ *v.* 2]. **1940** *S.P.E. Tract* LV. 196 Tickle the ivories. **1962** *Times* 10 Feb. 4/2 'Ivory-tickling' has become an outmoded and faintly derogatory description of piano-playing. **1974** *Times* 15 Feb. 14/7 Its cover portrays the Prime Minister, seated at the organ, tinkling one lot of ivories and flashing the other lot.

6. A tusk of an elephant, etc.

1894 SIR G. PORTAL *Mission Uganda* v. 88 They danced, .. swinging the great ivories from one shoulder to the other. **1897** MARY KINGSLEY *W. Africa* 325 Some of these private ivories are kept for years and years before they reach the trader's hands.

7. *slang.* (*sing.* and *pl.*) The teeth.

1782 MRS. COWLEY *Bold Stroke for Husb.* II. ii, Don Sancho, who.. complains of the tooth-ache, to make you believe that the two rows of ivory he carries in his head, grew there. **1811** *Lex. Bal.* s.v., How the swell flashed his ivories: how the gentleman showed his teeth. **1819** *Sporting Mag.* V. 7 A chattering blow upon the mouth, which loosened the ivory. **1848** LOWELL *Biglow Papers* Poems 1890 II. 147 He showed his ivory some, I guess, an' sez, 'You're fairly pinned'. **1898** *Tit-Bits* 18 June 230/1 His friend who gets one of his 'ivories' extracted with.. skill by the same dentist.

II. *attrib.* and *Comb.*

8. *simple attrib.*, passing into *adj.* **a.** Made or consisting of ivory. ***ivory gate***: see GATE *sb.*[1] 5.

1382 WYCLIF *Ps.* xliv. 9 [xlv. 8] Fro the yuer housis. **1533** BELLENDEN *Livy* v. (1822) 462 Thay sett doun in evore chiaris. **1596** SHAKS. *Tam. Shr.* II. i. 352 In Iuory cofers I haue stuft my crownes. **1613** PURCHAS *Pilgrimage* (1614) 457 The Ivory Image of Aiax. **1738** GLOVER *Leonidas* III. 148 The iv'ry car with azure sapphire shone. **1855** TENNYSON *The Letters* iii, She took the little ivory chest.

b. White or smooth as ivory.

a **1586** *Banks Helicon* 63 in *Montgomerie's Poems* 275 With yvoire nek, and pomellis round, And comlie intervall. **1592** SHAKS. *Ven. & Ad.* 230 Sometimes her arms infold him like a band.. 'Fondling', she saith, 'since I have hemm'd thee here Within the circuit of this ivory pale [etc.] '. **1624** QUARLES *Div. Poems, Sion's Sonn.* xii, Thy ivorie Teeth. **1652** H. C. *Looking-Gl. for Ladies* A iij, Let your Ivory fingers turn over these Leaves. **1786** tr. *Beckford's Vathek* (1868) 57 Refresh your delicate feet and your ivory limbs. **1879** *St. George's Hosp. Rep.* IX. 208 The complexion was typically 'ivory'. **1885** *Pall Mall G.* 23 June 8/1 The bridesmaids' dresses were composed of embroidered mousselaine de soie over ivory satin. **1897** OUIDA *Massarenes* xiv, She turned her ivory shoulder on him.

9. General comb.: **a.** attributive, as ***ivory broker, convoy, dealer, merchant***, etc. **b.** objective and obj. gen. as ***ivory-bearer, -carving, -hunter, -hunting, -turner, -turning***. **c.** similative, parasynthetic, and instrumental, as ***ivory-backed, -beaked, -faced, -hafted, -handled, -headed, -hilted, -studded, -tinted, -toned, -wristed***, adjs.; also ***ivory-like*** adj.

1887 J. ASHBY STERRY *Lazy Minstrel* (1892) 192 There's hair-dye for the gay old boys, And *ivory-backed brushes. **1864** TENNYSON *Islet* 12 A bevy of Eroses apple-cheek'd In a shallop of crystal *ivory-beak'd. **1898** *19th Cent.* 1021 The *ivory-bearers eluded the ivory-hunters, and moved on into the grass. **1887** *Pall Mall G.* 20 Aug. 10/2 The alleged news of the death of Mr. Stanley is said.. to have been brought by *ivory-brokers. **1839** *Chambers' Tour Holland* 22/1 Numerous cases displaying prodigies of Chinese skill, in *ivory-carving. **1885** *Pall Mall G.* 27 May 8/1 The story of an *ivory convoy making its way to Zanzibar. **1799** CORSE in *Phil. Trans.* LXXXIX. 212, I am credibly informed, by the *ivory-dealers in London, that the largest tusks generally come from Africa. **1886** STEVENSON *Dr. Jekyll* iv. (ed. 2) 41 An *ivory-faced and silvery-haired old woman opened the door. **1706** VANBRUGH *Mistake* IV. i. 296 There's thy *ivory-hafted knife again. **1813** *Examiner* 3 May 275/1 *Ivory-handled.. Knives and Forks. **1820** KEATS *St. Agnes* xi, The aged creature came, Shuffling along with *ivory-headed wand. **1900** *Q. Rev.* Apr. 307 White *ivory-hunters are scarce nowadays. **1898** *Dublin Rev.* July 168 The lessees also make lucrative speculations in *ivory-hunting. **1835–6** TODD *Cycl. Anat.* I. 460/1 The removal of an *ivory-like exostosis from the tibia. **1863** SPEKE *Discov. Nile* 101 The greatest man we found here was a broken-down *ivory-merchant called Serboko. **1715–20** POPE *Iliad* XIX. 430 The *iv'ry-studded reins return'd behind, Wav'd o'er their backs and to the chariot join'd. **1876** GEO. ELIOT *Dan. Der.* lxx, She was glowing like.. a delicate, *ivory-tinted flower. **1703** *Lond. Gaz.* No. 3902/4 Serjeant Jacob Rand,.. an *Ivory-Turner by Trade. *c* **1611** CHAPMAN *Iliad* I. 197 Th' *ivory-wristed Queen.

10. Special comb.: **ivory-agaric**, a species of mushroom, *Hygrophorus eburneus* (*Syd. Soc. Lex.* 1887); **ivory-barnacle**, a species of Acorn-shell, *Balanus eburneus* (*Cent. Dict.* 1890); **ivory-bill**, a species of woodpecker, *Picus* or *Campephilus principalis*: cf. next; **ivory-billed** *a.*, having a bill resembling ivory, as ***ivory-billed woodpecker*** (see IVORIST), and ***ivory-billed coot***, (*Fulica Americana*); **ivory board**, a kind of pasteboard with both surfaces smooth; **ivory-brown**, bone-brown obtained from ivory; **ivory dome** *U.S. slang*, a stupid person; **ivory-eater** (see quot.); **ivory-exostosis**, *Path.*, 'the form of bone tumour which is hard and dense like ivory' (*Syd. Soc. Lex.* 1884); **ivory-gull**, see GULL *sb.*[1]; **ivory-jelly**, a jelly made from ivory dust or turnings (*Syd. Soc. Lex.* 1887); **ivory-joint**, ? a morbid hardening of a joint; **ivory-line**, *Entom.*, a smooth yellowish-white space found on the elytra of many beetles; **ivory-nut**, the seed of the South American palm, *Phytelephas macrocarpa*, the albumen of which hardens into vegetable ivory: see sense 2; the Corozo-nut; hence **ivory-plant; ivory (nut) palm**, a South American palm of the genus *Phytelephas*, or a Micronesian one of the genus *Metroxylon*, both of which bear nuts yielding vegetable ivory; **ivory-paper**, a thick paper or thin cardboard with a finely prepared polished surface, used by artists; **ivory plum** *U.S.*, the wintergreen, *Gaultheria procumbens*, or the creeping snowberry, *Chiogenes hispidula*, or their fruit; **ivory-rat**, = *ivory-eater*; **ivory-saw** (see quot.); **ivory-shell**, a univalve of the genus *Eburna*, of an ivory colour; **ivory-space**, = *ivory-line*; **ivory-tablet** (see quot.); **ivory-tree**, an East Indian tree of the genus *Wrightia*, having wood of a texture and colour resembling ivory (Miller *Plant-n.* 1884); **ivory-type** (see quot. 1875); **ivorywood** *Austral.*, the tree *Siphonodon australe*, or its timber, which is used for drawing-instruments, etc.; **ivory-yellow**, a very pale yellow, almost white. Also IVORY-BLACK, -BONE, -WHITE.

1787 *Ellicott Almanac 1788* (Winchester, Virginia) sig. B2, The land fowls [of Kentucky] are turkeys, pheasants,.. the perraquet, *ivory-bill, woodcock, and the great owl. **1872** E. COUES *Key to N. Amer. Birds* 191 The ivory-bill and the flicker stand nearly at extremes of the family. **1893** NEWTON *Dict. Birds* 460 *Ivory-bill*, an abbreviation of Ivory-billed Woodpecker, so called from the colour of its beak, *Picus* or *Campephilus principalis*. **1893** *Ivory-billed [see *ivory-bill* above]. **1926** *Paper Terminol.* (Spalding & Hodge) 14 **Ivory boards*, superfine cardboard highly finished by means of bees-waxed rolls. **1962** F. T. DAY *Introd. to Paper* iv. 46 A large variety of boards is produced by the paper maker, in grades ranging from high class Bristol and Ivory boards to the cheaper kind of Triplex board. **1923** *Ivory dome [see DOME *sb.* 4 d]. **1861** DU CHAILLU *Equat. Afr.* xvi. 281 An.. animal of the squirrel kind, called by the natives the *mboco*, which eats ivory. I have called it the '*ivory-eater, *Sciurus eborivorus*'. **1885** *Life Sir R. Christison* I. 122 But eventually he was attacked with what appeared to be sub-acute rheumatism of both knee-joints, ending slowly in '*ivory-joints', or perhaps anchylosis. **1880** P. GILLMORE *On Duty* 11 In the south the veldt is covered with the *ivory needle thorn. **1844** W. PURDIE *Let.* 14 Dec. in *Compan. Bot. Mag.* (1847) LXXIII. 11 The *Phytelephas* (Vegetable *Ivory Palm) is procurable at Sta. Martha. *Ibid.* 12, I think of ascending the Magdalena, and myself collecting growing plants and seeds of the Ivory Palm. **1871** C. KINGSLEY *At Last* I. viii. 303 The ripe fruit [of the Moriche palm] contains first a rich pulpy nut, and at last a hard cone, something like that of the vegetable ivory palm. **1916** *Jrnl. Bombay Nat. Hist. Soc.* XXIV. 682 Names of the Tree [sc. *Phytelephas macrocarpa*]. English: Large-fruited Ivory Plant, Ivory Palm, Ivory nut Palm, Vegetable Ivory Plant. **1951** J. H. KRAEMER *Trees W. Pacific Region* 10 In this genus [sc. *Metroxylon*] are the sago palms and the ivory-nut palms. **1966** E. J. H. CORNER *Nat. Hist. Palms* xiii. 315 This anomalous species is the Caroline ivory-nut palm, *M[etroxylon] amicorum* of Micronesia. **1866** *Treas. Bot.* 884/1 The *Ivory Plant of South America.. producing the nuts known as.. Vegetable Ivory in commerce. **1828** J. NEAL *Rachel Dyer* 55 The more brilliant *ivory-plumbs or clustered bunch-berries rattled among the withered herbage. **1891** *Jrnl. Amer. Folk-Lore* IV. 149 *Gaultheria procumbens* seems to have an almost endless variety of epithets... The berries are called Ivory Plums. **1892** *Ibid.* V. 99 *Chiogenes serpyllifolia*, ivory plums. **1897** MARY KINGSLEY *W. Africa* 325 Ivories.. gnawed by that strange little creature.. the *ivory rat. This squirrel-like creature was first brought to Europe by Paul du Chaillu. **1875** KNIGHT *Dict. Mech.* 1207/2 **Ivory-saw*, a thin saw stretched in a steel frame for sawing ivory from the solid. **1873** ALDRICH *Marjorie Daw* vii, There is an exquisite *ivorytype of Marjorie. **1875** KNIGHT *Dict. Mech.* 1207/2 *Ivory-type* (Photography), a kind of picture in which two finished photographs are taken, one light in colour, made translucent by varnish, tinted on the back, and placed over a stronger picture, so as to give the effect of a photograph in natural colours. **1887** *Colonial & Indian Exhib. Rep. Col. Sect.* 429 *Ivory-wood. **1888** F. M. BAILEY *Queensland Woods* 29 Ivory-wood. A tall tree with straight erect stem, the bark of a light colour... Found in the dense scrubs both north and south in Queensland, and also in New South Wales. **1932** R. H. ANDERSON *Trees New South Wales* 145 Ivorywood.. is sometimes known as Native Guava. **1965** *Austral. Encycl.* II. 310/1 Though widely spread in coastal New South Wales and Queensland, the ivorywood is a comparatively rare tree.

ivory, dial. form of IVY.

ivory-black. A fine soft black pigment, obtained by calcining ivory in a closed vessel; sometimes loosely applied to bone-black.

1634 PEACHAM *Gentl. Exerc., Drawing* 90 With Ivory black as Elephants tooth burned. **1732** J. PEELE *Water-Colours* 53 The proper Black for Water-Colours is what they call Ivory-black. **1836** J. M. GULLY *Magendie's Formul.* (ed. 2) 21 He then dissolves the morphia in acetic acid and treats the solution with ivory-black, in order to withdraw all colour from it.

†**ivory-bone.** *Obs.* Forms: see IVORY and BONE. [Cf. BONE *sb.* 4 b.] = IVORY 1.

13.. *St. Gregory* (Vernon MS.) 195 in *Archiv Stud. neu. Spr.* LV, Tables riche heo tok to hire þat weore i mad of lueerbon. **1513** DOUGLAS *Æneis* I. ix. 21 Als gratius for to behald, I wene, As evor bone [**1555** euour bane] by craft of hand wele dycht. **1530** PALSGR. 235/1 Ivery bone, *yuoyre*. **1549** *Compl. Scot.* i. 20 Castell ylione.. hed al the portis of euoir bane. **1560** ROLLAND *Crt. Venus* II. 697 Thair Reillis all war maid of Euir bane.

ivory tower. [tr. F. *tour d'ivoire* (see below).] A condition of seclusion or separation from the world; in general, protection or shelter from the harsh realities of life. Also (with hyphen) *attrib.* Hence ***ivory-towered*** adj., ***ivory-toweredness***; ***ivory-towerish*** adj., somewhat ivory-towered; ***ivory-towerism, -towerist.***

[**1837** SAINTE-BEUVE *Pensées d'Août, à M. Villemain* 152 Et Vigny, plus secret, Comme en sa tour d'ivoire, avant midi rentrait.] **1911** BRERETON & ROTHWELL tr. *Bergson's Laughter* iii. 135 Each member [of society] must be ever attentive to his social surroundings.. he must avoid shutting himself up in his own peculiar character as a philosopher in his ivory tower. *a* **1916** H. JAMES *Ivory Tower* (1917) II. iii. 142 Doesn't living in an ivory tower just mean the most distinguished retirement? **1922** H. CRANE *Let.* 10 Dec. (1965) 108, I have grown accustomed to an 'ivory tower' sort of existence. **1936** E. POUND *Let.* Jan. (1971) 277 Ivory tower aesthetes. **1938** R. G. COLLINGWOOD *Princ. Art* vi. 120 The tendency was for each artist to construct an ivory tower of his own: to live, that is to say, in a world of his own devising. **1940** H. G. WELLS *New World Order* § 9. 133 We want a Minister of Education who can.. electrify and rejuvenate old dons or put them away in ivory towers, and stimulate the younger ones. **1945** A. HUXLEY *Let.* 2 Apr. (1969) 518 Between ivory-towerism and art for art's sake on the one hand and direct political action on the other lies the alternative of spirtuality. **1947** J. HAYWARD *Prose Lit. since 1939* 46 If [literature] fails in this task it will be reduced to the status of an art pursued for art's sake by isolated groups of writers, segregated from the world in their ivory towers and 'private worlds'. **1953** G. VANN *Water & Fire* iii. 50 That ivory-tower æstheticism which averts its gaze from the squalors of humanity. **1954** 'N. BLAKE' *Whisper in Gloom* vii.

94 I'm going to plunge you into reality, my little Ivory-Towerist. **1959** *20th Cent.* Nov. 401 British governments.. have been badly informed..and Britain's ivory-towered embassies may have to bear some of the blame. **1963** M. McCarthy *Group* vi. 120 We called you the Ivory Tower group. Aloof from the battle. **1963** *Daily Tel.* 12 Oct. 8/7 Pity the poor parson!.. If he eschews all worldly contact, he's accused of being ivory-towerish and out of touch. **1963** *Economist* 26 Oct. 355/1 Every don..however attached to academic ivory-toweredness. **1967** P. Nokes *Professional Task in Welfare Pract.* vii. 113 When I began teaching at the Prison Staff College..I soon became aware of a well established tradition that what was taught there was 'ivory-towered'. **1968** J. J. C. Smart *Between Sci. & Philos.* 17 It would be unwise to think that philosophy is exclusively a subject for inhabitants of ivory towers. **1972** *Science* 19 May 769/3 New realities which make it impossible for them to think and perform in such ivory-tower isolation.

'ivory-'white, *a.* and *sb.*

A. *adj.* White as ivory; of the colour of ivory.

1595 Spenser *Epithal.* 172 Her forehead yvory white. **1871** R. Ellis *Catullus* lxiv. 45 Thrones gleam ivory-white; cup-crown'd blaze brightly the tables. **1882** *Garden* 23 Dec. 553/1 Sepals and petals, ivory-white.

B. *sb.* **1.** The colour of ivory.

1897 *Daily News* 17 Sept. 6/7 Its warm brown contrasting pleasantly with the ivory-white of the cloth.

2. *ellipt.* Ivory-white porcelain; *spec.* a creamy-white porcelain anciently made in China.

†**ivray.** *Obs.* Also -aye. [a. F. *ivraie*, †*ivroie* (16th c. in Littré):—L. *ebriāca* drunken (sc. *herba*), in reference to its intoxicating qualities.] The weed Darnel, *Lolium temulentum*.

1578 Lyte *Dodoens* iv. xv. 469 Iuray is a vitious grayne that combereth or anoyeth corne, especially wheat. **1597** Gerarde *Herbal* i. li. §2. 71 Darnell is called..in English Darnell, of some Iuray and Raye. **1611** Cotgr., *Iuroye*, Darnell, Ray, Iueray. **1879** Prior *Plant-n.*, *Ivray.*

ivy ('aɪvɪ), *sb.* *Pl.* ivies ('aɪvɪz). Forms: α. 1 ífiȝ, ýfiȝ, 3 ivi, 4 yvi, 4–5 yve, yvy, 5–6 ivye, 5–7 ivie, 6 yvie, (ive), 4– ivy. β. 1 ifeȝn, 5 iwen, -yn, 5 iven, 6 yven, 9 *dial.* ivin, (hivin), ivvens. γ. 9 *dial.* ivory, ivery, iv'ry. [OE. *ífiȝ*, obscurely related to OHG. *ebahęwi*, *ebawi*, *ebah*, MHG. *ebe-höu*, *ep-höu*, early mod.G. (1561) *æbhöuw*, Ger. *ep-heu* (1600), *epheu* (1669), MLG. *îflôf*, LG. *eiloof*. The first element of these appears to be an OTeut. **ĭ̄ba*, of which no cognates are known. The second element in OHG. is app. *hęwi*, MHG. *höu*, Ger. *heu* hay; Kluge suggests that OE. *ífiȝ* may similarly go back to an earlier *ĭ̄f-heȝ*. But no explanation appears of the connexion with 'hay'.]

1. a. A well-known climbing evergreen shrub (*Hedera Helix*), indigenous to Europe and parts of Asia and Africa, having dark-green shining leaves, usually five-angled, and bearing umbels of greenish-yellow flowers, succeeded by dark berries; it is a favourite ornamental covering of walls, old buildings, ruins, etc. The plant was anciently sacred to Bacchus.

barren, creeping, small ivy (formerly also *earth-ivy*, and ground-ivy 2): a small, creeping, flowerless variety growing on hedgebanks. ***black, English ivy***: the common ivy, also termed *H. nigra*, from its black berries. ***Queensland ivy***, an Australian species having pinnate leaves. ***variegated ivy***, a variety having variegated leaves.

α. *a* **800** *Leiden Gloss.* 44 *Hederam*, ibaei. *Erfurt Gloss.* 392 *Hedera*, ifeȝ. *c* **1000** in Cockayne *Shrine* 139/27 Weal se is mid ifiȝe bewriȝen. *c* **1000** *Sax. Leechd.* I. 212 Eorð yfiȝ ..þysse wyrte þe man hederan nigran and oþrum naman eorð ifiȝ nemneþ. *a* **1250** *Owl & Night.* 27 On old stoc..was mid ivi al bi-growe. **1398** Trevisa *Barth. De P.R.* xvii. liii. (Bodl. MS.), Oftyn Poetes were crowned with Iuye: in token of noble witte & scharpe, for the yuye is alwei grene. **1578** Lyte *Dodoens* iii. xlix. 387 The blacke Iuye hath harde wooddy branches. **1597** Gerarde *Herbal* ii. ccci. 708 Creeping or barren Iuie is called..in English ground Iuie. **1624** Capt. Smith *Virginia* v. 170 The poysoned weed is much in shape like our English Iuy. **1764** Churchill *Gotham* i, The Ivy crawling o'er the hallow'd cell. **1814** L. Hunt *Feast Poets, Bacchus, or the Pirates* (1815) 156 And then an ivy, with a flowering shoot, Ran up the mast in rings. **1835** Hooker *Brit. Flora* I. 123 The Irish Ivy is much cultivated on account of the vastly larger size of its foliage, and its very rapid growth. **1837** Dickens *Pickw.* vi, Oh, a dainty plant is the Ivy green, That creepeth o'er ruins old! **1839** Tennyson *Lotos-eaters, Chor. Song* i, Here are cool mosses deep, And thro' the moss the ivies creep.

β. *a* **800** *Corpus Gloss.* 718 *Hedera*, ifeȝn. *c* **1425** *Voc.* in Wr.-Wülcker 644/26 *Hec edera*,..iwyn. *a* **1450** in Horstm. *Altengl. Leg.* (1881) 277 þan se þai a howse a lytyll þam fro Oure-growne wyt Iwen. **1483** *Cath. Angl.* 199/1 An Iven, *edera*. **1535** Coverdale *2 Macc.* vi. 7 They were constrayned to weere garlandes of yven. **1828** *Craven Dial.*, *Ivin*, Ivy. **1876–93** *Ivin* in north. dial. glossaries from Northumberland to Lincolnshire. **1884** *Cheshire Gloss.*, *Ivvens*, or Ivvy, ivy.

γ. **1877** *N.W. Linc. Gloss.*, *Ivory*, ivy. **1886** *S.W. Linc. Gloss.*, *Ivery*, *Iv'ry*, often used for Ivy; as ' The ivery had grown thruff the roof'. **1895** *E. Anglia Gloss.*, *Ivory*, ivy. **1895** Emerson *Birds* 56.

†**b.** Used as a sign that wine was sold within; cf. *ivy-garland* in 3 d, and ivy-bush. *Obs.*

1436 *Pol. Poems* (Rolls) II. 183 What nedeth a garlande, whyche is made of ivye, Shew a tavern wynelesse, also thryve I. **14..** *Why I can't be a Nun* 358 in *E.E.P.* (1862) 147 A fayre garlond of yve grene Whyche hangeth at a taverne dore, Hyt ys a false token as I wene, But yf there be wyne gode and sewer. **1612** W. Parkes *Curtaine-Dr.* (1876) 37 The Iuy is hung out in almost euery place, and open market, kept as vnder the allowance of authority.

c. *U.S.* = *poison ivy* (see sense 2).

1788 J. May *Jrnl.* 9 June (1873) 65, I have been clearing land for eight days, and now begin to feel the effects of poison—from ivy, doubtless. **1849** F. Parkman *Calif. & Oregon Trail* xiii. 205 In the morning Shaw found himself poisoned by ivy.

2. Applied, with distinctive addition, to various (usually climbing or creeping) plants of other genera.

American or **five-leaved ivy**, Virginia creeper, *Ampelopsis hederacea* or *quinquefolia*. **bindweed-leaved ivy**, the genus *Menispermum*, Moon-seed. **Boston** or **Japanese ivy**, *Ampelopsis tricuspidata*. **Colosseum** or **Kenilworth ivy**, Ivy-leaved Toad-flax (Miller *Plant-n.* 1884). **German ivy**, *Senecio mikanoides*, a variety of Groundsel (Webster 1864); *Yellow German ivy*, *S. scandens*; **Indian ivy**, *Scindapsus pertusus* (*Monstera deliciosa*) and other species (Miller); **Mexican ivy**, *Cobæa scandens* (*ibid.*); **(American) poison ivy**, *Rhus Toxicodendron* (*Treas. Bot.* 1866); **West Indian ivy**, *Marcgravia umbellata* (Miller). See also ground-ivy.

1588 Greene *Pandosto* (1607) 20 To see if perchance the sheepe was browzing on the sea Iuie. **1760** J. Lee *Introd. Bot.* App. 316 Ivy, Bindweed-leaved, *Menispermum*. **1866** *Treas. Bot.* 53/2 *Ampelopsis..hederacea*, the Virginian Creeper or American Ivy. *Ibid.* 632/2 *Ivy..German*, a garden name for *Senecio mikanoides*. **1879** Britten & Holland *Plant-n.*, *Five-leaved Ivy*, a common garden name for the Virginia creeper, *Ampelopsis hederacea*.

3. *attrib.* and *Comb.* **a.** simple attributive, as *ivy-bloom*, *-bud*, †*-crop*, *-crown*, *-shroud*, *-stem*, *-wood*, *-wreath*. **b.** instrumental, as *ivy-bound*, *-circled*, *-clad*, *-covered*, *-crowned*, *-gnarled*, *-hung*, *-mantled*, *-ridden*, †*-tapissed*, *-twined*, *-walled*, *-wimpled*, *-wound*, *-wreathed* adjs. **c.** similative, as *ivy-twisted* adj.

1821 Shelley *Prometh. Unb.* i. i. 745 The yellow bees in the *ivy-bloom. **1862** Barnes *Hwomely Rhymes* I. 201 Avore the walls were *ivy-bound. *a* **1593** Marlowe *'Come, live with me'* v, A belt of straw and *ivie buds. **1622** Drayton *Poly-olb.* xxvi. 118 An *Iuy-seeled Bower. **1875** W. McIlwraith *Guide Wigtownshire* 83 A small two-storied *ivy-clad tower. **1872** Jenkinson *Guide Eng. Lakes* (1879) 5 *The ivy-covered house passed on the left is 'The Knoll'. *c* **1000** *Sax. Leechd.* II. 214 *Ifiȝ croppena on þam monðe ȝegaderod þe we hatað ianuarius. *a* **1100** *Ags. Voc.* in Wr.-Wülcker 298/22 *Corimbus*, ifiȝcrop. *a* **1747** Holdsworth *Rem. Virgil* 26 The *Ivy crown is mentioned frequently by the ancients, as worn by the poets in those days. **1632** Milton *L'Allegro* 16 Whom lovely Venus..To *ivy-crowned Bacchus bore. **1813** Shelley *Q. Mab* ix. 128 Soothing notes Of *ivy-fingered winds. **1867** Mrs. Stowe *Knocking* in *Rel. Poems* 14 *Ivy-gnarled and weed-bejangled. **1858** Hawthorne *Fr. & It. Jrnls.* (1872) I. 58 Gray and *ivy-hung antiquity. **1597–8** Bp. Hall *Sat.* v. i. 9 Renowmed Aquine, now I..to thy hand yeeld up the *iuye-mace From crabbed Persius, and more smooth Horace. **1750** Gray *Elegy* 9 Save that from yonder *ivy-mantled tower The moping owl does to the moon complain. **1865** E. Burritt *Walk Land's End* 87 The silvery music of the old bells in the *ivy-netted tower. **1867** W. Cory *Lett. & Jrnls.* (1897) 197 Never have I seen ruins so ruinous, so *ivy-ridden. **1859** Tennyson *Enid* 322 Monstrous *ivy-stems Claspt the gray walls with hairy-fibred arms. **1675** Hobbes *Odyss.* (1677) 192 And in a basket sets on bread of wheat, And in an *ivy-tankard wine good store. **1602** Carew *Cornwall* 111 b, Onely there remaine the *Iuie-tapissed wals of the keepe. **1820** W. Tooke tr. *Lucian* I. 314 The *ivy-turned thyrsus in his hand. **1863** I. Williams *Baptistery* ii. xxiii. (1874) 74 In *ivy-walled solitude. **1621** S. Ward *Happiness of Practice* (1627) 9 Owles in *Iuy-woods. **1626** Bacon *Sylva* §3 Passing it thorow Ivy wood. **1644** Digby *Nat. Bodies* (1645) 183 The ivywood and divers others. **1896** 'M. Field' *Attila* ii. 36 The bowl of ivy-wood Our hero drinks from. **1866** J. B. Rose tr. *Ovid's Met.* 309 The thyrsus *ivy-wound.

d. Special comb.: **ivy-bells**, the Ivy-leaved Bell-flower, *Campanula hederacea* (Britten & Holland); **ivy-bind**, a climbing ivy stem; **ivy-bindweed**, Climbing Buckwheat, *Polygonum Convolvulus*; **ivy broom rape**, a species of *Orobanche*, with purple stem, parasitic upon ivy; **ivy-chickweed**, Ivy-leaved Speedwell, *Veronica hederifolia* (Britten & Holland); **ivy-dart**, the thyrsus; **ivy-fern** (see quot.); **ivy-garland**, a garland of ivy, formerly the sign of a house where wine was sold: cf. ivy-bush; **ivy-geranium**, the procumbent Ivy-leaved Pelargonium; **ivy-girl**, an effigy of a girl formed of ivy: see quots., and cf. *holly-boy* s.v. holly 3; **ivy (grape)-vine**, a species of vine, *Vitis indivisa* (Miller *Plant-n.* 1884); **ivy-gum**, the resinous juice which exudes from the ivy: cf. *gum ivy* (gum *sb.*[2] 3 b); **ivy-like** *a.*, like or resembling ivy; **ivy-owl** (see quot.); **ivy-resin** = *ivy-gum*; **ivy-twine** = *ivy-bind*; **ivy-vine**, the Virginia Creeper; **ivy-wort**, (*a*) Lindley's name for the natural order *Araliaceæ*, which includes the ivy and its congeners; (*b*) see quot. 1640 for *ivy-like*. Also ivy-bush, -leaf, -leaved, -tod, -tree.

1731 T. Cox *Magna Brit.* VI. 232/2 [The lightning] ran down in the Form of an *Ivy-bind, searing the Tree. **1578** Lyte *Dodoens* iii. liii. 394 This kinde of Bindeweede is called..Windweede, or *Iuybindweede. **1879** Britten & Holland *Plant-n.*, Ivy-Bindweed, *Polygonum Convolvulus*. *a* **1661** Holyday *Juvenal* 134 For in Pierian caves he never sings, Nor with an *ivy-dart divinely raves. **1865** Gosse *Land & Sea* (1874) 351 The curious *Ivy-fern, *Hemionitis palmata*, whose five-angled leaves, grovelling on the ground, clothed with a bristling crop of red down [etc.]. **1553** T. Wilson *Rhet.* (1580) 177 By an *Ivie garland, we judge there is wine to sell. **1894** *Daily News* 17 July 6/5 Drooping sprays of *ivy geranium, with its beautiful pointed leaves of brightest, glossiest green. **1736** Pegge *Kenticisms*, *Holly-boys* and **Ivy-girls*, in West Kent, figures in the form of a boy and girl, made one of holly, the other of ivy, upon a Shrove Tuesday, to make sport with. **1779** *Gentl. Mag.* XLIX. 137 The boys..in another part of the village, were assembled together and burning what they called an *Ivy Girl*, which they had stolen from the girls. **1855** Mayne *Expos. Lex.*, *Ivy-gum. **1861** Miss Pratt *Flower. Pl.* III. 103 In the south of Europe and north of Africa, an exudation is found on the old trunks of the Ivy, called ivy-gum. **1640** Parkinson *Theat. Bot.* v. xcv. 681 *Cymbalaria Italica Hederacea*, the Italian Gondelo or *Ivie like leafe. *Ibid.* 682 We may call it in English eyther Iviewort or the Ivie like leafe. **1842** H. Rogers *Ess.* I. i. 10 Wit..so disproportionate, that it conceals in its ivy-like luxuriance the robust wisdom about which it coils itself. **1678** Ray *Willughby's Ornith.* 102 The common brown or *Ivy-Owl. **1753** Chambers *Cycl. Supp.*, **Ivy-Resin*..is brought from Persia, and some other of the hot countries..It is said to be emollient and detergent, and to make a noble balsam for fresh wounds. **1597–8** Bp. Hall *Sat.*, *Defiance Envie* 19 Nor the low bush feares climbing *yvy-twine. **1867** Mrs. Stowe *Knocking* in *Rel. Poems* 12 The bolt is clogged and dusty; Many-fingered *ivy-vine Seals it fast with twist and twine. **1640** *Iviewort [see *ivy-like*]. **1866** *Treas. Bot.* 85/1 *Araliaceæ* (*Araliads*, *Ivyworts*), form a small natural order closely approaching umbellifers.

Hence **'ivy** *v. trans.*, to cover with or as with ivy (cf. ivied); in quot. *fig.*

1843 Lowell *Poems, Prometheus*, Earth with her twining memories ivies o'er Their holy sepulchres.

ivy, variant of *Ive* in herb Ive.

'ivy-,berry. Also ivenberry. **a.** The fruit or seed of the ivy.

c **1400** Maundev. (1839) xv. 168 It [a tree] is alle grene as it were Ivy Beryes. **1483** *Cath. Angl.* 199/1 An Iven bery, *cornubus*. **1530** Palsgr. 235/1 Ivy berry, *grayne de hierre*. **1634** Milton *Comus* 55 His clustering locks, With ivy-berries wreathed. **1971** *Country Life* 25 Mar. 667/3 The woodpigeons..had been on the ivy berries and the clover fields.

b. *U.S.* The wintergreen or checkerberry, *Gaultheria procumbens*.

1840 *Southern Lit. Messenger* VI. 518/2 There were the fringed polygula, the buttercup, wild geranium, bunch-plum, ivy-berry. **1892** *Jrnl. Amer. Folk-Lore* V. 100 *Gaultheria procumbens*, ivy-berry.

ivy-bush. A bushy branch of ivy; *fig.* a place of concealment or retirement. †**b.** *spec.* A bush of ivy or a representation of it, placed outside a tavern as a sign that wine was sold there; often in phrase ***good wine needs no ivy-bush***; hence, the tavern itself (*obs.*). Cf. bush *sb.*[1] 5. †Hence *fig.* A sign or display (of anything) (*obs.*).

1576 Fleming *Panopl. Epist.* 382 Hee is never from the Ivie bush: his lippes are alwayes staynd with the Juice of Bacchus his berries. **1580** Lyly *Euphues* Ep. Ded. (Arb.) 204 Where the wine is neat, ther needeth no Iuie-bush. **1591** Florio *2nd Fruites* 185 Womens beauty..is like vnto an Iuy bush, that cals men to the tauern, but hangs itselfe withoute to winde and wether. **1612** W. Parkes *Curtaine-Dr.* (1876) 12 Then Tobacco was an Indian, vnpickt and vnpiped, now made the common Iuy-bush of luxury. **1648** Jenkyn *Blind Guide* i. 14 This Ivye-bush of boasting doth but shew the badnesse of his wine. **1699** Locke *Educ.* (ed. 4) §94 An old Boy at his first appearance, with all the Gravity of his Ivy-Bush about him, is sure to draw on him the Eyes and Chirping of the whole Town Volery. **1738** Swift *Polite Conv.* i. 94 'Pr'y thee, how did the Fool look?' 'Look! Egad, he look'd for all the World like an Owl in an Ivy Bush'. **1823** A. Clarke *Mem. Wesley Fam.* 232 Mr. Wesley gave out the following line; 'Like to an owl in ivy-bush'. **1869** Hazlitt *Eng. Prov.* 262 Like an owl in an ivy-bush.

ivyl, obs. form of evil.

'ivy-'leaf. a. A leaf of ivy; †taken as the type of a thing of little value. ***to pipe in (with) an ivy-leaf*** (*fig.*), to console oneself (for failure, etc.) with some frivolous employment (*obs.*).

c **1000** *Sax. Leechd.* II. 326 Nim..ifiȝ leaf þe on eorþan wixþ. *c* **1374** Chaucer *Troylus* v. 1433 But, Troylus, thou mayst now, este or weste, Pipe in an ivy leefe, if that the leste. **1387–8** T. Usk *Test. Love* iii. vii. (Skeat) I. 50 Far wel the gardiner, he may pipe with an yue leafe, his fruite is failed. **1390** Gower *Conf.* II. 21 That all nis worth an yvy lefe. **1869** Hazlitt *Eng. Prov.* 425 *To pipe in an ivy leaf*, to go and engage in any sterile or idle occupation, to hang one's heels up.

b. *attrib.* = ivy-leaved *a.*

1909 *Daily Chron.* 5 June 9/5 Ivy-leaf geraniums can be depended on to produce a long succession of blooms. **1939** E. Bowen *Coll. Impressions* (1950) 64 A window-box gay with pink ivy-leaf geraniums. **1957** *Encycl. Brit.* X. 205/2 The ivy-leaf geranium, derived from *P*[*elargonium*] *peltatum*, has given rise to an important class of both double- and single-flowered forms adapted especially for pot culture, hanging baskets, [etc.].

Ivy League. Name given to a group of long-established eastern U.S. universities; also *attrib.* of the social and intellectual prestige or other characteristics of these universities, or of, relating to, or characteristic of the members or former members of these universities. So **Ivy Leaguer**, a member or former member of an Ivy League university.

[**1933** S. Woodward in *N.Y. Herald Tribune* 16 Oct. 18/1 The fates which govern [football] play among the ivy colleges and academic boiler-factories alike seem to be going

around the circuit.] **1939** *Princeton Alumni Weekly* 29 Sept., The 'Ivy League' is something which does not exist and is simply a term which has been increasingly used in recent years by sports writers, applied rather loosely to a group of eastern colleges. **1943** K. P. KEMPTON in *Sat. Even. Post* 22 May 14 (*title*) Ivy Leaguer. **1949** S. WOODWARD *Sports Page* xii. 132 For many years the colleges seemed to feel that there was something not quite nice about the press. It was fashionable, especially in the hallowed precincts of the Eastern Ivy League, to snub and bamboozle the sports writers. **1951** J. D. SALINGER *Catcher in Rye* xii. 103 My father wants me to go to Yale, or maybe Princeton, but I swear, I wouldn't go to one of those Ivy League colleges. *Ibid.* xvii. 133 The jerk had one of those very phoney, Ivy League voices, one of those very tired, snobby voices. **1959** *Listener* 12 Feb. 283/1 Hemingway's sense of Ivy-League social life and its complex snobberies. **1962** 'S. RANSOME' *Without Trace* v. 49 He could drop his natural guttersnipe talk and sound like an Ivy Leaguer whenever it suited him. **1965** *Times Lit. Suppl.* 25 Nov. 1053/1 James Purdy's Ivy-league rapist. **1970** *Daily Tel.* 28 Apr. 4/6 Rising costs are driving away middle-income students from some of America's Ivy League universities, turning the campuses into places for the poor, supported by scholarships, and the rich, admissions officers say. *Ibid.*, The Ivy League colleges are Brown, Columbia, Cornell, Dartmouth, Harvard, Pennsylvania, Princeton and Yale. **1973** S. ALSOP *Stay of Execution* (1974) II. 171 Waspish Ivy Leaguers like Roosevelt or Welles.

ivy-leaved, *a.* Having quinquangular leaves like those of the common ivy.

In many names of plants, as **ivy-leaved bellflower**, *Campanula hederacea*; **i. chickweed** or **speedwell**, Ivy-chickweed; **i. crowfoot**, *Ranunculus hederaceus*; **i. duckweed**, *Lemna trisulca*; **i. pelargonium**, a creeping species of *Pelargonium*; **i. toad-flax**, *Linaria Cymbalaria*.

1789 J. PILKINGTON *View Derbysh.* I. viii. 417 *Ranunculus hederaceus*, Ivy-leaved Crowfoot. **1861** MISS PRATT *Flower. Pl.* IV. 125 Ivy-leaved Toad-flax.. is a common plant on the walls of gardens. **1887** *Daily News* 11 July 3/7 A magnificent display of ivy-leaved pelargoniums.

'ivy-'tod. *arch.* [See TOD.] = IVY-BUSH.

1579 SPENSER *Sheph. Cal.* Mar. 67 At length within an Yuie todde.. I heard a busie bustling. **1603** DRAYTON *Heroic. Ep.* xiii. 158 Roosted all day within an Ivy Tod. **1798** COLERIDGE *Anc. Mar.* VII. v, When the ivy-tod is heavy with snow. **1885** TENNYSON *Balin* 330 The battlement over-topt with ivytods.

'ivy-'tree.

† **1.** A large plant of ivy. *Obs.*

1382 WYCLIF *1 Kings* xix. 4 Whanne he was comen, and satte vndir an yue tree. **1530** PALSGR. 235/1 Ivy tree, *hierre*. **1707** *Curios. in Husb. & Gard.* 71 Trunks of Ivy-Trees, that grew along on the Ground.

2. a. An evergreen tree of New Zealand (*Panax Colensoi*); also ***Otago ivy-tree***; **b.** A North American genus of evergreens, American Laurel, *Kalmia*.

1760 J. LEE *Introd. Bot.* App. 316 Ivy-tree of America, *Kalmia*. **1883** J. HECTOR *Hand-bk. New Zealand* 127 *Horoeka*, ivy-tree, an ornamental, slender, and sparingly-branched tree. Wood close-grained and tough. **1884** MILLER *Plant-n.*, *Panax Colensoi*, Otago Ivy-tree.

iw, obs. form of YEW.

† **i-wake**, *v. Obs.* In 3 i-wakien. [f. I-[1] + WAKE *v.*: cf. MHG. *gewachen*.] *intr.* To wake.

c **1205** LAY. 28082 Þa gon ich iwakien: Swiðe ich gon to quakien.

i-waked, -et, ME. pa. pple. of WAKE *v.*

† **i-'wald, i-weld**, *sb. Obs.* [OE. *ȝeweald* (= OS. *giwald*, OHG. *ga-, giwalt*, MHG. and Ger. *gewalt*, Du. *geweld*), f. *ȝe-*, I-[1] + root *wald-*, of *weald-an*: see WIELD *v.*] Power.

a **1000** *Cædmon's Gen.* 635 (Gr.) þonne he his ȝeweald hafað. *c* **1175** *Lamb. Hom.* 103 þe mon ne ah his modes iwald. *a* **1250** *Owl & Night.* 1541 Godd hit wot! heo nah iweld, Tha heo hine makie kukeweld.

† **i-walden**, *v. Obs.* [OE. *ȝewealdan* (= OS. *giwaldan*, OHG. *giwaltan*, MHG. *gewalten*, Goth. *gawaldan*), f. *ȝe-*, I-[1] + *wealdan*: see WIELD *v.*[1]] *trans.* To have power over; to sway, rule, control.

c **1000** ÆLFRIC *Hom.* II. 308 Ic..ȝewealde ealles middaneardes. *a* **1175** *Cott. Hom.* 231 Drihten.. alre sceafte ȝewalt. *c* **1205** LAY. 17213 Mid liste me mai ihalden þat strengðe ne mai iwalden.

i-walken, ME. pa. pple. of WALK *v.*[1]

i-walled, ME. pa. pple. of WALL *v.*

i-wan: see I-WON.

i-waned, ME. pa. pple. of WANE *v.*

i-war, i-ware, i-warre, obs. ff. AWARE.

i-warisd, ME. pa. pple. of WARISH *v.*

i-warned, ME. pa. pple. of WARN *v.*

† **i-'warness.** *Obs.* [f. *iwar*, obs. f. AWARE + -NESS.] Watchfulness, vigilance, wariness.

a **1250** *Owl & Night.* 1226 Grete duntes beoth the lasse, ȝef me i-kepth mid i-warnesse.

i-warpen, ME. pa. pple. of WARP *v.*

i-wasche(n, i-washe, i-wasshen, ME. pa. pple. of WASH *v.*

i-wasted, ME. pa. pple. of WASTE *v.*

i-watred, ME. pa. pple. of WATER *v.*

i-waxen, ME. pa. pple. of WAX *v.*

iwce, Iwe, obs. forms of JUICE, JEW.

i-wedded, -et, ME. pa. pple. of WED *v.*

† **i-'wede.** *Obs.* [OE. *ȝewǽde, -wéde* (= OHG. *ga-, giwâti*, MHG. *gewæte*), f. *ȝe-*, I-[1] + *wǽd, wǽde, wede*, WEED *sb.*] A garment, a weed.

c **950** *Lindisf. Gosp.* Matt. iii. 4 Ðe ilca soðlice iohannes hæfde ȝewede of herum ðæra camella. *c* **1000** ÆLFRIC *Hom.* II. 148 He nolde awendan.. his ȝewæda ðe he on westene hæfde. *c* **1175** *Lamb. Hom.* 109 On ete and on wete, and ec on iwedan. *c* **1205** LAY. 9450 On heo duden heore iweden. *Ibid.* 26754 Ne nime ȝe nenne stede No nanes cnihtes iwede.

i-weie, i-weye, ME. pa. pple. of WEIGH *v.*

i-weld, ME. pa. pple. of WELL *v.*

i-weld: see I-WALD.

† **i-welde**, *v. Obs.* Also ȝewilde(n. [OE. *ȝewieldan, -wyldan*, f. *ȝeweald*, I-WALD: see WIELD *v.*] *trans.* To exercise power over; to wield, rule; to subdue.

c **1000** *Ags. Gosp.* Mark v. 4 Hine nan man ȝewyldan ne mihte. *c* **1175** *Lamb. Hom.* 111 Iwisliche þa clennesse iwelt alle unþeawes. *c* **1205** LAY. 9029 Tou and twenti wintre þis lond he iwalde.

i-welled, ME. pa. pple. of WELL *v.*

i-wemmed, ME. pa. pple. of WEM *v.*, to stain.

† **i-wende**, *sb. Obs.* [ME.; origin obscure: perh. related to next.] ? Contrivances.

a **1250** *Owl & Night.* 651 Men habbet, among other i-wende, A rum-hus at hore bures ende.

† **i-'wende**, *v. Obs.* [OE. *ȝewęndan* (= OHG. *giwenten*, Goth. *gawandjan*), f. *ȝe-*, I-[1] + *węndan* to turn, WEND.]

1. *trans.* To turn; to change; to bring about.

Beowulf (Z.) 315 Guð-beorna sum wicg ȝe-wende. *a* **1000** *Cædmon's Gen.* 427 (Gr.) ȝif hit eower æniȝ mæȝe ȝewendan mid wihte, þæt [etc.]. *c* **1175** *Lamb. Hom.* 97 Matheus þet wes cachepol, þene he iwende to god-spellere. *a* **1225** *Ancr. R.* 254 Sansumes foxes, þet hefden þe nebbes euerichon iwend frommard oðer.

2. To turn oneself; to turn; to go. **a.** *refl.*

a **1000** *Boeth. Metr.* xxii. 113 Æȝhwilc..hine hræðe sceolde eft ȝewendan in to sinum modes ȝemynde. *c* **1275** *Passion Our Lord* 112 in *O.E. Misc.* 40 He hym vt iwende al bi þuster nyhte.

b. *intr.* To turn, wend one's way, go.

971 *Blickl. Hom.* 193 Hie..siþþan næfre to unrihtum ne ȝewendað. *c* **1000** ÆLFRIC *Hom.* I. 60 Drusiana þa aras.. and ..ham ȝewende. *c* **1175** *Lamb. Hom.* 97 Hit iwendeð from ufele to gode. *a* **1225** *St. Marher.* 2 Hire moðer wes iwend þe wei þe worldliche men.. schulen iwenden. *c* **1275** *Passion our Lord* 148 in *O.E. Misc.* 41 Vre louerd myd heom iwende to geth-semany. *a* **1300** *Floriz & Bl.* 61 Hire to feche ihc wille i-wende.

† **i-wene**, *v. Obs.* [OE. *ȝewénan* (= Goth. *gawênjan*), f. *ȝe-*, I-[1] + *wénan* to WEEN.] *trans.* and *intr.* To expect; to hope; to think, suppose.

a **1000** *Juliana* 453 (Gr.) Ic..me þyslicre ær þraȝe ne ȝewende! *c* **1000** *Ags. Ps.* (Th.) lxviii. 3 Ic on God minne ..ȝewene. *c* **1205** LAY. 20237 Al hit oðer iwarð: oðer he iwende. *c* **1275** *Ibid.* 17722 Ware his euere þe man.. þat wolde hit iwene þat he soch were.

i-wenet, ME. pa. pple. of WEAN *v.*

i-went, ME. pa. pple. of WEND *v.*

i-weorht, ME. pa. pple. of WORK *v.*

† **i-'wepen.** *Obs.* [f. I-[1] + *wepen*, WEAPON: cf. OHG. *giwâfani*, *gewâfene*, MHG. *gewâfen*, *-wæfen*.] Weapons, arms, equipment.

c **1205** LAY. 28388 He hehte his cnihtes alle mid alle heore iwepnen ut of burhȝe wenden.

i-wepened, i-wepned, ME. pa. pple. of WEAPON *v.*

i-wept, ME. pa. pple. of WEEP *v.*

i-werche: see I-WURCHE.

i-werned, ME. pa. pple. of WARN *v.*

i-werred, ME. pa. pple. of WAR *v.*

i-wersed, ME. pa. pple. of WORSE *v.*

i-weschen, i-wesscen, ME. pa. pple. of WASH *v.*

i-wet, ME. pa. pple. of WET *v.*

i-weve, ME. pa. pple. of WEAVE *v.*

† **i-whiles**, *adv.* and *conj. Obs.* In 4 i-whils, ewhils, ywhils. [f. WHILES: the nature of the prefix is obscure.] **A.** *adv.* In the mean time, meanwhile. **B.** *conj.* Whilst.

a **1340** HAMPOLE *Psalter* ix. 23, I whils þe wickid prides kyndeld is þe pore. *Ibid.* xxxix. 11 What profetabilte is in my blode: ywhils I descend in corupcioun. *Ibid.* xci. 14 Thai sall resayfe mykil mare when this life is endid and i whils thai sall be wele suffrand.

iwhillc, early ME. form of OE. *ȝehwylc*, EACH, q.v.

i-whited, ME. pa. pple. of WHITE *v.*

† **i-'wiht**, *a. Obs.* [f. I-[1] + ME. *wiht*: see WIGHT *a.*] Valiant, brave.

c **1205** LAY. 12175 He chæs of þan iwihte ten þusend cnihten.

† **i-wil**, *a. Obs.* [f. stem of WILL *v.*; cf. Goth. *gawilja*, *-jis* willing.] Pleasant, agreeable.

c **1205** LAY. 17122 Hit weoren him swiðe iwil þat he þerof wuste. *Ibid.* 29515 Þat him wes ful iwil.

iwil, obs. Sc. form of EVIL.

† **i-'will**, *sb. Obs.* Forms: 1 **ȝewil(l**, 2–3 **i-wil, i-wille**, 3–4 **ywyl, ywille**. [OE. *ȝewill* and *ȝewile*, f. *ȝe-*, I-[1] + stem of *will-an* to WILL.] Will, wish; pleasure.

c **888** K. ÆLFRED *Boeth.* iv, On yfelra manna ȝewill. *c* **1175** *Lamb. Hom.* 61 God..ȝife us to him god iwil. *Ibid.* 93 Þæt weorc wes bigunnen onȝen godes iwillan. *c* **1205** LAY. 6229 ȝif hit weore þin iwille and þu hit don woldest. *a* **1275** *Prov. Ælfred* 423 in *O.E. Misc.* 129 Ich telle him for a dote, þad sait[h] al is y-wille, þanne he sulde ben stille. **1340** *Ayenb.* 94 Hyer is myn ywyl to spekene of uirtue more openliche.

i-wilned, -et, ME. pa. pple. of WILNE *v.*

† **i-win**, *sb. Obs.* Also i-wyn. [OE. *ȝewin(n* (= OS. *giwin*, OHG. *gi-*, *gewin*, MHG. *gewin*, G. *gewinn*), f. *ȝe-*, I-[1] + *winnan* to labour; to suffer; to fight, contend; to win: see WIN *v.*]

1. Labour, toil; suffering. (Only in OE.)

c **900** tr. *Bæda's Hist.* II. i. (1890) 94 þis ȝewin & þissum ȝelic, þeos ȝemen þe wæs. *c* **1000** *Ags. Gosp.* Luke xxii. 44 He wæs on ȝewinne & hine lange ȝebæd.

2. Battle, war; contest, strife.

c **888** K. ÆLFRED *Boeth.* xxiv. §2 Sume.. tiliað þonne þæs æȝðer ȝe on sibbe ȝe on ȝewinne. *c* **1205** LAY. 9044 Ne bilæfde he næuer nænne.. þat heold feht and iwin Swa dude Kinbelin.

3. Gain, profit.

c **1000** *Ags. Ps.* (Th.) civ. 39 Hi folca ȝewinn fremdra ȝesæton. *c* **1275** *Duty of Christians* 91 in *O.E. Misc.* 144 Idelschipe and luþer iwyn.. We mote for-sake.

† **i-win, -winne**, *v. Obs.* Forms: 1 **ȝewinnan**, 2–4 **i-winne(n**, 4 **ywynne**. [OE. *ȝewinnan* (= OS. *gewinnan*, OHG. *gawinnan*, Ger. and Du. *gewinnen*), f. *ȝe-*, I-[1] + *winnan* to labour, struggle, suffer, WIN.]

1. *intr.* To struggle, contend, fight. (Only in OE.)

971 *Blickl. Hom.* 173 Hu hie wiþ Simone þæm dry fæstlice ȝefliton and ȝewunnon.

2. To gain by struggling or fighting, to win.

a **1000** *Boeth. Metr.* i. 17 Ða wæs Romana rice ȝewunnen. *a* **1100** *O.E. Chron.* an. 1090 Hu he mihte.. Normandiȝe of him ȝewinnan. *c* **1205** LAY. 2194 Brutlond heo wolden iwinnen. *Ibid.* 2560 Þus he iwon al þis lond. *a* **1250** *Prov. Ælfred* in *O.E. Misc.* 110 Þe mon þe on his youhþe swo swinkeþ, and worldes weole her iwinþ. **1297** R. GLOUC. (Rolls) 10687 [Hii] bilaye þe castel longe, ar hii him miȝte iwinne. *c* **1305** *St. Christopher* 194 in *E.E.P.* (1862) 65 Wel auȝte heo heuene iwinne. *c* **1380** *Sir Ferumb.* 478 Say him ..þat þov hem ywonne heer. *Ibid.* 4969 If we mowe þe tour ywynne.

i-wipet, ME. pa. pple. of WIPE *v.*

iwis, ywis (ɪ'wɪs), *a.*, *adv.*, and *sb. arch.* Forms: α. 1 **ȝewis**, 2–7 **iwis**, (4–5 **i-wis**, 4–7 **I-wis**, 4–9 **I wis**); 2–4 **iwiss**, (6 **I wys**), 3–5 **ywys**, 3–7 **ywis**, 4–6 **iwys, e-wis**, 6 **ywus, yewus**, 6–7 **iwus**, **I wus**. β. 3–6 **iwisse**, (3–4 **i wisse**, 4–7 **I wisse**), 4–5 **iwise, iwysse**, 4–7 **ywisse**, 5 **ywysse**, 6 **I wyse, yewisse**, 7 **I wusse**. Nearly every one of these forms occurs written continuously, hyphened, and as two words; in the two latter cases, those beginning with *i* have frequently a capital, *I-wis*, *I wis*, *I wisse*, etc. [α. OE. *ȝewis* adj. (= OHG. *giwis*, MHG. and Du. *gewis*, Ger. *gewiss* certain), of which the neuter was used adverbially in ME. β. ME. *iwisse* adv. corresp. to an OE. type **ȝewisse* = OHG. *ga-*, *giwisso*, MHG. *gewisse* certainly. After 14th c., when final *-e* ceased to have any value, the two forms were mere variant spellings, as is seen by the riming of *iwise* with *his* in *Cursor M.*]

A. *adj.* (*ȝewis*) Certain (subjectively and objectively). Only in OE.

c **888** K. ÆLFRED *Boeth.* xli. §4 Ic wundriȝe hwy swa mæniȝe wise men.. swa lytel ȝewis funden. *c* **900** tr. *Bæda's Hist.* IV. xxv. [xxiv.] (1890) 348 Þæt is ȝeseȝen þæt he wære ȝewis his seolfes forðfore. *a* **1000** *Guthlac* v. (Goodwin) 30 We syndon ȝewisse þines lifes. *c* **1000** *Gosp. Nicod.* iii, Myd ȝewyssum ȝesceade yrn & clypa.. þone [man].

B. *adv.* (*ȝewis*, *iwis*, and *iwisse*) Certainly, assuredly, indeed, truly. (Often with weakened sense as a metrical tag.)

The writing with capital I, and separation of the two elements, have led later authors to understand and use it erroneously as = *I wot*, *I know*, as if a present of *I wist*.

?*c* **1160** *Winteney Rule St. Benet* (1888) 39 Ic eam ʒewis wyrm & nængman. *a* **1175** *Cott. Hom.* 233 He is iwiss mihti. *c* **1175** *Lamb. Hom.* 15 ȝe hit maȝen witen iwis þet hit is al for ure sunne. *Ibid.* 55 Þet is al soð, ful iwis. *c* **1200** ORMIN 687 Þatt seȝȝde he ful iwiss forrþi þatt ta wass cumenn time. *c* **1205** LAY. 29481 Iwis ȝe beod Ænglisce englen ilicchest. *c* **1250** *Gen. & Ex.* 159 Ðe fifte day god made ywis of water, ilc fuel and eruerilc fis. *a* **1300** *Cursor M.* 876 (Cott.) For-þi þat thou has don þe mis, þiself þou wite þi wa, i-wis. *Ibid.* 2967 (Cott.) Bot herd it es to kepe, iwise [*v.rr.* I. wys, i wis, I wis] þe þing þat ilk man wald war his. *c* **1325** *Metr. Hom.* 17 And als Symond thoht this, Crist wist quat he thoht I wis. *c* **1340** *Cursor M.* 12749 (Fairf.) Of pantera come perpantera e-wis [*v.r.* i-wis]. *c* **1386** CHAUCER *Frankl. T.* 635 With my deth I may be quyt ywis. *c* **1440** *Generydes* 862 To sey yow myn intent I wis. **1519** *Interl. Four Elem.* (Percy Soc.) 12 Yet nothynge so grose as the yerth I wys. **1521** BRADSHAW *St. Werburge* II. 599 That prince Edmunde, the thyrde son e-wis Of Edwarde senior, true foundour shulde be. **1565** GOLDING *Ovid's Met.* I. (1593) 25 No marvell though thou be so proud and full of wordes ywus. **1578** CHURCHYARD *Disc. Queen's Entertainm.* K iij, The cace is aunswered thus: You are not ruld by loue of babes, nor womens willes yewus. **1598** MARSTON *Pygmal.* I. 140 And there (I wis) like no quaint stomack't man Eates vp his armes. **1616** BEAUM. & FL. *Scornful Lady* I. i, A comelier wear, I wus, it is than those dangling slops. **1748** THOMSON *Cast. Indol.* II. xlviii, To prove it were, I wis, To prove the beauteous world excels the brute abyss. **1829** HOOD *Epping Hunt* xviii, A well-bred horse he was, I wis. **1845** GUEST in *Proc. Philol. Soc.* II. 160 Till lately, our editors always converted the innocent adverb *i-wiss* (certainly) into *I wiss*, I know. **1865** SWINBURNE *Poems & Ball.*, *Masque Queen Bersabe* 48, I wis men shall spit at me.

β. *c* **1250** *Gen. & Ex.* 91 Ðo gan hem daȝen wel iwisse, Quan god hem ledde in-to blisse. *c* **1275** LAY. 19315 Mid moche blisse And richedom iwisse. *c* **1350** *Will. Palerne* 697 ȝis, i-wisse, was it sche, y wot wel þe soþe. *c* **1400** *Destr. Troy* 897 All cold it became & the course helde, Bothe of ymur & aire, after I-wise. *c* **1410** *Sir Cleges* 480 'Tell me trewth.. Knowyste thou of that man?' The harper seyd, 'Yee, I wysse'. **1535** FISHER *Ways Perf. Relig.* Wks. (1876) 368, I wisse it is a thing much more reasonable. **1565** JEWEL *Def. Apol.* (1611) 36 Yewisse, M. Harding, it greeveth you full sore they are so many. **1598** YONG *Diana* 10 For them the tender grasse in pleasant vales doth growe ywisse, Sweete shadowed riuer bankes tell me where my Syrenus is. **1663** COWLEY *Cutter Coleman St.* v. vi, An' these be your Visions! little did I think I wusse—O what shall I do?

γ. For aphetic form *wis* see WIS *adv.* For *in wis* (perh. in part an expansion of *iwis*), see WIS *sb.*

a **1240** *Ureisum* in *Lamb. Hom.* 187 As wis ase drope of þi deorwurþe blod mahte waschen a-wai alle folkes fulþe ase wis lifes louerd þe ilke fif wallen.. wascne mine fif wittes. *c* **1250** *Gen. & Ex.* 2521 An her endede to ful, in wis, ðe boc ðe is hoten genesis. **1579** TOMSON *Calvin's Serm. Tim.* 86/1 Alas, your sinnes are so horrible, that none can be more: yea wis, sinne?

†**C.** *sb.* [the adj. used absol.: cf. OHG. *giwissî*, MG. *gewisse* 'certainty', and the mod. *for certain.*] Certainty: in phr. *mid iwisse* with certainty, certainly (= prec. adv.); also *to iwisse* for certain. *Obs.*

a **1000** *Rule St. Benet* lxviii. (Schröer) 128 Wite se ʒingra mid ʒewisse, þæt hit him eal framað. *a* **1000** *Assmann's Angelsächs Homil.* 55 Forðan ðe we nyton to nanum ʒewisse. *a* **1200** *Moral Ode* 40 Þenne haueð he his mid iwisse. *c* **1205** LAY. 3545 Peniȝes þer buod an sunda To iwisse an hundrad punda. *Ibid.* 7607 Muchel wes þa blisse þat heo makeden mid iwisse. *a* **1300** *K. Horn* 432 He gan hire for to kesse Wel ofte mid ywisse. *c* **1315** SHOREHAM 23 Wanne eny prest his messe syngeth, I-lief hyt myd y-wysse.

iwisch, obs. form of JUICE *sb.*

†**i-'wisliche**, *adv. Obs.* [OE. *ʒewislíce*, f. *ʒewis* + *-líce* (= Du. *gewisselijk*): see IWIS and -LY².] Certainly; truly.

c **1000** *Ags. Gosp.* Luke x. 42 ʒe-wislice an þing is niedbehefe. *c* **1000** *Sax. Leechd.* III. 256 Ealle þa easternan.. tealdon þæt seo lenctenlice emniht is ʒewislice on duodecima kl. april. *c* **1175** *Lamb. Hom.* 111 Iwisliche þa clennesse iwelt alle unþeawes. *c* **1205** LAY. 26184 Whær he mihte þene kæisere iwisliche kepen.

†**i'wisse, iwise,** *v. Obs.* [OE. *ʒewísian*, later *ʒewissian* (= OS. *giwísian*, OHG. *gawîsan*, MHG. *gewîsen*); f. *ʒe-*, I-¹ + *wísian*, *wissian*, f. *wís*, WISE.] *trans.* To direct, instruct.

a **1000** *Cædmon's Gen.* 850 Bædon.. þæt.. him ʒewisade waldend se goda. *c* **1000** ÆLFRIC *Hom.* II. 130 Swa swa him Gregorius ær ʒewissode. —— *Josh.* iii. 8 Ðu ʒewissa ða sacerdas.. þæt hiʒ ʒebidon on þære ea. *c* **1175** *Lamb. Hom.* 119 Ðe helende us iwissie to his willan efre. *c* **1205** LAY. 1525 Brutus.. iwende forð rihtes To þon ilke weie þer him iwised wes. *a* **1300** *Prayer to Virgin* 3 in *O.E. Misc.* 195 Þu praie ihesu crist þi sone þat he me i-wisse. *c* **1315** SHOREHAM 122 Ase aungeles er he were y-bore Hys eldren hedde y-wysed.

Hence †**i-wissung**, direction, instruction.

c **1000** ÆLFRIC *On O.T.* (Sweet *Reader* (ed. 2) 65), For fela ʒewissungum ðe seo an boc hæfð. *c* **1175** *Lamb. Hom.* 93 Bi heore abbodes iwissunge.

i-wist(e, pa. pple. and pa. t. of I-WITE(N, *Obs.*

†**i-wit.** *Obs.* Also iwitt, ywit(t. [OE. *ʒewit(t* (= OHG. *gawitzi*, *gi-*, *gewizzi*, *gewizze*, MHG. *gewizze*, *-witze*), f. *ʒe-*, I-¹ + stem of *wit-an* to know; wit: cf. WIT *sb.*] Knowledge; understanding; wits, senses.

c **888** K. ÆLFRED *Boeth.* v. §3 Sio ʒedrefednes mæʒ þæt mod onstyrian, ac hio hit ne mæʒ his ʒewittes bereafian. *c* **1000** *Ags. Gosp.* Luke i. 77 To syllenne his folce hys hæle ʒewit. *a* **1175** *Cott. Hom.* 219 He ȝescop tyen engle werod.. Cherubim, ȝefildnesse of ywitte. *c* **1200** *Vices & Virtues* 19 He scolde sone bien ut of his iwitte. *a* **1250** *Owl & Night.* 772 For hit [the horse] non iwit ne kon, Hit berth on rugge grete semes.

†**i-wite, ywite,** (I-), *v.*¹ *Obs.* Also 4 ywyte. *Pa. t.* iwiste, iwuste. *Pa. pple.* iwist, iwust, iwiten. [OE. *ʒewit-an*, pa. t. *-wiste*, pa. pple. *witen*, f. *ʒe-*, I-¹ + *wit-an* to know, to WIT.]

1. *trans.* To understand, know, get to know, learn.

c **900** tr. *Bæda's Hist.* III. vi. [viii.] (1890) 174 Heo.. woldon ʒewitan hwæt þæt wære. *c* **950** *Lindisf. Gosp.* Matt. x. 26 Nowiht [is].. ʒehyded þæt ne se ʒewitten. *Ibid.* John ii. 9 Ða embehtmenn ʒeuiston ða ðe birladon þæt uæter. *c* **1000** *Apollonius* (Th.) 13 Ga and ʒewite hwæt se iunga man sy. *a* **1200** *Moral Ode* 382 (Lamb. MS.) Þo scullen more of him.. iwiten his mihte & his ore. *Ibid.* 17 (Trin. MS.) Elde me is bistolen on ar ich hit iwiste. *a* **1225** *Ancr. R.* 64 Iwiteð et ower meiden hwo hit beo þæt is icumen. *c* **1275** *Passion our Lord* 262 in *O.E. Misc.* 44 Iwyte at heom þat hit iherde, and nouht ne axe me. **1297** R. GLOUC. (Rolls) 224 Wane he wolde iwite ȝwat man þe child ssolde be. **1340** *Ayenb.* 29 Þou sselt ywyte þet þer byeþ zix zennes. **1393** LANGL. *P. Pl.* C. IV. 76 Let nat þy lyft half.. Ywite what þow delest with þy ryht syde. *c* **1460** *Launfal* 866 Ye schull y wyte, seyde the mayde, For sche cometh ryde.

2. To watch, guard, preserve.

c **1205** LAY. 13570 We habbeoð ibeon.. iwurðed þurh þinne stiwærd, þe haueð iwiten al þis ærd. *a* **1240** *Sawles Warde* in *Cott. Hom.* 247 Ne bið neauer his hus for þeos hinen wel iwist. **1297** R. GLOUC. (Rolls) 5540 In þe kinges tresorie þat suerd iwust ys. **1340** *Ayenb.* 212 Sire, ywyte ous, uor we spilleþ.

†**i-wite,** (iː-), *v.*² *Obs.* Also 3 i-whiten, -wihten. *Pa. t.* iwat, *Pa. pple.* iwiten. [OE. *ʒewítan*, to look at; to turn one's eyes towards a place with the intention of going thither; to depart, go away; to die, f. *ʒe-*, I-¹ + *wítan* to see: see WITE *v.*¹] *intr.* To go away, depart; to decease, die.

971 *Blickl. Hom.* 233 Gif we ʒewitaþ fram þe, þonne beo we fremde from eallum þæm godum þe þu us ʒeʒearwodest. *c* **1000** ÆLFRIC *Hom.* I. 64 Nacode we wæron acennede and nacode we ʒewitaþ. *c* **1175** *Lamb. Hom.* 93 Þa feol heo þer adun and iwat. *c* **1205** LAY. 13244 Wes i þere ilke wike þe ærchebiscop forð iwiten. *Ibid.* 17235 He sæt stille alse þeh he wolde of worlden iwiten. *Ibid.* 21311 Þe wulf heom to iwiteð and alle heom abiteð. *Ibid.* 25616 Þene beore he ismat þat he to þere eorþe iwhat.

i-wite(n, ME. pa. pple. of WITE *v.*, to blame.

†**i-'witness.** *Obs.* [OE. *ʒewitnes(s* (= OHG. *gawiʒnessi*), f. *ʒe-*, I-¹ + WITNESS.] Knowledge; witness, testimony; the act of witnessing.

c **888** K. ÆLFRED *Boeth.* xxxix. §2 Buton Godes willan & buton his ʒewitnesse. **971** *Blickl. Hom.* 153 Þa bletsode he eft Marian lichoman on Moyses boca ʒewitnesse. *c* **1175** *Lamb. Hom.* 91 Crist aras of deaðe, and on ure iwitnesse astah to heofene. *Ibid.* 131 Sancte iohannes baptiste, þe ure drihten ber iwitnesse. *a* **1225** *Leg. Kath.* 2491 To beoren hire witnesse [*v.r.* iwitnesse] of hire hwite meiðhad.

†**i-'witterli,** *adv. Obs.* [Cf. WITTERLY.] Certainly, of a truth.

c **1205** LAY. 17582 Þat wes a þan time tun swiðe hende. þat mon nu iwitterli clepeð seint Deouwi.

†**i-'wive, ywive,** *v. Obs.* [OE. *ʒewífian*, f. *ʒe-*, I-¹ + *wífian* to WIVE.] *intr.* To take a wife, to marry.

c **1000** ÆLFRIC *Judg.* iii. 6 And ʒewifodon him.. on þam hæþenum mædenum. *a* **1250** *Prov. Ælfred* 261 in *O.E. Misc.* 118 Wo is him þat vuel wif bryngeþ to his cotlyf, so him is alyue, þat vuele ywyueþ. **1297** R. GLOUC. (Rolls) 10888 He adde iwiued & an eir adde also.

i-wived, ME. pa. pple. of WIVE *v.*

iwlaht, pa. pple. of *wlecche v. Obs.*, to make lukewarm; cf. WLAK, WLACH *a.*

†**i-'won, i-wan.** *Obs.* [f. I-¹ + WON, hope, etc.]

1. Hope; expectation; resource; chance, fortune.

c **1205** LAY. 7706 Mid þere ȝeue he heom ouer-com þat was þa þat bezste iwan. **1297** R. GLOUC. (Rolls) 10790 As me þincþ turne aȝe uort god sende betere iwon [*rime* manie fon]. *a* **1300** *Leg. Rood* 26 He.. of-swonke is owe mete: he nuste no betere iwon. *c* **1300** *Beket* 1022 Ich have nou lither iwon. *Ibid.* 1712 Rathere he wolde thane deth afonge bote there were other iwon.

2. Fortune, substance, property.

c **1275** *Death* in *O.E. Misc.* 172 His freondes strіueð to gripen his i-won.

i-wonde(n, ME. pa. pple. of WIND *v.*

i-wonded, ME. pa. pple. of WOUND *v.*

i-wone: see I-WUNE.

i-woned, i-wont, ME. pa. pple. of WON *v.*: see WONT *a.*

i-wo(n)ne, ME. pa. pple. of WIN *v.*

i-woost, ME. pa. pple. of WIT *v.*

i-wope, ME. pa. pple. of WEEP *v.*

†**i-'worded,** *a. Obs.* [f. I-¹ + WORD + -ED².] Full of words, talkative, garrulous.

a **1225** *Ancr. R.* 78 Veole iwordede mon seið þe psalmwurhte, ne schal neuer leden riht lif on eorðe.

i-worpe(n, ME. pa. pple. of WARP *v.*

i-worred, ME. pa. pple. of WAR *v.*

i-worsed, ME. pa. pple. of WORSE *v.*

i-worð-, i-worschipped, ME. pa. pple. of WORSHIP *v.*

†**i-'worth, y'worth,** *v. Obs.* Forms: 1 **ʒeweorð-an, -wyrð-an,** 2 **ȝewurðen,** 2-3 **iwurðe(n, -þe(n,** 3 **iworþe(n,** 3-4 **yworþe.** *Pa. t.* 1 **ʒewearð,** *pl.* **-wurðon,** 2 **ȝewearð, -warð,** 2-3 **iwearð, iwarð,** 3 **iwærð, iwerð,** *pl.* **iwurðen,** 4 **yworþ.** *Pa. pple.* 1 **ʒeworden,** 2 **ȝewurðen,** 2-3 **iwurðen, iworðen,** 4 **yworthe, i-worth(e.** [OE. *ʒeweorð-an* (= OS. *giwerðan*, OHG. *gawerdan*, MHG. *gewerden*), f. *ʒe-*, I-¹ + *weorðan*, OS. *werðan*, Goth. *wairþan* to become: see WORTH *v.*]

1. *intr.* To become, or turn to (something); in *pass.* to be made or have become (something).

The complement of the predicate may be a sb., adj., pa. pple. (forming a passive voice), sb. in the dat. or with *to*, or a prep. phrase, as *mid cilde* with child.

a **900** CYNEWULF *Crist* 210 Ic his modor ʒewearð. *c* **1000** ÆLFRIC *Gen.* xxi. 18 He ʒewyrþ micelre mæʒþe. *c* **1000** *Ags. Gosp.* John i. 14 Ðæt word wæs flæsc ʒeworden. *a* **1175** *Cott. Hom.* 227 Þaðe he man ȝewarð, þa was he acenned of þe clene meidene. *c* **1175** *Lamb. Hom.* 89 Þa iwarð þat folc swiðe abluied. *c* **1205** LAY. 259 Hit iwerð þere.. þat þeos ȝunge wiman iwerð hire mid childe. *Ibid.* 3733 Cordoille com þat wourd, þat heo was iworðen widewe [*c* **1275** þat ȝeo was widewe iworþe]. *Ibid.* 18171 He wurðeliche iwarð him to kinge. *a* **1225** *Ancr. R.* 140 Hit schal iwurðen ful liht. *a* **1300** *Fragm. Sev. Sins* iv. in *E.E.P.* (1862) 17 Beþench þat þou salt iworþe & forroti to axen and erþe. *c* **1369** CHAUCER *Dethe Blaunche* 578, I wrechch.. of al þe blysse þat euer was maked.. Y worthe [*v.r.* I worþ] worste of al wyghtys. *c* **1380** *Sir Ferumb.* 2908 After euerech of hure strokes grute, ys body al swart y-worþ. *c* **1394** *P. Pl. Crede* 665 Þei wolden y-worþen so grete To passen any mans miȝt.

2. To happen, come to pass, come into being; to be made.

c **893** K. ÆLFRED *Oros.* v. x. §1 Eac on þæm ʒeare ʒewurdon moneʒa wundor. *c* **1000** *Ags. Gosp.* John iii. 9 Hu maʒon ðas þing ðus ʒeweorþan? *a* **1175** *Cott. Hom.* 223 He ne cweð naht ȝewurðe man.. ac he cweð: Uton ȝewurcan man to ure anlicnesse. *c* **1175** *Lamb. Hom.* 93 Ða iwearð þer muchel eie on godes folke. *c* **1205** LAY. 22735 Ich mai sugge hu hit iwarð. *Ibid.* 32240, Iwurðe þet iwurðe, iwurðe Godes wille! Amen. *a* **1225** *Ancr. R.* 52 Al þe wo þet nu is & euer ȝete was, & euer schal iwurðen. *c* **1230** *Hali Meid.* 33, I wurðe hit al þat ha habbe hire wil of streon. **1340** *Ayenb.* 262 Yworþe þi wil ase ine heuene and ine erþe.

3. To come, arrive, get to be (at a place).

c **1205** LAY. 9123 Fromward þeon londe of Jerusalem iwurðen heo beoð in Beðleem. *Ibid.* 29555 Þer heo iwurðen to [*c* 1275 Hii to him wende].

4. To befall, to happen to (a person).

Impers. with acc. or dat.

a **1000** *Judith* 260 (Gr.), Hu ðone cumbolwiʒan.. hæfde ʒeworden. *c* **1205** LAY. 2236 Sel þe scal iwurðen [*c* 1275 Wel þe sal bi-tyde]. *c* **1230** *Hali Meid.* 45 After þi word.. mote me iwurðen.

5. To come acceptably to; to please, be agreeable; to be agreed upon.

Impersonal, with acc. or dat., *ne mihte heom iwurðen*, they could not agree.

c **893** K. ÆLFRED *Oros.* IV. vi. §15 Hie ʒewearð þæt hie wolden to Romanum friþes wilnian. *a* **1000** *Andreas* 307 Hu ʒewearð þe þæs? **1014** *O.E. Chron.* (MS. E.), ʒewearþ him and þam folce on Lindesiʒe anes ðæt hi hine horsian sceoldan. *c* **1175** *Lamb. Hom.* 93 Hwi iwearð hine [Ananias & Sapphira] swa, þet ȝit dursten fondian godes? *c* **1205** LAY. 29427 Þa ne mihtte heom iwurðe wha þis lond scolde aȝen.

6. *let iwurðen*, let (a thing) be or go (as it will), let be, let or leave alone.

c **1205** LAY. 3343 Lauerd beo þeu stille, let me al iwurþen. *a* **1225** *Ancr. R.* 414 Marthe haueð hire mester, leteð hire iwurðen. **1297** R. GLOUC. (Rolls) 1535 He lete þe king al iworþe & to rome aȝen drou. **1340** *Ayenb.* 40 Þe ualse demeres, þet.. Zelleþ hare domes, oþer ham leteþ yworþe. **1377** LANGL. *P. Pl.* B. VI. 228 Late god take þe veniaunce; Theiȝ þei done yvel, Late þow god y-worþe! **1387** TREVISA *Higden* (Rolls) VI. 279 Bote we leteþ God i-worþe wiþ his owne privete.

i-worthe(n, ME. pa. pple. of WORTH *v.*

i-wost(e, ME. pa. pple. of WIT *v.*

i-wounde, ME. pa. pple. of WIND *v.*

i-wounded, ME. pa. pple. of WOUND *v.*

i-woven, ME. pa. pple. of WEAVE *v.*

i-woxe(n, ME. pa. pple. of WAX *v.*

i-wrapped, ME. pa. pple. of WRAP *v.*

†**i-'wrathe,** *v. Obs.* [OE. *ʒewráðian*, ME. *-ien*, f. *ʒe-*, I-¹ + *wráðian*: see WRATH *v.*] *trans.* To make angry or wroth; *refl.* to become angry.

c **1075** *O.E. Chron.* (MS. A.) an. 1070 Þa.. ʒewraðede hine se arcebiscop Landfranc. *c* **1205** LAY. 27698 Walwain þat bihedde.. and he hine iwraðede.

i-wraththed, -et, ME. pa. pple. of WRATH *v.*

i-wreied, -id, ME. pa. pple. of WRAY *v.*

i-wreken, ME. pa. pple. of WREAK *v.*

i-wrete, ME. pa. pple. of WRITE *v.*

i-wreþed, i-wreþþed, ME. pa. pple. of WRETHE *v.*, to anger.

i-wreyed, ME. pa. pple. of WRAY *v.*

i-wrien, i-wriȝen, ME. pa. pple. of *wrigh*, WRY *v.*, to cover, veil, conceal.

† i-'writ. *Obs.* [OE. *ȝewrit*, f. *wrítan* to WRITE: cf. WRIT.] Something written; a writing, a treatise.

c **893** K. ÆLFRED *Oros.* I. i. §6 þeah þe ȝewrito oft nemnen eal þa lond Media oþþe Asiria. **971** *Blickl. Hom.* 177 þa heht he .. rædan þæt ȝewrit beforan him. *c* **1175** *Lamb. Hom.* 133 Alswuche wise spekeð ðe eorðliche king wið iwilche cristene monne þe he to sendeð his halie iwriten. *a* **1250** *Prov. Ælfred* 103 in *O.E. Misc.* 108 þe mon þe on his youhþe .. leorneþ .. iwriten reden he may beon on elde wenliche lorþeu.

i-write, -en, ME. pa. pple. of WRITE *v.*

i-writhen, -wriðen, ME. pa. pple. of WRITHE *v.*, to bind.

i-wroht, i-wrouȝt, i-wrouht, ME. pa. pple. of WORK *v.*

i-wroken, ME. pa. pple. of WREAK *v.*

i-wryed, -yd, ME. pa. pple. of WRY *v.*, to twist.

i-wulc(h, obs. form of EACH.

i-wunde(n, ME. pa. pple. of WIND *v.*

i-wunded, ME. pa. pple. of WOUND *v.*

i-wundred, ME. pa. pple. of WONDER *v.*

† i-'wune, i-'wone. *Obs.* Also 3 ywune. [OE. *ȝewuna*, f. stem of *wun-ian*: see WON *v.* and WONT. Cf. Du. *gewoonte*.] Custom, habit, wont.

c **888** K. ÆLFRED *Boeth.* xxv, Heo .. ȝemonð þæs wildan ȝewunan hire eldrana. *c* **1175** *Lamb. Hom.* 55 Bute we bileuen ure ufele iwune. *c* **1205** LAY. 14017 þa Peohtes duden heore iwune. *a* **1250** *Owl & Night.* 475 Hit is gode monne iwone. *c* **1275** *Passion Our Lord* 207 in *O.E. Misc.* 43 Vyche day in þe temple wes myne ywune To techen eu godes lore.

i-wuned, -et, ME. pa. pple. of WON *v.*: see WONT *a.*

† i-'wuneliche, *adv. Obs.* [OE. *ȝewunelíce*, f. *ȝewunelic* customary (= OHG. *gewonelích*, G. *gewöhnlich*): see I-WUNE and -LY².] Customarily, usually.

c **900** tr. *Bæda's Hist.* IV. iv. (1890) 274 Is þæt þæt mynster .. þe ȝewunelice is Muigeo nemned. *c* **1175** *Lamb. Hom.* 131 Halic boc nemneð iwunliche ðreo þing to sede. *c* **1200** *Trin. Hom.* 152 Holi boc nemneð iwunelich þre þing to sed.

i-wunne(n, ME. pa. pple. of WIN *v.*

† i-'wurche, i-werche, *v. Obs. Pa. t.* iworhte, iwrohte, iwroughte. [OE. *ȝewyrc(e)an* (= OS. *giwirkjan*, OHG. *gawurchan*, *giwircan*, MHG. *gewirken*, Goth. *gawaurkjan*), f. *ȝe-*, I-¹ + *wyrc(e)an*: see WORK *v.*] *trans.* To work; to make; to do.

c **888** K. ÆLFRED *Boeth.* xxxiv. §6 þara lima ȝecynd is þæt hi ȝewercað ænne lichoman. **971** *Blickl. Hom.* 187 Het Neron ȝewyrcean mycelne tor of treowum. *c* **1000** *Ags. Ps.* (Th.) lxxvi. 11 þu eart ana God, þe æȝhwylc miht wundor ȝewyrcean. *a* **1175** *Cott. Hom.* 223 Uton ȝewurcan man to ure anlicnesse. *c* **1205** LAY. 3879 Remus & Romulus Rome iwrohten. *Ibid.* 17623 Passen at seint Deowi sorȝen iworhte. *Ibid.* 28995 Sexisce men .. seiden þat heo wolden wið hine grið iwurchen. *a* **1250** *Prov. Ælfred* 130 in *O.E. Misc.* 110 Bute he him of frumþe freond iwrche [*v.r.* bote he him fremede frend y-werche]. *c* **1374** CHAUCER *Troylus* III. 212 (261) Neuere I þis for coueytice Iwroughte.

† i-'wurht. *Obs.* [OE. *ȝewyrht* (cf. OS. *giwurht*, OHG. *gewurht*), f. *ȝe-*, I-¹ + stem **wurk-* of *wyrc(e)an* to work.] Work, deed; desert.

c **888** K. ÆLFRED *Boeth.* xxxix. §1 þæt hiora ælc ȝulde oðrum edlean ælces weorces æfter his ȝewyrhtum. *c* **1160** *Hatton Gosp.* John xv. 25 þæt syo spræce syo ȝe-fyllad .. þæt hyo hatedan me buton ȝe-werhtan. *c* **1205** LAY. 3066 þat heo hine nulde iwurði. *Ibid.* 29687 þene stude to iwurðien þer stod ure drihten.

i-wursed, ME. pa. pple. of WORSE *v.*

i-wurthe: see I-WORTH *v.*

i-wurþed, i-wurþeȝed, ME. pa. pple. of WORTHY *v.*

† i-wurthi, *v. Obs.* [OE. *ȝeweorþian, -wurþian, -wyrþian*, f. *ȝe-*, I-¹ + *weorþian*: see WORTHY *v.*] *trans.* To honour; to dignify; to hold in honour.

c **888** K. ÆLFRED *Boeth.* xiv. §3 Hu ne belimpð se weorðscipe þonne to þam þe hine ȝeweorðað? *c* **1205** LAY. (Th.) viii. 6 þu hine ȝewuldrast and ȝeweorðast. *c* **1205** LAY. 3066 þat heo hine nulde iwurði. *Ibid.* 29687 þene stude to iwurðien þer stod ure drihten.

i-wust, i-wuste, ME. pa. pple. and pa. t. of WIT *v.*

i-wympled, ME. pa. pple. of WIMPLE *v.*

i-wyped, ME. pa. pple. of WIPE *v.*

---

i-wyrshupped, ME. pa. pple. of WORSHIP *v.*

i-wys, i-wysse: see I-WIS.

iwyse, variant of JUISE *Obs.*, judgement.

ixia ('ɪksɪə). [L., a. Gr. *ἰξία*.]

‖ **1.** Name in Greek and Latin for the plant also called CHAMELEON (q.v., sense 3), a kind of thistle yielding an acrid resin. *Obs.*

1551 TURNER *Herbal* I. A v b, It is good against the poyson of ixia with wyne. **1601** HOLLAND *Pliny* II. 64 Most effectuall .. for them that haue drunke the gum of Chamælæon, called Ixia. **1706** PHILLIPS, *Ixia* or *Ixine*, a sort of Carduus; an Herb which some call Cameleon.

2. *Bot.* A genus of S. African iridaceous plants, with large showy flowers of various colours. Also extended to some allied plants, as a species of *Trichonema* cultivated in the Channel Islands.

1794 MARTYN *Rousseau's Bot.* xiv. 154 There are some very beautiful genera in .. this class, particularly the Ixia and Iris. **1804** CHARLOTTE SMITH *Conversations* II. 119 An almost endless variety of ixias. **1862** ANSTED *Channel Isl.* II. viii. (ed. 2) 175 The little species of ixia, *trichonema columnæ*, is particularly remarkable among the spring flowers. **1880** PARKMAN *France & Eng. Amer.* 58 From the grass gleams the blue eye of the starry ixia.

3. *Comb.* **ixia-lily**, a name for the plants of the genus *Ixiolirion* (N.O. *Amaryllideæ*), natives of Asia, with blue or violet funnel-shaped six-parted flowers.

1866 *Treas. Bot.* 682/2. **1884** MILLER *Plant-n.*

ixiolite ('ɪksɪəʊlaɪt). *Min.* [ad. Swed. *ixiolith* (Nordenskiöld, 1857), f. *Ixion* (see next) + Gr. *λίθος* stone (see -LITE): suggested by the association of Ixion and Tantalus in the infernal regions.] A variety of TANTALITE containing oxide of tin.

1861 BRISTOW *Gloss.* 193 Ixiolite .. usually occurs in rectangular prisms. **1892** DANA *Min.* (ed. 6) 734 Crystallized skögbolite and ixiolite are here included.

Ixionian (ɪksɪ'əʊnɪən), *a.* [f. L. *Ixiōni-us* adj. (f. *Ixiōn*, Gr. *Ἰξίων*: see below) + -AN.] Belonging to, or resembling that of, Ixion, a mythical king of Thessaly, who was punished in the infernal regions by being fastened to an eternally revolving wheel.

1678 CUDWORTH *Intell. Syst.* I. iii. §24. 169 Condemned to an Eternal Ixionian Fate.

ixodid (ɪk'sɒʊdɪd), *sb.* Pl. **ixodides**. [f. mod.L. family name *Ixodidæ*, f. the generic name *Ixodes* (P. A. Latreille 1795, in *Magazin encyclopédique* IV. 15), f. Gk. *ἰξώδης* sticky.] A tick of the family Ixodidæ. Also *attrib.* or as *adj.*, of or pertaining to a tick of this type.

1911 G. H. F. NUTTALL et al. *Ticks* II. 105 Leach called the Acarina *Monomerosomata*, and divided them into 11 families, one of which, Ixodides, included *Argas*, *Ixodes* and *Europoda.* *Ibid.* 113 The Argasid and Ixodid ticks were recognized as possessing very distinctive features. **1935** T. H. SAVORY *Arachnida* xiii. 146 The Ixodides possess a soft-skinned opisthosoma capable of great distension necessary for the alternate gorging and fasting that is inseparable from the life of a tick. **1952** BAKER & WHARTON *Introd. Acarology* iv. 144 The majority of ixodids usually parasitize different hosts in the immature and mature stages. *Ibid.*, Heavy infestation with ixodid ticks can cause anemia in domestic animals. **1965** B. E. FREEMAN tr. *Vandel's Biospeleol.* xv. 256 An ixodid parasitic on bats has been found frequently in Europe, Asia and Africa.

ixolite ('ɪksəlaɪt). *Min.* [ad. Ger. *ixolyt* (Haidinger, 1842), f. Gr. *ἰξός* mistletoe, bird-lime + *λίθος* stone (see -LITE).] A mineral resin occurring in bituminous coal, having a greasy lustre, and becoming soft and tenacious when heated.

1846 WORCESTER cites Dana. **1868** DANA *Min.* (ed. 5) 736 Ixolyte.

ixora (ɪk'sɔərə). [mod.L. (Linnæus in J. Burmann *Thesaurus Zeylanicus* (1737) 125), ad. *Iswara*, name of a Hindu divinity, = Skr. *īśvará* lord, master: so named because the flowers of some species are used as votive offerings.] An evergreen shrub or small tree of the genus so called, mostly native to tropical Africa and Asia and bearing clusters of white or brightly-coloured flowers.

1816 *Bot. Reg.* II. 154 (*heading*) Large-flowered scarlet Ixora. **1846** J. LINDLEY *Veget. Kingd.* 764 The fragrance or beauty .. of the Gardenias, Hindsias, Posoquerias, Ixoras .. &c. is unsurpassed. **1871** C. KINGSLEY *At Last* I. vii. 231 The air was .. almost too heavy with the fragrance of the 'white Ixora'. **1926** D. H. CAMPBELL *Outl. Plant Geogr.* vi. 214 In the upper forest [of Sarawak], a handsome Ixora .. was abundant. **1961** *Amateur Gardening* 21 Oct. Suppl. 29/3 For those with plenty of heat in the greenhouse the ixoras are well worth growing.

ixtle, ixtli: see ISTLE.

i-yarked, i-ȝarket, ME. pa. pple. of YARK *v.*, to prepare.

iye, obs. f. EYE.

---

† i-yeerid, ME. variant of YEARED.

c **1412** HOCCLEVE *De Reg. Princ.* 1858 þou of þe pryue seel art old I-yeerid.

i-yefen, i-ȝefen, ME. pa. pple. of GIVE.

† i-yell, i-ȝel, ME. variant of YELL, yelling.

c **1205** LAY. 17799 þer wes moni reolic spel þer wes gumene iȝel.

i-yelt, ME. pa. pple. of YIELD *v.*

i-yemed, i-ȝemed, ME. pa. pple. of YEME *v.*

i-yened, i-ȝened, ME. pa. pple. of YEAN *v.*, to bring forth.

i-yerned, i-ȝerned, ME. pa. pple. of YEARN *v.*¹

† i-'yeten, *pa. pple. Obs.* Also 3–4 i-'ȝet(t)e. [For *ȝe-eten*, *i-eten*, pa. pple. of EAT *v.*, and the early compound, ME. *ȝe-eten*, OE. *ȝe-etan* to eat up, consume (L. *com-edĕre*). Cf. mod.Ger. *gegessen*, for earlier *gessen* contr. for *ge-essen*.] Eaten.

c **1205** LAY. 6691 þæer heo hæfden wel iȝeten and seoððen idrunken. *a* **1300** *Fall & Passion* 33 in *E.E.P.* (1862) 13 Hi nad bot þat appil i-ȝette þat þe sin nas ido. **13** .. *Ipotis* 394 in Horstm. *Altengl. Leg.* (1881) 346 Whon wormes han I-ȝete þi syde. *a* **1400** *Octouian* 757 þo clement hadde y-ȝete a fyn.

† i-'yett, *v. Obs.* In 3 i-ȝetten. [f. I-¹ + ME. *ȝetten*: see YETTE.] *trans.* To grant, concede.

c **1205** LAY. 10792 Al him iȝette þat Gallus þer ȝer(n)de. *Ibid.* 14195 þe king him iȝette Swa Hengest ȝirnde.

† i-'yeve, *v. Obs.* In 3 i-ȝefuen. [f. I-¹ + ME. *ȝeven*, GIVE: cf. OHG. *gigeban*, *gegeben*, MHG. *gegeben*.] *trans.* To give.

c **1205** LAY. 21947 Heo þa iȝefuen ȝisles þan kingen.

i-yeve(n, i-ȝeve(n, i-ȝive(n, i-yove(n, i-ȝove(n, i-ȝyve, ME. pa. pple. of GIVE.

iyre, iys(e, obs. forms of IRE, ICE.

iyrne, iyron, obs. variants of IRON.

Iyyar ('iːjɑː(r)). Also Iyar, Jiar, Jyar, Yiar. [ad. Heb. *iyyār*.] The post-exilic name of one of the Jewish months, being the eighth of the civil and second of the ecclesiastical year; its pre-exilic name was *Zif*.

1737 W. WHISTON tr. *Josephus' Works* 910 The Romans began to raise their banks on the twelfth day of the month Artemisius (Jyar). **1738** A. CRUDEN *Compl. Concordance Holy Scriptures* s.v. *month*, *Zif* .. is the second month of the holy year, and .. answers to that which afterwards had the name *Jiar*, or *April*. **1902** *Encycl. Brit.* XXVI. 43/2 In 746 B.C. Calah rebelled, and on the 13th of Iyyar (April), in the following year, Pulu or Pul .. seized the throne. **1962** *New Jewish Encycl.* 229/2 Most of the *Sefirah* days occur during the month of Iyar. **1973** *Jewish Chron.* 9 Feb. 22/2 On May 7 this year the State of Israel will be 25 years old. (The Hebrew date is the fifth day of the month of Iyar.)

‖ **izar** ('ɪzə(r)). [Arab. *izār*, *izr'* veil, covering.] The outer garment of Muslim women, a long cotton mantle covering the whole person.

Also one of the two cloths of the ihram or pilgrim's dress.

1836 LANE *Mod. Egypt.* I. 52 Eezar. **1839** —— *Arab. Nts.* I. iii. 136 There accosted him a female wrapped in an izar. **1885** ALDRICH *Poems, Dressing the Bride* 21 The misty izar from Mosul. **1898** I. ZANGWILL *Dreamers of Ghetto* IV. viii. 121 Women and maidens .. raising their face-veils and putting off their shrouding izars as they sat at his feet.

izard ('ɪzəd, ‖izar). Also isard, izzard. [ad. F. *isard* (1553 in Hatz.-Darm.), Gascon *isart*: 'perh. of Iberian origin' (Darm.).] A capriform antelope allied to the chamois, found in the Pyrenees.

1791 CHARLOTTE SMITH *Celestina* IV. 195 The solitary hunter of the Izard. **1837** J. E. MURRAY *Summer Pyrenees* II. 59 The heights by which the troop of izards had passed over. **1841** *Penny Cycl.* XIX. 155/1 The recesses of the Pyrenees are the haunts of the izard, a variety of the chamois, of smaller size and brighter colour. **1882** *Cornh. Mag.* Jan. 57 We killed a lot of isards. **1886** R. BUCHANAN *Dream of Life* VIII. 165 And fleeter than the feet of swift izzards.

Comb. **1791** CHARLOTTE SMITH *Celestina* IV. 249 Equipped .. as Izard hunters, we reached this castle. **1846** *Blackw. Mag.* LIX. 369 They saw him .. spring from the ground with izard-like agility.

izard, variant of IZZARD.

Izarra (iː'zɑːrə). Also Izzara. [Basque, lit. 'star'.] A liqueur from the Pyrenees, brandy-based and flavoured with herbs.

1926 E. HEMINGWAY *Sun also Rises* xix. 243 The waiter recommended a Basque liqueur called Izzara .. made of the flowers of the Pyrenees... It looked like hair-oil and smelled like Italian *strega*. **1965** R. POSTGATE *Plain Man's Guide to Wine* (ed. 2) ix. 149 Name Izarra. Flavour Wild herbs. Origin France. **1971** *Good Food Guide* 397 Grapefruit sorbet with Izarra.

-ization, suffix forming nouns of action from vbs. in -IZE, q.v.

1865 DICKENS *Mut. Fr.* I. xi, He was not aware that he was driving at any *ization*.

izba, var. ISBA.

-ize (also written -ise), suffix forming vbs. = F. *-ise-r*, It. *-izare*, Sp. *-izar*, ad. late L. *-izāre*, *-izāre*, f. Gr. *-ίζειν*, formative derivative of vbs.

The Greek verbs were partly intrans., as βαρβαρίζειν to play the barbarian, act or speak as a barbarian, side with the barbarians, τυραννίζειν to side with the tyrants, partly trans. as καθαρίζειν to purify, clean, θησαυρίζειν to treasure up. Those formed on national, sectarian, or personal names were primarily intransitive, as Ἀττικίζειν to Atticize in manners, to speak Attic, Φιλιππίζειν to act or speak for Philip, to philippize, Ἑλληνίζειν to 'do' the Greek, act as a Greek, speak Greek, Hellenize; also, to make Greek. A few words of this form connected with or used in early Christianity, were latinized already in the 3rd or 4th c. by Christian writers: such were βαπτίζειν baptizāre, εὐαγγελίζειν euangelizāre, κατηχίζειν catechizāre, σκανδαλίζειν scandalizāre, ἀναθηματίζειν anathēmatizāre, χριστιανίζειν christiānizāre, ἰουδαίζειν iūdaizāre. Others continued to be formed both in ecclesiastical and philosophical use, e.g. canōnizāre, dæmonizāre, syllogizāre (Boethius Aristot. Anal.); and this became established as the normal form for the latinizing of Greek verbs, or the formation of verbs upon Greek analogies. In med.L. and the mod. langs. these have been formed also on L. or modern national names, and the use has been extended to the formation of verbs from L. adjs. or sbs. This practice prob. began first in French; in mod.F. the suffix has become *-iser*, alike in words from Greek, as baptiser, évangéliser, organiser, and those formed after them from L., as civiliser, cicatriser, humaniser. Hence, some have used the spelling *-ise* in Eng., as in French, for all these words, and some prefer *-ise* in words formed in French or Eng. from L. elements, retaining *-ize* for those of Gr. composition. But the suffix itself, whatever the element to which it is added, is in its origin the Gr. *-ιζειν*, L. *-izāre*; and, as the pronunciation is also with z, there is no reason why in English the special French spelling should be followed, in opposition to that which is at once etymological and phonetic. In this Dictionary the termination is uniformly written *-ize*. (In the Gr. *-ιζ-*, the *i* was short, so originally in L., but the double consonant z (= dz, ts) made the *syllable* long; when the z became a simple consonant, *-idz* became *īz*, whence Eng. (*-aiz*.))

In current English the following groups may be noted:

1. Words that have come down from Greek, or have been at some time adopted from Greek, or formed on Greek elements; **a.** with the trans. sense of 'make or conform to, or treat in the way of, the thing expressed by the derivation', as *baptize* (prob. the earliest -ize word in Eng.), *anathematize, anatomize, apostrophize, canonize, catechize, cauterize, characterize, christianize, crystallize, diphthongize, harmonize, idolize, monopolize, organize, phlebotomize, stigmatize, symbolize, systematize, tantalize*; **b.** with the intrans. sense 'to act some person or character, do or follow some practice', as *agonize, apologize, apostatize, botanize, dogmatize, geologize, philosophize, syllogize, sympathize, theorize*.

2. Words formed (in Fr. or Eng.) on Latin adjs. and sbs. (esp. on derivative adjs. in *-al*, *-ar*, *-an*, etc.), mostly with the trans. sense 'to make (that which is expressed by the derivation)', as *actualize, authorize, brutalize, civilize, colonize, consonantize, devocalize, eternize, etherealize, familiarize, fertilize, formalize, fossilize, humanize, immortalize, legalize, memorize, nationalize, naturalize, neutralize, patronize, pulverize, realize, satirize, scrutinize, secularize, signalize, solemnize, spiritualize, sterilize, terrorize, vocalize*; trans. or intrans., as *cicatrize, extemporize, moralize, particularize*; less frequently only intrans., as *temporize*.

3. Words from later sources, as *bastardize, foreignize, jeopardize, villanize, womanize* trans., *gormandize*, and such nonce-words as *cricketize, pedestrianize, tandemize*, intr.

4. Words formed on ethnic adjs., and the like, chiefly trans. but sometimes intrans., as *Americanize, Anglicize, Gallicize, Germanize, Latinize, Romanize, Russianize*.

5. Words formed on names of persons, sometimes with the intrans. Greek sense of 'to act like, or in accordance with', as in *Calvinize, Coryatize*, but usually in the trans. sense of 'to treat like, or after the method of, or according to the (chemical or other) process of'; as in *Boucherize, Bowdlerize, Burnettize, galvanize, Grangerize, macadamize, mesmerize, Rumfordize*; with many technical and commercial terms, and nonce-words such as *Gladstonize, Irvingize, Joe Millerize, Merry-Andrewize*, without limit.

6. From names of substances, chemical and other; in the trans. sense of 'to charge, impregnate, treat, affect, or influence with'; as *alcoholize, alkalize, carbonize, de-oxidize, hydrogenize, oxidize, ozonize, silverize*, etc.; so in nonce-words, as *Londonize* to make like London, etc.

Verbs in *-ize* have the usual derivative adjs. and sbs., as ppl. adj. in *-ed* (often more used than the vb.) as 'sensitized paper'; ppl. adj. in *-ing*, chiefly from the intrans. use, as 'Judaizing Christians', 'a philosophizing writer'; vbl. sb. in *-ing*, as 'the Bowdlerizing of Shakspere'; agent-noun in *-izer* (sometimes coexistent with a formation on the Greek type in -IST), as *colonizer* (colonist); noun of action in *-ization* (sometimes coexistent with one from Gr. in -ISM), as *civilization, organization* (organism).

The following are illustrations of some of the recent uses of the suffix:

1591 NASHE Introd. Sidney's Astr. & Stella in P. Penilesse (Shaks. Soc.) p. xxx, Reprehenders, that complain of my boystrous compound wordes, and ending my Italionate coyned verbes all in ize. **1611** FLORIO, Inpetrarcato, Petrarchized. **1618** J. TAYLOR (Water P.) Journ. Scotl., I haue a smacke of Coriatizing. **1682** D'URFEY Butler's Ghost II. 177 Ralpho..takes the Tongs..and snaps him by the Nose..surpriz'd, To be thus rudely dunstaniz'd. **1796** COLERIDGE Lett. I. 209 We might Rumfordize one of the chimneys. **1833** Blackw. Mag. XXXIV. 533 It is a taste that, to coin a word, insignificantizes everything—unpoetizes nature. **1840** New Monthly Mag. LIX. 492 Tandemizing, cricketizing, boatizing, et omne quod exit in izing, is not to be carried on without a considerable expenditure. **1858** Sat. Rev. V. 264/2 He has no fear of Tower-Hamletizing the land. Ibid. VI. 203/2 To Perkin-Warbeckize a pretender is the best, because not the most spirited, policy. **1861** T. L. PEACOCK Gryll Gr. viii, Arch-quacks have taken to merry-andrewizing in a new arena. **1866** Sat. Rev. 10 Nov. (L.), If a man..is funny, and succeeds in Joe-Millerizing somebody, he pleases somebody or other. **1876** PREECE & SIVEWRIGHT Telegraphy 164 Of the first class [Preservation of Timber] the three best known processes are: (a) Burnetising, (b) Kyanising, and (c) Boucherising. **1881** MAHAFFY in Academy 23 Apr. 295 She does not Irvingise Shylock. **1885** JEAFFRESON Real Shelley II. 192 The troop of nakedized children rushed downstairs. **1894** Westm. Gaz. 9/5 These instruments, before they are used, should always be strictly anti-septicized. **1897** A. LANG in Blackw. Mag. Feb. 187 To do this is not to Celticise but to Macphersonise. **1897** Westm. Gaz. 28 July 6/1 The word 'Klondykised' has been coined to express the conditions of persons who have caught the mania [for seeking gold at Klondyke]... The effect has been to 'Klondykise' nearly all the people of the town. **1898** L. A. TOLLEMACHE Talks w. Gladstone 114 note, It [the passage] is, as it were, Canning Gladstonized.

izekelle, obs. form of ICICLE.

Izeland, obs. form of ICELAND. *Izeland shock*, Iceland dog.

1638 DAVENANT Jeffereidos, The fleetest Izeland-Shock. **1694** R. L'ESTRANGE Fables 332 They..live like Izeland-shocks by shewing tricks for bread.

-izer, suffix of agent-nouns formed from vbs. in -IZE.

Izod ('aizɒd). The name of E. G. *Izod* (fl. 1903), British engineer, used *attrib.* with reference to a kind of impact test devised by him in which a notched specimen fixed at one end is broken by a blow from a pendulum hammer and the energy absorbed determined by the decrease in the swing of the pendulum.

1904 Proc. Inst. Mech. Engin. IV. 1225 A single-blow test of the Izod type. **1922** GLAZEBROOK Dict. Applied Physics I. 206/1 The brittleness in steel resulting from a high percentage of sulphur and phosphorus is well marked by the Izod test. Ibid., The form of notch selected, and sometimes called the Izod notch, is a 45° vee, 2 mm. deep, with a root radius of 0·25 mm. **1939** E. C. ROLLASON Metall. for Engineers i. 11 As a material with a low Izod figure offers a poor resistance to the development of a crack, a low Izod value indicates that in service there will be a greater chance of final failure before the crack is discovered. **1954** A. R. BAILEY Text-bk. Metall. xiii. 457 The Izod test..is standard in Great Britain. **1968** D. R. CLIFFE Technical Metallurgy vii. 152 The Izod machine is a cantilever type with the knife-edge of the hammer striking the specimen at the horizontal at a point 22 mm above the plane of gripping.

izzard ('izəd). arch. or dial. Also izzet, izzart, uzzard. [app. in origin the same word as *zed*: cf. EZOD, the dial. *izzet, uzzit*, and the form *ĕ'zed*, now or formerly in Scotl. for *zed*; also Languedoc *izeto*, the letter z (D'Hombras Dict.).] Old name for the letter Z.

1738 SWIFT Polite Conv. i. Wks. 1814 XI. 348 'Miss, what spells B double Uzzard?' 'Buzzard, in your teeth, Mr. Neverout.' **1755** JOHNSON Dict., Gram., zed, more commonly izzard or uzzard, that is s hard. **1773** GOLDSM. Stoops to Conq. IV. Wks. (1889) 668/2 Then there's an M, and a T, and an S, but whether the next be an izzard, or an R, confound me, I cannot tell. **1799** SOUTHEY Eng. Eclogues Poet. Wks. III. 78 Warbling house-notes wild from throat and gizzard, Which reach from A to G, and from G to Izzard. **1828** Craven Dial., Izzet, the letter z. **1834** HOOD Tylney Hall (1840) 269 A fiery izzard seemed written on the distant sky. a **1874** J. MOULTRIE Poems (1876) I. 167 In those days not a soul knew A from Izzard.

izzard, variant of IZARD.

‖izzat ('izʌt). Also izzut. [Urdu, ad. Arab. *'izzah* glory.] Honour, reputation, credit, prestige.

1857 H. LAWRENCE Let. 26 Feb. in Edwardes & Merivale Life Sir H. Lawrence (1872) II. xviii. 279 Man can but die once, and if I die in Oude, after having saved some poor fellow's hearths, or skins, or izzut (reputation), I shall have no reason for discontent. **1893** KIPLING Many Inventions 207 Thou hast done great wrong, and altogether lost thy izzat and thy reputation. **1922** Blackw. Mag. Feb. 201/1 Izzat, too, generally prescribes that he should be an hour or two late. **1924** E. M. FORSTER Passage to India iii. 31 The educated native..[is] trying to increase his izzat—in plain Anglo-Saxon, to score. **1953** —— Hill of Devi 27 In every remark and gesture, does not the Indian prince either decrease his own 'izzat' or that of his interlocutor? **1968** J. BARZUN Amer. University (1969) viii. 252 We saw how much faculties want presidents 'prestigious'. I suggest that instead of prestige we use the Hindi word izzat and see how absurd we are: 'Has he izzat? Have we enough izzat in the house? Our friends across the way are getting ahead of us in izzat.' Newspapers could then rank institutions izzat-wise.

J

J (dʒeɪ), the tenth letter of the alphabet in English and other modern languages, is, in its origin, a comparatively late modification of the letter I. In the ancient Roman alphabet, I, besides its vowel value in *ibīdem*, *mīlitis*, had the kindred consonantal value of modern English Y, as in *iactus*, *iam*, *Iouem*, *iūstus*, *adiūro*, *maior*, *peior*. Some time before the 6th century, this *y*-sound had, by compression in articulation, and consequent development of an initial 'stop', become a consonantal diphthong, passing through a sound (dj), akin to that of our *di*, *de*, in *odious*, *hideous*, to that represented in our phonetic symbolization by (dʒ). At the same time, the original guttural sound of G, when followed by a front vowel, had changed to that of palatal *g* (ɟ, gj), and then, by an advance of the point of closure, had passed through that of (dj), to the same sound (dʒ); so that *i* consonant and the so-called *g* 'soft' came to have, in the Romanic languages, the same identical value. In Italian, this new sound is represented by *g* before *e* and *i*, *gi* before *a*, *o*, and *u*. Thus, L. *gestus*, *Iēsūs*, *iam*, *iocāre*, *iūdicem*, are represented in Italian by *gesto*, *Gesù*, *già*, *giocare*, *giudice*. But in the other Romanic languages, the letter I was retained with the changed sound, so that, in these, *i* consonant and *g* 'soft' were equivalent symbols, distinguished only by derivation. In OF. the foregoing words were *gest*, *Iesu*, *ia*, *ioer*, *iuge*.

In OE., *i* consonant, so far as it was used, had (as still in all the continental Germanic languages) its Latin value (j), equivalent to OE. *ᵹe*, *ᵹi*, or *e* before certain vowels; thus we find *iá*, *iól*, *iow*, *iú*, *iuᵹoð*, *iung*, as occasional spellings of the words commonly written *ᵹeá*, *ᵹeól*, *eow*, *ᵹeó* (*ᵹió*, *ᵹiú*), *ᵹeoᵹoð* (*ᵹioᵹoð*), *ᵹeong* (*ᵹiong*, *ᵹiung*). This was especially the case with foreign proper names and other words known through Latin, as *Ianuarius*, *Iob*, *Iofes* (= Jove), *Iudéa*, *Iudéisc*, *iacinþ*, and the ethnic name *Iótas*, *Iútan* (rarely *Eotas*), now rendered 'Jutes'. But the French orthography introduced by the Norman Conquest brought in the Old French value of *i* consonant = *g* 'soft' (dʒ); a sound which English has ever since retained in words derived from that source, although in French itself the sound was subsequently, by loss of its first element, simplified to (ʒ).

From the 11th to the 17th c., then, the letter I i represented at once the vowel sound of *i*, and a consonant sound (dʒ), far removed from the vowel. Meanwhile, the minuteness and inconspicuousness of the small ı, and its liability, especially in cursive writing, to be confounded with one of the strokes of an adjacent letter, had led in mediæval Latin and general European writing, and thus also in English, to various scribal expedients in order to keep it distinct. (See I.) Among these, an initial ı was often prolonged above or below the line, or both; a final ı was generally prolonged below the line, and in both cases the prolonged part or 'tail' came at length in cursive writing to be terminated with a curve; thus arose the forms ȷ, *ȷ*, ȷ. The 'dot', used to individualize the minuscule i, was also used with the tailed form, and thus came the modern j, *j*. But this was at first merely a final form of i, used in Latin in such forms as 'filij', and in numerals, as j, ij, iij, vj, viij, xij. It was very little used in English, where *y* had previously been substituted for final *i*; and it was not till the 17th c. that the device of utilizing the two forms of the letter, so that i, *i*, should remain as the vowel, and j, *j*, be used for the consonant, was established, and the capital forms of the latter, J, *J*, were introduced.

The differentiation was made first in Spanish, where, from the very introduction of printing, we see j used for the consonant, and i only for the vowel. For the capitals, I had at first to stand for both (as it still does in German type, and in all varieties of Gothic or Black Letter); but before 1600 a capital J consonant began to appear in Spanish. (See, for example, Minsheu's Spanish Dictionary of 1599, where I and J are strictly distinguished, though the I and J words are put in one series.) In German typography, almost from the first, some printers employed a tailed form of the letter ȷ or j initially, to distinguish the consonant sound; but this was by no means generally established till much later. According to Watt (*Bibliotheca Britannica*), Louis Elzevir, who printed at Leyden 1595–1616, is generally credited with making the modern distinction of u and v, i and j, 'which was shortly after followed by the introduction of U and J among the capitals by Lazarus Zetzner of Strasburg in 1619'. In England, individual attempts to differentiate i and j were made already in the 16th c., as by Richard Day, who printed books in London after 1578, and George Bishop, who printed the translation of La Primaudaye's *French Academie* in 1586, with i, j, u, v, differentiated as in modern use, but had no capital J or U. The J j types are not used in the Bible of 1611, nor in the text of the Shakspere Folio of 1623 (but see JIG); these have I i for both values; but the latter has a capital Italic *J* in headlines in the proper names *John*, *Juliet*, *Julius*, and in the colophon, list of actors, etc., thus showing a tendency to use this (in its origin merely an ornamental variety of I) as a J. In Cotgrave's French-English Dictionary printed in 1611 (and in the reprint of it in 1632), the Roman type used for the French has no capital J, and uses I with both values, but it has the small j which is regularly used in the French words: thus Iustice, Ajuster. On the other hand, the italic type, in which the English is printed, has no small *j*, and uses *i* for both vowel and consonant; it has the two capitals, *I* and *J*, but uses them indiscriminately for the consonant: thus Ioyau: m. *A Jewell*; Ioyaulier: *m. A Ieweller*. Frequently *J* is used also for the vowel: thus Ingenieusement: *Jngeniously*; Ingenieux: *Ingenious*. Thus even when the types *I* and *J* were at hand, their use was not yet regulated. But during the decade which followed 1625, J, j, *J*, *j*, appear to have been gradually added to all founts of type, and the present usage of restricting I i to the vowel, J j to the consonant appears to have been generally established soon after 1630. (See, under U and V, the similar differentiation of U u vowel, and V v consonant, from the earlier V v initial, u medial and final.)

But though the differentiation of I and J, in form and value, was thus completed before 1640, the feeling that they were, notwithstanding, merely *forms of the same letter* continued for many generations; a vestige of it is still seen in the practice of many persons, who in script write the *I* form (𝒥) for both 𝒥 and 𝒥, and in the omission by printers of J and U from the signatures of the sheets of books. In Dictionaries, the I and J words continued to be intermingled in one series down to the 19th c. Dr. Johnson, indeed, under the letter I, says 'I is in English considered both as a vowel and consonant; though, since the vowel and consonant differ in their form as well as sound, they may be more properly accounted two letters'. Nevertheless, he proceeds to treat them practically as one, his first word *I* being followed by *Jabber*; *Jam* by *Iambick*, and this by *Jangle*; while the three last words of I are *Juxtaposition*, *Ivy*, *Jymold*. The same practice was followed by Todd, and by Richardson 1820, and even in some later dictionaries. Joddrell in 1820, Webster in 1828, separate I and J, as independent letters. The name of the letter, now *jay* (dʒeɪ), was formerly *jy* (dʒaɪ), riming with I, and corresponding to French *ji*; this is still common in Scotland and elsewhere.

In printing manuscripts or reprinting books produced before the differentiation of I and J, the earlier I has been treated in two different ways. The earlier editors, in most cases, introduced the modern usage into their texts, changing the I of the archetype, when it stood for the consonant, into J. Later editors more usually aim at reproducing the actual form of the original, and retain I with its twofold value. As our quotations are, in the main, from printed editions of MSS., and in some cases from later editions of printed books, they necessarily reflect these differences of editorial practice, and often show J before the 17th c.; it is to be remembered that this is usually due to the edition quoted, not to the original scribe or printer. But in our chronological lists of 'Forms', which precede the Etymology and Senses, these editorial J's have been disregarded, and the contemporary I alone given down to the date when J was actually in use.

In some modern editions of MS. or Black-letter books, in which the minuscule i of the original text is reproduced, we yet find a capital J introduced. This arises probably from the circumstance that the MS. or Italic *J*, or Black-letter 𝕵, is more like a J than an I in appearance, and is actually still used both for I and J.

No word beginning with J is of Old English derivation. Many are from Latin, chiefly through French; some from Greek, and a few from Hebrew and Arabic. There are also numerous modern words from distant languages, Eastern or Western, as *jaguar*, *jalap*, *jerboa*, *jungle*, *junk*. Besides these, many familiar or colloquial words of recent appearance and obscure history begin with this letter. On account of the phonetic equivalence of *i* consonant (i.e. *j*) and *g* 'soft' in words from Romanic, while in native English words, as *girl*, *get*, *g* was 'hard', there was a considerable tendency in Middle English to substitute *i* (= *j*) for *g* in words from French, as in *gemme*, *iemme*, *gentil*, *ientyl*, *gest*, *iest*, (and occasionally a counter tendency to use *g* for *i* (*j*), as in *iet*, *jet*, *geat*, *maiestie*, *majesty*, *magestie*), of which traces still remain in *gest*, *jest*, *sergeant*, *serjeant*, *jelly* from Fr. *gelée*, etc.

The regular and practically uniform sound of the letter J in English is the consonantal diphthong (dʒ). In the word *hallelujah* (also spelt *halleluiah*) it has the sound of Roman i-consonant (j). The same sound is retained in proper names or alien terms from German and other languages in which the Roman value of *j* is retained, as *Jena* (ˈjeːna), *Jaeger*, *Joachim*, *Jungfrau*, *junker*, *Janos*, *Jaroslav*, *Jassy*. In a few French words, distinctly recognized as alien, *j* has the French sound (ʒ), as *déjeuner*, *jeu d'esprit*. In the transliteration of Oriental names, as *Jāt*, *Jehangir*, *Jenghiz*, *Juggernaut*, *Jumna*, etc., *j* is used with its English value.

I. 1. The letter. The plural appears as *J*s, J's, *j*s, j's.

[**1573–80** BARET *Alv.* I *heading*, Now as concerning I consonant, which oftentimes vniustly vsurpeth the sound and place of G: me thinke it hath small reason: or rather I may say it is verie absurd, and much against both Art and reason.] **1591** PERCIVALL *Bibl. Hispan.*, *Gram*, B j b, j somewhat like the French *Desja*, *joieux*, *jouer*, but best like the Hebrew שׁ with his point on the right horne, or sh in English, as Ojo, *osho*. **1599** MINSHEU *Span. Gram.* 7 There be three kindes of I in the Spanish, that is, small i, Greeke y, and j, Jota or consonant... J jota or j consonant, which this toong taketh of the Arabique, is pronounced as in French *Jamais*, *Deja*, *Jehan*, in English like sh, as *Jardin*, a gardin, shardin. *Ibid.* 8 X is.. pronounced like J consonant, and the Spaniard often writeth one for another. *c* **1620** A. HUME *Brit. Tongue* iv. (1865) 13 For distinctiones of both sound and symbol, I wald commend the symbol and name of i and u to the voual sound;.. the symboles of j and v to the latin consonantes, and their names to be jod and vau; as, vain jestes. *Ibid.* v. 16 And j, for difference of the voual i, written with a long tail, I wald wish to be called jod or je. **1755** JOHNSON s.v. *I* (*the letter*): *J* consonant has invariably the same sound with that of *g* in *giant*; as *jade*, *jet*, *jilt*. **1896** A. WHYTE *Bible Characters* 190 Esau.. carved E. and J. into a true lover's knot under the handle of it. **1897** A. LANG in *Longm. Mag.* June 184 We carry the tails of our J's.. below the line.

2. A curve or figure of the shape of the letter.

1895 *Outing* (U.S.) XXVII. 211/1 A spur.. ran out toward the west and formed a large 'J' with the curve facing the south.

3. Short for **J-pen**, a broad-pointed pen, stamped with the letter J.

1885 SLADEN *In Cornwall*, etc. 178 The ink-pot.. with an old J nib in it stiff with rust. **1898** *Westm. Gaz.* 19 Jan. 3/1 A Visit to the J-Pen Club... Holding conclave with a group of brand-new Jays. *a* **1901** *Mod. colloq.* What pen do you write with? Do you use a J?

II. 4. Rarely used like the preceding letters to express serial order. In the signatures of the sheets of books, etc., the old order of the Roman alphabet, H, I, K, is usually retained. In the alphabetic designations of the batteries of the Royal Artillery A, B, C, etc., J is used for the tenth.

1884 *Whitaker's Alm.* 163 Field Artillery, 1st Brigade, A Battery, Dinapore;.. I, Ahmedabad; J, Dublin; K, Aldershot. **1899** *Ibid.* 195 Horse Artillery.. A Battery, *Umballa*;.. I, *Mhow*; J, *Bangalore*; K, *Rawal Pindi*. **1899** MACKAY *Introd. Lindesay of Pitscottie* (S.T.S.) 34 MS. J.. is at present in the library of Dupplin. **1900** *Dundee Advertiser* 12 Jan. 5 The transport Ujina sailed for Durban with J Battery Royal Horse Artillery and spare horses.

5. As a Roman numeral j was formerly used as a final form of i in j, ij, vj, and the like; this is retained in medical prescriptions.

c **1400** *Lanfranc's Cirurg.* 179 ℞ ladani ℥ j, & resolue it in ℥ iiij of oile of mirtilles.

6. a. In *Math.* and *Physics*, *J* is used to denote the Jacobian; also Joule's mechanical equivalent of heat; for *j* in Quaternions, see I (the letter) 6.

b. In *Electr.* *j* is used (in place of the mathematical symbol *i*, which is used for

electric current) to represent $\sqrt{(-1)}$, or an angular displacement of 90°.

1893 *Electrician* 15 Sept. 522/2 The next Paper was by Mr. C. P. Steinmetz on 'Complex Quantities and their Application in Electrical Engineering'. This Paper contained a novel method of the treatment of alternating currents... The device is to introduce the letter *j* in the expression of the sine curve, at first simply as a distinguishing index without mathematical meaning, and afterward as $j = \sqrt{(-1)}$. **1907** FRANKLIN & ESTY *Elem. Electr. Engin.* II. v. 90 It can be shown..by ordinary trigonometry that the components of a line whose length is $I\sqrt{R^2 + X^2}$ and which is θ degrees ahead of *I*, where θ is the angle whose tangent is X/R, are $e_1 = Ri_1 - Xi_{11}$ and $e_{11} = Xi_1 + Ri_{11}$. Therefore the term j^2Xi_{11}..must be equal to $-Xi_{11}$, or, in other words, we must have: $j^2 = -1$. **1945** '*Electr. Engineer*' *Ref. Bk.* I. 67 Considering *j* as a vector-operator, it is a means whereby a length in one direction is rotated anticlockwise by 90°. **1961** R. B. ANGUS *Electr. Engin. Fund.* xiii. 341 Since $j^2A = -A$.., then $j^2 = -1$ or $j = \sqrt{(-1)}$. *Ibid.* 343 The *j* is always placed to the left in the product. This practice helps avoid the overlooking of a *j*-term when real and *j*-terms are being grouped.

c. In *Physics* J and j represent quantized angular momentum.

j was first used by A. Sommerfeld (in *Ann. d. Physik* (1923) LXX. 33), in place of n_j, which had been used by W. Heisenberg (in *Zeitschr. f. Physik* (1922) VIII. 274) in place of Sommerfeld's original symbol n_i, which he introduced (in *Atombau und Spektrallinien* (ed. 3, 1922) vi. 446 and *Zeitschr. f. Physik* (1922) VIII. 269) as an empirical 'inner' quantum number (G. *innere Quantenzahl*) in describing the Zeeman effect. As this was interpreted in terms of later theory, *j* became the quantum number of the total angular momentum of an electron, corresponding to the resultant of its spin s and orbital momentum l; *J* is used similarly for an assemblage of electrons, and in molecular spectroscopy is the quantum number for angular momentum due to rotation of a molecule as a whole. Apart from these specific uses, j and J are often used as symbols for a general angular momentum.

jj-coupling, an approximation used in the quantum theory of the atom when the spin-orbit interaction of individual electrons is large compared with the remaining electrostatic interaction between one electron and another, so that spin and orbital angular momenta may be coupled to give a resultant j for each electron, and the resultants in turn coupled to give the total angular momentum J of the electrons. Cf. *LS-coupling*.

1924 *Phil. Mag.* XLVIII. 720 The X-ray atomic levels may be conveniently classified by means of three quantum numbers—*n* (total), *k* (azimuthal), and *j* (inner). **1929** *jj-coupling* [see COUPLING *vbl. sb.* 6f(ii)]. **1930** *Physical Rev.* XXXVI. 613 The resultant angular momentum of the molecule (quantum number *J*). **1955** TOWNES & SCHAWLOW *Microwave Spectroscopy* i. 5 As *J* increases and the molecule rotates faster, it stretches. **1957** M. E. ROSE *Elem. Theory Angular Momentum* i. 11 Consider the case of two spins (or angular momenta) j_1 and j_2. **1970** G. K. WOODGATE *Elem. Atomic Struct.* vii. 140 In the lower-lying configurations of neutral atoms the *j-j* coupling approximation is not often found, in other words the conditions for small electrostatic interaction are not often satisfied, even in heavy elements.

III. Abbreviations.

(Abbreviations given here with the full stop are frequently found without it.) **J.** stands for various proper names, as *John*, *James*, *Joseph*; *Jane*, *Jessie*, *Jemima*, etc.; **J**, joule; **J.A.**, Judge Advocate; **J.A.**, Justice of Appeal; **JCB**, a proprietary name for excavators and other earth-moving equipment made by the firm of J. C. Bamford (Excavators) Ltd.; **J.C.R.**, Junior Common Room; **JICTAR**, (with pronunc. 'dʒɪktɑː(r)), Joint Industry Committee for Television Advertising Research (replacing TAM); **j.n.d.**, just noticeable difference; **J.P.**, Justice of Peace; **Jr.**, **jr.**, Junior.

1951 *Symbols, Signs & Abbreviations* (R. Soc.) 14 Joule... *J. **1967** W. H. HAYT *Engin. Electromagn.* (ed. 2) ii. 32 The volt..having the label of joules per coulomb (J/C) or newton-meters per coulomb.., we shall..measure electric field intensity in..volts per meter (V/m). **1881** D. JONES *Notes Mil. Law* p. vii, **J.A.*, Judge Advocate. *Ibid.* v. 67 The J.A. and prosecutor must not be the same person. **1918** E. S. FARROW *Dict. Mil. Terms* p. x, *J.A.*, Judge Advocate. **1883** *Wharton's Law Lexicon* (ed. 7) 432 *J.A.*, Justice of Appeal. **1972** *Mod. Law Rev.* XXXV. I. 45 The dictum already referred to of Watermeyer J.A. came at the end of his judgment. **1960** *Trade Marks Jrnl.* 29 June 778/1 (*in figure*) **JCB*..Power-operated loaders and excavators, all for handling, transporting and loading earth, minerals and similar materials, and parts and fittings therefor... J. C. Bamford (Excavators) Limited, Lakeside Works, Rocester, Uttoxeter. **1972** *Police Rev.* 24 Nov. 1547/1 A query has recently arisen in my traffic section regarding the necessity for a provisional licence holder to be accompanied when driving a J.C.B. excavator on a road. **1985** *Financial Times* 18 Nov. 17/2 Dump trucks and JCBs are already flattening the site. **1892** *Isis* (Oxf.) 8 June 35/2 Only the Pres. of the *J.C.R. and the Captain of the Eleven retain their equanimity. **1914** C. MACKENZIE *Sinister St.* II. III. viii. 656 The editor rejected the frivolous attentions of his audience, and left the J.C.R. **1968** *Listener* 1 Aug. 147/1 The Student Council received the support..of the vast majority of JCRs. **1964** *World's Press News* 1 May 4/1 *JICTAR—Joint Industry Committee for Television Advertising Research—embraces the Incorporated Society of British Advertisers, the Independent Television Companies Association and the Institute of Practitioners in Advertising. **1968** *Guardian* 28 Sept. 9/1 JICTAR has replaced TAM as the index of response. **1982** *Listener* 16 Dec. 27/3 Other problems include the possibility that in rejuvenating the old JICTAR sample for BARB's birth last year, some faithful heavy viewers were lost and non-addicts put in their places. **1929** *Encycl. Brit.* VII. 420/1 The just noticeable difference, often called the '*j.n.d.', between the stimuli of two sensations. **1948** *Sci. News* VII. 14 Rubbers could be compared with one another with about three times as small a j.n.d. as that found for bitumens. **1732** *Calendar State Papers Amer. & W. Indies* (1939) 48 A dispute arising between two of his men on shore, Francis Squib and Jacob Taverner, *J.P's in that harbour, put them in the stocks. **1869** *Bradshaw's Railway Manual* XXI. 328 Directors..Sir Benjamin Morris, J.P. **1972** P. JOHNSON *Offshore Islanders* v. 291 The Local Government Act of 1888..replaced the old Quarter Sessions of JPs by democratically elected County Councils.

ja, obs. Sc. form of JAY, the bird.

‖**jaal-goat** ('dʒeɪəl-, 'jɑːəl'gəʊt). [ad. Heb. *yāʿēl* wild goat.] The wild goat of Mount Sinai, Upper Egypt, Abyssinia, etc. (*Capra jaala*).

1838 *Penny Cycl.* XI. 283/2 The Jaal Goat, *Capra jaela*, found in the mountains of Abyssinia, Upper Egypt, and Mount Sinai. *Ibid.* (*cut*) Jaal Goat, or Abyssinian Ibex.

jab (dʒæb), *v. colloq.* or *dial.* [var., orig. Sc., of JOB *v.*[1]] **a.** *trans.* To thrust with the end or point of something; to poke roughly; to stab.

1825–80 JAMIESON, To *Jab*, to prick sharply. *Ettr. For.* **1827** D. JOHNSON *Ind. Field Sports* 243 The hog..being jabbed with a spear. **1899** *Westm. Gaz.* 24 May 2/3 M. Mendès got jabbed in the lower part of his chest, seriously if not fatally.

b. To thrust (something) with an abrupt blow (*into* a thing or person).

1827 D. JOHNSON *Ind. Field Sports* 238, I disapprove of jabbing the spear into a hog. **1885** HOWELLS *Silas Lapham* I. 12 Jabbing the point of his penknife into the writing pad.

c. *absol.* or *intr.* To stab.

1827 D. JOHNSON *Ind. Field Sports* 238 When alone, it is fair to jab. **1892** R. KIPLING *Life's Handicap* 119 The Khusru Kheyl jab upwards from below, remember.

d. *trans.* To give (a person) a stabbing blow with the fist. Also *fig.*

1901 R. FITZSIMMONS *Physical Culture & Self-Defense* 114 Jab him, if you can, with your left. **1915** E. CORRI *30 Yrs. Boxing Referee* 38 Time and again he jabbed and patted Smith cleverly on the nose with his left hand. **1959** *Amer. Speech* XXXIV. 155 One may be shafted or jabbed by the opposite sex, a professor..or anyone else for any real or imagined injury.

e. *trans.* and *intr.* To inject or inoculate (a person) with a hypodermic needle; to use (a hypodermic needle) to make an injection. So '**jabbing** *vbl. sb. slang* (orig. *U.S.*).

1926 *Flynn's* 16 Jan. 638/2 Some stiffs uses mud but coke don't need any jabbin', cookin', or flops. You can hit it an' go. **1938** *Amer. Speech* XIII. 186/1 *To jab*, to take drugs hypodermically. **1948** PARTRIDGE *Dict. Forces' Slang* 100 *Be jabbed*, to be inoculated or vaccinated. **1956** S. LONGSTREET *Real Jazz* xviii. 114 Not all jazz-players smoke marijuana or opium, or sniff snow or jab a vein. **1968** J. R. ACKERLEY *My Father & Myself* xiii. 146 Dr Wadd..dashed in with a hypodermic syringe of digitalis and jabbed it so hastily, though successfully, into the back of one of his hands that it raised a large lump. **1968** 'L. BLACK' *Outbreak* ix. 82 Smith-road primary was jabbed. Why not our school?

jab (dʒæb), *sb. colloq.* or *dial.* [f. prec. vb.]

1. a. An act of jabbing; an abrupt blow with something pointed, or (in pugilistic slang) with the fist.

1825–80 JAMIESON, *Jab*, the act of pricking in this way [see JAB *v.*]. **1872** C. D. WARNER *Backlog Studies* 260 Giving the fire a jab with the poker. **1889** GUNTER *That Frenchman!* xi, A short, sharp, terrible jab of the masked man's unengaged left hand. **1899** *Blackw. Mag.* Feb. 198 The chief's son..made a tentative jab with a spear at the white man.

b. An injection with a hypodermic needle. *slang* (orig. *U.S.*).

1914 JACKSON & HELLYER *Vocab. Criminal Slang* 48 *Jab*, current amongst morphine and cocaine fiends. A hypodermic injection. **1959** *Punch* 13 May 658/3 Receiving the hypodermic jab intended for the bullock. **1972** G. DURRELL *Catch me a Colobus* i. 11 Can't you give me a jab of something to keep me going? **1973** *Times* 17 Apr. (Liberia Suppl.) p. ii/2 The visitor must..take precautions and submit to a variety of jabs.

2. A radio signal of momentary duration. *colloq.*

1932 *News Chron.* 23 Sept. 10/7 Another film I saw was of the flight of a jab of wireless energy on its journey from the East End to King's College, Strand. **1945** *Electronic Engin.* XVII. 679/3 For this purpose they devised a radio transmitter which sent out very short pulses, or jabs, of radio energy.

jabal, var. JEBEL.

jabber ('dʒæbə(r)), *v.* Also 5–6 **iaber**. [app. onomatopœic, with the form of a frequentative; with *jabber*, *jabble*, cf. *gab*, *gabber*, *gabble*; also *yabber*; the phonetic relation between these is not clear. An earlier form in the Promptorium MSS. is JAVER, which in Pynson's ed. became *jaber*.]

1. *intr.* To talk rapidly and indistinctly or unintelligibly; to speak volubly and with little sense; to chatter, gabble, prattle. Often applied, in contempt or derision, to the speaking of a language which is unintelligible to the hearer.

1499 *Promp. Parv.* 256/2 (Pynson), Iangelyn or iaberyn [*Harl. MS.* iaveryn], *garrulo*, *blatero*. *Ibid.* 487/1 Tateryn or iaberyn [*Harl. MS.* iaueryn, or speke wythe owte resone], *garrio*, *blatero*. **1655** FULLER *Ch. Hist.* I. iv. §23 Which Infant..doth not jabber so strangely, but that she is perfectly understood by her Parent. **1678** PHILLIPS (ed. 4), To *Jabber*, a word vulgarly used for to prattle, chat, or talk. **1748** SMOLLETT *Rod. Rand.* lvi, He had brought a gentleman who could jabber with her in French. **1866** MRS. H. WOOD *St. Martin's Eve* xxvii. (1874) 340 We have got two Flemish servants, and you should hear them jabbering.

b. To utter inarticulate sounds rapidly and volubly; to chatter, as monkeys, birds, etc.; to gibber or jibber.

c **1817** HOGG *Tales & Sk.* IV. 41 Allanson made some sound..as if attempting to speak, but his tongue refused its office, and he only jabbered. *a* **1859** MACAULAY *Hist. Eng.* xxiii. V. 76 The fool who jabbered at his feet, the monkey which grinned at the back of his chair. **1860** TROLLOPE *West Ind.* xx. 310 In the huge trees the monkeys hung jabbering. **1894** HALL CAINE *Manxman* v. iii. 289 On the top of the crag the sea-fowl were jabbering.

2. *trans.* To speak or utter rapidly and indistinctly; to express by jabbering. Often *contemptuously* = to speak (a foreign language), with the implication that it is unintelligible to the hearer.

1532 MORE *Confut. Tindale* VI. Wks. 665 Whatsoeuer the Iewes would iaber or iangle agayn. **1715** BENTLEY *Serm.* x. 348 They must jabber their *Credos* and *Pater-Nosters* at Home. **1716** ADDISON *Freeholder* No. 22 ¶2 He did not know what Travelling was good for, but to teach a Man..to jabber French, and to talk against Passive Obedience. **1854** H. MILLER *Sch. & Schm.* xviii. (1856) 383 A poor idiot,..used to come every day to the churchyard, to..jabber in broken expressions his grief.

Hence '**jabbering** *vbl. sb.* and *ppl. a.* ***jabbering crow***, a small species of crow common in Jamaica (*Corvus Jamaicensis*). '**jabberingly** *adv.*, in a jabbering manner (Hyde Clarke, 1855).

1499 *Promp. Parv.* 487/2 (Pynson), Taterynge or iaberinge [*Harl. MS.* iauerynge, *Winch. MS.* iaperynge], *garritus*. **1543** BALE *Course Rom. Fox* 43b, Latyne Iabberynge and wawlynge, accordynge to the offyce of saynt Antonynes personage. **1689** HICKERINGILL *Ceremony-monger* 29 His Singing-Boys with their alternate Jabberings and Mouthings. **1728** POPE *Dunc.* II. 237 'Twas chatt'ring, grinning, mouthing, jabb'ring all. *a* **1795** SIR W. JONES *Hymn to Lacshmí* Wks. 1799 VI. 364 Jabb'ring spectres o'er her traces glide. **1875** WHITNEY *Life Lang.* xiv. 292 To study the jabberings of monkeys.

jabber ('dʒæbə(r)), *sb.* [f. prec. vb.] The act of jabbering; rapid and indistinct or unintelligible talk; gabble, chatter; gibberish.

1727 SWIFT *Gulliver, Let. to Cousin Sympson* Wks. 1778 V. 7 Who only differ from their brother brutes in Houyhnhnmland, because they use a sort of Jabber. **1801** W. TAYLOR in *Monthly Mag.* XII. 586 A sea-port jabber, formed..by the mishmash of a hundred dialects. **1838** J. L. STEPHENS *Trav. Greece*, etc. 45/1 He..was utterly ignorant of any language but his own; despised all foreigners, and detested their 'jabber'. **1893** MRS. C. PRAED *Outlaw & Lawmaker* II. xvi. 85 Prepared for what she called a 'jabber'.

jabberer ('dʒæbərə(r)). [f. JABBER *v.* + -ER[1].] One who jabbers; a chatterer.

1678 BUTLER *Hud.* III. ii. 152 T' out-cant the Babylonian Labourers, At all their Dialects of Jabberers. **1818** KEATS *Lett.* Wks. 1889 III. 141 To daunt and dazzle the thousand jabberers about pictures and books. **1892** *Columbus* (O.) *Disp.* 24 Mar., The jabberer who sits near you..and annoys everybody around with senseless and endless talk.

'**jabberment**. *rare.* [f. as prec. + -MENT.] Jabbering; jabber; senseless and voluble talk.

1644 MILTON *Colast.* 25 We are com to his farewell, which is to bee a concluding taste of his Jabberment in law.

jabbernowl, variant of JOBBERNOWL.

jabbers, jabers ('dʒæbəz, 'dʒeɪbəz). Also **jap(p)ers**. Corruption of *Jesus*, used expletively (see BEJAB(B)ERS *int.*).

1821, etc. [see BEJAB(B)ERS *int.*]. **1934** A. P. HERBERT *Holy Deadlock* 311 'Be Jabers!' said the girl, 'is that the way you feel?' **1970** *Alberta Hist. Rev.* XVIII. III. 18/2 'Can you hit that man?' The gunner replied, 'Be japers, I'll ate what's left of him.'

jabberwock ('dʒæbəwɒk). The name of the fabulous monster in Lewis Carroll's poem *Jabberwocky*. Hence in allusive and extended uses, esp. 'incoherent or nonsensical expression'. So '**jabberwocky**, invented language, meaningless language, nonsensical behaviour; also as *adj.*, nonsensical, meaningless, topsy-turvy. Also '**jabberwock(y)** *v. intr.*, to write, speak, etc., in jabberwocky style.

1871 'L. CARROLL' *Through Looking-Glass* i. 22 The Jabberwock, with eyes of flame, Came whiffling through the tulgey wood. **1902** J. BUCHAN *Watcher by Threshold* iii. 38 It was the strangest jumble of vowels and consonants I had ever met... It was some maniac talking Jabberwock to himself. **1908** *Daily Chron.* 10 Apr. 4/7 Those exceptional modern folk who write with equal ease in the ordinary left-to-right manner and in 'Jabberwocky' fashion..right to left. **1917** [see CHRISTMAS-TREE 2]. **1926** *Glasgow Herald* 7 Oct. 5 From 'Jabberwocky' it is but a short step to the old-fashioned nursery-rhyme. **1931** E. WILSON *Axel's Castle* vi. 227 The dreaming mind does not usually speak—and when it does, it is more likely to express itself in the looking-glass language of 'Jabberwocky' than in anything resembling ordinary speech. **1939** *Times* 25 Feb. 15/5 It is all very Jabberwocky, and so far the writers of the movement [surrealism] have the advantage of the artists. **1953** H. MILLER *Plexus* (1963) ii. 57 Realizing in a short time that I was not in the least interested in all this jabberwocky, and thinking of Mona waiting for me to lunch with her, I

suddenly interrupted him. **1959** *Listener* 29 Jan. 226/1 His [*sc.* Skelton's] tendency to jabberwock (like Pound or Eliot, Skelton was a polylingual versifier). **1963** *Guardian* 22 July 5/5 He jabberwockied, pulling furiously at his ear-lobe as he talked. **1964** A. Swinson *Six Minutes to Sunset* vi. 126 Sometimes, to confuse the issue,..he would indulge in his own subtle form of jabberwocky. **1970** J. Fleming *Young Man, I think you're Dying* xii. 164 He was going to wear her down, intimidate her, tame and train her to obey, and a whole lot of other jabberwocky which he couldn't.. remember now. **1972** *Collector's Guide* Aug. 12/1 (Advt.), Worcester first period teapot stand 'Jabberwocky pattern'.

jabble ('dʒæb(ə)l), *v.*[1] Also 6 jabil. [f. as JABBER, with freq. or dim. ending -LE.] = JABBER *v.*

1570 Levins *Manip.* 126/45 Iabil, *garrire, multum loqui.* **1830** *Blackw. Mag.* XXVIII. 313 Thousands of birds, all jabbling and dabbling, and paddling.

'**jabble**, *v.*[2] *Sc.* [app. onomatopœic, with freq. or dim. ending -LE; cf. *dabble.*]

a. *trans.* To shake or mix up together (quot. 1760); to shake up or agitate (a liquid), to cause to splash. **b.** *intr.* To splash, plash, dash in small waves or ripples.

1760 Washington *Writ.* (1889) II. 163 All mix'd..by.. jabling them well together in a Cloth. **1825-80** Jamieson, To *Jabble*, 1. To cause agitation of the sea, as when the wind rises. 2. To agitate the liquid contents of a dish or vessel, so as to cause spilling. **1894** Crockett *Raiders* 286 The rippling tide..jabbling along the side of the boat.

jabble ('dʒæb(ə)l), *sb. Sc.* [f. prec. vb.] A slight agitated movement of water or other liquid; a splashing or dashing in small waves or ripples.

1831 *Mirror* XVII. 415/1 There is a perpetual 'jabble' against the cliffs on this coast. **1871** Blackie *Four Phases* i. 21 A plash and jabble of conflicting waters. **1883** Stevenson *Silverado Sq.* 4 The steamer jumped, and the black buoys were dancing in the jabble.

fig. **1896** 'Ian Maclaren' *K. Carnegie* 307 Carmichael's mind was in a jabble that day.

jabell, variant of JAVEL *Obs.*, worthless fellow.

‖**jabiru** ('dʒæbɪru:). Also **jaburu**, *Austral.* **jaberoo, jabiroo**. [Tupi-Guarani *jabirú*; also called *jabirú guaçú* (*guaçú* or *wassú* 'great').] A large wading bird of tropical and subtropical America (*Mycteria americana*), of the stork family. Also applied to the allied *Xenorhynchus australis*, *X. indicus*, and *X. asiaticus* (which is closely related to the tropical American *Jabiru mycteria*), and *Ephippiorhynchus senegalensis*, of the Old World.

[**1648** Marcgrave *Hist. Nat. Brasil.* 200 Iabiru Brasiliensibus, Belgis vulgo *Negro.* **1678** Ray *Ornith.* iii. iii. 276 Jabiru guacu [guaçú] of the Petiguares..I have eaten of it often.] **1774** Goldsm. *Nat. Hist.* (1862) II. vi. iv. 179 It will be proper to mention the Jabiru, and the Jabiru Guacu, both natives of Brazil. **1796** Stedman *Surinam* II. 343 The crane, or jabiru, of Surinam, I can best compare to a stork. **1860** G. Bennett *Gatherings of a Naturalist* 195 (Morris), In October, 1858, I succeeded in purchasing a fine living specimen of the New Holland Jabiru, or Gigantic Crane of the colonists (*Mycteria Australis*). **1896** Newton *Dict. Birds* s.v., Very nearly allied to *Mycteria*, and also commonly called Jabirus, are the birds of the genera *Xenorhynchus* and *Ephippiorhynchus*. **1912** A. Searcy *By Flood & Field* viii. 60 There were also Jaberoo, Spoonbill, Ibis and Spur-wing Plover. **1943** W. E. Harney *Taboo* 158 The jaberoo struts along its sands. **1946** I. L. Idriess *In Crocodile Land* xxxiii. 237 The call of the jabiru. **1952** *Coast to Coast 1951* 211 He had ridden up quietly, and the big, black-and-white, dark-blue-necked jabiroo, pacing slowly on its red-yellow legs at the further end of the lagoon, had not flown away. **1965** G. McInnes *Road to Gundagai* viii. 125 The brick walls dissolved into..polygonum swamps over which the long legged jabiroo flew creaking on its way. **1965** *Austral. Encycl.* V. 114/1 Sometimes the jabiru is quite solitary, hence perhaps the term 'policeman-bird', by which it is known in North Queensland.

Jablochkoff ('jæblɒtʃkɒf). The name of Paul *Jablochkoff* (1847-94), Russian physicist, used *attrib.* and in the possessive to denote an electric arc lamp invented by him (now obsolete) in which carbon rod electrodes were placed side by side and separated by an insulating material such as plaster of Paris, which gradually melted as the electrodes burned away.

1877 *Jrnl. Franklin Inst.* CIV. 295 Jablochkoff's electric candles burn for two or three hours without interruption. **1884** J. E. H. Gordon *Pract. Treat. Electr. Lighting* vii. 99 The lighting of the Avenue de l'Opera in Paris in 1878 by Jablochkoff candles first demonstrated the possibility of street lighting by electricity. **1894** R. M. Walmsley *Electr. Current* xii. 508 Because of the difference in the rate of burning of the positive and negative carbons in the ordinary arc, the Jablochkoff candle has to be supplied with alternate currents. **1922** S. G. Starling *Electricity* vi. 85 In that year [*sc.* 1876] Jablochkoff employed two parallel carbon rods, separated by an insulating material... These were called Jablochkoff's candles. They soon gave place to more convenient arc lamps.

‖**jaborandi** (dʒæbə'rændɪ, prop. ˌdʒaboran'di:). [Tupi-Guarani *jaburandí*, also *jaburandiba* (*iba* plant, tree).] The dried leaflets of a Brazilian plant *Pilocarpus pinnatifolius*, N.O. *Rutaceæ*, having diuretic and sudorific properties. Also applied to other plants having similar properties.

1875 H. C. Wood *Therap.* (1879) 513 *Jaborandi.* This drug, which has long been employed by the natives of South America, received its first notice, under the various names of *Jaborandi*, *Jaguarandy*, and *Jamguarandi*, from Dr. T. J. H. Langgard in his 'Diccionario de Medecina domestica', Rio Janeiro, 1865. **1875** *Pharmac. Jrnl.* 18 Sept. 227. **1877** Roberts *Handbk. Med.* (ed. 3) I. 35 Jaborandi might prove serviceable in some cases.

jaborine ('dʒæbəraɪn). *Chem.* [f. prec. + -INE.] An alkaloid contained, together with pilocarpine, in the leaves of jaborandi: see prec.

1887 *Syd. Soc. Lex.*, *Jaborin*,.. Its action resembles that of atropin... It is antagonistic to pilocarpin. **1896** *Allbutt's Syst. Med.* I. 226 Pilocarpine, when heated with dilute hydrochloric acid, is converted into jaborine.

‖**jabot** (ʒabo). [F. *jabot* gizzard, frill on a shirt front: 'origin unknown' (Hatz.-Darm.).]

1. A frill formerly worn by men on the front or bosom of the shirt, edging the opening.

1823 Scott *Quentin D.* Introd., His clean silk stockings.. the solitaire, the *jabot*, the ruffles at the wrist, and the *chapeau-bras*—all announced that La Jeunesse considered the arrival of a guest at the château as an unusual event. **1898** *Pall Mall G.* 12 Oct. 3/1 The costume is completed by a long waistcoat of cream satin, patterned with pink roses, a jabot of lace, pale blue satin knee-breeches [etc.].

2. An ornamental frill on a woman's bodice.

1881 *Truth* 19 May 686/2 The bodice of black and yellow striped silk, with frills and jabot of black lace. **1898** *Daily News* 7 May 8/4 The jabot has secured a fresh lease of life, and has elongated itself from the neck to the waist.

jaboticaba (dʒæbɒtɪ'kɑ:bə). Also **jabuticaba**. [Tupi.] An evergreen Brazilian tree, *Myrciaria* (or *Eugenia*) *cauliflora*, of the family Myrtaceæ, which bears clusters of white flowers and purple fruits directly on the trunk and branches; also, the fruit of this tree.

1824 H. E. Lloyd tr. *Spix & Martius's Trav. Brazil* II. iii. ii. 85 A light and agreeable wine is also prepared from the fruits of the jabuticaba (*Myrtus cauliflora*). **1862** *Chambers's Encycl.* IV. 161/1 *E[ugenia] cauliflora*, a Brazilian species,.. yields a very fine fruit of a black colour, about the size of a greengage plum, called the Jabuticaba. **1931** B. Miall tr. *Guenther's Naturalist in Brazil* iv. 79 In the Jaboticaba, a myrtle-tree, even the trunk looks as though beaded with the blue-black fruits, about the size of a damson, that seem to be nailed on to the bark. **1974** F. N. Howes *Dict. Useful Plants* 132 Jaboticaba (Braz[il]) *Myrciaria*, esp. *M. cauliflora*, (Braz. grape), fr[uit] ed[ible], used for wine and jelly.

jaca, early form of JACK *sb.*[4], the fruit.

jacal (hə'kɑ:l). Also **hackal, jackal(l), jucal**. [Mexican Sp., ad. Nahuatl *xacalli.*] A hut constructed of erect poles or stakes filled in with wattle and mud, a type common in Mexico and the south-western United States; an adobe house; also, the material or method used in building such a hut.

1838 'Texian' *Mexico v. Texas* 249 It was a little *Jacal*, or cabin, built with large unburnt bricks, called *adobes*, in the language of the country. **1844** J. J. Webb *Adventures in Santa Fe Trade* (1931) 104 In a valley..where the herders had a temporary corrall and *jacal* made of bushes laid upon poles. *Ibid.* 105 The *jacal* was *full*, packed so thick it was impossible to count them. **1850** J. W. Audubon *Western Jrnl.* (1906) 230 We..saw a comfortable (for this country), log and jacal built house. **1897** *16th Ann. Rep. U.S. Bureau Amer. Ethnol. 1894-95* 108 This method is known to the Mexicans as '*jacal*', and much used by them. It consists of a row of sticks or thin poles set vertically in the ground and heavily plastered with mud. **1900** R. B. C. Graham *Thirteen Stories* 127 A straw-thatched jacal. **1947** *Chicago Sun Bk. Week* 8 June 2/2 In the back alleys..are to be found.. primitive jacals.

‖**jacamar** ('dʒækəmɑ:(r)). [a. F. *Jacamar* (Brisson, 1760), ad. Tupi-Guarani *Jacamaciri.*] Any bird of the family *Galbulidæ*, natives of South America, having a general resemblance in appearance to the bee-eaters and in habits to the king-fishers.

[**1648** Marcgrave *Hist. Nat. Brasil.* 202 Iacamaciri Brasiliensibus, avis Alaudæ magnitudinis.] **1825** Waterton *Wand. S. Amer.* (1882) 26 A bird called Jacamar is often taken for a kingfisher. **1834** McMurtrie *Cuvier's Anim. Kingd.* 136 The *Jacamars* are closely allied to the king-fishers by their elongated sharp-pointed beak... They are solitary birds, that live in wet forests, feed on insects, and build on low branches. **1896** Newton *Dict. Birds*, *Jacamar*, a word formed by Brisson from *Jacamaciri*, the Brazilian name of a bird, as given by Marcgrave, and since adopted in most European tongues for the species to which it was first applied and others allied to it, forming the family *Galbulidæ* of ornithologists.

‖**jacana** ('dʒækənə), prop. **jaçana** (dʒasə'nɑ:). Also **jassana**. [Tupi-Guarani *jasaná*, in Pg. spelling *jaçaná*. (See Newton *Dict. Birds*.)] Any bird of the genus *Parra* (*Jacana*) or family *Parridæ* (*Jacanidæ*), consisting of grallatorial aquatic birds inhabiting the warmer regions of the world, having enormous straight claws, which enable them to walk on the floating leaves of aquatic plants.

[**1648** Marcgrave *Hist. Nat. Brasil.* 190 Iacana Brasiliensibus, gallina aquatica.] **1753** Chambers *Cycl. Supp.*, *Jacana*, the name of a Brasilian bird, a species of moor-hen. **1797** tr. *Buffon's Nat. Hist.* XIII. 243 (L.) The jacana..is most common in South America. **1820** Neuwied *Trav. Brazil* iii. 25 Large flocks appeared of Jassanas. **1888** R. Buchanan *City of Dream* ix. 195 And walking upon floating lotus leaves The red jacana screamed. **1895** C. Dixon in *Fortn. Rev.* Apr. 652 The Parridæ or jacanas, those curious long-toed birds that run over the floating vegetation of the marshes and swamps of the tropics.

‖**jacaranda** (dʒækə'rændə, prop. dʒakaran'dɑ:). [Tupi-Guarani *jacarandá.*] Name given to various trees of tropical America yielding fragrant and ornamental wood (called, in common with various other timbers, *rosewood*); esp. to those of the genus *Jacaranda* (N.O. *Bignoniaceæ*). **b.** The wood of any of these trees. **c.** A drug obtained from a tree of the genus *Jacaranda.*

1753 Chambers *Cycl. Supp.*, *Jacaranda*,..a name given by some authors to the tree the wood of which is the log-wood, used in dying and in medicine. **1830** Lindley *Nat. Syst. Bot.* 92 The fine Jacaranda or Rosewood of commerce ..is produced by a species of Mimosa. **1851** *Illustr. Catal. Gt. Exhib.* 1353 Writing table, of Jacaranda wood. **1887** *Syd. Soc. Lex.* s.v., Jacaranda, in the form of a fluid extract of the leaves of *J. procera*,..is given..in chronic catarrh of the bladder.

‖**jacare** ('dʒækəreɪ). [Tupi-Guarani *jacaré*, Pg. *jacaré.*] A South American alligator.

[**1648** Marcgrave *Hist. Nat. Brasil.* 242 Iacare Brasiliensibus, Cayman Æthiopibus in Congo, Crocodilus Latinis.] **1753** Chambers *Cycl. Supp.*, *Jacare*,..an animal found in the Brazils, and very little differing from the crocodile of the other parts of the world. **1869** R. F. Burton *Highlands Brazil* II. 177 Here a dog swimming across the stream showed little apprehension of the 'Jacare' (*Crocodilus Sclerops*). **1878** T. P. Bigg-Wither *Pioneering S. Brazil* II. 63 The *jacaré* a species of alligator..on the lower Ivahy.

†**jacatoo**, app. error for **cacatoo*, COCKATOO.

1654 Evelyn *Diary* 11 July, A rarely colour'd jacatoo or prodigious large parrot.

†**jacco**, obs. corrupt form of JACKAL *sb.*

1648-9 C. Walker *Relat. & Observ.* 14 The Clergy.. have ever held with the mighty as the Iacco hunts with the Lyon.

†**jace**, *sb. Obs.* According to Halliwell, A kind of fringe; but perh. = JESS, a pendent ribbon.

1399 Langl. *Rich. Redeles* iii. 130 With gyuleres joyffull ffor here grey Iaces And ffor her wedis so wyde.

†**jace**, *v. Obs. rare*$^{-1}$. Alteration of *chace*, app. for alliteration's sake.

1393 Langl. *P. Pl.* C. xx. 50 To Iusten in ierusalem he iacede awey ful faste [*v. rr.* iaced, iaside; *B.* chaced].

jacemine, obs. form of JASMINE.

jacent ('dʒeɪsənt), *a.* ? *Obs.* [ad. L. *jacēnt-em*, pr. pple. of *jacēre* to lie.] Lying; recumbent; *fig.* sluggish.

1611 Speed *Hist. Gt. Brit.* v. i. §12. 4 Countryes and Kingdomes farre iacent and remote. **1624** Wotton *Archit.* in *Reliq.* (1651) 224 Brick or squared Stones..laid in their lengths with sides and heads together, or their Points conjoyned..are more apt in swagging down to pierce with their points then in the jacent posture. **1656** Blount *Glossogr.*, *Jacent*, lying along, slow, sluggish. **1668** H. More *Div. Dial.* ii. xxvi. (1713) 174 My palate is something more surd and jacent. **1682** Wheler *Journ. Greece* iii. 282 A jacent Figure holding a reed in his right hand.

b. *Her.* = JESSANT 1.

1706 Phillips (ed. Kersey), *Jessant*, or *Jacent*,..us'd when in a Coat of Arms a Lion or other Beast is born over some Ordinary, as over a Chief Bend, or Fesse.

J-acid. *Dye Chem.* A crystalline dye intermediate, 2-amino-5-naphthol-7-sulphonic acid, $C_{10}H_9NO_4S$, used in coupling reactions with diazotized amines to form direct azo dyes.

1914 F. W. Atack tr. *A. Wahl's Manuf. Org. Dyestuffs* vii. 66 The third [*sc.* compound] is obtained by alkaline fusion of 2-naphthylamine-5:7-disulphonic acid, and is called 'J acid'. **1917** Fort & Lloyd *Chem. Dyestuffs* xvi. 159 There are certain peculiarities about J-acid and its azo derivatives. Thus coupled with diazobenzene derivatives cotton-dyeing properties are absent, but with diazonaphthalene derivatives are strongly marked. **1937** *Chem. Abstr.* XXXI. 3281 Absorption by cotton cellulose of J acid..was studied. **1971** R. L. M. Allen *Colour Chem.* v. 57 About 35 monoazo direct dyes are in use, most of them containing either a thiazole or a J acid residue.

jacinth ('dʒæsɪnθ, 'dʒeɪsɪnθ). Forms: 3-7 **iacinct(e, 4 iacynkt(e, -synkt, -cintt, 4-6 iacynct, iacynt(e, 4-7 iacynth, 6 iassink, 6-7 iacinth(e, iacint, (7-8 jacent, -int), 7- jacinth.** See also HYACINTH, and JACOUNCE. [ME. *iacynt*, *iacinct*, a. OF. *iacinte* or late L. *iacint(h)us*, *-inctus*, an alteration of *hiacint(h)us*, L. *hyacinthus*, a. Gr. *ὑάκινθος* HYACINTH; the *h* being lost and the initial *i* made consonantal; cf. mod.F. *jacinthe*, Pr. *jiacint*, Sp. *jacinto*, It. *giacinto* and *iacinto.*]

1. a. Among the ancients, a gem of a blue colour, prob. sapphire. **b.** In mod. use, a reddish-orange gem, a variety of zircon; also applied to varieties of topaz and garnet. (= HYACINTH 1.)

*c*1230 *Hali Meid.* 43, & tah is betere a briht iacinct þen a charbucle won. **1382** Wyclif *Song Sol.* v. 14 Goldene, and

ful of iacynctis. **1535** COVERDALE *Ezek.* xxviii. 13 Deckte with all maner of precious stones, with Ruby, Topas, Christall, Iacynte. **1555** EDEN *Decades* 236 Iacinthes growe in the Iland of Zerlam. They are tender stones and yelowe. **1567** MAPLET *Gr. Forest* 11 The Iacinct is blew, and of nigh neighborhoode with the Saphire. **1630** DRAYTON *Muses' Elys.* x. (R.), The yellow jacinth,.. Of which who hath the keeping, No thunder hurts nor pestilence. **1762–71** H. WALPOLE *Vertue's Anecd. Paint.* (1786) I. 154 The dagger, in her grace's collection, is set with jacynths. **1861** C. W. KING *Ant. Gems* (1866) 22 The greater part..of what are now termed Jacinths are only Cinnamon Stones of a reddish kind of Garnet.

†**c.** (In Wyclif's Bible, rendering L. *hyacinthus*): A dyed fabric of a blue or purple colour. *Obs.*

1382 WYCLIF *Exod.* xxv. 4 Iasynkt that is silk of violet blew. *Ibid.* xxviii. 15 The breest broche..thou shalt make with werk of dyuerse colours, after the weuyng of the coope, of gold, iacynkt [**1388** iacynt], and purpur.

d. The colour of the gem (see b above); in *Her.* name for the colour *tenné*, in blazoning by precious stones (= HYACINTH 1 c).

1572 J. JONES *Bathes Buckstone* 11 b, If it [the urine] be higher, then ambre or betwene it and iacincte, yellowish or chollerique red. **1572** BOSSEWELL *Armorie* II. 66 The fielde is of the Iacinthe. **1688** R. HOLME *Armoury* I. ii. 12/2.

e. = HYACINTH 3 b.

1854 L. A. MEALL *Moubray's Treat. Poultry* 288 Jacinth, ..slaty-blue, and pied on back and wings with white.

†**2.** A plant; = HYACINTH 2 (a and b). *Obs.*

[**1398** TREVISA *Barth. De P.R.* XVI. liii, An herbe of þe same name is liche þerto [the stone Iacinctus] in coloure.] **1567** MAPLET *Gr. Forest* 47 Iacinct is an Herbe hauing a purple flowre. **1597** GERARDE *Herbal* I. lxxvii. (1633) 106 The white-floured starry Iacinth. **1629** PARKINSON *Paradisi* xi. 122 Our English Iacinth or Hares-bels is so common everywhere. **1727** *Philip Quarll* 244 Junquils, Tuberoses, Jacents, and other delightful Flowers. **1760** J. LEE *Introd. Bot.* App. 315 Jacinth, *Hyacinthus.*

3. *attrib.* and *Comb.* (in senses 1 and 2).

1526 TINDALE *Rev.* ix. 17 Havynge fyry habbergions of a Iacynct colouore. *a* **1586** SIDNEY *Arcadia* I. Wks. 1725 I. 20 Her forehead Jacinth-like, her cheeks of Opal hue. *Ibid.* 107 The excellently fair queen Helen, whose jacinth-hair curled by nature..had a rope of fair pearl. **1591** PERCIVALL *Sp. Dict., Iacinto*, a iacint stone, a iacint flower. **1811** PINKERTON *Petral.* II. 129 Consisting of quartz and of jacint, so that it may be called jacint rock. **1842** TENNYSON *Morte d'A.* 57 Myriads of topaz-lights, and jacinth-work.

†**ja'cinthine**, *a.* (*sb.*) *Obs.* Forms: see prec. [ad. med.L. *iacint(h)inus*, *iacinctinus*, for L. *hyacinthinus.*] Consisting of jacinth; hyacinthine.

1382 WYCLIF *Exod.* xxv. 5 Skynnes iacynktynes. *Ibid.* xxvii. 37 A iacynctyne filete. **1430–40** LYDG. *Bochas* VIII. xii. (MS. Bodl. 263) lf. 379/2 Fourti stonis Iacynctyne.

B. *sb.* The hyacinth (flower).

1513 DOUGLAS *Æneis* XI. ii. 30 The purpour flour, hait iacynthyne [*ed.* 1555 iacinctyne].

So †**jacinthinous** (in 5 **-cinct-**) *a.*, of the colour of jacinth, dark purple.

1495 *Trevisa's Barth. De P.R.* XVII. cxi. 674 The fruyte of the oliue is fyrste..grene and thenne reddysshe other iacinctinous [*Bodl. MS.* iacinctines] and at the laste blacke.

jacitara (dʒæsɪ'tɑːrə). [Tupi.] In full, ***jacitara palm.*** A prickly climbing palm, *Desmoncus macroacanthus* or *D. orthacanthos*, native to the Amazon region.

1853 A. R. WALLACE *Palm Trees of Amazon* 74 The 'jacitara' never loses its hold, and it is only by deliberately extracting its fangs that the intruder can expect to depart unhurt. **1860** MAYNE REID *Odd People* 52 The grated pulp [of manioc]..is afterwards put into a long elastic cylinder-shaped basket or net, of the bark of the 'jacitara' palm. **1863** H. W. BATES *Naturalist on River Amazons* I. ii. 48 There is even a climbing genus of palms (*Desmoncus*), the species of which are called, in the Tupí language, Jacitára. *Ibid.* vii. 322 When the rolls [of tobacco] are sufficiently well pressed they are bound round with narrow thongs of remarkable toughness, cut from the bark of the climbing Jacitára palm tree. **1878** *Chambers's Encycl.* Suppl. X. 579/1 Jacitara palm, (*Desmoncus macroacanthus*), a palm found in the forests of the low lands of the Amazon district in South America. **1927** R. R. GATES *Botanist in Amazon Valley* vii. 167 Among climbers collected here was a small climbing palm called *jacitara* (*Desmoncus sp.*). The slender stem bears sharp spines in pairs, projecting backwards. **1931** B. MIALL tr. *Guenther's Naturalist in Brazil* v. 92 In Brazil there is another climbing palm, the Jacytára. I found it in Pernambuco, and was quite intimidated by its armament, which has earned it the name of 'the terrible'.

Jack (dʒæk), *sb.*[1] Forms: 3–5 **Iakke**, 3–7 **Iacke**, 5 **Iak**, 6–7 **Iack**, 7– **Jack**, **jack.** [A pet-name or by-name, used as a familiar equivalent of *John*; in ME. *Jakke, Jacce, Jacke*, a disyllable: cf. the analogous *Cebbe, Colle, Dawe, Geffe, Gibbe, Grigge, Hicke, Hobbe, Hogge, Hudde, Judde, Symme, Thomme, Watte*, mentioned along with *Jacke*, in Gower's *Vox Clamantis*, i. 783–91.

The actual origin is disputed. It has been generally assumed to be the same word as F. *Jacques*, in OF. also *Jaques, Jaqves* (:—**Jacbes*:—late L. *Jacobus*, for Jacōbus, Gr. Ἰάκωβος Jacob) James; also a familiar name for a peasant, a man of the lower orders (cf. JACQUERIE). But it has been used in Eng. from its earliest appearance as a by-name of *Johan, Jan*, John; and a strong case has been made out by E. W. B. Nicholson, M.A., Bodley's Librarian (*The Pedigree of Jack and of various allied names*, 1892), for its actual origination as a pet-form of that word. Cf. esp. the recognized diminutives *Jankin* and *Jackin* (as contained in the surnames *Jacken* (1327), *Jackins*, *Jackinson*), and the relation between *Dick* and *Dickin*, *Rob* and *Robin*, etc. The Scotch equivalent form of the name is JOCK[1], but this has not the transferred senses of *Jack.*]

I. Applied to a man, or the figure of one.

1. a. (As proper noun.) A familiar by-form of the name *John*; hence, a generic proper name for any representative of the common people.

[Occurs as a fore-name in the Worcestershire Lay Subsidy roll of 1276–82, which has also the variant or derivative *Jacky*. *Jakkes* occurs as a surname in Hants in 1279, and *Jak* as a surname in Norfolk in 1297.]

1362 LANGL. *P. Pl.* A. VII. 65 Saue Iacke þe Iogelour and Ionete of þe stuyues. **1390** GOWER *Conf.* II. 393 Therwhile he hath his fulle packe, They seie, 'A good felawe is Iacke'. **1414** *Hist. Monast. S. Augustini Cantuar.* (Rolls) 338 Mos enim est..Saxonum..verba ac nomina transformare.. ut pro Thoma *Tomme* sive *Tomlin*, pro Iohanne *Iankin* sive *Iacke*. **1546** HEYWOOD *Prov.* (1867) 29 Jacke would be a gentleman if he could speake frenche. **1589** PUTTENHAM *Eng. Poesie* III. xix. (Arb.) 228 We vse the like termes by way of pleasant familiaritie..as..*Mall* for *Mary*, *Nell* for *Elner*: *Iack* for *Iohn*, *Robin* for *Robert*. **1635** HEYWOOD *Hierarch.* IV. 206 Deckers but Tom; nor May, nor Middleton. And hee's now but Jacke Foord, that once were John. **1712** ADDISON *Spect.* No. 403 ¶5 Well Jack, the old Prig is dead at last. **1814** COLERIDGE *Lett.* II. 635 Jack, Tom, and Harry have no existence in the eye of the law, except as included in some form or other of the permanent property of the realm. **1840** MARRYAT *Poor Jack* viii, Thus did I become..the acknowledged..'Poor Jack of Greenwich'. **1892** I. TAYLOR in *Academy* 26 Mar. 302/3 In 1379..we find a Nicholaus Jakson Hughson, who must be the son of a man entered as Johannes Hughson. It seems impossible to avoid the conclusion that this Johannes Hughson was called Jak by his neighbours.

b. In conjunction with the female name *Gill* or *Jill*: see GILL *sb.*[4] 2.

[**14..** LYDG. *London Lyckpeny* 83 Some songe of Ienken and Iulyan for there mede.] *c* **1450** *Cov. Myst.* (Shaks. Soc.) 340 And I wole kepe the feet this tyde Thow ther come both Iakke and Gylle. *c* **1460** *Towneley Myst.* iii. 336 For Iak nor for Gille wille I turne my face. **1546** HEYWOOD *Prov.* (1867) 48 Al is well, Jack shall haue gill. **1661** NEEDHAM *Hist. Eng. Rebell.* 74 Princes are brav'd by Jack and Jill. **1670** RAY *Proverbs* 108 A good Jack makes a good Gill. **1852** LYTTON *My Novel* III. x, If Gill was a shrew, it was because Jack did not, as in duty bound, stop her mouth with a kiss.

c. ***cousin Jack***: familiar name for a Cornishman: see COUSIN *sb.* 5 b.

1890 BOLDREWOOD *Miner's Right* vi. 65 Cousin Jack Tressider, an opulent Cornish miner. *Ibid.* ix. 92 A short man, whose blue-black curly hair and deep-set eyes betrayed the Cousin Jack.

d. Used as a form of address to an unknown person. *colloq.* (orig. *U.S.*).

1889 BARRÈRE & LELAND *Dict. Slang* I. 490/2 *Jack* (American), it is common among schoolboys in Philadelphia to address a stranger as *Jack*. **1933** PARTRIDGE *Words, Words, Words!* I. 71 *Jack* is still very frequent among 'the common people' when, in addressing a stranger, one wishes to avoid the abruptness caused by omitting the unknown name. **1943** *N.Y. Times* 9 May II. 5/4 Jack, that man had them rolling in the aisles. **1966** S. KELLY in F. Shaw et al. *Lern Yerself Scouse* 76 Dawn taps yer winder [*sc.* window].. another day before yiz [*sc.* you], Jack. **1970** C. MAJOR *Dict. Afro-Amer. Slang* 70 *Jack*, term of address by one male to another.

2. †**a.** (As a common noun.) A man of the common people; a lad, fellow, chap; *esp.* a low-bred or ill-mannered fellow, a 'knave'. *Obs.*

1548 UDALL *Erasm. Par. Luke* vi. 65 A common poyncte of pleasure doyng, that euery iacke vseth. **1596** SHAKS. *Tam. Shr.* II. i. 290 A mad-cap ruffian and a swearing Iacke. **1600** SURFLET *Countrie Farme* I. xvi. 108 They send them [geese] to the medowes..vnder the custodie of some little small Iacke, who may keepe them from going..into any forbidden places. *a* **1640** DAY *Parl. Bees* v. (1881) 33 A halter stretch thee: such ill-tutord jacks Poyson the fame of Patrons. **1682** BUNYAN *Holy War* (Cassell) 354 But Mr. Unbelief was a nimble Jack; him they never could lay hold of. **1746** *Brit. Mag.* 75 Familiar both with peers and Jacks.

†**b.** Phr. ***to play the jack***: to play the knave, to do a mean trick. *Obs.*

1610 SHAKS. *Temp.* IV. i. 198 Your Fairy..Has done little better then plaid the Iacke with vs. **1611** BEAUM. & FL. *Knt. Burn. Pestle* Induct., If you were not resolved to play the Jacks, what need you study for new subjects, purposely to abuse your betters? **1668** PEPYS *Diary* 23 Feb., Sir R. Brookes overtook us coming to town; who played the jacke with us all, and is a fellow that I must trust no more.

c. Phr. ***every man jack*** (sometimes ***every Jack man***): every individual man. *colloq.*

1840 DICKENS *Barn. Rudge* xxxix, You don't mean to say their old wearers are all dead'... 'Every one of 'em... Every man Jack'. **1866** MRS. GASKELL *Wives & Dau.* i, Every man-jack in the place gave his vote to the liege lord. **1870** THORNBURY *Tour Eng.* II. xxviii. 233 They can't swim, not one man Jack of them.

d. A policeman or detective; a military policeman. Cf. JOHN 1 c. *slang.*

1889 CLARKSON & RICHARDSON *Police!* xxiii. 320 *A policeman*, a fly, Jack,..crusher, peeler. **1899** *Birmingham Daily Mail* 1 Nov., A couple of men who were in plain clothes in the tap-room of a public-house, and were suspected by the 'gaffer' of being 'Jacks'. **1919** W. H. DOWNING *Digger Dial.* 29 *Jack*, a military policeman. **1930** *Bulletin* (Sydney) 1 Jan. 11/2 Blue..looked up and saw two Jacks waiting. 'Where are you going?' demanded one M.P. **1941** *Argus* (Melbourne) *Week-End Mag.* 15 Nov. 1/4 *Jacks*, military police. **1946** F. SARGESON *That Summer* 102 We all had to stand there with a crowd of jacks in plain clothes standing round. **1967** J. GARDNER *Madrigal* viii. 199 You're not going to believe it. I haven't told all to the jacks naturally. **1971** J. WAINWRIGHT *Dig Grave* 45 These county coppers..couldn't get their minds unhooked from the words 'New Scotland Yard'—as if every jack in the Metropolitan Police District worked from *there*.

e. Slang phr. ***on one's jack*** = on one's own, alone (short for *on one's Jack Jones*: see 35 e below).

1931 'G. ORWELL' *Coll. Ess.* (1968) I. 71 *Jack, on his*: on his own. **1935** —— *Clergyman's Daughter* iii. 197 Michael went off on his jack an' left me wid de bloody baby. **1936** [see GRASS *sb.*[1] 12]. **1968** M. WOODHOUSE *Rock Baby* ix. 93 You're off on your jack then? **1973** R. PARKES *Guardians* x. 193, I thought I could go sneaking in there all on my jack and bring out the evidence.

3. a. (As proper or common noun.) A familiar appellation for a sailor. Also JACK-TAR, q.v.

1659 D. PELL *Impr. Sea* Proem. B iv, Hollanders..the Broom at the main... The English took it down, and laid it most sadly upon Jack-Sailors breech. **1706** *Wooden World Dissected* (1708) 94 Let us e'en turn about, and view honest Jack the Sailor. *Ibid.* 98 Here he and his Brother Jacks lie pelting each other with Sea-Wit. **1776** ABIGAIL ADAMS in *J. Adams' Fam. Lett.* (1876) 186 We drank tea..on board... Some of their Jacks played very well upon the violin. **1788** DIBDIN *Song, 'Poor Jack'*, There's a sweet little cherub that sits up aloft To keep watch for the life of poor Jack! **1840** R. H. DANA *Bef. Mast* xi. 25 There's nothing for Jack to do but to obey orders, and I went up upon the yard. **1860** L. OLIPHANT *Ld. Elgin's Mission to China* I. 154 Our Jacks presented a most grotesque appearance as they returned to their ships.

b. Phr. ***Jack ashore***: see quot. 1909. *slang.*

[**1875** R. ROWE (*title*) Jack afloat and ashore.] **1909** J. R. WARE *Passing Eng.* 158/2 *Jack ashore*, Jack elevated—practically drunk, and larky. **1920** CONRAD *Victory* (1921) Author's note p. xviii, It was long after the sea-chapter of my life had been closed, but it is difficult to discard completely the characteristics of half a lifetime, and it was in something of the Jack-ashore spirit that I dropped a five-franc piece into the sauceboat. **1970** E. MCGIRR *Death pays Wages* iv. 90 Jack Ashore does not check bills.

c. Colloq. phr. ***I'm all right, Jack***: a saying indicating selfish complacency on the part of the speaker.

1910 D. W. BONE *Brassbounder* iii. 37 It's 'Damn you Jack—I'm all right!' with you chaps. **1919** F. NINETTE *Tiddley Sailors* 26 They dodged as much work as possible and generally assumed the manner 'I'm all right Jack'. **1958** A. HACKNEY (*title*) Private life *or* I'm all right Jack. **1960** *News Chron.* 2 May 4/6 This 'I'm all right, Jack' attitude towards such relatives is deplorable. **1970** *Times* 17 Feb. 3/2 He adopted an 'I'm all right, Jack' attitude in leaving his convoy. **1971** JOHN & HUMPHRY *Because they're Black* (1972) x. 105 Right now it is, as I said before, dog eat dog. .. I'm all right, Jack, damn you.

4. a. Variously applied to a serving-man or male attendant, a labourer, a man who does odd jobs, etc. See also CHEAP *Jack*, STEEPLE-JACK, etc.

1836–7 DICKENS *Sk. Boz* (1850) 59/2 Having a chat with the 'jack,' who..seems to be wholly incapable of doing anything but lounging about. **1861** —— *Gt. Expect.* liv, A grizzled male creature, the 'Jack' of the little causeway. **1875** BARING-GOULD *Yorksh. Oddities* I. 131 He [a blind man] became skilful at bowls and bribed the jacks to give him hints as to the direction he was to throw. **1898** *Daily News* 18 Oct. 6/4, I asked Mr. Morris by what stages his steeplejacks attained the handsome sum of 5*l.* per week. His answer is that a jack (unless already trained) begins his career by labouring.

b. Colloq. shortening of *lumberjack* (LUMBER *sb.*[1] 4). *N. Amer.*

c **1900** in F. Rickaby *Ballads & Songs Shanty-Boy* (1926) 97 Every jack's a cant-hook man... They do some heavy loggin'. **1913** *Collier's* 18 Jan. 21/1 The breaking up of the lumber camps and the streaming southward of thousands of 'jacks'. **1947** *Sat. Even. Post* 8 Mar. 20/1 The red-bearded jack came on again, head low and shielded. **1961** W. E. GREENING *Ottawa* 101 The jacks who felled the trees and the workers who stripped them were called *piqueteurs*. **1973** L. GUTTERIDGE *Killer Pine* iv. 46, I had to fire thirty Jacks last fall... Lumberjacks.

5. *Cards.* Name for the knave of trumps in the game of all-fours; hence *gen.* any one of the knaves.

1674–80 COTTON *Compl. Gamester* ix, This game..is called *All Fours*, from highest, lowest, jack, and game, which is the set as some play it. *Ibid.*, He turns up a Card, which is Trump: if Jack (and that is any knave) it is one to the dealer. **1749** MARTIN *Eng. Dict.*, *Knave*,..a jack at cards. **1861** DICKENS *Gt. Expect.* viii, He calls the knaves, Jacks, this boy!

b. ***California jack***: 'a game of cards resembling all-fours' (*Cent. Dict.*). . Also ***Californian jack.***

1882 J. W. STEELE *Frontier Army Sk.* (1883) 50 Here is the down-east Yankee..turning his native cunning to account at poker and California jack. **1893** W. RALEIGH *Let.* 28 July (1926) I. 177 His losses at Californian Jack..were my gains. **1921** C. E. MULFORD *Bar-20 Three* iii. 39 For two hours they sat and played California jack in plain sight of the street.

6. A figure of a man which strikes the bell on the outside of a clock. (See *Jack of the clock*, in 37.)

As the name of a mechanical contrivance, this sense is transitional to the next group.

1498–9 in Kerry *Hist. Ch. St. Lawrence, Reading* (1883) 97 It. payed for the settyng of Jak with the hangyng of his bell and mendyng his hond, iiij[d]. **1594** SHAKS. *Rich. III*, IV. ii. 117 *K. Rich.* Well, let it strike. *Buck.* Why let it strike? *K. Rich.* Because that, like a Iack, thou keep'st the stroke Betwixt thy begging and my meditation. **1602** MIDDLETON *Blurt, Master Constable* II. ii, This is the night, nine the hour, and I the jack that gives warning. **1609** DEKKER *Gvlls Horne-bk.* iv, If Powles Iacks bee once vp with their elbowes, and quarrelling to strike eleuen. **1771** *Antiq. Sarisb.* 92 On the East side is a dial of near ten feet square, with quarter jacks under it. **1869** H. SYER CUMING in *Jrnl. Brit. Archæol. Assoc.* XXV. 278 There was an ancient clock in Old St. Paul's, with Jacks to strike the hours.

II. Applied to things which in some way take the place of a lad or man, or save human labour; also more vaguely to other things with which one has to do.

* *To separate contrivances, machines, utensils,* etc.

7. A machine for turning the spit in roasting meat; either wound up like a clock or actuated by the draught of heated air up the chimney (*smoke-jack*).

1587 *Lanc. Wills* (Chetham Soc.) II. 190 The iacke whiche turneth the broche. **1606** DEKKER *Sev. Sinnes* II. (Arb.) 20 It stood altogether like a Germane clock, or an English Iack or Turne-spit, vpon skrewes and vices. **1615** J. STEPHENS *Satyr. Ess.* 285 The winding up of a iacke is better then musicke to his eares in Lent. **1660** PEPYS *Diary* 23 Oct., After supper we looked over..his wooden jack in his chimney, which goes with the smoke, which indeed is very pretty. **1724** [see sense 11]. **1778** MAD. D'ARBLAY *Diary* Sept., Our roasting is not magnificent, for we have no jack. **1840** DICKENS *Barn. Rudge* xxix, Hugh..sent it twirling round like a roasting jack. **1844** ALB. SMITH *Adv. Mr. Ledbury* xv, I have hung [it]..to the bottle-jack, so that when I wind it up it will keep turning round. **1845** ELIZA ACTON *Mod. Cookery* (ed. 2) 155 A smoke-jack, by means of which several spits, if needful, can be kept turning at the same time.

8. A name for various contrivances consisting (solely or essentially) of a roller or winch.

1572 in *Lincolnsh. N. & Q.* I. 165 A Iack of wood for a towel and bason. **1623** T. SCOTT *Projector* 26 You should finde some Iacks faulty, and some cogges missing, whereby the wheele of Iustice is hindered in his circular course. **1703** MOXON *Mech. Exerc.* 51 The Wood-work belonging to the Jack, is a Barrel, or Spit-wheel and a Handing of the Winch. **1776** G. SEMPLE *Building in Water* 37 There were Sluices.. wound up and down by a Jack. **1794** *Rigging & Seamanship* 55 *Iron Jacks*, sometimes used instead of the table-wheel or back-frame wheel, differ from the latter by having an iron wheel with cogs, which work in the whirls.

9. A wooden frame for sawing wood upon.

1573 TUSSER *Husb.* (1878) 38 A Iack for to saw vpon fewell for fier. **1669** WORLIDGE *Syst. Agric.* (1681) 327 A *Jack*,..a Horse whereon they saw Wood. **1779** REES *Chambers' Cycl.*, *Jack* is used also for a horse or wooden frame to saw timber upon.

10. a. A machine, usually portable, for lifting heavy weights by force acting from below; in the commonest form, having a rack and a pinion wheel or screw and a handle turned by hand. Also called *lifting-jack* and *jack-screw*.

1703 MOXON *Mech. Exerc.* 161 *Jack*,..an Engine used for the removing and commodious placing of great Timber. **1780** HUNTER in *Phil. Trans.* LXXI. 65 The machine may be applied as a jack to raise great weights a little way from the ground. **1825** J. NICHOLSON *Operat. Mechanic* 282 Fig. 341 represents the common or simple hand jack. **1851** *Illustr. Catal. Gt. Exhib.* 236 Hydraulic lifting jack for railway engines and carriages. **1867** SMYTH *Sailor's Word-bk.*, *Double-jack*. See JACK-SCREW.

b. See quots.

1877 *N.W. Linc. Gloss.*, *Jack*..for supporting the axle-tree of a cart in order to remove one of the wheels. **1886** ELWORTHY *W. Somerset Word-bk.*, *Jack*, a contrivance, consisting of a lever and fulcrum, used in washing carriages, to lift one side so that the wheel..may run round freely; sometimes called a 'carriage-jack'.

11. A contrivance for pulling off boots; a bootjack. *rare* or *Obs.* (exc. in the compound).

1679 *Trials Wakeman*, etc. 22 He pull'd off his Boots.. upon the Frame of a Table, or else upon a Jack. **1724** WATTS *Logic* I. iv. §8 So foot-boys, who had frequently the common name of Jack given them, were kept to turn the spit, or to pull off their master's boots; but when instruments were invented for both these services, they were both called jacks.

12. *Mining.* **a.** 'A kind of water-engine, turned by hand, used in mines. *Staff.*' (Halliwell.) **b.** A wooden wedge or gad used in mining for assisting in the cleaving of strata. **c.** (See quot. 1851.)

1851 GREENWELL *Coal-trade Terms Northumb. & Durh.* 31 Whilst two pits or a pit and a staple are being sunk simultaneously by means of two gins, one of them, to prevent mistakes, is usually called a jack. **1858** SIMMONDS *Dict. Trade*, *Jack*,..a wedge. **1864** WEBSTER, *Jack*,..10. A wooden wedge used by miners to separate rocks after blasting.

13. In many names of instruments in which it is combined with a defining word: e.g. *lifting-jack, pegging-jack, shackle-jack, thill-jack*, etc. q.v. Also ***builder's jack***, a temporary staging or bracket projecting outwards from a window, used in cleaning, painting, or repairing; also called *window-jack* (Knight *Dict. Mech.* 1874). ***round jack***, 'a stand for holding a hat while the brim is trimmed to shape' (*Cent. Dict.*).

** *To parts of instruments or machines.*

14. In the virginal, spinet, and harpsichord: An upright piece of wood fixed to the back of the key-lever, and fitted with a quill which plucked the string as the jack rose on the key's being pressed down. (By Shaks. and some later writers erron. applied to the key.)

Also applied to a similar upright piece terminating in the 'tangent' in a clavichord, or serving to raise the damper, or the hammer, in early pianofortes; sometimes also to the hopper, or a part of it, in a modern pianoforte.

1598 FLORIO, *Saltarélli*, the iacks of a paire of virginals. *c* **1600** SHAKS. *Sonn.* cxxviii, How oft..Do I enuie those Iackes that nimble leape, To kisse the tender inward of thy hand. **1604** MIDDLETON *Father Hubbard's T.* Wks. (Bullen) VIII. 97 Her teeth chattered in her head, and leaped up and down like virginal-jacks. **1644** DIGBY *Nat. Bodies* xxxii. (1658) 335 Like the jack of a Virginall, which striketh the sounding cord. **1748** HARTLEY *Observ. Man* I. ii. 229 The Treble Notes of a Harpsichord would be overpowered by the Bass ones, did not the Bits of Cloth affixed to the Jacks check the Vibrations of the Strings in due time. **1896** A. J. HIPKINS *Pianoforte* 103 The merit of introducing in the square piano the 'hopper'—a jack with a spring and working in a notch or nose forming the front part of a lever, technically known as the 'underhammer'—belongs to John Geib, who in 1786 took out a patent for this improvement.

15. In various machines.

a. An oscillating lever, such as those in a stocking-frame or knitting-machine.

1764 CROKER, etc. *Dict. Arts* s.v. *Stocking*, The stocking-frame..the wheel by whose motion the jacks are drawn together upon the needles. **1829** *Glover's Hist. Derby* I. 242 The stocking-frame invented by the Rev. William Lea, or Lee..in 1589, was very simple, with jacks only. **1879** *Cassell's Techn. Educ.* VIII. 128/2 The stocking-frame has a series of vibrating levers, called *jacks*, which..throw the.. yarn into such curvatures as enable the needles to form the loops.

b. *Weaving.* = Heck-box: see HECK *sb.*[1] 8.

1875 in KNIGHT *Dict. Mech.*

attrib. **1844** WHITTIER *Swedenborg* Pr. Wks. 1889 III. 274 Each human being who watches beside jack or power loom feels more or less intensely that it is a solemn thing to live.

c. *Spinning.* A coarse bobbin and fly-frame operating on the sliver from the carding-machine and passing the product to the fine roving-machine, or fitting it therefor.

1875 in KNIGHT *Dict. Mech.*

d. *Telegr.*, etc. A socket or receptacle having one or more pairs of terminals and designed so that insertion of a suitable plug enables a device to be quickly introduced into a circuit.

1891 J. POOLE *Pract. Telephone Handbk.* vii. 128 The effect of inserting a plug in one of the jacks is that the end of the plug lifts the line spring R from pin Y. **1905** PREECE & SIVEWRIGHT *Telegraphy* (new ed.) xi. 233 The home sections and the multiple panels are made up of 'jacks', mounted in strips. *Ibid.* 234 The 'jacks' consist of two springs of unequal length and a collar or socket. **1926** J. L. PRITCHARD *Broadcast Reception* xi. 185 The last three jacks have filament controlling contacts by which the insertion of the plug automatically lights the filaments. **1970** *Toronto Daily Star* 24 Sept. 38/2 (Advt.), Lloyd's AM/FM digital clock radio... Features..earphone jack and solid-state circuitry. **1971** R. THOMAS *Backup Men* xiii. 119 Is there another jack in this room?.. Can you get another phone and plug it in?

16. In carriages: see quot.

1794 W. FELTON *Carriages* (1801) I. 78 Spring Jack. Fig. 11. This is a small engine fixed to the bottom of the spring. .. Its use is to heighten or lower the body. *Ibid.* 80 A pair of spring jacks.

*** *To things of smaller than the normal size.*

†**17.** A very small amount; the least bit; a whit. *Obs. colloq.*

1530 PALSGR. 233/2 Iacke or whitte *nicquet*, as I wyll nat gyve you a whyt.

18. a. In the game of *Bowls*, A smaller bowl placed as a mark for the players to aim at.

1611 SHAKS. *Cymb.* II. i. 2 Was there euer man had such lucke? when I kist the Iacke vpon an vp-cast, to be hit away? **1630** J. TAYLOR (Water P.) *Wit & Mirth* Wks. II. 193/2 The marke which they ayme at hath sundry names and Epithites, as a Blocke, a Iacke, and a Mistris. **1768–74** TUCKER *Lt. Nat.* (1834) I. 509 If I have a bowl in my hand and want it to touch the jack at the other end of the green. **1864** *Athenæum* No. 1920. 209/1 A bias that should reach the jack. **1875** 'STONEHENGE' *Brit. Sports* III. I. iii. §3. 683 The jack shall not be changed during a game, except by mutual consent of the players.

b. = JACK-STONE; usu. *pl.*; also, a game played with these (see also quot. 1908).

1900 S. R. CROCKETT *Little Anna Mark* xii. 97 Playing at quoits, tops, marbles, tic-tac-toe, jacks, knuckle-bones. **1908** *Dialect Notes* III. 323 *Jack*,..a piece of metal with five tines or protuberances, used in the game of jacks. *Jacks*, an indoor catching game played with small five-tined metal pieces. **1922** A. C. SIES *Spontaneous & Supervised Play* xix. 293 'Jacks' is a game in which throwing and catching are not the main centers of interest; rather are the attention and interest focussed on what is done between catches. **1960** H. MILLER *Nexus* (1964) i. 11 Do you know how to skate?.. Did you ever play jacks?

19. *slang.* **a.** A farthing. ? *Obs.* **b.** A counter made to resemble a sovereign: so ***half-jack***.

a **1700** B. E. *Dict. Cant. Crew*, *Jack*, a Farthing. **1851** MAYHEW *Lond. Labour* I. 349 The 'card-counters', or..the 'small coins', are now of a very limited sale. The slang name for these articles is 'Jacks' and 'Half Jacks'. *Ibid.*, It is hardly possible that any one who had ever received a sovereign in payment, could be deceived by..a Jack. **1873** *Slang Dict.*, *Jacks, and half-jacks*, card counters, resembling in size and appearance sovereigns and half-sovereigns.

c. Money. *slang* (orig. *U.S.*).

1890 M. TOWNSEND *Index U.S.A.* 427 The..verbal wealth of the United States language is illustrated in an inquiry for a loan of money; by using any of the following words in conjunction with the inquiry, *Have you any*.. Jacks, [etc.]. **1920** *Collier's* 28 Aug. 33/2 The fans which paid their jack to see a *fight* would be gypped. **1932** J. DOS PASSOS *1919* 24 This way every bastardly tourist with a little jack thinks he can hire you. **1945** 'N. SHUTE' *Most Secret* 111, I hadn't that much jack... I worked a passage home. **1960** A. PRIOR in *Pick of Today's Short Stories* XI. 184, I asked him..to think of the new suits he could get..when the jack came in.

d. *slang.* Also *jacks, jax.* Five pounds; a five-pound note. Cf. *Jack's alive* s.v. sense 37.

1958 F. NORMAN *Bang to Rights* III. 150 I'll bet you a jacks that I nick you. **1968** *Gloss. Brit. Argot*, *Jack*, five pounds. **1968** *Guardian* 13 Apr. 7/3 'That one,' says the dealer from Islington, 'that one we *know* she died in; so it'll cost you a jax.'.. Five quid for a shroud; cheap at the price. **1970** G. F. NEWMAN *Sir, You Bastard* viii. 230 'Couldn't lend me a Jack's, Terry, could you?' 'Sure.' He gave the DS a fiver. **1972** K. ROYCE *Miniatures Frame* v. 64 From under a pottery sugar jar..protruded two jacks.

20. A quarter of a pint: = the imperial gill, or half the northern GILL (q.v.). *local.*

1736 PEGGE *Kenticisms* s.v. *Tamsin*, *Jack*, a measure, and *Gill*, another. **1787** GROSE *Provinc. Gloss.*, *Jack*, half a pint. *Yorks.* **1796** MRS. GLASSE *Cookery* xxiii. 357 To a pound of sugar put a jack of water. **1855** ROBINSON *Whitby Gloss.*, *Jack*, a quarter of a pint measure. **1877** *N.W. Linc. Gloss.*, *Jack*, a quarter of a pint measure, and the quantity contained in one. Also in *Holderness, Sheffield, Mid. Yorksh. Gloss.*

21. *Building.* A small brick or 'bat' used as a closer at the end of a course. ? *Obs.*

1703 MOXON *Mech. Exerc.* 271 Imagine FEG to be a Stretcher, or a Stretching Archytrave..and imagining it to be thus divided; then EF is called a Header; or a heading Archytrave, and EG is called a Jak.

22. *Naut.* Short for *jack cross-tree* (see 34 b).

1840 R. H. DANA *Bef. Mast* xxiv, Though I could handle the brig's [fore-royal] easily, I found my hands full with this, especially as there were no jacks to the ship. **1867** SMYTH *Sailor's Word-bk.*, *Jack*,..also a common term for the jack or cross-trees. **1882** NARES *Seamanship* (ed. 6) 80 Rove through a block under the jack. *Ibid.* 84 The jack at the fore-top-gallant mast-head.

**** *To other things.*

23. A vessel used in soap-making.

c **1865** LETHEBY in *Circ. Sc.* I. 96/1 They are poured off into vessels called 'jacks'.

24. A post-chaise. *slang* or *colloq.*

1812 J. H. VAUX *Flash Dict.*, *Jack*, a post-chaise. **1816** PRESCOTT *Let.* in Ticknor *Life* (1864) 36 We travelled upon *jacks*, which is the pleasantest conveyance in the world both for its sociability and the little fatigue which attends it.

25. A schooner-rigged vessel used in the Newfoundland fisheries. Also *jack boat.*

1891 *Rep. U.S. Comm. Fish & Fisheries 1887* App. VI. 529 The jack varies from 5 to 15 tons; is schooner-rigged, carrying three sails as a rule. **1895** *St. Nicholas* Apr. 448/2 The gashers [were] dashing in and out among the punts and jacks (stoutly built two-stickers larger than gashers). **1908** *Daily Chron.* 8 Jan. 3/3 A little jack (much the same in rig as our North Sea smacks). **1937** *Beaver* June 29/2 Bill had a nice little jack (small fishing schooner, in this case with outriggers on the quarters instead of booms). **1951** *Maine Coast Fisherman* Oct. 26 A typical Newfoundland jack seen in the cruise to the Bras D'Or Lakes. **1954** *9th Census of Canada 1951* IX. Table 4 Jack boats... Bateaux 'Jack'. **1965** *National Fisherman* Mar. 24/2 The 'jack schooners' or 'jack boats' (so-called in Cape Breton), or 'two-spar boats' (as they are known in Newfoundland) were 40' to 50' from stemhead to taffrail. They were gaff-rigged on both masts and they usually carried a longish bowsprit. **1969** H. HORWOOD *Newfoundland* xx. 157 The sons of men who had built windjammers were confined to building trap skiffs and jack boats.

26. A portable cresset or fire-basket used in hunting or fishing at night. *U.S.*

1895 *Outing* (U.S.) XXVI. 61 Standing with my eyes below the level of the flaming jack.

27. A tablet of heroin. *slang.*

1967 M. M. GLATT et al. *Drug Scene* 115 *Jack*, heroin tablet. **1971** R. BUSBY *Deadlock* xii. 177 He's been cranking up on horse [*sc.* heroin]. His last jack is wearing off, and he's grovelling on the floor for another pill.

III. In names of animals. (Chiefly as an abbreviation of the fuller names treated under sense 38.)

28. Applied to the male of various animals, chiefly in comb.: see 38; also simply: **a.** A male hawk, *esp.* merlin (= *jack-merlin*).

1623 COCKERAM III. s.v. *Hawks*, A *Merlin*, the male is called a *Iack*. The *Castrill* male a *Iack*. **1727–41** CHAMBERS *Cycl.* s.v. *Hawk*, The female..is much larger, stronger, and more couragious than the male; which is distinguished therefrom by some diminutive name..that of the merlin, *jack*.

b. (Short for JACKASS 1.) A male ass, *esp.* one kept for breeding mules. *U.S.*

1799 WASHINGTON *Lett.* Writ. 1893 XIV. 197, I have two or three young Jacks..and several she asses, that I would dispose of. **1839–40** W. IRVING *Wolfert's R.* (1855) 189 A gentleman..took it into his head that it would be an immense public advantage to introduce a breed of mules, and accordingly imported three jacks to stock the neighbourhood. **1873** LONGF. *Wayside Inn, Monk of Casal-Maggiore* v, He leisurely untied From head and neck the halter of the jack.

29. Short for JACK-RABBIT.

1894 *Outing* (U.S.) XXIV. 386/2 The Doctor's experience with a jack rabbit was one of the most amusing of the hunt... One day he wounded a big jack, and as he went to pick it up, it arose upon its hind legs.

30. Name for various birds. **a.** Short for JACKDAW, *jack-curlew* (see 38), ***Cornish jack***, the Cornish chough, JACK-SNIPE. **b.** As the second element in various names, as CURLEW *jack*, JUMPING *jack*, WHISKY *jack*: see these words.

1803–4 HAWKER *Diary* (1893) II. 358 Curlew jacks (whimbrels). **1886** *Pall Mall G.* 15 Dec. 4/2 It may be said both of full snipe and jack that they afford not only the best, but the most legitimate kind of sport.

c. *Austral.* A laughing jackass, a kookaburra. Cf. JACKO, JACKY 1 c.

1898 MORRIS *Austral Eng.* 216/1 The bird is generally called only a *Jackass*, and this is becoming contracted into the simple abbreviation of *Jack*. **1934** *Bulletin* (Sydney) 14

Feb. 26/2 Jack came to the conclusion that it was, as tucker, a washout, and departed. **1949** *Geogr. Mag.* Feb. 374/1 Hence such names for the kookaburra as *laughing jackass*, *jack*.

31. Name of various fishes, etc. **a.** A young or small pike; also sometimes used generically as a name for the pike. (Pl. *jack* or *jacks.*)

1587 HARRISON *England* III. iii. (1878) II. 18 The pike as he ageth, receiueth diuerse names,.. from a pod to a iacke, from a iacke to a pickerell, from a pickerell to a pike. **1655** MOUFET & BENNET *Health's Improv.* (1746) 279 Old great Pikes are very hard, tough, and ill to digest; young ones, called Jacks, are contrariwise too waterish and moist. *a* **1658** CLEVELAND *Count. Com. Man* Wks. (1677) 97 The Jack may come to swallow the Pike, as the Interest often eats out the Principal. **1711** ADDISON *Spect.* No. 108 ⁋5 The Gentleman.. had the Pleasure of seeing the huge Jack, he had caught, served up for the first Dish. **1787** BEST *Angling* (ed. 2) 47 A method which I have taken more pikes and jacks with, than any other way. **1825** BROCKETT, *Jack*, a young male pike, under a foot in length. **1883** *Gd. Words* 12 Jack may be caught in the river Roding.

b. Also applied to several American fishes: as the pike-perch, *Stizostedium vitreum*; a scorpænoid fish, *Sebastodes paucispinis*; several carangoid fishes, esp. *Caranx pisquetos* and *Seriola carolinensis*; and the pampano, *Trachynotus carolinus*. (Cent. Dict.)

1897 *Outing* (U.S.) XXIX. 231/2 Other game fishes of Florida are the 'jack', or crevallé, also called carvalho.

c. With defining word. ***buffalo-jack***, the *Caranx pisquetos* (also called simply *jack*: see b). ***five-fingered jack***: popular name in U.S. for a starfish. ***goggle-eyed jack***: see GOGGLER 2. ***hickory-jack***: *(a)* the *Caranx pisquetos* or one of several other carangoid fishes (see b); *(b)* the hickory-shad, *Pomolobus mediocris*.

d. ***poor Jack*** (also ***dry*** or ***dried Jack***), a name for dried hake; also called *Poor John*.

1667 *Lond. Gaz.* No. 218/2 This week arrived here 9 English ships, whereof 4 with Pilchards, 4 with poor Jack, and one with Herrings. **1674** tr. *Scheffer's Lapland* xiii. 67 They pay.. half a pound of dried Jack. **1682** J. COLLINS *Making Salt Eng.* 93 That sort of Cod that is caught near the Shore, and on the Coast of Newfoundland and dryed, is called Poor-Jack. **1704** *Lond. Gaz.* No. 4026/3 Lading, consisting of.. Dry Codfish, Dry Jack, Hogslard. **1708** W. KING *Cookery* 103 Sometimes poor jack and onions are his dish And then he saints those friars who stink of fish.

†**32.** A kind of worm used as bait by anglers. *Obs.*

1681 CHETHAM *Angler's Vade-m.* iv. §8 (1689) 36 Crabtree-worm or Jack.

IV. 33. In names of plants. *pop.* or *colloq.*

a. A variety of polyanthus: 'one of the forms of the so-called "hose-in-hose" polyanthus, having the calyx more or less coloured, and partly assuming the character of the corolla' (Britten and Holland *Plant-n.* 1879). Cf. JACK-IN-THE-BOX 8 b.

b. Name for a single carnation fraudulently sold as a choice variety.

1878 *Gard. Chron.* 16 Mar. 340 (Britt. & Holl.) *Jacks* is the horticultural slang designation for single carnations, which are grown specially for the trading hawker.. and sold to the unsuspicious as best named varieties. **1882** *Garden* 16 Sept. 250/3 [He] has been victimised by the sharp dealers in single Carnations, usually called 'Jacks'.

V. Combinations and compounds.

34. a. Combinations denoting things, etc. (chiefly mechanical or other contrivances), or connected with those senses of the simple word which denote things: **jack-back** [BACK *sb.*[2]], *(a)* in *Brewing*, a vessel with a perforated bottom for straining the wort from the hops (also called *hop-back*: see HOP *sb.*[1] 5 b); *(b)* 'a tank which receives the cooled wort in a vinegar-factory' (Knight); **jack-engine** (*Coal-mining*), a donkey-engine; **jack-file** (see quots.); **jack-fishing**, *(a)* fishing for jack (sense 31); *(b) U.S.*, fishing at night by means of a jack or cresset; **jack-flyer**, the fly-wheel of a roasting-jack; **jack-hammer**, **jackhammer**, a portable rock-drill worked by compressed air; **jack-head pump**, 'a form of lift-pump for mines and deep borings, in which the delivery-pipe is secured to the cylinder by a goose-neck' (Knight *Dict. Mech.*); **jack-hunting** *U.S.*, hunting by means of a jack-light (sense 26); **jack-ladder** *Naut.*, *(a)* 'one with wooden steps and side ropes' (Knight), = JACOB'S LADDER 2; *(b)* = JACK-CHAIN 2; **jack-lamp**, *(a)* a Davy-lamp with a glass cylinder outside the gauze (Gresley *Gloss.* 1883); *(b) U.S.* = sense 26; **jack-lantern** *U.S.*, *(a)* = sense 26; *(b)* = JACK-O'-LANTERN 3; **jack-maker**, a maker of jacks, *i.e.* (usually) of roasting-jacks; **jack-pin** *Naut.*, a belaying-pin; **jack-pit** (*Coal-mining*), 'a shallow pit-shaft in a mine communicating with an overcast, or at a fault' (Gresley *Gloss.* 1883); **jack-plug** *Electr.*, a single-pronged plug for use with a jack (sense 15 d); **jack-pot**, *(a)* in draw-poker, a pot or pool that has to accumulate until one of the players can open the betting with a pair of jacks or better; hence *fig.*; also, any large prize, as from a lottery or a gambling machine; often, a prize that accumulates until it is won; ***to hit the jack-pot***: to win such a prize; to have an extraordinary stroke of luck, *(b)* (see quot. 1914); **jack-pulley**, the pulley of a roasting-jack; **jack-roll**, a winch or windlass turned directly by handles; **jack-roller** (see quots.); so ***jack-roll*** v. trans., ***jack-rolling***; **jack roving-frame** = JACK-FRAME 2; **jack shaft**, any of various kinds of auxiliary or intermediate shafts which are driven by another shaft or by a set of gears, esp. in locomotives and motor vehicles (see quots.); **jack-sinker**, each of a series of thin metal plates suspended from the front ends of the jacks in a stocking-frame or knitting-machine (see 15 a), and serving, in conjunction with the *lead-sinkers*, to form loops upon the thread; **jack-socket** *Electr.* = JACK *sb.*[1] 15 d; **jack-spinner**, a workman who operates a jack in spinning (see 15 c); **jack-towel**, a long towel with the ends sewed together, suspended from a roller. See also JACK-CHAIN, etc.

1764 CROKER, etc. *Dict. Arts* s.v. *Brew-house*, The *jack-back.. is placed something lower than the under-backs, and has a communication with them all; and out of this back the wort is pumped into the coppers. **1816** J. SMITH *Panorama Sc. & Art* II. 568 The jack-back, which receives the wort after it has been boiled with the hops. **1830** M. DONOVAN *Dom. Econ.* I. 175 The liquor is pumped.. into a large reservoir, called a jack-back, in which it is allowed to remain until all the yest has collected on the surface. **1883** GRESLEY *Gloss. Coal Mining*, **Jack Engine* (N.), the engine for raising men, débris, &c. in a sinking pit. **1688** R. HOLME *Armoury* III. 303/1 **Jack-File*, a broad File: with this Jack-Wheels have their Teeth cut in them. **1703** MOXON *Mech. Exerc.* 52 A Jack-file, is a broad File somewhat thin on both Edges, and stronger in the Middle. **1883** *Fisheries Exhib. Catal.* 54 Jack Tackle of every description.. Tackle for bottom and *jack fishing. **1731** MEDLEY *Kolben's Cape G. Hope* I. 327 She.. set her tongue a going with the fury of a *Jack-flyer. **1930** *Engineering* 24 Oct. 511/2 A battery of about 45 *jackhammers.. drilled two lines of holes. **1936** *Economist* 12 Oct. 714/1 While this may be possible with machine drills in development faces, it is difficult at the moment to see how such appliances could be used with mobile jackhammers in stoping. **1971** *Daily Tel.* 2 Aug. 20/5 A specially-designed percussion drill similar to a jack-hammer. **1972** *Southerly* XXXII. 102 He works a ship and has about the delicacy of a jackhammer. **1793** *Trans. Soc. Arts* (ed. 2) V. 210 In the manner of (what is called) a *Jack Head Pump. **1899** *Contemp. Rev.* May 669, I went out after dark to kill a deer by the unsportsmanlike method of *jack-hunting. **1886** *Encycl. Brit.* XXI. 345/1 From the rear end of the mill.. a '*jack ladder' is constructed of heavy timber. **1929** *Ibid.* XIV. 482/1 An endless spiked conveyor known as a jack ladder. **1888** *Harper's Mag.* Sept. 510 Occasionally a caribou is killed at night by the light of a *jack-lamp while seeking the grass growing in some boatable stream. **1881** *Pall Mall G.* 14 July 5/1, I have stood motionless on a flat rock.. amid the rushing water, with poised three-pronged spear behind a *jack-lantern, waiting for a sturgeon to come there. **1727** SWIFT *Petit. Colliers*, etc., The humble petition of the colliers, cooks, cook-maids, blacksmiths, *jack-makers, brasiers, and others. **1867** SMYTH *Sailor's Word-bk.*, **Jack-pins*, a name applied to the fife-rail pins. **1931** MOYER & WOSTREL *Radio Handbk.* 874 (Index), *Jack plugs. **1953** W. MACLANACHAN *Television & Radar Encycl.* 103/2 *Jack and Jack plug*, a socket with two or more contacts.. into which a jack plug with corresponding contacts can be inserted. **1973** Jack plug [see *jack socket* below]. **1881** *Harvard Lampoon* 6 Apr. 40/2 Poker-playing is not to be learned in one evening, and *Jack Pots are often a snake in the grass. **1884** *Virginia* (Nev.) *Chron.* 1 Oct. 3/3 Old Bill [the warden] just lays back until there is a good jack-pot of trout in hand, and then he makes a bold bluff and walks off with it. **1886** 'M. KERSHAW' *Colonial Facts & Fictions* 229 They call this [growing poker] pool a Jack Pot. **1887** *Grip* (Toronto) 21 May 10/2 What was written of.. was a jack-pot. **1895** *Harper's Mag.* Mar. 536 He suggested a round of jack-pots. **1897** *Star* 28 July 2/5 The jackpot was worth it, for Miller represented the accumulated prize as having risen to £21,160. **1902** L. MCKEE *Land of Nome* 123 On the occasion of his getting into a 'jack-pot' (some trouble) he had hunted Nome after me for legal advice. **1914** JACKSON & HELLYER *Vocab. Criminal Slang* 48 *Jackpot*, a dilemma; a difficult strait; a retribution; trouble; an arrest. **1923** G. ADE *Let.* 24 Oct. (1973) 97, I.. have been rather interested to learn that the Governor did not show you any degree of gratitude for your work in organizing the jack-pot. **1944** *Newsweek* 25 Dec. 67/1 The 'Vick's Vaper' had indeed hit the jack-pot. **1949** *Radio Times* 15 July 6/3 We saw our first American audience-participation show. The prizes included a diamond wrist watch... The jackpot was 1,250 dollars! **1956** N. STREATFEILD *Judith* II. 150 Those sort of weak good looks.. quite often hit the jackpot. **1959** *Maclean's Mag.* 4 July 34/3 Canada House receives SOS messages from 'distressed Canadians', the official designation for those who get themselves into various jackpots. **1962** *Sunday Times* Suppl. 10 June 10 There is always the chance that one or other number or artist will hit the jackpot. **1963** *Listener* 28 Mar. 568/3 Cabinet Ministers are hauled out in front of the cameras and asked increasingly impertinent leading questions. A week or two ago Mr. Butler copped one of these jackpots from Robert Mackenzie: did he, or did he not, want to be Prime Minister? **1967** *Times* 18 Dec. 5/6 A jackpot may be opened by any player who holds a pair of jacks or a higher ranking hand. **1970** *New Scientist* 14 May 341/1 Rolls-Royce landed a jack-pot order from the USA for the supply of aircraft engines. **1973** 'M. INNES' *Appleby's Answer* i. 10 It was nice to be fairly widely read... It would be even nicer if one day she contrived to hit the jackpot. **1675** J. SMITH *Chr. Relig. App.* II. 13 Such *Jack-pullies, and Weights.. Atoms, which our modern Wits have fancied for the Springs of his Motion. **1708** J. C. *Compl. Collier* (1845) 28 Sinking with *Jack Rowl, or by Mens winding up the Rowl. **1878** F. S. WILLIAMS *Midl. Railw.* 498 This was done by the aid of a 'jack roll', which is like the windlass over a common well. **1923** N. ANDERSON *Hobo* i. 5 The '*jack roller',.. the man who robs his fellows, while they are drunk or asleep. *Ibid.* iv. 51 '*Jack rolling' may be anything from picking a man's pocket in a crowd to robbing him while he is drunk or asleep. **1926** *Flynn's* 16 Jan. 638/1 Jack rollin' th' workstiffs was like takin' candy from th' kids. **1930** C. R. SHAW *Jack-Roller* vii. 85, I was in a predicament, for I had no money, and you can't enjoy life without dough. My buddy, being an old 'jack-roller', suggested 'jack-rolling' as a way out of the delima [*sic*]. **1955** *Publ. Amer. Dial. Soc.* XXIV. 171 Thieves who specialize.. on lumberjacks or other seasonal workers who get paid off in a lump sum at the end of the season are called jack rollers. **1844** G. DODD *Textile Manuf.* i. 31 The '*Jack roving-frame' in which the revolving can contained a bobbin whereon the roving was wound as fast as made. **1896** T. THORNLEY *Cotton Spinning Calculations* II. 70 The *jack shaft of the frame makes 298 revolutions per minute. **1901** J. BLACK *Illustr. Carpenter & Builder Ser.: Scaffolding* 72 The electric motor.. with jack-shaft and friction drive. **1907** R. B. WHITMAN *Motor-Car Princ.* ix. 146 The jack shaft.. is a shaft passing across the car, and bearing on its ends the sprockets by which the wheels are driven. **1925** A. W. JUDGE *Mechanism of Car* vii. 105 The object of the differential is to enable either jack shaft to rotate at a different speed to the other.. whilst transmitting the drive. **1936** W. STANIAR *Mech. Power Transmission Handbk.* v. 144 The jackshaft is used for ratio purposes and also to break up long center distances. *Ibid.* 145 Jack-shafts. Location.—Either between head and line shafts, or between line- and countershafts. **1940** *Chambers's Techn. Dict.* 465/2 *Jack shaft*, an intermediate shaft used in locomotives having collective drive; the jack shaft is geared to the motor shaft and carries cranks which drive the coupling rods on the driving wheels. **1950** *Engineering* 23 June 699/2 The final drive is through reduction gearing to a jackshaft which is fitted with pressed-on balanced cranks; thence the drive is by rods to the crankpins of the middle coupled wheels [of the Diesel locomotive]. **1962** *Diesel Traction* (Brit. Railways Board) 266 *Jackshaft*, a shaft with cranks at each end mounted across the frames for driving the road wheels through connecting rods. **1966** *McGraw-Hill Encycl. Sci. & Technol.* XII. 240/2 A countershaft, especially when used as an auxiliary shaft between two other shafts, is termed a jack shaft. **1875** *Ure's Dict. Arts* II. 817 The *jack sinkers falling successively from the loops on every alternate needle. **1970** J. EARL *Tuners & Amplifiers* i. 14 Modern amplifiers are often equipped with a *jack socket wired to accommodate stereo headphones. **1973** *Radio & Electronics Constructor* XXVI. 700/2 A suitable circuit for a miniature 2·5 mm. or 3·5mm. switched jack socket is given in Fig. 4, and this causes the speaker to be silenced when the jack plug is inserted. **1819** *Pantologia* s.v. *Printing*, The carrying-roller.. the receiving-rollers.. are connected by a piece of linen, woollen, or hair-cloth, in the manner of a *jack-towel, sewed round them. **1837** DICKENS *Pickw.* xxv, A clean jack towel behind the door.

b. In some uses *jack* has a diminutive force or meaning, denoting things which are smaller or slighter than the normal ones; as **jack-arch**, 'an arch whose thickness is only of one brick' (Gwilt *Archit.* 1842–76); **jack-block** *Naut.* (see quot.); **jack-bowl**, the jack at bowls; = sense 18; **jack-cross-tree** *Naut.*: see quot. 1867; **jack-rafter**, **-rib**, **-timber**, one shorter than the full length. (See also 18–22, 30, 31, 33 b, 38 b. and JACK *sb.*[3])

1885 *Harper's Mag.* Mar. 525/2 The windows are capped with *jack-arches of red brick. **1794** *Rigging & Seamanship* I. 168 **Jack-block*, a small block seized to the topgallant-mast-head, for sending the topgallant-yards up and down. **1697** R. PEIRCE *Bath Mem.* II. ii. 264 He had not Strength.. to throw the *Jack-Bowl half over the Green. **1803** *Sporting Mag.* XXII. 307 In shape and size like a jack-bowl, used on a bowling-green. **1840** R. H. DANA *Bef. Mast* xx. 61 The quarter boom-irons off her lower yards; her *jack-cross-trees sent down. **1867** SMYTH *Sailor's Word-bk.*, *Jack cross-trees*, single iron cross-trees at the head of long top-gallant masts, to support royal and skysail masts. **1757** LANGLEY *Builder's Jewell* 33 Which fill up with small and *Jack Rafters at Pleasure. **1881** YOUNG *Every man his own Mechanic* §1336. 615 It will be noticed that these rafters which are called jack-rafters decrease gradually in length. **1823** P. NICHOLSON *Pract. Build.* 110 In the construction of groins,.. the ribs that are shorter than the whole width are termed *Jack-ribs. *Ibid.* 225 **Jack Timber*, a timber shorter than the whole length of other pieces in the same range.

35. As the first element in a personal name used in a specific sense: **a.** ***Jack Adams***, a fool. **b.** Phr. ***before one can say Jack Robinson***: in a very short time, very quickly or suddenly. (See also JACK KETCH.)

a **1700** B. E. *Dict. Cant. Crew*, *Jack-adams*, a Fool. *a* **1704** T. BROWN *Lett. fr. Dead* II. Wks. 1760 II. 220 That from a quaker in the other world, I should be metamorphosed into a jack-adams in the lower one. **1867** SMYTH *Sailor's Word-bk.*, *Jack Adams*, a stubborn fool.

b. 1778 MISS BURNEY *Evelina* (1792) II. xxxvii, I'd do it as soon as say Jack Robinson. **1814** MRS. SHELLEY in Dowden *Life Shelley* (1887) I. 453 The white and flying cloud of noon, that is gone before one can say 'Jack Robinson'. **1903** [see DOGIE, DOGY]. **1942** G. MITCHELL *Laurels are Poison* xvii. 181 It'll be all over College before you can say Jack Robinson. **1956** N. MITFORD *Noblesse Oblige* 43 That picture will appear at Christies before you can say Jack Robinson, though there is no necessity whatever for such a sale.

c. ***Jack Scott*** = ***Jock Scott*** (see JOCK[1] 1).

1908 R. BAGOT *Anthony Cuthbert* xxix. 378 'There are some grilse come up. What do you think would be a good fly to use?'.. 'I should put on a small Jack Scott.' **1915** J. WEBSTER *Dear Enemy* 167 He.. got out his case of fishing-flies, and gallantly presented Betsy and me with.. a 'Jack Scott'.. to make hat-pins.

d. ***Jack Johnson*** [from the name of a noted American Negro boxer, whose nickname was 'The Big Smoke'], = BLACK MARIA 2.

1914 *Illustr. London News* 10 Oct. 504/1 The German 'Jack Johnson' siege-guns. *Ibid.* 505 The gigantic projectile which on bursting makes the black smoke called 'Jack Johnson'. **1919** [see BLACK MARIA 2]. **1962** J. B. PRIESTLEY *Margin Released* II. iii. 101 The German heavy batteries.. dropped 'Jack Johnsons' among us.

e. *Jack Jones*: rhyming slang for 'alone'; usu. in phr. ***on one's Jack Jones***: on one's own; alone. Cf. sense 2 e above.

1925 FRASER & GIBBONS *Soldier & Sailor Words* 130 Jack Jones, alone. **1935** 'G. ORWELL' *Clergyman's Daughter* ii. 156 A good night's kip all alone... All on your Jack Jones. **1958** P. SCOTT *Mark of Warrior* II. 168 You're on your jack jones again. What do you do? **1972** A. DRAPER *Death Penalty* xx. 134 You're on your Jack Jones. Ben's deserted you.

36. Prefixed to another noun denoting a person, a thing personified, a trade, or a quality, so as to form a *quasi*-proper name or nickname, often applied familiarly or contemptuously; as ***Jack Blunt*** (a blunt fellow), ***Jack boot(s*** (the 'Boots' at an inn), ***Jack bragger***, ***Jack breech***, ***Jack fellow***, ***Jack fiddler***, ***Jack fool***, ***Jack jailer***, ***Jack lord***, ***Jack lout***, ***Jack malapert***, ***Jack mate***, ***Jack meddler***, ***Jack monkey***, ***Jack Presbyter***, ***Jack Priest***; †**Jack Drum**: see DRUM *sb.*[1] 3 b; **Jack Dusty** *Naut. slang* (see quots.); **Jack Frost**, frost or frosty weather personified; †**jack-gentleman**, a man of low birth or manners making pretensions to be a gentleman, an insolent fellow, an upstart; so †***jack-gentlewoman*** (*rare*); **Jack Mormon** *U.S.*, a non-Mormon on friendly terms with Mormons; also, a nominal or backsliding Mormon; **Jack Nasty**, 'a term of reproach for a sneak or a sloven' (Davies); **Jack northwester**, the northwest wind; †**Jack-sauce**, a saucy or impudent fellow; **Jack Shalloo, Shilloo** *Naut. slang* (see quots.); **Jack sprat**, a little fellow, a dwarf; †**Jack-stickler**, a meddlesome or interfering person, a busybody; **Jack Strop** *Naut. slang* (see quots.).

1898 *Daily News* 17 Nov. 5/4 He was at once a *Jack Blunt and equal to a trick. **1803** *Censor* 1 March 31 Six-pence to the chamber-maid, six-pence to the ostler, and six-pence to the *jack-boot. **1824** *Hist. Gaming* 10 The Jack-boots of an Inn. **1579** TOMSON *Calvin's Serm. Tim.* 873/2 We shall see *iack-braggers, truce breakers, tratours full of crueltie & malice. **1522** SKELTON *Why not to Court* 331 No man dare come to the speche Of this gentell *Iacke breche. **1598** SHAKS. *Merry W.* II. iii. 65 Scuruy-*Iack-dog-Priest: by gar, mee vill cut his eares. **1591** GREENE *Disc. Coosnage* 26 With a broken pate or two he was paid, and like *Iacke drum, faire and orderly turned out of doores. **1608** TOPSELL *Serpents* (1658) 780 They made no more adoe, but gave her Jack-drummes entertainment, thrusting her out of doors by the head and shoulders. **1649** J. TAYLOR (Water P.) *Wand. to West* 16 The Hostes being very willing to give the courteous entertainement of Jack Drum, commanded me very kindely to get me out of dores. *c* **1931** W. N. T. BECKETT *Few Naval Customs* 18 The junior member of the Paymaster's Victualling staff is known as The Dusty Boy or *Jack Dusty. **1938** 'GIRALDUS' *Merry Matloe Again* 263 *Jack Dusty* , a ship's steward's assistant, *i.e.* any member of the supply branch below the rating of a petty officer. **1974** P. WRIGHT *Lang. Brit. Industry* x. 85 In the Second World War, destroyers had a *Jack Dusty*, a supply assistant who kept ledgers listing all the stocks. **1627** BP. WREN *Serm.* 17 Be *Iack-fellow, sit still, or be covered. **1597** *1st Pt. Return fr. Parnass.* v. i. 1397 The divell of the musition is he acquainted with but onlye *Iacke fidler. *c* **1386** CHAUCER *Miller's T.* 522 Go fro the wyndow, *Iakke fool she sayde. **1826** *Sporting Mag.* XVII. 376 *Jack Frost, however, put a veto on our morning's sport. **1872** C. HARDWICK *Trad. Lancash.* 53 The blustering of old Boreas, and the frigid embrace of 'Jack Frost'. **1667** *Answ. Quest. out of North* 13 What, Sir, do you think that it is fit for every *Jack-Gentleman to speak thus to a Bishop? **1710** *Answ. Sacheverell's Serm.* 9 They despised the Gentry at such a rate, that it was a common thing to call them Jack Gentleman. **1787** WOLCOTT (P. Pindar) *Ode upon Ode* Wks. 1812 I. 443 Yet men there are (how strange are Love's decrees!) Whose palates even *Jack-gentlewomen please. **1568** SKINNER tr. *Montanus' Inquis.* 24 a, As well *Iacke Iayler, as my Lord Judge. *a* **1689** BP. WARD in W. Pope *Life* (1697) 47, I met some *Jack Lords going into my Grove, but I think I have nettled them. *c* **1584** *Robin Conscience* 49 in Hazl. *E.P.P.* III. 229 To keepe open hovse for euery *Jack lovt. **1477–8** *Bk. Curtesye* (Caxton) 491 Playe not *Iack malapert [*Oriel MS.* Iakke malaperte], that is to saye Beware of presumpcion. *c* **1530** H. RHODES *Bk. Nurture* in *Babees Bk.* 80 Then will all your Elders thinke you be with him *Iack mate. **1602** *Withal's Dict.* 263/1 A *Iacke-medler, or busie-body, in euerie mans matter, *ardelio*. *a* **1563** BALE in Strype *Eccl. Mem.* III. xii. 114 He plays *jack monkey at the altar, with his turns and half-turns. **1845** *Quincy* (Ill.) *Whig* 30 Oct. 2/1 *Jack Mormons, and sympathizers abroad may croak and groan over the poor Mormons. **1846** Jack-mormon [see BIG-HEAD 3 b]. **1890** *Congress. Rec.* 2 Apr. 2941/2 In our country we have a *genus homo* called 'Jack-Mormon',..a class of individuals who do not belong to the Mormon church,..yet who are ever found doing the bidding of Mormon priests. **1947** *Time* 21 July 21/1 The number of backsliding 'jack-Mormons' is increasing. **1857** HUGHES *Tom Brown* I. iii. 67 The idea of equality or inequality..doesn't [enter their heads] till it's put there by *Jack Nastys or fine ladies' maids. **1550** BALE *Apol.* 28 He playeth the part of *Iack Nitigo, as yᵉ saying is, he seith but he wyll not se, or els that he seyeth a smal moate & letteth the great beame passe by. **1749** CAPT. STANDIGE in *Naval Chron.* III. 205 We experienced..uncommonly severe *jack northwesters. **1708** *Yorkshire-Racers* 14 *Jack Presbyter can cry, God save the King. **1598** SHAKS. *Merry W.* I. iv. 123 By gar, I vill kill de *Iack-Priest. *c* **1550** *Bk. Robin Conscience* 240 in Hazl. *E.P.P.* III. 242 *Jack savce..thov lovt, thov hoddie peake. **1599** SHAKS. *Hen. V*, IV. vii. 148 His reputation is as arrant a villaine and a Iacke sawce, as euer his blacke shoo trodd vpon Gods ground. **1702** VANBRUGH *False Friend* III. ii, Why how now, Jack-sauce? why, how now, Presumption? **1904** E. P. STATHAM *Story of 'Britannia'* iv. 70 This lad [*sc.* an officer cadet]..was already rather a favourite, being of the breezy type, which sailors call a '*Jack-shilloo'. **1929** F. C. BOWEN *Sea Slang* 73 *Jack Shalloo*, a braggart according to its old naval meaning. Nowadays it is applied to a happy-go-lucky, careless officer and hence a slack ship is called a Jack Shalloo ship. **1962** GRANVILLE *Dict. Sailors' Slang* 65/1 *Jack Shalloo*, naval officer whose aim in life is to be popular with the men. A corruption of *John Chellew*, an officer who earned himself the title Popularity Jack. **1611** SHAKS. *Cymb.* II. i. 22 Euery *Iacke-Slaue hath his belly full of Fighting. **1722** DE FOE *Col. Jack* (1840) 312, I should make myself full amends of *Jack Spaniard. *c* **1570** *Marr. Wit & Science* IV. i. in Hazl. *Dodsley* II. 357 Heard you ever such a counsel of such a *Jack sprat? *a* **1700** B. E. *Dict. Cant. Crew*, *Jack-sprat*, a Dwarf, or very little Fellow, a Hop-on-my-thumb. [*Nursery Rime*, Jack Sprat could eat no fat, His wife could eat no lean.] **1579** TOMSON *Calvin's Serm. Tim.* 853/2 Howe many *iacke sticklers are there nowe adayes..which..will needes shewe them selues to be somwhat by mouing troubles? **1643** HORN & ROBOTHAM *Gate Lang. Unl.* lxxxv. §837 A prying medler (busie-body, jack-stickler) crouds in and intrudeth..where it nothing concernes him. **1945** BAKER *Austral. Lang.* viii. 162 **Jack Strop*, a new recruit who tries to pass himself off as an old hand. **1946** J. IRVING *Royal Navalese* 98 *Jack Strop*, the Mess Deck's sobriquet for a conceited, opinionated sort of man.

37. Substantive phrases with specific senses. ***Jack among the maids***, a gallant, a ladies' man; ***Jack at a pinch*** (see quots.); †***Jack-hold-my-staff***, a servile attendant; ***Jack in office***, 'a consequential petty official' (Davies); also *attrib.* (cf. *Jack out of office*); ***Jack in the basket*** *Naut.*, a type of warning beacon (see quot. *a* 1865); ***Jack in the low cellar***, a rendering of Du. *Hans-in-kelder* (see HANS), an unborn child; ***Jack in the water*** (see quot. 1873); ***Jack of (at) all trades***, a man who can turn his hand to any kind (or to many kinds) of work or business; also rarely ***Jack of all work(s***; ***Jack of (on, o') both sides***, a person who sides first with one party and then with the other, a trimmer; †***Jack of Dover***, name of some dish, 'probably a pie that had been cooked more than once' (Skeat); ***Jack of straw***, a figure of a man made of straw (cf. JACKSTRAW 1); †***Jack of the clock*** or ***clock-house*** (also ***Jackaclock***, quot. 1689) = sense 6; also *transf.* applied to a person (see quots.); ***Jack of the dust***, 'a man on board a United States man-of-war appointed to assist the paymaster's yeoman in serving out provisions and other stores' (*Cent. Dict.*); †***Jack-o'-the-green*** (see quot.); †***Jack out of doors***, a person turned out of his former place; a homeless person, a vagrant; †***Jack out of office***, a person who has been dismissed from his office; one whose 'occupation is gone' (also rarely †***Jack out of service***); †***Jack-o'-wisp***, a will-o'-the-wisp; *transf.* a giddy or flighty person; ***Jack's alive***, (*a*) *Sc.*, a kind of game (see quot. 1825); *transf.* a lively run round (quot. 1894); (*b*) rhyming slang for 'five'; also, a five-pound note; ***Jack the Painter***, a kind of acrid green tea formerly used in the Australian bush; ***Jack the Ripper***, popular name for a murderer of women in London in 1888, who mutilated the bodies of his victims; also used *allusively*. See also JACK-A-LENT, JACK-IN-THE-BOX, JACK-IN-THE-GREEN, JACK-O'-LANTERN.

1785 J. TRUSLER *Mod. Times* I. 160 The Mayor..was a pleasant man, and *Jack among the maids. **1622** MABBE tr. *Aleman's Guzman d'Alf.* I. 130 When there was neede of my seruice..I was seldome or neuer wanting; I was *Iacke at a pinch. *a* **1700** B. E. *Dict. Cant. Crew*, *Jack at a Pinch*, a poor Hackney Parson. **1883** WHITCHER *Widow Bedott Papers* ii, Miss Coon..knows that the Major took her [to wife] 'Jack at a pinch'—seein' he couldent get such as he wanted, he took such as he could get. **1625** BP. MOUNTAGU *App. Cæsar* II. xvi. 217 As if..the man [were not] to bee made any more account of than **Iack hold my staffe*, by these Rabbies. **1678** MRS. BEHN *Sir Patient Fancy* v, Madam, in plain English I am made a John A-Nokes of, Jack-hold-my-staff,..to give Leander time to marry your Daughter. *a* **1700** B. E. *Dict. Cant. Crew*, **Jack in an Office*, of one that behaves himself Imperiously in it. *a* **1819** WOLCOTT (P. Pindar) *Advice Future Laureat* II, I hate a Jack-in-office martinet. **1836–9** DICKENS *Sk. Boz* xviii, A Jack-in-office, sir, and a very insolent fellow. **1887** BESANT *The World went*, etc. xiii, The clerks..gave this young officer..as much trouble as Jacks-in-office possibly can. *a* **1865** SMYTH *Sailor's Word-Bk.* (1867) 407 **Jack in the basket*, a sort of wooden cap or basket on the top of a pole, to mark a sand-bank or hidden danger. **1921** *Yachting Monthly* Mar. 299/1 How comfortingly the cocoa boiled on an even keel at dawn with Jack-in-the-basket in sight! **1941** *Beaver* Sept. 38/1 Jack-in-the-Basket. A beacon. The Moose River was well buoyed, and the many shoals were marked with high poles surmounted with long wicker baskets, or broom heads of willows. **1751** SMOLLETT *Per. Pick.* x, When his companions drank to the *Hans en kelderr*, or *Jack in the low cellar, he could not help displaying an extraordinary complacence of countenance. **1836–7** DICKENS *Sk. Boz, Tales* vii, *Jack-in-the-water. **1851** MAYHEW *Lond. Labour* I. 66 The lads, who act as jacks-in-the-water, were busy feeling in the mud for the fish that had fallen over board. **1873** *Slang Dict.*, *Jack-in-the-water*, an attendant at the watermen's stairs on the river and sea-port towns, who does not mind wetting his feet for a customer's convenience, in consideration of a douceur. **1618** MYNSHUL *Ess. Prison* 24 Some broken Cittizen, who hath plaid *Iack of all trades. **1651** CLEVELAND *Poems* 22 Thus Jack-of-all-trades hath devoutly showne The twelve Apostles on a Cherry-stone. **1687** M. CLIFFORD *Notes Dryden* i. 3 Your Writings are like a Jack of all Trades Shop, they have Variety, but nothing of value. **1770** *Gentl. Mag.* XL. 61 Jack at all trades, is seldom good at any. **1813** SCOTT *Let. to Joanna Baillie* 21 Mar. in *Lockhart*, Being a complete jack-of-all-trades, from the carpenter to the shepherd, nothing comes strange to him. **1820** *Sporting Mag.* VI. 159 My Jack of all works, who, by the by, is a universal gallant. **1878** S. WALPOLE *Hist. Eng.* I. 311 It would be unfair to say of Lord Brougham that he was 'Jack of all trades and master of none'. **1562** (*title*) A Godly and necessary Admonition concernyng Neutres, such as deserve the grosse name of *Iacke of both sydes. **1580** G. HARVEY in *Spenser's Wks.* (Grosart) I. 40 Claw-backes and Pickethanks: Jackes of bothe sides. **1656** EARL MONM. *Advt. fr. Parnass.* 338 That he hath won this universal good will by the vice of playing Jack of both sides. **1759** DILWORTH *Pope* 59 That he was a papist, a jack o' both sides. **1853** READE *Chr. Johnstone* xv, 'Are you ready, gentlemen?' said this Jack-o'-both-sides. *c* **1386** CHAUCER *Cook's Prol.* 23 Many a *Iakke of Douere hastow soold That hath been twies hoot and twies coold. **1621** FLETCHER *Wildgoose Chase* III. i. Wks. (Rtldg.) 551/1, I..would be married sooner to a monkey, Or to a *Jack of Straw, than such a juggler. **1563** *Ludlow Churchw. Acc.* (Camden) 114 For mendinge the chymes..and *jake of the clockehouse. **1593** SHAKS. *Rich. II*, V. v. 60 While I stand fooling heere, his iacke o' th' Clocke. **1661** COWLEY *Verses & Ess., Cromwell* (1669) 66 A Man, like that which we call Jack of the Clock-house, striking as it were, the hour of that fulness of time. **1689** *Diary* in *Topographer* (1790) 32 A new bell made for the Jackaclock at Gosford Gate. **1801** STRUTT *Sports & Past.* III. ii. 150. **1878** *Detroit Free Press* (Suppl.) 12 Jan. 2/4 Forward, on the gun-deck, the Paymaster's Steward, and his assistant, the *Jack of the Dust, were serving out small stores. **1882** J. W. DANENHOWER *Narr. 'Jeannette'* II. 41 He was doing duty at the time as paymaster's yeoman, or 'Jack of the Dust'. **1931** BROPHY & PARTRIDGE *Songs & Slang 1914–18* (ed. 3) 322 *Jacks alive*, the number 5, especially at House. **1938** F. D. SHARPE *Sharpe of Flying Squad* 331 *Jack's Alive*, a five-pound note. **1827** HONE *Every-day Bk.* II. 577 Formerly a pleasant character dressed out with ribands and flowers, figured at village May-games under the name of *Jack-o'-the-Green.. A Jack-o'-the-Green always carried a long walking stick with floral wreaths. **1603** FLORIO *Montaigne* I. vi. (1632) 13 At his returne [he] found the Towne taken, and himselfe *jack-out-of-doores [*sa place saisie*]. **1616** *Withal's Dict.* 569 Not altogether Iack out of doores, and yet no gentleman. **1553** BECON *Reliques of Rome* (1563) 159 Doth not this ceremony make Christ *Iacke out of office? **1579** TOMSON *Calvin's Serm. Tim.* 1031/1 They challenge such a power to them selues, that Iesus Christe is iacke out of office with them. **1591** SHAKS. *1 Hen. VI*, I. i. 175 For me nothing remaines: But long I will not be Iack out of Office. **1668** R. L'ESTRANGE *Vis. Quev.* (1708) 65 We should be but so many Jacks out of Office. **1540** COVERDALE *Confut. Standish* (1547) I vj, Gods good worde must weere the papyre and be *iack out of seruyce from other men. **1896** *Catholic Mag.* July 4 If she had been a *Jack-o'-wisp, in her young days...would Lady Mary have chosen her? **1825–80** JAMIESON, **Jack's alive*, a kind of sport. A piece of [lighted] paper or match is handed round a circle, he who takes hold saying, 'Jack's alive, he'se no die in my hand'. He, in whose hand it dies or is extinguished, forfeits a wad. **1894** ASTLEY *Fifty Years Life* II. 8 He gave her [a mare] 'Jack's alive' round the field. **1852** G. C. MUNDY *Our Antipodes* I. x. 329 Another notorious ration tea of the bush is called '*Jack the Painter'. This is a *very* green tea indeed. **1878** *Australian* I. 418 The billy wins, and 'Jack the Painter' tea Steams on the hob, from aught like fragrance free. **1945** BAKER *Austral. Lang.* iv. 83 *Jack the painter*..from the stain left round the drinker's mouth or in the billy (at least, that is the approved explanation). **1890** *Pall Mall Gaz.* 7 Mar. 5/1 A *Jack the Ripper outrage at Moscow. **1902** *To-Day* XXXV. 99/2 Now we know 'oo Jack the Ripper was! **1919** C. P. THOMPSON *Cocktails* 17 If only the officer would let him have a whack at her over the open sights, he'd do the Jack-the-ripper act on her in half a tick. **1958** HAYWARD & HARARI tr. *Pasternak's Dr. Zhivago* II. ix. 268, I expected to see a bashi-bazook or a revolutionary Jack the Ripper, but he was neither. **1959** 'H. CARMICHAEL' *Stranglehold* i. 13, I had to obtain a Home Office permit. And in case you still think I'm Jack the Ripper, here it is. **1972** A. E. LINDOP *Journey into Stone* (1973) ii. 21 There's a *lousy* fog... It's a Jack the Ripper's paradise.

38. In names of animals (sometimes signifying *male*, sometimes *small*, *half-sized*). **a.** Denoting the male of certain animals, as ***jack-ape***, ***-hare***; esp. of falcons, as ***jack-hobby***, ***-kestrel***, ***-merlin***. See also JACKASS. **b. jack crow**, a name for *Picathartes gymnocephalus*, a West African corvine bird; **jack curlew**, a name for two small species of curlew: (*a*) the Whimbrel, *Numenius phæopus*; (*b*) the *N. hudsonicus* of North America; **jack-fish**, a name for the pike; also for *Caranx pisquetos* and other carangoid fishes (see 31); **jack-in-a-bottle**, a name for the long-tailed titmouse, also called *bottle-tit*, from the shape of its nest; **Jack Russell (terrier)**, a small terrier named after John Russell (1795–1883), the so-called 'sporting parson'; **jack salmon** *U.S.*, a large freshwater fish, *Stizostedion vitreum*, also called walleyed pike; **jack-saw**, a name for the Goosander (*Mergus merganser*), 'from its saw-like bill' (Swainson *Prov. Names Birds* (1885) 163); **jack-sharp**, a northern dialect name for the STICKLEBACK; **jack-spaniard**, a large species of wasp found in the West Indies. See also JACKDAW, JACK-RABBIT, JACK-SNIPE.

1829 *Blackw. Mag.* XXVI. 636 That extreme 'facial development', which imparts it seems to the countenance of several of her ladyship's friends, the character of *jack-apes.

1897 Mary Kingsley *W. Africa* 23 One of the chief features of Free Town are the *jack crows. **1866** Montagu *Dict. Birds* s.v. *Wimbrel*, The Whimbrel has..in some parts.. obtained the name of *Jack Curlew, from a supposition that it is the male of that bird. **1884** Coues *Key N. Amer. Birds* 645 *Numenius hudsonicus* (Of Hudson's Bay), Hudsonian Curlew, Jack Curlew. **1847** Lytton *Lucretia* 32 A worthy object..which might well detain you from roach and *Jack-fish. **1887** J. Cummins *Hints Anglers*, If..Trout are well on the feed they will take the male or '*Jack' flies readily. **1742** Fielding *J. Andrews* III. vi, Swearing it was the largest *jack-hare he ever saw. **1885** Swainson *Prov. Names Birds* 31 British Long-tailed Titmouse..*Jack in a bottle. **1616** Surfl. & Markh. *Country Farme* 712 Of Merlins there are both male and female, the male is called *Iack-merlin. **1907** R. Leighton *New Bk. Dog* xxix. 317/1 In another decade or so the neglected Sealy Ham Terrier,..and the almost forgotten *Jack Russell strain, may have claimed a due recompense for their long neglect. *Ibid.* 318/1 'I have kept the Jack Russell type of terrier for nearly twenty years,' says Mr. Reginald Bates, 'and have used them for fox and badger digging.' **1931** *Times Lit. Suppl.* 13 Aug. 620/4 Perhaps the most popular is the 'Jack Russell' which..may now be considered a breed. **1965** B. Vesey-Fitzgerald *Dog Owner's Encycl.* 125 Jack Russell terrier. A small working terrier, named (for no very sound reason) after a West Country parson [*sc.* the Rev. John Russell of Devonshire] who, a century ago, was renowned for his working terriers. Any small Hunt terrier may be called a Jack Russell... There is no distinct type and the breed is not recognised by the Kennel Club. **1973** 'I. Drummond' *Jaws of Watchdog* i. 13 A little tubby man..with..the look of an overfed Jack Russell terrier. **1871** *Game Laws* (Pennsylvania) in *Fur, Fin & Feather* (1872) 122 The species commonly known as Susquehanna salmon, pike, perch, *jack salmon..shall henceforth not be taken..during their spawning time. **1920** *Outing* (U.S.) May 118/2 We always hope..to catch a few jack salmon. **1811** A. Clarke *Jrnl.* 12 June in *Acct. Life A. Clarke* (1833) II. 261, I went into the grounds where I had often sported, read, talked, searched for birds' nests, and caught *jack-sharps. **1876** I. Banks *Manchester Man* I. v. 81 He mun larn to tak' care on himsel' th' next time he marlocks among th' Jack-sharps. **1901** *Westm. Gaz.* 24 Apr. 8/1 A boy of ten was attempting to catch jacksharps when he fell from the embankment into the stream... (South-country readers will be interested to learn that jacksharps are the little fishes known to them as sticklebacks or tittlebats.) **1925** J. T. Jenkins *Fishes Brit. Isles* 124 There are numerous local names for this fish [*sc.* the three-spined stickleback], such as Jack Sharp, Prickleback, [etc.]. **1974** P. Wright *Lang. Brit. Industry* vii. 63 The worker pursuing his weekend hobby of angling may find round a pond *cockies* or *jacksharps*, 'sticklebacks' to the uninitiated. **1833** *Chambers's Edin. Jrnl.* 21 Sept. 269/3 The *jack-spaniard may be called the wasp of the West Indies; it is twice as large as a British wasp. **1843** Kirby & Sp. *Entomol.* (ed. 6) II. 80 The Jack-spaniard may be called the wasp of the West Indies, it is twice as large as a British wasp. **1855** Kingsley *Westw. Ho!* II. ix. 253 Sitting on the sandy turf, defiant of galliwasps and jack-spaniards. **1867** J. K. Lord *At Home in Wilderness* xviii. 299 A hornet, called by the packers a 'Jack-Spaniard',..builds a circular paper nest. **1938** *Trans. R. Entomol. Soc.* LXXXVII. 181 *Polistes* Latreille. Four species of this genus were collected in Trinidad. *P. canadensis* (L.). Typical form. 'Jack Spaniard'. Common throughout all settled areas. **1963** D. M. Douglass *Saba's Treasure* i. 14 You could as well discover the particular jack-spaniard that stung you a week ago.

39. In popular names of plants. Sometimes with the sense 'Dwarf, undersized', as ***jack bush***, ***Jack oak***; **jack-at-the-hedge**, local name in Ireland for Goose-grass or Clivers (Britten & Holland, *Appendix*); **jack bean**, a sub-tropical, climbing, leguminous plant of the genus *Canavalia*, esp. *C. ensiformis*; **jack-by-the-hedge** (also †*-of-the-hedge*, *-in-the-hedge*), the Hedge-garlic, *Sisymbrium Alliaria*; also locally applied to *Lychnis diurna*, *Tragopogon pratensis*, and *Linaria minor* (Br. & Holl.); **jack-go-to-bed-at-noon**, *Ornithogalum umbellatum* and *Tragopogon pratensis* (the latter also called simply *go-to-bed-at-noon*); **Jack-in-the-bush**, (*a*) local name for Hedge-garlic; (*b*) = Jack-in-the-green 1; **jack-in-the-hedge** = *Jack-by-the-hedge*, the hedge-garlic, *Alliaria petiolata*; **jack-in-the-pulpit** (*U.S.*), a North American araceous plant, *Arisæma triphyllum*, so called from the appearance of the upright spadix partly surmounted by the inclosing spathe; **jack-jump-about**, local name for *Angelica sylvestris*, *Ægopodium Podagraria*, and *Lotus corniculatus* (Br. & Holl.); **jack oak**, a North American species of oak (*Quercus nigra*); also called *black jack*; **jack of the buttery**, an old name for Stonecrop, *Sedum acre*; also called ***Creeping Jack***; **jack-pine**, any of several species of pine, esp. the Banksian pine, *Pinus banksiana*. See also Jack-in-the-box 8, Jack-in-the-green 2.

1885 'C. E. Craddock' *Prophet Gt. Smoky Mts.* xv. 280 He sat upon the cabin porch beneath the yellow gourds an the purple blooms of the *Jack-bean. **1951** *Dict. Gardening* (R. Hort. Soc.) I. 382/1 Jack Bean. Chickasaw Lima Bean. .. The young beans (about 4 to 6 in. long) are sometimes used like Scarlet Runners; the ripe seeds are said to be used as a substitute for coffee. **1812** J. Cutler *Top. Descr. Ohio* 96 The land in this distance is mostly clothed with *jack bushes and tall woods. **1536** Turner *Libellus* A ij a, *Alliaria*, ..*Iak of the hedge. **1578** Lyte *Dodoens* 639 In Englishe Sauce alone, and Iacke by the hedge. **1866** Rogers *Agric. & Prices* I. xxv. 627 Jack by the Hedge, or Sauce Alone..was a favourite condiment. **1875** *Sussex Gloss.*, Jack-in-the-hedge, *Lychnis diurna*. **1925** W. de la Mare *Broom-sticks* 312 Young spring flowers—primroses, violets, jack-in-the-hedge, stitchwort—in palest blossom starred the banks. **1941** A. L. Rowse *Poems of Decade* 111 The many and various scents of the flowers, Cuckoo-pint, cow-parsley and jack-in-the-hedge. **1853** A. Pratt *Wild Flowers* II. 47 The leaves and stems are often the only portions of the plant [*sc.* Yellow Goat's Beard] to attract the eye of the wanderer, for the flower is closed by mid-day. Several of its country names refer to this peculiarity, as Noontide, and *Jack-go-to-bed-at-noon. **1931** M. Grieve *Mod. Herbal* I. 360/1 The Goat's Beard opens its blossoms at daybreak and closes them before noon, except in cloudy weather, hence its old country name of 'Noon-flower' and 'Jack-go-to-bed-at-noon'. **1951** W. de la Mare *Winged Chariot* 9 How punctual they!.. As testifies 'Jack-go-to-bed-at-noon'. **1807** R. Southey *Lett. from Eng.* I. xiii. 146 A more extra-ordinary figure is sometimes in company, whom they call *Jack-in-the-Bush; as the name indicates, nothing but bush is to be seen, except the feet which dance under it. The man stands in a frame-work which is supported upon his shoulders, and is completely covered with the boughs of a thick and short-branched shrub. **1872** F. Kilvert *Diary* 10 May (1939) II. 196 He [*sc.* the sawyer] said wild garlic, called Jack-in-the-Bush, is a famous pot herb. **1837** H. Martineau *Society in Amer.* I. II. 211 Fine specimens of *Jack-in-the pulpit, and the moccassin-flower. **1884** M. E. Wilkins in *Harper's Mag.* Oct. 788/2 It would have been like looking at a jack-in-the-pulpit. **1894** Gibson *Ibid.* Mar. 565 Our well-known jack-in-the-pulpit, or Indian-turnip, with its purple-streaked canopy and sleek 'preacher' standing erect beneath it. **1906** *N.Y. Even. Post* (Suppl.) 16 June 2 In these woods I made acquaintance with Jack-in-the-pulpits, or, as the English call them, 'Lords and Ladies'. **1949** *Nature Mag.* Apr. 178 A few of these, like Indian turnip or jack-in-the-pulpit, cowslip and milkweed, may be considered mildly inedible. **1972** T. McHugh *Time of Buffalo* viii. 91 Soups were popular, some brewed with..buffalo meat, berries, fat, and the roots of jack-in-the-pulpits. **1816** U. Brown *Jrnl.* in *Maryland Hist. Mag.* (1915) X. 266 *Jack Oaks and other Scrub Wood. **1821** J. Fowler *Jrnl.* (1898) 15 The timber in the bottoms..is a kind of Jack oak and very low Cotton Wood. **1836** D. B. Edward *Hist. Texas* iv. 68 The post-oak and Jack-oak are considered in Texas as every man's property. **1901** Duncan & Scott *Hist. Allen & Woodson Counties, Kansas* 581 The 'jack oak hills' have been fenced. **1597** Gerarde *Herbal* II. cxlv. (1633) 518 Stone crop,..Wall pepper, Countrey pepper, and *Jacke of the Butteries. **1883** G. O. Shields *Rustlings in Rockies* xxxi. 285 This [country] is now grown up with scattering dwarf pines or, as the settlers call them, *jack-pines. **1925** *Chambers's Jrnl.* June 381/2 The jack-pine grows low and twisted. **1957** J. Kerouac *On Road* (1968) II. ix. 55, I..looked up and saw jackpines in the moon. **1965** G. McInnes *Road to Gundagai* xii. 210, I saw, moving majestically towards me and looming over the head of the crowd like a Douglas fir among jackpine, a prematurely grey giant about nine feet tall. **1969** T. H. Everett *Living Trees of World* 51/1 The range of the jack pine (*P. banksiana*), the most northern of eastern American pines, extends south from near the Arctic Circle to New York and Minnesota.

jack, *sb.*[2] Now *arch.* Forms: 4–6 **iakke**, **iak**, 4–7 **iacke**, 5–6 **iake**, 6 **iakk**, 6– **jack**. [a. F. *jaque*, in OF. also *jaques* (1375 in Hatz.-Darm.), in It. *giacco*, Ger. *jacke*, Du. *jak*, Sw. *jacka* jacket. Ultimate origin uncertain, but app. French: thought by some to be identical with the proper name *Jacques*, perh. as originally worn by the peasantry.

In sense 1 possibly ultimately of the same origin as Jack *sb.*[1], but not derived from that word in English, being of common European currency. Sense 2, and still more 3, are doubtfully placed here; both may belong to Jack *sb.*[1]]

1. † **a.** A short and close-fitting upper garment of men and women; a jacket. *Obs.*

1375 *Will of Thos. de Hemenhale* in *Promp. Parv.* 256 Unum iakke de rubio worstede. *c* **1375** in *Rel. Ant.* I. 41 Wommen..with her hornes..rydelid gownes, and rokettis, colers, lacis, iackes, pattokis, with her longe crakowis.

b. *esp.* A coat of fence, a kind of sleeveless tunic or jacket, formerly worn by foot-soldiers and others, usually of leather quilted, and in later times often plated with iron; sometimes applied to a coat of mail. (See Meyrick in *Archæol.* XIX. 224.) *arch.*

c **1380** *Sir Ferumb.* 3689 þorȝ-out ys scheld & is habreioun, Plates, & iakke & ioupoun, þorȝ-out al it ȝot. **1525** Ld. Berners *Froiss.* II. clxxxvii. 573 The kynge had on a iacke couered with blacke veluet, whiche sore chafed hym. **1549** *Compl. Scot.* xix. 163 Quhar for i exort ȝou that ȝe change ȝour sperutual habitis..in steil iakkis and in cotis of mailȝe, to deffend ȝour bodeis. **1562** *Lanc. Wills* (Chetham Soc.) I. 178 On jacke wi[th] a brest of plate..iijs. iiijd. **1573** Twyne *Æneid* x. (1584) Pvj, Through his golden plated Iacke he thrust into the side. **1578** Banister *Hist. Man* I. 8 Like..the yron plates of a iacke, one lying on an other. **1596** Spenser *State Irel.* Wks. (Globe) 639/1 The leather quilted jacke in iourneying and in camping, for that it is fittest to be under his shirte of mayle. **1622** Mabbe tr. *Aleman's Guzman d'Alf.* I. 94 They had brought with them good Iackes of Male. **1694** *Lond. Gaz.* No. 3035/3 Persons..arm'd with Blunderbuss's, Pistols,..Jackcaps, Leather Doublets and Jacks. **1828** Scott *F.M. Perth* xx, Some had the black-jack, or doublet, covered with small plates of iron of a lozenge shape. **1894** C. N. Robinson *Brit. Fleet* 91 The coats of livery, or 'jacks' as they were called, which the soldiers wore at Creçy.

† **c.** Phr. *to be on* (a person's) *jack*: to lay blows on him, to attack him; to be on his back, be down upon him. *Obs.*

1568 *Jacob & Esau* V. vi, If I wrought one stroke to day, lay me on the iacke. **1579–80** North *Plutarch*, *Themistocles* 127 That they..should stick to it like men, and lay it on the iacks of them. **1588** *Disc. Pres. Est. France* 18 So soone.. might the king of Nauar be sure that he would be vpon his iacke. **1600** Holland *Livy* VII. xxx. 269 They shall not.. stirre and put out their heads, but we will be streight upon their iacks [*ab tergo*]. **1631** J. Denison *Heav. Banquet* 241 All the Mariners are vpon the iacke of Ionas.

2. A vessel for liquor (either for holding liquor, or for drinking from); orig. and usually of waxed leather coated outside with tar or pitch (= Black jack 1); a (leathern) jug or tankard. *arch.*

'A Iacke of leather to drinke in, because it somewhat resembles a iacke or coat of maile' (Minsheu *Ductor* 1617).

1573 Tusser *Husb.* lxxxv. (1878) 175 Treene dishes be homely, and yet not to lack, where stone is no laster take tankard and iack. **1580** Hollyband *Treas. Fr. Tong*, *Hanap ou tasse à boire*, a tankard, a iacke. **1598** *Mucedorus* in Hazl. *Dodsley* VII. 218 To the buttery-hatch, to Thomas the butler for a jack of beer. **1633** *New Hampsh. Prov. Papers* (1867) I. 80, 1 jack of leather to drink in. **1680** *Lond. Gaz.* No. 1537/4 Two Drinking Jacks of Leather, edged round with Silver. **17..** *Song*, *''Twas merry in the Hall'*, And they each took a smack At the coal-black-Jack Till the fire burnt in their brain. **1826** Scott *Woodst.* ix, A large black leathern jack, which contained two double flagons of strong ale. **1885** *Standard* 25 Dec. 3/2 Water that I had in a tin jack.

† **3.** Name for some joint of mutton. *Obs.*

1466 *Mann. & Househ. Exp.* (Roxb.) 435 [Laid out] in a brest and a jakke of motone, v. *d.*

4. *Comb.*, as ***jack-maker***; **jack-cap**, a leathern cap to protect the head; **jack-coat**, a jacket or jack.

1575 *Estimate* in *St. Pap. Dom. Eliz.* CVI. No. 65 Cuttinge the cloth redie to be wrought by the Jackmakers. **1682** *Providence Rec.* (1894) VI. 96 Also a sarge jack coat, and a sarge paire of breeches. **1694** *Lond. Gaz.* No. 3014/4 Armed with Blunderbuss's, Pistols,..Quarterstaves, Jack-caps, with Dogs, Toyles, and Nets. **1713** *Ibid.* No. 5086/3 A Jackcoat and old Leather Breeches. **1769** *De Foe's Tour Gt. Brit.* II. 158 [Firemen] to whom they give Jack Caps of Leather, able to keep them from Hurt, if Brick or Timber, or any Thing not of too great a Bulk, should fall upon them.

jack (dʒæk), *sb.*[3] [Origin somewhat obscure; but most prob. a specific application of Jack *sb.*[1] (sense 34 b), said of and applied to things of smaller than the normal size; as if short for 'jack-flag', i.e. small flag (so called in contradistinction to the ensign): cf. the various uses of *jack* for *jack-bowl*, *jack-brick*, *jack-fish*, etc.; also the naval use in *jack* = *jack-cross-trees*.

Other conjectures have been offered, e.g. that the name is the F. *Jacques*, James, and that the jack was so called from King James I, who introduced the original union flag; or, that the word is prob. identical with jack *sb.*[2], the leathern surcoat having been (it is suggested) sometimes emblazoned with the cross of St. George. But app. neither of these conjectures covers the early use of the word.]

A ship's flag of smaller size than the ensign, used at sea as a signal, or as a mark of distinction; *spec.* the small flag which is flown from the jack-staff at the bow of a vessel (formerly at the sprit-sail topmast head), and by which the nationality of a ship is indicated, as in *British jack*, *Dutch jack*, *French jack*.

In British use the jack has been since the 17th c. (except under the Commonwealth) a small sized 'Union Flag' of the period (Union Jack), which has also been, since 1707, inserted in the upper canton of the ensign; hence, the name 'union jack' is often improperly applied to the union flag itself, when this is not carried or used as a jack. Every maritime nation has a jack of its own; this is usually, either as in Great Britain, the German Empire, Sweden, and the United States, the same as the canton of the ensign, or, as in France and the Netherlands, identical with the ensign, only smaller. (Prof. J. K. Laughton.)

1633 *Sailing Instruct.* (MS. Sloane 2682, lf. 51), You are alsoe for this present service to keepe in yo[r] Jack at yo[r] Boultspritt end and yo[r] pendant and yo[r] Ordinance. **1653** *Sail. Instr.* (MS. Sloane 3282, lf. 75 b), If y[e] cheife of y[e] squadron come by y[e] Lee and make a waft wth his Jack that then every shipp of his squadron beare und[r] his sterne and speake wth him. **1654** *Sail. Instr.* in G. Penn *Mem. Sir W. Penn* (1833) II. 59. **1665** *Ibid.* 599. **1667** Pepys *Diary* 22 June, That the Dutch did take her [the *Royal Charles*] with a boat of nine men..and presently a man went up and struck her flag and jacke. **1673** *Lond. Gaz.* No. 758/4 A Ship carrying the Hambrough Colours, who upon our Commanding him on Board with a Gun, immediately put up a Holland Ensign, and a Flushing Jack. **1673** Sir L. Jenkins *Let. to Earl of Arlington* in Wynne *Life* I. 91 All vessels whatsoever being in the King's service and wearing his colours, flag or Jack may have the same right done to them. **1678** Marvell *Growth Popery* Wks. 1875 IV. 275 A sorry yacht, but bearing the English jack, in August 1671. **1688** Sir J. Knatchbull *Diary* in *N. & Q.* 3rd Ser. VI. 2/2 He knew her to be a Custome-house boat by her Jack or pendant. **1694** Luttrell *Brief Rel.* (1857) III. 343 This day was published their majesties proclamation..prohibiting other than the kings ships to wear their majesties Jack, called the Union Jack. **1702** *Royal Proclam.* 18 Dec. in *Lond. Gaz.* No. 3871/1 All such Ships as have Commissions of Letters of Mart or Reprisals, shall, besides the Colours which may be worn by Merchants Ships, wear a Red Jack, with the Union Jack, described in a Canton of the upper Corner thereof next the Staff. **1707** *Lond. Gaz.* No. 4298/2 He entered into the Bay under French Jack and Pendent. **1712** E. Cooke *Voy. S. Sea* 119 The Signal is to shew a white Jack at the Main Top-mast Head. **1769** Falconer *Dict. Marine* (1776), *Jack*, a sort of flag colour or colours displayed from a mast erected on the outer end of a ship's bowsprit. In the British navy the jack is..a small union flag..but in merchant-ships this union is bordered with a red field. **1789** G. Keate *Pelew Isl.* 255 At day-light, an English jack was hoisted at the masthead. **1794** Nelson 30 July in Nicolas *Disp.* (1845) I. 463, I had established a signal with L'Amiable, a Dutch Jack inverted, when I wanted a boat. **1805** *Log 'Polyphemus'* 21 Oct. *Ibid.* (1846) VII. 156 *note*, A Spanish two-decker..hauled in her colours..and waved an English Jack from her traffle. **1855** M. Bridges *Pop. Mod. Hist.* 322 The British Jack obtained a complete triumph.

1890 *Cent. Dict.* s.v., In the United States naval service the jack is a blue flag with a white five-pointed star for each State in the Union. It is hoisted on a jack-staff at the bowsprit-cap when in port, and is also used as a signal for a pilot when shown at the fore. **1894** C. N. ROBINSON *Brit. Fleet* 89 The 'Jack' and the ensign still continue to be carried on staves at the extremities of the vessel.

jack, *sb.*[4] Also 7 giack(e, jawk, 9 jak. [ad. Pg. *jaca* (in Garcia De Orta, 1563), ad. Malayālam *chakka*. The earliest European representation of the word is *chaqui* in Friar Jordanus *c* 1328 (Hakl. Soc. 1863,13): see Yule.] **a.** The fruit of a tree (*Artocarpus integrifolia*) of the East Indies, resembling the bread-fruit, but larger and of coarser quality. Also the tree itself.

1613 PURCHAS *Pilgrimage* (1614) 505 Iacas are bigger.. and grow out of the bodie of the tree: they are of so many pleasant tastes, but hard to digest. **1634** SIR T. HERBERT *Trav.* 183 The Jacks or Giacks..deserve description...the Jacke is for bignesse comparable to a Pumpion. **1698** FRYER *Acc. E. India & P.* 67 This side is all covered with Trees of Cocoes, Jawks, and Mangoes. **1779** FORREST *Voy. N. Guinea* 319 Banka..abounds in coco nuts, limes, nankas or jacks, fish, turtle, and ratans. **1820** J. CRAWFURD *Hist. Indian Archipelago* I. IV. 122 Of the Jack fruit..two species occur in the Indian islands... The Jack is highly nutritious. **1824** H. E. LLOYD tr. *Spix & Martius's Trav. Brazil* I. II. i. 175 Brazil is indebted to the intercourse of the Portuguese with the East Indies..for the excellent fruits of the jaca, the mango, and the jambos. **1839** T. J. NEWBOLD *Pol. & Stat. Acct. Straits of Malacca* ii. 53 In the valley grow various fruit-trees, such as..the jack. **1859** TENNENT *Ceylon* II. VII. i. 111 The jak with broad glossy leaves and enormous yellow fruit. **1878** P. S. ROBINSON *Ind. Garden* (ed. 2) 49 The monstrous jáck that in its eccentric bulk contains a whole magazine of tastes and smells. **1919** *Nature* 25 Sept. 78/2 The native of the country is content with the fruit that is easily produced there and is already well known (in this case the durian, mango, sapodilla, mangosteen, jak, etc.). **1931** B. MIALL tr. *Guenther's Naturalist in Brazil* iv. 80 The fruits of the Jaca, as large as a man's head, seem to grow directly from the trunk and boughs. **1969** *Oxf. Bk. Food Plants* 114/2 Jak or Jack Fruit (*Artocarpus integrifolia*) is a related species with enormous fruits which can weigh up to 70 lb. each. In spite of their very strong odour, they are relished especially in Asia and may be eaten cooked or raw.

b. *Comb.*, as ***jack-fruit, -timber, -tree, -wood.***

1694 T. R. in *Phil. Trans.* XVIII. 280 A sort of large Club-Moss putting forth of the Jack-Trees and Mango's. **1789** SAUNDERS *Ibid.* LXXIX. 79 Jack and saul timber, are frequently to be met with in the forests and jungles. **1810** MARIA GRAHAM *Jrnl.* 101 (Y.) The jack-wood..at first yellow, becomes on exposure to the air of the colour of mahogany. **1830** M. SCOTT *Cruise Midge* (1859) 496 The cook having chosen to roast a jack fruit on a spit. **1869** A. R. WALLACE *Malay Archipelago* I. xvi. 362 There were also great numbers of a wild Jack-fruit tree (Artocarpus), which bore abundance of large reticulated fruit. **1900** W. W. SKEAT *Malay Magic* vi. 563 To dream about eating jack-fruit (*nangka*)..is an indication of great trouble impending. **1908** E. J. BANFIELD *Confessions of Beachcomber* I. i. 43 We have ..Jack fruit..in plenty. **1920** *Outward Bound* Oct. 44/1 The shameless stranger..issued from the saffron sunset, somewhere behind the spiky line of the mission jack fruit trees. **1921** E. M. FORSTER *Let.* 4 June in *Hill of Devi* (1953) 92 The Jack Fruits are ripening a little—they are extraordinary, with crocodile scales. **1947** *E. Afr. Ann. 1946-7* 23/2 Doors, mostly of local jack-fruit tree wood, are still being carved by Swahili craftsmen. **1962** *Housewife* (Ceylon) Apr. 23 The rich green foliage of mature plaintain and jak trees. **1966** D. FORBES *Heart of Malaya* ii. 27 A Malay kampong stands..half hidden by an assortment of fruit trees—durian, jack-fruit, mangosteen and rambutan. **1967** SINGHA & MASSEY *Indian Dances* xx. 175 It is said that he once had a vision in which Krishna asked him to carve his image from the wood of a certain jack-fruit tree. **1972** A. AMIN tr. *Ahmad's No Harvest but Thorn* II. 13 The handle of his *parang*, which was made of the heart-wood of a jack-fruit tree.

†**Jack**, *sb.*[5] *Obs.* Colloq. abbrev. of JACOBITE.

1695 B. BLAIRE in Sir. R. Blackmore *Hist. Conspir.* (1723) 180 Men of the greatest Acquaintance and Influence amongst the Jacks. ?*a* **1700** D'URFEY *Pills* (1719) I. 355 The Jacks are fierce, and Williamites are flesh'd. **1708** MRS. CENTLIVRE *Busie Body* I. i, We are all thought to be Politicians, or Whigs, or Jacks, or High-Flyers, or Low-Flyers, or Levellers. **1732** *Gentl. Mag.* II. 770 A Jack t'other Day in a Coffee-House prating, For Freedom as strongly as D'Anvers, debating.

jack, *sb.*[6] ? *Obs.* Abbreviation of JACOBIN *sb.*[3] (variety of pigeon). Also *Jack pigeon*.

1741 *Compl. Fam. Piece* III. 512 The Tame or House Pidgeons are called Barbels, Jacks, Crappers... The small Jack Pidgeon is a good Breeder. **1812** J. NOTT *Dekker's Gulls Hornbk.* 76 The jacobine, or jack vulgarly called.

jack, *sb.*[7] Short for JACK-BOOT. ***ankle-jack***: see ANKLE *sb.* 3. *colloq.*

1801 C. K. SHARPE *Corr.* 11 Apr. (1888) I. 108 His lordship..wears..boots nearly approaching to jacks. **1869** *Daily News* 13 July, A short jacket and voluminous knicker-bockers..with purple worsted stockings, low-up ankle jacks, and a wide-awake hat.

jack, *sb.*[8] Colloq. abbrev. of *Jacqueminot*, name of a variety of tea-rose.

1883 *Harper's Mag.* Jan. 241/1 The box contained a.. nosegay, with a 'Jack' rose in the centre.

jack, *sb.*[9] Colloq. abbrev. of JACKAL *sb.*

1892 *Daily News* 22 Jan. 5/4 The pack soon started a fine jackal, who led the hunt over the big paddy bunds and cactus fences... The jack was killed, and the Master presented the brush to Lady Harris.

jack, *sb.*[10], var. of JAKES.

jack (dʒæk), *a. Austral. slang.* [f. JACK *v.*[1] 3.] Tired *of* (something or someone); bored.

1901 E. DYSON *Gold Stealers* iv. 41 Oh, well, Twitter's jack of it, an' I don't think it's much fun. **1944** J. DEVANNY *By Tropic Sea & Jungle* xviii. 155 Too much of it makes you jack of it quick. **1959** BAKER *Drum* vi. 50 He was clearly a bore and they were jack of him. **1969** *Coast to Coast 1967-8* 4 He was willing to bet she'd get jack of it.

jack, (dʒæk), *v.*[1] [In senses 1, 2, from different senses of JACK *sb.*[1] Sense 3 may be merely onomatopœic: cf. CHUCK *v.*[2]]

1. *trans.* ***to jack up.*** **a.** To hoist with a jack (see JACK *sb.*[1] 10).

1885 *Pall Mall G.* 20 Mar. 6/1 To 'jack-up' a seven-ton engine and replace it on the rails. **1971** J. D. MACDONALD *Seven* (1974) iii. 46 When we decided to give up the apple stand, I said it might make a nice little cabin. My husband Ralph jacked it up and put it on a flatbed wagon and tractored it up through the west orchard. **1973** *Country Life* 18 Oct. 1190/1, I enjoy reminiscing over early motoring days... Jack up the back tyre to ensure easier starting.

b. *transf.* and *fig.* To raise, increase; to force or bolster *up*. *colloq.* (orig. *U.S.*).

1904 *N.Y. Tribune* 8 May 10 The management thought it saw a chance to jack up rents, and made a sudden announcement of a raise. **1939** J. P. MARQUAND *Wickford Point* x. 126 She had jacked up the price on the table d'hôte ten francs. **1959** *Economist* 7 Feb. 504/1 At his first trial, Cho Bong-Am got only five years, but a second trial jacked this up to capital punishment. **1964** *Ann. Reg. 1963* 44 Mr. Heath unveiled the plans to jack up the punctured local economies. **1971** *Daily Tel.* 26 July 15/7 Reinvestment would then jack up earnings per share and hence the value of the equity.

c. To arrange, organize, fix *up*; to put right, spruce *up*. *N.Z. slang.*

1942 *2 N.Z.E.F. Times* 12 Oct. 6/5 *Jack-up*, a term meaning to achieve the apparently impossible or to bring out of chaos; to arrange, inveigle, wangle or bolster up (a) Any transport (b) any alibi (c) leave (d) ED pay—usually without the prior knowledge or consent of authority. **1943** *Ibid.* 16 Aug. 6/5 Some of the pubs could do with a jacking up... Not enough service and civility. **1944** J. H. FULLARTON *Troop Target* xxvi. 187 I've jacked up a hot snack for the end of the shoot. **1945** E. G. WEBBER *Johnny Enzed in Middle East* 13/3 May take a year to jack it up again. **1956** D. M. DAVIN *Sullen Bell* I. iii. 24 I've jacked it up to stay the night with a friend of mine. **1960** B. CRUMP *Good Keen Man* 59 Harry decided to try his hand at jacking up a home brew. **1963** *Weekly News* (Auckland) 8 May 39/3 We jacked it up between ourselves that one evening we'd get Honey's gloves. **1971** *N.Z. Listener* 22 Mar. 13/1 I'll see you right at a boardin' place until you get jacked up.

2. *intr.* To hunt or fish at night with a jack (see JACK *sb.*[1] 26). *U.S.*

1881 *Harper's Mag.* Oct. 692/2 Gad went out 'jacking' with him, and jumped right over the bow of the boat to catch a deer. **1895** *Outing* (U.S.) XXVI. 61 Few have ever tried jacking for pickerel in the spring, by the light of a cedar wood or a kerosene blaze.

3. *dial.* or *colloq.* ***to jack up***: **a.** *trans.* (*a*) To do for, ruin. (*b*) To throw up, give up, abandon. (Cf. CHUCK *v.*[2] 2 b.) Also simply *to jack* (rare).

1873 *Slang Dict.*, *Jacked-up*, ruined, done for. **1880** *Daily Tel.* 9 Oct., The Liberal canvassers..became dissatisfied and threatened to 'Jack up' their books. **1881** M. REYNOLDS *Engine-Driving Life* 66 To burn a fire-box, burns your name into the locomotive superintendent's black-book, and there you are jacked up for ever. **1897** *Contemp. Rev.* Dec. 795 About 16 per cent 'jack it up' and go back to the slough and mire.

b. *absol.* or *intr.* To give up suddenly or promptly.

1873 *Slang Dict.* s.v. *Jacked up*, To *jack-up* is to leave off doing anything suddenly. **1875** PARISH *Sussex Dial. Gloss.*, *Jack-up*, to give up anything in a bad temper. **1881** *Leicestersh. Gloss.*, *Jack-up*..also, to become bankrupt or insolvent. **1889** BOLDREWOOD *Robbery under Arms* (1890) 135 [It] took a deal of punishment before he jacked up. **1898** —— *Rom. Canvass Town* 253 As a man, a gentleman, and a squatter, I 'jacked up' at the cookery.

4. Slang phr. ***to jack in***: to abandon, leave, give up, stop. Freq. in phr. ***to jack it in.***

1948 A. BARON *From City from Plough* i. 12 'What's your ol' woman do to you, Charlie?' 'Jacked me in for a civvy. I got home; no one there, no furniture, nothing.' **1958** F. NORMAN *Bang to Rights* III. 77 There was only fifteen of us on the hunger strike, I suppose the others must have got hungrey anyway they jacked it in. **1963** 'A. GARVE' *Sea Monks* v. 130, I ain't goin' to jack it all in now for Chris or anyone. **1972** K. ROYCE *Miniatures Frame* ix. 123 I'm beginning to wonder if it's worth it... Let me jack it in. **1973** *Times* 31 May 10/7 Private landlords jack-in the shaky business of letting.

5. ***to jack off*** (intr.): (*a*) to go away, depart; (*b*) to masturbate. *slang.*

1935 'G. ORWELL' *Clergyman's Daughter* ii. 109 Flo and Charlie would probably 'jack off' if they got the chance of a lift. *a* **1950** —— *Coll. Ess.* (1968) I. 71 *Jack off, to*, to go away. **1959** W. BURROUGHS *Naked Lunch* 74 He plummets from the eyeless lighthouse, kissing and jacking off in face of the black mirror. **1971** R. A. CARTER *Manhattan Primitive* (1972) xxiv. 237 You miserable little queer... You can jack off in Llewellyn's best hat for all I care. **1972** V. FERDINAND in A. Chapman *New Black Voices* 472 We might as well be jacking off, masturbating for our own self-gratification.

jack, *v.*[2] To take off the 'jacket' of a seal.

a **1795** G. LOW *Fauna Orcad.* (1813) 17 One party, armed with clubs, fall to knocking them on the head, and another set to jacking, i.e. cutting off the skin, together with the blubber on it.

Jack-a-dandy (ˌdʒækəˈdændɪ). Also 7 Iack O'Dandy. [See JACK *sb.*[1] 36, and cf. DANDY *sb.*[1]] A little pert or conceited fellow; a contemptuous name for a beau, fop, dandy.

1632 BROME *North. Lasse* III. ii, Ile throw him into the Dock rather then he shall succeed *Iack O'Dandy.* **1664** ETHEREDGE *Com. Revenge* II. iii, Leave her, she's only worth the Care Of some spruce Jack-a-dandy. **1754** RICHARDSON *Grandison* (1781) IV. xxix. 209 Notwithstanding all the Jack-a-dandies that have been fluttering about you. **1869** SPURGEON *J. Ploughm. Talk* 13 I'd sooner by half bend my back double with hard work than be a jack-a-dandy.

attrib. *a* **1791** GROSE *Olio* (1796) 98 Ere in this jack-a-dandy plight, I boasted an exclusive right. **1842** S. LOVER *Handy Andy* xix. 172 Tom did not understand French, but ..despised it as a jack-a-dandy acquirement.

Hence **Jack-a-ˈdandyism** [see -ISM].

1842 S. LOVER *Handy Andy* iv. 41 They call in Jack Growling, who scorns Jack-a-dandyism, and he gets a solitary guinea.

jackal (ˈdʒækɔːl), *sb.* Forms: 7 jaccal(l, jacal, jakhal, jackalle, chacall, (jagale, jacol, joecaul), 7-8 jack-call, 7-9 jackall, chacal, (8 shackal(l, siacalle, 9 shakal), 7- jackal. [Corruption of Turkish *chakāl*, ad. Pers. *shagāl*, or *shaghāl*, cognate w. Skt. *s'rgāla*, *ç'rgāla* jackal. Through Turkish also, F. *chacal* (formerly also in Eng.), whence Pg. *chacal*, It. *sciacal*, Ger. (Da., Sw.) *schakal*. The Du. *jakhals* was prob. from Eng.: cf. quot. 1694. The English word was formerly (as still in some dialects) stressed on the second syllable; the current form, and the obsolete *Jack-call*, show association with the proper name *Jack*, and names of animals containing it.]

1. An animal of the dog kind, about the size of a fox; one of various species of *Canis*, as *C. aureus* or *C. anthus*, inhabiting Asia and Africa, hunting in packs by night with wailing cries, and feeding on dead carcases and small animals; formerly supposed to go before the lion and hunt up his prey for him, hence termed 'the lion's provider'.

Described by Topsell, 1607 p. 439 as 'the second kind of hyæna'.

1603 W. BIDDULPH *Let.* in Purchas *Pilgrims* VIII. ix. (1625) 1337 About Scanderone there are many ravenous beasts about the bignesse of a Foxe, commonly called there Jackalles. **1615** G. SANDYS *Trav.* III. 205 Iaccalls..do lurke in the obscure vaults. **1617** MORYSON *Itin.* I. 247 A kind of beast little bigger then a Foxe..vulgarly called *Jagale*, used to..scratch the bodies of the dead out of their graves. **1659** D. PELL *Impr. Sea* 255 The Lyon..will not seek his prey himself, but sends his Caterer, or Jack-call to run about to seek it. **1667** DRYDEN *Ann. Mirab.* lxxxii, Close by, their Fire-ships, like Jackals, appear, Who on their Lions for the prey attend. **1672** W. DE BRITAINE *Dutch Usurp.* 33 They must not be like the Joe-caul, which provides food for the Lyon. **1682** WHELER *Journ. Greece* III. 264 An Habitation only for Wolves, Foxes, and Chacals. **1694** T. R. in *Phil. Trans.* XVIII. 276 Those Asiatick Foxes, vulgarly named by Travellers, Jakhals, or Jacals. **1702** W. J. *Bruyn's Voy. Levant* x. 39 A great many Siacalles, or Wild Dogs. **1753** HANWAY *Trav.* (1762) I. III. xxvi. 112 The shackalls in the woods bark'd and howl'd. **1818** JAS. MILL *Brit. India* II. vi. I. 266 He who has been bitten by a dog, a shakal, or an ass. **1831** MOIR in *Blackw. Mag.* XXIX. 914 From burial fields the midnight chacal cried. **1860** GOSSE *Rom. Nat. Hist.* 237 The shriek of the jackal bursting on the ear in the silence of night. **1885** BIBLE (R.V.) *Job* xxx. 29, I am a brother to jackals [1611 dragons], and a companion to ostriches.

2. *fig.* A person who acts like a jackal, *esp.* one who does subordinate preparatory work or drudgery for another, or ministers to his requirements.

a **1688** G. STRADLING *Serm. & Disc.* (1692) 384 Those lesser ones..are but so many Jack-calls to fetch him in store of prey. **1713** ADDISON *Guardian* No. 71 ¶7 A lion, or a master-spy, hath several jack-calls under him, who are his retailers in intelligence. **1739** CIBBER *Apol.* (1756) II. 146 (*Dial. old plays*) Alexander Goffe, the woman-actor at Blackfriers..used to be the jackall, and give notice of time and place. **1863** COWDEN CLARKE *Shaks. Char.* xviii. 460 [Richard's] cruelty and ingratitude towards his jackal, Buckingham, who wrought hard to help him to his bad eminence.

3. *attrib.* and *Comb.*, as ***jackal cry, -hunting, skin***; ***jackal-headed*** adj.; **jackal buzzard**, an African species of buzzard (*Buteo jackal*).

1680 MORDEN *Geog. Rect.*, *Lesser Tartary* (1685) 77 The Commodities..are Slaves..Chacal-Skins. **1823** BYRON *Juan* IX. xxvi, Nor give my voice to slavery's jackall cry. **1856** STANLEY *Sinai & Pal.* Introd. (1858) 43 Endless processions of jackal-headed gods. **1900** *Westm. Gaz.* 19 Apr. 4/3 His chapters..on jackal-hunting are excellent.

ˈjackal, *v.* [f. the sb.] *intr.* To play the jackal (see JACKAL 2); to do subordinate work or drudgery.

1900 KIPLING in *Daily Mail* 21 Apr. 4/5 For three months she had jackalled behind the army..and in that time had carried over thirteen hundred sick and wounded. **1914** A. DOBSON *18th Cent. Stud.* 204 Johnson..lost many of the papers lent to him by Percy. Malone, who jackalled for him, lost others. **1940** V. WOOLF *Writer's Diary* 6 Apr. (1953) 331, I..brooded quietly till the tyre punctured: we had to jackal in mid-road.

Jack-a-lantern: see JACK-O'-LANTERN.

jackaleg: see JOCKTELEG.

ˈJack-a-ˈLent. *arch.* Also -o'-Lent, -of Lent. [See A *prep.*]

1. A figure of a man, set up to be pelted: an ancient form of the sport of 'Aunt Sally', practised during Lent. Hence *fig.* a butt for every one to throw at. *arch.*

1598 SHAKS. *Merry W.* v. v. 134 See now how wit may be made a Iacke-a-Lent when 'tis vpon ill imployment. **1604** W. TERILO *Fr. Bacon's Proph.* 162 in Hazl. *E.P.P.* IV. 274 Ever upon Easter day, All Jack a Lents were cast away. **1633** B. JONSON *Tale Tub* IV. iii, Thou..Travell'dst to Hampstead Heath on Ash We'nesday. Where thou dist stand six weeks the Jack of Lent For boys to hurl, three throws a penny, at thee. **1682** SHADWELL *Medal* 295 Those Factious Few..Set up a Jack of Lent, and throw at it. **1813–49** *Brand's Pop. Antiq.* I. 101. **1863** *Chambers' Bk. of Days* I. 240/2.

2. *transf.* A puppet; an insignificant or contemptible person. *arch.*

1598 SHAKS. *Merry W.* III. iii. 27 You litle Iack-a-Lent, haue you bin true to vs? **1654** G. GODDARD in *Introd. Burton's Diary* (1828) I. 83 To make the Parliament a mere Jack-a-Lent, and as insignificant a nothing as the single person. **1702** VANBRUGH *False Friend* III. ii, What encouragement have I given you, Jack-a-Lent, to attack me with your tenders? **1884** T. HARDY *Wessex T., Interlopers at the Knap* (1889) 190 Can a jack-o'-lent believe his few senses on such a dark night, or can't he?

†**3.** A Lenten dish; a Lenten faster; Lent personified. *Obs.*

1643 *Char. Oxf. Incendiary* in *Harl. Misc.* (1745) V. 471/2 A Jack-a-Lent, made of a red Herring and a Leek. **1655** MOUFET & BENNET *Health's Improv.* (1746) 261 Sprats need no description, being one of Jackalent's principal Pages.

†**4.** = JACK-O'-LANTERN 2. *Obs.*

c **1717** *Lett. fr. Mist's Jrnl.* (1722) I. 99 The [Aurora Borealis] is as frequent in the Northern Countries as a Jack of Lent is here.

jackal(1), varr. JACAL.

jackanapes (ˈdʒækəneɪps). Forms: *α.* 5 Iac Napes (Nape), Iack (Iake) Napys, 5–6 Iack napis, 6 Iacke Napes (napes), Iack-, iackenapes. *β.* 6 Iack(e a napes, (Iack of Napes), 7–8 Jack-a-napes; 7 Jack-a-nape. *γ.* 6–7 Iack(e) an apes (Apes), Iack(e)-an-apes (-Apes), (7 Jack and Apes); 7 Jack an Ape, Jack-an-Ape, 9 jack-an-ape, jackanape. *δ.* 6–7 Iack(e)-anapes, 7 jacanapes, jackanaps, jackinapse, 7– jackanapes; 7 Jackanape. *Pl.* -apes, -apeses, (†-aps's). [Precise origin uncertain.

So far as yet found, the word appears first as an opprobrious nickname of William de la Pole, Duke of Suffolk (murdered 1450), whose badge was a clog and chain, such as was attached to a tame ape. Hence, in a poem of 1449 (see 2 a), in which other noblemen are denominated by their badges or heraldic emblems, as the Swan, fiery Cresset, Portcullis, Wheat-ear, etc., Suffolk is styled 'the Ape-clogge', and in somewhat later satirical invectives is referred to as an ape, and entitled *Jack Napes*; this being inferentially already a *quasi*-proper name for a tame ape, as it is seen to be in 1522. (The converse hypothesis, that Suffolk was for some other reason called 'Jack Napes', and that this nick-name was transferred from him to the ape, does not, on a review of the facts, seem probable.) But of *Jack Nape* or *Napes*, and its relation to *an ape* or *apes*, no certain explanation can be offered; it was perhaps, in its origin, merely a playful or whimsical name for a tame ape, and the *n-* might arise as in *nunckle* and *neye* (*birds-nie, pigs-ney*), or as in the by-names *Ned, Noll, Nell*, and the *-s* might be in imitation of the *-s* of surnames such as *Jakkes, Hobbes, Symmes*, etc., already in use, so that 'Jack Napes' parodied a human name and surname. If this was the standing of the name, it is easy to understand that it might never attain to literary use, till it became the nick-name of Suffolk. Be this as it may, the fact remains that *Jack Napes* is the earliest form, of which *Jack-a-Napes, Jack of Napes* (? Naples), *Jack-an-ape, Jack-and-apes*, are later perversions, app. attempts of 'popular etymology' to make the expression more intelligible. In accordance with this view, the original sense is here taken as 'ape', of which the use in 2 a is treated as a derived application, though it is in point of date the earliest use that has come down to us, and may possibly, with further evidence, have to stand first.]

1. Name for a tame ape or monkey.

†**a.** as the *quasi*-proper name of an ape. *Obs.*

1522 SKELTON *Why not to Court* 651 He grynnes and he gapis As it were iack napis. **1528** TINDALE *Obed. Chr. Man* 69 Noddinge, beckinge, and mowinge, as it were Iacke a napes. **1531** —— *Exp. 1 John* (1537) 23 He delyted in them, as we in yᵉ gestures of Iacke napes. **1546** BALE *Eng. Votaries* I. (1560) 4 b, They mocke and mow at them like Iack a napes. **1583** STUBBES *Anat. Abus.* II. (1882) 54 Women that haue as much knowledg in phisick or surgery as hath Iackeanapes. **1592** WARNER *Alb. Eng.* VII. xxxvii. (1612) 184 Iacke Napes, forsooth, did chafe because I [the Owle] eate my salue the Bat. **1613** W. BROWNE *Sheph. Pipe* Wks. 1869 II. 201 Some like him to a trimmed Asse And some to Iacke-an-Apes. **1674** *Camden's Rem.* (1870) Proverbs 321 Can Jack an Ape be merry when his clog is at his heel?

b. as common noun: An ape, a monkey. *arch.*

1526 SKELTON *Magnyf.* 2124 To mockynge, to mowynge, lyke a iackenapes. **1577** BRETON *Flourish on Fancie* in Park *Heliconia* I. 21 A sight of asses then There stoode in battell ray, With iackeanapeses on their backes. **1589** *Marprel. Epit.* B b, The Reader cannot chuse but haue as great delight therein, as a Iacke an Apes hath in a Whip. **1636** FEATLY *Clavis Myst.* xxxviii. 575 A Jack an Ape, a cat, or some such contemptible creature. **1660** HICKERINGILL *Jamaica* (1661) 81 Like fawning Curre, or mopping Jack-an-Ape. **1698** FRYER *Acc. E. India & P.* 7 Some brought Jackanaps's, such green Ones as are commonly seen in England to be sold. **1740** CHESTERF. *Lett.* (1792) I. lxiv. 180 Dressing him out like a jackanapes, and giving him money to play the fool with.

arch. **1828** SCOTT *F.M. Perth* xii, Had I but a rebeck or a guitar at my back, and a jackanapes on my shoulder. **1886** STEVENSON *Kidnapped* xvii. (1888) 163, I could see him climbing like a jackanapes.

2. Applied to a person compared to an ape.

†**a.** as *quasi*-proper name, applied to the Duke of Suffolk (whose badge was an ape's clog and chain). *Obs.*

[*c* **1449** *Pol. Poems* (Rolls) II. 222 The Rote is ded, the Swanne is goone, The firy Cressett hath lost his lyght;..The White Lioun is leyde to slepe Thorouȝ the envy of the Ape clogge (*gloss.* Southfolk).] **1450** *Ibid.* 224 (*Arrest Dk. Suffolk*), Jack Napys, with his clogge Hath tiede Talbot oure gentille dogge. Wherfore Beamownt, that gentille rache. Hath brought Jack Napis in an eville cache... [God] save the kynge and God forbede That he suche apes any mo fede. *Ibid.* 232 (*Death Dk. Suffolk*), Jac Napes wolde one the see a maryner to ben, With his cloge and his cheyn, to seke more tresour... For Jac Napes [*also* For Jac Nape] soule *Placebo* and *Dirige*.

†**b.** as *quasi*-proper name of a man using the tricks, or displaying the qualities, of an ape. *Obs.*

1534 *Lett. & Pap. Hen. VIII* (Rolls) VII. 39 As he played at cards with me..[he] said I played Jacke Napes with him. **1573** G. HARVEY *Letter-Bk.* (Camden) 120, I, quoth Iack a napes, by these ten bones, Nothinge happens amiss to a præparid minde. **1575–6** BP. BARNES *Let.* in *Eccl. Proc. Bp. Barnes* (Surtees) Pref. 10 Churlish people..who shew but, as the proverb is, Jack of Napes charity in their hearts. **1600** O. E. *Repl. Libel* I. vii. 159 It was nothing else, but a loftie tricke of iacke an apes.

c. as common noun: One who is like an ape in tricks, airs, or behaviour; a ridiculous upstart; a pert, impertinent fellow, who assumes ridiculous airs; a coxcomb. (The current use.) Also, playfully, A pert forward child, a 'monkey'.

c **1555** HARPSFIELD *Divorce Hen. VIII* (Camden) 291 This the Divell's Jackanapes made pastime to Lucifer. **1592** GREENE *Upst. Courtier* H j b, A iollie light timberd Iacke a Napes, in a sute of watchet Taffata. **1601** SHAKS. *All's Well* III. v. 88 *Hel.* Which is he? *Dia.* That Iacke an-apes with scarfes. **1610** *Histrio-m.* VI. 56 Now stands at every door a Iack and Apes, And tels me 'tis too late, his Lord hath din'd. *a* **1654** SELDEN *Table-T.* (Arb.) 96 They tell him he's a Jackanapes, a Rogue and a Rascal. **1709** *Tatler* No. 86 ⁋3 Upon which the pert Jackanapes Nick. Doubt tipp'd me the Wink. **1748** CHESTERF. *Lett.* (1774) I. 349, I always put these pert jackanapeses out of countenance. **1820** SCOTT *Abbot* iv, She hath favoured, doth favour, and will favour, this jackanapes. **1850** KINGSLEY *Alt. Locke* iv, A whiskered Jackanapes, like that officer..set to command grey-headed men before he can command his own temper.

†**3.** Applied contemptuously to a crucifix. *Obs.*

1562 BULLINGHAM *Let.* in Foxe *A. & M.* (1583) 1935, I will rather have these knees pared of, then I will kneele to yonder Iacknapes.

4. *Mining.* 'The small guide pulleys of a whim' (Gresley *Gloss. Coal Mining* 1883).

†**5.** ***jackanapes on horseback***: name for a proliferous variety of marigold, daisy, etc. in which additional flower-heads spring from the principal one; also for a monstrous variety of cowslip or oxlip in which the calycine segments are converted into leaves. *Obs.*

1597 GERARDE *Herbal* II. ccxliii. §7. 602 *Calendula maior prolifera*..This fruitfull or much bearing Marigolde, is..called of the vulgar sort of women Iacke an apes a horse backe. *Ibid.* cclx. §2. 635 Oxelip..whose flowers are curled and wrinckled after a most strange maner, which our women haue named, Iacke an apes on horsebacke. **1629** PARKINSON *Paradisi* v. 12 Double daisies..both white and red, both blush and speckled or party-coloured, besides that which is called Iacke-an Apes on Horsebacke. **1688** R. HOLME *Armoury* VII. 70/2 The Jack-an-Apes on Horse-back, or the fantastick Cowslip, hath the flower all green and jagged, like to a Juli flower.

6. *attrib.*

1598 SHAKS. *Merry W.* I. iv. 113 You, Iack 'Nape: giue-'a this Letter to Sir Hugh, by gar it is a shallenge..I will teach a scuruy Iack-a-nape Priest to meddle, or make. **1622** MASSINGER & DEKKER *Virg. Mart.* II. i, All my fear is of that pink-an-eye jack-an-apes boy, her page. **1660** PEPYS *Diary* 5 July, This morning my brother Tom brought me my jackanapes coat with silver buttons. **1813** MAR. EDGEWORTH *Patron.* (1832) I. iii. 44 The squire..declared that he would not be brow-beat by any..jackanapes colonel. **1881** BESANT & RICE *Chapl. of Fleet* II. xvii, Any jackanapes lawyer..might think it fine thus to insult..a harmless nobleman.

Hence (*nonce-wds.*) **ˈjackaˌnapery**, action characteristic of a jackanapes; **ˈjackaˌnapish**, **jackaˈnapsian** *adjs.*, having the character of a jackanapes.

1842 *Fraser's Mag.* XXVI. 448 That monument of congenial jackanapery reared..in caricature of an Elizabethan mansion. **1880** 'VERN. LEE' *Belcaro* vi. 151 Calling in Offenbach or Lecocq to rewrite that air in true jackanapsian style. **1884** *J. Bull's Neighb.* vii. 50 Go into a *bureau de poste*, and see how you will be insulted by the jackanapish officialism there.

jackaroo (dʒækəˈruː), *sb. Australian colloq.* Also **jackeroo**. [A derivative of JACK *sb.*¹, app. with the ending of *kangaroo*.] A man newly arrived from England to gain experience in the bush (see quot. 1885); an inexperienced young colonist. Now esp. a cadet or novice on a sheep-station or cattle-station.

1878 'R. BOLDREWOOD' *Ups & Downs* vii. 72 If these here fences is to be run up all along the river, any Jackaroo can go stock-keeping. **1880** W. SENIOR *Travel & Trout* 19 (Morris) Jackaroos—the name given to young gentlemen newly arrived from home to gather colonial experiences. **1880** A. C. GRANT *Bush Life in Queensland* (1881) I. 53 The young Jackaroo woke early next morning. **1885** H. FINCH-HATTON *Advance Australia* 85 (Morris) Before starting on their own account to work a station, they go into the bush to gain colonial experience, during which process they are known in the colony as 'jackaroos'. **1911** C. E. W. BEAN *'Dreadnought' of Darling* xi. 99 In the bachelors' quarters there will probably live..one or two 'jackeroos' —young Australians, or sometimes young Englishmen, learning the work of a sheep run by taking an ordinary part in it. **1918** *Chambers's Jrnl.* Apr. 267/2 The tracker's methods are noted in the following true story of a lost 'jackeroo' (a 'new chum' learning station work). **1936** I. L. IDRIESS *Cattle King* xxxii. 287 Some of the blacks told me he was coming with a couple of young jackeroos. **1956** 'N. SHUTE' *Beyond Black Stump* ii. 45 At the age of sixteen David had gone as a jackeroo upon a sheep station, to learn the business. **1962** *Coast to Coast 1961–62* 28 Coorabin's Royal Hotel had afforded her plenty of practice in turning on a stare that caused the invitations of commercial travellers, boundary-riders and jackaroos to trail off before they were half spoken. **1968** *TV Times* (Austral.) 28 Aug. 30/1 Jackaroo. 45 min. documentary. The jackaroo is..an apprentice to the rural industry, and in theory is in training to become a manager or owner. **1969** *West Australian* 5 July 58/2 (Advt.), 2 Jackaroos or Junior Stockmen with riding experience 16/18 years for West Kimberley Cattle Station.

Hence **jackaˈroo** *v. intr.*, to lead the life of a jackaroo; to gain experience of bush-farming.

1878 'R. BOLDREWOOD' *Ups & Downs* xix. 239 A year or two more Jackerooing would only mean the consumption of so many more figs of negro-head. **1887** DAYNE *In Name of Tzar* 134 Ah, wouldn't I break you in, if I had you jackerooing at Bundoolumoonoung for six months. **1890** BOLDREWOOD *Col. Reformer* (1891) 91 Perhaps the young one's going jackerooing at Jedwood. **1890** 'TASMA' *In her Earliest Youth* 152 (Morris) There's nothing for them to do but to go and jackaroo up in Queensland. **1911** C. E. W. BEAN *'Dreadnought' of Darling* xxxiv. 302 A houseful of bachelors—three or four young fellows jackerooing (that is to say, learning colonial experience) under a bachelor manager. **1936** A. RUSSELL *Gone Nomad* ii. 12 My graduation in jackerooing, or, as I usually call this period of my life, my 'pack-mule and damper days', had begun. **1967** *Coast to Coast 1965–6* 161 Young and old..jackerooed for thirty bob and tucker.

jackass (ˈdʒækæs), *sb.* [f. JACK *sb.*¹ 38 + ASS *sb.*]

1. A male ass, a he-ass.

1727 ARBUTHNOT *Coins* 128 Pliny relates from Varro that a Jack-ass for a Stallion was bought for 3,229*l.* 3*s.* 4*d.* **1774** GOLDSM. *Nat. Hist.* (1776) II. 385, I have seen a jack-ass, from that country, above fifteen hands high. **1803** A. YOUNG in *A. Hunter's Georg. Ess.* III. 197 The Earl of Egremont, early in 1800 established a team of six Jack-asses for carting. **1815** SCOTT *Guy M.* viii, She often contrived to..give him a ride upon her jackass. **1899** MORLEY in *Westm. Gaz.* 26 May 9/1 The old Greeks, when disputing and debating about idle contentions, had an expression that they were contending for the shadow of a jackass.

2. Applied opprobriously to a stupid or foolish person, a dolt, a blockhead: = ASS *sb.* 2.

1823 SCOTT *Peveril* vii, I..began..to think I had borne myself something like a jackass in the matter. **1870** DICKENS *E. Drood* iv, The purest Jackass in Cloisterham.

3. laughing jackass (also in mod. use simply *jackass*): the Giant Kingfisher of Australia (*Dacelo gigas*), so called from its loud discordant cry.

The name is also given to a kind of owl (*Sceloglaux albifacies*) in New Zealand, and *jackass* or *Derwent jackass* to a shrike (*Cracticus cinereus*) in Tasmania.

1798 D. COLLINS *N.S. Wales* 615 (Morris) Bird named by us the Laughing Jackass. **1833** STURT *S. Australia* II. iv. 100 He returned with..a laughing jackass..a species of king's-fisher, a singular bird, found in every part of Australia. **1847** LEICHHARDT *Jrnl.* x. 326 The laughing Jackass (*Dacelo cervina*, Gould) of this part of the country, is of a different species from that of the eastern coast. **1848** H. W. HAYGARTH *Bush Life Australia* xii. 130 The silence..was broken in a startling manner by the loud note, ha! ha! ha! of the 'laughing jackass'. **1859** H. KINGSLEY *G. Hamlyn* xviii. 148 Below us, in the valley, a mob of jackasses were shouting and laughing uproariously. **1880** MRS. MEREDITH *Tasman. Friends & Foes* 110 (Morris) We, too, have a 'jackass', a smaller bird, and not in any way remarkable, except for its merry gabbling sort of song. **1882** T. H. POTTS *Out in the Open* 122 (ibid.) *Athene Albifacies*, wekau of the Maoris, is known by some up-country settlers as the big owl or laughing jackass.

4. *Naut.* **a.** A kind of heavy rough boat used in Newfoundland. (Smyth *Sailor's Word-bk.* 1867.) **b.** = *hawse-bag*: see HAWSE *sb.*¹ 5. (*U.S.*)

1891 in H. PATTERSON *Illustr. Naut. Dict.* **1907** A. T. MAHAN *From Sail to Steam* iv. 96 The absurd-sounding, but legitimate, message to have the jackasses put in the hawse-holes. **1918** F. RIESENBERG *Under Sail* ii. 29 'Jackasses' were then bowsed into the hawse holes *for fair*. **1948** R. DE KERCHOVE *Internat. Maritime Dict.* 368/1 Jackasses are a most effective method of making hawseholes watertight in ships using stocked anchors.

5. *attrib.*, (in sense 2) as ***jackass author***, etc.; *Comb.*, as ***jackass-driver***, ***-headed*** adj.; **jackass barque**, a sailing ship having the same sails as a barquentine but rigged in a manner varying in some respect from the orthodox barquentine rig; **jackass brandy** *U.S. slang*, home-made brandy; **jackass brig**, 'a brig with square topsail and topgallant-sail instead of a gaff-topsail' (*Cent. Dict.*); **jackass copal**, the raw copal of Zanzibar: see quots.; **jackass-deer**, an African antelope, the singsing; **jackass-fish**, a fish of the Australian seas (*Chilodactylus macropterus*),

highly esteemed as food; **jackass frigate** (see quot. and cf. *donkey-frigate*: FRIGATE *sb.* 2 b, quot. 1867); **jackass penguin**, a common species of penguin (*Spheniscus demersus*), so called from its cry; **jackass pick** (see quot.); **jackass rabbit** = JACK-RABBIT; **jackass-rigged** *a.*, of a schooner, having three masts with square sails set on the foremast and having no main topmast; **jackass schooner**, a schooner which is jackass-rigged.

1884 J. FITZPATRICK *To an Old Printer*, And many a *jackass author has his wit Saved from damnation's literary pit. **1861** *Mitchell's Maritime Reg.* 890 On the 10th instant there was launched from the building-yard of Messrs. J. and J. Hall, at Arbroath, a beautifully modelled *jackass barque, named the Princess Alice, of 190 tons N.N.M. **1923** F. C. BOWEN *Ships for All* ii. 39 The sails of a barquentine and of a jackass barque are precisely the same. **1969** B. LANDSTRÖM *Sailing Ships* 178 It sometimes occurred that a ship was rigged, for example, with a fore-and-aft sail on the lower mainmast and square sails on the top and topgallant masts. .. In England all such types of pseudo-barques were called *jackass barques*. **1920** *Federal Reporter* (U.S.) CCLXXVIII. 42 Intoxicating liquors, to wit, one pint bottle of *jackass brandy. **1921** *Dialect Notes* V. 109 *Jackass brandy*, a home-made brandy with a powerful 'kick'. **1923** *San Francisco Examiner* 18 Feb. 16/7 A still in operation and a stock of jackass brandy close by. **1883** R. B. DIXON *Fore & Aft* 191 The potatoes would have to be paid for before that '*jackass brig' could sail. **1887** G. DAVIS *Recoll. Sea Wanderer's Life* 231 She is what is called a jackass brig. She has one mast square rigged and the other is schooner rigged, with topsail. **1926** *Sea Breezes* VIII. 214 There was a jackass brig, no main course, main yard high up, rigged like a topsail schooner on main mast. **1860** READE *Cloister & H.* lv. (1896) 157 A dog as big as a *jackass colt. **1872** R. F. BURTON *Zanzibar* I. 357 These places supply only the raw or unripe Copal, locally called Chakazi, and by us corrupted to *Jackass. **1887** *Sci. Amer.* 28 May 340/2 The raw, or true, copal is called chackaze, corrupted by the Zanzibar merchant to jackass copal. **1829** GEN. P. THOMPSON *Exerc.* (1842) I. 143 Your poor industrious *jackass-driver. **1898** MORRIS *Austral English*, *Morwong*, the New South Wales name for the fish *Chilodactylus macropterus*; also called the Carp and *Jackass-fish. **1833** MARRYAT *P. Simple* xiii, 'What do you mean by a *jackass frigate'? inquired I. 'I mean one of your twenty-eight gun ships, so called, because there is as much difference between them and a real frigate, like the one we are sailing in, as there is between a donkey and a race-horse. **1851** *Voy. to Mauritius* i. 10 The skipper looks anxiously toward the man of war, a jackass frigate, lying lower down the harbour. **1883** BLACK *Shandon Bells* xii, To be jumped upon by a *jackass-headed old idiot like that. **1863** G. KEARNEY *Links in Chain* ix. 195 The famous *Jackass Penguin. **1865** *Reader* 29 Apr. 486/2 Commonly called the 'Jackass Penguin', from its habit, while on shore, of throwing its head backwards, and making a loud strange noise like the braying of that animal. **1874** J. H. COLLINS *Metal Mining* 60 When the pick is much used as a lever, the head is frequently formed .. with a projecting wing to afford increased support to the helve. This is called a *jackass pick. **1851** AUDUBON *Vivip. Quadr. N.A.* II. 97 All ideas of blue mountains, vast rolling prairies, etc., were cut short by a *jackass-rabbit bounding from under our horses' feet. **1883** *Leisure Hour* 475/2 Jackass rabbits (the Californian hare), and numbers of .. grey .. land squirrels .. scampered .. over the flats. **1810** *Sporting Mag.* XXXVI. 168 To have *jackass racing upon particular days. **1883** E. F. KNIGHT *Cruise 'Falcon'* (1887) 32 October 19th .. passed a *jackass-rigged craft. **1898** A. ANSTED *Dict. Sea Terms* 239 There is another class of trading schooner, with three masts... When it sets square sails on the fore-mast it is sometimes called *jackass* rigged. **1929** H. W. SMYTH *Mast & Sail* (new ed.) 520 **Jackass schooner*, still used occasionally of a schooner without main-topmast. **1951** H. BENHAM *Down Tops'l* v. 71 'Jackass' schooners .. were so called because they were square rigged forward like a tops'l schooner, but had a ketch's mizzen. **1961** F. H. BURGESS *Dict. Sailing* 122 A 'jackass schooner' has no main topmast.

Hence **'jackass** *v. intr.*, to ride a jackass; **ja'ckassery**, the character of a jackass (see 2), gross folly or stupidity; (with *pl.*) something characteristic of a jackass, a piece of folly; **jackassifi'cation**, the action of making a jackass of, stultification; **'jackassism** = *jackassery*; **jackassness**, the quality of being a jackass, gross foolishness. (All more or less *nonce-wds.*)

1893 LELAND *Mem.* I. 228 Driving in a Russian telega, or *jackassing in Egypt. **1833** *Fraser's Mag.* VII. 618 The genius of *jackassery is not always to rule us. **1889** MRS. RANDOLPH *New Eve* II. xiii. 206 He will clothe his body after the latest jackasseries of the masher. **1822** *Blackw. Mag.* XII. 57 Acting on the principle of the general *jackassification of mankind, .. he abuses them right and left. *a* **1845** BARHAM *Ingol. Leg.*, *Wedding-Day* 46 Calling names, whether done to attack or to back a schism, Is .. a great piece of *jack-ass-ism. **1803** SOUTHEY *Lett.* (1856) I. 238 The crimes of pedantry, stupidity, *jackassness. **1885** MRS. PIRKIS *Lady Lovelace* I. v. 74 To convey such news .. was the very essence of Jackassness.

'jack-bird. [Echoic: influenced by JACK *sb.*[1]]

1. A local name for the fieldfare.

1885 SWAINSON *Prov. Names Birds* 6 Fieldfare (*Turdus pilaris*) .. Jack bird. From its cry. Cf. *Chack chack* (Luxemburg), *Claque* (Normandy).

2. 'A bird of the South Island of New Zealand, *Creadion cinereus*' (Morris *Austral Eng.*).

1873 SIR W. BULLER *Birds N. Zealand* (1888) I. 23 (Morris) I have .. adopted the name of Jack-bird, by which it is known among the settlers in the South Island. Why it should be so called I cannot say, unless this is an adaptation of the native name *Tieke* .. the equivalent, in the Maori vernacular, of our Jack.

jack boat: see JACK *sb.*[1] 25.

jack-boot, 'jackboot. [Sense of *jack* uncertain: taken by some as JACK *sb.*[2], but may be JACK *sb.*[1]]

a. A large strong boot the top of which came above the knee, serving as defensive armour for the leg, worn by cavalry soldiers in the 17th and 18th centuries; also, a large boot coming above the knee, worn by fishermen and others, and also *spec.* by German soldiers during the Nazi regime.

1686 *Lond. Gaz.* No. 2182/4 He had a light bob Periwig .. and a pair of Jack-Boots. **1712** ADDISON *Spect.* No. 435 ¶6 Should they meet a Man on Horseback, in his Breeches and Jack-Boots. **1712** E. COOKE *Voy. S. Sea* 74 Leather, so dress'd that it is not inferior to Iron, like our Jack-Boots. **1771** MACKENZIE *Man Feel.* (1886) 41 Two jack-boots concealed, in part, the well-mended knees of an old pair of buckskin breeches. **1824** W. IRVING *T. Trav.* I. 17 A meagre but fiery postilion, who with tremendous jack-boots and cocked hat was floundering on before him. **1861** SALA *Dutch Pict.* xii. 181 Jack-boots with long brass spurs. **1942** *R.A.F. Jrnl.* 2 May 36 Either the British way shall survive or the Nazi jackboot and whip shall take its place. **1955** *Times* 13 June 8/5 There were jackboots to be seen, iron crosses were pinned to the pockets of a few green shirts.

b. *fig.* Military oppression; rough bullying tactics. Also *attrib.*

1768 J. MORDAUNT *Let.* 10 May in E. Hamilton *Mordaunts* (1965) ix. 215 Some insults were offer'd to some of the Lords & Commons in their Coaches as they went down with a Cry of Wilkes & Liberty & no Jack Boot. **1910** *Westm. Gaz.* 14 Feb. 5/1 A large numerical majority .. excluded from power and honour by a mere jack-boot minority. **1968** *Sat. Rev.* 26 Oct. 36 The writers' trials and the jackboot on Prague have made it quite clear that Brezhnev and Kosygin's views on liberalism are akin to Stalin's. **1968** 'R. SIMONS' *Death on Display* vii. 105 He also objected strongly to what he called your jack-boot methods when you interviewed Mrs Hurd. **1970** *Times* 18 Mar. 26 This .. attempt by the Government to bludgeon this Bill through with jackboot tactics.

Hence **'jack-booted** *a.*

1846 R. FORD *Gatherings from Spain* xxii. 300 The clumsy look of a French jackbooted postilion. **1939** 'N. BLAKE' *Smiler with Knife* iv. 60 Silent, jack-booted watchers standing outside frightened houses. **1946** *R.A.F. Jrnl.* May 175 The once-jackbooted Germans. **1972** J. ROSSITER *Rope for General Dietz* ii. 28 He stood .. with his jackbooted legs apart .. as if to underline what they'd done in the name of Nazi justice.

jack-boot, -boots (= the 'Boots' at an inn): see JACK *sb.*[1] 36.

†'jack-boy. *Obs.* [f. JACK *sb.*[1] + BOY.] A boy employed in menial work; *spec.* a stable-boy, groom, or postillion. Cf. JOCKEY.

[**1401** *Pol. Poems* (Rolls) II. 62 Jacke boy, .. fayne thou woldist witen.] **1573** TUSSER *Husb.* lxxxvii. (1878) 177 Rather make lackey of Iack boie thy wag. **1596** SHAKS. *Tam. Shr.* IV. i. 43 Why Iacke boy, ho boy, and as much newes as thou wilt. **1600** SURFLET *Countrie Farme* v. vii. 668 They must haue the stones gathered off in winter .. by little Iackboyes and girles. **1812** J. H. VAUX *Flash Dict.*, *Jack-boy*, a postillion. **1849** tr. *Meinhold's Sidonia* II. 152 She .. uttered coarse and shameful words, such as the most shameless groom or jack-boy would scarce pronounce.

jack-chain. [f. JACK *sb.*[1] 7: because used in roasting-jacks.] **1.** A chain each link of which consists of a double loop of wire, resembling a figure of 8, but with the loops in planes at right angles to each other; the links are not welded.

1639 W. CARTWRIGHT *Royall Slave* I. ii, If you'l make use of any ornaments, I've a couple of jack-chains at your service. **1676** WYCHERLEY *Pl. Dealer* I. i, Here you see .. a great Lord [bowing] to a Fishmonger, or Scrivener with a Jack-chain about his neck. **1801** *Trans. Soc. Arts* XIX. 125 Six lengths of jack-chain. **1892** *Pall Mall G.* 23 Sept. 6/2 Much stronger than ordinary welded or jack chains.

2. *Logging.* (See quot. 1905.)

1905 *Terms Forestry & Logging* (U.S. Dept. Agric. Bureau Forestry) 40 *Jack chain*, an endless spiked chain, which moves logs from one point to another, usually from the mill pond into the sawmill. **1957** in *Brit. Commonwealth Forest Terminol.* II. 97.

jackdaw ('dʒækdɔː). [f. JACK *sb.*[1] 38 b + DAW. Formerly stressed *jack-'daw* (in J. 1755, Walker 1791, Todd 1818; still in Scotl.) Ash 1775 has '*Jackdaw*.]

1. The common name of the DAW (*Corvus monedula*), one of the smallest of the crow family, which frequents old buildings, church towers, etc.; it is easily tamed and taught to imitate the sound of words, and is noted for its loquacity and thievish propensities.

1543 BALE *Course Rom. Foxe* 87 Not all vnlyke vnto Isopes choughe, whom we commonlye call Iacke dawe. **1553** T. WILSON *Rhet.* (1580) 223 Some cackles like a Henne, or a Iacke Dawe. **1601** HOLLAND *Pliny* I. x. xxix. 285 Choughes and iack dawes: the veriest theeves .. especially for silver and gold. **1672** WILD *Poet. Licent.* 32 And may the Jack-daws still the Steeples hold. **1769** G. WHITE *Selborne* xxii. (1875) 75 Jackdaws building with us under the ground in rabbit-burrows. **1840** BARHAM *Ingol. Leg.*, *Jackd. Rheims* 12 In and out Through the motley rout That little Jackdaw kept hopping about. **1879** JEFFERIES *Wild Life in S.C.* 283 The jackdaw .. could not keep silence to save his life, but must talk after his fashion.

b. A species of grackle or 'blackbird' (*Quiscalus major*) of the Southern United States.

1884 COUES *Key N. Amer. Birds* 412 Boat-tailed Grackle, Jackdaw. Of large size, with long, much keeled and graduated tail.

2. *fig.* Applied contemptuously to a loquacious person.

1605 *Tryall Chev.* II. i. in Bullen *O. Pl.* (1884) III. 289 Bowyer a Captayne? .. a very Jackdaw with his toung slit. **1719** D'URFEY *Pills* I. 6 With City-Jack-daws; That make Staple-Laws, To measure by Yards and Ells.

3. *attrib.* and *Comb.*, in reference to the Fable of the Jackdaw decked out with peacock's feathers, or to the furtive and secretive habits of the bird.

1739 MELMOTH *Fitzosb. Lett.* (1763) 49 Jack-daw poets with their stolen feathers. **1890** *Athenæum* 19 Apr. 498/2 In the Bodleian Library, where they now rest, thanks to the jackdaw-like propensities of Mr. Secretary Pepys.

jacked (dʒækt), *a.* [f. JACK *sb.*[2] + -ED[2].]

†a. Clothed in or armed with a jack (see JACK *sb.*[2] 1). Obs. **b.** Hardened and thickened as leather for jack-boots.

1461 J. PASTON in *P. Lett.* II. 36 The peple was jakkyd and saletted, and riottously disposid. **17..** ? E. WARD *Welsh Monster* 3 Their brown Skins, from Knee to Foot, Are jack'd like Trooper's stubborn Boot. **1841** JAMES *Brigand* xix, Dagger or sword point will not well make its way through the jacked doublings of those hides. **1849** —— *Woodman* vii, Made of double jacked leather.

jackeen (dʒæ'kiːn). *Anglo-Irish.* [Irish dim. of JACK *sb.*[1]] A contemptuous designation for a self-assertive worthless fellow.

1840 *Fraser's Mag.* XXII. 320 A buckeen, a jackeen, a squireen, or any of the intermediate classes. **1892** *Q. Rev.* July 138 'Jackeens' loitering about the Dublin Theatres. **1897** SIR C. G. DUFFY *ibid.* Sept. 451 In manner and bearing he is a superb Jackeen.

jacker ('dʒækə(r)). [f. JACK *v.*[1] + -ER.] **a.** One who jacks, in various senses; e.g. one who hunts or fishes with a jack; one who jacks or throws.

b. ***jacker-off***, ***-up***: see quots. 1921.

1881 in *Instructions to Census Clerks* (1885) 70. **1904** *Westm. Gaz.* 28 Apr. 4/1 It was in the lace factory that the lad was set to work as a 'jacker-off'. **1921** *Dict. Occup. Terms* (1927) §399 *Jacker-off* (lace); takes off from bobbins, waste lengths of unused threads, and winds them on to large wooden bobbins, using a small winding machine. *Ibid.* §688 *Jacker-up* (lead pencil making); places a number of glued pencils together in a clamp, and screws down clamp to make glueing secure; removes pencils when clamping is complete. **1924** J. MARCHANT *Dr. John Clifford* i. 5 Three-fourths of the children were jackers-off or 'piecers'.

jackeroo: see JACKAROO.

jacket ('dʒækɪt), *sb.* Forms: 5 iaquet, -ette, 5–6 iaket, -ette, 6 iakett, iackett(e, iakket, iacquet(e, -quit, iakquet, 5–7 iacket, 7– jacket. [a. OF. *jaquet*, *jacquet*, dim. of *jaque*: JACK *sb.*[2]]

1. a. An outer garment for the upper part of the body: orig. the same as, or a shorter form of the jack; now, an outer garment with sleeves, reaching no lower than the waist, worn by boys (as an ***Eton jacket***) and by men in certain occupations; also a short coat without tails (as a ***Norfolk jacket***), worn in shooting, riding, cycling, etc.

Also as second element in *shooting-*, *smoking-*, *tennis-jacket*, and the like.

1462 *Mann. & Househ. Exp.* (Roxb.) 149 Ffor makynge off a jaket off crymysyn clothe ffor my sayd lurd, ij.*s.* iiij.*d.* **1464** *Nottingham Rec.* II. 377 Rede clothe to make jakettes of to þe saudeours. *c* **1483** CAXTON *Dialogues* 33/40 Donaas the doblet maker Hath performed my doublet And my Iaquet [F. *paltocque*]. **1527** in *Lanc. Wills* (Chetham Soc. 1854) 5 Item I giff my white chamlett iakett to be a vestiment to our lady chapell aforsaid. **1530** PALSGR. 233/2 Iacket that hath but four quarters, *jacquette*. **1548** UDALL, etc. *Erasm. Par. John* 116 The souldiers thought good that it [Christ's seamless coat] should bee kept whole vncut, and that sum of them shoulde haue the whole iacket to whose lotte it shoulde chaunce. **1580** HOLLYBAND *Treas. Fr. Tong*, *Hoqueton*, a Iacket, a cote of armor. **1599** THYNNE *Animadv.* (1875) 31 A comone garmente .. suche as we call a Ierken or Iackett withoute sleues. **1697** DAMPIER *Voy.* I. 427 Some of them have Iackets made of Plantain leaves, which were as rough as any Bear's-skin. **1706** PHILLIPS, *Jacket*, a sort of Garment in Use among Country-People. **1767** T. HUTCHINSON *Hist. Mass.* II. ii. 163 The women put on their husbands hats and jackets. **1834** L. RITCHIE *Wand. by Seine* 144 The royal archers led the way, clothed in jackets of vermilion, red, white, and green. **1841** EMERSON *Lect. on Times* Wks. (Bohn) II. 260 Before the young American is put into jacket and trousers, he says 'I want something which I never saw before'. **1897** HALL CAINE *Christian* xi, You were only a boy in jackets.

b. That worn by a jockey in horse-racing; now a loose-fitting blouse of silk or satin, of the owner's distinctive racing colours. Hence, ***to send in his jacket, take away his jacket, retain his jacket***, etc. See J. Rice *Hist. Brit. Turf* 1879.

1856 H. H. DIXON *Post & Paddock* v. 83 The Duke of Bedford .. very nearly requested him [Chifney senior] to send in his jacket. *Ibid.* vi. 89 Sam [Chifney] .. mounted the magnificent 'purple jacket with scarlet sleeves, and gold-braid buttons' of the Prince. *Ibid.* xii. 214 Jockey Club law does not acknowledge such a process as 'sending in a jacket'. .. But if masters .. force a senior jockey to retain their jacket, they are bound to give him their mounts, and not to .. prevent him from seeking for more considerate masters elsewhere. *Ibid.*, He thought nothing .. of putting a silk jacket into his pocket, and riding 70 or 80 miles to a meeting,

to oblige a friend. **1894** DOYLE *S. Holmes* (1899) 16/2, I glanced at the card to see the entries. It ran:—..4. Colonel Ross's Silver Blaze (black cap, red jacket).

c. A woman's outer garment analogous to that of boys or men, either loose or close-fitting, and of varying length.

1756 *Connoisseur* No. 103 ¶5 Her usual dishabille..is, an ordinary stuff jacket and petticoat. **1862** MISS YONGE *C'tess Kate* vii. (1880) 69 To the detriment of that young lady's muslin jacket.

d. Locally in U.S., = waistcoat. (*Cent. Dict.*)

e. Applied to something worn or fastened round the body for other purposes than clothing; as a *strait-jacket*, a *swimming jacket*.

f. Phrases. †*to line one's jacket* (obs.): see quot. 1611. ***to dust, swinge, thrash, trim,*** etc. (a person's) ***jacket***, to give him a beating. Also in phrases referring to breadth or narrowness of opinions, etc. (quots. 1792, 1896). See also DUST *v.*[1] 6 b.

1611 COTGR. s.v. *Accoustrer*, He stuffes himselfe soundly, hee lines his iacket throughly with liquor. **1687** T. BROWN *Saints in Uproar* Wks. 1730 I. 74 I'll substantially thrash your jacket for you. **1740** *Christmas Entertainm.* ii. (1883–4) 12, I will swinge his Jacket for him. **1792** BURKE *Corr.* (1844) III. 367 They were not able to make a schism in their short and narrow jacket. **1845** BUCKSTONE *Green Bushes* I. 13 I'll dust your jacket if you do that again. **1896** *Daily News* 30 Apr. 6/1 He had 'widened the jacket' of his Scotch theological training by mastering the results of the most advanced German speculation.

†**g.** *Mil. colloq.* (See quots.) *Obs.*

1898 *Geogr. Jrnl.* May 556 Lieut. Tanner obtained his 'jacket', and was the *beau ideal* of a horse-artillery officer. **1908** *Westm. Gaz.* 15 Oct. 5/3 Unitl 1895..a 'jacket'—i.e., a post in the Royal Field Horse Artillery—might be given to an officer of Field Artillery or of Garrison Artillery. **1909** J. R. WARE *Passing Eng.* 158/2 *Jacket* (Military), a soldier who wears a jacket (chiefly cavalry or horse artillery). **1925** FRASER & GIBBONS *Soldier & Sailor Words* 130 *Jacket, to get the*: colloquial for an appointment to the Royal Horse Artillery.

2. a. An outer covering, coating, or casing of any kind placed round a vessel, as a pipe, steam-cylinder, or boiler, to protect it, prevent escape of access of heat, etc. See also STEAM-JACKET.

1815 *Specif. J. Kilby's Patent* No. 3920, I enclose my brewing vessel in another vessel which I call the case or jacket. **1837** *Chambers' Misc.* VI. No. 136. 16 The enclosing of the cylinder in a jacket or drum of wood. **1852** W. BRANDE *Lect. Arts* 213 Heating a fluid by means of a steam-warmed jacket or coil. *c* **1865** J. WYLDE in *Circ. Sc.* I. 307/1 The crucible is to be covered by the plumbago jacket. **1898** P. MANSON *Trop. Diseases* xxi. 334 The evaporation is best done in a vessel like a glue-pot, in which the milk is not boiled, but is surrounded by a jacket of boiling water.

b. A paper cover or wrapper issued with a bound book, usually with the title printed upon it. See also *dust-jacket* (DUST *sb.*[1] 8 e).

1894 *Month* May 116 It was arrayed in a handsome purple 'jacket', and bore the crown and monogram of George III. **1895** H. FROWDE *Let.* 26 June, Paper jackets are being printed for it, worded as shown.

c. *U.S.* 'A folded paper or open envelop containing an official document, on which is indorsed an order or other direction respecting the disposition to be made of the document, memoranda respecting its contents, dates of reception and transmission, etc.' (*Cent. Dict.*)

d. *Ordnance.* A coil or cylinder of wrought iron or steel placed around the barrel of a gun to strengthen or protect it.

1876 *Engineering* XXI. 17 This improvement consists in the addition of a steel jacket to the body of the gun from the breech to beyond the trunnions. **1888** O. E. MICHAELIS tr. *Monthaye's Krupp & De Bange* ii. 24 The tube..is encircled by a single band or jacket (Mantel, in German), shrunk on. **1902** *Kynoch Jrnl.* Apr.–May 79/2 A second gun..having a jacket of cast steel. **1972** *Internat. Defense Rev.* Feb. 61 Sheathing the gun tube in an insulating jacket of cloth, plastic material or aluminum plate.

3. a. The natural (usually hairy) covering or 'coat' of various animals; the fleece (of a sheep), hair (of a dog), fur (of a cat), etc.; also the skin (of a seal, fish, etc.).

1613 PURCHAS *Pilgrimage* (1614) 560 These kindes of Serpents..The Scythale is admirable in her varied Iacket. *c* **1847** COCKS in *Knowledge* (1883) 188/2 Herds of *Actinia bellis* in prime condition—jackets as red as a Kentish cherry. **1865** *Jrnl. R. Agric. Soc.* Ser. II. I. II. 242 The recent high price of long wool has tempted some flockmasters to neglect the form, in their eagerness to secure a heavy jacket. **1880** *Standard* 20 May 3 As fast as one [seal] is clubbed or shot the skinner with the sharp knife turns it out of its 'jacket', as the skin with the attached blubber is styled. **1882** *Daily News* 28 Jan. 2/2 A two-pound perch boiled in its own jacket, and served up with parsley sauce. **1898** *Ladies' Field* 6 Aug. 378/2, I have seen her in July with a magnificent jacket, while every other cat had next to none.

b. The skin of a potato (when cooked with the skin on).

1856 *Farmer's Mag.* Nov. 378 Potatoes..boiled unpeeled—or as we say, 'in their jackets'. **1894** HALL CAINE *Manxman* 31 A pot of potatoes in their jackets.

c. *Path.* A formation coating some organ.

1897 *Allbutt's Syst. Med.* IV. 119 This white jacket, which may be a quarter of an inch thick, easily peels off the subjacent liver.

d. A young seal; so called from the rough fur. *Newfoundland.*

4. *attrib.* and *Comb.*, as ***jacket-collar, -pocket, -stuff, -suit***; **jacket-bodice**, a dress-bodice coming down over the skirt like a jacket; also a jacket-shaped under bodice; **jacket crown** *Dentistry*, a crown (CROWN *sb.* 28 b), often of porcelain or vinyl, fitted over an existing natural crown, which is usually ground down to receive it; **jacket potato**, a potato cooked in its jacket, i.e. unpeeled; **jacket poultice**, a poultice placed between two folds of stuff; **jacket wise** *adv.* or *advb. phr.*, in the manner of a jacket.

1810 *Splendid Follies* I. 119 The laundress..had left a deep triangular singe in the very centre of the *jacket-back. **1889** *Tablet* 3 Aug. 167 Over her *jacket-bodice she wears a woollen shawl. **1838** DICKENS *O. Twist* x, Oliver..was at once lugged along the streets by the *jacket-collar, at a rapid pace. **1903** H. J. GOSLEE *Princ. & Pract. Crowning Teeth* viii. 129 The so-called *jacket crown is often a most useful style of construction. **1963** [see *bridge-work* (BRIDGE *sb.*[1] 11 b)]. **1966** L. DEIGHTON *Billion-Dollar Brain* xix. 197 One of my jacket crowns is loose. **1806** *Naval Chron.* XV. 453 The crew lost their *jacket knives. **1833** MARRYAT *P. Simple* xxix, He thrust the first book into his *jacket-pocket which he could lay his hand on. [**1902** WRIGHT *Eng. Dial. Dict.* (s.v. *jacket*), *Jackutty-taters*, potatoes boiled with their skins on.] **1928** GALSWORTHY *Swan Song* I. v. 37 A young woman was handing him '*jacket' potatoes. **1967** M. SUMMERTON *Memory of Darkness* iv. 56 You'll fare better on Rosie's stew and my baked jacket potatoes. **1898** *Allbutt's Syst. Med.* V. 149 A *jacket poultice of linseed is a common and for the most part a good application. **1643** DAVENANT *Unfort. Lovers* Wks. (1673) 133 What skirt's in fashion now; the *Jacket-way, Down to the hams? **1598** HAKLUYT *Voy.* I. 387 Aloft their shirts they weare a garment *iacket wise.

Hence ˈ**jacketless** *a.*, without a jacket; ˈ**jackety** *a. colloq.*, of the nature of a jacket.

1852 R. S. SURTEES *Sponge's Sp. Tour* (1893) 49 His coat was a light jackety sort of thing, with little pockets behind. **1862** MRS. H. WOOD *Channings* vi, Her son..burst into the room jacketless. **1891** HARDY *Tess* xxix. *ad fin.*, Tess had come out with her milking-hood only, naked-armed and jacketless.

ˈ**jacket,** *v.* [f. prec. sb.]

1. a. *trans.* To cover with or enclose in a jacket (in various senses of the sb.).

1861 *Times* 13 May 5/4 The cylinders [of the Mooltan's engines] are 'jacketed', as it is termed,—that is, there is an upper pair of 43 inches' diameter, in which the dry steam is first used, at a pressure of 20 lb., and an outer cylinder of 96 inches' diameter, where it is worked expansively. **1884** F. J. BRITTEN *Watch & Clockm.* 65 The 'ice-box' is also a metal chamber..jacketed all over with a non-conductor. **1889** FARMER *Americanisms* s.v., In Government offices, to *jacket* a document is, after scheduling, to enclose it with other papers referring to the same subject. **1899** *Westm. Gaz.* 25 Feb. 1/3 A Bible jacketed in American cloth upon the table. **1900** *Ibid.* 15 Aug. 7/1 Unfortunately, there are forty-five waiters to only forty jackets,..perhaps..the managers will be able to scrape together sufficient money to jacket the unhappy five.

b. *slang.* (See quot.)

1812 J. H. VAUX *Flash Dict.*, To jacket a person..is more properly applied to removing a man by underhand and vile means from any birth or situation he enjoys, commonly with a view to supplant him.

c. To enclose (a person) in a strait-jacket.

1856 C. READE *Never too Late* I. xv. 276 He found himself surrounded, jacketed, strapped, and collared. **1905** J. LONDON *Jacket* (1915) 52 They told me plainly that they would jacket me to death if I did not confess.

2. *dial.* or *colloq.* To beat, thrash. (Cf. the phrases s.v. JACKET *sb.* 1 f.) See also JACKETING 3.

1875 *Sussex Gloss.* s.v., 'I'll jacket him when he comes in'. **1877** *N.W. Linc. Gloss.* **1896** in FARMER *Slang*.

jacketed (ˈdʒækɪtɪd), *a.* [f. prec. sb. or v. + -ED.] Clothed, covered, or surrounded with a jacket (in various senses of the sb.).

1552 HULOET, Iacketed, *tunicatus*. **1831** CARLYLE *Sart. Res.* I. x, Those jacketed Gouda Cows. **1860** *All Year Round* No. 54. 79, I have seen baby London short-coated, and frocked, and breeched, and jacketed. **1884** *Health Exhib. Catal.* 66/1 Jacketed Pans, for soups [etc.].

ˈ**jacketing.** [f. JACKET *sb.* or *v.* + -ING[1].]

1. = JACKET *sb.* 2.

1881 GREENER *Gun* 309 This pipe is surrounded by a water jacketing, and kept cool by a running stream of water.

2. Material, as cloth, etc. for making jackets.

1882 in OGILVIE.

3. *colloq.* A beating. Also *fig.*

1851 MAYHEW *Lond. Labour* I. 92, I don't work on Sundays. If I did, I'd get a jacketing. **1894** 'J. S. WINTER' *Red Coats* 29 The very worst 'jacketing' which the Colonel was capable of administering.

Jackey: see JACKY.

Jackfield (ˈdʒækfiːld). The name of a village in Shropshire, used *attrib.* to denote a kind of black-glazed pottery of a type manufactured there in the 18th century. Also *ellipt.* as *sb.*

1904 A. H. CHURCH *Eng. Earthenware* (rev. ed.) xv. 115 Collectors of English earthenware are generally inclined to assign the black so-called 'Jackfield ware' to Whieldon. Possibly the black glaze..may have been added at Jackfield. **1967** *Sunday Times* 5 Mar. 47/1 Leeds pottery dates from about 1750, and though the creamware is the commonest product, the factory also produced some rather nasty shiny black earthenware called 'Jackfield'. **1968** *Canad. Antiques Collector* Oct. 5/2 A smaller exquisitely modelled Jackfield ware jug.

jack-frame. [f. JACK *sb.*[1] 8 + FRAME.]

1. The frame in which a jack or winch is fixed.

1703 MOXON *Mech. Exerc.* 41 The Nuts will not draw the Fore and Backsides close.., then the whole Jack Frame will not stand fast and firm together.

2. *Cotton Manuf.* A contrivance consisting of a rotating can containing a bobbin, formerly much used for giving a twist to the roving as delivered by the drawing rollers, and simultaneously winding it upon the bobbin. Also called *jack-in-a-box*.

1875 KNIGHT *Dict. Mech.* s.v., The jack-frame was superseded by the Bobbin and Fly-frame.

jack-fruit: see JACK *sb.*[4] b.

Jack-in-the-box, Jack-in-a-box. Also 6 Iacke of the boxe.

†**1.** A name for a sharper or cheat; *spec.* 'a thief who deceived tradesmen by substituting empty boxes for others full of money' (Nares). *Obs.*

1570 *Satir. Poems Reform.* xxii. 78 Jak in the bokis, for all thy mokis a vengeance mot the fall! Thy subteltie and palȝardrie our fredome bringis in thrall. **1612** DEKKER *Cryer of Lanthorne*, etc. xi, This Iacke in a Boxe or this Deuill in mans shape..comes to a Golde-smithes stall. **1623** MIDDLETON, etc. *Sp. Gipsy* IV. i, Jack in boxes nor Decoyes, Puppets, nor such poore things. **1639** GLAPTHORNE *Argalus* v. Wks. 1874 I. 61 These women..toungs that lie worse than false clocks, By which they catch men like Jacks in a box. *a* **1700** B. E. *Dict. Cant. Crew*, *Jack in a Box*, a Sharper, or Cheat. **1725** in *New Cant. Dict.*

†**2.** Applied contemptuously to the consecrated host, with an allusion to its reservation in the pyx.

1555 RIDLEY *Last Exam.* in Foxe *A. & M.* (1583) 1759 Rayling billes agaynst the sacramente, termynge it 'Iacke of the boxe', 'the sacramente of the halter', 'round Robin', with like vnseemely termes.

3. The name of some gambling games.

1592 NASHE *Summer's Last Will* (1600) G iij, When I should haue beene at schoole, I was close vnder a hedge..playing at spanne counter or Iacke in a boxe. **1664** J. WILSON *Cheats* IV. i. Dram. Wks. (1874) 67 Did not I..teach you your top, your palm, and your slur, Shew'd you the mystery of jack-in-the-box, and the frail die?

b. 'A game in which some article, of more or less value, is placed on the top of a stick standing in a hole, and thrown at with sticks. If the article be hit so as to fall clear of the hole, the thrower takes it.' (Farmer *Slang*.)

1836–7 DICKENS *Sk. Boz, Greenw. Fair* (1850) 67/2 The allurements of the stout proprietress of the 'Jack-in-the-box, three shies a penny'.

†**4.** A street pedlar stationed in a portable stall or box. *Obs.*

1699 E. WARD *Lond. Spy* III. 13 Here and there a Jack in a box, like a Parson in a Pulpit, selling Cures for your Corns, Glass Eyes for the Blind.

5. A kind of firework.

1635 J. BABINGTON *Pyrotechnia* xxxvii. 45 Another, which I call Iack in a box. **1841** J. T. HEWLETT *Parish Clerk* II. 44 Jacks-in-the-box, and all sorts of fireworks. **1892** *Pall Mall G.* 1 Nov. 5/2 There is more attraction to the ordinary child in a handful of 'blue devils',..'Roman candles', and a 'jack-in-the-box' than a grand Crystal Palace show.

6. A toy consisting of a box containing a figure with a spring, which leaps up when the lid is raised. Also *fig.*

1702 *Infernal Wanderer* (N.), Up started every one in his seat, like a Jack in a box, crying out *Legit aut non Legit*. **1833** MARRYAT *P. Simple* lxiv, Could he have jumped up twenty times, like Jack-in-the-Box. **1856** READE *It is never too late* lxx, Two figures..came bounding like Jacks-in-the-box out of the gloom into the red light. **1899** *Westm. Gaz.* 14 Oct. 8/1 Battles are won by resolute, enthusiastic men, not by jacks-in-boxes.

7. Applied to various mechanical contrivances. †**a.** A self-acting valve for relieving water-mains from accumulations of air. *Obs.* **b.** A screw-jack or lifting-jack, esp. one used in stowing cargo on board ship. **c.** A kind of screw-press: see quot. 1801. **d.** An instrument with a small but powerful screw, used by burglars to break open safes or doors. **e.** = JACK-FRAME 2.

1726 DESAGULIERS in *Phil. Trans.* XXXIV. 82 This machine which from its make we call Jack in a Box will be useful where ever water is to be conveyed a great way in Pipes. **1801** J. J. MOORE *Vocab. Sea Phrases*, *Jack in the box*, a large wooden male screw, turning in a female one, which forms the upper part of a strong wooden box, shaped like the frustrum of a pyramid. It is used..as a press. **1824** *Ann. Reg.* (1825) 8 Apr. 49/1 [He] with the assistance of hand-spikes and a hand screw, called by the sailors, 'Jack in the Box',..threw over the stone. **1841** JONES *Specif. Patent* No. 8988. 2 This differential movement now commonly called the 'Jack-in-the-box' is governed by the varying rotation of the pinion D. **1850** CHUBB *Locks & Keys* 23 Some years ago, one of Chubb's locks, fixed on a common iron safe, was forced open by a burglar's instrument, called a 'Jack-in-the-Box'.

8. a. A West Indian tree, *Hernandia sonora*, bearing large nuts that rattle in their pericarps when shaken. **b.** A local appellation of the wild arum, *Arum maculatum*; cf. *Jack-in-the-pulpit* s.v. JACK *sb.*[1] 39; also, of a hose-in-hose variety of primrose (Britt. & Holl.); cf. JACK *sb.*[1] 33 a.

1752–9 MILLER *Gard. Dict.* s.v. *Hernandia*, The Hernandia..with a large umbilicated Ivy Leaf, commonly called in the West-Indies, Jack-in-a-Box. **1756** P. BROWNE *Jamaica* 373 *Jack-in-a-box*, the cups that sustain the nuts are

very large, and as they move in the wind, keep a whistling noise, which is often frightful to unwary travellers. **1819** REES *Cycl.* s.v. *Hernandia*, The whistling hernandia.. in the West Indies is frequently denominated the Jack-in-a-box tree.

9. A fisherman's name for a hermit-crab. *U.S.*

Jack-in-the-green.

1. A man or boy inclosed in a wooden or wicker pyramidal framework covered with leaves, in the May-day sports of chimney-sweepers, etc.

1801 STRUTT *Sports & Past.* IV. iii. §20 Jack in the Green .. consists of a hollow frame of wood or wicker work, made in the form of a sugar loaf, but open at the bottom, and sufficiently large and high to receive a man.. who dances with his companions. *a* **1845** HOOD *Sweep's Compl.* 63. **1855** DICKENS *Dorrit* I. xxi. **1895** H. B. WHEATLEY *Pepys' Diary* VI. 296 *note*, The editor saw a jack-in-the-green with men dressed as milkmaids dancing round it on May 1st of the present year.

attrib. **1897** MARY KINGSLEY *W. Africa* 529 The heads of his society.. go out to meet him in their canoes, and bring him in his Jack-in-the-Green dress ashore.

2. 'A variety of *Primula vulgaris* [the primrose], in which the calyx is transformed into leaves' (Britten & Holland *Eng. Plant-n.*).

1876 *Gard. Chron.* 8 Apr. 472.

Jack Ketch. Also 7 Kitch, 8– Catch, jack-Ketch. [From the name of John or 'Jack' Ketch (sometimes written *Catch* and *Kitch*), the common executioner 1663 (?)–1686. Partly on account of his barbarity at the executions of William Lord Russell, the Duke of Monmouth, and other political offenders, partly perhaps from apt association with the vb. *Ketch*, CATCH, his name became notorious, was given to the hangman in the puppet-play of Punchinello, introduced from Italy shortly after his death, and became a common appellation. See *Dict. Nat. Biog.* s.v.] An appellation for the common executioner or hangman.

[**1673** R. HEAD *Canting Acad.* 13 Jack Kitch, the proper name of the Common Hangman that is now in being. **1682** DRYDEN *Dk. of Guise* Epil. 30 'Jack Ketch', says I, 'is an excellent Physician.. But hanging is a fine dry kind of death.' **1683** (*title*) The Apologie of John Ketch Esquire. **1685–6** LUTTRELL *Diary* 20 Jan., Jack Ketch, the hangman for affronting the Sherifs of London.. is turn'd out of his place, and one Rose, a butcher, put in. **1702** T. BROWN *Lett. fr. Dead* 48 From Charon to the Most Illustrious and High-born Jack Ketch, Esq.] **1705** HICKERINGILL *Priest-cr.* II. iii. 28 A Priest-ridden Magistrate to be the Jack Ketch, and do the Priest's drudgery. **1755** WESLEY *Wks.* (1872) II. 349 He is then a kind of jack-catch, an executioner-general. **1812** *Examiner* 19 Oct. 666/2 A few dozen lashes well laid on by Jack Ketch.. may be a very appropriate punishment. [**1849** MACAULAY *Hist. Eng.* v.] **1889** CLARK RUSSELL *Marooned* (1890) 75 If they seize the vessel, it is piracy—a criminal act which ends with Jack Ketch.

jack-knife ('dʒæknaɪf), *sb.* [app. of U.S. origin: perh. associated with some sense of JACK *sb.*[1], but cf. *jackleg* knife s.v. JOCKTELEG.]

1. A large clasp-knife for the pocket: see also quot. 1867.

1711 *Official Rec. Springfield, Mass.* (1898–9) IX. 39 One Dozen of Jack Knives, at six pence the knife. **1776** *Militia Act, New Hampsh.* in *Outing* (1895) XXVII. 80/1 A hundred buckshot, a jack-knife and tow for wadding, six flints, one pound of powder. **1825** J. NEAL *Bro. Jonathan* II. 227 Ever in Jerusalem?—I was—got a jackknife, that.. emperor Titus .. he lost it, one afternoon. **1861** DICKENS *Gt. Expect.* xl, Taking out his great horn-handled jack-knife.. and cutting his food. **1867** SMYTH *Sailor's Word-bk.*, *Jack-knife*, a horn-handled clasp-knife with a laniard, worn by seamen. **1870** EMERSON *Soc. & Solit.*, *Work & Days* Wks. (Bohn) III. 69 The old school-house, and its porch, somewhat hacked by jack-knives.

2. In a telephone station: = JACK *sb.*[1] 15 d.

3. *Swimming.* In full, *jack-knife dive.* A kind of dive executed by first doubling up and then straightening the body before entering the water.

1922 *Country Life* (U.S.) July 60/3 All variety dives fall into four main groups—somersaults, twists, gainers, jack-knives. **1928** *Radio Times* 11 May 274/2 Doing jack-knife and swallow dives from incredible heights. **1942** J. D. CARR *Seat of Scornful* xiv. 191 That's not a jack-knife, you ass... A jack-knife dive is where you bend double and touch your toes in mid-air, and then straighten out before you hit the water. **1956** J. SYMONS *Paper Chase* x. 60 His long legs drawn up like those of a jack-knife-diving swimmer.

4. The accidental folding up of an articulated lorry.

1966 *Times* 29 Sept. 11/6 A 'jack-knife' is an ugly complaint of 'artics' as these articulated monsters [*sc.* lorry and trailer] are known familiarly in the trade. The trailer and lorry fold up like a Boy Scout's jack-knife.

Hence **jack-knife** *v.*, (*a*) *trans.* to cut with a jack-knife; (*b*) *intr.* to double up like a jack-knife; *spec.* of the sections of an articulated lorry: in an accident, to fold together like a jack-knife; (*c*) to do a jack-knife dive. So **'jack-knifing** *vbl. sb.*

1806 *Balance* (Hudson, N.Y.) 22 July 228 (Th.), A sailor .. Jacknifed (as he termed it) the poor creature [*sc.* a cat] in several places about the head. **1855** BOYD *Oakw. Old* I, The stage-yankee's method of recording things, in jackknifed notches on a softwood stick. **1888** *Century Mag.* June 251/2 The practice.. of dodging shots, 'jack-knifing' under fire. **1889** *Amer. Ann. Deaf* Oct. 277 Desks ink-stained and jack-knifed like those of a country school. **1897** H. PORTER *Campaigning w. Grant* ix. 141 One of their amusements in camp.. was to throw stones and chips past one another's heads, and raise a laugh at the active dodging and bending the body low or 'jack-knifing' as the men called it. **1920** T. S. ELIOT *Ara Vos Prec* 22 The sickle motion from the thighs Jackknifes upward at the knees Then straightens down from heel to hip. **1949** *Sun* (Baltimore) 4 Aug. 1/8 An automobile crashed into a tractor-trailer truck that jackknifed in a driving rain. **1955** T. STERLING *Evil of Day* v. 50 He.. jack-knifed into a chintz armchair. **1958** *Times* 12 Apr. 7/7 Nobody envies Joe Cree his new 'artic.', for there is always the danger that, on ice, the rear will swing round, or jack-knife. **1964** [see FIN *v.* 4]. **1968** *New Scientist* 14 Mar. 573/3 Jack-knifing accidents to articulated vehicles are all too common... The vehicle folds up—jack-knifes—at the kingpin, which is the hinge between the two parts. **1971** *Rand Daily Mail* 27 Mar. 8/2 This was particularly so in the case of drivers, where jackknifing of the upper torso onto the steering wheel rim could lead to serious injuries. **1971** *New Scientist* 12 Aug. 359/2 Commercial vehicles.. need them [*sc.* antilock brakes] most urgently because of their widely varying states of load and their tendency to jack-knife if articulated.

jack-leg, jackleg ('dʒæklɛg), *a.* and *sb. U.S. colloq.* and *dial.* [f. JACK *sb.*[1] + *-leg* as in BLACK-LEG 2, 3.] Used as a term of contempt or depreciation: **A.** *adj.* Incompetent, unskilled; unscrupulous, dishonest. Freq. used of lawyers and preachers. **B.** *sb.* An incompetent or unskilled or unprincipled person.

1850 *Amer. Rev. Mag.* XI. 465/2 A party of some twenty of the most notorious rode up, headed by what is there [*sc.* in Texas] known as a 'jack-leg' lawyer. **1853** 'P. PAXTON' *Stray Yankee in Texas* xiii. 137 A sorter jack-leg lawyer. *Ibid.* xxviii. 284 In the Texan vocabulary, all men who have a mere inkling of any trade or profession are called 'jack-legs'. *Ibid.*, These men were 'jack-leg' carpenters. **1891** *Harper's Mag.* June 160/1 Once I was called a jack-leg and shyster. **1902** W. N. HARBEN *Abner Daniel* ii. 16 The Atlanta jack-leg lawyer is akin to the Tompkins family some way. **1943** R. OTTLEY *New World A-Coming* 86 The cultists were augmented by a number of herb doctors, clairvoyants, and 'jackleg' preachers. **1958** P. OLIVER in P. Gammond *Decca Bk. Jazz* i. 19 The wandering evangelists, and 'Jack-leg' preachers. **1974** *Amer. Speech* 1971 XLVI. 70 One innovation possibly attributable to population shift is *jackleg preacher*, which Carlson heard from a black informant in Roxbury.

So **'jack-legged** *a.*

1839 *Congress. Globe* App. 127 A set of jack-legged pettifogging lawyers. **1892** *Congress. Rec.* 27 May 4777/1 He goes away, and a jack-legged [army] officer could do nothing except to mark him as a deserter.

jackleg: see JOCKTELEG.

jack-light, *sb. U.S.* [f. JACK *sb.*[1] 26 + LIGHT.] A light carried in a jack or cresset for hunting or fishing at night. Also *attrib.* Hence **jack-light** *v.*, to hunt or fish with a jack-light.

1883 *Chicago Advance* 30 Aug., By night, it is called 'jacklighting' the deer. *Ibid.*, William sat just behind the jack-light for two long hours. *Ibid.*, Once after that in a jack-light hunt. **1895** *Outing* (U.S.) XXVI. 63/2 Dark banks so suggestive of jack-lighting experiences.

jack-line. [f. JACK *sb.*[1], in various senses: cf. JACK-CHAIN.] A kind of thin rope or line used for various purposes: see quots.

1615 E. S. *Brit. Buss* in Arb. *Garner* III. 642 Every string must be fifty fathom long, and about the bigness of a jack-line. **1665** J. WILSON *Projectors* I. Dram. Wks. (1874) 227, I shall be an alderman,.. I think a brass jack-line would hang as well o' my shoulders as on another man's. **1686** PLOT *Staffordsh.* 337 A round wooden box which receives a Jack-line, that goes also through another box which turnes a second spindle above in the Chimney. **1794** *Rigging & Seamanship* I. 64 Jack-line is made of bar hemp, and has 9 threads, 3 in a strand. **1851** *Illustr. Catal. Gt. Exhib.* 514 Sash and jack-lines, made from Indian spun hemp. **1858** KIPPING *Sails & Sail-making* 57 Through these eyes a small-sized rope is reeved, and this is called the *Jack-line*.

jackman ('dʒækmən). *Sc.* [app. f. JACK *sb.*[1] 4 + MAN. Referred by Scott, and writers after him, to JACK *sb.*[2]] An attendant or retainer kept by a nobleman or landowner. *Obs.* exc. *Hist.*

1567 *Gude & Godlie B.* (S.T.S.) 197 Preistis, leif ȝour pryde.. And Iakmen be ȝour syde. *a* **1572** KNOX *Hist. Ref.* Wks. 1846 I. 37 The Bischop of Brechin, having his placeboes and jackmen in the toun, buffated the Freèr, and called him Heretick. **1637–50** ROW *Hist. Kirk* (1842) 172 Familie exercises, prayer, and the word, and singing of psalms.. are profaned and abused, by calling on the cook, stewart, or jackman, to performe that religious duetie, the masters of families ashamed so to honour God in their awin persons. **1820** SCOTT *Monast.* ix, The chiefs and landed proprietors retaining in their service what were called jack-men, from the 'jack', or doublet quilted with iron, which they wore as defensive armour. **1849** JAS. GRANT *Kirkaldy of G.* iv. 35 A train of swash-bucklers or stout jackmen.

¶ Erroneously put for JARKMAN, q.v.

Jacko ('dʒækəʊ). *Austral. slang.* [f. JACK *sb.*[1] 30 c + -O[2].] A kookaburra (= JACK *sb.*[1] 30 c).

1941 BAKER *Dict. Austral. Slang* 38 *Jacko*, a kookaburra. **1942** C. BARRETT *On Wallaby* iv. 80 Were they only having a close-up view, having mistaken the moving figure among the dunes for a Jacko?

Jack-o'-'lantern, Jack-a-lantern, *sb.* Forms: 7– J. with a (the) l., 8 o', -a-, of l.; 7–8 lanthorn, 8– lantern; 8– Jack-lantern, -horn.

†**1.** A man with a lantern; a night watchman.

1663 STAPLETON *Slighted Maid* III. 48, I am an Evening dark as Night, Jack-with-the-Lantern, bring a Light. **1698–1700** E. WARD *Lond. Spy* II. (1709) 32 Each Parochial Jack-a-Lanthorn was Croaking about Streets the Hour of Eleven. *a* **1704** T. BROWN *Lett. fr. Dead* Wks. 1760 II. 195 Who should come by before I could get up again, but the constable going his rounds, who quickly made me centre of a circle of jack of lanthorns.

2. An ignis fatuus or will-o'-the-wisp; = *friar's lantern* (FRIAR *sb.* 9 b); *fig.* something misleading or elusive.

1673 RAY *Journ. Low C.* 410 Those reputed Meteors.. known in England by the conceited names of Jack with a Lanthorn, and Will with a Wisp. **1749** FIELDING *Tom Jones* XII. xii, Partridge.. firmly believed.. that this light was a Jack with a lantern, or somewhat more mischievous. **1750** S. HALES *Earthquakes* 10 Plenty of inflammable sulphureous Matter in the Air, such as *Ignes fatui*, or Jack-a-Lanterns. **1775** SHERIDAN *Rivals* III. iv, I have followed Cupid's Jack-a-lantern, and find myself in a quagmire. **1862** H. MARRYAT *Year in Sweden* II. 67 As a mist rises, Jack-o'-lantern flits his pale light over the swamp. **1870** LOWELL *Study Wind.* 5 Supplying so many more jack-o'-lanterns to the future historian.

attrib. **1750–1** *Student* II. 352 It.. is.. of a mere Jack-lanthorn nature, neither here nor there. **1817** COLERIDGE *Biog. Lit.* 293 The characters in this act frisk about, here, there, and everywhere, as teasingly as the Jack o'Lantern lights which mischievous boys.. throw with a looking-glass on the faces of their opposite neighbours.

3. A lantern made of the rind of a large turnip or a pumpkin, in which holes are cut to represent eyes, nose, and mouth; a turnip- or (in U.S.) pumpkin-lantern. *North Eng.*, *Sc.*, and *U.S.*

1837 HAWTHORNE *Twice-Told Tales* 222 Hide it [*sc.* the great carbuncle] under thy cloak, say'st thou? Why, it will gleam through the holes, and make thee look like a jack-o'lantern! **1959** I. & P. OPIE *Lore & Lang. Schoolch.* xii. 269 As soon as it is dark on Hallowe'en they take the lighted 'Jack-o-lanterns' and put them on their gateposts.

Hence **jack-o'-lantern** *v. intr.* (*nonce-wd.*), to play or move erratically like a will-o'-the-wisp.

1891 G. MEREDITH *One of our Conq.* I. iv. 52 His Puckish fancy jack-o'-lanterning over it.

jack-o-leg: see JOCKTELEG.

Jack-o'-lent: see JACK-A-LENT.

jackonet: see JACONET.

'jack-,plane. [f. JACK *sb.*[1] + PLANE.] A long heavy plane used by joiners for coarse work.

1812–16 J. SMITH *Panorama Sc. & Art* I. 109 The Jack-plane used by joiners, is generally about 17 inches in length. **1825** J. NICHOLSON *Operat. Mechanic* 582 The jack-plane is used for taking away the rough occasioned by the saw, and removing all superfluous and other uneven parts. **1876** T. HARDY *Ethelberta* (1890) 380 That comes from the jack-plane, and my pushing against it day after day and year after year.

Hence **jack-plane** *v. trans.*, to smooth with a jack-plane.

1872 'MARK TWAIN' *Innoc. Abr.* xii. 76 Surely the.. smooth.. turnpikes are jack-planed and sand-papered every day.

jack-pot: see JACK *sb.*[1] 34 a.

'jack-'pudding. *arch.* [JACK *sb.*[1] 36.] A buffoon, clown, or merry-andrew, *esp.* one attending on a mountebank.

1648 C. WALKER *Hist. Independ.* I. 21 The Junto-men, the Hocus-Pocusses, the State-Mountebanks, with their Zanyes and Jack-puddings! **1664** ETHEREDGE *Com. Revenge* III. iv, Sir, in a word, he was Jack-pudding to a mountebank. **1711** ADDISON *Spect.* No. 47 ¶6. **1752** FIELDING *Covent Garden Jrnl.* No. 10 Writers are not.. to be considered as mere jackpuddings, whose business it is only to excite laughter. **1826** SCOTT *Woodst.* xxviii, What make you in that fool's jacket, and playing the pranks of a jack-pudding? **1881** BESANT & RICE *Chapl. of Fleet* I. x. (1883) 75 They were again jocund,.. the jester and Jack-pudding of the feast.

attrib. **1668** T. ST. SERFE *Taruga's Wiles* A iv, Be gone with your Jack-Pudding Speech! **1836–48** B. D. WALSH *Aristoph.*, *Knights* II. iv, You rascal, how you worry me with your jack-pudding nonsense.

Hence **jack-'puddinghood**, the character of a jack-pudding, buffoonery.

1749 H. WALPOLE *Lett. to Mann* 3 May, Grossatesta, the Modenese minister, a very low fellow, with all the jack-puddinghood of an Italian.

'jack-'rabbit. *U.S.* [Short for *jackass-rabbit* (see JACKASS 5); so called from its long ears.] One of several species of large prairie-hares (*Lepus campestris*, *L. callotis*, etc.), with remarkably long ears and legs. Also *attrib.* and *fig.*

1863 N. S. KEITH *Let.* 24 Aug. in *Colorado Mag.* (1940) XVII. 69 We saw wolves, buffalos, antelopes, jack-rabbits, prairie-dogs innumerable, deer, and birds of various sizes. **1882** *Harper's Mag.* Nov. 869 The jack-rabbits speed to their holes with long kangaroolike bounds. **1897** MISS HARRADEN *Hilda Strafford* 215 She would never again go.. chasing the jack-rabbits and the cotton-tails. **1906** *Chambers's Jrnl.* July 538/1 For miles one may ride without seeing a living thing larger than a jack-rabbit. **1929** W. FAULKNER *Sartoris* III. iv. 206 The mules flapped their jack-rabbit ears. **1961** 'E. LATHEN' *Banking on Death* (1962) vii. 57 He was thrown backward by a jack-rabbit start from a stop sign. **1962** *Amer. Speech* XXXVII. 269 *Jack rabbit*, a motorist who is proficient at watching the cross-street traffic light; when it turns yellow, he starts up and is into the intersection before the light in front of him has turned green. **1963** D. P. MANNIX *All Creatures Great & Small* xi.

180 We saw our first live jackrabbit just at dawn while crossing the plains of Nebraska. A big, white-tailed jack with black-and-white squares like signal flags on his long ears bolted across the road. **1972** *Guardian* 16 Dec. 10/1 You surely have hit the jack-rabbit on the head with a fire-iron.

ˈjack-ˌscrew. A lifting-jack with a screw; = JACK *sb.*[1] 10.

1769 FALCONER *Dict. Marine* (1789), *Verin*, an instrument nearly similar to a jack-screw. **1840** R. H. DANA *Bef. Mast* xxix. 99 The jack-screws which are used in stowing cotton.

jackshay, -shea (ˈdʒækʃeɪ). *Australia.* [Origin unknown.] A tin quart-pot.

1881 A. C. GRANT *Bush Life Queensland* I. 209 (Morris) Hobbles and Jack Shays hang from the saddle dees. *Note*, A tin quart-pot, used for boiling water for tea, and contrived so as to hold within it a tin pint-pot. **1890** *Melbourne Argus* 14 June 4/1 His ration bags are beside his head, and his jackshea . . stands by the fire. **1893** MRS. C. PRAED *Outlaw & Lawmaker* III. 140 The tin billys, and pint pots and jackshays, strung together by a saddle strap.

†**jacksmith** (ˈdʒæksmɪθ). *Obs.* [f. JACK *sb.*[1] 7 + SMITH.] A maker of roasting-jacks.

1678 *Lond. Gaz.* No. 1280/4 Next door to the Jack Smiths in Philpot Lane, London. **1723** *Lond. Gaz.* No. 6196/7 Ralph Simson, . . Jacksmith. **1800** MALONE in *Dryden's Works* (1808) XVIII. 127 *note*, The celebrated watchmaker [Mr. Tompion] who was originally a jacksmith.

jack snipe, ˈjack-ˌsnipe. [See JACK *sb.*[1] 29, 34 b.] A small species of snipe, *Scolopax (Gallinago) gallinula*; also called *half-snipe*. Also applied to the common American or Wilson's snipe, *Gallinago Wilsoni*, the Dunlin, *Tringa alpina* (Shetland), and the pectoral sandpiper of N. America, *Tringa maculata*.

1663 KILLIGREW *Parson's Wed.* III. ii. in *Com. & Trag.* (1664) 109 Provide me then the Chines fry'd, and the Salmon Calvered . . and an Assembly of Woodcocks, and Jack-snipes. **1766** PENNANT *Zool.* (1768) II. 359 The Jacksnipe. . . Its weight is less than two ounces, inferior by half to that of the snipe. **1883** *Century Mag.* Oct. 921/1 The Wilson's snipe . . very closely resembles the jack snipe of Europe. **1889** R. S. S. BADEN-POWELL *Pigsticking* 52 Like the particular tussock always tenanted by a jack snipe.

Jacksonian (dʒækˈsəʊnɪən), *a.*[1] [See -IAN.] Pertaining to or characteristic of Andrew Jackson (1767–1845), seventh president of the United States, a prominent leader of the Democratic party. Also as *sb.*, a follower of Jackson. Hence **Jackˈsonianism.**

1824 *Amer. Sentinel* (Georgetown, Ky.) 18 Oct. 3/1 At Mount-sterling . . they collected together six Jacksonians. **1824** *Commentator* (Frankfort, Ky.) 23 Oct. 3/2 The old Jacksonian aristocratic leaven of the Adams faction. **1906** W. CHURCHILL *Coniston* v. 51 He . . preached the word of Jacksonian Democracy in all the farmhouses round about. *Ibid.* 57 The conscientious Jacksonians who were misguided enough to believe in such a ticket. **1929** *Encycl. Brit.* I. 156/2 Up to this point Adams's career had been almost uniformly successful, but his presidency (1825–29) was in most respects a failure, owing to the virulent opposition of the Jacksonians. *Ibid.* IV. 585/1 Calhoun, . . during the remainder of the Jackson regime, was a severe critic of Jacksonianism. **1966** AUDEN *About House* 16 A Proustian snob or a sound Jacksonian Democrat. **1973** *New Yorker* 28 Apr. 146/2 Douglas's creed was Jacksonianism, which to him meant a United States expanding over the whole continent and demonstrating that a democracy could not only survive but prosper.

Jacksonian (dʒækˈsəʊnɪən), *a.*[2] *Med.* [f. the name of John Hughlings *Jackson* (1834–1911), English physician and neurologist: see -IAN.] Designating a form of epilepsy (and the associated convulsions, fits, etc.) in which the seizures are usually confined to one side of the body (in which case consciousness is retained) and begin at one site (usually a digit or the angle of the mouth), progressing from there to neighbouring parts.

1877 *Brit. & Foreign Med.-Chirurg. Rev.* LIX. 51 The epithet 'Jacksonian' is even being introduced in France by Charcot to be applied to epilepsy or convulsions of a localised and partial character. **1878** *Glasgow Med. Jrnl.* X. 92 Dr. Robertson showed a patient who suffers from Jacksonian Epilepsy. **1878** *Brit. Med. Jrnl.* 28 Dec. 959/1 (*heading*) Jacksonian convulsions. **1890** *Jrnl. Nerv. & Mental Dis.* XVII. 56 The Jacksonian spasm confined chiefly to the left hand and arm. **1933** W. R. BRAIN *Dis. Nervous Syst.* iii. 224 Jacksonian attacks may occur at long intervals, or with great frequency, even up to several hundreds a day—serial Jacksonian epilepsy. **1960** W. G. LENNOX *Epilepsy* I. vii. 212 Most authorities, including Penfield . . , use the term Jacksonian to cover all forms of local motor seizures. **1969** H. H. JASPER et al. *Basic Mechanisms Epilepsies* xix. 517/1 Particular interest was centered in Jacksonian seizures.

ˈjack-staff. *Naut.* [f. JACK *sb.*[3] + STAFF.]

1. A short staff, usually set upon the bowsprit or at the bow of a ship, on which the flag called the jack (JACK *sb.*[3]) is hoisted.

1692 *Capt. Smith's Seaman's Gram.* I. xiv. 65 Jack staff and Jack. **1794** *Rigging & Seamanship* I. 175 The Jack-staff is a short staff erected on the aftside of the bowsprit-cap, to expand the jack. **1880** PREBLE *Hist. of Flag* (ed. 2) v. 509 The stars and stripes for the stern, the boat-flag for the jackstaff, and two blue flags for the wheel-houses.

2. Used (? erron.) for JACOB'S STAFF (sense 2 a).

1891 J. WINSOR *Columbus* xi. 261 Whether the cross-staff or Jackstaff, a seaboard implement somewhat more convenient than the astrolabe, was known to Columbus is not very clear.

jackstay (ˈdʒækstei). *Naut.* [f. JACK *sb.*[1] 34 + STAY.] **a.** A rope, rod, or batten placed along a yard or gaff to bend the sail to. **b.** A rod or rope running up and down on a mast, on which the square-sail yard travels.

1840 R. H. DANA *Bef. Mast* Gloss., *Jack-stays*, ropes stretched taut along a yard, to bend the sail to. *c* **1860** H. STUART *Seaman's Catech.* 19 What is the use of jackstays? To bend the sails to. **1875** BEDFORD *Sailor's Pocket Bk.* VI. (ed. 2) 227 A jackstay should be fitted round the boat, underneath the rubbing strake for the rain awning to be laced down to.

ˈjack-stone, ˈjackstone. [A variant of CHECKSTONE; perh. associated with JACK *v.*[1]] A small round pebble or stone; esp., in *pl.*, a set of pebbles tossed up and caught in the game of dibs.

1814 BRACKENRIDGE *Jrnl. Voy. Missouri* in *Views Louisiana* 251 The women . . amuse themselves with a game something like jack-stones: five pebbles are tossed up in a small basket, with which they endeavor to catch them again as they fall. **1885** *Truth* 28 May 853/1 She had a passion for gathering jack-stones and forming mosaics with them in the garden.

ˈjack-ˈstraw, ˈjackstraw. [See JACK *sb.*[1], in various senses. *Jack Straw* was the name or nickname of one of the leaders in the Rising of the Commons in 1381.

c **1386** CHAUCER *Nun's Pr. T.* 574 Certes he Iakke Straw and his meynee Ne made neuere shoutes half so shille. **14..** *Pol. Poems* (Rolls) I. 230 Jak Strawe made yt stowte. **1568** GRAFTON *Chron.* II. 342 But Fabian, . . Polidore, and many Aucthours doe impute Iack Straw to be chiefe.]

1. A 'man of straw'; a man of no substance, worth, or consideration.

1596 NASHE *Saffron Walden* 126 Those worthlesse Whippets and Iack Strawes. *a* **1605** POLWART *Flyting w. Montgomerie* 155 Iacstro, bee better anes inginde, Or I sall flyte against my sell. **1692** WASHINGTON tr. *Milton's Def. Pop.* Pref., M.'s Wks. (1847) 342 Thou . . an inconsiderable fellow and a jack-straw, and who dependest upon the good-will of thy masters for a poor stipend.

attrib. **1754** RICHARDSON *Grandison* (1812) VII. 63 (D.), I command you on your obedience to accept of this; I will not be a jackstraw father.

2. One of a set of straws, or strips of ivory, bone, wood, or the like, used in a game in which they are thrown on the table in a heap, and have to be picked up singly without disturbing the rest of the heap. Also, in *pl.*, the game thus played.

1801 MAR. EDGEWORTH *Belinda* xix, 'Mr. Percival', said Belinda, 'condescending to look at a game of jack-straws!' **1810** —— *Early Lessons, Harry & Lucy* (1829) IV. 81 Playing a game at Jack-straws, or, as some call them *spillikins*. **1845** MRS. BROWNING in *Lett. Mr. & Mrs. Browning* (1899) I. 267, I . . have no sort of presence of mind (not so much as one would use to play at Jack straws).

3. As a type of worthlessness; cf. *straw*.

1828 C. CROKER *Fairy Leg.* (new ed.) 434 The only thing about this place that's worth one jack-straw. **1885** T. HEALY in *Leeds Mercury* 16 Dec. 8/1 The Protestants of the North do not care a jackstraw about England.

4. Local name for the Whitethroat, and for the Blackcap, from the construction of their nests.

1885 SWAINSON *Prov. Names Birds* 23 Whitethroat (*Sylvia cinerea*). . . It forms its nest of fine pieces of grass, bits of straw, feathers and wool, hence it is called . . Winnell straw, or Jack straw (Salop). *Ibid.* 24 Blackcap (*Sylvia atricapilla*) . . builds its nest of hay, roots, and hair, in a low bush or hedge, hence its names Jack straw (Somerset) [etc.].

5. The flower-spikes of the common plantain (*Plantago lanceolata*). *local.*

1863 MISS PLUES *Rambles in Search of Wild Fl.* 238 We used to call the spikes 'Jack straws', and many a good game I have had with them fighting my fifty against my neighbour's fifty.

jacksy (ˈdʒæksɪ). *slang.* Also **jacksie, jacksy-pardo, -pardy, jaxey, jaxie.** [f. JACK *sb.*[1] + -SY.] The posterior, backside, arse.

1896 FARMER & HENLEY *Slang* IV. 33/1 *Jacksy-pardy*, the posteriors. **1943** HUNT & PRINGLE *Service Slang* 40 *Jacksie*, service slang for 'rear', 'tail', or 'bottom'. **1959** K. WATERHOUSE *Billy Liar* v. 78 Why don't you tell the boring little man to stick the job up his jacksy? **1963** *Sunday Times* 15 Sept. 29/8 Tonbridge boys many years ago said 'a root on the Jaxie (or Jacksie)' for 'a kick in the pants'. **1966** B. NAUGHTON *Alfie* xxxvi. 206 She's sitting there on her jacksie, reading one of those colour things out of a newspaper. **1970** A. DRAPER *Swansong for Rare Bird* i. 9 The amount of love in our house you could stick up a dog's jacksie and he wouldn't even yelp.

Jack-ˈtar. [See JACK *sb.*[1] 3.] A familiar appellation for a common sailor.

1781 G. PARKER *View Society* I. 53 Our house in this place [Gosport] was chiefly supported by Jack-tars. **1822** LAMB *Elia* Ser. I. *Old Actors*, A downright concretion of a Wapping sailor—a jolly warm-hearted Jack Tar.

attrib. **1892** W. S. GILBERT *Foggerty's Fairy* 179 He had mixed it [brandy and water] on the Jack-tar principle of 'half-and-half'.

jack-up (ˈdʒækʌp). [f. JACK *v.*[1] 1.] In full, *jack-up rig*. A type of drilling rig for use in an offshore oil-field the legs of which are lowered to the sea bed from the operating platform.

1965 *Oil & Petroleum Year Bk.* 511 (Advt.), Santa Fe's offshore operations now include drilling services from fixed platforms, jack-ups and the semi-submersible Blue Water No. 2. **1967** *Ocean Industry* Dec. 11/1 Husky's New Jack-up Rig Designed for North Sea Husky Oils new $10-million jack-up *Gulftide* was christened October 6. **1970** *New Scientist* 29 Oct. 219/2 In the North Sea . . of the dozen or so mobile rigs usually operating the most common types are the semi-submersible and the jack-up. *Ibid.*, Jack-ups are . . very vulnerable when jacking up or down to move location. **1972** *Times* 23 Nov. 23/2 The discovery was made by the new jack-up rig Zapata Nordic which is under long term contract to Shell.

†**ˈjack-weight.** *Obs.* [JACK *sb.*[1] 7.] A weight forming part of the mechanism in an obsolete form of a roasting-jack.

1659 *Lond. Chanticleers* xii. in Hazl. *Dodsley* XII. 352 A woman's anger should be like jack-weights—quickly up and quickly down. *a* **1784** JOHNSON *Acc. Early Life*, I remembered a little dark room behind the kitchen, where the jack-weight fell through a hole in the floor, into which I once slipped my leg. **1814** *Last Act* I. iii, A short thick squat cutt of a mon, fit for the devil's jack-weight.

Jacky, jackey (ˈdʒækɪ). [f. JACK *sb.*[1] + -Y *dim.*]

1. a. A diminutive or pet form of Jack in various senses; *spec.* a sailor.

1835 HOOD *Dead Robbery* iii, The stiff'un . . Starts sudden up, like Jacky-in-a-box. **1893** *Funk's Stand. Dict.*, *Jacky*, a sailor. **1897** *Outing* (U.S.) XXX. 358/1 A warm clasp of the hand . . from the wealthiest owner as well as from the poorest 'Jackey' in port. **1909** *Daily Chron.* 1 Oct. 1/6 The place of honour . . was given to the British 'jackies', who were easily the most popular.

b. Also *Jacky-Jacky*. A white man's name for an Aboriginal. *Austral. slang.*

1928 'BRENT OF BIN BIN' *Up Country* ii. 35 He was . . going to . . outdo Jacky-Jacky as a swell. **1944** W. E. HARNEY *Taboo* (ed. 3) 87 Such was the view of the boss—not how good a cattle-man you were, but how cheap and good were your methods with the 'jackies'—the name given to the natives out there. **1969** *Sun-Herald* (Sydney) 13 July 52/1 'Jackie Jackie' is dead. There is a new and growing spirit in the Aboriginal community.

c. *Austral.* A kookaburra. Cf. JACK *sb.*[1] 30 c.

1934 *Bulletin* (Sydney) 11 July 21/2 Jacky left hurriedly and didn't return for his dinner. *Ibid.* 17 Oct. 20/4 Cockatoos are the latest-feeders among the bush birds, bar the jacky.

2. *slang.* Gin.

1799 *Morn. Herald* in *Spirit Pub. Jrnls.* (1800) III. 352 Got up at eight o'clock—had a drap of Jackey. **1825** BROCKETT, *Jackey*, English gin. **1832** W. STEPHENSON *Gateshead Local Poems* 37 Sometimes she would pawn her smock, To get a drop of Jacky.

3. *Comb.*, as **ˈjacky-bird, jacky-breezer**: see quots.; **Jacky** (or **Jackie**) **Howe** (see quot. 1965); *Austral.* and *N.Z. slang*; cf. *Jimmy Howe* s.v. JIMMY[2]; **jacky-screamer**: see quot.; **Jacky Winter** *Austral.*, the brown flycatcher, *Micrœca fascinans*.

1897 R. KEARTON *Nature & Camera* 277 A live one [starling] called a 'Jackey-bird' is secured to a 'flue' or 'play-stick', which can be moved up and down by means of a string which the fowler holds in his left hand. **1840** SPURDENS *Suppl. Voc. East A.*, *Jacky-breezer*, the dragon-fly. **1930** *Bulletin* (Sydney) 9 Apr. 19/2 It took nine bars of soap to wash his 'Jacky Howe' flannel. **1948** V. PALMER *Golconda* xi. 85 In his sleeveless Jackie Howe he swaggered around showing the punctures on his burly arm. **1965** *N.Z. Listener* 26 Feb. 15/2 *Jackie Howe*, the familiar navy or black woollen singlet worn by Australian and New Zealand shearers and bushmen. It is named after Jackie Howe, an Australian shearer who in 1892 established a world shearing record by shearing 321 Merinoes with hand shears in 8 hr 40 min. **1867** WOOD *Pop. Nat. Hist.*, *Birds* 40 When flying, the Swift screams continually, and is sometimes called the Jacky-screamer in consequence. **1898** MORRIS *Austral. Eng.* 218/2 Jacky Winter . . the vernacular name in New South Wales of the Brown Flycatcher, *Micrœca fascinans*, a common little bird about Sydney. **1911** LUCAS & LE SOUËF *Birds Austral.* 272 Jacky Winter is indeed seldom molested by even the thoughtless schoolboys. **1936** F. D. DAVISON *Children of Dark People* 5 Jacky winters . . flitted among the bushes. **1969** A. BELL *Common Austral. Birds* (ed. 2) 22 Post Boy, Jacky Winter, Spinks—half-a-dozen unofficial names suggest the friendly feeling towards this quiet, confidential, contented bird.

jackyard (ˈdʒækjɑːd). *Naut.* [See JACK *sb.*[1] 34 b.] A spar used in fore and aft rigged craft, chiefly yachts, to spread the foot of a large gaff-topsail out beyond the peak. Also *attrib.*

1873 'VANDERDECKEN' *Yachts & Yachting* 186, I have never seen a jack yard used with a jib-headed gaff-topsail. **1882** *Standard* 11 Aug. 6/6 Lorna and Chittywee last, the latter with a large jackyardtopsail set. **1896** *Daily News* 18 Aug. 3 All carried jackyards above their mainsails. **1931** *Rudder* Mar. 82/2 The topsail might be termed half a club topsail, having a jack yard or club at the luff only.

Hence **jackˈyarder**, a jackyard topsail.

1892 *Daily News* 8 Aug. 3/7 The yachts . . reached out the river under full lower canvas, jackyarders, and jib topsails. **1894** *Times* 24 July 10/2 It was astounding that Britannia with jackyarder aloft came scathless out of the squall.

Jacob (ˈdʒeɪkəb). [a. Heb. *yaʿăqōb*, in Gr. Ἰάκωβος, L. *Jacōbus*, whence also came Eng. *James*.] A personal name and surname; used also in derived and transferred senses, partly referring to JACOB'S LADDER.

†**1.** = JACOBUS, the gold coin. *Obs.*

1662 PEPYS *Diary* 23 Nov., A poulterer..hath left £800 per annum..and 40,000 Jacobs in gold.

†**2.** *slang.* **a.** A housebreaker carrying a ladder.

1712–53 *Thief-Catcher* 25 Rogues called Jacobs; these go with Ladders in the Dead of the Night, and get in at the Windows.

b. A ladder.

1708 *Mem. John Hall* 21 *Jacob*, a Ladder. **1796** GROSE *Dict. Vulgar T.*, *Jacob*, a ladder: perhaps from Jacob's dream. **1803** *Sporting Mag.* XII. 54 A Jacob is a ladder.

c. A simpleton.

1811 *Lex. Balatr.*, *Jacob*, a soft fellow, a fool. **1812** J. H. VAUX *Flash Dict.*, *Jacob*,..a simple half-witted person.

3. The possessive *Jacob's* occurs in the following: **Jacob's coat, membrane** (*Anat.*), the layer of rods and cones of the retina of the eye (named after Arthur Jacob, an Irish ophthalmic surgeon, died 1874); **Jacob's shell**, the scallop-shell *Pecten Jacobæus*, the emblem of St. James the Greater, and worn by pilgrims who had visited his shrine; **Jacob's stone**, a name applied to the coronation stone of the Scottish kings at Scone, now in Westminster Abbey, fabled to be the stone of Jacob's pillow (Gen. xxviii. 11); **Jacob's ulcer**, 'a term for *Lupus* or rodent ulcer of the eye' (from Arthur Jacob, above-named). Also JACOB'S LADDER, JACOB'S STAFF.

1842 E. WILSON *Anat. Vade M.* 453 *Jacob's Membrane ..is seen as a flocculent film when the eye is suspended in water. **1879** HARLAN *Eyesight* ii. 18 This external layer, called Jacob's membrane. **1756–7** tr. *Keysler's Trav.* (1760) III. 212 In the Adriatic are likewise found the species called *Jacob's shells, or Pectines. **1637** HEYWOOD *Royal King* I. i. Wks. 1874 VI. 7 If I survive Englands Inheritance, Or euer liue to sit on *Iacob's Stone.

4. [f. Genesis xxx. 40 A.V. 'Jacob did separate the lambs, and set the faces of the flocks toward the ring-straked'.] A variety of two- or four-horned piebald sheep, believed to have been introduced from Spain in the eighteenth century, and since used as an ornamental park breed.

1913 H. J. ELWES *Guide Primitive Breeds of Sheep* 30 'Spanish' or Piebald Sheep... These sheep are called by various names—'Syrian', 'Persian', 'Zulu', 'Barbary', 'Jacobs', and 'Spotted'. **1970** *Observer* (Colour Suppl.) 26 Apr. 35/2 The black and white Jacobs..are another rare breed of sheep. **1972** *Kent Life* July 28/2 Ten years ago the number of Jacob Sheep in Britain could be counted in dozens. Today the National Agricultural Centre calculates that there are more than 3,000 sheep in 132 flocks. **1973** *Times* 14 Apr. 14/5 Most horned breeds are hill breeds. Exceptions are Dorset..and Jacob.

Jacobæa (dʒækəˈbiːə). [mod.L. (R. Dodoens in *Trium Priorum de Historia Stirpium* (1553) 15), perh. f. G. popular name of the plant *S. Jacobs kraut*.] **1.** The ragwort, *Senecio jacobæa*, formerly called St. James's wort, or a related purple-flowered species from South Africa, *S. elegans*.

[**1578** H. LYTE tr. *Dodoens's Niewe Herball* 69 Jacobea. S. James' worte. Jacobea marina. S. James' worte of the Sea. .. The first kinde of S. James worte, hath long, browne, red, crested or straked stalkes. **1728** R. BRADLEY *Dictionarium Botanicum* I. s.v., Jacobæa, in English, Ragwort, is of different Sorts. *Ibid.*, James-wort, or Ragwort, is Jacobæa, which see.] **1789** W. AITON *Hortus Kewensis* III. 193 Elegant Groundsel, or Purple Jacobea. Nat[ive] of the Cape of Good Hope. **1884** W. MILLER *Dict. Eng. Names Plants* 69/2 Jacobæa, Purple. *Senecio elegans*. *c* **1903** E. T. COOK *Cent. Bk. Gardening* 27/1 The botanical name of the Jacobaea is Senecio elegans. **1972** W. T. STEARN in *A. W. Smith's Gardener's Dict. Plant Names* (rev. ed.) 371/3 Jacobea. *Senecio jacobaea*.

2. Jacobæa lily = *Jacobean lily* s.v. JACOBEAN *a.* 2 b.

1752 P. MILLER *Gardeners Dict.* (ed. 6) s.v. Amaryllis. The third Sort, which is commonly called Jacobæa-lily, is now become pretty common. **1760** [see JACOBEAN *a.* 2 b.]. **1789** W. AITON *Hortus Kewensis* I. 416 Jacobea Lily. Nat[ive] of South America. Cult[ivated] 1658, in the Oxford garden. **1864** L. H. GRINDON *Brit. & Garden Bot.* 644 Perhaps the commonest [Amaryllid] is the 'Jacobæa-lily', *Amaryllis formosissima*, easily told by its dark hue. **1962** *Jrnl. Roy. Hort. Soc.* LXXXVII. 284 (*title*) The Jacobaea Lily —*Sprekelia formosissima*.

Jacobean (dʒækəˈbiːən), *a.* (*sb.*) Also **-æan**. [f. late and mod.L. *Jacōbæus* (f. *Jacōbus*: see JACOB).]

A. *adj.* **1. a.** Of or pertaining to the reign or times of James I of England; *spec.* in *Arch.*, a term for the style which prevailed in England in the early part of the 17th cent., consisting of very late Gothic with a large admixture of Palladian features; also *transf.* in other arts, as Engraving, etc.

1844 F. A. PALEY *Church Restorers* 171, I have seen Jacobean doors added to ancient churches. **1867** F. G. LEE 1636 & 1866 in *Ess. Reunion* 128 Most of the Jacobean divines, apparently, could not look beyond the confines of the English nation. **1874** PARKER *Goth. Archit.* I. ii. 20 What are called Jacobean Gothic buildings of the time of James I. are often very good examples of the Perpendicular style. **1880** WARREN *Book-plates* iii. 22 The Jacobean style was most prevalent on our book-plates about 1730.

b. In the furniture trade, designating wood of the colour of dark oak, or the colour itself; also denoting furniture made in mock-Jacobean style.

1918 *Heal & Son Catal.* 28 Jacobean refectory table in dark oak. **1928** *Daily Mail* 31 July 1/2 It can be obtained in Light Brown or Jacobean coloured solid oak. **1930** *Daily Express* 8 Sept. 2 This fine Chest is..finished Jacobean colour. **1974** *Times* 8 Apr. 13/3 Philips can provide you with a colour television set in a Jacobean chest. *Ibid.* 18 May 5/5 (Advt.), Reproduction styling in Jacobean oak, walnut, white or ivory and gilt finishes.

2. a. Of or pertaining to the apostle St. James the Less or the Epistle written by him.

1883 *Pulpit Treas.* June 108 The Jacobean definition of religion must be recovered [Jas. i. 27]. **1898** W. S. LILLY in *19th Cent.* Sept. 516 A doctrine in which the Pauline and Jacobean pronouncements are unobtrusively blended.

b. ***Jacobean lily***, a bulbous plant (*Sprekelia formosissima*, N.O. *Amaryllidaceæ*), a native of Mexico, named after St. James.

1770–74 A. HUNTER *Georg. Ess.* (1803) III. 125, I have no where seen it more manifest than in the Jacobean Lily. **1846** J. BAXTER *Libr. Pract. Agric.* (ed. 4) I. 119 In the Jacobæan lily, Linnæus noticed a drop of transparent liquid protruding every morning from the stigma.

3. Of or pertaining to Henry James (1843–1916), American novelist and critic.

1906 M. BEERBOHM *Around Theatres* (1953) II. 442, I cannot imagine two minds..more divergent than the Shavian and the Jacobean. Mr. James must excuse my invention of this adjective. **1932** Q. D. LEAVIS *Fiction & Reading Public* III. iii. 264 Those interested will even find a telegram in Jacobean English in *The Great Good Place*. **1958** *Times* 6 Mar. 13/5 The masterly Jacobean answer to this insult is laid up in the Lubbock volumes of James's letters.

B. *sb.* A statesman or writer of the time of James I.

1885 *Athenæum* 21 Nov. 661/2 Milton's chance of leadership would have been slight if..the age needed a prosaic reaction from the extravagances of the Jacobeans.

Jacobethan (dʒækəˈbiːθən), *a.* [Blend of JACOBEAN *a.* and ELIZABETHAN *a.*] Of design: that displays a combination of the Elizabethan and Jacobean styles. Also *transf.* and *ellipt.* as *sb.*

1933 J. BETJEMAN *Ghastly Good Taste* iv. 53 The style in which Gothic predominates may be called, inaccurately enough, Elizabethan, and the style in which the classical predominates over the Gothic, equally inaccurately, may be called Jacobean. To save the time of those who do not wish to distinguish between these periods of architectural uncertainty, I will henceforward use the term 'Jacobethan'. *Ibid.* 54 To me the appeal of Jacobethan is indeed remote... Jacobethan architecture may be ugly, but it is never dull. **1945** *Archit. Rev.* Nov. 124/3 Westcombe Park Road.. shows an early tendency towards those ornamental features which long afterwards gave the names of 'sham Tudor' and 'Jacobethan' to a rather pathetic phase in domestic design. **1966** *Listener* 22 Dec. 928/1 The hacienda-Jacobethan garage with which the inhabitants of Sompting are so rightfully delighted. **1969** J. GROSS *Rise & Fall Man of Lett.* i. 13 Archaisms, hand-picked quotations, artful Jacobethan echoes. **1974** *Times Lit. Suppl.* 7 June 602/4 The specimen quoted is a pseudo-archaic piece of 'Jacobethan' prose, modelled on the style of the King James Bible.

Jacob Evertsen (ˈjækəb ˈeɪvɜːtsən). *S. Afr.* Also **Jacob Evertson, jacopever.** [Name of a 17th-c. Dutch sea-captain.] Any of several marine food fishes distinguished by reddish skin and large eyes, esp. *Sebastichthys capensis*.

1727 J. G. SCHEUCHZER tr. *Kæmpfer's Hist. Japan* I. I. xi. 136 *Ara* is what the Dutch in the Indies call *Jacobs Ewertz*. **1798** S. H. WILCOCKE tr. *Stavorinus's Voy. E. Indies* II. II. iii. 352 There is likewise, it is said, a large fish near the pier-head at Amboyna, to which the name of Jacob Evertsen has been given. **1801** J. BARROW *Acct. Trav. S. Afr.* I. i. 31 The *Scorpœna Capensis*, here called Jacob Evertson, is a firm, dry fish, but not very commonly used. **1853** L. PAPPE *Synopsis Edible Fishes Cape of Good Hope* 14 *Sebastes Capensis*... Called Jacob Evertsen, after a Dutch Captain, remarkable for a red face and large projecting eyes. **1927** *Ann. S. Afr. Mus.* XXI. 908 *Sebastichthys capensis* (Gmel.). Jacob Evertson; Jacopever... Red, shading to orange below; several silvery-white or pinkish irregular spots on sides. *Ibid.* 910 *Sebastosemus capensis* (G. and v. B.). Spiny Jacopever. **1973** *Farmer's Weekly* (S. Afr.) 18 Apr. 102 In the very early days of the Colony, the Dutch East India Company had as captain of one of its ships a certain Jacob Evert. When the local fishermen caught a fish with a red face, bulging eyes and thick lips they named it jacopever.

Jacobian (dʒəˈkəʊbɪən), *a.*[1] and *sb.* *Math.* [f. *Jacobi*, proper name + -AN.]

A. *adj.* Pertaining to or named after the mathematician K. G. J. Jacobi (1804–51), professor at Königsberg in Prussia; discovered, introduced, or investigated by Jacobi; as ***Jacobian determinant, Jacobian ellipsoid of equilibrium, Jacobian function, Jacobian system of differential equations.*** **B.** *sb.* (short for *Jacobian determinant.*) An important functional determinant, named after Jacobi.

The constituents of the determinant are the differential coefficients of any number of functions ($u, v, w, ..$) with respect to the same number of variables ($x, y, z, ..$); it vanishes when the functions are connected by any relation of the form F ($u, v, w, ..$) = 0. It is usually denoted by $\frac{d(u, v, w, ..)}{d(x, y, z, ..)}$.

1852 SYLVESTER in *Camb. & Dubl. Math. Jrnl.* VII. 71–2. **1881** *Encycl. Brit.* XIII. 31 Such functional determinants are now more usually known as *Jacobians*, a designation introduced by Professor Sylvester, who largely developed their properties, and gave numerous applications of them in higher algebra, as also in curves and surfaces.

Jacobian (dʒəˈkəʊbɪən), *a.*[2] *rare.* [f. L. *Jacōb-us* + -IAN: cf. JACOBEAN.] **a.** Of or pertaining to the patriarch Jacob. **b.** = JACOBEAN 1 a.

1865 F. H. LAING in Manning *Ess. Relig. & Lit.* I. 208 The race of Israel proper, the genuine Jacobian breed. **1883** *Wallenstein in the Drama* in *Westm. Rev.*, Dramatic work of the Elizabethan and Jacobian times.

Jacobic (dʒəˈkəʊbɪk), *a.* *rare.* [f. L. *Jacōb-us* + -IC.] = JACOBEAN 2 a.

1871 BOLTON tr. *Delitzsch's Comm. Ps.* I. 234 The Old Testament conception [of righteousness]..is (so to speak) more Jacobic than Pauline.

Jacobin (ˈdʒækəbɪn), *sb.*[1] and *a.*[1] Also 4 **-yn**, 6 **-yne**, 6–9 **-ine**. [a. F. *Jacobin* (orig. an adj., *frère jacobin*, 13th c. in Godef. *Compl.*), ad. med.L. *Jacōbīnus*, f. *Jacōbus*: see JACOB.]

A. *sb.* **1.** A friar of the order of St. Dominic; a Dominican. Also *attrib.* or as *adj.*

Originally applied to the French members of the order, from the church of *Saint Jacques* (S. Jacobus) which was given to them, and near which they built their first convent (Littré).

a **1325** *Trental St. Gregory* 12 in *Anglia* XIII. 303 To mynour ne to frere Austyn To caryne [*read* carme] ne to Jacobyn. *c* **1330** R. BRUNNE *Chron.* (1810) 258 Frere Hugh of Malmcestre was a Jacobyn. *c* **1400** *Rom. Rose* 7458 Thow woldest..have sworne..That he, that whilome was so gaie, And of the daunce Iolly Robin, Was tho become a Iacobin. *a* **1550** *Freiris Berwik* 29 in *Dunbar's Poems* 286 Twa of the Jacobyne freiris. **1681** DRYDEN *Sp. Friar* II. ii, This jacobin, whom I have sent to, is her confessor. **1758** JORTIN *Erasm.* I. 135 They behold the Jacobins fighting for their Thomas. **1818** A. RANKEN *Hist. France* VI. I. 233 It was a soldier in disguise and not a jacobin monk. **1833** ALISON *Europe* (1847) II. vi. 184 The club Breton..established its sittings in the library of the Convent of the Jacobins, in the Rue St. Honoré, which gave its name, since become imperishable, to the club.

2. A member of a French political club or society established in 1789, at Paris, in the old convent of the Jacobins (sense 1), to maintain and propagate the principles of extreme democracy and absolute equality.

1790 BURKE *Fr. Rev.* 158 They have, it seems, found out in the academies of the Palais Royal, and the Jacobins, that certain men had no right to the possessions which they held. **1794** J. GIFFORD *Louis XVI* 296 The new republican clubs, of which the Jacobins became the most noted. **1837** CARLYLE *Fr. Rev.* III. VII. iv, Gone are the Jacobins; into invisibility; in a storm of laughter and howls.

b. *transf.* A sympathizer with the principles of the Jacobins of the French Revolution; an extreme radical in politics or social organization. About 1800, a nickname for any political reformer.

1793 BURKE *Corr.* (1844) IV. 200 With the Jacobins I shall keep no terms. **1812** T. AMYOT *Life Windham* in *W.'s Speeches* (1812) I. 29 Parties, which..were branded with the reproachful titles of 'Alarmists' and 'Jacobins'. **1821–30** LD. COCKBURN *Mem.* 81 Jacobins..soon became the common nickname..given, not only to those who had admired the dawn of the French liberation, but to those who were known to have any taste for any internal reform. **1888** MRS. H. WARD *R. Elsmere* 542 'Why am I here?' the little Jacobin said to herself fiercely as she waltzed.

fig. **1822** BYRON *Juan* VI. xiii, Consign'd To those sad hungry jacobins the worms, Who on the very loftiest kings have din'd.

B. *adj.* **a.** Of or belonging to the Jacobins or Dominican friars. **b.** Pertaining to the Jacobins of the French Revolution; hence, ultra-democratic.

1795 WINDHAM *Sp.* 27 Mar., The cry of peace proceeded from the Jacobin party in this country. **1806** FESSENDEN *Democr.* I. 68 [They] swore to have the pure reality, Essence of Jacobin equality. **1837** CARLYLE *Fr. Rev.* III. VII. iv, Billaud from the Jacobin tribune says, 'The lion is not dead; he is only sleeping'. *a* **1886** J. KER *Lect. Hist. Preach.* viii. (1888) 139 They..gave name to the famous Jacobin party in the French Revolution, because their sittings were held in the Jacobine or Dominican monastery.

Hence ˈ**Jacobinly** *adv.*

1848 CRAIG, *Jacobinly*, after the manner of Jacobins.

†ˈ**Jacobin**, *sb.*[2] and *a.*[2] *Obs.* Also 6 **-yn**, 7 **-ine**. [= OF. *Jacobin*, ad. med.L. *Jacōbīnus*, f. *Jacōbus*: see JACOBITE[1].]

A. *sb.* A member of a Monophysite sect in Syria, Mesopotamia, etc.; = JACOBITE *sb.*[1] **B.** *adj.* Of or pertaining to this sect.

1517 TORKINGTON *Pilgr.* (1884) 24 Ther com to vs Jacobyns and other feynyd Cristen Peple. **1653** BAXTER *Chr. Concord* 40 Of all which (with the other smaller parties, as the Copties, the Jacobines, &c.) it is hard to say which are the more ignorant. **1727** A. HAMILTON *New Acc. E. Ind.* I. iv. 35 Its present Possessors are Nestorian and Jacobin Monks. **1768** HUME *Ess. & Treat.* (1809) II. 430 The Jacobins denied the immaculate conception.

jacobin (ˈdʒækəbɪn), *sb.*[3] Forms: 7–9 **Jacobine**, 8– **-in**. [a. F. *Jacobine*, fem. of *Jacobin* (JACOBIN *sb.*[1] 1); so called from their cowl or hood.]

1. An artificial breed of the domestic pigeon, with reversed feathers on the back of the neck, suggesting a cowl or hood.

1688 R. HOLME *Armoury* II. 244/1 The Jacobines..or Cop Headed Pigeons..have..Feathers..almost like a Monks-hood. **1766** PENNANT *Zool.* (1768) I. 218. **1851–61** MAYHEW

Lond. Labour II. 64 His pigeon-cote..is no longer stocked with carriers, dragoons, horsemen, jacobins.

2. A humming-bird of the genus *Heliothrix*, having neck-feathers resembling a hood.

1843 *Penny Cycl.* XXV. 272/2 13th Race. The Jacobins. Bill short, straight; tail ample or graduated.

†**3.** A kind of French soup (F. *soupe à la Jacobine*, Littré). *Obs.*

1706 Phillips, *Jacobine*, a kind of French Potage with Cheese.

†'**Jacobine**[1]. *Obs. rare.* [f. Jacob + -ine[1].] A descendant of Jacob; an Israelite.

a **1625** Boys *Wks.* (1630) 800 All true beleeuers are the sons of Jacob, and the Church of these true Jacobines and Israelites are the land of the Lord.

†'**Jacobine**[2]. *Obs. rare.* [f. L. *Jacōb-us* + -ine[1].] = Jacobus.

1612 Sir R. Boyle in *Lismore Papers* (1886) I. 6 Lent Mr leonard chichester..in gold, a Iacobyne xxijs.

Jacobinic (dʒækəʊ'bɪnɪk), *a.* [f. Jacobin *sb.*[1] + -ic.] Of, pertaining to, or characteristic of the French Jacobins; ultra-democratic.

1793 *Hist.* in *Ann. Reg.* 274/2 Every method..that Jacobinic invention could suggest, or Jacobinic energy employ. **1802** A. Hamilton *Wks.* (1886) VII. 325 To rise to power on the ladder of Jacobinic principles. **1881** *Athenæum* 20 Aug. 233/2 Throughout the Jacobinic period the notion was widely current that as the people was sovereign, any crowd that might gather in the street..was sovereign.

Jaco'binical, *a.* [f. as prec. + -al[1].] = prec.

1793 Mad. D'Arblay *Lett. to Dr. Burney* 19 Feb., Perhaps all may be Jacobinical malignity. **1821-30** Ld. Cockburn *Mem.* i. (1874) 59 Trousers or gaiters..he described as Jacobinical. **1871** Morley *Crit. Misc.* I. 62 Reason like Condorcet's, streaked with jacobinical fibre.

Hence **Jaco'binically** *adv.*

1821 *Blackw. Mag.* X. 752 Patting them on their heads (rather jacobinically greasy for our taste). **1887** *Daily News* 28 June 5/1 The present House of Commons has no 'mandate', as Lord Salisbury Jacobinically calls it, to coerce Ireland.

Jacobinism ('dʒækəbɪnɪz(ə)m). [f. Jacobin *sb.*[1] + -ism.] The doctrine or practice of the French Jacobins; ultra-democratic principles.

1793 Burke *Rem. Policy Allies* Wks. VII. 122 The true principles of legitimate government in opposition to jacobinism. **1798** Coleridge *Satyrane's Lett.* ii. in *Biog. Lit.* (1882) 262 The whole system of your drama is a moral and intellectual Jacobinism. **1801** M. Cutler in *Life*, etc. (1888) II. 44 Jefferson's speech,..a mixed medley of Jacobinism, Republicanism, and Federalism. **1821-30** Ld. Cockburn *Mem.* 82 Jacobinism was a term denoting everything alarming and hateful, and every political objector was a Jacobin.

b. A Jacobinical trait or notion.

1888 Mrs. H. Ward *R. Elsmere* 510 A solitary eccentric life..had developed in him a good many crude Jacobinisms.

Jacobinize ('dʒækəbɪnaɪz), *v.* [f. as prec. + -ize.] *trans.* To render Jacobin, to imbue with revolutionary or ultra-democratic ideas. Hence ˌ**Jacobini'zation**, the action of Jacobinizing.

1793 Burke *Rem. Policy Allies* Wks. VII. 183, I think no Country can be aggrandized whilst France is jacobinised. **1798** W. Taylor in *Monthly Review* XXVI. 548 Surely this author will not admit that a domestic Jacobinization was the only defence against foreign subjection. **1836** Arnold *Let.* in Stanley *Life* (1844) II. viii. 61 A most unprincipled system of agitation,—the Tories actually doing their best to Jacobinize the poor, in the hope of turning an outbreak against the Whig government to their own advantage.

Jacobite ('dʒækəbaɪt), *sb.*[1] and *a.*[1] [ad. med.L. *Jacōbīta*, f. *Jacōbus*: see Jacob and -ite.] A member of a Monophysite sect taking its name from Jacobus Baradæus, of Edessa, who revived the Eutychian heresy in the 6th cent. Also *attrib.*, or as *adj.*

c **1400** Maundev. (1839) x. 121 There ben othere that ben clept Surienes..thei maken here confessioun right as the Iacobytes don. *c* **1511** *1st Eng. Bk. Amer.* (Arb.) Introd. 30/2 Iacobyten named also of on ketter Iacob... These be kytte and chrystened with a byrnynge yren. **1640** Bp. Hall *Episc.* II. xviii. 194 The Jacobite Christians..have a Patriarch of their own. **1645** Pagitt *Heresiogr.* (1661) 21 The Iacobites ..mark their children with a hot Iron with the signe of the Cross, alluding to the words of Saint Iohn, He shall baptize you with the holy Ghost and with fire. **1867** E. B. Elliott *Mem. Ld. Haddo* xv. (1868) 252 Egyptian Christians of the Eutychian or Jacobite persuasion.

†'**Jacobite**, *sb.*[2] *Obs.* [ad. med.L *Jacōbīta*, f. *Jacōbus*: see -ite.] = Jacobin *sb.*[1] 1.

c **1550** Bale *K. Johan* (Camden) 18 Jacobytes, Mynors, Whyght Carmes, and Augustynis. **1614** Selden *Titles Hon.* 174 In a Monasterie of the Iacobits at Paris..the Epitaph, of Humbert is thus conceiued. **1818** A. Ranken *Hist. France* IV. IV. 317 They granted..to the Dominicans or Jacobites certain rights.

†'**Jacobite**, *sb.*[3] *Obs.* [f. Jacob + -ite.] A descendant of Jacob, an Israelite; also applied to the 17th c. Puritan refugees. (See N. & Q. 9th ser. III. 323.)

1658 *Sir F. Gorges' Amer. painted to the Life* I. xxiii. 46 Jaccobbites. *Ibid.* III. ii. 200 Hearing that prophane Esau had mustered up all the bands..to come against his brother Jacob, these wandering race of Jacobites deemed it now high time to implore the Lord.

Jacobite ('dʒækəbaɪt), *sb.*[4] and *a.*[2] [f. L. *Jacōbus* James (see Jacob) + -ite.]

A. *sb.* An adherent of James II of England after his abdication, or of his son the Pretender; a partisan or supporter of the Stuarts after the Revolution of 1688.

1689 E. Bohun (*title*) The Doctrine of Passive Obedience, and Non-Resistance, no way concerned in the Controversies now depending between the Williamites, and the Jacobites. **1690** Luttrell *Brief Rel.* Apr. (1857) II. 36 A private form of prayers is printed here, used amongst the Jacobites, for King James in his afflictions. **1736** Bolingbroke *Patriot.* (1749) 169 Every Jacobite at this time..is a rebel to the constitution under which he is born. **1814** Scott *Wav.* xxix, The sanguine Jacobites, during the eventful years 1745-6, kept up the spirits of their party by the rumour of descents from France.

B. *adj.* †**1.** Pertaining to James I of England; in *Jacobite piece* = Jacobus. *Obs.*

1611 in *Crt. & Times Jas. I* (1849) I. 147 There is speech of finding some little remedy, by raising gold,..the angel and sovereign to eleven shillings, and the Jacobite piece to two and twenty.

2. a. Of or pertaining to the adherents of James II and his family: see A.

1692 *Song* in *12th Rep. Hist. MSS. Comm.* App. v. 320 At Kingsland near the City There met a Jacobite crew. **1697** J. Dennis (*title*) A Plot and no Plot, or Jacobite Credulity; a Comedy. **1788** H. Walpole in *Walpoliana* xix. 10 Atterbury was nothing more or less than a Jacobite priest. **1892** *Guardian* 10 Feb. 184/2 On Monday, the Marquis de Ruvigny placed on the spikes of the gate at Westminster Abbey a wreath with the following inscription 'In memory of the martyrdom of Mary..from the Legitimist Jacobite League'.

b. Of glass or pottery: bearing inscriptions and emblems which indicate Jacobite sympathies.

1936 *Burlington Mag.* Oct. p. xxiii/1 There are also many specimens of engraved glasses including Jacobite specimens with their symbolic references. *Ibid.* 175/1 A series of Jacobite glasses. **1957** Mankowitz & Haggar *Conc. Encycl. Eng. Pott. & Porc.* 117/2 Jacobite pottery. **1960** H. Hayward *Antique Coll.* 150 *Jacobite glasses*, propaganda glasses bearing emblems and mottoes of a cryptic character associated with the Jacobite cause. **1970** *Canad. Antiques Collector* Oct. 29/2 The emblems to be found on these Jacobite glasses include a rose..and the Latin word 'Fiat'.

Hence '**Jacobitely** *adv.*

1706 Hearne *Collect.* 7 May (O.H.S.) I. 241 He was.. look'd upon as Jacobitely inclin'd.

Jacobite ('dʒækəbaɪt), *sb.*[5] [f. as Jacobite *sb.*[4]] An admirer of Henry James (1843-1916). Cf. Jacobean *a.* 3.

1909 Beerbohm *Around Theatres* (1953) II. 541 There, in those six last words, is quintessence of Mr. James; and the sound of them sent innumerable little vibrations through the heart of every good Jacobite in the audience. **1961** L. Auchincloss *Reflections of Jacobite* p. vii, I have called myself a Jacobite because so much of my lifetime's reading has been over the shoulder of Henry James.

Jaco'bitic, *a. rare*—0. = next.

1855 in Hyde Clarke *Eng. Dict.* Also in mod. Dicts.

Jacobitical (dʒækəʊ'bɪtɪkəl), *a.* [f. Jacobite *sb.*[4] + -ical.] Pertaining to the Jacobites or adherents of the Stuarts; holding Jacobite principles.

1779 H. Swinburne in *Crts. Europe close last cent.* (1841) I. 255, I drew my wife's attention to this undeserving object of all her Jacobitical adoration [the Young Pretender carried home drunk]. **1814** Scott *Wav.* v, A few songs, amatory and Jacobitical. **1855** Macaulay *Hist. Eng.* xxi. IV. 685 Of all the counties of England Lancashire was the most Jacobitical.

Hence **Jaco'bitically** *adv.*

1855 in Hyde Clarke *Eng. Dict.* Also in mod. Dicts.

'**Jacobitish**, *a. rare.* [f. as prec. + -ish.] = prec. adj. Hence '**Jacobitishly** *adv.*

1703 *Moderation a Virtue* 35 Her Jacobitish false Brethren. **1846** Macfarlane *Cab. Hist. Eng.* XV. 126 The ..Earl of Clarendon, with a 'Jacobitish secretary', was sent in his stead. **1883** Omond *Ld. Advoc. Scot.* II. 47 Lawyers in Scotland being Jacobitishly inclined.

Jacobitism ('dʒækəbaɪtɪz(ə)m). [See -ism.]

1. The principles of the Jacobites or adherents of James II and his family; adherence to or sympathy with the Stuart cause.

1700 Wagstaff (*title*) The Present State of Jacobitism in England. **1707** Hearne *Collect.* 23 Dec. (O.H.S.) II. 82 His charging ye University..wth Jacobitism. **1814** Scott *Wav.* v, Sir Everard's Jacobitism had been gradually decaying. **1839** Ld. Brougham *Statesm. Geo. III* (L.), Since Jacobitism and divine right were exploded.

2. The doctrines of the Jacobite sect of Christians.

1882-3 Schaff *Encycl. Relig. Knowl.* I. 17 Abulfaraj..son of a Jewish physician, who had embraced Jacobitism.

jacobsite ('dʒeɪkəbzaɪt). *Min.* [f. *Jakobsberg*, place-name + -ite.] An oxide of iron and manganese, belonging to the spinel group, found at Jakobsberg in Sweden.

1869 *Latest News* 17 Oct., Jacobsite is a new mineral described before the French Academy of Sciences by M. Damour. **1872** Dana *Min.* App. i. 8 Jacobsite..does not lose weight when ignited.

'**Jacob's** '**ladder.** Also (in sense 2) jacob-ladder. [In reference to Gen. xxviii. 12.]

1. A common garden plant, rarely found wild in Britain (*Polemonium cæruleum*) having corymbs of blue (or white) flowers; so called from the ladder-like appearance of its closely pinnate leaves.

Popularly or locally applied also to Solomon's Seal, and various other plants.

1733 Miller *Gard. Dict., Polemonium*..Greek Valerian, or Jacob's Ladder. **1794** Martyn *Rousseau's Bot.* xvi. 189 Greek Valerian or Jacob's Ladder. **1882** *Garden* 3 June 380/2 A white Jacob's-ladder..with purple throat,..a very delicate flower.

2. *Naut.* A rope ladder with wooden steps for ascending the rigging from the deck.

1840 Marryat *Poor Jack* xxviii, The youngster runs to the jacob-ladder of the main-rigging. *c* **1860** H. Stuart *Seaman's Catech.* 31 It is used..for Jacob's ladders. **1882** Nares *Seamanship* (ed. 6) 179 Let go the..jacob's ladder lanyards. **1898** *Daily News* 9 May 6/4 One [gun] cut the Jacob's ladder of the Vicksburg adrift.

3. In fig. allusions to Gen. xxviii. 12.

1831 Carlyle *Sart. Res.* II. v, Like mysterious priestesses, in whose hand was the invisible Jacob's-ladder, whereby man might mount into very heaven. **1890** L. C. D'Oyle *Notches* 88 It seemed to climb the very edge of the gray bank of clouds,..a veritable Jacob's Ladder, stretching away into the heavens,..meet for angels' feet to tread.

4. A frequent local name or nickname of a high and steep flight of steps.

c **1895** Proposals to do away with the bridge over the reservoir and railway at Oxford, known as Jacob's Ladder. **1900** *Daily News* 13 Mar. 5/1 A feature of the island [St. Helena] is 'Jacob's Ladder', a wooden staircase of 699 steps, with an average slope of 39 degrees to the vertical.

5. An elevator consisting of a series of bucket-shaped receptacles fixed upon an endless chain.

1845 G. Dodd *Brit. Manuf.* 5th Ser. ii. 31 The hops are raised to the boiler by a contrivance something like the buckets of a dredging-machine; it is called a 'Jacob's ladder'. **1853** *Househ. Words* VII. 491/1 The malt..being precipitated up a curious contrivance called a 'Jacob's ladder'. **1860** *Ure's Dict. Arts* (ed. 5) II. 589 It [*sc.* the bloom] is squeezed four times before it leaves the rolls and falls upon the Jacob's ladder. **1884** W. H. Greenwood *Steel & Iron* xvi. 303 The puddled ball..falling from the bottom shoot of the machine on to a Jacob's ladder or other elevator.

Jacob's membrane, etc.: see Jacob 3.

Jacobson ('dʒeɪkəbsən). The name of Ludwig Levin *Jacobson* (1783-1843), Danish anatomist and physician, used in the possessive or with *of*-adjunct to designate structures investigated by him, as **Jacobson's nerve**, the tympanic nerve, a branch of the glosso-pharyngeal (ninth cranial) nerve; **Jacobson's organ**, an organ which is only vestigial in adult man but is a well-developed olfactory organ in many vertebrates, notably snakes and lizards, occurring as (one of) a pair of sacs or tubes in communication with the mouth (or in some cases the nose).

1836-9 R. B. Todd *Cycl. Anat. & Physiol.* II. 495/2 The most important of these is a small branch which proceeds from the ganglion into the tympanum (*ramus tympanicus nervi glosso-pharyngei*; nerve of Jacobson). **1860** Gray *Anat.* (ed. 2) 524 The tympanic branch (Jacobson's nerve), arises from the petrous ganglion. **1871** T. H. Huxley *Man. Anat. Vertebrated Animals* ii. 72 In the latter case they are the canals of Stenson... Glandular diverticula of the mucous membrane, supplied with nervous filaments from both the olfactory and the fifth pair, may open into these canals. They are called..the 'organs of Jacobson'. **1888** Rolleston & Jackson *Anim. Life* 346 A portion of the nasal cavity becomes separated off from the nose proper. It is known as Jacobson's organ, and is supplied by the fifth nerve as well as by the olfactory. **1888** W. R. Gowers *Man. Dis. Nervous Syst.* II. 212 The gangliform enlargement also receives a twig from the nerve (small petrosal) which connects the otic ganglion, through the nerve of Jacobson, with the glosso-pharyngeal. **1896** Kirkaldy & Pollard tr. *Boas's Text Bk. Zool.* 333 In some Reptiles and most Mammals, there is a peculiar saccular or tubular paired organ, Jacobson's organ, in close connection with the olfactory apparatus. **1951** C. K. Weichert *Anat. Chordates* vi. 254 Although the function of Jacobson's organ is obscure, it is believed to aid in the recognition of food, since it is best developed in animals which hold food in their mouths. **1954** T. L. Peele *Neuroanat. Basis Clin. Neurol.* ix. 217/2 By way of the tympanic branch of the glossopharyngeal (Jacobson's nerve) sensory fibers are supplied to the medial surface of the ear drum, to the tympanic cavity, to the eustachian tube in part, and to mastoid cells. **1965** R. & D. Morris *Men & Snakes* viii. 195 Snakes, like lizards, possess a..Jacobsen's [*sic*] Organ. This is a scent-sensitive pair of pits lying in the roof of the mouth.

Hence †**Jacob'sonian** *a.* (*obs.*).

1878 A. Macalister *Introd. Syst. Zool. & Morphol. Vertebr. Animals* iii. 16 In connexion with this 5th pair [of nerves] there may be six separate ganglia:..5th, Cloquet's, on the Jacobsonian organ. **1893** Gunn & Hensman in H. Morris *Treat. Human Anat.* vii. 928 In the septal cartilage above the opening of Stenson's canal there is a small pouch which presents a minute opening below. This is the representative of the Jacobsonian organ. A strip of cartilage underneath this..is known as the Jacobsonian cartilage.

Jacob's staff. [In sense 1, from St. James (*Jacobus*), whose symbols in religious art are a pilgrim's staff and a scallop shell. In the other senses the name is app. more or less fanciful.]

†**1.** A pilgrim's staff. *Obs.*

Sometimes perhaps with a reference to Gen. xxxii. 10.

*a*1548 HALL *Chron., Hen. VIII*, 10 Like two pilgrems from sainct Iames,..with palmers hattes on their helmettes, wyth long Iacobs staves in their handes. 1590 SPENSER *F.Q.* I. vi. 35 In his hand a Iacobs staffe, to stay His weary limbs upon. 1656 BLOUNT *Glossogr., Jacobs Staff*, a Pilgrims staff, so called from those who..go on pilgrimage to the city of S[t] Jago, or S[t] James Compostella in Spain.

2. a. An instrument formerly used for taking the altitude of the sun; a cross-staff. **b.** An instrument for measuring distances and heights, consisting of a square rod about three feet in length with a cursor which slips on the staff. **c.** A straight rod shod with pointed iron, and having a socket-joint at the summit for supporting a surveyor's circumferentor instead of a tripod. (In mod. Dicts.)

1559 W. CUNNINGHAM *Cosmogr. Glasse* 106 The Astronomers staffe, also called Iacobes staffe. 1613 M. RIDLEY *Magn. Bodies* 105 Having a Iacobs-staffe at sea and a quadrant at land take the altitude of the Sunne. 1777 HOOLE *Comenius' Vis. World* (ed. 12) 129 A geometrician measureth the height of a tower, or the distance of places either with a quadrant or a Jacob's-staff. 1867 SMYTH *Sailor's Word-bk., Jacob's Staff*, or *Cross-staff*, a mathematical instrument to take altitudes, consisting of a brass circle, divided into four equal parts by two lines cutting each other in the centre; at each extremity of either line is fixed a sight perpendicularly over the lines..The cross is mounted on a staff or stand for use.

fig. *a*1613 OVERBURY *A Wife* (1638) 132 He..dares beleeve nothing above *primum mobile*, for 'tis out of the reach of his Jacobs staffe. *a*1734 NORTH *Exam.* I. ii. §16 Erecting a Jacob's Staff to take the Altitude of these wise Doings.

†**3.** A staff containing a concealed sword or dagger. *Obs.*

1596 THOMAS *Lat. Dict., Dolo*, a great sparre or staffe with a small head of iron and a sword within it: a Iacobs staffe. 1606 HOLLAND *Sueton.* xiii. 159 Found there were likewise twaine..with a staffe having a blade in it [*dolone*] (*margin* Some cal this a Iacobs-staffe) and a Hunters wood-knife waiting for him. 1656 in BLOUNT *Glossogr.*

4. A plant, the Great Mullein or Aaron's Rod.

1879 BRITTEN & HOLLAND *Plant-n.*, Jacob's Staff, *Verbascum Thapsus.*

Jacobus (dʒəˈkəʊbəs). Pl. **-uses**, (7 **-us**, 7–8 **-usses**, **-us's**). [a. L. *Jacōbus* James: see JACOB.] The current (but not official) name of an English gold coin, struck in the reign of James I.

Originally issued in 1603, under the name of the *Sovereign*, and current for 20*s*. In 1604 there was a second issue known as the *Unite*, which being 1/10 lighter, the value of the Sovereign rose to 22*s*. In 1612 the current value of the Unite was raised by statute to 22*s*., and the earlier piece rose to 24*s*.

1612 in *Crt. & Times Jas. I* (1849) I. 197 The prince having entreated him to provide him £1000, in so many Jacobus pieces. *a*1618 RALEIGH *Obs.* in *Rem.* (1661) 200 The English Iacobus goeth for three and twenty shillings in Merchandizing. 1678 MARVELL *Let. to Mayor of Hull* Wks. 1776 I. 346 The Jacobus's cost twenty three and eight-pence a piece. 1754 RICHARDSON *Grandison* (1781) II. xx. 216 In the second purse were 115 Jacobus's. 1855 MACAULAY *Hist. Eng.* xv. III. 585 His salary was..eight thousand Jacobuses, equivalent to ten thousand pounds sterling.

jacoby (ˈdʒækəʊbɪ). An anglicized form of F. *jacobée*, L. *Jacobæa* (*Senecio Jacobæa*, Ragwort), applied to the Purple Ragwort (*S. elegans*), also called *Purple Jacobæa*, from the Cape of Good Hope.

jacol, obs. form of JACKAL *sb.*

jacolatt, -let, obs. forms of CHOCOLATE.

jaconet (ˈdʒækənɪt). Forms: 8 jaconot, jackonet, 9 jacconot, -et (jacounet, -onite). [Corruption of Urdū *Jagannāthī*, from *Jagannāth* (Juggernaut) or *Jagannāthpūrī* in Cuttack, where orig. manufactured.] A cotton fabric originally imported from India, but now manufactured in England. The application of the name has undergone change; in the trade it now means 'A plain cotton cloth of medium thickness or weight, lighter than a shirting, and heavier than a mull'.

1769 *Publ. Advertiser* 14 Nov. 3/3, 260 Dozen Book and Jaconot Muslins and clear Lawns. 1808 C. SIMEON in W. Carus *Life* x. (1847) 250, I was buying the shawl and jaconet for her. 1851 *Illustr. Catal. Gt. Exhib.* 482 India jaconets. Cambric of various qualities. 1891 *Times* 8 Oct. 4/1 Moderate enquiry exists for mulls, jacconets, and dhooties.

†**jaˈcounce, jaˈgounce.** *Obs.* Also 5 iaconct. [a. OF. *jacunce* (*Roland*, 11th c.), *jagonce* (*Rom. Rose*):—pop. L. type *iacunti-us* for **hiacynti-us*, in cl. L. *hyacinthius* (sc. *lapis*), adj. from *hyacinthus*. With *jaconct* cf. *jacinct*, *jacynct* under JACINTH.] The jacinth or hyacinth (precious stone).

?*a*1366 CHAUCER *Rom. Rose* 1117 Rubyes there were, saphires, iagounces [Fr. *Rubis i ot, saphirs, iagonces*], And emeraudes, more than two ounces. ?*a*1400 LYDG. *Chorle & Byrde* (Roxb.) 12 Ther is a stone whiche callid is a Iagounce ..Whiche of fyn gold peyseth an ence. ?*c*1400 —— *Æsop's Fab.* i. 54 Hid in the dunghill he founde a Iaconct [*editor* Jaconet, *v.r.* iacynct] stone. *Ibid.* 99 The best Iaconct in Ethiope is founde. *a*1529 SKELTON *Sp. Parrot* 365 More precious then the ryche iacounce.

Jacquard (dʒəˈkɑːd, ˈdʒækəd). The surname of Joseph Marie Jacquard of Lyons, who, at the beginning of the 19th c., invented an apparatus to facilitate the weaving of figured fabrics in the loom, superseding the ruder heddle or heald appliance previously used. Hence many attrib. uses and combinations, as ***Jacquard apparatus, attachment, engine, machine, mechanism,*** applied to this apparatus; also **Jacquard loom**, a loom fitted with this apparatus, for the weaving of figured fabrics; ***Jacquard fabric, muslin, stripes,*** etc., those woven or produced on the Jacquard loom; ***Jacquard-figured*** adj., ***-weaving***, etc. **b.** Also *ellipt.* as *sb.* = Jacquard apparatus, etc.

1841 *Encycl. Brit.* (ed. 7) XXI. 828 The draw-loom has of late years been to a considerable extent superseded by the Jacquard engine. 1842 S. C. HALL *Ireland* II. 330 *note*, The Jacquard machine, introduced a few years ago by some of the leading manufacturers. 1843 *Penny Cycl.* XXVII. 178/2 The Jacquard apparatus was first intended for and applied to silk-weaving. 1851 *Illustr. Catal. Gt. Exhib.* 482 A new arrangement of the Jacquard loom. *Ibid.* 506 Specimens of Jacquard figured silk fabrics. *Ibid.* 1279 Shawls with muslin Jacquard stripes. *Ibid.*, Muslin from the loom, white jacquard, needle work spots. 1875 KNIGHT *Dict. Mech.*, *Loom-card*, a pierced pattern-card for Jacquard weaving. 1890 *Cent. Dict.* s.v. *Loom*, The Jacquard attachment is a device for forming sheds or openings for the passage of the shuttle between the warp-threads. 1897 *Sketch* 26 May 181/1 The application of a Jacquard to looms, lace and hosiery machines. *Ibid.* 181/2 Deteriorations are impossible with the Jacquard.

Jacqueminot (ʒakmino). [Name of the Vicomte J. F. *Jacqueminot* (1787–1865), French soldier.] In full ***Général Jacqueminot***. A red-flowered, hybrid perpetual variety of rose; also, formerly used for a colour resembling that of the flower.

1857 T. RIVERS *Rose Amateur's Guide* (ed. 6) 98 We must not forget to rank under our crimson flag General Jacqueminot, which..is so glorious in its colour. 1881 C. C. HARRISON *Woman's Handiwork* I. 12 Contrast the works of art of quondam florists..with the sumptuous modern assembling of Maréchal Neil [*sic*] or glowing Jacqueminot roses. 1893 W. ROBINSON *Eng. Flower Garden* (ed. 3) 644/2 General Jacqueminot and many other H.Ps. do not usually bloom after the month of August. 1895 *Montgomery Ward Catal.* 6/3 French crepon... Colors: Beige,..heliotrope, magenta or jacqueminot. 1908 *Daily Chron.* 10 Mar. 3/2 English roses have..arrived.., and include the beautiful Jacqueminot. 1920 E. WHARTON *Age of Innocence* I. ix. 69 He tried to analyse the trick, to find a clue to it in..the fact that only two Jacqueminot roses (of which nobody ever bought less than a dozen) had been placed in the slender vase. 1955 C. C. HURST in G. S. Thomas *Old Shrub Roses* ix. 87 In 1852 'Jules Margottin' and the famous 'Général Jacqueminot' arrived... 'The General', with its brilliant scarlet-crimson flowers and damask fragrance was a fertile tetraploid.

‖**Jacquerie** (ʒakri). Also anglicized, 6–9 **-ery**. [F., in OF. *jaquerie*, peasants or villeins collectively, spec. as in Eng.; f. *Jacques* James, old term for a French villein or peasant: cf. JACK *sb.*[1]] *Hist.* The revolt of the villeins or peasants of northern France against the nobles in 1357–8; hence, Any rising of the peasantry.

1523 LD. BERNERS *Froiss.* I. clxxxii. 217 They called hym kyng Iaques Goodman, and so therby they were called companyons of the Iaquery. 1548 THOMAS in Strype *Eccl. Mem.* (1721) II. App. 65 The Jaquerie that sprang in Beauvoisine and other countries of France, in the year 1358. 1791 BURKE *App. Whigs* Wks. VI. 219 That furious insurrection of the common people in France called the Jacquerie. 1882 *Spectator* 8 Apr. 457 There is too much reason to believe that in many districts of Ireland the anti-landlord agitation..has changed an agrarian movement into a true jacquerie. 1892 *Review of Rev.* 15 Jan. 17/1 In Russia ..villages scattered here and there in the midst of great steppes do not afford material even for successful jacquery.

jacques, obs. form of JAKES.

jactance (ˈdʒæktəns). *rare.* [a. F. *jactance* (13th c. in Godef. *Compl.*), ad. L. *jactāntia*, f. *jactāntem*, pr. pple. of *jactāre*: see JACTATION and -ANCE.] Boasting; vainglorious speaking.

1491 CAXTON *Vitas Patr.* (1495) 4 Vayn glory or iactaunce. 1502 *Ord. Crysten Men* II. v. (W. de W. 1506) 95 It is arrogance, iactans, & ypocrysye. 1526 *Pilgr. Perf.* (W. de W. 1531) 92 Iactance is, whan a man sercheth for the prayse or laude of other, bostyng hym selfe of ony euyll dede. 1828 [J. R. BEST] *Italy* 163 Let there be no jactance in an epitaph. 1885 *Edin. Rev.* Apr. 550 She even asks, with a little unnecessary jactance, 'Don't you imagine [etc.]'.

jactancy (ˈdʒæktənsɪ). [ad. L. *jactāntia*: see prec. and -ANCY.] Boastfulness, vainglory; boasting.

1623 COCKERAM, *Iactancie*, boasting. 1841 *Fraser's Mag.* XXIII. 223, I speak not this in any jactancy or self-laudation. 1884 SIR S. ST. JOHN *Hayti* ii. 51 Rigaud had,.. with his usual jactancy, marched on Port-au-Prince to expel the English.

ˈ**jactant**, *a. rare.* [ad. L. *jactānt-em*, pr. pple. of *jactāre*: see next.] Boasting, boastful.

1839 *Tait's Mag.* VI. 353 The jactant self-importance assumed by the cock-pigeon of the dove-cote.

jactation (dʒækˈteɪʃən). [ad. L. *jactātiōn-em*, n. of action from *jactāre* to throw, toss about, discuss, boast of, *refl.* to talk boastfully, make an ostentatious display, freq. of *jacĕre* to throw; cf. F. *jactation* (Cotgr.).]

1. A tossing or swinging of the body to and fro; *spec.* in *Path.* = JACTITATION 2.

1680–90 TEMPLE *Ess., Health* Wks. 1731 I. 282 Jactations ..help or occasion Sleep, as we find by the common Use and Experience of rocking froward Children in Cradles, or dandling them in their Nurses Arms. 1751 BP. LAVINGTON *Enthus. Methodists* (1754) II. iii. 96 Various Tumults of Mind, and Jactations of Body. 1887 *Syd. Soc. Lex.*, *Jactation.* Same as *Jactitation.*

2. Boasting, bragging, ostentatious display.

1576 WOOLTON *Chr. Manual* (Parker Soc.) 91 If we use them with excess, filthy pleasure, vain jactation..we abuse Gods gifts. 1604 T. WRIGHT *Passions* I. vi. 26, I could adde ..Envy, Emulation..Iactation or Boasting. 1825 *Lond. Mag.* I. 379 There is no surer sign of vulgarity than jactation of gentility. 1886 SAINTSBURY in *Macm. Mag.* July 171 The tedious burlesque, the more tedious jactation which disfigure his work.

†**jacˈtator.** *Obs. rare*[−0]. [a. L. *jactātor*, agent-n. from *jactāre*: see prec.]

1656 BLOUNT *Glossogr.*, *Iactator*, a cracker or boaster. 1721 BAILEY, *Jactator*, a Boaster or Bragger.

ˈ**jactitate**, *v. rare.* [f. ppl. stem of L. *jactitāre*: see next.] *intr.* To toss restlessly about: see JACTITATION 2. Hence ˈ**jactitating** *ppl. a.*

1822–34 *Good's Study Med.* (ed. 4) IV. 150 The stertor, the insensibility, and the jactitating struggle of the limbs, form a picture of agony.

jactitation (dʒæktɪˈteɪʃən). [ad. med.L. *jactitātiōn-em* (in Canon Law) a false declaration tending to some one's detriment, n. of action f. L. *jactitāre*, in sense 'to throw out publicly, to utter', freq. of *jactāre*: see JACTATION. The senses follow or are influenced by L. *jactātio*. So in F. (Littré).]

1. Public or open declaration, esp. of a boastful sort; ostentatious affirmation; boasting, bragging.

1632 *High Commission Cases* (Camden) 304 This jactitation or gloriacion of adultery is as much as a confession of the fact. 1655 FULLER *Ch. Hist.* II. v. §46 The Arch-bishop sent his Mandate to the Abbot and Convent of Glassenbury, henceforward to desist from any jactitation of Dunstan's Corpse. 1766 J. IBBETSON *Plea Subscr.* 39 *Art.* (T. Suppl.), Shall the jactitation of his friends be instead of a public revocation on his own part? [1842 *Blackw. Mag.* LI. 684 What Johnson would call his perpetual 'jactitation' about the infinite wealth of the Indus.]

b. *Law.* ***jactitation of marriage***: see quots.

1685 H. CONSETT *Pract. Spir. Crts.* 252 The Defendant being cited in a Cause of Jactitation or Boasting of Marriage. 1773 *Gentl. Mag.* XLIII. 101 The long contested cause of Jactitation, brought by the Hon. Thomas Harvey against his lady, after a cohabitation of eighteen years. 1883 *Wharton's Law Lex.* (ed. 7) 432/1 The suit of jactitation of marriage.. which is not known to modern practice, may still be brought in the Divorce Court by the express terms of 20 and 21 Vict. c. 85, s. 6, when a person falsely boasts that he or she is married to another whereby a reputation of their marriage may ensue. The party injured sues for the purpose of having perpetual silence enjoined upon the unjustifiable boaster. 1892 *Daily News* 12 July 2/4 The case of 'Thompson v. Rourke' ..is a suit marked 'Jactitation', and is of a very novel character, it being thirty years since such a case was before the Court.

2. *Path.* A restless tossing of the body: a symptom of distress in severe diseases. **b.** A twitching or convulsive movement of a limb or muscle.

1665 HARVEY *Advice agst. Plague* 3 A perpetual restlesness, with anguishing jactitations, or throwing ones self from one part of the bed to the other. 1809 *Med. Jrnl.* XXI. 115 Voice querulous with constant moaning; jactitation; pulse..feeble. 1844 B. G. BABINGTON tr. *Hecker's Epidemics Mid. Ages* (Syd. Soc.) 318 An insufferable itching came on over the whole body, accompanied by distressing jactitation. 1861 T. J. GRAHAM *Pract. Med.* 426 There may be jactitation of the extremities.

†**3.** Discussion; bandying to and fro. *Obs.*

1761 STERNE *Tr. Shandy* IV. xxix, After much dispassionate enquiry and jactitation of the arguments on all sides,..it has been adjudged for the negative.

†ˈ**jacture.** *Obs.* [ad. L. *jactūra* loss, detriment, f. ppl. stem of *jacĕre* to throw, throw away; see -URE. So OF. *jacture* (1306 in Godef.).] Loss, injury, detriment.

1515 HEN. VIII *Let. to Ponynges* 22 July, Which iacture wronge, and preiudice we cannot ne woll suffre to passe. 1563–87 FOXE *A. & M.* (1596) 904/1 To repaire the piteous iacture and decay, that the church and sea Apostolick hath so long suffered. 1657 TOMLINSON *Renou's Disp.* 666 Oyl will endure a whole dayes coction without sensible jacture.

jacu (dʒəˈkuː). [Pg., f. Tupi *jacú*.] A large, turkey-like, South American game bird of the genus *Penelope*, esp. *P. marail* or *P. jacquacu*; cf. GUAN.

1824 H. E. LLOYD tr. *Spix & Martius's Trav. Brazil* II. IV. ii. 227 Several species of wood-hens, particularly the pretty Jacú (*Penelope Marail, leucoptera*). 1876 *Encycl. Brit.* IV. 227/2 The gallinaceous *jacús*, the *hoccus*, and different kinds of pigeons, haunt the woods [of Brazil]. 1933 P. FLEMING *Brazilian Adv.* I. xvi. 137 There were a lot of the birds called *jacú*, a kind of stringy, dowdy pheasant with

subfusc plumage. **1964** A. L. THOMSON *New Dict. Birds* 175/2 There are 12 species of guans, some of them with the names 'jacu' and 'camata'.

† **'jaculable**, *a. Obs. rare*—⁰. [ad. L. *jaculābil-is*, f. *jaculā-ri*: see next.]

1656 BLOUNT *Glossogr.*, *Jaculable*, fit to be thrown, that may be cast or darted. **1721** in BAILEY.

jaculate ('dʒækjʊleɪt), *v. rare.* [f. L. *jaculāt-*, ppl. stem of *jaculārī* to dart, hurl, f. *jaculum* a dart, f. *jacĕre* to throw.] **a.** *trans.* To dart, hurl. **b.** *intr.* (for *refl.*) To dart forward.

1623 COCKERAM, *Iaculate*, to dart. **1634** SIR T. HERBERT *Trav.* 20 They know accurately how to jaculate their Darts of blacke Ebony. **1860** EMERSON *Cond. Life* i. (1861) 27 Do you suppose, he can be estimated by his weight in pounds, ..this reaching, radiating, jaculating fellow?

jaculation (dʒækjʊ'leɪʃən). *rare.* [ad. L. *jaculātiōn-em*, n. of action from *jaculārī*: see prec. Cf. F. *jaculation* (16th c.).] The action of darting, hurling, or throwing; a hurl, a throw.

1608 J. KING *Serm.* 5 Nov. 20 It was well and strongly strung with 36 barrels of gunpowder..for the more uiolent iaculation, uibration, and speed of the arrows. **1667** MILTON *P.L.* VI. 665 Hills..encounterd Hills Hurl'd to and fro with jaculation dire. **1837** *Blackw. Mag.* XLII. 543/1 As far as one could cast a lance, at one or three successive jaculations.

jaculator ('dʒækjʊleɪtə(r)). [a. L. *jaculātor*, agent-n. from *jaculārī* to JACULATE: cf. F. *jaculateur* (16th c. in Godef.).]

1. One who throws or hurls; a thrower of the dart or javelin. *rare.*

1796 *Mod. Gulliver* Pref. 4 The serpent would..have spent its venom on the breast of the..malicious jaculator. **1804** T. TAYLOR *Plato's Wks.* V. 136 This same mean person, like a skilful jaculator, will hurl a sentence worthy of attention.

2. A fish (*Toxotes jaculator*) which has the power of shooting a drop of water at insects that come near it; = ARCHER 5. Also *jaculator fish*.

1763 SCHLOSSER in *Phil. Trans.* LIV. 89 Governor Hommel gives the following account of the Jaculator or shooting fish. **1773** *Gentl. Mag.* XLIII. 220. **1897** *Alden's Juvenile Gem* (N.Y.) Mar. 79/1 The jaculator fish,..in the lakes of Java, uses its mouth as a squirtgun and is a good marksman.

jacula'torial, *a. rare.* [f. as next + -AL¹.] Having the faculty of darting.

1856-8 W. CLARK *Van der Hoeven's Zool.* II. 456 *Sagittilingues*,..Tongue jaculatorial.

jaculatory ('dʒækjʊlətərɪ), *a. rare.* [ad. late L. *jaculātōri-us*, f. ppl. stem of *jaculārī* to dart, throw, JACULATE: cf. F. *jaculatoire* (16–17th c. in Godef. *Compl.*).] Pertaining to throwing or darting; that is thrown or darted.

1616 BULLOKAR, *Iaculatory*, that which is suddenly cast from one, like a dart. **1795-8** T. MAURICE *Hindostan* (1819) III. v. iv. 242 The foe..having formed no conception of the jaculatory strength of those engines,..retired in confusion.

† **b.** *jaculatory prayer*, a short prayer 'darted up' to God (L. *preces jaculatoriæ* (Jerome); F. *oraison jaculatoire*). *Obs.* Cf. EJACULATORY 3.

1624 BP. MOUNTAGU *Immed. Addr.* 34. **1626** T. H[AWKINS] *Caussin's Holy Crt.* 333 Learne a little to talke with God by iaculatory prayers. **1649** JER. TAYLOR *Gt. Exemp.* II. Disc. xi. 150 We may be very much helped by iaculatory prayers and short breathings.

† **'jacule**. *Obs. rare.* [ad. L. *jaculus* a darting serpent, f. *jacĕre* to throw. Cf. OF. *jacule* a dart.] A serpent that darts on its prey.

[**1398** TREVISA *Barth. De. P.R.* XVIII. ix. (Bodl. MS.), þe serpent þᵗ hat *Iaculus* fleeþ as a darte..and ȝif he meteþ wiþ any beeste he þroweþ hym silfe þere vpon and sleeþ it.] **1572** BOSSEWELL *Armorie* II. 62 b, N. beareth Azure, a Iacule d'Argent. [**1774** GOLDSM. *Nat. Hist.* IV. 106 The manner of progression in the swiftest serpent we know, which is the jaculus, is by instantly coiling itself upon its tail and darting from thence to its full extent.]

jacu'liferous, *a.* [f. L. *jacul-um* dart + *-fer*-bearing + -OUS.] (See quot.)

1855 MAYNE *Expos. Lex.*, *Jaculiferus*, having prickles, or spine-like darts, as those seen on the flanks of the *Diodon*: jaculiferous. **1887** in *Syd. Soc. Lex.*

jacutinga (dʒækjuː'tɪŋgə). Also 9 jaco-. [f. Pg. *jacutinga* (formerly *jacú-tinga*), Brazilian name of a kind of guan (*jacu*) (probably the black-fronted piping guan, *Pipile jacutinga*) whose plumage the ore is said to resemble.] A name given to various kinds of soft gold-bearing iron ore found in Brazil (see quot. 1963).

1846 *Trans. R. Geol. Soc. Cornwall* VI. 227 In both mines [*sc.* Itabira and Santa Anna, in Brazil] the directions and inclinations of the gold-bearing beds conform to the configuration of the neighbouring mountain, as well as to the structure of the contiguous rock;—a circumstance of common occurrence in jacotinga formations. **1851** *Edin. New Philos. Jrnl.* L. 61 These [strata] are followed by the *Jacotinga*, the principal auriferous rock, which is for the most part composed of specular iron-ore and oxide [*printed* oixide] of manganese. **1869** R. F. BURTON *Explor. Highlands Brazil* I. 301 The mysterious Jacutinga. The name is evidently derived from the well-known Penelope called Jácu-tinga (P. Leucoptera) from the white spots upon its crested head and blue-black wings. This substance of iron-black, with metallic lustre, sparkles in the sun with silvery mica... The constituents are micaceous iron schist and friable quartz mixed with specular iron, oxide of manganese, and fragments of talc. **1908** J. M. MACLAREN *Gold* 649 With the itabirite are associated thin beds..of sandy micaceous and limonitic iron-ore containing yellowish talc and earthy oxides of manganese. These beds are generally friable, and appear to be a decomposition product of itabirite. The rock is locally known as jacutinga. **1934** BAIN & READ *Ores & Industries S. Amer.* vi. 112 In places this [*sc.* itabirite] contains narrow veins of native gold, or of gold-bearing quartz, giving rise to what are known as jacutinga ores, which are peculiar to Minas Geraes. **1963** *Prof. Papers U.S. Geol. Survey* No. 341-C. 104/2 The term 'jacutinga' is now used indiscriminately for soft high-grade hematite, soft itabirite, or both, depending entirely upon the locality within the Quadrilátero Ferrífero. In short, it has only a local, not a general meaning and should not be used in scientific description without precise definition.

Jacuzzi (dʒə'kuːzɪ). orig. and chiefly *U.S.* Also jacuzzi. The proprietary name of a kind of bath or bathing-pool incorporating underwater jets of warm water, and used for both therapeutic and leisure purposes. Cf. *whirlpool bath* s.v. WHIRLPOOL².

1966 *New Yorker* 19 Feb. 107/1 Now I will go take my Jacuzzi bath!.. You know what it is, a Jacuzzi?.. The brochure that comes with it describes it as a hydromassage. **1973** *Los Angeles Times* 30 Sept. (Home Mag.) 18/2 You'll hear this kind of pool called a 'Jacuzzi', because the Jacuzzi firm pioneered in this application of the hydro-jet. **1976** *National Observer* (U.S.) 10 July 8/5 Just a few extras, including a 74-by-54-foot swimming pool, a gymnasium, sauna, Jacuzzi pool, tennis and handball courts. **1976** *Honolulu Star Bull.* 21 Dec. F-5/7 (Advt.), Hawaii Kai: luxury 1 bdrm, oceanview, pool jacuzzis & saunas. **1978** *Official Gaz.* (U.S. Patent Office) 13 June TM88/1 Jacuzzi Bros Inc., Little Rock, Ark... *Jacuzzi*... For Hydro-therapy products... Therapeutic whirlpool baths and parts thereof. **1978** J. KRANTZ *Scruples* xii. 329 The large, plant-bordered Jacuzzi in one corner of the two-story living room. **1979** *Tucson Mag.* Apr. 58/2 It offers the sauna and Jacuzzi facilities common to most. **1981** *Times Lit. Suppl.* 14 Aug. 923/1 The spread of jacuzzis in the United States has been facilitated by [the] recognition that they too are tax-deductible if medically prescribed for the relief of back pain. **1984** *Sunday Tel.* (Colour Suppl.) 22 Jan. 7/1 You'll still hear 'anyone for tennis?', but you're as likely to hear 'anyone for a jacuzzi?'

jad (dʒæd), *sb. local.* [Origin unknown: cf. JUD.] In the Bath-stone quarries: 'A long deep holing or cutting made for the purpose of detaching large blocks of stone from their natural beds' (Gresley *Gloss. Coal Mining*, 1883). Hence **jad** *v. trans.*, to form a jad in; **'jadder**, a stone-cutter (Halliw. 1847–78); **'jadding** *vbl. sb.*, also *attrib.*

1871 MORGANS *Mining Tools* 148 The 'jadding pick'.. serves for cutting in long and deep holings, juds, or 'jads', for the purpose of detaching large blocks of stone from their natural beds. *Ibid.* 153 When the face of any heading from which the stone is to be worked away has been properly jadded under the roof, the side saw-cuts are proceeded with.

jad, obs. variant of JADE *sb.*¹ and ².

‖**jadam** ('dʒadam). [Malay.] A type of silver or brass niello ware from the Malay Peninsula and Sumatra: used esp. for decorating belt-buckles.

1907 F. SWETTENHAM *Brit. Malaya* vii. 138 The most original and artistic work of all is called *chûtam* or *jâdam*, and it was made originally in the Province of Ligor. **1908** L. WRAY in A. Wright *20th Cent. Impressions Brit. Malaya* 244/1 The art of enamelling is also known to the Malays. The ware is called *Jadam*, which is equivalent to niello in England. **1910** C. W. HARRISON *Illustr. Guide Federated Malay States* II. 166 *Jadam* is the fashion in Rembau where the women wear large belt-buckles of it called *pinding*. but it is also made in boxes of all shapes. It may be of silver or of brass filled with enamel. **1953** C. A. GIBSON-HILL *Malay Arts & Crafts* §Silverwork, A form of silverware called *Jadam*, in which the hollows of the pattern were filled in with black enamel to give a smooth surface, used to be made in the western Malay states, principally in Negri Sembilan. The art is said to have come from Sumatra... In Malaya *jadam* work was used mostly for the production of decorated waist buckles.

jade (dʒeɪd), *sb.*¹ Also *Sc.* 8 jad, 9 jaud. [Of unknown origin; often assumed to be a doublet of YAUD (Icel. *jalda* mare), but app. without reason.]

1. A contemptuous name for a horse; a horse of inferior breed, e.g. a cart- or draught-horse as opposed to a riding horse; a roadster, a hack; a sorry, ill-conditioned, wearied, or worn-out horse; a vicious, worthless, ill-tempered horse; rarely applied to a donkey.

c **1386** CHAUCER *Nun's Pr. Prol.* 46 Be blithe though thou ryde vp-on a Iade, What thogh thyn hors be bothe foule and lene. **1530** PALSGR. 233/2 Iade a dull horse, *galier*. **1576** GASCOIGNE *Steele Gl.* (Arb.) 79 When horsecorsers beguile no friends with Iades. **1589** *Pappe w. Hatchet* (1844) 35 If like a restie Iade thou wilt take the bitt in thy mouth, and then runne ouer hedge and ditch, thou shalt be broken. **1600** J. PORY tr. *Leo's Africa* II. 309 You are much deceived..that thinke mine asse to be dead: for the hungrie iade knowing his masters necessity hath wrought this sleight. **1605** VERSTEGAN *Dec. Intell.* vii. (1628) 205 Not fit for Gentlemens horses, but for Carters iades. **1666** CHAS. II in Julia Cartwright *Henrietta of Orleans* (1894) 237, I shall have much ado to mounte my selfe with so much as jades for this summer's hunting. *a* **1680** BUTLER *Rem.* (1759) II. 495 The swiftest Race-horse will not perform a long Journey so well as a sturdy dull Jade. **1709** POPE *Ess. Crit.* 604 False steps but help them to renew the race, As, after stumbling, Jades will mend their pace. **1816** SCOTT *Antiq.* i, The expected vehicle, pressing forward with all the despatch to which the broken-winded jades that drew it could possibly be urged. **1819** L. HUNT *Indicator* No. 11 (1822) I. 82 He palmed upon the owners a sorry jade of an ass.

b. Sometimes used without depreciatory sense, playfully, or in generalized sense: = Horse.

1553 BALE *Vocacyon* in *Harl. Misc.* (Malb.) I. 362 The Kearnes, the Galloglasses, and the other brechelesse souldiers, with horses and their horse gromes, sum time iij waitinge vpon one jade. **1584** R. SCOT *Discov. Witchcr.* XVI. viii. (1886) 408 You shall not heare a butcher or a horsse-courser cheapen a bullocke or a jade. **1602** MARSTON *Antonio's Rev.* III. i. Wks. 1856 I. 104 The black jades of swart night trot foggy rings Bout heavens browe. **1653** H. MORE *Antid. Ath.* III. ix. (1712) 118 Cantius his Horse ..(which was a lusty-bodied Jade). *a* **1825** FORBY *Voc. E. Anglia*, *Jade*, a horse. We do not always use it in a contemptuous sense, as it is in general use... A clown will somtimes call a fine hunter 'a brave jade'. Cart horses are very commonly called so, though they be by no means despicable. Nay, even fine teams of Suffolk punches.

c. In figurative applications.

a **1577** GASCOIGNE *Weedes* ii. *Compl. Green Knt.*, And bad Repentance holds the reines, to rule the brainsicke iade. **1583** GOLDING *Calvin on Deut.* iii. 17 They play the ouer-pampered Iades which fall to kicking against their maisters. **1599** SHAKS. *Much Ado* I. i. 145 You alwaies end with a Iades tricke. **1657** H. CROWCH *Welsh Trav.* 8 Fortune often plaies the Jade. **1768** GOLDSM. *Good-n. Man* I. i, That same Philosophy is a good horse in the stable, but an errant jade on a journey.

2. A term of reprobation applied to a woman. Also used playfully, like *hussy* or *minx*.

1560 *Nice Wanton* in Hazl. *Dodsley* II. 179 Such a jade she is, and so curst a quean, She would out-scold the devil's dame I ween. **1584** R. W[ARDE] *Three Ladies Lond.* I. *Ibid.* VI. 257 When I could not thrive by all other trades, I became a squire to wait upon jades. **1590** SPENSER *F.Q.* II. xi. 31 The Squyre..Snatcht first the one, and then the other Iade [the hags Impotence and Impatience]. **1668** PEPYS *Diary* 14 Jan., [Mʳˢ] Pierce says she [Miss Davis] is a most homely jade as ever she saw. **1711** ADDISON *Spect.* No. 130 ¶1 You see now and then some handsome young Jades among them [the Gipsies]. **1712** *Ibid.* No. 343 ¶7 Being marry'd to an expensive Jade of a Wife. **1780** S. CRISP *Let.* in *Mad. D'Arblay's Diary* 27 Apr., Sarah Marlborough,.. though much of the jade, had undoubtedly very strong parts. **1786** BURNS *Ordination* iv, How..Zipporah, the scauldin jad, Was like a bluidy tiger. **1790** —— *Tam o' Shanter* 182 A souple jade she was, and strang. **1812** CRABBE *Tales* xiii. 246 A lying, prying, jilting, thievish jade. **1824** SCOTT *Redgauntlet* Let. x, Are ye at it again wi' the siller, ye jaud? **1849** SAXE *Poems, Times* 73 A laughing jade, of not ungentle mold. **1883** *Times* 1 Jan. 4/2 A procession of scamps and jades, who marched through Paris wearing in mockery vestments robbed from the churches.

b. Applied to Fortune, Nature, etc. personified.

1594 CAREW *Huarte's Exam. Wits* xiii. (1596) 218 These crie out vpon fortune, and call her blind buzzard, and iade. **1791** WOLCOTT (P. Pindar) *Loyal Odes* VI. ii, But error, what a meretricious jade. **1807** W. IRVING *Salmag.* (1824) 123 Confound the Jade,..what a pity nature had not been of the masculine instead of the feminine gender. **1812** H. & J. SMITH *Horace in Lond.* 119 When Fortune, fickle jade's unkind. **1871** C. GIBBON *Lack of Gold* xiii, Poverty is a stern jade to fight.

c. Rarely applied to a man: usually in some figure drawn from sense 1.

1596 SHAKS. *Tam. Shr.* I. ii. 249 *Gre.* What, this Gentleman will out-talke vs all. *Luc.* Sir giue him head, I know hee'l proue a Iade. **1608** SYLVESTER *Du Bartas* II. iv. IV. *Decay* 893 A iolly Prater, but a Iade to doe. **1616** S. WARD *Coale from Altar* (1627) 49.

3. *attrib.* and *Comb.*

1599 MARSTON *Sco. Villanie* II. Proem. 193 Though roguie thoughts do force some iade-like moile. **1752** FIELDING *Amelia* I. v, Had not Fortune played one of her jade tricks.

Hence **'jadeship**, the personality of a jade; **'jadery**, behaviour characteristic of a jade.

1612 *Two Noble K.* v. iv. [vi.], The hot horse..seekes all foule meanes Of boystrous and rough Iadrie to dis-seate His Lord. **1621** J. TAYLOR (Water P.) *Taylors Motto* Wks. (1630) II. 44/1 Marry gep With a horse night-cap doth your Iadeship skip? Although you kicke..and spurn, Yet all your Colts-tricks will not serue your turn.

jade (dʒeɪd), *sb.*² Also 8 jadde, 9 jad. [= F. *le jade* (1667 in Hatz.-Darm.), for *l'ejade* (Voiture, 1633) = It. *iada* (Florio, 1598), ad. Sp. *ijada* in *piedra de ijada* or *yjada* (Monardes, 1569), lit. 'colic stone', f. *ijada*, *yjada*, 'the small ribs, the collike, the flanke' (Minsheu); cf. the synonym NEPHRITE, f. Gr. νεφροί kidneys, reins.

The transformation of F. *l'ejade* fem. into *le jade* masc. was an error made when the word was as yet unfamiliar: see *Athenæum*, 20 Oct. 1900.]

1. A name given to two distinct minerals which from their hardness have been used for implements and ornaments. **a.** *nephrite*, a silicate of lime and magnesia, a hard, translucent stone, in colour light green, bluish, or whitish; **b.** *jadeite*, a silicate of sodium and aluminium, closely resembling nephrite in appearance. Sometimes also applied to SAUSSURITE. *oceanic*, *oriental jade* (see quot. 1881).

[**1569** MONARDES *Cosas de las Indias*, (*heading*) De la Piedra de la Yjada. *Ibid.*, Tiene esta piedra por propriedad oculta,..de preservar que no caygan en el dolor de la Yjada.] **1595** RALEIGH *Discov. Guiana* 24 A kinde of greene stones,

which the Spaniards call *Piedras Hijadas*, and we vse for spleene stones. **1598** FLORIO, *Iada*, a kinde of precious stone like an emerauld. **1633** VOITURE *Wks.*, *Let. to Mdle. Paulet* (1665) 47 Ainsi pour ce coup, l'Ejade a eu pour vous vn effet que vous n'attendiez pas d'elle.] **1657** J. D[AVIES] tr. *Voiture's Lett.* xxiv. 37 So that for this time, *L'Ejade* hath had for you an effect which you expected not from it. *Ibid.* xlii. 79, I perceive there must be found out for me some more substantial remedies than the Ejade [*mispr.* Ejacle]. **1727–41** CHAMBERS *Cycl.*, *Jade*, a greenish stone, bordering on olive colour, much esteemed for its hardness. .. This stone applied to the reins is said to be a preservative from the nephritic colic. **1751** SIR J. HILL *Materia Med.* (J.), The jade is a species of the jasper, and of extreme hardness ..it takes a very elegant polish. It is used by the Turks for handles of sabres. **1777** G. FORSTER *Voy. round World* I. 161 A piece of green nephritic stone, or jadde. **1823** RUTTER *Fonthill* 51 A sceptre of jad, brought from China. **1863** LYELL *Antiq. Man* 20 Here, also..hatchets and wedges of jade have been observed. **1868** DANA *Min.* (ed. 5) 293 Jadeite is one of the kinds of pale stones used in China for making ornaments, and passing under the general name of jade or nephrite. **1875** *Ure's Dict. Arts* III. 6 A third mineral, originally described by H. B. de Saussure as a jade, was termed Saussurite by T. de Saussure: this was the *jade tenace* of Haüy and the early French mineralogists. **1881** F. W. RUDLER in *Encycl. Brit.* XIII. 540/1 Under the name of 'oceanic jade', M. Damour has described a fibrous variety found in New Caledonia and in the Marquesas Islands.. differing from ordinary nephrite in the proportion of lime and magnesia which it contains. *Ibid.* 540/2 If this oceanic jade be recognized as a distinct variety, the ordinary nephrite may be distinguished as 'oriental jade'.

c. A colour resembling that of jade; jade-green. Also *attrib.*

1921 H. WALPOLE *Young Enchanted* IV. iv. 391 The faint jade of the fading light. **1926** M. LEINSTER *Dew on Leaf* iii. 42 The jade rabbit (moon) nibbles the clouds. **1928** *Manch. Guardian Weekly* 31 Aug. 175/3 A faint breeze blowing in from a North Sea of misty jade. **1972** *Guardian* 5 Dec. 11/2 Toga dress..in..midnight blue, jade, red, sapphire.

2. a. *attrib.* (as a material of ornaments and implements, especially of prehistoric times).

1865 LUBBOCK *Preh. Times* (1869) 155 A square chamber, in which were eleven beautiful jade celts. **1875** *Ure's Dict. Arts* III. 7 The so-called jade pebbles of Iona are nothing more than serpentinous marble. **1880** OUIDA *Moths* II. 92 She sent a malachite cabinet and some grand jade vases. **1881** *Nature* 20 Oct. 599/1 This is the first find of jade implements in graves in Russia. **1881** F. W. RUDLER in *Encycl. Brit.* XIII. 540/2 Jade celts have been found by Dr. Schliemann among the relics of the oldest of the cities at Hissarlik.

b. *Comb.*, as ***jade-carver***, ***-quarry***; ***jade-coloured***, ***-green*** adjs. Also JADE-STONE.

1868 G. M. HOPKINS *Jrnl.* 19 July (1959) 178 The Aar sallow and jade-coloured. **1875** *Ure's Dict. Arts* III. 7 The jade-quarries on the Kara-kash River have been visited and described by Dr. Cayley. **1880** *Daily Tel.* 18 Sept., The rarest handicraft of the jeweller, the jade-carver. **1892** R. KIPLING in *Pall Mall G.* 24 Mar. 3/2 The jade-green rivers with the oily swirls in them that run through the bush. **1926** A. HUXLEY *Essays New & Old* 17 The brown or jade-coloured water.

jade (dʒeɪd), *v.* [f. JADE *sb.*[1]]

1. *trans.* To make a jade of (a horse); to exhaust or wear out by driving or working hard; to fatigue, weary, tire.

1606 SHAKS. *Ant. & Cl.* III. i. 34 The nere-yet beaten Horse of Parthia, We haue iaded out o' th' Field. **1615** G. SANDYS *Trav.* 64 Horses, which are beautifull to the eye,.. but quickly iaded if held to a good round trot. **1798** MILLER in Nicolas *Nelson's Disp.* (1846) VII. p. clvii, My people were so extremely jaded, that, as soon as they had hove our sheet anchor up they dropped under the capstan-bars, and were asleep in a moment. **1837** J. E. MURRAY *Summer in Pyrenees* I. 306 Our horses were jaded—perfectly 'done up'. **1857** RUSKIN *Arrows of Chace* (1880) I. 43 Contemplation of works of art without understanding them jades the faculties and enslaves the intelligence.

2. *intr.* To become tired or worn out; to grow dull or languid; to flag.

1620 SANDERSON *Serm.* (1637) 261 As an horse that is good at hand, but naught at length, so is the Hypocrite; free and fiery for a spurt, but he jadeth and tyreth in a journey. **1737** BRACKEN *Farriery Impr.* (1757) II. 27 He [a horse] will be apt to jade and tire in any Exercise. **1794** BURNS in Shairp *Burns* vii. (1879) 159 When I feel my Muse beginning to jade, I retire to the solitary fireside of my study. **1856** CAPERN *Poems* (ed. 2) 154 We sit and pass the chilly night, The interest never jading.

†**3.** *trans.* To befool; to jape. *Obs.*

1601 SHAKS. *Twel. N.* II. v. 178, I do not now foole my selfe, to let imagination iade mee. **1613** —— *Hen. VIII*, III. ii. 280 If we liue thus tamely To be thus Iaded by a peece of Scarlet, Farewell Nobilitie. *a* **1626** FLETCHER *Woman's Prize* I. iii, On my wedding-night, am I thus jaded? **1679** *Poor Robin's Intelligence* in *Sporting Mag.* 61 Whosoever takes a horse upon his word is sure to be jaded.

†**4.** *intr.* To play the jade: see JADE *sb.*[1] 2. *Obs.*

1641, **1766** [see JADING below].

Hence ˈ**jading** *vbl. sb.* and *ppl. a.*

1641 *Pol. Ballads* (Wilkins) I. 8 You grow poor, As any common whore That long hath been without her jading. **1670** G. H. *Hist. Cardinals* I. I. 11 They..feel his goad at their sides, which keeps them both from tripping and jading. **1766** FORDYCE *Serm. Yng. Wom.* (1767) I. ii. 65 Lament too late the jading course thou hast run. **1845** DARWIN *Voy. Nat.* xxi. (1873) 501 The jading feeling of constant hurry.

jaded (ˈdʒeɪdɪd), *ppl. a.* [f. JADE *v.* + -ED[1].]

1. Worn out or exhausted; fatigued; fagged out.

1693 SIR C. SEDLEY *Prol. to H. Higden's Wary Widdow*, Their Jaded Muse is distanc'd in the Course. **1798** BLOOMFIELD *Farmer's Boy, Summer* 106 Unwittingly his jaded eyelids close. **1809** BYRON *Eng. Bards & Sc. Reviewers* 145 Each spurs his jaded Pegasus apace. **1865** LECKY *Ration.* (1878) II. 319 Charming away the weariness of the jaded mind.

2. Dull or sated by continual use or indulgence.

1631 BRATHWAIT *Eng. Gentlew.* (1641) 305 Former times were not so jaded to fashions as to esteeme nothing formall, but what was phantasticall. **1744** ARMSTRONG *Preserv. Health* II. 158 To spur beyond Its wiser will the jaded appetite. **1828** W. SEWELL *Oxf. Prize Ess.* 39 Nature was tortured in every way to stimulate the jaded palate.

†**3.** ? Regarded with contempt. *Obs.*

1593 SHAKS. *2 Hen. VI*, IV. i. 52 The honourable blood of Lancaster Must not be shed by such a iaded Groome.

Hence ˈ**jadedly** *adv.*, in a jaded or fatigued manner; ˈ**jadedness**, the state of being worn out.

1885 HOWELLS *Silas Lapham* (1891) II. 132 Lapham listened jadedly, and answered far from the point. **1896** A. J. WILSON in *Westm. Gaz.* 27 Apr. 8/1 Days..saddened by incessant toil, performed in weakness of body and jadedness of brain. **1899** MISS HARRADEN *Fowler* vi. 49 The worldliness fled from her soul, the jadedness from her spirit.

jadeite (ˈdʒeɪdaɪt). *Min.* [Named 1863; f. JADE *sb.*[2] + -ITE.] One of the two minerals commonly included under the name of JADE (q.v.), of which it is the hardest and most highly prized variety. Hence **jadeitic** (dʒeɪˈdɪtɪk) *a.*, approximating to jadeite in composition.

1865 LUBBOCK *Preh. Times* iv. (1878) 82. **1868** [see JADE *sb.*[2] 1]. **1875** *Ure's Dict. Arts* III. 6 Jadeite is a mineral closely resembling true nephrite in external characters,..it is essentially a silicate of alumina and soda. *Ibid.* 7 In prehistoric times, jade and jadeite were used for amulets and ornaments. **1965** *Prof. Papers U.S. Geol. Survey* No. 525. 25 (*heading*) Composition of jadeitic pyroxene from the California metagraywackes. **1971** I. G. GASS et al. *Understanding Earth* viii. 116/1 A notable feature of the overall mineralogy of meteorites is the absence of phases, such as..jadeitic pyroxenes, indicative of high pressure.

jade-stone. Also jad-stone. [f. JADE *sb.*[2] + STONE.] = JADE *sb.*[2]

1775 in ASH. **1812** I. MILNER in *Life* xxiv. (1842) 496 Many thanks for securing me the Turkey stone, or Jad stone. **1848** *Assoc. Archit. Soc. Rep.* (1850–1) I. 165 A rude Celt, formed of Jade stone. **1895** *Pall Mall Mag.* Feb. 277 A piece of beautifully carved, pale-green jadestone.

attrib. **1851** *Illustr. Catal. Gt. Exhib.* 1424 Nephrite or jade-stone cup. **1861** SWINHOE *N. China Camp.* 307 Enamelled jars, and an infinity of jadestone curiosities.

†**jadge, jedge.** *Sc. Obs.* [Cf. F. *jauge* = ONF. *gauge* GAUGE.] A Scotch form of GAUGE. So †ˈ**jadgerie**, the action of gauging; the office of a gauger.

1617 *Sc. Acts Jas. VI*, 28 June (Jam.) The same Measure and Firlot being found agreeable with the said Jedge. **1621** *Ibid.* (1814) 669 (Jam.) Confermes the gift made..to the saidis provest, etc. of Edinburgh of the jadgerie of salmon, herring, and quhyit fische packit..within the kingdome of Scotland.

jadish (ˈdʒeɪdɪʃ), *a.* [f. JADE *sb.*[1] + -ISH[1].] Of the nature of, or having the characteristics of, a jade; of or pertaining to a jade. **a.** Of a horse.

1589 R. HARVEY *Pl. Perc.* 18 Such Iadish trickes make a sound horse to be suspected. **1633** T. ADAMS *Exp. 2 Peter* ii. 21 A horse of the best mettle, when he falls into the hands of a currier, and is made a pack-horse, becomes dull and jadish. **1737** BRACKEN *Farriery Impr.* (1757) II. 91 He [a horse] will be apt to tire, and grow jadish, before he has travelled many Miles. **1768–74** TUCKER *Lt. Nat.* (1834) II. 677 A less fault for the horse to be a little too mettlesome than jadish. *a* **1843** SOUTHEY *Comm.-pl. Bk.* IV. 412 The Eclipses [horses] jadish, speedy and uncertain.

b. Of a person, *esp.* a woman.

1573 G. HARVEY *Letter-bk.* (Camden) 141 There is not a Besse..That hath such iadysh qualityes. *c* **1600** DAY *Begg. Bednall Gr.* I. ii. (1882) 20 Sirra Horse-Courser, I'll course you one day for you[r] Jadish tricks. **1658** DEKKER, etc. *Witch Edmont.* IV. i, This jadish Witch, mother Sawyer. **1727** BAILEY vol. II, *Jadish*,..also lewd, as a Jade or Strumpet.

Hence ˈ**jadishly** *adv.*; ˈ**jadishness**.

1593 *Tell-Troth's N.Y. Gift* 41 He begins to be jadishly tired. **1594** CAREW *Huarte's Exam. Wits* iii. (1596) 30 Amongst horses are found many iadishnesses, and good qualities. ? *a* **1640** *Lady Alimony* I. iii, My legs have been taught to pace iambics, and jadishly to interfere upon any condition. **1659** TORRIANO, *Cavallinità*, coltishness, jadishness, jadish condition.

jadoo (ˈdʒɑːduː). Also jadu. [Hind. *jādū* enchantment.] Magic, conjuring. *Comb.* ˈ**jadoo-,wallah** [WALLAH], a Hindu conjurer.

1886 KIPLING *Plain Tales from Hills* (1888) 126 If there was any *jadoo* afoot. **1890** *Q. Rev.* July 244 The Indian conjurers, or Jadoo-walla. **1924** J. A. TYSON *Barge of Haunted Lives* iv. 93 These took me before a jaboowallah [*sic*], who..had performed some of his tricks before me at Rajiid.

‖**j'adoube** (ʒadub). *Chess.* [Fr., = I adjust.] An expression used when a player wishes to touch a chessman without making a move.

1808 J. H. SARRATT *Treat. Game of Chess* I. 3 If a player *touch* one of his adversary's pieces, without saying '*J'adoube*', he may be compelled to take it. **1847** H. STAUNTON *Chess-Player's Handbk.* 36 A Piece or Pawn touched must be played, unless at the moment of touching it the player say '*J'adoube*', or words to that effect. **1967** *Chess* 11 Dec. 99/2 You may adjust a piece if you previously warn your adversary you are going to do so by saying 'j'adoube'.

jady (ˈdʒeɪdɪ), *a.* [f. JADE *sb.*[1] + -Y[1].] Of a horse: Like a jade; tricky, jadish.

1873 *Daily Tel.* 26 May 8/3 Somerset..has become so jady that at exercise he bolts, and is up to other shifty tricks to avoid work. **1891** H. S. CONSTABLE *Horses, Sport & War* 31 Some of the 'jadiest' mares bred the stoutest horses.

Jaeger[1] (ˈjeɪgə(r)). The proprietary name of an all-wool clothing material manufactured originally by Dr. [Gustav] Jaeger's Sanitary Woollen System Co. Ltd.; also, a garment made of this material. Also *attrib.* and *fig.*

1887 G. B. SHAW *Let.* 8 Feb. (1965) 163 Seeing me arrive, clad in an irresistible new Jaeger samite. **1893** K. SANBORN *Truthful Woman in S. California* 121, I really suffered during a drive, although encased in the heaviest of Jaeger flannels. **1905** CHESTERTON *Heretics* x. 140 Those who talk to us with interfering eloquence about Jaeger and the pores of the skin. **1925** *Trade Marks Jrnl.* 7 Oct. 2200 Jaeger... Cloths and stuffs of wool, worsted or hair. The Jaeger Company, Limited,..London,..merchants. **1932** THORNE SMITH *Bishop's Jaegers* (1934) 2 If they could not be called things of beauty, these brave long jaegers of the Bishop's, they did..represent the highest expression of the drawers-maker's craftsmanship. **1936** R. LEHMANN *Weather in Streets* I. i. 12 A grubby jaeger shroud lay over the first suburbs. **1942** N. BALCHIN *Darkness falls from Air* vii. 127 The inspector was wearing a roll-necked Jaegar [*sic*] pull-over. **1973** A. MORICE *Death & Dutiful Daughter* v. 53 Betsy's old Jaeger dressing-gown.

Jaeger[2] (ˈjeɪgə(r)). The name of E. R. *Jaeger* von Jastthal (1818–1884), Austrian ophthalmologist, used in the possessive (or occas. *attrib.*) to designate a series of short passages printed in type-faces of different sizes and used for testing visual acuity at reading distances.

1869 *Trans. Amer. Ophthalm. Soc., 4th and 5th Ann. Meeting* 68 In Jaeger's Schrift-Scalen the numbering is altogether arbitrary and irregular. **1884** G. HARTRIDGE *Refraction Eye* iii. 45 Snellen and Jaeger's are the types most commonly in use. **1897** NORRIS & OLIVER *Syst. Dis. Eye* II 28 Jaeger's Schriftscalen consisted of a very complete set of reading tests printed in several languages. **1907** J. H. PARSONS *Dis. Eye* ix. 161 Jaeger's near test types..are simply the ordinary printers' founts of type, from the smallest upwards (nonpareil, minion, etc.). **1962** H. C. WESTON *Sight, Light & Work* (ed. 2) viii. 224 Another series of test types has been selected by the British Faculty of Ophthalmologists and either this or the Jaeger series is readily obtainable.

Jaffa (ˈdʒæfə). The modern name of Joppa, a port in Israel, used *attrib.* or *absol.* to designate an oval, thick-skinned variety of orange first cultivated near Jaffa, and later introduced to other parts of Israel and suitable regions elsewhere.

1881 A. H. MANVILLE in T. W. Moore *Treat. & Handbk. Orange Culture in Florida* (ed. 2) 110 Jaffa and other recently imported varieties have not been fruited long enough in the State to determine their qualities. **1909** *Westm. Gaz.* 20 Apr. 7/2 The practice of 'faking' oranges by boiling and greasing them and selling them as Jaffas. *a* **1916** 'SAKI' *Toys of Peace* (1919) 134 We have some very fine Jaffa oranges. **1943** WEBBER & BATCHELOR *Citrus Industry* I. v. 511 In Florida, however, the Jaffa develops a fruit of very good quality. **1962** J. FLEMING *When I grow Rich* xix. 207 Oven-hot rolls, ice-cold Jaffa juice, fragrant hot coffee. **1973** 'D. JORDAN' *Nile Green* xx. 76 The orange-juice they serve..in the Beirut St Georges isn't Israeli but I'm sure they'd produce the Jaffas if you insisted. **1974** W. GARNER *Big Enough Wreath* iv. 43 El Al's flying in fresh-picked Jaffa oranges. *Ibid.*, Miss Cleverley's..face showed no more emotion than a Jaffa.

jag (dʒæg), *sb.*[1] Forms: 5–7 **iagge**, (6 **iaggue**), 6–7 **iagg, iag**, 7– **jagg, jag**. [*Jag.* sb. and vb. are found from *c* 1400. From the uncertain date of the *Morte Arthur* (MS. *c* 1440) in which the vb. first occurs, it does not appear whether the sb. or the vb. is the primary word. The sb., with the adj. *jagged*, but not the vb., is in the Promptorium *c* 1440. The formation appears to be onomatopœic; in some senses it coincides with DAG *sb.*[1] and [3], DAG *v.*[1] and [2], and in some approaches *tag* and *rag*.

There are no cognates in Teutonic or Romanic, and the Celtic *gàg* 'split, rent, fissure', sometimes compared, cannot (in our present knowledge) be connected phonetically. It is possible that the two notions of 'cut or slash', and 'pierce', ought to be referred to separate words (cf. DAG. *v.*[1] and [2]); but in our ignorance of the facts, they are here left together. In the vb. the sense 'pierce, prick', is essentially northern, and is the only sense known in Sc.]

1. One of the dags or pendants made by cutting the edge of a garment, as was done for ornament in the 14th and 15th cents.; also, a slash or cut made in the surface of a garment, to show a different colour underneath.

14.. W. STAUNTON *Vis. Patrick's Purg.* 1409 (MS. Reg. 17 B XLIII. lf. 136 b), I saw summe there with colors of gold abowte here neckis,..summe with mo iagges on here clothis than hole cloth. *Ibid.* lf. 141 Thilk serpentes, snakes, todes, and other wormes, ben here iaggis and daggis. *c* **1440** *Promp. Parv.* 255/2 Iagge, or dagge of a garment, *fractillus*. **1530** PALSGR. 233/2 Iagge a cuttyng, *chicqueture*. **1552** HULOET, Iagge of a garmente, *lacinia*. **1573–80** BARET *Alv.* I 5 A Iag, garse, or cut, *Incisūra, Lacinia*. **1577** HARRISON *England* II. vii. (1877) I. 170 What should I saie of their [women's] doublets..full of iags and cuts. **1609** HOLLAND *Amm. Marcell.* 11 To the end, that these inner garments, thus beset with long iagges and purfles, might shine againe with

varietie of threads seene quite through. **1613** T. MILLES tr. *Mexia's, etc. Treas. Anc. & Mod. T.* I. 960/1 To wear such rich garments, Imbroydered with Veluet, in a thousand iagges and cuts. **1715** tr. *Pancirollus' Rerum Mem.* II. xxiv. 203 Severus never wore any Garment of Velvet, which we now see daily tatter'd into Iags, even by the meaner sort.

†**b.** An attached pendant or fringe. *Obs.*

1600 J. PORY tr. *Leo's Africa* II. 143 Whereupon they sowe iags of partie-coloured silke, and upon every iag a little ball or button of silke, whereby the saide hanging may..be fastened unto a wall. **1606** HOLLAND *Sueton.* 19 He..who used to goe in his Senatours purple studded robe, trimmed with a iagge or frindge at the sleeve hand. *Ibid.* 186 As he was rising up, first the hem (*margin* Iag, welt or fringes) or edge of his Gowne stuck to the seate.

2. A shred of cloth; in *pl.* Rags, tatters. Also *transf.* and *fig.* A scrap, fragment. *Obs.* exc. *dial.*

1555 W. WATREMAN *Fardle Facions* II. i. 113 Pluckyng from eche of their garmentes a litle iaggue. **1637** HEYWOOD *Royall King* III. i. Wks. 1874 VI. 39 Wee have store, of ragges; plenty, of tatters; aboundance, of jagges. **1658** CLEVELAND *Rustick Rampant* Wks. (1687) 415 To preserve a Shred, or jagg of an incertain ragged Estate. *a* **1670** HACKET *Abp. Williams* I. ¶146 The latter of the two letters,..whereof..some Jaggs will suffice to be recited. **1800** MAR. EDGEWORTH *Belinda* (1830) II. xxiv. 156, I saw..black jags of paper littering the place. **1886** ELWORTHY *W. Somerset Word-bk.*, *Jags*, tatters.

3. A protruding bristle, hair, or fibre; a hairy, bristly, or thread-like outgrowth or projection. Now said *dial.* of the beard of an ear of corn; in *Sc.* a prickle, as of a thorn or furze.

1519 HORMAN *Vulg.* 167 b, Some dagswaynys haue longe thrummys and iagges on bothe sydes: some but on one [cf. *Cath. Januensis* s.v. *Fractillus*, 'fractillus dicitur etiam villus in tapeto vel aliâ a veste villosâ']. **1562** TURNER *Herbal* II. C iij a, The roote..beneth it hath many yealowe iagges or berdes lyke heres. **1609** C. BUTLER *Fem. Mon.* iii. (1623) F j, First take away all those staring strawes, twigs, and other offensiue jagges that are fast in the Hiue, making them inside as smooth as may be. **1616** SURFL. & MARKH. *Country Farme* 556 It shall thus lye in the couch till you see it begin to sprout and put forth little white jags or strings which is called the coming of the malt. **1683** A. SNAPE *Anat. Horse* I. xxvi. (1686) 54 Then parting into many jags as it were, they [ligaments] end near the *clitoris*. **1880** JEFFERIES *Gt. Estate* 8 The despised oats were coming out in jag..in jag means the spray-like drooping awn of the oat.

4. A sharp projection or tooth on an edge or surface; one of the teeth, denticulations, or divisions of a leaf; a sharp or rugged point of rock, etc.

1578 LYTE *Dodoens* I. xxxii. 45 The thirde kinde [of Stork's Bill]..hath..small leaues, cut as it were in little iagges or peeces. **1608** TOPSELL *Serpents* (1658) 666 Their other feet are broader, with many jags and notches like a saw. **1753** CHAMBERS *Cycl. Supp.* s.v. *Papilio*, [They] have one of the jaggs of the wing far extended beyond the rest of the verge. **1831** *Blackw. Mag.* XXX. 129 The cliffs touch the clouds with their jags. **1892** H. HUTCHINSON *Fairway Island* 98 Clutching an outstanding jag of the rock.

5. A jagged piece of metal fitted on the end of the ramrod of a rifle, and used, with some tow or rag fastened to it, to clean the barrel; now superseded by the 'pull-through'.

1844 *Regul. & Ord. Army* 96 *note*, One Ball-drawer, One Brass Jagg, to each Rifle. **1879** *Martini-Henry Rifle Exerc.* 61 Screw the jag on to the cleaning rod, wrap a damp rag round the jag, so as to cover it. **1880** *Daily Tel.* 6 May 5/8 A private..shot himself..with a blank cartridge and the jag of his ramrod. **1890** *Rep. Magazine Rifle* §19 in *Times* 6 Dec. 15/4 The jag in the Martini-Henry rifle is an extra part, and has to be screwed on to the rod.

6. 'A barb or dovetail which resists retraction.'

1875 in KNIGHT *Dict. Mech.* [Cf. JOG.]

7. *Sc.* A prick with anything sharp.

1818 SCOTT *Hrt. Midl.* ix, Affliction may gie him a jagg, and let the wind out o' him. *Mod. Sc.* A tailor gave an elephant a jag with his needle. His bare legs were a' jags wi' rinnin' through the whuns.

8. *attrib.* and *Comb.*, as **jag-armed** *a.* armed with jags or prickles; **jag-bolt**: see quot. (hence **jag-bolt** *v.*, to fasten with a jag-bolt); **jag-spear**, a barbed spear; **jag-tail** (see quot.).

1819 W. TENNANT *Papistry Storm'd* (1827) 73 *Jag-arm'd nettles soon, I trow, The passers-by shall sting. **1793** SMEATON *Edystone L.* §42 *note*, *Jag or bearded bolts or spikes, are such as with a chissel have a beard raised upon their angles. *Ibid.* §48 The uprights were also *jag-bolted and trenailed to one another. **1864** in McLennan *Prim. Marriage* (1865) 304 Their long *jag-spears. **1741** *Compl. Fam.-Piece* II. ii. 347 Your Bait, which should be a Red Worm, or a Worm called the *Jag-tail, which is of a pale flesh Colour, with a yellow Jag on his Tail.

jag, *sb.*² *dial.* and *U.S.* Forms: 6–9 jagg, 9 *Sc.* jaug, 8– jag. [Origin unknown.]

1. a. A load (usually a small cart-load) of hay, wood, etc.

1597 *1st Pt. Return fr. Parnass.* II. i. 747 You shall have my carte to carrie home a iagg of haye when you wonn. **1636** *Plymouth Col. Rec.* (1855) I. 40 The quantity of two loade or jaggs of hey at the Iland Creeke. **1688** R. HOLME *Armoury* III. 73/1 A Jagg of Hay is a small Load of Hay. **1700** in Sir J. Cullum *Hist. Hawsted*, etc. (1813) Voc. s.v., Carried the widow Smith one jagg of thorns—12*s*. *a* **1825** FORBY *Voc. E. Anglia*, *Jag*, an indefinite quantity, but less than a load, of hay or corn in the straw. **1828** *Craven Dial.*, *Jag*, a large cart load of hay. In Cheshire, however,..jag or jagg means a parcel, a small load of hay or corn. *a* **1862** THOREAU *Cape Cod* x. (1894) 326 Their companion a cow, their wealth a jag of drift-wood. **1893** *Essex Rev.* II. 125.

b. A load for the back; a pedlar's wallet.

(According to Jamieson, A leather bag or wallet; a pocket; a saddle-bag.)

1787 GROSE *Prov. Gloss.*, *Jag*, a parcel or load of any thing, whether on a man's back, or in a carriage. *Norf.* **1824** SCOTT *St. Ronan's* ii, There's nae room for bags or jaugs here.

c. As much liquor as a man can carry; a 'load' of drink. Also, a drinking bout; the state or a period of being drunk. *dial.* and *colloq.*

1678 J. RAY *Coll. Eng. Proverbs* (ed. 2) 87 Proverbiall Periphrases of one drunk... He has a jagg or load. **1872** J. GLYDE *Norfolk Garland* I. 149 He has got his jag, *i.e.*, as much drink as he can fairly carry. **1891** *Pall Mall G.* 15 Sept. 6/3 A 'saccharine jag' appears to be the latest thing in the way of Yankee intoxication. **1892** *Voice* (N.Y.) 4 Aug., Others with the most picturesque 'jags' on, hardly able to keep their feet. **1894** [see GIN *v.*³]. **1895** *N.Y. Dramatic News* 26 Oct. 7/2 An ability to acquire a 'jag' in a wonderfully short space of time and with a single drink. **1904** [see HANG-OVER 2]. **1921** E. WALLACE *Law Four Just Men* iv. 112 He had been on a jag the night before and had finished up in what he called an opium house. **1924** [see CROOK *v.*¹ 1 d]. **1934** WODEHOUSE *Right Ho, Jeeves* xix. 250, I took the whole thing as a great compliment, proud to feel that any drink from my cellars could have produced such a majestic jag. **1966** *Listener* 28 Apr. 619/1 Sid Chaplin's *Saturday Saga*, the account of two miners on a memorable jag.

d. *transf.* and *fig.* A period of indulgence in a particular pastime, emotion, interest, etc.; = FIT *sb.*² 4 a; freq. with defining word prefixed, as ***crying jag***; *spec.* (see quot. 1946). *colloq.* (orig. *U.S.*).

1913 J. LONDON *Valley of Moon* (1914) I. xv. 119 'Aw, it's only one of his cryin' jags,' Mary said. **1924** P. MARKS *Plastic Age* xix. 213 One had a 'crying jag'. *Ibid.* xxii. 254 A girl got a 'laughing jag' and shrieked with idiotic laughter. **1933** S. HOWARD *Alien Corn* III. 97 Isn't seventy-one fifty cheap for the jag I've got tonight? **1945** S. LEWIS *Cass Timberlane* (1946) xlix. 347 Now you're beginning to get over your love-jag, maybe you can see that Jinny is as..tricky and grabbing as a monkey. **1946** MEZZROW & WOLFE *Really Blues* 375 *Jag*, a state of extreme stimulation, produced by marihuana or some other stimulant. **1958** *Spectator* 4 July 15/2 The British public are on an enormous clean-clothes jag. **1972** *New Yorker* 26 Aug. 38/3 A neurotic habit..may be overt, like a temper tantrum or a crying jag. **1973** *Times Lit. Suppl.* 8 June 631/3 The Kennedy years..launched the Americans on a jag of hope and fear.

2. A train of trucks in a coal-mine.

1900 *Daily News* 9 Feb. 3/1, I crept rapidly alongside the moving 'jag'. *Ibid.* 14 Feb. 3/1 The work of the driver is to hook the pony to the 'jags' or trains of loaded little trucks, marshalled by the putters.

3. A portion or quantity; a 'lot'. *U.S.*

1834 C. A. DAVIS *Major Downing's Lett.* 168 (Bartlett) As there was very little money in the country, the bank bought a good jag on't in Europe. **1888** *Missouri Republican* (Farmer *Amer.*), One broker..caught a jag of 2,000 or 3,000 shares. **1890** *Boston Jrnl.* 10 May 2/2 Farmer (to new hand)—'Hans, you may give the roan critter a jag of feed'.

Jag (dʒæg), *sb.*³ Colloq. abbrev. of *Jaguar* (the proprietary name of a make of motor car). See also *gin-and-Jag* s.v. GIN *sb.*² 2 b.

1959 J. DRUMMOND *Black Unicorn* xxi. 146 'He will meet us opposite the clock-tower in Point Road. I gave him a little word-picture of the Jag.' The Jaguar was a long cream drop-head. **1962** *Times Lit. Suppl.* 19 Oct. 805/4 Stephen, the boss's son, with his Jag, to Wilf, the miner's son, with his typewriter. **1968** J. FLEMING *Kill or Cure* vii. 88 People with lots of money, living in the Jag belt. **1974** T. ALLBEURY *Snowball* x. 55 They've bought a car. A Jag—second-hand.

jag (dʒæg), *v.*¹ Forms: 5–7 iagge, (5 iogge), 8 jagg, 6– jag. [See JAG *sb.*¹]

†**1.** *trans.* To pierce with a sharp instrument, to stab. *Obs.* exc. as in b.

? *a* **1400** *Morte Arth.* 2087 Sir Loth..Enjoynede with a geaunt, and jaggede hym thorowe. *Ibid.* 2891, 2893 Thorowe a jerownde schelde he jogges hym thorowe,..Ioyntes and gemows, he jogges in sondyre. **1507** DUNBAR *Sevin Deidly Sinnis* 41 Sum iaggit vthiris to the heft, With knyvis that scherp cowd scheir. **1607** TOPSELL *Four-f. Beasts* (1658) 283 First, turn up his upper lip, and jagge it lightly with a launcet, so as it may bleed. *a* **1611** BEAUM. & FL. *Philaster* v. iv, Jag him, Gentlemen. **1809** SOUTHEY in *Q. Rev.* II. 37 He saw them jag the cocoa-shell for the purpose.

b. *Sc.*, *north. Eng.*, and *U.S. dial.* To prick with something sharp, as with a spur or thorn.

a **1700** in J. Watson *Coll. Poems* (1706) I. 39 (Jam.) He bade her ride, And with a spur did jag her side. **1819** *Blackw. Mag.* V. 640* May ne'er a thorn hae power to jag the hide upon his shins. **1852** R. S. SURTEES *Sponge's Sp. Tour* I. 286 He now whipped and jagged the old nag, as if intent on catching the hounds. **1883** C. F. SMITH *Southernisms* in *Trans. Amer. Philol. Soc.* 50, *Jag*, 'to prick or pierce with a thorn or any sharp-pointed thing'. Common in various parts of the South. **1893** in *Northumbld. Gloss.*

†**c.** *absol.* or *intr.* To pierce, thrust, prick. *Obs.*

? *a* **1400** *Morte Arth.* 2909 Gyawntis forjustede with gentille knyghtes Thorowe gesserawntes of Iene jaggede to the herte. **1513** DOUGLAS *Æneis* VIII. Prol. 99 Sum garris wyth a ged staf to iag throw blak jakkis.

2. *trans.* To slash or pink (a garment, etc.) by way of ornament.

? *a* **1400** *Morte Arth.* 905 A jupone of Ierodyne jaggede in schredez. **1530** PALSGR. 589/1, I jagge or cutte a garment, *je chicquette*. **1577** tr. *Bullinger's Decades* (1592) 139 To what ende doe wee iagge and gash the garmentes? **1708** MOTTEUX *Rabelais* IV. lii. (1737) 211 His Journey-men..did jagg it and pink it at the bottom. **1839** BAILEY *Festus* v. (1852) 57 Like a black block of marble, jagged with white.

3. To make indentations in the edge or surface of; to make ragged or uneven by cutting or tearing; to make rugged or bristling. ***to jag in***, to indent with cuts.

1568 TURNER *Herbal* III. 5 Angelica hath leves somethinge lyke lovage, but not so far iagged in. **1615** tr. *De Monfart's Surv. E. Indies* 22 When they take any prisoner, who by chance hath his garments cut or iag'd, they say hee did teare them of purpose. **1692** BENTLEY *Boyle Lect.* viii. 292 Jagged and torn by the impetuous assaults of Waves. **1748** THOMSON *Cast. Indol.* II. 699 The ground..Was jagg'd with frost or heap'd with glazed snow. **1764** GRAINGER *Sugar Cane* III. 243 Three long rollers..With iron cas'd, and jagg'd with many a cogg. **1899** *Westm. Gaz.* 26 May 5/2 A doctor was called, who said the man had jagged the windpipe.

4. *trans.* To dovetail or join by 'letting in'. *U.S.*

1894 *Outing* (U.S.) XXIV. 23/1 The ribs..run around full length, except at the trunk where they will be jagged into the piece holding the trunk to the keel.

5. *Naut.* To lay in long bights, as a rope, and tie with stops. *U.S.*

jag, *v.*² *dial.* [f. JAG *sb.*²] *trans.* To carry in a cart, or on a pack-horse. Hence **'jagging**.

1747 [see JAGGER² 2]. **1847–78** HALLIWELL, *Jag*, to carry hay, &c. *West.* **1879** MISS JACKSON *Shropsh. Word-bk.*, *Jag*, to carry hay, &c. in a cart. **1881** RAYMOND *Mining Gloss.*, *Jagging*, a mode of carrying ore to the reduction-works in bags on horses, mules, etc. **1887** *S. Chesh. Gloss.*, *Jag*, to cart.

jag, Sc. var. JOG, JOUG.

jagale, obs. var. JACKAL *sb.*

Jagannāth, the more systematic spelling of JUGGERNAUT.

Jagatai (dʒægə'tɑːɪ). [The native name of Turkestan, f. *Jagatai*, a son of Jenghiz Khan, who inherited it.] The branch of the Turkic group of languages spoken in Turkestan. Also *attrib.* Also **Jaga'taic**. Hence **Jaga'taian** *a.*, pertaining to Turkestan or the dialects spoken there.

1843 *Penny Cycl.* XXV. 406/1 Jagatáï, [spoken] in the greater part of independent Turkistán... The Jagatáï language has a valuable literature. **1867** *Chambers's Encycl.* IX. 589/2 The former [*sc.* Eastern Turkish] is mainly represented by the Uigur (Jagatai). *Ibid.* 590/1 The Eastern [Turkish] or Jagataian [literature]. **1908** T. G. TUCKER *Introd. Nat. Hist. Lang.* 134 (*d*) *Uiguric*, including *Uigur* proper, *Jagataic*, and *Turkoman*, the dialects spoken in the parts of Turkestan not occupied by the Kirghiz. **1929** *Encycl. Brit.* XXII. 920/1 The Uzbeg (Jagatai Turkish) tongue. **1962** A. TIETZE in Householder & Saporta *Probl. Lexicogr.* 266 Jagatai and other non-Ottoman Turkic languages.

jagatī ('dʒʌgətiː). Also **gagatî**. [Skr.] A Vedic metre of twelve syllables.

1843 [see GĀYATRĪ]. **1869** MAX MÜLLER tr. *Rig.-Veda-Sanhita* p. cxxx, I maintain by no means that this was the actual origin of Ǵagatî metres... Theories..would wish us to look upon the hendecasyllabic Trishṭubh as originally a dodecasyllabic Ǵagatî, only deprived of its tail. **1937** M. D. SHASTRI *Ṛgveda-Prātiśākhya* III. 137 All that is light by nature is related to light syllables, and a Jagatī, one should know, has light syllables. **1969** *Language* XLV. 251 A cadence of four or five syllables depending on whether the pāda is in triṣṭubh meter (typically 11 syllables) or jagatī (12 syllables).

‖**jäger, jaeger** ('jeːgə(r)). Also 8–9 **jager, iager**, and anglicized YAGER, q.v. [G. *jäger* hunter, f. *jagen* to hunt, chase. Cf. CHASSEUR.]

1. A (German or Swiss) huntsman or hunter.

1809 [see YAGER]. **1823** W. IRVING in *Life & Lett.* (1864) II. 139 The king has his forest masters; his chasseurs, piqueurs, jägers, &c. **1859** H. KINGSLEY *G. Hamlyn* iv. (1894) 16, I..ran at full speed up to the jager, and offered him five shillings if he would come down and shoot the bird. **1880** OUIDA *Moths* II. 337 A jäger brought to the hotel a grand golden eagle.

2. A rifleman or sharpshooter in a corps of German soldiers, or one forming part of a German or Austrian army. Orig. applied to the members of various bodies of light infantry, recruited mainly from foresters and armed with a huntsman's equipment, but the *jägers* subsequently formed certain special battalions (for the most part organized as riflemen) in the German and Austrian armies, and the name is still retained in the official title of some regiments.

1776 in F. Moore *Songs & Ball. Amer. Rev.* (1856) 125 *note*, [The British Government] has..succeeded in raising a legion of Jagers. **1783** SIR H. CLINTON *Narrative* 112 Detachments from four British battalions, and Iagers, artillery and cavalry. **1815** WELLINGTON *Let. to Alten* 6 June in Gurw. *Desp.* XII. 446 You shall have the field Jägers in your division. **1837** ALISON *Europe* (1847) IX. xl. 112 The Austrian army consists of..twenty battalions of grenadiers, the corps of jagers of thirteen battalions [etc.]. **1892** *Nation* (N.Y.) 6 Oct. 259/1 These jägers were good shots, and generally fired at gilt uniforms and epaulets.

attrib. **1844** W. SIBORNE *Waterloo* I. v. 110 The two jäger-companies in the wood.

3. An attendant upon a person of rank or wealth, dressed in a huntsman's costume. Cf. CHASSEUR 3.

1831 DISRAELI *Yng. Duke* II. viii, Supervised by his Jager, who stood behind his chair. **1835** *Court Mag.* VI. 193 The old Iager or garde-chasse who accompanied her. **1884** Q. VICTORIA *More Leaves* 279 He saw poor Macdonald the

Jäger here.. and, being in want of a Jäger, inquired after him and engaged him.

attrib. **1896** A. H. BEAVAN *Marlb. Ho.* vii. 114 A handsome dark young fellow.. clad in picturesque jäger costume.

4. A predatory sea-bird belonging to the family *Laridæ*, and subfamily *Stercorariinæ* or *Lestridinæ*; a skua-gull.

1838 *Encycl. Brit.* (ed. 7) XVI. 633/1 The skua.. the pomarine jager.. and Richardson's jager, which is common on our coasts in autumn. **1839** *Penny Cycl.* XIII. 337/1 *Lestris Parasiticus* (Arctic Jager). **1853** KANE *Grinnell Exp.* xiii. (1856) 99 The Fulmar petrel, a solitary jager. **1880** *Libr. Univ. Knowl.* (U.S.) VIII. 829 The jägers or gull hunters, so called because they pursue the smaller gulls, and rob them of.. food. **1894** *Outing* (U.S.) XXIII. 366/2 We also killed some jaegers and small bladder-nosed seals.

jagerant: see JESSERANT.

Jagernaut, -not, Jaggarnat, obs. ff. JUGGERNAUT.

jagery, jagg: see JAGGERY, JAG.

jagged ('dʒægɪd, dʒægd), *a.*[1] Also 6 geagged. [f. JAG *sb.*[1] and *v.*[1] + -ED. Now usually disyllabic as adjective, monosyllabic as participle.]

1. Of a garment, etc.: Cut into jags by way of ornament; pinked, slashed.

c **1440** *Promp. Parv.* 255/2 Iaggyd, or daggyd, *fractillosus.* **1459** *Paston Lett.* I. 476 Item, j jagged huke of blakke sengle. *Ibid.* 480. **1519** HORMAN *Vulg.* 112 He hath a pleasure in geagged clothynge [*laciniosa veste*]. **1547** BOORDE *Introd. Knowl.* xxvii. (1870) 190 My rayment is iagged and kut round a-bout. **1641** MILTON *Ch. Govt.* I. vi, She might go jagg'd in as many cuts and slashes as she pleas'd for you.

2. Having the edge irregularly cut, gashed, or torn, into deep indentations and acute projections; torn or worn to a ragged or uneven edge.

1577 STANYHURST *Descr. Irel.* iii. in *Holinshed* (1587) II. 21/2 The Irish feare a ragged and iagged blacke standard that the citizens haue. **1596** SPENSER *F.Q.* v. ix. 10 An vncouth vestiment Made of straunge stuffe, but all to-worne and ragged;.. his breech was all to-torne and iagged. **1684** T. BURNET *The. Earth* I. 130 The shores and coasts of the sea .. go in a line uncertainly crooked and broke, indented and jag'd as a thing torn. **1797** COLERIDGE *Christabel* I. 282 Amid the jagged shadows Of mossy leafless boughs. **1835-6** TODD *Cycl. Anat.* I. 455/1 [The] extremities [of the bone] are always jagged, pointed and uneven. **1840** DICKENS *Barn. Rudge* lix, Having borrowed a notched and jagged knife.

b. *Her.* (See quot.)

1828-40 BERRY *Encycl. Herald.* I. Gloss., *Jagged*.. is said of the division of the field, or of the outlines of an ordinary, which appear rough by being forcibly torn asunder.

3. Having the margin naturally furnished with deep irregular indentations and projecting points; laciniated: esp. of leaves, petals, and the like.

1523 FITZHERB. *Husb.* §20 Golds hath a shorte iagged lefe. **1685** J. CHAMBERLAYNE *Coffee, Tea & Choc.* 38 Its branches are covered with white and yellow flowers jagg'd and pick'd from top to bottom. **1740** P. COLLINSON in Darlington *Mem. Bartram & Marshall* (1849) 137 A very pretty dwarf Gentian, with a large blue flower, the extremity of the flower-leaves, all notched or jagged. **1767** GOOCH *Treat. Wounds* I. 421 The *Morsus Diaboli*, a jagged body, ridiculously so called, resembling a fringe. **1870** HOOKER *Stud. Flora* 49 *Dianthus cæsius*,.. petals jagged and bearded.

b. In names of plants: Having jagged leaves or flowers.

1548 TURNER *Names Herbs* s.v. *Verbenaca*, The leaues are deaplyer endented... It may be called in english geagged Bugle. **1688** R. HOLME *Armoury* II. 88/2 Jagged Germander hath the flowers spiky. **1776-96** WITHERING *Brit. Plants* (ed. 3) III. 603 *Geranium dissectum*.. Jagged Cranesbill. Road sides; borders of fields, ditch banks.

4. Irregularly and sharply pointed.

1651 BIGGS *New Disp.* ¶80 All ice beginning, maketh jagged pikes, after the fashion of a Nettle-leafe. **1856** STANLEY *Sinai & Pal.* iv. (1858) 205 Two jagged points, or 'teeth of the cliff'. **1862** MERIVALE *Rom. Emp.* (1865) VII. lx. 306 Frowning cliffs and jagged pinnacles. **1900** *Blackw. Mag.* July 117 The quick jagged spear of the lightning flashed forth.

jagged (dʒægd), *a.*[2] *slang* (chiefly *U.S.*). [f. JAG *sb.*[2] I c + -ED[2].] Drunk, intoxicated.

1737 *Pennsylvania Gaz.* 6-13 Jan. 1/3 He's Jagg'd. **1902** *Telegram* (Winnipeg) 20 Aug. 7/4 Miller was pretty well jagged. **1904** 'O. HENRY' in *N.Y. World Mag.* 1 May 8/2 What I want is a masterful man that slugs you when he's jagged, and hugs you when he ain't jagged. **1956** *Amer. Speech* XXXI. 279 *Jagged*, adj. In the sense of intoxicated .. [it] is probably not of American origin.

b. Intoxicated by, or under the influence of, drugs.

1938 C. HIMES *Black on Black* (1973) 175 She made him smoke pot and when he got jagged.. she put him out on the street. **1973** BOYD & PARKES *Dark Number* xiii. 151 Solange is—was—God help her, a heroin addict. When we first met, she was all jagged up. She was a reject on the junk heap.

jaggedly ('dʒægɪdlɪ), *adv.* [f. JAGGED *a.*[1] + -LY[2].] In a jagged manner; with sharp indentations.

1698 WALLIS in *Phil. Trans.* XX. 7 His Cloaths on one Shoulder cut jaggedly to the Skin. **1846** DANA *Zooph.* (1848) 281 Jaggedly dentate. **1891** OLIVE SCHREINER *Dreams* 33 The old thin hands cut the stones ill and jaggedly.

jaggedness ('dʒægɪdnɪs). [f. as prec. + -NESS.] The quality or state of being jagged; sharp and rough unevenness of edge or outline.

1530 PALSGR. 233/2 Iaggednesse, *chicqueture.* **1606** PEACHAM *Art Drawing* 43 First draw rudely your leaves.. before you give them their veins or iaggednesse. **1890** TALMAGE *Fr. Manger to Throne* 36 The boldness and jaggedness of the scenery.

jagger[1] ('dʒægə(r)). [f. JAG *v.*[1] + -ER[1].] One who or that which jags; *spec.* a jagging-iron, also a toothed chisel.

In quot. 1562, prob. error for *iagges*: see JAG *sb.*[1] 4.

[**1562** TURNER *Herbal* II. Hj a, Lupine hath.. a lefe with v. or seuen iaggers, which altogether, when as they are growen out, haue the lykenes of a ruel of a spor, or of a sterr.] **1825-80** JAMIESON, *Jagger*, a prickle, that which jags. *Fife.* **1864** WEBSTER, *Jagger*,.. a jagging-iron. **1875** KNIGHT *Dict. Mech.*, *Jagger*.. 2. A toothed chisel. **1892** *Voice* (N.Y.) 15 Sept., Mix the eggs with flour.. cut them the shape of a long narrow leaf.. cut them with a jagger so they will be notched.

'jagger[2]. *dial.* [f. JAG *sb.*[2] or *v.*[2] + -ER[1].]

1. a. A carrier, a carter. **b.** A pedlar, a hawker.

1514 BARCLAY *Cyt. & Uplondyshm.* 14 Coblers, or tynkers, or else costard iaggers. **1822** SCOTT *Pirate* v, A stout, vulgar little man, who had.. the humble appearance of a pedlar, called 'jagger' in these islands. *Ibid.* xviii, The jagger, or travelling merchant, as he styled himself.. on one pony, and his pack of goods.. forming the burden of another. **1868** HOLME LEE *B. Godfrey* xlvii. 262 There's the jagger's bell—Ralph promised to buy me a comb. **1887** *S. Chesh. Gloss.*, *Jagger*, a carter, esp. a man who makes his living by carting for other people, e.g. fetching their coal.

2. *Mining.* A man who carries ore on pack-horses from a mine to the place where it is smelted. Also, a boy who has charge of the 'jags' or trains of trucks in a coal-mine.

1747 HOOSON *Miner's Dict.*, *Jaggers*, this includes both the Men and Horses, that are imploy'd to carry the Ore on the Horses Backs, from the Mine to the Place where it is Smelted, yet we say seperately Jagger-Lads, and Jagging-Horses. **1870** *Swaledale Gloss.*, *Jagger*, a driver of pack-horses. **1900** *Daily News* 9 Feb. 3/1 The trains of trucks.. are called 'jags', and the lads who attend to them are consequently called 'jaggers'.

3. *Comb.*, as *jagger-galloway*, *jagger-horse*.

1825 BROCKETT, *Jagger-galloway*, a pony with a peculiar saddle for carrying lead, etc. **1870** *Swaledale Gloss.*, *Jagger-horse*, a pack-horse.

† **'jagger**[3]. *Obs.* Forms: α. 7-8 yager, (yawger, yagger). β. 8 jagger, (jaggar, jagar). [a. Du. *jager*, abbreviation of *haringjager*, f. *haring* herring + *jagen* to chase, dog, pursue.] A sailing-vessel which followed a fishing fleet in order to bring the fish from the busses and to supply these with stores and provisions.

α. **1615** E. S. *Brit. Buss* in Arb. *Garner* III. 636 A Yager (which is a caravel or a merchant's ship employed to seek out the said Herring Busses, and to buy of them their herrings upon the first packing). **1622** MALYNES *Anc. Law-Merch.* 242 Lading their ships twice or thrice before they come to Yarmouth, sending them away by the Merchants ships that send them victuals, barrels, and more salt and nets if they need any; which ships are called Yagers, that is to say Hunters or Doggerbotes, and these ships do carry them, and sell them in the East countries. **1733** P. LINDSAY *Interest Scot.* 196 Those who have Yagers to attend them, &c. continue fishing until their Yagers bring their second Fleet of Nets. **1762** *Gentl. Mag.* 339 The first caught herrings.. arrived in Holland in a yagger.

β. **1751-66** POSTLETHWAYT *Dict. Trade* (ed. 3), Jaggers, or store ships, commonly provide them with everything that is necessary. **1753** *Scots Mag.* Aug. 417/1 A jagger from the busses at Shetland arrived at London. **1773** *Gentl. Mag.* XLIII. 573 They were discovered by a jagar coming from Iceland with fish.

b. *Comb.*

1824 HEBER *Jrnl.* (1828) I. 236 The large pulwars with sails.. reminded me of the Manks jagger-boats.

† **'jaggered**, *a. Obs. rare*⁻¹. [f. JAGGER *sb.*[1] + -ED[2].] Having jags or short barbs directed backwards so as to resist drawing out.

1627 CAPT. SMITH *Seaman's Gram.* ii. 5 Rag bolts are so iaggered that they cannot be drawne out.

Jaggernaut, variant of JUGGERNAUT.

jaggery ('dʒægərɪ). Forms: 6 **gagara**, 6-8 **jagra**, 7 **jeggery**, **jagre**, **jaggaree**, 7-8 **jaggory**, 8 **jagree**, 9 **jagory**, **-ery**, **jaggeree**, **-ary**, (**jaghery**, **-ari**), 7- **jaggery**. [a. Indo-Port. *jágara*, *jagra*, *jagre*, ad. Canarese *sharkare*, Urdū *shakkar*, Skr. *çarkarā*: see SUGAR.]

1. A coarse dark brown sugar made in India by evaporation from the sap of various kinds of palm.

1598 HAKLUYT *Voy.* II. I. 252 Sugar which is made of the nutte called Gagara: the tree is called the palmer. **1598** tr. *Linschoten's Voy.* 102 Of the aforesaide *Sura* they likewise make Sugar, which is called *Iagra.* **1631** in *Cal. Colon. Pap., E. Ind.* (1892) 161 Half a hhd. of jaggery, given to him by Capt. Weddell. **1681** R. KNOX *Hist. Ceylon* 15 The which Liquor they boyl and make a kind of brown Sugar, called Iaggory. **1732** PIKE in *Phil. Trans.* XXXVII. 231 Dissolve 20 lb of Jaggery, which is course Sugar (or thick Molasses) in Water. **1831** TRELAWNEY *Adv. Younger Son* cxv. III. 224 Cargoes of coir, oil, jaggeree, ghee, and cocoa-nuts. **1897** *Daily News* 29 Jan. 5/7 The Government have stopped irrigation in the case of all the 'jaghari' sugar-cane crops. **1899** F. T. BULLEN *Log Sea-waif* 204 Jaggery, or palm sugar —looking like bags of black mud, and almost as nice to handle.

2. *jaggery palm*, a palm-tree that yields jaggery, esp. *Caryota urens.*

1859 *All Year Round* No. 32. 130 The tusked elephant is able to rip open the stems of the jaggery palms and young palmyras to extract the mealy core. **1890** SARAH J. DUNCAN *Social Departure* 234 Brown 'jaggery' sugar, got from the jaggery palm.

jagging ('dʒægɪŋ), *vbl. sb.*[1] [f. JAG *v.*[1] + -ING[1].] The action of JAG *v.*[1] in its different senses; indenting, piercing; also *concr.* a jagged edge, an indented border, a fringe, etc.

1502 *Privy Purse Exp. Eliz. York* (1830) 14 Six tapettes for the sompter horses with the lynyng grayling jagging. **1593** NASHE *Christ's T.* (1613) 146 Not your pinches, your purles, your floury iaggings, superfluous enterlacings, and puffings vp. **1626** BACON *Sylva* §590, I account the Iagging of Pinkes, and Gilly Flowers, to be like the Inequality of Oake-Leaues, of Vine-Leaues, or the like. **1776** DA COSTA *Elem. Conchol.* 13 The jaggings or toothings of the contour. **1815** POLEHAMPTON *Gallery Nat. & Art* (1821) V. 186 The gum.. is obtained by wounding the bark in different parts of the body of the tree, or by what has been called jagging.

b. *Comb.* **jagging-board** *Metall.*, an inclined board on which ore-slimes are washed, as in a buddle; **jagging-iron**, an instrument used for ornamenting pastry, etc., now made in the form of a wheel with teeth, set in a handle.

1598 FLORIO, *Speronélle*, a brasen toole with a spoone at one end, and a rowell or little spur at the other, that cookes vse to cut out or marke their paste meates, called a iagging iron. **1718** MRS. MARY EALES *Receipts* 84 When you use it, cut it with a Jagging-Iron in long Slips.

jagging, *vbl. sb.*[2]: see JAG *v.*[2]

jaggory, obs. form of JAGGERY.

jaggy ('dʒægɪ), *a.*[1] [f. JAG *sb.*[1] + -Y[1].] Abounding in or characterized by jags; jagged; in *Sc.*, prickly.

1717 ADDISON tr. *Ovid* Wks. 1758 I, Three tongues he brandish'd when he charg'd his foes; His teeth stood jaggy in three dreadful rows. **1849** RUSKIN *Sev. Lamps* iii. §16. 82 Four branches of thistle leaves.. throwing their jaggy spines down. **1865** E. BURRITT *Walk to Land's End* 425 The narrow road between these dark, jaggy, craggy heights.

'jaggy, *a.*[2] *Sc.* [f. *jag*, var. of JOG *v.* and *sb.* + -Y[1].] Having a jerking motion, jolting.

1842 *Blackw. Mag.* LI. 241 The jaggy motion and the continuous rumble of the vehicle.

jaghari, -ery: see JAGGERY.

‖**jaghire** (dʒɑːˈgɪə(r)). *E. Indies.* Also 7 **jahghir**, **jaggea**, **jageah**, 8 **jaguir(e**, **-ere**, **jagghire**, 9 **jaghir**, **-eer**, **jagir**, **-eer**, (**jagier**, **jahgeer**). [a. Urdū (Pers.) *jāgīr*, f. *jā* place + *gīr* holding, holder.] An assignment of the king's or government's share of the produce of a district to a person or body of persons, as an annuity, either for private use or for the maintenance of a public (esp. military) establishment; also, the district so assigned, or the income derived from it.

1684 J. PHILLIPS tr. *Tavernier's Voy.*, etc. II. 70 The lands in the Kingdom being the King's propriety.. are given.. as benefices which they call Jah-ghirs to men of the militia for their pay or pension [etc.]. **1698** FRYER *Acc. E. India & P.* 120 Being in the Jaggea or Diocess of another. *Ibid.* 134 Were the ways free, it would enrich his Jageah beyond the Bunder at Surat. **1753** HANWAY *Trav.* (1762) II. Gloss., *Jaguirs*,.. lands assigned to governors. **1764** *Newcastle Chron.* No. 1. 2/1 Lord Clive.. is.. to have the payment which have been stopped of his jaghire. **1778** FOOTE *Nabob* I. i, Should it be more agreeable to the parties, Sir Matthew will settle upon Sir John and his Lady, for their joint lives, a jagghire. **1800** *Asiat. Ann. Reg., Misc. Tr.* 291/2 This is the head town of a pergunnah of eight lacks of rupees, held in jaghire from the Peshwa. **1845** STOCQUELER *Handbk. Brit. India* (1854) 146 The revenue of the college [was] fixed at 30,000 rupees per annum, instead of the original jaghir. **1897** LD. ROBERTS *41 Yrs. India* lxviii. (1898) 533 Jagirs were sanctioned annually for a limited number of specially distinguished native officers.

attrib. **1763** SCRAFTON *Indostan* (1770) 24 The Jaghire lands, which are lands bestowed by the crown out of its demesnes to the Omrahs, for the support of their forces. **1801** R. PATTON *Asiat. Mon.* 203 The jagheer grants of the sovereign form an additional proof of his proprietary rights. **1818** JAS. MILL *Brit. India* I. II. v. 188 The collector in the jaghire district at Madras.

Hence ‖**jaghirdar** (dʒɑːˈgɪədɑː(r)). [Urdū *jāgīrdār*, f. *jāgīr* + Pers. *-dār* possessor.] The holder of a jaghire.

1794 BURKE *Sp. agst. W. Hastings* Wks. XV. 385 The jaghirdars, the holders of jaghires, form the body of the principal Mahometan nobility. **1872** COLIN VALENTINE in *Mem. Mrs. Valentine* vii. (1882) 114 It makes me one of the Jagirdars of the Rajah.

jagory, jagra, jagre, -ee: see JAGGERY.

jagounce, variant of JACOUNCE, *Obs.*

‖**jagt** (jakt). [a. Da. *jagt* (cf. Norw., Sw. *jakt*) YACHT *sb.*] In Scandinavia, a small single-masted coastal vessel, rigged either with square sails or as a cutter or sloop.

1861 J. LAMONT *Seasons with Sea-Horses* ii. 22 We saw two small vessels, which we made out to be a brig and a sloop, or 'jagt', at some distance amongst the ice. **1906** H.

W. Smyth *Mast & Sail* iii. 44 Square-rigged Nordland jaegts which formerly were so characteristic a feature of the Norwegian coastline. *Ibid.* 51 The old Nordland 'jaegt' which formerly did so much of the coast-wise trade of Norway. **1925** A. Moore *Last Days Mast & Sail* vi. 181 Amundsen's ship, the *Gjoa*, in which he made the North-West Passage, was described in the English papers as a sloop, and she was one according to the old definition; but in the list of the Bureau Veritas for 1907 she is called a *Jagt*. **1971** *Mariner's Mirror* LVII. 152 In Schleswig-Holstein the *Jachten* doubtless were of the classical Danish *jagt* design in hull and rig; carvel-built keel craft with transom stern and outside rudder, convex stem, and pole-masted gaff sloop rig.

jaguar ('dʒægwɑː(r), 'dʒægjuːɑː(r)). Also 8 **jaguara.** [a. Tupi-Guarani *yaguara, jaguara* (ja-, ʒawaːra).

According to writers on Tupi-Guarani, *jaguara* or *jagua* is orig. a class-name for all carnivorous beasts, including the tiger (i.e. jaguar), the puma, etc., more recently also extended to dogs, the specific name of the jaguar being *jaguareté*, where *-eté* is a Tupi augmentative, generally rendered 'true'. De Lery (1580), cited by Hatz.-Darm., gave the native name as *jan-ou-are* (app. a misprint or misreading of *jau-ou-are*). The etymological meaning of the Tupi word is disputed: see Skeat in *Trans. Philol. Soc.* 1885, 89; also Burton *Highlands of Brazil* II. 21, *Hans Stade* xliii.]

A large carnivorous quadruped of the cat kind (*Felis onca*), inhabiting wooded parts of America from Texas to Paraguay. It is yellowish-brown in colour, and is marked with ocellated spots.

1604 E. Grimstone tr. *D'Acosta's West Ind.* v. iv, They ascribe power to another starre, which they called Chuquinchincay (which is as much as iaguar), over tigres, beares, and lyons. [**1648** Marcgrave *Hist. Nat. Brasil.* vi. x, Jagvara Braziliensibus, nobis Tigris.] **1753** Chambers *Cycl. Supp.*, *Jaguara*, a Brasilian animal, accounted by Marggrave a species of tyger: but..approaching to the leopard in the shape of its variegations. **1771** *Gentl. Mag.* XLI. 589 In this state it [the Armadillo] braves the claws of the Jaguara. **1774** Goldsm. *Nat. Hist.* I. 146 The jaguar or panther of America. **1796** Stedman *Surinam* II. xviii. 50 It has even happened that the jaguar has carried off young negro women at work in the field. **1875** Nicholson *Man. Zool.* lxxix, Of the large Spotted Cats, the largest is the Jaguar.

‖**jaguarete.** Also 8 **-ette, -etta.** [See prec.: Montoya 1639 has '*Yaguarete* tigre'.] Adaptation of the Guarani specific name for the jaguar; long mistaken by European writers for a distinct species or variety, and applied by some to the Black Jaguar.

1753 Chambers *Cycl. Supp.*, *Jaguarete*,..the name of a Brasilian beast of prey, accounted by Marggrave a species of tyger, but improperly; its roundish spots arguing it of the lynx or leopard kind... It much resembles the creature called Jaguara, but is larger. **1774** Goldsm. *Nat. Hist.* (1862) I. xiv. 234 The sixth class..comprehends the Cat, the Lion, the Panther, the Leopard, the Jaguar, the Cougar, the Jaguarette, the Lynx, the Ounce, and the Catamountain. **1839** *Penny Cycl.* XIII. 435/2 There is a black variety of the Jaguar.. *Felis nigra* of Erxleben, and probably the Jaguarete of Marcgrave. **1852** Th. Ross *Humboldt's Trav.* I. vi. 230 This fact..prove[s] that the great jaguar of Terra Firma, like the jaguarete of Paraguay,..does not flee from man when it is dared to close combat.

‖**jaguarondi** (dʒægwə'rɒndɪ, jægwɑː-). Also **jaguarundi, yaguarundi.** [Native name in Tupi-Guarani; written by Montoya *Tesoro de la lengua Guarani* 1639, *yagua-rundi*: cf. jaguar.] A wild cat (*Felis yaguarundi*, Desmarest), larger than the common cat, dark brown or brownish grey in colour, with a long body and tail, inhabiting America from Texas to Paraguay.

1885 in *Cassell's Encycl. Dict.* **1897** L. Robinson *Wild Traits in Tame Animals* 239 Possibly also in [the case] of the male and female jaguarondi..it occasionally exists. **1906**, **1955** [see eyra]. **1959** A. S. Leopold *Wildlife Mexico* 482 Little is known of the jaguarundi. **1964** L. S. Crandall *Managem. Wild Mammals in Captivity* 368 The jaguarundi is a shy, secretive creature.

jaguere, -ire: see jaghire.

‖**Jah** (dʒɑː). The form in which the Heb. *Yah*, shortened form of *Yahwe(h* (Jahveh) Jehovah, is represented in the English Bible.

1539 Bible (Great) *Ps.* lxviii. 4 Oh synge vnto God,.. prayse ye him in his name Ia [**1611** Iah] and reioyse before hym. **1613** Purchas *Pilgrimage* (1614) 154 In the name of Iah the God of Israel. There is none like to Iah our God. **1758** C. Wesley *Hymn, 'Lo! He comes'* iv, Jah, Jehovah, Everlasting God, come down.

Jahve, Jahveh: see Jehovah.

Jahvism ('jɑːvɪz(ə)m). Also **Jahveism, -ehism, Yahwiz'm** ('jɑːveɪɪz(ə)m, 'jɑːhwɪz(ə)m). [f. *Jahveh, Jahve, Yahwe(h*, transliterations, according to different systems, of the Heb. *Yhwh* (previously represented by Jehovah) + -ism.] The religion of Jahveh; the system of doctrines and precepts connected with the worship of Jahveh. **b.** The use of *Jahve(h)* as a name for God.

1867 J. Martineau tr. *Ewald's Israel* 536 *note*, We purposely adopt the term Jahveism as the antithesis to Christianity, rather than Mosaism. **1877** J. E. Carpenter tr. *Tiele's Hist. Relig.* 86 Such zealous champions of Jahvism as Saul and David. **1879** Newman Smyth *Old Faiths in New Light* iv, Even the rationalistic Kuenen..rejects the possibility of an Egyptian origin for the Javehism of Moses. **1882** *Athenæum* 14 Oct. 490/2 He is still ready to see in Yahwism too much the creation of the prophets. **1900** R. H. Charles *Eschatol.* 13 Preprophetic Yahwism from Moses to the 8th century.

So **'Jahvist** ('jɑːvɪst), (*a*) A worshipper of Jahveh or Yahweh; (*b*) The writer of the (non-Deuteronomic) portions of the Hexateuch which are marked by the use of *Jahveh* (*Jehovah*) as the name of God, instead of *Elohim*; = Jehovist 2. **Jah'vistic** *a.*, of or pertaining to Jahvism, or to the authorship of the Jahvist.

1874 tr. *Kuenen's Relig. Israel* I. 344 The stricter Jahvistic party which was led by the prophets of Jahveh. **1885** *Athenæum* 16 May 623/2 The Elohistic account is separated from the Jahvistic by a longer break. **1892** W. E. Addis *Docum. Hexat.* Introd. 29 Hupfeld convinced inquirers that ..three documents have been used in the compilation of Genesis: viz. that of the 'Priestly Writer', of the Elohist, and of the Jahvist. **1894** A. Lang in *Contemp. Rev.* Aug. 171 The rebuke and the prediction are a..Jahvehistic gloss and interpolation. **1899** R. H. Charles *Hibbert Lecture* Syllabus, Yahwistic eschatology starts from the new value set on the individual.

jai alai ('haɪlaɪ, 'haɪəlaɪ, haɪə'laɪ). [Sp., f. Basque *jai* festival + *alai* merry.] = pelota.

1910 I. A. Wright *Cuba* i. 7 (*caption*) Ball Players on the Court. General Leonard Wood, a Jai Alai enthusiast among them. **1923** W. Stevens *Let.* 4 Feb. (1967) 234 In the evening I went to see a game of jai alai, the Spanish national game. **1947** M. Lowry *Under Volcano* i. 9 Its jai-alai courts are grass-grown and deserted. **1972** *Times* 8 Aug. (Asian Suppl.) p. vii/8 Do not forget to see a game of *jai-alai* [in the Philippines]. **1973** *Times* 28 May (Macao Suppl.) p. iii/3 The fast and furious Basque ball and racquet game of Jai Alai (or Pelota Basque in Portuguese) is the latest of Macau's diversions for the visitor. The opulent new Jai Alai Centre on the Outer Harbour offers the last word in de luxe comfort for fans or gamblers betting on the matches, plus nightclub, restaurant and bar facilities.

‖**Jai Hind** (dʒaɪ hɪnd), *int.* [Hindi, f. *jai* long live! + *Hind* India.] In India, a salutation: used in exchange of greetings, at a public meeting, etc.

1948 A. Moorehead *Rage of Vulture* v. 76 The Indians.. raised their cry of 'Jai Hind', and it really meant 'Expel the British'. And finally they have expelled us. They go on crying 'Jai Hind', and now it means exactly what it says—'Long Live India'. **1969** *Commerce* (Bombay) 26 July 170/3 We remain committed to the freedom and progress of the people of this great country. Jai Hind.

jail, gaol (dʒeɪl), *sb.* Forms: α. 3–4 **gayhol(e,** 5 **gayll(e, gaille,** 5–7 **gayole, gayl(e, gaile,** 6 **gaiell, gaill,** 6–7 **gaole, goale,** 7–8 **goal,** 7– **gaol.** β. 4 **iaiole,** 4–7 **iaile, iayle,** 5 **iayll,** 6–7 **iaole,** 7–8 **jayl,** (7 **jale),** 7– **jail.** γ. 6 **geyle, geayle, (gial),** 7 **geale.** [ME. had two types, from Northern or Norman Fr., and Central or Parisian Fr. respectively: 1) ME. *gay(h)ole, -ol, gayll(e, gaill(e, gayl(e, gaile*, a. ONF. *gaiole, gayolle, gaole* (mod. Picard *gayole*, Walloon *gaioule*); 2) ME. *jaiole, jayle, jaile, jayll*, a. OF. *jaiole, jaole, jeole, geole*, cage, prison, F. *geôle* prison (Besançon *javiole* cage for fowls) = obs. It. *gaiola*, Sp. *gayola* (also, from F., *jaula* cage, cell), Pg. *gaiola* cage:—Romanic and pop.Lat. *gaviōla (med.L. *gabiola*, 1229 in Brachet) for *caveola, dim. of *cavea* hollow, cavity, den, cage, coop: see cage. Of the two types, the Norman Fr. and ME. *gaiole, gaole*, came down to the 17th c. as *gaile*, and still remains as a written form in the archaic spelling *gaol* (chiefly due to statutory and official tradition); but this is obsolete in the spoken language, where the surviving word is *jail*, repr. Old Parisian Fr. and ME. *jaiole, jaile*. Hence though both forms *gaol, jail*, are still written, only the latter is spoken. In U.S. *jail* is the official spelling. It is difficult to say whether the form *goal(e*, common, alike in official and general use, from the 16th to the 18th c., was merely an erroneous spelling of *gaol*, after this had itself become an archaism, or was phonetic: cf. mod.F. *geôle* (ʒol).

1668 R. L'Estrange *Vis. Quev.* (1708) 6 Some again are.. boring their very Noses with hot Irons, in reage that they cannot come to a Resolution, whether they shall say Face or Visage; whether they shall say Jayl or Gaol; whether Cony or Cunny.]

1. a. A place or building for the confinement of persons accused or convicted of a crime or offence; a prison. Now, a public building for the detention of persons committed by process of law.

α. *c* **1275** *11 Pains Hell* 219 in *O.E. Misc.* 153 In helle is a deop gayhol. *c* **1290** *S. Eng. Leg.* I. 187/105 Heo setten him in a swyþe deork put, þat in þe gayhole was. *c* **1380** *Sir Ferumb.* 1970 To my Gayhol goþ anon & þe fyue þat buþ þer Bryngeþ hem out euerechon. **1463** *Bury Wills* (Camden) 17, I wille the presoneres in the Gayle haue o day brede, mete, and drynkke, and eche persone *jd*. **1494** Fabyan *Chron.* vii. 380 The duke of Burgoyne..wᵗ the prouost of Paris, came vnto the Gayole, and there receyued the sayd Peter. *a* **1548** Hall *Chron., Hen. VI* 170 b, He was committed to the gayle of Newgate. **1572** *Act 14 Eliz.* c. 5 §38 To such sufficient persons dwellinge nighe the said Goales. **1647** Clarendon *Hist. Reb.* v. §51 To be committed to the Common Goal of Colchester. **1689** *Wonderful Predict. Nostradamus* 3, Beer shall fail The Great one Cold, and famish't in a Gaol. **1779** J. Burgoyne *Let. to Constituents* (ed. 3) 15 The goals..were resorted to for other recruits. **1846** McCulloch *Acc. Brit. Empire* (1854) II. 497 At that period the gaols were.. depositories of pestilence. **1848** *Act 11 & 12 Vict.* c. 42 §21 To remand the party accused..to the common gaol or house of correction, or other prison, lock-up house, or place of security in the county.

β. *a* **1300** *Cursor M.* 13174 (Cott.) A sargant sent he to Iaiole [*Laud MS.* Iayle] And iohan hefd comanded to cole. *a* **1400–50** *Alexander* 4321 Nouthire Iugement ne Iayll ne Iustice of aire. *c* **1440** *Generydes* 1572 Generydes was brought out of the Iayle. **1566** Painter *Pal. Pleas.* I. 42 He was sent to the iaole and examined vpon interrogatories. **1596** Shaks. *Tam. Shr.* v. i. 95 Call forth an officer: Carrie this mad knaue to the Iaile. **1674** Milton *Samson* 949 This jail I count the house of liberty. **1743–5** Bp. Pococke *Trav.* (1756) II. 184 The jayl was in the gatehouse adjoyning. **1860** Emerson *Cond. Life, Wealth* Wks. (Bohn) II. 352 A dollar in a university is worth more than a dollar in a jail.

γ. **1688** W. Fleming in *12th Rep. Hist. MSS. Comm.* App. vii. (1890) 224 Hee will get noe body to undertake the geale nor under gealership.

b. Without the article, as in the phrases 'to send to jail', 'in jail', 'let out of jail': = imprisonment, confinement in prison.

1447 Bokenham *Seyntys* (Roxb.) 77 O damysel worthily born And to oft me semyth distressyd in gayle. **1593** Q. Eliz. *Boeth.* iv. pr. v. 89 Geayle, lawe, and other tormentes for due punishment..pertayne to wicked Citizens. **1596** Spenser *State Irel.* Wks. (Globe) 620/1 Committed to goale. **1732** Law *Serious C.* xiii. (ed. 2) 216 To redeem a prisoner out of Jayl. **1863** Kingsley *Water-Bab.* i. 8 Having been sent to gaol by him twice.

c. *transf.* and *fig.* Place of confinement.

c **1400** *Rom. Rose* 4745 A swete helle it [love] is..A plesaunt gayl and esy prisoun. **1591** Spenser *Ruines of Time* 296 His happie soule to heaven went Out of this fleshlie gaole. **1593** Q. Eliz. *Boeth.* ii. pr. vii. 39 If the mynde.. dissolued from earthly gial, all freed seekes heauen. **1635** Heywood *Hierarch.* vi. 356 Each one his gaile About him had, beeing fastned to a beame. **1764** Grainger *Sugar Cane* ii. 214 Small eggs appear..alas, too soon They burst their filmy gaol, and crawl abroad.

2. *attrib.* and *Comb.*, as ***jail-fee, -gang, -gate, -guard, -keeper, -mate, -official, -rat, -room, -spy, -yard; jail-bleached, -like*** adjs.; **jail-bait** *slang* (orig. *U.S.*), a girl who is under the legal age of consent; **jail-break** orig. *U.S.*, the act of escaping from a jail; †**jail damp**, the noxious exhalation formerly common in jails; **jail distemper** = jail-fever; **jail-house** (*U.S.*), a jail; **jail money**, money paid for the maintenance of a jail.

1934 J. T. Farrell *Calico Shoes* 48 She's not hard on the eyes but she's *jail bait. **1957** J. Braine *Room at Top* xxiv. 198 I'm not interested in little girls. Particularly not in jail-bait like that one. **1972** A. Draper *Death Penalty* vi. 45 She looks young enough to be jail bait. **1871** Hay *Pike County Ball.* (1880) 33 Shadowed by his *jail-bleached hair. **1910** J. Hart *Vigilante Girl* xix. 266 Hamlin did not yet know of the *jail-break. **1952** J. Steinbeck *East of Eden* 440 Not with her holding that jail-break over him. **1973** E. Hyams *Final Agenda* ii. 24 He..led a jail-break of seventeen political prisoners. **1636** in *Crt. & Times Chas. I.* (1848) II. 244 That *goal-damp of Hereford hath already killed a great many that were at the last assizes. **1745** Reid in *Phil. Trans.* XLIII. 228 Two Convicts in Newgate..very ill of the putrid, infectious, malignant Fever, commonly call'd the *Gaol Distemper. **1799** *Med. Jrnl.* I. 90 A new and enlarged edition of Dr. J. C. Smyth's work on the jail-distemper..is nearly ready. *a* **1715** Burnet *Own Time* (1724) I. 271 They would not..pay their fines set on them, [not] so much as the *jayl fees. **1828** P. Cunningham *N.S. Wales* (ed. 3) II. 321 A single magistrate can..sentence..to the *jail gang or tread-mill. **1623** Drumm. of Hawth. *Cypress Grove* Wks. (1711) 123 When the *jail-gates were broken up. **1626** Bernard *Isle of Man* (1627) 82 The Chiefe-Gaoler is..made the *Gaole-keeper by the Sheriffe. *a* **1743** Savage *Love in Veil* iii. i, Can it..fail to tempt such fellows as jail-keepers to be perfidious to their trust? **1865** Dickens *Mut. Fr.* i. xv, With a *jail-like upper rim of iron and spikes. **1828** P. Cunningham *N.S. Wales* (ed. 3) II. 298 The prisoners would never be able to know who their *jailmates were. **1600** *Stanford Churchw. Acc.* in *Antiquary* (1888) May 212 To the Constable of the hundred for *gayole money..ijˢ. vjᵈ. **1821** Scott *Kenilw.* iii, Thou gallows-bird—thou *jail-rat—thou friend of the hangman. *a* **1683** Oldham *Poems* (1698) 197 (Jod.) The Town can scarce afford them *jail-room now. **1818** Cobbett *Pol. Reg.* XXXIII. 625 The suffering people of Lancashire..were driven by hundreds into jails and *jail-yards.

jail, gaol (dʒeɪl), *v.* Forms: see jail *sb.* [f. prec.] *trans.* To confine in or as in a jail; to imprison, confine.

α. **1622** Bacon *Hen. VII* 215 The Dislike the Parliament had of Gaoling of them. **1635** Heywood *Hierarch.* ix. 569 Unwilling To be so goald [they] struggle. **1718** *Entertainer* No. 41. 280 A Design to imprison and Gaol him for Life. **1887** *Times* 29 Aug. 4/5 Several of whom..have been gaoled for their share in the knavery.

β. **1604** T. Wright *Passions* vi. 324 They..enforce him as a iudge, like prisoners, to iayle them by iustice. **1633** T. Adams *Exp. 2 Pet.* ii. 22 The other are jailed up in the dark ..dungeon of hell. **1787** *Hist. Pelham, Mass.* (1898) 375 Day, Colton, Clark and Brown, jailed—the others not found. **1875** Tennyson *Q. Mary* iii. v, One, whose bolts, That jail you from free life, bar you from death. **1889** C. King *Queen of Bedlam* 265 The scoundrel had a wife in Denver, where he was finally tracked and jailed.

Hence **'jailing, 'gaoling** *vbl. sb.* and *ppl. a.*

1622 [see above]. **1705** Hickeringill *Priest-cr.* iv. (1721) 213 Content to..do the Priests Drudgery in Gaoling and Burning. **1862** C. J. Vaughan *Bk. & Life* 40 Not the jailing of the evil nature, but rather the exercising of the good, is the true aim and work of youthful discipline. **1869** Tennyson *Pelleas & Ettarre* 336, I will..tame thy jailing princess to thine hand.

'jailage, 'gaolage. *rare.* [ad. F. *geôlage*, f. *geôle* JAIL: see -AGE.] The jailer's fee.

1853 JAMES *Agnes Sorel* II. 162 It is the gaolage due.

jail-bird, gaol-bird ('dʒeɪlbəd). Forms: see JAIL *sb.* [With allusion to a caged bird.] A prisoner in jail; esp. one who has been long, or is often, in jail, a habitual criminal; also, as a term of reproach, an incorrigible rogue.

α. **1618-61** HOLYDAY *Juvenal* 24 *Servitia* and *Ergastala*, in Florus, signify Slaves and Gaol-Birds. **1692** WASHINGTON tr. *Milton's Def. Pop.* vi. M.'s Wks. (1851) 169 Thou Goal-bird of a Knight,..thou everlasting scandal to thy Native Countrey! **1701** DE FOE *True-born Eng.*, *Fine Speech* 124 In Print my Panegyricks fill the Street, And hired Goal-Birds their Huzza's Repeat. **1860** H. GOUGER *Imprisonment Burmah* xx. 226 We had now become old gaol-birds.

β. **1603** J. DAVIES *Microcosmos*, etc. *Sonn. to Lady Rich* (1878) 99/1 It made thee subiect to a Iaile's controule. But, such a Iaile-bird heauenly Nightingale. **1685** *Mischief of Cabals* 21 The bare oaths of a pack of Jayl-birds. **1751** SMOLLETT *Per. Pic.* IV. ciii, She bestowed on him the epithets of spendthrift, jailbird and unnatural ruffian. **1883** *Contemp. Rev.* Aug. 172 The one thing most dreaded by the old jail-bird is work requiring bodily exertion.

'jail-de,liver, *v. nonce-wd.* [A back-formation from JAIL-DELIVERY in sense 2.] *trans.* To deliver from jail.

1631 R. H. *Arraignm. Whole Creature* i. 8 It dissolves the very workes of the devill, Iaile-delivers his prisoners.

'jail-de,livery, gaol-delivery. [See DELIVERY.]

1. The clearing a jail of prisoners by bringing them to trial, esp. at the assizes; hence, the judicial process by which every prisoner awaiting trial in a jail is either condemned or acquitted at the assizes. See DELIVER *v.*[1] 2 c.

1464 *Nottingham Rec.* II. 377 Paied to the Justices of Deliuerance for the Gaole Delyuere. **1487** *Act 3 Hen. VII*, c. 4 §2 The next generall gaille delyvere of the same gailles in every Shire. *a* **1548** HALL *Chron.*, *Hen. VIII* 243 b, [He] came before the Justices of Gaole delivery at Newegate. **1618** L. PARSONS in *Lismore Papers* (1887) Ser. II. II. 154 My lord deputy intends..to make a priuate jaole deliuery at Corck of all the pirats lately taken. **1769** BLACKSTONE *Comm.* IV. 267 They have..a commission of general gaol delivery; which empowers them to try and deliver every prisoner, who shall be in the gaol when the judges arrive at the circuit town, whenever indicted, or for whatever crime committed. **1858** BEVERIDGE *Hist. India* II. v. v. 380 A court of oyer and terminer and jail-delivery was undoubtedly competent to try crimes.

fig. **1579-80** NORTH *Plutarch*, *Coriolanus* (ed. Nutt) II. 184 But my only demaunde consisteth, to make a gayle deliverie of all evills. **1860** EMERSON *Cond. Life*, *Considerations* Wks. (Bohn) II. 417 It was..a general jail-delivery of all the rowdies of the rivers.

b. ellipt. for *Sessions*, *Court*, or *Commission of jail-delivery*.

1612 DAVIES *Why Ireland*, etc. (1747) 109 At a goal deliuery at Waterford before Iohn Wogan. **1670-1** MARVELL *Corr.* Wks. 1872-5 II. 371 He had given orders to the Judges to adjourn the Goale Delivery at the Old Bailey till the 10th of March.

2. Deliverance from jail or imprisonment.

1592 DAVIES *Immort. Soul* (1599) 100 Were it knowne to all, What life our Soules do by this death receaue, Men would it birth, or Gaole deliuery call. *a* **1661** FULLER *Worthies* I. (1662) 37 To..imploy the charity of well affected people for a General Goale Delivery, of all English Captives, in Tunis, Tripoli, [etc.]. **1780** BURKE *Sp. Bristol previous to Election* Wks. III. 378 The legislature has been obliged to make a general arbitrary jail-delivery. **1818** SCOTT *Hrt. Midl.* li. *note*, Ratcliffe..was released by the Porteous Mob when under sentence of death;..the Highlanders made a similar jail-delivery in 1745. **1826** —— *Woodst.* xxxvii, The inferior personages of the grand jail-delivery at Woodstock Lodge.

jailer, jailor, gaoler ('dʒeɪlə(r)). Forms: α. 3 gayholer, 4-6 gailer, 4-7 gayler, 5 gaylere, 6 gaylour, -or, 6-7 gailor, 7 goaler, 7- gaoler. β. 4 iaioler, iaoler(e, iailere, iaylar, 4-5 iaylere, 4-6 iayler, 4-7 iailer, (5 iaylarde, 6 ioyler), 6-7 iayl-, iailour, 7-8 jaylor, -our, 7- jailer, jailor. γ. 5 geil-, geyl-, geayl-, geyel-, 7 gealer. [Two types corresp. to *gaol*, *jail*: 1) *gayholer*, *gayler*, *gailer*, etc., a. ONF. *gayolierre*, *gaiolere*, accus. *gaioleor*, f. *gaiole*; 2) *jaioler*, *jaoler(e*, *jailer(e*, etc., a. OF. *jaioleur*, *jeolier* (F. *geôlier*), f. *jaiole*, *jeole*, *geole*: see JAIL *sb.* and -ER[2] 2.] One who has charge of a jail or of the prisoners in it; a jail-keeper.

α. *c* **1290** *S. Eng. Leg.* I. 98/204 He let nime alle þe gayholers: and tormenti heom ful sore. *c* **1320** *Sir Beues* 1652 A wente quik out of prisoun Be þe rop þe gailer com adoun. **1465** *Mann. & Househ. Exp.* (Roxb.) 179 The gaylere that was att Colchester. **1530-1** *Act 22 Hen. VIII*, c. 12 The sayde Gaylour or Keper of pryson. **1611** SHAKS. *Cymb.* v. iv. 204 Thou shalt be then freer than a Gaoler. **1765** BLACKSTONE *Comm.* I. ix. 346 *margin*, Goalers are also the servants of the sheriff. **1859** DICKENS *T. Two Cities* II. ii, Two gaolers..went out, and the prisoner was brought in.

β. *a* **1300** *Cursor M.* 4434 (Cott.) Son was ioseph halden dere wit þe maister iailere [*Gött.* iaolere]. *Ibid.* 17319 (Cott.) þair Iailers [*Gött.* iaioleris] to þaim þai cald. *c* **1380** *Sir Ferumb.* 1183 þe Amyral..clepede ys iayler þer a-stede. *c* **1420** *Chron. Vilod.* st. 731 Bot þe Iaylardes folowedon þis theff full fast. **1526** TINDALE *Acts* xvi. 23 They cast them into preson, commaundynge the ioyler [**1534** iayler; **1611** Iaylour] to kepe them surely. *a* **1625** BOYS *Wks.* (1630) 262 As a cunning Iailour..he will be sure to keepe the prison doore fast. **1705** STANHOPE *Paraphr.* III. 416 This was the Faith of St. Paul's Jaylor and his Family. **1840** DICKENS *Barn. Rudge* lxxi, Their jailers had been regular in bringing food and candles.

γ. *c* **1375** *Sc. Leg. Saints*, *Adrian* 159 With geileris þane cane he trete. **1485** CAXTON *Chas. Gt.* 89 Brutamont the geayler made Olyuer & his felawes to auale doun in to a pryson. [**1688** Gealer: see JAIL *sb.* 1 γ.]

b. *transf.* and *fig.*

1514 BARCLAY *Cyt. & Uplondyshm.* (Percy Soc.) 33 Jaylers of justyce. **1607** SHAKS. *Cor.* v. i. 65 His Iniury The Gaoler to his pitty. **1642** FULLER *Holy & Prof. St.* IV. xxi. 352 A slavish fear, the jaylour of the soul. **1821** *Examiner* 1 Apr. 200/1 That we should act as the perpetual gaolers of Napoleon was most horrible and disgraceful. **1864** CONINGTON *Æneid* (1866) 7 The jailor-monarch of the wind.

jaileress, gaoleress ('dʒeɪlərɪs). Also 8-9 Jailoress. [f. prec. + -ESS.] A female jailer.

1748 RICHARDSON *Clarissa* (1811) II. xii. 72 My saucy gaoleress assured me, that all my oppositions would not signify that pinch of snuff. **1796** *Plain Sense* III. 67 He would find such a jailoress as he desired. **1863** SALA *Capt. Dangerous* I. x. 285 Knocked about by the Turnkeys, or abused by the Gaoleress.

'jailering, 'gaolering. *rare.* Also 9 jailoring. [See -ING[1] 1 c.] The occupation of a jailer.

1837 CARLYLE *Fr. Rev.* I. v. vi, Jail, Jailoring and Jailor, all three..must finish. **1897** *Daily News* 18 Nov. 2/1 'Ah!' says the Sergeant..and smoothes down that hair of his which anxious years of gaolering have dyed to its whitish hue.

jailership, gaolership ('dʒeɪləʃɪp). Also 7-9 jailorship. [f. JAILER, etc. + -SHIP.] The office or function of a jailer.

1485 *Rolls Parlt.*, VI. 349/1 The Office of Jailershipp of the Chekergate, and Burgesgate, of oure Towne of Dynbigh. **1611** COTGR. *Chepage*,..Goalership. **1688** [see JAIL *sb.* 1 γ]. **1831** TYTLER *Hist. Scot.* (1864) IV. 114 She [Mary, Queen of Scots] was removed..to the severer jailership of Paulet.

'jailery. *nonce-wd.* [f. JAIL *sb.* + -ERY.] Confinement, imprisonment.

1825 HONE *Every-day Bk.* I. 691 The decent jailery of a light wicker cage.

jail-fever, gaol-fever ('dʒeɪl'fiːvə(r)). [f. JAIL, GAOL *sb.* + FEVER *sb.*] A virulent type of typhus-fever, formerly endemic in crowded jails, and frequent in ships and other confined places.

[**1750** PRINGLE *(title)* Observations on the Nature and Cure of Hospital and Jail Fevers.] **1753** J. PRINGLE in *Phil. Trans.* XLVIII. 42 Cases of the true goal-fever arising from the gaol itself. **1780** *Gentl. Mag.* Dec. 578/1 No signs of a jail-fever were ever discovered in the Russian prisons. **1800** *Med. Jrnl.* IV. 356 The gaol fever is seldom to be met with except on board of ships or in crowded towns. **1887** *Syd. Soc. Lex.*, *Gaol fever*, a term for a very infectious and fatal fever which at various times..has broken out in crowded, dirty prisons... There is no doubt that this was Typhus fever generated in the prison out of the filth, and overcrowding, and bad diet and close foul air. **1898** BESANT *Orange Girl* II. xxii, Her cheek grew pale and thin: her eyes became unnaturally bright: I feared gaol-fever.

'jailish, *a. rare.* [f. JAIL *sb.* + -ISH[1].] Akin to or suggestive of a jail; jail-like.

1751 SMOLLETT *Per. Pic.* IV. xcix, A sort of jailish cast contracted in the course of confinement.

Jain, ‖Jaina (dʒeɪn, 'dʒeɪnə), *sb.* and *a.* [Hindī *jaina*:—Skr. *jaina* of or pertaining to a Buddha or saint, f. *jina* a Buddha, a (Jain) saint, lit. 'overcomer', f. root *ji* conquer, overcome.]

A. *sb.* A member of a non-Brahminical East Indian sect, established about the sixth century B.C., the principal doctrines of which closely resemble those of Buddhism. **B.** *adj.* Of or pertaining to the Jains or their religion.

1805 COLEBROOKE in *Asiatic Res.* (1808) V. 483 In the books of the Jainas. *Ibid.*, A treatise by a Jaina author. **1809** C. MACKENZIE *ibid.* IX. 244 *heading*, Account of the Jains. *Ibid.*, Books on the laws, customs, ceremonies and regulations of the Jain religion. **1832** H. H. WILSON *ibid.* XVII. 243 Every province of Hindustan can produce Jain compositions, either in Sanscrit or its vernacular idiom. **1839** *Penny Cycl.* XIII. 73/1 The religious ritual of the Jainas is very simple. **1881** RHYS DAVIDS in *Encycl. Brit.* XIII. 543/2 Jains, the most numerous and influential sect of heretics, or nonconformists to the Brahmanical system. **1881** *Athenæum* 30 July 142/2 The Jaina religion is closely connected with Buddhism.

Hence **'Jainism**, the religious system of the Jains; **'Jainist** *sb.* and *a.* = JAIN.

1816 G. S. FABER *Orig. Pagan Idol.* II. IV. vi. 486 The Jainist or Mahimanian. *Ibid.* III. VI. iii. 469 Among the Buddhic sect of the Jainists. **1858** J. M. LUDLOW *Brit. India* I. 66 The three great forms of religious worship which.. have sprung from Hindooism..Buddhism, Jainism, and the Sikh faith. **1893** *Nation* (N.Y.) 9 Mar. 182/2 Unfortunately there is no contemporary literature to appeal to, for the Jainist books also are of the later date.

jaiole, jaiolere, obs. forms of JAIL, JAILER.

jaip, jaiper, Sc. forms of JAPE, JAPER.

Jaipur ('dʒaɪpʊə(r)). The name of a former Indian native state and its capital city, now capital of the State of Rajasthan, used *attrib.* to designate products of this State. Hence **Jaipuri**, the dialect of this region.

1889 KIPLING in *Macm. Mag.* Dec. 152/1 The cedar sliding doors were fitted with hasps of translucent Jaipur enamel. **1901** *Jrnl. R. Asiatic Soc.* 787 Sixteen real dialects spoken over the area in which Rājasthānī is a vernacular.. fall into four main groups, which may be called Mēwātī, Mālwī, Jaipurī, and Mārwārī. *Ibid.* 788 Jaipurī may be taken as representing the dialects of Eastern Rājputānā, as far east as Gwāliōr. **1931** A. U. DILLEY *Oriental Rugs & Carpets* Pl. 37 *(caption)*, Agra copy of Jaipur plant rug. **1957** *Encycl. Brit.* XVIII. 957/2 Rajasthani language..has several dialects, the principal of which are Jaipuri, Marwari, Mewati and Malvi. **1963** *Listener* 28 Feb. 365/2 Then there is Jaipur work.

jak, var. JACK *sb.*[4]

jake (dʒeɪk), *sb.*[1] *U.S. colloq.* [Prob. the personal name *Jake*, abbrev. of *Jacob*.] A rustic lout or simpleton: usually ***country jake***.

a **1854**, etc. [see *country jake* s.v. COUNTRY 16]. **1884** G. W. PECK *Peck's Boss Bk.* 68 A masher, like many of the Jakes of the present day. **1915** *Dialect Notes* IV. 199 He's no jake even though he did come from a Nebraska farm. **1941** H. S. TRUMAN *Let.* 5 Oct. in M. Truman *Harry S. Truman* (1973) viii. 142 You'd think I was Cicero or Cato. But I'm not. Just a country jake who works at the job.

jake (dʒeɪk), *sb.*[2] *slang* (orig. *U.S.*). [Abbrev. form of *Jamaica* (*ginger*).] An alcoholic beverage made from Jamaica ginger. **b.** Methylated spirits used as an alcoholic drink.

1926 [see HIP *a.*]. **1932** *Fortn. Rev.* Mar. 324 Over twenty-five per cent. are 'jake' or 'feke' drinkers... They drink methylated spirits. **1935** H. NEVILLE *Sneak Thief on Road* II. 162 That's pure meths... They call it Blue Billy or jake, and it's known among all tramps and kip-houses and wherever men have empty lives. **1939** J. STEINBECK *Grapes of Wrath* x. 131 He would drink jake or whisky until he was a shaken paralytic.

jake (dʒeɪk), *a. slang* (orig. *U.S.*). [Origin obscure.] Excellent, admirable, fine, 'O.K.'

1914 JACKSON & HELLYER *Vocab. Criminal Slang* 48 As an adjective 'jake' means good; satisfactory; acceptable; all-right. **1921** P. & T. CASEY in *Adventure* (U.S.) 18 May 40/2 Well, if it *is* Jerrold, everything's jake. **1924** P. MARKS *Plastic Age* xxii. 247 She said the whole college seemed jake to her. **1924** WODEHOUSE *Bill the Conqueror* vi. 130 Everything was jake with Horace. **1930** [see BY *prep.* 33 e]. **1943** *2 N.Z.E.F. Times* 10 May 5/1 She'll be Jake on the counter. **1947** D. M. DAVIN *Gorse blooms Pale* 190 We'll just give [the tea] a minute to draw and she'll be jake. **1958** R. FRANCE *Race* 100 'Will you be all right..if I lie down in the wheelhouse?'..'I'm jake. You have a rest.' **1958** 'A. GILBERT' *Death against Clock* viii. 105 'If it's about the election we vote conservative here.' 'Jake by me,' said Mr. Crook politely. **1967** *Southerly* XXVII. 149 'Is she [*sc.* a train] on time?'..'She's jake tonight mate.' **1970** *N.Z. Listener* 12 Oct. 12/4 Long as there's plenty of beer, she'll be jake.

So **jake(a)loo, jakerloo** *a. Austral.* and *N.Z. slang*, in the same sense.

1919 W. H. DOWNING *Digger Dial.* 29 Jake-aloo. **1936** N. MARSH *Death in Ecstasy* xvii. 211 It'll all come out what the Australians call 'jakealoo'. **1936** 'R. HYDE' *Passport to Hell* xi. 174 Jakeloo, Starkie; she's a little beauty, clean through my arm. **1938** X. HERBERT *Capricornia* xii. 169 'Lambkin, you're not wounded, are you?'..'Na—ow! I'm jakerloo.' 'You're what?' she demanded, looking scared. 'Jakerloo Mum, jakerloo.' 'What—not a disease, my darling?' 'Na —ow—that's French for "I'm good-o".' **1965** G. MCINNES *Road to Gundagai* viii. 123 Jakeloo! Let's have the names then, *and* the addresses.

jake, earlier form of JAUK *v. Sc.*, to trifle.

jakes (dʒeɪks). Forms: 6 iacques, 6-7 iaxe, iakes, iaques, 7 jacks, 7-8 jaques, 7- jakes (also 6 iake, 8 jack). *Plural*, 6 iaxes, 7 jakeses, jaqueses, 8 jakes's; also in same form as *sing.* [Origin unascertained; it has been suggested to be from the proper name *Jaques*, *Jakes*; or from *Jakke*, 'Jack', quasi *Jakkes*, 'Jack's'.

('Gakehouse' in 1438 *Tintinhull Churchw. Acc.* (Som. Rec. Soc.) p. 179, is an editorial misreading of 'Bakehouse'.)]

1. a. A privy.

153. in Ellis *Orig. Lett.* Ser. III. III. 84 The Iaques was very well doon. **1538** *Inv.* in J. W. Clark *Barnwell* Introd. 24 The jakes of the dorter. **1549** BALE *Journ. Leland* Pref. Bj, A great nombre of them whych purchased those superstycyouse mansyons, reserued of those Lybrarie bokes, some to serue theyr iakes, some to scoure theyr candlestyckes. **1552** HULOET, Siege, iacques, bogard, or draught, *latrina*. **1570** LEVINS *Manip.* 12/13 Iake, *forica*. **1596** HARINGTON *Metam. Ajax* Pref. (1814) 14 Because I will write of a Jakes. **1620** *Naworth Househ. Bk.* 145 To a tyller for tylling the jacks, vjd. **1634** *Documents agst. Prynne* (Camden) 12 They..dragged his carckesse throughe the cittye, and cast it into the common jakes. **1649** R. HODGES *Plain Direct.* 12 Let the hous bee made a jakes for Mr. Jaques. **1657** *Manchester Crt. Leet Rec.* (1887) IV. 202 Noe close stoole, Jackes, Carrion or garbage be cast vpon the Ackers Middinge. **1701** C. WOLLEY *Jrnl. New York* (1860) 26 The more unhealthful it may prove, by reason of Jaques, Dunghills and other excrementitious stagnations. **1727** P. WALKER *Life of Peden* in *Biogr. Presb.* (1827) I. 144 He [Arius] went..into a common Jack and purg'd out all his Inwards. **1788** V. KNOX *Winter Even.* I. II. xv. 211 His book is a nasty book, and fit only for the jakes. **1855** KINGSLEY *Westw. Ho* (1861) 168 The fox..that..jumped down a jakes to escape the hounds. **1913** L. WOOLF *Village in Jungle* iv. 54 The headman's brother is to marry a sweeper of jakes! **1922** JOYCE *Ulysses* 68 He kicked open the crazy door of the jakes. **1969** *Listener* 26 June 902/3 He is at his best when not occupied with symbols..but concerned to tell how the

keeper of an 'underground jakes' mistakes a police stool-pigeon for a real poof.

b. *transf.* and *fig.*

1579 TOMSON *Calvin's Serm. Tim.* 967/1 What vermine, I pray you, is there of Monkes, and Priestes, and all that Cleargie?..that filthie and stinking iaxe hath filled the world so full. **1637** GILLESPIE *Eng. Pop. Cerem.* Ep. B iij, Cast forth as things accursed into the Iakes of eternall detestation. **1660** *Life & Death Mrs. Rump* 2 Hell..that stinking poysonous place called the Ile of Jaqueses. **1701** DE FOE *True-born Eng.* 194 We have been Europe's Sink, the Jakes where she Voids all her Offal Out-cast Progeny. **1753** SMOLLETT *Ct. Fathom* (1784) 13/1 Who eagerly explore the jakes of Rabelais, for amusement. **1829** BENTHAM *Petit. Justice* 173 The jakes, of late so notorious by the name of the Secondary's Office in the city of London.

2. Excrement; filth. *s.w. dial.*

1847–78 HALLIW., *Jakes*..applied in Devon to any kind of filth or litter. **1880** in *East & West Cornw. Glossaries.* **1886** in ELWORTHY *W. Somerset Word-book.*

3. *attrib.* and *Comb.*, as ***jakes door, jakes-like*** adj.; †**jakes-barreller**, †**jakes-farmer, jakes-man**, a man employed to clean out privies; so †**jakes-farming**; †**jakes-house** = jakes.

1596 NASHE *Saffron Walden* 155 Like a *iakes barreller and a Gorbolone. **1557–8** *Louth Rec.* (1891) 110 One locke to the *Jakes dore. **1591** PERCIVALL *Sp. Dict.*, *Privadero*, a *iakes farmer. *a* **1618** SYLVESTER *Tobacco Battered* 267 Iakes-farmers, Fidlers, Ostlers, Oysterers. **1639** HORN & ROB. *Gate Lang. Unl.* lviii. §624 The common draught-house..which the jakes-farmer..makes cleane. **1577** tr. *Bullinger's Decades* (1592) 890 A doonghill God,..a god of the *iakeshouse. **1606** SYLVESTER *Du Bartas* II. iv. I. *David* 1251 Flames from his eies, from's mouth coms *Iakes-like fumes. **1630** DAVENANT *Cruel Brother* Wks. (1673) 475 On that branch appears a Hang-man, Then a *Jakes-man, then, a Tinker.

jakkalsbessie ('jakəlsˌbɛsɪ). *S. Afr.* [Afrikaans, f. *jakkals* jackal + *bessie* berry.] Either of two trees, the evergreen *Diospyros mespiliformis* or *Sideroxylon inerme*, or their fruit. Also *attrib.*

1854 L. PAPPE *Silva Capensis* 22 *Sideroxylon inerme.* Lin. (*Melkhout.*)... The fruit (*Jackalsbesjes*) are edible. **1917** R. MARLOTH *Dict. Common Names of Plants* 42 Jakkalsbessie. *Diospyros mespiliformis*, but also *Sideroxylon inerme* (milkwood). **1932** WATT & BREYER-BRANDWIJK *Medicinal & Poisonous Plants S. Afr.* 137 The Zulus take an infusion of the bark of *Sideroxylon inerme* L., White milkwood, Wit melkhout, Jakkals-bessie..to dispel bad dreams. **1953** [see GEELHOUT]. **1963** S. CLOETE *Rags of Glory* 377 Here and there a giant tree, a baobab, jakkals-bessie, or fig, stood out—a blob dropped on the carpet. **1969** T. H. EVERETT *Living Trees of World* 285/1 A fine African member of the genus [*Diospyros*] is the jakkalsbessie, West African ebony or Transvaal ebony (*D. mespiliformis*), which becomes 70 feet tall with a trunk diameter of 3 feet. **1973** PALMER & PITMAN *Trees of Southern Africa* III. 1795 The bar at Leydsdorp is made out of a solid piece of jakkalsbessie timber.

Jakun (dʒɑːˈkuːn). [Native name.] An aboriginal people of the southern part of the Malay peninsula; a member of this people; also, their language. Also *attrib.* or as *adj.*

1839 T. J. NEWBOLD *Pol. & Stat. Acct. Straits of Malacca* I. vii. 421 The Jakuns do not differ materially from the Malay in colour or physiognomy. **1883** *Encycl. Brit.* XV. 323/2 The aborigines..are divided into a great many tribes, of which the best known are the Jakuns, widespread in the south. **1906** SKEAT & BLAGDEN *Pagan Races Malay Peninsula* I. II. v. 235 An old Jakun, who was singularly free from superstition. *Ibid.* II. III. vi. 196 In the Semang tribes the office of chief medicine-man appears to be generally combined with that of chief, but amongst the Sakai and Jakun these offices are sometimes separated. *Ibid.* IV. i. 405 It may be that before their decay, the other Jakun dialects resembled it [*sc.* Kenaboi] more than they do now... Kenaboi must be regarded either as the best specimen of Jakun recorded or else as not being Jakun at all. **1935** *Discovery* Sept. 262/2 The Jakun, straight haired and akin to the Malay, occupy Southern Johore. **1947** R. O. WINSTEDT *Malays* 14 A Jakun (or Proto-Malay) marriage ceremony..requires the groom to walk or run after his bride three or seven times round a hillock. **1958** *Listener* 13 Nov. 793/3 Ethnically, they [*sc.* the aborigines of Malaya] were divided into Jakun (proto-Malays), Negritos, and a group that was primarily Caucasoid. **1972** A. AMIN tr. *Ahmad's No Harvest but Thorn* iii. 18 If the *jakuns* come out what can we say?

jāl, var. JOL.

jalap ('dʒæləp, 'dʒɒləp), *sb.* Also 7–8 jallap, jallop, jollop. [= F. *jalap*, ad. Sp. *jalapa*, in full *purga de Jalapa*, from *Jalapa* formerly *Xalapa*, a city of Mexico, in Aztec *Xalapan* (pronounced ʃaˈlaːpan), lit. 'sand by the water' f. *xalli* sand + *atl* water + *pan* upon. (Skeat in *Trans. Philol. Soc.* 1889.) Aztec names in *-an*, with accent on penult, uniformly lost the *n* in Spanish.]

1. A purgative drug obtained from the tuberous roots of *Exogonium* (*Ipomœa*) *Purga* and some other convolvulaceous plants; the active principle is the resin contained in the tubers (***resin of jalap***).

1675 GREW *Disc. Tastes* v. §6 Jalap hath a special property of irritating the Glandulous Parts of the Mouth, and Throat. **1681** tr. *Willis' Rem. Med. Wks.* Vocab., *Jalap*, a purging drug. **1782** WOLCOTT (P. Pindar) *Odes to R.A.'s* iii. Wks. 1812 I. 19 The Lad, who would a Pothecary shine, Should powder claws of crabs, and jalap, fine. **1866** *Treas. Bot.* 626/1 Although the best jalap is obtained from *Exogonium purga*, yet many species of *Ipomæa* supply it, though of an inferior quality. **1880** J. W. LEGG *Bile* 175 Next to Colocynth as a cholagogue Röhrig sets jalap.

2. The Mexican climbing plant *Exogonium Purga*, with salver-shaped purplish flowers; also applied to some allied plants yielding a similar drug.

false or *garden j.*, *Mirabilis Jalapa*; *E. Indian j.*, *Ipomæa Turpethum*; *male j.*, *jalap tops*, *I. orizabensis* (*I. batatoides*); *Mechoacan j.*, *I. Jalapa*; *wild j.*, *Convolvulus panduratus.* (Miller *Plant-n.*)

1698 G. THOMAS *Pensilvania* 19 Poke-Root, called in England Jallop. **1725** BRADLEY *Fam. Dict.*, *Night-shade*, a Plant which the Learned Father Plumier..calls Jalap. **1809** *Med. Jrnl.* XXI. 394 Houstoun..had travelled into that part of Spanish America where jalap grows spontaneously. **1860** TYLOR *Anahuac* xii. 317 In the neighbouring forests grows the 'purga de Jalapa', which we have shortened into jalap. **1876** HARLEY *Mat. Med.* (ed. 6) 501 Jalap is now grown in the open air in botanical gardens in the south of England, and on the continent.

3. *attrib.*, as ***jalap plant, root, tuber***; **jalap-stalks, jalap-wood** (see quot. 1865–72).

1811 A. T. THOMSON *Lond. Disp.* (1818) 626 Macerate the jalap root in the spirit for four days. **1865–72** WATTS *Dict. Chem.* III. 436 Spurious, woody or fusiform jalap, jalap-wood, or jalap-stalks,..the root of *Convolvulus orizabensis*, is sometimes mixed with genuine jalap. **1866** *Treas. Bot.* 484/1 *E*[*xogonium*] *Purga*..furnishes the true Jalap tubers of commerce.

Hence **jalap** *v. trans.*, to dose or purge with jalap.

1768 FOOTE *Devil on 2 Sticks* III. Wks. 1799 II. 277 Yesterday..we bled the west ward, and jalloped the north. **1854** SURTEES *Handley Cross* (1898) II. 275 Captain Doleful again had recourse to the jalaped Tent [wine].

jalapin ('dʒæləpɪn). *Chem.* [f. mod.L. *jalāpa* (see prec.) + -IN.] A glucoside resin, one of the purgative principles of officinal jalap and allied plants; the resin of jalap-stalks. So **ja'lapic** *a.* in ***jalapic acid***, $C_{68}H_{59}O_{35}$, an acid produced by dissolving jalapin in aqueous solutions of the alkalis or alkaline earths. Its salts are **'jalapates**.

1832 *Encycl. Brit.* (ed. 7) VI. 467/1 Jalappin..was first obtained by Mr. Hume in 1824. **1865–72** WATTS *Dict. Chem.* III. 439 Jalapin is a colourless amorphous resin, translucent when in thin plates. *Ibid.* 437 Jalapate of lead..Hydrate of lead dissolves in boiling aqueous jalapic acid, forming an amorphous, easily soluble salt.

jalapinolic (ˌdʒæləpɪˈnɒlɪk), *a. Chem.* [tr. G. *jalappinolsäure* jalapinolic acid (W. Mayer 1854, in *Ann. d. Chem. u. Pharm.* XCII. 128), f. *jalappin* (now *jalapin*) JALAPIN + *-ol* -OL: see -IC.] ***jalapinolic acid***: the dextrorotatory form of 11-hydroxyhexadecanoic acid, $CH_3(CH_2)_4CHOH(CH_2)_9COOH$, a crystalline derivative of palmitic acid obtained by hydrolysis of jalapin.

1855 *Chem. Gaz.* 15 Mar. 115 The oxidation of convolvulinolic and jalapinolic acids by nitric acid. **1928** *Jrnl. Amer. Chem. Soc.* L. 1749 The resin from Orizaba root yields on hydrolysis an hydroxyhexadecanoic acid, jalapinolic acid. **1964** *Phytochemistry* III. 289 The aglycons most frequently obtained from convolvulaceous glycosidic acids have been (+)-11-hydroxyhexadecanoic acid (jalapinolic acid) and convolvulinolic acid.

jale, obs. form of JAIL.

‖**jaleo** (xaˈleo). [Sp., lit. 'halloo'.] A lively Andalusian dance, or the clapping that accompanies it.

1865 H. O'SHEA *Guide to Spain* p. xlv, The dances differ in each province... Andalucia is the land of the *jaleo de Jerez.* **1893** *Funk's Stand. Dict.*, *Jaleo*, a vivacious Spanish dance. **1967** 'LA MERI' *Spanish Dancing* (ed. 2) v. 69 Probably because of the centuries of dancing to a percussive sound, the *jaleo* accompanying the dance has developed into an art in itself.

jalloped, var. JOLLOPED *a. Her.*, wattled.

jalme, obs. Sc. f. JAMB.

jalopy (dʒəˈlɒpɪ). *colloq.* (orig. *U.S.*). Also †gillopy, jalapa, jollopy; jallopy, jaloppi(e), -y. [Origin unknown.] A battered old motor vehicle; also, an old aeroplane.

1929 HOSTETTER & BEESLEY *It's a Racket!* 229 *Jaloppi*, a cheap make of automobile; an automobile fit only for junking. **1936** J. STEINBECK *In Dubious Battle* vi. 90 Mac and Jim circled the buildings and went to the ancient Ford touring car. 'Get in, Jim. You drive the gillopy.' **1937** *Time* 17 May 35/1 They announced they would burn..used cars at the fair grounds... The huge pile of jalopies was touched off while firemen..looked on. **1938** P. GALLICO in *Sat. Even. Post* 8 Oct. 8/3 He..made a living out of the Red Arrow Hangar down at one end of the field, teaching beginners how to hoist a couple of training jalopies around the field without killing themselves. **1941** AUDEN *New Year Let.* III. 68 And in jalopies there migrates A rootless tribe from windblown states. **1951** WODEHOUSE *Old Reliable* xxi. 233 This afternoon we'll go out in my jalopy and start pricing ministers. **1955** M. E. B. BANKS *Commando Climber* vi. 114 Perhaps a succession of broken down jalopies has impaired my faith in the internal combustion engine. **1973** A. HUNTER *Gently French* ii. 22 He'd get in the jalopy beside him, start trying to pressure him.

jalous, jalousie, obs. ff. JEALOUS, JEALOUSY.

jalouse (dʒəˈluːz), *v. Sc.* [a. F. *jalouser* to regard with jealousy (13–14th c. in Godef. *Compl.*), f. *jaloux, -ouse* JEALOUS.]

1. *trans.* To suspect; to be suspicious about.

1816 SCOTT *Old Mort.* xxxviii, 'I will tell ye', said Jenny. 'I jaloused his keeping his face frae us, and speaking wi' a made-like voice'.

2. To suspect (that a thing is so); to have a suspicion of; to surmise, guess. (With *simple obj.* or *obj. cl.*; also *absol.*)

1816 SCOTT *Antiq.* xvi, He jaloused their looking into his letters at Fairport. **1827** —— *Surg. Dau.* ii, I am jalousing that the messenger and his warrant were just brought in to prevent any opposition. **1883** BLACK *Shandon Bells* xxxii, I jalouse there'll be more grey nor red in my beard by that time. **1893** CROCKETT *Stickit Minister* 119 Never for a minute did I jaloose what was comin'.

¶ **3.** (*Misused by southern writers.*) **a.** To regard with jealousy. **b.** To begrudge jealously.

1879 A. REED *Alice Bridge* 343 The Queen..ever jaloused favourites of the King. **1881** PALGRAVE *Lady Catherine's Lament*, O Queen! O Woman! does thy rage Jalouse me one caress? **1886** R. F. BURTON *Arab. Nts.* (abr. ed.) I. 44 He jaloused him and planned to do him a harm.

‖**jalousie** (ʒaluzi). [F., = jealousy; also as here.] A blind or shutter made with slats which slope upwards from without, so as to exclude sun and rain, and admit air and some light.

[**1591** PERCIVALL *Sp. Dict.*, *Gelosia*, iealousie, also a window lid. **1598** FLORIO, *Gelosia*, iealousie,..a letteise window or drawing window.] **1766** DUCHESS OF NORTHUMBERLAND *Diary* 23 Oct. (1926) 76, Rows of Seats with Jalousies in Front that they [*sc.* the women] may not be seen. **1824** *Blackw. Mag.* XV. 462 We have jalousies not only to our windows but to our breasts. **1833** MARRYAT *P. Simple* xxx, Houses after houses..with their green jalousies, dotting the landscape. **1851** *Ord. & Regul. R. Engineers* xix. 90 The Galleries, instead of being always open to the Sun and Weather, should have Jalousies, in fixed and moveable portions. **1859** TENNENT *Ceylon* (ed. 2) II. 153 Their floors are tiled, and the doors and windows formed of Venetian jalousies. **1961** I. FLEMING *Thunderball* xxiv. 254 Inside the small room, the jalousies threw bands of light and shadow over the bed. **1974** K. BENTON *Craig & Tunisian Tangle* v. 47 Tall windows shielded against the sun by wooden jalousies.

Hence **'jalousied** *a.*, provided with a jalousie.

1847 MRS. SHERWOOD *Life* xvii. 317 Vast doorways, having their green jalousied doors. **1889** *Pall Mall G.* 30 Aug. 3/1 Crooked, ill-paved streets, of tall jalousied houses.

jalpaite ('dʒælpəaɪt). *Min.* [ad. G. *jalpait* (A. Breithaupt 1858, in *Berg- und hüttenmännische Zeitung* 17 Mar. 85/2), f. *Jalpa*, the name of a locality in Mexico (probably the town of that name in southern Zacatecas): see -ITE[1].] A sulphide of silver and copper, Ag_3CuS_2, of a light metallic-grey colour when freshly fractured.

1868 J. D. DANA *Syst. Min.* (ed. 5) ii. 39 Jalpaite is a cupriferous silver-glance from Jalpa, Mexico. **1925** *Mineral. Abstr.* II. 519 Jalpaite..., as narrow veins in hornstone, gave analyses agreeing closely with the formula $3Ag_2S.Cu_2S$. **1968** *Amer. Mineralogist* LIII. 1539 Jalpaite from Silver Plume and Boulder County, Colorado probably formed at some temperature below 117°C.

jam (dʒæm), *sb.*[1] Also 9 jamb. [f. JAM *v.*[1]]

1. a. The action of jamming; the fact or condition of being jammed, or tightly packed or squeezed, so as to prevent movement; a crush, a squeeze; a mass of things or persons tightly crowded and packed together so as to prevent individual movement; a block in a confined street, river, or other passage; *spec.* in logging, an accumulation of logs in a river. Also *attrib.*

1805 *Deb. Congress U.S.* 7 Apr. 1076 Its overflowing [is] occasioned by a jam of timber choking the river. **1806–7** J. BERESFORD *Miseries Hum. Life* (1826) xv. i, To be locked up in the very heart of the most crowded of all the rooms, by that elegant jam of human kind which constitutes the great charm of your torments. **1812** H. & J. SMITH *Rej. Addr.*, *Theatre* 19 All is bustle, squeeze, row, jabbering, and jam. **1827** LONGF. in *Life* (1891) I. viii. 123, I have been several times to her evening jams; but, as it was Lent, there was no dancing. **1836** *Bytown* (Ottawa) *Gaz.* 9 June 4/3 A canoe with nine men..were engaged in taking some timber in a jam at the head of Colton's shoots. **1838** J. T. HODGE in C. T. Jackson *2nd Rep. Geol. Pub. Lands* 65 In descending we find it..overgrown for miles with elder bushes, and obstructed by jams of trees. **1848** THOREAU *Maine W.* (1894) 3 Here is a close jam, a hard rub, at all seasons. **1858** CARLYLE *Fredk. Gt.* x. ii. II. 592 There being a jam of carriages, and no getting forward for half the day. **1860** *Chamb. Jrnl.* XIV. 241 There was a jam of people. **1863** *Sat. Rev.* 305 There are two great centres and *nuclei* of jam, and crush, and obstruction. **1891** C. ROBERTS *Adrift Amer.* 83 The 'gorge' or 'jamb' was occasioned by some of these large pieces of ice getting piled in such a manner across the river as to form a sort of barrier or dam which backed the water up to a flood level. **1905** *Terms Forestry & Logging* (U.S. Dept. Agric. Bureau Forestry) 40 *Jam, to break a*, to start in motion logs which have been jammed. **1910** S. E. WHITE *Rules of Game* I. xii. 69 'Where's the drive, doctor?' asked the lumberman. 'This is the jam camp,' replied the cook. 'The jam's upstream a mile or so.' **1929** *Encycl. Brit.* XIV. 482/1 A log jam in the Montreal river, Ontario, Canada. **1955** *Times* 31 May 4/3 From all around the capital came reports of traffic jams. **1968** R. M. PATTERSON *Finlay's River* 32 So they made a risky crossing of the Parsnip [River] on a jam, wondering as they did so whether the ice-bridge over the deepest water would not give way beneath them. **1971** *Daily Tel.* (Colour Suppl.) 22 Oct. 22/1 There would be fewer frayed tempers and thus far fewer accidents—not to mention fewer jams.

b. The tight squeezing of one or more movable parts of a machine into or against another part so that they cannot move; the blocking or stopping

of a machine from this cause. Also *fig.*, an awkward or difficult situation; trouble; = FIX *sb.* 1; freq. in phr. ***in a jam*** (*colloq.*, orig. *U.S.*).

1890 *Times* 6 Dec. 12/4 The cocking tumbler can be slewed round, with a consequent jam, by a contact which a soldier in the hurry of battle would not notice. *Ibid.* 15/4 No jam would ensue, unless the soldier tried to use his rifle both as a single-loader and as a magazine arm at the same time. **1914** *San Francisco Call* 26 Oct. 7, I knew we'd get in a jam coming here. **1926** *Clues* Nov. 159/1, I think some one single-duked us, but if so I'll shiv the heel. There'll be plenty of jam. **1927** WODEHOUSE *Small Bachelor* vi. 93 'I've gone and got myself into the devil of a jam.' 'A position of embarrassment?' 'You said it!' **1938** R. D. FINLAYSON *Brown Man's Burden* 81 Henare would give his whole-hearted sympathy and his last shilling to anyone in a bit of a jam. **1950** [see CLEANER 2]. **1958** *New Statesman* 12 Apr. 459/3 He knew instinctively that in a jam it was not done to let down one's own side.

c. *attrib.* and *Comb.* (mainly in words of the American lumber-trade), as **jam-boom**, a boom on a river for jamming or blocking the floating logs sent down the stream for transportation; **jam-breaker**, one who unfixes or breaks up a jam of floating logs (Funk, 1893); so **jam-breaking** (ibid.); **jam-nut**, an auxiliary nut screwed down upon the main nut to hold it (Webster, 1864); **jam-weld** (*Forging*), 'a weld in which the heated ends or edges of the parts are square butted against each other and welded' (Knight *Dict. Mech.* 1875).

1879 *Lumberman's Gaz.* 1 Oct., From the jam-boom to the head of the sorting works is a distance of seven miles.

2. Jamming (of broadcasts, devices, etc.), or an instance of this. Hence **ˈjam-proof** *a.*, proof against jamming. Cf. JAM *v.*[1] 3 c.

1914 P. VAUX *Sea-Salt & Cordite* 129, I don't like this wireless jam! **1927** W. E. COLLINSON *Contemp. Eng.* 113 The trouble caused by jams, atmospherics, and howlings. **1964** *Ann. Reg. 1963* 185 It was said..that the needles in orbit round the earth could provide an inexpensive and jam-proof global communications system. **1972** *Sci. Amer.* June 17/1 These communications must be jam-proof; the potential attacker cannot be allowed to hope that a communications failure might prevent a retaliatory strike.

3. [This sense may belong to JAM *sb.*[2]] Jazz or similar music simultaneously extemporized by a number of performers; a period of playing such music. Freq. *attrib.*, esp. as **jam session**, a gathering of musicians to improvise jazz; also *transf.* and *fig. colloq.*

1929 *Melody Maker* Jan. 75/3 There are many variations on this rhythm..which make excellent breaks—or 'jams' as they now call them when they are taken by the whole band, the word 'break' being used only when it is intended to signify that it is played by one instrument or a section moving together or unaccompanied. **1933** *Fortune* Aug. 90/1 The jazz musicians' jam sessions where the players vie with one another in hot solos. **1935** *Swing Music* July 120/2 The best Chicagoans very often had 'jam' sessions. **1935** *Vanity Fair* (N.Y.) Nov. 71/3 Extremely hot ensemble improvisations are *jams*. **1937** *Amer. Speech* XII. 46/2 A jam band depends entirely on improvisation, using no written music. **1944** *Theology* XLVII. 278 This contemporary jam session gives enormous pleasure to the participants. But we [*sc.* the Church of England] have had little enough success in charming the ear of the nation to the extent of persuading it to come and join the band. **1949** *Chicago Daily News* 25 Mar. 33/2 One of his ambitions reportedly was to sit in on a jam session with some of our jazz musicians. **1959** R. GANT *World in Jug* 116 Everyone sat back to hear Mitch give a muted chorus which had them roaring again as we went into a final jam. **1967** 'LA MERI' *Spanish Dancing* (ed. 2) vi. 78 Martinez called bulerias 'the Cachucha of the gitanos', while Argentinita described it as a 'flamenco jam-session'. **1969** S. GREENLEE *Spook who sat by Door* xx. 170 He..moved to the stereo. 'Let's see if I can remember the jams you dig.' **1972** *Jazz & Blues* Feb. 18/3 Several musicians told me how much they enjoyed the jam sessions.

jam (dʒæm), *sb.*[2] Also 8 **giam, jamm.** [perh. a deriv. of JAM *v.*[1] in sense 'to bruise or crush by pressure': cf. quots. 1747, 1781 below.]

1. a. A conserve of fruit prepared by boiling it with sugar to a pulp.

1730–6 BAILEY (folio), *Jam* of Cherries, Raspberries, &c. (prob. of *J'aime*, i.e. I love it; as Children used to say in French formerly, when they liked any Thing) a Sweetmeat. **1747** MRS. GLASSE *Cookery* 286 To Make Rasberry Giam. Take a pint of this Currant Jelly, and a Quart of Rasberries, bruise them well together, set them over a slow fire [etc.]. **1755** JOHNSON, *Jam* (I know not whence derived), a conserve of fruits boiled with sugar and water. **1781** MRS. BOSCAWEN in *Corr. Mrs. Delany* Ser. II. III. 25 The trotting of his horse will make my strawberries into jamm before they reach the hand of yr fair niece. **1845** ELIZA ACTON *Mod. Cookery* xxi. 467 To preserve both the true flavour and the colour of fruit in jams and jellies, boil them rapidly until they are well reduced [etc.]. **1862** MRS. H. WOOD *Mrs. Hallib.* II. iv, Scarcely had Cyril begun to enjoy his black currant jam.

b. *transf.* and *fig.* Something good or sweet, esp. with allusion to the use of sweets to hide the disagreeable taste of medicine, or the like; ***real jam, jam and fritters*** (*slang*), a real treat. Colloq. phrases: ***to have*** (or ***like, want***) ***jam on it***: to have, etc., something exceedingly pleasant or easy; ***jam tomorrow***: something pleasant promised or expected for the future, esp. something that one never receives; ***money for jam***: see MONEY *sb.* 6 h.

1871 'L. CARROLL' *Through Looking-Glass* v. 94 The rule is, jam to-morrow and jam yesterday—but never jam to-day. **1874** HOTTEN *Slang Dict.* 268 *Real jam*, a sporting phrase, meaning anything exceptionally good. **1882** T. A. GUTHRIE *Vice-Versâ* xiv, Ah!.. I thought you wouldn't find it all jam! **1885** *Punch* 3 Jan. 4/1 Without Real Jam—cash and kisses—this world is a bitterish pill. **1896** *Pall Mall G.* 6 Jan. 4/1 Its [a sermon's] repetition in the guise of a play could only be justified if the jam were nice enough to make us forget the powder. **1897** MARY KINGSLEY *W. Africa* 295 Exposing yourself as a pot shot to ambushed natives would be jam and fritters to Mr. MacTaggart. **1919** *Athenæum* 8 Aug. 727/2 'Having jam on it' (*i.e.*, something nice and easy, a 'cushy' job). **1925** FRASER & GIBBONS *Soldier & Sailor Words* 130 'You want jam on it', *i.e.*, You expect too much. **1936** J. CURTIS *Gilt Kid* 23 You want jam on it, you do. **1939** A. HUXLEY *After Many a Summer* II. iii. 201 The entire capital outlay had already been amortized, so that everything from now on would be pure jam. **1946** J. IRVING *Royal Navalese* 99 The ironical suggestion made to a sailor already 'moaning' about his job—'Do you want jam on it?' **1951** 'J. WYNDHAM' *Day of Triffids* xii. 225 Just put the Americans into the jam-tomorrow-pie-in-the-sky department awhile. **1962** *Listener* 29 Nov. 925/1 Dr Leavis sees C. P. Snow as a gross materialist concerned only with jam tomorrow. **1970** *Times* 21 Feb. 6/8 Freedman says he can break even during the 10 weeks, with the jam to follow in the summer. **1972** *Daily Tel.* 30 Mar. 22/6 Ultramar has ever been the 'jam tomorrow' stock par excellence, with not a penny paid out in dividends. Instead, shareholders get scrip issues. **1973** G. MITCHELL *Murder of Busy Lizzie* i. 14 'I think Greece might be a very good idea—later on.' 'Never jam today!' muttered Margaret. **1974** O. MANNING *Rain Forest* I. vi. 87 Hugh.. was free to leave at six... Pedley..said: 'You've got jam on it: walking home in the sunset.'

c. *attrib.* and *Comb.*, as ***jam-boiler, -factory, -maker, -making, -pot, -pudding, -puff, -tart, -tin***; ***jam-like*** adj.; **jam-buttie, -butty**, a butty (BUTTY[2]) spread with jam; **jam-jar**, (*a*) a jar designed for holding jam; (*b*) rhyming slang for 'motor-car' (see also quot. 1943).

1927, 1965 Jam-buttie, butty [see BUTTY[2]]. **1970** *Times* 29 Jan. 9/8 You could have knocked us all down with a jam buttie when she [*sc.* Gracie Fields] first took up with those foreigners. **1972** *Observer* (Colour Suppl.) 16 Jan. 17/4, I am sluggish and sapped of energy and living on an occasional 'jam butty'. **1883** 'ANNIE THOMAS' *Mod. Housewife* 118 A kind of jam custard and pastry-pudding peculiar to the district, and known as 'Bakewell Pudding'. **1895** *Army & Navy Co-op. Soc. Price List* 785 [Cut glass] Jam Jar. **1902** M. BARNES-GRUNDY *Thames Camp* iv. 67 Jane went on with her jam-jar trap [for wasps]. **1934** P. ALLINGHAM *Cheapjack* xiii. 163 Have you got a jam-jar—a car? **1943** C. H. WARD-JACKSON *It's a Piece of Cake* 38 *Jam jars*, armoured cars. **1962** R. COOK *Crust on its Uppers* i. 23 Parking this dreadful great orange-and-cream jamjar..slap under a no-parking sign. **1967** N. FREELING *Strike Out* 81 A few brushes in a jam-jar. **1899** *Westm. Gaz.* 4 Apr. 1/3 His jam-like proposal will not make any the more palatable the powder of the Bill, which he is so anxious to see administered. **1896** *Daily News* 19 Dec. 8/4 A firm of jam makers were ready to give 24,000*l.* at once for the site. **1908** G. JEKYLL *Children & Gardens* ii. 12 In the kitchen the children..learn the elements of even more serious cookery, such as jam making. **1968** P. JENNINGS *Living Village* 122 Most wives buy cakes and preserves, a few still do their own baking and jam-making. **1887** *Pall Mall G.* 5 Sept. 3/1 His stand-up collar was of the kind which the gilded youth of London describe as a jam-pot. **1892** *Daily News* 16 Sept. 3/3 The new autumn bonnets have the small, high crowns known as 'jam-pot'. **1841** THACKERAY *Gt. Hoggarty Diamond* (1849) ix. 100 My dear wife..vowed she would cook all the best dishes herself (especially jam pudding, of which..I am very fond). **1864** SALA in *Daily Tel.* 30 Mar., Spending their abundant green-backs..in jam-puffs— huge triangular cocked hats of pastry. **1906** E. DYSON *Fact'ry 'Ands* xii. 161 Gets 'is quid a week..solderin' jam-tins. **1956** *Coast to Coast 1955–6* 59 He had one of the jam-tins in his hand.

2. Affected manners; self-importance; freq. in phr. ***to lay*** (or ***put***) ***on jam***. *Austral. slang.*

1882 *Sydney Slang Dict.* 5/1 *Jam* (*putting on*), assuming fast airs of importance. **1901** 'M. FRANKLIN' *My Brilliant Career* (1966) xxvi. 159 People who knew how to conduct themselves properly, and who paid one every attention without a bit of fear of being twitted with 'laying the jam on'. **1924** LAWRENCE & SKINNER *Boy in Bush* 46 Don't y' get sidey..puttin' on jam an' suchlike. **1945** BAKER *Austral. Lang.* vi. 119 Terms like..jam and guiver, connoting 'side' or affectation.

Hence **ˈjamless** *a.*, without jam.

1894 *Cornh. Mag.* May 499 She thrives..on jamless bread and butter.

‖**jam** (dʒɑːm), *sb.*[3] ? *Obs.* [f. JAMA[1].] A kind of dress or frock for children.

1793 W. HODGES *Trav. India* 3 This [long muslin] dress is in India usually worn both by Hindoos and Mahomedan and is called Jammah; whence the dress well known in England, and worn by children is usually called a jam. **1821** SOUTHEY in *Life & Corr.* (1849) I. 44, I had a fantastic costume of nankeen..trimmed with green fringe; it was called a vest and tunic, or a *jam*. **1879** LOUISA POTTER *Lancash. Mem.* 50 A little boy's dress she always called a 'Jam'.

‖**Jam** (dʒɑːm), *sb.*[4] Also **jám, jām.** ['Of obscure origin' (Yule).] A hereditary title of certain princes and noblemen in Sind, Kutch, and Saurashtra.

1727 A. HAMILTON *New Acct. E. Indies* I. xi. 115 The *Jams* to the Eastward, who being Borderers, are much given to Thieving, and they rob all whom they are able to master. **1843** SIR C. NAPIER *Let.* in G. Smith *Life J. Wilson* (1878) 440 Jam.—You have received the money of the British for taking charge of the dawk. **1849** E. B. EASTWICK *Dry Leaves* 12 A small sea-port belonging to the Jám of Nowanaggar. **1899** *Daily News* 26 July 3/2 The late Jam [of Nowanaggar] was permitted by the Government of India to disinherit his son by a Mohammedan lady,..he selected Kumar Ranjitsinghji as his son by adoption. **1913** A. G. GARDINER *Pillars of Society* 293 And so, 'hats off' to the Jam Sahib—the prince of a little State, but the king of a great game. **1958** L. F. R. WILLIAMS *Black Hills* 70 Certain chiefs.. whose original early title of Jam is by tradition associated with the mighty Iranian monarch Jamshed.

jam (dʒæm), *v.*[1] Also 8–9 **jamb**, *dial.* **jaum.** [app. onomatopœic, and akin to CHAM, CHAMP.]

1. *trans.* To press or squeeze (an object) tightly between two converging bodies or surfaces; to wedge or fix immovably in an opening, either by forcing the object in, or by the narrowing or closing in of the sides.

1719 DE FOE *Crusoe* I. xiii, The Ship..stuck fast, jaum'd in between two Rocks. **1753** WASHINGTON *Jrnl.* Writ. 1889 I. 38 We were jammed in the Ice, in such a Manner that we expected every Moment our Raft to sink, and ourselves to perish. **1769** FALCONER *Dict. Marine* (1789) X iv b, A cask, box, &c. is..said to be jammed, when it is..wedged in between weighty bodies, so as not to be dislodged without.. difficulty. **1794** *Rigging & Seamanship* I. 153 The blocks are ..jambed up..with wedges in a clave. **1818** SCOTT *Hrt. Midl.* ii, Wilson..jammed himself so fast, that he was unable to draw his body back again. *c* **1860** H. STUART *Seaman's Catech.* 14 The rammer is jammed in the gun. *fig.* **1865** CARLYLE *Fredk. Gt.* XX. i, No end to his contrivances..especially when you have him jammed into a corner.

b. To make fast by tightening.

1726 G. ROBERTS *4 Years Voy.* 111 When the Shark had ..got his Head through the Noose, to hale, and thereby jam the running knot taut about him. *Ibid.*, I jamm'd the Snare by a sudden Jirk of the Rope, and haled him up. **1755** FALCK *Day's Diving Vessel* 49 Run a jewel down, and jam all the sweeps amidships.

c. To block or fill up (a passage or avenue) by crowding or crushing into it.

1866 MRS. GASKELL *Wives & Dau.* xv. (1867) 153 Heavy box after heavy box jammed up the passage. **1868** TENNYSON *Lucretius* 169 As crowds that in an hour Of civic tumult jam the doors, and bear The keepers down.

d. To bruise or crush by pressure.

1832 MARRYAT *N. Forster* xiii, His hand was severely jammed by the heel of a topmast. **1840** SPURDENS *Suppl. Forby's Voc. E. Anglia* (E.D.S.), *Jam*, to bruise by compression. 'He jamm'd his finger in the door.' **1880** *Times* 17 Dec. 5/6 The mate got his hand jammed, and received some other slight injuries. **1882** J. B. BAKER *Scarborough* 502 Two men had each a leg jammed off.

e. *dial.* (*Eng.* and *U.S.*) To press hard or make firm by treading, as land is trodden hard by cattle.

1787 W. MARSHALL *Norfolk* (1795) II. Gloss. (E.D.S.), *Jam*, to render firm by treading; as cattle do land they are foddered on. **1890** in *Cent. Dict.* as U.S. dial.

2. *intr.* To become fixed, wedged, or held immovably; to stick fast.

1706 S. SEWALL *Diary* 6 Mar. (1879) II. 156 The Ice jam'd and made a great Damm. **1834** M. SCOTT *Cruise Midge* xix. (1859) 382 The sumpter-mule..came down rattling past us like a whirlwind, until she jammed between the stems of two of the cocoa-nut trees. **1848** THOREAU *Maine W.* (1894) 33 Just above McCauslin's, there is a rocky rapid, where logs jam in the spring. **1860** *Merc. Marine Mag.* VII. 180 The cable jammed on the windlass.

3. *trans.* To cause the fixing or wedging of (some movable part of a machine) so that it cannot work; to render (a machine, gun, etc.) unworkable, by such wedging, sticking, or displacement.

1851 *Illustr. Catal. Gt. Exhib.* 362 Immediately after the first shock..the screw was jammed or locked. **1885** *Pall Mall G.* 24 Jan. 1/2 The term 'jammed'..when used in connection with a machine gun means that the gun ceased to operate from some disarrangement of the parts. **1890** *Times* 6 Dec. 12/4 When the extractor grips a refractory cartridge the gun is jammed. **1891** LD. HERSCHELL in *Law Times Rep.* LXV. 593/1 Her propeller got foul of a rope, so that the shaft was jammed, and the engines could not be worked.

b. *intr.* Of a machine, gun, etc.: To become unworkable through the wedging, sticking, or displacement of some movable part.

1885 *Manch. Exam.* 25 Mar. 6/1 From five to twenty-five per cent of the rifles would jam after firing one or two rounds. **1889** *Spectator* 21 Sept., If the guns jam, the swords break, and the bayonets curl up, we cannot say that there is necessarily safety in the multitude of stores. **1892** *Law Times Rep.* LXVII. 251/2 [There can be no] doubt that this machinery did jam, and that it was the jamming which caused the collision.

c. *trans.* To cause interference with (radio or radar signals) so as to render them unintelligible or useless, esp. deliberately; to prevent reception of (a transmitter or station) by such means. Also *transf.*

1914 P. VAUX *Sea-Salt & Cordite* 46 Communications became regularly jammed. *Ibid.* 47 We'll stop this jamming, wherever it's coming from. **1914** *Wireless World* July 246/1 Electricity in our language..is not 'juice'; neither is radio interference 'jamming'. **1920** *Discovery* Apr. 116/2 When the reception of a message is thus interfered with by other messages being sent at the same time, the message is said to be 'jammed'. *Ibid.*, The jamming of a message may also be caused by stray ether disturbances in the atmosphere itself. **1920** *Telegraph & Telephone Jrnl.* VI. 165/1 As the number of aeroplanes multiplied 'jambing'—the great drawback of wireless—became more acute. 'Jambing'..refers to the general mix up which results from the reception of two or more sets of signals at once in the same instrument. **1926** E. F. SPANNER *Naviators* x. 124 The Admiral had answered the Japanese C.-in-C. by sending out jamming signals immediately the British scout had been driven down. **1939** *War Illustr.* 7 Oct. 126/2 Gramophone records of pledges

given by Hitler in his public speeches have been broadcast from France—and jammed by the Germans! **1947** *Amer. Speech* XXII. 154/1 Allied bombers jammed (rendered ineffective) German radar equipment by dropping quantities of metal foil when over enemy targets. **1947** *Jrnl. R. Aeronaut. Soc.* LI. 432/2 We developed a jamming screen for the purpose of blinding the enemy's early warning system and so preventing him from obtaining information of our approach. **1955** *Times* 18 Aug. 9/2 In 1933 the Vienna transmitters were put on to jam Nazi attacks on the Dolfuss Government from the Munich transmitters. Between 1934 and the outbreak of the war the device was copied wholesale. **1959** *Ann. Reg. 1958* 235 Jamming of Western broadcasts continued. **1970** *Daily Tel.* 16 Apr. 1 The Post Office is jamming broadcasts by the pirate radio ship North Sea International. **1971** *Sci. Amer.* June 132/2 Any sonar can be jammed, and clever moving jammers would pretty surely beat the art of beam shaping. **1971** *New Scientist* 2 Sept. 536/3 In 1942 they investigated the severe jamming of army radar stations, and concluded that radio waves of amazing intensity are emitted by the Sun.

4. *trans.* To press, squeeze, or crowd (a number of objects) together in a compact mass; to pack with force or vigour; to force together.

1768 WALES in *Phil. Trans.* LX. 112 [The ice] consisted of large pieces close jambed together. **1871** L. STEPHEN *Playgr. Europe* v. (1894) 121 The masses..were crumbled and jammed together so as to form a road. **1885** *Manch. Exam.* 14 Feb. 5/4 To jam them together in one or two rooms like sheep in a fold. **1886** R. C. LESLIE *Sea-painter's Log* x. 195 In these pockets nearly all the soles of a catch are found jambed together.

5. To thrust, ram, or force violently *into* a confined space.

1793 SMEATON *Edystone L.* §53 A part of a chain..was jammed in so fast..that it remained so. **1841** L. HUNT *Seer* (1864) 84 He has a small foot..and he would squeeze, jam, and damn it into a thimble. **1848** DICKENS *Dombey* iv, Everything was jammed into the tightest cases. **1855** CHAMIER *My Travels* I. i. 12 All these..useless articles were jammed into a bag. **1863** GEO. ELIOT *Romola* vi, Ruined porticoes and columns..jammed in confusedly among the dwellings of Christians. **1887** SIR R. H. ROBERTS *In the Shires* ii. 22 Hats are jammed tightly on the head.

fig. **1829** SCOTT *Jrnl.* 19 May, I have no turn for these committees, and yet I get always jamm'd into them. **1876** G. MEREDITH *Beauch. Career* III. xii. 214 He wants to jam the business of two or three centuries into a life-time.

b. To thrust, push, dash, or drive (anything) violently or firmly *against* something, or in some direction, as *down*, *in*.

1836 *Boston Herald* 12 Apr. 1/6 He jammed her against the bannisters. **1861** HUGHES *Tom Brown at Oxford* ii. (1889) 12 [He] passed close under the bows..the steersman having jammed his helm hard down. **1877** *N.W. Linc. Gloss.*, *Jaum*, to strike another's head against any hard object, such as a wall. **1887** T. N. PAGE *Ole Virginia* (1893) 158 Polly jambed the door back, and returned to his side.

c. To apply or put (a brake) *on* violently.

1925 *Morris Owner's Manual* 11 Jambing on the brakes at the last moment.

6. *intr.* To play in a 'jam' or 'jam session' (see JAM *sb.*[1] 3); to extemporize. Also *trans.*, to improvise (a tune, etc.). *colloq.* (orig. *U.S.*).

1935 *Stage* Sept. 46/2 *Jam*, to improvise hot music, usually in groups. **1936** *Delineator* Nov. 11/2 He just comes on in here once in a while because he likes to jam. **1951** E. PAUL *Springtime in Paris* xi. 203 Pierre Braslavsky could sit in anywhere old-school jazzmen are jamming. **1955** L. FEATHER *Encycl. Jazz* 132 He was seen in the Norman Granz film, *Jamming the Blues*. **1958** R. HORRICKS in P. Gammond *Decca Bk. Jazz* ix. 115 This became an important factor in Kansas City jamming. *Ibid.* 117 The legendary Art Tatum loved to jam with the resident jazz musicians. **1960** *Melody Maker* 31 Dec. 5/3 They just wanted me to jam a blues for the fourth number. **1971** *It* 2–16 June 19/1 They've been jamming together at a studio in Greenwich Village.

Hence **jammed** (dʒæmd) *ppl. a.*, squeezed, blocked up; **'jammedness**, jammed condition; **'jamming** *vbl. sb.* and *ppl. a.*

(In first quot. the form and meaning are uncertain.)

[**1617** J. TAYLOR (Water P.) *London to Hamburgh* C iv, The chaine was shorter then the halter, by reason whereof hee was not strangled, but by the gamming of the chaine which could not slip close to his necke he hanged in great torments.] **1769** FALCONER *Dict. Marine* (1789), *Jamming*, the act of inclosing any object between two bodies, so as to render it immoveable. **1887** W. CRANE in *Pall Mall G.* 16 Nov. 2/2 The mounted men charging into this jammed crowd every now and then. **1887** A. A. WRIGHT in *Boston Acad.* June 5 Browning's conciseness is more than conciseness; it is jammedness.

jam (dʒæm), *v.*[2] *colloq.* [f. JAM *sb.*[2]: cf. *butter* vb.] **1.** To spread with jam.

1852 MUNDY *Our Antipodes* (1857) 130 The slices of bread looked as if they had been first jammed and then well scraped.

2. *trans.* To make into jam. Hence **jammed** *ppl. a.*[2]; **'jamming** *vbl. sb.*[2]

1854 THOREAU *Walden* 256 The cranberries,..destined to be *jammed*. **1905** *Daily Chron.* 2 Dec. 4/4 Apples, pears, plums, berries, &c. (fresh or dried, or jammed, or tinned, or bottled). **1949** *Hansard Commons* 16 May 12 'Jamming sugar' is a term very frequently used by housewives. **1969** *Islander* (Victoria, B.C.) 21 Sept. 8/1 In many kitchens there is jamming, jelly and pickle making, perking.

jam (dʒæm), *adv.* and *a.* orig. *U.S.* Also **jamb.** [f. JAM *v.*[1]] **A.** *adv.* **1.** Closely; in close contact or with firm pressure. Often with *up* (*against*).

1825 J. NEAL *Bro. Jonathan* II. 52 He had been sitting, for two or three hours,..'jam up' in a back seat. **1842** *American Pioneer* I. 184 The next moment the sloop ran jamb against it. **1852** MRS. STOWE *Uncle Tom's Cabin* I. 49 'It'll stand, if it only keeps jam up agin de wall!' said Mose. **1932** *Kansas City* (Missouri) *Star* 24 May 18 His Chevrolet..[ran] jam up against a house.

2. *jam up*: thoroughly, perfectly, excellently; right up *to*; so ***jam-full*** adj.: packed full, completely filled; ***jam-packed*** adj.: tightly packed; closely crowded or squeezed together; hence (as a back-formation) ***jam-pack*** v. trans., to pack tightly, fill.

1835 D. CROCKETT *Acct. Col. Crockett's Tour* 192 [Andrew Jackson] went jam up for war; but the cabinet got him down to half heat. **1846** *Congress. Globe* 22 May 852 Their notion is that we go jam up to 54° 40′, and the Russians come jam down to the same. **1858** S. A. HAMMETT *Piney Woods Tavern* xiv. 146 The regular stage was jam full, and there was an extra put on, and that was jam full, and a leetle more. **1866** C. H. SMITH *Bill Arp* 61 Linton played his part of the programme jam up. **1893** G. B. SHAW *Let.* 27 Apr. (1965) 392 Friday & Saturday are jam full. **1925** R. LARDNER in *Liberty* 28 Mar. 5/1 This place is jam-packed Saturdays, from four o'clock on. **1928** WODEHOUSE *Money for Nothing* v. 96 How can you be poor, when that gallery place you showed us round yesterday is jam full of pictures worth a fortune an inch? **1936** F. CLUNE *Roaming round Darling* xxi. 214 Eventually we were jampacked in, with the ladies alternately sitting on the Poet's knees. **1938** *State Jrnl.* (Lincoln, Nebr.) 5 May 14 The foursome finally got a chance to try the floor of the ballroom before the crowd, which later jampacked it, got there. **1947** J. BERTRAM *Shadow of War* 262 It was jam-packed with neglected cargo. **1958** *Archit. Rev.* CXXIV. 383 In surprising and welcome contrast to the jam-packed streets. **1970** N. ARMSTRONG et al. *First on Moon* xiii. 322 They passed the rock boxes through to me, and I handled them as if they were absolutely jampacked with rare jewels.

B. *adj.* Usu. ***jam-up***. Excellent, perfect; thorough. *colloq.*

1832 *Boston Transcript* 6 Aug. 1/1 Do you like jam spruce beer, Miss? **1839** F. TROLLOPE *Dom. Manners Amer.* (ed. 5) 270, I must have everything jam. *Ibid.* 273 That's a jam gal. **1841** *Southern Lit. Messenger* VII. 54/2 Introduced him to the 'jam-up little company' in his command. **1855** T. C. HALIBURTON *Nat. & Human Nat.* II. ix. 261 In Paradise..connubial bliss, I allot was rael [*sic*] jam up. **1946** MEZZROW & WOLFE *Really Blues* i. 4, I got my first chance to play in a real man-size band, with jam-up instruments.

jam, variant of JAMB.

‖**jama**[1], **jamah** ('dʒɑːmə). *E. Ind.* Also *erron.* **jamma(h.** [Urdū (Pers.) *jāmah* garment.] The long cotton gown worn by Hindus.

1776 *Trial Thomas Fowke* 1 He said, he had that instant made his escape..His jammah was torn. **1800** *Asiat. Ann. Reg., Misc. Tr.* 257/1 They were in plain muslin jamahs and coloured turbans and kummerbunds. **1832** HERKLOTS tr. *Quaroon-e-Islam* App. xi, The Mohummudans tie their jāmas on the right side; the Hindoos, on the left.

jama[2] ('dʒɑːmə). Colloq. abbrev. of *pyjama*. Usu. *pl.*

1960 *Galaxy Mag.* Feb. 120/2, I groped under the bed for the paper bag that had my jamas in it. **1969** E. GÉBLER *Shall I eat you Now?* 59 She pulled her skirt on up over her pyjama trousers, and rolled the jama legs up. **1969** *Guardian* 26 Aug. 7/1 Pyjamas..in the language of lingerie..are now called 'jamas.

jama, jamabandi, varr. JUMMA, *jummabundi*.

jamadar, variant of JEMADAR.

Jamaica (dʒə'meɪkə). **a.** The name of a large West Indian island. Used *attrib.* in the names of things native to or imported from that island, as ***Jamaica bark***, ***bilberry***, ***birch***, ***buckthorn***, ***cherry***, ***ebony***, ***fan-palm***, ***shorts***. Also **Jamaica ginger**, white ginger (see GINGER *sb.* 1); **Jamaica pepper**, a name of ALLSPICE; **Jamaica wood** = BRAZILETTO.

1801 T. DANCER *Med. Assistant* 363 **Jamaica bark*... These [species] are indigenous species of the Jesuits or Peruvian bark. **1811** W. J. TITFORD *Sk. Hortus Bot. Amer.* 60 *Jamaica bilberry, or Whortle Berry. **1942** A. L. SIMON *Conc. Encycl. Gastron.* V. 40/2 Jamaica Bilberry. The edible berry of a Jamaica mountain shrub. *Ibid.*, *Jamaica Cherry. A West Indian Fig, globose and no bigger than a cherry. **1946** Jamaica cherry [see CERIMAN]. **1756** P. BROWNE *Jamaica* 299 *Jamaica Ebony (*Brya Ebenus*). This shrubby tree is common in all the lower hills. **1818** *Public Ledger* LVIII. 4/5, 20 Bags and 10 Casks *Jamaica Ginger. **1870** Jamaica ginger [see GINGER *sb.* 1]. **1920** *T. Eaton & Co. Catal.* Spring & Summer 367/3 Ginger, Jamaica, powdered. **1777** G. FORSTER *Voy. round World* I. 586 On both sides the ground was covered with a thin perennial *Jamaica-grass. **1660** HICKERINGILL *Jamaica* (1661) 12 A kind of Pepper, that tastes like Cloves, and very Aromatick (known by the name of *Iamaica-Pepper). **1959** *Sears, Roebuck Catal.* Spring/Summer 333/3 *Jamaica shorts. One pocket. **1972** *Evening Telegram* (St. John's, Newfoundland) 23 June 2/6 (Advt.), 500 only Ladies Jamaica Shorts. **1656** *Cromwell's Bk. Rates, Woods,* Brazeletto or *Jamaica wood. **1789** *Act 27 Geo. III*, c. 13 Sched. s.v. *Wood*, Brazilletto or Jamaica Wood for Dyers use.

b. *ellipt.* for *Jamaica coffee*, *rum*, etc.

1775 ADAIR *Amer. Ind.* 339 A large dose of old Jamaica and qualified mercury. **1848** DICKENS *Dombey* xvii, I'd bet a gill of old Jamaica..that I know. **1899** *T. Eaton & Co. Catal.* Spring & Summer 171/3 Coffees... Finest Santos and Jamaica with chicory. **1910** S. R. CROCKETT *Dew of their Youth* II. xviii. 142 My grandfather got his ale, of the sort just then beginning to be made—called 'Jamaica', because a quantity of the cheap sugar refuse from the hogsheads was used in its production. **1938** S. V. BENÉT *Thirteen o'Clock* 206 He bought his Jamaica personal and in the jug. **1964** *Women's Wear Daily* 30 Nov. 36 From short-shorts to slacks—with Jamaicas, Nassaus, Bermudas, knee pants in between. **1969** *Sears Catal.* Spring/Summer 41D Package of 3 Jamaicas [*sc.* shorts]. (Above-the-knee length.)

Jamaican (dʒə'meɪkən), *sb.* and *a.* [f. JAMAICA + -AN.] **A.** *sb.* A native or inhabitant of Jamaica; the form of English spoken there.

1693 *Truest & Largest Acct. Earthquake in Jamaica* 23 God curb'd their Malice, restrain'd their Power, and gave the Jamaicans a Signal Victory over them. **1770** W. GUTHRIE *New Geogr. Gram.* 613 The Jamaicans were undoubtedly very numerous, until reduced by earthquakes. **1902** J. D. HOOKER in L. Huxley *Life J. D. Hooker* (1918) II. 408 The Jamaicans do not deserve the sacrifice England is making in respect of its fruit trade. **1960** R. B. LE PAGE *Jamaican Creole* x. 116 'English with a Jamaican accent'..one could well call Standard Jamaican. *Ibid.* 120 The grammar of Standard Jamaican is not very greatly different from that of Standard English. **1970** *Sunday Times* (Colour Suppl.) 6 Dec. 39/1 Everyone's English accent..had lapsed comfortably into Jamaican during the flight. **1971** I. F. HANCOCK in J. Spencer *Eng. Lang. W. Afr.* 114 *Jamaican Creole*: spoken in one form or another by about one million Jamaicans.

b. A Jamaican cigar.

1964 I. FLEMING *You only live Twice* ii. 27 The best of the Jamaicans are quite up to the Havanas these days. They've got the outer leaf right at last. **1971** 'A. YORK' *Infiltrator* x. 144 Lucinda carefully pierced his cigar... 'I like these stogies... Better than your Jamaicans.'

B. *adj.* Of or pertaining to Jamaica or the Jamaicans.

1881 *Handbk. Jamaica* IV. 131 The Calipeva or 'Jamaica Salmon'..ranks among three specially Jamaican dainties. **1907** W. JEKYLL (*title*) Jamaican song and story. **1913** [see *gros Michel* s.v. GROS *a.*]. **1955** *Caribbean Q.* IV. II. 125, 4 Jamaican plums, hard round sugar sweets, a roast corn. **1971** [see the *sb.*, above]. **1972** 'B. GRAEME' *Tomorrow's Yesterday* xiv. 145 He..pushed a box of cigars across the table. 'Do you smoke these? They are not too bad. Jamaican.'

Hence **Ja'maicanism**, a Jamaican word or idiom.

1961 [see CHINCHY *a.*]. **1963** *Amer. Speech* XXXVIII. 136 The cultural and historical setting in which these Jamaicanisms have developed. **1967** F. G. CASSIDY in *Amer. Speech* XLII. 190 (*title*) Some new light on old Jamaicanisms.

‖**jaman** ('dʒɑːmən). *E. Ind.* Also **jamun, -oon.** [Hindī *jāmun, jāman.*] The fruit of *Eugenia Jambolana*; = JAMBOLAN. (Sometimes confounded with the Rose-apple or JAMBO, *Eugenia Jambos.*) Also *attrib.*

1826 LEYDEN & ERSKINE tr. *Mem. Baber* 325 (Y.) Another is the jaman..Its fruit resembles the black grape, but has a more acid taste, and is not very good. *Ibid.*, *note* (Y.), The jâman has no resemblance to the rose-apple; it is more like an oblong sloe than anything else. **1838** *Penny Cycl.* X. 65/2 The Clove tree, the Rose apple, and Jamoon of India, formerly included in Eugenia. **1842** *Ibid.* XXIII. 483/1 *S[yzygium] Jambolanum*..planted near villages..chiefly on account of its fruit, which is sometimes called Java plum by Europeans, but Jamoon by the natives. **1914** *Indian Forester* XL. 268 *Eugenia Jambolana*, Lam. Jam, Jamun, H[indi]. **1958** J. CAREW *Black Midas* x. 206 Get you mango,..soursop, starapple and sweet jamoon. **1965** 'LAUCHMONEN' *Old Thom's Harvest* x. 133 Everybody make their cake and ginger-beer and jamoon and rice wine. **1969** S. M. SADEEK *Windswept & Other Stories* 32 Rance lay under the jamoon tree.

jamb (dʒæm). Forms: 4–7 **iambe,** 7– **jamb, jambe;** also 5 **iamne, iawmbe,** 5–6 **iawme,** 6 **ialme, iamme,** 6–7 **iaumbe, iame,** 7 **jaume, jayme, jeame, geaum,** 7–9 **jam, jaum,** 8–9 **jaumb, jawm.** [a. F. *jambe* = ONF. *gambe*, Pr. *camba*, Cat., It. *gamba* leg:—late L. *gamba* 'hoof', in later pop. L. 'leg'; referred by Diez to an earlier *camba* (as in OSp., Pr., and Sard.), from Celtic *camb-* crooked, bent. In senses 1, 1 b, still spelt *jambe*. The dial. pronunciation from Cumbria and Yorkshire to Shropsh. is (dʒɔːm, dʒɒm).]

1. *Her.* A leg; = GAMB.

1725 COATS *Dict. Her.*, *Jamb*, is the French Word signifying a Leg, or Shank, and some English Heralds have made Use of it in that Sense. **1882** CUSSANS *Her.* vi. (ed. 3) 87 A Leg, styled heraldically a Jambe, or Gambe, which is usually represented as erased, or torn from the body.

b. *Armour.* A leg-piece made of metal or cuir-bouilli; cf. JAMBEAU.

[*c* **1386**: see JAMBEAU *v.rr.*] **1834** PLANCHÉ *Brit. Cost.* 138 The greaves or jambs for the legs. **1860** FAIRHOLT *Costume Eng.* (ed. 2) 111 In the armoury of Lord Londesborough is a jambe and solloret of this era.

2. *Arch.* Each of the side posts of a doorway, window, or chimney-piece, upon which rests the lintel; a cheek; esp., in popular use, (*pl.*) the stone sides or cheeks of a fire-place.

1428 in Heath *Grocers' Comp.* (1869) 6 Unwroughte Stapylton stone..for wyndowes, wyndow jambes and sills. *c* **1467–9** *Durham Acc. Rolls* (Surtees) 642 Factura unius Iambe in fenistra australi. **1501** DOUGLAS *Pal. Hon.* III. xvii, Subtill muldrie wrocht mony day agone, On Buttereis, Ialme, Pillaris and plesand springis. **1565** GOLDING *Ovid's Met.* XII. (1593) 284 Yet caught he upon his shoulders twaine A stone the iawme of either doore. **1584** R. SCOT *Discov. Witchcr.* v. i. (1886) 73 He [a mouse] was killed comming out of the hole of a jamme in a windowe. **1611** CORYAT *Crudities* 303 In one of the higher chambers there is the fairest chimney for clauy and ieames that ever I saw. **1611** COTGR., *Ante*,..the cheeke, or iaumbe of a doore. **1663** GERBIER *Counsel* 7 Three Inches broader than the breadth of his James and Cornish. **1719** D'URFEY *Pills* (1872) VI. 142 To the Jawm of a Chimney spend I my breath. **1725** W.

HALFPENNY *Sound Build.* 13 Door, or Window, whose Jaums..splays more or less. **1793** SMEATON *Edystone L.* §286, I set about leading the door hooks into the jambs. **1833** J. LARDNER *Manuf. Metal* II. 170 The front of the stove, generally cast in a single plate, and fitting within the jambs, or chimney bottom. **1870** F. R. WILSON *Ch. Lindisf.* 61 Two narrow lights..corbelled out towards the top of the jaumbs. **1889** D. C. MURRAY *Danger. Catspaw* 108 She was clinging to the jamb of the door.

fig. **1848** CLOUGH *Bothie* v. 25 Perfect as picture.. Through the great granite jambs, the stream, the glen, and the mountain.

3. Each of the two side-pieces or cheeks of anything. *rare.*

c **1400** *Destr. Troy* 939 Jason..gyrd of his hede, Vnioynis the Iamnys þat iuste were to-gedur: Gyrd out the grete tethe. *Ibid.* 11114 Pirrus..flang at hir with a fyne swerd, Share of þe sheld at a shyre corner; Vnioynet the Iawmbe of þe iust arme, þat hit light on þe laund. **1864** RAWLINSON *Anc. Mon.* II. vii. 62 The jambs of the spear-head were exceedingly short.

†**4.** A projecting 'wing' of a building. *Obs.*

1597 in Craufurd *Univ. Edinb.* (1808) 41 Thereafter the lower schoole in the south jambe was appointed for the Humanity. *c* **1600** *Hist. Kennedys* in Paterson *Hist. Ayrsh.* (1863) p. cxi, [They had effected a breach] in the wall of the jayme. **1793** *Statist. Acc. Scot.* VIII. 311 It [the Church] has a large *jam*, very commodious for dispensing the Sacrament.

5. A projecting columnar part of a wall; a columnar mass or pillar in a quarry or mine.

1687 *Hist. Sir J. Hawkwood* xv. 33 We..bolted the Door on the inside, and so hid ourselves in a Nook, or behind the Geaum of the Wall, to expect the event. *a* **1825** FORBY *Voc. E. Anglia*, *Jamb*, a mass of masonry in a building, or of stone or other material in a quarry or pit, standing upright, and more or less distinct from neighbouring or adjoining parts. **1875** KNIGHT *Dict. Mech.*, *Jamb*, a pillar of ore in a mine.

†**6.** An angular turn or corner in a street or way. *Obs.*

1567 FENTON *Trag. Disc.* 165 They came deuisynge merely together till they were at the iaumbe or torne of a streete. **1579** —— *Guicciard.* IV. (1599) 179 Gurlin remembring that from a part or Iawme of Stampace bending towards the towne, there was a way that led to the gate of the sea.

7. *Mining.* A bed of clay or stone running across a mineral vein or seam.

1721 BAILEY, *Jam, Jamb*, a thick Bed of Stone which hinders the Miners in their pursuing the Veins of Oar. **1747** HOOSON *Miner's Dict.* K iij b, These Jaums are sometimes found in the Top of the Lime. **1787** MARSHALL *Norfolk* (1795) II. Gloss. (E.D.S.), *Jam*, a vein or bed of marl or clay.

8. *attrib.* and *Comb.*, as ***jamb-lining, -post, -shaft, -splay, -stone***, etc.

1823 P. NICHOLSON *Pract. Build.* Gloss. 587 *Jamb-post*, a post fixed on the side of a door, etc., and to which the jamb-lining is attached. **1825** J. NICHOLSON *Operat. Mechanic* 538 In every pier, between windows and other apertures, every alternate jamb-stone ought to go through the wall with its bed perfectly level. **1879** SIR G. SCOTT *Lect. Archit.* I. 281 This, if the arch were made slightly segmental, would die into the jamb-splay. **1898** J. T. FOWLER *Durh. Cathedr.* 49 Windows..deeply recessed within, and flanked by jamb-shafts of the local Frosterley marble.

jamb, variant of JAM *v.*[1]; obs. form of YAM.

jambalaya (dʒæmbəˈleɪə). orig. *U.S.* Also **jambalayah, jambolaya.** [Louisiana Fr., f. Provençal *jambalaia.*] A dish composed of rice together with shrimps, chicken, turkey, etc. Also *fig.*

1872 *New Orleans Times* 28 June, Those who brought victuals, such as gumbo, jambalaya, etc., all began eating and drinking. **1905** 'O. HENRY' in *Munsey's Mag.* July 467/2 Terrapines,..jambolaya, and canvas-covered ducks. **1916** *Dialect Notes* IV. 269 The show was a regular jambalaya of stunts. **1949** B. A. BOTKIN *Treas. S. Folklore* IV. i. 552 Louisianians [grow lyrical] over the superiorities of the Cajun and Creole cuisine—gombo, jambalaya, bouillabaisse. **1961** *Listener* 14 Dec. 1050/2 *Jambalaya*..is based on a creole mixture of ham chunks, prawns, and rice, highly flavoured and simmered in chicken stock. **1973** L. HELLMAN *Pentimento* (1974) 78 The dinner was wonderful: jambalaya, racoon stew, and wild duck.

†**jambart.** *Obs. rare.* Var. of JAMBER.

1850 BOUTELL in *Gentl. Mag.* CXX. II. 45 The lower limbs have jambarts or front-guards of plate or leather.

jambe, var. JAMB.

jambé, var. JAMBY *a.*

†**jambeau** (ˈdʒæmbəʊ). *Obs.* exc. *Hist.* Forms: *Pl.* 4–5 **iambeaus, -beux, -bieux,** 5 **iaumbeuxe,** 6 **giambeux,** 7–9 **jambeux, -beaux.** [In form repr. AF. **jambeau* deriv. of *jambe* leg.] A piece of armour for the leg; *pl.* leggings; a pair of jambes.

c **1380** *Sir Ferumb.* 5615 Be ys iambeaus forþ he swarf & ys oþer spore þanne he carf, Adoun riȝt by the hele. *c* **1386** CHAUCER *Sir Thopas* 164 Hise Iambeux [*so* 3 *texts*; *Cambr.* Iambieux, *Petw.* Iaumbeuxe, *Corp. & Lansd.* Iambes] were of qwyrboilly, His swerdes shethe of Yuory. **1590** SPENSER *F.Q.* II. vi. 29 A large purple streme adowne their giambeux falles. **1700** DRYDEN *Palamon & Arc.* III. 35 With jambeux arm'd, and double plates of steel.

†**jambee.** *Obs.* Also 8 **jumbee.** [f. *Jambi* a district, town, and large river of Sumatra, lying due south of Singapore.] A species of *Calamus* or *Dæmonorops* from the district of Jambi; a cane or walking-stick made of this, fashionable in the time of Queen Anne.

1704 *Lond. Gaz.* No. 4059/4 The following Goods, viz... Jumbee Canes,..Dragon's Blood Canes. **1709** STEELE *Tatler* No. 142 ¶¶5–6 Yours [a cane] is a true Jambee, and Squire Empty's only a plain Dragon. This Vertuoso has a Parcel of Jambees now growing in the East Indies. **1885** DOBSON *Select. fr. Steele* 479 *note*, A Jambee..is a knotty bamboo of a pale brown hue.

†**ˈjamber, -bier.** *Obs.* Also 4 **iaumber, iamber,** 7 **jamar.** [ME. a. AF. *ja(u)mbere* = F. *jambière*, armour that covers the leg, deriv. of *jambe* leg.] Armour for the legs; a greave. Hence †**jambered (jamar'd)** *a.*, armed with greaves.

13.. *Guy Warw.* (A.) II. cxviii, Þe..swerd doun gan glide ..þat gambisoun & iambler Boþe it karf atvo y-fere. *c* **1330** R. BRUNNE *Chron. Wace* (Rolls) 10026 Hym self was armed fynly wel Wyþ sabatons, & spores, & iaumbers of stel. *c* **1400** *Sege Jerus.* 1114 Fyf hundred fiȝtyng men,..In jepouns & jambers, Jewes þey wer. **1601** HOLLAND *Pliny* XVI. xxxix. I. 489 The mourrions, iambriers, or grieues, of braue men in times past. **1668** GLANVILL *Plus Ultra* 66 [The microscope] represents that little Creature [a flea] as bristled and jamar'd ..if the mentioned bristles and jamars are in the Glass, and not in the Animal, they would appear..in all the small Creatures..look'd on through the Microscope. **1706** PHILLIPS, *Jambier*, a Greave or Leg-piece; an Armour for the Leg.

†**jamble**, *v.*, obs. var. of JANGLE.

1715 HEARNE *Rem.* 28 May (1869) II. 2 This being the duke of Brunswick, commonly called King George's birthday, some of the bells were jambled in Oxford, by the care of some of the whiggish fanatical crew. **1726** *Ibid.* 20 Oct. II. 605 This being the Coronation-day of George Duke of Brunswick, commonly called King George, there was mighty jambling of bells very early in the morning.

‖**jambo, jambu** (ˈdʒæmbəʊ, -buː). *E. Ind.* Also **jamboo, jambos, jumboo.** [Various vernacular forms repr. Skr. *jambu, jambū* 'rose-apple', and its derivatives *jambula, jambūla*, etc.] A name given in different parts of the East Indies and Malay Archipelago to several species of *Eugenia* (N.O. *Myrtaceæ*), and their fruits; esp.

a. *Eugenia Jambos* (*Jambosa vulgaris*), the Rose Apple.

1598 tr. *Linschoten's Voy.* I. (Hakluyt Soc.) II. 29, 30 (Stanf.) Of Iambos. In India ther is another fruit that for the beautie, pleasant taste, smell, and medicinable vertue thereof, is worthie to bee written of... The Iambos tree taketh deepe roote. **1613** PURCHAS *Pilgrimage* (1614) 505 The Iambos..smelleth like a Rose, is ruddie; and the tree is never without fruit or blossomes. **1775** MASSON in *Phil. Trans.* LXVI. 270 No Indian fruits, except the guyava and jambo. **1851** *Illustr. Catal. Gt. Exhib.* 1319 Jambo, Rose apple (*Eugenia jambos*).

b. *Eugenia Jambolana*, the Java Plum, also called JAMBOLAN and JAMAN.

1835 BURNES *Trav. Bokhara* (ed. 2) II. 36 They consisted of the peach,..mango, jamboo, bair, date,..and apple. **1866** LIVINGSTONE *Jrnl.* (1873) I. vii. 172 We got some wretched wild fruit like that called 'jambos', in India. **1879** SIR E. ARNOLD *Lt. Asia* VI. (1881) 143 The books Tell how jambu-branches, planted thus Shoot with quick life in wealth of leaf and flower.

c. *Eugenia malaccensis*, the Malay Apple, and kindred species, native to the Malay archipelago.

1727 A. HAMILTON *New Acc. E. Ind.* I. xxi. 255 Their Jambo Malacca is very beautiful and pleasant. **1772–84** COOK *Voy.* (1790) I. 280 The jamboo is a fruit that has but little taste, but is of a cooling nature: it is considerably less than a common-sized apple,..its shape is oval, and its colour a deep red. **1789** G. KEATE *Pelew Isl.* 257 *note*, It is the Jamboo Apple, the *Eugenia Malaccensis* of Linnæus. **1812** MARIA GRAHAM *Jrnl. Resid. Ind.* 22 (Y.) The jumboo, a species of rose-apple, with its flowers like crimson tassels covering every part of the stem. **1883** MRS. BISHOP *Sk. Malay Pen.* v. in *Leisure Ho.* 198/2 Clusters of a species of jambu, a pear-shaped fruit.

So ‖**jambol, jambul** [Skr. *jambula, jambūla*: see JAMBO]; also **jambolan** = JAMBO b.

1613 PURCHAS *Pilgrimage* (1614) 505 But of these, also the Carambolas, Iambolijns and other Indian fruits, I leave to speake. **1866** *Treas. Bot.* 634/2 Jambolan-tree, *Calyptrantes Jambolana.* **1880** C. R. MARKHAM *Peruv. Bark* 32 By the roadside..there were roses, daturas, and jambol-trees (*Eugenia Jambolanum*) with heads of graceful flowers. **1887** *Syd. Soc. Lex.*, *Jambul*, the *Syzygium jambolanum.*

jambok, var. SJAMBOK, a powerful whip.

†**jambon.** *Obs.* [Fr. (ʒɑ̃bɔ̃): see GAMMON.]

1. = GAMMON 2.

1655 MOUFET & BENNET *Health's Improv.* (1746) 150 The Normans..whose Bacon flitches and Jambons Varro extolleth. **1668** R. L'ESTRANGE *Vis. Quev.* (1708) 206, I would not affront the Jambon; for Water upon Gammon, would be false Heraldry.

†**2.** A mollusc of genus *Pinna* (F. *jambonneau*).

1753 CHAMBERS *Cycl. Supp.*, *Jambon*,..a kind of sea-shell, resembling a ham of bacon. It is a species of pinna marina.

jambone (ˈdʒæmbəʊn). *Euchre.* ? *Obs.* (See quots.)

1864 W. B. DICK *Amer. Hoyle* (1866) 83 A party who plays Jambone plays a lone hand with his cards exposed upon the table. **1886** *Euchre: how to play It* 42 A Jambone is to play a lone hand with the cards exposed on the table, and to give to that adversary who is entitled to the lead, or whose first play it is, the privilege of calling one of the exposed cards to the first trick played, or if the jambone player has the lead, to call upon him to lead any one of the exposed cards.

jamborandi, variant of JABORANDI.

jamboˈree. **a.** A noisy revel; a carousal or spree. orig. *U.S. slang.*

1868 *N.Y. Herald* 10 July 8/3 The Seventh regiment has gone on a jamboree to Norwich, Connecticut. **1872** *Scribner's Mag.* IV. 363 (Farmer) There have not been so many dollars spent on any jamboree. **1878** W. H. DANIELS *That Boy* xv. 236 He enjoyed a drinking bout or a jamboree as well as if he couldn't write the finest poetry in the language. **1895** W. O'BRIEN *On the Eve* 25/2 The Orange bad boys who..would be making the air of Belfast hideous about this time of the year with their annual jamboree over the July anniversaries. **1955** H. SPRING *These Lovers fled Away* iii. 90 There was some jamboree or other at the Assembly Rooms. **1959** *Economist* 27 June 1144/1 This is sufficiently important, and difficult, to warrant a top-level western conference this year—not merely another Atlantic jamboree. **1960** A. HUXLEY *Let.* 17 July (1969) 893 Meet me in Boston with the Microbus and drive me..to Hanover, where you might stay for all or part of the Jamboree (at which I am to receive an honorary degree). **1973** G. SCOTT *Water Horse* (1974) v. 33 Even the most respectable souls milled around the countryside..holding all sorts of jamborees.

b. *Euchre.* A lone hand containing the five highest cards. ? *Obs.*

1886 *Euchre: how to play It* 45 *Jamboree* signifies the combination of the five highest cards, as, for example, the two Bowers, Ace, King, and Queen of trumps in one hand, which entitles the holder to count sixteen points. The holder of such a hand simply announces the fact, as no play is necessary; but should he play the hand as a Jambone, he can count only eight points, whereas he could count sixteen if he announced it as a Jamboree.

c. The name given to the 1920 International Rally of Boy Scouts, and now applied to any large scout rally. Also *attrib.*

1919 *Times* 17 Oct. 9/6 The Council of the Boy Scouts Association announce that a 'Jamboree' will be held at Olympia, for about eight days next August. **1931** *Mag. Univ. Students' Union* Apr. 2 The Jamboree spirit was marvellous. **1955** *Times* 20 Aug. 9/3 The four-year cycle for jamborees is being broken in order to commemorate in 1957 the fiftieth anniversary of scouting.

jambosine (ˈdʒæmbəʊsaɪn). *Chem.* [f. Bot.L. *jambosa* (see JAMBO) + -INE[5].] An alkaloid, $C_{10}H_{15}NO_3$, obtained from the root bark of *Jambosa vulgaris* (*Syd. Soc. Lex.* 1887).

jambu: see JAMBO.

†**ˈjamby**, *a.* *Obs.* Also 5 **jambé.** [a. F. *jambé* legged, well-legged.] Strong on the legs.

? *a* **1400** *Morte Arth.* 373, I salle be at journee with gentille knyghtes, On a jamby stede fulle jolyly graythide. *Ibid.* 2895 One a jambe stede this jurnee he makes.

‖**jamdani** (dʒɑːmˈdɑːniː). *E. Ind.* Also **-danee.** [Pers. *jāmdānī.*] 'A species of fine cotton cloth with spots or flowers woven in the loom'.

1858 SIMMONDS *Dict. Trade*, *Jamdanee*, a flowered Dacca wove muslin.

James (dʒeɪmz). [a. OF. *James* (*Gemmes*, **Jaimes*) = Sp. *Jaime*, Pr., Cat. *Jaume*, *Jacme.* It. *Giacomo*:—popular L. **Jacomus*, for *Jacobus*, altered from L. *Iaˈcōbus*, a. Gr. Ἰάκωβος, ad. Heb. *yaʕăqōb* Jacob, a frequent Jewish name at all times, and thus the name of two of Christ's disciples (St. James the Greater and St. James the Less); whence a frequent Christian name.]

I. A Christian name of men: hence in various transferred senses. (See also JEAMES.)

1. a. A sovereign. *slang.* (Cf. JACOBUS.) **b.** ***James Royal***, a Scottish silver coin of James VI, the Sword dollar.

1567 in Keith *Hist. Ch. & St. Scot.* App. (1734) 150 That thair be cunyeit ane Penny of Silver callit the James Ryall, ..of Weicht an Unce Troyis-weicht,..havand on the ane Syde ane Swerd with ane Crown upoun the same. **1858** A. MAYHEW *Paved w. Gold* III. xvii. 365 The firm..was in the habit of pricing its ' half-James' and 'James' (*i.e.* half and whole sovereigns) at 2*s.* 10*d.* and 7*s.* **1893** P. H. EMERSON *Signor Lippo* xxi, He gives him the half-James, and told him never to bother him no more.

2. A burglar's crow-bar; = JEMMY *sb.* 6.

1812 J. H. VAUX *Flash Dict.*, *Jemmy* or *James*, an iron-crow. **1885** *Pall Mall G.* 29 May 11/2 The uses and varieties of the James will be at once understood when it is explained that it is used as a lever of the third order. **1896** A. MORRISON *Child Yago* 319 He wondered what had become of the james and the gimlets.

3. A sheep's head; = JEMMY *sb.* 7.

1827 *Becher's Every Nt. Bk.* 38 (Farmer) Hear us, great James, thou poetry of mutton; Delicious profile of the beast that bleats. **1870** *Lond. Figaro* 2 July (ibid.), Club your pence, and you may attain to the glories of Osmazome and James—that is, of baked sheep's head.

II. St. James, either apostle of the name; esp. St. James the Greater, chosen as the Patron Saint of Spain, whose shrine at Compostella was a famous centre of pilgrimage. ***St. James's day, St. James's tide*** (dial. ***James-mass***), the 25th of July, dedicated to St. James the Greater.

a **1225** *Ancr. R.* 192 For þi, seið sein Iame, 'Omne gaudium [etc.]'. *c* **1386** CHAUCER *Shipman's T.* 355, I thanke yow by god and by seint Iame. *a* **1568** ASCHAM *Scholem.* I. (Arb.) 36 Thies yong scholers be chosen commonlie, as yong apples be chosen by children, in a faire garden about S. Iames tyde. **1641** *Churchw. Acc. St. Margaret's, Westminster* (Nichols 1797) 47 Paid to the singing men of the Abbie towards their feast at S[t] James's tide. **1701** *Lond. Gaz.* No. 3718/4 The Fairs held at the City of Bristol at St. James-

Tide.. will not begin before the 25th of July. **1898** *Westm. Gaz.* 25 July 10/1 There is a popular saw that 'Whoever eats oysters on St. James's Day will never want money', and this is due to an indistinct connexion with the saint of the scallop shell.

b. St. James's wort (also dial. ***James wort, James-weed***), Ragwort, *Senecio Jacobæa.*

1578 LYTE *Dodoens* I. xlviii. 69 S. Iames worte groweth almost euery where, alongst by wayes and waterish places, and.. in the borders of fieldes. **1579** LANGHAM *Gard. Health* (1633) 577 Saint James wort, it hath a speciall vertue to heale wounds. **1597** GERARDE *Herbal* II. xxvi. §1. 218 Saint Iames his woort or Ragwoort.

III. Also, a surname; hence, **James's powder**, a febrifuge very popular during the latter part of the 18th century and at the beginning of the 19th; prepared by Dr. Robert James (1703–1776).

*a*1776 R. JAMES *Dissert. Fevers* (1778) 94 Suppose a patient or his friends, should insist upon trying James's Powders, a little confederacy might easily blast all hopes. **1801** H. SWINBURNE in *Crts. Europe* (1841) II. 304 They say his [Geo. III's] illness was brought on by his taking a most extraordinary dose of James's powders of his own accord.

James Bond (ˌdʒeɪmz ˈbɒnd). The name of the hero of a series of novels by the British writer Ian Fleming (1908–64), used allusively (freq. *attrib.* or as *adj.*) of adventurous, sophisticated men resembling the hero, or of situations similar to those in the novels. So **James 'Bondish** *a.*

1966 *Economist* 19 Mar. 1115/1 There was nothing James Bondish about his arrival, for Mr Smith's external relations department was informed well in advance. **1967** *Guardian* 23 Dec. 14/2 The escape itself was James Bond with the merest trace of Keystone Cops. **1968** *Ibid.* 23 Feb. 7/4 This fast James Bond stuff doesn't blend happily with the more realistic comedy. **1968** K. BIRD *Smash Glass Image* iv. 54, I should love to deck myself out as a two-fisted James Bond because that would impress you. **1970** *Motoring Which?* Apr. 43/2 Aston Martin DB5—very powerful James Bond car. **1972** G. LYALL *Blame the Dead* vii. 47 People who.. go running around France playing James Bond with unlicensed Walthers.

Jamesian (ˈdʒeɪmzɪən), *a.* (*sb.*) [f. *James* + -IAN.]

1. Of or pertaining to the American philosopher and psychologist William *James* (1842–1910) or his works. Also as *sb.*, a follower or admirer of William James.

1875 C. WRIGHT *Let.* 18 July in R. B. Perry *Tht. & Char. W. James* (1935) I. 532 He rather attracts me by the Jamesian traits. **1935** R. B. PERRY *Tht. & Char. W. James* II. 668 While there are very few pure Jamesians, in the sense of direct descent, the world is full of mixed Jamesians, who acknowledge their common relationship to him without feeling any bond with one another. **1955** KOESTLER *Trail of Dinosaur* 249 The Jamesian view that a transcendental faith was a biological necessity for man. **1964** *Amer. Philos. Q.* I. 115/1 Elements in the German phenomenology of the 1930's.. are clearly repugnant to the post-Jamesian American philosophical temper.

2. Of or pertaining to the American (later naturalized British) writer Henry *James* (1843–1916) or his works. Also as *sb.*, a follower or admirer of Henry James.

1905 *Daily Chron.* 7 Sept. 3/1 The plot.. is Jamesian.. in its tenuity. **1954** *Essays in Crit.* IV. 371, I am not a good enough Jamesian to decide the other claim. **1958** *Listener* 17 July 98/1 For Jamesians, it is the first thrilling scent of the great chase. **1972** J. SYMONS *Bloody Murder* xvi. 235 The motivations of his characters seem at times to be of Jamesian complexity.

James-Lange (ˈdʒeɪmzˈlæŋə). *Psychol.* The names of W. *James* (1840–1900) and C. G. *Lange* (1834–1900), used *attrib.* to designate a theory propounded by each of them separately that the response to an emotional stimulus is, in the first place, an organic reaction rather than a mental awareness of the emotion.

1909 H. R. MARSHALL *Consciousness* I. App. A. 109 It is not correct to say either that the emotions cause the instinctive reaction.. nor to say that the instinctive reactions cause the emotions, as the common statement of the James-Lange theory implies. **1914** M. PRINCE *Unconscious* xiv. 423 The James-Lange theory is disregarded here as untenable. **1918** E. JONES *Papers on Psycho-Anal.* (ed. 2) xxvii. 485 The occurrence of the abortive anxiety attacks.. stands in direct conflict with the James-Lange hypothesis. **1933** G. MURPHY *Gen. Psychol.* v. 75 Such evidences might even lead to a partial confirmation of the James-Lange view. **1949** D. O. HEBB *Organization of Behavior* x. 237 Just such an inconsistency of thought has led to an endless, and pointless, debate on the James-Lange theory of emotion. **1970** H. C. SHANDS *Semiotic Approaches to Psychiatry* xx. 307 The James-Lange notion is an interpretation of a communicational process involving feedback from one's own behavior.

Jameson (ˈdʒæmiːsən, ˈdʒeɪ-, ˈdʒɪ-). The proprietary name of a brand of Irish whiskey. Also, a drink of this whiskey.

[**1877** *Trade Marks Jrnl.* 28 Feb. 568/1 W. Jameson & Co. Distillers. Dublin. William Robertson, on behalf of self and partners, William Jameson and James Jameson, trading as Wm. Jameson and Co.,.. Dublin; whiskey distillers.] **1922** JOYCE *Ulysses* 176 We'll take two of your small Jamesons after that. **1948** W. STEVENS *Let.* 7 Sept. (1967) 613 Perhaps if I could have that bottle of Jameson.. on the reading stand, I could really get somewhere. **1965** *Trade Marks Jrnl.* 24 Mar. 414/1 Jameson.. Irish whiskey.. John Jameson & Son Limited,.. Dublin.

jamesonite (ˈdʒeɪmsənaɪt). *Min.* [Named 1825 after Professor Jameson, of Edinburgh (1773–1854).] Sulph-antimonide of lead, usually occurring in fibrous masses; feather-ore.

1825 HAIDINGER tr. *Mohs' Min.* I. 451. **1868** DANA *Min.* (ed. 5) 91 Jamesonite occurs principally in Cornwall.

Jamestown-weed, var. JIMSONWEED.

Jamie Green (ˈdʒeɪmɪ griːn). *Naut.* [Proper name, orig. unknown.] The name of a type of sail found on tea-clippers. Cf. *Jimmy Green* (JIMMY² 8).

1866 CAPT. KEAY *Jrnl.* 20 June in B. Lubbock *China Clippers* (1914) App. H. p. xxi, About 5.30 a.m., all stay-sails and fore-topmast and topgallant stunsails set and Jamie Green. **1927** G. BRADFORD *Gloss. Sea Terms* 109/2 *Jamie Green*, a sail set beneath the bowsprit and jib-boom of a tea clipper. The halyard hauled the sail to the end of the jib-boom and the tack to the lower end of the martingale boom. **1934** P. MITCHELL *Deep Water* I. xxiii. 184 They.. had.. Jamie Greens for under the jib boom, ringtails, watersails, and an extra flying jib. **1961** F. H. BURGESS *Dict. Sailing* 123 *Jamie Green*, a sail set under the jib-boom, to the dolphin striker.

jamme(e, obs. form of YAM.

jammer (ˈdʒæmə(r)). [f. JAM *v.*¹ + -ER¹.] A transmitter used for jamming.

1947 *Jrnl. R. Aeronaut. Soc.* LI. 428/1 We could.. dispose our limited number of transmitters along the tracks usually followed by the beam-flying enemy bombers and site our relatively low-powered jammers where they would produce their greatest effect. **1957** *B.B.C. Handbk.* 39 Jamming by the Communist authorities is more efficient than the wartime efforts of the Germans and Italians, but except in certain centres of population where local jammers are used, it is not completely effective. **1965** H. KAHN *On Escalation* vii. 141 The Soviets might even use shipboard jammers. **1971** [see JAM *v.*¹ 3 c].

jammy (ˈdʒæmɪ), *a.* [f. JAM *sb.*² + -Y¹.] Covered with jam, sticky. Also *fig.* (*colloq.*), excellent; very lucky or profitable; easy, 'soft'. Hence **'jamminess**.

1853 D. G. ROSSETTI *Let.* 2 Nov. (1965) I. 161 The frame for my water-colour.. is.. jammy, nobby, stunning, jolly, splendacious. **1895** *Punch* 12 Oct. 180/1 The way as that Sam chewed the rag was just jammy. **1899** KIPLING *Stalky & Co.* 228 Jam for the Sixth! Jam for us! Either way it's jammy! **1908** 'I. HAY' *Right Stuff* xi. 205 We had disposed of grouse sandwiches.. and jammy scones. **1915** D. O. BARNETT *Lett.* 170 If I get a 'jammy' one as it is called, I shall be back pretty soon. **1920** *Chambers's Jrnl.* X. 862/2 She was aroused by the.. jammy caresses of her blue-eyed nephews. **1929** W. DEEPING *Roper's Row* 179 There was a jamminess about these meals and about the ladies' fingers. **1932** A. J. WORRALL *Eng. Idioms* 32 I don't know any one like him. He's jammy. **1955** M. ALLINGHAM *Beckoning Lady* x. 137 The twins, jammy-faced and excited. **1973** 'TREVANIAN' *Loo Sanction* (1974) 130 'I almost always win. Isn't that odd?' The Sergeant regarded the slim body... 'I'd say you were bloody jammy.'

jam-packed, *a.*: see JAM *adv.* 2.

‖**'jampan**. *E. Ind.* Also **jampaun**, **jompon**, **janpan**, etc. [Bengālī *jhāmpān*, Hindī *jhappān*.] A kind of sedan chair, carried by four men, used in the hill-country of India.

1832 MUNDY *Pen & Pencil Sk.* I. 284 We therefore persuaded him to take the jampaun and return. **1836** BP. WILSON *Diary in Life* (1860) II. xv. 108 We ordered our ponies and johnpons. **1845** STOCQUELER *Handbk. Brit. India* (1854) 248 The usual mode of travelling is by 'jampauns'—a conveyance not unlike a large clumsy chair, having a top from which curtains are suspended. They are carried by four men by means of poles fixed to the sides. **1872** MRS. VALENTINE in *Mem.* iii. (1882) 37 We have a sort of chair called a 'Jhampan', carried by four men. **1886** YULE *Anglo-Ind. Gloss.*, *Jompon.* **1887** FIFE-COOKSON *Tiger Shooting* 139 At a hill-station ladies are carried in jampans, which are open doolies.

Hence ‖**jampa'nee** [Hindī *jānpānī*], a bearer of a jampan.

1859 LANG *Wand. India* 11 Ladies and gentlemen on horseback, and ladies in janpans—the janpanees dressed in every variety of livery. **1879** *Times* 17 Aug. (Y.), Every lady on the hills keeps her jampan and jampanees.. just as in the plains she keeps her carriage and footmen.

jamrosade (ˈdʒæmrəʊzeɪd). [app. f. JAMBO, with addition or mixture of *rose* + -ADE.] The fruit of the East Indian tree *Eugenia Jambos*; the Rose-apple.

1866 *Treas. Bot.* 635/1 *Jamrosade*, the Rose Apple, *Eugenia Jambos.* **1887** in *Syd. Soc. Lex.*

jams (dʒæmz), *sb. pl.* [Shortened from PYJAMAS, PAJAMAS *sb. pl.*] A garment, derived from PYJAMAS, worn as leisure-wear, and *spec.* as a type of swimming-trunks.

1966 *Telegraph* (Brisbane) 3 Feb. 18 It's the season of the hubba hubba jams—and that's.. a patio fashion stopper. It is snug.. just-above-the-knee jams worn with a covered camisole top... Jams can be worn with a bikini top or a frilly feminine flip-top style. **1968** *N.Y. Times* 22 Jan. 36 There will also be ascots (which can double as belts), walking shorts, swim trunks and surfers' 'jams', knee-length trunks with drawstring waists. **1970** *New Yorker* 14 Mar. 34/3 He wore His-'n-Hers flowered at-home jams. **1971** *Telegraph* (Brisbane) 29 Dec. 31 (Advt.), Boys' cotton floral swim jams... Cord tie at waist. Hip pocket detail. **1971** *U.S. Trademark 920, 266* (U.S. Patent Office), *Jams.* Surf Line Hawaii, Ltd... For: Men's swimming trunks.

jam-tree. *Austral.* Also **jamwood**. = *raspberry jam tree* (s.v. RASPBERRY 6).

1934 T. WOOD *Cobbers* vii. 91 Jam trees grow here [*sc.* in Western Australia], and blackboy, that strange fascination. **1941** *Coast to Coast* 46 The wheat.. rippled up the hillside and lost itself.. in the shadow of a jam-tree belt. **1947** *Coast to Coast 1946* 202 Old Tom Caseley had just finished whittling the fifty-seventh link in his jamwood chain when he died. **1962** A. UPFIELD *Will of Tribe* iv. 39 He.. dismounted and neck-roped the horse to a stout desert jamwood. **1965** *Austral. Encycl.* IX. 219/2 Myall wood has a peculiar violet-like fragrance, while jamwood is reminiscent of raspberries.

jam-up, *sb. colloq.* [JAM *sb.*¹ + UP *adv.*¹] = JAM *sb.*¹ 1.

1941 J. M. CAIN *Mildred Pierce* xi. 229 To forestall the possibility of another jam-up. **1961** *Time* 14 Apr. 105/3 The jam-up at the post-office when the social security checks arrive. **1970** *Globe & Mail* (Toronto) 28 Sept. 22/4 Larry Foubert of Weston ended up on the infield grass after a jam-up at the north end of the track. **1973** 'D. JORDAN' *Nile Green* xi. 46 There was the usual jam-up.. and the auto horns blared in frustration.

‖**jamwar** (ˈdʒɑːmwɑː(r)). *E. Ind.* Also **jame-**. [Pers. *jāmahwār* cloth, garment; a kind of chintz; a flowered sheet or shawl.]

1721 C. KING *Brit. Merch.* I. 299 Ginghams 375 Pieces Jam Warrs 10 Pieces. **1722** *Lond. Gaz.* No. 6079/7 A Parcel of.. strip'd Herba Cotton, Jamwars.

jam-weld: see JAM *sb.*¹

†**jan**. *Thieves' Cant. Obs.* A purse.

1610 ROWLANDS *Martin Mark-all*, *Ian*, a purse. **1621** B. JONSON *Gipsies Metamorph.* ¶1 To *nip a Ian*, and *cly the jark.*

Jan., abbreviation of JANUARY.

janapa (ˈdʒænəpə). Also **-um**. [Tamil.] = SUNN.

1851 *Illustr. Catal. Gt. Exhib.* IV. 882/2 *Crotolaria juncea*.. is cultivated in most parts of India for its fibre, which.. is called *sun* and *sunnee* in different parts of India, but, in the Madras peninsula, *janapum.* **1866** LINDLEY & MOORE *Treas. Bot.* II. 635/1 *Janapa*, an Indian name for Sunn Hemp.

janders, -dies, -dise, obs. ff. JAUNDICE.

jane¹ (dʒeɪn). Also 5 **iayne**. [From OF. *Janne(s*, F. *Gênes*; cf. ME. *Janewey*, GENOWAY.]

†**1.** A small silver coin of Genoa introduced into England towards the end of the 14th century: cf. GALLEY-HALFPENNY. *Obs.*

c **1386** CHAUCER *Sir Thopas* 24 His Robe was of Syklatoun That coste many a Iane [*v.r.* Iayne]. —— *Clerk's T.* 943 O Stormy peple.. Ay ful of clappyng deere ynogh a Iane. **1590** SPENSER *F.Q.* III. vii. 58 [She] flat refusd to have adoe with mee, Because I could not give her many a Jane. **1671** SKINNER *Etymol. Ling. Angl.* C cccc j b, *Jane*.. q.d. nummus Genuensis, vel Januensis.

2. = JEAN, the fabric, q.v.

Jane, jane² (dʒeɪn). *slang* (orig. *U.S.*). [Female Christian name.] A woman, girl, girlfriend.

1906 *Dialect Notes* III. 142 'It's the magazine over yonder with a red Jane on it.' 'Going to take your Jane to the show?' **1916** C. J. DENNIS *Moods of Ginger Mick* 79 She's like some fat ole Jane 'oo loves to smile. **1923** [see DAME 2 c]. **1924** P. MARKS *Plastic Age* 149, I met a bunch of janes down at Bar Harbour. **1929** 'G. DAVIOT' *Man in Queue* iii. 30 He has a new 'jane'. He probably wants money. **1941** *Coast to Coast* 129, I was trailing round with a high-class little jane in those days. **1958** 'A. GILBERT' *Death against Clock* x. 145 She didn't see that it could, and for once I agree with a jane. **1967** E. S. GARDNER *Case of Queenly Contestant* (1973) xiii. 150 'Who was this jane? Anybody I know?' 'No one you know. .. She had been a nurse in San Francisco.'

Janeite (ˈdʒeɪnaɪt). Also **Jane-ite**, **Janite**. [f. the Christian name of *Jane* Austen (1775–1817), novelist + -ITE¹.] = AUSTENITE¹.

1896 G. SAINTSBURY *Hist. 19th Cent. Lit.* 129 It did not apparently occur to this critic that he (or she) was in the first place paying Miss Austen an extraordinarily high compliment—a compliment almost greater than the most enthusiastic 'Janites' have ventured. **1924** KIPLING *Debits & Credits* (1926) 147 (*title*) The Janeites. **1927** *Observer* 5 June 6/3 Clearly he is *not* a Janeite. **1928** *Daily Tel.* 7 Aug. 3/3 The best page of her book by far is her spirited defence of Jane Austen, which will endear her to the 'Jane-ites' for all time. **1947** W. J. BLYTON in *Eng. Lang. & Lit.* vii. 111/1 Men as masculine as Scott and Kipling have been Jane-ites and have been enthralled by her sly humour and fidelity to reality. **1972** N. FREELING *Long Silence* II. 149 Arlette was not a Janeite, and.. it was accidentally that she let slip.. that Piet used to call her 'Bates'.

†**Jane-of-apes**. *Obs. humorous nonce-wd.* [f. after *Jack-of-apes*, with the female name *Jane.*] The female counterpart of a Jackanapes.

1623 MASSINGER *Bondman* III. iii, But we shall want A woman... No, here's a Jane-of-apes shall serve.

Janever(e, -wer, obs. forms of JANUARY.

janewey, variant of GENOWAY, Genoa. *Obs.*

‖**jangada** (dʒæŋˈgɑːdə). Also 6 **gyn-**, **gingatho**, 7 **gingatha**, **-ada**, **-ado**, (**jergado**), 8 **jungodo**, **jungada**, **janjade**. [Pg. *jangada* (1504 in Correa), ad. Malayālam *changāḍam*, in Tuḷu *jangāla* raft, junction of two boats, ferry-boat, ad. Skr. *saṃghāṭa*, 'fitting and joining together (of timber), joinery'. Taken by the Portuguese

from East Indies to South America, where it is now chiefly used.]

A float or raft consisting of four or five logs fastened together, and furnished with a seat and lateen sail, so as to form a rude fishing-boat: used in the northern parts of Brazil and Peru. **b.** *orig.* A raft, used in the East Indies, often formed of two or more boats fastened together; a JANGAR.

1598 PHILIPS tr. *Linschoten's Voy.* 1472 Some tooke bords, deals, and other peeces of wood, and bound them together (which yᵉ Portingals cal *Iangadas*)..all hoping to saue their liues. **1600** HAKLUYT *Voy.* III. 776 There came aboord vs two Indians vpon a *Gyngatho.* **1625** PURCHAS *Pilgrims* I. v. 631 Their Boat being split in pieces, made a *Gingada* of Timber. **1760-72** tr. *Juan & Ulloa's Voy.* (ed. 3) I. 181 These Balzas, called by the Indians, Jungadas [*note*, They are the same that are called Catamorans in the East Indies]. **1846** G. GARDNER *Brazil* 79. **1893** *Daily News* 27 May 5/3 To create a fresh sensation by importing a 'Jangada' from Pernambuco for use on our own river.

jangal: see JUNGLE *sb.*

‖**jangar.** *E. Ind.* Also jungar. [a. Tamil *jangar* = Tuḷu *jangāla*: see JANGADA. (An early form of this word intermediate between Skr. *saṃghāṭa* and the mod. Dravidian forms occurs in the *Periplus* of Arrianus (A.D. 124), in the Gr. spelling *σάγγαρον*.)] A raft; = JANGADA b.

1800 WELLINGTON *Suppl. Desp.* (1858) I. 519 There are two rivers..It will be proper to have a jungar upon each of them. **1886** YULE & BURNELL *Anglo-Ind. Gloss.*, *Jangar*, a raft. Port. *jangada.*

jang(g)a, varr. JONGA.

jangle ('dʒæŋg(ə)l), *v.* Also 4-6 iangil(l, -el(e, 5 -ille, -ylle, (changel, yangle): see also GANGLE. [a. OF. *jangler* (12th c.), *jengler*, *gengler*, in same senses; ulterior origin obscure. (Referred by some to an Old Nether-frankish **jangelôn* repr. by MDu. *jangelen*; but this is improbable.) In senses 3, 5, app. influenced by JINGLE *v.*]

I. *intr.* †**1.** To talk excessively or noisily; to chatter, babble, prate; said also of birds. Often applied contemptuously to ordinary speaking. *Obs.*

a **1300** *Cursor M.* 27620 O pride es iangling o foly, and namliest of licheri. *c* **1330** R. BRUNNE *Chron. Wace* (Rolls) 4098 þenne come Saxoyns, men of Angle, Als þey couþe on þer speche iangle. *c* **1386** CHAUCER *Man of Law's T.* 676 Thy mynde is lorn, thou iangliest as a Iay. ? *c* **1475** *Sqr. lowe Degre* 51 The iay iangled them amonge, The larke began that mery songe. *c* **1480** *Lyt. Childr. Lyt. Bk.* 90 in *Babees Bk.* 22 Aryse up soft & stylle, And iangylle nether with Iak ne Iylle. **1569** BP. PARKHURST *Injunctions*, Whether there be..any that walk vp and downe, iangling and talking in the tyme of Common praier. **1604** T. WRIGHT *Passions* I. x. 41 In halfe an houre five men will bee wearie with conference..but three women will iangle, and never lacke new subiects to discourse vpon. **1642** ROGERS *Naaman* 489 To prate and jangle, play and be merry, and tell tales. **1774** GOLDSM. *Nat. Hist.* III. III. VI. iii. 175 It was usual to hear the two nightingales Jangling and Talking together.

2. To speak angrily, harshly, or discordantly; to grumble, murmur; to contend, dispute, wrangle, squabble. *arch.*

13.. *E.E. Allit. P.* C. 90 Raykes bylyue Ionas toward port Iaph, ay Ianglande for tene þat he nolde þole, for no-þyng, none of þose pynes. **1382** WYCLIF *Exod.* xvii. 2 The which ianglynge aȝens Moyses, seith, ȝif to us water, that we drynken. *c* **1470** HENRY *Wallace* VI. 920 Schyr, we jangill bot in wayne. **1514** BARCLAY *Cyt. & Uplondyshm.* (Percy Soc.) p. li, Some braule and some jangle when they be beastly fed. **1588** SHAKS. *L.L.L.* II. i. 225 Good wits wil be iangling, but gentles agree. **1692** WASHINGTON tr. *Milton's Def. Pop.* viii. M.'s Wks. (1851) 194 It is not worth while to jangle about a French word. **1797** MAD. D'ARBLAY *Lett.* 3 Apr., Thus they go on, wrangling and jangling. **1849** ROBERTSON *Serm.* Ser. I. viii. (1866) 146 They..jangle about..the breadth of a phylactery.

†**b.** To parley (*with* a thing or person). *Obs.*

c **1440** HYLTON *Scala Perf.* (W. de W. 1494) II. xxiii, Jangill not therwith..but smyte [it] oute of thyne herte. *a* **1684** LEIGHTON *Comm. 1 Pet.* iii. 15 It suffers us not to stand to jangle with each trifling grumbling objection.

c. quasi-*trans.* With *out.* To go on jangling till it exhausts itself.

1840 CARLYLE *Heroes* ii. (1872) 58 *Homoiousion, Homoousion*, vain logical jangle..may jangle itself out, and go whither and how it likes.

3. To make a discordant or unmusical noise; to sound or 'jingle' harshly or discordantly.

1494 *Lett. Rich. III & Hen. VII* (Rolls) I. 394 The changelyng of bellis. **1581** J. BELL *Haddon's Answ. Osor.* 320 The Belles from the Turrettes on highe make a wonderfull ianglyng. **1678** OTWAY *Friendship in F.* v. i, The Bells shall jangle out of Tune all Day. **1732** MRS. DELANY *Lett., to Mrs. A. Granville* 345, I was placed at the harpsichord, and after jangling a little, Mr. Wesley took his fiddle and played to his daughters' dancing. **1875** MANNING *Mission H. Ghost* viii. 214 All its notes jangle in discord.

II. *trans.* **4.** To speak or utter in a noisy, babbling, discordant, or contentious manner.

1377 LANGL. *P. Pl.* B. IV. 155 Madame, I am ȝowre man. What so my mouth iangleth. **1412-13** HOCCLEVE *Ball. to Hen. V*, 37 Thogh my conceit be smal, And..my wordes..clappe and iangle foorth, as dooth a iay. **1545** HEN. VIII in Hall *Chron.* (1809) 866 How unreverently that moste precious iuel the worde of God is disputed rimed song and iangeled in every Alehouse. **1597** GERARDE *Herbal* Pref., Anything they shall..either murmure in corners, or iangle in secret. *c* **1709** PRIOR *Protogenes & Apelles* 6 Ere monkish rhymes Had jangled their fantastic chimes. **1841** T. A. TROLLOPE *Summ. W. France* I. xvii. 284 The bell..is clanging and jangling its last angry summons to tardy passengers. **1843** CARLYLE *Past & Pr.* III. ix, That..Life-theory which we hear jangled on all hands of us.

5. To cause (a bell, etc.) to give forth a harsh discordant sound; to cause to ring, jingle, or clang inharmoniously.

1604 SHAKS. *Ham.* (2nd Qo.) III. i. 166 Like sweet bells iangled out of time, and harsh. **1641** J. JACKSON *True Evang. T.* III. 189 They jangle all out of tune the sweet Bels of reason and judgement. **1848** CLOUGH *Amours de Voy.* II. 109 Jangling a sword on the steps, or jogging a musket Slung to the shoulder behind. **1883** LD. R. GOWER *My Remin.* I. vii. 122 Bell-ringers would come..and jangle their changes before an admiring..audience.

†**6.** To speak angrily to, to scold. *Obs. rare.*

c **1430** *Pilgr. Lyf Manhode* II. li. (1869) 83 What gost thou thus jangelinge me?

†**7.** To jape. *Sc. Obs.*

c **1470** HENRY *Wallace* VI. 150 So said the prest that last janglyt thi wyff.

Hence '**jangled** *ppl. a.*

1868 FARRAR *Silence & V.* ii. (1875) 36 That jangled dissonance in what should be the sweet music of men's lives. **1880** BARING-GOULD *Mehalah* xxviii. (1884) 391 The jangled clash of bells. **1886** STEVENSON *Dr. Jekyll* viii. 70 A ferocity of accent that testified to his own jangled nerves.

jangle ('dʒæŋg(ə)l), *sb.* [In ME. a. AF. and OF. *jangle* sb. from *jangler*; in later use immediately from the Eng. vb.]

†**1.** Idle talk, chatter, jabber; an idle word. *Obs.*

1340-70 *Alex. & Dind.* 462 But swiche wordus of wise we wilnen to lere, þere nis no iargoun no iangle ne iuggementis falce. *c* **1386** CHAUCER *Pars. T.* ¶576 And he answerde, do manye goode werkes, and spek fewe Iangles.

2. Contention, altercation, bickering.

1641 MILTON *Ch. Govt.* I. ii, Then in such a cleere text as this may we know too without further jangle. **1672** MARVELL *Reh. Transp.* I. 302 Having made the whole business of State their Arminian jangles. **1751** MRS. DELANY *Lett., to Mrs. Dewes* 55 If these jangles were to happen often, it would greatly embitter the pleasure I have in Don.'s company. **1876** MISS YONGE *Womankind* xviii. 144 This ought to be frankly owned..if for no other reason than to prevent jangles.

3. Discordant sound, ring, or clang.

1795 GIFFORD *Mæviad* 106 The mad jangle of Matilda's lyre. **1834** HT. MARTINEAU *Farrers* iii. 40 The jangle of cans at the stall where hot coffee was sold. **1871** B. TAYLOR *Faust* (1875) I. Prelude 6 And the discordant tones of all existence In sullen jangle are together hurled.

4. Confused and noisy talk; the mingled din of voices. (A kind of blending of senses 1 and 3.)

1839 CARLYLE *Chartism* vi. 146 Infinite sorrowful jangle. **1866** *Cornh. Mag.* Nov. 516 The gay jangle went on, and the laughter and music poured out to where Catherine was sitting. **1884** *Chr. Commw.* 23 Oct. 20/3 When the chaff of sputter and jangle of platitude and puerility has been sifted away.

jangler ('dʒæŋglə(r)). [a. OF. *jangleor*, nom. *janglere*, f. *jangler* to JANGLE: see -ER² 3.] One who jangles: †**a.** A chatterer, idle talker, or prater; a story-teller, a jester (*obs.*); **b.** A noisy disputant.

1303 R. BRUNNE *Handl. Synne* 9307 For Ianglers, þys tale y tolde, þat þey yn cherche here tunges holde. **1377** LANGL. *P. Pl.* B. x. 31 Iaperes and iogeloures and iangelers of gestes. *c* **1386** CHAUCER *Manciple's T.* 239 A Iangler is to god abhomynable. **1422** tr. *Secreta Secret., Priv. Priv.* 227 Tho that haue ribbis bocchynge outwardes..bene yanglours, and folis in wordys. **1491** CAXTON *Vitas Patr.* (W. de W. 1495) I. xl. 60 a/1 Yf ony were a Iangeler, a Lyar, or Chyder; she warnyd her for to amende her. **1551** T. WILSON *Logike* (1580) 56 b, A brablyng iangeler without all reason. **1604** T. WRIGHT *Passions* IV. i. 107 Ianglers and praters deserue to be registred in the catalogue of fooles. **1651** W. CARTWRIGHT *Ordinary* II. ii. in Hazl. *Dodsley* XII. 240 You snyb mine old years, sans fail I wene you bin A jangler and a golierdis. **1884** *Chr. Commw.* 23 Oct. 20/3 Any other clique of junior janglers and wranglers.

†'**jangleress.** *Obs.* [a. OF. *janglerresse* fem. of *jangleor*: see prec. and -ESS.] A female jangler.

c **1386** CHAUCER *Merch. T.* 1062 For sithen he seyde that we been Iangleresses..I shal nat spare for no curteisye To speke hym harm þat wolde vs vileynye. —— *Melib.* ¶119 Thise wordes been vnderstonde of wommen þat been Ianglerresses and wikked. *c* **1430** *Pilgr. Lyf Manhode* II. lxxvii. (1869) 104 Why hast thou leeued the counseil of thilke berkinge lyere Oiseuce the jangeleresse?

†'**janglery.** *Obs.* Also 5 ianglory. [a. OF. *janglerie*, f. *janglere*, -*eor* JANGLER: see -ERY 1 b.] Idle talk, babbling; wrangling.

c **1374** CHAUCER *Troylus* v. 755 This purpos wol I hold, and þis is best, No fors of wykked tonges Ianglerye. *c* **1386** —— *Melib.* ¶96 It is written, the Ianglerye of wommen ne can nothing hide, save that which they wot not. **1483** CAXTON *Gold. Leg.* 248/2 Ther was a nonne in Sabyne whiche..eschewed not the Ianglerye of her tonge. **1631** WEEVER *Anc. Fun. Mon.* 685 Ianglery, buffonnerie, and such other vices.

attrib. **1583** STANYHURST *Æneis* II. (Arb.) 46 To what purpose do I chat such ianglerye trim trams?

'**jangling,** *vbl. sb.* [f. JANGLE *v.* + -ING¹.] The action of the vb. JANGLE, in its various senses; now chiefly, wrangling, noisy altercation; dissonant or discordant din of voices, bells, etc.

a **1300** [see JANGLE *v.* 1]. *c* **1330** R. BRUNNE *Chron. Wace* (Rolls) 11604 þe kyng..þen lifte his hed, When þei hadde þer ianglyng leued. *c* **1386** CHAUCER *Pars. T.* ¶332 Ianglynge is whan men speken to muche biforn folk and clappen as a Mille and taken no Kepe what they seye. **1463** *Paston Lett.* II. 133 If ony questions or jangelyng schuld be mad. **1526** TINDALE *1 Tim.* i. 6 From the which thynges some have erde, and have turned vnto vayne iangelynge. **1581** [see JANGLE *v.* 3]. **1663** PEPYS *Diary* 8 June, After dinner my wife and I had a little jangling, in which she did give me the lie. **1686** *Lond. Gaz.* No. 2193/3 Nothing but Lamentations, and the Jangling of Bells for help, is heard. **1713** STEELE *Guardian* No. 73 ¶8 They lose their respect towards us from this jangling of ours. **1812** *Sporting Mag.* XXXIX. 188 The ring was in confusion by the janglings of betting men. **1879** FARRAR *St. Paul* (1883) 459 The harsh jangling of their timbrels.

'**jangling,** *ppl. a.* [f. as prec. + -ING².] That jangles, in various senses of the verb.

c **1374** CHAUCER *Boeth.* III. met. ii. 53 (Camb. MS.) The Iangelynge [*v.r.* Iangland] bryd þat syngeth on the heye braunches. **1382** WYCLIF *Prov.* xxi. 19 Betere is to dwelle in desert lond, than with a ianglende womman and wratheful. *c* **1460** J. RUSSELL *Bk. Nurture* 36 in *Babees Bk.*, As Iangelynge as a Iay. **1576** FLEMING *Panopl. Epist.* 175 *note*, A thing proper to iangling sophisters..in their quarrelling exercises. **1667** MILTON *P.L.* XII. 55 A jangling noise of words unknown. **1836** W. IRVING *Astoria* II. 288 The lord and master has much difficulty in maintaining harmony in his jangling household. **1882** W. B. WEEDEN *Soc. Law of Labor* 4 Freed from the conditions of this jangling modern time.

jangly ('dʒæŋglɪ), *a.* [f. JANGLE *v.* + -Y.] Harsh-sounding, inharmonious, discordant.

18.. JOEL BENTON *April Blackbird* (Cent.), Answering back with jangly scream. **1892** ATKINSON *Moorland Parish* 14 There was a piano in the parish, old-fashioned and jangly.

†'**Janian,** *a. Obs. rare.* [f. JAN-US + -IAN.] Janus-like; two-faced.

1598 MARSTON *Pygmal.* i. Wks. (1764) 137 Yee vizarded-bifronted-Ianian rout.

So '**Janiform** *a.* (*erron.* Januform.)

1814 SYD. SMITH *To Jeffrey* Mem. 1855 II. 115 The statue was to be Januform, with Playfair's face on one side and Stewart's on the other. **1892** W. RIDGEWAY *Orig. Metallic Currency* 318 The Janiform head, male and female, on the obverse of the coins of Tenedos.

janissarian, -sary: see JANIZARIAN, -ZARY.

janitor ('dʒænɪtə(r)). [a. L. *jānitor*, f. *jānua* door, entrance: with agent-suffix -*tor*.]

1. a. A door-keeper, porter, ostiary.

c **1630** RISDON *Surv. Devon* §44 (1810) 50 One John, sir-named *Janitor*, of his office, who..was to keep the prison. **1686** PLOT *Staffordsh.* 429 The Keys for Sᵗ Peter, reputed the Ianitor of heaven. **1746** SMOLLETT *Advice* 34 The gaunt, growling janitor of hell. **1762** C. PARKIN *Topogr. Freebridge* 144 He is to lay down the cap and cloak, and give it to the janitor to keep. **1876** FARRAR *Marlb. Serm.* v. 47 Even the heathen saw that toil is the janitor at the gate of virtue.

b. A caretaker of a building, esp. a school, who has charge of the cleaning, heating, etc., of it. Also *attrib.*

1708 C. MORTHLAND *Acct. Govt. Church of Scotl.* 18 When a Student enters the University [of Edinburgh] he must pay Half a Crown to the Porter or Janitor and Seven Pence to his Servant. **1835** DR. NEILL in J. J. Audubon *Ornith. Biogr.* III. 313 A cock-heron..had been..kept for some weeks in a cellar in the old College, and then presented to me by the late Mr John Wilson, the janitor. **1868** *Mich. Agric. Rep.* VII. 22 Expenses for wood, furniture, janitor work, &c. **1884** H. BUTTERWORTH *Zigzag Journeys Western States* 50 He was employed merely as janitor at Yule [school]. **1952** *Manch. Guardian Weekly* 4 Dec. 13 The Civil Service now protects janitors and chauffeurs. **1954** *Press & Jrnl.* (Aberdeen) 7 Apr., The Education Committee..had recommended that a janitor be appointed, and that he be responsible for all janitorial and cleaning work at the school, including maintenance of the gardens. **1961** *Evening Standard* 12 Sept. 19/1 Janitor required for building in W.1. area. **1968** *Globe & Mail* (Toronto) 13 Feb. 31/6 (Advt.), Prestige offices, full janitor services.

†**2.** An usher in a school. (Cf. DOCTOR *sb.* 1 b.)

1584 in Grant *Burgh Sch. Scotl.* App. 543. **1876** *Ibid.* II. xiv. 491 In 1661 the doctor or Janitor of the grammar School of Cupar had from every bairn at the School his meat day about, or 2*s.* daily.

Hence '**janitoress,** '**janitress** = JANITRIX; **jani'torial** *a.*, of or pertaining to a janitor; '**janitorship,** the office of janitor.

1806 LAMB *Lett.* (1888) I. 240 The gray-haired Janitress at my door. **1866** J. FISHER *Where shall we get Meat* 121, I ..told the janitoress that I did not think there was a Protestant church in the world into which a person would not be permitted to enter and worship. **1885** *Chicago Advance* 3 Dec. 779 This lesson in janitorial science. **1893** *Columbus* (O.) *Dispatch* 12 July, The janitorships heretofore have largely been given to men who were known as political hustlers. **1894** *Daily Tel.* 18 Oct. 5/7 Restored to consciousness by the janitress of the house.

janitrix ('dʒænɪtrɪks). [L. fem. of *janitor.*] A female janitor.

1841 WARREN *Ten Thous. a Year* I. i. 24 The complaisant old janitrix shut the door in their faces.

Janivare, -veer(e, -ver(e, obs. ff. JANUARY.

jani'zarian, *a. rare.* [f. JANIZARY, -ISSARY + -IAN.] Of or pertaining to the janizaries.

1796 BURKE *Regic. Peace* i. Wks. VIII. 199 The Janisarian republick of Algiers.

janizary, janissary ('dʒænɪzərɪ, 'jænɪ-). Forms: *α.* 6 genys-, genez-, gianniz-, ienes-,

ianess-, ianits-, ianitzarie, 6–7 genis-, ianis(s-, ianiz(z-, ienis-arie, 7 janazary, 7- janis(s-, janizary. *β.* 6 ianniz-, ianis-, giannizz-er, 6–7 ianizer(e, ianizar(e, 7–8 janisar, 7- janizar. *γ.* 8 yenesherre, 9 yanizari. [Ultimately ad. Turkish *yeñi-tsheri*, f. *yeñi* new, modern + *tsheri* soldiery, militia. Variously adopted in European langs., e.g. 15–16th c. Lat. *Ienizari, Ianizari*, It. *ianizzero, giannizzero* (pl. *-eri*), Sp., Pg. *genizaro, ianizaro*, F. *janissaire* (in 15th c. *jainusere*), Ger. *janitschar*, Du. *janitsaar*. The Eng. forms reflect the L., It., Sp., or Fr. channels, through which they were derived; the attempt to represent the Turkish word directly was rare.]

1. One of a former body of Turkish infantry, constituting the Sultan's guard and the main part of the standing army. The body was first organized in the 14th century, and was composed mainly of tributary children of Christians; after a large number of them had been massacred in 1826, the organization was finally abolished.

α. **1529** MORE *Dyaloge* IV. xv. X ij a/2 Mammolukes & genysaryes about yᵉ turke and sowdeyn. **1562** SHUTE *Cambine's Turk. Wars* 36 b, Upon the death of Mahomethe, the Gianizzaries marched with all spede to Constantinople. **1579** J. JONES *Preserv. Bodie & Soule* I. xxxix. 87 As his Ienesaries are instructed al too Heathenly. **1585** T. WASHINGTON tr. *Nicholay's Voy.* II. xxiv. 65 b, The Sarail of the Azamoglans or Ianissaries. **1586** T. B. *La Primaud. Fr. Acad.* (1589) 407 Being advertised..of the valure of a yong Ianitsarie. *Ibid.* 718 The Pretorian souldiours (who were to the emperours as the Ianitzaries are to the Turke). **1702** W. J. *Bruyn's Voy. Levant* xxv. 107 The Janizaries..compos'd partly of Tributary Children, and partly of voluntary Renegades. **1717** LADY M. W. MONTAGU *Let. to Pope* 12 Feb., We were met..by an aga of the janisaries. **1832** tr. *Sismondi's Ital. Rep.* xi. 241 The new militia of the janissaries was, at the same time, the best infantry in Europe. **1866** FELTON *Anc. & Mod. Gr.* II. II. v. 343 The place called the At Midan is memorable in recent history for the slaughter of the janizaries.

β. *a* **1548** HALL *Chron., Hen. VIII*, 191 b, Thei were firste robbed of the Ianizeres, and..shamfully slain. **1572** W. MALIM in Hakluyt *Voy.* (1599) II. I. 127 The Lieutenant of Mustafa, and the Aga of the Giannizzers. **1597** BP. HALL *Sat.* IV. iv, Then falls to praise the hardy Ianizar That sucks his horse side, thirsting in the war. **1598** FLORIO, *Ianizzeri*, the Turkes gard, Ianizers. **1713** *Lond. Gaz.* No. 5106/1 The Janisar Aga..went to the King. **1821** SHELLEY *Hellas* 240 The Janizars Clamour for pay.

γ. **1704** J. PITTS *Acc. Mohometans* 160 The *Cull Ougles*, that is, the Sons of the *Yenesherres*, or Soldiers.

2. By extension, any Turkish soldier; *esp.* one of an escort for travellers in the East.

1615 tr. *De Monfart's Surv. E. Ind.* 3 Trauellers..become as poore wretched slaues subject to all injuries..from which their very Ianisaries and Gardes cannot alwayes defend them. **1642** HOWELL *For. Trav.* (Arb.) 83 He may go to Venice, where he may agree with a Janizary to conduct him in company of a Caravan all the way through the Continent of Greece as farre as Constantinople. **1775** CHANDLER *Trav. Asia M.* (1825) I. 100 Our janizary was unwilling to go then. **1812** BYRON *Ch. Har.* II. App. D i, The traveller whose janissary flogs them. **1847** DISRAELI *Tancred* III. vi, Eva.. mounted her horse;..before whom marched her janissary armed to the teeth.

3. In various allusive and figurative uses, from prec. senses.

a. 1565 JEWEL *Repl. Harding* (1611) 6 Such eloquence might better become some of your yonger Iannizers. **1599** NASHE *Lenten Stuffe* 32 Being not much behinde in the check-roule of his *Ianissaries* and contributories, with Eagle-soaring Bullingbrooke. **1663** *Flagellum or O. Cromwell* (1672) 145 Volleys of Acclamations, were given at the close of this mock solemnity, by Cromwel's Janizaries. **1679** *Establ. Test* 26 The Romish Janizaries are the tribute Children of all Europe. **1810** JEFFERSON *Writ.* (1830) IV. 153 The shipping interest, commercial interest, and their janizaries of the navy. **1867** FREEMAN *Norm. Conq.* I. vi. 581 The King had now at his command a body of Janissaries.. ready to carry out his personal will.

b. 1612 T. LAVENDER *Trav. Four Englishm.* Pref. C j b, The heauenly Ierusalem..Iesus Christ being our Pilot and Ienisarie to conduct vs thereunto. **1659** D. PELL *Impr. Sea* To Rdr. d iv, Let this Epistle be thy Janisary, or Pole-star to the perusal of this book.

4. *attrib.* and *Comb.* **janizary music** [G. *janitscharenmusik*] = *Turkish music* (TURKISH *a.* 2 b); **janizary pedal**, a pedal attached to some old pianofortes, etc., having an arrangement of drums and cymbals connected with it, by which a sound as of martial music was produced.

1642 SIR E. DERING *Sp. on Relig.* xvi. 121 Monks, Fryers, and Secular Priests, with his Janizary Jesuits. **1812** SIR R. WILSON *Priv. Diary* I. 123 Even under Janissary prejudice and despotism civilization is advancing. **1888** F. MOSCHELES tr. *Mendelssohn's Lett. to I. & C. Moscheles* 54 He must have a cradle song with drums and trumpets and janissary music. **1896** A. J. HIPKINS *Descr. & Hist. Pianoforte* 106 Drum and triangle (for Janissary music). **1900** *Pall Mall Gaz.* 21 May 4/2 Even Mozart condescended to employ the 'Janissary pedal' in one or two of his sonatas. **1922** J. RIVIERE tr. *Freud's Introd. Lect. Psycho-Anal.* 75 The little bells, shaken violently, begin their familiar janizary music.

Hence **janiza'resque** *a.*, in the style of a janizary.

1835 *New Monthly Mag.* XLV. 5 A most trenchant and janissaresque style of handling his cleaver.

jank (dʒæŋk), *v. Sc.* [Derivation obscure: cf. Sw. and Norw. dial. *janka* to totter, go slowly, hesitate.] *intr.* To trifle, shuffle.

1697 CLELAND *Poems* 19 (Jam.) Now he's rewarded for such pranks, When he would pass, it's told he janks. **1808–18** JAMIESON, *Jank*, to trifle. *Loth.*

So **jank** *sb.*, a shuffle.

1705 *Observator* No. 4. 22 His pretending to bring Witnesses from the East Indies, seem'd liker a fair Jank than any proper Defence.

‖**janken** ('dʒaŋkɛn). [Jap.] A Japanese children's game played with the hands. Now principally used in sport to decide ends, etc.

1936 E. K. VENABLES *Behind Smile in Real Japan* viii. 269 The ceremony which is the Oriental equivalent of tossing up... *Jan-ken-poh*, as it is called, is used in all such cases of decision by chance. **1964** *Japan* (Jap. Nat. Commission for Unesco) 831/2 *Janken* is the only form of the game which remains today as a means to decide the dealer in card games, the server in a match, and so on. **1967** D. & E. T. RIESMAN *Conversations in Japan* 157 *Janken* (games of three: paper, scissors, and stone). **1972** *Nat. Geographic* CXLI. 689/2 There was the ritual with children of *jan ken pon*, a game in which fist and fingers represent paper, rock, or scissors.

janker ('dʒæŋkə(r)). *Sc.* [Derivation unknown: it appears to be an agent-n. Cf. JINKER *sb.*] A long pole on wheels, used for carrying logs, also casks or other heavy weights.

1823 *Edin. Even. Courant* 26 July (Jam.), A janker..was passing along with a log of wood. **1828** STEUART *Planter's G.* 492 In Edinburgh, Glasgow, and other great towns in this kingdom, a Pole or beam, from fifteen to thirty feet long, of great strength, and fortified with iron, when mounted on a Crossbar with a pair of high Wheels at each end, is called 'a Janker'; and the immense logs of wood, which are transported by means of it..are swung under the axle and.. pole. **1891** *Scot. Leader* 21 Jan. 5 A man..attempted to jump on to a janker, used for carrying logs, but fell to the ground.

jankers ('dʒæŋkəz). *Services' slang.* [Origin unknown.] Punishment for defaulters; the defaulters themselves; the cells in which they are placed. Also *attrib.* (occas. in *sing.* form).

1916 J. N. HALL *Kitchener's Mob* 35 The 'jankers' or defaulters' squad was always rather large. **1919** *Athenæum* 25 July 664/2 The advent of the Royal Navy Division introduced to the Army the sailor's slang word 'jankers', the equivalent of the soldier's 'clink', punishment cells. *Ibid.* 8 Aug. 727/2 When doing C.B. or 'time' he [*sc.* the soldier] was doing 'jankers' or 'Paddy Doyle'. *a* **1935** T. E. LAWRENCE *Mint* (1950) II. xxii. 160 A week before my last jankers. **1936** F. RICHARDS *Old-Soldier Sahib* ii. 54, I was now a defaulter, or 'on jankers' as the troops called it. **1946** *Penguin New Writing* XXVII. 72, I stepped into the hall of B.H.Q. over two janker-wallahs. *Ibid.* 73 He broke off to bawl out the jankermen. **1960** T. RATTIGAN *Ross* I. ii. 20 None of your lip, Parsons, now—unless you want a dose of jankers. **1965** J. PORTER *Dover Two* ix. 122, I pulled her leg about it a bit, you know, said something about having her put on jankers if she was late again. **1971** *Sunday Mail Mag.* (Brisbane) 25 July 6/2 Jankers can be painful. It usually means confined to barracks and menial tasks. *Ibid.*, My first jankers was for causing a fire.

jann (dʒɑːn). Also jan. [a. Arab. *jānn* demon.] = JINN *sb.*

1777 J. RICHARDSON *Dict. Persian, Arabic & Eng.* I. 667 That race of creatures called by the Arabians *Jan* or *Jinn*. **1891** E. S. HARTLAND *Sci. Fairy Tales* x. 256 Hasan is favoured with the sight of 'ten virgins'... He fell madly in love with the chief damsel, who turns out to be a daughter of a King of the Jann. **1931** A. WILSON in E. S. Stevens *Folk Tales Iraq* p. xiv, Stories in which *jānn*, or fairy-folk, don at will the appearance of birds.

jannet, obs. form of JENNET.

janney ('dʒænɪ). *Newfoundland.* Also janny, jenny, johnny. [Prob. var. JOHNNY, JOHNNIE.] A Christmas mummer in Newfoundland. Hence as *v. intr.*, to act as a janney; to dress *up* as a janney.

1896 *Jrnl. Amer. Folklore* IX. 36 *Old teaks* and *jannies*, boys and men who turn out in various disguises and carry on various pranks during the Christmas holidays. **1925** *Dialect Notes* V. 335 *Johnnies*, Christmas mummers. Also *jennies*. **1964** *Canad. Jrnl. Linguistics* Fall 44 At Christmas time it was usual for people to..'janny up'—dress up as mummers. **1969** J. D. A. WIDDOWSON in Halpert & Story *Christmas Mumming in Newfoundland* 218 Janneys 'janney up', but mummers 'rig out' or 'dress up'.

jannock ('dʒænək), *sb. north. Eng.* Forms: ? 5, 6–8 janock(e, 6 jannacke, janok(e, 7 janack, 7- jannock. [A north. Engl., esp. Lancash., word, of obscure origin. Not *Sc.*] A loaf of leavened oaten bread.

? *a* **1500** *Chester Pl.* vii. 120 A Ianock [*v.r.* jannacke] of Lancashyre. **1584** COGAN *Haven Health* vii. (1636) 30 Of Oates they make bread..some in broad Loaves which they cal Ianocks. **1655** MOUFET & BENNET *Health's Improv.* (1746) 331 Had Galen seen the Oaten Cakes of the North, the Janocks of Lancashire, and the Grues of Cheshire, he would have confessed that Oats and Oatmeal are not only Meat for Beasts, but also for tall, fair and strong Men and Women. *c* **1746** J. COLLIER (Tim Bobbin) *View Lanc. Dial.* Wks. (1862) 40 'Twur Seign Peawnd t'a tuppunny Jannock, I'd bin os deeod os o Dur Nele. **1818** SCOTT *Rob Roy* xiv, Mattie [in Northumberland] gae us baith a drap skimmed milk, and ane o' her thick ait jannocks that was as wat and raw as a divot. O for the bonnie girdle cakes o' the North! **1825** BROCKETT, *Jannock*, leavened oat bread. **1855** E. WAUGH *Lancash. Life* (1857) 58 Content with water-pottage, buttermilk, and jannock, till he was between thirteen and fourteen years of age.

attrib. **1694** THORESBY *Diary* (Hunter) I. 268 Jannock bread and clap-cakes the best that gold could purchase.

jannock ('dʒænək), *a.* (*adv.*) *dial.* Also jonnock, jonnik, jonnic(k, jannic, jenick. [A modern dial. word: thought by some to be connected with prec., but of much more recent history, wider diffusion (Northumberland to Hampshire, Norfolk to Cornwall), and greater phonetic diversity. (Not *Sc.*)] Fair, straightforward; genuine.

1828 *Craven Dial.* s.v., 'That isn't Jannock', i.e. not fair, a phrase in use..when one of the party is suspected of not drinking fairly. **1863** in Robson *Bards of Tyne* 80 Frank an' free an' jenick tee, We eat the breed we buy. **1867** *N. & Q.* 3rd Ser. XI. 146/1 Eh Sam, Bill's a reet un, he's gradely jannock. **1885** HALL CAINE *Shadow of Crime* xxi. (1899) 65 You've got a deal too much talk to be jannic. **1897** *Manch. Guardian* 28 Oct., The people of Lancashire were jannock.. and they wanted any Government that they might support to be jannock also.

b. as *adv.*

1857 BORROW *Romany Rye* (1872) 111 Unless you choose to behave jannock. **1894** C. N. ROBINSON *Brit. Fleet* 475 Ready to act jonnic all round.

janpan, -ee, variants of JAMPAN, -EE.

†**Jan'senian.** *Obs. rare.* [f. *Jansen* (see below) + -IAN.] = JANSENIST.

1653 *Nicholas Pap.* (Camd.) II. 10 They were to have gone upon the account of the Jansenians. **1657** BAXTER *Acc. Pres. Th.* 33 The Jansenians, and other Dominicans.

Hence †**Jan'senianism** = JANSENISM.

Jansenism ('dʒænsənɪz(ə)m). [f. as next + ISM.] The doctrinal system of the Jansenists.

1656 BLOUNT *Glossogr.*, *Jansenism* or *Jansenianism*, the Tenets and Opinion of Cornelius Jansenius late Bishop of Ypres. **1669** GALE (*title*) True Idea of Jansenisme, both historick and Dogmatick. **1756** NUGENT *Gr. Tour, France* IV. 11 Jansenism was thought in great measure suppressed. **1816** MARY SCHIMMELPENNICK *Abbé de St. Cyran* I. 196 Jansenism may then be said to be in doctrine the Calvinism, and in practice the Methodism of the Romish church.

Jansenist ('dʒænsənɪst), *sb.* (*a.*) [f. the surname *Jansen* + -IST.] A member of that school or party in the Roman Catholic Church holding the doctrines of Cornelius Jansen, bishop of Ypres in Flanders (died 1638), who maintained after St. Augustine the perverseness and inability for good of the natural human will.

The Jansenists were a powerful body in the R.C. Ch. in the 17th and 18th centuries, but were strongly opposed by the Molinists and other Jesuits, and their doctrines were condemned by several popes, especially by Clement X in the Bull *Unigenitus*.

1664 T. BARLOW in *Evelyn's Mem.* (1857) III. 143 Discovered to the world by the pious pains of the Jansenists. *a* **1715** BURNET *Own Time* II. 436 The Jansenists..were looked on as the most zealous asserters of the liberties of the Gallican Church. **1892** *Nation* (N.Y.) 20 Oct. 308/1 It is probable that the Jansenist was hardly less narrow than the Jesuit.

b. *attrib.* or *adj.* Of, pertaining to, or holding the doctrine of, Jansenism or the Jansenists.

1860 J. GARDNER *Faiths of World* II. 201/2 A Jansenist divine of such piety and power as Quesnel. *Ibid.* 203/2 Thus closed the last public attempt made by the Jansenist church of Utrecht to become reconciled to Rome.

Hence **Janse'nistic, -ical** *adjs.*, = JANSENIST *a.*; **'Jansenize** *v. intr.*, to follow the doctrines of the Jansenists.

1745 A. BUTLER *Lives Saints, S. Vincent of Paul* (1847) VII. 306 Gerberon the Jansenistical historian. **1756** NUGENT *Gr. Tour, France* IV. 11 The present disputes between the parliament and the clergy, have revived the drooping spirits of the Jansenistical party. **1837** HALLAM *Hist. Lit.* III. ii. §4 *note*, The Jansenizing Gallicans of the eighteenth century. *Ibid.* (1847) III. 273 This..cannot be reckoned entirely a Jansenistic controversy. **1882–3** SCHAFF *Encycl. Relig. Knowl.* II. 1145 By the bull *Unigenitus*..a hundred and one propositions from Quesnel's New Testament were condemned as Jansenistic.

†**jant**, variant of GENT *a. Obs.*

c **1648–50** BRATHWAIT *Barnaby's Jrnl.* III. H iij, Where were dainty ducks and gant [*ed. 2,* **1716** jant] ones, Wenches that could play the wantons.

jant, jante, -ee, obs. ff. JAUNT *sb.*, JAUNTY *a.*

jantil, jantyl(l, obs. forms of GENTLE.

c **1400** TREVISA *Higden* (Rolls) I. 245 þe gentil [*Add. MS.* 24194 jantil] men and noble. *Ibid.* VIII. 149 He wolde.. wiþstonde gentil [*MS. Cott. Tib. D. VII.* iantyl] men.

jantily, jantiness, janty, var. JAUNTILY, etc.

‖'**janua.** [Lat., = 'gate': formerly often used in the titles of treatises.] A gate or introduction (to some branch of learning).

1644 MILTON *Educ.* ¶ 1 To search what many modern *Janua's* and Didacticks..have projected.

January ('dʒænjuːərɪ). Forms: *α.* 3–4 Ieniuer, 3–5 Ieneuer, -e, 4 Ianewer, Genuer, 4–5 Ianyuer, -e, Ianeuer, -e, -ver, Ianiuer, -e, Ianuuer, Ianver, 6 Ianivare, 7 Ianiuere; *Sc.* 7–8 Janiveer, (9 -vier); *β.* 5 Ienuare, 5–7 Ianuar(e; *Sc.* 7–8 Januar, 8 Janwar; *γ.* 4–7 Ianuarie, -ye, 5 Ianuari, 5–7 -ary,

(-arij); 7- January. [In early form a. ONF. *Jenever*, *Genever*, = mod.F. *Janvier*:—L. *Jānuārium*, nom. *Jānuārius* (*mensis*), i.e. the month of JANUS, as presiding over the entrance into the year. Whence also It. *Gennajo*, *Gennaro*, Pr. *Genovier*, *Januer*, Sp. †*Jenero*, *Enero*, Pg. *Janeiro*. The later forms show gradual conformation to the L.; which was sometimes used unchanged in OE.]

1. The first month of the year according to the modern reckoning. Abbreviated Jan.

α. [*c* **1120** P. DE THAUN *Livre des Creatures* (Wright) 858 Mais tut tens en Genever femes l'an cumencer.] *c* **1290** *S.E. Leg.* I. 76/202 In þe Monþe of Ieneuer. **1297** R. GLOUC. (Rolls) 7259 In þe verþe day of Ieniuer [*later v.rr.* Ianyuere, ianewer, Ieneuere, Ianuuer]. **13..** *K. Alis.* 57 Genuer was theo endleft [month]. **1387** TREVISA *Higden* (Rolls) III. 73 Pompilius.. putte Ianeuer and Feuerrer to þe bygynnynge of þe ȝere. **1483** CAXTON *Gold. Leg.* 145 b/1 His feste is the xv day of Ianyuer. **1556** *Chron. Gr. Friars* (Camden) 16 The xxiiij. day of Janivare. **1604** DEKKER *1st Pt. Honest Wh.* Wks. 1873 II. 69 Hee's more cold then a Cittizens countrie house in Janiuere. **1651** CLEVELAND *Poems, Yng. Man to Old Woman* 16 December meeting Ianiveer. *Old Rime*, If the grass grow in Janiveer, It grows the worse for't all the year. **1834-51** MARY HOWITT *Sk. Nat. Hist.* (ed. 7) 117 First of the months comes Janivier, The coldest month of all the year.

β. [**14..** *Chaucer's Merch. T.* 561 (Corpus) þis hastyf Ianuare [so *Petw.*, *Lansd.*; *Ellesm.*, *Hengw.*, *Harl.*, *Cambr.* Ianuarie].] **1432-50** tr. *Higden* (Rolls) III. 73 Pompilius.. addede Ianuare and Februare to the begynnenge of the yere. **1570** *Ane Tragedie* 1 in *Satir. Poems Reform.* x. 82 In Januar the thre and twentie day. **1784** BURNS *There was a lad* ii, 'Twas then a blast o' Janwar win' Blew hansel in on Robin.

γ. [*a* **1000** *Menologium* 10 (Gr.) Forma monað hyne folc mycel Ianuarius ȝerun heton.] [*c* **1386** CHAUCER *Merch. T.* 451 This mayden.. Mayus highte.. Shal wedded be vn-to this Ianuarie.] **1495** *Trevisa's Barth. De P.R.* IX. ix. 354 The fyrste hyghte Ianuari, and hath that name of a god feyned that hyghte Ianus. **1579-80** NORTH *Plutarch, Numa*, Numa tooke away the moneth of Marche from the first place, and gave it unto Ianuary. **1674** JEAKE *Arith.* (1696) 229 The Commonalty begin the Year the First Day of January, the Lawyers the Five and Twentieth Day of March. **1788** PRIESTLEY *Lect. Hist.* III. xiv. 110 By act of parliament in one thousand seven hundred and fifty-two, the first day in January was appointed to be the beginning of the year for all purposes. **1891** *Pall Mall G.* 15 Jan. 1/2, Few Januaries have been preceded by such a week as Christmas, 1891.

2. *attrib.*, as ***January sale***.

1896 in G. Eley *Ruined Maid* (1970) 24/1 A friend of mine .. bought at a January sale six yards of brocade in pale electric blue. **1936** *Discovery* Oct. 320/2 A rush.. which must have equalled the January sales of our own days. **1967** E. G. COUSINS *Death in Quiet Place* xiv. 177 Mollie's getting so used to Town that she's threatening to stay on over the January Sales.

januay, -ey, januway, var. GENOWAY, *Obs.*

Januform: see JANIFORM s.v. JANIAN *a.*

Janus (ˈdʒeɪnəs). **1. a.** The name of an ancient Italian deity, regarded as the doorkeeper of heaven, as guardian of doors and gates, and as presiding over the entrance upon or beginning of things; represented with a face on the front and another on the back of his head; the doors of his temple in the Roman Forum were always open in time of war, and shut in time of peace. Often used allusively, and in attributive and other relations.

1508 DUNBAR *Gold. Targe* 120 Ianus, god of entree delytable. **1598** HAKLUYT *Voy.* I. 488 Certaine idoll puppets .. which they fasten to the doore of their walking houses, to be as Ianusses or keepers of their house. **1667** MILTON *P.L.* XI. 129 Four faces each Had, like a double Janus. **1713** *Lond. Gaz.* No. 5118/6 Janus's Gate is now shut. **1814** CARY *Dante, Paradise* VI. 83 Composed the world to such a peace That of his temple Janus barr'd the door.

b. *attrib.* and *Comb.*, referring to the two-faced figure, as ***Janus face***, ***glance***, ***line***, ***word***, etc.; ***Janus-faced***, ***-like***, ***-visaged*** adjs.

1654 WHITLOCK *Zootomia* 549 An Experiment it is with a *Janus face. **1711** SHAFTESB. *Charac.* II. i. §3 This Janus-face of writers, who with one countenance force a smile, and with another show nothing beside rage and fury. **1682** SIR T. BROWNE *Chr. Mor.* III. §3 Bivious Theorems and *Janus-faced Doctrines. **1841-4** EMERSON *Ess., Friendship* 172 A friend is Janus-faced: he looks to the past and the future. **1648** SANDERSON *Serm. Heb.* xii. 3 §35 Every affliction, *Janus-like, hath two faces, and looketh two ways. **1875** JOWETT *Plato* (ed. 2) III. 150 The Janus-like character of the Republic. **1822** SHELLEY *Triumph of Life* 94 A *Janus-visaged Shadow.

2. a. Designating materials with a double facing, or things having a two-way action, as ***Janus-beaver***, ***-cloth***, ***-cord***, ***-lock***.

1851 *Illustr. Catal. Gt. Exhib.* III. 486/2 Fur Janus beaver. *Ibid.* v. 1468/2 Janus locks. *a* **1877** KNIGHT *Dict. Mech.* II. 1210/2 *Janus-cloth*, a fabric having each side dressed, and different colors on the respective sides. Such fabric is used for reversible garments. **1881** in A. Adburgham *Shops & Shopping* (1964) vi. 64 Mourning materials such as Victoria Cords, Janus Cords, Cashmere, and so on. **1960** CUNNINGTON & BEARD *Dict. Eng. Costume* 259/2 *Janus cord*, a black rep of wool and cotton, the fine cord showing equally on both sides. Much used for mourning.

b. *Dye Chem.* Applied to a group of basic azo dyes that contain a quaternary ammonium group, often with safranine as the diazo component, and are capable of dyeing cotton directly; **Janus** (also **janus**) **green (B)**, either of the two basic dyes obtained by coupling diazotized safranine or dimethylsafranine with dimethylaniline, of little importance as dyes but extensively used as biological stains.

1898 *Jrnl. Soc. Dyers & Colourists* XIV. 146 The first eight patterns.. were dyed with Janus Colours on Union linings. *Ibid.* (Table), Janus Black I. Janus Blue R... Janus Green G. Janus Green B. **1926** *Stain Technol.* I. 35 The use of janus green to stain mitochondria has long been known. While using it to study the mitochondria in *Trichomonas buccalis* it was found to stain flagella also. **1928** C. E. MULLIN *Acetate Silk* x. 142 Some of the Janus dyes are also applicable to acetate silk, however most of them give rather dull shades. **1949** N. G. HEATLEY in H. W. Florey et al. *Antibiotics* I. iii. 118 The test organism was *Welchii perfringens* strain HA, the indicator was janus green. **1971** D. R. BAER in K. Venkataraman *Chem. Synthetic Dyes* IV. iv. 165 Derivatives of (*m*-aminophenyl) trimethylammonium chloride.. formed part of the Janus range of colors which were of limited use on rayon, silk-wool unions, and on cotton. **1971** E. GURR *Synthetic Dyes* 128 There are apparently two types of Janus green B, one from the USA and the other of European origin. *Ibid.* 129 Both types of Janus green are employed as oxidation-reduction indicators.

jaole, jaoler(e, obs. forms of JAIL, JAILER.

jaour, obs. form of GIAOUR.

Jap, *sb.* Colloquial abbreviation of JAPANESE. Also as *adj.*; spec. ***Jap silk*** = HABUTAI.

As *sb.* and *adj.* the word *Jap* has strong derogatory connotations and is now falling into disuse.

c **1880** (Remembered in colloquial use in London.) **1890** *Lit. World* 11 July 23 The fearlessness of death, which makes a Jap submit to the loss of his own life rather than to permit the death of a father to go unavenged. **1893** *Athenæum* 20 May 639/3 Directly a good demand arises for a book, the Japs print for themselves. **1895** *Montgomery Ward Catal.* 37/3 Ladies' short silk waists, made of plain colored Habutai Jap silk. **1896** *Westm. Gaz.* 3 Nov. 6/3 Fifty years ago it was only a few gardeners.. who grew chrysanthemums, and.. only about twelve distinct varieties of 'Japs' were to be found. **1900** in *American Mail Order Fashions* (1961) 18 Jap braid edge. **1902** *To-Day* 14 May 95/1 Printed Jap silks are lovely. **1914** *Dialect Notes* IV. 136 This is a Jap Kimona. **1921** [see CHOW *sb.* 1]. **1936** *Times* 3 Jan. 10/3 The most jealously limited edition of an unacted Swinburne drama, 50 copies only on jap vellum. **1940** [see DAGO, DAGO 1]. **1944** *Living off Land* viii. 156 The Jap pearlers have landed on his coasts. **1951** *Good Housek. Home Encycl.* 251/2 Many attractive natural silk fabrics.. jap and spun silks and ninons. **1959** [see JEW *sb.* 3 a]. **1970** G. F. NEWMAN *Sir, You Bastard* viii. 211 Nice little tape-recorder... Snazzy Jap job.

jap (dʒæp), *v. U.S. slang.* [f. JAP *sb.*] *trans.* To make a sneak attack on; also, to queer the pitch of (a person).

In restricted use.

1957 *New Yorker* 21 Sept. 135/1 'They japped us,' a third boy said, meaning that the Cherubs had taken them by surprise. **1958** H. E. SALISBURY *Shook-up Generation* (1959) ii. 29 An uncertain area where one side or another may at any sudden moment 'jap' an unwary alien. **1971** D. E. WESTLAKE *I gave at the Office* 170 Joe would hate me forever and would probably jap me with Mr. Clarebridge.

jap, dial. form of JAUP.

Japan (dʒəˈpæn), *sb.* (*a.*) Also 6 Giapan, 7 Japon. [Like the other European forms (Du., Ger., Da., Sw. *Japan*, F., Sp. *Japon*, Pg. *Japão*, It. *Giappone*, app. ad. Malay *Jăpung*, *Japang*, ad. Chinese *Jih-pŭn* (= Japanese *Ni-pon*), 'sun-rise', 'orient', f. *jih* (Jap. *ni*) sun + *pŭn* (Jap. *pon*, *hon*) origin. The earliest form in which the Chinese name reached Europe was app. in Marco Polo's *Chipangu*, in Pigafetta *Cipanghu*. The existing forms represent Pg. *Japão* and Du. *Japan*, 'acquired from the traders at Malacca in the Malay forms' (Yule).]

I. In primary sense. **1. a.** The insular empire so called, on the east of Asia.

1577 EDEN & WILLIS (*title*) The History of Travayle in the West and East Indies, and other countreys.. as Moscovia, Persia,.. China in Cathayo and Giapan. **1613** J. SARIS *Voy. to Japan* (Hakl. Soc.) 1, January 14, 1612.. we wayed out of the roade of Bantam for Japan. **1613** PURCHAS *Pilgrimage* v. xiv. 440 That you may at last bee acquainted with Iapon. **1653** H. COGAN tr. *Pinto's Trav.* xliv. 173 It is the custome of those of Jappon [*de Japão*] to be exceeding kind and courteous.

†**b.** A native of Japan, a Japanese. *Obs.*

1613 J. SARIS *Voy. to Japan* (Hakl. Soc) 1 My Companye 81 persons, viz., 74 English, 1 spanniar, 1 Japan, and 5 swarts. **1623** *St. Papers Col.* 1622-4, 208 The Japons lying in irons.

II. Transferred applications, often with lower-case initial. (Elliptical uses of III.)

2. a. A varnish of exceptional hardness, which originally came from Japan. The name is now extended to other varnishes of a like sort, *esp.* to (*a*) a black varnish obtained by cooking asphaltum with linseed oil, used for producing a black gloss on metal and other materials; (*b*) a varnish-like liquid made from shellac, linseed-oil and turpentine, and used as a medium in which to grind colours and for drying pigments.

1688 PARKER & STALKER *Treat. Japanning* Pref., True, genuine Japan.. stands unalterable, when the wood which was imprisoned in it, is utterly consumed. *Ibid.* v. 19 Of Black Varnishing or Japan. *Ibid.* 21 You cannot be over-nice and curious in making white Japan. **1761** FITZGERALD in *Phil. Trans.* LII. 150, I had it varnished over several times with strong varnish, or japan. **1851** *Illustr. Catal. Gt. Exhib.* 624 Japan is applied with a brush.

b. *fig.* Specious semblance, 'veneer'.

1856 EMERSON *Eng. Traits, Manners* Wks. (Bohn) II. 50 But this japan costs them dear. **1866** READE *Griffith Gaunt* (1887) 34 Thin japan of venal sympathy.

3. a. Japanese work; work in the Japanese style; esp. work varnished, and adorned with painted or raised figures.

17.. *Tom Thumb* III. 153 in Hazl. *E.P.P.* II. 239 The inward parts were all japon [*pr.* japan]. **1742** H. WALPOLE *Lett. to Mann* (1857) I. 192 He little thought that what maintained him for a whole session would scarce serve one of his younger grandsons to buy japan and fans for princesses at Florence! **1798** JANE AUSTEN *Northang. Abb.* II. vi, She looked closely at the cabinet... It was Japan, black and yellow Japan of the handsomest kind. *Ibid.* II. x, She did not love the sight of japan in any shape.

†**b.** Applied to a black varnished cane. *Obs.*

1678 *Quack's Acad.* in *Harl. Misc.* (Park) II. 33 You must always carry a caduceus or conjuring japan in your hand, capped with a civet-box.

4. a. Japanese porcelain. †**b.** Japanese silk.

1729 MRS. DELANY *Autobiog. & Corr.* 5 Dec. (1861) I. 227, I saw nothing extraordinary but the fine japan you so much despised. **1752** FOOTE *Taste* II. Wks. 1799 I. 22 That piece of China.. is the right old Japan of the pea-green kind. **1782** *Europ. Mag.* II. 68 Where's the old China? Show me the Japan! **1810** *Splendid Follies* I. 170 Miss Betty brought up the rear in a robe of transparent japan.

5. *Entom.* Short for *Japan moth*: see 6.

1832 J. RENNIE *Consp. Butterfl. & Moths* 195 *Adela*.. The Copper Japan... Very uncommon. Near London.

III. *attrib.* and *Comb.* or as *adj.*

6. *attrib.* Of, belonging to, native to, or produced in Japan; passing into *adj.* = JAPANESE. Frequent in names of natural or artificial products; as ***Japan anemone***, ***euonymus***, ***gold***, ***porcelain***, ***ware***, etc.

1673 RAY *Journ. Low C.* 28 A Japan Letter, written to the Dutch Governour. *a* **1680** ROCHESTER *Poems* (1702) 71 Kiss me thou curious picture of a man; How odd thou art, how pretty, how japan! **1699** LUTTRELL *Brief Rel.* (1857) IV. 581 Monday last the old East India company began their sale of images, japan ware, china. **1819** G. SAMOUELLE *Entomol. Compend.* 249 Japan-moths. **1861** DELAMER *Fl. Gard.* 128 *Pyrus Japonica*—Japan Pear,—which bears scarlet blossoms early in spring, is really a Quince, and is now removed to the genus *Cydonia*.

b. Special Comb.: **Japan anemone**, one of several varieties or hybrids of *Anemone hupehensis*, bearing large pink or white flowers; **Japan camphor** = *tub-camphor* (see TUB *sb.* 10); **Japan cedar** = CRYPTOMERIA; **Japan clover**, a leguminous annual introduced into the southern United States in 1840 from China and Japan; **Japan current** = KUROSHIWO; **Japan earth** = *Terra japonica*, CATECHU; **Japan-ink** (see quot. 1848); **Japan lacquer (tree)** (see LACQUER *sb.* 2 b, 4); **Japan lily**, any of several species of *Lilium* native to Japan, esp. *L. japonicum*; **Japan moth**, a moth of the genus *Adela*; **Japan paper** = *Japanese paper*; **Japan pepper** = *Japanese pepper* (see PEPPER *sb.* 3); **Japan quince** (see JAPONICA); **Japan rose**, a name once used for the camellia; later = *Japanese rose*; **Japan varnish (tree)** = *varnish sumach* (see VARNISH *sb.*[1] 5); = *Japan lacquer*; **Japan wax** = *Japanese wax*.

1847 *Curtis's Bot. Mag.* LXXIII. 4341 (*heading*) Japan Anemone. **1870** W. ROBINSON *Wild Garden* I. 28 The Japan Anemone and A. hybrida.. grow so strongly that they will take care of themselves. **1882** *Garden* 1 Apr. 213/2 Japan Anemones.. seem here to enjoy both the shelter and partial shade. **1908** G. JEKYLL *Colour in Flower Garden* ix. 81 The pink colourings are the wide-headed *Sedum spectabile*, pink Japan Anemone and a few pale pink Gladioli. **1882** R. BENTLEY *Man. Bot.* (ed. 4) 642 Commercial camphor is derived entirely from the island of Formosa and Japan,.. the latter [being known] as *Japan* or *Dutch Camphor*. **1852** Japan cedar [see CRYPTOMERIA]. **1900** M. THORN in W. D. Drury *Bk. Gardening* xi. 488 *C. japonica* (Japan Cedar) is a charming tree. **1884** MILLER *Plant-n.*, *Lespedeza*,.. 'Hoop-koop'-plant, Japan Clover. **1865** D. PAGE *Handbk. Geol. Terms* (ed. 2) 263 *Japan current*, that branch of the equatorial current of the Pacific which trends northward along the Japan coasts. **1885** [see KUROSHIWO]. **1936** RUSSELL & YONGE *Seas* (ed. 2) x. 231 The Japan Current or 'Kuro Shiwo' corresponding to our Gulf Stream. **1718** QUINCY *Compl. Disp.* 107 Japan Earth.. is very austere upon the Palate. **1807** HERSCHEL in *Phil. Trans.* XCVII. 209 A.. strip of card, discoloured with japan ink. **1848** CRAIG, *Japan Ink*, a superior kind of black writing ink, generally glossy when dry. **1835** W. J. HOOKER *Compan. Bot. Mag.* I. 268/1 The so much celebrated Japan lacquer or varnish. **1880** C. E. BESSEY *Bot.* xx. 535 Japan Lacquer, so much used by the Japanese in the manufacture of many wares, is obtained.. from *Rhus vernicifera*, and probably other species. **1884** W. MILLER *Dict. Eng. Names Plants* 241/1 Japan Lacquer-, or Varnish-, Tree. **1911** *Encycl. Brit.* XXVI. 70/2 *Rhus vernicifera* is the Japan lacquer or varnish-tree. **1813** *Curtis's Bot. Mag.* XXXVIII. 1591 (*heading*) White one-flowered Japan Lily. **1854** C. M. YONGE *Heartsease* I. iv. 56 You should go and look at the Japan lilies. **1625** PURCHAS *Pilgrimes* III. II. v. 339 Nothing gave him such content as two Bookes of Iapon paper, smooth and hard bound in Europæan manner. **1914** *Photo-Era* Feb. 102/1 There are certain tricks to produce a soft print from a sharp negative, one of which is to put a piece of Japan paper between the

plate and the sensitive paper in the printing-frame. **1974** *Country Life* 17 Jan. 75/1 The exquisite *Le Bain* of 1905, a dry point (an impression from the edition of 27 or 29 on Japan paper). **1866** Japan pepper [see PEPPER *sb.* 3]. **1914** W. J. BEAN *Trees & Shrubs Hardy in Brit. Isles* II. 692 *Z[anthoxylum] piperitum*, De Candolle. Japan Pepper... The seeds when ground are used by the Japanese as pepper. **1850** W. HOWITT *Year-bk. Country* 24 In gardens..come forth the vernal crocus, various hellebores, the Japan quince. **1916** L. H. BAILEY *Pruning-Manual* 222 *Chænomeles japonica* (Japan quince). **1789** W. AITON *Hortus Kewensis* II. 460 Camellia... Japan Rose. **1793** B. EDWARDS *Hist. Brit. Colonies W. Indies* I. 204 *Camellia japonica*, Japan Rose. **1895** W. ROBINSON *Eng. Flower Garden* (ed. 4) 732/1 It [*Rosa acicularis*] has a showy fruit, which differs from that of the Japan Rose, for, instead of being roundish and smooth, it is long and Pear-shaped. [**1727** J. G. SCHEUCHZER tr. *Kæmpfer's Hist. Japan* I. I. ix. 114 The *Urusi* or *Varnish-Tree* is another of the noblest and most useful Trees of this country.] **1789** J. BELKNAP *Let.* 13 Mar. in W. Parker & J. P. Cutler *Life M. Cutler* (1888) II. 252, I have sent for the seeds of the Japan varnish tree. **1843** *Penny Cycl.* XXVI. 147/2 The Japan varnish of Kæmpfer and Thunberg is Rhus vernix. **1889** W. ROBINSON *Eng. Flower Garden* (ed. 2) 788/2 Others in cultivation..include *R[hus] vermicifera*, or Japan Varnish Tree. **1859** Japan wax [see *Japanese wax* s.v. JAPANESE *a.* b]. **1887** *Colonial & Indian Exhib. Rep. Col. Sect.* 275 Myrtle wax..which, like Japan wax, is rather a fat than a true wax. **1969** R. MAYER *Dict. Art Terms & Techniques* 201/2 Japan wax is sometimes called vegetable wax.

7. *attrib.* and *Comb.*, in sense 2; Of, pertaining to, or adorned with japan, as ***japan cabinet***, ***frame***, ***ground***, etc. Also similative and parasynthetic as ***japan-black***, ***japan-headed*** adjs.

1681 *Secr. Serv. Money Chas. & Jas.* (Camden) 42 For two japan cabinets..100.0.0. **1688** PARKER & STALKER *Treat. Japanning* xiii. 36 There are two sorts of Bantam, as well as Japan-work. *Ibid.*, The Japan-Artist works most of all in Gold, and other metals. **1697** *Lond. Gaz.* No. 3250/4 Lost.., a large Silver Japan headed Cane, the ground of it Shagreen, and the Japan Work most of it gilt. **1712** ARBUTHNOT *John Bull* III. i, She had laid aside your carving, gilding, and japan work, as being too apt to gather dirt. **1855** MRS. GASKELL *North & S.* xiv, Go to my little japan cabinet ..and in the second left-hand drawer you will find a packet of letters. **1883** *B'ham Daily Post* 11 Oct., Japan-stovers and Polishers, used to Cash-boxes and Coal-vases.

japan (dʒəˈpæn), *v.* Also 8 japon. [f. prec., sense 2.]

1. *trans.* To lacquer with japan; to varnish with any material that gives a hard black gloss.

1688 PARKER & STALKER (*title*) A Treatise of Japanning and Varnishing. *Ibid.* xi. 35 They may be Japanned, and look well. **1697** DAMPIER *Voy.* (1729) I. 400 Laquer which is used in Japanning of Cabinets. **1762** GOLDSM. *Cit. W.* lv, A square table that had been once japanned. **1816** J. SMITH *Panorama Sc. & Art* II. 37 Made of copper, or tinned iron plates japanned within and without.

2. *transf.* To make black and glossy as in japanning; to polish or cover with black.

1714 [see JAPANNING *vbl. sb.*]. ?**1730** *Royal Remarks* 7 'Dear Jack' has exhausted his splendid Shilling, and now cries 'Japan your shoes, your Honour'. **1812** W. COMBE *Dr. Syntax* x. ix, His gaiters, too, were fresh japann'd. **1818** SCOTT *Rob Roy* v, The monsters of heraldry..grinned and ramped in red freestone, now japanned by the smoke of centuries. **1865** CARLYLE *Fredk. Gt.* XIX. viii. (1873) VIII. 265 Japanning people with pitch to cure them of every malady.

3. *slang.* To make clerical, to ordain. (With reference to the black coat.)

1756 *Connoisseur* No. 105 ¶3 He had been double-japanned (as he called it) about a year ago, and was the present incumbent of —. **1796** GROSE *Dict. Vulg. T.* s.v. **1826** *Sporting Mag.* XVIII. 283 My friend's son had just been ordained Deacon, or, in the language of the day, 'japanned'. **1879** J. PAYN *High Spirits* II. 106 He had passed his 'voluntary', and was to be 'japanned' in a fortnight.

Japanese (dʒæpəˈniːz), *a.* and *sb.* [f. JAPAN + -ESE: in F. *Japonnais*, Sp. *Japonés*, etc.]

A. *adj.* a. Of or pertaining to Japan.

[**1588** R. PARKE tr. *Mendoza's Hist. China* 375 There is no nation so abhorred of the Chinos as is the Iapones.] **1719** DE FOE *Crusoe* II. xiii, Japanese merchants. **1769** FALCONER *Dict. Marine* (1789), *Fayfena*, a sort of Japonese galley. **1860** MRS. CARLYLE *Lett.* III. 72 The Japanese trays are for the new drawing-room. **1884** *Pall Mall G.* 4 July 4/2 What more picturesque than the Japanese umbrellas?

b. Special collocations: **Japanese anemone** = *Japan anemone*; **Japanese ape** = *Japanese monkey*; **Japanese artichoke** = *Chinese artichoke*; **Japanese beetle**, a scarabæid beetle, *Popillia japonica*, which has become a pest of foliage and grasses in eastern North America; **Japanese camphor** = *Japan camphor*; **Japanese cedar** = CRYPTOMERIA; **Japanese cherry**, an ornamental flowering tree belonging to a variety or hybrid of several species of *Prunus* native to Japan; **Japanese current** = KUROSHIWO; **Japanese flower**, a piece of coloured paper which unfolds like a flower when placed in water; **Japanese garden**, a garden in which clipped shrubs, water, bridges, rocks, stepping-stones, raked gravel, stone lanterns, etc., are used in a formal design, without masses of bright colour; **Japanese gold thread** (see quot. 1880); **Japanese iris**, a variety of *Iris kæmpferi* or *I. lævigata*; **Japanese lantern** = *Chinese-lantern* (see CHINESE *a.* 2); **Japanese larch**, *Larix leptolepis*, which was introduced to Britain in 1861; **Japanese lily** = *Japan lily*; **Japanese macaque** = *Japanese monkey*; **Japanese maple**, a variety of *Acer palmatum* or *A. japonicum*, cultivated esp. for its decorative foliage; **Japanese medlar** = LOQUAT; **Japanese monkey**, a large monkey, *Macaca fuscata*, which is native to Japan; **Japanese pagoda tree**, *Sophora japonica*, the scholar tree; **Japanese paper**, paper made by hand, originally and chiefly in Japan, from the bark of the mulberry-tree; **Japanese pepper** (see PEPPER *sb.* 3); **Japanese print**, a coloured print made in Japan from a wood-block; **Japanese quince** = JAPONICA; **Japanese rose**, any of several species of *Rosa* native to Japan, esp. *R. rugosa*; **Japanese screen**, an embroidered screen made in Japan; **Japanese silk** = *Jap silk*; **Japanese spaniel**, a breed of small, black-and-white or brown-and-white, long-coated dog; **Japanese stitch** (see quot. 1880); **Japanese tissue (paper)**, a type of strong thin transparent paper; **Japanese vellum** (see quot. 1923); **Japanese waltzing mouse**, a mutant of *Mus musculus bactrianus*, a house mouse native to Central and Eastern Asia; also **Japanese waltzer**; **Japanese wax**, a yellow wax obtained from the berries of certain plants of the genus *Rhus*; **Japanese wolf**, *Canis lupus hodophylax*, a subspecies of the common wolf.

c **1908** E. J. COOK *Century Bk. Gardening* 71/1 The Japanese Anemone..was originally seen only in its pink-blossomed form. **1913** C. MACKENZIE *Sinister St.* I. I. vi. 87 All along the paths were masses of flowers, phloxes and early Michaelmas daisies and Japanese anemones. **1969** H. R. FLETCHER *Story R. Hort. Soc.* x. 151 All the 'Japanese anemones'..are now grouped under the hybrid name of *A. x elegans.* **1883** *List Animals* (Zool. Soc.) (ed. 8) 22 *Macacus speciosus*... Japanese Ape. **1966** R. & D. MORRIS *Men & Apes* i. 18 The famous three wise monkeys, See-no-evil, Hear-no-evil, and Speak-no-evil..are based on the Japanese ape (*Macaca fuscata*), a delightful monkey with a short, stumpy tail and a bright pink face that flushes scarlet when the animal is sexually active. **1905** tr. *Vegetable Garden* (Vilmorin-Andrieux et Cie) 671 Chinese or Japanese Artichoke... These rhizomes..are white, watery and tender. **1970** SIMON & HOWE *Dict. Gastron.* 40/2 Artichokes, Japanese or Chinese. These are small tubers which one writer describes as looking like 'petrified worms'. **1919** *Rev. Appl. Entomol.* A. VII. 101 Eradication work in connection with a Japanese beetle (*Popillia japonica*) has been systematically undertaken. **1922** *Jrnl. Econ. Entomol.* XV. 303 An efficient contact spray will no doubt have considerable application in the control of the Japanese beetle at this time. **1936** *Discovery* XVII. 36/1 The Japanese Beetle (*Popillia japonica*)..accidentally introduced into America in the larval stage in a shipment of Japanese iris in 1916, has now invaded the eastern coastal states. **1972** SWAN & PAPP *Common Insects N. Amer.* xx. 431 The Asiatic Garden Beetle..is similar in habits to the Japanese beetle.. but it flies only at night. **1727** J. G. SCHEUCHZER tr. *Kæmpfer's Hist. Japan* I. 179 Japanese boil'd Camphire may be had for one single Catti of the true Bornean Camphire. *Ibid.*, The Japanese Camphire-tree. **1880** *Encycl. Brit.* XIII. 574/2 *Cryptomeria* (Japanese cedar). **1954** *New Biol.* XVI. 97 The Japanese Cedar or Sugi, a tree found in China and Japan and, in the latter country, an important and abundant timber tree. **1901** L. H. BAILEY *Cycl. Amer. Hort.* III. 1452/2 Japanese Flowering Cherry. **1913** W. P. WRIGHT *Garden Trees & Shrubs* xxvi. 215 The double Japanese Cherries..have beautiful rosy flowers. **1925** *Jrnl. R. Hort. Soc.* L. 73 (*title*) Notes on Japanese cherries. **1951** *Dict. Gardening* (R. Hort. Soc.) II. 1085/2 It is only comparatively recently that the Japanese Cherries have been widely planted. **1972** G. CHADBUND *Flowering Cherries* I. 16 As far as we know none of the upright garden varieties of Japanese cherries were introduced into the western world until 1894. **1926** *Daily Colonist* (Victoria, B.C.) 16 Jan. 1/3 Similar conditions..gave rise to the belief that the Japanese current had changed its course. **1972** *Islander* (Victoria, B.C.) 26 Mar. 16/1 The fickle Japanese current which sweeps in a circular motion across the Pacific. **1917** N. DOUGLAS *South Wind* xxii. 271 Those Japanese flowers.. those paper flowers, I mean, which we used to put in our finger-bowls... They look like shrivelled specks of cardboard. But in the water they begin..to unfold themselves into unexpected patterns of flowers of all colours. **1968** D. HOPKINSON *Incense-Tree* iv. 42 A Japanese flower in a glass of water slowly uncurling to reveal its coloured pattern. **1863** R. ALCOCK *Capital of Tycoon* I. iv. 103 We..gained a fine suite of apartments looking on to as beautiful a specimen of Japanese garden..as can well be conceived. **1902** C. H. TOWNSEND in G. Brown *European & Japanese Gardens* 162 The composition of the Japanese garden depends chiefly upon the arrangement of its trees, boulders, paths, streams, bridges and other artificial structures. It is, least of all, a flower garden, and is probably best understood when regarded as a reduced copy of the scenery of a country—conveying the impression produced by a picture. **1912** MRS. B. TAYLOR *Japanese Gardens* iv. 53 Seldom does a Japanese garden lack water, or the appearance of water, in its scenery. **1920** W. J. LOCKE *House of Baltazar* I. 13 The Japanese garden with its pond of great water-lilies and fairy bridge across. **1957** M. G. SIMS tr. *Yoshida's Gardens of Japan* I. 7 Much in the Japanese garden is merely symbolical of nature. *Ibid.* 9 The Japanese garden is monochrome, the European polychrome. **1971** S. ELIOVSON *Gardening the Japanese Way* 26 Another misconception is that Japanese gardens are composed only of sand and stone. **1972** T. ITO (*title*) The Japanese garden —an approach to nature. **1880** L. HIGGIN *Handbk. Embroidery* i. 8 '*Japanese gold thread*', which has the advantage of never tarnishing, is..made of gilt paper twisted round cotton thread. **1883** W. ROBINSON *Eng. Flower Garden* 155/2 *I* [*ris*] *Kæmpferi* (Japanese Iris). The large number of varieties in cultivation under this name have sprung from *I. lævigata* and *I. setosa.* **1900** L. H. BAILEY *Cycl. Amer. Hort.* II. 822/1 There are few handsomer flowers than good forms of the white Japanese Iris. **1936** *Discovery* XVII. 86/2 An iris garden with special emphasis on Japanese Iris. **1895** *Brit. Warehouseman* Feb. 26/1 Japanese lanterns and Kakemonos (wall-pictures) are shown. **1901** *Daily Colonist* (Victoria, B.C.) 2 Oct. 10/2 There, added to the the effect of the bunting drapings and clusters of flags, three long strings of Japanese lanterns stretch from the roof. **1966** G. BAXT *Queer Kind of Death* (1967) xii. 174 The garden will be festooned with Japanese lanterns. **1861** *Gardeners' Chron.* 12 Jan. 23/1 The Japanese larch, *A[bies] leptolepis* of Zuccarini, is represented with cones four times larger than those sent home by Mr. Veitch. **1914** W. J. BEAN *Trees & Shrubs Hardy in Brit. Isles* II. 8 The Japanese larch has been almost, although not wholly, immune from the attacks of larch canker. **1957** M. HADFIELD *Brit. Trees* 46 In Britain the European and Japanese larches have been planted extensively. **1870** J. C. PATTESON *Let.* 21 Dec. in C. M. Yonge *Life J. C. Patteson* (1874) II. xii. 488, I have *such* Japanese lilies making ready to put forth their splendours. **1943** R. GODDEN *Rungli-Rungliot* 45 What else is there in the garden? Wild coffee flowers, roses, Japanese lilies. **1894** H. O. FORBES *Hand-bk. Primates* II. 14 Nothing is known of the habits of the Japanese Macaque. **1967** J. R. & P. H. NAPIER *Handbk. Living Primates* 405 Japanese macaque. Yellowish-brown shaggy fur. **1898** W. ROBINSON *English Flower Garden* (ed. 6) 379/1 The varieties of the Japanese Maple (*A. palmatum*) and its numerous forms..have been found of much interest for the garden. **1904** *Jrnl. R. Hort. Soc.* XXIX. 328 The popularly known 'Japanese Maples' are varieties of the two species *Acer palmatum* and *Acer japonicum.* **1973** C. LLOYD *Foliage Plants* x. 172 The beautiful but slow growing Japanese maple of the golden foliage is the corner piece at the back. **1866** LINDLEY & MOORE *Treas. Bot.* I. 462/1 The Loquat, or Japanese Medlar..is a native of Japan and the southern parts of China. **1950** G. BRENAN *Face of Spain* iv. 80 The Japanese medlars with their fish-shaped leaves and thick snake-like branches. **1972** A. F. SIMMONS *Growing Unusual Fruit* 179 It [*sc.* the loquat] arrived in the Mediterranean area in the nineteenth century, under the name of the Japanese medlar. **1872** *Proc. Zool. Soc.* 780 (*heading*) Observations on the Macaques.—IV. The Japanese Monkey. **1932** S. ZUCKERMAN *Social Life Monkeys* xix. 310 The Japanese monkeys are confined together. **1961–2** *Primates* (Inuyama, Japan) III. II. 3 The Japanese monkey is an endemic species which usually inhabits the thick forests of the mountains which cover the greater part of the Japanese Islands. **1924** L. H. BAILEY *Man. Cultivated Plants* 413 Japanese Pagoda-Tree. Round-headed deciduous tree attaining 60 ft., with spreading branches. **1973** *Times* 20 Feb. 16/3 The 152-year-old scholar tree, or Japanese pagoda tree, at Oxford University Botanic Garden is being felled because it is dying. **1727** J. G. SCHEUCHZER tr. *Kæmpfer's Hist. Japan* II. App. ii. 25 The Japanese paper is very tight and strong, and will bear being twisted into ropes. **1822** F. SHOBERL tr. *Titsingh's Illustr. Japan* II. 319 Two hundred and thirty-four different flowers, painted with great truth on thin Japanese paper. **1877** *Trans. Asiatic Soc. Japan* V. 77 The kites are constructed of Japanese paper which is both thin and strong. **1905** F. H. COLLINS *Author & Printer* 190/2 *Japanese paper*, hand-made in Japan with vellum surface. Used for proofs of etchings and engravings. **1958** J. R. BIGGS *Woodcuts* 90 The best Japanese papers are made from the fibres of the mulberry tree. *a* **1963** S. PLATH *Ariel* (1965) 59 My head a moon Of Japanese paper. **1861** R. BENTLEY *Man. Bot.* II. 503 The fruit of *X[anthoxylum] piperitum* is employed by the Chinese and Japanese as a condiment... It is commonly termed in commerce, Japanese Pepper. **1972** Y. LOVELOCK *Vegetable Bk.* III. 344 The most important among these [members of the genus *Zanthoxylum*] include Chinese pepper (*Z. bungei*) and Japanese pepper (*Z. aromaticum*). *c* **1895** A. BEARDSLEY *Lett.* (1971) 98 All the books I have left behind are at your disposal. Also a set of erotic Japanese prints. *a* **1922** T. S. ELIOT *Waste Land Drafts* (1971) 33 line 140 A touch of art is given by the false Japanese print, purchased in Oxford Street. **1972** *Country Life* 5 Oct. 805/1 William Burges was collecting Japanese prints in the 1850s. **1900** L. H. BAILEY *Cycl. Amer. Hort.* I. 427/1 Rarer kinds..are grafted in the greenhouse in early spring, on stock of the Japanese or common Quince. **1972** A. F. SIMMONS *Growing Unusual Fruit* 152 A species known often as *Cydonia sinensis* and classed with the Japanese quince or japonica..does not, however, belong to the same genus. **1883** W. ROBINSON *Eng. Flower Garden* 244/1 The palm for hardiness and decorativeness in exposed situations must be given to another Japanese Rose (Rosa rugosa). **1922** T. G. W. HENSLOW *Rose Encycl.* xiv. 176 The Japanese Rose (*R. Rugosa*). These roses are gaining in popularity every day. **1956** B. PARK *Collins Guide to Roses* xi. 196 *R[osa] rugosa.* The Ramanas Rose. The Japanese Rose. The typical form has deep purplish-pink single flowers. **1872** D. G. ROSSETTI *Let.* 18 Dec. (1967) III. 1108 If you could look in at Hewitt's one day, would you see what Japanese screens he has, and what he wants for them? **1881** C. C. HARRISON *Woman's Handiwork* III. 151 A Japanese screen in the house is a liberal education to the follower of art-needlework. **1935** C. ISHERWOOD *Mr. Norris changes Trains* xv. 254 In addition to the etchings and the Japanese screen, Arthur gave her three flasks of perfume. **1973** *Country Life* 22 Nov. 1691 A few delectable painted Japanese screens..averaged about £750 each. **1873** *Young Englishwoman* May 258 How to clean a white Japanese silk, which has got soiled in the wearing. **1895** *Montgomery Ward Catal.* 79/3 Ladies' Japanese Silk Chemisette. [**1863** R. ALCOCK *Capital of Tycoon* I. xv. 309 First I am to find a pair of well-bred Japanese dogs, 'with eyes like saucers, no nose, the tongue hanging out at the side, too large for the mouth, and white and tan if possible'.] **1880** H. DALZIEL *Brit. Dogs* III. 444 At the New York Dog Show ..they [*sc.* Japanese pugs] were classed as Japanese spaniels. **1894** R. B. LEE *Hist. & Descr. Mod. Dogs Gt. Brit. & Ireland* (*Non-Sporting Division*) xiii. 302 These little dogs are now called and identified as Japanese spaniels because they are supposed to have originally been brought from Japan. **1948** C. L. B. HUBBARD *Dogs in Brit.* 253 The native Japanese spaniel is quite distinct from the Pekingese of China. **1971** F. HAMILTON *World Encycl. Dogs* 524 One such rarity is what is known in its country of origin, Japan, as the Chin; in Britain as the Japanese; and in the Americas as the Japanese

Spaniel. **1880** L. HIGGIN *Handbk. Embroidery* v. 51 *Japanese Stitch* is a modification of stem.. taking very long stitches, and then bringing the needle back to within a short distance of the first starting-place. **1900** *Knowledge* 1 Dec. 285/1 Japanese tissue paper used by dentists. **1936** *Discovery* May 157/2 Paste a good quality Japanese tissue on to both sides of the document. **1888** C. T. JACOBI *Printers' Vocab.* 68 *Japanese vellum paper*, thick handmade paper with a vellum surface manufactured in Japan. **1923** H. A. MADDOX *Dict. Stationery* 41 *Japanese Vellum*, a stout toned printing or cover paper with smooth surface and of exceptional strength made from long Japanese fibre by natural methods. **1952** J. CARTER *ABC for Bk.-Collectors* 109 Japanese vellum is a very costly paper, hand-made in Japan from the inner bark of the mulberry tree. **1902** *Biometrika* II. 101 (*title*) Note on the results of crossing Japanese waltzing mice with European albino races. **1904** [see WALTZING *vbl. sb.* and *ppl. a.*, WALTZER b]. **1943** H. GRÜNEBERG *Genetics Mouse* iv. 50 Most stocks of Japanese waltzing mice are homozygous for it [*sc.* the gene for 'recessive' or piebald spotting]. *Ibid.* 85 Japanese waltzers differ slightly, but significantly, from albino mice in their temperature of choice. **1964** G. DURRELL *Menagerie Manor* vii. 141 Rich people who do nothing all day long but revolve from one cocktail party to another, like a set of Japanese waltzing mice. **1859** L. OLIPHANT *Narr. Earl of Elgin's Mission China & Japan* II. 257 Hitherto the most successful cargo brought to this country from Japan has been one of Japanese wax. Mr. Simmonds.. gives the following account of Japan wax:—'Rhus succedanea, the species which furnishes the Japan wax, has long been grown in our greenhouses, having been introduced from China nearly a century ago.' **1951** Japanese wax [see HENEICOSANE]. **1878** *Proc. Zool. Soc.* 788 Judging from the present specimen the Japanese Wolf, although nearly allied to *Canis lupus*, would seem to be a distinct species, to be recognized by its smaller size and shorter legs. **1968** R. & A. FIENNES *Nat. Hist. Dog* 160 Japanese wolves are very like the common northern wolves, but they are smaller.

B. *absol.*, or as *sb.* **1.** A native of Japan.

Formerly as true sb. with pl. in *-es*; now only as adj. used absol. and unchanged for pl.: a *Japanese*, two *Japanese*, the *Japanese*.

1604 E. G[RIMSTONE] *D'Acosta's Hist. Indies* v. xxv. 401 A Iapponois reported this after hee was christened. **1613** R. COCKS in J. Saris *Japan* (Hakl. Soc.) 151 The King made Proclamation that no Iapenese should receiue any of our people into their houses. **1665** *Sir T. Roe's Voy. E. Ind.* in G. Havers *P. della Vale's Trav. E. Indies* 375, I have taken special notice of divers Chinesaas and Japanesaas there. **1693** SIR T. P. BLOUNT *Nat. Hist.* 105 The Japponeses prepare [tea].. quite otherwise than is done in Europe. **1707** PSALMANAZAR (*title*) Dialogue between a Japanese and a Formosan. **1839** *Penny Cycl.* XIII. 93/2 All travellers who have been acquainted with both nations prefer the Japanese to the Chinese.

2. The Japanese language.

1828 in WEBSTER. **1861** HOFFMANN (*title*) Shopping-dialogues in Dutch, English, and Japanese. **1880** MAX MÜLLER *Ess.* (1881) II. 338 A Chinese vocabulary with Sanskrit equivalents and a transliteration in Japanese.

Japaneseness (dʒæpəˈniːznɪs). [f. JAPANESE *a.* + -NESS.] The quality or state of being Japanese, or of displaying Japanese characteristics.

1965 *New Statesman* 19 Mar. 462/2 There is no point in trying to skirt the sheer Japaneseness of Ozu's film. **1967** D. & E. T. RIESMAN *Conversations in Japan* 8 The wife being the one to bear the burden of Japaneseness.

Japanesery (dʒæpəˈniːzərɪ). [f. JAPANESE *a.* and *sb.* + -ERY, after F. *japonaiserie* (see JAPONAISERIE).] Japanese characteristics or fashion; also *pl.*, Japanese ornaments, knick-knacks, etc.

1885 *Daily News* 30 Apr. 4/8 The 'Mikado' may even bring in a little agreeable Japanesery. **1894** W. J. LOCKE *At Gate of Samaria* ix. 103 Cheap Japaneseries that had lent it the suggestion of artistic atmosphere the girl of eighteen had craved. **1906** E. NESBIT *Man & Maid* viii. 179 Bright, picturesque cushions and screens and Japaneseries. **1929** BLUNDEN *Near & Far* Pref., Those, however, who go from England to Japan without succumbing first to Japanesery will find that there is no great gulf between the old experiences and the new. **1958** *Spectator* 14 Feb. 204/2 One very soon starts longing for a bit of simple Japanesery without all that *obtrusive* local detail.

Japanesey, Japanesy (dʒæpəˈniːzɪ), *a.* [f. JAPANESE *a.* and *sb.* + -Y[1].] Having or inclining to a Japanese character.

1890 B. H. CHAMBERLAIN *Things Japanese* 144 Criticism is not at all a 'Japanesey' thing. **1891** S. J. DUNCAN *Amer. Girl in London* 55 Her parlour was Japanesy, too, in places. **1901** 'C. HOLLAND' *Mousmé* xxiii. 328 He.. has referred to.. their figures as '*petite*' and Japanesy. **1923** E. F. WYATT *Invis. Gods* I. ii. 17 The Japanesy shadows of the black scrub pine. **1925** *Glasgow Herald* 8 May 10 High-art, Japanesy tenements. **1941** *Penguin New Writing* X. 23 The stained Japanesey walls. **1971** *Country Life* 16 Dec. 1720/3 A trifle too fussy, too obviously Japanesey?

Japanesque (dʒæpəˈnɛsk), *a.* and *sb.* [f. JAPAN *sb.* + -ESQUE.]

A. *adj.* Japanese in style or manner.

1883 G. ALLEN in *Colin Clout's Cal.* 36 Delicate pink-white blossom, standing out in true Japanesque relief. **1894** *Westm. Gaz.* 27 July 3/2 Like one of those patiently-wrought pieces of cloisonné-work with which a Japanesque age has made us all familiar.

B. *sb.* A design or ornament in Japanese style.

1884 *Price List*, Tapestry Curtains. Designs, Early English, Japanesques, Persian, &c., with suitable dados. **1898** ROSS in *B. Jonson's Volpone* p. xl, He began.. his so-called Japanesques long before seeing any real Japanese art.

Hence **Japaˈnesquely** *adv.*, in a Japanesque way. **Japaˈnesquery**, Japanesque tone or spirit.

1892 *Black & White* 6 Aug. 157/1 That 'Flower watching' is Japanesquely pretty. **1895** G. ALLEN in *Westm. Gaz.* 21 June 3/2 Its Japanesquery is delightful.

Japanism (dʒəˈpænɪz(ə)m). [f. JAPAN + -ISM.] The study of or devotion to things Japanese.

1888 *Harper's Mag.* Feb. 334 Japanism—a new word coined to designate a new field of study, artistic, historic, and ethnographic.

Japanize (ˈdʒæpənaɪz), *v.* [f. as prec. + -IZE.] *trans.* To make Japanese. Hence **Japaniˈzation**.

1890 MISS DUNCAN *Soc. Depart.* 157 Foreigners are becoming so Japanised. **1894** *Chicago Advance* 5 Apr., 'In order to Christianize Japan, we must Japanize Christianity,' is a prevalent sentiment in that country. **1895** *Curr. Hist.* V. 301 Such an alliance could amount to nothing less than the Japanization of China.

japanned (dʒəˈpænd), *ppl. a.* Also with capital initial. [f. JAPAN *v.*]

1. Varnished, lacquered, or adorned with japan or in Japanese style.

1693-4 in *12th Rep. Hist. MSS. Comm.* App. v. 338 The tortoise-shell room, and the japanned room. **1717** BULLOCK *Woman is a riddle* I. i. 6 A japan'd cane, and a brush'd beaver. **1727** A. HAMILTON *New Acc. E. Ind.* II. lv. 305 Their lackt or japon'd Ware is.. the best in the World. **1851** *Illustr. Catal. Gt. Exhib.* 1356 Specimens of japanned tea-trays.

b. Polished with blacking.

1750 *Student* I. 93 A white Hand.. being the same to a Fiddler as japan'd pumps are to a Dancer. **1848** THACKERAY *Bk. Snobs* Pref. (1892) 3 He wore japanned boots and moustachios.

2. Made or become Japanese.

1889 W. CORY *Lett. & Jrnls.* (1897) 540 The 'nice' drivel of talk in Japanned parlours. **1895** *Westm. Gaz.* 26 Nov. 7/1 More will be heard later of these japanned Chinese.

3. *japanned leather* (see quot. *a* 1877); *japanned peacock, peafowl*, the black-winged peafowl, *Pavo cristatus* mut. *nigripennis*.

1814 R. HERON *Jrnl.* in *Proc. Zool. Soc.* (1835) 54 The hens.. would not suffer a japanned peacock to touch them. **1851** *Illustr. Catal. Gt. Exhib.* IV. 1252/1 Japanned leather, grained calf-skin for boots and shoes, and trimmings. **1855** J. C. MORTON *Cycl. Agric.* II. 698/2 The Japanned peafowl, as it ought to be styled, instead of the *Japan* pea-fowl. *a* **1877** KNIGHT *Dict. Mech.* II. 1211/1 *Japanned leather*, leather treated with several coats of Japan varnish and dried in a stove. **1894** A. NEWTON *Dict. Birds* III. 699 The 'japanned' Peacock, often erroneously named the Japanese or Japan Peacock,.. has received the name of *P[avo] nigripennis*, as though it were a distinct species. *Ibid.* 701 The 'japanned' bird is not known to exist anywhere as a wild race.

Japanner (dʒəˈpænə(r)). [f. JAPAN *sb.* and *v.* + -ER[1].]

I. †**1.** A native of Japan; a Japanese. †**b.** A Japanese ship. *Obs.*

1614 J. SARIS *Japan* (Hakl. Soc.) 198 The Towne where the Iapanners haue their chiefe residence and Mart, is called Matchma. **1673** DRYDEN *Amboyna* v. i, With the aid Of ten Japanners, all of them unarmed. **1719** DE FOE *Crusoe* II. xiii, Two Japanners, I mean ships from Japan. **1725** —— *Voy. round World* (1840) 100 Seven or eight Chinese or Japanners. **1764** *Mem. G. Psalmanazar* 213 The young Japaner had been presented to the Archbishop of Canterbury.

II. 2. (With lower-case initial.) One who japans, one who follows the trade of varnishing with japan.

1695 LUTTRELL *Brief Rel.* (1857) III. 513 To find out the author, who is a japanner. *c* **1790** IMISON *Sch. Art* II. 1 Take japanners gold size of the best sort. **1846** *Art-Union Jrnl.* 59 Formerly the japanner was limited to iron plates.

†**b.** *humorous.* A shoe-black. *Obs.*

1725 DE FOE *Everybody's Business* (1841) 20 These are called the black-guard, who black your honour's shoes, and incorporate themselves under the title of the Worshipful Company of Japanners. **1734** POPE *Hor. Ep.* I. i. 156 They.. Prefer a new Japanner to their shoes.

japanning (dʒəˈpænɪŋ), *vbl. sb.* [f. JAPAN *v.* + -ING[1].] The action of japanning or varnishing with japan; the material used in japanning, japan. Also *attrib.*

1688 [see JAPAN *v.* 1]. **1714** GAY *Trivia* II. 166 And aids with soot the new japanning art. **1745** ELIZA HEYWOOD *Fem. Spectator* (1748) IV. 47 We have them copied in painting, in japanning, and in embroidery. **1757** MRS. DELANY *Lett.*, *to Mrs. Dewes* 462 On the water is a Chinese vessel.. as.. gay as carving, gilding, and japanning can make it. *c* **1817** HOGG *Tales & Sk.* VI. 93 Covered with pitch or black japanning. **1839** *Penny Cycl.* XIII. 94/2 Japanning is the art of producing a highly varnished surface on wood, metal, or other hard substance, sometimes of one colour only, but more commonly figured and ornamented.

Japannish (dʒəˈpænɪʃ), *a.* [f. JAPAN *sb.* + -ISH.] Somewhat Japanese; Japanesque.

1851 CARLYLE *Sterling* vi, A splendour hovering between the raffaelesque and the japannish.

Japano- (ˈdʒæpənəʊ), used as combining form of JAPANESE, esp. in adjs. meaning 'belonging to Japan (and some other country)'. Also **ˈJapanophile**, a lover of Japan or the Japanese.

1904 *Daily Chron.* 10 May 5/2 The Japano-Russian war. **1905** D. SLADEN *Playing Game* II. iii. 185 Under the influence of the Japanophile Jevons. **1906** *Daily Chron.* 21 May 7/5 The Japano-Korean treaty. **1910** *Westm. Gaz.* 3 Feb. 3/1 The Japano-Chinese war of 1894-5. **1973** *Record* (Oxf. Univ. Press) XVIII. 5/1 We.. made our way to.. Tokyo where TK greeted us in his Japano-Oxford accent and bore us off to the Palace Hotel.

Japaˈnolatry. [See -LATRY.] Excessive devotion to or worship of Japanese art and customs.

1890 *Spectator* 6 Dec. 832/2 The curious japonolatry which is current in some literary and artistic circles. **1895** *Athenæum* 24 Aug. 249/3 Examples of the Japanolatry characteristic of this rococo age.

Japaˈnology. [See -LOGY.] That branch of ethnology which relates to Japan, its people, history, art, etc. Hence **Japaˈnologist**, a student of Japanology.

1881 tr *Nordenskiöld's Voy. 'Vega'* II. xvi. 321 The learned Japanologist, Mr. E. M. Satow.

jape (dʒeɪp), *sb.* Also 5 **chape, iappe,** 6 **iaip,** 7-9 *Sc.* **jaip.** [See JAPE *v.*]

†**1.** A trick, a device to deceive or cheat. *Obs.* since *c* 1515, but used by Scott.

13.. *E.E. Allit. P.* B. 864, & ȝe ar iolyf gentylmen your iapes ar ille. *Ibid.* C. 57 Did not Ionas in Iude suche Iape sum-whyle? *c* **1380** WYCLIF *Wks.* (1880) 12 ȝif þei maken wyues and oþer wymmen hure sustris bi lettris of fraternite or oþere iapes. *c* **1386** CHAUCER *Prol.* 705 With feyned flaterye and Iapes He made the person and the peple his Apes. **1496** *Dives & Paup.* (W. de W.) I. lvii. 99/1 The fende sholde dysceyue hym by Illusions & by Iapes. **1501** DOUGLAS *Pal. Hon.* I. lxviii, Sair I dred me for some vther iaip. **1820** SCOTT *Monast.* x, Subjecting yourself.. to the japes and mockeries of evil spirits.

†**b.** Something used to deceive; a means of deception; a deception, fraud. *Obs. rare.*

c **1400** *Destr. Troy* III. 890 Iason for all þo Iapes hade nere his ioy lost, Hade his licour ben to laite. **1513** DOUGLAS *Æneis* II. v. [iv.] 65 Turnand quhelis thai set in, by and by, Vnder the feit of this ilk bisnyng iaip [the wooden horse]. *c* **1600** BUREL *Pilgr.* in Watson *Coll. Poems* (1706) II. 22 (Jam.) To haue an hole he had grit hast, Yit in the wood thair wes nane wast, To harberie that iaip.

†**c.** With reference to sexual intercourse. *Obs.*

13.. *E.E. Allit. P.* B. 272, & en-gendered on hem Ieauntez with her Iapez ille. ? *a* **1600** J. T. *Grim the Collier* (1662) Prol., Heard you not never how an actor's wife.. Coming in's [the devil's] way did chance to get a jape.

2. A device to amuse; a merrry or idle tale; a jest, joke, gibe. *Obs.* generally before 1600 (not used by Spenser, Shaks., or their contemporaries, and recorded in 17th c. Dicts. as an 'Old Word'); revived in 19th c. in literary use by Lamb, Barham, etc. See note to the vb.

c **1340** *Cursor M.* 21911 (Fairf.) To here how rouland faȝt & oliuere or of oþer iapis to roun. **1377** LANGL. *P. Pl.* B. xx. 144 þanne lowgh lyf.. and helde holynesse a iape and hendenesse a wastour. *c* **1386** CHAUCER *Pard. Prol. & T.* 66, I preche so as ye han herd bifoore, And telle an hundred false Iapes moore. *c* **1400** MAUNDEV. (Roxb.) v. 17 þai broght him furth.. and made dance before þam and make iapes. *c* **1400** *Promp. Parv.* 257/1 Iape, *nuga, frivolum, scur(r)ilitas.* **1494** FABYAN *Chron.* VII. ccxxv. 252 He set all at noughte, & made of it a scoffe or a iape. *c* **1510** MORE *Picus* Wks. 14 The sayinges of wisemen thei repute for Iapes and very fables. **1611** R. BRADLEY *Paneg. Verses* in *Coryat's Crudities*, A crue of Apes Sporting themselves with their conceited Iapes About a Pedler that lay snorting by. **1678** PHILLIPS (ed. 4) App., *Jape* (old word), a jest, jeer or sport. **1819** W. TENNANT *Papistry Storm'd* (1827) 20 All hail, sweet son o' Nox! Father o' daffin, jaips, and jokes! **1830** LAMB *Album Verses, To Louisa M*——v, The scoff, the banter, and the jape, And antics of my gamesome Ape. **1840** BARHAM *Ingol. Leg.*, *'Leech of Folkstone'*, The bystanders well-pleased with the jape put upon him. **1882** BESANT *All Sorts* viii. (1884) 70 The coy giggle of the young lady to whom he has imparted his latest merry jape.

†**3.** A trifle, toy, trinket, plaything. *Obs.*

1436 *Pol. Poems* (Rolls) II. 172 The grete galees of Venees.. Be wel laden wyth.. Apes and iapes, and marmusettes taylede, Nifles, trifles, that litelle have availede. **1488** in Tytler *Hist. Scot.* (1864) II. 391 Item twa tuthpikis of gold, with a chenye,.. ane hert of gold, with uther small Iapis. **1526** SKELTON *Magnyf.* 1148 *Fol.* In faythe I wolde thou had a marmosete. *Fan.* Cockes harte I loue suche iapes. **1570** *Satir. Poems Reform.* xiii. 134 God wait gif ȝe be Iaips to hald in stoir, Or bony byrdis to keip in to ane Cage.

4. *Comb.*, as †**jape-worthy** *a. Obs.*, ridiculous.

c **1374** CHAUCER *Boeth.* v. pr. iii. 122 (Camb. MS.) What difference is ther bytwixe the prescience and thilke Iape-worthi dyuynenge of tyresye the dyuynor.

jape (dʒeɪp), *v.* Also 5 **iaape, iappe,** 6 **iaip,** (**gape**), 7 **jap.** [*Jape* sb. and vb. are known from the 14th c.; it is not certain whether the vb. or the sb. came first; their derivation is obscure.

In form the vb. agrees with OF. *japer*, mod.F. *japper* to yelp (as a dog), whence there was also the (rare) sb. *jap*, and *japerie* yelping: but there appears no approach of sense between this and the Eng. word. On the other hand, *jape* is nearly identical in sense with OF. *gaber*, 'to mock, deride, laugh at', whence there were the sbs. *gab* and *gabe*, also *gaberie*, 'mockery, raillery, pleasantry', *gabere, gabeor*, 'mocker'; but (notwithstanding a single instance of *jaber* in Godef.), no known phonetic laws enable us to connect *gabe-* and *jape-*. The suggestion has been made that the two French verbs are combined in the English vb.; but of such a process we have no evidence.

From its use in sense 2, the vb. began to be held impolite or indecent in 16th c. (so in Bale, Speght's *Gloss.* to Chaucer, and esp. Puttenham), was avoided by polite writers, and soon became obsolete. The sb. had the same fate. Both have been revived in 19th c., in sense 2 of the sb., 4 of the vb.]

†**1.** *trans.* To trick, beguile, befool, deceive. *Obs.*

1362 LANGL. *P. Pl.* A. I. 65 Fader of falsness.. Iudas he Iapede with þe Iewes seluer. *c* **1386** CHAUCER *Knt.'s T.* 871

Thus hath he iaped thee ful many a yer, And thou hast maked hym thy chief squier. *c* **1400** *Beryn* 3458 He hath but I-Iapid us, and scornyd her to fore. *c* **1430** LYDG. *Min. Poems* (Percy Soc.) 186 Y wyl bewar.. That of no Fowlar y wil no more be Iaped. **1463** MARG. PASTON in *P. Lett.* II. 142, I wold not he shuld iape hyr, for she menythe good feythe, and yf he wolle not have hyr, late me wete in haste.

†2. To seduce (a woman); to know carnally. *Obs.*

1382 *Pol. Poems* (Rolls) I. 270 Sle thi fadre, and iape thi modre, and thai wyl the assoile. *a* **1400–50** *Alexander* 4415 Iupitir a Iettoure þat Iapid many ladis. *c* **1530** *Hickscorner* in Hazl. *Dodsley* I. 171 He iaped my wife, and made me cuckold. **1576** *Durham Depos.* (Surtees) 312 He had rather that any man should gape his owne wif then kysse Jane Slaiter mowthe.

†**b.** *intr.* To have carnal intercourse. *Obs.*

a **1450** *Cov. Myst.* xii. (Shaks. Soc.) 118 Goddys childe! thou lyist, in fay: God dede nevyr jape so with may. **1572** GASCOIGNE *To Barth. Withipoll* Wks. (1587) 151 First in thy jorney iape not overmuch. What laughest thou Bat bycause I write so plaine?.. Methinks plaine dealing biddeth me to cast Thys bone at first amid my doggrell rime. **1589** PUTTENHAM *Eng. Poesie* III. xxii. (Arb.) 260.

†3. *trans.* To mock, deride, insult. *Obs.* in 16th c., but occasionally used in 18–19th c.

c **1440** *Jacob's Well* 191 But þou iapyst god & scornyst him. *c* **1450** *Mirour Saluacioun* 118 Xristis visage hidde was dispisid Japed and all bespitted. **1730** FENTON *Knt. of Shield*, Urge not the wags to sneer and jape us. **1822** T. MITCHELL *Arist.* II. 179 The sons of Pronapus.. Oft jape us.

4. *intr.* To say or do something in jest or mockery; to jest, joke, jeer; to make game, make fun, sport. *Obs. c* 1550; revived in 19th c.

c **1374** CHAUCER *Troilus* I. 262 (318) Repentynge hym þat he hadde euere y-Iaped Of loues folk. *Ibid.* II. 1115 (1164) And he gan at hym self to Iape faste. *c* **1450** *Merlin* iv. 66, I trowe ye do but iape. **1483** CAXTON *G. de la Tour* A v b, There was a grete noyse and the men and wymmen iaped togeder eche with other. **1523** LD. BERNERS *Froiss.* I. ccxxxiii. 324 Howe is it that my lorde the prince iapeth and mocketh thus with me? **1530** PALSGR. 589/2, I dyd but jape with hym, and he toke it in good ernest. **1552** HULOET, Iape or iest. **1858** MORRIS *Sir P. Harpdon's End* 68 What have I done that he should jape at me? **1879** GREEN *Read. Eng. Hist.* xxvii. 142 The Host in the Tales japes at him for his lonely, abstracted air.

Hence '**japing** *vbl. sb.* and *ppl. a.*; '**japingly** *adv.*, in a japing manner; †'**japing-stick**, a laughing-stock, a butt for jokes.

c **1380** WYCLIF *Serm.* Sel. Wks. I. 410 Sum men.. feden her wittis wiþ sensible þingis and ȝaping of childis gamen. *c* **1380** in *Rel. Ant.* II. 50 How mowen thei be more takyn in idil than whanne thei ben maad mennus japynge stikke, as when thei ben pleyid of japeris? *a* **1420** HOCCLEVE *De Reg. Princ.* 3768 Demostenus his hondes ones putte In a wommans bosome japyngly. *c* **1440** *Generydes* 6135 Generides in Iaping said agayn. **1494** FABYAN *Chron.* VI. clviii. 147 Bernulphus.. made thereof dyuerse scoffys and iapynge rymes. **1664** COTTON *Scarron.* I. Wks. (1765) 25 And said in merry kind of japping Indeed sirs have I ta'ne you napping?

japer ('dʒeɪpə(r)). [f. prec. + -ER¹.]

†1. A trickster, deceiver, seducer, impostor. *Obs.*

1362 LANGL. *P. Pl.* A. Prol. 35 Iapers and Iangelers Iudas Children, Founden hem fantasyes and fooles hem maaden. **1393** *Ibid.* C. XVIII. 310 Thei seien soþliche.. That Iesus was bote a Iogelour, a Iaper a-monge þe comune. *c* **1440** *York Myst.* xxxii. 43 It is Jesus þat japer þat Judas ganne selle vs. *a* **1450** *Knt. de la Tour* (1868) 33 Ye are but a mocker, and a iaper of ladies, and that is a foule tache. **1470–85** MALORY *Arthur* VIII. xl, Me semeth by his countenaunce he sholde be a noble knyght and no Iaper.

2. One who japes or jokes; *esp.* a professional jester. *Obs.* since 16th c.; revived in 19th c.

1377 LANGL. *P. Pl.* B. IX. 90 He is worse þan Iudas þat ȝiueth a iaper, siluer, And biddeth þe begger go for his broke clothes. *Ibid.* x. 31 Iaperes and iogeloures and iangelers of gestes. **1387** TREVISA *Higden* (Rolls) VII. 453 He [archebishope Rauf] usede more lawhynge and playenge þan it semede his staate and his age, and he was nyh i-cleped a iapere. *c* **1440** *Promp. Parv.* 257/2 Iaper, *nugax, nugaculus*. *c* **1475** *Pict. Voc.* in Wr.-Wülcker 806/20 *Hic nugator*,.. a chaper. **1550** BALE *Eng. Votaries* II. 72 b, And Treuisa addeth.. in fyne Englysh, that thys hawtie prelate [abp. Rauf] was a great Iaper: the terme is sumwhat homelye. **1869** *Blackw. Mag.* Dec. 687/1 Japers, who were an inferior kind of minstrel, also made their appearance in these plays. **1884** A. LANG in *Harper's Mag.* Nov. 894/1 Sydney Smith's fame is dwindling into that of a japer of japes.

†**japery** ('dʒeɪpərɪ). *Obs.* [f. prec.: see -ERY.]

1. Trickery, deception.

1496 *Dives & Paup.* I. xxxiv. (W. de W.) 73/2 That they suffre only by fantasy by dreme & by Iapery of the fende.

2. Jesting speech; ribaldry; a jest.

c **1340** *Cursor M.* 10131 (Trin.) þis book is of no iaperie [*Cott.* ribodi] But of god & oure ladie. *c* **1386** CHAUCER *Pars. T.* ¶ 576 (Harl.) After þis comeþ þe synne of Iapers þat ben þe deueles apes For þay maken folk to laughen at here iapes or iaperie as folk doon at þe gaudes of an ape. *c* **1449** PECOCK *Repr.* II. ii. 138 This seiyng is to be cast aside as a iaperi. *a* **1533** LD. BERNERS *Huon* xxvii. 85 The hoste.. beleuyd that those wordes had bene spoken in iapery.

Japhetian (dʒə'fiːʃɪən), *a.* and *sb.* [f. *Japheti* or *Japheth* + -IAN.] **A.** *adj.* = next. **B.** *sb.* A descendant of Japheth, one of the sons of Noah.

1850 J. JORDAN in *Chr. Sabbath* ii. 52 They were derived from a different family of Japhetians than the Greeks. *Ibid.* 53 The Hindus are not of Shemitic but of Japhetian origin. **1887** I. TAYLOR in *Nature* 20 Oct. 597/2 The pre-scientific Japhetian theory and the Caucasian theory.. have long been abandoned.

Japhetic (dʒə'fɛtɪk), *a.* Also Japetic. [f. *Japheth* (or L. *Japetus*) + -IC.] Of or belonging to Japheth, one of the sons of Noah; descended or supposed to be descended from Japheth: sometimes applied to the Indo-European family.

1828 WEBSTER s.v., The Japhetic nations, which people the North of Asia and all Europe. Japhetic languages. **1842** PRICHARD *Nat. Hist. Man* 136 The Indo-European or Japetic people. **1865** W. SMITH *O. Test. Hist.* (1876) 37 The allusion to the light complexion of the Japhetic races. **1877** DAWSON *Orig. World* xii. 260 A spontaneous growth of the Japetic stock scattered by the Cushite empire.

So **Japhetite** ('dʒeɪfɛtaɪt), also **Japhethite**, a descendant of Japheth.

1863 J. G. MURPHY *Comm. Gen.* ix. 25 The Persians, the Macedonians, and the Romans, who were all Japhethites. **1877** DAWSON *Orig. World* xiii. 268 The Japhetites of the Bible include none of the black races.

japing, -ly: see under JAPE *v.*

'**japish**, *a.* [f. JAPE *sb.* + -ISH¹.] Of the nature of a jape; inclined to jest. Hence '**japishly** *adv.*, '**japishness**.

1882 *Sat. Rev.* 4 Nov. 598/2 Surely a man of some japishness.. might be fished out here and there. **1888** *Ibid.* 15 Dec. 714/2 Stockton's *Bee-man of Orn* is a collection of *Märchen*, writ japishly, and of varying value.

Japlish ('dʒæplɪʃ). [f. JAP(ANESE *sb.* + ENG)LISH *sb.*] A blend of Japanese and English spoken in Japan: either the Japanese language freely interlarded with English expressions or the English language spoken in an unidiomatic way by a Japanese speaker. Also *attrib.* or *adj.*

1960 *N.Y. Times* 25 Dec. 3/5 (*caption*) New traffic instructions, written in 'Japlish', cause linguistic bewilderment. **1963** *Harper's Mag.* Jan. 54 A great many Japanese speak English nowadays (or at least 'Japlish', as the American colony calls it), and their words are usually understandable. **1966** *Time* 22 July 30 Japanese sometimes sounds like Japlish: *masukomi* for mass communications, *terebi* for TV, *demo* for demonstration and the inevitable baseballisms *pray bollu, storiku* and *hitto*. **1970** *Times* 26 Nov. 12 A word of warning to tourists and others: the Japlish veneer can be deceptive. The Japanese may use more English words, but they still think like Japanese. **1970** *Bull. Inst. Res. Lang. Teaching* (Tokyo) CCXCIII. 13 There are, moreover, hosts of 'Japlish'.. words and expressions, such as '*old miss*'.. (meaning 'old maid' or 'spinster').

Japon, obs. form of JAPAN.

‖**japonaiserie** (ʒapɔnɛzri). [Fr.] = JAPANESERY.

1896 S. R. CROCKETT *Cleg Kelly* xxvii. 195 The little alcove.. was cobwebbed with the latest artistic Japonaiseries of the period. **1902** *Westm. Gaz.* 11 Aug. 12/2 His earlier passion for Gothic art had been succeeded by one for *japonaiseries*. **1905** W. STEVENS *Let.* 21 Aug. (1967) 84 The japonaiserie of the pines. **1966** *New Statesman* 8 July 64/2 This.. enthralling piece of contemporary *japonaiserie* [*sc.* a film] circles round a gentle young wife.

japonate ('dʒæpəneɪt). *Chem.* [f. JAPON-IC + -ATE¹ 1 c.] A salt of japonic acid.

1838 T. THOMSON *Chem. Org. Bodies* 117 The Japonates do not crystallize, but dry into hard masses.

†**Ja'ponian**, *a.* and *sb. Obs.* [f. *Japon*, JAPAN.]

A. *adj.* Of or relating to Japan; Japanese.

1613 PURCHAS *Pilgrimage* (1614) 526 A Iaponian King had erected three thousand.. Temples, with houses adjoyned for the Bonzii. **1738** [G. SMITH] *Curious Relations* II. 278 After his death the Japonian Army withdrew from Coria.

B. *sb.* A native of Japan.

1600 HAKLUYT *Voy.* III. 857 The Iaponians being furnished with brazen ordinance. **1627** tr. *Bacon's Life & Death* (1651) 21 The Japonians are longer-liv'd than the Chineses. **1679** *Confinement* 32 His Neighbours slight him, and there's not a Man, But looks as strange, as a Japonian.

So †'**Japonite** *sb.*, a Japanese.

1613 PURCHAS *Pilgrimage* (1614) 525 Between him and the King of China hapned warres about the Kingdome of Coray, which the Iaponites left upon his death.

Japonic (dʒə'pɒnɪk), *a.* [f. as prec. + -IC.] Of or pertaining to Japan; Japanese.

Japonic earth: catechu, terra japonica. *japonic acid*: $C_{12}H_{10}O_5$, a form of tannic acid obtained from catechu.

1673 RAY *Journ. Low C., Milan* 245 Chinese and Japonic manuscripts. **1710** T. FULLER *Pharm. Extemp.* 104 Powder'd Japonic Earth. **1789** W. BUCHAN *Dom. Med.* (1790) 275 The size of the nutmeg of *diascordium*, or the japonic confection. **1838** T. THOMSON *Chem. Org. Bodies* 116 By this absorption of oxygen, the catechuic acid is changed into japonic acid. **1859** FOWNES *Man. Chem.* 457 Japonic acid is a black and nearly insoluble substance, soluble in alkalies and precipitated by acids.

Hence **Ja'ponically** *adv.*, in Japanese style; **Ja'ponicize** *v.*, to make Japanese, to Japanize.

1889 *Academy* 27 July 656 A sort of tale.. illustrated 'japonically'. **1890** *Athenæum* 30 Aug. 284/1 Japanese place-names.. japonicized in pronunciation.

japonica (dʒə'pɒnɪkə). [mod.L., fem. of *japonicus* pertaining to Japan.] A name used for various plants originally native to Japan, esp. formerly the camellia (*C. japonica*); now usually designating a spring-flowering, deciduous shrub of the genus *Chænomeles*, esp. *C. japonica*, the Japanese quince, or its fruit.

1819 KEATS *Let.* 13 Mar. (1931) II. 309, I would put it [*sc.* a globe of gold-fish] before a handsome painted window and shade it all round with myrtles and Japonicas. **1851** H. MELVILLE *Moby Dick* I. xli. 299 Whiteness refiningly enhances beauty,.. as in marbles, japonicas, and pearls. **1859** A. VAN BUREN *Jottings of Sojourn in South* 134 That richest and sweetest blossomed of tropical shrubs—the japonica—that never blossoms only in winter. **1910** 'O. HENRY' *Strictly Business* (1917) ix. 91 You put me in mind of a japonica in a window. **1933** A. OSBORN *Shrubs & Trees for Garden* xxxv. 318 *C[ydonia] japonica* (Japanese Quince), of which there are varieties with flowers of many shades of white, yellow, pink and red, is often known as 'Japonica'. **1963** W. BLUNT *Of Flowers & Village* 46 The japonica has had no less than five different names during my lifetime. **1969** *Listener* 9 Jan. 45/2 The Japonica is strangled with convolvulus.

b. The fruit of the Asian plant *Zizyphus jujuba* (*Z. sinensis*); cf. JUJUBE.

1874 LINDLEY & MOORE *Treas. Bot.* II. Suppl. 1308/1 Japonica. A market name for the fruits of *Zizyphus sinensis*, which are occasionally sold in Covent Garden as dessert fruits. **1887** R. BENTLEY *Man. Bot.* (ed. 5) II. 517 Another Japanese species, *Z[izyphus] sinensis*, yields the fruits known as Japonicas.

Hence **ja'ponicadom** *U.S.* (see quot. 1860). *Obs.*

1851 A. O. HALL *Manhattaner* 123 The general society of New Orleans is still in a chaotic state, and she has no located, acknowledged empire of Japonicadom. **1860** BARTLETT *Dict. Amer.* (ed. 3), *Japonicadom*, a word invented by N. P. Willis to denote the upper classes of society.

Japonize ('dʒæpənaɪz), *v.* [f. as JAPONIC *a.* + -IZE.] *trans.* = JAPANIZE.

1899 *Eng. Hist. Rev.* Apr. 224 *note*, Many place-names all over Japan are of Ainu origin, japonised.

So '**Japonism**, Japonizing action or practice; following of the Japanese fashion.

1890 *Sat. Rev.* 29 Mar. 380/1 Cockney Japonism, applying an impossible Fuji-no Yama on a ground of saffron.

jaquenette, altered form of JACONET.

jaques, obs. form of JAKES.

jar (dʒɑː(r)), *sb.*¹ Forms: 6 gerre, 6–7 iarre, 7–8 jarr, 6– jar. [Goes with JAR *v.*¹ Sense 7 appears to be independently taken from the vb.; and in sense 8 there may be an independent operation of the same echoic or onomatopœic process which gave rise to the vb. and sb.]

I. A sound or vibration.

1. A harsh inharmonious sound or combination of sounds; †*spec.* in *Mus.*, A discord (*obs.*).

1553 T. WILSON *Rhet.* (1580) 169 Composition.. is an apte joynyng together of woordes in suche order, that neither the eare shall espie any gerre, nor yet [etc.]. **1586** W. MASSIE *Marriage Serm. at Trafford*, A litle iarre in musick is not easily espied. **1600** SHAKS. *A. Y. L.* II. vii. 5 If he compact of iarres, grow Musicall, We shall haue shortly discord in the Spheares. **1655** MOUFET & BENNET *Health's Improv.* (1746) 359 When the Jars of Crowders shall be thought good Music. **1781** COWPER *Conversat.* 902 With rash and awkward force the chord he shakes, And grins with wonder at the jar he makes. **1841** D'ISRAELI *Amen. Lit.* (1867) 278 The critic's fastidious ear listens to nothing but the jar of rude rhymes.

†**2.** A vibration or tick of the clock; cf. JAR *v.*¹ 2. *Obs. rare.*

1611 SHAKS. *Wint. T.* I. ii. 43, I loue thee not a Iarre o' th' clock, behind What Lady she her Lord.

3. A quivering or grating sound; a tremulous or harsh vibration of sound.

1669 HOLDER *Elem. Speech* (J.), The impulse.. shakes and agitates the whole tongue, whereby the sound is affected with a trembling jar. **1813** SCOTT *Rokeby* v. iv, Bolt and bar Resumed their place with sullen jar. **1885** R. L. & F. STEVENSON *Dynamiter* ii. 9 House after house echoed upon his passage with a ghostly jar.

4. A vibration or tremulous movement resulting from concussion, *esp.* a movement of this kind running through the body or nerves; a thrill of the nerves, mind, or feelings caused by, or resembling the effect of, a physical shock.

c **1815** JANE AUSTEN *Persuas.* xii, She.. ran up the steps to be jumped down again. He advised her against it, thought the jar too great. **1822–34** *Good's Study Med.* (ed. 4) I. 371 Such exercise as gives a general jar to the animal frame, as riding a hard-trotting horse. *a* **1853** ROBERTSON *Lect.* i. (1858) 100, I know what it is to feel the jar of nerve gradually cease. **1871** R. H. HUTTON *Ess.* II. 131 It is a jar to the mind, like coming down three steps without notice.

II. 5. Discord, want of harmony, disagreement; a divergence or conflict of opinions, etc.; †a discrepancy of statement (*obs.*).

1548 UDALL, etc. *Erasm. Par. John* x. verse 19 There fel a newe iar in opinions among the people. **1593** BILSON *Govt. Christ's Ch.* 21 The iarre in the number of the Judges, I labour not to reconcile. **1612** T. TAYLOR *Comm. Titus* i. 16 Not.. admitting discord, and iarre in things whereof the one should be as the true exposition of the other. **1893** in Barrows *Parlt. Relig.* II. 837 [If] there has been no such jar in the original creation as the doctrine of sin implies.

6. a. Discord manifested in strife or contention; variance, dissension, quarrelling.

1546 J. HEYWOOD *Prov.* II. ii. (1867) 47 Alone to bed she went. This was their beginnyng of iar. **1590** SPENSER *F.Q.*

II. ii. 26 He maketh warre, he maketh peace againe, And yett his peace is but continual iarre. **1658** *Whole Duty Man* xv. ¶2 The continual conversation that is among them . . will be apt to minister some occasion of jar. **1781** COWPER *Expostul.* 294 Thy senate is a scene of civil jar. **1850** TENNYSON *In Mem.* xciv, They can but listen at the gates, And hear the household jar within.

b. A dissension, dispute, quarrel. Now used chiefly of petty (esp. domestic) broils.

1583 BABINGTON *Commandm.* v. (1590) 186 Brawles, iarres, and vnkindnesse betwixt man and wife before their children and seruants. **1682** BUNYAN *Holy War* xi, Now there were no jars, no chiding . . in all the Town of Mansoul. **1700** DRYDEN *Pal. & Arc.* II. 418 The vanquish'd party shall their claim release, And the long jars conclude in lasting peace. **1848** BRIGHT *Sp., Ireland* 25 Aug., Ireland has long been a land of jars and turmoil. **1853–7** TRENCH *Proverbs* i. 20 Women's jars breed men's wars. **1887** JESSOPP *Arcady* i. 5 Once or twice a family jar put two households at war.

c. *at (a) jar*, † *at jars*: at discord, in a state of dissension or variance. † *to fall at jar*: to fall out, to quarrel (*obs.*). Cf. AJAR². Now *rare.*

1552 *Acts Privy Counc. Eng.* 23 July (1892) 102 A letter to the Mayour and townes men of Excestre willing them . . to contynnewe in frendship with . . the gentlemen with whome they were lately at jarre. **1586** J. HOOKER *Hist. Irel.* in *Holinshed* II. 82/2 The citizens and Ormond his armie fell at some iar. **1603** KNOLLES *Hist. Turks* (1638) 122 The German Princes were still at a jarre about the choice of their Emperors. **1674** N. FAIRFAX *Bulk & Selv.* 74 An hugger-mugger of meddlesom beings all at jars. **1784** J. BARRY in *Lect. Paint.* vi. (1848) 220 The hues of colour in the sky and distance must frequently be at jar with the light and shade of the advanced parts. **1859** I. TAYLOR *Logic in Theol.* 139 The life seen and temporal, and the life eternal are at a jar.

III. 7. A method of connecting the bit and the rods or cable in an apparatus for drilling rocks by impact, by means of which at each up-stroke a jar of the bit is produced which jerks it upwards though it may be tightly wedged in the hole.

a **1864** GESNER *Coal, Petrol.*, etc. (1865) 28 The downward stroke of the walking-beam releases the Auger Stem and Bit for an instant as the Jars slide together, and they fall the distance necessary to penetrate the rock, and are again lifted by the Jars on the upward stroke. **1881** RAYMOND *Mining Gloss., Jars*, a part of percussion-drilling apparatus for deep holes . . which by producing at each up-stroke a decided jar of the bit jerks it up. **1883** *Century Mag.* July 330/1 The 'jars', two heavy bars linked together.

IV. 8. A representation of the harsh vibratory sound made by certain birds and insects, used to form their popular names, as JAR-BIRD, JAR-FLY, JAR-OWL; hence transferred to the animal, etc., as in EVE-JAR, NIGHT-JAR.

V. 9. *attrib.* and *Comb.*, as **jar ramming** *Founding* = *jolt ramming* (s.v. JOLT *sb.* 5).

1909 *Iron Age* LXXXIV. 1165/1 The working foundry-man has carried this development, especially as applied to what are known as jolt or jar ramming machines, far beyond what was anticipated. **1912** *Jrnl. Iron & Steel Inst.* LXXXVI. 546 A jar-ramming moulding-machine with a roll-over device, which also lowers the mould away from the pattern, is described. **1934** LAING & ROLFE *Man. Foundry Pract.* v. 102 (*heading*) Jolt- or jar-ramming.

jar (dʒɑː(r)), *sb.*² Forms: 6–7 iarre, 7–8 jarr, 7– jar. [a. F. *jarre* (16th c. in Godef. *Compl.*) = Pr. *jarro*, Sp., Pg. *jarra, jarro*, It. *giara* (formerly also *giarra, zara*), a. Arab. *jarrah*, earthen water-vessel. (The Eng. may be in part directly from Sp.)]

1. A vessel of earthenware, stoneware, or glass, without spout or handle (or having two handles), usually more or less cylindrical in form. Orig. used only in its eastern sense of a large earthen vessel for holding water, oil, wine, etc. (See quots.)

Leyden jar, an electrical condenser consisting of a cylindrical glass jar lined inside and outside nearly to the top with tin foil, the inner coating being connected at the top with a brass rod which ends in a knob.

1592 J. TWITT in Hakluyt *Voy.* (1600) III. 568 Wee descryed a frigat . . wherein were 22. iarres of copper-money. **1613** PURCHAS *Pilgrimage* (1614) 469 At the dore there is a great iarre of water, with a . . Ladle in it, and there they wash their feete. **1628** DIGBY *Voy. Medit.* 48, I found that . . hanging some lead in the iarres, it continued perfect good. **1660** BOYLE *New Exp. Phys. Mech.* xxv. 199 The Glass did . . fall down to the bottom of the Jar. **1718** LADY M. W. MONTAGU *Let. to Abbé Conti* 19 May, The galleries . . are adorned with jars of flowers. **1750** FRANKLIN *Lett.*, etc. 25 Dec., Wks. 1840 V. 255 The shock from two large glass jars, containing as much electrical fire as forty common phials. **1832** *Hand-bk. Nat. Philos.* II. *Electr.* viii. 34 (U.K.S.) This instrument having been made known principally through the experiments of Kleist, Cuneus, and Muschenbroeck, at Leyden, the name of the *Leyden phial*, or *jar*, was generally applied to it. **1846** GROTE *Greece* II. xxiii. (1862) II. 563 The jars and pottery of Korkyra enjoyed great reputation.

2. a. Such a vessel and its contents; hence, as much as a jar will hold, a jarful. Formerly a measure of capacity varying according to the commodity.

1598 FLORIO, *Giara, Giarra*, . . also a certaine measure of liquid things, which we call a iarre. **1656** BLOUNT *Glossogr., Jar* (Span. *Jarro* . .), with us it is most usually taken for a vessel of twenty Gallons of Oyl. **1706** PHILLIPS, *Jarr of Oil*, an Earthen Vessel containing from 18 to 26 Gallons; A Jarr of green Ginger is about a Hundred Pounds Weight. **1732** POPE *Ep. Bathurst* 56 Sir, Spain has sent a thousand jars of oil. **1848** L. HUNT (*title*) A Jar of Honey from Mount Hybla.

† **b.** *Electr.* A unit of capacity (see quot. 1920¹). *Obs.*

[**1834** W. S. HARRIS in *Rep. Brit. Assoc. Adv. Sci. 1833* 387 The unit of measure consists of a small electrical jar, having a discharging electrometer. **1889** A. W. POYSER *Magn. & Electr.* xiii. 139 Harris's unit jar.—This instrument is used for measuring the charge given to a Leyden jar.] **1920** *Admiralty Handbk. Wireless Telegr.* iii. 68, 1 farad = . . 9 x 10^8 (nine hundred million) 'jars'. *Ibid.*, The jar is a Service unit, and is very useful when dealing with small capacities. *Ibid.* viii. 245 Provide a condenser composed of two elements of 100 jars each. **1932** *Admiralty Handbk. Wireless Telegr. 1931* vi. 338 The low reactance of even minute capacities and the easy shunt paths they provide . . may best be realised by giving a comparative table of the reactances of a capacity of 1 jar and an inductance of 100 microhenries at various frequencies.

c. A drink (of beer, etc.). *colloq.*

1925 S. O'CASEY *Juno & Paycock* I, in *Two Plays* 42 *Boyle.* An' now, Mr. Bentham, you'll have to have a wet. *Bentham.* A wet? *Boyle.* A wet—a jar—a boul! **1941** BAKER *Dict. Austral. Slang* 38 *Jar*, a pint or 'handle' of beer. **1961** C. WILLOCK *Death in Covert* i. 8 'Have a jar, Goss,' he said, and poured him at least three fingers of whisky. **1966** P. MOLONEY *Plea for Mersey* 56 Whan lads frae Scotty Road gang far, Untae the boozer for a jar. **1969** V. CANNING *Queen's Pawn* iii. 41 Hot morning. Care for a jar? They keep good beer. **1972** *Observer* 26 Nov. 26/4 The painter, Raymond Piper, took us for a jar at his local. **1973** *New Society* 6 Sept. 563/1 A great place to meet old friends and make new ones, to knock back the jars and sit gossiping into the early hours.

3. *attrib.* and *Comb.*, as *jar radiation, jar-like* adj.; † **jar-glass**, a low glass vessel shaped like a gallipot.

1602 PLAT *Delightes for Ladies* (1605) §52 Put it vp in gally pots or iarre glasses. **1652** CULPEPPER *Eng. Physic.* 256 Take a flat glass, we call them jarr glasses, strew in a lair of fine sugar. **1694** SALMON *Bate's Dispens.* (1713) 274/2 Keep it in a Jarglass or Gally-pot, tyed close over with a wet Bladder, for Vse. **1880** A. WILSON in *Gentl. Mag.* CCXLVI. 42 These animals are given to eject water from their jar-like bodies. **1892** *Pall Mall G.* 5 May 6/2 The discharges of a Leyden jar were sent through the primary wire of an oil induction coil. The wave-length of the jar radiation was three hundred metres.

jar, *sb.*³ *arch.* or *colloq.* [Later form of *char*, CHARE *sb.*¹, turn, turning: see AJAR¹.] In the phrases *on (upon) the jar*, † *on (a) jar*, † *at jar*, on the turn, partly open, AJAR¹: cf. CHARE *sb.*¹ 2 b.

1674 N. FAIRFAX *Bulk & Selv.* 7 The fulfilledness or perfection of the will in the next life, will not be in a standing at jar, and wavering alike towards good and evil. **1707** J. STEVENS tr. *Quevedo's Com. Wks.* (1709) 45 Finding a Door upon the jar. **1767** H. BROOKE *Fool of Qual.* (1859) I. 311 The door was on the jar, and, gently opening it, I entered and stood behind her unperceived. **1777** SHERIDAN *Sch. Scand.* II. ii, She never absolutely shuts her mouth, but leaves it always on a-jar, as it were, thus. **1794** MRS. A. M. BENNETT *Ellen* II. 112 She found . . the hall door on jar. **1837** DICKENS *Pickw.* xxxiv, 'I see Mrs. Bardell's street door on the jar'. 'On the what?' exclaimed the little judge. 'Partly open, my Lord', said Serjeant Snubbin.

jar (dʒɑː(r)), *v.*¹ Forms: 6–7 iarr(e, 6 gerre, ier, charre, 7–8 jarr, 6– jar. [This vb. and its accompanying sb. JAR¹ are known only from the 16th c. In origin prob. echoic, varying with *gerre, charre*, representing (with trilled *r*) a continued harsh vibratory sound. Words phonetically akin are *churr, chirr, chark* (OE. *cearcian*), *chirk*, etc., with various verbs expressing vocal sound in other languages.]

I. 1. *intr.* To make or emit a harsh grating sound; to make a musical discord; to sound harshly or in discord with other sounds. Also *fig.*

1526 SKELTON *Dk. Albany* 378 Ye muse somwhat too far, All out of joint ye iar. **1542** UDALL *Erasm. Apoph.* 76 b, Thei would bestowe greate labour and diligence to sette the strynges in right tune, and had maners gerryng quite and clene out of all good accorde or frame. **1576** FLEMING *Panopl. Epist.* 115 Iarringe, and snarringe at me like dogs. **1598** DRAYTON *Heroic. Ep.* xi. 124 The British Language, which our Vowels wants, And iarres so much vpon harsh Consonants. **1602** MARSTON *Antonio's Rev.* IV. v. Wks. 1856 I. 131 The strings of natures symphony Are crackt and jar. **1642** FULLER *Holy & Prof. St.* I. viii. 21 Though with the clock they have given the last stroke, yet they keep a jarring, muttering to themselves a good while after. **1658** tr. *Porta's Nat. Magic* VI. xiii. 189 If it . . ring clearly, it is whole; if it do jar, it is cracked somewhere. **1709** ADDISON *Tatler* No. 157 ¶10 She jarrs and is out of Tune very often in Conversation. **1734** WATTS *Reliq. Juv.* iv. (1789) 10 Rivers of peace attend his song . . He jars; and, lo! the flints are broke. **1816** BYRON *Ch. Har.* III. iv, Perchance my heart and harp have lost a string, And both may jar.

† **b.** To produce a harsh or grating sound on or as on a musical instrument. *Obs.*

1581 J. BELL *Haddon's Answ. Osor.* 93 Many other good men iarryng alwayes upon the same stryng, mistooke the note as I did. **1594** NASHE *Unfort. Trav.* Wks. 1883–4 V. 185 Brauely did he drum on this Cutwolfes bones . . iarring on them quaueringly with his hammer. **1603** DRAYTON *Bar. Wars* III. xlviii, Which like the tunes of the Celestials are . . Compar'd with which Arion did but iar.

† **2.** *intr.* Of a clock (or, of minutes): To tick. Also (in quot. 1593) *trans.* To cause to tick. *Obs.*

1593 SHAKS. *Rich. II*, v. v. 51 My thoughts, are minutes; and with Sighes they iarre Their watches on vnto mine eyes. *c* **1594** KYD *Sp. Trag.* IV. in Hazl. *Dodsley* V. 122 The bells tolling . . the minutes jarring, and the clock striking twelve. **1609** HEYWOOD *Brit. Troy* IV. cvii, He heares no waking clocke, nor watch to iarre.

3. *intr.* To strike against something (or each other) with a grating sound, or so as to cause vibration; to clash. Const. *upon, with, against.*

1665 [see JARRING *ppl. a.* 2]. **1713** STEELE *Guardian* No. 143 ¶1 He came . . encumbered with a bar of cold iron . . it banged against his calf and jarred upon his right heel, as he walked. **1810** SCOTT *Lady of L.* II. xvii, As broad-sword upon target jarred. **1877** MRS. OLIPHANT *Makers Flor.* xiii. 327 His boat of life had already jarred upon the soft shores of the eternal land.

4. *intr.* With reference to the sensation caused by discordant sound: To sound harshly *in* (*obs.*), or fall with harsh effect *on*, the ear. Hence, To strike with discordant or painful effect *upon* the nerves, feelings, mind, conscience, etc.

1538 STARKEY *England* I. ii. 63 Hyt sounyth veray yl, hyt jarryth in myn yerys, to gyue such powar to blynd fortune. **1850** MERIVALE *Rom. Emp.* (1865) II. xiii. 108 Of all his audacious innovations, none, perhaps, jarred more upon the prejudices of his countrymen. **1851** THACKERAY *Eng. Hum.* i. (1863) 57 His laugh jars on one's ear after seven score years. **1874** GREEN *Short Hist.* vi. §5. 322 The iniquity of the proposal jarred against the public conscience. **1875** W. S. HAYWARD *Love agst. World* 78 There was something in her manner . . which jarred painfully on his feelings.

5. *intr.* Of the body affected: **a.** To vibrate audibly; to resound, clatter, or rattle with a grating or grinding sound. **b.** Hence (without reference to sound) To vibrate, shiver, or shake, from an impact or shock.

1735 WESLEY *Wks.* (1830) I. 21 The ship shook and jarred with so unequal grating a motion. **1742** PLANT in *Phil. Trans.* XLII. 40 We had a great Shock; it made my House shake much, and the Windows jar. **1791** COWPER *Iliad* xx. 203 The incumber'd earth jarr'd under foot. **1879** *Cassell's Techn. Educ.* IV. 102/1 May be applied to the doors and windows . . where subject to jar or vibrate.

6. *trans.* To cause to sound discordantly.

1633 tr. *Bp. Hall's Occas. Medit.* §80 When once they [bells] jarre, and check each other . . how harsh and unpleasing is that noise. **1839–40** DE QUINCEY *Casuistry* Wks. 1858 VIII. 300 Every impulse of bad health jars or untunes some string in the fine harp of human volition. **1863** WHITTIER *Andrew Rykman's Prayer* 107, I alone the beauty mar, I alone the music jar.

7. To cause to vibrate; to shake into vibration; to trill. In quot. 1568 to grind (the teeth).

1568 T. HOWELL *Arb. Amitie* (1879) 101 And breake the bragges of curssed curres, that iarre their teeth at thee. **1790** WALKER *Pronounc. Dict.* Introd. §419 The rough *r* is formed by jarring the tip of the tongue against the roof of the mouth near the fore teeth. **1820** W. IRVING *Sketch Bk., Westm. Abb.* (1859) 129 It [the music] fills the vast pile, and seems to jar the very walls. **1859** W. COLLINS *Q. of Hearts* (1875) 53 The blow must have jarred the hand of Shifty Dick up to his very shoulder. **1860** O. W. HOLMES *Prof. Breakf.-t.* vii. (Paterson) 150 A sudden gust . . jars all the windows.

b. To cause the nerves or feelings to vibrate painfully, to send a shock through.

1789 MRS. PIOZZI *Journ. France*, etc. I. 12 The fine paved road . . jars the nerves terribly. **1795** SOUTHEY *Joan of Arc* v. 393 Discord of dreadful sounds That jarr'd the soul. **1821** BYRON *Cain* III. i. 135 Since That saying jars you, let us only say—'Twere better that he never had been born.

8. To injure by concussion or impact.

1875 MANNING *Mission H. Ghost* viii. 214 If you take in hand a musical instrument that has been broken or jarred, all its notes jangle in discord. **1898** P. MANSON *Trop. Diseases* 359 This blood comes from the wall of an abscess jarred and torn by the succession of the harassing cough.

b. To roughen, as by concussion or impact.

18.. O. BYRNE *Artisan's Handbk.* 338 (Cent.) The face of the polishing-lap is hacked or jarred.

9. To drill by impact, as a rock; to use a drill-jar upon: cf. JAR *sb.*¹ 7. (Funk.)

10. To drive by a jarring sound.

1820 BYRON *Mar. Fal.* III. ii. 540 Man, thou hast struck upon the chord which jars All nature from my heart.

II. 11. *intr.* To be out of harmony or at discord in character or effect; to be at variance; to disagree; to conflict. Of persons (*obs.*), or of opinions, statements, systems, etc.

1541 R. COPLAND *Galyen's Terapeut.* 2 E iij, In this thynge almost all the maysters of medycyne do agre, albeit that in sondry thynges they iarre. **1563** A. BROOKE (*title*) Agreemente of sondry Places of Scripture, seeming in shew to iarre. **1579** TOMSON *Calvin's Serm. Tim.* 49/2 The Gospell is not a doctrine iarring from the lawe that Moses published in Gods name. **1667** MILTON *P.L.* v. 793 Orders and Degrees Jarr not with liberty, but well consist. **1764** CHURCHILL *Gotham* III. 577 Making those jar, whom Reason meant to join. **1873** M. ARNOLD *Lit. & Dogma* (1876) 168 This verse . . jars with the words which precede and follow.

b. To come into conflict, to clash.

1621 BURTON *Anat. Mel.* I. i. II. xi. (1651) 30 They often jar, Reason is overborne by Passion. **1711** STEELE *Spect.* No. 174 ¶1, And yet those Interests are ever jarring. **1851** G. BRIMLEY *Ess., Wordsw.* 140 Clashing sympathies jarred the more harshly within him.

12. *intr.* To be at strife or active variance; to quarrel; to dispute, bicker, wrangle.

1550 LATIMER *Last Serm. bef. Edw. VI* Serm. (1562) 125 They will ier now a dayes one with an other, excepte they haue all. *Ibid.* 125 b, When they haue ierred they haue both gon to wracke. **1587** HIGGINS in *Mirr. Mag., Brennus* xxxi, O rather now, my sonnes, leaue of to iar. *c* **1592** MARLOWE *Jew of Malta* II. ii, We will not jar about the price. **1697** DRYDEN *Virg. Georg.* IV. 94 If intestine Broils allarm the Hive, . . The Vulgar in divided Factions jar. **1742** YOUNG *Nt. Th.* II. 176 Body and soul, like peevish man and wife, United jar, and yet are loth to part. **1840** LADY C. BURY *Hist.*

of *Flirt* xi, We were everlastingly jarring and saying disagreeable things to each other.

†13. *trans.* To bring to disunion or discord. *Obs.*

c1615 SYLVESTER tr. *H. Smith's Map of Man*, We build and batter, ioyne and iarre, We heap and scatter, make and marre. 1628 FELTHAM *Resolves* II. [I.] lxxii. 208 'Giue it to the fairest', was it, which jarr'd the Goddesses.

Hence **jarred** (dʒɑːd), *ppl. a.*

1892 ANNE RITCHIE *Rec. Tennyson*, etc. III. vii. 211 He was in a jarred and troubled state. 1899 LD. ROSEBERY in *Daily News* 28 Oct. 6/5 This little island..viewed..with such jarred ambition by the great Empires of the world.

jar (dʒɑː(r)), *v.*² [f. JAR *sb.*²] *trans.* To preserve (fruit) in a jar; to bottle. Also *transf.*

1747 H. GLASSE *Art of Cookery* xviii. 152 (*heading*) To jar Cherries. 1962 *Guardian* 24 Dec. 4/3 There's no point in jarring it away. You have to buy clothes with anything you get.

‖**jarabe** (xa'rabe). Also **jarave**. [Amer. Sp., a. Sp. *jarabe* syrup.] One of several Mexican pair dances in which the man dances the zapateado steps.

1834 A. PIKE *Prose Sk. & Poems* 103 In the jarabes, or singular dances of the fandango, her first partner was always Rafael. 1903 C. LUMHOLTZ *Unknown Mexico* II. xxii. 382 Professional male and female dancers, engaged as special attractions, execute the national dance, *jarave*. 1932 H. CRANE *Let.* 12 Apr. (1965) 408 Someone dances a *jarabe*, a dance that is all vibrant gristle. 1964 *Spectator* 3 Apr. 450/1 The typical dance [of Mexico], the *Jarabe*, slightly Spanish in origin.

‖**jararaca** (dʒɑːrə'rɑːkə). [Native name in Tupi-Guarani.] A venomous serpent of Brazil (*Bothrops Jararaca*) of the family *Crotalidæ*.

1613 PURCHAS *Pilgrimage* (1614) 842 Snakes, as the Iararaca, of..foure kinds, of muskie sent, one ten spannes long. 1708 tr. *Nieuhoff's Brazil* in Pinkerton *Voy.* (1808) XIV. 714 The serpent Jararaka is short, seldom exceeding the length of an arm to the elbow. 1825 A. CALDCLEUGH *Trav. S. Amer.* I. ii. 40 The jararáca is sometimes..six feet in length.

†**jarbe**. *Sc. Obs.* [app. var. of GERBE; a. F. *gerbe*, OF. *jarbe* sheaf.] Apparently 'a knot in form of a sheaf' (Jam.).

1578 *Inv. R. Wardr.* (1815) 264 A belt of knottis of perll and reid curall and jarbes of gold contening xliii knottis of perll. 1579 *Ibid.* 288 Ane belt of knottis of perll amatistes and jarbis of gold betuix.

'**jar-bird**. [JAR *sb.*¹ 8.] Local name of the Nuthatch.

1768 G. WHITE *Selborne* xvi. (1875) 60 My countrymen talk much of a bird that makes a clatter with his bill against a dead bough, or some old pales, calling it a jar-bird... It proved to be the *Sitta europæa* (nuthatch).

‖**jarde**. *Farriery. Obs.* [F. *jarde*, ad. It. *giarda*, med.L. *giarda, jarda*.] = JARDON.

1727 BAILEY vol. II, *Jardees, Jardons*. 1755 JOHNSON, *Jardes* (French), hard callous tumours in horses, a little below the bending of the ham on the outside.

jarden, obs. form of JORDAN (almond).

‖**jardinière** (ʒardinjɛr). [F., = a female gardener, a gardener's wife, a pot or stand for flowers.] **1.** An ornamental receptacle, pot, or stand for the display of growing flowers within doors, or on a window-sill, balustrade, or other part of a building; also for the display of cut flowers for the decoration of the table, etc.

1841 LADY BLESSINGTON *Idler in France* I. 121 Small *jardinières* are placed in front of each panel of looking-glass. 1873 MISS THACKERAY *Wks.* (1891) I. 465 'Take care, you will knock over the jardinière', cried Mrs. Palmer. 1884 F. BOYLE *Borderland* 321 Superb old braziers lately fashionable as jardinières.

2. *Cookery.* (See quot. 1877). So *jardinière soup*, vegetable soup.

1841 THACKERAY in *Fraser's Mag.* June 723/1 They.. served us..Jardinière cutlets (particularly seedy). 1846 A. SOYER *Gastronomic Regenerator* 40 [Sauces.] Jardinière. 1846 C. E. FRANCATELLI *Mod. Cook* 234 Fill the centre of the *entrée* with a *jardiniere* of vegetables. 1877 *Cassell's Dict. Cookery* 338/1 Jardinière.—This is a garnish made of cooked vegetables, which gives its name to the dish with which it is served. Thus, fillet of beef à la jardinière, mutton à la jardinière, goose à la jardinière, simply mean fillet of beef, mutton, and goose served with a garnish à la jardinière. *Ibid.*, Jardinière Soup. 1907 G. A. ESCOFFIER *Guide Mod. Cookery* 357 Prepare the fillet as directed under 'Filet de Bœuf Jardinière'. Set it on a long dish and surround it with a *Macédoine* garnish. The latter comprises the same ingredients as the '*Jardinière*'. *Ibid.* 512 *Sauté* the *suprêmes* in butter. Dish and surround with small heaps of vegetables, arranged very neatly, as explained in the case of the *Jardinière* garnish. 1969 R. & D. DE SOLA *Dict. Cooking* 128/1 Vegetables served in a savory sauce or soup, usually labelled *à la jardinière*.

‖**jardon**. *Farriery. Obs.* [F. *jardon*, ad. It. *giardone*, augmentative of *giarda* JARDE.] A callous tumour on the leg of a horse, a little below the bending of the ham on the outside.

c1720 W. GIBSON *Farrier's Guide* II. lxxviii. (1738) 234 All those hard Tumors..whether they be Spavins, Jardons, Curbs, or any other kind. 1797 *Sporting Mag.* X. 11 A Jardon is a swelling on the outside of the hock, proceeding from a kick or some accident.

jardyne: see JORDAN (almond).

†'**jarecork**. *Obs.* [f. *jare*, of unascertained origin + CORK *sb.*²] A kind of purple or red dye-stuff, obtained from various lichens.

1483 *Act 1 Rich. III*, c. 8 Que nul tinctour nauter person tinct..ascun drap launs ouesque orchel ou corke appell' iarecorke sur peine de forfeiture et perdicion de xls. 1483 tr. *Act 1 Rich. III*, c. 8 §3 Diers..usen to die great quantite as well of fyne as of course Clothes with Orchell and Corke brought from beyonde the See called Jarecork.

¶ In Cowell's *Interpreter* 1607, this word was misprinted *Iarrock*, and this blundered form was handed down as 'a kind of cork so called', in the law dictionaries of 17th and 18th c., and in the general dictionaries of Phillips, Coles, Bailey, and Ash, still appearing in those of Halliwell and Wright.

jarfalcon, etc., obs. forms of GYRFALCON.

'**jar-fly**. [JAR *sb.*¹ 8.] A winged insect of the family *Cicadidæ*, so called from the shrill jarring sound which it produces.

1880 *New Virgin.* I. 110 Insects... There is the thing they call the 'jar-fly', for instance... It makes a noise like a watchman's rattle.

jarful ('dʒɑːfʊl). [f. JAR *sb.*² + -FUL.] As much as a jar will contain.

1866 *Daily Tel.* 16 Jan. 7/3 The New Year's allocution of the Emperor Napoleon..seems to have been as mellifluous as a jarful of Narbonne honey.

†**jarg**, *v.* Chiefly *Sc. Obs.* Also 6 **girg**. [Echoic: cf. JAR *sb.*¹ and *v.*¹, CHARK, CHIRK.]

1. *intr.* Of a door or gate: To make a creaking noise, to grate, jar, vibrate.

1513 DOUGLAS *Æneis* I. vii. 57 The brasin durris iargis on the marble hirst. *Ibid.* VI. ix. 88 At last with horrible soundis trist Thai wareit portis, iargand on the hirst, Warpit wp braid. *Ibid.* VII. xi. 33 Wythin that girgand hirst also suld he Pronunce the new weyr. a1600 DRAYTON *Mortimer.* N ij, The iargging casements which the fierce wind dryues, Puts him in mind of fetters, chaynes, and gyues.

2. *fig.* 'To waver, to flinch' (Jam.).

a1614 J. MELVILL *Mem.* (Wodrow Soc.) 69 He..nevir jarged a jot ather from the substance of the cause, or forme of proceiding thairin. *Ibid.* 142 Mr. Andro [Melvill] never jarging, nor daschit a whit, withe magnanimus courage.. planlie tauld the King and Counsall, that [etc.].

Hence **jarg** (also **jerg, jirg, girg**) *sb. Sc.*, a creaking noise.

1820 HOGG *Wint. Even. T.* II. 42 (Jam.) Thilk dor gyit ay ..thilk tother jerg. 1825-80 JAMIESON, *Jarg, Jerg*, a harsh grating sound, as that of a rusty hinge. 1893 CROCKETT *Stickit Minister* 148 The sofa gied an awfu' girg.

†**jargaunt**, *a. Obs. rare.* [Form and origin uncertain: the MSS. read *chargaunt, chariant*. Cf. JARGON *sb.*¹ and *v.*] ? Chattering.

1412-20 LYDG. *Chron. Troy* II. xvii. (1555) L j b/1 And yet they be as Iargaunt as a pye.

†'**jargle**, *v. Obs.* Also 6 **iargol**. [a. OF. *jargoillier, -ouiller, -oullier* (also *gar-*) to warble as a bird, murmur as a brook, chatter, prob. f. an onomatopœic base *jarg-, garg-*: see JARGON *sb.*¹] *intr.* To utter a harsh or shrill sound; to chatter, jar. Hence †'**jargling** *vbl. sb.* and *ppl. a.*

1549 *Compl. Scot.* vi. 39 The iargolyne of the suallou gart the iay iangil. 1597-8 BP. HALL *Sat.* IV. iv, Her husband's rusty iron corselet; Whose iargling sound might rocke her babe to rest. 1600 *Eng. Helicon* F iv, Harke, sweete Phil, how Philomell, That was wont to sing so well, Iargles now in yonder bush, Worser than the rudest T[h]rush.

†**jargogle**, *v. Obs. trans.* To confuse, jumble.

1692 LOCKE *3rd Let. Toleration* iii. 92, I fear, that the jumbling of those good and plausible Words in your Head.. might a little jargogle your Thoughts, and lead you hoodwink'd the round of your own beaten Circle.

jargon ('dʒɑːgən), *sb.*¹ Also: 4 **iargoun, girgoun, -un**, 5 **gargoun**, (7 **ier-, jur-, gergon, jargone**). [a. OF. *jargon, -oun, gargon, ghargun, gergon*, warbling of birds, prattle, chatter, talk; = It. *gergo, gergone*; cf. Sp. *gerigonza*, formerly *girgonz* (Diez), Pg. *geringonça*. Of uncertain origin (see Littré, & Diez s.v. *gergo*); perh. containing the same radical *garg-, jarg-* as *jargoillier*: see JARGLE.]

1. The inarticulate utterance of birds, or a vocal sound resembling it; twittering, chattering.

This early sense, which became obsolete in the 15th cent., has been revived in modern literature, sometimes with a mixture of sense 5; cf. JARGON *v.* 1.

c1386 CHAUCER *Merch. T.* 604 He was al coltissh ful of ragerye And ful of Iargon [*v.rr.* Girgoun, -un] as a flekked pye. 1390 GOWER *Conf.* II. 264 Sche [Medea] made many a wonder soun..And riht so as hir jargoun strangeth, In sondri wise hir forme changeth. c1425 *Seven Sag.* (P.) 3148 Thre ravenes hyghte adoun, And made a gret gargoun. 1830 LONGF. *Return of Spring* 6 With beast and bird the forest rings, Each in his jargon cries or sings. 1853 KANE *Grinnell Exp.* xliii. (1856) 396 The snow-birds increase in numbers. ..It is delightful to hear their sweet jargon.

2. A jingle or assonance of rimes. *rare.*

1570 LEVINS *Manip.* 163/42 Iargon, rime, *fabula, metrica*. 1891 C. JAMES *Rom. Rigmarole* 103 Later that evening some Power sent me to my writing-table, with a jargon of rhymes in my head.

3. Unintelligible or meaningless talk or writing; nonsense, gibberish. (Often a term of contempt for something the speaker does not understand.)

1340-70 *Alex. & Dind.* 462 Swiche wordus of wise we wilnun to lere, þere nis no iargoun, no iangle, ne iuggementis falce. 1624 BEDELL *Lett.* iii. 66 Which we must remember the Romanists vnderstand by this Iargon. 1658 BRAMHALL *Consecr. Bps.* iii 42 It had bene a thousand times more materiall then all this Iargon. 1678 CUDWORTH *Intell. Syst.* I. v. 651 When Religion and Theology..is made Philosophy, then is it all meer jargon and insignificant nonsence. 1722 QUINCY *Lex. Physico-Med.* (ed. 2) 12 Alchymy ..is found to be mere Jargon and Imposture. 1816 J. WILSON *City of Plague* II. iii. 100 Cease, cease that jargon About sights seen in the city. 1876 FAWCETT *Pol. Econ.* IV. vii. (ed. 5) 628 The laws of rating [in the case of railways and water-works] are simply a mass of heterogeneous and contradictory jargon.

†**4.** A conventional method of writing or conversing by means of symbols otherwise meaningless; a cipher, or other system of characters or signs having an arbitrary meaning. *Obs.*

1594 BACON in *Life & Lett.* (1862) I. 284 The letters aforesaid, written in jargon or verbal cipher. 1643 *5 Yrs. K. James* in *Harl. Misc.* (Malh.) V. 398 They had cyphers and jargons for the king and queen, and great men of the realm; things seldom used but either by Princes or their Confederates. 1678 BUTLER *Hud.* Lady's Answ. to Knt. 76, I..can unriddle, by their tones, Their mystic cabals, and jargones. 1708 BURNET *Lett.* (ed. 3) 250 She [a deaf child] had formed a sort of Jargon in which she could hold conversation.

5. A barbarous, rude, or debased language or variety of speech; a 'lingo'; used esp. of a hybrid speech arising from a mixture of languages. Also applied contemptuously to a language by one who does not understand it.

1643 SIR T. BROWNE *Relig. Med.* II. §8 Besides the Jargon and Patois of severall Provinces, I understand no lesse then six Languages. 1697 tr. *C'tess D'Aunoy's Trav.* (1706) 131 She now mixes Italian, English, and Spanish with her own natural Language, and this makes such a Jargon [etc.]. 1725 DE FOE *Voy. round World* (1840) 203 Others had the Levant Jargon, which they call Lingua Frank. 1755 JOHNSON *Dict.* Pref. §86 A mingled dialect, like the jargon which serves the traffickers on the Mediterranean and Indian coasts. 1874 SAYCE *Compar. Philol.* ii. 67 They [the pagans of antiquity] could discover in a foreign language nothing but a barbarous jargon. *Ibid.* v. 184 The Negro jargon of the United States. 1874 GREEN *Short Hist.* vi. §3. 288 'Oxford Latin' became proverbial for a jargon in which the very tradition of grammar had been lost.

6. Applied contemptuously to any mode of speech abounding in unfamiliar terms, or peculiar to a particular set of persons, as the language of scholars or philosophers, the terminology of a science or art, or the cant of a class, sect, trade, or profession.

1651 HOBBES *Leviath.* IV. xlvi, *Abstract essences* and *substantiall formes*. For the interpreting of which Iargon, there is need of somewhat more than ordinary attention. 1704 *Swift's T. Tub* Bookseller to Rdr., It would..pass for little more than the cant or jargon of the trade. 1717 BULLOCK *Woman is a riddle* II. 18, I see, Mr. Vulture, you are a perfect master in the jargon of the Law. 1762 KAMES *Elem. Crit.* (1833) 485 Space and time have occasioned much metaphysical jargon. 1825 LYTTON *Zicci* ii, I should tell you in their despicable jargon that my planet sat darkly in your house of life. 1889 JESSOPP *Coming of Friars* vii. 324 The jargon of the German mystic was exactly what he wanted in his present state of mind.

7. A medley or 'babel' of sounds.

1711 ADDISON *Spect.* No. 165 ¶1 Our Soldiers..send us over Accounts of their Performances in a Jargon of Phrases, which they learn among their conquered Enemies. 1806-7 J. BERESFORD *Miseries Hum. Life* (1826) IV. i, That savage jargon of yells, brays and screams familiarly but feebly termed 'The cries of London'. 1837 CARLYLE *Fr. Rev.* I. III. viii, Dissonant hubbub there is; jargon as of Babel.

b. *transf.* Any mixture of heterogeneous elements. *rare.*

1710 ADDISON *Whig Exam.* No. 4. 37 Such a Jargon of Ideas, such an Inconsistency of Notions, such a Confusion of Particles that rather puzzle than connect the Sense.

8. *attrib.* and *Comb.*

1727-46 THOMSON *Summer* 1544 The gloom Of cloister'd monks and jargon-teaching schools. 1729 SAVAGE *Wanderer* I, Sudden a thousand different jargon-sounds, Like jangling bells, harsh-mingling grate the ear. 1770 BARRINGTON in *Phil. Trans.* LX. 60 Little Mozart..immediately began five or six lines of a jargon recitative proper to introduce a love song. 1887 H. KNOLLYS *Sk. Life Japan* 281 At the end of four months I should have been able..to go ahead with what I may call jargon fluency.

Hence '**jargonal** *a.*, of the nature of jargon or sound without sense; '**jargonish** *a.*, resembling or characteristic of a jargon.

1816 *Q. Rev.* XVI. 28 That inflated and jargonish style which has of late prevailed. 1831 in *Mirror* XVII. 299/1 Away, then, with the jargonal pretence that English singers cannot acquire a good and pure Italian pronunciation.

jargon, jargoon ('dʒɑːgən, dʒɑː'guːn), *sb.*² [a. F. *jargon* (1762 in *Dict. Acad.*), ad. It. *giargone* (Hatz.-Darm.). Ulterior derivation obscure: Hatz.-Darm. compare OF. *jagonce, jargunce* (in St. Brandan), variants of *jacinth* (see JACOUNCE); but most etymologists identify it ultimately with ZIRCON, Pg. *zarcão*, Arab. *zarqūn*. (Both the

hyacinth or jacinth and the jargon are varieties of zircon.)]

A translucent, colourless, or smoky variety of the mineral zircon, found in Sri Lanka.

α. **1769** *Pub. Advertiser* 29 May 3/4 Rough and polished Emeralds..Topazes, Jargoons. **1815** HONE *Every-day Bk.* I. 1526 These borders are studded with..jargoon diamonds. **1883** CHURCH *Prec. Stones* iv. 28 The diamond and the jargoon do not improve or bring out each other's qualities, for they have too many points in common. **1884** F. J. BRITTEN *Watch & Clockm.* 215 The Zircon, the Hyacinth, and the Jargoon are silicates of zirconia.

β. **1797** *Monthly Mag.* III. 206 The hyacinth..consists.. more than six-tenths of its weight of a peculiar earth, now known under the name of jargon, zircon, or circonia. **1868–72** WATTS *Dict. Chem.* V. 1079 The name *hyacinth* includes the bright-coloured varieties of zircon;..the greyish or brownish kinds are called zirconite. A variety from Ceylon, which is colourless, or has only a smoky tinge, and is therefore sold for inferior diamonds, is sometimes called *jargon*.

jargon ('dʒɑːgən), *v.* Also 4 iargoune, 5 -onne, (7 gargon). [a. OF. *jarg-*, *gargonner*, *-ouner*, F. *jargonner*, to warble, chatter, jabber, talk, f. *jargon* JARGON *sb.*[1]]

1. *intr.* To warble, twitter, chatter. *Obs.* from 15th to 19th c.: see JARGON *sb.*[1] 1.

?*a* **1366** CHAUCER *Rom. Rose* 716 These birdes..Laies of loue, full well souning Thei songen in her iargoning. **1390** GOWER *Conf.* II. 318 She withall no word may soune But chitre and as a brid iargoune. **1480** CAXTON *Ovid's Met.* XIV. xiii, The birdes that iargonned on the ryver..made her to slepe. **1798** COLERIDGE *Anc. Mar.* v. xvi, All little birds that are How they seem'd to fill the sea and air With their sweet jargoning! **1849** LONGF. *Kavanagh* xv. Pr. Wks. 1886 II. 335 A cage, in which sundry canary-birds..were jargoning together. **1892** A. LANG *Grass of Parnassus* 108 Far in dim fields cicalas jargoned.

b. *trans.* To utter by warbling, warble.

1894 *Tablet* 22 Dec. 966 Never mavis or merle Jargoned such roundelays.

2. *intr.* To utter jargon; to talk unintelligibly.

1570 LEVINS *Manip.* 164/42 Iargon, *nugari*. **1823** *Blackw. Mag.* XIII. 69 If he jargons thus, he can expect nothing else. **1850** CARLYLE *Latter-d. Pamph.* ii. 29 Disappear, I say; away, and jargon no more in that manner.

b. *trans.* To utter in a jargon; to prate about in a jargon.

1805 [see below]. **1825** J. WILSON *Noct. Ambr.* Wks. 1855 I. 31 In such slang he jargons the characters of Shakespeare and Milton.

Hence **'jargoned** *ppl. a.*, **'jargoning** *vbl. sb.* and *ppl. a.*; **'jargoner**, one who uses jargon.

?*a* **1366** [see 1]. **1623** COCKERAM, *Gargoning*, strange speaking. **1798** [see 1]. **1805** ROBERDEAN in *Spirit Publ. Jrnls.* (1806) IX. 249 The jargon'd phrase. **1837** CARLYLE *Fr. Rev.* I. III. iv, Mere idle jargoning, and sound and fury. **1875** HOWELLS *Foregone Concl.* 18 His ear was taken by the vibrant jargoning of the boatmen. **1890** O. CRAWFURD *Round the Calendar in Portugal* 28 He [the serin] fills the air of spring and early summer with his eager jargoning. **1893** W. G. COLLINGWOOD *Life Ruskin* I. 110 He took it out of the hands of adepts and initiated jargoners.

jargonal, -ish: see under JARGON *sb.*[1]

jargoneer (dʒɑːgə'nɪə(r)). [f. JARGON *sb.*[1] + -EER.] One who uses jargon.

1913 A. QUILLER-COUCH *On Art of Writing* (1916) 90 A Jargoneer would have said that 'among the beneficent qualities of sleep its capacity for withdrawing the human consciousness from the contemplation of immediate circumstances may perhaps be accounted not the least remarkable'. **1923** *19th Cent.* Nov. 786 Your true jargoneer must have at least two languages in the same word. **1947** I. BROWN *Say Word* 92 Among the jargoneers of our time.. the advertisers of women's garments have a notable place. **1973** *N.Y. Law Jrnl.* 4 Sept. 5/1 Another miserable heritage of Watergate has been the bilge loosed on the public by.. psychopathic jargoneers..and belly-achers.

jargonelle (dʒɑːgə'nɛl). Also -el. [a. F. *jargonelle* 'a very gritty variety of pear' (Littré), dim. of *jargon* JARGON *sb.*[2]]

An early ripening variety of pear.

Orig. applied, as in Fr., to an inferior variety, but already by 1733 transferred to that called in Fr. *Cuisse Madame*.

1693 EVELYN *De la Quint.* III. I. 123 Here is a particular List of those [Pears] which I know to be so Bad, that I Counsel no Body to Plant any of them. Summer-Pears..8. The Jargonnelle. **1733** MILLER *Gard. Dict.* s.v. *Pyrus*, Jargonelle..is certainly what all the French Gardeners did formerly call the Cuisse Madam. **1858** O. W. HOLMES *Aut. Breakf.-t.* iv. (1865) 32 Some are ripe at twenty, like human Jargonelles, and must be made the most of, for their day is soon over. **1858** MRS. OLIPHANT *Laird Norlaw* I. 22 The white gable wall of the manse, obscured with the branches of its jargonel tree. **1894** *Times* 25 Oct. 10/2 That prettiest and earliest of all pears, the Jargonnelle.

b. Short for *jargonelle pear essence*, Amylacetate, $C_5H_{11}.C_2H_3O_2$, used as flavouring for confectionery.

jargonesque (-'ɛsk), *a. rare*⁻¹. [f. JARGON *sb.*[1] + -ESQUE: cf. mod.F. *jargonnesque* (R. Estienne in Littré).] Characterized by the use of jargon, composed in jargon.

1884 *St. James's Gaz.* 28 June 7/1 The plan of the book is to make a vocabulary of the jargonesque ballads [i.e. Villon's ballads in *jargon*].

jargonic (dʒɑː'gɒnɪk), *a.*[1] [f. JARGON *sb.*[1] + -IC.] Pertaining to or of the nature of a jargon.

1819 'R. RABELAIS' *Abeillard & Heloisa* 189 Enveloping jargonic slang. **1834** DISRAELI *Rev. Epick* I. xvii, Jargonic strife! Man fights for syllables And worships words. **1894** *Sat. Rev.* 24 Mar. 309 Villon's Coquillards of 1450, seem to have taken their jargonic name from the scallop-shells of Compostella.

jargonic (dʒɑː'gɒnɪk), *a.*[2] [f. JARGON *sb.*[2] + -IC.] Pertaining to the mineral jargon.

1796 KIRWAN *Elem. Min.* (ed. 2) I. 14 Jargonic Earth, or *Jargonia*..has..been found only in the stone called Jargon, or Circon, of Ceylon. **1828** in WEBSTER. **1847** in CRAIG.

'jargonist. *rare.* [f. JARGON *sb.*[1] + -IST.] One who affects or uses a jargon.

1782 MISS BURNEY *Cecilia* IV. ii, 'And pray of what sect', said Cecilia, 'is this gentleman?' 'Of the sect of jargonists', answered Mr. Gosport. **1829** *Examiner* 178/1 One of the most crotchety sophists, and afflicting jargonists in Parliament. **1878** F. HALL in *Nation* XXVI. 345/1.

jargonize ('dʒɑːgənaɪz), *v.* [f. JARGON *sb.*[1] + -IZE. Cf. OF. *gargoniser* to jargon (1495 in Godef.).] **a.** *intr.* To talk jargon or a jargon. **b.** *trans.* To bring (*into* a condition) by means of jargon; to translate into jargon. Hence **'jargonizing** *ppl. a.*; also **jargoni'zation**, the action of jargonizing or using a jargon.

1803 J. BRISTED *Pedestr. Tour* II. 583 As there is no..book by which the jargon may be learned, the candidate for a diploma must be taught to jargonize by an animal called a grinder, whose business it is to drill into the head of his pupil ..the questions and answers, which will pass and re-pass in the examining rooms during the time of jargonization. **1808** BENTHAM *Sc. Reform* 23 Principle and practice of jargonization. **1812** *Religionism* 68 Cecil's jargonizing pupils all. **1825** *Blackw. Mag.* XVII. 604 He used to pay the *Morning Chronicle* sometimes to let him jargonize in their columns. **1825** *Examiner* 607/1 A prevalent desire..to jargonise the weak and unprincipled family of the Stuarts into a portion of sentimental public favour. **1887** A. BIRRELL *C. Brontë* 180 Novels are supposed to treat of life, and life refuses to be jargonized.

†**jark.** *Old Cant.* A seal.

1561 AWDELAY *Frat. Vacab.* 4 A Counterfaite Lisence, which they call a Gybe, and the seales they call Iarckes. **1673** R. HEAD *Canting Acad.* 78 They [counterfeit sailors] have alwaies a Counterfeit Pass or License which they call a Gybe, and the Seals thereunto Jarkes. **1818** SCOTT *Hrt. Midl.* xxix, 'This is a jark from Jim Ratcliffe', said the taller, having looked at the bit of paper.

Hence †**'jarkman**, an educated beggar, who fabricates counterfeit passes, licences, and certificates for others.

1561 AWDELAY *Frat. Vacab.* 5 A Iarkeman [*mispr.* 1575 Iackeman] is he that can write and reade, and sometime speake latin. He vseth to make counterfaite licences which they call Gybes, and sets to Seales, in their language called Iarkes. **1567** HARMAN *Caveat* xv. 60 These two names, a Iarkeman and a Patrico, bee in the olde briefe of vacabonds. .. A Iarkeman hathe his name of a Iarke, which is a seale in their Language, as one should make writinges and set seales for lycences and pasporte. **1622** FLETCHER *Beggar's Bush* II. i, Come, princes of the ragged regiment..Jarkman, or patrico, cranke, or clapperdudgeon, Frater, or abram-man. **1624** BP. MOUNTAGU *Gagg* iii. 35 A counterfeit passe made by some jarkman under an hedge for a rogue. **1834** H. AINSWORTH *Rookwood* III. v. (*Oath Canting Crew*), No jarkman, be he high or low.

¶ Following the misprint in the 1575 ed. of quot. 1561, *jackman* has been sometimes taken as the right form.

1608 DEKKER *Belman Lond.* D iij, Some in this Schoole of Beggars practise writing and reading: and those are called Iackmen. **1673** R. HEAD *Canting Acad.* 81.

‖**jarl** (jɑːl), *sb. Hist.* Also yarl. [ON. (= OE. *eorl* EARL), orig. 'a man of noble birth'; hence used as the title of hereditary Norse and Danish chieftains; later, of the royal liegemen next in rank to the king whom they followed.] An old Norse or Danish chieftain or under-king.

Applied by modern historians to those of Scandinavia, and to those of Orkney, Shetland, and the Western Isles of Scotland. The OE. contemporary form was *eorl*, applied to Danish leaders and to viceroys or governors of the great divisions of the kingdom under Cnut, whence EARL, q.v.

1820 S. TURNER *Anglo-Sax.* (ed. 3) I. IV. iii. 479 Then humble kingdoms, jarls, and nobility appeared. **1829** TYTLER *Hist. Scot.* (1864) II. 40 These northern districts [of Scotland] had for many centuries been more accustomed to pay their allegiance to the Norwegian yarls, or pirate kings. **1839** KEIGHTLEY *Hist. Eng.* I. 38 Five Danish Kings and seven Iarls were slain. **1861** J. A. H. MURRAY *Week in Orkney* 12 Sigurd, the first Jarl, in alliance with Thorstein the red, Norse Jarl of the Hebrides, conquered all Scotland north of the Grampians.

Hence **'jarldom**, the territory governed by a jarl; **'jarless**, the wife of a jarl; **'jarlship**, the office or function of a jarl.

1820 TURNER *Anglo-Sax.* (ed. 3) I. IV. iii. 480 Among their little kingdoms and jarlldoms. **1847** I. A. BLACKWELL in *Percy's Transl. Mallet's North. Antiq.* 141 *note*, We are not told whether Sigurd's fair Countess or Jarless accompanied him. **1861** J. A. H. MURRAY *Week in Orkney* 11 Ridding them of the piratical Vikings, and bestowing the jarlship of them upon Sigurd brother to Rognvald. *Ibid.* 28 When Rolf the Ganger, the third successor to the Jarldom, found Orkney too narrow a sphere.

†**jarl**, *v. Obs. rare.* Also iarle. [app. a derivative of JAR *v.*[1]] *intr.* To quarrel, fall out.

1580 SIDNEY *Lett. R. Sidney* 18 Oct. in A. Collins *Sidney Collect. Lett.* (1746) I. 285 The odd 30*l.* shall come with the Hundred, or els my Father and I will iarle. *a* **1586** —— *Arcadia* II. (1622) 224 What if Lælaps a better morsell find Then you earst knew? rather take part with him Then iarle.

'jarless, *a.* [f. JAR *sb.*[1] + -LESS.] Free from jar or jars; causing no jar.

1876 BLACKIE *Songs Relig. & Life* 67 Nor can the well-timed courses Of earths and moons Ring to the stroke of blind unthinking forces Their jarless tunes. **1888** *Pall Mall G.* 31 Jan. 5/2 The smooth, jarless, but sadly suggestive hammock.

jarlite ('jɑːlaɪt). *Min.* [f. the name of C. F. *Jarl*, 20th-century Danish mining official: see -ITE[1].] A colourless to greyish-white fluoride of sodium, strontium, and aluminium, $NaSr_3Al_3F_{16}$, found as monoclinic crystals at Ivigtut, Greenland.

1933 R. BØGVAD in *Meddelelser om Grønland* XCII. VIII. 3 The mineral has been named jarlite, after Mr. C. F. Jarl, by whose courtesy I have been enabled to carry out the present investigations. **1949** *Amer. Mineralogist* XXXIV. 386 Jarlite ..occurs as colorless, flat crystals about 1mm. in size, often fused in the shape of a fan and growing with thomsenolite in vugs in the cryolite.

Jarman, obs. form of GERMAN *a.*[1]

Jarnsey, obs. form of JERSEY[1].

jarool (dʒə'ruːl). Also jarul. [Hind., a. Bengali *jarūl*.] A deciduous tree, *Lagerstrœmia speciosa*, of the family Lythraceæ, which is native to tropical Asia and bears large panicles of purple flowers; also, the wood of this tree.

1850 J. D. HOOKER *Himalayan Jrnls.* (1854) II. xxxi. 327 These forests are frequented by timber-cutters, who fell jarool (*Lagerstrœmia Reginæ*), a magnificent tree with red wood, which, though soft, is durable under water, and therefore in universal use for boat-building. **1889** G. S. BOULGER *Uses of Plants* VII. 188 Among numerous proposed teak substitutes we can..mention..the Jarúl. **1922** J. S. GAMBLE *Man. Indian Timbers* (ed. 2) 373 The Jarúl tree is never likely to be important beyond its use for local requirements. **1962** *Wealth of India* (Council Sci. & Industr. Res. India) VI. 24 Jarul is a constructional timber of considerable commercial importance, particularly in North-East India.

jarosite ('dʒærəʊsaɪt). *Min.* [Named 1852 from Barranco Jaroso, in Spain: see -ITE.] A hydrous sulphate of iron and potassium, occurring usually in yellowish rhombohedral crystals.

1854 DANA *Min.* (ed. 4) 389 Jarosite..may be isomorphous with alunite. **1883** M. F. HEDDLE in *Encycl. Brit.* XVI. 402/2 Jarosite..fibrous in nodules or incrusting.

jarovization (jærəʊvaɪ'zeɪʃən). Also iarovization. [ad. Russ. *yarovizátsiya*: see VERNALIZATION.] = VERNALIZATION.

[**1933** WHYTE & HUDSON in *Bull. Imperial Bureau Plant Genetics* No. 9. 3 The Russian word 'Jarovizatzia', referred to in German publications as 'Jarowisation', has here been translated by the latinized equivalent 'vernalization' in consultation with the School of Slavonic Studies, London, and Miss M. V. Cytovich.] **1934** *Biol. Abstr.* VIII. 1655/2 Discussion is given of..the process of vernalization (or iarovization) by means of which an early development of the reproductive phase of many plants..was obtained. **1946** *Nature* 19 Oct. 548/1 Vol. 1, No. 1 [of *Genetica Agraria*] contains papers on such subjects as..Jarovization of the potato and resistance to rust in wheat.

jar-owl, jarr-owl. [JAR *sb.*[1] 8.] A local name of the goatsucker or night-jar.

1832–5 JESSE *Gleanings* (1843) 297 The Caprimulgus is known in different parts of England by the names of the dor-hawk,..jarr-owl, churn-owl,..and night-jarr.

jarr(e, obs. forms of JAR *sb.* and *v.*

jarraff: see GIRAFFE.

jarrah ('dʒærə). [Anglicized adaptation of *Jerryhl*, the native name in West Australia; called in Sir Geo. Grey's Glossary (1840) *djarrail*, in Mr. G. F. Moore's (1884) *djarryl*. (Morris *Austral English*.)] The mahogany gum-tree (*Eucalyptus marginata*) of West Australia; the timber of this tree, remarkable for its durability. Also *attrib.* as ***jarrah-forest, -timber, -tree, -wood.***

1866 *Treas. Bot.* 635/2 *Jarrah*, a durable West Australian wood, like mahogany, the produce of *Eucalyptus rostrata*. **1873** TROLLOPE *Austral. & N. Zeal.* II. 102 It may be that after all the hopes of the West-Australian Micawbers will be realized in jarrah-wood. **1894** *Q. Rev.* July 180 Jarrah and other Australian hardwoods..used for street-paving in London. **1897** *Illustr. Lond. News* 1 May 598 Jarrah..is especially suitable for submarine structures such as jetties and wharves, as it resists the ravages of the *teredo navalis*.

jarring ('dʒɑːrɪŋ), *vbl. sb.* [f. JAR *v.*[1] + -ING[1].] The action of the vb. JAR.

1. The production or utterance of a harsh grating, creaking, or vibratory sound; a sound of this kind; harsh dissonance; discordant sound.

1555 W. WATREMAN *Fardle Facions* II. viii. 187 Certeine saluages with dogges heades..that make a very terrible charringe with their mouths. **1567** DRANT tr. *Horace, Art Poetry*, What though sum iudges cannot marke the iarringe of a rime. **1653** H. COGAN tr. *Pinto's Trav.* lxix. 281 It was a most dreadfull thing to hear the discord and jarring of

those barbarous Instruments. **1820** BYRON *Mar. Fal.* I. i. 11 He hears the jarring of a distant door.

2. Vibration caused by concussion; agitation of the nerves or feelings, as from a physical shock.

1775 *Phil. Trans.* LXV. 192 The great jarring [was] consequent upon taking off the old rafters. **1873** J. RICHARDS *Wood-working Factories* 152 The jarring communicated to the foot is disagreeable, and often injurious in heavy work. **1880** LE CONTE *Sight* 11 Coarse vibrations are perceived by the nerves of common sensation as a jarring. **1893** *Winning of May* iii, The sense of leisure and culture..rested her nerves after their long jarring in cramped noisy quarters.

3. Discordant or conflicting action.

1581 J. BELL *Haddon's Answ. Osor.* 172 b, By what meanes can you forge unto us such a crafty devise of iarryng, in so uniforme an agreement of Iudgement, betwixt Luther and Calvine? **1695** WOODWARD *Nat. Hist. Earth* (1702) 60 Natural Things will continue..without Jarring, Disorder, or Invasion of one another. **1772** SIR J. REYNOLDS *Disc.* v. (1876) 365 A harsh jarring of incongruent principles.

4. Quarrelling, disputing, wrangling.

1574 STUDLEY tr. *Bale's Pageant Popes* III. 49 After wrangling and iarring betwene him and Theophilact. **1649** CROMWELL *Let.* Nov. in *Carlyle*, If the Father..be so kind, why should there be such jarrings and heart-burnings amongst the children? **1719** D'URFEY *Pills* (1872) I. 32 Strange jarring I know 'Twixt the High Church and Low. **1837** CARLYLE *Fr. Rev.* II. v. iv, Nothing but untempered obscure jarring; which breaks forth ever and anon into open clangour of riot.

'jarring, *ppl. a.* [f. JAR *v.*^{1} + -ING^{2}.] That jars.

1. Sounding with harsh or rough vibration; grating; hence, inharmonious, discordant, out of tune; grating upon the ear or (*transf.*) the feelings or nerves.

1552 HULOET, Iarrynge or discordyng, *discrepans, dissonus* [etc.]. *a* **1592** H. SMITH *Serm.* (1637) 451 A note above Ela is a jarring note, and alwayes makes a discord in the harmony. **1626** BACON *Sylva* §169 A Bell, if it haue a Rift in it,..giueth a Hoarse and Iarring Sound. **1667** MILTON *P.L.* II. 880 Op'n flie With impetuous recoile and jarring sound, Th' infernal dores. **1773** *Phil. Trans.* LXIII. 283 The wild note..of the bulfinch..is a most jarring and disagreeable noise. **1803** T. BEDDOES *Hygëia* III. ix. 201 Creaking wheels, jarring windows.

2. Striking with a concussion; causing vibration.

1665 R. HOOKE *Microgr.* vi. 13 Another Instance of the strange loosening nature of a violent jarring Motion. *a* **1732** GAY (J.), My knees tremble with the jarring blow. **1830** HERSCHEL *Stud. Nat. Phil.* 238 The jarring effect of a blow.

3. Discordant, conflicting, clashing.

1661 BOYLE *Style of Script.* (1675) 95 Writings, alledg'd..to countenance their jarring opinions. **1762** FALCONER *Shipwr.* Proem 1 While jarring int'rests wake the world to arms. **1849** MACAULAY *Hist. Eng.* ii. I. 226 Their jarring inclinations and mutual concessions gave to the whole administration a strangely capricious character.

4. Quarrelling, disputing, wrangling.

1628 FORD *Lover's Mel.* II. i, A young lady contracted to a noble gentleman..being hindered by their jarring parents, stole from her home. **1780** COWPER *Nightingale & Glow-worm* 27 Hence jarring sectaries may learn Their real interest to discern. *a* **1832** MACKINTOSH *Wks.* (1846) II. 474 The suspicion and jealousy of jarring parties.

Hence **'jarringly** *adv.*, in a jarring manner. **'jarringness,** the quality of being jarring.

1583 BABINGTON *Commandm.* i. (1590) 34 That they [the strings of an instrument] sounde iarringlie and out of tune. **1832** LYTTON *Eugene A.* I. x, The answer sounded jarringly on the irritated nerves of the disappointed rival. **1865** *Pall Mall G.* 22 Apr. 11 Self-complacency which implies jarringness to others, and pococurantism.

jarrit: see JERID, Moorish dart.

jarrock, erroneous form of JARECORK.

jarry ('dʒɑːrɪ), *a. rare.* [f. JAR *sb.*^{1} + -Y.] Abounding in jarring or jars.

1583 STANYHURST *Æneis* I. (Arb.) 19 Theese flaws theyre cabbans wyth stur snar iarrye doe ransack.

Jarsey, obs. form of JERSEY^{1}.

jarvey ('dʒɑːvɪ), *sb. colloq.* Also **jarvy, jarvie.** [By-form of *Jarvis* or *Jervis*, personal name.]

1. A hackney-coachman. Now frequently applied to the driver of an Irish car.

[**1796** GROSE *Dict. Vulg. T.*, *Jarvis*, a hackney coachman. **1812** J. H. VAUX *Flash Dict.*, *Jervis's upper benjamin*, a box, or coachman's great coat.] **1820** *Blackw. Mag.* VI. 391 To see him through the jar of jarvies pushing. **1862** SALA *Accepted Addr.* 184, I seek in vain for the old jarvey with his many-caped Benjamin. **1882** SERJT. BALLANTINE *Exper.* ii. 19 The driver [of a hackney-coach] was called a jarvey, a compliment paid to the class in consequence of one of them named Jarvis having been hanged.

†**2.** A hackney-coach. *Obs.*

1819 *Blackw. Mag.* V. 639/2 He had a large loaf stuck upon the pole of the Jarvie in which he travelled. **1841** MOTLEY *Corr.* (1889) I. iv. 76 The droskies, the most awkward and inconvenient of all jarvies. **1868** H. C. R. JOHNSON *Argent. Alps* 163 A most wonderful and antique coach, something like an enormous ghost of one of the London jarveys of fifty years ago.

Hence **'jarvey** *v. intr.*, to act the jarvey, to drive a carriage.

1826 *Sporting Mag.* XIX. 18 No one can pronounce that person a 'good whip' who has only been seen jarveying along a turnpike level road.

jas, var. JAZZ *sb.*

jasane, variant of GESINE *Obs.*, lying-in.

jasbo, var. JAZZBO.

†**jasch.** *Sc. Obs. rare*$^{-1}$. [app. onomatopœic: cf. mod.Sc. *jass* a dash, the noise of a severe blow (Jamieson).] The dash of a wave.

1513 DOUGLAS *Æneis* XI. xii. 70 That with hys bulrand iaschis and out swak With hym he sowkis and drawis mony stane.

jasey ('dʒeɪzɪ). Also **jasy, jazey, jazy,** *Sc.* **jeezy.** [According to Forby = *Jersey*: see quot. 1825.] A humorous or familiar name for a wig, esp. one made of worsted.

c **1780** G. PARKER *Life's Painter* 157 Wig, Jasey. **1797** MARY ROBINSON *Walsingham* IV. 8 Dash my jasey, if I wasn't threatened with the pillory. **1824** SCOTT *Redgauntlet* ch. xx, The old gentleman in the flaxen jazy. *a* **1825** FORBY *Voc. E. Anglia*, *Jasey*, a contemptuous name for a wig, or even a bushy head of hair, as if the one were actually, and the other apparently, made of Jersey yarn, of which this is the common corrupt pronunciation. **1848** THACKERAY *Van. Fair* lxii. **1899** BESANT *Orange Girl* II. xviii, He wore the old jasey with a broken pigtail.

Hence **jaseyed** ('dʒeɪzɪd) *a.*, wigged.

1883 L. WINGFIELD *A. Rowe* I. ix. 203 Was ever jaseyed person so perfidious?

jasmine, -in ('dʒæsmɪn, 'dʒæz-), **jessamine, -in** ('dʒɛsəmɪn). Forms: α. 6 **gesmine, iasmyne,** 6–7 **iesmin(e, iasmine,** 7 **iassmine,** 7– **jasmin(e.** β. 6 **gessemine,** (**gethsamine**), **iacemine,** 6–7 **iesemin(e, iessemine, -yne,** 7 **jesamin, -an, jeci-, geci-, gessamin(e, jasemine,** 8 **jessemin, jas(s)amine,** 7– **jessamine,** 8– **jessamin.** γ. 6 **gelsemine,** 6–7 **gelsomine,** 7 **jelsomine,** (**gelsom**). [Of this there are 3 types: α. *jasmin(e*, corresp. to F. *jasmin*, †*josmin* (Paré 16th c.), Sp. *jazmin*, †*jasmin*, Pg. *jasmim*, Ger. *jasmin*, Du. *jasmijn*, It. *ge'smino*, Bot.L. *jasminum*; β. *jessamin(e*, in 16th c. also *gessemine*, = obs. 16th c. F. *jas(s)emin, jessemin, josimin, gensemin*; α and β are united by such forms as *gesmine, jesmin*; γ. *gel-, jelsomine* = It. *gelsomino*. Of these α and β are both in current use, *jessamine* being the more popular, and also frequent in the poets, *jasmine* more common with botanical writers; γ is *obs.* All the European forms derive from the Arabic *yās(a)mīn*, adopted from Pers. *yāsmīn*, also *yāsman*, and *yāsam*, with which cf. Gr. ἴασμη, ἰασμέλαιον, ἰάσμινον μύρον, name of a Persian perfume, prob. oil of jasmine, in Dioscorides.]

1. a. *orig.* The plant *Jasminum officinale*, a climbing or ascending shrub with fragrant white flowers, long naturalized in Southern Europe, and grown in England since the 16th c.; hence, **b.** Any species or plant of the botanical genus *Jasminum*, comprising shrubs, often of climbing habit, chiefly natives of the warmer regions of the Old World, with white or yellow salver-shaped flowers; several of which are cultivated for their beauty and fragrance, while some yield an oil used in perfumery. Also the flower of any of these.

Next to the Common or White Jasmine, the ordinary 'jessamine' of English literature, the best known is the Yellow-flowered, *J. fruticans*; other species are cultivated, the total number known being about ninety.

α. **1578** LYTE *Dodoens* VI. ii. 657 Iasmine groweth in maner of a hedge or quickeset. **1597** GERARDE *Herbal* II. cccxxix, The yellow Iasmine differeth not from the common white Gesmine. **1663** COWLEY *Verses & Ess.*, *Garden* (1669) 117 Who, that has Reason, and his Smell, Would not among Roses and Jasmin dwell? **1676** DRYDEN *Aurengz.* IV. i. 1655 What sweets so e'er Sabean springs disclose, Our Indian Jesmine or the Syrian rose. **1796** COLERIDGE *Refl. having left place Retirem.* 6 In the open air Our myrtles blossomed; and across the porch Thick jasmins twined. **1807** CRABBE *Par. Reg.* III. 315 Where jasmine trails on either side the door. **1882** *Garden* 9 Sept. 233/2 The golden Jasmine (*Jasminum aureum*) is really golden.

β. **1548** TURNER *Names of Herbes* 44 Iasminum otherwise called Iasme. **1562** —— *Herbal* II. 19 b, Iesemin or Gethsamine, as I suppose is called in Greke iasme, and it is the flower wher of the oyle called in Dioscorides oleum iasminum is made. **1563** HYLL *Art Gard.* (1593) 13 That sweet tree or floure named Iacemine. **1597** GERARDE *Herbal* II. cccxxv, There be found at this day fower sorts of Iasmine: ..White Gessemine..Great White Gessemine..Yellow Iasmine..Blew Iasmine. **1594** SPENSER *Amoretti* lxiv, Yong blossomed Iessemynes. **1622** MABBE tr. *Aleman's Guzman d'Alf.* II. II. x. 200 Gecimines, Muske-roses, & other sweet flowers. **1637** MILTON *Lycidas* 143 The tufted crowtoe and pale gessamine. **1657** R. LIGON *Barbadoes* (1673) 15 Other kinds..good to smell to, as Mirtle, Jesaman. **1707** *Curios. in Husb. & Gard.* 252 If we graft the Spanish Jessemin..on Spanish Broom, the Flowers of the Jessemin will grow yellow. **1719** YOUNG *Revenge* IV. i, In yonder arbour bound with jessamin. **1838** DICKENS *O. Twist* xxxiv, A cottage-room, with a lattice-window: around which were clusters of jessamine and honeysuckle.

γ. **1597** GERARDE *Herbal* II. cccxxv, Iasmine or Gelsemine. **1598** FLORIO, *Gelsomino*,..gelsomine or gesmine. *a* **1649** DRUMM. OF HAWTH. *Poems* 130 Simplicity, more white than Gelsomine. **1652** C. B. STAPYLTON *Herodian* XIV. 115 Light Torches, Gelsoms, Odours and Musk Roses.

c. With qualification, applied to plants of various other genera: as **Arabian j.** = *night j.* (see below); **bastard j.,** the genus *Cestrum*, natives of S. America and the W. Indies; **Cape j.,** *Gardenia florida* and *G. radicans*; **Carolina j.,** *Gelsemium nitidum*; **Chili j.,** *Mandevilla suaveolens*; **French j.,** *Calotropis procera*, a shrub found in Southern Asia and Africa, also called *French Cotton*; **ground j.,** *Passerina Stelleri* (*Treas. Bot.* 1866); **night j.,** *Nyctanthes Arbor-tristis*, a shrub or small tree of Southern Asia, allied to the jasmine, with fragrant night-blooming flowers; **red. j.,** *Plumieria rubra*, a W. Indian shrub with fragrant red flowers; **wild j.,** 'of Jamaica, a species of *Pavetta*' (*Treas. Bot.*); 'of the W. Indies, *Faramea odoratissima* and the genus *Ixora*' (Miller); see also quot. 1879.

1760 J. LEE *Introd. Bot.* App. 315 Jasmine, Arabian, *Nyctanthes.* [Eight others named.] **1772–84** COOK *Voy.* (1790) V. 1723 The..odoriferous gardenia, or Cape Jasmine. **1794** MARTYN *Rousseau's Bot.* xvi. 209 Cestrum or Bastard Jasmine..requires a stove to keep it alive in these northern countries. **1866** *Treas. Bot.* 715/1 *Mandevilla*..a climbing shrub, a native of Buenos Ayres, whence it was first introduced, under the name of Chili Jasmine. **1879** BRITTEN & HOLLAND *Plant-n.*, Jessamine, Wild, *Anemone nemorosa. Dumfriessh.*

2. A perfume derived from the flowers of the jasmine or jessamine.

1670 *Moral State Eng.* 16 They would daub their Heads with a whole pot of Jasmine at once. **1688** R. HOLME *Armoury* III. 128/2 To put Jecimin on the palms of your hands and rub it on the hair. *Mod. Price List*, Perfumery.. Jasmin.

3. *attrib.* and *Comb.*, as *jasmine* or *jessamine bower, flower, grove, leaf, wood*; *j. bordered* adj.; †**j.-butter,** an ointment perfumed with jasmine; **j.-tea,** tea perfumed with jasmine; also *ellipt.*; †**j.-water,** a perfume made from jasmine-flowers. Also in names of plants resembling jasmine, as **j.-box,** the genus *Phillyrea*; **j.-mango, j.-tree** = red jasmine (see 1 b); **j.-wood,** *Ochna Mauritiana* (Miller *Plant-n.* 1884).

1883 F. M. PEARD *Contrad.* xviii, Standing together in the *jessamine-bordered window. **1750** JOHNSON *Rambler* No. 78 ¶2 The fragrance of the *jessamine bower is lost after the enjoyment of a few moments. **1678** PHILLIPS (ed. 4), With the flowers whereof *Jesemin Butter is made. **1644** EVELYN *Diary* 15 Oct., The perfumes of Orange, Citron and *jassmine flowers. **1727–46** THOMSON *Summer* 761 From *jasmine grove to grove. **1832** TENNYSON *Margaret* v, Let your blue eyes dawn Upon me thro' the *jasmine-leaves. **1933** N. WALN *House of Exile* I. iii. 44 We finished our meal with..cups of *jasmine tea..served without milk or sugar. **1967** V. C. CLINTON-BADDELEY *Death's Bright Dart* 64 Neither Lapsang..nor Jasmine, was what he wanted. **1967** S. KNIGHT *Window on Shanghai* 119 Just broke off to.. make myself a cup of jasmine tea which smells delicious. **1972** *Korea Herald* 17 Nov. 5/1 Between sips of jasmine tea they haggle. **1749** LADY LUXBOROUGH *Lett. to Shenstone* 14 Mar., I send you half the *jessamine-water I have left. **1712** tr. *Pomet's Hist. Drugs* I. 61 This Wood..bears the Name of *Jessamine-Wood from its Flowers. **1870** DISRAELI *Lothair* lxxvi, A large pipe of cherry or jasmine wood.

Hence **'jasmined, 'jessamined** (-ɪnd) *a.*, adorned with jasmine or jessamine.

1827 G. DARLEY *Sylvia* 17 The jasmined cottage in the glen. **1840** W. KENNEDY *Poems* 41 The trellised porch.. Was jessamined and honeysuckled o'er.

†**jasp** (dʒɑːsp, -æ-). Now *rare* or *Obs.* Also 4–7 **iaspe,** 5–6 *Sc.* **iesp.** [a. F. *jaspe* (Ph. de Thaun, 12th c.), = Sp., Pg. *jaspe*, ad. L. *iaspis*: see JASPER.] = JASPER *sb.*^{1} 1.

a **1310** in Wright *Lyric P.* v. 25 Ase saphyr in selver semly on syht, Ase jaspe the gentil that lemeth with lyht. **1382** WYCLIF *Isa.* liv. 12, I shal sette iasp [**1388** iaspis] thy pynacles. *c* **1440** *Promp. Parv.* 257/2 Iaspe, stone, *iaspis.* **1517** TORKINGTON *Pilgr.* (1884) 70 A box with grene Iaspys. **1535** STEWART *Cron. Scot.* II. 569 As iesp, iasink, and margareis mony one. **1591** SPENSER *Vis. Bellay* ii, The floore of Iasp and Emeraude was dight. **1648** GAGE *West. Ind.* xii. (1655) 44 Wrought of Marble, Iaspe, and other black stone, with veines of red. **1900** *Daily News* 15 Apr. 5/5, I have seen the most expensive map in the world... The 86 departments of France are represented by as many varieties of Siberian jasp.

b. jasp-opal = *jasper-opal* (see JASPER *sb.*^{1} 3 b).

1868 DANA *Min.* (ed. 5) 199 *Jasp-opal*..Opal containing some yellow oxyd of iron and other impurities, and having the color of yellow jasper with the lustre of common opal.

'jaspachate (-keɪt), **'jaspagate.** *Min.* [a. F. *jaspagate*, ad. L. *iaspachātes* (Pliny), a. Gr. ἰασπαχάτης, f. ἴασπ-ις jasper + ἀχάτης AGATE.] The same as *agate jasper*: see JASPER *sb.*^{1} 1.

'*Iaspachates* must have been an agate in which bluish and greenish shades (Iaspis) predominated' (Dana *Min.* 195).

1748 SIR J. HILL *Hist. Fossils* 489* Greenish brown Variegated Agate. The Jasp-Agate of the Antients. **1811** PINKERTON *Petral.* I. 99 Opake; sometimes translucent on the edges, but it then passes to jaspagate. **1828** WEBSTER, *Jaspachate*, a name anciently given to some varieties of agate jasper.

jaspé ('dʒæspeɪ, ‖ʒaspe). Also **jaspe.** [Fr., pa. pple. of *jasper* to marble.] Resembling jasper; mottled or variegated.

1851 *Illustr. Catal. Gt. Exhib.* III. 500/2 Printed and embroidered 'jaspé' cashmere. **1908** *Ladies' Field* 24 Oct. 318/1 The Ghiberti damask has a *jaspé* ground. **1923** *Weekly Dispatch* 11 Feb. 16 Harmonising shades of Pink, Blue, Mauve, Brown and Green on Cream, Jaspe, Black or Grey backgrounds. **1931** *Daily Express* 23 Sept. 4/1 New clasp in Imitation Jaspe Shell. **1961** J. I. M. STEWART *Man who won*

Pools 36 Crossing the jaspé lino. **1968** J. Arnold *Shell Bk. Country Crafts* 274 Products of horn are obtainable in four colours:—a mottled horn called 'Jaspé', [etc.].

jasper (ˈdʒɑːspə(r), -æ-), *sb.*¹ Also 4–5 **iaspre**, 5 **iaspere**, 6 **iaspar**. [a. OF. *jaspre* (15th c. in Littré) var. of *jaspe* = Sp., Pg. *jaspe*, Pr. *jaspi*, It. *iaspide*, ad. L. *iaspis*, *iaspid-em*, a. Gr. ἴασπις, ἰασπιδ- jasper, a word of oriental origin: cf. Heb. *yashpeh* (Exod. xxviii. 20), Assyrian *asphū*; Pers. *yashm*, and *yashp* (Pers. and Arab. *yashb*, and *yashf*) jasper.

In med.L. *diasprus*, *-um*, was used both for jasper and diaper; It., Sp., and Pg. *diaspro* have also the sense 'jasper'.]

1. A kind of precious stone. **a.** As rendering of Gr. ἴασπις or L. *iaspis*, name among the ancients for any bright-coloured chalcedony except carnelian, the most esteemed being of a green colour. **b.** In modern use, an opaque cryptocrystalline variety of quartz, of various colours, usually red, yellow, or brown, due mostly to the admixture of iron oxide.

agate jasper, 'an agate consisting of jasper with veinings and cloudings of chalcedony' (1868 Dana *Min.* (ed. 5) 195). ***banded, striped,*** or ***ribbon jasper***, a variety having the colours in broad stripes. ***Egyptian jasper***, a variety much used in ancient art, occurring in nodules with zones of brown, yellow, or red. ***porcelain jasper***, a kind of baked indurated clay.

13.. *E.E. Allit. P.* A. 998 Iasper hyȝt þe fyrst gemme. *c* **1330** *Owayn* 37 Jaspers topas and cristal Margarites and coral. *c* **1374** Chaucer *Troylus* ii. 1180 (1229) Doun she sette here by hym on a ston Of Iaspre vp-on a quysshon gold y-bete. *c* **1400** Maundev. (Roxb.) xi. 43 Þare was..a boist of grene iasper with foure figures and viii. names of oure Lord þerin. **1526** Tindale *Rev.* xxi. 18 The byldinge of the wall of hit was of iaspar. **1555** Eden *Decades* 115 He founde many of the precious stones cauled Smaragdes, calcedones, and Iaspers. **1688** R. Holme *Armoury* ii. 39/2 The Jasper is somwhat green, yet specked with bloody spots. **1794** Sullivan *View Nat.* I. 446. **1805–17** R. Jameson *Char. Min.* (ed. 3) 232 Glistening minerals. Gray copper ore, porcelain jasper. **1855** Longf. *Hiaw.* iv. 47 Oaken arrows, Tipped with jasper. **1861** C. W. King *Ant. Gems* (1866) 18 The true antique Jasper, vermillion coloured, is only to be met with in antique examples. **1868** Dana *Min.* (ed. 5) 195 *Porcelain jasper* is nothing but baked clay, and differs from true jasper in being B.B. fusible on the edges.

2. Short for *jasper-ware* (see 3 b).

1825 J. Nicholson *Operat. Mechanic* 476 In Messrs. Riley's shining black biscuit porcelain, the ware is of a jet black jasper, or porcelain body. **1832** G. R. Porter *Porcelain & Gl.* 17 *Jasper*,..a white porcelainous biscuit of exquisite delicacy and beauty [among Wedgwood's inventions]. **1894** Smiles *J. Wedgwood* xiv. 153 The material was called jasper from its resemblance to that stone. The jasper ware was made of white porcelain bisque.

3. *attrib.* and *Comb.* **a.** Simple *attrib.* or *adj.* Made or consisting of jasper.

1718 Prior *Pleasure* 34 On the jasper steps to rear the throne. **1822** Hazlitt *Table-t.* Ser. ii. xviii. (1869) 372 Are not pictures and statues as much furniture as gold plate or jasper tables?

b. *Comb.*, as ***jasper-glitter***; ***jasper-hued***, ***-like*** adjs.; **jasper-dip**, **jasper-wash**, a kind of ceramic decoration introduced by Wedgwood, in which jasper-ware is used for the surface, the body being of coarser material; **jasper-opal**, an impure opal containing iron oxide and having the colour of yellow jasper; **jasper-pottery**, **jasper-ware**, a fine kind of porcelain invented by Wedgwood, and used by him for his cameos, and other most delicate work; †**jasper stone** = sense 1 a.

1894 Smiles *J. Wedgwood* xiv. 154 He afterwards invented his *jasper-dip in 1777. **1850** Mrs. Browning *Poems* II. 426 Her hair had grown just long enough To catch Heaven's *jasper-glitter. **1822–34** *Good's Study Med.* (ed. 4) IV. 401 [Calculi] purple *jasper-hued, red, brown, crystalline. **1887** *Pall Mall G.* 19 July 5/2 Red Etruscan is the unmeaning trade name of this *jasper-like stone. **1843** Portlock *Geol.* 208 Associated with it, but sparingly, *jasper-opal is found. **1825** J. Nicholson *Operat. Mechanic* 483 The *jasper pottery..is extremely beautiful; and is formed of blue and porcelain clay, Cornish-stone, Cork-stone, (sulphate of barytes), flint, and a little gypsum, tinged with cobalt calx. **1509** Hawes *Past. Pleas.* iv. v, Of *iasper stones it was wonderly wrought. **1611** Bible *Rev.* xxi. 11 Like a iasper stone, cleare as christal. **1863** Gladstone *Glean.* (1879) II. 206 Of the ware which I believe is called *jasper-ware.

jasper (ˈdʒæspə(r)), *sb.*² *U.S. colloq.* [Male Christian name.] A person, fellow: usu. with contemptuous overtones; *spec.* a rustic simpleton, 'hick'. Also (with capital initial) used as a nickname (see quot. 1929, 1952).

1896 H. M. Blossom *Checkers* x. 229 After supper..I went over to the only shanty in the place that looked like a store, and opened the door. There were a lot of 'Jaspers' sitting around the stove, chewing Tobacco and swapping lies. **1914** 'B. M. Bower' *Flying U Ranch* 174 Some uh you boys help me rope him—like him and that other jasper over there done to Andy. **1929** T. Gordon *Born to Be* 236 *Zigaboo, Dingo, Jasper*, nicknames for Ethiopians. **1952** Granville *Dict. Theatr. Terms* 103 *Jasper*, the traditional name for the villain of the piece in melodrama. **1963** 'M. Corrigan' *Why do Women* —— ? xxiii. 173 If that dark jasper calls on you again, try and keep him here. **1970** *New Yorker* 17 Oct. 40/3 What's with those jaspers?

† **ˈjasper**, *v. Obs. rare.* [f. jasper *sb.*¹: cf. F. *jasper* vb. (in same sense), f. *jaspe* sb.; also Sp., Pg. *jaspear* to speckle like jasper, to sprinkle with green and vermilion; to marble.]

1. *intr.* To have a speckling or clouding of various colours like some kinds of jasper; to be variegated.

1620 Shelton *Quix.* ii. xxxi. 206 Don Quixote's face was in a thousand colours, that Iaspered vpon his browe.

2. *trans.* To variegate with different colours; to marble, to speckle.

1799 G. Smith *Laboratory* II. 427 How to imitate a Black Jasper, or variegated Black Marble... Lay it with a brush on what you want to be jaspered, whether a column, a table, or any thing else.

ˈjasperated, *ppl. a.* [f. jasper *sb.*¹ + -ate + -ed.] 'Mixed with jasper' (Webster, 1828).

jaspered (ˈdʒɑːspəd, -æ-), *a.* [f. jasper *sb.*¹ or *v.* + -ed. Cf. F. *jaspé*, Sp. and Pg. *jaspeado* 'speckled or coloured like jasper'.] Marbled, speckled.

1620 Shelton *Quix.* ii. xxxii. 218 Don Quixote was not very well pleased to see him so ill dressed with his iasperd towell [*la jaspeada toalla*]. **1730** Rutty in *Phil. Trans.* XXXVI. 267 The second makes them of an Ash Colour and Marbled, or Iaspered. **1780** J. T. Dillon *Trav. Spain* (1781) 304 A slaty stone, jaspered with blue and green.

ˈjasperite. *Min.* [See -ite.] A red jasper rock occurring near Lake Superior. (*Cent. Dict.*)

jasperize (ˈdʒɑːspəraɪz, -æ-), *v.* [f. jasper *sb.*¹ + -ize.] *trans.* To convert by petrifaction into jasper, or into a form of silica resembling jasper.

1887 *Nature* 17 Nov. 68/2 The Arizona agatized or jasperized wood shows the most beautiful variety of colours of any petrified wood in the world.

ˈjasperoid, *a.* and *sb.* [f. jasper *sb.*¹ + -oid.]

A. *adj.* Like jasper in appearance or structure.

1876 *Forest & Stream* 13 July 375/2 A piece of basaltic or jasperoid rock of suitable shape. **1965** G. J. Williams *Econ. Geol. N.Z.* xii. 176/1 The lode..lies immediately alongside and to the south-east of a belt of banded jasperoid chert.

B. *sb. Petrol.* A rock in which silica, in the form of fine-grained quartz or chalcedony, has replaced some of the original constituents (usually the carbonate of limestone).

1898 J. E. Spurr in *Monogr. U.S. Geol. Survey* XXXI. 219 He [*sc.* the writer] has become impressed with the widespread occurrence of this variety of quartz, which arises from the replacement of some original rock, ordinarily limestone or dolomite, by silica from circulating waters; and there seems to be need of some term which may specifically indicate it. For this use the word 'jasperoid' is suggested. Jasperoid may then be defined as a rock consisting essentially of cryptocrystalline, chalcedonic, or phenocrystalline silica, which has formed by the replacement of some other material, ordinarily calcite or dolomite. **1928** W. Lindgren *Mineral Deposits* (ed. 3) xiii. 207 Silicification of limestone, argillaceous shale and rhyolite is..a very common process taking place frequently with preservation of texture. The quartz will usually be fine-grained. Silicified limestones are called jasperoids. **1944** *Proc. Prehist. Soc.* X. 12 The cherts and jasperoids probably came from the conglomerates at Bankrom. **1968** *Prof. Papers U.S. Geol. Survey* No. 600-B. 112/1 Sixty-eight samples of jasperoid associated with base- and precious-metal ore deposits in 25 western mining districts.. were analysed for gold.

ˈjasperous, *a.* [f. as prec. + -ous.] = next.

1851 *Illustr. Catal. Gt. Exhib.* 999 Red ochre, resulting from the decomposition of jasperous ore of iron.

jaspery (ˈdʒɑːspərɪ, -æ-), *a.* [f. as prec. + -y.] Of the nature of, resembling, or containing jasper.

1843 Portlock *Geol.* 525 The small cavities are filled with red jaspery agate. **1882** Geikie *Text-bk. Geol.* iv. viii. §2. 579 The calcareous and marly shales are changed into hard, almost jaspery, shales or slates.

jaˈspidean, *a. Obs.* [f. as next + -an.] = next.

1796 Kirwan *Elem. Min.* (ed. 2) I. 358 A jaspidean cement. **1807** Headrick *Arran* 56 Their fracture jaspidean, white, and sparkling.

jaspideous (dʒæˈspɪdiːəs), *a.* [f. L. *iaspide-us* (f. *iaspid-em* jasper) + -ous.] Of the nature of jasper; jaspery.

1804 Watt in *Phil. Trans.* XCIV. 283 The formation of secondary spheroids, in the heart of the compact jaspideous substance. **1833** Lyell *Princ. Geol.* III. 369 In Arthur's Seat and Salisbury Craig..a sandstone is seen to come in contact with greenstone, and to be converted into a jaspideous rock.

‖**jaspis** (ˈdʒæspɪs). [L. *iaspis* jasper, a. Gr. ἴασπις jasper.] = jasper *sb.*¹ 1 a; rarely 1 b.

1382 Wyclif *Rev.* iv. 3 Lijk the siȝt of a stoone iaspis, and to sardyn. **1390** Gower *Conf.* III. 112 Ther sitten fyve Stones mo..Iaspis and Elitropius And Dendides and Iacinctus. **1569** *Vis. Bellay* ii. in *Spenser's Wks.* (Globe) 700/1 The floor was Jaspis, and of Emeraude. **1640** Wilkins *New Planet* ii. (1684) 119 A Loadstone, rather than a Jaspis, Adamant, Marble, or any other. **1745** A. Butler *Lives Saints* (1836) I. 20 The shrine is..supported by four high pillars, two of marble and two of jaspis.

ˈjaspoid, *a.* [f. Gr. ἰασπ-ις jasp + -oid.] Resembling jasper. (Mayne *Expos. Lex.* 1855.)

† **jaˈsponyx.** *Obs.* [a. L. *iasponyx* (Pliny), a. Gr. ἰασπόνυξ, f. ἴασπ-ις jasper + ὄνυξ onyx.] An onyx stone partaking of the characters of jasper; 'an old name for clouded jasper' (A. H. Chester).

1616 Bullokar, *Iasponyx*, a precious stone, white of colour, and hauing red strakes. **1748** Sir J. Hill *Hist. Fossils* 492* The Jasponyx of the antients, Or Horney Onyx with green Zones.

jaspure (ˈdʒæspjʊə(r)). [a. F. *jaspure* (1680 in Hatz.-Darm.), f. *jasper* to jasper + -ure.] Decoration with spots or clouds of various colour; marbling.

1890 in *Cent. Dict.*

† **jass**, *v. Obs. rare.* [var. *chass*, chase: cf. jace.] *trans.* To chase.

1577 B. Googe *Heresbach's Husb.* 118 b, They [mares in foal] must bee kept in the house, and neyther labored nor iassed vp and downe, nor suffered to take colde.

jass, error for **iass*, eyas.

1679 *Lond. Gaz.* No. 1436/4 Lost of his Majesties,..an Entermewed Jass Faulcon,..with the Kings Varvels. **1706** Phillips, Jass-hawk. **1755** Johnson, *Jashawk* (probably *ias* or *eyas* hawk), a young hawk.

jass, var. jazz *sb.*

jassid (ˈdʒæsɪd), *a.* and *sb.* [f. mod.L. family name *Jassidæ* f. the generic name *Iassus* (*Jassus*) (J. C. Fabricius *Systema Rhyngotorum* (1803) 85), f. L. *Iāsus* a town in Asia Minor.] **A.** *adj.* Of or pertaining to a homopterous insect of the family Jassidæ, sometimes considered equivalent to the Cicadellidæ, and including several pests of cereals, fodder crops, etc. **B.** *sb.* A leaf-hopper, a small, jumping insect of this kind, which attacks the leaves of plants.

1892 *Trans. Amer. Entomol. Soc.* XIX. 307 Mr. Howard Ewarts Weed..has brought to light many new and interesting members of the little-known Jassid fauna of the 'Mississippi Bottoms'. **1895** *Insect Life* VII. 323 The half-clothed jassid (*Eutettix seminudus* Say) was often taken on the stalk of the cotton, and was observed to feed upon the juices of the plant. **1918** *Agric. Gaz. New South Wales* 568 (*title*) The apple-leaf Jassid (*Empoasca australis*). **1926** *Proc. U.S. Nat. Museum* LXVIII. 1 (*title*) Revision of the American leaf hoppers of the Jassid genus *Typhlocybe*. **1956** *Nature* 11 Feb. 282/2 The influence of sprayed areas in reducing populations of jassids infesting adjacent unsprayed cotton was elucidated recently.

jassink, obs. f. jacinth.

Jat¹ (dʒɑːt). Also 7 **Jett**, **Jutt**, 8 **Jaut**. [Hindi *Jāṭ*.] A member of an Indian tribe settled in the Punjab, Sind, and North-West Provinces. Also *attrib.*

1622 in W. Foster *Eng. Factories India 1622–3* (1908) 90 [There] goeth with the carts 27 Jutts, etc. for their safer passadge. *Ibid.* 111 A Jett whome some tymes you have [app]roved off for trusty. **1787** C. Hamilton *Hist. Relation of Rohilla Afgans in N. Provinces of Hindostan* 104 By similar means he procured the assistance of Soorâj Mull with a number of Jâts. **1797** *Encycl. Brit.* VIII. 529/1 The Jauts, or Jats. **1845** *Encycl. Metrop.* XXIII. 781/2 The Ják'har, Shiyág'hs and Punyás..are all of Jat origin. **1880** *Encycl. Brit.* XIII. 597/2 Early Ját settlements on the shores of the Persian gulf. **1901** *North Amer. Rev.* Feb. 301 The Jats are the most important people in the Punjab. **1946** J. H. Hutton *Caste in India* i. iv. 33 The Jats who form perhaps the most important element in the population of the Punjab may be either Hindu or Sikh or Muslim, though..the typical Punjab Jat is probably a Sikh. The Jat is a typical yeoman, devoted to agriculture and..takes a lower social level than the Rajput. *Ibid.* 34 The Sikh of Rajput or Jat origin. **1956** Singh & Seti in Aiyappan & Ratnam *Soc. in India* xxii. 241 The Sardars..have been converted from the higher castes of Hindus and Jats. **1964** A. Swinson *Six Minutes to Sunset* iii. 49 Some retired Jat and Sikh police officers. **1972** *Nat. Geographic* Oct. 535/1 Each of the three basic divisions of the Sikhs—Jats, non-Jats, and untouchables—lives behind boundaries that the others cross with difficulty.

jat² (dʒɑːt). Also **jāt**, **jāti**. [Hind. *jāt*.] A caste, tribe, sect.

[**1855** H. H. Wilson *Gloss. Judicial & Revenue Terms* 234 *Ját*, H., and in most dialects; corruptly, *Jaut*... Caste, clan, tribe, occupation, kind, sort.] **1873** E. Balfour *Cycl. India* (ed. 2) III. 151/2 *Jat* or Jet or Jut or Zat, pronounced thus variously in different parts of India, means a race, a tribe, a clan, a manner, a kind. **1894** M. Dyan *All in Man's Keeping* I. i. 5 Are they not all one jât or caste? **1909** M. Diver *Candles in Wind* viii. 80 She's another 'jāt' [*note*, class] from us altogether. **1931** N. K. Dutt *Orig. & Growth Caste in India* i. 6 Many castes or jatis were produced by a series of crosses..between members of the four varnas. **1960** A. C. Mayer *Caste & Kinship in Cent. India* iii. viii. 152 *Jat*, the general word for species, is the most commonly used term for 'caste'... You ask a man..'what is your *jat*'. **1971** *Illustr. Weekly India* 4 Apr. 11/3 Besides, they have helped in removing a number of malpractices in the community like child marriage, polygamy and in settling *Jati* disputes.

jat' (jætj), *sb.*³ Also **ěti**, **iet**, **jat**, **jet'**, **yat**, etc. [ad. OSl. *jatĭ*; cf. quot. 1964.] The name of the characters ѣ and ѣ of the Slavonic Glagolitic and Cyrillic alphabets; the sound represented by these characters, or the Common Slavonic sound from which it developed.

1763 W. Massey *Origin & Progress of Letters* (*tables facing* 114) Yat..iet. **1883** I. Taylor *Alphabet* II. 196 (*table*) Yet. **1887** M. Gaster *Ilchester Lectures on Greeko-Slavonic Lit.* 214 (*table*) ěti. **1950** *Slavistična Revija* III. 257 In both alphabets *jat'* as a letter is distinct from the other vowel-symbols. **1955** R. Jakobson *Slavic Languages* (ed. 2) 14, *ě*

(called *jat'*, the reflex of *ē* and *oi*). **1964** M. Samilov *Phoneme jat' in Slavic* 11 One of the main reasons for disagreement is the extreme diversity of the reflexes of *jat'* (as the Glagolitic and Cyrillic letter for the sound **ě* has been called)... The old name for the Glagolitic ѣ and Cyrillic ѣ seems to have been *ěd'* or *jad'* 'food'. **1965** G. Y. Shevelov *Prehist. of Slavic* xi. 164 Long *ₑa* has traditionally been denoted in Slavistics by *ě* (and known as *jat'*).

Jataka ('dʒɑːtəkə). [Skr. *jātaka* engendered by, born under, f. *jātá*, pa. pple. of *jan* to produce.] In Buddhist literature, a story of one or other of the former births of the Buddha; also, the name of the Pāli collection of these stories. Also *attrib.*

1828 *Asiatic Researches* XVI. 427 *Játaka*, treat of the actions of former births. **1861** V. Fausböll *Five Játakas* Pref., We.., in the Játaka, meet with some of the Comical stories that are well known all over Europe under different names. **1876** *Encycl. Brit.* IV. 430/1 Jātaka stories.. containing..the oldest known versions of many of the nursery songs, and fairy tales, and comic stories, and fables, which are the common property of Europe in the present day. **1876** J. Fergusson *Hist. Indian & Eastern Archit.* I. 88 Bas-reliefs.. representing some scene or legend of the time, and..inscribed..with the title of the jataka or legend. **1951** G. De *Significance of Jātakas* p. xii, Prof. Rhys Davids..has observed..that a typical Jātaka is one which has..an introductory episode,..the story of the past being the Jātaka proper in prose. **1956** M. Wickramasinghe *Buddhist Jataka Stories & Russ. Novel* p. ix, The linguistic, religious and sociological aspects of the Jataka Stories have attracted the attention of Western Orientalists. *Ibid.* i. 3 There are two kinds of narratives in the Jataka Book.

jatha ('dʒɑːtə). *India.* Also **jathā**. [Hind. *jathá*.] An armed or organized band, *spec.* of Sikhs.

1922 *Glasgow Herald* 9 Sept. 9 There is no waning in Sikh fanaticism, and organized jathas, or companies, come forward increasingly. A jatha of Sikh women wearing daggers has been formed. **1924** *Ibid.* 31 Mar. 11 A continuous procession of martyr jathas from Amritsar to Jaito. **1964** H. Singh *Heritage of Sikhs* xviii. 156 A Jatha of 150 Sikhs came to make obeisance at the Gurdwara. **1964** A. Swinson *Six Minutes to Sunset* x. 181 The Sikh leaders [in 1947] sat at the feet of Master Tara Singh and listened as he roused them to violence. His plan was to form murder gangs known as *jathas*. **1966** K. Singh *Hist. Sikhs* II. iv. xiii. 203 *Jathās* of 100 Akalis each were formed. They first took an oath..to remain non-violent.

jati, jâti ('dʒɑːtɪ). [Skr. *jāti*.] (See quots.)

1891 C. R. Day *Mus. & Mus. Instruments S. India* iii. 36 The different degrees of time are termed Tâlas, of which there are seven, each being sub-divided into five 'jâtis', or kinds; so that there are in use no less than thirty-five distinct measures. **1914** A. H. F. Strangways *Mus. Hindostan* iv. 112 There are seven modes (*mūrchanā*) of each of the two *grāmas*, i.e. fourteen in all; but only seven of these fourteen are in practical use under the name of *jātīs*, species. **1967** Singha & Massey *Indian Dances* ii. 42 The adavus are combined in the tirmanas with complex rhythm patterns known as *jatis*. Jatis are a combination of long and short syllables. **1968** A. Daniélou *Rāga-s of N. Indian Mus.* ii. 55 The classes obtained by grouping the modes according to the number of their notes are sometimes known as *jāti-s*.

jāti, var. djati, jat².

jato ('dʒeɪtəʊ). *Aeronaut.* orig. *U.S.* Also **Jato, JATO**. [f. the initial letters of *jet-assisted take-off*.] **a.** A take-off assisted by a jato unit. **b.** An auxiliary, usually detachable, unit of one or more jet engines (usually rockets) for providing temporary extra thrust when an aircraft takes off. Usu. *attrib.*, esp. in *jato unit*.

1944 *Sci. News Let.* 7 Oct. 229/3 Of particular value on the restricted area of carrier flight decks, JATO, as jet-assisted take-offs are known in the Navy, will also be extremely useful for lifting heavily-laden flying boats from the water. **1950** J. V. Casamassa *Jet Aircraft Power Syst.* v. 94 The application of the 1,000-lb thrust of a single JATO rocket motor to an aircraft traveling at a take-off speed of 115 mph at sea level is equivalent to an additional 395 engine-brake-horsepower for the duration of the thrust. **1951** Coggins & Pratt *Rockets, Jets, Guided Missiles & Space Ships* iv. 35/1 When the Jato unit burned out the pilot could push a release lever and drop the empty cylinder. *Ibid.* 35/2 Jatos were being used to help Navy fighters go almost straight up into the air. **1962** F. I. Ordway et al. *Basic Astronautics* ii. 21 During World War II he worked for the U.S. Navy on propellant pumps, jatos, and liquid propelled engines. **1965** C. N. Van Deventer *Introd. Gen. Aeronaut.* vi. 125/1 JATO (jet-assisted takeoff) is sometimes used to accelerate to the required flying speed. **1967** *Propulsion* (Amat. Rocket Assoc. U.S.) ii. 39 Jato units permit aircraft to take off with a heavier payload or to utilize unusually short airfields. **1973** W. T. Gunston *Bombers of West* i. 36 We flew an F-80 jet at Muroc.., and with it also experienced JATO take-offs.

jatoba (dʒætə'bɑː). [Tupi.] = courbaril.

1890 Billings *Med. Dict.* I. 726/1 *Jatoba*, resin of *Hymenæa courbaril*. **1933** P. Fleming *Brazilian Adv.* ii. ii. 191 We landed on a beach strewn with *jatobá* nuts, of which we subsequently made a dish as nauseous as any I have ever tasted.

jaud, Sc. f. jade *sb.*¹

†**jau dewin.** *Obs.* Also **-wine, wyne.** [Origin obscure.] A term of reproach.

1340–70 *Alex. & Dind.* 659 þᵉ iaudewin iubiter ioiful ȝe holde, For he was wraþful i-wrouht & wried in angur. *c* **1362** *Durham Acc. Rolls* (Surtees) 565 Cuidam Istrioni Jestour Jawdewyne in festo Natalis D'ni, 3*s.* 4*d.* **1401** *Pol. Poems* (Rolls) II. 86 Thou jawdewine, thow jangeler, how stande this togider.

jaueler, jaueling, obs. ff. javeler, javelin.

jauk (dʒɔːk), *v.* *Sc.* Also 6–7 **jake.** [Origin obscure: cf. jank.] *intr.* To trifle, delay, dawdle.

1568 *'Say weill is trewly ane wirthy guid Thing'* in *Bannatyne Poems* (1885) ii. 231 Say weill him self will sumtyme adwance, Bot do weill dois nowdir jake nor prance. **1600** J. Melvill *Diary* (Wodrow Soc.) 435 They haid jaked on manie dayes. **1785** Burns *Cotter's Saturday Nt.* vi, An' ne'er tho' out o' sight, to jauk or play. **1825–80** Jamieson, *To Jank*, to trifle, to dally, in walking or work.

jaul, obs. form of jowl *v.*

jaul, var. jol.

jaum, jaumb(e, variants of jamb.

‖**jaun** (dʒɔːn). *East Ind.* In Calcutta, a small palanquin-carriage, such as is used by business men in going to their offices. (Yule.)

1851 H. M. Parker *Bole Ponjis* II. 215 Who did not know that Office Jaun of pale Pomona green? **1882** *Calcutta Englishman* 2 Dec. 4/3 A..very roomy Office Jaun, very comfortable and easy running. **1893** *Blackw. Mag.* Oct. 499 An occasional run in an office Jaun to the Customhouse.

jaunce (dʒɑːns, dʒɔːns), *v.* *Obs.* or *arch.* [prob. derived from OF.

Palsgrave has 'I gestyll a horse to and fro in the stabyll, *Je jance.* He hath gestylled my horse in the stabyll tyll he hath made hym all on a water: *il a jancé mon cheual a lestable tant quil la mys tout en eaue.*' Cotgrave has '*Iancer un cheval*, to stirre a horse in the stable till hee sweat withall; or (as our) to iaunt; (an old word).' Neither of these writers uses the Eng. *jaunce* to render *jancer*, nor is the sense assigned by them that used by Shaks. But Palsgr. has 'I gawance a horse up and downe upon the stones and make hym gambalde and flynge, *je pourbondis.* And you gaunce your horse up and downe thus upon the stones, he wyll be naught within a whyle: *si vous pourbondissez vostre cheual en ce poynt*,' etc. (OF. *Pourbondir* = *caracoler* and *faire carcacoler*, Godef.) This *gawnce* or *gaunce* appears to agree in meaning with Shakspere's *jaunce*, but hardly with *jancer*, as explained by Palsgr. and Cotgr. If the words are the same, the only possible inference seems to be that there was an OF. **jancer* (? ONFr. *gancer*) to prance as a horse, to make a horse prance, the existence of which is as yet known only from Palsgr. and Cotgr. (both Englishmen), who perhaps did not clearly understand its meaning. See also jounce *v.*]

a. *trans.* ? To make (a horse) prance up and down. **b.** *intr.* ? To prance as a horse. Hence '**jauncing** *ppl. a.*, ? prancing.

1593 Shaks. *Rich. II*, v. v. 94 Spur-gall'd, and tyrd by iauncing Bullingbrooke. **1598** —— *Rom. & Jul.* ii. v. 53 (2nd Qo.) Beshrewe your heart for sending me about To catch my death with iaunsing vp and downe. **1792** [S. Henley] *Ess. new ed. Tibullus* 29 Behold Him sit, in conscious state, the jauncing steed. **1868** Browning *Ring & Bk.* xi. 108 Just so wend we, now canter, now converse, Till, 'mid the jauncing pride and jauntly port, Something of a sudden jerks at somebody.

†**jaunce**, *sb.* *Obs.* exc. *dial.* [? app. related to jaunce *v.* But in the Shaks. quot. possibly only a scribal error or misprint for *iaunte*.] = jaunt *sb.*¹ 1.

1598 Shaks. *Rom. & Jul.* ii. v. 26 (2nd Qo.) Fie how my bones ake: what a iaunce [*1st Qo.* and *1st Fol.* iaunt] have I? **1875** *Sussex Gloss.*, *Jaunce*, a weary journey. 'I doant justly know how far it is to Hellingly, but you'll have a middlin' jaunce before you get there.'

jaunder ('dʒɑːndə(r)), *sb.* *Sc.* Also **jauner, janner.** [Origin unknown.] Idle talk.

a **1794** *Lass of Ecclefechan* ii. in *Burns' Wks.*, O haud your tongue and jauner [*rime* wander]. **1821** *Blackw. Mag.* Dec. 321 (Jam.) What but harm can come of this senseless jauner? **1866** Mrs. Carlyle *Lett.* III. 333, I never read such stupid, vulgar janners.

jaunder ('dʒɑːndə(r)), *v.* *Sc.* Also **jauner, janner.** [Goes with prec.: the vb. may be the earlier.] *intr.* To talk in an idle manner.

1808–18 Jamieson, *To jawner*, to talk foolishly. **1825–80** *Ibid.*, *Jander, Jaunder.* **1817** *Edin. Monthly Mag.* June 248 They war just jaunderin wi' the bridegroom for fun. **1831** Carlyle in Froude *Life* (1882) II. 213 To janner about at great length.

jaundice ('dʒɔːndɪs, 'dʒɑːndɪs), *sb.* Forms: α. 4–6 **iaunes,** 4–5 **iawnes,** 4 **iaunys, iaunyce,** 9 *dial.* **jaunis, -us.** β. 4–7 **iaund-,** 5 **iawnd-,** 5–7 **iand-,** 6 **gaund-, giaund-,** 7–8 **jand-,** 4–6 **-is, -ys,** 5–6 **-yes, -es, -yce,** 6–7 **-ies, -ise, eis,** 7 **-ize,** 7– **jaundice.** γ. 5 **iawndres;** 6–7 **iaun-, ian-,** 7 (9 *dial.*) **jaun-, janders.** [ME. a. F. *jaunice, jaunisse*, in 12th c. *jalnice* (Hatz.-Darm.), lit. 'yellowness', f. *jalne, jaune* yellow: see -ice¹. The *d* in the form *jaundice* is a phonetic accretion as in *astound, sound, thunder*, etc. The ending of the word in *-s* led to its frequent treatment from the 15th c., and esp. in the 17th, as a plural in *-yes, -ies, -ers*, as in other plural names of diseases, cf. *measles, mumps, glanders*.]

1. A morbid condition caused by obstruction of the bile, and characterized by yellowness of the conjunctiva, skin, fluids, and tissues, and by constipation, loss of appetite, and weakness.

Three varieties (*yellow, black*, and *green*) are recognized and distinguished according to the colour of the skin in each case. Yellow vision, often referred to as a characteristic of this state, though the source of much literary allusion, occurs only in rare instances.

α. **1303** R. Brunne *Handl. Synne* 3980þe ye þat ys ful of Jawnes Alle þenkeþ hym ȝeloghe yn hys auys. **1340** Hampole *Pr. Consc.* 700 Many yvels,..Als fevyr, dropsy, and Iaunys. **14..** in *Rel. Ant.* I. 51 For hym that is in the jaunes: tak wormot. **1483** *Cath. Angl.* 194/1 *Iawnes*, ubi *gulsoghte.* **1547** Boorde *Brev. Health* clxxviii. 63 In Englyshe it is named the iaunes, or the gulsuffe. **1825** Brockett, *Jaunis, Jaunus.* **1893** *Northumbld. Gloss.*, *Jaunis, Jenis* (N.), *Jaanis* (T.), *Jonas* (W.-T.)

β. **1387** Trevisa *Higden* (Rolls) II. 113 A pestilence of þe ȝelowe yuel þat is i-cleped þe jaundys. *c* **1440** *Promp. Parv.* 258/1 Iawndyce, sekenesse, *hicteria.* **1494** Fabyan *Chron.* iii. lx. 39 Yᵉ yelowe euyl called the Iaundyes. *a* **1530** Heywood *Love* (Brandl) 1208 He is infecte with the blak iawndes. **1555** Eden *Decades* 121 The Spanyshe inhabitours are all pale and yelowe, like vnto them that haue the yelowe giaundyes. **1597** A. M. tr. *Guillemeau's Fr. Chirurg.* 29 b/2 The liver vayn is phlebotomized agaynst the yellowe gaundise. **1606** Shaks. *Tr. & Cr.* i. iii. 2 What greefe hath set the Iaundies on your cheekes? **1656** Stanley *Hist. Philos.* I. iv. 4 To him that hath the yellow jaundies, all things seem yellow. **1693** Dryden *Juvenal* vi. (1697) 154 From him your Wife enquires the Planets Will, When the Black Jaundies shall her Mother kill. **1725** N. Robinson *Th. Physick* 162 After the fiftieth Year, a Jaundice happening upon a schirrous Liver or Spleen, always turns to the Black Jaundice, and kills the Patient. **1732** Arbuthnot *Rules of Diet* 256 A very excellent Remedy in Jaundices and Dropsies. **1875** H. C. Wood *Therap.* (1879) 448 Dr. Mosler has been led to try forced enemata in catarrhal and other jaundices. **1888** *Poor Nellie* 274 He had an attack of the jaundice.

γ. **1432–50** tr. *Higden* (Rolls) II. 113 An infirmitie reignenge in Wales..was callede the iawndres [L. *ictericia*]. **1528** Paynell *Salerne's Regim.* 4 Whey is..holsome for them that haue the ianders. **1563–4** Randolph *Let. to Cecil* 15 Jan. in *Calr. Scott. Pap.* II. (1900) 34 Yellowe ganders. **1607** Topsell *Four-f. Beasts* (1658) 500 Very profitable against the yellow-jaunders. **1676** *Phil. Trans.* XI. 712 A very malign Fever, which..is followed with the Jaunders. **1879** Miss Jackson *Shropsh. Word-bk.*, *Jaunders.* **1881** *Leicestersh. Gloss.* s.v., The 'black janders' designates its more malignant form.

b. Applied to other diseases in which the skin is discoloured or which resemble jaundice in some way, as ***white jaundice*** = chlorosis; ***blue jaundice*** = cyanosis.

1727–41 Chambers *Cycl.*, *Chlorosis*, a feminine disease, vulgarly called the green-sickness, white-jaundice, etc. **1855** Mayne *Expos. Lex.*, *Icterus Albus*, White jaundice. **1887** *Syd. Soc. Lex.*, *Jaundice, blue*, a synonym of Cyanosis.

†**2.** A disease of trees, in which there is discolouration of the leaves. Cf. icterus 1 b. *Obs.*

1616 Surfl. & Markh. *Country Farme* 405 Trees that haue the iaundise, or else are otherwise any way sicke. **1664** Evelyn *Sylva* 69 Mice, Moles, and Pismires cause the Jaundies in Trees, known by the discolour of the Leaves and Buds. **1669** Worlidge *Syst. Agric.* (1681) 223 The Jaundies, or Langor of Trees.

3. *transf.* and *fig.* In various phrases referring to the colour and reputed yellow or disordered vision of jaundiced persons.

1629 Symmer *Spir. Posie* i. i. 8 Envie hath the yellow Iaundies. **1663** Cowley *Verses & Ess.*, *Greatness* (1669) 125 The Love of Gold, (That Jaundice of the Soul, Which makes it look so Guilded and so Foul). **1687** Dryden *Hind & P.* iii. 73 And jealousie, the jaundice of the soul. **1700** —— *Sigism. & Guisc.* 542 These were thy thoughts, and thou couldst judge aright, Till interest made a jaundice in thy sight. **1825** Waterton *Wand. S. Amer.* iv. i. 298 He must be sorely afflicted with spleen and jaundice, who, on his arrival at Saratoga, remarks, there is nothing here worth coming to see.

4. *attrib.* and *comb.*, as ***jaundice colour, hue,*** etc.; ***jaundice-faced, jaundice-tinctured*** adjs.: **jaundice-berry, -tree,** the Barberry, *Berberis vulgaris*.

1598 E. Gilpin *Skial.* (1878) 43 Their iaundice looks, and raine-bow like disclosed, Shall slander them with sicknes ere their time. **1607** Walkington *Opt. Glass* 160 Some iaundice-fac'd idiot. **1682** Creech *Lucretius* (1683) iv. 112 Whatever Jaundice-eyes do view, Look..as those, and yellow too. **1821** Clare *Vill. Ministr.* II. 132 The jaundice-tinctur'd primrose, sickly sere. **1858** Hogg *Veg. Kingd.* 34 The bark of the Berberry..is said..to have proved highly efficacious in the cure of jaundice; hence, in some parts of the country, we have heard the plant called the Jaundice Berry. **1887** *Westm. Rev.* June 281 Mr. Chamberlain's views of the Irish people have become suffused with a jaundice colour.

jaundice ('dʒɔːn-, 'dʒɑːndɪs), *v.* [app. a back-formation from jaundiced.]

1. *trans.* To affect with jaundice; usually *fig.* To affect with envy or jealousy; to tinge the views or judgement of.

1791 Mrs. Radcliffe *Rom. Forest* v, Her perceptions were jaundiced by passion. **1867** O. W. Holmes *Guard. Angel* xxiv. (1891) 289 She..wanted to crush the young lady, and jaundice her mother, with a girl twice as brilliant.

2. To tinge with yellow, to make yellow.

1892 *Harper's Mag.* June 104/1 The sulphur weighted and jaundiced the atmosphere.

jaundiced ('dʒɔːn-, 'dʒɑːndɪst), *a.* [f. jaundice *sb.* + -ed².]

1. Affected with jaundice; coloured yellow.

1640 Bp. Hall *Episc.* iii. ii, Jaundised eies seeme to see all objects yellow, blood-shoten, red. **1709** Pope *Ess. Crit.* ii. 359 All looks yellow to the jaundic'd eye. **1804** Abernethy *Surg. Obs.* 60 [I have] seen the bone of the tooth tinged with bile like the other bones in persons deeply jaundiced. **1845** Budd *Dis. Liver* 379 It sometimes happens that the cornea, or the humors of the eye, become jaundiced, and all objects appear yellow. The notion..formerly prevailed that this is

generally the case..but it happens, on the contrary, very rarely. **1883** *Times* 27 Aug. 3/6 He is beginning to look better, though still jaundiced and aged.

2. Yellow-coloured.

1640 BROME *Antipodes* v. x. liv, My husband presents jealousie in the black and yellow jaundi[c]ed sute there. **1838** LYTTON *Alice* VII. iii, A comely matron.. in a jaundiced satinet gown. **1849** RUSKIN *Sev. Lamps* ii. §16. 44 The barred windows with jaundiced borders and dead ground square panes.

3. *fig.* In reference to the yellow appearance and (reputed) yellow vision of jaundiced people; coloured or disordered by envy, jealousy, spleen, etc.

1699 GARTH *Dispens.* VI. 244 Here jealousy with jaundic'd look appears. **1787** BENTHAM *Def. Usury* xiii. 151 The fact is too manifest for the most jaundiced eye to escape seeing it. **1800** COLQUHOUN *Comm. Thames* xi. 310 Reason loses her faculties..the mind becomes jaundiced. **1837** WHEWELL *Hist. Induct. Sc.* (1857) II. 149 He was naturally querulous and jaundiced in his views. **1882** MRS. OLIPHANT *Lit. Hist. Eng.* I. 21 [Here] he was again miserable enough, to take his own jaundiced account of it.

jaundy, var. JAUNTY *sb.*

‖**jaune** (dʒɔːn), *a. Obs.* exc. as Fr. Also 5 **jawne**. [a. F. *jaune*, OF. *jalne*:—L. *galbinum* greenish-yellow. Naturalized in ME.; but in mod.E. (ʒon) only a borrowing of the French word.]

a. Yellow.

1430-40 LYDG. *Bochas* I. xx (1554) 36b/1 If they want freshnesse of colour And haue their faces Iawne. *c* **1475** *Partenay* 971 Wine of Tourain, And of Bewme also, Which iawne colour applied noght vnto. **1859** READE *Love me little* i, I won't be known by my colours like a bird. I have made up my mind to wear the jaune.

b. In the names of pigments: ***jaune brill(i)ant***, cadmium yellow (alone or in a mixture with white lead); ***jaune jonquille*** (see quot. 1960).

1851 H. WATTS tr. *Gmelin's Hand-bk. Chem.* V. 57 Sulphide of Cadmium.—Found native in the form of Greenockite. Prepared as a pigment known by the name of *Jaune brillant.* **1895** *Montgomery Ward Catal.* 252/3 Artists tube oil colours... Jaune Brilliant. **1910** B. RACKHAM *Bk. of Porc.* iv. 56 On a ground of yellow (*jaune jonquille*) are rococo-bordered panels. **1924** F. W. WEBER *Artists' Pigments* 30 Mixtures of Cadmium Yellow and Lead White are offered under the name *Jaune Brilliant.* **1948** KIRK & OTHMER *Encycl. Chem. Technol.* II. 736 Cadmium sulfide (cadmium yellow, jaune brilliant). **1960** R. G. HAGGAR *Conc. Encycl. Cont. Pott. & Porc.* 234/2 *Jaune jonquille*, a yellow ground colour introduced at Sèvres in 1753. It is of great intensity and beauty and somewhat different from the shade of yellow employed at Meissen.

Jaune Desprez (ʒon depre). The name of Monsieur *Desprez*, nineteenth-century French horticulturist, used to designate a variety of yellow climbing rose developed by him about 1830.

1837 T. RIVERS *Rose Amateur's Guide* 82 Jaune Desprez, or the new French Yellow Noisette, is a well-known and much esteemed rose... This was originated by M. Desprez about seven years since. **1867** H. KINGSLEY *Silcote of Silcotes* I. x. 93 Clinging to the house itself, hung the deep dark porch..with festoons of Jaune d'Esprez, and Dundee Rambler. **1869** S. R. HOLE *Bk. about Roses* ix. 134 Jaune Desprez, Noisette.—Phoebus, what a name!..Yellow Desprez, moreover, is not yellow, but buff or fawn colour, deliciously fragrant. **1955** C. C. HURST in G. S. Thomas *Old Shrub Roses* ix. 82 In 1830 'Lamarque' and 'Jaune Desprez' appeared... yellowish Noisettes which, selfed, gave Yellow Climbing Teas.

jaunes, -is, obs. forms of JAUNDICE.

†**jaunette**, *sb. Obs.* Also 5-7 **ionet**, 7 **janet**. [a. F. *jaunet, jaunette*, dim. of *jaune* yellow.] In ***flower jaunette, janet*** or ***jonet flower***, a name originally applied to some yellow flowers, as marsh-marigold, yellow water-lily, and species of St. John's wort (see Cotgr., *Jaulnette*); afterwards vaguely extended to other flowers, including app. the Red Campion or Scarlet Lychnis.

1423 JAS. I *Kingis Q.* xlvii, The plumys eke like to the floure-Ionettis. **1480** CAXTON *Ovid's Met.* XIII. iv, Of hys bloode grewe a flour iaunette lyke unto the lylye, sauf of colour. **1570** *Satir. Poems Reform.* xv. 13 ȝe Baselik and Ionet flouris, ȝe Gerofleis so sweit. *a* **1605** MONTGOMERIE *Misc. Poems* xxxv. 39 Hir comelie cheeks of vive colour Of rid and vhyt ymixt Ar lyk the sanguene jonet flour Into the lillie fixt. **1673** WEDDERBURN *Gloss.* 18 *Caryophyllata*, a janet-flower.

†ˈ**jaunish, jawnish**, *a. Obs. rare*$^{-1}$. [f. *jawne*, JAUNE *a.* + -ISH.] Yellowish.

1597 LOWE *Chirurg.* (1634) 200 If it proceede of..choller, it is jawnish coloured, with some tumor.

†**jaunsel**, *v. Obs. rare*$^{-1}$. [deriv. of JAUNCE *v.*] *intr.* To trot or jaunt about.

1590 NASHE *Pasquils Apol.* C ij b, Mounted upon their doole geldings, with theyr wives behinde them, ryding and iaunsling from place to place to feaste among the gentlemen of the Shyre.

jaunt (dʒɔːnt, dʒɑːnt), *v.* Also 6 **iant**. [Of obscure origin; in 1 it appears to be more or less identical in sense with JAUNCE *v.*; but the phonetic relation is obscure: cf. JAUNCE *sb.*]

I. †**1.** *trans.* (?) To make (a horse) prance up and down; to exercise or tire a horse by riding him up and down. *Obs.*

1570 B. GOOGE *Pop. Kingd.* IV. 45 a, Then followeth Saint Stephens day, whereon doth euery man His horses iaunt and course abrode, as swiftly as he can. **1573** TUSSER *Husb.* (1878) 177 For euerie trifle leaue ianting thy nag, but rather make lackey of Jack boie thy wag. **1611** COTGR., *Iancer vn cheval*, to stirre a horse in the stable till hee sweat withall: or (as our) to iaunt: an old word.

†**2.** *intr.* (?) To prance. *Obs. rare.*

1598 SYLVESTER *Du Bartas* II. i. IV. *Handy-crafts* 466 Th' angry Steed..All side-long iaunts, on eyther side he justles, And's waving Crest courageously he bristles.

†**3.** *trans.* To carry up and down on a prancing horse; to 'cart about' in a vehicle. *Obs. rare.*

1574 STUDLEY tr. *Bale's Pageant Popes* VI. 126b, He [Boniface VIII] was set vpon an vnbroken coult with his face to the horse tayle, and so caused to ride a gallop and iaunted til he were breathlesse. **1818** COBBETT *Pol. Reg.* XXXIII. 120 To get into a Grecian car, and to be drawn, with Minerva at his back..four or five miles through the streets of London..after having quietly suffered himself to be jaunted about in this manner [etc.].

†**4.** *intr.* Of a person: To trot or trudge about (with the notion of exertion or fatigue); to run to and fro. *Obs.* or *arch.*

1575 *Appius & Virginia* in Hazl. *Dodsley* IV. 150 Why did I ride, run, and revel, And for all my jaunting now made a javel? **1592** SHAKS. *Rom. & Jul.* II. v. 53 (1st Qo.) Sending me about To catch my death with iaunting up and downe. **1706** PHILLIPS, *To Jaunt*, to go, trot, or trudge up and down. **1771** FOOTE *Maid of B.* III. Wks. 1799 II. 231 Running forwards and backwards to town, and jaunting to see all the fine sights. **1892** *Cornh. Mag.* Oct. 337 The one omnibus jaunts about seeking travellers.

5. *intr.* To make a short journey, trip, or excursion; to take a jaunt, now, esp., for pleasure. Also †***jaunt it.***

1647 STAPYLTON *Juvenal* x. 183 He, to his Moores..o're the Pyren mountains jaunts. **1766** GARRICK in *G. Coleman's Posth. Lett.* (1820) 292 We are jaunting it for a few days. **1803** E. S. BOWNE in *Scribner's Mag.* (1888) II. 178/1, I am most tired of jaunting. **1848** C. C. CLIFFORD tr. *Aristophanes, Frogs* 37 He'd to the market jaunt. **1895** *Daily News* 13 Feb. 5/5 The Lord Mayor and the Sheriffs [of Dublin] jaunting over to London with the petition presented themselves..at the door of the House.

II. Influenced by JAUNTY *a.*

6. *intr.* To move jauntily: cf. JAUNT *sb.*[1] 3. *rare.*

1890 R. BRIDGES *Shorter Poems* II. 8 Jaunt and sing outright As by their teams they stride.

Hence ˈ**jaunting** *vbl. sb.*, also used *attrib.*: cf. JAUNTING-CAR; ˈ**jaunting** *ppl. a.*; ˈ**jauntingly** *adv.*, [from sense 6] jauntily.

a **1616** BEAUM. & FL. *Wit at sev. Weap.* v. ii, 'Las I'm weary with the walk, My jaunting days are done. **1813** J. C. HOBHOUSE *Journey* 858, I have seen a circle of French gentlemen..after the manner of our jaunting citizens, amusing themselves with a Jew conjuror. **1840** HOOD *Up the Rhine* 7 In hopes the jaunting about a bit will make her forget the loss of her husband. **1839** *New Monthly Mag.* LVI. 70 With his forage-cap jauntingly cocked over one eye.

jaunt (dʒɔːnt, dʒɑːnt), *sb.*[1] Also 8 **jant**. [Goes with JAUNT *v.*, which is evidenced a little earlier.

In sense 1, it varied with *jaunce*, whether as a real variant or from scribal confusion of *t* and *c* is uncertain.]

1. A fatiguing or troublesome journey. (Now only as an ironical use of 2: cf. *a dance.*)

1592 SHAKS. *Rom. & Jul.* II. v. 26 (1st Qo.) Lord how my bones ake: Fie what a iaunt [*2nd Qo.* iaunce, *1st Fol.* iaunt] haue I had. **1599** *Warn. Faire Wom.* II. 270 Where have I been? where I have had a jaunt Able to tire a horse. **1695** WOODWARD *Nat. Hist. Earth* (1702) 215 This Part have I run over: and led my Reader a long and tedious Jaunt in tracing out these..mineral Bodies. **1727** BAILEY vol. II, *A Jaunt*, a tedious, fatiguing Walk. **1752** J. STEWART in *Scots Mag.* (1753) 552/1, I arrived here, after a very troublesome jaunt. **1756** WASHINGTON *Lett.* Writ. 1889 I. 360 Last night I returned from a very long and troublesome jaunt on the Frontiers. **1879** BROWNING *Ivan Ivanov.* 52 This rough jaunt—alone through night and snow.

2. An excursion, a trip, or journey, *esp.* one taken for pleasure.

1678 R. L'ESTRANGE *Seneca's Mor.* (1702) 413 The next day they take the same Jaunt over again. **1708** MOTTEUX *Rabelais* v. xliii. (1737) 186 She..made him take a Jant [*le feit cheminer*] nine Times round the Fountain. **1725** G. ROCHFORT *Let. to Swift* in *S.'s Wks.* (1841) II. 577 If you have not got rid of your cold, I would prescribe a small jaunt to Belcamp this morning. **1736** H. WALPOLE *Corr.* (1820) I. 8, I have been a jaunt to Oxford. **1768-74** TUCKER *Lt. Nat.* (1834) I. 67 Your idle jaunts, taken for amusement only. **1809** PINKNEY *Trav. France* 120 The French gentry of late have become so fond of jaunts of pleasure. **1866** CARLYLE *Remin.* I. 203 He was on his marriage jaunt.

†**3.** Jaunty carriage of the body. *Obs. rare*$^{-1}$.

1721 AMHERST *Terræ Fil.* xlvi. (1726) 256 He has a delicate jaunt in his gait.

†**jaunt**, *sb.*[2] *Obs. rare*$^{-0}$. [F. *jante* (12th c. in Hatz.-Darm.).] A felloe of a wheel.

1706 PHILLIPS, *Jaunts*, the Fellows of a Wheel. **1721** in BAILEY; and in mod. Dicts.

jauntily (ˈdʒɔːntɪlɪ), *adv.* [f. JAUNTY *a.* + -LY[2].] In a jaunty, gay, or airy manner; with an air of sprightly self-assertion.

1828 WEBSTER, *Jantily.* **1837** DISRAELI *Venetia* I. xvi. (1871) 77 His hat was rather jauntily placed on his curly red hair. **1876** LOWELL *Among my Bks.* Ser. II. 4 Voltaire.. jauntily forgives Bayle for having been right. **1877** MRS. OLIPHANT *Makers of Flor.* vi. 167 He then enters into his.. treatment of his own wife which he expounds jantily.

jauntiness (ˈdʒɔːntɪnɪs). [f. as prec. + -NESS.] The quality of being jaunty; self-satisfied sprightliness; airiness; perkiness.

1712 ADDISON *Spect.* No. 530 ¶4, I felt a certain Stiffness in my Limbs, which entirely destroyed that Jauntyness of Air I was once Master of. **1838** DICKENS *Nich. Nick.* xix, That indescribable air of jauntiness and individuality which empty garments..will take. **1884** *Chr. Commw.* 23 Oct. 21/5 The paper was marred by a jauntiness which did not become the subject.

jaunting-car (ˈdʒɔːntɪŋkɑː(r), ˈdʒɑːnt-). [f. *jaunting* vbl. sb. (see JAUNT *v.*) + CAR.] A light, two-wheeled vehicle, popular in Ireland, now carrying four persons seated two on each side, either back to back (***outside jaunting-car***) or facing each other (***inside jaunting-car***), with a seat in front for the driver. Formerly made for a larger number of passengers: see quot. 1801.

1801 FELTON *Carriages* (ed. 2) II. App. 5 There has been introduced some of a foreign description, called German Waggons, and Jaunting Carrs. *Ibid.* 6 The Jaunting Carr is a one horse carriage..so contrived as to carry many passengers; intended for gentlemen to go a pleasuring with their families, they driving themselves..The body is made to project over the wheels, is of a round form, and capacious enough to hold five or six persons comfortable, besides the driver, forming, as it were, a small apartment, and will even afford a small table to stand in the middle. **1829** *Blackw. Mag.* XXV. 771/2 There is a vehicular machine, peculiar, I believe, to Ireland called 'an outside jaunting-car!' **1842** S. LOVER *Handy Andy* i, He..drove out the nurse and children on the jaunting-car. **1883** S. C. HALL *Retrospect* II. 303 In general there was no way of travelling except by the old jaunting-car. **1894** HALL CAINE *Manxman* 351 A company of jolly fellows in a jaunting-car.

jaunty (ˈdʒɔːntɪ), *a.* Forms: α. 7 **jentee, juntee, shauntee**, 7-8 **jante(e, jauntee**, 8 **jantée**, 8-9 **janté**. β. (7 **ganty**), 7-9 **janty**, 8 **jantie**, 8- **jaunty**. [First found in 17th c., in forms *jantee* (in 8 also *jantée, janté*) and *janty*, anglicized phonetic representations of F. *gentil* (pronounced ʒɑ̃ti), noble, gentle, genteel; at first app. with final stress (dʒanˈtiː), but soon treated like an Eng. adj. in *-y*, and with the F. *a* lengthened as in *chant, aunt, haunt.* Cf. GENTEE, GENTY.]

†**1.** Of persons, their manners, etc.: Well-bred; gentlemanly; genteel. *Obs.*

α. **1674** J. WRIGHT *Mock Thyestes* 109 'Twould be most redicule, and he That does it, not at all jentee. **1675** CROWNE *Country Wit* I. i. 11 See how finely bred he is, how juntee and complaisant. *a* **1676** DK. NEWCASTLE *Humorous Lovers* 20 He is very jantee indeed, and of a humour now in fashion. **1713** MRS. CENTLIVRE *Wonder* II. i, Now, in my mind, I take snuff with a very jantee air. *a* **1750** T. GORDON *Another Cordial* (1751) II. 138 They look upon a Jantee air and Mien to be excellent Virtues. **1752** FIELDING *Amelia* v. vii, Mrs. Ellison..said, so Captain, my jantee [*mod. ed.* jaunty] serjeant was very early here.

β. **1663** KILLIGREW *Parson's Wedd.* I. iii, 'Tis true, 'tis a good ganty way of begging. **1667** DRYDEN *Maiden Queen* v. i, Save you Monsieur Florimel. Faith, methinks you are a very janty fellow. **1709** MRS. MANLEY *Secret Mem.* 229 [She] had something jantie in her Mein and Conversation. **1712** STEELE *Spect.* No. 503 ¶2 Whether it is reasonable that ..such a Creature as this shall come from a janty Part of the Town, and give herself such violent Airs. *c* **1830** MRS. SHERWOOD in *Houlston Tracts* III. No. 81. 3 She had..what my mother called a very jaunty genteel air.

†**b.** Of things: Elegant, stylish, 'smart'. ? *Obs.*

α. **1678** SHADWELL *Timon* Epil., This Jantee slightness to the French we owe. **1687** SETTLE *Refl. Dryden* 10 A Discourse so jauntee that 'tis the first you have met with yet, that has been all clear wit, and no Billingsgate. **1708** MOTTEUX *Rabelais* IV. xlviii, With a jantee pair of Canvass Trowzers. *a* **1770** C. SMART *Fables* xvi, A bag-wig of a jauntee air, Trick'd up with all a barber's care. **1771** T. HULL *Hist. Sir W. Harrington* (1797) II. 226 A true jauntee manner of dressing is, to be sure, a vast advantage.

β. **1662** *Hobbes Considered* 54 A new Gin, or other janty device. **1713** GAY *Guard.* No. 149 ¶7 We owe most of our janty fashions now in vogue, to some adept beau among them. **1760** WARTON *Oxford Newsman's Verses* 9 What tho' they dress so fine and ja'nty? **1864** A. LEIGHTON *Myst. Leg. Edinburgh* (1886) 153 Then every one knew how janty the bachelor had to make himself.

2. Easy and sprightly in manner; having or affecting well-bred or easy sprightliness; affecting airy self-satisfaction or unconcern.

1672 SHADWELL *Miser* III. Wks. 1720 III. 48 Just that free and janty mein, that very easy and unconstrain'd motion which she describ'd. **1700** FARQUHAR *Inconstant* I. ii, Turn you about upon your heel with a jaunty [*ed.* 1786 janté] air. **1712** STEELE *Spect.* No. 454 ¶4 This sort of Woman is usually a janty Slattern. **1840** DICKENS *Barn. Rudge* lviii, He wore a jaunty cap and jacket. **1862** SALA *Seven Sons* II. i. 25 He saw..the jaunty little man coming across the high street.

b. Lively, brisk.

1719 D'URFEY *Pills* III. 228 Brisk and of a Jantee Meen. **1755** HERVEY *Theron & Aspasia* I. i. 10 However jauntee and alert the various methods of modern trifling may seem. **1819** *Sporting Mag.* IV. 155 A quick and janté motion of the finger and thumb. **1866** LIVINGSTONE *Last Jrnls.* ix. (1873) I. 229 The ladies have a jaunty walk. **1875** JOWETT *Plato* (ed. 2) III. 106 The old imitate the jaunty manners of the young.

jaunty ('dʒɔːntɪ), *sb. Naut. slang.* Also **jaundy, jonty.** [Said to be a sailor's corruption of GENDARME.] The master-at-arms on board ship.

1902 KIPLING *Traffics & Discov.* (1904) 197 The other jaunty is now pursuin' us on his lily feet. **1903** 'L. YEXLEY' *Grog Time Yarns* 3 The Chief of the Police—the Master-at-Arms—is always referred to as the 'Jonty'. **1909** J. R. WARE *Passing Eng.* 159/2 *Jaundy*, master-at-arms. **1927** *Blackw. Mag.* Oct. 457/1 Mounting the rope ladder in that awful sea ..proved a bit of a task to the unaccustomed Jonties. **1928** *Weekly Dispatch* 27 May 14 The sailor spun a yarn that would make the hardest-hearted jonty (master-at-arms) weep.

jaup, jawp, *v. Sc.* and *north. dial.* Also **jap, jaap, jalp.** [app. echoic: the Sc. spelling *au, aw*, in early 16th c. suggests an original *jalp* (cf. *haud, yaud* from *hald, yald*), which is an apt echo of the sound made by agitated water. The vowel now varies dialectally as (ɑː, a, ɔː, ɒ).]

1. *intr.* To dash and rebound like water with splashing of the vicinity; to move with splashing; to splash; to make a light splashing sound.

1513 DOUGLAS *Æneis* VII. x. 101 A rok of the see,..Fra wallis feill, in all thair byr and swecht Iawping about his skyrtis wyth mony a bray. **1787** BURNS *To a Haggis* viii, Auld Scotland wants nae skinking ware That jaups in luggies. **1825** BROCKETT s.v., The water went jauping in the skeel. **1828** *Craven Dial.*, *Jaupe*, to dash like water. **1886** *S.W. Linc. Gloss.* Suppl., *Jaup*, to splash, make a splashing noise; said of the sound made by water or any liquid in a bucket or barrel: 'How it jaups about'.

2. *trans.* **a.** To cause (water or liquid) to splash or move with splashing. **b.** To splash or bespatter (a person or thing) with water, wet mud, or the like, rebounding from a breaking wave, wet or muddy ground, etc.

1721 KELLY *Sc. Prov.* 283 Ride fair and jaap nane. ? *a* **1800** *Rosmer Hafmand* 110 in Child *Ballads* (1857) I. 428 Rosmer sprang i' the saut sea out, And jawp'd it up i' the sky. *a* **1801** R. GALL *Poems* (1819) 25 Sandie frae his doughty wark Came hame a' jaupit i' the dark. **1825–80** JAMIESON, To *Jawp, Jaap, Jalp*, to bespatter with mud. *Mod. Sc.* The laddie ran through the mud and jaupit hissel' up to the neck.

jaup, jawp, *sb. Sc.* and *north. dial.* [Goes with JAUP *v.*] The splash of water against any surface, or one of the drops or spurts of water which this scatters on adjacent bodies; a spot of water or wet mud splashed upon the clothes from wet or muddy ground, etc.

1513 DOUGLAS *Æneis* V. iii. 44 Weill far from thens standis a roche in the see,..Quhilk, sumtyme with the boldnand wallis quhite, Is by the iawp of fludis coverit quyte. *Ibid.* VIII. i. 136, I am God Tibris,..Quhilk,..with mony iaup and iaw Bettis thir brayis, schawand the bankis down. **1786** BURNS *Brigs of Ayr* 126 Then down ye'll hurl,..And dash the gumlie jaups up to the pouring skies! **1880** *Antrim & Down Gloss.*, *Japs*, splashes or sparks of water or mud. **1893** *Northumbld. Gloss.*, *Jaup*, a splash or smut of mud or dirt of any kind adhering to any article. A spurt of water.

b. (See quots.)

1811 WILLAN *W. Riding Gloss.* (E.D.S.), *Jop*, the sound of water agitated in a narrow or irregular vessel. **1877** *N.W. Linc. Gloss.*, *Jaup*, the sound produced by liquid shaken in a half-empty cask.

Java ('dʒɑːvə). **a.** The name of a large island in the Malay archipelago. Used *attrib.* in the names of things connected with it in origin, as **Java almond**, *Canarium commune* (Miller *Plant-n.* 1884); **Java ape-man** = *Java man* (below); **Java canvas**, a loosely-woven linen cloth with an even mesh used in embroidery; **Java man**, the fossil hominid, *Homo erectus* (formerly *Pithecanthropus erectus*) whose remains were first found by E. Dubois in Java in 1891; cf. PITHECANTHROPE b; **Java plum**, *Eugenia Jambolana*: see JAMBO b; **Java sparrow**, a kind of Weaver-bird (*Amadina oryzivora*). Also ellipt., **Java**, a variety of domestic fowl.

1931 STUBBS & BLIGH *Sixty Centuries Health & Physick* 3 Pithecanthropus, the Java ape-man. **1872** *Omen* 26 Oct. 342/2 Antimacassar (Java canvas). **1878** *Cassell's Family Mag.* 494/2 The materials used for these curtains are many—velvet,.., Java canvass,..and serges. **1882** CAULFEILD & SAWARD *Dict. Needlework* 278/1 *Java canvas*, a close make of canvas, having an appearance of being plaited, and made in many sizes and degrees of fineness. *Ibid.*, *Java canvas work*, this Embroidery is named from the material upon which it is worked and is used for mats, work cases, music cases. **1932** D. C. MINTER *Mod. Needlecraft* 246 Two 4"squares of Java canvas. [**1896** E. DUBOIS in *Nature* 16 Jan. 247/1, I could find no place for the fossil Javanese form, which I consider as intermediate between Man and the Anthropoid apes.] **1911** A. KEITH *Anc. Types of Man* xiv. 136 One is compelled to believe that the human brain had attained a greater size than that of the Java man at the end of the Pliocene Period. **1945** *Anthropol. Papers Amer. Mus. Nat. Hist.* XL. 62/2 Considering..the complexity of the problem of Java man.. I deem it best to put aside the Sangiran Mandible of 1939 for the present. **1965** M. H. DAY *Guide to Fossil Man* 224 The features of this femur..suggest strongly that Java man was capable of standing and walking erectly. **1842** Java plum [see JAMAN]. **1861** MAYHEW *Lond. Labour* II. 82 The Java sparrows are chiefly in demand for the aviaries of the rich in town and country. **1893** NEWTON *Dict. Birds*, *Java Sparrow*, one of the best known of exotic cage-birds, *Padda* or *Munia oryzivora*,..family *Ploceidæ*.

b. *ellipt.* Coffee from Java; also (*slang*) any sort of coffee.

1850 L. H. GARRARD *Wah-to-Yah* xiii. 169 Partaking of the nectar-like Java. **1926** J. BLACK *You can't Win* vi. 67 We went back to the fire and discussed breakfast. 'Nothing but Java,' said the bum that had the coffee. **1945** G. MILLAR *Maquis* ii. 29 Later on, to wake you up a bit.., we'll give you a nice cup of Java, strong and hot. **1956** H. GOLD *Man who was not with It* (1965) xxv. 235 Lots a guys come in for chatter and java, friend.

javaite ('dʒɑːvəaɪt). *Geol.* [f. JAVA + -ITE[1], rendering Du. *javaniet* (see etym. of JAVANITE).] Any tektite from the tektite field of Java.

1938 *Mineral. Abstr.* VII. 78 The tektites ('javaites') from Solo in central Java..the form of balls or drops. **1961** *Sci. Amer.* Nov. 63/1 Those [tektites] from Java, Indo-China and the Philippines are designated javaites, indochinites and philippinites respectively. **1964** *Geochim. & Cosmochim. Acta* XXVIII. 761 Rhenium and osmium abundances have been determined in two australites, two javaites, one philippinite, two indochinites, two moldavites and one bediasite.

Javan ('dʒɑːvən), *a.* and *sb.* [f. JAVA + -AN.] **A.** *adj.* Of Java. **B.** *sb.* A native of Java.

1606 SCOTT (*title*) An exact Discovrse..of the East Indians, as well Chyneses as Iauans. **1613** PURCHAS *Pilgrimage* (1614) 541 A Iavan King..which had a hundred wives. **1817** [see BANTENG, BANTING]. **1883** G. ALLEN *Colin Clout's Garden* xii. 69 The Javan and Indian fauna. **1892** in G. T. Wrench *Restoration of Peasantries* (1939) v. 59 The Javans have escaped the fatal gift of proprietary right which has been the ruin of so many tens of thousands of our peasantry in India. **1893** W. B. WORSFOLD *Visit to Java* x. 172 The average size of the Javan coffee plantation is from 400 to 500 acres. **1910** *Encycl. Brit.* VII. 795/2 The Javans are perhaps unique in their distinct and graceful gestures of the hands and fingers [in dancing]. **1939** G. T. WRENCH *Restoration of Peasantries* v. 58 They [*sc.* the Dutch] made no effort to impose the methods of their civilization upon the Javans for their good. *Ibid.*, They stood aside from indifference and lack of interest in their Javan subjects. **1962** *Times* 20 Dec. 9/6 Some such as..the Javan Rhinoceros are on the verge of extinction. **1964** R. PERRY *World of Tiger* xiii. 192 The reputations of some Javan tigers as man-eaters have served to scare poachers away from the haunts of the lesser one-horned rhino. **1965** R. MCKIE *Company of Animals* xiii. 184 Two species of rhinoceros..have lived in the jungles of Malaya for thousands of years. One, known as the Javan, has one horn on its snout. **1966** C. A. W. GUGGISBERG *S.O.S. Rhino* v. 125 The 300 to 400 bantengs (*Bibos javanicus*) and the numerous Javan deer (*Rusa timorensis*).. frequent the more open parts of the reserve.

‖**javanais** (ʒavanɛ). [Fr.] A form of French *argot* or slang in which *av* or *va* is introduced after each syllable of word.

1925 P. RADIN tr. *Vendryes's Lang.* 255 French children often employ *javanais* in the school. **1939** L. H. GRAY *Foundations of Lang.* 31 The relatively recent French *loucherbème* and *javanais*.

Javanese (dʒɑːvə'niːz, dzæv-), *a.* and *sb.* [f. JAVAN + -ESE.] **A.** *adj.* Of or pertaining to Java, Javan. **B.** *sb.* A native of Java (formerly with pl. *Javaneses*); also, the language of central Java, belonging to the Malayan family.

1704 CHURCHILL *Collect. Voy.* III. 724/1 The Javaneses and Mardykers. **1811** J. LEYDEN in Scott *Biog. Notices* (1880) II. 192 *note*, We will be joined by all the Malays and Javanese. **1836** N. WISEMAN *Twelve Lect. Sci. & Revealed Relig.* I. i. 47 Among these languages [*sc.* the vernacular Indo-Chinese languages on the continent] he [*sc.* J. Leyden] reckons the Bugis, Javanese, Malayu,..and others. *Ibid.* 48 Javanese..is peculiarly deficient in grammatical forms. **1841** *Penny Cycl.* XIX. 467/2 The scapula of the Javanese Rhinoceros. **1847** F. A. KEMBLE *Let.* 23 June in *Rec. Later Life* (1882) III. 204 Patagonians, Javanese, from the Cordilleras, from Peru..—the flower tribes of the whole earth. **1858** FABER tr. *Life Xavier* 340 Malay and Javanese soldiers. **1869** *Month* June 612 Javanese servants and porters. **1933** [see FORMOSAN *a.* and *sb.*]. **1961** P. KEMP *Alms for Oblivion* v. 85 The peoples of Indonesia, many of whom differed widely in language, religion and culture from the Moslem Javanese. *Ibid.* 86 The full fury of Javanese chauvinism was reserved for the Eurasians. **1964** R. PERRY *World of Tiger* ii. 26 A Javanese tiger..carried off a girl. **1969** *Word* XXV. 323 All masculine names are either first names (in Javanese terminology *nama alit*, little names) or second names. **1973** D. MAY *Laughter in Djakarta* i. 7 He peered into the warm Javanese night from the betjak—the bicycle rickshaw—in which he was riding. *Ibid.* 18 The other, Subekto, evidently a Javanese like Sumitro, laughed softly.

javanicin (dʒɑː'vænɪsɪn, dʒɑːvə'naɪsɪn). *Pharm.* [f. mod.L. *javanic-um* (f. JAVA), specific epithet (see def.) + -IN[1].] A red, crystalline, bicyclic compound, $C_{15}H_{14}O_6$, isolated from the fungus *Fusarium javanicum* and having antibacterial properties.

1946 H. R. V. ARNSTEIN et al. in *Nature* 16 Mar. 333/2 One pigment formed red laths with a coppery lustre, m.p. 208° (decomp.).. It had the molecular formula $C_{15}H_{14}O_6$, and as it does not seem to have been encountered before, the name 'javanicin' is proposed for it. **1949** ABRAHAM & FLOREY in H. W. Florey et al. *Antibiotics* I. vii. 306 Germination of lettuce seeds was entirely suppressed by a concentration of 1 in 20,000 of javanicin. **1967** E. PARYSKI tr. *T. Korzybski's Antibiotics* II. iii. 1320 Gram-negative micro-organisms..are very slightly sensitive to javanicin.

javanite ('dʒɑːvənaɪt). *Geol.* [f. JAVAN *a.* and *sb.* + -ITE[1]; before coining the word in Eng. von Koenigswald had previously coined its Du. equivalent, *javaniet*, in *Natuurkundig Tijdschrift voor Nederlandsch-Indië* (1936) XCVI. 285.] = JAVAITE.

1957 G. H. R. VON KOENIGSWALD in *Proc. Kon. Nederl. Akad. van Wetensch.* B. LX. 371 Here for the first time we will give a survey of the types we can distinguish among the javanese tektites, for which the name 'Javanites' is proposed. *Ibid.* 380 The Javanites (nom. nov.) from Java. **1963** J. A. O'KEEFE *Tektites* i. 1 Accepted varieties [of tektites] are.. javanites from Java. **1964** *Geochim. & Cosmochim. Acta* XXVIII. 793 Forty-two tektites and two 'amerikanites' were..analysed for major elements. Included were 7 moldavites, 1 bediasite, 2 javanites, 15 philippinites, 12 inidochinites and 5 australites.

‖**ja'var.** *Obs.* [F. *javart*, in Cotgr. *iavard, iavar, iavarre.*] 'A swelling in the hollow of the pastern of a horse' (Cotgr.).

1616 SURFL. & MARKH. *Country Farme* 142 For the Iauar, take Pepper,..and make an emplaister to be layd vpon the place. *Ibid.* 144 For the Iavar in the houghs or hams.

javel[1] ('dʒæv(ə)l). ? *Obs.* Also 5–7 **-ell**, (5 **iawvell**, 6 **iavelle, -all**), 6–7 **-il**(1, 6–7 *Sc.* **ievel**(1, 6 **iefwell, ieffell**). [Derivation obscure: cf. CAVEL *sb.*[2], HAVEL *sb.*[1]] A low or worthless fellow; a rascal.

13.. *E.E. Allit. P.* B. 1495 þe lorde..Displesed much ..þat his iueles so gent wyth iaueles wer fouled. *c* **1440** *York Myst.* xxx. 235 O, what javellis are ye þat jappis with gollyng? **1500–20** DUNBAR *Poems* lx. 15 Fowll jow-jowrdane-hedit jevellis. **1534** MORE *Treat. Passion* Introd., Wks. 1272 How much more abhominable is that pieuish pride in a lewde vnthriftye iauell. *a* **1572** KNOX *Hist. Ref.* Wks. 1846 I. 82 Pack you, Jefwellis [*v.r.* jeffells], gett yow to your chargeis. **1591** SPENSER *M. Hubberd* 309 Whenas Time ..Expired had the terme, that these two iavels Should render up a reckning of their travels. *c* **1648–50** BRATHWAIT *Barnabees Jrnl.* IV. I. vij, Should this Javell dye next morrow, I partake not in his sorrow. [**1825** J. WILSON *Noct. Ambr.* Wks. 1855 I. 3 Javel or Devil or how shall we call thee?]

†'**javel**[2]. *north.* and *Sc. Obs.* In 5 **iavelle**, 5–6 **iauill**, 6 **gavyll, gavil.** [A by-form of JAIL: cf. dial. F. *javiole* and med.L. *gabiola, gaviola*, with cognate forms, under JAIL. (But the *v* may be a *u*, or a scribal vagary.)] = JAIL.

1483 *Cath. Angl.* 194/1 A Iavelle, *gaola*, ubi a presone. **1558** *Wills & Inv. N.C.* (Surtees 1835) 185, I bequithe to the presoners of Duresme gavyll to be distributed in allmes x[s]. **1577** HOLINSHED *Chron.*, *Scot.* 430/2 The heads..were taken downe beside the place where they were fastned on a gavil [*ed.* 1587 iauill].

†'**javel**[3]. *Obs.* Also 7 **iauil.** [a. F. *javelle* = ONF. *gavelle* GAVEL *sb.*[2]] A quantity of stalks of flax, corn, etc. laid in the sun to dry; = GAVEL *sb.*[2]

1601 HOLLAND *Pliny* II. 4 When they be sufficiently watered..then must the foresaid iauils or stalkes bee hung out a second time to be dried in the sun. **1611** COTGR., *Enjaveler*, to make vp corne into Iauels, or Gauels.

†'**javeler.** *north.* and *Sc. Obs.* Also 6 **ievellour**, 6–7 **iavel(l)our.** [cf. JAVEL[2].] = JAILER.

c **1450** *St. Cuthbert* (Surtees) 5044 For Iauelers was he rad, And besyd him to eschape. **1500–20** DUNBAR *Poems* xxxviii. 34 The presone [is] brokin, the jevellouris fleit and flemit. **1536** BELLENDEN *Cron. Scot.* (1821) II. 402 The javellouris quhilkis kepit the presoun quhare he was,.. pressit down ane hevy burd on his wambe. *a* **1605** MONTGOMERIE *Sonn.* lv, My pairties ar my javellour and my judge.

javelin ('dʒævəlɪn, 'dʒævlɪn), *sb.* Also 6 **iavelyn(e, -ynge, -inge, -en,** *Sc.* **ievilling, (geweling, iaivelin),** 6–7 **iaveling, -ine,** 7 **javlin.** [a. F. *javeline* (15th c. in Hatz.-Darm.); from the radical *javel-*, found also in JAVELOT.]

1. a. A light spear thrown with the hand with or without the help of a thong; a dart.

1513 [see *javelin spear* in 4]. **1530** PALSGR. 233/2 Iavelyn a speare, *jauelot.* **1535** COVERDALE *1 Sam.* xix. 10 Saul..had a iauelynge in his hande... And Saul thought with the iauelinge to sticke Dauid fast to the wall. **1592** SHAKS. *Ven. & Ad.* 616 (Globe) With javelin's point a churlish swine to gore. **1667** MILTON *P.L.* XI. 658 Others from the Wall defend With Dart and Jav'lin. **1774** GOLDSM. *Nat. Hist.* (1776) III. 227 When the hunters approach him [the lion], they either shoot or throw their javelins. **1874** BOUTELL *Arms & Arm.* i. 2 The arrow—either discharged from the bow or thrown as a javelin from the hand.

b. *Her.* A charge consisting of a short spear with a barbed head.

1882 CUSSANS *Handbk. Her.* vii. (ed. 3) 122 When a plain Spear is intended, it must be blazoned as a Javelin.

†**c.** As rendering of L. *jaculus*, a serpent that darts on its prey; cf. DART *sb.* 4. *Obs. rare*$^{-1}$.

1718 ROWE tr. *Lucan* IX, Fierce from afar a darting javelin shot, For such, the serpent's name has Afric taught.

d. *fig.*

1850 MRS. BROWNING *An Island* v, Where the grey rocks strike Their javelins up the azure. **1856** ELIZ. WARNER *Hills Shatemuc* 242 The speaker was a well dressed and easy mannered man of the world, but with a very javelin of an eye. **1867** WHITTIER *Tent on Beach* 197 Piercing the waves along its track With the slant javelins of rain.

†**2. a.** A pointed weapon with a long shaft used for thrusting; a pike or half-pike; a lance. *Obs.*

1520 *Rutland Papers* (Camden) 43 And lx of his [the king's] gard on horsbacke, with javelyns. *a* **1548** HALL *Chron.*, *Hen. VIII*, 235 b, Every man havyng a iavelyn or slaughsword to keepe the people in aray. **1576** *Extracts Aberdeen Reg.* (1848) II. 27 Ane halberd, dence aiks, or geweling. **1656** BLOUNT *Glossogr.*, *Javeline*, a weapon of a size between the Pike and Partisan. *a* **1839** PRAED *Poems*

(1864) II. 422 And see thy javelin's point be bright, Thy falchion's temper true.

b. One who bears a 'javelin'; = JAVELIN-MAN 1.

1849 MACAULAY *Hist. Eng.* iii. I. 338 There were the halls where the judges, robed in scarlet and escorted by javelins and trumpets, opened the king's commission twice a year.

†**3.** A fish: app. the pilchard or anchovy (both caught in immense numbers at Venice, and preserved for exportation). *Obs. rare.*

1655 MOUFET & BENNET *Health's Improv.* (1746) 244 Javelings or Sea-darts are plentiful in the Venetian Gulf, and all the Adriatic Sea.

4. *attrib.* and *Comb.*, as ***javelin-bearer, -head, -spear; javelin-darting, -proof*** adjs.; **javelin-bat**, a South American vampire, *Phyllostoma hastatum*; **javelin-fish**, a species of hæmulonid fish (*Pomodasys hasta*) (Funk); **javelin-snake**, a snake-like lizard of the genus *Acontias* = *dart-snake* (DART *sb.* 4, 8); also applied to various species of *Bothrops*, an American genus of *Crotalidæ* or rattlesnakes; **javelin-throwing**, the throwing of a javelin as an athletic field event; also *ellipt.* as ***javelin.***

1861 HULME tr. *Moquin-Tandon* II. IV. i. 212 It has been asserted that..the Vampire and the *Javelin Bat..could destroy a man by sucking his blood. **1552** HULOET, *Iauelyn bearer, *lancearius.* **1813** BYRON *Br. Abydos* I. ix, Nor mark'd the *javelin-darting crowd. **1552** HULOET, *Iauelyn head, *sicilites.* **1866** CONINGTON *Æneid* II. 664 Screened by a pent house *javelin-proof. **1835** *Penny Cycl.* IV. 529/1 These bones are absent in the fourth subgenus, *Acontias* (*Javelin-Snake) of Cuvier. **1847** CARPENTER *Zool.* §502 The *Acontias*, or Javelin Snake, of Southern Africa, is nearly allied to our Slow-worm. **1861** HULME tr. *Moquin-Tandon* II. V. i. 257 The most formidable species is the Javelin Snake properly so called, or Yellow Viper of Martinique (*Bothrops Lanceolatus*). **1513** DOUGLAS *Æneis* XII. iv. 14 The braid hed brangland on the *ievilling speyr. **1902** *Daily Chron.* 7 Apr. 3/1 Professors in a university to teach *javelin-throwing. **1906** *Westm. Gaz.* 3 May 10/2 Very pretty was the javelin-throwing, the long thin spear being launched high into the air. **1958** *Times* 20 Aug. 2/6 Mrs. Zatopkova..won the women's javelin with a new European record of 183 ft. 9½ in. **1964** J. J. WALSH *Understanding Paraplegia* xix. 128 Throwing and catching a medicine ball, javelin-throwing, and shot-putting, were all of use. **1974** *Country Life* 14 Feb. 292/1 The big breakthrough..came from young Charles Clover in the javelin as he threw 278 ft 7¼ in.

javelin ('dʒævəlɪn, 'dʒævlɪn), *v.* [f. prec. sb.] *trans.* To strike or pierce with or as with a javelin.

1859 TENNYSON *Vivien* 934 Out of heaven a bolt..struck, Furrowing a giant oak, and javelining With darted spikes and splinters of the wood The dark earth round. **1898** *Atlantic Monthly* Apr. 502/2 The lightning began to javelin the pines about the cottage.

javelineer (dʒæv(ə)lɪ'nɪə(r)). Also 6-7 **-ier, -er.** [a. obs. F. *javelinier*: see JAVELIN and -EER¹.]

1. A soldier armed with a javelin.

1600 HOLLAND *Livy* VIII. viii, The forefront of the vantgard, were iaveliniers called Hastati. *a* **1656** USSHER *Ann.* vi. (1658) 208 Before this battalian..there went six thousand slingers, and javeliners. **1828** LEWIS tr. *Boeckh's Pub. Econ. Athens* (1842) 267 Grecian and Barbarian javelineers.

2. = JAVELIN-MAN 1.

1879 BROWNING *Ned Bratts* 64 Judges the prime of the land, Constables, javelineers.

javelin-man. [f. JAVELIN *sb.* + MAN.]

1. One of a body of men in the retinue of a sheriff who carried spears or pikes (JAVELIN *sb.* 2), and escorted the judges at the assizes.

1705 *Lond. Gaz.* No. 4154/1 The High Sheriff of Hampshire, with about 90 Javelin Men,..received Her Majesty. **1832** *Boston Herald* 7 Feb. 3/3 The javlin-men and special constables ranged themselves in front of the Court-house. **1871** BESANT & RICE *Ready Money Mortiboy* xiii, The twelve javelin men, walking in martial array by the side of the carriage. **1890** *Daily News* 16 July 2/8 An amendment, practically abolishing javelin men and substituting police was inserted on the motion of Lord Belper.

2. A soldier armed with a javelin; = JAVELINEER 1.

1846 H. TORRENS *On Milit. Lit. & Hist.* I. 76 Clouds of skirmishers, javelin-men, bowyers, and slingers. **1850** MERIVALE *Rom. Emp.* vi. (1865) I. 276 Caesar brought into the field javelinmen from Numidia.

Javelle (ʒa'vɛl). Also **Javel, javelle.** [ad. *Javel*, name of the village near (now a suburb of) Paris where the solution was first made as a bleach.] ***eau de Javelle*** (also ***water of Javelle, Javelle('s) water***): an aqueous solution containing potassium hypochlorite and used as a bleach or a disinfectant; also applied to a similar solution of sodium hypochlorite, which has largely replaced it in modern use. Cf. LABARRAQUE.

1807 J. A. CHAPTAL *Chem. Arts & Manuf.* III. v. 98 What is known at Paris by the name of *eau de javelle*, is oxy-muriatic acid, combined with an alkali. It is used for taking out the stains of fruit, &c. from linen. **1815** S. PARKES *Chem. Ess.* IV. xii. 57 Some manufacturers at Javelle near Paris announced..that they had discovered a particular liquor which they called the Lye of Javelle, having the property of bleaching cloth by a few hours immersion. This composition..was found to be..a solution of the oxy-muriate of potash. *Ibid.* 61 The manufacturers of Javelle,..having been disappointed in their commercial prospects at home, came over to England, and settled at Liverpool for the purpose of manufacturing the solution of oxy-muriate of potash, which they proposed to sell to the English bleachers in bottles, and which they still denominated the Liquor de Javelle. **1875** *Ure's Dict. Arts* (ed. 7) I. 787 When a weak solution of caustic potash or soda is saturated with chlorine, it affords a bleaching liquor, still used by some bleachers and calico-printers for delicate processes. The chloride of potash is known as Water of Javelle, and the chloride of soda as Labarraque's Liquor... These so-called chlorides are now generally considered to be mixtures or compounds of chlorides and hypochlorites. **1888** J. P. REMINGTON *Pract. Pharmacy* xxxii. 422 Solution of chlorinated soda..is sometimes substituted for *Eau de Javelle* (Javelle's water), a French preparation made with potassium carbonate instead of sodium carbonate. **1892** A. BROTHERS *Photogr.* IV. 260 As a reducing agent for negatives which are too dense and for removing the last traces of sodium thiosulphate, the following solution, which forms *eau de javelle*, may be used:—Chloride of lime 2 ounces. Potassium carbonate 4 ounces. Water 40 ounces. **1928** *Daily Express* 19 Dec. 5 Javelle water, made by dissolving half a pound of washing soda in a quart of cold water, adding four ounces of bleaching powder. **1951** A. GROLLMAN *Pharmacol. & Therapeutics* xxv. 517 Compounds which give off chlorine have long been used as disinfectants, e.g., potassium hypochlorite (Javelle water), alkaline sodium hypochlorite (Labarraque's solution). **1958** L. DURRELL *Balthazar* vi. 117 It's all right..and smells fashionably of armpits and *eau de javel.* **1967** *Martindale's Extra Pharmacopoeia* (ed. 25) 314/2 Eau de Javel (Fr[ench] P[harmacopoeia]) is a concentrated solution of sodium hypochlorite. **1969** B. WEIL *Dossier IX* iii. 22 The bathroom with shower, redolent of *Eau de Javel.*

†'**javelot.** *Obs.* [a. OF. *javelot*, It. *giavelotto*; in ONF. *gavelot*, Breton *gavlod*, MHG. *gabilôt* (Diez). See also GAVELOT.

The original source of F. *javel-*, ONF. *gavel-*, in *javelot, javeline*, and their cognates, is uncertain, and beset with many difficulties; opinion at present favours a Celtic origin; see GAVELOCK, and cf. Diez and Thurneysen s.v. *giavelotto.*]

A small spear or javelin thrown with the hand or from a catapult.

1489 CAXTON *Faytes of A.* I. xiv. 38 Sperys, dartys, and iauelots. **1675** *Phil. Trans.* X. 282 Catapultæ and Balistæ: the former casting Javelots: the latter stones. **1693** URQUHART *Rabelais* III. Prol., They sharpned and prepared Spears,..Javelins, Javelots and Trunchions. **1708** MOTTEUX *Rabelais* V. ix. (1737) 35 Javelins, Javelots, Darts, Dartlets.

†**javelo'tier.** *Obs. rare.* Also **-ott-.** [a. obs. F. *javelotier*, f. *javelot* JAVELOT.] A soldier armed with a javelot or javelin; a javelineer.

1600 HOLLAND *Livy* XXI. xxi. 405 Hee [Hannibal] sent for fresh supplie out of Affricke, specially of Archers and Iavelotiers, and those lightly armed. *Ibid.* XXVI. iv. 585 Hereupon began the manner..to entertaine such light armed iavelottiers called Velites, euen among the Legions.

†'**javer,** *v.* *Obs.* exc. *dial.* Also 5 **chauer,** 9 **javver.** [app. onomatopœic: cf. JABBER *v.*] *intr.* = JABBER *v.* 1.

c **1440** *Promp. Parv.* 80/2 Clenchyn a-ȝen or chaueryn a-ȝen, for prowde herte, *obgarrio. Ibid.* 257/1 Iangelyn or iaueryn a-ȝen, þat ys clepyd clenchyng a-ȝen, *oggarrio.* [See also JABBER *v.* 1.] **1839** A. BYWATER *Sheffield Dial.* (1877) 98 To bawl to t' Orishmen, or javver abaht chetch rates. **1876** *Mid. Yorksh. Gloss.*, Javver. [In various Yorkshire dialects, in sense To talk idly, garrulously, or noisily.]

Hence **javer, javver** *sb.* (*dial.*)

1869 *Lonsdale Gloss., Javver*, idle talk. **1876** *Mid. Yorksh. Gloss., Javver*, bold, assuming talk. **1876** *Whitby Gloss., Javver*, 'jaw' or talk; impudence.

javil, -ill, variants of JAVEL *sb.*

jaw (dʒɔː), *sb.*¹ Forms: α. 4-5 **iow,** 4-6 **iowe;** β. 5-7 **iawe,** 7- **jaw;** (5 **geaw, gowe, gew,** 7 **gagh**). [A word of difficult etymology, on the origin of which the evidence known to us affords conflicting indications. It occurs in the form *jow(e* from *c* 1375; *c* 1483 we find *jaw(e*, which before long superseded *jowe*; from 1530 to *c* 1675 there was a collateral CHAW(E. Chaucer rimed *jowe* with *clowe* (= *jaw, claw*), which shows that the sound was not (uː), and thus that the word was not the F. *joue* cheek.

If, notwithstanding the want of evidence, and in spite of the late exemplification of *ch* forms in *chaw(e*, it may be assumed that *jowe* was preceded by a ME. **chowe*, representing an unrecorded OE. **céowe, ceówe* wk. fem., this would be identical with OHG. *kiuwa, chiuwa*, early MHG. *chiwe, chouwe*, MHG. *kiuwe, couwe*, early mod. and dial. Ger. *keu, käu, koie* (Grimm); MDu. *couwe*, Kilian *kouwe, keeuwe*, Du. *kieuw*; going back to OTeut. **kewwôn*, deriv. of *kewwan* to CHEW. The later *chawe, jawe* would then be parallel to mod.Ger. *kaue*, MDu. *cauwe*, Kilian *kauwe*, and to Ger. *kauen*, Du. *kauwen*, 16th c. Eng. CHAW *v.*, beside OHG. *kiuwan*, MHG. *kiuwen*, MDu. *kouwen*, and OE. *céowan* CHEW, the phonetic relations of which are not clearly settled. The spelling with *j* may have been influenced by association with F. *joue* cheek; though the frequent passage of *ch* into *j* in other words shows that this need not be assumed. Cf. the phonetic development of OE. *céafl*, ME. *chavel, chaul, chol, chowl*, JOWL: also Marston's JAWN for *chawn* sb. and vb.]

1. a. One of the bones (or sets of bones) forming the framework of the mouth, and the seizing, biting, or masticating apparatus of vertebrates; in *sing.* more frequently the ***lower*** or ***under*** (†***nether***) ***jaw***, the inferior maxillary or mandible, than the ***upper*** (†***over***) ***jaw***, or superior maxillary; cf. JAW-BONE.

The *dropping* or *falling* of the jaw is a mark of death, dejection, or chagrin: see JAW-FALLEN, CHOP-FALLEN.

α. **1382** WYCLIF *Judg.* xv. 16 In the cheek boon of an asse, that is, in the iow of the colt of assis, I haue doon hem awey. **1398** TREVISA *Barth. De P.R.* V. xvi. (1495) 121 The Cocadryll meuyth the ouer Iowe [*Bodley MS.* þe ouer gowe] ayenste kynde of all other beestes and holdyth the nether Iowe [*Bodley MS.* þe neþir iowe] still and meuyth it not. **1484** CAXTON *Fables of Æsop* 2 He had a grete hede large vysage longe Iowes. **1486** *Bk. St. Albans* C vij a, For booches that growe in a hawkis Iowe.

β. *c* **1450** *Trevisa's Barth. De P.R.* V. xlii. (Bodl. MS.), No beeste haþ an euen gut but he haue teeþ in ayþer iawe. **1509** HAWES *Past. Pleas.* XLIII. (Percy Soc.) 210 Dyd not kyng Davyd a lyons jawe tere? **1600** E. BLOUNT tr. *Conestaggio* 270 The bullet hitting him under his right iawe. **1611** BIBLE *Job* xli. 2 Canst thou..bore his iawe through with a thorne? **1774** GOLDSM. *Nat. Hist.* (1776) VII. 218 Their teeth are.. numerous, and..perfectly inoffensive: they lie in either jaw. **1819** SHELLEY *Peter Bell* I. x, There was a silent chasm Betwixt his upper jaw and under. **1866** G. MACDONALD *Ann. Q. Neighb.* xxx. (1878) 528 The jaw fell, and the eyes were fixed.

b. The parts of certain invertebrates used for the ingestion of food.

1870 H. A. NICHOLSON *Man. Zool.* 163 The Medicinal Leech (*Sanguisuga officinalis*)..has its mouth furnished with three crescentic jaws. **1877** T. H. HUXLEY *Man. Anat. Invertebr. Animals* i. 56 In the Arthropoda, what are usually termed jaws are modified limbs. **1902** *Encycl. Brit.* XXV. 696/1 The jaws of Peripatus are formed by the axis or corm itself. **1932** BORRADAILE & POTTS *Invertebrata* xviii. 567 The lantern [of echinoids] consists of five composite jaws, each clasping a tooth. **1971** J. E. SMITH et al. *Invertebr. Panorama* iv. 55 The gut [of leeches] has a muscularized blood-sucking pharynx often armed with piercing jaws.

2. In *pl.* The bones and associated structures of the mouth including the teeth, regarded as instruments of prehension, crushing, and devouring; hence, the cavity formed by these parts; the mouth, fauces, throat.

α. *c* **1374** CHAUCER *Boeth.* I. pr. iv. 9 (Camb. MS.) Yit drowh I hym owt of the Iowwes of hem þat gapeden. **1398** TREVISA *Barth. De P.R.* XVII. xxiii. (Tollem. MS.), It abateþ swellynge of iowes [*tumorem faucium sedat*] and helpeþ woundes of þe longes. *c* **1430** *Stans Puer* 31 in *Babees Bk.* 29 To enbrace [*v.r.* enboce] þi iowis with breed, it is not dewe; with ful mouþ speke not lest þou do offence. **1483** CAXTON *Gold. Leg.* 195/1 There apperyd on hir no sygne of lyf sauf that hyr Iowes were a lytel reed. **1513** DOUGLAS *Æneis* XI. xiii. 69 With ane hydduus wolfis gapand iowis.

β. *c* **1483** *Chaucer's H. Fame* III. 696 (ed. Caxton) Euyl thryft come on your Iawes [*rime* clawes; *Fairf. and Bodl. MSS.* Iowes, -ys, clowes, -ys]. **1573** GASCOIGNE *Hearbes, Voy. to Holland*, At last the Dutche with butter bitten iawes ..Gan aunswere thus. **1590** SPENSER *F.Q.* III. viii. 33 The hungry Spaniells..With greedy iawes her ready for to teare. **1608** D. T[UVIL] *Ess. Pol. & Mor.* 69 Many haue had the victory snatcht (as it were) out of their iawes,..for not making a..bridge for the..enemy to passe over. **1732** LEDIARD *Sethos* II. VII. 103 [No] form..discern'd but sparkling eyes and flaming jaws. **1735** SOMERVILLE *Chase* III. 147 From his wide Jaws His Tongue unmoisten'd hangs.

3. *transf.* chiefly in *pl.* The two sides of a narrow pass, fissure, gorge, or channel; the narrow 'mouth' or entrance into a valley, gulf, or sea; the fauces or entrance into the 'throat' of a flower, etc.

1387 TREVISA *Higden* (Rolls) I. 167 Cesariensis, þat haþ.. in þe west þe ryuer Malua, and in þe norþ þe gewes of þe grete see. **1618** BOLTON *Florus* (1636) 271 Being commanded by Cæsar to guard the jawes of the Adriatick gulph. **1655** F. W. *Obs.* in *W. Fulke's Meteors* 165 The Ground perhaps open with those inundations, and the Gold fall into the gaping jaws of the Earth, and so stick there. **1776** J. LEE *Introd. Bot.* Explan. Terms 395 *Faux*, the Jaws gaping between the Divisions of the Corollæ, where the Tube terminates. **1810** SCOTT *Lady of L.* V. iii, The guide, abating of his pace, Led slowly through the pass's jaws. **1851** MAYNE REID *Scalp Hunters* xxxvii. 283 The ridge that formed the southern jaw of the chasm. **1883** SYMONDS *Ital. Byways* i. 4 The torrent, foaming down between black jaws of rain-stained granite.

4. *pl.* Applied to the seizing or holding members of a machine or apparatus, arranged in pairs, and usually capable of an opening and closing movement; *spec. Naut.* the semicircular, concave, or forked end of a boom or gaff which clasps the mast with its projecting ends or 'horns'.

1789 *Trans. Soc. Arts* VII. 209 Bringing the jaws of the cap to embrace the stern-post. **1825** J. NICHOLSON *Operat. Mechanic* 370 The end of the paper is at that time lying even with the extremity of the teeth *i i*, and the jaws of the tongs closing immediately that the rod *j* is put in motion. **1830** E. S. N. CAMPBELL *Dict. Mil. Sc.* 39 *Cock*, that part of a musquet lock which sustains the two pieces of iron, called jaws, between which the flint is fixed. **1835** MARRYAT *Pirate* viii, The jaws of the main-gaff were severed. **1877** RAYMOND *Statist. Mines & Mining* 421 Krom's laboratory crusher.. In this machine (unlike any other) both jaws oscillate on centers, fixed some distance from the crushing faces. **1881** YOUNG *Every man his own Mechanic* 238 The joiner's vice.. is furnished with 9 in. jaws to open 12 in.

5. *fig.* (in *pl.*) The seizing action or capacity of any devouring agency, as death, time, etc.

1563 *Mirr. Mag.* Induction xxxii, And first within the portche and iawes of Hell. *c* **1580** SIDNEY *Ps.* XXX. iii, The graves moist hungry jawes. **1595** SHAKS. *John* V. ii. 116 To winne renowne Euen in the iawes of danger, and of death. **1654** FULLER *Two Serm.* 41 Mustering of Men in this case, was but casting away so many into the Gaghs of Death. **1703** MAUNDRELL *Journ. Jerus.* (1732) 16 Which great strength has preserv'd it thus long from the jaws of time. **1855** TENNYSON *Charge Lt. Brigade* iii, Into the jaws of Death, Into the mouth of Hell Rode the six hundred.

6. Vulgar loquacity; *esp.* 'cheeky' or impudent talk; also, *colloq.*, a talk, a speech, a lecture, an

address; a long talk, incessant chatter. Frequent in the phrases *to hold* or *stop one's jaw* (where the sense may at first have been literal, as in *to open, loose,* or *work one's jaws*: cf. also *to hold one's tongue*).

1748 SMOLLETT *Rod. Rand.* iii, None of your jaw, you swab,..else I shall trim your laced jacket for you. **1753** FOOTE *Eng. in Paris* I. Wks. 1799 I. 37 Hold your jaw and dispatch. **1772** —— *Nabob* III. Wks. 1799 II. 318 Let's have no more of your jaw! **1800** LD. METCALFE in *Fortn. Rev.* (1885) June 757 Tremendous jaw from my tutor. **1836** COL. HAWKER *Diary* (1893) II. 94 A rich jaw between..Read and Buckle, who met afloat after a previous quarrel. **1842** F. J. FURNIVALL in *F. J. Furnivall: Personal Rec.* (1911) p. xi, Had a jaw with Young, which ended, as it began, in nothing. *a* **1845** HOOD *Tale Trumpet* xx, Parliamentary jabber and jaw. **1846** *Swell's Night Guide* 123/1 *Jaw*, abusive language. **1861** D. G. ROSSETTI *Lett.* (1965) II. 387 We would go to a theatre afterwards or else have a jaw here. **1868** FREEMAN in W. R. W. Stephens *Life & Lett.* (1895) I. 354 When they talk of right and law, we bid them hold their jaw. **1888** D. C. MURRAY in *Illustr. Lond. News* Christmas No. 11/2, So long as a man has the sense to hold his jaw at the right time. **1916** G. B. SHAW *Pygmalion* I. 115 Come with me now and lets have a jaw over some supper. **1964** *Guardian* 2 Mar. 7/6 So before the show starts the promoter gives me a bit of a jaw. **1968** J. R. ACKERLEY *My Father & Myself* viii. 79 He invited the two of us into the billiard-room of Grafton House..for a 'jaw'. **1972** *Times Lit. Suppl.* 14 Apr. 420/3 Without these things, committee work is just endless jaw and empty substitute.

7. *attrib.* and *Comb.*, as *jaw-arch, -break, -calipers, -chasm, -forceps, -gape, -line, -man, -muscle, -opening, -sheath, -work*; *jaw-cracking, jaw-locked, jaw-tied* adjs.; **jaw-bit** (*U.S.*), a short bar placed beneath a journal box to unite the two pedestals in a car-truck (*Cent. Dict.* 1890); **jaw-chuck**, a chuck in a lathe furnished with jaws for seizing an object; **jaw clutch**, a claw clutch or a dog clutch; **jaw-crusher** (*Mining*), an ore-crushing machine similar to the jaw-breaker; **jaw-foot** = *foot-jaw* (see FOOT *sb.* 35); **jaw-footed** *a.*, provided with a jaw-foot; **jaw-jerk** *Med.*, a jerk (JERK *sb.*[1] 2 b (*a*)) of the lower jaw elicited by a downward blow on it when the mouth is open; **jaw-lever**, a veterinary instrument for opening the mouth and administering medicine to cattle (Simmonds *Dict. Trade* 1858); **jaw-piece** (*Arch.*), †(*a*) = JOWPY, JOPY; (*b*) (see quot. 1886); **jaw-process** = GNATHOBASE; **jaw-rope** (*Naut.*), the rope which fastens the two horns or prongs of the boom or gaff round the mast; **jaw-smith, jawsmith** *U.S. slang*, a talkative person; esp. a loud-mouthed demagogue; **jaw-spring** (*U.S.*), a journal spring; **jaw-tackle** (*slang*), the muscles of the jaws; the mouth, etc., as employed in talking; **jaw-wedge** (*U.S.*), a wedge to tighten the axle-box in an axle-guard (Webster, 1864).

1879 tr. *Haeckel's Evol. Man* II. xviii. 111 The foremost of these pairs of gill-arches changes into the *jaw-arch which gives rise to the upper and lower jaws. **1896** A. MORRISON *Child Jago* 311 His chin fell on his chest, as by *jaw-break. **1900** *Animal World* XXXI. 18/2 They [larvæ of *Libellula*] then advance..until within half an inch of their prey, when out shoot the *jaw-calipers, and the object is seized. **1880** G. MEREDITH *Egoist* II. 105 The gaping *jaw-chasm of his greed. **1875** KNIGHT *Dict. Mech.* s.v. *Chuck*, [figure] *k* is an independent *jaw chuck. **1893** LANGMAID & GAISFORD *Elem. Less. Steam Machinery* vi. 62 A common form of this fitting is the *jaw clutch. **1907** Jaw clutch [see *change-speed* (CHANGE *sb.* 12 a)]. **1911** *Encycl. Brit.* XVIII. 927/1 A clutch of this description can be made to engage without difficulty, there being no fixed positions or steps such as one associates with the ordinary jaw-clutch. **1936** W. STANIAR *Mech. Power Transmission Handbk.* vii. 267 Jaw Clutches.—This type of clutch is employed for moderate and heavy rough driving... It consists of a square or spiral jaw portion which is keyed to the driving shaft and a sleeve portion equipped with square or spiral jaws into which the driving portion can be engaged. With this type of clutch..the pick-up is instantaneous, resulting therefore in shock. **1966** *McGraw-Hill Encycl. Sci. & Technol.* III. 224/1 Although square jaw clutches are the strongest and most elementary to construct, the difficulty of engagement limits their use... A modification..to permit more convenient engagement and to provide a more gradual movement of the mating faces toward each other produces the spiral jaw clutch. **1883** *Illustr. Lond. News* 8 Dec. 551/1 (Farmer) Such *jaw-cracking jokes. **1877** RAYMOND *Statist. Mines & Mining* 421 A similar manner to that in which the *jaw-crusher operates so effectually on large pieces of ore. **1871** T. R. JONES *Anim. Kingd.* (ed. 4) 422 The term *jaw-feet has now, by common consent, become the appellation by which they are distinguished. **1883** A. WILSON in *Longm. Mag.* II. 48 The curious jaws, jaw-feet, and legs of the armoured crustacean. **1900** *Animal World* XXXI. 18/2 The snatch of their *jaw-forceps is so quick it takes good eyesight to see it. **1898** G. MEREDITH *Odes Fr. Hist.* 11 Lyrical on into death's red roaring *jaw-gape. **1886** A. DE WATTEVILLE in *Brain* VIII. 518 It does not appear to be generally known that a '*jaw-jerk' can be readily elicited... The phenomenon is clearly of the same nature as that of the 'knee-jerk', and is due to the sudden stretching of the masseter and other muscles of mastication. Hence the name I have ventured to give to it, in preference to the longer and less accurate term mandibular (or masseteric) tendon-reaction (or reflex). **1968** PASSMORE & ROBSON *Compan. Med. Stud.* I. xxiv. 12/2 This jerk [*sc.* the knee jerk] is one of a whole family of tendon jerks... They include the Achilles tendon or ankle jerk..the biceps and triceps jerks.., and the masseter-temporalis or jaw jerk. **1936** J. CURTIS *Gilt Kid* xiv. 144 Perhaps his *jaw-line was a little tenser. **1971** *Chatelaine* Aug. 41/2 Tweezing stragglers over nose bridge and applying tawny blusher from brows to jawline livened her skin and slimmed her face. **1807** E. S. BARRETT *Rising Sun* III. 130 Their tongues.. were, for some minutes, *jaw-locked, after beholding this dismal portent. **1894** DOYLE *Round the Red Lamp* 203 He was himself a *jawman, 'a mere jawman', as he modestly puts it, but in point of fact he [a surgeon] is too young..to confine himself to a specialty. **1890** W. JAMES *Princ. Psychol.* I. x. 301 In *effort* of any sort, contractions of the *jaw-muscles and of those of respiration are added to those of the brow and glottis. **1929** W. FAULKNER *Sound & Fury* 140 My jaw-muscles getting numb. **1958** E. FISCHER-JØRGENSEN in Saporta & Bastian *Psycholinguistics* (1961) 131/2 Slow *jaw-opening might rather be combined with a fortis-lenis difference. *a* **1548** HALL *Chron., Hen. VIII*, 73 b, The *iawe pece of the said selyng: whiche pece was guilte with fine Golde. *Ibid.* 156 b, The Iawe peces and crestes were karved wyth Vinettes and trailes of savage worke, and richely gilted with gold and Bise. **1886** WILLIS & CLARK *Archit. Hist. Univ. Cambr.* I. 283 A 'jaw-piece' or triangular piece of wood..interposed between [the principal] itself and the spars forming the roof. **1881** *Jaw process [see GNATHOBASE]. **1902** *Encycl. Brit.* XXV. 697/1 The usual uniramose limb found in the various classes of Arthropoda.. varies as to the presence or absence of the jaw-process. **1833** MARRYAT *P. Simple* li, I..disengaged the *jaw-rope and small gear about the mast. **1886** F. GUILLEMARD *Cruise 'Marchesa'* I. 230 The jaw-rope had carried away. **1875** HUXLEY in *Encycl. Brit.* I. 770/1 [The] horny *jaw-sheaths [of *Siren*] might be compared to those of the Anuran tadpole. **1887** *Chicago Tribune* 13 May 5/2 George Schilling, Socialist and *jawsmith. **1910** Jawsmith [see HOT AIR 2]. **1942** BERREY & VAN DEN BARK *Amer. Thes. Slang* §422 Talker,..*jawsmith* (esp. a public speaker). **1831** TRELAWNEY *Adv. Younger Son* I. 290 Van would have countermanded this, had I not clapped my hand as a stopper on his *jaw-tackle. **1884** *Bread-winners* 210 He had never worked a muscle in his life except his jaw-tackle. **1756** TOLDERVY *Hist. Two Orphans* III. 75 My *jaw-ty'd tongue no speech could lend. *Ibid.* III. 166 Come, come..no more of your *jaw-work here. **1802** *Morn. Her.* in *Spirit Pub. Jrnls.* (1803) VI. 29 An event..conducive to jaw-work in every sense of the word.

jaw (dʒɔː), *sb.*[2] *Sc.* and *north. dial.* [Goes with JAW *v.*[2], the two appearing together early in 16th c. Origin unknown.]

1. The rush or dash of a wave; a surging or dashing wave, a billow.

1513 DOUGLAS *Æneis* I. iii. 21 Heich as ane hill the iaw of watter brak. *Ibid.* VIII. i. 136, I am God Tibris..Quhilk.. wyth mony iaup and iaw Bettis thir brayis, schawand the bankis down. **1606** tr. *Rollock's Lect. 2 Thess.* 118 The sey when it flowes on a rock, immediatelie the iaw returnes backe againe in the sey. **1768** ROSS *Helenore* (1866) 231 Sae we had better jook until the jaw Gang o'er our heads. ? *a* **1800** *Sir Patrick Spence* viii. (Child), They had not saild upon the sea A league but merely three, When ugly, ugly were the jaws That rowd unto their knee. **1868** G. MACDONALD *R. Falconer* III. 65 Tak guid tent 'at ye ride upo' the tap o' 't, an' no lat it rise like a muckle jaw ower yer heid; for it's an awfu' thing to be droont in riches. **1893** *Northumbld. Gloss.*, Jaa, Jaw.

2. A quantity of water or other liquid dashed, splashed, or thrown out; an outpour of water, etc.

a **1816** PICKEN in *Whistle-Binkie* (1890) I. 149 Wi' jaws o' toddy reeking hot Will keep the genial current warm. **1825-80** JAMIESON s.v., The cow has gi'en a gude jaw the day. **1899** CROCKETT *Kit Kennedy* 57 Giein' a pot a bit syne [= rinse] wi' a jaw o' water.

Hence (or from JAW *v.*[2]) **jaw-box, jaw-tub,** *Sc.*, a kitchen sink with sides; also JAW-HOLE.

1880 *Antrim & Down Gloss.*, *Jaw tub, Jaw box*, a scullery sink.

jaw (dʒɔː), *v.*[1] [f. JAW *sb.*[1]]

†**1.** *trans.* To seize or devour with the jaws; to use the jaws upon. *Obs.*

1612 *Two Noble K.* III. ii, I wreake not if the wolues would jaw me, so He had his fill.

2. *slang.* **a.** *intr.* To use the vocal organs; to speak, talk. (A vulgar, contemptuous, or hostile equivalent for *speak.*)

1748 SMOLLETT *Rod. Rand.* xxiv, He swore woundily at the lieutenant..whereby the lieutenant returned the salute, and they jawed together fore and aft a good spell. **1760** C. JOHNSTON *Chrysal* (1822) III. 299 Will you stand jawing here? **1801** M. G. LEWIS *Tales Wonder*, *Sailor's T.* iv, In vain I begg'd, and swore, and jaw'd; Nick no excuse would hear. **1885** T. A. GUTHRIE *Tinted Venus* viii. 98 What's the good of jawing at him?

b. *trans.* To address censoriously or abusively; to scold or 'lecture' (a person).

1810 *Sporting Mag.* XXXVI. 262 He was then very abusive and noisy; he kept jawing us. **1833** MARRYAT *P. Simple* xi, I have been jawed for letting you go. **1896** *Chicago Advance* 30 July 141/1 In politics we jaw one another partly for the fun of it.

3. *to jaw away*: to cut to the shape of jaws, or in a concave curve.

1802 *Naval Chron.* VIII. 470 The top-most part of the cap was cut to fit the rudder, and the after part jawed away, so as to work on the stern-post.

jaw (dʒɔː), *v.*[2] *Sc.* Also 7 jae. [See JAW *sb.*[2]]

1. *intr.* To rush in waves; to dash or pour; to splash; to surge.

1513 DOUGLAS *Æneis* v. Prol. 53 Bot my propyne coym fra the pres fuit hait, Vnforlatit, not iawyn fra tun to tun. ? *a* **1800** *Sir Roland* 91 in Child *Ballads* I. (1857) 345 For now the water jawes owre my head, And it gurgles in my mouth.

2. *trans.* To pour or dash (water) in waves; to throw or dash (liquid) in quantity.

c **1680** R. LAW *Mem.* (1818) 177 When it [the elephant] drinks..it jaes in the water in it's mouth as from a great spout. **1725** RAMSAY *Gentle Sheph.* I. i, Tempest may cease to jaw the rowan flood. **1787** BURNS *American War* i, Then up they gat the maskin-pat, And in the sea did jaw, man.

Hence ˈ**jawing** *ppl. a.*

? *a* **1800** *Lass of Lochroyan* 43 in Scott *Minstr. Scot. Bord.*, The stately tower..Whilk stood aboon the jawing wave.

‖**jawan** (dʒəˈwɑːn). Also **juwan**. [a. Urdu *jawān*.] An Indian soldier.

1839 M. TAYLOR *Confessions of Thug* I. i. 6 Chumpa was busy cooking and the Juwans were all out of the way. **1923** *Blackw. Mag.* July 22/1 The cool deliberately-aimed fire of the jawans lashed them each time. **1962** *Listener* 29 Nov. 895/2 For the public, the cult of the Indian soldier, the Jawan, remains unshaken. **1965** P. ROBINSON *Pakistani Agent* i. 9 A *jawan* in a dark-green uniform..was resting upright against the wall of the cargo shed, with his rifle propped up next to him. **1969** *Amrita Bazar Patrika* 5 Aug. 1/1 Ten persons, including five Security Force personnel, were killed and three jawans were wounded in two incidents of ambush in far-flung areas of the State in the last 48 hours. **1971** *Sunday Times* 13 June 12/2 One of the *jawans* (privates) crouched in the back of the Toyota Land Cruiser called out sharply: 'There's a man running, Sahib.'

jawar, jawari, variant of JOWAR, JOWARI.

jawbation: see JOBATION.

jaw-bone, jawbone (ˈdʒɔːbəʊn). [f. JAW *sb.*[1] + BONE.] **1.** Any bone of the jaws; *spec.* each of the two forming the lower jaw in most mammals, or the whole bone formed by their combination in others.

c **1489** CAXTON *Sonnes of Aymon* xxvi. 562 He gaff constans soo grete a stroke vpon the ere, that he bare it awaye wyth all the iawe bone. **1551** BIBLE *Judg.* xv. 15 He founde a iaw-bone of a rotten asse..and slewe a thousande men therewith. **1626** BACON *Sylva* §750 The Iaw-Bones haue no Marrow Seuered, but a little Pulpe of Marrow diffused. **1709** STEELE *Tatler* No. 129 ¶7 It [a tooth] belong'd to the Jaw-Bone of a Saint. **1793** HOLCROFT tr. *Lavater's Physiog.* III. xx. 104 The Chinese..appear to have broad cheeks with projecting jaw-bones. **1870** BRYANT *Iliad* II. XVII. 190 The javelin entered underneath the ear By the jaw-bone. *Mod.* A pair of whale's jaw-bones forming a gateway.

2. An animal's jaw-bone used as a musical instrument; also, castanets or a jew's harp.

[**1790** W. BECKFORD *Descr. Acct. Jamaica* II. 387 Their musical instruments..consist of..the jaw-bone of an animal, from which is produced a harsh and disagreeable sound.] **1844** in C. Cist *Cincinnati Misc.* (1845) I. 14/2 Fowler..found the truant..at a dance house..playing the *jaw bones* or Castanets. **1952** B. ULANOV *Hist. Jazz in Amer.* (1958) v. 46 By the end of the 1880s New Orleans Negro musicians were no longer playing jawbones, hide-covered casks, or bamboo tubes. **1970** P. OLIVER *Savannah Syncopators* 109 *Jawbone*, jawbone of a mule, ass, cow or other domestic animal used as a rattle. A North American plantation instrument. The jawbone was also struck or played with a nail or length of iron.

3. Credit. *N. Amer.* (orig. *Canadian*) *slang.*

1862 *Times* 21 Oct. 9/4 Individuals who, in digger's parlance, live on jawbone (credit). **1885** A. S. HILL *From Home to Home* 413 His ready money gone, he has nothing to live on but 'jawbone', *i.e.* credit. **1941** J. SMILEY *Hash House Lingo* 33 *Jawbone*, credit. **1970** *New Yorker* 31 Oct. 130/3 A young Canadian..started this film on a small grant..and apparently finished it on jawbone and by deferring processing costs. **1971** A. P. MCINNES *Dunlevy* 54 No jawbone credit is allowed and all bets must be matched with goods.

Hence **jawboning** *U.S. slang*, name applied to a policy, first associated with the administration of President Lyndon Johnson (1963–1969), of urging management and union leaders to adopt a policy of restraint in wage and price negotiations. Also in extended use. Also (as a back-formation) **jaw-bone** *v.*

1966 *N.Y. Times* 2 Jan. IV. 2 Every price increase that happens to catch the public's eye must be 'jawboned' to death by the Government. **1969** *Time* 19 Sept. 32 Since June, Feather has been jawboning his union chiefs on the virtues of labor discipline on the shop floor. **1969** *Time* 10 Oct. 57 As for jawboning, Nixon's Republican advisers consider it unfair and almost immoral to single out individual companies or industries. **1970** *Daily Tel.* 19 June 15 Policy will almost certainly concentrate on 'jawboning', the American tactic of trying belatedly to talk both sides of industry out of outlandish wage and price increases. **1970** *Harper's Mag.* Mar. 48 Lecturing business and labor on their responsibilities to hold down prices and wages—jawboning as it was called in the Johnson Administration—has been foregone. **1970** *Times* 7 Nov. 7/1 He criticized the Nixon Administration's decision on coming to office to drop the practice of 'jawboning', or presidential persuasion, on the prices and wages front.

ˈ**jaw-ˌbreaker.** *colloq.*

1. A word hard to pronounce; a word of many syllables.

1839 LEVER *H. Lorrequer* xix, I'd rather hear the Cruiskeen Lawn..than a score of your high Dutch jawbreakers. **1886** D. C. MURRAY *1st Person Sing.* xviii. 136 It's a jawbreaker at first for an Englishman. **1887** SAINTSBURY *Hist. Elizab. Lit.* i. 14 You will find no 'jawbreakers' in Sackville.

2. A machine with powerful jaws for crushing ore, etc.

1877 RAYMOND *Statist. Mines & Mining* 421, I speak of the rolls as more applicable for completing the crushing of the ore as it comes in small pieces from the jaw-breaker.

So ˈ**jaw-breaking** *a. colloq.*, hard to pronounce; hence ˈ**jaw-ˌbreakingly** *adv.*

1824 *Blackw. Mag.* XVI. 191 Entitled by a name most jaw-breakingly perplexing. **1842** THACKERAY *Miss Tickletoby's Lect.* i. Wks. 1886 XXIV. 13 He conquered a great number of princes with jaw-breaking names. **1883** *Gd. Words* Sept. 592/2 A little plant that has a jaw-breaking name.

jawed (dʒɔːd), *a.* [f. JAW *sb.*[1] + -ED[2].] Having or furnished with jaws.
a **1529** SKELTON *E. Rummyng* 38 Iawed like a jetty. **1887** E. D. COPE *Origin Fittest* xi. 316 *note*, The metamorphosis of the jawed Neuroptera is little more marked.

'jaw-fall.
1. Falling of the jaw; *fig.* dejection. *rare.*
1660 M. GRIFFITH *Fear of God & King* 29 For a time they had an Inter-regnum, and no King in Israel, besides divers other horrid jawfalls in government.
†**2.** Dislocation or subluxation of the lower jaw so that it cannot be shut. *Obs.*
1788 RUSH in Pettigrew *Lettsom* (1817) II. 432 The locked-jaw, or as it is usually called among the planters, the jaw-fall, is a very common disease among the children of the slaves.

'jaw-ˌfallen, *a.* [f. JAW *sb.*[1] + FALLEN *pa. pple.*] Having the lower jaw fallen or hanging loose; chop-fallen; dejected.
1603 FLORIO *Montaigne* I. xl. (1632) 128 The wench offered him was jaw-falne, long-cheekt, and sharpe-nosed. *a* **1691** FLAVEL *Sea-Deliv.* (1754) 165 We were jaw-fallen and starved with the extreme cold. **1748** RICHARDSON *Clarissa* (1811) III. 54 (D.) The people..seemed by their jaw-fallen faces and goggling eyes to wonder at beholding a charming young lady.

jaw-hole[1] ('dʒɔːˌhəʊl). [f. JAW *sb.*[2], *v.*[2] + HOLE.] A hole into which dirty water or other liquid is 'jawed' or thrown; an open entrance to a sewer, house-drain, or cesspool.
1760 *City Cleaned & County Improv.*, Jaw-holls or water-spouts of timber [etc.]. **1815** SCOTT *Guy M.* i, Piloting with some dexterity along the little path which bordered the formidable jaw-hole, whose vicinity the stranger was made sensible of by means of more organs than one. **1824** —— *St. Ronan's* xxviii, That odoriferous gulf, ycleped, in Scottish phrase, the jawhole; in other words, an uncovered common sewer.

'jaw-hole[2]. [JAW *sb.*[1]] A gaping fissure or opening; an abyss.
1840 T. A. TROLLOPE *Summer in Brittany* II. xxxiv. 187 A sort of jaw-hole, or abyss, moreover, is still pointed out between Huelgoat and Cairhax, which this vixen of a princess used as a second—or rather first—Tour de Nesle. **1876** *Whitby Gloss.*, *Jaw-hooal*, a fissure or opening in the land, as the mouth of a stream. The arched entrance to a cavern.

Jawi ('dʒɑːwɪ). [Malay.] Formerly, the Malay vernacular; now, the Malay language written in Arabic script.
1808 *Asiatick Researches* X. iii. 164 The *Basa Jawi* or written language of composition, is nearly the same in all [dialects]. **1812** W. MARSDEN *Gram. Malay Lang.* p. xiv, *Jāwī* or *bhā sa jâwī* is..employed in writings to denote the vernacular language of the Malays, especially that of books, as distinguished from all foreign languages. **1920** R. O. WINSTEDT *Colloquial Malay* (ed. 2) 138 The Malay word spelt in Arabic characters is a puzzle to be solved by the possession of a large vocabulary. And it is impossible to draw up a logical system of *Jawi* spelling. **1964** M. TAIB BIN OSMAN in Wang Gungwu *Malaysia* III. xv. 210 Traditional literature as known today is the literature written in the Perso-Arabic script known as *Jawi*. **1972** *Straits Times* (Malaysian ed.) 24 Nov. 21/1 A tombstone found in the same area has inscriptions in Jawi, stating that it was erected in 1292.

jawing ('dʒɔːɪŋ), *vbl. sb. slang.* [f. JAW *v.*[1] + -ING[1].] A vulgar or contemptuous equivalent for *speaking*.
1788 *De Foe's Voy. round World* (1840) 313 They would chop off his head, and put a stop to his jawing. **1810** *Sporting Mag.* XXXV. 78 Mary Jordan and her acquaintances were fighting and jawing. **1871** DIXON *Tower* III. xviii. 190 Two hours were spent in drinking, jawing, and accepting terms. **1874** LISLE CARR *Jud. Gwynne* I. iii. 83 Nigh blowing the roof off..with her everlasting jawing.
b. *attrib.*, as **jawing-tackle**, the jaws, etc., as used in speaking: = *jaw-tackle* (JAW *sb.*[1] 7).
1859 READE *Love me little* xxii, Ah, Eve, my girl, your jawing-tackle is too well hung.

jaw-jaw ('dʒɔːdʒɔː), *v.* [Redupl. form of JAW *v.*[1]] *intr.* To talk in a tedious manner or at great length.
Quot. 1831 is an isolated early example.
1831 M. EDGEWORTH *Let.* 14 Apr. (1971) 523 Mrs. Sotheby is *jaw-jawing* in the drawing room to that poor victim Fanny. **1954** *Times* 28 June 8/1 [W. S. Churchill at a White House lunch] Eden's two words are pretty good words. To jaw-jaw is always better than to war-war. **1969** *Manch. Guardian Weekly* 13 Dec. 12 The novelty of the reaction to the latest call for a European Summit is not in any changed assessment of the super-Powers' intentions, but in the feeling that it is time at last to start jaw-jawing.

jaw-jaw ('dʒɔːdʒɔː), *sb.* [Redupl. form of JAW *sb.*[1] 6.] Talking, often with the implication of lengthy and sterile discussion.
1958 *Times* 31 Jan. 6/7 He [*sc.* Mr. H. Macmillan] believed, in the words of Sir Winston Churchill, that 'jaw jaw is better than war war'. **1960** *Economist* 22 Oct. 326/3 The easy going jaw-jaw policy introduced to Lancaster House by Mr Macleod has been successful enough so far. **1963** *Daily Tel.* 7 Aug. 10/2 We seem to be entering an era of 'jaw-jaw'. **1969** *Listener* 10 July 59/2 Here..is one idea..which might actually enliven the jaw-jaw on Radio-4.

jawl, var. JOL.

'jawless, *a.* [f. JAW *sb.*[1] + -LESS.] Without jaws; *spec.* without a lower jaw, as the lamprey.
1708 MOTTEUX *Rabelais* IV. xv. (1737) 60 The jawless Bum shrug'd up his Shoulders. **1968** *Times* 19 Dec. 4/8 Lampreys, like hagfish, are surviving members of the jawless fishes, the first group of vertebrates to evolve. **1972** *Sci. Amer.* Nov. 61/3 Primitive jawless ostracoderms belonging to the orders Anaspida and Thelodonti.

jawm(e, dial. form of JAMB.

†**jawn,** obs. var. of CHAWN *sb.*, chine, fissure, and of CHAWN *v.*, to gape.
1598 MARSTON *Sco. Villany* I. iii. Cviij, To stop his iawning chaps. **1602** —— *Antonio's Rev.* II. ii. Wks. 1856 I. 94 Defyance to thy power, thou rifted jawne.

jawndes, -dres, jawnes, obs. ff. JAUNDICE.

jawne, jawnish, var. JAUNE, JAUNISH, *Obs.*

jawp, variant of JAUP *v.* and *sb.*, splash.

jaw's harp, jaws harp, varr. JEWS' HARP.
1880 GROVE *Dict. Mus.* II. 34/1 *Jew's-harp*, possibly a corruption of Jaw's-harp. **1927** *Melody Maker* Aug. 811/1 When I tune my 'Jaws Harp' as a 'Jujulele', I do not seem to get the *full* banjolic effect. **1958** P. OLIVER in P. Gammond *Decca Bk. Jazz* i. 23 Cheap guitars, jaw's harps and harmonicas became available in greater numbers in the 'nineties.

'jaw-tooth. A molar tooth. Cf. CHEEK-TOOTH.
1601 HOLLAND *Pliny* II. 440 If the grinders and great iaw teeth do ake, this is a speciall medicine for them. **1611** BIBLE *Prov.* xxx. 14 There is a generation, whose teeth are as swords, and their iaw-teeth as kniues. **1678** CUDWORTH *Intell. Syst.* I. v. 670 The former teeth were made..thin and sharp, by means whereof they became fit for cutting; but the jaw-teeth thick and broad, whereby they became useful for the grinding of food. **1789** MADAN *Persius* (1795) 39 *note*, Grinding food between the jaw-teeth. **1837** WHEELWRIGHT tr. *Aristophanes* II. 8 In wrestlers' fashion, plying his jaw-teeth.

jawy ('dʒɔːɪ), *a. rare.* [f. JAW *sb.*[1] + -Y.] Of or pertaining to the jaw; forceful in language.
1654 GAYTON *Pleas. Notes* II. iii. 42 The dulapes and the jawy part of the face. **1898** *Academy* 15 Oct. 92/1 It is material detail: forceful, stunning, jawy detail.

jax: see JACK *sb.*[1] 19 d.

jaxe, obs. form of JAKES.

jaxey, jaxie, varr. JACKSY.

jay (dʒeɪ). Also 5–6 *Sc.* **ia,** 5–7 **iaye.** [a. OF. *jay*, mod.F. *geai*, in ONF. *gai*, *gay* = Pr. *gai* (*jai*), Sp. *gayo*, med.L. *gaius*, *gaia* (Papias); of uncertain origin: some refer it to OHG. *gâhi* adj. quick; hence, lively. It cannot be identified with F. *gai* adj. 'gay', which has *g*, not *j*, in Central F.]
1. a. The name of a common European bird, *Garrulus glandarius*, in structure and noisy chattering resembling the magpie, but in habits arboreal, and having a plumage of striking appearance, in which vivid tints of blue are heightened by bars of jet-black and patches of white. Hence used as the English name of the genus *Garrulus*, and applied with distinguishing additions to the other species.
a **1310** in Wright *Lyric P.* 52 Heo is dereworthe in day,..Gentyl, jolyf so the jay. *c* **1386** CHAUCER *Manciple's T.* 28 And taughte it speke as men teche a Iay. **1412–13** HOCCLEVE *Ball. to Hen. V*, 37 My wordes..clappe and iangle foorth, as dooth a iay. **1530** LYNDESAY *Test. Papyngo* 725 The gentyll Ia, the Merle, and Turtur trew. **1590** SPENSER *F.Q.* II. viii. 5 Decked with diverse plumes, like painted Iayes. **1596** SHAKS. *Tam. Shr.* IV. iii. 177 What is the Iay more precious then the Larke? Because his feathers are more beautifull. **1746–7** HERVEY *Medit.* (1818) 43 Not long ago I happened to spy a thoughtless jay; the poor bird was idly busied in dressing his pretty plumes. **1766** PENNANT *Zool.* (1768) I. 173 Jays..may be brought to imitate the human voice. **1880** A. R. WALLACE *Isl. Life* ii. 20 There are, so far as yet known, twelve species of true jays. **1893** NEWTON *Dict. Birds* 470 Doubts may be expressed whether these birds are not more nearly related to the Pies than to the Jays.
b. In more extended sense, applied to birds of the sub-family *Garrulinæ* or family *Garrulidæ*, among which are the ***Canada jay*** (*Perisoreus canadensis*), the ***grey jay, green jay, Siberian jay***, etc.
1688 J. CLAYTON in *Phil. Trans.* XVII. 991 The *Pica Glandarea*, or Jay, is much less than our English Jay..it has both the same Cry, and suddain jetting Motion. **1838** *Encycl. Brit.* (ed. 7) XVI. 584/2, A most magnificent bird is the Columbia jay. **1855** LONGF. *Hiaw.* xiii. 100 Jays and ravens, Clamorous on the dusky tree-tops. **1886** YULE *Anglo-Ind. Gloss.*, *Jay*, the name usually given by Europeans to the *Coracias Indica*, Linn., the *Nīlkant* or 'blue-throat' of the Hindus, found all over India. **1893** NEWTON *Dict. Birds* 469 The *Lanius infaustus* of Linnæus..the Siberian Jay of English writers, which ranges throughout the pine-forests of the north of Europe and Asia. *Ibid.*, The Canada Jay, or 'Whiskey Jack'..presents a still more sombre coloration.
c. Also, the **blue jay**: (*a*) a North American jay, *Cyanocitta cristata*; (*b*) = ROLLER *sb.*[2] 1.
(*a*) **1709** *Gleanings Anc. Rec. Bristol, R.I.* 18 Mar. in *Narragansett Hist. Reg.* (1885) III. III. 211 The same order shall extend to the killing of blew Jawes [*sic*]. **1731** M. CATESBY *Nat. Hist. Carolina* I. 15 The Blew Jay is full as big, or bigger than a Starling. **1792** J. BELKNAP *Hist. New Hampshire* III. 173 The blue jay, the wood pecker and the partridge..are then seen flying. **1838** *Encycl. Brit.* (ed. 7) XVI. 584/2 The blue jay of America is an almost universal inhabitant of the western woods. **1885** 'C. E. CRADDOCK' (Miss Murfree) *Proph. Gt. Smoky Mount.* viii, He saw..the white tips of the tail-feathers of a fluttering bluejay. **1886** *Harper's Mag.* Nov. 877/2 The bell note of the blue-jay comes up from some mysterious haunt. **1961** O. L. AUSTIN *Birds of World* 226/2 Essentially a woodland species fond of open forest, the Blue Jay has become a common resident of the parks and suburbs of most North American cities.
(*b*) **1878** T. J. LUCAS *Camp Life & Sport S. Afr.* vi. 83 Conspicuous among them [*sc.* the birds] were..the beautiful blue jay, and the Kaffir finch. **1896** H. A. BRYDEN *Tales S. Afr.* viii. 185 Please don't forget the blue jay [*fn.* the 'roller' is usally called 'blue jay' by colonists] feathers. **1911** *Encycl. Brit.* XV. 298/1 The birds known as blue jays in India and Africa are rollers. **1964** A. L. THOMSON *New Dict. Birds* 411/2 'Blue Jay' is a misnomer in India for *Coracias benghalensis*.
2. Applied to other birds: **a.** The Jackdaw (app. from a French mistransl. of *κόλοιος* or *graculus* in the fable of the jackdaw decked in peacock's plumes). **b.** The Cornish chough, also termed ***Cornish jay***. **c.** The Missel thrush. *local.*
1484 CAXTON *Fables of Æsop* II. xv, The xv fable is of the Iaye and of the pecok. **1552** HULOET, Iaye, byrde, *gracus, graculus*. [**1565** COOPER *Thesaurus* s.v. *Graculus*, They are much deceyued that haue taken *Graculus* for a Iaye.] **1628** WITHER *Brit. Rememb.* Pref. 129 The Jay that vaunts In others plumes. **1706** PHILLIPS, *Jay*, or *Jack-daw*, a kind of chattering Bird. **1750** POCOCKE *Trav. Eng.*, etc. (Camden) 135 About Penzance, in the rocks, are jays with red bills and legs, called a Cornish jay, and by Pliny *Pyrrhocorax*. **1880** *Antrim & Down Gloss.*, *Jay*, the missel thrush is called the jay here. The jay does not occur.
3. *transf.* **a.** An impertinent chatterer. **b.** A showy or flashy woman; one of light character. **c.** A person absurdly dressed; a gawk or 'sight'. **d.** A stupid or silly person; a simpleton. Also *attrib.* or as *adj.*, dull, unsophisticated; inferior, poor (*U.S. colloq.*).
1523 SKELTON *Garl. Laurel* 1262 For the gyse now adays Of sum iangelyng iays Is to discommende What they cannot amende. **1598** SHAKS. *Merry W.* III. iii. 44 We'll teach him to know Turtles from Iayes. **1611** —— *Cymb.* III. iv. 51 Some Iay of Italy..hath betraid him. **1639** CHAPMAN & SHIRLEY *The Ball* II. ii, *Sol.* Mr. Bostock, madam. *Luc.* Retire, and give the jay admittance. **1884** *Pall Mall G.* 29 Dec. 4/2 The intending larcenist will strike up a conversation with a likely looking Jay in a public conveyance ..and win his friendship. **1886** BARING-GOULD *Mehalah* vii. 91 You stood by..and listened while that jay snapped and screamed at me. **1888** *N.Y. Herald* Sept. (Farmer *Americanisms*), Never..have I been annoyed in the slightest way by any of the so-called jays. **1889** *Daily Even. Bulletin* (San Francisco) 13 July 1/6 Smith has a poor opinion..of St. Joseph, which he alludes to as a 'jay' town of the worst description. **1891** H. C. BUNNER *Short Sixes* 91 'T ain't neuralogy, you jay pillbox, she's *cooked*! **1898** *Westm. Gaz.* 7 Oct. 4/2 'Kharki is not exactly a blanket; besides, we are jays enough as it is, and if we had had our old things on we should have been regular jays'. **1900** *Dundee Advertiser* 30 July 4 An underbred undergraduate—called in America a 'jay'. **1900** ADE *More Fables* (1902) 185 It was a Shame to String these Jay Amateurs. *a* **1911** D. G. PHILLIPS *Susan Lenox* (1917) II. ii. 23 Gee, what awful jay things we work off on them, sometimes! They can't see the dress for the figure. **1916** H. L. WILSON *Somewhere in Red Gap* viii. 348 Them jay New York newspapers would fall for it. **1942** BERREY & VAN DEN BARK *Amer. Thes. Slang* §21/10 Small; insignificant,..*jay*. *Ibid.* §30/4 Poor; mean; contemptible, ..*jay*. *Ibid.* §45/3 Small country town; 'hick' town,..*jay town*.
4. *Angling.* Name of a variety of artificial fly.
1867 F. FRANCIS *Angling* xi. (1880) 432 The Blue Jay..is the Blue Doctor dressed with jay.
5. *Coal-mining.* (See quot.)
1829 *Glover's Hist. Derby* I. 59 Strong jay or roof coal. *Ibid.* 60 Black jay, a sort of cannel coal.
6. *attrib.* and *Comb.*, as **jay-black, -like** adjs.; **jay-feather**, esp. in Sc. phrase ***to set up one's jay-feathers*** (see quot.); **jay pie, jay-piet**, (*a*) the jay; (*b*) locally, the Missel thrush; **jay-teal**, locally, the common teal. Also JAY-BIRD, etc.
1706 *Lond. Gaz.* No. 4236/8 Stolen..a black Mare, but not *Jay-black. **1825–80** JAMIESON s.v., She made sic a rampaging, that I was obliged to set up my *jay-feathers at her, *Roxb.* The expression contains a ludicrous allusion to the mighty airs of a jackdaw, when in a bad humour. **1880** DK. ARGYLL in *Fraser's Mag.* Jan. 49 The large Belted Kingfisher..was passing with a *Jay-like flight over the creeks..of the Hudson. **1880** *W. Cornwall Gloss.*, **Jay-pie*, a jay. **1885** SWAINSON *Prov. Names Birds* 2 Missel Thrush ..the harsh note it utters when alarmed has caused it to receive the names of..Jay (North of Ireland), Jay pie (Wilts). **1895** CROCKETT *Men Moss Hags* xxxix. 282 Yet I saw as it had been the waft of a *jaypiet's wing among them. **1885** SWAINSON *Prov. Names Birds* 158 Common Teal ..*Jay teal (Kirkcudbright).

'jay-bird. A jay: in some parts of England, the Common Jay; in N. Amer., the Blue Jay.
1661 *Early Rec. Dedham, Mass.* (1894) IV. 41 En Dani Fisher is creditor to the Towne for his sonne catching of Jaybirds. **1832** J. P. KENNEDY *Swallow Barn* II. iii. 55 A scream of jay-birds heard at intervals. **1851** MAYNE REID *Scalp Hunters* xxxii. 247, I could hear the shrill voices of the jay-birds. **1881** *Leicestersh. Gloss.*, *Jay-bird*, the jay. **1890** L.

C. D'Oyle *Notches* 81 The only signs of life were an occasional jay-bird, or an eagle. **1893** *Wiltsh. Gloss.*, *Joy-bird*, the Jay. **1896** J. C. Harris *Sister Jane* 84, I hear a flutter in the chaneyberry tree and look up and see a jaybird. **1972** D. Delman *Sudden Death* (1973) iii. 74 The corpus was naked as a jaybird.

Jaycee ('dʒeɪ'siː). orig. *U.S.* [f. J + C, initial letters of *junior chamber*.] A colloquial name for a member of a junior chamber of commerce. Also **Jaycee-ette, Jaycette**, a female member of such an organization. Also *attrib.*

1946 in *Amer. Speech* XXI. 295. **1952** *Ibid.* XXVII. 75 *Jaycee-ettes* are the wives of Jaycees—members of the United States Junior Chamber of Commerce. **1969** *Sun-Herald* (Sydney) 13 July 77/1 Blue and white—Jaycee colours—was the theme for decorations at Menzies Sydney Hotel when the Combined Sydney Metropolitan Jaycees held their 2nd annual ball last night. **1971** *Illustr. Weekly India* 25 Apr. 20/3 Through his association with the Jaycees he met Paru, a fellow-Jaycee, whom he married. **1972** *Malay Mail* 25 May 2/3 (*headline*) Four Malaysian Jaycees for Asian youth voyage. **1973** *Sunday Advocate-News* (Barbados) 25 Feb. 14/1 Mrs. Hazel Ann Edwards..[was] named the 1972 Jaycette of the Year... Mrs. Edwards.. received her award at the annual Jaycees of Barbados Awards dinner. **1974** *Ibid.* 3 Mar. 5/7 Yesterday Mr. Mann toured projects of the Jaycees and met members of the State Board, Bridgetown Jaycees and Jaycettes at Viamede.

jay-hawk, *v.* *U.S.* [A back-formation from next.] *trans.* To harry as a jay-hawker; to 'raid'.

1866 *Standard* 27 Oct. 3/2 A war of neighbourhoods..of lynchings and jay-hawkings, of rapine and outrage without parallel. **1893** *Scribner's Mag.* XIII. 381/2 Every man suddenly discovering that somebody has jayhawked his boots or his blanket.

'jay-ˌhawker. *U.S.* A name given to members of the bands who carried on irregular warfare in and around eastern Kansas, in the free soil conflict, and the early part of the American civil war, and who combined pillage with guerilla fighting: hence, generally, a raiding guerilla or irregular soldier.

1865 *Pall Mall G.* No. 143. 5/1 Jay-hawkers, cut-throats, and thieves. **1867** A. D. Richardson *Beyond the Mississippi* x. 125 Found all the settlers justifying the 'Jay-hawkers', a name universally applied to Montgomery's men, from the celerity of their movements and their habit of suddenly pouncing upon an enemy. **1888** *St. Louis Globe Democrat* 20 Jan. (Farmer *Americanisms*), He was connected with what is known as the Jayhawker war that raged on the borders of Kansas about twenty-five years since. **1900** R. Kipling in *Times* 15 Mar. 8/1 Suppose that you who read these lines had been out with Rimington's jay-hawkers or somebody else's fly-by-nights, riding hard and sleeping light for weeks.

jayl(e, jayler, etc., obs. forms of jail, etc.

†**Jayne**, variant of Geane *Obs.*, Genoa.

1488 *Naval Accts. Hen. VII* (1896) 79 Hausers of Jayne.. vij.

jay-walker ('dʒeɪwɔːkə(r)). orig. *U.S.* [f. jay 3 d + walker *sb.*[1]] A pedestrian who crosses a street without regard to traffic regulations. Hence **'jay-walk** *v. intr.*; **'jay-walking** *vbl. sb.*

1917 *Harper's Mag.* June 70/2 The Bostonian..has reduced 'a pedestrian who crosses streets in disregard of traffic signals' to the compact *jaywalker*. **1919** S. Lewis *Free Air* 257 He had..been cursed by a policeman for jaywalking. **1933** *Bulletin* (Sydney) 1 Nov. 23/4 His car brushed plaintiff, who was jay-walking. **1937** *Times* 25 Jan. 8/2 In many streets like Oxford Street, for instance, the jaywalker wanders complacently in the very middle of the roadway as if it was a country lane. **1957** C. Brooke-Rose *Lang. of Love* 15 She jay-walked through the traffic-jam of St. Giles, vaguely hoping to be run over. **1970** P. Laurie *Scotland Yard* v. 123 A quarter of all London's accidents involve pedestrians—we have no effective jay-walking law. **1972** *Police Rev.* 24 Nov. 1528/3 Realising his mistake, [he] pulls back quickly, narrowly missing the jay-walker. **1973** *Scotsman* 7 Aug. 8/3 Although there are penalties for jay-walking they do not seem to be much needed. Indeed a friend of mine from another part of Canada once jay-walked in the city I refer to and said that she would never do so again because she had been so embarrassed when all the traffic stopped for her.

jazerant, jesserant ('dʒæzərənt, 'dʒɛs-). Now only *Hist.* Forms: α. 5 **iessera(u)nt(e, -and, -ance, iestraunt**, 5–6 **iestern(e**, 8 **jazerent**, 9 **-an, -ant.** β. 5 **gessera(u)nt(e, -an, -en, (geseran)**, 6 **gesseron**; see also gesteron. [a. OF. *jaseran, -ant, jaz-, jac-, jesseran, jasiran*, in Roland (11th c.) *jazerene* = Pr. *jazeran*, Pg. *jazerão*; in Sp. *jacerina*, Pg. *jazerina*, It. *ghiazzerino*; orig. an adj., in OF. *osberc jazerenc, hauberc jazerant*, in Sp. *cota jacerina*. Generally agreed to be of Saracen origin, and according to Diez prob. identical with Sp. *jazarino* Algerian, f. Arab. (*al-*) *jazīrah* 'the island', in pl. *Al-jazā ir*, Algiers, in the old Arabic writers *Jazīrah beni Mazighanan*.]

'A light coat of armour composed of splints or small plates of metal rivetted to each other or to a lining of some stout material' (Fairholt).

α. ?*a* **1400** *Morte Arth.* 4238 Thorowe jopowne and jesserawnte of gentille mailes. *a* **1400–50** *Alexander* 2450 (Ashm.) Ȝarkid to þe ȝatis & ȝode to þe wallis, Sum in Iopons, sum in Iesserantis [*Dublin MS.* Iesserauntez] sum Ioyned all in platis. **1466** *Mann. & Househ. Exp.* (Roxb.) 353 He schal make my mastyr a jestrawnt. **1470–85** Malory *Arthur* xiii. vi, Thenne syr Galahalt..dyd vpon hym a noble Iesseraunce. **1577** Holinshed *Chron. Scot.* 32 Armed in iacks and light iesternes. **1795** Southey *Joan of Arc* vii. 184 At all points arm'd A jazerent of double mail he wore. **1823** Scott *Quentin D.* ii, Underneath his plain habit, the Scotsman observed that he concealed a *jazeran*, or flexible shirt of linked mail. **1834** Planché *Brit. Costume* 194 The jazerant or jazerine jacket was frequently worn in lieu of the breast and back plates. This defence was composed of small overlapping plates of iron covered with velvet, the gilt studs that secured them forming the exterior ornament.

β. ?*a* **1400** *Morte Arth.* 2909 Thorowe gesserawntes of Iene jaggede to the herte. **1422** *Will of Salwayn* (Somerset Ho.), A Habirgon of gesseran. **1423** Jas. I *Kingis Q.* cliii, Lytill fischis..That In the sonne on thaire scalis bryght As gesserant, ay glitterit In my sight. **1465** *Paston Lett.* II. 214 Your gesseren and gaunteletts shall be send hom by the next caryours. **1530** Elyot *Gov.* i. xvii, Armed as he was in a gesseron.

†**'jazul, -al, -el.** [A corruption of Sp. *azul* blue.] Lapis lazuli; = azure 1.

1616 Bullokar, *Iazul*, a precious stone of a blew, azure colour. **1678** Phillips (ed. 4), *Jazul* [*edd.* **1696, 1706** jazal]. **1727** Bailey, *Jazal.* **1818** Todd, *Jazel.*

jazy, variant of jasey, a wig.

jazz (dʒæz), *sb.* orig. *U.S. slang.* Also †**jas, jascz, jass, jasz, jaz.** [Origin unknown: see quots. for some of the many suggested derivations. Cf. jazzbo.] **1.** A kind of ragtime dance (see quot. 1919[2]); hence, the kind of music to which this is danced; (the usual sense) a type of music originating among American Negroes, characterized by its use of improvisation, syncopated phrasing, a regular or forceful rhythm, often in common time, and a 'swinging' quality (see quots.); loosely, syncopated dance-music.

Connection with Amer. Eng. *jasm* 'energy, enthusiasm' (see Mathews *Dict. Amer.* s.v.) cannot be demonstrated.

1909 C. Stewart *Uncle Josh in Society* (*gramophone-record*), One lady asked me if I danced the jazz. **1913** *Bulletin* (San Francisco) 6 Mar. 16 The team which speeded into town this morning comes pretty close to representing the pick of the army. Its members have trained on ragtime and 'jazz'. **1917** *Sun* (N.Y.) 5 Aug. iii. 3/6 Variously spelled Jas, Jass, Jaz, Jazz, Jasz and Jascz. The word is African in origin. It is common on the Gold Coast of Africa and in the hinterland of Cape Coast Castle. *Ibid.* 3/7 Jazz is based on the savage musician's wonderful gift for progressive retarding and acceleration guided by his sense of 'swing'. **1918** *Era* 11 Sept. 21 John Lester's Frisco Five. The Jollities of 'Jazz'. **1919** *Punch* 12 Mar. 193/1 'Whitehall,' says a society organ, 'has succumbed to the Jazz, the Fox-trot and the Bunny-hug.' **1919** 'Monsieur Pierre' *How to Jazz* 7 The Jazz is a three-step dance done to four-beat time. The three steps fall on the first three beats of the bar, the third being prolonged to last two beats, namely, the third and fourth. There are three distinct movements, which may be described as the Straight Jazz, the Side Jazz and the Jazz-Roll. **1920** V. Lindsay *Daniel Jazz* 1 Daniel was the chief hired man of the land. He stirred up the jazz in the palace band. **1921** W. Le Queux *Secret Telephone* 48, I was thoroughly enjoying a delightful jazz with the child. **1922** C. Engel *Discords Mingled* (1931) 147 Jazz is rag-time, *plus* 'blues', *plus* orchestral polyphony; it is the combination, in the popular music current, of melody, rhythm, harmony, and counterpoint. **1925** *Amer. Mercury* Sept. 7 According to tradition, jazz has taken its name from Jasbo Brown, an itinerant Negro player along the Mississippi, and later, in Chicago cabarets. **1927** [see Beethovenized *ppl. a.*]. **1928** Galsworthy *Swan Song* i. iv. 26 'The faster you can move your legs, the more you think you're dancing.'..'You don't like jazz?' queried the young lady. 'I do not,' said Soames. **1930** Auden *Poems* 41 In a hot room with the sagging melody of jazz. **1933** *Fortune* Aug. 47/2 Their use of 'jazz' includes both Duke Ellington's Afric brass and Rudy Vallée crooning *I'm a Dreamer, Aren't We All?* **1934** S. R. Nelson *All about Jazz* i. 23 It has been suggested that jas, jass, jaz, jazz, jasz, or jascz were originally part of the patois of the Negro in his native Africa. **1937** *Amer. Speech* XII. 180 Mr. Preston Jackson, negro trombonist of note, says that the 'Creole Jazz Band' was in New Orleans in 1911. Almost as early as that was the 'Original Dixieland Jass Band' which was the first of the lot to have the name printed on a phonograph record, 1917... The word 'Jass' was a verb of the negro patois meaning 'to excite' with an erotic and rhythmic connotation. Later becoming pronounced 'Jazz', it was used attributively to describe bands which by the intensity of their rhythm produced excitement. **1950** *N.Y. Times* 30 June 21 Dr. Bender..was stumped by the word 'jazz'. In..three years..he..tracked it to the West Coast of Africa, the contact point for the slave trade with colonial America. He said that the word meant 'hurry up' in the native tongue, and was first applied in the Creole dialect to mean 'speed up' in the syncopated music in New Orleans. **1952** B. Ulanov *Hist. Jazz in Amer.* viii. 82 When ..[Brown's] band came to Chicago, directly from New Orleans, the word 'jass' had a semi-sordid sexual connotation. Chicago Musicians Union officials..thought that labeling this group a jass or jazz band would be a very successful smear. But..the term caught on, and Brown's Dixieland Band became Brown's Dixieland Jass Band. **1955** L. Feather *Encycl. Jazz* 50 Improvisation has always been the life blood of jazz. There are critics today who still claim that true jazz cannot be written down. This is not literally true, but it is true that orchestrated jazz, if it is to remain jazz, must retain the same rhythmic feeling, the same concept of phrasing, that is inherent in improvised jazz... Just as the three basic elements of music as a whole are melody, harmony and rhythm, the three additional elements essential to jazz may be said to be syncopation, improvisation and inspiration. **1955** J. Jones in Shapiro & Hentoff *Hear Me Talkin' to Ya* 358 What is jazz? The closest thing I can get to saying what jazz is, is when you play what you feel. All jazz musicians express themselves through their instruments and they express the types of person they are, the experiences they've had during the day, during the night before, during their lives. D. Brubeck *Ibid.* 361 When there is not complete freedom of the soloist, it ceases to be jazz... If it's spontaneous, it's going to be rough, not clean, but it's going to have the spirit which is the essence of jazz. **1956** M. Stearns *Story of Jazz* (1957) xxii. 282 We may define jazz tentatively as a semi-improvisational American music distinguished by an immediacy of communication, an expressiveness characteristic of the free use of the human voice, and a complex flowing rhythm; it is the result of a three-hundred-years' blending in the United States of the European and West African musical traditions. **1968** A. Dankworth *Jazz* 1 Most jazz is in the form of melodic or rhythmic variations upon a theme. The theme is usually a twelve-bar blues melody, the chorus of a popular dance-tune, or a specially composed theme. **1970** *Melody Maker* 12 Sept. 35/1 The essential motive of all jazz, at least through the end of the 1950s, was to relate to the audience through a steadily pulsing improvisational concept—in other words, to swing. Today we find young jazzmen effecting radical alterations in this objective. Much of the jazz presented by today's innovators avoids the free-flowing 4/4 or 3/4 essence in favour of a beat that is often heavier though not necessarily cruder.

†**b.** A piece of jazz music. *U.S. Obs.*

1920 *Harvey's Weekly* 24 July 14/2 That isn't a keynote; it's a jazz. **1921** *Ladies' Home Jrnl.* Jan. 50 All the latest popular hits..all this season's jolliest jazzes.

c. *spec.* A passage of improvised music in a jazz performance.

1926 [see break *sb.*[1] 9 c].

2. *transf.* Energy, excitement, 'pep'; restlessness, excitability.

1913 *Bulletin* (San Francisco) 6 Mar. 16 What is the 'jazz'? Why it's a little of that 'old life', the 'gin-i-ker', the 'pep', otherwise known as the enthusiasalum. **1922** *Dialect Notes* V. 142 *Jazz*,..animation, animal good spirits. 'She's just full of jazz.' **1923** L. J. Vance *Baroque* vi. 34 Only about enough heroin to give every man, woman and child in N'York the jazz for a week. **1924** Galsworthy *White Monkey* ii. iii. 145 With all the jazz there is about, she'd appreciate somebody restful. **1928** 'J. Sutherland' *Knot* xii. 163 'What is really the matter?' she asked. 'You look extraordinarily queer, and you ought to be full of jazz.'

3. Meaningless or empty talk, nonsense, rot, 'rubbish'; unnecessary ornamentation; anything unpleasant or disagreeable.

1918 *Dialect Notes* V. 25 *Jazz*, talk; 'gas'. College students. **1930** E. Pound *XXX Cantos* vii. 27 'Toc' sphinxes, sham-Memphis columns, And beneath the jazz a cortex, a stiffness or stillness, Shell of the older house. **1936** *Harper's Mag.* Apr. 567 The word jazz has been used to describe every disagreeable phenomenon since the year 1916, when it came into common use. **1944** *Metronome* Apr. 22 Some of them [*sc.* swing musicians] use the noun 'jazz' to denote corn, especially those who are opposed to the Dixieland type of music and sum it up derogatorily with the word 'jazz'. **1953** D. Wallop *Night Light* iii. 153 What do you call that jazz, alpaca or something? **1958** 'E. McBain' *Killer's Choice* (1960) iii. 31 'How was school today, darling?' 'Oh, the same old jazz,' Monica said. **1962** M. Barrett *Return of Cornish Sailor* x. 129 All this jazz about your poppa and..his old ship, all that stuff. **1969** C. F. Burke *God is Beautiful, Man* (1970) 20, I asked one of the young men if he understood what had been read from the Bible. His response was that he 'didn't get that jazz'. **1971** B. Malamud *Tenants* 165, I read all about that formalism jazz in the library and it's bullshit.

b. Colloq. phr. ***and all that jazz***: and all that sort of thing; et cetera.

1959 F. Astaire *Steps in Time* (1960) i. 3 But it's nice to hear, 'How does the old boy do it...why isn't he falling apart?' And all that jazz. **1960** *Punch* 9 Mar. 345/1 Politics, world affairs, film stars' babies and all that jazz, the things that the adult world seems obsessed with, do not interest us at all. **1968** B. Turner *Sex Trap* ix. 69 Always been a good girl and all that jazz, but a bit stage-struck. **1972** J. Porter *Meddler & her Murder* x. 132 Come to identify the body.. and all that jazz.

4. *slang.* Sexual intercourse. Cf. jazzing *vbl. sb.* 2.

[**1924** *Étude* Sept. 595/3 If the truth were known about the origin of the word 'Jazz' it would never be mentioned in polite society... The vulgar word 'Jazz' was in general currency in those dance halls thirty years or more ago.] **1927** *Jrnl. Abnormal & Social Psychol.* XXII. i. 14 The word *jazz*... Used both as a verb and as a noun to denote the sex act,..has long been common vulgarity among Negroes in the South, and it is very likely from this usage that the term 'jazz music' was derived. **1950** A. Lomax *Mister Jelly Roll* (1952) 47 Winding Boy is a bit on the vulgar side. Let's see —how could I put it—means a fellow that makes good jazz with the women.

5. *attrib.* and *Comb.*, as ***jazz ballet, band, banjo, club, cult, dance, -dancing, drum, -drummer, -drumming, fan, festival, joint, king, -land, -lover, music, musician, opera, orchestra, -player, queen, record, scene, -singer, song, tune***; ***jazz-conscious, mad*** adjs.; ***jazz-loving, -minded, -oriented, -struck, -tinged*** ppl. adjs.; **jazz age** (freq. with capital initials), the era of jazz; *spec.* (see quot. 1959); **jazz baby**, a girl who is interested in jazz; a flapper; **jazz poem**, a poem that is read aloud to the accompaniment of jazz; so ***jazz poetry***; **jazz-rock**, music that has the characteristics of both jazz and 'rock' music. Also jazzman.

1922 F. Scott Fitzgerald (*title*) Tales of the jazz age. **1926** Whiteman & McBride *Jazz* vii. 137 The jazz age has been the subject of profound and careful condemnation. **1959** T. Griffith *Waist-High Culture* (1960) iii. 31 In the years between the Armistice and the stock-market crash, came the period we used to call..the Jazz Age. **1920** F.

Scott Fitzgerald in *Metropolitan* Oct. 65/2 Evylyn and Ben followed singing a drowsy song about a Jazz baby. **1964** M. McLuhan *Understanding Media* (1967) ii. xxxi. 348 Baseball.. will always remain a symbol of the era of the hot mommas, jazz babies.. and the fast buck. **1961** Webster, Jazz ballet. **1972** *Times* 16 May 14/8 We have a jazz ballet by a Canadian choreographer, set to music that uses a string quartet and a rock quartet. **1916** *Ragtime Rev.* Oct. 6/3 The 'Jaz' bands that are so popular at the present time. **1916** *Variety* 27 Oct. 12/4 The Jazz Band is composed of three or more instruments and seldom plays regulated music. **1917** *Era* 20 Aug. 20 Holborn Empire... Frank Powell and The Magleys and the Jazz Band. **1919**, etc. [see Dixie[2] 1 c]. **1956** M. Stearns *Story of Jazz* (1957) vii. 71 The 101 Ranch, a cabaret which employed many jazz-bands, was particularly famous. **1923** Jazz banjo [see banjolin]. **1917** *Spiker* 25 Dec. 10/3 H. Williams, Rickard, Putney, Short, Hermann and Duncan were the Jazz Club entertainment committee. **1958** *New Statesman* 25 Jan. 102/3 Our native music.. still flourishes nightly in the jazz-clubs, though best in those where musicians.. like to drop in for a little drinking, gossiping, watching the dancers.. and perhaps sitting in with the band. **1968** A. Diment *Great Spy Race* vii. 114 Past the pub with built-in Jazz Club. **1956** M. Stearns *Story of Jazz* (1957) xxiii. 286 With the arrival of jazz-conscious American troops, the murmur of interest grew to a rhythmic roar. **1933** *Fortune* Aug. 47/3 The jazz cult is apathetic to nine-tenths of modern dance music. **1919** *Punch* 30 Apr. 333/3 An early bather was seen executing the Jazz-dance on the beach at Ventnor on Easter Monday. **1963** *Spectator* 27 Dec. 852/1 In America the jazz-dance.. has a validity as.. a pop-art expression of one side of the national culture. *Ibid.*, The so-called jazz-dancing which has insidiously crept into our ballet repertory. **1919** *Observer* 16 Mar. 14/4 There has been a good deal of curiosity concerning the origin of the term 'Jazz'. Authorities on Jazz dancing say it is a word used by niggers to denote a scramble. **1922** *Encycl. Brit.* XXX. 796/1 The music.. consists of various combinations, the most common of which perhaps is:—piano, violin, alto or tenor saxophone, banjo and jazz-drum. **1925** *Chambers's Encycl.* VI. 302/2 The jazz-drummer, a sort of one-man band, provides the characteristic feature of jazz, which is noise. **1930** *Melody Maker* Feb. 123/2 Murray Pilcer—Britain's first 'jazz' drummer and still going strong. **1956** B. Edwards in S. Traill *Play that Music* vi. 59 There have been five major stages in jazz-drumming during the last three and a half decades. **1958** D. Halperin in P. Gammond *Decca Bk. Jazz* xx. 241 Calling the young man.. a jazz-fan would be off-centre: he is, rather, a jazz convert. **1961** *Observer* 16 July 5/5 He caught on, first with his fellow college intellectuals and jazz fans (whom he still calls 'my people') and then with a wider audience. **1959** 'F. Newton' *Jazz Scene* xi. 184 'Jazz festivals'—in Newport, Conn., in Nice, Cannes, San Remo and other European holiday resorts. **1970** *New Statesman* 9 Oct. 454/3 The crowd was very similar.. to the audience that came to the Beaulieu jazz festivals. **1942** Berrey & Van den Bark *Amer. Thes. Slang* §366/4 Dance hall,.. *jazz joint*. *Ibid.* §576/27 *Jazz King*, Paul Whiteman, jazz orchestra leader. **1920** *Quill* Sept. 6 They're the best jazz kings in the jazzy world. **1958** *Daily Herald* 24 Mar. 2/4 Gladys Hampton, wife of jazz-king Lionel, arrived in London yesterday. **1942** Berrey & Van den Bark *Amer. Thes. Slang* §578/2 *Jazzland*, the world of jazz. **1947** *Penguin Music Mag.* May 30 'You can't make a gentleman out of jazz'—a perfectly true statement, and one which all jazz-lovers will applaud. **1974** *Guardian* 22 Mar. 14/6 The European jazz lover can go to Harlem or New Orleans. **1956** M. Stearns *Story of Jazz* (1957) xvii. 201 Jazz-loving record buyers wore out the grooves. **1924** 'J. Sutherland' *Circle of Stars* xxvi. 273 Far more dangerous to a silly, headstrong child than the jazz-mad boys she chose as habitual companions. **1955** L. Feather *Encycl. Jazz* vii. 141 A style that was found palatable by many non-jazz-minded people. **1917** *Sun* (N.Y.) 5 Aug. iii. 3/7 Jazz music is the delirium tremens of syncopation. **1922** W. J. Locke *Tale of Triona* v. 51 The crash of jazz music welcomed them. **1941** B. Schulberg *What makes Sammy Run?* iii. 46 It made me realize again how true jazz music was, how it echoed everything that was churning inside us. **1973** *Listener* 19 Apr. 522/2 The excitement in jazz music is usually concerned with nerve. **1917** *Sun* (N.Y.) 5 Aug. iii. 3/7 The jazz musicians and their auditors have the most rhythmic aggressiveness. **1969** Jazz musician [see bit *sb.*[2] 4 i]. **1924** *N.Y. Times* 18 Nov. 23/1 Irving Berlin, Jerome Kern and George Gershwin might submit.. a jazz opera to.. the Metropolitan Opera House. **1970** *New Yorker* 29 Aug. 22/2 Recently, I [*sc.* Rolf Liebermann] commissioned a jazz opera, because I think that is a way to make contact with.. young people. **1916** *Variety* 27 Oct. 12/4 The low cost makes it possible for all the smaller places to carry their Jazz orchestra. **1925** *Scribner's Mag.* July 45/1 The faint echo of a jazz orchestra in the background. **1955** Keepnews & Grauer *Pict. Hist. Jazz* xv. 155/2 The personnel were primarily jazz-oriented musicians. **1918** *Quill* June 31 (Advt.), Music and Entertainment by the original Jackson Jazz Players. **1958** *New Statesman* 25 Jan. 102/3 Jazz-players and promoters.. are so much more difficult to handle than the good old-fashioned pit and palais musicians. **1960** *Guardian* 21 Nov. 7/7 A 'jazz poem' read at a recital of modern poetry and jazz. **1959** *Listener* 26 Mar. 567/3 In the current craze for jazz poetry a mistaken attempt is made to bend the verse to the last of the music. **1922** *Canad. Mag.* June 96 What will they make of a literature which is garnished with references to 'snuggle puppers' and 'jazz queens' and 'flappers' and 'face dancers'? **1923** H. Crane *Let.* 5 Dec. (1965) 159 We had a Victrola... Lots of jazz records, etc. **1970** *Americana Ann.* 578 The year [*sc.* 1969] was flooded with such new combinations as jazz-rock, folk-rock, and country-rock. **1974** *Down Beat* 18 July 26/3 Here are two exploratory jazz-rock albums. **1959** 'F. Newton' (*title*) The jazz scene. **1969** Jazz scene [see bit *sb.*[2] 4 i]. **1927** (*film-title*) The jazz singer. **1929** A. Huxley *Do what you Will* 57 He is employed as a jazz-singer on the music-hall stage. **1923** H. Crane *Let.* 9 May (1965) 133 Marvelous jazz songs, jokes, etc. **1947** R. de Toledano *Frontiers of Jazz* vii. 82 The jazz-struck kids who are today the core of the non-commercial white bands. **1955** L. Feather *Encycl. Jazz* vii. 227 A honey-toned, jazz-tinged, original song stylist. **1918** F. Hunt *Blown in by Draft* vi. 144 This, he felt deep in his heart, might be a fighting army, but it was a jazz tune army. **1926** [see classic *sb.* 1 c].

6. *attrib.*, passing into *adj.* Of grotesque or fantastic design, marked by vivid or riotous colouring; also, lively, sophisticated, unconventional.

1919 *Punch* 7 May 357 Jazz stockings are the latest thing. **1919** *Current Opinion* Aug. 98/3 Boston is only slightly Jazz. **1922** *Glasgow Herald* 14 Dec. 5 He has some justification for using this jazz language. **1923** *Daily Mail* 5 May 8 Jazz patterns in dress. **1927** R. H. Wilenski *Mod. Movement in Art* iii. 165 The 'jazz' curtains and sunshades.. and the prevalence of bright tints in the theatre. **1928** E. Weekley *Eng. Lang.* 76 The rather jazz-patterned idiom which is now spoken. **1930** J. Collier *His Monkey Wife* xiv. 198 Drawing a jazz silk dressing-gown about her shoulders, she went to the bathroom. **1938** S. M. Bessie (*title*) Jazz journalism: the story of the tabloid newspapers. **1957** H. Croome *Forgotten Place* 15 A jazz-patterned carpet on the floor.

jazz (dʒæz), *v.* orig. *U.S. slang.* [Cf. prec.]

1. *trans.* To speed or liven *up*; to render more colourful, 'modern', or sensational; to excite.

1917 *Sun* (N.Y.) 5 Aug. iii. 3/6 In the old plantation days when the slaves were having one of their rare holidays and the fun languished some West Coast African would cry out, 'Jaz her up', and this would be the cue for fast and furious fun... Curiously enough the phrase 'Jaz her up' is a common one to-day in vaudeville and on the circus lot. **1919** *Amer. Mag.* Nov. 69/1 For ways that is dark and tricks which is vain, the daughters of Eve is peculiar, to jazz up a line of Bret Harte's. **1923** *Daily Mail* 27 Mar. 8 My colour scheme is rather fetching, don't you think? X—a famous artist—jazzed it up for me. **1923** Wodehouse *Inimitable Jeeves* xv. 195 It's rather too late to alter the thing [*sc.* a little fairy play] entirely, but at least I can jazz it up. **1926** [see gas *sb.*[2]]. **1959** *Times Lit. Suppl.* 2 Oct. 557/3 The 'honesty' and the depth of the rejection here carry no conviction and the attempt to jazz it up leads Mr. Sillitoe where we would expect it to lead him—to bluster and sentimentality. **1967** *Surfabout* IV. iii. 33/2, I could hardly sleep at all; man, I was jazzed just listening to the hissing swells as they smoothly broke through the night. **1974** *Guardian* 13 June 10/5 He.. jazzes the mixture up with a series of film-makers' cliches that one can only describe as stylised film school.

b. To play (music, or an instrument) in the style of jazz. Freq. const. *up*.

1919 E. Scott *All about Latest Dances* 76 The nigger bands at home 'jazz' a tune; that is to say, they slur the notes, they syncopate, and each instrument puts in a lot of little fancy bits on its own. **1922** C. Sandburg *Slabs of Sunburnt West* 6 Listen while they jazz the classics. **1934** *Hound & Horn* VII. 599 The saxophone.. can be as 'hot' as the clarinet when it is 'jazzed up'. **1934** C. Lambert *Music Ho!* ii. 74 A Frenchman or an Italian might have felt some embarrassment about jazzing up the classics. **1965** *Listener* 20 May 738/2 He had jazzed up Weill's music in the modern American manner.

2. *intr.* To play jazz; to dance to jazz music. Hence *transf.*, to move in a grotesque or fantastic manner; to behave wildly (see also quot. 1918[2]).

1918 F. Hunt *Blown in by Draft* vi. 143 Ole Hen Sauser.. started, walking up and down the black and white ivories until he had the brown box rocking and swaying and jazzing like eight electric pianos. **1918** *Dialect Notes* V. 25 *To jazz.* 1. To talk to kill time. 2. To walk about to kill time. Rare. 'I *jazzed* around all forenoon.' **1919** E. Scott *All about Latest Dances* 80 When the band is 'jazzing' along. **1919** *Punch* 23 Apr. 318/1 She did not ask whether I could jazz, mainly, I think, because I had already danced with her. **1922** *Dialect Notes* V. 142 You mustn't expect to pass your quizzes if you keep jazzing around like this. **1923** *Daily Mail* 18 Apr. 8 There are a good many present-day books that just give the reader a view of the protagonists jazzing across the pages in a vivid pattern of action, passion or crime. **1934** S. Spender *Vienna* ii. 23 Where radio crazily jazzes. **1966** 'J. Hackston' *Father clears Out* 19 Chester.. waltzed, jazzed, did Catherine wheels, [etc.].

3. *trans.* and *intr.* To have sexual intercourse (with). *slang.*

1927 [see jazz *sb.* 4]. **1929** T. Wolfe *Look Homeward, Angel* (1930) ii. xiv. 176 Jazz 'em all you like,.. but get the money. **1930** J. T. Farrell in *This Quarter* July–Sept. 193 'She's cute. I jazzed her too,' O'Keefe said. **1931** G. Irwin *Amer. Tramp & Underworld Slang* 109 *Jazz*,.. to have intercourse. **1948** H. MacLennan *Precipice* (1949) i. 81 My sister was being jazzed by half the neighbourhood cats by the time she was fifteen. **1968** B. Foster *Changing Eng. Lang.* ii. 114 The original verb 'jazz' denoting the human male's most important generic activity (itself probably an African word).

jazzbo ('dʒæzbəʊ). *U.S. slang.* Also jasbo, jazz-bo. [Origin unknown; perh. a corruption of the name *Jasper*; cf. jazz *sb.*] (See quots.)

1917 *Sun* (N.Y.) 5 Aug. iii. 3/7 'Jasbo' is a form of the word [*sc.* jazz] common in the varieties, meaning the same as 'hokum', or low comedy verging on vulgarity. **1919** *Quill* June 9 Have you heard Jazzbo the chocolate syncopated Hobohemian at the Moulin Rouge Cave? **1923** H. C. Witwer *Fighting Blood* ix. 272, I merely commence to stutter an apology, when the old jazzbo [= fellow] shuts me off kind of angrily. **1923** *N.Y. Times* 9 Sept. vii. 2/1 *Jazzbo*, bladder and slapstick comedy. **1926** Whiteman & McBride *Jazz* v. 122 Sousa.. says jazz slid into our vocabulary by way of the vaudeville stage, where at the end of a performance, all the acts came back on the stage to give a rousing, boisterous *finale* called a 'jazzbo'. **1942** Berrey & Van den Bark *Amer. Thes. Slang* §438/1 Dissolute person,.. *jazz-bo*. *Ibid.* §583/18 *Jazz-bo*, *jazzbo*, a negro performer, esp. in a minstrel show. *Ibid.* §868/3 *Jazzbo*, a colored American soldier. **1944** [see jigaboo]. **1957** J. Kerouac *On Road* (1958) ii. i. 113 He dodged a mule wagon; in it sat an old Negro plodding along... He slowed down the car for all of us to turn and look at the old jazzbo moaning along.

jazzed (dʒæzd), *ppl. a.* [f. jazz *v.* + -ed[1].] Played in the style of jazz; hence, enlivened; made more colourful, 'modern', or sensational. Freq. with *up*.

1919 E. Scott *All about Latest Dances* 75 Certain steps and movements already in practice may be more or less adaptable to 'jazzed' music. **1926** *Bulletin* 9 June 5 Some of our own jazzed thoroughfares. **1929** *Musical Times* Feb. 129 The music is jazzed-up, restless stuff. **1958** E. Borneman in P. Gammond *Decca Bk. Jazz* xxi. 270 The real Cuban rumba.. had next to nothing to do with the jazzed-up sones which had passed under the name 'rumba' in the U.S. **1969** *Listener* 16 Jan. 85/2 Denouncing his inaugural lecture at the University of Malaya (or rather, a tendentious and jazzed-up version of part of the lecture which had appeared in the local Singapore press). **1972** *Country Life* 7 Dec. 1587 (Advt.), Jazzed up drinks aren't quite our style.

jazzer ('dʒæzə(r)). orig. *U.S. slang.* [f. jazz *v.* + -er[1].] One who plays or dances to jazz; a jazz fan.

1919 *Current Opinion* Aug. 99/3 The 'klaxon' in particular.. as one of the Jazzers explains,.. reminds them that they have an automobile. **1922** *Public Opinion* 5 May 418/2 The son of an agricultural labourer has won the second prize as the best jazzer in the village. **1927** *Musical Times* Nov. 978 In the hands of jazzers, syncopation is a ruthless and mechanical defiance of strict time. **1928** A. Huxley *Point Counter Point* xxiii. 418 A real complete human being. Not a newspaper reader, not a jazzer, not a radio fan. **1935** *Punch* 22 May 620/2 D'ye think the earliest jazzer Who coined the ragtime strain Was the ill-starred Belshazzar, Or was it Tubal Cain? **1973** *Melody Maker* 31 Mar. 18 Most of the musical action for jazzers is, then, in the studios, away from the public gaze.

Jazzercise ('dʒæzəsaɪz). *U.S.* Also jazzercise. [Blend of jazz *sb.* and exercise *sb.*: cf. dancercise.] A proprietary name for a programme of physical exercises arranged to be carried out in a class to the accompaniment of jazz music; also, exercise of this kind.

1977 *Official Gaz.* (U.S. Patent Office) 13 Sept. TM107/1 Jazzercise. For educational services—namely, conducting a class in dance and exercise... First use Nov. 1, 1974. **1982** *Washington Post* 19 July B1/1 These memories of summer past made me think of one of my favorite meals,.. fasting, 'jazzercise' and yogurt. **1983** *N.Y. Post* 4 Oct. 20 Jazzercise.. a fun way to aid in elevating the heartrate to improve the cardiovascular system. **1984** *New Yorker* 27 Aug. 36/1 She wanted to know whether in the jazzercise routine done to the words 'I want a man with a slow hand' your hips bumped left or right on 'hand'.

jazzetry ('dʒæzətrɪ). [f. jazz *sb.* + po)etry.] The reading aloud of poetry accompanied by jazz; a recital of poetry accompanied by jazz.

1959 *Daily Mail* 17 Feb. 4 A hybrid art-form.. known variously as jazzetry, jazz-poetry readings or.. just J. & P. **1959** C. Logue in *Encounter* June 86 A jazzetry, using two narrative poems of mine and some short epigrammatic fables will have been given at the Royal Court. **1963** *Spectator* 26 July 113 A new art form had been developed called (by Lindsey Anderson) 'jazzetry' and consisting of poetry read to a jazz accompaniment.

jazzify ('dʒæzɪfaɪ), *v.* [f. jazz *sb.* + -ify.] *trans.* To render jazzy; = jazz *v.* 1 a and b. So **jazzifi'cation**; **'jazzified** *ppl. a.*

1922 [see *crazy flying* s.v. crazy *a.* 6]. **1927** *Daily Express* 9 Nov. 9 In 'Hit the Deck',.. British bluejackets kneel down, and, with arms uplifted to heaven, jazzify a negro spiritual. **1928** *Daily Tel.* 28 Feb. 15/1 We had already seen our musical taste jazzified, and our British standards of art and life were being jazzified by foreign films. **1958** E. Borneman in P. Gammond *Decca Bk. Jazz* xxi. 270 The mambo, of course, was part of the gradual 'jazzification' of Cuban folk-music that had begun with the so-called 'rumba'.

jazzily, jazziness: see jazzy *a.*

jazzing ('dʒæzɪŋ), *vbl. sb.* (and *ppl. a.*). orig. *U.S. slang.* [f. jazz *v.* + -ing[1], [2].] **1.** The playing of jazz music; jazz dancing. Also *attrib.* or as *ppl. adj.*

1918 *Red Cross Mag.* Oct. 53/1 When I was singing this, one poor fellow.. endeavored to keep time to my jazzing by wiggling his toes! **1919** *Lit. Digest* 26 Apr. 28/1 The negro loves anything that is peculiar in music, and this 'jazzing' appeals to him strongly. **1920** P. Gibbs *Realities of War* viii. v. 437 There was an epidemic of dancing, Jazzing, card-playing, theatre-going. **1920** *Glasgow Herald* 26 Feb. 9 This business woman of 1920 has nothing of the jazzing featherhead about her appearance. **1920** *Chambers's Jrnl.* 28 Aug. 617/1 Good jazzing partners were scarce. **1922** Chesterton *Ballad St. Barbara* 75 Of earth's other tributes are plenty to choose, Tobacco and petrol and Jazzing and Jews. **1928** D. L. Sayers *Unpleasantness at Bellona Club* vii. 80 They had a much better time than they have now, with all this jazzing and short skirts and pretending to have careers. **1938** *Life* 26 Dec. 52/2 Whiteman's new-fangled jazzing of the classics.

2. Sexual intercourse. *slang.*

1958 Murtagh & Harris *Cast First Stone* xiv. 205 She asked if I wanted to do a little jazzing... I said, 'How much?' 'Two dollars,' she said.

jazzist ('dʒæzɪst). orig. *U.S.* [f. jazz *sb.* + -ist.] = jazzer.

1926 Whiteman & McBride *Jazz* viii. 181 Jazzists chuckle over lowbrows who say they can't abide classical music and highbrows who squirm when they hear jazz. **1927** *Radio Times* 1 July 1/1 Whether the jazzist ever listens to oratorio with an appreciative ear is possibly a doubtful point. **1941** *New Yorker* 1 Mar. 44/2 Basie makes effective use of tone-shading, a technique which some of our noisier jazzists might do well to cultivate.

jazzman, jazz man ('dʒæzmæn). orig. *U.S.* [f. JAZZ *sb.* + MAN *sb.*¹] A man who plays jazz.

1926 *Amer. Mercury* Apr. 392/1 Alfredo Casella..bore public testimony in writing that the American jazz men have invented effects that he and his colleagues never dreamt of. **1935** *Vanity Fair* (N.Y.) Nov. 38/1 Our jazz-men have had no attention. **1939** W. HOBSON *Amer. Jazz Mus.* 30 Traditionalists accuse the jazz players..and the jazz men accuse the traditionalists. **1970** [see JAZZ *sb.* 1]. **1972** J. L. DILLARD *Black English* vi. 262 New Orleans jazzmen.

jazzophile ('dʒæzəʊfaɪl). *U.S.* [f. JAZZ *sb.* + -O + -PHIL, -PHILE.] A devotee of jazz.

1941 *Jazz Information* Nov. 24/2 Many hardshelled jazzophiles. **1959** *Look* 21 July 76/2 But 3,000 brave jazzophiles sat patiently through three hours of liquefied jazz.

jazzy ('dʒæzɪ), *a.* orig. *U.S.* [f. JAZZ *sb.* + -Y¹.] Pertaining to or resembling jazz; characterized by jazz; spirited, lively, exciting; vivid, gaudy. Hence in more pejorative senses: 'corny', false, phoney.

1919 *Quill* Apr. 8 Gil Boag promises the Jazziest dance of the season. **1920** *Collier's* 13 Mar. 57/2 Bergstrom's two-piece orchestra was in the throes of its jazziest fox-trot number. **1922** *Dialect Notes* V. 142 She's the jazziest girl in Pem East. **1924** GALSWORTHY *White Monkey* I. ix. 76 'Whom do you think to meet him, besides Alison?' 'Nothing jazzy.' *Ibid.* III. iii. 238, I should like to change my bedroom curtains to blue... The present curtains really are too jazzy. **1925** *Chambers's Jrnl.* 466/2 To sing some jazzy stuff called 'Alexander's Rag Time Band'. **1925** D. H. LAWRENCE *Refl. Death Porcupine* 82 Inside it, the worms will jig the same jazzy dances. **1928** 'J. SUTHERLAND' *Knot* xv. 204, I may be frivolous and modern and jazzy and all the things you clever people hate. **1934** [see CORNINESS]. **1937** *Amer. Speech* XII. 46/2 *Jazzy*, outmoded, showy, ostentatious style of playing. **1944** *Metronome* Apr. 22 Most musicians use the adjective 'jazzy' to denote 'corny'. **1957** *Sunday Mail* (Glasgow) 10 Feb. 11 Poor ole-fashioned jazz is almost a dirty word with the kids. So Jazzy means phoney or false. **1959** *Times Lit. Suppl.* 2 Oct. 556/3 The jazzy ebullience of the United States seems curiously out of date. **1961** C. MCCULLERS *Clock without Hands* vii. 149 Hard as it was for Jester to make up jazzy hurtful remarks, he was learning to do it. **1963** N. & J. KANTROWITZ in A. Dundes *Mother Wit* (1973) 351 *Jazzy motherfucker*..describes someone fluent, glib, animated. **1967** E. SHORT *Embroidery & Fabric Collage* ii. 54 Beach clothes can take bold areas of really 'jazzy' colours. **1967** *Melody Maker* 27 May 10/3 The material he works over on eleven tracks isn't the jazziest ever. **1971** *Homes & Gardens* Aug. 32 Jazzy colours are confined to the bathrooms and kitchen, where they make a vibrant contrast to the other rooms. **1973** B. BROADFOOT *Ten Lost Years* xxvii. 311 He bought a new car, the jazziest in Calgary.

Hence **'jazzily** *adv.*; **'jazziness.**

1921 J. C. LINCOLN *Galusha the Magnificent* xv. 253 They danced jazzily in the hotel parlor and on the porches. **1927** *Melody Maker* Sept. 847/2 Quite as full of jazziness of song and dance as it is now. **1928** *Ibid.* Feb. 183/2 The slow tempo and complete absence of 'jazziness' is the ideal treatment for a melody number. **1928** *Gramophone* VI. 300/1 With a musically artistic legato rhythmic swing and not 'jazzily'. **1951** *Archit. Rev.* CIX. 220/2 The freedom of handling, the faith in elementary cubic forms, the occasional jazziness of detail. **1959** *Encounter* Nov. 60/1 When the ballets met with resistance, it often hinged on this question of jazziness. **1968** D. E. ALLEN *Brit. Tastes* v. 126 These jazzily unnerving designs and patterns.

J-curve: see J-SHAPED *a.*

jeabard, obs. form of JEOPARD *v.*

†**'jealisom**, *a. dial. Obs.* [f. JEALOUS *a.* + -SOME.] Jealous; having jealousy.

1599 PEELE *Sir Clyom.* Wks. (Rtldg.) 518/1 They'll be so jealisom over them, that cham in doubt Ich shall not keep Jack my boy till seven years go about.

jealous ('dʒɛləs), *a.* Forms: α. 3-4 gelus(e, 4 -os, 4-5 -ows, 4-6 -ous(e, 5 -uce, 6 gealous. β. 4-5 ielus, 4-7 -ous(e, 6 -ose, (-oux); 6-7 iealous(e, 7- jealous. γ. 5 ielius, 6 -ious, -yus, -yous, 6-7 iealious. δ. 4-6 ialous(e, 6 -ouss. ε. 5-6 iolyce, -yous, -ious, -yus, ioyluse. [ME. *gelos*, etc., a. OF. *gelos* (12th c. in Hatz.-Darm.), mod.F. *jaloux, -ouse*, = Pr. *gelos*, It. *geloso*, Sp. *zeloso*:—late L. *zēlōs-us*, f. late L. *zēl-us* a. Gr. ζῆλος emulation, zeal, jealousy: see -OUS. The Romanic *j* or *ge* for Gr. ζ, shows the analysis of Gr. ζ as dz, dʒ, dj, di, evidenced in other words, in late L.]

†**1.** Vehement in feeling, as in wrath, desire, or devotion: **a.** Wrathful, furious (*rare*); **b.** Devoted, eager, zealous. *Obs.*

1382 WYCLIF *Deut.* xxix. 20 The woodnes of hym [the Lord] shal wax feers, and gelows aȝens that man. **1535** COVERDALE *Ecclus.* li. 18, I will be gelous to cleue vnto the thinge yᵗ is good. **1560** BIBLE (Genev.) *1 Kings* xix. 10, I haue bene very ielous for the Lord God of hoste. **1661** MARVELL *Corr.* Wks. 1872-5 II. 66 Mr. Recorder and Mr. Vaux, persons as jealous in your service as I myselfe.

†**2.** Ardently amorous; covetous of the love of another, fond, lustful. *Obs.* (But cf. 4.)

c **1430** *Syr Gener.* 1070 The Quene had a ful licorous eye And a hert ful amerous; On Generides she wax gelous. **1555** BRADFORD in Strype *Eccl. Mem.* (1721) III. App. xlv. 130, I sawe certayne letters sent from th' Emprour..wherin was contayned theise privities..the good simple Quene is so jelous over my sonne..we shall make her agree vnto all our requestes [etc.].

3. Zealous or solicitous for the preservation or well-being of something possessed or esteemed; vigilant or careful in guarding; suspiciously careful or watchful. Const. *of* (*for, over*).

1387-8 T. USK *Test. Love* III. v. (Skeat) l. 38 Some maner of ielousy, I wot wel is euer redy in al the hertes of my trew seruauntes, as thus: to be ielous ouer him self, lest he be cause of his owne disease. **1526** TINDALE *2 Cor.* xi. 2, I am gelous over you with godly gelousy. **1555** POLE in Ellis *Orig. Lett.* Ser. I. II. 192 Myn helth..wherof I am the more jelose now then I am commonly at other tymes. **1665** BOYLE *Occas. Refl.* II. xiv. (1848) 142, I am..brought..to set a high Value upon Health, and be a very Jealous Preserver of so great a Blessing. **1738** WESLEY *Ps.* XIII. vii, Be jealous for thy glorious Name. **1828** SCOTT *F.M. Perth* xxvii, The chief is young, and jealous of his rank. **1888** BRYCE *Amer. Commw.* I. xxv. 378 The people, jealous of their hardly-won liberties.

4. Troubled by the belief, suspicion, or fear that the good which one desires to gain or keep for oneself has been or may be diverted to another; resentful towards another on account of known or suspected rivalry: **a.** in love or affection, esp. in sexual love: Apprehensive of being displaced in the love or good-will of some one; distrustful of the faithfulness of wife, husband, or lover. Const. *of*, arch. *over* (the beloved person, or the suspected rival); also *of* (the attentions of another, etc.).

a **1250** *Owl & Night.* 1075 He was so gelus of his wive, That he ne miȝte..I-so that man with hire speke. *a* **1300** *Cursor M.* 1794 O lauerdschipp was þar na strijf, Was naman Ielus of his wijf. *c* **1386** CHAUCER *Miller's T.* 38 Ialous [*v.rr.* ielous, gelous] he was, and heeld hire narwe in cage For she was yong and wylde and he was old. **1398** TREVISA *Barth. De P.R.* XII. xvii. (MS. Bodl.) lf. 121 b/1 The Cock..fiȝteþ for heere [a hen] specialliche as þouȝe he were Ielous. *a* **1450** *Knt. de la Tour* (1868) 23 She loued hym so moche that she was ielous ouer alle women that he spake with. **1484** CAXTON *Fables of Alfonce* (1889) 12 A blynd man whiche had a fayre wyf of the whiche he was moche Jalous. **1592** GREENE *Upst. Courtier* Bj, The yellow daffadil, a flowre fit for gelous Dottrels, who through the bewtie of their honest wiues grew suspitious. **1611** BIBLE *Num.* v. 30 When the spirit of ielousie commeth vpon him, and hee be ielous ouer his wife. **1717** LADY M. W. MONTAGU *Let. to C'tess Mar* 1 Apr., It is impossible for the most jealous husband to know his wife when he meets her. **1819** BYRON *Juan* I. clv, So young a husband's jealous fears. **1888** MISS BRADDON *Fatal Three* I. iii, Mrs. Fausset..had been jealous of the new-comer, and resentful of her intrusion from the outset.

b. in respect of success or advantage: Apprehensive of losing some desired benefit through the rivalry of another; feeling ill-will towards another on account of some advantage or superiority which he possesses or may possess; grudging, envious. Const. *of* (the person, or the advantage).

c **1385** CHAUCER *L.G.W.* Prol. 331 Ffor hate or for Ielous ymagynyng. *c* **1477** CAXTON *Jason* 32 Alle were ialous of him. But Iason neuer thought on none of them. **1563** B. GOOGE *Eglogs* vii. (Arb.) 59 You iudge but of malicious hart, and of a Ialouse brayne. *c* **1601** SIR C. HATTON in *Hatton Corr.* (Camden) 2 My many iealious observers prevent my presence. *a* **1732** ATTERBURY *Serm. Isa.* xl. 22 (Seager) It is certain that they looked upon it with a jealous eye. **1838** THIRLWALL *Greece* xxiii. III. 289 Several of the leading persons in the state were jealous of his glory. **1897** *Eng. Hist. Rev.* Jan. 152 The Church was, as early as 1254, becoming jealous of the civil law.

c. In biblical language, said of God: Having a love which will tolerate no unfaithfulness or defection in the beloved object.

a **1225** *Ancr. R.* 90 Vnderstond, ancre..hwas spuse þu ert; & hu he is gelus of alle þine lates. **1382** WYCLIF *Exod.* xx. 5, I forsothe am the Lord thi God, strong gelows [**1388** a stronge gelouse louyere]. **1535** COVERDALE *Ibid.*, For I the Lorde thy God am a gelouse God. —— *Josh.* xxiv. 19 He is an holy God, mightie, and gelous, which spareth not youre trangressions and synnes. **1617** MORYSON *Itin.* III. 6 Our very God is in a good sence said to be iealous:..you shall ever find the chastest Weomen, desiring an husband vertuously iealous. **1853** MAURICE *Proph. & Kings* vii. 119 God is contemplated as jealous over his people.

5. Suspicious; apprehensive of evil, fearful. Const. *of*, or with subord. clause. Now *dial.*

c **1532** DU WES *Introd. Fr.* in Palsgr. 921 A man doutfull and suspect of jelous (*soupeconeus*). **1593** SHAKS. *Lucr.* 800 Let not the iealous daie behold that face. **1607** MIDDLETON *Five Gallants* I. i, My master is very jealous of the pestilence. **1622** WITHER *Mistr. Philar.* in Arb. *Garner* IV. 420 Never did the jealous 'st ear Any muttering rumour hear. *a* **1639** WOTTON in *Reliq.* (1651) 524 The jealous Trout, that low did lie, Rose at a wel-dissembled Flie. **1755** B. MARTIN *Mag. Arts & Sc.* III. xiii. 398, I am jealous of some baneful Experiment to follow. **1868** ATKINSON *Cleveland Gloss.*, *Jealous*, apprehensive, ready to anticipate something..more or less unpleasant in its nature.

†**b.** Doubtful, mistrustful. *Obs.*

1601 SHAKS. *Jul. C.* I. ii. 162 That you do loue me, I am nothing iealous. **1682** SCARLETT *Exchanges* 216 When..the Acceptant afterwards repents, and is jealous whether the Drawer will really accept of his Re-draughts.

6. Suspiciously vigilant against, or to prevent, something (expressed or understood); vigilant in scrutinizing.

1601 R. JOHNSON *Kingd. & Commw.* (1603) 215 They are very iealous to shew themselves fearefull or base minded in worde or deede. **1632** J. HAYWARD tr. *Biondi's Eromena* 51 The Princesse..was jealous lest her griefe [for her brother's death] should grow to be displeased with her, for adventuring her selfe to the gust of a curious sight. **1709** STRYPE *Ann. Ref.* I. l. 499 They were very jealous of any Popish prince to become her husband. **1797** MRS. RADCLIFFE *Italian* lxi. (1824) 641 He examined with a jealous eye the emotions he witnessed. **1843** POE *Purloined Let.* Wks. 1864 I. 268 The most jealous scrutiny of the microscope. **1866** ROGERS *Agric. & Prices* I. xxi. 549 Measures [of weight, etc.] were subject to jealous supervision.

b. *transf.* Requiring suspicious or careful vigilance: delicate, ticklish. ? *Obs.*

1600 E. BLOUNT tr. *Conestaggio* 127 The difficultie..to finde a trustie person in so dangerous and iealous a cause as this is. **1672** MARVELL *Reh. Transp.* I. 267 Nor shall I dwell too long upon so jealous or impertinent a subject.

†**7.** *jealous glass*, an old name for glass which is translucent, but cannot be seen through: see quots., and cf. JALOUSIE. *Obs.*

1703 T. N. *City & C. Purchaser* 153 *Jealous Glass*..is a sort of wrinkled Glass of such a Quality, that one cannot distinctly see what is done on the other side of it. **1726** R. NEVE *Builder's Dict.* s.v. *Glass*, This Jealous Glass..is commonly used in and about London, to put into the lower Lights..where the Windows are low against the Street. [**1879** *Centenary Birmingham Libr.* 32 A curious question arose [in 1821] as to the use of 'jealous glass' in the windows towards the bank, as provided by the original lease.]

8. *Comb.*, as ***jealous-headed***, ***-eyed***, etc.

1679 M. RUSDEN *Further Discov. Bees* 122 To answer these jealous-headed persons. **1704** STEELE *Lying Lover* II. i. **1719** SAVAGE *Love in Veil* I. i. 9 Some jealous pated Father or Brother must interfere. **1815** *Woman's Will* II. i, I am told he is a cursed silly, jealous-pated fellow.

†**jea'louse**, *v. Obs.* or *dial.* Also 7 jealouze, 9 jealous. [ad. F. *jalouser*, with spelling conformed to JEALOUS. Now chiefly *Sc.* and *north. dial.* and spelt JALOUSE, q.v.] *trans.* To suspect (a thing or person); to have a suspicion *that*: see JALOUSE *v.* 2.

1682 BUNYAN *Holy War* xiv, It was jealoused that they were too familiar with them. **1682** FLAVEL *Fear* 32 A guilty conscience..distrusts all, doubts and jealouzeth all. **1703** D. WILLIAMSON *Serm. bef. Gen. Assembly Edinburgh* 48 With attestations justly jealoused. **1718** *Wodrow Corr.* (1843) II. 377 But I jealouse, if the Lord take him away, it will be so sudden. **1721** WODROW *Suffer. Ch. Scot.* I. 7 The Brethren ..did very much fear and jealouse Mr. James Sharp. **1827** CARLYLE in Froude *Life* (1882) I. xxii. 430 Will you be good neighbours or bad? I cannot say... I jealouse you. **1876** *Whitby Gloss.* s.v., 'I jealous'd it'.

Hence †**jea'loused** *ppl. a.*, suspected.

1695 J. SAGE *Article* Wks. 1844 I. 268 She assisted the Scottish subjects against their native Sovereign (her jealoused competitrix).

†**jealous-hood.** So printed in the 4th Folio of Shakspere (1685), and taken by some as a single word, with the sense 'jealousy'.

All the quartos and the first three folios have the two words *jealous hood*, which is presumably the true reading; old Capulet, in applying the phrase to his wife, either using *hood* as the type of the female head, or alluding to the use of a hood as a disguise for a jealous spy. Cf. the personal application of *chaperon*; also *mad-cap*, *sly-boots*, etc.

[**1592** SHAKS. *Rom. & Jul.* IV. iv. 13 A iealous hood, a iealous hood [**1685** jealous-hood], Now fellow, what there?] **1846** WORCESTER, *Jealous-hood*, Jealousy *Shak.* So later Dicts.

jealously ('dʒɛləslɪ), *adv.* [f. JEALOUS *a.* + -LY².] In a jealous manner.

†**1.** Zealously, eagerly. *Obs.*

1388 WYCLIF *Joel* ii. 18 The Lord louyde gelousli his lond. **1549** COVERDALE, etc. *Erasm. Par. Gal.* iv. Ccij b, Some ielously wooe you and as it were enuiyng at me, labor to wynne your fauor.

2. In a way characterized by jealousy (in mod. senses); with watchful care for preservation; with apprehension of rivalry, or (*esp.*) of loss or damage.

1718 STRYPE *Whitgift* III. xxiii, He had always hoped that her Majesty's safety..should be jealously preserved. *a* **1788** MICKLE *Siege Marseilles* III. v, He stamps the ground; then jealously casts round His burning eyes, as if he fear'd his thoughts Were listen'd to. **1857** KEBLE *Euchar. Adorat.* 31 Surely it is natural that we should..jealously guard them, and scrupulously make the most of them. **1868** FREEMAN *Norm. Conq.* II. vii. 29 They were doubtless jealously watched.

†**3.** Suspiciously, distrustfully. *Obs.* (exc. *dial.*)

1628 DIGBY *Voy. Medit.* 84 But seeing they wrought jealously of me. (Still common dialectally.)

'jealousness. Now *rare.* [f. as prec. + -NESS.] The quality of being jealous; jealousy; suspicion.

c **1380** WYCLIF *Serm.* Sel. Wks. I. 88 Chana, þat is gelousnes. **1382** —— *Num.* v. 15 If the spiryt of gelousnes stire the man aȝens his wijf. —— *Song Sol.* viii. 6 Strong is as deth looue, hard as helle ielousnesse. *c* **1420** *Avow. Arth.* lxiv, Of jelusnes be thou bold. *a* **1626** BACON *War with Spain* in *Harl. Misc.* (Malh.) IV. 135 Not out of umbrages, light jealousness, apprehensions afar off, but out of clear foresight of imminent danger. **1900** *Longm. Mag.* June 141 Jealousness does not seem to be the distinguishing feature of Louise's early training.

†**jealouste.** *Obs.* [from OF. type **jalousetė*, f. *jaloux, -ouse*: see -TY.] Jealousy; zeal.

1382 WYCLIF *Num.* v. 15 The sacrifice of gelouste it is. —— *Ps.* lxxviii[i.] 5 Shal be tend vp as fyr thi jelouste? —— *Isa.* lix. 17 Couered with the mantil of ielouste.

jealousy ('dʒɛləsɪ). Forms: α. 3-5 gelusie, -usye, 4-6 gelosie, -osy(e, -ousie, -ousy(e, 5 -owsye, -ozye, 6 (gelacy) gealosie, -osy(e, -ousy. β. 4

ielesye, 4–7 ielousie, -ousy, (4–5 -ousye, 5 -acy, 5–6 -osy(e, 6 -usy, -owsy); 6–7 iealousie, -sye, 7– jealousy. γ. 4 ialusy(e, 4–6 -ousie, -ousye, 6 -owsye. δ. 5 iolysye. [a. OF. *gelosie, jalousie* (= Pr. and It. *gelosia*), f. *gelos* JEALOUS: see -Y.] The quality of being jealous.

†**1.** Zeal or vehemence of feeling against some person or thing; anger, wrath, indignation. *Obs.*

c **1400** *Apol. Loll.* 25 þe gelousy [**1382** WYCLIF *Wisd.* v. 18 ielouste] of Him schal tak armor, & arme þe crature to venge Him on þe wickid. **1535** COVERDALE *Deut.* xxix. 20 His wrath and gelousy shall smoke ouer soch a man. **1611** BIBLE *Ps.* lxxix. 5 How long, Lord, wilt thou be angry, for euer? shall thy ielousie burne like fire? **1649** BP. REYNOLDS *Hosea* i. 32 The Lord shewing the jealousie of his Justice.

†**2.** Zeal or vehemence of feeling in favour of a person or thing; devotion, eagerness, anxiety to serve. *Obs.*

1436 *Pol. Poems* (Rolls) II. 165 He hadde a manere gelozye To hys marchauntes, and lowede hem hartelye. **1483** CAXTON *Gold. Leg.* 170b/1 The Iuge wyste not who had wrong for the ialousye of Iustyse that he had. *Ibid.* 442/1 The swete percepcyon of thy precious body whiche by Ialousye of loue I doo take be to me eschewyng of dampnacion. **1565** T. STAPLETON *Fortr. Faith* 20 This shall the gelousy of the Lorde of Hostes bringe to passe.

3. Solicitude or anxiety for the preservation or well-being of something; vigilance in guarding a possession from loss or damage.

1387–8, 1526 [see JEALOUS *a.* 3]. **1601** R. JOHNSON *Kingd. & Commw.* (1603) 109 A citie holden by the Genoise, with great iealousie, by reason of the neighborhoode of the great Duke. **1639** T. BRUGIS tr. *Camus' Mor. Relat.* 160 Of a love intirely pure, and..with a holy jealousie of the protection of her integrity. **1738** BOLINGBROKE *On Parties* Ded. 23 There is a plain and real Difference between Jealousy and Distrust. .. Men may be jealous, on Account of their Liberties, and I think They ought to be so, even when They have no immediate Distrust that the Persons, who govern, design to invade them. **1856** EMERSON *Eng. Traits, Aristocracy* Wks. (Bohn) II. 83 The jealousy of every class to guard itself, is a testimony to the reality they have found in life.

4. The state of mind arising from the suspicion, apprehension, or knowledge of rivalry: **a.** in love, etc.: Fear of being supplanted in the affection, or distrust of the fidelity, of a beloved person, esp. a wife, husband, or lover.

1303 R. BRUNNE *Handl. Synne* 1896 But where þe wyfe haþ gelousye, þer beþ wrdys grete and hye. c **1375** *Sc. Leg. Saints, Laurentius* 698 þe feynd..gert hyme fal In Ialusy, Venand his wyf had mysdone Vith a ȝunge knycht. c **1386** CHAUCER *Knt.'s T.* 441 The fyr of Ialousie [*v.rr.* ielusye, gelousie, gelesie, Ielousie, -sye] vp sterte With Inne his brest and hente him by the herte. **1432–50** tr. *Higden* (Rolls) IV. 349 For contempte of vice of iolysye. **1535** COVERDALE *Song Sol.* viii. 6 Loue is mightie as the death, and gelousy as the hell. **1611** BIBLE *Num.* v. 29 This is the law of ielousies, when a wife goeth aside to another in stead of her husband. **1711** ADDISON *Spect.* No. 170 ¶2 Jealousy is that Pain which a Man feels from the Apprehension that he is not equally beloved by the Person whom he entirely loves. **1871** DALE *Ten Commandm.* ii. 63 Jealousy is but the anger and pain of injured and insulted Love.

b. in respect of success or advantage: Fear of losing some good through the rivalry of another; resentment or ill-will towards another on account of advantage or superiority, possible or actual, on his part; envy, grudge.

c **1425** LYDGATE *Assembly of Gods* 640 Malyce, Frowardnes, Gret Ielacy. **1470–85** MALORY *Arthur* VIII. xiii, There befelle a Ialousye..betwyxe kynge Marke and sir Tristram, for they loued bothe one lady. **1549** COVERDALE, etc. *Erasm. Par. Rom.* xi. 30 To folowe your godlynes, though it be but euen for enuie and malice, as the propertie of them is to be gyuen to a ialowsye. **1650** SIR R. STAPYLTON *Strada's Low C. Warres* VI. 21 Lest this warrelike Preparation might beget a Ielousy in the minds of princes, his Majesty satisfied them by his Ambassadours. a **1715** BURNET *Own Time* II. (1724) I. 208 This drew a jealousy on me from the Bishops. **1836** W. IRVING *Astoria* I. 90 There were feuds between the partners themselves, occasioned.. by jealousy of rank. **1870** FREEMAN *Norm. Conq.* (ed. 2) I. iv. 163 We see traces of strong local diversities, sometimes rising into local jealousies. **1879** MCCARTHY *Own Times* II. xxv. 232 [Turkey] reckoning on the mutual jealousies of the cabinets.

c. In biblical language, attributed to God: see JEALOUS *a.* 4c, and quot. 1860 below.

a **1225** *Ancr. R.* 90 Ich am gelus of þe, Syon, mi leofmon, mid muche gelusie. **1611** BIBLE *Deut.* xxxii. 16 They prouoked him to iealousie with strange gods. **1622** DONNE *Serm.* i. 3 a, Iealous of his iealousie, He will not have his iealousie despised nor forgotten. **1860** PUSEY *Min. Proph.* 102 'Jealousy' is used..in the O.T. of that attribute in God, whereby He does not endure the love of His creatures to be transferred from Him, or divided with Him. *Ibid.* 373 God's jealousy is twofold. It is an intense love, not bearing imperfections or unfaithfulness in that which It loves, and so chastening it; or not bearing the ill-dealings of those who would injure what It loves, and so destroying them.

5. Suspicion; apprehension of evil; mistrust. Now *dial.* †*to have in jealousy*: to be suspicious of, suspect, mistrust (*obs.*).

c **1385** CHAUCER *L.G.W.* 722 (*Thisbe*) Maydenys been I-kept for gelosye Ful streyte lyst they dedyn sum folye. **1523** PACE *Let. to Hen. VIII* in Strype *Eccl. Mem.* (1721) I. App. xi. 22 Against such persons as are had in a jelosie of revolting. **1541** *Act 33 Hen. VIII*, c. 24 §1 Some gelosie of their affection and favor towardes their kinsmen..hath bene conceyued and had against them. **1659** D. PELL *Impr. Sea* 323 Sailing..without any mistrust or jealousy of Sands. **1702** J. LOGAN in *Pa. Hist. Soc. Mem.* IX. 82 Through a jealousy of the vessel being crank. **1714** C'TESS COWPER *Diary* (1864) 36 He had some little Jealousy, before he went, that the fine Lady was Lady Harriet Vere. **1793** SMEATON *Edystone L.* §264 Some suspicion of the Polparra Fishermen, as having cut away the buoy..; a jealousy I should not have given way to. **1893** STEVENSON *Catriona* xi. 119, I judged it was beyond the course of nature they could have any jealousy of where I was.

6. = JALOUSIE.

1834 M. SCOTT *Cruise Midge* xviii. 288, I..peered through the open jealousies, or blinds, on the scene below.

7. *attrib.*

1611 BIBLE *Num.* v. 25 Then the Priest shall take the ielousie offering out of the womans hand. **1899** S. BUTLER *Shaks. Sonn.* 98 The jealousy series must be dated in the spring months of 1585–6.

Jeames. †**a.** Obs. form of the personal name JAMES. **b.** In mod. use (after Thackeray), a ludicrous name for a liveried footman (pron. dʒiːmz). Hence **Jeames-ism** *nonce-wd.*, flunkeyism.

c **1600** NORDEN *Spec. Brit., Cornw.* Ded., To the most high and mightie Prince Ieames, by diuine prouidence, kinge of Englande, Scotland, Fraunce, and Irelande. *Ibid.* (1728) 22 That is betwene St. Jeames tide and the feast of All Saynts. **1846** THACKERAY (*title*) The Diary of C. Jeames de la Pluche, Esq. **1859** —— *Virgin.* xxxvii, Jeames with his cocked hat and long cane, [is] passing out of the world. **1875** JAS. GRANT *One of the '600'* xv, She and her family.. attended by a tall 'Jeames' in plush. **1883** *Athenæum* 13 Oct. 459/1 'Students of the social history and manners of courts' —which seems to be the latest modern euphemism for 'Jeames-ism' in literature.

jean (dʒeɪn). Forms: α. 6 ieen, iene, ge(a)ne, ieane, ieyne, ienne, 7 ieine, 7– jean; β. 7– jane. In early use with capital initial. [app. the same as ME. *Gene, Jene, Jeyne, Jayne, Jane*, in OF. *Janne(s*, mod.F. *Gênes*, med.L. *Janua*, Genoa, a city of Italy; cf. JANE[1], a coin of Genoa, and GEANE.]

†**1.** = GEANE, Genoa; *attrib.* = GENOESE. *Obs.*

1495 *Naval Acc. Hen. VII* (1896) 262 Cables..of Jeane makyng. c **1524** *Churchw. Acc. St. Mary Hill, London* (Nichols 1797) 127 A carpet of Jeen makyng. **1607** MARKHAM *Caval.* II. 59 Some horsmen vse that bytt, which wee call the Bastonet or Ieine bytt, which is made with.. great rough rings, made high like wheeles.

2. a. A twilled cotton cloth; a kind of fustian. Orig. ***jene (ge(a)ne, geanes) fustian***, shortened to *jeanes, jean*, etc.

The form *jeans* is used in U.S.

α. **1567** in Swayne *Sarum Church-w. Acc.* (1896) 113, ij yerdes of Jene fustyan. **1575** *Richmond. Wills* (Surtees) 233, vij. yeards of geanes fustion..xvj yeardes of geane fustion. **1577** *Ibid.* 269, ij yardes of whitt geanes. **1589** in H. Hall *Soc. Eliz. Age* (1886) 210 Gene fustian. **1589** *Acc.-Bk. W. Wray* in *Antiquary* XXXII. 78 White Jennes, iijs. vjd. **1622** *Househ. Bks. Ld. W. Howard* (Beck *Draper's Dict.*), A quarter of jean for my Ladie's stockins, 3*d.* **1766** W. GORDON *Gen. Counting-ho.* 427, 2 pieces ½ yard wide white jean. **1802** *Brookes' Gazetteer* (ed. 12) s.v. *Leigh*, Considerable manufactures, particularly of fine jeans. **1862** in Bryant & Gay *Hist. U.S.* (1880) IV. 531 A million yards of jeans. c **1885** *Weldon's Pract. Needlewk.* IV. 3/1 Executed ..on a ground of white satin jean.

β. **1612** *Two Noble K.* III. v, You most coarse freeze capacities, Ye jaue judgments [*Dyce reads* 'jane']. **1662** *Stat. Ireland* (1765) II. 407 Fustians called janes. **1835** *Blackw. Mag.* XXXVIII. 164 A new suit of olive jane.

b. *pl.* Garment of this material. Now usu. close-fitting trousers of this (or other) material. See also *blue-jean* s.v. BLUE *a.* 13.

1843 R. S. SURTEES *Handley Cross* I. xiii. 276 Septimus arrived flourishin' his cambric, with his white jeans strapped under his chammy leather opera boots. **1846** S. F. SMITH *Theatr. Apprenticeship* 48 My friend in the jeans and white hat. **1873** 'MARK TWAIN' & WARNER *Gilded Age* (1874) i. 19 They were dressed in homespun 'jeans', blue or yellow. **1879** *Birmingham Weekly Post* 26 Apr. 2/7 The cook, in his spotless 'jeans,' made the usual enquiry. **1904** G. V. HOBART *Jim Hickey* ii. 35 Wouldn't we be a nice pair of turtles to stand around with coin in our jeans and see a nice girl like Amy getting the ice? **1923** J. GALSWORTHY *Captures* 62 He wore, not white ducks, but blue jeans. **1936** WODEHOUSE *Laughing Gas* xvii. 187 No doubt this fiend in butler's shape was even now on his way east with the stuff in his jeans, gone beyond recall. **1957** *Times* 12 Nov. (Canada Suppl.) p. xv/4 For miles and miles of suburban area you will rarely see a young woman out of blue jeans, shorts or slim-jim pants during the day. **1958** *Economist* 11 Jan. 94/1 Girls in tight jeans and dazzle socks. **1958** *Daily Herald* 24 Mar. 2/6 In bright red jeans and thick nautical sweater, secretary Fiona stood on the deck of her Thames-side barge. **1969** I. & P. OPIE *Children's Games* xi. 317 Little girls, dressed in T-shirts and jeans.

c. *attrib.* and *Comb.* Made of jean, as ***jean boot, cap, coat, trousers***, etc. Also ***jean-clad, -jacketed*** adjs. **jean-age** [cf. TEEN-AGE *a.*], the age at which a young person is likely to wear jeans; so ***jean-aged*** adj.; ***jean-ager***.

1960 *Guardian* 15 Sept. 9/1 A full-house audience, ranging from the peerage to the jean-age. **1967** *Observer* (Colour Suppl.) 30 Apr. 34/2 (*heading*) Up to jean-age. *Ibid.*, The most comprehensive analysis yet of the difficult jean-age years. **1962** *Times Lit. Suppl.* 18 May 359/2 Mr. Kerouac is..far more than the mere apostle of jean-aged, teen-aged..American youth. **1959** *Design* Oct. 29/2 Pony-tailed jean-agers. **1961** *Times Lit. Suppl.* 1 Dec. p. iv (*heading*) Tales for jean-agers. **1849** THACKERAY *Pendennis* I. xxiv. 231 His jean-boots, with tips of shiny leather. **1858** LYTTON *What Will He do?* I. i, 'You are a keen observer', said he of the jean cap. **1885** *Harper's Mag.* Dec. 132 The jeans-clad mountaineers. *Ibid.* A leather belt girded his brown jeans coat. **1801** T. S. SURR *Splendid Misery* II. 141 Habited in..a jean grey frock. **1860** *Observer* 16 Sept. 3/6 The disinterested and brave liberator of Italy, in his red shirt, in a dirty pair of jean trowsers, and worn-out boots. c **1871** J. ALBERY *Dramatic Works* (1939) I. 234 He..wears ..brown, soiled jean trousers.

Hence **jeaned** *a.*, clad in jean trousers.

1970 'E. LINDALL' *Gathering of Eagles* iii. 30 Van Jordan stood up and looked down at him, legs wide and hands on her jeaned hips. **1971** D. WALLIS *Bad Luck Girl* I. i. 8 She forked out a length of jeaned thigh to fall against his own.

jeand(e, jeant(e, obs. ff. GIANT.

jean(n)ette (dʒəˈnɛt). Also **jean(n)et.** [f. JEAN + -ETTE.] A name for various types of material resembling jean (see quot. 1950).

1785 *Daily Universal Reg.* 1 Jan. 4/2 Half-ell printed jeanets. **1862** *Illustr. Catal. Internat. Exhib., Industr. Dept., Brit. Div.* II. No. 3667 Spinners and manufacturers of jeannettes. **1882** CAULFEILD & SAWARD *Dict. Needlework* 278/2 *Jeanette*, a variety of jean, coarser in quality, yet not so closely woven. Some Jeanettes are twilled. **1950** *'Mercury' Dict. Textile Terms* 286 *Jeanettes*, a cloth similar to jean, but usually finer yarns... There is very little difference between jeans and jeanettes. Many makers make no distinction at all. *Jeannet*, a strong coarse fabric, made with cotton warp and wool weft in a twill weave, especially for working clothes for use in cold weather.

jeapard, obs. f. JEOPARD *v.*

jear, -e, obs. f. JEER *sb.*[1]

jeast, obs. f. GIST *sb.*[2] and *v.*, JEST *sb.* and *v.*

c **1567** in *Hist. Northumbld.* (1899) V. 201 In the springe tyme..they have ther cattell jeasted in Shilbottell-wood.

jeat(e, obs. form of JET.

jeaund(e, jeaunt(e, obs. forms of GIANT.

jebat, jebbet, jebet, etc., obs. ff. GIBBET.

jebel (ˈdʒɛbəl). Also **djebel, djibel, gebel, jabal.** [a. colloq. Arab. *jebel*, classical Arab. *jabal* mountain.] A hill or mountain; freq. in specific names.

[**1600** J. PORY tr. *Leo Africanus' Geogr. Hist. Afr.* II. 58 (*heading*) Of the mountaine of Iron, commonly called Gebelelhadih. **1834** *Penny Cycl.* II. 210/1 The mountainous region in the interior is distinguished by the appellation of Jabal, 'the Hills'.] **1844** A. W. KINGLAKE *Eothen* xxvii. 387 For a part of two days I wound under the base of the snow-crowned Djibel el Sheik. **1848** H. MARTINEAU *Eastern Life* I. iv. 53 It [*sc.* the causeway] extends from the river bank to the town, and thence on to the Djebel (mountain) with many limbs from this main trunk. **1920** *Blackw. Mag.* Nov. 667/1 An enormous waste of rocky jebels and broad sandy plains. **1924** *Ibid.* Oct. 562/1 The mountains or gebels, to give them their local name, are honeycombed with caves. **1927** *Chambers's Jrnl.* 535/1 A low-lying bank of white mist wound itself round the gaunt jabal. **1942** F. STARK *Lett. from Syria* 186 He thought I was referring to the Intelligence in the Jebel Druse! **1968** *New Scientist* 30 May 447/3 Swarms of desert locusts have whirled up like djinns from the moist jebels on both sides of the Red Sea. **1970** *Guardian* 3 Aug. 3/1 The annual monsoon..hits the Jebel, the mountain range behind Salala.

jeberd, jeblet, obs. ff. JEOPARD, GIBLET.

Jebusite (ˈdʒɛbjuzaɪt). Name of a tribe of Canaanites, dispossessed of Jerusalem by David. In 17th c., a nickname for Roman Catholics, esp. Jesuits.

1535 COVERDALE *Judg.* i. 21 Ye Iebusites [WYCLIF Iebuse, Iebusei] dwelt amonge the children of Ben Iamin at Ierusalem vnto this daye. **1583** FULKE *Defence* (1843) 568 Your Jebusites, that must be called 'fathers'. **1604** *Supplic. Masse-Priests* C viij, Henry Sammier a Iebusite disguised in the habit of a souldier. **1681** DRYDEN *Abs. & Achit.* 213 And proves the King himself a Jebusite.

Hence **Jebusite** *v.*, **Jebuˈsitic, -ˈitical, -itish** *a.*

1608 A. WILLET *Hexapla Exod.* 62 The desperate plot.. Iebusited by that wicked seede and seminarie of Satan. **1613** PURCHAS *Pilgrimage* (1614) 18 Ignatius and his Colony of Iesuites..that Iebusiticall societie. **16..** SEMPILL *Pick Tooth for Pope* in *Harp Renfrewshire* Ser. II. (1873) 8 Your Jebusitish Jesuits. **1681** DRYDEN *Abs. & Achit.* 663 And suited to the temper of the times, Then groaning under Jebusitick crimes. **1898** E. S. WALLACE *Jerusalem* i. 20 The Jebusitic occupation was of later date.

jebytt, obs. form of GIBBET.

jecimin, -my, obs. ff. JASMINE, JESSAMY.

†ˈ**jecorary**, *a. Obs. rare.* [ad. F. *jécoraire* (Cotgr.), f. L. *jecur, jecor-* liver: see -ARY.] Belonging to the liver; hepatic.

1684 tr. *Bonet's Merc. Compit.* I. 14 To Breathe the Jecorary, or Cephalick Vein. *Ibid.* VI. 181 The place must be the right jecorary vein.

†**jectiˈgation.** *Obs.* [a. F. *jectigation* 'wagging, shrugging' (Cotgr.), f. med.L. *jectigāre*, f. *jact-, ject-*, ppl. stem of L. *jacĕre* to throw.] A wagging, a tremulous movement.

a **1693** URQUHART *Rabelais* III. xix. 159 With various Jectigation of his Fingers, and other Gesticulations. *Ibid.* III. xlv. 370 Shrugging of the Shoulders, and Jectigation of the whole Body. **1730–6** BAILEY (folio), *Jectigation*, a Trembling or Palpitation felt in the Pulse of a sick Person. **1855** MAYNE *Expos. Lex.*, [as a term anciently used]..: jectigation.

jectour, variant of JETTER, *Obs.*

jedge, variant of JADGE *Sc., Obs.*

jee (dʒiː), *v. Sc.* [Origin obscure: cf. GEE *v.*[1]]

1. *intr.* To move, to stir; to move to one side; to move to and fro (quot. 1727).

1727 RAMSAY *Bessy Bell & Mary G.* iv, Our fancies jee between you twae, Ye are sic bonny lasses. **1789** Ross *Helenore* (ed. 3) 60 She never jee'd [*ed.* 1768 budg'd], till he was out o' sight. **1896** J. LUMSDEN *Poems* 123 A gloom fell owre the hame when Willie jeed awa.

2. *trans.* To cause to move, to move; to move aside, shift, or displace slightly.

1722 RAMSAY *Three Bonnets* IV. 224 Wha wi' havins jees his bonnet. **1825–80** JAMIESON, 'Ye're no able to jee it;' You cannot move it. **1838** J. STRUTHERS *Poetic T.* 81 A lassie.. Staw up our stair Syne jee't the door.

jee, *sb. Sc.* [f. prec. vb.] 'A move, motion' (Jam. 1880). ***on the jee***: off the straight, AJEE.

1829 *Blackw. Mag.* XXV. 560 You canna gie your head a jie to the ae side, without [etc.]. **1893** STEVENSON *Catriona* xxiii. 276 To set you on the jee.

jee, *adv.* and *int.* **a.** The verb-stem used adverbially or as an exclamation: see JEE *v.* 1 (*Sc.*). **b.** = GEE *int.*[1], a word of command to a horse.

1785 BURNS *Vision* I. vii, When click! the string the snick did draw; And jee! the door gaed to the wa'. **1880** JAMIESON, *Jee, jee-up*, a call to a horse to move. **1898** T. HARDY *Wessex Poems* 137 Only the creak of the gibbets Or waggoner's jee.

jeel (dʒiːl), *sb.*[1] *Sc.* Variant of GEILL, jelly.

a **1774** FERGUSSON *Election* Poems (1845) 40 There whang his creams and jeels Wi' life that day. **18..** *Song, Jenny's Bawbee* (Jam. Suppl.), His suit he press'd sae weel, That Jenny's heart grew saft as jeel.

So **jeel** *v. Sc. intr.* [F. *geler*], to set as jelly, to congeal, to 'jell'.

1896 IAN MACLAREN *Kate Carnegie* 205 Setting saucers of black jam upon the window-sill to 'jeel'.

jeel, *sb.*[2] *I. of Man.* [Manx *jeeyl, jeeill, jeell*, Ir. *díoghbhail* damage, loss, OIr. *dígbail* diminution.] Damage; mischief.

1887 HALL CAINE *Deemster* xxiii. 147 We came out to sea just to help you out of this jeel. **1890** —— *Bondman* xxii. II. 279 In all this jeel with the girl and the Governor.

jeep (dʒiːp), *sb.* orig. *U.S.* [f. the initials *G.P.* (dʒiː piː) '*g*eneral *p*urpose', prob. influenced by the name 'Eugene the Jeep', a creature of amazing resource and power, first introduced into the cartoon strip 'Popeye' on 16 March 1936 by his creator E. C. Segar.] A small, sturdy, four-wheel-drive army vehicle, used chiefly for reconnaissance; a similar vehicle in non-military use; hence (*colloq.*) any vehicle. Also *attrib.* and *Comb.*

For an earlier application in 1937 of the term to a commercial motor vehicle, see 1944 *Amer. N. & Q.* May 26/2 and June 43/1.

1941 *Amer. Speech* XVI. 166/2 *Jeep*, a term applied to bantam cars, and occasionally to other motor vehicles; in the Air Corps, the Link trainer; in the Armored Force, the 1½ ton command car. **1941** J. DANIELS *Tar Heels* 47 Beer wagons moved on the road with the brown jeeps of soldiers and marines. **1942** *News Chron.* 7 Apr. 4/5 The light armoured car which hauls the gun and carries the gun crew is called a jeep. **1942** *R.A.F. Jrnl.* 3 Oct. 24 The Canadians ..put their dollars on a Jeep. There were a few of these contraptions beetling about the countryside. **1943** *Archit. Rev.* XCIV. 52 The Jeep is no family car, but it has points that private-car designers might well study. **1945** *Trade Marks Jrnl.* 22 Aug. 423/2 Jeep... Motor cars, and parts thereof.. Willys-Overland Motors Inc.., Toledo, State of Ohio, United States of America; manufacturers. **1946** *R.A.F. Jrnl.* May 174 The men and machines, drivers and Jeeps.. have finished their job. **1950** G. GREENE *Third Man* iv. 37 A jeep came tearing round the corner and bowled him over. **1952** MORIN & SMITH tr. *Herzog's Annapurna* ii. 30 The jeep now took us along a dusty stony road. **1954** D. DODGE *Lights of Skaro* vi. 213 We were picked up by a jeep-load of soldiers. **1955** *Sci. News Let.* 18 June 396/3 The cosmetic preparations women use to remove superfluous hair might help speed recovery from jeep disease. This is the slow-healing painful infection at the base of the spine which thousands of World War II soldiers developed from riding in jeeps. Doctors called it pilonidal sinus. **1958** *Punch* 22 Jan. 141/1 We flew over more icebergs and then landed at Gander, Newfoundland, where people in woolly tartan jackets drove around in jeeps. **1960** *Guardian* 25 Feb. 9/4 The arrival of jeep-loads of armed police. **1966** F. SHAW et al. *Lern Yerself Scouse* 64 Here comes the police jeep. **1967** WODEHOUSE *Company for Henry* ix. 155 Repeated inquiries as to whether his darned jeep couldn't do more than three miles an hour. **1971** *Country Life* 19 Aug. 431/1 There are no paths, pony tracks or jeep roads to this inaccessible spot. **1973** *Daily Mirror* 24 Jan. 15 On the US side, ADSIDS (air delivered seismic intrusion detectors) dropped by plane, could tell a Communist jeep from a truck. **1973** J. LEASOR *Host of Extras* vii. 127 The Jeep driver started his engine... The Jeep shuddered.

jeep (dʒiːp), *v.* orig. *U.S.* [f. the sb.] *intr.* To travel by jeep. So **'jeeping** *vbl. sb.*

1942 *Time* 28 Sept. 57 Yanks: drinking English tea; jeeping in the Middle East. **1945** *Picture Post* 14 Apr. 7 Sometimes, it took us hours to jeep a few miles. **1959** *Times Lit. Suppl.* 27 Feb. 115/4 Jeeping across the mountains on sheep tracks, ingeniously harrying the Germans. **1966** M. R. D. FOOT *SOE in France* xii. 406 An attempt to harass the impending German retreat by jeeping and ambushing.

jeepable ('dʒiːpəb(ə)l), *a.* [f. JEEP *sb.* + -ABLE.] Negotiable by jeep.

1944 *Daily Tel.* 12 July 4/6 A new word is now being used on the maps of the South-East Asia Command. It designates tracks impassable to vehicles other than jeeps. These are marked as 'jeepable'. **1946** G. HANLEY *Monsoon Victory* vii. 71 The infantry battalions took off their jackets and started to lay thousands of logs across the mud in an endeavour to make the road even 'Jeepable'. **1960** D. MORAES *Gone Away* 195 There are two passes into Tibet: the Jelep La and the more strategically important Nathu La, to which a jeepable road has been constructed from Gangtok. **1967** *Guardian* 19 Jan. 9/4 Now at least many roads are jeepable.

jeepers ('dʒiːpəz), *int. slang* (orig. *U.S.*). Also **jeepers-creepers** (-'kriːpəz). [Corruption of JESUS.] = JEEZ(E *int.*

1929 W. D. EDMONDS *Rome Haul* ii. 24 Jeepers! A cat would n't stand no show at all. *Ibid.* 30 Spinning swore. 'I'll bet that's right. Jeepers Cripus! How can they expect us to help a marshal if he don't let us know who he is?' **1930** *Amer. Speech* VI. 98 *Jeepers*, an expression of astonishment. 'By Jeepers!' **1937** *Sat. Even. Post* 13 Feb. 13/2 Jeepers Creepers! Where are you going to find a couple of goats and a red wagon on Christmas Eve in three hours? *Ibid.* 82/2 Jeepers, what a story! **1938** MERCER & WARREN (*song-title*) Jeepers creepers. **1939** A. HUXLEY *After Many a Summer* II. ix. 265 'Jeepers Creepers!' he said to himself, remembering the expression on Mr. Stoyte's face. **1940** 'N. BLAKE' *Malice in Wonderland* I. vii. 94 'I think you're very pretty.' 'Jeepers-creepers! Put some conviction into your voice, my pet.' **1959** C. MACINNES *Absolute Beginners* 57, I put my head around the door, and jeepers-creepers, nearly had a fit. **1972** J. AIKEN *Butterfly Picnic* vii. 129 Jeepers, Fernand, we had a bullfight... It was real great!

jeepney ('dʒiːpnɪ). *Philippine Islands.* [f. JEEP *sb.* + JIT)NEY.] A jitney bus converted from a jeep.

1961 in WEBSTER. **1963** *New Yorker* 8 June 137 A flock of jeepneys—United States Army surplus jeeps the Filipinos have converted into buses. **1972** *Asian* 26 Nov.–2 Dec., The Philippine *jeepney*, the jeep bus (which derives its name from the New Orleans *jitney*, or five cent ride..).

jeer (dʒɪə(r)), *sb.*[1] *Naut.* Forms: 5 iere, 7 ieare, ieere, 7–8 **gear**, 8–9 **geer**, **jear**, 7– **jeer**. [Origin unascertained.] Tackle for hoisting and lowering the lower yards. (Usually in *pl.*)

1495 *Naval Acc. Hen. VII* (1896) 188 Jeres for the Mayne takell. *Ibid.* 206 There is employed.. iij hausers of vj ynch compas for makyng of ij mayne liftes and a mayne Jere. **1626** CAPT. SMITH *Accid. Yng. Seamen* 15 The cat harpings, a Ieare, leatch lines. **1672** NARBOROUGH *Jrnl.* 9 Sept., Captain Fowles comander of his Ma^{stie} Ann was dismissed from his comande for beatinge one Mr Murfeild comander of a collier at the Jers. **1712** W. ROGERS *Voy.* 34 He was lash'd to the Main-Geers and drub'd. **1725** DE FOE *Voy. round World* (1840) 87, I caused him to be brought to the gears, with a halter about his neck, and be soundly whipped. **1762** FALCONER *Shipwr.* II. 320 Jears, lifts, and brails, a seaman each attends. *c* **1860** H. STUART *Seaman's Catech.* 24 How will you reeve the jeers? They are usually rove with a reeving line, a becket is fitted in one end of the reeving line, and both ends of the jeers.

b. *Comb.*, as ***jeer-bitt, -block, -capstan, -pulley.***

1495 *Naval Acc. Hen. VII* (1896) 203 Jere poleyes vith a shyver of Brasse. **1626** CAPT. SMITH *Accid. Yng. Seamen* 13 A Ieare capsterne is only in great ships to hoyse their sayles. **1706** PHILLIPS, *Jeer*, or *Jeer-Rope*, a piece of Hawser made fast to the Main-Yard and Fore-Yard in great Ships, its use being to help to hoise up the Yard. **1768** J. BYRON *Narr. Patagonia* (ed. 2) 8 The straps of the fore jeer blocks breaking, the fore-yard came down. **1867** SMYTH *Sailor's Word-bk.*, *Jeer-bitts*, those to which the jeers are fastened and belayed.

jeer (dʒɪə(r)), *sb.*[2] Forms: see JEER *v.* [f. next.]

1. An act of jeering; a derisive speech or utterance; a scoff, flout, gibe, taunt.

1625 B. JONSON *Staple of N.* IV. i, Fitt. Madrigall, a ieere! *Mad.* I know. **1642** SLINGSBY *Diary* (1836) 82 [Lord Hotham] sending ye town a jear y^t w^n he comes he finds y^m still in their beds. **1650** FULLER *Pisgah* II. vii. 159 An impudent and unseasonable jeer, 'Had Zimri peace that slew his Master?' **1686** AGLIONBY *Painting Illustr.* 145 Half afraid he had put a Jear upon him, and that he should be Laughed at. **1729** SWIFT *Grand quest. debated* 187 But the Dean, if this secret should come to his ears, Will never have done with his gibes and his jeers. **1821** BYRON *Sardan.* I. ii. 366 With his savage jeers. **1880** SPURGEON *J. Ploughm. Pict.* 16 A blow is much sooner forgotten than a jeer.

†**b.** The action of jeering; mockery, scoffing, derision. *Obs.*

1660 F. BROOKE tr. *Le Blanc's Trav.* 388 The statue of the Sun..a Spaniard took and gam'd away in a night, whereupon one said by way of jeer, that he had plaid away the Sun before he was up. **1676** MARVELL *Mr. Smirke* 4 With the utmost extremity of Jeere, Disdain, and Indignation. **1753** L. M. tr. *Du Boscq's Accompl. Woman* I. 228 Socrates was naturally given to jeer and railing.

†**2.** Phr. ***in a jeer***, (?) in a huff, in a pet. *Obs.*

1579–80 NORTH *Plutarch, Cicero* (1895) V. 341 This Nepos..being Tribune, left in a geere [*ed.* 2 iear] the exercise of his office, and went into Syria to Pompey, upon no occasion: and as fondly againe he returned thence upon a sodaine.

3. *attrib.* and *Comb.*

1633 SHIRLEY *Triumph Peace* 266 Yet there be some.. mean to show Themselves jeer majors: some tall critics have Planted artillery and wit-murderers. **1659** FULLER *App. Inj. Innoc.* (1840) 363 That he may have the benefit of his own jeer-prayers to himself.

jeer (dʒɪə(r)), *v.* Forms: 6 **geare, gyre, gyere**, 6–7 **geere, giere**, 7 **geer, jear(e, jeere**, 7– **jeer**. [Origin unascertained: appears *c* 1550.

(Among derivations which have been suggested, are Ger. *scheren* to shear, fig. to plague, tease, vex (cf. Du. *gekscheren* 'to shear the fool', to jest, banter); Du. *gieren* 'stridere, strepere' (Kilian), 'to cry, to roar, or bray' (Hexham), 'cum stridore et strepitu alicui illudere' (Junius); both of these show some similarity of sense, but, phonologically, *jeer* could only be an illiterate corruption of either. On the French side *giries*, in Norman patois 'grimaces, affectations hypocritiques', in Rouchi 'tromperie, mauvaise plaisanterie', has been suggested as allied; but it is obvious that this is inadequate to account for the Eng. verb. A suggestion that *jeer* may have originated in an ironical use of *cheer* is plausible and phonetically feasible (cf. JASS, JAWN), but lies beyond existing evidence.)]

1. *intr.* To speak or call out in derision or mockery; to scoff derisively. Const. *at*.

1553 [implied in JEERER]. **1561** [see JEERING *vbl. sb.*]. **1577–87** HOLINSHED *Chron.* III. 1146/2 Some papists resorted thither to geere at him, some of his friends to mourne for him. **1581** J. BELL *Haddon's Answ. Osor.* 264 b, Therefore this Portingall Pasquill doth giere at Haddon by way of mockage. **1590** SPENSER *F.Q.* II. vi. 21 But when he saw her toy, and gibe, and geare, And passe the bonds of modest merimake, Her dalliaunce he despis'd. **1607** HIERON *Wks.* I. 430 Ishmael giereth at Isaac. **1650** FULLER *Pisgah* II. v. 125 Smile good Reader, but doe not jeer at my curiosity herein. *a* **1771** GRAY *Char. Christ Cross Row*, Here Grub-street Geese presume to joke and jeer. **1887** *Spectator* 21 May 675/1 The meeting only jeered at him, and he was unable to make his voice heard.

2. *trans.* To address or treat with scornful derision; to deride, flout, openly mock or scoff at.

1590 SHAKS. *Com. Err.* II. ii. 22 Yea, dost thou ieere & flowt me in the teeth? **1633** PRYNNE *Histrio-m.* Ep. Ded., Do they not deride and jeare religion? *c* **1645** HOWELL *Lett.* (1650) II. lxx. 108, I am heer for my good qualities as your cosin Fortescue geer'd me not long since. **1712** ARBUTHNOT *John Bull* III. ii, Some odd humours.. for which John would jeer her. **1821** CLARE *Vill. Minstr.* I. 190, I jeer my weakness, painfully repent. **1852** MISS YONGE *Cameos* I. xli. 351 The mob pelted him and jeered him by his assumed name of King Arthur.

3. quasi-*trans.* To drive (*into, out of*, etc., something) by jeering.

a **1661** FULLER *Worthies, Staffordsh.* (1662) III. 47 A Fool of Mans making, jeered into it by general Dirision. **1677** GILPIN *Demonol.* (1867) 5 So far from being jeered out of our religion, that [etc.]. *a* **1810** TANNAHILL *Poet. Wks.* (1846) 20 I'll jeer my ancient wooer hame. **1833** HT. MARTINEAU *Manch. Strike* viii. 88 They would jeer me off the stand.

jeerer ('dʒɪərə(r)). Forms: see JEER *v.*; also 6 **girar**. [f. JEER *v.* + -ER[1].] One who jeers or calls out in derision; a mocker, scoffer.

1553 in Strype *Eccl. Mem.* (1721) III. App. xi. 28 All ar not gyrers and mockers. **1562** LEIGH *Armorie* (1597) A iv, Such girars nowe be, who seeming to contemne all thinges, become themselues a contempt to all men. **1569** FOXE *A. & M.* (1583) 2105 Henry Smith.. beyng now a foule gierer and a scornfull scorner of that religion which before he professed ..strangled himselfe. **1637** JACKSON *Treat. God's Forewarn.* Wks. 1844 VI. 131 He..doth either jeer our Saviour or make him to be a jeerer of the sons of affliction. **1837** MAJOR RICHARDSON *Brit. Legion* iii. (ed. 2) 61 The grumbler and the jeerer sat side by side upon the road.

jeerga, var. JIRGA.

jeering ('dʒɪərɪŋ), *vbl. sb.* [f. as JEERER + -ING[1].] The action of the verb JEER; the utterance of derisive mockery; scoffing.

1561 BP. COX *Let. to Parker* in Strype *Parker* II. viii. (1711) 109 What rejoicing and ieering the Adversaries make. **1625** B. JONSON *Staple of N.* IV. i, Call you this ieering! I can play at this. **1724** RAMSAY *Throw the Wood* ii, Their jeering ga'es aft to my heart wi'a knell. **1867** SMILES *Huguenots Eng.* ii. (1880) 27 These jeerings of the towns-folk reached his ears as he passed along the streets.

jeering, *ppl. a.* [f. as prec. + -ING[2].] That jeers; scornfully mocking, derisively scoffing.

1581 J. BELL *Haddon's Answ. Osor.* 258 b, Here is no want of any thing nowe, but of some gyering Gnato, which may lowt this Thraso out of hys paynted coat. **1593** SHAKS. *Lucr.* 1812 Esteemed..As seelie ieering idiots are with Kings. **1598** B. JONSON *Ev. Man in Hum.* I. ii, Such petulant, geering gamsters that can spare No.. subject from their jest. **1762** LLOYD *Hare & Tort.* Poems 37 Friend tortoise, quoth the jeering hare, Your burthen's more than you can bear. **1828** CARLYLE *Misc., Goethe* (1872) II. 198 Even in these trivial, jeering, withered, unbelieving days.

jeeringly, *adv.* [f. prec. + -LY[2].] In a jeering manner; in the way of scornful derision.

1637 LAUD *Sp. Star-Chamber* 14 June 56 The King and his Chappell are most jeeringly and with scorne abused. **1845** LD. CAMPBELL *Chancellors* (1857) III. liv. 76 He jeeringly advises him not to be too much cast down.

†**'jeery**, *a. Obs. rare.* [f. JEER *sb.*[2] + -Y.] Of the nature of a jeer; scornfully derisive.

1606 DEKKER *Seven Sinnes* VII. (Arb.) 44 The Courtiers giues you an open scoffe, ye clowne a secret mock, the Cittizen..a ieery frump.

jeet, obs. form of JET.

Jeeves (dʒiːvz). The name of a character in the novels of P. G. Wodehouse represented as the

perfect valet, used allusively. Hence **'Jeevesian, Jeeves-like** *adjs.*, resembling Jeeves.

1930 E. WAUGH *Labels* iii. 46 The stewards.. maintained a Jeeves-like standard of courtesy and efficiency. **1952** 'R. GORDON' *Doctor in House* xiii. 149 I'll.. get my evening clothes out, and appear as the Jeeves of the chafing dish. **1957** M. SUMMERTON *Sunset Hour* i. 7 That dummy Jeeves we've hired for the evening. **1962** *Observer* 24 June 24/8 A periphrastic and Jeevesian repetition. **1970** *Times* 8 Apr. 18/3 (Advt.), Jeeves required to attend the needs of wealthy bachelor. **1972** *Listener* 27 Jan. 125/2 His Jeeves-like valet. **1972** E. ROUTLEY *Puritan Pleasures of Detective Story* xii. 140 Wimsey is buried in a trench and rescued by his batman. The batman becomes his Jeeves. In Bunter there is about 70 per cent Jeeves.

Jeez(e (dʒiːz), *int. slang* (orig. *U.S.*). Also **Geez(e), Jese, Jez,** and with lower-case initial. [Corruption of JESUS.] = GEE *int.*²

1923 G. EMERY in A. H. Quinn *Contemp. Amer. Plays* 252 Gee-z—it's a cold night, I'll tell the world. **1930** J. DOS PASSOS *42nd Parallel* I. 73 Jez we got to get us women. **1932** L. GOLDING *Magnolia St.* III. vi. 546 'Jeeze!' he said. 'It's going to be a swell party!' **1934** J. BROPHY *Waterfront* i. 17, I wish you wouldn't say, Jeez. **1937** N. MARSH *Vintage Murder* xxi. 238 'Aw, Geeze!' said Wade disgustedly. 'What a case!' **1939** I. BAIRD *Waste Heritage* iii. 40 He muttered, 'Jese, Eddy, I don't know whether I ought to aplogise to you or turn you over to the cops.' **1946** 'S. RUSSELL' *To Bed with Grand Music* iii. 45 Jeez, I certainly am proud to be seen out with you. **1965** D. LODGE *Brit. Mus. is falling Down* x. 164 Geeze, was that you? What were you doing up there? **1968** A. HAILEY *Airport* I. iii. 43 At an adjoining table, a woman said loudly, 'Geez! Lookit the time!' **1970** *Private Eye* 2 Jan. 12 Jeez, that's nice of you to say so. **1971** *Melody Maker* 18 Dec. 30/6 Jeez, this travels.

jeff (dʒɛf), *sb.*¹ *Circus slang.* A rope.

1854 DICKENS *Hard T.* vi, Tight-Jeff or Slack-Jeff, it don't much signify; it's only tight-rope and slack-rope.

jeff (dʒɛf), *sb.*² Also **Jeff Davis.** [f. *Jefferson Davis* (1808–89), president of the Confederate States 1861–5.] A derogatory term for a man, usu. a 'hick' or a bore; esp. used by American Blacks of white men. Also *attrib.*, as ***jeff artist, hat.***

1870 O. LOGAN *Before Footlights* 202, I thought perhaps they imagined I was a female Jeff Davis, and were going to make a '*charge a la bayonette*' instanter. **1917** E. E. CUMMINGS *Let.* 4 June (1969) 26, I escaped repairing with the bums, mutts and Jeffs. **1938** C. CALLOWAY *Hi De Ho* 16 *Jeff*, a pest, a bore, an icky. **1946** MEZZROW & WOLFE *Really Blues* (1957) 375 *Jeff Davis*, an unenlightened person, a hick from down South; sometimes shortened to *jeff*. **1952** BERREY & VAN DEN BARK *Amer. Thes. Slang* (ed. 2) (1954) 391/3 *Jeff Davis, jeff*, a Southern 'hick'. **1969** *Publ. Amer. Dial. Soc.* LI. 29 Names used exclusively by Negroes.. jeff, jeffer, jeff davis, jeff artist. **1970** C. MAJOR *Dict. Afro-Amer. Slang* 70 *Jeff*,.. a white person;.. a dull person; a horrible square. **1973** *Black World* Apr. 57 He wears a jeff hat and a light raincoat.

jeff, *v. Printers' slang. intr.* 'To throw or gamble with quadrats as with dice' (Jacobi *Printers' Vocab.* 1888). Hence **'jeffing** *vbl. sb.*

1837 *Baltimore Commercial Transcript* 7 Nov. 2/1 (Th.), We move that the printers of the U.S. divide off in halves, and 'jeff' to see which shall go to digging ditches or picking stone coal for a living. **1841** W. SAVAGE *Dict. Art of Printing* 428 *Jeff.* See *Throw.* **1875** J. SOUTHWARD *Dict. Typogr.* (ed. 2) 58 *Jeffing*, throwing with quads... One of.. [the party interested] takes up the quads, shakes them.. and throws them.. after the manner of throwing dice, when the number of quads with the nicks appearing uppermost are counted,.. the highest thrower being the winner. **1884** J. GOULD *Letter-Press Printer* (ed. 3) 166/1 *Jeff*, to throw for a choice with quadrats instead of dice. **1888** *Amer. Humorist* (Farmer), He never set any type except in the rush of the last day, and then he would smouch all the poetry, and leave the rest to jeff for the solid takes. **1892** A. POWELL *Southward's Pract. Printing* (ed. 4) lxv. 577 In the old companionship system, the fat [*sc.* easy work] is distributed by 'jeffing', or 'throwing quads'. **1942** BERREY & VAN DEN BARK *Amer. Thes. Slang* § 526 *Jeff*, to play dice with em quadrates. **1947** E. HOWE *London Compositor* 24 A custom [*sc.* playing at quadrats] known in the nineteenth century as 'Jeffing'. **1967** F. J. M. WIJNEKUS *Elsevier's Dict. Printing & Allied Industr.* 177/2 *Jeffing*, gambling with nine one-em quadrates, i.e., to throw quards [*sic*] like dice, using the nick side, appearing uppermost, representing one and the other sides blanks. It is a very old custom, but now almost entirely out of practice.

jefferisite ('dʒɛfərɪsaɪt). *Min.* [Named 1866, after W. W. Jefferis, of Westchester, Pennsylvania: see -ITE.] A hydrous silicate of aluminium, iron, and magnesium, in foliated crystals, like mica, exfoliating in a remarkable manner when heated.

1866 *Amer. Jrnl. Sc.* Ser. II. XLI. 248 Jefferisite, a new mineral species. **1890** *Ibid.* Ser. III. XL. 455 The analogies between kerrite and jefferisite are perfectly clear.

Jeffersonian (dʒɛfə'səʊnɪən), *a.* and *sb. U.S. Hist.* and *Politics.* [f. the name of Thomas Jefferson, President of the United States 1801 to 1809.]

A. *adj.* Pertaining to President Jefferson, or holding the political doctrines held by or attributed to him (now called DEMOCRATIC, q.v.).

1800 *Connecticut Courant* 6 Oct. 1/3 The Jeffersonian party boast, that the increase of Jacobinism has been great in the Northern part of the United States, within the last year. **1806** *Balance* (Hudson, N.Y.) V. 35/3 Occlusion.. is a Jeffersonian word. **1813** *Niles' Reg.* IV. Suppl. 65/1 This is true Jeffersonian, Madisonian, democratic economy. **1838** *U.S. Mag & Democratic Rev.* Jan. 145 Jeffersonian republicanism. **1856** OLMSTED *Slave States* 302 A resolute determination.. not to be driven from the Jeffersonian creed upon Slavery. **1888** BRYCE *Amer. Commw.* II. III. liii. 333 One of these two parties carried on, under the name of Democrats, the dogmas and traditions of the Jeffersonian Republicans. *Ibid.* 342 In applying Jeffersonian doctrines the slave-holders stopped when they came to a black skin. **1972** *Science* 16 June 1223/3 The group takes a Jeffersonian view of the virtues of rotation in office and recommends that a committee member's service be limited to a 3-year term. **1972** *Listener* 21 Dec. 858 They didn't say: 'Yessir, Mr Jefferson, we are going to conquer the North-West for Jeffersonian democracy.'

B. *sb.* A supporter or follower of Jefferson; an adherent of the political doctrines held by or attributed to him: a Democrat.

1799 *Spectator* (N.Y.) 3 Apr. 1/1 Rouse, ye insurgents, rioters, refugees, and deserters! Ye friends to liberty and equality... Ye Jeffersonians, Gallatonians, Nicholites. **1803** *Fredericktown* (Maryland) *Herald* 30 Apr. 3/3 A thorough going Jeffersonian. **1880** *Libr. Univ. Knowl.* (N.Y.) I. 91 The Jeffersonians were eager for discriminations against England. **1888** BRYCE *Amer. Commw.* II. III. liii. 326 The Jeffersonians had more faith in the masses and in leaving things alone, together with less respect for authority. **1948** *Antioch Rev.* Spring 10 American Federalists openly sympathized with British Tories and American Jeffersonians with French Girondists.

Hence **Jeffer'sonianism,** the political doctrines held by or attributed to Jefferson.

1876 H. C. LODGE in *N. Amer. Rev.* CXXIII. 137 Ultimately Jeffersonianism must have prevailed, but at the time of its actual triumph it came too soon.

jeffersonite ('dʒɛfəsənaɪt). *Min.* [Named 1822, after President Jefferson: see prec. and -ITE.] A greenish-black variety of pyroxene, containing some zinc and manganese.

1822 *Amer. Jrnl. Sc.* V. 402 Jeffersonite.. has a great resemblance to pyroxene. **1852** SHEPARD *Min.* 199 Jeffersonite.. abounds in iron and manganese.

Jeffrey ('dʒɛfrɪ). The name of John *Jeffrey* (d. ?1854), British plant-collector, used *attrib.* or in the possessive to designate *Pinus jeffreyi*, a large pine with a spreading head of drooping branches, collected by him in California in 1852.

1858 G. GORDON *Pinetum* 198 *Pinus Jeffreyii*, Hort. Jeffrey's Pine... A noble tree, growing 150 feet high. **1908** N. L. BRITTON *N. Amer. Trees* 25 Black Pine, *Pinus Jeffreyi* A. Murray, also known as Jeffrey's pine.. occurs on dry volcanic mountains from southern Oregon through California. **1931** *Discovery* XII. 92/1 The insect [*sc.* the pandora moth] attacks only pines, its principal hosts being western yellow pine (*Pinus ponderosa*) and Jeffrey pine (*P. jeffreyi*). **1942** N. A. BOWERS *Cone-bearing Trees Pacific Coast* 107 As compared with the Yellow Pine, the Jeffrey cones are much denser; they are shaped like the old-fashioned beehive. **1965** *Listener* 20 May 742/3 There are a good many specimen trees of considerable age—Jeffrey's pine, the Bishop pine. **1967** N. T. MIROV *Genus Pinus* iii. 159 *Pinus jeffreyi*, commonly known as 'Jeffrey pine', has been considered by some botanists as a variety of *P. ponderosa*, while other specialists maintain it to be an independent species.

jeg (dʒɛg). [With sense 1 cf. JACK *sb.*¹ 31; with 2 cf. *jedge*, JADGE.]

†**1.** = JACK *sb.*¹ 31, a young pike. *Obs.*

1611 COTGR., *Lanceron*, a leg, or Iacke; a Pickerell thats about a foot long. **1708** MOTTEUX *Rabelais* IV. lx. (1737) 246 [in a list of fish, shell-fish, etc.] Jegs.

2. (See quot.)

1875 KNIGHT *Dict. Mech.*, *Jeg*, a templet or gage.. for verifying shapes of parts in gun and gun-stock making.

† **'jegget.** *Obs. rare*⁻⁰.

1736 AINSWORTH *Lat. Dict.*, A jegget [sausage], *Tucetum.*

jegotte, obs. form of GIGOT¹.

jehad: see JIHAD, a Muslim religious war.

je-ho, var. of GEE-HO: in quot. used as *sb.*

1731 ? ARBUTHNOT *Acc. Ginglicutt's Treat. Scolding Ancients* 25 Like the Je-ho to loitering Horses.

Jehoshaphat (dʒɪ'hɒʃəfæt, -səfæt). orig. *U.S.* Also **Jehosaphat,** etc. A biblical name (2 Sam. viii. 16, etc.) used interjectionally as a mild expletive. Freq. ***jumping Jehoshaphat.***

1857 S. A. HAMMETT *Sam Slick in Texas* xxiv. 161 'Jehosophat!'.. 'Easy over the stones, Joe,' ses I. **1866** MAYNE REID *Headless Horseman* vi. 39 Geehosofat! what a putty beest it air! *Ibid.* xviii. 100 By the jumpin' Geehosofat, what a gurl she air sure enuf! **1876** [see GREAT *a.* 12 c]. **1898** J. D. BRAYSHAW *Slum Silhouettes* 123 'Oh, Jehosephat!' cried the old man, with a chuckle. **1935** G. HEYER *Death in Stocks* iv. 41 'Great jumping Jehoshaphat!' he exclaimed. 'Who did it?' **1972** *Guardian* 16 Dec. 10/1 Why Jeehosophat, Houston, you surely have hit the jack-rabbit on the head.

‖**Jehovah** (dʒɪ'həʊvə). [The English and common European representation, since the 16th c., of the Hebrew divine name *Yhwh*. This word (the 'sacred tetragrammaton') having come to be considered by the Jews too sacred for utterance, was pointed in the O.T. by the Masoretes with the vowels ' (= ă), ō, ā, of *ădōnāi*, as a direction to the reader to substitute ADONAI for the 'ineffable name'; which is actually done by Jerome in the Vulgate translation of Exodus vi. 3, and hence by Wyclif. Students of Hebrew at the Revival of Letters took these vowels as those of the word *Yhwh* (IHUH, JHVH) itself, which was accordingly transliterated in Latin spelling as IeHoVa(H), i.e. *Iehoua(h.* It is now held that the original name was IaHUe(H), i.e. *Jahve(h*, or with the English values of the letters, *Yahwe(h*, and one or other of these forms is now generally used by writers upon the religion of the Hebrews. The word has generally been understood to be a derivative of the verb *hāwāh* to be, to exist, as if 'he that is', 'the self-existent', or 'the one ever coming into manifestation'; this origin is now disputed, but no conjectured derivation which has been substituted has found general acceptance.

The following is cited as the first use of the form *Iehoua* (*Jehova*):—

1516 P. GALATINUS *De Arcanis Cath. Veritatis* II. lf. xlviij, Non *enim* hę quatuor literę [*yhwh*] si, ut punctatę sunt, legantur, Ioua reddunt: sed (ut ipse optime nosti) Iehoua efficiunt.]

1. The principal and personal name of God in the Old Testament; in English versions usually represented by 'the LORD'. Hence in modern Christian use, = God, the Almighty.

1530 TINDALE *Exod.* vi. 3, I appeared vnto Abraham Isaac and Iacob an allmightie God: but in my name Iehouah [*Wyclif* Adonay] was I not knowne vnto them. **1539** BIBLE (Great) *Ps.* lxxxiii. 18 They shall know that thou (whose name is Iehoua) art only the most hyest ouer all the earth. **1600** HEYWOOD *Edw. IV*, Author to Bk. 24 If then the world a theater present.. In which Iehove does as spectator sit. **1667** MILTON *P.L.* VII. 602 Great are thy works, Jehovah, infinite Thy power. **1738** POPE *Univ. Prayer* 4 Father of All! in ev'ry Age, In ev'ry Clime ador'd, By Saint, by Savage, and by Sage, Jehovah, Jove, or Lord! **1821** BYRON *Cain* I. i, All hail! Jehovah, with returning light, all hail! **1860** PUSEY *Min. Proph.* 77 It is better to own ignorance, how this Name of God is pronounced, than to use the name Jehovah, which is certainly wrong, or any other, which can only be conjectural.

β. Examples of recent forms of the word.

1869 J. E. CARPENTER tr. *Ewald's Hist. Israel* II. 130 Jahveh alone was the true defence. **1892** MONTEFIORE *Hibbert Lect.* 45 Yahveh, to the Israelite, was emphatically the God of Right. **1899** R. H. CHARLES *Eschatol., Heb., Jew. & Chr.* 8 As the natural God, Yahwe was the invisible Head of the nation.

2. ***Jehovah's Witness,*** a member of a fundamentalist millenary sect, the Watchtower Bible and Tract Society, founded *c* 1879 (under the name 'International Bible Students') by Charles Taze Russell (1852–1916), which rejects institutional religion and refuses to acknowledge the claims of the State when these are in conflict with the principles of the sect. Occas. ***Jehovah Witness.***

[**1932** J. F. RUTHERFORD *Health & Life* (Watchtower Bible & Tract Soc.) 7 This commandment is written, in Isaiah 62:10, directed to Jehovah's faithful witnesses.] **1933** M. S. CZATT (*title*) The International Bible Students, Jehovah's Witnesses. **1941** H. G. WELLS *You can't be too Careful* IV. i. 223 A single declared Fascist or Communist or Jehovah's Witness or Single Taxer. **1944** G. B. SHAW *Everybody's Pol. What's What?* v. 46 May he choose.. a tribal idol as the sect called Jehovah's Witnesses now do? **1955** W. GADDIS *Recognitions* II. i. 305 It's like Jehovah's Witnesses when you sit down at a table there, everybody comes over. **1961** *Times* 5 May 20/6 A rhesus-positive baby whose father, a Jehovah Witness, refused to consent to a blood transfusion. **1962** *Lancet* 7 Apr. 747/2 Jehovah Witnesses will usually accept their own blood at operation, though they would not take that of a donor. **1973** *Guardian* 14 Mar. 7/4 A mother who divorced her husband because of his adultery is to lose her children because of her religious beliefs. She is a Jehovah's Witness. *Ibid.*, To bring up the children under the Jehovah Witness cult would tend to isolate them.

Hence †**Je'hovian, Je'hovic** *adjs.*, of or pertaining to Jehovah. †**Je'hovism,** the relation of Jehovah to his people and church.

1822 C. WELLS *Stories after Nature* (1891) 218 His inveteracy of purpose was in its depth Satanic, as a saint's is Jehovian. **1872** D. BROWN *Life John Duncan* xi. 228 On this Jehovism Mr. Duncan would at times wax grand. **1884** G. F. PENTECOST *Out of Egypt* iii. 46 As He announced the unspeakable Jehovic name, he at the same time interpreted it.

Jehovist (dʒɪ'həʊvɪst). [f. JEHOV(AH + -IST.]

†**1.** One who holds that the vowel-points annexed to the word Jehovah in Hebrew represent the actual vowels of the word; opposed to ADONIST. *Obs.*

1753 CHAMBERS *Cycl. Supp.* s.v. *Adonists*, Adonists stands opposed to Jehovists [see also ADONIST].

2. A name applied by Hebraists to the author (or authors) of those non-Deuteronomic parts of the Hexateuch in which the divine name is the word *Yhwh*, rendered 'Jehovah'; opposed to ELOHIST.

Now more usually JAHVIST or *Yahwist*, in accordance with more recent notions as to the form of the name.

1844 M. STUART *O.T. Canon* (1849) §3. 50 The Jehovist (proh pudor! to form such a sacrilegious appellation) i.e. the one who employs Jehovah [to designate the Godhead]. **1856** DAVIDSON *Horne's Introd.* II. 598 A twofold tradition seems to have been worked up by the Jehovist [in *Gen.* xxxvii.

23–30]. **1862** —— *Introd. to O.T.* I. 30 In biographies the difference between the Elohist and Jehovist is remarkable. **1885** tr. *Wellhausen's Hist. Israel* 333 With the Jehovist also the genealogy underlies the narrative as its skeleton.

Hence **Jeho'vistic** *a.*, of or pertaining to the Jehovist or Jehovists, characterized by the use of the name 'Jehovah'; also (rarely) pertaining to the religion of Jehovah. In both senses more recent writers use JAHVISTIC (or *Yahwistic*).

1841 RYLAND *Hengstenberg on Pentat.* (1847) I. 335 No instance occurs in this chapter [Gen. xii.] where, even in the Jehovistic connection, Elohim is required. **1856** DAVIDSON *Horne's Introd.* II. 623 A plan can be discovered in the Jehovistic as well as in the Elohistic document. **1885** tr. *Wellhausen* in *Encycl. Brit.* XVIII. 506/1 The second Elohist is preserved only in extracts embodied in the Jehovistic book. **1885** tr. *Wellhausen's Hist. Israel* 91 Not only in the Jehovistic but also in the Deuteronomic legislation the festivals rest upon agriculture.

Jehu ('dʒiːhjuː). *humorous.* [In allusion to 2 Kings ix. 20 'the driving is like the driving of Jehu the son of Nimshi, for he driveth furiously'.] **a.** A fast or furious driver. **b.** A driver, a coachman.

1682 DRYDEN *Medal* 119 But this new Jehu spurs the hot-mouth'd horse. **1682** S. PORDAGE *Medal Rev.* 124 And if these Jehu's who so fiercely drive, In their sinister Arts proceed and thrive. **1694** CONGREVE *Double-Dealer* III. iii, Our Jehu was a hackney-coachman When my lord took him. **1759** GOLDSM. *Bee* No. 5 (*Reverie*), He assured the Coach-man that.. his baggage.. was perfectly light. But Jehu was inflexible. **1826** *Sporting Mag.* XVII. 243 'Team' and 'Drag' are terms very generally made use of by Gentlemen Jehus. **1877** M. M. GRANT *Sun-Maid* ii, He admired Gilbert as a Jehu.

c. *attrib.* and *Comb.*

1755 *Man* xxxiii. 2 There came behind me a Jehu driver of a phaeton. **1830** N. .S. WHEATON *Jrnl.* 338 He manages his fiery steeds in a very Jehu-like style.

Hence **'Jehu** *v.*, to drive (*trans.* and *intr.*).

1822 GALT *Sir A. Wylie* II. viii. 77 Miss Julia and Mr. Mordaunt jehuing awa in a chaise and four. **1825** *Examiner* 266/2 He himself was Jehu-ing this four-wheeled carriage.

jehup *v.*: see GEE-UP.

jeig, obs. Sc. f. JIG.

jeine, obs. form of JEAN.

jeistiecor ('dʒiːstɪkɔː(r)). Scotch form of JUSTAUCORPS, a close-fitting garment: cf. CHESTICORE.

1818 SCOTT *Rob Roy* vi, It's a sight for sair een to see a gold-laced jeistiecor in the Ha' garden sae late at e'en.

jeit, obs. Sc. form of JET.

jejunal (dʒiː'dʒuːnəl), *a.* [f. JEJUN-UM + -AL¹.] Of or pertaining to the jejunum.

1887 in *Syd. Soc. Lex.* **1897** *Allbutt's Syst. Med.* III. 819 Jejunal intussusceptions.

†**jeju'nation.** *Obs.* [ad. late L. *jejūnātiōnem* (Tertull.), n. of action from *jejūnāre* to fast.] Fasting, abstinence from food.

1623 COCKERAM, *Ieiunation*, fasting. **1632** LITHGOW *Trav.* x. 445 Restrained to a relenting ieiunation. **1658** in PHILLIPS.

jeju'nator. *rare.* [late L., agent-n. from *jējūnāre* to fast.] A faster.

1858 *Earnest Exhort. Chr. Unity* v. 400 The recipients of the jejunator's acts of bounty.

jejune (dʒiː'dʒuːn), *a.* [ad. L. *jējūn-us* fasting.] †**1.** Without food, fasting; hungry. *Obs.*

a **1619** FOTHERBY *Atheom.* II. ii. §2 (1622) 199 When their Bellies are distended, and full; yet their appetites are ieiune, and emptie. **1670** J. BEALE in *Phil. Trans.* V. 1162 Poor and jejune people, who are accustomed to drinks almost as weak as water. *a* **1754** J. MᶜLAURIN *Serm. & Ess.* (1755) 156 That cold, jejune, lifeless frame.

2. Deficient in nourishing or substantial (physical) qualities; thin, attenuated, scanty; meagre, unsatisfying; (of land) poor, barren.

1646 SIR T. BROWNE *Pseud. Ep.* III. xxi. 162 Jejune or limpid water, and nearer the simplicity of its Element. *a* **1652** J. SMITH *Sel. Disc.* v. 146 Those jejune and insipid morsels. **1696** WHISTON *The. Earth* IV. (1722) 352 They might never see such a Poor, Jejune, and Degenerate State of the Vegetable Kingdom. **1708** J. PHILIPS *Cyder* I. 54 Not from the sable ground expect success, Nor from cretaceous, stubborn and jejune. **1833** J. RENNIE *Alph. Angling* 5 That they [fish] are best pleased with such jejune diet may easily be confuted.

3. a. Unsatisfying to the mind or soul; dull, flat, insipid, bald, dry, uninteresting; meagre, scanty, thin, poor; wanting in substance or solidity. Said of thought, feeling, action, etc., and *esp.* of speech or writing; also *transf.* of the speaker or writer. (The prevailing sense.)

1615 [implied in JEJUNELY]. **1647** H. MORE *Song of Soul* II. iii. I. xiii, Jejune exilities. *a* **1652** J. SMITH *Sel. Disc.* ii. 41 A forced and jejune devotion, void of inward life and love. **1656–63** BULLOKAR *Eng. Expos.* s.v., When we say of an Oration, Sermon, or any Discourse, that it is *Jejune*, we mean Sorry, paltry, and very dangerous stuff. **1671** R. BOHUN *Wind* 49 Have employed so much time in such empty and jejune speculations. *c* **1705** BERKELEY *Comm.-pl. Bk.* Wks. 1871 IV. 478 The short jejune way in mathematiques will not do in metaphysiques. **1758** BLACKSTONE in *Comm.* I. 16 He gives what seems.. a very jejune and unsatisfactory reason. **1818** HALLAM *Mid. Ages* iii. I. (1872) I. 395 The chroniclers of those times are few and jejune.

b. Puerile, childish; also, naïve.

¶ This use may owe its origin to the mistaken belief that the word is connected with L. *juvenis* young (comp. *junior*), or F. *jeune* young.

1898 G. B. SHAW *Arms & Man* II. 29 His jejune credulity as to the absolute value of his concepts. **1975** *Economist* 22 Nov. 14/1 Is anybody.. now so jejune as not to realise that the state ownership of the deadweight of present nationalised industries must prevent Labour governments from being able to follow.. their social policies. **1982** *N.Y. Times Mag.* 8 Aug. 10 Other people.. write in to correct you if you define the word..'jejune' as 'childish'. **1982** M. HOWARD *Eppie* (1983) xxxiii. 271 Mother seemed jejune, at times, with her enthusiasms and her sense of mission.

†**4.** *jejune gut*: = JEJUNUM. *Obs.*

1696 PHILLIPS (ed. 5), *Jejune Gut*, the second of the small Guts, so called, because it is frequently empty.

jejunely (dʒiː'dʒuːnlɪ), *adv.* [f. prec. + -LY².] In a jejune manner; meagrely, insipidly.

1615 SIR E. HOBY *Curry-Combe* ii. 100 The Knight saw how Ieiunely his Aduersary pleaded for Purgatory. **1665** BOYLE *New Exp. Cold* Pref., Wks. 1772 II. 475 Other learned writers.. have handled it exceedingly jejunely. **1805** SYD. SMITH *Elem. Sk. Mor. Philos.* (1850) 170. **1850** SIR H. TAYLOR *Sicil. Summer* I. ii, And teach us, not jejunely what we are, But what we may be when the Parian block Yields to the hand of Phidias.

jejuneness (dʒiː'dʒuːnnɪs). [f. as prec. + -NESS.] The quality of being jejune.

1. Deficiency of (physical) substance; thinness, meagreness, attenuation.

1626 BACON *Sylva* §799 The Ieiunenesse or extreme Comminution of Spirits. **1703** *Art Vintners & Wine-Coopers* 5 The grand and proxim Cause seems to be their Jejuneness and poverty of Spirits.

2. Emptiness of interest or intellectually satisfying quality; baldness, meagreness, poverty.

1655 FULLER *Ch. Hist.* VIII. i. §41 Many much admiring the jejunenesse of his discourse. **1796** BURKE *Let. to Noble Lord* Wks. VIII. 48 The jejuneness and penury of our municipal law. **1886** STUBBS *Lect. Hist.* xv. 339 The pages of the annalist, where there are any, are so dull that we scarcely complain of their jejuneness.

je'junery. *nonce wd.* [f. JEJUNE + -ERY.] Fasting; jejune writing.

1846 LANDOR *Wks.* II. 157/2 For these forty good verses you will pardon, 'After forty days' fasting had remained'... Very much like the progress of Milton himself in this jejunery.

jejunity (dʒiː'dʒuːnɪtɪ). [ad. L. *jējūnitās* emptiness of stomach, fasting, meagreness, f. *jējūnus* JEJUNE.] = JEJUNENESS.

1623 COCKERAM, *Ieiunitie*, barrennesse, or slendernesse of stile. **1719** BENTLEY *Epist., to S. Clarke* 18 Nov., Pray extend your Spartan jejunity to the length of a competent letter. **1891** *Sat. Rev.* 5 Dec. 641/1 Criticism.. exempt from impertinence and from servility, from jejunity and from *fronde*.

jejuno- (dʒiːˌdʒuːnəʊ), used as combining form of JEJUNUM, as in **jeˌjuno-duo'denal** *a.*, belonging to the jejunum and the duodenum; **jeˌjuno'ileum** [prob. ad. F. *jéjuno-iléon* (J. Cruveilhier *Traité d'Anat. path.* (1849) I. 718)], the small intestine exclusive of the duodenum; the jejunum and ileum considered together; **jeˌjunojeju'nostomy** [-STOMY], the operation of joining, and creating a passage between, two parts of the jejunum so that the intervening part is bypassed; **jeju'nostomy** [-STOMY], the operation of attaching the jejunum to the abdominal wall and making an opening, through which the patient may be fed, directly into the jejunum from the exterior; also, the opening thus made.

1897 *Allbutt's Syst. Med.* III. 591 The jejuno-duodenal orifice is narrowed. **1876** DUNGLISON *Dict. Med. Sci.* (rev. ed.) 561/2 Jejunoileum. **1955** R. T. SHACKELFORD *Bickham-Callander Surg. Alimentary Tract* II. vii. 999 The jejunoileum.. is coiled in a complicated fashion. **1925** DORLAND *Med. Dict.* (ed. 13) 595/2 Jejunojejunostomy. **1955** R. T. SHACKELFORD *Bickham-Callander Surg. Alimentary Tract* I. ii. 330 Most surgeons do not perform jejunojejunostomy routinely with antecolic gastrojejunostomy. **1885** *Brit. Med. Jrnl.* 5 Dec. 1063/2 For the operation of jejunostomy, as he [*sc.* C. H. Golding-Bird] termed the one that he detailed, he claimed that.. it was.. the best palliative operation for pyloric cancer. **1948** T. H. SOMERVELL *Surg. Stomach & Duodenum* xxvii. 500 The patient is well nursed, and nourished through the jejunostomy. **1971** CAREY & ALBERTIN *Ellison's Atlas Surg. Stomach & Duodenum* ix. 125 Even though parenteral hyperalimentation has decreased the need for jejunostomy, it remains a valuable procedure. *Ibid.* 130 Feedings through the jejunostomy should not be attempted until the return of normal bowel activity.

‖**jejunum** (dʒiː'dʒuːnəm). *Anat.* Also 6 ieiunium. [Mediæval application of L. *jējūnum*, neuter of *jējūnus* JEJUNE *a.* (sc. *intestinum*). So F. *jejunum* (1541 in Hatz.-Darm.).] The second part of the small intestine, between the duodenum and ileum, the limits of which, where it passes into the ileum, are ill-defined.

[**1398** TREVISA *Barth. De P.R.* v. xlii. (1495) 158 The seconde subtyll gutte in latyn is callyd ieiunium to vnderstonde in englyssh, fastynge, for he is alwaye voyde of mete and drynke, that gutte putteth of al thynges fro it selfe, and holdith no thynge to his owne fedynge.] **1541** R. COPLAND *Guydon's Quest. Chirurg.* H iv, After this is the gut that hyght Ieiunium, bycause it is alwayes emptye for the greate multytude of messerayke veynes that be aboute it contynually suckynge it. **1706** *Phil. Trans.* XXV. 2302 The *cæcum*.. red coloured like the *jejunum* in a Man. **1831** R. KNOX *Cloquet's Anat.* 613 The jejunum occupies the two upper fifths of the small intestine, and the ileum the rest of its extent. It is easy enough to see that such a division is arbitrary and has no sufficient foundation.

Jekyll ('dʒɛkɪl, 'dʒɛk(ə)l). The name of the hero of R. L. Stevenson's story, 'Strange Case of Dr. Jekyll and Mr. Hyde' (published 1886), who appears as a benevolent and respectable character under the name of *Jekyll* and the opposite under the name of *Hyde*: used allusively in reference to opposite sides of a person's character or to persons or things of a dual character, alternately good and evil. Also *attrib.* (Cf. HYDE.)

? **1885** F. STEVENSON *Let.* in J. Pope-Hennessy *R. L. Stevenson* (1974) ix. 179 While one side represents an angel, the devil must have posed for another... Plainly Jekyll and Hyde. **1887** *Puck* (U.S.) XXII. 188 Is that you, Livingston? .. No, m' dearsh, it'sh Doct' Hyde. Mist' Jekyll didn't.. g-g' out t'night! **1902** *Daily Chron.* 22 May 3/4 While the left lobe is the Jekyll of the intellect. the right, on occasion at least, is apt to play the part of Hyde. **1905** *Strand Mag.* Apr. 455/2 Meeting a young and winsome feminine counterpart of Dr. Jekyll and Mr. Hyde in real life is a very plesant, if novel, experience. **1915** 'I. HAY' *First Hundred Thousand* xiv. 187 When he is good he is very good indeed, and when he is bad he is horrid. He is either Jekyll or Hyde. *Ibid.*, But we encountered surprisingly few Hydes. Nearly all were Jekylls—Jekylls of the most competent and courteous type. **1929** W. J. LOCKE *Ancestor Jorico* xviii. 253 Suppose it pleased him to lead a Jekyll and Hyde sort of life? **1931** *Times Lit. Suppl.* 2 July 522/1 Turner was a case of Jekyll and Hyde in real life and oscillated continuously between the Victorian respectability of Bloomsbury.. and the Rabelaisian society of the London Docks. **1945** A. J. P. TAYLOR *Course German Hist.* 146 A Jekyll and Hyde policy, the bureaucrat Jekylls confident until too late that they could always shake off the Pan-German Hyde at their convenience. **1971** L. P. DAVIES *Shadow Before* xi. 128 We are all a mixture of good and evil, Jekyll and Hyde, if you like.

‖**jelab** ('dʒɛləb). Also jelib, jellab. [ad. Arab. *jilyāb* a tunic.] A hooded cloak worn in Morocco.

1849 W. S. MAYO *Kaloolah* (1850) 170 The jelib, the haick, the barnouse and kaftán. **1889** HALL CAINE *Scapegoat* (1891) I. Introd. 17 His dress was hardly less brilliant—a chocolate jellab over a kaftan of several colours.

jelacy, jelesye, obs. forms of JEALOUSY.

jeldi, var. JILDI.

jelefloure, obs. form of GILLYFLOWER.

‖**jelick** ('dʒɛlɪk, *prop.* 'jɛlɪk). Also jellick. [Turkish *yelek* waistcoat.] A vest or bodice worn by Turkish women.

1816 R. TULLY *Narr. 10 Yrs.' Resid. Tripoli* 31 Over it [her chemise] she wore a gold and silver tissue jelick, with coral and pearl buttons, set quite close together down the front. **1821** BYRON *Juan* III. lxx, Of all the dresses I select Haidée's: she wore two jelicks—one was of pale yellow;.. With buttons form'd of pearls as large as peas All gold and crimson shone her jelick's fellow.

jelious, jelius, obs. forms of JEALOUS.

jell (dʒɛl), *v.* orig. *U.S. colloq.* [Back-formation from JELLY *sb.*¹] **1.** *intr.* To become a jelly; to congeal or jelly. Also *fig.*, to take definite or satisfactory shape; = CRYSTALLIZE *v.* 5. Cf. GEL *v.* Hence **jelled** *ppl. a.*

1830–40 [Remembered by F. Hall]. **1869** L. M. ALCOTT *Little Women* II. 60 The jelly won't jell. **1874** MISS ALCOTT *Little Women Wedded* v, She reboiled, resugared, and restrained, but that dreadful stuff wouldn't *jell*. **1879** *Scribner's Mag.* XIX. 823/1 One of the gravest questions in the domestic economy, whether the jelly will 'jell'. **1902** *Fortn. Rev.* June 1021 (*heading*) Why a nerve tends to 'jell'. **1908** *Daily Chron.* 20 Mar. 3/3 [He] remarked of his countrywomen's minds that they 'didn't jell'; but he possibly, and mistakenly, thought he was talking American. **1937** *Maclean's Mag.* 15 Apr. 17/3 Davis shook his head, but the look of innocent disclaimer in his cherubic eyes didn't quite jell. **1956** K. FARRELL *Cost of Living* 138 'Not going well?' 'Hardly going at all. Even the cat book doesn't quite jell.' **1958** K. AMIS *I like it Here* ix. 113 His uncertainty.. now felt more or less permanently jelled. **1958** *Observer* 18 May 10/5 Let jell in cool larder. **1959** P. H. JOHNSON *Unspeakable Skipton* iv. 26 They did the music by itself, later, at the Wigmore Hall, but it didn't jell. **1970** *Times* 5 Dec. 21/1 The present Parliament is only two parliamentary months old.., and although it will jell in time, it has not yet done so. **1972** *Times Lit. Suppl.* 12 Jan. 45/5 Somehow his case against RTZ as a sort of Hydra does not quite jell. **1972** *Village Voice* (N.Y.) 1 June 24/3 These detective novels were written very fast, read extremely well, and, as Himes told me: 'They worked. They jelled.'

2. *trans.* = JELLIFY *v.* 1. Also *fig.*, to give shape to; to make clear and definite.

1905 *Dialect Notes* III. 62 *Jell*, make or turn into jelly. **1935** *Forres Gaz.* 6 Nov. 4/5 To jell (to firm jelly). **1941** A. J. CRONIN *Keys of Kingdom* (1942) ii. 20 The tea was delicious, the scones and bannocks home-made, the preserves jelled by Elizabeth's own hands. **1948** *Newsweek* 10 May 58/3 The studio also ordered that no scripts be

bought unless it was certain they could be jelled onto film. **1968** J. M. Ziman *Public Knowl.* v. 91 The course work is too rich a diet, and the knowledge it contains has been jelled too soon.

jell (dʒɛl), *sb.* orig. *U.S.* [f. the vb.] A jelly or gel.

1870 'F. Fern' *Ginger-Snaps* 262 My excellent country friends put up pounds and quarts of 'jell' every fall. **1951** *Good Housek. Home Encycl.* 423/1 Allow it to boil briskly, without stirring, until a jell is obtained on testing. **1959** *Listener* 11 June 1043/1 The sticky jells given by other starches such as tapioca and arrowroot.

jellaba(h), jellibee, varr. GALABIYA. Cf. JELAB.

1904 A. E. W. Mason *Truants* xxv. 233 A black jellaba and cap, such as the Jews must wear in Morocco. **1922** Joyce *Ulysses* 742 Longbearded jews in their jellibees. **1964** *Punch* 19 Feb. 278/3 'He had always a bottle of whisky under his jellaba,' Si Mohammed went on. **1969** *Daily Tel.* (Colour Suppl.) 24 Jan. 17/2 A girl called Susy in a jellabah like John Hanson in *Desert Song*.

jellettite ('dʒɛlɪtaɪt). *Min.* [Named 1853 after Rev. Prof. Jellett of Dublin: see -ITE.] A green variety of lime-iron garnet.

1853 Apjohn in *Jrnl. Geol. Soc., Dublin* V. 120 This mineral, which is undoubtedly new, it is proposed to call Jellettite, after the distinguished mathematician through whose means it has been made the subject of chemical and mineralogical examination. **1868** Dana *Min.* (ed. 5) 269 *Jelletite* is green garnet, light or dark, and yellowish-green, from the moraine of the Findel glacier near Zermatt.

jellico ('dʒɛlɪkəʊ). Also jeelyco. Corruption of ANGELICA; applied also to another umbelliferous plant, *Sium helenianum*, of St. Helena.

1853 Johnston *Bot. E. Bord.* 86 *Angelica sylvestris.* Jeelyco: Ground-Ash. **1879** Britten & Holland *Plant-n.*, Jeelico, *Angelica sylvestris.* **1884** Miller *Plant-n.*, 'Jellico', of St. Helena, *Sium helenianum*.

jellied ('dʒɛlɪd), *a.* [f. JELLY *sb.*¹ and *v.* + -ED.]

1. Turned into jelly; brought to, or having, the consistence of jelly; congealed, coagulated.

1593 Nashe *Christ's T.* (1613) 61 Slimy flood-gates for thicke iellied gore to sluce out by. **1601** [? Marston] *Pasquil & Kath.* iii. 185 Thou'lt serue to make him gellide broaths. **1710** T. Fuller *Pharm. Extemp.* 13 Hydropic Ale..melting down the gelly'd Lympha. **1819** Shelley *Cenci* iv. iii, My breath Comes..lighter, and the jellied blood Runs freely thro' my veins.

†**2.** Flavoured with jelly, sweet. *Obs.*

a **1658** Cleveland *Poems* (1677) 6 Now to the melting Kiss that sips The Jellied Philtre of her Lips; So Sweet there is no Tongue can prays't.

3. Coated with jelly; made or cooked inside jelly.

1895 'M. Ronald' *Century Cook Bk.* iv. 171 Jellied veal..a good cold dish to use with salad. *Ibid.* v. 182 Jellied boned chicken. A braised boned chicken may be..jellied as follows. **1907** *Daily Chron.* 6 June 5/5 'Jellied eel! 'Ave a plate; lovally jelly,' shouts a third. **1908** *Ibid.* 6 July 3/4 She ..knows the secrets of jellied eels. **1911** *Daily Colonist* (Victoria, B.C.) 26 Apr. 10/5 (Advt.), Jellied Ham per lb. 40¢. **1960** *Good Housek. Cookery Bk.* (rev. ed.) 84/2 Jellied eels. *Ibid.* 157/2 Jellied sheep's tongues. *Ibid.* 524/1 Jellied eggs.

jellify ('dʒɛlɪfaɪ), *v.* Also jellyfy. [See -FY.]

1. *trans.* To convert into jelly; to reduce to the consistence of jelly.

1806 Southey *Lett.* (1856) I. 374 My solids seem to be jellified by so much shaking. **1866** Blackmore *Cr. Nowell* lvii. (1883) 396 A little snake, semi-transparent and jellified.

2. *intr.* To become or turn into a jelly.

1880 Miss Bird *Japan* II. 201 Soap jellyfies, ink turns mouldy.

Hence '**jellified** *ppl. a.*; also **jellifi'cation**, the action of 'jellifying'.

1864 Sala in *Daily Tel.* 1 Nov., A bundle of jellyfied seaweed. **1881** *Sat. Rev.* 24 Sept. 383/2 In process of jellification. **1883** *Hardwich's Photogr. Chem.* (ed. Taylor) 374 The washing of the jellified emulsion to remove from it the crystallizable salts.

jellily, *adv.*: see after JELLY *a.*

Jell-o, Jello ('dʒɛləʊ). Chiefly *N. Amer.* [f. JELLY *sb.*] The proprietary name of a powder used to make a fruit-flavoured gelatin dessert; loosely (with lower-case initial), jelly.

1934 *Trade Marks Jrnl.* 11 July 907 *Jell-o.* Brand of Jelly Powder... Jell-o can be placed in the refrigerator as soon as dissolved... The Jell-o Company of Canada Limited.. Montreal, Canada; Manufacturers. **1936** *Amer. Speech* XI. 40 *Nervous pudding, Shivering Liz,* or *Shimmy* for jello.. describe neatly. **1945** *New Yorker* 1 Dec. 36/2 Carola.. learned to prefer salt fish and bean curd..to Jello and cereal. **1961** *Guardian* 29 Mar. 12/4 All the side dishes of salad and jello were there. **1971** *Black Scholar* Sept. 44/2 Her firm young breasts quivering like a dish of molded jello. **1972** *Sat. Rev.* (U.S.) 27 May 7/2 Herb Edelman's well-turned contribution as the agent with a heart of jello.

jelloid. [f. JELLY: see -OID.] A preparation of some drug in gelatine; a gelatine tabloid.

1898 *Allbutt's Syst. Med.* V. 514 Little lozenges containing iron, called 'jelloids'.

jellop, jelloped: see JOLLOP, JOLLOPED.

jelly ('dʒɛlɪ), *sb.*¹ Forms: 4 geli, 5 gelle, 5–6 gele, gely(e, iely, 5–9 gelly, 6 gelley, (chely, gelu), 6–7 gellie, -ye, iellie, 7– jelly. [ME. *gelé*, a. F. *gelée* frost, also (14th c. in Littré) jelly:—L. *gelāta* frozen, congealed, pa. pple. of *gelāre* to freeze, used subst. in Romanic: see -ADE.]

1. a. An article of food, consisting chiefly of gelatin, obtained from various animal tissues, as skin, tendons, bones, etc., by boiling and subsequent cooling, having a characteristic soft stiff homogeneous consistence, and usually semitransparent. Also, in later use, a preparation of the juice of fruit, or other vegetable substances, thickened into a similar consistence.

1393 [see *jelly-cloth* in 4]. **14..** Lydg. *Hors, Shepe, & G.* (Roxb.) 19 Of the shepe..Of whos hede boylled..Ther cometh a gely [*MS. Lamb.* 306 Iely] and an oynement. *c* **1430** *Two Cookery-bks.* 25 Gelye de chare. *Ibid.* 26 Gelye de Fysshe..Do as þou dedyst be þat oþer Gelye. **1523** Fitzherb. *Husb.* §44 Tyll it begyn to waxe thycke lyke a gelly. **1525–6** in Nichols *Progr. Q. Eliz.* (1823) I. 252 *note*, All honest manner and good order,..in wine, brawn, chely, or other vitails. *a* **1548** Hall *Chron., Hen. VIII,* 80b, Spices, fruites, ielies, and banket viandes. **1602** Plat *Delights* (1605) §58 A white gelly of Almonds. **1657** R. Ligon *Barbadoes* (1673) 37 Jelly which we make of the flesh of young pigs, calves feet, and a cock. **1732** Arbuthnot *Rules of Diet* i. in *Aliments*, etc. 249 The Jelly or Juice of Red Cabbage, bak'd in an Oven. *Ibid.* 252 Robs and Gellies of Garden Fruits. *c* **1850** *Arab. Nts.* (Rtldg.) 179 She desired some thick jelly made from chickens..to be served up.

†**b.** The substance GELATIN, which forms the basis of animal jellies. *Obs.*

1800 tr. *Lagrange's Chem.* II. 414 A mucous matter, exceedingly soluble in warm water, which is known under the name of *Jelly*. **1805** W. Saunders *Min. Waters* 13 Animal gelly which is easy of solution. **1839** G. Bird *Nat. Phil.* 373 Jelly, solutions of gum, and albuminous fluids, allowed to evaporate spontaneously, so as to leave an indurated mass. **1855** Mayne *Expos. Lex.*, *Jelly*, common name for the substance gelatine.

c. A table-jelly.

1728 E. Smith *Compleat Housewife* (ed. 2) 146 *To make Riben Jelly*..run the Jelly into little high Glasses..one Colour must be thorough cold before you put another on.. colour red with Cochineal, green with Spinage..and sometimes the Jelly by it self. **1845** E. Acton *Mod. Cookery* (ed. 2) xx. 438 A great variety of..excellent jellies for the table may be made with clarified isinglass, clear syrup, and the juice of..fresh fruit. **1851** *Illustr. Catal. Gt. Exhib.* iii. 650/1 Moulds for jellies, cakes, &c. **1916** *Punch* 6 Dec. 394/2 He shook all over like a badly-set jelly. **1930** C. Mackenzie *April Fools* vii. 152 Mr. Wenlow, balanced like a pale jelly on the edge of a chair in the drawing-room. **1974** *Radio Times* 4 Apr. 42/4 (Advt.), Rowntrees strawberry flavour jelly.

2. a. *gen.* Anything of the consistence of jelly; a gelatinous substance of any kind. ***glycerin(e) jelly***, any of various mixtures of glycerol and gelatin, principally used as mounting media in microscopy; cf. JELLY *sb.* 2d; ***royal jelly***, the secretion produced by honey bees to feed the larvae of the colony, esp. those that will become queens.

c **1600** Donne *Progr. Soul* xxiii, A female fishes sandie Roe With the males jelly newly lev'ned was. **1605** Timme *Quersit.* iii. 178 Take of..the ielly or sperme of frogges, which is to be found in standing waters. **1605** Shaks. *Lear* iii. vii. 83 *Ser.* My Lord, you haue one eye left... *Corn.* Lest it see more, preuent it; Out vilde gelly. **1631** Massinger *Beleeve as you list* iii. ix, How my jelly quakes! **1673** Ray *Journ. Low C.* 121 One would verily have thought, that.. Stone had been broken or bruised whilst a Gelly..and so hardened. **1676** D'Urfey *Mad. Fickle* ii. i. (1677) 14, I could have beaten the Woman into a Jelly. **1793** Beddoes *Math. Evid.* 124 Those masses of animated jelly, which one sees at times scattered along the sea shore. **1817** Kirby & Spence *Introd. Entomol.* II. xix. 130 They will select one or more to be educated as queens; which..being fed with royal jelly for not more than two days..will come forth complete queens. **1846** G. E. Day tr. *Simon's Anim. Chem.* II. 203 The pus becomes so viscid as to form a tenacious jelly. **1859** *Q. Jrnl. Microsc. Sci.* VII. 257 The bottle of glycerine jelly is put into a cup of hot water, until liquefied. **1880** *Amer. Monthly Microsc. Jrnl.* I. 208/1, I have used such a medicine dropper to hold and apply glycerin jelly, with great satisfaction. **1886** F. R. Cheshire *Bees* I. vi. 82 In the case of the queen larva..that secretion, commonly, though, as I hold, erroneously, called royal jelly, is added unstintingly. **1954** C. G. Butler *World of Honeybee* iv. 46 It has come to be believed that any female honeybee larva..that is fed exclusively on royal jelly always develops into a queen bee. **1958** J. R. Baker *Princ. Biol. Microtechnique* xiii. 255 Preparations mounted in glycerine-jelly, balsam, or other commonly-used media. **1973** L. Hellman *Pentimento* (1974) 230 He was always having mysterious operations... He took royal jelly.

fig. **1651** N. Bacon *Disc. Govt. Eng.* ii. xl. (1739) 178 Lordship, once bringing therewith both Authority and Power unto Kings,..in these latter days is become a mere Jelly.

b. *spec.* Applied to the alga *Nostoc*, which appears as a jelly-like mass on dry soil after rain, and was popularly supposed to be the remains of a fallen 'star' or meteor.

a **1641** Suckling *Poems, Farew. to Love*, As he whose quicker eye doth trace A false star shot to a mark't place Do's run apace, And thinking it to catch, A gelly up do's snatch. **1649** Jer. Taylor *Gt. Exemp.* i. Prelim. Exhort. ¶7 Stand staring upon a Meteor or an inflamed gelly. **1656** H. More *Enthus. Tri.* 45 That the Starres eat,..that those falling Starres, as some call them, which are found on the earth in the form of a trembling gelly, are their excrement. **1678–9** Dryden & Lee *Œdipus* ii. i, The shooting stars end all in purple jellies. **1679** Dryden *Sp. Friar* Ded., When I had taken up what I supposed a fallen star, I found I had been cozened with a jelly. **1740** Somerville *Hobbinol* iii. 266 Like that falling Meteor, there she lies, A Jelly cold on Earth. **1766** Pennant *Zool.* (1768) II. 424 The Winter Mew ..The gelatinous substance, known by the name of Star Shot, or Star Gelly, owes its origin to this bird,..being nothing but the half digested remains of earth-worms, on which these birds feed. [**1875** Bennett & Dyer tr. *Sachs' Bot.* 215 Nostoc..consists, when mature, of a large number of moniliform threads..imbedded in a glutinous jelly, and thus united into colonies.]

c. A jelly-fish.

1882 *Harper's Mag.* Jan. 181/1 One of these large jellies was observed..moving lazily along, its disk encircled by a halo twenty-feet in diameter, while the train of gleaming tentacles stretched away two hundred feet or more.

d. A mixture of gelatin and glycerin used for mounting microscopic objects.

1856 Carpenter *Microscope* 246 This Composition, when cold, forms a very stiff jelly. *Ibid.* (1891) 443 When used, the jelly must be liquified by gentle warmth, and it is useful to warm both the slide and the cover-glass previous to mounting.

e. *slang.* A pretty girl; a girl-friend.

1889 Barrère & Leland *Dict. Slang* I. 496/1 *Jelly*, or *All jelly*, a buxom, good-looking girl. **1931** W. Faulkner *Sanctuary* iii. 23 Gowan goes to Oxford a lot... He's got a jelly there. He takes her to the dances. *Ibid.* iv. 36 Don't think I spent last night with a couple of your barber-shop jellies for nothing.

f. A gelatinous contraceptive substance.

1931 F. W. S. Browne tr. *T. H. van de Velde's Fertility & Sterility in Marriage* iii. xiv. 348 The most important chemical contraceptives are the lubricant jellies. **1935** E. F. Griffith *Mod. Marriage* iv. 84 There are numberless chemical substances, made up either in the form of tablets or jellies... These are introduced into the vagina and are intended to kill the sperms. **1937** —— *Voluntary Parenthood* iii. 46 Many other devices have been invented to carry the chemical, such as jellies, ointments, foaming tablets and foaming jellies... All these solubles, jellies and tablets are unsatisfactory and if used by themselves are liable to fail in a high percentage of cases. **1943** in T. H. van de Velde *Ideal Marriage* (1947) 148 Arrangements have now been made for the manufacture of Dr. Van de Velde's Jellies ('Eugam'): Lubricant, Contraceptive and Proconceptive. **1949** *New Gould Med. Dict.* 529/1 *Contraceptive jelly*, any one of a number of viscous substances introduced into the vagina to prevent conception. **1970** *Which? Contraceptives Suppl.* (ed. 3) 58 (*heading*) Spermicidal creams, jellies and pastes. **1972** *Guardian* 9 June 5/5 Her doctor..prescribed a diaphragm and a contraceptive jelly but the jelly was seized by the [Irish] customs authorities.

3. *ellipt.* A jelly-glass. (Cf. *a salt.*)

1709 *Lond. Gaz.* No. 4595/4 There is lately brought over a great Parcel of..German Cut and Carv'd Glasses, viz. Jellies, Wine and Water Tumblers [etc.].

4. *attrib.* and *Comb.*, as ***jelly-broth, -dish, -glass, -mould, -pot; jelly-boned, -like*** adjs.; **jelly baby**, a soft gelatinous sweet in the shape of a baby; **jelly bean** orig. *U.S.*, (*a*) a bean-shaped sweet with a gelatinous centre and a hard sugar coating; (*b*) *slang*, an unpleasant, weak, or dishonest person; *spec.* a pimp; **jelly-belly**, a fat person; hence **jelly-bellied** *a.*; †**jelly-blood**, clotted blood (*obs.*); **jelly-cloth**, a cloth for straining jelly; **jelly-dog** (*slang*), a harrier (so called from being used to hunt hares, which are eaten with currant jelly); hence ***jelly-dogging***, hunting with harriers; **jelly-lichen**, a lichen of gelatinous texture, such as *Collema*; **jelly-nut** (see quot.); **jelly paint**, a non-drip paint with the consistency of jelly; **jelly-plant**, an Australian seaweed: see quot. 1866; †**jelly-poke** = JELLY-BAG; **jelly powder**, (*a*) a kind of explosive (see quot. *a* 1884); (*b*) a crystalline powder used in the preparation of table-jellies; **jelly roll** *U.S.*, a cylindrical cake containing jelly or jam; freq. in *transf. slang* senses: (*a*) a lover; (*b*) sexual intercourse; (*c*) the female genitalia or vagina.

1945 Dylan Thomas in *Listener* 20 Dec. 734/2 A bag of moist and many-coloured *jelly-babies. **1950** 'R. Crompton' *William—the Bold* i. 13 'Jelly babyth are nithe, too,' said the small shrill voice behind them. **1972** *Guardian* 27 Dec. 9/1 A lady going round Europe buying..jelly babies. **1905** *Chicago Daily News* 5 July 11/5 *Jelly beans, assorted, per lb., 9 c. **1919** *Dialect Notes* V. 65 Mary is such a jelly-bean that she never gets her lessons. **1923** Wodehouse *Adv. Sally* 223 What's the idea, you jelly bean? **1929** W. Faulkner *Sound & Fury* 202 Are you hiding out in the woods with one of those damn slick-headed jellybeans? **1935** A. J. Pollock *Underworld Speaks* 63/2 *Jelly bean*, a pimp (ellyjay eanbay). **1940** C. McCullers *Heart is Lonely Hunter* (1943) i. iii. 32 She..took from her shirt pocket a blue-coloured jelly bean. **1972** M. J. Bosse *Incident at Naha* i. 56, I went into the kitchen for jelly beans, which taste good after you've been blowing grass. **1899** Kipling *Stalky & Co.* 214 He was..a Flopshus Cad, an Outrageous Stinker, a *Jelly-bellied Flag-flapper (this was Stalky's contribution). **1938** *Times Lit. Suppl.* 26 Nov. 753/2 The most jelly-bellied of them is Nabucet, a flowery and despicable humbug. **1950** M. Lowry *Let.* 23 June (1967) 213 She (*sc.* Russia]..lives in a state of constant 'war effort', with its attendant..'jelly-bellied flag-flapping'. **1896** Farmer & Henley *Slang* IV. 44/1 **Jelly-belly*, a fat man or woman. **1903** [see EH *int.* 3]. **1935** L. A. G. Strong *Tuesday Afternoon* 88 If ever I want a ginger-chinned jelly-belly's advice,..I'll ask for it. **1583** Stanyhurst *Æneis* iv. (Arb.) 120 Thee blackned *gellyeblud, hardning, Shee skums with napkins. **1590** Spenser *F.Q.* iii. iv. 40 They softly wipt away the gelly blood From th' orifice. **1912** D. H. Lawrence *Let.* 3 July (1962) I. 134 Curse the blasted, *jelly-boned swines. **1961** *Spectator* 17 Nov. 698 It is so spineless and 'jelly-boned'. *a* **1648** Digby *Closet Open.* (1669) 156 Make a very good *gelly-broth of Mutton. **1393** *Earl Derby's Exp.* (Camden) 234 Et pro iij. vergis tele pro j *gelicloth, xviijs. *c* **1480** *Guild Acc.* in Blades *Caxton* (1882) 79, ix dosen *gely

dishes. **1897** W. .E. NORRIS *Marietta's Marriage* 4 We have no hounds hereabouts, except the *jelly-dogs. **1889** R. S. S. BADEN-POWELL *Pig-sticking* 20 You..would prefer a gallop with the Quorn..to a day's '*jelly dogging'. **1738** STUART in *Phil. Trans.* XL. 8 A wine or *jelly glass, or any such vessel tapering towards the bottom. **1774** GOLDSM. *Nat. Hist.* (1818) IV. 361 Studded with little *jelly-like drops. **1835–6** TODD *Cycl. Anat.* I. 512/2 The..jelly-like body of the Polypifera. **1860** *All Year Round* No. 74. 557 Looking at schools too often as if they were *jelly-moulds, and the young mind a jelly. **1885** LADY BRASSEY *The Trades* 361 The cocoanuts are called '*jelly-nuts' before the flesh is ripe and has hardened, and while it still can be scraped off in the form of a delicious thin pulp. **1958** *Listener* 28 Aug. 323/1 If anyone were to ask me what has been the most interesting new development for the do-it-yourself painter over the last year or two I think I would say the dripless, or *jelly, paints. .. Some complain that the jelly paints do not cover up the surface underneath. **1866** *Treas. Bot.* 473/1 *Eucheuma speciosum* is the *Jelly-plant of Australia, and is one of the best species for making jelly, size, cement, etc. **1516–17** *Durham Acc. Rolls* (Surtees) 106 Pro una uln. panni lanei pro le *gelypoke, 8*d.* *c* **1865** G. GORE in *Circ. Sc.* I. 233/1 Coat the inside of a glass jar or earthen *jelly-pot with wax. *a* **1884** KNIGHT *Dict. Mech.* Suppl. 511/2 **Jelly powder*, so called from its resemblance to calf's-foot jelly. It consists of 94% or 95% of nitro-glycerine and 5% or 6% collodion cotton, so mixed as to assume a gelatinous form. **1895** *Army & Navy Co-op Soc. Price List* 16 Table Jelly powder..in packets. **1921** *Daily Colonist* (Victoria, B.C.) 6 Apr. 6/1 Lipton's and Shirriff's Jelly Powders, per packet..10¢. **1895** 'M. RONALD' *Century Cook Bk.* xxi. 468 **Jelly Rolls.* Make a layer of Genoese..press it through a pastry bag in lines onto the tins... Before it has had time to cool, cut off the hard edges, spread it with..any jelly or jam, and roll it up evenly; then roll it in paper and tie, so it will cool in a round, even shape. **1914** W. C. HANDY *St. Louis Blues* (song), I'm most wile 'bout mah Jelly-Roll. **1919** S. & C. WILLIAMS (*song-title*) I ain't gonna give nobody none o' this jelly roll. **1927** *Jrnl. Abnormal & Social Psychol.* XXII. 13 By far the most common of these terms is *jelly roll*. As used by the lower class Negro it stands for vagina, or the female genitalia in general, and sometimes for sexual intercourse. *Ibid.* 14 Angels in heaven do the sweet jelly roll. **1929** T. WOLFE *Look Homeward, Angel* (1930) xxii. 324 'What yo' want?' she asked softly. 'Jelly roll?' **1964** *Amer. Folk Music Occasional* I. 12 Negro blues where women are sweet food (*biscuit-roller..jelly roll baker*). **1970** G. GREER *Female Eunuch* 265 If a woman is food, her sex organ is for consumption also, in the form of..*cake-* or *jelly-roll*. **1971** B. MALAMUD *Tenants* 205 Irene Lost Queen I miss To be between Your Jelly Roll. **1974** *Amer. Speech 1971* XLVI. 79 Jelly-filled doughnut, *bismarck*, *jelly roll*.

jelly (ˈdʒɛlɪ), *sb.*^{2} *slang.* Also **gelly**. [Shortening of the pronunciation of GELIGNITE, influenced by its jelly-like appearance.] Gelignite.

1941 in BAKER *Dict. Austral. Slang*. **1948** D. L. G. MUNDY *There's Gold in them Hills* x. 128 Put a charge of 'gelly' under it. **1955** [see CREEP *v.* 5 b]. **1960** *Observer* 24 Jan. 5/2 A hut where they knew gelly was kept. *Ibid.* 5/3 There was always the gelly and oxy-acetylene if necessary. **1971** *Guardian* 28 Aug. 1/1 Stolen 'gelly' found.

jelly (ˈdʒɛlɪ), *a. Sc.* Now *rare.* Also 6–8 **gelly**. [Origin unknown: the sense agrees fairly with some of the uses of JOLLY; but the phonetic change which this would involve has no parallel.] Good, worthy, excellent; having a high opinion of oneself, proud, haughty.

c **1560–73** [see GELLY]. **1596** DALRYMPLE tr. *Leslie's Hist. Scot.* I. 7 The woddes selfes..are verie jocund and jellie, and gif we myt speik it, in a maner peirles in pleisour. **1638** A. CANT *Serm.* in Kerr *Covenants & Covenanters* (1895) 103 Numbers mocked and thought themselves over jelly to come in. *a* **1758** RAMSAY *To Hamilton* iii, A jelly sum to carry on A fishery's designed. **1787** SHIRREFS *Jamie & Bess* I. i, The Provost o' the Town, A jelly man, well worthy of a crown. **1828** *Courteous Knt.* in Whitelaw *Bk. Sc. Ballads* (1875) 163 'Leave off your pride jelly Janet', he said. 'Use it not ony mair'. **1871** W. ALEXANDER *Johnny Gibb* xl. (1873) 226 An aunt o' the bride's was there to welcome the fowk; a richt jellie wife in a close mutch.

Hence ˈ**jellily** *adv.*, worthily, excellently.

18.. *Bonny Bee-ho'm* in *Jamieson's Popular Ball.* (1806) I. 189 And jellily dance the damsels, Blythe-blinkin' in your ee.

jelly (ˈdʒɛlɪ), *v.* [f. JELLY *sb.*^{1}]

1. *intr.* To come to the consistence of jelly; to 'set' as jelly; to congeal, solidify, coagulate.

1601 HOLLAND *Pliny* II. 354 It will neuer iellie and grow to any thick consistence in Summer, vnlesse there be wax put into it. **1750** E. SMITH *Compl. Housew.* (ed. 14) 201 You may know by setting some in a spoon to try if it will jelly. **1770** HEWSON in *Phil. Trans.* LX. 376 The blood..very soon jellies or coagulates. **1822–34** *Good's Study Med.* (ed. 4) IV. 308 The secreted fluid..commonly..jellies upon exposure to heat.

2. *trans.* To convert into jelly; to cause to 'set' or coagulate; to reduce to the consistence of jelly.

1601 HOLLAND *Pliny* II. 334 A liue Wolfe sodden in oile til the said oile be gellied to the height or consistence of a cerot. **1770** HEWSON in *Phil. Trans.* LX. 374 In a few minutes the whole will be jellied or coagulated. **1876** G. MACDONALD in *Macm. Mag.* XXXIV. 351 They, jellied with fear, have uttered no challenge.

Hence ˈ**jellying** *vbl. sb.* and *ppl. a.*

1673 MARVELL *Appleton Ho.*, The jellying stream compacts below. *a* **1697** AUBREY *Nat. Hist. Surrey* (1719) II. 194 The Jellying of some Parts of the Earth in *Aqua Fortis*. **1871** NAPHEYS *Prev. & Cure Dis.* I. ii. 75 The jellying of fruits.

ˈ**jelly-bag.** A bag for straining jelly through.

1602 PLAT *Delights* (1605) §28 Let it run through a gelly bagge into a bason. **1750** JOHNSON *Rambler* No. 51 ¶15 She is pressing the jelly-bag or airing the Store-room. **1806** *Culina* 114 Run it through a jelly-bag.

ˈ**jellydom.** *nonce-wd.* [See -DOM.] A state of jelly; gelatinous condition.

1877 J. HAWTHORNE *Garth* I. II. vi. 47 He advanced from infant jellydom to the solid flesh of babyhood.

ˈ**jelly-fish.**

†**1.** An oceanic fish of the genus *Plagyodus* or *Alepisaurus*, family *Scopelidæ*. *Obs.*

1707 W. FUNNELL *Voy. Round World* 8 The Jelly-fish was about fourteen Inches long..with a very sharp set of Teeth. .. That part of him which is without small spots, is a perfect green Jelly, whence he was called by us a *Jelly-fish*.

2. a. The popular name of various acalephs, medusas, or sea-nettles, from their gelatinous structure.

1841 *Encycl. Brit.* (ed. 7) XXI. 1013 Acalephæ.—Sea-jellies... Jelly-Fish; Sea-Blubbers. **1861** J. R. GREENE *Man. Anim. Kingd., Cœlent.* 127 The large 'jelly-fishes' which, during summer and autumn, occur so abundantly in our seas, are, with few exceptions, the reproductive zoöids of *Aurelia*, *Cyanea*, and *Chrysaora*. **1873** MIVART *Elem. Anat.* i. 9 More than 99 per cent of water enters into the total composition of a Jelly fish.

b. *fig.* A person of 'flabby' character, or deficient in energy, steadfastness, or 'backbone'.

1883 PH. S. ROBINSON *Sinners & Saints* i. 11 Chicago is nearly terrific... Its astonishing resurrection from its ashes and its tremendous energy terrify jelly-fishes like myself. **1910** [see GABFEST]. **1928** [see FACE *v.* 6]. **1966** C. ACHEBE *Man of People* viii. 88 Max's unfortunate..presentation of me as a kind of pitiable jellyfish.

c. *attrib.*, usually in *fig.* sense.

1889 *Catholic News* 16 Nov. 3/2 Language is at first in the Jelly-fish condition. **1891** *Daily News* 5 Nov. 5/4 We have.. thousands of jellyfish sermons preached every year.

jellygraph (ˈdʒɛlɪgrɑːf, -æ-). [f. JELLY *sb.* + -GRAPH.] An appliance used for multiplying copies of writing, etc., of which the essential part is a sheet of jelly. Also *attrib.* Hence ˈ**jellygraph** *v. trans.*, to copy with a jellygraph; ˈ**jellygraphed** *ppl. a.*

1900 H. G. WELLS *Love & Mr. Lewisham* xxv. 241 A letter of atrociously jellygraphed advices from Messrs. Danks & Wimborne. **1902** WODEHOUSE *Pothunters* xii. 182 On Sunday we jellygraph it—it'll have to be a jellygraphed number this time. **1904** *Sat. Rev.* 9 Jan. 40 It is better 'jellygraphing' questions for some one else's form than [etc.]. **1919** *Brit. Jrnl. Photogr. Alm.* 615/1 Jellygraph mixture for enlarging easel. **1936** 'G. ORWELL' *Keep Aspidistra Flying* iii. 58 They ran an unofficial monthly paper..duplicated with a jellygraph. **1972** W. A. PANTIN *Oxf. Life* iv. 52 We can trace the belated triumph of the typewriter..over the older methods of manuscript, jellygraph, and printed fly-sheet.

jelopher, obs. form of GILLYFLOWER.

jelose, -ous, -osy, etc., obs. ff. JEALOUS, -OUSY.

jelot, obs. variant of GILLOT. (Cf. JILLET.)

c **1550** C. BARNSLEY *Treat. agst. Woman*, For a stewde strumpet can not so soone gette up a light lewde fashyon, But everye wanton Ielot wylle lyke it well, and catche it up anon. *Ibid.*, Ducke, Ielot, ducke pretye minions.

jelsomine, obs. variant of JASMINE.

jeltron, variant of SHELTRON, shelter, *Obs.*

jelutong (dʒɛˈluːtɒŋ). Also 9 **jolo-, julu-**; 20 **jela-, jelo-**. [Malay.] A Malaysian tree of the genus *Dyera*, esp. *D. costulata*, which produces a latex when tapped; the latex or the light-coloured wood from a tree of this kind.

1836 J. LOW *Diss. Soil & Agric. Penang* iv. 205 *Julutong*—very white. These woods are used chiefly by undertakers. **1885** *Spons' Mechanics' Own Bk.* 164 Jolotong... Well adapted for patterns and mouldings, excellent for carving purposes. **1900** W. W. SKEAT *Malay Magic* 205 Other haunted trees..are the Jawi-jawi, the Jĕlotong, and Bĕrombong. **1904, 1927** [see GUTTA^2 2]. **1940** E. J. H. CORNER *Wayside Trees Malaya* I. 144 The *Jelutong* is deciduous partly or wholly. **1947** H. BARRON *Mod. Rubber Chem.* (ed. 2) iii. 27 Jelutong is obtained by tapping. **1970** *Timber Trades Jrnl.* 21 Mar. 54/1 Few sales of jelutong or kapur have been made, but meranti is said to be selling fairly well.

†**jelyf.** *Obs.* Also **geliffe**. A false form of the word JELLY found in 15–16th c., perh. in imitation of *jolif*, archaic form of *jolly*.

c **1450** *Songs & Carols* (1856) 76, I have a jelyf of Godes sonde Withoutyn fyt it can stonde. **1577** HARRISON *England* II. vi. (1877) I. 148 In such cases [merchants' feasts] also geliffes, conserues, suckets, codinacs, marmilats [etc.].

jem, obs. form of GEM.

‖**jemadar** (ˈdʒɛmədɑː(r)). *E. Indies.* Also 8 **jemmahdaur**, 8–9 **jemautdar**, 9 **jemat-, jummah-, jemma-, jemi-, jamadar**. [Urdū *jamaʿdār*, f. Pers. (Arab.) *jamāʿat* body of men, *jamaʿ* collection, aggregate + Pers. *dār* holder.]

A native officer in a Sepoy regiment, ranking next below a subahdar, and corresponding to a lieutenant; the name is also given to certain officers of police and other civil departments, and to the head of a body of servants.

1763 ORME *Hist. Mil. Trans.* (1803) I. 257 (Y.) The jemautdars, or captains of these troops, received his bribes. **1788** *Gentl. Mag.* LVIII. I. 67/2 M'Culloch..sent in a flag of truce with a Jemmahdaur. **1799** WELLINGTON in *Suppl. Desp.* (1858) I. 353 The Jemadar's party of the Bengal volunteers. **1800** *Asiatic Ann. Reg., Misc. Tr.* 24/1 Their jemidars were in actual correspondence with the Shah Zadah. **1826** HOCKLEY *Pandurang Hari* v, The principal officers are called *jummahdars*. **1836** *Encycl. Brit.* (ed. 7) XII. 495/1 *Jamadar*, an officer of horse or foot, in Hindustan. **1897** LD. ROBERTS *41 Yrs. India* xlvii, The Jemadar of the Pathan Company knew who the culprits were.

jemble, obs. form of GIMBAL, a hinge.

1588 in *Archæol.* XLI. 366 For a pare of Jembles for the stoole dore xd.

jemcrack, obs. form of GIMCRACK.

†**je'mello.** *Obs.* (See quot.) Cf. JUMBAL.

1688 R. HOLME *Armoury* III. 83/1 *Jemelloes* is a Paste made like Butter, of fine Sugar, Yolks of Eggs, Musk, Carraway seeds searsed [etc.].

‖**je m'en fiche** (ʒəmɑ̃fiʃ), *phr.* [Fr.] I couldn't care less; I don't care at all. Hence **je-m'en-fich(e)ism(e)**, indifference.

1889 E. DOWSON *Let.* 10 Mar. (1967) 48 As for *esprit*—je m'en fiche—there never was a woman spirituelle before she was thirty. **1902** W. JAMES *Varieties Relig. Experience* ii. 36 *Je m'en fiche* is the vulgar French equivalent for our English ejaculation 'Who cares?' And the happy term *je m'en fichisme* recently has been invented to designate the systematic determination not to take anything in life too solemnly. **1905** A. BENNETT *Sacred & Profane Love* III. iii. 251 'Oh!' with a disdainful gesture. '*Je m'en fiche.* Let him go.' **1916** A. HUXLEY *Let.* Dec. (1969) 117 Old Birrell came down.. professing an almost total je-m'en-ficheisme about the war. **1921** GALSWORTHY *To Let* II. ii. 139 Why want to know anything of that 'small' mystery—*Je m'en fiche*, as Profond says? **1923** A. HUXLEY *Antic Hay* v. 69 His divining eyes pierced through the veil of cynical *je-m'en-fichisme* to the bruised heart beneath. **1968** W. GARNER *Deep, Deep Freeze* ix. 240 As they say in this part of the world, *je m'en fiche*. **1970** R. HAUGHTON *Love* i. 25 The school of Anglo-Saxon 'je m'en fiche-ism'.

‖**je m'en fous** (ʒəmɑ̃fu), *phr.* [Fr.] = prec. Hence **je-m'en-foutism(e)**.

1918 A. BENNETT *Pretty Lady* xxi. 134 'But, madame, it is raining terribly.' '*Je m'en fous.* Run for a taxi.' **1936** 'G. ORWELL' *Keep Aspidistra Flying* x. 269 At the bottom of all his feelings there was a sulkiness, a je m'en fous in the face of the world. **1954** *Landfall* VIII. I. 27 The Sydneysider's traditional lounging *jemenfoutism*. **1959** *Guardian* 5 Nov. 6 France..has gone from despair and j'menfoutisme to optimism. **1964** *Ibid.* 4 Dec. 11/3 There is a species of *je m'en foutisme* in Godard that I like. **1966** *Ibid.* 9 Dec. 7/3 Happiness, they appear to say, is square, happiness is corny —and *je m'en fous*.

jemeow, -ew(e, -mow, obs. ff. GEMEW, GEMOW.

1518–19 in Swayne *Sarum Church-w. Acc.* (1896) 64 Makynge of Jemeows viij*d.*

jemer, jemmar, var. GIMMER^1, a hinge.

Jemima, jemima (dʒɪˈmaɪmə). [Female Christian name.] **1.** A made-up tie. Also *attrib.*

1899 SOMERVILLE & 'ROSS' *Some Experiences Irish R.M.* v. 97 We indulged in..'Jemima' ties with diagonal stripes. **1920** *Glasgow Herald* 3 Apr. 4, I have never learned the knack of fixing a dress tie, and I have not the moral courage to wear a jemima.

2. *pl.* Elastic-sided boots; the British name for *Congress boots*.

1902 *M.A.P.* 29 Mar. 323/1, I spoke of Mr. Chamberlain's having fallen from sartorial grace to the extent of wearing 'Jemimas'. **1906** *Westm. Gaz.* 31 Dec. 3/1 A pair of well-preserved 'jemimas'. They are a kind of footgear the immortal Teufelsdröckh himself might have worn, unless he had a weakness for bluchers. **1927** *Glasgow Herald* 24 Aug. 8 The old-fashioned, long obsolete elastic-sided boots, known for some obscure reason as 'Jemimas'. **1961** *Times* 2 Oct. 13/4 The..Dame would at last be caught in the mangle out of whose rollers protruded the struggling feet in the supposedly ludicrous Jemimas.

jemme, obs. form of GEM.

jemmel, obs. form of GEMEL, a hinge.

?**16..** in Blunt *Dursley* 60 (Glouc. Gloss) For a payre of Jemmels for the Raile Door that goeth before the Communion Table £1. 0. 8.

jemmy (ˈdʒɛmɪ), *sb.* Also 9 **jimmy**. [A pet-form and familiar equivalent of the name JAMES. But in sense 1 associated with, and in 2 and 3 prob. derived from, JEMMY *a.*]

†**1.** A dandy or fop; a finical fellow. *Obs.*

1753 *Scots Mag.* Oct. 490 The scale..consists of eight degrees; Greenhorn, Jemmy, Jessamy, Smart [etc.]. **1764** *Low Life* 65 The Jemmies, Brights, Flashes, Puzzes, Pizzes and Smarts of the Town.

b. In phr. ***Jemmy Jessamy (Jessamine)*** *attrib.*, dandified, foppish, effeminate. See JESSAMY 4.

1786 *Pogonologia* 51 You pretty fellows of the present day, Jemmy Jessamy persons, jolly bucks. **1806–7** J. BERESFORD *Miseries Hum. Life* (1826) VI. i, A Jemmy Jessamy lover in a wood. **1823** E. NARES *Heraldic Anom.* (1824) II. 356 Who is this Jemmy Jessamine Gentleman?—I am Charmoleus the Dandy, universally admired for my shape and figure and complexion.

†**2.** A kind of riding-boot; also *jemmy boot*.

1753 FOOTE *Eng. in Paris* I. Wks. 1799 I. 39 When I hunt with the King..I'll on with my Jemmys; none of your black bags and jack boots for me. **1771** SMOLLETT *Humph. Cl.* 10

June Let. i, Who..made his appearance in a pair of new jemmy boots.

†**3.** A light cane, a switch. *Obs. rare*⁻¹.

1753 *Scots Mag.* Oct 490/2, I..carried in my hand a little switch, which, as it has been long appendant to the character that I had just assumed, has taken the same name, and is called a Jemmy.

4. *plur.* 'A species of woollen cloth. *Aberd.*' (Jam. 1808–18).

5. A great-coat.

1837 DICKENS *Pickw.* ii, But if I'd been your friend in the green jemmy—damn me—punch his head,—'cod I would.

6. A crowbar used by burglars, generally made in sections screwing together.

1811 *Lex. Bal.*, *Jemmy*, a crow..much used by house-breakers. Sometimes called Jemmy Rock. **1828** P. CUNNINGHAM *N.S. Wales* (ed. 3) II. 223 As expert a burglar as ever handled a *jemmy*. **1851** D. JERROLD *St. Giles* vii. 59 Fame, won by highway pistol, or burglar's jemmy. **1889** D. C. MURRAY *Danger. Catspaw* 26 A complete set of jemmies, of all sizes.

7. A sheep's head as a dish.

1836 DICKENS *Sk. Boz, 7 Dials*, The man in the shop, perhaps, is in the baked 'jemmy' line. **1851–61** MAYHEW *Lond. Labour* II. 48 (Farmer) They..had a 'prime hot jemmy' apiece. **1884** HENLEY & STEVENSON *Deacon Brodie* IV. i, You're all jaw like a sheep's jimmy.

jemmy ('dʒɛmɪ), *a. Obs.* exc. *dial.* Also 9 **gemmy, gimmy, jimmy.** [deriv. of *jim*, GIM *a*] Spruce, neat, smart; neatly-made; dexterous.

1750 COVENTRY *Pompey Litt.* II. iv. (1785) 58/1 His great ambition was to be deemed a 'jemmy fellow'. **1756** *Connoisseur* No. 112 ¶7 The jemmy frock with plate buttons. **1771** P. PARSONS *Newmarket* II. 89 His jemmy turn'd-down boots. *a* **1825** FORBY *Voc. E. Anglia*, *Gim, gimmy*, spruce, neat, smart. **1828** LAMB in *Life & Lett.* (1876) II. 341 A smart cock'd beaver and a jemmy cane!

b. *Comb.*, as ***jemmy-stitched, -worked.***

1762 T. JEFFERSON *Corr.* Wks. 1859 I. 181 They carried away my jemmy-worked silk garters. **1817** MRS. ROSS *Balance of Comfort* (ed. 3) I. xxiii. 246 Only a piece of muslin rag, neatly jemmy-stitched.

Hence **'jemmily** *adv.*; **'jemminess.**

1756 F. GREVILLE *Maxims*, etc. 125 Its fort shall be either convenience or jemminess. **1818** TODD, *Jemminess*, spruceness. A colloquial expression; not much used in serious writing. **1837** *New Monthly Mag.* LI. 194 A stick to be carried jemmily under the arm, in Portsmouth fashion.

Jemmy O'Goblin, var. *Jimmy O'Goblin* (s.v. JIMMY² 5).

1889 in BARRÈRE & LELAND *Dict. Slang.*

jemowe, obs. variant of GEMEW, GEMOW.

Jena ('jeɪnə). The name of a city in East Germany, used *attrib.* to designate glass made there, which originated in the experiments of Ernst Abbe and Otto Schott and became famous for its high quality and the special kinds that were developed.

1892 *Work* IV. 145/2 The new Schott Jena glass. **1902** J. D. & A. EVERETT tr. *Hovestadt's Jena Glass* i. 20 The introduction of Jena glass into practical optics was initiated by Abbe, who was now enabled, with the help of the technical resources of Zeiss' optical works, to realise his long-cherished plans for the improvement of the microscope. *Ibid.* vii. 189 Results for 29 different Jena glasses. **1902** [see ANASTIGMAT]. **1908** W. ROSENHAIN *Glass Manuf.* i. 7 Another instance of these refractory glasses is to be found in the Jena special thermometer glasses..; the best of these glasses show little or no plasticity at temperatures approaching 500°C. **1941** *Jrnl. Inst. Petroleum* XXVII. 434 The solution was sucked off via a Jena-glass immersion filter. **1954** G. W. MOREY *Properties Glass* (ed. 2) iii. 78 The first Jena 'Geräte' glass, made before 1910.., differed from the ordinary soda-lime glass in the substitution of magnesia and zinc oxide for lime, and in having a small content of B_2O_3. Later..the soda content was reduced and the magnesia largely removed, with increase in the zinc oxide, alumina and boric oxide.

jenepere, obs. Sc. form of JUNIPER.

jenequen, var. HENEQUEN [Sp. *jeniquen*].

‖**je ne sais quoi** (ʒənsɛkwa). [Fr., = I know not what.] An indescribable or inexpressible something. Also *attrib.*

1656 BLOUNT *Glossogr.*, *Je-ne-scay-quoi*, four French words, contracted as it were into one, and signifies *I know not what*, we use to say they are troubled with the *Je-ne-scay-quoy*, that faign themselves sick out of niceness but know not where their own grief lies, or what ayls them. **1671** AUBREY *Countrey Revell* II. iii, Seemed to give a mournefull *je n'scay quoy*. **1696** D'URFEY *Don Quix.* III. IV. 38 Some sweet alluring *Jen Scay Quoy*, Some pleasing pretty tickling Toy. *a* **1734** NORTH *Exam.* III. viii. § 14 (1740) 592 Now this Word Post has a *je ne sçai quoi* Sound of a deep Design. **1745** *Gentl. Mag.* 324 So refined a *Je-ne-scay-quoy* was about 'em, For goddesses there was no reason to doubt 'em. **1774** FOOTE *Cozeners* III. Wks. 1799 II. 185 There is, besides, an elegance, a *je ne scai quoi*, in your son's air. **1881** W. S. GILBERT *Patience* II, A..*Je-ne-sais-quoi* young man. **1894** SIR E. SULLIVAN *Woman* 71 Her famous nepenthe was simply the irresistible fascination of her 'Je ne sais quoi'.

jenette, jenit, obs. forms of GENET¹.

Jenever(e, -iver, obs. forms of JANUARY.

Jenewey, variant of GENOWAY *Obs.*, Genoa.

jenful, variant of GINFUL *a. Obs.*, deceitful.

c **1400** *Sege Jerus.* (E.E.T.S.) 66/1133 But Jon þe jenfulle, þat þe Jewes ladde..forsoke þe profre.

jenick, variant of JANNOCK *a.*, honest.

jenite, variant of YENITE *Min.*

†**'jeniver.** *Obs.* [a. F. *genèvre* (now *genièvre*):—L. *juniper-um.*] = JUNIPER.

1585 T. WASHINGTON tr. *Nicholay's Voy.* II. x. 43 b, Mount Ida..clothed with al maner of trees, as.. Terebinths, Ieniuers and other trees.

jenkin ('dʒɛŋkɪn), *Coal-mining. north.* Also **-ing.** 'An opening cut into a slice taken off a pillar from six to eight feet in width, in the *board and pillar* system of working coal' (Gresley *Gloss. Coal-mining T.* 1883).

1851 GREENWELL *Coal-trade terms Northumb. & Durh.* 31 Wherever practicable, when a jenking is necessary, it should be driven loose sided; a fast jenking very frequently causing a creeping to take place. **1893** HESLOP *Northumbld. Gloss.*, *Jenkin.*

jenkinsite ('dʒɛŋkɪnzaɪt). *Min.* [Named 1852 after its discoverer J. Jenkins.] A variety of hydrophite, found as a fibrous incrustation on iron ore.

1852 *Amer. Jrnl. Sc.* Ser. II. XIII. 392 Jenkinsite.. Occurs implanted upon massive magnetite.

Jenne, variant of GEANE *Obs.*, Genoa.

1479 J. PASTON in *P. Lett.* III. 259, ij Pottys of tryacle of Jenne.

Jennerian (dʒɛ'nɪərɪən), *a. Med.* [f. the name of Edward *Jenner* (1749–1823), English physician, who in 1796 vaccinated a subject with cow-pox against small-pox and thereby laid the foundations of vaccination in medicine and of the science of immunology: see -IAN.] Of, pertaining to, or commemorating Jenner; made by or following the methods of Jenner.

1801 *Med. & Physical Jrnl.* VI. 5 The Jennerian Inoculation is universally adopted by the medical gentlemen of this town and neighbourhood. **1805** W. ROWLEY *Cow-Pox Inoculation No Security against Small-Pox* p. v, The names of..those who formed the principals in the Royal Jennerian Institution, etc. are omitted. **1824** MILL *Prefaces to Liberty* (1959) 72 The great spiritual physicians who would vaccinate the nation with hypocrisy to prevent the eruption of infidelity, are not acting on a true Jennerian analogy. **1911** G. B. SHAW *Doctor's Dilemma* p. lxvi, To this day the law which prescribes Jennerian vaccination is carried out with an anti-Jennerian inoculation because the public would have it so. **1951** W. R. LEFANU *Bio-Bibliogr. E. Jenner* ii. 59 The text was included in Jones' and Crookshank's Jennerian collections.

jennet¹ ('dʒɛnɪt). Forms: α. 5–6 **genett,** 6 **gynnet,** 6–7 **ginnet,** 6–8 **gennet(te,** 6–9 **genet,** 7 **ganet,** 7–9 **ginet,** 8 **gennett.** β. 5 **iennet(te,** 6 **ienete, -ate, iannet, ionet,** 6–7 **ienet(t,** 7– **jennet.** [a. F. *genet* (in 15th c. also *ginet*) in same sense, a. Sp. *jinete*, †*ginete*, 'a light horseman that rideth *a la gineta*' (F. *à la genette*), i.e. 'with the legs trussed vp in short stirrups, with a target and a ginnet launce' (Minsheu, 1599). In Fr. and Eng. (also in It. *gianetto* masc., *gianetta* fem.) transferred from the horseman to his horse, a sense unknown to Sp. dictionaries until quite recently. The Sp. use appears in our sense 2, which is however later in Eng. Dozy derives the Sp. word from Arab. *Zenāta* 'a great Berber nation noted for the valour of its cavalry'; other conjectures have been made.]

1. A small Spanish horse.

α. **1463** *Mann. & Househ. Exp.* (Roxb.) 178 Item ffor a genett that my mastyr lent hym into the northe contry. **1557–87** HOLINSHED *Chron.* III. 834/1 The countie Galeas came into the place on a genet trapped in blew satten. *c* **1645** HOWELL *Lett.* (1645) III. 109 The proudest Don..prancing upon his ginet in the streets. **1670** DRYDEN *1st Pt. Conq. Granada* I. i, (Each Brandishing his Bull-spear in his Hand) Did their proud Gennets gracefully command. **1774** GOLDSM. *Nat. Hist.* (1862) I. I. i. 250 Next to the Barb, travellers generally rank the Spanish genette. **1870** DISRAELI *Lothair* iv. 10 The dames and damsels vaulted on their barbs and genets.

β. ?*c* **1475** *Sqr. lowe Degre* 749 Iennettes of Spayne, that ben so wyght, Trapped to the ground with velvet bright. **1550** LYNDESAY *Sqr. Meldrum* 1711 Ane man in armour bricht, Upon ane ionet or ane cursour wicht. **1565** JEWEL *Repl. Harding* (1611) 310 The Sacrament must be caried before him, whither so euer he goe, vpon a faire white Iannet. **1580** LYLY *Euphues* (Arb.) 405 In seeking to trie your louer like a Ienet, you tyre him like a Iade. *a* **1674** MILTON *Hist. Mosc.* i. Wks. (1851) 479 The Emperor rides into the Field..with all his Nobility, on Jennets and Turky Horses. **1764** CHURCHILL *Times* Wks. 1776 III. 78 Watch not their steps—They're safe without thy care, Unless, like Jennets, they conceive by air. **1838** PRESCOTT *Ferd. & Is.* I. I. v. 252 Isabella, royally attired, rode on a Spanish jennet.

†**2.** A (Spanish) light horseman. *Obs.* exc. *Hist.*

1676 *North's Plutarch* Add. Lives 76 He [Cortez] was made Lieutenant of a company of Gennets. [**1838** PRESCOTT *Ferd. & Is.* II. II. ii. 406 The Spanish *ginetes* succeeded in throwing the French gendarmerie into some disorder.]

3. *attrib.*, as ***jennet-bit, -fashion, -lance.***

1599 MINSHEU *Sp. Dict.*, *Gineta lança*, a ginnet launce. **1600** J. PORY tr. *Leo's Africa* II. 364 They fight on horse-backe after the Gynnet fashion, they use lances with two heads, and darts and arrowes. **1600** E. BLOUNT tr. *Conestaggio* 197 A thousande foote, and five hundreth horse, after the Genette manner. **1611** COTGR., *Genet*, a kind of bit with a round port..a Genet-bit.

†**jennet**². *Obs.* **a.** = GINNET, a carpenter's adz. **b.** App. some part of the fixture of a bell.

1562 in Rogers *Agric. & Prices* III. 576/2, 11 axes..8 jennets..12 augers. **1615–16** in Swayne *Sarum Church-w. Acc.* (1896) 166, xij Jennetes for the Gudgins of the third bell, 6*d.*

jennet, obs. variant of GENET¹.

jenneting ('dʒɛnɪtɪŋ). Forms: 7 **iennit-, jenit-, jenet-, junit-, junet-, genet-, ginniting,** 8 **jenit-, junetin, gen(n)iting, jeunetting,** 9 **gennetting, geniton, juneating,** 8– **jenneting.** [app. from F. *Jean* or *Jeannet*, in *pomme de Saint-Jean* 'S. John's apple, a kind of soone-ripe Sweeting' (Cotgr.): cf. *pomme de Jeannet* in Norman patois. The termination is conformed to that of *sweeting, hasting*, etc. Etymological ingenuity in the 17–18th c. saw in the word a reference to *June*, and 'improved' it into *Juniting* and *June-eating.*] A kind of early apple.

1601 HOLLAND *Pliny* I. 540 The Apple trees..the hastie kind that bringeth sweet Iennitings. **1625** BACON *Ess.*, *Gardens* (Arb.) 556 Early Peares, and Plummes in Fruit; Ginnitings; Quadlins. **1655** MOUFET & BENNET *Health's Improv.* (1746) 301 Junitings are the first kind of Apples which are soonest ripe, coming in and going out with the Month of June. **1741** *Complete Fam.-Piece* II. i.i. 383 Apples [July]..White Jeunetting, Margaret Apple. **1803** *J. Abercrombie's Ev. Man his own Gard.* 671 Apples, Jenneting, or June eating; smallest early ripe. **1833** TENNYSON *Blackbird* iii, With that gold dagger of thy bill To fret the summer jenneting.

b. ***jenneting pear***: An early pear; = F. *poire de la Saint-Jean.*

1695 WESTMACOTT *Script. Herb.* 11 The Fruit..is about the bigness of a small Jeneting Pear.

jenny ('dʒɛnɪ). [A female personal name, pet-form or familiar equivalent of *Janet* (or, by confusion with *Jinny* or *Jeanie*, of *Jane*), and so serving as a feminine of *Jack*. Hence, like *Jack*, used as a feminine prefix, and as the name of machines.]

I. 1. The female name: hence, sometimes applied derisively to a man who concerns himself with purely feminine matters.

Mod. Sc. 'He is a regular jenny'.

2. Used as a prefix to denote a female animal, as ***jenny-ass***, and *esp.* in names of birds, as ***jenny-hooper, -howlet***, and sometimes loosely applied without reference to sex.

1600 SURFLET *Countrie Farm* I. xxii. 122 To preuent the danger of owles and iennye [*printed* ienupe, *ed.* 1616 Iennie] whuppers. **1632** BROME *North. Lasse* III. ii. Wks. 1873 III. 53, I should not be so fond to mistake a Jennie Howlet for a Tassel Gentle. **1828** *Craven Dial.*, *Jinny-Hullet*, an owl. **1847–78** HALLIWELL, *Jenny-Hooker*, an owl. *North.* It is also called a Jenny-howlet. **1885** SWAINSON *Prov. Names Birds* 34 Blue Titmouse..Jenny tit (Suffolk).

b. Short for *jenny ass, jenny wren.*

1808 E. S. BARRETT *Miss-led General* 22 A jackass and his jenny will do well enough for a lord and lady. **1881** *Leicestersh. Gloss.*, *Jenny* and *Jenny-wren*, the wren. **1885** SWAINSON *Prov. Names Birds* 35 Wren..Familiar names. Kitty, Jenny (General).

3. ***creeping Jenny***, the plant *Lysimachia Nummularia* or Moneywort.

1882 *Garden* 12 Aug. 138/2 The common Money-wort, or Creeping Jenny as it is called. **1883** *Pall Mall G.* 1 Oct. 3/2 Vases..with fuchsia centres and pendent border of creeping jenny.

II. In names of machinery, etc.

4. Short for SPINNING-JENNY.

[**1789** *Trans. Soc. Arts* I. 34 The construction of this Kind of Machine, called a Spinning Jenny.] **1796** MORSE *Amer. Geog.* I. 440 The filling of the cotton goods is spun with jennies. *Ibid.* 386 The operation of the jenny is nearly the same as the roving billy. **1859** SMILES *Self-Help* 32 The work-people..made a desperate effort to destroy all the jennies; and a mob rose and scoured the country round Blackburn, demolishing the machines wherever they could find them.

5. A locomotive crane which runs backwards and forwards, and is used for moving heavy weights.

1861 *Ann. Reg.* 17 The jenny, which is three or four tons in weight, fell on the top of the boiler. **1878** F. S. WILLIAMS *Midl. Railw.* 508 A jenny, or crane, is placed on a movable platform extending from one stage to the other.

6. A pair of compasses, having the point of one leg bent inwards, so as to be applied to an edge at right angles to the surface on which the other leg is fixed. Also called *oddlegs* or *moffs*.

Mod. Price-list Engineers' and Joiners' Tools.

7. *Billiards.* Name of a particular stroke.

1856 CRAWLEY *Billiards* (1859) 17 The *Jenny*..is made by a losing hazard into the middle pocket, from a ball lying near to the cushion. **1873** BENNETT & CAVENDISH *Billiards* 149 Strokes..sometimes called Jennys. **1899** *Daily News* 31 Mar. 3/3 He then scored two brilliant jennies—short and long—and after another loser gave a safety miss.

8. *Comb.*, as ***jenny-minder, -spinning***; **jenny-bank, jenny-gates** (see quots.); **jenny-long-legs** *Sc.*, a daddy-long-legs; **jenny-mony-feet** *Sc.*, a centipede (Jam.).

1852 *Jrnl. R. Agric. Soc.* XIII. II. 275 The cross-beam in the outhouses was called the *jenny-bank, from its being the usual domicile of the barn-owl. **1829** *Glover's Hist. Derby* I. 58 Cross-gates or *jenny-gates are then driven, which are passages not only giving admission to the pure air, but serving for different roads to the works. **1899** *Daily News* 9 Jan. 7/2 Bolt-maker, *Jenny-minder, Yeast-seller. **1825** J. NICHOLSON *Operat. Mechanic* 385 The carding-engine used in *jenny-spinning.

jenny, variant of GINNY, *Obs.*

jennyrickshaw, variant of JINRICKSHA.

'jenny-spinner.
1. A popular name in the north of the crane-fly or daddy-long-legs.
1817 *Edinb. Even. Courant* 1 Sept. (Jam.), The worm which so much injured the oat crop this season is the progeny of the fly..with long legs and body, called jenny-spinners. It belongs to the order diptera, and the genus tipula. **1825** BROCKETT, *Jenny-spinner*, or Long-legg'd tyalyur. **1893** *Northumbld. Gloss., Jenny-spinner*..the insect called daddy-long-legs or Harry-long-legs.
2. A child's teetotum.
1824 MACTAGGART *Gallovid. Encycl., Jennie Spinner*, a toy. **1825** BROCKETT, *Jinny-spinner*, a play-thing among children.
3. One who spins with a jenny.
1828 *Blackw. Mag.* XXIV. 871 The Cotton Lords claim the superiority for Arkwright, the jenny-spinner.

jenny wren ('dʒɛnɪ 'rɛn). [See JENNY 2.]
1. A popular, and esp. nursery, name for the wren (also locally *kitty wren*): sometimes regarded in nursery lore as the wife, bride, or sweetheart of Robin Redbreast.
1648 EARL WESTMORELAND *Otia Sacra* 137 The finch, the sparrow, Jenny Wren. **1828** *Craven Dial., Jenny Wren*, the wren. An opinion prevails..that this diminutive bird is the female of the Robin Redbreast. **1863** *Sat. Rev.* 283 He gives up the ripeness of his studies, and the last growth of his artistic skill to our robin red-breasts and jenny wrens.
2. *U.S.* A name for Herb Robert, *Geranium Robertianum.*
1890 in *Cent. Dict.*

jenoper, obs. form of JUNIPER.

jent, -e, obs. forms of GENT *a.*

†**jen'tacular.** *a. Obs.* [f. L. *jentācul-um* breakfast (f. *jentāre* to breakfast) + -AR.] Of or belonging to breakfast.
1721 AMHERST *Terræ Fil.* App. 318 Nothing more..can be expected from those jentacular confabulations. **1811** A. KNOX in *Corr. w. Jebb* (1834) II. 44, I therefore wish to close at this ante-jentacular hour.

†**jen'tation.** *Obs. rare.* [ad. L. *jentātiōn-em*, n. of action from *jentāre*: see prec.] Breakfast.
1599 A. M. tr. *Gabelhouer's Bk. Physicke* 36/1 Administre heerof to the Patient fasting..2 howers before his ientatione. **1604** R. CAWDREY *Table Alph., Ientation*, breakefast.

jentel, -ile, -ill, jentylle, obs. ff. GENTLE.

jentew, obs. form of GENTOO.

†**jenticulate**, *v. Obs. rare*⁻⁰. [Erroneously for **jentaculate*: cf. *jentacular.*] *intr.* To breakfast (Cockeram, 1623). Hence †**jenticulation**, breakfast (Phillips, 1658).

jentman, obs. form of GENTMAN.

jentrie, -tery, obs. forms of GENTRY.
1422 tr. *Secreta Secret., Priv. Priv.* 191 Of this grette Ientrie alle men mervelith.

jenuper, jenyper, -re, obs. ff. JUNIPER.

jeobard, -berdye, obs. forms of JEOPARD, -Y.

jeobet(te, jeobit, obs. forms of GIBBET.

jeofail ('dʒɛfeɪl), *sb.* Also 6 ieo-, (yeo-), ioe-, ieoyfaile, ieofall. [AngloFr. *jeo fail, jo faill*, I am at fault, I mistake.]
Law. A mistake or oversight in pleading or other legal proceeding; also, an acknowledgement of such error. *Obs.* exc. *Hist.*
1541 *Act 32 Hen. VIII*, c. 30 Thissues haue ben misioyned and a Ieofall [*orig. draft* Yeofaile]. *Ibid.*, Any myspleading lacke of colour insufficient pleading or ieofaile notwithstanding. **1622** MALYNES *Anc. Law-Merch.* 465 The Writ of Error..was heretofore vsuall to prolong suits in Law, before the Statute of Ieofaile was made, meaning in good French *I'ay failly.* **1624** *Act 21 Jas. I*, c. 13 An Act for the further reformation of Jeofails. **1768** BLACKSTONE *Comm.* III. xxv. 407 Mistakes are also effectually helped by the statutes of amendment and *jeofails*: so called, because when a pleader perceives any slip in the form of his proceedings, and acknowledges such error (*jeo faile*) he is at liberty by those statutes to amend it. **1810** BENTHAM *Packing* (1821) 137 Here we see—alas!—a jeofail: a jeofail in the shape of a misrecital. **1879** *Act 42-3 Vict.* c. 59 Sched. II, 32 Hen. VIII. c. 30 Mispleading Jeofayles, &c. [**1883** *Act 46-7 Vict.* c. 49 §4 The enactments mentioned in Part II of the schedule to the Civil Procedure Acts, Repeal Act, 1879, are hereby repealed.]
†**b.** *transf.* and *fig.* A mistake or error generally. (In first quot. Failure, discomfiture.) ? *Obs.*
1546 J. HEYWOOD *Prov.* (1867) 82 Pouertee brought that ioye to ioefaile. **1641** 'SMECTYMNUUS' *Vind. Answ.* xi. 111 The Acts of Dioclesian Maxim..You doe as good as passe by..which is greater Jeofaile then our Maximilian. **1644** J. GOODWIN *Innoc. Triumph.* (1645) 22, I conceive it to be a jeofaile in Theologie, a mistake in stead of a truth. **1828** *Edin. Rev.* XLVIII. 511 These flaws and jeofails are not nature's doings, but our own.
Hence †'**jeofail** *v. intr.*, to fail to meet an obligation. *Obs. rare*⁻¹.
1599 HAYWARD *1st Pt. Hen. IV*, 27 The Lords..sent him word, that if hee did ieofaile with them, and not come according to appointment, they would chuse another King.

†'**jeopard**, *sb. Obs. rare.* Also 4 ioparde, iupred, 6 iupert. [? Shortened from JEOPARDY, or with final vowel mute.] = JEOPARDY.
13.. *E.E. Allit. P.* A. 601 Of more & lasse in godez ryche ..lys no Ioparde [*rime* rewarde] For þer is vch mon payed in-liche. *Ibid.* B. 491 þen watz þer ioy in þat gyn where Iupred er dryȝed. **1508** DUNBAR *Poems* viii. 62 Iulius, in iupert, in wisdom and expence, Most fortunable chiftane, bothe in yhouth and eild. **1611** COTGR., *Hasard*, hazard, aduenture, ieopard, fortune, chance.

jeopard ('dʒɛpəd), *v.* Forms: see JEOPARDY; also 5 iouperd, geoparde, ieoparte, 7 jeabard, -poard, 9 jipper. [Back-formation from JEOPARDY.
No example from 1654 to 19th c. Marked *Obs.* by Johnson 1755. F. Vesey in *Decl. Eng. Lang.* 1841, censures Johnson for including it, and says 'it is quite out of use', and its attempted revival 'indicates rather a spirit of research than good taste'.]
1. *trans.* To put in jeopardy; to expose to loss, injury, or death; to hazard, risk, imperil. †Often in alliterative phr. *to jeopard a joint*, sc. of a finger, as opposed to the whole body (*obs.*).
c **1374** CHAUCER *Troylus* IV. 1538 (1566) And er þat ye Iuparten so youre names Beth nought to hasty. **1412-20** LYDG. *Chron. Troy* II. x. F 3, Day by day his life he gan Ieoparte, Tofore their walles for to preue his mighte. *c* **1440** *Generydes* 4480 Nay, god defende it..That ye shall iupert me so in this case. **1494** FABYAN *Chron.* VII. ccxxxviii. 276 To ieoberde his propre persone agayne Crystes enemyes. **1530** PALSGR. 596/1, I juparte, I put in daunger or adventure. **1535** COVERDALE *Judg.* v. 18 Zabulons people ioperde their life vnto death. *a* **1548** HALL *Chron., Hen. VII*, 7 Taryenge draweth and ieopardeth perell. **1556** J. HEYWOOD *Spider & F.* lvii. 105 Rather then ieberd in war; goods life and all. **1563** *Homilies* II. *Excesse of apparell* ¶6 Manye a one ieopardeth his beste ioynte to maintayne him self in sumptuous rayment. **1570** LEVINS *Manip.* 31/5 Ioparde, *periclitari.* **1600** DEKKER *Fortunatus* Wks. 1873 I. 153 My ten duckets are like my ten fingers, they will not jeopard a joynt for you. **1623** COCKERAM II, To Hazard, *Ieobard.* *a* **1625** FLETCHER *Wom. Pleased* III. ii, Are not you three now going to be sinfull, to jeabard a joynt or so? **1654** in Hammond *Answ. Animadv. Ignat.* iii. §3. 64, I dare not be so bold with my soul as to jeopard it in that manner. **1822** SCOTT *Nigel* xxx, This man Gregory is not fit to jipper a joint with him. **1838** PRESCOTT *Ferd. & Is.* (1846) II. II. i. 249 To jeopard the interests of the Spanish sovereigns. **1867** FREEMAN *Norm. Conq.* I. vi. 513 As ready to jeopard his life and fortune..as ever his..forefathers had been. **1896** EDITH THOMPSON *Red Mirko* i. in *Monthly Packet* Christm. No. 86, I will jeopard my own head rather than throw him over.
†**b.** with *inf.* To risk doing something. *Obs.*
1456 *Paston Lett.* I. 408 The toun arose, and wold have jouperdit to have distressed the Duke of Somerset. **1479** *Ibid.* III. 259, I dar well juperde to take a dystres. **1535** COVERDALE *2 Sam.* xv. 20 Thou camest yesterdaye, and to daye thou iuperdest to go with vs. **1554** KNOX *Godly Let.* D ij, Why will you ieoperde to lese the lyfe euerlastinge?
†**c.** *intr.* (for *refl.*) To risk oneself, to run the risk; to venture, adventure. *Obs.*
1430-40 LYDG. *Bochas* III. i. (1558) 40 b, It were foly with suche one to ieoparte. **1509** BARCLAY *Shyp of Folys* (1874) II. 251 Who that dare auenture or ieparde for to rowe Vpon the see swellynge by waues great and hye. **1530** PALSGR. 561/2, I geoparde, I adventure..I coulde have gotten a goodly botye one daye..if I durst have geoparded. **1536** BELLENDEN *Cron. Scot.* III. x, To ieoperde aganis sa huge multitude of peple. **1577** HOLINSHED *Chron.* I. *Scot.* 236/1 In nowise to ieoparde with them in any pight field. **1598** R. BERNARD tr. *Terence* (1607) 88, I ieoparded almost farre enough.
†**2.** *trans.* To stake, bet. *Obs.*
c **1470** *Pol. Poems* (Rolls) II. 287 The kyng schold be enrychyd for his parte..I dare playnly joparte. *c* **1563** *Jack Jugler* in *Four Old Plays* (1848) 17, I durst ieoperd an hunderid pounde That sum bauderie might now within be founde. **1579** FULWELL *Art Flatterie* H iij (N.), I dare ieobard my cappe to fortie shillings, thou shalt have but a colde suite. **1579-80** NORTH *Plutarch, Alexander*, I am content (quoth Alexander) to ieopard the price of the horse.
†**3.** *Venery.* (Meaning uncertain: see quots.) *Obs.*
1575 GASCOIGNE *Wordes of Hart* in Turberv. *Venerie* 139 He ieopardes and rechates: ahlas he blowes the fall And soundes that deadly dolful mote, whiche I muste die withall. **1897** D. H. MADDEN *Diary Master W. Silence* iv. 50 The huntsman, now that scent is lost for a time, at all events, jeopards with his horn, an ancient usage that places the prospects of the chase indeed in jeopardy... I have sought in vain for any explanation of this term of art.
Hence '**jeoparded** *ppl. a.*, '**jeoparding** *vbl. sb.* Also '**jeoparder**, one who puts in jeopardy.
1534 MORE *Let.* in Roper *Life* (1731) 122, I could not swere without the jubarding of my soule to perpetual dampnacion. **1611** COTGR., *Hasardeur*, a hazarder, venturer, ieoparder, aduenturer. **1783** AINSWORTH *Lat. Dict.* (Morell) I, A jeoparding, *periclitatio.*

†**jeopardious**, *a. Obs.* [f. JEOPARDY + -OUS.] Fraught with danger or risk; = JEOPARDOUS I.
1502 ATKYNSON tr. *De Imitatione* I. xxiii. 172 It is fere-full to dy, but parauenture it is more ieoperdyous to lyue lenger. **1526** TINDALE *Acts* xxvii. 9 When moche tyme was spent and saylynge was nowe ieoperdeous [**1535** COVERD. ioperdous]. **1540** HYRDE tr. *Vives' Instr. Chr. Wom.* (1592) E vij, He was never infected with any sore or ieoperdious sickenes. *a* **1548** HALL *Chron., Hen. VIII* 211 b, It was both ieopardeous for yᵉ kyng & for his whole realme.

jeopardize ('dʒɛpədaɪz), *v.* [f. JEOPARD *v.* or JEOPARD-Y + -IZE.] *trans.* To put into jeopardy; to jeopard.
1646 N. B[ARNET] *Regenerate man's growth in Grace* 47 We doe..*Jeoperdize* our soules safety. **1828** WEBSTER, *Jeopardize*..(This is a modern word used by respectable writers in America, but synonymous with *jeopard*, and therefore useless.) **1834** SIR H. TAYLOR *2nd Pt. Artevelde* III. ii, That he should jeopardize his wilful head Only for spite at me! **1846** TRENCH *Mirac.* xx. (1862) 330. **1862** STANLEY *Jew. Ch.* (1877) I. xiii. 246 Ready to jeopardise their lives for the nation. **1885** S. L. LEE in *Dict. Nat. Biog.* I. 13/1 Abbot found it difficult to steer a course that should not jeopardise either his loyalty or his honesty.
Hence '**jeopardized** *ppl. a.*, exposed to risk.
1864 SKEAT *Uhland's Poems* 328 No one would bide, But fast to his jeopardized fort did ride. **1898** *Westm. Gaz.* 4 May 2/3 A new terror has been added to the already jeopardised existence of the German journalist.

†'**jeopardless**, *a. Obs.* Also 6 ieopardiles. [f. JEOPARD-Y + -LESS.] Free from risk or peril.
1549 COVERDALE, etc. *Erasm. Par. 1 Cor.* vii. 18 b, Rather had I haue in you that, whiche is of lesse perfeccion, so that it bee ieoperdlesse. *Ibid.*, *Gal.* v. 18 It is neither wel done, nor ieopardiles to beare with it any lynger. **1652** URQUHART *Jewel* Wks. (1834) 247 For foyles, and every thing else befitting that jeopardless monomachy.

†'**jeopardous**, *a. Obs.* Forms: see JEOPARDY; also 5 jowpertous. [f. JEOPARD-Y + -OUS: cf. JEOPARDIOUS.]
1. Fraught with risk or danger; hazardous, risky, perilous, dangerous.
1451 *Paston Lett.* I. 212 It had be right jowpertous and ferefull. **1474** SIR J. PASTON in *P. Lett.* III. 115 It had been jopertous to leve moche plate wyth hyr. **1489** *Act 4 Hen. VII*, c. 3 §1 To the Iubardoue abydyng of his moost noble persone. **1502** HEN. VII in Ellis *Orig. Lett.* Ser. I. I. 54 Shippes sailyng into so jeoperdous and ferre parties. **1545** RAYNOLD *Byrth Mankynde* II. iii, This is a very ieopardous labour. **1584** COGAN *Haven Health* clxxx. (1636) 165 Lamprayes..bee..lesse jeopardous [than eels]. *a* **1661** FULLER *Worthies, Cornwall* (1662) 202 This his Goodly, Valiant, and Jeopardous enterprise (as it is termed).
2. Addicted to risks; venturesome, daring.
1494 FABYAN *Chron.* VII. ccxxx. 261 Guy,..as a lustye and iuperdous Knyght, put hymselfe in adventure dyuerse wayes and tymes. **1593** NASHE *Christ's T.* (1613) 121, I will not bee so vnweaponed ieopardous, to ouerthrow both thy cause and my credite at once.
Hence †'**jeopardously** *adv.*; †'**jeopardousness.**
1494 FABYAN *Chron.* VII. 554 The erle..fledde, and so lepynge ieopardously into the howse of an olde woman, escapyd. **1523** LD. BERNERS *Froiss.* I. ccclviii. 581 He.. aduentured hymselfe oftentymes ryght ieoperdously. **1552** HULOET, Ieopardouslye, *periculose.* **1730-6** BAILEY (folio), *Jeopardousness*, Hazardousness.

jeopardy ('dʒɛpədɪ), *sb.* Forms: α. 3 iuperti, 4 ieupartie, -tye, 4-5 iupartie, -tye, 5 ieperte, ioparte, -perte, 5-6 iupertie, ioperty, -partie, 6 iuberte, ioberty. β. 4 ieupardye, 4-6 iuperdy(e, 5 iupurdy, iepardye, ieberde, 5-6 iupardy(e, iubardie, -berdy, iopardie, -perdye, 6 ioberdie, ieoperde, -pardie, -berdye, -bardie, 7 jobardy, 7- jeopardy. [ME. *iuparti*, etc., a. OF. *iu parti*, later *ieu* (*geu*) *parti*, lit. 'divided play or game, even game', hence 'uncertain chance, uncertainty', orig. a term of chess and similar games, in med.L. *jocus partitus*, Cat. *joch partit*, Sp. *juego de partido.* It has been suggested that the Eng. change of *-parti* to *-pardy* was partly influenced by association with F. *perdre* to lose, but it was evidently mainly phonetic, like the occasional change of *p* to *b* in *jubertie, joberdie, jeobardie*, etc.
Johnson says erroneously 'a word not now in use'; it was in continuous use during the 18th c.]
†**1.** *Chess*, etc. A problem. *Obs.*
The regular name for this down to 1500.
[**12..** *MS. Cott. Cleop.* B. IX. lf. 4 Les gius partiz numeement ke me vnt apris diuerse gent. **12..** *MS. Royal* 13 A xviij lf. 161 Icy comencent les iu partiez des Eschez.]
c **1369** CHAUCER *Dethe Blaunche* 666 But god wolde I had ones or twyes Y-kond [*Skeat* y-koud] and knowe the Ieupardyes That kowde the Greke Pictagoras, I shulde haue pleyde the bet at ches. **1412-20** LYDG. *Chron. Troy* II. xi. (MS. Digby 230) lf. 58 b/1 Of þe chesse þe pleie moste glorious,..þouȝ a man studied al his liue He shal ay finde diuerse fantasies Of wardes makinge and newe Iuparties. *a* **1500** *MS. Ashmole* 344 (Bodl.) lf. 18 b, Thys ys a Iupertie to do a man mate the. *Ibid.* 19 a, At v. draughtis shall this Iupertie be plaiede.
†**b.** A device, trick, stratagem. *Obs.*
1375 BARBOUR *Bruce* XIV. 421 He thoucht than on a Iuperdy, And gert his menȝhe halely Dicht thame in the presoners dray. *c* **1450** HOLLAND *Howlat* 789 Thus iowkit with iuperdyss the iangland Ia. *c* **1480** HENRYSON *Mor. Fab.* (Maitl. Cl.) 16 In his minde hee kest The juperties, the wayis and the wile, By what meanes hee might this Cocke beguyle. **1536** BELLENDEN *Cron. Scot.* IV. xiii, Be quhais wisdome and ilhand ieoperdis the Romanis wer stoppit..fra ony forthir conques on the Scottis.

†**2.** A position in a game, undertaking, etc. in which the chances of winning and losing hang in the balance; an even chance; an undecided state of affairs; uncertainty; chance.

[*c* **1250** BRACTON IV. i. §32 Nec potest [ballivus] transigere, nec pascisci, nec jocum partitum facere. **1292** BRITTON II. xvii. §8 Mes ne mie en jeupartie de perdre ou de gayner, tut le voillent les parties.] *c* **1374** CHAUCER *Troylus* II. 416 (465) For myn estat now lyth in Iupartye And eek myn emes lyf lyth in balaunce. **1390** GOWER *Conf.* III. 200 Pompeie..A werre had in ieupartie Ayein the king of Ermenie. *c* **1450** LYDG. *Secrees* 305 A twix two [I] stood in Iupartye To what party my penne I shulde applye. *c* **1470** HENRY *Wallace* v. 173 He wist nocht weill giff thai war tayne or slayne Or chapyt haile be ony ieperte. ? *c* **1475** *Sqr. lowe Degre* 83 And [it] were put in ieoperde, What man shoulde wynne that lady fre. **1597** BACON *Coulers Good & Evill* v. Ess. (Arb.) 146 By imputing to all excellencie in compositions..a casualty or ieopardy.

3. Risk of loss, harm, or death; peril, danger. *c* **1374** CHAUCER *Troylus* v. 916 For Troye is brought in swich a Iupartye That it to save is now no remedye. **1390** GOWER *Conf.* I. 92 For which he schal in that degree Stonde of his lif in jeupartie. **1471** MARG. PASTON in *P. Lett.* III. 30, I schuld send ȝow mony therefore, but I dar not put yt in joperte, ther be so many theves stereng. **1472** *Presentm. Juries* in *Surtees Misc.* (1888) 25 In payn of the jeberde þt may fall thar off. **1513** DOUGLAS *Æneis* IX. iii. 162 Thair lyfe is now in iuperty, thai rave. **1526** TINDALE *1 Cor.* xv. 30 Why stonde we in ieoperdy every houre? **1537** *Nottingham Rec.* III. 375 He puttes the towne in grete danger and juberte. **1556** J. HEYWOOD *Spider & F.* i. 60 The more he wrange, the faster was he wrapt And all to thencrease of his ieoberdee. **1663** BUTLER *Hud.* I. i. 696 If any yet be so fool-hardy, T'expose themselves to vain Jeopardy. **1768** BLACKSTONE *Comm.* III. xxii. 326 Under a tyrannical sway trade must be continually in jeopardy. **1805** WORDSW. *Waggoner* I. 131 As chance would have it, passing by I saw you in that jeopardy. **1857** BUCKLE *Civiliz.* I. vii. 439, I think ..that if the colonists had been defeated, our liberties would have been for a time in considerable jeopardy.

†**b.** A deed involving peril; a daring exploit. *a* **1300** *Siriz* 276 in Wright *Anecd. Lit.* (1844) 9 For I shal don a juperti, And a ferli maistri. **1375** BARBOUR *Bruce* x. 145 Interludys, and iuperdyss That men assayit on mony viss. **1536** BELLENDEN *Cron. Scot.* IV. xvi, Maist forsy and strang beistis be thair awin ieoperdyis, ar oft slane. **1816** SCOTT *Ballad* in *Antiq.* xl, Now here a knight that's stout and good May prove a jeopardie.

jeopardy ('dʒɛpədɪ), *v. rare.* [f. prec. sb.] *trans.* = JEOPARD *v.* 1.

1460 *Paston Lett.* II. 87 Yf ye dar joperdie your suyrtie of c. marc I shall come and se you. **1836** *Fraser's Mag.* XIV. 272 He did wrong in jeopardying his well-earned histrionic fame. **1848** THACKERAY *Van. Fair* xviii, She would have seen..how entirely her character was jeopardied [*later ed.* jeopardized].

jepsyon, jeptyon, obs. ff. GIPSY (Egyptian).

jequirity (dʒɪ'kwɪrɪtɪ). Also **-erity.** [a. F. *jéquirity*, a. Tupi-Guarani *jekiriti*. For its introduction to European Pharmacy, see De Wecker in *Annales d' Oculistique* LXXXVIII (1882) 26.] A woody twining shrub, *Abrus precatorius* or Indian liquorice, indigenous to India, but now found in most tropical countries, the parti-coloured seeds of which, called ***jequirity beans***, are variously used for ornament, for weights, and in medicine. Also *attrib.*

1882 *Nature* XXVII. 192/1 (Acad. of Sc., Paris, 11 Dec.) Factitious purulent ophthalmia produced by the liquorice liana, or jequirity. **1887** MOLONEY *Forestry W. Afr.* 316 Crabs' Eyes, Jequerity, Prayer Beads, Jumble Beads... Recently these seeds have been brought into notice, under the name of 'Jequerity'. **1897** *Allbutt's Syst. Med.* II. 853 The serum of animals rendered immune to the toxic proteids of jequirity and castor-oil seeds.

jer (jɛr). Also ier, yeer, yer(r). Pl. jers, jery. [ad. OSl. *jerŭ* and *jerĭ*, Russ. *er* (pl. *éry*) and *er´*.] The name of either member of the pairs of characters Ⱏ, Ⱐ and ъ, ь of the Slavonic Glagolitic and Cyrillic alphabets, sometimes distinguished according to their Slavonic names as jerŭ (yerŭ, jer) and jerĭ (yerĭ, jer´) respectively; one or both of the sounds represented by these characters, or the Common Slavonic sounds from which they developed. Also *attrib.* (jerek, yerek in quots. 1861, 1883, referring to the second member of each pair, are from the deriv. seen in Russ. *érik.*)

1763 W. MASSEY *Origin & Progress of Letters* (*tables facing* 114) Yerr... Yeer.. ier. **1861** *Grammatography Based on the German compilation of F. Ballhorn* 58 (*table*) Jer... Jerek. *Ibid.* 61 (*table*) Yerr... Yer. **1883** I. TAYLOR *Alphabet* II. 196 (*table*) Yer... Yerek. **1949** *Archivum Linguisticum* I. 158 The left-to-right characters, viz. *jestŭ, kako, onŭ, ukŭ*, and the left-inclined, *jerŭ* and *jerĭ*..are significant. **1949** ENTWISTLE & MORISON *Russian & Slavonic Languages* 66 Peter the Great's Russian 'civil alphabet'..retained the two *jers* which had no longer an alphabetical value. *Ibid.* 82 In Russian the *jers* continued to be distinguished as back/front vowels, and so developed into the open vowels *o/e* respectively. **1952** *Word* VIII. 323 Leskien..thought that the spellings indicated a change in the quality of the consonant preceding the jer-letter. *Ibid.* 325 The category of jer-phonemes had been sharply reduced as to occurrence. **1955** H. G. LUNT *Old Church Slavonic Gram.* 30 A jer is weak in a syllable followed directly by a non-reduced vowel or pause... A jer is strong only in a syllable directly before a weak jer... When the jers were lost as a category, the weak jers simply disappeared, and the strong jers were replaced by another vowel. **1969** *Language* XLV. 558 The rule specifying sequences of obstruents as fricative + stop was eliminated by the time the jers were lost.

jerapigre, obs. form of HIERA PICRA.

jerarchy, obs. form of HIERARCHY.

‖**jerboa** (dʒə'bəʊə, 'dʒɜːbəʊə). Forms: 7 **jerbuah,** 8 **gerbo, gerbua, yerbua, jeribo,** 8– **jerboa.** [mod.L. *jerbōa*, a. Arab. *yarbūʻ*, in Barbary *yerbōʻ*, the flesh of the loins, also the animal; whence F. *gerbo, gerboise*, Sp. *gerbasia*.]

1. A small rodent quadruped, *Dipus sagitta*, found in the deserts of Africa; it is of the size of a rat, has very long hind legs and short fore legs, and a long tufted tail, and is remarkable for its powers of jumping. Hence, any Jumping-mouse of the genus *Dipus*, or of the family *Dipodidæ*, representatives of which are found in various arid regions.

1662 J. DAVIES *Olearius' Voy. Ambass.* VII. 415 We saw also, neer Terki, a kind of Field-mice, which in the Arabian Language are called *Jerbuah*. **1702** W. J. *Bruyn's Voy. Levant* lxxviii. 287, I was presented with a small Animal called *Gerbo*, which was brought for a rarity from Barbary. **1752** H. WALPOLE *Corr.* (1837) I. 182 Mr. Conway has brought lady Ailesbury..a *Jeribo*..a composition of a squirrel, a hare, a rat, and a monkey, which altogether looks very like a bird. **1774** GOLDSM. *Nat. Hist.* II. 432 The *gerbua*, though, properly speaking, furnished with but two legs, is one of the swiftest animals in the world. **1813** BINGLEY *Anim. Biog.* (ed. 4) I. 399 The Jerboas seem, in many respects both of conformation and habit, much allied to the kanguroos. **1853** KINGSLEY *Hypatia* xxi, A jerboa sprang up from a tuft of bushes at his feet.

2. *Comb.* **jerboa-mouse,** a North American rodent of the genus *Dipodomys*, one of the pouched-mice or kangaroo-rats of the South-western U.S. and Mexico.

jere, in ***good jere***, alteration of GOODYEAR, q.v.

1821 SCOTT *Kenilw.* xv, 'Who the good jere would have thought this!'

jereed: see JERID.

jeremeievite, -ieffite (jɛrɛ'meɪjɛvaɪt, -faɪt). *Min.* [Named 1883 after Jeremejev or Yeremeieff, a Russian mineralogist + -ITE.] A transparent colourless borate of aluminium occurring in hexagonal prisms.

1883 *Amer. Jrnl. Sc.* Ser. III. XXV. 478 Jeremeieffite, a new mineral. **1892** DANA *Min.* 875 Jeremejevite. **1896** A. H. CHESTER *Names Min.*, Jeremeievite.

jeremiad (dʒɛrɪ'maɪæd). Also **-ade.** [a. F. *jérémiade* (1762 in Hatz.-Darm.), f. *Jérémie*, L. *Jeremias* Jeremiah, in reference to the 'Lamentations of Jeremiah' in the Old Testament.] A lamentation; a writing or speech in a strain of grief or distress; a doleful complaint; a complaining tirade; a lugubrious effusion.

1780 HAN. MORE in W. Roberts *Mem.* (1834) I. 186 It has been long the fashion to make the most lamentable *Jeremiades* on the badness of the times. **1791–1823** D'ISRAELI *Cur. Lit.*, *Prediction*, I have been occasionally struck at the Jeremiads of honest George Withers. **1844** W. H. MAXWELL *Sports & Adv. Scotl.* xv. (1855) 140 The lady commenced a Jeremiade. **1875** HELPS *Ess.*, *Convers. Railway Carriage* 192, I could sit down, and mourn, and utter doleful Jeremiads without end.

Jeremiah (dʒɛrɪ'maɪə). The name of a Hebrew prophet (see JEREMIAD), used allusively to denote a person given to lamentation or woeful complaining.

1781 GIBBON *Decl. & Fall* III. 620 The vague and tedious lamentations of the British Jeremiah [*sc.* Gildas]. **1902** *Daily Chron.* 15 Oct. 3/1 This talk about the rate-payers only came from municipal Jeremiahs. **1905** *Ibid.* 1 Sept. 5/7 The Jeremiahs have been on the rampage; the dismal and the doleful would-be experts [etc.]. **1928** *Daily Express* 23 Feb. 3/5 There are always Jeremiahs who go about saying that we have never had such bad times. **1928** *Observer* 22 July 16/3 The Socialists are..bound to be confirmed Jeremiahs by the necessity of their propaganda. **1963** *Times* 22 Apr. 8/5 Mr. Selwyn Lloyd..wanted to see Young Conservatives 'rise up in protest against the Jeremiahs, defeatists, pessimists, denigrators', [etc.]. **1973** *Listener* 15 Nov. 655/1, I am not going to try to play the role of prophet, least of all Jeremiah.

Jeremianic (ˌdʒɛrɪmaɪ'ænɪk), *a.* [f. JEREMIAH, after *Messianic*.] Of or pertaining to the prophet Jeremiah or the book of the Old Testament which bears his name.

1880 *Encycl. Brit.* XIII. 628/1 Brought into its present form by a captivity prophet, working on a Jeremianic basis. **1891** T. K. CHEYNE *Orig. Psalter* 151 A group of literary works which we may call Jeremianic. **1921** J. MOFFATT *Approach to New Testament* ii. 62 The Jeremianic prediction of the new covenant has been fulfilled in Christianity.

jerfalcon, etc., obs. forms of GYRFALCON.

Jericho ('dʒɛrɪkəʊ). [Name of a town in Palestine, where David bade his servants tarry until their beards were grown: see *2 Sam.* x. 5.] Used in slang or colloq. phrases for a place of retirement or concealment, or a place far distant and out of the way.

1635 HEYWOOD *Hierarch.* IV. 208 Who would,..I know, Bid such young boyes to stay in Iericho Vntill their Beards were growne, their wits more staid. **1648** *Mercurius Aulicus* 2–30 Mar., Let them all goe to Jericho, And ne're be seen againe. **1758** A. MURPHY *Upholsterer* II, He may go to Jericho for what I cares. **1840** BARHAM *Ingol. Leg.*, *Grey Dolphin*, His kick was tremendous, and when he had his boots on would—to use an expression of his own,..'send a man from Jericho to June'. **1859** THACKERAY *Virgin.* xvi, She may go to Bath, or she may go to Jericho for me. **1898** J. ARCH *Story of Life* xiii. 310 To enable them to do without the strong arm of the labourer and to send them to Jericho, if they had nowhere else to go to.

‖**jerid, jereed** (dʒə'riːd), *sb.* Forms: 7 **tzirid,** 8 **jarrit,** 9 **dsjerid, djer(r)id, djereed, jerreed, jerrid, jareed,** 8– **jerid,** 9 **jereed.** [Arab. *jarīd* midrib of the palm-leaf, rod, shaft, javelin.] A wooden javelin, about five feet long, used in games by Persian, Turkish, and Arabian horsemen. Also, A game in which this is used.

1662 J. DAVIES *Olearius' Voy. Ambass.* VI. 297 They also often Exercise themselves at the *Tzirid*, or Javelin. **1775** R. CHANDLER *Trav. Asia M.* (1825) I. 233 Galloping from all sides,..throwing at each other the *jarrit* or blunted dart. **1799** W. G. BROWNE *Trav. Africa*, etc. xi. 152 Here they shoot at a mark, and throw the jerid. **1811** SCOTT *Don Roderick* xxv, The Moor his jerrid flings. **1813** BYRON *Giaour* ix, Swift as the hurl'd on high jereed. **1819** T. HOPE *Anastasius* (1820) I. xi. 214 Flinging the djereed. **1853** LAYARD *Nineveh & Babylon* xi. 245 They played the Jerid with their long spears, galloping to and fro on their well-trained mares.

Hence †**je'rid** (**gereed, gerede**) *v. intr.*, to throw the jerid.

1698 FRYER *Acc. E. India & P.* 110 Tilting and Gereeding, that is, Casting of Darts. *Ibid.* 397 Here they Gerede, or cast Darts.

jerk (dʒɜːk), *sb.*[1] Also 6–7 **ierke, girke,** 7–9 **jirk.** [*Jerk* sb. and vb. are known from *c* 1550; app. echoic. See also YERK, which in some senses appears to be synonymous with this.]

†**1. a.** A stroke with a whip or wand, a stripe, a lash. *Obs.*

1555 W. WATREMAN *Fardle Facions* II. xi. 256 To the manne..foure score ierkes or lasshes with a skourge. **1594** *Contention* v. 154 After the Beadle hath hit him one girke, he leapes ouer the stoole and runnes away. **1612** BRINSLEY *Lud. Lit.* xxix. 288 Sometimes in greater faults, to giue three or fowre ierkes with a birch, or with a small redde willow where birch cannot be had. **1629** Z. BOYD *Last Battell* 1216 Let me giue him a girke with my rodde. **1742** RICHARDSON *Pamela* III. 334 Many a Jirk has the Dog had from me. **1796** MORSE *Amer. Geog.* I. 221 The Indians..imagine that it [a coach-whip snake] is able to cut a man in two with a jerk of its tail.

†**b.** *fig.* A lash of sarcasm; a cutting gibe.

1590 NASHE *Pasquil's Apol.* I. A iv b, The dislike that some had of the ierke which I gaue to Fryer Sauanarol. **1642** MILTON *Apol. Smect.* i, Who he is..under whose contempt and jirk these Men are not deservedly fallen? *a* **1700** B. E. *Dict. Cant. Crew*, *Gybe*,..also Jerk or Jeer. **1741** tr. *Laval's Hist. Ref.* IV. VIII. 912 He..omitted not to slide into his Speech some Jerks against the Doctrine..of the Jesuits.

2. a. A quick suddenly arrested movement; a sharp sudden pull, throw, push, thrust, or twist.

1575 GASCOIGNE *Weeds, Fruit of Fetters, Continence*, The stiffe and strongest arme Which geues a ierke and hath a cunning loose; Shoots furdest stil. **1633** B. JONSON *Love's Welcome, Welbeck*, His Jade gave him a Jerk. **1664** POWER *Exp. Philos.* I. 21 Little whitish Animals, which move up and down the water with jerks. **1706** BAYNARD *Cold Baths* in Sir J. Floyer *Hot & Cold Bath.* II. 302 To leave that and other Vices *gradatim*, and not at a jerk. **1776–96** WITHERING *Brit. Plants* (ed. 3) IV. 344 Seeds on the upper surface only: discharged by jerks. **1807** ROLAND *Fencing* 96, I may, with this smart sudden jirk from my wrist, strike your blade in such a manner as will leave your body quite exposed. **1871** L. STEPHEN *Playgr. Europe* iii. (1894) 84 He..brought me with a jerk into a sitting position.

b. (*a*) *Physiol.* An involuntary spasmodic contraction of a muscle, due to reflex action of nerves, as from external stimulus: usually with qualification, as ***knee-jerk, chin jerk***. (*b*) (in pl. ***the jerks***). Involuntary spasmodic movements of the limbs or features, esp. resulting from religious excitement.

1805 DOW *Jrnl.* in H. Mayo *Pop. Superst.* (1851) 125, I have seen all denominations of religion exercised by the jerks. **1822** SOUTHEY in *Q. Rev.* XXVIII. 6 The Jerks are not confined to a peculiar sect, or order. **1849** H. MAYO *Pop. Superst.* (1851) 124 The convulsions were commonly called 'the jerks'. **1874** E. EGGLESTON *Circuit Rider* xii. (1895) 89 These Methodis' sets people crazy with the jerks, I've hearn tell. **1895** G. N. STEWART *Man. Physiol.* xii. 625 The interval which elapses between the tap and the jerk ($\frac{5}{100}$ to $\frac{4}{100}$ second) is distinctly shorter than the reflex time of the extremely rapid lid-reflex. **1936** M. G. EGGLETON *Muscular Exercise* viii. 181 The jerk is equally readily obtained if the skin has been de-sensitized by application of a local anæsthetic. **1968** PASSMORE & ROBSON *Compan. Med. Stud.* I. xxiv. 14/1 The presence of a normal jerk shows that the receptors are sensitive..and the responding muscle is in order.

c. *fig.* in reference to literary style.

1818 HAZLITT *Eng. Poets* i. (1870) 16 The jerks, the breaks, the inequalities and harshnesses of prose are fatal to the flow of a poetical imagination. **1883** S. C. HALL *Retrospect* I. 322 His wit was more like a jerk than the flow it had once been.

d. Colloq. phr. ***physical jerks***, physical or gymnastic exercises.

1919 [see sense 2 e below]. **1930** E. RAYMOND *Jesting Army* I. i. 7 It was the parade for 'Physical Jerks'. *Ibid.* 14 Now the whole family party must go out into the garden to do physical jerks. **1966** A. SACHS *Jail Diary* ii. 24 In the afternoon, I am busy doing physical jerks. *Ibid.* 25 My physical jerks period.

e. Colloq. phr. ***to put a jerk in it***, to act vigorously, smartly, or quickly.

1919 *Athenæum* 25 July 664/2 'Physical jerks' dates from war-time, as does also the admonition 'put a jerk in it', which is the equivalent of the ante-bellum 'jump to it'. **1921** N. KENT *Quest M. Harland* II. viii. 241 'I like to see young people enthusiastic. Put a jerk in it, can't you?' 'A—a *what?*' stammered Anthea, tottering. 'Put a jerk in it,' repeated Roger. **1939** C. DAY LEWIS *Child of Misfortune* III. ii. 271 Put a jerk in it. I'm meeting my boy at the second house at the Royal. **1974** 'J. ROSS' *Burning of Billy Toober* xv. 147 If you put a jerk into it, you'll probably have something for me by lunchtime.

f. The name of a dance characterized by jerking movements.

1966 *N.Y. Times Mag.* 9 Jan. 106/2 There is the Watusi, basically a side-to-side stumble, the Shake, and the Jerk—whose movements come as no surprise to old fans of burlesque. **1969** N. COHN *AWopBopaLooBop* (1970) ix. 85 Dance-crazes bossed pop right up until the Beatles broke... The Jerk and the Block. **1972** T. KOCHMAN *Rappin' & Stylin' Out* 161 Names for dances (Rock and Roll,..Jerk, and Black Power Stomp) all embody kinetic elements.

3. *fig.* A short sharp witty speech; a sally.

1588 SHAKS. *L.L.L.* IV. ii. 129 Smelling out the odoriferous flowers of fancy, the ierkes of inuention. **1606** *Choice, Chance*, etc. (1881) 49 At last, one merry fellowe comes out with his ierke. **1630** J. TAYLOR (Water P.) *J. Garret's Ghost* Ded., Wit and Mirth: Chargeably Collected ..Made vp and fashioned into Clinches, Bulls, Quirkes, Yerkes, Quips and Ierkes. *a* **1652** BROME *Novella* IV. i. Wks. 1873 I. 155 Sir, use your jerks and quillets at the bar. **1889** A. H. BULLEN *Musa Proterva* Pref., Some happy jerk of fancy or playful sally of wit.

†**4.** A short abrupt series of notes (of a bird). *Obs.*

1766 PENNANT *Zool.* (1768) II. 333 They [the call-birds] invite the wild ones by what the bird-catchers call short jerks. **1773** BARRINGTON in *Phil. Trans.* LXIII. 252 The short bursts of singing birds, contending with each other (called *jerks* by the bird-catchers), are equally distinguished from what I term *song*, by their not continuing for four seconds. **1794** PRISC. WAKEFIELD *Mental Improv.* (1801) I. 58 The invitation is given by what is called Jerks, in the language of the birdcatchers.

5. *slang* (orig. *U.S.*). Someone of little or no account; a fool, a stupid person. Cf. JERKWATER b.

1935 A. J. POLLOCK *Underworld Speaks* 63/2 *Jerk*, a boob; chump; a sucker. **1938** *New Republic* 7 Sept. 129/1 A jerk not only bores you but pats you on the shoulder as he does so. **1945** *Daily Express* 11 Sept. 2/4 See this lighter? A dying Jerry gave it to me. I gave the jerk a smoke from my last cigarette. **1950** [see *brown-noser* s.v. BROWN *a.* 7]. **1956** L. MCINTOSH *Oxford Folly* 85 Julian sounds a dismal little jerk when you sum him up like that. **1958** *Listener* 15 May 802/1 If..the sponsors get eight letters saying that their comedian is an idiot, or a foul-mouthed jerk, they're terrified. **1971** J. BALL *First Team* (1972) xxiv. 382 '*I say* you're a nigger!' ..'And I say that you're a goddamned jerk.'

6. *Physics.* Rate of change of acceleration (with respect to time).

1955 J. S. BEGGS *Mechanism* iv. 122 Since the forces to produce accelerations must arise from strains in the materials of the system, the rate of change of acceleration, or jerk, is important. **1964** A. G. FADELL *Calculus* vii. 195 In the automobile industry the concept of a jerk is used as a 'comfort index'. *Ibid.*, Free fall has an ideal comfort index, namely zero of jerk. **1973** *Nature Physical Sci.* 19 Feb. 140/1 Large values of jerk (third derivative of the position of *m*) can occur if *M* is sufficiently large.

jerk, *sb.*² Also 8-9 jirk. [f. JERK *v.*²: see also JERKY.] Jerked meat, charqui.

1799 J. SMITH *Acc. Remark. Occurr.* (1870) 116 We jirked the lean, and fryed the tallow out of the fat meat, which we kept to stew with our jirk as we needed it. **1851** W. DE HASS *Hist. Early Settlements* VII. iii. 389 As soon as daylight appeared, the captain started to where they left some jerk hanging on the evening before.

jerk (dʒɜːk), *v.*¹ Also 6 gierk, 6-7 girk(e, ierck(e, ierke, 7-8 jirk. [See JERK *sb.*¹]

†**1. a.** *trans.* To strike with or as with a whip, switch, or wand; to scourge, whip, lash, switch.

1550 COVERDALE *Spir. Perle* vi. (1588) 48 Than he beateth and gierketh vs a little with a rod. **1563** FOXE *A. & M.* (1583) I. 72/1 Whip him with scourges, iercke him with rods. **1593** G. HARVEY *New Letter* C ij b, I may..chearne him like a dish of butter or girke him like a hobling gig. **1607** WALKINGTON *Opt. Glass* 89 They..are worthy to bee iirkt with..lashes. **1611** COTGR., *Fouetter*, to scourge,..yerke or ierke. **1673** F. KIRKMAN *Unlucky Citizen* 281 He now being naked, [they] Slapt and Jerkt him with all their strength. **1709** *Brit. Apollo* II. No. 52. 3/2 An Ox cheek Old Woman..he firk'd, And.. a Fruiterer Jirk'd.

†**b.** *fig.* To lash with satire or ridicule. *Obs.*

1602 *2nd Pt. Return fr. Parnass.* I. ii. 260 Acute Iohn Davis, I affect thy rymes, That ierck in hidden charmes these looser times. **1613-16** W. BROWNE *Brit. Past.* II. i, My busied pen Shall ierke to death this infamy of men. **1710** E. WARD *Brit. Hud.* x. 114 A Third Man..with much Pleasure Jirks the Church, As if his Words were Rods of Birch.

2. a. To move (anything) by a sharp suddenly arrested motion, like that with which a whip is wielded; to thrust, pull, or shake by such a motion; to give a sudden thrust, push, pull, or twist to. Often with an adv. of direction or its equivalent.

1589 NASHE *Almond for Parrat* 5 b, Would you not laugh to see Cli. the Cobler, and New. the souter, ierking out theyr elbowes in euerie Pulpit? *a* **1661** HOLYDAY *Juvenal* viii, Though some grave friend..jerk his whip for notice [*virgâ prior annuit*]. **1780** *Puritan* in Steevens *Suppl. Shaks.* II. 580 Let him play a little; we'll jerk him up of a sudden. **1849** H. MAYO *Pop. Superst.* (1851) 81 To..jerk and swing the limbs. **1863** A. J. HORWOOD *Yearbks. 30 & 31 Edw. I* Pref. 37 The rope broke not by reason of the holders moving or jerking it, but by reason of its weakness. **1865** LOWELL *Ode Harvard Commem.* iv, We poor puppets, jerked by unseen wires. **1875** W. S. HAYWARD *Love agst. World* 18 He jerked the horse's mouth roughly.

b. To throw or toss with a quick sharp motion, esp. with a sudden twitching or snatching action.

1786 MAD. D'ARBLAY *Diary* 4 Nov., I had the greatest difficulty to save myself from being suddenly jerked into the middle of the room. **1851** D. JERROLD *St. Giles* vi. 59 [He] jerked a bow, and in a few moments was free. **1858** LONGF. *M. Standish* iv. 138 Then from the rattlesnake's skin, with a contemptuous gesture, Jerking the Indian arrows, he filled it with powder and bullets. **1865** CARLYLE *Fredk. Gt.* XXI. ii. (1872) IX. 276 Excellent sound masonries; which have an over-tendency to jerk themselves into pinnacles. **1883** MOMERIE *Personality* Introd. (1886) 15 The primeval chaos of ὁμοιομερῆ was, so to speak, jerked into a number of distinguishable objects, by a movement.

3. *fig.* To utter or throw out (words or sounds) abruptly, or sharply and shortly.

1602 MARSTON *Antonio's Rev.* I. iii. Wks. 1856 I. 83 How your cornet jerketh up His straind shrill accents. **1860** PUSEY *Min. Proph.* 407 He speaks as if the one word, jerked out, as it were, wrung forth from his inmost soul, was Violence. **1883** S. C. HALL *Retrospect* I. 145 His sentences seemed jerked out. **1889** P. H. EMERSON *Eng. Idyls* 46 ''Bout-four-an'-a-half-mile', jerked out Ben, between strong pulls at his pipe.

4. a. *intr.* To give a jerk; to jerk a bow or nod; to move with a jerk.

1606 *Sir G. Goosecappe* II. i. in Bullen *O. Pl.* III. 32 Your dauncers legges bow for-sooth, and Caper, and jerke and Firke, and dandle the bodie aboue them. **1693** G. STEPNEY in *Dryden's Juvenal* viii. (1697) 204 Nor blush, shou'd he some Grave Acquaintance meet, But, (proud of being known) will Jerk and Greet. **1782** MRS. E. BLOWER *G. Bateman* III. 7 He..making but one step..to the street door, jerked out of the house. **1833** HT. MARTINEAU *Berkeley the Banker* I. vii. 136 The door jerked open. **1889** BARRIE *Window in Thrums* xx. 191 Jess's head jerked back involuntarily.

b. *intr.* To move the limbs or features in an involuntary spasmodic manner. Cf. JERKER¹ 1 b.

1874 E. EGGLESTON *Circuit Rider* xiv. (1895) 104 He..was seized with that curious nervous affection which originated in these religious excitements... He jerked violently—his jerking only adding to his excitement, which in turn increased the severity of his contortions.

†**5.** *intr.* To aim satire; to sneer, carp, gird. *Obs.*

a **1643** W. CARTWRIGHT *Ordinary* IV. v, You must be jerking at the times, forsooth. **1649** MILTON *Eikon.* viii. Wks. (1851) 395 By the way he jerkes at some mens reforming to models of Religion. *a* **1704** T. BROWN *Pindar. Petit. Lds. Council* Wks. 1730 I. 62 Prologues so witty, That jirk at the city.

†**6.** *intr.* Of a bird: To utter a short sharp abrupt series of notes. *Obs.*

1766 PENNANT *Zool.* (1768) II. 334 The bird catchers frequently lay considerable wagers whose call-bird can jerk the longest. **1773** BARRINGTON in *Phil. Trans.* LXIII. 263 A very experienced catcher of nightingales hath informed me, that some of these birds have jerked the instant they were caught.

7. *trans.* To serve (soda, beer, etc.) at a soda-fountain, bar, etc. Cf. *soda-jerker*. *U.S. colloq.*

1883 G. W. PECK *Peck's Bad Boy* xiii. 126 Well, I must go down to the sweetened wind factory, and jerk soda! **1884** J. MILLER *Memorie & Rime* 20 They stared at me, but went on jerking beer behind the counter. **1935** *Amer. Mercury* May 102/1 They had spent their tender years jerking sodas. **1949** WODEHOUSE *Uncle Dynamite* iv. 54, I also jerked soda.

8. ***to jerk off*** (trans. and intr.), to masturbate. *slang.*

1937 in PARTRIDGE *Dict. Slang.* **1947** A. BERNSTEIN *Home is the Hunted* 152 Big enough for a bush and jerking off like crazy, disconcerted and embarrassed by the riches of manhood flooding through your bones, veins, and gizzard. **1969** P. ROTH *Portnoy's Complaint* 177 She will jerk off one guy, but only with his pants on. **1971** B. MALAMUD *Tenants* 202 The mother..dies unattended, of malnutrition, as Herbert jerks off in the hall toilet.

Hence **jerked** (dʒɜːkt) *ppl. a.*

1867 A. J. ELLIS *E.E. Pron.* I. 5 Jerked utterance. *Ibid.*, Jerked whisper.

jerk (dʒɜːk), *v.*² Also 8 jirk. [Corrupted from American Sp. *charque-ar* in same sense, f. *charque*, *charqui*, ad. Quichua (Peruvian) *ccharqui* 'dried flesh, unsalted, in long strips'. The verb in Quichua was *ccharquini* 'to prepare dried meat, to jerk', whence perh. the early cognate JERKIN *sb.*³ The word is now used in all parts of Spanish America, and was app. found by English navigators in Spanish use in the W. Indies. (See Skeat, *Trans. Philol. Soc.* 1885, 94.)]

trans. To cure (meat, esp. beef) by cutting it into long thin slices and drying it in the sun.

1707 SLOANE *Jamaica* I. p. xvi, They [the wild hogs] are shot,..cut open, the bones taken out, and the flesh gash'd on the inside into the skin, filled with salt, and exposed to the sun, which is called Jirking. **1748** *Anson's Voy.* III. ii. 305 He..was sent here with twenty-two Indians to jerk beef. **1760-72** tr. *Juan & Ulloa's Voy.* (ed. 3) II. 329 Killing cattle; more for the sake of their hides, and tallow, than their flesh; of which, nevertheless, they jerk great quantities for the use of such ships as sail from Pernambuco. **1807** P. GASS *Jrnl.* 19 At 12 we stopped to jirk our meat, and again proceeded at two. **1859** R. F. BURTON *Centr. Afr.* in *Jrnl. Geog. Soc.* XXIX. 202 When a bullock is killed they either jerk the meat, or dry it upon a dwarf platform of sticks raised above a slow and smoky fire. **1863** *Lit. Times* 4 July (*Tracks across Australia*), Two of the horses were slaughtered for food—one jerked, the other boiled down.

Hence **jerked** (dʒɜːkt) *ppl. a.*, **'jerking** *vbl. sb.*

1712 W. ROGERS *Voy. round World* 199 They export.. Rice, Cotton, and some dry'd Jerkt Beef. **1726** SHELVOCKE *Voy. round World* 116. **1812** J. J. HENRY *Camp. agst. Quebec* 47 Preserve our provisions by jerking. **1851** MAYNE REID *Scalp Hunters* xxvii. 201 Yonder goes the jerking-line! **1865** *Leeds Merc.* 22 Feb., Experiments are being made in Aldershott camp with the South American 'jerked beef' with a view to its introduction in the army.

jerk, *v.*³: see JERQUE *v.*

jerker¹ ('dʒɜːkə(r)). [f. JERK *v.*¹ + -ER¹.]

1. One who jerks: in senses of the verb.

1596 NASHE *Saffron Walden* 133 Yea Madam Gabriela, are you such an old ierker. **1598** FLORIO, *Frustatore*, a whipper, a scourger, a ierker. **1651** TRIPLETT *On Dr. Gill* (in D'Urfey *Pills* (1719) IV. 263), Take heed..Lest you taste of his Lash, For I have found him a Jirker.

b. *spec.* One who makes involuntary spasmodic movements of the limbs or features, caused by religious excitement. Cf. JERK *sb.*¹ 2 b (*b*).

1851 S. JUDD *Margaret* viii. (1871) 41 The jumpers of Wales were outdone by the jerkers of Kentucky. **1889** *Pop. Sci. Monthly* June 148 Examples of this in America are seen in the 'Jumpers', 'Jerkers', and various revival extravagances.

2. *U.S.* A fish, the river-chub, *Hybopsis kentuckiensis*, also called *hornyhead*.

1890 in *Cent. Dict.*

jerker², variant of JERQUER.

jerkily ('dʒɜːkılı), *adv.* [f. JERKY *a.* + -LY².] In a jerky manner; by fits and starts.

1874 BURNAND *My time* i. 6 His head would drop forward, jerkily. **1885** E. M. THOMPSON in *Librar. Mag.* July 4 Their nest progressed very slowly and jerkily.

jerkin¹ ('dʒɜːkın). Also 6 ierkynge, -yn, 6-7 -en, 7 jerking. [Recorded soon after 1500: origin unknown.

(It has been conjecturally associated with Du. and Western LG *jurk*, 'girl's or child's frock'; but, besides the facts that Eng. *j* does not correspond to Du. *j* (= *y*), and that a jerkin is not a frock, *jurk* is merely a mod. Du. word, unknown to Kilian, Hexham, and other 17th c. lexicographers, and is itself of unknown origin.)]

a. A garment for the upper part of the body, worn by men in the sixteenth and seventeenth centuries; a close-fitting jacket, jersey, or short coat, often made of leather. Since *c* 1700 used in literature mainly historically, or in reference to foreign countries; and some dialects for a waistcoat, an under vest, or a loose jacket. Whence in modern use, usu. a sleeveless jacket or waistcoat (see quots.).

1519 *Presentm. Juries* in *Surtees Misc.* (1888) 33 For stellyng a jerkynge. **1532-3** *Act 24 Hen. VIII*, c. 13 No man, vnder the saide degrees..weare..any silke, other than.. veluet in their sleueles cotes, iakettes, ierkyns, coifes, cappes. **1556** W. TOWRSON in Hakluyt *Voy.* (1589) 101 [They] haue their skinne of their bodies raced with diuers workes in maner of a leather Ierkin. **1576** GASCOIGNE *Steele Gl.* Epil. (Arb.) 83 What are they? women? masking in mens weedes? With dutchkin dublits, and with Ierkins iaggde. **1599** THYNNE *Animadv.* (1875) 31 A common garmente daylye vsed suche as we call a Ierken or Iackett without sleues. **1606** SHAKS. *Tr. & Cr.* III. iii. 266 A plague of opinion, one may weare it on both sides, like a leather Ierkin. **1616** SIR R. BOYLE in *Lismore Papers* (1886) I. 135 Iohn nagle sent me ffrize for a Ierkin and breeches for my own wearing. **1726** SWIFT *Gulliver* I. i, By good luck, I had on me a buff jerkin, which they could not pierce. **1808** SCOTT *Marm.* I. viii, Last, twenty yeomen two and two, In hosen black, and jerkins blue. **1820** W. IRVING *Sketch Bk.* (1859) 25 His dress was of the antique Dutch fashion—a cloth jerkin, strapped round the waist—several pair of breeches, the outer one..decorated with rows of buttons down the sides, and bunches at the knees. **1828** *Craven Dial.*, *Jerkin*, a waistcoat. **1843** BORROW *Bible in Spain* xxv. 147 A shabby-looking fellow, dressed in a jerkin and wearing a high-crowned hat, attended as domestic. **1868** FREEMAN *Norm. Conq.* II. ix. 389 With nothing but his javelin and his leathern jerkin. **1935** E. WEEKLEY *Something about Words* 44 Until the War one vaguely associates *jerkin* with the costume of Robin Hood, but after the War 'army jerkins' were to be had cheap. **1957** M. B. PICKEN *Fashion Dict.* 187/2 *Jerkin*, jacket, short coat, or doublet, sometimes of leather. Occasionally, waistcoat without sleeves. Also straight woolen pull-over. **1963** *Austral. T.V. Times* 18 Apr. 10/1 *Jerkin*, a sort of zipper jacket. **1974** *Guardian* 4 Apr. 11/2 It is legal to shoot clouts, which used to be the jerkins of longbowmen hung on a stick.

b. *Comb.*, as ***jerkin-maker***.

c **1565** J. SPARKE in Hakluyt *Voy.* III. 504 They..doe iagge their flesh..as workemanlike as a Ierkinmaker with vs pinketh a ierkin. **1589** *Nottingham Rec.* IV. 58 Thomas Rogers, de Nottingham, iyrkynmaker.

Hence **'jerkined** (-ınd) *a.* [-ED²], wearing a jerkin.

1852 MISS YONGE *Cameos* (1877) III. xii. 98 Five hundred red jerkined men.

†**'jerkin**². Also 6 gircken, 7 girking. [deriv. (? dim.) of *jer-* in *jerfalcon*, GYRFALCON.] The male of the gerfalcon.

1539 *Act 31 Hen. VIII*, c. 12 Any faucon, gerfaucon, Ierkin, sacre or sacret. *a* **1605** MONTGOMERIE *Poems* xviii. 25 Thair wes a gentle girking gay. **1616** SURFL. & MARKH. *Country Farme* 713 The male to the Gerfaulcon is that which is called the Ierkin, being a much lesse bird.

†**'jerkin**³, *sb.* or *a. Obs.* In *jerkin beef* = jerked beef: see JERK *v.*²

1612 CAPT. SMITH *Map Virginia* 17 As drie as their ierkin beefe in the West Indies. **1657** R. LIGON *Barbadoes* (1673) 39 Jerkin Beef, which is hufled, and slasht through, hung up and dryed in the Sun.

jerkiness ('dʒɜːkɪnɪs). [f. JERKY *a.* + -NESS.] The quality of being jerky.

1856 BRIMLEY *Ess.*, *Proctor* 243 To the same feature.. we are inclined to attribute the jerkiness of the verse. **1866** G. MACDONALD *Ann. Q. Neighb.* vi. (1878) 83 Impulse was always predominant, giving a certain jerkiness, like the hopping of a bird.

†**jerki'net.** *Sc. Obs.* In 7-8 girkienet, 8 jerke-, jirkinet. [f. JERKIN¹ + -ET¹.] A sort of jacket or blouse worn by women of the humbler classes.

c **1689** *Depred. Clan Campbell* (1816) 32 Item.. 2 shirts, 3 girkienets, 2 playds. **1725** *Willie Winkie's Test.* in Whitelaw *Bk. Sc. Song* (1875) 540/1 A jerkenet, scarce worth a louse. *a* **1794** *Old Chorus* in *Burns' 'My Lady's Gown'*, Jenny's jimps and jirkinet.

jerking ('dʒɜːkɪŋ), *vbl. sb.* [f. JERK *v.*¹ + -ING¹.]

a. The action of JERK *v.*¹, q.v.

1552 *Harl. MS.* 353 lf. 121 She sayd.. that the kinge shewed himself an unnaturall nephew, and withall did wishe that she had had the ierkinge of him. **1641** WILKINS *Math. Magick* II. iv. (1648) 78 The jerking of a Switch like the letter Q. **1820** SCOTT *Abbot* xix, My lady's favour stood between your skin and many a jerking. **1851** *Illustr. Catal. Gt. Exhib.* 248 The breaks are successively brought into action.. so as to avoid the danger of sudden jerking. **1875** H. C. WOOD *Therap.* (1879) 519 Children with.. nervous symptoms, such as starting, jerkings, etc.

b. The action of JERK *v.*¹ 8. Also with *off*.

1889 BARRÈRE & LELAND *Dict. Slang* I. 497/2 *Jerking*, masturbation. **1960** E. L. WALLANT *Human Season* ix. 94 Another thing bothers me is your jerking off in bed at night. **1969** F. NORMAN *Banana Boy* 108 'Ninety-nine change hands,' he would laugh when he came into the kitchen after a hard night's jerking-off. **1972** *Screw* 12 June 12/1 Such sexual behavior as homosexuality, jerking off, [etc.].

jerking ('dʒɜːkɪŋ), *ppl. a.* [f. as prec. + -ING².] That jerks: in various senses of JERK *v.*¹

1602 *2nd Pt. Return fr. Parnass.* I. i. 92, I, Iuuenall: thy ierking hand is good, Not gently laying on, but fetching bloud. **1672** MARVELL *Reh. Transp.* I. Wks. 1776 II. 62 Triplet.. in his turn avenged himself of his jerking pedagogue. **1830** MARRYAT *King's Own* xxxii, The violent jerking motion of the vessel. **1854** HOOKER *Himal. Jrnls.* I. xvii. 376 Three sharp jerking shocks of earthquake.

Hence **'jerkingly** *adv.*, in a jerking manner.

1880 J. E. BURTON *Handbk. Midwives* §42. 29 The limbs begin to move jerkingly.

jerkin-head. *Arch.* [Of uncertain origin: perh. for *jerking-*, from JERK *v.* (as if the slope were jerkily interrupted). Cf. KIRKIN-HEAD, the earlier existence of which suggests that *jerkin-head* originated in some error.] (See quots.)

1842-76 GWILT *Archit.* (ed. 7) Gloss., *Jerkin Head*, the end of a roof not hipped down to the level of the opposite adjoining walls, the gable being carried higher than the level of those walls. *Ibid.*, *Shread Head*, the same as Jerkin Head. **1868** *Chambers' Encycl.* V. 697 *Jerkin-head*, a form of roofing which is half-gable, half-hip. The gable generally goes as high as the ties of the couples, above which the roof is hipped off.

jerkish ('dʒɜːkɪʃ), *a. rare.* [f. JERK *sb.*¹ + -ISH.] Characterized by jerks; jerky.

1885 *Manch. Exam.* 18 Mar. 5/6 'No', said Lord Edmond, in his jerkish manner, 'the Government have no information'.

jerk-line ('dʒɜːklaɪn). *N. Amer.* [f. JERK *v.*¹ 2.] A rope used in place of reins to guide a team of horses, etc. Also *attrib.*

1888 M. GRIGSBY *Smoked Yank* xix. 156 The driver rode on the nigh wheel mule, and drove the leader with a jerk-line. **1907** S. E. WHITE *Arizona Nights* III. iv. 287, I bet that Sang would get a wiggle on him.., if he had a woman ahold of his jerk line. **1910** J. HART *Vigilante Girl* x. 140 This train of animals was driven by a 'jerk line' instead of reins. **1937** J. STEINBECK *Of Mice & Men* ii. 61 He was a jerkline skinner.. capable of driving ten, sixteen, even twenty mules with a single line to the leaders. **1960** A. DOWNS *Wagon Road North* 43 Sometimes there were so many horses or mules hitched to a freight wagon that the use of reins was impractical. Under these circumstances a 'jerk-line' was used. This was a single line connected to the bridles of the lead horses.

jerk-off ('dʒɜːkɒf), *a.* [f. vbl. phr. *to jerk off* (JERK *v.*¹ 8).] Erotic; encouraging masturbation.

c **1957** in N. Mailer *Advts. for Myself* (1961) 310 They turn their backs.. on.. the grandeurs of the past, restrict their horizon to.. tripe.. jazz magazines and jerk-off magazines. **1965** *New Society* 30 Dec. 21/1 It would prove Screeches was not a 'jerk-off' press but was serious.

jerk-off ('dʒɜːkɒf), *sb.* [Perh. f. prec. but cf. JERK *sb.*¹ 5.] = JERK *sb.*¹ 5.

1968-70 *Current Slang* (Univ. S. Dakota) III-IV. 75 *Jerk off*,.. a rustic; a simpleton. **1972** J. MILLS *Report to Commissioner* 145 I'm sitting there alone.. feeling like the biggest jerk-off in the history of the world. **1972** R. A. WILSON *Playboy's Bk. Forbidden Words* 172 A jerk or jerk-off is a fool. **1973** W. SHEED *People will always be Kind* I. xiv. 182 You know perfectly well that the jerk-offs do all the talking at meetings.

jerksome ('dʒɜːksəm), *a. rare.* [f. as JERKISH *a.* + -SOME.] = JERKY *a.*

1880 BLACKMORE *Mary Anerley* lvii. (1881) 435 With females jolting up and down, upon no springs except those of jerksome curiosity.

jerkwater ('dʒɜːkˌwɔːtə(r)). *U.S.* [f. JERK *v.*¹] In full, ***jerkwater train.*** A train on a branch railway (see quot. 1945). Also *attrib.*

1878 F. H. HART *Sazerac Lying Club* 16, I wish I may be run over by a two-horse jerk-water if there was a sage-hen in sight. **1905** *Dialect Notes* III. 84 The St. Paul branch is a jerkwater railroad. *Ibid.*, *Jerkwater* (*train*), train on a branch railway. 'Has the jerkwater come in yet?' **1909** *Sat. Even. Post* 15 May 9/3 The farther along Thorpe got in the list the more disgusted he became with the prospect of living on jerk-water trains. **1920** *Bulletin* 22 June 10/1 This Oriental who, with perfect self-possession.. descended from the jerk-water train carrying a modern suitcase. **1926** J. BLACK *You can't Win* xx. 303, I followed the pay-roll aboard the jerkwater train that carried it to the waiting miners. **1941** *Sun* (Baltimore) 7 Mar. 12/7 In the early days of railroads the small boilers of the locomotives required frequent refilling, and water tanks were very few. Every train crew carried a leather bucket on a long rope with which they 'jerked water' from the streams along their track. As locomotives increased in size the small 'jerk-water' engines were relegated to branch-line service. Today no train crew carries a bucket, but the name 'jerk water' still sticks and has become part of our national heritage of American slang. **1945** J. L. MARSHALL *Santa Fe, Railroad that built an Empire* 68 The Santa Fe was the Jerkwater Line—because train crews, when the water got low, often had to stop by a creek, form a bucket brigade and jerk water from the stream to fill the tender tank.

b. Used *attrib.* or as *adj.* in sense 'small, insignificant, inferior'. *colloq.*

1897 *Chicago Tribune* 25 July 15/2 John J. Ingalls regards the Swiss Mission as a jerkwater job, and would not take it if it were offered to him. **1911** H. S. HARRISON *Queed* xviii. 225 The spring found West stronger and more contented with his lot as president of a jerkwater college. **1923** J. DOS PASSOS *Streets of Night* 130 Perkinville, a little jerkwater town back in South Dakota. **1936** *Jrnl. Genetic Psychol.* XLIX. 492 It was one of those jerkwater towns that have one lawyer, one drug store and no traffic cops. **1950** BLESH & JANIS *They all played Ragtime* (1958) 3 Vaudeville teams —from the jerkwater acts to specialists like Ben Harney. **1970** R. LOCKRIDGE *Twice Retired* (1971) v. 68 It won't be easy for him to get another job if he's fired... Maybe at some jerkwater college at half what he's getting now.

jerky ('dʒɜːkɪ), *a.* and *sb.*¹ [f. as JERKSOME *a.* + -Y.]

A. *adj.* Characterized by jerks or sudden abrupt or twitching movements; often *fig.*, spasmodic.

1858 O. W. HOLMES *Aut. Breakf.-t.* i. (1891) 6 They are the talkers that have what may be called jerky minds. **1875** W. HOUGHTON *Sk. Brit. Insects* 101 They move rapidly through the water by jerky motions. **1887** *Spectator* 26 Mar. 422/1 A style which is so jerky that it may be described as dislocated.

B. *sb.* A springless wagon; a shaky jolting vehicle. *U.S.*

1884 W. SHEPHERD *Prairie Exper.* 108 The liveliest travelling was by jerky, the ordinary American farm-waggon without springs. **1894** *Outing* (U.S.) 398/1 Now a wabbling, jumping 'jerky' does the stage work for the line.

'jerky, *sb.*² *U.S.* [ad. American Sp. *charqui*, *charque* (Pg. *xarque*), from native Peruvian *ccharqui*: see CHARQUI and JERK *v.*²] Jerked beef.

1890 in *Cent. Dict.* **1893** E. COUES *Lewis & Clark* I. 31 The word as a verb is now generally spelled *jerk*, and jerked meat is known as *jerky*.

‖**jerm** (dʒɜːm). Also 7 germo, 7-8 germe, 9 djerm. [Arabic *jarm*; in It. *germa*, F. *djerme*.] A small one- or two-masted vessel with large lateen sails used on the Egyptian coast; formerly applied to larger trading vessels in the Levant.

1632 LITHGOW *Trav.* III. 118 In Salonica I found a Germo, bound for Tenedos, in which I imbarked. **1660** F. BROOKE tr. *Le Blanc's Trav.* 281 At Roussetta we.. imbarked by night in a Germe, and the next day were in Alexandria. **1799** *Naval Chron.* II. 325 His Lordship set out from Alexandria in a *germe*, or open boat. **1800** *Ibid.* XXIV. 222 Spoke a Jerm from El-Aarish. **1819** T. HOPE *Anastasius* (1820) I. xv. 292 On board one of the country djerms.

jerm-, obs. spelling of GERM- in various words.

†**'jernie**, *int. Obs.* [a. F. *jerni*, *jarni*, shortened form of *jarnidieu*, corruption of *je renie Dieu* I renounce God.] Used as a profane oath. Hence †**jernie** *v. intr.*, to utter this oath.

1678 OTWAY *Friendship in F.* v. i, Jernie what a Bush of Bryars and Thorns is here? *a* **1680** BUTLER *Rem.* (1759) I. 84 Although he Iernie and blaspheme, When they miscarry, Heav'n and them.

jeroboam (dʒɛrəʊ'bəʊæm). [So called in allusion to *Jeroboam*, 'a mighty man of valour' (1 Kings xi. 28), 'who made Israel to sin' (xiv. 16).] A large bowl or goblet; a very large wine-bottle.

1816 SCOTT *Bl. Dwarf* xiii, Or make a brandy jeroboam in a frosty morning. *a* **1825** FORBY *Voc. E. Anglia*, *Jeroboam*, a capacious bowl or goblet; otherwise, and more generally, called a *Joram*. **1889** *Daily News* 27 July 5/5 Enormous bottles of fabulous content called 'Jeroboams', which some say contain 10, others 12 ordinary bottles.

Je'ronymite, variant of HIERONYMITE.

1777 W. DALRYMPLE *Trav. Sp. & Port.* lv, The convent.. is inhabited by the Jeronymites. **1893** FOREMAN *Trip to Spain* 28 A convent built for the Jeronymite monks of Belem.

jeropiga, -pigia, var. GEROPIGA, HIERA PICRA.

1852 *Min. Evid. Import Duties on Wines, Sel. Committee Ho. Comm.* 16 Jeropiga, of first-rate quality, is composed of two-thirds must or grape juice and one-third spirit.

jerownde, obs. form of GYRONNY *a. Her.*

jerque (dʒɜːk), *v.* Also 9 jirk. [Origin obscure: it has been conjecturally referred to It. *cercare* to search, which suits the form and sense; but historical evidence is wanting.

The agent noun JERQUER, *jerker*, is evidenced back to 1706, and ought to be formed from the vb.; but the latter is not known so early, nor does it appear how either word was connected with Italy.]

trans. **a.** To search (a vessel) for unentered goods: see next. **b.** *now*, To examine or search a ship's papers in order to ascertain whether the captain's and the customs officer's lists of cargo agree, and to see that all the cargo has been duly 'entered' and described.

1819 *Smugglers* I. 125 McGroul and McBain engaged to meet him.. as soon as the Hazard was fairly in the harbour, and assist in *jirking* the vessel. **1843-63** WATERSTON *Cycl. Commerce*, *Jerquing*, the search of a ship performed by a custom-house officer (called a jerquer), to ascertain if there are any unentered goods concealed. **1867** SMYTH *Sailor's Word-bk.*, *Jerquing a vessel*, a search performed by the jerquer of the customs, after a vessel is unloaded, to see that no unentered goods have been concealed.

jerquer ('dʒɜːkə(r)). Also 8 (*erron.*) jerguer, 9 jerker. [See prec. vb.] 'A custom-house officer, a searcher' (Simmonds, 1858); in the London Custom House, A clerical officer who examines and checks a ship's papers, to see that all the cargo has been duly entered and described.

1706 PHILLIPS, *Jerguer*, an Officer at the Custom-House, who oversees the Actions and Accounts of the Waiters. **1707** J. CHAMBERLAYNE *St. Gt. Brit.* III. 498 Four Examiners of the Out-Port Books 200*l.* Three Jerquers at 100*l.* each, 300*l.* **1812** J. SMYTH *Pract. of Customs* (1821) 7 The Warrants, Books, &c. are to be delivered to the Jerquer (or Surveyor, in those Ports where there is not a Jerquer), within one month after the clearing of the Ship by the Tide-surveyor. **1862** SALA *Ship-Chandler* (L.), I've heard tell that she's three parts slaver and one part pirate; and I wonder the custom-house jerkers don't seize her whenever that gibbet-face Stoneyard has the impudence to put into Longport.

jerreed, jerrid, variants of JERID, JEREED.

jerrican, jerrycan ('dʒɛrɪkæn). Also jerry can, jerry-can. [f. JERRY *sb.*² + CAN *sb.*¹] A five-gallon (usu. metal) container for petrol, water, etc., of a type first used in Germany and later adopted by the Allied forces in the war of 1939-45.

1943 *Hutchinson's Pict. Hist. War* 17 Feb.-11 May 258 Mules carrying 'jerricans' to British troops... Jerricans are a special type of petrol container for transporting water. **1944** [see JERRY *sb.*²]. **1944** *Times* 25 Nov. 8/3 The Germans had a very efficient five-gallon petrol can. The Eighth Army captured some of the cans. They were sent back to England, and the British started manufacturing them. They were called jerricans. **1955** M. E. B. BANKS *Commando Climber* v. 87 We counted our burden of spuds a privilege in comparison to the jerrycan of red wine which was foisted on to one unfortunate. **1958** *Punch* 9 July 60/2 It [*sc.* sea-water] is collected *each week*.. and rushed to Paris in white plastic jerricans. **1969** *New Yorker* 4 Oct. 55/1 Foreigners flying into Biafra now bring their own food and, if the pilot permits it, their own gasoline in jerry cans. **1972** D. HASTON *In High Places* x. 109 Water is the only problem: you have to bring big jerry-cans in from Cassis.

jerry ('dʒɛrɪ), *sb.*¹ [Familiar variant of the proper name *Jeremy* or *Jeremiah* (in Ireland treated as equivalent to *Diarmaid*). Variously applied; mostly in slang or vulgar speech.]

1. A machine for shearing cloth.

1883 *Almondbury & Huddersfield Gloss.*, *Jerry*, the common name of a machine for finishing cloth, by which all the rough portions are removed. **1885** *Taylor's Patent* No. 2784 (*title*) Jerrys or machines for shearing fabrics.

2. *Printers' slang.* The noise made by beating chases, etc., on an apprentice finishing his time, or on other occasions.

1888 JACOBI *Printers' Vocab.* 68. **1894** D. C. MURRAY in *My First Bk.* 196 The compositors performed what they called a 'jerry' in the blunderer's honour.

3. Short for ***jerry-shop*** (a contraction, it is said, of *Tom-and-Jerry-shop*, from the cant name of a mixture of liquors): A low beer-house.

1851-61 MAYHEW *Lond. Labour* II. 255 (Farmer) An advance of 5/. made to him by the keeper of a beer-shop, or, as he called it, a jerry. **1873** *Slang Dict.*, *Jerry shop*, a beer-house. Contraction of 'Tom and Jerry'. **18..** CARLYLE in Froude *Life* (Cent.), A worse than jerry-shop over the way raged like Bedlam or Erebus.

4. Short for ***jerry hat***: A round felt hat.

1841 *Punch* I. 98 Those unassuming castors designated 'Jerrys'. **1851** *Illustr. Catal. Gt. Exhib.* 275 Showing the manufacture of felt caps or jerries.. Finished felt cap or

jerry. **1865** *Sat. Rev.* 4 Feb. 146/1 Large light whiskers, a jerry hat, and green cutaway coat.

5. Short for JERRY-BUILDER.

1890 in *Cent. Dict.*

6. *Comb.* **jerry-come-tumble, jerry-go-nimble,** a tumbler, an antic, a performer (equestrian or other); also *transf.*; **jerrycummumble, jerry-mumble** *vbs. trans.*, to shake or tumble about; **jerry-sneak,** a mean sneaking fellow, a hen-pecked husband. See also JERRY-BUILDER, etc.

1823 SCOTT *Quentin D.* xiv, I [a hangman] never quarrel with my customers—my *jerry-come-tumbles, my merry dancers. **1785** GROSE *Dict. Vulg. Tongue*, **Jerrycummumble*, to shake, towzle, or tumble about. **1876** T. HARDY *Far fr. Madding Crowd* viii, They took me..into a large *jerry-go-nimble show, where there were women-folk riding round. **1721** CIBBER *Rival Fool* III, I'gad I'll fetch one then, shall *jerrymumble you. **1764** FOOTE *Mayor of G.* (Dram. Pers.), *Jerry Sneak, a henpecked husband. **1824** MISS MITFORD *Village* Ser. I. (1863) 223 A little insignificant, perking, sharp-featured man, with a Jerry-Sneak expression in his pale whey-face. **1844** W. H. MAXWELL *Sports & Adv. Scotl.* xxviii. (1855) 226 A..landlady..was mated to a Jerry Sneak.

Jerry ('dʒɛrɪ), *sb.*[2] *colloq.* (orig. *Mil. slang*). [Prob. alteration of GERMAN *a.*[2] and *sb.*[2], perh. infl. by JERRY *sb.*[1]] A German; *spec.* a German soldier; a German aircraft; also, the Germans or German soldiers collectively. Also *attrib.* or as *adj.* Cf. FRITZ[1].

1919 J. B. MORTON *Barber of Putney* ii, There was three Jerries waiting for 'im to get tired and chuck it. **1925** FRASER & GIBBONS *Soldier & Sailor Words* 131 *Jerry over*, 'Lights out!' The word passed along the lines at the Front at night on the nearing overhead of an enemy aeroplane. *Ibid.*, *Jerry up*, a warning call on the approach of a German aeroplane. **1929** E. W. SPRINGS *Above Bright Blue Sky* 272 If you have many chaps like him, it won't take long to chase Jerry back to the Rhine. **1931** W. V. TILSLEY *Other Ranks* 8 The way they referred to the Germans—almost affectionately. Old Fritz, or Old Jerry! Might be an ally! **1941** *Southern Daily Echo* (Southampton) 26 Mar., Last time the enemy was generally called the *Hun* by the people at home, and *Jerry* by the soldiers. The latter is the term which remains in use in the present war. **1942** *Tee Emm* (Air Ministry) II. 58 Net result: all square—instead of one Jerry down. **1943** [see BAG *sb.* 18 (*c*)]. **1944** G. NETHERWOOD *Desert Squadron* xii. 118 The well known Jerry boat, the canvas and leather affair, was soon put into active service by our men and also the petrol container known as the 'Jerrycan'. **1955** J. THOMAS *No Banners* xx. 198, I thought you were a Jerry, trailing me. **1961** W. VAUGHAN-THOMAS *Anzio* viii. 185 They almost felt a sympathy for the Jerries under that merciless rain of explosions. **1972** *Daily Mail* 4 May 3/3 Give us a Jerry paper, love... There's a German bloke on top wants one.

jerry ('dʒɛrɪ), *sb.*[3] *slang.* [Prob. abbrev. of JEROBOAM.] A chamber-pot.

[**1827** W. MAGINN *Whitehall* II. iv. 140 The naval officer ..came into the Clarendon for a Jerry [= jeroboam]of punch. **1850** *Sessions Papers Cent. Criminal Court* (Surrey cases) May 124, I went into the *jerry* [= water-closet], but they had got there before me.] **1859** HOTTEN *Dict. Slang* 53 *Jerry*, a chamber utensil. **1932** J. CARY *Aissa Saved* xvii. 96 A thin handsome young man carrying a tin jerry in his hand and a broken kettle among the tatters on his back. **1939** 'G. ORWELL' *Coming Up for Air* IV. vi. 271 A bed not yet made and a jerry under the bed. **1968** *Canad. Antiques Collector* Dec. 10/1 Young English ladies and gentlemen were beginning to find it offensive to have the old man keep a jerry in the sideboard.

jerry ('dʒɛrɪ), *sb.*[4] *Austral.* and *N.Z. slang.* [Cf. JERRY *a.*[2] and *v.*] Phr. ***to take a jerry (to)***: to investigate and understand (something), to 'tumble' *to* (something).

1919 W. H. DOWNING *Digger Dial.* 30 *Take a jerry*, change (for the better) one's course of conduct. **1937** PARTRIDGE *Dict. Slang* 437/1 *Jerry*,..a recognition, discovery, 'tumble'. **1969** *Landfall* XXIII. 328 It was time this country—ah! Took a jerry to itself. Ha ha.

'jerry, *a.*[1] [prob. short for JERRY-BUILT.] Constructed unsubstantially of bad materials.

1882 *Lanc. Gloss.*, *Jerry*, bad, defective, and deceptive;.. a jerry building is one that is badly built, although it may look well outwardly. **1892** LD. EGERTON in *Times* 31 Aug. 9/4 A jerry canal would never have commanded the confidence of the public. **1899** *Westm. Gaz.* 6 Apr. 4/3 No matter how jerry the main structure of a house may be, if it is nicely decorated and finished inside..they [the public] will rent or buy it readily.

So **'jerryism,** jerry-building.

1885 *Peterhead Sentinel* 24 June, The cheap jerryism of the building yards. **1885** *Aberdeen Jrnl.* 30 Dec., The Penedo..broke in two and foundered in a couple of minutes. This..is a very violent illustration of jerryism.

jerry ('dʒɛrɪ), *a.*[2] *U.S. slang.* [Origin unknown.] Phr. ***to be*** (or ***get***) ***jerry (on, on to, to)***: to be aware (of); to be 'wise' (to); to understand.

1908 K. MCGAFFEY *Sorrows of Show Girl* 200 She accepted the attentions of the comedian which his wife was not supposed to be jerry to. **1921** *Adventure* (U.S.) 18 May 25/1 I've got a strong hunch that thousand bucks is all stowed away, neat as pie, in the pendulum box o' that clock. I'm wise, Kid; I'm jerry. **1926** *Flynn's* 16 Jan. 639/1, I know that th' fly was jerry because he gave me th' once over as I was comin' out. **1942** BERRY & VAN DEN BARK *Amer. Thes. Slang* § 149/7 Know; be aware of, *be hep,—jerry,—on,—onto,—wise to.* *Ibid.* § 149/12 Knowing; cognizant; aware of, ..*jerry.*

jerry ('dʒɛrɪ), *v.* *slang* (chiefly *Austral.* and *N.Z.*). [Cf. JERRY *sb.*[4]] *intr.* To understand, realize; to 'tumble' *to* something.

1917 *Digger* 4/3 The excuse was so full of Mer(r)it that the officer failed to 'Jerry' to it. **1918** *Chrons. N.Z.E.F.* 21 June 221/1 Unless the sergeant jerries to your lurk. **1925** FRASER & GIBBONS *Soldier & Sailor Words* 131 *Jerry, to*, to understand, *e.g.*, 'Do you Jerry it, man?' **1959** G. SLATTER *Gun in my Hand* viii. 91 Tried to cut me out with me sheila. Hadn't jerried to it before.

'jerry-'builder. [Origin not ascertained.

That *jerry-builder* and *jerry-built* originated in some way from the name *Jerry* is probable; but the statement made in a letter to the newspapers in Jan. 1884, that they commemorate the name of a building firm on the Mersey, has on investigation not been confirmed. The earliest example yet found is that of *jerry-built* 1869.]

A speculating builder who 'runs up' unsubstantially built houses of inferior materials.

1881 YOUNG *Every Man his own Mechanic* 536 It is unfortunately too often the habit of builders—or rather jerry builders—to use the worst possible description of bricks. **1886** BESANT *Childr. Gibeon* II. xvii, The jerry-builder walks there alone and wonders how long his houses are likely to stand. **1890** *Guardian* 15 Oct. 1605/1 Even Norman Cathedrals reveal the 'jerry builder'.

So **'jerry-build** *v. trans.*, to build unsubstantially and of bad materials; **jerry-'building,** the speculative building of houses, etc. of bad materials and unsubstantial workmanship.

1885 J. E. C. MUNRO *Legal Posit. Landlords & Tenants* 164 To put an end to the jerry building. **1890** SIR N. BARNABY in *Daily News* 15 Nov. 6/2 As to jerry-building of the ships... He would say that anything in the nature of jerry-building was absolutely impossible at any dockyard in the United Kingdom. **1893** G. ALLEN in *Westm. Gaz.* 19 Dec. 2/1 It takes half a year to jerry-build a dingy street.

'jerry-'built, *a.* [See prec.]

Built unsubstantially of bad materials; built to sell but not to last. Also *fig.*

1869 *Lonsdale Gloss.*, *Jerry-built*, slightly, or unsubstantially built. **1875** RUSKIN *Fors Clav.* V. 263 Rows of jerry-built cottages are creeping up. **1900** G. C. BRODRICK *Mem. & Impr.* 316 It would soon be overspread by vulgar jerry-built villas. **1901** *Daily Chron.* 13 Aug. 3/2 In an age of jerry-built books it is refreshing to come across a volume that has taken forty years to compile. **1903** *Ibid.* 20 Feb. 3/2 Fiction, he said, was now jerry-built. **1933** J. BAILLIE *And Life Everlasting* (1934) i. 15 That great cataclysm undoubtedly came as a rude shock to many jerry-built philosophies of life.

jerrycan: see JERRICAN.

jerrymander, erron. form of GERRYMANDER.

jersey[1] ('dʒɜːzɪ). Also 6 iarzie, ierdseie, iarnsey, 7–9 jars(e)y, and with capital initial. The name of the largest of the Channel Islands: used *attrib.* and *ellipt.*, esp. in reference to the knitting of stockings and other worsted articles, which was long a staple industry of Jersey.

1. *attrib.* Of Jersey; of Jersey worsted. Hence also used of fine machine-knitted fabric generally.

1583 STUBBES *Anat. Abus.* I. (1879) 57 Nether-stocks.. not of cloth..for that is thought to base, but of Iarnsey worsted. **1603** in Brand *Hist. Newcastle* (1789) II. 231 [Not] to weare..worsted or Jersey stockings. **1693** *Lond. Gaz.* No. 2914/4 One fine Knit Jersey Night Gown..3 pair of Knit Jersey Breeches. **1704** *Ibid.* No. 4030/4 Light-coloured Jersey Stockings. **1881** *Queen* 8 Jan. (Advt.), Boy's jersey suit. **1938** D. BAKER *Young Man with Horn* I. iv. 38 His brother Henry..was selling jersey knits. **1959** *Observer* 22 Mar. 18/4 Some lovely short evening dresses were in silk jersey and had to be bought therefore, a little surprisingly, in the jersey wear department. **1966** *Economist* 9 Apr. 175/1 Acrylics (woolly, fluffy fibres used in knitwear mostly) and polyesters (mostly used in wool mixes, now bulked in jersey-knits) are bound to follow the same course as nylon. **1969** N. FREELING *Tsing-Boum* vi. 36 A nearly new jersey cocktail dress with the boutique label of a couturier. **1972** *Sci. Amer.* Dec. 4/2 The fabric is a plain knitted jersey... It was knitted ..of a spun, staple yarn.

2. *sb.* **a.** Jersey knitted work; Jersey worsted; worsted generally.

1587 *Acc. Death Mary Q. Scots* (*Bodl. MS. e Museo* 178, lf. 21 b), Her hose wer wosted..wrought with syluer about the Clockes, and whit Iarzie vnder them. **1587** HARRISON *England* II. vii. (1877) I. 170 The women's diverslie coloured nether stocks of silke jerdseie. **1882** BECK *Draper's Dict.* 175 Jarsey is still the local name for worsted in Lancashire.

†**b.** Wool which has been combed and is ready for spinning. *Obs.*

1657 *Golden Fleece* (N.), The present practice..which daily carrieth away of the finest sorts of wools ready combed into jarsies for worke. **1688** R. HOLME *Armoury* III. 286/1 *Jersey*, is the finest Wool taken out of other sorts of Wool by Combing it with a Jersey-Comb. **1781** *Specif. G. Dundas' Patent* No. 1288 (*title*) New Method of Spinning of Jersey. **1790** P. LUCKOMBE *Eng. Gazetteer* s.v. *Kettering*, A charity-school of 20 girls employed in spinning jerseys.

3. a. A woollen knitted close-fitting tunic, with short or long sleeves; applied esp. to that worn as a sole covering of the body in athletic exercises and sports; also, to a similar woollen garment worn either as an outer tunic by seamen, children, etc., or as an under-shirt or under-vest; also, to a close-fitting knitted tunic or jacket worn by women.

1836–48 B. D. WALSH *Aristoph., Knights* 215 But though you saw poor People [Δῆμος] here..had no flannel-waistcoat, ne'er Have you given him a jersey. **1857** HUGHES *Tom Brown* I. v, Now each house has its own uniform of [football] cap and jersey, of some lively colour. **1861** —— *Tom Brown at Oxf.* ii. (1889) 15 Here's this rough jersey which I use instead of a coat. **1880** MISS BRADDON *Just as I am* vii, She was not the kind of woman to encase herself in a boating Jersey because the fashion book told her that Jerseys were universally worn. **1889** RAWLINSON *Phoenicia* 356 A close-fitting tunic with short sleeves, like a modern 'jersey'.

b. A man wearing a jersey. ***blue jersey***, a seaman, a bargee.

1889 A. T. PASK *Eyes Thames* 57 You pass some dingy anchored craft in which the blue jerseys are smoking.

4. One of a breed of cattle of the Channel Islands; a cow of the island of Jersey. Also *attrib.* or as *adj.*

1842 *Guide to Island of Jersey* v. 94 The English reader need scarcely be told in what great estimation the Jersey Cows and Heifers are held... The Jersey cow is small and slender in its make, with short crumpled horns. **1845** *Jrnl. R. Agric. Soc.* V. 47 The Jersey cow is a singularly docile and gentle animal. **1875** [see ALDERNEY]. **1881** SHELDON *Dairy Farming* 25/1 The term 'Jerseys' is now taking the lead of the others. **1885** *Pall Mall G.* 2 Oct. 9/1 An exceptionally fine lot of Jerseys were shown. **1964** G. DURRELL *Menagerie Manor* ii. 35 You have vivid mental pictures of an escaped tiger stalking your pedigree herd of Jersey cows.

5. *Comb.*, as (sense 2) ***jersey-comb, -comber, -weaver, -wheel***; (sense 3) ***jersey-shaped*** adj.; (sense 4) ***Jersey cream, milk***; **Jersey elm,** *Ulmus stricta* var. *sarniensis*, a variety of elm of more erect growth than the parent species; **Jersey lily,** a nickname for Li(l)lie or Lily Langtry (1852–1929), an actress born in Jersey.

1688 Jersey-Comb [see 2 b]. **1720** *Lond. Gaz.* No. 5881/5 Humphry Maden,..Jarsy-comber. **1895** *Montgomery Ward Catal.* 110/1 Williams' Medicated Jersey Cream Toilet Soap; contains pure, rich cream from Jersey Cows. **1971** 'J. J. MARRIC' *Gideon's Art* iv. 35 The butler..offered more of the delicious apricot and peach flan, more of the rich Jersey cream. **1838** J. C. LOUDON *Arboretum* III. 1376 The Jersey Elm: is a free-growing variety, differing very little from the species. **1914** W. J. BEAN *Trees & Shrubs Hardy in Brit. Isles* II. 620 A yellow-leaved form of the Jersey elm originated in the nurseries of Messrs Dickson at Chester in 1900. **1957** M. HADFIELD *Brit. Trees* 242 The Jersey Elm is not infrequently seen planted as a street or ornamental tree, but is believed to be indigenous only to the Channel Islands. **1971** *Country Life* 8 Apr. 823/1 It should be widely known that the Jersey elm (*Ulmus stricta sarniensis*) is not immune to elm disease. **1882** W. HAMILTON *Aesthetic Movement* 103 *La bella Donna della mia Mente* exists, but she is not the Jersey Lily, though I have grovelled at her feet. **1895** M. BEERBOHM in *Yellow Bk.* IV. 275 To have strained my eyes for a glimpse of the Jersey Lily. **1930** W. S. MAUGHAM *Cakes & Ale* xii. 145 She had..a fringe on the forehead with a bun at the nape of the neck as you may see in old photographs of the Jersey Lily. **1972** *Times* 3 July 14/8 The Millais portrait ..showed her [*sc.* Lily Langtry] holding a lily in one hand which earned her the nickname [Jersey Lily]. **1881** *Jrnl. R. Agric. Soc.* 2nd Ser. XVII. 234 Jersey milk is considered too rich [for a calf]. **1970** E. MCGIRR *Death pays Wages* vi. 115 Her own breakfast..was Jersey milk and sliced banana. **1634** *Canterbury Marriage Licences* (MS.), Nicholas Du Sor, jarsey-weaver. **1718–19** *Overseers' Acc. Holy Cross, Canterbury*, A jarsey wheel a cloath basket. **1884** J. M. COWPER *Our Parish Bks.* 113 Spinning Wheels or jersey-wheels, were provided.

Hence **'jerseyed** *a.*, wearing a jersey.

1869 *Pall Mall G.* 29 Sept. 10 Blue-jerseyed boatmen and newspaper boys. **1890** *Daily News* 17 Nov. 6/2 Red-jerseyed Salvationists serve there all day alone.

Jersey[2] ('dʒɜːzɪ). *U.S.* = *New Jersey*, the name of the state situated south of New York, used *attrib.* and *Comb.* to denote people or things coming from or associated with New Jersey, as ***Jersey girl, maid***; ***Jersey-built, -made*** adjs.; **Jersey blue,** (*a*) a colonial New Jersey soldier (so called from his blue uniform); (*b*) a native or inhabitant of New Jersey; (*c*) a breed of chicken; **Jersey justice,** strict or severe justice; **Jersey lightning** *colloq.*, a strong kind of apple-jack, peach-brandy, or whisky; **Jersey pine,** the scrub pine, *Pinus virginiana*; **Jersey tea,** the red-root, *Ceanothus americanus*, the leaves of which were used as a substitute for tea; **Jersey wag(g)on,** a light carriage formerly used in New Jersey.

1758 C. REA *Jrnl.* 16 July in *Essex Inst. Hist. Coll.* (1881) XVIII. 110 Excepting ye Yorkers and Jersy Blews all ye Provincials didn't loose more than 100 men. **1849** J. F. COOPER *Sea Lions* I. i. 3 Distinctions..exist between the eastern and the western man,..the Buckeye or Wolverine, and the Jersey Blue. **1850** D. J. BROWNE *Amer. Poultry Yard* 77 The Jersey-Blue Fowl..is another large mongrel of a bluish cast. **1942** C. WEYGANDT *Plenty of Pennsylvania* 277 We have no native breeds of fowls in Pennsylvania as New Jersey had its Jersey Blues. **1829** R. C. SANDS *Writings* (1834) II. 121 Trim Jersey-built wagons. **1770** *Boston Gaz.* 7 May (Th.), A likely active Jersey girl. **1903** *N.Y. Tribune* 18 Oct. 8 Even with a faithful judge..'Jersey justice' did not shine as brilliantly as usual. **1948** *Collier's* 20 Nov. 78/3 Pellechia is having dealings with Jersey justice. **1852** *Alta California* (San Francisco) 23 Aug. 2/5 The rumsellers dealt out Jersey lightning by the gallon. **1872** G. P. BURNHAM *Mem. U.S. Secret Service* p. vi, *Jersey lightning*, a peculiar New Jersey drink; 'blue ruin'. **1970** *Observer* 19 Apr. 9/4 This urbane and sophisticated man came to believe that after repeal Jersey Lightning would capture the fancy of the

whole country, and become a standard national drink. **1778** *Boston Gaz.* 25 Aug. 373 Handy, light, Jersey made waggon. **1713** *Boston News-Let.* 5 Oct. 2/2 A Jersey Maids times for four years and an half very good Servant to be disposed of. **1743** J. F. GRONOVIUS *Flora Virginica* 191 The common Jersay-Pine. **1908** N. L. BRITTON *N. Amer. Trees* 46 Jersey Pine—*Pinus virginiana* Miller... This tree grows in poor rocky or sandy soil from southern New York to Indiana. **1971** *Country Life* 23 Dec. 1773/1 A singular collection of conifers, some species such as the Jersey pine (*Pinus virginiana*) being planted in considerable numbers. **1759** P. MILLER *Gardeners Dict.* (ed. 7) s.v. Ceanothus. New Holland Dogwood with female cornel leaves commonly called New Jersey Thea grows naturally in most Parts of North America, from whence great Plenty of the Seeds have been of late Years brought to Europe, by the Title of New Jersey Thea, where I have been informed the inhabitants dry the leaves of this Shrub to use as Thea. **1808** H. MUHLENBURG *Let.* 5 July in E. Rowland *Life W. Dunbar* (1930) 203 Red Root or Jersey Tea we call the Ceanothus americanus a little shrub with white Flowers, cordate leaves —Some times the sanguinaria is called so. **1870** *Amer. Naturalist* IV. 583 The *Ceanothus*, or Jersey tea, is a frequent inhabitant of the prairies. **1948** *Green Bay* (Wisconsin) *Press-Gaz.* 13 July 11/4 Jersey tea, the shrub whose leaves were the 'tea' used by the colonists after the Boston tea party. **1811** R. SUTCLIFF *Travels N. Amer.* p. viii, Jersey waggons.. are made very light, hung on springs with leather braces, and travel very pleasantly. **1835** J. J. AUDUBON *Ornith. Biogr.* III. 606 Fishermen gunners passed daily.. with Jersey wagons, laden with fish, fowls, and other provisions. **1944** *Sat. Rev.* (U.S.) 14 Oct. 24/2 The vagabond Reverend Mason Weems 'bumping along in his Jersey wagon'.

Jerseyman ('dʒɜːzɪmən), *sb.*[1] Now *rare.* A native or inhabitant of New Jersey, U.S.A.

1679 *Rec. Early Hist. Boston* (1881) VII. 58 Thomas Begretia [entertained] at James Wardens, Jersiman. **1839** *Southern Lit. Messenger* V. 800/2 A Jerseyman is pre-eminently calculated to make a good traveller. **1873** C. G. LELAND *Egypt. Sk.-Bk.* 45 The last number of the *Anglo-American* contains the names of half-a-dozen as veritable Jerseymen as ever drank apple-jack. **1878** *Harper's Mag.* 318/2 'Pretty hard times,' said the Jersey-man; 'but I want three hundred dollars in cash.' **1949** *Hist. & Philos. Soc. Ohio Bull.* Apr. 74 They were especially obnoxious to the Pennsylvanians and Jerseymen.

Jerseyman ('dʒɜːzɪmən), *sb.*[2] A native or inhabitant of Jersey (one of the Channel Islands).

1825 J. C. LOUDON *Encycl. Agric.* 1129/2 The treasure highest in a Jersey-man's estimation, is his cow. **1842** *Guide to Island of Jersey* x. 144 There is an independence of character in a Jerseyman. **1973** A. GREY *Some put their Trust in Chariots* v. 23 Jerseymen turn every statement into a question with that little word 'Ay?'

jert, *sb. Obs.* or *dial.* Also 8- jirt. = JERK *sb.*[1]

1568 *Jacob & Esau* I. i, Come on, ye must haue three iertes for the nonce. **1607** MARKHAM *Caval.* II. (1617) 40 Giue him a Ierte or two vpon the nether part of his buttocks. **1611** COTGR., *Attainte*, a gentle nip, quip, or iert. **1785** BURNS *2nd Ep. to Lapraik* ix, She's gien me monie a jirt an' fleg.

jert, *v. Obs.* exc. *dial.* Also 9 jirt. [A phonetic variant or parallel form of JERK.]

1. = JERK *v.*[1]

1566 DRANT *Horace* A vij, They ierted vp their horse with whippes. **1599** NASHE *Lenten Stuffe* 42 An other tower.. that is not so wide as a belfree, and a Cobler cannot iert out his elbowes in. **1600** —— *Summer's Last Will* in Hazl. *Dodsley* VIII. 52, I jerted my whip, and said to my horses but *hay*. **1616** SURFL. & MARKH. *Countrey Farme* 134 You shall on the suddaine chocke him in the weekes of the mouth, and iert his head vp aloft. *a* **1693** URQUHART *Rabelais* III. xx. 165 Withdrawing himself.. with a jerting turn towards the left hand. **1826** J. WILSON *Noct. Ambr.* Wks. 1855 I. 117 That only gars you jirt out the words.

2. *dial.* To throw a stone by jerking the arm against the hip: = HAUNCH *v.*[3]

In most north. Eng. dial. glossaries.

Jerusalem (dʒə'ruːsələm). The city in Palestine (Israel) so called; the Holy City. **1.** Hence *attrib.* or *ellipt.* in the following, among other uses: **Jerusalem cherry** = WINTER CHERRY 1 b; **Jerusalem jump** (see quot.); **Jerusalem letters**, letters or symbols tattooed on the arm or body, such as pilgrims or visitors to Jerusalem sometimes bore, in testimony or memory of their visit; **Jerusalem pony** and ellipt. **Jerusalem**, a donkey (in reference to Christ's riding into J. on an ass). Also in numerous plant-names and other combinations, as *Jerusalem* ARTICHOKE, CROSS, etc.: see these words.

1884 W. MILLER *Dict. Eng. Names Plants* 251 *Solanum Pseudo-Capsicum.* *Jerusalem Cherry, Winter-Cherry Capsicum. **1887** G. NICHOLSON *Illustr. Dict. Gardening* III. 455/1 *S*[*olanum*] *Pseudo-capsicum* (false Capsicum). Jerusalem Cherry. A few handsome hybrids have been raised from this species. **1902** L. H. BAILEY *Cycl. Amer. Hort.* IV. 1679/1 [*Solanum*] *Pseudo-Capsicum*, Linn. Jerusalem Cherry... An old-fashioned plant.. grown for its showy berry-like fruits, which persist a long time. **1969** *Northwest* (*Sunday Oregonian Mag.*) 14 Dec. 19/3 Christmas potted plants are just as important a part of the scene. Poinsettias, cyclamens, chrysanthemums, Christmas peppers, Jerusalem cherries, foliage plants, dish gardens, and others are among them. **1615** G. SANDYS *Trav.* 159 They bare five crosses gules, in forme of that which is at this day called the *Ierusalem crosse. **1697** DAMPIER *Voy.* 514 The Jerusalem Cross is made in Mens Arms, by pricking the skin, and rubbing in a pigment. **1877** W. JONES *Finger-ring* 265 Two signet-rings, also bearing as a device the 'Jerusalem Cross'. **1887** LANG *Myth, Rit. & Relig.* II. 240 The Voodoo-dance is consecrated as the '*Jerusalem Jump'. **1760–72** H. BROOKE *Fool of Qual.* (1809) II. 16 If heaven should ever bless me with more children,.. I have determined to fix some indelible mark upon them, such as that of the *Jerusalem-Letters. **1716** *Lond. Gaz.* No. 5400/4 He is.. well set, with a Scar on his right Cheek, and the *Jerusalem Mark on his Arm. **1806** in H. Martin *Brighton* (1871) 156 The *Jerusalem ponies have been in high requisition all the morning. **1840** *P. Parley's Ann.* I. 218 Mrs. Button.. at last thought of trying her Jerusalem poney in the streets. **1878** *Daily News* 16 Sept. 3/1 Jerusalems, alias living donkeys, are plentiful in the market.

2. *fig.* An ideal or heavenly city; *spec.* = CITY 3 b; freq. ***the new Jerusalem.***

1382, etc. [see CITY 3 b]. **1535** [see NEW *a.* 5 c]. **1601** *Song of Mary Mother of Christ* 38 Ierusalem my happy home, when shall I come to thee. **1804–8** W. BLAKE *Milton* Pref., in *Compl. Writings* (1972) 481, I will not cease from Mental Fight, Nor shall my Sword sleep in my hand Till we have built Jerusalem In England's green & pleasant Land. **1933** J. BUCHAN *Prince of Captivity* I. ii. 70 For the first time Adam told another of.. his childhood home and its lonely peace... 'Ah,' he said, 'it is as I guessed. We have each our Jerusalem.' **1959** A. HUXLEY *Let.* 10 Jan. (1969) 863 The nature of these visions is often paradisal and the descriptions of them remind one irresistibly of the description of the New Jerusalem in the Apocalypse. **1968** *Listener* 21 Mar. 377/3 Both men indeed looked forward to the same new Jerusalem —a society in which the state would wither away, bureaucracy would be no more.

3. Used as an exclamation, usu. of surprise.

1840 *Spirit of Times* 8 Aug. 276/2 By Jerusalem! **1868** READE & BOUCICAULT *Foul Play* III. xvii. 199 'What is your name, when you are ashore?' 'Robert Penfold. The Reverend Robert Penfold.' 'The Reverend!—Jerusalem.' **1872** [see GEEWHILLIKINS *int.*]. **1898** J. D. BRAYSHAW *Slum Silhouettes* 179 Jee-roosalem! You can't stand there; the police won't allow it. **1914** CHESTERTON *Wisdom of Father Brown* i. 19 'Jerusalem!' ejaculated Brown suddenly. **1968** J. F. STRAKER *SIN & Johnny Inch* i. 19 He consulted his watch. 'Jerusalem! It's nearly three hours.' **1974** P. LOVESEY *Invitation to Dynamite Party* ii. 27 'He kept.. buying me whisky.' Jerusalem! Cribb blinked. 'You were on spirits that night, then?'

jervine ('dʒɜːvaɪn). *Chem.* [Formerly also in mod.L. form *jervīna*: f. Sp. *jerva* the poisonous root of *Veratrum.*] A crystalline alkaloid occurring, together with veratrine, in the roots of *Veratrum album* and *V. viride.* Also called *jervia.*

1838 T. THOMSON *Chem. Org. Bodies* 282 (*heading*) Of Jervina. **1846** WORCESTER, *Jervine.* **1865–72** WATTS *Dict. Chem.* III. 444 Jervine is colourless and crystalline... It is insoluble in water, soluble in alcohol. **1875** H. C. WOOD *Therap.* (1879) 156 Jervia still lessened the pulse-rate.

†**jeryne.** *Obs. rare*[−1]. [perh. a. OF. *geron, giron*, front part of the dress, lap.] An article of dress or armour.

?*a* **1400** *Morte Arth.* 903 Sir Arthure.. Armede hym in a actone with orfraeez fulle ryche, Aboven one þat a jeryne of Acres owte over.

jes, jes' (dʒɛs), colloq. shortening of JUST *adv.*; freq. in American (esp. Black English) writings. Cf. JEST.

1851 MRS. STOWE *Uncle Tom's Cabin* (1852) I. iv. 41 Missis let Sally try to make some cake t'other day, jes to *larn* her, she said. **1886** in H. BAUMANN *Londinismen* 85/2. **1895** *Southern Workman* XXIV. 15/3 Ef I was starvin' an' had jes one ginger-cake, I would give you half. **1925** ODUM & JOHNSON *Negro & his Songs* ii. 39 Ef you want to see old Satan run, Jes fire off dat gospel gun. **1929** *Amer. Mercury* XVIII. 48/1 This big sargent wus jes' too mean to live. **1938** R. E. BASS in B. A. Botkin *Treas. S. Folklore* (1949) III. i. 457 He jes rared back and 'lowed, 'I ain't never told a lie in my life.' **1962** *Jrnl. Amer. Folklore* LXXV. 311 They thinks that science has solved jes' about ever'thin. **1966** *Massachusetts Rev.* VII. 659 He be sittin' theah at crop time, jes' afigurin' an' areckonin'. **1969** 'J. MORRIS' *Fever Grass* vi. 65 You jes talked a whole lotta sense.

jesamin, jesemin(e, jesmin(e, obs. forms of JASMINE.

jesing, var. GESINE *Obs.*, childbed.

jess (dʒɛs), *sb.* In pl. **jesses** ('dʒɛsɪz). Forms: *α.* 4 (*sing.* and *pl.*) **ges**; 5 (in *pl.* sense) **gesse**, 6 **iesse**; *β.* (*pl.*) 4–8 **gesses**, 5 **iessis, -ys**, (7 **chesses, gests**), 6– **jesses**. [ME. *ges*, a. OF. *ges* (*gez, getz*) nom., sing. and pl., of *get* (*giet, geet, gest, gect*), mod.F. *jet* 'cast' (= Pr. *get*, It. *getto, geto*):—L. *jact-us* throw, cast, f. *jacĕre* to throw. Both sing. and pl. were orig. as in OF. *ges*, but the pl. was soon conformed to the Eng. type as *gesses.* The sing. does not occur in our mod. examples.]

A short strap of leather, silk, or other material, fastened round each of the legs of a hawk used in falconry; usually bearing on its free end a small ring or *varvel* to which the swivel of the leash is attached.

1340 *Ayenb.* 254 Alsuo ase me ofhalt þane uoȝel be þe ges þet he ne vly to his wylle. **1398** TREVISA *Barth. De P.R.* XII. ii. (Tollem. MS.), Hire feet beþ fastenid with gesses þat þey may not fle frely to euery brid. **1486** *Bk. St. Albans* B iv b, Sett yowre honde and be sure of the gesse. *Ibid.* B v b, Hawkys haue aboute ther legges Gesse made of leder most commynly, som of silke. **1530** PALSGR. 183 *Vngz gietz*, a payre of gesses for a hauke. *Ibid.* 234/1 Iesses for a hauke, *get.* *c* **1560** *Parlt. Byrdes* 142 in Hazl. *E.P.P.* III. 174 Kepe him in a payre of Jesse. That he flye not to no byrde about. **1615** G. SANDYS *Trav.* 209 [They] make tame Doves the speedy transporters of their letters; which they wrap about their legs like iesses. **1671** *Lond. Gaz.* No. 623/4 A Falcon lost.. with the Kings Varvels upon her Gesses. **1685** COTTON tr. *Montaigne* I. 504 We commend.. a hawk for her wing, not for her gests and bells. **1774** GOLDSM. *Nat. Hist.* (1862) II. II. v. 47. **1828** SIR J. SEBRIGHT *Obs. Hawking* 9–10 Slips of light leather, seven or eight inches long, and a quarter of an inch wide, are to be made fast to each of his legs. These are called *jesses.* **1874** TENNYSON *Merlin* 123 Their talk was all of training, terms of art, Diet and seeling, jesses, leash and lure.

b. In figurative applications.

1590 MARLOWE *Edw. II*, II. ii, Soar ye ne'er so high, I have the jesses that will pull you down. **1604** SHAKS. *Oth.* III. iii. 261 If I do proue her Haggard, Though that her Iesses were my deere heart-strings, I'ld whistle her off, and let her downe the winde To prey at Fortune. **1630** BRATHWAIT *Eng. Gentlem.* Ded., Intangled with the light chesses of vanity. **1849** JAMES *Woodman* xvii, Methinks you are one who would find even gesses of silk or gold cord difficult to wear.

¶ Erroneously defined in Dictionaries.

1706 PHILLIPS, *Jesses*, Ribbons hanging down from Garlands or Crowns. **1828** WEBSTER adds 'in falconry'; repeated by OGILVIE, CASSELL, *Cent. Dict.*, FUNK.

jess, *v.* [f. JESS *sb.*] *trans.* To put the jesses on (a hawk). Also *fig.*

1860 WHYTE MELVILLE *Holmby Ho.* 263 With her own fair hands, she jessed and hooded 'Dewdrop', and took her from her perch. **1894** G. EGERTON *Keynotes* ii. 45 My heart had been a free, wild, shy thing, jessed by my will.

jess, var. GEST *sb.*[4] *Obs.*, stage of a journey.

1596 J. NORDEN *Progr. Pietie* (Parker Soc.) 47 *heading*, The first resting-place or jess in this progress.

jessamine, another form of JASMINE, q.v.

†**jessamy**, *sb. Obs.* Also 7 **jessamie, jes(s)imy, jecimy, gessamy, gessamy, -imy.** [Corrupt. of *jessamine.*]

1. = JASMINE 1.

1633 EARL MANCH. *Al Mondo* (1636) 6 Meditation is.. as he that smells the Violet, the Rose, the Jessamie, and the Orange flowers dividually. **1733** MORTIMER in *Phil. Trans.* XXXVIII. 179 She gnawed the Jessamy likewise, but least of all some Holly Trees.

2. A yellow colour like that of yellow jasmine.

1750 E. SMITH *Compl. Housew.* (ed. 14) 293 If you colour them [gloves], scrape some of the following colours amongst the white-lead;.. for a jessamy, yellow-oaker.

3. A perfume or cosmetic made from jasmine.

1671 EACHARD *Obs. Answ. Cont. Clergy* 146 A little pot of double refin'd Jesimy and a box full of specifick perfum'd Lozenges.

4. A man who scents himself with perfume or who wears a sprig of jessamine in his buttonhole (?); a dandy, a fop. See JEMMY *sb.* 1 b.

1753 HAWKESWORTH *Adventurer* 20 Oct. 176 You have frequently used the terms Buck and Blood,.. but you have not considered them as the last stages of a regular procession .. the scale consists of eight degrees; Greenhorn, Jemmy, Jessamy, Smart, Honest Fellow, Joyous Spirit, Buck, and Blood. *Ibid.* 177 My labour.. recommended me to the notice of the ladies, and procured me the gentle appellation of Jessamy. **1802** MRS. J. WEST *Infidel Father* I. 88 If men became Jessamys, and Women Amazons. *Ibid.* I. 296 The half pagan half democratic dress of clerical jessamies.

5. *attrib.* That is a jessamy, as *j. fopling*; of a jessamy, as ***jessamy air*** (see 4), ***plant***; also **jessamy-butter** = *jasmine-butter* (see JASMINE 3); **jessamy-chocolate**, (?) chocolate perfumed with jasmine; **jessamy gloves**, (?) gloves of a light yellow colour.

1657 REEVE *God's Plea* 123 How much girdles, gorgets,.. rose powders, gessamy butter, complexion waters do cost in our daies. **1666** PEPYS *Diary* 27 Oct., I did give each of them a pair of jesimy plain gloves, and another of white. **1675** T. DUFFETT *Mock Temp.* III. i. 22, 3 Ounces of Jessimy-butter ..and 6 pair of Jessimy-Gloves. **1696** *Lond. Gaz.* No. 3181/4 Spanish Gessimy Plants. **1697** *Ibid.* No. 3302/4 Jessamy-Chocolate, with other Perfumes and Spirits; all newly come from Florence. **1756** W. TOLDERVY *Hist. Two Orphans* III. 106 A severe punishment to the fribbled jessamy waiter. **1800** *Spirit Pub. Jrnls.* (1801) IV. 357 The steel-clad baron and the jessamy fopling. **1837** *Old Commodore* II. 124 A slighter figure now appears.. with a gentle jessamy air.

Hence †**jessamy** *v. trans.*, to anoint or perfume with 'jessamy' (sense 3).

1688 R. HOLME *Armoury* III. 128/2 Terms of Art used in Barbing and Shaving.. Jecimy the Hair, is to put Jecimin on the palms of your hands and rub it on the hair.

jessant ('dʒɛsənt), *a. Her.* Forms: 6 **iesaunt, iezante, gesante**, 8 **gessant**, 7– **jessant.** (See also JACENT *a.* b.) [In sense 1, a. OF. *gesant* (later *gisant*) lying, pr. pple. of *gésir*:—L. *jacēre* to lie. Sense 2 is perh. a different word.]

1. Said of a charge represented as lying over another and partly covering it, so that the latter appears on both sides of, or above and below, the former.

1610 GUILLIM *Heraldry* III. xv. (1660) 194 A Lyon Jessant .. is not subjected to the primary Charge, but is borne over both the Field and Charge, and is therefore called a *Lyon Jessant, à jacendo*, because of such lying all over. **1706** [see JACENT b]. **1725** BRADLEY *Fam. Dict.*, *Jessant*, a Term in Heraldry, when in a Coat of Arms, a Lyon or other Beast is born over some Ordinary.. that Lyon or Beast is blazoned *Jessant* or *Jacent*, that is, Lying over all.

2. Said when a charge (as an animal) is represented with another (as a branch or flower) in its mouth or as if issuing from it.

Jessant stands between the two names, e.g. *a hart gessant a branch of dittany*, as if agreeing with the first and governing the second; but it is explained by Chambers and later writers as if agreeing with the second, and = Shooting or springing forth (? for Fr. *issant*, ISSANT). ***jessant-de-lis***, abbrev. of ***jessant a fleur de lis***, or in pl. ***jessant fleurs-de-lis***.

1572 BOSSEWELL *Armorie* II. 58, G. Beareth Sable, a Dromede passante d'or, gesante a branche of the Date tree propre. *Ibid.* 59 An Harte regardante d'Argente, iezante a branche of Dictamie propre. **1610** GUILLIM *Heraldry* III. xxvi. (1660) 257 The Field is..a Leopards head..Jessant a flower de lis. **1727-41** CHAMBERS *Cycl. Jessant*, in heraldry, is applied to a flower-de-luce, or the like figure, seeming to spring, or shoot out of some other charge... The word is formed from the obsolete French *jesser*, to rise or spring out. **1766** PORNY *Heraldry* (1787) Gloss., *Jessant*, this word signifies *shooting forth*, as vegetables do; it is also used to express the bearing of Fleurs-de-lis coming out of a Leopard's head, or out of any other Bearing. **1882** CUSSANS *Handbk. Her.* vi. (ed. 3) 103 *Jessant*: Shooting, or springing out of.

Jesse[1] ('dʒɛsiː). [Name of the father of David (1 Sam. xvi. 12).] A genealogical tree representing the genealogy of Christ, from 'the root of Jesse' (cf. Isa. xi. 1); used in churches in the Middle Ages as a decoration for a wall, window, vestment, etc., or in the form of a large branched candlestick. Also *attrib. Obs.* exc. *Hist.*

1463 *Bury Wills* (Camden) 39 The Jesse set vndir our lady with the virgenys afore hire. **1549** *Churchw. Acc. Ely* (Nichols 1797) 137 A coope of white silke with jessy rooles and prophetes. **1706** PHILLIPS, *Jesse*,..In old Records a large Brass Candlestick, branched out into several Sconces, such as are us'd in Churches. This useful Devise was first call'd *Arbor Jessæ*, and *Stirps Jessæ*, from its resemblance to the Genealogical Tree of Jesse. **1836-45** *Gloss. Archit.* (ed. 4) 217 It was..wrought into a branched candlestick,.. called a Jesse,..in the year 1097 Hugo de Flori, abbot of St. Augustine's, Canterbury, bought for the choir of his church a candlestick of this kind—'*Candelabrum magnum in choro æreum quod* Jesse *vocatur in partibus emit transmarinis*'. **1848** RICKMAN *Archit.* p. xxxviii, The Jesse window, Dorchester, Oxfordshire [is] a very rich and fine example. **1899** *Q. Rev.* Jan. 169 Interesting chapters on Jesse windows and Story windows.

Jesse[2] ('dʒɛsiː). *U.S. slang.* (? *Obs.*) Also jesse, jessie, jessy. [Perh. derived from a jocular interpretation of 'There shall come a rod out of the stem of Jesse' (Isa. xi. 1).] ***to give*** (a person) ***Jesse***: to treat or handle severely; to beat or scold soundly. Similarly ***to catch*** or ***get Jesse***.

1839 *Spirit of Times* 19 Oct. 396/3 If I thought he had been shot and creesed in that savigerous sorta fashion, I'd give him jessy with my butcher knife. **1840** *Daily Even. Transcript* (Boston) 12 Feb. 1/1 If any of you ever come to Saco, I kalkilate you'll get *jesse*. **1846** *Spirit of Times* 4 July 223/3 One of the combatants 'caught Jessie'. **1846** D. CORCORAN *Pickings* 126 Threatening to give Miss Martin 'jessy' when she would next meet her. **1865** A. H. STEPHENS *Diary* 29 Sept. (1910) 518 While I thought I was giving you Jesse on hearts, you were giving me fits on spades. **1946** *Amer. Speech* XXI. 153/1 Thornton's latest citation for *give him Jesse* is from 1865... In February, 1946, I heard the expression used in a game of bridge by a player from Sidney, Nebraska, when her partner was ruffing an opponent's suit.

†**jesse**, obs. abbrev. of *jessamine*: see JASMINE.

1597 GERARDE *Herbal* II. cccxv. 747 Called..in English Iasmine, Gessemine, and Iesse. **1611** COTGR., *Iasmin*,.. Jessemine, Jelsomine, Jesse.

Jessean (dʒɛ'siːən), *a.* ? *Obs.* [f. JESSE[1] + -AN.] Belonging to Jesse, or to King David, his son.

1605 SYLVESTER *Urania* xvii, Tuning now the Iessean Harp again. **1623** COCKERAM, *Iessean Harpe*, Dauids musicke. *a* **1754** W. HAMILTON *Contemplation*, The blest Jessean Lyre.

jessed (dʒɛst), *a.* [f. JESS *sb.* or *v.* + -ED.] Of a hawk: Furnished with or wearing jesses; in *Her.* having the jesses of a specified tincture.

1610 GUILLIM *Heraldry* III. xx. (1611) 161 He beareth Sable, a Goshawke Argent..armed Iessed and belled. **1766** PORNY *Heraldry* (1777) Dict., *Jessed*, this is said of a Hawk or any other Bird, whose Jesses..are of a Tincture different from the rest. **1877** RUSKIN *Fors Clav.* VII. lxxv. 78 You will like better to see the eagle free than the jessed hawk. **1882** CUSSANS *Handbk. Her.* vi. (ed. 3) 92 When the Jesses, or straps with which the bells were attached, are Flotant, or hanging loose, they are Belled and Jessed.

jessemin, jessimy, obs. ff. JASMINE, JESSAMY.

jesserant (-ance, -aunce): see JAZERANT.

Jessie ('dʒɛsɪ). *colloq.* Also Jessy, and with lower-case initial. [Female proper name.] A cowardly or effeminate man; a male homosexual.

1923 G. BLAKE *Mince Collop Close* i. 20 He was a big Jessie,...but she liked him. **1938** [see GO-ROUND]. **1958** K. AMIS *I like it Here* ii. 31 Darling, you really don't have to convince me that you're not a jessie. **1958** M. DICKENS *Man Overboard* iv. 59 Don't listen to those timid old Jessies at Southampton. **1971** G. SIMS *Deadhand* II. ii. 88 Duff had been scathing about 'soft jessies who couldn't get their fat heads down'. **1973** D. LEES *Rape of Quiet Town* xix. 153 The implication that J. Plummer Esquire was a soft jessie—because he had a rotten objection to getting himself killed.

jest (dʒɛst), *sb.* Also 4-6 ieste, 6 gest, 6-7 ieast. See also GEST *sb.*[1] [a. OF. *geste, jeste*, ad. L. *gesta* doings, exploits: see GEST *sb.*[1], of which this is a variant spelling.]

†**1.** A notable deed or action; an exploit. *Obs.*

a **1300**, etc. [see GEST *sb.*[1] 1]. **1534** WHITINTON *Tullyes Offices* I. (1540) 35 The noble iestes at home. *a* **1548** HALL *Chron., Hen. VIII*, 4 b, Settyng furthe the iestes, actes and deedes, of the nobilitie. **1594** LODGE *Wounds Civ. War* in Hazl. *Dodsley* VII. 186 Now, by my sword, this was a worthy jest. **1604** E. G[RIMSTONE] tr. *D'Acosta's Hist. Ind.* I. vii. 22 These two authors agree in their ieasts.

†**2.** A narrative of exploits; a story, tale, or romance, originally in verse. *Obs.*

a **1300**, etc. [see GEST *sb.*[1] 2]. **13..** *K. Alis.* 30 Here a noble jeste of Alisaundre theo riche kyng. **1387-8** T. USK *Test. Love* Prol. (Skeat) l. 2 Men..that..so moche swalowen the deliciousnesse of iestes and of ryme.

†**3.** An idle tale. *Obs.*

c **1470** [see GEST *sb.*[1] 3 b]. *a* **1577** GASCOIGNE *Memories, R. Courtop*, Thus this foolishe iest, I put in dogrell rime. **1585** T. WASHINGTON tr. *Nicholay's Voy.* IV. xxiv. 140 Alexander taking it for a iest would not beleeve it. **1611** COTGR., *Bourde*, a ieast, fib, tale of a tub. **1620** T. PEYTON *Glass Time* I. (1623) 50 The paradise of Rome's fantastike braine Is but a iest a little wealth to gaine.

4. A mocking or jeering speech; a taunt, a jeer. Also, in milder sense, A piece of raillery or banter. ***to break a jest*** (also in sense 5): see BREAK *v.* 23.

a **1548** HALL *Chron., Hen. V*, 77 b, [He] fled to Burges in Berrie,..and therefore in a Iest he was commonly called the kyng of Burges and of Berries. **1551** ROBINSON tr. *More's Utop.* To P. Giles (1895) 10 An other is so narrow in the sholders That he can beare no iestes nor tawntes. **1588** SHAKS. *L.L.L.* IV. iii. 174 Too bitter is thy iest. Are wee betrayed thus to thy ouer-view? **1599** —— *Much Ado* V. i. 189 You breake iests as braggards do their blades, which God be thanked hurt not. **1670** A. ROBERTS *Adv. T.S.* 27 He cast a Jest upon every one of us, which gave the Company a great deal of Mirth. **1791** COWPER *Iliad* II. 258 Might he but set the rabble in a roar, He cared not with what jest. **1871** FREEMAN *Norm. Conq.* IV. xviii. 233 That their return to Normandy was owing to the importunities of their wives would be an obvious jest at the time.

5. A saying intended to excite laughter; a witticism, joke.

1551 ROBINSON tr. *More's Utop.* I. (1895) 73 He himself was oftener laughed at then his iestes were. **1576** FLEMING *Panopl. Epist.* 152 *note*, He forgot..who exceeded al other in uttering delightsome ieastes with a convenient grace. **1640** QUARLES *Enchirid.* iv. 83 Let not thy laughter hand-sell thy owne Jest. **1751** JOHNSON *Rambler* No. 141 ¶8 The hapless wit has his labours always to begin..and one jest only raises expectation of another. **1864** TENNYSON *Aylmer's F.* 440 The jests, that flashed about the pleader's room, Lightning of the hour.

b. *transf.* Something the recital of which causes amusement; a ludicrous event or circumstance.

1593 SHAKS. *2 Hen. VI.* I. i. 132 A proper iest, and neuer heard before, That Suffolke should demand a whole Fifteenth. **1598** —— *Merry W.* II. ii. 116 *Fal.* Has Fords wife, and Pages wife acquainted each other, how they loue me. *Qui.* That were a iest indeed. **1632** LITHGOW *Trav.* I. 32 Now I remember here of a pretty jest, for he and I going in [etc.]. **1737** POPE *Hor. Ep.* II. i. 318 To complete the Jest, Old Edward's Armour beams on Cibber's breast.

6. a. The opposite of earnest or seriousness; trifling sport, fun. Chiefly in phrases, as ***in jest***: not seriously, without serious intention, in joke, in fun.

1551 T. WILSON *Logike* (1580) 68 Reasonyng in ieste after this sorte, and yet meanyng good earnest. **1593** SHAKS. *Rich. II*, V. iii. 101 His eyes do drop no teares: his prayres are in iest. **1617** MORYSON *Itin.* III. 83, I complaining therof to my Host, he betweene ieast and earnest replied [etc.]. **1635** J. HAYWARD tr. *Biondi's Banish'd Virg.* 163 In loves schoole, wherein who-so studies in jest, may learne in good earnest. **1838** THIRLWALL *Greece* xxxviii. V. 72 Epaminondas.. never permitted himself to utter a falsehood even in jest. **1847** TENNYSON *Princ.* IV. 541 The jest and earnest working side by side.

b. Jesting, joking, merriment; ridicule.

1597 BACON *Ess., Discourse* (Arb.) 16/1 Some thinges are priuiledged from iest, namely Religion, matters of state, great persons,..and any case that deserueth pittie. **1602** SHAKS. *Ham.* V. i. 204 Alas poore Yorick,..a fellow of infinite Iest, of most excellent fancy. **1632** MILTON *L'Allegro* 26 Haste thee, Nymph, and bring with thee Jest and youthful Jollity. **1771** *Junius Lett.* xlix. 257 A hopeful subject of jest and merriment between them. **1854** PATMORE *Angel in Ho.* I. II. ix. (1879) 231 In joy's crown danced the feather jest.

c. A thing that is not serious or earnest; a jocular affair.

a **1732** GAY *Epitaph*, Life is a jest, and all things shew it, I thought so once, and now I know it. **1822** BYRON *Werner* II. i, Oh, thou world! Thou art indeed a melancholy jest!

7. A sportive action, prank, frolic; a trick played in sport, a practical joke. Now *rare*.

1578 N. BAXTER *Calvin on Jonah* Compl. 3 Guy of Warwicke, Scoggins gests and Gargantua. **1590** SHAKS. *Mids. N.* III. ii. 239 Hold the sweete iest vp: This sport well carried, shall be chronicled. **1613** HEYWOOD *Braz. Age* Wks. 1874 III. 238 If Vulcan in this ieast hath pleas'd the Gods, All his owne wrongs he freely can forgiue. **1698** FRYER *Acc. E. India & P.* 110 March begins with a Licentious Week of Sports..nor are they to be offended at any Jest or Waggery. **1807-8** W. IRVING *Salmag.* (1824) 60 Students famous for their love of a jest—set the college on fire, and burnt out the Professors.

†**8.** An amusing or entertaining performance; a pageant, masque, masquerade, or the like. *Obs.*

1599 KYD *Sp. Trag.* I. (1602) C j, But where is old Hieronymo our Marshall? He promised vs..To grace our banquet with some pompous iest. *Stage direction*, Enter Hieronymo with a Drum, three Knightes..then he fetches three Kinges, etc. **1601** MUNDAY *Downf. Earl Huntington* I. iii. in Hazl. *Dodsley* VIII. 114 My rival..Hath cross'd me in this jest, and at the court employs the players should have made us sport.

9. An object of or matter for jesting or derision; a laughing-stock.

1598 SHAKS. *Merry W.* III. iii. 161 Why then make sport at me, then let me be your iest. **1606** HIERON *Wks.* I. 46 [He] scorneth it, [the Word] and maketh a very ieast of it. **1777** SHERIDAN *Sch. Scand.* V. ii, To be the standing jest of all one's acquaintance. **1809** MALKIN *Gil Blas* I. v. ¶6 My father and mother were a standing jest. **1878** B. TAYLOR *Deukalion* II. iii. 69 Lowly virtue is the jest of fools.

10. *Comb.*, as ***jest-killer***, ***-monger***; †***jest-monging*** adj.; **jest-wise** *adv.*, in a jesting manner; **jest-word**, a word of jesting; *transf.* an object of jesting or ridicule (cf. *byword*).

1599 MARSTON *Sco. Villanie* III. xi. 227 Tuscus, that iest-mounging youth Who nere did ope his Apish gerning mouth But to retaile and broke anothers wit. **1681** W. ROBERTSON *Phraseol. Gen.* (1693) 754 A witless jestmonger. **18..** JOANNA BAILLIE (O.), Some witlings and jest-mongers still remain For fools to laugh at. **1843** WHITTIER *Chr. Slave* 11 The jest-word of a mocking band. **1844** MRS. BROWNING *Vis. Poets* ccxli, Because Anacreon looked jest-wise.

jest (dʒɛst), *v.* Also 6 gest(e, geast, ieste, 6-7 ieast. [f. prec.: = GEST *v.*[1], of which this is a variant spelling.]

†**1.** *intr.* To tell a tale, to recite a romance.

1340-1440 [see GEST *v.*[1] 1].

2. *intr.* To utter gibes or taunts; to give utterance to ridicule; to scoff, jeer, mock.

1526 TINDALE *3 John* 10 Iestynge on vs with malicious wordes. **1530** PALSGR. 562/1, I geste, I rayle upon one, *je raffarde*. I love nat his condyscions, for he doth but jeste upon other men. **1535** COVERDALE *Job* xxvii. 23 Than clappe men their hondes at him, yee and ieast of him. **1563** WINȜET *Four Scoir Thre Quest.* Wks. 1888 I. 73 Ȝe schaw ȝour arrogance only..to be lachin and gestit at. **1660** F. BROOKE tr. *Le Blanc's Trav.* 313 He..made an oath he would never jest at spirits again.

b. *trans.* To jeer at; to ridicule; to banter.

1721 RAMSAY *Content* 248 Be not aghast; Come briskly on, you'll jest them when they're past; Mere empty spectres. **1775** ADAIR *Amer. Ind.* 427, I jested them in commending the swiftness of their horses. **1800** W. TAYLOR in *Monthly Mag.* VIII. 728 Mock'd by the madman, jested by the fool. **1830** JAMES *Darnley* xx, He jested his companion upon his gravity.

3. *intr.* To speak or act in a trifling manner or not seriously; to trifle.

1530 PALSGR. 562/1, I gest, I bourde or tryfyll with one, *je bourde*. I sayd it nat in good earnest, I dyd but..jeste with you. **1560** DAUS tr. *Sleidane's Comm.* 63 b, God forbydde I should ieste in these weyghtie matters. **1607** SHAKS. *Cor.* I. iii. 103 Verily I do not iest with you; there came newes from him last night. **1650** FULLER *Pisgah* II. xiii. 270 The most sportfull fishes dare not jest with the edged-tools of this Dead-sea. *a* **1873** LYTTON *Pausanias* I. i. (1876) 51 'Jest not, Pausanias; you will find me in earnest', answered Uliades, doggedly.

4. *intr.* To say something amusing or facetious; to make witty or humorous remarks; to joke.

1553 T. WILSON *Rhet.* (1580) 137 Other can ieste at large, and tell a rounde tale pleasauntly. **1641** J. JACKSON *True Evang. T.* I. 34 Now was Severus the Emperour, an Emperour of his own name, as they jested upon him, Severe was his name, and severe his nature. **1710** STEELE *Tatler* No. 215 ¶2 Because Mirth is agreeable, another thinks fit eternally to jest. **1725** RAMSAY *Gent. Sheph.* III. iv, Well jested, Symon. **1855** MACAULAY *Hist. Eng.* xvii. IV. 97 He drank: he jested: he was again the Dick Talbot who had diced and revelled with Grammont.

†**b.** *intr.* To disport or amuse oneself; to make merry; ? to act in a masque or play. *Obs.*

1593 SHAKS. *Rich. II.* I. iii. 95 As gentle, and as iocond, as to iest, Go I to fight. **1632** J. HAYWARD tr. *Biondi's Eromena* 29 To the end that those of the House..seeing them jest (beating one the other with pillowes) might beleeve that thence began the first noise.

c. quasi-*trans.*, usually with adverb or phrase expressing result.

a **1562** G. CAVENDISH *Wolsey* (1893) 214 The matter was gested and laughed owte merylye. **1634** MASSINGER *Very Woman* V. iv, Do not jest thyself Into the danger of a father's anger. **1712** STEELE *Spect.* No. 358 ¶1 Thus they have jested themselves stark naked, and ran into the Streets, and frighted Women. **1802** *Oracle* in *Spirit Pub. Jrnls.* (1803) VI. 291, I have jested away all my friends. **1811** LAMB *Ess., Edax on Appetite*, That freak..jested me out of a good three hundred pounds a year.

jest (dʒɛst), colloq. and dial. var. JUST *adv.* Cf. JES, JES'.

1815 D. HUMPHREYS *Yankey in Eng.* I. 22 I'm rather in a strait, jest now. **1890** KIPLING *Barrack-Room Ballads* (1892) 19 Jest send in your Chief an' surrender. **1896** in G. F. NORTHALL *Warwickshire Word-Bk.* 119. **1908** A. J. DAWSON *Finn* xix. 293 Jest you remember, my boy, that where I sleeps I breakfast. **1971** M. BABSON *Cover-up Story* x. 112 Hell, it was jest a thought. **1973** *Black World* June 63 Jest git on da good foot.

jest, variant of GIST *sb.*[3], JET *sb.*[4]

jest-book ('dʒɛstbʊk). [f. JEST *sb.* + BOOK *sb.*] A book of jests or amusing stories.

1750 H. WALPOLE *Lett.* (1845) II. 367 You will think my letters are absolute jest-and-story books. **1781** COWPER *Truth* 307 The Scripture was his jest-book, whence he drew *Bons-mots* to gall the Christian and the Jew. **1876** *N. Amer.*

Rev. CXXIII. 58 Various collections of jestbooks, as those containing the jokes of Bertaldo and Gonnella.

† **'jest-'earnest.** *Obs.* In phr. *in jest-earnest*: in earnest under colour of jesting.

1642 Fuller *Holy & Prof. St.* v. ii. 362 Such blows in jest-earnest are most dangerous. **1660** —— *Mixt Contempl.* (1841) 200 Hereupon one in jest-earnest said, that formerly they put down bishops and deans, and now they had put down chapters too.

je'stee. *rare.* [f. jest *v.* + -ee: cf. jester.] One who is the object of a jest; a butt.

1759 Sterne *Tr. Shandy* I. xii, The Mortgager and Mortgagee differ..not more in length of purse, than the Jester and Jestee do in that of memory. **1831** *Fraser's Mag.* IV. 180 'Immense arrogance', shout the eclipsed; 'unprofitable jests', grunt the jestees.

jester ('dʒɛstə(r)). Forms: 4-5 iestour, (6 iesture), 6 gester, -ar, (*Sc.* geister), (7 gestor), 6-7 ieaster, iester, 7- jester. [f. jest *v.* + -er[1]; a variant spelling of gester.]

1. A professional reciter of romances. *arch.*

c **1380-1496** [see gester]. **1814** Scott *Ld. of Isles* ii. ii, Harper's strain And jester's tale went round in vain. *a* **1861** Mrs. Browning *Summing up in Italy* viii, Some pale feudal jester.

2. A mimic, buffoon, or merry-andrew; any professed maker of amusement, esp. one maintained in a prince's court or nobleman's household.

[*c* **1362** *Durham Acc. Rolls* (Surtees) 565 Cuidam Istrioni Jestour Jawdewyne in festo Natalis D'ni, 3*s.* 4*d.*] *c* **1510** Barclay *Mirr. Gd. Manners* (1570) Eiij, Seke not to get glory nor lawdes vnto thee Of a common gester or bourder hauing name. **1551** Robinson tr. *More's Utop.* i. (1895) 77 The cardinal..sent away the iester by a preuy beck. **1569** *Nottingham Rec.* IV. 133 To Lockewood, the Quen's Iester ijs. **1573-80** Baret *Alv.* G 164 A Gester, or dizard faining and counterfeiting all men's gestures, *pantomimus.* **1694** Luttrell *Brief Rel.* 13 Nov. (1857) III. 399 Mr. Henry Killigrew has a warrant to be jester to the King, with £300 per ann. to be setled on him. **1762-71** H. Walpole *Vertue's Anecd. Paint.* (1786) V. 66 A small whole length of Archee, the king's jester. **1858** Doran *Crt. Fools* 162 The jester was now a higher personage than the fool.

3. One who jests, or speaks or acts in jest; a person given to uttering jests or witticisms; a joker.

c **1510** More *Picus* Wks. 11/1 The flesh chaungeth..the rauenous extorcioner in to a wolfe,..yᵉ mocking gester in to an ape. **1530** Palsgr. 224/2 Gestar a scoffer, *raillevr.* **1598** Shaks. *Merry W.* ii. i. 218, I heare the Parson is no Iester. **1605** —— *Lear* v. iii. 71 Iesters do oft proue Prophets. **1728** Young *Love Fame* ii. 124 Dull is the jester, when the joke's unkind. **1866** Lowell *Biglow Papers* Introd., There is no imputation that could be more galling to any man's self-respect than that of being a mere jester.

Hence **'jestership**, the office of a jester.

1858 Doran *Crt. Fools* 134 Patch was thus promoted to a court jestership. **1899** *Academy* 3 June 610/2 The triumph of my career was a jestership to a bishop.

jestern(e, obs. forms of jazerant.

'jestful, *a.* [See -ful.] Full of jesting.

1831 *Fraser's Mag.* II. 695 His courteous, though quaint and jestful manners. **1892** *Welsh Rev.* I. 756 Though my tones were jestful, I felt in reality little mirth.

† **je'sticular**, *a. Obs.* = gesticular 1.

1619 T. Morrice *Apol. Schoole-masters* C vij b, A young man who will vse verball and iesticular complements.

jesticulation, obs. form of gesticulation.

jesting ('dʒɛstɪŋ), *vbl. sb.* [f. jest *v.* + -ing[1].] The action of the vb. jest; joking, pleasantry; trifling; ridicule.

1526 Tindale *Eph.* v. 4 Nether folishe talkyng, nether gestinge. **1548** Udall *Erasm. Par. Luke* xvi. 25 For thy iestynges and songes [thou hast] continuall wepyng. **1606** Shaks. *Tr. & Cr.* i. ii. 224 Looke you what hacks are on his Helmet... There's no iesting. *a* **1679** Hobbes *Rhet.* ii. xiv. (1681) 71 Jesting is witty contumely. **1700** Dryden *Pal. & Arc.* i. 285 Jesting, said Arcite, suits but ill with pain. **1891** F. M. Crawford *Cigarette-Maker's Rom.* i, Vjera cast an imploring look on Dumnoff, as though beseeching him not to continue his jesting.

attrib. **1573-80** Baret *Alv.* I 32, I had almost fallen into a shrewd sporting, or iesting matter, ere I was ware. **1712** Arbuthnot *John Bull* iii. ii, A rope and a noose are no jesting matters! **1855** Macaulay *Hist. Eng.* xv. (1889) II. 175 He will find that these are no jesting matters.

jesting ('dʒɛstɪŋ), *ppl. a.* [f. jest *v.* + -ing[2].] That jests; jocose; trifling; †scoffing, jeering.

1551 Robinson tr. *More's Utopia* i. (1895) 73 A certein iesting parasite, or scoffer. **1625** Bacon *Ess., Truth* (Arb.) 499 What is Truth; said jesting Pilate; And would not stay for an Answer. **1700** Dryden *Pal. & Arc.* i. 284 Speakst thou in earnest, or in jesting vein? **1868** Freeman *Norm. Conq.* II. viii. 287 In revenge for a jesting and not very intelligible ballad sung against him.

'jesting-beam. *Building.* A beam introduced into a building for ornament, not for use.

In mod. Dicts.

jestingly ('dʒɛstɪŋlɪ), *adv.* [f. jesting *ppl. a.* + -ly[2].] In a jesting manner; by way of joke or merriment; in jest, not seriously.

1568 Grafton *Chron.* II. 58 The king receyved him after a certayne maner..taunting him iestingly and merily. **1647** H. More *Song of Soul* iii. ii. xli, Thus jestingly he flung out what was true. **1722** De Foe *Relig. Courtsh.* i. ii. (1840) 38 He told me he kept a chaplain, and jestingly told me, he was devout enough for all the rest of the house. **1883** Froude in *Mrs. Carlyle's Lett.* II. 256 She had taken the harder parts of her lot lightly and jestingly.

† **'jesting-stock.** *Obs.* [f. jesting *vbl. sb.* + stock *sb.*: cf. *gazing-stock, laughing-stock.*] An object of jest or ridicule; a laughing-stock.

1535 Coverdale *Job* xvii. 6, I am his gestinge stocke. **1577** tr. *Bullinger's Decades* (1592) 214 Wee are to all the heathen a iesting stocke to laugh at. **1632** Massinger *City Madam* iv. iv, He's your 'kind brother' now; but yesterday, Your slave and jesting-stock.

jestour, jestraunt, obs. ff. jester, jazerant.

† **'jestress.** *Obs. rare*⁻¹. [f. jester + -ess.] A female jester.

1557 *Tottell's Misc.* (Arb.) 177 O Temerous tauntres that delightes in toyes,..Ianglyng iestres, depraueres of swete ioyes.

jesture, obs. form of gesture.

† **'Jesuist.** *Obs. rare.* [See -ist.] = next, 1.

1602 H. Ely in *Archpriest Controv.* (1898) II. 200 This said Runagate Iesuist. *c* **1645** Howell *Lett.* (1655) IV. xii. 35 Giving advice..to expell the Iesuists.

Jesuit ('dʒɛzjuːɪt), *sb.* Also 6-7 -ite. [ad. mod.L. *Jēsuīta*, f. *Jēsū-s* + *-īta*: see -ite.]

1. A member of the 'Society of Jesus', a Roman Catholic order founded by Ignatius Loyola in 1533, and sanctioned by Paul IV in 1540.

The object of the Society of Jesus was to support the Roman Church in its struggle with the 16th c. Reformers and to propagate the faith among the heathen. Hated and feared by Protestants, the Order, with its authoritarian constitution and its principle of total obedience to papal commands, became suspect to many in Roman Catholic countries too—more especially when Jesuit schools and confessionals came to exercise great influence on rulers and high society. By their enemies, the Jesuits were accused of teaching that the end justifies the means, and the lax principles of casuistry put forward by a few of their moralists were ascribed to the Order as a whole, thus giving rise, not only in English but in French and other languages, to sense 2, and to the opprobrious sense attached to *Jesuitical, Jesuitry*, and other derivatives.

1559 in *Cecil Papers* (Hist. MSS. Comm.) I. 153 Yᵉ multitud of Iesuitts and seminaryes secrettly comen into yᵉ realm. **1565** T. Stapleton *Fortr. Faith* 52* The deuoute and lerned company of the Iesuites, men prouided of God bothe to staie heresy and to enlarge Christendom. **1583** Stubbes *Anat. Abus.* ii. (1882) 6 The diuels agents..by the name of Iesuites..a name verie blasphemously deriued from the name of Iesus. **1588** Hunsdon in *Border Papers* (1894) I. 367 The suffering of the Bisshope of Doubleane and a nombre of Jessewittes within his realme. **1602** T. Fitzherbert *Apol.* 47 a, Against a Martyn Luther and his cursed crue of vitious Apostates he raysed an Ignatius de Loyola with his blessed company, of vertuous, and Apostolical priests, commonly called Iesuites. **1647** Cowley *Mistr., Prophet* i, Teach Jesuits that have travell'd far, to Lye, Teach Fire to burn, and Winds to blow. **1769** Blackstone *Comm.* IV. viii. 104 We might call to witness the black intrigues of the Jesuits, so lately triumphant over Christendom, but now universally abandoned by even the Roman catholic powers. **1838** Macaulay *Ess., Temple* (1887) 445 That new brood of Oxonian sectaries who unite the worst parts of the Jesuit to the worst parts of the Orangeman. **1846** McCulloch *Acc. Brit. Empire* (1854) II. 253 The only class of Christians at present proscribed on account of religious opinions are the Jesuits, and members of orders bound by monastic or religious vows. **1846** W. F. Hook *Church Dict.* (ed. 5) 491 The Jesuits assume neither the name, quality, nor way of living, of monks. They call themselves an *order of priests*... The end of their institution is the salvation of souls: they preach, instruct youth, read lectures, and dispute and write against heretics. **1913** G. P. Gooch *Hist. & Historians in 19th Cent.* xxvi. 530 Renan sharply castigates the futility of the Priestly Code and the sterile scholasticism of its commentators. Nehemiah is described as the first Jesuit, who turned Jerusalem into a tomb. **1914** [see boyo]. **1932** E. Bevan *Christianity* ix. 191 Jesuits were trained by a severe discipline, not to live in retirement from the world, but to mingle with the world in order to conquer it for the Church. **1934** H. H. Gowen *Hist. Relig.* xxxix. 598 The Jesuits as a body, by their splendid training, their broad-minded knowledge of human nature, and by their extraordinary personal devotion, did much to win for the Roman Churches territory far larger in area than ..had been lost. **1939** [see iconology 1]. **1953** J. E. Neale *Elizabeth I & her Parliaments* vii. i. 370 The Jesuits came, as it were, direct from England's capital enemy, the Pope. **1959** L. Hanke *Aristotle & Amer. Indians* viii. 108 The efforts of another Jesuit, Antonio Vieira, in the seventeenth century to protect the natives of Brazil. **1972** J. P. Kenyon *Popish Plot* i. 22 The Jesuits..aimed to draw England into the revitalized Church Universal of the Counter-Reformation.

2. *transf.* A dissembling person; a prevaricator. Also *fig. depreciatory.*

1640 A. Leighton *Pet. to Parlt.* in Chandler *Hist. Persec.* (1736) 367 Apprehended in Black-Fryers,..and..dragged along (and all the way reproached by the name of Jesuit and Traitor). **1692** Washington tr. *Milton's Def. Pop.* iii. M.'s Wks. (1851) 90 Your self are more a Jesuit than he, nay worse than any of that Crew. **1777** J. Adams in *Fam. Lett.* (1876) 306 To humble the pride of some Jesuits, who call themselves Quakers. **1851** Gallenga *Italy* 45 He was himself a Jesuit in all but the cunning. [**1852** Thackeray *Esmond* I. v. 99 Father Holt wore more suits of clothes than one. All Jesuits do. You know what deceivers we are, Harry.] **1855** C. Kingsley *Westward Ho!* III. ii. 34 Eustace is a man no longer; he is become a thing, a tool, a Jesuit. **1856** J. W. Carlyle *Jrnl.* 11 Apr. in *Lett. & Memorials* (1883) II. 271 'I'll tell you what to do,' said this Jesuit of a baker; 'Go and join the Methodists' chapel for six months; make yourself agreeable to them, and you'll soon have friends that will help you in your object.' **1878** *N. Amer. Rev.* CXXVI. 504 The political Jesuits of the South. *c* **1879** E. Dickinson *Poems* (1955) III. 1015 The Jesuit of Orchards He cheats as he enchants. **1907** G. B. Shaw *Major Barbara* iii. 285 Charles Lomax: you are a fool. Adolphus Cusins: you are a Jesuit. Stephen: you are a prig. Barbara: you are a lunatic. **1923** D. L. Sayers *Whose Body?* ii. 40 Gentlemen, we are not Jesuits, we are straightforward Englishmen. You cannot ask a British-born jury to convict any man on the authority of a probable opinion. **1947** V. S. Pritchett in *Horizon* May 241 Rubashov and Gletkin are a sad pair of Jesuits consumed and dulled as human beings by their casuistry. **1948** D. Shub *Lenin* vii. 152 In July 1916, Viacheslav Menzhinsky, later chief of the Soviet secret police,..wrote: Lenin is a political Jesuit who over the course of many years has molded Marxism to his aims of the moment.

3. A kind of dress worn by ladies in the latter part of the 18th century: see quot. 1885.

1767 *Trial Ld. Grosvenor* (Fairholt). **1775** *Misc.* in *Ann. Reg.* 193/2 Under the titles of hats, bonnets, sacks, jesuits, brunswicks, poloneses, muffs, &c. **1885** *Fairholt's Costume Eng.* (ed. 3) Gloss., *Jesuit*, a dress worn by ladies in 1767, buttoning up to the neck, a kind of indoor morning gown.

4. *attrib.* and *Comb.* **a.** *attrib.* or *adj.* That is a Jesuit; of or belonging to the Society of Jesus; Jesuitical. **b.** *Comb.*, as †*Jesuit-founder.*

1613 Purchas *Pilgrimage* (1614) 171, I had beene reading the life and precepts of Ignatius Leiola the Iesuite-founder. **1660** F. Brooke tr. *Le Blanc's Trav.* 215 Instructed by the Jesuite Fathers. **1764** Churchill *Gotham* ii. 394 If..from the Jesuit school some precious knave Conviction feign'd. **1844** H. H. Wilson *Brit. India* I. 475 To the Jesuit missionaries succeeded those of the Lutheran church. **1874** J. R. Green *Short Hist. Eng. People* vii. 402 The torture and death of the Jesuit martyrs sent a thrill of horror through the whole Catholic Church. **1922** Joyce *Ulysses* 220 Father Conmee..thought..of the book that might be written about jesuit houses. **1939** *Times Lit. Suppl.* 14 Jan. 20 One of the most heroic members of one of the most heroic bodies in the history of the world, the Jesuit mission to the Hurons. **1950** *Chambers's Encycl.* VIII. 273/1 In 1872 supervision of schools was reserved exclusively for the government of Prussia and the Jesuit Order was banned from Germany altogether. **1953** J. E. Neale *Elizabeth I & her Parliaments* vii. i. 370 The Jesuit mission to England led by two distinguished and contrasting men, Parsons and Campion. **1956** *Atlantic Monthly* Nov. 43/2 It was a form of answer well known to the examiners—the famous Jesuit equivocation. **1966** D. Johnson *France & Dreyfus Affair* xiii. 220 The tighter the organisation of the group, Assumptionist or Jesuit, the greater the hostility towards Dreyfus. **1972** J. P. Kenyon *Popish Plot* vi. 182 The suspicion that he had designs on the family estate, which should have descended to his Jesuit brother, now in Newgate.

c. Special genitival combinations. **Jesuits' bark**, the medicinal bark of species of *Cinchona*, Peruvian bark (introduced into Europe from the Jesuit Missions in S. America); also applied to the bark of *Iva frutescens* (*false* or *bastard Jesuits' bark*). **Jesuits' drops**, 'name given to a preparation of garlic, Peruvian balsam, and sarsaparilla' (Mayne *Expos. Lex.* 1855). **Jesuits' nut**, a name for the seed of *Trapa natans.* † **Jesuits' powder** (F. *poudre des Jésuites*), an old name for powdered Peruvian bark. **Jesuits' tea**, an infusion of the leaves of *Psoralea glandulosa*, a South American leguminous shrub.

1694 Salmon *Bate's Disp.* (1713) 250/2 *Cortex Peruvianus* or *Jesuits Bark in fine Powder newly made. **1714** *Phil. Trans.* XXIX. 48 Three Ounces of Jesuits Bark. **1760** J. Lee *Introd. Bot.* App. 305 False Jesuit's Bark, *Iva.* **1799** J. Robertson *Agric. Perth* 316 A gentleman..told me, that a little warm milk with some Jesuit bark would cure the trembling. **1880** C. R. Markham *Peruv. Bark* 14 In 1670 these fathers sent parcels of the powdered bark to Rome... Hence the name of 'Jesuits' bark', and 'Cardinal's bark'. **1783** Pott *Chirurg. Wks.* II. 228 He had for a month before been taking *Jesuit's drops and other quack medicines. **1866** *Treas. Bot.* 1161/1 The seeds..of *T[rapa] natans*—called *Jesuit's nuts at Venice, and Chataigne d'Eau by the French—are ground into flour and made into bread in some parts of Southern Europe. **1659** *Merc. Pol.* No. 553 *Advt.*, The Feaver bark, commonly called the *Jesuites powder which is so famous for the cure of all manner of agues. *a* **1715** Burnet *Own Time* iii. (1724) I. 474 The fits did not return after the King [Chas. II] took *Quinquina*, called in England the *Jesuits powder*. **1866** *Treas. Bot.* 935/2 In Chili the leaves of *P[soralea] glandulosa*, there called Culen, are used as a substitute for tea under the name of *Jesuit's Tea; but their infusion..appears to be valued more for its medicinal properties.

d. Use *attrib.* to designate a type of Chinese 18th-century export porcelain decorated with religious pictures copied from European designs.

1882 W. W. Old *Indo-European Porc.* 5 Dealers as a rule calling it [*sc.* Indo-European porcelain] 'Jesuit china', a general impression has prevailed that it was the work of the converts to the early Romish missions in China and Japan. **1898** W. G. Gulland *Chinese Porc.* 12 Christianity has left little mark on the ceramics of China;..few pieces display biblical subjects or Christian emblems, and such are known as 'Jesuit China'. **1900** F. Litchfield *Pott. & Porc.* vii. 114 This is called 'Jesuit china', because it is said that it was painted to the order of..the Jesuit missionaries. **1927** W. B. Honey *Guide Later Chinese Porc.* viii. 67 'Jesuit china' was ..probably copied from designs supplied by the merchants. **1952** M. Anderson *Story Chinese Porc.* 46 Flat-edged plates with biblical subjects painted in a grey-black are the usual features of these 'Jesuit' pieces. **1962** D. Imber tr. *Beurdeley's Porc. E. India Co.* 141/2 The Roman Catholic creed was foremost in Europe at the time, but the great reformers, Calvin and Luther, are also represented on different plates and servers. The British Museum has a plate

representing John of Leyden, the leader of the Anabaptists. It will be clear, then, that the title *Jesuit porcelain* cannot be maintained in the light of the facts.

'Jesuit, *v.* [f. prec. sb.]

†**1.** *intr.* To act the Jesuit. *Obs. rare.*

1601 *Archpr. Controv.* (1898) II. 164 Yf we would have Jesuited and caried so small a respect to charity.

†**2.** *trans.* To make a Jesuit of; to imbue with Jesuit principles. Chiefly in *pa. pple. Obs.*

1601 (*title*) Important Considerations which ought to move all Trve and sovnd Catholickes who are not wholly Iesuited. **1621** in *Crt. & Times Jas. I* (1849) II. 274 He is.. popishly affected, and even jesuited.

†**3.** To dose with Jesuits' bark: see prec. 4 c. *Obs. nonce-use.*

1689 Harvey *Curing Dis. by Expect.* iv. 32 The course of bleeding.. purging and Jesuiting.

4. Used by Freeman for: To alter (an ancient church) into the Renaissance style, in which the Jesuits commonly built their churches, *c* 1560–1680.

1872 Freeman in W. R. W. Stephens *Life & Lett.* (1895) II. 59 St. Michael's has been Jesuited inside. **1876** —— *Hist. Sk., Ancona* 155 That [taste] which condemned the north transept and the crypt below it to be mercilessly Jesuited. **1891** —— *Sk. fr. French Trav.* Ser. iv. 76 A systematic Jesuiting which the church underwent.

†**Jesuital**, *a. Obs. rare.* = Jesuitical 1.

1672 Stillingfl. *Idol. Ch. Rome* (ed. 2) 374 What spight the Jesuital order bears to the authority of Bishops.

†**'Jesuited**, *a. Obs.* [f. Jesuit *sb.* or *v.* + -ed.] Made or become a Jesuit; influenced or corrupted by Jesuits; imbued with the principles or character of the Jesuits; Jesuitical. (Frequent in 17th c.)

1601 A. Copley (*title*) An Answere to a Letter of a Iesuited Gentleman. **1660** T. M. *Hist. Independ.* iv. 82 Sir Henry Vane himself with his Jesuited and poysonous breath sought to infect him. *a* **1716** Blackall *Disc. Matt.* v. 10 Wks. 1723 I. 126 A Jesuited Papist.. may think that he does God and Religion good Service, by raising a Rebellion against his Prince, whom he accounts a Heretick. **1834** *Gentl. Mag.* CIV. i. 139 Denouncing him as the most Jesuited Papist alive, and stating that he retained a Jesuit in his house.

Jesuitess ('dʒɛzjuːɪtɪs). [f. Jesuit *sb.* + -ess: cf. F. *jésuitesse*.] A female Jesuit; a member of an order of nuns established on the principles of the Jesuits, but not recognized by papal authority, and suppressed by Pope Urban VIII.

1600 W. Watson *Decacordon* (1602) 44 You shall haue a yong Iesuitesse ready to flie in his face, to cast the house out at the window. **1616** Sir D. Carleton *Lett.* (1775) 68 Mrs. Ward and her fellow.. at Liege.. having bought a house.. which they intend to make a college of Jesuitesses. **1645** Evelyn *Diary* 6 May, There was now at Rome one Mrs. Ward, an English devotee, who much solicited for an Order of Jesuitesses. **1898** *Weekly Reg.* 9 July 43 The Congregation popularly miscalled Jesuitesses was suppressed by Urban VIII. in 1631.

Jesuitic (dʒɛzjuː'ɪtɪk), *a.* Now *rare.* [f. as prec. + -ic: cf. F. *jésuitique*.]

1. = next, 1.

1804 W. Taylor in *Ann. Rev.* II. 254 The other secret directors of the jesuitic interest. **1888** *Biblioth. Sacra* Jan. 194 The Jesuitic maxim, that 'he who has the schools has the future'.

2. = next, 2.

1640 R. Baillie *Canterb. Self-convict.* Postscr. 2 In these Jesuiticke arts ye prove so excelent. **1788** H. Walpole in *Walpoliana, Caution to yng. Auth.* 23 Pope was, perhaps, too refined and Jesuitic a professor of authorship. **1840** Carlyle *Heroes* vi. (1858) 361 A hypocrite shrouding himself in confused Jesuitic jargon!

Jesuitical (dʒɛzjuː'ɪtɪkəl), *a.* [See -ical.]

1. Of or pertaining to the Jesuits; belonging to the Society of Jesus; Jesuit.

1600 W. Watson *Decacordon* (1602) 230 The most dangerous infections, and.. irremedilesse poyson of the Iesuiticall doctrine. **1647** *Mass. Col. Rec.* (1854) III. 112 The secrit practises of those of the Jesuiticall order. **1748** *Anson's Voy.* iii. x. 413 The behaviour of the Magistrates.. at Canton, sufficiently refutes these jesuitical fictions. **1837** Hallam *Hist. Lit.* iii. iv. §14 Productions so little regarded as those of the jesuitical casuists. **1848** *Jesuitism in Church* iv. 41 Jesuitical principles are by no means confined to those who openly adhere to the rule of Loyola. *c* **1905** H. A. Henderson *Shall we tolerate Jesuits?* vii. 24 An influx of Jesuitical religious Orders. **1932** G. F.-H. Berkeley *Italy in Making* I. xvi. 238 The head of a Jesuitical society, the *Amicizia cattolica*. **1943** H. J. Muller *Sci. & Crit.* 195 It has therefore incorporated the Jesuitical principle that the end justifies the means. **1947** C. J. Cadoux *Philip of Spain & Netherlands* vii. 147 The need of money for.. launching his Jesuitical seminaries.. caused the pope great financial difficulty.

2. Having the character ascribed to the Jesuits; deceitful, dissembling; practising equivocation, prevarication, or mental reservation of truth. Often used in sense 'hair-splitting', keenly analytical.

1613 Purchas *Pilgrimage* (1614) 530 Easie it may be indeed to seared Iesuiticall Consciences, that account Treason Religion. **1771** Smollett *Humph. Cl.* 13 July, All which Mr. Lismahago answered with a sort of jesuitical reserve. **1817** Coleridge *Biog. Lit.* II. xxiii. 288 The low cunning and Jesuitical trick with which she deludes her husband. **1829** *Jesuitism & Methodism* I. viii. 119 She trusted.. to preserve Cordelia from being perverted, by Jesuitical craft, from the true light. **1871** Smiles *Charac.* vii. (1876) 207 Their jesuitical cleverness in equivocation. **1925** T. Dreiser *Amer. Trag.* (1926) II. iii. xxvi. 327 'Hesitating fatally but not criminally at the one time in his life when he should not have hesitated'—a really strong if jesuitical plea which was not without its merits and its weight. **1932** E. Bevan *Christianity* ix. 192 Two things especially brought odium upon the name of Jesuit. One is the suspicion of vast subterranean intrigue carried on to gain worldly power..; and the other is the belief that the Jesuits cultivate an immoral casuistry—whence the adjective 'jesuitical'—and especially teach that a good end justifies any kind of means. **1950** *Nation* (N.Y.) 16 Dec. 595 If they insist on debating jesuitical verbal formulas instead of effective and enforceable agreements.. then no worth-while end would be served by attempting to bargain with them. **1971** M. Hastings *Jesuit Child* i. i. 14 People only call a man jesuitical when they are beaten in an argument. **1972** *New Yorker* 29 Apr. 112/2 The film ['Loot'] is made up of people who regard themselves as lone wolves with a unique hold on sense who have to put up with the Jesuitical twitterings of everybody else. **1974** *Daily Tel.* 17 Dec. 12 An argument of such Jesuitical subtlety that one would have thought it could impress no one of moderate common sense or sanity.

Jesu'itically, *adv.* [f. prec. + -ly².] In a Jesuitical manner; with equivocation or mental reservation; with cunningly dissembled policy.

1624 F. White *Repl. Fisher* 570 Your protestation.. must be vnderstood Iesuitically, with mentall limitation. **1726** Amherst *Terræ Fil.* xxxiii. 177 If you have ever so many ugly [qualities], they will be either palliated, or jesuitically interpreted into good ones. **1855** Macaulay *Hist. Eng.* xiv. III. 453 To reason more Jesuitically than the Jesuits themselves. **1946** *Protestant* (Boston, Mass.) Oct.–Nov. 48 Yet so jesuitically has the argument of 'discrimination' been presented that it has taken in even some well-intentioned progressive citizens. **1962** *Punch* 7 Feb. 253/3 'It's an ancient highway, a bit of old England,' he pleads jesuitically, caring nothing for the means so that his end be achieved. **1974** I. Murdoch *Sacred & Profane Love Machine* 240 Monty in black linen jacket and white shirt, his dark hair well combed and neat, his black shoes ludicrously well polished, was looking his most jesuitically untouchable.

†**'Jesuitish**, *a. Obs.* [See -ish¹.] Belonging to, or characteristic of, the Jesuits; Jesuitical.

1600 W. Watson *Decacordon* (1602) 242 His most Turkish, Iesuitish, Puritanian, and barbarous designements. **1614** Bp. Hall *Recoll. Treat.* 524 The ten Patriarchs of the Iesuitish Religion. **1695** Sage *Article* Wks. 1844 I. 303 Disingenuous and Jesuitish fetches.

Jesuitism ('dʒɛzjuːɪˌtɪz(ə)m). [f. as prec. + -ism: cf. F. *jésuitisme*.]

1. The system, doctrine, principles, or practice of the Jesuits.

1609 Bp. W. Barlow *Answ. Nameless Cath.* 254 It is one point of Iesuitisme. **1817** Lady Morgan *France* v. (1818) II. 49 In their contests on Jansenism and Jesuitism. **1862** Max Müller *Chips* (1880) I. ix. 185 Even Christianity has been depraved into Jesuitism and Mormonism. **1897** J. McCabe *Twelve Yrs. in Monastery* ix. 187, I have met very many priests who quite accept the Protestant Alliance version of Jesuitism. **1901** W. C. Copeland *Empire's Greatest Danger* is. 58 How can one prove that the origin of this particular 'genius' of Jesuitism belongs to Mussulman monasticism? *c* **1905** H. A. Henderson *Shall we tolerate Jesuits?* viii. 32 Jesuitism is too deadly a danger for us as a Protestant nation to tolerate. **1913** J. McCabe *Candid. Hist. Jesuits* vii. 167 (*heading*) The first century of Jesuitism.

2. Principles or practice of such a character as those ascribed to the Jesuits; Jesuitry.

1613 Purchas *Pilgrimage* (1864) 54 After this they tried experiments: First by poyson, and this was the Iesuites Iesuitisme. **1749** J. Wesley *Jrnl.* 2 June (1912) III. 404 A gentlewoman informed me that Dr. B had averred to her.. that it [*sc.* Methodism] was all Jesuitism at the bottom. Alas for poor Dr. B.! **1829** *Jesuitism & Methodism* I. xi. 187 Had he been present,.. spite of Jesuitism and priestly pride, it is probable his secret would have escaped him. **1838** *Fraser's Mag.* XVIII. 751 A piece of Protestant jesuitism, quite worthy of Loyola. **1863** Kinglake *Crimea* (1876) I. xii. 193 The mere inverted Jesuitism of a man resolved to do good that evil might come. **1956** *Time* 2 Jan. 58/2 Her plans to give 'freedom' to Bavaria were blocked by what she called 'the cloven foot of Jesuitism'. **1970** *Guardian* 25 July 7/2 Both Catholics and Communists suffered from Jesuitism, from a belief that the ends justified the means, and the Church would be willing to come to agreement when the terms suited its books.

3. A Jesuitical quibble or equivocation. *rare.*

1749 Bp. Lavington *Enthus. Method. & Papists* (1754) I. ii. xxxiii, Be open and sincere, consistent and uniform. Affect not Jesuitisms. **1781** S. A. Peters *Hist. Conn.* 289, I hope Mr. Neal did not mean to quibble, as the New-Englanders generally do, by a jesuitism, viz. that religion is peaceable and admits not of quarrels.

Jesuitize ('dʒɛzjuːɪˌtaɪz), *v.* [See -ize.]

1. *intr.* To play the Jesuit; to propound Jesuitical doctrines.

1644 R. Harwood *K. David's Sanct.* 14 Either the Jesuite doth Platonize, or Plato did Jesuitize, when he first sent abroad his *Deos intermedios*. **1825** *Blackw. Mag.* XVIII. 234 The opinions of universities either Jesuitizing like Bossuet, or trembling before the coming storm.

2. *trans.* To imbue with Jesuit principles; to make Jesuitical. Hence '**Jesuitized** *ppl. a.*

1679 C. Nesse *Antid. Popery* 151 Which all jesuitiz'd papists have received. **1830** Southey in *Q. Rev.* XLIII. 31 How nearly Jesuitized Christianity had become the ruling religion in Japan. **1885** Mrs. H. Ward tr. *Amiel's Jrnl.* II. 92 A population jesuitised by education.

Jesuitocracy (-'ɒkrəsɪ). *nonce-wd.* [See -cracy.] The rule or government of Jesuits.

1851 Kingsley *Yeast* v, Results of a century of Jesuitocracy, as they were represented on the French stage in the year 1793.

†**'Jesuitrice, -trix.** *Obs.* [irreg. f. Jesuit *sb.*, after Fr. fem. agent-nouns in *-trice*, Lat. *-trix*.] = Jesuitess.

1629 Wadsworth *Eng. Span. Pilgr.* iii. 30 These.. are growne to a faction, about the Iesuitrices or wandring Nuns, some allowing, some disliking them vtterly. *c* **1665** R. Carpenter *Pragm. Jesuit* 27/2 You have seen Mrs. Ward and her Jesuitrices, as tender-hearted people call them.

Jesuitry ('dʒɛzjuːɪtrɪ). [f. Jesuit *sb.* + -ry.]

1. The principles, doctrine, or practices of the Jesuits, or such as are ascribed to them; subtle casuistry or prevarication; the doctrine that the end justifies the means.

1832 Coleridge *Table T.* (1851) 190 The honest German Jesuitry of Dobrizhoffer. **1837** Carlyle *Fr. Rev.* III. ii. vii, Justifying, *motivant*, that most miserable word of theirs, by some brief casuistry and jesuitry. **1847** G. E. Corrie 3 May in Holroyd *Mem.* xi. (1890) 249. **1891** Sidgwick *Elem. Politics* 196 The general indignation caused by Jesuitry. **1901** W. C. Copeland *Empire's Greatest Danger* vi. 40 Belgium cleared its borders of Jesuitry in 1818. **1911** *Encycl. Brit.* XV. 340/1 A certain characteristic, which soon began to manifest itself in an impatience of episcopal control, showed that the quality of 'Jesuitry', usually associated with the Society, was singularly lacking in their dealings with opponents. **1944** *Atlantic Monthly* Nov. 75/1 Humanism considered as an intellectual discipline-for-discipline's-sake.. is a prime specific for such ills as bigotry and puritanism and jesuitry and vulgarity.. and the complacency of the bourgeois mind. **1951** R. Hall *Short Hist. Ital. Lit.* 261 The words *Jesuitry* and *Jesuitical* have become proverbial in reference to dishonestly subtle dialectics and hypocritical condonement of evil practice. **1972** *Times Lit. Suppl.* 22 Dec. 1551/1 Casuistry like Jesuitry is a perfectly respectable word, but it has acquired a sinister connotation.

2. *nonce-use.* (See Jesuit *v.* 4.)

1881 Freeman *Subj. Venice, Zara* 130 The triforium has an air of Jesuitry; but it seems to be genuine, only more or less plastered.

Jesus ('dʒiːzəs). [a. L. *Iēsū-s*, a. Gr. Ἰησοῦς, ad. late Heb. or Aram. *yēshūăʕ*, *Jeshua*, for the earlier *y'hōshūăʕ*, *Jehoshua* or *Joshua* (explained as 'Jah (or Jahveh) is salvation': cf. *y'shūʕāh* 'salvation, deliverance', and Matt. i. 21), a frequent Jewish personal name, which, as that of the Founder of Christianity, has passed through Gr. and L. into all the languages of Christendom.

In OE. rendered by *hǽlend* 'saviour' (see healend); but during the ME. period regularly used in its OF. (objective) form *Iesu* (*Jesu*). The (L. nom.) form *Iesus* (*Jesus*) was rare in ME., but became the regular Eng. form in 16th c. Yet in Tindale's New Test., 1525–34, the form *Iesu* was generally used where the Gr. has Ἰησοῦ, the Vulgate *Iesu*, in the vocative and oblique cases. This was, as a rule, retained by Coverdale 1535, and in the Great Bible 1539, also, in the vocative instances, in the Bishops' Bible 1568; but in representing the Gr. oblique cases, this has *Iesus*. *Iesu* disappeared from the Geneva 1557 (exc. in one place), and from the Rhemish 1582, and the version of 1611. *Jesu* was frequent in the earlier forms of the Book of Common Prayer, and survives in one place; in later use it occurs in hymns, rarely in nom. or obj., but frequently in the vocative. In hymns, the possessive *Jesus'* is commonly sung ('dʒiːzjuːz).

In ME. the name was rarely written in full, being usually represented by the abbreviations ihu, and ihc, ihs, ihus, or ihu, etc.: see IHS. These have been commonly expanded by modern editors as *Ihesu*, *Ihesus*, forms which occur occasionally in MSS. and in early 16th c. printed books.]

1. a. The proper name.

a **1175** *Cott. Hom.* 235 Ures hlafordes to-cyme þes helendes iesu [*ed.* ihesu] cristes. *c* **1240** *Ureisun* in *Lamb. Hom.* 200 Iesu soð god, soð mon, & soð meidenes bern. *Ibid.* 202 þet mei iesu þis baldeliche seggen to þe. **1377** Langl. *P. Pl.* B. Prol. 165 Were þere a belle on here beiȝ, bi Iesu [*ed.* Ihesu], as me thynketh, Men myȝte wite where þei went, and awei renne. *c* **1435** *Torr. Portugal* 1450 For Iesu love that died on rood. **1526** Tindale *Matt.* i. 1 The boke off the generacion off Ihesus Christ. [So i. 16; *elsewhere usually* Iesus.] —— *Matt.* viii. 29 O Iesu the sonne off God. [So Coverd., *Great B.*, *Bps'.*, *Geneva*; *Rhem.*, and 1611 Iesus.] —— *Luke* xvii. 13 Iesu master, have mercy on vs. [So Cov., *Gr.*, *Bps'.*; *Gen.*, *Rh.*, 1611 Iesus.] [So also *Acts* vii. 59.] —— *Luke* xviii. 38 Iesus the sonne of David, have mercy on me. [Cov., *Gr.*, *Bps'.* Iesu; *Gen.*, etc. Iesus.] —— *Rev.* xxii. 20 Even soo: come lorde Iesu [so Cov., *Gr.*; *Bps'.*, *Gen.*, etc. Iesus.] —— *Luke* viii. 28 What have I to do wyth the Iesus the sonne off the moost hyest? [So all later versions.] —— *Rev.* xxii. 21 The grace of oure lorde Iesus [**1534** Iesu, so Cov., *Gr.*; *Gen.*, *Bps'.*, etc. Iesus] Christ be with you all. —— *Rom.* xv. 17 Wheroff I maye reioyse in Christ Iesu. [So Cov., *Gr.*; *Gen.*, *Bps'.*, etc. Iesus.] —— xv. 30 For oure lorde Iesu [**1534** Iesus: so all later versions] Christes sake. **1544** *Supplic. to Hen. VIII* (E.E.T.S.) 57 Through thy Sone Ihesus Christe. **1552** *Bk. Com. Prayer, Gen. Confess.*, According to thy promyses declared vnto mankynde, in Christe Iesu oure Lorde. [So in mod. Pr. Bk.] **1633** G. Herbert *Temple, Jesu*, Jesu is in my heart, his sacred name Is deeply carved there. **1740** C. Wesley *Hymn*, Jesu, lover of my soul, Let me to thy bosom fly. **1779** Cowper *Olney Hymns* xlix. 2 Lord, my soul with pleasure springs When Jesus' name I hear. **1827** Keble *Chr. Y., St. Stephen's Day* v, Jesu, do Thou my soul receive. **1881** N. T. (R.V.) *John* xii. 9 They came, not for Jesus' [**1611** Iesus] sake only.

b. Used as (or as part of) an oath or as a strong exclamation of surprise, disbelief, dismay, or the like; also in various phrases, as *by Jesus*,

Jesus (H.) Christ, *Jesus wept*. Cf. GEE *int.*², JEEZ(E *int.*

1377 LANGL. *P. Pl.* B. III. 154 Bi iesus [*ed.* Ihesus], with here ieweles, ȝowre iustices she shendeth. **1592** SHAKES. *Rom. & Jul.* II. iv. 31 Iesu a very good blade, a very tall man. *Ibid.* v. 29 Iesu what hast? can you not stay a while? **1676** ETHEREDGE *Man of Mode* III. i. Wks. (1888) 283 Jesu! madam, what will your mother think is become of you? **1753** GRAY *Long Story* in *Six Poems* 22 Jesu-Maria! Madam Bridget, Why, what can the Viscountess mean? **1922** JOYCE *Ulysses* 38 Jesus! If I fell over a cliff. *Ibid.* 39 Yes, sir. No, sir. Jesus wept: and no wonder, by Christ. *Ibid.* 131 By Jesus, she had the foot and mouth disease and no mistake! **1923** *Dialect Notes* V. 212 *Jesus Christ*, an expletive or exclamation common to both men and women and considered by neither as in any wise profane. **1924** *Ibid.* 264 Jesus Christ, Jesus H. Christ, holy jumping Jesus Christ. **1936** S. SASSOON *Sherston's Progress* IV. iii. 273 Someone gasping by, carrying a bag of rations—'Jesus, ain't we there yet?' **1943** 'C. DICKSON' *She died a Lady* xvi. 135 Have we heard about him?.. Jesus H. Christ! **1966** A. LA BERN *Goodbye Piccadilly* vi. 66 It's you she's describing, your clothes, everything. Oh, Jesus wept! **1968** B. HEALEY *Murder without Crime* iii. 59 Jesus! It's murder out there. **1970** T. LEWIS *Jack's Return Home* 223 'Jesus Christ!' he says softly. 'Jesus H. Christ.' **1974** I. MURDOCH *Sacred & Profane Love Machine* 94 He's so spineless... He just wants to be let off and I let him off. Jesus wept!

†**2.** A figure or representation of Jesus Christ, as a CRUCIFIX or ECCE HOMO, or an emblem or device such as the letters IHS, etc. *Obs.*

1487 *Will of Laurence* (Somerset Ho.), My Jhus of gold.

3. *attrib.* and *Comb.*, as ***Jesus-worshipper***; ***Jesus-like*** adj.; **Jesus day**, the festival of the Name of Jesus, 7 Aug.; **Jesus mass**, a votive mass in honour of the Name of Jesus.

1540 Ihc masse [see IHS]. **1546** *Acc.* in Sharp *Cov. Myst.* (1825) 214 Paid to þe mynstrell on Jhesus day at Smyths tavern xijd. **1641** SIR E. DERING *Sp. on Relig.* xi. 40 He is not afraid to call Christians Iesu-worshippers. *a* **1711** KEN *Urania* Poet. Wks. 1721 IV. 474 No Grace on earth more Jesus-like appears Than Charity. **1886** *Archæol. Cantiana* XVI. p. lviii, The Jesus altar and Jesus mass are often mentioned in wills of parishioners [of Sandwich].

b. Used *attrib.* or *Comb.* to designate a fervently evangelical type of Christian, or a group of such people, or things characteristic of them.

1970 *Catholic Worker* Feb. 2/3 He still spoke contemptuously of Jesus-shouters. **1970** *N.Y. Times* 22 Feb. 64 They gladly accept the name Jesus Freaks and have long hair and other marks of hip culture. **1971** *New Scientist* 3 June 588/1 Its Jesus shops, symbols of the brand of freaked-out Christianity that has replaced Flower Power as a culture. **1971** *Listener* 9 Sept. 324/1 The Jesus people, offering religion as a substitute for the drug cult among young people, arrived from America. **1971** *Daily Colonist* (Victoria, B.C.) 12 Dec. 4/1 Certainly the sect seems to have outfreaked all its competitors in the 'Jesus Freak' movement. **1972** *Sat. Rev.* (U.S.) 6 May 58/2 (*heading*) Meditations on the Jesus Movement. *Ibid.*, The Jesus revolution is simply the most recent, popular, and obvious expression of that need. *Ibid.*, The Jesus-cults.. offer the young.. an instantaneous and push-button forgiveness. **1972** *Awake!* 8 Nov. 3/1 Also called 'Jesus freaks', or 'Street Christians', they put up Jesus posters, wear Jesus buttons, and emblazon their car bumpers with stickers that say: 'Honk, if you love Jesus.' **1973** *Times* 3 Mar. 6/3 Dr Ramsey said: 'I welcome Jesus Freaks as a genuine religious movement.'

jesyne, variant of GESINE *Obs.*, childbed.

jet (dʒɛt), *sb.*¹ and *a.* Forms: α. 4–5 **gete**, 4–6 **geet**, 4–7 **get**, 5 **geete**, **geyte**, **geitt**, 5–6 **gett**, 6 **gette**, **gete**, **geytt**, (**gate**, **giette**), 6–7 **geat(e**. β. 4–6 **ieet**, 5 **iet(e**, 6–7 **ieit**, **ieate**, **iet**, 6–8 **ieat**, **jett**, 7 **jette**, 7– **jet**. [ME. a. OF. *jaiet* (12th c. in Hatz.-Darm.), *jayet* (F. *jais*):—L. *gagātēs*, a. Gr. γαγάτης: see GAGATE. In Du. *git*. The Eng. may partly represent the OF. fem. *jayete*, *geiete*, Walloon *gayète* (Godef.).]

A. *sb.* **1.** A hard compact black form of 'brown coal' or lignite, capable of receiving a brilliant polish. It is used in making toys, buttons, and personal ornaments; and has the property of attracting light bodies when electrified by rubbing.

α. *a* **1387** *Sinon. Barthol.* (Anecd. Oxon.) 22 *Gagates*, lapis est qui trahit paleas et cortices tritici, i. geet. **1398** TREVISA *Barth. De P.R.* XVI. xlix. (Tollem. MS.), Get is calde Gagates, and is a boystous ston. *c* **1420** *Pallad. on Husb.* IV. 694 Take oxon yonge.. Their lippes and their eyen blaak as gete. **1502** ARNOLDE *Chron.* (1811) 191 By troy weyght is bought and solde golde syluer perlys gette. **1513** DOUGLAS *Æneis* X. iii. 40 The blak terebynthine Growis by Orycia, and, as the geit dois schyne. **1599** DALLAM *Trav.* (Hakl. Soc.) 80 Neagers that weare as blacke as geate. *a* **1661** FULLER *Worthies* (1840) III. 392 The virtues of geat are hitherto concealed. **1688** R. HOLME *Armoury* III. 251/2 Get, a stone,.. some write Jeat.

β. *c* **1386** CHAUCER *Nun's Pr. T.* 41 His Coomb was redder than the fyn coral.. His byle was blak and as the Ieet [*v.rr.* iet, gete] it shoon. **1463** *Bury Wills* (Camden) 15 A peyre of smale bedys of jeet. **1657** TRAPP *Comm. Esther* i. 9 Having faculty attractive with the Jeat, and retentive with the Adamant. **1784** COWPER *Task.* I. 122 The bramble, black as jet. **1838** JAMES *Robber* i, The buttons were of polished jet. **1875** *Ure's Dict. Arts* III. 8 Jet occurs in the Upper Lias shale in the neighbourhood of Whitby in Yorkshire, in which locality this beautiful substance has been worked for many hundred years. **1894** ROSCOE & SCHORLEMMER *Chem.* I 688 Jet is a black variety of brown coal, compact in texture, and taking a good polish. Hence it is largely used in jewellery.

†**b.** A piece of jet. *Obs.*

1598 B. JONSON *Ev. Man in Hum.* III. iii, Your lustre too'll.. Draw courtship to you, as a iet doth strawes. **1607** HEYWOOD *Fayre Mayde* Wks. 1874 II. 35 The drawing vertue of a sable jeat.

c. *dial.* Camel-coal, bituminous shale.

1893 *Northumbld. Gloss.*, *Jeat, jead, jit*, cannel coal, bituminous shale, jet.

†**2.** Black marble. *Obs.*

c **1440** *Sir Degrev.* 1461 Alle þe wallus of geete. **1591** GREENE *Maiden's Dr.* 2, I saw a silent spring railed in with jeat. *c* **1620** T. ROBINSON *Mary Magd.* 11 The battelments of smoothest Iett were made. **1648** J. RAYMOND *Il Mercurio Ital.* 95 [A statue of] Seneca bleeding to death, of Jet.

3. The colour of jet; a deep glossy black.

c **1450** *Songs & Carols* (1856) 31 His comb is of red corel, his tayil is of get. **1637** MILTON *Lycidas* 144 The pansy freaked with jet. **1711** STEELE *Spect.* No. 41 ¶3 Never Man was so enamoured.. of.. the bright Jett of her Hair. **1850** DOBELL *Roman* i. Poet. Wks. 1875 I. 3 Closer yet, eyes of jet.

†**4.** *Old Cant.* A lawyer. ***autem jet***, a clergyman. (App. referring to the black gown.)

c **1700** *Street Robberies Consider'd*, *Jet*, Lawyer. **1737** *Bacchus & Venus* (Cant. Dict.), *Jet*, a Lawyer. *Autem Jet*, a Parson. **1785** in GROSE *Dict. Vulg. T.*

B. *attrib.* or as *adj.* **1.** Made or consisting of jet.

1444 *Test. Ebor.* (Surtees) II. 106 To yᵉ vicar of Milton a pare of get bedds. **1596** NASHE *Saffron Walden* O iv, These ieat droppes which diuers weare at their eares instead of a iewell. *Mod. Price List.* Jet goods. Cut jet buttons. Black elastic belts, jet, silver and oxydised clasps.

fig. **1649** FULLER *Just Man's Funeral* 1 Jet memories (onely attracting straws and chaff unto them).

2. Of the colour of jet, jet-black.

1716 LADY M. W. MONTAGU *Let. to Lady Rich* 1 Dec., All the women have.. snowy foreheads and bosoms, jet eyebrows. **1792** S. ROGERS *Pleas. Mem.* II. 330 As the coot her jet-wing loved to lave. **1834** H. AINSWORTH *Rookwood* III. ii. (1878) 160 Hair, of the jettest dye.

b. *spec.* in names of certain animals and plants, as **jet ant**, a kind of ant (*Formica fuliginosa*); **jet slug**, a kind of slug; †**jet-wood**, ebony.

1607 TOPSELL *Four-f. Beasts* 193 The Ethyopians payed for a tribute vnto the king of Persia euery 3. yeare twenty of these [elephants'] teeth hung about with gold and Iet-wood. **1746** MILES in *Phil. Trans.* XLIV. 356 Five Species of Ants have occurred to the Observation of our Author... 2. The Jet Ant. **1747** GOULD *Eng. Ants* 3 The Red and Jet Ants are of an equal Largeness. *Ibid.* 23 The Queen of the Jets I had never the Pleasure of seeing. **1882** *Garden* 30 Dec. 579/1 The Jet Slug.. about 2½ inches long.

C. *Comb.*, as ***jet-miner***, ***-worker***; ***jet-embroidered***, ***jet-like*** adjs.; **jet-coal**, cannel-coal; **jet-glass**, black-coloured glass made into cheap jewellery in imitation of jet; **jet-rock**, a bituminous shale containing jet; **jet-seam** (see quot. 1891).

1606 SYLVESTER *Du Bartas* II. iv. I. *Tropheis* 1078 One-while set in a black Jet-like Chair. **1851** in *Illustr. Lond. News* 5 Aug. (1854) 119 Jet-miner. **1875** *Ure's Dict. Arts* III. 8 The jet-miner.. finding the jet spread out.. follows it with great care. *Ibid.*, The best jet is obtained from a lower bed of the upper lias formations. This bed.. is known as jet rock. *Ibid.* 10 The jet workers complain of the great scarcity of designs in jet. **1891** *Labour Commission Gloss.*, *Jet Seam*, a bed of Durham coal of a coarse cannel species, nearly approaching to a black shale. *Jet coal* burns with a bright flame, but loses little bulk in the fire. **1891** *Daily News* 24 Feb. 5/8 The daintiest little collars are jet-embroidered upon black silk muslin.

†**jet**, *sb.*² *Obs.* Forms: 4–5 **gett**, **get**, (4 **aget**), 4–6 **gette**; 4–5 **iett(e**, 4–6 **iet**. [app. a substitution of *jet* = F. *jet* throw, cast, for certain senses of CAST *sb.* This sense of *jet* may prob. have been in Anglo-Fr.; but is not recorded in Godefroy, his nearest sense being that of 'proposal, project', illustrated chiefly from Flanders.]

1. A device, a contrivance; = CAST *sb.* 24.

13.. *E.E. Allit. P.* B. 1354 In notyng of nwe metes & of nice gettes, Al watz þe mynde of þat man, on misschapen þinges. *c* **1380** *Sir Ferumb.* 1681 Al of marbre y-mad ys sche wyþ a quynte iet. *c* **1386** CHAUCER *Can. Yeom. Prol. & T.* 724 With this stikke aboue the Crosselet That was ordeyned with that false Iet [*v.rr.* gett(e] He stired the coles. *c* **1440** *Promp. Parv.* 191/2 Get, or gyn (*K.* gett, or gyle, *S.* gette, or gyty), *machina*.

2. Fashion, style, mode, manner. Cf. CAST *sb.* 25. Phr. ***of the new jet***, ***of the best jet***, etc.: cf. *after the newest cast*.

c **1325** *Poem Times Edw. II* 118 in *Pol. Songs* (Camden) 329 He adihteth him a gay wenche of the new jet, *sanz doute*. *c* **1330** R. BRUNNE *Chron. Wace* (Rolls) 4024 After Sysilly com Glegabret, A syngere of the beste get. *c* **1386** CHAUCER *C.T.* Prol. 682 Hym thoughte he rood al of the newe Iet. **1399** LANGL. *Rich. Redeles* III. 159 þe leesinge so likyde ladies and oþer That þey Ioied of þe Iette, and gyside hem þer-vnder. *a* **1420** HOCCLEVE *De Reg. Princ.* 449 There is another newe gette, A foule waste of clothe and excessyfe. *c* **1440** *Promp. Parv.* 191/2 Get, or maner of custome, *modus*, *consuetudo*. *a* **1450** *Knt. de la Tour* (1868) 31 Now a dayes and a woman here of a newe gette, she wille neuer be in pees tille she haue the same. **1526** SKELTON *Magnyf.* 458 What? would ye, wyves, counterfet, The courtly gyse of the newe iet.

jet (dʒɛt), *sb.*³ Also 7–8 **jett**. See also JUT *sb.* [Partly from JET *v.*²; in sense 3, app. connected or associated with JET *v.*¹; partly (senses 4–6) from senses of F. *jet*, f. *jeter* to throw, cast.]

I. †**1.** A projection, protruding part; = JETTY *sb.* 2. *Obs.*

1610 G. FLETCHER *Christ's Vict.* II. xiii, Pillars that.. rise with goodly grace and courage bold To beare his Temple on their ample ietts.

II. †**2.** A sudden darting movement; a dart, spring, 'sprint'. *Obs.*

1647 H. MORE *Song of Soul* I. I. lii, Their jets [of sparrows], their jumps, that mirour doth disclose. *Ibid.* II. iii. III. lxxi, So could I.. prove.. why Saturn moves Ofter in those back jets then Jove doth shoot.

†**3.** An affected movement or jerk of the body; a swagger. *Obs.*

1687 SEDLEY *Bellam.* I. Wks. 1722 II. 100 Yonder goes an odd Fellow with a very pretty Wench: what a Toss she has with her head, and a Jett with her Breech. **1712** BUDGELL *Spect.* No. 277 ¶17 The genteel Trip, and the agreeable Jett, as they are now practised at the Court of France. **1719** D'URFEY *Pills* I. 222 She.. has got the Town Jett with her Bum too.

III. 4. a. A stream of water or other liquid shot forward or thrown upwards (either in a spurt or continuously), esp. from a small orifice; hence, any similar emission of liquid, steam, or gas; more rarely, a shower of solid bodies, as stones, etc.

1696 PHILLIPS (ed. 5), *Jet*,.. a spouting forth of Waters. **1728** POPE *Dunc.* II. 177 Thus the small jett which hasty hands unlock, Spirts in the gardner's eyes who turns the cock. **1821** SOUTHEY *Vis. Judgem.* iv, Turrets and pinnacles sparkled, Playing in jets of light. **1825** HONE *Everyday Bk.* I. 1185 Lighted by.. a single hoop.. with little jets of gas. **1846** RUSKIN *Mod. Paint.* I. II. v. ii. §2 A jet of spray leaps hissing out of the fall. **1854** RONALDS & RICHARDSON *Chem. Technol.* (ed. 2) I. 379 In a tank, where it is heated, by means of a jet of steam. **1869** PHILLIPS *Vesuv.* ix. 252 Jets of solid stones are thrown up with violence.

b. *transf.* and *fig.*

1822–34 *Good's Study Med.* (ed. 4) II. 8 The stream of nervous power, thus communicated by jets from the sensorial fountain. **1877** 'H. A. PAGE' *De Quincey* II. xvi. 28 He would brighten up.. with little jets of humour.

c. *Astr.* (i) A thin, well-defined stream of luminous material extending from the nucleus in the head of a comet.

1866 W. LOCKYER tr. *Guillemin's Heavens* (ed. 2) 293 If we look at the drawings.. of the comet of 1862.. we shall be astonished at the rapidity of the changes of position and form of the luminous jets which successively were emitted from the nucleus... M. Chacornac was able to distinguish the formation of thirteen.. jets, similar to jets of steam. **1888** C. A. YOUNG *Textbk. Gen. Astron.* (1889) xvii. 404 In the case of a very brilliant comet, its head is often veined by short jets of light which appear to be continually emitted by the nucleus. **1931** *Publ. Lick Observatory* (Univ. Calif.) XVII. 481 Secondary nuclei were found showing all the properties of the primary nucleus, namely, halos, jets, and streamers. **1966** *McGraw-Hill Encycl. Sci. & Technol.* III. 314/1 At smaller distances [from the sun] (less than 0·5 AU) there may be profuse emission of material but distinguishable features, such as jets, are seldom observed.

(ii) A spicule or similar structure in the solar chromosphere.

1948 *Astrophysical Jrnl.* CVIII. 130 An interpretation of the chromospheric spicules as a system of superthermic jets is presented. **1951** *Monthly Notices R. Astron. Soc.* CXI. 630 The solar chromosphere exhibits an intricate fimbriate structure that consists of very small prominences in contact with the photosphere. For brevity, these chromospheric details will be called 'jets'. *Ibid.*, 'Spicule', introduced by W. O. Roberts.., apparently refers to the largest of the jets that appear in the Sun's polar regions. **1953** G. P. KUIPER *Sun* v. 212 The chromosphere seems composed of a more or less homogeneous layer, from which emerge fine streaks or spikes... Roberts has introduced the name spicules for these fine details, Lyot and Mohler call them jets.

(iii) A narrow strip extending radially outwards from some galaxies and quasars and usually differing from the rest of the galaxy or quasar in the radiation it emits.

1954 *Astrophysical Jrnl.* CXIX. 221 NGC 4486 has a unique peculiarity which has been known for a long time. In the center of the nebula.. is a straight jet, extending from the nucleus in position angle 290°... Several strong condensations are in the outer parts of the jet, which extends about 20" from the nucleus and has an average width of about 2". **1966** *Nature* 13 Aug. 698/2 The synchrotron radiation of the jet of 3C 273 is detectable optically but not in the radio wave-lengths. **1967** *Internat. Astron. Union Symposium* XXXI. 442 A well-known feature of M87 is a jet, about 1000 pc long, emitting polarized light via the synchrotron mechanism. **1972** *Physics Bull.* Apr. 202/2 An example is galaxy M87, the famous 'jet' galaxy showing a high velocity jet of matter flying from its centre.

d. = JET STREAM.

1953 *Q. Jrnl. R. Meteorol. Soc.* LXXIX. 236 The wind components perpendicular to this axis were evaluated on each sounding at 50-mb intervals below and above the level of the jet. **1957** *Ibid.* LXXXIII. 222 The local and shallow nature of the near-discontinuity surface compared to the upper-temperature gradients in the jet certainly suggests a minor role for the front in the overall mechanics of the waves. **1963** tr. *E. R. Reiter's Jet-Stream Meteorol.* iv. 167 (*heading*) The structure of the frontal zone in the region of the polar-front jet. **1968** *Jrnl. Atmospheric Sci.* XXV. 1169/1 An equatorial jet can be driven by a convergence of momentum flux. **1970** *Nature* 17 Jan. 254/2 Thermal convection on a global scale in the lower atmosphere of Jupiter redistributes angular momentum so as to produce a well defined westerly jet at high level astride the equator... On Earth, equatorial jets are found in the lower stratosphere and in the oceans.

5. a. A spout or nozzle for emitting water, gas, etc.

1825 J. NICHOLSON *Operat. Mechanic* 216 Two other branch-pipes, supplied with gas from the gasometer, and ending in a jet at each end. **1851** *Illustr. Catal. Gt. Exhib.* 389 Garden-engine.. with jet and spreader, for watering

plants, greenhouses [etc.]. **1887** *Encycl. Brit.* XXII. 500/2 The oil is injected in the form of a spray..by a steam jet arranged in such a way that air will be drawn into the furnace along with the petroleum. **1901** *Motor-Car World* II. 42/1 Sometimes the jet gets stopped up, causing the engine to cease working. **1929** NEWTON & STEEDS *Motor Vehicle* vii. 108 [In a Diesel engine] the jet must also be so disposed and directed that a stream of liquid is not likely to impinge on the cylinder wall or piston, where rapid carbonization would occur. **1943** A. P. FRAAS *Aircraft Power Plants* vii. 116 The simple carburetor has been used to meter fuel to gasoline engines from the time they first came into use. Essentially, it consists of two orifices in parallel. The first, the air venturi, meters the air flow. The second, the fuel jet, meters the fuel flow. **1963** C. CAMPBELL *Sports Car Engine* vi. 97 This is a simple auxiliary carburettor with an air jet and a fuel jet feeding into a passage leading to the engine side of the throttle plate.

b. *Pyrotechnics.* A rocket-case filled with a burning composition, and attached to the circumference of a wheel or the end of a movable arm to communicate motion.

c. [Ellipt. use.] A jet plane or a jet engine.

1944 *Flight* 10 Feb. 153/2 The advantages of the jet are so great that I am sure their development will be rapid. **1944** *Collier's* 22 Apr. 13/3 The jet..is capable of faster flight at low altitudes than any airplane with conventional engines and propeller. **1948** 'N. SHUTE' *No Highway* i. 7 The Mark I model..had radial engines, though now they all have jets. **1957** *Economist* 31 Aug. 697/1 In military air weapons, the jet is now giving way to the rocket motor. **1973** *Observer* 14 Jan. 7/2 The enormous capacity of the latest generation big jets can be filled only by promotional and concessionary fares.

6. *Metal-casting.* **a.** A channel or tube for pouring melted metal into a mould. **b.** The small projecting piece of metal remaining in the aperture through which the liquid metal was poured.

1875 KNIGHT *Dict. Mech.*, *Jet*, the sprue of a type, which is broken therefrom when the type is cold.

7. Phrases. ***at a single jet***, at a single effort of the mind; ***at the first jet***, at first impulse. [After F. *d'un seul jet, du premier jet*.]

1838 SIR W. HAMILTON *Logic* xxiv. (1866) II. 20 A long definition is..burthensome..to the understanding, which ought to comprehend it at a single jet. **1880** *Times* 19 Jan. 4 It is always desirable that an etching should be a first thought..A certain spontaneity and freshness seems to belong to all work done at the first jet.

8. A large ladle.

1727 BRADLEY *Fam. Dict.* s.v. *Brewing*, Mix it again with your Hand Jett. **1742** *Lond. & Country Brew.* I. (ed. 4) 50 Others..for Butt or Stout-beer will..mix it once, and beat it again with the Hand-bowl or Jett. *a* **1825** FORBY *Voc. E. Anglia*, *Jet*, a very large ladle to empty a cistern.

9. *Comb.*, as *jet-hole*, ***speed***, ***velocity***; *jet-like* adj.; **jet boat** *N.Z.* (see quot. 1968); **jet-break**, the mark left, as on a metal type, by a jet or sprue when removed after casting; **jet engine**, an engine utilizing jet propulsion to provide forward thrust, esp. an aircraft engine that takes in air and ejects hot compressed air and exhaust gases; so ***jet-engined*** adj.; **jet flap** *Aeronaut.*, a jet of gas from a jet engine ejected downward as a sheet through a slot in the trailing edge of an aircraft wing, so as to act as a flap and increase the lift; **jet injector** *Med.*, an instrument for giving injections without breaking the skin by means of a fine jet of fluid forced through it under pressure; **jet motor** = *jet engine* above; **jet pipe**, a pipe or duct from which a jet of fluid is expelled; *spec.* the exhaust duct of a jet engine; **jet-pump**, a pump in which fluid is impelled by a jet of air, steam, etc.; **jet turbine**, a turbojet engine. Also JET STREAM.

1963 J. HAMILTON (*title*) White water, the Colorado jet boat expedition, 1960. **1967** A. & D. REID *Paddle Wheels on Wanganui* p. x, Canoes, rafts and jetboats notwithstanding, there can be no equal to the experience of shooting a long twisting rapid in..a Wanganui riverboat in its heyday. **1968** *Times* 31 Aug. 7/5 The jet boat is..a simple enough contraption—a strong glass fibre hull..; a powerful and reliable inboard engine; and..a highly developed water pump. Water is sucked in through a flat grating..and projected violently out the back to supply propulsion and steering. **1970** *N.Z. Listener* 27 Feb. 1 (*caption*) The experimental jetboat on the Waimakariri River, 1951. **1975** *N.Z. News* 8 Jan. 9/3 Another development of consequence in New Zealand has been the invention of the jet boat... Propelled and steered by its water jet, the [Sir William] Hamilton jet boat can make 180-degree turns in its own length. **1943** *Jrnl. R. Aeronaut. Soc.* XLVII. 413 In general, the jet engine performance is given not in h.p. but in kg. of thrust. **1950** *Sci. News* XV. 72 The ordinary jet engine uses oxygen from the air, but the rocket carries its own oxygen supply with it in some form. **1952** A. Y. BRAMBLE *Air-Plane Flight* x. 156 There are, at present, three types of air-plane jet 'engine'—(*a*) rocket, (*b*) turbo-jet, (*c*) athodyd. **1969** *Jet Engine* (Rolls-Royce Ltd.) (ed. 3) i. 4/1 Although a rocket engine..is a jet engine, it has one major difference in that it does not use atmospheric air as the propulsive fluid stream. **1952** *Lancet* 15 Nov. 967/2 In jet-engined aeroplanes the high sonic frequencies predominate. **1960** *Guide Civil Land Aerodrome Lighting* (*B.S.I.*) 30 Where a runway is used by large jet-engined aircraft, blister type fittings are advisable as elevated fittings can be blown over by the jet efflux. **1958** *Spectator* 7 Feb. 160/3 The vast amount of British work on blown flaps, jet flaps, jet lift and boundary layer control. **1963** *Engineering* 5 Apr. 493/1 The principle of the jet flap was..patented in 1952 by the National Gas Turbine Establishment and is a technique whereby the power of jet engines installed for propulsion can also be used greatly to increase the wing lift at low speeds. **1879** *Cassell's Techn. Educ.* IV. 74/1 The most brilliant light from common gas is produced by a burner in which the jet-holes are very numerous. **1947** *Current Res. Anesthesia & Analgesia* XXVI. 223 Figure 2 shows position of the jet injector for anesthetizing the skin preparatory to insertion of lumbar puncture needle. **1965** *Brit. Med. Jrnl.* 25 Dec. 1541/1 High-pressure jet injectors..throw the material to be injected with considerable force through a very fine nozzle. **1973** *Lancet* 28 Apr. 927/2 Contacts of the early cases were vaccinated by intradermal injection, but two jet injectors were ordered for the vaccination of the 5 and 6-year-old children. **1883** R. A. PROCTOR in *19th. Cent.* Nov. 876 They have been classified according to the various forms of cloud-like and jet-like prominences. **1944** *Discovery* Nov. 346/2 This is the Whittle aircraft, with a gas-turbine jet-motor. **1950** J. V. CASAMASSA *Jet Aircraft Power Syst.* v. 89 The Aerojet motor is a true rocket, since its propellent charge contains both the fuel and the oxygen necessary to burn it. Consequently, this jet motor delivers its rated power independent of altitude or atmospheric conditions. **1946** *Jrnl. R. Aeronaut. Soc.* L. 317/1 After compression in the compressor, the air is circulated through a radiator or heat exchanger situated in the jet pipe of the engine. **1966** *McGraw-Hill Encycl. Sci. & Technol.* X. 227/2 Jetting consists of displacing the soil at the pile tip by means of a quantity of water or air through an internal or external jet pipe, which also lubricates the sides of the pile as it rises to escape. **1966** D. STINTON *Anat. Aeroplane* vii. 126 The thrust of a turbojet is frequently augmented by burning additional fuel in the jetpipe, thus utilizing unburnt air. **1875** KNIGHT *Dict. Mech.*, *Jet-pump*... It acts by the pressure of a column of air passing through an annular throat; or conversely, an annular jet around a central orifice. **1934** *Aircraft Engineering* VI. 170/2 At the maximum pressure end the difference between the static pressure inside the [wind] tunnel and atmospheric at a jet speed of 200 ft./sec. is about 45 lb./sq. ft. **1945** *Sci. Amer.* June 365 Jet turbines have extremely low oil consumption ratings. **1949** *Punch* 14 Sept. 286/3 Emerging miraculously from its dive, the monster..flashes low across the runway, the whiffling roar of its jet-turbine manfully pursuing. **1935** in *Aeronaut. Jrnl.* (1970) LXXIV. 130/2 The jet velocity resulting from a useful heat drop of 250 units is..2320 ft/s. **1966** *McGraw-Hill Encycl. Sci. & Technol.* XIV. 159/1 Under these conditions, afterburning to an exhaust temperature of 3460°R provides an increase in jet velocity of ..1·5.

IV. 10. Combs. in which *jet* represents 'jet engine', as ***jet efflux***, ***fuel***; ***jet-assisted***, ***-powered*** adjs.; esp. in the designations of aircraft (and occas. other forms of transport) powered by jet engines, as ***jet aeroplane***, ***aircraft***, ***air liner***, ***airplane***, ***bomber***, ***fighter***, ***lifter***, ***liner***, ***plane***, ***tanker***, ***trainer***. Also **Jetfoil** (also **jetfoil**), a type of passenger-carrying hydrofoil with a stabilization and control system based on that of an aircraft (proprietary in the U.S.); **jet lift**, lift (vertical thrust) provided by a jet engine. (For *jet engine*, *motor*, etc., see sense 9.) Also JET PROPULSION.

1951 'J. WYNDHAM' *Day of Triffids* ii. 36 Also I must buy an aeroplane—a jet aeroplane, very fast. **1944** *Flight* 3 Feb. 130/1 Now about the jet aircraft. Instead of the jets coming out of the tail, shape the aircraft like an orange pip and have several jets coming out of the shoulders, pressing air against and all round the fuselage. **1954** *Economist* 11 Sept. 12/2 On multi-engined jet aircraft the horizontal tail must also be placed away from the jet blast. **1959** *Daily Tel.* 23 Feb. 11/8, I have seen films of man's experience of weightlessness in a jet aircraft. **1970** *Times* 25 Feb. 8/6 The first Whittle jet was tested three years later [*sc.* in 1937].., and the first British jet aircraft flew in 1941. **1947** *Jrnl. R. Aeronaut. Soc.* LI. 178/2 With regard to the comfort of jet air liners, he wondered whether people were being misled. **1959** *Daily Tel.* 2 Mar. 16/4 The new large jet airliners are probably as fast, and can fly as high, as most jet bombers now in service. **1944** *Collier's* 22 Apr. 13/1 Few standard conveniences for upper stratosphere flying had yet been built into the jet airplane. **1944** Jet-assisted [see JATO]. **1957** *Jane's Fighting Ships 1957–8* 413 The missile is using jet-assisted rocket bottles to launch it. **1952** *Oxf. Jun. Encycl.* X. 56/2 One of the first tactical jet bombers to go into service was the English Electric *Canberra*. **1965** H. KAHN *On Escalation* x. 200 In a jet-bomber and ballistic-missile age, events go so fast. **1960** Jet efflux [see *jet-engined* adj. in 9]. **1966** D. STINTON *Anat. Aeroplane* 244 The position of the fin was an initial argument against mounting the engine above the boom, because of the hot jet efflux playing on the surfaces. **1944** *Sat. Even. Post* 6 May 20/2 The British had flown a jet plane successfully, and now the USAAF proposed to develop a twin-engined jet fighter of its own. **1955** *Ann. Reg. 1954* 149 An outstanding item in Canadian mutual aid within N.A.T.O...was the transfer of 164 Sabre jet fighters to Greece and Turkey. **1964** M. MCLUHAN *Understanding Media* II. xxvii. 272 The two pilots of one Canadian jet fighter. **1972** *Aviation Week & Space Technol.* 16 Oct. 17/2 Boeing Co. has launched a commercial hydrofoil production program after receiving orders..for 11 100-ton boats powered by a water jet propulsion system... The boat, which Boeing is calling the Jetfoil, is being designed to cruise at 50 mph. **1974** *Times* 27 Feb. 16 Macao is about an hour away by hydrofoil and when the jetfoils are introduced later this year the time will be cut to 45 minutes. **1976** *Official Gaz.* (U.S. Patent Office) 17 Feb. TM155/2 The Boeing Company, Seattle... *Jetfoil* for watercraft—namely, hydrofoil boats. **1979** *Daily Tel.* 23 Apr. 21/8 Using ultrasonic sensors to measure approaching wave-heights, and both vertical and horizontal gyros, to compensate for pitch and roll, a computer keeps the Jetfoil absolutely stable. **1982** *Observer* 3 Oct. 25/5 By now you could feel the West close by..a jetfoil ride across a small stretch of the South China Sea. **1953** *Ann. Reg. 1952* 164 Agreement was also reached on financing the first half of the..programme for air-fields, communications, and jet-fuel supplies. **1966** *McGraw-Hill Encycl. Sci. & Technol.* I. 178/2 Volatility is the most important consideration in the selection of jet fuels; combustion qualities are of secondary concern. **1958** Jet lift [see *jet flap* in 9]. **1968** *New Scientist* 25 July 167/1 Jet lift, as a means of personal mobility, has been a tempting idea since Rolls-Royce began using the Flying Bedstead about 15 years ago... This invites speculation as to whether paratroopers, deployed from a transport aeroplane, might subsequently be gathered back into it with the help of their individual jet-lift belts. **1954** P. MASEFIELD in *Listener* 30 Sept. 511/2 The commercial jet-lifters are yet to come. **1967** *Times Rev. Industry* Feb. 68/2 As long as a decade ago, technically competent enthusiasts were saying that another form of vertical take-off and landing (VTOL) transport, the jet-lifter, was just round the historical corner. **1949** *Birmingham* (Alabama) *News-Age-Herald* 13 Nov. A. 18/3 But there is much work yet to be done before the combination of the jetliner and the helibus can be fully utilized. **1961** A. MILLER *Misfits* i. 12 A great jet liner roars over, flying quite low. **1970** *New Scientist* 23 Apr. 172/2 The cruising speed would be competitive with current jetliners at Mach 0·93. **1971** *Daily Tel.* (Colour Suppl.) 30 July 25 This frenetic era of automated jetliners and impersonal airports. **1944** G. SMITH *Gas Turbines & Jet Propulsion for Aircraft* (ed. 3) 104 He believed the jet plane would be used in the near future. **1944** *War Illustr.* 10 Nov. 404/3 The first enemy jet-plane to fall in Allied lines was shot down over Nijmegen on October 5 by six R.A.F. Spitfires; it was a Me 262. **1964** M. MCLUHAN *Understanding Media* II. xviii. 177 The effect of ..jet-plane speeds. **1956** W. A. HEFLIN *U.S. Air Force Dict.* 281/1 *Jet-powered*, powered by one or more jet engines. **1957** *Encycl. Brit.* I. 246/2 Aeroplanes are either propeller driven or jet powered. **1959** *Daily Tel.* 2 Mar. 16/4 The United States Air Force already has a large number, probably about 400, Boeing KC-135 jet tankers. **1967** *Times* 28 Feb. (Canada Suppl.) 27 Jet tankers are also needed for long distance inflight refuelling of the CF5. **1959** *Daily Tel.* 23 Feb. 11/8 The first such experiments were conducted by a pilot and a doctor in a T-33 jet trainer.

11. In numerous combinations (in which *jet* represents 'jet plane') relating to locomotion by means of jet aircraft, as ***jet route***, ***transport***, ***transportation***, ***travel***, ***traveller***; ***jet-borne*** adj. Also **jet age**, the age or era of travel by jet aircraft; **jet hop**, a short or rapid flight by a jet aircraft; also as *v. intr.*; **jet lag**, the delayed effects (esp. temporal disorientation) suffered by a person after a long flight on a (jet) aircraft; **jetport** [after AIRPORT], an airport served by jet aircraft; **jet set**, a smart set of wealthy people who conduct business by jet travel, or who make frequent journeys, e.g. to holiday resorts, by jet aircraft; also in weakened senses; so **jet-setter**.

1952 R. WALKER (*title*) Jet age. **1953** *Sci. News Let.* 21 Feb. 122/1 A weird-looking, skin-tight 'space suit' now clothes the jet-age test pilot. **1958** *New Statesman* 21 June 804/2 The uppermost deck of this air-pier or jet-age jetty is an open public area— 'waving base' in official terminology —that gives one a grandstand or pierhead view of the comings and goings. **1963** *PMLA* LXXVIII. I. p. v, Air France ground hostesses threaten to work in civilian clothes unless their employer comes up with jet age fashions. **1971** *Guardian* 12 June 12/3 You can cleanse yourself immediately of most jet-age pollution in the..local Turkish bath. **1968** *N.Y. Times* 21 Apr. IV. 1 Johnson..climbed aboard his jetborne White House for the flight back to his Texas ranch. **1963** *Times* 26 Feb. 8/6 A certified real Orient just a jet-hop away. **1969** J. MANDER *Static Soc.* i. 27 As he jet-hops from country to country, it is the similarities that strike him. **1969** 'A. CADE' *Turn up Stone* i. 23 The long journey, jet-lag and the heat had given him a headache. **1971** *Times* 16 Apr. 7 (Advt.), A team of scientists has researched the phenomenon of 'jet lag' thoroughly. The disorientation of a jet flight has been proved to upset..decision-making. **1972** *Sat. Rev.* (U.S.) 10 June 15/2 The news of Nixon—booked into Salzburg to fight jet lag for a weekend on his way to the summit meeting in Moscow. **1973** *Observer* 3 June 29/1 They had the dazed, sleep-walking look of people still confused by jet-lag. **1961** *N.Y. Times* 1 June 37/1 (*caption*) New study backs jetport in Morris. **1972** *Fortune* Jan. 40D/3 (Advt.), A fourth major jetport to serve the New York metropolitan area. **1970** *Times* 27 Feb. 3/8 (*heading*) Windsor on jet route. **1951** *San Francisco Examiner* 5 Aug. 5/1 You're strictly jet set..if you stake your claim in the dunes..*never* descend to ocean level except for a quick dunk. **1956** *N.Y. Times Mag.* 4 Nov. 14 This is the Soviet 'Jet Set', an element of the younger generation... The term was originated by a young member of a foreign embassy staff in Moscow and refers to the Soviet youth who are attracted by things foreign. **1963** *Amer. Speech* XXXVIII. 206 *Jet set* (analogous to *smart set*), rhyming slang term referring to the sophisticated, well-to-do skiers who go abroad by jet just for skiing vacations in the best known resorts. **1964** *Sat. Rev.* (U.S.) 10 Oct. 70/1 The Jet Set..has rediscovered St. Tropez. **1966** *Daily Tel.* 24 Oct. 13/6 Clothes for the jet set, for you who seek the sun in winter. **1970** *Americana Ann.* 694 His campaign managers created a new image of him [*sc.* Pierre Trudeau] as the youthful, debonaire, 'with-it' man of the jet-set age. **1972** *House & Garden* Dec.–Jan. 126/2 Even in the jet-set hotels..local dishes are presented. **1965** *N.Y. Times* 13 June 17 (*caption*) Jet-setter Mrs...and model.. prepare for ABC's fall special, 'The Wild, Wild East'. **1966** *Time* 9 Dec. 88/3 In swarmed the jet-setters (Gloria Guinness, Lee Radziwill, Count and Countess Rudolfo Crespi). **1973** *Daily Tel.* 22 Sept. 19/8 The crowd.. naturally included show business celebrities and jet-setters who had paid £40 for court-side seats. **1949** *Flight* 29 Sept. 438/2 A large jet transport might take five years to develop to the production stage. **1961** L. MUMFORD *City in Hist.* xvi. 505 Jet transportation brings an area twelve hundred miles away as near as one sixty miles distant today. **1962** *Daily Tel.* 13 June 11/1 What with jet travel, the Common Market and [etc.]. **1964** M. MCLUHAN *Understanding Media* II. x. 94 The jet traveler..might just as well be in a cocktail lounge.

jet, *sb.*[4] Also 8 jett, (jest), jut. [By-form of GIST, a. Law Fr. *gist*, mod.F. *gît* in the legal phrase *action gist* or *gît* 'action lies', taken subst. as the 'lie' of the action; cf. the following:

1613 FINCH *Nomotechnia* 7 [II] ne girra le foundation de son edifice sur estates, tenures, les gists de briefes ou tiel [i.e. the lie of writs (the cases in which a writ will lie) or the like].]

That wherein the action lies, the real point of an action at law; hence, the substance or pith of a matter; = GIST *sb.*³

α. **1748** RICHARDSON *Clarissa* (1811) III. lxii. 363 Here comes the jet of the business. *Ibid.* VIII. x. 54 To point out..where the jet of our arguments lieth. **1777** SHERIDAN *Sch. Scand.* III. i, *Sir Pet.* But Rowley, I don't see the jest [*some later edd.* jet] of your scheme. **1795** tr. *Moritz' Trav. Eng.* 57 The jett, or principal point in the debate, is lost in these personal contests. **1813** DICKINSON 5 May in *Hansard's Parl. Deb.* XXV. 1141 The story of the loaf was the whole jet of the case. **1818** COBBETT *Pol. Reg.* 483 This is the jet of all her reasoning. **1872** R. RAINY *Lect. Ch. Scot.* iii. (1883) 140 The very jet of the quarrel lay here.

β. **1772** NUGENT tr. *Hist. Friar Gerund* II. ii. 287 The whole jut of the business consists in advancing boldly a proposition. *Ibid.* III. iii. 481 All the jut of which..consists in its being very like that vulgarism.

†**jet**, *v.*¹ *Obs.* Forms: 5 gette, 5–7 iett(e, 6 get, 6–7 iet(t, 7–8 jet. [In form, app. a. Anglo-F. *gettre* (Bozon), in 15th c. F. *getter, jetter*, mod.F. *jeter* to throw, cast, etc.; but the senses appear to be those belonging to the L. *jactāre sē, jactārī* 'to carry oneself confidently or conceitedly, to talk boastfully of oneself, to boast, brag, vaunt oneself, make an ostentatious display', sense not recorded in French. The sb. *jetter*, corresp. to L. *jactātor* 'an ostentatious displayer of himself, a boaster, a braggart' (senses also absent from F. *jetteur*), was app. in earlier use than the vb., and possibly contributed to the currency of the latter.]

I. Of gait and motion.

1. *intr.* To assume a pompous gait or make a vaunting display in walking; to walk or move about in an ostentatious manner; to strut, swagger. Said also of animals, as a prancing horse, a peacock, a turkey, etc. Often with *up and down*.

a **1420** HOCCLEVE *De Reg. Princ.* 428 Þogh he iette forth among þe prees, And ouer loke euery pore wight. **1432–50** tr. *Higden* (Rolls) VIII. 149 The seide William wente iettynge in the stretes [HIGDEN *pompatice procedebat*, TREV. wente wiþ greet boost and array], and moche peple drawynge to hym. *c* **1440** *Promp. Parv.* 192/2 Gettyn, *verno, lassivo, gesticulo.* *a* **1529** SKELTON *E. Rummyng* 51 And yet she wyll iet..In her furred flocket. **1530** PALSGR. 563/2, I get, I use a proude countenaunce and pace in my goyng, *je braggue.* **1548** UDALL *Erasm. Par. Luke* xix. 150 The Pharisee, he goeth jetting bolt upright. **1587** M. GROVE *Pelops & Hipp.* (1878) 41 They [horses] prauncing iette, to shew themselues which best might tread the land. **1601** HOLLAND *Pliny* I. 291 Others..cast out their feet before them, staulk and jet as they go, as Storks and cranes. **1649** W. M. *Wand. Jew* (Halliw. 1857) 59 Your Wife [shall be] pointed at, for jetting in stolne feathers. **1669** WORLIDGE *Syst. Agric.* (1681) 304 The Wicked Crow aloud fowl-weather threats, When alone on dry sands she proudly jets.

b. To move along jauntily, to caper, to trip.

1557 PHAER *Æneid* VII. T iv, Girt in skinnes they iett, wᵗ vinetree garlonds borne on prickes. **1604** T. WRIGHT *Passions* IV. ii. §3. 134 To trip, to iet, or any such like pase, commeth of lightnesse. **1632** T. MORTON *New Eng. Canaan* (1883) 180 Cleare running streames..jetting most jocundly where they doe meete and hande in hande runne downe to Neptunes Court. *a* **1700** B. E. *Dict. Cant. Crew, Jetting along*, or *out*, a Man Dancing in his Gate.

c. quasi-*trans.* *to jet it.* (Cf. *to trip it.*)

1526 SKELTON *Magnyf.* 974 Mary, thou iettes it of hyght. **1592** NASHE *P. Penilesse* (ed. 2) 10 b, Mistris Minx..iets it as gingerly as if she were dancing the Canaries. *a* **1624** BP. M. SMITH *Serm.* (1632) 229 They iet it not onely in soft clothing, but in cloth of gold and of siluer. *a* **1634** RANDOLPH in *Ann. Dubrensia* (1877) 20 Where..harmlesse Nimphes, jet it with harmlesse Swaynes. **1672** *Maypole Dance in Westm. Drollery* 80 Then ev'ry man began to foot it round about; And ev'ry Girl did jet it, jet it, jet it, and out.

2. *intr.* To stroll; sometimes simply a humorous equivalent of *walk* or *go.* (In quot. 1546, to 'depart', to die.)

1530 PALSGR. 563/2, I get up and downe, I loyter as an ydell or masterlesse person dothe, *je vilote.* **1546** J. HEYWOOD *Prov.* II. iv. (1867) 49 God forbyd wyfe, ye shall fyrst iet. I will not iet yet (quoth she), put no doutyng. *a* **1571** JEWEL *On 2 Thess.* (1611) 134 Poore soules came creeping and crying out of Purgatory, and ietted abroad. **1600** *Maides Metam.* III. i. in Bullen *O. Pl.* I. 137 Ioculo, whither iettest thou? Hast thou found thy maister? **1706** PHILLIPS, *To Jet*, to run up and down. *a* **1777** *Robin Hoode & Q. Kath.* xix. in Child *Ballads* v. cxlv, Thus he ietted towards louly London.

3. *trans.* To traverse ostentatiously; to parade.

1557 NORTH tr. *Gueuara's Diall Pr.* 262 b/2, I ietted the stretes, I sang balladеs. **1576** GASCOIGNE *Steele Gl.* (Arb.) 63 In towne he ietted euery streete, As though the god of warres ..Might wel (by him) be liuely counterfayte. **1581** SAVILE *Tacitus, Hist.* II. lxxxviii. (1591) 105 The Tribunes also.. with multitudes of armed men went squaring and ietting the streetes.

II. Of behaviour. **4.** *intr.* To act or behave boastfully, to vaunt, to brag.

c **1514** BARCLAY in *Cyt. & Uplondyshm.* (Percy Soc.) p. lxvii, They laude their verses, they boast, they uaunt, and jet. **1581** J. BELL *Haddon's Answ. Osor.* 490 On this maner ietteth forth this Buskine Portingall. *a* **1592** GREENE *Alphonsus* v. Wks. (Rtldg.) 247/1 Jason did jet whenas he had obtain'd The golden fleece by wise Medea's art. **1664** *Flodden F.* II. 20 King James for joy began to jet So huge an army to behold.

5. *intr.* To revel, roister, riot; to indulge in riotous living.

1514 BARCLAY *Cyt. & Uplondyshm.* (Percy Soc.) 2 In the towne & cyte so long jetted had he, That from thens he fledde for det & poverte. **1530** PALSGR. 570, I go a jettynge or a ryottynge, *je raude.* **1584** R. SCOT *Discov. Witchcr.* XII. xvii. (1886) 216 A certeine sir John..once went abroad a jetting, and..robbed a millers weire. **1640** in Balfour *Scot. Ballads* 37 That he may jet in dancing and whooring.

jet (dʒɛt), *v.*² Forms: 6–8 jett, (8 jeat), 7– jet; see also JUT *v.* [a. F. *jeter* (14–16th c. also *jetter*, Cotgr. *jecter*) to throw, cast; to fling, dart, thrust, push, cast metal, etc. = Pr. *gitar, getar*, Sp. *jitar, jetar*, It. *gittare, gettare*:—late L. or Com. Rom. type **jettare*:—*jectare* 'unexplained alteration' of cl. L. *jactāre*, freq. of *jacĕre* to throw, cast.]

I. †**1. a.** *intr.* To shoot prominently forward; to project, protrude, jut. Const. *out, over. Obs.*

1593 NASHE *Christ's T.* (1613) 76 Thy streets were paued with Marble, and thy houses ietted out with Iaphy and Cedar. **1615** G. SANDYS *Trav.* 116 The houses..jetting over aloft like the poopes of ships, to shadow the streets. **1640** tr. *Verdere's Romant of Rom.* III. vii. 28 A Window, that jetted upon the Garden. **1657** R. LIGON *Barbadoes* (1673) 83 Some ..bear fruits which jett out from the stem a little. **1749** L. EVANS *Mid. Brit. Colonies* (1755) 8 *note*, Spurs we call little Ridges jetting out from the principal Chains of Mountains. **1762** BP. FORBES *Jrnls.* (1886) 228 A moss-grown Ruine, jetting into the North Side of the Lake.

fig. **1655** FULLER *Ch. Hist.* IX. v. §2 Enough hereof at this time, having jetted out a little already into the next year. **1662** GURNALL *Chr. in Arm.* verse 18. I. xviii. (1669) 362/2 That thy faith may not jet beyond the foundation of the promise.

†**b.** *intr.* (*transf.*) To encroach *on* or *upon.*

1588 SHAKS. *Tit. A.* II. i. 64 (Qos.) Thinke you not how dangerous It is to iet [*Fos.* set] vpon a Princes right? **1594** —— *Rich. III*, II. iv. 51 (Qos.) Insulting tyranny beginnes to iet [**1623** *Folio* Iutt] Upon the innocent and lawlesse throane. *c* **1590** *Play Sir T. More* (1844) 2 It is hard when English-mens pacience must be thus jetted on by straungers. **1636** HEYWOOD *Loves Mistr.* I. Wks. 1874 V. 104 A..foole, Who spights at those above him,..and his equalls jets upon.

†**2.** *trans.* To build *out* (part of a house, etc.); to cause to project, to furnish with projections.

1632 *Manchester Crt. Leet Rec.* (1886) III. 192 John Gryffin hath Jetted out his chamber Windowes over the Lords Wast. **1667** *Obs. Burn. London* in *Sel. fr. Harl. Misc.* (1793) 449 Magistrates..have suffered them..to incroach upon the streets, and to jet the tops of their houses, so as from one side of the street to touch the other. **1714** DERHAM *Phys.-Theol.* III. iv. (ed. 2) 79 That..it [the earth] should be jetted out everywhere into Hills and Dales..is a manifest Sign of an especial Providence.

II. **3.** To throw, cast, toss. *Obs.* exc. *dial.*

1659 D. PELL *Impr. Sea* 407 As the ball that is jetted to and fro upon the racket. *Ibid.* 414 They have no mind to bee jetted up to the Heavens in a storm. **1877** *N.W. Linc. Gloss.*, *Jet*, to throw with a jerk.

†**4.** *intr.* To spring, hop, bound, dart. *Obs.*

1635 QUARLES *Embl.* III. i, Like as the haggard, cloister'd in her mew,..Jets oft from perch to perch. **1647** H. MORE *Song of Soul* II. iii. III. xxxiv, Not more heavie then dry straws that jet Up to a ring, made of black shining jeat. **1827** MONTGOMERY *Pelican Isl.* VII. 174 He hoped to see..The wingless squirrel jet from tree to tree.

†**5.** *intr.* To move or be moved with a jerk or jerks; to jolt or jog. *Obs.*

a **1635** CORBET *Poems* (1807) 95, I on an ambling nag did jet,..And spur'd him on each side. **1676** WISEMAN *Surg.* (J.), Upon the jetting of a hackney-coach she was thrown out of the hinder seat.

†**6.** *intr.* Of a bird: To move the tail up and down jerkily. *Obs.*

1657 R. LIGON *Barbadoes* (1673) 60 As she [a bird] sits on a stick, jets, and lifts up her train, looking with so..merry a countenance. **1783** AINSWORTH *Lat. Dict.* (Morell) v, *Todeo, -ere*,..to jet up and down like a wagtail.

III. **7.** *intr.* To spout or spurt forth; to issue in a jet or jets, or curve in the form of a *jet d'eau.*

1692 RAY *Dissol. World* II. ii. 96 Springs break out after great rains which jet and spout up a great height. **1730** A. GORDON *Maffei's Amphith.* 168 Pipes, by which..they caused odoriferous Liquor to spring up from the bottom to the top of the Amphitheatre, which then jetted and spread itself in the Air. *a* **1854** H. REED *Lect. Brit. Poets* iii. (1857) 101 That quiet humour which is forever jetting out of Chaucer's pages. **1862** TYNDALL *Mountaineer.* xi. 90 We.. observe the smoke of a distant cataract jetting from the side of the mountain.

8. *trans.* To emit or send forth in a jet or jets.

1708 MOTTEUX *Rabelais* I. iv. 158 The Three Graces, with their Cornucopia's,..did jet out the Water [*earlier edd.* jert, orig. *jectoyent l'eau*] at their Breasts, Mouth, Ears, Eyes. **1814** SCOTT *Ld. of Isles* I. xviii, Conflicting tides that foam and fret, And high their mingled billows jet. **1849** DANA *Geol.* vii. (1850) 356 The lavas may be jetted from a vent in small ejections.

9. *Building.* To loosen and remove (sand, gravel, etc.), or to sink (a pile), by the technique of jetting (see JETTING *vbl. sb.*² 4).

1956 H. L. NICHOLS *Mod. Techniques Excavation* v. 58/2 In peat, the points are jetted down and sand pumped in the hole around them. *Ibid.* vi. 25/2 If the cover should be left off, and the vertical pipe filled with dirt.., it may be jetted out by the use of an engine-driven water pump.

Hence '**jetted**, †**jet**, *ppl. a.*

1709 MRS. MANLEY *Secret Mem.* (1736) II. 49 In that Chamber was a large jet-out Window. **1762** USTICK in *Phil. Trans.* LII. 512 Every one of the windows of the church, (excepting one in the jet-out north-isle). **1864** S. FERGUSON *Forging of Anchor* ii, Hurrah! the jetted lightnings are hissing high and low.

jet (dʒɛt), *v.*³ [f. JET *sb.*³] *intr.* To travel by jet plane. Also *trans.* (and *refl.*), to convey by jet plane or jet engine. So '**jetted** *ppl. a.*

1946 *All Hands* June 50 A Martin Marauder was jetted into the air for the scientist-spectators. **1949** *Sat. Rev.* (U.S.) 8 Jan. 17, I rather think Captain Osborne will be the first of us to go jetting to the moon. **1951** A. C. CLARKE *Sands of Mars* vii. 81 They jetted themselves slowly out across the surface of Deimos. **1956** F. POHL *Alternating Currents* (1966) 96 We can't jet home through normal space because we don't have the fuel. **1959** *Time* 23 Mar. 20/3 Jetting home to Moscow..Krushchev exuded confidence. **1962** *Daily Tel.* 13 June 11/1 There's no rest for the 'jetted' British businessman. **1966** *Guardian* 7 June 12/6 In the last few days, Brown has jetted over an area the size of Europe. **1968** *Daily Tel.* 28 Sept. 9/6 (Advt.), Clarksons jet you to top resorts like Alpbach, Auffach, [etc.]. **1971** *Radio Times* 21 Oct. 71/3 Perhaps I'd been lucky to catch him in today, before he jetted off to Tokyo or the Bahamas? **1973** *Daily Tel.* (Colour Suppl.) 10 Aug. 7/2 But Beer now jets between Santiago and his Surrey home.

jetavator ('dʒɛtəveɪtə(r)). *Astronautics.* Also **jetevator**. [f. (irreg., in the case of *jetavator*) JET *sb.*³ + EL)EVATOR.] A ring-shaped deflector surrounding the exit nozzle of a rocket engine which can be swivelled into the exhaust gases to divert them and so alter the direction of the thrust.

1960 *Aeroplane* XCVIII. 176/2 The missile is powered by a solid-propellent Aerojet rocket motor fitted with 'jetavator' deflectors of the kind developed for Polaris. **1961** *Flight* LXXIX. 13/2 The use of swivelling nozzles is claimed to be lighter than the Polaris system of fixed nozzles plus jetevators, and undoubtedly minimizes drag. **1967** *Propulsion* (Amat. Rocket Assoc. U.S.) ii. 45 A jetavator consists of a ring surrounding the exhaust-nozzle exit. The ring is mounted so that it can be moved into the jet exhaust as needed.

'**jet-'black**, *a.* [f. JET *sb.*¹ + BLACK *a.*] Black like jet; absolutely black; glossy black.

c **1475** *Bk. of Curtesye* 45 (Oriel MS.) Youre nayles loke they be not geet blake. **1693** TATE in *Dryden's Juvenal* ii. (1697) 32 With Jet-black Pencils one his Eye-brows dyes. **1777** POTTER *Æschylus, Persians* 478 That led his dark'ning squadrons..On jet-black steeds. **1875** W. S. HAYWARD *Love agst. World* 100 Balthazar was jet black.

‖**jet d'eau** (ʒɛdo). Also 8 jette d'eau. Pl. **jets d'eau** (ʒɛːdo). [F., = 'jet of water'; see also JETTEAU.] An ornamental jet of water ascending from a fountain or pipe. Also, the fountain or pipe from which such a jet issues.

1706 PHILLIPS, *Jet d'Eau*, the Pipe of a Fountain that casts up the Water into the Air. **1720** WILCOCKS in Ellis *Orig. Lett.* Ser. II. IV. 322 The King is mightily pleased with a new *jette d'eau* in Herrenhausen gardens. **1776** H. SWINBURNE in *Crts. Europe close last Cent.* (1841) I. 92 The orange groves in the King's garden, watered by *jets d'eau*, in the style of those..in Italy. **1808** PIKE *Sources Mississ.* III. (1810) 256 In the centre of the square was a Jet d'eau, which cast forth water from eight spouts. **1858** LARDNER *Hand-bk. Nat. Phil., Hydrost.*, etc. 94 The water will..rise to a certain height forming a natural *jet d'eau.*

jete, obs. form of JET.

‖**jeté** (ʒəte). Also erron. **jété, jetée, jetté.** [F. *jeté*, pa. pple. (sc. *pas* step) of *jeter* to throw.] A ballet-step, having a wide variety of forms, in which a spring is made from one foot to land on the other. So **jeté en tournant** (ɑ̃ turnɑ̃), a leap executed with a turning movement. Cf. GRAND JETÉ.

1830 R. BARTON tr. *Blasis' Code of Terpsichore* II. vi. 78 *Entrechats* are generally begun with an *assemblé, coupé*, or *jetté.* **1877** [see CONTRETEMPS 3]. **1927** *Dancing Times* Apr. 9 All dancers know that the coupé cannot be done alone, as the position of the foot which is being 'cutaway' depends entirely upon the step which follows the coupé. I am therefore taking the 'coupé-dessous', followed in the first instance by a 'posé', and afterwards the 'coupé-dessous' followed by a 'jeté'. **1930** CRASKE & BEAUMONT *Theory & Pract. Allegro in Classical Ballet* 95 Execute a *Jeté en Tournant*, that is:—With a slight spring, change the position of the feet so that the *right* foot is *sur le cou de pied devant.* **1953** *Ballet Ann.* VII. 59 She took off with a wonderful *jeté* and landed only a few inches from his nose. **1958** *Observer* 28 Sept. 18/5 A special salute is due to Yelle Bettencourt's splendid *jétés.* **1961** *Times* 28 Dec. 12/7 M. Jean-Paul Andreani is quite electrifying with his *jétés en tournant.*

‖**jetee** (dʒɛ'tiː). [Native name.] A shrub growing in certain hilly districts in India.

1866 *Treas. Bot.* 637/2 *Jetee*, an Indian name for *Marsdenia tenacissima*, whose fibres are made into bowstrings.

jetevator, var. JETAVATOR.

jeton. [See JETTON.] **1.** ('dʒɛtən) = JETTON.

1933 H. G. WELLS *Shape of Things to Come* II. §11. 229 Today our museums contain hundreds of thousands of specimens of these improvised European coins of lead, nickel, tin and all sorts of alloys, *jetons* or checks of wood. **1969** R. C. BELL *Board & Table Games* II. x. 138 Many of these casting-counters, or *jetons*, simulated coins, and cause difficulty to collectors of medieval money.

2. (ʒətɔ̃). A metal disc used, chiefly in France, instead of a coin for insertion in a public telephone box. Also *attrib.*

1942 E. PAUL *Narrow St.* xi. 82 In order for a client to use the phone he had to buy from her a metal disc or *jeton.* **1957** *Times* 16 Oct. 11/7 The French *jeton* system for calls from

public telephone boxes. *Jetons* were introduced in France because of frequent changes in the local call tariff (15 changes in 20 years) and in the diameter and material of the coinage. **1962** A. Williams *Long Run South* vi. ii. 193 An old crone sold him a jeton and he dialled the number of the house in the Viale Piemonte. **1972** *Times* 4 Jan. 14/8 (*heading*) Use the nickel sixpence as a jeton [for telephone coin boxes].

jet propulsion. [JET *sb.*[3]] The ejection of a usu. high-speed jet of gas (or liquid) as a source of propulsive power, esp. for aircraft.

1867 *Ann. Rep. Aëronaut. Soc.* 50 In spite of the costly experiments.. made to revive the system of jet propulsion, it was clear to him that the screw propeller must be much superior. **1877** C. B. Mansfield *Aerial Navigation* ii. xiii. 453 One of the great advantages attending the system of pump or jet propulsion in the air is that, however the force be generated, the direction in which it is applied may be instantly altered, without shifting the position of the actual instrument of motion. **1886** *Ann. Rep. Aëronaut. Soc.* 67 (*heading*) Jet propulsion for aëronautical purposes. **1892** J. H. Cotterill *Appl. Mech.* (ed. 3) 572 The efficiency of jet propulsion [of ships] can hardly be estimated as greater than ·33. **1920** *Chambers's Jrnl.* June 415/1 In the case of lifeboats liable to ground on sandbanks.. jet-propulsion has obvious advantages. **1935** Balmer & Wylie *After Worlds Collide* iv. 75 The most energetic members of the colony were working upon a small metal jet-propulsion [air]ship. **1944** *Time* 24 Jan. 66 This.. drawing illustrates.. the operation of a propellerless, jet-propulsion airplane. **1945** *Daily Express* 4 June 4/8 America's car manufacturers are secretly experimenting to produce the first jet-propelled car, using exhaust gases from the present car to boost power by jet propulsion. **1953** J. Y. Cousteau *Silent World* xi. 106 The octopus was downright terrified... It made off by slow jet propulsion, exuding spurts of its famous ink. **1962** F. I. Ordway et al. *Basic Astronautics* x. 392 Jet propulsion may be divided into two categories: ducted or air-breathing engines and rocket engines.

So **jet-propelled** *a.*, having or employing a means of jet propulsion; also *fig.*, very fast, frenzied; also (as a back-formation) **jet-propel** *v. trans.* (chiefly *fig.*).

[**1867** J. Bourne *Treat. Screw Propeller* (new ed.) p. cxix/3 Johnson's jet propeller.] **1877** W. H. White *Man. Naval Archit.* xiv. 612 Jet-propelled vessels, when moving ahead at full speed, derive their steering power from the reaction of the water in the wake upon the rudder. **1904** R. Kennedy *Mod. Engines & Power Generators* I. ii. 104 The Viper and Vixen, twin screw vessels of about the same tonnage.. were built as fair competitors with the jet propelled Waterwitch. **1922** *Flight* XIV. 276/2 *Many* of the inventions imagined by Jules Verne.. have already been realised, so who shall say that the design for a jet-propelled monoplane seaplane described by M. Maurice Armende.. will not materialise—some day? **1936** *Daily Sketch* 17 Nov. 13/4 In visualising a jet-propelled aeroplane of the future, the mind immediately thinks of a large hole in the tail, from which would come a blast of whatever gases were being released. **1944** A. Huxley *Let.* 9 July (1969) 507 One can be safe in betting that, within ten years, there will be rockets, or jet-propelled flying bombs,.. capable of flying any distance up to five thousand miles. **1945** F. Whittle in *Proc. Inst. Mech. Engin.* CLII. 422/2 At the beginning of 1940 the Air Ministry.. began to work on the assumption that there was a good chance of getting jet propelled fighter aircraft into production for use in the war. **1947** *Sci. News* IV. 35 When Sir Malcolm Campbell makes his next attempt on the world's speed record, he will be using a true 'jet-propelled' speedboat. **1949** *Sat. Rev.* (U.S.) 25 June 17/2 It was that courage.. that jet-propelled her onward and upward to stardom and marriage to Florenz Ziegfeld, Jr. **1950** in *Amer. Speech* (1956) XXXI. 285 They have learned to jet-propel bodies, but they haven't taken the first step in jet-propelling the human spirit. **1954** 'N. Blake' *Whisper in Gloom* i. i. 15 If the jet-propelled craft he had built failed to jet-propel itself. **1958** A. Huxley *Let.* 22 June (1969) 850 Time, as one advances in life, seems to become jet propelled. **1959** *Encounter* Aug. 35 He was lit up and jet-propelled by a sort of crazy, electric frenzy. **1960** *Times* 6 Aug. 9/5 On the same disc.. is Mendelssohn's concerto which Heifetz carries by assault. He lays into the triplets of the first movement.., plays the slow movement with a fair amount of elbow-power, and jet-propels the fairies through the last. **1962** *Economist* 19 May 672/1 Dr Nkrumah's phrase about achieving a 'jet-propelled' rate of economic growth. **1969** *Daily Tel.* 13 Feb. 22/8 The book conveys the period of music-making in the 1920s and 1930s and its air of domesticity far removed from today's jet-propelled bustle.

jetsam ('dʒɛtsəm). *Law.* Forms: 6 iottsome, 7 jettson, jetsen, jetzon, jotsom, -um, -on(e, 7-9 jetson, (8 jettezoon), 9 jetsom(e, -um, (jettison), 7- jetsam. [Orig. *jetson*, syncopated form of *jetteson*, JETTISON; but soon perverted to *jetsom(e* (? perh. by association with native words in *-some*), *jetsam*: cf. FLOTSAM. The fuller form *jettison* having been restored for sense 1, *jetsam* remains as the accepted form in sense 2.]

†**1.** The throwing of goods overboard; = JETTISON *sb. Obs.*

[**1600** Coke *Rep.* v. 106 b, Ietsam est quant le nief est in perill d'être merge et pur disburden le niefe les biens sont iects in le mere.. et nul de ceux byens que sont appeles Ietsam Flotsam ou Lagan sont appeles wreck cy longe come ils remain in ou sur la mere, mais si ascun de eux sont mise al terre per le mere, donques ils seront dit wreck.] **1641** *Termes de la Ley* 187 b, *Ietsam* is when a Ship is in perill to be drowned, and to disburden the Ship the Mariners cast the goods into the sea,.. but if any of them are driven to land by the sea, there they shall bee said wrecke, and passe by the graunt of wrecke. **1755** [see JETTISON *sb.*]. **1839** Bouvier *Law Dict.*, *Jettison, Jetsam*, the casting out of a vessel, from necessity, a part of the lading; the thing so cast out. **1883** *Wharton's Law Lex.* (ed. 7), *Jactus*, or *Jactura mercium* (a throwing away of goods), jetsam.

2. Goods thrown overboard from a ship in distress in order to lighten the vessel (and afterwards washed ashore).

The last clause is no part of the etymological meaning, but is found as early as 1570, having apparently originated from taking the word as 'that which is *thrown* or *cast ashore* by the sea'. This is directly opposed to the quot. from Coke in sense 1, and its transl. in *Les Termes de la Ley*. But it is the sense given in recent Law-books. Spelman and Blackstone took the meaning as 'merchandise thrown overboard and sunk in the sea'. Both explanations evidently arose in the attempt to distinguish *jetsam* from *flotsam*, in the phrase *flotsam and jetsam*. Etymologically *flotsam* should mean that which is afloat in consequence of a wreck or from the action of the wind or sea itself, *jetsam* that which has been thrown overboard to save the ship, without reference to whether it floats or sinks.

(In quot. 1570 the word appears to be used as adj. or adv.)

1570 in Boys *Sandwich* (1792) 775 [At a special brotherhood held at Sandwich: Decreed to give the Lord Warden of free gift and not otherwise the third part] of all wrecks and fyndalls floating and the half of all wrecks and fyndalls jottsome, viz. dryuen to the londe yshore. **1591** *Articles conc. Admiralty* 21 July §6 Any ship, yron, leade, or other goods floating or lying under the water or in the depth, of which there is no possessor or owner, which commonly are called Flotzon, Jetson, and Lagon. **1607** Cowell *Interpr.* s.v. *Flotsen*, Ietson is a thing cast out of the shippe being in daunger of wrecke, and beaten to the shore by the waters, or cast on the shore by the marriners. [**1626** Spelman *Gloss.* s.v. *Flotson*, Iotsone id quod sidet et moratur in fundo.] **1670** Blount *Law Dict.*, *Jetsen, Jetzon* and *Jotson*,.. Is any thing cast out of a ship being in danger of Wreck, and driven to the Shore by the Waves. **1678** Phillips (ed. 4), *Jetson* or *Jetsam*, that which being cast over board in time of Shipwrack, is found lying on the shore, and so belongs to the Lord,.. Flotsam is that which is espied floating on the Sea. **1708** *Termes de la Ley* 794 *Jettezoons*, This is mentioned in Policies of Insurance, and signifies Goods thrown into the Sea in a great Storm. **1765** Blackstone *Comm.* I. viii. 292 If they continue at sea, the law distinguishes them by the.. appellations of *jetsam, flotsam, and ligan.* Jetsam is where goods are cast into the sea, and there sink and remain under water. **1875** Tennyson *Q. Mary* iii. iii, These.. range with jetsam and with offal thrown Into the blind sea of forgetfulness. **1883** *Wharton's Law Lex.* (ed. 7), *Jetsam, Jettison*, or *Jetson*, goods or other things which having been cast overboard in a storm, or after shipwreck, are thrown upon the shore. **1894** *Act 57-8 Vict.* c. 60 §510 In this Part of this Act..'wreck' includes jetsam, flotsam, lagan, and derelict found in or on the shores of the sea or any tidal water.

b. *transf.* and *fig.*

1861 *All Y. Round* 1 June 235 Turkey buzzards were searching for flotson and jetson in the shape of dead Irish deck hands. **1878** *N. Amer. Rev.* CXXVI. 486 These are the mere flotsam and jetsam thrown up by the self-moving Gulf-Stream of Republican destiny. **1898** *Daily News* 18 Apr. 5/1 What a line of flotsam and jetsam it is!.. that mass of human wreckage. **1900** *Ibid.* 7 Apr. 8/2 His line of retirement.. was marked for miles by the jetsam of a hurried retreat—bags of flour, mealies, bran, and odds and ends of all sorts.

†**'jet-stone.** *Obs.* [f. JET *sb.*[1] + STONE.]

1. The mineral jet (JET *sb.*[1] 1).

1552 Huloet, Ieate stone, *gagates*. **1596** Dalrymple tr. *Leslie's Hist. Scot.* I. 47 In Ingland the Jeit stane is abundant. **1611** J. Davies *Commend. Poem Coryat's Crudities* 6 It giues wits edge, and drawes them too like Ietstone. **1748** tr. *V. Renatus' Distemp. Horses* 42 Of Jeatstone, male and female, three ounces each.

2. A piece of black marble or other black stone.

1598 Yong *Diana* 103 In the middes of the garden stoode a Ieat-stone vpon fower brazen pillers: and in the mids of it a tombe framed out of Iaspar. **1613** Purchas *Pilgrimage* (1614) 546 In the morning.. he is at his Beads,.. in a private faire roome, upon a faire Jet-stone.

jet stream. [f. JET *sb.*[3] + STREAM *sb.*] **a.** A fast-moving, relatively narrow stream of fluid that is present as a current in an atmosphere or ocean; *spec.* in *Meteorol.*, a strong wind confined to a narrow region of the atmosphere, esp. one in the upper troposphere at middle latitudes that blows in an approximately horizontal direction, predominantly from west to east.

1947 *Bull. Amer. Meteorol. Soc.* XXVIII. 255 During periods of reasonably straight west wind circulation over the North American continent, there exists normally, at levels between 5 km and 15 km above sea level, a fairly narrow zone of extremely strong west wind circulation (jet stream), reaching its maximum intensity and sharpness at the tropopause level. **1950** *Time* 29 May 70/2 Six miles up, where the air is thin and cold, a fearful wind zigzags round the earth at 200 m.p.h. Meteorologists call it the 'jet stream'. **1957** G. E. Hutchinson *Treat. Limnol.* I. iv. 225 The jet-stream mechanisms believed to maintain circulation in the region of the westerlies. **1963** tr. *E. R. Reiter's Jet-Stream Meteorology* iv. 271 (*heading*) Jet streams in the oceans. *Ibid.*, The current does not spread out.. but it remains concentrated in a narrow band of high velocities—the oceanic jet stream. **1971** *New Scientist* 8 Apr. 90/2 In the tropopause.. there is a meandering hemispheric band of high speed westerly winds, called the jet streams.

b. A jet of fluid (JET *sb.*[3] 4), esp. one ejected by a jet engine.

1955 *Sci. News Let.* 5 Mar. 160/3 Graphite lubricant is propelled in a jet-stream reaching many often inaccessible trouble spots. **1955** *Ibid.* 26 Mar. 200/1 These air whirlpools are not caused by either the propeller backwash or jet stream, but by the action of the plane's wings. **1959** S. N. Samburoff tr. *Feodosiev & Siniarev's Introd. Rocket Technol.* vii. 232 The presence of the jet stream.. introduces certain specific peculiarities into rocket aerodynamics. **1962** H. E. Newell *Express to Stars* iii. 29 It takes a force to expel material into a jet stream.. and by Newton's law of reaction there must be a reaction force.

jett, jette, obs. forms of JET.

jettage ('dʒɛtɪdʒ). *local.* [f. JETT-Y *sb.* + -AGE, after *wharfage, cranage*, etc.] Dues levied on vessels for the use of the jetty or pier (as at Hull).

1833 *Inq. Municipal Corpor., Hull*, Freemen as well as non-freemen pay Jettage. The charge for Jettage is not made unless with goods landed at or taken in at Hull or within the Harbour. **1844** McCulloch *Dict. Commerce* 505 Dues payable to the Corporation of Hull. On Vessels entering inwards and outwards.. *Jettage.*—Under 100 tons, 13*s.* 6*d.* **1852** *Hull Shipping Dues Act* 2209 Certain dues called.. jettage dues.

‖**jettatura** (jɛtə'tʊərə). [ad. It. *iettatura.*] The evil eye (see EVIL *a.* 6); bad luck. So **jetta'tore** [ad. It. *iettatore*], a person who brings bad luck.

1855 Mrs. Gaskell *Accursed Race* in *Househ. Words* 25 Aug. 78/2 Their glance, if you meet it, is the jettatura, or evil eye. **1882** C. M. Yonge *Unknown to Hist.* II. iii. 34 'Tis not only the *jettatura* wherewith the Queen Mother used to reproach me. Men need but bear me good will, and misery overtakes them. **1892** A. Lang *Bks. & Bookmen* (new ed.) 122 The superstitious might have been excused for crediting him with the gift of *jettatura*,—of the evil eye. **1921** *Glasgow Herald* 29 July 6 This simple remedy is much in use throughout Italy to-day as an antidote to the evil power of the Jettatore.

jette, jettee: see JETTY *sb.*

†**jetteau** (dʒɛ'təʊ). *Obs.* A form app. arising from confusing It. *getto* (*d'acqua*) and F. *jet d'eau*: see JETTO, JET D'EAU.

1705 Addison *Italy* (1767) 297 One might easily make a great variety of jetteaus.. in a garden that has the river Inn running by its walls. **1725** Bradley *Fam. Dict.* s.v. *Reservatory*, In order to make Jetteaus, one of the greatest Ornaments of a Garden. *a* **1763** Shenstone *Ess.* 103 Squirts up his rivulet in jetteaus.

jetted ('dʒɛtɪd), *a.*[1] [f. JET *sb.*[1] + -ED[2].] Ornamented with jet; trimmed with jet beads.

1888 *Daily News* 26 Mar. 3/3 A thickly jetted apron covered the front of the petticoat. **1893** *Pall Mall G.* 2 Feb. 1/2 The bretelles are of jetted velvet.

jetted ('dʒɛtɪd), *a.*[2] *Tailoring.* [app. f. JET *v.*[2]] Of a pocket: having no flap, but an outside seam on either edge, called the **jetting**.

1923 *Daily Mail* 23 Apr. 8 The skirt pockets, which are finished in jetted fashion. **1928** [see FLAPLESS *a.*]. **1933** J. E. Liberty *Pract. Tailoring* v. 38 *Jettings.* These are strips of material about 9 in. long and 2 in. wide. They.. are made up in two forms, flat jettings,.. and as a narrow piping.

†**'jetter**[1]. *Obs.* Forms: α. 4-5 gettour, 4-6 getter, (5 gettare, 6 -ar); β. 4 iectour, 5 iettoure, -ir, 6 iettar, 4-7 ietter. [ME. a. AF. *gettour = (in form) OF. *geteor, -our, -eur, getteur, jetteur* (also, 15th c., (after Lat.) *gecteur, jecteur*) thrower, caster (= It. *gettatore*):—pop.L. *jettātōr-em* = cl.L. *jactātōr-em* 'one who makes an ostentatious display of himself, a boaster, a braggart', agent-n. from *jactāre*: cf. JET *v.*[1] The sense in Eng. (prob. in AFr.) was app. taken from L. *jactātor*, as no similar sense is recorded in continental French.]

One who boasts, vaunts, or makes an ostentatious display; a swaggering or roystering fellow; a braggadocio, bully, 'blade', 'spark'.

α. **1303** R. Brunne *Handl. Synne* 761 þys gentyl men, þys gettours þey ben but Goddys turmentours. *c* **1380** Wyclif *Sel. Wks.* III. 281 Grete festis of riche men, as officeris of þe bischop and getteris of countre. —— *Wks.* (1880) 23 þei.. hanten tauernys of wyn and ale, aboute strumpetis.. and gay squyeris and opere getteris. *c* **1440** *Promp. Parv.* 192/1 Gettare, *gestulator, gestuosus.* **1494** Fabyan *Chron.* vii. 616 This yere.. was a great affray in Fletestrete, atwene ye getters of the innys of court, and the inhabytauntes of the same strete. **1530** Palsgr. 225/1 Gettar a braggar, *fringuereau.* *a* **1533** Ld. Berners *Gold. Bk. M. Aurel.* (1546) H, The hatred that this emperour had to trewandes, reuelers, getters, iuglers, gesters.

β. *c* **1380** Wyclif *Wks.* (1880) 242 Many ietteris of contre þat wolen make hem self gentel men and han litel or nouȝt to lyue onne. —— *Sel. Wks.* III. 195 Manye whanne þei ben drounken comen hom.. fro here cursed strumpatis and jectouris of contre, and chiden. *a* **1400-50** *Alexander* 4415 Iupiter [was] a Iettoure þat Iapid many ladis. *Ibid.* 4504 Dame Iuno was a iettir and ioyned full of iree. **1530** Palsgr. 234/1 Iettar of nyght season, *brigvevr.* **1611** Cotgr., *Fringuereau*, a ietter, spruce minion, gay fellow, compt youth.

jetter[2]. [JET *sb.*[1]] A digger of jet.

1614 *N. Riding Rec.* (1884) II. 67 Fr. Trewett, jeater.

'jetter[3]. [JET *v.*[2] + -ER[1].]

1. *Cornish Mining.* (See quot.)

1778 Pryce *Min. Cornub.* Gloss., *Pokkers* and *Jetters*, are blocks or pullies, over which the sweep rods of some engines move and play.

2. That which jets or throws out; in quot., a geyser.

1869 Baring-Gould *Orig. Relig. Belief* (1878) II. i. 2 Sprinkled with boiling water from a jetter in Iceland.

jettied ('dʒɛtɪd), *a. rare.* [f. JETTY *sb.* + -ED[2].] Furnished with jetties.

1882 *Harper's Mag.* LXV. 613 Instead of scouring out the jettied pass, it was scouring out the other two.

† **ˈjetting**, *vbl. sb.*^{1} *Obs.* [f. JET *v.*^{1} + -ING^1.]
a. Pompous walking, strutting. **b.** Wanton revelry, riot. **c.** Walking, strolling.

c **1440** *Promp. Parv.* 192/2 Gettynge in iolyte, *gestus.* **1509** BARCLAY *Shyp of Folys* (1874) I. 221 These folys as it were rorynge swyne With theyr gettynge and talys of vycyousnes Trouble all suche seruyce, that is sayd. **1546** J. HEYWOOD *Prov.* II. v. (1867) 57 Besyde his iettyng into the towne, to his gyls, With calets he consumeth hym selfe and my goodes. **1609** HOLLAND *Amm. Marcell.* XXVIII. i. 328 He affected to imitate the Bracmans, who..keepe a stalking and stately ietting among the altars. **1654** J. P. *Tyrants & Protectors* 15 May we not well remember..their man-like apparel,..their jetting, their strutting, their leg-making?

jetting (ˈdʒɛtɪŋ), *vbl. sb.*^{2} [f. JET *v.*^{2} + -ING^1.]
†**1.** Projection or jutting out; a projection. *Obs.*

1669 WORLIDGE *Syst. Agric.* (1681) 237 If it be a Wall for Fruit-trees, those Nooks or Corners in the Jettings out..are secure places for the more tender Trees. **1754–64** SMELLIE *Midwif.* II. 7 The protrusion or jetting forwards of the last Vertebra of the loins. **1760** WESLEY *Wks.* (1872) III. 16 A jetting out of the rock..gave me a very convenient pulpit.

2. a. A spouting or spurting forth; a jet.

1702 W. J. *Bruyn's Voy. Levant* xxxvi. 144 The Pipes and Cocks, and Generally all that is useful to the Jettings of Water. **1849** DANA *Geol.* iii. (1850) 243 A jetting of scoria, which has formed a pseudo-conglomerate.

b. (See quot. 1957.)

1941 *Nature* 5 Apr. 422/2 Work in Britain has been concentrated mainly on chemical means of protecting the host by the use of dips. Jetting has been tried in Scotland, but protective dusts have not been experimented with on a large scale. **1957** *New Biol.* XXII. 99 Mr. A. J. Gillespie, a woolgrower in Queensland, suggested jetting. This consisted of spraying the breech of the sheep with a jet of fluid delivered at a pressure of up to 120 lb per square inch from a nozzle whose aperture varied between 3/64 and 5/64 of an inch. A solution of sodium arsenite was the most popular jetting fluid.

3. A jerky moving up and down. (Cf. JET *v.*^{2} 6.)

1874 E. COUES *Birds N.W.* 68 Its habits are somewhat peculiar..such as the continual jetting of the tail.

4. *Building.* The loosening and removal of sand, gravel, etc., by directing jets of water or compressed air on to it, esp. so as to make a hole for pile-driving; the sinking of a pile by this means.

1942 *Amer. Speech* XVII. 280/1 *Jetting*, the act of pushing aside the mud or sand at the foot of a pile by a jet of compressed air or water. **1948** D. W. TAYLOR *Fund. Soil Mech.* xx. 647 Jetting often aids greatly in getting piles to the desired final grade. **1951** G. P. TSCHEBOTARIOFF *Soil Mech.* xv. 445 It is not always possible to drive piles..through a compact layer of sand without serious damage to the piles... Jetting of the piles has to be used then. **1956** H. L. NICHOLS *Mod. Techniques Excavation* v. 60/1 Jetting with high pressure water, or less commonly, compressed air, is used in making deep narrow holes for setting piles, installing vertical drains, obtaining soil samples, and for various other purposes. **1966** *McGraw-Hill Encycl. Sci. & Technol.* X. 228/1 Open-type piles are usually cleared of soil by jetting.

ˈjetting, *vbl. sb.*^{3} [f. JET *v.*^{3} + -ING^1.] Travelling in a jet plane.

1966 in WEBSTER. **1971** *Guardian* 9 Sept. 11/3 It is work which involves much jetting about,..lecture tours across the States, visits to North Vietnam.

† **ˈjetting**, *ppl. a.*^{1} *Obs.* [f. JET *v.*^{1} + -ING^2.] Ostentatious in gait or demeanour; strutting; boastful, vaunting.

c **1430** *A.B.C. of Aristotle* in *Babees Bk.* 12 To iettynge, ne to iangelinge, ne iape not to ofte. **1586** J. HOOKER *Hist. Irel.* in *Holinshed* II. 103/2 A Thrasonicall Golias..in ietting and daring wise chalenged anie one of the English armie. **1604** DRAYTON *Owle* 595 A ietting Iay accomplished and brave. **1631** BRATHWAIT *Eng. Gentlew.* (1641) 316 With a jetting and strutting pace.

Hence † **ˈjettingly** *adv.*

c **1440** *Promp. Parv.* 192/2 Gettyngly, *gestuose.*

jetting (ˈdʒɛtɪŋ), *ppl. a.*^{2} [f. JET *v.*^{2} + -ING^2.]
†**1.** Projecting, protruding, jutting. *Obs.*

a **1661** FULLER *Worthies* (1840) III. 396 Some drop, some stream down, partly over, partly through a jetting rock. **1707** SLOANE *Jamaica* I. p. xcviii, His belly a little jetting out or prominent. **1812** SCOTT *Rokeby* II. xv, Yon earth-bedded jetting stone.

†**2.** Darting, flitting. *Obs.*

1688 J. CLAYTON in *Phil. Trans.* XVII. 991 The *Pica Glandarea*, or Jay, is much less than our English Jay..it has both the same Cry, and suddain jetting Motion.

3. Spouting, spurting.

1886 R. F. BURTON *Arab. Nts.* (abr. ed.) I. 5 They came to a jetting fountain. **1898** ZANGWILL *Dreamers Ghetto* viii. 308 He strikes a dagger into his own heart, to sprinkle mockingly with the jetting black blood the ladies and gentlemen around.

† **ˈjettish**, *a.* *Obs. rare.* [f. JET *sb.*^{1} + -ISH^1.] Jet-like; jet-black.

1599 R. LINCHE *Fount. Anc. Fict.* H iv, A most perfect jettish hue.

jettison (ˈdʒɛtɪsən), *sb.* *Maritime Law.* Also 5 ietteson. [a. AF. *getteson*, in OF. *getaison*:—L. *jactātiōn-em*, action of throwing, f. *jactāre* to throw: see JET *v.*^{3} and -ISON. In spoken use, syncopated in 16th c. to *jetson* (cf. *benison*, *benzown*, *venison*, *ven'son*), and this further corrupted to *jetsome*, JETSAM, which also took a concrete sense, in consequence of which writers on Marine Insurance have restored the earlier form as *jettison* to distinguish the action.]

The action of throwing goods overboard, esp. in order to lighten a ship in distress.

[*Liber Niger Admiralitatis* (Rolls) I. 126 Quant il avient que len face getteson dune nef il est bien escript a Rome que toutes les marchandizes et denrees continues en la nef devoient partir au gette.] **1425** *Rolls Parlt.* IV. 304/1 Wool ..taken uppon þe see be Enemys, or lost be Jetteson, or be any oþer mysaventure. **1755** MAGENS *Insurances* I. 55 Whatever the Master of a Ship in Distress..deliberately resolves to do..in throwing Goods overboard to lighten his Vessel, which is what is meant by Jettison or Jetson. *Ibid.* II. 182 Ammunition, and Stores, Wages or Hire, and Cloaths of Seamen, shall not contribute towards the Jettison. **1843–63** WATERSTON *Cycl. Commerce* s.v. *Average*, A jettison, or other loss on which average is claimed. **1880** *Times* 30 Dec. 12/1 The Mars..was got off by a tug, after jettison of a portion of the cargo. **1882** *Ibid.* 29 Mar. 5/3 To regain his course..the aeronaut made jettison of all his ballast.

b. *fig.* 'Throwing overboard'.

1887 *Sat. Rev.* 6 Aug. 174/1 It illustrates more forcibly than any election that has yet taken place the jettison of convictions, of honour, of patriotism. **1900** *Q. Rev.* Apr. 321 Mere modernity..involved the complete jettison of every restraining principle in language, metre, and morals.

ˈjettison, *v.* [f. prec. sb.] **1. a.** *trans.* To throw overboard (cargo, articles of merchandise, etc.), esp. in order to lighten a ship in distress.

1848 ARNOULD *Mar. Insur.* (1866) II. III. iv. 778 The goods in such case are as much sacrificed for the general safety as though they were jettisoned. **1880** *Times* 13 July 10 The vessel experienced such severe weather that she was compelled..to jettison about 1000 cases petroleum. **1890** *Times* 23 Aug. 4/6 The jettisoning of timber is hazardous. *fig.* **1874** A. ROBERTSON *Nuggets*, etc. 177 When my patience was nearly all jettisoned I heard the sharp ting of a bell. **1895** *Westm. Gaz.* 27 Mar. 3/1 Count Tolstoy.. jettisons a chapter here, a verse there, an Epistle there.

b. To release or drop from an aircraft or spacecraft in flight; *spec.* to drop (a bomb) intentionally from an aircraft elsewhere than over an assigned target.

1934 [implied in JETTISONABLE *a.*]. **1942** D. M. CROOK *Spitfire Pilot* 66 Enemy bombers showed a much greater tendency to jettison their bombs. **1942** *R.A.F. Jrnl.* 18 Apr. 14 'C for Charlie's' pilot jettisoned his guns rather too near the wife of a senior officer who happened to be below. *Ibid.* 34 The crew went to their ditching stations... No fuel was jettisoned. **1946** TAYLOR & ALLWARD *Spitfire* 101/1 The hood..could be jettisoned. **1955** *Times* 10 Aug. 8/7 The world's fastest aircraft..was jettisoned by its mother aircraft after an explosion at 30,000 ft. **1974** *Flight International* 29 Aug. (Suppl.) 11/1 Surface-to-air missiles often use a booster to produce a high initial acceleration and push the missile clear of its launcher, the booster then being jettisoned.

2. *intr.* To drop off, or fall away from, an aircraft or spacecraft in flight.

1962 J. GLENN in *Into Orbit* 138 The escape tower, which we would not need once we got above the atmosphere, would jettison when the boosters dropped off and lighten the load even more.

Hence **ˈjettisoned** *ppl. a.*, **ˈjettisoning** *vbl. sb.*

1889 LD. WATSON in *Law. Rep.* 14 App. Cases 606 Every owner of jettisoned goods becomes a creditor of ship and cargo saved. **1950** *Engineering* 10 Feb. 158/1 Landing operations..could take the form of 'jettisoning' operations. **1957** J. S. HUXLEY *Relig. without Revelation* ix. 209 This wholesale jettisoning.

jettisonable (ˈdʒɛtɪsənəb(ə)l), *a.* [f. JETTISON *v.* + -ABLE.] Capable of being jettisoned from an aircraft or spacecraft; designed to be readily detachable in flight.

1934 *Shell Aviation News* No. 34. 18/1 As a result, the machine can be used for a variety of purposes... It is fitted with a 'jettisonable' fuel tank riveted with duralumin. **1946** *Aeroplane Spotter* 14 Dec. 290/1 The pilot and test engineer are housed in a conical nose section which is jettisonable and contains a decelerating parachute in case of emergency. **1956** *Spaceflight* I. 24/1 The second stage..is a new rocket; the final stage and the satellite package are enclosed within its jettisonable nose. **1961** E. BROWN *Wings on my Sleeve* x. 113 The undercarriage consisted of a retractable skid mounted on the jettisonable two-wheel chassis which was automatically dropped when the skid was retracted on take-off. **1963** A. SMITH *Throw out Two Hands* v. 52 The balloon commander is all,..the passenger is nothing more than jettisonable ballast.

† **ˈjetto.** *Obs.* [ad. It. *getto* (*d'acqua*) jet of water.] A jet d'eau.

1644 EVELYN *Diary* 22 Oct., The garden has..fountaines, especialy one of five jettos. **1685** *Phil. Trans.* XV. 1093 Two shells to receive the Water from the Jetto's. **1699** EVELYN *Acetaria* Plan, Fountains, Jetto's, Cascades.

jetton (ˈdʒɛtən). [a. F. *jeton* (13–14th c. in Hatz.-Darm.), f. *jeter* to throw, cast, to cast up (accounts), calculate: see JET *v.*^{2}]

A piece of metal, ivory, or other material, bearing an inscription or device, formerly used as a counter in casting up accounts and in card-playing. Also applied to medals or tokens of various kinds.

1762–71 H. WALPOLE *Vertue's Anecd. Paint.* (1786) II. 259, I have a good medal of Cardinal Richelieu, by Warin, who died in 1675, as I learn from a jetton of him by Dacier. **1769** SNELLING (*title*) View of the Origin, Nature, and Use of Jettons or Counters, especially those known by the name of Black Money and Abbey Pieces. **1819** J. MILLINGEN (*title*) Medallic History of Napoleon, a Collection of all the Medals, Coins, and Jettons relating to his Actions and Reign. **1868** G. STEPHENS *Runic Mon.* II. 535 There was also a class of Jettons commonly called Abbey-Counters, with similar or cognate instructive stamps.

jettoure, jettson, obs. ff. JETTER, JETSAM.

jetty (ˈdʒɛtɪ), *sb.* Forms: α. 5 get(t)ey, gette(e, gete(e, getty, 6 git(t)ie, 6–7 gettie. β. 5–6 iette, 7–9 jettee, (8 -ée, 8–9 jetée). γ. 6 iettye, 6–7 -ie, 7– jetty. See also JUTTY. [a. OF. *getee*, *jetee* the action of throwing, a thrown out or projecting part of a building (1392 in Godef.), a structure of wood or stone made to straighten the bed of a stream, or to protect the entrance of a harbour (1450 in Godef. *Compl.*), subst. use of fem. of pa. pple. of *jeter* to throw: see JET *v.*^{2} From the 18th c. sometimes treated as French and written with *-ée*.]

1. a. A mole, pier, or the like, constructed at the entrance of a harbour, or running out into the sea or a lake, so as to defend the harbour or coast; a similar structure running into a river so as to divert the current from a threatened part of the bank; an outwork of piles or timber protecting a pier, a starling. **b.** A projecting part of a wharf; a landing-pier, a timber pier of slight construction.

α. **1412–20** LYDG. *Chron. Troy* II. xxi. (MS. Digby 230) lf. 99/1 He vnwarly smet vpon the londe On the getees [*MS. Digby* 232 Gettys] and þe drye sonde þat hise shipes sheuered alle asoundre. **1450** *Rolls Parlt.* V. 187/1 In makyng and repairyng of a Getey, in defensyng of the seid Towne of Melcombe ayenst the flowyng of the See. **1541** *Act 33 Hen. VIII*, c. 33 The maintenance..of the..clowes sloweses gettiez gutters goottes and other fortresses.

β. **1478** W. BOTONER *Itin.* (Nasmith 1778) 125 Mem. from Pensance to Seynt Yves jette 6 myle. **1713** STEELE *Englishm.* No. 31 Two Peer Heads, commonly called the Jettées. **1772** HUTTON *Bridges* 95 Jettee, the border made around..a pier, being the same with Sterling. *Ibid.* 99 To surround a stone pier with a sterling or jettee. **1791** R. MYLNE *Rep. Thames & Isis* 52 There should be several Jettees thrown up, to confine the Stream, where it spreads too wide. **1804** *Burgomasters' Petit.* in Allnutt *Improv. Navig. Thames* (1805) 10 Such Jettees or Weir Hedges create very rapid and dangerous Currents. **1887** J. BALL *Nat. in S. Amer.* 267 Until the jetée ..should be finished.

γ. **1692** RAY *Dissol. World* (1732) 221 There were found Jettys, as they call them to keep up the old River-Bank. **1755** ROBERTSON in *Phil. Trans.* XLIX. 353 Near the borders of the dock, bason, and jetties. **1867** HERSCHEL *Fam. Lect. Sc.*, *Volcanoes* 38 Three thousand people had taken refuge on a new stone quay or jetty just completed at great expense. **1875** J. H. BENNET *Winter Medit.* II. xi. 337 A small and secure harbour, but so narrowed by the jetty that..the entrance is..difficult.

c. *transf.* and *fig.*

1587 GOLDING *De Mornay* viii. (1617) 112 [They] did serue rather for a Banke or Iettie against the ouerflowing of the Germanes. **1833** J. HODGSON in J. Raine *Mem.* (1858) II. 314 Jetties or binks of hard rock here and there protrude from the line of the perpendicular scars.

†**2.** A projecting part of a building; *esp.* an overhanging upper storey. *Obs.*

c **1440** *Promp. Parv.* 192/1 Getee of a solere (*K., H., P.* gete), *techa, procer.* **1462** in C. Welch *Tower Bridge* (1894) 108 Large gettes hangeing over the strete there. **1598** FLORIO, *Barbacane*,..an outnooke or corner standing out of a house, a iettie. **1657** HOWELL *Londinop.* 393 They [Wardmote Inquest] are to inquire..if any Porch, Pent-house, or Jetty be too low, in letting of Passengers that ride, or Carts. **1664** EVELYN tr. *Freart's Archit.* 137 Such monstrous jetties and excessive Superstructures as we many times find under Balconies. **1677** *Boston Rec.* (1881) VII. 109 The widdow Walker hath set vp 4 posts vpon the towne land to support the Gettie of her house.

transf. **1615** CROOKE *Body of Man* 433 The round head they call in Greeke στρογγύλον because it hath no προβολή or ietty eyther in the forehead or in the nowle.

†**3.** A bulwark or bastion. *Obs.*

1550 EDW. VI *Lit. Rem.*, *Jrnl.* (Roxb.) 307 At the west gitie [of Cales] there should bee another gittie which should defend the vitaylers of the towne..frome shott from the sandhills. **1736** T. PRINCE *New Eng. Chronol.* an. 1622, Made four bulwarks or jetties, whence we can defend the whole town. **1867** R. PALMER *Life Philip Howard* 52 Henry VI granted them land..to build a tower and jettee.

4. *attrib.* and *Comb.*, as ***jetty-end***; **jetty-head** (see quot. 1769); †**jetty-wise** *adv.*, in the manner of a jetty or projection.

1667 C. MERRET in *Phil. Trans.* II. 465 The Garret-windows are Jetty-wise. **1769** FALCONER *Dict. Marine* (1789), *Jetty-head*, a name..given, in the royal dock-yards, to that part of a wharf which projects beyond the rest; but more particularly the front of a wharf, whose side forms one of the cheeks of a dry or wet dock. **1884** STEVENSON *Lett.*, *To C. Monkhouse* 16 Mar. (1899) I. 311, I at the jetty end, and one or two of my bold blades keeping the crowd at bay.

jetty (ˈdʒɛtɪ), *a.*^{1} Also 5 **geaty**, 7 **ieaty, jettie.** [f. JET *sb.*^{1} + -Y.]
1. Of the colour of jet; jet-black.

1586 MARLOWE *1st Pt. Tamburl.* IV. i, His..ietty feathers menace death and hell. **1607** WALKINGTON *Opt. Glass* Ep. to Rdr. 4 Venus had her mole..Cynthia her spots, the Swan her ieaty feete. **1724–5** SWIFT *Receipt to Stella* 41 Your jetty locks with garlands crown'd. **1810** SCOTT *Lady of L.* II. i, At morn the black-cock trims his jetty wing.

b. quasi-*adv.* in *comb.*, as **jetty-black**, jet-black.

1477–8 *Bk. Curtesye* (Caxton) 44 Your naylis loke they be not gety blacke [*Hill MS.* gety blake, *Oriel MS.* geet blake]. **1622** DRAYTON *Poly-olb.* XXVI. 410 Among the Moors the

jettiest black are deem'd The beautifull'st of them. **1697** DRYDEN *Virg. Georg.* III. 136 His horny Hoofs are jetty black and round.

2. Of the nature or composition of jet.

1875 *Ure's Dict. Arts* III. 9 The jetty matter appears to have first entered the pores of the bone, and there hardened.

Hence **'jettiness**.

1776 PENNANT *Zool.* (1812) I. 441 (Reed Bunting) On the return of spring [the head] resumes its pristine jettyness.

† **'jetty**, *a.*^{2} *Obs. rare.* [f. JET *sb.*^{3} or *v.*^{2} + -Y.] Characterized by jetting or jutting; swelling.

c **1611** CHAPMAN *Iliad* II. D iij b, Twise twentie Iettie sailes with him the swelling streame did take.

jetty ('dʒɛtɪ), *v.*^{1} [f. JETTY *sb.*]

† **1.** *intr.* To project, jut: said of a part of a building. Cf. JET. *v.*^{2} 2, JUTTY *v. Obs.*

1598 FLORIO, *Porgere*, to iut, to iettie, or butte forth, as some parts of a building do, further then the rest. **1609** HEYWOOD *Brit. Troy* XV. lxvi, Some Greekes the Pallace scale, The Laders cleaue unto the iettying stones. **1615** G. SANDYS *Trav.* 120 Goodly buildings, having galleries.. which ietty over, sustained upon pillars.

† **2.** *trans.* To furnish with projections (see quot.). *Obs. rare*$^{-0}$.

1598 FLORIO, *Adentellare*,.. It is properly to ietty out or indent stones or timber of any vnfinished building, that another may the easier be ioyned vnto, or that finished.

3. To furnish with a jetty or starling. *rare.*

1889 *Sci. Amer.* 16 Feb. 105/2 The expense will be but moderate, by jettying with brush and pile, and finally strengthening of stone.

† **'jetty**, *v.*^{2} *Obs. rare.* In 6 **iettie**. [app. an extension of JET *v.*^{1} or ^{2}] *intr.* To move about briskly.

1573 TUSSER *Husb.* (1878) 159 Concerning how prettie, how fine and how nettie, Good huswife should iettie From morning to night.

jetzon, obs. form of JETSAM.

‖ **jeu** (ʒø). Pl. **jeux** (ʒø:). [F.:—L. *jocum* jest, joke, play, sport.] The French for 'play' or 'game'; occurring in several phrases, occasionally used in Eng.

a. † **jeu de dames** (ʒø də dam), in ME. *iew-de-dame*, the game of draughts: see DAM *sb.*^{3} (*obs.* exc. as Fr.).

c **1380** *Sir Ferumb.* 2225 Summe of hem to iew-de-dame; & summe to tablere.

b. jeu d'esprit (ʒø dɛspri): a play or playful action in which some cleverness is displayed; now usually, a play of wit in literary composition; a witty or humorous trifle.

1712 ADDISON *Spect.* No. 305 ⁋16 Whether any such Relaxations of Morality, such little *jeux d'esprit*, ought not to be allowed in this intended Seminary of Politicians. **1798** (*title*) The Spirit of the Public Journals for 1797, being an Impartial Selection of the most exquisite Essays and *Jeux d'Esprits*.. that appear in the Newspapers. **1855** KINGSLEY *Heroes* Pref. 21 The few scholars who may happen to read this hasty *jeu d'esprit*. **1889** *Spectator* 14 Dec. 849 Recollections of the *jeux d'esprit* and audacious onslaughts which made the guerilla warfare of the Fourth Party.. as little acceptable to the leaders of the Tory Opposition.. as it was to Mr. Gladstone.

c. jeu de mots (ʒø də mo), a play on words, a pun.

1749 LADY LUXBOROUGH *Lett. to Shenstone* 29 Nov., It consists.. of puns (or as the French properly call it, *Jeu de mots*) upon his name. **1823** SCOTT *Peveril* xxxvii, 'I have heard your Grace indulge in the *jeu de mots*', answered the attendant. **1898** *Westm. Gaz.* 27 July 3/2 Of course, many *jeux de mots*—as distinguished from *jeux d'esprits*—would be sacrificed.

d. jeu de paume (ʒø də pom) [Fr., lit. 'game of palm (of the hand)']: tennis (not lawn-tennis); also, a tennis court; also *fig.*

1789 A. YOUNG *Jrnl.* 20 June in *Trav. France* (1792) I. 115 The resolution.. was to assemble instantly at the *Jeu de paume*, and there the whole assembly took a solemn oath. **1880** GEO. ELIOT *Let.* 7 Oct. (1956) VII. 329 Johnnie gets a game of real tennis—jeu de paume—every day. **1910** *Encycl. Brit.* X. 450/1 Fives and racquets are probably both descended from the *jeu de paume*, of which they are simplified forms. **1939** A. TOYNBEE *Study of Hist.* IV. 161 Warfare now is no longer just a *jeu de paume* among a party of kings. **1940** E. POUND *Cantos* lviii. 74 Playing at jeu de paume and escrime. **1970** *Guardian* 3 June 9/2 The story that the *jeu de paume* has been played by members of the opposing army with a living infant as the ball, goes back hundreds.. of years.

e. jeu de règle (ʒø də rɛgl) [Fr., lit. 'game of rule']: in the game of *Écarté* (see quot. 1963).

1850 *Bohn's Hand-bk. Games* 261 On this principle all '*Jeux de Regles*' are played without changing (although there be a few which can scarcely reckon in their favor 2 to 1). **1934** *Neuphilol. Mitt.* XXXV. III/IV. 132 Écarté..*jeu-de-règle*, hand which should be played without taking cards. **1963** G. F. HERVEY *Handbk. Card Games* 61 There are certain stock hands, called *jeux de règle*, holding which a player should play and not propose, and equally refuse the opponent's proposal.

f. jeu de société (ʒø də sɔsjete) [Fr., lit. 'game of society']: (freq. in *pl.*) a game or amusement at a party.

1827 *Edin. Rev.* XLVI. XCII. 382 To these pantomimes succeeded ballets, and such *jeux de société* as 'La Peur'.. a sort of dumb show. **1854** THACKERAY *Newcomes* I. xxviii. 271 These little diversions and *jeux de société* can go on anywhere. **1932** H. NICOLSON *Diary* 1 Jan. (1966) 104 He.. had been kept up doing *jeux de société* till 8 am. **1963** A. ZAINA in B. Sewell *Two Friends* 78 The two duologues.. were obviously destined to be a *jeu de société*... Perhaps it was performed at one of the Raffalovich parties.

jeuk, obs. form of JOUK *v. Sc.*

jeuk skei: see JUKSKEI.

‖ **jeune fille** (ʒœn fij). [Fr.] A young girl. Used *attrib.* or as *adj.*: characteristic of an *ingénue*.

1802 H. ECKERSALL *Jrnl.* 4 July in Malthus *Trav. Diaries* (1966) 296 Les jeunes filles who were sitting near us were much diverted but did not look as if they would take his advice. *a* **1855** C. BRONTË *Professor* (1857) I. xii. 191, I took these sketches in the second-class school-room of Mdlle. Reuter's establishment, where about a hundred specimens of the genus 'jeune fille' collected together, offered a fertile variety of subject. **1888** E. DOWSON *Let.* 13 Nov. (1967) 19 It is not les filles de l'opéra or horizontales that I protest against—it is les jeunes filles de société. **1892** [see ENFANT GÂTÉ]. **1903** H. JAMES *Ambassadors* VI. xiv. 189 It will really be a chance for you.. to see the *jeune fille*—I mean the type —as she actually is. **1926** C. BEATON *Diary* in *Wandering Yrs.* (1961) 110 Miss Wilberforce plays safe in a *jeune fille* frock. **1928** D. H. LAWRENCE *Phoenix II* (1968) 519 Talking to an intelligent girl, the famous '*jeune fille*'.. you find.. that she, the innocent girl in question, is flinging all sorts of fierce questions at your head. **1946** 'S. RUSSELL' *To Bed with Grand Music* ix. 115, I always think romance is rather *jeune fille*. **1974** *Times* 30 Apr. 8/6 The dresses are ravishing—*jeune fille* dresses of the right sort, drifting and romantic.

‖ **jeune premier** (ʒœn prəmje). [Fr., lit. 'first young man'.] An actor who plays the part of the principal lover or young hero. So **jeune première** (prəmjɛr), the performer of the corresponding female part.

1852 *Blackw. Mag.* Nov. 600/2 The *prima donna* and *jeune premiere* of the troop. **1877** *Sat. Rev.* 24 Nov. 662/2 What the *jeune premier* would necessarily be when acting the part of a ruined country gentleman. **1888** *Athenæum* 3 Nov. 588/2 Theology always plays a part, albeit in the form of the *jeune premier*, the handsome curate with Broad Church instead of agnostic views. **1896** MRS. H. WARD *Sir G. Tressady* xiii. 283 Ancoats always seems to me the *jeune premier* in his own play. **1902** *Sat. Rev.* 13 Sept. 329/2 [He] plays him with no more intelligence than would suffice for the part of a quite ordinary jeune premier. **1924** 'R. CROMPTON' *William—the Fourth* iv. 71 William.. has eloped with a *jeune première* and a bear-skin. An entire Christmas pantomime is searching the village for him. **1946** MRS. BELLOC LOWNDES *Let.* 1 Jan. (1971) 269 Lord Rosebery.. was the *jeune premier* of that generation. **1958** L. DURRELL *Mountolive* xv. 272 Mountolive was now irradiated by an appalling sense of futility as he sat (like some ageing *jeune premier*) and listened to the torrent of Nur's excuses. **1960** *Guardian* 20 May 8/4 He.. became a highly successful jeune premier in light comedy and revue.

‖ **jeunesse** (ʒœnɛs). [Fr.] Young people; the young.

1781 H. WALPOLE *Let.* 25 July (1904) XII. 31 All the *jeunesse* strolled about the garden. We ancients.. retired from the dew. **1858** TROLLOPE *Doctor Thorne* II. xv. 309 'La jeunesse' was beginning to get a lesson; experience.. sometimes comes early in life. **1884** H. JAMES in *Atlantic Monthly* Sept. 310/2 In the early days of October when the whole *jeunesse* of the country is going back to school. **1947** *Horizon* Oct. 11 As if the wonderful *jeunesse* of America were suddenly to retain their idealism.

‖ **jeunesse dorée** (ʒønɛs dɔre). [Fr., lit. = gilded youth.] Orig. applied in France to the group of fashionable counter-revolutionaries formed after the fall of Robespierre; now *gen.*, young people of wealth and fashion.

1830 W. HAZLITT *Life Napoleon Buonaparte* I. viii. 383 The volatile genius of this people [*sc.* the French].. decked out the youth of the city [*sc.* Paris] (*La Jeunesse Dorée*) in the Chouan uniform. **1836** *Edin. Rev.* LXIII. 460 The indefatigable opponents of the ancient rudeness, the *jeunesse dorée* of Germany. **1837** [see GILT *ppl. a.* 2]. **1845** *Encycl. Metrop.* XIII. 374/1 These young men, who were commonly known as the 'Jeunesse dorée', no longer permitted the Jacobins to hold assemblies in the public places. *Ibid.*, The Jeunesse dorée and the Thermidorians had on their side the tradesmen. **1886** *Athenæum* 11 Sept. 329/2 We shall not envy the *jeunesse dorée* of the period these so-called sports. **1888** *N. & Q.* 7th Ser. V. 190/1 *Jeunesse dorée* answers, perhaps, rather to Disraeli's expression of 'curled darlings' than to 'dandy'. **1910** D. SCHWANN *Bk. Bachelor* 47 Mason.. received the guests, who were the fine flower of dramatic and critical Bohemia, with a sprinkling of the *jeunesse dorée* of Society and high finance. **1939** N. MONSARRAT *This is Schoolroom* I. i. 28 One of the favourite children, the *jeunesse dorée*. **1965** *New Statesman* 9 Apr. 568/2 The *jeunesse dorée* would have to go out and work for their living. **1969** J. MANDER *Static Soc.* v. 134 Those Country Clubs where the *jeunesse dorée* of Lima, Caracas and Bogota cavort. **1974** D. SMITH *Look back with Love* x. 90 The love-life of the Old Trafford *jeunesse dorée*.

jeupardy, -partie, obs. forms of JEOPARDY.

jeuse, obs. form of JUICE.

jevel(l, Sc. f. JAVEL^{1}, *Obs.*

jevellour, obs. Sc. f. JAILER.

jevilling, obs. Sc. f. JAVELIN.

Jew (dʒ(j)u:), *sb.* Forms: *Sing.* 3 **Gyu**, 4 **Giu, Gyw, Iu, Iuu, Iuw(e, Ieu, Ieuu, Ieuȝ**, 4–5 **Iwe**, 4 (6 *Sc.*) **Iow**, 4–7 **Iewe**, 5 **Ieue**, 5–6 **Iue, (Ive)**, 4–7 **Iew**, 7– **Jew**. *Plur.* 2 **Giwis**, 3 **Giws, Gius, Gyu(e)s**, 3–4 **Gywes, Giwes, Geus**, 4 **Iuu(e)s, Iuwis, Iow(e)s, Ioues, Iewis, -ys, -us**, 4–5 **Iuwes**, 4–6 **Iues**, 4–7 **Iewes**, 5 **Iuys**, 6 *Sc.* **Iowis, Iouis**, 4–7 **Iews**, 7– **Jews**; β. 4 **Iuen**. [ME. a. OF. *giu, gyu, giue*, earlier *juieu, juiu, jueu*:—L. *iūdæum* (nom. *-us*) Jew (cf. F. *dieu, ebreu*:—L. *deum. hebræum*); in later F. *juif*, fem. *juive*. L. *iūdæus* was a Gr. *ἰουδαῖ-ος*, f. Aramaic *y'hūdāi*, corresp. to Heb. *y'hūdī* Jew, f. *y'hūdāh* Judah, name of a Hebrew patriarch and the tribe descended from him. (The OE. equivalent was *Iudeas* Jews, Early ME. *Iudeow, Iudew*: see JUDEW.)]

1. a. A person of Hebrew descent; one whose religion is Judaism; an Israelite.

Orig. a Hebrew of the kingdom of Judah, as opposed to those of the ten tribes of Israel; later, any Israelite who adhered to the worship of Jehovah as conducted at Jerusalem. Applied comparatively rarely to the ancient nation before the exile (cf. HEBREW *sb.* 1), but the commonest name for contemporary or modern representatives of this group, now spread throughout the world. The word 'Jew' is also applied to groups, e.g. the Falashas in Ethiopia, not ethnically related to persons of the main European groups, the Ashkenazim and the Sephardim.

c **1275** *Passion our Lord* 351 in *O.E. Misc.* 47 Pilates hym onswerede, am ich Gyv þenne? *a* **1300** *Cursor M.* 3944 (Cott.) O sinnu etes neuer Iuu [*v.rr.* ieuu, iew]. *Ibid.* 11072 (Cott.) It halus bath Iu and sarzine. *c* **1310** in Wright *Lyric P.* (Percy Soc.) 100 Ich holde me vilore then a Gyw [*rimes* bowe, trowe, now]. *c* **1340** *Cursor M.* 4532 (Trin.) þerynne a iewes childe we fonde. *Ibid.* 18579 (Trin.) And namely leue herof no iwe For al þus dud þei wiþ ihesu. **1387** TREVISA *Higden* (Rolls) VI. 385 Charles Grossus was i-poysoned of a Iewe [*v.r.* Iuw]. *a* **1400** *Pistill of Susan* 2 þat was a Ieuȝ ientil, and Ioachin he hiht. *c* **1440** *Promp. Parv.* 266/2 Ive, *judeus*. **1530** PALSGR. 235/1 Jue a man of jurye, *jvif*. **1572** *Satir. Poems Reform.* xxxi. 173 Mair nor in Jurie dois the Jow. **1596** SHAKS. *Merch. V.* III. i. 61 What is the reason? I am a Iewe; Hath not a Iew eyes? **1615** G. SANDYS *Trav.* 52 His mother a Iew both by birth and religion. **1775** SHERIDAN *Rivals* II. i, She shall have a skin like a mummy, and the beard of a Jew. **1820** BYRON *Blues* I. 77 You forget Lady Lilac's as rich as a Jew. **1940** AUDEN *Another Time* 116 He [*sc.* Sigmund Freud] Was taken away from his old interest To go back to the earth in London, An important Jew who died in exile. **1956** I. MURDOCH *Flight from Enchanter* ix. 126 'Of course, you realize that I could rescue you with my little finger,' said Mrs Wingfield. 'I'm as rich as a Jew!' **1970** R. D. ABRAHAMS *Positively Black* iii. 76 The Englishman is arrogant and overbearing, the American is a check-writing millionaire who doesn't mind the cost, the Jew tries to push down the entry price into heaven. **1970** *Times* 28 Jan. 10/4 At the heart of the matter lies the rabbinical definition of a Jew: a person born of a Jewish mother, or a person who has converted to Judaism according to rabbinical law. **1974** J. R. BAKER *Race* xiv. 234 From the traditional religious point of view, a Jew was a person born of a Jewish mother, but this formula suffers from the defect that the defined word is included in adjectival form in the definition. The same flaw occurs in part of the new definition enacted by the Israeli Parliament in.. 1970, according to which a person is a Jew if he or she is the offspring of a Jewish mother or has been converted to the Jewish faith by the Orthodox Rabbinate or by the Rabbis of the Jewish Reform Movement or by the Rabbis of the Jewish Conservative Movement.

plural. *c* **1175** *Lamb. Hom.* 9 Alswa hefden þe giwis heore sinagoge. *c* **1250** *Old Kent. Serm.* in *O.E. Misc.* 26 Hi.. askede wer was se king of gyus þet was i-bore. *Ibid.*, King of geus. *a* **1300** *Cursor M.* 142 O þe Iuus [*v.rr.* iewes] and moyses. *Ibid.* 19129 (Gött.) þar badd þai iuen suld þaim ȝeme. *a* **1340** HAMPOLE *Psalter* xxvii. 5 þe iowes sloghe crist. **1387** TREVISA *Higden* (Rolls) VIII. 53 þat he schulde doo þe Iewes [*v.r.* Iuwes] out of Engelond. **1482** CAXTON *Trevisa's Higden* (Rolls) IV. 369 þe Iuwes accused Pilatus to Tiberius. **1533** GAU *Richt Vay* 30 Ve prech Iesu Christ crucifeit, sclander to the Iowis and folie to the gentils. **1548–9** (Mar.) *Bk. Comm. Prayer* (Coll. Good Friday), Haue mercy upon all Iewes, Turkes, Infidels, and heretikes. **1611** BIBLE *2 Kings* xvi. 6 At that time Rezin king of Syria.. draue the Iews from Elath. **1619** SANDERSON *Twelve Serm.* (1632) 2 In Rome there lived in the Apostles times many Iewes. **1710** etc. [see FALASHA]. **1776** GIBBON *Decl. & F.* xv, The same .. abhorrence for idolatry which had distinguished the Jews from the other nations of the ancient world. **1968** L. ROSTEN *Joys of Yiddish* 142 Relentless persecution of Jews, century after century, in nation after nation, left a legacy of bitter sayings: 'Dos ken nor a goy.' ('That, only a *goy* is capable of doing'). **1971** B. MALAMUD *Tenants* 50 The Jews got to keep us bloods stayin weak. **1974** J. R. BAKER *Race* xiv. 232 In various parts of the world today there are communities that practise the Jewish faith in one form or another, but are ethnically distinct from the Jews of Europe and North America.

gen. plur. *a* **1225** *Ancr. R.* 394 Uorto acwiten ut his leofmon of Giwene honden. *a* **1225** *Juliana* 62 Ant þoledest pinen ant passiun þurh giwes read on rode. *a* **1300** *Cursor M.* 4532 (Cott.) þar in a Iuen child [*Trin.* iewes childe] we fand. *c* **1300** *Ibid.* 19289 (Edin.) þe iuwin folc felune. *Ibid.* 21696 (Edin.) Mang þe Iuwis lede. *c* **1350** *Childh. Jesus* 616 (Mätz.) Giwene children feole.. Him siweden. *c* **1449** PECOCK *Repr.* III. iii. 291 If Cristen preestis weren Iewen preestis. **1653** GREAVES *Seraglio* 150 In the Kings Seraglio, the Sultana's are permitted to employ divers Jewes-women about their ordinary occasions.

b. *Jew's eye*: proverbial expression for something valued highly.

1592 G. HARVEY *Pierce's Super.* 85 A souerain Rule, as deare as a Iewes eye. **1596** SHAKS. *Merch. V.* II. v. 43 There will come a Christian by, Will be worth a Iewes eye. **1833** MARRYAT *P. Simple* ii, Although the journey.. would cost twice the value of a gold seal, yet, that in the end it might be worth a Jew's eye. **1844** WILLIS *Lady Jane* I. 212 From dome to floor, Hung pictures.. Each 'worth a Jew's eye'.

c. *Black Jew* (see quot. 1967); also = FALASHA.

1807 C. BUCHANAN *Jrnl.* 4 Feb. in *Christian Res. in Asia* (1811) 192 The resident Jews are divided into two classes, called the Jerusalem or *White* Jews; and the Ancient or *Black* Jews. The White Jews reside at this place [*sc.* Cochin]. The Black Jews have also a Synagogue here; but

the great body of that tribe inhabit towns in the interior of the province. *a* **1817** T. DWIGHT *Trav. New-Eng.* (1823) III. 174 The black Jews in Hindostan. **1822** *Imperial Mag.* IV. 358 A copy of the Hebrew Pentateuch..found in one of the Black Jews' Synagogues, at Cochin. **1843** J. C. MAITLAND *Lett. from Madras* xviii. 178, I told him about the first preachers, the Black Jews, the Syrian Christians, &c. **1892** G. M. RAE *Syrian Church in India* x. 150 These black Jews are converts to the faith from among the people of the land. **1907** I. ZANGWILL *Ghetto Comedies* 155 The black Jews..surrounded by all those millions of Hindoos. **1930** H. NORDEN *Africa's Last Empire* 185 The black Jews among whom he works. **1964** [see FALASHA]. **1967** D. T. KAUFFMAN *Dict. Relig. Terms* 77/1 *Black Jews*, in India, term applied to brown-skinned Jews to distinguish them from a group known as 'White Jews'. Sometimes used also for Negro Jewish groups. **1974** J. R. BAKER *Race* xiv. 232 The Falasha or 'black Jews' of Ethiopia are members of the Aethiopid subrace, a hybrid taxon.

d. A ship's tailor. Hence also **jewing** *vbl. sb.* and *ppl. a. Naut. slang.*

1916 *Chambers's Jrnl.* May 278/2 They [*sc.* ships' tailors] were still known as 'jews'. *Ibid.*, The term 'jewing', as sewing is still called. **1945** 'TACKLINE' *Holiday Sailor* x. 102 There was the 'Jewing-bloke', who undertook tailoring repairs. *Ibid.*, The 'Jewing-bloke' had a rather ancient Singer sewing machine, bought when ashore at Alexandria with..pay in his pocket. **1946** J. IRVING *Royal Navalese* 100 A sailor-tailor is known as a 'Jew'. **1962** GRANVILLE *Dict. Sailors' Slang* 66/1 *Jewing firm*, ship's tailoring 'firm' run by one or more ratings who repair and make clothing.

2. a. *transf.* and *offensive.* As a name of opprobrium: *spec.* applied to a grasping or extortionate person (whether Jewish or not) who drives hard bargains.

In medieval England, Jews, though engaged in many pursuits, were particularly familiar as money-lenders, their activities being publicly regulated for them by the Crown, whose protégés they were. In private, Christians also practised money-lending, though forbidden to do so by Canon Law. Thus the name of Jew came to be associated in the popular mind with usury and any extortionate practices that might be supposed to accompany it, and gained an opprobrious sense.

1606 *Sir G. Goosecappe* v. i. in Bullen *O. Pl.* III. 77 If the sunne of thy beauty doe not white me like a shippards holland, I am a Iewe to my Creator. **1700** BP. PATRICK *Comm. Deut.* xxviii. 37 Better we cannot express the most cut-throat dealing, than thus, You use me like a Jew. **1830** COLERIDGE *Table-t.* 16 May, Jacob is a regular Jew, and practises all sorts of tricks and wiles. **1844** D. KING *Ruling Eldership* II. i, It is undesirable..that he pass in the commercial circle for what is there termed a Jew. **1846** *Swell's Night Guide* 123/1 *Jew*, an overreaching fellow. *c* **1861** E. DICKINSON *Poems* (1955) I. 160 'Twould be 'a Bargain' for a *Jew*! *Say*—may I have it—Sir? **1906** J. M. SYNGE *Lett. to Molly* (1971) 31 What have I done that you should write to me as if I was a dunning Jew? **1920** T. S. ELIOT *Ara Vos Prec* 14 The jew is underneath the lot. Money in furs. **1931** T. R. G. LYELL *Slang* 428 Why waste your time asking him for a subscription? He's a perfect Jew where money's concerned. **1944** *Britannica Bk. of Year* 693 In March 1943 there were tirades from Bangkok radio against the 'Jews of Siam' (probably Chinese), who were accused of profiteering. **1952** G. BONE *Came to Oxf.* xi. 34 There is a curious fallacy, rather wide-spread, that a borrower of money is an innocent and hapless person, while a lender is a shark, a harpy, a 'Jew'. **1964** H. BROTZ *Black Jews of Harlem* iii. 54 Occasionally the Black Jews forget they are Jews when complaining about the fact that 'the Jews' own all or most of Harlem!

b. A pedlar.

In this use not depreciatory.

1803 G. COLMAN *John Bull* III. ii. 32 Here is two poets, and a poll-parrot, the best image the Jew had over his head, over the mantle-piece. **1963** 'E. MCBAIN' *Ten Plus One* (1964) iv. 42 There was a guy who used to come around to the door selling stuff, and my mother called him 'The Jew'... For her, 'Jew' was synonymous with pedlar. **1970** J. H. GRAY *Boy from Winnipeg* 43 For us, however, 'Jew' was just another generic word that often included the peddlers who were Greek or Italian. When we scrounged bottles it was to sell to 'the Jew', who was anybody that came along buying junk.

3. *attrib.* and *Comb.* **a.** *attrib.* or as *adj.* That is a Jew, Jewish, as ***Jew boy***, ***butcher***, ***girl***, ***man***, ***pedlar***, ***physician***, ***trooper*** (such expressions now mainly in offensive use but not originally opprobrious); of or relating to Jews, as ***Jew bill***, ***hatred***, ***toll***. **b.** objective, similative, etc., as ***Jew-drowning***, ***-hater***, ***Jew-dear***, adj.; ***Jew-like*** adj. and adv., ***-looking*** adj.

1765 BLACKSTONE *Comm.* I. x. (1793) 375 Very high debates about the time of the famous *Jew-bill; which enables all Jews to prefer bills of naturalization in parliament, without receiving the sacrament. **1796** P. COLQUHOUN *Treat. Police of Metropolis* (ed. 3) vi. 125 *Jew Boys..go out every morning loaded with counterfeit Copper, which they exchange for bad Silver, to be afterwards coloured anew, and again put into circulation. **1817** M. EDGEWORTH *Harrington* iii. 45 Mowbray easily engaged me to join him against the Jew boy; and a zealous partizan against Jacob I became. **1873** TROLLOPE *Eustace Diamonds* II. liii. 361 You used to be very wicked, and say he was once a Jew-boy in the streets. **1929** D. H. LAWRENCE *Let.* 10 Oct. (1962) II. 1208, I do hate John's Jewish nasal sort of style—so uglily moral... Spring doesn't only come for the moral Jew-boys—for them perhaps least. **1948** J. BALDWIN in *Commentary* Oct. 334/2 Jules Weissman, a Jewboy, had got the room for me. **1954** Jewboy [see IKEY *sb.* and *a.*]. **1959** N. MAILER *Advts. for Myself* (1961) 50 Jewboy, blond Jewboy Wexler perched by the cellar window, tackling Japs with machine-gun bullets. **1968** *Daily Mail* 9 Feb. 3/3 Angry viewers rang the BBC last night to complain about an 'anti-Semitic' remark on the TV programme *Softly, Softly*. In last night's episode..the detective tells the man: 'You always were a great one for putting things in your wife's name, Bob, just like a Jewboy heading for bankruptcy.' **1972** *Observer* 7 May, Mrs Lane Fox dismisses what she calls the country set, who call their children 'the brats', talk about 'thrashing them into shape', support Enoch Powell and still refer to 'jew boys'. **1974** *New Society* 3 Jan. 11/2 A car's desirability also creates the opposite reaction, in that envy is easily turned to resentment and aggression towards, for instance, the 'jewboy', the 'poser', the 'toffee nose' and the 'business classes' who sport expensive and powerful cars. **1849** W. S. MAYO *Kaloolah* (1887) p. viii, Oil, garlic, salt fish, and *Jew brandy. **1613** PURCHAS *Pilgrimage* (1614) 213 Thus you see the *Iew-butcher had need be no botcher, but halfe a Physitian in Anatomizing. **1755** J. SHEBBEARE *Lydia* (1769) I. 274 [He] must have had this *jew-craft among his reasons for endeavouring to naturalize the Jews. **1899** A. WHITE *Modern Jew* 122 There are many instances of the drollery of *Jew-drowning in the annals of monkish historians. **1796** E. WYNNE *Diary* 11 Dec. (1937) II. ix. 139 Before having ever seen us she declared that we were all excepting the youngest, like little crows and *Jew girls. **1930** E. POUND *XXX Cantos* x. 45 Wives, jew-girls, nuns. **1971** B. MALAMUD *Tenants* 50 Jewgirls are the best whores. **1899** *Westm. Gaz.* 18 Sept. 2/2 The nature of the wounds roused amongst the *Jew-haters the old story of the blood sacrifice. **1898** *Nat. Rev.* Aug. 807 Outside Russia, *Jew hatred is a matter with which Governments have no direct concern. **1808** COBBETT *Pol. Reg.* XIII. 172 Through the means of a *jew-like commerce with the revolted slaves. **1905** JOYCE *Let.* 29 Oct. (1966) II. 127 For a *Jewman it's better than having to bathe. **1922** —— *Ulysses* 336 I'll brain that bloody jewman for using the holy name. **1938** W. B. YEATS *John Kinsella's Lament* in *London Mercury* Dec. 114 Though stiff to strike a bargain Like an old Jew man. **1771** SMOLLETT *Humph. Cl.* 20 Apr. Let ii, I was cheapening a pair of spectacles with a *Jew-pedlar. **1731** *Gent. Mag.* I. 403 Dr. Bass, a noted *Jew Physician in St. Mary Axe. *a* **1680** BUTLER *Rem.* (1759) II. 84 And crucify his Saviour worse Than those *Jew-Troopers, that threw out, When they were raffling for his coat.

c. Special Combs.: **Jew-bail**, insufficient bail, 'straw-bail'; **'Jew-baiting** *sb.* [= Ger. *Judenhetze*], systematic harrying or persecution of Jews; so **Jew-bait** *v. nonce-wd.*, **Jew-baiter**, **Jew-baiting** *a.*; **Jew-bush**, a euphorbiaceous plant of the genus *Pedilanthus*; **Jew-cart** (see quot.); **Jew-lizard**, a large Australian lizard, *Amphibolurus barbatus*; **Jew plum** = OTAHEITE APPLE; **Jew Tongo**, a language spoken among Bush Negroes in Surinam, possessing a structure largely derived from West African languages and a vocabulary largely derived from English.

1785 GROSE *Dict. Vulg. T.*, **Jew Bail*. **1797** MARY ROBINSON *Walsingham* IV. 283 He..did the deep ones with Jew-bail, till they were up to the trick. **1892** *Sat. Rev.* 18 June 700/2 [He] is always going about Jew-baiting and to *Jew-bait with pen or sword. **1883** *Pall Mall G.* 19 Nov. 3/1 [They] are now in full possession of the case of the German *jew-baiters against the Jews. **1907** I. ZANGWILL *Ghetto Comedies* 85 She's honest... She won't fall back on the old Jew-baiter. **1945** W. S. CHURCHILL *Victory* (1946) 145 Julius Streicher, most notorious of Jew-baiters, was captured by the Americans. **1960** C. DAY LEWIS *Buried Day* vi. 116 The same herd instinct that produces Teddy Boys, Jew-baiters and Ku-Klux-Klansmen. **1974** G. MITCHELL *Javelin for Jonah* xi. 133 Benjy was unlucky enough to fall foul at school of a ring of young Jew-baiters. **1883** *Evening Post* (N.Y.) 21 Apr., The *Jew-baiting in Germany; the bloody persecutions in Russia. **1898** *Nat. Review* Aug. 807 In the Empire of the Tsar..Jew-baiting is a matter of high State policy. **1922** JOYCE *Ulysses* 202 Shylock chimes with the jewbaiting that followed the hanging. **1939** *Ann. Reg. 1938* 203 The brutalities began on April 23, and it was clear that the scheme of Jew-baiting had been worked out in readiness for the 'Anschluss'. **1969** J. MANDER *Static Soc.* iii. 99 The American, however ugly, is no Jew-baiting *Gauleiter*. **1830** LINDLEY *Nat. Syst. Bot.* 105 The *Jew Bush, or Milk plant. **1840** MARRYAT *Poor Jack* xviii, Then we have what we call *Jew Carts, always ready to take [stolen] goods inland, where they will not be looked after. **1847** LEICHHARDT *Jrnl.* iii. 89 A small Chlamydophorus (*Jew lizard of the Hunter [River]) was also seen. *a* **1884** J. SERVICE *Thir Notandums* (1890) 205 From beneath a log the green Jew-lizard, or the iguana peeps. **1913** W. HARRIS *Notes Fruit & Veg. in Jamaica* 18 The *Jew Plum..was introduced to Jamaica in 1782 and again in 1792. **1920** W. POPENOE *Man. Tropical & Subtropical Fruits* iv. 156 Jew-plum is another name for the ambarelle, used in Jamaica. **1971** *Caribbean Q.* XVII. II. 14 Different name, same referent..golden apple/Jew plum/pomme-citerre. **1933** L. BLOOMFIELD *Lang.* xxvi. 474 Two creolized forms of English are spoken in Suriname (Dutch Guiana). One of these.., more divergent from ordinary types of English, is known as *Jew-Tongo. **1968** W. J. SAMARIN in J. A. Fishman *Readings Sociol. of Lang.* 666 Amerindian pidgins... Saramakan (Jew Tongo, Ningre-Tongo).

d. Genitival Combs.: **Jews' apple**, a name for the Egg-plant or its fruit; **Jews' frankincense**, a plant of the genus *Styrax*, or the resin obtained from it (storax or benzoin); **Jews' houses**, name given to the remains of ancient tin-smelting furnaces in Cornwall; †**Jew's letter**, a text inscribed in Hebrew upon a phylactery, regarded as the outward symbol or badge of a Jew; †**Jews' lime**, a synonym of *Jews' slime* (see below); **Jews' mallow**, a name for *Corchorus olitorius* (N.O. *Tiliaceæ*), one of the plants from which the fibre called jute is obtained, used as a pot-herb in Egypt, Syria, and other countries; †**Jews' money**, a popular name for ancient Roman coins found in some parts of England; **Jews' myrtle**, a name for Butcher's Broom, and for a variety of the common Myrtle; **Jews' pitch**, †**Jews' slime**, names for asphalt or bitumen (cf. Gen. xi. 3); **Jews' thorn** = *Christ's thorn* (see CHRIST 5); **Jews' tin**, name for lumps of tin found in ancient smelting-furnaces (*Jews' houses*) in Cornwall.

1884 MILLER *Plant-n.*, *Solanum esculentum*, *Jew's-Apple, Mad-Apple... *S. Melongena*,..Egg-plant, Jew's-Apple. **1760** J. LEE *Introd. Bot.* App. 315 *Jew's Frankincense, *Styrax*. **1851** *Illustr. Catal. Gt. Exhib.* 162 In the reign of King John, the mines [were] principally in the hands of the Jews..remains of furnaces, called *Jews' houses, have been discovered, and small blocks of tin, known as Jews' tin, have..been found in the mining localities. **1589** R. HARVEY *Pl. Perc.* (1860) 32 *Iewes letter scrible scrable ouer the Copurtenaunce of a mans countenaunce. **1598** FLORIO *Worlde of Wordes* To Rdr. A vj, A fouler blot then a Iewes letter..in the foreheads of Cælius and Curio. **1731–3** MILLER *Gard. Dict.* s.v. *Corchorus*, **Jews Mallow*, ..sown in great Plenty about Aleppo as a Pot-herb, the Jews boiling the Leaves of this Plant to eat with their Meat. **1887** MOLONEY *Forestry W. Afr.* 289 'Jews' Mallow' or 'Jute' (*Corchorus olitorius*, L.)—Annual. This is one of the species that affords the well-known fibre of commerce called 'Jute'. **1577** HARRISON *England* II. xxiv. (1877) I. 360 Some peeces or other are dailie taken vp, which they call Borow pence, Dwarfs monie..*Iewes monie, and by other foolish names not woorthie to be remembred. **1856** *N. & Q.* Ser. II. I. 432/2 In some parts of Kent it [*Ruscus aculeatus*] is called '**Jews' Myrtle*'; and it is the popular belief, that the crown of thorns..was composed of its branches. **1756** P. BROWNE *Jamaica* 40 Asphaltum, *Jew's pitch. **1816** TINGRY *Varnisher's Guide* (ed. 2) 1 Asphaltum..issues in a liquid form from the bottom of the lake Asphaltis in Judæa; and hence the name of Jew's pitch. **1607** TOPSELL *Four-f. Beasts* 188 *Iewes lime drunk in water..prescribed for a remedy of this euill. **1639** HORN & ROB. *Gate Lang. Unl.* x. §104 Salt-peter, brimstone, Jew's slime, patrol, bole-armoniak,..are called mineral juyces. **1597** GERARDE *Herbal* Index, *Iewes thorne, that is Christs thorne. [III. xxvi. 1153 This shrubbie thorne *Paliurus* was the thorne wherewith they crowned our Sauiour Christ.] **1851** *Jews' tin [see *Jews' house*].

Jew, jew, *v. colloq.* [f. JEW *sb.* (sense 2).] *trans.* To cheat or overreach, in the way attributed to Jewish traders or usurers. Also, to drive a hard bargain, and *intr.*, to haggle. Phr. *to jew down*, to beat down in price; also *transf.* Hence **'Jewing** *vbl. sb.*

These uses are now considered to be offensive.

1824 C. HARDING *Diary* 29 Apr. in *Sketch* (1929) 75 He is a country clergyman; and, from his Jewing disposition, I should judge he had more taste in tithes than pictures. **1825** *Constitutional Adv.* (Frankfort, Kentucky) 15 Dec. 3/1 We hope, for the honour and character of the state, that neither the legislature nor the people, will Jew the items of expence. **1833** L. DOW *Dealings of God* (1849) 189 If they [*sc.* the Jews] will *Jew* people, they cannot flourish among Yankees, who are said to '*outjew*' them in trading. *a* **1845** BARHAM *Ingol. Leg.*, *Bro. Birchington* lxv, Is it that way you'd Jew one? **1847** W. IRVING *Let.* 30 Apr. in *Life & Lett.* (1864) IV. 19 Some mode of screwing and jewing the world out of more interest than one's money is entitled to. **1848** W. BAGLEY *Let.* 14 Mar. in N. E. Eliason *Tarheel Talk* (1956) 279, I Jewed old Galloway down to 1·50 for ploughs. **1851** H. MAYHEW *London Labour* I. 368/1 Some of the ladies in the squares..sets to work Jewing away as hard as they can, pricing up their own things, and downcrying yourn. **1854** D. G. ROSSETTI in Rossetti *Ruskin, Rossetti*, etc. (1899) 15 But as to his doings And jawings and jewings, William brought me the news. **1870** *Congress. Globe* 7 July 5340/1 This bill supposes that Congress..is ready to commence jewing down the pay of its General. **1872** *Chicago Tribune* 14 Oct. 8/2 The prices [for lodging] asked vary—the lodger being generally asked as much as it is thought he will give. If he jews, he will get it for comparatively little. **1883** G. M HOPKINS *Let.* 6 Dec. (1938) 195 You will I know say..that Jew is a reproach because the Jews have corrupted their race and nature, so that it is their vices and their free acts we stigmatise when we call cheating 'jewing'—and that you mean that Disraeli in 1871 overreached and jewed his constituents. **1891** *Daily News* 2 Nov. 7/3 He'd take care he didn't 'Jew' him again. **1897** [see HIGHLAND *a.* 2 b]. **1908** *Dialect Notes* III. 324 *Jew*, to beat down the price. 'I tried to jew him, but he wouldn't jew.' **1926** *Market Growers Jrnl.* 1 July 3, I make my retail prices about half way between grocery store wholesale and retail prices, and do not stand for any 'jewing' down. **1937** *Scribner's Mag.* Apr. 25 Thought we might get the divorce a little under fifty dollars. Maybe we might jew the young man down. **1939** A. POWELL *What's become of Waring* v. 140 Then we can meet again and jew each other down. **1946** W. G. HAMMOND *Remembrance of Amherst* 121 Both here and at the mountain top we were unmercifully jewed for all the refreshments. **1947** L. Z. HOBSON *Gentleman's Agreement* i. 9 Now she was describing the large new house she and Dick wanted to buy. 'Did you close the sale on the old place?' Mrs. Green asked. 'Not yet. That cheap Pat Curran keeps trying to Jew us down.' **1968** L. ROSTEN *Joys of Yiddish* 142 Just as some Gentiles use 'Jew' as a contemptuous synonym for too-shrewd, sly bargaining ('He tried to Jew the price down,' is about as unappetizing an idiom as I know), so some Jews use *goy* in a pejorative sense. **1970** R. LOWELL *Notebk.* 69 This embankment, jewed—No, yankeed—by the highways down to a grassy lip. **1971** R. THOMAS *Backup Men* xxi. 184, I say how much and he says this much and I say it's not enough so we jew around with each other until we make a price. **1972** *Harper's Mag.* May 83 Jew the fruitman down for his last Christmas tree. **1972** *New Society* 11 May 301/1, I got jewed down..over the cheap offer.

Jewdom ('dʒ(j)uːdəm). *rare.* [f. JEW *sb.* + -DOM, after *Christendom*.] The Jewish world or community; the religious system of the Jews.

1869 BARING-GOULD *Orig. Relig. Belief* (1878) I. x. 202 The existence of the Jews as a nation was annihilated, but Jewdom survives to this day. **1881** EMERSON in *Scribner's Mag.* XXII. 89 Coupled..with the utmost impatience of Christendom and Jewdom and all existing presentments of the good old story. **1891** *Field* 14 Feb. 241/2 On the glass..

are nine figures for Jewdom, Heathendom, and Christendom, three..heroes for each.

jewel (ˈdʒ(j)uːəl), *sb.* Forms: α. 3–6 iuel, -e, 4 iuwele, 4–5 -el(l, iuell(e, (ieueal), 5 iuall, iwell, (yewel), 5–6 *pl.* iuelx, 6 *Sc.* iwale. β. 4–5 iowel, 4–6 iowell(e, 5 -aile, (yowele), 6 ioell, *Sc.* iowalle. γ. 3 gywel, 4 gewel, 5 -elle; 4 iywel, iewile, 4–5 iewele, (5 iewle), 4–6 -elle, 5–7 -ell, 4–7 iewel, 7– jewel. δ. 4 ioyel, *pl.* ioiax, ioyaus, 5 *pl.* ioyaulx, 6 ioyelle, (ioywell). [a. AF. *juel, jeual*, = OF. *joel* (nom. sing. and obj. pl. *joeaus, joiaus*), 12th c. in Hatz.-Darm., 13–14th c. *jouel*. 14– 15th c. *joiel*. *joiau*, mod.F. *joyau*: cf. Pr. *joell, joyel*, Cat. *joyell*, Sp. *joyel*, It. *gioiello*; all app. from Fr.

The etymology of the Fr. word is still a matter of dispute; some see in it a deriv. of L. *gaudium* (quasi **gaudiellum*), whence F. *joie*, joy; others of L. *jocāre*, whence F. *jouer* to play, or of the cognate *jocus*, F. *jeu* play, through a deriv. *jocāle*. Cf. also JUELET. The med. L. was (13th c.) *jocāle*, pl. *jocālia*. See Diez, Littré, Schéler, Hatz.-Darm., Koerting *Lat. Rom. Wbch.* s.v. *jocālis*.]

1. a. An article of value used for adornment, chiefly of the person; a costly ornament, *esp.* one made of gold, silver, or precious stones. *Obs.* in *gen.* sense; now restricted to a small ornament containing a precious stone or stones, worn for personal adornment (cf. sense 2): see also b.

α. *c* **1290** *Beket* 1110 in *S. Eng. Leg.* I. 138 Noble ȝiftes and oþur Iueles. *c* **1330** R. BRUNNE *Chron.* (1810) 154 Richard.. gaf him a faire Iuelle, þe gode suerd Caliburne. **1362** LANGL. *P. Pl.* A. III. 151 Barouns and Burgeis heo bringeþ to serwe, Heo buggeþ with heore Iuweles. **1390** GOWER *Conf.* III. 312 Of gold he leide Sommes grete And of jeueals a strong beyete. **1460** *Lybeaus Disc.* 877 Well ryche and reall.. Wyth many a juall. **1475** *Bk. Noblesse* (Roxb.) 32 For no sight of juelx and riches of cheynes of golde or nouches. *a* **1548** HALL *Chron., Hen. V* 79 b, Garnished with precious stones and decked with Iuelx bothe radiant and pleasant. *Ibid., Hen. VIII* 209 Diverse precious Iuelles and greate horses. **1560** DAUS tr. *Sleidane's Comm.* 3 b, An hat set with golde, pearle, and precious Iwels.

β. *c* **1330** R. BRUNNE *Chron.* (1810) 152 A noþer iowelle fairer & worþi. *c* **1375** *Sc. Leg. Saints, Nycholas* 499 Of oure Iowelys als tak ȝe, & berys hyme. *c* **1400** MAUNDEV. (Roxb.) xxx. 135 Full of gold and of iowailes and precious stanes. *c* **1440** *Promp. Parv.* 264/1 Iowel, or iuelle, *Iocale*. **1502** *Will of Myrfyn* (Somerset Ho.), My basyn of siluer there to remayne for euer as a Iowell to be occupied at the high awter. **1508** KENNEDIE *Flyting w. Dunbar* 278 The Croce of Halyrudhouse, and vthir iowellis. **1570** *Satir. Poems Reform.* xxiii. 37 Thairfoir that hauld and worthie house of stone He gaif to the with Iowallis mony one.

γ. **1297** R. GLOUC. (Rolls) 10460 þe king offrede him a marc, & anoþer gywel þer to. *c* **1300** *Beket* (Percy Soc.) 1118 Noble ȝiftes and gewels. *c* **1380** WYCLIF *Serm.* Sel. Wks. III. 50 Ȝyvyng of jewelis to bigge chirchis. *c* **1400** *Destr. Troy* 1368 Gemys ne gewellis, ne no ioly vessell. **14..** *Lat.-Eng. Vocab.* in Wr.-Wülcker 590/30 *Iocale*, a iewel. **1477** EARL RIVERS (Caxton) *Dictes* 125 To haue fayre horsses and riche gownes, and other Iewles. **1568** GRAFTON *Chron.* II. 194 Piers of Gavestone..had at the last the guydyng of all the kinges Iewelles and treasure. **1601** SHAKS. *Twel. N.* III. iv. 228 Heere, weare this Iewell for me, tis my picture. **1613** PURCHAS *Pilgrimage* (1614) 767 Attire of Beares skins, hanged with Beares pawes, the head of a Wolfe, and such like iewells. **1655** FULLER *Ch. Hist.* IX. iii. §2 A Iewell (sometimes taken for a single precious stone) is properly a collective of many, orderly set together to their best advantage. **1762–71** H. WALPOLE *Vertue's Anecd. Paint.* (1786) I. 37 *note*, King Alfred's jewel, found at Athelney in Somersetshire,.. I call it a jewel, because it seems to have been used as jewels were after-wards, appendent to ribbands.

δ. **1340** *Ayenb.* 118 He hise loueþ mid al his herte, and hire brengþ of his ioiax. *Ibid.* 216 Ich hatie þe toknen of prede and þe blisse of agrayþinges and of ioyaus. **1485** CAXTON *Paris & V.* 15 He dyd doo sette these thre Ioyaulx or Iewels in the baners. **1502** *Priv. Purse Exp. Eliz. of York* (1830) 44 Wayting upon the Quenes joyelles.

b. An ornament worn as the badge of an Order of honour, or as a mark of distinction or honour.

1672 [see GEORGE 3]. **1888** *Encycl. Brit.* XXIII. 201/2 The jewel of the order [Teutonic Order] consists of a black and white cross, surmounted by a helmet with three feathers. **1894** S. L. YEATS *Honour of Savelli* ix, My cross of St. Lazare... I sat staring at the jewel and at the diamonds on it.

2. a. A precious stone, a gem; *esp.* one worn as an ornament. (The prevailing modern sense: in early use often difficult to separate from sense 1.)

1590 SHAKS. *Mids. N.* III. i. 161 Ile giue thee fairies to attend on thee, And they shall fetch thee Iewels from the deepe. **1596** SPENSER *F. Q.* IV. viii. 6 Amongst the rest a iewell rich he found That was a Ruby of right perfect hew. **1607** SHAKS. *Cor.* I. iv. 56 Thou art left Martius, A Carbuncle intire, as big as thou art, Weare not so rich a Iewell. **1613** PURCHAS *Pilgrimage* (1614) 214 A Ring of pure gold, with-out any Iewell in it. **1655** [see 1 γ.]. **1718** LADY M. W. MONTAGU *Let. to C'tess Mar* 10 Mar., According to the common estimation of jewels..her whole dress must be worth above a hundred thousand pounds sterling. *a* **1861** MRS. BROWNING *King's Gift* ii, That necklace of jewels from Turin.

fig. **1593** SHAKS. *Rich. II*, I. iii 267 A foyle, wherein thou art to set The precious Iewell of thy home returne. **1869** FREEMAN *Norm. Conq.* III. xii. 186 One of the proudest jewels in his continental coronet.

b. *Watch-making.* A precious stone, usually a ruby, used for a pivot-hole, on account of its hardness and resistance to wear.

1825 [see *jewel-hole* in 5]. **1875** KNIGHT *Dict. Mech.* 1213 The balance jewel always has an end-stone, or cap, the balance running on the end of its pivot in order that it may have the utmost freedom... Rubies are used as jewels in good watches..but cheaper stones, such as crystals, garnets, etc., and even glass of hard quality, are often used.

c. Applied to an imitation, in glass or enamel, of a real gem; as those worn on women's dresses in the end of the 19th c.; also, an ornamental boss of glass in a stained-glass window.

1889 *Harper's Mag.* July 255/1 Mosaic glass has rapidly improved in the past century... The 'jewels' cut from pieces of a rich colored glass add effectively to the brilliancy of recent designs. **1891** *Daily News* 23 Mar. 2/2 Can such a display be anything but vulgar? Its sole redeeming point is that the 'jewels' do not even pretend to be real. **1897** *Ibid.* 14 Dec. 8/7 Some of the newest evening bodices have a shaped piece of guipure laid on the front, and often glittering with inexpensive 'jewels'.

3. *fig.* Applied to a thing or person of great worth, or highly prized; a 'treasure', 'gem'. ***jewels of the crown***, a rhetorical phrase for the colonies of the British Empire (*temporary*).

13.. *E.E. Allit. P.* A. 278 A Iuel to me þen watz þys geste, & Iuelez wern hyr gentyl sawez. **1340** *Ayenb.* 156 þet is þe vifte ioyel and þe vifte stape. *a* **1450** *Mankind* (Brandl) 426 Ȝe xall not choppe my Iewellys [—my privyte (cf. 414)] and I may. **1529** *Supplic. to King* (E.E.T.S.) 39, I wolde not commytt my best beloued ioywell and treasure [sheep] vnto the, vnlesse thowe loue me hartely. **1589** NASHE *Almond for Parrat* 9 b, Learning is a iewel my maisters, make much of it. **1598** SHAKS. *Merry W.* II. ii. 213 Vnlesse Experience be a Iewell, that I haue purchased at an infinite rate. **1673** DRYDEN *Amboyna* IV. i, Oh, 'tis a jewel of a husband. **1694** SALMON *Bate's Dispens.* (1713) 620/2, I commend it as a Jewel, to sweeten their Milk and Pap withal. **1762** FOOTE *Orators* II. Wks. 1799 I. 217 Oh, my jewel, I know him well enough. **1858** MRS. CARLYLE *Lett.* II. 387 She is quite a jewel of a servant. **1872** R. ELLIS *Catullus* xxxi. 1 O thou of islands jewel and of half-islands, Fair Sirmio. **1901** P. MANSON in *Daily Mail Year Bk.* 101, 10 or 15 years hence that region [*sc.* West Africa] would be regarded as one of the richest jewels in the crown of England. **1931** *N. & Q.* 5 Sept. 166/2 Those irritations against tyranny and stupidity which lost us those jewels of the Crown [*sc.* the American colonies].

†**4.** *Naut.* A heavy ring, sometimes weighted, used to press together the two parts of a cable or rope which is laid round an article and then rove through the ring. Also *attrib.* *Obs.*

1750 BLANCKLEY *Naval Expos.* 82 *Jewel*, Made not unlike the Ring of an Anchor, and of Substance, that its Weight may carry it down, to purchase anything that is heavy under Water, when two parts of a Cable or Rope are put through it..and as they heave, the Jewel slides down, jams the Bite, so as that it may not slip off the Purchase the Rope is about. **1755** FALCK *Day's Diving Vessel* 29 Then a jewel, well parcelled with about an hundredweight of stones together with a messenger of jewel-rope, was let over the hawser, and run down, in order to jam the sweep.

5. *Comb.* **a.** *appositive*, as *jewel-bud*, *-fire*, *-stone*. **b.** *attrib.* Of or for jewels, as *jewel-box*, *-case*, *-casket*, *-coffer*, *-hunger*, *-merchant*, *-mine*, *-tint*. **c.** instrumental, similative, etc., as *jewel-coloured*, *-enshrined*, *-gleaming*, *-headed*, *-like*, *-loving*, *-proof*, *-studded* adjs. **d.** Special Combs.: †**jewel-darling** *a.*, as dear or highly prized as a jewel; **jewel-hole** (*Watch-making*), a hole drilled in a jewel for a pivot; **jewel-office** = JEWEL-HOUSE; **jewel-setter**, an instrument for setting a jewel; **jewel-stand**, a small stand for the toilet-table for placing jewels on or in; **jewel-weed** *U.S.*, either of two annual herbs, *Impatiens capensis*, with orange flowers, or *I. pallida*, with yellow flowers, native to eastern and central North America.

1831 *Society* I. 169 Her ladyship's *jewel-box, which was ostentatiously produced, was exhibited. **1845** G. MURRAY *Islaford* 56 Every *jewel-bud shone like a star. **1860** EMERSON *Cond. Life, Beauty* Wks. (Bohn) II. 439, I did not know you were a *jewel-case. **1899** CROCKETT *Kit Kennedy* 368 This jewel-case Mary had given Dick on his birthday. **1601** HOLLAND *Pliny* II. 602 The first that euer was known to haue any such at Rome, was Scaurus,..vntill Pompeius the Great met with the *jewel-casket of K. Mithridates. *a* **1835** MRS. HEMANS *Poems, Child reading the Bible*, Where *jewel-colour'd pebbles lay Beneath the shallow tide. **1643** R. WILLIAMS *Key Lang. Amer.* 173 Man stakes his *Iewel-darling soule. **1899** E. PEACOCK in *Month* May 541 The *jewel-enshrined miniature. **1848** LD. TENNYSON in *Mem.* (1897) I. 273 *Jewel-fires in the waves from the oar, which Cornish people call 'bryming'. *a* **1868** A. I. MENKEN *Infelicia* (1883) 48 The poorest worm would be a *jewel-headed snake if she could. **1825** J. NICHOLSON *Operat. Mechanic* 508 The *jewel-hole should be as shallow as possible, so as not to endanger cutting the pivot. *a* **1586** SIDNEY *Arcadia* (1622) 248 Her heart held it, as so *jewel-like a treasure that it would scarce trust her owne lippes withall. **1608** SHAKS. *Per.* v. i. 111 Her eyes as jewel-like, And cased as richly. **1859** LANG *Wand. India* 70 A band of robbers attacked the *jewel-merchant. **1698** A. BRAND *Emb. Muscovy to China* 84* One of the Masters of the *Jewel-Office belonging to the Czar of Muscovy. **1739** LADY HARTFORD *Corr.* (1805) I. 51 On Saturday my lord Townshend gave up the jewel-office. **1618** FLETCHER *Loyal Subject* III. ii, An honest mind I hope, 'tis petticoat proof, Chain proof, and *jewel-proof; I know 'tis gold proof. **1871** B. TAYLOR *Faust* (1875) II. III. 166 Beauty complete With gold and pearl and *jewel-stone. **1818** A. EATON *Man. Bot.* (ed. 2) 283 *Impatiens..nolitangere* (*jewel-weed, touch-me-not). **1869** J. G. FULLER *Uncle John's Flower-Gatherers* 223, I have seen..the wild jewel-weed in our meadow. **1884** MILLER *Plant-n., Impatiens fulva*, Spotted Jewel-weed. **1907** *St. Nicholas* July 842/2 A sudden thrust of the lantern into this clump of jewel weed near our path, produces a shower of miniature drops. **1951** R. FROST *Coll. Poems* 143 It will be found Either to have gone groping underground.. Or flourished and come up as jewel-weed. **1968** *Herb Grower Mag.* (Falls Village, Connecticut) XXI. II. 23 Jewelweed is our favorite [name] for the plant which makes its own gleaming droplets, poised to defy gravity even on leaves tipped downwards, out of rain, dew or even tap water that falls upon the foliage.

jewel, *v.* [f. prec. sb.]

1. *trans.* To furnish or adorn with jewels.

1601 B. JONSON *Poetaster* IV. i, You are as well jewell'd as any of them: your ruff and linen about you is much more pure than theirs. **1853** MOTLEY *Corr.* (1889) I. v. 151 Some few of the high Court ladies were well jewelled also.

b. *Watch-making.* To fit with jewels for the pivot-holes (JEWEL *sb.* 2 b). Usually in *pa. pple.*

1804 *Nicholson's Jrnl.* VII. 204 *margin*, Jewelling the holes of timekeepers is injurious. **1844** DICKENS *Mart. Chuz.* xiii, A gold hunting watch,..jewelled in four holes. **1851** *Illustr. Catal. Gt. Exhib.* 1266 An eight-day watch,..8 holes jewelled in rubies. **1858** O. W. HOLMES *Aut. Breakf.-t.* vi. (1883) 112 If a watch tells us the hour and minute, we can be content..though it is not enamelled nor jewelled.

2. *fig.* To bedeck as with jewels; to begem.

1859 SALA *Tw. round Clock* (1861) 44 The cut flowers, too, ..are here, jewelling wooden boards, and making humble wicker-baskets, iridescent. **1897** B. HARRADEN *Hilda Strafford* i. 18 That tender rosy tint..jewelled the mountains and the stones.

jewel, dial. variant of JOWEL, of a bridge.

ˈjewel-block. *Naut.* [perh. a sailors' fanciful appellation.] The name given to each of two small blocks suspended at the extremities of the main and fore-topsail yards, through which the halyards of the studding-sails are passed.

1769–89 FALCONER *Dict. Marine* s.v., The haliards, by which those studding-sails are hoisted, are accordingly passed through the jewel-blocks. *c* **1860** H. STUART *Seaman's Catech.* 19 Jewel blocks are not on royal yards, unless royal studding sails are used.

ˈjewel-house. A house, building, or chamber in which jewels are kept; a treasury. Now *rare*. **b.** *spec.* The room in the Tower of London in which the crown jewels are kept; the jewel-office.

1530 PALSGR. 235/1 Iowell house. **1546–7** *Acts Privy Council Eng.* 14 Mar., iiijˣˣ ounzes of demi souveraine gold deliverde to R. D. and J. A. Yeomen of the Jewelhowse. **1548** UDALL *Erasm. Par. Luke* xxi. 1 Called Gazophylacium, that is to saie, the Iewelhouse or sextrie, or treasourie in the whiche the Iewels of the temple wer kept. **1613** SHAKS. *Hen. VIII*, IV. i. 111 The King ha's made him Master o' th' Iewell House. *a* **1652** BROME *Queenes Exch.* v. Wks. 1873 III. 549, I have heard of them that robb'd my brothers Jewel-house. **1706** PHILLIPS, *Master of the Jewel-House*,..has Charge of all Plate us'd for the King or Queen's Table, or by any great Officer attending the Court; as also of all Plate in the Tower of London, of Chains, loose Jewels, etc. **1815** T. THOMSON (*title*) Collection of Inventories and other Records of the Royal Wardrobe and Jewelhouse.

c. *fig.* A repository of 'treasures'.

1594 PLAT (*title*) Iewell House of Art and Nature.

jewelled, -eled (ˈdʒ(j)uːəld), *a.* [f. JEWEL *sb.* or *v.* + -ED.]

1. Set or adorned with jewels; *spec.* of a watch (JEWEL *v.* 1 b); also of pottery (JEWELLING 3).

a **1601** ? MARSTON *Pasquil & Kath.* II. 129 More soft and cleere Then is the jewell'd tip of Venus eare. **1742** COLLINS *Ecl.* iii. 65 On Persia's jewell'd throne. **1804** *Nicholson's Jrnl.* VII. 204 So far from jewelled holes being advantageous in Clockwork, they are absolutely injurious. **1820** SCOTT *Abbot* xiii, The gemmed ring and jewelled mitre had become secular spoils. **1899** T. M. ELLIS *Three Cat's-Eye Rings* ii. 43 The..corridors were glittering with jewelled women.

2. *fig.* Glistening like or as with jewels.

1818 KEATS *Endym.* III. 312 Jewell'd sands Took silently their foot-prints. **1884** *B'ham Weekly Post* 20 Sept. 1/4, I do not like the coloured, almost jewelled, effect of the oxides of different metals used in the construction of this screen. **1898** *Pall Mall Mag.* May 22 The blue of her eyes was scintillant and jewelled.

jeweller, -eler (ˈdʒ(j)uːələ(r)). Forms: 4 iuweler, 4–5 iueler, -e, -our, 4–7 iueller(e, 5 iouelere, iowel(l)er, iewellere, 6 iuellere, -ar, 6–9 jeweler, 6– jeweller. [a. AF. *jueler* = OF. *juelier* (1438 in Godef.), f. *juel*: in mod.F. *joaillier*.]

1. An artist who works in precious stones, etc.; a maker of jewels; a dealer in jewels or jewellery.

13.. *E.E. Allit. P.* A. 264 If þou were a gentyl Iueler. **1382** WYCLIF *Jer.* xxiv. 1 Jeconye, the sone of Joachym,..and the smyth, and his iueler [1388 goldsmith]. *c* **1440** LYDG. *Secrees* 554, I was nevir noon expert Ioweler. **1530** PALSGR. 235/1 Juellar, *lapidaire*. **1601** SHAKS. *All's Well* v. iii. 297 The Ieweller that owes the Ring is sent for. **1621** BURTON *Anat. Mel.* I. ii. III. xv. (1651) 139 A most expert Jueller, and an exquisite Philosopher. **1718** LADY M. W. MONTAGU *Let. to C'tess Mar* 10 Mar., It is for jewellers to compute the value of these things. **1832** W. IRVING *Alhambra* II. 114 The jeweller saw that it had an Arabic inscription, and was of the purest gold.

2. ***jeweller's*** (or ***jewellers'***) ***rouge***, a fine preparation of ferric oxide used as rouge.

1839 [see ROUGE *sb.*[1] 2]. **1886** *Encycl. Brit.* XXI. 13/2 Jeweller's rouge for polishing gold and silver plate is a fine red oxide of iron prepared by calcination from sulphate of iron. **1947** J. C. RICH *Materials & Methods Sculpture* vii. 210 For the final stages of polishing, a chamois skin can be used to apply a fine buffing powder or jeweller's rouge.

jewellery, jewelry (ˈdʒ(j)uːəlrɪ, ˈdʒ(j)uːələrɪ). Forms; 4 iuelrye, 5 *Sc.* iowalre; 8– jewellery,

jewelry. [ME. a. OF. *juelerye* (1434 in Godef. *Compl.*), f. *joel, juel*: see JEWEL and -ERY. In mod.Eng. app. two new formations, from JEWELLER (cf. mod.F. *joaillerie* from *joaillier* jeweller), and from JEWEL: see -ERY and -RY. Not in Johnson or Todd.]

Jewellers' work; gems or ornaments made or sold by jewellers; esp. precious stones in mountings; jewels collectively, or as a form of adornment.

In commercial use commonly spelt *jewellery*; the form *jewelry* is more rhetorical and poetic, and unassociated with the jeweller. But the pronunciation with three syllables is usual even with the former spelling.

13.. *E.E. Allit. P.* B. 1309 Bot þe ioy of þe iuelrye so gentyle & ryche, When hit watz schewed hym so schene, scharp watz his wonder. *c* **1470** HENRY *Wallace* VI. 615 The jowalre, as it was thiddir led, Palȝonis and all thai leiffit quhen thai fled. **1786** BURKE *Charges W. Hastings* IV. xlviii, Even jewellery and goods she finds..lose their value the moment it is known they come from her. **1814** SOUTHEY *Roderic* xviii, The proud array Of ermines, aureate vests, and jewelry. **1828** WEBSTER, *Jewelry*. **1842** TENNYSON *Morte d' Arthur* 58 Jacinth-work Of subtlest jewellery. **1872** YEATS *Techn. Hist. Comm.* 336 The most delicate steel jewellery has displaced ornaments in wood or brass.

fig. **1817** COLERIDGE *Alice du Clos* 69 Smit by the sun the mist in glee Dissolves to lightsome jewelry—Each blossom hath its gem! **1885-6** SPURGEON *Treas. Dav.* Ps. cxl. Introd., Few short psalms are so rich in the jewelry of precious faith. **1898** DAVIDSON *Last Ballad*, And brimming stars hung from the sky Low down, and spilt their jewellery.

jewelless ('dʒ(j)u:əllɪs), *a.* [f. JEWEL *sb.* + -LESS.] Destitute of jewels; not jewelled.

1865 EMMELINE LOTT *Governess in Egypt* I. 157 The Prince..took hold of her right hand, which was jewelless, as also were her ears.

jewelling, jeweling ('dʒ(j)u:əlɪŋ). [f. JEWEL *sb.* or *v.* + -ING¹.]

1. The action or art of working in, or adorning something with, jewels. Also *attrib.*

1613 PURCHAS *Pilgrimage* I. vii. 31 He taught to make womens ornaments, and how to looke faire, and Iewelling. **1673** O. WALKER *Educ.* 34 Rodulfus the Emperor gave his mind to Jewelling. **1750** tr. *Leonardus' Mirr. Stones* 43. **1851** *Illustr. Catal. Gt. Exhib.* 1283 Engraving, chasing in relief, jewelling, and enamel painting.

2. *Watch-making.* The employment of jewels for the pivot-holes in a watch; also *concr.*

1804 [see JEWEL *v.* 1 b]. **1884** F. J. BRITTEN *Watch & Clockm.* 102 Facio..introduced watch jewelling (Patent No. 371, May 1704). **1885** *Pall Mall G.* 21 May 6/2 A watch selling at £3 has no extra jewelling..there are grades from 'plain jewelled' up to 5½ pairs of extra jewels.

3. *Pottery.* Decoration with small bosses of translucent glaze, or with rounded projections of the body covered with glaze, as some kinds of porcelain.

4. *concr.* A trimming on a dress consisting of (real, or commonly, imitation) jewels.

1891 *Truth* 10 Dec. 1240/2 A most lovely tea-gown..in white satin set into a yoke of turquoise jewelling. **1896** *Daily News* 21 Nov. 6/3 If the jewelling were garnet and jet commingled, the effect would be very good.

jewelly, -ely ('dʒ(j)u:əlɪ), *a.* [f. JEWEL *sb.* + -Y.]

1. Abounding in, adorned with, or wearing jewels. Also *fig.*

1765 JOHN BROWN *Chr. Jrnl.* (1814) 137 The splendid wealth of the jewelly tribe. **1862** M. B. EDWARDS *John & I*, xxxix. (1876) 290 Glimpses..of jewelly orchards and vine-yards. **1881** G. MACDONALD *Mary Marston* II. ix. 157 Jewelly Tom was idling away time.

2. Resembling a jewel, jewel-like; having the brilliancy of a jewel. Also *fig.*

1822-56 DE QUINCEY *Confess.* (1862) 26 This incident.. I look back upon..as a jewelly parenthesis of pathetic happiness. **1880** M. B. EDWARDS *Forestalled* I. I. vi. 90 The little town was garlanded with fiery crescents and stars of jewelly light and lustre. **1885** C. MONKHOUSE in *Mag. of Art* Sept. 471/1 Walls..lit with jewelly glass.

jewelry: see JEWELLERY.

jewes, -esse, var. JUISE *Obs.*, judgement.

Jewess ('dʒ(j)u:ɪs). Forms: 4 Iuwesse, Iuesse, 4-7 Iewesse, (6 Iewes, -as), 7- Jewess. [f. JEW *sb.* + -ESS: cf. OF. *Juise* (Godefroy).] A female Jew; a Jewish woman.

1388 WYCLIF *Acts* xvi. 1 Timothe, the sone of a Jewesse cristen. *a* **1400** *Pistill of Susan* 41 For gentrise and Ioye of þat Iuwesse. **1526** TINDALE *Acts* xxiv. 24 Felix and his wyfe Drusilla which was a iewes [**1534** Iewas, **1539** CRANMER Iewesse, **1611** Iew]. **1613** PURCHAS *Pilgrimage* (1614) 214 *note*, For the Virgin Mary, say they, wore the Ring on her middle finger, and therefore all Iewesses refuse that, and use the forefinger. **1820** SCOTT *Ivanhoe* xxiv, The Jewess Rebecca awaited her fate. **1876** GEO. ELIOT *Dan. Der.* xvii, I am English-born. But I am a Jewess. **1922** JOYCE *Ulysses* 756 As if we met somewhere I suppose on account of my being jewess looking after my mother. **1927** E. O'NEILL *Lazarus Laughed* II. ii. 84 And why should you plead for them, Jewess? **1936** G. B. SHAW *Millionairess* II. 39 'Are you ..[an] Italian aristocrat..?'..'My ancestors were moneylenders to all Europe..we are now bankers to all the world.'..'Jewess, eh?' **1970** J. UPDIKE *Bech: a Book* 35 'Is she also a typical Rumanian beauty?' 'I think..she is a typical little Jewess.'

Jewessy ('dʒ(j)u:ɪsɪ), *a. depreciatory.* [f. JEWESS + -Y¹.] Resembling or characteristic of a Jewess.

1930 J. B. PRIESTLEY *Angel Pavement* iv. 151 And there were two or three [girls] worth looking at, the flashy young Jewessy type.

'jew-fish. [app. f. JEW *sb.* + FISH: as to origin of name, see quot. 1697.] A name given to various fishes, chiefly of the family *Serranidæ*.

Among these are *Promicrops guasa, Epinephelus nigritus, Megalops atlanticus*, and *Paralichthys dentatus*, of the Atlantic coast of U.S.; *Stereolepis gigas* of the Californian coast; *Polyprion americanus* or *P. couchi* of Madeira; and *Sciæna antarctica* and *Glaucosoma hebraicum* of Australia. (*Cent. Dict.* and Morris *Austral Eng.*)

1679 T. TRAPHAM *Discourse State of Health in Jamaica* 65 The Jew fish crowds to be one of the first three of our most worthy Fish. **1697** DAMPIER *Voy.* (1729) I. 249 The Jew-fish is a very good Fish, and I judge so called by the English, because it hath Scales and Fins, therefore a clean Fish, according to the Levitical Law. **1764** GRAINGER *Sugar Cane* III. 608 Can Europe's seas..Aught so delicious as the Jew-fish show? **1775** ROMANS *Florida* App. 20 Jew-fish are very abundant both within and without the river. **1847** LEICHHARDT *Jrnl. Austral.* ii. 40 The water holes abounded with jew-fish and eels. **1883** E. M. RAMSAY *Food Fishes N.S. Wales* 16 (Fish. Exh. Publ.) The most important of this family is the Jew-fish (*Sciæna antarctica*), which attains to a large size, exceeding 5 feet in length. **1890** *Boston* (Mass.) *Jrnl.* 13 Apr. 2/3 The largest jewfish ever caught on the Gulf coast..weighed 348 pounds, was 6 feet in length and 8 feet in circumference just back of the gills. **1968** J. E. RANDALL *Caribbean Reef Fishes* 60 Jewfish. *Epinephelus itajara*... Tropical western Atlantic and eastern Pacific... Highly esteemed as food. **1972** *Nature* 7 Apr. 266/2 The groupers (some species are known as jewfishes and hinds) are well represented in American warmer seas.

jewge, obs. form of JUDGE.

†**'Jewhead.** *Obs. rare.* In 4 Iuhede. [f. JEW *sb.* + *-hede*, -HEAD.] The condition or profession of a Jew; Judaism.

a **1300** *Cursor M.* 4248 Men war þar o sarzin lede, And Ioseph held ai his Iuhede.

jewhil(l)iken(s), -kin(s), varr. GEEWHILLIKINS.

Jewhood ('dʒ(j)u:hʊd). *rare.* [f. JEW *sb.* + -HOOD.] = JEWHEAD.

1851 CARLYLE *Sterling* II. iii. (1872) 110 Abstruse vague speculations..about Will, Morals, Jonathan Edwards, Jew-hood, Manhood.

jewing ('dʒ(j)u:ɪŋ). [From a supposed resemblance to the hooked nose of a Jew: see -ING¹.] Name for the caruncIulations or wattles at the base of the beak in some varieties of domestic pigeon.

1886 *Century Mag.* May 104 The jewing [in the barb pigeon] is three small knobs of cere in the middle of the lower mandible, and each side of the gape of the mouth.

jewis, -ise, variant of JUISE *Obs.*, judgement.

Jewish ('dʒ(j)u:ɪʃ), *a.* [f. JEW *sb.* + -ISH. The OE. equivalent was *Iudeisc*, early ME. *Judewish*.]

1. Of, belonging to, or characteristic of, the Jews; Israelitish, Hebrew.

a **1546** JOYE in Gardiner *Declar. Joye* (1546) 81 b, This scismatyke iewissh Hieroboam. **1549** COVERDALE, etc. *Erasm. Par. Col.* ii. 16 In obseruyng of dayes, and in other Iewyshe rules. **1582** N. T. (Rhem.) *Tit.* i. 14 Not attending to Iewish fables [WYCLIF fables of iewis; TINDALE, etc. iewes fables]. **1596** SHAKS. *Merch. V.* I. iii. 113 You..spet vpon my Iewish Gaberdine. **1829** MILMAN *Hist. Jews* II. 85 The Jewish Exodus, or deliverance from Egypt. **1874** GREEN *Short Hist.* II. v, A Jewish Medical School seems to have existed at Oxford. **1925** P. GIBBS *Unchanging Quest* xiv. 109 These peasants think the Duma will..kill all the *Koulaks*, or Jewish moneylenders. **1935** [see ARMENOID *a.*]. **1941** *Time* 24 Feb. 102/3 Alfred Rosenberg last fortnight opened in Frankfurt am Main what Nazis call 'the biggest library in the world dealing exclusively with the Jewish problem'. **1951** A. POWELL *Question of Upbringing* ii. 96 Yes—and have you seen it? A Jewish old clothes man would think twice about wearing it. **1957** *Oxf. Dict. Chr. Ch.* 1093/2 The Jewish problem arose at a later date than in Spain, and it was not until 1536 that, under the influence of the civil power, the Inquisition was set up. **1968** L. ROSTEN *Joys of Yiddish* 141 It is important to note that the idea of respect for others and the values of a pluralistic society form an old, integral part of Judaism and Jewish tradition. **1970** I. SIEFF *Memoirs* vi. 113 In February we submitted a memorandum to the Peace Conference. It asked that Palestine 'Shall be placed under such political, administrative, and economic conditions as will ensure the establishment therein of the Jewish national home.' **1970** *Times* 24 Jan. 7/1 It is now declared that under the law of Israel a person may be of Jewish nationality although not of Jewish religion, whereas under Rabbinic law the two are inseparable. **1973** *Times* 17 July 15/2 PLO leaders seek to identify a community of culture interest between the Palestinian Arabs and these oriental Jews whom they call 'Jewish Arabs'. **1973** *Daily Mail* 4 Oct. 4/5 The strain of anguish and uncertainty shows in the face of this Jewish woman as she waits with her grandson at a railway station before going to Schoenau transit camp in Austria. **1974** [see JEW *sb.* 1]. **1974** *Publishers Weekly* 18 Feb. 12/2, I do not see why writers should be given ethnic identities when the habit of so designating individuals has been abandoned generally. I suppose it is because of the new use of the term 'Jewish writers'. But those are writers—I believe—who concentrate on the experience of being Jewish in America.

2. *fig.* Chiefly referring to the extortion or overreaching attributed to Jewish money-lenders. (Offensive.)

1606 DEKKER *Sev. Sinnes* VI. (Arb.) 40 Brokers yat shaue poore men by most iewish interest. **1801** BP. OF LINCOLN in G. Rose *Diaries* (1860) I. 426 Soane's office has offered only 19,000*l*...which is a *Jewish* offer. **1852** THACKERAY *Esmond* III. vi, You ask a Jewish price for it, Mr. Graves.

3. *Comb.*, as *Jewish-looking*,

1874 LISLE CARR *Jud. Gwynne* II. viii. 194 A Jewish-looking gentleman in faultlessly-made clothes.

'Jewishly, *adv.* [f. prec. + -LY².] In a Jewish manner; after the custom of the Jews; like a Jew.

1558 BP. WATSON *Sev. Sacram.* vii. 37 We maye not Iewishlye doubte whether it be done. **1613** PURCHAS *Pilgrimage* (1614) 226 Unchristian Christians, who Iewishly hate the name of a Jew. **1661** R. L'ESTRANGE *Interest Mistaken* 34 Persue and Jewishly sell and betray his Sacred Person.

'Jewishness. [f. as prec. + -NESS.]

†**1.** The religious system of the Jews; Judaism.

1549 COVERDALE, etc. *Erasm. Par. Gal.* iv. 21 Suche of you, as are contented to fall backe to Iewishnes. **1550** BALE *Apol.* 60 Christ will not have hys pure Gospell myngled with Iewyshnesse. **1627** W. SCLATER *Exp. 2 Thess.* (1629) 222 It sauours of Iewishnesse, rather then Christianity.

2. Jewish quality or character.

1822 *New Monthly Mag.* IV. 70 An air of Jewishness, or an old-clothesman-like expression. **1899** *Speaker* 10 Feb. 133/2 The Jews of this country..are rapidly losing all their Jewishness.

Jewism ('dʒ(j)u:ɪz(ə)m). [f. JEW *sb.* + -ISM.]

†**1.** The religious system of the Jews; Judaism.

1579 J. STUBBES *Gaping Gulf* E iv b, To maintaine therein thopen exercise of Turcisme, arrianisme, iewisme, papisme, anabaptisme, and such monstrous professions. **1653** MILTON *Hirelings* Wks. (1851) 357 Superstitions fetch'd from Paganism or Jewism. **1800** *Asiat. Ann. Reg., Hist. India* 5/1 The channels through which Christianity and Jewism were communicated to the nations of the Indian peninsula.

2. An idiom or characteristic of the Jews. *rare.*

1841 *Blackw. Mag.* L. 617 We search in vain for the remotest inkling of Jewism of any kind. **1884** L. GRONLUND *Co-op. Commw.* ii. 50 'Jewism', to our mind, best expresses that special curse of our age, Speculation.

jewkry, obs. form of JOUKERY, trickery.

jewlep, -lip, obs. forms of JULEP.

Jewless ('dʒ(j)u:lɪs), *a. rare.* [f. JEW *sb.* + -LESS.] Destitute of Jews.

1882 FREEMAN in W. R. W. Stephens *Life* (1895) II. 254 Meanwhile Aberdeen..abideth altogether Jewless. **1897** *Daily News* 8 Feb. 2/1 It was generally supposed that from 1290 to 1655 this was a Jewless England. Mr. Wolf and Mr. Sydney Lee have, however, proved..that the Hebrew race was represented in that interval.

Jewling ('dʒ(j)u:lɪŋ). *rare.* [f. JEW *sb.* + -LING.] A little or young Jew.

1613 PURCHAS *Pilgrimage* (1614) 213 Everie of the youthes holdeth a pot in his hand..they wish joy to each other: and the Iewlings presently breake their earthen pots. **1879** BARING-GOULD *Germany* II. 258 The Count..turned 'the stupid Jewling' out of his house.

†**'Jewly**, *adv. Obs rare.* [f. as prec. + -LY².] In the manner of a Jew; in the Jewish language.

1382 WYCLIF *Isa.* xxxvi. 11 Ne speke thou to vs Iewly [1388 bi the langage of Iewis]. —— *Gal.* ii. 14 If thou.. lyuest hethenli, and not Iewly [**1388** Iewelich].

jewmew, variant of GEMEW *Obs.*, twin.

Jewry ('dʒ(j)ʊərɪ). Forms: 3-4 Giw-, Gywerie, -ye, 4 Iuery, -ie, 4-5 Iuwery, -ie, Iewery, -ie, -ye, (Iurye, 4-7 Iurie, Iury, 5 Iure, Iwry), 5-6 Iewry(e, (6 *Sc.* Ioure), 6-7 Jewrie, 7- Jewry. [a. AF. *juerie* = OF. *juierie, juerie, jurie* (13th c.), mod.F. *juiverie*: see JEW and -ERY.]

†**1.** The land of the Jews, Judea; sometimes extended to the whole of Palestine. *Obs.* or *arch.*

a **1350** *Harl. MS.* 4196 in *Archiv Stud. neu. Spr.* LVII. 79 Als custum was in þe iury. **1387** TREVISA *Higden* (Rolls) III. 89 þis Nabugodonosor..wente into Iuda, þat is þe Iewerie, and took Ierusalem. *c* **1440** *Promp. Parv.* 267/2 Ivrye, where Ivys dwelle [*v.r.* Iwry], *Iudea.* **1526** TINDALE *John* vii. 1 Iesus went about in Galile, and wolde not goo about in iewry. **1533** GAU *Richt Vay* 41 O thow bethleem effrata thow art litil amangis ane thowsand of Ioure. **1539** BIBLE (Great) *Ps.* lxxvi. 1 In Iewry is God knowne; his name is greate in Israel. **1606** SHAKS. *Ant. & Cl.* I. ii. 28 A Childe.. to whom Herode of Iewry may do Homage. **1671** *True Nonconf.* 19 It may be considered that Antiochus his title to Jurie is not obnoxious to any particular exception. **1708** J. PHILIPS *Cyder* II. (1807) 97 Drawn from the north to Jewry's hallow'd plains. **1742** YOUNG *Nt. Th.* IX. 1662 'Tis unconfin'd To Christian land, or Jewry.

attrib. **1597-8** BP. HALL *Sat.* I. viii. 4 Parnassus is transform'd to Sion hill, And Iury-palmes her steepe ascents done fill.

2. The district inhabited by Jews in a town or city; the Jews' quarter; the Ghetto. (Hence the *Old Jewry* in London.) *Obs.* exc. *Hist.*

In 1225, *in Giwerie* = in pawn to the Jews: cf. 1386.

a **1225** *Ancr. R.* 394 Ne telleð me him god feolawe þet teið his wed ine Giwerie uorto acwiten ut his fere? God Almihti leide himsulf uor us ine Giwerie,..uorto acwiten ut his leofmon of Giwene honden. **1297** R. GLOUC. (Rolls) 9920 Þer was mani a wilde hine þat..wende in to þe gywerie and woundede and to drowe. *c* **1386** CHAUCER *Prioress' T.* 37

Ther was in Asye in a greet Citee Amonges cristene folk a Iewerye Sustened by a lord of that contree For foule vsure and lucre of vileynye. **1598** B. Jonson *Ev. man in Hum.* I. i[i], Hast thou for-sworne all thy friends i' the old Iewrie? **1670–98** Lassels *Voy. Italy* II. 50, I saw on my left hand the great back door of the Jewry; for here the Jews live all together in a corner of the town, and are locked up every night. **1844** *Fraser's Mag.* XXX. 423/1 To assign them a peculiar quarter, as the Israelites were once confined to their Jewry. **1876** Green *Stray Stud.* 336 Here [Oxford] as elsewhere the Jewry was a town within a town.

†**3.** The Jewish religion, Judaism. *Obs.*

13.. *S. E. Leg.* (MS. Bodl. 779) in *Archiv Stud. neu. Spr.* LXXXII. 346/4 Al his kyn byleued al on þe gywerye. **1382** Wyclif *Gal.* i. 14, I profitide in Iurye aboue many myn euene eeldis. *c* **1449** Pecock *Repr.* I. xiii. 69 Conuertid fro Iewry into Cristenhode. **1552** Huloet, Iewrye, *iudaismus.*

4. The Jewish people, nation, race, or community; the Jews collectively.

c **1330** R. Brunne *Chron.* (1810) 247 Now comes a new pleynt, to destroie þe Juerie. **1340** *Ayenb.* 7 þis word zeterday þet þe iurie clepeþ sabat. *c* **1400** *Apol. Loll.* 100 Wer þer þre sectis among þe Iury, Phariseis and Esseis, and Saduceis. *c* **1460** *Towneley Myst.* xx. 640 Most gentyll of Iure to me that I fynde. **1641** Jackson *True Evang. T.* 2 This Prophecy hath been contained neither within the limits of Jury nor Christendome. **1893** Zangwill *Childr. Ghetto* Proem, That long cruel night in Jewry which coincides with the Christian Era. **1899** *Westm. Gaz.* 11 Aug. 7/1 All three parties call upon the judges [In the Dreyfus trial]..to remember that the real issue 'is between Catholic France and Cosmopolitan Jewry'.

†**jewse.** *Obs.* App. an erratic form of joist.

1610 *Engl. Eliza* in *Mirr. for Mag.* 866 Th' iron barres in sunder they did rent, Beate downe the posts, and all the iewses brent.

Jew's-ear. [Erroneous rendering of med.L. *auricula Judæ* Judas's ear; so called from its shape, and from its being frequently found on the elder, on which tree Judas Iscariot was reputed to have hanged himself.]

1. An edible cup-shaped fungus (*Hirneola* or *Exidia Auricula-Judæ*) growing on the roots and trunks of trees, chiefly the elder, and formerly in repute as a medicine; also locally applied to species of *Peziza* (Britten & Holl. 1879).

1544 Phaer *Regim. Lyfe* (1560) T j b, Take the musherom yt groweth upon an elder tree, called in englyshe Iewes eares. **1597** Gerarde *Herbal* III. lxxi. 1233 There groweth oftentimes vpon [elders] a certaine excrescence called *Auricula Indæ* or Iewes eare. **1634** Heywood & Brome *Witches Lanc.* III. Wks. 1874 IV. 209 All the Sallets are turn'd to Iewes-eares. **1646** Sir T. Browne *Pseud. Ep.* II. vi. 101 Jews eares..an excrescence about the roots of Elder, and concerneth not the Nation of the Jews, but Judas Iscariot, upon a conceit, he hanged on this tree. **1694** Salmon *Bate's Dispens.* (1713) 705/2 Let the Throat be anointed with Oil of Jews-Ears; which is made by boiling the Jews-Ears..in Oyl-Olive till they are crisp, and pressing out the Oyl, and repeating the boiling in like manner with fresh Jews-Ears, to the third time. **1694** Motteux *Rabelais* IV. lx. (1737) 245 Sallats, a Hundred Varieties, of Creeses,..Sives, Rampions, Jew's Ears. **1882** *Garden* 2 Sept. 207/2 There are several tree-growing edibles besides the two just mentioned. Of such is the Jew's ear.

2. Locally applied to the Tomato (Britten & Holl.).

Jews' harp. (Also sometimes with small j.) [A variant of Jews' trump, q.v.]

1. A musical instrument of simple construction, consisting of an elastic steel tongue fixed at one end to a small lyre-shaped frame of brass or iron, and bent at the other end at right angles; it is played by holding the frame between the teeth and striking the free end of the metal tongue with the finger, variations of tone being produced by altering the size and shape of the cavity of the mouth. Called also *Jews' trump.*

double Jews'-harp: one having two tongues.

1595 R. Duddeley in Hakluyt *Voy.* III. 576 If they would bring him hatchets, kniues, and Iewes-harps, he bid them assure me, he..would trade with me. *c* **1596** Raleigh *ibid.* 665 Wee should send them Iewes harpes: for they would giue for euery one two Hennes. **1626** Bacon *Sylva* §116 As for the Iewes Harpe, it is a sharpe Percussion; And besides, hath the vantage of penning the Aire in the Mouth. **1742** Fielding *J. Andrews* I. vii, Thou canst make a mole hill appear as a mountain; a Jew's-harp sound like a trumpet. **1762** B. Thornton (*title*) An Ode on St. Cecilia's Day, adapted to the ancient British musick, viz. the Saltbox, the Jews-harp, the Marrow-bones and Cleavers. **1774** Pennant *Tour Scotl. in* 1769 I. 194 The trump, or Jew's harp, would not merit the mention among the Highland instruments of Musick, if it was not to prove its origin and antiquity. **1787** Hawkins *Johnson* 477 They..are lovers of music and dancing, but know no instrument save the jews' harp. **1820** Byron *Blues* I. 60 The Jews' harp he nick-names his lyre. **1836** Smart *Dict.*, Jew's harp. **1865** Lubbock *Preh. Times* xiii. (1869) 443 Their musical instruments are..a Jew's-harp made of a strip of bamboo. **1880** Grove *Dict. Music*, Jew's harp. **1882** Ogilvie, **1885** Cassell, **1890** *Cent. Dict.*, Jews'-harp. **1893** Leland *Mem.* I. 206 Quite as marvellous ..was the Doctor's own performance on the single and double Jew's harp.

2. *transf.* **a.** *Naut.* 'The shackle for joining a chain-cable to the anchor-ring' (Smyth *Sailor's Word-bk.* 1867), shaped like the frame of the musical instrument. **b.** *attrib.* Applied to a staple of similar form.

1750 Blanckley *Naval Expos.* 83 *Jews Harps*, are made of Iron, and of such Substance and suitable Strength, as to be sufficient to hold the Pendant Chain where the Moaring Cable is bent to the Ring, and secured by a Forelock. **1794** *Rigging & Seamanship* II. 281 A link called a jew's harp, through which the bridle or hawser of a ship, when moored, is passed. **1794** W. Felton *Carriages* (1801) I. 76 It is fixed on the axletree by a Jew's harp staple.

Hence **Jews'-harper**, one who plays the Jews' harp.

1790 *By-stander* 105 Joah called the Muses ballad-singers, Apollo a jews-harper.

†'**Jewship.** *Obs. rare.* [f. Jew *sb.* + -ship.] The condition or profession of a Jew; Judaism.

1535 Coverdale *Gal.* i. 13 Ye haue herde of my conuersacion afore tyme in the Ieweshippe how that..I.. preuayled in the Ieweshippe aboue many of my companyons in my nacion. **1549** Coverdale, etc. *Erasm. Par. 1 Tim.* iv. 1 Whiche shall departe from the synceritie of fayth..and slyde backe vnto a certayne Ieweship.

Jews' stone, Jewstone. [In senses 1, 2, rendering med.L. *lapis Judaicus* (*Lanfranc's Cirurgie* 278, and Minsheu *Ductor*).]

1. The fossil spine of a large sea-urchin, found in Syria, formerly used in medicine. ? *Obs.*

1633 Hart *Diet of Diseased* III. xx. 312 Some medicines.. are esteemed good against the stone..of this kind is the Iewes stone, goats blood [etc.]. **1751** Sir J. Hill *Mat. Med.* 302 *Lapis Judaicus*, The Jews Stone,..is no other than the Spine of a large *Echinus Marinus* of a peculiar Species. **1888** *Syd. Soc. Lex.*, *Jew's stone*, see *Lapis judaicus* [a stone found in Palestine, and formerly used as a diuretic and lithontriptic, as well as in fluxes].

2. A crystallized form of iron pyrites (also called *marcasite*), formerly used as a gem. ? *Obs.*

1617 Minsheu *Ductor*, Marchesite..etiam Iewes stone. **1658** Phillips, *Jewstone*, a kind of stone called also a Marchesite. **1863** Geo. Eliot *Romola* I. vii, The 'Jew's stone', with the lion-headed serpent enchased in it.

3. Applied locally to various hard rocks.

1839 Murchison *Silur. Syst.* I. xxv. 313 *Jew stone*..This quarriers' term is evidently used to designate all hard unmanageable rocks of uneven and splintery fracture. **1885** *Cassell's Encycl. Dict.*, *Jew-stone.* 1. *Geol.* A local name for a black basalt found on the Clee Hills. **1890** *Cent. Dict.*, *Jews'-stone*..local name of a limestone-bed belonging to the White Lias (Rhætic) in Somersetshire.

Jews' trump, Jew's-trump. Now *rare.* Also 6 **Iues trounk**, 9 *dial.* **Jew-trump.** [An earlier name than the now usual *Jews' harp*, and formerly equally common in England. In Scotland and N. of England the instrument is still called simply trump, agreeing with the Fr. name *trompe* (Littré), which is now however mostly displaced by *guimbarde.* Although no early example of F. *trompe* in this sense has been adduced, it is probable that the name *trump* came from France, esp. as in the Customs Rates of 1545 they are called *Iues trounks*, a mistranslation perh. due to the fact that the *trompe* of the elephant is also called in Eng. *trunk.* The first element was certainly *Jews* from the first; conjectures that this was an alteration of *jaws*, or of F. *jeu*, are baseless and inept. But the attribution of the instrument to the Jews occurs, so far as is known, only in English, and there is no actual evidence as to its origin.

More or less satisfactory reasons may be conjectured: e.g. that the instrument was actually made, sold, or sent to England by Jews, or supposed to be so; or that it was attributed to them, as a good commercial name, suggesting the trumps and harps mentioned in the Bible. As the instrument was neither a trump nor a harp, the ingenuity which conferred upon it these names may well have distinguished it as the trump or harp of the Jews. See also article by Rev. C. B. Mount in *Notes & Queries*, 23 Oct. 1897, p. 322.]

= Jews' harp 1.

1545 *Rates of Customs*, Iues trounks the grose iijs. iiijd. **1583** *Ibid.* C vij, Iewes trumps the groce *xs.* **1591** *News fr. Scotl.* (Roxb.), Geillis Duncan..did goe before them playing this reill or daunce uppon a small trumpe called a Jewes trump, untill they entred into the Kirk of North Barrick..the king..sent for the saide Geillis Duncan, who upon the like trump did play the saide daunce before the kinges majestie. **1592** G. Harvey *Pierce's Super.* 85 An vniversall reformation be proclaimed with the sound of a Iewes trumpe. **1613** R. Harcourt *Voy. Guiana* in *Harl. Misc.* (Malh.) III. 178 Knives, beads, jews trumps and such toys as well contented [S. American Indians]. *a* **1625** Fletcher *Lover's Progr.* I. i, Playing on a gytterne or a Jewes Trumpe. **1678** Rymer *Trag. last Age* 139 Our ears are rapt with the tintamar and twang of the Tongs and Jewstrumps. **1762** Sterne *Tr. Shandy* V. xv, I'll stake my Cremona to a Jew's trump. **1796** Pegge *Anonym.* (1809) 48 **1877** *N.W. Linc. Gloss.*, Jew-trump. **1882** Ogilvie, **1885** Cassell, **1890** *Cent. Dict.*, Jews'-trump. **1901** *Eng. Dial. Dict.*, Jew's trump or trunk.

†**b.** Applied to a usurer: cf. Jew *sb.* 2. *Obs.*

1605 Chapman, etc. *Eastw. Ho* II, O 'tis a notable jews trump! I hope to live to see dog's meat made of the old usurer's flesh.

Jewy ('dʒ(j)uːɪ), *a. depreciatory.* Also **Jewey.** [f. Jew *sb.* + -y¹.] Resembling or characteristic of a Jew or the Jews; having the characteristics attributed to Jewish people. Also as *sb.*

1904 Fowler & Felkin *Kate of Kate Hall* xvii. 194 They [*sc.* the noses] are as like as two peas, and both, to my mind, a bit Jewy. **1914** E. Pugh *Cockney at Home* 67 You're a dirty, bloomin' tyke, Jewey. **1919** 'W. N. P. Barbellion' *Jrnl. Disappointed Man* 154 That mean, Jewy, secretive, petty creature, J. M. W. Turner. **1922** Joyce *Ulysses* 287 Jesus, I had to laugh at the little jewy getting his shirt out. *Ibid.* 299 I'm told those Jewies does have a sort of a queer odour coming off them for dogs. **1930** J. B. Priestley *Angel Pavement* iv. 184 A neat dark Jewy sort of chap.

jewys, jewyse, var. juise *Obs.*, judgement.

Jeyes(') fluid (dʒeɪz). [f. *Jeyes*, the name of the manufacturing company.] The proprietary name of a disinfectant consisting of a saponified solution of phenols, resins, and other ingredients. Also *Jeyes(') disinfecting fluid.*

[**1888** *Trade Marks Jrnl.* 18 July 995/2 [In] sickness always use Jeyes' disinfectants... Jeyes' Sanitary Compounds Company, Limited,..London,.. manufacturers.] **1900** *Encycl. Medica* III. 31 Cresol or methyl phenol with its derivatives forms the chief constituent of..'Jeyes' Fluid' and a host of similar mixtures. **1911** *T. Eaton & Co. Catal.* Spring & Summer 175/4 Jeyes' Disinfecting Fluid. **1933** D. L. Sayers *Murder must Advertise* iv. 72 'It's the boy that goes round with the disinfectant, sir.' 'Ah, of course! Spray with Sanfect and you're safe.' 'That's right, sir, except that they use Jeyes' Fluid.' **1957** S. Locket *Clin. Toxicol.* xix. 490 Phenolic substances and cresols are contained in a number of disinfectants, e.g... Izal, Jeyes' Disinfecting Fluid and Creolin. For sanitary purposes varying mixtures with soap and alkali are used. **1973** *Times* 19 June 1/3 Jeyes Fluid will rise by a maximum of 20 per cent.

jeyst, var. gest *sb.*⁴ *Obs.*, stage of a journey.

‖**jezail** (dʒəˈzaɪl, -ˈeɪl). *E. Ind.* Also **juzail.** [Pers. *jazā'il*, a large musket or rifle (used with a rest), a swivel-gun, wall-piece; according to Redman, corrupt. of *jazā'ir*: cf. *jazā'irī* a matchlockman, one of the guard of the Safawī kings.] A long and heavy Afghan musket.

1838–42 Gen. A. Abbott *Jrnl. Afghan War* (1879) ii. 167 The assailants had flint locks to their juzails. **1862** Beveridge *Hist. India* III. viii. iv. 414 The Afghan jezails carrying much farther than the British muskets, poured in a fire which could not be returned. **1881** Palgrave *Vis. Eng.*, *Valley of Death* ix, The one who out-slipp'd the jezail and the knife! **1889** R. Kipling *Departm. Ditties*, etc. (1899) 67 Two thousand pounds of education Drops to a ten-rupee jezail [*rime* defile]. **1892** —— *Barrack-r. Ballads* 84 All night the cressets glimmered pale On Ulwar Sabre and Tonk Jezail.

attrib. **1892** *Pall Mall G.* 21 Apr. 4/3 Colonel Durand himself receiving a very serious wound in the groin with a *jezail* bullet—a garnet enclosed in lead.

Hence ‖**je'zailchee** [f. prec. with Turkī agential suffix *chī*], a soldier carrying a jezail.

1862 Beveridge *India* III. viii. v. 434 It was deemed necessary '..to get rid..of the detachment of jezailchees'.

Jezebel ('dʒɛzəbəl, -bɛl). Also 6 **Iesabelle**, 7 **Jezabel, Jesebel.** Name of the infamous wife of Ahab king of Israel (1 Kings xvi. 31, xix. 1, 2, xxi; 2 Kings ix. 30–37); hence used allusively for a wicked, impudent, or abandoned woman (cf. Rev. ii. 20) or for a woman who paints her face.

1558 Knox *First Blast* (Arb.) 39 He hath raised vp these Iesabelles [our mischeuous Maryes] to be the vttermoste of his plagues. **1679** T. Oates (*title*) Witch of Endor, or the witchcrafts of the Roman Jesebel. **1711** Budgell *Spect.* No. 175 ¶2 A Jezebel..appears constantly dress'd at her Sash, and has a thousand little Tricks and Fooleries to attract the Eyes of all the idle young Fellows. **1771** Smollett *Humph. Cl.* 18 July Let. i, Mrs. Jenkins was..insulted with the opprobrious name of painted Jezebel. **1891** S. Mostyn *Curatica* 113 Oh! you abandoned Jezebel!

Hence **Jezebelian** (-'biːlɪən), †**Jezebelical** (-'bɛlɪkəl), **Jezebelish** ('dʒɛzəbəlɪʃ) *adjs.* (*nonce-wds.*), of the character of, or resembling, Jezebel.

1625 Purchas *Pilgrims* I. I. 63 That painted Iezabel, whose fouler wrinkles, her Iezabelicall, Iesuiticall Parasites still labour with renewed and refined Arts also to playster and fill vp a fresh. **1896** *Westm. Gaz.* 28 July 4/2 Remarks on her Jezebelish appearance [so much paint and powder].

‖**jeziah** ('dʒɛzjə). *E. Ind.* Also 7 **jid-, judge(e)a**, 8 **jezia, jezzeea.** [Pers. (Arab.) *jizyah* poll-tax.] The poll-tax imposed by Islamic law on non-Muslim subjects; *spec.* that exacted by the Mogul emperors in India.

1683 *Vizier's Let.* in W. Hedges *Diary* 18 July (1887) I. 101 Our last order for taking Custome, and Jidgea. **1686** *Fort St. Geo. Cons.* in *Notes & Extr.* I. (1871) 49 (Y. Suppl.) That the Poll-money or Judgeea lately ordered by the Mogul would be exacted of the English and Dutch. **1753** Hanway *Trav.* (1762) II. xiv. vii. 371 *note*, This tax, called the jeziah, was wont to be paid by those who were not mahommedans. **1815** Elphinstone *Acc. Caubul* (1842) II. 71 He also levies the Jezzeea, or tax on Hindoos. **1862** Beveridge *Hist. India* I. I. vi. 142 The *jezia* or capitation tax on infidels.

jhampan, variant of jampan.

‖**jheel, jhīl** (dʒiːl). *E. Ind.* Also 9 **jeil, jeel.** [Hindī *jhīl.*] A pool or lagoon (in India) often of vast extent, left after an inundation.

1805 *Lond. Gaz.* Extraord. No. 27 Apr., We found the enemy very strongly encamped..a large *jeel* of water extending to their right. **1824** Heber *Jrnl.* (1828) I. 207. **1845** Stocqueler *Handbk. Brit. India* (1854) 336 'The pigs' come out of their own accord, to take the air or wallow in some neighbouring jheel. **1885** *Encycl. Brit.* XVIII. 71/2 Numerous shallow ponds or *jhīls* mark the former beds of

the shifting rivers. These *jhils* have great value, not only as preservatives against inundation, but also as reservoirs for irrigation. **1899** *Westm. Gaz.* 28 Jan. 7/3 A performance which would not be amiss in the best snipe jheels of India.

jhoom, varr. JOOM, JÚM.

‖**jhow** (dʒhaʊ). *E. Ind.* Also 9 jow, jhao, jhau. [Hindī *jhā'u, jhau, jhāwu*, Skr. *jhāwuka*.] A shrubby tamarisk (*Tamarix indica*), frequent in the marshes of the Indian rivers, and used for basket-making and other purposes. Also *attrib.*

1827 D. JOHNSON *Ind. Field Sports* 274 *Jow*, or dagger grass jungles that are nearer. **1862** BEVERIDGE *Hist. India* III. VIII. vii. 489 A low, but in some places thick jhow jungle. **1889** R. S. S. BADEN-POWELL *Pigsticking* 92 In countries like Bengal, where long grass, jhao, thick crops, etc., are common.

jhula ('dʒu:la). *India.* Also joolah. [Hind., Hindi *jhūlā* swing, swing-rope.] A simple suspension bridge used in the Himalayas.

1830 A. S. H. MOUNTAIN *Mem. & Lett.* (1857) 114 Our chief object in descending to the Sutlej was to swing on a Joolah bridge. **1844** J. C. STOCQUELER *Hand-bk. India* 458 The rustic bridge is supplanted.. by *jhulas*, formed by ropes stretched across, constituting a species of loose parapet. **1923** *Blackw. Mag.* Aug. 259/2 A *jhula* or swinging rope-bridge.

jhum, varr. JOOM, JÚM.

jiao (dʒaʊ). Also **chiao**. [Chinese.] A unit of currency and coin of China.

1949 *Whitaker's Almanack* 905/2 By Presidential Decree of August 19, 1948, the Chinese National Dollar currency.. was replaced by a new currency named the *Gold Yuan*... The subsidiary coinage consists of *fen* (cents) and *Chiao* (tenths of a *yuan*). **1962** R. A. G. CARSON *Coins* 544 The coinage of Nationalist China in Formosa, issued since 1949 in various values of the chiao in aluminium and bronze. **1971** *Whitaker's Almanack* 980 China—*Renminbi* or *Yuan* of 10 *Jiao* or 100 *Fen*. **1973** *Times* 21 Mar. (China Trade Suppl.) p. iii/6 The subsidiary units are jiao (10 jiao = 1 yuan).

jib (dʒɪb), *sb.*[1] Also 7 gibb, 7–8 jibb, 8 gib, jyb. [Origin uncertain; the name has been only in English.

Possibly an abbreviation of *gibbet*, with reference to its suspension from the mast-head. Connexion with JIB *v.*[2] is also plausible; but the vb. has not as yet been found so early.]

1. a. *Naut.* A triangular stay-sail stretching from the outer end of the jib-boom to the fore-topmast head in large ships, and from the bowsprit to the mast-head in smaller craft. *flying jib*, a second sail of similar shape set before the jib on the *flying jib-boom* (but *c* 1700–1750 applied to the only jib of large vessels); in some large vessels more jibs, in extreme cases as many as six, are carried, the outermost being the *jib of jibs*: see quot. 1867.

'No Tudor ship carried anything in the form of a fore-sail or jib. It was not till long afterwards that any nation adopted them for square-rigged vessels—a fact that is very remarkable, since they were certainly used by small craft at the end of the 16th century.' (J. Corbett *Successors of Drake* (1900) 424.) 'In 1688 jibs were part of the ordinary stores at Woolwich, and must therefore have been used in the large ships before that date.' (M. Oppenheim.)

1661 *Inventory Swallow Ketch* (S. P. Dom. Chas. II. xxxv. 10. 1), One new Gibb.. One ould Gibb. **1694** *Acct. Stores sent to Streights Fleet* 31 July (Navy Board Lett. XXIX. 834), For preserving the sailes—Jibbs Two, Mizen Tops[11] 1. **1711** W. SUTHERLAND *Shipbuild. Assist.* 117 There is another Sail call'd a flying Gib. **1712** E. COOKE *Voy. S. Sea* 16 Her flying Jyb loose. **1726** G. ROBERTS 4 *Yrs. Voy.* 280 My Fore-sail and Jibb were patched out of the Pieces of the Main-Sail. **1750** BLANCKLEY *Naval Expos.* 140 Those [sails] which are not bent to the Yards, are, the Flying Jibb, Fore, Fore-top, Main.. and Mizon Top-mast Stay Sails. **1794** *Rigging & Seamanship* I. 83 Before the mast is a foresail, a jib, and a flying jib. **1867** SMYTH *Sailor's Word-bk.*, *Jib of Jibs*, a sixth jib on the bowsprit, only known to flying-kitemen: the sequence being—storm, inner, outer, flying, spindle, jib of jibs. **1878** *Masque of Poets* 53 The jib swung loose in the sudden gale.

b. ***the cut of one's jib*** (*colloq.*): one's personal appearance, countenance, or look; see CUT *sb.* 16 c.

Orig. a sailor's figure of speech, suggested by the prominence and characteristic form of the jib of a ship.

1823–1881 [see CUT *sb.* 16 c]. **1824** SCOTT *St. Ronan's* i, If she disliked what the sailor calls the cut of their jib. **1853** LYTTON *My Novel* IV. xxiii, Not know an Avenel! We've all the same cut of the jib, have not we, father? **1896** GUY BOOTHBY *In Strange Comp.* II. iv. 48/1, I like the cut of your jib, or you wouldn't be sitting there opposite me.

2. *dial.* The under lip (in phr. *to hang the jib*). Also, The mouth, face, or nose.

a **1825** FORBY *Voc. E. Anglia*, *Jib*, the under-lip. Of a whimpering child it is said 'he hangs his jib'. **1852** R. S. SURTEES *Sponge's Sp. Tour* i. 2 They cock up their jibs and ride along with a 'find any fault with either me or my horse, if you can' sort of air. **1865** B. BRIERLEY *Irkdale* I. 255 (*Lancash. dial.*) Cock up thy jib, an' let's have another smeawtch, an' then I'se goo whoam.

3. *Comb.*, as **jib-down-haul**, a rope used to haul down the jib; **jib-guy**, a stout rope which supports the jib-boom; **jib-halyard**, the halyard for raising and lowering the jib; **jib-head**, an iron fastened to the head of a Jib which has been shortened at the top; **jib-headed** *a.*, shaped like a jib, said of a topsail; **jib-header**, a topsail shaped like a jib; **jib-iron** = *jib-traveller*; **jib-netting**, a triangular netting fixed under the jib-boom to hold the jib when temporarily hauled down and to prevent men from falling into the sea while furling, etc. the jib; †**jib-sail** = JIB 1; **jib-sheet**, one of the ropes by which the jib is trimmed, stretching from its clew to the bows of the ship; **jib-stay**, the stay on which the jib is set; **jib topsail** (see quot. 1961); **jib-traveller** (see quot. 1794).

1825 H. B. GASCOIGNE *Nav. Fame* 54 While some to Let the anchor go prepare, The slack *Jib-down-haul in the Waste they bear. **1868** KINGLAKE *Crimea* (1877) IV. xiii. 390 When the movement of each ship had ceased, the *jib-guys of the two were.. touching. **1726** G. ROBERTS 4 *Yrs. Voy.* 169 So I unreev'd the.. Main Haliards, and *Jibb Haliards, and bent them. **1861** *Times* 16 Aug., The Christabel had a *jib-headed topsail up, and completed her race with much less labour than her rival had done. **1881** *Standard* 22 June 3/7 All having jibheaded topsails and whole mainsails set. **1899** *Daily News* 19 July 5/7 The Britannia.. substituted a jackyarder for a *jibheader. **1752** BEAWES *Lex Merc. Rediv.* 268 Lying too, with her *Gib Sail hauled to windward and her Mizzen Sail set. **1861** SMILES *Engineers* II. 36 In this situation the jibsail was blown to pieces. **1825** H. B. GASCOIGNE *Nav. Fame* 51 Starboard the helm, the slack *Jib-sheet haul Aft. **1828** M. SCOTT *Tom Cringle* xix, In a minute the jibsheet was again hauled over to leeward, and away she was like an arrow, crowding all sail. **1875** BEDFORD *Sailor's Pocket Bk.* (ed. 2) iii. 59 If under sail and about to tack, let fly the jib-sheet. **1752** CHAMBERS *Cycl.* s.v. *Ship* (Plate), Flying *Jibb Stay and Sails. *c* **1860** H. STUART *Seaman's Catech.* 48 Let go the jibstay. *a* **1865** SMYTH *Sailor's Work-Bk.* (1867) 411 *Jib topsail. **1866** CAPT. KEAY *Jrnl.* in B. Lubbock *China Clippers* (1914) App. H. p. xxii, Again bent the spare flying-jib for a jib topsail set on fore-royal stay well up. **1892** *Rudder* Sept. 202 The Princess had her jib topsail hoisted. **1927** G. BRADFORD *Gloss. Sea Terms* 92/2 *Jib-topsail*, a light jib set aloft in a similar manner to other head sails. It is hoisted on the outer of the head stays with its tack well up above the jib-boom instead of being fast to it. **1929** A. J. VILLIERS *Falmouth for Orders* 219 There were rumours that the captain intended to bend royal-stays'ls and a jib-tops'l, and a water-sail under the bowsprit. **1936** B. ADAMS *Ships & Women* xi. 239 While Pat O'Brien went out to the boom end to furl the jib topsail I stood on the forecastle head. **1961** F. H. BURGESS *Dict. Sailing* 123 *Jib topsail*, a light triangular sail, set above the jib; it is hanked to the topmast stay and sometimes called 'jib o' jib'. **1794** *Rigging & Seamanship* I. 179 The **Jib-traveller* is a circular iron hoop, with a hook and shackle, used to haul out the tack of the jib.

jib (dʒɪb), *sb.*[2] Also 8–9 gib. [app. an abbreviation of *gibbet*: see GIBBET *sb.*[1] 3.] The projecting arm of a crane; also applied to the boom of a derrick.

1764 FERGUSON in *Phil. Trans.* LIV. 24 This crane.. might be built in a room eight feet in width; the gib being placed on the outside of the room. **1804** *Naval Chron.* XII. 116 Mr. I. Bramah has invented a new jib. **1825** J. NICHOLSON *Operat. Mechanic* 284 The jib, or gibbet, as it is called, from a resemblance to that machine, is a triangular frame of wood, one side being perpendicular, and supported on pivots at the top and bottom, so that the whole moves round on these as a vertical axis of motion. **1851** *Illustr. Catal. Gt. Exhib.* 230 The projection or radius of the jib of these cranes is 32 feet. **1875** KNIGHT *Dict. Mech.* 688/1 The jib or movable spar of the derrick is hinged to and near the foot of the post, its top being held by a chain which passes over pulleys to a winch on the post, so that the inclination of the jib may be adjusted as required. **1895** *Mod. Steam Engine* 56 The jib is adjustable at any angle, and the crane is made to hoist, lower and turn round in either direction by steam.

b. *Comb.*, as *jib-beam*, *-pole*; **jib-crane**, a crane fitted with a jib; **jib-frame**, 'the upright frame at the sides of a marine-engine, connecting the cylinder, condenser, and the framing' (Knight *Dict. Mech.* 1875).

1792 *Trans. Soc. Arts* X. 222 Hung on a pulley, at the end of the gib-beam. **1873** *Daily News* 17 Sept. 7/1 The stone was lifted up by a jib crane for the purpose of placing the mortar. **1898** *Westm. Gaz.* 4 July 6/1 A powerful electric travelling jib crane running on a large elevated track controlling the entire length. **1898** *Daily News* 17 May 2/6 The jib poles did not go against the brick pier.

jib (dʒɪb), *sb.*[3] [f. JIB *v.*[2]]

1. A jibbing horse, a jibber.

1843 YOUATT *Horse* xv. 317 The mare was a rank jib in single harness. **1851** H. MAYHEW *Lond. Labour* I. 189 (Farmer) Frequently young horses that will not work in cabs—such as jibs—are sold to the horse-slaughterers as useless. **1890** BOLDREWOOD *Squatter's Dream* iv. 43 Jack was borne off by two jibs and a bolter in the Warroo mail.

2. The state of being at a standstill.

1893 G. D. LESLIE *Lett. to Marco* xx. 134 My picture is at present in a state of jib, owing to a child's head in it which I cannot get right.

jib (dʒɪb), *sb.*[4] *slang.* Also gib, jibb. [Origin unknown.] A first-year student at Trinity College, Dublin.

Unknown to the present generation of TCD students (1973).

1827 in J. E. Walsh *Trinity College in 19th Cent.* (1901) 21 About a hundred young jibbs.. forced the gates and sallied out into the streets. **1839** C. J. LEVER *Confessions H. Lorrequer* xiii. 99 During all this melée tournament, I perceived that the worthy jib as he would be called in the parlance of Trinity, Mr. Cudmore, remained perfectly silent. **1902** W. M. DIXON *Trinity College, Dublin* vi. 137 It was a proud thing for a 'gib' to present himself to a crowd round the door, hear many a cry, 'Make way for the gentleman of the College!' **1922** JOYCE *Ulysses* 160 And the Trinity jibs in their mortarboards.

jib (dʒɪb), *v.*[1] *Naut.* Also 7 gib, 9 gibb, jibb: see also GYBE. [Etymology obscure; the same sense is expressed by Da. *gibbe*, Sw. dial. *gippa*; cf. also Du. *gijpen*, Ger. *giepen*, prob. from a LG. original. But, as in GYBE *v.*, the phonetic change of (g) to (dʒ) is unexplained.]

1. *trans.* To pull (a sail or yard) round from one side of the vessel to the other, as in tacking, etc.

1691 T. H[ALE] *Acc. New Invent.* 126 The place and fitting of the Shrowd so as to make way for the gibbing of the Yards. **1776** COOK *2nd Voy.* II. iii. (1842) I. 426 In changing tacks, they have only occasion to shift or jib round the sail. **1834** M. SCOTT *Cruise Midge* (1863) 15 It could be hooked and unhooked, as need were, when she tacked and it became necessary to jib the sail. **1865** *Examiner* 18 Mar. 163 A movement of the boys when the boat was jibbing her sail may have upset her.

2. *intr.* Of a sail, etc.: To shift or swing round from one side of a vessel to the other; = GYBE *v.* 1.

1719 DE FOE *Crusoe* I. ii, The Boom gibbed over the Top of the Cabin. **1804** *Naval Chron.* XI. 169 The sail gibbed, the boat upset. **1831** TRELAWNEY *Adv. Younger Son* II. 199, I saw the Boston schooner's main-sail jib.

b. *transf.* Of other things: To swing round.

1891 *Daily News* 23 July 7/2 The arm of the crane could swing round, or gibb, on each side, and deliver the stone on a truck.

jib, *v.*[2] Also jibb, *rarely* gib. [A recent word of uncertain derivation: not in Todd 1818, Webster 1828, or Craig 1847. Thought by Forby (*a* 1825) to be transf. from the jibbing of a sail, and so to be identical with JIB *v.*[1] But this is very doubtful.

Jib has a curious resemblance to OF. and mod. dial. F. *giber* to kick, sometimes said of horses; whence *regiber* (mod.F. *regimber*), early ME. *regibben* in Ancr. R., to kick as a wanton beast; but it is not possible to connect *jib* historically with these words.]

1. *intr.* Of a horse or other animal in harness: To stop and refuse to go on; to move restively backwards or sideways instead of going on; to balk stubbornly.

1811 JANE AUSTEN *Lett.* (1884) II. 95 The horses actually gibbed on this side of Hyde Park Gate. **1816** SCOTT *Antiq.* ii, Miss Grizie Oldbuck was sometimes apt to jibb when he pulled the reins too tight. *a* **1825** FORBY *Voc. E. Anglia*, *Jib*, to start suddenly and violently aside, generally from the collar; and to refuse to draw or go forward. It is said of a horse metaphorically from the jibbing of a sail. **1826** DISRAELI *Viv. Grey* VI. ii, The horses have jibbed, and will not stir. **1845** FORD *Handbk. Spain* I. 48 In the best regulated teams it must happen that some one will occasionally start, gib, and bolt.

2. *transf.* and *fig.* **a.** To stop short in some action; to refuse to proceed or advance; to draw back, back out.

1812 *Sporting Mag.* XXXIX. 139 Nanny jibbed a bit in the twelfth round. **1827** SCOTT *Jrnl.* 16 Mar., I had settled to finish the review, when, behold.. I jibb'd. **1845** EMPSON *Let.* in *Corr. M. Napier*, Many Whigs, however, will jib, from fear of their constituents. **1894** SIR E. SULLIVAN *Woman* 110 When there is no compulsion there is no gibbing.

b. To start aside; to shy *at*.

1882 T. A. GUTHRIE *Vice Versa* vi. 123 The boys taking the parts of ladies jibbing away from their partners in a highly unladylike fashion. **1896** OUIDA *Massarenes* xv, There are people who jib at you still, you know: when once you were one of us, they wouldn't dare.

Hence **jibbing** *vbl. sb.* and *ppl. a.*

1844 ALB. SMITH *Adv. Mr. Ledbury* xlii. (1886) 130 The playful vagaries of jibbing horses. **1861** G. F. BERKELEY *Sportsm. W. Prairies* xv. 247 A succession of jibbings and rearings. **1862** WHYTE MELVILLE *Ins. Bar* x. (ed. 12) 363 A backward swain is like a jibbing horse.

jib, *v.*[3] *Sc. trans.* To fleece; to strip; to milk closely, drain to the dregs. Hence **jibbings**, the last strainings of milk from a cow; afterings.

1728 RAMSAY *Vision* viii, Our trechour peirs thair tyranns treit, Quha jyb them, and thair substance eit. **1824** MACTAGGART *Gallovidian Encycl.*, *Jibb*, to milk closely. *Jibbings*, the last milk that can be drawn out of a cow's udder. **1828** CARLYLE *Let.* in Froude *Life* (1882) II. ii. 27 Jane the lesser.. furnishes butter and afterings (jibbings) for tea.

‖**jibbah** ('dʒɪbə). Also djebba, djibba(h), jibbeh, jibba. [A variant (following the pronunc. current in Egypt) of JUBBAH.] **a.** An outer garment, worn by Egyptian Muslims, consisting of a long cloth coat with sleeves reaching nearly to the wrists. Occas. (outside the Middle East) worn by women as a type of smock.

1848 J. RICHARDSON *Trav. Sahara* I. xiv. 386 Feel glad I took the advice of the Governor of Ghadames, and purchased a quantity of warm woollen clothing, heik, bornouse, and jibbah. **1892** *Daily News* 20 Oct. 5/6 He again returned, wearing a clean jibbeh patched with pieces of the vestments belonging to our Mission church at El Obeid. **1896** *Ibid.* 3 Feb. 6/4 A man dressed in the Mahdist 'jibba' appeared before Slatin's fort, with a summons to surrender. *Ibid.* 23 Oct. 2/1 They had turned their tattered djebbas inside out. **1898** DOYLE *Trag. Korosko* v. 123 Then he laid his black forefinger upon the breast of his jibbeh. **1904** *Daily Chron.* 27 July 8/2 The djibbah is produced in full, warm

reds, purples, blues, and orange hues. **1909** H. G. Wells *Ann Veronica* vii, A purple djibbah with a richly embroidered yoke. **1922** [see ABAYA]. **1927** *Spectator* 17 Dec. 1081/1 The books..are sold by ladies in djibbas. **1963** *Punch* 27 Feb. 302/2 A girl going into the senior school [at Roedean]..could wear her djibbah until she left at eighteen.

b. *Comb.*, as ***jibbah-clad***.

1898 *Daily News* 5 Sept. 5/8 The Dervishes..broke and fled, leaving the field white with jibbah-clad corpses, like a meadow dotted with snowdrifts.

jibber ('dʒɪbə(r)), *sb.* [f. JIB *v.*² + -ER¹.]

a. A horse that jibs.

1847 in Halliwell. **1871** Le Fanu *Checkmate* II. xiii. 123 There are kickers and roarers, and bolters and jibbers. **1879** Sala *Paris herself again* (1880) II. xiv. 233 His horse was a miserable jibber.

b. One who jibs.

1936 F. D. Davison *Children of Dark People* x. 147 He said you'd got lost and he'd been sent out by the elders of the tribe to look for you; the old jibber! **1961** F. H. Burgess *Dict. Sailing* 123 *Jibber*, one who has second thoughts about attempting something, and then refuses to make the effort.

jibber, *v.* [Related to JABBER and GIBBER.] *intr.* To speak rapidly and inarticulately; to chatter unintelligibly. Also **jibber-jabber** *sb.* and *v.*

1824 Scott *Redgauntlet* Let. xi, The jackanape..jibbered and cried as if it was mocking its master. **1883** Hall Caine *Cobw. Crit.* i. 16 A jibbering disposition to 'break into ecstasies'. **1898** *Westm. Gaz.* 25 May 3/2 The proud passenger..may jibber with fright. **1900** *Ibid.* 12 Sept. 4/2 They decline to learn..and jibber when corrected. **1922** A. Haddon *Green Room Gossip* ix. 240 The jibber-jabber was entertaining, not because the utterances were those of ordinary human beings, but because they were the voice of Shaw. **1945** L. Shelly *Jive Talk Dict.* 26 *Jibber jabber*, senseless talk. **1948** *Bulletin* (Philadelphia) 23 Mar. 24/5 Time for Congress to quit jibber-jabbering.

jibbet(t, jibbong, obs. ff. GIBBET, GEEBUNG.

jibbings: see JIB *v.*³

jib-boom. *Naut.* [f. JIB *sb.*¹ + BOOM *sb.*²] A spar run out from the end of the bowsprit, to which the tack of the jib is lashed, and beyond which is sometimes extended the ***flying jib-boom***.

1748 *Anson's Voy.* II. ix. 226 One of the sail-makers mates was fishing from the end of the gib-boom. **1752** Chambers *Cycl.* s.v. *Ship* (Plate), *Flying Jibbboom* [no simple jib-boom shown]. **1769** Falconer *Dict. Marine* (1776), *Jib-Boom*,.. This boom..is nothing more than a continuation of the bowsprit forward, to which it may be considered as a top-mast. **1833** Marryat *P. Simple* xxxv, To prepare for action, and keep close order, which means, to have your flying jib-boom in at the starn windows of the ship a head of you. **1878** *Masque of Poets* 55 Out on the jibboom in a gale He went in the darkness to furl a sail.

jibby-horse. [cf. dial. (E.Angl.) *jibby*, a girl dressed in showy finery.] (See quot. 1825.)

[*c* **1440** *Promp. Parv.* 192/2 Gybbe, horse, *mandicus*.] **1601** Sir W. Cornwallis *Ess.* II. xxxvi. (1631) 110 Knowledge disdaines the rattles and gibby horses of the world. *a* **1825** Forby *Voc. E. Anglia*, *Jibby-horse*, a showman's horse decorated with particolored trappings, plumes, etc. It is sometimes transferred to a human subject.

jib-crack, obs. variant of GIMCRACK.

jib-door. [Origin unascertained.] A door flush with the wall in which it stands, and usually painted or papered so as to be indistinguishable from it.

1800 Mrs. Hervey *Mourtray Fam.* II. 159 Emma..darted out through a gib-door, covered with pictures, which had struck her eye while he was speaking. **1820–22** Pyne *Wine & Walnuts* (1824) II. ix. 132 The delighted bookseller opened a jib door..that went from the side of the shop to a steep narrow staircase. **1852** Lomax & Gunyon *Encycl. Archit.* s.v., The use of a jib-door is to preserve the symmetry of an apartment, where only one door is wanted, nearer to one end of the partition than the other.

jibe, variant of GIBE *sb.* and *v.*, GYBE *v.*

jibe (dʒaɪb), *v.* Chiefly *U.S.* Also **gibe.** [Origin obscure: perh. phonetically related to *chime*: see CHIME *v.* 8, 9 c.] *intr.* To chime *in* (*with*); to be in harmony or accord; to agree.

1813 *Sporting Mag.* XLII. 122 It however curricle-izes or gibes in but too well with the passing anecdotes of the day. **1855** *Doesticks* xiv. 113, I attempting to sing the words of 'Old Hundred', while the lady played the Jenny Lind polka, which didn't seem to jibe. **1860** Bartlett *Americanisms* 245 To *jibe* [*ed.* **1877** to *gibe*], to suit, agree, harmonize. **1871** 'Mark Twain' *Screamers* xxix, The piece you happened to be playing..didn't seem to gibe with the general gait of the picture that was passing at the time. **1894** *Nation* (N.Y.) LIX. 311/1 The dislike..of Trilby's posing for the 'altogether', doesn't jibe with the author's authoritative declaration that to all artists..'nothing is so chaste as nudity'. **1959** [see GYBE]. **1970** *New Yorker* 28 Nov. 101/1, I didn't jibe with my mother as a personality, but there was no other woman..I could relate to. **1973** *Word 1970* XXVI. 16 The first does not jibe with the patterning of meanings.

jiblet, variant of GIBLET.

‖**jiboya** (dʒɪ'bɔɪə). [Tupi *giboia* (*boia* = serpent).] A Brazilian name of the great BOA, also called *boiguaçú*.

1613 Purchas *Pilgrimage* (1614) 842 [*Brazil*] Of Snakes without venome, he numbereth the *Giboya*, some of which are twentie foote long, and will swallow a Deere whole. *Ibid.* 839 *Iaboya*. [**1648** W. Piso *De Med. Brasil.* III. 41 Boiguaçu sive Iiboya, serpentium omnium facile maximus.] **1712** W. Rogers *Voy.* 52 That Monster call'd Jiboya, or the Roebuck-Serpent, which I enquir'd after. **1774** Goldsm. *Nat. Hist.* VII. 225. **1839** *Encycl. Brit.* (ed. 7) XX. 145/1 *Boa constrictor*, Linn...is met with in Surinam and Brazil, in woody districts... It is..commonly known by the name of *Jiboya*.

‖**jicara** ('hikara). Also **jicaro.** [Amer. Sp. *jícara*, *jícaro*, ad. Nahuatl *xicalli*.] A Central American name for the *calabash-tree* (s.v. CALABASH 7) or its fruit (CALABASH 2).

1859 J. Froebel *Seven Years' Travel in Central Amer.* I. vi. 91 On the market place..many interesting and highly creditable articles of Indian skill and industry are offered for sale..*jicaras* and *guacales* (cups and basins made of calabashes) ornamented with reliefs. **1892** C. F. Lummis *Tramp across the Continent* 149 Each bore upon her head a big, flaring basket—the rush *chiquihuite* of home make, or the elegantly woven Apache *jicara*. **1924** *Chambers's Jrnl.* Sept. 615/1 They saw a woman carrying a jicara gourd. **1927** D. H. Lawrence *Mornings in Mexico* 73 He bargained..for a carved *jicara*. **1943** Record & Hess *Timbers of New World* 78/2 The shells [of calabash fruits] are used by the natives for making cups, dishes, and other household utensils, and some of them are ornately carved or painted... Common names: Calabash..jícaro. **1964** Little & Wadsworth *Common Trees Puerto Rico & Virgin Islands* 490/2 Calabash-tree... Widely planted in Puerto Rico and through the tropics for the fruits... Other common names..jicaro, jícara (Central America).

Jicarilla (hika'riʎa). Also **Jiccarilla.** [Mexican Sp. (dim. of prec.).] In full, ***Jicarilla Apache***. An Apache people in New Mexico and nearby states; a member of this people; also, the name of their language. Also *attrib.* or as *adj.*

1850 *Ex. Doc. 31st U.S. Congress 1 Sess. Senate* No. 64. 57 The vocabulary as distinctly shows the kindred character of the language of the Navajos and of the Ticorillas [*sic*] branch of the Apache. **1858** D. C. Peters *Life Kit Carson* xv. 416 The Jiccarillas..had broken out in open defiance of the authorities. **1871** *Republican Rev.* (Albuquerque, New Mexico) 1 Apr. 2/1 News also came on Sunday of the murder of Francisco, the lawyer of the Jicarilla Apache tribe. **1911** *Anthropol. Papers Amer. Mus. Nat. Hist.* VIII. 8 A large number of texts was secured from Cas Miria, a Jicarilla now about seventy years of age and nearly blind. *Ibid.*, This shift..has taken place in the Lipan, Jicarilla, and Kiowa-Apache. **1944** J. Adair *Navajo & Pueblo Silversmiths* vi. 97 The Jicarilla Apache move down to the southern edge of their reservation in the winter. **1971** *Observer* 24 Jan. 32/5 The land-rich Jicarilla tribe in New Mexico. *Ibid.*, The Jicarillas didn't ask for an *anti*-Western with a trendy social message.

†**jie,** obs. Sc. var. of JEE *v.*, to move, turn.

1728 Ramsay *Vision* xxii, Ay jieand, and flieand, Round lyk a wedder-cock.

jiff. *colloq.* Short for JIFFY.

1797 Mrs. A. M. Bennett *Beggar Girl* (1813) III. 281 'Twould raise a mutiny in a jiff. **1894** Wilkins & Vivian *Green Bay Tree* I. 76 I'll be back in two jiffs. **1899** E. J. Chapman *Drama 2 Lives, Amphioxus & Ascid.* 83 He grasps the creature in a jiff.

jiffle ('dʒɪf(ə)l), *v.* Now *dial.* [Origin obscure: cf. JUFFLE *v.*] *intr.* To shuffle, to fidget. Also as *sb.*

1674 Fairfax *Bulk & Selv.* 134 Jogging on in a jiffling way, they lag behind at every bearing, as they come up more or less at every jetting. **1799** W. Taylor in *Monthly Mag.* VII. 139 You limp'd and jiffled for a long while after. **1825–80** Jamieson, *To jiffle*, to shuffle. *Perths.* **1877** *N.W. Linc. Gloss.*, *Jiffle*, to fidget. **1895** *E. Anglian Gloss.*, *Jiffling*, fidgety. **1963** S. Marshall *Exper. in Educ.* iii. 93, I have usually been aware of a discreet rustling (and jiffling) among my audience, and..little note-books and pencils have appeared. **1968** G. J. Barrett *Guilty, be Damned!* ix. 104 Fenton's stomach squirmed, and he jiffled in his seat. **1971** B. W. Aldiss *Soldier Erect* 13 Ann was working our gramophone,..and Sylvia was standing beside her, jiffling to the tunes. *Ibid.*, I prowled round the perimeter of the little conversations, attracted by Sylvia's jiffle.

jiffy ('dʒɪfɪ). *colloq.* Also 8 **jeffy**, 9 **jiffey.** [Origin unascertained.] **1.** A very short space of time: only in such phrases as ***in a jiffy***, in a trice.

1785 *Munchhausen's Trav.* xxiii. (1792) 96 In six jiffies I found myself and all my retinue..at the rock of Gibralter. **1796** Grose *Dict. Vulgar Tongue* s.v., It will be done in a jeffy: it will be done in a short space of time, in an instant. **1833** Marryat *P. Simple* xiii, We were ordered to South America; and the trade winds took us there in a jiffey. *a* **1845** Hood *T. Trumpet* xxxv, In half a jiffy, or less than that. **1880** Spurgeon *J. Ploughm. Pict.* 100 They have wonderful plans for doing everything in a jiffy.

2. *Comb.* The proprietary name *Jiffy* in **Jiffy (book) bag**, a type of large envelope padded to protect the contents; also *fig.*; also *ellipt.* as *Jiffy*; **Jiffy pot**, a type of small pot in which seeds may be sown (see quot. 1972); also **jiffy-quick** *adv.*, in a jiffy.

1956 *Library Jrnl.* 1 June 1384/1 Book handling equipment... Mailing bags: Jiffy, Triangle. *Ibid.* 1388/1 Jiffy book bag. **1968** *New Scientist* 10 Oct. 77/1 Dr. Pratt has recently been using 'Jiffy bags' for his outer-jackets—those patent padded envelopes used for mailing books. **1969** *Trade Marks Jrnl.* 2 July 1084/2 Jiffy... Padded paper bags, cushioned paper pads and padded paper in sheet or roll form, all being wrapping and packaging materials for industrial use, for protecting goods in transit. Jiffy Packaging Company Limited,..Winsford, Cheshire; manufacturers. **1973** 'D. Halliday' *Dolly & Starry Bird* xvi. 249 Maurice..had backed discreetly into a Jiffy bag of deliberate ignorance. **1957** *Trade Marks Jrnl.* 4 Dec. 1278/1 Jiffapot [*sic*]... Hormonal peat in the form of propagating pots for plants. **1959** *Greenhouse* IV. iv. 243 (Advt.), These tomato plants grew up side by side,..'B' in a standard clay pot, 'A' in a Jiffy Pot... Exhibit 'A' forged ahead... Ideal for root cuttings too—hyacinths start evenly in Jiffy Pots. **1965** G. V. Williams *Econ. Geol. N.Z.* xvi. 256/2 It is of interest to note that 25 million 'jiffy pots' are used annually for horticultural purposes in New Zealand. **1968** *Trade Marks Jrnl.* 27 Mar. 484/2 Jiffypots... Flower, planting and transplanting pots made of peat. Odd Smaaberg Melvold and Leif Fraas Koxvold, trading as Me-Kox Industri Melvold & Koxvold, Østre Akers Vei 210 Grorud, near Oslo, Norway; manufacturers and merchants. **1972** *Guardian* 16 Dec. 12/7 Jiffy pots are..made of peat and wood pulp, through which plant roots can grow. **1927** *Ladies' Home Jrnl.* Dec. 34/3 A waxed surface that..you can dust up jiffy-quick promises spick-and-span floors with but little trouble.

jig (dʒɪg), *sb.*¹ Forms: 6 *Sc.* ieig, 6–7 iyg, iigge, iygge, gigge, 7 gig, ijgge, 7–8 jigg, 7– jig. [Origin uncertain. Often assumed to be identical with OF. *gigue* a kind of stringed instrument, a rude fiddle, It. and Sp. *giga*, MHG. *gîge*, Ger. *geige*; but as to this there are difficulties: the OF. word had none of the senses of *jig*, it was also obs. long before *jig* is known to have existed; moreover, mod.F. *gigue* the dance, and dance tune (exemplified 1680) is not a continuation of OF. *gigue*, but is said by Darmesteter to have been simply adopted from Eng. *jig*. In this uncertainty as to the origin and history of the word, the order of senses here presented is provisional; those in 6 are in part directly from the stem of JIG *v.*

Apparently the only way in which *jig* could be connected with OF. *gigue*, would be its formation from JIG *v.*, the derivation of the latter from F. *giguer*, *ginguer* 'to leap, frolic, gambol', and the formation of this from OF. *gigue*. But not one of these steps is certain: in particular the senses and chronology of JIG *v.* offer difficulties.]

1. a. A lively, rapid, springy kind of dance. Freq. as ***Irish jig*** (also *v. intr.*).

c **1560** A. Scott *Poems* (S.T.S.) iv. 58 Sum luvis, new cum to toun, With jeigis to mak thame joly; Sum luvis dance vp and doun, To meiss thair malancoly. **1599** Marston *Sco. Villanie* x, The Orbes celestiall Will daunce Kemps Iigge. **1599** Shaks. *Much Ado* II. i. 78 Wooing..is hot and hasty like a Scotch ijgge (and full as fantasticall). **1624** Bp. Hall *Serm. Hampton Crt.* Sept., Surely jiggs at a Funeral..are things prodigiously unseasonable. **1634** Milton *Comus* 952 All the swains that there abide With jigs and rural dance resort. **1775** A. Burnaby *Trav.* 21 When the company are pretty well tired with country dances, it is usual to dance jiggs. **1780** A. Young *Tour in Ireland* II. xvii. 75 The irish jig, which they can dance with a most *luxuriant* expression. **1843** Lever *J. Hinton* xvii. (1878) 124 The whole party would take hands and dance round the table to the measure of an Irish jig. **1919** [see FOX-TROT *v.*].

†**b.** ***St. Vitus's jig***: St. Vitus's dance, chorea.

1702 Baynard *Cold Baths* II. (1709) 377 A Youth that had lost the use of his Limbs by a sort of a Chorea sancti Viti (called Saint Vitus's Jigg).

c. [f. JIG *v.*] Fidgety movement: in phr. ***on the jig***. (*colloq.*)

1881 Jefferies *Wood Magic* I. ii. 25 The sight of the white steam, and the humming of the fly-wheel, always set Bevis 'on the jig', as the village folk called it, to get to the machinery.

2. The music for such a dance; a rapid lively dance-tune; *spec.* one in triple rhythm (usually 6–8 or 12–8) used as the last movement of a suite (oftener in the Fr. form GIGUE or It. GIGA).

1588 Shaks. *L.L.L.* IV. iii. 168 To see great Hercules whipping a Gigge, And profound Salomon tuning a Iygge. **1593** Donne *Sat.* iv. 147 As fidlers still, Though they be paid to be gone, yet needs will Thrust one more iig upon you. **1621** Burton *Anat. Mel.* II. ii. VI. iii, The sound of those Gigges and Hornpipes. **1649** Lovelace *Poems* (1864) 128 In the same key with monkeys jiggs Or dirges of proscribed piggs. **1674** Playford *Skill Mus.* Pref. 9 Our late solemn Musick is now justled out of esteem by the new Corants and Jigs of Foreigners. **1747** H. Walpole *Lett.* (1846) II. 177 They sing to jigs, and dance to church music. **1878** Browning *Poets Croisic* cxix, What some player-prig Means for a grave tune though it proves a jig.

†**3.** A song or ballad of lively, jocular, or mocking (often scurrilous) character. (In 17th c. applied in mockery to metrical versions of the Psalms).

1570 Foxe *A. & M.* (ed. 2) I. 470 The Scottish Gigges and rymes were these, Long berdes hartles, Paynted hoodes, witles. **1590** Marlowe *Edw. II*, II. ii, The fleering Scots, To England's high disgrace, have made this jig; 'Maids of England, sore may you mourn, For your lemans you have lost at Bannocksbourn, With a heave and a ho!' **1611** Florio, *Chiarantana*, a kinde of Caroll or song full of leapings like a Scotish gigge. **1621** Molle *Camerar. Liv. Libr.* v. ii. 322 In praise of him certaine jygges were made. **16..** *Roxb. Ball.* II. 257 *Man in Moon*, In wine we call for bawdy jiggs, Catzoes, rumbillows, whirligigs. *c* **1657** *Cent. Art. agst. Clergy* in J. Walker *Suffer. Clergy* (1714) 82 The singing of Hopkins's Psalms, which he called Hopkins's jiggs. **1673** R. Leigh *Transp. Reh.* 17 Having had our Geneva Jigg, let us advance.

†**4.** A light performance or entertainment of a lively or comical character, given at the end, or in an interval, of a play. *Obs.*

Perhaps originally mainly consisting of song and dance (quot. 1632), but evidently sometimes of the nature of a farce.

a **1592** Greene *Jas. IV*, I. Interl., Here see I good fond actions in thy jig. **1602** Shaks. *Ham.* II. ii. 522 He's for a

Iigge, or a tale of Baudry. **1611** COTGR., *Farce*,..the Iyg at the end of an Enterlude, wherein some pretie knauerie is acted. **1632** D. LUPTON *Lond. & Country* xx, Most commonly when the play is done, you shal haue a Iigge or dance of all trads, they mean to put their legs to it, as well as their tongs. **1654** GAYTON *Pleas. Notes* IV. iii. 187 Untill the sad Catastrophe shews the Play to be a jig, all mockery and mirth. **1700** *Playhouse Advt.* in *Flying Post* 4 July, Miss Evans's Jigg and Irish dance. **1728** POPE *Dunc.* III. 238 A fire, a jigg, a battle, and a ball. **1864** SHAW *Hist. Eng. Lit.* vi. (1875) 125 At the end of the piece, or occasionally perhaps between the acts, the clown or jester performed what was called a *jig*.

5. A piece of sport, a joke; a jesting matter, a trifle; a sportive trick or cheat. ***the jig is up*** (or ***over***) = 'the game is up', it is all over. Now *dial.* or *slang*.

1592 NASHE *P. Penilesse* (ed. 2) 38 Let not your shops be infected with anie such goose gyblets or stinking garbadge, as the Iygs of newsmongers. **1627** E. F. *Hist. Edw. II*, (1680) 66 As with a Jigg of State might catch them naked. **1663** *Flagellum, or O. Cromwell* (1672) 27 When the Major now perceived the Jig, and how Kitchinman had fooled him, he could have pulled the Hair off his Head. **1688** BUNYAN *Jerus. Sinner Saved* (1886) 103 By jiggs, and tricks, and quirks, which he helpeth them to. **1735** DYCHE, *Jig*,..an arch merry trick. **1777** *Maryland Jrnl.* 17 June (Th.), Mr. John Miller came in and said, 'The jig is over with us.' **1800** *Aurora* (Philadelphia) 17 Dec. (Th.), As the Baltimore paper says, 'The Jigg's up, Paddy.' **1848** JONES *Sk. Trav.* 14 (Farmer), I know'd the jig was up. **1861** THACKERAY *Four Georges* iv. (1862) 224 Her jigs, and her junketings, and her tears. **1894** HOWELLS in *Harper's Mag.* Feb. 380 The die is cast, the jig is up, the fat's in the fire, the milk's spilt. **1923** E. WALLACE *Missing Million* xii. 100 It was almost like the last spiteful act of a man who knew the jig was up. **1961** WODEHOUSE *Service with a Smile* (1962) ix. 134 You're in the soup, Miss Briggs. The gaff has been blown, and the jig is up. **1965** *New Yorker* 18 Sept. 56 O.K., Frankie, the jig's up! **1974** *Nature* 15 Feb. 420/3 The weight of opinion seems to be that the jig is up for the map's supporters.

6. a. A name variously applied in different trades to mechanical contrivances and simple machines for performing acts or processes, some of which arise directly from uses of JIG *v.*, while in others the sense is little more than 'dodge', 'device', 'contrivance': see the quots. *spec.* **b.** A machine or contrivance for jigging or dressing ore by shaking it up jerkily in a fluid medium (see JIG *v.* 5) = JIGGER *sb.*[1] 3 b. **c.** A contrivance of various kinds for catching fish: see quots., and cf. GIG *sb.*[4] **d.** *Coal-mining.* A steep tramway on which the loaded trucks as they descend draw up the empty trucks by means of a cable passing round a drum or worked by wheels; also called *jinny*. **e.** A device for accurately guiding and positioning a drill or other tool in relation to the workpiece, or for positioning the parts of an object during assembly, and used when a large number of similar articles have to be made with high precision; = TEMPLET[1] 2 b. **f.** *Dyeing* = JIGGER *sb.*[1] 5 n.

a. 1875 KNIGHT *Dict. Mech.*, *Jig*. 1. A handy tool. The name is applied to various devices, and in many trades small and simple machines are called jigs. In the armorer's set of tools we find cited,—Drilling-jig. Filing-jig. Milling-jig. Shaving-jig. Tapping-jig. **1881** GREENER *Gun* 432 By means of jigs, callipers, and other tools the exact size of the stock and its angle with the barrel is obtained.

b. 1849 *Ex. Doc. 31st U.S. Congress 1 Sess. House* No. 5. III. 479 Assay and analysis of the washed metals from the jigs at the Boston and Pittsburg Company's mine. **1877** RAYMOND *Statist. Mines & Mining* 424 No principle has yet been discovered which is better adapted to the separation of minerals than the intermittent and impulsive action of some fluid medium on the crushed ore. The best results thus far obtained are from machines known as 'jigs', which employ the above principle. **1953** F. B. MICHELL in *Symposium Recent Devel. Mineral Dressing* (Inst. Mining & Metall.) 263 The jig is by no means obsolete and in the United States, indeed, it is finding increased use for the treatment of those fractions which are too fine for economical concentration by dense media.

c. 1846 *Knickerbocker* XXVII. 513 See that your jigs are in perfect order, for if we do get hold of 'em, our lines and hooks will have to take it, I guess, for a spell. **1858** *N.Y. Tribune* 22 July (Bartlett), A long, stout line, at the end of which was a shining, spoon-shaped piece of pewter, terminated by a large hook. This apparatus he called a jig. **1873** *Forest & Stream* 2 Oct. 122 The Shoals are fished with a 'jig', a three-pronged harpoon, fastened to a long wooden handle. **1883** *Fisheries Exhib. Catal.* 195 Jigs and drails for the capture of cod,..mackerel jigs formerly extensively used. **1897** R. KIPLING *Capt. Courageous* 145 Every soul aboard hung over his squid-jig—a piece of lead painted red and armed at the lower end with a circle of pins bent backward like half-opened umbrella ribs. **1897** *Outing* (U.S.) XXX. 258/1 Harry..leaned over to watch critically the action of the bone jigs, as they played in the water. They darted from side to side without whirling, thus closely imitating a wounded fish.

d. 1866 *Daily Tel.* 26 Jan. 6/3 The spot where it was ignited was shown to be the first level on the north side near the top of the jig. **1893** *Labour Commission Gloss.*, *Jigs*, term used in North Staffordshire in the steep measures to describe the road down which the trams are sent, the full trams pulling the empty ones up.

e. 1894 W. L. LINEHAM *Text-bk. Mech. Engin.* vi. 274 Jigs are an extension of the template principle. Instead of thin plates, castings of an inch or so in thickness are used, supplied with holes where needed, the object being to guide the drill to its proper place on the work without the necessity of lining-out. **1903** W. H. VAN DERVOORT *Mod. Machine Shop Tools* xxvii. 410 Jigs are manufacturing tools of, as a rule, high first cost and their economy depends very largely on the number of pieces to be drilled. **1912** R. W. A. BREWER *Motor Car Construction* ii. 13 Modern competition has made jig work absolutely essential. **1942** B. A. SHIELDS *Princ. Flight* iii. 91 The airplane fuselage is built in a jig. **1947** BRYANT & DICKINSON *Jigs & Fixtures for Mass Production* i. 4 In the machine shop, a jig is usually an appliance which guides a cutting tool... In the automotive industry, a jig is a work-holding device wherein all positions for assembly or fabrication operations are prelocated. **1967** M. CHANDLER *Ceramics in Mod. World* iv. 127 (*caption*) Assembling a large post insulator in a jig.

f. 1942 WHITTAKER & WILCOCK *Dyeing with Coal-Tar Dyestuffs* (ed. 4) iv. 67 The jig or jigger is a machine designed for dyeing piece goods at full width. **1963** MEITNER & KERTESS tr. *Schmidlin's Preparation & Dyeing Synthetic Fibres* xii. 108 High-temperature pressure jigs are mainly used for heavier fabrics.

7. Applied ludicrously to a horse, a person, etc. *colloq.*

1706 *Wooden World Dissected* (1708) 54 Up he [a sailor] hoists himself a Trip upon his Jig of a Horse, and sticks as close..as if he was got cross a Yard-arm. **1781** BENTHAM *Wks.* (1843) X. 103 This Lord and Lady Tracton are the queerest jigs you ever saw.

8. *Comb.*, as (senses 1–4) *jig-dancer*, *-given* adj., *-like* adj., *-maker*; **jig-backed** *a.*, having a twist in the back; **jig borer**, (*a*) a machine for drilling holes in or machining the surfaces of a component (esp. a jig (sense 6 e)), usually having a vertical spindle mounted above a table which can be accurately positioned relative to the spindle; (*b*) (see quot. 1972); so **jig-boring** *vbl. sb.*; hence (as a back-formation) **jig-bore** *v. trans.*, to drill (a hole) by means of a jig borer; **jig box**, the box or sieve of a jig (sense 6 b); **jig-brow** (*Coal-mining*), an underground incline on which a jig or jinny (see 6 d) works, also called *jinny-road*; **jig button**, a steel bush used for accurate positioning of a jig plate when making jigs on a lathe; **jig-chain** (see quot.); **jig-clog**, a clog worn in dancing a jig; **jigman**, one who works an ore-dressing jigger; **jig-mould**, a mould into which melted lead is poured to form the shank of a jig (sense 6 c); **jig-pin**, 'a pin used by miners to hold the turn-beams, and prevent them from turning' (Webster, 1828); **jig plate**, (a part of) a jig consisting of a steel plate which carries the bushes which guide the drill; **jig-time**, *colloq.* (chiefly *U.S.*) in phrase ***in jig-time*** expressing a very short space of time. See also JIG-SAW.

1821 *Sporting Mag.* VIII. 262 It was discovered that, from a wrench, she [a mare] was also *jig-backed. **1939** C. B. COLE *Tool Making* 258 The bushing plate is made from cold-rolled steel, and this is laid out carefully and the hole *jig-bored for the drill bushing. **1967** A. J. LISSAMAN *Metrology* vi. 71 The holes in the plate would be jig-bored prior to the fitting of the bushes and the centre distances would need to be checked, both after jig-boring, and after the fitting of the drill bushes. **1932** GWIAZDOWSKI & LORD *Econ. Tool Engin.* xiii. 189 A Swiss firm..developed a large *jig borer that derives its accuracy from its lead screws. **1941** W. C. DURNEY *Machine Shop Pract.* v. 149 In the majority of modern engineering establishments, manufacturing jigs and fixtures in any quantity, these pieces of vital auxiliary apparatus are usually machined up in jig borers. **1959** *Times* 5 Oct. (Switzerland Suppl.) p. vii/3 Over one thousand SIP jig-borers are installed in the United Kingdom to-day. **1972** *Classification of Occupations & Directory Occupational Titles* (Department of Employment) III. 290/2 *Jig borer*, [one who] sets up and operates a jig boring machine to drill and bore holes in workpieces to extra fine limits of accuracy. **1932** GWIAZDOWSKI & LORD *Econ. Tool Engin.* xiii. 183 (*heading*) *Jig-boring methods. **1935** H. J. DAVIES *Precision Workshop Methods* vii. 115 A large proportion of the time occupied in jig-boring..is taken up in the initial setting up of the discs or buttons on the work. **1970** W. J. PATTON *Mod. Manuf.* vii. 157 Jig-boring machines are not production machines but toolmaking equipment for the accurate location and drilling of holes. **1902** *Encycl. Brit.* XXXI. 371/2 The pulsating current is obtained by placing a vertical longitudinal partition..extending part of the way down to the bottom of the *jig box. **1951** A. F. TAGGART *Elem. Ore Dressing* x. 190 The supporting reactions of the relatively rigid screen and sidewalls of the jig box are familiar. **1881** RAYMOND *Mining Gloss.*, *Jig-brow*. **1900** *Daily News* 11 Jan. 7/3 Then we went to the face, up some of the 'jig brows', the roads running off at right angles from this pony track. **1877** *Jig-brow [see DIP *sb.* 5 b]. **1932** GWIAZDOWSKI & LORD *Econ. Tool Engin.* xiii. 184 (*caption*) Toolmaker's *jig buttons. **1964** S. CRAWFORD *Basic Engin. Processes* v. 134 Fig. 19 (a) shows a sectional view of a jig-button, a small cylindrical steel bush accurately ground on the circumference and end faces, the hole being about $\frac{1}{8}$ inch larger in diameter than the retaining screw. These buttons can be set by end measurement. **1881** RAYMOND *Mining Gloss.*, **Jig-chain*, a chain hooked to the back of a skip and running round a post, to prevent its too rapid descent on an inclined plane. **1897** *Daily News* 5 Feb. 9/5 A card, on which he was described as 'the champion clog and *jig dancer'. **1611** B. JONSON *Catiline* Ded., Posterity..shall know, that you dare, in these *jig-given times, to countenance a legitimate Poem. **1835** *Court Mag.* VI. 24/2 It is a *jig-like sort of tune. **1899** *Daily News* 20 Apr. 5/3 With the exception of a jig-like presto,..the Fantasia is less remarkable for idea or effect than for skilful instrumentation. **1602** SHAKS. *Ham.* III. ii. 131 Oh God, your onely *Iigge-maker: what should a man do, but be merrie. **1633** FORD *Love's Sacr.* II. i, Petrarch was a dunce, Dante a jigmaker. **1849** *Ex. Doc. 31st U.S. Congress 1 Sess. House* No. 5 III. 469 The heavier metals are thrown out to be farther cleansed by the *Jigmen. **1921** *Dict. Occup. Terms* (1927) 18/1 *Jigger, jigman*; controls by levers and generally attends to jig, i.e., water concentration machine used to separate larger portions of ore from rock, stones, etc., with which it is found. **1929** F. H. ROLT *Gauges & Fine Measurement* II. vi. 108 Three discs are..attached to the *jig plate by screws passing through loosely fitting holes. **1970** W. J. PATTON *Mod. Manuf.* v. 79 Drill bushings are inserted into a jig plate and used to guide the drill bit. **1916** H. L. WILSON *Somewhere in Red Gap* vii. 314 Kate has about four more of 'em licked to a standstill in *jigtime. **1922** JOYCE *Ulysses* 313 Confident of knocking out the fistic Eblanite in jigtime. **1947** S. J. PERELMAN *Westward Ha!* (1949) x. 123 We completed the return journey in jig time; some mysterious metamorphosis..had endowed me with the agility of a lizard. **1962** K. ORVIS *Damned & Destroyed* xiv. 100 Then he gets it out of his possession in jig-time. **1968** L. W. ROBINSON *Assassin* (1969) xvi. 203 If I was you, I'd see Gracie Hutchinson... She'd solve your problem in jig time.

jig (dʒɪg), *sb.*[2] *U.S. coarse slang.* Also **jigg(s.** [Origin unknown, but perhaps the same word as prec.] A Black person, a Negro.

Like JIGABOO, a term that gives offence.

1924 F. J. WILSTACH *Slang Dict. Stage* (Typescript in N.Y. Public Libr.), *Jiggs*, Negro actor. **1927** K. NICHOLSON *Barker* III. i. 128 You go along and give 'em a hand, too. Nat Brody's there and a crew of jigs. **1931** *Amer. Mercury* Nov. 352/2 *Jig*, a Negro.—*Jigband*, the sideshow band. **1932** J. T. FARRELL *Young Lonigan* iii. 113 Janitor's jobs were for jiggs, and Hunkies, and Polacks, anyway. **1933** *Fortune* Aug. 47/1 A couple of jigs got on the bus with a doghouse. **1935** E. HEMINGWAY *Green Hills Afr.* (1936) II. vi. 163 This jig we call Othello falls in love with this girl. **1939** *New Yorker* 7 Oct. 22/3 He said if a jig band..could be a big success in Paris why not a fellow like you. *Ibid.*, They even made this jig a liutenant [*sic*]. **1950** BLESH & JANIS *They all played Ragtime* (1958) i. 23 Tom Ireland recalls that up to that time ragtime piano was called 'jig piano', and the syncopating bands, like Joplin's were called 'jig bands'. This term, taken from jig dances, even came a little later to be a designation for the Negro himself. **1969** S. GREENLEE *Spook who sat by Door* xiii. 116, I don't have to worry about no jig lieutenants! **1972** 'H. HOWARD' *Epitaph for Joanna* iv. 51 The photograph..showed..a Negro orchestra... I'd never seen the jig band before.

jig (dʒɪg), *v.* Also 7 gig, (gidge). [Closely related to JIG *sb.*[1] (q.v.), but not known so early. In some senses it aproaches obs. F. *giguer* (15th c.) to gambol, freak, sport, nasalized *ginguer* to leap, kick, wanton (which is app. not related to OF. *gigue*); but this resemblance may be merely accidental, or due to parallel onomatopœic influence, the large number of words into which *jig-* enters indicating that it has been felt to be a natural expression of a jerking or alternating motion. See the words following, and cf. FIG, FRIG. Some of the senses evidently arose independently from JIG *sb.*[1], and the historical order of the whole is unascertained.]

1. a. *trans.* To sing or play as a jig, or in the style of a jig (see JIG *sb.*[1] 2, 3). ? *Obs.*

1588 SHAKS. *L.L.L.* III. i. 11 To Iigge off a tune at the tongues end, canarie to it with the feete, humour it with turning vp your eie. **1633** FORD *Love's Sacr.* III. i, Make thy moan to ballad-singers and rhymers; they'll jig out thy wretchedness and abominations to new tunes.

b. *trans.* To dance (a jig or other lively dance).

1719 D'URFEY *Pills* IV. 100 We Jig the Morris upon the Green. **1802** MRS. J. WEST *Infidel Father* III. 151 A gentleman..jigged country dances the same evening for six hours. **1837** CARLYLE *Fr. Rev.* III. v. iv, While this brave Carmagnole-dance has hardly jigged itself out.

c. *intr.* To dance a jig; to dance in a rapid, jerky, lively fashion. Also ***to jig it***.

1672 *Maypole Dance* in *Westminster Drollery* II. 80 For Willy has gotten his Jill, And Johnny has got his Joan, To jig it, jig it, jig it, jig it, Jig it up and down! **1713** STEELE *Guardian* No. 147 ¶2 The bride thoughtlessly jigging it about the room. **1764** FOOTE *Mayor of G.* II. Wks. 1799 I. 187 Are all the women engaged? why then my *locum tenens* and I will jig together. **1798** JANE AUSTEN *Northang. Abb.* viii, I suppose you and I are to stand up and jig it together again. **1883** *Cornh. Mag.* June 718 The country dances commenced, in which the *beau monde*..bobbed, capered, jigged and grinned.

d. (*to jig it.*) To play the fiddle briskly.

1780 MAYNE *Siller Gun* II. xxiv, Jock Willison, a Sutor bred, Wha, for the fiddle, left his trade, Jigg'd it far better than he sped.

2. a. *intr.* To move up and down or to and fro with a rapid jerky motion; in quot. 1886 of a fish = JIGGER *v.*[1]

1604 SHAKS. *Ham.* III. i. 150 (2nd Qo.) You gig [*Fol.* gidge] and amble, and you list, you nickname Gods creatures, and make your wantonnes ignorance. **1713** C'TESS WINCHELSEA *Misc. Poems* 28 Phillis..Kept time with every thrilling Close, And jigg'd upon her seat. **1869** BLACKMORE *Lorna D.* xxx, The girls' feet were already jigging. **1876** T. HARDY *Ethelberta* (1890) 121 His hands under his coat-tails, and his person jigging up and down upon his toes. **1886** H. P. WELLS *Amer. Salmon Fisherman* 160 He [a 32 lb. salmon] begins to jig—a series of short, heavy and sudden jerks.

b. *trans.* To move (any thing) with a light jerky motion; to jerk to and fro or up and down.

1710 *Duncay Gray* in Whitelaw *Bk. Sc. Song* (1875) 82, I maun sit the leelang day An' jeeg the cradle wi my tae. **1834** M. SCOTT *Cruise Midge* (1863) 60 The rushing water.. closing in on the rudder making it cheep as it was jigged from side to side with a buzzing gurgle. **1888** *Sci. Amer.* 29 Dec. 403/2 When the carriage [of a sawmill] is to be jigged back, the lever manipulating the rock shaft is moved from the saw.

3. *intr.* To move in unison *with*; to agree, 'jump', chime *with*. *rare*.

1838 *Fraser's Mag.* XVII. 63 My manhood cannot to it stoop: It jigs not with my wants or wishes.

†**4.** *trans.* To put *off* with a trick (see JIG *sb.*[1] 5). *Obs.*

1633 FORD *Love's Sacr.* III. iii, Do not think the gloss Of smooth evasion.. Shall jig me off; I'll know't, I vow I will.

5. To dress (ore) so as to separate the coarser and finer portions, by shaking it under water in a sieve or a box with perforated bottom, or by means of a machine operating in a similar way.

1778 PRYCE *Min. Cornub.* 235 This coarser size.. is jigged pure and clean, if it be well given for Ore. *Ibid.* Gloss. s.v. *Jigging*, In the Lead Mines, the Jigged Ore goes by the name of Peasy. **1855** *Cornwall* 228 The ores are now given to boys, who jig them, or shake them in a sieve under water, by which means the ore or heavy part keeps at the bottom, whilst the spar, or refuse, is scraped from the top. **1875** J. H. COLLINS *Metal Mining* 112 The best ore when so crushed is ready for sale, but the seconds has next to be 'jigged'... The sieves are made to move up and down for a few minutes with a peculiar jerking motion while dipping in water.

6. a. To catch (a fish) by jerking a hook into its body; to catch with a jig (see JIG *sb.*[1] 6 c). **b.** *intr.* To fish with a jig.

1883 CHAS. HALLOCK *Sportsman's Gazetteer* (rev. ed.) 243 Keep the line constantly in motion, and half the time you will 'jig' them in the belly, tail or side, as the finny mass moves over the hook.

7. To shape an earthen vessel with a jigger (see JIGGER *sb.*[1] 5 a).

1865 [see JIGGING *vbl. sb.* 2].

8. In *Well-boring*, To bore with the aid of a spring-pole, which jerks up the rods and drill after the stroke. (*U.S.*)

9. *trans.* To provide or equip with jigs (sense 6 e). Also *absol.*

1900 *Machinery* (N.Y.) Dec. 130/1 There are many other considerations.. which cannot be overlooked when the question of 'To jig or not to jig' arises. **1927** *Observer* 16 Oct. 26 A sound financial scheme always includes writing off the heavy cost of jigging and tooling up a factory to manufacture a given type during the first year of its production. **1957** *Times* 23 Aug. 3/6 There was lying idle floor space jigged and tooled to produce six Britannia fuselages a month.

jigaboo ('dʒɪgəbuː). *U.S. coarse slang.* Also jiggabo, jijjiboo, zigabo, etc. [Related to JIG *sb.*[2] after BUGABOO.] A Black person, a Negro.

Like JIG *sb.*[2], a term that gives offence.

1909 WESTON & BARNES *I've got Rings on my Fingers* (song), So come to your na-bob, and next Pat-rick's Day Be Mis-tress Mum-bo Jum-bo Jij-ji-boo J. O'Shea. **1929** *Sat. Even. Post* 13 Apr. 54/4 Jigaboo (underworld). **1929** T. GORDON *Born to Be* 236 *Zigaboo, Dinge, Jasper*, nicknames for Ethiopians. **1930** *Amer. Mercury* Dec. 456/1 Me broad's squawkin' the jiggabo hop tries to make her. **1935** J. T. FARRELL *Studs Lonigan* iv. 87 Yes, but the pupils are all jiggabooes, and the parish is very poor now, I guess. **1935** D. RUNYON *Money from Home* 6, I will take Follow You and that ziggaboo jock of his in the Gold Vase for mine against any horse and any amateur rider in the world. **1940** W. R. BURNETT *High Sierra* vi. 35 'Yeah,' said Red, 'I think the zigaboo has got your cabin all set.' **1944** *Amer. Speech* XIX. 174 Such vulgar synonyms for Negro as.. jazzbo, jigabo (with the variants, jibagoo, jig, zigabo, zigaboo, zig). **1961** J. H. GRIFFIN *Black like Me* (1962) 57 The Negro.. hearing himself referred to as nigger, coon, jigaboo! **1970** L. SANDERS *Anderson Tapes* lix. 160 The tall one.. was a jigaboo. **1973** *Washington Post* 11 Mar. 6/6 'All that is left back there is a bunch of boos'—short for 'jigaboos', a derogatory term for blacks.

jig-a-jig, jig-a-jog. [See also JIG-JIG.] Imitative words expressing reiteration or alternation of light, short, jerky movements (see JIG *v.* 2, JOG *v.* 3); they may be used: **1. a.** as *adv.* = with a jigging or jogging motion; **b.** as *adj.* = having such a motion; **c.** as *sb.* = such motion itself; **d.** as *vb.* = to move in such a way.

1602 DEKKER *Satirom.* Wks. 1873 I. 221 Thou shalt be carted, drawne I meane, Coacht, Coacht, thou shalt ryde Iigga-Iogge. **1614** B. JONSON *Barth. Fair* Induct., Hee would ha' made you such a Iig-a-iogge i' the boothes, you should ha' thought an Earthquake had been in the Fayre. **1659** TORRIANO, *Baccoláre*,.. to play at titter-totter, giggajoggie. **1837** MARRYAT *Olla Podr.* xxix, It was a regular jig-a-jig. *Ibid.*, The whole company.. were jig-a-jigging up and down.

2. as *sb.* In the sense 'sexual intercourse'; also as *vb.*, to copulate. *slang.*

1896 FARMER & HENLEY *Slang* IV. 54/2 *Jig-a-jig*, to copulate. **1932** L. GOLDING *Magnolia St.* II. xiv. 468 This was.. the red lamp district... The women stopped... 'Jig-a-jig, Johnny? Very nice!' they said. **1935** AUDEN & ISHERWOOD *Dog beneath Skin* I. v. 58 Come wiv me. Good Jig-a-Jig. **1953** A. BARON *Human Kind* xvii. 124 He put his hand on her knee. 'You like jig-a-jig?' **1966** 'E. LINDALL' *Time too Soon* (1967) iv. 49 This woman's master has jig-a-jig with my blood sister.

jigamaree (ˌdʒɪgəmə'riː). *dial.* or *colloq.* Also jigg-, gig-. [An arbitrary humorous formation f. JIG *sb.*[1] (senses 5–6): cf. JIGGUMBOB, also *whigmaleerie*, and the like.]

1. (See quots.)

1847–78 HALLIWELL, *Jiggamaree*, a manœuvre. *Var. dial.* **1864** WEBSTER, *Jiggamaree*, a sportive or cunning trick; a maneuver. (*Colloq. and low.*) **1890** *Cent. Dict.*, *Jigamaree.*

2. A fanciful contrivance, which the speaker thinks ridiculous or worthless.

1844 *Major Jones's Courtship* (Bartlett), Mary was sewin' something mighty fine with ruffles and jigamarees all around it. **1848** JONES *Sk. Trav.* 9 (Farmer) Byin' fineries and northern gigamarees of one kind or another. *a* **1860** *N.Y. Spirit of the Times* (Bartlett), The 'housekeeper's friend', that ere jigamaree the wimmin scrubs with, instead of going on their hands and knees as they used to.

jigambob, variant of JIGGUMBOB.

†**jigga'lorum.** *Obs. colloq.* [Cf. JIGAMAREE.] A fanciful thing of little value; a trifle.

1613 H. KING *Halfe-pennyw. Wit* Ded. A ij b, I see my inferiours.. torment the Print daily with lighter trifles and Iiggalorums then my russet Hermit is.

jiggambob, jiggembob, var. JIGGUMBOB.

jig(g) by jowl: see CHEEK *sb.* 5.

jigger ('dʒɪgə(r)), *sb.*[1] Also 6 gygger, 7 giger, 8 jiger, 8–9 gigger. [In some senses, agent-noun from JIG *v.*; the relationship of others is obscure.]

I. 1. a. One who 'jigs' or dances a jig. Also, in dial., An odd-looking person, a 'guy'. Cf. JIG *sb.*[1] 7.

1675 COTTON *Scoffer scofft* 168 *Venus*... O how I'le trip it at thy wedding. *Paris.* Nay, you'r a jigger, we all know. **1825** BROCKETT, *Jigger*, an airy, swaggering person. 'A comical jigger'. **1880** *Jamieson's Dict.*, *Jigger*, a term of reproach or disrespect.

b. In full, *jigger coat.* A woman's short loosely-fitting jacket.

1957 M. B. PICKEN *Fashion Dict.* 190/2 *Jigger coat*, short semi-tailored, informal coat. **1966** *Olney Amsden & Sons Ltd. Price List* 30, 50 numbers Pinarettes, Aprons and Jiggers. **1968** J. IRONSIDE *Fashion Alphabet* 36 *Jigger*, a jacket popular in the 1930s—loose, finger-tip length, often with a tuxedo front. **1974** *Times* 12 Feb. 11/7, I thought this little mink jigger.. was a coming look.

c. *N.Z.* (See quot. 1971.)

1961 *Countryman* LVIII. iii. 500 The axeman has to insert at least two 'jiggers' or steps. **1966** *Wanganui* (N.Z.) *Photo News* 4 June 43/2 (*caption*) Champion axeman Sonny Bolstad is watched by the Queen Mother as he competes in a jigger chop. **1971** F. C. FORD-ROBERTSON *Terminol. Forest Sci.* 252/2 *Jigger(-board)* (New Zealand).., a short board or plank, its end notched into the bole, on which the cutter stands so as to enable him to fell the tree at a level not reachable from the ground.

II. 2. *Naut.* **a.** A small tackle consisting of a double and a single block and a fall, used for various purposes; *esp.* one used to hold on the cable when it is heaved into the ship.

1726 G. ROBERTS *4 Yrs. Voy.* 119 To enable the little Boy to hold on, I made him a Jigger with a Block fix'd to the Cable, and a Rope reev'd through it, so that having a double Purchase [etc.]. **1769** FALCONER *Dict. Marine* (1789) s.v., The jigger is.. useful when the cable is either slippery with mud.., or when it is stiff and unwieldy. **1840** R. H. DANA *Bef. Mast* xxii. 66 The sails were furled with great care, the bunts triced up by jiggers. **1847** KEY *Recov. H.M.S. Gorgon* (1866) 28 Bousing the casks close to the ships side with a jigger.

b. A small sail: see quot. 1867.

1831 [implied in *jigger-mast*: see 8]. **1867** SMYTH *Sailor's Word-bk.*, *Jigger*,.. a small sail rigged out on a mast and boom from the stern of a cutter, etc. **1894** *Times* 1 June 11/4 To steady her.. a jigger was run up at the stern.

c. Short for *jigger-mast*: see 8.

1880 *Times* 23 Oct. 5/4 She has four masts, the fore and main masts carrying yards, a large spread of fore and aft canvas being provided for the mizzenmast and the jigger.

d. A small vessel of the smack type furnished with a 'jigger' sail: see b; a similar vessel used as a fishing-vessel on the N.E. coast of N. America.

1860 BARTLETT *Dict. Amer.*, *Jigger*, a small fishing vessel. New England. **1875** KNIGHT *Dict. Mech.*, *Jigger*.. 3.. *e.* A fishing-vessel whose rig corresponds to that of a cutter, excepting a small mizzen in the stern. **1891** *Times* 16 Oct. 9/6 The jigger Petril, of Port Bannatyne, with gravel, is supposed to have foundered, as she has not been heard of since leaving Blairmore.

3. *Mining.* **a.** One who dresses or 'jigs' ore; see JIG *v.* 5. **b.** An apparatus for dressing ore and separating it into layers of varying fineness; consisting wholly or essentially of a sieve, or a box with holes, which is shaken up and down in water, or into which water is forced.

1778 PRYCE *Min. Cornub.* 234–5 The jigger holds a coarse wire sieve.. while another person throws the unclean Ore into the sieve, which the jigger dips into the water and shakes twice or thrice. *Ibid.* Gloss. s.v. *Jigging*, [The larger particles of ore] lie at the bottom of the Jigging-sieve or Jigger. **1874** RAYMOND *Statist. Mines & Mining* 499 The mining laboratory now contains.. a little hand-jigger, a rotary pulverizer, and a fan-blower.

4. A contrivance for catching fish: = JIG *sb.*[1] 6 c. Also, in ice-fishing (*Canad.*).

1815 *Sporting Mag.* XLV. 153 Cod lines and pouting, and jigger likewise. **1884** *Weekly Scotsman* 23 Feb. 1/6 The method of capturing them [cuttle or squid] is known as jigging, the jigger consisting of a number of hooks radiating from a fixed center of lead. No bait is used. The jigger is lowered to the bottom where it is constantly kept moving up and down till the squid is felt upon it. **1946** *Beaver* June 17/1 The jigger is a wooden plank with a slot in the middle through which a wooden arm controlled by a metal lever, moves. **1972** D. PRYDE *Nunaga* i. 16 The ice is eight feet thick on the lakes and it's almost impossible to set a net without a jigger. We had a jigger in here once and showed the Eskimos how to use it to string a net under the ice, but no one ever bothered to make one.

5. The name of numerous mechanical contrivances or devices, used in many trades and operations. Among these may be specified: **a.** *Pottery.* A horizontal lathe used in china-making. **b.** *Mining.* A hook or similar contrivance for attaching hutches or trams to a hauling rope, or for coupling them to each other. **c.** A loose chain used as a warehouse crane. **d.** A small roller, or set of rollers fitted in a suspended oscillating frame, used for graining leather. **e.** A shoemaker's tool for polishing the edge of the sole of a boot. **f.** A machine for hardening and condensing a felted fabric by repeated quick blows from rods, by a rapidly vibrating platen or platens, or by an intermittent rolling action. **g.** *Billiards.* A slang name for the supporting rest, used when the ball is too far off to be reached by the cue if rested on the hand. **h.** A cooper's drawing-knife with a hollowing blade. (Knight *Dict. Mech.*) **i.** A small street-railway car, drawn by one horse. *U.S.* **j.** A machine worked by electricity and indicating by means of a pointer dial the prices at which sales are made on 'change. *U.S.* **k.** *Mint.* 'A small weight which it is necessary, in certain cases, to add to a given number of coins to make an exact pound in weight'. (*W. J. Hosking*, Royal Mint.) **l.** Any small mechanical contrivance; a 'thingummy'. *U.S. colloq.* **m.** *Golf.* A short iron-headed club used for approaching shots. **n.** *Dyeing.* A device for dyeing piece goods by passing them back and forth through a dye-bath over a set of rollers. **o.** A bicycle or small motor vehicle or hand-car. †**p.** *Radio.* A high-frequency transformer used in early spark transmitters to couple the aerial circuit to the circuit in which the oscillations were generated; an oscillation transformer. *Obs.* **q.** A light vehicle, esp. one that moves on rails. *dial.* and *N.Z.* (see *E.D.D.*, sense 4). **r.** A ouija. **s.** A device for administering electric shocks (see quot. 1973).

a. *a* **1825** J. NICHOLSON *Operat. Mechanic* 463 For forming saucers, and other small circular articles, there has been recently introduced a small vertical shaft, called a *jigger*, on the top of which is a turned head, suited to receive the mould on which the saucers, &c. are to be formed. **1881** *Porcelain Works, Worcester* 21 The mould that gives the form to the face of the plate or saucer is fixed on a horizontal lathe called a jigger.

b. 1888 *N. & Q.* 7th ser. VI. 322/2, *Jigger*, an apparatus for attaching hutches to a haulage rope, which holds by twisting or biting the rope.

c. 1891 *Labour Commission Gloss.*, *Jigger boy*, name given (at the Millwall Docks) to a boy working a jigger or loose chain. *Ibid.* s.v. *Work*, A jigger,.. a loose chain worked not through the medium of a crane, but by hydraulic or steam power. **1900** *Dundee Advert.* 21 Aug. 5 An increased charge for the use of the hydraulic jiggers.

d. 1883 HALDANE *Workshop Receipts* Ser. II. 374/1 A grain or polish is given to the leather, either by boarding or working under small pendulum rollers, called 'jiggers', which are engraved either with grooves or with an imitation of grain.

e. 1850 J. STRUTHERS *Poet. Wks.* I. Autobiog. 38 A tool highly esteemed among them called a jigger.

g. 1847 ALB. SMITH *Chr. Tadpole* xli. (1857) 347 The long cue and the 'jigger'.

l. 1874 HOTTEN *Slang Dict.* 203 Jigger has many meanings, the word being applied to any small mechanical contrivance. **1926** *Amer. Speech* I. 628/2 The term jigger has long been used of small mechanical devices... In America, jigger is often used as an indefinite name, not too dignified, of the same order as thingumbob. **1944** H. WENTWORTH *Amer. Dial. Dict.* 328 *Jigger*, thingemajig.

m. 1893 H. G. HUTCHINSON *Golfing* 21 The learner will probably do better.. to employ..—supposing that he finds he cannot play the short approaches with sufficiently dead loft off an ordinary iron—much-laid-back approaching cleek. On some links these are a great deal used, under the name of jiggers. **1931** *Punch* 1 July 717/2 *Fully-equipped Visitor.* This looks a weird sort of hole. What on earth does one take here? *Local player.* One takes a jigger, if that's all one has. **1970** H. TAYLOR *Golf Dict.*, *Jigger*, an iron club, of value in all kinds of golfing situations.

n. 1893 E. KNECHT et al. *Man. Dyeing* II. ix. 694 The modern jigger consists of a wooden or cast-iron dye vessel heated by steam and provided with water supply and waste-pipe. In the vessel are three rollers.. at the top and two.. at the bottom, which guide the pieces in their passage through the dye-liquor. **1915** T. BEACALL et al. *Dyestuffs & Coal-Tar Products* iv. 82 The machine most frequently met with in the dyeing of cotton cloth is the jigger. In this machine the cloth in full width is passed through the dye liquor several times over guide rollers. **1963** MEITNER & KERTESS tr. *Schmidlin's Preparation & Dyeing Synthetic Fibres* xi. 90 Although a discontinuous machine the automatic jigger is very suitable for de-sizing, boiling-off, bleaching and dyeing of heavy fabrics sensitive to creasing.

o. 1897 H. G. WELLS in *Humours of Cycling* 7 'Pretty Jigger!' said the Bounder... 'Nice-looking machine you've got.' **1930** 'E. BRAMAH' *Little Flutter* iv. 52 My little jigger is no good for a job like this. **1958** *Globe Mag.* (Toronto) 9 Aug. 18/1 A jigger carrying eight men came belting around the mountains and ran smack into a moose. **1973** *Courier-Mail* (Brisbane) 28 July 17/11 It takes a little time, too, to absorb the antique public school language... Jigger—a bicycle.

p. 1902 *Encycl. Brit.* XXXIII. 230/2 The plugs of the sensitive tube.. are joined to the terminals of the secondary circuit S'S' of a small transformer, called a 'jigger'. **1906** J. A. FLEMING *Princ. Electr. Wave Telegr.* vii. 437 If the oscillation transformer, or jigger, is not wound to suit the wave length employed, so far from being a benefit, it prevents any signals being received at all. **1924** P. J. RISDON

Wireless xii. 116 The oscillating current in the primary circuit induces, through the 'jigger' coils, as they were called, another current of the same frequency in the aerial circuit. **1937** in 'DECIBEL' *Wireless Terms Explained* 41

q. **1904** 'G. B. LANCASTER' *Sons o' Men* 158 Two men sat on the little iron jigger that straddled the wooden tram-line. **1918** *N.Z.E.F. Chrons.* 8 Nov. 179/1 At last I commenced the second stage—this time on a 'jigger', a frame on two rubber-tyred wheels which holds the stretcher. **1949** E. DE MAUNY *Huntsman in Career* 162 Chancey.. went off on the jigger down the narrow track into the bush each morning.

r. **1916** O. LODGE *Raymond* 186 Jigger. (A kind of Ouija.)

s. **1972** *Sunday Sun* (Brisbane) 26 Nov. 1/2 Battery operated jiggers are being used on mentally retarded children..to bring them into line. The electric shock treatment is followed by..lollies if they behave. **1973** *Sunday Mail Mag.* (Brisbane) 25 Feb. 14/1 Occasionally, a blue spark would flash forth as a recalcitrant beast was touched with the 'jigger' (a battery-operated device carried over the shoulder and imparting an electric shock through an insulated rod held in the hand).

III. Various slang uses. (Possibly not related to the foregoing.)

6. a. A door.

1567 HARMAN *Caveat* (1869) 85 Dup the gygger..open the doore. **1659** *Caterpillers anatomized*, Gigers jacked, locked doors. **1812** J. H. VAUX *Flash Dict.*, *Jigger*, a door. **1851** MAYHEW *Lond. Labour* I. 314 Such men are always left outside the jigger (door) of the houses.

b. A prison or cell.

1896 MAX PEMBERTON *Puritan's Wife* xiii. 116, I would sooner have been in the gigger at Newgate.

c. A passage between or at the back of houses; a back entry or alley. *Merseyside.*

1902 in *Eng. Dial. Dict.* **1966** [see *knee-trembler* s.v. KNEE *sb.* 14]. **1966** P. MOLONEY *Plea for Mersey* 21 'A seen a scuffer up a jigger wid a rozzer' ('I saw two policemen in the side entry'). **1967** A. HENRI in *Penguin Mod. Poets* X. 16 A Polish gunman..collapses down a back jigger.

7. a. An illicit distillery.

1824 *Compl. Hist. Murder Mr. Weare* 241 He said that Probert and two others were in the jigger at Gill's Hill. *Ibid.* 251, I kept a private jigger there, and it was never discovered. **1851** MAYHEW *Lond. Labour* I. 387 They carry about their persons pint bladders of 'stuff', or 'jigger stuff' (spirit made at an illicit still).

b. A drink of spirits, a dram. Also, a small glass or metal cup, a measure used in mixing cocktails; the contents of such a glass or measure. (*U.S.*)

1836 W. O'BRYAN *Narr. Trav. U.S.* 107 These canal labourers have a boy to supply them with Whiskey, called a *Jiggar boss*, who goes on the canal and carries a half gill (half noggin) of Whiskey to every man sixteen times a day! **1870** J. H. B. NOWLAND *Early Reminisc. Indianapolis* 361 By jiggers was meant a small cup of whiskey, say about a gill; they had cups made on purpose for this use. **1879** *N.Y. Herald* 21 Nov. 8/2 A jigger..is a conical metal cup in which to mix fancy drinks. **1889** *Lisbon* (Dakota) *Star* 15 Feb. 3/1 After giving him two small 'jiggers', the civilities were brought to an end. **1892** A. E. LEE *Hist. Columbus* (Ohio) I. 335 The 'jigger' was a dram of less than a gill, taken [5 times a day]. **1946** E. HOLDING *Innocent Mrs. Duff* 17 On a shelf there was a fine array of bottles, with jiggers of two sizes, swizzle sticks, glass mixers. **1946** 'P. QUENTIN' *Puzzle for Fiends* (1947) viii. 62 A jigger of liquor clutched between thumb and first finger. **1952** S. KAUFMANN *Philanderer* (1953) vii. 114 What I came out to ask you is, do you have any gin in the house and could you spare me a jigger? **1971** R. DENTRY *Encounter at Kharmel* ix. 148 A baker's dozen perversions for a jigger of vodka.

IV. 8. *attrib.* and *Comb.*, as (senses 5 a, b) *jigger-boy*; **jigger-block** (see quot., and cf. sense 2 a); **jigger-board** *N.Z.* = JIGGER 1 c; **jigger-dubber** (*slang*), a turnkey (cf. sense 6); **jigger mast** *Naut.*, (*a*) a small mast at the stern, on which a jigger (sense 2 b) is hoisted; (*b*) the aftermost mast of a four-masted merchant ship; **jigger-pump**, (*a*) a force-pump mounted on a portable stand and usually connected with a hose, used for watering flower-beds, etc.; (*b*) see quot; **jigger-saw** = JIG-SAW *sb.*; **jigger-tackle** *Naut.* = sense 2 a; **jigger-yard** *Naut.*, a yard on which the jigger (sense 2 b) is extended.

1859 F. A. GRIFFITHS *Artil. Man.* (1862) 107 If the strap be continued, so as to form a tail, at the end of the block which has no hook, the block is called a tail or *jigger block; and if a tackle have its moveable block so furnished, it is called a 'jigger tackle'. **1944** R. GILBERD in *N.Z. New Writing* III. 55 We would have given you..nerves to stand the narrow insecurity of the *jigger-board. **1961** B. CRUMP *Hang on a Minute* 42 During the next few weeks Jack learned about scarfing, backing, limbing, deeing, sniping, jigger-boards, platforms, toms, strops, drives, triggers, and saw and axe sharpening. **1963** N. HILLIARD *Piece of Land* 176 The best thing of the day to watch, the three-tier jigger-board chop. **1869** *Good Words* 1 Mar. 172/2 A plaster-of-Paris cast is placed on a disc which a handle-turning '*jigger-boy' causes to revolve. **1921** Jigger boy [see JIGGERER]. **1781** G. PARKER *View Soc.* II. 69 *Jigger-dubber is a term applied to Jailors or Turn-keys. **1831** TRELAWNEY *Adv. younger Son* xxiv, This dow had a large mast forward, and a *gigger-mast aft. **1835** SIR J. ROSS *Narr. 2nd Voy.* Explan. Terms 16 *Jigger mast*, a small mast at the stern, with a sail resembling a lug sail. **1879** BLACK *Macleod of D.* xxxiv. 305 The red ensign clung to the jigger-mast. **1894** *Westm. Gaz.* 15 May 7/2 Owing to the frightful rolling of the ship the steel masts gave way, all coming down, with the exception of the lower foremast, the mizen lower mast, the jigger lower mast and topmast, and the bowsprit. **1847–78** HALLIWELL, **Jigger-pump*, a pump used in breweries to force beer into vats. **1888** *Lockwood's Dict. Mech. Engin.* 197 **Jigger saw*, or *jig saw*. **1957** *N.Z. Timber Jrnl.* Sept. 61/1 *Jigger saw*, a reciprocating saw. A fret or scroll or jig saw, used for pierced and tracery work. **1769** FALCONER *Dict. Marine* (1789), **Jigger Tackle*, a light..tackle, consisting of a double and single block. **1797** *Gazetteer* in *Spirit Pub. Jrnls.* (1799) I 76 D—n me! if I would not get a jigger-tackle upon you. **1842** J. F. COOPER *Jack o' Lantern* I. 182 Three fair, handsome flags rose to the end of the Fen-Follett's *jigger-yard.

jigger ('dʒɪgə(r)), *sb.*[2] Also 8 chiger, 9 chigger, jigga. [Corruption of CHIGOE.]

1. Also *jigger flea* = CHIGOE. The Latin name of the insect is now *Tunga penetrans*.

1756, 1810, 1830, 1868 [see CHIGOE]. **1781** SMEATHMAN in *Phil. Trans.* LXXI. 170, I know nothing similar, except in the *pulex penetrans* of Linnæus, the jigger of the West Indies. **1826** KIRBY & SP. *Entomol.* (1856) IV. 53, I am speaking of the celebrated Chigoe or Jiggers, called also Nigua, Tungua, and Pique. **1897** MARY KINGSLEY *W. Africa* 205 A touch of fever on him and jiggers in his feet. **1899** *Blackw. Mag.* Nov. 635/1 Several Sepoys were suffering from that African pest the 'jigger'. **1947** H. VAUGHAN-WILLIAMS *Visit to Lobengula* xxvii. 176 Arthur's feet suffered badly from jigger fleas—horrid little tiny insects that burrow under the skin and lay a bunch of eggs there in a capsule. **1953** *New Biol.* XIV. 120 *Tunga penetrans*, the tropical jigger flea of man, is the best-known of these [burrowing fleas]. **1962** GORDON & LAVOIPIERRE *Entomol. for Students of Med.* xxxv. 217 Both the male and the female jigger flea are blood-suckers.

2. Applied in U.S. to various harvest-ticks, such as *Leptus americanus* and *L. irritans*, which fasten on the human skin and cause great irritation.

jigger ('dʒɪgə(r)), *v.*[1] *colloq.* [? frequentative of JIG *v.*] **1.** *intr.* To make a succession of rapid jerks; said of a fish struggling to free itself from the hook.

1867 F. FRANCIS *Angling* ix. (1876) 328 When a fish 'jiggers' or keeps up a constant 'jag, jag, jag', at the line, it is a very unpleasant..symptom. **1891** A. LANG *Angling Sk.* 118 He [a salmon] came slowly up, and 'jiggered' savagely at the line. **1895** *Daily News* 1 Aug. 6/4 When he jiggers, a fish puts all he knows into a series of short rapid tugs.

2. orig. *pass.*, usu. with *up*: to be tired out, exhausted; so, to be 'done for', devitalized. Also *actively*: to break, destroy, ruin. *dial.* and *slang.*

1862 C. C. ROBINSON *Dial. Leeds* 332 *Jigger'd up*, Av tramp'd a matter o' fotty mile to-daay, an' am fair jigger'd up. *a* **1865** SMYTH *Sailor's Word-Bk.* (1867) 412 *Jiggered-up*, done up; tired out. **1885** B. BRIERLEY *Ab-o' th-Yate in Yankeeland* v. 42 A generation or two would see it jiggered up if it wurno' for th' fresh blood ut's bein sent into it. **1895** 'G. MORTIMER' *Like Stars that Fall* xii. 167 Bates will jigger us if he can... I wouldn't trust that fellow. **1896** *Yorks. Weekly Post* 6 June 6/8 T'chap wor reight jiggered up. **1923** *Daily Mail* 13 June 12 I've 'jiggered' up my Rolls-Royce. **1949** E. DE MAUNY *Huntsman in Career* 150 He jiggered up his ankle last Saturday. **1969** *Telegraph* (Brisbane) 19 May 8/1 The firing pin's jiggered and the sights are sloppy.

Hence '**jiggering** *vbl. sb.* and *ppl. a.*

1867 F. FRANCIS *Angling* ix. (1876) 328 I have lost many a jiggering fish.

jigger, *v.*[2] *slang* or *colloq.* [Origin disputed. It has been referred to JIGGER *sb.*[2], and to JIGGER *sb.*[1] sense 6 b: cf. next.] Used as a vague substitute for a profane oath or imprecation, esp. in asseverations. (Only in passive.) Also '**jiggering** *ppl. a.* and intensive *adv.*

1837 MARRYAT *Dog-Fiend* xxxvi, I'm jiggered if he don't tell a lie. **1861** DICKENS *Gt. Expect.* xvii, 'Well, then', said he, 'I'm jiggered if I don't see you home'. This penalty of being jiggered was a favourite supposititious case of his. He attached no definite meaning to the word that I am aware of. **1886** MRS. BURNETT *Lit. Ld. Fauntleroy* ii. (1892) 23 'Well', said Mr. Hobbs, 'I'll be—jiggered!' This was an exclamation he always used when he was very much astonished or excited. **1903** *Daily Chron.* 14 Sept. 3/3 Once you've made up your mind, as you may say, about a young man, you've got to be jiggerin' well careful you don't go and lose him. *a* **1950** X. HERBERT in Murdoch & Drake-Brockman *Austral. Short Stories* (1951) 301 Take the lot. Take the rintin' jiggerin' lot!

jigger, *v.*[3] *slang.* [app. f. JIGGER *sb.*[1] sense 6 b.] *trans.* To shut *up*, imprison.

1887 HALL CAINE *Deemster* xxxiii, Poor Mastha Dan had been..jiggered up in Peel Castle.

'**jigger,** *v.*[4] *Pottery.* [f. JIGGER *sb.*[1] 5 a.] *trans.* To shape with a jigger.

1931 W. H. WARBURTON *Hist. Trade Union Organization in Potteries* xi. 208, I will try and get the price you want for this article, but you must remember that this..is being jiggered by a firm in the next town at a much less price. **1967** M. CHANDLER *Ceramics in Mod. World* ii. 63 Shaping methods..include..throwing, jollying or jiggering, plastic pressing, and extrusion.

'**jigger,** *v.*[5] *Book-binding.* [? f. JIGGER *sb.*[1]] *trans.* To rub (a tool) backwards and forwards along a line or other impression in a leather binding, in order to polish it. Hence '**jiggering** *vbl. sb.*

1880 J. W. ZAEHNSDORF *Art of Bookbinding* xxii. 114 The lines impressed on the back must now have their gloss given to them. This is done by *giggering* the pallets over them. **1901** D. COCKERELL *Bookbinding* xv. 224, I have found that a tool guided by a straight-edge, and 'jiggered' backwards and forwards, makes by far the best lines for blind-tool work. **1946** E. DIEHL *Bookbinding* II. xxiii. 352 It [*sc.* the fillet] is then pushed over the line a few times with a 'jiggering' motion, until the line is polished. **1951** L. TOWN *Bookbinding by Hand* x. 229 The tool can be put down again and rocked slightly. This gives a polished surface as well as a darkened one, and is known as 'jiggering'. **1963** B. C. MIDDLETON *Hist. Eng. Craft Bookbinding Technique* xii. 167 The tools are usually rocked or jiggered to produce a polish.

jiggerer ('dʒɪgərə(r)). [f. JIGGER *sb.*[1] 5 + -ER[1].] One who uses or works with a jigger (in various trades).

1881 *Instructions to Census Clerks* (1885) 84 Coal Miner ..Loader, Jiggerer, Trammer, Hooker-on. *Ibid.* 88 China, Porcelain, Manufacture:..Jigger or Gigger Turner, Jiggerer. **1921** *Dict. Occup. Terms* (1927) §043 *Jigger, jigger boy, jiggerer*..attaches or detaches tubs, singly or in pairs, to or from endless rope, by placing rope in fork of 'jigger', or double crook, in socket at one side or end of tubs. *Ibid.* §105 *Jigger, jiggerer*, makes flat-ware such as plates, saucers; presses bat of clay on top of mould, already revolving on vertical spindle. **1931** W. H. WARBURTON *Hist. Trade Union Organization in Potteries* xi. 205 By this scheme his hollow-ware pressers would employ female assistants in the same way as did his hollow-ware jiggerers and 'jolliers'.

jiggery-pokery ('dʒɪgərɪ'pəʊkərɪ). *colloq.* [Cf. Sc. *joukery-pawkery* (see JOUKERY, JOOKERY b).] Deceitful or dishonest 'manipulation'; hocus-pocus, humbug.

1893 in DARTNELL & GODDARD *Gloss. Words Wiltshire* 86. **1926** E. F. SPANNER *Naviators* ix. 104, I thought..it was some more jiggery-pokery to keep down the expenditure this financial year. **1943** *Mind* LII. 304, I share with Gray the feeling that there's some *jiggery pokery* here and that what you are doing is not what one tends to feel you are doing. **1973** G. MITCHELL *Murder of Busy Lizzie* ii. 23 Business reasons could make any alliance respectable..so long as there was no jiggery-pokery.

jigget ('dʒɪgɪt), *v. colloq.* Also 9 jiggit. [dim. of JIG *v.*] *intr.* To move about with a jerky or shaky motion; to jig; to hop or skip about; to shake up and down; to fidget. Hence '**jiggeting** *vbl. sb.* and *ppl. a.*

1687 MRS. BEHN *Lucky Chance* II. ii, Come, my Lady Fulbank, the night grows old upon our hands, to dancing, to jiggeting. **1709** T. BAKER *Fem. Tatler* No. 15 She..has a languishing Eye, a delicious soft Hand, and two pretty jiggetting Feet. **1818** MISS MITFORD in L'Estrange *Life* (1870) II. 35 He is..always jiggeting about from one great house to another. **1862** MISS YONGE *C'tess Kate* iv. (1864) 55 There's Aunt Barbara coming down the lane in the baker's jiggetting cart. **1898** R. KIPLING *Fleet in Being* i. 4 At eight knots you heard the vicious little twin-screws jiggitting like restive horses; at seventeen they pegged away into the sea like a pair of short-gaited trotting ponies on a hard road.

jigget, jiggetai, var. GIGOT[1], DZIGGETAI.

jiggety ('dʒɪgɪtɪ), *a. colloq.* Also jiggity, jiggoty. [f. JIGGET *v.* + -Y; cf. *rickety*.] Characterized by jiggeting; having a jerky unsteady movement.

1883 G. H. BOUGHTON in *Harper's Mag.* Apr. 687/1, I would not fix on a bustling, jiggity steamer as the best place ..to sketch..on. **1876** H. E. SCUDDER *Dwellers in Five-Sisters Court* ii. 30 Mr. le Clear appeared and received the jiggoty Miss Pix's welcome in a smiling and well-bred manner.

'**jigginess.** *rare.* [f. assumed adj. **jiggy* (f. JIG *sb.*[1] or *v.* + -Y) + -NESS.] The quality of being like a jig, or having a 'jigging' or jerky movement.

1869 T. HOOD *Rules Rhyme* 47 A too frequent repetition of rhyme at short intervals gives a jigginess to the verse.

jigging ('dʒɪgɪŋ), *vbl. sb.* [f. JIG *v.* + -ING[1].] The action of the verb JIG. **1. a.** The dancing of jigs; light, rapid, jerky movement, etc.: see JIG *v.* 1, 2.

1641 MILTON *Reform.* II. Wks. (1851) 48 That men should bee..pusht forward to gaming, jigging, wassailing, and mixt dancing is a horror to think. **1668** ETHEREDGE *She Would if She Could* III. i. Wks. (1888) 164 The natural inclination they have to jigging will make them very ready to comply. **1806** SURR *Winter in Lond.* (ed. 3) II. 207 Suggesting that such jigging and romping was inconsistent with the elegance that should distinguish the amusements of the higher orders. **1849** THACKERAY *Let.* in *Scribner's Mag.* (1887) I. 681/1, I..go out feeling deucedly lonely in the midst of the racketting and jigging.

b. Of a fish: = *jiggering*: see JIGGER *v.*[1]

1886 H. P. WELLS *Amer. Salmon Fisherman* 152 Of all the performances of the salmon, none demoralizes me like jigging..a series of short heavy jerks to the line at intervals of 3 or 4 seconds.

2. In technical senses: see JIG *v.* 5–9.

1778 PRYCE *Min. Cornub.* Gloss., *Jigging*, is a method of dressing the smaller Copper and Lead Ores by a peculiar motion of a wire sieve in a kieve or vat of water, where the smallest particles pass through the Jigging-sieve. **1865** *Daily Tel.* 18 Apr. 5 Machinery..has already been designed to execute one part of potters' work, *jigging*. **1884** *Weekly Scotsman* 23 Feb. 1/6 The method of capturing them is known as jigging, the jigger consisting of a number of hooks radiating from a fixed center of lead. **1903** W. H. VAN DERVOORT *Mod. Machine Shop Tools* xxvii. 410 No class of work in the manufacturing shop presents as many possibilities for jigging as does the work handled in the drilling machine. **1945** LEA & SIMONS *Machining of Steel* xii. 107 A fraction of a minute per part saved in large-scale production by better jigging soon outweighs any appreciable resultant increase in the cost of the jig.

3. *attrib.* and *Comb.*, as **jigging-party** (*dial.*), a dancing-party; **jigging-machine**, a machine for jigging (usually in sense 5 of the verb: = JIGGER *sb.*[1] 3 b); **jigging-sieve**, a sieve for jigging ore: see sense 2 above, quot. 1778.

1872 T. HARDY *Greenwood Tree* vii, [On Christmas-day night] a jigging party looks suspicious. **1884** *West. Morn. News* 30 Aug. 1/6 Crusher, jigging machine and jiggers. **1890** *Melbourne Argus* 29 May 9/8, I recommend that some jigging machinery be put up at once, to concentrate ore now at grass for smelting.

jigging (ˈdʒɪgɪŋ), *ppl. a.* [f. JIG *v.* + -ING[2].] That jigs, in various senses (see JIG *v.*); dancing jigs, moving jerkily; singing, playing, or composing jigs; of the style of a jig (see JIG *sb.*[1] 1–3).

1586 MARLOWE *1st Pt. Tamburl.* Prol., Jigging veins of rhyming mother-wits. **1592** CHETTLE *Kinde-Harts Dr.* (1841) 16 Men brought vppe to an honest handicraft, of which the realme more need then iygging vanities. **1601** SHAKS. *Jul. C.* IV. iii. 137 What should the Warres do with these Iigging Fooles? **1629** DAVENANT *Albovine* v. Dram. Wks. 1872 I. 94 Leave off your jigging motion when you mix Yourselves in a salute. **1839** MARRYAT *Diary Amer.* Ser. I. I. 119 One of the leaders then burst out into a hymn to a jigging sort of tune. **1862** THACKERAY *Four Georges* ii. 85 Never was such a brilliant, jigging, smirking Vanity Fair.

jiggish (ˈdʒɪgɪʃ), *a.* [f. JIG *sb.*[1] + -ISH[1].]

1. Inclined to jigging, dancing, or frolicking; of light or frivolous disposition (quot. 1634).

1634–40 HABINGTON *Castara* I. (Arb.) 16 She is never sad, and yet not jiggish. **1815** J. SCOTT *Vis. Paris* iii. (ed. 2) 39 Crowds of both sexes.. gratifying the jiggish propensities of their minds by the sound of fiddles.

2. Resembling or of the nature of a jig or light dance; suitable for a jig.

1709 ADDISON *Tatler* No. 157 ¶7 That Musical Instrument which is commonly known by the Name of a Kit, that is more jiggish than the Fiddle it self. **1712** STEELE *Spect.* No. 276 ¶3 This Man makes on the Violin a certain jiggish Noise to which I dance. **1756** COWPER in *Connoisseur* No. 134 ¶5 The tunes themselves have also been new-set to jiggish measures. **1789** T. TWINING *Aristotle's Treat. Poetry* (1812) I. 249 *note*, 'A jiggish measure' would be weak, to the force of the original [Greek].

jiggle (ˈdʒɪg(ə)l), *v.* [dim. or frequentative of JIG *v.*] To move backwards and forwards, or up and down, with a light unsteady motion; to move in a rapid succession of slight jerks; to rock or jerk lightly. **a.** *trans.*

1836 SIR G. HEAD *Home Tour* 13 The more the child cried the more she jiggled it. **1887** JESSOPP *Trials Country Parson* (1890) i. 23 We know that the fellow was jiggling the poor brute's teeth out of his mouth at the time.

b. *intr.*

1846 WORCESTER, *Jiggle v. n.*, to practise affected or awkward motions, to wriggle. *Mrs. Farrar.* **1880** *Jamieson's Dict.*, To *Jiggle*, v.n., to rock or shake backwards and forwards. Shetl. **1887** JESSOPP *Arcady* i. 10 He shambles to the next brewery with any beast of burden that can jiggle along.

Hence ˈ**jiggling** *vbl. sb.*; also ˈ**jiggle** *sb.*, a 'jiggling' movement; a light rapid rocking.

1888 *N. Amer. Rev.* Jan. 59 It is only a little wilder jiggle. **1894** R. KIPLING *Seven Seas* (1896) 225 There aren't a wave for miles an' miles Excep' the jiggle from the screw. **1894** *Times* 1 Mar. 3/5 The chief novelties claimed in the plaintiffs' invention were the use of narrower jiggling sieves, in proportion to the lateral area of the machine; a deflector [etc.]. *Ibid.*, The jiggling of the sieve caused the heavier particles to fall through and the larger but lighter to pass off over the tail.

jiggoty, var. JIGGETY *a.*

jiggumbob (ˈdʒɪgəmbɒb). *colloq.* ? *Obs.* Also 7 **jig(g)am-, jiggem-, jigum-, jiggobob, jig-em-bob, giggam bobb, gigg-em-, giggom-, giggum-, gingam-, gingumbob.** [A humorous formation from JIG *sb.*[1] or *v.*: cf. *kickumbob, thingumbob.*] Something odd or fanciful; a bauble, toy, knick-knack; something which one does not choose to name or specify: = THINGUMBOB. (Rarely applied to a person.)

1613 BEAUM. & FL. *Coxcomb* IV. vii, What Giggombob have we here? *a* **1627** MIDDLETON *Wom. beware Wom.* II. ii, On with her chain of pearl, her ruby bracelets, Lay ready all her tricks and jiggembobs. **1629** MASSINGER *Picture* V. iii, Shall we have More jiggobobs yet! **1638** BROME *Antipodes* III. v. Wks. 1873 III. 285 Tumbles all Our jigambobs and trinckets to the wall. **1671** SHADWELL *Humorists* v, I'll be quit with him and that Jig-em-bob my Niece. **1678** BUTLER *Hud.* III. i. 108 The Enemy.. Had rifled all his Pokes and Fobs Of Gimcracks, Whims and Jiggumbums, Which he by hook or crook had gather'd. *a* **1700** B. E. *Dict. Cant. Crew*, *Gingumbobs*, Toies, or Baubles.

ˈ**jiggy-**ˈ**joggy**, *adv.* = JIG-A-JOG, JIG-JOG.

1600 DEKKER *Gent. Craft* ii. (1862) 13 Faith, then.. I'll go jiggy-joggy to London and be here in a trice, young Mistress.

jig-jig, jig-jog, *adv.*, etc. **1.** = JIG-A-JIG, JIG-A-JOG I.

1836 SMART, *Jig-jog*, a jolting motion, a jog, a push. **1864** WEBSTER, *Jig-jog*, having, or pertaining to, a jolting motion. **1870** MISS BROUGHTON *Red as a Rose* (1878) 151 Jig-jog through life alongside of Bob. **1885** G. ALLEN *Babylon* xi, That.. drawing-master.. with his formal little directions of how to go jig-jig for a pine-tree, and to-whee, whee, whee, for an oak.

2. as *sb.* = JIG-A-JIG, JIG-A-JOG 2.

1935 A. J. POLLOCK *Underworld Speaks* 64/1 *Jig-jig*, a lewd act. **1948** G. GREENE *Heart of Matter* I. I. i. 2 The boys' refrain... 'Captain want jig jig, my sister pretty girl school-teacher, captain want jig jig.' **1971** B. W. ALDISS *Soldier Erect* 125 'Hello, sweetheart. You like jig-jig?' 'That's the idea. Let's look at you first.'.. She said something—... All we had in common was the word, the call-sign, 'jig-jig'.

jigot, var. GIGOT, haunch of mutton, etc.

‖**jigotai** (dʒigoˈtai). *Judo.* [Jap.] In Judo, a defensive posture.

1950 E. J. HARRISON *Judo* 102 *Jigotai*, self-defensive posture. **1957** TAKAGAKI & SHARP *Techniques Judo* I. ii. 12 *Jigo-tai*.. is assumed by spreading your legs wide apart and bending your knees to lower your body.

jigs, var. GIGGS *Obs.*, mouth-disease in horses.

jig-saw, *sb.* orig. *U.S.* Also **gig-saw, jigsaw.** [f. JIG *v.* + SAW.] **a.** A vertically reciprocating saw driven by a crank, mounted in various different ways. Also *attrib.*, of a type of architectural decoration using fretwork patterns.

1873 J. RICHARDS *Wood-working Factories* 128 With respect to jig saws, the band saw and duplicating machines have driven the most of them out of use. **1875** KNIGHT *Dict. Mech.*, *Gig-saw*, a thin saw to which a rapid vertical reciprocation is imparted, and which is adapted for sawing scrolls, frets, etc. **1892** KIPLING *Lett. of Travel* (1920) 21 The jig-saw days, when it behoved respectability to use unlovely turned rails and pierced gable-ends. **1928** E. O'NEILL *Strange Interlude* III. 86 The room is one of those big, misproportioned dining rooms that are found in the large, jigsaw country houses scattered around the country as a result of the rural taste for grandeur in the eighties. **1966** M. M. PEGLER *Dict. Interior Design* 245 *Jigsaw detail*, a cutout or fretwork design made with a jigsaw. It was used for the enhancement of buildings of the mid and late 19th century. The bargework was often made with a jigsaw. The 'gingerbread' or 'steamboat Gothic', late Victorian period was jigsaw work in its most aggravated form. **1968** J. ARNOLD *Shell Bk. Country Crafts* 274 Salad-forks, for example, are cut without previous marking by a hand jig-saw.

b. In full, *jig-saw puzzle.* A puzzle formed by cutting into small irregular pieces (orig. with a jig-saw) a picture mounted on a sheet of wood, cardboard, or the like. (Now the usual sense.) So *jig-saw map.* Also *transf.* and *fig.*

1909 *Daily Mirror* 17 Aug. 4/4 A jigsaw map of England. *Ibid.*, These jigsaw geography puzzles should be introduced into all the Council schools in London. **1910** *Punch* 9 Mar. 172 (*caption*) What if the jig-saw epidemic spreads? **1915** *Morning Post* 15 Apr. 2/4 A kind of verbal jig-saw. **1919** E. SHACKLETON *South* i. 11 Pack-ice might be described as a gigantic and interminable jigsaw-puzzle devised by nature. **1935** W. S. MAUGHAM *Don Fernando* x. 213 The various particulars fit like the pieces of a jig-saw puzzle. **1947** *People* 22 June 4/3 How can this jigsaw be pieced together? Many of the facts are now known as a result of most painstaking police inquiries. **1955** A. HUXLEY *Let.* 25 Sept. (1969) 766 All this jigsaw work entailed in shaping a play for stage production is extremely boring. **1964** M. CRITCHLEY *Developmental Dyslexia* ix. 57 Constructional tasks which embrace spatial concepts include the assembling of jigsaw puzzles, a game which may not be easy for some of these dyslexics. **1972** *Oxford Times* 11 Aug. 3 As the excavation proceeds more and more tiny pieces of the archaeological jigsaw puzzle will be discovered. **1974** G. MARKSTEIN *Cooler* xl. 149 Sylvia was turning into the little jigsaw piece that often remained the hardest one to find.

Hence **jig-saw** *v. trans.*, to cut or shape with a jig-saw; also, to fit together the pieces of a jig-saw puzzle. Freq. *fig.*

1873 J. RICHARDS *Wood-working Factories* 128 What may be said of jig-sawing need not consume much space here. **1883** HOWELLS *Woman's Reason* (Tauchn. 1884) I. 213 Designs jig-sawed out of white-wood. **1938** *Times* 2 Feb. 13/4 Jig-sawing is one of the few pastimes in which bludgeoning methods definitely do not pay. **1963** *Harper's Bazaar* Jan. 29/3 It taxed all Miss Molesworth's expertise to jigsaw the requirements into a pleasing ensemble. **1966** *Punch* 18 May 720 I've often cut his articles into line sentences, mixed them up, and tried to jigsaw them together, a most difficult thing to do until you've caught the drift of his mind. **1967** *Listener* 9 Feb. 207/3 The interviews through which Lowry's character was jigsawed together were wholly fascinating. **1973** *Guardian* 27 Feb. 11/5 We.. jig-sawed our bits together into one consecutive piece, typing on maddening French machines.

‖**jihad, jehad** (dʒiːˈhɑːd). Also **jahad.** [Arab. *jihād* struggle, contest, spec. one for the propagation of Islam.] A religious war of Muslims against unbelievers in Islam, inculcated as a duty by the Koran and traditions.

1869 *M. Wilks' Sk. S. India* (ed. 2) II. xlviii. 381 The projects of Jehad—holy war. **1875** KAYE *Sepoy War* III. iv. 167 To collect money and preach the Moslem Jehad. **1880** GEN. ROBERTS in *Daily News* 14 Feb. 2/4 The Mollahs have been preaching a *jehad* or religious war.

b. *transf.* A war or crusade for or against some doctrine, opinion, or principle; war to the death.

1880 J. COWEN in *Daily News* 2 Feb. 6/5 The political *jehad* that was being preached against doctrines which.. had right and justice to sustain them. **1880** *Sat. Rev.* 6 Mar. 305 His last attempt to stir up a kind of moral jehad against the Government. **1886** *19th Century* XX. 505 An economical government bargained to abolish the deer [in the New Forest]. So the edict went forth, and a 'Jihad' against the deer was proclaimed.

jildi (ˈdʒɪldɪ). *Mil. slang* (orig. *Anglo-Indian*). Also **jeldi, jildy, juldie,** and other varr. [ad. Hind. *jaldi* quickness.] Haste, as in phrases ***on the jildi***, in a hurry, and to ***do*** or ***move a jildi.*** So **jildi** *a.*, quick; **jildi, juldily** *adv.*, quickly; **jildi** *v. trans.* and *absol.*, to hurry.

1890 KIPLING *Barrack-Room Ballads* (1892) 24 You put some *juldee* in it Or I'll *marrow* you this minute. **1919** W. H. DOWNING *Digger Dial.* 59 *Jeldi*, hurry; run. *Ibid.* 30 *Jeldy* (Hind.), quickly. **1926** *Scots Observer* 30 Oct. 21/1 Wullie.. would have seen.. that the rabbits were moving juldie into the thistles and long grass as he came along. Juldie! What's that? Hindustani for quick. **1929** [see FUCK *v.* 3]. **1930** R. BLAKER *Medal without Bar* vii. 47 Come on. We'll catch 'im if we jildi. **1930** BROPHY & PARTRIDGE *Songs & Slang 1914–18* 132 *Jildi*, quick, look sharp, hurry. Also used in the phrase 'on the jildi', e.g. 'Get them bags filled on the jildi.' **1948** PARTRIDGE *Dict. Forces' Slang* 102 *Jildi*, hurry! Also *get a jildi on.* (Indian Army.) *Ibid.*, *Do a jildi move*, to beat a hasty retreat. General Army slang... Among tank men: to take evasive action. **1957** M. K. JOSEPH *I'll soldier no More* (1960) 14 Hey, Antonio, where's me rooty? And make it juldy, see? **1972** J. BROWN *Chancer* i. 12, I went out jilty.. and there he was.

jill (dʒɪl), *v.* [Presumably var. of GILL *v.*[2]: cf. quot. 1855 s.v.] *intr.* Of a boat: to move *about*, to move *around*; to idle around.

1955 *Times* 18 July 9/6 In the early morning light Falmouth bay looked as lovely as ever, with its rounded green hills and little fishing boats jilling about under sail off the Manacles. **1956** W. GOLDING *Pincher Martin* i. 18 Survivors, a raft, the whaler, the dinghy, wreckage may be jilling about only a swell or two away hidden in the mist and waiting for rescue with at least bully and perhaps a tot. **1964** F. CHICHESTER *Lonely Sea & Sky* xxix. 303 After breakfast I took over for an hour or two until we had cleared the point, when I gratefully lowered all sail and *Gipsy Moth* jilled along. **1972** *Guardian* 23 Sept. 5/4 Bosun dinghies jilling around the windless Medway... Picture by Peter Johns.

jill, variant of GILL *sb.*[3], *sb.*[4], *sb.*[6], *v.*[2]

jillaroo (dʒɪləˈruː). *Austral.* Also **jilleroo.** [Jocular formation from JACKAROO *sb.*] A female station-hand. So as *v. intr.*, to work as a jillaroo.

1945 BAKER *Austral. Lang.* iii. 62 The past few years have given us a variant [of jackeroo] in *jillaroo*, a female station-hand.., especially used during World War No. 2 for a Land Girl. **1945** *Salt* 26 Feb. 16/1 Miss Garraty is our new 'jilleroo'. **1964** *Pix* 22 Aug. 41 Dr. Davies said *Pix* should have called Miss Lukis a jenniroo or jennyroo. That might be all right for West Australians but the word used in the Eastern States is jillaroo. **1969** *Courier-Mail* (Brisbane) 15 Aug. 7/3 A part-time model, jilleroo and cattle judge was named the top under-21 Rural Youth member yesterday. **1970** *Sunday Mail Mag.* (Brisbane) 28 June 6/2 Isabel has been jillarooing all over Australia for the last four years.

jillet (ˈdʒɪlɪt). *Sc.* [dim. of the female name *Jill* or GILL (*sb.*[4]): see also GILLOT, JELOT.] A giddy or flighty young woman; a jilt; sometimes, a familiar or contemptuous term for a girl or young woman, a wench.

1755 JOHNSON s.v. *Jilt*, Perhaps from.. *gillet*, or *gillot*, the diminutive of *gill*, the ludicrous name for a woman. 'Tis also called *jillet* in Scotland. **1786** BURNS *On a Scotch Bard gone to W. Indies* vi, A jillet brak his heart at last, Ill may she be! **1808–25** JAMIESON, *Jillet*, a giddy young woman, implying the idea of levity. **1828** SCOTT *F.M. Perth* xxxi, Hark you, were it not well to receive that coy jillet with something of a mumming?

jill-flirt, variant of GILL-FLIRT.

jilliflower, jilliver, var. of GILLYFLOWER.

jillion (ˈdʒɪljən). orig. *U.S.* [Fanciful formation after BILLION, MILLION.] Very many, a great many.

1942 BERREY & VAN DEN BARK *Amer. Thes. Slang* §18/6 *Indefinite number*, jillion. **1945** L. SHELLY *Jive Talk Dict.*, *Jillion*, a lot of people or money. **1950** *Time* 13 Feb. 10/1 After Spindletop, in the superlatives of the oilfields, came a jillion jackpots—roaring booms at Electra, Ranger, Burkburnett, Desdemona and Mexia proved that oil was where you found it. **1957** *New Yorker* 2 Nov. 141/1 'Oh, I've got a jillion,' he replied. 'A jillion ties and no wife. I have ties from many parts of the world.' **1963** 'R. L. PIKE' *Mute Witness* (1965) vi. 100, I bet I've hit about a jillion travel agencies today. **1971** *Physics Bull.* Nov. 682/3 Gamesters with 'game theories' of a jillion different maliciously fixable kinds.

jills (dʒɪlz). *slang.* [Shelta.] Used with a possessive pronoun: ***my jills*** = 'I', ***his jills*** = 'he', etc.

1906 E. DYSON *Fact'ry 'Ands* ix. 117 'They thort his jills had done er get,' said the packer. **1940** *N. & Q.* 15 June 421/1 In the current slang of the Variety profession and other Bohemian circles, 'jills', coupled with a possessive pronoun, stands for 'I', 'you', 'he', etc., according to the possessive pronoun prefixed... So 'my jills', 'your jills', 'his jills'.

jilt (dʒɪlt), *sb.* Also 7–8 **gilt.** [In sense 1 = GILLOT 1, of which it is perh. a syncopated form (though analogies are wanting). Sense 2 appears to be influenced by JILT *v.*, whence also sense 4.]

†**1.** A woman who has lost her chastity; a harlot or strumpet; a kept mistress. *Obs.*

1672 WYCHERLEY *Love in Wood* Dram. Pers., Mrs. Crossbite an old cheating Jilt, and Bawd to her Daughter. **1683** KENNETT tr. *Erasm. on Folly* 59 He whose wife is a common jilt.. and yet swears she is as chast as an untouch'd virgin. **1702** *Eng. Theophrast.* 36 Is he not as vile a wretch, as she a mercenary gilt? **1815** W. H. IRELAND *Scribbleomania* 232 A Jilt most consummate, and impudent Doxie.

2. 'A woman who gives her lover hopes, and deceives him' (J.); one who capriciously casts off a lover after giving him encouragement. (The current sense.)

1674 BLOUNT *Glossogr.* (ed. 4), *Gilt* or *Jilt*, a Cheat, or Woman that has defeated her Gallant in his Amours. **1680** OTWAY *Orphan* I. i. 66 Dilatory Fortune plays the Jilt With the brave noble honest gallant Man, To throw herself away on Fools and Knaves. **1712** STEELE *Spect.* No. 288 ¶1 When

you spoke of the Jilts and Coquets. **1751** SMOLLETT *Per. Pic.* III. lxxxi, Lord W—m..was waiting in expectation of my coming, and might..imagine I was playing the jilt. *a* **1845** BARHAM *Ingol. Leg.*, *Marie Mignot* v, They'll teach you the guilt Of coquetting and ogling, and playing the jilt.

b. Rarely applied to a man.

1865 *Sat. Rev.* 19 Aug. 240/2 The offences of the jilt, whether man or maiden, are not, it is true, the most grievous that can be committed against society.

3. *Sc.* A contemptuous term for a girl or young woman: = JILLET.

1816 SCOTT *Old Mort.* viii, Though she's but a dirty jilt. **1818** —— *Hrt. Midl.* xxix, His wheat-close, you crazed jilt!

†**4.** ? A deception: cf. JILT *v.* 2. *Obs.*

1683 E. HOOKER *Pref. Pordage's Mystic Div.* 63, I beleev it wil be a slurr and blurr, or a base-foul Jilt upon themselvs.

Hence ˈ**jiltish** *a.*, having the character of, or characteristic of, a jilt; ˈ**jiltship** (*nonce-wd.*), a mock title for a jilt.

1690 CROWNE *Eng. Frier* IV. 31, I let him know how your Jiltship has serv'd him. **1787** BURNS *Addr. for Miss Fontenelle* 33 The wretch in love, Who long with jiltish arts and airs hast strove. **1897** BLACKMORE in *Blackw. Mag.* June 780 Eyes..wavering jiltish, deceitful.

jilt (dʒɪlt), *v.* Also 7 **gilt**. [A 'new cant word' in 1674; origin not recorded; connexion with GILLOT, or JILT *sb.* in sense 1, is doubtful.]

1. *trans.* To deceive after holding out hopes in love; to cast off (a lover) capriciously; to be faithless to; to play the jilt towards. Orig. said only of a woman; in later use also of a man.

1673 [see JILTING below]. **1674** BLOUNT *Glossogr.* (ed. 4), *Jilt*, is a new canting word, signifying to deceive and defeat ones expectation, more especially in the point of Amours. **1675** WYCHERLEY *Country Wife* I. i. Wks. (Rtldg.) 71/2 He can no more think the men laugh at him than that women jilt him. **1690** LOCKE *Hum. Und.* IV. xx. (1695) 403 Tell a Man, passionately in Love, that he is gilted; bring a score of Witnesses of the Falshood of his Mistress, 'tis ten to one but three kind Words of hers shall invalidate all their Testimonies. **1747** WESLEY *Wks.* (1872) II. 78 You shortly after jilted the younger, and married the elder sister. **1816** SCOTT *Old Mort.* xxxviii, Your mistress seems much disposed to jilt you. **1865** *Spectator* 11 Feb. 153 If the man jilts the woman he is fined,..as men are liable to be fined on conviction of open treason.

b. *absol.* or *intr.* To play the jilt.

1696 CONGREVE *Epil. to Southerne's Oroonoko*, She might have learnt to cuckold, jilt, and sham, Had Covent Garden been in Surinam. *a* **1736** YALDEN *Poet. Wks.* (1833) 65 The nymph, when she betrays, disdains your guilt, And, by such falsehood taught, she learns to jilt. **1739** *Matrimony* 3 Where have you [wife] been Jilting all the Day?

2. *gen.* To deceive, cheat, trick, delude (*obs.*); to cheat (one's) expectation; to prove false or faithless to (any one): to 'throw over' or discard for another. (Now chiefly *fig.* from 1.)

1660 *No Droll but a Rational Account* 8 Treacherous telltales, that frequent clubs and Coffee-houses, whose chief business is to jilt others into discourse. *a* **1700** B. E. *Dict. Cant. Crew*, *Hedge-Tavern*, a jilting sharping tavern. **1782** MISS BURNEY *Cecilia* VIII. iii, He is waiting for me at the inn: however,..if you will give me some tea here, I shall certainly jilt him. **1851** THACKERAY *Eng. Hum.* iv. 181 But Fortune shook her swift wings and jilted him too.

Hence ˈ**jilted** *ppl. a.*, ˈ**jilting** *vbl. sb.* and *ppl. a.*; also **jilˈtee**, one who is or has been jilted; ˈ**jilter**, one who jilts, a jilt.

1673 DRYDEN *1st Pt. Marr. à la Mode* IV. i[i], It [masquerading] was invented first by some jealous Lover, to discover the Haunts of his Jilting Mistress. **1708** *Brit. Apollo* No. 99. 3/2 Those cruel Jilters. **1833** L. RITCHIE *Wand. by Loire* 141 Is it necessary..that you insult the jilted suitor? **1894** *Pall Mall Mag.* July 397 It is difficult to believe that..the jilter, not the jiltee is to be admired.

jilt-flirt, erron. form of GILL-FLIRT.

jim, jimal, obs. forms of GIM, GIMMAL.

jim (dʒɪm). *Austral. colloq.* [f. *Jimmy O'Goblin.*] A pound, a pound note.

1906 E. DYSON *Fact'ry 'Ands* xvi. 214 He was tearin' ratty t' raise another jim. **1919** V. MARSHALL *World Living Dead* in Baker *Austral. Lang.* (1945) xvii. 310 Half a jim (10s.). **1959** BAKER *Drum* 120 *Jim*, the sum of £1.

jimbang, variant of JINGBANG.

jimber-jaw (ˈdʒɪmbədʒɔː). *U.S. colloq.* [var. of *gimbal-jaw*: see GIMBAL 5.] A projecting lower jaw. So ˈ**jimber-jawed** *a.* = *gimbal-jawed*.

1848–60 BARTLETT *Dict. Amer.*, *Gimbal-jawed* or *jimber-jawed*, whose lower jaw is loose and projecting. **1885** MISS MURFREE *Prophet Gt. Smoky Mount.* iii. 71 The long chin, of the style familiarly denominated jimber-jawed. **1889** FARMER *Americanisms*, *Jimber-jaw*.

jimbol, jimcrack, obs. ff. GIMBAL, GIMCRACK.

Jim Crow[1], **Jim-crow, jim crow** (ˈdʒɪm ˈkrəʊ). [From the refrain of a popular old Negro song, 'Wheel about and turn about and jump Jim Crow'.]

Orig. *U.S.*, but the main current senses (1 f, and its *attrib.* and verbal uses, with *Jim Crowism*) are used throughout the English-speaking world, although chiefly in U.S. contexts.

1. The name of a Negro plantation song of the early nineteenth century; also, a stage presentation of a song and dance first performed by Thomas D. Rice (1808–60) and subsequently by other actors dressed as 'nigger minstrels'.

c **1832** T. D. RICE (*title*) Jim Crow. Celebrated comic song or ballad. **1832** *Amer. Sentinel* (Philadelphia) 11 Sept. 3/1 (Advt.), Mr. Rice will appear and sing Jim Crow. **1835** *Vade Mecum* (Philadelphia) 28 Mar. 2/7 'Ditanti Palpita', 'Jim Crow', 'Old Hundred', with two or three waltzes played in *different* keys usually form the *Hotchpotchiana* of their delicious entertainment. **1837** *New Yorker* 16 Dec. 610/2 The impulse of despair must have tempted them to strike up 'Jim Crow'. **1841** THACKERAY in *Britannia* 15 May 315/4 The organ-man..struck up two beautiful melodies, viz., 'Getting up Stairs', and 'Jim Crow'. **1926** *N.Y. Times* 26 Dec. VII. 8/2 From 'Old Jim Crow' to 'Black Bottom', the negro dances..are African in inspiration.

b. Phr. *to jump Jim Crow*: to execute the dance that was part of a theatrical (or street) performance of Jim Crow; to jump about. Also *fig.*, to change one's political principles, to desert one's party.

1833 *Sk. & Eccentr. D. Crockett* 41 You nebber get to Heben till you jump Jim Crow. **1836** *Louisville* (Kentucky) *Jrnl.* 16 Sept., A Mr. Collier of Virginia has 'jumped Jim Crow'. **1840** *Log Cabin Song-Bk.* 38 Fo he's the man to jump Jim Crow, And prove that black is white. **1857** *Observer* 12 Apr. 2/4 A street clown once told him (Mr. Mayhew) that..he jumped 'Jim Crow' for twelve hours in the mud and wet of the streets, and he carried home..the sum of 15 d. **1922** GALSWORTHY *Windows* I. 19 Not much balance about us. We just run about and jump Jim Crow.

c. A Negro character in the Jim Crow song; T. D. Rice or another performer of the Jim Crow act; in England, a street performer of this type of act (see b).

1835 *Vade Mecum* (Philadelphia) 24 Jan. 3/7 Jim Crow is in the town, about to 'wheel about' for the edification of the Brandywine. Daddy Rice will surprise them. **1851** H. MAYHEW *London Labour* I. 4/1 The street-actors—as clowns, 'Billy Barlows', 'Jim Crows', and others. **1861** *Ibid.* III. 121/1 A few minutes afterwards I saw this man dressed as Jim Crow, with his face blackened, dancing and singing in the streets as if he was the lightest-hearted fellow in all London. **1867** *Atlantic Monthly* Nov. 608/2 As a national or 'race' illustration, behind the footlights, might not 'Jim Crow' and a black face tickle the fancy of pit and circle?

d. A turncoat. (Cf. the *fig.* sense of b.)

1837 *New Yorker* 16 Dec. 610/2 An engraving of the veritable Jim Crow is to be seen in every print-shop, with the exception that the face of Lord Lyndhurst usurps that of Rice, his lordship being placed in that peculiar attitude which the Liberals denominate 'turning about—wheeling about' from political consistency and common sense. **1840** J. ROMILLY *Diary* 13 Nov. (1967) 204 The blackg[ds] in the gallery hooted & called him Jim Crow.

e. A Black person, a Negro. *depreciatory.*

1838 'UNCLE SAM' in *Bentley's Misc.* IV. 582 Don't be standing there like the wooden Jim Crow at the blacking maker's store. **1841** H. PLAYFAIR *Hugo Playfair Papers* I. 3 A portmanteau and carpet-bag..were snatched up by one of the hundreds of nigger-porters, or Jim Crows, who swarm at the many landing-places to *help* passengers. **1948** *Sat. Rev.* (U.S.) 27 Mar. 36/1 Jim Crow works at the depot.

f. Racial discrimination, *spec.* against Blacks in the U.S. More usually *attrib.*, or as *Jim Crowism* (below).

1943 R. OTTLEY *New World A-Coming* 69 Negro soldiers had suffered all forms of Jim Crow, humiliation, discrimination, slander, and even violence at the hands of the white civilian population. **1946** J. H. BURMA in A. Dundes *Mother Wit* (1973) 625/2 To the Negro any joke is particularly humorous if it shows Jim Crow 'backfiring' on a Southerner. **1958** J. ASMAN in P. Gammond *Decca Bk. Jazz* xiv. 166 The difficulties facing any studio recordings by Negro artists are almost insurmountable in the Southern States, where Jim Crow is predominant, even to the present time. **1969** *N.Y. Times* 16 Jan. 40/5 Those of them who are young and loud want segregated colleges... It's Jim Crow when we want it... Why don't they think of it as James Eagle? **1971** *Black Scholar* June 4/1 The historical literature ..suggests that Jim Crow was directed more at the black male than the black female. **1973** A. DUNDES *Mother Wit* 231 Since white southerners obviously spoke in dialect.. this practice was little more than another insidious form of Jim Crow. **1973** *Freedom-ways* XIII. 30 One hundred years of frustration and battle have not resulted in victory over Jim Crow and racism.

2. An implement for bending or straightening iron rails by the pressure of a screw.

1875 in KNIGHT *Dict. Mech.*

3. *attrib.*, as (sense 1 a) ***Jim Crow song***; (sense 1 b) ***jim-crow planing-machine*** (see quot. 1875); (sense 1 c) ***Jim Crow boots, dance, hat***; (sense 1 e) ***Jim Crow line***; (sense 1 f) ***Jim Crow bill, car, college, conditions, law, school, town.*** Also (with possessive case) **Jim Crow's nose** = *John Crow('s) nose* (JOHN CROW).

1835 *Knickerbocker* V. 47 Some jolly slaves..were waiting to take us into a ferry-boat, which they rowed, singing some Jim Crow song. **1842** *Liberator* (Boston) 21 Jan. 10/1 It is this spirit that compels the colored man to..ride in the 'Jim-Crow car'. **1847** *Chicago Jrnl.* 7 Oct., We do not mean *Jim Crow* dances and poor songs worse sung. **1851** G. S. COOPER *Jrnl. Expedition Auckland to Taranaki* 58 A man in a common shooting jacket, a Jim Crow hat, trowsers rather the worse for wear and a pair of moustaches. **1851** MRS. STOWE *Uncle Tom's Cabin* (1852) II. xx. 33, I thought she was rather a funny specimen in the Jim Crow line. **1866** LINDLEY & MOORE *Treas. Bot.* II. 638/1 Jim Crow's nose. A West Indian name for *Phyllocoryne*. **1875** KNIGHT *Dict. Mech.* 1216/1 The jim-crow planing-machine is furnished with a reversing tool, to plane both ways, and named from its peculiar motion, as the tool is able to 'wheel about and turn about'. **1887** C. B. GEORGE *40 Yrs. on Rail* viii. 160 An educated colored man..found, on going from Boston to Salem, his home, that he must ride in the Jim Crow car. **1900** *Morning Leader* 19 Dec. 5/5 'Jim-Crow' Cars. In many Southern States there are laws compelling the railroad companies to run on their trains separate cars for colored people..which are called 'Jim-Crow' cars. **1902** A. H. LEWIS *Wolfville Days* xvi. 235 An' whyever don't you-all wear leather chapps that a-way, instead of them jimcrow boots an' trousers? **1903** *Sun* (N.Y.) 29 Nov. 7 The members of the committee have arranged with the parents of negro children to send them all to the Jim Crow school, thus entirely separating the white and negro pupils. **1904** *Nation* (N.Y.) 17 Mar. 202 The Jim Crow bills now before the Maryland Legislature. **1904** *Richmond* (Virginia) *Times-Despatch* 25 May 10 Violating the Jim Crow law by allowing negroes to ride in the same car with whites. **1926** A. NILES in W. C. Handy *Blues* 20 'Jim Crow' songs with syncopated airs..were current long before the Civil War. **1931** W. FAULKNER *Sanctuary* xix. 167 It was full too, the door between it and the jim crow car swinging open. **1949** L. FEATHER *Inside Be-Bop* i. 3 Big band jazz had been played by Negro orchestras, frequently under Jim Crow conditions. **1957** W. C. HANDY *Father of Blues* xiv. 195 Having spent much time in Jim Crow towns, I was under the illusion that these Negro musicians would jump at the chance to patronize one of their own publishers. **1960** *New Left Rev.* Sept.–Oct. 39/2 The Uncle Tom presidents of the captive Jim Crow colleges. **1971** *Black World* Mar. 75/1 Black people will continue to see themselves under jim crow conditions. **1973** A. DUNDES *Mother Wit* 397 Riding on Jim Crow cars could literally make a Negro sick.

So **Jim Crow** *v. trans.*, to segregate persons ethnically, to discriminate against (Blacks or other non-whites); so **Jim Crowing** *vbl. sb.*; **Jim Crowism**, the institution of segregation, the practice of 'racial' discrimination; also, the act of deserting one's political party.

1837 *N.Y. Mirror* 7 Oct. 118/1 Then, to counterbalance this good, you have entailed upon those British islands the curse of Jim Crowism. **1841** *Times* 21 June 5/6 His propensities to what they call 'Jim Crowism' in politics. **1921** *United Free Ch. Miss. Rec.* Jan. 2/1 [S. Africa] The picture he gives of the 'jimcrowing' and ostracizing of the natives in public places and the working of the pass-laws up-country is dark enough. **1923** *Nation* (N.Y.) 15 Aug. 155 But they are not 'jim crowed'. **1925** *Amer. Mercury* Jan. 87/2 In his celebrated Atlanta speech he justified all the forms of Jim-Crowism. **1932** E. WILSON *Devil take Hindmost* iii. 17 The Negroes..are discriminated against by a general policy of Jim Crowism. **1942** C. HIMES *Black on Black* (1973) 216 Out of the bootings and the lynchings and the jim-crowings ..will come our strength. **1948** *Sat. Rev.* (U.S.) 24 July 16/3 It is to his eternal credit that he ripped through the Jim Crowism of our national game by giving a fine Negro athlete a chance to play in organized baseball. **1955** L. FEATHER *Encycl. Jazz* i. 22 The Negro musician was Jim Crowed from the day he first became aware of music. **1969** C. HIMES *Blind Man with Pistol* i. 16 It was obviously a jim-crowed convent, and no one ever dreamed that white Catholics would act any different from anyone else who was white. **1971** *Rand Daily Mail* (Johannesburg) 4 Dec. 4/2 Since I visited South Africa, the Government has opened the door to dozens of prominent Blacks and ensured that they were not Jim Crowed. (Jim Crowed means treated like Blacks in the old segregationist United States South.)

Jim Crow[2] (ˈdʒɪm ˈkrəʊ). *colloq.* [Coined by W. S. Churchill; cf. CROW *sb.*[1] 8 and CROW'S NEST.] A roof-top spotter of enemy aircraft; also his look-out post (see also quot. 1943).

1940 W. S. CHURCHILL *Into Battle* (1941) 278 Our plan must be to use the siren..as an alert and not as an alarm, and to have a system of highly trained what I may call Jim Crows or look-out men, who will give the alarm when immediate danger is expected at any point. **1941** *Battle of Britain Aug.–Oct. 1940* (Ministry of Information) 21 Except when roof-watchers—the Prime Minister's 'Jim Crows'—signalled that danger was imminent, life went on as usual and still does. **1943** HUNT & PRINGLE *Service Slang* 41 *Jim Crow*, normally used to describe the corps of roof-spotters guarding our large buildings. Now taken into service slang to denote the man on watch when 'unofficial business', such as cards, is being transacted. **1952** R. SHERBROOKE-WALKER *Khaki & Blue* v. 43 An anti-aircraft post, with a good view of the sky, had already been installed on top of one of the forts. To convert this into 'Jim Crow', it was turned into a post de luxe.

ˈ**jim-ˈdandy**, *sb.* and *a.* *U.S. colloq.* [Cf. DANDY *sb.*[1] (and *a.*).] **A.** *sb.* An excellent person or thing. **B.** *adj.* Remarkably fine, outstanding.

1887 *Courier-Jrnl.* (Louisville, Kentucky) 12 Jan. 2/1 Dear Sir: Though a stranger to you (yet a Democrat), let me say you are a 'Jim Dandy'. **1888** *Inter-Ocean* (Chicago) 14 Feb. (Farmer), George C. Ball came upon the floor yesterday arrayed in a jim-dandy suit of clothes. **1902** O. WISTER *Virginian* xxvii. 346 He must have been a jim-dandy of a boy. **1904** W. N. HARBEN *Georgians* ix. 87 Right thar I baked pies—open-top jim dandies, too. **1912** *Collier's* 21 Dec. 23/2 Prince Albert rolls up the jim dandiest cigarette. **1919** H. L. WILSON *Ma Pettengill* iv. 119, I bet you made a jim-dandy good report. **1941** J. STUART *Men of Mountains* 154 He said the blue-tick hound was a jim-dandy possum dog. **1953** *New Yorker* 7 Feb. 92/2 When one suffers from headaches,..Anacin is the jim-dandy remedy. **1963** *Spectator* 12 July 45 The new GPO tower building is a jim-dandy, it excites and pleases me. **1972** B. GARFIELD *Line of Succession* (1974) ii. 128 Your voting record on foreign affairs was fine, jim-dandy.

ˈ**jim-ˈhickey.** [Cf. HICKEY *sb.*] = prec. sb.

1895 S. CRANE *Red Badge of Courage* xxi. 207 Th' lieutenant, he ses: 'He's a jimhickey,' an' th' colonel, he ses: 'Ahem! ahem! he is, indeed, a very good man.' **1907** J. MASEFIELD *Tarpaulin Muster* xii. 131 Them topsails had a good look along the yard..or there was a jim hickey of a stink raised.

Jiminy, Jimminy, now the usual form of GEMINI (sense 4). Used esp. in phrases *Jiminy*

Christmas (see CHRISTMAS *sb.* 1 c) and *Jiminy cricket*.

1803 G. COLMAN *John Bull* I. i. 5 *Den.* A customer... *Mrs. B.* Jemmeny! and so there is. *c* **1816** [see CRIMINE, -INY *int.*]. **1848** in *Amer. Speech* (1935) X. 40 *By Jiminy Cricket*, an exclamation of surprise. **1863** [see GEMINI 4]. **1890** *Dialect Notes* I. 49 Jimminy Cripes! and Jimminy Christmas! are forms of oaths overheard. **1894** J. T. MOORE *Songs & Stories from Tennessee* (1897) 18 Jiminy! But didn't we hab a good time on de road? **1897** [see CHRISTMAS *sb.* 1 c]. **1930** J. DOS PASSOS *42nd Parallel* II. 147 Jimminy criskets [*sic*], what I couldn't do to a watermelon, Joe. **1934** W. SAROYAN *Daring Young Man* (1935) 123 He was telling her. Jiminy crickets. **1940** N. MARSH *Surfeit of Lampreys* (1941) x. 139 'I am completely baffled.' 'Jiminy cricket!'

jim-jam ('dʒɪmdʒæm). [A reduplicated term, of which the elements are unexplained; perhaps only whimsical: cf. *flim-flam*, *trim-tram*, *whim-wham*, etc. Connexion with the first element of *gimcrack* is possible, but the latter is not found till later.]

1. A fanciful or trivial article, a gimcrack, a knick-knack. *colloq.*

a **1550** *Image of Hypocr.* in *Skelton's Wks.* (1843) II. 446 These be as knappishe knackes As ever man made, For iavells and for iackes, a iymiam for a iade. **1565** HARDING in Jewel *Def. Apol.* (1611) 381 To shew vs.. whether he had some iimjam made for him to take it vp, hold it and put it on handsomely. **1592** NASHE *P. Penilesse* 13 A thousand iymiams and toyes haue they in theyr chambers. **1890** KIPLING *Phantom 'Rickshaw* 85 There was half a dozen big stone idols. Dravot he goes to the biggest.. and says: 'That's all right.. all these old jim-jams are my friends.'

2. *pl.* Fantastic ways, peculiarities. *colloq.*

1899 *Daily News* 16 Dec. 8/3 Oh, that's all right. Every regiment has its little jim-jams.

3. *pl.* **a.** Delirium tremens. *slang.*

1885 J. RUNCIMAN *Skippers & Shellbacks* 42 I'll die on the flags with the jim-jams before I'll wet my lips with it again. **1897** *Blackw. Mag.* May 702 One man was just recovering from an attack of the jim-jams.

b. The fidgets, jitteriness; a fit of depression. *colloq.*

1896 'MARK TWAIN' in *Harper's Mag.* Sept. 537 They gave me the jimjams and the fantods and caked up what brains I had. **1904** *Strand Mag.* Dec. 770/2 By Gosh, look there. Enough to give a fellow the jim-jams, isn't it? **1926** GALSWORTHY *Silver Spoon* I. vi. 44 Who was the old buffer? .. he gave me 'the jim-jams'. **1931** C. MACKENZIE *Buttercups & Daisies* xiii. 169, I reckon if you put him in the upper circle at *Charley's Aunt* he'd give half the audience the jim-jams and upset the whole piece. **1946** K. TENNANT *Lost Haven* (1947) xix. 332 'There *is* someone out there,' he said. 'Or else I'm giving myself the jim-jams.' **1961** R. M. PATTERSON *Buffalo Head* vi. 223 The sides gave me the jim-jams merely to look at them: on the south, sliding rock and then a drop of 2000 feet down.

jimmal, jimmer: see GIMMAL, GIMMER[1].

jimmies, *sb. pl. colloq.* = JIM-JAM 3 and 3 b.

1900 J. C. HARRIS *On Wing of Occasions* 42 Take 'im to the hospital, Tim; 'tis the only way to clear the jimmies from his head. **1921** A. MASON *Flying Bo'sun* xxvi. 216 Riley,.. you drank too much Scotch last night; be careful that you don't get the Jimmies and jump overboard. **1928** *New Yorker* 22 Dec. 18/3 Him popping down the chimney—well, frankly, it gives me the jimmies. **1945** BAKER *Austral. Lang.* x. 199 *Britts up, to have the*, to be alarmed. From 'to have the wind up' and 'have the sh-ts', by rhyming slang on the name of the former lightweight boxing champion of the world, Jimmy Britt, who was on vaudeville tour in Australia during World War No. 1. *To have the jimmies* is an extension. **1961** P. WHITE *Riders in Chariot* xi. 415 She was not accustomed to see the grey light sprawling on an empty bed; it gave her the jimmies.

Jimminy: see JIMINY.

jimmy[1] ('dʒɪmɪ), dial. and colloq. pronunciation of JEMMY *sb.*, occurring in most of the senses of that word, and in numerous other slang, dialectal, and local uses, for which see Dictionaries and Glossaries dealing with such uses. Now the more usual form in the U.S. Also as *v. trans.*, to open with a jemmy.

1848 G. W. M. REYNOLDS *Mysteries of London* IV. cxcv. 369/1, I have got my own clasp-knife.. and a small jimmey. **1854** *Alta California* (San Francisco) 23 Feb., Officer Powers,.. upon examining the lock, found it had been broken open with a 'jimmy'. **1893** J. HAWTHORNE *Confessions of Convict* iii. 49 We took the safe.. and carried it.. to the basement... We jimmied it open in no time. *Ibid.* xi. 172, I have drilled holes in large safes so accurately that the bolts could be 'jimmied' without leaving a mark. **1904** G. H. LORIMER *Old Gorgon Graham* viii. 159 You can't break a big merchant with a jimmy and a stick of dynamite. **1905** *N.Y. Even. Post* 22 Dec. 3 The thieves jimmied the front door. **1922** R. PARRISH *Case & Girl* xxxii. 247 Finally we jimmied open the back door of this garage. **1973** 'E. MCBAIN' *Let's hear It* xiii. 194 The patrolman.. was examining a door and jamb for jimmy marks. **1973** *Sat. Rev. Society* (U.S.) May 42/2 Any attempt to jimmy the doors, hood, or trunk will cause the horn to begin sounding. **1973** P. B. AUSTIN tr. *Sjöwall & Wahlöö's Locked Room* v. 24 The door was equipped with a jimmy-proof lock. *Ibid.* xxiii. 186 [He] had brought with him every thinkable jimmy and other tool for opening the door.

Jimmy[2] ('dʒɪmɪ). [A male personal name, pet-form and familiar equivalent of the name JAMES.] In various transferred senses:

1. In full, **Jimmy Grant**. Rhyming slang for *immigrant* or *emigrant*. *Austral.*, *N.Z.*, and *S. Afr.*

1845 E. J. WAKEFIELD *Adventure N.Z.* I. xi. 337 The profound contempt which the whaler expresses for the 'lubber of a *jimmy-grant*', as he calls the emigrant. **1850** *McLean Papers* VIII. 177 (MS.), I consider Davy has done a foolish thing in selling his farm... I am glad it has not as usual fallen into the hands of 'Jimmies', usurpers of the soil. **1859** H. KINGSLEY *Recoll. G. Hamlyn* II. ix. 154 'What are these men that we are going to see?' 'Why one,' said Lee, 'is a young Jimmy (I beg your pardon, sir, an emigrant), the other two are old prisoners.' **1878** A. AYLWARD *Transvaal of To-Day* xi. 216, I was a raw emigrant, and still what Natalians call a '*Jimmy*'. **1922** *Daily Mail* 11 Dec. 8 With his wife and child he had just come over as a 'Jimmie-grant'. **1948** F. IRVINE-SMITH *Streets of my City* ii. 32 At the close of 1840, there were 2,500 settlers, or in whaler parlance, 'Jimmy Grants', upon its shores.

2. Jimmy Ducks, Jimmy Dux. Also **Jemmy Ducks**. A sailor who had charge of the livestock carried on merchant ships to serve as food on long voyages. *Naut. slang* (*Obs.* exc. *Hist.*).

1849 H. MELVILLE *Redburn* I. ix. 97 He in the rudest kind of manner laughed aloud in my face, and called me a 'Jimmy Dux'. **1850** —— *White Jacket* I. iii. 12 These fellows are all Jimmy Duxes—sorry chaps, who never put foot in ratlin, or venture above the bulwarks. **1890** R. C. LESLIE *Old Sea Wings* xiii. 177 The ship's butcher and his mate, 'Jemmy Ducks', formed an important part of the economy of our old East Indiamen. *Ibid.* 182 A gay rooster, after an exciting chase round the decks by Jemmy Ducks, escaped overboard. **1928** J. MASON *Before Mast in Sailing Ships* 13 One of our men had deserted an Orient Liner in Sydney, and had been a 'Jimmy Ducks' on that vessel. **1938** W. E. DEXTER *Rope-Yarns* v. 32 'Sails' or 'Jimmy Ducks' was the first one to get round.

3. Jimmy Low *Austral.*, a name for red mahogany, *Eucalyptus resinifera*.

1887 *Colonial & Indian Exhib. Rep. Col. Sect.* 428 Jimmy Low is usually a large tree, yielding timber of a rich red colour. **1888** F. M. BAILEY *Queensland Woods* 65 'Jimmy Low'. Forest Mahogany of N.S.W. Usually a very large tree with a rough, reddish, fibrous bark. **1904** J. H. MAIDEN *Forest Flora N.S.W.* I. 67 In Queensland it [sc. *Eucalyptus resinifera*] is often called 'Jimmy Low', after the late Mr. James Low, of Maroochie River, a locality for some of the finest specimens in that State. **1945** BAKER *Austral. Lang.* xii. 215 Among popular names for various trees noted by Morris were Jemmy Donnelly, Jimmy Low and Roger Gough.

4. Jimmy (also **Johnny**) **Wood(s, Woodser**, a solitary drinker; a drink taken on one's own; also *transf.*; so **Jimmy Woods** *nonce vb.*, to drink alone. *Austral.* and *N.Z. slang.*

The usual form is *Jimmy Woodser*.

1892 B. H. BOAKE in *Bulletin* (Sydney) 7 May 15/1 At the thought the heart beats quicker Than an old Bohemian's should... Bah! I'll go and have a liquor With the genial 'Jimmy Wood'. **1898** *Ibid.* 17 Dec. Red Page/2 The use of Christian names in this form of slang seems to have originated the Australian.. *Jimmy-Woodser*, a solitary drinker. **1900** H. LAWSON *Verses Pop. & Humorous* 67 The old Jimmy Woodser comes into the bar, Unwelcomed, unnoticed, unknown. **1928** J. DEVANNY *Dawn Beloved* II. xxxiv. 307 Duke preferred to drink alone.., Jimmy Woodsing, as the miners called it. **1930** *Bulletin* (Sydney) 19 Feb. 51/4 'You have your holiday.' 'Oh, no,' she told him.. 'I'm getting too old for Jimmy Woodsers, thanks.' **1933** *Press* (Christchurch, N.Z.) 28 Oct. 17/7 *Jimmy* or *Johnny Woodser*, slang. A drink by yourself. It is a common expression up-country in New Zealand. **1942** *2 N.Z.E.F. Times* 21 Dec. 18/2 You'll find me lonesome in a Naafi, a-drinkin' to me sins, A-sippin' like a Jimmy Woodser. **1945** BAKER *Austral. Lang.* ix. 171 A *Jimmy Woodser* is not only a lone drinker, but also a drink consumed by such a person. **1957** D. NILAND *Call me when Cross turns Over* i. 9 I'm a real Jimmy Woodser now. On my own. The first bird on the family tree and the last.

5. In full, **Jimmy O'Goblin** (also with lower-case initials). Rhyming slang for 'sovereign', twenty shillings. Cf. GOBLIN[2], JEMMY O'GOBLIN. *slang.*

1899 A. E. W. MASON *Miranda of Balcony* xv. 206, I want one thousand jimmies per annum. **1931** T. H. DEY *Leaves from Bookmaker's Bk.* xi. 180 Here's another story of a lost 'Jimmy o' Goblin'. **1932** D. L. SAYERS *Have his Carcase* xi. 128 Three hundred golden sovereigns... Three hundred round, golden jimmy o' goblins. **1934** E. WAUGH *Handful of Dust* ii. 35 He had won five Jimmy-o-goblins at ten to three at Chester. **1956** C. SMITH *Deadly Reaper* xiv. 108 Her first husband left her half a million. Yes, sir, five hundred thousand jimmy o'goblins. **1959** *Spectator* 3 July 5/2 The proposed sale of the Watford firm S. G. Brown Ltd., at present owned by the Admiralty.. is a most unlikely haunt of businessmen, if the thirty-eight million jimmy-o'goblins they were wasting on obsolete warships a month or so ago is anything to go by. **1967** C. WATSON *Lonelyheart 4122* xv. 149 'The money's paid in—five hundred nice shiny Jimmy O'goblins.' (Dear God! Where had she last come across that one? Sapper? Henty?) **1973** *Times* 28 June 16/2 He.. had made a profit of some six million jimmy-o-goblins.

6. In full, **Jimmy the One**. First Lieutenant. *Naut. slang.* Also in various other applications (see quots.).

1916 'TAFFRAIL' *Pincher Martin* viii. 147 Th' Bloke, an' Jimmy the One, an' most o' th' other officers made a bit too. **1935** WODEHOUSE *Luck of Bodkins* viii. 80 'By rights I ought to just go to Jimmy the One.'.. 'The chief steward, sir?' **1945** [see FLANNEL *sb.* 1 f]. **1953** E. HYAMS *Gentian Violet* v. 76 He became second in command of a very old destroyer and as such he was perhaps the only Jimmy-the-One in the Royal Navy who was not detested by the ship's company. **1962** 'E. PETERS' *Funeral of Figaro* i. 10 He was.. used to being Number One or Jimmy the One [in a theatre]. **1970** *Guardian* 19 Aug. 16/8 Smith told Petty Officer David Lewis, 'We are going to have a sit-in and give the "Jimmy" a hard time.'

7. dismal Jimmy: see DISMAL *a.* 7.

8. Jimmy Green = JAMIE GREEN; a sail under the jib-boom.

1913 E. K. CHATTERTON *Ships & Ways of Other Days* xii. 265 The reader will remember we called attention some time back to those spritsails which seem so curious to us moderns. They were also known as 'water sails' and as 'Jimmy Greens', both appellations being due, obviously, to the unhappy knack they possessed of scooping up the sea. **1933** *Sea Breezes* XVII. 186 A 'Jimmy Green' was set along the bowsprit and jibboom under the head sails. **1944** J. MASEFIELD *New Chum* 155 Once one came by with an odd triangular yardless topsail, then, very rare, but now in use again. We were told that it would be called a Jimmy Green if set above a royal.

9. In full, **Jimmy Riddle**. Rhyming slang for *piddle*.

1937 in PARTRIDGE *Dict. Slang.* **1959** R. FULLER *Ruined Boys* i. 10 Come and have a Jimmy Riddle. **1964** J. SYMONS *End of Solomon Grundy* I. ii. 34, I must do a Jimmy Riddle before I go. **1966** 'L. LANE' *ABZ of Scouse* 56 Said of a person with a weak bladder: 'e's got ther jimmy riddles. **1971** D. CLARK *Sick to Death* vii. 154 Mrs D. was in there having a jimmy.

10. Jimmy Howe *Austral.* and *N.Z.*, = *Jacky Howe* s.v. JACKY 3.

1937 E. HILL *Great Austral. Loneliness* xl. 301 A weird figure in a flour-bag, Jimmie Howe, with shoes of raw-hide laced with pandanus, Leng carried no luggage.

jimmy, dial. form of JEMMY *a.*

†**jimp** (dʒɪmp), *sb.*[1] *Sc. Obs.* Forms: 5 **gimp**, 6 **gymp(e, iymp, iimp**. [Perh. connected with JIMP *a.*]

1. A minute or subtle point; a trifling distinction; a quirk, subtlety; a tittle.

c **1470** HENRYSON *Mor. Fab.* XII. (*Wolf & Lamb*) xvi, O man of law, let be thy subteltie, With nyce gimpis, and fraudis intricait. **1513** DOUGLAS *Æneis* I. Prol. 124 For ane iymp or a bourd, I pray ȝou note me nocht at euery wourd. **1563** WINȜET *Wks.* (1890) II. 15 To eschew al occasioun of wane stryfe.. for Iimpis of Grammar or sik triflis. **1596** DALRYMPLE tr. *Leslie's Hist. Scot.* IX. 226 In the leist iot or iimp tha neuer brak the papes authoritie.

2. A trick, prank.

1572 *Satir. Poems Reform.* xxxi. 132 Nor with the hous of Guyis to mell, Quha is als godles as thair sell, And kens thair gymps, I trow.

jimp, *sb.*[2]: see JUMP *sb.*[2]

jimp (dʒɪmp), *a.* (*adv.*) *Sc.* and *north. dial.* Forms: 6 **gymp**, (**gympt**), 8–9 **gimp**, 8– **jimp**. [Known in Sc. since *c* 1500; origin obscure. It has been compared with GIM *a.*, 'smart, spruce', of the same age, and with JUMP *a.*, exact, precise, which appears later; but in neither case is the sense congruous.]

1. Slender, slim, delicate, graceful, neat. (A Scotch or northern word, introduced in 19th c. into English literature.)

1508 DUNBAR *Tua Mariit Wemen* 69 Gymp, iolie, and gent, richt ioyus, and gentryce, I suld at fairis be found. **1513** DOUGLAS *Æneis* VI. x. 45 Apon his harp.. Now with gymp fingeris doing stringis smyte. *Ibid.* XII. Prol. 121 Gymp gerraflouris thar royn levys vnschet. *a* **1550** *Christis Kirke Gr.* iii, Of all thir madynis.. Wes nane sa gympt as Gillie. **1719** LADY WARDLAW *Hardy Knute* I. 27 Her girdle shawed her middle gimp. **1788** BURNS '*O, were I on Parnassus' hill*' ii, I see thee dancing o'er the green, Thy waist sae jimp, thy limbs sae clean. **1844** WILLIS *Lady Jane* II. 598 Satin waistcoat.. Becoming to a youth so jimp and slim. *a* **1845** BARHAM *Ingol. Leg.*, *Knt. & Lady* xii, Then his left arm he placed Round her jimp, taper waist. **1893** *Northumbld. Gloss.*, *Gimp* (g soft), thin, neat in figure.

2. Scanty; barely full; bare (measure).

1768 ROSS *Helenore* I. 6 An' howsoon as the jimp three raiths was gane. **1868** ATKINSON *Cleveland Gloss.*, *Jimp*,.. 3. small, scanty, deficient in measure. *Mod. Sc.* I fancy he has given you but jimp measure to-day.

3. *Comb.*, as *jimp-waisted*.

1826 J. WILSON *Noct. Ambr.* Wks. 1855 I. 192 That bonny dark-haired.. jimp-waisted lassie.

B. *adv.* Barely, scarcely.

1814 SCOTT *Diary* 10 Aug. in *Lockhart*, These islanders.. are sober, good-humoured, and friendly—but jimp honest. **1893** STEVENSON *Catriona* xv, He had jimp said the word.

Hence '**jimply** *adv.*, slenderly, scantily; '**jimpness**, slenderness.

1816 SCOTT *Old Mort.* xxxvii, We are jimply provided for in beds rather. **1885** *Chamb. Jrnl.* II. 43 Not of the jimpness engendered of corsets, but of nature.

jimsonweed. *U.S.* Also 7–9 **Jamestown-weed**, 9– **jimpsonweed.** [f. Jamestown, in Virginia.] The Thorn-apple, *Datura Stramonium*. Also *ellipt.* as **jim(p)son**.

1687 J. CLAYTON in *Phil. Trans.* XLI. 160 Several of them [the Soldiers] went to gather a Sallad.. and lighting in great Quantities on an Herb called Iames-town-weed, they gathered it; and by eating thereof in plenty, were rendered apish and foolish. **1700** J. LAWSON *Carolina* (1718) 78 James-Town-Weed.. is excellent for curing Burns and asswaging Inflammations. **1812** *Cramer's Almanac 1813* (Pittsburgh) 26 James'-town weed.. also known by the name of Jimson, and Thorn-Apple. **1842** *Amer. Pioneer* I. 314 She said her principal dressings were made of.. the leaves of stramonium, or 'jimson'. **1880** 'MARK TWAIN' *Tramp Abr.* I. 220 The village jokers came creeping stealthily through the jimpson weeds and sunflowers. **1892** *Harper's Mag.* LXXXIV. 936/2 The front yard was overrun with cockle-burs and 'jimsonweed'. **1911** C. HARRIS *Eve's Second Husband* xiv. 299 Clumps of sweet jimson and borders of balsam and pinks. **1930** R. BASS in A. Dundes

Mother Wit (1973) 382 He cures.. headaches with a poultice of jimson-weeds. **1934** *Amer. Ballads & Folk Songs* 23 Mike was pilin' ties near the ditch by the road Out among the jimpson where the boys ain't mowed. **1943** R. PEATTIE *Great Smokies* 118 Jimson root for ulcers. **1954** C. J. HYLANDER *Macmillan Wild Flower Book* 360 Jimsonweed is a stout plant, growing to a height of five feet, with ovate lobed leaves and white or violet, trumpet-shaped flowers up to four inches in length.

jimswinger ('dʒɪmswɪŋə(r)). *Southern U.S.* Also **jim swinger, jim-swinger.** [Origin unknown.] In full, ***jimswinger coat.*** A swallow-tailed coat, esp. a frock coat.

1890 *Dialect Notes* I. 389 *Jim-swinger*, long-tailed coat, especially a 'Prince Albert'. **1898** P. L. DUNBAR *Folks from Dixie* 52 He walked to church, flanked on one side by Aunt Caroline.. and on the other by her husband stately in the magnificence of an antiquated 'Jim-swinger'. **1912** H. & W. B. CRUMPTON *Adv. Two Alabama Boys* 78, I was a tall, slim, awkward lad, about eighteen years old, thin as a match, pale as a ghost and had on a long Jim Swinger. **1933** C. MILLER *Lamb in Bosom* v. 47 If you were a lawyer,.. you wore a jimswinger coat. **1950** *Publ. Amer. Dial. Soc.* XIV. 75 *Cut-away and Jim swinger*, formal clothes. Suwannee backwoods. **1951** E. PAUL *Springtime in Paris* i. 9 She wore indoors and out a strictly tailored swallow-tail coat, the kind American Negroes call a 'Jimswinger'. **1972** *News & Observer* (Raleigh, North Carolina) 30 Dec. 4/1 Jim-swinger coat.. and brogans have almost vanished.

[**jimwhiskee**, error for TIM-WHISKY, q.v.]

jin, variant of GIN *sb.*² and ³, JINN.

Jina ('dʒɪnə). Also **Gina.** [Skr.: see JAIN.] Title given to Mahavira or to any other of the twenty-four Jain tirthankars or to one of the five Dhyani Buddhas; a sculptured representation of such a saint.

1807 *Asiatick Researches* IX. 303 The first chapter [of a vocabulary of synonymous terms, by an author of the Jaina sect] begins with the synonyma of a *Jina* or deified saint. **1833** *Ibid.* XVII. 250 Notwithstanding the sameness of the general character and identity of generic attributes, the twenty-four *Jinas* are distinguished from each other in colour, stature, and longevity. Two of them are red, two white, two blue, two black, the rest are of a golden hue, or a yellowish brown. The other two peculiarities.. observe a series of decrement from *Rishabha*, the first *Jina*, who was five hundred poles in stature, and lived 8,400,000 great years to Mahávina the 24th, who had degenerated to the size of man, and was not more than forty years on earth. **1875** M. WILLIAMS *Indian Wisdom* vii. 129 Twenty-four Jinas or 'perfect saints' raised to the rank of gods have appeared in the present Avasarpini cycle. **1884** *Sacred Bks. East* XXII. I. 201 The Venerable One had become an Arhat and Gina, he was.. omniscient. **1901** V. A. SMITH *Jain Stûpa of Mathurâ* xviii. 46 The Jina shown in the plate is Pârśvanâth. **1915** A. M. STEVENSON *Heart of Jainism* iii. 39 Mahāvīra now added to his titles those of *Jina* (or Conqueror of the Eight Karma, the great enemies), from which Jainism derives its name, [etc.]. **1924** B. BHATTACHARYA *Indian Buddhist Iconogr.* i. 2 The Jinas (victorious ones) are Vairocana, Ratnasambhava, Amitābha, Amoghasiddhi and Aksobhya, whose colours respectively are white, yellow, red, green and blue. **1971** *Illustr. Weekly India* 11 Apr. 8/1 (*caption*) Risabha and Vardhamana are the most honoured among the twenty-four Tirthankaras and the Jain scriptures narrate in detail the life of these two Jinas.

Jindyworobak (ˌdʒɪndɪ'wɒrəʊbæk). [Austral. Aboriginal word.] A member of a group founded in 1938 by R. C. Ingamells (1913-55) to promote Australianism in literature, art, etc. Also *attrib.* or as *adj.*

1938 (*title*) Jindyworobak anthology. **1958** *N. & Q.* Oct. 459/1 Roland Robinson, the Jindyworobak, is a perspicuous observer of natural beauty. **1959** *Times Lit. Suppl.* 2 Jan. 9/1 This book demonstrates that, while in the direct Jindyworobak line, he is no fanatic.

jing (dʒɪŋ), *sb.*¹ *rare.* [Echoic; cf. *ping, ting*, etc.] A sharp ring, a jingle.

a **1653** G. DANIEL *Idylls* iv. 93 The cag'd Squirrell, with a Iing of Bells.

jing, *sb.*² orig. *Sc.* In the asseveration ***by jing!*** (rarely ***by jings!***) = BY JINGO.

1785 BURNS *Halloween* ix, While Willie lap, and swoor by jing. **1809** [see GOOD *a.* 19]. **1850** [A common asseveration apparently in all parts of Scotland (*By jingo* not in use).]**1881** 'MARK TWAIN' *Let.* 16 Dec. (1917) I. 412 By jings! the postman will be here in a minute. **1925** T. DREISER *Amer. Tragedy* II. iii. 184 Well, by jing, if it ain't Tom. **1941** BAKER *Dict. Austral. Slang* 39 *By jings!*, an exclamation, derived from 'by jingo!'

jing, *v. rare.* [Cf. JING *sb.*¹] *intr.* To ring.

1884 R. BUCHANAN *Eng. Huswife's Gossip* Poems 95/1 Her tongue was like a bell upon a sheep—Her very motion seemed to make it jing.

jingal, jingko, variant of GINGALL, GINGKO.

jingbang ('dʒɪŋ'bæŋ). *slang.* Also **jimbang.** [Origin not recorded.] In phr. ***the whole jingbang***: the whole lot, company, concern, or affair.

1866 W. GREGOR *Banffsh. Gloss.*, *Jingbang*, the whole number. *a* **1884** PEERIE *Nugæ Eccles.* i. 22 Here they come —the whole jingbang. **1886** STEVENSON *Kidnapped* vii. (1891) 61 The chief mate.. was.. 'the only seaman of the whole jing-bang'. **1890** BOLDREWOOD *Col. Reformer* (1891) 183 The best thing.. is to leave the whole jimbang in his hands altogether. *Ibid.* 321, I.. bought the whole jimbang right out.

jingle ('dʒɪŋg(ə)l), *v.* Also 4-6 **gyngle**, 5 **gyngel, gingelle**, 6 **gingil, iyngel, iengle**, 7-9 **gingle.** [Imitative: cf. *dingle, tinkle*, Du. *jengelen*, and G. *klingeln.* There does not appear any original association with JANGLE.]

1. *intr.* To give forth a mingling of ringing sounds, as by the striking together of coins, keys, or other small metallic objects; it expresses a more prolonged and continuous sound than *clink*, and a more complicated one than *tinkle.*

c **1386** CHAUCER *C.T.* Prol. 170 Whan he rood men myghte his brydel heere Gynglen in a whistlynge wynd als cleere And eek as loude as dooth þe Chapel belle. **1530** PALSGR. 566/1, I gyngyll, I make a noyse, as thinges of metall do whan they be shaked togyther. **1555** W. WATREMAN *Fardle Facions* II. x. 213 To haue a great sort of siluer sounded belles, gynglyng aboute their horse neckes. **1583** STUBBES *Anat. Abus.* I. (1879) 147 Their bels iyngling. **1607** MIDDLETON *Five Gallants* II. iii, To hear my money gingle in other men's pockets. **1628** EARLE *Microcosm.*, *A Gallant* (Arb.) 39 Hee.. takes great delight in his walke to heare his Spurs gingle. **1653** A. WILSON *Jas. I*, 110 Her chains gingled as she came. **1824** BYRON *Juan* XV. lxx, The glasses jingled, and the palates tingled. **1870** DISRAELI *Lothair* xxi. I. 173 The bells.. gingled. **1871-4** J. THOMSON *City Dreadf. Nt.* IX. ii, The harness jingles, as it passes by.

b. *transf.* and *fig.* (Cf. *ring.*)

1659 D. PELL *Impr. Sea* 76 How.. their roaring oaths gingle in their mouthes. **1867** *Fortn. Rev.* Oct. 379 There is not one word in the whole quotation but jingles false.

c. To proceed or move with a jingling sound.

1732 POPE *Ep. Bathurst* 37 From the crack'd bagg the dropping Guinea spoke.. gingling down the back-stairs. **1870** EMERSON *Soc. & Solit.*, *Clubs* Wks. (Bohn) III. 93 To fairly disengage the mass, and send it jingling down, a good bowlder. **1894** MRS. RITCHIE *Chapters from Mem.* iii. 36 A yellow carriage jingled by.

d. quasi-*trans.* with *it.*

1631 BRATHWAIT *Whimzies* II. *Pedler* 19 Here the Guga-girles gingle it with his neat nifles.

2. *trans.* To cause (something) to emit a mingling of ringing sounds.

1508 KENNEDY *Flyting w. Dunbar* 506 Bot gif it war to gyngill Iudas bellis. **1515** BARCLAY *Egloges* iii. (1570) C ij/1 The kitchin clarke.. Iengling his counters. **1615** G. SANDYS *Trav.* 172 Fannes of brasse, hung about with rings, which they gingle in stops according to their marchings. **1760** GOLDSM. *Cit. W.* xlv, Another.. gingles several bells fixed to his cap. **1874** BURNAND *My time* xi. 93 Jingling his keys in one pocket.

3. *intr.* **a.** Of prose or verse: To sound with alliteration, rimes, or other repetitions.

1670 EACHARD *Cont. Clergy* 67 Then comes the joy of joyes, when the parts jingle, or begin with the same letter; and especially if in Latin. **1780** HOWARD *Prisons Eng.* 115 In this chamber on the wall is inscribed a gingling verse,.. *Ad mala patrata, sunt atra theatra parata.* **1855** MACAULAY *Hist. Eng.* xv. III. 535 Compositions of all sorts, from sermons with sixteen heads down to jingling street ballads.

b. To play with words for the sake of sound; (*depreciatively*) to rime.

1642 FULLER *Holy & Prof. St.* II. xvi. 113 Rich in Latine, though he doth not gingle with it in every company. **1708** OCKLEY *Hist. Saracens* Pref. (1848) 18 At other times jingling upon words. **1714** POPE *Let.* 13 July, I should be sorry and ashamed, to go on jingling to the last step. **1785** BURNS *First Ep. Lapraik* ix, Whene'er my Muse does on me glance, I jingle at her.

c. *trans.* To rime. (*depreciative.*)

1894 F. HALL in *Nation* (N.Y.) LVIII. 252/1 Carlyle.. I have more than once seen spoken of as having first jingled *end* with *mend.*

Hence **'jingle-'jingle**, reduplication of the vb.-stem, used *advb.* = with continued jingling.

1664 COTTON *Scarron.* iv. Poet. Wks. (1765) 85 Gingle gingle went her Bridle.

jingle ('dʒɪŋg(ə)l), *sb.* Also 6-9 **gingle**, 7 **yingle**, 9 **gingell.** [f. prec. vb.]

1. a. A noise such as is made by small bells, a chain of loose links, or loose pieces of metal when struck; a sound intermediate between clinking and ringing.

1599 B. JONSON *Ev. Man out of Hum.* Pref. 35 The gingle of his spurre, and the ierke of his wande. **1678** OTWAY *Friendship in F.* 18 We know when a certain Spark of this Town is at hand by the new fangled gingle of his Coach. **1791** MRS. INCHBALD *Simp. Story* I. vii. 75 The gentle gingle of a teaspoon. **1826** DISRAELI *Viv. Grey* v. vi, No other sound was heard, except the jingle of the dollars and Napoleons. **1833** HT. MARTINEAU *Three Ages* II. 73 Mrs. Reade heard the jingle of the chain. **1874** SYMONDS *Sk. Italy & Greece* (1898) I. ii. 30 The continual jingle of our sledge-bells.

b. Applied depreciatively to other sounds.

1827 CARLYLE *Misc.*, *Richter* (1869) I. 7 The jingle of the household operations seemed not at all to disturb him. **1842** THOREAU *Excurs.*, *Nat. Hist. Mass.* (1863) 46 The gingle of the song-sparrow salutes us from the shrubs and fences. **1865** M. ARNOLD *Ess. Crit.* v. 184, I hear nothing but the.. scolding and the jingle of the piano.

2. a. Something that jingles; a jingling bell; anything adapted to produce a jingling sound.

1615 G. SANDYS *Trav.* 173 Who instead of musicall instruments, have sawcers of brasse (which they strike against one another) set about with gingles. **1625** BACON *Ess.*, *Plantations* (Arb.) 534 If you Plant, where Sauages are, doe not onely entertaine them with Trifles, and Gingles; But vse them iustly. **1825** HONE *Every-day Bk.* I. 1248 The tambourine,.. and the Turkish jingle, used in the army.

b. *Austral. slang.* Money. Cf. *jingle-boy.*

1906 E. DYSON *Fact'ry 'Ands* viii. 99 Ther Elder dug in 'n' brought up er 'andful iv jingle. **1941** BAKER *Dict. Austral. Slang* 39 *Jingle*, money.

3. a. The affected repetition of the same sound or of a similar series of sounds, as in alliteration, rime, or assonance; any arrangement of words intended to have a pleasing or striking sound without regard to the sense; a catching array of words, whether in prose or verse. Chiefly contemptuous.

c **1645** HOWELL *Lett.* (1892) II. 658 In the perusal of these Parables.. you shall find no gingles in them. **1663** BP. PATRICK *Parab. Pilgr.* 157 Frivolous hearers, who are more pleased with little gingles, and tinkling of words than with the most perswasive arguments. *a* **1680** BUTLER *Rem.* (1759) II. 261 As if that old Gingle were logically true. **1717** ADDISON *Spect.* No. 297 ¶ 16 Milton.. often affects a kind of Jingle in his Words, as in the following Passages.. 'And brought into the World a World of Woe'. **1791** *Gentl. Mag.* 26/2 Several pages of his sermons consisting of a series of verbal quibbles and jingles. **1837-9** HALLAM *Hist. Lit.* I. I. i. §35. 32 This gingle is certainly pleasing in itself. **1879** FARRAR *St. Paul* I. 534 Their so-called philosophy had become little better than a jingle of phrases.

b. A short verse or song in a radio or television commercial or in general advertising.

1930 A. FLEXNER *Universities* I. xxv. 165 Let the psychologists study advertising.. in order to understand what takes place when a jingle like 'not a cough in a carload' persuades a nation to buy a new brand of cigarettes. **1949** *Life* 28 Mar. 36/1 She abhors the jingle's suggestion that she be taken home and squeezed. **1959** *Punch* 10 June 769/1 He says I can't possibly get on in the jingles business without going to Oxford. *Ibid.* 17 June 815/2 Channel 9 already gets into hot water when its 'natural breaks' happen to clip a speech in mid-sentence: its life would not be worth living if it saw fit.. to substitute a jingle for the heavyweight's knock-out hook. **1968** *Listener* 26 Sept. 421/3 Certainly those hideous jingles could go: it made good sense for Radio London or Radio Caroline, as new, commercial stations, to tell us that they were wonderful, but the BBC could spare itself that reassurance. **1972** D. RAMSAY *Little Murder Music* 76 Colby was working a jingle date. *Ibid.*, The jingle, a singing commercial for a detergent, was being recorded.

4. A covered two-wheeled car used in Cornwall, the south of Ireland, and in Australia. Also *attrib.*

1806 CARR *Stranger Irel.* v. 111, I mounted a jingle at the great jingle stand at the corner of Bagot Street. **1824** T. C. CROKER *Researches S. Ireland* ii. 34 Jingles.. have been established between the principal towns. These are carriages on easy springs,.. to contain six or eight persons. **1829** *Blackw. Mag.* XXV. 772/2 Ultimately the gingle was almost abandoned for the jaunting-car. **1842** THACKERAY *Fitz-Boodle's Pap.* Pref., I got it.. from.. a jingle-driver. **1862** CLARA ASPINALL *Three Yrs. Melbourne* 122 (Morris) Gentlemen who have lived in India will persist in calling this vehicle a jingle;.. it is a kind of dos-a-dos conveyance, holding three in front, and three behind, it has a water-proof top to it.. and oilskin curtains to draw all round. **1874** A. I. THACKERAY *Let.* 12 July (1924) viii. 158 You come to a most detestable little object called Bude.. and then you.. come home in a little thing called a Jingle. **1887** *Cassell's Picturesque Australasia* I. 64 The jingle has been ousted by the one-horse waggonette. **1892** *Pall Mall G.* 17 Aug. 2/3 Queenstown is full... The jingle men, as they are called here .. are making their fortunes. **1906** *Daily Chron.* 10 Mar. 4/4 When I asked one of the drivers how to reach the Cornish border, he offered to convey me.. in a jingle-cart. **1924** C. MACKENZIE *Heavenly Ladder* ii. 34 He saw the black-coated train toiling up Pendhu hill,.. some leading the ponies in the jingles. **1942** A. L. ROWSE *Cornish Childhood* vii. 189, I was sent to put the donkey into the shay or jingle.

5. An American name for the shell of the saddle-oyster, *Anomia.* Also *attrib.*

1887 *Fisheries U.S.* Sect. v. II. 543 A more fragile shell, such as a scallop, mussel, or jingle (*Anomia*) is certainly better. **1889** *Pall Mall G.* 9 Aug. 3/3 A large collection of scallop and jingle shells—gold and silver shells the little people call them.

6. *attrib.* and *Comb.* (see also senses 4 and 5), as ***jingle-bell***, etc. (see quots.); **jingle-boy** (*slang*), a coin, *spec.* a sovereign; also, a man who has plenty of money in his pockets.

1887 *Bicycling News* 21 May 99/1 My light was burning brilliantly and my *jingle bell going at the time. **1894** *Outing* (U.S.) XXIV. 71/1 The captain of the launch pulls the 'jingle bell' for full speed ahead. *a* **1700** B. E. *Dict. Cant. Crew*, **Jingle-boxes*, Leathern Jacks tipt and hung with Silver Bells formerly in use among Fuddle Caps. *c* **1600** DAY *Begg. Bednall Gr.* v. (1881) 111 Come, old fellow, bring thy white Bears to the Stake, and thy yellow *gingle boys to the Bull-ring. *a* **1652** BROME *Covent Gard.* I. Wks. 1873 II. 16 There is a Gallant now below, a Gingle boy indeed, that has his pockets full of crowns that chide for vent. **1891** FARMER *Slang*, *Canary*,.. 2... a sovereign. *English Synonyms*.. Yellow hammer; shiner; gingleboy; monarch. *a* **1700** B. E. *Dict. Cant. Crew*, **Jingle-brains*, a Maggot-pated Fellow.

jingle, obs. form of JUNGLE *sb.*

jingled ('dʒɪŋg(ə)ld), *ppl. a. U.S. slang* (now *rare*). [f. JINGLE *v.* + -ED¹.] Intoxicated, fuddled.

1908 G. H. LORIMER *Jack Spurlock* xii. 315 Old Mrs. Corliss was purple with pleasure at having so plausible a pretext for getting comfortably jingled. **1917** [see BLOTTO *a.*] **1942** in BERREY & VAN DEN BARK *Amer. Thes. Slang* § 106/7.

'jingle-'jangle, *sb.* [Varied reduplication of *jingle*: cf. *dilly-dally, dingle-dangle, ding-dong, clink-clank*, etc.] **a.** An alternating jingle of sounds; a sentence or verse characterized by this. **b.** Something that makes a continuous and

alternating jingle; a jingling ornament or trinket.

1640 *King & poore North. Man* 179 in Hazl. *E.P.P.* IV. 300 With so many jingle jangles about ones necke, as is about yours. **1694** MOTTEUX *Rabelais* v. vii. (1737) 22 The everlasting Jingle Jangle of the Bells. **1851** HAWTHORNE *Twice-told T.* II. xii. 191 The variety of rapid vehicles; and the jingle jangle of merry bells. **1864** *N. Brit. Rev.* Dec. 432 It was then he [Caracalla] made use of his famous jingle-jangle.. 'Inter Divos? Sit Divus.. dummodo non sit vivus': Let him [Geta] be a god, but don't let him live.

So **'jingle-'jangle** *v.*, to jingle with alternation of sounds; to proceed with such jingling.

1899 *Westm. Gaz.* 13 Feb. 3/1 Such a paltry collection of commonplace tunes, handled clumsily, as jingle-jangles and drums its way through the piece.

jingler ('dʒɪŋglə(r)). [f. JINGLE *v.* + -ER[1].]

1. One who or that which jingles; a rimer.

1599 B. JONSON *Ev. man out of Hum.* II. v, I had spurres of mine own before: but they were not ginglers. **1672** EACHARD *Hobbs's State Nat.* 30 Thou shalt see that thou art ten times more an Owl, than I am a cheat and jingler. **1803** T. G. FESSENDEN *Terrible Tractoration* II. (ed. 2) 89 *note*, The wolf always makes it his first object to silence this jingler [the bell wether]. **1884** J. G. BOURKE *Snake Dance Moquis* xi. 119 A fringe of small bells, or jinglers, of lead and tin.

†**2.** *slang.* (See quot.) *Obs. rare*—⁰.

a **1700** B. E. *Dict. Cant. Crew*, *Jinglers*, Horse-Coursers frequenting Country Fairs.

3. A local name for the Golden-eyed Duck.

1829 COL. HAWKER *Diary* (1893) I. 360 The golden-eye is here provincially called gingler or ginging-curre, from the noise of its wings. **1888** G. TRUMBULL *Names & Portraits Birds* xxiii. 79 At Pleasantville.. *Jingler*; at Baltimore and on the Patapsco River, *Whiffler*.

†**'jinglespur.** *Obs.* In 7 gingle-. One who jingles his spurs; a cavalier.

1604 *Meeting Gallants at Ordinarie* (Percy Soc.) 9 Signior Ginglespur, the fine gallant I mette in Powles.

jinglet ('dʒɪŋglɪt). *U.S.* [f. JINGLE *sb.* or *v.* + -ET[1].]

1. The loose metal ball which serves as the clapper of a globular sleigh-bell.

1881 *Sci. Amer.* XLIV. 323 This sand core, with the jinglet inside, is placed in the mould of the outside, and the melted metal is poured in, which fills up the space between the core and the mould. **1884** in *Chicago Advance* 7 Feb. 83 This little iron ball [in a sleigh bell] is called 'the jinglet'. When you shake the sleigh bell it jingles.

2. 'Any small jingling appendage, esp. one shaped like a sleigh-bell' (Funk, 1893).

jingling ('dʒɪŋglɪŋ), *vbl. sb.* Also **gingling.** [f. JINGLE *v.* + -ING[1].] The action of the vb. JINGLE, q.v.

14.. *Chaucer's Nun's Pr. Prol.* 28 (Harl. MS.) Gingling [*6-text*, clynkyng] of þe bellis þat on ȝour bridil hong on euery syde. *c* **1440** *Promp. Parv.* 195/1 Gyngelynge of gay harneys.., *resonancia*. **1583** STANYHURST *Æneis* III. (Arb.) 75 With theese Gods gingling [*voce deorum*], with sight moste geason apaled. **1601** WEEVER *Mirr. Mart.* E j, Jingling of fetters had no merie sound. **1655** FULLER *Ch. Hist.* I. iii. §1 The puddle-Poet did hope, that the jingling of his rhyme would drown the sound of his false quantity. **1731** A. HILL *Adv. Poets* xxiii, Shame on your Jyngling, ye soft Sons of Rhyme! **1842** TENNYSON *Locksley Hall* 105 The jingling of the guinea helps the hurt that Honour feels.

b. *attrib.*, as **jingling match**, a diversion in which all the players are blindfolded except one, who keeps ringing a bell in each hand, while the others try to catch him.

c **1786** COWPER *Let.* Wks. 1835 V. 355 All who are attached to the jingling art. **1801** STRUTT *Sports & Past.* IV. iii. §31 Jingling match.. a diversion common enough at country wakes and fairs. **1805** *Sporting Mag.* XXV. 304 A smock-race and a jingling-match were to take place. **1888** *Daily Tel.* 23 Apr. 5/4 We hear nowadays less and less of.. gingling and whistling matches.

jingling ('dʒɪŋglɪŋ), *ppl. a.* [f. as prec. + -ING[2].]

1. That jingles: see the verb.

1557-8 PHAER *Æneid* VI. R j b, From thens wer howlings heard.. and gyngling noyse of draggyng chaynes. **1570** B. GOOGE *Pop. Kingd.* IV. 48 b, A hundred gingling belles do hang, to make his courage more. **1610** SHAKS. *Temp.* V. i. 232. **1634** HEYWOOD *Witches Lanc.* IV. i. Wks. 1874 IV. 218, I wanted but a paire of gingling spurs to make you mend your pace. **1789** BURNS *On Capt. Grose's Peregrin.* vi, Auld nick-nackets: Rust airn caps and jinglin jackets. **1840** CARLYLE *Heroes* iii. (1858) 252 Whatsoever is not sung is properly no Poem, but a piece of Prose cramped into jingling lines,—to the great injury of the grammar, to the great grief of the reader, for most part!

2. jingling Johnny, (*a*) *slang* = *Chinese pavilion*; (*b*) *Austral.* and *N.Z. slang*, one who shears sheep by hand; *pl.* hand shears.

a. 1904 H. G. FARMER *Mem. R. Artillery Band* ii. 51 An instrument known as the 'Jingling Johnnie', and tambourines were employed. **1920** G. B. SHAW *How to become Mus. Critic* (1960) 311 Every scorer of ballets could scatter pearls from the *pavillon chinois* (alias Jingling Johnny) over the plush and cotton velvet of his harmonies. **1970** *Times* 24 Aug. 20/5 (Advt.), French Pavillon Chinois (jingling Johnny) for sale. Recently restored. £100 o.n.o. **b. 1934** L. G. D. ACLAND in *Press* (Christchurch, N.Z.) 20 Jan. 15/7 *Jingling Johnnies*, old time slang term for hand shearers. **1941** BAKER *Dict. Austral. Slang* 39 *Jingling johnnies*, hand shears. **1945** [see DAGGER *sb.*[2] a]. **1965** J. S. GUNN *Terminol. Shearing Industry* I. 33 *Jingling Johnny*, originally a swagman or bagman but in many districts this was also another name for a hand-shearer.

Hence **'jinglingly (ging-)** *adv.*

1840 BROWNING *Sordello* v. 953 Some shape.. Approached, out of the dark, ginglingly near.

jingly ('dʒɪŋglɪ), *a.* [f. JINGLE *sb.* + -Y[1].] Characterized by jingle or affected recurrence of words or sounds.

a **1806** K. WHITE *Rem.* (1811) II. 249 It [has] a set of chiming and jingly terminations. **1885** E. D. GERARD *Waters of Hercules* xxvi, The jingly prayer rambled on.

jingo ('dʒɪŋgəʊ); *int.*, *sb.*, and *a.* Also 7 jeingo. [Appears first *c* 1670 as a piece of conjuror's gibberish, usually *hey* or *high jingo!*, prob. a mere piece of sonorous nonsense with an appearance of mysterious meaning. In 1694 *by jingo* occurs in Motteux's transl. of Rabelais, where the Fr. has *par Dieu*: this, being contemporary with the conjuror's term, may be presumed (though not proved) to be the same word, substituted, as in many other cases, for a sacred name: cf. *by golly*, *gock*, *gom*, *gosh*, *jabers*, etc. In Scotland, *by jing* (or *jings*) has long been in common use.

A recent conjecture, since *jingo* began to attract attention, would identify it with the Basque word for 'God', given by Van Eys and Larramendi as *Jinko*, *Jainko* (*Yinko*, *Yainko*), *Jincoa*, *Jaincoa*; the suggestion being that this may have been caught up from Basque sailors. Such an origin is not impossible, but is as yet unsupported by evidence. The grotesque notion that the word is short for *St. Gengulphus* is merely a joke of the author of the *Ingoldsby Legends*.]

A. *interj.* and *sb.*

I. †**1.** (Usually ***hey*** or ***high jingo!***) A conjuror's call for the appearance of something: the opposite of *hey presto!*, by which a thing is bidden to be gone. Hence, an exclamation of surprise at the appearance of something. *Obs.*

1670 EACHARD *Cont. Clergy* 34 He.. falls a flinging it out of one hand into the other, tossing it this way and that; lets it run a little upon the line, then *tanutus, high jingo, come again!* **1672** *Pasquil on Stair Family* in *Bk. Scot. Pasquils* (1868) 180 Jeingo! the taws. Presto, begon: a mace. **1679** OLDHAM *Sat. Jesuits* IV. (1685) 89 Where spiritual Jugglers their chief Mast'ry shew: Hey Jingo, Sirs! What's this? 'tis Bread you see; Presto be gone! 'tis now a Deity. **1707** FENTON *Fair Nun*, He.. turns it round and round, and eyes it, Heigh jingo, worse than 'twas before! **1722-30** RAMSAY *Fables, Monk & Miller's Wife*, [He] Cries, Rhadamanthus husky mingo, Monk, horner, hipock, jinko, jingo, Appear in likeness of a priest.

2. ***by jingo!*** a vigorous form of asseveration. Also intensified, ***by the living jingo!*** *colloq.* or *vulgar*.

1694 MOTTEUX *Rabelais* IV. lvi. 219 By jingo [Rab. *Par Dieu*], quoth Panurge, the Man talks somewhat like, I believe him. **1760** MURPHY *Way to Keep Him* I. ii, Their husbands care no more for them, no, by jingo, no more than they care for their husbands! **1766** GOLDSM. *Vic. W.* ix, One of them.. expressed her sentiments.. in a very coarse manner when she observed, that by the living jingo she was all of a muck of sweat. **1773** —— *Stoops to Conq.* v. ii, By jingo, there's not a pond or slough within five miles of the place, but they can tell the taste of. **1800** W. B. RHODES *Bomb. Fur.* I. (1830) 8 Does he, by jingo? **1837** MARRYAT *Dog-fiend* xxx, No, by the living jingo! not till he treats us. **1878** G. W. HUNT *Song* (Chorus), We don't want to fight, yet by Jingo! if we do, We've got the ships, we've got the men, and got the money too. **1888** J. PAYN *Myst. Mirbridge* xiii, That was a parting shot he took at you, by jingo!

II. [Derived from the expression 'by Jingo!' in the refrain of the music-hall song, quoted in sense 2, 1878, which became the Tyrtæan ode of the party ready to fight Russia in 1878.]

3. A nickname for those who supported and lauded the policy of Lord Beaconsfield in sending a British fleet into Turkish waters to resist the advance of Russia in 1878; hence, one who brags of his country's preparedness for fight, and generally advocates or favours a bellicose policy in dealing with foreign powers; a blustering or blatant 'patriot'; a Chauvinist.

1878 G. J. HOLYOAKE in *Daily News* 13 Mar. 3/4 The Jingoes in the Park. *Ibid.*, The Jingoes—the new tribe of music hall patriots who sing the jingo song. **1879** *Truth* 22 May, The Jingoes ought to rejoice and be glad that their 'tall talk' did not drive us into a war with Russia last year. **1880** GRANT DUFF in *19th Cent.* Apr. 667 Our interest in Russia is that the Muscovite Jingoes should learn a little more geography. **1881** *Gentl. Mag.* Jan. 46 The Jingo is the aggregation of the bully. An individual may be a bully; but, in order to create Jingoism, there must be a crowd. **1897** LD. SALISBURY in *Times* 19 Jan., A well-working arbitration system would be an invaluable bulwark to defend the Minister from the jingoes. **1898** *Times* 18 Jan. 6/1 (N.Y. Corresp.) A school of politicians.. who, like the jingoes, are apt to use the word American aggressively, as the jingoes do.

4. The jingo spirit or policy personified.

1898 L. STEPHEN *Stud. Biogr.* I. iii. 104 Nobody.. could be less given to the worship of Jingo.

B. *adj.*

†**1.** [from sense A. 2.] Exhibiting vulgar dash; suggestive of the man who asseverates *by jingo!*

1859 MILLAIS *Let.* 28 Apr. in *Life* (1899) I. 342 It is very good (well painted), but egregiously vulgar and commonplace, but there is enough in it of a certain 'jingo' style to make it a favourite.

2. [from sense A. 3.] Of or pertaining to the political jingo; characterized by jingoism.

1879 *Truth* 22 May, The consummation of the Jingo policy. **1879** *Scotsman* 1 Dec. 4 In the height of the Jingo fever in London, mobs, carefully organised, broke the windows of Mr. Gladstone's house. **1882** *Daily News* 19 July 5/5 He [M. Lockroy] is intensely Jingo, very hostile to M. de Freycinet. **1896** *Ibid.* 20 Jan. 7/6 Sentiment in Washington is overwhelmingly Jingo. **1900** E. C. BRODRICK *Mem. & Impr.* 198 The imperialism of the so-called 'Jingo' party, which seemed to measure national greatness by the constant annexation of new territories.

Hence **'jingo** *v. trans.*, to drive by the jingo spirit; **'jingodom**, the realm or domain of jingoes; **jingo'esque** *a.*, jingo in style or manner; **'jingoish** *a.* = JINGO B. 2.

1898 *Daily News* 28 Feb. 5/7 A member of the Cabinet stated in an interview to-day that President McKinley.. would not be jingoed into war. **1895** *Nation* (N.Y.) 19 Dec. 441/3 The resemblance of Jingodom in this to an Indian village is very remarkable. **1885** *Glasgow Herald* 3 Aug. 6/2 The continental press.. is essentially Jingoesque. **1892** GOLDW. SMITH in *19th Cent.* Sept. 348 There is nothing more jingoish in tone than were the speeches of Lord Palmerston and Lord Russell. **1896** *Nation* (N.Y.) 3 Dec. 421/3 Jingoish ideas of America's past and future.

jingoism ('dʒɪŋgəʊɪz(ə)m). [f. prec. A. 3 + -ISM.] The policy or practices of the jingoes.

1878 A. HAYWARD in *Corr.* (1886) II. 291 Another year must pass away before 'Jingoism' receives its death-blow. **1881** *Gentl. Mag.* Jan. 46 We call it Jingoism in England; in France it is called Chauvinism; and in the United States, Bunkum. **1882** LD. DERBY in *Standard* 5 Jan. 2/3 'Jingoism'.. of which I suppose the leading idea to be that no State can be in a healthy condition that is not occasionally pitching into its neighbour. **1885** *Pall Mall G.* 17 Jan. 1/1 The essential infamy of Jingoism was its assertion as the first law of its being that might was right. **1895** *Times* 1 Nov., The President.. puts himself on record against the empty bluster which is the note of jingoism.

So **'jingoist** = JINGO A. 3 (also *attrib.*); **jingo'istic** *a.*, given to or characteristic of jingoism; jingo in style or spirit.

1884 *Ch. Times* 28 Nov. 915/2 Of an amusingly Jingoist turn. **1890** *N. Lindsey Star* 31 May 5/4 Terrible jingoists when in opposition. **1885** *Spectator* 18 July, We are not all Jingoistic noodles in New Zealand. **1894** MAX O'RELL *Jn. Bull & Co.* 97 When the Englishman is in his cups, he grows conservative and jingoistic.

jingol, variant of GINGALL.

'jingo-'ring. *Sc.* Also jing-go-ring, jing-a-ring. [With the first element, cf. JINK *v.*[1]] A girls' game in which they join hands in a circle, and move to music round a central girl, singing the ditty of which the beginning is cited in quot. 1841.

1841 in R. Chambers *Pop. Rhymes Scot.* 268 'Here we go the jingo-ring, The jingo-ring, the jingo-ring, Here we go the jingo-ring, About the merry-ma-tanzie.' **1865** *Cornh. Mag.* Mar. 358 Little folk, that play at jing-a-ring. *a* **1872** W. MILLER *Hairst* in *Whistle-Binkie* II. 346 (Jam. Suppl.) An' han' in han' they jink about Like weans at jingo-ring.

jingsing, variant of GINSENG.

jink (dʒɪŋk), *sb.*[1] orig. *Sc.* [cf. JINK *v.*[1]]

1. a. The act of eluding; a quick turn so as to elude a pursuer or escape from a guard. Used esp. of a tricky turn in Rugby Football, or in Aeronautics. Also *transf.* and *fig.* ***to give the jink***, to give the slip by way of a trick.

1786 BURNS *Bard gone to W. Ind.* i, Our billie's gien us a' the jink An' owre the sea. **1818** SCOTT *Hrt. Midl.* xxx, Now, lass, if ye like, we'll play them a fine jink: we will awa out and take a walk; they will mak unco wark when they miss us, but we can easily be back by dinner time. **1889** R. S. S. BADEN-POWELL *Pigsticking* 125 In pursuit of a small wild boar.. She followed his every 'jink' or jump striving to get him under her forefeet. *a* **1914** J. E. RAPHAEL *Mod. Rugby Football* (1918) 122 [Poulton Palmer's] 'jink' is all by itself in modern-day Rugger. **1921** E. H. D. SEWELL *Rugby Football* vi. 126 The defender.. moves to *his* left as the dummy pass is made, thus making wider the gap which the attacker widens still further by his jink to the defender's right. **1943** HUNT & PRINGLE *Service Slang* 41 *Jinks*, quick turns in the air, a form of aerobatics and of avoiding action. **1959** V. FUCHS *Antarctic Adv.* xii. 168 Suddenly,.. below them, they spotted vehicle tracks in the snow. From the outward flight they remembered that except for one 'jink' these led in a straight line from South Ice—and the 'jink' was only about a quarter of a mile from the station. **1969** P. DICKINSON *Pride of Heroes* 164 A jink in his train of thought made Pibble wonder who the next heir was.

b. A 'turn' or 'point' in an argument.

1823 GALT *R. Gilhaize* I. xiv. 158 At this jink o' their controversy, who should come in.. but Winterton.

2. *Cards.* The winning of a game of spoil-five, twenty-five, or forty-five, by taking all the tricks in one hand.

1887 *Standard Hoyle* 225 Jinks, or, as it is sometimes called, Jink Game, is derived from Spoil-five. The game is won when all five tricks are taken. **1894** 'HOFFMANN' *Card & Table Games* (1898) 248 A player making all five tricks is said to make a 'jink', and wins the game, whether at twenty-five or forty-five.

3. high jinks: app. orig. high pranks.

†**a.** A name given to various frolics formerly indulged in at drinking parties. *Sc. Obs.*

They mostly consisted in deciding by the throw of dice who should perform some ludicrous task for the amusement of the company, or who should empty a large bowl of liquor, failure in either case entailing a forfeit. See Hone *Year-bk.* (1892) 566; also Ramsay's note to quot. 1711, and the full context of quot. 1815.

a **1700** B. E. *Dict. Cant. Crew*, *Highjinks*, a Play at Dice who Drinks. **1711** RAMSAY *Elegy Maggy Johnstoun* iv, Often in Maggy's, at hy-jinks We guzzled scuds, Till we could

scarce, wi' hale-out drinks, Cast off our duds. **1815** SCOTT *Guy M.* xxxvi, The revel had lasted since four o'clock, and, at length.. the frolicsome company had begun to practise the ancient and now forgotten pastime of *high jinks*. This game was played in several different ways. **1822–30** LD. COCKBURN *Mem.* 225 There were no *High Jinks*, or sprightly sayings, or songs; but a good deal of kindly personal banterings. **1837** LOCKHART *Scott* May an. 1795, The evening ended in the full jollity of *High Jinks*. **1890** MRS. OLIPHANT *Roy. Edinb.* IV. i. 409 He only learned to rhyme from the necessity of taking his part in the high jinks of the club.

b. Lively or boisterous sport; romping games or fun; free or unrestrained merry-making. (Also simply *jinks*.)

1842 BARHAM *Ingol. Leg., Bros. Birchington* xvii, High Jinks going on night and day at 'the court'. *a* **1845** HOOD *Forge* ii, Smiling with faces full of glee, As if about to enjoy High Jinks. **1851** DIXON *W. Penn* iii. (1872) 25 The Navy Gardens were a scene for romps and jinks. **1861** HUGHES *Tom Brown at Oxf.* i. (1889) 7 All sorts of high jinks go on on the grass plot. **1896** J. D. COLERIDGE *Eton in Forties* iv. 295 The high time for jinks was during the Windsor fair.

c. See quot.

1785 GROSE *Dict. Vulg. T.*, *High Jinks*, a gambler at dice, who, having a strong head, drinks to intoxicate his adversary, or pigeon [*ed.* 1823 adds: chaps always on the look out to rob unwary country men at cards, &c.].

d. *attrib.* in form *high-jink*.

1853 W. JERDAN *Autobiog.* IV. iii. 33 In the midst of these high-jink enjoyments, it must not be thought that the real business.. was quite neglected.

e. Hence **high-'jinking**.

1891 *Pall Mall Gaz.* 22 Oct. 2/1 On board we were very jovial and had much high jinking. **1904** *Daily Chron.* 13 July 8/1 It is evening—eight o'clock—and the festival is at its very top notch of high-jinking.

jink, *sb.*² *rare.* [var. of CHINK *sb.*³ Cf. JINK *v.*²] The sharp metallic sound of a coin, or the like, striking against a hard substance; *transf.* (*slang*) 'chink', coin.

c **1775** *Roxb. Ball.* (1890) VII. 85 No race we shall have I think, for C—s is come without his jink. **1898** WATTS-DUNTON *Aylwin* (1900) 126/1 'Quid seems to jink all right, anyhow',..'though I'm more used to the jink of a tanner than a quid'.

jink (dʒɪŋk), *v.*¹ orig. *Sc.* [app. onomatopœic, expressing the idea of nimble motion.]

1. a. *intr.* To move with quick sudden action; to move or dart with sudden turns; to move jerkily to and fro. In senses 1 and 2, now esp. in Rugby Football and Aeronautics; cf. JINK *sb.*¹ 1. *to jink in*, to make a sudden indirect or clandestine dart in. *to jink one's way*, to advance by means of jinks.

1785 BURNS *2nd Ep. to Davie* ii, Hale be your heart, hale be your fiddle; Lang may your elbock jink an' diddle. *a* **1810** TANNAHILL *Poems, Midges dance aboon the burn*, The merry wren, frae den to den, Gaes jinking through the thorn. **1816** SCOTT *Antiq.* xxv, My lord couldna tak it weel your coming blinking and jinking in, in that fashion. **1834** M. SCOTT *Cruise Midge* xxi, Jink out of the room, will ye, for I am very drowsy. **1932** *Daily Tel.* 19 Mar. 17/2, I can see him jinking his way past our mid-field players. **1942** E. WAUGH *Put out More Flags* iii. 243 If they come in now from the rear the cars may jink round and give the other companies a chance to get out. **1944** *R.A.F. Jrnl.* Aug. 288 The aircraft crossed in front of them, jinking steadily at high speed. **1961** R. JEFFRIES *Evidence of Accused* i. 14 A rabbit.. jinked away under the rhododendron bush.

b. To wheel or fling about in dancing; to dance.

1715 RAMSAY *Christ's Kirk Gr.* II. xxiv, Was n'er in Scotland heard or seen.. Sic dancing and sic jinkin'. **1804** TARRAS *Poems* 12 (Jam.) Then Tullie gart ilk carlie jink it, Till caps an' trenchers rair't and rinkit. **1894** CROCKETT *Raiders* 17 Here we were, jinking hand in hand under the trees in the moonlight.

2. *intr.* To make a quick elusive turn, so as to dodge a pursuer or escape from a guard.

1785 BURNS *Addr. to Deil* xx, But, faith! he'll turn a corner jinkin, An' cheat you yet. —— *Halloween* vi, But Rab slips out, an' jinks about, Behint the muckle thorn. **1827** *Blackw. Mag.* XXI. 650 He jinks under your elbow, and starts off. **1887** BLACK *In Far Lochaber* ii, Then ye jink round the corner and call it by another name. **1889** R. S. S. BADEN-POWELL *Pigsticking* 68 The boar.. will often make a feint of jinking to one side, and will dart off in exactly the opposite direction. *Ibid.*, When the boar.. sees the spear point being lowered in his direction he will 'jink', or suddenly turn sharply to the right or left. *a* **1914** J. E. RAPHAEL *Mod. Rugby Football* (1918) 103 This is a method which.. should not be copied by the ordinary performer—except perhaps when 'jinking'. **1927** WAKEFIELD & MARSHALL *Rugger* 93 A curious jinking side-step. **1940** *Aeroplane* 30 Aug. 235/2 One example of Air Ministry verbosity is the continual use of the phrase 'took evasive action', instead of saying 'dodged' or 'jinked'. **1942** *R.A.F. Jrnl.* 18 Apr. 3 You boost and you dive and you jink. **1959** V. FUCHS *Antarctic Adv.* xii. 169 The visibility was about a hundred yards, but where the tracks jinked sharply right, he closed the throttle. **1963** I. FLEMING *On H.M. Secret Service* xvii. 189 Bond.. put on all the speed he could, crouching low and jinking occasionally to spoil the man's aim. **1969** G. MACBETH *War Quartet* 35 Untailed, I jinked, Flipped over in a half-roll. **1973** *Times* 1 Jan. 17/2 Hales scored two tries, but I only saw the first of them, and a good one it was as he jinked inside his man.

3. *trans.* To elude or escape by dodging; to dodge. Cf. JOUK *v.*² 3.

a **1774** FERGUSSON *Hame Content* Poems (1788) II. 107 There the herds can jink the show'rs 'Mang thriving vines an' myrtle bow'rs. **1889** R. S. S. BADEN-POWELL *Pigsticking* 180 In such a way as to cause him to jink his pursuers.

4. To trick, cheat, diddle, swindle.

1785 R. FORBES *Poems Buchan Dial.*, *Ulysses Answ. Ajax* 15 For Jove did jink Arcesius. **1832** M. SCOTT in *Blackw. Mag.* XXXII. 22 The gipsy, after all, jinked an old rich goutified coffee-planter. **1885** RUNCIMAN *Skippers & Sh.* 146 When they find he means to jink them.

5. *intr.* (*Cards.*) To win a game of spoil-five or forty-five by taking all the tricks in one hand.

1887 *Standard Hoyle* 221 (*Spoil-five*), Sometimes spoils are dispensed with altogether, and the game is made a fixed number (either twenty-five or forty-five),.. at Twenty-five or Forty-five who wins all five tricks wins the game. This is called *jinking* it. Properly the jink belongs only to these games, but sometimes by agreement jinking is allowed at Spoil-five.

jink (dʒɪŋk), *v.*² [Cf. CHINK *v.*³] *trans.* and *intr.* To chink; to make, or cause to make, a short metallic sound. Hence **jinking** *vbl. sb.*

1828 *Craven Dial.*, *Jink*, to chink or jingle. **1848** *Fraser's Mag.* XXXVIII. 83 A dog barked, and jinked his chain upon the stones. **1888** AMÉLIE RIVES *Quick or Dead?* (1889) 20 An old spinet.. from which Miss Fridiswig used to coax forth ghastly jinkings (this spinet could not utter anything so liquid as a jingle). **1898** [see JINK *sb.*²].

jinker ('dʒɪŋkə(r)), *sb.*¹ Chiefly *Sc.* [f. JINK *v.*¹ + -ER¹.] One who or that which jinks; one who suddenly eludes or dodges; one who is nimble and sprightly; a dodging beast.

1724 RAMSAY *Tea-t. Misc.*, *Clout the Caldron* ii, I am a gentle jinker. **1786** BURNS *To auld mare* vii, That day ye was a jinker noble, For heels an' win'! —— *Ep. to Logan* x, Ochon for poor Castalian drinkers, When they fa' foul o' earthly jinkers. **1889** R. S. S. BADEN-POWELL *Pigsticking* 89 A pig, and particularly a 'jinker', is more quickly reached with it.

jinker ('dʒɪŋkə(r)), *sb.*² *Australia.* [Variant of JANKER.] A contrivance, used in the Australian bush, consisting of two pairs of wheels, having their axle-trees joined by a long beam, under which tree-trunks are suspended by chains. Also, in *Trotting*, a sulky.

1894 *Melbourne Argus* 7 July 8/4 (Morris) A rather novel spectacle was to be seen to-day on the Ballan road in the shape of a five-roomed cottage on jinkers. **1916** J. B. COOPER *Coo-oo-ee* i. 1 Often the wheels of the jinkers bogged in a soak on the track. **1941** BAKER *Dict. Austral. Slang* 39 *Jinker*, a trotting sulky. **1941** *Coast to Coast* 185 Then would come a decision, a harnessing of the old horse to the jinker and a trip to the township. **1966** 'J. HACKSTON' *Father clears Out* 15 We hated the horse that was tied to the man's jinker.

jinker, *v.* *Austral.* *trans.* To manipulate with a jinker (see JINKER²).

1903 R. BEDFORD *True Eyes & Whirlwind* 240 Waiting for a fine day to jinker those trees out of the bush.

jinket ('dʒɪŋkɪt), *v.* *colloq.* [dim. of JINK *v.*]

1. *intr.* To indulge in (high) jinks. (Or ? To junket.)

1742 FIELDING *J. Andrews* IV. xiii, Tom.. is just come from the George; where it seems Joseph and the rest of them are a jinketting.

2. ? To dance *about* or *round*. Also *fig.*

1823 SCOTT *St. Ronan's* ii, He has her aften jinketing about, and back and forward, wi' a' the fine flichtering fools that come yonder. **1894** *Superfluous Woman* (ed. 4) II. 170 Lassies weary in time of jinketing round.

'**jinkle**, *v.* *rare.* [dim. or freq. of JINK *v.*¹] *intr.* To move with sudden turns or swervings.

1852 R. S. SURTEES *Sponge's Sp. Tour* lx. (1893) 324 Our friend jinkled and jolted, and bumped and jumped in the.. style that characterizes country conveyances. **1899** *Contemp. Rev.* Dec. 800 It [a rabbit] diverts itself with queer sidelong cavorts, piaffes, jinklings and somersaults.

‖**jinn** (dʒɪn), *sb.* (prop. *pl.*) Also 7 **dgen**, 9 **ginn, dschin, djin, jin.** [a. Arab. *jinn*, collect. pl., demons, spirits, angels; sing. *jinnī* (see next).] In Muslim demonology, an order of spirits lower than the angels, said to have the power of appearing in human and animal forms, and to exercise supernatural influence over men. More commonly used as a *sing.* to denote one of this class.

a. (as *sing.*) **1684** *Tavernier's Trav.* II. 67 Some *Dgen* or evil spirit. **1822** BYRON *Juan* VI. xlviii, Giaours, and Ginns, and Gouls in hosts. **1838** TORRENS *Arab. Nts.* I. 16 Tale of the Merchant and the Jin [**1841** LANE I. 44 Story of the Merchant and the Jinnee]. *a* **1845** HOOD *Drop of Gin* i, Ghost and vampyre, demon and Jin! **1859** BEATON *Jews in East* I. ix. 317 The Dschins grew weary or refractory.

b. (as *pl.*) **1841** LANE *Arab. Nts.* I. Notes to Introd. 30 The species of Jinn is said to have been created some thousands of years before Adam. **1884** J. PAYNE *Tales fr. Arabic* I. 272 Arise, let us depart this place, for it is full of Jinn and Marids.

‖**jinnee** (dʒɪ'niː). Also fem. ji'nneeyeh. [a. Arab. *jinnī*, fem. *jinnīyeh*, demon or spirit. A more frequent spelling in English is *genie*: see GENIE 1 b.] The sing. of prec.

[**1713** tr. *Arab. Nts.* I. 14 It was one of those malignant Genies, that are Mortal Enemies to Mankind.] **1841** LANE *Arab. Nts.* I. Introd. 8 It was a Jinnee of gigantic stature, broad-fronted and bulky, bearing on his head a chest. *Ibid.* 54 As soon as my wife awoke, she shook herself, and became transformed into a Jinneeyeh. **1885** BURTON *Arab. Nts.* I. 27 O Jinni, thou Crown of the Kings of the Jann! **1900** F. ANSTEY *Brass Bottle* iv. 43 Seeing that, though a Jinneeyeh, she was of the believing Jinn. **1900** *Westm. Gaz.* 6 Nov. 2/2 The Jinnee turns his rooms into an Arabian Palace.

jinny ('dʒɪnɪ). A female proper name (also *Jeanie*), pet-form of *Jane*; used locally in transferred uses. (Cf. JENNY.)

1. *Mining.* A stationary engine used to let down or draw up trucks on an inclined plane; also = **jinny-road**, a self-acting inclined plane; = JIG 6 d.

1877 [see DIP *sb.* 5 b]. **1881** RAYMOND *Mining Gloss.*, *Jinny-road*, a gravity plane underground. **1888** *Sheffield Gloss.*, *Ginny*, an engine by means of which a load is let down an inclined plane. A term used in coal-mining. **1891** *Labour Commission Gloss.*, *Jinny*, a self-acting incline where the full tubs of coal pull the empty ones up.

2. A name given in Long Island, U.S., to a bird, *Strepsilas interpres*, the Turnstone.

1888 G. TRUMBULL *Names & Portr. Birds* 186 At Moriches, *Maggot-snipe*; at Amityville, *Jinny*.

‖**jinricksha, jinrikisha** (dʒɪn'rɪkʃə, -'rɪkɪʃə), *sb.* Also **-rickisha, -riksha,** (**jenny-, jinnyrickshaw**). [a. Japanese *jin-riki-sha* (*j* = (ʒ)), f. *jin* man + *riki* strength, power + *sha* vehicle.] A light two-wheeled hooded vehicle having springs and two shafts, drawn by one or more men. First used in Japan *c* 1870, but now common in other parts of the world; colloq. shortened to *rickshaw*.

1874 LADY HERBERT tr. *Hübner's Ramble* (1878) II. iv. 280 The Jinriksha only came into fashion a year or two ago. **1876** *Times* 18 Aug. (Stanf.), We take seven jin-rick-shas, each with two runners, to convey ourselves and baggage. **1880** MISS BIRD *Japan* I. 18 The *kuruma* or jin-ri-kisha consists of a light perambulator body, an adjustible hood of oiled paper, a velvet or cloth lining and cushion, a well for parcels under the seat, two high slim wheels, and a pair of shafts connected by a bar at the ends. **1895** C. ROPER *Zigzag Travels* II. 169 It is curious to remember that these jinrikishas are not really Japanese at all. They were invented by a missionary, W. Goble, about 1870.

Hence **jin'ricksha** *v.* *intr.*, to ride in a jinricksha.

1890 *Pall Mall G.* 5 Feb 3/1 Chumming with Chinamen, jinrickshaing with Japanese,.. palavering with Peruvians.

jinshang, jinsing, variants of GINSENG.

jintawan (dʒɪn'tɑːwən). [Malay.] A kind of caoutchouc derived from *Urceola elastica*, a woody climbing plant of the family Apocynaceæ; also, the plant itself.

1851 *Illustr. Catal. Gt. Exhib.* IV. 877/2 Raw caoutchouc from Assam, Singapore (*Urceola elastica*, the Jintawan of the Malays). **1853** URE *Dict. Arts* (ed. 4) I. 984 The said apparatus may be used also for purifying caoutchouc and jintawan. **1880** *Encycl. Brit.* XII. 817/1 Besides the orange.. we have the rambutan,.. the jintawan,.. and the jambosa.

jintee, obs. form of JAUNTY.

jinx (dʒɪŋks). orig. *U.S.* Also **ginks, jinks.** [app. f. JYNX 2.] A person or thing that brings bad luck or exercises evil influence; a hoodoo, a Jonah. Also *attrib.* and *Comb.*

1911 *Chicago Daily News* 19 Sept. 6/3 Dave Shean and 'Peaches' Graham.. have not escaped the jinx that has been following the champions. **1919** *Oxf. Mag.* 7 Mar., Will some one remove the jinx? On Friday, February 28, we lost to Oriel and Merton by 3 goals to nil. On Saturday, March 1, .. we lost to Queen's by 1-0. **1926** ANDERSON & STALLINGS *What Price Glory* III, in *Three American Plays* 88 This town is a jinx for me. **1927** A. MILLER *Colfax Bk.-Plate* xiv. 172, I thrust that jinx of a book back into the lowest left-hand drawer. **1931** *Collier's* 26 Sept. 57/3 They say he is a jinx to them and they cannot beat him in any manner, shape, or form. **1932** J. T. FARRELL *Young Lonigan* iv. 157 Young Corbett who was born with a horse shoe in his hands.. put a jinx on Terrible Terry. **1948** MENJOU & MUSSELMAN *It took Nine Tailors* 96 There has never been such a jinx picture as that one. **1955** E. POUND *Classic Anthol.* III. 179 Jinx on the remnants everywhere. **1958** *Times Lit. Suppl.* 24 Jan. 41/4 The family jinx, in this case dark strangers who erupt into the bourgeois marriages of three generations, leaving behind an illegitimate child and the torturing memory of a bliss that might have been. **1962** *Times* 19 Feb. 3/7 A jinx-ridden Thomas somehow contrived to miss the kick. **1969** *Daily Colonist* (Victoria, B.C.) 30 Nov. 8/4 A man and two boys went fishing Friday, and Mary went along. The boat capsized, and apparently she alone survived. 'I'm either a jinx, or very lucky,' she says. **1972** 'E. LATHEN' *Murder without Icing* (1973) xxiii. 198 I'm beginning to think that damned team is a jinx... It's been a bad-luck team from the beginning.

So **jinx** *v.* *trans.* (freq. *pass.*) to cast a spell on, to bring bad luck upon; **jinxed** *ppl. a.*

[**1912** C. MATHEWSON *Pitching in a Pinch* xi. 244 He outjinxed our champion jinx killer.] **1917** *Amer. Mag.* Apr. 43/1 What do you mean—humming love songs when their darn pitcher is forcing in runs? You jinxed my ball club. **1934** J. T. FARRELL *Young Manhood* iv. 61, I know they ain't loaded. But use these ones. Them damn things is jinxed! **1946** E. O'NEILL *Iceman Cometh* (1947) III. 147 I's an ole gamblin' man and I knows bad luck when I feels it!.. But it's white man's bad luck. He can't jinx me! **1956** D. BARNHAM *One Man's Window* 26 He told me he was 'jinxed'. He explained that on his last three trips [in a fighter aircraft] he had been in trouble. **1962** K. ORVIS *Damned & Destroyed* xi. 73 I'm jinxed. No fix. All blew up. **1972** G. DURRELL *Catch me a Colobus* vii. 152 I'm damned if I'm going to take up all my animals and myself and my wife in a jinxed plane. No, I'm afraid I'll have to get another charter flight.

jip. ? = GIP, GIPSY; cunning rogue.

1728 RAMSAY *Twa Cut-purses* 29 The jip wha stood aboon them a' His innocence began to shaw.

jip, obs. form of GYP *sb.*

jipijapa ('hiːpɪ'hɑːpə). Also jipi-japa, jippa-jappa, jippi-jappa. [Name of a town in Ecuador.] a. The palm-like tree, *Carludovica palmata*, native to tropical America, or the fibre produced from its leaves. b. A Panama hat. Also *attrib.*

1858 P. L. SIMMONDS *Dict. Trade Products* 273/2 (s.v. *Panama-hats*), In Central America where they are made, the palm is called Jipijapa. **1877** *Encycl. Brit.* VI. 155/1 Straw hats, usually known as jipijapa or Panamá hats. **1901** *Amer. Anthropologist* III. 206 Ecuador is the real home of the hats wrongly designated under the name of 'panama'... Everywhere in Latin America the hat is known under the name of *jipijapa*, in honor of the city where its manufacture was first started. **1901** *Daily Chron.* 7 Feb. 4/6 The Jippi-Jappa plant, known sometimes as 'the broom thatch'. **1953** V. BELL in *Caribbean Anthol. Short Stories* 72 He could almost see her there in her usual seat at the back of the church in her white linen dress and her jippi-jappa hat. **1961** F. G. CASSIDY *Jamaica Talk* vi. 115 The best known Jamaica-made hat is the *jipi-japa*..from the name of the town..in Ecuador. **1965** I. FLEMING *Man with Golden Gun* iv. 51 There were only two other passengers..Cubans, perhaps, with jippa-jappa luggage. **1972** D. SALE *Love Bite* iv. 52 Shops crammed with liqueur, tweeds, English doeskin, jippa-jappa straw goods.

jipper ('dʒɪpə(r)). *dial.* Also gipper. Gravy; dripping; stew. So as *v. trans.*, to baste.

1822 SCOTT *Fortunes of Nigel* III. vi. 176 This man Gregory is not fit to jipper a joint with him. **1886** W. H. LONG *Dict. Isle of Wight Dial.* 31 Thee'st lat all the jipper out of the pudden. **1896** FARMER & HENLEY *Slang* IV. 59/2 *Jipper* (nautical), gravy. **1900** *N. & Q.* 9th Ser. V. 295 The *chef de cuisine* was an old navy pensioner, and his instructions were: 'Mind you jipper them [*sc.* thrushes] well.' From him I learned to call gravy 'jipper', and bread and dripping 'bread-and-jipper'. **1904** *Daily Chron.* 12 Aug. 3/7 The mysteries of Irish stew, or 'gipper', as it is mysteriously termed in camp. **1909** H. G. WELLS *Tono-Bungay* II. iii. 195 They [*sc.* shavings] might be anything. Soak 'em in jipper,—Xylo-tobacco!

jipper, dial. or corrupt form of JEOPARD *v.*

jippo. = GIPPO².

1929 *Papers Mich. Acad. Sci., Arts & Lett.* X. 303 *Jippo*, fat. **1931** W. V. TILSLEY *Other Ranks* 119 Every morning, a good thick slice of bread and toasted cheese or bacon. Plenty of jippo (if you were pally with the orderly man). **1937** D. JONES *In Parenthesis* v. 118 He's with his longe ladel To test the jippo.

jippo, variant of GIPPO¹, tunic. *Obs.*

jirble ('dʒɜːb(ə)l), *v.* Chiefly *Sc.* [Imitative of the characteristic sound.] *intr.* and *trans.* To spill (a liquid) by shaking or unsteady moving of the vessel; to pour out unsteadily; hence, to pour (liquid) from vessel to vessel.

1760 *City Cleaned & Country Improven* 9 Two men-scavengers with the sting and say can carry more water conveniently than ten single persons can do with an open jirbling tub between their hands. **1819** W. TENNANT *Papistry Storm'd* (1827) 164 Frae the bottle o' his pride He jirbles out a dram. **1824** SCOTT *St. Ronan's* x, It's the jinketing and the jirbling wi' tea and wi' trumpery that brings our nobles to ninepence.

jirga ('dʒɪəgə). Also jeerga, jirgah. [Pushtu.] An assembly or council of the headmen of Pathan or Baluchi tribes.

1843 F. SALE *Jrnl. Disasters Afghanistan* p. xii, *Jeerga.* An assembly or council—a diet. **1894** M. DYAN *All in Man's Keeping* I. iv. 75 All large issues had to be referred to his Jeerga. **1906** *Westm. Gaz.* 14 May 3/2 They can..mobilise as easily as a Pathan jirga. **1908** *Ibid.* 24 Feb. 7/1 Afridis other than Zakka Khels are collecting at Chora for a jirgah. **1926** *Chambers's Jrnl.* Apr. 293/2 He eyed the elders of Pir Mahommed, assembled in *jirga.* **1935** *Pathfinder* July 125/1 The 'jirga', that is the council of the headmen of each tribe, would meet us at each new boundary..to..see if they would let us pass or not. **1967** A. SWINSON *N.-W. Frontier* xv. 326 This triumph seemed to expend the tribesmen's energy and soon the jirgas came in to sue for peace. **1972** *Times of India* 28 Nov. 11/5 The paper quoted Mr. Bhutto as telling a tribal jirga at Landikotal..that unfortunately Pakistan did not accept this offer.

jirk, jis, obs. forms of JERK, GIS.

jism (dʒɪz(ə)m). *slang* (orig. *U.S.*). Also chism, gism, jizz, etc. [Origin unknown.] a. Energy, strength. b. Semen, sperm.

In sense b often regarded as a taboo-word.

1842 *Spirit of Times* 29 Oct. 409/3 At the drawgate Spicer tried it on again, but his horse was knocked up—'the gism' and the starch was effectively taken out of him by the long and desperate struggles he had been obliged to maintain. **1899** B. W. GREEN *Word-bk. Virginia Folk-Speech* 85 Chism, chissum, seminal fluid. **1937** J. WEIDMAN *I can get it for you Wholesale!* xxxii. 314 'Step on it, will you?' 'Sure...' 'All right,..but put a little jism into it, will you?' **1942** C. MORLEY *Thorofare* (1943) xxxvii. 137 One of the same fields that the Major said had had the jizzum leached out of it by tobacco. **1955** T. STERLING *Evil of Day* vii. 76 The man had more jisum than he'd counted on. **1959** W. BURROUGHS *Naked Lunch* 90 The Moslems must have blood and jissom. .. See, see where Christ's blood streams in the spermament. **1967** S. BECKETT *Stories & Texts for Nothing* 85 A week will be ample, a week in spring, that puts the jizz in you. **1968** J. UPDIKE *Couples* iv. 311 Georgene would wash herself before and after. Said his jizz ran down her leg, too much of it. **1969**

P. ROTH *Portnoy's Complaint* 132 You've got to..work round downtown Newark dripping gissum down your forehead. **1972** *Screw* 12 June 35/3 At last I felt my gism rushing up like electricity and I..felt the love bolt burst out of my cock into her vacuum-sucking mouth.

jist (dʒɪst), colloq. and dial. var. JUST *adv.* Cf. JEST.

c **1820** in *Amer. Speech* (1941) XVI. 157/1 *Jist*, just. **1835** A. B. LONGSTREET *Georgia Scenes* 29 His eyes don't look like it; but he *jist as live go agin* the house with you, or in a ditch, as anyhow. **1839** [see LOP *v.²* 2 b]. **1848** TROLLOPE *Kellys & O'Kellys* II. iii. 69 You must do more than jist ask her. **1931** D. L. SAYERS *Five Red Herrings* xxv. 283 'I was jist thinkin', then,' said Duncan, '..whether it was not, after all, possible.' **1941** *Sat. Even. Post* 10 May 36/2 Jist taste a grain o' patience. *Ibid.* 112/3, I jist saw a quare thing.

jist, variant of GIST *v.* and *sb.²*

1828 *Craven Dial., Jist*, cattle taken to depasture at a stipulated price, from agist. *Jist*, to take cattle to grass.

jit¹ (dʒɪt), abbrev. JITNEY 1.

1913 *Awgwan* (Univ. of Nebraska) 3 June 10 We went to the second jit show. **1915** G. BRONSON-HOWARD *God's Man* IV. iv. 264 Keeping tab on you and knowing how much you snatch to the last jit. **1926** J. BLACK *You can't Win* xx. 318 A 'jit', as the Southern negro affectionately calls his nickel. **1931** J. T. FARRELL in *New Rev.* (Paris) I. 24 Say Vinc lemme take a nickel will yuh?.. You'll lemme take a jit won'tcha?.. I'll give yuh the jitney back with a nickel interest. **1946** B. TREADWELL *Big Bk. of Swing* 124/2 Jit, five-cent piece.

jit² (dʒɪt). *U.S. slang. depreciatory.* [Origin unknown.] A Black person, a Negro.

1931 G. IRWIN *Amer. Tramp & Underworld Slang* 110 *Jit.* .. A negro, or, more usually, a negress, and seemingly a term of derision. **1936** MENCKEN *Amer. Lang.* (ed. 4) 296 For Negro..jit. **1942** BERREY & VAN DEN BARK *Amer. Thes. Slang* §385/14 *Negro*, jit.

jitney ('dʒɪtnɪ). *N. Amer.* [Origin unknown.] 1. A five-cent piece, a nickel. *slang.*

1903 *Cincinnati Enquirer* 2 May 11/5 [In St. Louis] a 'crown guy' is a policeman, a 'gitney' is a nickel, and 'mug's landing' is the Union Station. **1915** *Nation* (N.Y.) 4 Feb. 142/1 The word 'jitney'..is the Jewish slang term for a nickel. **1916** *Chambers's Jrnl.* June 400/1 Five cents..is the charge for any distance, and as the colloquial name for this coin is a 'jitney', this form of traffic has become known as 'jitney competition'. **1931** 'D. STIFF' *Milk & Honey Route* 177 Beer or wine at a jitney a throw. **1947** W. SAROYAN *Jim Dandy* I. i. 11 Call that money? A jitney? A nickel?

2. In full *jitney bus, omnibus.* An omnibus or other motor vehicle which carries passengers for a fare, orig. five cents. So, on account of the low fare or the poor quality of these buses, used *attrib.* to denote anything cheap, improvised, or ramshackle.

1914 *Let.* 28 Nov. in *Nation* (N.Y.) (1915) 14 Jan. 50/3 This autumn automobiles, mostly of the Ford variety, have begun in competition with the street cars in this city [*sc.* Los Angeles]. The newspapers call them 'Jitney 'buses. **1915** *N.Y. Even. Post* 16 Apr., The jitney wears out the streets and should contribute to their repair. **1916** *Daily Colonist* (Victoria, B.C.) 6 July 4/5 The daily jitney service between Nanaimo and South Wellington has been discontinued. Hereafter cars will run on Saturdays only and the fare has been raised from 25 cents to 50 cents. **1916** H. L. WILSON *Somewhere in Red Gap* ii. 59 He..sells these jitney pianos and phonographs and truck like that. **1917** E. FROST *Lett.* (1972) 13, I hired McGrath, the jitney driver, to bring us home. **1919** M. A. VON ARNIM *Christopher & Columbus* xxxi. 400 He had come in the jitney omnibus to the nearest point. **1920** [see DAIQUIRI]. **1921** *Daily Colonist* (Victoria, B.C.) 25 Mar. 2/4 The decision of the Provincial Legislature to prohibit the sale of near beer will affect 58 jitney bars in this city, according to City Licence Inspector Charles Jones. **1923** F. PARSONS *Everybody's Business* 215 Railroads can solve the problem..in the jitney. **1925** *Amer. Speech* I. 152/1 That bastard word 'jitney' is still used in outlying places, where a 'jitney dance' means a nickel dance. **1933** *N.Y. Herald Tribune* 5 Dec. 17/3 We refer to the jitney economists, the boys who play the money tunes only by ear. **1946** E. O'NEILL *Iceman Cometh* (1947) I. 36 He never worries in hard times because there's always old friends from the days when he was a jitney Tammany politician. **1947** E. A. McCOURT *Music at Close* 108 He would go to the jitney dance held in the big open space behind the town hall unless an outdoor floor had been set up. **1967-8** *Bahamas Handbk. & Businessmen's Ann.* (ed. 7) 197 There are jitneys on New Providence..which travel over unscheduled and not necessarily prescribed routes picking up and dropping off passengers. **1973** *Philadelphia Inquirer* (Today Suppl.) 7 Oct. 8/2 From the museum a jitney carries visitors to the Mills.

jito ('dʒiːtəʊ). Also gito. [Jap.] In the Japanese feudal system: a military land steward (see also quot. 1974).

1845 *Encycl. Metrop.* XX. 472/2 A military commander.. appoints the *gitos*, or revenue officers,..who are stationed in every township to levy the portion of the produce claimed by the Crown. **1902** L. HEARN *Kottō* viii. 65 The Jitō of the district, with a hunting party. **1974** *Encycl. Brit. Macropædia* X. 64/2 In 1185..Yoritomo appointed military governors (*shugo*) in all the provinces and military stewards (*jitō*) in both public and private landed estates... The *jitō* collected taxes, supervised the management of landed estates, and maintained public order.

jitter ('dʒɪtə(r)), *sb. colloq.* [Origin unknown.] 1. *pl.* (usu. *the jitters*). Extreme nervousness, nervous incapacity; a state of emotional and (often) physical tension; agitation.

1929 P. STURGES *Strictly Dishonorable* II. 123 *Isabelle.* Willie's case of the jitters—. *Judge.* Jitters? *Isabelle.* You know,

he makes faces all the time. **1930** *N.Y. Press* 2 Apr. 6/4 The game is played only after the mugs and wenches have taken on too much gin and they arrive at the state of jitters, a disease known among the common herd as heebie jeebies. **1931** *Charlottesville* (Virginia) *Progress* 23 Mar. 12/8 Swift moving elevators and roller coasters also give her the jitters. **1931** *Harper's Mag.* Mar. 420/2 How much of a price did we pay next day for a very good party? How many kinds of 'jitters'? I know my hostess called me up to say she had the jitters and her husband an awful hangover. **1932** E. WILSON (*title*) The American jitters. **1933** *Passing Show* 15 July 14/1 Oh Heck, tell some photographer that The very sight of a camera nowadays gives me the jitters. **1934** *Redbook Mag.* June 38/2 You begin to have the 'jitters'. Your placid disposition has given way to irritability, sarcasm and dissatisfaction. **1936** 'P. QUENTIN' *Puzzle for Fools* vi. 44 My old jitters had returned and I had started to shake. **1937** *Daily Herald* 12 Jan. 15/5 All this chatter about royal play has been to give players..the jitters. **1939** F. M. FORD *Let.* 23 May (1965) 324 All the publishers here have the jitters so badly that they won't look at anything new at all. **1945** *Univ. of Colorado Stud.* Ser. B. II. iv. 42 The cures of General Semantics are not limited, fortunately, to those suffering from platform jitters. **1957** *Economist* 7 Sept. 759/1 The recession jitters now afflicting significant numbers of economists..seem to be better founded on economic evidence than did the others. **1971** B. W. ALDISS *Soldier Erect* 229 The signal came, the machine-gun fire stopped... Geordie was next to me, not showing a sign of his earlier jitters.

b. **jitter party** *Mil. slang* (see quot. 1948).

1948 PARTRIDGE *Dict. Forces' Slang 1939–45* 102 *Jitter party*, a party of Japanese sneaking around the perimeter of a camp and trying to cause panic with strange noises and grenades. **1956** W. SLIM *Defeat into Victory* xviii. 430 Only a few jitter parties prowled about the perimeter. **1962** *Times* 16 Oct. 14/6 Still less was anyone to return the unaimed small-arms fire so often indulged in after nightfall by Japanese 'jitter-parties'.

2. Chiefly *Electronics.* Random or irregular variation in the shape or timing of a regularly repeated pulse; the resulting unsteadiness of an image in a cathode-ray tube. Also in *Cinemat.*, jerkiness of the picture.

1943 *Electronic Engin.* XVI. 55/2 Absence of 'jitter' or hum derived from fluctuations of the H.T. supply potential. **1954** *Ibid.* XXVI. 37/2 V_6..failed to fire properly..and caused considerable 'jitter' in the output pulse length. **1959** HALAS & MANWELL *Technique Film Animation* xix. 231 The main danger of rostrum tracks and pans is strobing, or jitter. *Ibid.* 339 *Jitter*, uncontrolled movement on the screen caused by faulty animation, tracing or camera work. **1960** J. D. HAIGH *Radiolocation Techniques* v. 76 If the displayed picture is to be..free from 'jitter' echoes must appear in exactly the same position at each recurrence of the time-base. **1966** *Jrnl. Acoustical Soc. Amer.* XXXIX. 920 The principal experimental parameters are the mean interval between pulses and root-mean-square deviation or jitter about this interval. **1966** R. J. ROSS *Television Film Engin.* i. 5 Very slight errors in registration cause vertical or horizontal unsteadiness in screen presentations, commonly known as jitter or weave.

So **'jitteriness; 'jittery** *a.*, nervy, jumpy, upset, 'on edge'; also *transf.*

1931 H. CRANE *Let.* 1 May (1965) 369 I'm too jittery to write a straight sentence. **1936** 'P. QUENTIN' *Puzzle for Fools* iv. 26 A slight return of jitteriness. **1937** *Daily Mirror* 27 Feb. 10/4 Stop being so jittery. What if we have missed the bus? There will be another later. **1941** *Penguin New Writing* X. 23 Jittery light sprang on the screen. **1946** *Mind* LV. 137 There is the effect of their [*sc.* the Wittgensteinians'] therapy upon practical philosophers. Under its attack, the latter tend, in general, to become 'jittery' and to retreat into worried silence. **1950** H. E. BATES *Scarlet Sword* ii. 17 An atmosphere of tense and growing jitteriness. **1957** *Listener* 12 Dec. 968/2 An impression of weakness and jitteriness. **1963** A. ROSS *Australia 63* viii. 153 Barrington made 33, in his more jittery manner, before flicking at an outswinger and being caught at slip. **1970** B. W. ALDISS *Moment of Eclipse* 47 Nobody gets jittery down there? **1972** *Jrnl. Social Psychol.* LXXXVIII. 279 Clutched-up, jittery, stirred-up, fearful.

jitter ('dʒɪtə(r)), *v. colloq.* [Origin unknown.] 1. *intr.* To move in an agitated manner; to exhibit alarm, to act in a nervous way, to get the 'jitters'.

1931 A. M. MACKENZIE *Cypress in Moonlight* IV. iv. 226 Her lace cap jittered tremulously till her earrings rattled. **1932** *Brevities* (N.Y.) 5 Dec. 16 (*heading*) Jittering junkies sniff sexy joy flakes. **1936** M. ALLINGHAM *Flowers for Judge* xxi. 301 You've been jittering around the Continent like an agitated tourist. **1938** *N. & Q.* 5 Mar. 172/1 My daily paper this morning points out that the total of the workless is higher, and adds, 'But don't jitter!' **1959** 'P. QUENTIN' *Shadow of Guilt* vii. 67 My thoughts jittered around Chuck. **1960** 'S. HARVESTER' *Chinese Hammer* vi. 64 There was a funny atmosphere about him. He jittered. **1966** *Electronics* 17 Oct. 109 If the error signal during the measurement period is too low, the antenna may jitter. **1970** *New Yorker* 28 Feb. 73/1 He sat there quietly, taking part in the dinner, but I knew that under the table his leg was jittering wildly.

2. *trans.* To propel by nervous energy; to fluster.

1932 E. HEMINGWAY *Death in Afternoon* ii. 18 His effort to be statuesque while his feet jittered him away out of danger was very funny to the crowd. **1951** C. SIMAK *Time & Again* (1956) xvi. 78 He knew that I would catch and he thinks he can jitter me.

3. *trans.* To subject (a series of pulses, or some characteristic of it) to rapid variation. So **'jittered** *ppl. a.*

1960 J. D. HAIGH *Radiolocation Techniques* xvii. 251 In order that an aircraft might be able to identify the responses to its own transmissions its pulse recurrence frequency was 'jittered' automatically. **1966** *Jrnl. Acoustical Soc. Amer.* XXXIX. 920/2 Jittering the interval between pulses might

also eliminate perceptual differences. *Ibid.* 922/1 Assumptions of ideal distributions were used to obtain power-density spectra of jittered pulse-train signals.

jitterbug ('dʒɪtəbʌg), *sb.* orig. *U.S.* Also jitter bug, jitter-bug. [f. JITTER *v.* + BUG *sb.*² 3 a.]

1. A jittery or nervous person; an alarmist; an attack of the jitters. Also as *adj.*

1934 C. CALLOWAY et al. (*song title*) Jitter bug. **1934** —— in *Song Hits Mag.* (1939) Nov. 19 They're four little jitter bugs. He has the jitters ev'ry morn, That's why jitter sauce was born. **1939** *Times* 30 Jan. 13/5 It [*sc.* the Government] is the only body capable of giving the information which would largely dispel the apprehensions of the 'Jitter-bugs', who, though perhaps few in number, are vocal and often influential. **1941** N. MARSH *Death & Dancing Footman* (1942) iv. 65 One man will keep his head in a crisis where another will go jitter-bug. *Ibid.* 76 Nick had a jitter-bug and wanted to make off. **1944** [see *bomb-happiness*]. **1966** E. H. JONES *Margery Fry* xiv. 193 Sir Samuel Hoare denounced the 'jitterbugs' who feared war... Five days after..German troops moved unresisted into Czechoslovakia.

2. A jazz musician; a devotee of jazz; a person who dances the jitterbug.

1937 *Down Beat* Feb. 9/4 (*heading*) 'Jives of the jitter-bugs.' High and low-down on the swing men. **1938** *Manch. Guardian Weekly* 2 Sept. 188/3 A 'jitterbug' is a person keen on swing. **1939** *Times* 27 Jan. 7/5, I am told that in the U.S.A. there is a class of people who sit listening in hysterical excitement to what is called 'hot-music' and waiting for the final crash. Americans in their forcible language call them the 'Jitter-bugs'. There are many people in Europe to-day who seem to be behaving in much the same way. **1942** *Dancing Times* May 411/2 Equally pleasing to Jitterbugs and some rhythm dancers will be 'Russian Salad'. **1951** E. PAUL *Springtime in Paris* xii. 218 On the corner, the Nest of Vipers nightly harboured jitterbugs and Lindy hoppers whose antics shamed the praying mantis.

3. A dance, popular esp. in the early 1940s, performed chiefly to boogie-woogie and swing music, and consisting of a few standardized steps augmented by much improvisation.

1939 R. CHANDLER in *Sat. Even. Post* 14 Oct. 11/1 This jitterbug music gives me the backdrop of a beer flat. I like something with roses in it. **1943** *Dancing Times* Sept. 560/1 The wildest Jitterbug yet is danced by Dorothy Lamour. **1969** N. COHN *A Wop Bopa Loo Bop* (1970) ix. 81 With old favourites like the jitterbug and the jive..the girls spun like tops and everyone got fast flashes of knicker. **1971** *Daily Tel.* 1 Nov. 9/1 To pop music..she performed movements reminiscent of the jitterbug of a generation ago.

'jitterbug, *v.* orig. *U.S.* [See prec., sense 3.] *intr.* To dance to jitterbug.

1939 *Amer. Mag.* Sept. 160 Susy Shag..begins thinking seriously of marrying the guy she's been jitterbugging with. **1949** N. MARSH *Swing, Brother, Swing* v. 77 D'you jitter-bug? **1951** J. D. SALINGER *Catcher in Rye* x. 80 The band was starting a fast one. She started jitterbugging with me. **1955** C. FOX in *Jazzbook 1955* 4 They jitter-bugged down the aisles to the exhilarating music, horrifying their parents and bringing worried frowns to the faces of the jazz purists of those days. **1972** *Jazz & Blues* Nov. 5/1 They jitterbugged to 'One O'Clock Jump' and stomped their feet to 'Maple Leaf Rag'. **1973** *Washington Post* 5 Apr. B.2 The happiest part..is a salute to the big bands of the '40s, with Miss Adams in a snood and Candoli jitterbugging in a zoot suit.

Hence **'jitterbugging** *vbl. sb.* and *ppl. a.*

1938 *Call-Bulletin* (San Francisco) 8 Dec. 17/1 'Jitter-bugging is just a phase,' he said... 'It isn't music. This town wants real music and nothing else will do.' **1939** *San Francisco Examiner* 17 Sept. 2/2, I love ballroom dancing and I usually do just that, but at times I find it a job to express my joy of living by doing a little jitter-bugging. **1940** GRAVES & HODGE *Long Week-End* xxii. 390 Jitterbugging had then [1939] just come over from the United States..an ecstatic mode of dancing to fast swing music in which the two partners could perform absolutely any..acrobatic feat they liked. **1942** A. P. JEPHCOTT *Girls growing Up* iii. 63 The slick, apparently assured, smoking, jitterbugging town girl of sixteen still regards friendliness as the all-important feature of any group with which she intends to associate. **1952** M. MCCARTHY *Groves of Academe* (1953) ii. 20 He did not dance, but..vigorously nodded with approval when a jitter-bugging pair desisted. **1973** G. DURRELL *Beasts in my Belfry* v. 105 The only folk dances I have ever witnessed were danced by elderly, aesthetic ladies with fringes and strings of beads and they were nothing like the gnus' wild jitterbugging.

jiu-jitsu, -jutsu, varr. JU-JITSU *sb.*

jiva ('dʒiːvə). *Hindu* and *Jain Philos.* [Skr. *jīvá* living being, life, and highest personal principle of life.] Life, the soul, the self; the vital principle.

1807 *Asiatick Researches* IX. 290 The *Jainas* conceive the soul (*Jíva*) to have been eternally united to a very subtil material body. **1885** E. BALFOUR *Cycl. India* (ed. 3) II. 442/2 *Jiva.* Sansk. Life, the soul. **1887** W. J. WILKINS *Mod. Hinduism* viii. 101 All beings possessed of jiva are of two kinds: those who can move and those who cannot. **1915** A. M. STEVENSON *Heart of Jainism* 176 As long as the jiva or ātmā is fettered by karma, so long must it undergo rebirth, and it must be remembered that karma is acquired through good as well as through evil actions. **1951** H. ZIMMER *Philosophies of India* III. i. 229 Jainism regards the life-monad (*jiva*) as pervading the whole organism; the body constitutes, as it were, its garb; the life-monad is the body's animating principle. *Ibid.* 277 Some vegetables, such as trees, are provided with a collectivity of jīvas. **1971** *Times Weekender* (Ceylon) 3 Oct. 4/3 As the macrocosmic reality it is called Braman and its manifestation through human beings is the microcosmic reality known as the atman or soul or jiva.

Jivaro ('hiːvərəʊ). [ad. Sp. *jíbaro*, f. a native name.] An Indian people of Ecuador and Peru; a member of this people; also, the language of this people or a group of related languages of which this is the principal. Also *attrib.* or as *adj.* So **'Jivaran, Jiva'roan** *adjs.*

1862 *Intellectual Observer* Mar. 134 On the eastern side of the Republic of Ecuador..live a tribe of Indians called Jivaros. *Ibid.* 135 It is in the forests among these rivers that the Jívaro Indians now make their homes. **1902** *Encycl. Brit.* XXV. 374/1 The families of..South America are.. Jivaroan, [etc.]. **1927** K. G. GRUBB *Lowland Indians of Amazonia* v. 77 The Jivaro live in communal houses divided into numerous sub-tribes. *Ibid.*, The Jivaro language has been attested by a variety of documents. **1934** WEBSTER, Jivaran. **1957** *Encycl. Brit.* VII. 941/1 The Cayapa-Colorados and the Jivaro [languages] still survive owing to their existence in inaccessible regions. *Ibid.* XIII. 69/2 *Jivaran*, an independent linguistic stock of South American Indians, so called from the best known tribe, the Jivaros. The Jivaran tribes live in eastern Ecuador and the adjacent portions of Peru. **1962** N. MAXWELL *Witch-Doctor's Apprentice* i. 3 That was my first long jungle trip and I was lucky enough to get to a tribe of Jívaros who had never seen a white woman before. **1969** *Times* 24 Jan. 6/7 Jivaro give the seeds to refractory children so that during their visions the ancestral spirits may come to admonish them.

jive (dʒaɪv), *sb. slang* (orig. *U.S.*). [Origin unknown.] **1.** Talk or conversation; *spec.* talk that is misleading, untrue, empty, or pretentious; hence, anything false, worthless, or unpleasant; vaguely, 'stuff'; = JAZZ *sb.* 3 a.

1928 R. FISHER *Walls of Jericho* 301 *Jive*, pursuit in love or any device thereof. Usually flattery with intent to win. **1929** T. GORDON *Born to Be* 236 *Jive*, a misleading remark. **1932** MUSE & ARLEN *Way down South* 50 Thus the enamoured customer completed his meal, without ever having taken his eyes off that tantalizing brown, with her suave Birmingham jive. **1935** *Swing Music* Autumn 55/2 Maybe you think that that is all jive. You are wrong if you do. It is the way I felt about these new records. **1946** MEZZROW & WOLFE *Really Blues* iii. 37, I used to hear a lot of medical jive. *Ibid.* 375 *Jive* n., confusing doubletalk, pretentious conversation, anything false or phony. *Jive that makes it drip*, clouds that produce rain. **1954** L. ARMSTRONG *Satchmo* x. 150 There was lots of just plain common shooting and cutting. But..that jive didn't faze me at all. *Ibid.* xii. 193, I bought a lot of cheap jive at the five and ten cents store to give to the kids. **1956** M. STEARNS *Story of Jazz* (1957) v. 50 The attitude of several modern jazzmen, born and bred in the South, is striking: 'This hoodoo jive is nowhere,' they say, 'but man, watch out!' **1960** in P. Oliver *Blues fell this Morning* vii. 197 I'm evil and mean and funny, so don't come back with that line of jive. **1972** M. J. BOSSE *Incident at Naha* iii. 152 Maybe some of his Christian sentiments sound corny today, but..he had cut through a lot of the jive of his own time, and he had, like, the balls to fight injustice. **1973** *Black World* Oct. 36/2 Everything that we do must be aimed toward the total liberation, unification and empowerment of Afrika... Anything short of that is jive.

2. Jazz, esp. a type of fast, lively jazz; 'swing'.

1928 (*title of gramophone record by Cow Cow Davenport*) State Street Jive. **1937** *New Yorker* 17 Apr. 31/3 The music of hot bands..is referred to as *swing* or *jive*, of which, in turn, there are several kinds. **1939** *San Francisco News Let.* 1 Sept. 12/2 Fats Waller..is the King of Jive and gets off some fine stuff. **1946** *N. & Q.* 13 July 20/1 Mr. Mitchell Parish, the American song-writer,..told me that he uses *jive* to describe syncopated music played noisily, and (usually) fast, with great emphasis on rhythm. **1959** 'F. NEWTON' *Jazz Scene* i. 12 In Sophiatown and the rest of the South African ghettoes the 'jive bands' play what is patently jazz. **1960** *Down Beat* 9 June 15 Regarding the word jive, Wilson said, it is nothing more than an obsolete slang term for jazz.

b. Lively and uninhibited dancing to dance-music or jazz; *spec.* 'jitterbugging'.

1943 *Dancing Times* Dec. 117/1 The rhythm of the Jive is not an entirely new one. **1957** C. MACINNES *City of Spades* I. iv. 24 I'll teach you..bop steps, and jive, and all. **1958** *Listener* 20 Nov. 848/1 Jive and tribal dancing. **1969** H. HORWOOD *Newfoundland* x. 69 The jive..is still the universal dance of..outport youngsters.

3. A variety of American English associated with the Harlem area of New York; slang used by American Blacks, or by jazz musicians and their followers. Also *attrib.*, as *jive talk.*

1938 C. CALLOWAY *Hi De Ho* 16 *Jive.* 1. Harlemese speech or lingo. 2. To kid along, to blarney, to give a girl a line. **1943** *Time* 26 July 56/2 A jive-talk glossary that is strictly Dracula has been put out by Parents' Institute. **1944** D. BURLEY (*title*) Original handbook of Harlem jive. E. CONRAD in *Ibid.* 5 Jive is one more contribution of Negro America to the United States. *Ibid.* 6 Jive talk may have been originally a kind of 'Pig Latin' that the slaves talked with each other, a code—when they were in the presence of whites. **1960** *Time & Tide* 24 Dec. 1599/2 Jive-talk is nothing new. It goes back at least to the thirties when for the first time a brand of jazz, swing, grew to be a cult. Jive was originally the patois of Harlem, not jazz musicians' slang; but with time the distinction was lost. **1965** *Economist* 4 Sept. 888/2 Some common American jive-words (nappy, funky) are left out [of the *Penguin English Dictionary*]. **1971** *Black World* June 92/2 All the rest of that jive talk about white liberals and Rhett Butler is part of another conversation, Sam. **1971** *Melody Maker* 13 Nov. 31/1 That is if you forget the usual jive phrases that whittle their way into his conversation. **1973** *Times Lit. Suppl.* 1 June 604/4 A narrative tone which frequently coincides with the fast, obscene jive-talk of his characters.

4. Marijuana, or a cigarette containing it.

1938 *Call-Bulletin* (San Francisco) 19 Mar., The cigarettes are variously called sticks, reefers, tea gyves, Mary Anns and goofy butts. **1952** *N.Y. Times* 29 Apr. 25 So Diane smoked jive, pod, and tea. **1955** *U.S. Senate Hearings* (1956) VIII. 4168 'Sticks', 'reefers', 'jive sticks'. **1963** 'D. RUTHERFORD' *Creeping Flesh* ii. 124 'Jive' originally meant marijuana. **1972** *Lancet* 16 Sept. 565/1 She was convinced that only in the institution could she 'make it without jive', for she invariably used heroin whenever she was sent home.

jive (dʒaɪv), *v. slang* (orig. *U.S.*). Also **gieve.** [Cf. prec.] **1. a.** *trans.* To mislead, to deceive, to 'kid'; to taunt or sneer at. Also *intr.*, to talk jive, to talk nonsense, to act foolishly.

1928 L. ARMSTRONG (*title of gramophone record*) Don't jive me. **1929** W. THURMAN *Blacker the Berry* 128 But I jived her along, so she ditched him, and gave me her address. **1934** *Amer. Speech* IX. 26/2 *Gieve..*, to mislead with words; to take into one's confidence. *Ibid.* 27/1 *Jive*, see *gieve*. **1938** *Ibid.* XIII. 317/1 *To jive around*,..'to fool around'. **1939** J. DOLLARD in A. Dundes *Mother Wit* (1973) 281/2 Willy kept 'jiving' him until Jimmy finally left. **1944** D. BURLEY *Orig. Handbk. Harlem Jive* 71 Jive is a distortion of that staid, old respectable English word 'jibe'... In the sense in which it came into use among Negroes in Chicago about the year 1921, it meant to taunt, to scoff, to sneer. *Ibid.*, A highly effective manner of talking about each other's ancestors and hereditary traits..called 'Jiving' someone. **1946** MEZZROW & WOLFE *Really Blues* vi. 70 Monkey wasn't jiving about that bartender. **1950** A. LOMAX *Mr. Jelly Roll* (1952) iv. 170, I..jived the expressman to hank my trunks to the station by telling him my money was uptown. **1969** J. MCPHERSON in A. Chapman *New Black Voices* (1972) 162, I don't need no money. Nobody's jiving me. I'm jiving them. You know I can still pull in a hundred in tips in one trip [as a waiter on a train]. **1973** *Black World* Mar. 57 Lawd, don't jive Miz Jackson,..Ride on King Jesus!

b. *intr.* To make sense; to fit in. *U.S.* Cf. JIBE *v.*

1943 *Amer. Speech* XVIII. 153/2 *Doesn't jive*, doesn't make sense. **1955** W. GADDIS *Recognitions* II. i. 308 His analyst says he's in love with her for all the neurotic reasons in the book. It don't jive, man. **1973** *To our Returned Prisoners of War* (Office of U.S. Secretary of Defense) 7 *Jive*, verb meaning fit in, go with, to make sense.

2. *intr.* **a.** To play 'jive' (JIVE *sb.* 2 a).

c **1938** N. E. WILLIAMS *His Hi De Highness of Ho De Ho* 35/2 'Jiving', meaning to improvise. **1942** BERREY & VAN DEN BARK *Amer. Thes. Slang* §579/9 Play 'hot jazz'; 'swing', ..*jive*. **1947** AUDEN *Age of Anxiety* (1948) ii. 44 The juke-box jives rejoicing madly.

b. To dance the 'jive' (JIVE *sb.* 2 b).

1939 *San Francisco News Let.* 1 Sept. 12/2 If you should dance to the rhythms of either gentleman you will be jiving. **1957** *Observer* 13 Oct. 3/4 Young people from the East End and the West End came there [the Humphrey Lyttelton Club] to jive or listen. **1958** *New Statesman* 4 Jan. 10/2 A couple began a little hesitantly to jive.

Hence **'jiver,** one who jives; **'jiving** *vbl. sb.* and *ppl. a.*

1936 *N.Y. World-Telegram* 6 Oct. 16/1 High jiving—tall, if you know what I mean, talk. *c* **1938** [see 2 above]. **1939** BLIND BOY FULLER (*song title*) Jivin' Big Bill Blues. **1939** *San Francisco Examiner* 18 Aug. 3 (*heading*) Jiving deluxe. **1943** *N.Y. Times* 9 May II. 5/7 I'm a jivin jitter-bug. **1943** *Gramophone* Aug. 47/2 Lawd, don't cut out 'Jazz'! I'll write you as many letters as Robert Mackenzie likes, but..don't forget the 'jiver', sir, don't forget the 'jiver'! **1944** S. J. PERELMAN *Crazy like Fox* (1945) 163 A jiving, hot-hosing jitterbug. **1947** M. H. BOULWARE *Jive & Slang of Students in Negro Colleges*, *Jiver*,..a flatterer. **1951** 'A. GARVE' *Murder in Moscow* iii. 46 Her daughter..had won a prize for jiving at some South London *palais*. **1959** *Spectator* 12 June 856/1 One..finds the jazz virtuoso Stephane Grapelly performing to an admiring crowd of jivers. **1973** *Black World* Mar. 85 Jiving, bopping, napping, signifying, sounding—all modes of Afro-American expression—seek to affirm the vitality of the Black American experience. *Ibid.* May 84/1 He comes down hard on white racists, but he also attacks Black 'jivers' who seek to exploit their brethren under the guise of Blackness.

jive (dʒaɪv), *a. U.S. slang.* [f. the sb.] Used, chiefly by American Blacks, in the primary sense 'not acting correctly' but with a wide range of connotations ('pretentious', 'deceitful', etc.).

[**1959** *Esquire* Nov. 70 *Jive*, to fool, to kid. The adjective is bogus.] **1971** E. E. LANDY *Underground Dict.* 112 *Jive*,.. not acting right; doing something wrong—e.g. *You never showed up. You're a jive dude.* **1973** E. BULLINS *Theme is Blackness* 131 Kiss ma ass ya jive mathafukker! **1973** *Black World* June 61 Huh? Awh, Sistuh, u sho is jive. *Ibid.* 79/1 The hero..is ' hip', but not 'jive'. *Ibid.* Sept. 53, I been confused, fucked up, scared, phony And jive To a whole/lot of people.

jive, erron. spelling of GYVE *v.* and *sb.*

In mod. editions of some works.

jive-ass ('dʒaɪvæs, -ɑːs). *U.S. slang.* Also **jiveass.** [f. JIVE *sb.* + ASS (= ARSE *sb.*).]

a. A person who loves fun or excitement. **b.** A deceitful or pretentious person. Freq. *attrib.*

A word of fluid meaning and application.

1964 R. S. GOLD *Jazz Lexicon* 169 Jive-ass mother-fucker. **1969** C. BROWN in A. Chapman *New Black Voices* (1972) 181 'You jiveass nigger,' Reb said, laughing. 'No, I'm telling the truth.' *Ibid.* 184 He became a hustler, a jiveass, a jazz player. **1970** *New York* 16 Nov. 42/1 This happens to be a jive-ass af-*flu*-ent neighborhood. **1973** *Black World* Aug. 55/2 Silly-ass so-called hangups of jive-ass white folks. *Ibid.* 67/1 Jive-ass jivers. Stupid. Looking clever.

jivey ('dʒaɪvɪ), *a. slang* (chiefly *U.S.*). Also **jivy.** [f. JIVE *sb.* + -Y¹.] Jazzy, 'swinging', lively (see also quot. 1954); also, misleading, phoney, pretentious.

1944 [in the popular song *Mairzy Doats* by M. Drake, A. Hoffman, and J. Livingston]. **1953** BERREY & VAN DEN BARK *Amer. Thes. Slang* (1954) §149/13 'Knowing'; 'hep'

(manifesting knowledge of what is proper or fashionable) ..*jivey*. **1955** KEEPNEWS & GRAUER *Pict. Hist. Jazz* xv. 187 Stuff Smith, one of the jiviest. *Ibid.* xix. 248 Bassist Slam Steuart was..primarily a jivey Swing man who hummed solos loudly as he played. **1972** M. J. BOSSE *Incident at Naha* ii. 85 I'm not sure I would have accepted that sort of jivey explanation, but Mrs. Halliday did. **1972** *Jazz & Blues* Dec. 28/1 This coupling finds him in jivey mood.

jiwan (dʒɪ'wɑːn). [Skr. *jívana* a son; cf. Hindi *jawān*.] = JAWAN; also, an Indian youth.

1914 KIPLING *New Army* (1915) 49 The trouble in India was that all the young men—the mere *jiwans*—wanted to come out at once. **1924** *Blackw. Mag.* Aug. 227/1, I met the Gurkha officer in the back of beyond with two or three of his *jiwans*. *Ibid.* 232/2, I ruled over as jolly a crowd of students as a Principal of a College can hope to collect, north-country lads—Sikh, Muhammadans, and Hindus... At cricket..we had an English professional..who coached them... He became attached to my *jiwans*.

Jixi, Jixie ('dʒɪksɪ). *temporary*. [f. *Jix*, nickname of *Joynson-Hicks* (see below) + *-i*, after TAXI.] A two-seater taxi-cab licensed in 1926 while Sir William Joynson-Hicks (1865–1932) was Home Secretary.

1926 *Westm. Gaz.* 7 Apr., Jixi is the name given by the Westminster Gazette, and now used by everyone, to 2-seater taxicabs. **1926** *Punch* 21 Apr. 438/2 The Home Secretary explained to Sir F. Meyer that the police have licensed two types of 'Jixi'. **1927** *Observer* 3 Apr. 9 The first 'Jixie' or two-seater taxicab will probably be seen on the streets of London at the end of the present week.

jizz (dʒɪz). [Etym. unknown.] The characteristic impression given by an animal or plant.

GUISE *sb.* 5 is coincident in sense but the phonetic relationship remains unexplained and the two words may therefore be unrelated.

1922 T. A. COWARD *Bird Haunts & Nature Memories* 141 A West Coast Irishman was familiar with the wild creatures which dwelt on or visited his rocks and shores; at a glance he could name them, usually correctly, but if asked how he knew them would reply 'By their "jizz".' What is jizz?..We have not coined it, but how wide its use in Ireland is we cannot say... Jizz may be applied to or possessed by any animate and some inanimate objects, yet we cannot clearly define it. A single character may supply it, or it may be the combination of many. *Ibid.* 143 Jizz, of course, is not confined to birds. The small mammal and the plant alike have jizz. **1950** *Brit. Birds* XLIII. 29 Miss Quick obviously looks at her birds more than once and does so with an artist's eye for those peculiarities of shape, outline and stance which give a species its 'jizz'. **1960** *Times* 14 June 14/7 The boy could name any bat at a glance..(an indefinable accomplishment which the late T. A. Coward..once described as 'jizz' when speaking of bird identification). **1966** D. MCCLINTOCK *Compan. Flowers* ix. 117, I know only too well the problem of trying to express what there is in a plant that enables me, or you, to tell it from another at sight. The word I use for these intangible characteristics, that defy being put into words, is jizz.

jizz, var. JISM.

‖**jnana** (dʒə'nɑːnə). *Hinduism*. Also **jnyana**. [Skr. *jñāna*, f. *jñā* to know.] Spiritual knowledge, as a means of salvation.

1827 *Trans. R. Asiatic Soc.* I. 576 *Vásudéva*, or *Bhagavat*, ..has six especial attributes,..1st. Knowledge (jnyána), or acquaintance with everything animate or inanimate constituting the universe. **1875** M. WILLIAMS *Indian Wisdom* iii. 59 Jnāna, 'knowledge of universal truth'. **1916** T. A. GOPINATHA RAO *Elem. Hindu Iconogr.* II. I. 273 Siva was seated facing south when he taught the *rishis yōga* and *jñāna*. **1945** A. HUXLEY *Let.* 10 Apr. (1969) 520 There is gnosis or jnana after death only for those who have chosen to pay the price..of gnosis during life. **1971** *Illustr. Weekly India* 11 Apr. 15/4 The essence of the world is religion..the essence of religion is knowledge (*jnana*).

b. *Comb.*, as **jnana-marga** [Skr. *mārga* road, path], the way to salvation through spiritual knowledge or asceticism.

1877 M. WILLIAMS *Hinduism* i. 11 Popular Hindûism.. though supposed to accept this creed as the way of true knowledge (*Jnāna-mārga*)..adds to it two other..ways. **1883** —— *Relig. Thought & Life in India* iii. 63 The way of love and faith (bhakti-mārga)..superseded the other two ways of salvation—knowledge and works (jñāna-mārga and karma-mārga). **1937** [see *bhakti-marga*]. **1945** A. HUXLEY *Let.* 21 Jan. (1969) 513 The three types of religion enumerated in the *Bhagavad Gita*, (karma marga, the way of works or action; Bhakti marga, the way of devotion; and jnana marga, the way of knowledge) correspond precisely to the three extremes of somatotonic, viscerotonic and cerebrotonic temperament. **1963** *Listener* 28 Mar. 550/2 In earliest times, in pre-Buddhist texts such as the first *Upanisads* is described what later became known as *Jnana-marga*, or the way of knowledge, in which the realization of the identity of the individual self or soul with the Universal, the absolute, Brahma, was sought.

‖**jnani** (dʒə'nɑːnɪ). *Hinduism*. [Skr., f. JNANA.] A worshipper or devotee of *jnana-marga*.

1885 E. BALFOUR *Cycl. India* (ed. 3) II. 442/2 *Jnani*, or divine Buddhas, are five. **1916** T. A. GOPINATHA RAO *Elem. Hindu Iconogr.* III. I. 242 The silent *jñānis* destroying the threefold bond..behold the sacred and are filled with bliss. **1962** BRAHMACHARINI USHA *Ramakrishna-Vedanta Wordbk.*, *Jnani*. 1. One who follows the path of knowledge and discrimination to reach the impersonal Reality; a non-dualist. 2. A knower of Brahman. **1969** *Indian Music Jrnl.* V. Suppl., Arunagiri completed the song, got cured of his ailments and became a Jñānî and a yōgēsvara.

jo (dʒoː). *Sc.* Also **joe** (*anglicized* joy). [In sense 1, Sc. form of JOY, F. *joie*. (In some dialects of 16th c. Sc., *oy*, *oi* ran together with *ō*: hence *jone* = *join*; *rois* = *rose*, etc.) In sense 2 app. the same word, and sometimes in 16th c. spelt *joy*.]

†**1.** Joy, pleasure. *Obs.*

c **1560** A. SCOTT *Poems* (S.T.S.) xxiv. 13 Hir court hes [*pr.* he] jo, quhair evir thay go. **1567** *Gude & Godlie B.* (S.T.S.) 53 Now lat vs sing with myrth and Jo [*rime* principio]. **1570** *Satir. Poems Reform.* xvii. 180 God may conuert our cair In plesure and in Jo [*rimes* wo, fo, no].

2. As a term of endearment: A sweetheart, darling, beloved one.

a **1529** SKELTON *Agst. Scottes* 91 Kynge Jamy, Jemmy, Jocky my jo, Ye summond our kynge,—why dyd ye so? [**1535** LYNDESAY *Satyre* 1302 Iennie, my Ioy [*Pinkerton* joe] quhair is thy dadie? **1563** FOXE *A. & M.* (1583) 1266 [Treigton, Bp. of Dunkelden] 'My ioy Deane Thomas, I loue you wel'. **1573** SEMPILL in *Satir. Poems Reform.* xxxix. 255 Alace, my Joyis! ȝe had bot lytill skill. *a* **1605** MONTGOMERIE *Misc. Poems* iii. 73 Judge of ȝour self by Julius, my joyes, Quhais fenȝeid freinds wer worse then open foes.] **1686** G. STUART *Joco-ser. Disc.* 49 My Joe, quo' she, I need no' speer What wind it was that blew you here. **1725** RAMSAY *Gent. Sheph.* I. i, Dear Roger, when your Jo puts on her gloom, Do ye sae too and never fash your thumb. **1790** BURNS *Song, 'John Anderson'* i, John Anderson, my jo. **1816** SCOTT *Old Mort.* xxxviii, It's Miss Edith's first joe, your ain auld maister, Cuddie. **1830** GALT *Lawrie T.* IX. ii. (1869) 408 It might have been one of the servant girls with her jo. **1893** STEVENSON *Catriona* iii. 28 Just twa o' my old joes, my hinny dear.

jo, variant of JOE, Portuguese coin.

joab, joal, obs. forms of JOBE, JOWL.

Joachimite ('dʒəʊəkɪmaɪt). *Ch. Hist.* [f. the name of *Joachim*, abbot of Fiore in Calabria (*c* 1132–1202) + -ITE[1].] A heretical follower of the Italian mystic, Joachim of Fiore. Also **'Joachimist, 'Joachist, 'Joachite, 'Joachitist**; so **'Joachimism, 'Joachism**.

1797 *Encycl. Brit.* IX. 290/2 *Joachimites*, in church history, the disciples of Joachim, a Cistertian monk. **1842** K. H. DIGBY *Mores Catholici* XI. xiii. 478 The execrable book, entitled the eternal Gospel,..whose adherents, termed Joachimites, as it was ascribed to Joachim, were again condemned by the Council of Arles. **1874** J. H. BLUNT *Dict. Sects* 242/1 As early as 1260 the Council of Arles spoke of the Joachitist error as spreading like a cancer. **1906** G. G. COULTON *From St. Francis to Dante* 104 The Pope.. insisted on his resignation, partly on account of his Joachism. *Ibid.* 108 A great orator and a great Joachite. **1913** E. G. GARDNER *Dante & Mystics* vi. 192 The Joachists went considerably beyond what Joachim himself had taught. **1913** A. G. F. HOWELL *S. Bernardino of Siena* i. 10 They cultivated the Joachite literature. **1926** E. HUTTON *Franciscans in Eng.* ix. 141 A sect of Joachists had arisen among the 'spiritual' party within the Franciscan Order. **1929** E. C. MESSENGER tr. *Guiraud's Mediæval Inquisition* v. 143 In 1247, a friar with Joachimist tendencies, John of Parma was elected minister general of the Order. *Ibid.*, Peter John Olivi..expounded a modified Joachimism which was henceforth the doctrine of the Spirituals. **1931** H. BETT *Joachim of Flora* v. 112 These Joachites maintain that the future age of the Holy Spirit shall be enlightened with a more perfect law. **1932** *Speculum* VII. 260 These works.. beside throwing some lights on several problems of the Joachite tradition, were..useful in awakening more interest in the subject. *Ibid.* 267 Grundmann's work is..epoch-making in the studies on Joachim and Joachism. **1947** H. R. WILLIAMSON *Arrow & Sword* x. 158 The Joachists..had taken their master's ideas to their logical conclusion. *Ibid.*, It is possible that the *Divine Comedy*..is the classic Joachist apologia.

Joan (dʒəʊn). Also 5–7 **Ione**, 7 **Ioane**. [A female proper name, orig. *Joanna* or *Johanna*, fem. of *Jo(h)annes* John; hence in transf. uses.]

1. A generic name for a female rustic.

[*c* **1490** *Promp. Parv.* 264/2 (MS. H.) Ione, *Johanna*.] **1588** SHAKS. *L.L.L.* III. i. 207 Some men must loue my Lady, and some Ione. **1595** —— *John* I. i. 184 Now can I make any Ioane a Lady. **1612** WARNER *Alb. Eng.* XIV. xci. Fj, Many a countrie Ione. *a* **1700** B. E. *Dict. Cant. Crew*, *Joan*, a *homely Joan*, a Coarse Ord'nary Woman. **1802** MRS. SHERWOOD *Susan Grey* 48 You are such a dowdy, such a country Joan, no one will look upon you.

2. Name for a close-fitting cap worn by women in the latter half of the 18th century.

1756 COWPER in *Connoisseur* No. 134 ¶7 A grocer's wife attractd our eyes, by a new-fashioned cap, called a Joan. **1762** *Poetry* in *Ann. Reg.* 208 Now loose in a mob, now close in a Joan.

joanna (dʒəʊ'ænə). Also **joano**, **johanna**, and other varr. Rhyming slang for 'piano'.

1846 *Swell's Night Guide* 34 As a sort of whipper-in, music is provided—viz.,..a joano. **1912** A. N. LYONS *Clara* iii. 28 All the time a party down below was bangin' out a song called 'Bedelia' on a old johanner. **1923** J. MANCHON *Le Slang* 168 *Johannah, johanner*, un piano. **1961** S. PRICE *Just for Record* ix. 89 He gets up from the joanna-stool. **1972** *Listener* 20 July 92/2 The old Jo-anna intrudes its amateurish thumpings.

Joannite: see JOHANNITE[1].

joaquinite (wɑː-, wəʊ'kiːnaɪt, 'dʒəʊəkwɪnaɪt). *Min.* [f. *Joaquin*, the name of a ridge in San Benito County, California: see -ITE[1].] A honey-yellow to brown silicate of sodium, barium, iron, and titanium that occurs as small, isolated, orthorhombic crystals.

1909 G. D. LOUDERBACK in *Bull. Dept. Geol. Univ. Calif.* V. 376 Joaquinite... A honey yellow or light brown substance in small generally individual crystals or crystal grains..which is believed to be a new mineral. **1932** *Amer. Mineralogist* XVII. 308 (*heading*) The chemical nature of joaquinite. *Ibid.* 312 There are, therefore, 4 molecules of composition $NaBa(Ti, Fe)_3Si_4O_{15}$ in the unit cell of joaquinite. **1967** *Ibid.* LII. 1762 An apparently new rare-earth mineral of the joaquinite group occurs in nephelin—syenite pegmatites of Ilimaussaq alkaline massif (S. Greenland). Optical and X-ray properties are the same, as for standard joaquinite $Na\ Ba\ Ti_3\ Si_4\ O_{15}$ from California, but the chemical analysis is quite different... The formula is $NaBa_2Fe^{2+}Ce_2Ti_2Si_8O_{26}(OH)$.

joar, variant of JOWAR, millet.

joar, var. JOHAR.

joate, obs. form of JOT *sb.*[1]

†**job**, *sb.*[1] *Obs.* [Of unascertained origin; some have thought it an assibilated form of GOB *sb.*[1]; but, beside the phonetic difficulty, the approximation of sense is only distant.]

1. A small compact portion of some substance; a piece, lump; a stump, block; a tassel.

c **1400** *Destr. Troy* 11941 Robbet þere Riches..Gemmes, & Iewels, Iobbes of gold. **1587** GOLDING *De Mornay* xii. 210 Sometimes [God] letteth vs goe alone by our selues..and then stumble we at the next iob yt we meete with. **1659** E. BURROUGH *Reign Whore* 11 Why must you have a soft Cushion with silken Jobs at the corners to lean on?

2. A cart-load, or what a horse and cart can bring at one time.

[It is not clear whether the essential notion is that of the mass or amount carried by a cart, or that of which the carrying constitutes a single job. In the latter case this would belong rather to JOB *sb.*[2], and might perh. be the link uniting the two words.]

1560 *Stanford Church-w. Acc.* in *Antiquary* (1888) Apr. 168 For faching a Jobbe of thornes and mending the hedges aboute the churche howsse xd. **1571** *Ibid.* 170 For iij Jobbs of Strawe and the Caryage vijs. iiijd. [Cf. *Jobbel, Jobbet*, a small load, generally of hay or straw: widely used in Midland and Southern dialects.]

job (dʒɒb), *sb.*[2] Also 7–8 **jobb**. [Of obscure origin: prob. in colloquial use some time before it appeared in literature. Possibly connected with prec., sense 2.]

1. a. A piece of work; *esp.* a small definite piece of work done in the way of one's special occupation or profession.

a **1627** MIDDLETON *Mayor Quinborough* IV. i, I cannot read, I keep a Clark to do those jobbs for need. **1688** *New Jersey Archives* (1881) II. 29 Old Smith I keep doeing jobs vp and down. **1721** BAILEY, *Jobb*, a small Piece of Work. **1726** SWIFT *Corr.* Wks. 1841 II. 583, I am strongly tempted to send a parcel to be printed..and make a ninepenny job for the bookseller. **1798** BLOOMFIELD *Farmer's Boy* I. 56 He.. never lack'd a job for Giles to do. **1806–7** J. BERESFORD *Miseries Hum. Life* (1826) II. xxxiv, Carpenter whom you have..entreated to come himself for the purpose of doing a variety of jobs. **1833** HT. MARTINEAU *Berkeley the Banker* I. v. 108 This, you see, was a pretty long job, and a profitable one, she says. **1866** G. MACDONALD *Ann. Q. Neighb.* iii. (1878) 36 Well, well, Rogers, Simmons shall have the job.

b. *Thieves' slang.* A theft or robbery; any criminal deed, esp. one definitely arranged beforehand.

1722 DE FOE *Moll Flanders* (1840) 224 It was always reckoned a safe job when we heard of a new shop. **1800** W. B. RHODES *Bomb. Fur.* i. (1830) 11, I knocked him down, then snatch'd it from his fob, Watch, Watch, he cried, when I had done the job. **1815** SCOTT *Guy M.* xxxiii, I thought the job was clayed over and forgotten. **1884** *Public Opinion* 5 Sept. 301/1 He..found..stolen property sufficient to connect the thief with several 'jobs'.

c. *Printing.* A small piece of work of the miscellaneous kind, as the printing of posters, handbills, cards, etc.

1795 *Let. of Compositors of London* in E. Howe *London Compositor* (1947) i. 76 That all jobs, not exceeding one sheet, be paid at the rate of six pence per thousand. **1800** in J. Johnson *Typogr.* II. 578 That every article under one sheet be considered a job. *Ibid.*, All jobs in foreign languages to be paid sevenpence halfpenny per thousand. **1810** *Ibid.* 582 Jobs of one sheet or under (except Auctioneers' Catalogues and Particulars) to be cast up at sevenpence per thousand. **1841** W. SAVAGE *Dict. Art of Printing* 428 Any thing which printed does not exceed a sheet, is termed a Job, and is paid for extra to the compositor, because there is no return of furniture or of letter: he has generally to put up fresh cases, and has some additional trouble in getting the right letter, and in making up the furniture. **1960** P. M. HANDOVER *Printing in London* vii. 183 In general, however, both the Bagford and Johnson Collections [*sc.* of ephemera] reveal that during the eighteenth century the letterpress printers made little effort to extend the range of jobs.

d. Phr. *by the job*.

1733 BERKELEY *Let. to Tom Prior* 1 May in Fraser *Life* (1871) 207, I do not design to hire one [gardener]..but only employ him by the job. **1792** WOLCOTT (P. Pindar) *Odes Condol.* Wks. 1812 III. 108, I thank my stars, I am not like the Mob Whom Nature fabricated by the job. **1865** LIVINGSTONE *Zambesi* xviii. 351 The teacher said he was paid by the job.

2. A piece of work, or transaction, done for hire, or with a special view to profit.

1660 PEPYS *Diary* 2 June, I will do you all the good jobs I can. **1664** EVELYN tr. *Freart's Archit.* App 119 Workmen, who from..some lucky jobb (as they call it) do generally ingrosse all the work they can hear of. **1727–38** GAY *Fables* II. xiii, Then marriage (as of late profest) Is but a money job at best. **1778** *The Saints* 4 Their Faith's a Dream, their Preaching but a Job. **1852** MRS. STOWE *Uncle Tom's C.* viii. 56 You see Mr. Haley's a puttin' us in a way of a good job, I reckon.

3. a. A public service or trust turned to private gain or party advantage; a transaction in which duty or the public interest is sacrificed for the sake of private or party advantage. ***jobs for the boys***: see BOY *sb.*[1] 6 d.

1667 PEPYS *Diary* 10 Apr., It [Tangier] hath been hitherto . . used as a jobb to do a kindness to some Lord. **1724** SWIFT *Drapier's Lett.* iii. Wks. 1755 V. II. 46, I never can suppose, that such patents . . were originally granted with a view of being a jobb for the interest of a particular person to the damage of the publick. **1735** POPE *Donne Sat.* iv. 142 Who makes a Trust or Charity a Job, And gets an Act of Parliament to rob. **1769** *Junius Lett.* vii. 31 It would have been more decent in you to have called this dishonourable transaction by its true name; a job, to accommodate two persons. **1807–8** SYD. SMITH *Plymley's Lett.* x. (ed. 11) 171 If Ireland is gone, where are jobs? where are reversions? **1888** BRYCE *Amer. Commw.* III. lxxxvi. 153 Even when jobs are exposed by the press, each particular job seems below the attention of a busy people.

†**b.** Personal profit; private interest. *Obs.*

1661 BAXTER *Mor. Prognost.* I. xcv. 24 Those dangerous Extreams, that seem to serve some present Exigence and Jobb. **1785** BURKE *Sp. Nabob Arcot* Wks. IV. 275 Territories, on the keeping of which . . the defence of our dominions, and, what was more dear to them, possibly, their own job, depended.

4. a. Anything one has to do; a 'business', affair, operation, transaction, matter to be done. *spec.* a paid position of employment, a situation (sense 6 b).

1694 R. L'ESTRANGE *Fables* cccxxxii. (ed. 6) 345 A Widow . . had a Twittering towards a second husband: and she took a Gossiping Companion of hers to her Assistance, how to Manage the Jobb. **1791** MRS. RADCLIFFE *Rom. Forest* ii, I've had a hard job to find my way back. **1858** in *Amer. Speech* (1965) XL. 130 But when he gets a good fat job For dat am all he cares. *a* **1861** T. WINTHROP *Edwin Brothertoft* (1862) 38, I will find you a fat job and plenty of pickings! **1879** BROWNING *Martin Relph* xvii, 'Tis an ugly job: but soldiers obey commands. **1883** [see FAT *a.* 9 b]. **1889** R. S. S. BADEN-POWELL *Pigsticking* 49 To drive them out is naturally a very difficult job. *Ibid.* 80, I was carried into camp and my wounds sewn up and dressed, a job which took nearly four hours. **1931** *Daily Express* 13 Oct. 5/2 When I got my job as social secretary . . I got a large salary and lived in luxury. **1940** G. D. H. & M. COLE *Counterpoint Murder* xv. 237 He was in the same job up to about a week ago. **1974** *New Statesman* 17 May 701/3 After the Tory general election defeat of 1964, the outgoing Chancellor of the Exchequer . . told a newspaper gossip writer: I shall have to get a job and earn some money.

b. Phr. ***to do the job for***, or ***to do*** (a person's) ***job***: (*a*) to do what is required by him; (*b*) *slang*, to 'do for', ruin, destroy; ***to make a job of***: to transact or manage successfully; ***bad job***: a thing on which labour is spent in vain, a failure (see also 5 below); ***job of work***: a task, piece of work; ***to have a job*** (***to***): to have difficulty (in doing something); similarly, ***to be a job***: to present difficulties; also, ***(to be) the devil's (own) job***; ***to get on with the job*** [GET *v.* 63 f], to proceed with one's work, to continue with one's affairs; ***just the job*** (colloq.): exactly what is wanted, the very thing.

1557 in A. Feuillerat *Documents Revels Court Ed. VI & Q. Mary* (1914) 236 Doinge certen Iobbes of woorke. **1694** MOTTEUX *Rabelais* IV. xli. (1737) 165 The Sausage's Job being done. **1719** DE FOE *Crusoe* I. xviii, Had they thought fit to have gone to sleep there, . . they had done the job for us. **1855** MOTLEY *Corr.* (1889) I. vi. 172, I should not like him to read it till he can do it all at once, and make a job of it. **1862** BORROW *Wild Wales* I. xix. 210 The minister of the parish . . had frequently entered into argument with him, but quite unsuccessfully and had at last given up the matter, as a bad job. **1865** H. KINGSLEY *Hillyars & Burtons* lxix, He had given up religion as a bad job. **1865** DICKENS *Mut. Fr.* III. ix, Bella . . heaved a little sigh, and gave up things in general for a bad job. **1873** TROLLOPE *Eustace Diamonds* I. xix. 252 Arthur did not go on the search, because he had a job of work to do. *Ibid.* III. lxxii. 251 The barrister who will have the cross-examining of her . . will have a job of work on his hand. **1878** [see COAST *v.* 14]. **1887** G. H. DEVOL *Forty Yrs. a Gambler* 267 For ten or fifteen years during my early life, the sporting men of the South tried to find a man to whip me, but they couldn't do it, and finally gave it up as a bad job. **1907** J. M. SYNGE *Tinker's Wedding* I. 1 It's the divil's job making a ring. **1922** F. H. BURNETT *Robin* xviii. 154 'You propose to suggest that she shall marry *you?*' . . 'Yes. It will be the devil's own job . . she has abhorred me all her life.' **1928** M. WALSH *While Rivers Run* xx. 279 ' A sound job of work!' boasted Alistair. 'We have arriven.' **1931** A. HUXLEY *Let.* 24 Aug. (1969) 351 It has been a job writing the book and I'm glad it's done. **1931** 'P. WILLIAMS' *Word of To-morrow* IV. xvi. 263 Tramps . . who wouldn't do an honest job of work not if it was offered them. **1935** *Punch* 21 Aug. 208/3, I had a job to find the meter, and I can't think why they want to hide it behind a table. **1941** *London Opinion* June 48 (*caption*) I'll have a job explaining things to my wife. **1942** 'A. BRIDGE' *Frontier Passage* viii. 131 Why the hell couldn't all the extremists . . allow sensible people . . to get on with the job?—the job being to live the good life. **1943** HUNT & PRINGLE *Service Slang* 42 *Just the job*, if you see anything that you like, whether it is something in a shop window or a new billet, this is what you say, meaning of course that it suits you all right. **1944** R. LEHMANN *Ballad & Source* 55 My riding lessons had been given up as a bad job. **1959** 'J. ROSS' *Boy in Grey Overcoat* ii. 21, I thought . . she'd be just the job. **1960** H. PINTER *Dumb Waiter* 148 Just the job. We should have used it before. **1966** *Listener* 1 Sept. 300/2, I have had quite a job to get a copy [of a book]. **1969** *Ottawa Commons Debates* 24 July 11570/2 If the opposition accords so little respect to parliament that it defines governing as evil, that getting on with the job is regarded as tyranny, then I am happy to be given the chance to join issue. **1973** E. PAGE *Fortnight by Sea* ix. 98 If Mrs Barratt could possibly see her way to letting us stay on . . it really would be just the job.

c. A consignment of goods to be sold cheaply as bargains, a job lot.

1858 *Illustr. News World* I. 257/3 Butcher's meat, the week's gathering, to be sold by the job. **1905** *Daily Chron.* 18 Nov. 3/7 As soon as a girl can do a corset, which is at all passable, even if we have to put it into the 'jobs'—that is, lots for selling cheap—she can earn much more.

d. ***on the job***: (*a*) hard at work, busy (also in extended senses, committing a crime, engaged in sexual intercourse, etc.); (*b*) (of a racehorse) out to win and well backed; (*c*) = *by the job* (sense 1 d); (*d*) used as *attrib. phr.* (hyphenated): done or occurring while a person is at work.

1882 W. BURNOT *Old Mother Goose* iii. 12 He will have to hide his nob. Come along, we're on the job. *a* **1889** in Barrère & Leland *Dict. Slang* (1889) I. 502/1 Trainers and jockeys . . very easily gathered whether a particular horse . . was 'out for an airing' or was on the job. **1890** LLOYD GEORGE *Let.* 7 Aug. (1973) 32, I am on the job Saturday or Monday. **1891** *Licensed Victuallers' Gaz.* 23 Jan. (Farmer & Henley), There was a long wrangle over the choice of referee, for no one cared to occupy that thankless post when the Lambs were on the job. **1892** E. J. MILLIKEN *'Arry Ballads* 3 'Arry is fair on the job. **1901** *To-Day* 22 Aug. 115/1 'This cook . . is very good.' 'She is, but she is only here on the job.' **1909** *Post & Paddock* 22 Nov. 1/3 Their denunciations of horses 'not trying', being 'out for an airing', or 'not on the job' on every occasion when their speculations go wrong. **1914** G. ATHERTON *Perch of Devil* I. iv. 22 She was 'on the job' every minute until the cottage was 'on wheels'. **1922** JOYCE *Ulysses* 466 Mother Slipperslapper. (*Familiarly.*) She's on the job herself tonight with the vet. **1922** *N. & Q.* 9 Sept. 206/2 To be 'on the job' is for a horse to be 'busy', to be 'out', *i.e.*, backed and trying. **1937** *Burlington Mag.* June p. xxvi/1 The slippery pickpocket is depicted 'on the job'. **1947** [see BIOTECHNOLOGY]. **1958** *Times* 24 Mar. (Careers in Industry Suppl.) p. vi/4 Everyone should receive the training appropriate to his particular aptitude—which may range from the on-the-job training to a university course. **1966** ' L. LANE' *ABZ of Scouse* 78 *On ther job*: engaged in sexual intercourse. **1971** *Optometry Today* 17 On-the-job accidents and injuries could be appreciably reduced if every worker had maximum visual efficiency for the task at hand. **1972** *Daily Tel.* (Colour Suppl.) 16 Nov. 94/3 'Why the hell did you play Eric Clapton's *Easy Now?* . . Didn't you realise it was all about some guy on the job?' And I said, 'Yeah. How many songs aren't?' **1973** *Amer. Speech 1969* XLIV. 243 This approach . . falls short of giving the reader an accurate idea of the large role that railroad language plays in on-the-job communication.

e. A commission to back a racehorse; so, a horse on which such bets are placed.

1889 BARRÈRE & LELAND *Dict. Slang* I. 502/1 'He has got the job', he has the putting on of the stable money. **1907** *Favourite* 16 Nov. 9/2 Elfin Revel was a big starting-price job for the Croxteth Plate. **1911** *Turf* 10 Oct. 1/1, I am not now referring to s.p. jobs.

f. *colloq.* A term of wide application, often with suggestions of excellence, to describe something, esp. something manufactured (as a motor vehicle, aircraft, etc.); also *joc.* of persons, esp. a pretty girl.

1927 D. HAMMETT in *Black Mask* May 14/2 She's a tough little job who was probably fired for dropping her chewing gum in the soup the last place she worked. **1928** *Daily Mail* 7 May 6/4 [U.S. slang] *A job*, always used when a particular aeroplane is mentioned. **1930** 'A. ARMSTRONG' *Taxi* xii. 164 The fare is 'the rider' or 'the job'. **1930** *Engineering* 18 July 79/3 The motorship press would hail with delight the figures given . . as showing the fuel cost of Diesel engines to be almost half that of any of the steam jobs. **1938** *Harper's Mag.* Jan. 141/2 There was an antiquated high-wing monoplane job. **1939** *Ottawa Jrnl.* 25 July 7/3 He was just about to sit down to a good breakfast in Texas opposite a young woman who was a first class job. **1942** BERREY & VAN DEN BARK *Amer. Thes. Slang* §81.2 *Automobile*, . . job. **1942** *R.A.F. Jrnl.* 30 May 23 The bath was a limited affair: a quick sponge job from a gallon or so of warm water. **1942** *Gen* 1 Sept. 12/2 A 'ropey job' is likely as not to be a blonde who proved uncollaborative. **1946** BRICKHILL & NORTON *Escape to Danger* v. 50 A rather imposing moustache. It was one of those bushy black jobs. **1948** C. DAY LEWIS *Otterbury Incident* i. 2 It [*sc.* a chronometer] was one of those super Swiss jobs. **1964** 'A. GILBERT' *Knock, knock, who's There?* i. 9 You make good contacts in a pub. . . There was a job called the Admiral Box where I'd never been. **1972** G. LYALL *Blame the Dead* xvii. 117 The only desk was Steen's own oiled-teak job. **1973** *Daily Tel.* 22 June 9 (Advt.), Its suspension's almost identical to that of a £2,966 Mercedes 220. (Not to mention a few other equally pricey jobs.)

5. An 'affair', 'business', occurrence, state of things: esp. in ***good job***, ***bad job***, a fortunate or unfortunate event, fact, or condition of affairs.

a **1700** B. E. *Dict. Cant. Crew*, *Badjob*, an ill bout, bargain, or business. **1802** STEPHENSON in *Naval Chron.* VII. 49 It would be a bad job. **1859** LANG *Wand. India* 404 'We are, unfortunately, very much in debt.' 'That's a bad job', said my Lord. **1876** W. S. GILBERT *Trial by Jury* ad fin., So we've finished with the job, And a good job too! **1886** FENN *Master Cerem.* vii, It is a jolly good job the old woman is dead. **1888** J. PAYN *Myst. Mirbridge* (Tauchn.) II. xxvii. 281 She would make the best of a bad job. **1923** *Spectator* 9 June 972/2 The novel ends, therefore, with Derek making the best of a bad job. **1930** J. B. PRIESTLEY *Angel Pavement* ii. 65 Girls *are* a bit silly . . and it's a good job for the men they are. **1942** *Punch* 9 Sept. 215 (*caption*) It's a good job that pig-headed old fool of a farmer ignored our instructions, or we'd have been running on ploughed land. **1950** T. S. ELIOT *Cocktail Party* II. 111 *Edward*: Lavinia, we must make the best of a bad job. That is what he means. *Reilly*: . . The best of a bad job is all any of us make of it.

†**6.** Short for *job-carriage*, *job-horse*: see 7. *Obs.*

1808 *Sporting Mag.* XXXI. 10 It happens . . that the horses are only Jobs. **1819** MOORE *Tom Crib* 10 C—nn—g came in a job. **1863** *Sat. Rev.* 361 Those jobs which the Most Noble Master of the Horse thought fit to harness to the shabby landau which held the future King and Queen of England.

7. *attrib.* and *Comb.* Hired or used, not in the way of constant employment, but by the job or particular piece of work, or for a limited time; as ***job-carriage***, ***-coach***, ***-coachman***, ***-doctor***, ***-gardener***, ***-horse***; (now chiefly in sense 4), as ***job assessment***, ***assignment***, ***centre***, ***content***, ***-counselling***, ***definition***, ***description***, ***discrimination***, ***displacement***, ***enlargement***, ***enrichment***, ***evaluation***, ***-hungry*** adj., ***hygiene***, ***insecurity***, ***mobility***, ***opportunity***, ***placement***, ***reservation***, ***-rich*** adj., ***rotation***, ***satisfaction***, ***security***, ***-seeking***, ***situation***, ***specification***, ***structuring***, ***study***. Also **job analysis**, analysis of the essential factors of a particular piece of work and the necessary qualifications of the person who is to perform it; so *job analyst*; **job book** (see quot.); **job-broking**, dealing in jobs; **job-buyer**, one who buys job lots; **job case** (*Printing*), a type case used in job printing with boxes for both upper- and lower-case types; **Job Corps** *U.S.*, 'an organization . . that operates rural conservation camps and urban training centers for poor youths' (Random House Dict.); **job creation**, the provision of new opportunities for paid employment, *esp.* as part of a policy to provide work for those who are currently unemployed; also *attrib.*; so **job-creating** *vbl. sb.* and *ppl. a.*; **job fount, font** (*Printing*), see quots. 1888, 1894; **job-hopping**, the act or practice of changing from one job to another; so **job-hop** *v. intr.*; **job-hopper**; **job house** (*Printing*), = *job-office*; **job lot**, a lot or parcel of goods, of sundry kinds or qualities, bought as a speculation with a view to profit; hence applied depreciatively to any miscellaneous lot of things, persons, etc.; **job note** (see quot.); **job-office** (*Printing*), an office at which only job-work is done (see 1 c); **job press** (*Printing*), a small press designed for job-printing; **job-price**, (*a*) a price paid for things hired or work done by the job; (*b*) a price paid for things bought as a job lot; **job-print**, **-printing**, the printing of job-work (see sense 1 c); so **job-printer**; **job sharing**, a working arrangement in which two or more people are employed on a part-time basis to perform a job which would otherwise have been available only to a person able to work full-time, and share the renumeration and other benefits; hence (as a back-formation) **job-share** *v. intr.*, to be employed under such an arrangement; also as *sb.*, job-sharing; an instance of this; **job-sharer**; **job sheet**, a sheet on which are recorded details of a job that has been done; **job shop**, (*a*) a workshop where small pieces of work are performed; (*b*) = *job-office*; (*c*) (see quot. 1972); **job-type**, type (of a special or ornamental kind) used in job-work; **job watch** (*Naut.*) = *hack-watch*, HACK *sb.*[3] 6; **job-work**, (*a*) work done and paid for by the job; piece-work; (*b*) the printing of jobs (sense 1 c).

1923 J. D. HACKETT in *Managem. Engin.* May, **Job analysis*, the determination of the essential factors in a specific kind of work and of the qualifications of a worker necessary for its competent performance. **1929** *Encycl. Brit.* XIII. 78/2 This 'questionnaire method' has received severe condemnation from scientists and should be used sparingly by investigators in the field of job analysis. **1962** H. C. WESTON *Light, Sight & Work* (ed. 2) viii. 239 This is subsequently fitted to a job visual standards profile based on the results of job-analysis. **1946** R. H. WARNHOFF *Automobile Accessory Industry* 18 **Job analyst*. Performs detailed job analysis and job evaluation studies. **1971** *State Service* Nov. 340/2 The job analyst . . assesses the post. **1959** *Gloss. Terms Work Study* (*B.S.I.*) 26 **Job assessment*, the process of ascertaining the relative value of a job by examination of the job analysis and job description. **1964** G. L. COHEN *What's Wrong with Hospitals?* i. 17 Through *job-assignment, nurses gain expertise but also become frustrated. **1824** J. JOHNSON *Typogr.* II. 487 By means of a *Job Book, an Employer or Overseer will be enabled . . to discover not only every charge that had been made upon a Job, but also for whom, the number printed, and the size and description, together with the full charge. **1701** DE FOE *Freeholder's Plea* in *Misc.* (1703) 178 That the Scandalous Mechanick Upstart Mistery of *job-broking should thus grow upon the Nation. **1903** *Daily Chron.* 7 Oct. 10/1 E. H. . . described as a '*Job buyer'. **1805** *Naval Chron.* XIII. 183 The horses to be put to the *job carriage which he used. **1894** *Amer. Dict. Printing & Bookmaking* 308/2 **Job case*, a lower case condensed into two-thirds of its usual width, half of the boxes in the upper case being placed by its side. **1946** A. MONKMAN in H. Whetton *Pract. Printing & Binding* ii. 20/1 The two best double cases are the California Job Case . . and the Improved Double Case. **1972** *Jrnl. Printing Hist. Soc. 1971* VII. 39 By 1860 the full size job case was generally available as a printers' supplier's stock item on both sides of the Atlantic. **1972** *Times* 8 Sept. 15/1 Forget about the Government employment exchanges . . think about the bright, new offices with a new image and a sign outside

saying *job centre. **1973** *Guardian* 23 May 6/4 Britain's first Job Centre will be opened this afternoon. Job Centres are the modern version of what have.. been called employment exchanges or.. labour exchanges. **1827** HONE *Every-day Bk.* II. 461 Some were in *job-coaches, at two guineas a day. **1852** R. S. SURTEES *Sponge's Sp. Tour* iii. 9 He condescended to take a place as *job coachman in a livery-stable. **1969** J. ARGENTI *Managem. Techniques* 153 The use of a computer to analyse trends in *job content. **1965** MRS. L. B. JOHNSON *White House Diary* 3 Feb. (1970) 234 Dr. Otis Singletary.. director of the *Job Corps.. says that applications to join are coming in about six thousand a day. **1965** *Economist* 4 Sept. 884/1 Over forty of the Job Corps centres are already in operation. **1970** *Times* 1 June 9/1 The separation of benefit from *job counselling. **1962** *Economist* 19 May 688/2 More '*job-creating' projects were approved than during all of the previous six months. **1976** *Time* 20 Dec. 42/2 Both advocated spending of an additional $5 billion by the government on job-creating programs. **1985** *Times* 18 Apr. 16/7 Getting job-creating small businesses going. **1973** E. F. SCHUMACHER *Small is Beautiful* III. 195 What proportion of national income.. can one reasonably expect to be available for the establishment of this capital fund for *job creation? **1976** *Ann. Rep. Manpower Services Comm. 1975–76* iii. 23/1 On 24 September, as part of a package of measures designed to alleviate unemployment, the Government provided £30 million for the implementation of a job creation scheme. **1986** *Tribune* 12 Sept. 3/1 Labour-controlled local councils are making detailed plans for job creation by local authorities. **1967** A. BATTERSBY *Network Analysis* (ed. 2) iv. 68 It will always be more convenient to go on using existing *job-definitions for which data on performance and cost are already known. **1951** J. M. FRASER *Psychol.* II. xi. 126 Once we have drawn up a complete and realistic description of a job we can work out from it a specification of the kind of person who is likely to do it satisfactorily. It is very important that.. each quality laid down in it should be linked with some aspect of the actual duties shown in the *job description. **1972** *Accountant* 28 Sept. 385/1 Essential records are.. those for employee turnover, performance appraisals, dynamic job descriptions/specifications. **1970** G. GREER *Female Eunuch* 297 A protest against *job discrimination. **1964** *Job displacement [see ACROSS *prep.* 2c]. **1835** *Court Mag.* VI. 207/1 A *job-doctor, or one whose engagement is likely to terminate with a particular service. **1954** *Time* 12 Apr., *Job enlargement (a phrase coined by Yale's Human Relations Expert Charles R. Walker) was formally born in 1943. On a trip through International Business Machine Corp.'s plant at Endicott, N.Y., I.B.M. President (now Chairman) Thomas J. Watson spotted a young woman standing idly by a milling machine. She explained that she was waiting for the 'machine inspector' (there was a 'setup man', whose task it was to adjust the machine for each new operation, and an inspector, who okayed the adjustment). Actually, she was able to adjust the machine herself, but it was against the plant rules to do so. **1966** T. LUPTON *Managem. & Social Sci.* ii. 32 It might well be possible to look at individual jobs to see whether it is possible to make them less rigidly paced and repetitive and not lose output, by '*job enlargement' for example. **1972** *Listener* 7 Sept. 301/1 A growing interest in the idea of work-structuring or '*job enrichment'. **1957** *Encycl. Brit.* XXIII. 272/1 Where *job evaluation wage rate systems prevail jobs are analyzed and defined in terms of basic attributes and requirements. **1973** *Times* 17 Jan. 13/3 Some techniques that until recently were virtually unheard of in the [hotel] industry are now beginning to make their appearance, such as job evaluation and formal performance appraisals. **1888** C. T. JACOBI *Printers' Vocab.* 68 **Job fount*, a small fount of type used for displaying purposes. **1894** *Amer. Dict. Printing & Bookmaking* 308/2 *Job font*, a small font of type used for display, distinct from a book font. **1972** *Jrnl. Printing Hist. Soc. 1971* VII. 39 A more efficient use of the full size case in accommodating the caps, figures and points only job fonts came with the devising of the treble case. **1883** 'ANNIE THOMAS' *Mod. Housewife* 30 Contenting ourselves with the services of a '*job gardener'.. whose crops were always late and poor. **1970** *Time* 19 Jan. 43 He *job-hopped, serving briefly as operating vice president of Servo-mechanisms Inc. and later organizing his own law firm in Los Angeles. **1967** *Time* 13 Oct. 63 Boyden's prospects are rarely aware that Boyden is aware of them as potential *job hoppers. **1953** *Britannica Bk. of Year* 639/2 **Job-hopping*, a policy of changing jobs so as to place a higher value on one's services. **1972** *Times* 22 Sept. 22/6 Increased job-hopping tendencies among young male graduates. **1790** H. M. WILLIAMS *Julia* II. xxii. 51 You had *job horses. **1849** THACKERAY *Pendennis* xxxiv, The sight of Dr. Slocum's large carriage, with the gaunt job-horses, crushed Flora. **1825** T. C. HANSARD *Typographia* 700 But, that it [*sc.* a kind of printing machine] could be introduced into a book-work house, or even a *job-house, to execute all the variety of sizes of works and pages, was a thing which I could never believe. **1841** W. SAVAGE *Dict. Art of Printing* 428 *Job house*, a printing office, the general run of business in which is the printing of Jobs; namely, cards, shop bills,.. play bills,.. and all other things of a similar description. **1888** C. T. JACOBI *Printers' Vocab.* 68 *Job house*, a term applied to printing offices distinct from book or newspaper offices. **1894** *Amer. Dict. Printing & Bookmaking* 309/1 *Job house*, a term applied in England to printing-offices where the chief kind of work done is in jobs. **1946** *Job-hungry [see GADGET 2]. **1966** T. LUPTON *Managem. & Social Sci.* iii. 63 Good environmental conditions—so called '*job hygiene', i.e. good welfare facilities, meals, lighting, heating, good mates. **1959** *Listener* 25 June 1095/2 The very notion of a *job insecurity.. is alien to the Russians. **1851** MAYHEW *Lond. Labour* I. 272 Some few of them [pocket-books] may, however, have been damaged, and these are bought by the street-people as a '*job lot', and at a lower price. **1864** *Reader* 3 Dec. 707/3 Called 'job lots', because the articles included in them are not resold in the state in which they were purchased, but jobbed away, or, in other words, sold to different customers, as opportunity may offer. **1879** *Print. Trades Jrnl.* No. 26. 16 Job lots of paper and job lots of leather and sometimes old covers. **1891** *Law Times* XC. 395/1 Defendant.. saw two cows belonging to Kidd among a job lot of cattle. **1966** I. JEFFERIES *House-Surgeon* iii. 26 Rosalind.. was used to even more *job-mobility than most people would regard as desirable. **1972** *Accountant* 12 Oct. 441/2 To cope with the problems presented by job mobility it was proposed to concentrate employees' records in ten computer centres. **1803** in *Naval Chron.* XV. 58 What is the nature of a *job note? It is.. an actual statement of the work performed by job and task, with the prices of the labour set against each article. **1882** T. MACKELLAR *Amer. Printer* (ed. 13) 301 A useful thing to have in a *job office is Ame's Paper and Card Scale. **1894** *Amer. Dict. Printing & Bookmaking* 309/2 *Job office*, a printing-house where the chief work is in jobs. **1971** *Wall St. Jrnl.* 22 July IV. 1/1 While thousands of 1971 graduates pound the pavements in pursuit of jobs, an exclusive little group here has found alluring *job opportunities popping up on all sides. **1963** *New Society* 7 Nov. 7/2 The private employment agencies, who handle a lucrative *job-placement business. **1894** *Amer. Dict. Printing & Bookmaking* 309/2 **Job press*, a press on which job-work is done. It is, however, in practice usually limited to the treadle-machines, which do not print a sheet larger than 14 or 15 by 21 [inches]. **1936** GREENHOOD & GENTRY *Chronol. Bks. & Printing* (rev. ed.) 111, 1850.. Gordon of New York is awarded a patent for first 'job' press. **1971** R. W. & E. W. POLK *Pract. Printing* (ed. 7) xv. 115 Most of the small presses for general job work are of the platen type. These presses are often classified as job presses. **1853** R. S. SURTEES *Sponge's Sp. Tour* (1893) 12 Mr. Buckram's *job price, we should say, was as near twelve pounds a month,.. as he could screw, the hirer, of course, keeping the animals. **1886** *Daily News* 26 July 2/5 Home buyers.. not infrequently supply their wants from accumulated stocks at 'job' prices. **1921** C. E. MULFORD *Bar-20 Three* vi. 77 A hard-riding courier, relaying twice, carried the work of the *job-print toward Mesquite. **1884** J. GOULD *Letter-Press Printer* (ed. 3) 132 For *job-printers the small platen machines are invaluable. **1960** P. M. HANDOVER *Printing in London* vii. 194 Without the lavish production of publicity material fashionable since the second world war many job printers would be unable to meet the necessary cost of new machines and the rising cost of labour and rent. **1825** *New Lisbon* (Ohio) *Patriot* 29 Oct. 1/4 *Job Printing, Neatly and expeditiously done at this office. **1859** *Abridgments of Specifications relating to Printing* (Patent Office) 365 The main object of this invention is to carry on 'job printing'.. without the necessity of employing skilled labour. **1892** A. POWELL *Southward's Pract. Printing* (ed. 4) xxix. 266 Bookwork is almost always executed in black ink; while in job printing any colour is permissible. **1924** *Southward's Mod. Printing* (ed. 5) I. Job Design Suppl. 2 (following p. 336), Fine book and job printing a speciality. **1960** P. M. HANDOVER *Printing in London* viii. 196 As job printing in London followed a course separate from that of periodicals, .. so the course of book printing was equally distinct. **1969** *Times* 19 Nov. 30/2 Some form of *job reservation [in South Africa] imposed either by legislation or custom will persist for some time to come. **1971** *Sunday Express* (Johannesburg) 28 Mar. 4/3 Sir Francis de Guingand.. said he found job reservation difficult to understand. **1972** *Sat. Rev.* (U.S.) 6 May 39/1 Industrialized and *job-rich Morgan City. **1963** R. STEWART *Reality of Management* II. vii. 119 The companies which use *job rotation as a conscious policy are likely to have a general policy of moving people in their early years and later to practise selective job rotation. **1955** BRAYFIELD & CROCKETT in *Psychol. Bull.* LII. 397/1 We have not attempted to define such terms as *job satisfaction or morale. Instead, we have found it necessary to assume that the measuring operations define the variables involved. **1972** *Accountant* 21 Sept. 346/1 Prinny.. would attend the first course to assess its suitability in terms of personal job-satisfaction. **1959** *Listener* 25 June 1095/1 A number of other attitudes towards *job security. **1972** *Sat. Rev.* (U.S.) 6 May 39/1 *Job-seeking itself can be costly. **1972** *Guardian* 22 July 1/8 The report will ask for a massive injection of Government money into the docks industry... There [were].. also proposals for *job-sharing schemes. **1981** *Job-sharing* (Equal Opportunities Commission) 8 A small survey of *job-sharers known to the Commission was carried out in January 1980. *Ibid.* 18 If I hadn't been able to job-share, I'd have left the job. **1982** *Computerworld* 8 Nov. 11/2 One programmer/analyst may prefer coding while his *job-share partner may prefer the design aspects of the job. **1985** *Marketing Mag.* (N.Z.) July 44/3 Maybe the concept of job sharing on a major scale.. will make increasing sense. **1987** *New Musical Express* 14 Feb. 15/4 What is wrong with the world? This is job-share schemes gone mad! **1970** P. LAURIE *Scotland Yard* v. 116 The ambulance crew which we met on the way are in Sister's office drinking tea and filling out their *job-sheets. **1974** 'J. ROSS' *Burning of Billy Toober* xvi. 149 Completing job sheets and questionnaires. **1851** H. MELVILLE *Moby Dick* III. xl. 233 When I kept my *job-shop in the Vineyard. **1963** *Times* 15 Feb. 7/1 The west coast and international editions of the *New York Times* are printed in 'job shops', commercial printing offices working on a contract basis. **1967** *Electronics* 6 Mar. 28 (Advt.), Whether you have an in-plant plating operation or a job shop, we'll help you select a process. **1972** *Times* 7 June 27/5 The Butts Centre.. will feature a job shop—the officially approved title of a room full of advertising boards where people can browse. **1951** J. M. FRASER *Psychol.* II. xi. 120 We are confronted then with two variables, the job and the individual... Our task is to match up one with the other, to find the individual who will fit neatly into the *job situation. **1923** J. D. HACKETT in *Managem. Engin.* May, **Job specification*, a record of the essential factors in a given piece of work and of the human qualifications necessary for its performance. **1970** *Times* 11 May 9/1 The company has begun the groundwork for *job structuring. **1951** J. M. FRASER *Psychol.* II. xi. 128 The *job-study provides a complete factual description of the job and the conditions in which it is carried out. **1882** T. MACKELLAR *Amer. Printer* (ed. 13) 304 Capitals and lower-case *job types should not be laid together in the same boxes. **1888** Job type [see *book type* (BOOK *sb.* 19)]. **1892** A. POWELL *Southward's Pract. Printing* (ed. 4) viii. 53 Job types are laid in upper and lower cases, in double cases, or in half cases, according to the extent of the founts. **1867** SMYTH *Sailor's Word-bk.*, **Job-watch*, or *Hack-watch*, for taking astronomical sights, which saves taking the chronometer on deck or on shore to note the time. **1803** R. PERING in *Naval Chron.* XV. 58, I conceive.. *job work [in royal dockyards] to consist in pulling to pieces and repairing. **1832** *Reg. Deb. Congress U.S.* 5 May 2766 The occasional advertising and job-work for the Government. **1859** *Abridgments of Specifications relating to Printing* (Patent Office) 390 This invention relates to an arrangement of machinery intended chiefly for printing 'job work' with great expedition. **1887** JESSOPP *Arcady* vi. 176 Once or twice I had come upon him doing job-work for the small employers. **1892** A. POWELL *Southward's Pract. Printing* (ed. 4) xxix. 266 It is obvious that there is hardly any limit to the modes in which job work may be executed. **1948** *Words into Type* 543 *Job work*, miscellaneous printing—all except newspaper, magazine, or book work. **1966** BERRY & POOLE *Ann. Printing* 256/1 The extravagant style of American job work.

job (dʒɒb), *sb.*³ Also 6–7 iobbe. [f. JOB *v.*¹] An act of 'jobbing'; an abrupt stab with the point or sharp end of anything; a peck, dab, thrust; a jerk or wrench of the bit in a horse's mouth.

1560 DAUS tr. *Sleidane's Comm.* 339 Nicholas Quercey toke the with his wife.. and gaue the a iobbe with hys Dagger. **1583** GOLDING *Calvin on Deut.* ciii. 635 A iob with his beake is not so great a matter. **1607** MARKHAM *Caval.* II. (1617) 198 With his contrary spur to giue him a good stroake or Iobbe to bring him with spirit againe into the managing path. **1611** COTGR., *Vn rabat de bride*, a iob, or checke which a horse giues himselfe with his bridle. **1885** *Eng. Illustr. Mag.* Apr. 505 It requires a good job to drive the point of a large hook in beyond the barb.

†**b.** *Comb.* **job-nut**, name of a game in which hazel-nuts are perforated and strung through, in order to be knocked against each other: see COB-NUT 2. *Obs.*

1659 *Lady Alimony* II. v. D ij b, All his games.. Are yert-point, nine pins, job-nut, or span counter.

Job (dʒəʊb), *sb.*⁴

1. Name of an ancient patriarch, whose story forms a book of the Old Testament; used in proverbial phrases as a type (*a*) of destitution, (*b*) of patience.

1553 T. WILSON *Rhet.* (1580) 210 Tushe, thou art as poore as Iob. **1749** FIELDING *Tom Jones* x. viii, You would provoke the patience of Job. **1822** BYRON *Werner* I. i. 401 He's poor as Job, and not so patient. **1884** W. E. NORRIS *Thirlby Hall* vi, My uncle bore it with the patience of Job.

Comb. **1878** BROWNING *La Saisiaz* 355 Job-like couched on dung and crazed with blains. **1891** *Critic* (U.S.) 5 Sept. 114/2 There is no sound of lamentation or Job-cry in it.

2. Phrases with *Job's*. **Job's cat, turkey** *U.S. joc.*, used as types of poverty; **Job's comforter**, one who, like Job's friends, under the guise of administering comfort, aggravates distress (cf. Job xvi. 2); **Job's news**, news of disaster; so **Job's post**, a messenger who brings such news: see Job i. 13–19; **Job's tears** (also †*Job's drops*), name for a species of grass (*Coix Lacryma*), having round shining grains resembling tears, and used as beads.

1854 S. SMITH *Way down East* 184, I should rather be as poor as *Job's cat all the days of my life. **1738** SWIFT *Pol. Conversat.* iii, *Lady Sm.* I think your Ladyship looks thinner than when I saw you last. *Miss*.. Your Ladyship is one of *Job's comforters. **1882** MRS. CROKER *Proper Pride* III. i. 22 You are a Job's comforter with a vengeance. **1831** CARLYLE *Sart. Res.* III. v, This, we think, is but *Job's news to the human reader. **1837** —— *Fr. Rev.* III. III. iv, It was Friday .. when this *Job's-post from Dumouriez, thickly preceded and escorted by so many other Job's-posts, reached the National Convention. **1597** GERARDE *Herbal* I. lix. §4. 82 In English it is called *Iobs Teares or Iobs Drops, for that euery graine resembleth the Drop or Teare that falleth from the eie. **1772–84** COOK *Voy.* (1790) IV. 1291 Job's tears, mosses, and several kinds of fern. **1857** HENFREY *Elem. Bot.* 426 *Coix Lacryma*, the hard grains of which are known by the name of 'Job's-tears'. **1824** *The Microscope* 22 May 42/2 We have seen fit to say 'the patience of *Job's turkey', instead of the common phrase, 'as patient as Job'. **1871** E. EGGLESTON *Hoosier Schoolmaster* (1872) iv. 22 But laws! don't I remember when he was poorer nor Job's turkey! **1951** *Publ. Amer. Dial. Soc.* xv. 58 Poor as Job's turkey.

job (dʒɒb), *v.*¹ Also 5–7 iobbe, 7–8 jobb: see also JAB. [app. onomatopœic, expressing the sound or effect of an abruptly arrested stab.]

1. *trans.* To pierce to a small depth with a forcible but abruptly arrested action, as with the point of something; to peck, dab, stab, prod, punch; to hurt a horse's mouth with the bit; in pugilistic language, to strike with a sharp or cutting stroke.

c **1490** *Promp. Parv.* 36/1 (MS. K.) Byllen or iobbyn as bryddys (*H.*, *P.* iobbyn with the byl), *rostro*. *c* **1537** *Thersites* in *Four Old Plays* (1848) 79 Jynkyn Jacon that iobbed iolye Jone. **1560** DAUS tr. *Sleidane's Comm.* x. 130 Then caught he a boore speare.. and as he laie iobbed him in with the staffe heade [*iacentem pila transverberat*]. **1741** E. SMITH *Compl. Housew.* (1750) 199 With a small bodkin job the oranges as they are boiling, to let the Syrup into them. **1818** *Sporting Mag.* II. 189 He measured his distance accurately, and jobbed his adversary about the head. **1844** DICKENS *Mart. Chuz.* xxxiii, He had 'jobbed out' the eye of one gentleman. **1860** READE *Cloister & H.* xxiv, He.. drew his long knife, and.. prepared to job the huge brute as soon as it should mount within reach. **1884** BARING-GOULD *Mehalah* v. 63 Let the horse go, but don't job his mouth in that way.

2. To thrust (something pointed) abruptly into something else. †*to job faces*, ludicrously used for 'to kiss' (*obs.*).

1573 TUSSER *Husb.* (1878) 89 If peacock and turkey leaue iobbing their bex. **1600** HEYWOOD *1 Edw. IV*, III. i, What the dickens is it loue that makes ye prate to me so fondly? By my fathers soule, I would I had iobd faces with you. **1674** JOSSELYN *Voy. New Eng.* 186 Two crooked bones growing upon the top of the heart, which as she bowed her body.. would job their points into one and the same place. **1741** *Compl. Fam. Piece* III. 511 Immediately jobb a Penknife into the Throat. *a* **1795** *Robin Hood & Maid Marian* xiv. in Child *Ballads* (1888) III. v. cl. 219/2 With kind embraces, and jobbing of faces. **1845** STOCQUELER *Hand-bk. Brit. India*

(1854) 337 In some parts of India our sportsmen throw the spear—in others they thrust or job it.

3. *intr.* To peck (*at*) as a bird; to thrust (*at*) so as to stab or pierce; to penetrate *into*.

1566 DRURY *Let. to Cecil* 27 Mar. (P.R.O., St. Pap. Dom., Borders II. 131 b), In Iobbying att hym [Rizzio] so meny att onse. **1579–80** NORTH *Plutarch, Nicias* 457 Upon that palm-tree sate certain crows many daies..and never left pecking and jobbing at the fruit of it. **1603** HOLLAND tr. *Plutarch's Rom. Quest.* (1892) 33 After he [the woodpecker] hath jobbed and pecked into it [the oak] as farre as to the very marrow and heart thereof. **1703** MOXON *Mech. Exerc.* 169 The Tool will job into softer parts of the Stuff. **1882** JESSOPP in *19th Cent.* Nov. 733 Pigmies of the Meiocene..jobbing at the eyes of some mammoth floundering in a hole.

job (dʒɒb), *v.*[2] Also 8 jobb. [f. JOB *sb.*[2]]

1. *intr.* To do jobs or odd pieces of work; to do piece-work, work by the piece.

1694 MOTTEUX *Rabelais* IV. Prol., By his Hatchet he earn'd many a fair Penny of the..Log-Merchants, among whom he went a Jobbing. *c* **1820** MRS. SHERWOOD *Penny Tract* 7 in *Houlston Juvenile Tracts*, Cutting fruit-trees, and jobbing about in different gardens. **1825** HONE *Every-day Bk.* I. 873 He had worked..and still jobbed about.

2. *trans.* Chiefly in colloq. phr. ***that job's jobbed***.

1840 MARRYAT *Poor Jack* xix, That job's jobbed, as the saying is. **1847** DE QUINCEY *Secret Societies* Wks. 1863 VI. 240 'Then', said Pyrrhus, 'next we go for Macedon; and after that job's jobbed, next, of course, for Greece'. **1864** WEBSTER s.v., To job work.

3. To let out (a large piece of work) in separate portions to different contractors or workmen.

1882 in OGILVIE.

4. To hire (less usually, to let out on hire) for a particular job, or for a definite time (a horse, carriage, etc.). Also *absol.*, and in phr. *to job it*.

1786 WOLCOTT (P. Pindar) *Birthday Ode* xliv, Whitbread, d'ye keep a coach, or job one, pray? Job, job, that's cheapest; yes, that's best, that's best. **1829** HOOD *Epping H.* xxxi, Some had horses of their own, And some were forced to job it. **1848** THACKERAY *Van. Fair* xlviii, She went to the livery-man from whom she jobbed her carriage. **1861** MAYHEW *Lond. Labour* III. 358/1 The masters of whom I have spoken will job a carriage duly emblazoned..with the proper armorial bearings..and job coachmen and grooms as well. *Ibid.*, Very few noblemen at present bring their carriage-horses to town;..they nearly all job, as it is invariably called.

5. To let or deal with for profit.

1726 in *Swift's Corr.* Wks. 1841 II. 583 Your interest with me..procured Dr. Ellwood the use of that chamber, not the power to job it. **1812** SCOTT *Let. to Southey* 4 June in *Lockhart*, The clergy..have a strange disposition to job away among themselves the rewards of literature. **1838** LYTTON *Alice* II. iii, These old ruins are my property, and are not to be jobbed out to the insolence of public curiosity.

6. a. To buy and sell (stock or goods) as a broker; to deal with as a middleman; to buy from one person and sell to another at a profit. ***to job off***: to sell goods at very low prices.

1670 [implied in JOBBER[2] 3]. **1711** J. DENNIS *Pub. Spirit* 29 Stocks are jobb'd by People in the City, who have no real Stock but their Impudence. **1864** WEBSTER s.v., To job goods. **1890** WALT WHITMAN in *Pall Mall G.* 26 Aug. 7/2 The Essays are remarkably fine specimens of type, paper, and press-work—Chapman and Hall their English publishers—and jobb'd here by Scribners, New York. **1903** *Lett. that bring Business* 68 We have had some very unpleasant experiences in the past through our goods being held on consignment for months, and then jobbed off at suicidal prices. **1936** *Economist* 22 Feb. 400/1 Motor spirit.. has been comparatively easy to sell, while heavier oils have either been 'jobbed off' or used for 'cracking' into lighter oils. **1955** *Times* 22 Aug. 7/6 The bottom has dropped out of the rice market and hard decisions are being taken about jobbing off as cattle fodder a million tons of surplus rice.

b. *intr.* To buy and sell stock; to deal or speculate in stocks.

1721–2 AMHERST *Terræ Fil.* No. 12 (1754) 59 Those persons, who could not raise money enough..jobb'd in these little bubbles. **1781** JUSTAMOND *Priv. Life Lewis XV*, I. 84 This Nobleman had jobbed to advantage in the Quincampoix- street. **1809** R. LANGFORD *Introd. Trade* 116 If he has lost..certain sums..in..jobbing in the funds. **1890** *Spectator* 15 Nov., The Bourses of the world have begun to job in currency.

c. ***to job backwards***: to engage retrospectively in calculations, e.g. of profits on Stock Exchange transactions, that presume knowledge of subsequent events. Freq. *transf.*

1919 D. LLOYD GEORGE *Let.* 8 July in A. J. P. Taylor *My Darling Pussy* (1975) 27 The election was muddled but it is no use jobbing backwards. **1931** *Economist* 21 Mar. 621/1 Calculations based on 'jobbing backwards' on a Fixed Trust holding are altogether illusive. **1939** *War Illustr.* 18 Nov. p. ii/1, I notice that in his [*sc.* Lloyd George's] writings about this later, and quite possibly greater, War he shows a sad inclination to 'job backwards', as they say on the Stock Exchange. By jobbing backwards I have no difficulty in proving how I could have been worth £20,000,000, whereas if I die, or get bombed, before this war finishes I shall figure for ever so much less than that, having lost a considerable fortune by declining values of stocks and shares. **1959** *Times* 4 Sept. 11/4 Did he [*sc.* the Prime Minister] not actually say 'We never job backwards'? This is a Stock Market term meaning, in this context, 'We let bygones be bygones.' **1959** *Observer* 11 Oct. 15/3 Meanwhile, jobbing backwards, how much was one inclined to overestimate the effect of those excellently produced Labour Party telecasts? **1968** J. M. ZIMAN *Public Knowl.* iii. 31 All too often it becomes an exercise in 'jobbing backwards': it tells us how we ought to have derived our result if only we had known the answer before we began.

7. *intr.* To turn a public office or service, or a position of trust, improperly to private or party advantage; to practise jobbery.

1732 POPE *Ep. Bathurst* 141 Statesman and Patriot ply alike the stocks,..And Judges, job, and Bishops bite the town. **1826** SCOTT *Jrnl.* 20 Jan., I daresay he jobs, as all other people of consequence do, in elections and so forth. **1844** P. HARWOOD *Hist. Irish Rebell.* 47 *note*, He found it necessary to bribe and job on a larger scale than the boldest of his predecessors. **1869** *Spectator* 17 Apr. 469/2 If left unfettered he would job.

8. a. *trans.* To make a 'job' of (JOB *sb.*[2] 3, 4 b); to deal with in some way; *esp.* to deal with corruptly for private gain or advantage.

1825 SCOTT *Fam. Lett.* 25 Aug. (1894) II. xxiii. 344 The local magistrates..seem to have jobb'd the matter sadly. **1881** BLACKMORE *Christowell* ix, He meant to do his duty to his own kin, instead of founding charities to be jobbed by aliens. **1889** *Spectator* 28 Sept., They would regard this power as certain to be jobbed, and will accordingly never give it.

b. To give *away* by jobbery; to get (a person) *into* some position by jobbery.

1720 RAMSAY *Wealth* 50 How..these..Have jobb'd themselves into sae high a state. **1849** *Tait's Mag.* XVI. 141/2 The Colonial Office had all but jobbed away Vancouver's Island. **1864** SALA in *Daily Tel.* 30 Sept., The nominee may have been jobbed into the place to serve some dirty purpose. **1899** *Daily News* 20 July 7/2 [He] was then jobbed into the post of director of the deaf and dumb asylum.

9. To put *off* by artifice: cf. *fob off*.

1876 WEISS *Wit. Hum., & Shaks.* xi. 379 When you try jauntily to job off suspicion before other persons, the cheek grows pale with dread of being contradicted. **1887** *Pall Mall G.* 23 Aug. 6/1 The policy of Scotland-yard, he [Mr. Pickersgill] said, was to 'job off' complaints made against the police.

10. To cheat; to betray; = FRAME *v.* 10. *slang* (orig. *U.S.*).

1903 A. H. LEWIS *Boss* viii. 100 Twelve honest dullards who called themselves a jury, despite his protestations that he was 'being jobbed', instantly declared him guilty. **1904** *McClure's Mag.* Nov. 64/1 Now she was coming back, swearing she'd been 'jobbed', the judge had been bought, and the jury corrupted. **1926** J. BLACK *You can't Win* xxiii. 353 It has always been a question with me where this framing and jobbing started; whether the defense originally began it..or whether it was the other way round. *Ibid.* 366, I was in the district attorney's office..and I know you got 'jobbed'. I'll take your case for nothing. **1972** C. DRUMMOND *Death at Bar* v. 110 Funny you not minding Alwyn jobbin' your mum, not to mention your lawful wedded hubby. **1972** J. PHILIPS *Vanishing Senator* (1973) I. ii. 11 'Peter is troubled by the possibility that Jeremy Lloyd was jobbed by the Justice Department.'.. 'You think Lloyd is innocent?' **1973** K. GILES *File on Death* ii. 28 You want to watch or they'll job you on that.

job, obs. form of JOBE *v.*

† **'jobard.** *Obs.* Also 5 iobbard. [a. F. *jobard*, f. *jobe* silly.] A stupid fellow, a fool.

14.. LYDG. *Min. Poems, Hors, Shepe & G.* (Percy Soc.) 119 Looke of discrecioune sette jobbardis upon stoolis, Whiche hathe distroyed many a comunalté. **14..** *Seven Maysters* in *MS. Cantab. Ff.* ii. 38 lf. 150b, þo seyde þe Emperour Sodenmagard, þen was þe Erle a nyse Iobarde.

jobardy, obs. form of JEOPARDY.

jobation (dʒəʊ'beɪʃən). *colloq.* [f. JOBE *v.* + -ATION. Dialectally, usually *jawbation*, as if derived from *jaw, jawing*.] The action of the verb JOBE; a rebuke, reproof, *esp.* one of a lengthy and tedious character; a 'talking to', a 'lecture'. Also, a long discussion.

1687 J. SMITH *Let.* 1 Aug. in Granville *Rem.* (1865) 137, I had far rather venture to be liable to a jobation for not having done my part. **1714** C. JOHNSON *Country Lasses* IV. ii, You see I have stood your jobation very patiently. **1785** R. CUMBERLAND *Observer* No. 95 ¶4 Neither will I disguise the frequent *jobations* I incurred for neglect of college duties. **1861** HUGHES *Tom Brown at Oxf.* xlii. (1889) 412 Don't be angry at my jobation; but write me a long answer. **1877** *Holderness Gloss., Jawbation*, a long and tedious harangue; a prolonged disputation. **1888** J. PAYN *Myst. Mirbridge* I. xvi. 268 Fathers..deliver a didactic harangue, which the recipient terms a jobation. **1916** 'TAFFRAIL' *Pincher Martin* v. 75 Well, after a lot of jawbation we got him into the boat. **1925** P. GIBBS *Unchanging Quest* vii. 51, I used to watch Katherine while all this jawbation was in progress. **1938** H. G. WELLS *Apropos of Dolores* iv. 227 They aren't happy until the hand's been played [*sc.* at bridge] and the jawbation begins.

jobbe, variant of JUBBE, *Obs.*, a large vessel.

jobbed (dʒɒbd), *ppl. a.* [f. JOB *v.*[2] + -ED[1].] Hired, as a horse or carriage, for a particular job or for a definite time.

1883 LD. R. GOWER *My Remin.* I. xi. 188 We had some pleasant..rides on jobbed horses. **1899** *Westm. Gaz.* 22 June 7/2 Driving about in jobbed carriages and pairs.

jobber[1] ('dʒɒbə(r)). *dial.* [f. JOB *v.*[1] + -ER[1].] One who or that which 'jobs', pecks, pokes, thrusts, etc.: see quots. and cf. NUT-JOBBER.

1580 HOLLYBAND *Treas. Fr. Tong* s.v. *Grimpereau*, Some do call that birde a nut iobber. **1868** ATKINSON *Cleveland Gloss., Jobber*, a small spade or iron tool for cutting up thistles from their roots.

jobber[2] ('dʒɒbə(r)). [f. JOB *v.*[2] + -ER[1].]

1. One who does jobs or odd pieces of work; one employed to do a job; a hack; one employed by the job, as distinguished from one continuously engaged and paid wages; a piece-worker.

1706 PHILLIPS (ed. Kersey), *Jobb*, a small piece of Work. *Jobber*, he that undertakes such Jobbs. **1733** SWIFT *On Poetry* 312 These are not a thousandth part Of jobbers in the poet's art. **1791–1823** D'ISRAELI *Cur. Lit., B. Jonson on Transl.*, Our translators have usually been the jobbers of booksellers. **1803** W. TAYLOR in *Ann. Rev.* I. 424 Sailors and soldiers are improvident for the same reason as jobbers in a manufactory. **1841** D'ISRAELI *Amen. Lit.* (1867) 523 To this humiliated state of jobbers of old plays, were reduced the most glorious names.

2. One who lets out horses, etc. on hire for a particular job, or for a period; a job-master.

1848 THACKERAY *Van. Fair* xxxvii, Nobody in fact was paid. Not the blacksmith who opened the lock;..nor the jobber who let the carriage. **1872** *Daily News* 25 Mar., The Hampstead donkey drivers and Greenwich mule jobbers.

3. One who buys goods, etc. in bulk from the producer or importer, and sells them to retail dealers, or to consumers; a broker, a middleman; a small trader or salesman.

In many compounds, as HOUSE-, LAND-JOBBER, etc., q.v.

1670 *Act 22 & 23 Chas. II*, c. 2 §2 Jobber, Salesman or other Broker or Factor, who doe or shall commonly buy or sell Cattell for others. *c* **1680** *Popish Plot* 1 They have 100000*l.* in ready Money..used in Trade by Graziers, Jobbers, and Bankers. **1769** *De Foe's Tour Gt. Brit.* I. 245 A Fair for Cattle and Lambs,..of late..much lessened in that respect, owing principally to the Jobbers about Horsham, who ingross great Numbers and send them to Smithfield Market. **1805** R. W. DICKSON *Pract. Agric.* (1807) II. 659 What the Yorkshire jobbers call *runts*. **1862** MERIVALE *Rom. Emp.* (1865) III. xxvi. 216 Ventidius..had been for a time a jobber of beasts of burden to the public officers. **1887** JESSOPP *Arcady* vii. 213 In Norfolk a cattle dealer is commonly called a jobber. **1898** *Archæol. Jrnl.* LV. 186 One of the Irish jobbers who every autumn bring over Irish bred geese for sale to the farmers to fatten on their stubbles against Christmas.

4. A member of the Stock Exchange, who deals in stocks or shares on his own account; one who acts as a middleman between holders and buyers of stocks or shares; a STOCK-JOBBER; called, in the Stock Exchange itself, a *dealer*.

1719 (*title*) The Anatomy of Exchange Alley..by a Jobber. **1720** SWIFT *Fates Clergymen* Wks. 1755 II. II. 28 Acquainted with jobbers in Change-alley. **1812** L. HUNT in *Examiner* 14 Sept. 577/1 This is one of the old tricks of the Stock-jobbers... But the jobbers do not appear to have thought it worth their while. **1897** *Daily News* 27 Sept. 6/6 The jobber exists to create a free market in securities... If the jobber were eliminated the trouble and worry of the broker would be so much increased that he would be forced at least to double his commissions.

5. One who improperly uses a public office, trust, or service for private gain or party advantage; a perpetrator of corrupt jobs.

1739 HILDROP *Lett. Commandm.* 18 An absolute Discouragement to all Sorts of Jobbers, Gamesters, Fortune-hunters, and Jockeys. *a* **1745** SWIFT *Corr.* (1766) III. 299 Every squire, almost to a man, is..a racker of his tenants; a jobber of all public works. **1794** G. ROSE *Diaries* (1860) I. 194 He is an atrocious jobber. **1885** FLETCHER in *Collect.* (O.H.S.) I. 183 Possibly it was what would now be called a 'job'. But, if so, the jobbers had been warned.

b. ***borough-jobber***: see BOROUGH 7 c, BOROUGH-MONGER.

1758 JOHNSON *Idler* No. 7 ¶22 Captain Grim, who never owed any of his advancement to borough-jobbers, or any other corrupters of the people. **1874** GREEN *Short Hist.* x. §2. 744 Others were 'close boroughs' in the hands of jobbers like the Duke of Newcastle.

jobbernowl ('dʒɒbənəʊl). *colloq.* Also 6–7 iobbernowle, -noul(e, iobernol(e, 7 job(b)ernoll, 7–9 jobbernol(e, 8 -knowl, 9 (in Dicts.) jabbernowl. [app. f. *jobbard*, JOBARD + NOLL, OE. *hnol*, head; but evidence of the historical connexion is incomplete.]

1. A blockish or stupid head; a ludicrous term for the head, usually connoting stupidity.

1599 MARSTON *Sco. Villanie* II. vi. 200 His guts are in his braines, huge Iobbernoule, Right Gurnets-head. **1656** EARL MONM. *Advt. fr. Parnass.* 356 Submit your jobernols to the sacred precepts of Nature. **1678** BUTLER *Hud.* III. ii. 815 And, like the World, Men's Jobbernoles Turn round upon their Ears, the Poles. **1794** GIFFORD *Baviad* (1811) 32 Nothing from thy jobbernowl can spring But impudence and filth. **1827** *Blackw. Mag.* XXII. 480 The Giant, heightened by the ell-long bonnet and feather on his huge jobbernowl.

2. A stupid person, a blockhead.

1592 NASHE *4 Lett. Confut.* E iv, Gaffer Iobbernoule,.. how dost thou? **1653** URQUHART *Rabelais* I. Prol., A certain sneaking jobernol alledged that his [Horace's] verses smelled more of the wine then oile. **1711** E. WARD *Quix.* I. 94 How hard His Brother Jobbernole had far'd. **1823** *Blackw. Mag.* XIV. 512 Ministers, who are regularly called asses,..dunder-pates, jobbernowls. **1890** HALL CAINE *Bondman* xx. II. 242 The numbskull!.. The jobbernowl!

3. *attrib.* or as *adj.* Stupid, dunderheaded.

1828 *Examiner* 4/2 Misled by the jobbernol applause of an audience. **1838** J. P. KENNEDY *Rob of Bowl* xv. 172 Our jobbernowl English..have gone back to their old sport.

Hence **'jobbernowlism**, the condition, or something characteristic, of a jobbernowl; stupidity; a stupid act, remark, etc.

1652 URQUHART *Jewel* Wks. (1834) 265 A more sanctified brother, whose zealous jobernolisme would never have affected..Plato, Euclid, or Aristotle. **1824** *Blackw. Mag.* XVI. 289 Gabble pretty jobbernowlisms on the sky gods.

jobbery ('dʒɒbərɪ). [Cf. JOBBER[2] and -ERY.]
1. Jobs or small pieces of work collectively; job-work. *rare*. (In quot. *attrib.*)
1832 J. H. NEWMAN *Lett.* (1891) I. 294 Coal, which the foreign jobbery heavers are conveying into the vessel.
2. The practice of corruptly turning a public office, trust, etc. to private gain or advantage; the perpetration of jobs (see JOB *sb.*[2] 3).
1837 SIR F. PALGRAVE *Merch. & Friar* Ded. (1844) 7 A notable example of the ancient mode of Parliamentary jobbery. **1852** MISS YONGE *Cameos* (1877) III. xxiv. 225 He was now staining the honour of that seat by his intrigues and jobbery. **1861** GOLDW. SMITH *Irish Hist.* 184 Inveterate habits of official jobbery and party corruption. **1893** *Times* 26 Apr. 9/5 Incited by his friends [he] aspired to wider opportunities of jobbery.

jobbing ('dʒɒbɪŋ), *vbl. sb.*[1] [f. JOB *v.*[1] + -ING[1].] The action of JOB *v.*[1]; stabbing, thrusting, etc.
1573, *a* **1795** [see JOB *v.*[1] 2]. **1814** *Sporting Mag.* XLIV. 71 His adversary was not to be pinked away by left-handed jobbing. **1889** R. S. S. BADEN-POWELL *Pigsticking* 82 No jobbing or spurring would induce the horse to move.
b. *attrib.* Used for 'jobbing' or thrusting, as *jobbing-knife*, *-spear*.
1870 tr. *Erckmann-Chatrian's Waterloo* 122 These men with their jobbing-knives in their leather belts. **1889** R. S. S. BADEN-POWELL *Pigsticking* 89 Two kinds of spear are used in India, the long or 'underhand' spear, and the short or 'jobbing' spear.

jobbing, *vbl. sb.*[2] [f. JOB *v.*[2] + -ING[1].] The action of JOB *v.*[2]
1. a. The doing of jobs or small pieces of work. b. *spec.* (*Printing*), the printing of jobs (JOB *sb.*[2] 1 c.); also *attrib.* and *Comb.* as JOB *sb.*[2] 7, ***jobbing case***, ***fount***, ***office***, ***press***, ***printer***, ***printing***, ***type***, ***work***.
1800 *D. Corpor. Acc.* in Tomlinson *Doncaster* (1887) 255 For sundries as per jobbing bill. **1841** W. SAVAGE *Dict. Art of Printing* 428 Jobbing is an extensive business in London. **1856** KANE *Arct. Expl.* II. x. 105 Able to do much useful jobbing. **1861** *Bookseller* 26 Oct. Advt., The Founts of Type are..adapted for..every description of First-class Jobbing and Bookwork. **1872** *Printers' Register* Apr. 114/1 The difficulty often experienced in laying Jobbing Founts. **1884** J. GOULD *Letter-Press Printer* (ed. 3) 78 Every compositor should endeavour to make himself acquainted with the composition of miscellaneous work, as it is a great source of annoyance to find that a man who is put on to assist cannot earn his wages, but is in fact a hindrance to others in a jobbing office. **1888** C. T. JACOBI *Printers' Vocab.* 68 *Jobbing cases*, double cases made with upper and lower in one. They are sometimes made treble. **1892** A. POWELL *Southward's Pract. Printing* (ed. 4) vi. 41 Jobbing Type is so called because it is used for 'jobs', i.e., for work like cards, circulars, letter headings, and advertisements. **1924** *Southward's Mod. Printing* (ed. 5) I. ii. 9 (*caption*) Small jobbing office. *Ibid.* v. 37 The ordinary arrangement causes the 49 boxes, in seven rows, for the capitals, to be much too small for jobbing founts. For this reason, double cases are now being made with only five or six rows of boxes. *Ibid.* li. 328 Jobbing work is a term applied to every kind of printing except book-work and newspaper work. **1946** A. MONKMAN in H. Whetton *Pract. Printing & Binding* vii. 75/1 There is still a wide variety of work available to the general or jobbing printer. **1960** P. M. HANDOVER *Printing in London* vii. 172 (*heading*) Jobbing. *Ibid.* vii. 173 The range of jobbing is so great that it would be possible to confine the following pages to a single subject, such as printed games. **1960** G. A. GLAISTER *Gloss. Bk.* 204/1 *Jobbing types*, types used for jobbing printing. **1966** BERRY & POOLE *Ann. Printing* 236/2 This [*sc.* Gordon's 'Alligator' Press 1851] was a jobbing press with a platen standing fixed at an angle of 45 degrees. *Ibid.* 248/2, 1870..A collection of 'artistic' jobbing work..the work of Oscar H. Harpel..was published in Cincinnati. *Ibid.* 253/2, 1880..The [Printers' International Specimen] Exchange was commenced with the object of fostering good jobbing printing. **1972** *Jrnl. Printing Hist. Soc.* 1971 VII. 38 *Double case, improved double case, improved jobbing case*, British terms for full size job cases which put the lower case letters in the left two thirds and the capitals in the right third of the case. *Ibid.*, Most printers both in America and in Britain were forced to add more and more of the new letters to their stores of type in order to remain competitive in the jobbing printing business. *Ibid.*, J. L. Ringwalt [and others] ..offer succinct but accurate accounts of the forces that brought about the design and production of these new jobbing types. **1973** *Univ. of Stirling Press Room* (Univ. of Stirling Library), The Press Room contains a large assortment of printing types, jobbing cases, galleys, chases, composing sticks, rules and leads. **1973** *Times Lit. Suppl.* 7 Dec. 1500/3 These principles underlie the construction of most of the presses now operating, from jobbing presses to the largest newspaper machine.
2. The buying of goods or stock from one person and selling to another in order to profit; the practice of a middleman or stock-jobber. (See also STOCK-JOBBING.)
1735 BOLINGBROKE *Lett. Hist.* ii. (1752) 39 Amassing immense estates by the management of funds, by trafficking in paper, and by all the arts of jobbing. **1754** *Ess. Manning Fleet* 34 Regulations..to prevent..the Monopoly of Tickets, and the..jobbing of them. **1790** BURKE *Fr. Rev.* 170 The jobbing of the public funds. **1825** HONE *Every-day Bk.* I. 174 Forced to an undue price by the arts of jobbing.
3. The action of using a public office or service for private gain or party advantage; the perpetration of corrupt jobs; jobbery.
1780 A. YOUNG *Tour in Ireland* II. ix. 41 Lists and tables of the names of all persons who have obtained presentments, ..should be given freely by the jurymen, to all their acquaintance, that every man might know, to whose carelessness or jobbing, the public was indebted for bad roads. **1784** J. BARRY in *Lect. Paint.* iv. (1848) 166 The influence and jobbing by which the doing of them is obtained. **1838** LYTTON *Alice* III. i, No jobbing was too gross for him. He was shamefully corrupt in the disposition of his patronage. **1861** MAY *Const. Hist.* I. vi. 322 The costly..contracts, which this system of Parliamentary jobbing encouraged.
4. *attrib.* (See also sense 1 b.)
1775 T. MORTIMER *Ev. Man his own Broker* 14 Rash engagements in jobbing contracts. **1873** J. RICHARDS *Wood-working Factories* 144 A planing, moulding, and general jobbing machine. **1889** *Daily News* 6 Dec. 3/1 Out of this post-horse system..has grown this jobbing system, which is revolutionizing the customs of all who 'keep their gig'.

jobbing, *ppl. a.* [f. JOB *v.*[2] + -ING[2].] That 'jobs', in various senses: see JOB *v.*[2]
1. That does jobs; employed in odd or occasional pieces of work.
1705 *Double Welcome* xlii, A starving Mercenary Priest, A Jobbing, Hackney, Vicious Pulpit Jest. **1746** T. LANGLEY *Builder's Jewel* Introd. (1757) A ij, Apprentices..bound to Jobbing Masters, who know but little. **1836–7** DICKENS *Sk. Boz, Scenes* v, A jobbing man—carpet-beater and so forth. **1850** *Beck's Florist* 298, I never had a jobbing gardener that did not want to get in the saddle himself, and put you on the pillion. **1881** YOUNG *Every man his own Mechanic* § 187 It is an easy matter..to find a jobbing carpenter.
2. Dealing as a middleman.
1896 *Proc. New-Eng. Hist. Geneal. Soc.* 105 He was one of the prominent jobbing merchants of this city.
3. Using means to secure private gain or advantage in connexion with a public service, etc.; given to jobbery.
1792 BURKE *Corr.* (1844) IV. 27 The sentiments of the nation must finally decide the dispute between them and the jobbing ascendancy. *a* **1859** MACAULAY *Hist. Eng.* xxiii. V. 70 Covered with the mansions of his jobbing courtiers.

jobbing-master. *rare*. = JOBMASTER.
1851 MAYHEW *Lond. Labour* I. 362 These articles are usually sold at the several mews, stable-yards, and jobbing-masters' in and about the metropolis. **1960** G. E. EVANS *House in Furrow* xv. 193 A jobbing-master at The Rampant Horse, kept about six horses for use in broughams and so on.

jobbish ('dʒɒbɪʃ), *a.* [f. JOB *sb.*[2] + -ISH[1].] Of the nature of a job (see JOB *sb.*[2] 3); characterized by jobbery.
1792 BURKE *Corr.* (1844) III. 436 Power is a very corrupting thing, especially low and jobbish power. **1829** SCOTT *Jrnl.* 2 June, I think it [a sale of property] has been a little jobbish. **1834** *Fraser's Mag.* IX. 503 Such a court was incapable, stupid, abominable, jobbish.

'jobbism. *nonce-wd.* [-ISM.] = JOBBERY 2.
1807 JEFFREY in Ld. Cockburn *Life* (1852) I. 177, I cannot dissemble my suspicions of jobbism.

jobble ('dʒɒb(ə)l), *sb.* = JABBLE *sb.*
1847 SIR J. C. ROSS *Voy. S. Seas* I. 41 We found a harassing jobble of a sea. **1899** F. T. BULLEN *Way Navy* 71 Fog again, thick drizzling rain, and a confused jobble of a sea this morning.

† **'jobble**, *v. Obs. rare*[−1]. [Cf. prec. and JABBLE *v.*[2]] *intr.* To move unevenly like a choppy sea. Hence ppl. adj. **'jobbling** (*jobling*).
1630 J. TAYLOR (Water P.) *Odcombes Compl.* To Rdrs., Wks. II. 59 T' accompany his all-lamented here In hobling, iobling, rumbling, tumbling verse.

† **jobe** (dʒəʊb), *v. Obs. colloq.* Also 8 **joab**, **job**. [f. JOB *sb.*[4], in allusion to the lengthy reproofs addressed to Job by his friends.] *trans.* To rebuke, reprove, or reprimand, in a long and tedious harangue; to 'lecture'.
1670 RAY *Proverbs* 207 In the University of Cambridge, the young scholars are wont to call chiding Jobing. **1683** SIR J. BRAMSTON *Autobiog.* 205 The Kinge had talked earnestly to the Duke and jobed him (that was the word) soe that the teares stood in his eyes. **1709** *Tatler* No. 71 ¶ 8 What bright Man says, I was Joab'd by the Dean. **1721–2** AMHERST *Terræ Fil.* No. 33 (1726) 178 A former president of St. John's college..would frequently Job his students for going constantly three or four times a day to chapel. **1794** *Gentl. Mag.* Dec. 1085 In consequence of an intimation from the tutor relative to his irregularities, his own father came from the country to *jobe* him.

joberdie, **-ertye**, obs. forms of JEOPARDY.

jobernol, **-nole**, **-noll**, obs. ff. JOBBERNOWL.

'job-hunter. *colloq.* [f. JOB *sb.*[2] + HUNTER 1 b.] One who seeks employment. So **'job-hunting** *vbl. sb.* and *ppl. a.*, and (as back-formations) **'job-hunt** *v.* and *sb.*
1928 *Daily Tel.* 13 Nov. 9/3 His abrupt departure without returning to Washington will serve as a notice to job-hunters ..that he intends to make up his own mind about all important appointments. **1930** H. CRANE *Let.* 16 Mar. (1965) 349 I've really never known so discouraging a time job-hunting. **1946** *Vogue* June 88/2 Hardly anyone's prepared to job-hunt till they've had their demobilisation leave. **1956** W. H. WHYTE *Organization Man* (1957) ix. 113 Job-hunting seniors. **1965** H. WAUGH *Girl on Run* (1966) x. 63 If the idea falls through, then you can job hunt. **1970** *Physics Bull.* Mar. 106/1, I launched into my own 'job hunt': the only way to see the full picture was to go out and see industry for myself. **1972** M. JONES *Life on Dole* II. v. 120 Every day, they..study the advertisements. Then they go job-hunting. **1973** *Sci. Amer.* Apr. 63/2 (Advt.), How to job hunt for a 20% to 50% salary increase.

Jobism ('dʒəʊbɪz(ə)m). *nonce-wd.* [f. JOB *sb.*[4] + -ISM.] A vehement lamentation like that of Job.
1855 MRS. CARLYLE *Lett.* II. 268, I am tempted to break out into Jobisms about my bad nights.

† **jobler**. *Obs. nonce-wd.* [f. **jobble* vb. as dim. of JOB *v.*[2]: perh. for rime's sake.] One who does jobs or small pieces of work; = JOBBER[2] 1.
1662 *Mock Remonstr.* in *Rump* I. 79 Weavers Dyers Tinkers Coblers And many other such like Joblers.

jobless ('dʒɒblɪs), *a.* and *sb.* [f. JOB *sb.*[2] + -LESS.]
1. Free from jobbery. *rare*.
1807–8 SYD. SMITH *Plymley's Lett.* xlvi. (ed. 11) 130, I ask him his opinion of a jobless faith, of a creed which dooms a man..to a lean and plunderless integrity.
2. Out of work, unemployed. Also as *sb. collect.*
1923 *Glasgow Herald* 25 Oct. 7 The demand that would ensue for land users would mean jobs for jobless men. **1937** *Times Lit. Suppl.* 16 Oct. 755/2 The later episodes showing the graduates of the college being set free into a jobless world full of depression are not so agreeable. **1958** *Economist* 1 Nov. 415/1 One-sixth to one-fourth of the labour force has been jobless for several months. **1970** *Times* 7 Sept. 16 (*headline*) Jobless total must go higher says Paish. **1971** *Nature* 8 Oct. 369/2, 4·4 per cent of the engineers who do not possess a degree of any kind were jobless in the summer.
So **'joblessness**, the state of being out of work.
1923 *Public Opinion* 30 Mar. 304/1 He means not the fear of foremen so much as the fear of joblessness. **1964** *Economist* 11 Jan. 110/1 The realities behind joblessness.

jobling: see JOBBLE *v.*

Jo block, colloq. abbrev. of *Johansson block* (see JOHANSSON). Also *fig.*
1936 H. D. BURGHARDT *Machine Tool Operation* (ed. 2) I. xi. 274 Size blocks may be used also instead of the pin gauge for spacing the holes. The most accurate of these gauges are the Johansson gauge blocks or 'Jo-blocks', which measure accurately in millionths of an inch. **1942** F. H. COLVIN *Gages* viii. 96 Standard measuring blocks, once known largely as 'Jo' blocks from the name of the first maker, Johannsen. **1957** R. A. HEINLEIN *Door into Summer* (1960) ii. 41, I had known Ricky half her life and if there ever was a human being honest as a Jo block, Ricky was she. **1966** G. W. MICHALEC *Precision Gearing* xi. 564 Using a very accurate input for positioning the carriage, such as master Jo-blocks.., the output can be observed and plotted.

'jobman. *rare*[−1]. [f. JOB *sb.*[2]] = NEXT.
1812 *Sporting Mag.* XXXIX. 280 His coachman was the servant of a jobman.

jobmaster, **job-master** ('dʒɒb,mɑːstə(r), -æ-) [f. JOB *sb.*[2] + MASTER *sb.*]
1. A man who keeps a livery stable and lets out horses and carriages by the job or for a definite period: cf. JOB *sb.*[2] 7.
1802 *Sporting Mag.* XX. 182 A very respectable job-master and hackney-man. **1886** *Leeds Merc.* 9 Mar. 5/4 A meeting of coachbuilders and jobmasters of Leeds. **1893** *Spectator* 29 July 136 A jobmaster..who had a great many horses in his stable.
2. A master printer who does job-work.
1824 J. JOHNSON *Typogr.* II. 578 Job Masters' Resolutions.
So **'job-mistress**, a woman who lets out horses and carriages.
1885 *Law Rep.* 14 Queen's Bench Div. 893 The defendants..hired the horses and a driver from a job-mistress.

jobmonger ('dʒɒb,mʌŋgə(r)). [f. as prec. + MONGER.] = JOBBER[2] 5.
1900 *Daily News* 24 May 4/6 The slum-owner, the corrupt contractor and the municipal jobmonger.

'jobmongering, *vbl. sb. rare*. [f. JOBMONGER + -ING[1].] The action or practice of a jobmonger.
1901 *Daily Chron.* 18 Dec. 5/1 Has Tammany no synonym? Or what about jobmongering? **1927** *Glasgow Herald* 24 Mar. 4 The intriguing and jobmongering of the Base.

jobsmith ('dʒɒbsmɪθ). [f. JOB *sb.*[2] + SMITH.] A smith who does miscellaneous jobs.
1831 J. HOLLAND *Manuf. Metal* I. 156 The comprehensive designation of 'jobsmith' which he [the blacksmith] mostly assumes.

† **'jobson**. *Obs.* [The surname *Jobson* used as a typical name: cf. *Hodge*. (Perh. associated with JOB *sb.*, *v.*)] A country fellow, a lout.
1660 *Chas. II.'s Esc. fr. Worcester* in *Select. fr. Harl. Misc.* (1793) 380 They had much ado..to order his steps, and straight body, to a lobbing Jobson's gate, and were forced every foot to remind him of it. **1661** K. W. *Conf. Charac.*, *Detracting Empirick* (1860) 65 His first adventures are upon the sweaty toes and butter teeth of country jobsons.

jobster ('dʒɒbstə(r)). [f. JOB *sb.*[2] + -STER.] = JOBBER[2].
1892 W. W. GREENER *Breech-Loader* 117 If unable to send [a damaged gun] to the makers, avoid advertising jobsters. **1897** *N.Y. Times* 15 Nov., The Hawaiian jobsters are astir again... They seem to feel sure of the administration. **1901** *Westm. Gaz.* 7 May 2/2 All the jobsters, speculators, South African financiers, all the coal and steel owners, who in 1899 cheered on the war. **1913** R. M. LA FOLLETTE *Autobiogr.* 167 He was not in favor of the spoilsman or the jobster. **1964** R. M. BUCK *Grim Truth about Fluoridation* iv. 23 (*heading*) Federal jobsters disagree.

job-trot: see JOG-TROT.

jocalat, obs. form of CHOCOLATE.

† **'jocant**, *a. Obs.* Forms: 5 iocande, 5–6 iocaunt(e, 6–7 iocant. [In form *jocant*, app. ad. L. *jocānt-em*, pr. pple. of *jocārī* (rarely *jocāre*) to

jest, joke; but, in form *jocande*, prob. a corruption of *joconde*, JOCUND.] Mirthful, merry, jocund.

c 1440 *Gesta Rom.* xxxi. 116 (Harl. MS.) When the knyght harde this, he was iocaunt & murye. 1494 FABYAN *Chron.* VI. clxxxvi. 186 Iocande and mery tydynges out of Englande. 1563-87 FOXE *A. & M.* (1596) 218/2 The moonks [of Canterbury] on the other side were as brag and iocant. 1628 J. ROUS *Diary* (Camden) 28 The duke..was very jocant and well pleased. 1687 J. NORRIS *Coll. Misc.* 87 And as they sung and play'd, the jocant orbs danc't round.

So †'**jocantry** [cf. *pleasantry*], mirth, merriment. *Obs.*

16.. H. MORE, Such Jocantry..is but like the dancing of men and women in an unswept room. 1664 —— *Myst. Iniq.* II. I. xv, Two notorious Specimens of that Jocantry and Festivity, as I may so speak, that is sometimes observable in Divine Providence.

†'**jocatory**, *a. Obs.* [f. L. *jocāt-*, ppl. stem of *jocārī* to joke: see -ORY.] Characterized by joking; jocular.

1576 FLEMING *Panopl. Epist.* Epil. Bivb, An epistle.. Jocatorie. 1586 A. DAY *Eng. Secretary* II. (1625) 67 And next..will we passe unto the title *Jocatorie*. The letters of this sute are such as of some pleasant conceited vaine, do proceed from one familiar friend..to another. 1656 BLOUNT *Glossogr.*, *Iocatory*, pertaining to jesting.

Jocism ('dʒəʊsɪz(ə)m). [ad. F. *Jocisme*, acronym from the initial letters of *Jeunesse Ouvrière Chrétienne*, Christian working youth, set up by Joseph Cardijn in Belgium in 1924, and subsequently extended in Europe: see -ISM.] An organization which aimed at spreading Christianity amongst working people. So '**Jocist** *sb.* and *a.*

1935 *Catholic Worker* Nov. 3/2 It is necessary to have study circles exclusively for the young wage-earners... Let us see how the Jocists (Catholic working youth) run theirs. 1939 *Theology* XXXIX. 432 Jocism has as its final end the conquest of the entire working class, the whole world, for Christ and His Church. *Ibid.* 437 The apex of the Jocist organization. 1951 *Scottish Jrnl. Theol.* IV. 160 This theory, sometimes derided by its opponents as 'Jocist romanticism', has been the main support, particularly in Anglo-Catholic circles, of much Christian social doctrine. 1960 *Rev. Politics* XXII. 339 From the beginning Mounier was against any political movement by a specifically confessional group (such as the Jocist movement).

Jock[1] (dʒɒk). *Sc.* Also 6 Iok. [The Scotch equivalent of JACK.]

1. a. A by-form of the name John; sometimes a generic name for any man of the common people, and thus used in association with Jean or Jenny; also prefixed, like Jack, to other words as in *Jock Fuil* = Jack Fool. **Jock Scott**, a kind of artificial fly used by anglers.

1508 DUNBAR *Poems* vi. 73 To Iok Fule, my foly fre Lego post corpus sepultum. *a* 1605 POLWART *Flyting w. Montgomerie* 789 Iock Blunt, deid runt! I sall dunt whill I slay thee. 1867 F. FRANCIS *Angling* x. (1880) 350 Jock Scott ..is a first-rate killer. 1885 W. H. RUSSELL in *Harper's Mag.* Apr. 769/2 [They] see him cast a 'Doctor' or 'Jock Scott' straight as an arrow. 1898 *Daily News* 14 Mar. 4/7 The proverb says..that 'there is a silly Jock for every silly Jenny'.

b. A Scottish (or †northern English) sailor; a Scottish soldier or a member of a Scottish regiment; any Scotsman. Freq. as a nickname. *slang.*

1788 GROSE *Dict. Vulgar T.* (ed. 2), *Jock*,..a jeering appellation for a north-country seaman, particularly a collier. *a* 1865 SMYTH *Sailor's Word-Bk.* (1867) 413 *Jocks*, Scotch seamen. 1914 R. HODDER *Brit. Regiments* 17 'The Jocks.' The origin of this name for the Scots Guards is obvious. 1918 H. MATTHEWS in Murdoch & Drake-Brockman *Austral. Short Stories* (1951) 242 And he had to admit that some of the Jocks and Tommies from France were fine fellows. 1925 FRASER & GIBBONS *Soldier & Sailor Words* 132 *Jocks*, Scotsmen in general. Men of a Highland regiment. 1930 BLUNDEN *De Bello Germanico* 17 An interminable stream of displeased and ejaculatory Jocks repeat the act. 1952 'J. TEY' *Singing Sands* vii. 101 Mr. Mackay had been in North Africa with the Jocks. 1965 *New Statesman* 16 Apr. 606/3 Why can't the Jocks support their team without dressing up like that? 1968 *Scottish Field* Feb. 35/1 All the infantry officers..attached tremendous importance to the Scottishness of their regiments. Kilts, trews, bonnets, pipe bands..have helped enormously to make the Jock the man he is. *Ibid.* 37/2 The Scots Guards could be described as typical Jocks. 1970 G. M. FRASER *General danced at Dawn* 46 Who knows your Jocks aren't my matelots?

2. A countryman, a rustic, a clown.

a 1568 SEMPILL in *Satir. Poems Reform.* xlvi. 61 Scho will ressaif no landwart Jok. 1803 SIR A. BOSWELL *Poet. Wks.* (1871) 15, I ken't the day when there was nae a Jock But trotted about upon honest shanks-naigie. *Mod.* The country Jocks and Jennies at the fair.

jock[2] (dʒɒk). Colloq. abbrev. of JOCKEY (senses 5 a and c).

1826 *Sporting Mag.* XVIII. 385 A neat horseman, and quite at the top of the tree amongst Northern jocks. 1856 H. H. DIXON *Post & Paddock* xii. 211 Many clever young jocks ..have ridden as many races by the time they are twenty. 1894 J. K. FOWLER *Recoll. Old Country Life* xv. 176, I don't think he performed as a gentleman jock over that celebrated course. 1952 in Wentworth & Flexner *Dict. Amer. Slang* (1960) 294/1 Already the jukes and jocks are dinning our ears with Christmas songs. 1972 *Islander* (Victoria, B.C.) 9 Jan. 14/4 Jocks..are pretty much a thing of the past.

jock[3] (dʒɒk). *coarse slang.* [Origin unknown; perh. f. an old slang word *jockum*, *-am* penis (Farmer & Henley).] The genitals of a man (or †of a woman). So †**jock-gagger**, a man living upon the earnings of a prostitute (*Obs.*).

a 1790 H. T. POTTER *New Dict. Cant & Flash* (1795) 36 *Jock*, private parts of a man or woman. 1809 G. ANDREWES *Dict. Slang & Cant*, *Jock-gagger*, a sort of fellows who live on the prostitution of their wives, &c. 1846 *Swell's Night Guide* 123/1 *Jock*, man's privates. 1960 J. CROSS *Backward Sex* iii. 73 Sprigs clattering on the floor, knees, jocks, backsides and shouting as everybody dressed. 1966 'L. LANE' *ABZ of Scouse* 56 *Jocks*, testicles. 1972 *Dict. Contemp. & Colloq. Usage* (Eng.-Lang. Inst. Amer.) 17/1 *Jock*,..*vulgar*, the penis.

jock[4] (dʒɒk). *dial.* and *slang.* [Origin unknown.] Food. (See also *E.D.D.*)

1879 *Yorkshireman's Comic Ann.* 33 Monny a shift he wor put to to get jock eniff. 1881 B. PRESTON *Dial. & Other Poems* 3 An' bumps 'em dahn i' t'corner chair, An' gloars reyt hard at t'jock. 1966 H. SHEPPARD *Dict. Railway Slang* (ed. 2) 7 *Jock*, food. 1974 P. WRIGHT *Lang. Brit. Industry* vi. 59 Food becomes..*jock*.., and contrasts oddly with officialese.

jock[5] (dʒɒk). *N. Amer. slang.* **1.** Abbrev. of JOCK-STRAP 1.

1952 B. MALAMUD *Natural* (1963) 68 He located his jock, with two red apples in it, swinging from a cord. 1973 W. McCARTHY *Detail* ii. 87 He found the Beretta..as well as the jock strap. He quickly took off his trousers, put on the jock.

2. Abbrev. of JOCK-STRAP 2.

1963 [see JOCK-STRAP 2]. 1968 *N.Y. Times* 12 May IV. 13 An obstacle to such trust is the attitude of some students and faculty members who, for example, smear all anti-strike students with the blanket label of 'jocks'. 1969 C. DAVIDSON in Cockburn & Blackburn *Student Power* 351 The administration will try by a whole range of 'divide and rule' tactics such as fostering the 'Greek-Independent Split', sexual double standards, intellectuals *vs* 'jocks', [etc.]. 1970 *Globe Mag.* (Toronto) 26 Sept. 2/1 On the sundeck are the clubbers, the sweats, the jocks. 1972 *Time* 2 Oct. 41/2 Rocks for jocks, elementary geology course popular among athletes at Pennsylvania.

jocker ('dʒɒkə(r)). *N. Amer. slang.* [f. JOCK[3] + -ER[1].] **a.** A tramp who is accompanied by a youth who begs for him or acts as his catamite. **b.** A male homosexual.

1893 'J. FLYNT' in *Cent. Mag.* Nov. 107/2 Subject to the whims and passions of various 'jockers', or protectors. 1913 'A No. 1' *Trail of Tramps* 72 A simple-faced chap..played the deaf and dumb game, for which purpose his jocker had forced him to learn the sign language. 1923 [see GUNSEL 1]. 1931 'D. STIFF' *Milk & Honey Route* iii. 34 While it is true that the punk serves the jocker..it is not accurate to call this exploitation. *Ibid.* xiv. 161 Whenever a man travels around with a lad he is apt to be labeled a 'jocker' or a 'wolf'. 1935 A. J. POLLOCK *Underworld Speaks* 64/2 *Jocker*, one who practices sodomy (ockerjay). 1950 H. E. GOLDIN *Dict. Amer. Underworld Lingo* 111/1 *Jocker*, an active pederast. 1972 B. RODGERS *Queens' Vernacular* 156 *Jocker* is synonymous with wolf: his role in prison parodies the husband's relationship in a marriage. 1972 J. WAMBAUGH *Blue Knight* (1973) iv. 54 Roxie hustles the guys who want a queen, and the kid goes after the ones who want a jocker. This jocker would probably become a queen himself.

jockette (dʒɒ'kɛt). [f. JOCK[2] + -ETTE.] Occas. used for: a female jockey.

1969 *N.Y. Times* 17 Jan. 21/3 The male riders, determined not to let the so-called jockettes compete against them, continue to bellow 'Vive la Différence!' 1972 *Sunday Express* 11 June 16/4 That leaves Mr. Rippon about as much chance of displacing him as jockette Miss Meriel Tufnell has of dislodging Lester Piggott from his chosen mount in the St. Leger. 1973 *Times* 17 Oct. 13/3 We have now reached the stage when theoretically a 'jockette' could ride in the 1975 Derby.

jockey ('dʒɒkɪ), *sb.* Also 6-7 iocky, 7-9 jockie. [dim. or pet-form of JOCK[1]; cf. JACKY: originally Sc. and northern Eng.]

1. a. A diminutive or familiar by-form of the name Jock or John, usually with the sense 'little Jock, Jacky, Johnny'; hence, applicable (contemptuously) to any man of the common people (chiefly Sc.); also, a lad; an understrapper. (Cf. JACK *sb.*[1] 2.)

a 1529 SKELTON *Agst. Scottes* 90 Kynge Iamy, Iemmy, Iocky my io. 1594 SHAKS. *Rich. III*, v. iii. 304 Iockey [*a* 1548 HALL *Chron.* Iack] of Norfolke, be not so bold, For Dickon thy maister is bought and sold. *a* 1670 HACKET *Abp. Williams* II. (1693) 142 What could Lesly have done then with a few untrain'd, unarmed Jockeys, if we had been true among our selves? 1795 BURKE *Let. to W. Elliot* Wks. VII. 351 A jockey of Norfolk [see quot. 1594] who was inspired with the resolute ambition of becoming a citizen of France. 1848 DICKENS *Dombey* vi, 'You're Dombey's jockey, a'nt you?' said the first man. 'I'm in Dombey's House, Mr. Clark', returned the boy.

b. *transf.* Of a thing. Cf. *fellow*, *lad*, *chap.*

1827 COLERIDGE *Table-t.* 24 June, Some apple dumplings were placed on the table, and my man..burst forth with 'Them's the jockies for me!'

2. A strolling minstrel or beggar; a vagabond. *Sc. Obs.* exc. *Hist.*

1683 G. MARTINE *Reliq. Divi Andreæ* (1797) §1 They are called by others and by themselves jockies, who go about begging and use still to recite the sluggornes. 1685 G. SINCLAIR *Satans Invis. World* xvii, He..turned a vagrant fellow like a Jockie, gaining Meal, Flesh, and Money by his Charms. 1815 SCOTT *Guy M.* vii, The tribes of gypsies, jockies, or cairds.

†**3. a.** One who manages or has to do with horses; one who deals in horses, a horse-dealer. *Obs.* or *dial.*

1638 BROME *Antipodes* I. v. Wks. 1873 III. 246 Let my fine Lords Talk o' their Horse-tricks, and their Jockies, that Can out-talke them. 1668 PEPYS *Diary* 4 Dec., I, and W. Hewer, and a friend of his, a jockey, did go about to see several pairs of horses, for my coach. 1721 BAILEY, *Jockey*, one who manages and deals in Horses. 1749 SMOLLETT *Gil Blas* I. ii. I. 7 If I had a mind to sell my mule, he was acquainted with a very honest jocky who would buy her. 1768-74 TUCKER *Lt. Nat.* (1834) I. 659 Perhaps I design to buy a horse for my riding... I know there are enow to be had in town, and the jockeys will cheat one egregiously. 1841 MACAULAY *Ess.*, *Hastings* (1887) 648 The crime..was regarded by them in much the same light in which the selling of an unsound horse, for a sound price, is regarded by a Yorkshire jockey.

b. (From the character attributed to horse-dealers.) A crafty or fraudulent bargainer; a cheat. (Cf. JOCKEY *v.* 1.)

1683 TRYON *Way to Health* 615 They are meer Jockies in the Art of Wiving, and will Higgle for the other Hundred Pound in Portion. 1777 *Gamblers* 6 The growing Jockey, or the man of Dice. 1790 BAILEY, *Jockey*,..also a cheat.

†**4.** One who rides or drives a horse; a postillion, courier; a charioteer. *Obs.*

1643 *Char. Oxford Incendiary* in *Harl. Misc.* (1745) V. 473/1 Two of Gondemar's Jockies, that posted between Whitehall and Madrid. 1702 ADDISON *Dial. Medals* i. 16 The wise Ancients..heapt up greater Honours on Pindar's Jockies than on the Poet himself. 1850 [The usual name in South of Scotland for a postillion].

5. a. *spec.* A professional rider in horse-races. (The chief current sense.)

dumb jockey: see DUMB *a.* 6 (quot. 1853).

1670 EVELYN *Diary* 22 July, We return'd over Newmarket Heath,..the jockies breathing their fine barbs and racers, and giving them their heates. 1693 *Lond. Gaz.* No. 2845/4 A Jockey's Saddle stitched with green Silk. 1703 *Ibid.* No. 3928/4 A Plate of 30*l.* value will be run for on Nottingham Course, Jockies to ride, to carry 10 Stone weight. 1780 COWPER *Progr. Error* 221 Prepares for meals as jockies take a sweat. 1820 COMBE *Dr. Syntax*, *Consol.* x, The jockies whipp'd, the horses ran. 1878 *N. Amer. Rev.* CXXVII. 210 As jockeys meet upon a race-course.

b. *transf.* A driver of a motor vehicle. Freq. preceded by a sb. used *attrib.* So ***garage jockey***, a garage attendant. Chiefly *N. Amer.*

1912 *Collier's* 28 Sept. 11/2 Some are, so to speak, 'gentlemen jockeys', and own, enter, and drive their own cars for the fun of the thing. 1929 D. RUNYON in *Hearst's International* Nov. 72/2 Jerking me into the cab and telling the jockey to go to the Penn Station. 1936 *Daily Herald* 5 Aug. 8/4 Here is a short list of busmen's slang phrases: ..*Jockey* (*Driver*). 1942 BERREY & VAN DEN BARK *Amer. Thes. Slang* §723/2 *Automobile racer*, auto *or* buzzer jockey, ..speed jockey,..suicide jockey. *Ibid.* §723/4 *Motorcycle racer*, broadsider, jockey,..motor jockey. *Ibid.* §765/2 *Commercial driver* (*bus, taxicab, truck*),..jockey, motor jockey. *Ibid.* §765/5 *Truck driver*, truck jockey *or* spinner... *Spec.* juice jockey, a gasoline-truck driver; grunt-and-squeal jockey, a stock hauler;..suicide jockey, a nitro-glycerine hauler. 1945 *Amer. Speech* XX. 148/1 *Jeep jockey*, truck driver. 1954 *Chicago Tribune* 20 July A. 17/1 Trolley jockey gets even with slowpokes. 1968 *Drive* Spring 113 The driver of any heavy-load vehicle is known as the pilot or jockey. 1970 *Globe & Mail* (Toronto) 25 Sept. 37/3 (Advt.), Executive 2 bedroom, 2 baths professionally decorated, overlooking rose garden, pool treed ravine. Doorman and car jockey. 1972 *Nat. Geographic* Aug. 209/1 Sweat-streaked truck jockey. 1973 J. CLEARY *Ransom* i. 33 There had been no trouble with the garage jockey. He had been lounging in a chair in the tiny office.

c. = *disc-jockey*.

1963 B. W. ALDISS *Airs of Earth* 69 We stayed with the jocular jockey, hoping to catch a news bulletin, as I drove south. 1971 *Daily Tel.* 5 Jan. 10/1 The same 30 turns. Different jockeys. Different stations, but no real choice. 1972 P. BLACK *Biggest Aspidistra* III. iv. 179 *Housewives' Choice*, a favourite shop-window for records and jockeys from 1946 to 1967.

6. 'A self-acting apparatus carried on the front tub of a *set*, for releasing it from the hauling rope at a certain point' (*Midland Coal Field*).

1882 GRESLEY *Gloss. Coal Mining.*

7. Short for *jockey boot*, *pulley*, *sleeve*, *wheel*: see 9.

1851-61 MAYHEW *Lond. Labour* II. 49 (Hoppe) Top-boots (they're called Jockeys in the trade). 1896 *Godey's Mag.* Feb. 211/1 Jockeys cut in fanciful shape are set into the shoulders of many of the sleeves. 1960 CUNNINGTON & BEARD *Dict. Eng. Costume* 118/2 *Jockey*,..a flat trimming applied over the outer part of the shoulder of a dress and having the lower border free. 1963 A. GERNSHEIM *Fashion & Reality* I. 27 By 1841 tight sleeves were..often headed by a *mancheron* (later called jockey).

8. *attrib.* and *Comb.* **a.** *attrib.* (*a*) That is a jockey, as (senses 3-5) ***jockey-boy***, ***-groom***, ***-lord***, ***-parson***, ***-rider***; (sense 1) ***jockey-pedlar***. (*b*) Belonging to or used by a jockey, as ***jockey-frock***, ***-pad***, ***-seat***, ***-whip***; also ***jockey-back***, ***-leg***: applied to a style of boot. (*c*) Practised by a jockey (sense 3 b), fraudulent, cheating, as ***jockey trade***, ***trick***. **b.** *Comb.*, as ***jockey-cut***, ***jockey-like*** adjs.

1909 *Boot Catal.*, Gentleman's brown calf lace, whole golosh, *jockey back. 1816 *Sporting Mag.* XLVIII. 36 The anecdote..of poor Jack Clark the *jockey-boy, struck us most forcibly. 1827 LYTTON *Pelham* ii, The men..wore *jockey-cut coats. 1806 SURR *Winter in Lond.* II. 93 His outer garment was a *jockey frock. 1708 *Lond. Gaz.* No. 4441/4 John Hague, a *Jockey-Groom,..has lately ran away without accounting..for Mony receiv'd by him. 1862 *Illustr. Catal. Internat. Exhib.*, *Industr. Dept.*, *Brit. Div.* II.

No. 4658, Skins, kips, fronts, shoe legs, *jockey legs, cordovan, grained calf. **1765** *Universal Mag.* XXXVII. 371/1 The State Jockeys..all, *jockey-like, whip to get the best places. **1679** SHADWELL *True Widow* 7 He is a dry-jester to Gameing and *Jocky-Lords. **1759** JOHNSON *Idler* No. 62 ¶10, I grew ashamed of the company of jockey lords. **1875** KNIGHT *Dict. Mech.*, **Jockey-pad*,..a knee-pad on the forepart of a saddle. **1837** MRS. SHERWOOD *Henry Milner* III. ii. 33 A sporting parson is quite as good as a *jockey parson surely. *a* **1670** HACKET *Abp. Williams* II. (1692) 223 England deserved worse and heard worse than these *jockey pedlars [Scots] that chaffered away their King. **1678** BUTLER *Hud.* III. ii. 1690 Force, enough to fly, And beat a Tuscan Running Horse, Whose *Jocky-Rider is all Spurs. **1867** BAKER *Nile Tribut.* x. (1872) 161 The latter with a regular *jockey-seat riding most comfortably. **1770** in F. Chase *Hist. Dartmouth College* (1891) I. 149 It can't prosper,..it's all a *jockey trick from first to last. **1801** WOLCOTT (P. Pindar) *Ep. to Ct. Rumford* Wks. 1812 V. 144 Try every jockey trick to pass thy fame. **1804** *Europ. Mag.* XLV. 58/2 Time..changes the youth to Harlequin, transforms his *jockey-whip to a wooden sword.

9. Special Combs.: **jockey-bar** (see quot.); **jockey-boot**, a top-boot formerly worn by jockeys; **jockey-box**, 'a box in a wagon, underneath the driver's seat, for carrying small articles' (*Cent. Dict.* 1890); **jockey briefs, shorts**, short under-drawers for men; **jockey-cap**, a peaked cap of the style worn by jockeys; **jockey-cart** *local* [from its motion], a spring-cart; **jockey club**, (*a*) a club or association for the promotion and regulation of horse-racing; *spec.* the Jockey Club established at Newmarket, which is the supreme authority in Great Britain on all matters connected with horse-racing; (*b*) a toilet-water releasing chiefly rose and jasmine scents; **jockey-coat**, a kind of great-coat (?formerly worn by horse-dealers); **jockey-gear**, a set of jockey-wheels (see below) with their connected mechanism; **jockey-pulley**, a small wheel which 'rides' upon the top edge of a larger one, used for obtaining a high speed, or for keeping a rope in the groove of a grooved wheel; an 'idle' pulley or wheel which 'rides' upon the belt or rope between two working pulleys so as to increase its contact surface upon these and to tighten it up when slack; **jockey-sleeve**, (*a*) a sleeve like that of a jockey-coat; (*b*) a sleeve or free casing riding on a spindle or shaft, and carrying part of a train of mechanism; used in some forms of electric arc-lights; **jockey spider** *Austral.*, a venomous black spider, *Latrodectus hasseltii*, the female of which is distinguished by a red stripe on the upper side of its abdomen; also = KATIPO; also ellipt. *jockey*; **jockey-stick** *U.S.* (see quots.); **jockey strap** = JOCK-STRAP 1 ?*obs.*; **jockey-wheel**, (*a*) = JOCKEY-PULLEY; (*b*) a small adjustable wheel at the nose of a caravan.

1887 *So. Chesh. Gloss.*, **Jockey-bar*, the broad flat top bar of a kitchen grate. **1894** HALL CAINE *Manxman* II. i. 51 The kettle was singing on the jockey-bar. **1683** *Lond. Gaz.* No. 1810/4 A pair of *Jockey-Boots. **1725** SWIFT *Receipt to Stella*, All the squires from nine miles round,..With jocky boots and silver spurs. **1851** *Illustr. Catal. Gt. Exhib.* 525 Jockey, hunting..and dress boots. **1966** J. GARDNER *Amber Nine* ix. 130 He stripped to his *jockey briefs. **1748** *Anson's Voy.* II. vi. 193 Having on a *jocky cap, one side of the peak was shaved off..by a ball. **1837** MRS. SHERWOOD *Henry Milner* III. iii. 43 Two young 'squires in jockey caps. **1840** MRS. F. TROLLOPE *Michael Armstrong* xvii. (D.), [No] conveyance more rough and rude than Sir Matthew's *jockey-cart, which was constructed with excellent and efficient springs. **1775** (*title*) An Appeal to the *Jockey Club; or, a True Narrative of the late Affair between Mr. Fitzgerald and Mr. Walker. **1809** *Sporting Mag.* XXXIII. 108 The unerring scales of the Jockey-Club. **1855** G. W. S. PIESSE *Art of Perfumery* 122 Jockey Club Bouquet. **1859** in Bartlett *Dict. Amer.* (1860) 396, I..used cologne, hair oil, and scented my handkerchief with 'jockey-club'. **1886** COVENTRY & WATSON *Racing* iii, Tradition..assigns to the year 1750 the origin of the Jockey Club. **1907** *Yesterday's Shopping* (1969) 521/1 Highly concentrated Essences... Jockey Club, Maiglöckchen, [etc.]. **1941** W. A. POUCHER *Perfumes, Cosmetics & Soaps* (ed. 6) II. vii. 281 Jockey Club. .. Bergamot oil... Jasmin... Rose... Tuberose... Mace oil... Civet extract. **1973** *Sat. Rev. World* (U.S.) 6 Nov. 29/2 The following..of our own exclusive scents..are presently available: 1 Jockey Club, 2 Number Six, [etc.]. *a* **1745** SWIFT *Helter Skelter* 10 With whips and spurs so neat; And with *jocky-coats complete. **1752** in *Scots Mag.* (1753) July 344/2 He was dressed in a long dun jocky coat. **1818** SCOTT *Hrt. Midl.* xiii, His dress was also that of a horse-dealer—a close-buttoned jockey-coat, or wrap-rascal, as it was then termed, with huge metal buttons. **1893** *Jrnl. R. Agric. Soc.* Dec. 715 A *jockey pulley attached to the main frame is arranged to take up the slack of the chain. **1896** E. T. CARTER *Mot. Power Electr. Mach.* 508 The advantage in the use of a jockey pulley is that the arc of contact of the belt on the working pulleys can be increased beyond what is obtainable with a free belt, thus shortening the necessary distance between the pulley centres. **1951** G. MARX *Let.* 18 Jan. (1967) 194, I remember in 1932 telling Truman to stick to the haberdashery business, that there was a fortune in shirts and *jockey shorts. **1968** J. R. ACKERLEY *My Father & Myself* 210, I took to wearing tight jockey shorts. **1971** B. MALAMUD *Tenants* 210 The bridegroom, in a smoked raffia skirt from waist to knees over his jockey shorts. **1692** *Lond. Gaz.* No. 2767/4 A buff-colour Cloth Coat with *Jockey-sleeves. **1933** *Bulletin* (Sydney) 15 Nov. 20/4 *Latrodectus*, which we call the 'redback' or '*jockey'. **1936** K. C. MCKEOWN *Spider Wonders Austral.* xi. 155 In the Jockey Spider the red stripe is a direct and unmistakable warning. **1942** C. BARRETT *On Wallaby* ii. 30 An infant bitten by a 'jockey'..died six hours later. **1944** *Living off Land* vi. 129 The red-back spider, or katipo, also called the 'jockey' spider, definitely is harmful. **1965** *Austral. Encycl.* VIII. 236/2 The best-known Australian member [of the comb-footed group of spiders] is the red-back, red-spot, or jockey spider, *Latrodectus hasseltii*, with a distribution from Arabia to New Guinea, the whole of Australia, the Pacific Islands, Hawaii and New Zealand; in the last-named country it is called 'katipo' (night-stinger). **1887** E. B. CUSTER *Tenting on Plains* xii. 352 [In driving a prairie schooner] a small hickory stick, about five feet long, called the *jockey-stick, not unlike a rake-handle, is stretched between a pilot [mule] and his mate. **1968** R. F. ADAMS *Western Words* (rev. ed.), *Jockey stick*, in freighting, a hickory stick,..stretched between a pilot mule or horse and its mate. **1896** *Crescent* (Brooklyn, N.Y.) 1 Dec. 33/1 (Advt.), Suspensories, *Jockey Straps. **1909** *Spalding's Athletic Library* (N.Y.) Group XV. No. 333 (Advt.), Bike Jockey Strap Suspensory. **1952** *Motor Manual* (ed. 34) xiii. 248 Car and caravan can be connected or disconnected in a matter of a few seconds. To help this operation, the forward end of the van chassis is provided with a *jockey wheel to take the forward weight. **1966** *Caravanning* ('Know the Game' Series) 12 The nose weight of a caravan can vary from a few pounds to over a hundredweight. On most vans there is a telescopic jockey wheel to facilitate raising the nose.

Hence **'jockeydom**, (*a*) the world of jockeys, jockeys collectively; (*b*) the position or occupation of a jockey; **'jockeyish** *a.*, like a jockey, 'horsy'; **'jockeyism**, the style, phraseology, or practice of jockeys.

1869 *Punch* 10 July 10/1 The dearest interests of jockeydom stand in jeopardy. **1878** L. WINGFIELD *Lady Grizel* I. ii. 28 A man who never..spends his nights at hazard, or affects jockeydom at Newmarket. **1838** *Fraser's Mag.* XVII. 326 But this, though sufficiently jockeyish, leaves out Hector himself, to make room for his horses. **1802** *Sporting Mag.* XX. 273 The slang of jockeyism. **1827** LYTTON *Pelham* lxi, A mixture of slang and jockeyism.

jockey ('dʒɒkɪ), *v.* [f. prec. sb.]

1. a. *trans.* To play the jockey with (see prec. 3 b); to gain the advantage of by adroit management or trickery; to trick, outwit, overreach, take in, 'do'.

1708 *Yorkshire-Racers* 3 And as you jockey'd us, we jockey'd you. *c* **1740** A. ALLEN *MS. Dict.* s.v., To jockey a Man, is to impose upon, to cheat, overreach; to deal wth any one, as Jockeys usually doe wth all ye world. Nor is there any more deceitful race of Men than Jockeys, in their Sale of Horse flesh. **1785** R. CUMBERLAND *Observer* No. 96 ¶6 Let us see if any bishop shall jockey us with the like jade's trick for the future. **1848** THACKERAY *Van. Fair* xxxiv, The way in which she jockied Jos, and which she described with infinite fun. **1865** DICKENS *Mut. Fr.* II. iii, Whether the business in hand be to..promote a railway, or jockey a railway.

b. With *adv.* or *prep.* To get (*out*, *in*, *away*, etc.) by trickery; to cheat or do *out of*.

1719 T. GORDON *Cordial Low Spirits* I. 117 They would at any time Jockey away a small Tenement in Abraham's Bosom, for a rich Manor in England. **1772** *Town & Country Mag.* 83 When he finds that I have jockied him out of his mistress. **1840** THACKERAY *Paris Sk.-bk.*, *Caricatures*, Penniless Directors,..jockeying their shares through the market. **1855** —— *Newcomes* xxxiii, When his Majesty, Louis XIV. jockeyed his grandson on to the throne of Spain. **1865** *Sat. Rev.* 25 Feb. 217/2 Having been jockeyed into a miscarriage of justice.

c. To play tricks with; to manage or manipulate in a tricky way.

1890 *Nature* 16 Oct. 587 In Foucault's pendulum a very slight jockeying can make the thing go as we wish. **1893** *Evid. Crt. Martial H.M.S. Victoria*, Admiral Tryon disapproved of any jockeying the engines. **1894** J. KNIGHT *Garrick* vii. 104 Quin..had been controlled or jockeyed.

d. *intr.* To play the jockey, play tricks, act fraudulently; to aim at an advantage by adroit management or artifice. Freq. in phr. *to jockey for position*, to try to gain an advantageous position (in a race, contest, etc.).

a **1835** *Comic song, 'The Fox went out'*, He cut up the goose with a carving knife, And the little ones jockeyed for the bones, O! **1855** THACKERAY *Newcomes* lxii, An event for which she had been jockeying ever since she set eyes on young Newcome. **1899** *Daily News* 21 Oct. 3/4 When the preparatory gun was fired..both yachts were jockeying under their mainsails, jibs, and staysails. **1908** *Daily Chron.* 16 July 8/1 The fastest time was that by J. Matthews..but that counts for little in a cycle race owing to the..jockeying ..for position in the final sprint. **1955** *Times* 27 July 6/7 In Alberta when there was no jury, congestion was caused by lawyers jockeying for position in order to appear before the right judge. **1969** AUDEN *City without Walls* 105 They're jockeying for position round the first bend.

2. a. *intr.* To ride as a jockey (in quot. 1767 contemptuous). **b.** *trans.* To ride (a horse) in a race, as a jockey.

1767 ANNA SEWARD *Poems*, etc. (1810) I. p. cxcvii, She reads no curtain-lectures upon his jockying over to Nottingham to read the news three times a week. **1825** *Sporting Mag.* XVI. 273 Eclipse was then jockeyed by Sam Merrit. **1837** [see JOCKEYING 2].

jockeying ('dʒɒkɪɪŋ), *vbl. sb.* [f. JOCKEY *v.* + -ING[1].] The action of the verb JOCKEY.

1. Horse-dealing; the riding and management of race-horses. Also *attrib.*

a **1770** C. SMART *Duellist* 58 A thousand trifles not worth naming, In whoring, jockeying, and gaming. **1837** MRS. SHERWOOD *Henry Milner* III. iii. 33 Unless Mr. Dalben thinks of bringing him up in the jockeying line.

2. Adroit management for the purpose of gaining an advantage, esp. an unfair one; trickery, cheating.

1779 G. WILLIAMS *Let.* 28 Feb. in *Essex Inst. Hist. Coll.* (1907) XLIII. 202 The Makers of Money sent it to there servants to purchas goods and thay knew it was to be out of circulation in a few months. It would be called by some Jockeing. **1807–8** W. IRVING *Salmag.* (1824) 293 In their zeal to get a good seat..a vast deal of jockeying and unfair play was shown. *c* **1810** MARIA EDGEWORTH *Stories of Ireland* v, It's not called swindling amongst gentlemen, who know the world: it's only jockeying—fine sport—and very honourable, to help a friend, at a dead lift. **1858** O. W. HOLMES *Aut. Breakf.-t.*, *Race of Life*, That turf where there is no more jockeying. **1897** W. M. RAMSAY in *Brit. Weekly* 20 May 78 No one among us will ever look back to it without blushing for the jockeying by which it was effected.

jockeyship ('dʒɒkɪʃɪp). [See -SHIP.]

1. a. The art of a jockey; skill in horse-racing. (Cf. *horsemanship*.) **b.** The practice of jockeying; trickery, artifice, adroit management for unfair advantage.

a **1763** SHENSTONE *Ess. Envy* Wks. 1764 II. 111 To vie in jockey-ship or cunning at a bett. **1784** COWPER *Task* II. 276 We justly boast At least superior jockeyship, and claim The honours of the turf as all our own. **1787** BENTHAM *Def. Usury* ix. 87 Jockey-ship, a term of reproach..frequently applied to the arts of those who sell horses. **1846** J. W. CROKER in *C. Papers* 22 Aug. (1884), Newmarket does not afford more..instances of jockeyship, than could be found in the secret history of episcopal promotion. **1894** *Daily News* 16 Apr. 3/7 This defeat was probably due to the inferior jockeyship of his rider.

2. As a mock title for a jockey.

1781 COWPER *Conversat.* 420 If neither horse nor groom affect the squire, Where can at last his jockeyship retire?

3. Jockeys collectively.

c **1820** CHALMERS *Serm.*, The full assembled jockeyship of half a province muster together.

Jocko ('dʒɒkəʊ). Also **Jacko.** [a. F. *jocko*, erroneously made by Buffon out of *engeco*, properly *ncheko*, the native name of the chimpanzee in the Gaboon country, West Africa.] The chimpanzee; sometimes used as a familiar name for any ape (perh. influenced by *Jack* or *Jackanapes*).

[**1625** BATTEL *Angola* in *Pinkerton's Voy.* XVI. 332 The largest of them is called Pongo in their language, and the other Engeco. **1766** BUFFON *Hist. Naturelle* (1837) III. 590 Jocko, Enjocko, nom de cet animal a Congo, et que nous avons adopté. *En* est l'article que nous avons retranché.] **1777** P. THICKNESSE *Year's Journey* II. xl. 68 My monkey.. rode postilion upon my sturdy horse... Jocko put whole towns in motion. **1778** *Ibid.* (ed. 2) II. xlv. 106, I have seen an animal of the Jocko kind, when chained to a spot, contrive to get his food, which was out of his reach, by an address which many human creatures would have perished for want of abilities to put in practice. **1847** SAVAGE in *Boston Jrnl. Nat. Hist.* V. 422 Their local name for the Chimpanzee is Enche-eko, as near as it can be anglicised, from which the common term Jocko probably comes. [**1861** DU CHAILLU *Equat. Africa* xx. 359 In the Gaboon country the Chimpanzee is called Nshiego, in the interior it is known as the Ncheko. *Ibid.* 362 The Chimpanzee is called Engeco by Battel, 1625;..Enjocko, Jocko, by Buffon, 1766; Inchego, by Bowdich, 1819; Enche-eco, by Savage, in 1847; Ntchego, by Franquet, in 1852; Nchego, by Aubry Lecomte, 1854–57; most of which are variations again of the Camma name, which, according to our English mode of spelling, should be, as I have given it, Nshiego..the negro name for the true Chimpanzee.] **1863** HUXLEY *Man's Place Nat.* i. 14 Thus it was that Andrew Battell's 'Engeco' became metamorphosed into 'Jocko', and, in the latter shape, was spread all over the world, in consequence of the extensive popularity of Buffon's works.

jock-strap ('dʒɒkstræp). [f. JOCK[3] + STRAP *sb.*]

1. A supporter or protector for the male genitals, worn esp. by sportsmen; also (occas.), a CACHE-SEXE.

1897 *U.S. Patent Office Index* 27 Bennett, Charles F., Chicago, Ill. Combined jock-strap and suspensory. **1911** *T. Eaton & Co. Catal.* Spring & Summer 179/2 Athletic Support. Sharp & Smith's Bike-Jock Strap, being made entirely of elastic. **1929** T. WOLFE *Look Homeward, Angel* (1930) II. xiv. 191 The checking of overcoats, evening wraps, jock-straps, and jewellery. **1933** E. E. CUMMINGS *eimi* 52 Do I seriously..seem to see your human mind squatting in your magic jockstrap, freely watching Hitchy Goomy Gitchie Koo (the sickest medicine-man of them all) turn your ailments into formulas? **1935** *New Statesman* 14 Sept. 357/1 (Advt.), The Linia Belt, including a Linia Jock Strap. **1936** H. MILLER *Black Spring* 247 The night is cold but the queen is naked save for a jock-strap. **1947** 'A. P. GASKELL' *Big Game* 15, I had to undo my pants and look to see whether I'd put on my jock-strap. **1954** *Dancing Times* Mar. 400 Articles for Sale. Jock straps for either sex in pink, white or black. **1960** *Guardian* 23 Sept. 26/7 A Nubian chauffeur in a leopard-skin jockstrap. **1969** *Daily Tel.* 7 Mar. 21/1 It is the first play in which I remember to have encountered an actor with a jockstrap which squeaks when pushed.

2. An athletic (as distinguished from an æsthetic or intellectual) man (esp. one at a university); a 'hearty'. *N. Amer. slang.*

1956 *Amer. Speech* XXXI. 192 A healthy, athletic young man addicted to sports may wince under the pointed *jockstrap marine*. **1963** *Ibid.* XXXVIII. 169 A college athlete: jock (81), animal (32)... The full synecdoche itself, jockstrap, was also reported once.

Hence **'jock-strapped** *a.*; **'jock-strapper**.

1960 *Spectator* 23 Sept. 432 Even prints biographical notes on its jock-strapped heroes. **1967** N. MAILER *Cannibals & Christians* I. 14 Scranton had none of the heft of a political jockstrapper like Goldwater.

jockteleg ('dʒɒktəlɛg). *Sc.* and *north. dial.* Also α. 7 Jock the Leg, 8- jocte-, jactaleg, 9 jockta-, joktaleg, jock-to-, jock-tae-leg. β. 8-9 jacklag, jack-o-legs, 9 jacka-, jacki-, jackylegs, jocka-, jocke-, jockylegs. [The α forms are Sc., and the original; the β forms are Engl. dial. See *Note* below.] A (large) clasp knife.

α. **1672** *Acc.-bk. Sir J. Foulis* (1894) 6 For a Jock the Leg Knife 00l. 08s. 0d. Scots. **1727** RAMSAY *Twa Cut-purses*, Sma' gimcracks that pleas'd their nodles Sic as a joctaleg, or sheers. **1785** BURNS *Halloween* v, An' gif the custock's sweet or sour, Wi' joctelegs they taste them. **1789** —— *Peregrin. Capt. Grose* viii, It was a faulding jocteleg, or lang-kail gullie. **1818** SCOTT *Rob Roy* xxxii, After John Highlandman's sneckit this ane wi' his joctaleg. **1833** *Fraser's Mag.* Oct. 398 In a hole he had..jock-to-legs, keelavine-pens..or whatever else he could purloin. **1885** JAS. GRANT *Royal Highlanders* (Rtldg.) 229 A large knife—like the genuine jockteleg of the days of old.

β. **1777** *Horæ Subsecivæ* 227 (E.D.D.) Jack-lag-knife. **1787** GROSE *Prov. Gloss.*, *Jack-o-legs*, a clasp knife. (*North.*) **1822** BEWICK *Mem.* 26, I involuntarily got my 'Jackleg knife'. **1825** BROCKETT, *Jackalegs, Jockelegs*, a large clasped knife. **1847-78** HALLIWELL, *Jack-lag-knife*, a clasped knife. *Glouc.*

[*Note.* Lord Hailes *Spec. Sc. Gloss.* (*c* 1776) 18, says 'The etymology of this word remained unknown till not many years ago an old knife was found having this inscription *Jacques de Liege*, the name of the cutler'. A similar statement is made by Smiles *Industr. Biog.* (1863) 101, and Jevons *Coal Question* (1866) 91. The former says 'Jacques de Liege, a famous foreign cutler whose knives were as well known throughout Europe, as those of Rodgers or Mappin are now'. On the face of it this account is plausible: it was not uncommon in Sc. for *de* to be corrupted to *the*, e.g. *the Bruce*; the change of *d* to *t* after *k* is also phonetically simple. But, for the present, Scottish antiquaries have failed to find any confirmation, in knife or document, of Hailes's statement; and inquiries made for us at Liege have been equally unsuccessful in finding any trace of *Jacques* the cutler.]

jock-trot: see JOG-TROT.

†'**joco.** *Obs.* [Cf. It. *gioco* 'any kind of game or play' (Florio):—L. *jocus* jest.] = JOKE *sb.*

1663 *Flagellum, or O. Cromwell* (1672) 160 The like Joco's and Frisks he would have with other Company.

jocolatte, -let, obs. forms of CHOCOLATE.

jocond(e, obs. form of JOCUND.

jocose (dʒəʊ'kəʊs), *a.* [ad. L. *jocōs-us* full of jesting or joking, f. *jocus*: see JOCO and -OSE.]

1. Of persons, or their dispositions, etc.: Full of jokes: given to joking; playful, sportive, waggish.

1673 KIRKMAN *Unlucky Citizen* 247 It was enough to depress and tame the most Jocose and bravest spirit in the World. **1709** SHAFTESBURY *Ess. Wit & Humour* I. §3 When they vouchsafe to quit their Austerity, and be Jocose and pleasant with an Adversary. **1787** WESLEY *Wks.* (1872) XIII. 263 Jocose Clergymen..cannot but dislike those who are steadily serious. **1882** L'ESTRANGE *Friendships Miss Mitford* I. vii. 176 That she was so far heart-whole was evident, for she could be jocose on the subject.

2. Of speech, writing, or action: Of the nature of a joke, or characterized by jokes; spoken, written, or done in joke; playful in style or character.

1699 BENTLEY *Phal.* 287 The Greek *Satyrica* was only a jocose sort of Tragedy. *a* **1708** BEVERIDGE *Priv. Th.* I. (1730) 118 There are some Words, that are purely jocose, spoken with no other Intent, but only to promote Mirth and divert Melancholy. **1838** DICKENS *Nich. Nick.* v, So he gave her three or four with a kind of jocose gallantry. **1859** GEO. ELIOT *A. Bede* xix, He caught the sound of jocose talk and ringing laughter from behind the hedges.

jocosely (dʒəʊ'kəʊslɪ), *adv.* [f. prec. + -LY².] In a jocose manner; playfully; in joke.

?**1712** BROOME (J.), Spondanus imagines that Ulysses may possibly speak jocosely, but in truth Ulysses never behaves with levity. **1728** CURL in *Pope's Dunc.* II. 3 *note*, What the Gentlemen of the long robe are pleased jocosely to call mounting the Rostrum for one hour. **1807-8** W. IRVING *Salmag.* (1824) 279 We have more than once, in the course of our work, been most jocosely familiar with great personages. **1879** MCCARTHY *Own Times* II. xix. 54 He protested against having serious things treated jocosely.

jocoseness (dʒəʊ'kəʊsnɪs). [f. as prec. + -NESS.] Jocose quality or character; mirthfulness of disposition or style; waggishness.

1706 *Reflex. upon Ridicule* 385 He talks with the same liberty, familiarity, and jocoseness. **1778** MAD. D'ARBLAY *Diary* Sept., She has really some drollery about her,..and is very fond of jocoseness. **1859** G. MEREDITH *R. Feverel* xxi, The Baronet..thought proper in his wisdom to water the dryness of his sermon with a little jocoseness.

jocoserious (dʒəʊkəʊ'sɪərɪəs), *a.* [f. *joco-* as comb. form of L. *jocus* joke, jest + SERIOUS.] Half jocular, half serious; partly in jest and partly in earnest; blending jokes and serious matters. Hence **jocoseri'osity** (*nonce-wd.*).

a **1661** FULLER *Worthies, Suffolk* III. (1662) 61 Mr. Brounrig was appointed to perform the Joco-serious part thereof. **1737** M. GREEN *Spleen* 176 Drink a joco-serious cup With souls who've took their freedom up. **1819** *Ann. Reg.* 21/2 The right hon. gentleman went on in this joco-serious strain. **1885** E. JOHNSON in *Browning Society Papers* VII. 29 Our own poet has lately characterized himself as a *jocoserious* genius; and in fact this jocoseriosity seems of much the same quality with the eironeia of the Greek.

jocosity (dʒəʊ'kɒsɪtɪ). [f. L. type **jocōsitās*, f. *jocōsus* JOCOSE: see -ITY. Cf. It. *giocosità* (1611 in Florio), Sp. *jocosidad*.] Jocose quality or disposition, mirthfulness; *esp.* as exhibited in speech or action: mirth, merriment.

1646 SIR T. BROWNE *Pseud. Ep.* VII. xvi. 372 A laugh there is of contempt or indignation, as well as of mirth and Jocosity. **1778** MAD. D'ARBLAY *Diary* 26 Aug., A curious trait..of Dr. Johnson's jocosity. **1874** HELPS *Soc. Press.* xiv. (1875) 199 A low-minded creature, whose only idea of wit or jocosity is to give others pain.

b. A jocose saying or act; a piece of jesting.

1859 MASSON *Brit. Novelists* i. 42 Early fabliaux, passing from mouth to mouth as rude jocosities. **1865** *Sat. Rev.* 29 July 151/1 A fabricator of small jocosities affecting the manner of a great humourist.

jocound(e, obs. form of JOCUND.

†'**jocular**, *sb. Obs.* Also 5 ioculer. [a. OF. *joculer*, altered form (after L.) of *jougler*, *jougleur*: see JUGGLER.] A professional jester or minstrel.

1432-50 tr. *Higden* (Rolls) II. 171 Thei be as ioculers [*histriones*] in behauor. **1498** *Privy Purse Exp. Hen. VII* Aug., My Lord of Oxford's Iocular. *a* **1552** LELAND *Collect.* I. 235 A sothsayer, and iocular, and minstrelle. **1806** SOUTHEY in *Ann. Rev.* IV. 536 The Normans had joculars or minstrels.

jocular ('dʒɒkjʊlə(r)), *a.* [ad. L. *joculāris* facetious, f. *joculus*, dim. of *jocus* joke, jest.]

1. Of persons or their dispositions: Disposed to joking or jesting; speaking or acting in jest or merriment; mirthful, merry.

1626 B. JONSON *Fort. Isles* 56 My name is Johphiel..An airy jocular spirit. *a* **1661** FULLER *Worthies, Warwickshire* (1662) 126 Though his [Shakespeare's] Genius generally was jocular, and inclining him to festivity, yet he could..be solemn and serious. **1716** ADDISON *Drummer* II. i, He, he, he! pardon me for being jocular. **1836** W. IRVING *Astoria* III. 46 He joined, with the best grace he could assume, in the merriment of the jocular giant.

2. Of speech or action: Of the nature of, or containing, a joke; said or done in joke; comic, humorous, funny.

1674 *Govt. Tongue* 128 Many can sooner forgive a solemn deep contrivance against them, then one of their jocular reproches. *a* **1687** PETTY *Pol. Arith.* (1690) 65 To..interpose a jocular, and perhaps ridiculous digression. **1719** D'URFEY *Pills* (1872) II. 12 You that delight in a jocular Song. **1826** *Sheridaniana* 160 Sheridan made some jocular reply. **1871** R. ELLIS *Catullus* l. 6 Launched one arrowy metre and another, Tenders jocular o'er the merry wine-cup.

Hence '**jocularness** = next (Bailey vol. II, 1727).

jocularity (dʒɒkjʊ'lærɪtɪ). [ad. med.L. *joculāritās*, f. *joculāris*: see prec. and -ITY.] The quality of being jocular, mirthfulness; jocular speech or behaviour, jesting, mirth, fun.

1646 SIR T. BROWNE *Pseud. Ep.* VII. xvi. 372 When men could..persist unalterable at all effortes of Jocularity. **1751** JOHNSON *Rambler* No. 101 ¶1, I..applied my faculties to jocularity and burlesque. **1881** GOLDW. SMITH *Lect. & Ess.* 259 The jocularity which was always struggling with melancholy in his mind.

b. with *pl.* A jocular act or remark, a joke.

1848 DICKENS *Dombey* vii, Little jocularities, of which old Joe Bagstock was the perpetual theme.

jocularly ('dʒɒkjʊləlɪ), *adv.* [f. JOCULAR *a.* + -LY².] In a jocular manner; jestingly; in joke.

1655 STANLEY *Hist. Philos.* I. (1701) 42/2 Riddles..which she used jocularly, like Dice upon occasions, only contesting with such as provoked her. **1791** BOSWELL *Johnson* Oct. 1778 He has sometimes suffered me to talk jocularly of his group of females. **1828** D'ISRAELI *Chas. I*, I. ii. 16 Henry..jocularly placed the Archbishop's cap on his head.

†'**joculary**, *sb. Obs. rare.* [app. an altered form of OF. *jouglerie*, *jogelerie*, with assimilation to L. *joculator*: cf. JOCULAR *sb.*] The art or practice of jesters or jugglers; jugglery.

a **1500** *Bernard. de cura rei fam.* (E.E.T.S.) 216 A mane, he says, quhik al his fantasy Has geffyne to vice and vesy ioculary. *Ibid.* 231 The instrumentis pertenande ioculary War neuer plesande to god ȝeit sekyrly.

†'**joculary**, *a. Obs.* [ad. L. *joculāri-us* ludicrous, f. *jocul-us*: see -ARY.] = JOCULAR *a.*

1605 BACON *Adv. Learn.* II. x. §13 With Arts voluptuarie, I couple practises iocularie. *a* **1661** FULLER *Worthies, Cornwall* I. (1662) 198 This is a joculary and imaginary Court, wherewith men make merriment to themselves.

joculator ('dʒɒkjʊleɪtə(r)). *Obs.* exc. *Hist.* [a. L. *joculātor* jester, joker, agent-n. from *joculārī* to jest, joke, f. *joculus*: see JONGLEUR, JUGGLER.] A professional jester, minstrel, or jongleur.

a **1500** *Bernard. de cura rei fam.* (E.E.T.S.) 223 A mane to lach at ioculatouris fantasy. **1652** GAULE *Magastrom.* 87 Lawes..enacted against..prophesiers, predictors, circulatours, joculators, or jugglers! **1782** BURNEY *Hist. Mus.* (1789) II. iv. 355 The bounty of our first Norman sovereign to his Joculator or Bard. **1858** DORAN *Crt. Fools* 117 No monarch more needed a joculator than..Bolingbroke.

†'**joculatory**, *a. Obs.* [ad. L. *joculātōri-us*, f. *joculātor*: see prec. and -ORY.] Characteristic of, or having the character of, a jester; jocular.

1623 COCKERAM, *Ioculatorie*, merrily spoken. **1652** GAULE *Magastrom.* 348 They conclude them to be but joculatory pranks. **1661** K. W. *Conf. Charac., Cambridge Minion* (1860) 79 She..can if need be sing you a merry song and be pretty joculatory.

Hence †'**joculatorily** *adv. Obs.*

1623 COCKERAM II, Merrily, *Ioculatorily*. **1652** GAULE *Magastrom.* 210 How, then, dare prophane men offer to do such a thing joculatorily, jugglingly?

jocund ('dʒɒkənd, 'dʒəʊkənd), *a.* Also 4-6 iocounde, 4-7 iocunde, (5 ioycounde), 5-6 iocond(e, 6 iocound, (gioconde), 7-8 jocond. [a. OF. *jocund*, *jocond* (also *ju-*) = Sp. *jocunde*, It. *giocondo*, ad. late L. *jocund-us*, modification (after *jocus* joke, jest) of L. *jūcundus* pleasant, agreeable, delightful, f. *juv-āre* to help, aid, delight, please. Hence the etymological form is JUCUND; the application of *jocund* to persons has been affected by association with *jocus*. Now exclusively a literary word.]

Feeling, expressing, or communicating mirth or cheerfulness; mirthful, merry, cheerful, blithe, gay, sprightly, light-hearted; pleasant, cheering, delightful. (Of persons, actions, things, etc.)

?*c* **1380** CHAUCER *To Rosemounde* 5 Therwith ye ben so mery and so iocounde. *c* **1386** —— *Can. Yeom. Prol.* 43 He is ful iocunde also, dar I leye. **1388** WYCLIF *1 Sam.* xxv. 36 The herte of Nabal was iocounde, for he was drunkun greetli. **1509** HAWES *Past. Pleas.* XXVII. (Percy Soc.) 127 An hevy herte it wolde make jocunde. **1514** BARCLAY *Cyt. & Uplondyshm.* (Percy Soc.) 10 His jocunde jestes made me oftetyme full gladde. **1592** SHAKS. *Rom. & Jul.* III. v. 9 Iocond day Stands tipto on the mistie Mountaines tops. **1632** MILTON *L'Allegro* 94 And the jocond rebecks sound. **1677** W. HUGHES *Man of Sin* III. iii. 94 To avoid more Ink-shed in these Tales of Blood-shed, let's fall on some that are of a Jocunder Humour. **1750** GRAY *Elegy* vii, How jocund did they drive their team afield! **1814** SCOTT *Ld. of Isles* I. xvii, Be laughter loud and jocund shout, And bards to cheer the wassail rout. **1843** PRESCOTT *Mexico* (1850) I. 202 His careless manners and jocund repartees might well seem incompatible with anything serious.

†**b.** Feeling pleasure at some particular event or circumstance; joyful, glad, well-pleased. *Obs.*

?*a* **1400** *Morte Arth.* 2897 Gerarde es jocunde, and joyes hym þe more! *c* **1440** *Gesta Rom.* I. xx. 69 (Harl. MS.), I am more iocund þen any man may trowe, þat I se the hole. **1578** FLORIO *1st Fruites* 52 Gioconde was the Emperor Gratian, when he read the Posies of Ausonius.

c. *Comb.*

1863 COWDEN CLARKE *Shaks. Char.* ii. 45 Rosalind is one of the most enchanting among jocund-spirited heroines. **1866** CARLYLE *Remin.* II. (1881) I. 131 Irving was very good and jocund-hearted.

†'**jocundary**, *a. Obs.* [f. late L. *jocund-us* + -ARY: cf. *secondary*.] Jocund, mirthful, jocular. Hence †'**jocundarily** *adv. Obs.*, jestingly.

1618 DEKKER (*title*) The Owles Almanacke; prognosticating many strange accidents..by Jocundary Merrie-braines. **1624** FORD *Sun's Darling* III. i, Poor folly, honest folly, jocundary folly, forsake your lordship! **1660** *Trial Regic.* 155, I have found him jocundarily scoffing at it.

jocundity (dʒəʊ'kʌndɪtɪ). [ad. late L. *jocunditās*, f. *jocund-us* JOCUND: cf. OF. *jocond-*, *jocundite*, It. *giocondità*.]

1. Jocund quality or condition; mirthfulness, gaiety; mirth, merriment, glee.

c **1420** *Pallad. on Husb.* III. 1121 Vngreyned grape in high iocundite Me may suppe of. *c* **1510** BARCLAY *Mirr. Gd. Manners* (1570) Eiij, But mingle so in measure mirth and iocunditie. **1560** ROLLAND *Crt. Venus* III. 661 Iudas..With Thamar lay in his Iocunditie. **1685** BAXTER *Paraphr. N.T., John* ii. 9 Marriages among the Jews were celebrated with great Feasting, where moderate jocundity was thought seasonable. **1764** *Mem. G. Psalmanazar* 160, I have seen many of them go up to the gallows..with a seeming jocundity, as if they were mounting the guard. **1882** J. HAWTHORNE *Fort. Fool* I. xviii, He overflowed with jocundity, though he was neither a wit nor a humourist.

b. A merry act or saying; a pleasantry.

a **1734** NORTH *Exam.* I. ii. §27 (1740) 43 The more Liberties he [Shaftsbury] took in the way of Pleasures and Jocundities..the more acceptable he was to the King.

†**2.** Pleasure, delight, joy, happiness (of a high or spiritual kind). *Obs.*

c **1450** tr. *De Imitatione* III. lii. 124 Noon anxiete, blisful iocundite, swete companye & plesant to beholde. **1492** RYMAN *Poems* lxxxii. 7 in *Archiv Stud. neu. Spr.* LXXXIX. 251 In blisse with me thy place shall be Replete with alle iocundite. **1628** J. HUME *Jewes Deliv.* v. 76 He is joy and jocunditie to such as mourne.

'**jocundly**, *adv.* [f. JOCUND + -LY².] In a jocund manner; cheerfully, cheerily, merrily, gaily; with mirth or glee; with a light heart.

1471 *Arriv. Edw. IV* (Camden) 11 When ethar party welcomyd and jocundly receyvyd othar with perfect frindlynes. *c* **1510** BARCLAY *Mirr. Gd. Manners* (1570) Eiij, Iocundly iesting with wordes of wantonnes. **1566** DRANT *Horace, Sat.* II. i, He woulde ieste uery iocondlye. **1600** HOLLAND *Livy* 1361 They..clad themselves in the skins of the goats which they had sacrificed, and then fell to hopping and dauncing full jocundly. *a* **1716** SOUTH *Serm.* (1717) III. 498 He is ruined jocundly and pleasantly, and damned according to his Heart's desire. **1821** BYRON *Sardan.* I. ii. 637 At least we'll wear our fetters jocundly.

ˈjocundness. [f. as prec. + -NESS.] The quality or state of being jocund.

1. = JOCUNDITY 1.

1482 *Monk of Evesham* (Arb.) 86 He shewid alwey in wordys and countenans gladnes and iocundnes. **1548** UDALL *Erasm. Par. Luke* v. 34 Where reason would that al thinges should be ful of mirth and iocoundnesse. **1635** SWAN *Spec. M.* v. §2 (1643) 178 Casting away..the clouds of the mind, and begetting jocundnesse in the heart.

†**2.** = JOCUNDITY 2. *Obs.*

1426 AUDELAY *Poems* 26 Ther is no tong that con tel,.. That joye, that jocundnes, that Ihesus wyl joyn hym to. **1625** USSHER *Answ. Jesuit* 264 Where is light and life, where is glory and jocundnesse, where is joy and exultation.

†**ˈjocundry.** *Obs.* Also 7 jocondrie. [f. JOCUND *a.* + -RY: cf. *pleasantry*.] **a.** Jocund action or behaviour, merriment. **b.** Jocund disposition, cheerfulness.

1634 MILTON *Corrections of Comus* Wks. 1738 I. 8 And favour our close Jocondrie, Till all thy Dues bee done, and nought left out. **1655** tr. *Mdme. Scuderi's Artamenes* IV. VIII. II. 111 No person upon Earth had a sweeter Jocundry of mind then she. **1670** E. R. *Ne Plus Ultra* 39 By way of jocundry.

jod (dʒɒd, jəʊd), *sb.* [med.L. (German, etc.) spelling of Heb. *yōd*, the name of the letter י (*y*, *i*), the smallest letter of the square Hebrew alphabet: cf. IOTA, JOT.] = IOTA 2, JOT *sb.*¹

1596 H. CLAPHAM *Briefe Bible* I. 55 Neither might he [Moses] Adde, detract or Alter any iod thereof. **1610** DONNE *Pseudo-mart.* 277 The Canons..inflict an Anatheme vppon any Lay-man, which shall so much as dispute vpon, the text, or any one Iod of the Epistle of Pope Leo. *c* **1629** —— *Serm.* IV. cx. 515 No Iod in the Scripture shall perish, therefore no Iod is superfluous. **1851** LONGF. *Gold. Leg.* III. *Nativity* viii, As surely as the letter Jod Once cried aloud, and spake to God.

†**jod,** *v. Obs. trans.* To strike, knock.

?**14..** *Stasyons Jerus.* 139 in Horstm. *Altengl. Leg.* (1881) 357 We fond þe holys in þe stone, There-in þei Joddyd hym onne þe gronde.

jodel: see YODEL.

jodhpurs (ˈdʒɒdpəz, ˈdʒəʊd-), *sb. pl.* Also jodhpor, jodpor(e, judhpur, etc. [Name of a town and district in Rajasthan, a state in north-western India.] **1. a.** Riding-breeches reaching to the ankle, combining breeches and gaiters. Also *attrib.* in *sing.* **b.** Indian trousers cut loosely at the top but close-fitting below the knee.

1899 G. W. STEEVENS *In India* iv. 28 The Jodhpur riding-breeches—breeches and gaiters all in one piece, as full as you like above the knee, fitting tight below it, without a single button or strap..are on the way to be world-famous. **1913** E. M. FORSTER *Let.* 1 Jan. in *Hill of Devi* (1953) 21 My legs were clad in Jodpores made of white muslin. **1925** *Vogue* 1 Sept. 66 Judhpur. **1927** *Daily Express* 14 Nov. 5/2 These ski-ing suits are made with a plain, well-cut coat and jodhpurs or trousers. **1928** *Ibid.* 2 May 13 Finding some new jodhpors in his room, [he] could not resist trying them on. **1931** *Times* 7 May 17/5 Princess Elizabeth of York is shown dressed for a ride with her fair curls shining and wearing a yellow jumper pulled down over her jodhpurs. **1952** R. S. SUMMERHAYS *Elements of Riding* (ed. 3) xv. 87 Jodhpurs..are less expensive than breeches. **1957** *Encycl. Brit.* XIII. 80/2 The Jodhpur style of riding breeches (also seen, made of cotton, as normal walking garb in northern India) comprises breeches and gaiters in one. **1969** G. GREENE *Travels with my Aunt* I. iii. 19 Men..in tweed coats ..split horsily behind, gathered round a girl in jodhpurs. **1973** 'B. MATHER' *Snowline* xvii. 203 The Ismailis..dress in a distinctive style—jodhpurs, silk frock-coats and small embroidered skull-caps.

2. jodhpur boot, an ankle-high boot, orig. as worn with jodhpurs.

1939 E. HEMINGWAY *Fifth Column* II. iii. 61 *Dorothy Bridges*, wearing..a tweed skirt, wool stockings and jodhpur boots. **1972** *Police Rev.* 10 Nov. 1472/1 (Advt.), Angel (Reg. Brand) Best Jodhpur Boot.

Hence **ˈjodhpured** *a.*, wearing jodhpurs.

1969 *Daily Tel.* 8 Sept. 10/5 Small, pig-tailed Thelwell girls in voluminous riding-macs that flap round the bottoms of their plump, jodhpured legs. **1971** D. FRANCIS *Bonecrack* vii. 94, I watched the trim jodhpured figure walk off.

Jōdo (ˈdʒəʊdəʊ). Also Jō-do. [Jap., lit. 'purified land'.] **a.** A Japanese Buddhist sect which teaches salvation through absolute faith in the Buddha Amida and constant repetition of a formulaic prayer invoking his name. **b.** One of the heavens of Buddhist faith; *spec.* the Western Paradise, where the Buddha Amida resides. Also *attrib.* or as *adj.*

1727 J. G. SCHEUCHZER tr. *Kæmpfer's Hist. Japan* I. IV. iii. 287 Zealous persons, chiefly the followers of the Sect of Siodo. **1886** B. NANJIO *Short Hist. Twelve Jap. Buddhist Sects* ix. (*title*) The Jō-do-shū, or Pure Land sect. **1895** W. E. GRIFFIS *Relig. Japan* ix. 268 The Japanese technical term, '*tariki*', or relying upon the strength of another, renouncing all idea of *ji-riki* or self-power is the substance of the Jō-dō doctrine. **1911** B. H. CHAMBERLAIN *Jap. Poetry* IV. 215 *Jōdo*, literally, 'the Pure Land', is one of the Buddhist heavens fabled to exist in the West. **1938** D. T. SUZUKI *Zen Buddhism & its Influence on Jap. Culture* I. iii. 37 The Jōdo appeals naturally more to plebeian requirements because of the simpleness of its faith and teaching. **1970** J. W. HALL *Japan from Prehist. to Mod. Times* vi. 74 In the tenth century new and more accessible teachings began to gain currency among the aristocracy. Among these was the worship of Amida, the Buddha of the Pure Land (Jōdō) or Western Paradise.

jods (dʒɒdz, dʒəʊdz), colloq. abbrev. of JODHPURS *sb. pl.* Also (in *sing.*) *attrib.*

1959 J. VERNEY *Friday's Tunnel* xxvii. 258, I had nothing on but a sopping shirt and jods. *Ibid.* 259 The thought of riding reminded me of gob-stoppers. I found three left in my jod pocket. **1960** E. H. CLEMENTS *Honey for Marshal* ii. 43 Better take her jods! Your children do ride, don't they?

joe (dʒəʊ), *sb.*¹ Also 8 jo. Abbreviation of *Joannes* or JOHANNES, a Portuguese gold coin.

1772 in F. Chase *Hist. Dartmouth College* (1891) I. 262 *note*, Let Mr. Ripley have a guinea, half a jo, and 9 coppers. **1783** WOLCOTT (P. Pindar) *Odes R. Academ.* vii. Wks. 1790 I. 75 Or Sol's bright orb—be sure to make him glow Precisely like a guinea, or a jo. **1833** MARRYAT *P. Simple* xxxi, I think they were half a joe, or eight dollars each. **1840** BARHAM *Ingol. Leg.*, *Hand of Glory* vii, The fair rose-noble, the bright moidore, And the broad Double-Joe from ayont the sea.

Joe (dʒəʊ), *sb.*² *colloq.* or *slang.* [Familiar abbreviation of the name *Joseph*.]

1. a. Short for *Joe Miller*: see 4.

1834 SOUTHEY *Doctor* xvi. I. 159 Of what use a story may be even in the most serious debates may be seen from the circulation of old Joes in Parliament. **1882** *Athenæum* 9 Sept. 337/2 Such venerable Joes as the 'Lapsus linguæ' story.

b. phr. ***not for Joe (Joseph)***, by no means, not on any account.

1844 C. SELBY *London by Night* (1886) II. i. 9/1 *Jack.* Who's to pay? *Ned.* Whichever you please. *Jack.* Oh! in that case you may as well settle it. *Ned.* Not for Joseph! You asked me to tea. *c* **1867** *Broadside Ballad* in Farmer & Henley *Slang* (1896) IV. 76/2 Not for Joe...Not for Joseph, if he knows it. **1928** GALSWORTHY *Swan Song* II. xiii. 219 Not if he knew it—not for Joe.

c. *int.* (See quots. 1855¹ and 1862.) So as *v. trans.* (See quot. 1861.) *Austral.* and *N.Z. slang.*

1855 W. HOWITT *Land, Labour & Gold, or Two Yrs. in Victoria* I. xxii. 400 The well-known cry of 'Joe! Joe!'.. which means..one of the myrmidons of Charley Joe, as they familiarly style Mr. [Charles Joseph] La Trobe [Governor of Victoria]. **1855** C. R. THATCHER in Stewart & Keesing *Old Bush Songs* (1957) 111 Should a body 'Joe' a body For having on a hat? **1861** T. MCCOMBIE *Austral. Sk.* 135 To 'Joey' or 'Joe' a person on the diggings, or anywhere else in Australia, is grossly to insult and ridicule him. **1862** E. HODDER *Memories N.Z. Life* 188 As [the diggers] descried us approaching on the rocks, a simultaneous cry of 'Joe! Joe!' was raised. This is a popular cry on the New Zealand diggings and is used to hail any 'new chums' who may appear. It had its origin at the Australian diggings, where licenses were granted to all who held claims... When the police came upon the ground, to inspect licences, the cry of 'Joe!' was raised. **1871** C. L. MONEY *Knocking about in N.Z.* vii. 103 The word 'Joe' expresses derision usually bestowed on new chums on the diggings, or any man acting, or dressing, or speaking in any way considered as outré by the diggers themselves. *Ibid.*, Among the first to 'Joe' me at the beginning. **1917** 'H. H. RICHARDSON' *Fortunes R. Mahony* I. i. 11 An odd figure..crying at the top of her voice: 'Joe, boys!—Joe, Joe, Joey!'

2. A fourpenny piece: = JOEY¹.

1882 in OGILVIE.

3. Joe Manton. 'A name given to fowling-pieces made by Joseph Manton, a celebrated London gunsmith' (Farmer *Slang*).

1816 SCOTT *Antiq.* xxxix, It's a capital gun; it's a Joe Manton, that cost forty guineas. **1885** W. H. RUSSELL in *Harper's Mag.* Apr. 771/1 Malachy..shot with a Joe Manton.

4. Joe Miller. [From the name of Joseph Miller, a comedian (1684–1738), attached to a popular jest-book published after his death.]

a. A jest-book. **b.** A jest or joke; *esp.* a stale joke, a 'chestnut'. Hence (*nonce-wds.*) **Joe-ˈMillerism**, the practice of retailing stale jokes; **Joe-ˈMillerize** *v. trans.*, to render jocular or comic, to turn into a joke (see -IZE, quot. 1866).

[Miller's chief reputation was made for him after his death by John Mottley, who was commissioned by a publisher, T. Reid, in 1739 to compile a collection of jests, and unwarrantably entitled his work 'Joe Miller's jests, or the Wit's Vade-mecum'. *Dict. Nat. Biog.* s.v. *Joseph Miller*.]

1789 G. PARKER *Life's Painter* xii, What..should not be found in every common jest book or a Joe Miller, p. 14. **1816** SCOTT *Antiq.* xxxix, A fool and his money are soon parted, nephew: there is a Joe Miller for your Joe Manton. **1870** RAMSAY *Remin.* (ed. 18) p. xxx, Many of the anecdotes are mere Joe Millers. **1882** OGILVIE, *Joe-Millerism.*

5. *colloq.* **a.** A fellow, 'guy', chap; (in certain countries) an American. Cf. *G.I. Joe, Holy Joe.*

1846 *Swell's Night Guide* 123/1 *Joe*, an imaginary person, nobody, as Who do those things belong to? Joe. **1906** E. DYSON *Fact'ry 'Ands* viii. 92 Why, man, it's meat 'n' beer t' them Joes what go in fer bringin' ther wanderers 'ome. **1932** *Amer. Speech* June 333 *Joe*, term used to designate anyone whose real name is unknown. When used with a place or profession 'Joe' indicates a perfect example of the type connected with that place or profession. **1945** 'A. BOUCHER' in M. & G. Gordon *Pride of Felons* (1964) 80 The customers are mostly elderly Italian businessmen who are good Joes. **1947** *Amer. Speech* XXII. 55/1 *Joe*, name given by the natives [in the Pacific] to any American. **1952** S. SELVON *Brighter Sun* iv. 55 In Trinidad... All Americans..are known as 'Joes'. **1957** J. OSBORNE *Entertainer* viii. 71 While everyone else is sitting on their hands you're the Joe at the back cheering. **1962** E. LACY *Freeloaders* vii. 133 Way I see it, Gil is an American... We joes have to stick together. **1969** M. PUGH *Last Place Left* xvi. 110 A few of his men were Irish moleskin joes from the hydro-electric operation. **1972** J. BURMEISTER *Running Scared* xii. 169 Be a good Joe and take the pills. Please. **1973** *Publishers Weekly* 26 Mar. 65/2 The average Joe probably thinks that cyclists..are eccentric folk.

b. Joe College. 'A college boy; *esp.* one devoted to amusement' (Webster, 1961).

1932 *Amer. Speech* June 333 'Joe College' is a perfect specimen of the college man. Often used with 'himself'. **1964** *Ibid.* XXXIX. 193 The net effect of the publications on college slang has been to encourage the image of perky Joe College.

c. Joe Bloggs, Joe Blow (*U.S.*), **Joe Do(a)kes:** names applied to a hypothetical average or ordinary man.

c **1941** KENDALL & 'VINEY' *Dict. Army-Navy Slang*, Joe Blow...means any soldier. **1943** *Amer. Speech* XVIII. 109 *Joe Doakes*, generic term for all ball players. **1945** L. LANE *How to become a Comedian* x. 92 He would ask the conductor if he had seen 'Joe Dokes' last night. **1956** B. HOLIDAY *Lady sings Blues* (1973) ix. 90 But just let me walk out of the club one night with a young white boy of my age, whether it was John Roosevelt, the President's son, or Joe Blow. **1968** *Jazz Monthly* 15/1 All these items are essentially jazz-tinged versions of Joe Doakes's favourite melodies. **1969** *Guardian* 6 Mar. 7/2 LSD can be taken by Joe Bloggs on a lump of sugar. **1970** C. MAJOR *Dict. Afro-Amer. Slang* 71 *Joe Blow*, ..horn-blowing musician..came to mean any male person. **1971** *Daily Tel.* 27 July 13/5 In too many cases these forms arrive on the desk of a busy executive who concludes that Joe Bloggs down the corridor must have signed the order. **1973** K. GILES *File on Death* iv. 98 Joe Bloggs, the honest garage mechanic.

d. Joe Soap: name applied to a 'dumb' person, a mug; also, more generally, a quite ordinary person, any person.

1943 HUNT & PRINGLE *Service Slang* 41 *Joe Soap*, the 'dumb' or not so intelligent members of the forces. The men who are 'over-willing' and therefore the usual 'stooges'. **1966** 'L. LANE' *ABZ of Scouse* 56 *Joe Soap*, whozit, whatzisname. When asked by the police to account for the possession of a stolen article the answer often is *I got guv it by Joe Soap.* **1968** 'B. MATHER' *Springers* xi. 111, I sat there like Joe Soap on guard; feeling guilty if I dozed off. **1969** *Guardian* 31 Mar. 15/8 Socialists have become..over-eager to find out what Joe Soap is doing in order to tell him not to do it. **1972** J. BROWN *Chancer* ix. 118 Who do you think I am, moosh? Joe Soap?

6. Joe Blake. *Austral. rhyming slang.* A snake.

1927 M. TERRY *Through Land of Promise* ix. 123 I'll bet you what you like there are Joe Blakes in this camp. **1934** *Bulletin* (Sydney) 22 Aug. 20/2 At Bob's prompting Billy sneaked up quietly and quickly behind Joe Blake, and, seizing the tail firmly, gave a terrific swing round his head. **1970** *Sunday Mail Mag.* (Brisbane) 11 Jan. 3/1 We've camped..with the Joe Blakes, the goannas, the flies, and 4000 skinny jumbucks.

7. A French Canadian. *Canad. slang.*

1963 R. I. MCDAVID *Mencken's Amer. Lang.* 368 Frog is not applied in Canada to a French Canadian, who is a Canuck or simply Joe, and prefers to be called a Habitant. **1966** *Globe & Mail* (Toronto) 19 Apr. 6/6 Their waspish counterparts in Quebec always refer to 'pea-soupers' or 'Joes'. The word 'Frog' in that connection went out of fashion 50 years ago.

joe (dʒəʊ), *sb.*³ *U.S. colloq.* [Origin unknown.] Coffee.

1941 J. SMILEY *Hash House Lingo* 34 *Joe*, coffee. **1944** K. D. MCCRACKEN *Baby Flat-Top* 87 Quartermasters..are inexhaustible in furnishing the Officer of the Deck with anything from the true wind and the relative humidity to a flashlight and a pot of Joe. **1953** C. M. KORNBLUTH *Syndic* (1964) viii. 80 Get me a mug of joe, sailor... Go get the coffee. **1963** 'E. MCBAIN' *Ten plus One* (1964) v. 48 'Would you like some coffee?' Carella asked. 'Is there some?' 'Sure. .. Can we get two cups of joe?'

joe, variant of JO *Sc.*, darling, sweetheart.

joe-caul, obs. perversion of JACKAL *sb.*

joell, obs. form of JEWEL.

joe-pye weed. *N. Amer.* Also joe pye. [See quot. 1893.] Either of two tall, perennial herbs, *Eupatorium purpureum* or *E. maculatum*, belonging to the family Compositæ, and bearing clusters of purplish flowers.

1818 A. EATON *Man. Bot.* (ed. 2) II. 245 *Eupatorium ..purpureum* (purple thoroughwort, or joe-pye). *Ibid. Eupatorium..verticillatum* (joe-pye's weed). **1866** LINDLEY & MOORE *Treas. Bot.* II. 638/1 Joe-pye weed. An American name for *Eupatorium purpureum.* **1893** F. T. DANA *Wild Flowers* iii. 210 Joe-Pye-Weed. Trumpet-Weed. *Eupatorium purpureum*... 'Joe Pye' is said to have been the name of an Indian who cured typhus fever in New England by means of this plant. **1895** K. D. WIGGIN *Village Watch-Tower* 42 Purple asters and gay Joe Pye waved their colors by the road-side. **1903** E. C. WALTZ *Pa Gladden* vii. 144 In other Septembers the slope..was lovely with..joepye-weed. **1949** *Nature Mag.* Apr. 187/2 Later the cowslips are replaced by purple loose-strife and that butterfly magnet, Joe-pye weed. **1954** C. J. HYLANDER *Macmillan Wild Flower Bk.* 412 Joe-Pye-weed is found from New England south to North Carolina and New Mexico.

joes (dʒəʊz), *sb. pl. Austral. slang.* [Origin unknown.] Depression of spirits, the blues.

1916 C. J. DENNIS *Moods of Ginger Mick* 27 'E's got the joes reel bad. *a* **1938** —— in *Penguin Bk. Austral. Ballads* (1964) 235 It gimme Joes to sit an' watch them two! **1957** V. PALMER *Seedtime* xx. 138 What I saw in the sugar country gave me the joes.

Joey¹ (ˈdʒəʊɪ). Also joey. [Diminutive from JOE *sb.*²: see -Y.] **1.** A fourpenny piece: see quot. 1876. *Obs. slang* or *colloq.*

1865 H. KINGSLEY *Hillyars & B.* xlii, A young man as has owed me a Joey. **1876** E. HAWKINS *Silver Coins Eng.* 421 In

1836 it was resolved to issue groats for general circulation... The legend, FOUR PENCE.. These pieces are said to have owed their existence to the pressing instance of Mr. [Joseph] Hume, from whence they for some time bore the nick-name of Joeys. **1834** BLACKMORE *Tommy Upm.* I. 288 Here is the eightpence—a couple of Joeys, as you call them.

2. A threepenny bit. *slang.*

1936 'G. ORWELL' *Keep Aspidistra Flying* i. 7 A Joey. He took out the miserable little threepenny-bit. **1945** BAKER *Austral. Lang.* v. 109 *3d.*,..joey. **1965** *Australasian Post* 4 Mar. 46 *Threepence*, 'joe' or 'joey', though these..two words are now rarely heard. (A 'joey' was originally London slang for a fourpenny bit; and later was transferred to the English threepence). **1966** F. SHAW et al. *Lern Yerself Scouse* 33 *Joey*, threepence.

joey[2] ('dʒəʊɪ). [Native Austral. *joè*: see quot. 1839.] A young kangaroo; also *gen.* a young animal or child. See also quot. 1887.

1839 W. H. LEIGH *Reconnoit. Voy. S. Austral.* 93–4 (Morris) Here [in Kangaroo Island] is also the wallaba... The young of the animal is called by the islanders a joè. **1845** MOORE *Tasman. Rhymings* (1860) 15 He was a 'joey' which, in truth, Means nothing more than that the youth Who claims a Kangaroo descent Is by that nomenclature meant. **1866** *Cornhill Mag.* Dec. 762 Large flocks of kangaroo..the larger males..towered above the flying bucks, flying does and joeys, the half-grown bucks, does, and young ones. **1887** *All Year Round* 30 July (Farmer), Joey..is applied indifferently to a puppy, or a kitten, or a child, while a wood-and-water-joey is a hanger about hotels, and a doer of odd jobs.

Joey[3] ('dʒəʊɪ). *colloq.* [Familiar abbrev. of the name of the clown *Joseph* Grimaldi (1779–1837).] A clown.

1896 G. B. SHAW *Our Theatres in Nineties* (1932) II. 105 Its [*sc.* philosophic comedy's] common Joeys with red-hot poker and sausages. **1926** *Amer. Speech* Feb. 283/2 I'm through with bein' a joey. Gettin' too old, thought I would never troupe again. **1962** D. H. LAURENCE in G. B. Shaw *Platform & Pulpit* p. xiii, Thus was created a paradox of the public simultaneously decrying Shaw for playing a 'Joey' rôle and seeking desperately to set a jester's cap upon his head. **1973** J. WAINWRIGHT *Devil you Don't* 121 A pensioner—gnarled hand gripping a walking-stick, grey hair peeping from beneath an old-fashioned flat cap, pullover, frayed jacket and baggy trousers—like a Joey, without make-up.

jog (dʒɒg), *sb.*[1] Also 7–8 jogg. [f. JOG *v.*]

1. The act of jogging a thing or person (see JOG *v.* 1, 2); a shake; a slight push; a nudge.

1635 QUARLES *Embl.* IV. iv. (1718) 202, I have none to guide me With the least jog. **1693** EVELYN *Refl. Agric.* xviii. 69 in *De la Quint. Compl. Gard.*, To pull up the Weight, and give a little Jog to the Pendulum. **1725** DE FOE *Voy. round World* (1840) 330 A little breeze of wind..which..gave them a kind of a Jog on their way towards the shore. **1755** RAMSAY *To James Clerk* 72 Should dreary care then stunt my muse, And gar me aft her jogg refuse? **1881** BESANT & RICE *Chapl. of Fleet* I. xii, The man Roger gave the dazed bridegroom a jog in the ribs. **1896** *Westm. Gaz.* 20 Feb. 1/2 The perpendicular jog usually experienced in dog-carts.. and also the side-to-side jog due to a horse with each step pulling first against one trace, then against the other.

2. a. The act of jogging or moving mechanically up and down. **b.** The act of jogging along (see JOG *v.* 4); a slow measured walk, trot, or run; also *transf.*, *e.g.* of the rhythm of verse.

1611 COTGR., *Cahot*, the iumpe, hop, or iog of a coach, etc., in a rugged, or vneuen, way. **16..** in W. Blundell *Crosby Rec.* 135 Sir Humphrey Stapleton..hath hit very right of the jog of an English style in his version of 'Strada'. **1667** H. MORE *Div. Dial.* v. xxv. (1713) 483 Not caring to bespatter others in this high jogg, as he himself was finely bespattered from others. **1889** MRS. OLIPHANT *Poor Gentleman* xlviii, A carriage..was coming along with the familiar jog of a hack carriage which is paid for at so much an hour. **1890** 'BOLDREWOOD' *Col. Reformer* (1891) 319 The slow, hopeless, leg-weary jog to which most of the horses.. had long been reduced. **1948** *Oxf. Pocket Bk. Athletic Training* iii. 32 A very slow jog, where the runner lands flat-footed with a slight jarring action. **1969** [see JOG *v.* 4].

jog, *sb.*[2] Also 8 jogg. [In sense 1 var. of JAG *sb.*[1]; in senses 2 and 3, cf. JOGGLE *sb.*[2]]

1. A projecting point on an edge or surface; = JAG *sb.*[1] 4; a protuberance, swelling. *rare.* ? *Obs.*

1715 tr. *Pancirollus' Rerum Mem.* II. App. 440 The Beginnings..are a little rude..till the little Jogs are rubbed off by Experience and Time. **1744–50** W. ELLIS *Mod. Husbandm.* III. II. 73 (E.D.S.) Hogs..jogged under their throats..we discharge by cutting, or running a red-hot iron through the bunch or jogg. *Ibid.* IV. I. 127.

2. A right-angled notch, recess, or step, in a surface; any space cut out by such a notch. *U.S.*

'In the States, *jog* is used to signify any deviation from a straight line or even surface' (Farmer *Americanisms*, 1889).

1881 MORGAN *Contrib. Amer. Ethnol.* 157 The thickness of the main wall..diminishing every story by retreating jogs on the inside, from bottom to top. **1884** B. B. WARFIELD in *Chr. Treas.* Feb. 91/1 The parts historically dovetail together, jog to jog, into one connected and consistent whole. **1893** MAHAN *Sea Power & Fr. Rev.* iii. 80 Her [Spain's] maritime advantages were indeed diminished by the jog which Portugal takes out of her territory.

3. *Cryst.* A step in a dislocation where it passes from one atomic plane to another.

1951 N. F. MOTT in *Proc. Physical Soc.* LXIV. B. 733 Supposing one of the expanding dislocation loops..cuts a screw dislocation, pictured as perpendicular to the plane of the paper. This will normally happen several times in the expansion of a loop in a real crystal. The loop will then necessarily contain what we call a 'jog', i.e. a point where the dislocation jumps from one slip plane to an adjacent one. **1955** *Rep. Conf. Defects Crystalline Solids 1954* (Physical Soc.) 391 If the section of the dislocation between the two parallel planes has a length of the order of the atomic distance, it is called a dislocation jog. **1960** *New Scientist* 6 Oct. 915/3 There is a theory based on the strain fields round the dislocations and the way they attract and repel each other, and a theory based on the way they get kinky ('jogs' is the technical word) when they cut through each other. **1966** C. R. TOTTLE *Sci. Engin. Materials* iv. 98 If the jog climbs, by moving into another slip plane, point defects are created, but the screw dislocation containing the jog can continue to slip.

jog (dʒɒg), *v.* Forms: 6–7 iogge, 7 jogg, 7– jog, (9 *Sc.* jag). [Known only from 16th c.; origin unascertained: app. onomatopœic, and akin to SHOG, which is to some extent synonymous and of earlier appearance.

The suggestion of a Celtic origin is not tenable. English phonology knows nothing of a change of *go* to *jo*. And the alleged Welsh *gogi*, given by Pughe as 'to shake, agitate', has no existence (Prof. Rhys).

For a vb. *jog, jogge*, which appears in Piers Plowman, varying with *jagge*, and *jugge*, see JUG *v.*[4] *Jogis* in *Wars of Alexander* I. 1507 (where the two texts differ widely, and are both corrupt) is evidently an error for some other word.]

1. a. *trans.* To shake or move (a heavy body) with a push or jerk; to throw *up* with a jerk; to shake *up*.

1548 COOPER *Elyot's Biblioth.*, *Succutio*, to shake a thyng, to iogge vp, to lifte as the horse that trotteth harde lifteth one at euery steppe in the saddle. **1591** LYLY *Sappho* IV. iii, I thinke all her teeth will be loose, they are so often jogged against her tongue. **1640** BP. REYNOLDS *Passions* xvii. 182 The Seamans needle which is jogged and troubled, never leaves moving till it finde the North point againe. *a* **1648** DIGBY *Closet Open.* (1677) 109 Perfectly sweet cream, that hath not been jogged with carriage. *a* **1770** CHATTERTON *Exhibition* in *Harper's Mag.* (1883) July 236/1 The prudent Mayor jogged his dinner down. **1878** CLARK RUSSELL *Wreck 'Grosvenor'* vi, Large masses of this froth..were jogged clean off the water, and struck the deck or sides of the ship with reports like the discharge of a pistol.

b. *fig.*

1642 FULLER *Holy & Prof. St.* III. x. 175 What wonder is it if agitation of businesse jog that out of thy head? **1688** BUNYAN *Jerusalem Sinner* (1886) 119 Art thou jogged, and shaken, and molested at the hearing of the Word? *a* **1734** NORTH *Lives, Ld. Guildford* (1745) 239 This very project of getting the general gaol delivery of recusants..was jogged upon his lordship to have had it been moved by him.

2. a. To give a slight push to, so as to shake; to nudge; esp. so as to arouse to attention.

1589 GREENE *Menaphon* (Arb.) 45 Doron iogde Melicertus on the elbowe, and so awakte him out of a dreame. *c* **1620** Z. BOYD *Zion's Flowers* (1855) 12 Though I him jog and shake, its all in vaine. **1643** PRYNNE *Sov. Power Parlt.* App. 195 Shall he pull those by the eares who are asleepe, or onely jogge them by the sides? **1663** BUTLER *Hud.* I. iii. 765 He jogg'd his good Steed nigher And steer'd him gently toward the Squire. **1725** POPE *Odyss.* XIV. 545 Sudden I jogg'd Ulysses, who was laid Fast by my side. **1889** J. K. JEROME *Idle Thoughts* 32 A bored-looking man, with a fashionably-dressed woman jogging his elbow.

b. *fig.*: esp. *to jog the memory*.

1601 SIR W. CORNWALLIS *Disc. Seneca* (1631) 10 Providence..jogs him, if vaine pleasures lull him in sensuality. *a* **1764** LLOYD *Poems, Shakespeare*, Jog them, lest attention sink, To tell them how and what to think. **1778** (*title*) An Antidote to Popery; or, the Protestant's Memory jogg'd in Season. **1825** LAMB *Elia* Ser. II. *The Convalescent*, Jogging this witness, refreshing that solicitor. **1840** LADY C. BURY *Hist. of Flirt* xi, I jogged his memory by reverting to our water-party. **1874** C. KEENE *Let.* in *Life* vii. (1892) 165, I often jog him up with a letter, but he never answers.

3. *intr.* To move up and down or to and fro with a heavy unsteady motion; to move about as if shaken.

1586 BRIGHT *Melanch.* xl. 268 When the meate is perceaued to be loose and iogge in the stomach. **1611** COTGR., *Cahoter*, to iumpe, iog, or hop, as a coach in vneuen way. **1676** HOBBES *Iliad* I. 50 His bow and quiver both behinde him hang, The arrows chink as often as he jogs. **1852** MRS. SMYTHIES *Bride Elect* viii, His sisters-elect, jigging and jogging in a mad polka. **1858** GREENER *Gunnery* 370 One projection..would make the ball jog and oscillate much after the manner that has been described. **1865** DICKENS *Mut. Fr.* III. xiv, Mr. Venus listened to these lamentations in silence, while Mr. Boffin jogged to and fro.

4. a. *intr.* To walk or ride with a jolting pace, 'to move with small shocks like those of a low trot' (J.); to move on at a heavy or laboured pace, to trudge; hence, to move on, go on, be off. More recently, to run at a gentle pace (esp. as part of a 'keep-fit' schedule).

1565 [see JOGGING *vbl. sb.*]. **1590** GREENE *Mourn. Garm.* (1616) 38 He bade his man bee iogging. **1596** LAMBARDE *Peramb. Kent* (ed. 2) 229 This Iade..driuen (as it were) by some diuine furie, neuer ceassed iogging till he came at the Abbay church doore. **1596** SHAKS. *Tam. Shr.* III. ii. 213 There lies your way, You may be iogging whiles your bootes are greene. **1630** DEKKER *2nd Pt. Honest Wh.* Wks. 1873 II. 145 Has thy husband any Lands?..any Ploughs iogging? **1663** BUTLER *Hud.* I. i. 631 Few miles on Horseback had they jogged. *a* **1754** FIELDING *Fathers* I. ii, A Knight of the Shire used to jog to town with a brace of geldings. **1821** CLARE *Vill. Minstr.* I. 26 The load jogg'd homeward down the lane. **1833** L. RITCHIE *Wand. by Loire* 182 You may see the farmer and his fraternity jogging to market..on their respective steeds. **1876** GREEN *Stray Stud.* 51 The women sing as they jog down the hill-paths. **1968** 'E. V. CUNNINGHAM' *Margie* ix. 156 Fenton, who was jogging in place to keep his circulation up, explained that they were in a local elevator. **1969** *Age* (Melbourne) 24 May 17/4 Latest to join the 'jog' set is Sir Reginald Sholl, who was seen jogging around Fawkner Park. **1970** N. ARMSTRONG et al. *First on Moon* ii. 37 There would be little time..to read or jog on the beach.

b. esp. with *on*, *along*.

1611 SHAKS. *Wint. T.* IV. iii. 132 Iog-on, Iog-on the foot-path way, And merrily hent the Stile-a. *c* **1631** MILTON *2nd Poem Univ. Carrier* 4 While he might still jog on and keep his trot. **1697** DAMPIER *Voy.* (1729) I. 172 We jogged on after this with a gentle gale. **1758** CAPT. TYRREL in *Naval Chron.* X. 359 Whilst I made all the sail I could, they were jogging on under their foresails and top-sails. **1797** MRS. RADCLIFFE *Italian* xii. (1824) 596 But Paulo..jogged merrily along. **1892** ANNE RITCHIE *Rec. Tennyson*, etc. III. iv. 187 Our old white horse jogged steadily on.

c. *fig.* In reference to time, or continued action of any kind. Chiefly *jog along, on*.

1677 HORNECK *Gt. Law Consid.* iv. (1704) 142 Unwillingness to lose a temporal advantage makes them jogg on in a course which perhaps they do dislike. **1683** KENNETT tr. *Erasm. on Folly* 23 To jog sleepingly through the world..cannot properly be said to live. **1698** FRYER *Acc. E. India & P.* 282 Through all these Scenes, Time keeps jogging on. **1702** C. MATHER *Magn. Chr.* I. iii. (1852) 57 So they jogged on till the day twelvemonth after their first arrival. **1803** SCOTT *Fam. Lett.* 6 Mar. (1894) I. i. 18 My worldly matters jog on very well. **1847** A. BRONTË *Agnes Grey* xxii. 325 They're jogging along as usual, I suppose. **1893** F. F. MOORE *I forbid Banns* (1899) 14, I want things to jog along as quietly as possible. Jogging along is true happiness, if people only knew it.

Hence '**jogging** *ppl. a.*

1886 STEVENSON *Kidnapped* i, He..set off..by the way that we had come at a sort of jogging run.

jog *v.*, obs. form of JAG *v.*[1]; see also JUG *v.*[4]

jog, jogg, *sb.* and *v.*: see JOUGS.

jogah ('dʒəʊgə). *slang.* Also jogar. [Origin unknown.] = BUSKER[2].

1928 *Radio Times* 2 Nov. 302/1 'Varda the polone,' murmurs a 'jogah'. **1952** GRANVILLE *Dict. Theatr. Terms* 104 *Jogar*, a street-singer, or queue entertainer.

jogee, jogi, varr. YOGI.

jogeler, -our, obs. forms of JUGGLER.

‖**joget** ('dʒɒgət). Also *erron.* jogget. [Mal. *joget.*] A Malay popular dance, in which a couple improvises to the accompanying music. Also *attrib.*, and *transf.*, the place where such dancing occurs.

1895 F. A. SWETTENHAM *Malay Sk.* vii. 45 Dancing girls ..perform what is called the 'Jôget'—a real dance with an accompaniment of something like real music, though the orchestral instruments are very rude indeed. **1900** W. W. SKEAT *Malay Magic* vi. 513 The *Joget*, a kind of dramatic and symbolical dance. **1910** R. J. WILKINSON *Papers on Malay Subjects: Life & Customs* III. 22 The *ronggeng*, *gamboh* and *joget* come from Java. **1959** P. BROWN *As Far as Singapore* vi. 125 'It is the Malayan *jogget* dancing.'.. It was rather like an Oriental version of jiving, with the boy and girl facing each other and executing intricate steps to the rhythmic music, but never actually touching each other. **1963** J. KIRKUP *Tropic Temper* xv. 163 The place where the dancing is done is called a joget. **1966** D. FORBES *Heart of Malaya* vii. 89 We were shown..an entertainment at court, providing the occasion for more music and for *joget* dances. **1972** M. SHEPPARD *Taman Indera* 92 (*caption*) The Trengganu palace *Joget* dancers in an 18th century dance. **1972** *Straits Times* (Malaysian ed.) 23 Nov. 4/4 Among the dances to be performed are..Joget.

jogg(e: see JAG *v.*[1], JOG, JOUGS, JUG *v.*[4]

jogged, *a.* [f. JOG *sb.*[2] + -ED[2].]

a. Having a protuberance or swelling. ? *Obs.*

1744–50 [see JOG *sb.*[2] 1].

b. *Cryst.* Having a jog or jogs.

1962 *Phil. Mag.* VII. 83 Jogged dislocations can advance only if the jogs glide conservatively along the Burgers vector direction or by producing lines of point defects. **1973** *Nature* 3 Aug. 276/2 Bowed, looped and jogged dislocations.

jogger ('dʒɒgə(r)). [f. JOG *v.* + -ER[1].] One who or that which jogs (see the verb); a person who pushes or nudges, or who moves slowly and heavily; one who jogs at a gentle pace for physical exercise; an instrument or appliance for giving a jog or slight push to some part of mechanism.

a **1700** DRYDEN (J.), They with their fellow joggers of the plough. **1884** R. JEFFERIES in *Pall Mall G.* 8 Aug. 4/2 A hand was placed on my elbow... The fair jogger beamed yet more sweetly..and went on among the crowd. **1888** *Sci. Amer.* 2 June 340/3 A receiving-table for cylinder printing presses, designed to facilitate the accurate piling of the sheets without the use of the ordinary form of jogger. **1895** *N.B. Daily Mail* 11 Mar. 4 Members who represent a 'happy medium' between the old 'joggers' and the new 'jumpers'. **1968** *Times* 24 May (N.Z. Suppl.) p. viii/5 The caption refers to the runner as 'a jogger out for his morning run'. In New Zealand the noun jogger is an acceptable..word because so many people..run for fitness. **1968** *Chicago Tribune* 9 July 1. 12/1 Joggers have become an almost familiar sight thruout America in the last year. **1969** *Age* (Melbourne) 24 May 17/4 Ken Myer is a well-known jogger around the Toorak area.

jogging, *vbl. sb.* [f. JOG *v.* + -ING[1].]

1. The action of the vb. JOG.

1565 COOPER *Thesaurus*, *Succussatura*, a ioggynge: a trottinge. **1581** MULCASTER *Positions* xii. (1887) 61 Sore shaking or hard iogging doth [trouble] the wearied body. **1660** H. MORE *Myst. Godl.* I. vi. 17 A kinde of jogging or stirring up which is used to recover or prevent ones falling into a swoon. **1787** BEST *Angling* (ed. 2) 12 Lead it [the line] in such manner as will sink the bait..and permit its motion, without any violent jogging on the ground. **1884** *St. James's*

Gaz. 21 Mar. 4/2 The official memory requires frequent jogging. **1948** K. S. DUNCAN *Oxf. Pocket Bk. Athletic Training* iii. 33 The runner should start any piece of jogging with the slow jog style. **1968** *Courier-Mail* (Brisbane) 4 May 4/6 Jogging enthusiasts say that it improves posture and waistline. **1972** *Publishers Weekly* 3 Apr. 64/1 His whole-hearted commitment to jogging..on five mile jaunts around New York's Central Park.

2. *attrib.* Designating: (*a*) a garment, etc., designed for jogging as light physical exercise, e.g. ***jogging shoes, suit***; (*b*) a place for jogging, as ***jogging path, track***, etc. Chiefly *U.S.*

1976 *New Yorker* 17 May 35/2 You will always be in good taste with a pair of Adidas jogging shoes. **1978** *Detroit Free Press* 5 Mar. A19/1 (Advt.), Jogging suits and separates. *Ibid.* D17/1 You can unwind with our pool,..squash courts and outdoor jogging track. **1979** *Globe & Mail* (Toronto) 26 Apr. T1/3 In the United States, there are about half a dozen jogging bras on the market. **1984** *New Yorker* 13 Feb. 5/2 QE2 has countless pleasant surprises aboard for you... To stimulate your..body,..hydrocalisthenics, saunas, jogging deck. **1986** *Daily News* (N.Y.) 23 May (Real Estate Suppl.) 2/2 The homes are all located in a community that boasts a swimming pool, tennis courts, clubhouse, jogging path, and more. **1986** *Philadelphia Inquirer* 11 July 34C/2 Other recreational facilities include two lighted tennis courts, a swimming pool and a jogging trail.

joggle ('dʒɒg(ə)l), *sb.*[1] [f. JOGGLE *v.*[1]] An act, or the action, of joggling; a slight shake, a jog, a jolt; a shaking loosely from side to side.

1727 BAILEY vol. II, *A Jog, a Joggle*, a push or shove. **1822** GALT *Sir A. Wylie* xxxiv, She grippit wi' me like grim death at every joggle the coach gied. **1864** LOWELL *Fireside Trav.* 280 Just as the guides had progued..the donkeys into a brisk joggle. **1893** BARING-GOULD *Cheap-Jack Z.* I. vii. 109 Get into the waggon and drive along... I can't abear the joggle, answered the Cheap Jack.

joggle, *sb.*[2] *Masonry* and *Carpentry*. [Origin uncertain; perh. from *jog* = JAG, a projection.] A joint at the meeting of two adjacent pieces of stone or timber, so constructed as to produce a pressure transverse to that by which they are held together, and thus to prevent them from sliding on one another; a notch in one piece, or a corresponding projection in the other, or a small piece let in between both, for this purpose.

1703 [see b]. **1793** SMEATON *Edystone L.* §240 When a smaller piece of stone, of any shape, is let in between two larger stones, partly into one, and partly into the other, so as to prevent their shifting place with respect to each other, those pieces of stone are termed Joggles. **1823** P. NICHOLSON *Pract. Build.* 128 Joggles are the points at the meeting of struts, king-posts, queen-posts, and principal rafters. **1845** PARKER *Gloss. Archit.* I. 218 Almost every sort of jointing, in which one piece of stone is let or fitted into another, is called a joggle: what a carpenter would call a rebate is also a joggle in stone. **1847** SMEATON *Builder's Man.* 110 The method of securing the joints of masonry by means of joggles..consists in sinking a cavity in the two pieces in such a manner as to make them correspond with each other, and inserting in that cavity a piece of metal, stone, or even wood, so that any lateral thrust may not be able to separate them. **1869** SIR E. REED *Shipbuild.* xx. 456 The joggles for the continuous longitudinal angle-irons are cut out.

b. *Comb.*, as ***joggle-beam, -joint, -piece, -post, -truss, -work*** (see quots.).

1703 T. N. *City & C. Purchaser* 122 Crown-post..is also call'd a King-piece, or Joggle-piece. **1823** P. NICHOLSON *Pract. Build.* 225 *Joggle-piece*, a truss-post, with shoulders and sockets for abutting and fixing the lower ends of the struts. **1858** *Skyring's Builders' Prices* (ed. 48) 88 Joggle joints to 3 inch landings in cement. **1875** KNIGHT *Dict. Mech., Joggle-beam*,..a built beam, the parts of which are joggled together... *Joggle-work*,..work in which the courses are secured by joggles..so as to prevent their slipping on each other.

joggle ('dʒɒg(ə)l), *v.*[1] [app. dim. or freq. of JOG *v.*: but found earlier in our quots. Cf. SHOGGLE.] To jog continuously or repeatedly.

1. *trans.* To shake to and fro, as by repeated jerks; to cause to move from side to side.

1513 DOUGLAS *Æneis* x. vii. 55 The ilk schaft stak in hys cors anone: Pallas it jogglyt, and furth drew in hy. **1583** STANYHURST *Æneis* III. (Arb.) 89 Guts of mounten yrented From roote vp hee iogleth. **1640** WILKINS *New Planet* VIII. (1707) 244 The Earth is firm and stable from all such Motions whereby it is joggled or uncertainly shaken. **1738** WHELER in *Phil. Trans.* XLI. 108 Striking or jogling the Vessel would make them subside. **1837** BREWSTER *Magnet.* 169 Something chanced to joggle the magnets..and they instantly rushed together. **1853** MRS. BUTLER in *Recoll. G. Butler* v. (1892) 87 If he was long in replying I drove the dog-cart over some lumps on the roadside, and this joggled the answers out of him.

2. *intr.* To move to and fro with a succession of short jerky movements; to shake or rock about, as something loose or unsteady; *dial.* to jog *along*.

1683 MOXON *Mech. Exerc.* x. §3. 178 That they may neither joggle nor tremble in working. **1706** *Phil. Trans.* XXV. 2253 That the Wheel may turn about upon the Pin.. tight to the Ruler without joggling. **1825** BROCKETT, *Joggle*, to shake, to totter. **1869** MRS. STOWE *Old-Town folk* xx. 239 My grandmother's broad shoulders joggling with a secret laugh. **1883** MISS BROUGHTON *Belinda* I. iii. 37 They are.. joggling tranquilly along in the sunshine.

Hence '**joggling** *vbl. sb.*[1] and *ppl. a.* '**joggling-board**: see quot. 1883; **joggling-table**, (*a*) a machine in which ore is made to separate according to its specific weight, by the joggling or shaking of an inclined table on which it is spread; (*b*) *Printing* (see quot. 1947).

1828 MOIR *Mansie Wauch* xiii. (1849) 87 Wearied with the joggling of the cart. **1849** *Ex. Doc. 31st U.S. Congress 1 Sess. House* No. 5. I. 435 It is probable that a set of joggling and sleeping tables will be added to the washing machinery. **1860** RUSSELL *Diary India* II. i. 7 Camels slung along at their utmost joggling stride. **1883** C. F. SMITH *Southernisms* in *Trans. Amer. Philol. Soc.* 50 *Joggle*, 'to shake up and down or move up and down on a plank suspended between supports at each end'... Joggling is a favorite amusement of children in South Carolina, and the joggling-board..is a common sight. **1947** *Jrnl. R. Aeronaut. Soc.* LI. 319/1 Offset lithographic process... The mat surface is obtained by placing the template on a joggling table... When the table is joggled or agitated by a lever.., the constant scouring action ..produces a delicate mat surface.

joggle, *v.*[2] *Masonry* and *Carpentry*. [f. JOGGLE *sb.*[2]] *trans.* To join or fit together by means of a joggle; to fasten with a joggle.

1820 DAWSON TURNER *Tour Normandy* II. 33 The stones immediately over the entrance are joggled into each other, the key-stone having a joggle on either side. **1861** SMILES *Engineers* II. VI. iv. 41 Sixteen pieces forming each circle, all joggled and cramped, so as to secure perfect solidity. **1869** SIR E. REED *Shipbuild.* ii. 34 One way would be to joggle the butt-strap over the keel angle-iron.

Hence '**joggled** *ppl. a.*; '**joggling** *vbl. sb.*[2], the action of the verb; also *concr.* a joggle, or work consisting of joggles.

1823 P. NICHOLSON *Pract. Build.* 339 Joggled-joints. **1858** *Skyring's Builders' Prices* (ed. 48) 85 Sunk joggling to 3 inch and 4 inch landings, set in cement. **1865** G. E. STREET *Goth. Archit. Spain* 83 The joggling of the joints of stone-work. **1899** *Hist. Northumbld.* V. 87 A fire-place with a skilfully joggled flat arch.

joggly ('dʒɒglɪ), *a. dial.* or *colloq.* [f. JOGGLE *v.*[1] + -Y; cf. *jumpy*, etc.] Characterized by, or causing, joggling movement; shaky, unsteady.

1828 *Craven Dial., Joggly*, shaking, unsteady. 2. Rough, as joggly road. **1897** CROCKETT *Sir Toady Lion* 242 A joggly and much-rutted cart-track.

'**jog-,jog**, *adv.* and *a.* [f. JOG *v.*]

A. *adv.* With a jogging motion or pace.

*c*1780 COWPER *Yearly Distr.* 13 For then the farmers come jog, jog. **1840** BROWNING *Sordello* I. 177 Quietly through the town they rode, jog-jog.

B. *adj.* Characterized by jogging; = JOG-TROT B.

1837 W. E. FORSTER 10 July in Reid *Life* (1888) I. iii. 87 Enslavement to the common jog-jog way of doing things.

jog(o)ler(e, -our(e, obs. forms of JUGGLER.

jog-trot, *sb., a., adv.* [f. JOG *v.* or *sb.*[1] + TROT: cf. quot. 1631 in JOG *v.* 4 b.

The Sc. *job-trot, jock-trot*, are earlier, and possibly distinct in origin.]

A. *sb.* ('*jog-'trot*).

1. *lit.* A jogging trot; a slow regular jerky pace (usually of a horse, or on horseback).

1796 GROSE *Dict. Vulg. T.* s.v., To keep on a jogg-trot; to get on with a slow but regular pace. **1812** *Sporting Mag.* XXXIX. 102 They ride..some in a jog-trot. *a* **1863** THACKERAY *D. Duval* ii, Madame..rode entirely away from me, saying that she could not afford to go at my clerical jog-trot. **1866** in Engel *Nat. Mus.* viii. 291 Off they [Palanquin-men] set in a nasty jog-trot, which rattled every bone in my body.

2. *fig.* A slow, dull, monotonous, or easy-going progression in any action; a uniform unhurried pace or mode of doing anything, kept up continuously or pertinaciously.

[**1709** M. BRUCE *Serm. Soul-confirm.* 15 You that keeps only your old Job-troot, and does not mend your pace, you will not wone at Soul-confirmation.] **1756** *World* No. 193 ¶3 They contented themselves indeed with going on a jog trot in the common road of application and patience. **1843** LEVER *J. Hinton* xxxii, There was nothing to break the monotonous jog-trot of daily life. **1887** SAINTSBURY *Hist. Elizab. Lit.* i. 8 Nor does he [Grimald] ever fall into the worst kind of jog-trot.

B. *adj.* ('*jog-trot*).

1. *lit.* Of the nature of a jog-trot, jogging; adapted for jogging along (quot. 1857).

1797 HOLCROFT *Stolberg's Trav.* III. lxxix. (ed. 2) 204 The stiff jog trot pace of our hack horses. **1857** HUGHES *Tom Brown* i. Pleasant jog-trot roads, running through the great pasture-lands. **1885** BLACK *White Heather* i, The jog-trot clatter of the horses' feet.

2. *fig.* **a.** Of action, or manner of acting: Uniform and unhurried; kept up steadily without haste, and without interruption or variation; according to routine; monotonous, humdrum.

[**1693** *Scotch Presbyt. Eloq.* (1735) 116 To preach the old Jock-trot Faith and Repentance]. **1826** SCOTT *Jrnl.* 17 Feb., A regular jog-trot way of busying themselves in public matters. **1877** T. A. TROLLOPE *Peep beh. Sc. at Rome* xvii. 228 Numbers..regret that the old jog-trot ways of the old jog-trot days were ever deserted. **1879** HINGSTON *Austral. Abr.* i. 3 A steady jog-trot trade is now done.

b. Of persons: Acting in a jog-trot way; easy-going; keeping up a monotonous routine.

[**1709** M. BRUCE *Serm. Soul-confirm.* 16 Your Old Job-troot Curats and your Old Job-troot Professors.] **1766** GOLDSM. *Vic. W.* xx, Honest jog-trot men, who go on smoothly and dully, and write history and politics, and are praised. **1876** F. E. TROLLOPE *Charming Fellow* II. xii. 191 A steady, jog-trot old fellow, who did his daily task like a horse in a mill.

C. *adv.* ('*jog-trot*). At a jog-trot pace.

1845 CARLYLE *Cromwell*, There came a man riding jog-trot through Stratford-at-the-bow. *Mod. Dial., Northampt.*, He got on the old mare and went off jog-trot, about three miles an hour.

Hence '**jog-'trot** *v. intr.*, to go or move at a jog-trot, *lit.* and *fig.* (also ***to jog-trot it***); hence '**jog-'trotting** *ppl. a.* Also **jog-'trottism** (*nonce-wd.*), jog-trot principles or practice; **jog-'trotty** *a.* (*nonce-wd.*), of a jog-trot character.

1837 *Blackw. Mag.* XLII. 419/1 He merely desired to keep the even tenor of his way, and jog-trot it through life. **1852** DICKENS *Bleak Ho.* xvii, It's rather jog-trotty and hum-drum. **1870** MISS BRIDGMAN *Rob. Lynne* II. viii. 162 To..be driven along the..roads at the Rector's jog-trotting pace. **1879** *Tinsley's Mag.* XXIV. 176 Prosaic, matter-of-fact jog-trottism stands awed. **1900** *Westm. Gaz.* 16 Feb. 3/2 He..compared..the War Office to a four-wheeled cab that jog-trotted on neither better nor worse year in year out. **1968** *Courier-Mail* (Brisbane) 4 May 4/6 The latest American keep-fit craze—jogging. The idea is to jog-trot for 50 yards, then walk 50 yards and repeat this sequence until you are tired.

joguler, -or, -(o)ur, obs. ff. JUGGLER.

jogyll, obs. form of JUGGLE *v.*

johachidolite (dʒəʊhæ'tʃɪdəlaɪt). *Min.* [f. *Jōhachidō*, Japanese name for the village of Sāng-pal-dong in Kilchu Co., North Hamgyong Province, Korea: see -LITE.] A colourless hydrous fluoborate of sodium, calcium, and aluminium, $Na_4Ca_6Al_8B_{10}O_{25}(OH, F)_{20}$.

1942 IWASE & SAITO in *Sci. Papers Inst. Physical & Chem. Res.* (Tokyo) XXXIX. 302 Investigation on chemical composition and determination of some physical constants convincingly demonstrate that the blue fluorescent mineral here studied is a new mineral species for which we would like to present the name jōhachidōlite after Jōhachidō district, where we have come across it. **1968** *Amer. Mineralogist* LIII. 2082 (*heading*) Johachidolite, a revised chemical formula.

Johannean (dʒəʊ'hænɪən), *a.* [f. L. *Johannē-s* (see next) + -AN.] = JOHANNINE.

1847 W. SMITH tr. *Fichte's Characteristics Present Age* 98 The Johannean Jesus knows no other God than the true God. **1881** FAIRBAIRN *Stud. Life Christ* xii. 199 The discourse to Nicodemus is much more elementary than the great Johannean discourses. **1892** J. HUTCHISON *Our Lord's Signs* Introd. 5 Dr. Martineau rejects entirely the Johannean authorship.

Johannes, Joannes (dʒəʊ'æniːz). Also 9 joanese. [a. L. *Joannes* (see JOHN), in the legend of the coin.] The name by which the Portuguese *dobra de quatro escudos* or *peça* of Joannes or João V (1703–1750), a gold coin of the value of 6,400 reis, or about 36*s.* sterling (also commonly called *João*), was known in the British American Colonies, etc. (Also familiarly *jo*, or JOE *sb.*[1]) So ***Double Johannes, Half Johannes***.

This coin was formerly largely current in New England, and in 1725 it was ordered by proclamation to pass current in Ireland for 40*s.*

1758 *Essex Inst. Hist. Coll.* (1881) XVIII. 102, I this day delivered one Johannes to Major Gage. **1765** *New Hampsh. Prov. Papers* (1873) VII. 77 Be it Enacted..That one Guinea shall be valued at Twenty-eight shillings,..a Double Johannes or gold coin of Portygal of the value of Three pounds twelve shillings sterling at four pounds sixteen shillings. **1768** *Ibid.* 175 Counterfeit coin, mostly Dollars, Pistareens and Joannes. **1797** SIR H. PARKER in *Naval Chron.* X. 126 The pattern johannes, which the maker values at 4*s.* 9*d.* **1839** *Penny Cycl.* XV. 324 *Joanese, Johanes*, or *Joe*, a Portuguese gold coin, of 6400 rees. **1849** FREESE *Comm. Class-bk.* 85.

Johannine (dʒəʊ'hænaɪn), *a.* [f. as prec. + -INE[1].] Of, belonging to, or having the character of, the apostle John. (In quot. 1874, Of or pertaining to John the Baptist.)

1861 *Nat. Rev.* Oct. 434 The Johannine 'Word made flesh', however, involves no miraculous conception, or birth from a Virgin. **1874** H. R. REYNOLDS *John Bapt.* i. 18 To imitate the mission of the Baptist, to repeat his work..a Johannine Christianity. **1888** MRS. H. WARD *R. Elsmere* 305 On..the Johannine authorship of the Fourth Gospel. **1894** IAN MACLAREN *Bonnie Brier Bush, A Highland Mystic* i. 64 Johannine men are subject to sudden flashes of anger, and Donald blazed.

Johannisberger (dʒəʊ'hænɪsbɜːgə(r)). Also -berg. [Ger. f. *Johannisberg* (lit. John's Mount), a castle and village on the Rhine above Rüdesheim.] A fine white wine produced at Johannisberg in the Rheingau.

1822 J. WILSON *Noct. Ambr.* i, Two aums of Johannisberg. **1831** DISRAELI *Yng. Duke* II. xiii, The Johannisberger quite converted them. They no longer disliked the young Duke. **1853** S. WHITING *Mem. Stomach* 112 From the Johannisberg, with the golden seal..down to the poverty-stricken Marsala. **1888** *Century Mag.* Apr. 875/1 This brief but finished composition stood in the same relation to the usual 'magazine story' that a glass of Johannisberg occupies to a draught of table d'hôte *vin ordinaire*. **1958** A. L. SIMON *Dict. Wines* 93/2 Plain Johannisberg..is never one of the best wines of Johannisberg. **1967** A. LICHINE *Encycl. Wines* 437/1 The estate-bottled (*Originalabfüllung*) Schloss Johannisberg is divided into three grades of quality and price.

Johannite[1] (dʒəʊˈhænaɪt). Also 6 **Iohannit**, 7–8 **Joannite**. [a. med.L. *Jo(h)annitæ* (plural), a. Gr. Ἰωαννῖται, f. *Jo(h)annes*, Ἰωάννης, John: see -ITE.]

†**1.** A member of the order called the Knights of St. John. *Obs.*

1563–87 FOXE *A. & M.* (1596) 181/2 About the yeare of our Lord 1128, the order of the Knights of the Rhodes called Iohannits..rose up. **1708** *Termes de la Ley* 387b, Hospitallers..an Order of Knights..called the Joannites or Knights of St. John of Jerusalem.

†**2.** A disciple of John the Baptist. *Obs.*

1659 GELL *Ess. Amendm. Transl. Bible* 165 Most men leap over John Baptist's head, commence Christians, per saltum, before they have been Johannites.

3. A follower or adherent of John Chrysostom after his deposition from the patriarchate in 404.

1680 BAXTER *Answ. Stillingfl.* xlix. 70 You confess the Joannites separation. **1681** —— *Answ. Dodwell* 107 Did Cyril's Counsel against the Joannites win them, or harden them?

joˈhannite[2]. *Min.* [ad. Ger. *johannit*; so named by Haidinger, 1830, in honour of the Archduke Johann: see -ITE.] Uranium sulphate containing some copper, found in green druses.

1835 SHEPARD *Min.* I. 288 Johannite..dissolves easily in water. **1892** DANA *Min.* 978 Johannite... In a glass tube at a low heat does not change.

johannsenite (dʒəʊˈhænsənaɪt). *Min.* [f. the name of Albert *Johannsen* (1871–1962), American geologist: see -ITE[1].] A brown, greyish, or greenish silicate of calcium and manganese, $CaMnSi_2O_6$, which often occurs with partial substitution of ferrous iron for manganese.

1932 *Amer. Mineralogist* XVII. 575 The Mineralogical Society of America... List of papers to be presented Wednesday, December 28, 1932... W. T. Schaller.—Johannsenite, a new manganese pyroxene. **1963** W. A. DEER et al. *Rock-Forming Min.* II. 75 Johannsenite, the manganese analogue of diopside and hedenbergite, occurs in metasomatized limestones, and is found less frequently as a vein mineral.

Johansson (jəʊˈhænsən). Also erron. **Johannson**, **Johannsen**. The name of Carl E. *Johansson*, 20th-century Swedish armaments inspector, used *attrib.* to designate a type of steel block originated by him which is made with flat, parallel faces and of a designated length to a high degree of accuracy, and forms one of a set of different sizes used in making up standard lengths.

1918 D. T. HAMILTON *Gages* i. 3 (*heading*) Johansson reference blocks. **1920** *Proc. Inst. Mech. Engin.* Nov. 1102 A gauge of known length is made up by wringing together a series of Johansson gauges. **1932** HARDY & PERRIN *Princ. Optics* xxviii. 577 A set of Johansson gauges used in conjunction with a plane test glass..can be used for the extremely accurate measurement of thickness. **1935** O. W. BOSTON *Engin. Shop Pract.* II. ix. 448 So-called master gage blocks with very hard, smooth, flat, and parallel surfaces in the form of Johansson gages..which are known as Swedish gages as they were made in Sweden, but which are now owned and made by the Ford Motor Company. **1941** A. W. JUDGE *Aircraft Engines* II. iv. 141 The inside walls..receive a micro-finish..guaranteed to be accurate within 2 micro-inches..longitudinally; this corresponds to the surface finish of Johannson gauge blocks. **1943** S. H. LEBOWITZ *Pre-Service Course Machine Sci.* vi. 149 When two adjoining surfaces of solids are sufficiently smooth and plane, they cohere from relatively slight pressure. This fact can be demonstrated with Johansson gage blocks. **1968** J. A. RANKIN *Workshop Processes & Materials* II. ix. 156 Slip gauges, often called Johannsen gauges after their originator, are rectangular blocks of steel with a cross-section of about 1¼ in. by ⅜ in. which are hardened before being finished to size.

johar (ˈdʒəʊhɑː(r)). Also **jauhar**, **joar**. [ad. Hindi *jauhar*, f. Skr. *jatu-griha* a house built of combustible materials.] The sacrificial burning of Rajput women to avoid their being captured by the enemy.

1802 C. JAMES *New Mil. Dict.*, *Joar*, a general massacre of the women and children, which is sometimes performed by the Hindoos, when they find they cannot prevent the enemy from taking the town. **1907** *Westm. Gaz.* 27 Nov. 2/1 The last siege of Chitor, terminated by the greatest of the Johars. **1919** V. A. SMITH *Oxf. Hist. India* 350 The women were immolated on funeral pyres to save them from dishonour, a dread rite known as *jauhar*, and usually practised by Rājpūts when hard pressed. **1965** *Handbk. for Travellers India* (ed. 20) p. xlviii, Three times Chitor suffered the horrors of sack. Time after time, when all hope was lost, the fatal *johar* was commanded. The women committed their bodies to the flames, and the men, arrayed in bridal robes of saffron, sallied out and died fighting.

johl, var. JOL.

John (dʒɒn). Forms 2–6 **Iohan**, 3–5 **Ion**, 4 **Ioan**, **Ioon**, 4–6 **Ihon**, 4–7 **Iohn**, 5 **Ione**, 6 **Iohne**, 7– **John**. [= OF. *Jehan*, F. *Jean*:—L. *Joannes* (later *Johannes*), a. Gr. Ἰωάννης, ad. Heb. *yōḥānān*, in full *yʼhōḥānān* Johanan, or Jehohanan, explained as 'Jah (or Jahveh) is gracious'.]

1. a. A masculine Christian name, that of John the Baptist and John the Evangelist; hence, from early ME. times one of the commonest in England. **b.** Also used as a representative proper name for a footman, butler, waiter, messenger, or the like, and in other ways: see quots., and cf. JACK, JOHNNY (of which the transferred use is much more marked).

[*c* **1160** *Hatton Gosp.* John i. 6 Man wæs fram gode asend þæs name wæs Iohannes.] *c* **1175** *Lamb. Hom.* 127 He is þet soðe lomb alswa Sancte Iohan þe baptist cweð. *c* **1200** ORMIN 707 Forr att te come off Sannt Iohan Bigann all ure blisse. *Ibid.* 714 Sannt Iohan Bapptisste comm Biforenn Cristess come. *a* **1225** *Ancr. R.* 78 þæt was sein Iohan, in his moder wombe. *Ibid.* 106 He iseih his deorewurðe moder teares, & sein Iohannes euangelistes, & te oðre Maries. *c* **1275** *Passion our Lord* 223 in *O.E. Misc.* 43 Ion hedde enne mantel of cendal hym abute. **1297** R. GLOUC. 7147 Seint Ion þe ewangelist. *Ibid.* 9924 Richard..ȝef is broþer Ion [*rime* anon] þe erldom of gloucestre. *Ibid.* 11751 Sir Ion le fiz Ion. *a* **1300** *Cursor M.* 167 (Cott.) Sithen o þe baptist Iohan [*Fairf.* Ioan, *Gött.* iohn, *Trin.* Ion] þat Iesu baptist in flum Iordan. *Ibid.* 171 Siþen o Ions [*v.rr.* Iones, ionis] baptisyng. **1377** LANGL. *P. Pl.* B. v. 415 Al þat euere Marke made Mathew, Iohn [**1393** C. VIII. 24 Iohan] and Lucas. *c* **1380** WYCLIF *Serm.* Sel. Wks. I. 325 On Seint Ihones day. *Ibid.*, Ioon cam to blisse wiþouten killing. *c* **1440** *Promp. Parv.* 264/2 Ion, propyr name (*S.* Ione, *P.* Iohn), *Johannes.* **1549** LATIMER *3rd Serm. bef. Edw. VI* (Arb.) 77 Some saye, you are Iohan Baptiste.

b. 1633 B. JONSON *Tale Tub* IV. ii, All constables are truly Johns for the King, Whate'er their names, be they Tony or Roger. **1838** COL. HAWKER *Diary* (1893) II. 141, I knocked down 16 geese and sacked 'every man John' of them. **1848** THACKERAY *Bk. Snobs* ii, Suddenly..her Majesty's own crimson footmen, with epaulets and black plushes, came in. It was pitiable to see the other poor Johns slink off at this arrival! **1883** J. P. GROVES *Fr. Cadet to Captain* ii. 15 My ignorance of the manners and customs of Sandhurst cadets prevented my knowing that 'John' was a generic title applied to all first-termers.

c. A policeman; (less commonly) a detective. In full, **johndarm** (ˈdʒɒndɑːm) [ad. F. *gendarme*]. Also with suffixed quasi-surname, as ***John Dunn*** (Austral.), ***John Hop*** (Austral. and N.Z.), ***John Law*** (U.S.). Cf. JONNOP. [Austral., N.Z., and U.S. *john* perh. shortened directly from *John Hop* (rhyming slang for COP *sb.*[5]) and *John Law.*] *depreciatory.*

1633 [sense 1 b]. **1858** S. A. HAMMETT *Piney Woods Tavern* vi. 63 He larnt that time to let the John Darmes hunt thar own varmint. **1901** *Westm. Gaz.* 18 Sept. 8/2 'George Johns are sure to visit the old girl to see if anyone has got to her... Brake the cab then shift it again as the John will be sure to tell the porter of that.'.. Detective-sergeant Stevens said the word 'Johns' on the paper signified 'detectives'. **1905** *Munsey's Mag.* July 466/2 Somebody hollers that the johndarms are coming. **1906** E. DYSON *Fact'ry 'Ands* viii. 99 'Twas near two hours afore I see His Whiskers steamin' back, 'n' he had er John in tow... Ther policeman was fer me. **1907** J. LONDON in *Cosmopolitan* May 17/2 A lot of my brother hoboes had been gathered in by John Law. **1918** *Chrons. N.Z.E.F.* 19 July 280 In view of the fact that the camp 'John Hops' were off duty. *Ibid.* 22 Nov. 206 'Never mind about that,' said the John—and dumped him in the cell. **1925** [see FINK *sb.*[2]]. *c* **1926** 'MIXER' *Transport Workers' Song Bk.* 94 'Tis us..The wily 'John Hop' loves to track. **1933** *Bulletin* (Sydney) 31 May 12/3 Even on beat duty a John Hop..can cogitate. **1939** H. HODGE *Cab, Sir?* xv. 222 A policeman is the usual cockney 'Grass'... Or sometimes 'Johndarm'—thus proving we know French. **1940** R. CHANDLER *Farewell, my Lovely* xxxix. 302 'The johns tied me to it?' 'I don't know.' **1941** BAKER *Dict. Austral. Slang* 39 *John Dunns*, policemen. **1941** W. G. DAVIS *Phenomena in Crime* xix. 254 Bogies, busies, gendarmes, johns... Detectives. **1961** P. WHITE *Riders in Chariot* xi. 380 'I'll fetch the johns in the mornin'!' she shrieked. 'Layin' into a white woman!' **1965** G. MCINNES *Road to Gundagai* xi. 187 Then we would climb the steps, leaving our bicycles chained to a lamp post (courtesy of John Hops). **1965** M. SHADBOLT *Among Cinders* xxi. 202 Bill Halloran... He's the local john. **1968** K. WEATHERLY *Roo Shooter* 23, I didn't tell the John to sweep your cell out.

d. (With lower-case initial.) A lavatory, water-closet. *slang* (chiefly *U.S.*).

[**1735** *Harvard Laws* in W. Bentinck-Smith *Harvard Bk.* (1953) 146 No freshman shall mingo against the College wall or go into the fellows' cuzjohn.] **1932** *Amer. Speech* VII. 333 *John, johnny*, a lavatory. **1946** 'J. EVANS' *Halo in Blood* xvi. 181, I..made a brief visit to the john. **1959** C. MACINNES *Absolute Beginners* 54 'You poor old bastard,' I said to the Hoplite, as he sat there on my john. **1972** *Last Whole Earth Catalog* (Portola Inst.) 247/3 Every time you take a dump or a leak in a standard john, you flush five gallons of water out with your piddle. **1973** *Black World* June 19 They gave me my Status Symbol The key to the white Locked John.

e. In full, ***John Chinaman.*** A Chinaman; the Chinese collectively. *depreciatory.*

1818 B. HALL *Acct. Voy. Corea* ii. 92 This interpreter is called 'John' by all the parties. **1826** *Ibid.* (rev. ed.) i. 37 The seamen..not caring whether John Chinaman, as they called him, understood them or not. **1834** *Amer. Railroad Jrnl.* III. 189/1 They are required to..ascertain the height of John Chinaman in a breath. **1853** *Alta California* (San Francisco) 20 Apr. 2/2 The May Adams brought 118 'Johns' from the terrestrial kindgom of heaven. **1854** C. A. CORBYN *Sydney Revels of Bacchus, Cupid & Momus* 125 They came to the determination of giving wretched John Chinaman such a dose that prussic acid is fool to it. They committed John for trial at the Quarter Sessions. **1858** *Brit. Colonist* (Victoria, B.C.) 27 Dec. 4/3 The Johns had a high time, drinking brandy and eating fried hog. **1865** *Dunedin Punch* 16 Sept. 119 John Chinaman is to immigrate here. **1869** J. R. BROWNE *Adv. Apache Country* 308 John Chinamen, with long tails rolled up on the backs of their heads, running distractedly through the crowd in search of their lost bundles. **1872** [see CHINAMAN 2]. **1921** R. WATSON *Spoilers of Valley* 310 John always was a better truck farmer anyway. **1933** *Bulletin* (Sydney) 8 Mar. 10 Old John Chinaman, patient, hardworking, scrupulously honest. **1970** *Brewer's Dict. Phr. & Fable* (rev. ed.) 591/2 *John Chinaman*, a Chinaman or the Chinese as a people.

f. A ponce; the client of a prostitute. *slang* (orig. *U.S.*).

a **1911** D. G. PHILLIPS *Susan Lenox* (1917) II. vi. 154 A John's a sucker—a fellow that keeps a girl. **1928** [see CREEP *v.* 5b]. **1953** W. BURROUGHS *Junkie* (1972) ii. 27 Mary was describing the techniques she used to get money from the 'Johns' who formed her principal source of revenue. **1967** M. M. GLATT et al. *Drug Scene* 117 *John*, prostitute's customer. **1972** *New York* 24 Apr. 38/3 Many working girls, when they are new in the city, spend at least a few months with a madam to meet the better johns. **1973** *Times* 22 Mar. 8/7 The customers (Johns or tricks) are the usual solitary, bored, out-of-town..men.

g. Abbrev. of *John Thomas* (*b*).

1934 *Neuphilol. Mitt.* XXXV. 130 Here [at public-school] his first linguistic experience will be with mumfordish and swear-words (e.g...*john* 'penis'..). **1948** D. BALLANTYNE *Cunninghams* II. xvi. 241 How often did the nurse find him with his old john lying limply? **1972** C. MURRY *Private View* I. 33 The tip of old John brushed against the inside of my thigh.

†**2.** A plant: old name for a variety of pink; usually SWEET JOHN, q.v. *Obs.*

1572 PLAT *Floures Philos.* Addr. to Rdr., The Iohn so sweete in shewe and smell, distincte by colours twaine, Aboute the borders of their beds in seemelie sighte remaine. **1597** GERARDE *Herbal* II. clxxiv. 478 Of Sweete Iohns, and Sweete Williams. *Armeria alba*, White Iohns. *Armeria rubra*, Red Iohns.

†**3.** ***Sir John***: a familiar or contemptuous appellation for a priest: from SIR as rendering L. *dominus* at the Universities. Cf. also MESS JOHN. ***Sir John Lack-latin***: see LACK-LATIN A. *Obs.*

c **1386** CHAUCER *Nun's Pr. Prol.* 44 Com neer thou preest, com hyder thou sir Iohn. **1553** PILKINGTON in Strype *Eccl. Mem.* (1721) III. I. xii. 114 Who is meeter for any of these businesses than Sir Iohn Lack-latin? **1721** *Ibid.* xxxiii. 253 Instead of a faithful and painful teacher, they hire a Sir Iohn, which hath better skill in playing at tables, or in keeping of a garden, than in God's word. **1594** ? GREENE *Selimus* Wks. 1881–3 XIV. 264 But our Sir Iohn beshrew thy hart, For thou hast ioynd vs, we cannot part. **1653** BAXTER *Worc. Petit. Def.* 30 Most would have a Masse-Priest or Reading Sir John, that would humour them for a little.

4. Prefixed to another word, so as to form a name or nickname, or used in a phrase with specific sense. Such are *John Blunt* (cf. JACK *sb.*[1] 36), ***John Cheese***; **John-a-dogs**, ? a dog-whipper; **John-a-dreams**, a dreamy fellow; one occupied in idle meditation; **John-a-droyne** (?); **John-a-nods**, one who is nodding, or not quite awake; **John Barleycorn**: see BARLEY-CORN 1 b; **John Birch Society** (see BIRCHER); hence **John Bircher** = BIRCHER; **John boat** (also **Jon boat**) *U.S.*, a small, flat-bottomed boat for use principally on inland waterways; **John Citizen**, the ordinary man (esp. considered as a member of the community); **John Collins**, a Collins (see COLLINS[2]) made with a base of gin or whisky; a *Tom Collins*; **John Company**, a humorous appellation of the East India Company, taken over from the name *Jan Kompanie*, by which the Dutch E.I.C., and subsequently the Dutch government, are known to natives in the East: see quot. 1785; **John Doe**, (*a*) (*Eng.* and *U.S. Law*), the name given to the fictitious lessee of the plaintiff, in the (now obsolete) mixed action of ejectment, the fictitious defendant being called *Richard Roe*; (*b*) name given to an ordinary or typical citizen (see also quot. 1942); **John Down**, a Newfoundland name for the fulmar; **John Dringle** (?); **John-go-to-bed-at-noon**, a popular name for the Goat's-beard, *Tragopogon pratensis* (also simply *go-to-bed-at-noon*: see GO *v.* VIII.), or other flowers which close about midday, as the Pimpernel and the Star-of-Bethlehem; **John Hancock** *U.S. colloq.*, a signature; **John Henry** *U.S. local slang* = prec.; †**John-hold-my-staff**, †**John-of-all-trades**, †**John-out-of-office** = corresp. phrases with *Jack* (JACK *sb.*[1] 37); **John Innes (compost)**, one of a group of composts prepared according to formulæ developed at the John Innes Horticultural Institution in the late 1930s; **John Q. Public** *U.S. colloq.*, the general public, or a member of this; **John Roscoe**, a gun (*U.S. slang*); see also ROSCOE; **John Scott**, an artificial fly: = *Jock Scott*; **John Thomas**, (*a*) a generic name for a livery servant; (*b*) *slang*, the penis; **John Thomson's man**, *Sc.* [origin lost: Jamieson suggested *Joan Thomson's man*, but this is not the form exemplified], a proverbial appellation for a man who is guided by his wife; †**John Trot**, a man of slow or uncultured intellect, a bumpkin, a clown. For CHEAP *John*, POOR JOHN, etc., see the other words.

1613 JACKSON *Creed* II. xxviii. §5 Never to swerve from the beadle of beggars or *John-a-dogs his determinations and resolutions in any point of logic, philosophy, or metaphysics. **1602** SHAKS. *Ham.* II. ii. 594, I, a dull and muddy-metled Rascal, peake Like *Iohn a-dreames. **1876**

HENLEY *Bk. Verses* (1888) 91 Kate-a-Whimsies, John-a-Dreams, Still debating, still delay. **1562** J. HEYWOOD *Prov. & Epigr.* (1867) 214 Hogis head in hogstowne is no *Iohn a droyne. **1596** NASHE *Saffron Walden* P j b, That poor Iohn a Droynes his man,..a great big-boand thresher. **1603** HARSNET *Pop. Impost.* xxiii. 160 Hee would say The Apostle wrote like a good plaine *Iohn a Nods. **1608** ARMIN *Nest Ninn.* (1880) 57 His name is Iohn,..but neither *Iohn a nods*, nor *Iohn a Dreames.* **1961** *John Bircher [see BIRCHER]. **1961** *Listener* 20 Apr. 684/1 The patriots of the right—and they seem to be mushrooming belligerent societies round the country, as witness the sudden, and alarmingly widespread, rise of the John Birch Society. **1963** *Ibid.* 21 Feb. 350/2 The line taken by the interviewer, whose questions might have been drafted by the John Birch Society, so puritanical did they sound. **1967** *Boston Sunday Herald* 30 Apr. I. 1/1 A strange hybrid bird is hovering..over the town of Lincoln. Is it a dove? Is it a hawk? No, it's a John Bircher who may be somebody's pigeon. **1973** W. MCCARTHY *Detail* iii. 201 We have covered every John Bircher and nut that has sworn to kill the President. **1508** DUNBAR *Tua mariit wemen* 142 For all the buddis of *Iohne Blunt, quhen he abone clymis. **1905** *N.Y. Even. Post* (Sat. Suppl.) 2 Sept. 3/1 Two men came down the Mississippi in an Illinois *Jon-boat, paddling slowly with rough-whittled boards. **1917** H. KEPHART *Camping & Woodcraft* II. 134 We..hit upon what we conceived to be a brilliant scheme for transporting a gallon of whiskey inconspicuously in our John-boat. **1921** *Rudder* Feb. 7 Their scope of understanding..ranges from the 150-foot schooner to the ten-foot 'john boat'. **1965** A. J. MCCLANE *Standard Fishing Encycl.* 441/2 The original john boat..was made of clear pine boards 20 feet long and 18 inches wide. *a* **1568** ASCHAM *Scholem.* I. (Arb.) 54 If thou be thrall to none of theise, Away good Peek goos, hens *Iohn Cheese. **1924** H. H. CURRAN (*title*) *John Citizen's job. **1931** T. E. GREGORY in W. Rose *Outl. Mod. Knowl.* 626 If John Citizen buys a house out of his own savings, [etc.]. **1937** *Evening News* 12 Mar. 8/1 No Government department has yet thought of issuing a pamphlet extolling the virtues of John Citizen, who, as taxpayer, every year takes a stronger weight and never complains. **1958** *Daily Tel.* 8 Aug. 11/4 When all is quiet John Citizen says what a great humanitarian he is. **1965** MRS. L. B. JOHNSON *White House Diary* 13 July (1970) 296, I would depend upon that man if I were John Citizen looking on from my living room. **1865** *Australasian* 25 Feb. 8/7 That most angelic of drinks for a hot climate—a *John Collins... Take a bottle of sodawater, a wineglassful of gin, a lump of sugar, a piece of ice, with a slice of lemon—mix well together. **1913** R. BROOKE *Let.* 3 Aug. in *Coll. Poems* (1918) p. lxxxvi, I believe I could do a deal in Real Estate,..over a John Collins, with a clean-shaven Yankee. **1928** T. M. HEALY *Lett. & Leaders* I. x. 142 Two barmen who..served me with a 'John Collins' [in U.S.]. **1962** John Collins [see COLLINS[2]]. [**1785** tr. *Sparrmann's Voy. Cape G. Hope*, etc. x. II. 21 The ignorant Hottentots and Indians not having been able to form any idea of the Dutch East-India Company,..the Dutch from the very beginning in India, politically gave out the company for one individual powerful prince, by the christian name of *Jan* or *John*... On this account I ordered my interpreter to say farther, that we were the children of *Jan Company*, who had sent us out to view this country.] **1808** *Life Ld. Minto in India* (1880) 184 (Y.) Preparations to save *Johnny Company's cash. **1832** MARRYAT *N. Forster* xli. (Rtldg.) 223 John Company will some day find out the truth. **1886** MRS. LYNN LINTON *Paston Carew* ii, He was offered a position in India, in the service of John Company, under whose flag, as we know, the pagoda-tree was worth shaking. **1768** BLACKSTONE *Comm.* III. xviii. 274 The security here spoken of..is at present become a mere form: and *John Doe and Richard Roe are always returned as the standing pledges for this purpose. [**1825** 'O'HARA FAMILY' (*title*) Tales, containing..John Doe.] **1841** S. WARREN *Ten Thousand a Year* viii, John Doe further says that one Richard Roe (who calls himself—'a Casual Ejector') came and turned him out, and so John Doe brings his action against Richard Roe. **1852** DICKENS *Bleak Ho.* (1853) xx. 195 It is reported at the public offices that his father was John Doe. **1882** FARRAR *Early Chr.* II. 506 So common was it [the name Gaius] that it was selected in the Roman law-books to serve the familiar purpose of John Doe and Richard Roe in our own legal formularies. **1900** (*title*) The bridge manual..by John Doe [pseudonym of Francis Reginald Roe]. **1928** M. H. WESEEN *Crowell's Dict. Eng. Gram.* 355 John Doe. Properly used in legal actions as the name of a fictitious plaintiff. Richard Roe is the corresponding name of a fictitious defendant. By extension these names are used loosely as substitutes for real names in other affairs. **1932** John Doe [see JONES 1]. **1935** M. M. ATWATER *Murder in Midsummer* xxi. 196 Serve on them one of the John Doe warrants with which you have been provided. **1938** S. ROBERTSON in *For Men Only* Feb. 50 (*heading*) John Doe... crosses the Styx. **1940** L. E. FRAILEY *How to write Better Business Lett.* ii. 14 You start thinking: 'Here's a salesman, John Doe.' **1941** *N.Y. Times* 13 Mar. 25/2 (*title*) Meet John Doe, screen play by Robert Riskin... 'John Doe'..Gary Cooper. **1942** BERREY & VAN DEN BARK *Amer. Thes. Slang* §442/3 *One whose name is not known*,.. Joe Doe, Joe Zilch, John Doe, John Henry, John Smith. **1957** B. & C. EVANS *Dict. Contemp. Amer. Usage* 259/2 John Doe is a fictitious person in legal proceedings, usually the plaintiff. The corresponding fictitious defendant is Richard Roe. **1972** *N.Y. Law Jrnl.* 31 Oct. 15/4 USA v. Jose Valenzuela-Correa,..John Doe. **1973** *Washington Post* 18 Apr. III. 1/8 They didn't include any small guys struggling down here. I think they should have had some John Doe on there. **1852** *Arctic Miscellanies* 10 On the banks of Newfoundland, where this bird is known by the name of '*John Down', it attends the fishing vessels for the offal of the cod fish. **1893** A. NEWTON *Dict. Birds* II. 471 John-Down, the name given to the Fulmar by Newfoundland fishermen. **1917** T. G. PEARSON *Birds of America* I. 80 Fulmar. *Fulmarus glacialis glacialis*... [Also called] Molly Hawk; John Down; Sea Horse. **1957** W. L. MCATEE *Folk-Names Canad. Birds* 4 Fulmar... John Down (Sailor's name, significance unknown. Nfld.). **1597** *1st Pt. Return fr. Parnass.* III. i. 918 Everie *Iohn Dringle can make a booke in the commendacions of temperance against the seven deadlie sinns. **1758** PULTNEY in *Phil. Trans.* L. 508 Our country people long since called it **John-go-to-bed-at-noon.* **1897** WILLIS *Flow. Plants* II. 373 The flower-heads..close up at midday, whence its common name of 'John-go-to-bed-at-noon'. [**1846** HOLMES in R. W. Griswold *Passages from Corr.* (1898) 221 Avoiding..the pretentious boldness of *John Hancock..I subscribe myself Yours very truly.] **1903** ADE *People you Know* 150 After he got through filling in the Blank Spaces with his John Hancock, he didn't have a Window to hoist or a Fence to lean on. **1937** *N. & Q.* 6 Mar. 178/1 There is also a popular phrase for signature, 'John Hancock', as in, 'Go ahead. Put down your John Hancock.' **1937** *Greensboro* (N. Carolina) *News* 23 Dec., Lindberg's *John Hancock* is worth ten to twenty-five dollars on the market. **1972** *Listener* 7 Dec. 784/1 Even today an American handing you a contract is apt to say: 'And now if you will just give us your John Hancock.' **1914** *Dialect Notes* IV. 109 **John Henry* or *John Hancock*, autograph. **1951** *Publ. Amer. Dial. Soc.* xv. 56 Put your John Henry on that. **1974** T. BARLING *Shooter Man* iii. 20 Sign your John Henry there... Your name is Balkin. You'd better get used to it. **1682** 15 *Comf. Matrimony* vi. 47 The poor Gentleman at home is like *John Hold-my-staff, she must Rule, Govern, Insult, Brawl. **1939** *Ann. Rep. John Innes Hort. Inst. 1938* XXIX. 17 A great many enquiries about the *John Innes composts have been received. The John Innes Base Fertiliser is now being widely used. **1939** LAWRENCE & NEWELL *Seed & Potting Composts* 9 These composts are the outcome of experiments to meet the practical needs of cultivation at the John Innes Horticultural Institution. *Ibid.* 10 In the John Innes composts the gardener has soil mixtures which, properly used, always give excellent results. **1951** *Good Housek. Home Encycl.* 94/2 The compost for..practically all house plants should be that known as 'John Innes'. **1959** *Listener* 12 Nov. 850/1 The standard John Innes compost is excellent. **1970** *Nature* 25 July 377/1 These results show that fertilizer is crucial for satisfactory growth, particularly slow acting types such as John Innes base. **1973** *Country Life* 29 Mar. 864/3 Acidanthera corms are being potted..in 7 or 8 in. pots of John Innes No. 2 compost. **1639** MAYNE *City Match* II. v, You mungrel, you *John of all Trades. **1672** R. WILD *Declar. Lib. Consc.* 3 A Good King..who sees no reason for putting down Haberdashers, and Johns of all Trades. **1563** FOXE *A. & M.* (1583) 2113 Who now (God be thanked) is *Iohn out of office, and glad of his Neighbours good will. **1937** *N. & Q.* 6 Mar. 177/2 'John Citizen'..is not so frequent in American usage as '*John Q. Public'... It is probably a play on the name of an early president, John Q(uincy) Adams. **1938** S. CHASE *Tyranny of Words* xiv. 175 There is no 'public'... Calling it 'John Q. Public' does not help. **1972** M. KAYE *Lively Game of Death* ix. 49 My main concern at that moment was to play John Q. Public by phoning the cops. **1938** D. RUNYON *Furthermore* iii. 54 The joke is, I will not be asleep in the sack, and my hands will not be tied, and in each of my hands I will have a *John Roscoe, so..I pop out blasting away. **1973** A. S. NEILL *Neill! Neill! Orange Peel!* (rev. ed.) II. 130 The USA.., where anyone can carry a gun, or, to be topical, should I say a Betsy or a John Roscoe? **1867** F. FRANCIS *Angling* x. (1880) 375 *John Scott..is a very tasty-looking fly. **1500–20** DUNBAR *Poems* lxii. 4 God gif ȝe war *Johne Thomsounis man. **1637** R. MONRO *Exp. Scots Regim.* II. 30 Some will alleage, he was Iohn Thomsons man. I answer, it was all one, if shee was good: for all stories esteeme them happie, that can live together man and wife, without contention. **1816** SCOTT *Old Mort.* xxxviii, 'The deil's in the wife!' said Cuddie; 'd'ye think I am to be John Tamson's man, and maistered by women a' the days o' my life?' **1712** STEELE *Spect.* Nos. 296 and 314 [Letters signed] *John Trott. **1753** FOOTE *Eng. in Paris* Epil., The merest John Trot in a week you shall zee *Bien poli, bien frizé, tout à fait un Marquis.* **1762** COLMAN *Mus. Lady* II. i, Our travelling gentry..return from the tour of Europe as mere English boors as they went—John Trot still. **1879–80** *Pearl* (1970) 76 As around her fair form I a firm hold took, And *John Thomas I silently buried. **1928** D. H. LAWRENCE *Lady Chatterley* xiv. 253 'John Thomas! John Thomas!' and she quickly kissed the soft penis. **1957** L. DURRELL *Justine* 249 She had neatly tied his dresstie to his John Thomas, a perfect bow. **1972** *Times Lit. Suppl.* 7 July 783/3 The grotesquely coy accounts of sex, during which Tony tells us that his 'John Thomas' was 'up and raring to go'.

5. St. John's, in composition. **†St. John's berry**, the barberry. **St. John's bread**, the fruit of the carob-tree (see CAROB 1); also the tree itself. **†St. John's disease**, **†St. John's evil**, a name for epilepsy. **†St. John's grass** = *St. John's-wort*. **†St. John's seal**, the plant Solomon's Seal. **St. 'John's-wort**, the common English name for plants of the genus HYPERICUM.

1561 HOLLYBUSH *Hom. Apoth.* 22 b, *S. Ihons berries called in Latine Berberis. **1591** PERCIVALL *Sp. Dict.*, *Algarrova*, Carobes, or *S. Iohns bread. **1597** GERARDE *Herbal* III. lxxv. 1241 This of some is called S. Iohns bread, and thought to be that which is translated Locusts, whereon S. Iohn did feed. **1706** PHILLIPS, *St. John's Bread*, a kind of Shrub. **1883** *Harper's Mag.* Sept. 622/2 The St.-John's-bread-tree, which does not bear until seventy years of age. **1616** SURFL. & MARKH. *Country Farme* 42 To preserue one from the Falling sicknesse, otherwise called *S. Iohns disease. **1607** TOPSELL *Four-f. Beasts* (1658) 339 Against the falling sickness, called *Saint Johns-evill. **1538** TURNER *Libellus* B j b, Hypericon..uulgus appellat *Saynt Iohns gyrs. **1597** GERARDE *Herbal* II. cl. §3. 433 S. Iohns woort, or S. Iohns grasse. **1567** MAPLET *Gr. Forest* 61 *Saint Iohnes seale, of Ruellius Salomons seale: of Monardus, Saint Maries seale. **14..** *Voc.* in Wr.-Wülcker 590/31 *Iperica*, *seynt Iohnys worte. **1551** TURNER *Herbal* I. E iij, Great saint Iohnes wurte. *Ibid.*, A kynde of hyperici, called in englishe saint Iohns grass, or saynt Iohns wurt. **1625** K. LONG tr. *Barclay's Argenis* I. ii. 4 Asswaging the heat with Oyle extracted from St. John's-woort. **1794** MARTYN *Rousseau's Bot.* xxv. 373 Upright St. John's Wort is an elegant species growing in woods and heaths. **1861** DELAMER *Fl. Gard.* 102 The large St. John's Wort..has a very showy flower, almost filled with a silky tasselled tuft of stamens with red anthers... Tutsan is a hardy shrubby St. John's Wort.

†'Johnanapes. *Obs. rare.* = JACKANAPES.
1633 SHIRLEY *Bird in Cage* II. i, Do I look like a Johnanapes?

†'John-a-'nokes. *Obs.* Forms: 6 **Iohn at Noke, of the Nokes, -a-noke,** 7 **John-a-noakes, an Okes, a Noke,** 7–8 **-a-Nokes,** 7–9 **a Nokes.** [orig. *John atten Oke*, i.e. *John* (who dwells) *at the oak*.] A fictitious name for one of the parties in a legal action (usually coupled with JOHN-A-STILES as the name of the other); hence sometimes used indefinitely for any individual person.

1531 *Dial. on Laws Eng.* II. ix. 19 If a man haue lande for terme of lyfe of Iohan at Noke and make a lease. **1581** SIDNEY *Apol. Poetrie* (Arb.) 53 Doth the Lawyer lye then, when vnder the names of Iohn a stile and Iohn a noakes [*Wks.* (1622) 520 Iohn of the Stile, & Iohn of the Nokes] hee puts his case? **1642** HOWELL *For. Trav.* (Arb.) 79 Nor indeed is he capable to beare any Rule or Office in Town or Countrey, who is utterly unacquainted with John an Okes, and John a Stiles, and with their Termes. **1714** *Spectator* No. 577 ¶6 The humble Petition of John a Nokes and John a Stiles, Sheweth, That your Petitioners have had Causes depending in Westminster-Hall above five hundred Years. **1815** SCOTT *Guy M.* xlii, Adventurers who are as willing to plead for John a'Nokes as for the first noble of the land.

'John-apple. = APPLE-JOHN.
1609 N. F. *Fruiterers Secr.* Epist., Iohn-Apples be in some places called Dewzings or long-lasters. **1676** WORLIDGE *Cyder* (1691) 203 The John-Apple, or Deux-ans, so called from its durableness, continuing two years before it perisheth. **1708** J. PHILIPS *Cyder* I. 29 John-Apple whose wither'd rind entrencht With many a furrow aptly represents Decrepid Age. **1711** STEELE *Spect.* No. 52 ¶3 She has not a Face like a John-Apple. **1754** RICHARDSON *Grandison* (1781) III. v. 32 Like a withering John-apple that has never ripened kindly. **1884** HOGG *Fruit Manual* 244.

†'John-a-'stiles. *Obs.* Forms: 6 **John at Stile, of the Stile,** 6–7 **-a-stile,** 7 **-a-Stiles, -a-Styles,** 7–8 **a Stiles.** [orig. *John atte Stile*, i.e. *John* (who dwells) *at the stile*.] (See JOHN-A-NOKES.)

1531 *Dial. on Laws England* I. vi. 12 If a man be out-lawed, and after by his wyll byqueth certayne goodes to Iohn at Style. **1581, 1642** [see JOHN-A-NOKES]. **1687** R. L'ESTRANGE *Answ. Diss.* 34 Here is an Imperial Prerogative over-ruled by a Pamphlet; A Cause given against the King by John-a-Styles. **1714** FORTESCUE-ALAND *Pref. Fortescue's Abs. & Lim. Mon.* 51 Taking Goods in *Withernam*..is no more than to take other Goods of John a Stiles in lieu of Goods which he took under colour of distress.

John Bull. [Name of a character representing the English nation in Arbuthnot's satire (see quot. 1712).]

1. A personification of the English nation; Englishmen collectively, or the typical Englishman.

[**1712** ARBUTHNOT (*title*) Law is a Bottomless Pit. Exemplified in the Case of the Lord Strutt, John Bull, Nicholas Frog and Lewis Baboon: who spent all they had in a Law-suit. **1714** POPE *Key to Lock* (*sub init.*), If an honest believing nation is to be made a Jest of, we have a story of John Bull and his wife.] **1778** J. ADAMS in *Fam. Lett.* (1876) 350 France..assisted the American cause, for which John Bull abused and fought her. But John will come off wretchedly. **1788** W. SKERRETT in *15th Rep. Hist. MSS. Comm.* App. x. 99 The French treat their slaves much better than we do..John Bull does not endeavour to conciliate their affections. *a* **1805** A. CARLYLE *Autobiog.* ix. 374 A horse-race we met with near Chester-le-Street. This we could not resist, as some of us had never seen John Bull at his favourite amusement. **1822** BYRON *Vis. Judgm.* lix, Here crash'd a sturdy oath of stout John Bull. **1899** CLIFFORD in *Daily News* 3 Jan. 8/5 John Bull was now an Imperialist, and dwelt very much abroad.

attrib. **1824** BYRON *Juan* xv. lxxi, Roast beef in our rough John Bull way.

b. (with *a* and *pl.*) An individual Englishman who exemplifies the national character; a typical Englishman.

1772 MAD. D'ARBLAY *Early Diary* (1889) I. 148 Both, like true John Bulls, fought with better will than justice for Old England. **1785** BOSWELL *Tour to Hebrides* 11 He [Johnson] was..at bottom much of a John Bull; much of a blunt true-born Englishman. **1815** CROKER in *C. Papers* (1884) I. iii. 71 The Prince of Bavaria..is, it seems, a great John Bull, and is highly flattered at being told that he speaks English like an Englishman. **1840** DICKENS *Barn. Rudge* xlvii, By some he was called..'a thorough-bred Englishman', by some 'a genuine John Bull'.

2. A kind of game of chance played by a number of persons in which a coin is pitched so as to fall on a board divided into sixteen numbered compartments.

1801 STRUTT *Sports & Past.* III. vii. §14.

Hence **John-'Bullish** *a.*, typically English; hence ***John-'Bullishness***; **John-'Bullism**, the typical English character; a typically English act, utterance, or characteristic; **John-'Bullist**, one who favours the English.

1802 SOUTHEY *Lett.* (1856) I. 207–8 My taste has always been right English, and I grow more *John-Bullish every time I look into a newspaper. **1842** *Blackw. Mag.* LI. 188 This John Bullish stolidity is very high, and mighty. **1854** HAWTHORNE *Eng. Note-bks.* (1883) I. 480 His face was intelligent, dark, pleasing, and not at all John-Bullish. **1895** *Nation* (N.Y.) 14 Nov. 345/3 The stolid *John Bullishness with which England refuses arbitration of the whole question. **1796** MAD. D'ARBLAY *Camilla* VII. xi, This true *John Bullism Lynmere had neither sense to despise, nor humour to laugh at. **1847** B. BARTON *Select.*, etc. (1849) 32 A finer sample of John Bullism you would rarely see. **1851** J. H. NEWMAN *Cath. in Eng.* 25 Anglo-maniacs or *John Bullists, as they are popularly termed.

John Canoe (dʒɒn kəˈnuː). *W. Indies* (and †*U.S.*). Also (with various local pronunciations) **John Connú, Johnkannau, joncanoe, jonkanoo,** etc. [f. a W. African lang.] **a.** The chief dancer, or one of several dancers, in a Christmas celebration. **b.** Any of various masks or structures worn or carried on the head by the dancer at Christmas time. **c.** The celebration itself.

See also Cassidy and Le Page *Dict. Jamaican Eng.* s.v.

1774 E. Long *Hist. Jamaica* II. III. iii. 424 The masquerader..dances at every door, bellowing out *John Connú*! **1816** M. G. Lewis *Jrnl. W. India Proprietor* (1834) 51 The John-Canoe is a Merry-Andrew..bearing upon his head a kind of pasteboard house-boat. **1825** R. Bickell *W. Indies as they Are* 214 The crowds of Slaves..making John Canoe, as they term it, according to the customs of Africa. **1826** A. Barclay *Pract. View Slavery W. Indies* 11 One or two Joncanoe-men, smart youths, fantastically dressed. **1826** C. R. Williams *Tour through Jamaica* 25 This [model of a] house is called the Jonkanoo. **1844** W. Bagley *Let.* 18 Dec. in N. E. Eliason *Tarheel Talk* (1956) 279 On Christmas day..four young fellows blacked themselves & dressed up in negro clothes..& the fiddler would play & the rest dance. They acted the part of 'John Cunners' very well. **1861** H. Jacobs *Incidents Life Slave Girl* 179 Every child rises early on Christmas morning to see the Johnkannaus. **1929** M. Beckwith *Black Roadways* ix. 155 The instruments which I saw used in the John Canoe performance [were] identical with those accompanying the myal dance. **1952** M. Kerr *Personality & Conflict in Jamaica* 144 These dances..are usually called the John Canoe Dance. **1961** F. G. Cassidy *Jamaica Talk* xii. 256 The John Canoe dancing, recently revived, has had a complex history, and the meaning of the name is uncertain. **1962** S. Wynter *Hills of Hebron* ii. 36 The mask on the face of a 'junkonoo' dancer, striped black and white with slits for eyes and huge white teeth. **1966** *Punch* 5 Jan. 27/2 The wild revelry of the Junkanoo Parade. **1972** E. Hargreaves *Fair Green Weed* xii. 172 John Kanoos. .. They're rather like old-fashioned mummers, they go round at Christmas time.

John Crow (dʒɒn krəʊ). [Reduction, in folk pronunciation, of *carrion crow*.] In Jamaica, a name for the red-headed turkey vulture, *Cathartes aura*. Hence **John Crow('s) nose,** a parasitic plant, *Scybalium jamaicense*, which bears bright red flowers.

1826 C. R. Williams *Tour through Jamaica* 82 The dead carcass of a mule, on which a score of john-crows were holding an inquest. **1864** A. H. R. Griesbach *Flora Brit. W. Indian Islands* 785 John-Crow's-nose. **1893** A. Newton *Dict. Birds* II. 470 In Jamaica, within a few years, the John-Crow, though there protected by human law, has been nearly extirpated by the introduction of the Mongoose. **1963** Robertson & Gooding *Bot. for Caribbean* xvi. 122 In the rain-forests of the West Indies, several members of the family Balanophoraceae occur as parasites on the roots of trees. An example is the John Crow Nose (*Scybalium jamaicense*), which occurs in Jamaica, Cuba and Puerto Rico. **1963** A. L. Thomson *New Dict. Birds* 867/1 The Turkey Vulture *Cathartes aura* (also called 'Turkey Buzzard' and 'John Crow' in the United States) is regarded as a pest on the Peruvian guano islands. **1972** E. Hargreaves *Fair Green Weed* viii. 88 The john-crows hadn't yet caught sight of him, and given warning by their insistent, wheeling flight.

John Dory (dʒɒn ˈdɔːrɪ). Also 8 j. dorée, J. Dorey, 9 J. Doree. [In sense 2 formed by prefixing the name *John* to *dorée* or dory, the name of the fish, which it bore for 300 years before this addition.

Doubtless a humorous formation; possibly suggested by 'a very popular old song or catch' printed in 1609, and often alluded to in 17th c., the subject of which is the career of John Dory, captain of a French privateer: see Nares. The guesses which purport to explain the name from an assumed Fr. *jaune dorée*, or from a bogus Italian *janitore*, in allusion to the Sp. name *San Pedro*, are only ingenious trifling.]

1. Used as a proper name.

1609 *Deuteromelia* in Hawkins *Hist. Mus.* App. 23 John Dory bought him an ambling nag to Paris for to ride a. **1645** Milton *Colast.* Wks. (1851) 363 Then asks my opinion of John a Nokes, and John a Stiles..I for my part think John Dory was a better man then both of them. **1655** Sir J. Mennis *Musarum Delic.* 17 But I to Paris rid along Much like John Dory in the song Upon a holy Tide.

2. A popular name of a fish, *Zeus faber*, formerly called simply the *dorée* or *dory*.

1754 Fielding *Voy. Lisbon* Wks. 1784 X. 274 The only fish which bore any price was the john dorée, as it is called. **1771** Smollett *Humph. Cl.* 30 Apr., Your cook..has committed felony on the person of that John Dory; which is mangled in a cruel manner. **1863** Ansted *Ionian Isl.* 25 The John dory, sole and other flat fish are common enough.

Johne (ˈjoːnə). The name of Heinrich Albert *Johne* (1839–1910), German veterinary surgeon, used in the possessive to designate **Johne's bacillus,** *Mycobacterium johnei*, first recognized by him in 1895, which causes **Johne's disease,** an infectious enteritis of cattle and sheep, characterized by diarrhœa and progressive emaciation.

1907 J. M. Fadyean in *Jrnl. Compar. Path. & Therapeutics* XX. 53, I have therefore ventured to suggest that in this country the disease might in future be known as Johne's disease. Similarly, the causal organism would be known as the bacillus of Johne's disease. **1910** *Proc. R. Soc.* B. LXXXIII. 158, I have also succeeded in isolating and growing the acid-fast bacillus found in the intestine of cows in Jöhne's [*sic*] disease... Jöhne's bacillus grows somewhat more easily than Hansen's lepra bacillus. **1913** Twort & Ingram *Monogr. Johne's Dis.* iii. 29 'Johne's disease' should be the name given to the disease of sheep produced by an infection of Johne's bacillus in the gut and mesenteric glands. **1943** *Jrnl. Compar. Path. & Therapeutics* LIII. 140 Lesions could be produced with various saprophytic acid fast bacilli and killed cultures of Johne or tubercle bacilli suspended in saline. **1945** *Ibid.* LV. 41 (*title*) Ovine paratuberculosis (Johne's disease of sheep). **1972** *Jrnl. Compar. Path.* LXXXII. 333 (*title*) *Corynebacterium renale* as a cause of reactions to the complement fixation test for Johne's disease.

Johnian (ˈdʒəʊnɪən), *sb.* (*a.*) *Camb. Univ.* [f. John + -ian.] **A.** *sb.* A member or student of St. John's College, Cambridge.

1655 Fuller *Hist. Camb.* (1840) 143 The Johnians, having intelligence by their emissaries, that the property of the person was altered. **1712** Henley *Spect.* No. 396 ¶2 The Monopoly of Puns in this University has been an immemorial Privilege of the Johnians. **1829** Praed *Vicar* ad fin., The doctrine of a gentle Johnian..Whose phrase is very Ciceronian. **1885** *Athenæum* 7 Feb. 179/1 He..is nothing if not a Cambridge man and a Johnian.

B. *adj.* Of or belonging to St. John's College, Cambridge.

1785 Grose *Dict. Vulg. T.* s.v. *Hog*, Jonian hogs; an appellation given to the members of St. John's College, Cambridge. **1886** *Pall Mall G.* 19 June 4/2 By all the benefactors' merits, who bade us be, and raised our Johnian towers.

Johnny, Johnnie (ˈdʒɒnɪ). [Familiar diminutive of the name *John*: see -ie, -y.]

1. a. Applied humorously or contemptuously to various classes of men: A fellow, chap; *spec.* a nickname given to Englishmen in the Mediterranean, to the Confederate soldiers in the American civil war, etc.; in recent use chiefly denoting a fashionable young man of idle habits.

1673 Hickeringill *Gregory F. Greyl* 46 As if it was such a marvel, Jonye should be chous'd when he comes to commence gentleman. **1724–27** ?Ramsay *Bonny Tweedside*, Where she that is bonny May catch her a johnny, And never lead apes below. **1803** *Naval Chron.* IX. 417 The Johnnys rubbed their hands. **1824** Byron *Let. to Murray* 25 Feb., The English Johnnies, who had never been out of a cockney workshop before! **1842** E. E. Napier *Excurs. Shores Medit.* I. 226 Addressing us as 'Johnny', [they] were very officious in offering their services. 'Johnny' is, in this part of the country, the national appellation of an Englishman by the lower orders of Spaniards. **1865** R. H. Kellogg *Life & Death in Rebel Prisons* 194 The 'cheekiest' thing that had been done by the 'Johnnies'..was an attempt to secure the services of our men as artillerists. **1889** *Daily News* 15 July 3/1 An idle and vacuous young aristocrat, of the class popularly known as 'Johnnies'. **1894** H. Gardener *Unoff. Patriot* 310 It took..the entire regiment hitched to one of the cannon to pull it along the road the Johnnies retreated over. **1900** [see crumpet 4 b]. **1930** [see cool *v.* 3 e]. **1960** M. Spark *Bachelors* i. 9 He felt himself to be, not the amiable johnnie he had by then..affected to be. **1965** A. Nicol *Truly Married Woman* 42 Why are you always trying to be fair, you Johnnies?

b. [Cf. John 1 c.] A policeman. Also *Johnny Darby*, *Johnny Hop*. *slang.*

a **1852** H. Mayhew *London Labour* (1861) II. 154/1 The 'Johnny's' on the water are always on the look out, and..we has to cut our lucky. **1886** *Graphic* 30 Jan. 130/1 Constables used to be known as 'Johnny Darbies', said to be a corruption of the French *gensdarmes*, and they are still occasionally called 'Johnnies'. **1898** W. T. Goodge in M. Davitt *Life & Progress Australasia* xxxv. 192 A policeman is a 'johnny', Or a 'copman' or a 'trap'. **1923** D. H. Lawrence *Kangaroo* xvi. 357 Somers knew that Johnny Hops was Australian for a policeman. **1935** H. Neville *Sneak Thief on Road* 347 Johnny, a policeman. A Lincoln johnny, a stupid and impudent policeman.

c. (*a*) = John 1 e; (*b*) a soldier of the Indian Army (before 1947); (*c*) a Gurkha; (*d*) = *Johnny Turk*; (*e*) an Arab; (*f*) an onion-seller from Brittany.

1857 T. B. Gunn *Physiology of N.Y. Boarding Houses* 275 He's seed the *Johnnies* goin' into that there doorway next block. **1858** *Leisure Hour* 27 May 326/1 Sepoys..known as Johnnys. **1888** Kipling *Wee Willie Winkie* (1889) 103 The Highlander..turning to a Gurkha, said, 'Hya, Johnny!' **1897** I. Scott *How I stole over 10,000 Sheep in Austral. & N.Z.* 46 His name was Lim Hung Ching...this Johnny knowing he would have no show in such a scotch town if he sent in his tender with his own name,..signed it Angus McPherson. **1916** *Anzac Book* 50 What should we at Anzac have done without 'Johnnie' and his sturdy little mules? **1925** Fraser & Gibbons *Soldier & Sailor Words* 132 *Johnny*, a Turk. (As a Service nickname, dating from the Crimean War.) **1948** Partridge *Dict. Forces' Slang* 103 *Johnny*, soldiers' word for Arab. It rebounded, as Arabs also used the name for British soldiers. **1960** *Guardian* 8 Mar. 8/7 Any time now we shall have the Johnnies [from Brittany] coming around in small vans. **1967** J. Caird *Murder Scholastic* xi. 130 She heard the knock at the door... It could be a tradesman..or Onion Johnny, or a tramp. **1969** S. Mays *Fall out Officers* xxii. 173 'Now we are all the fighting brothers,' said Johnny with delight.

2. Applied to various animals. **a.** A sportsman's name for a tiger. **b.** A sailor's name for a penguin, *Pygoscelis papua*, the gentoo (*sb.*[2]). **c.** Local American name of two fishes, *Oligocottus maculosus*, abundant on the western coast of the United States, and *Etheostoma nigrum*, a kind of darter. (*Cent. Dict.*)

1815 *Sporting Mag.* XLV. 9 We entered the jungle, and soon caught sight of three Johnnies. **1879** H. N. Moseley *Notes by Naturalist on 'Challenger'* vii. 175 One [sort] was a penguin called by the sealers the 'Johnny' (*Pygoscelis tæniata*), the 'Gentoo' of the Falklands. **1893** A. Newton *Dict. Birds* II. 471 Johnny, the South-Sea sealers' name for a Penguin, *Pygoscelis papua* or *tæniata*, one of the widely-distributed species. **1898** *Daily News* 19 Apr. 6/2 Reading the following paragraph on penguins—or Johnnies as they are familiarly called. **1954** W. B. Alexander *Birds of Ocean* (ed. 2) 155 At the Falkland Islands it [*sc.* the gentoo penguin] is usually known as the 'Johnny'.

3. ***Johnny Armstrong*** joc. slang (see quot. 1962); ***Johnny-come-lately*** orig. *U.S.*: (*a*) a newcomer; (*b*) = *Johnny Raw*; (*c*) *fig.* and *attrib.*; ***Johnny Crapaud*** [i.e. toad], also ***Johnny Crapeau***: (*a*) nickname for a Frenchman or French Canadian; (*b*) (*Obs.*) the French nation; ***Johnny Head-in(-the)-Air***: nickname for a man with 'his head in the clouds', unconscious of his surroundings; cf. head *sb.* 40; ***Johnny Magorey*** (see quots.); ***Johnny Newcome***: (*a*) = *Johnny Raw*; (*b*) a newcomer of any kind; ***Johnny-on-the-spot***: a person who is available when needed, or 'at the psychological moment'; quasi-*adj.*, present, in readiness; ***Johnny Raw***: nickname for an inexperienced youngster: a raw recruit; a new hand; a novice; ***Johnny Reb***: a *U.S.* (Northern) name for a 'rebel' or Confederate soldier in the American Civil War; ***Johnny Turk***: a Turkish soldier; any Turk; ***Johnny Woodser*** = *Jimmy Woodser* (Jimmy[2] 4).

1922 *N. & Q.* 9 Sept. 206/2 *Johnny Armstrong*, the action of 'pulling' or restraining a horse. **1962** Granville *Dict. Sailors' Slang* 66/2 *Johnny Armstrong*, any hard work involving pulling or hauling. **1839** C. F. Briggs *Adv. H. Franco* I. 249 'But it's Johnny Comelately, aint it, you?' said a young mizzen topman. **1924** 'R. Daly' *Outpost* xiv. 139 He may be an old barbarian, but he's entitled to more consideration than these Johnny-come-lately's who cruise along the coast after trade. **1933** *Press* (Christchurch, N.Z.) 28 Oct. 17/7 *Johnny-come-lately*, nickname for a cowboy or any newly-joined hand or recent immigrant. **1946** M. Shulman *Zebra Derby* iii. 22 Postwar planning in these United States was no Johnny-come-lately. **1952** E. Coxhead *Play Toward* iii. 88 The Midlands are..all Johnny-come-latelys who coined money out of the war. **1953** *Amer. Scholar* XXIII. 17 The excessive power and renown of many Johnny-come-lately anti-Communists. **1972** *Listener* 16 Nov. 671/2 Here [in Utah] man himself is a Johnny-come-lately. [**1818** 'A. Burton' *Adv. Johnny Newcome* III. 131 Jean Crappeau's mighty stout, He surely means to fight it out.] **1834** W. N. Glascock *Naval Sketch-Bk.* 2nd Ser. II. 137 Mister Bull and Johnny Crappo..have ..suddenly taken for each other..a fit of affection. **1839** *Spirit of Times* 31 Aug. 312/1 Poor Johnny Crapeau has been the favorite mark for every shaft of ridicule. **1840** J. F. Cooper *Pathfinder* II. vi. 201 We are no Johnny Crapauds to hide ourselves behind a..fort on account of a puff of wind. **1851** J. F. W. Johnston *Notes N. Amer.* II. 6 These Ayrshire emigrants appear to be shrewd enough to buy out Johnny Crapaud. **1887** *Gentl. Mag.* Feb. 135 Those vessels went armed, too, as befitted the majesty of the bunting under which old Dance had gloriously licked Johnny Crapeau. **1915** G. Parker *Money Master* xxiii. 323 Yet, raging as he was, and ready to take the Johnny Crapaud..by the throat, he was not yet sure that Jean Jacques was not armed. **1919** W. A. Fraser *Bulldog Carney* 70 Them Johnnie Crapeaus from Quebec. **1965** G. R. Stevens *Incompleat Canadian* 142 'Johnny Crapeau', esteemed alike for his good temper..and ebullient spirits. **1848** *English Struwwelpeter* (ed. 4) 21 (*title*) The story of Johnny Head-in-Air. **1913** C. Mackenzie *Sinister St.* I. I. ii. 23 Much of his morning walk was passed in a dream... Nanny used to jeer at him, calling him Little Johnny Head-in-Air. **1929** C. Day Lewis *Transitional Poem* I. 14 What happier place For Johnny Head-in-Air, Who never would hear Time mumbling at the base? **1942** J. Pudney *Dispersal Point* 24 Do not despair For Johnny-head-in-air; He sleeps as sound As Johnny Underground. **1958** B. Nichols *Sweet & Twenties* xvi. 225 Yet he was not a Johnny-Head-in-the-Air; he had a shrewd grasp of the contemporary scene. **1870** G. M. Hopkins *Jrnl.* 4 Apr. (1959) 198 The following Irish expressions..Johnny Magoreys (seeds of the hip). **1922** Joyce *Ulysses* 172 Poisonous berries. Johnny Magories. **1815** (*title*) The military adventures of Johnny Newcome, with an account of his campaigns on the Peninsula and in Pall Mall. **1818** 'A. Burton' (*title*) The adventures of Johnny Newcome in the navy; a poem, in four cantos. **1833** *United Service Jrnl.* XI. I. 59 On first landing at Port Royal, a Johnny Newcome (as all strangers are there called)..will at once imagine himself transported into the community of Bedlamites. **1839** Barham *Ingol. Leg.* (1840) 1st Ser. 308 Now to young 'Johnny Newcome' she seems to confine hers, Neglecting the poor little dear out at dry-nurse. **1865** J. H. A. Bone *Petroleum & Petroleum Wells* 40 The Johnny Newcomes had to fight their way back to the bar, and deposit seventy-five cents for the bit of blue paste-board. **1961** F. H. Burgess *Dict. Sailing* 125 *Johnny Newcome*,..a new hand or a landsman, unused to the sea. **1896** Johnny-on-the-spot [see case *sb.*[2] 1 d]. **1902** 'D. Dix' *Fables of Elite* 43 Because they had never Tried it, they thought they were Johnny on the Spot, and could do anything. **1914** Wodehouse *Man Upstairs* 102 'I must be close at hand. I must be—what's your expression?—' 'Johnny-on-the-spot.' **1916** *Daily Colonist* (Victoria, B.C.) 23 July 7/5 We have our eyes on some splendid billets, and will be 'johnny on the spot' when the present residents move out. **1944** E. Bennett-Bremner *Front-Line Airline* (1945) viii. 50 Qantas Empire Airways have been called upon to conduct searches for missing aircraft, and it was only natural, therefore, that being 'Johnny-on-the-spot' they should be asked to join in when aircraft went missing. **1961** J. McCabe *Mr. Laurel & Mr. Hardy* (1962) ii. 57 Suddenly they needed a fat boy for a comedy sequence. He was Johnny-on-the-spot and he was hired at $5 a day. **1968** *Globe & Mail* (Toronto) 13 Jan. 42/7 He..was johnny-on-the-spot to rap in Mike Walton's rebound. **1813** Col. Hawker *Diary* (1893) I. 68 A grand attack was made on the Johnny raws of Blandford. **1823** in Hone *Every-day Bk.* II. 1395 There were some Johnny Raws on board. **1886** Stevenson *Kidnapped* (1888) 39 You took me for a country Johnnie Raw, with no more mother-wit or courage than a porridge-stick. **1865** *Nation* (N.Y.) I.

584 They said he was a Johnny Reb. **1948** Johnny Reb [see GREY, GRAY *sb.* 1 c]. **1919** *Mr. Punch's Hist. Gt. War* 24 Now it is the turn of 'Johnny Turk', who has had his knock on the Suez Canal. **1972** E. AMBLER *Levanter* ii. 22 'Johnny Turk is a gentleman,' he used to say. **1933** Johnny Woodser [see JIMMY² 4].

4. (With lower-case initial.) = JOHN 1 d. *slang* (chiefly *U.S.*).

1932 [see JOHN 1 d]. **1934** J. O'HARA *Appointment in Samarra* (1935) iv. 98 Kitty Hofman came in the johnny. **1946** C. S. ARCHER *China Servant* ii. 32 He left a smell of stale tobacco where-ever he went. Even in the johnny. **1969** L. GREENBAUM *Out of Shape* (1970) xviii. 136 You're not going to find me in aisle four next to the toilet paper and the johnny mop. **1971** D. CONOVER *One Man's Island* 65 Why, oh, why, do little boys (and big ones) rush to a johnny when nature provides opportunity everywhere?

5. Johnny-jump-up *N. Amer.*, a name used for several kinds of wild or cultivated pansy or violet; **Johnny penguin** = JOHNNY 2 b.

1842 *Knickerbocker* XIX. 115 Mr. Ketchup had now kissed little Chip and stuck a johnny-jump-up in his cap. **1872** E. EGGLESTON *End of World* i. 12 Julia..was hoeing a bed in which she meant to plant some johnny-jump-ups. **1929** F. A. POTTLE *Stretchers* (1930) iii. 48 Under foot the ground teemed with lupine and phlox and those large scentless violets which the natives call 'Johnny-jump-ups'. **1972** T. A. BULMAN *Kamloops Cattlemen* xii. 75 Green grass, buttercups and Johnny-jump-ups were much in evidence. **1879** H. N. MOSELEY *Notes by Naturalist on 'Challenger'* viii. 189 The whole beach of Christmas Harbour [in Kerguelen's Land] was covered with droves of the Johnny Penguin. **1882** *Encycl. Brit.* XIV. 49/1 All parts of the coast [of Kerguelen's Land] and even the lower slopes are covered with penguins of various species, mainly the Johnny penguin..rock-hopper..and king penguin. **1968** SHACKLETON & STOKES *Birds Atlantic Ocean* 20/2 Affectionately known as 'Johnny' penguin, the gentoo is the only penguin with white on top of its head.

'johnny-cake. Also Johhny-cake. [Origin uncertain; referred to in 1775, and by some later writers, as *journey-cake*, which may be the original form.

The cake is said to be of Negro origin.]

a. *U.S.* A cake made of maize-meal, in the Southern States toasted before a fire, elsewhere usually baked in a pan. Also *W. Indies*, a scone or dumpling (cf. quot. 1831). **b.** *Australia.* A cake made of wheat-meal, baked on the ashes or fried in a pan.

1739 *S. Carolina Gaz.* 22 Dec. 4/2 (Advt.) (Th. Suppl.), New Iron Plates to cook Johnny Cakes or gridel bread on. **1775** ROMANS *Florida* 125 Notwithstanding it [rice] is..only fit for puddings,..or to make the wafer-like bread called journey cakes in Carolina. **1793** J. BARLOW *Hasty Pudding*, Rich Johnny-Cake, this mouth has often tried. **1831** JANE PORTER *Sir E. Seaward's Narr.* I. 229 My dear helpmate made us some johnny cakes, a West Indian sort of tea-bread. **1861** MRS. MEREDITH *Over the Straits* v. 154 The dough-cakes fried in fat, called 'Johnny-cakes'. **1868** G. CHANNING *Early Recoll. Newport, R.I.* 25 The 'journey-cake', vulgarly called Johnny-cake,—how can I sufficiently describe it? **1890** *Melbourne Argus* 16 Aug. 13/1 Here I, a new chum, could..make a sweet and wholesome johnny cake. **1892** *Nation* (N.Y.) 3 Mar. 168/2. **1893** in C. Sullivan *Jamaica Cookery Bk.* **1952** S. SELVON *Brighter Sun* vi. 109 Over there, nastiness and poverty, a tin cup of weak tea and a johnny cake or a roti. **1972** J. HEWITT *N.Y. Times Heritage Cook Bk.* 96 Massachusetts johnnycakes usually have wheat flour and corn meal in them.

Johnson ('dʒɒnsən). A common surname, used in *low slang* to designate: **a.** The penis. Also *Jim Johnson*.

1863 W. B. CHEADLE *Jrnl. Trip across Canada* (1931) 108 Neck frozen. Face ditto; tights ditto; Johnson ditto, & sphincter vesicae partially paralyzed. **1972** *Screw* 12 June 10/3 So I went to take my turn with the hopes of somehow getting my *Jim Johnson* wet.

b. A man who is kept by a prostitute or prostitutes, a ponce.

1960 'J. ASHFORD' *Counsel for Defence* v. 66 You got Legs off... He was a Johnson.

Johnson bar ('dʒɒnsən bɑː(r)). *U.S.* [Origin unknown.] A long heavy lever used to reverse the motion of a steam locomotive. Also *transf.* (see quot. 1971).

1930 *Railroad Man's Mag.* II. 471/1 *Johnson bar*, reverse lever on a locomotive. **1943** *Railroad Mag.* XXXIV. 58/1 He jerked two short ones from his chime, eased the Johnson bar down to the first corner and dropped his left hand on the throttle. **1959** P. RANSOME-WALLIS *Conc. Encycl. World Railway Locomotives* 508 *Johnson bar*, reversing lever. **1971** M. TAK *Truck Talk* 93 *Johnson bar*, the emergency brake handle.

Johnsonese (dʒɒnsəˈniːz), *sb.* (*a.*) [f. the surname *Johnson* + -ESE.] The language or style of Dr. Johnson, or an imitation of it: see next, A.

1843 MACAULAY *Ess., Mad. D'Arblay* (1887) 766 It is a sort of broken Johnsonese. **1865** *Pall Mall G.* 5 Aug. 9/2 As the Rector of Marylebone lately expressed it in his extraordinary Johnsonese,..'the juvenile branches of our population are greatly dependent on this nutritious diet' [milk]. **1898** L. STEPHEN *Stud. Biogr.* I. ii. 58 Who clothed the utterances of every orator..in sonorous Johnsonese.

B. *adj.* In the style of Dr. Johnson.

1882 *Athenæum* 2 Dec. 729/1 A country clergyman who in 1784..protested vehemently against the Johnsonese language and the Johnsonian criticism of poetry.

Johnsonian (dʒɒnˈsəʊnɪən), *a.* and *sb.* [f. as prec. + -IAN.]

A. *adj.* Of, belonging to, or characteristic of Dr. Samuel Johnson (1709–84), a celebrated English man of letters and lexicographer; applied esp. to a style of English abounding in words derived or made up from Latin, such as that of Dr. Johnson.

1791 BOSWELL *Johnson* (1831) I. 154 The concluding line is much more Johnsonian than it was afterwards printed. **1866** MISS MULOCK *Noble Life* x. 172 In prolix and Johnsonian style. **1886** RUSKIN *Præterita* I. xii. 415 Johnsonian symmetry and balance in sentences.

B. *sb.* A student or admirer of Dr. Johnson.

1887 *Athenæum* 25 June 825/1 Many of its most distinguished members have been as enthusiastic Johnsonians as Dr. Birkbeck Hill.

Hence **John'sonianism**, Johnsonian style, or a Johnsonian phrase; **John'sonianly** *adv.*, in a Johnsonian style. So also **'Johnsonism** = *Johnsonianism*; **'Johnsonize** *v. trans.*, to clothe in or imbue with the style or language of Dr. Johnson. (All more or less *nonce-wds.*)

1791 BOSWELL *Johnson* (1831) I. p. xlii, I have Johnsonised the land; and I trust they will not only talk but think Johnson. **1807** T. HORNE tr. *Goede's Trav. Eng.* II. 142 In England, the Johnsonianism is a prevalent disease. **1856** WEBSTER, *Johnsonism.* *c* **1890** A. MURDOCK *Yoshiwara Episode*, etc. 78 Pompous, meaningless, and empty Johnsonianisms.

Johnsoniana (dʒɒnsəʊnɪˈeɪnə, -ˈɑːnə). [f. *Johnson* (see JOHNSONIAN *a.* and *sb.*) + -IANA.] Sayings, etc., of or about Dr. Samuel Johnson; matters connected with Dr. Johnson.

1776 (*title*) Johnsoniana; or, a collection of Bon Mots, etc., by Dr. Johnson and others. **1909** *Daily Chron.* 14 Sept. 3/2 [Mr. Reade's] latest compilation of Johnsoniana. **1928** *Daily Tel.* 12 June 17/3 Miss Anna Seward's delightful Johnsoniana. **1952** *Bull. John Rylands Libr.* XXXV. 211 (*title*) Johnsoniana from the Bagshawe muniments.

Johnson noise. *Electronics.* [Named after John Bertrand *Johnson* (b. 1887), naturalized U.S. physicist, who published an account of it in 1928.] Electrical noise caused by the random thermal motion of conduction electrons.

1931 *Proc. IRE* XIX. 1407 Finally..an irreducible minimum of noise is encountered, commonly referred to as 'Johnson' or circuit noise. **1947** [see *flicker noise* (FLICKER *sb.*³ 4)]. **1958** CONDON & ODISHAW *Handbk. Physics* v. iii. 31/1 This voltage fluctuation, called Johnson noise, which places a limit on the ultimate sensitivity of amplifiers, provides a method for measuring thermodynamic temperature. **1973** *Physics Bull.* Oct. 596/2 Any electrical resistor exhibits a Johnson noise voltage, with a mean square amplitude proportional to absolute temperature.

johnstrupite ('jɒnstrjuːpaɪt, 'dʒɒnstrəpaɪt). *Min.* [ad. G. *johnstrupit* (W. C. Brögger 1890, in *Zeitschr. f. Krystallogr. u. Mineral.* XVI. 75), f. the name of J. F. *Johnstrup* (1818–1894), Danish geologist: see -ITE¹.] A brownish green hydrous silicate and fluoride of several metals.

1890 *Jrnl. Chem. Soc.* LVIII. 1077 In addition to the minerals previously known, the author [*sc.* Brögger] has found..johnstrupite. **1906** J. P. IDDINGS *Rock Minerals* II. 458 Mosandrite and johnstrupite occur in nephelite-syenites and closely related rocks, chiefly in the region of the Langesund fjord, Norway; also in the aphanitic and lava equivalents in other localities. **1959** *Mineral. Abstr.* XIV. 105/1 Calculations of the unit cell contents..give the following formulae:..johnstrupite $(Ca, Na, Ce)_{12}$ $(Ti, Mg, Al, Zr)_3Si_7O_{31}H_2F_{4-5}$... The authors conclude that mosandrite and johnstrupite are varieties of the same species. **1965** *Ibid.* XVII. 287/1 Selective concentration of B ..has been observed in specimens of..mosandrite and johnstrupite.

Johnswort. = *St. John's-wort* (JOHN 5).

1753 J. HEMPSTEAD *Diary* (1901) 611 Wee pulld up the yellow Blossoms (alias Johnsworth) in the upper end & back Side the Lot. **1819** *Mass. Hist. Soc. Coll.* 2nd Ser. VIII. 170 In July the lover of plants is gratified with..two species of pyrala, the small geranium, several species of hypericum or John's wort. **1874** *Rep. Vermont Board Agric.* II. 390 It is very desirable that the dairyman's pastures should be well stocked with good nutritious grasses, not wild grass of the low boggy pasture, or johnswort, or daisies, but June or blue grass and clover.

joiaux, joiax, obs. pl. of JEWEL.

joice, obs. form of JOIST, JUICE.

‖**joie de vivre** (ʒwa də vivr). [Fr., = joy of living.] A feeling of healthy enjoyment of life; exuberance, high spirits.

1889 E. DOWSON *Let.* 1 Apr. (1967) 58, I do not suppose 'la joie de vivre' will be revealed to me any more at Limehouse than in the Temple. **1901** 'L. MALET' *Hist. R. Calmady* III. v. 204 The hungry all-compelling *joie de vivre* which is begotten whensoever youth thus seeks and finds youth. **1907** *Westm. Gaz.* 5 Feb. 4/2 The new *joie de vivre* of motoring. **1917** S. McKENNA *Sonia* vi. 263 It was only when the twanging banjos changed to rag-time that the majority of our neighbours sheepishly unbent and put forth an assumption of *joie de vivre.* **1925** A. P. HERBERT *Laughing Ann* 82 The simple mind and manly air, Not Brains so much as Breeding, With *joie de vivre* and *savoir faire*, Are constantly succeeding. **1935** *Discovery* Jan. 28/2 Song is an outlet for any of a bird's emotions.., but chiefly *joie de vivre.* **1944** *Burlington Mag.* Sept. 216/2 Many delightful travel impressions have also been noted by him in spirited pen and wash drawings, glistening with *joie-de-vivre.* **1955** *Times* 16 Aug. 5/3 She is excitable, but rather in the sense of joie de vivre. Children play with her, ride on her back, twist her tail and do anything that might aggravate a ferocious dog. **1964** R. CHURCH *Voyage Home* i. 10 Suffering acutely from the effort to ignore the bursts of *joie-de-vivre* from the corridors. **1974** I. MURDOCH *Sacred & Profane Love Machine* 96 He had laughed at Sophie's spiteful jokes, of which the sheer *joie de vivre* had seemed to lessen the bite.

join, *sb.* [f. JOIN *v.*¹] An act of joining, or the fact of being joined; *concr.* the formation or the place in which two things or parts of a thing are joined, a line of junction, a joining. Also *join-up.*

1825 ESTHER HEWLETT *Cottage Comf.* v. 36 Saving sixpence..by having a join, which a good needlewoman can do in half an hour. **1884** H. R. HAWEIS *Musical Mem.* iii. 89 The obvious join between the neck and the head of old violins. **1894** COOK *Old Touraine* II. 187 To hide the join of the old masonry with the new. *Mod.* Let us see what sort of a join you have made. That is not a very good join. **1945** A. LUNN *Third Day* v. 47 If we are expected to accept the hypothesis of a second-century compiler who worked his heterogeneous materials into an artistic unity with..skill we may ask why the join-ups between the 'we' sections and the rest of the *Acts* are so inartistic. **1969** *Sun* 22 July 1/2 On the join-up, Eagle and Columbia ended their separate existences [as space vehicles] and became Apollo-11 again.

join (dʒɔɪn), *v.*¹ Forms: 3–7 ioin, 7– join; also 4–5 ioign, ioygn, 4–6 ione, 4–7 ioyn, (5 iony-on, iunge, 5–6 yoyn, iune), 7–8 joyn. [ME. a. OF. *joign-* stem of *joindre* (= It. *giugnere*):—L. *jungĕre* to join: root *jug-* = Gr. ζυγ-, Skt. *yuj-*, Indo-Eur. *yug-*, whence OTeut. *juk-*, Eng. *yoke.* The rimes show the pronunciation (dʒaɪn) in 17–18th c.; this is still dialectal.]

I. *trans.* To put together, to unite one thing to another, in any kind of connexion physical or immaterial.

1. a. To put (things) together, so that they become physically united or continuous; to fasten, attach, connect, unite (one thing to another); also, to connect by means of something intervening or attached to each, *e.g.* two islands by a bridge.

1297 R. GLOUC. (Rolls) 1616 þe soule þoru godes grace out of helle he broȝte, & to is bodi is ioinede, & ȝef him cristendom. **1382** WYCLIF *Job* xli. 7 Oon to oon is ioyned. *c* **1440** *Promp. Parv.* 264/1 Ioynyn, or ionyon, *jungo, compagino.* **1483** *Cath. Angl.* 199/2 To Iunge (*A.* Iune), *adiungere, apponere.* **1613** PURCHAS *Pilgrimage* (1614) 876 Some of them are..strangely ioyned without morter. **1615** G. SANDYS *Trav.* 120 Onely a lake when the River overfloweth; joyned thereunto by a chanell. **1617** MORYSON *Itin.* I. 77 Consisting of many Ilands joyned with Bridges. **1704** POPE *Windsor For.* 400 Seas but join the regions they divide. **1726** LEONI *Alberti's Archit.* II. 114/1 Joyn the ends of the Timbers together. **1825** J. NICHOLSON *Operat. Mechanic* 567 Fig. 569 shews how two pieces may be joined by..a niche. **1885** WATSON & BURBURY *Math. The. Electr. & Magn.* I. 244 The pairs are said to be joined in series.

†**b.** To harness (horses, etc. together, or to a vehicle, or the vehicle to the horses); to yoke.

1377 LANGL. *P. Pl.* B. XIX. 260 Grace gaue Piers a teme, ..And ioigned to hem one Iohan most gentil of alle, þe prys nete of Piers plow, passyng alle other. **1382** WYCLIF *Jer.* xlvi. 4 Ioyneth hors, and steȝeth vp, ȝee hors men. **1484** CAXTON *Fables of Æsop* III. ii, I haue ioyned and bound [a bull and an ox] bothe to gyder. **1621** G. SANDYS *Ovid's Met.* II. (1626) 24 He bade the light-foot Houres without delay To joyn his Steeds. **1728** NEWTON *Chronol. Amended* i. 144 It was Erechtheus that first joyned a chariot to horses.

†**c.** To combine in a mixture. *Obs.*

c **1400** *Lanfranc's Cirurg.* 24 He [the ligament] is ioyned wiþ senewis to make cordis and brawnes. **1526** *Pilgr. Perf.* (W. de W. 1531) 3, & so ioyned with the golde, it is of more fresshe colour. **1530** PALSGR. 593/1 All the worlde can nat joyne fyre and water togyther. **1626** BACON *Sylva* §50 Pistachoes..joyned with Almonds in almond milk,.. are an excellent nourisher.

d. *Geom.* To connect (two points) by a straight line; to draw the straight line between.

1660 BARROW *Euclid* I. vii, If D falls without the triangle ACB, let CD be joined. *Ibid.* xvi, Join FC, and IC; and produce ACG. **1825** J. NICHOLSON *Operat. Mechanic* 686 Describe a circle, cutting the ellipsis in the four points k, l, m, n; join k, l, and m, n. **1885** LEUDESDORF *Cremona's Proj. Geom.* 72 The straight line which joins a pair of corresponding points.

2. To put or bring into close contact, cause to touch each other. ***to join hands***: see 19.

c **1369** CHAUCER *Dethe Blaunche* 393 A whelpe..Hylde doun hys hede and ioyned hys erys. *c* **1450** *Merlin* 333 Kynge Boors..ioyned his feet and lept vpon the deed bodyes of men..that he hadde slain. **1552** HULOET, Ioyne lyppes, *collabello.* **1609** BIBLE (Douay) *Num.* xxii. 25 The asse..ioyned her-selfe close to the wal, and brused the foote of him that ridde. **1662** R. MATHEW *Unl. Alch.* §85. 115 Alwayes ready to join my shoulder unto him that is ready to fall. **1717** POPE *Eloisa* 349 O'er the pale marble shall they join their heads.

3. To put together, combine, unite (immaterial things, or one *with* or *to* another or a person).

1340 *Ayenb.* 247 þe yefþe of wysdom..þet is alsuo y-goyned to god. *c* **1374** CHAUCER *Boeth.* II. pr. vi. 43 (Camb. MS.) The yiftes of fortune..neyther they ne Ioignen hem nat alwey to goode men, ne makyn hem alwey goode to whom they ben I-ioigned. **1423** JAS. I *Kingis Q.* cxxxiii, Lat wisedom ay vnto thy will be Iunyt. **1553** T. WILSON *Rhet.* (1580) 169 When we have learned usual and accustomable wordes to set forthe our meanyng, wee ought to ioyne them

together in apt order. **1560** DAUS tr. *Sleidane's Comm.* 247 b, That they..may ioyne theyr prayers with his, that is, with God and religion. **1604** E. G[RIMSTONE] TR. *D'Acosta's Hist. Ind.* III. xxii. 187 By reason of continuall moisture ioyned to the heate of the burning Zone. *a* **1626** BACON *New Atl.* 15 That King also still desiring to joyn Humanity and Policy together. **1690** LOCKE *Hum. Und.* II. xxxiii. §18 Two Ideas that they have been accustom'd so to join in their minds as to substitute one for the other. **1882** HINSDALE *Garfield & Educ.* II. 248 The disaster that may be brought upon us by ignorance and vice in the citizen when joined to corruption and fraud in the suffrage.

†**4.** To put (something) to another thing or things, so as to increase the amount or number; to add, annex; to add in contribution. *Obs.*

13.. *E.E. Allit. P.* A. 1008 Ȝet Ioyned Iohan þe crysolyt, þe sevenþe gemme in fundament. **1526** *Pilgr. Perf.* (W. de W. 1531) 1 b, Ioynynge also therto the goostly exercyse and experyence of holy fathers. **1585** T. WASHINGTON tr. *Nicholay's Voy.* II. ix. 42 b, Terpandre the famous Musition, which ioined the seventh string to the quadricord. **1610** SHAKS. *Temp.* I. ii. 231 Who, with a Charme ioynd to their suffred labour I haue left asleep. **1645** USSHER *Body Div.* (1647) 411 Those five other Sacraments..joyned by the Papists, are superfluous. **1693** DRYDEN *Juvenal* Ded. to Ld. Dorset, Obsolete Words may then be laudably reviv'd.. when their Obscurity is taken away, by joyning other Words to them, which clear the Sense. **1709** POPE *Ess. Crit.* 346 While expletives their feeble aid do join.

5. a. To bring or put (persons, troops, etc.) into one body or company; to unite, combine. *to join forces*, *fig.* to combine efforts.

1560 DAUS tr. *Sleidane's Comm.* 224 b, That he myghte ioyne the munition of hys brother..and hys owne to gether. **1596** DALRYMPLE tr. *Leslie's Hist. Scot.* VIII. 60 Tha conclude, and propones to June thair forces against the Erle Douglas. **1615** J. STEPHENS *Satyr. Ess.* 341 His first..is to joyne forces, and make up his defects of pollicy..by partaking in anothers projects. **1715** VANBRUGH *Country Ho.* I. Wks. (Rtldg.) 462/2 Let's join companies. **1748** *Anson's Voy.* II. xi. 256 All the ships being joined, the Commodore made a signal to speak with their Commanders.

†**b.** *refl.* To attach oneself *to*, associate oneself *with*, or go into the company *of*; to go up *to*. *Obs.*

13.. *K. Alis.* 4030 He a knyght of Grece slowgh..And joined him us among. **1382** WYCLIF *Acts* viii. 29 Come to, and ioyne thee to this chare. *a* **1400–50** *Alexander* 1284 He ..Ioynes him to Iosaphat: full ioyles he rydes. **1600** E. BLOUNT tr. *Conestaggio* 167 Seeing these men..to flie,..and to ioine themselves with the Governors his adversaries. **1611** BIBLE *Acts* viii. 29 Then the Spirit saide vnto Philip, Goe neere, and ioyne thy selfe to this charet. [So **1881** (R.V.).]

6. a. To link or unite (persons, etc. together, or one *with* or *to* another) in marriage, friendship, or any kind of association, alliance, or relationship; to unite, associate, ally.

1297 R. GLOUC. (Rolls) 7257 Normandie þoru þe king & þoru þe quene engelond Iioyned were þo kundeliche as in one monnes hond. **1340** *Ayenb.* 88 Þis loue and þis wylnynge þet ioyneþ and oneþ zuo þe herte to god. **1362** LANGL. *P. Pl.* A. II. 106 An ȝif þe Iustise wol Iugge hire to be Ioynet with Fals, ȝit be-war of þe weddyng. *a* **1548** HALL *Chron., Hen. V* 65 Any waie or meane by the whiche he might reconcile and ioyne in amitee the twoo greate and mightie kynges of Englande and of Fraunce. **1548–9** (Mar.) *Bk. Com. Prayer, Matrimony*, We are gathered together..to ioyne together this man and this woman in holy matrimonie. **1611** BIBLE *Matt.* xix. 6 What therefore God hath joyned together, let not man put asunder. **1678** WANLEY *Wond. Lit. World* V. i. §96. 468/1 He was joined Emperour with his Father in his Fathers life-time. **1719** YOUNG *Revenge* IV. i. Wks. 1757 II. 166 Life is the desart, life the solitude; Death joins us to the great majority. **1844** LINGARD *Anglo-Sax. Ch.* (1858) II. xii. 226 With these learned foreigners, the king joined four Anglo-Saxons.

b. *refl.* To unite, associate, or ally oneself (*with*, *to*); to enter into alliance.

1535 COVERDALE *Exod.* i. 10 Yf there shulde ryse vp eny warre agaynst vs, they might ioyne them selues also vnto oure enemies. *a* **1548** HALL *Chron., Hen. IV* 8 The best felowe and companion that a man in aduersitie can associat or ioyne him self withal. **1611** BIBLE *Luke* xv. 15 He went and ioyned himselfe to a Citizen of that Countrey. **1642** ROGERS *Naaman* 11 Prone to joyne themselves purchasers with God, in this great worke. **1882** R. L. STEVENSON *New Arabian Nights* I. 95 You join yourselves to persons of condition..for no other purpose than to escape the consequences of your crimes. **1904** S. J. WEYMAN *Abbess of Vlaye* ii. 41 Had I known of what sort they were to whom I was joining myself.

II. *intr.* To come or be put together in any kind of connexion physical or immaterial.

7. To come or be brought into material contact or connexion; to become connected or fastened together; to combine, unite physically.

c **1330** *Arth. & Merl.* 5426 Alle the other com after tho, Ioinand bi hond to and to. **1481** CAXTON *Myrr.* I. xvii. 51 Therfore behoueth us to Ioyne to the erthe. **1530** PALSGR. 592/2 The ryver of Tames begynneth where Tame and Yse ioyne togyther. **1593** SHAKS. *3 Hen. VI*, II. i. 29 See, see, they ioyne, embrace, and seeme to kisse. **1615** G. SANDYS *Trav.* 101 Long taild (being thicke where it joynes to the body). **1632** J. HAYWARD tr. *Biondi's Eromena* 150 Two timber-beams, joyning angle-wise under it. **1639** T. BRUGIS tr. *Camus' Mor. Relat.* 308 All he could doe, was to make the Serpents head joyne to the tayle, I meane, make the first day of the yeare touch the last without borrowing. **1665** HOOKE *Microgr.* 6 In twisting into a thread they joyn, and lie so close together, as to lose their own, and destroy each others particular reflections. **1774** GOLDSM. *Nat. Hist.* (1776) VI. 198 The female joins with the male, as is asserted, *more humano*, and once in two years feels the accesses of desire. **1828** D'ISRAELI *Chas. I*, I. iv. 90 Parallel lines can no more join together in politics than in geometry. *Mod. colloq.* I tried to fit the pieces together, but they wouldn't join.

8. (Expressing the resulting condition.) To be in contact; to be contiguous or adjacent; to adjoin. †Const. *to*, *upon*, *with*.

c **1325** *Coer de L.* 4082 Under the brygge there is a swyke, Corven clos, joynand queyntlyke. *c* **1350** *Will. Palerne* 751 Þat preui pleyng place..Ioyned wel iustly to meliors chamber. *c* **1374** CHAUCER *Troylus* v. 813 Here browes Ioyneden y-fere. **1387** TREVISA *Higden* (Rolls) VII. 307 Þey haveþ þrittene celles.. bote þey joyneþ al to gidres. *c* **1400** MAUNDEV. (Roxb.) vi. 22 Araby..ioynes apon Ydumee. **1480** CAXTON *Descr. Brit.* 21 Cornewayle is in englond and ioyneth to deuenshire. **1526** TINDALE *Acts* xviii. 7 Iustus.. whose house ioyned harde to the sinagoge. **1585** T. WASHINGTON tr. *Nicholay's Voy.* II. xiii. 47 Two sides are washed by the sea, and the thyrd ioyneth vnto the firme land. **1632** LITHGOW *Trav.* 24 Whose breadth is narrow, and where it joyneth with both seas, it is but sixty miles. **1781** S. A. PETERS *Hist. Conn.* 164 The houses are..well built, but, as I have observed in general of the towns on Connecticut, do not join. **1796** MORSE *Amer. Geog.* I. 443 It joins to the sea on the east side of the island. *Mod.* On the side where the two gardens join.

9. Of non-physical contact: †**a.** To come close together in time; to follow or precede something else immediately. *Obs.* **b.** To come together or exist together, in operation, as associated qualities, etc.

c **1400** *Destr. Troy* 11882 The last Ioy of ioly men Ioynys with sorow. **1593** Q. ELIZ. tr. *Boeth.* II. met. vi. 37 O grevous hap whan wicked Sword To cruel Venom Joingnes. **1639** S. DU VERGER tr. *Camus' Admir. Events* 53 The condition of a souldiour, and that of a merchant are not used to joyne together. **1697** DRYDEN *Virg. Georg.* IV. 713 Three flashes of blue Light'ning gave the sign Of Cov'nants broke, three peals of Thunder join. **1709** POPE *Ess. Crit.* 361 Where Denham's strength and Waller's sweetness join [*rime* line]. **1850** TENNYSON *In Mem.* xxxvi, Tho' truths in manhood darkly join.

10. †**a.** To attach oneself *to*, associate oneself *with* (= 5 b). *Obs.* **b.** Of two or more: To come together, come into company.

a **1375** *Joseph Arim.* 407 Hiderward he ioynes, With sixti þousent..of clene men of Armes, And Fifti þousend fotmen. *c* **1400** *Destr. Troy* 512 His comaundment to kepe sho hir course held, and Ioynet by Iason iustly to sit. *a* **1548** HALL *Chron., Hen. V* 50 His horsmen..to ioyne with him against the rereward of Fraunce. **1600** E. BLOUNT tr. *Conestaggio* 255 That such as followed the kings partie.. might ioine with them. **1679** PENN *Addr. Prot.* II. 87 Philip joyn'd to him and askt him, If he understood what he read? **1706** PHILLIPS, *To Joyn*, to..come together, to agree. **1855** MACAULAY *Hist. Eng.* xviii. IV. 235 These orders had been given before it was known at Versailles that the Dutch and English fleets had joined.

†**11.** *Astrol.* To come into conjunction. Also *pass.* To be in conjunction. See CONJUNCTION 3.

c **1391** CHAUCER *Astrol.* II. §4 And that he be nat retrograd ne combust, ne ioigned with no shrewe in the same signe. **1509** HAWES *Past. Pleas.* XXXIII. (Percy Soc.) 161 Whan clere Diana joyned with Mercury, The crystall ayre and assured firmament Were all depured. **1697** DRYDEN *Virg. Georg.* I. 460 Observe the starry Signs, Where Saturn houses, and where Hermes joins.

12. To come together or meet in conflict; to engage in conflict, encounter. ? *Obs.*

13.. *Gaw. & Gr. Knt.* 97 Oþer sum segg hym bi-soȝt of sum siker knyȝt, To Ioyne wyth hym in iusting in Ioparde to lay. *c* **1400** *Destr. Troy* 12965 Þat he might ryde with þat Orest & his ranke oste, To Ioyne with Engest for his vniust werkes. **1530** PALSGR. 593/1 Thoughe he be called never so peryllous, I dare joyne with hym. **1560** DAUS tr. *Sleidane's Comm.* 82 b, When both armies were ready to ioyne in battel. **1597** SHAKS. *2 Hen. IV*, I. ii. 233 Looke you pray..that our Armies ioyn not in a hot day. **1600** E. BLOUNT tr. *Conestaggio* 289 The captaine with great dexteritie to avoide the shotte, ioyned with them towards the prooe, and boorded the gallion. **1712–14** POPE *Rape Lock* III. 29 Straight the three bands prepare in arms to join.

13. a. To enter into association or alliance, to combine in action or purpose (= 6 b).

13.. *E.E. Allit P.* B. 726 Schal þay falle in þe faute þat oþer frekez wroȝt & ioyne to her iuggement her iuise to haue? **1563** WINȜET *Four Scoir Thre Quest.* Wks. 1888 I. 136 We will nocht only nocht iwne with ȝow generalie in religioun,..bot aluterlie fle ȝour cumpanie. **1581** MULCASTER *Positions* v. (1887) 34, I do thinke that all my countreymen will ioyne with me, and allow their children the vse, of their letter and penne. **1613** PURCHAS *Pilgrimage* (1614) 820 *note*, Negro-slaves..ioyning with the Indians, used to robbe the Spaniards. **1745** *Col. Rec. Pennsylv.* V. 5 Their own security will oblige them to join with the enemy.

b. with *const.* To associate oneself or take part *in* an action, or *to do* something.

1560 DAUS tr. *Sleidane's Comm.* 39 Desyring them to ioyne with hym in disputation. **1584** POWELL *Lloyd's Cambria* 111 The princes to ioine in their enterprise. **1672–5** COMBER *Comp. Temple* (1702) 36 The People vocally joyned in the Hymns and Psalms. **1711** STEELE *Spect.* No. 19 ¶2 He makes it his business to join in Conversation with Envious Men. **1815** SHELLEY *Demon of World* I. 218 The elements of all that human thought Can frame of lovely or sublime, did join To rear the fabric of the fane. **1896** *Law Times Rep.* LXXIII. 689/2 He..insisted that S. Lord..must join in the conveyance to him.

c. also absol. *to join in* (the action being understood from the context).

1785 GOUV. MORRIS in Sparks *Life & Writings* (1832) III. 459 The government joins in and agrees to the depreciation. *Mod.* Some of them were singing. Presently other voices joined in.

III. *trans.* To form (a resulting whole) by the combination of parts.

14. To construct or compose (a whole) by putting parts together; *esp.* to make (wooden furniture, etc.) in this way, as a JOINER (see also JOINED 2). In quot. *c* 1400, To unite the edges of (a wound) in order to healing; in quot. *c* 1386, To compound (a word). *Obs.* exc. in phrases: see 21.

c **1340** *Cursor M.* 21270 (Fairf.) þe qu[h]elis ar ioyned with mani a dowle. *c* **1386** CHAUCER *Sec. Nun's T.* 95 Cecile, as I writen fynde, Is ioyned by a manere conioynynge Of heuene and lia. *a* **1400–50** *Alexander* 4458 For iolite of Iupiter ȝe ioyen vp templis. *c* **1400** *Lanfranc's Cirurg.* 34 Brynge þe parties of þe wounde togideris, þat it may be weel ioyned. **1530** PALSGR. 316/2 Joyned as a stole or any other thynge is by the joyners crafte. **1600** SHAKS. *A. Y. L.* III. iii. 88 This fellow wil but ioyne you together, as they ioyne Wainscot.

IV. *trans.* To come into contact, contiguity, company, or union with. *ellipt.* for *join oneself to* (5 b), *join to* (10 a).

15. a. To come or go into local contact or association with; to go to and accompany (a person); to come to and take up one's post in (one's regiment, ship, or the like).

1713 STEELE *Englishm.* No. 29. 186 A young Fellow joyns us from t'other End of the Room. **1748** *Anson's Voy.* II. xiv. 283 It would have been impossible..to have prevented their joining us. **1793** NELSON 26 Jan. in Nicolas *Disp.* (1845) I. 298, I think the Ship will be commissioned within a fortnight and I shall join her directly. **1833** MARRYAT *P. Simple* xli, I reported myself to the admiral, and joined my brig. **1838** LYTTON *Alice* I. iii, Then she joined her mother and Mrs. Leslie at breakfast. **1838** THIRWALL *Greece* II. 83 Here they seem to have been joined by other fugitives and soldiers of fortune.

b. To associate or ally oneself with, attach oneself to, take part with (a person, party, etc.); to become a member or associate of (a society, staff of workers, etc.); to take part with another or others in (an action).

to join the (great or silent) majority, to die: see MAJORITY.
1714 GAY *Trivia* III. 70 Injur'd Tenants Joyn the Hunters' Cries. **1738** POPE *Epil. Sat.* ii. 41 Or, if a Court or Country's made a job, Go drench a Pick-pocket, and join the Mob. **1781** COWPER *Hope* 741 Rocks, groves, and streams, must join him in his praise. **1845** M. PATTISON *Ess.* (1889) I. 23 I..promise..to join the other bishops in all that they shall decide in conformity with the canon law. **1860** TYNDALL *Glac.* I. xxiii. 164 He..asked me whether I would join him in an ascent of the Dom. **1874** GREEN *Short Hist.* v. §1. 220 The blind King of Bohemia, who had joined Philip's army. *Mod.* Ten new members have joined the society. How long is it since he joined your staff? Many converts have joined the church.

c. *absol.* (in sense a or b).

1844 LEVER *T. Burke* xxi, When do you join?—where is your regiment? **1896** *Daily News* 28 Dec. 6/3 An old convict was brought in whilst we were there. He had only 'joined' that day. *Mod.* Is he a member of our society? When did he join?

d. *to join up*: to enlist in the army.

1916 'BOYD CABLE' *Action Front* 5 Just joined up to get a finger in the fighting? **1922** D. H. LAWRENCE *England, my England* 40 Egbert went and joined up immediately as a private soldier. **1934** J. T. FARRELL *Young Manhood* i. 20 He stepped up to a beefy-faced sergeant... 'We came to join up.' **1943** J. B. PRIESTLEY *Daylight on Saturday* xxxviii. 301, I wish you'd leave here—join up or something.

16. Of a thing: **a.** To become or be connected or continuous with (something else); **b.** to be adjacent to, to adjoin.

1702 ADDISON *Dial. Medals* (1727) 82 The two hands that joyn one another are Emblems of Fidelity. **1837** SIR F. PALGRAVE *Merch. & Friar* (1844) 90 The bare-worn places join one another, all the grass between them is destroyed. **1855** TENNYSON *Brook* 48, I chatter, chatter, as I flow To join the brimming river. **1860** TYNDALL *Glac.* I. viii. 57 A rivulet..was joined by the stream whose track I had pursued. *Mod.* The Cherwell joins the Thames just below Oxford. His land joins mine.

V. *Phrases*, from prec. senses.

†**17.** ***to join action***: To enter upon a debate or dispute. *Obs.*

1588 GREENE *Perimedes* D iij, Perymides hearing his wife to alledge such sound reasons for Gamsters, thought to ioyne action with her in this manner. You resemble wife those subtill Lawyers, that onely alledge that clause in their euidence, which best serues for the proofe of their plea.

18. a. ***to join battle*** (formerly also ***the battle***): to come together, as opposing forces, and begin a battle (cf. sense 12); to enter upon a battle, or (*fig.*) a contest of any kind.

1455 *Battle of St. Albans* in *Paston Lett.* I. 332 They joynid batayle anon; and it was done with inne di. houre. **1539** BIBLE (Great) *1 Sam.* iv. 2 When they ioyned yᵉ battel, Israel was put to the worse. —— *1 Kings* xx. 29 In the vii. daye the battayle was ioyned. **1605** CAMDEN *Rem.* 190 That morning that he was to ioyne battell with Harold. **1673** LEYCESTER *Antiq. Gt. Brit.* II. II. iv. 122 Both Armies meet near the Town of Lincoln, and being put in order, joyn Battel. **1770** LANGHORNE *Plutarch* (1879) I. 29/2 After the battle was joined, [he] routed his army, and took his city. **1893** R. WILLIAMS in Traill *Soc. Eng.* I. i. 33 When two armies were on the point of joining battle.

†**b.** *intr.* said of the battle. *Obs.*

c **1650** *Earles of Chester* 182 in Furniv. *Percy Folio* I. 280 Vpon the plaine before the towne, the battell Ioyned couragiouslye. **1667** MILTON *P.L.* VI. 108 On the rough edge of battel ere it joyn'd. **1697** DRYDEN *Virg. Georg.* II. 382 Legions in the Field their Front display..Before the Battel joins. **1702** ROWE *Tamerl.* I. i. 396 The tumult of the Battle That hastes to joyn.

19. ***to join hands*** (from 2): **a.** *lit.* (*a*) To fold or clasp one's hands together; (*b*) of two persons, To grasp each the hand of the other, in token of amity, or *spec.* of marriage; (*c*) of a third person

(*e.g.* the priest officiating at marriage), To cause two persons to grasp each other's hand.

1513 MORE in Grafton *Chron.* (1568) II. 761 Eche forgave other, and ioyned their hands together, when.. their hartes were farre a sunder. **1548–9** (Mar.) *Bk. Com. Prayer, Matrimony*, Then shal the prieste ioyne theyr ryght handes together, and say; Those whome god hath ioyned together: let no man put a sundre. **1595** SHAKS. *John* II. i. 532 If thou be pleas'd withall, Command thy sonne and daughter to ioyne hands. **1613** PURCHAS *Pilgrimage* (1614) 532 His hands ioyned in a praying gesture. **1817** COLERIDGE *Sibyl. Leaves, Three Graves*, When the Vicar joined their hands. *a* **1835** MRS HEMANS *Tubal Cain* 50 And men.. In friendship joined their hands. **1861** J. EDMOND *Children's Church at Home* iv. 60 The bridegroom and bride joined hands.

b. *fig.* (*j. hands, j. hand in hand*): To associate, to combine in some action or enterprise; to enter into alliance for some particular end.

1598 FLORIO *Ital. Dict.* Ep. Ded. 1 May it please your Honors to ioyne hand in hand. **1603** KNOLLES *Hist. Turks* 626 Most part of Graecia.. readie to have rebelled and ioyned hands with the Christians. **1713** S. PYCROFT *Brief Enq. Free-think.* 35 The former argue.. The latter urge.. So that one wou'd think they had join'd Hands. **1886** MRS. LYNN LINTON *P. Carew.* xx, A banker.. who joins hands with the lawyer in his ruin of thousands.

20. *to join issue* (†*join in issue*): see ISSUE *sb.* 13. Also elliptically *to join.*

1632 MASSINGER *City Madam* III. ii, There Sir I joyn with you. A due decorum must be kept, the Court Distinguished from the City.

21. With various objects, expressing the result or the nature of the joining: as *to join †affinity, company, concert, † encounter, † unity*, etc.

c **1400** *Destr. Troy* 13831 The coniunctoun vniust is Ioynit vs betwene. **1593** *Tell-Troth's N.Y. Gift* 8 To joyne unity with the whole world. **1611** BIBLE *2 Chron.* xviii. 1 Iehoshaphat.. ioyned affinitie with Ahab. **1632** LITHGOW *Trav.* VIII. 364 Who intending to visit Fez, joyned company with me. **1738** WESLEY *Ps.* CIV. IV. x, 'Till with my Song the list'ning World Join Concert. **1859** REEVE *Brittany* 235 At St. Malo, we joined company, quite accidentally.

22. *to join the ladies*: to go into the room to which the ladies have retired after dinner.

1848 *Punch* XIV. 204/1 (*caption*) Walter, I think you had better join the ladies. **1921** J. M. BARRIE (*title*) Shall we join the ladies? **1956** N. MARSH *Off with his Head* (1957) x. 212 'Join the ladies?' Dr. Otterley suggested, and they did so. **1974** N. FREELING *Dressing of Diamond* 95 And that, thought Richard grinning, will be denounced as 'sexual fascism'... And shall we now join the ladies?

23. *if you can't beat them, join them*: a semi-proverbial assertion applied to a situation where a person crosses to another side or party because he is unable to defeat them by opposition alone.

1955 [see EPISTEMOLOGICAL *a.*]. **1970** *Times* 26 Nov. 12/3 Gale will also be applying for a ticket to the Parliamentary lobby for himself: 'If you can't beat them, join them.'

†join, *v.*^{2} *Obs.* [Aphetic for *ajoyne* (ADJOIN *v.* ¶), for ENJOIN.]

1. *trans.* To enjoin or impose (penance, a task, etc.) upon a person. Const. *to* (the person), or with simple dative. = ENJOIN 2.

1303 R. BRUNNE *Handl. Synne* 11782 Blelyche in penaunce for to do Alle þat he ioyneþ þe vnto. **1432–50** tr. *Higden* (Rolls) VII. 291. *c* **1440** *Jacob's Well* 112 þat makyth a man noȝt gladly to do penaunce þat þe preest ioyneth hym. **1528** TINDALE *Obed. Chr. Man* Wks. (1573) 155 They ioyne them penaunce, as they call it.

2. To enjoin or charge (a person) *to* (the task), or with inf. or subord. clause; rarely with complement (quot. *c* 1400). = ENJOIN 2 c, e.

13.. *E.E. Allit. P.* B. 877 Who Ioyned þe be Iostyse our iapez to blame. *c* **1400** *Rom. Rose* 2355 First, I ioigne the, here in penaunce,—That.. Thou set thy thought in thy loving To last withouten repenting. *a* **1450** *Knt. de la Tour* (1868) 52 And they that dede the dede were ioyned to penaunce. **1563** LORD J. GRAY in Ellis *Orig. Lett.* Ser. II. II. 273, I wolde I were the Queenes Confessor this Lent, that I might joine her in pennaunce to forgeve and forget. **1563** *Homilies* II. *On Rogat. Week* III, Remember.. your duetie of thankes... Stil ioyne your selfe to continue in thankes geuinge.

Hence **†joined** *ppl. a.*

c **1475** *Partenay* 5145 To go and do ioyed pennaunce.

join-, the verb-stem used in combination, as in **†join-hand** *sb.*, cursive handwriting, JOINING-HAND; whence **†join-hand** *v. intr.*, to write 'join-hand'; **†join-work**, work of joining, operation of combining (*obs.*).

a **1652** BROME *Queen & Conc.* IV. iii. Wks. 1873 II. 88, 3. *Girl.* Pray shall I have a *Joyn-hand Copy next? *Eul.* No child, you must not Joyn-hand yet. **1711** ADDISON *Spect.* No. 7 ¶1 A little Boy.. told her, that he was to go into Join-hand on Thursday. **1768–74** TUCKER *Lt. Nat.* (1834) II. 75 The four elements.. by their different commixtures produce other secondary elements,.. which being mingled .. generate all the grosser bodies.. By this wonderful *join-work the stores of nature are supplied.

joinable (ˈdʒɔɪnəb(ə)l), *a.* *rare*$^{-0}$. [a. OF. *joignable*, in 15th c. *joinnable*, f. *joindre* to JOIN: see -ABLE.] Capable of being joined.

1483 *Cath. Angl.* 199/2 Iuneabylle, *jungibilis.*

joinant (ˈdʒɔɪnənt), *a.* Forms: 4–5 ioynant, 5 ioyn(e)aunt, iunant, 9 joinant. [a. F. *joignant*, pr. pple. (used adj.) of *joindre* to join: see -ANT^1.]

†1. Adjoining, adjacent: = JOINING *ppl. a.* 2. *Obs.*

c **1386** CHAUCER *Knt's T.* 202 The grete tour.. Was euene ioynant to the gardyn wal. **1447–8** SHILLINGFORD *Lett.* 86 A cloyster joynaunt to the seide Cathedrall Churche.

2. *Her.* = CONJOINED c.

1828–40 BERRY *Encycl. Her.* I. Gloss., *Joinant*, a term in Heraldry, which signifies the same as *conjoined.*

joinder (ˈdʒɔɪndə(r)). [a. F. *joindre* to JOIN, pres. inf. taken subst.] The act of joining; conjunction, union.

1601 SHAKS. *Twel. N.* v. i. 160 A Contract of eternall bond of loue, Confirm'd by mutuall ioynder of your hands. **1884** J. SHARMAN *Hist. Swearing* viii. 155 This incongruous and perfectly irrelevant joinder of words. **1887** S. D. HORTON *Silver Pound* p. xi, The reason of this joinder of subjects is apparent.

b. *spec.* in *Law*, in various connexions: see quots.

1607 COWELL *Interpr.*, *Ioynder* is the coupling of two in a suite or action against another. **1768** BLACKSTONE *Comm.* III. xxi. 315 Upon either a general, or such a special demurrer, the opposite party avers it to be sufficient, which is called a joinder in demurrer, and then the parties are at issue in point of law. **1848** WHARTON *Law Lex.*, *Joinder in action*,.. *Joinder in pleading.* **1883** *Ibid.* (ed. 7) s.v. *Parties*, The Judicature Act, 1875, Ord. XVI., has made very full provisions as to the joinder of parties and the consequences of misjoinder and nonjoinder. **1875** *Rules Supreme Crt.* XIX. xxi, Such joinder of issue shall operate as a denial of every material allegation of facts.

joined (dʒɔɪnd), *ppl. a.*^{1} [f. JOIN *v.*^{1} + -ED^1.]

1. Put together, connected, combined, united, etc.: see the verb.

1483 *Cath. Angl.* 199/2 Iuned, *coniunctus.* **1704** *Addr. Canterbury* 15 Aug. in *Lond. Gaz.* No. 4047/2 The Joyn'd Forces of Your Majesty's Enemies. **1742** RICHARDSON *Pamela* IV. 201 Pointing to the Backs of three Chairs, which I had placed in a join'd Row. **1885** *Athenæum* 21 Mar. 375/3 A new shorthand, with joined vowels.

2. Put together, as a whole; constructed by joining the parts; *spec.* of furniture, etc., Made by a joiner. ? *Obs.* *joined stool*: see JOINT-STOOL.

1434 [see JOINT-STOOL 1]. **1520** SIR R. ELYOT *Will* in *T. Elyot's Gov.* (1883) I. App. A. 312 Al my beddyng and naprye.., except my ioyned presse. **1560** *Trinity Coll. Inv.* in Willis & Clark *Cambridge* (1886) III. 361 Item three Joyned trustles vnder the highe table. Item a joynid Chare for the maister. **1588** *Will* in *Trans. Cumb. & West. Arch. Soc.* X. 41 One coverlett one blanckett and also one ioyned bedstead. **1699** DAMPIER *Voy.* II. 62 In laying on the lack upon good and fine joyned work they frequently spoil the joynts, edges, or corners of drawers of cabinets.

3. That has joined, or become a member of, some society; received into membership.

1849 C. BRONTE *Shirley* viii. 110 Praise God!.. I'm a joined Methody! **1889** *Tablet* 2 Nov. 691 A 'joined member' of the Wesleyan Society.

†joined, *ppl. a.*^{2}: see JOIN *v.*^{2}, to enjoin.

joiner (ˈdʒɔɪnə(r)), *sb.* Forms: 4–6 ioynour, -or, -ar, (5 ionyowre, ionour, iunour), 5–7 ioyner, (6 ioigner), 6–7 ioiner, 7–8 joyner, 7– joiner. [ME. *ioynour*, a. AF. *joignour*, OF. *joigneor*, f. *joigner* to JOIN: subseq. conformed to agent-nouns in *-er*: see -OR, -ER^1.]

1. a. One who joins, connects, unites: see JOIN *v.*^{1}

1483 *Cath. Angl.* 199/2 A Ionour, *junctor*,.. *confederator.* **1503** HAWES *Examp. Virt.* XIII. viii, O ioyner of vertue and well of vnyte. *a* **1619** FOTHERBY *Atheom.* II. i. §8 Some, Housewrights; some, Shipwrights;.. some, the Ioyners of smaller workes. **1642** C. VERNON *Consid. Excheq.* 38 The two Deputy Chamberlaines, being Joyners of the Tallies.

b. One who makes a habit of joining societies, etc. Cf. JOIN *v.*^{1} 15 b. *colloq.* (orig. *U.S.*).

1890 *Ann Arbor* (Mich.) *Reg.* 13 Mar., Ypsilanti is a good place for 'jiners'. There are.. 100 societies and organizations that a person can join. **1923** R. MACAULAY *Told by Idiot* 36 That was Stanley's headlong manner of entering into movements. She was a great and impetuous joiner. **1957** *Times Lit. Suppl.* 15 Nov. 690/2 He is not a 'joiner', that [is] he resists the temptation to cash in on stock fashionable attitudes. **1967** W. MURRAY *Sweet Ride* vii. 109 I'm not a joiner, you know? I mean, all they do is party, party, party all the time. **1971** *Guardian* 6 July 8/5 You could not see Bogart as a marcher or a singer or a joiner—he was strictly solo. **1973** C. MULLARD *Black Brit.* III. vii. 78 Sadly, this meant that people who were not 'joiners', but who might have been active in race relations, were not considered.

2. a. A craftsman whose occupation it is to construct things by joining pieces of wood; a worker in wood who does lighter and more ornamental work than that of a *carpenter*, as the construction of the furniture and fittings of a house, ship, etc.

1386 *Pat. Roll 9 Rich. II*, I. memb. 3. 10 Jan., Joynour. **1412–20** LYDG. *Chron. Troy* II. xi, For eche caruer and curious ioyner. **1428** *E.E. Wills* 82 Y be-quethe to Iohn Hewet, Ioynour, my cosyn.. vjs. viijd. **1523** *Act 14 & 15 Hen. VIII*, c. 2 Vsing any of the misteries.. of smithes, joigners, or coupars. **1563** SHUTE *Archit.* Aij b, Enbroderers, Caruers, Ioynars, Glassyers. **1649** FULLER *Just Man's Fun.* 23 Let.. the most exquisite Joyner make the coffin. **1710** *Tatler* No. 252 ¶4 What Method is to be taken to make Joiners and other Artificers get out of a House they have once entered. **1872** YEATS *Techn. Hist. Comm.* 43 The workshops.. of joiners and cabinet-makers.

b. In possessive case, denoting tools used specially by joiners: see quot. 1875. *joiner's work*: (*a*) the work or occupation of a joiner; (*b*) woodwork made by a joiner.

1530 PALSGR. 234/2 Ioyners worke, *menvserie.* **1647** CLARENDON *Hist. Reb.* I. §199 Inclosing it with a Rail of Joiners Work. **1823** P. NICHOLSON *Pract. Build.* 236 The Joiner's Bench is composed of a platform or top, supported by four substantial legs [etc.]. **1825** J. NICHOLSON *Operat. Mechanic* 582 Rebates are also used for ornamenting mouldings, and for many other purposes in joiners' work. **1874** MICKLETHWAITE *Mod. Par. Churches* 130 English joiners' work of the fifteenth century. **1875** KNIGHT *Dict. Mech.* 1217/1 Joiner's-chisel.. Joiner's-clamp.. Joiner's-gage.. Joiner's-plane.

3. *transf.* A machine for doing various kinds of work in wood.

1875 in KNIGHT *Dict. Mech.*

4. *Comb.* **joiner-work** = *joiner's work*: see 2 b. (In quot. 1875 *fig.*)

1562 in *Our Eng. Home* (1861) 161 *note*, Buffet stoles of joyner worke. **1875** LOWELL *Wks.* (1890) IV. 280 There is a passage.. that comes near being fine; but the far greater part is mere joiner-work. **1893** EARL DUNMORE *Pamirs* I. 278, I admired all the joiner-work; the patterns.. were thoroughly Chinese.

Hence **ˈjoiner** *v. intr.*, to do the work of a joiner; **ˈjoinering**, the work of a joiner, or a piece of this.

1839 CARLYLE *Chartism* x. 183 They are twenty-four millions.. weaving, delving.. joinering. **1884** *Manch. Exam.* 17 Nov. 5/2 [He] had a workshop wherein he did carpentering and joinering. **1888** *Pall Mall G.* 24 May 2/1 We found them busy joinering in a room in which, save for uniform of the warder, there was nothing to indicate that the prisoners were not ordinary carpenters.

joinery (ˈdʒɔɪnərɪ). [f. JOINER + -Y^3: see -ERY.]

1. The art or occupation of a joiner; the construction of wooden furniture, fittings, etc.; also *concr.* such articles collectively; things made by a joiner.

1678 MOXON *Mech. Exerc.* iv. (1683) I. 59 Joynery is an Art Manual whereby several Pieces of Wood are so fitted and joyned together by straight Lines, Squares, Miters or any Bevel, that they shall seem one intire Piece. *c* **1695** J. MILLER *Descr. New York* (1843) 31 The trades of joinery, carpentry, masonry. **1794** STEDMAN *Surinam* (1813) II. xxviii. 347 Chests, cupboards, lockers, and all sorts of joinery. **1879** *Cassell's Techn. Educ.* III. 183 The higher branches of joinery approach cabinet-making and wood-carving.

2. *transf.* and *fig.* Work analogous to that of a joiner; the process or product of joining or fitting parts together.

1774 BURKE *Sp. Amer. Taxation* Wks. 1880 I. 425 Lord Chatham.. made an administration, so checkered and speckled; he put together a piece of joinery, so crossly indented. **1826** MISS MITFORD *Village* Ser. II. (1863) 317 That hideous piece of female joinery, a patch-work counterpane. **1828** CARLYLE *Misc., Goethe* (1872) I. 186 Mind.. reasoned of as.. some curious piece of logical joinery.

3. *attrib.*

1727 BRADLEY *Fam. Dict.* s.v. *Frames*, Wooden Joinery Work of a triangular Form. **1875** *Carpentry & Join.* 106 Gloucester, in which town were then steam joinery works.

join-hand: see JOIN-.

joining (ˈdʒɔɪnɪŋ), *vbl. sb.* [f. JOIN *v.*^{1} + -ING^1.]

1. The action of the verb JOIN, or the fact of being joined. **a.** Connexion, combination, union.

1398 TREVISA *Barth. De P.R.* XVI. xix. (Bodl. MS) 172 b/1 Glew.. is good to Ioynynge of schippis. **1540** *Act 32 Hen. VIII*, c. 30 §1 Ioynyng of issues, and other pleadynges. **1620** T. GRANGER *Div. Logike* 178 Syntaxis is a part of Grammar, that teacheth the true joyning of words together. **1726** LEONI *Alberti's Archit.* I. 9/2 The joyning of those two Arches, intersecting each other, makes an Angle. **1856** EMERSON *Eng. Traits, Aristocracy* Wks. (Bohn) II. 77 Time and law have made the joining and moulding perfect.

b. The action of coming together in conflict; engagement, encounter. Also *joining of battle.*

c **1400** *Rowland & O.* 454 Thies kene knyghtis to-gedir gan glide,.. theyre Ioynynge was so harde that tyde. **1549** *Compl. Scot.* To Rdr. 14 Befor the iunyng of ane battel. **1613** PURCHAS *Pilgrimage* (1614) 352 That his souldiers should in the first ioyning with the enemie sing certaine Hymnes. **1618** BOLTON *Florus* II. vi. (1636) 96 An huge earthquake at the joyning of the battels.. had forewarned our rash General of the event.

c. The occupation or work of a joiner; joinery.

1680 MOXON *Mech. Exerc.* xi. §3 (1683) I. 193 The Office of Smoothing Plains in Joyning and Carpentry.

2. quasi-*concr.* **a.** An instance of such action or state; the place where two things or parts of something join or are joined; a junction, joint.

1382 WYCLIF *Col.* ii. 19 Al the body by bondis and ioynyngis to gidere vndirmynistrid and maad. **1483** *Cath. Angl.* 199/2 A Iunynge, *compages, compago, iunctura.* **1530** PALSGR. 235/1 Ioyning of bordes, *joincture.* **1611** BIBLE *1 Chron.* xxii. 3 Dauid prepared yron.. for the nailes for the doores of the gates, and for the ioynings. **1764** REID *Inquiry* vi. §22 (1801) 395 In the steeple.. the joinings of the stones are clearly perceptible. **1859** GULLICK & TIMBS *Paint.* 149 These joinings are unavoidable: these divisions.. are among the tests of fresco painting properly so called.

b. Something that joins or connects two things; a piece forming a junction.

c **1384** CHAUCER *H. Fame* III. 97 Eke the halle and euery boure, Wythouten peces or ioynynges. **1816** KIRBY & SP. *Entomol.* (1843) I. 424 Each group connected with those next it by slight joinings of wax.

3. *attrib.* or *Comb.*, as **joining-place** (in quot. = place for joining battle); †**joining-work** = joiner's work; see JOINER 2 b.

1513 DOUGLAS *Æneis* X. viii. 47 Formast he bownys to the ioynyng place. **1562** *Richmond Wills & Inv.* (Surtees 1853) 162 One counter of joynyng work.

joining, *ppl. a.* [f. as prec. + -ING².]

1. That joins; connecting, uniting, etc.

1483 *Cath. Angl.* 199/2 Iunynge, *coniungens.* *a* **1631** DONNE *Poems* (1650) 60 Our hopes joyning blisse. **1885** LEUDESDORF *Cremona's Proj. Geom.* 13 Produce the joining line to cut *OI* in *I'*.

2. Adjoining, adjacent, contiguous: see JOIN *v.* 8. Now *rare* or *Obs.*

c **1385** CHAUCER *L.G.W.* 1962 (*Ariadne*) The tour.. Was Ioynynge in the wal to a foreyne. **1530–77** H. RHODES *Bk. Nurture* in *Babees Bk.* 67 Other that syt ioyning by them. **1616** *Marlowe's Faust.* 1228, I have a castle joining near these woods. **1747** MRS. DELANY *Life & Corr.* (1861) II. 473 A pretty field.. joining to my garden. **1858** HAWTHORNE *Fr. & It. Jrnls.* (1872) I. 10 The Tuileries joining to the Louvre.

†**joining-hand.** *Obs.* [f. prec. sb. or adj. + HAND *sb.* 16.] Handwriting in which the successive letters of each word are joined; cursive writing.

1583 HOLLYBAND *Campo di Fior* 339 First I will write you, A, b, c, Then syllables: Then ioyning hande. **1612** BRINSLEY *Lud. Lit.* 31 Vnder them both a line or two of ioyning hand. **1809–12** MAR. EDGEWORTH *Mad. de Fleury* xi, The youngest .. had but just begun to learn joining-hand.

†'**joiningly,** *adv. Obs.* [f. JOINING *ppl. a.* + -LY².] In the way of junction or connexion, jointly, unitedly; in the way of contiguity, adjacently.

c **1430** *Pilgr. Lyf Manhode* II. xvii. (1869) 81 Hadde j not yit lerned that thou and Rude entendement weren oon ioyningeliche [F. *conioynctement*]. **1562** J. HEYWOOD *Prov. & Epigr.* (1867) 99 We two hauyng.. Dwelt wall to wall, so ioygninglie That whispering soundeth through welny.

†'**joinpee, joynpee,** *adv. Obs. rare*⁻¹. [a. F. *joint* joined + *pié, pied* foot.] With the feet joined or put close together.

c **1430** *Pilgr. Lyf Manhode* IV. ix. (1869) 180, I strogle and lepe diches joynpee [*les piez ioincts*].

join stool (*joyne stoole*): see JOINT-STOOL.

joint (dʒɔɪnt), *sb.* Forms: 3–7 ioynt, 4–6 ioynte, iointe, (ioynct(e, 5 geynt(t)e, iuynt, iunte, ionte, yonte, yuncte, 6–7 ioinct, ioint, 7 jonct, 8 *Sc.* junt), 7– joint. [a. OF. *joint* and *jointe*, sb. use of *joint, -te* (:—L. *junctum, juncta*), pa. pple. of *joindre* to join.]

I. The place or part at which two things or parts are joined or fitted together; a junction.

1. An arrangement, structure, or mechanism in an animal body, whereby two bones (or corresponding parts of an invertebrate animal) are fitted together, either rigidly, or (*esp.*) so as to move upon one another; an articulation.

c **1290** *S. Eng. Leg.* I. 186/42 Euerech Ioynt and senue. **1388** WYCLIF *Dan.* x. 16 My ioynctis ben vnknit. *c* **1400** *Lanfranc's Cirurg.* 19 In bringyng to her placis ioyntis þat ben oute. **1422** tr. *Secreta Secret., Priv. Priv.* 227 Tho men whych haue the neke wel dystyncted by his yontes. *c* **1460** *Towneley Myst.* xxiii. 307 It will breke ilk ionte in hym. **1553** EDEN *Treat. Newe Ind.* (Arb.) 15 There be some men which thincke that Elephantes haue no ioyntes in theyr legges. **1582** STANYHURST *Æneis* III. (Arb.) 75 A cold sweat saltish through my ioynctes fiercely dyd enter. **1593** SHAKS. *Rich. II,* III. iii. 75 How dare thy ioynts forget To pay their awfull dutie to our presence? **1665** MANLEY *Grotius' Low C. Warres* 299 For avoiding the Gout, and other pains of the Joynts. **1726** LEONI *Alberti's Archit.* III. 34/1 The Joynt of the Wrist. **1873** MIVART *Elem. Anat.* ii. 23 The contiguous surfaces of such movable bones form the joints.

2. Phr. *out of joint.* **a.** *lit.* Said of a bone displaced from its articulation with another; dislocated; also of the part or member affected.

to put any one's nose out of joint: see NOSE.

1393 LANGL. *P. Pl.* C. x. 215 He.. is lame, oþer his leg out of ioynte. *c* **1400** *Lanfranc's Cirurg.* 62 Whanne.. þe boon.. is to-broke atwo and dislocate—þat is to seie out of ioynte. **1535** COVERDALE *Ps.* xxi[i.] 14 All my bones are out of ioynt. *a* **1586** SIDNEY *Arcadia* II. 109 Had her shoulder put out of joinct. **1652** CULPEPPER *Eng. Physic.* 3 It helpeth to strengthen the members that be out of joynt. **1712** ARBUTHNOT *John Bull* III. x, He had like to have shook his shoulder out of joint.

b. *fig.* Disordered, perverted, out of order, disorganized. (Said of things, conditions, etc.; formerly also of persons in relation to conduct.)

1415 HOCCLEVE *To Sir J. Oldcastle* 200 Thow haast been out of ioynt al to longe. **1513** MORE in Grafton *Chron.* (1568) II. 766 They might peradventure bring the matter so farre out of ioynt, that it should never be brought in frame againe. **1602** SHAKS. *Ham.* I. v. 188 The time is out of ioynt: Oh cursed spight, That euer I was borne to set it right. **1842** TENNYSON *Locksley Hall* 133 All things here are out of joint. **1871** LOWELL *Pope* Pr. Wks. 1890 IV. 18 The loyalty of everybody both in politics and in religion had been put out of joint.

3. A part of the stem of a plant from which a leaf or branch grows (esp. when thickened, as in grasses, so as to resemble a knee- or elbow-joint); a node.

1523 FITZHERB. *Husb.* §138 Se that it haue a good knot or ioynte and an euen. **1552** HULOET, Ioynt of a cane, rede, strawe, or suche lyke, *geniculum, nodus.* **1688** R. HOLME *Armoury* II. 84/2 The knot or joynt from whence a years growth proceeds. **1698** FRYER *Acc. E. India & P.* 105 Its Leafs are small, and come out at its Joints. **1863** FR. A. KEMBLE *Resid. in Georgia* 87 From each of the notches or joints of the recumbent cane. **1866** *Treas. Bot.* 516/2 G[*aleopsis*] *Tetrahit*.. is well marked by its hispid stem, which is singularly swollen beneath the joints.

4. a. That wherein or whereby two component members or elements of an artificial structure or mechanism are joined or fitted together, either so as to be rigidly fixed (as *e.g.* bricks, stones, pieces of timber, rails, lengths of pipe, etc.), or so that one can move upon the other while still remaining connected with it (as in a hinge, pivot, swivel).

universal joint, a contrivance by which one of two connected parts of a machine is made capable of moving freely in any direction with respect to the other.

c **1420** *S. Etheldred* 718 in Horstm. *Altengl. Leg.* (1881) 298 þat ston was well ygraue euery geyntte. *c* **1440** *Promp. Parv.* 264/2 Ioynte, or knytty[n]ge to-gedur, what so they be, *compago.* **14..** *Voc.* in Wr.-Wülcker 590/46 *Junctura*, a Juynt. **1550** *Churchw. Acc. St. Mich., Cornhill,* For new joynts and ij cramps to Mr. Machyns pewe dore. **1589** NASHE *Pasq. & Marforius* 9 The ioyntes of that house begin to gape. **1613** PURCHAS *Pilgrimage* (1614) 876 Stones.. so cunningly layed that one could not see the ioints. **1703** T. N. *City & C. Purchaser* 51 Let Care be taken that Bricks be not laid Joynt on Joynt. **1831** BREWSTER *Nat. Magic* xi. (1833) 275 The part.. to which the quadrants are attached, moves on a joint. **1856** S. C. BREES *Gloss. Terms* 463 The universal joint is of great use for conveying angular motion when it can be applied in couplings. **1884** W. C. SMITH *Kildrostan* I. iii. 174 There is no armour but it has its joints, And where the joints are there the arrow sticks. **1893** *Law Times* XCV. 62/2 The joints of the pipes were not properly cemented.

b. *to break joint:* see BREAK *v.* 31. †*breaking joint,* an arrangement of bricks, stones, timbers, etc. in which the joints are not continuous (*obs.*).

1663 GERBIER *Counsel* 44 That the Bording be with breaking Joynts. **1856** OLMSTED *Slave States* 666 Planting is done by laying the cuttings.. three always together, with the eyes of each a little removed from those of the others—that is, all 'breaking joints'.

c. *Bookbinding.* The flexible cloth or leather which forms the junction between the spine and the sides of the binding of a book; also the projection along the edge of this junction.

1835 J. HANNETT *Bibliopegia* 104 The volume being laid upon the table or press, with the head towards the workman and the upper board open, the guard or false end paper must be removed and all other substances cleared out of the joint with the folder. **1861** *Chambers's Encycl.* II. 226/2 Coming to his hands flat and solid, and with its joints well formed. **1894** *Amer. Dict. Printing & Bookmaking* 313/2 *Joints*, the projection formed in backing to admit the millboards. The leather or cloth placed from the projection to the millboard is called a joint. **1901** D. COCKERELL *Bookbinding* xii. 165 Ensure that there is enough leather in the turn-in of the joint to allow the cover to open freely. **1951** L. TOWN *Bookbinding by Hand* xvi. 203 If a slight amount of moisture is still present the leather will bed itself very neatly into position in the joint. **1967** V. STRAUSS *Printing Industry* x. 673/2 Backing does not give the book a new back but provides the joints of the back.

5. *Geol.* A crack or fissure intersecting a mass of rock; usually occurring in sets of parallel planes, dividing the mass into more or less regular blocks.

1601 HOLLAND *Pliny* II. 611 The Bactrian Emerauds.. be in chinks and ioints (as it were) of rocks in the sea. **1761** CATCOTT *Treat. Deluge* III. (1768) 306 The tops of rocks and summits of the highest mountains are sometimes divided by joints into separate pieces. **1833** LYELL *Princ. Geol.* Gloss. s.v., The partings which divide columnar basalt into prisms are joints. **1882** GEIKIE *Text-bk. Geol.* IV. II. 501 All rocks are traversed more or less distinctly by vertical, or highly inclined planes termed Joints.

†**6.** A connecting point of time. *Obs. rare.*

a **1638** MEDE *Wks.* (1672) 585 To shew the connexion of that vision of the book with the joynt which begins the seventh Trumpet. *a* **1679** T. GOODWIN *Knowl. Father & Son* in Spurgeon *Treas. Dav.* Ps. cii. 24, I note these several joints of time, because the Scripture notes them.

II. One of the parts or sections by the longitudinal union of which a body is made up.

7. A portion of an animal or plant body connected with another portion by a joint or articulation (see 1–3); *esp.* such a portion or section of a limb, or of the stem of a plant, an internode.

1377 LANGL. *P. Pl.* B. XVII. 175 Þe paume hath powere to put oute alle þe ioyntes, And to vnfolde þe folden fuste. *c* **1420** *Pallad. on Husb.* v. 162 Kitte out a ioynt of reed, and in the side Therof let make an hole. *c* **1420** *St. Etheldred* 880 in Horstm. *Altengl. Leg.* (1881) 302 þat ston was y-shape as mete for hurre body.. þat no geynte of hurre body lay þerinne amys. **1606** SHAKS. *Tr. & Cr.* IV. v. 233, I haue with exact view perus'd thee Hector, And quoted ioynt by ioynt. **1697** DRYDEN *Virg. Past.* II. 45 Of seven smooth Joints a mellow Pipe I have. **1828** STARK *Elem. Nat. Hist.* II. 303 Antennæ short, of nine joints. **1869** HUXLEY *Phys.* i. (ed. 3) 7 The several joints of the fingers and toes have the common denomination of *phalanges*.

8. *spec.* One of the portions into which a carcass is divided by the butcher, consisting of one or more bones (e.g. that of the leg or shoulder) with the meat thereon; *esp.* as cooked and served at table.

1576 GASCOIGNE *Flowers* Wks. (1587) 40 An olde frutedish is bigge ynough to hold a ioynte of meate. **1592** NASHE *P. Penilesse* (ed. 2) 21 There being one ioynt of flesh on the table. **1617** MORYSON *Itin.* III. 115 They serve small peeces of flesh (not whole joints as with us). **1726** SWIFT *Gulliver* III. ii, The joints that were served to his majesty's table. **1883** MATTIEU WILLIAMS in *Knowledge* 11 May 274 A single wing rib, or other joint of three to five pounds weight.

†**9.** *gen.* A portion, 'article', item. *Obs. rare.*

1303 R. BRUNNE *Handl. Synne* 5093 Y rede we þanke hym of euery poynt, Syn we may nat forbere þe lest Ioynt.

III. Something constructed with a joint or joints.

†**10.** (*app.*) A snuff-box (with a hinged lid). *Obs.*

c **1701** CIBBER *Love makes Man* III. iii, Sir, I have lost my Snuff-box... I'll go to Paris, split me.. They make the best joynts in Europe there.

11. *Betting slang.* An outside bookmaker's paraphernalia of list-frame, umbrella, etc., some of which are joined together in movable pieces.

1899 *Daily News* 15 Mar. 5/5 It was positively ridiculous to see the police knocking down bookmakers' 'joints' every time the inspector came round, and looking passively on all the rest of the time.

b. ***flat joint, set joint, strong joint:*** see the adjs.

IV. †**12.** = JOINTURE 4. *Obs.*

1513 BRADSHAW *St. Werburge* I. 1900 Whiche place was gyuen to her Ioynt and dowry By Tombert her husbande. *Ibid.* 1951 Whiche (as afore is sayd) was her Ioynt and dowry.

†**13.** A coming together, meeting; the action of joining battle; attack, onset. *Obs.*

c **1540** tr. *Pol. Virg. Eng. Hist.* (Camden No. 29) 68 At the first ioncte [L. *in primo congressu*] many fell on both sides.

14. *slang* or *colloq.* (chiefly *U.S.*). A partnership or union, or a place of meeting or resort, esp. of persons engaged in some illicit occupation; *spec.* (in America) a place illegally kept (usually by Chinese) for opium-smoking, an opium-den; also applied to illicit drinking-saloons. More generally, a place; a house.

1821 *Real Life in Ireland* xvii. 199, I had my education at the boarding-school of Phelim Firebrass..; and when I slipt the joint, and fang'd the arm, he strengthened the sinews. **1877** *Sessions Papers Cent. Criminal Court* 25 Oct. 631 The *joints*—that means the offices where the swindle was carried on—that is a cant word. **1880** *Weekly Times* 4 Jan. 8/3 They soon found him a 'joint' to do... Doing a 'joint' means effecting a burglarious entrance. **1883** *Harper's Mag.* Nov. 945/1, I have.. smoked opium in every joint in America. **1885** *Homilet. Rev.* Aug. 179 A few months since the police made a raid on a 'joint' at No. 44 Clinton Place, and found seven men there smoking the drug. **1885** *Daily Tel.* 18 Aug. 3/2 (Farmer) This class of thieves, when they agree on a partnership or joint, as the slang phrase is, work one for the other as they best can. **1887** *Lippincott's Mag.* (U.S.) Aug. 290 The student, upon reaching his 'joint', as the club is called, hurriedly bolts a few mouthfuls of breakfast and swallows a cup of coffee. **1899** ROWNTREE & SHERWELL *Temperance Prob.* iii. 197 There were from sixty to eighty 'joints' (i.e. illicit liquor places) in the city. **1904** *Sun* (N.Y.) 6 Mar. 7/4 Of course, there are no saloons in Kansas; no one would dream of calling them by that name. They are all 'joints', whether the drinks are passed over a polished counter by a white aproned attendant, or shoved through a hole in the wall by a dirty fist. **1905** 'H. MCHUGH' *You can search Me* 20, I took Clara J. to the St. Regis to dinner... It's a swell joint, all right. **1912** *Maclean's Mag.* Sept. 69/2 Mr. Kelley, to whom few streets were unfamiliar, knew the place exteriorly as a 'Dago joint'. *a* **1922** T. S. ELIOT *Waste Land Drafts* (1971) 59 line 50 So the men.. thought Of home, and dollars, and the pleasant violin At Marm Brown's joint, and the girls and gin. **1925** H. L. FOSTER *Trop. Tramp with Tourists* 32 Been to Havana? Good Lord! I've been to that damned joint with Cook, Clarke, Frank, Raymond-Whitcomb, and the American Express. **1934** WODEHOUSE *Right Ho, Jeeves* xiv. 167 Hanging out in a joint called Kingham Manor. **1935** A. SQUIRE *Sing Sing Doctor* v. 73 In cities the market for brothels, gambling joints, & narcotic dens is better. **1946** F. SARGESON *That Summer* 55, I found a joint that was kept by a Mrs. Clegg. **1953** G. LAMMING *In Castle of my Skin* xiv. 282, I see one or two things change round this joint... I mean the village. **1959** 'A. GILBERT' *Death takes Wife* xv. 198 Put down money for a joint you didn't frisk in advance. **1959** 'M. M. KAYE' *House of Shade* iii. 31 He turns the joint upside down until he finds it. **1974** *Listener* 13 June 766/2 A rather pokey, smokey little jazz joint in San Francisco.

b. *Fairground slang.* A stall, tent, etc., in a circus or fair; a concession stand. orig. *U.S.*

1927 *Amer. Speech* June 414 A carnival concession is known as a joint or store. **1931** *Amer. Mercury* Nov. 353/1 *Joint*, any concession stand, or novelty spindle. **1934** P. ALLINGHAM *Cheapjack* ii. 16 'You can build up yonder... Where's your joint?'.. It took some time to discover that by a 'joint' he meant my tent. **1968** D. BRAITHWAITE *Fairground Archit.* 22 The tober is a composite of many elements—roundabouts, booths, joints, and transport vehicles. *Ibid.* 68 Joints fall into roughly three categories—round ones, generically termed hoop-las, side-stuff,.. and casual stalls for vending.

c. A marijuana cigarette; also, hypodermic equipment used by drug addicts.

1935 A. J. POLLOCK *Underworld Speaks* 65/1 *Joint*, a complete hypodermic outfit consisting of syringe and needles (ointjay). **1938** *Amer. Speech* XIII. 186/1 *Joint.* The hollow needle, or a substitute... The hypodermic outfit including all accessories... The opium smoker's outfit complete. **1952** G. MANDEL *Flee Angry Strangers* 171 You got a couple of joints to take along?.. I know I'll want to get on. Take some pod, Dinch. **1967** M. M. GLATT et al. *Drug Scene* i. 5 In Britain, cannabis is.. almost always smoked in

the form of a cigarette which is referred to as a smoke, joint or reefer. **1970** *Times* 28 Apr. 10/8 (*caption*) Please fasten your seat belts and extinguish your joints. **1971** *Black Scholar* Sept. 33/1 When the shower stopped he lit two joints and went to the bathroom. **1972** *Daily Tel.* 3 Apr. 8 The making of the joint seemed to be as much a part of the ritual as smoking it.

d. Prison. *U.S. slang.*

1953 W. BURROUGHS *Junkie* (1972) xii. 124 He said even the best thieves spend most of their time in the joint. **1969** C. F. BURKE *God is Beautiful, Man* (1970) 27 She made things so rotten for him that the king threw him in the joint. **1972** J. WAMBAUGH *Blue Knight* (1973) i. 28 He was a no-good asshole and belonged in the joint.

V. 15. *attrib.* and *Comb.*, as (in sense 1) ***joint-adhesion***, ***-disease***, ***-pain***, ***-stiffening***; ***joint-like***, ***-racking*** adjs.; (in sense 4) ***joint-collar***, ***-end***, ***-maker***, ***-making***, ***-pin***, ***-splice***, ***-strip***, ***-test***; (sense 5) ***joint-face***, ***-filling***, ***-surface***; **joint-bedded** *a.* (*Masonry*), of a stone: placed so that its natural bed (or horizontal surface) forms a vertical joint of the work; distinguished from *face-bedded*, in which the horizontal surface is made to form the face of the work; **joint bolt**, a bolt for holding together the two parts of a joint; *spec.* (see quots. *a* 1884, 1964); **joint box**, a junction-box, esp. one designed to be filled with an insulating material; **joint-chair** (*Railways*), a chair (see CHAIR *sb.* 12) supporting the rails at a joint; **joint-coupling**, 'a form of universal joint for coupling sections of shafting' (Knight); **joint-evil**, a name of *Elephantiasis nodosa*; **joint-file**, a small file of circular section, used for dressing the holes in hinge-joints; **joint-fir**, a name for plants of the N.O. *Gnetaceæ*; **joint-hinge**, the same as a strap-hinge; **joint-ill** (see quot.); **joint mouse** *Med.* [tr. G. *gelenkmaus* (see quot. 1886)], a loose fragment (as of cartilage or bone) floating in the cavity of a joint; usu. *pl.*; **joint-oil**, the secretion which lubricates the joints between the bones, synovia; **joint-pipe**, a small section of gas- or steam-pipe, forming a connexion between two lengths of pipe; **joint-plane** *Geol.*, a plane in rock in which a joint exists or is liable to form; also, an exposed surface that was once such a plane; **joint-pliers**, a small kind of pliers used by watchmakers and mathematical instrument makers; **joint-rule**, a rule made of pieces jointed or hinged together so as to fold up; **joint-saw**, a saw with a curved working face, used in making the joints of compasses and the like; **joint set** *Geol.*, a group of parallel joints; †**joint-sick**, *a.*, diseased in the joints; so †**joint-sickness**, disease of the joints; gout; **joint-snake** = *glass-snake* (see GLASS *sb.*[1] 16); †**joint-sponge**, a morbid spongy concretion in the joints (*obs.*); **joint system** *Geol.*, a group of two or more intersecting joint sets; **joint-vetch**, a leguminous plant of the genus *Æschynomene*, so called from its jointed seed pods; **joint-water**, synovia (= *joint-oil*); *esp.* a flux of this in diseases of the joints; **joint-wire**, tubular wire, used for hinge-joints in watches, etc., a solid wire being passed through it to form the joint; **joint-wood** = JOINTER[2] 3 q.v. See also JOINT-ACHE, -GRASS, etc.

1896 *Allbutt's Syst. Med.* I. 381 The forcible breaking up of *joint-adhesions. **1883** *Stonemason* Jan., A great advantage is gained by working all string courses, cornices, and copings '*joint-bedded' with the exception of quoins which should be placed on their natural bed. **1844** H. STEPHENS *Bk. Farm* II. 75 The top bar..swells out in the middle, where it is perforated for the *joint-bolt of the lever. *a* **1884** KNIGHT *Dict. Mech.* Suppl. 514/2 *Joint bolt*, a bolt used for fastening two timbers, one endwise to the other... Used commonly as a fastening for a bed-rail to the bed-post. **1964** J. S. SCOTT *Dict. Building* 159 *Handrail bolt* or *joint bolt*, a bolt threaded at both ends. **1901** *Chambers's Jrnl.* Dec. 845/2 A new form of *joint-box for forming connections. **1907** J. F. C. SNELL *Distrib. Electr. Energy* v. 269 Joint boxes must be used to connect lengths of cables or conductors equivalent to, or larger than 7-16 S.W.G. **1929** G. W. STUBBINGS *Underground Cable Systems* v. 50 A cast-iron joint box must provide a compound-tight chamber for the filling compound. **1966** J. F. WHITFIELD *Electr. Installations & Regulations* vi. 120 There is some saving in cable but extra man-hours are needed for joint-box connections. **1856** S. C. BREES *Gloss. Terms* 100 The chairs for receiving the ends of two rails are termed *joint, or double chairs. **1889** G. FINDLAY *Eng. Railway* 44 Up to the year 1847 the ends of the rails rested on joint chairs. **1680** MOXON *Mech. Exerc.* xi. §7 (1683) I. 201 The *Joynt-Coller is made of two Iron Cheeks..moving upon a Joint. **1897** *Allbutt's Syst. Med.* III. 73 Neural arthritis comprises all *joint diseases which are the sequel of central or peripheral nerve-lesions. **1677** MOXON *Mech. Exerc.* ii. (1683) I. 19 Put the *Joint-end of the Hinge into the Fire. **1669** B. WELLIS (*title*) Treatise on the *Joint Evil. **1683** TRYON *Way to Health* xix. (1697) 419 Leprous Scabby Diseases, Joint-evils, and that which they call the Kings Evil. **1744** MITCHELL in *Phil. Trans.* XLIII. 144 *Lepra Arabum*, two Species of which are called, the *Yaws*, and the *Joint-Evil*. **1912** *Jrnl. Geol.* XX. 76 The cliff face is in many parts composed of projecting and re-entrant angles formed by the *joint faces of large area meeting in obtuse angles. **1931** *Times Lit. Suppl.* 11 June 466/2 A block of which the bounding joint-faces slope downwards and towards each other will be squeezed upwards. **1961** *Amer. Jrnl. Sci.* CCLIX. 502 The convergence of plumose and radial structures toward the center of the joint face strongly suggests that joints are fractures initiated at a point. **1916** F. H. LAHEE *Field Geol.* viii. 223 By their shape and relations to the surface of unconformity, these *joint fillings may indicate something of the original character and arrangement of the fractures in which they were formed. **1965** G. J. WILLIAMS *Econ. Geol. N.Z.* xiv. 230/1 Soft white veinlets and joint-fillings of crystalline laumontite are abundant in greywackes throughout New Zealand. **1866** *Treas. Bot.* 538/1 *Gnetaceæ.* (*Joint Firs.)..Small trees or creeping shrubs..with jointed stems and branches. **1892** DALZIEL *Dis. Dogs* (ed. 3) 14 Anthrax..a disease of cattle, known in the vernacular as..'*joint ill'. *a* **1661** FULLER *Worthies, Wiltsh.* 145 The *joint-like knots..will fat swine. **1725** *Lond. Gaz.* No. 6380/12 James Low,..*Jointmaker. **1900** *Daily News* 25 Aug. 5/1 The old system of *joint-making by 'junction pieces' or splicing and soldering, has also been abandoned. **1886** H. MARSH *Dis. Joints* xv. 185 On account of the manner in which these bodies change their site, and slip out of reach, the Germans have suggestively called them '*joint-mice' (*gelenk-mäuse*). **1920** R. STOCKMAN *Rheumatism & Arthritis* ix. 115 'Joint-mice', if present, can be felt, and slip from under the fingers in a very characteristic fashion. **1952** E. F. TRAUT *Rheumatic Dis.* ix. 194 A detached portion of the internal meniscus constitutes a loose body or joint mouse. **1961** R. D. BAKER *Essent. Path.* xxi. 560 (*caption*) Aching, weakness and locking, inability to extend left knee, began 11 years previously, following which joint mice were removed on two occasions. **1887** MIVART in *Encycl. Brit.* XXII. 111/1 An albuminous fluid called 'synovia', and commonly known as '*joint-oil'. **1653** R. SANDERS *Physiogn.* bj, Foot-gout, knee-gout, and all *joint-pains whatsoever. **1710** T. FULLER *Pharm. Extemp.* 433 Water of Millepedes..is useful..in scorbutic Joint-pains. **1825** J. NICHOLSON *Operat. Mechanic* 74 The *joint-pins must either have nuts and screws, or other proper fastenings, to keep them in their several places. *Ibid.*, To drill both the arm frames..and the circle..together, that the joint pin-holes in all three may correspond exactly with each other, and particularly from the centre of each. **1855** J. PHILLIPS *Man. Geol.* ii. 44 The cleavage and *joint planes in these beds are not parallel to the general cleavage. **1905** J. GEIKIE *Struct. & Field Geol.* x. 144 Common household coal..is divided by three sets of planes disposed at right angles to each other: namely (*a*) planes of bedding..and (*b*) and (*c*) joint-planes. **1944** A. HOLMES *Princ. Physical Geol.* vi. 76 The joint pattern may also control the course of rivers, the joint planes themselves commonly forming the walls of steep-sided gorges and canyons. **1970** R. J. SMALL *Study of Landforms* iv. 122 The spectacular cliffs on the east side of the A'Chir ridge coincide with near-vertical joint-planes. **1667** MILTON *P.L.* XI. 488 Dropsies, and Asthma's, and *Joint-racking Rheums. **1708** J. PHILIPS *Cyder* II. 77 Joint-racking Gout..and pining Atrophy. **1680** MOXON *Mech. Exerc.* xi. §7 (1683) I. 201 Moving upon a Joint..as the two insides of the *Joynt-Rule Carpenters use. **1692** *Capt. Smith's Seaman's Gram.* II. 160, I have no other Instrument but my Two Foot Joynt Rule. **1931** C. M. NEVIN *Princ. Struct. Geol.* v. 144 That it [*sc.* tension] is the effective stress which caused the actual break has not been proven for dip and strike *joint sets. **1942** *Bull. Geol. Soc. Amer.* LIII. 392 The relationships of the joint sets to other structures indicates their age. **1965** P. C. BADGLEY *Struct. & Tectonic Princ.* iv. 117/1 A close relationship exists between these lineament patterns and regional joint sets. *a* **1618** J. DAVIES *Wit's Pilgr.* (1878) 41/1 How, from this *Ioynt-sick Age to bite the Gowt? **1545** ELYOT *Biblioth.*, *Arthetica passio*,..the *ioynte syckenesse: the goute. **1684** T. GHYLES (*title*) Treatise of the Joint Sickness, or Gout. **1796** MORSE *Amer. Geog.* I. 221 The *joint snake..is a great curiosity, [breaking into pieces when struck, without bleeding]. **1658** A. FOX *Wurtz' Surg.* I. vi. 26 A *Joint-sponge is nothing else but a moisture of the sinew-water, which groweth on and turneth hard, and settleth there. **1943** *Bull. Geol. Soc. Amer.* LIII. 396 On most of the more planar *joint surfaces featherlike or flamelike markings..are found. **1961** *Amer. Jrnl. Sci.* CCLIX. 493 Freshly exposed joint surfaces commonly are marked with faint ridges that form plume-like or radial patterns. **1973** E. E. WAHLSTROM *Tunneling in Rock* v. 102 Joint surfaces that are smooth..commonly display slickensides and contain crushed materials. **1929** C. R. LONGWELL *Pirsson's Textbk. Geol.* (ed. 3) I. xii. 315 In many places there are two prominent sets of joints, approximately at right angles to each other and each set nearly vertical. Such a combination of two or more intersecting sets constitutes a *joint system. **1952** VON ENGELN & CASTER *Geology* xiv. 191 Joint systems are commonly much more distinctively and conspicuously developed in sedimentary than in other classes of rocks. **1973** E. E. WAHLSTROM *Tunneling in Rock* v. 99 Regional geological studies often reveal a systematic geometrical relationship between joint systems and faults and folds. **1829** J. C. LOUDON *Encycl. Plants* 1284 *Arthrolobium...* *Joint-Vetch. **1884** W. MILLER *Dict. Eng. Names Plants* 156/1 *Æschynomene..hispida.* Sensitive Joint-Vetch. **1599** A. M. tr. *Gabelhouer's Bk. Physicke* 324/2 How we shoulde restrayne the fluxion of the Synnue, or *Ioyntewater. **1658** A. FOX *Wurtz' Surg.* II. xiv. 102 The joynt water, that is, the humidity of joynts and sinews. **1753** CHAMBERS *Cycl. Supp.*, *Joint Water*, a term used by our farriers, for..a running of a clear ichor from the Joints, when they are either wounded or ulcerated.

joint, *sb.*[2] *Obs. rare.* [Aphetic f. ENJOINT.] That which is enjoined, injunction, charge.

c **1475** *Partenay* 5019 In that doubte ye noght, in no maner point, Sin ye me commaunde, gree to such a ioynt.

joint (dʒɔɪnt), *a.* Forms: 4-7 **ioynt**, 5-7 **ioint**, (5 **yont**, 6 **iont**, **ioncte**), 7-8 **joynt**, 7- **joint**. See also JUNCT. [a. F. *joint* (:—L. *junctum*), pa. pple. of *joindre*:—L. *jungĕre* to join. In sense 2 often, in other senses occasionally, hyphened to the following sb.]

1. Put together, joined, combined, united.

†**a.** Const. as *pa. pple.* or in predicate. *Obs.*

c **1340** *Cursor M.* 10625 (Trin.) þe witt þe vertu of hir ioynt [*Laud* to hir ioynt] May no mon write wiþ penne poynt. **1390** GOWER *Conf.* I. 253 Whan Pride is with Envie joint. *c* **1400** *Rom. Rose* 2037, I..knelide doun with hondis joynt. *c* **1590** GREENE *Fr. Bacon* ix. 185 Next to him, And joint with him Castile and Saxony are welcome. **1727** *Wodrow Corr.* (1843) III. 280 The Presbytery of Glasgow.. are joint and unanimous for what I know.

b. as adj. in attributive relation. Rarely of material things; usually of the actions or attributes of two or more persons, etc. *spec.* Of the lives of two or more persons: Continuing together in time until one lapses, contemporaneous, concurrent.

1606 SHAKS. *Tr. & Cr.* II. ii. 193 For 'tis a cause that hath no meane dependance, Vpon our ioynt and seuerall dignities. **1641** J. JACKSON *True Evang. T.* II. 120 By their joynt endeavours. **1765** BLACKSTONE *Comm.* I. iii. 214 They therefore settled the crown, first on king William and queen Mary..for their joint lives. **1853** J. H. NEWMAN *Hist. Sk.* (1873) II. I. ii. 59 Civilized by the joint influences of religion and of chivalry. **1883** SIR E. KAY in *Law Times Rep.* XLIX. 261/1 During the joint lives of the trustees.

2. a. Of a person or persons: United or sharing *with* another, or among themselves, *in* some possession, action, liability, etc.; having or doing (what is expressed by the noun) together or in common.

Often hyphened to the following sb., esp. in words of legal or technical use.

1424-5 *E.E. Wills* (1882) 60 Now I declare here my laste wille, als wel to my saide feffez as to my ioint feffes. **1568** BIBLE (Bishops') *Rom.* viii. 17 Heyres of God and ioyntheyres [**1611** ioynt heires] with Christe. **1586** T. B. *La Primaud. Fr. Acad.* I. 106 Joint-laborers with him for honor and glorie. **1607** SHAKS. *Cor.* v. vi. 32, I..Made him ioynt-seruant with me. **1698** F. B. *Free but Modest Censure* 4 Joint-partners in the same Principles. **1708** HEARNE *Collect.* 13 Nov. (O.H.S.) II. 151 Having Two Churches, and Two Joint-Rectors. **1817** W. SELWYN *Law Nisi Prius* (ed. 4) II. 920 Joint owners of property insured for their joint use and on their own account. **1828** P. BINGHAM *Rep. Court Common Pleas* IV. 70 (Adamson v. Jarvis 1827), The Plaintiff and Defendant..must..be both considered as joint tort feasers, and the present action is nothing else but an attempt by one tort feaser to recover contribution from another. **1878** F. S. WILLIAMS *Midl. Railw.* 201 The directors..agreed with the G.N. and Manchester, Sheffield and Lincolnshire lines in becoming joint-owners of the Stockport and Woodley Junction. **1886** [see TORTFEASOR]. **1908** J. C. MILES in E. Jenks *Digest Eng. Civil Law* II. i. 337 Persons are joint tort-feasors when one aids, counsels, or joins the other in the commission of a tort. **1920** H. CRANE *Let.* 28 Jan. (1965) 32, I am enraged at Mencken and Nathan..the joint authors. **1925** J. A. HOLDEN *Bookman's Gloss.* 63 Joint author, a person who writes a book in collaboration with one or more associates. **1935** *Act 25 & 26 Geo. V* c. 30 §6 Any tort-feasor liable in respect of..damage may recover contribution from any other tort-feasor who is..liable in respect of the same damage, whether as a joint tort-feasor or otherwise. **1957** J. G. FLEMING *Law of Torts* xxviii. 744 The common law.. does attach some significance to the distinction between 'joint' and 'several' tortfeasors. **1967** *Anglo-Amer. Catal. Rules: Brit. Text* 267 *Joint author*, a person who collaborates with one or more associates to produce a work in which the contribution of each is not separable from that of the others. **1971** *Mod. Law Rev.* XXXIV. VI. 674 The accessory after the fact has become, perhaps more appropriately, something more like the joint-tortfeasor.

b. *joint family*, a type of extended family in which married children share the family home, living under the authority of the head of the family. Also *attrib.*

1876 W. K. SULLIVAN in *Encycl. Brit.* V. 799/2 Beside the 'joint and undivided family' there was another kind of family which we might call the 'joint family'. This was a partnership composed of three or four members of a sept whose individual wealth was not sufficient to qualify each of them to be an aire, but whose joint wealth qualified one of the co-partners as head of the joint family to be one. **1889** C. N. STARCKE *Primitive Family* II. ii. 139 Polyandry belongs to the category of facts which have to do with the ordinary family communism, and especially with the joint family group. **1937** *Jrnl. R. Anthrop. Inst.* LXVII. 137 Members of the owner's joint-family and lineage. **1953** J. H. WEAKLAND in Mead & Métraux *Study of Culture at Distance* X. v. 423 Dissent among the brothers of a Chinese joint family is concealed from the public. **1957** *Encycl. Brit.* XII. 235/2 The striking feature of Hindu society and Hindu law is the joint family. It is the form, no doubt, in which the Aryan patriarchal family has survived. **1968** G. D. MITCHELL *Dict. Sociol.* 77 Extended family is sometimes used not merely to include but as a synonym for joint family. It is more useful to restrict this last term to a form of family which has a number of distinctive characteristics: co-residence, commensality and often some common family cult. **1971** *Illustr. Weekly India* 11 Apr. 23/2 (*caption*) The house was full of Tagore relatives who all lived together as a traditional Bengali joint-family.

3. a. Of a thing, action, etc. (in *sing.*): Held, done, made, etc. by two or more persons, parties, or things, in conjunction; of or belonging to more than one at once; common to two or more.

1424-5 *E.E. Wills* (1882) 60 Diuers men haf ioint astate whit me in diuerce of my purchace be wey of truste. **1503-4** *Act 19 Hen. VII*, c. 25 *Preamble*, As if the seid persones.. had a iont astate..wt the seid suruiuours. **1587** GOLDING *De Mornay* v. 56-7 By the iointworking of the vnderstanding and will together. **1597** SHAKS. *2 Hen. IV*, v. ii. 55 A ioynt burthen, laid vpon vs all. **1634** W. TIRWHYT tr. *Balzac's Lett.* (vol. I) 69 You remember..what our ioynt opinion hath beene. **1698** FRYER *Acc. E. India & P.* 345 The joint Advantage both of the Emperor and his Subjects. **1762-71** H. WALPOLE *Vertue's Anecd. Paint.* (1786) II. 117 In one corner Henry VII. and Ferdinand are conferring amicably on a joint throne. **1767** BLACKSTONE *Comm.* II. 183 The remaining grand incident of joint-estates, viz. the doctrine of survivorship. **1778** *N.Y. Laws* 27 Mar., The joint Committee..[shall] canvas and estimate the votes. **1855**

MACAULAY *Hist. Eng.* xxi. IV. 553 It was determined that a joint committee of the two Houses should be appointed. **1869** *Bradshaw's Railway Manual* XXI. 80 The companies should enter into a joint purse agreement with the Irish North Western. **1871** FREEMAN *Norm. Conq.* IV. xviii. 250 All hopes of joint action were at an end. **1884** Joint account [see *N.E.D.*, s.v. ACCOUNT *sb.* 2]. **1886** G. C. BRODRICK *Hist. Univ. Oxf.* xviii. 213 A vote of censure on Dr. Hampden.. was defeated in Convocation by the Proctors' joint-veto. **1909** WEBSTER, Joint sitting. **1936** T. S. ELIOT *Coll. Poems 1909–1935* 138 The fletchers and javelin-makers and smiths Have appointed a joint committee to protest against the reduction of orders. **1937** *Discovery* May 139/1 The formal invitation of the Indian Science Congress Association for the British Association to send a party to hold a joint session in India. **1942** N. BALCHIN *Darkness falls from Air* x. 184 You'll want some money... Use the joint account. **1952** H. NICOLSON *King George V* ix. 132 It was agreed.. that if.. an irreconcilable conflict arose between the House of Commons and the House of Lords, the matter should be settled by a Joint Sitting of both Houses. **1964** W. DUFF *Indian Hist. Brit. Columbia* I. 73 Of great and growing importance in recent years has been the development of 'joint' or 'integrated' schools. **1965** H. I. ANSOFF *Corporate Strategy* ii. 16 Joint-venture opportunities. **1966** *Rep. Comm. Inquiry Univ. Oxf.* I. 83 A statutory 'joint' committee of Council, the General Board, and the Council of the Colleges. **1966** T. LUPTON *Managem. & Social Sci.* iii. 63 The term Joint Consultation is usually used to describe the formal machinery through which the managers and the workers in a firm.. discuss their common problems. **1972** WODEHOUSE *Pearls, Girls, & Monty Bodkin* iv. 50 He and his wife have a joint account, and he can't draw a cheque without her approval. **1973** *Oxf. Univ. Gaz.* 16 May 866/1 A universal system of joint appointments is in my view unnecessary.

b. ***joint denial***: the negation of each of two or more stated propositions; 'neither.. nor..'.

1940 W. V. QUINE *Math. Logic* i. 45 A joint denial, e.g. 'Neither is Jones away nor is Smith ill',.. is true just in case its components are both false. *Ibid.* 49 The definability of denial, conjunction, and alternation in terms of joint denial was first pointed out by Sheffer in 1913. **1954** I. M. COPI *Symbolic Logic* viii. 256 The other operator which suffices for a functionally complete logic is that of 'joint denial'. **1960** S. KÖRNER *Philos. of Math.* ii. 40 All truth functions.. can be introduced by definition if we start either (a) with the single notion of alternative denial.., or else (b) with the single notion of joint denial.

†**4.** Made up of parts joined, fastened together, or combined (see also JOINT-STOOL); continuous, uninterrupted (quot. 13..); *fig.* with reference to an unopened rose (quot. *c* 1450). *Obs.*

13.. *E.E. Allit. P.* C. 355 On to þrenge þer-þurȝe [Niniue] watz þre dayes dede. þat on Iournay ful Ioynt Ionas hym ȝede Er euer he warpped any worde. *c* **1429** in Willis & Clark *Cambridge* (1886) II. 445 It' pro lj ped' de joyntable vj^s iiij^d ob. *c* **1450** LONELICH *Grail* xliii. 480 Al Ioint & Clos In Al manere tyme as was the Rose. *a* **1711** KEN *Edmund* Poet. Wks. 1721 II. 301 O're the Stone Bridge, cross the Joint-Current laid.

†**5.** = JOINTED *a.* 1. *Obs.*

1685 *Lond. Gaz.* No. 2054/4 Lost.. a Joynt Cane, wrought with a Gold Head on it.

†**6.** Used *advb.* = JOINTLY. *Obs.*

1424–5 *E.E. Wills* (1882) 61 Als wel þo þat stande enfeffed by me, as þo þat ben ioint feffed with me. *a* **1691** BOYLE *Hist. Air* xiii. (1692) 67 Our so much joint-esteemed friend Mr. Mercator.

7. *Comb.*, as **joint-awned**, having a jointed awn.

1787 *Fam. Plants* I. 348 Seeds numerous.. joint-awn'd with a long style.

joint (dʒɔɪnt), *v.* [f. JOINT *sb.*]

1. *trans.* To connect by a joint or joints; to fasten, fit together, unite. **a.** *lit.* material things.

1611 SHAKS. *Cymb.* v. iv. 142 Branches, which being dead many yeares, shall after reuiue, bee ioynted to the old Stocke, and freshly grow. **1691** RAY *Creation* II. (1692) 53 The fingers are strengthened with several Bones, jointed together for motion. **1793** SMEATON *Edystone L.* 193 The manner of jointing the five courses of stone. **1889** R. S. S. BADEN-POWELL *Pigsticking* 94 Those which are jointed and soldered together.

b. *fig.* (usually with direct allusion to the literal sense).

1547 *Homilies* I. *Contention* ¶ 2 We cannot be ioynted to Christ our Head, except we be glued with concord and charitie one to another. *a* **1634** RANDOLPH *Muse's Looking-glass* III. ii, He, with the pegs of amity and concord,.. Joints 'em together. **1673** TEMPLE *Obs. United Prov.* Wks. 1731 I. 58 They seem to be a sound Piece of the State, and fast jointed in with the rest.

c. To fill up the joints of stone, brickwork, etc. with mortar or the like; to point; to represent with (imitation) joints (quot. 1823).

1703 MOXON *Mech. Exerc.* 247 They joint the long Joints, and also the Cross Joints. **1793** SMEATON *Edystone L.* §209 They joint the paving with mortar. **1823** RUTTER *Fonthill* 9 The walls and ceiling have been jointed to represent stone. **1897** *Daily News* 4 Sept. 6/1 They threw us a lot of red-lead, and each man carried a large piece.. ready to joint into any leak or crack he came across.

d. *Carpentry*, etc. To prepare (a board, stave, etc.) for being joined to another, by planing its edge with a jointer (see JOINTER² 1).

1815 *Niles' Reg.* IX. 36/1 The power is given by one or two horses, which with a man and a boy can dress and joint.. the staves necessary for one hundred barrels. **1864** WEBSTER, *Joint*, 1.. To prepare so as to fit closely; to fit together;.. as to joint boards. **1875** KNIGHT *Dict. Mech.* s.v., To *joint* is to plane straight the edges of boards. *Ibid.* s.v., *Jointer-plane* (*Coopering*), The inclined sole being presented upward for the staves, which are jointed thereon.

2. *intr.* for *refl.* To fit exactly into each other as in the joints of masonry, etc.

1695 TEMPLE *Introd. Hist. Eng.* 38 A small round Tower built of Stone.. so exactly Cut, as every one to Joynt into another. **1726** LEONI *Alberti's Archit.* I. 55/1 Bricks lying sideways, with their heads joynting into each other.. as a Man locks his right hand fingers into his left.

3. a. *trans.* To divide (a body or member) at a joint or into joints; to dismember, disjoint.

1530 PALSGR. 592/2, I joynte, I cut meate by the joyntes to make it meter for the potte or spytte. **1591** PERCIVALL *Sp. Dict.*, *Acodar vides*, to ioynt vines, to prune vines, *Ceniculare.* **1596** SPENSER *F.Q.* v. xi. 29 Her huge taile.. He with his sword it strooke, that without faile He ioynted it. **1697** DRYDEN *Æneid* IX. 1040 He joints the Neck: And with a stroke so strong The Helm flies off; and bears the Head along. **1709** *Brit. Apollo* II. No. 59. 2/1 A Person is Joynting a piece of Meat,.. he finds it difficult to Joynt. **1898** R. KEARTON *Wild Life at Home* 78 'Jointing' two large worms, [she] flew off at once to her chicks with them.

†**b.** *fig.* To 'cut off' from or deprive *of* something. *Obs.*

1573 G. HARVEY *Letter-bk.* (Camden) 30, I shal be contentid to be bard of mi mastership and iointid of my fellowship too. **1642** ROGERS *Naaman* 290 Threaten their poore children to joynt them of this or that land or portion.

4. *intr.* To form joints.

1772 *Carroll Papers* in *Maryland Hist. Mag.* (1919) XIV. 287, I am apprehensive it will be too thick and Joint if the weather proves warme. **1904** *Topeka* (Kansas) *Daily Capital* 1 June 8 Wheat has not done well, though it is jointing now.

joint-ache. An ache or pain in the joints.

1576 BAKER *Jewell of Health* 60 The water of Iuniper beries.. auayleth against all ioyntaches proceeding of colde. **1657** W. COLES *Adam in Eden* lix, It is good for the Sciatica and Joynt-Aches.

b. *transf.* Applied to a disease of trees.

1601 HOLLAND *Pliny* XVII. xxiv. I. 538 No trees are exempt from the worme, the blasting, and the ioint-ach [*dolor membrorum*].

jointed ('dʒɔɪntɪd), *a.* [f. JOINT *sb.* + -ED².]

1. a. Furnished with, constructed with, or having joints (see the various senses of the sb.). *spec.* in *Geol.*: cf. JOINT *sb.* 5.

1413 *Pilgr. Sowle* (Caxton 1483) IV. xxxii. 81 They ben wel ioynted and myghtely boned. *a* **1547** SURREY *Æneid* IV. (1557) G ij b, The throwing spirit, and iointed limmes to loose. **1667** MILTON *P.L.* VII. 409 Or under Rocks thir food In jointed Armour watch. **1721** POPE *Let. to E. Blount* 3 Oct., I saw her sober over a Sampler, or gay over a joynted Baby. **1821** J. MACCULLOCH *Geol. Classification of Rocks* viii. 129 In a few instances, from the extreme shortness of the prisms, the columnar passes to a tabular, or a lamellar and jointed structure. **1863** D. T. ANSTED *Gt. Stone Bk.* ix. 133 The harder kinds of sand-rock are always jointed. **1880** HUXLEY *Crayfish* i. 24 The crayfish has a jointed and segmented body. **1968** R. W. FAIRBRIDGE *Encycl. Geomorphol.* 489/2 The contrast between granite that is widely jointed and that which is closely jointed and generally shattered is easily seen in many localities.

b. In *comb.* with qualifying word: Having joints of a specified kind.

1591 SPENSER *Muiopot.* 121 Beeing nimbler ioynted then the rest. **1797** M. BAILLIE *Morb. Anat.* (1807) 188 This head is placed upon a narrow jointed portion of the worm. **1842** TENNYSON *Locksley Hall* 169 Iron-jointed, supple-sinew'd, they shall dive, and they shall run. **1895** *Outing* (U.S.) XXVI. 369/1 My single short-jointed rod.

2. *Bot.* Having or appearing to have joints; separating readily at the joints; as a specific vernacular name.

1597 Iointed Glassewoort [see GLASSWORT]. **1793** T. MARTYN *Lang. Bot.* s.v. Jointed... Applied to the root.. —to the stem or culm, in corn and grasses— to the leaves, when one leaflet grows from the top of another. **1821** S. F. GRAY *Nat. Arrangement Brit. Plants* II. 160 Leaves.. knotty, jointed, or smooth. **1839** J. LINDLEY *Sch. Bot.* 4 If a stem is swelled at the part where the leaves grow, and capable of being snapped across, or apparently so, it is called *articulated* or *jointed*, as in Stellaria Holostea, and Geraniums. **1843** C. C. BABINGTON *Man. Brit. Bot.* 31 *Raphanus Raphanistrum* (L.).. Jointed Charlock. **1913** C. PETTMAN *Africanderisms* 234 Jointed cactus, *Opuntia pusilla*, a dangerous weed. **1971** J. E. LOUSLEY *Flora Isles of Scilly* 268 *J[uncus] articulatus* L. Jointed Rush. Native.

Hence **'jointedly** *adv.*, connectedly; **'jointedness**, quality or state of being jointed.

1846 WORCESTER, *Jointedly*, in a jointed manner. *Smith.* **1877** *Tinsley's Mag.* XX. 207 When he could talk faintly and jointedly. **1881** WHITNEY in *Proc. Amer. Philol. Assoc.* 22 Articulation, in this its literal sense of jointedness.

jointenant, obs. form of JOINT-TENANT.

†**jointer**¹. *Obs.* [? f. JOINT *a.* (or *joint-* in JOINTURE) + -ER¹.] A joint possessor; one who holds a jointure.

1566 J. STUDLEY tr. *Seneca's Agamemnon* (1581) 147 b, Thou that dost rule with him, made jointer of his mace. *c* **1590** GREENE *Fr. Bacon* x. 8 Ile make thy daughter ioynter of it all, So thou consent to giue her to my wife.

jointer² ('dʒɔɪntə(r)). [f. JOINT *v.* + -ER¹.] One who or that which joints.

1. Name of various tools. **a.** *Carpentry*, etc. A long kind of plane used in dressing the edges of boards, staves, etc. in preparation for jointing them; also, a machine used in jointing staves.

1678 MOXON *Mech. Exerc.* iv. §4 (1683) I. 65 The Joynter is made somewhat longer than the Fore-plane.. Its Office is to follow the Fore-plane, and to shoot an edge perfectly straight,.. especially when a Joynt is to be shot. **1875** *Carpentry & Join.* 25 The carpenter uses this jack plane first, and, subsequently, his longer trying plane, and still longer jointer, to put the final touches. **1885** J. RICHARDS *Wood-Working Machinery* 147 The first and leading tools are bench planes, a set of which should consist of one 26-inch jointer.. one 24-inch jointer.. one 22-inch foreplane [etc.]. **1900** C. G. WHEELER *Woodworking for Beginners* xvi. 448 The jointer.. is more accurate for making a surface level and true, or for shooting the edges of boards. **1953** W. COVENTON *Woodwork Tools* ii. 48 The trying plane .. will be used for finishing the jointing, unless there is much jointing to do in hardwood, when it will pay to follow with a steel panel and jointer plane. **1958** G. H. LOVE *Theory & Pract. Woodwork* ii. 28 Working on the assumption that the longer the surface, the longer the plane required to true it, we have the jointer, a plane which is even longer than the trying plane. **1959** *Handyman & Home Mechanic* I. 36/2 Steel trying planes are often known as jointers, and are similar to steel jack planes except in length.

b. *Masonry.* A tool used for filling with mortar or for marking the joints between courses of brick or stone work.

1703 MOXON *Mech. Exerc.* 247 A Jointer of Iron, with which, and the foresaid Rule, they joint the long Joints,.. the Cross Joints.. being done with the Jointer without the Rule. **1812–16** J. SMITH *Panorama Sc. & Art* I. 194 The iron tool used along with the jointing-rule, to mark the joints of brick-work, is called a jointer; its form is nearly that of the letter ∽, though its flexure is not in proportion so considerable.

c. A bent piece of iron inserted into a wall to strengthen a joint.

1864 in WEBSTER.

2. A workman employed in jointing; *esp.* one who makes the junctions between parts of an electric wire, etc.

1876 PREECE & SIVEWRIGHT *Telegraphy* 235 Not only should the jointer's hands be scrupulously clean, but he should see that the wires to be joined are equally so, the copper being scraped bright and clean. **1895** *B'ham Weekly Post* 16 Mar. 4/8 There are plenty of excavators, but the pipe jointers are very scarce.

3. In the West Indies, a common name of *Piper geniculatum.*

1847 GOSSE *Birds of Jamaica* 73 The deserted provision-grounds are overgrown with a thicket, almost impenetrable, of jointer, or jointwood.

4. *Comb.* **jointer-plane** = sense 1 a.

1823 P. NICHOLSON *Pract. Build.* 245 The Jointer-Plane is the longest of all the planes... It is used for shooting the edges to boards perfectly straight, so that their juncture may scarcely be discernible when their surfaces are joined together. **1881** YOUNG *Every man his own Mechanic* §244 Trying-planes and Jointer-planes differ from the jack-plane in being longer and set with a finer cut.

joint-grass. [f. JOINT *sb.* 3 + GRASS.] A local name for the herbs Horsetail (*Equisetum*), and Lady's Bedstraw (*Galium verum*) (Britten and Holland); also, in southern U.S., the grass *Paspalum distichum* (Cent. Dict.).

1790 W. MARSHALL *Midl. Countries* (1796) II. Gloss. (E.D.S.), *Joint-grass*, yellow bedstraw. **1835** W. G. SIMMS *Partisan* 55 Rebellion grows like joint-grass when it once takes root. **1894** J. M. COULTER *Bot. W. Texas* III. 499 Joint grass... Moist places throughout Texas and across the continent.

joint-heir, etc.: see JOINT *a.* 2.

jointing ('dʒɔɪntɪŋ), *vbl. sb.* [f. JOINT *v.* + -ING¹.] The action of the verb JOINT.

1. The action of connecting or uniting by a joint; also *fig.*

1642 FULLER *Holy & Prof. St.* II. x. 90 An excellent Chirurgeon he was at joynting of a broken soul. **1899** *Westm. Gaz.* 28 Aug. 8/1 The old piles.. showing the tool marks and evidences of morticing and jointing.

b. *concr.* The structure of a joint or junction.

1668 CULPEPPER & COLE *Barthol. Anat.* I. iii. 6 It defends the ends of Gristles, the Joyntings of the greater Bones. **1696** J. EDWARDS *Exist. & Prov. God* II. 94 Their joyntings and closures are wonderful. **1833** *Act 3 & 4 Will. IV*, c. 46 §116 The said Commissioners shall.. form the jointing with the other pipes to be added thereto with proper and sufficient materials. **1885** *Athenæum* 22 Aug. 247/2 Another wall.. of fine squared white stone drafted at the jointings, so that it looks panelled.

2. The action of dividing at the joints, or into 'joints'; dismemberment, disjointing.

1591 in Pitcairn *Crim. Trials* I. 233 Thair taking vp the bwreit people, and junting of thame, quhairof scho maid inchantit powder for Witchcraft. **1603** HOLLAND *Plutarch* 750 About cutting it up, quartering, jointing, seething and rosting.

3. The formation of joints or cleavage planes in rocks, etc.; the nature or arrangement of these.

1698 MOLYNEUX in *Phil. Trans.* XX. 217 The universal Jointing of the whole Causway, is certainly otherwise. **1784** TWAMLEY *Dairying* 27[The cheese] when released from the Press, will heave, or puff up, by Splitting or Jointing, according as the Nature or State of the Curd happens to be. **1865** GEIKIE *Scen. & Geol. Scot.* vi. 119 In one part the solid granite is only beginning to show its lines of jointing.

4. *attrib.* and *Comb.*, as **jointing-plane**, (*a*) a plane of 'jointing' or fissure, as in a rock; (*b*) = JOINTER² 1 a; **jointing-rule**, a long flat ruler used for guiding the jointer (JOINTER² 1 b) in marking the joints of brickwork.

1900 *Daily News* 10 May 6/4 *Jointing boxes and aigrettes used in the re-arrangement of the lightning conductors of St. Paul's Cathedral. **1854** HOOKER *Himal. Jrnls.* I. xvii. 406 Whose surfaces are no doubt, cleavage and *jointing planes. **1875** KNIGHT *Dict. Mech.*, *Jointing-plane*, a plane with a long stock, used to true the edges of boards or staves which

are to be accurately fitted together. **1703** MOXON *Mech. Exerc.* 247 A *Jointing Rule..whereby to run the long Joints of the Brick-work. **1823** P. NICHOLSON *Pract. Build.* 386 The Jointing-Rule is about eight or ten feet long, and about four inches broad.

'jointist. *U.S.* [f. JOINT *sb.* 14 + -IST.] The keeper of a 'joint' or illicit drinking-saloon.

1889 in *Voice* (N.Y.) 5 Sept., The Grand Jury had found nineteen indictments against jointists. **1893** *Arena* (U.S.) Mar. 467 In Kansas..the liquor seller is the sneaking boot-legger, skulking jointist, criminal and outlaw.

jointless ('dʒɔɪntlɪs), *a.* [f. JOINT *sb.* + -LESS.] **a.** Without joints, or the use of joints; having no joints, stiff, rigid.

1559 W. BALDWYN in *Mirr. Mag.* To Rdr., Looking for his strong jointless olyphants. *a***1603** T. CARTWRIGHT *Confut. Rhem. N.T.* (1618) 500 Your knees..are ioyntlesse and Elephant-like in your obedience unto his precepts. **1748** RICHARDSON *Clarissa* (1811) VI. viii. 38 'Let me die here', were her words, remaining jointless and immovable. **1867** *Nat. Encycl.* I. 92 The pods are jointless.

b. In one piece; without a seam or joint of any kind.

1909 *Prosp. Rubber-Tanned Leather Co.* 2 May, Automobile tyres in seamless and jointless bands. **1921** *Dict. Occup. Terms* (1927) §571 'Composition' or jointless floors.

jointly ('dʒɔɪntlɪ), *adv.* [f. JOINT *a.* + -LY².] In a joint manner; so as to be joined.

†**1.** So as to be joined in space; together (in position); in contact; adjacently. *Obs.*

*c***1375** *Lay Folks Mass Bk.* (MS. B.) 58 And þer-with ioyntly hold þi handes. **1574** tr. *Littleton's Tenures* 18 b, The tenaunt shall..hold his handes iointly together betweene the handes of his Lord. **1582** STANYHURST *Æneis* III. (Arb.) 88 But neere joynctle brayeth with rufflerye rumboled Ætna. **1710** PRIDEAUX *Orig. Tithes* iv. 180 That whole Paragraph..being joyntly added, any Reader may compare them.

†**b.** Continuously in space or time. *Obs.*

*c***1400** *Destr. Troy* 1538 This Cite was sothely, to serche it aboute, þre iorneys full iointly to ioyne hom by dayes. **1548** G. WISHART tr. *Conf. Fayth Sweserland.* in *Wodrow Misc.* (1844) 13 Yf there by any good that remayneth in man after the fall, that same beynge joyntelie made weaker and weaker by our vyce tournes to the worse.

†**2.** Together, in union; concordantly, harmoniously; at the same time, simultaneously. *Obs.*

1362 LANGL. *P. Pl.* A. II. 127 To loke if þe lawe wole Iugge ȝou Ioyntely to be Ioyned for euer. *a***1400–50** *Alexander* 1470 All þe iewis of ierusalem he Ioyntly a-sembles. **1545** BRINKLOW *Lament.* (1874) 84 Loke..how iointly ye agre with the saide people of Iuda! **1593** SHAKS. *Lucr.* 1846 Then jointly to the ground their knees they bow. *a***1693** URQUHART *Rabelais* III. xlii. 352 They..went joyntly to a..Tent.

†**b.** In conjunction with this. *Obs.*

1656 M. BEN ISRAEL *Vind. Judæorum* in *Phenix* (1708) II. 405 Your Worship desir'd jointly to know what Ceremony or Humiliation the Jews use in their Synagogues, toward the Book of the Law.

3. In conjunction, combination, or concert; unitedly; conjunctly: opp. to *severally* or *separately*. (The only current sense.)

1340 HAMPOLE *Pr. Consc.* 5850 Þarfor men sal yhelde acount ioyntly Of bathe togyder, þe saule and þe body. *c***1430** *Pilgr. Lyf Manhode* III. vii. (1869) 139 Soothliche this is weylinge and sorwe ioyntliche. **1469** *Waterf. Arch.* in *10th Rep. Hist. MSS. Comm.* App. v. 307 The saide Maire..byndith them yontly and severally to stand by this acte. **1491** *Act 7 Hen. VII*, c. 23 §4 Landes..wherof she..was seised or possessed in her owne right..or jointly with her said husband. **1593** SHAKS. *2 Hen. VI*, IV. iv. 52 The Rascall people..Ioyne with the Traitor, and they ioyntly sweare To spoyle the City. **1676** DRYDEN *Aurengz.* II. i. 15 Where'er you lead, We joyntly vow to own no other Head. **1767** BLACKSTONE *Comm.* II. xii. 193 A devise to two persons, to hold jointly and severally, is said to be a joint-tenancy. **1875** BRYCE *Holy Rom. Emp.* App. B. (ed. 5) 450 The relation of Schleswig to Holstein, and of both jointly to the Danish crown.

†**'jointmeal,** *adv. Obs.* [f. JOINT *sb.* + -MEAL.] Joint by joint.

1548 COOPER *Elyot's Biblioth.*, *Articulatim*, from ioinct to ioinct, ioynct meale. **1600** HOLLAND *Livy* XLV. xxx. 1221 They seemed like creatures dismembred & plucked asunder joint-meale.

joint-owner, -partner, etc.: see JOINT *a.* 2.

jointress ('dʒɔɪntrɪs). [f. JOINTER¹ + -ESS.] A widow who holds a jointure; a dowager.

1602 SHAKS. *Ham.* I. ii. 9 Our Queene Th' Imperiall Ioyntresse of this warlike State. **1697** *Lond. Gaz.* No. 3296/4 Part being in present possession, and the other in Reversion after the death of a Joyntress. **1707** *Ibid.* No. 4320/3 One Estate..subject to a Jointure, which the Jointress is willing to sell. **1892** *Law Times Rep.* LXVII. 490/2 Since the hearing..one of the jointresses had died and her jointure of 1000*l.* a year had ceased.

†**joint-ring.** *Obs.* A finger-ring made of two separable halves: = GEMEL 4, GIMMAL 1. Cf. the description in Dryden *Don Sebastian* v. i:

'Those rings..a curious artist wrought them With joints so close as not to be perceived: Yet are they both each others counterpart; Her part had Juan inscribed, and his had Zaida ..and in the midst A heart divided in two parts was placed'.

1604 SHAKS. *Oth.* IV. iii. 73 Marry I would not doe such a thing for a ioynt Ring,..nor any petty exhibition. **1703** *Lond. Gaz.* No. 3897/4 Lost or stolen,..a Box,..in which were..3 Rose Stone Rings, 24 Joint Rings.

joint stock, joint-stock. *Comm.* [f. JOINT *a.* + STOCK.]

1. Stock or capital contributed and owned by a number of persons jointly; capital divided into shares; a common fund.

1615 E. S. *Brit. Buss* in Arb. *Garner* III. 655 For the good government and sincere disposition of this Joint Stock. **1694** LUTTRELL *Brief Rel.* (1857) III. 400 The merchants of Amsterdam are fitting out with a joint stock 15 privateers of 40 guns each. **1711** *Lond. Gaz.* No. 4868/3 The Joynt Stock of a Corporation to be erected to carry on a Trade in the South Seas. **1779** HERVEY *Nav. Hist.* II. 200 A kind of open trade was carried on from England to the east, which greatly affected the merchants who traded on the joint stock. **1806** HUTTON *Course Math.* I. 124, X, Y, and Z made a joint-stock for 12 months. **1883** *Wharton's Law-Lex.* (ed. 7) s.v. *Joint-Stock Company*, The common property of the members, applicable to the purposes of the company, is called its joint-stock, and hence the name.

2. *attrib.* (*joint-stock*). Holding a joint stock; formed or conducted on the basis of a joint stock; as ***joint-stock bank, company, companyship, firm.***

1776 Joint-stock company [see COMPANY *sb.* 7]. **1808** H. DAY (*title*) A Defence of Joint Stock Companies. **1825** SCOTT *Fam. Lett.* (1894) II. xxi. 278 The people are all mad here about joint-stock companies. **1843** *Ainsworth's Mag.* IV. 110 It is a pleasant privilege of the honourable corps.. that a sort of joint-stock-companyship prevails among them. **1844** DISRAELI *Coningsby* VIII. i, When he received a deputation on sugar duties or joint-stock banks. **1853** MRS. GASKELL *Cranford* xii. 225 Her poor opinion of joint-stock banks in general. **1893** BITHELL *Counting-ho. Dict.* s.v., A Joint Stock Company is defined by Act of Parliament to be 'A Company consisting of seven or more members having a permanent paid up or nominal capital of fixed amount, divided into shares, also of fixed amount, and formed on the principle of having for its members the holders of shares of such capital, and no other persons'. This definition excludes companies consisting of six or fewer members, whose affairs fall under the Law of partnership. **1964** GOULD & KOLB *Dict. Social Sci.* 550/1 The modern business corporation or joint stock company originated in the 18th century. **1969** *Lebende Sprachen* XIV. 97/2 Clearing arrangements have been agreed with the joint stock banks, so that money can be readily transferred from a giro account to a bank account. **1972** *Accountant* 5 Oct. 413/1 Sweden's national pension fund, it has been recommended, should be free to invest approximately 1 per cent of its resources in selected joint-stock companies.

Hence **joint-'stock** *v. trans.*, to turn into joint stock, or into a joint-stock company; **joint-'stockery**, dealing in, or formation of, joint stocks; **joint-'stockism**, the system or principle of joint-stocks. (All more or less *nonce-wds.*)

1894 SIR E. SULLIVAN *Woman* 99 Let some clever person invent something better, patent it, *joint-stock it, and get some good names on the direction, and he will have an immense success. **1899** *Contemp. Rev.* June 870 We refine the method of stealing, that is all—joint-stock it, and sometimes call it a dividend. **1864** *Realm* 6 Apr. 3 They are themselves so immersed in *joint-stockery, that they fancy all the rest of mankind are similarly inclined. **1856** *Tait's Mag.* XXIII. 304 *Joint-stockism has been successfully applied to many other branches of business. **1890** G. B. SHAW *Fab. Ess.* 137 The transfigured joint stockism of the present Co-operative movement.

joint-stool ('dʒɔɪntstu:l). Forms: α. 5–7 ioyned, ioyn'd, ioynd, ioin'd s. (with or without hyphen: see forms of STOOL); β. 7 joyne-stoole; γ. 6–7 ioynt, 8 joynt-, 7–9 **joint-stool.** [In sense 1, orig. *joined stool.* In sense 2, f. JOINT *sb.* 4.]

1. A stool made of parts joined or fitted together; a stool made by a joiner, as distinguished from one of more clumsy workmanship. (Cf. JOINED 2.) *Obs.* exc. *Hist.*

Frequently mentioned in 16–18th c. as an article of furniture; also in allusive or proverbial phrases expressing disparagement or ridicule, of which the precise explanation is lost.

1434 *E. E. Wills* (1882) 102 Also a litil Ioyned stoll for a child, & a nother Ioyned stoll, large for to sitte on, whanne he cometh to mannes state. **1512** *Nottingham Rec.* III. 114 Duo scabella vocata joyned stoles. **1594** LYLY *Moth. Bombie* IV. ii, *Accius.* You neede not be so lustie: you are not so honest. *Selina.* I crie you mercie, I tooke you for a ioynt stoole. **1596** SHAKS. *Tam. Shr.* II. i. 199 *Kath.* I knew you at the first, You were a mouable. *Petr.* Why, what's a mouable? *Kath.* A ioyn'd stoole. **1611** COTGR., *Selle*,..any illfauored, ordinarie..stoole, of a cheaper sort then the ioyned, or buffet-stoole. **1634** *Withal's Dict.* 553 *Ante hoc te cornua habere putabam*, I cry you mercy, I tooke you for a joynd stoole. **1638** BAKER tr. *Balzac's Lett.* (vol. III.) II. xii, Fitter to be read upon a Joyne-stoole, than pronounced at a Tribunall. **1712** ARBUTHNOT *John Bull* III. i, He used to lay chairs and joint-stools in their way, that they might break their noses by falling over them. **1784** COWPER *Task* I. 19 Joint-stools were then created; on three legs Upborne they stood. Three legs upholding firm A massy slab, in fashion square or round. **1820** SCOTT *Monast.* xv, As passive an instrument of my accommodation as this ill-made and rugged joint-stool on which I sit. **1859** JEPHSON *Brittany* ii. 9, I seated myself on a joint-stool on the deck.

2. *Mech.* 'A block holding up the ends of parts which belong in apposition, as railway rails, ways of vessels, etc.' (Knight *Dict. Mech.* 1875).

joint-tenant. Forms: 6 ioynt tenaunt, ioyntenaunt(e, iointenaunte, 7 joyntenant, joyn-tenant, 7–8 jointenant; 7 joynt-tenant, 8– joint-tenant, joint tenant. [f. JOINT *a.* + TENANT.] One who holds an undivided estate in the same right jointly with another or others, with a *jus accrescendi*, whereby the interest of each passes at his death to the survivors or survivor, till the whole remains in a single hand.

This right of survivorship distinguishes joint-tenants from *tenants in common.*

1531 *Dial. on Laws Eng.* II. xxv. 55 The ioynt tenaunt hathe ryght to the hole goodes. **1574** tr. *Littleton's Tenures* 57 a, If two or three disseise another of anye landes..to theire owne use, then the disseisoures be iointenauntes. **1659** *Termes de la Ley* s.v., If one Joyntenant grant that which belongs to him to a Stranger, then the other Joyntenant and the Stranger are Tenants in common. **1767** BLACKSTONE *Comm.* II. xii. 184 While it [the joint-tenancy] continues, each of two joint-tenants has a concurrent interest in the whole; and therefore, on the death of his companion, the sole interest in the whole remains to the survivor.

fig. **1621** QUARLES *Div. Poems, Esther* (1638) 91 These brave ioyntenants that surviv'd To see a little world of men unliv'd. **1645** —— *Sol. Recant.* viii. 23 Nay, Heaven and Hel May sooner..turn Joynt-tenants in one perfect Line. **1733** POPE *Ess. Man* III. 152 In nature's state..Man walked with beast, joint-tenant of the shade.

So **joint-'tenancy**, the holding of an estate by two or more joint-tenants.

1613 SIR H. FINCH *Law* (1636) 364 The writ abating for some cause that cannot be imputed to the Plaintifes folly: as for..Ioyntenancie, and such like. **1767** BLACKSTONE *Comm.* II. xii. 179 An estate in joint-tenancy is where lands or tenements are granted to two or more persons, to hold in fee-simple, fee-tail, for life, for years, or at will. **1844** WILLIAMS *Real Prop.* vi. (1875) 132 Any estate may be held in joint tenancy.

jointure ('dʒɔɪntjʊə(r)), *sb.* Forms: 4–7 ioynt-, ioint-, ioynct-, (4 ioyngt-, 5 ioyntt-), -ure, -er, (4–6 -our, 5–6 -or(e, 6 -yre, -ur; 5 iuntor, yonture, 6 ionctour, gintur); 7 joinct-, 7–8 joynt-, 7– jointure. [a. F. *jointure*:—L. *junctūra*, f. *junct-*, ppl. stem of *jungĕre* to join; see -URE.]

†**1.** Joining, junction, conjunction, union. *Obs.*

*c***1374** CHAUCER *Boeth.* II. pr. v. 32 (Camb. MS.) Ioyngture of sowle and body. **1550** VERON *Godly Sayings* (1846) 47 Lette hym notte goo from the joynture and compage of the members. **1601** HOLLAND *Pliny* I. 326 That place where the ioincture is of the shoulders to the nape of the neck. **1606** FORD *Fame's Memorial* x, To..sympathize in ioincture with thy courage.

2. *concr.* A joining, a junction, a joint. Now *rare.*

1382 WYCLIF *Ezek.* xxxvii. 7, I prophecied..and loo! a styryng to gydre, and bones wenten to boones, eche to his ioynture. *c***1400** *Lanfranc's Cirurg.* 109 Þei ben bounde togidere bi oon ioynture, þe which þat strecchiþ from bifore to bihynde to þe lenkþe of þe heed, þe which is clepid sagittales. *Ibid.* 157 Alle þese boonys..þat ben in ioynturis, as þe schuldris, elbowis [etc.]. **1413** *Pilgr. Sowle* (Caxton 1483) IV. xxxi. 80 The necke..is the ioynture of the hede and the body and maketh them bothe one. **1594** DANIEL *Cleopatra* III. ii, Her disioyned Iointures as undone, Let fall her weak dissolved Limbs Support. **1609** BIBLE (Douay) *1 Chron.* xxii. 3 Yron for the nayles of the gates, and for the ioyninges and ioynctures. **1726** LEONI *Alberti's Archit.* III. 30/1 The jointures and commissures of both halves shou'd perfectly tally to each other. **1888** *Harper's Mag.* Aug. 332 A wall whose every jointure is being attacked by vigorous little weeds.

†**3.** The holding of an estate by two or more persons in joint-tenancy. *Obs.*

[**1533–4** *Act 25 Hen. VIII*, c. 13 §7 Euerie personne.. which..shall haue iuncture in vse or in possession..of or in any manours.] **1574** tr. *Littleton's Tenures* 57 b, He that surviveth shal have onely the whole tenancy after such estate as he hath if yᵉ iointure bee continued. **1601–2** FULBECKE *1st Pt. Parall.* 30 If lands be giuen to two, and the heirs of one of them, this is a good iointure, & the one hath freehold & the other fee simple, and if hee which hath the fee die, he that hath the frehold shal haue the entierty. **1660** BONDE *Scut. Reg.* 223 If Lands are given to the King and a subject, or if there be two jointenants and the Crown descend to one of them, the Jointure is severed, and they are Tenants in Common. **1767** BLACKSTONE *Comm.* II. xii. 180 Such..an estate is called an estate in joint-tenancy, and sometimes an estate in jointure.

4. *spec.* **a.** *orig.* The holding of property to the joint use of a husband and wife for life or in tail, as a provision for the latter, in the event of her widowhood. Hence, by extension, **b.** A sole estate limited to the wife, being 'a competent livelihood of freehold for the wife of lands and tenements, to take effect upon the death of the husband for the life of the wife at least' (Coke upon Littleton, 36 b).

1451 *Rolls Parlt.* V. 218/1 This Acte shall not extende to the prejudice of..the Quene of hir Dower, joyntour or freeholder, to hir by you graunted. *a***1466** *Paston Lett.* II. 79 The maner of Estlexham, the qwych is parte of my juntor. **1513** MORE *Rich. III*, Wks. (1557) 58 Yᵗ she might be restored vnto such smal landes as her late husband had giuen her in iointure. **1535** *Act 27 Hen. VIII*, c. x. §4 In every suche case every woman maryed havyng such Ioynter ..shal not clayme to have eny Dower of the residue of the Landes..that..were her said husbondes. **1556** *R. Arden's Will* in French *Shaks. Geneal.* (1869) 470, I will that my wyfe shall have butt iij.*li.* vjs. viij.*d.* and her gintur in Snytterfylde. **1684** WOOD *Life* 11 May (O.H.S.) III. 95 He had married a widow of 700 li. per annum joynter. **1767** BLACKSTONE *Comm.* II. viii. 137 A jointure..strictly speaking, signifies a joint estate, limited to both husband and wife, but in common acceptation extends also to a sole estate, limited to the wife only. **1876** DIGBY *Real Prop.* vi. 295 It became a common practice for a man upon his marriage to convey lands to feoffees to the joint use of

himself and his wife for life or in tail, by which means a provision for the remainder of her life was secured to the wife. This was called a jointure.

†**c.** Used as equivalent to *dowry*: see DOWRY 2.

1494 FABYAN *Chron.* VII. ccxxix. 259 For the withholdyng of the dowre, or ioyntoure, of his firste doughter, maryed vnto Wyllyam ye Kynges sone. **1580** LYLY *Euphues* (Arb.) 280, I am perswaded yat my faire daughter shal be wel maryed, for there is none, that will or can demaund a greater ioynter then Beautie. **1598** FLORIO, *Indotato*, without a dowrie or iointer. **1615** J. STEPHENS *Satyr. Ess.* 364 She would make likewise a thousand pound Joyncture of her behaviour only, and Court-carriage.

5. *Comb.*, as **jointure-castle, -house**, one settled upon a woman as a jointure (sense 4); †**jointure-water** = *joint-water*, synovia (see JOINT *sb.* 15).

1599 A. M. tr. *Gabelhouer's Bk. Physicke* 324/2 We must not to suddaynly restrayne the Synnue, or Ioyncture-water. **1773** JOHNSON in *Boswell* 18 Sept., Most of the great families of England have a secondary residence, which is called a jointure-house. **1830** MISS MITFORD *Village* Ser. IV. (1863) 273 Leaving the great town in which she had hitherto resided, and coming to occupy the family jointure-house at Oakhampstead. **1852** MISS YONGE *Cameos* (1877) III. ix. 73 Within this castle lay the little King, who was thus conveyed to her jointure castle at Stirling.

'jointure, *v.* [f. prec. sb.] *trans.* To settle a jointure upon; to provide with a jointure: see prec. 4.

a **1634** RANDOLPH *Poems* (1638) 6 But what fond virgin will my love preferre, That only in Parnassus joynture her? **1667-8** PEPYS *Diary* 10 Feb., She to have £600 presently, and..to be joyntured in £60 per annum. **1762** FOOTE *Lyar* III. Wks. 1799 I. 313 She'll be easily jointur'd. **1885** *Law Rep.* 28 Chanc. Div. 205 Trusts which gave *A.* and *B.* respectively..powers of jointuring their wives.

jointured ('dʒɔɪntjʊəd), *a.* [See -ED.]

1. Provided with a jointure; holding a jointure.

1766 BURROW *Rep.* I. 215 Even jointured ladies of manors, might make voluntary grant, and incumber their posterity.

2. Of an estate: Saddled with a jointure.

1818 CRUISE *Digest* (ed. 2) IV. 192 The charges the jointured estate was to be freed from.

'jointureless, *a.* [f. JOINTURE *sb.* + -LESS.] Without a jointure; not provided with a jointure.

c **1611** CHAPMAN *Iliad* IX. 150 Of all three, the worthiest let him take All ioynturelesse, to Peleus court; I will her ioyncture make; And that so great, as neuer yet, did any maide preferre.

jointuress ('dʒɔɪntjʊərɪs). [Altered form of JOINTRESS, after *jointure*.] = JOINTRESS.

a **1693** AUBREY *Lives* (1898) I. 136 He [Butler] maried a good jointuresse, the relict of Morgan, by which meanes he lives comfortably. **1711** *Lond. Gaz.* No. 4905/3 The Reversion and Fee-Simple Estate, after the Death of a Jointuress. **1848** WHARTON *Law Lex.*, *Jointress*, or *Jointuress*.

jointweed ('dʒɔɪntwiːd). Popular name of different weeds having conspicuously jointed stems. **a.** In U.S., *Polygonum articulatum*. **b.** Locally in Eng., various species of Horsetail (*Equisetum*); also the common Mare's-tail (*Hippuris vulgaris*).

a. 1866 *Treas. Bot.* **1884** MILLER *Plant-n.*
b. 1879 BRITTEN & HOLLAND *Plant-n.*

'joint-worm.

1. A tape-worm; as consisting of a series of joints.

1706 MRS. CENTLIVRE *Basset-Table* III. Eiij, 'Tis the Joint-Worm, which the Learned talk of so much,..or Vulgarly in English the Tape-Worm.

2. *U.S.* The larval form of several species of chalcid flies belonging to the genus *Harmolita* (or *Tetramesa*), which forms galls near joints on grain stems, causing them to bend.

1851 *Southern Planter* (Richmond, Virginia) July 197/2 Joint worm has injured White Flint most, Early Purple Straw next, and Mediterranean least. **1851** A. FITCH in *Cultivator* VIII. 322/1, I first observe, lying upon the infested stalk, the insect to which you allude in your letter, as perhaps having been hatched from the joint-worm. **1852** T. W. HARRIS *Insects Injurious to Vegetation* (ed. 2) 443 The ravages of the joint-worm in the wheatfields of Virginia are said to have been first observed in Albemarle county, about four or five years ago. **1882** *Illinois Entomol. Rep.* XI. 81, I have obtained another specimen of this species from a gall in a stalk, produced evidently by the regular joint-worm. **1918** *U.S. Dept. Agric. Farmers' Bull.* No. 1006. 2 This jointworm can be controlled in Virginia, Tennessee, and Kentucky by plowing down wheat stubble deeply after harvest. **1972** SWAN & PAPP *Common Insects N. Amer.* xxi. 537 The Rye Jointworm, *T[etramesa] secale*, occurs in eastern U.S., westward to Utah and Alberta.

jointy ('dʒɔɪntɪ), *a.* [f. JOINT *sb.* + -Y.] Full of joints; having numerous joints.

1578 LYTE *Dodoens* II. cvii. 296 The..stalke is thicke, and ioyntie. **1747** HOOSON *Miner's Dict.* Eij b, When it lies in a Body of considerable thickness, it is more Brickle and Joynty. **1855** G. MEREDITH *Shav. Shagpat* 332 They were as jointy grasshoppers through the action of the Flea.

join-work: see JOIN-.

†**joise,** *v. Obs.* Forms: 4 iois(s)en, iosyen; *Sc.* 4-6 ioys, 5-6 iois, 6 iose, ioyse, ioise, 7 ioiss, (9 joyse). [a. OF. *joiss-*, lengthened stem of *joir*: see JOY *v.* and REJOICE.]

1. *refl.* and *intr.* To rejoice.

c **1320** *Seuyn Sag.* (W.) 92 That thai made so grete josying. *a* **1325** *Prose Psalter* cxlix. 2 Ioisen þe douȝters of Syon in her kynge. **1340** *Ayenb.* 25 þus him ioisseþ and him glorifieþ þe wreche ine his herte.

2. *trans.* (*Sc.*) To enjoy the possession or use of.

a **1400** *Burgh Laws* c. 41 (*Sc. Stat.* I.) þan sall þe man ioys [*gaudebit*] all þe gudis of þat lande. **1508** DUNBAR *Tua mariit wemen* 201, I wend I iosit a gem, and I hafe ane geit gottin. **1615** in *Proc. Soc. Ant. Scot.* (1896) XXX. 56 To use and exerce the said office..als frelie..as vmquhile Schir William McDougall..bruikit and joissit the samen of before. [*c* **1817** HOGG *Tales & Sk.* V. 152 To be peaceably brooked, joysed, set, used and disposed of by him and his aboves, as specified.]

joise, joissh, obs. forms of JOIST, JUICE.

joist (dʒɔɪst), *sb.*^{1} Forms: α. 4 **gieste**, 4-6 **gyste**, **geste, gyest**, 5-6 **giste**, (5 **gyyst**), 6 **geist, gyst**, 6-7 **geast(e**, 7 **geest**. β. 7-8 **gise** (*pl.* **gises, gise**, 7 **jyce**). γ. 5-6 **iest(e**, 6- 7 **ieast**, 7 *Sc.* **jest, jeist**. δ. 5-6 **ioyste**, 6-7 **ioyst**, 7 **ioist**, 7-8 **joyst**, 7- **joist**. ε. 6 **ioyse** (**ioysse**), 6-7 **ioise, ioyce**, 7 **ioice** (**iuice**), **joyse**, 7-8 **joyce** (*pl.* **joyces, joyce**), 8 **joice**. [ME. *giste, gyste*, a. OF. *giste*, one of the beams supporting a bridge, in mod.F. *gîte* one of the small beams supporting a platform for artillery, a bed of mineral, etc., f. OF. *gesir* (mod.F. *gésir*):—L. *jacēre* to lie.

The later form *joist* has parallels in HOISE, HOIST, FOIST *sb.*^{3}, and JOIST *sb.*^{2}. These developments of *oi* from *i* are of earlier date than the interchange of (aɪ) and (ɔɪ) in *boil, bile*, etc., and their phonetic history is as yet obscure.]

1. One of the timbers on which the boards of a floor or the laths of a ceiling are nailed, and which themselves stand on edge parallel to each other stretching horizontally from wall to wall, or resting on supporting beams or girders; also, A timber which similarly supports the floor of a platform, a bridge, or other structure.

In a large floor the main joists (*binding joists*) are sometimes more widely apart, and are crossed by smaller ***bridging joists*** which bear the boards of the floor; in such a case there may be light joists beneath to bear the laths (*ceiling joists*). See also TRIMMING *joist*.

α. [**1294** *Pat. Roll 22 Edw. I*, m. 3 in *Calr.* 102 Ad voltam vel gistas.] **1379** *Mem. Ripon* (Surtees) III. 100 Pro j gyste pro le flore in clocher—*3d.* **1448** in Willis & Clark *Cambridge* (1886) II. 8 The Gistes shall be on the one part squar vj inches and on the other part viij inches. **1535** COVERDALE *Jer.* xxii. 14 The sylinges and geastes maketh he off Cedre. *a* **1651** CALDERWOOD *Hist. Kirk* (Wodrow Soc.) III. 77 They drew down manie of Alex Clerks geests lying in the street.

β. **1674** PETTY *Disc. Dupl. Proportion* 54 Which saving of stuff is the reason of dividing Plank into Girders, Gise, and Board. *Ibid.*, 17 Gises of 9 inches deep. **1699** *Boston Rec.* (1881) VII. 237 From out side to out side of the Jyce of said Bridge. **1711** W. SUTHERLAND *Shipbuild. Assist.* 42 Which Girder contains but half the Stuff of the 17 Gise.

γ. **1413-14** in Willis & Clark *Cambridge* (1886) II. 441 Item pro xv Jestys longitudinis xiij ped'. **1581** *Hull Charterho. Acc.* in *N. & Q.* 6th Ser. VIII. 217/1, 1 ieast, 2 sparres, 1 furdeale. **1673** WEDDERBURN *Voc.* (Jam.), *Tignus*, a jest.

δ. **1494** FABYAN *Chron.* VI. cxcvi. 201 Sodenly the ioystes of the lofte fayled, and the people fell downe. **1523** LD. BERNERS *Froiss.* I. cxxv. 150 They came to Poyssey, and founde the brige broken, but the arches and ioystes lay in the ryuer. **1658** ROWLAND *Moufet's Theat. Ins.* 899 Under the next ceiling between the joysts. **1667** PRIMATT *City & C. Build.* 78 The fourth being a Cross Joyst or Girder. *Ibid.* 81 Binding-Joysts with their Trimming-Joysts, thickness five inches, depth equal to their own floors. **1708** SWIFT *Baucis & Phil.* 58 The kettle to the top was hoist, And there stood fasten'd to a joist. **1823** P. NICHOLSON *Pract. Build.* 118 When the supporting timbers of a floor are formed by one row laid upon another, the upper row are called bridging joists, and the lower row are called binding joists. **1899** R. KIPLING *Stalky & Co.* 76 The floor-joists of one room are the ceiling-joists of the room below.

ε. **1570** LEVINS *Manip.* 215/46 Ioyse of a house, *trabula*. **1600** J. PORY tr. *Leo's Africa* II. 125 The tops of these temples..are made of ioises and planks. **1613** SIR R. BOYLE in *Lismore Papers* (1886) I. 23, I rec^d out of ffrance..20 square Ioyce. **1633** T. STAFFORD *Pac. Hib.* III. viii. (1810) 560 To make Ioyces for the platforme. **1663** GERBIER *Counsel* 43 That the Joyses be framed $2\frac{1}{2}$ or three Inches under the top of the Summers. **1703** S. SEWALL *Diary* 25 Sept. (1879) II. 89 The Beams and Joyce of the old Hall Floor are laid.

†**2.** A beam, plank, or deal. *Obs.*

1375 BARBOUR *Bruce* XVII. 597 Of gret gestis ane sow thai maid. **1661** *Sc. Acts Chas. II* (1814) VII. 252/2 Jeists of oak ilk tuentie peices.

†**3.** (See quot. 1598.) *Obs.*

1502 ARNOLDE *Chron.* (1811) 85 That the brewars..fill up the vessels after thei be leyde on the gyest. **1552** HULOET, Ioysse, whervpon great vessell are couched, or set, *incitega*. **1598** FLORIO, *Rincalzo*,..a thing laide vnder a barrell to keepe it from rouling or falling... Some call it a ioyce.

†**4.** A mass of mineral in its natural bed. (F. *gîte*.) *Obs.*

1829 *Glover's Hist. Derby* I. 101 A quantity of very white, striated or fibrous gypsum is dug in the Chellaston pits, in thin beds, called joists.

5. *attrib.* and *Comb.*, as *joist-hole*; †**joist-tree**, a joist, beam.

1566 in Peacock *Eng. Ch. Furniture* (1866) 95 Item the rood lofte sold to Johnne okelye and Robarte harwood and thei haue made a ioyce tree for a chamber. **1886** MRS. CADDY *Footst. Jeanne D'Arc* 109 The joist holes are also visible.

joist (**joyest, joyse**), *sb.*^{2}, obs. and dial. ff. GIST *sb.*^{2}, agistment. [As to the *oi* from *i*, see prec.]

1558 *Nottingham Bor. Rec.* (1889) IV. 118 For pyche to merke kye with all, at the first joyest taken in-to the Cow-pasture. **1621** *Naworth Househ. Bk.* (Surtees) 158 Rec. of Henry Wilson for joyse cattle at Mosedall, xx^{li}. **1854** *Jrnl. R. Agric. Soc.* XV. I. 234 The farmers keep no sheep, but a man called a 'joist' shepherd brings his flock, and has the run of the stubbles and other food.

joist (dʒɔɪst), *v.*^{1} Forms: see JOIST *sb.*^{1} [f. JOIST *sb.*^{1}] *trans.* **a.** To furnish with joists. **b.** To fix on joists.

a **1615** *Brieue Cron. Erlis Ross* (1850) 20 He caused to joist and loft the chamber. **1635** BRERETON *Trav.* (Chetham Soc.) 95 A fair long gallery joiced, not boarded. **1839** SOUTHEY in *Q. Rev.* LXIII. 423 Large holes..in which the several floorings were joisted.

joist, *v.*^{2}, obs. and dial. f. GIST *v.*, to agist.

1601 HOLLAND *Pliny* XXI. x, By joisting and laying in of the said beasts. **1767** A. YOUNG *Farmer's Lett. to People* 238 The common price of joisting a horse is one shilling and six-pence per week in clover. **1851** *Jrnl. R. Agric. Soc.* XII. II. 408 Many of the labourers keep a cow, or 'joist' one upon a neighbouring farmer's land.

joisting ('dʒɔɪstɪŋ). [f. JOIST *sb.*^{1}: see -ING^1 1 g.] The timber-work of joists supporting a floor or the like; the mass or structure of joists.

1651 *Ayr Presbyt. Rec.* in *Lit. Scott. World* iv. (1894) 43 The flooring and gisting to be directly the height of the place of repentance. **1893** *Westm. Gaz.* 30 Oct. 4/2 About 12ft. by 12ft. of the flooring and joisting was involved in the flames.

'joistless, *a.* [f. JOIST *sb.*^{1} + -LESS.] Having no joists.

1861 BP. SMITH *Ten Weeks Japan* xix. 273 The houses.. were..joistless structures unfastened with clamps and ligatures at the angles.

joit, obs. Sc. form of JOT *sb.*^{1}

Jokari (dʒə'kɑːrɪ). The proprietary name of a game played with bat and ball.

The name is registered for a number of games, etc. (see quot. 1973).

1953 *N.Y. Times* 2 Aug. 43L (Advt.), Jokari requires little space. You use paddles and a ball that's fastened to the Jokari center control box on a long rubber cable. **1960** 'A. GARVE' *Golden Deed* xxiv. 161 A bald, plump man..was playing Jokari with an equally plump youth on the grass outside the door... Mellanby waited till the ball had come to rest. **1961** B. W. ALDISS *Primal Urge* ii. 34 That podgy creature who..played Jokari from a sitting position. **1963** I. FLEMING *On H.M. Secret Service* i. 11 Two golden girls in exciting bikinis packed up the game of Jokari which they had been so provocatively playing. **1973** *Trade Marks Jrnl.* 4 Apr. 665/1 Jokari... Games (other than ordinary playing cards), playthings, gymnastic and sporting articles (other than clothing), and parts..of all the aforesaid goods. R. & J. Travis Limited, Fenbright Works,..Berkhamsted, Hertfordshire; manufacturers and merchants.

joke (dʒəʊk), *sb.* Also 7 **joque, joc**, 8 **joak**. [Appeared in second half of 17th c., app. originally in slang or colloquial use: cf. JOKING *vbl. sb.*, quot. 1670; app. ad. L. *joc-us* jest, joke, sport: cf. It. *gioco* 'game, play, sport, jeast' (Florio).]

1. a. Something said or done to excite laughter or amusement; a witticism, a jest; jesting, raillery; also, something that causes amusement, a ridiculous circumstance.

practical joke, a trick or prank played upon some person usually in order to have a laugh at his expense. Phr. ***to cut, crack a joke; to turn a matter into a joke***, etc.; ***a joke is a joke***: a joke is not to be taken seriously (freq. with the implication that the matter referred to is too serious for jokes); ***joke over***: the joke is finished (usu. implying that the speaker is not amused by the words or behaviour of the person addressed).

1670 EACHARD *Cont. Clergy* 34 To have the right knack of letting off a joque, and of pleasing the humsters. **1683** KENNETT tr. *Erasm. on Folly* 19 Coming off with so many dry joques and biting Repartees. **1683** DR. EDW. HOOKER *Pref. Ep. to Pordage's Myst. Div.* 15 Jocs, or Witticisms, Railleries and Drolleries, Quirks and Quillets. **1726-46** THOMSON *Winter* 623 The simple joke that takes the shepherd's heart. **1741** FIELDING *Ess., Conversat.*, Tossing men out of their chairs, tumbling them into water, or any of those handicraft jokes. **1741** WATTS *Improv. Mind* I. xviii. §17 A merry joak upon the stage. **1748** RICHARDSON *Clarissa* Wks. 1883 VII. 410, I..should not forbear to cut a joke, were I upon a scaffold. **1749** SMOLLETT *Gil Blas* III. i. ¶5 The best joke of all was, I did not know my master's name. **1790** BEATTIE *Moral Sc.* I. i. §7 The practice of turning every thing into joke and ridicule is a dangerous levity of imagination. **1804** M. WILMOT *Let.* 4 June in *Russ. Jrnls.* (1934) I. 104 Such are the practical Jokes of the Great. **1824** J. HOGG *Private Mem. Justified Sinner* 356 Nane o' your practical jokes on strangers an' honest foks. **1837** DICKENS *Sk. Boz* 2nd Ser. 123 A joke's a joke: and even practical jests are very capital in their way, if you can only get the other party to see the fun. **1838** T. C. HALIBURTON *Clockmaker* 2nd Ser. xvii. 253 A joke is a joke, but that's no joke. **1849** [see PRACTICAL *a.* 1]. **1870** E. PEACOCK *Ralf Skirl.* I. 186 All practical jokes do seem to be particularly foolish to those who suffer from them. **1892** [see *bear-fight*]. **1930** R. GORE-BROWNE *By Way of Confession* vi. 52 'Goes too far, 'e does!' agreed an elder with a walrus mustache. 'A joke's er joke.' 'And politics is politics!' The retort came from a skinny-necked man. **1941** [see COD *v.*^{3}]. *a* **1953** E. O'NEILL *Long Day's Journey* (1956) I. 25 No, Mary, a joke is a joke, but —. **1961** PARTRIDGE *Dict. Slang* Suppl. 1153/2 Joke over! or when do we laugh? **1965** G. M. WILSON *Devil's Skull* ix. 112

'Telephone!' He laughed again. 'All right, joke over,' said Lovick, nettled. **1967** C. WATSON *Lonelyheart 4122* xviii. 180 All right. Joke over. Now just what is it you think you're up to? **1972** *Listener* 2 Nov. 614/1 Midnight feasts, practical jokes and all the fun of the dormitory.

b. ***black joke*** (see quot. 1796). Also ***coal-black joke***. *slang*.

1729 C. COFFEY *Beggar's Wedding* I. iv. 17 (*heading*) Hunter with Musick. Air X. Coal-black Joak. *c* **1734** in Hearne *Collect.* (O.H.S.) II. 463 His black Jokes or smutty Songs. **1748** SMOLLETT *R. Random* II. liii. 186 He whistled one part and hummed another of Black Joke. **1796** GROSE *Dict. Vulgar T.* (ed. 3) *Black Joke*, a popular tune to a song, having for the burden, 'Her black joke and belly so white': figuratively the black joke signifies the monosyllable. **1808** S. W. RYLEY *Itinerant* I. iv. 91 A blind fiddler, mounted on a three footed stool, rasped away very *seriously* the black *Joke*. *c* **1835** *Song*, '*Oxford Freshman*', Next night I got drunker than ever, And sang the Black Joke at his [my Tutor's] door. **1970** P. O'BRIAN *Master & Commander* ix. 252 He decided..to sit it out until the drum beat to quarters, ..humming the Black Joke.

2. *transf.* An object of or matter for joking; a laughing-stock.

1791 'G. GAMBADO' *Ann. Horsem.* x. (1809) 109, I am the joke of the road wherever I go. **1823** J. F. COOPER *Pilot* xvi, I shall be the standing joke of the mess-table, until some greater fool than myself can be found.

3. Something not earnest or serious; a jesting matter. ***no joke***, a serious matter.

1726 GAY *Let. to Swift* 22 Oct., I wish, I could tell you, that the cutting of the tendons of two of his fingers was a joke; but it is really so. **1737** POPE *Hor. Ep.* II. ii. 261 Link towns to towns with avenues of oak, Enclose whole downs in walls, 'tis all a joke! Inexorable Death shall level all. **1809** MALKIN *Gil Blas* IX. viii. ¶8 And indeed it was no joke. **1890** *Guardian* 29 Oct. 1711/1 An Irish faction fight is evidently no joke.

4. *attrib.* and *Comb.*, as ***joke book***, ***joke-capping***; ***joke-exchanging***, ***-loving***, ***shop***, ***-worthy*** adjs.; **joke-fellow**, one with whom a joke is shared.

1951 J. STEINBECK *Burning Bright* 23 His malformed wisdom, his pool-hall, locker-room, joke-book wisdom. **1973** T. TOBIN *Lett. of George Ade* 174 This rare pamphlet is in the Ford joke book tradition. **1883** T. WRIGHT *Unknown Public in 19th Cent.*, Opportunities for using them in the way of joke-capping. **1821** GALT *Sir A. Wylie* III. xxiv. 197 That English Lord and his Leddy mak him joke-fellow wi' themselves. **1947** K. P. KEMPTON *Short Story* 189 At a joke shop in town he had bought one of those spark-plug bombs with the idea of hitching it to a friend's jalopy. **1951** J. M. FRASER *Psychol.* iii. 28 Any 'joke-shop' will furnish examples of similar bits of apparatus designed to suggest a misleading total situation. **1967** V. C. CLINTON-BADDELEY *Death's Bright Dart* 122 Sinister in the silence gleamed the window of the Joke Shop. **1973** E. PAGE *Fortnight by Sea* ix. 101 One of those joke shops, you know, rubber poached eggs, exploding cigars. **1866** *Ch. & State Rev.* 17 Aug. 518 A very joke-worthy subject.

joke (dʒəʊk), *v.* [f. JOKE *sb.*, or ad. L. *jocārī* to jest, to joke: cf. It. *giocare*, also JOKE *sb.*]

1. a. *intr.* To make jokes, to jest.

[*Joking* is attributed to Milton in Warton's ed. of M.'s *Poems* 1785, p. 375; thence in Todd, and Globe ed. p. 575. But the actual reading (*Apol. Smect.* i. (1642) 26) is *jesting*, which remains in all edd. of the Prose Wks.]

1670 [see JOKING *vbl. sb.*]. **1723** STEELE *Consc. Lovers* IV. i, Your Honour is pleas'd to joke with me. **1768–74** TUCKER *Lt. Nat.* (1834) II. 337 They quote Elijah for a precedent, who joked upon the four hundred priests of Baal. **1823** F. CLISSOLD *Ascent Mt. Blanc* 10 The guides, who had so reluctantly agreed to ascend, now merrily joked upon our novel situation. **1858** HAWTHORNE *Fr. & It. Jrnls.* II. 286 The benchers joke with the women passing by, and are joked with back again.

b. ***you are*** (or ***have got to be***) ***joking***, etc.: in phrases indicative of incredulity. Cf. also HAVE *v.* 7d.

1907 G. B. SHAW *John Bull's Other Island* II. 36 Youre joking, Mr. Keegan: I'm sure yar. **1967** PARTRIDGE *Dict. Slang* Suppl. 1204/2 *You're, he is*, etc. *joking, of course.* A c.p. of modified optimism. **1967** N. LUCAS *C.I.D.* xiii. 195 'Norman, would you be interested in meeting Charlie de Silva?' 'Probably,' I replied, 'but where do I have to go, Paris, New York..' 'You're joking. He's skint.' **1968** M. STEWART *Wind off Small Isles* i. 26 'If I've got to turn on sand—' 'You could reverse up.' 'You've got to be joking.' **1972** *Times* 29 Sept. 15/5 'We can consider ourselves fortunate in the character of the Prime Minister.'.. In the parlance of the day, you must be joking, mate.

2. *trans.* To make the object of a joke or jokes; to poke fun at; to chaff, banter, rally.

1748 SMOLLETT *Rod. Rand.* lvii, Miss Snapper.. pretended to joke me upon my passion for Narcissa. **1768** BOSWELL *Corsica* (ed. 2) 282, I often joked them with the text which is applied to their order. **1789** MRS. PIOZZI *Journ. France* II. 28 Sir Joseph Banks joked her about Otoroo. **1838** P'CESS ELIZABETH in *Lett.* (1898) 344 She loves to joke others. *a* **1847** MRS. SHERWOOD *Lady of Manor* III. xix. 100 It is my wish never to be joked upon subjects of this kind.

3. *trans.* To get or put (*out* or *away*) by joking.

1863 COWDEN CLARKE *Shaks. Char.* x. 268 A fellow who will joke and laugh the money out of your pocket. **1891** *Harper's Mag.* July 194/1 The question was joked away between them.

joke, variant of JOUK *v.*[1] *Obs.*

jokee (dʒəʊˈkiː). *colloq.* [f. JOKE *v.* + -EE.] One on whom a joke is played.

1869 M. BROWNE *Chaucer's Eng.* I. 275 The practical joker..who was also, in due course, very frequently the jokee too. **1880** *Punch* LXXIX. 189/1 The fun is fast and the jokees [are] furious.

jokeless (ˈdʒəʊklɪs), *a.* [-LESS.] Devoid of jokes, lacking humour or wit.

1846 D. JERROLD *Chron. Clovernook* Wks. 1864 IV. 419 The jokeless..become physically forlorn.

jokelet (ˈdʒəʊklɪt). [f. JOKE *sb.* + -LET.] A little joke, a small witticism.

1847 ALB. SMITH *Chr. Tadpole* xv. (1879) 136 The lecturer to enliven his subject made some small witticism —or jokelet. **1875** MISS BRADDON *Str. World* I. i. 17 Justina began to laugh, as if it had been a green-room jokelet.

joker (ˈdʒəʊkə(r)). [f. JOKE *v.* + -ER[1].]

1. One who jokes; a jester; a merry fellow. Freq. in ***practical joker***.

1729 T. COOKE *Tales, Proposals*, etc. 118 St. Patrick's Dean, of holy Men the Pest, A scurril Joker, and of all the Jest. **1807–8** SYD. SMITH *Plymley's Lett.* Wks. 1859 II. 164/1 Thou shalt be laid low by a joker of jokes, and he shall talk his pleasant talk against thee. **1830** G. COLMAN *Random Rec.* II. vi. 205 It convinced me that he was no practical joker. **1879** MCCARTHY *Own Times* II. xviii. 12 The temptation to schoolboys and practical jokers of all kinds was irresistible. **1887** *Spectator* 9 Apr. 491/2 Some confirmed jokers,—verbal contortionists. **1899** BEERBOHM *More* 70 Scores of licensed practical jokers. **1926** A. CONAN DOYLE *Hist. Spiritualism* I. vii. 153 The contemptible crew of practical jokers and ill-natured researchers who visited her found her a ready victim. **1950** T. S. ELIOT *Cocktail Party* II. 104 Are you a devil Or merely a lunatic practical joker?

2. *slang.* Man, 'fellow', 'chap'. Also *transf.* to animals (esp. *Austral.* and *N.Z.*).

1811 *Sporting Mag.* XXXVIII. 50 Six jokers on horse-back were standing stock still. **1844** DICKENS *Mart. Chuz.* xli, You were another sort of a joker, in those days, you were! **1868** *Auckland Punch* No. 2. 7/1 If Louis Napoleon could be prevailed on to bring over his Zouaves, and join the mounted marines, together with some Indian jokers. **1888** J. D. WICKHAM *Ramblings* xv. 92 The driver of this coach was the joker that wanted to charge me a shilling. **1891** C. ROBERTS *Adrift Amer.* 136 We spotted some very fine turkeys, and my hungry companion said at once, 'There is a good feed for two men on one of those jokers'. **1894** *Times* 14 Feb. 3/2 We managed to get the sick joker out of his bunk, but we could not get him aft. **1895** [see BEST *a.* 5b]. **1941** *Coast to Coast* 197 We'd get tired of tramping around the mines listening to well-fed jokers say 'No'. **1949** [see CLEAN *v.* 6b]. **1951** *Landfall* V. 21 There are about a dozen brush in the place and about three times as many jokers. **1963** *Australasian Post* 14 Mar. 51/2 Mr Dingleton turned out to be a tall, rather thin, pleasant-looking joker with big feet. **1970** *N.Z. Listener* 12 Oct. 13/5 Their benevolent guff's even harder for a decent-spirited joker to accept.

3. a. Something used in playing a trick.

1858 O. W. HOLMES *Aut. Breakf.-t.* ii. (1883) 30 The thimble-rigger's 'little joker'. **1895** *Rev. of Rev.* Jan. (Farmer), These little jokers were attached to the left thumbs of certain judges of election as the ballots were being counted. These jokers are made of rubber and have a cross on them.

b. An odd card in a pack, either left blank or ornamented with some design, used in some games, counting always as a trump and sometimes as the highest trump. Also in fig. phr. ***joker in the pack***: a person whose behaviour is unexpected or unpredictable.

1885 J. B. GREENOUGH *Queen of Hearts* iii. (Cent.), The White Knight, called the Joker, otherwise the Best Bower. **1894** *St. James's Gaz.* 19 July (Farmer), The game of poker is played with a pack of fifty-three cards, the fifty-third card being called the joker... American manufacturers of playing-cards are wont to include a blank card at the top of the pack; and it is, alas! true that some thrifty person suggested that the card should not be wasted. This was the origin of the joker. **1894** MASKELYNE *Sharps & Flats* 223 In euchre you can hold the joker every time. **1963** *Times* 25 Feb. (Canada Suppl.) p. ii/2 Mr. Caouette is a joker in the pack; his group's tally of 26 federal seats reflects a morbid situation. **1973** G. SIMS *Hunters Point* vi. 47 Fred Wheeler may be the joker in the pack. He might have got Dave involved in something wild. **1974** *Times* 9 May 4/1 Although the Government has a majority of four votes over the Conservatives, there are 37 'jokers in the pack'.

4. A clause unobtrusively inserted in a legislative enactment and affecting its operation in a way not immediately apparent. Also *transf.* of a clause, etc., in a contract, administrative order, etc., which frustrates its intention or puts one of the parties at a disadvantage; *fig.*, a drawback, a 'snag', a trick. *U.S.*

1904 *N.Y. Even. Post* 11 May 1 They are all nervous over the possibility that there may be a hitherto unperceived joker in the present bill. **1906** *Ibid.* 30 Apr. 6 The Malby 'joker' to the Adirondack Reserve bill. **1914** S. H. ADAMS *Clarion* 241 Even her simple mind grasped the joker in the contract. **1928** *Daily Express* 17 July 8/2 The surtax was slipped into the Finance Act of 1927 very much as a 'joker' is occasionally insinuated into an American Tariff Act—that is to say, surreptitiously, without anybody except those in the know being aware of the significance of what was happening. **1935** A. J. POLLOCK *Underworld Speaks* 65/1 *Joker* (*nigger in the wood pile*), laws, investigations, vice abatements, controversies, political appointments, newspaper articles, speeches or contracts arranged for..so that the looters in on the in will be financially benefited. **1942** E. PAUL *Narrow St.* xiv. 100 Early in 1926 Painlevé introduced a bill to reorganize the French army from thirty-two to twenty divisions. To this was attached a joker, increasing the term of universal compulsory military service from one year to eighteen months. **1947** *Harper's Mag.* Nov. 441/1 The order also contains this crucial joker: The charges shall be stated as specifically and completely as..security conditions permit. **1953** *Congress. Rec.* XCIX. App. A5292/2 A postal rate increase bill..had within it a 'joker' which seriously affected the nonprofit publications of organized labor in all parts of America.

Hence **ˈjokeress**, a female joker. †**ˈjokery**, jesting, raillery.

1740 *Apol. Life Mr. T. C., Comedian*, When he spoke, that seriousness of Joakery was discharged and a dry drolling levity took possession of him. **1858** DORAN *Crt. Fools* 66 She was the duly-appointed jokeress, if I may so speak, to the Duchess. **1970** *Daily Tel.* 21 May 6/5, I could find very little to make me laugh..although it has all the ingredients of current jokery.

jokesman (ˈdʒəʊksmən). *nonce-wd.* [f. *joke's*, possess. of JOKE *sb.* + MAN: cf. *spokesman*.] A professional joker.

1882 *Sat. Rev.* 4 Nov. 598/2 To preserve the spirits of the Liberal party a jokesman was necessary.

jokesmith (ˈdʒəʊksmɪθ). [f. JOKE *sb.* + SMITH: cf. *rimesmith*.] A manufacturer of jokes.

1813 SOUTHEY *Lett.* (1856) II. 336 (D.), I feared to give occasion to the jests of newspaper jokesmiths. **1820** —— *Devil's Walk* (D.), My jokesmith Sidney, and all his kidney. **1886** *Sat. Rev.* 20 Mar. 400/1 To judge from the tone of the untimely jokesmith's letter.

jokesome (ˈdʒəʊksəm), *a.* [f. as prec. + -SOME.] Characterized by jokes, facetious, jocular.

1810 H. V. ELLIOTT *Let.* in Bateman *Life* i. (1870) 16 Light and jokesome Terpsichore. **1885** B. L. FARJEON *Sacred Nugget* I. I. xiii. 185 He would indulge in jokesome reminiscences.

Hence **ˈjokesomeness**, humorousness.

1880 BLACKMORE *Mary Anerley* lvii. (1881) 435 Her husband excelled in jokesomeness.

jokester (ˈdʒəʊkstə(r)). [f. JOKE *v.* + -STER: cf. *punster*.] A petty joker.

1877 *Daily News* 11 Oct. 5/6 Set in fashion by pious jokesters. **1899** *Ibid.* 13 Oct. 6/3 The opportunities which Sir Charles's fanaticism furnished to the satirists and jokesters of his time.

jokey: see JOKY *a.*

jokiness (ˈdʒəʊkɪnɪs). [f. JOKY *a.* + -NESS.] A joking style or manner.

1869 D. G. ROSSETTI *Let.* 26 Aug. (1965) II. 720 His letters remind one by their ponderous jokiness of Holman Hunt. **1966** *Punch* 26 Jan. 138/3 Very short chapters and much coy jokiness about methods of fiction add to the Shandean charm. **1971** *Daily Tel.* (Colour Suppl.) 8 Jan. 6/2 The jokiness at a first night of an amateur theatrical company. **1974** *Times* 11 May 9/8 The self-conscious jokiness and triviality that is the bane of newscasting on British television.

joking (ˈdʒəʊkɪŋ), *vbl. sb.* [f. JOKE *v.* + -ING[1].]

a. The action of the vb. JOKE; jesting. Phr. ***joking apart*** [APART *adv.* 5b].

1670 EACHARD *Cont. Clergy* 33 Punning, quibling, and that which they call joquing, and such other delicacies of wit. **1694** R. L'ESTRANGE *Fables* ccccii. (1708) 430 Singing and Joaking was his Delight. **1745** S. CIBBER *Let.* 18 July in D. Garrick *Private Corr.* (1831) I. 35 But joking apart, I long till you come that we may consult together. **1841** J. ELLIOTSON *Let.* 4 Aug. in Dickens *Lett.* (1969) II. 345 Joking apart, you make me ashamed with your overflowing of the *milk* of kindness. **1853** MRS. GASKELL *Cranford* vi. 101 The captain of the school in the art of practical joking. **1860** Practical joking [see BITE *sb.* 9]. **1888** HENTY *Cornet of Horse* vii. 64, I..have put up more than once with practical jokings. **1918** C. MACKENZIE *Early Life Sylvia Scarlett* II. i. 256 No, joking apart, I think it would be a great effort. **1931** 'G. TREVOR' *Murder at School* xiii. 254 Joking apart, you had some ingenious ideas. **1973** *Times* 17 Nov. 11/8 Joking apart, this is the kind of show difficult to write about without..spoiling the jokes.

b. ***joking relationship*** (Anthropol.), a relationship of familiarity between specific persons which is sanctioned in certain tribal groups.

1920 R. H. LOWIE *Primitive Soc.* (1921) v. 95 Of a distinct character is the joking-relationship of the Crow and Hidarsa. **1933** E. E. EVANS-PRITCHARD *Ess. Social Anthropol.* (1962) vii. 151 One way in which intimacy and equality are expressed between the partners [*sc.* blood-brothers] is by each publicly insulting the other, a custom commonly described by ethnologists as a 'joking relationship'. *Ibid.* 152 A 'joking relationship' may grow up between two clans. **1958** A. R. RADCLIFFE-BROWN *Method in Social Anthropol.* I. v. 119 The expression of opposition between the moieties may take various forms. One is the institution to which anthropologists have given the not very satisfactory name of 'the joking relationship'. **1964** GOULD & KOLB *Dict. Social Sci.* 358/1 A joking relationship is a relationship between two persons (sometimes between two groups) in which one is by custom permitted (and in some cases obliged) to tease or make fun of the other, who must take no offence... Obscenity..and the taking of property are common forms.

joking (ˈdʒəʊkɪŋ), *ppl. a.* [f. JOKE *v.* + -ING[2].] That jokes. Hence **ˈjokingly** *adv.*

1700 TOLAND *Life Harrington* in *Oceana* 24 Harrington jokingly said, That they had an excellent faculty of magnifying a Louse, and diminishing a Commonwealth. **1714** GAY *Sheph. Week, Tuesday*, In joking talk. **1893** LIDDON, etc. *Life Pusey* I. iv. 90 His friends..used to say jokingly 'you are looking towards Canterbury'.

jokish (ˈdʒəʊkɪʃ), *a.* [f. JOKE *sb.* + -ISH[1].] Given to joking, jocular.

1785 O'KEEFE *Fontainebleau* III. i. (L.), Oh, dear, how jokish these gentlemen are!

jokist ('dʒəʊkɪst). [f. JOKE *sb.* + -IST.] A professed or habitual joker.

1873 'MARK TWAIN' & WARNER *Gilded Age* xxxvi. 331 And here is The Jokist's Own Treasury. **1882** *Pall Mall G.* 8 June 3/2 Elaborate inventions palmed off upon an uncritical public by unscrupulous 'jokists'. **1893** *Daily Tel.* 24 Apr. 5/4 Theodore Hook, the king of practical jokists.

‖**jokul**, *prop.* **jökull** ('jœkʊl). Also yokul. [Icel. *jökull* icicle, hence ice, glacier:—**jakulo-z*, dim. of *jaki* (:—**jakon*) piece of ice: cf. ICKLE *sb.*, ICICLE.] In reference to Iceland: A mountain permanently covered with snow and ice; a snow-mountain.

1780 VON TROIL *Iceland* 233 The fire is generally contained in these mountains covered with ice, or, as they are called in the country, *jokuls*. **1835** *Encycl. Brit.* (ed. 7) XII. 146/1 The great range of yokuls to the eastward of Mount Hecla. **1862** *Lond. Rev.* 23 Aug. 163 Will the Alpine Club..console themselves with the jokuls of Iceland? **1890** HALL CAINE *Bondman* III. i, Under the feet of the great Vatna Jökull.

joky ('dʒəʊkɪ), *a.* Also jokey. [f. JOKE *sb.* + -Y.] Inclined to joke, jocular. Also, subject to jokes, ridiculous.

1825–80 JAMIESON, *Jokie*, jocular, fond of a joke, as, 'He's a fine jokie man'. **1894** H. GARDENER *Unoff. Patriot* 39 Feel jokey to-day, do you, you ridiculous Bob White? **1964** 'N. BLAKE' *Sad Variety* viii. 149 'Leake,' I said, 'your mind's as jokey as your clothes.' **1970** *Homes & Gardens* May 145/1 Despite the jokey reputation that middle-class British hotels enjoy, they compare very well indeed for comfort with their European and US counterparts. **1972** *Times Lit. Suppl.* 1 Sept. 1014/4 Crops up again in less joky moments. *Ibid.* 1021/1 A jokey 'textbook' tricked out with comic diagrams. **1974** *Times Lit. Suppl.* 11 Oct. 1142/4 The use of anachronism..is now a joky, selfconscious device.

‖**jol** (dʒəʊl). Also djōl, jāl, jaul, jawl, johl, jōl. [Arab.] The local name (often with capital initial) for a barren, much dissected, limestone plateau south of Wadi Hadhramaut in the Arabian peninsula; also applied (often with captial initial) to different regions within this plateau, and (with lower-case initial) to the individual blocks of tableland into which the whole plateau is dissected.

By some writers the plateau itself is designated by the plural form.

1904 D. G. HOGARTH *Penetration of Arabia* II. ix. 217 The guides conducted Hirsch through the cultivated coastal district..up to bare down-land, 'Jol', rising to six thousand five hundred feet. *Ibid.* 219 At the head of this [*sc.* a valley] he found himself once more on the downs of the Jol, a wild, arid, broken country. **1921** *Handbk. Arabia* (Admiralty, Naval Intelligence Div.) I. vii. 218 Physically the Hadhramaut may be divided into four main horizontal belts: ..(*b*) a broad belt of downs or plateaux (jāl) diversified by a few outstanding peaks. **1932** VAN DER MEULEN & VON WISSMAN *Hadramaut* iii. 53 Our way now led over the *djōl* as far as Wādī Dōᶜan. The *djōl* consists of vast table-lands of reddish-brown limestone. *Ibid.* xvi. 210 This *djōl* differed little in character from that which we had crossed on our way to Wādī Dōᶜan. **1936** F. STARK *Southern Gates Arabia* ix. 87 The Jōl has usually been dismissed by travellers as a piece of dull dreariness, a plateau where heat and cold are alike unbearable. **1940** —— *Winter in Arabia* iii. 14 Our lorry.. began to climb long broken ridges that lead to the tilted plateau of the jōl. *Ibid.*, Jōl—waterless steppe plateau. **1945** *Antiquity* XIX. 189, I expect that these stone-age people lived very much the life that the Beduins of the northern jols of the Hadhramaut on the edge of the Rub'al Khali live today. **1946** *Western Arabia & Red Sea* (Geogr. Handbk. Ser. B.R. 527, Admiralty, Naval Intelligence Div.) ii. 32 To the north the land rises to 3,500 feet between the wadi and the desert, but to the south altitudes of 6,000 feet and more are attained. These barren *jōls* are dissected into detached blocks of tableland by an extraordinarily intricate network of canyons and valleys. **1958** *Geogr. Jrnl.* CXXIV. 165 This is Wādī Hadramaut..which is enclosed by the precipices of the limestone strata of a wide and barren table land, the Jaul. **1961** *U.S. Board on Geogr. Names, Gazetteer no.* 54: *Arabian Peninsula* p. vi, Jawl..plateau, plain. **1966** J. LUNT *Barren Rocks Aden* ix. 139 We were now on the *johl*, as the Arabs call the mountainous plateau which lies between the coast and the Wadi Hadhramaut, and between the Wadi Hadhramaut and the Empty Quarter. **1966** W. C. BRICE *S.-W. Asia* xii. 253 Further inland, in the districts known as the Jols, the limestone surface..is scored with a maze of ravines.

jole, variant of JOWL.

jolely, joliflich, jolile, etc., obs. ff. JOLLILY.

jolie, jolif, -ife, etc., obs. ff. JOLLY.

‖**jolie laide** (ʒɔli lɛd). [Fr., fem. sing. of *joli* pretty + *laid* ugly.] A woman or girl who is attractive in spite of not being pretty. Occas. *joli laid* (lɛ), applied to a man.

1894 LADY MONKSWELL *Diary* 12 May in E.C.F. Collier *Victorian Diarist* (1944) I. 243 Mrs. Flower is a 'jolie laide' of about 50, rather charming. **1949** N. MITFORD *Love in Cold Climate* I. viii. 87 One was a beauty or a *jolie-laide* and that was that. **1960** D. HOLMAN-HUNT *My Grandmothers & I* i. 6 The lazy young ladies who came to stay were called *jolies laides*. **1961** *Times* 10 Oct. 16/1 The arrival in the house ..of a jolie-laide innocent looking for the Y.W.C.A. **1966** *Observer* 20 Mar. 25/4 He has the *joli-laid* face of a boxer. **1972** *Times* 22 June 12/5 Sexual teases like *jolie-laide* Israeli Drora. **1973** R. RENDELL *Some lie & Some Die* xi. 95 He had an ugly attractive face, *joli laid*.

jolifte, -ivete, -ite, etc., obs. ff. JOLLITY.

†'**jolious**, *a. Obs. rare.* Also 6 iolyous. [f. *joly*, *jolie*, JOLLY + -OUS.] Jolly.

1560 ROLLAND *Crt. Venus* Prol. 64 Iocund with Ioy, and Iolyous to Iaip. *Ibid.* I. 315 O Lustie lufe, thy lufesome obseruance So Ioyous is,..So Iolious, repleit of all plesance.

jolious, obs. form of JEALOUS.

joll(e, obs. form of JOWL.

jolley ('dʒɒlɪ). *Pottery.* Also jolly. [Of unknown origin.] A variety of jigger (see JIGGER *sb.*[1] 5 a). So '**jolleying**, '**jollying** *vbl. sb.*, the act of using a jolley; '**jollied** *ppl. a.*, manufactured by jolley; '**jollier**[1], **jollyer**, one who makes pottery by means of a jolley.

1881 *Instructions to Census Clerks* (1885) 88 Earthenware ..manufacture... Jollier. Jolly Maker. **1891** *Pop. Sci. Monthly* Dec. 168 A 'jolly'..consisting of a table on which is a revolving mold [etc.]. **1901** W. P. RIX tr. *Bourry's Treat. Ceramic Industries* iv. 182 In jollying, the body is compressed, and forced to become stretched out by means of a profile, having the outline of the article to be made. *Ibid.* 213 The heads of jolleys are arranged so as to receive the moulds, the placing and removal of which must be done very rapidly. **1915** A. B. SEARLE *Clays & Clay Products* xv. 118 As plates and saucers are always made 'upside down' the profile forms the 'bottom' of the plate. The machines used for this work are known as *jiggers* and *jolleys*. **1921** *Dict. Occup. Terms* (1927) § 105 *Bowl maker*,..a jollier who makes bowls by jolleying process. *Ibid.*, *Cup maker*, a jollier who makes cups on a single or double cup jolley. **1934** J. B. PRIESTLEY *Eng. Journey* 213 If Bennett had been either a master potter on the one hand, or a 'thrower' or 'jollyer' on the other. *Ibid.* 220 If you work at the stuff [*sc.* potter's clay] inside a mould, you are, I believe, either 'jollying' or 'jiggering'. **1951** *Electronic Engin.* XXIII. 337 Automatic jollying machines have now been developed for the production of plates, cups and saucers. **1960** H. POWELL *Beginner's Bk. Pott.* I. i. 14 A good investment for a fairly small cash outlay is the jigger, or jolley (no one seems to know which name is correct). **1972** N. FRENCH *Industr. Ceramics: Tableware* iii. 26 The extreme precision and expense of mould-making normally offsets the advantages of jolleying.

'**jollier**[2]. *U.S.* [f. JOLLY *v.* 2 c.] One who 'jollies' or flatters others; a jovial or sociable person.

1896 ADE *Artie* ix. 78 He's one o'f the biggest jolliers that ever come over the hills. **1901** MERWIN & WEBSTER *Calumet 'K'* i. 12 Oh, he's a good-looking young chap... He's a great jollier. **1904** 'No. 1500' *Life in Sing Sing* 250/1 Jollier, flatterer. **1905** *N.Y. Even. Post* 12 Oct. 2 He was talkative, and as the attendants say, 'quite a jollier'. **1946** W. A. WHITE *Autobiogr.* 443, I was errand boy, peacemaker, jollier, fixer, horse-trader.

jollification (ˌdʒɒlɪfɪ'keɪʃən). *colloq.* [f. JOLLY *a.* + -FICATION.] The action of jollifying or making merry; merrymaking, jollity; a merrymaking.

1809 W. IRVING *Knickerb.* VI. i. (1849) 313 For some time this war of the cupboard was carried on to the great festivity and jollification of the Swedes. **1818** SCOTT *Let. to Morritt* 5 Nov. in *Lockhart*, We had a grand jollification here last week. **1863** COWDEN CLARKE *Shaks. Char.* viii. 200 She rates Sir Toby..soundly,..twitting him with his jollifications. **1872** HARDWICK *Trad. Lanc.* 117 There existed no impediment to unlimited jollification.

jollify ('dʒɒlɪfaɪ), *v. colloq.* [f. as prec. + -FY.]

1. *trans.* To make jolly or merry; to make slightly intoxicated: cf. JOLLY *a.* 3 b.

1824 *Blackw. Mag.* XV. 600 Such things serve as shoeing-horns to draw on more bottles by jollifying the host.

2. *intr.* To make merry; *esp.* to indulge in drinking.

1830 *Fraser's Mag.* I. 212 Noah was about performing a religious rite at the very moment that he jollified. **1865** *Pall Mall G.* 29 Dec. 3 The tens of thousands who jollified at Sydenham on Boxing Day. **1880** BLACKMORE *Mary Anerley* I. vi. 66 Here will they all jollify together; while the sky holds a cloud, or the locker a drop.

jollily ('dʒɒlɪlɪ), *adv.* Forms: see JOLLY *a.*; also 4 ioliflich, iolely. [f. JOLLY *a.* + -LY[2].] In a jolly manner.

1. Cheerfully, gaily, merrily, jovially; †spiritedly, gallantly, boldly, insolently (*obs.*).

13.. *K. Alis.* 4753 (4737) Who þat haþ trewe amye Ioliflich he may hym in here afyȝe. *c* **1380** WYCLIF *Wks.* (1880) 99 Redi..to werre jolily aȝenst cristene men. *c* **1420** *Anturs of Arth.* xxxix, So iolyly thes gentille iustede one were. **1547** HOOPER *Answ. Gardiner's Bk.* X. iv, Lord, I knew thy trewthe, and Iolyly pratyd of the same. **1581** J. BELL *Haddon's Answ. Osor.* 36 b, Wherein you triumph so Iollylye. **1670** MILTON *Hist. Eng.* VI. Wks. (1847) 560/1 Sitting jollily at dinner. **1788** FRANKLIN *Autobiog.* Wks. 1840 I. 200 Having done a good day's work, they spent the evening jollily. **1865** KINGSLEY *Herew.* ix, Baldwin was silent, thinking and smiling jollily.

†**2.** Amorously; licentiously. *Obs.*

c **1400** *Rom. Rose* 7031 Prelat lyuyng iolily Or prest that halt his quene hym by.

†**3.** Finely, handsomely, gaily. *Obs.*

1375 BARBOUR *Bruce* IX. 201 Men arayit Iolely. **1426** AUDELAY *Poems* 16 He is a gentylmon and jolyle arayd. *a* **1640** PEACHAM in Ellis *Spec. Eng. Poets* II. (R.), Their heads full jollily they dight.

4. Excellently, splendidly; finely; delightfully. Now *slang* or *colloq.*

c **1563** *Jack Jugler* in *4 Old Plays* (1848) 34 You wold pommile him ioylile a-bout the pate. **1668** H. MORE *Div. Dial.* II. ix. (1713) 113 You come off jollily, methinks,.. apologizing thus in the general. *a* **1822** SHELLEY tr. *Faust* II. 23, I see one yonder burning jollily. **1878** M. C. JACKSON *Chaperon's Cares* II. ix. 117 When one meets nice people and gets on jollily with them.

†'**jolliment.** *Obs. rare.* [irreg. f. JOLLY *a.* + -MENT.] Mirth, merriment, jollity.

1590 SPENSER *F.Q.* II. vi. 3 To feede her foolish humour, and vaine iolliment. **1596** *Ibid.* IV. xi. 12 Triton his trumpet shrill before them blew, For goodly triumph and great iollyment.

jolliness ('dʒɒlɪnɪs). [f. JOLLY *a.* + -NESS.] The state or quality of being jolly, in the various senses of the adj.; jollity.

c **1386** CHAUCER *Sqr.'s T.* 281 In this Iolynesse I lete hem til men to the soper dresse. *c* **1430** *Pilgr. Lyf Manhode* IV. xiv. (1869) 183 þat is a perile to which jolyfnesse [F. *jeunesse*] led me. *c* **1450** *Merlin* 475 For the jolynesse that was in hym and the myrthe. **1530** PALSGR. 235/1 Iolynesse, *joliueté*. **1601** SIR W. CORNWALLIS *Ess.* II. xlvi. H h viij, This life of armes which custom hath taught to put on a gallant iollinesse in his outward behauiour. **1682** BUNYAN *Holy War* 336 At his own table, among his own guests..in the midst of his jolliness. **1894** *Yellow Bk.* I. 82 Times of jolliness and glad indulgence.

†'**jollitry.** *Obs.* [irreg. alteration of next; ? after *gallantry*, *pleasantry*, etc.] = JOLLITY 1, 2.

?*c* **1685** *Debtford Plumb Cake* in *Bagford Ball.* (1876) 72 Mark I pray what came to pass, which spoiled their jollitry. **1732** *Gentleman Instr.* (ed. 10) 537 (D.) To strain jollitry not into annual..but into a daily madness. **1736** LEDIARD *Life Marlborough* I. 273 The officers were celebrating the Festival..in Mirth and Jollitry.

jollity ('dʒɒlɪtɪ). Forms: α. 4 iolif-, -yf-, -ive-, -yvete. β. 4–6 ioli-, ioly-, (5 golly-), 6–7 ioyli-, ioyly-, iolli-, 7– jolli-; 4–5 -te, 4–6 -tee, 6 -tye, -ti, 6–7 -tie, 6– -ty. [a. OF. *jolivete*, *joliete*, *jolite*, f. *jolif*, *joli*: see JOLLY *a.* and -TY.]

1. The quality or condition of being jolly, light-hearted, or festive; exuberant mirth or cheerfulness; †levity, giddiness (*obs.*).

a **1310** in Wright *Lyric P.* xxx. 89 Wymmon with the jolyfte, thou thench on Godes shoures. **1382** WYCLIF *Judith* x. 3 She clothide hir with the clothis of hir jolite. *a* **1400–50** *Alexander* 3537 Quen al þe iolite of Giugne and Iulus was endid. *a* **1450** *Knt. de la Tour* (1868) 73 The doughter of Iacob whiche for lyghtnes and iolyte of herte lefte the hous of her fader. **1509** BARCLAY *Shyp of Folys* (1570) 105 Omnia fert ætas, both health and iolitie. **1670** MILTON *Hist. Eng.* v. Wks. 1738 II. 86 A Youth, through jollity of mind unwilling perhaps to be detain'd long with sad and sorrowful Narrations. **1756** BURKE *Subl. & B.* III. xxv, The passion excited by beauty is..nearer to a species of melancholy, than to jollity and mirth. **1871** R. ELLIS *Catullus* lxi. 238 O happiest Lovers, jollity live with you.

2. Merrymaking, festivity, revelry; *pl.*, Festivities, festive dissipations or enjoyments.

a **1300** *Cursor M.* 28147 Caroles, iolites, and plaies. Ic haue be-haldyn. *c* **1440** *Gesta Rom.* xxvi. 100 (Harl. MS.) The knyght yede to the tornement *scil.* as ofte as a man goþe to the Iolytees of worldlye speculacions. *c* **1470** HENRYSON *Mor. Fab.* ii. (*Town & C. Mouse*) 292 Thus as thay sat in all their jolitie. **1579** LYLY *Euphues* (Arb.) 109 For all my treasure spente on Iewells and spylte in iolytye, what recompence shall I reape besides repentaunce? **1627–77** FELTHAM *Resolves* I. xiii. 21 It comes, like an arrest of Treason in a Jollity. *a* **1674** CLARENDON *Hist. Reb.* x. §170 Not keeping company with the other Officers of the Army in their jollities, and excesses. **1750** JOHNSON *Rambler* No. 80 ⁋7 Winter brings natural inducements to jollity and conversation. **1849** MACAULAY *Hist. Eng.* iii. I. 321 The coarse jollity of the afternoon was often prolonged till the revellers were laid under the table.

†**3.** Pleasure, enjoyment; esp. sexual pleasure, lust. *Obs.*

c **1330** R. BRUNNE *Chron.* (1810) 50 Knoute of his body gate sonnes þre, Tuo by tuo wifes, þe þrid in jolifte. *a* **1340** HAMPOLE *Psalter* ii. 10 Enuye couartis iolifte and oþer vices. *c* **1374** CHAUCER *Boeth.* III. pr. vii. 62 (Camb. MS.) Of whyche bestys al the entencyon hasteth to fulfylle hyr bodyly Iolyte. *c* **1386** CHAUCER *Sir Thopas* 132 Nedes moste he fighte..For paramour and Iolitee Of oon that shoon ful brighte. *a* **1450** *Knt. de la Tour* (1868) 41 [Thei] that.. thought more on her iolytees and the worldes delite.. thanne thei dede on the seruice of God. **1615** CROOKE *Body of Man* 242 In gelt men..all vigour of lust and desire of ioylity is extinguished.

†**4.** Insolent presumption or self-confidence; presumptuous self-reliance. *Obs.*

a **1340** HAMPOLE *Psalter* xxiv. 7 The trespasis of my ȝouthed that is my iolifte and fole hardynes. **1549** LATIMER *4th Serm. bef. Edw. VI* (Arb.) 112 The pore wyddowe.. wyth. ii. or thre wordes shall bryng hym downe to the grounde, and destroye his iolitye. **1581** *Confer.* II. (1584) H, This he spake with great iolitie and scoffingly. **1614** RALEIGH *Hist. World* II. v. iii. §6. 375 In this iollitie of conceit, he determined to fight.

†**5.** Gallantry, bravery. *Obs.*

c **1540** tr. *Pol. Verg. Eng. Hist.* (Camden) I. 89 Wee will returne unto Carausius..renomed throwghe his jolitee in warfare.

†**6.** A beauty, grace, or personal accomplishment. *Obs.*

1484 CAXTON *Chivalry* 46 Yf by beaute of facion, or by a body fayr grete or wel aourned, or by fayr here..and by the other Iolytees shold a Squyer be adoubed Knyght..lowe and vyle mayst thou make Knyghtes.

†**7.** A state of splendour, exaltation, or eminent prosperity; splendour, magnificence; finery of dress or array. *Obs.*

1549 LATIMER *4th Serm. bef. Edw. VI* (Arb.) 113 He shewed him al the kyngedomes of the worlde, and all theyr iolitye. **1565** JEWEL *Def. Apol.* (1611) 363 In the time of Pope Boniface the Eight, when the Authority of the Bishop of Rome was in greatest iollity. *c* **1600** SHAKS. *Sonn.* lxvi, To

behold..needie Nothing trimd in iollitie. **1620** SANDERSON *Serm. on 1 Kings* xxi. 29 (1689) 152 To proclaim judgement against an oppressing King [Ahab] in the prime of his Jollity. **1698** FRYER *Acc. E. India & P.* 109 The Jollity and Pomp of the Heathens is much allayed by the Puritanism and unlimited Power of the Moors.

†**8.** Pleasantry, jocularity; joke, jest. *Obs.*

1581 SAVILE *Tacitus, Hist.* II. lxviii. (1591) 92 Two souldiers,..vpon a iolity challenged one another to wrestle. **1596** BP. W. BARLOW *Three Serm.* Ded. 82 Others in their iollitie haue reported that they could neuer salute the Sunne in England. **1608** D. T. *Ess. Pol. & Mor.* 106 They must.. out of the humour of their jollities, give vent.

jollo ('dʒɒləʊ). *Austral. slang.* [app. f. JOLL(IFICATION + Austral. termination -O².] A party, esp. one at which liquor is drunk. Cf. JOLLY *sb.*⁴

1934 *Bulletin* (Sydney) 25 July 46/3 Most..came to the wedding jollo to drink the beer and admire the bride's new fawn coat-and-skirt. **1966** BAKER *Austral. Lang.* (ed. 2) xi. 230 Australians have a fair selection of terms to describe drinking and drinking bouts, such as..jollo [etc.].

Jollof, Jolof, varr. WOLOF.

jollop ('dʒɒləp), *sb.*¹ Also jowlop, ? jellop: see JOLLOPED. [app. f. JOWL², *joll, jole* + **lop*, LAP *sb.*¹ 2: cf. DEWLAP, which also occurs in the same or a cognate sense (1 b).

(It is tempting to conjecture that *dewlap* itself, of which the first element is unexplained, may have originated in some popular perversion of *jowlap* or *jewlap*; but at present this is not supported by evidence or analogy.)]

The wattle of a cock, turkey, or other fowl.

1705 BOSMAN *Guinea* 262 His Bill is Yellow; from whence to the Head grows out on each side a red Jollop. **1866** H. CLARK *Introd. Her.*, Jellop [see JOLLOPED]. **1890** *Cent. Dict.*, Jewlap.

jollop ('dʒɒləp), *sb.*² *slang.* [See JALAP *sb.*] **a.** A purgative, a medicine. **b.** Strong liquor, or a drink of this.

1920 *Contemp. Rev.* Aug. 250 We may imagine them [*sc.* smugglers *c* 1820] stowing away their precious booty in *caches*, then a jollop of brandy all round. **1955** D. NILAND *Shiralee* 146 He nutted out some jollop for her cough. **1961** C. WILLOCK *Death in Covert* ii. 32 'Tell 'em up at the house to bring out the jollop.' The keeper uttered this in a tone that made it quite clear that he considered serving refreshment something completely outside his duties. **1966** 'L. LANE' *ABZ of Scouse* 57 If yer don't wallop yer jollop yer'll get ther beezers in yer belly.

†'**jollop,** *v. Obs. rare*⁻¹. *intr.* To gobble as a turkey-cock.

1688 R. HOLME *Armoury* II. 310/2 (Of the Voices of Birds) The Turky Cock Jollopeth.

¶ Hence, erron. **jollop** *sb.* 'the cry of a turkey', in HALLIWELL; whence in *Cent. Dict.* and FUNK as 'Prov. Eng.' Not in *Eng. Dial. Dict.*

jollop, obs. form of JALAP.

jolloped ('dʒɒləpt), *a. Her.* Also jowlopped, ?jellop(p)ed. [f. JOLLOP *sb.*¹ + -ED²: cf. DEWLAPPED.] Of a cock, etc., borne as a charge: Having the wattles of a specified tincture different from that of the body and head; = WATTLED.

1610 GUILLIM *Heraldry* III. xx. 164 He beareth Gules three Cockes Argent, Armed Crested and Iellopped Or, by the name of Cocke. *Ibid.* xxi. 164 Three Capons Sable, Armed, Crested, and Iow-Lopped Or. *Ibid.* xxvi. 182 Hee beareth, Sable, a Cockatrice displaied, Argent, crested, membred, and iollopped, Gules, by the name of Buggine. **1622** PEACHAM *Compl. Gent.* xvi. (1634) 178 Three Cockes Gules, Armed, Crested, and jellopped, Sable. **1766** PORNY *Heraldry* Gloss., *Jollopped* or *Jowlopped*, term used to signify the gills of a Cock, when bor'n of a different Tincture from his Head. **1864** BOUTELL *Heraldry, Hist. & Pop.* x. 64 A Game-cock is..jowlopped of his Wattles or simply wattled. **1866** H. CLARK *Introd. Her.* (ed. 18), *Jellop, Jelloped*, terms occasionally used..to describe the comb of a cock, etc. when borne of a tincture different from that of the head. **1890** *Cent. Dict.*, Jewlapped.

jollopy, var. JALOPY.

†'**jollux.** *Obs. slang.* [f. JOLLY *a.*: cf. dial. *jollus* fat, fleshy, *jollock* jolly, hearty, *sb.* (slang) a parson.] (See quot.)

a **1797** W. MASON *Ode to Sir Fl. Norton* 12 And find it the same easy thing To hit a Jollux or a king. (Poems (1810) 419/1 *Note*, A phrase used by the *bon ton* for a fat person.)

jolly ('dʒɒlɪ), *a.* and *adv.* Forms: α. 4 iolife, -iffe, -yfe, -ef, 4-5 iolyf, 4-6 iolif. β. 4-6 iolye, 4-7 ioly, (5 iuly, yoly), 5-6 ioyly, 5-7 iolie, 6 iollie, iolly, ioylye, 7 jollie, 7- jolly. [ME. *jolif, jolyf, joly*, a. OF. *jolif, joli*, gay, festive, lively, merry, amorous, gallant, brave, finely dressed, handsome, fair, pretty, = It. *giulivo* merry, pleasant, cheerful, glad, gay (in Florio *giolivo* 'iollie, pleasant, ioyous, blithe, bonnie, buckesome'), OCat. *joliu* (Littré). For the loss of the final *f* in F. and Eng. cf. *hasty, tardy*. In 15-16th c. app. associated with *joy*, whence the spelling *joyly*.

The origin of OF. *jolif* is uncertain. French etymologists have generally followed Diez in referring it to ON. *jól* (= OE. *ȝeól*) YULE, or to a cognate German name (indicated by Gothic *Juleis* November) for the midwinter feast of the northern nations, whence (in ON.) for 'a feast' generally; thus **jōl-īvus, jôl-if* would be = festive. But the historical and phonetic difficulties involved, whether the word is supposed to have been taken into F. from Norse after 900, or to have been Common Romanic, are such as to render this conjecture extremely doubtful. M. Paul Meyer suggests that OF. *jolif* might be after all:—L. **gaudīvus*, f. *gaudēre* to rejoice, *gaudium* joy, with change of *d* to *l*, as in *cigāda*, Pr. *cigala*, F. *cigale*, *Vadensis*, F. *Valois*, and some other words.]

A. *adj.* **I. 1.** Of gay and cheerful disposition or character; bright, lively; joyous, gladsome; mirthful. Now *arch.* and chiefly of time.

α. *a* **1310** in Wright *Lyric P.* xvi. 52 Heo is dereworthe in day, Graciouse, stout, ant gay, Gentil, jolyf so the jay. ? *a* **1366** CHAUCER *Rom. Rose* 435 Ne she was gay fresh ne Iolyf But semed be ful ententyf To gode werkes.

β. *c* **1380** WYCLIF *Wks.* (1880) 169 Preiere is betre herd of god bi..stille devocion..þan bi..ioly chauntynge þat stireþ men & wommen to daunsynge. **1582** STANYHURST *Æneis* III. (Arb.) 73 Wee..with iollye tumult, where should that cittye be setled Streight ways demaunded. *c* **1636** MILTON *Sonn. Nightingale*, While the jolly Hours lead on propitious May. **1647** MAY *Hist. Parl.* I. ii. 18 Though the times were jolly for the present..they could not chuse but feare the sequell. **1750** DODD *Poems* (1767) 28 The jolly choir of maidens trim, Daughters of pleasance. **1871** R. ELLIS *Catullus* lxi. 11 Come, for jolly the time, awake.

†**2.** In more physical sense: Having the freshness and lively spirits of youth or good health; fresh, lively, sprightly, spirited. *Obs.*

α. **13..** *Seuyn Sag.* 2565 Hit was a knight..And [had a] yong jolif wif. *c* **1380** *Sir Ferumb.* 1582 A doȝty iolyf bacheler a ȝong man & a wiȝt þat is of body fresch & fier. *c* **1450** *Bk. Hawking* in *Rel. Ant.* I. 300 That hawke was never so jolyfe and so luste afore.

β. *c* **1325** *Song of Yesterday* 75 in *E.E.P.* (1862) 165 An hounde þat is likyng, and Ioly And of sekenesse hol and sounde. *c* **1386** CHAUCER *Miller's T.* 77 Wynsynge she was as is a ioly colt. *c* **1450** *Merlin* 47 Thei be yonge men and Iolye, and have grete nede of counseile. **1523** LD. BERNERS *Froiss.* I. ccxxix. 308 Therle of Marche was as then a ioly yong herty knight. **1586** BRIGHT *Melanch.* xxviii. 160 The bloude getteth a farther egernesse, and these iolie spirits be wasted.

3. a. In high spirits; exhilarated, joyful; †glad *of* or pleased *at* something. Chiefly *predicative*.

c **1305** *St. Swithin* 117 in *E.E.P.* (1862) 46 þis gode man of þis tokning: iolyf was ynouȝ. **1393** LANGL. *P. Pl.* C. xiv. 20 Iob by-cam a iolif man and al hus ioye newe. *c* **1400** *Destr. Troy* 249 Iason was Ioly of his Iuste wordes. **1600** HOLLAND *Livy* x. 358 The Tuscans..got hart and were very iolie, saying that the Gods were in favour of them. **1656** *Nicholas Papers* (Camden) III. 266 Though some are soe jollie at the French entertaynement. **1780** JOHNSON *Lett. to Mrs. Thrale* 30 May, Taylor, who is gone away brisk and jolly, asked me when I would come to him. **1863** KINGSLEY *Water-Bab.* i, And then shook his ears, and was as jolly as ever.

b. *euphem.* Exhilarated with drink, slightly intoxicated.

1652 C. B. STAPYLTON *Herodian* 56 In his Tipsy Cups when he was Jolly. **1741** H. WALPOLE *Lett. H. Mann* (1834) I. 36 Young Churchill and a dozen more grew jolly, stayed till seven in the morning and drank thirty two bottles. **1884** PAE *Eustace* 33 I'm never more than jolly, and can take care of myself precious well.

4. Indulging in, or fond of, conviviality and social merriment; festive; jovial. ***the jolly god***, Bacchus. ***jolly fellow, jolly dog***, a person of convivial tastes and habits: cf. FELLOW *sb.* 3 a.

1375 BARBOUR *Bruce* I. 332 The quhethir he glaid was and Ioly, And till swylk thowlesnes he ȝeid As the courss askis off ȝowtheid. **1483** CAXTON *G. de la Tour* C iij, Them..that so moche waste their good to be iolif and repayre their carayn. **1550** CROWLEY *Epigr.* 35 b, To lyue lyke a Lorde, and make iolye chere. *a* **1661** FULLER *Worthies* (1840) II. 532 He was a jolly gentleman, both for camp and court, a great reveller. **1697** DRYDEN *Alexander's Feast* 49 The jolly god in triumph comes. **1750** *The Student*, There is another set..who assume to themselves the name of jolly fellows and ridicule every body who has the folly to be sober. **1799** LD. MELBOURNE in *M. Papers* (1889) 5 Miller himself is a little jolly dog. **1813** *Sporting Mag.* XLI. 88 A decent-looking man..who had sacrificed too freely to the jolly God. **1843** THACKERAY *Crit. Rev.* Wks. 1886 XXIII. 87 He became a viveur and jolly dog about town. **1871** R. ELLIS *Catullus* xlvii. 6 They, my jolly comrades Search the streets.

II. †**5. a.** Of cheerful courage; high-hearted, gallant; brave. *Obs.*

c **1330** R. BRUNNE *Chron.* (1810) 333 With jolif men of gest toward þe North he schoke, To chace Kyng Robyn. **13..** *E.E. Allit. P.* B. 300 The Iolef Iapheth watz gendered þe þryd. **1375** BARBOUR *Bruce* XI. 524 Thai war all ȝong men and Ioly, And ȝarnand till do cheuelry. *c* **1400** *Beryn* 2440 A trewe visage He had, & a manly, And Iuly was he. **1523** LD. BERNERS *Froiss.* I. ccccxlii. 779 The same season there dyed ..the gentyll and ioly duke Vincelyns. **1590** SPENSER *F.Q.* I. i. 1 Full jolly knight he seemd, and faire did sitt, As one for knightly giusts and fierce encounters fitt. **1642** ROGERS *Naaman* 29 The only season of working a jolly and stout heart to crouch and creepe.

b. *jolly roger*: see ROGER² 4.

†**6.** Overweeningly self-confident; flushed with success or prosperity; full of presumptuous pride; defiantly bold, arrogant, overbearing. *Obs.*

a **1340** HAMPOLE *Psalter* cxlvi. 12 Proude men & iolif [*v.r.* ioly], nouþere dredis him na has hope in him. **1474** CAXTON *Chesse* I. i, Evilmerodach, a Iolye man without Iustyse and cruel. **1566** STAPLETON *Ret. Untr. Jewel* IV. 111 Thinke you to outface us with ioyly bragges? **1573** G. HARVEY *Letter-bk.* (Camden) 45 M. Brown..amongst other of his iolly vaunts ..made this bost. **1648** SANDERSON *Serm.* II. 232 It concerneth every one of us..not to be too high-minded or jolly for any thing that is past. **1666** SANCROFT *Lex. Ignea* 40 Our Mountain which we said in our jolly pride should never be removed.

III. †**7. a.** Amorous; amatory; wanton, lustful.

1382 WYCLIF *Amos* vi. 4 ȝe sleepen in beddis of yuer, and wexen wijld [*gloss* or iolyf] in ȝour beddis. *c* **1385** CHAUCER *L.G.W.* 1192 *Dido*, So prikyth hire thes newe iolye wo. **1390** GOWER *Conf.* III. 36 Thou in al thi lust jolif The bodily delices soghtest. *c* **1425** *Seven Sag.* (P.) 235 The emperour was jolyf of blode, And hare councel undirstood. **1483** CAXTON *Gold. Leg.* (1495) 256 He sholde send to her all the yonge men that were Ioly for to enforce and to make her do theyr wyll. **1645** MILTON *Tetrach.* Wks. (1847) 181/2 (Gen. ii. 18) In the Song of Songs, which is generally believed, even in the jolliest expressions, to figure the spousals of the church with Christ.

b. Of animals: In heat. *Obs.* exc. *dial.*

1500-20 DUNBAR *Poems* lxxxiv. 8 Quhone the biche is jolie and on rage. **1535** STEWART *Cron. Scot.* 1947 Quhen ane[s] iolie persauit wes ane beist..Scho suld be keipit closlie vndir cuir. **1884** *Chesh. Gloss.*, *Jolly*, maris appetens.

IV. †**8. a.** Bright or gay in appearance; brilliant, showy, splendid. *Obs.*

13.. *E.E. Allit. P.* A. 841 Thys Iherusalem lombe hade neuer pechche, Of oþer huee bot quyt [= white] Iolyf. *c* **1380** WYCLIF *Sel. Wks.* III. 520 Jolye and gaye sadeles. *a* **1440** *Sir Eglam.* 1200 Mony knyghtys herde of bone That yoly colourys bare. **1535** COVERDALE *Job* xl. 10 Vp, decke the in thy ioly araye. **1688** SOUTH *Serm., Prov.* xii. 22 An apple of Sodom..with a florid jolly white and red.

†**b.** Of immaterial things: Fine; fair; specious.

a **1500** *Bernardus de cura rei fam.* (E.E.T.S.) 198 Trast hym nocht, suppose he were þi brudyr, Bot gef a ioly worde ay for ane vdyr. **1557** *Tottel's Misc.* (Arb.) 202 Then finenesse thought by trainyng talke to win that beauty lost. And whet her tonges with ioly wordes. **1562** JEWEL *Apol. Ch. Eng.* IV. (1600) 146 Thus with a gay, and iollie shewe, deceiue they the simple. **1576** FLEMING *Panopl. Epist.* 245 Those, which by outward gesture and habite of the body, make a jollie shew.

†**9.** Finely or 'bravely' dressed; = *Sc.* 'braw'.

c **1386** CHAUCER *Frankl. T.* 199 A squier..That fressher was and Iolyer of array As to my doom than is the Monthe of May. **1483** CAXTON *G. de la Tour* C iij b, [I] spared myn araye on holy dayes for to shewe me fresshe and ioly tofore men of astate. **1508** DUNBAR *Tua mariit wemen* 67 With silkis arrayit, Gymp, iolie and gent. **1593** R. HARVEY *Philad.* 5 His multitude of rude Scythians and sheepheardes could do more Actes than all the fine gay troopes and rankes of Baiazete,.. vnlesse it be an infallible Item that the iolliest men are euer greatest actors by sea and land.

10. Good-looking; handsome; fair, pretty. Now only *dial.*

? *a* **1366** CHAUCER *Rom. Rose* 829 So noble he was of his stature, So fair, so Ioly, and so fetys. *c* **1475** *Partenay* 343 Then spak the moste gentillest of thaim thre, The most good-lokest And iolyest to se. **1565** GOLDING *Ovid's Met.* XIII. (1567) A a ij b, I know my selfe too bee A iollye fellow. For euen now I did behold and see Myne image in the water sheere. **1648** BEAUMONT *Psyche* IV. iv, When all the glorious Realm of pure Delight, Illustrious Paradise waited on the feet Of jolly Eve. **1650** J. REYNOLDS *Flower Fidel.* 20 This jolly Nymph..very joyfully conducted them through the Woods.

11. Healthy and well developed; of large make and fine appearance; well-conditioned; plump. Rarely of a plant. *dial.* and *colloq.*

a **1661** FULLER *Worthies* (1840) III. 363 A dainty dame in her youth, and a jolly woman in her age. **1683** *Lond. Gaz.* No. 1848/8 A brisk jolly Man, brown hair'd. **1707** *Curiosities in Husb. & Gard.* 205 One of these Branches..was grown to be a very Jolly Plant. **1712** STEELE *Spect.* No. 485 ¶3 He is that Sort of person which the Mob call a handsome jolly Man. **1749** *Phil. Trans.* XLVI. 234 The Lady was brought to bed of a fine jolly Boy. **1825** BROCKETT, *Jolly*, stout, large in person. 'A jolly landlady'. **1887** *Kent Gloss.*, *Jolly*, fat; plump; sleek, in good condition.

V. 12. a. Used as a general expression of admiration: Splendid, fine, excellent.

1548 UDALL, etc. *Erasm. Par. Mark* viii. 31 To haue hym greatly estemed, and taken for a ioly felowe of euery body. **1576** FLEMING tr. *Caius' Eng. Dogs* in Arb. *Garner* III. 239 This dog..taketh the prey with a jolly quickness. *c* **1620** C. MORE *Life Sir T. More* (1828) 316 This said jolly invention of Sir Thomas More's. **1697** DRYDEN *Virg. Past.* III. 146 Graze not too near the Banks, my jolly Sheep. **1805** WORDSW. *Waggoner* I. 118 My jolly team, he finds that ye Will work for nobody but me! **1859** FARRAR *J. Home* 264 (Hoppe) They all drank his health with the usual honours: ..For he's a jolly good fe-el-low, Which nobody can deny.

b. *ironically.* (Cf. 'pretty', 'fine', Sc. 'bonny'.)

The term *jolly fellow* was often thus used in the sixteenth cent., sometimes with allusion to sense 6, and is still applied in the same way dialectally.

1534 MORE *Treat. on Passion* Wks. 1303/2 Here shall you see Iudas play the ioylye marchaunt I trowe. **1546** GARDINER *Declar. Art. Joye* 42 b, Is not he a ioylye workeman that wolde deuise to haue god done, otherwyse then he hath? **1586** FERNE *Blaz. Gentrie* 71 Mary, a iolly peece of worke it were, to see plow-men gentlemen. *c* **1620** Z. BOYD *Zion's Flowers* (1855) 82 They're jolly praters, but are Jades to doe. **1645** MILTON *Colast.* Wks. (1851) 343 It was my hap at length..to finde not seeking..a jolly slander, call'd *Divorce at pleasure.* **1881** *Leicester Gloss.* s.v., 'A jolly fellow' = 'a fine fellow', in the sense of one who prides himself on something he has no occasion to be proud of.

13. a. Exceedingly pleasant, agreeable, or 'nice'; delightful. Now *colloq.*

1549 LATIMER *5th Serm. bef. Edw. VI* (Arb.) 142 A ioly praye for oure holye father. **1579-80** NORTH *Plutarch, Sertorius* (1676) 493 The heat of Summer is nourished and inforced by the melting of the ice and snow, and so bloweth a joly coole winde. **1600** SHAKS. *A.Y.L.* II. vii. 183 This Life is most iolly. **1610** FLETCHER *Faithf. Sheph.* I. i, Sports, delights and jolly games That Shepherds hold full dear. *c* **1704** PRIOR *Henry & Emma* 122 A Shepherd now along the Plain He roves; And with his jolly Pipe, delights the Groves. **1865** KINGSLEY *Herew.* xv, How jolly it will be to see them. **1888** *Poor Nellie* 57 By Jove! but it is awfully jolly out here! **1890** 'L. FALCONER' *Mlle. Ixe* iii. (1891) 86 Good-bye, Mrs. Merrington; so jolly of you to give a dance. **1891** E. PEACOCK

N. Brendon I. 138 What was, by universal consent, the jolliest room in the house.

b. Also *ironically.*

1916 GALSWORTHY *Sheaf* i. 13 'Jolly for my new coat!' I said.

14. Used as an admiring intensive, deriving its meaning from the context: Admirably great, large, big, etc.; *ironically* 'fine', 'nice'. Now *colloq.*

1559 *Mirr. Mag., Salisbury* xxiv, With erles, lordes and captaynes ioly store. **1579** SPENSER *Sheph. Cal.* Sept. 165 Indeede, thy Ball is a bold bigge curre, And could make a jolly hole in theyr furre. *a* **1661** FULLER *Worthies* (1840) III. 514 This king had four-and-twenty daughters, a jolly number. **1855** DARWIN in *Life & Lett.* (1887) I. 405 Are not these a jolly lot of assumptions? **18..** F. W. ROBINSON *Wrayford's Ward*, etc., *Tito's Troubles*, The fate that loomed before Tito..was..set down as a 'jolly shame'. **1880** MRS. RIDDELL *Myst. Palace Gard.* xxx. (1881) 293 The jolly row there was between him and the mater. *Mod. slang,* 'I should call you a jolly fool, if you did.'

B. *adv.*

1. In a jolly manner; merrily, pleasantly.

1615 WITHER *Sheph. Hunt.* in *Juvenilia* (1633) 385 Willy, thou now full jolly tun'st thy Reeds. **1856** EMERSON *Eng. Traits, Race* Wks. (Bohn) II. 31 They eat and drink, and live jolly in the open air.

2. a. Qualifying an adj. or adv.; orig. appreciatively, then ironically, with intensive force: Extremely, very. Now *colloq.*

1549 COVERDALE, etc. *Erasm. Par. Phil.* iii. 5, I thought my selfe a iolye fortunate man [*pulchre mihi videbar felix*], aswell for the nobylitie of my kyndred..as also for my strayte obseruyng of ye law. *c* **1555** HARPSFIELD *Divorce Hen. VIII* (Camden) 171 The..25 chapter..maketh a jolly impertinent process. **1596** SHAKS. *Tam. Shr.* III. ii. 215 'Tis like you'll proue a iolly surly groome. *c* **1645** HOWELL *Lett.* VI. 43 Prince Rupert having got a jolly considerable Army in Holland. **1647** TRAPP *Comm. Matt.* iv. 1 All was jolly quiet at Ephesus before St. Paul came hither. **1838** DICKENS *O. Twist* ix, 'He is so jolly green', said Charley. **1898** R. KIPLING in *Morn. Post* 8 Nov. 5/1 My friend, you made a mistake, and you jolly well know it.

b. Formerly also *jolly and* ——; cf. Sc. *braw and* ——, *gay and* ——; in *braw and able, braw and soon, it is gay and late.*

1565 T. STAPLETON *Fortr. Faith* 37 Is not your doctrine a ioyly and holesom doctrine? *Ibid.* 40* Is not this religion of protestants like to be a ioyly and sounde religion? **1575** LANEHAM *Lett.* 58, I am of woont iolly & dry a mornings.

C. *Comb.*, as ***jolly-cheeked, -faced, -timbered, jollylike*** adjs.; **jolly-boys**, 'a group of small drinking vessels connected by a tube, or by openings one from another' (Farmer *Slang* 1896); **jolly-tail** *Austral.*, a small fresh-water fish of the genus *Galaxias*, esp. *G. attenuatus.*

1587 M. GROVE *Pelops & Hipp.* (1878) 48 As if Alexandrus were With all his iolilyke royaltie, in place among them there. **1594** LODGE *Wounds Civ. War* III. i. in Hazl. *Dodsley* VII. 145 Aristion is a jolly-timber'd man. **1819** W. TENNANT *Papistry Storm'd* (1827) 118 The jollie-cheekit moon. **1892** P. L. SIMMONDS *Commercial Dict. Trade Products* (rev. ed.) Suppl. 463/2 *Jolly-tail*, a small fresh-water fish of Australia..highly esteemed as a delicacy for the table. There are several species. **1898** F. C. GOULD in *Westm. Gaz.* 8 Dec. 2/1 Jolly-faced farmers. **1898** E. E. MORRIS *Austral Eng.* 224/1 Jolly-tail, *n.* a Tasmanian name for the larger variety of the fish *Galaxias attenuatus*, Jenyns, and other species of *Galaxias.* **1951** T. C. ROUGHLEY *Fish Austral.* (rev. ed.) 156 It [*sc.* whitebait] is composed mainly of the young fry of small fish called minnows or jollytails (*Galaxias attenuatus*). **1965** *Austral. Encycl.* V. 141/2 Jollytails, small freshwater fishes (*Galaxias*) rarely attaining a length of 8 inches.

jolly ('dʒɒlɪ), *sb.*[1] *slang.* [JOLLY *a.* used as sb.]

1. A royal marine. ***tame jolly***, a militiaman.

1829 MARRYAT *F. Mildmay* xi, The jollies fired tolerably well. **1841** —— *Poacher* xxvi, 'Jollies! what are they?' 'Why, marines, to be sure'. **1867** SMYTH *Sailor's Word-bk.* s.v., *Tame jolly*, a militiaman: *royal jolly*, a marine. **1896** R. KIPLING *Seven Seas* 176 I'm a Jolly—'Er Majesty's Jolly—Soldier and Sailor too.

2. A cheer.

1871 *Daily Tel.* 7 Mar. (Farmer), On a suggestion to give him a jolly, which appears to be the local phrase, they cheered the hero loud and long. **1894** *Daily News* 27 July 8/1 The Chairman..called upon those who benefited by it to give those gentlemen a 'jolly', a request which was carried out with amazing vigour.

3. A word of praise or favourable notice, esp. one uttered for some ulterior purpose, as to further the sale of goods; also, A sham purchaser (see quot. 1867).

1856 H. MAYHEW *Gt. World London* 46 (Farmer) The dependents of cheats; as jollies and 'magsmen', or the confederates of other cheats. **1867** *Morning Star* 25 Dec., The man Kelly was what is termed a 'jolly', that was, a person paid to bid so as to induce strangers to believe that he was a bonâ fide purchaser. **1873** *Slang Dict.* 205 'Chuck Harry a jolly, Bill', i.e. go and praise up his goods, or buy of him, and speak well of the article.

jolly ('dʒɒlɪ), *sb.*[2] [Short for JOLLY-BOAT.] = JOLLY-BOAT.

1829 MARRYAT *F. Mildmay* xxii, There is the jolly for you: send the boat off as soon as you have landed. **1887** W. RYE *Norfolk Broads* 74 We took the jolly across the broad. **1889** *Blackw. Mag.* CXLVI. 172 The jolly was half full of water.

Jolly ('dʒɒlɪ, 'jɒlɪ), *sb.*[3] The name of P. von *Jolly* (1809–1884), German physicist, used *attrib.* (†or in the possessive) to denote a balance invented by him, used esp. in determining the specific gravities of minerals, in which the elongation of a helical spring when a body is hung on it indicates the weight of the body.

1882 A. GEIKIE *Text-bk. Geol.* II. ii. 93 Jolly's spring balance is a simple and serviceable instrument. **1906** J. P. IDDINGS *Rock Minerals* ii. 92 By means of a Jolly balance or spring..the specific gravity of a crystal may be found with approximate accuracy. **1964** J. SINKANKAS *Mineral. for Amateurs* vii. 187 In the homemade Jolly balance shown.., a specimen attached by thread to the lower hook of the spring carries it down a certain distance which can be measured.

jolly, *sb.*[4] *colloq.* Short for JOLLIFICATION; so, a thrill of enjoyment or excitement, as in phr. ***to get one's jollies***. Also *jollyo, jolly-up.* Cf. JOLLO.

1905 in *Dialect Notes* (1908) III. 325 Justice Brewer's jolly. **1907** F. H. BURNETT *Shuttle* xxiii. 237 If you can give 'em a jolly and make 'em laugh, they'll listen. **1920** *Spectator* 4 Dec. 740/1 Every age must be allowed an occasional 'jolly'. **1921** GALSWORTHY *To Let* II. iv. 154 Come and have a 'jolly' with us. **1924** M. NEWMAN *Consummation* IV. xv. 197 Troops fed to the teeth with..relentless routine, broken only by the occasional horror of a 'show' (what Bossy called a 'jolly'). **1927** *Amer. Speech* II. 277/1 *Jolly-up*, informal dance. **1932** E. WAUGH *Black Mischief* iv. 140 Why can't the silly mutt go off home and leave us to have a jolly up. **1957** M. SHULMAN *Rally round the Flag, Boys!* (1958) ix. 100 If she wasn't so goddam busy..then he wouldn't be thinking about getting his jollies elsewhere! **1962** in Wentworth & Flexner *Dict. Amer. Slang* Suppl. (1967) 686/1 The owner of this place gets his jollies by walking around most of the day in a Sioux war bonnet. **1963** *Daily Tel.* 3 Oct. 20/2 Many parents rejoice inwardly at..their sons being immured under a régime of spartan rigour, but if the compensating jolly-up in the holidays is carried beyond a certain point the whole exercise becomes..unrealistic. **1966** D. FRANCIS *Flying Finish* v. 64 You couldn't just go up alone for an afternoon's jolly in an airliner. **1968** *Surfer Mag.* Jan. 18/2 The announcer acted like this is where all of the surfers go after dark to get their jollies. **1970** V. C. CLINTON-BADDELEY *No Case for Police* iv. 78, I had gone for a jollyo to one of the rather swell hotels. **1971** 'W. HAGGARD' *Bitter Harvest* xiv. 145 It would be a splendid wedding, the sort of big jolly Charles Russell enjoyed.

jolly ('dʒɒlɪ), *v.* [f. JOLLY *a.* and *sb.*[1]; cf. OF. *jolyer.*]

1. *intr.* To make merry, enjoy oneself. *rare.*

1610 G. FLETCHER *Christs Tri.* I. xxxv, They jolly at his grief, and make their game. **1839** THACKERAY *Fatal Boots* xii, Home at half-past three to dinner—when I jollied, as I call it, for the rest of the day.

2. *slang.* **a.** *trans.* To treat with rough merriment, ridicule, or horseplay; to chaff; to abuse.

1873 *Slang Dict., Jolly*, to abuse or vituperate. **1879** *N. & Q.* 5th Ser. XI. 406 Jolleying is a common term among workmen in London, and is used to express nearly every description of verbal ridicule and abuse. **1885** RUNCIMAN *Skippers & Sh.* 146 The way they hustled us and jollied us was cruel. **1924** H. DE SELINCOURT *Cricket Match* vii. 219 Their main effort seems not to be..jollied out for a depressing total.

b. To cheer.

1891 *Licensed Victuallers' Gaz.* 9 Feb. (Farmer), The ring of spectators..cheered and jollied both lads vociferously.

c. To treat (a person) in a pleasant, agreeable manner, with the object of keeping him in good humour or of obtaining a favour from him. Const. *up, along*, etc. Also with *impers.* obj. orig. *U.S.*

1890 H. PALMER *Stories of Base Ball Field* 81, I jollied him along as strong as I could. **1893** GUNTER *Miss Dividends* 232 You've left her alone all to-day—you ain't been near to jolly her up. **1894** *Outing* (U.S.) XXIV. 60/1 It was very difficult to beg off. I jollied the trio as best I could. **1895** *Nebraska State Jrnl.* 23 June 3/1 They jollied Hiram Ebright and touched up the players. **1899** *Harper's Mag.* XXVIII. 529/2 We want you to jolly them up a bit. **1901** *Daily Colonist* (Victoria, B.C.) 19 Oct. 2/5 It is now asserted that the message was an artful device of the astute Mr. Bratnober, who wanted to keep Mr. Macdonald 'jollied up' until the time should come to dispense with his services. **1908** G. H. LORIMER *Jack Spurlock* v. 91 Our customers expect the boys to have a little snap and jolly their grub along. **1929** E. WILSON *I thought of Daisy* iv. 253, I thought that I'd jolly him along a little. **1938** E. WAUGH *Scoop* II. i. 124 We've got to..make contacts, dig up some news sources, jolly up the locals a bit. **1943** J. B. PRIESTLEY *Daylight on Saturday* xi. 68 He had seen himself arranging sports and entertainments ..and generally jollying everybody along. **1958** 'A. GILBERT' *Death against Clock* 10 Her clothes were varying shades of brown, jollied up with a purple scarf. **1959** *Times* 28 July 11/2 Mr. Maurice Browning..jollies things along briskly enough, with enthusiastic aid from the audience. **1973** H. MCCLOY *Change of Heart* iv. 40 He protested, he argued, he even tried to jolly them along. They only became bolder.

d. *intr.* To make a sham bid at an auction; see JOLLY *sb.*[1] 3.

1869 *Echo* 11 Oct., Dealers who if they chance to see a likely purchaser in the crowd will forthwith commence to make false offers—termed 'jollying'—for their own horses when brought up for auction.

jolly-boat ('dʒɒlɪbəʊt). [Known only from 18th c.: origin uncertain.

It has been supposed to be a perversion of JOLYWAT or *gellywatte*, an earlier name app. for the same or a similar ship's boat of small size. On the other hand the first element bears a strong (written) resemblance to a name (of unknown origin and uncertain age) applied to small boats of various kinds in many Teutonic langs.: e.g. Da. *jolle* (17th c.), Sw. *jol, jolle, julle*, LG. *jolle, jölle, gölle, gelle* (in Fischer 1741 *jol* or *jelle*, Brem. Wbch. *jelle*, E. Fris. *jül, jülle*, Wang. *jel*), Du. *jol* (1682 in Winschooten; Hexham, 1678, has the dim. *jolletjen* 'small bark or boat'). But in all these langs. the *j* is = Eng. *y*, and the actual corresponding word is F. *yole*, Eng. *yawl.* (An alleged F. *jol, jelle*, seems only to be the Teutonic word mentioned as a foreign word in an *Encyclopédie* of the 18th c.) Hence the exact historical relations of these words remain unascertained.]

A clincher-built ship's boat, smaller than a cutter, with a bluff bow and very wide transom, usually hoisted at the stern of the vessel, and used chiefly as a hack-boat for small work.

1727–41 CHAMBERS *Cycl.* s.v. *Boat*, The several boats, and their names are, a jolly boat, a long boat,..a yaul, boats for ships. **1775** DALRYMPLE in *Phil. Trans.* LXVIII. 397 Sent jolly boat and yawl in search of him. **1809** W. IRVING *Knickerb.* (1861) 51 A little round Dutch boat, shaped not unlike a tub, which had formerly been the jolly-boat of the Goede Vrouw. *c* **1860** H. STUART *Seaman's Catech.* 9 Jolly boat or dingey, is used on all calls for market, or going round the ship squaring yards, or for any similar purpose.

†'**jollyhead.** *Obs. rare*^−1^. [f. JOLLY *a.* + -HEAD.] Jollity, merriment.

1596 SPENSER *F.Q.* VI. xi. 32 Despoyled of those ioyes and iolly-head, Which with those gentle shepheards here I wont to lead.

jolt (dʒəʊlt), *v.* Also 6–7 **ioult.** [Etymology obscure: see Note below.]

†**1.** *trans.* To butt or push with the head, elbow, or other blunt part; to give a push or knock to; to nudge. *Obs.*

1611 COTGR., *Coudéer*, to iog or ioult with the elbow. *Ibid., Tabuter*, to ioult, butt, or push. **1778** MAD. D'ARBLAY *Diary* 18 June, I jolted Mr. Crisp, who, very much perplexed, said,..that it was a novel.

2. a. To shake up from one's seat or place with a sudden jerk or succession of jerks, esp. in locomotion; to carry or transport with jolts. (Chiefly in *passive.*)

1599 [see JOLTING *ppl. a.*]. **1607** DEKKER & WEBSTER *Westw. Hoe* II. iii. D.'s Wks. 1873 II. 311 O fie vpont: a Coach? I cannot abide to be iolted. **1796** BURKE *Regic. Peace* iii. Wks. VIII. 268 We are yet to be jolted and rattled over the loose misplaced stones. **1851** *Illustr. Catal. Gt. Exhib.* 247 Their object is to advance by steps as in walking, without jolting the carriage. **1877** BLACK *Green Past.* xlvi. (1878) 370 We were once more jolted over the unmade roads.

b. To startle, to surprise. Cf. JOLT *sb.* 2 b.

1872 'MARK TWAIN' *Roughing It* (1873) ii. 27 She would launch a slap at him that would have jolted a cow. **1875** —— in *Atlantic Monthly* Feb. 219, I said I didn't know. 'Don't know?' His manner jolted me. **1919** H. CRANE *Let.* 27 Dec. (1965) 28 Yes, the last word will jolt you. **1972** *Guardian* 23 Dec. 17/2 Those mega-million pound takeover bids which jolt the City.

3. To move or throw (anything) *up* with a jerk; to force *out* in a jerky manner.

a **1845** HOOD *The Desert-Born* 189 My scanty breath was jolted out with many a sudden groan. **1896** *Liberal Mag.* Dec. 507 The contest between State-aid and Rate-aid ended in jolting the two up together in one scheme.

4. *intr.* Of a vehicle, etc.: To receive an abrupt and rough jerk in moving; to move along with a succession of jolts, as on an uneven road.

a **1703** POMFRET *Last Epiph.* Poems (1790) 138 The globe shall..backward jolt, distorted with the wound. **1750** JOHNSON *Rambler* No. 34 ¶6 He whipped his horses, the coach jolted again. **1855** MACAULAY *Hist. Eng.* xiv. III. 430 Waggons laden with the sick jolted over the rugged pavement.

5. *intr.* Of a person: To ride with constant jolts.

1730 MRS. DELANY *Lett., to Mrs. A. Granville* 266 Good-night; I have jolted all over the city, and am so tired I can only say I am..Yours, M.P. **1880** DIXON *Royal Windsor* III. xxi. 210 To jolt along the road was painful.

6. *intr.* To move up and down or to and fro in a jerky manner.

1788 MAD. D'ARBLAY *Let. to Mr. Twining* 20 Jan., The shoulders..jolting up and down in the convulsions of a hoarse laugh. **1849** H. MAYO *Pop. Superst.* (1851) 125 With head, limbs, and trunk twitching and jolting in every direction.

[*Note.* The etymology of *jolt* vb. and sb., and their derivatives, and of words apparently allied in form and sense, is, in the present state of the evidence, involved in obscurity and difficulty. *Jolt-head* is known in 1533; *jolt-headed* (in the form *cholt-headed*) in 1552; *jolting pate*, app. in the sense of *jolt-head* in 1579; while the simple vb. and sb. *jolt*, are not known till 1599. But JOT *v.*[1], largely identical in sense with *jolt*, is quoted at least from 1530, and may be a century earlier. Sense 1 of *jolt*, both in sb. and vb., has evident affinities with *joll*, JOWL *sb.*[4], *v.*[1], and perh. with JOWL *sb.*[3]; but the other senses of *jolt* vb. coincide with those of *jot* vb. *Jolt* has thus the appearance of an alteration of *jot*, influenced by *jowl*, and perh. by *jolt-head*, which latter is evidently related in some way to JOWL *sb.*[4] or JOWL *sb.*[3]: the form *cholt-headed* esp. recalls the *cholle* form of the latter. (Cf. also the mod. dial. *cholter-, chowter-headed* = JOLTER-HEADED.) It has been suggested that *jolt-head* may have been a phonetic variant of **jolled-* or **jowl'd head*, and that *jolt* vb. was a back-formation from it, perh. through *jolting pate*: but this has obvious difficulties, phonetic and semantic. Further evidence may harmonize facts, which are at present somewhat contradictory.]

jolt (dʒəʊlt), *sb.* Also 7 **ioult.** [See prec.]

†**1.** A knock (of the head, etc.) against something. *Obs. rare.*

1599 MINSHEU *Sp. Dict., Coxorrón*,..iolts of the head against the wall. **1618** HOLYDAY *Juvenal* ii. 22 He..Who Mars his shields, staid with close thong, oft bears With jolts and sweat.

2. a. An abrupt shock or jerk which throws a person (or thing) up, to fall again by his (or its) own weight; esp. one received by a moving vehicle, or by a person driving or riding on a rough road.

1632 SHERWOOD *Cotgr.*, The ioult of a coach in vneuen way. **1688** EVELYN *Diary* 12 Feb., My daughter Evelyn going in the coach..a jolt (the doore being not fast shut) flung her quite out. **1763** WILKES *Corr.* (1805) II. 33 My wound has been a good deal fretted by the vile jolts through the rascally towns of Stroud, Rochester, Chatham, &c. **1876** LOWELL *Among my Bks.* Ser. II. 135 A series of jolts and jars, proving that the language had run off the track.

b. *fig.* A surprise; a shock which disturbs one's mental composure.

1884 'MARK TWAIN' *Huck. Finn* v. 30, I was scared now, ..but in a minute I see I was mistaken. That is, after the first jolt,..he being so unexpected. **1905** D. G. PHILLIPS *Plum Tree* 3 I'd like to give him a jolt. **1924** H. T. LOWE-PORTER tr. *Mann's Buddenbrooks* I. vi. 208 Oh, no! I know they gave you a jolt yesterday—a very, very stimulating jolt.

c. A blow in boxing. Also in phr. *to pass a jolt*, to deliver a blow. Also *fig.*

1908 S. E. WHITE *Riverman* xvii. 160 Murphy blocked, ducked, and kept away, occasionally delivering a jolt as opportunity offered. **1912** [see HAY-MAKER 4]. **1916** C. J. DENNIS *Songs Sentimental Bloke* 124 *Jolt, to pass a*, to deliver a short, sharp blow. **1950** J. DEMPSEY *Championship Fighting* vii. 26 Best of all the punches is the 'stepping straight jolt'. **1954** F. C. AVIS *Boxing Reference Dict.* 60 *Jolt*, a kind of jab punch that brings up short an advancing opponent.

3. A jerky movement, an abrupt jerk.

1849 H. MAYO *Pop. Superst.* (1851) 124 The exercise commonly began in the head, which would fly backwards and forwards, and from side to side, with a quick jolt.

4. a. A drink of liquor. *slang* (chiefly *U.S.*).

1904 *McClure's Mag.* Mar. 560/2, I stopped at a blacksmith's shop..and had my arm dressed and a big jolt of whiskey. **1920** F. SCOTT FITZGERALD *This Side of Paradise* (1921) II. iv. 252 We'll take you to some secluded nook and give you a wee jolt of Bourbon. **1935** G. BLUNDEN *No More Reality* xxxiii. 344 'Take another jolt, sport,' said Clarrie with a grin. **1957** A. MACNAB *Bulls of Iberia* xii. 125 'You've been drinking.'..'I shoved in a couple of jolts on the way here.' **1959** T. GRIFFITH *Waist-High Culture* (1960) 231 Jolts of whiskey or vodka. **1973** R. THOMAS *If you can't be Good* (1974) xvi. 145 She took two green plastic glasses... I poured a generous jolt into both of them.

b. A prison sentence. *slang* (orig. *U.S.*).

1912 D. LOWRIE *My Life in Prison* ii. 17 A professional 'pete' man had..returned exultingly to the jail with a six-year 'jolt'. **1926** J. BLACK *You can't Win* xv. 197 He was in good spirits and condition after 'stopping his jolt' in the stir and anxious to start 'rooting'. **1928** [see BOOK *sb.* 10 d]. **1936** 'D. HUME' *Meet Dragon* ix. 96 They are only too ready to turn King's evidence...you'd take a very stiff jolt.

c. = BANG *sb.*[3]; a quantity of a drug in the form of a cigarette, tablet, etc. *slang* (chiefly *U.S.*).

1916 T. BURKE *Limehouse Nights* 19 A little later he would take a jolt of opium at the place at the corner of Formosa Street. **1926** J. BLACK *You can't Win* xii. 162 He wouldn't give us a jolt if we had the horrors... Given a sufficient quantity of hop, no fiend is ever at a loss for a sound reason for taking a jolt of it. **1929** D. HAMMETT *Dain Curse* (1930) xxi. 233 You can take your jolt in front of me. I won't blush. **1955** *U.S. Senate Hearings* (1956) VIII. 4164 Terms used in the traffic pertaining to the alkaloid morphine are as follows: ..jolt,..a dose. **1970** K. PLATT *Pushbutton Butterfly* (1971) vi. 58 Her LSD cap would cost about two dollars and fifty cents for the jolt.

5. *attrib.* and *Comb.*, as **jolt ramming** *Founding*, a method of packing the sand around a pattern in which the moulding box, pattern, and sand are repeatedly lifted by machine and allowed to fall; freq. *attrib.*; **jolt-squeeze** *Founding*, simultaneous or successive jolting of a moulding box and 'squeezing' of the sand in it (i.e. application of pressure at the top), as a means of packing the sand around a pattern; usu. *attrib.*

1909 *Iron Age* LXXXIV. 1165/1 Today we have pneumatic jolt-ramming machines in successful service with lifting capacities from 10 to 15 tons. *Ibid.* 1165/2 How to adapt our foundry methods to this new principle of jolt-ramming green sand molds. **1926** *Jrnl. Iron & Steel Inst.* CXIII. 568 The whole of the mould and core are rammed on a Mumford jolt ramming machine. **1950** J. S. CAMPBELL *Casting & Forming Processes* xii. 104 Jolt ramming packs the lower portions of the sand next to the pattern best. **1931** *Jrnl. Iron & Steel Inst.* CXXIII. 602 (*heading*) A novel combination jolt-squeeze moulding machine. **1955** HEINE & ROSENTHAL *Princ. Metal Casting* iv. 53 Match-plate molding using jolt-squeeze machines is perhaps the simplest method of speeding up the molding of small castings. **1971** W. B. PARKES *Clay-Bonded Foundry Sand* viii. 235 For most moulds, all that is needed is a simultaneous jolt-squeeze of a few seconds.

jolter (ˈdʒəʊltə(r)), *sb.*[1] [f. JOLT *v.* + -ER[1].] One who or that which jolts; a jolting carriage.

1611 COTGR., *Secoueur*, a shaker, tosser, swinger, ioulter. **1843** *Knickerbocker* XXI. 39 The traveller has but to express a wish to visit a distant plantation, and his..luggage is placed in the donkeyed jolter. **1852** R. S. SURTEES *Sponge's Sp. Tour* (1893) 146 It was two o'clock before Mr. Spraggon was again in his jolter.

jolter, *sb.*[2] Also joulter. App. a variant of JOWTER, a hawker, pedlar.

Perhaps only an individualism of the writers; the form is not in *E.D. Dict.* and the word not cited from Ireland.

1841 S. C. HALL *Ireland* II. 157 A jolter, a man selling oysters, brooms and sundries, was as welcome to the servants' hall, as a pedlar with shawls and laces to the drawing room. **1845** MRS. S. C. HALL *Whiteboy* x. 85 The widdy sould them [ducks] to a Cork joulter for eightpence a couple.

ˈjolter, *v. rare.* [Frequentative of JOLT *v.*: see -ER[5].] *intr.* and *trans.* To jolt, to move with continuous jolting.

1828 LAMB *Wife's Trial* i, I am jolter'd, bruised, and shook to death, With your vile Wiltshire roads. **1864** SALA in *Daily Tel.* 13 Oct., The luggage! It was coming joltering in a van to the place where we couldn't get a bed.

jolter-head, jolterhead. Also *dial.* cholter-head, chowter-head. [An extension of JOLT-HEAD.]

1. (ˈdʒəʊltəˈhɛd) = JOLT-HEAD 1.

a **1700** B. E. *Dict. Cant. Crew*, *Jolter-head*, a vast large Head; also Heavy and Dull. **1822** HAZLITT *Table-t.*, *Merry England* (1852) 61 They judge of the English character in the lump, as one great jolter-head, containing all the stupidity of the country. **1823** MOORE *Fables Holy Alliance* ii. 10 The Easterns, in a Prince, 'tis said, Prefer what's called a jolter-head. **1829** SCOTT *Diary* 18 Mar. in *Lockhart*, A misshapen dwarf, with a huge jolter-head.

2. (ˈdʒəʊltəhɛd) = JOLT-HEAD 2.

1620 SHELTON *Quix.* IV. xviii, Who was that Iolter-head that did subscribe or ratify a warrant for the attaching of a Knight? *a* **1818** LEWIS, etc. *Ct. Hamilton's Fairy Tales* (1849) 68 While my jolter-head of a Genius laboured with both his body and soul. **1881** *Spectator* 26 Feb. 275 A clerk so low..that Prince Bismarck can disavow him as a jolter-head without remark. **1897** *E.D. Dict.*, *Cholter-head.*

jolter-headed (ˈdʒəʊltərˌhɛdɪd), *a.* Also *dial.* cholter-. [f. prec. + -ED[2].] = JOLT-HEADED.

1748 RICHARDSON *Clarissa* (1811) VI. xxvi. 111 Half-a-dozen jolter-headed crop-eared boys. **1765** *Treat. Dom. Pigeons* 69 The Dutch tumbler is..larger, often feather-leg'd, and more joulter-headed. **1821** SCOTT *Kenilw.* xxvii, How didst thou come off with yonder jolter-headed giant? **1876** *Whitby Gloss.*, *Cholter-headed*, stultified, heavy headed.

Hence **jolterˈheadedness.**

1852 DICKENS *Lett., to W. Collins* Dec. I. 294 The jolter-headedness of the conceited idiots who suppose that volumes are to be tossed off like pancakes.

jolter-pate. *rare*[−1]. [f. *jolter-* in *jolter-head* + PATE.] = JOLTER-HEAD 1, JOLTING *pate*.

1822 SCOTT *Nigel* viii, Her little conceited noddle or her father's old crazy calculating jolter-pate.

jolt head, jolt-head. ? *Obs.* Also 6 cholt-, iolte-, ioulte-, iollt-, 7 ioult-. [Origin obscure: see note to JOLT *v.*]

†**1.** *prop.* **jolt head** (ˈdʒəʊltˈhɛd): A large, clumsy, or heavy head; a stupid head. *Obs.*

1533 MORE *Debell. Salem* Wks. 993/1 A mastyffe hath..a greate iolte head, and a great mosel. **1605** B. JONSON *Volpone* v. viii, Your red saucy cap, that seemes (to me) Nayl'd to your iolt-head. **1680** *Lond. Gaz.* No. 1531/4 The other a darker Bay with a jolt head. **1701** GREW *Cosm. Sacra* I. v. §25 He must then have had a Jolt Head.

2. (ˈdʒəʊlthɛd.) A heavy-headed or thick-headed person; a blockhead. Also *attrib.*

1573 G. HARVEY *Letter-bk.* (Camden) 126 Take him for a ioultehedd and a senseless brute. **1653** URQUHART *Rabelais* Prol. (Rtldg.) 18 Hearken, Joltheads. **1767** STERNE *Tr. Shandy* IX. xxv, Ninny-hammers, goose-caps, jolt-heads. *attrib.* **1664** *Flodden F.* I. 7 At home is left none in the Land, But joult-head Monks and brosten Fryers.

jolt-headed (ˈdʒəʊltˌhɛdɪd), *a.* ? *Obs.* [f. prec. + -ED[2].] Having a 'jolt head', i.e. a large, clumsy, or heavy head; thick-headed. Now only *fig.*

1552 HULOET, Cholt headed felow, whose heade is as greate as a betle or mall, *tuditanus*. **1655** MOUFET & BENNET *Health's Improv.* (1746) 274 A kind of jolt-headed Gudgeons. **1865** tr. *Hugo's Hunchback* v. iii. (Chapman & Hall) 169 'Twas cruel to make a Tantalus of the jolt-headed cub.

ˈjoltiness. [f. JOLTY *a.* + -NESS.] The condition of being jolty.

1891 'L. MALET' *Wages of Sin* IV. iii. 78 Oh! the joltiness of this conversational road. **1905** *Westm. Gaz.* 9 May 4/2 The existing motor-'buses..with their perpetual pulling up, their joltiness, and malodorousness.

†**jolting**, *a. Obs.* [app. from first element of JOLT-HEAD, with ppl. ending. See note to JOLT *v.*] In *jolting pate* = JOLT-HEAD 1, 2.

1579–80 NORTH *Plutarch, Pericles*, This tyranne here, this heauy iollting pate. **1650** BULWER *Anthropomet.* i. 7 Cratinus jesting at his monstrous joulting pate.

jolting (ˈdʒəʊltɪŋ), *vbl. sb.* [f. JOLT *v.* + -ING[1].] The action of the vb. JOLT; the process of being jolted; a shaking in a carriage, etc.

1641 WILKINS *Math. Magick* II. ii. (1648) 161 Whether.. Unevenness of the Ground, will not cause such a jolting of the Chariot. **1713** DERHAM *Phys.-Theol.* I. iii. (1727) 25 *note*, They..found him dead, and that he had been brought thither in the same Posture on Horseback, notwithstanding the jolting of the Horse. **1881** BESANT & RICE *Chapl. of Fleet* I. iii. (1883) 16 The best thing to cure a crying fit is a good jolting..in a country cart.

jolting (ˈdʒəʊltɪŋ), *ppl. a.* [f. JOLT *v.* + -ING[2].] That jolts (in senses of the vb.).

1599 MARSTON *Sco. Villanie* I. iii. 183 Hurried In ioulting Coach. **1772** *Poetry* in *Ann. Reg.* 221 From jolting stones An easy litter sav'd my bones. **1889** *Spectator* 14 Dec. 839 His unusually unmusical and even jolting verse.

Hence **ˈjoltingly** *adv.*, in a jolting manner, so as to jolt.

1843 *Fraser's Mag.* XXVII. 657 Off they started most joltingly. **1859** CORNWALLIS *New World* I. 151 We drove joltingly over a rough lava plain deeply furrowed.

ˈjoltless, *a.* [f. JOLT *sb.* + -LESS.] Free from jolts.

1808 MOORE *Corruption* v, Court and Commons jog one joltless way. **1898** *Spectator* 5 Feb. 190/1 To keep his part of the machine in steady and joltless motion.

jolty (ˈdʒəʊltɪ), *a.* [f. JOLT *sb.* + -Y.] Characterized by jolting; having or causing jolts.

1834 M. SCOTT *Cruise Midge* (1859) 417 The wains..were rumbling and rattling on their jolty axle trees. **1867** LE FANU *Tenants Malory* lxi. (1871) 354 Going slowly down the jolty hill. **1896** MARIE CORELLI *Mighty Atom* xi, The coach would be too jolty for him.

Joly (ˈdʒɒlɪ). The name of John *Joly* (1857–1933), Irish physicist, used *attrib.* and in the possessive to denote apparatus and processes devised by him, as **Joly('s) method, process** *Photogr.*, a process of colour photography using a screen (*Joly screen*) ruled with a repeating sequence of adjacent orange, blue-green, and blue lines placed in front of the plate in the camera and a screen similarly ruled with red, green, and blue lines placed in contact with the transparency when it is being projected; **Joly's steam calorimeter**, a device for determining the specific heat of a substance by measuring the weight of steam that condenses on a known mass of the substance in raising its temperature to that of the steam.

1894 T. PRESTON *Theory of Heat* v. 236 (*heading*) Joly's steam calorimeter. **1902** *Encycl. Brit.* XXXI. 686/1 (*heading*) Joly's process. **1906** E. J. WALL tr. *König's Natural-Color Photogr.* 20 In 1904 Professor Wood improved his process and applied it to positives obtained by the Joly process... Gratings were ruled with three sets of lines in bands corresponding to the width of the red, green, and blue lines of the Joly screen. **1909** S. E. BOTTOMLEY *Photogr. in Princ. & Pract.* xxvi. 207 At the time the Joly process was put on the market, a suitable panchromatic emulsion was not obtainable, and to this cause alone must be ascribed its non-success. **1938** W. J. SPARROW *Heat* vii. 139 Joly's steam calorimeter may be used (*a*) to find the specific heat of a solid.., (*b*) to determine the specific heat of a gas at constant volume. **1940** *Chambers's Techn. Dict.* 469/1 *Joly screen*, a colour mosaic consisting of ruled lines. **1958** H. BAINES *Sci. of Photogr.* xx. 246 Fig. 6 illustrates the reproduction of a red colour by the Joly and similar methods... The Joly experiments showed the possibility of colour photography using a mosaic screen. **1963** A. E. E. MCKENZIE *Second Course Heat* ii. 32 Joly's steam calorimeter measures heat in terms of the mass of steam condensed on a body.

joly, joly-: see JOLLY, JOLLI-.

jolyce, -yous, -ysye, obs. ff. JEALOUS, -OUSY.

†**ˈjolyvet.** *Obs. rare*[−1]. [a. OF. *jolivet*, *jollyvet*, dim. of *jolif*, *-ve* gay, pretty, JOLLY.] A gay or pretty little creature.

1413 *Pilgr. Sowle* (Caxton) I. xxii. (1859) 28 The byrd that syngeth on the braunche on hye, And sheweth hym self a lusty iolyuet, Vnto the deth is smyten sodeynly.

†**ˈjolywat.** *Obs.* Also 5 iolywet, 6–7 gellywatte. [Of obscure origin and uncertain form, the earlier instances having *joly-*, the later *gelly-*.

Conjectured by some to be a corruption of Sp. and Pg. *galeota*, F. *galiote*, Du. *galjoot* (GALLIOT[1]). But this is extremely doubtful. It is difficult to comprehend how *galeota* could be transformed into *jolywat*; and the *things* differ even more than their *names*, for the *galliot* was an independent vessel with sails and many rowers, while the *jolywat* was a ship's boat of small size. It is true that the Pg. *galeota* appears to have become *galleywat* or GALLIVAT, in the East Indies, but this, like the original, was a vessel of 60 or 70 tons with sails and 40 or 50 rowers, carrying sometimes 8 guns—a very different thing from the *jolywat*, to say nothing of the impossibility of any connexion between an Indo-Portuguese word and an English word before 1500. The variation *jolly-*, *gelly-*, reminds us of the numerous forms of the Scandinavian and Low German word *jol*, *jolle*, *gelle*, cited under JOLLY-BOAT; but the evidence for this as yet does not carry us back to the date of *jolywat*.]

A ship's boat of small size; ? = JOLLY-BOAT.

1495–7 *Naval Accts. Hen. VII* (1896) 143 The Soueraigne with her grete bote and Iolywet. *Ibid.* 181 The Soueraignes grete Bote and Iolywat. *Ibid.* 272 (The Regent) Cokke Botes Belongyng to the seid Ship j, Botes called Iolywates j. **1513** in Oppenheim *Admin. Roy. Navy* (1896) 80 For the boat 40 [men]; the cok, 20; the gelly-watte 10. **1613** DOWNTON in Purchas *Pilgrims* (1625) I. 501 As soone as I anchored, I sent ..Master Spooner, and Samuell Squire in my Gellywatte to sound the depths within the sands.

Jomon (ˈdʒəʊmən). Also Jōmon. [Jap.] Used *attrib.* in *Jomon pottery* to denote a kind of very early hand-made Japanese pottery; hence applied to the early neolithic or pre-neolithic culture which is characterized by this pottery.

1946 G. B. SANSOM *Japan* (rev. ed.) i. 1 Two main types of neolithic culture are distinguished. One is known as the Jōmon ('rope-pattern') type, because the pottery which characterises it was made by coiling or has a coil as conventional decoration. **1957** *Encycl. Brit.* XII. 901/1 The Jomon is classified as Neolithic. *Ibid.*, The Jomon ('cord-

pattern') cultures have handmade pottery with patterns formed by rolling or pressing a cord-wrapped stick.. into the still wet clay. **1960** B. LEACH *Potter in Japan* vii. 156 The earliest Jomon pots are long pre-Ainu and are estimated to be upwards of 6,000 years old. **1970** J. KIRKUP *Japan behind Fan* 27 Rare Haniwa and Jomon figures.

jompe, jompre, obs. ff. JUMP, JUMPER.

Jon (dʒɒn), abbrev. JONATHAN 3.
1931 *Daily Tel.* 21 May 5/1 Jons 10s 6d–12s 6d.

Jonah ('dʒəʊnə). Also **Jonas.**
1. The name of a Hebrew prophet, the subject of the Book of Jonah; used allusively, in senses thence derived.
1612 T. LAVENDER *Trav.* Pref. to Rdr. C j, [He] thought it best to make a Ionas of him, and so cast both him and his books into the Sea. **1663** J. SPENCER *Prodigies* (1665) 369 They were always presumed the Jonas's which raised all the storms in the State. **1679** *Establ. Test* 9 One of the Jonahs that was.. heaved over the Decks to allay the Tempest. *a* **1885** H. CONWAY *Living or Dead* viii, You must be very lucky in love.. for you are a regular Jonah at cards. **1887** *Spectator* 5 Nov. 1479 To make a Jonah of the one of its members who is probably least in fault.
2. Jonah-crab, a large crab (*Cancer borealis*) of the eastern coast of North America.
1893 in FUNK.
Hence **jonah** *v. trans.*, to bring ill luck to.
1887 BLACK *Sabina Zembra* 282, I seem to Jonah everything I touch. **1897** R. KIPLING *Captains Courageous* 97 A Jonah's anything that spoils the luck... I've known a splittin'-knife Jonah two trips till we was on to her.

Jonathan ('dʒɒnəθən). [A personal name; orig. that of the son of Saul, king of Israel.]
1. (esp. in phrase ***Brother Jonathan.***) A generic name for the people of the United States, and also for a representative United States citizen.
Understood to have originated in the expression *Brother Jonathan* (cf. 2 Sam. i. 26), said to have been applied to Jonathan Trumbull, Governor of Connecticut, by General Washington, who often sought his advice. Hence it is believed to have been applied at first to a New Englander, and at length, like Yankee, in the wider sense.
1816 'QUIZ' *Grand Master* I. 25 May she all Europe's arms withstand, Keep France and Jonathan in awe. **1816–18** F. HALL *Trav. Canada & U.S.* 330 A humorous publication entitled 'John Bull and Brother Jonathan'. **1820** SYD. SMITH *Wks.* (1840) I. 372 We can inform Jonathan what are the inevitable consequences of being too fond of glory: Taxes upon every article which enters into the mouth. **1825** SCOTT *Fam. Lett.* (1894) II. 384 But I do not suppose brother Jonathan would like much so large a fortune passing out of his continent to gild a Marchioness's coronet in Britain. **1848** LOWELL *Biglow P.* Poems 1890 II. 36 To move John [Bull] you must make your fulcrum of solid beef and pudding; an abstract idea will do for Jonathan.
2. See quot.
1847–78 HALLIWELL, *Jonathan*, an instrument used by smokers to light their pipes with.
3. A red-skinned variety of dessert apple, first introduced in the United States.
1831 J. BUEL in *Gardeners' Mag.* VII. 239 Besides the Newton, I know of none except the Aesopus, the Pownal, the White and the New, or Jonathan. **1831** *Catal. Fruits in Garden of Hort. Soc.* (ed. 2) 18 Apples... Jonathan. **1845** A. J. DOWNING *Fruits Amer.* 113 The Jonathan is a very beautiful dessert apple... The original tree of this new sort is growing on the farm of Mr. Philip Rick, of Kingston, New York. **1879** *Chicago Tribune* 3 May 10/3 Our best winter apples are.. Jeniton, Jonathan, Red Canada, Wythe. **1924** *Glasgow Herald* 23 Dec. 5 In 1922 the price realised for Jonathans did not pay the cost of packing. **1932** [see DELICIOUS *a.* 2 b]. **1950** SMOCK & NEUBERT *Apples & Apple Products* ix. 233 Jonathan spot occurs primarily on Jonathan apples. **1959** [see DELICIOUS *a.* 2 b]. **1963** A. LUBBOCK *Austral. Roundabout* 68 The crimson-cheeked Jonathan apples.
Hence **Jonathani'zation**, an Americanizing.
1854 EMERSON in *Corr. w. Carlyle* II. cxxxviii. 235 Come and see the Jonathanization of John. **1894** *Sat. Rev.* 15 Dec. 652/1 The Jonathanization of John is going on.. symptoms of American corruption and misrule.

joncade, -ate, jonckett, obs. ff. JUNKET.

jonct(e, obs. forms of JOINT *sb.* and *a.*

Jone, obs. form of JOAN, JOIN, JUNE *sb.*

Jones (dʒəʊnz). **1.** One of the commonest British family names, used esp. in the plural to designate one's neighbours or social equals, as in phrase ***to keep up with the Joneses***: see KEEP *v.* 57 j; now usu. with allusion to this phrase.
1879 E. J. SIMMONS *Mem. Station Master* (1974) vi. 83 There is a considerable amount of importance attached to this public place of meeting—the railway station. The Jones's who don't associate with the Robinsons, meet there. Mr Jones would not like the station master to touch his cap to the Robinsons, and pass him without notice. **1932** E. C. HARWOOD *Cause & Control of Business Cycle* x. 124 Why.. does John Doe choose to speculate on margin?.. An ages-old desire to get something for nothing; keeping up with the Joneses; [etc.]. **1955** J. CANNAN *Long Shadows* vii. 106 On a higher scale you're simply outdoing the Joneses. **1959** 'L. GIBB' (*title*) The Joneses: how to keep up with them. **1959** *Times* 18 Sept. 14/5 By addressing Mr. and Mrs. Jones through The Reader's Digest, you thus exert a selling leverage [etc.].. that's Jonesmanship. **1962** *Friend* 29 June 801/1 What we decide will be affected by whether we think morals are something stuck on to people by outside pressure (law, custom, tradition, and 'what the Joneses do') or whether they are an outcome of our nature. **1967** *Guardian* 3 Jan. 4/7, I pretended not to hear.. but in the end you follow the Jones. **1967** G. HOUSEHOLD *Courtesy of Death* 38 Dunton.. avoided any nonsense of competing with Joneses.
2. *slang.* A drug addict's habit.
1968 *Sun Mag.* (Baltimore) 13 Oct. 19/4 Soon you're out to keep from getting the Jones. **1970** C. MAJOR *Dict. Afro-Amer. Slang* 71 *Jones*, a fixation; drug habit; compulsive attachment. **1971** *Black World* Mar. 54/1, I don't have a long jones. I ain't been on it too long. **1971** E. E. LANDY *Underground Dict.* 113 *Jones*, the habit of a drug addict—eg. *His jones is heavy.* **1974** *Publishers Weekly* 12 Aug. 50/2 Knows the reality of Detroit's heroin sub-culture as few of those who are not 'Jones men' do. ('Jones' stands for both heroin and the habit.)

Jonesian ('dʒəʊnzɪən), *a.* [f. name of Daniel *Jones* (1881–1967), English phonetician + -IAN.] Used to designate the phonetic system or the system of classifying phonemes adopted by Daniel Jones. Hence as *sb.*, an adherent or follower of Jones.
1951 *Language* XXVII. 334 Neither 'pure' phonetics nor Jonesian phonemics stands the ghost of a chance. **1953** A. MARTINET in *Anthropol. Today* 578 A Jonesian origin of the Bloomfieldian phoneme might account for the opinion. **1964** Y. R. CHAO in D. Abercrombie et al. *Daniel Jones* 40 Linguists trained under the Jonesian cardinal vowels. **1965** *Language* XLI. 308 Linguists who are neither Firthians nor Jonesians. **1969** *Ibid.* XLV. 109 A reaction against Jonesian and Bloomfieldian phonemics.

jonet(t, var. JAUNETTE, GENET.

jong[1] (jɒŋ). *S. Afr.* [Afrikaans *jong* a coloured servant, f. Du. *jong* a young person.] Formerly, a young male slave; now a coloured male servant; also used as a familiar term of address to any person.
1615 W. PEYTON in R. Raven-Hart *Before Van Riebeeck* (1967) 71 One of the Condemned menn (with twoe other of the Peppercornes companye) caryed awaye her pinasse the next night, at which instant twoe yeongers of my Shipps companye allsoe conserted to carry awaye my boat. **1812** A. PLUMPTRE tr. *Lichtenstein's Trav. S. Afr.* I. viii. 119 A Hottentot.. takes it extremely amiss if he is addressed by the words *Pay* or *Jonge*, as the slaves are. **1846** J. C. BROWN tr. *Arbousset & Daumas's Narr. Tour N.-E. of Cape Good Hope* xxiii. 253 Tied his *jong*, or young bushman slave, to the wheel of his wagon, where he was severely flogged. **1886** G. A. FARINI *Through Kalahari Desert* xvii. 279 These slaves were called 'yungs' or 'boys'. **1912** *East London* (Cape Province) *Dispatch* 13 Feb. 3 (Pettman), Presently a couple of jongs came along with dainty cigarettes in their mouths. **1926** E. LEWIS *Mantis* I. v. 88 And then, another time (so Dan wrote to his father), he'd make you feel a piccanin yourself, a proper little *jong* that'd never been beyond the dorp. **1939** S. CLOETE *Watch for Dawn* v. 65 Where is your whip, jong? **1953** J. COLLIN-SMITH *Locusts & Wild Honey* II. iv. 155, I.. shouted into the house for the 'jong', the coloured houseboy, to bring me coffee. **1956** A. G. MCRAE *Hill called Grazing* vii. 55 Now look here, *jong*, I've got all these pigs yere on my farm, man. *Ibid.*, Now, if I can't get a permit to sell them, man *jong*, I'll have to drive them up on to the main road. **1960** D. LYTTON *Goddam White Man.* i. 10 The sergeant at the police station says—'Watch it jong.' **1973** *Sunday Tribune* (Durban) 1 Apr. 20 Jong, I've had enough of this!

jong[2] (dʒɒŋ). Also **dzong.** [ad. Tibetan *rdzoṅ* fortress.] A Tibetan building (also, a territorial and administrative division) constituting a prefecture, freq. also serving as a fortress, a monastery, or both. Hence **'dzongpön, 'jongpen, jong-pon**, a prefect; **jong-nyer**, a sub-prefect.
[**1888** *Encycl. Brit.* XXIII. 340/2 A valley to the southeast.. contains the towns of Pena-jong and Gyangtse-jong.] **1904** *Times* 11 May 5/1 The Tibetans have strongly fortified the jong. **1904** *Daily Chron.* 21 May 5/4 The collection and equipment of the local levies are conducted by various Jongpen. **1911** *Encycl. Brit.* XXVI. 922/1 The administrative subdivisions of the Lhasa country.. are called *jong*, or 'prefecture', each of which is under the rule of two *jong-pon*. *Ibid.*, There are 123 sub-prefectures under *jong-nyer*. **1921** *Glasgow Herald* 13 July 9 The Jongpen of the district rode out to meet us with a few followers. **1938** F. S. CHAPMAN *Lhasa* iii. 33 The *Dzongpön* (fort commander) of Phari came in for tea. *Ibid.* iv. 49 The dzong is.. on the summit of a volcano-like rock six or seven hundred feet high. *Ibid.* v. 83 He is.. magistrate, or dzongpön, of a district called Purang. **1960** 'S. HARVESTER' *Chinese Hammer* xi. 99 Phari Dzong, Hog Fort, a large square grey fortress. **1960** *Times* 9 June 15/6 The castle-monastery (the *dzong*) which rears high above the floor of the wide valley. **1966** *Times* 17 June 13/5 The great *dzong*.. rears up on the side of the valley, inward-leaning walls around a keep.

jonga ('dʒɒŋgə). Also **jangga.** [f. Doulla-Bakweri (Cameroons) *njaŋga* crayfish.] In Jamaica, a small freshwater prawn, *Macrobrachium jamaicensis.*
See Cassidy & Le Page *Dict. Jamaican Eng.* s.v. *jangga* for oral uses of the word.
1893 C. SULLIVAN *Jamaica Cookery Book* 4 Jonga Soup. *Ibid.* 8 Jongas are a kind of small cray-fish which are often found in our mountain rivers. **1929** M. W. BECKWITH *Black Roadways* 51 Fresh-water shrimps, called *jonga*, from the mountain streams. **1967** *Amer. Speech* XLII. 191 *Jangga*, the river prawn *Macrobrachium jamaicense* [sic]. This word is usually found in print as *jonga*, an unfortunate misrepresentation which has probably led would-be explainers astray. Its actual pronunciation among the folk may always be respelled *jangga*. **1969** 'J. MORRIS' *Fever Grass* iii. 31 They're even canning *jongas* from the head-waters of the Martha Brae. **1971** E. JONES in J. Figueroa *Caribbean Voices* I. 4 Up in de hills, where de streams are cool, An' mullet an' janga swim in de pool.

jonglery ('dʒɒŋglərɪ). [ad. F. *jonglerie*, f. *jongleur*: see next and -ERY. Cf. JUGGLERY.] The performance of a jongleur.
1616 BULLOKAR *Eng. Expos.*, *Ionglerie*, iugling. **1841** LEVER *C. O'Malley* xiv. 79 These feats of *jonglerie* usually terminated in a row. **1841** *Tait's Mag.* VIII. 309 The minstrel found it necessary to unite mimicry and jonglery with his rhymes.

‖**jongleur** (ʒɔ̃glœr). [F. *jongleur* (anciently a minstrel, now a juggler or tumbler), altered or erroneous form of *jougleur*, in OF. *jogleor*:—L. *joculātōr-em* jester: see JUGGLER. (Hatz.-Darm. suggest that the *n* was due to influence of OF. *jangler*.)] The Norman French term (technically used by modern writers) for an itinerant minstrel, who sang and composed ballads, told stories and otherwise entertained people: = JUGGLER 1.
1779 W. ALEXANDER *Hist. Women* (1782) I. vii. 232 It was that of the Troubadours, or Poets, who composed sonnets in praise of their beauty; and of the Jongleurs who sung them at the courts and castles of the great. **1835** LYTTON *Rienzi* VII. viii, A minstrel, or jongleur.. with a small lute slung round him, was making his way.. through the throng. **1855** MILMAN *Lat. Chr.* XIV. iv. (1864) IX. 189 The Jongleurs (the reciters of the merry and licentious fabliaux).
b. = JUGGLER 2.
a **1851** MOIR *Poems, The dark Waggon* xv, On stage his sleights the jongleur shows.

joning ('dʒəʊnɪŋ), *vbl. sb.* [Origin unknown.] A name given by American Blacks to a game characterized by the exchange of insults; 'playing the dozens'.
1970 H. E. ROBERTS *Third Ear* 12/2 *Signifying*,.. language behavior that makes direct or indirect implications of baiting or boasting, the essence of which is making fun of another's appearance, relatives or situation. Variations include joning, playing the dozens. **1971** C. M. KERNAN in A. Dundes *Mother Wit* (1973) 312 The verbal insult game known in other regions as.. 'Joning'. **1972** J. L. DILLARD *Black English* vi. 260 There are, of course, some characteristic topics, speech styles, and modes of discourse. One of the more interesting is called *jonin'* by the Washington community—*sounding* or *the dozens* elsewhere.

jonk, -et, jonkry, obs. ff. JUNK, -ET, JUNKERY.

jonnop ('dʒɒnəp). *Austral. slang.* [Contraction of *John Hop* (JOHN 1 c).] A policeman.
1938 X. HERBERT *Capricornia* xxiv. 353 But even the jonnops don't treat the Binghis anything like they used to. **1963** A. LUBBOCK *Austral. Roundabout* 45 He's not a bad sort for a jonnop. **1966** BAKER *Austral. Lang.* vii. 142 England was originally responsible for the word cop, which Australia elaborated into the now-obsolete copman and copperman and which, by a process of rhyme, gave us the popular Australianisms john hop, jonnop and hop.

jonour, obs. form of JOINER.

jonque: see JONQUIL 3.

jonquil ('dʒʌŋkwɪl, 'dʒɒnkwɪl). Also 6–7 iunquilia, 7–8 junquil(l, 8 jonquille, *Sc.* jonckeel. [ad. mod.L. *jonquilla* = F. *jonquille*, It. *gionchiglia*, or Sp. *junquillo*, dim. of *junco*, L. *juncus* rush; so called from the rush-like leaves. Walker pronounces *junkwill*; so all the poets down to Wordsworth; Smart 1836 has *jung'kwil.*]
1. A species of Narcissus (*N. Jonquilla*), having long linear leaves and spikes of fragrant white and yellow flowers; the rush-leaved Daffodil.
Hence extended to allied species, as **large j.**, *Narcissus odorus*; **small j.**, *N. pusillus*; **Queen Anne's j.**, *N. pusillus plenus*.
1629 PARKINSON *Parad.* ix. 90 The great *Junquilia* with the large flower or cup. **1633** JOHNSON *Gerarde's Herbal* I. lxxxiv. §17. 129 There is also another Rush Daffodil or *Iunquilia*. **1664** EVELYN *Kal. Hort.* (1729) 198 *March*.. Flowers in Prime or yet lasting. Junquills. **1696** —— *Corr.* 28 Oct. (1871) 725 Beds of Tulips, Carnations,.. Jonquills, Ranunculas. **1699** GARTH *Dispens.* VI. 70 And hence Junquils derive their fragrant Dew. **1713** C'TESS WINCHELSEA *Misc. Poems* 90 Now the Jonquille o'ercomes the feeble Brain. **1730** SWIFT *Panegyr. on Dean*, The crocus and the daffodil, The cowslip soft, and sweet jonquil. **1819** WORDSW. *Sonn. to Snowdrop*, This border thickly set With bright jonquils. **1821** SHELLEY *Epipsych.* 450 And from the moss violets and jonquils peep. **1882** *Garden* 18 Mar. 182/1 A sheaf of slender Jonquils.
2. A pale yellow colour like that of the jonquil. [F. *jonquille*.]
1791 HAMILTON *Berthollet's Dyeing* I. I. I. iv. 67 The silk assumed a fine jonquille yellow. **1816** J. SMITH *Panorama Sc. & Art* II. 543. **1851** *Illustr. Catal. Gt. Exhib.* 498 Jonquil, apricot, and cerulean blue.. corded poplin.
3. A canary-bird of jonquil colour. Abbreviated *jonque*.
1865 *Derby Mercury* 25 Jan., The goldfinch mules were exceedingly good, the first prize in jonques being given to a choice specimen. **1891** C. L. MORGAN *Anim. Life & Intell.* 225 It does not answer to pair two jonquils.

Jonsonian (dʒɒn'səʊnɪən), *a.* [f. the name of Ben *Jonson* (? 1573–1637), English dramatist + -IAN.] Of, pertaining to, or characteristic of

Jonson or his works. So **Jon'sonianly** *adv.*, in the manner of Jonson or his works.

1886 J. A. SYMONDS *Ben Jonson* 153 The most truly Jonsonian of all these places.. was the Old Devil Tavern at Temple Bar. **1909** G. G. GREENWOOD *In re Shakespeare* ii. 76, I here leave the Jonsonian riddle. **1928** C. J. SISSON *Eliz. Dramatists* iv. 43 The Jonsonian comedy of humour. **1931** *Times Lit. Suppl.* 21 May 405/1 But the 'laws of dramatic art' have already ceased to look Aristotelian or Jonsonian. **1947** *Partisan Rev.* Mar.–Apr. 176 They are monsters in the Jonsonian manner; a human trait has been carried in them to the point of inhumanity. **1948** F. R. LEAVIS *Great Tradition* v. 235 Bounderby.. remains Jonsonianly consistent in his last testament and death. **1959** *Times* 26 Nov. 6/5 Mr. Raymond Raikes's production took pleasure in the Jonsonian tumult. **1973** M. R. BOOTH *Eng. Plays of 19th Cent.* IV. 2 The father.. may be a traditional Jonsonian 'humours' character with a dominant eccentricity.

jont(e, obs. forms of JOINT *sb.* and *a.*

jonty, var. JAUNTY *sb.*

Jonval ('ʒɔ̃val). *Engin.* The name of Nicolas Joseph *Jonval*, nineteenth-century Frenchman, used *attrib.* and *absol.* to denote an obsolete kind of reaction turbine (see quots.), patented by him in 1841.

1851 *Jrnl. Franklin Inst.* LII. 419 The advantage of the Jonval Turbine over the over-shot wheel, using the same amount of water, is consequently seven per cent. **1894** W. J. LINEHAM *Textbk. Mech. Engin.* xi. 724 The Jonval turbine, like the Fourneyron, is a pressure turbine; but while the latter works best above tail water, the Jonval is always drowned or else connected to tail water by a 'suction' tube. **1909** H. LOUIS *Dressing of Minerals* xii. 491 For lower falls turbines are best employed; a twin Jonval parallel-flow turbine.. offers many advantages, amongst which may be reckoned the fact that the turbine itself may be situated 10 to 15 feet above the level of the tailwater. **1957** *Encycl. Brit.* XXII. 580/2 In.. the Fourneyron, the guide vanes were inside the runner, and the water flowed outward. This was followed by the Jonval turbine, in which the guide vanes are above the runner and the water flows axially into and through the wheel. Both types are now obsolete.

jooar, variant of JOWAR, Indian millet.

joobba, joobey, variants of JUBBAH.

jook, var. spelling of JOUK.

jook, var. JUKE *sb.*

‖**joom, júm** (dʒuːm). *E. Indies.* Also jum, and *erron.* jh-. [Arakanese. The name is native to the Hill country, east of Chittagong; but applied by Anglo-Indians to the same system in other parts.] A system of cultivation practised in the hill forests of India and Indo-China, under which a tract is cleared by fire, occupied and cultivated for a time, and then abandoned for another tract, which is similarly treated; a tract so treated. Also *attrib.* Hence **joom, júm**, *v.* to clear a joom.

1855 H. H. WILSON *Ind. Gloss.* 242 *Jum, Joom*, a Mug village, or one belonging to a forest race on the east of Chittagong; any hill or forest village on the east of Bengal. **1869** *Jrnl. Bot.* VII. 157 Joom cultivation is the term used to designate the rude cultivation practised by most of the hill tribes of India. **1876** SIR W. HUNTER *Statist. Acc. Bengal* VI. 46 The sign of manhood among the Chakmás is when a lad is sent out to cut his first *júm*. *Ibid.* 67 Restrictions being placed on *júming* (the hill mode of cultivation). *Ibid.*, The people have there better *júming* lands. **1885** G. C. WHITWORTH *Anglo-Ind. Dict.* 140 *Jumāh*, a cultivator on the *jum* system. **1886** YULE & BURNELL *Hobson-Jobson* 351/2 Jhoom, Jhūm. **1895** W. R. FISHER *Schlich's Man. Forestry* IV. 350 Jhuming, or the thorough burning of branchwood on the soil. *Ibid.* 543 In *jhums*, or cultivations on forest clearings, where the branches and undergrowth are burned. **1897** LD. ROBERTS *41 Yrs. India* xl, We came across a large number of these jooms. **1921** J. H. HUTTON *Angami Nagas* II. 72 Good jhum land, cleared once in twelve or fifteen years. *Ibid.*, The Lhotas, Semas, Aos, and trans-Dikhu and trans-Tizu tribes cultivate only by 'jhuming'. **1927** *Blackw. Mag.* June 816/2 Crops are grown by a simple method known as 'Jhoom'. *Ibid.*, A fresh patch of jungle is then cut down, and the 'Jhooming' process repeated. **1936** *Nature* 5 Sept. 408/1 A fisher folk, who.. practised a rude form of agriculture, comparable to jhuming, but not terracing or systematic irrigation. **1937** *Times Lit. Suppl.* 20 Feb. 123/2 The low-caste Indian addicted to *jhum* cultivation. **1946** ALI & LAMBERT *Assam* 16 One or two tribes have adopted terrace cultivation, but the others depend on the *taungya* or *jhuming* system, which is very wasteful.

jop, dial. form of JAUP.

joparde, -ardie, -arte, -erte, obs. forms of JEOPARD, JEOPARDY.

jope, jopee, joppe, -y, jopy: see JOWPY.

jopen, jopoun, var. of GIPON *Obs.*

†**joppe**, *sb. Obs. rare*⁻⁰. [Known only from *Promp. Parv.*, which equates it with a med.L. *joppus*, used also as one of the renderings of *javel*, and cited from earlier med.L. glossaries.] A fool. Hence †**'joppery**, folly.

c **1440** *Promp. Parv.* 265/1 Ioppe, or folte, *Joppus*, C[ampus] F[lorum] *joppa*. [Cf. Iavel, *Joppus, gerro*, Ugutio.] *Ibid.* 264/1 Iopperye, or foltery, *Jopperia*.

†**jopper**, *v. Obs. rare*⁻¹. [Onomatopœic, with frequentative ending.] *intr.* To jolter or jolt.

1607 MIDDLETON *Phœnix* II. iii, Take heed the coach jopper not too much.

joque, obs. form of JOKE.

joram: see JORUM.

jordan[1] ('dʒɔːdən). Forms: 4–6 iurdan(e, iordan, 5 iurdone, 6 yordan, iourden, 6–7 iorden, 7 jur-, jor-, jourdon, jordain, 7–9 jurden, 8 jourdan, 7– jordan. [Origin uncertain.

The suggestion has been made that *Jordan* is short for *Jordan-bottle*, and meant orig. a bottle of water brought from the Jordan by crusaders or pilgrims; that it was thence transferred to 'a pot or vessel used by physicians and alchemists', and thence to the chamber utensil. But the earlier steps of this conjecture app. rest upon nothing but the later form of the word (which may actually be a corruption of something else), and the external probabilities of such an origin. It is remarkable that, though the early accentuation and spellings indicate a French origin, no trace of the word has been found in Old French; nor does the med.L. *jurdānus* appear to be known outside England. The river Jordan is in L. *Jordānēs*, a word necessarily familiar to the author of the *Promp. Parv.* and other glossarists, who used not this, but *jurdanus* for the 'jurdan'.]

†**1.** A kind of pot or vessel formerly used by physicians and alchemists. *Obs.*

As figured in Sloane MS. 73, and elsewhere, it has somewhat the shape of the bulb of a retort, or of a Florence flask with the neck cut off midway between the widest part and the mouth, and the top expanded somewhat to a rim. Possibly it was often used to hold urine for purposes of diagnosis, which would naturally lead to sense 2. Skeat puts the Chaucer example in sense 2.

[**1384–5** *Acc. Rolls Durham* (Surtees) 265, j mortarium ereum cum pila ferrea, j stillatorium plumbeum cum olla erea sibi convenienti, j postenet, j jurdanus, j dorsorium antiquam.] *c* **1386** CHAUCER *Doctor-Pardoner Link* 19 (C. 305) Thyne vrynals and thy Iurdones [*v.rr.* Iurdanes, Iordans, Iordanes] Thyn ypocras and eek thy Galiones And euery boyste ful of thy letuarie. **14..** *Sloane MS.* 73 lf. 133 b (*olim* 138 b), Make a good lute.. and þerwiþ daub þi Iordan al aboute.. and putte al þi mater in þe Iordan and hange it ouer þe fier by þe necke þᵗ þe glas be almoost an hond brede fro þe coolis.

2. A chamber-pot. Now *vulgar* or *dial.*

1402–3 *Acc. Rolls Durham* (Surtees) 217, 1 lectus de plumis; 7 iordan; 7 cappe pro noctibus. **1404** *Ibid.* 398, 1 fethyr-bed, 5 pulvinaria, 5 cathedre, 5 nyght chares, 5 iordan. **1440** *Promp. Parv.* 267/1 Iurdone, pyssepotte, *iurdanus*. **1596** SHAKS. *1 Hen. IV*, II. i. 22. **1622** B. JONSON *Masque Augurs*, Her Hand-maid with a Iorden. **1711** PUCKLE *Club* (1817) 92 Glasses, bottles, candlesticks, chairs, stools, and jordans were converted into weapons. **1751** SMOLLETT *Per. Pickle* xlvii, Snatching up an earthen chamberpot... shaking his jordan at the imaginary guard. **1888** *Sheffield Gloss.*, Jordan, *madula*.

3. Applied derisively to a person. (With the first quot. cf. the L. uses of *matula* a vessel, pot; *spec.* a chamber-pot, urinal; *fig.* a term of abuse, Foolish, silly fellow, noodle.)

1377 LANGL. *P. Pl.* B. XIII. 82, I shal iangle to þis Iurdan with his iust wombe To telle me what penaunce is. **1500–20** DUNBAR *Poems* l. 38 Thairfoir Quhentyne was bot ane lurdane That callit him ane full plum Jurdane.

†**4.** *slang.* A blow with a staff. *Obs.* [Perh. unconnected with the above. Cf. Gen. xxxii. 10.]

a **1700** B. E. *Dict. Cant. Crew*, *Jordain*, a great Blow or Staff.

5. *attrib.*, as *jordan-pot* = sense 1 or 2.

1577–87 HOLINSHED *Chron.* (1807–8) II. 754 A lewd fellow that tooke vpon him to be skilfull in physicke.. was set on horssebacke, with his face towards the taile,.. and so was led about the citie, with two jorden pots about his necke.

Jordan[2] ('dʒɔːdən). The name of a river in Palestine, the crossing of which is used (after Num. 33:51) in pietistic language to symbolize death.

1684 BUNYAN *Pilgr.* II. 222 Mr. Stand-fast.. went down to the River.. he said.. my Foot is fixed upon that, upon which the Feet of the Priests.. stood while Israel went over this Jordan. **1707** I. WATTS *Hymns & Spiritual Songs* II. No. LXV. 139 Could we but climb where Moses stood, And view the Landskip o're, Not Jordan's Stream, nor Death's cold Flood Should fright us from the Shore. **1772** W. WILLIAMS *Hymn*, '*Guide me, O Thou Great Jehovah*', When I tread the Verge of Jordan. **1786** S. STENNETT (*title of hymn*), On Jordan's stormy banks I stand. *c* **1871** in J. W. Johnson *Bk. Amer. Negro Spirituals* (1925) 63, I look'd over Jordan, an' what did I see... A band of angels comin' after me. *a* **1890** in Barrère & Leland *Dict. Slang* (1890) II. 368/1 (s.v. *T'other*), And I saw a mighty charret a comin'.., To take us to de odder side of Jordan... Jordan am a hard road to trabble. **1944** D. VAN DE VOORT in B. A. Botkin *Treas. Amer. Folklore* v. 682 Everybody thought that when Wiley's pappy died he'd never cross Jordan because the Hairy Man would be there waiting for him.

Jordan[3] ('dʒɔːdən). *Math.* [Name of Marie Ennemond Camille *Jordan* (1838–1922), French mathematician.] ***Jordan curve***, any curve that is topologically equivalent to a circle, i.e. is closed and does not cross itself; so ***Jordan('s) (curve) theorem***, the theorem that any Jordan curve in a plane divides the plane into just two distinct regions having the curve as their common boundary.

1900 W. F. OSGOOD in *Trans. Amer. Math. Soc.* I. 310 By a Jordan curve is meant a curve of the general class of continuous curves without multiple points, considered by Jordan, *Cours d'Analyse*, vol. I, 2d edition, 1893, p. 90. **1919** *Ann. Math.* XXI. 180 (*heading*) A proof of Jordan's theorem about a simple closed curve. **1939** M. H. A. NEWMAN *Elem. Topology of Plane Sets of Points* vi. 132 Theorem 2·3. (Jordan's Theorem for a polygon.) A simple polygon determines two domains, of each of which it is the frontier. **1947** COURANT & ROBBINS *What is Math.?* (ed. 4) v. 246 The Jordan curve theorem is quite simple to prove for the reasonably well-behaved curves, such as polygons or curves with continuously turning tangents, which occur in most important problems. **1965** S. BARR *Exper. Topology* i. 13 A Jordan curve can be drawn on the side of the torus and still divide it into two, but not if it circles, or goes through the hole.

jordan almond. Also 5 iarden, iardyne. [In ME. *jardyne almaunde*, app. from F. or Sp. *jardin* garden; in later times associated with the Jordan.] A fine variety of almond, now coming chiefly from Malaga. Also simply *jordan*.

c **1440** *Promp. Parv.* 257/2 Iardyne almaunde, *amigdalum jardinum*. *c* **1460** J. RUSSELL *Bk. Nurture* 774 Creme of almond Iardyne & mameny. **1469** in *Househ. Ord.* (1790) 103 Item, Jardens and Valaunces 330 lb.—4*l.* 2*s.* 6*d.* **1615** MARKHAM *Eng. Housew.* II. ii. (1668) 101 Take the best Jordan Almonds. **1769** MRS. RAFFALD *Eng. Housekpr.* (1778) 13 Put in half a pound of Jordan almonds beat fine. **1888** *Pall Mall G.* 24 Jan. 5/2 With the Malaga raisins go the Jordan almonds, with which they are always eaten.

Jordanian (dʒɔː'deɪnɪən), *a.* and *sb.* [f. *Jordan* + -IAN.] **A.** *adj.* Of or pertaining to the Hashemite kingdom of the Jordan (see JORDAN[2]), formerly Transjordan. **B.** *sb.* A native or inhabitant of Jordan. Hence **'Jordanize** *v. trans.*, to render Jordanian in character; **ˌJordani'zation**.

1950 *Encycl. Brit. Bk. of Year* 371/1 On Aug. 26 the Jordanian minister in London announced that a firm of British irrigation engineers.. were now engaged in drafting practical schemes of irrigation for the Jordan valley. **1953** *Daily Tel.* 10 Mar. 6/5 The refugees, sometimes aided by Jordanian.. officials, 'infiltrate' into Israel. **1955** *Times* 12 May 11/7 As totally inaccessible to Jordanians as Siberia or Tibet. **1959** *Chambers's Encycl.* XIII. 745/1 There is.. a national guard, to which all Jordanians between 20 and 40 years of age are liable to be called for service. **1960** A. RAMATI *Rebel against Light* v. 110 Then the Jordanian guns opened fire again, but this time at another part of the city. **1962** *Oxf. Univ. Gaz.* 9 Mar. 776/2 The British School in Jordanian Jerusalem, where a further lecture was given. **1969** *Listener* 6 Mar. 305/1 The dignity, pride, reticence.. of the Jordanian and Palestinian Arab. **1970** *Times* 13 May 11/2 Israel hawks have often spoken of the 'Jordanization' of Lebanon. **1972** *Times* 27 June 9/1 They asserted that the main aim of the 'Israeli aggressors' was to 'Jordanize' Lebanon. **1972** *Guardian* 11 Oct. 4/2 Jordanians, like Israelis, wanted.. peace, the newscaster assured viewers.

jordanite[1] ('dʒɔːdənaɪt). *Min.* [Named 1864 after Dr. Jordan: see -ITE.] A sulph-antimonide of lead, occurring in twin crystals, of a grey colour and brilliant metallic lustre.

1868 DANA *Min.* (ed. 5) 88 Jordanite.. approaches closely sartorite in its planes and angles.

Jordanite[2]. [f. the proper name *Jordan* (see below) + -ITE[1].] A believer in the doctrines of Jordan, a 20th-century Jamaican preacher who found followers in Guyana.

1934 E. WAUGH *Ninety-two Days* ii. 43 The Jordanites are one of the many queer sects that flourish among negroes. They derive their name not.. from the river, but from a recently deceased Mr. Jordan from Jamaica. **1958** J. CAREW *Black Midas* iv. 60 Processions of torch bearing Jordanites passed by the house. **1965** 'LAUCHMONEN' *Old Thom's Harvest* ix. 113 Brother Polo.. was done up in flowing white cotton gown like the Jordanite sect wear.

Jordanon ('dʒɔːdənən). [f. the name of Alexis *Jordan* (1814–1897), French botanist.] = MICROSPECIES.

1916 J. P. LOTSY *Evolution by Means of Hybridization* i. 23 Forms from which we know nothing else than that they breed true to type, may consequently not be designated as species but must receive another name; as such I propose *Jordanons*. **1963** DAVIS & HEYWOOD *Princ. Angiosperm Taxon.* xi. 378 The formation of numbers of morphologically uniform populations, all easily separable from each other and eligible for consideration as distinct taxa.. is well known to the practising taxonomist who often refers to the populations as microspecies or Jordanons after the nineteenth-century French botanist who described so many breeding lines as distinct 'true' species.

jordeloo, var. of GARDYLOO.

jordisite ('dʒɔːdɪsaɪt, 'jɔːd-). *Min.* [ad. G. *jordisit* (F. Cornu 1909, in *Zeitschr. f. Chem. u. Ind. d. Kolloide* IV. 190/2), f. the name of E. F. A. *Jordis* (1868–1917), German chemist: see -ITE[1].] A black amorphous sulphide of molybdenum, MoS_2.

1910 *Mineral. Mag.* XV. 423 Jordisite... A black, powdery, colloidal form of molybdenum sulphide. **1951** *Amer. Mineralogist* XXXVI. 614 The present study.. indicates that Cornu was correct in his statement that ilsemannite is derived from a black colloidal molybdenum sulfide, and although Cornu did nothing to establish the name 'jordisite', the occurrence in Oregon should confirm the name as a valid one for the mineraloid. **1966** *Prof. Papers U.S. Geol. Survey* No. 550-B. 120/1 Much of the jordisite occurs in medium-grained to coarse-grained sandstone.

joree (dʒəˈriː). *U.S.* [Echoic, from the call of the bird.] = *ground robin* (GROUND *sb.* 18 b).

1884 J. C. HARRIS *Mingo* 179 We seem to agree, Brother Brannum, like the jay-bird and the joree—one in the tree and t'other on the ground. **1938** M. K. RAWLINGS *Yearling* iv. 35 Jorees flew from the denseness. **1955** *Sci. News Let.* 23 Apr. 271/2 Other names by which he [*sc.* the towhee or ground robin] is known include swamp robin, joree, bush-bird and turkey sparrow.

†**jorn**, *v. Obs.* Pa. pple. in Sc. with latinized ending **jornat**. [Aphetic f. *aiorn, ajorn* ADJOURN.] *trans.* = ADJOURN 1, 2.

c **1330** R. BRUNNE *Chron.* (1810) 322 þei com vnto þe kyng, for pes if it mot tide, Vpon þer askyng, he iorned þam to bide. **1460** CAPGRAVE *Chron.* (Rolls) 266 Than mad the Kyng to crye, that this Parlement schuld be jorned tyl aftir Cristmasse. **15..** *Chart. Aberd. MS.* 153 (Jam.) The said Androw Elphinstoun hes bene lauchfullie procest, jornat, and summond to this court. *Ibid.*, Beand lauchfullie procest and jornat be the said reverend ffathyr.

‖**jornada** (dʒɔːˈnɑːdə). [Sp. (xorˈnaða), = It. *giornata*, F. *journée*, JOURNEY, lit. day's space, work, or journey; in Sp. also 'an act in a Comedy' (Minsheu, 1599).]

†**1.** An act of a play; a book or canto of a poem. *Obs.*

1656 FLECKNOE (*title*) Diarium, or Journall; divided into 12 Jornadas in Burlesque Rhyme or Drolling Verse. **1667** DRYDEN *Ess. Dram. Poesie* Dram. Wks. 1725 I. 30 The Spaniards at this day allow but three Acts, which they call *Jornadas*, to a Play. **1833** LONGF. *Outre-Mer* Pr. Wks. 1886 I. 197 The second act, or *jornada*, discovers Eusebio as the leader of a band of robbers.

2. In Mexico, etc.: A march or journey performed in a day; *spec.* a journey across a tract where there is no water and consequently no place to halt; also, the waterless district thus traversed. Also **journada, -ado**.

1828 in *Missouri Hist. Rev.* (1914) VIII. 190 At 4 p.m. we entered *Jornada*. **1844** J. J. WEBB *Adv. Santa Fe Trade* 156 Stopping over for a few hours.. to prepare for the journey of fifty miles to the Arkansas, without water, [we] started into the *jornada*. *Ibid.* 119 Whether..to..travel a longer distance and through two *jornadas*. **1845** J. C. FRÉMONT *Rep. Exploring Expedition* 260 The caravans sometimes continue below to the end of the river, from which there is a very long *jornada* of perhaps sixty miles. **1850** B. TAYLOR *Eldorado* v. (1862) 49 The route led in a zigzag direction across the mountain chain from one watering-place to another, with frequent *jornadas* (journeys without water). **1851** MAYNE REID *Scalp Hunt.* xlii. 327 The events that occurred to us in the passage of that terrible *jornada*. **1859** MARCY *Prairie Trav.* xi. 52 In some localities 50 or 60 miles, and even greater distances, are frequently traversed without water; these long stretches are called by the Mexicans 'journadas', or day's journeys.

jornall, jorney, obs. ff. JOURNAL, JOURNEY.

†**jornay.** *Obs. rare.* [a. OF. *jornée, journée*: see JOURNEY.] ? = next.

1540 *Ld. Treas. Acc. Scotl.* in Pitcairn *Crim. Trials* I. 300 *Item, to T.A. to be iij Jornayis and iij Comparisonis to the Kingis grace.

†**jornet.** *Obs. rare.* Also 6 **-ette**. [app. corrupted from OF. *journade* 'habillement de dessus, sorte de casaque..servant aux hommes et aux femmes' (Godef.); ad. Prov. *jornada*, the corresp. OF. being *jornée*: see prec.] A kind of cassock or cloak formerly worn by both sexes; 'a loose travelling cloak' (Fairholt); in 15-16th century worn by men over armour.

1502 *Will of Walsh* in Fairholt *Costume* (1885) II. Gloss. 262 Gown doublett, jacket salett, and iornett with bullions. **1539** WRIOTHESLEY *Chron.* (Camden) I. 95 The constables in jornets of white satten. **1598** STOW *Surv.* 75 In bright harnesse, some ouergilte, and euery one a Iornet of Scarlet thereupon.

‖**joro** (ˈdʒoːro). [Jap. *jorō, jōro.* a prostitute.] In Japan: a prostitute.

1884 [see HININ]. **1891** A. M. BACON *Jap. Girls & Women* x. 289 Below the géisha in respectability stands the jōrō, or licensed prostitute. **1899** J. LONDON *Let.* 22 Feb. (1966) 17 My last posed foto was taken in sailor costume with a Joro girl in Yokohama. **1959** N. MAILER *Advts. for Myself* (1961) 109 The Americans..did not want geisha girls. They wanted a *joro*, a common whore.

joroffle, jorour, obs. ff. GILLYFLOWER, JUROR.

‖**jorram, iorram** (ˈjʊrəm). *Sc.* Also **jurram**. [Gaelic *iorram, iurram.*] A Gaelic boat-song: improperly extended to other songs or choruses.

1774 PENNANT *Tour Scotl. in 1772.* 291 Our boat's crew.. gave a specimen of marine musick, called in the Erse, *Jorrams*. **1805** in Jamieson *Scot. Songs* (1870) 366 The cronach stills the dowie heart The jurram stills the bairnie. **1814** *Saxon & Gael* I. xiii. 170 What would they think to hear..the girls sing a *jorram* at a waulking? **1818** SCOTT *Hrt. Midl.* xlvi, The jorram, or melancholy boat-song of the rowers, coming on the ear with softened and sweeter sound. **1891** *Scottish Rev.* Oct. 331 The *iorram* was intended to be sung by the rowers.

jorrour, obs. form of JUROR.

jorum (ˈdʒɔərəm). [Origin uncertain.

It has been conjectured to be the same as the name of *Joram* who 'brought with him vessels of silver, and vessels of gold, and vessels of brass', 2 Sam. viii. 10. Cf. JEROBOAM. (It can scarcely be connected with WFlem. *djooren, djoorn*, half a pint.)]

A large drinking-bowl or vessel; also, the contents of this; *esp.* a bowl of punch.

1730 FIELDING *Auth. Farce* III. air xiii, The usurer is a swallow, sir, That can swallow gold by the jorum. **1773** GOLDSM. *Stoops to Conq.* I. ii, Then come put the jorum about, And let us be merry and clever. **1785** GROSE *Dict. Vulg. T.*, *Jorum*, a jug, or large pitcher. **1791** BURNS '*O May, thy morn*' ii, Here's to them that, like oursel, Can push about the jorum. **1823** LOCKHART *Reg. Dalton* I. xi. (1842) 69 A huge jorum of mulled port. **1838** DICKENS *O. Twist* xxxvii, The host smiled..and shortly afterwards returned with a steaming jorum. **1868** MISS BRADDON *Run to Earth* III. ix. 148, I know how to brew a decent jorum of punch when I give my mind to it.

b. *fig.* A large quantity.

1872 *St. James's Mag.* Dec. 632 Treated to a jorum of gossip.

‖**jōruri** (ˈdʒoːruri). [Jap., f. the name of Lady *Jōruri*, whose story was one of the most popular subjects for recitation.] **1.** A type of dramatic recitation to musical accompaniment, associated with the Japanese puppet theatre. Also *attrib.* or as *adj.*

1890 B. H. CHAMBERLAIN *Things Japanese* 342 The plays given at these [kabuki] theatres originated..partly in marionette dances accompanied by explanatory songs, called *jōruri* or *gidaiyū*. **1911** *Encycl. Brit.* XV. 170/1 The Jōruri is a dramatic ballad, sung or recited to the accompaniment of the *samisen* and in unison with the movements of puppets. **1965** W. SWAAN *Jap. Lantern* xv. 175 *Joruri* singing or chanting or recitation derives from an ancient form of metrical story-telling analogous to that of the Greeks and the mediaeval bards.

2. In full, ***ningyo-jōruri*** [Jap. *ningyo* doll]. The Japanese puppet drama.

1950 *Chambers's Encycl.* VIII. 60/2 The *jōruri* (puppet play) arose from recitations..which were combined in the early 17th century with marionette performances. **1954** F. BOWERS *Jap. Theatre* i. 30 The word *Joruri* applies specifically to musical dramas which developed from this style of chanting, and which retain for their accompaniment a combination singer-narrator and one or more samisen players. **1959** E. ERNST *Three Jap. Plays* 36 It is not clear when the puppets were added to jōruri, but it is thought that puppet *jōruri* performances were given in 1596 in the city of Kyoto. **1966** C. J. DUNN *Early Jap. Puppet Drama* 4 The name *bunraku* has widely displaced *jōruri* as the name of the puppet drama.

jose, variant of JOISE, *Obs.*, to possess.

jose, josing: see JOWSE, etc.

joseite (ˈdʒəʊziːaɪt). *Min.* [Named 1853 from San Jose in Brazil: see -ITE.] Native celluride of bismuth, found in greyish black laminated masses.

1868 DANA *Min.* (ed. 5) 31 Joseïte. **1883** *Encycl. Brit.* XVI. 381 Joseite.

Joseph (ˈdʒəʊzɪf). [A proper name repr. Heb. *yōsēph*, name of one of the twelve sons of Jacob, and of later Israelites, esp. of the husband of Mary the mother of Jesus Christ (*St. Joseph*); hence in derived uses.]

1. In allusion to the patriarch Joseph, Gen. xli. 48-57.

1849 E. B. EASTWICK *Dry Leaves* 16 These evil Josephs raise the price of corn so high that the unfortunate poor are placed beyond hope.

2. A long cloak, worn chiefly by women in the eighteenth century when riding, and on other occasions; it was buttoned all the way down the front and had a small cape. [See quot. 1708.]

1659 *Caterpillers of this Nation anatomized*, *Joseph*, a cloak. **1688** SHADWELL *Sq. Alsatia* II. i. *ad fin.*, Hide me, give me my Joseph. **1708** *Brit. Apollo* No. 104. 2/1 Why is a great Coat call'd a Joseph? From the..upper Coat, which..Joseph left behind him. **1766** GOLDSM. *Vic. W.* xvi, Olivia would be drawn as an Amazon..dressed in a green joseph, richly laced with gold, and a whip in her hand. **1807** CRABBE *Par. Reg.* III. 323 In the dear fashions of her youth she dress'd; A pea-green Joseph was her favourite vest. *a* **1825** FORBY *Voc. E. Anglia*, *Joseph*, a very old fashioned riding coat for women, scarcely now to be seen. **1861** GEO. ELIOT *Silas M.* xi, Seated on a pillion, and attired in a drab joseph and a drab beaver-bonnet.

3. In names of flowers, as **Joseph and Mary**, Lungwort (*Pulmonaria officinalis*); **Joseph's coat** (in ref. to Gen. xxxvii. 3), a cultivated variety of *Amarantus tricolor*, with variegated leaves; **Joseph's flower** (in ref. to the bearded figure of St. Joseph in art), Goat's-beard.

1578 LYTE *Dodoens* II. xvii. 167 This hearbe is now called ..in English Goates barde, Iosephs floure,..and Go to bedde at Noone. **1597** GERARDE *Herbal* II. ccxli. 596 Goates bearde is called..in low Dutch Iosephes bloemen..in English Goats beard, Iosephs flower. **1866** *Treas. Bot.* I. 48/1 In the gardens of the Southern United States, these hues are so richly developed as to have procured for it [*Amaranthus tricolor*] the appellation of Joseph's Coat.

4. A violin made by Joseph Guarnieri del Gesù (1698-1744). Cf. GUARNERIUS.

1875 G. HART *Violin* VI. 95 How is this 'Joseph', unaccustomed to elbow his legitimate namesakes in the world of fiddles, to maintain the character he has assumed? **1879** GROVE *Dict. Mus.* I. 637/2 The value of a good 'Joseph' now varies from £150 to £400. **1968** *Encycl. Brit.* X. 986/2 It was not until Paganini played on the 'Joseph' that the taste of amateurs turned from the sweetness of the Amati and the Stradivari violins in favour of the more robust tone of the Giuseppe Guarneri.

Josephine (ˈdʒəʊzɪfɪn, -aɪn), *a.* [See -INE[1].] Of or belonging to Joseph II (1741-90), Emperor of Austria, and to the ecclesiastical measures introduced by him.

1882-3 SCHAFF *Encycl. Relig. Knowl.* 527 In Austria the Josephine traditions were still continued [in concordat of 1855]. **1886** W. S. LILLY *Chapt. Europ. Hist.* I. 270 Germany..crushed by Hohenzollern militarism or Josephine doctrinairism.

Hence ˈ**Josephinism**, the ecclesiastical policy of the Emperor Joseph II; also ˈ**Josephism**[1].

1882-3 SCHAFF *Encycl. Relig. Knowl.* II. 1847 The Emperor [Joseph II] went on with that whole series of ecclesiastical reforms which is generally comprised under the name of Josephinism. **1891** *Amer. Eccl. Rev.* Feb. 123 The quintessence of the theology of Jansenism, Josephinism, Febronianism, and in our own times Doellingerism. **1880** *Sat. Rev.* No. 1310. 702 Josephism.

josephinite (ˈdʒəʊzɪfɪnaɪt, dʒəʊzɪˈfiːnaɪt). *Min.* [f. *Josephine*, the name of the county in southwestern Oregon where it was first found: see -ITE[1].] The terrestrial (as opposed to meteoric) alloy of nickel and iron, having about 67 to 77 per cent of nickel.

1892 W. H. MELVILLE in *Amer. Jrnl. Sci.* CXLIII. 509 (*heading*) Josephinite; a new nickel-iron. *Ibid.* 514 The placer gravel, in which josephinite is found. **1905** *Ibid.* CLXIX. 415 It is seen from a glance at the analyses of the alloys from the five different localities, that there is a certain uniformity in composition, but that they are not a definite compound of iron and nickel is evident, nor would this be expected... It seems unfortunate that so rare a substance should have received three distinct names, awaruite, josephinite, and souesite, and it is urged that awaruite, which has priority, should alone be used. **1950** *Mineral. Mag.* XXIX. 390 The occurrences of native nickel-iron regarded as magmatic secretions from peridotites (awaruite, josephinite, souesite, &c.) are certainly formations of extremely low temperatures.

Josephite[1] (ˈdʒəʊzɪfaɪt). [f. the name *Joseph* (see below) + -ITE[1].] A member of either of two orders of St. Joseph, the Priests of the Mission of St. Joseph (founded *c* 1640), or a teaching institute founded in 1817 by Constant-Guillaume van Crombrugghe (1789-1865). Also *attrib.* or as *adj.*

1846 in N. French *Works* I. p. lvi, At the end of the street, there is a large building yet occupied as a school, and now held by the Josephites. **1897** ADDIS & ARNOLD *Cath. Dict.* (ed. 5) 531/2 *Josephites.* Two communities bear, or have borne, this name. The first was founded by Jacques Cretenet at Lyons... At the Revolution it was suppressed. The second.., founded in 1817 at Grammont in Belgium. **1898** C. H. BOWDEN *Simple Dict. for Catholics* 18 *Josephites*, a teaching institute..for the education of the commercial and industrial classes. **1973** *Daily Colonist* (Victoria, B.C.) 28 June 43/1 The 50-year-old former Josephite priest was parolled last December.

Josephite[2] (ˈdʒəʊzɪfaɪt). Also **Josephine**. [f. the name of St. *Joseph* (1439-1515), Abbot of Volokolamsk, a Russian zealot.] A member of an ascetic and caesaro-papist party formed among Russian Orthodox monks in the sixteenth century. Hence **Josephism**[2], **Josephitism**, the doctrines of this party.

1944 B. H. SUMNER *Survey Russ. Hist.* iv. 187 The Josephines won the day in the church council of 1503. **1946** G. P. FEDOTOV *Russ. Relig. Mind* p. xii, The study of the conflict between the Josephites and the Trans-Volgans led at least one of our scholars to deeper inquiry. **1947** R. M. FRENCH tr. *Berdyaev's Russ. Idea* i. 7 Fedotov explains this as due to the fatal influence of 'Josephism' which has distorted the portrait of Christ among the Russian people, so that the Russian people wants to take shelter from the frightful God of Joseph Volotsky behind Mother Earth. **1950** G. P. FEDOTOV *Treas. Russ. Spirituality* p. xiii, Josephitism degenerated into static ritualism. **1953** K. S. LATOURETTE *Hist. Christianity* xxvii. 618 Probably it was inevitable that the Josephites and the Non-Possessors should clash. *Ibid.* xl. 905 The Josephites..believed in the possession of property by the monasteries and the Church. They were ascetic, approved works of charity, and stressed ritual... The Josephites believed in the maintenance of a close tie between Church and State. **1963** T. WARE *Orthodox Church* vi. 117 Russia needed both the Josephite and the Transvolgian forms of monasticism.

Josephson (ˈdʒəʊzɪfsən). *Physics.* The name of Brian David *Josephson* (b. 1940), British physicist, used *attrib.* to denote an effect predicted by him in 1962, whereby an electric current (***Josephson current***) can flow from one superconducting metal to another with no potential difference between them if they are separated by a sufficiently thin layer of an insulator (owing to tunnelling by coherent pairs of electrons), the application of a potential difference causing the current to oscillate with a frequency equal to the voltage multiplied by $2e/h$ (e = the electronic charge, h = Planck's constant). So **Josephson junction**, a metal-insulator-metal junction exhibiting this effect.

1963 ANDERSON & ROWELL in *Physical Rev. Lett.* X. 231/1 There are..four experimental points suggesting that this is indeed the Josephson effect. **1966** *Physical Rev.* CXLI. 366/2 The Josephson junction behaves as a parametric

inductance element in which the voltage is proportional to the frequency. **1966** *McGraw-Hill Encycl. Sci. & Technol.* XIII. 301/2 If a very small voltage difference is maintained between the two sides of the barrier.. the Josephson current should oscillate. Its frequency should be 4·836 × 10^{14} cycles per second per volt of potential difference. **1969** J. E. MERCERAU in R. D. Parks *Superconductivity* I. viii. 399 Such structures of two superconductors nearly in contact (weakly connected) are now called Josephson junctions... The device provides a unique opportunity to study the coupling of electromagnetic and quantum waves. **1972** *Physics Bull.* Aug. 457/1 The Josephson effects have led to new types of galvanometer, magnetometer and computer memory elements, to new methods of harmonic mixing of two frequencies and of harmonic generation, and to simple oscillators.

josh (dʒɒʃ), *v. slang.* (orig. *U.S.*) Also joss. [Cf. *Josh Billings*, pseudonym of an American humorist.] **1.** *trans.* To make fun of, chaff, banter, ridicule.

1852 *Lantern* (N.Y.) I. 199/2 The squint eyed chap's been jossin' ye. **1891** *Century Mag.* Nov. 63 'Oh go away.. I fear that you are joshing me'. **1895** *Weekly Examiner* 19 Sept. 4/2 The boys joshed Mr. Durrant some about it. **1921** WODEHOUSE *Indiscretions of Archie* vi. 54 Are you trying to josh me? **1927** J. DEVANNY *Old Savage* 30 They jossed him in the usual way about his proverbial amours. **1940** L. A. G. STRONG *Sun on Water* 58 Though every now and then she'd remember and clap a hand to her mouth, we'd soon josh her out of it. **1950** C. M. KORNBLUTH in D. Knight *100 Yrs. Sci. Fiction* (1969) 249 A humorous sergeant, the Mindworm was pleased to note, joshed the loafer out of his temper. **1972** P. H. KOCHER *Master of Middle-Earth* (1973) v. 107 When Pippin and Merry are reunited with their comrades.. Gimli joshes them over and over as 'truants' who had to be rescued.

2. *intr.* To indulge in banter or ridicule.

1845 *St. Louis Reveille* 19 Apr. 2/4 Look out in future, and if you must *Josh*, why, give a *private* one. **1887** F. FRANCIS *Saddle & Mocassin* 185 He.. liked nothing better than to.. chin and josh [*note*, chat and joke] with them in his funereal fashion. **1905** *Amer. Illustr. Mag.* Dec. 214, I was jus' joshin', mother, 'cause I 'spect all your plans are made. **1958** J. G. MACGREGOR *North-West of 16* xiv. 195 Each, according to his outlook on life, grumbled or whined, laughed or 'joshed'. **1963** *Guardian* 25 Jan. 9/4 The bearded Alberts tootle and joss with a goon-like ebullience. **1966** J. DOS PASSOS *Best Times* (1968) i. 13 I'd huddle in acute misery while he joshed with the waiters.

Hence **'josher**, **'joshing** *vbl. sb.* and *ppl. a.*, **'joshingly** *adv.*

1864 in *Ohio Arch. & Hist. Q.* LII. 175 The Bay was rough; thirty minutes out and the boys began to get sick. There was a good deal of joshing. **1899** F. NORRIS *McTeague* iv. 57 What a josher was this Marcus! Sure, you never could tell what he would do next. **1909** R. A. WASON *Happy Hawkins* xxii. 263 Dick was smilin' now.. an' makin' funny, joshin' remarks. **1921** *Daily Colonist* (Victoria, B.C.) 25 Mar. 4/3 Indifference is blazingly conspicuous by the small audiences that attend pre-election meetings; also the joshing manner in which the electors speak to and about the candidates. **1924** WODEHOUSE *Bill the Conqueror* xvii. 273 Miss Stryker formally stamped him with the seal of her approval as 'a good kid'. And.. it is but a step from being a good kid to being.. a great old josher. **1948** V. PALMER *Golconda* xi. 85 It was only Donovan's energy and easy joshing that carried the day with them. **1957** —— *Seedtime* 122 Donovan had said joshingly to the.. conductor.. 'Well, how's this strike of yours going?' **1959** J. THURBER *Years with Ross* ii. 21 The intramural joshing turns up everywhere in the crumbling documents. **1966** H. MARRIOTT *Cariboo Cowboy* viii. 75 This P.G.E., or 'Please Go Easy' as some smart joshers called it, started its way at Squamish on Howe Sound. **1970** B. SPOCK *Decent & Indecent* 18 There has been a trend in social gatherings to substitute loud joshing and playful insults for conversation. **1972** P. DICKINSON *Lizard in Cup* xi. 172 Buck maintained his peculiar brand of joshing bonhomie.

josh (dʒɒʃ), *sb. U.S. slang.* [f. the vb.] A piece of banter or badinage; a good-natured or bantering joke. Also as *adj.*, ridiculous.

1878 F. H. HART *Sazerac Lying Club* 57 Be there anything in this.. or aint it only one of them 'joshes' they get up in the *Reveille* sometimes? **1896** ADE *Artie* iii. 30 That ain't no josh, neither. **1908** G. H. LORIMER *Jack Spurlock* iii. 40 First, I sat there chuckling, but by and by I began to forget the josh end of it I had joined [the union] for, and to remember my own grievances against the house. **1948** *Sat. Rev.* (U.S.) 12 June 19/1 We found him tired-eyed and peaked,.. not a man for josh and chatter. **1959** J. THURBER *Years with Ross* ii. 20, I shall spare you the *New Yorker's* prospectus, drawn up in.. 1924, except for.. 'There will be a personal mention column... This will contain some josh.'

Joshua[1] ('dʒɒʃuːə). [f. the Christian name of Sir *Joshua* Reynolds (1723–92), English painter.] In full, *Sir Joshua.* **a.** A portrait painted by Reynolds. **b.** A woman resembling those depicted in the portraits of Reynolds.

[**1866** A. J. MUNBY *Diary* 6 July in D. Hudson *Munby* (1972) 227 One [girl] with a rose in her bosom.. looked like a masterpiece of Sir Joshua.] **1875** G. H. LEWES *Diary* 8 July in Geo. Eliot *Lett.* (1956) VI. 155 Lady Clementina Mitford —quite a Gainsborough or Sir Joshua—charmed me with her beauty. **1972** 'M. INNES' *Open House* xi. 102 It's a poor class of thing to my eye—me 'aving been in places with Joshuas and the like on the walls.

Joshua[2] ('dʒɒʃuːə). *U.S.* [prob. f. the name of the Old Testament leader of the Israelites, in allusion to the branching shape of the tree, compared with that of Joshua brandishing a spear: see Josh. 8:18.] In full **Joshua palm, tree,** or **yucca**. A small evergreen tree, *Yucca brevifolia*, bearing clustered white flowers and found in western, desert regions.

1867 W. H. JACKSON *Diary* 15 Feb. (1959) I. 134 Sage brush is used for cooking and the cactus or Joshuas, as I hear them called, for other fires. **1897** G. B. SUDWORTH *Nomencl. Arborescent Flora U.S.* 106 *Yucca arborescens*... Joshua Yucca... Common names... The Joshua (Utah). Joshua Tree (Utah, Ariz., N. Mex.). **1946** E. S. GARDNER *D.A. Breaks Seal* 3 Joshua palms, thrusting up grotesque spine-covered arms, made the scenery resemble some fantastic reconstruction of life on another planet. **1948** A. HUXLEY *Ape & Essence* (1949) 12 A strangely gesticulating Joshua-tree, rough-barked, or furred with dry prickles. **1955** *Sci. Amer.* Apr. 69 (*caption*) Joshua trees (Yucca brevifolia) grow among the fantastic rock formations of the Joshua Tree National Monument in southern California east of Los Angeles. These plants are characteristic of high steppe-desert vegetation in the southwestern U.S. **1964** GLEASON & CRONQUIST *Nat. Geogr. Plants* xxii. 408 Some of the most interesting plants of the Sonoran Floristic Province are giant Joshua (*Yucca brevifolia*) [etc.].

joskin ('dʒɒskɪn). *slang.* [Cf. *bumpkin*, and *joss* dial. to bump.] A country bumpkin.

1811 *Lex. Bal.* s.v., The drop-cove maced the joskin of twenty quid, the ringdropper cheated the countryman of twenty guineas. **1819** LAMB *Let. to Manning*, I hate the Joskins. **1885** *Fortn. in Waggonette* 38 In nine cases out of ten a country joskin was much more useful and informing than even the great Bacon's maps. **1887** FARRELL *How He Died* 87 The best thing she could do Was to go back.. and marry The joskin that followed the plough.

joss[1] (dʒɒs). Also 8 josse, 9 jos. [app. derived from Pg. *deos* god: cf. in same sense Du. *joosje*, dim. of **joos*.

In Javanese, the name given to a Chinese idol or image is *dejos*, i.e. dēyos (Prof. Kern in *De Indische Gids* XI. (1889) 1218), taken in 16th c. from Pg. *deos*. Quot. 1771 (though erroneous in details) indicates how *dejos* might be reduced to *jos*. Hence the Du. and Eng. forms of the word. The latter has been carried from Bantam or Batavia to the Chinese seaports, where it has become the 'pidgin'-English term; it is not Chinese, nor of Chinese origination.]

a. A Chinese figure of a deity, an idol. Loosely used of those of neighbouring peoples. Also, (*colloq.*) luck: ***bad, good joss.***

1711 LOCKYER *Acc. Trade India* 181 (Y.), I know but little of their Religion, more than that every Man has a small Joss or God in his own House. **1727** A. HAMILTON *New Acc. E. Ind.* II. liii. 266 Their Josses or Demi-gods are, some of human Shape, some of monstrous Figures. **1771** J. R. FORSTER tr. *Olof Toreen's Voy. China* (1750–52) in *Osbeck's Voy.*, etc. II. 232 The sailors, and even some books of voyages.. call the pagodas, Yoss-houses: for, on enquiring of 2 Chinese for the name of the idol, he answers, *Grande Yoss*, instead of *Gran Dios.* **1840** MALCOM *Trav.* 29/1 The 'Jos' was delineated in a large picture surrounded by ornamental paper-hangings. **1899** F. T. BULLEN *Log of a Sea-waif* 45 He might as well have appealed to a bronze joss. **1913** *Chambers's Jrnl.* Aug. 590/2 This comprises a good 'joss' for the voyage, and may be likened to a system of 'blessing'. **1915** KIPLING *Fringes of Fleet* 48 Mines are all Joss. You either hit 'em or you don't. **1948** PARTRIDGE *Dict. Forces' Slang* 104 Bad joss your leave being stopped.

b. *Comb.*, as *joss-candle*, *-god*; *joss-like* adj.; **joss-house**, a Chinese temple or building for idol-worship; **joss-man**, a priest of a Chinese religion; *slang*, of any other religion (see also quot. 1948); **joss-paper**, gold and silver paper, cut into the shape of coins and ingots and sometimes inscribed with prayers, burned by the Chinese at funerals and other religious ceremonies; **joss-pidgin**, a religious ceremony; **joss-pidgin-man**, a minister of religion; **joss-stick**, a thin cylinder or stick of fragrant tinder mixed with clay, used by the Chinese as incense, etc.

1898 *Tit-Bits* 21 May 154/2 The avidity with which they polished off *joss candles was a sight for the gods. **1826** HONE *Every-day Bk.* 28 Nov. I. 1526 A lion-like *jos-god figure, called Sing. **1771** *Yoss-house [see above]. **1831** *Edin. Rev.* LIII. 224 On the panels of the jos house, or temple, are painted figures seated upon broadswords. **1869** *Spectator* 6 Nov. 1290 To tax Chinamen to support churches was just as unfair as to tax Christians for the support of joss-houses. **1913** *Chambers's Jrnl.* Aug. 590/2 A missionary is known as a European '*joss-man'. **1948** PARTRIDGE *Dict. Forces' Slang* 104 *Jossman*, a term used on China-side for Plymouth gin... (From the picture of the monk on the bottle.) All holy men are 'jossmen' to the Chinese. **1964** *Navy News* Nov. 12/4, I was watch aboard and tried to get a sub, but no joy. I asked the Jossman if I could go ashore, and he told me to go to... **1970** *Islander* (Victoria, B.C.) 17 May 5/2 The jossman picked up hammer and nails and, with great care, fixed the eyes, exactly 15 feet from the bow [of a junk]. **1884** MISS GORDON CUMMING in *Pall Mall G.* 11 Sept. 1/2 Quantities of *joss paper inscribed with prayers for good luck were burned on each altar. **1886** YULE & BURNELL *Hobson-Jobson* 354/1 Joss-house-man or *Joss-pidgin-man is a priest, or a missionary. *a* **1889** *Mary Coe* in Barrère & Leland *Dict. Slang* (1889) I. 508/1 Allo tim he make joss-pidgin, Wat you fan-kwei cally 'ligion. *a* **1889** *The Rebel Pig* in *Ibid.* I. 508/1 When dey talkey pig look all-samee like he joss-pidgin-man. **1926** M. LEINSTER *Dew on Leaf* iv. 45 He do joss-pidgin. **1845** J. R. PETERS *Misc. Remarks upon Chinese* 111 Every one has a shrine and Jos, or representation of one, before which a *jos stick is kept continually burning. **1876** C. G. LELAND *Pidgin-Eng. Sing-Song* 43 Burnee joss-stick, talkee plitty. **1879** I. L. BIRD *Let.* 4 Jan. in *Golden Chersonese* (1883) 49 There is a recess outside each shop, and at dusk the joss-sticks.. fill the city with the fragrance of incense. **1883** MRS. BISHOP *Sk. Malay Penins.* iii. in *Leisure Ho.* 83/2 Joss-sticks burn incessantly. **1974** *Times* 15 Aug. (India Suppl.) p. iv/9 The sandalwood-based joss sticks.. were produced to the tune of 5,000 tonnes last year.

Hence **'jossish** *a.*, resembling a joss, joss-like.

1834 BECKFORD *Italy* II. 159 A little jossish old woman, with a head as round as a humming-top.

joss[2] (dʒɒs). *dial.*, *Austral.*, and *N.Z.* [Eng. dial., of unknown origin.] = BOSS *sb.*[6]

c **1860** in H. Maxwell *Evening Memories* (1932) xviii. 323 Come where the boss is a deuce of a joss, Come to the pub next door! *a* **1876** E. LEIGH *Gloss. Words Dial. Cheshire* (1877) 111 *Joss*, a foreman. Used in Macclesfield. **1877** F. ROSS et al. *Gloss. Words Holderness* 81/2 *Joss*, a head man; a superior. *a* **1922** H. LAWSON in *Penguin Bk. Austral. Ballads* (1964) 149 Must I turn aside from my destined way For a task your Joss would find me? **1948** V. PALMER *Golconda* iv. 28 'Then why don't you go to the Golconda Mining Company?' asked Donovan slyly. 'Tilburg Kloss is there, a big joss from down south.' **1955–6** —— in *Coast to Coast* 36 A big joss among the young bucks and gins.

joss, var. JOSH *v.*

†**jossa.** *Obs.* [Conjectured by Prof. Skeat to be an adv. = 'Down here', repr. an OF. **jos-ça*, for the actual OF. *ça jus.* But it may be a sb. (in vocative) or vb. (in imper.).]

c **1386** CHAUCER *Reeve's T.* 181 Keepe, keepe, stand, stand, Iossa warderere, Ga whistle thou and I shal kepe hym heere.

joss-block, jossing-block. *local.* [f. *joss* vb. dial., to mount (a horse).] (See quots.)

1706 PHILLIPS, *Jossing-block*, a Block to get up on Horse-back. **1847–78** HALLIWELL, *Joss-block, jossing-block*, a horse-block. **1887** *Antiquary* Oct. 146 There was an old wooden step—*jossing-block* is the local [Kentish] name.

josser ('dʒɒsə(r)). *slang.* [f. JOSS + -ER[1].]

1. A clergyman or minister of religion, 'padre'. *Austral.*

1887 J. FARRELL *How he Died* 22 The reverend josser.. hammering the pulpit. **1889** BARRÈRE & LELAND *Dict. Slang* I. 507/1 *Josser*,... a priest... Australian slang designated those who ministered in them [*sc.* joss-houses] *jossers*, and then extended this term it had created to mean ministers of any religion. **1941** BAKER *Dict. Austral. Slang* 40 *Josser*, a parson. **1973** G. ROSE *Clear Road to Archangel* iii. 35 The old josser, all black robe and beard and upside-down hat and silver cross, addressed himself to me. In German.

2. a. A simpleton; a soft or silly fellow. So, in flippant or contemptuous use, a fellow, an (old) chap (see also quots. 1933 and 1946).

1886 *Broadside Ballad, 'I took it On'* in Farmer & Henley *Slang* (1896) IV. 77/1, I took it on, Of course I was a josser. **1890** *Punch* 22 Feb. 85/2 These 'Equality' jossers would spile it; if arf their reforms they can carry. **1894** WILKINS & VIVIAN *Green Bay Tree* I. vii. 176 The josser next me, who had won his money. **1901** *Westm. Gaz.* 30 Mar. 8/2 The old josser asked me where the fire was, and I said: 'Jolly well go and find out yourself, you old bounder!' **1902** STRONG & OSBOURNE *Memories of Vailima* (1903) 61 Though he had known and liked Mr. Stevenson all this time, it was only the other day.. that it came over him all of a heap—'*he's* the josser that wrote *Treasure Island*'. **1904** 'G. B. LANCASTER' *Sons o' Men* 184 There's a big josser at Gatefield—Hunt, I s'pose. He gits what he wants. **1911** G. B. SHAW *Getting Married* 244 *Reginald*: Boxer is rather a fine old josser in his way. **1933** E. SEAGO *Circus Company* iii. 29 One of their number would speak of a subject not meant for a 'gajo's' ears, to be checked immediately.. 'Nante palari before the josher [*sic*] cul.' *Ibid.* 294 *Josser*, outsider. **1936** F. CLUNE *Roaming round Darling* vi. 53 Meanwhile, a hard-boiled josser, with beard and gun complete, has seated himself on a post to see we didn't get away with his wire fence (for a towline). **1938** 'R. HYDE' *Nor Years Condemn* xv. 270 Some josser with a necktie tells 'em he's got a job waiting. **1946** G. TYRWHITT-DRAKE *Eng. Circus & Fair Ground* vi. 67 A 'josser' is an amateur, or in fact any one of the public who does not belong to the profession.

b. *attrib.*

1891 *Daily News* 29 June 2/4 Any 'josser' policeman would be enabled.. to pry into their show. **1893** *Standard* 29 Jan. 2 (Farmer & Henley), Now suppose we are on the road ..and we meet a josser policeman?

jostle, justle ('dʒɒs(ə)l, 'dʒʌs(ə)l), *v.* Forms: 5 iustil, 6 iussell, iustell, ioustle, 6–7 iustle, 7 jussel(l, jusle, josle, jostel, 7– justle, jostle. [f. JOUST *v.* + freq. suffix -LE. *Justle* was usual in the 17th c.; and the main form in the 18th (Johnson has *justle* as the main form and *jostle* as a variant); it has now largely yielded to *jostle*.]

I. *intr.* †**1.** To come into collision in the tournament; to just or tilt. *Obs.*

1580 HOLLYBAND *Treas. Fr. Tong, S'Entr'essayer à la jouste*, to tryе one an other at iustling. **1600** R. CAWDRAY *Treas. Similies* 398 No man iustleth with two Speares together. **1706** PHILLIPS, *To Just*, or *Justle*, to run a Tilt. **1759** tr. *Adanson's Voy. Senegal* 289 The horsemen themselves greatly added to those sports.. feigning by their gesture and attitude, sometimes a combat, and other times a justling, a chace, or dance.

†**b.** *transf.* To encounter sexually. *Obs. rare*$^{-1}$.

c **1400** *Destr. Troy* 12738 Engest, with his Iapis, hade Iustilet hir with, And getyn in his gamyn on the gay lady, A doghter þat was dere.

2. To knock or push *against*, to come into collision *with*; also *absol.* to push and shove; to push one against another as in a crowd.

1546 J. HEYWOOD *Prov.* II. v, Each of his ioyntes agaynst other iustles. **1591** *Durham Depos.* (Surtees) 332 One that, having a burthen of wood on his back.. did then jussell upon a strainger.. which then was rydeing out of the towne. **1611**

Bible *Nahum* ii. 4 The charets shall rage in the streets, they shall iustle one against another in the broad wayes. **1699** Pomfret *Eleazar's Lament.* 49 The num'rous throng Was forc'd to jostle as they pass'd along. **1795** Burke *Let. to W. Elliot* Wks. VII. 367 Nor am I of force to win my way, and to justle and elbow in a crowd. **1817** Scott *Rob Roy* v, All tramped, kicked, plunged, shouldered, and jostled. **1893** *Times* 18 May 5/6 Her Majesty's Justices jostled with mayors and aldermen.

fig. **1639** Fuller *Holy War* ii. ii, The clergy of that age, who counted themselves to want room except they justled with princes. **1876** Green *Stray Stud.* 190 The old world of feudalism jostling with the new world of commerce. *a* **1894** Froude *Counc. Trent* iii. (1896) 54 As in most human things, the commonplace jostled against the sublime.

b. To contend for a place, the best path, or the wall, by pushing another away from it; hence, to vie or struggle *with* some one *for* some advantage.

1614 T. Adams *Serm. Ps. lxvi.* 12 Wks. 608 It were more braue for them to iustle with champions that will not giue them the way. **1681–6** J. Scott *Chr. Life* (1747) III. 369 With whose legislative Power it never justled for the Wall. **1726** De Foe *Hist. Devil* i. x. (1840) 133 Nations and tribes began to jostle with one another for room. **1822** Lamb *Elia* Ser. i. *Decay Beggars*, None jostle with him for the wall, or pick quarrels for precedency.

3. To make one's way by pushing or shoving; to push one's way. Also ***to jostle one's way***.

1612–15 Bp. Hall *Contempl., O.T.* xvii. i, Adonijah..will underworke Salomon and justle into the not yet vacant seat of his father David. **1687** Dryden *Hind & P.* iii. 1186 Eager of a name, He thrusts about, and justles into fame. **1790** A. Wilson *Poems, to Andrew Clarke*, While bustling business justles through the mind. *c* **1819** Scott in *Croker Papers* (1884) I. v. 139 It requires a strong man to jostle through a crowd. **1832** Ht. Martineau *Homes Abroad* ix. 122 Condemned to jostle their way in the world.

II. *trans.* **4.** To shake or drive by pushing; to come into rough collision with, to knock or push against; to elbow, hustle.

1575 R. B. *Appius & V.* in Dodsley *O. Pl.* (1825) XII. 361 What if case that cruelty should bussell me and jussell mee. **1591** Sylvester *Du Bartas* i. ii. 533 Som boistrous winde, with stormy puff Joustling the clouds. **1610** Shaks. *Temp.* iii. ii. 29, I am in case to iustle a Constable. **1712** Steele *Spect.* No. 454 ⁋4 The Coachmen took care to meet, jostle, and threaten each other for Way. **1717** Prior *Alma* iii. 177 Each still renews her little labour, Nor justles her assiduous neighbour. *a* **1861** Clough *Early Poems* xi. 6 Who standeth still i' the street Shall be hustled and justled about. **1870** Mrs. Riddell *Austin Friars* xii, When a woman mixes among a crowd, she must expect to be jostled and pushed by the sterner sex.

fig. **1580** Lyly *Euphues* (Arb.) 430 Enuie not thy betters, justle not thy fellowes. *a* **1764** Lloyd *Temple Favour* Poet. Wks. 1774 II. 143 Far from the colleges of taste, I jostle no poetic name. **1880** A. H. Huth *Buckle* I. iv. 224 Rampant theories jostled each other in the race for power.

5. To push, drive, or force, roughly or unceremoniously, *from*, *out of*, or *into* some place, condition, etc. *lit.* and *fig.*

1602 Marston *Ant. & Mel.* ii. Wks. 1856 I. 25 It would ..Justle that skipping feeble amorist Out of your loves seat. **1610** Shaks. *Temp.* v. i. 158 Howsoeu'r you haue Beene iustled from all sences. **1645** Fuller *Good Th. in Bad T.* (1841) 5 Must the new foe quite justle out the old friend? **1692** Bentley *Boyle Lect.* ii. 25 That dead senseless Atoms can ever justle and knock one another into Life and Understanding. **1713** Addison *Guardian* No. 106 ⁋4 We justled one another out by turns, and disputed the post for a great while. **1871** Tyndall *Fragm. Sc.* (1879) I. i. 9 One atom can jostle another out of its place.

6. *Racing.* To push against (a competitor) so as to retard him. Often in ***to cross*** (cross the path of, get in front of) ***and jostle***. Also *absol.*

1723 *Lond. Gaz.* No. 6167/8 Jostling allowed on by the two foremost Horses for these Plates and no other Horse. **1747** *Gentl. Mag.* 536 He marks, what dog sagacious vies, And just'ling strains to win the prize. **1754** *Articles rel. to H.M.'s Plates* in Pond *Sport. Calendar*, As many of the Riders as shall cross jostle or strike..shall be made incapable of riding any Horse in His Majesty's Plates hereafter. **1776** Mrs. Harris in *Priv. Lett. Ld. Malmesbury* I. 348 They all rode exceedingly well... Jostling was allowed, and Mr. Hanger declared he would jostle and whip whoever came near. **1858** *Rules Racing* §42 in Blaine *Encycl. Rur. Sports* (1870) 374 If in running for any race one horse shall jostle or cross another, such horse is disqualified for winning the race, whether such jostle or cross happened by the swerve of the horse, or by the foul and careless riding of the jockey, or otherwise.

fig. **1807–8** W. Irving *Salmag.* (1824) 139 We must be crossed and jostled by these meddling incendiaries. **1850** Merivale *Rom. Emp.* (1865) I. ii. 71 A thousand intrigues crossed and jostled one another in the forum.

7. To cause (one thing) to push against another; to bring (things) into collision. *lit.* and *fig.*

1641 Milton *Reform.* i. (1851) 66 Where do the Churches ..clash and justle Supremacies with the Civil Magistrate? **1678** Moxon *Mech. Exerc.* No. 6 §35 (1683) I. 102 You must jostle them one upon the other, that the Glew may very well touch and take hold of the Wood. **1765** A. Dickson *Treat. Agric.* ii. (ed. 2) 246 They are justling the furrow-cattle upon the plowed land.

jostle, justle (ˈdʒɒs(ə)l, ˈdʒʌs(ə)l), *sb.* [f. jostle *v.*] An act or bout of jostling.

†**1.** A just or joust; a struggle, tussle. *Obs.*

1607 Middleton *Phœnix* v. i, There was a villanous raven seen..in hard justle With a young eaglet. **1609** Heywood *Brit. Troy* xiv. xxiii. 363 His armour..besprinkt with gore ..he is wel-nye lame With often iustles.

2. A shock or encounter, a collision; a push or thrust that shakes; the action of a pushing or elbowing crowd. *lit.* and *fig.*

1611 Cotgr., *Gorrette*,..a iustle, iurre; thumpe, or thwacke. **1625** Fletcher *Nice Valour* iii. ii, For what a lamentable folly 'tis, If we observe 't, for every little justle.. we must fight forsooth. **1641** W. Mountagu in *Buccleuch MSS.* (Hist. MSS. Comm.) I. 288 He is fast riveted on that side, if the Commons give him not a jostle. **1710** *Tatler* No. 250 ⁋10 All such as have been aggrieved by any ambiguous Expression, accidental Justle, or unkind Repartee. **1869** Mrs. Whitney *Hitherto* ix. 117 This little sportive justle and antagonism. **1881** *Nation* (N.Y.) XXXII. 428 In the jostle of South African nationalities and civilizations.

jostle, mod. dial. f. jussel, a dish.

jostlement (ˈdʒɒs(ə)lmənt). [f. jostle *v.* + -ment.] Jostling.

1859 Dickens *T. Two Cities* ii. xii, To the jostlement of all weaker people. **1880** Miss Bird *Japan* I. 216 Free from the jostlement of a foreign settlement.

ˈjostler, ˈjustler. *rare.* [f. as prec. + -er^1.] One who jostles; in quot. one who tilts.

1599 Minsheu *Sp. Dict.* 11, A Iustler or tilter, *Iustador.*

jostling, justling (ˈdʒɒslɪŋ, ˈdʒʌslɪŋ), *vbl. sb.* [f. jostle *v.* + -ing^1.] The action of the verb jostle; †the shock of the tournament; clashing; collision; knocking or pushing about.

1580 [see jostle *v.* 1]. **1587** Golding *De Mornay* xiv. (1617) 223 What else is violence, but a justling of two bodies together? **1610** Holland *Camden's Brit.* i. 265 Martiall justlings or torneaments, were much practised. **1642** Fuller *Holy & Prof. St.* iii. xxiv. 220 There is much justling for precedency. **1705** Hearne *Collect.* 5 Oct. (O.H.S.) I. 52 Mr. Dalton..met with some High-Constable, who not giving way, there was some Justleing. **1768** Sterne *Sent. Journ.*, *Snuff-box*, In the jostlings of the world. **1843** Carlyle *Past & Pr.* ii. xvi, His life is but a labour and a journey; a bustling and a justling, till the still Night come.

ˈjostling, ˈjustling, *ppl. a.* [f. jostle *v.* + -ing^2.] That jostles: see the vb.

1562 Phaer *Æneid* viii. Ccij b, A man wold thinke y^t mountaines meete In seas, or iustling wods w^t wods. **1600** J. Lane *Tom Tel-troth* 124 When iusling Iacks to walls their betters drive. **1716** Swift *Pethox*, As Epicurus shows, The world from justling seeds arose. **1758** Home *Agis* i, Through justling multitudes. **1851** D. Jerrold *St. Giles* xxvi. 265 To moralise upon the hubbub and the jostling crowd.

jot (dʒɒt), *sb.*^{1} Forms: α. 6–7 iote, (6 ioate, *Sc.* ioyt, ioit), 7 jote; β. 6–7 iot, (6 iott(e, 7 jott), 7– jot. [ad. L. *iōta* (read as *jōta*, cf. Sp. *jota*, Ger. *jota* and *jot, jodt, jott*), a. Gr. ἰῶτα name of the letter I, ι, the smallest in the alphabet; see iota, and cf. jod. The 16th c. *iote* is shown by the metrical quots. to have been monosyllabic, i.e. = *jōte*.]

The least letter or written part of any writing; hence, generally, the very least or a very little part, point, or amount; a whit. Often in the phrase *jot or tittle*: see quot. 1526. (Usually with negative expressed or implied.)

1526 Tindale *Matt.* v. 18 One iott or one tytle [Wyclif oon. i. or titil] of the lawe shall not scape. **1538** Bale *God's Promises* iii. in Dodsley *O. Pl.* I, I wyll not one iote, Lorde, from thy wyll dyssent. **1540–54** Croke *Ps.*, etc (Percy Soc.) 48 There shall remayne of theym no iote. **1563** *Homilies* ii. *Good Works* 1, Not giltie of transgressing any iot of Gods law. **1570** B. Googe *Pop. Kingd.* ii. 19 b, And Ioseph ruled Egypt well, obseruing euery iotte Of Moyses lawe, and chastly kept his minde from any spotte. *a* **1572** Knox *Hist. Ref.* Wks. 1846 I. 107 Yf, in any joyt, he sufferred the authoritie of the Pape to be violated. **1579** Fenton *Guicciard.* xii. (1599) 578 Not breaking one ioate of their order. **1596** Shaks. *Merch. V.* iv. i. 306 This bond doth giue thee heere no iot of bloud. **1652** Row *Lett.* 27 May in *Hist. Kirk* App. iii. (Wodrow Soc.) 545 Befor I brake my word in a jote to you. **1657** Thornley tr. *Longus' Daphnis & Chloe* 200, I swear I will not lie a jott. **1768** H. Walpole *Hist. Doubts* 31 The Solomon that succeeded him was not a jot less a tyrant. **1868** G. Duff *Pol. Surv.* 80 He seems never to have..abated one jot of his claim.

†**jot,** *sb.*^{2} *Obs. rare*$^{-1}$. [f. jot *v.*^{1}] A jolt.

1647 H. More *Song of Soul* i. ii. xxxix, Frequent jot Of his hard setting jade.

†**jot,** *sb.*^{3} *Obs. rare.* [Origin and meaning obscure: cf. *jolthead* and joppe.] ? A person of small intelligence, or of low condition.

1362 Langl. *P. Pl.* A. xi. 301 Souteris and seweris suche lewide iottis [*v.r.* iuttis] Percen wiþ a pater noster þe paleis of heuene. [So B. x. 460 iottes, iuttes.]

jot, *v.*^{1} *Obs.* exc. *dial.* [app. onomatopœic: cf. jog, jopper. The final *t* naturally expresses sudden interruption of action. For relation to jolt, see that vb.] To jog, jolt, bump. **a.** *trans.* **b.** *intr.* (The first quot. is doubtful.)

[*a* **1425** *Langl.'s P. Pl.* A. ii. 157 (MS. Trin. Coll. Camb. R. 3. 14) Fabulers and Faytours as Folis iotten [*v.r.* þat on Fote rennen].] **1530** Palsgr. 593/1, I iotte, I touche one thynge agaynst another.. What nedest thou to iotte me with thyne elbowe? **1556** J. Heywood *Spider & F.* xxiv. 45 Nowe is iuste iustice, so iotted out of iointe. *c* **1611** Chapman *Iliad* xvi. 360 Numbers beneath their axle-trees..Made th' after chariots jot and jump in driving over them. **1643** Horn & Rob. *Gate Lang. Unl.* xlii. §453 A trotter jotteth [*marg.* shaketh] the rider. *a* **1825** Forby *Voc. E. Anglia*, *Jot*, *Jotter*, to jolt roughly.

jot, *v.*^{2} [app. f. jot *sb.*^{1}: the original sense being prob. to make the smallest mark with pen or pencil. Cf. dot *v.*^{1} 4. App. orig. Scotch, and in English familiarized by Scott and writers in *Blackwood*.] *trans.* To write down in the briefest and most hasty form, to make a short note or jotting of. Usually ***to jot down***; the simple vb. is *rare*.

1721 Ramsay *Addr. Thanks* xi, What will they have to crack about, Or jot into their journal? **1818** Todd, *Jot*, to set down; to make a memorandum of. *Modern.* **1822** Galt *Provost* xxxv. 254 Many of the things that I have herein jotted down. **1827** Scott *Jrnl.* 12 Feb., I have jotted down his evidence elsewhere. **1827** [see jotter]. **1832** G. Downes *Lett. Cont. Countries* I. xi. 165 Rude sketches of trees, rocks, and other materials of future pictures. These were evidently jotted down during his rambles. **1841** D'Israeli *Amen. Lit.* (1867) 581 He must have jotted down a mass. **1871** Waddell *Ps.* lxxvii. 6 The Lord he sal count whan he jots the folk that siclike was born tharin. **1890** Gross *Gild Merch.* II. 241 Accounts..too roughly jotted down to be very intelligible.

Hence ˈ**jotty** *a.*, of the nature of jottings or fragmentary notes.

1844 H. Taylor *Let.* in *Autobiog.* (1885) II. ii. 10 Reading Alice's jotty journal. **1888** G. J. Holyoake in *Co-operative News* 8 Sept. 9/1 The narrative is dreadfully jotty, jerky and confused.

jot, *v.*^{3}, var. or error for jet *v.*^{1}, to strut.

c **1560** A. Scott *Poems* (S.T.S.) iv. 81 Moir gentrice is to jott vndir ane silkin goun, Nor ane quhyt pittecott, and reddyar ay boun.

‖**jota** (ˈxota). [Sp.] A Spanish folk dance in $\frac{3}{4}$ or $\frac{3}{8}$ time. Also, the music of this dance.

1846 A. Robinson *Life in California* iii. 23 Singing or whistling the air of some favorite '*jota*'. **1850** E. G. Buffum *Six Months in Gold Mines* 143 Often have I seen little girls, scarce six years of age, flying through a *cotillon*..or dancing with great skill their favourite *jotah* or *jarabe*. **1902** *Encycl. Brit.* XXVII. 374/2 The *Jota* is the national dance of Aragon. **1912** J. E. C. Flitch *Mod. Dancing & Dancers* xiii. 195 The Spanish dance is intensely national. The snapping of the castanets, the short and insolent skirt, the exciting rhythm of the music, do not alone suffice for the performance of the *jota* or *fandango*, as some foreign artists would appear to suppose. **1922** J. Hergesheimer *Bright Shawl* (1923) 12 The air..was Liszt's Spanish Rhapsody. The accent of its measure, the jota, was at once perceptible and immaterial. **1960** *Spectator* 16 Dec. 988 Antonio's own solo numbers have vitality, and the company's final *jota* is attractive. **1967** 'La Meri' *Spanish Dancing* (ed. 2) ii. 36 It is said that the Jota, 'the fastest dance in the world', is less a dance than an endurance contest.

jotsom, -on, -um, jottsome, obs. ff. jetsam.

jotter. [f. jot *v*^{2} + -er.] **1.** One who jots.

1827 *Blackw. Mag.* XXII. 451 All the jottings that ever were jotted down on his jot-book, by the most inveterate jotter.

2. A small pad or exercise book used for setting down notes, memoranda, etc.; a memorandum book.

1882 Ogilvie *Imp. Dict.*, *Jotter*,..the book in which notes or memoranda are made. **1916** A. S. Neill *Dominie's Log* xii. 132 More attention..should be paid to neatness of method and penmanship in copybooks and jotters. **1930** *Times Educ. Suppl.* 29 Nov. 487/2 The present practice is to supply to all primary schools a sufficient supply of 'Second' readers and jotters sufficient for free issue to all pupils. **1968** M. Woodhouse *Rock Baby* vii. 75 A scribbled list on a desk jotter.

jotting (ˈdʒɒtɪŋ), *vbl. sb.* [f. jot *v.*^{2} + -ing^1.] The action of jot *v.*^{2}; usually *concr.* Something jotted down; a brief hasty note or sketch.

1808–18 Jamieson, *Jotting*, a memorandum. **1814** Scott *Wav.* lxxi, I'll mak a slight jotting the morn. **1818** Todd, *Jotting*, a memorandum; as, cursory jottings. Of very recent usage. The Scotch also employ this word. **1823** *Caled. Merc.* 29 Mar. (Jam.), Here his Lordship read the judgment, and the paper called Jottings respecting John Dalgleish's settlement. **1841** D'Israeli *Amen. Lit.* (1867) 581 We have had perhaps too many of these jottings.

‖**jotun** (ˈjəʊtən), prop. **jötun** (ˈjœtən). [ON. *jǫtunn* + OE. *eoten*, eten:—OTeut. **itunoz* giant.] One of a supernatural race of giants in Scandinavian mythology.

1842 Prichard *Nat. Hist. Man* 207 The epithet of *Jotnar*, or Jotuns..of frequent occurrence in the Sagas. **1865** Baring-Gould *Werewolves* iv. 38 Attributes..appropriate to trolls and jötuns. **1869** Lowell *Pict. fr. Appledore* v, A great mist-jotun you will see Lifting himself up silently.

jou, variant of jow *v.*, obs. form of Jew.

‖**joual** (ʒwɑl). *Canada.* [Dialectal Canad. Fr., ad. F. *cheval* horse.] 'Uneducated or dialectal Canadian French considered as debased or inferior by educated French Canadians, characterized by regional pronunciations, non-standard grammar, and often, especially in cities, by numerous English words and syntactical arrangements' (*Dict. Canadianisms*).

[**1959** *Le Devoir* (Montreal) 21 Oct. 4/6 Faut-il expliquer ce que c'est que *parler joual*?... Tout y passe: les syllabes mangées, le vocabulaire tronqué ou élargi, toujours dans le même sens, les phrases qui boitent, la vulgarité virile, la voix qui fait de son mieux pour être canaille.] **1962** M. Chapin tr. *Impertinences of Brother Anonymous* 27 Our pupils talk joual, write joual, and don't want to talk or write any other way. Joual is their language. *Ibid.* 30 To be understood, I often

must have recourse to one or another joual expression. **1963** *Maclean's Mag.* 16 Nov. 54/3 [I] have less trouble with workers' *joual* than with Montreal cabdrivers. **1965** *New Statesman* 10 Dec. 931/1 The uneducated [in Quebec] often speak a *patois* which is not even a genuine dialect so much as a lazy slurring—it is known as *joual*, which reproduces the pronunciation of *cheval*. **1972** *Evening Telegram* (St. John's, Newfoundland) 5 Aug. 36/7 Michel Tremblay's play, Les Belles-Soeurs, done in the joual. **1972** *Islander* (Victoria, B.C.) 15 Oct. 15/1 The French is mere tokenism, too; a few words or sentences of high-school français and joual sandwiched between paragraphs of English. **1973** *N.Y. Times* 22 Apr. 14/3 There are six million Canadians whose native language is French, but much of what they say would be baffling to a Parisian because many of them speak a patois known as '*Joual*', its name drawn from the way some rural people in Quebec pronounce the word 'cheval' or horse. **1975** *Canadian Forum* (Toronto) Oct. 7/2 In some of his books he lapses into *joual*.

†**joucat** ('dʒuːkət). *Sc. Obs.* Also 6 ioucatte, iowcat, iucat. [Deriv. unknown.] An obsolete Scotch measure, the same as a Scotch gill.

1587 *Sc. Acts Jas. VI*, c. 114 Be just calculation and comptrolment, the samin extended to 19 pintes, and a jucat. *Ibid.*, They therefore.. decernis and ordanis the Firlot to be augmented,.. And to conteine nine-tene pintes, and twa Ioucattes. **1892** P. COCHRAN *Mediæv. Scotl.* viii. 164 [In] 1587.. the Commissioners discovered that an error had been made in 1457 with regard to the contents of the firlot which should contain 19 pints and a 'jowcat' or gill.

jouelere, obs. form of JEWELLER.

joug, sing. of JOUGS; var. JUG *sb.*² and *v.*²

‖**jough** (dʒəʊx). [Manx, = Gaelic *deoch* drink.] Drink.

1887 HALL CAINE *Deemster* xv. 89 A long pint of Manx jough. **1890** —— *Bondman* I. x. 223 Collared head, and beef, and pinjeen, and Manx jough.

jougler, obs. form of JUGGLER.

jougs (dʒugz, dʒʌgz), *sb. pl. Sc.* Rarely in sing. joug. Forms: (6 jorgs), 7 jog(g)s, 8–9 jougs (9 jugg(s, jagg). [app. a. F. *joug* or L. *jugum* yoke: the sense seems to be confined to Sc. The pl. form app. refers to the construction of the collar in two hinged halves adapted to be locked together.]

An old Scottish instrument of punishment, analogous to the pillory; it consisted of an iron collar, which was locked round the culprit's neck, and was attached by a chain to a wall or post.

1596 in *Collect. Lives Reformers Ch. Scot.* (1848) II. 72 The Session [of Glasgow] appoint jorgs and branks to be made for punishing flyters. **1646** BP. MAXWELL *Burd. Issach.* in *Phenix* (1708) II. 262 Making them stand in 'jogs', as they call them,—pillorys.. fix'd to the two sides of the main door of the parish-church. **1661** *Kirk Session Rothesay* in A. Edgar *Old Ch. Life Scotl.* Ser. I. 311 If hereafter she should be found drunk, she should be put in the joggs. **1771** PENNANT *Tour Scotl. in* 1769 (1790) 173 Observed on a pillar of the door of Calder church, a joug, i.e. an iron yoke or ring, fastened to a chain. **1814** SCOTT *Wav.* x, He set an old woman in the jougs (or Scottish pillory). **1851** D. WILSON *Preh. Ann.* (1863) II. IV. x. 518 The jougs, which consists of an iron collar, attached by a chain to a pillar or tree, forms the corresponding judicial implement to the English stocks. **1882** *Cornh. Mag.* Feb. 206 Offenders were put into the jugg and severely flogged at the church door. **1884** C. ROGERS *Soc. Life Scotl.* I. viii. 354 Those who cheated in the market were.. borne by the executioner to the Cross, and thereto.. made fast with a jagg or iron collar.

Hence **joug, jog**, *v.*, to confine in the jougs.

1632 *Act* in Barry *Orkney* (1805) App. 474 The Baillie of the paroch.. shall cause him be jogged at the church, upon Sunday, from 8 in the morning till 12 hours at noon.

†**jouisance, -issance**. *Obs.* Forms: 5 ioys-, 6 ioyss-, ioyis-, iouiss-, iouys(s)-, 6–7 iouis-, 7 jouis(s)-, jovyss-, 7–8 *arch.* jovis-; 5–6 -aunce, 6–8 -ance. [a. late OF. *jouissance*, f. *jouissant*, pr. pple. of *jouir* to enjoy: see -ANCE. (Exemplified in Fr. only from 1534 by Hatz.-Darm.) The spelling *jovi-*, a misreading of *ioui-*, has been erroneously introduced by editors into Spenser and some other 16–17th c. texts.]

1. The possession and use *of* something affording advantage: = ENJOYMENT I.

1483 CAXTON *G. de la Tour* E vj b, He may not be peasyble to the reame ne haue the ioysaunce of it. **1539** *St. Papers Hen. VIII*, I. 599 He concluded that the Duk of Sax shuld have the joyssance of all them. **1603** FLORIO *Montaigne* I. xxxviii. (1632) 122 In full jouyssance of them.

2. Pleasure, delight (= ENJOYMENT 2); merriment, mirth, festivity.

1579 SPENSER *Sheph. Cal.* May 25 To see those folkes make such iouysaunce. *Ibid.* Nov. 2 When shall it please thee sing.. songs of some iouisaunce? **1594** CAREW *Tasso* (1881) 119 For such their comming, mirth and iouyssance. **1597** *Pilgr. Parnass.* IV. 489 Till you have tasted of this ioyisance. **1633** J. DONE *Hist. Septuagint* 126 All the Company betook them to make cheare and to jouisance. **1657** REEVE *God's Plea* 98 We cannot abdicate wonted jovisances. **1750** DODD *Poems* (1767) 45 They rioted in jovisaunce secure.

†**jouise**, *v. Obs. rare*⁻¹. [ad. F. *jouir, jouiss-*: see -ISH².] *refl.* To rejoice oneself; with *of*: To have the enjoyment of, to enjoy (F. *se jouir de*).

1597 A. M. tr. *Guillemeau's Fr. Chirurg.* *v, Let them iouise and ioy themselves of their privileadge.

jouk, jook (dʒuk), *sb.*¹ *Sc.* Forms: 6 iouk, iowk, iuike, 8- jouk, jook. [f. JOUK *v.*²]

1. A sudden elusive movement; a quick turn out of the way; *fig.* a 'dodge'. ***to give*** (a person) ***the jouk***: to give the slip, to elude, escape from.

1513 DOUGLAS *Æneis* XI. xiii. 101 With mony a curs [= course] and iowk, abowt, abowt, Quhair euir he fled scho followis in and owt. **1583** *Leg. Bp. St. Androis* 964 To George Durrie he played a iuike, That will not be foryet this oulke. **1871** C. GIBBON *Lack of Gold* xxix, He has given the lass the jouk.

2. A bow or curtsy, a jerked obeisance.

1567 *Gude & Godlie B.* (S.T.S.) 193 For all ȝour Joukis and ȝour noddis, ȝour hartis is hard as ony stone. **1768** ROSS *Helenore* (1866) 202 She.. hailst her with a jouk. *Ibid.* 239 The honest shepherd.. wondering at the kindness, gae a jook.

3. A place into which one may dart for shelter; a shelter from a blow, a storm, etc. *Mod. Sc.*

1808–18 in JAMIESON.

†**jouk**, *sb.*² *Obs.* In 7 iuke. [a. OF. *joc, jouc, juc*, roosting of a fowl, from *jokier, jouquier* (see next).] The state of roosting; ***at juke***, at roost. (OF. *au jouc*.)

1626 BRETON *Fantasticks, Twelue of the Clocke* F ij b, The Beasts of the field take rest after their feed, and the Birds of the Ayre are at Iuke in the Bushes.

†**jouk**, *v.*¹ *Obs.* Forms: 4–5 iouke, ioyke, 4–6 iowke, 5–6 ioke, 6 ieouke, 7 jouk, juke, jook. [a. OF. *jok-ier, joqu-ier, jouq-ier* (3 sing. pr. *joke, jouque*) to be at roost, at rest, to lie down, mod.F. *jucher*, Walloon *joukî*, Namur *joker*. Ulterior derivation unknown.]

1. *intr.* Of birds: **a.** To perch, sit (upon branches). **b.** *Falconry.* To roost, to sleep upon its perch.

a **1400** *Pistel of Susan* 82 Þe Briddes.. On peren and pynappel, þei ioyken in pees. **1486** *Bk. St. Albans* A v (1496 a iij) The kyndeli termis that belong to hawkis... The .v. youre hauke Ioukith [*Rel. Ant.* I. 296 joketh], and not slepith. *Ibid.* C viij (1496 c iij) She Ioykith when she slepith. **1575** TURBERV. *Faulconrie* 121 Make her jeouke all nyght in payne and in a moyste or colde place, and so shall she watch moste of the nyght. *c* **1575** *Perf. Bk. Sparhawkes* (ed. Harting) 32 Or elles sodenly awake her from jokin. **1672** SKINNER, To juke or jug as birds doe, *se in pertica ad dormiendum componere*. **1886** HARTING *Gloss. Perf. Bk. Sparhawkes* 44 *Jokin*, sleeping: now obsolete.

2. *intr.* To lie asleep or at rest; to lie close, lie, (?) to lurk; also, more vaguely, To abide, remain.

13.. *E.E. Allit. P.* C. 182 Ionas þe Iwe.. Iowked in derne. *c* **1374** CHAUCER *Troylus* V. 409 For certes it noon honour is to the To wepe and in þi bed to Iowken þus. **1377** LANGL. *P. Pl.* B. XVI. 92 And þanne spakke *spiritus sanctus* in Gabrieles mouthe To a mayde þat hiȝte Marye.. þat one Ihesus a iustice sone moste iouke in her chambre, Tyl *plenitudo temporis*. *c* **1400** *Sege Jerus.* (E.E.T.S.) 300 Schal neuer kyng of ȝour kynde with croune be ynoyntid, Ne Jewe for Jesu sake [i]ouke in ȝou more. *a* **1400–50** *Alexander* 4202 And saue þe Iolite of Iuly þai Iowke in þ a strandis.

¶**b.** *pseudo-arch.* To doze.

a **1652** BROME *Eng. Moor* III. ii. Wks. 1873 II. 44 *Buz.* Hey ho. I am very sleepy. *Nat.* See he jooks already.

jouk, jook (dʒuk), *v.*² *Sc.* and *north.* Forms: 6 iouk, iouck, iuke, iowk, 7 jowk, 8 juck, jeuk, 8–9 jook, 9 juik. 7- jouk. [A Scottish word of uncertain origin.

It has been compared with DUCK *v.*, senses 2, 4 of which coincide with senses 1, 4 of this; and it is noteworthy that the sb. *duck* is in many parts of Scotl. *Jook* or *jouk*; but this seems an inadequate explanation, since the sb. is in other parts (dʏk) or (døk), and the vb. to *duck* (in water) is generally (duk): see DUCK *v.* The forms coincide to some extent with those of JOUK *v.*¹ (which is not Sc.), but the sense seems to be essentially distinct, coinciding to some extent with that of JINK *v.*¹]

1. *intr.* To bend or turn the body with a quick adroit movement downward or to one side, in order to avoid a missile or blow; to dodge; to duck.

1513 DOUGLAS *Æneis* X. ix. 39 And jowkit in vnder the speyr has he. **1535** STEWART *Cron. Scot.* 4530 It is oure lait to juke quhen that the heid Is fra the hals. **1721** KELLY *Scot. Prov.* i. 92 Juck, and let a Jaw go o'er you. **1785** BURNS *To Jas. Smith* xxv, I jouk beneath Misfortune's blows As weel's I may. **1820** SCOTT *Abbot* xvi, But we must jouk and let the jaw gang by. **1888** BARRIE *Auld Licht Idylls* (1892) 146 The grey old man would wince, as if 'joukin' from a blow.

b. *transf.* and *fig.* To swerve for a moment.

1513 DOUGLAS *Æneis* VIII. iv. 120 This rolk.. Hercules it smyttis wyth a mychty touk Apon the richt half, for to mak it jouk. **1573** DAVIDSON *Commend. Vprichtnes* 152 in *Satir. P. Ref.* xl, He.. did not iouk ane ioit from vprichtnes.

2. *intr.* By extension: To dart or spring with an adroit elusive movement out of the way or out of sight; to hide oneself by such action; to skulk.

a **1510** DOUGLAS *Conscience* 21 For Sciens baith and faythfull Consciens Sa corruptit ar with this warldis gude, That falset ioukis in everie clerkis hude. **1560** ROLLAND *Crt. Venus* I. 55, I Iowkit than but dout quhen I thame sa v, Behind the Bus, Lord bot I liggit law! **1637** RUTHERFORD *Lett.* (1862) I. 439, I think it manhood to play the coward and jouk in the leeside of Christ. **1780–1808** MAYNE *Siller Gun* III, As he strack, The supple tailor skips and springs —Aye jouking back. *c* **1790** BURNS *Past. Poetry* vi, Come forrit, honest Allan! Thou need na jouk behint the hallan. **1886** STEVENSON *Kidnapped* (1888) 165 Jouk in here among the trees.

b. *fig.* To dart in and out (of sight).

a **1810** TANNAHILL *Poems, Gloomy winter's now awa'*, 'Neath the brae the burnie jouks. **1894** CROCKETT *Raiders* (ed. 3) 155 The reed lowe jookin' through the bars.

3. *trans.* To evade, elude, 'dodge', by ducking, bending, or springing aside.

1812 RANKEN *Poems* 36 Fain wad he the bargain jeuket, But his honour was at stake. **1894** CROCKETT *Raiders* (ed. 3) 165 Ye micht possibly hae juiked the blunderbush. *Mod. Sc.* Every sodger at first tries to jouk the bullets.

4. *intr.* To bend the body adroitly (without any notion of dodging). †**a.** To bend oneself supply as a tumbler or acrobat. *Obs.*

c **1450** HOLLAND *Howlat* 789 Thus iowkit with iuperdyss the iangland Ia.

b. To bow in salutation or obeisance; *esp.* to make a quick jerky bow: cf. JERK *v.*¹ 4.

1567 *Ps.* lxxxiii. in *Gude & Godlie B.* (S.T.S.) 105 Quhilk can not do, bot drink, sing, Iouk and beck. **1686** G. STUART *Joco-ser. Disc.* 13, I jowkt to her, she baikt to me. **1728** RAMSAY *Step-daughter's Relief* vii, Sax servants shall jouk to thee. **1795** BURNS *Heron Ballads* I. iv, But why should we to nobles jouk?

c. *fig.* To cringe, fawn; to dissemble.

1573 DAVIDSON *Commend. Vprichtnes* Prol. in *Satir. Poems Reform.* 276 That our watche men faint not, nor begin to iouk or flatter with the world for feir of Tyrannis. **1821** GALT *Ayrsh. Legatees* Let. xxxii. 274, I saw no symptoms of the swelled legs that Lord Lauderdale, that jooking man, spoke about.

Hence '**jouker**, one who jouks.

1573 DAVIDSON *Death Knox* 34 in *Satir. Poems Reform.* xli, Thair ioukers durst not kyith thair cure, For fear of Fasting in the Fratour.

jouk(e, obs. form of JUCK.

jouk, var. JUKE *sb.*

joukery, jookery ('dʒukərɪ). *Sc.* and *north.* In 6 ioukrie, 7 jewkry, 8 jouckry, 9 jookery, joukry, -rey. [f. JOUK *v.*²: see -ERY.] Dodging; 'underhand dealing, trickery'; 'deceit' (Jam.).

1563 *Ressoning betuix Crosraguell & Knox* B iij b (Jam.) Keip your promes, and pretex na ioukrie be my Lorde of Cassillis writing. **1822** GALT *Provost* v. 38, I was so displeased by the jookerie of the bailie.. that we had no correspondence on public affairs, till long after.

b. *Comb.* **joukery-cookery** [cf. COOK *v.*¹ 3 c], 'artful management' (Jam.); **joukery-pawkery** [PAWKY], clever trickery, jugglery, legerdemain.

1822 GALT *Sir A. Wylie* I. xxi. 182 As ye're acquaint wi' a' the *jookery-cookery of newsmaking. —— *Provost* xiv. 112 Nothing could be more manifest than that there was some jookerie cookerie in this affair. **1686** G. STUART *Jocoser. Disc.* 59 Deil fetcht was it but *Jewkrypawkry. **1785** R. FORBES *Poems Buchan Dial., Ajax's Speech* 5 The sin o' Nauplius.. His jouckry-pauckry finding out, To weir did him compell. **1816** SCOTT *Bl. Dwarf* x, That here has been some jookery-paukery of Satan's in a' this. **1871** W. ALEXANDER *Johnny Gibb* xxxvii, There's been mair joukry-pawkry wi' Dawvid nor ye're avaar o'.

jouking ('dʒukɪŋ), *vbl. sb. Sc.* [f. JOUK *v.*² + -ING¹.] The action of JOUK *v.*²; evasive movement or action, dodging, eluding, bending.

1513 DOUGLAS *Æneis* X. xiv. 144 This irksum traysing, jowking, and delay. **1573** DAVIDSON *Commend. Vprichtnes* 51 in *Satir. Poems Reform.* xl, With iouking thay will jangil craftelie. **1631** RUTHERFORD *Lett.* (1862) I. 73 Innocency and uprightness.. shall hold its feet.. when jouking will not do it. **1871** W. ALEXANDER *Johnny Gibb* xxiii, A bit canny joukin to let the jaw gae owre's.

joul(e, obs. form of JOWL.

joule (dʒuːl) *Physics.* Also Joule. [Named 1882, after Dr. J. P. Joule, an English physicist.]

1. An electrical unit, being the amount of work done (or of heat generated) by a current of one ampère acting for one second against a resistance of one ohm. Later adopted as the M.K.S. unit of energy and work in non-electrical contexts also; it is equal to 10 million ergs, and is now incorporated in the International System of Units, in which it is given the equivalent definition of the work done when the point of application of a force of one newton is displaced through a distance of one metre in the direction of the force.

Although some people of this name call themselves (dʒaʊl) and others (dʒəʊl) (D. Jones *Everyman's Eng. Pronouncing Dict.* (ed. 11, 1956), G. M. Miller *BBC Pronouncing Dict. British Names* (1971)), it is almost certain that J. P. Joule (and some at least of his relatives) used (dʒuːl). For evidence on this point see *Nature* (1943) CLII. 354, 418, 479, 602.

1882 *Athenæum* 26 Aug. 274/2 Dr. Siemens proposes to add to these [electrical] units four new ones, as follows: (1) a Watt.. (2) a Weber.. (3) a Gauss.. (4) a unit of heat, to be called a 'Joule', and to be defined as the quantity of heat generated by an ampère flowing through an ohm for one second. *Ibid.* 2 Sept. 310/2 Two of his units were unanimously approved—namely, (1) the watt.. (2) the joule. **1886** J. A. FLEMING *Short Lect. to Electr. Artisans* v. 87 An amount of work equal to 10 million ergs is called one joule. Hence one foot-pound = 1·356 joules, or one joule = ·7373 foot-pound. **1889** *Rep. Brit. Assoc. Adv. Sci. 1888* 56 It was

also agreed to adopt the name 'Joule' for 10^7 C.G.S. units of work. Thus a Joule is equal to 10^7 ergs. It is the work done in one second by a power of one Watt. **1893** *Operator & Electr. World* 2 Sept. 175/1 The several governments represented by the delegates of this International Congress of Electricians.. hereby recommended to formally adopt as legal units of electrical measure the following... As a unit of work the joule, which is 10^7 units of work in a C.G.S. system. **1896** *Rep. Brit. Assoc. Adv. Sci. 1896* 154 The amount of heat required to raise the temperature of 1 gramme of water 1° C. of the scale of the hydrogen thermometer, at a mean temperature which may be taken as 10° C. of that thermometer, is 4·2 Joules. **1923** N. SHAW *Forecasting Weather* (ed. 2) i. 24 Observations for nine stations within greater London, comprising measures of atmospheric pollution at Richmond and South Kensington, total solar radiation at South Kensington in joules, and its average and maximum rate in milliwatts. **1949** *Nature* 19 Mar. 428/1 It was also agreed [by the ninth International Conference of Weights and Measures] that the unit of heat should be the 'Joule'. **1951** *Engineering* 11 May 577/1 The international units, as realised in the various national laboratories, differed by small amounts, but it has been agreed that the mean international joule of the various laboratories is equal to 1·00019 absolute joules. *Ibid.* 577/3 If the value of the 15-deg. calorie is taken as 4·1855 absolute joules, a B.Th.U. is equal to 1054·54 absolute joules. **1963** [see CALORIE]. **1970** *Daily Tel.* 4 May 3 Adoption of the metric system and loss of the calorie as a unit of energy may increase the hazard of obesity, Prof. J. B. M. Coppock, an expert on nutrition, said yesterday... There was a danger of losing the calorie for another unit, the joule, which was little understood outside physics and engineering... It would be years before the public.. could adjust to a new jargon.

2. Used *attrib.* and in the possessive as the personal name to designate quantities, effects, etc., discovered by Joule or arising out of his work: **Joule** (†or **Joule's**) **effect**, (*a*) the heating effect of an electric current flowing through a resistance (described by *Joule's law* (a)); (*b*) a change in the linear dimensions (esp. length) of a body when it is subjected to a magnetic field; **Joule's equivalent** = mechanical equivalent of heat: see EQUIVALENT *sb.* 3 c; **Joule heating**, the heating that occurs when an electric current flows through a resistance; **Joule's law**, (*a*) the law that the heat produced by an electric current i flowing through a resistance R for a time t is proportional to i^2Rt; (*b*) a law concerning ideal gases, now usually given in the form: the internal energy of a given mass of a gas depends only on its temperature; **'Joule,meter**, a meter in which the Joule is used as the unit of work or energy.

¶ See also JOULE-KELVIN, JOULE-THOMSON.

1879 *Encycl. Brit.* VIII. 57/2 In general the Peltier effect is.. mixed up with Joule's effect, and makes itself felt by producing a disturbance at the junction. **1914** *Physical Rev.* IV. 499 If the change in length of *AC* is measured as the field, *H*, is varied, we have the ordinary longitudinal Joule effect, whereas if *DB* or the length normal to the page is measured we have the transverse Joule effect. **1931** S. R. WILLIAMS *Magn. Phenomena* ii. 108 In the Joule effect the changes in length are.. very small. *Ibid.* 111 (*heading*) Transverse Joule effect—change in dimensions normal to the magnetic field. **1933** J. E. PHILLIPS *Intermediate Magn. & Electr.* xiii. 303 The Peltier effect.. is proportional to the first power of the current, while the Joule effect varies as the square of the current. **1939** L. F. BATES *Mod. Magn.* x. 303 The existence of a Joule effect in non-ferromagnetic substances was first proved by Kapitza. **1966** F. BRAILSFORD *Physical Princ. Magn.* vi. 143 Additional to the high-field volume change is the Joule effect involving changes in linear dimensions in relatively low fields, which in most cases may be 10 to 100 times greater than those due to the volume magnetostriction. **1853** W. J. M. RANKINE in *Trans. R. Soc. Edin.* XX. 192 This last quantity.. is.. one-ninth of the value according to Mr Joule's equivalent. W. THOMSON in *Ibid.* 298 In terms of Joule's mechanical equivalent of heat. **1912** H. A. PERKINS *Introd. Gen. Thermodynamics* ii. 19 The numerical constant connecting heat energy.. and mechanical energy.. is known as 'Joule's equivalent'. **1958** A. J. WOODALL *Heat* v. 99 Joule's equivalent is, of course, expressible in different units. **1929** J. A. RATCLIFFE *Physical Princ. Wireless* iv. 57 The known forms of A.C. galvanometer, which depend on Joule heating. **1971** *Physics Bull.* Apr. 207/3 Some of the power generated is wasted by joule heating within the element. **1855** W. THOMSON in *Proc. Philos. Soc. Glasgow* III. 286 We thus have an equation between the diminution of the electrical energy in any infinitely small time, and the expression according to Joule's law for the heat generated in the same time in the discharges multiplied by the mechanical equivalent of the thermal unit. **1879** *Encycl. Brit.* VIII. 57/1 The current of the battery heats the pile in part uniformly according to Joule's law. **1887** *Ibid.* XXII. 480/1 Joules law... When a gas expands without doing external work, and without taking in or giving out heat, its temperature does not change... We must therefore conclude that the internal energy of a given mass of a gas depends only on its temperature, and not upon its temperature or volume. **1945** R. H. FRAZIER *Elem. Electr.-Circuit Theory* i. 21 Ohm's law and Joule's law are interdependent; either can be derived from the other. **1951** C. L. BROWN *Basic Thermodynamics* vi. 83 For a perfect gas the internal energy is a function of temperature only. This statement, known as Joule's law after its formulator, can be expressed symbolically as $u = f(T)$.

joulean, Joulean ('dʒuːlɪən), *a. Physics.* Chiefly *U.S.* [f. prec. + -AN.] Of or pertaining to Joule heating.

1891 *Electrician* 27 Feb. 507/2 The waste in Joulean heating. **1903** C. O. MAILLOUX tr. *Boy de la Tour's Induction Motor* p. xii, Joulean effect. This term is used.. to denote the loss of power (watts), and the heating, due to ohmic resistance. **1937** M. W. ZEMANSKY *Heat & Thermodynamics* xiv. 268 A phantom experiment in which the two irreversible phenomena, namely, Joulean dissipation and heat conduction are absent. **1952** A. HUND *Short-Wave Radiation Phenomena* I. i. 3 The electric field component along the conductor surface accounts for the joulean heat loss in the conductor. *Ibid.* II. ix. 1196 This energy is dissipated in the thin skin as joulean heat. **1960** E. M. & E. W. PUGH *Princ. Electr. & Magn.* vi. 179 The joulean heat produced in the windings of an electro-magnetic generator.

Joule-Kelvin (dʒuːl 'kɛlvɪn). [See next.] = next.

1909 *Cent. Dict.* Suppl. s.v. *Effect*, Joule-Kelvin effect. **1916** I. B. HART *Student's Heat* xvi. 320 The liquefaction of hydrogen is achieved as a result of the fact that at 200 atmospheres and a temperature of −200° C. the Joule-Kelvin effect changes from a heating to a cooling. **1937** M. W. ZEMANSKY *Heat & Thermodynamics* xiv. 246 One of the most important commercial applications of the Joule-Kelvin effect involves the transition of a liquid at room temperature and at high pressure (15 to 20 atm) into a mixture of liquid and vapor at a temperature about 30°C colder. **1965** W. C. REYNOLDS *Thermodynamics* viii. 216 Show that the Joule-Kelvin coefficient for a perfect gas is zero.

Joule-Thomson (dʒuːl 'tɒmsən). The names of James Prescott *Joule* (1818–89), English physicist, and Sir William *Thomson*, Lord Kelvin (see KELVIN), used *attrib.* with reference to an effect discovered jointly by them, viz. the change of temperature of a gas that occurs when it expands through a porous plug or a throttle without doing external work, the gas being heated or cooled according as it is initially above or below its inversion temperature (which is above room temperature for most gases).

1899 *Proc. Physical Soc.* XVI. 454 He desires to indicate the relation which must exist between the formula assigned to the Joule-Thomson effect, considered as a function of the temperature, and the particular form adopted for the characteristic equation of a gas. *Ibid.* 464 The Joule-Thomson results.. were necessary for the establishment of the thermodynamic scale [of temperature]. **1930** *Engineering* 7 Feb. 163/3 The first commercial pure oxygen which Carl Linde put on the market in 1902 was prepared by the application of the Joule-Thomson effect. **1957** G. E. HUTCHINSON *Treat. Limnol.* I. iii. 207 The amount of change in temperature per unit change of pressure is known as the Joule-Thomson coefficient. **1966** D. G. BRANDON *Mod. Techniques Metallogr.* 221 Miniaturized liquid-hydrogen refrigerators based on Joule-Thomson cooling are now available commercially.

joult, joulthead, obs. ff. JOLT, JOLT-HEAD.

joulter, *a. rare.* [Deduced from *joulter-head*, JOLTER-HEAD.] Clumsily stupid.

1854 *Blackw. Mag.* LXXVI. 22 He seems to have a collection of these puns.. stowed away in his joulter jaws.

jouncat, obs. form of JUNKET.

jounce (dʒaʊns), *v.* [Of obscure origin: it has been compared to JAUNCE *v.*, which it partly approaches in use, but with which it can scarcely be phonetically connected. Several words in *-ounce*, as *bounce*, *flounce*, *pounce*, *trounce*, are of obscure history.]

1. *intr.* To move violently up and down, to fall heavily against something; to bump, bounce, jolt; to go *along* with a heavy jolting pace.

c **1440** *Promp. Parv.* 265/2 Iowncynge, or grete vngentylle mevynge [*v.rr.* iownsynge.. ioyuncynge], *strepitus.* **1711** S. SEWALL *Diary* 11 Aug. (1879) II. 321 One of the Porters stoop'd to take up his Hat, by which means the.. Head of the Coffin jounc'd upon the Ground. *a* **1825** FORBY *Voc. E. Anglia*, *Jounce*, to bounce, thump, and jolt, as rough riders are wont to do. **1885** HOWELLS *Silas Lapham* (1891) I. 60 The mare jounced easily along. **1886** HALL CAINE *Son of Hagar* I. viii, The lawyer was jouncing along towards the house with a lantern in his hand. **1888** *Atlantic Monthly* Feb. 267 [The blue jay] stamped his feet, and jounced (the only word to describe a certain raising and violent dropping of the body without lifting the feet). **1967** C. O. SKINNER *Madame Sarah* viii. 171 The train.. swayed, rocked, jounced and hustled a couple of passengers from their seats. **1969** *New Yorker* 12 Apr. 118/3 The drill, which is a percussive one, jounces up and down. **1971** D. E. WESTLAKE *I gave at the Office* (1972) 55 The two trucks jouncing off along the narrow dirt road through the swamp.

2. *trans.* To jolt, bump, or shake up and down, as by rough riding; to give (a person) a shaking.

1581 MULCASTER *Positions* xxiv. (1887) 96 Set him.. vpon a trotting iade to iounce him thoroughly or vpon a lame hakney to make him exercise his feete, when his courser failes him. **1834** *New Monthly Mag.* XLII. 314 You have become a little used to the bouncings and jouncings that greet your first attempts to go to sleep. **1893** *Chicago Advance* 31 Aug., At every step of the [camel's] long, ungainly legs the rider is bounced and jounced around and up and down. **1897** R. KIPLING *Captains Courageous* 209 We weren't runnin' for a record. Harvey Cheyne's wife.. were sick back, an' we didn't want to jounce her. **1902** H. L. WILSON *Spenders* xiv. 148 Then I jounced Hank. **1910** *N. Y. Even. Post* 4 Aug. (Th.), The raft was jounced about so severely that it broke its anchorages. **1972** *Time* 17 Apr. 40/3 The rover's seat belts have been redesigned to anchor passengers more comfortably during the jouncing ride in the moon's weak gravity.

Hence **jounce** *sb.*, a bump, a jolt, in which a thing is raised and allowed to fall by its weight; a jolting pace.

1787 GROSE *Prov. Gloss.*, *Jounce*, a jolt or shake, A jouncing trot, a hard rough trot. *Norf.* **1813** SIR J. CULLUM *Hist. Hawsted* (ed. 2) Vocab. (E.D.S.), *Jounce*, a jolt, a shock, or shaking bout. **1876** MRS. WHITNEY *Sights & Ins.* II. xvii, She made straight for a bench.. sat herself down upon it with a jounce. **1892** *Harper's Mag.* Aug. 341/1 You saw large individuals of the leisure class toiling it in their daily foot-jounce. **1893** ZINCKE *Wherstead* 261 A jolt, or a shake, is a 'jounce'.

joun(c)k, obs. form of JUNK *sb.*[3]

joup(e, jouperd, obs. ff. JUPE, JEOPARD.

‖**jour**[1] (ʒur). [OF. and F. *jour*:—L. *diurnum* neut. sing. (used in pop. L. as sb.) of *diurnus* of or pertaining to the day, f. *diēs* day.]

†**1.** A day. *Obs.*

c **1450** *Merlin* 67 On the xi^e iour of Pentecoste, the kynge satte at mete, and with hym the Duke of Tintagel. **1538** *Churchw. Acc. St. Giles, Reading* 56 M^d that ther is owyng Thomas Clere which he hathe Accompted for dewe uppon Joure.

2. *pl.* (See quot. 1882.) [F. *jour*: cf. DAY *sb.* 4.]

1865 F. B. PALLISER *Hist. Lace* xiii. 181 Twined among them appear a variety of 'jours', filled up with patterns of endless variety, the whole wreathed and garlanded like the decoration of a theatre. **1882** CAULDFEILD & SAWARD *Dict. Needlework*, *Jours*, a term used by lacemakers to denote the open stitches that form the Fillings in Needle and Pillow Laces. **1953** M. POWYS *Lace & Lace-Making* iv. 27 *Binche*, Modern Belgian Lace... As a filling in the center is the Fond à la Mariage or honeycomb, mode or jour.

3. jour de fête = *fête-day*.

1806 C. WILMOT *Let.* 21 Oct. in *Russ. Jrnls.* (1934) II. 234 The gift of their Wives on such a *Jour de Fête* or *Jour de Nom.* **1864** MRS. GASKELL *French Life* in *Fraser's Mag.* Apr. 439/2 The gowns they wear on jours de fêtes. **1869** C. SCHREIBER *Jrnl.* 17 May (1911) I. 4 Jour de Fête, no shops open.

jour[2] (dʒɜː(r)), U.S. colloq. abbrev. of JOURNEYMAN.

1835 *Gent's. Vade-Mecum* (Philadelphia) 27 June 3/1 The *jours* are in the habit of *spouting* their work from one week to another. **1854** B. P. SHILLABER *Life & Sayings Mrs. Partington* 146 '*I* wouldn't be so bothered about *my* meals,' said a jour printer to a brother typo. **1868** E. E. HALE *If, Yes & Perhaps* 35, I stopped at one or two cabinet-makers, and talked with the 'jours' about work. **1898** *Milwaukee Sentinel* 16 Jan. II. 2/7 Where the hundreds of old time-honored 'jours'.. have gone to, no one seems able to decide.

jour, var. GIAOUR.

jourer, obs. f. JUROR.

journal ('dʒɜːnəl), *a.* and *sb.* Forms: 5 iurnalle, 5–7 iornall, 6–7 iournal(l, -el(l, 7 journall, (giornal), 7– journal. [a. OF. *jur-*, *jor-*, *journal*, *-el* daily (*livre*, *registre*, *papier journal* a day-book); as sb. a day, a day's work (so in AF.); a measure of land, a breviary, etc. (= Sp., Pg *jornal*, It. *giornale*):—late L. *diurnāl-em* of or belonging to a day, DIURNAL.]

†**A.** *adj. Obs.*

1. Performed, happening, or recurring every day; daily, diurnal.

1590 SPENSER *F.Q.* I. xi. 31 Phœbus.. his faint steedes watred in Ocean deepe, Whiles from their iournall labours they did rest. **1611** SHAKS. *Cymb.* IV. ii. 10 So please you, leaue me, Sticke to your Iournall course. **1637** BASTWICK *Litany* II. 3 This is their journall practice. **1658** R. WHITE tr. *Digby's Powd. Symp.* (1660) 144 To see a hand.. mark the journall houres.. upon the flat of a quadrant.

2. Of or belonging to one day, restricted to the day; ephemeral. *rare.*

1685 *Gracian's Courtier's Orac.* 72 There are some who dayly differ from themselves. Their understanding is even journal, and much more their will and conduct.

B. *sb.* **I.** A book or record.

†**1.** *Eccl.* A service-book containing the day-hours: = DIURNAL *sb.* 1. *Obs.*

1355–6 *Durham Acc. Rolls* (Surtees) 121 Ad repar. unius Jurnal. *c* **1440** *Promp. Parv.* 268/1 Iurnalle, lytylle boke, *diurnale.* **1454** *Test. Ebor.* (Surtees) cxlii, Also I wyte to y^e said Thomas my jornenall that I bere in my slefe dayly. **1549** *Act 3 & 4 Edw. VI*, c. 10 §1 All Books called.. Couchers, Journals, Ordinals.. shall be.. abolished.

†**2. a.** A book containing notices concerning the daily stages of a route and other information for travellers; = ITINERARY. (Cf. JOURNEY *sb.* 2, 3.)

1552 HULOET, Itinerary booke wherein is wrytten the dystaunce from place to place, or wherin thexpenses in iourney be written, or called other wyse a iournall, *hodœporicum.* **1613** PURCHAS *Pilgrimage* II. x. §2 It is written in an auncient Iournall of Burdeaux [marg. *Itinerarium Burdigal.*] that not farre from the Images there is a stone.

†**b.** A record of travel: = ITINERARY *sb.* 2. (Now only as in 4 a and c.)

1600 J. PORY tr. *Leo's Africa* To Rdr. A iij. It is.. nothing else but a large Itinerarium or Iournal of his African voiages. **1700** LAWSON (*title*) Journal of a thousand Miles' Travel among the Indians. **1783** FRANKLIN in *Lett. Lit. Men* (Camden) 425 Containing the Journal of the first Aerial Voyage perform'd by Men.

attrib. **1792** A. YOUNG *Trav. France* 1 The journal form hath the advantage of carrying with it a greater degree of credibility; and, of course, more weight.

3. A daily record of commercial transactions, entered as they occur, in order to the keeping of accounts. **a.** In a general sense = DAY-BOOK. **b.**

In Book-keeping by Double Entry, A book in which each transaction is entered, in systematic form, with statement of the accounts to which it is to be debited and credited, so as to ensure correct posting in the ledger. These entries are either made at first-hand, or are 'journalized' from a *waste-book* or *day-book*, in which they have been entered as they occur, without consideration of the special accounts concerned.

Thus the waste-book entry, 'John Smith paid his acct of £100 due 3 months hence less discount at 5%—£98 15*s*., 0*d*.', would be entered in the journal as 'Dr. *Cash* £98 15*s*., *P. & L. Discount* £1 5*s*.; Cr. *John Smith* £100'.

1540 *Househ. Ord.* (1790) 228 The said Cofferer shall yearly within one moneth after the expirement of every yeare, make a *stett* in his booke called the Journall, for entring any Debentures or other Payments into the same. **1588** J. MELLIS *Briefe Instruct.* B viij b, The parcels of the Iournall ought to bee written..in shorter sentence, without superfluous words, than be the parcels in ye Inuentory or Memorial. **1611** FLORIO, *Giornale*, a iournall or day-booke, such as Shop-keepers vse. **1622** MALYNES *Anc. Law-Merch.* 363 The Iournall he [the Spaniard] calleth Manuall,..and vnto this they keepe a Borrador or Memorial, wherein all things are first entred, and may vpon occasion be blotted, altered, or (by error) be miscast, or not well entred. **1760** JOHNSON *Idler* No. 95 ¶9 He made two mistakes in the first bill,..and dated all his entries in the journal in a wrong month. **1836** *Penny Cycl.* V. 164/2 He..posts to their credit the several sums which he finds in the journal, carefully stating in his ledger the page in the journal where the entry came from, and in the journal the folio of the ledger where the entry is gone to. **1882** BITHELL *Counting-Ho. Dict.* 162 The journal is..one of the principal books, in contradistinction to those which are auxiliary or accessory.

4. A daily record of events or occurrences kept for private or official use. **a.** A record of events or matters of personal interest kept by any one for his own use, in which entries are made day by day, or as the events occur. (In quots. 1670, 1781, a single day's record.) Now usually implying something more elaborate than a *diary*.

1610 HOLLAND *Camden's Brit.* I. 18 Cæsar hath in his Iournels or Day-books [*in ephemeridibus*] written [etc.]. **1670** DRYDEN *1st Pt. Conq. Granada* III. i, Good heaven, thy book of fate before me lay, But to tear out the journal of this day. **1781** COWPER *Conversat.* 276 An extract of his diary—no more, A tasteless journal of the day before. **1825** SCOTT *Jrnl.* 20 Nov., I have all my life regretted that I did not keep a regular Journal. **1855** MACAULAY *Jrnl.* 10 Jan., I am getting out of the habit of keeping my journal.

b. A register of daily transactions kept by a public body or an association; *spec.* in pl. ***Journals***, the record of the daily proceedings in one or other of the Houses of Parliament, kept by the Clerk of the House.

1647 CLARENDON *Hist. Reb.* I. §7 Having carefully perused the Journals of both Houses. **1769** BURKE *Late St. Nat.* Wks. II. 51 We find by an account of the Journals of the house of commons in the following session, that [etc.]. **1775** J. ADAMS in *Fam. Lett.* (1876) 127, I hope the Journal of the Session will be published soon. **1817** *Parl. Deb.* 374 The Speaker's Reprimand was ordered to be entered on the Journals.

c. *Naut.* A daily register of the ship's course, the distance traversed, the winds and weather, etc.; a log or log-book.

1671 R. BOHUN *Wind* 77 What I could not..collect from many reviews of our Seamens Journals. **1706** PHILLIPS, *Journal*..in *Navigation*, a Book in which a particular Account is kept of the Ship's Way, the Changes of the Wind, and other remarkable Occurrences. **1769** FALCONER *Dict. Marine* (1789) Y b, In all sea-journals, the day..terminates at noon. **1867** SMYTH *Sailor's Word-bk.*, *Journal*, synonymous at sea with *log-book*.

d. *Mining.* A record of the strata passed through in drilling a bore-hole or sinking a shaft.

†**5.** A record of public events or of a series of public transactions, noted down as they occur day by day or at successive dates, without historical discussion. Also in *pl. Obs.*

1565 COOPER *Thesaurus* s.v. *Commentarius, Diurni commentarij*, a iournall, conteynyng thynges for euery daye. **1617** MORYSON *Itin.* II. 84 That his Lordship purposed to imploy me in the writing of the History or Journall of Irish affaires. **1651** N. BACON *Disc. Govt. Eng.* II. xxviii. (1739) 130 Nor [are] they good Historians, that will tell you the bare Journal of Action, without the Series of Occasion. **1687** RYCAUT *Contn. Knolles' Hist. Turks* II. 95 Memoirs, Giornals, or Historical Observations of their Times.

6. A daily newspaper or other publication; hence, by extension, Any periodical publication containing news or dealing with matters of current interest in any particular sphere. Now often called specifically a *public journal*.

1728 POPE *Dunc.* I. 42 Hence Journals, Medleys, Merc'ries, Magazines. **1785** CRABBE *Newspaper* 170 Our weekly journals o'er the land abound. **1791–1823** D'ISRAELI *Cur. Lit., Lit. Jrnls.*, The Monthly Review, the venerable (now the deceased) mother of our journals, commenced in 1749. **1800** *Med. Jrnl.* III. 107 To the Editors of the Medical and Physical Journal. *Ibid.*, To merit insertion in your very useful Journal. **1865** *Sat. Rev.* 7 Jan. 15/2 The opinion of this journal has been already more than once expressed on the subject. **1890** *Spectator* 21 June 875 The personalities and weedy gossip of the Society journals.

II. Other senses.

†**7.** A day's travel; a journey. *Obs.*

1617 MORYSON *Itin.* II. 272 The Lord Deputy..in his journall towards Cilkenny Knighted three Irish men. **1633** B. JONSON *Underwoods* xciii, Now sun looke, And..tell In all thy age of journals thou hast tooke, Saw thou that paire became these rites so well?

†**8.** Provision for a journey. (In quot., the viaticum.) *Obs.*

1629 R. HILL *Pathw. Piety, Communic. Instr.* 35 If any departed without receiuing this journall, he was not to be interred in Christian Buriall.

9. As much land as can be ploughed in a day. Properly the Fr. word *journal* (ʒurnal), a land-measure varying in different departments.

1656 BLOUNT *Glossogr.*, *Journal*,..as much land as a Team of Oxen can plough up in one day. **1792** A. YOUNG *Trav. France* 305 From Calais to Bolougne and Montreuil the good land lets at 24 liv. the journal or arpent of Paris. **1882** *Contemp. Rev.* Jan. 13 The hiring price of land was from 45 to 50 francs a journal for the best.

10. in *Machinery.* The part of a shaft or axle which rests on the bearings. (Sometimes erroneously identified with 'bearing'.)

Originally used in a more restricted application: 'It was proposed by Buchanan, in his *Treatise on Millwork*, to apply the word *gudgeon* only to the bearing part at the end of a shaft or axle, which is exposed to bending action alone, and not to twisting action; and *journal* to an intermediate bearing part through which a twisting moment is or may be exerted; but the custom of using the word "journal" in both senses indiscriminately is so prevalent, that it is impracticable to carry out Buchanan's suggestion'. (Rankine *Machinery & Millwork* (1869) III. iii. §460.) [*Journal* or *journey* in this sense appears to have arisen in the Scotch workshops. No explanation of its origin has been found.]

1814 R. BUCHANAN *Shafts of Mills* 24 *note*, *Journals*, or *journeys*, are gudgeons subject to torsion. **1823** —— *Millwork* 145 In the case of the small pinion..a much greater stress would be thrown on the journeys (or journals) of the shaft. **1848** CRAIG, *Journal*, in Mechanics, that portion of a shaft which revolves on a support situated between the power applied and the resistance. **1851** *Illustr. Catal. Gt. Exhib.* 247 The lower chamber of the axle-box, which contains the journal and bearing, is cast in one piece. **1860** C. D. ABEL *Constr. Machin.* 75 The bearing or journal should always be placed as near as possible to the gearing. *Ibid.* 78 For upright shafts the diameter of the bottom journal which has to carry the weight of the shaft and gearing should be determined by the amount of pressure [etc.]. **1881** *Design & Work* 24 Dec. 449/2 Those parts of a shaft which revolve or work in these blocks are known indifferently as necks, bearings, gudgeons, and journals. **1894** *Harper's Mag.* Apr. 662 The oilers moved here and there,..feeling and examining every journal, rod, and crank.

III. 11. *Comb.* **a.** General combinations, as ***journal-wise*** adv. (adj.).

1741 RICHARDSON *Pamela* (1824) I. 54 Having written it [the account] journal-wise, to amuse and employ her time. **1742** *Ibid.* III. 415 At last I end my Journal-wise Letters as I may call them. **1839** R. M. M'CHEYNE in *Mem.* iv. (1872) 104, I would have written journalwise.

b. Special combinations: in senses 2 and 4: **journal-letter**, a letter written as a diary; (cf. sense 11 a, quot. 1742); in sense 3 (Book-keeping): **journal-entry**, a formal entry in the journal; in sense 10: **journal-bearing**, the support of a shaft or axle; **journal-box**, the box or structure enclosing the journal and its bearings; **journal-brass**, a journal-bearing of brass, also of white metal, etc.; **journal-packing**, any mass of fibrous material saturated with oil or grease, and inserted in a journal-box to lubricate the journal.

1875 KNIGHT *Dict. Mech.* 1219/2 The circular system of anti-friction wheels for a *journal-bearing is described in Tate's English patent, 1802. *Ibid.*, A journal-bearing for a vertical shaft with journal box, in one piece. **1864** WEBSTER, **Journal-box*. **1874** RAYMOND *Statist. Mines & Mining* 497 Each journal-box of the friction rollers is held in position by adjusting-screws, by which it can be moved horizontally to or from the center line of the machine. **1888** *Scribner's Mag.* 183/1 The other end is supported in a journal-box out of view on the other side of the machine. **1836** *Penny Cycl.* V. 165/2 If..the *journal entries already given are properly posted into a ledger. **1756** J. HANWAY *Jrnl. Eight Days Journey from Portsmouth* III. 9 You see I have begun my *Journal Letters, with the solemnity of a dedication. **1869** L. M. ALCOTT *Little Women* II. x. 141, I shall keep a journal-letter, and send it once a week. **1906** *Daily Chron.* 26 Oct. 3/3 Fanny's journal-letters to her dear 'Daddy Crisp'..are delightful and vivid effusions. **1964** *Listener* 17 Dec. 983/2 Sir Edward Marsh's long journal-letters..reveal that he was often silly.

journal (ˈdʒɜːnəl), *v.* [f. JOURNAL *sb.*] Chiefly in pa. pple. **journaled**.

1. *trans.* To record in a journal.

1803 J. KENNY *Society* 107 Oft o'er the journal'd tale she cast her eye. **1892** *Idler* May 461 His journaled impressions of America.

2. In *Machinery.* To provide with or fix as a journal: see JOURNAL *sb.* 10.

1875 KNIGHT *Dict. Mech.* 986/1 The grains..are placed..in a glazing-barrell; this is journaled at the ends, and is caused to rotate for some ten or twelve hours. **1881** *Metal World* No. 12. 178 Plates in which pivots or small shafts are journaled as in clock work.

†ˈ**journalary**, *a. Obs. rare.* [f. JOURNAL + -ARY.] Of or belonging to each day; occurring or dealt with day by day.

c **1740** WARBURTON *Serm.* I *John* iv. 20 Hence the origin of friendship,..which, while we are advancing towards..a Whole, teacheth us by the way all our journalary duties to particulars. **1762** —— *Doctr. Grace* II. ix, [As] Mr. Wesley hath amply shewn in the journalary history of his adventures.

ˈ**journal-book.** [f. JOURNAL *a.* + BOOK *sb.*, after F. *livre journal*, OF. *papier journal*, but the first element is now felt as JOURNAL *sb.*, as if the sense were 'book containing, or consisting of, a journal'.] A day-book of any kind; a diary of events; a book containing daily records.

1603 FLORIO *Montaigne* II. xviii. (1897) IV. 184 So are the Jornal bookes [F. *papiers journaux*] of Alexander the great..greatly to be desired. **1659** RUSHW. *Hist. Coll.* I. 54 His Majesty did this present day..*manu sua propria* take the said Protestation out of the Journal-book of the Clerk of the Commons House of Parliament. **1682** GREW *Anat. Plants* Pref., Of this, entry was made in their [the Royal Society's] Journal Book. **1726** SWIFT *Gulliver* I. ii, My comb and silver snuff-box, my handkerchief and journal-book. **1807** *Edin. Rev.* IX. 305 Every traveller carries a Journal-book as regularly as a portmanteau.

journalese (dʒɜːnəˈliːz). *colloq.* [f. JOURNAL *sb.* + -ESE.] The style of language supposed to be characteristic of public journals; 'newspaper' or 'penny-a-liner's' English.

1882 *Pall Mall G.* 6 Apr. 2/1 Translated from 'Journalese' into plain English. **1893** *Athenæum* 30 Dec. 901 It is sad..to find [him] guilty of such journalese as 'transpired'. **1893** R. KIPLING *Many Invent.* 166, I..refrained from putting any journalese into it.

†ˈ**journalet** *Obs.* *rare*$^{-1}$. [f. as prec. + -ET^{1}.] A little journal.

1776 T. TWINING in *Country Clergyman 18th Cent.* (1882) 41 Next in my little journalet stands our expedition to Ealand.

‖**journalier** (ʒurnalje), *a.* and *sb. rare.* [F. *journalier* daily, a day-labourer, f. *journal* JOURNAL.]

†**A.** *adj.* Of newspapers: Published daily. *Obs.*

1714 E. LEWIS *Let. to Harley* 7 May in *Dk. Portland's Papers* (Hist. MSS. Comm.) V. 436 Since you left us we have several new journalier papers, viz., the 'Reader', the 'Monitor', the 'Patriot', and the 'Muscovite'.

B. *sb.*

1. (? dʒɜːnəˈlɪə(r)), A newspaper writer, a journalist. (Not in F.)

1712 SWIFT *Pub. Spirit Whigs* Wks. 1738 VI. 46 This Writer is reported to be what the French call a Journalier. **1883** *Hartford Courant* (U.S.) June, The statement made by a Broadway travelling commission firm to a journalier.

2. A day-labourer.

1891 G. MEREDITH *One of our Conq.* xxxi, A tight-packed [third class] carriage of us poor journaliers would not have obstructed them with as much as a sneer.

ˈ**journalish,** *a.* *rare*$^{-1}$. [f. JOURNAL *sb.* + -ISH^{1}.] Of the character of a journal.

1712 SWIFT *Jrnl. Stella* 8 Feb., I never saw such a letter..so saucy, so journalish.

journalism (ˈdʒɜːnəlɪz(ə)m). [a. F. *journalisme* (1781 in Hatz.-Darm.), f. *journal* JOURNAL: see -ISM.]

1. The occupation or profession of a journalist; journalistic writing; the public journals collectively.

1833 *Westm. Rev.* Jan. 195 (Reviewing a French work '*Du Journalisme*') 'Journalism' is a good name for the thing meant..A word was sadly wanted. *Ibid.* 196 The power of journalism is acknowledged..to be enormous in France. **1837** CARLYLE *Fr. Rev.* II. I. iv, Great is Journalism. Is not every Able Editor a Ruler of the World, being a persuader of it? **1880** G. MEREDITH *Tragic Com.* (1881) 112 Journalism for money is Egyptian bondage. No slavery is comparable to the chains of hired journalism. *a* **1881** CARLYLE in *Westm. Gaz.* (1894) 26 Feb. 7/1 [He [L. Stephen] remembered Carlyle..saying to a young man who told him that he wrote for the papers,] 'Journalism is just ditchwater'. **1887** M. ARNOLD in *19th Cent.* May 638 We have had opportunities of observing a new journalism which a clever and energetic man has lately invented. **1891** *Pall Mall G.* 11 Sept. 6/1 It was Matthew Arnold who christened the 'New Journalism' (that much abused and much misapplied name) and identified it with Mr. Stead.

b. With *a* and *pl.* A piece of 'journalese'.

1893 *Pall Mall G.* 30 Jan. 7/1 A rather pleasant Indian novel, which would be better without some cheap journalisms.

2. The keeping of a journal; the practice of journalizing. *rare*$^{-0}$.

1848 CRAIG, *Journalism*, the keeping of a journal.

journalist (ˈdʒɜːnəlɪst). [f. JOURNAL *sb.* + -IST. Cf. F. *journaliste* (Dict. Acad. 1718).]

1. One who earns his living by editing or writing for a public journal or journals.

1693 *Humours Town* 78 Epistle-Writer, or Jurnalists, Mercurists. **1710** TOLAND *Refl. Sacheverell* 16 They [the Tories] have one Lesley for their Journalist in London, who for Seven or Eight Years past did, three Times a Week, Publish Rebellion. **1812** L. HUNT in *Examiner* 31 Aug. 545/1 The congratulations of friends and brother-journalists. **1898** *Times* 18 Oct. 13/5 The writer is a 'newspaper woman'—which is, she tells us, 'the preferred American substitute for the more polite English term "lady journalist"'.

attrib. **1881** SAINTSBURY *Dryden* v. 103 As we should put it in these days, he [Dryden] had the journalist spirit.

2. One who journalizes or keeps a journal.

1712 ADDISON *Spect.* No. 323 ¶2 My following correspondent..is such a Journalist as I require... Her

Journal..is only the picture of a Life filled with a fashionable kind of Gaiety and Laziness. **1775** MICKLE *Dissert. Lusiad* App. (R.), The force..is thus..described by Hernan Lopez de Castaneda, a contemporary writer, and careful journalist of facts. **1828** WEBSTER, *Journalist*, the writer of a journal or diary. **1848** in CRAIG; and in mod. Dicts.

journalistic (dʒɜːnəˈlɪstɪk), *a.* (*sb.*) [f. prec. + -IC.]

1. Of or pertaining to journalists or journalism; connected or associated with journalism.

1829 CARLYLE *Misc., Germ. Playwrights* I. 297 The journalistic office seems quite natural to him. **1879** GEO. ELIOT *Theo. Such* ii. 42 Journalistic guides of the popular mind. **1882** C. PEBODY *Eng. Journalism* xii. 87 The old habits of the journalist, the old journalistic way of looking at public questions..still distinguish his speeches.

2. Addicted to journalism. *rare.*

1833 *Westm. Rev.* Jan. 195 'The Frenchman', he [a French writer] again remarks, 'is beyond all others journalistic'. *Ibid.* England may be maintained to be as 'journalistic' as any part of the globe.

B. as *sb.* in *pl.* ***journalistics***, matters pertaining to journalism; the practice of journalism. *nonce-use.*

18.. CARLYLE (L.), It is a well-known fact in journalistics that a man may not only live but support wife and children by his labours in this line, years after the brain..has been completely abstracted.

journaˈlistically, *adv.* [f. prec. + -AL^1 + -LY^2.] In a journalistic manner; in the matter of public journals or journalism; by means or through the medium of public journals.

1870 *Even. Standard* 26 Oct., Certainly the aggregate of articles in this journalistically barren land has been unprecedented. **1891** *Pall Mall G.* 9 Oct. 6/3 The Quakers are waking up journalistically. **1894** *Athenæum* 21 July 97/1 To establish a 'Court of Honour' in matters journalistically professional.

ˈjournalizable, *a. rare.* [f. next + -ABLE.] Fit to be journalized.

1858 HAWTHORNE *Fr. & It. Jrnls.* II. 717 Few things journalizable have happened during the last month.

journalize (ˈdʒɜːnəlaɪz), *v.* [See -IZE.]

1. *trans.* To enter in a journal or book for daily accounts; *spec.* in *Book-keeping*, to make a journal entry in which the Dr. and Cr. accounts are specified, in order to its being posted to the proper accounts in the ledger.

1766 W. GORDON *Gen. Counting-ho.* 17 To journalize the inventory. **1786** W. LARKINS *Let.* in *Burke's Wks.* XIV. 225 He requested me to form the account of his receipts and disbursements, which you will find journalised in..the Honourable Company's general books of the year 1781–2. **1816** *Gentl. Mag.* LXXXVI. I. 345 A Waste-book..in which transactions are hastily entered, until more leisurely journalised in a proper form. **1849** FREESE *Comm. Class-bk.* 101 From the books above specified, the accounts are organised in the Journal, or as it is termed, journalised; and thence posted into the Ledger.

2. To enter, record, or describe in or as in a private journal.

1775 J. JEKYLL *Corr.* 29 July (1894) ii. 39 A little tour I had made for a week, and which I shall journalise after I have thanked you. **1777** JOHNSON *Let. to Mrs. Thrale* 29 Sept., He [Boswell] kept his journal very diligently; but then what was there to journalize? **1844** P. HARWOOD *Hist. Irish Rebell.* 61 *note*, He journalises the following note of a conversation. **1860** HAWTHORNE *Fr. & It. Jrnls.* II. 303, I would gladly journalize some of my proceedings, and describe things and people.

3. *intr.* To make entries in or keep a journal. (In first quot., to write letters in journal form.)

1774 MAD. D'ARBLAY *Early Diary* Sept. (1889) I. 312 Willingly..do I comply with your request of journalizing to you during my stay at this place. **1843** HAWTHORNE *Amer. Note-bks.* (1883) 334 After dinner, I..began to journalize. **1856** KANE *Arct. Expl.* I. xix. 239, I have too much to attend to in my weak state to journalize.

4. To engage in journalism; to do the work of a journalist.

1864 *Realm* 13 Apr. 3 A writer who is also an actor in politics..is a healthier man than the journalist who journalises *in sæcula sæculorum*.

Hence **ˈjournalizing** *vbl. sb.* and *ppl. a.* Also **ˈjournalizer**, one who journalizes.

1796 LAMB *Lett.* (1888) I. 25 To-day's portion of my journalising epistle has been very dull. **1818** LADY MORGAN *Autobiog.* (1859) 9 Journalising is a dangerous temptation to the garrulity of women. **1836** *Penny Cycl.* V. 164/1 The act of digesting these original entries is called Journalizing, because they are collected together in a book called The Journal. **1837** LOCKHART *Scott* Nov. an. 1825, Though not a regular journalizer, he kept a brief diary.

†**ˈjournally**, *adv. Obs.* [f. JOURNAL *a.* + -LY^2.] Every day; daily, diurnally.

1553 LYNDESAY *Dial. Exper. & Courteour* 372 All men begynnis for tyll de The day of thare Natiuitie;..journelly thay do proceid, Tyll Atrops cut the fatell threid. **1592** BURGHLEY *Let.* in *Unton's Corr.* (Roxb.) 281 To repeate your advertisements unto us..verie perticularly and journallie.

[**journ-chopper**, a blundered representation of *yern-chopper*, yarn-dealer, in Cowell; reproduced more and more corruptly in succeeding law dictionaries down to Wharton's, 1883, as **journey-chopper**, **journey-hopper**. See YARN-CHOPPER.]

journey (ˈdʒɜːnɪ), *sb.* Forms: 3–5 iurn-, 3–7 iorn-, iourn-, (5 iowrn-, iern-); 3, 6 -eie, 3–6 -e, -ay, 3–7 -ey, 4–7 -ee, 5–7 -y, -eye, 6 -aye, 6–7 -ie; 7 jorney(e, journee, -y, 7– journey. [a. OF. *jornee* (12th c.), *journee*, F. *journée* day, day's space, day's travel, work, employment, etc. (in OF. also travel, a conference, etc.) = Pr., Sp., Pg. *jornada*, It. *giornata*:—pop.L. **diurnāta*, f. *diurnum* day, sb. use of neut. of *diurnus* of the day, daily, f. *dies* day. For the suffix *-ata*, *-ada*, *-ee*, *-ey*, see -ADE. OF. *journee* corresponded in various senses with med.L. *diēta*; hence *journey* and DIET *sb.*^{2} agree in some of their senses.]

I. †**1. a.** A day. *Obs.*

c **1305** in *Rel. Ant.* II. 178 Thi dawes beth i-told, thi jurneis beth i-cast. *c* **1400** MAUNDEV. (1839) xxiii. 254 All the cytees..senden hym riche presentes so þat at þat iourneye [F. *celle jurne*] he schall haue more þan lx chariottes charged with gold and syluer. **1422** tr. *Secreta Secret., Priv. Priv.* 155 The thyrde dyshonoure was, that euery man myght..myssayne the Prynce for that Iorney. **1656** BLOUNT *Glossogr.*, *Journee*, a day or whole day.

†**b.** *Law.* ***journeys accounts*** (med.L. *diētæ computātæ* 'days counted'), the number of days (usually fifteen) after the abatement of a writ within which a new writ might be obtained. *Obs.*

1613 SIR H. FINCH *Law* (1636) 364 The writ abating for some cause that cannot be imputed to the Plaintifes folly:..himselfe bringing another with speed in the same Court against the same partie, we call it a writ purchased by Iourneys accompts. **1641** *Termes de la Ley* 191 b, If it be purchased by Iournies accounts (that is to say, within as little time as hee possibly can after the abatement of the first Writ)..And fifteen dayes have been held a convenient time for the purchase of the new Writ. **1883** *Wharton's Law Lex.*, *Journey's accounts*, the shortest possible time between an abatement of one writ and the issuing of another.

†**c.** An appointed day; in phr. ***to give*** (***assign***) ***journey of battle, treaty***, to agree to or fix on a day for battle or negotiation. (Cf. OF. *mettre journée*.) (This has associations with senses 7 and 8.) *Obs.*

c **1500** *Melusine* 80, I gyue you iourney of batayll at the requeste of the knight straunger on suche day that he shall assigne. *Ibid.* 291 They had Counseyll that they shuld requyre king Vryan iourney of traytye vpon fourme of peas..And the iourney was assygned by thaccorde of bothe partes on the iii^{de} day.

II. 2. A day's travel; the distance travelled in a day or a specified number of days.

†**a.** *simply.* An ordinary day's travel, the distance usually travelled in a day. As a measure of distance, varying with the mode of travel, etc.; usually estimated in the Middle Ages at 20 miles.

c **1250** *Gen. & Ex.* 1291 Fro Bersabe iurnes two Was ðat land ðat he bed him to [*MS.* two]. *c* **1290** *S. Eng. Leg.* I. 41/234 þis holie Man ladde þene dede forth..Fyftene Iorneies grete are day..To þe mount of Ioie. *a* **1300** *Cursor M.* 9192 (Cott.) Þe tune o niniue, þat was of vmgang thre iorne [*Gött.* jornays thrie]. *c* **1330** R. BRUNNE *Chron.* (1810) 154 Tancrez was fulle hend, conueied him tuo journez. *c* **1400** MAUNDEV. (1839) xvii. 178 A 52 jorneyes fro this Lond..there is another Lond..that men clepen Lamary. *a* **1533** LD. BERNERS *Huon* xxi. 63 The most surest way is hense a .xl. iurneys, & the other is but .xv. iurneys.

b. With qualification: ***a*** (or ***one***) ***day's journey*** = a.; ***two, three*** (etc.) ***days' journey***, the distance travelled in the number of days specified.

c **1340** *Cursor M.* 11741 (Trin.) Of þritti dayes Iourney þro þou shal haue but a day to go. *c* **1400** MAUNDEV. (Roxb.) v. 15 Fra Beruch three day iourneez es þe cytee of Sardyne. **1422** tr. *Secreta Secret., Priv. Priv.* 200 God sente the prophete Ionas to the grete Cite of Nynyvee, wyche was a thre-dayen Iornay. **1560** J. DAUS tr. *Sleidane's Comm.* 188 b, Trent is..thre dayes Iorney on this syde Venise. **1698** FRYER *Acc. E. India & P.* 231 A whole Day's Journy. *Ibid.* 261 Sending at least Twelve Days Journy for their Fuel. **1841** LANE *Arab. Nts.* I. 102 The King said to him, How many days' journey distant?

†**c.** The portion of a march or expedition actually done in one day, or accomplished each day; a stage of a journey. *Obs.* or merged in 3.

c **1489** CAXTON *Sonnes of Aymon* vii. 156 They dyde soo moche by there iourneys that they cam to saynt Iames in Galyce. *a* **1548** HALL *Chron., Hen. VI* 177 They set forward the King, and by easy iorneys brought him to London. **1617** MORYSON *Itin.* To Rdr. ¶5 For the First Part of this Worke, it containes onely a briefe narration of daily journies. **1759** JOHNSON *Rasselas* xxxvii, We travelled onward by short journeys.

d. The daily course of the sun through the heavens. (Now taken as *fig* from 3.)

1613 PURCHAS *Pilgrimage* (1614) 464 The Sunne, in his daily journey round about this vast Globe. **1667** MILTON *P.L.* v. 559 Scarce the Sun Hath finisht half his journey. **1694** PRIOR *Hymn to Sun* 3 As thou dost thy radiant journies run. **1719** WATTS *Ps.* LXXII. II, Jesus shall reign where'er the sun Does his successive journies run.

3. a. A 'spell' or continued course of going or travelling, having its beginning and end in place or time, and thus viewed as a distinct whole; a march, ride, drive, or combination of these or other modes of progression to a certain more or less distant place, or extending over a certain distance or space of time; an excursion or expedition to some distance; a round of travel. Usually applied to land-travel, or travel mainly by land, in contradistinction to a *voyage* by sea.

The normal word for this in English, often qualified by an adj., or phrase, as a *long, short, quick, slow, good, bad, cold, dangerous, difficult, easy, interesting, pleasant, prosperous, successful, tedious, uncomfortable journey*; a *j. by railway, railway j., j. on foot; j. to London, to the continent, into the country*, etc. Phrases: ***to make*** or ***undertake a j.***; ***to take one's j.***, to set out and proceed on one's way.

a **1225** [see b]. *c* **1375** *Leg. Rood* (1871) 123 When he was þus cumen hame ogayn, Of his iorne he was ful fayne. *c* **1380** *Sir Ferumb.* 4029 To morwe let ous our iorne take, Hamward aȝen to ryde. **1382** WYCLIF *Acts* ix. 3 Whanne he made iourney, it bifel, that he cam nyȝ to Damaske. **1503** HAWES *Examp. Virt.* IX. vii, So forth I went walkynge my iournay. **1526** TINDALE *Luke* xv. 13 Not longe after the yonger sonne..toke his iorney into a farre countre. *a* **1533** LD. BERNERS *Huon* cvii. 360 Within a shorte tyme they had sayled a great iourney. *a* **1548** HALL *Chron., Edw. IV* 223 Kyng Edwarde..made a iorney into Kente. **1617** MORYSON *Itin.* III. 151 And at parting..they wish him a happy journey. **1649** SIR E. NICHOLAS in *N. Papers* (Camden) 149 When you arrive att your jorneyes end. **1667** TEMPLE *Let. to Sir J. Temple* Wks. 1731 II. 42 My Sister took a very strong Fancy to a Journey into Holland. **1713** STEELE *Guard.* No. 8 ¶4 Being tired..with so many long and tedious journies. **1763** HUME in Calderwood *Life* viii. (1898) 139 A journey to Glasgow will be one of the first I shall undertake. **1841** LANE *Arab. Nts.* I. 89 When he had made his journey, and accomplished his business. **1888** RUSKIN *Præterita* I. vi. 188 On longer days of journey we started at six.

b. *fig.*, esp. the 'pilgrimage' or passage through life.

a **1225** *Ancr. R.* 352 Þe pilegrim iðe worldes weie..monie þinges muwen letten him of his jurneie. *c* **1400** *Rom. Rose* 4993 Where Elde abit, I wol thee telle..If Deth in youthe thee not slo, Of this iourney thou maist not faile. **1533** MORE *Debell. Salem* ii. Wks. 934/2 That murmur and discencion against the clergy was than already farre gone onwarde in hys vnhappye iurney. **1535** COVERDALE *Ps.* ci[i]. 23 He hath brought downe my strength in my iourney. **1672** GREW *Idea Philos. Hist. Pl.* §3 If we consider how long and gradual a Journey the Knowledge of Nature is. **1768–74** TUCKER *Lt. Nat.* (1834) II. 645 This life..is a journey, or rather one stage of our journey through matter. **1844** DICKENS *Mart. Chuz.* (Househ. ed.) 375/1 We used to toast a quicker journey to the old man, and a swift inheritance to the young one.

†**c.** *transf.* Any course taken or direction followed; *spec.* (in making a mine), the line along which the gallery is carried. *Obs.*

1571 DIGGES *Pantom.* I. xxxv. L iij b, You may make by the former preceptes moste certeine plattes of your iorneis. **1591** *Ibid.* (ed. 2) xxxvi, Finde out the true distance of the place whither you meane to carrie the mine:..how many degrees from the East, Weast, or other principal Quarters of the Heauens the iourney lyeth. **1578** BANISTER *Hist. Man* I. 32 The beginning and iourney of yᵉ greatest nerue.

d. *dial.* The load or amount carried at one journey: cf. GANG *sb.*^{1} 7.

1859 *Jrnl. R. Agric. Soc.* XX. II. 314, I can..in a few hours have a journey of corn ready for market.

e. The travelling of a vehicle along a certain route between two fixed points and at a stated time.

1851 *Illustr. London News* 25 Oct. 526/1 If they..obtained ..12 passengers at 2d. each per journey, the profit would be 19s. 3d. per diem. **1878** *Porcupine* XX. 507/2 The conductor ..shouts, 'Journey's end.' **1908** *Daily Chron.* 4 Jan. 1/7 London Motor Bus Strike... The company is determined to insist on the journey system of payment. **1909** *Westm. Gaz.* 8 Sept. 2/1 The journey-time to Glasgow is 8¾ h. **1954** *Gloss. Highway Engin. Terms* (*B.S.I.*) 55 *Journey time*, the overall time taken to travel between two specified points on a route, excluding the times of any stoppages other than those due to interruptions of traffic.

†**4.** A military expedition, a campaign, etc. Sometimes, Any military enterprise, as a siege. *Obs.*

c **1380** WYCLIF *Sel. Wks.* III. 349 Þis laste journe þat Englishemen maden into Flandres. **1417** in Ellis *Orig. Lett.* Ser. II. I. 56 Your saide Lifetenaunte..made many greate jernies and hostinges uppon one of the strongest Irishe enimies of Leynstre. *a* **1548** HALL *Chron., Hen. VI* 101 b, Thei lefte that iourney for a tyme, and returned to the Castle ..and besieged the same. **1601** R. JOHNSON *Kingd. & Commw.* (1603) 62 The Spanish king never enterprised anie sole iourney against the Turke. **1617** MORYSON *Itin.* II. 49 Other Deputies used to make some two or three iournies in a Summer against the rebels.

III. A day's work.

5. A day's labour; hence, a certain fixed amount of daily labour; a daily spell or turn of work (see quots.). *Obs.* exc. *dial.* † ***in journey***, at work as a day-labourer (*obs.*).

a **1300** *Cursor M.* 5870 (Gött.) Fra þat time nedis had þ ai, Do tua iorneys apon a day. **1393** LANGL. *P. Pl.* C. XVII. 5 When here deuer is don and his daies iourne, þen may men wite what he is worþ. **1502** *Ord. Crysten Men* (W. de W. 1506) IV. xxx. 349 They that holdeth werkemen in Iourney. *a* **1548** HALL *Chron., Hen. VI* 97 Ordinaunces..against the excessive taking of Masons..and other laborers for their daily iorneis. **1552** HULOET, Iourney with cattell at cartynge, plowynge, *opera*. **1706** PHILLIPS, *Journey*..Among Farmers a Days Work, in ploughing, sowing, reaping, etc. **1875** *Sussex Gloss.*, *Journey*, a day's work. **1881** *I. Wight Gloss.*, *Journey*, a day's work at plough.

fig. **1387** TREVISA *Higden* (Rolls) VII. 29 For þat nyȝtes iornay sche axede fredom for here mede.

†**6.** A day's doings or business. Hence, generally, Business, affair. *to wish one a good*

journey, to wish one well through a business. *Obs.*

a **1352** MINOT *Poems* iii. 9 Thare he made his mone playne ..And all that land, untill this day, Fars the better for that jornay. *c* **1400** MAUNDEV. (Roxb.) xxiv. 113 In þe meen tyme þe Grete Caan died; and forþi þe iournee chaunged efter to þe werse. *c* **1435** *Torr. Portugal* 2579 Euer we will be at youre will, What iurney ye will put us tyll. *c* **1475** *Partenay* 141 Do it at your owne lesire; For all the labour and iornay is your. **1672** W. MOUNTAGU in *Buccleuch MSS.* (Hist. MSS. Comm.) I. 317 The trial..stands appointed for the 2nd of May; so wish your Lordship a good journey.

†**7.** *esp.* A day's performance in fighting; a battle, a fight; = DAY 10. ***to keep the journey***, to keep the field, to continue the fight. *Obs.*

c **1330** R. BRUNNE *Chron.* (1810) 18 Adelwolf his fader saued at þat ilk iorne. **1375** BARBOUR *Bruce* XIII. 323 He did mony a fair Iourne, On sarisenis thre derenȝeis did he. *c* **1440** LONELICH *Grail* xiv. 75 A wondirful knyht..That Al this day hath kept the Iorrne Aȝ en thy fowre batailles. **1455** *Paston Lett.* I. 336 Alle the Lordes that dyed at the jorney arn beryed at Seynt Albones. *c* **1500** *Melusine* 231 Lordes, barons, auaunce, the iourney is oure, For they may not vs escape. *a* **1548** HALL *Chron.*, *5 Hen. VIII* (1809) 550 The Frenchmen call this battaile the iourney of Spurres because they ranne away so fast on horsbacke. **1601** HOLLAND *Pliny* I. 171 What crowne could haue bin gained and woon at the iourney of Cannæ. **1617** MORYSON *Itin.* II. I. ii. 84 The Rebels lost in this iourney above 800.

†**8.** A meeting held on an appointed day, *esp.* for public business; = DIET *sb.*[2] 5. *Obs.*

c **1500** *Melusine* 291 Thenne came to the iourney of traytye that was assigned the saudants and theire Counseyll. **1529** J. HACKET *Let. to Wolsey* (*Cott. Galba MS. B.* ix. 157). Som prolongassion of [the] iourne of Spirs. **1586** T. B. *La Primaud. Fr. Acad.* I. 632 They hold their generall councell, called a iourney or a diet.

9. A round or turn of work, such as is done at one time, in a day or a shorter space.

a. At the *Royal Mint.* (*a*) The coinage of a certain weight of gold or silver, orig. representing the amount of one day's work: viz. 180.0321 Troy ounces of gold (701 sovereigns or 1402 half-sovereigns), or 720 oz. of silver. (*b*) The parts of the surfaces of a pair of rolls used to roll fillets down to the thickness of the coin required; supposed to have been so called because after a day's work it is necessary to select another portion of the surface owing to wear.

a **1600** *Harl. MS.* 698 lf. 157 Of every iournie of silver contayning xxx lb. wt. tooe peaces [shall be taken]. *Ibid.* lf. 169 Certaine pec's of ev'ry iorny that was coyned the same moneth. **1789** *Chron.* in *Ann. Reg.* 230 The pix is a box kept at the Mint into which one piece of every journey is put. A journey is the technical term for the coinage of a certain weight of gold. **1852** A. RYLAND *Assay Gold & S.* 83 *note*, The Trial of the Pix is an important and ceremonious proceeding... Several coins are taken at random from a certain weight, called a journey, and are assayed by the jury. **1867** *Chamb. Jrnl.* No. 38. 105 Every distinct melting or coinage is technically called a *journey*;..or rather the entire coining at one time is made up into journeys, each of one hundred and eighty ounces, or fifteen pounds of standard gold.

b. *Glass-making.* A round of work in the course of which a certain quantity of raw material is converted into glass.

1875 *Ure's Dict. Arts* II. 652 This waste is first of all calcined..from 24 to 30 hours being the period of a journey ..in which the materials could be melted and worked into bottles. **1886** *Leeds Merc.* 28 Sept., If all things were favourable a man could make 57 dozens of bottles on 'a journey', as it was called, in seven hours.

c. *slang.* A turn of work; a 'turn'; a time or occasion.

1884 *Longm. Mag.* V. 179 'Well', said the policeman..'as for him, he's got safe enough off, this journey!'

†**10.** *Machinery.* **a.** = JOURNAL *sb.* 10. **b.** See quot. 1833. *Obs.*

1814–1823 [see JOURNAL *sb.* 10]. **1833** J. HOLLAND *Manuf. Metal* II. 226 This carriage, with the forms of types properly secured upon it, is adapted to move backwards and forwards upon steady guides or journeys.

c. A set of trams in a colliery.

1883 W. S. GRESLEY *Gloss. Terms Coal Mining* 144 *Journey*, a train or set of trams all coupled together running upon an engine plane. **1896** MRS. H. WARD *Sir G. Tressady* xxiv. 553 The 'journey' of trucks..was standing laden in the entrance of the mine. **1901** *Daily Chron.* 8 Nov. 11/3 He was caught by the 'journey' and killed. **1921** *Dict. Occup. Terms* (1927) §043 *Journey rider*,.. rides on trams or tubs on haulage planes. **1967** *Gloss. Mining Terms* (*B.S.I.*) x. 14 *Train* (*journey, set, trip*), a number of tubs or cars coupled together.

11. *attrib.* and *Comb.*, as ***journey-bee***, ***-guider***, ***-hack***, ***-milkman***, ***-speed***; †***journey-bated*** adj.; **journey-book**, an itinerary or road-book; **journey-money**, travelling expenses; **journey-pride** *dial.*, excitement or alarm occasioned by the prospect of travelling; so **journey-proud** *a.*; **journey-ring**, a kind of ring-dial or portable sun-dial; **journey-weight** = sense 9 a. Also JOURNEYMAN, etc.

1596 SHAKS. *1 Hen. IV*, IV. iii. 26 So are the Horses of the Enemie In generall *iourney bated, and brought low. **1714** MANDEVILLE *Fab. Bees* (1725) I. 16 Their clergy, rouz'd from laziness, Laid not their charge on *journey-bees. **1610** HOLLAND *Camden's Brit.* I. 358 Mentioned by Antonine the Emperour in *Journey-booke. **1890** BOLDREWOOD *Col. Reformer* (1891) 327 As good a stock horse and *journey hack as ever you crossed. **1891** T. HARDY *Tess* (1900) 43/1 His *journey-milkmen being more or less casually hired. **1883** —— in *Longm. Mag.* July 266 The carter gets what is called *journey-money, that is, a small sum, mostly a shilling, for every journey taken beyond the bounds of the farm. **1899** R. KIPLING *Stalky* 186 Here's your journey-money. Good-bye. **1914** 'I. HAY' *Lighter Side School Life* iv. 95 You've been a long time getting your journey-money. **1936** 'R. HYDE' *Check to your King* vii. 84 Vigneti is parcelled off to Guadeloupe, supplied by his Sovereign Chief with a thousand francs journey-money. **1960** G. E. EVANS *Horse in Furrow* v. 69 Wagoners and horsemen on long journeys..even where they had adequate journey-money,..often preferred to sleep out. **1938** *Times* 21 Dec. 10/4 '*Journey-pride'..will be familiar to your west-country readers. The adjective is still more useful, for 'feeling-upset-physically-and-mentally-with-anticipatory-excitement-and/or-anxiety' can all be expressed by 'journey-proud'. **1902** *Eng. Dial. Dict.*, **Journey-proud*, excited like children, at the prospect of a journey. **1908** *Daily Chron.* 5 Nov. 4/7 In Cheshire,..a village good-wife, describing her farm-labourer husband's first visit to Manchester, declared that he was 'that journey-proud that he couldn't eat a bite o' breakfast'. **1956** *Sunday Times* 3 June 2/6 The lengthy German phrase for holiday anxiety... People who suffered from it used to be described in Yorkshire..as being journey proud. **1877** W. JONES *Finger-ring* 452 A brass ring-dial, probably of the kind formerly designated as '*journey rings'. **1888** *Pall Mall G.* 4 Aug. 1/2 This gives a mere gross '*journey-speed', i.e. speed including stops. **1883** *Encycl. Brit.* XVI. 483/2 The finished coins are delivered to the mint master in weights called '*journey weights', supposed to be the weight of coin which could be manufactured in a day when the operations of coining were performed by the hand. [Abolished 1901.]

journey ('dʒɜːnɪ), *v.* Forms: 4–6 iorn-, 4–7 iourn-; 4–7 -ey, -ay, 5–6 -ie; 7–8 journy, 7– journey. [a. AF. *journey-er*, OF. *jo(u)rnoyer*, *-ier*, *-éer* to travel, to put off (a person), etc., f. *journee*, *jornee* JOURNEY *sb.*]

I. 1. *intr.* To make or proceed on a journey; to travel.

c **1330** R. BRUNNE *Chron. Wace* (Rolls) 14071 He iorneyed þen fro land to land. *a* **1400–50** *Alexander* 2249 A gentilman full ioyles þen iornays hym after. *c* **1470** *Golagros & Gaw.* 230 Thus iournait gentilly thyr cheualrouse knichtis. *c* **1470** HENRY *Wallace* VIII. 976 Quhen Wallace thus throw ȝorkschyr jowrnat was. **1539** BIBLE (Great) *Acts* ix. 3 And when he iorneyed..he was come nye to Damasco. **1667** MILTON *P.L.* IV. 173 Satan had journied on, pensive and slow. **1813** COLERIDGE *Remorse* II. ii. 77 Think'st thou I journied hither To sport with thee? **1894** J. T. FOWLER *Adamnan* Introd. 54 He..journeyed south and settled at Clonmacnoise.

fig. **1526** *Pilgr. Perf.* (W. de W. 1531) 251 b, Yᵉ heuenly Ierusalem to the whiche we iourney. *a* **1568** ASCHAM *Scholem.* II. (Arb.) 129, I would haue a good student passe and iorney through all authors.

†**b.** To travel by ordinary daily stages: cf. JOURNEY *sb.* 2 c. *Obs.*

1756 MRS. CALDERWOOD *Jrnl.* (1884) 4 Finding that journying was too little exercise, we took post horses in our own chaise at Belfoord.

†**c.** ***to journey it***: to make the journey. *Obs.*

c **1680** W. MOUNTAGU in *Buccleuch MSS.*, *Montagu Ho.* (Hist. MSS. Comm.) I. 333 After that time it will be too late to journey it.

2. *trans.* To travel, traverse. ? *Obs.*

1531 ELYOT *Gov.* I. xi, Realmes, cities, sees, ryuers, and mountaynes, that..can nat be iournaide and pursued. **1720** GAY *Poems* (1745) II. 151 When..the pale moon had journey'd half the skies. **1808** SCOTT *Marm.* VI. vi, In a palmer's weeds arrayed..I journeyed many a land.

†**3.** To take (a horse) through a journey; to ride or drive. *Obs.*

1590 MARLOWE *2nd Pt. Tamburl.* III. v, You shall have bits, And harness'd like my horses, draw my coach... I shall have occasion shortly to journey you. **1607** TOPSELL *Four-f. Beasts* (1658) 318 'The Pains'..breedeth in the pasterns for lack of clean keeping and good rubbing after the horse hath been journyed.

†**4.** *intr.* To engage in a battle. *Obs.*

c **1475** *Rauf Coilȝear* 485 Haue he grace to the gre in ilk Iornaying.

5. *trans.* (*Royal Mint.*) To weigh or count coins into 'journeys': see JOURNEY *sb.* 9 a.

II. †**6.** *Sc. trans.* To remand (a person) for justice, or put off (a matter in litigation) to another day; to adjourn. Cf. JORN *v. Obs.*

1478 *Acta Audit.* (1839) 75/2 Þai war lauchfully Journait to the ferd court before hir bailȝe. **1493** *Acta Dom. Conc.* (1839) 302/1 James lord of abernethy..protestit It sulde turne him to na preiudice quhill he wer ordourly Journayit. **1609** SKENE *Reg. Maj.* 106 Quhatsomever parte be journeyed in quhatsomeuer Court, and the Baillie of that Court assignes ane certaine day and steid to them, for to receaue fulfilling of judgement, or dome be them asked.

Hence **'journeyed** *ppl. a.*, travelled; **'journeying** *ppl. a.*

1553 T. WILSON *Rhet.* (1580) 164 Some far iourneyed gentleman at their retourne home..will ponder their talke with oversea langage. **1739** G. OGLE *Gualtherus & Griselda* 21 A Fairer, not the journeying Sun surveys. **1847** EMERSON *Poems, Sphinx* 29 The journeying atoms..Firmly draw, firmly drive, By their animate poles.

journey-cake: see JOHNNY-CAKE.

journey-chopper, -hopper: see JOURN-CHOPPER.

journeyer ('dʒɜːnɪə(r)). [f. JOURNEY *v.* + -ER[1]. With *iourneor* in first quot. cf. OF. *journeor* a day-labourer.] One who journeys, a traveller.

1566 PAINTER *Pal Pleas.* I. Pref. 11 Which..the iourneors on horsback [may use] for a chariot or lesse painful meane of trauaile. **1647** LILLY *Chr. Astrol.* lii. 370 Note, the ascendant is for the Journier. **1655** DIGGES *Compl. Ambass.* 262 So is the Journeyer slain by the Robber. **1855** CHAMIER *My Travels* III. x. 219 The most entertaining journeyer along the high-road of life I ever knew.

journeying ('dʒɜːnɪɪŋ), *vbl. sb.* [f. JOURNEY *v.* + -ING[1].] The action of the vb. JOURNEY; travelling; †engagement in a battle (*obs.*).

c **1330** *Arth. & Merl.* 3515 No lete thai neuer jornaying, Til thai com to Ban the king. *c* **1475** [see JOURNEY *v.* 4]. **1526** TINDALE *2 Cor.* xi. 26 In iorneyinge [**1611** -ings] often. **1611** BIBLE *Num.* x. 28 Thus were the iourneyings of the children of Israel, according to their armies. **1780** COWPER *Lett.*, *to J. Hill* Wks. 1837 XV. 61 A time of year when journeying is not very agreeable.

attrib. **1890** BOLDREWOOD *Col. Reformer* (1891) 70 A good journeying pace.

journeyman ('dʒɜːnɪmən). [f. JOURNEY *sb.* 5 + MAN.]

1. One who, having served his apprenticeship to a handicraft or trade, is qualified to work at it for days' wages; a mechanic who has served his apprenticeship or learned a trade or handicraft, and works at it not on his own account but as the servant or employee of another; a qualified mechanic or artisan who works for another. Distinguished on one side from *apprentice*, on the other from *master*.

1463–4 *Rolls Parlt.* V. 506/2 Aswell householders as journeymen, Servauntes and Apprenticez. **1481** in *Eng. Gilds* (1870) 332 If any of the Jornaymen of the saide crafte be electe Warden. **1550** *Disc. Common Weal Eng.* 56 To give my Iorney men ijᵈ a daye more. **1608** *Vestry Bks.* (Surtees) 214 No younge man, journamen nor prentice. **1758** JOHNSON *Idler* No. 26 ¶8 My mistress..rose early in the morning to set the journeymen to work. **1849** MACAULAY *Hist. Eng.* viii. II 274 The government appears to have had no hold on such a man, except the hold which master bakers and master tailors have on their journeymen. **1863** W. G. BLAIKIE *Better Days Work. People* ii. (1864) 81 The journeyman tyrannises over the apprentice.

2. *fig.* (chiefly depreciatory): **a.** One who is not a 'master' of his trade or business. **b.** One who drudges for another; a hireling, one hired to do work for another.

a **1548** HALL *Chron.*, *Hen. V* 54 b, Every iorneiman of their faction..put all their..diligence to avance forward their sect and part. **1588** *Marprel. Epist.* (Arb.) 30 Nonresidents with their iourneimen the hedge priests. **1602** SHAKS. *Ham.* III. ii. 37, I haue thought some of Natures Iouerney-men had made men, and not made them well. *a* **1670** HACKET *Abp. Williams* I. (1692) 20 He attended at them..and acted in them *vivâ voce*, and did not put off the work to journey-men. **1705** HICKERINGILL *Priest-cr.* II. vi. 62 A Lord being too Great to Pray to God himself, when he keeps a Journey-man or Chaplain to do that drudgery for him. **1762–71** H. WALPOLE *Vertue's Anecd. Paint.* (1786) IV. 237 The colouring was worse..than that of the most errant journey-men to the profession. **1817** (May) *Title of Print*, A Master Parson and his Journeyman.

3. *Astron.* More fully, ***journeyman clock***: a secondary clock in an observatory, used generally as an intermediary in the comparison of standard clocks.

1764 MASKELYNE in *Phil. Trans.* LIV. 373, I fixed up a little clock there, which may be called a journeyman or secondary clock, having a pendulum swinging seconds. **1787** SMEATON *ibid.* LXXVII. 330 *note*, The journeyman clock was generally set to the transit clock on Sunday mornings... The journeyman will generally agree with the transit clock to 2″ in 24 hours. **1890** J. SERVICE *Sk. Jas. Dunlop* in *Thir Notandums* 162 The journeyman employed was compared with a sidereal clock.

b. = *impulse dial* (IMPULSE *sb.* 6 b).

1904 GOODCHILD & TWENEY *Technol. & Sci. Dict.* 384/1 *Master clock*, the timepiece controlling and actuating by electricity a series of dial works, or 'journeymen', at different points in the circuit. **1923** [see *impulse clock* (IMPULSE *sb.* 6 b)]. **1938** J. W. PLAYER *Britten's Watch & Clock Maker's Handbk.* (ed. 14) 159 Secondary clocks, sometimes called impulse clocks, dial works, or journeyman clocks, are simple constructions.

4. *attrib.* and *Comb.*, as ***journeyman tailor***, ***work***; ***journeyman-like*** adj. and adv.

1467 in *Eng. Gilds* (1870) 407 Alle jorneymen straungers comynge to the seid cite. **1615** J. STEPHENS *Satyr. Ess.* 424 Journy-man-like hee trauailes from place to place, seeking to be set on worke before he hath learnt his trade. **1657** R. LIGON *Barbadoes* (1673) 109 You may hire poor Journy-men Taylors, here in the City. **1764** *Low Life* (ed. 3) 29 Journeymen Clergymen putting on their best Bands and Cassocks. **1825** COBBETT *Rur. Rides* (1885) II. 97 A journeyman parson comes and works in three or four churches of a Sunday. **1864** M. ARNOLD in *Cornh. Mag.* Aug. 172 To raise the standard amongst us for what I have called the journeyman-work of literature.

'journey,woman. *rare.* [f. as prec.] A woman working at a trade for daily wages.

1732 FIELDING *Miser* I. ii. No journeywoman sempstress is half so much a slave as I am. **1843** C. ELIZABETH *Wrongs Wom.* I. 99 The journeywomen..receive very poor wages.

journey-work ('dʒɜːnɪwɜːk). [f. JOURNEY *sb.* 5 + WORK.]

1. Work done for daily wages or for hire; the work of a journeyman.

1601 SIR W. CORNWALLIS *Ess.* II. l N n v b, The next.. worke iorney worke..and trust themselues onely to their hire. **1712** ARBUTHNOT *John Bull* III. iv, When she could not get bread for her family, she was forced to hire them out at journey work to her neighbours. **1768–74** TUCKER *Lt. Nat.*

(1834) II. 489 He may better qualify himself to act as a master, by doing journeywork in the interim.

2. *fig.* (chiefly depreciatory). Work delegated to a subordinate or done for hire; servile, inferior, or inefficient work; hackwork.

1614 T. ADAMS *Devil's Banquet* 55 Machiauell will no longer worke Iourney-worke with the Deuill, he will now cut out the garment of damnation himselfe. **1714** SWIFT *Corr.* Wks. 1841 II. 514 They would not give the dragon [Lord Oxford] the least quarter, excepting only a pension, if he will work journeywork by the quarter. **1859** GEN. P. THOMPSON *Audi Alt.* II. lxxxix. 64 Fancy decent and reverend men set to such a job of journey-work by virtue of their offices. **1880** SWINBURNE *Stud. Shaks.* App. (ed. 2) 235 The swift impatient journeywork of a rough and ready hand.

So **'journey-,worker, journey-,workman**, a journeyman.

1755 *Phil. Trans.* XLIX. 172 Servants, journey-workmen, and young people, that are to push into life. **1886** T. HARDY *Woodlanders* iv, Besides the itinerant journey-workers there were also present [etc.].

jous(e, jousy, obs. forms of JUICE, JUICY.

joust (dʒaʊst, formerly dʒuːst), **just** (dʒʌst), *sb.* Forms: 3-4 ioust, 7- joust; 4-7 iust, 7- just, (6-9 giust). [a. OF. *juste, joste, jouste*, F. *joute*, f. *juster*, etc. JOUST *v.* For the spelling and pronunciation, see JOUST, JUST, *v.*]

1. A combat in which two knights or men-at-arms on horseback encountered each other with lances; *spec.* a combat of this kind for exercise or sport; a tilt. Usually in pl. *jousts, justs*, a series of such encounters, as a spectacular display; a tournament.

1297 R. GLOUC. (Rolls) 2898 Vor þer nas so god kniȝt non ..þat in ioustes ssolde sitte þe dunt of is lance. *c* **1320** *Sir Beues* (A.) 3785 And to þe iustes þai gonne ride. *c* **1380** WYCLIF *Wks.* (1880) 10 Whanne lordis ben fro hom in werris, in iustis. *a* **1533** LD. BERNERS *Huon* xxi. 62, I was a yonge knyght and hauntyd the iustes and tornoys. **1590** SPENSER *F.Q.* I. i. 1 For knightly giusts and fierce encounters fitt. **1593** SHAKS. *Rich. II*, v. ii. 52 What newes from Oxford? Hold those Iusts and Triumphs? **1635** J. HAYWARD tr. *Biondi's Banish'd Virg.* 192 Right joyfull..to light on by the way so solemne jousts. **1645** EVELYN *Diary* 2 May, There had been in the morning a Just and Tournament of severall young gentlemen. **1709** STRYPE *Ann. Ref.* I. xv. 191 Great justs were made: the French King himself justing. **1755** JOHNSON, *Just*, mock encounter on horseback; tilt; tournament. *Joust* is more proper. **1776** MICKLE tr. *Camoens' Lusiad* 330 At just and tournay with the tilted lance. **1801** STRUTT *Sports & Past.* III. i. 113 The just was a separate trial of skill, when only one man was opposed to another. **1808** SCOTT *Marm.* I. xiv, Seldom hath pass'd a week but giust Or feat of arms befel. **1830** JAMES *Darnley* xxi. 93 Just after just, tourney after tourney. **1838** PRESCOTT *Ferd. & Is.* (1846) III. xi. 44 The knights..defied one another to jousts and tourneys. **1859** TENNYSON *Enid* 537 Down to the meadow where the jousts were held.

fig. **1598** SYLVESTER *Du Bartas* II. ii. III. *Colonies* 553 Less powrfull in the Paphian Ioust For Propagation. **1846** H. ROGERS *Ess.* I. iv. 203 He entered the lists in those intellectual jousts, as they may be called.

†**b.** *pl.* as *sing.* A tournament. *Obs.*

1377 LANGL. *P. Pl.* B. XVII. 50 Coming fro..Ierico To a iustes in iherusalem. *a* **1512** FABYAN *Chron.* VII. 687 Chief chalengeour, at a royall iustyce and turney. **1568** GRAFTON *Chron.* II. 303 The king did holde a royall Iustes in Smithfielde in London. **1593** PEELE *Order Garter* 44 As if the God of war Had held a justs in honour of his love. **1641-74** BAKER *Chron.* an. 1400, They would publish a solemn Justs to be holden at Oxford.

†**2.** Applied to the ancient Grecian games. *Obs.*

1387 TREVISA *Higden* (Rolls) I. 37 Olympades, þat beeþ þe tymes of here iustis and tornementis. **1388** WYCLIF *2 Macc.* iv. 18 Whanne iustus, doon oonys in fyue ȝeer, was maad solempli in Tire.

joust (dʒaʊst, formerly dʒuːst), **just** (dʒʌst), *v.* Forms: 3-7 iust(e, 4-7 ioust(e, (5 youst, yust, iowst, iost, 6 iuyst), 7- just, joust. [a. OF. *juste-r* (11th c.), *joster* (12th c.), *jouster* (13th c.) = Pr. *justar, jostar*, Sp., Pg. *justar*, It. *giostrare*:—late pop.L. *juxtāre* to approach, come together, meet, f. *juxtā* near together. The sense 'approach, join', remained in OF.

The historical Eng. spelling from the 13th c. is *just*: cf. the cognate *adjust*:—L. *adjuxtāre*. Under later French influence, *joust* was used sometimes by Gower, Caxton, Spenser, and Milton, was preferred by Johnson, and used by Scott, and is now more frequent; but the pronunciation remained as in the historical spelling; the pronunciation (dʒaʊst) (formerly dʒuːst) is recent, and suggested by the spelling *joust*.]

†**1.** (?) To join, to ally oneself. *Obs. rare.*

c **1250** *Gen. & Ex.* 1589 Esau wifuede us to dere Quan he iusted & beð so mat, Toc of kin ðe canaan bi-gat.

†**2.** *intr.* To join battle, encounter, engage; *esp.* to fight on horseback as a knight or man-at-arms.

c **1300** *Cursor M.* 21910 (Edinb.) Mikil leuer war him to here Hu roland iuste [*Gött.* iusted], and oliuere. *c* **1330** R. BRUNNE *Chron. Wace* (Rolls) 4379 Knyghte iustede, archers drowe On boþe parties fol manie þey slowe. *c* **1380** *Sir Ferumb.* 105, I wil kuþe on hem my miȝt and dyngen hem al to douste Wheþer þay wille on fote fiȝt ouþer on horse iouste. *c* **1440** *Bone Flor.* 459 Fyfty of them issewed owte, For to juste in werre. **1667** MILTON *P.L.* I. 583 And all who since, Baptiz'd or Infidel Jousted in Aspramont or Montalban.

3. *spec.* To engage in a joust or tournament; to run at tilt with lances on horseback.

13.. *Guy Warw.* (A.) 872 Oȝaines sir Gij þer com Gayer, To iuste wiþ him he drouȝ him ner. *c* **1386** CHAUCER *Knt.'s T.* 1628 Al that Monday Iusten they and daunce. **1390** GOWER *Conf.* III. 63 To se..The lusti folk iouste and tourneie. **1485** CAXTON *Chas. Gt.* 41 Sende to Iuste ayenst me somme of thy barons. *c* **1489** —— *Sonnes of Aymon* i. 32 They Iousted moche worthyly but Reynawde iousted beste vpon his horse bayarde. *a* **1548** HALL *Chron., Hen. VIII* 85 The kyng..in his owne person Iusted to all comers. **1608** SHAKS. *Per.* II. i. 116 There are Princes and Knights come from all partes of the world to Iust and Turney for her loue. **1755** JOHNSON, *To joust* and *to just.* **1773-83** HOOLE *Orl. Fur.* XXVI. 524 Every chief..He call'd to joust, and dar'd them to the field. **1805** WORDSW. *Prelude* IX. 455 Methought I saw a pair of knights Joust underneath the trees. **1825** MACAULAY *Ess., Milton* (1851) I. 15 Knights, who vowed to joust without helmet or shield. **1868** FREEMAN *Norm. Conq.* II. viii. 261 Not justing with his lance as in a mimic tourney.

b. With adverbial accusative.

a **1661** FULLER *Worthies, Essex* (1662) 330 An Englishman challenged any of the French, to just a course or two on horse-back with him.

4. In various fig. applications. (In quot. 1639, To copulate.)

1377 LANGL. *P. Pl.* B. XX. 133 He iugged til a iustice and iusted in his ere, And ouertilte al his treathe. **1549** *Compl. Scot.* vi. 58 Lyik tua gait buckis iustand contrar vthirs. **1591** SYLVESTER *Du Bartas* I. i. 515 Auster and Boreas justing furiously Under hot Cancer. **1608** *Ibid.* II. iv. IV. *Schisme* 941 So fare these miners; whom I pittie must That their bright valour should so darkly joust. **1639** T. DE GREY *Compl. Horsem.* 51 His justing, howsoever without fruit,..is but once only in the whole course of his life. **1824** BYRON *Def. Transf.* I. ii, The lion and his tusky rebels..brought to joust In the arena.

joust, obs. form of JUST *sb.*², a pot.

jouster ('dʒaʊstə(r), formerly 'dʒuːstə(r)), **juster** ('dʒʌstə(r)). [a. AF. *justour* = OF. *justeor, justeur*, f. *juster* JOUST *v.*¹; for suffix, see -ER² 3.] One who jousts or fights on horseback with a spear, in battle or (esp. in later use) in tournament; a tilter; hence, †an antagonist.

c **1330** R. BRUNNE *Chron. Wace* (Rolls) 7657 Þey ar fighters and noble iustours. **13..** *K. Alis.* 3325 Iustere he is, with the beste, He can his launce thorugh threste. **14..** tr. *Secreta Secret., Priv. Priv.* 215 In the ryght hande of thyne enemys, the Swerde mene; In the lyfte hande, the Iusters wyth Speris. **1470-85** MALORY *Arthur* x. xvii, A passyng good knyȝt, and the best Iustar that euer I sawe. **1598** YONG *Diana* 491 Let him that hath prooued himselfe so weake a iuster, row in my place. **1820** SCOTT *Monast.* xxvii, No..plumed jouster of the tilt-yard. **1856** BOKER *Poems, Leonor de Guzman* III. i, Like two brave jousters at a course of spears.

†**b.** A horse for jousting; a charger. *Obs.*

13.. *K. Alis.* 1400 (Lincoln's Inn MS.) Seven and twenty hundredis asondre, Strong in felde, apon iusters..And fif hundred fot men, Y fynde. *Ibid.* 1867 The knyghtis redy on iusters. [MS. Laud Misc. 622 (a better text) reads *destrers* in both passages.]

jouster, hawker of fish: see JOWTER.

jousting ('dʒaʊstɪŋ, formerly 'dʒuːstɪŋ), **justing** ('dʒʌstɪŋ), *vbl. sb.* [f. JOUST *v.* + -ING¹.] The action of the verb JOUST; fighting or tilting on horseback with a lance; *spec.* a tournament.

13.. *Coer de L.* 252 The fyrste yere that he was kyng, At Salybury he made a iustynge. *c* **1400** MAUNDEV. iii. (1839) 17 A fair place for iustynges or for other Pleyes and Desportes. *c* **1440** LONELICH *Grail* lii. 635 Sire knyht, ȝoure Iostyng lost han ȝe. **1556** *Chron. Gr. Friars* (Camden) 8 The kynge made a gret justynge be syde Kyngstone uppon Temes. **1622** BACON *Hen. VII* 106 The King..kept Triumphes of Iusting and Tourney during all that Moneth. **1823** PRAED *Poems, Troubadour*, There was a jousting at Chichester. **1892** *Athenæum* 11 June 757/1 Major abhors the dangerous jousting with the spear.

fig. **1519** HORMAN *Vulg.* 103 In that erthquake, there was a great hurlyng and iustynge of one house ageynst an other.

b. *attrib.* and *Comb.*, as ***jousting-field, -horse, -place, -spear***.

1478 BOTONER *Itin.* (Nasmith 1778) 212 Via eundo..per le justyng-place ab antiquis diebus. **1485** CAXTON *Paris & V.* 7 He ordeyned a Ioustyng place wythin his cyte of Uyenne. **1530** PALSGR. 235/2 Justyngehorse, *cheual de jouste*. **1773-83** HOOLE *Orl. Fur.* XL. 461 With armour try'd, and swords of temper wrought And jousting spears. **1854** PATMORE *Angel in Ho.* XI. i, They made her face the jousting field Of joy and beautiful alarm.

†**joute, jowte.** *Obs.* Also 5 iouute, eowte, iute. [In form identical with OF. *joute* (*jote, jute*) vegetable, pot-herb (L. *olus*), later esp. beet; in med.L. *juta* (cf. *jutta* in Du Cange).] In *pl.*, Pot-herbs; usually, soup or pottage made chiefly of vegetables. (Cf. Sc. *kale*.)

1377 LANGL. *P. Pl.* B. v. 158, I was þe priouresses potagere ..And made hem ioutes of iangelynge. **1390** GOWER *Conf.* III. 162 To gadre some [herbs] In his gardin, of whiche his joutes He thoghte have. *c* **1400** MAUNDEV. viii. (1839) 58 Þei..lyuen porely & sympely, with ioutes & with Dates [Fr. *des ioutes et des dates*]. *c* **1440** *Anc. Cookery* in *Househ. Ord.* (1790) 426 Joutes on Flesh Day. Take cole, and borage, and lang de beeff, and parsell, and betes, and arage, and avence, and vyolet, and saveray, and fenelle, and sethe hom;..hewe hom smalle..put thereto gode brothe..and serve hit forthe. *c* **1440** *Promp. Parv.* 265/2 Iowtys, potage, *brassica,..juta*. **1513** *Bk. Keruynge* in *Babees Bk.* 274 Than serue potage, as wortes, Iowtes, or browes.

Jove ('dʒəʊv). [ad. L. *Jov-em* acc. (other oblique cases *Jovis, Jovi, Jove*) of OL. *Jovis*, for which in the classical period the compound *Juppiter*, *Jūpiter* (= *Jovis-pater*) was substituted; in It. *Giove*.]

1. a. A poetical equivalent of *Jupiter*, name of the highest deity of the ancient Romans: = JUPITER 1. **b.** Colloquially used in the asseveration ***by Jove***: cf. L. *pro Juppiter, pro Jovem*.

c **1374** CHAUCER *Troylus* III. 673 (722) Ioue ek for þe loue of faire Europe, The whiche in forme of bole a-way þow fette. **1599** SHAKS. *Hen. V*, II. iv. 100 Therefore in fierce Tempest is he comming, In Thunder and in Earth-quake, like a Ioue. **1672** WILKINS *Nat. Relig.* 51 Believing but one supreme Deity, the Father of all other subordinate powers: ..whom they called Jupiter or Jove, with plain reference to the Hebrew name Jehovah. **1738** POPE *Univ. Prayer* i, In ev'ry clime adored By saint, by savage, and by sage, Jehovah, Jove, or Lord! **1886** SIR T. MARTIN tr. *Faust* 120, I even upheaved the glorious seat of Jove.

b. **1575** R. B. *Appius & Virginia* in Hazl. *Dodsley* IV. 124 By Jove, master merchant..Would get but small argent, if I did not stand His very good master. **1588** SHAKS. *L.L.L.* v. ii. 495 By Ioue, I alwaies tooke three threes for nine. **1698** FARQUHAR *Love & Bottle* III. i, *Luc.* Did you ever see me before? *Roeb.* Never, by Jove. **1818** MISS FERRIER *Marriage* ix, 'Venus and the Graces, by Jove', exclaimed Sir Sampson. **1885** MISS BRADDON *Wyllard's Weird* I. i. 24 By Jove! here comes the Coroner.

c. In names of plants, as **Jove's beard** = JUPITER'S BEARD (*Treas. Bot.* 1866); **Jove's fruit**, a variety of wild Allspice or Feverbush (*Lindera melissæfolia*), growing in the southern United States (*ibid.*); **Jove's nut** (*dial.*), the acorn (Halliw. 1847-78).

2. The planet Jupiter (*poetic*). Hence (like *Jupiter*) **b.** *Her.* = Azure; **c.** *Alch.* Tin.

c **1374** CHAUCER *Troylus* III. 576 (625) Saturne and Ioue in Cancro Ioyned were. **1562** LEIGH *Armorie* (1597) 129 The Torse is by nature wreathed with pure colours of wise Ioue and Pale Luna, Manteled of the first. **1599** T. M[OUFET] *Silkwormes* 45 When Ioue they turne to Sol or Luna fine. **1732** POPE *Ess. Man* I. 42 Ask..Why Jove's satellites are less than Jove. **1784** COWPER *Tiroc.* 634 The moons of Jove, and Saturn's belted ball.

3. *Comb.*, as ***Jove begotten, -born, -like***, etc., adjs.

1613 HEYWOOD *Silv. Age* III. i. Wks. 1874 III. 123 Yet in her wombe the Ioue-bred Issue striues. **1634** MILTON *Comus* 676 Not that Nepenthes, which the wife of Thone In Egypt gave to Jove-born Helena. **1725** POPE *Odyss.* XXIV. 581 The Jove-descended Maid. **1774** *Epist. to Sir W. Chambers* Her. Postscr. 84 So when o'er Crane Court's philosophic gods The Jove-like majesty of Pringle nods. **1848** BUCKLEY *Homer's Iliad* 115 There Jove-beloved Hector entered.

†**jo'vencel.** *Obs.* [a. OF. *jovencel*, mod.F. *jouvenceau* = It. *giovincello*:—late L. **juvencellus* (cf. cl. L. *juvenculus*), dim. of *juvencus* young.] A young man, a youth.

c **1489** CAXTON *Blanchardyn* iii. 18 The Iouencel blanchardyn, Ioyful and gladde. **1490** —— *Eneydos* xxxvi. 124 One of the Iouencellys that thus dyde sporte hym selfe there.

[**joves.** Error for F. *joues* cheeks of a battery.

1883 WILHELM *Mil. Dict.*, *Joves* (Fr.), the two sides in the epaulment of a battery which form the embrasure are so called. [*Joves*, which is an error for F. *joues* (old-print spelling *IOVES*), is entered in *Century Dict.* (**1890**, citing *Wilhelm*) as an English word ('Origin not ascertained'). Hence in some later Dicts.]]

jovial ('dʒəʊvɪəl), *a.* [a. F. *jovial* (Rabelais, *a* 1553), ad. It. *gioviale* 'borne vnder the planet Ioue' (Florio, 1598), ad. L. *joviāl-is* of or pertaining to Jupiter, f. *Jovi-s*: see JOVE and -AL¹.]

†**1.** Of or pertaining to Jove; Jove-like, majestic.

1604 DRAYTON *Owl* 220 When this princely jovial fowl [the eagle] they saw. **1610** HEALEY *St. Aug. Citie of God* III. xxvii. (1620) 137 Merula the Iouiall Flamine cut his owne veines and so bled himselfe out of their danger. **1611** HEYWOOD *Gold. Age* III. Wks. 1874 III. 50 All that stand Sink in the weight of his high Iouiall hand.

2. Of or belonging to the planet Jupiter; also *absol.* as *sb.* An inhabitant of Jupiter.

1665 R. HOOKE *Microgr.* 240 The highest of Jupiter's Moons is between twenty and thirty Jovial Semidiameters distant from the Center of Jupiter. **1690** LEYBOURN *Curs. Math.* 450 b, Saturn..hath several..lesser Planets, like the Jovial Satellites. *a* **1734** NORTH *Lives, Guildford* (1826) II. 183 Applying Jovial observations to marine uses, for finding longitudes at sea. **1870** PROCTOR *Other Worlds* 122 There must be four moons visible above the horizon of the Jovials.

†**3.** *Her.* Azure in colour. *Obs.*

1610 HOLLAND *Camden's Brit.* I. 173 In Ioviall blew mantles, as a man would say in the colour of iust Iupiter.

†**4.** *Alchemy.* Of tin. *Obs.*

1694 SALMON *Bate's Dispens.* 337/1 This Jovial Bezoartick is one of the best Preparations that can be made of Tin.

†**5.** *Astrol.* Under the influence of, or having the qualities imparted by, the planet Jupiter, which as a natal planet was regarded as the source of joy and happiness. Also *absol.* as *sb.* *Obs.*

1590 SPENSER *F.Q.* II. xii. 51 Therewith the Heauens alwaies Iouiall, Lookte on them louely. **1605** TIMME *Quersit.* I. xi. 47 There are starres which haue their most colde and moyst spirites;..others hote and moyst, as the Iovialls. **1646** SIR T. BROWNE *Pseud. Ep.* (J.), The fixed stars are astrologically differenced by the planets, and are esteemed

martial or jovial, according to the colours whereby they answer these planets. **1656** CULPEPPER *Eng. Physic.* s.v. *Endive*, A fine cooling, clensing, jovial plant. **1656** STANLEY *Hist. Philos.* v. (1701) 207/1 According to that Star..the Aspect of one is Saturnine, of another Jovial, &c. in their looks were read the nature of their Souls. **1661** LOVELL *Hist. Anim. & Min.* Isagoge, The Joviall, are the Hart, bull, elephant, lamb and sheep. **1863** MISS SEWELL *Chr. Names* I. 363 The word *jovial* is an allusion to the supposed influence of the planet Jupiter.

6. Characterized by hearty mirth, humour, or good fellowship; merry, jolly; convivial.

1596 DRAYTON *Legends* iv. 223 As meerely Ioviall in my selfe was I. **1605** SHAKS. *Macb.* III. ii. 28 Be bright and Iouiall among your Guests to Night. **1631** R. BOLTON *Comf. Affl. Consc.* (1635) 293 The joviall, good-fellow-mirth of carnall men. **1685** DRYDEN *Misc.* II. Pref., Some of them [odes of Horace] are..jovial (or, if I may so call them) Bacchanalian. **1789** W. BUCHAN *Dom. Med.* (1790) 265, I have often known the quinsey prove fatal to jovial companions. **1833** I. TAYLOR *Fanat.* iv. 72 Men of the present age are..merry or jovial rather than joyous. **1898** H. CALDERWOOD *Hume* iii. 28 A jovial spirit characterised even literary gatherings.

†Hence **jovia'lissime**, *a. Obs.* [after L. or It. superlatives in *-issimus, issimo*], most jovial.

1652 URQUHART *Jewel* Wks. (1834) 231 The exuberant diversitie of his jovialissime entertainment.

†'jovialist. *Obs.* [f. prec. + -IST.]

1. A person born under the planet Jupiter.

1569 J. SANFORD tr. *Agrippa's Van. Artes* 50b, She pronounceth this man a Saturniste or Iouialist. **1589** WARNER *Alb. Eng.* (1597) 319 Aeneas, for personage the Iouilist, for wel-spoken the Mercurilist. **1647** LILLY *Chr. Astrol.* xv. 84 We must describe..a Jovialist, to be one of a comely stature [etc.]. **1653** R. SANDERS *Physiogn.* 151 So much for the Saturnines; now for the Jovialists.

2. A person of a jovial or convivial disposition.

1596 FITZ-GEFFRAY *Sir F. Drake* (1881) 31 What marvell then though some base humorists..Extenuate the work of Iovialists. **1650** A. B. *Mutat. Polemo* 25 The great mirth of the Jovialists. *a* **1656** BP. HALL *Satan's Fiery Darts quenched* III. v, Let the jovialists of the world drink wine in bowles, and feast themselves without feare.

3. A satellite of Jupiter. *rare.*

1664 POWER *Exp. Philos.* III. 163 What then must we think of the Secondary Planets, as the..four Jovialists?

4. *attrib.* or as *adj.* = JOVIAL.

1610 J. DAVIES *Commend. Poems* (1878) 5 There shall thy Iouialist Mechanicalls Attend this Table all in Scarlet Cappes.

jovialistic (dʒəʊvɪə'lɪstɪk), *a.* [f. as prec.: see -ISTIC.] = JOVIAL *a.* 5.

1883 *Wallenstein in Drama* in *Westm. Rev.*, The combination of saturnine and jovialistic influences promises greatness, but predicts danger.

joviality (dʒəʊvɪ'ælɪtɪ). [ad. F. *jovialité* (1624 in Hatz.-Darm.), f. *jovial*: see -ITY.] The quality of being jovial; hearty mirth, humour, or good-fellowship; jollity, festivity, conviviality.

1626 BERNARD *Isle of Man* (1627) 67 Where Iovialitie taketh his place, there joy will bid him welcome. **1788** H. WALPOLE *Remin.* i. 13 His majesty, fond of private joviality. **1846** WRIGHT *Ess. Mid. Ages* I. v. 183 A description of the jovialities of an English drinking party of the twelfth century. **1887** MISS BRADDON *Like & Unlike* i.

jovialize ('dʒəʊvɪəlaɪz), *v.* [f. JOVIAL *a.* + -IZE.]

1. *trans.* To make jovial; to cause to be jolly.

1614 C. BROOKE *Leg. Rich. III*, vii, Here I began to jouialize my spirit. **1780** MAD. D'ARBLAY *Diary* 5 June, A spirit, a gaiety, and an activity that jovialised us all. **1860** L. HUNT *Autobiog.* xxii. 391 Lamb, whose countenance, a little jovialized, he engrafted upon an active little body.

†**2.** *intr.* To be jovial, to make merry. *Obs.*

1634 BRERETON *Trav.* (Chetham Soc.) 51 At a great assembly, to feast and jovialize it. **1640** G. ABBOTT *Job Paraphr.* 134 No mens children lead merrier lives than theirs, dancing and joviallizing. *a* **1675** LIGHTFOOT *Rem.* (1700) 102 Their wicked inhabitants prospered and jovialized.

jovially ('dʒəʊvɪəlɪ), *adv.* Also 7 giovially. [-LY².] In a jovial manner; †under the influence of Jupiter; with jollity or hearty mirth.

1603 FLORIO *Montaigne* II. xii. (1634) 305 So are they more or lesse merrily and Giovially, or rudely and Saturnally incorporated. **1621** BURTON *Anat. Mel.* II. iii. III. (1676) 203/1 The rich man lives like Dives Iovially heere on Earth. **1632** BROME *North. Lasse* Ded., A Countrey Lass..that Minerva-like was a brayn-born Child, and Jovially begot. **1704** C. JOHNSON *Epil. Cory's Metamorphosis*, Let us but Jovially jog on together. **1861** DICKENS *Lett.* (ed. 2) II. 146 We dined together jovially. **1875** W. S. HAYWARD *Love agst. World* 44 'That's right', said the old squire, jovially.

jovialness ('dʒəʊvɪəlnɪs). [f. JOVIAL *a.* + -NESS.] Jovial quality, joviality.

1658 HEWYT *Serm.* 32 Swearing with such persons, is but a grace and lustre to their speech..drunkenness, jovialness, or good fellowship. **1764** in *Ann. Reg.* 173/1 By way of ridicule of their jovialness and hospitality, when a man was in liquor, they would call him *as drunk as a lord.*

jovialty ('dʒəʊvɪəltɪ). Now *rare.* [f. as prec. + -TY, shortened form of -ITY: cf. *regality, royalty.*] = JOVIALITY.

1621 H. FARLEY *St. Paule's Ch.*, Ride on, likewise, yee worthy knights, With jovialty and pleasure. **1685** BAXTER *Paraphr. N.T. 1 Peter* iv. 3 In the Bacchanals and Jovialties of their Idolatry. **1855** SINGLETON *Virgil* I. 259 (*Æn.* I. 635) The gifts and jovialty of the god.

Jovian ('dʒəʊvɪən), *a.* (*sb.*) [f. L. *Jovi-s* JOVE + -AN: cf. L. *Joviānus* as a personal name, and obs. F. *jovien* (Palsgr.).]

1. Of, belonging to, of the nature of Jove; Jove-like.

1530 PALSGR. 316/2 Jovyen of the nature of Jupiter, *Jouien.* **1599** MARSTON *Sco. Villanie* I. iii. 185 Nay, shall a trencher slaue..magnificate Lewde Iouian lust? **1822–56** DE QUINCEY *Confess.* (1862) 126 A splendid pluralist..would never stoop from his Jovian attitude. **1893** *Times* 5 Jan. 13/6 With Jovian recklessness he played with the artificial lightning which he generated. **1894** SIR E. SULLIVAN *Woman* 70 Helen..is the only woman to whom a Jovian parentage is allowed.

2. Of or belonging to the planet Jupiter.

1794 G. ADAMS *Nat. & Exp. Philos.* IV. xliii. App. 175 The Jovian system... The motion of Jupiter's four moons or satellites. **1867–77** G. F. CHAMBERS *Astron.* VIII. 769 Shadow of a Jovian satellite.

B. *sb.* One who resembles or imitates Jove.

1598 MARSTON *Pygmal.* v. 161 Would damned Iouians, be of all men praised, And with high honors vnto heauen raised?

Jovi'centric, *a. Astron.* Referred to Jupiter as a centre; viewed as from the centre of Jupiter.

1864 in WEBSTER. **1867–77** G. F. CHAMBERS *Astron.* Vocab. 917.

Jovinianist (dʒəʊ'vɪnɪənɪst). [f. med.L. *joviniānista*, f. *Joviniān-us* Jovinian: see -IST.] A follower or adherent of Jovinian, a Milanese monk in the end of the 4th century, who denied the virginity of Mary, opposed certain forms of celibacy and asceticism, and maintained the equality of all sins, rewards, and punishments. Also *attrib.*

1864 in WEBSTER. **1874** J. H. BLUNT *Dict. Sects* s.v., Augustine states that the Jovinianist heresy was quickly extinguished. **1882** J. LL. DAVIES in *Dict. Chr. Biog.* III. 465/2 It is..stated that the emperor [Theodosius] 'execrated' the impiety of the Jovinianists.

So **Jo'vinian** = prec.; **Jo'vinianish** *a.*

1585–7 T. ROGERS *39 Art.* (1607) 277 Being once baptized, we can no more be tempted, as thought the Jovinians. **1614** BP. HALL *No Peace with Rome* xiii, The monkes of Burdeaux ..haue vpbraided vs with the opinion of a certain stoicall and Iouinianish parity of sinnes.

jovisa(u)nce, variant of JOUISANCE.

†'jovy, *a. Obs.* [ad. L. *Jovi-us*, f. *Jovis* JOVE.] Jovial, merry.

1426 LYDG. *De Guil. Pilgr.* 11154 And now I lepe Iouy pe; Now I sterte, & now I ffle. **1610** B. JONSON *Alch.* v. v, Thou art a Iouy Boy! **1621** FLETCHER *Wild Goose Chase* III. i. Wks. (Rtldg.) 554/1 In those daies I thought I might be jovy. **1667** DRYDEN *Sir M. Mar-all* v. i, Let 'em come in, and we'll be jovy.

jow (dʒaʊ), *sb. Sc.* and *north. dial.* [app. a dialect form of JOWL *sb.*⁴ In south. Sc. and north. Eng. the diphthong is (ou), in central Sc. (ʌu); these are the dial. representatives of the standard Eng. (əʊl).]

1. A knock, push.

1790 MRS. WHEELER *Westmld. Dial.* i. 38 They gav her a jow an she fell oa my Knee.

2. *Sc.* A single stroke or pull in the ringing of a bell; the ringing, tolling, or sound of a bell.

17.. *Barbara Allen* vii, And ev'ry jow that the dead-bell gied, It cry'd woe to Barbara Allen. **1818** SCOTT *Br. Lamm.* xxiv, That's another jow of the bell to bid me be ready. **1833** CARLYLE *Let.* 18 Nov. in Froude *Life* II. xvi. 378 The jow of the old bell went far into my heart.

3. *Sc.* The dashing of a wave on the shore; the wave thus dashed; = JAW *sb.*²

1820 in *Edin. Mag.* May (Jam.), Wi' swash an' swow, the angry jow Cam lashan' doun the braes.

jow (dʒaʊ), *v. Sc.* and *north. dial.* [Cf. JOWL *v.*¹, to which this answers phonetically: see prec. It is not certain that the word is the same in all the senses.]

1. *trans.* To knock, strike (esp. the head).

1802 MRS. WHEELER *Westmld. Dial.* iii. (ed. 2) 94 Yee er sae knockd an jowd. **1863** *Lancash. Fents, New Shirt* 11 If aw wurt jow mi yed till aw seed blue leets flyin' eawt on't. **1882** in *Lanc. Gloss.* **1886** in *Chesh. Gloss.*

2. To ring or toll a bell, esp. without giving it a full swing (see quot. 1825). *Sc.*

1516 [see JOWING below]. *a* **1572** KNOX *Hist. Ref.* Wks. 1846 I. 46 He..caused immediatlie to jow the bell, and to give significatioun that he wald preach. **1816** SCOTT *Bl. Dwarf* ii, If ye'll just gar your servant jow out the great bell in the tower. **1825–80** JAMIESON s.v., Sometimes a bell is said to be jowed, when it receives only half the motion, so that the tongue is made to strike only on one side.

b. *intr.* Of a bell: To toll or ring. *Sc.*

1785 BURNS *Holy Fair* xxvi, Now Clinkumbell, wi' rattling tow Begins to jow and croon. **1824** SCOTT *Redgauntlet* x, There is the council bell clinking in earnest: and if I am not there before it jows in, Bailie Laurie will be trying some of his manœuvres. **1858** WHITTIER *From Perugia* xi, There! the bells jow and jangle the same blessed way That they did when they rang for Bartholomew's day.

3. *intr.* To move from side to side with a slow or rocking motion. *Sc.*

1816 SCOTT *Antiq.* xxvi, He kens weel eneugh wha..keeps a' tight thack and rape, when his coble is jowing awa in the Firth.

Hence **'jowing** *vbl. sb.* and *ppl. a.*

1516 *Council Rec. Edin.* (Jam.), That all maneir of persouns..compeir..to the said Presidentis, at jowyng of the common bell. **1813** SCOTT *Rob Roy* xiv, Yon's the curfew, as they ca' their jowing-in bell.

Jow, variant of JEW, JHOW.

jow(e, obs. forms of JAW.

jowaile, joweler, -re, etc., obs. ff. JEWEL, etc.

‖**jowar, jawar** (dʒaʊ'ɑː(r)). *E. Ind.* Also joar, jooar, juar. [Hindī *jawār.*] = next.

1800 *Asiatic Ann. Reg., Misc. Tr.* 289/2 In the Khereef they have a good deal of rice, also Jooar (*Holcus Sorghum*). **1884** *Health Exhib. Catal.* p. xliii, Samples of bajra and jowar. **1886** A. H. CHURCH *Food Grains Ind.* 85 Joār is one of the most important rainy-season crops of India. **1900** *Blackw. Mag.* May 640/2, I happened to be perched on a muchan in the middle of a jawar field.

‖**jowari, jawari** (dʒaʊ'ɑːriː). *E. Ind.* Also jawarri, jewary, -arree, jawaree, jowaree, -r(r)y, juarree, juwarree. [Hindī *jawārī.*] Indian millet, *Sorghum vulgare*, extensively cultivated in India. Also *attrib.*

1800 WELLINGTON in Gurw. *Desp.* (1837) I. 175 Jowarry, of which there is an abundance everywhere. **1801** *Ibid.* I. 359 Jowarry straw is the best kind of forage for horses and cattle. **1813** J. FORBES *Oriental Mem.* I. 194 The soil..produces juarree, bajeree, natchee, and some inferior grains. **1849** E. B. EASTWICK *Dry Leaves* 131 A vast plain, which..is clothed with a gigantic grain, the Jawári, or *Holcus sorgum.* **1858** R. HUNTER in Mitchell *Mem R. Nesbit* 405 The chief grain cultivated in the Deccan is jowaree or the great millet.

jowce, obs. form of JUICE.

jowder: see JOWTER.

†'jowel. *Obs.* Also 8 jewell. [Origin uncertain: cf. F. *jouelle* yoke, '*jouelles* arched, or yoaked vines; vines so vnderpropped, or fashioned that one may goe vnder the middle of them' (Cotgr.).] app. One of the piers or supporters of a wooden bridge. (See recent explanations in quots. 1788, 1828.)

1516 in *12th Rep. Hist. MSS. Comm.* App. VII. 6 To the ..bulding of new a brige of xxj jowelles adionyng the wallis of the forsaid Citie [Carlisle] standing over the river of Eden. *Ibid.*, Ther is bulded fyve jowelles and oon landstaple..tymber is right skant to be gotten in any parte within xx myles of the saide Citie. **1570** LEVINS *Manip.* 56/14 Iowels of a bridge, *columnæ.* **1745** *N. Riding Rec.* VIII. 252 The jewells or supporters of Whitby bridge are not wide enough for the ship to come through. **1788** W. MARSHALL *Yorksh.* II. Gloss. (E.D.S.), *Jewel*, the starling of a wooden bridge. **1828** *Craven Dial.*, *Jowel*, the space betwixt the piers of a bridge.

jower (dʒaʊə(r)), *v. dial.* and *local U.S.* Also jour, jowr. [? Onomatopœic.] *intr.* **a.** To growl; to scold; to mutter or grumble in an undertone. **b.** To use a boorish dialect with a growling sound. Hence **'jowering** *vbl. sb.* and *ppl. a.*

1628 R. HAYMAN *Quodlibets* II. 37 You may our cursings, swearing, iouring mend. **1724–42** DE FOE *Tour Gt. Brit.* (ed. 3) I. 303 As this Way of boorish Speech is in Ireland called the Brogue upon the Tongue, so here 'tis named Jouring... The Difference is not so much in the Orthography, as in the Tone and Accent; their abridging the Speech, *Cham*, for *I am*; *Chill*, for *I will*..and the like. **1746** *Exmoor Scolding* 26 (E.D.S.) Ya purting, tatchy, stertling, jowering, prinking, mincing Theng. **1821** SCOTT *Kenilw.* xx, [She] answered his petition..with a volley of vituperation, couched in what is there called the *jowring* dialect. **1879** MISS JACKSON *Shropsh. Word-bk.*, *Jour*, obsols., to mutter, or grumble in an undertone; generally used in the participial form—*jouring.* **1883** C. F. SMITH *Southernisms* in *Trans. Amer. Philol. Soc.* 50 *Jower* or *jour*, quite common in the South in the sense of persistent quarrelling or scolding. **1888** ELWORTHY *W. Som. Word-bk.*, *Jowering*, growling, grumbling.

jowk, obs. form of JOUK *v.*

jowl, jole (dʒəʊl, dʒaʊl), *sb.*¹ Forms: *α.* 1 ceafl, (? ceáfl), 3 cheafl, chefl, chæfl, (? chouel), 3–4 chauel, chavel, cheuel, chevel, 4 chawl, chaul, 4–5 chavyl(l, 4–7 chaule, 5 chawylle, 6 chall(e, 5–7 chawle; 9 *dial.* chole. *β.* 6 ioule, 7 jowle, joll, 9 jole, jowl. [OE. *ceafl* (? *ceáfl*), corresp. to OS. **kaƀal* (only in dat. pl. *kaflun*), mod.Flem. *kavel*, Du. *kevel* gum; cf. MHG. *kivel*, Ger. dial. *kiefel*, *kiffel* = *kiefe, kiefer* jaw, chap; a deriv. of an ablaut stem *kef-, kaf-*, whence also ON. *kjaptr* (Sw. *käft*, Sc. CHAFT, q.v.). The OE. *ceafl* regularly gave ME. *chavel*, whence *chauel, chawl.* The later *jowle, jowl, joul, joll, jole*, is not a regular development; even with change of *ch* to *j, chawl* would have given *jawl.* But these forms coincide with the *j* forms in JOWL² and ³, and they first appear late in the 16th c., contemporaneously with those of JOWL², from *cholle, chowle.* From that time onward the three words have run together in form, although in this word *ch* forms have come down dialectally to the present day.

The origin of the *j*, first in JOWL *sb.*³, and then in JOWL *sb.*¹ and ², is at present unaccounted for; there is no OF. or other Romanic word to the influence of which it can plausibly be referred. This, with the obscurity which attaches to the origin of JOWL *sb.*² and JOWL *sb.*³, and the fact that all are in

recent use levelled under the form *jowl*, makes the group a very puzzling one.]

1. A jawbone, a 'chaft'; a jaw; esp. the under jaw; *pl.* Jaws.

α. *a* **1000** *Whale* 59 in *Exeter Bk.*, Oð þæt se wi 'a ceafl ȝefylled byð. *c* **1000** ÆLFRIC *Hom.* I. 572 Ða leon.. ðærrihte mid grædiȝum ceaflum hi ealle totæron. *c* **1205** LAY. 6507 Þat deor to-dede his chæfles [*c* **1275** vndude his choules (? cheules)]. *Ibid.* 26056 Arður.. þen chin him of-swipte mid alle þan cheuele. *c* **1220** *Bestiary* 513 Ðis cete ðanne hise chaueles lukeð, Ðise fisses alle in sukeð. *a* **1300** *Cursor M.* 7510 (Cott.) Þair chauelis [*Gött.* chaulis; *Trin.* chaules] cleue in twa. *c* **1380** WYCLIF *Serm.* Sel. Wks. II. 169 Mannis soul mut have two chauelis, boþe þe over and þe neþere, and þes moten eete Cristis bodi. *Ibid.* 170 Þe over chawl. **1483** *Cath. Angl.* 60/2 A Chawylle (Chavylle; *vbi* A chafte). **1489** MARG. PASTON in *P. Lett.* III. 349 My lord.. had qwestyond John a Lowe of this fych.. and he answerd, as for the nedyr chavyll therof, he had put it in sewrte. **1523** FITZHERB. *Husb.* §75 The .ix. propertyes of an oxe... The fyfte [is] to be wyde betwene the challes. **1601** HOLLAND *Pliny* II. 326 If one take a tooth out of one of the chawles of a dead horse, it will ease his owne that aketh. **1614** MARKHAM *Cheap Husb.* I. i. 4 Let your hunting horse haue a large leane head, wide nostrils, open chauld, a big weasand. **1617** —— *Caval.* I. 28 His tusks worne close to his chaule. [**1861** E. WAUGH *Birtle Carter's T.* 23 Are yo noan flayed o' throwin' yo're choles off th' hinges?]

β. **1598** SYLVESTER *Du Bartas* II. i. IV. *Handie-crafts* 410 [Of a horse] a lean bare bonny face, Thin joule, and head. **1658** SIR T. BROWNE *Gard. Cyrus* iii, That prominent jowle of the Spermaceti whale. **1699** FARQUHAR *Love & Bottle* III. i, It has made my Jolls rhime in my head. **1808** J. BARLOW *Columb.* I. 73 The Dragon dips his fiery-foaming jole. **1828** SCOTT *Jrnl.* 2 Feb., My portrait is like, but I think too broad about the jowls. **1892** BESANT *Ivory Gate* (1893) 268 His mouth was too large and his jowl too heavy.

b. *transf.* A toothed projection from the front of a cart, used for reaping the ears of corn (an ancient reaping machine).

c **1420** *Pallad. on Husb.* VII. 34 A squared carre on whelis too they make.. His chaule aforn, that shal ete vp the whete, Is not right high.. That iowe is toothed thicke as the mesure Of eres wol not passe hem vpward bende.

†**2.** Idle or malicious talk; = JAW *sb.*[1] 6. ***to lead chawle***, to give mouth. *Obs.*

a **1225** *Ancr. R.* 72 Þet heo [our thoughts].. ne uallen aduneward, & to uleoten ȝeond te world, ase deð muchel cheafle. *Ibid.* 76 Of the worldes maðelunge, & of hire chefle. *c* **1315** SHOREHAM 150 That other reyson was for the devel, That he schal to mys-wende hys chevel. **1589** R. ROBINSON *Gold. Mirr.* (Chetham Soc.) 346 And cald vpon the houndes that were of choyce, Who leade no chawle, the game they found so warme.

3. The cheek, a cheek. (In late use often blending with JOWL *sb.*[2])

1668 WILKINS *Real Char.* II. vii. 177 Cheek, Jole. **1711** STEELE *Spect.* No. 32 ⁋2 If his Sides are as compact as his Joles, he need not disguise himself to make one of us. **1713** —— *Guard.* No. 42 ⁋3 The merit of his wit was founded upon the shaking of a fat paunch, and the tossing up of a pair of rosy jowls. **1885** J. L. ROBERTSON *White Angel*, etc. 15 He has such a good crop of hair on his jowls.

4. Here perhaps belongs the phrase ***cheek by jowl***, in earlier usage ***cheek by cheek***: see CHEEK *sb.* 5.

In this the *j* form is known from 1577, which is somewhat earlier than it is known in sense 1 above. The 17th c. variants *cheek by chole, chowl*, agree in form better with JOWL *sb.*[2] or [3]. But it is probable that, by the time the phrase came into use, all three sbs. were already felt as one. The following examples supplement those under CHEEK.

1577 HANMER *Anc. Eccl. Hist.* VIII. XXV. 165 Cheeke by iole with the Emperour. **1589** *Hay any work* (1880) 46 That maidenly Doctor, (who sits cheek by ioll with you). **1590** SHAKS. *Mids. N.* III. ii. 338 Follow? Nay, Ile goe with thee cheeke by iowle. **1660** S. FISHER *Rusticks Alarm* Wks. (1679) 336 Howbeit they may.. set up their meer Transcriptions, so as to make them sit cheek by chole with the first Hand-writings. **1678** *Trans. Crt. Spain* 172 There to find Father Nitard cheek to jowl with me. **1818** SCOTT *Rob Roy* xiv, In puir auld Scotland's Parliament they a' sate thegither, cheek by choul. **1820** W. IRVING *Sketch Bk.* II. 146 The dragon and the grass-hopper actually lie, cheek by jole. **1880** BROWNING *Dram. Idyls* II. *Doctor* —— 159 Old and young, rich and poor—crowd cheek by jowl.

5. *Comb.*, as †**chawle-bone**, a jawbone.

1430–40 LYDG. *Bochas* I. xix. (MS. Bodl.) 78/2 Off an Asse cauhte a chaule bon, And a thousand he slouh off hem anon. *c* **1440** *Promp. Parv.* 70/2 Chavylbone, or chawlbone, *mandibula.* **1523** FITZHERB *Husb.* §86 Betwene his chall bones.

jowl, jole (dʒəʊl, dʒaʊl), *sb.*[2] Forms: α. 4–5 **cholle, choll, chol,** 7 **chowle.** β. 6 **ioule,** 7 **iowle, jowle,** 9 **jole,** 7– **jowl.** [ME. *cholle, choll, chol*, coincides in sense with OE. *ceolur*, CHOLLER, a deriv. of same stem as OE. *ceolu, ceole*, ME. *cheole*, CHEL throat (cf. OLG. *kela*, OHG. *chela*, Du. *keel*, Ger. *kehle* throat). But the etymological relation of ME. *cholle* to these words is difficult to determine; and it does not appear possible to refer it to any OE. type. The 17th c. *chowle* was a regular development of ME. *cholle*: cf. *bowle*, BOWL *sb.*[1] from ME. *bolle*; but the *j* forms, which, as in JOWL *sb.*[1], appear late in the 16th c., are not accounted for. See prec., and next.]

The external throat or neck when fat or prominent; the pendulous flesh extending from the chops to the throat of a fat person, forming a 'double' chin; the dewlap of cattle; the crop or the wattle of a bird, etc.; = CHOLLER.

α. *c* **1320** *Sir Beues* (MS. A.) 2665 Þar þe dragoun gan ariue .. Eiȝte toskes at is mouþ stod out, Þe leste was seuentene ench about, Þe her, þe cholle vnder þe chin. *Ibid.* 2879 A hitte hem so on þe cholle, And karf ato þe brote bolle. *c* **1394** *P. Pl. Crede* 224 His chyn with a chol lollede As greet as a gos eye growen all of grece. **1646** SIR. T. BROWNE *Pseud. Ep.* V. i. 234 The chowle or crop adhering unto the lower side of the bill, and so descending by the throat.

β. **1591** PERCIVALL *Sp. Dict.*, *Cerbiguillo*, the necke of a bull, any fat necke or ioule. **1807** VANCOUVER *Agric. Devon* (1813) 327 Its head is small, clean, and free from flesh about the jaws;.. throat free from jowl or dewlap. **1827** D. JOHNSON *Ind. Field Sports* 25 Jungle fowl.. the cocks are of a black red with large combs and joles. **1868** ATKINSON *Cleveland Gloss.*, *Jowl*, .. 2. The fleshy appendages which, in a fat person, hang down from the jaws, forming, as it were, part of the flesh of the throat. **1871** NAPHEYS *Prev. & Cure Dis.* III. vi. 786 The pendulent jowls of the pig.

jowl, jole (dʒəʊl, dʒaʊl), *sb.*[3] Forms: α. 4–5 **choll(e,** 5 **choule.** β. 5–6 **iolle,** 5 **iol,** 6–7 **iole,** 7 **jolle, joule, (geoule),** 7– 8 **joll, joul, joal,** 7–9 **jole, jowl.** [The forms agree generally with those of JOWL *sb.*[2]; but the *j* forms appear here much earlier, and the *ch* forms disappear before 1500; in sense 2, the *ch* forms are not evidenced at all. For these reasons, and on account of the complete distinction of sense, this is treated provisionally as a distinct word; but its origin remains unknown.

The chronology of the forms of this word, and of JOWL *sb.*[1] and [3], suggests that it was in this word that the *j* forms originated, and that hence they passed in the 16th c. to the two others in which *ch* was original, so as to level all three under the form *jowl, jole.* But no extrinsic source of either *jolle* or *cholle* in the sense 'head' has been found.]

†**1.** The head of a man or beast. (In quot. 1562 applied app. to the head or top of an engine of war.) *Obs.* or ? *dial.*

α. *a* **1400** *Minor Poems fr. Vernon MS.* 501/314 So harde raced he þat Rolle, Þat he chopped his Cholle Aȝeyn þe Marbel-ston [cf. AUDELAY 77 So hard Rofyn rogud his roll, That he smot with his choule Aȝayns the marbystone]. *c* **1400** *Ywaine & Gaw.* 1994 Sunder strake he the throte boll That fra the body went the choll, By the lioun tail the hevid hang yit, For tharby had he tane his bit.

β. *c* **1440** *Promp. Parv.* 264/2 Iol, or heed (*K, S, P.* iolle), *caput.* **1562** PHAER *Æneid* IX. Ee ij b, Wher their engine ioynes his iolle, A huge vnweldie weight ye troians rumbling did doun rolle. **1783** WOLCOTT (P. Pindar) *Lyric Odes* V. iv, St. Dennis, when his jowl was taken off, Hugg'd it, and kiss'd it. **1795** —— *Pindariana* Wks. 1812 IV. 227 Leeds and Hawkesbury join'd their jowls together. **1825** BROCKETT, *Jowl*, the head.

2. *spec.* The head of a fish; hence (as a cut or dish), the head and shoulders of certain fish, as the salmon, sturgeon, and ling.

c **1430** *Two Cookery-bks.* 61 Jollys of Samoun. *c* **1460** J. RUSSELL *Bk. Nurture* 622 The Iolle of þe salt sturgeoun thyn take hede ye slytt. **1530** PALSGR. 235/1 Iolle of a fysshe, *teste.* **1607** BEAUM. & FL. *Woman-Hater* I. ii, For the Captain of the Guards Table, three chines of Beef, and two joals of Sturgeon. *c* **1645** HOWELL *Lett.* I. V. xvi, Two geoules of sturgeon. **1659–60** PEPYS *Diary* 20 Jan., Went.. to the Swan in Fish Streete.. where we were very merry at our Jole of Ling. **1719** S. SEWALL *Diary* 25 Mar. (1882) III. 216, I present his Excellency with a Joll of the Salmon. **1732** POPE *Ep. Cobham* 241 Mercy on my Soul! Is there no hope? Alas! —then bring the Jowl. **1747** MRS. GLASSE *Cookery* ix. 89 To dress a jole of pickled salmon. **1853** SOYER *Pantroph.* 225 The jole and belly were thought the most delicate parts. **1859** THACKERAY *Virgin.* ix, I have kept for your Excellency the jowl of this salmon.

jowl, joll (dʒəʊl), *sb.*[4] Now *dial.* Also 6 **iole.** [f. JOWL, JOLL *v.*[1]]

1. A bump; a blow, esp. on the head; a knock, a stroke.

c **1520** MORE *Mery Geste* 259 The wenche behinde lent him.. Many a iole about the nole with a great battill dore. **1877** *N.W. Linc. Gloss.*, *Jowl*, a jolt, a knock. **1883** G. C. DAVIES *Norfolk Broads* xix. (1884) 143 The wherrymen seize the opportunity.. to plunge the spears into the mud, and so get a good many eels. The strokes of the spear are called 'jowles'.

2. A knock on the wall of a coal-pit, given as a signal, or to ascertain its thickness: cf. JOWL *v.*[1] 4.

1851 GREENWELL *Coal-trade Terms Northumb. & Durh.* 32 *Jowl*, a sort of 'tattoo', beaten alternately upon the face of two places or drifts near holing, or intended to hole into each other, by a person in each place, for the purpose of ascertaining, by the sound, their relative positions.

3. *pl.* ***jowls***, a game resembling hockey.

1855 ROBINSON *Whitby Gloss.* s.v. *Jowl*, The game of 'Jowls'.. appears to have no more aim in it than that of sending the projectile from place to place by way of bodily exercise.

4. A single stroke of a bell; the tolling, knell, or clang of a bell: cf. JOW *sb.* 2. Chiefly *dial.*

1822 SCOTT *Nigel* x, The dinner-bell is going to sound —hark, it is clearing its rusty throat with a preliminary jowl. **1883** THOMSON *Leddy May* 4 (E.D.D.) The deid-bell rings wi' solemn jowl.

jowl, joll (dʒəʊl), *v.*[1] Now *dial.* Forms: 5 **cholle;** 6 **iolle, geolle,** 7 **joule, jowle,** 5– **joll,** 8– **jowl,** (9 **joul, jole**). [perh. f. JOWL *sb.*[3], the notion being app. to knock a head or ball; cf. also note to JOLT *v.* Sense 5 may be of distinct origin.]

1. *trans.* To strike (a ball) with a stick.

c **1430** *Pilgr. Lyf Manhode* IV. ix. (1869) 181 A crooked staf me lakketh for to cholle with, and a bal to pleye me with. **1855** ROBINSON *Whitby Gloss.*, *To Jowl*, to strike from the ground with a long stick or a boy's bat, a piece of wood or a ball, to a distance.

2. To bump; to strike, knock, or push; esp., to dash (the head, etc.) against something.

c **1470** *Pol. Poems* (Rolls) II. 276 There was jollyng, ther was rennyng for the sovereynte. **1519** HORMAN *Vulg.* 138, I geolled my heed ageynst the walle. **1530** PALSGR. 593/1, I iolled hym aboute the eares tyll I made my fyste sore. **1556** J. HEYWOOD *Spider & F.* ii. 103 Many a flie the flap hath iobde and iolde. **1601** SHAKS *All's Well* I. iii. 50 They may ioule horns together. **1602** —— *Ham.* V. i. 84 That Scull.. how the knaue iowles it to th' grownd. **1640** GENT *Knave in Gr.* II. i. D iv, Yester night a scurvy boy did so joule my head and the wall together. *a* **1811** CUMBERLAND in T. Mitchell *Aristoph., Clouds* II. 52 Who is he that jowls them [the clouds] thus together But Jove himself? **1863** MRS. TOOGOOD *Yorksh. Dial.*, He jouled his head against the wall. **1865** *Leeds Merc.* 7 Mar., She also 'joled' my head against the bed post.

†**3.** *intr.* To strike or bump *against* something.

1770 ARMSTRONG *Imitations* 85 Now they mount On the tall billow's top, and seem to jowl Against the stars.

4. *trans.* To strike (the wall of a coal-pit) as a signal or to ascertain the thickness of the wall.

1825 BROCKETT, *Jowl*, to knock, or rather to give a signal by knocking. **1862** *Times* 21 Jan., The men [imprisoned in the pit] have not been heard 'jowling' since 1 o'clock yesterday afternoon.

5. *intr.* and *trans.* To toll, knell, or ring slowly, as a bell; = JOW *v.* 2. Chiefly *dial.*

1872 E. PEACOCK *Mabel Heron* II. 120 Candles were lighted and bells were jowled. **1888** DOTTIE *Rambles* 88 (E.D.D.) It [the bell] kept on jowlin.

jowl, *v.*[2] *Obs.* exc. *dial.* In 5–6 **ioll,** 7 **jole, jaul, jawl.** [Origin obscure.] *intr.* To talk noisily or angrily. Hence ˈ**jowling** *vbl. sb.*

[*c* **1440** *York Myst.* XXX. 235 O, what javellis are ye þat jappis with gollyng [*read* jollyng].] ? *a* **1550** *Image Ipocr.* IV. 580 Thus the people seyne, With words true and playne How they iest and ioll. **1606** *Wily Beguiled* in Hawkins *Eng. Drama* III. 317 Well, I'll not stay with her: stay, quotha? To be yauld and jaul'd at. *Ibid.* 342 Her father o' th' other side, he yoles at her and joles at her. **1632** I. L. *Womens Rights* 180 The poore woman can haue no quiet her husband keepes such a iawling. [In mod. s.w. dialect: see *Eng. Dial. Dict.*]

†**jowl,** *v.*[3] *nonce-wd.* [f. JOWL *sb.*[1]] *trans.* To place 'cheek by jowl'.

1654 GAYTON *Pleas. Notes* III. i. 66 Sancho was cheek by jowle at dinner, and now he is jowl'd with him after dinner.

jowled (dʒəʊld), *a.* [f. JOWL *sb.*[1] + -ED[2].] Having jowls or jaws (of a specified kind).

1861 DICKENS *Gt. Expect.* III. 65 Drummle glanced at me, with an insolent triumph on his great-jowled face. **1897** R. KIPLING *Captains Courageous* 248 The crowd about the town-hall doors—blue-jowled Portuguese.

jowler[1] (ˈdʒəʊlə(r), ˈdʒaʊlə(r)). *Obs.* exc. *dial.* [f. as prec. + -ER[1].] A heavy-jawed dog. Used also as quasi-proper name for a dog of this kind.

1679 MULGRAVE *Ess. Satire* 109 Jowler lugs him still Through hedges, ditches. **1719** D'URFEY *Pills* II. 331 With deep mouth'd Jowlers too, and Rocks. **1721** BAILEY, *Jowler* a Dog's Name. **1755** JOHNSON, *Jowler*, the name of a hunting dog or beagle. **1826** J. WILSON *Noct. Ambr.* Wks. 1855 I. 138 When the jowlers tear him to pieces, he shows fecht, and gangs aff with a snarl.

jowler[2]. *Merseyside slang.* = JIGGER *sb.*[1] 6 c.

1961 PARTRIDGE *Dict. Slang* Suppl. 1154/1 *Jowler*, a lane between back-to-back houses: Liverpool. **1966** S. KELLY in F. Shaw et al. *Lern Yerself Scouse* 80 When I was young half of me time was spent Up jowlers.

jowlop, jowlopped: see JOLLOP, JOLLOPED.

†ˈ**jowl-piece.** *Arch. Obs.* Also 6 **ioull-, iooll-.** [f. JOWL *sb.* (it is doubtful which) + PIECE.] = JOWPY.

1533 *Hampton Court Acc.*, To J. H. painter.. for laying of the ioull-pecys rownde abowght the haull with green merbyll in oyle.. to R. S. moulder of Antykeworke, for a trayle of antyk sett in the great Ioull-pece.. for a creste goyng uppon the hedde of the sayd iooll pece.

jowly (ˈdʒəʊlɪ), *a.* [f. JOWL *sb.*[1] + -Y.] Having large or prominent jowls.

a **1873** LYTTON *Ken. Chillingly* I. viii, The face of the rural man is coarse-grained and perhaps jowly. **1896** *Chamb. Jrnl.* XIII. 585/1 A coarse, open-faced, jowly man.

jowpoun, obs. form of JUPON.

†**jowpy, jopy.** *Arch. Obs.* Forms: 4 **iowpe,** 5 **iowpye, iopee, iope, ioppe, ioppy,** 5–6 **iopy.** [A word recorded from Cambridge and East Anglia; app. orig. *jow-pece*, f. *jow* earlier form of JAW *sb.*[1]: cf. the later *jaw-piece* s.v. JAW *sb.*[1] 7, and JOWL-PIECE.] A cornice extending between the principals of a Gothic roof, and usually supporting the feet of the secondary principals.

1374 in Willis & Clark *Cambridge* (1886) I. 238 Wyndbems, suchlates Asthelers Corbels jowpes balkes summers. **1413–14** *Ibid.* II. 441 Item pro cariagio vnius trabis cum j jopy v[s]. **1432–3** *Ibid.* 446 Pro vj joppyes precii joppe xij[d]. **1438** in J. Gage *Suffolk* (1838) 140 Having atwix iche two princeapals a purloyne a iope and iiij sparrys. **1448–9** in Willis & Clark *Cambridge* (1886) II. 10 The walplates of the seid hall shalbe.. vij inches of Thiknes with jopees from bem to bem. **1452** *Ibid.* I. 282 Also Jowpyes xvj[ne] inche in brede with a Batylment by nethe with a Crest above... Item atte euery end of the sengulers atte the Jowpye shalbe an Angell. **1466** *Ibid.* III. 93 Alle the gistes .. shal rest vpon the crosse dormauntes and on the said

ioppijs. **1504** in J. Gage *Suffolk* 150 Item, paid to Lyng for coloryng my closet, and the jopys in the hall 6s. 8d.

jows(e, obs. forms of JUICE.

jowser ('dʒaʊzə(r)), variant of DOWSER, one who uses the divining rod. So **jowsing**, †**josing**.

1797 BILLINGSLEY *View Agric. Somerset* 22 By the help of the divining-rod vulgarly call'd *josing*. **1839** DE QUINCEY *Mod. Superst.* Wks. 1862 III. 323 These people are locally called *jowsers*. **1886** ELWORTHY *W. Som. Word-bk.* s.v. *Dowse*, In some parts of the country the operation is called *Jowsing*, and the operator a *Jowser*.

jowte, obs. form of JOUTE.

jowter ('dʒaʊtə(r)). *dial.* Also jowder, -ler, chowter, chowder; and (? orig. fem.) jowster, jouster. A fish-hawker (Cornwall, Devonsh.). Also, A hawker or pedlar of any kind.

1550 in Strype *Eccl. Mem.* (1721) II. App. QQ. 142 (Cornwall) Item, when the fisher or jowtar bring any fish to the market, that then they sel the same at reasonable prices. **1602** CAREW *Cornwall* 131 b, When plenty of fish is vented to the fish-drivers, whom we call Jowters. **1630** in Westcote *Devon* (1845) 378 Fishing is a very commodious employment..where they take sufficient..and send by divers called Jouters, into the inland countries. **1808** *Monthly Mag.* II. 545 Chowter. **1848** C. A. JOHNS *Week at Lizard* 47 The *jowsters*, or hawkers are miles away. **1857** KINGSLEY *Two Y. Ago* xiv, Mr. Treluddra, principal 'jowder', i.e. fish-salesman, of Aberalva. **1863** C. A. JOHNS *Home Walks* 187 The majority [of the Lobsters] being purchased at a set rate by the 'jowders', fish salesmen. **1880** *W. Cornwall Gloss.*, *Chowter*, a female fish-vendor. More commonly *jouster*. Generally, those who go about the country in carts. **1888** ELWORTHY *W. Som. Word-bk.*, *Jowder, jowler*, a hawker, pedlar.

joy (dʒɔɪ), *sb.* Forms: 3-6 ioie, ioi, 3-7 ioye, ioy, (3 ioiȝe, 4 ioȝe, ioyȝe, yoi, yoe, goye, 5 yoye, yoy), 7 joye, 7- joy. [ME. a. OF. *joie, joye* joy, jewel, F. *joie* (= Pr. *joia*, Sp. *joya*, Pg. *joia* jewel, It. *gioja* joy, jewel):—pop.L. **gaudia* fem. for L. *gaudia*, pl. of *gaudium* joy; cf. Pr. *joi*:—L. *gaudium*.]

1. a. A vivid emotion of pleasure arising from a sense of well-being or satisfaction; the feeling or state of being highly pleased or delighted; exultation of spirit; gladness, delight.

a **1225** *Ancr. R.* 218 Auh efter þe spreoue, on ende,—þeonne is þe muchele ioie. *a* **1240** *Lofsong* in *Cott. Hom.* 213 Al mi woa on eorðe schal turnen me to ioie. **1340** *Ayenb.* 226 More wes tocne of wepinge and of zorȝe þanne of goye and of ydele blisse. *Ibid.* 75 Ioye wyþoute ende. *c* **1440** *York Myst.* xxx. 387 þi joie is in japes. **1535** COVERDALE *Ps.* cxxvi. 5 They that sowe in teeres, shal reape in ioye. **1611** BIBLE *Job* xxxviii. 7 When the morning starres sang together, and all the sonnes of God shouted for ioy. **1651** BP. HALL *Solil.* 27 There is little difference betwixt joy and happiness. **1754** RICHARDSON *Grandison* IV. iv. 39, I have joy in the joy of all these good people. **1785** BOSWELL *Tour Hebr.* 30 Oct., Joseph..reported that the earl 'jumped for joy'. **1802** WORDSW. *Resol. Indep.* vii, I thought..Of him who walked in glory and in joy Following his plough, along the mountain-side. **1820** KEATS *Ode Melancholy* iii, Joy, whose hand is ever at his lips Bidding adieu. **1867** JEAN INGELOW *Dominion* 29 It is a comely fashion to be glad—Joy is the grace we say to God.

b. with *a* and *pl.*: an instance or kind of this.

a **1300** *Cursor M.* 23366 Ne hert mai think þaa ioies sere, þat iesu crist has dight til his. *c* **1450** *Cov. Myst.* 261 There joye of alle joyis to the is sewre! *c* **1620** DONNE *Serm.* (ed. Alford) IV. 272 This third Ioy..is not a collateral Ioy..but it is a fundamental Ioy, a radical Ioy. **1697** DRYDEN *Virg. Georg.* IV. 749 Averse from Venus, and from nuptial Joys. **1855** TENNYSON *Maud* I. v. 3 A joy in which I cannot rejoice, A glory I shall not find.

c. The expression of glad feeling; outward rejoicing; mirth; †jubilant festivity.

a **1300** *Cursor M.* 3014 Isaac wel es for to sai A man þat takens ioy and plai. *c* **1400** MAUNDEV. (1839) xxviii. 286 Whan thei dyen, thei maken gret feste and gret ioye and reuell. **1535** COVERDALE *Ps.* cxxvi. 2 Then shall oure mouth be fylled with laughter, and oure tonge with ioye. **1552** HULOET, Ioye made for victorie, as bonefyres wyth bankettes, *epinicium*. **1611** BIBLE *Isa.* lii. 9 Breake foorth into ioy, sing together, yee waste places. **1800** WORDSW. *Idle Shepherd-boys* 1 The valley rings with mirth and joy.

†**d.** ***maiden of joy***, a courtesan (F. *fille de joie*). *Obs.*

1585 T. WASHINGTON tr. *Nicholay's Voy.* IV. xxv. 141 The lively drafts..of a mayden of ioy or a common woman.

†**e.** *ellipt.* An expression of sympathetic joy, a congratulation. Cf. phr. *to give one (the) joy*. *Obs.*

1656 FINETT *For. Ambass.* 11 In conclusion, a joy pronounced by the King and Queen, and seconded with congratulation of the Lords there present.

f. Used *interjectionally*, as an expression of joy.

1719 DE FOE *Crusoe* I. xv. (1840) 266 Friday..in a kind of surprise falls a-jumping and dancing..'O joy!' says he. **1803-6** WORDSW. *Intimations* ix, O joy! that in our embers Is something that doth live. **1817** MOORE *Lalla R.*, *Par. & Peri*, Joy, joy for ever! my task is done, The gates are passed, and heaven is won.

g. *colloq.* Result, satisfaction, success. Esp. with negative, and freq. *ironical*.

1945 *Tee Emm* (Air Ministry) V. 53 There's even less joy in sending us the money. **1945** C. H. WARD-JACKSON *Piece of Cake* (ed. 2) 40 *Joy*, satisfaction. Thus, 'Johnnie took the new kite up this morning—had bags of joy', or 'no joy at all'. **1946** BRICKHILL & NORTON *Escape to Danger* xxxiii. 294 At 9.15 the workers had been down nearly forty minutes and still 'no joy'. **1961** S. PRICE *Just for Record* ii. 17, I..tried to get a taxi. No joy, so back into the studio. **1961** H. R. WILLIAMSON *Wicked Pack Cards* ix. 94 Did you get any joy at the picture gallery? **1971** D. BAGLEY *Freedom Trap* vii. 147 He reported, 'No joy!' *Ibid.* viii. 178 'Any joy there?' She looked up. 'There's not much more than I told you last night.' **1972** R. FIENNES *Ice Fall in Norway* vi. 86 It was becoming late—we tried to locate Patrick's position again, but without joy. **1973** *Scotsman* 7 Aug. 8/2 Parking the car in this bay we started to look for a path and a break in the barbed wire—again with no joy.

2. A pleasurable state or condition; a state of happiness or felicity; *esp.* the perfect bliss or beatitude of heaven; hence, the place of bliss, paradise, heaven; = BLISS 2 c, GLORY 7. *Obs.* or *arch.*

c **1275** *Passion Our Lord* 586 in *O.E. Misc.* 54 þer is my vader and eke heore, and ioye euer ilyche. **1297** R. GLOUC. (Rolls) 535 þer abbeþ kinges & mani oþere ofte ibe in ioie. *c* **1320** *Cast. Love* 1519 þat he wone wiþ vs wiþ-Inne, And aftur þis lyf to Ioye wende. *c* **1400** MAUNDEV. (Roxb.) xxxi. 141 þai go to þe ioy of Paradys [*il vait en paradis*]. **1422** tr. *Secreta Secret., Priv. Priv.* 150 Therfor Sholde a man lytill cowete..the honnoure, the yoy, or the gladnysse of this worlde. **1552** *Bk. Com. Prayer, Morn. Prayer*, So that at the last we may come to hys eternall ioye. *c* **1646** MILTON *Sonn. Mrs. Thomson*, Thy works, and alms..Followed thee up to joy and bliss for ever. [**1870** J. ELLERTON *Hymn*, '*When the day of toil is done*' iv, Bring us, where all tears are dried, Joy for evermore.]

3. a. A source or object of joy; that which causes joy, or in which delight is taken; a delight.

Joys of Mary (*R.C. Ch.*), special occasions of joy to the mother of Jesus Christ. The mediæval church reckoned five; lists differ; an early 14th c. poem (Wright *Lyric P.* (1844) 95) has the Annunciation, Nativity, Epiphany, Resurrection, and her Assumption; later R.C. writers make seven, adding as second and fifth, the Visitation and Finding in the Temple, and making the seventh the Ascension.

c **1275** *Luve Ron* in *O.E. Misc.* 97 His sihte is al ioye and gleo, he is day wyþ-ute nyhte. **1382** WYCLIF *Phil.* iv. 1 My britheren moost dereworthe..my ioye and my crowne. *c* **1430** *Hymns Virg.* 67 Quod man, y pleie, y wrastile, y sprynge, þese ioies wolen neuere wende me fro. **1539** BIBLE (Great) *Ps.* xlviii. 2 The hyll of Sion is a fayre place, & the ioye of the whole earth. **1611** BIBLE *Isa.* xxxii. 14 The forts and towers shall be for dens for ever, a joy of wild asses, a pasture of flocks. **1818** KEATS *Endym.* I. 1 A thing of beauty is a joy for ever. **1876** OUIDA *Winter City* vi. 151 You can see no horizon from it; that alone is the joy of the moor-land.

a **1310** in Wright *Lyric P.* 89 Al thourh that levedy gent and smal, heried by hyr joies fyve. *Ibid.* 96 The thridde joie of that levedy That men clepeth the Epyphany. **1463** *Bury Wills* 17 Oure ladyes fyve joyes. **1674** BREVINT *Saul at Endor* 281 They allow but 40 daies Pardon for saying seven *Paters* and *Aves* to the honor of the seven Joies.

b. Used (esp. *dial.*) as a term of endearment for a sweetheart, child, etc.; a darling: cf. JO 2.

1590 SHAKS. *Mids. N.* IV. i. 4 While I..kisse thy faire large eares, my gentle ioy. **1606** —— *Ant. & Cl.* I. v. 58 His remembrance lay In Egypt with his ioy. **1789** BLAKE *Songs Innoc.*, *Infant Joy* 7 Pretty joy! Sweet joy but two days old. **1875** B. L. FARJEON *Love's Vict.* xxv, She instructed her eldest joy how to behave. **1876** *Whitby Gloss.* s.v., 'My bonny joy!' my pretty dear.

†**4.** The quality which causes joy; quality or faculty of delighting; = DELIGHT *sb.* 3. *Obs. rare.*

a **1400** *Pistill of Susan* 41 þus þis dredful demers on dayes þider drewe, Al for gentrise and Ioye of þat Iewesse. **1483** *Cath. Angl.* 197/2 Ioy,..*amenitas*.

†**5.** Joyful adoring praise and thanksgiving; = GLORY 4. Rendering L. *glōria* (Gr. $\delta\acute{o}\xi\alpha$), esp. in the doxologies. *Obs.*

When OE. *wuldor*, early ME. *wulder*, became obs., and L. *gloria*, OF. *glorie, gloire*, was not yet adopted, Eng. had no word distinctly representing L. *gloria*. Hence *bliss* and *joy* were used naturally at first of the glory of heaven (see sense 2 above, BLISS 2 c, GLORY 4), and extended to this sense in which *gloria, gloire* represent Gr. $\delta\acute{o}\xi\alpha$: cf. BLISS 3.

a **1300** *Cursor M.* 11260 On hei be ioi, and pes on lagh. *c* **1374** CHAUCER *Boeth.* v. pr. vi. 139 (Camb. MS.) þe Iuge þat seeþ and demeþ alle þinges. (To whom be goye and worshipe bi Infynyt tymes Amen.) **1387** TREVISA *Higden* (Rolls) VII. 289 *Gloria Patri* etc. þat is, Ioye to þe Fadir. *a* **1400** *Prymer* (1891) 17 Ioyȝe be to the fadir, and to the sone, and to the holy goost. **1483** *Cath. Angl.* 197/2 Ioy, *adoria..doxa, doxula*.

†**6. a.** A jewel. (F. *joie*, Godef.) *Obs.*

1599 BRETON *Miseries Manillia* II, Here my sweete Mistresse, take this Pearle-ioye Set it in the ring that hangeth at mine eare. **1611** FLORIO, *Gioia*, a ioy, a gemme, a iewell.

†**b.** In E. Indian use from Pg. *joia*. *Obs.*

1800 *Asiat. Ann. Reg.*, *Chron.* 17/1 Shaik Ishmail was convicted of breaking into the house of Pittamber Narrain, and stealing from thence a variety of gold and silver joys. **1809** MARIA GRAHAM *Jrnl. Resid. India* (1812) 3 To murder these helpless creatures for the sake of their ornaments or *joys*. **1824** *Sk. India* (ed. 2) 78 Groups of dancing-girls, covered with joys.

7. *Astrol.* ***Joys of the Planets***: see quots.

[*a* **1400-50** *Alexander* 704 And how þe mode Marcure makis sa mekill ioy.] **1658** PHILLIPS, *Joyes* of the Planets, are when they are in those houses where they are most powerful and strong, as Saturn joyeth in Scorpio. **1706** PHILLIPS, *Joys of the Planets*..are certain Dignities that befall them, either by being in the place of a Planet of like Quality or Condition, or when they are in a House of the Figure agreeable to their own Nature. **1819** JAS. WILSON *Compl. Dict. Astrol.*, *Joys of the Planets*..Every planet, according to Ptolemy, is in his joy when another is dignified in any of his dignities... They are also said in modern astrology to have their joys in certain houses according to their nature, whether good or evil, thus ♄ joys in the 12th, ♃ in the 11th.

†**8.** Isolated obsolete uses. **a.** A stage-play.

c **1440** *Promp. Parv.* 264/1 Ioy, or pley þat begynnythe wythe sorow, and endythe wythe gladnes, *comedia*. Ioy, or pley þat begynnythe wythe gladnesse, and endythe wythe sorow, *tragedia*.

b. (See quot.)

1600 DYMMOK *Ireland* (1843) 9 Joye is when their idle men require meat and drinke out of meale tymes..it is as much to say as a benevolence.

9. In various phrases:

†**a.** ***to have joy of***, to be highly pleased or delighted with. †**b.** ***to make joy***, to rejoice. With indirect obj., To give a glad welcome. †**c.** ***to take joy***, to take pleasure, be glad, rejoice. **d.** ***to wish*** (arch. ***give***) ***one*** (†***the***) ***joy of***, to express sympathetic joy or give one's good wishes to a person on a happy occasion; to congratulate. Often *ironical*. Cf. JOY *v.* 5 b. **e.** ***God give you joy, joy go with you***, etc., ejaculations expressive of good wishes.

a. 1297 R. GLOUC. (Rolls) 253 Al þe kun þat him iseiȝ adde of him ioye inou. *c* **1386** CHAUCER *Melib.* ¶ 768 They were so ..rauysshed and hadden so greet ioye of hire, that wonder was to telle. *c* **1450** *Merlin* 184 Whan Gawein vndirstode the speche of his brother, he hadde of hym hertely ioye, and moche he hym preysed. **1586** A. DAY *Eng. Secretary* II. (1625) 60, I trust you shall have joy of me, and..I doubt not but so to behave my selfe, that I shall well deserve this good liking..of my master.

b. *c* **1300** *Havelok* 1209 Hise children..maden ioie swiþe mikel. *c* **1320** *Cast. Love* 1771 in *Minor Poems fr. Vernon MS.*, The apostlys and the martiris, The confessors and the virginis, Alle wolle him ioy makyn. **1483** CAXTON *Gold. Leg.* 79/1 Thenne ranne the dogge..and cam home as a messager fawnyng and makyng ioye with hys tail. **1590** SPENSER *F.Q.* I. iii. 32 Such ioy made Vna when her knight she found.

c. *c* **1600** SHAKS. *A.Y.L.* IV. i. 90 *Ros.* Am not I your Rosalind? *Orl.* I take some ioy to say you are. **1611** —— *Wint. T.* V. i. 80 Such As..it should take ioy To see her in your armes.

d. 1599 SHAKS. *Much Ado* II. i. 200, I wish him ioy of her. **1631** T. ADAMS in *Lett. Lit. Men* (Camden) 147, I wish you much joy in the execution of that hopefull employment. **1638** W. MOUNTAGU in *Buccleuch MSS.*, *Montagu Ho.* (Hist. MSS. Comm.) I. 277 Sir Christ. Yerlverton gave him first joy of his office. *c* **1710** CELIA FIENNES *Diary* (1888) 141 Ye Earle having just marry'd his Eldest daughter..there was Company to wishe her joy. **1806-7** J. BERESFORD *Miseries Hum. Life* (1826) IV. Introd., I give you joy of having found out that. **1855** THACKERAY *Newcomes* ii, Newcome, my boy..I give you joy. **1885** J. PAYN *Heir Ages* xlvi, You will even go the length of wishing them joy of their bargain.

e. *a* **1440** *Sir Eglam.* 608 Syr, yf you yoye of yowre chylde. *c* **1460** *Towneley Myst.* xiii. 550 So god..gyf me Ioy of my chylde! **1588** SHAKS. *L.L.L.* v. ii. 448 God giue thee ioy of him. **1596** —— *Merch. V.* III. ii. 190 To cry good ioy, good ioy my Lord and Lady. **1603** —— *Meas. for M.* v. i. 532 Ioy to you Mariana. **1742** POPE *Dunc.* IV. 54 Joy to great Chaos! let Division reign. **1824-46** LANDOR *Imag. Conv.* Wks. I. 171 There we leave her, and joy go with her.

10. *Comb.* objective and obj. genitive, as ***joy-killer***, ***-maker***; ***joy-bringing***, ***-dispelling***, ***-inspiring*** adjs.; instrumental, etc., as ***joy-bright***, ***-encompassed***, ***-rapt***, ***-resounding***, ***-wrung*** adjs.; ***joy-bereft***, ***-mixt*** adjs.; attrib., of or expressing joy, as ***joy-gift***, ***-night***, ***-note***, ***-offering***, ***-tear***; **joy-bells**, **-fire**, bells rung, or a bonfire lighted [F. *feu de joie*], to celebrate a joyful event; **joy-firing**, lighting of joy-fires; the firing of celebratory shots (cf. FEU DE JOIE 2); **joy-flight**, an aerial joy-ride; so **joy-flying**; **joy-gun**, a gun fired to celebrate a joyful event; **joy-house** *slang*, a brothel; **joy juice** *U.S. slang*, alcoholic drink; †**joy-making**, merrymaking; **joy-plank**, a plank leading from the stage to the audience in a theatre, for the use of performers; **joy-popper** *slang* (orig. *U.S.*), an occasional taker of illegal drugs; hence [back-formations] **joy-pop**, (an inhalation or injection of) a drug; **joy-pop** *v. intr.*, **joy-popping** *vbl. sb.*; †**joy-sop**, a sop made by dipping cake in wine; **joy-stick** (*a*) *slang*, the control-lever of an aeroplane; the controls of another vehicle; also *attrib.*, *transf.*, and *fig.*; (*b*) a small lever that can be moved in each of two dimensions to control the movement of an image on a television or VDU screen; also *Comb.*; **joy-weed**, a plant of the genus *Alternanthera* (Miller *Plant-n.* 1884); **joy-wheel**, a form of amusement consisting of either (*a*) a gigantic wheel-shaped structure, as on a fairground, on which passengers are carried in cars rotating round the axis, or (*b*) (see quot. 1954).

1836 MAYNE *Siller Gun* v. xliv, When now, in tune, The *joy-bells chime. **1894** MRS. FR. ELLIOT *Roman Gossip* i, Every church echoes joy-bells to the deep boom of Saint Peter's. **1586** WARNER *Alb. Eng.* I. ii, Cybell, *ioy-bereft, And Vesta..Did both lament. **1744** AKENSIDE *Pleas. Imag.* III. 91 Chief of the glance Of wishful envy draws their *joy-bright eyes. *c* **1600** DAVISON *Ps.* cxxv, Peace, *joy-bringing peace And plentie shall for euer dwell With God's owne chosen Israell. **1811** W. R. SPENCER *Poems* 54 Through all her *joy-deserted seats. **1871** B. TAYLOR *Faust* (1875) II. III. 169 The *joy-encompassed path of Song. **1845** CARLYLE *Cromwell* (1871) I. 53 Old London was..in a blaze with *joy-fires. **1864** —— *Fredk. Gt.* XVII. vii, Such a '*joy-firing' for Lobositz. **1926** T. E. LAWRENCE *Seven Pillars* (1935) cxvii. 635 The shooting he heard was joy-firing. **1923** *Daily Mail* 7 Aug. 8/2 The '*joy flights' in three-seater Avros, at 5s. a time. **1928** *Daily Express* 3 July 12 Strict regulations were made against joy-flights during the war. **1851** MRS. BROWNING *Casa Guidi Wind.* II. 123 And foiled The *joy-guns of their echo. **1940** R. CHANDLER *Farewell, my Lovely* iii. 24, I ain't been in a *joy house in twenty years. **1970** 'B. MATHER' *Break in Line* iii. 43 All right—so you're a sailor in a joy-house with a sore foot. **1819** SHELLEY *Cyclops* 170 The

Bacchic dew Of *joy-inspiring grapes. **1960** WENTWORTH & FLEXNER *Dict. Amer. Slang* 297/2 **Joy-juice*, liquor. **1974** *Black World* Mar. 56/2 He could hear the others as in a dream, laughing, telling dirty jokes, playing cards and swizzling joy-juice. **1858** DORAN *Crt. Fools* 336 To place.. the German fools or *joy-makers before a foreign public. *c* **1330** R. BRUNNE *Chron.* (1810) 56 In alle his *joy makyng ..He felle dede doun colde as any stone. **1748** THOMSON *Cast. Indol.* I. xlvii, Oh..fill with pious awe and *joy-mixt woe the heart. **1925** T. DREISER *Amer. Tragedy* I. I viii. 53 Being invited by them to a *joy-night supper—a 'blow-out' as they termed it..he decided to go. **1928** *Daily Mail* 7 Aug. 12/7 It was a 'joy night', although many people were still unable to believe that they could..buy a packet of cigarettes openly. **1898** *Athenæum* 27 Aug. 281/3 No *joy-peal was rung. **1924** *Illustr. London News* 27 Dec. 1265/2 The picture of the Grand Ballet at Florence in 1616..shows a method of presentation which was in vogue here in Revues a year or two ago, and is still continued in the Cabarets; performers leaving the stage by means of steps and '*joy-planks'. **1970** J. B. PRIESTLEY *Edwardians* III. 247 (*caption*) Shirley Kellogg leading the chorus along the joy plank in *Hullo Ragtime!* at the London Hippodrome in 1912. **1939** *Detective Fiction Weekly* 18 Mar. 59/1 If you should happen to hear anybody speaking of a suey-pow or a *joy-pop or of gowing out the lemon bowl,..bring him right here. **1951** *Time* 26 Feb. 24/3 A sniff of heroin is a 'snort of horse', and an injection under the skin a 'joy pop'. **1954** BECKHARDT & BROWN *Violators* viii. 238 Every now and then he would 'joy-pop' (take an occasional injection) but he thought he could avoid the 'hook' (addiction) by 'spacing his shots'. **1962** K. ORVIS *Damned & Destroyed* v. 41, I take a joy-pop once in a while. *Ibid.* vii. 51 So you're handling a bit of hot stuff as well as joy-popping? **1964** D. WARNER *Death of Dreamer* I. i. 8 Each junkie is taking an average of twenty joy-pops a day. The joy-pops are sold in one-grain packets, called decks by the junkies. **1936** *Amer. Speech* XI. 123/1 **Joy-popper*, a person, not a confirmed addict, who indulges in an occasional shot of dope. However, joy-popping is usually the beginning of a permanent addiction. If the joy-popper has trouble establishing the desire and pleasure from indulging it, he is called a student. **1949** N. ALGREN *Man with Golden Arm* I. 24 They called those using the stuff only occasionally 'joy-poppers' and wished them all great joy. For the 'joy-poppers' had no intention of becoming addicts in the true sense. **1972** J. BROWN *Chancer* ii. 30 The weekend ravers and joy-poppers..for whom smoke and amphetamines alone were not enough. **1648** HERRICK *Hesper.*, *Twelfe Night* iii, Let us make *Joy-sops with the cake. **1910** R. LORAINE *Diary* 9 Apr. in W. Loraine *Robert Loraine* (1938) vi. 105 In order that he shall not blunder inadvertently into the air, the central lever—otherwise the *cloche*, or *joy-stick is tied well forward. **1916** Joy-stick [see *control lever*]. **1932** AUDEN *Orators* II. 52 *Joystick*—Pivot of power And responder to pressure And grip for the glove. **1936** *Amer. Speech* XI. 123/1 *Joy stick*, an opium pipe. **1948** PARTRIDGE *Dict. Forces' Slang* 104 *Joysticks*, the two levers by which the steering of tanks and some other tracked vehicles was controlled. **1950** G. BARKER *News of World* 44 My love, my love, lift up your joystick hand. Dismiss the dividing Grief. **1952** A. TUSTIN *Automatic & Manual Control* 467 Both hands held at approximately elbow height a joystick that could be rotated or deflected about a universal coupling, to control the spot movement in elevation and traverse. *Ibid.* 468 The joystick controlled the movements of the spotlight. **1964** S. DUKE-ELDER *Parsons' Dis. Eye* (ed. 14) x. 98 (*caption*) Joystick lever for horizontal course and fine adjustments. **1967** *Times Rev. Industry* Mar. 43/3 The system is simply operated by a keyboard and joystick—no computer programming knowledge is needed. **1969** G. MACBETH *War Quartet* 34 Easing the joy-sticks to their mid-riffs. **1978** J. MILLER *Body in Question* (1982) viii. 339 By using a joystick, subjects can track a moving spot on a television set with a follow spot of their own. **1983** *Your Computer* (Austral.) Aug. 14/2 Standard features of the Fox-640 include a Forth programming system card, joystick port, [etc.]. **1985** *Personal Computer World* Feb. 244/3 The game is joystick-controlled and has three skill levels. **1911** *Oxford Times* 9 Sept. 10/6 A new form of amusement to Oxford, known as the '*Joy Wheel'. **1942** 'M. INNES' *Daffodil Affair* I. i. 7 Perhaps twenty times it passed to and fro, as if outside some great joy-wheel were oscillating idly in a derelict amusement park. **1954** *Engineer* 27 Aug. 282/2 A once-popular novelty, now obsolete, was the 'Joywheel', or 'Devil's Disc'. This consisted of a power-driven spinning disc, slightly domed and having a smooth surface. It was surrounded by a stationary padded circular platform, which in turn was surrounded by a padded wall. Riders sat on the disc while it was stationary and, as it accelerated, were eventually thrown off against the padding. **1968** D. BRAITHWAITE *Fairground Archit.* 65 A panoramic 'Joy Wheel' using kinetoscope effects to create the illusion of a race between motor-car and train.

joy (dʒɔɪ), *v.* Forms: 3-6 ioyen, 4-5 ioie(n, 4-7 ioye, ioy, (5 ioi), 7 joye, 7- joy. [ME. a. OF. *joir* to rejoice, enjoy, welcome, etc., F. *jouir* = Pr. *gaudir, gauzir, jauzir*:—pop.L. **gaudīre* = L. *gaudēre* to rejoice.]

†**1.** *refl.* To experience joy; to find or take pleasure; to enjoy oneself; to rejoice. *Obs.*

c **1260** *Somer is comen* in *Rel. Ant.* I. 100 This day beginniz to longe, And this foules everichon ioye hem wit songe. **1614** MERITON *Chr. Assur. House* 13 To joy our selves in things uncertaine is but an induction of griefe. **1712** ADDISON *Spect.* No. 517 ¶2 He has never joyed himself since.

2. *intr.* To feel or manifest joy; to be glad; to rejoice, exult. Occas. with *it* or cognate obj.

a **1300** *Cursor M.* 17976 Wiþ cry þei ioyeden euerychone. *a* **1325** *Prose Psalter* xl[i]. 12 Myn enemy ne shal nouȝt ioien up me. **1483** CAXTON *Gold. Leg.* 387/1 Al the celestyal courte ioyed and songen thys verce. *a* **1533** LD. BERNERS *Huon* xliv. 147, I shall neuer ioy in my herte vnto the tyme I haue slayne the. **1602** *Narcissus* (1893) 422 Ah, the poore rascall, never ioyd it since. **1605** CHAPMAN *All Fooles* I. i, To ioy one ioy, and thinke both one thought, Liue both one life. **1715-20** POPE *Iliad* III. 37 So joys a lion, if the branching deer Or mountain-goat, his bulky prize, appear. **1885** MISS BRADDON *Wyllard's Weird* xxiv, She had..sympathised and sorrowed and joyed with them.

b. To rejoice or delight: const. *in* (†*of, at, with*), *to do* something, or with clause.

1303 R. BRUNNE *Handl. Synne* 1990 Makayre ioyede þat þey were so stable. *a* **1340** HAMPOLE *Psalter* v. 14 Ioy sall all in þe þat lufis þi name. *c* **1450** tr. *De Imitatione* III. iii. 66 þei ioy more at vanyte þan þou at trouþe. *c* **1470** HENRYSON *Mor. Fab.* iii. (*Cock & Fox*) 537 Prydfull he was, and joyit of his sin. **1495** *Trevisa's Barth. De P.R.* XVIII. lxxxii. (W. de W.) Ff ij b/2 Some bestys Ioye of theyr owne colours. **1549** COVERDALE, etc. *Erasm. Par. 1 Pet.* iv. 11 If they do repent, it is to be ioyed at. **1590** MARLOWE *2nd Pt. Tamburl.* v. iii, I joy, my lord, your highness is so strong. **1690** CHILD *Disc. Trade* (1694) 255 This is sufficient to make us little to joy in foreigners money. **1741** RICHARDSON *Pamela* II. 345 O my good old Acquaintances, said I, I joy to see you. **1837** HOWITT *Rur. Life* III. vi. (1862) 274 Back to the scenes in which he early joyed.

c. *Astrol.* Of a planet: see JOY *sb.* 7.

1658, 1819 [see JOY *sb.* 7]. **1855** SMEDLEY *Occult Sci.* 311 Cogent reasons are given why the planets should joy in these houses rather than others.

†**d.** *trans.* To rejoice at. *Obs.*

1602 WARNER *Alb. Eng.* IX. xlv, Edward Duke of Buckingham, whose end That Prelate ioyde, the people moend. **1607** TOURNEUR *Rev. Trag.* IV. ii. Wks. 1878 II. 105 Thou shalt not joy his death. **1647** R. STAPYLTON *Juvenal* xv. 86, I joy it, and I thinke it self does so.

3. *trans.* To fill with joy; to gladden, delight.

†**a.** quasi-*impers.*: with *of* or clause. *Obs.*

1303 R. BRUNNE *Handl. Synne* 12110 The syxte grace of shryfte to neuene Hyt ioyeth alle þe court of heuene. *c* **1400** *Destr. Troy* 214 It Ioyes me, Iason, of þi iust werkes. *c* **1590** GREENE *Fr. Bacon* x. 20 It joys me that such men..should lay their liking on this base estate. **1651** CROMWELL in Ellis *Orig. Lett.* Ser. II. III. 366 It joyes mee to heere thy soule prospereth. **1703** ROWE *Fair Penit.* I. i. 320 It joys my heart that I have found you.

b. With ordinary subject. *arch.*

c **1450** *Cov. Myst.* (Shaks. Soc.) 68 God wol be man, Mankend to save, and that joyth me. **1573** TUSSER *Husb.* (1878) 68 For his sake that ioyed vs all with his birth. **1667** PEPYS *Diary* 2 Sept., Which did mightily joy me. **1807-8** W. IRVING *Salmag.* ix. (1860) 209 O, how these strangers joy'd my sight. **1845** MRS. S. C. HALL *Whiteboy* ix. 76 The barrel was..smooth enough to joy the heart of a Red Indian.

†**c.** *passive. to be joyed*, to be rejoiced or delighted, to find joy or delight. *Obs.*

1382 WYCLIF *Ecclus.* xxv. 10 A man that is ioȝid [L. *jucundatur*, 1388 is myrie] in sones lyuende. **1486** *Surtees Misc.* (1888) 53 Gretely gladdit and joyed of the commyng of his moost riall persone. **1617** MORYSON *Itin.* II. 273 How joied we are that so good event hath followed. **1676** HOBBES *Iliad* XIX. 165, I am joy'd The counsel you have given us to hear. **1725** POPE *Odyss.* VII. 355 My soul was joy'd in vain; For angry Neptune rouz'd the raging main.

4. To derive enjoyment from; to possess or use with enjoyment; to enjoy. †Formerly, also, in weaker sense, To have the use or benefit of: = ENJOY 4, JOISE 2. **a.** *trans. arch.*

c **1320** *Sir Tristr.* 47 A forward fast þai bond þat ich a man schul ioien his. *c* **1400** *Apol. Loll.* 77 He schal ioi it as his oune. **1515** BARCLAY *Egloges* iv. (1570) C iv/2, I graunt thee Codrus to ioy my armony. **1590** SPENSER *F.Q.* II. x. 53 Him succeded Marius, Who ioyd his dayes in great tranquillity. **1667** MILTON *P.L.* IX. 1166 Who might have liv'd and joy'd immortal bliss. **1700** DRYDEN *Cymon & Iph.* 544, I will be there, And join'd by thee intend to joy the fair. **1866** ALGER *Solit. Nat. & Man* IV. 282 He was at home, with the things he joyed.

†**b.** *intr.* with *of.* (F. *jouir de.*) *Obs.*

1502 *Ord. Crysten Men* (W. de W. 1506) IV. viii. 189 Who useth, or ioyeth wyttyngely of lettres or of graces so graunted. *a* **1533** LD. BERNERS *Gold. Bk. M. Aurel.* (1546) B iv b, Yf that age was glorious in ioyeng of his persone, no lesse it is to vs to ioye of his doctrines. **1564** *Brief Exam.* *iv b, Howe lytle we shall ioy of them, and vse them.

†**5.** *trans.* To salute or greet with expressions of joy, welcome, or honour; in early use, to give glory to, glorify, extol. *Obs.*

1387-8 T. USK *Test. Love* I. x. (Skeat) l. 76 If thou laudest and ioyest any wight, for he is stuffed with soche maner richesse. *c* **1450** *Merlin* 579 'Sir', seide Merlin, 'I wolde ye dide ioy and honour these lordes that here be assembled to diffende youre reame'. **1693** DRYDEN *Persius* i. (1697) 412 Met by his trembling Wife, returning home, And Rustically Joy'd, as Chief of Rome. **1725** POPE *Odyss.* XIV. 489 The faithful servant joy'd his unknown lord.

†**b.** To give or wish (a person) joy of something; to congratulate. Const. *of* (*in*). *Obs.*

1483 *Cath. Angl.* 197/2 To Ioy,..*coletari*..*congaudere, gratari*. **1603** KNOLLES *Hist. Turks* (1621) 885 Embassadours from their neighbour princes, came to joy them of this victorie. **1660** PEPYS *Diary* 22 Aug., In the House..I met with Mr. G. Montagu, and joyed him in his entrance [as M.P.] for Dover. **1701** ROWE *Amb. Step-Moth.* IV. i. 1578, I come to joy you of a Crown.

†**c.** *intr.* To offer honour or salutation *to.* *Obs.*

1482 *Monk of Evesham* (Arb.) 47 Then this goldsmyth.. wyth an enarrabulle gestur and behauing of gladnes ioyde to my leder and..ofte bowde done al hys body worshippyng and greting hym with innumerable thankys.

†**6.** *trans.* To convert into joy. *Obs. nonce-use.*

1645 RUTHERFORD *Trial & Tri. Faith* ix. (1845) 105 To the saints..hell (to speak so), is heavened, sorrow joyed.

Hence **joyed** (dʒɔɪd) *ppl. a.* [cf. OF. *joï* rejoiced, delighted], rejoiced, delighted; †taking delight *in*.

1491 *Act 7 Hen. VII*, c. 15 Persones of evyll riotous and sedicious dispositions joyed in rumor and rebellious novelries. **1640** LADY GORING in *Lismore Papers* Ser. II. (1888) IV. 150 Truly hee waes the Most Ioyed man in the World. **1655** H. VAUGHAN *Silex Scint.* II. *Palm-Sunday* ii, Put on your best array; Let the joy'd road make holy-day. **1821** CLARE *Vill. Minstr.* I. 9 Each varied charm how joy'd would he pursue.

joyance ('dʒɔɪəns). Chiefly *poet.* Also **-aunce**. [f. JOY *v.* + -ANCE.

App. formed by Spenser; rare before 1800, and considered 'obsolete' by Johnson; reintroduced by Coleridge and Southey, and in 19th cent. a favourite word with poets and writers of imaginative prose. The corresponding word derived from OF. was the obsolete JOUISANCE.]

1. The state of feeling or action of showing joy; rejoicing; delight; enjoyment.

1590 SPENSER *F.Q.* III. xii. 18 Chearfull, fresh and full of ioyance glad, As if no sorrow she ne felt, ne drad. **1607** *Trag. Nero* K ij b, Though Iulia..made great ioyance, that it should be so. **1742** SHENSTONE *Schoolmistr.* 228 Ne for his fellows' joyaunce careth aught. *c* **1796** COLERIDGE *Autumnal Even.* 24 Chaste Joyance dancing in her bright-blue eyes. **1820** SHELLEY *To a Skylark* 76 With thy clear keen joyance Languor cannot be. **1859** TENNYSON *Elaine* 1314 Then would I..Estate them with large land and territory..To keep them in all joyance.

b. Enjoyment *of* something. *rare.*

1596 SPENSER *F.Q.* VI. xi. 7 Which gave him hope..That he in time her joyance should obtaine. **1850** MRS. BROWNING *Poems* I. 20 God, Who gave the right and joyaunce of the world Both unto thee and me,—gave thee to me.

2. The action of enjoying or disporting oneself; disport, festivity, merrymaking.

c **1586** SPENSER *Astrophel* 25 His sports were faire, his ioyance innocent. **1662** GUNNING *Lent Fast* 168 They abstained from..public joyances. **1797** SOUTHEY *King Charlemain* xi, Now merriment, joyaunce, and feasting again Enliven'd the palace of Aix. **1878** *Masque Poets* 20 There too are jousts and joyance rare And beauteous ladies debonair.

3. Joyous character or quality; delight, charm.

1847 DISRAELI *Tancred* I. i, The..illusion of an illimitable distance of sylvan joyance. *a* **1865** BAMFORD *Poems, Farew. Cottage*, Where I..met early spring with her buskin of dew, As o'er the wild heather a joyance she threw.

'**joyancy.** [f. JOYANT; cf. prec. and see -ANCY.] The quality or state of being joyant; joyousness.

1849 J. WILSON in *Blackw. Mag.* LXVI. 381 In a rapture of aimless joyancy. **1866** CARLYLE in *Remin.* (1881) I. 202 One heard too that in Irving there was visible a certain joyancy and frankness of triumph.

'**joyant,** *a. rare.* [f. JOY *v.* + -ANT, after *joyance.*] Feeling or showing joy; joyous.

1834 MUDIE *Brit. Birds* (1841) II. 6 It [the lark] is in fact more joyant in the sun. **1844** LD. HOUGHTON *Mem. Many Scenes, Dream Gondola* 97 O joyant earth! beloved Grecian sky! **1876** J. ELLIS *Cæsar in Egypt* 126 The joyant day-dreams of my rising life.

joyaus, obs. pl. of JEWEL.

joyce, obs. form of JOIST, JUICE.

Joycean ('dʒɔɪsɪən), *a.* and *sb.* Also **Joycian**.

A. *adj.* Of, pertaining to, or characteristic of the Irish writer James *Joyce* (1882-1941), or his work. **B.** *sb.* An admirer or follower of Joyce.

1927 *New Republic* 20 July 236 Joycean passages and bursts of purple lyricism. **1932** *Times Lit. Suppl.* 26 May 386/3 The modified 'Joycean' language is clever and expressive. **1935** *Discovery* Dec. 378/2 The verbatim description of one 'disturbed case' by another, with its progressive lapse into Joycian language. **1938** PARTRIDGE *World of Words* vi. 161 The Joyceans are artificial, but, except at the cost of a highly gymnastic cerebration, unintelligible. **1953** M. LOWRY *Lett.* (1967) 330 Even Bernard de Voto had to interpolate that he was 'a good Joycean—he hoped'. **1965** *Times Lit. Suppl.* 11 Mar. 199/3 This particular 'deviation' has a rather Joycean flavour to it, as it combines the meaning and the effect of exorbitance in one word. **1966** *Listener* 2 June 805/3 The hero's name, Strumienski, would delight any Joycean: it is derived from 'stream'. **1971** *Ibid.* 16 Sept. 381/2 There was a fine Joycian slide into a muck wake. **1971** *Daily Tel.* (Colour Suppl.) 3 Dec. 9/2 The lecturer..led his summer school audience down the howling avenues of Joycean puns.

joycounde, joyel(le, obs. ff. JOCUND, JEWEL.

joyeusity, variant of JOYOUSITIE.

†**joyfnes.** *Obs. rare.* [Cf. OF. *joefnesce* (13th c.), early form of *jeunesse* youth.] Youth.

13.. *Gaw. & Gr. Knt.* 86 Arthure..watz so Ioly of his Ioyfnes & sumquat child gered.

joyful ('dʒɔɪfʊl), *a.* [f. JOY *sb.* + -FUL. For earlier native synonyms, see BLISSFUL, BLITHE.]

1. Of persons, their feelings, etc.: Full of joy; having and showing a lively sense of pleasure or satisfaction; elated with gladness, delighted. †Formerly const. *of*.

c **1290** *S. Eng. Leg.* I. 50/112 Ȝeot was heore heorte glad, and Ioyful, þo huy him founde. **13..** *E.E. Allit. P.* A. 288 Were I at yow by-ȝonde þise wawez, I were a Ioyful Iueler. *c* **1400** *Destr. Troy* 974 Medea the mayden..Was ioyfull of Iason, aioynit hym to. **1535** COVERDALE *Ps.* xcix. [c.] 1 O be ioyfull in God (all ye londes). **1590** SHAKS. *Com. Err.* I. i. 51 A ioyfull mother of two goodly sonnes. **1632** J. HAYWARD tr. *Biondi's Eromena* 75 Polimero taking him..for the Admirall, was the joyfullest man in the world. **1725** POPE *Odyss.* IX. 72 Sad for their loss, but joyful of our life. **1841** LANE *Arab. Nts.* I. 87 He passed the night happy and joyful on account of his recovery. **1876** M. M. GRANT *Sun-Maid* i, Ah, Monsieur, they are all joyful to receive you.

2. Of action, speech, looks, etc.: Expressing or manifesting joy; indicative of gladness.

c **1340** *Cursor M.* 20516 (Fairf.) He..saide til ham wiþ ioiful steyuen comis wiþ me. **1535** COVERDALE *Ps.* lxiii. 5 When my mouth prayseth the with ioyfull lippes. **1611** BIBLE *Ps.* lxvi. 1 Make a ioyfull noise vnto God, all yee lands. **1632** J. HAYWARD tr. *Biondi's Eromena* 68 Being the first time that a ioyfull looke was seene in that Court, sithence the departure of the Princesse. **1756–7** tr. *Keysler's Trav.* (1760) IV. 32 He was received..amidst the joyful acclamations of almost all Italy. **1842** TENNYSON *Captain* 30 Then the Captain's colour heighten'd, Joyful came his speech.

3. Of things, events, etc.: Fraught with, attended by, or causing joy; gladsome, delightful.

1297 R. GLOUC. (Rolls) 786 Nere neuere king ne quene glad wanne hii him seie Ac to þe Ioiuol day hopede wanne he ssolde deie. *c* **1400** MAUNDEV. (Roxb.) ix. 34 He was putt oute of þat ioyfull place. **1480** CAXTON *Chron. Eng.* ccxxvi. 232 All thynges and wethers fallen to me ioyfull and lykyng and gladsum. *a* **1592** H. SMITH *Serm. Luke* xix. 6 Wks. 1867 II. 158 This was the joyfullest news that ever came to Zaccheus's house. **1680** BURNET *Rochester* 143 It was one of the joyfullest things that befe him. *a* **1808** HURD *Serm. Rev.* xix. 10 Wks. 1811 V. 24 Contemplating with grateful admiration so joyful a state of things.

4. *O* (or *oh*) *be joyful*, an alcoholic drink. *slang.*

1823 P. EGAN *Grose's Dict. Vulgar T.* (rev. ed.), *O be joyful*, good liquor; brandy. *Sea term.* **1830** *Greensborough* (N. Carolina) *Patriot* 4 Aug. 4/2 They didn't come to, till the old woman and her darter poured some o be joy full down their throates. **1846** L. CRAWFORD *Hist. White Mts.* iv. 45, I was loaded..with a plenty of what some call..'O-be-joyful'. **1865** *London Jrnl.* 8 Apr. 222/3 Like a great many other clever fellows, he was too much addicted to the 'O be joyful!' **1934** T. S. ELIOT *Rock* ii. 77 Well, boys, what do you say to a pint of Oh be Joyful? **1968** *Listener* 21 Mar. 369/3 It's a lively scene on this part of the Oldham Road: some very jolly pubs, Dutton's O Be Joyful ales in little bottles.

joyfully (ˈdʒɔɪfʊlɪ), *adv.* [f. prec. + -LY².] In a joyful manner.

1. With a feeling or manifestation of joy; with joy; with much gladness.

c **1330** *Arth. & Merl.* 4681 Ther thai setten ioifulliche. *a* **1340** HAMPOLE *Psalter* xxv. 8 A sted in þe whilk þou wold ioyfully wonne. **1413** *Pilgr. Sowle* (Caxton 1483) v. xiv. 105 Ioyfully takyng eueriche other by the hand. **1568** GRAFTON *Chron.* II. 488 He was receyved most ioyfully and honourably, namely by the Citezens of London. **1615** J. STEPHENS *Satyr. Ess.* 322 She hearkens joyfully to the numerous footing of horses. **1860** WILKIE COLLINS *Dead Secret* II. iii, 'In two months', she exclaimed joyfully, 'I shall see the dear old place again'.

2. So as to occasion joy; with happy outcome or result.

c **1400** *Destr. Troy* 993 Pelleus..had pyne at his hert, þat Iason of his Iorney Ioifully hade sped. **1549** COVERDALE, etc. *Erasm. Par. Cath. Epist.* Ded., The Lorde Iesus..Ioyfully preserue yowre longe prosperous healthe in hym. **1602** SHAKS. *Ham.* II. ii. 41 Th' Ambassadors from Norwey, my good Lord, Are ioyfully return'd. **1883** F. M. CRAWFORD *To Leeward* iv. 42 However the tale ends, we would have made it end yet more joyfully.

ˈ**joyfulness.** [See -NESS.] The quality or state of being joyful; gladness; lively happiness.

c **1485** *Digby Myst.* (1882) IV. 1554 In Ioye of this Ioyfullnese, A songe of comforte lete vs expresse. **1526** *Pilgr. Perf.* (W. de W. 1531) 261 All the collettes and orysons after this tyme be of ioyfulnesse. **1611** BIBLE *Ecclus.* xxx. 22 The ioyfulnes of a man prolongeth his dayes. **1794** MRS. RADCLIFFE *Myst. Udolpho* lvi, With..the joyfulness of pure benevolence. **1849** RUSKIN *Sev. Lamps* ii. §19. 49 The record of..trials and heartbreakings—of recoveries and joyfulnesses of success.

joygne, obs. form of JOIN.

joying (ˈdʒɔɪɪŋ), *vbl. sb.* [f. JOY *v.* + -ING¹.]

1. The action of JOY vb.; rejoicing; enjoyment.

c **1300** *Havelok* 2087 He dide unto the borw bringe Sone anon, al with ioynge, His wif, and his serganz thre. *c* **1450** LONELICH *Grail* lii. 829 Thanne that damysele Made gret Ioyeng. *c* **1560** INGELEND *Disobed. Child* Epil., How short a feast is this worldly joying. **1633** P. FLETCHER *Poet. Misc.* 65 Our sweet retired joying.

†2. *transf.* An object or source of joy. *Obs.*

1388 WYCLIF *Ps.* xxxi[i]. 7 Þou, my fulli ioiynge, delyuere me fro hem þat cumpassen me! *c* **1430** *Hymns Virg.* 28 Ihesu, my king and my ioiynge!

†ˈ**joyingly**, *adv. Obs.* [f. *joying*, pr. pple. of JOY *v.* + -LY².] With joy, joyfully.

c **1430** *Christ's Compl.* in *Pol. Rel. & L. Poems* 199 Ioiyngly þou woldist it take anoon. *c* **1450** tr. *De Imitatione* III. lxii. 144 Suffre paciently, if þou can not suffre ioingly.

joyke, obs. form of JOUK *v.*¹

joyless (ˈdʒɔɪlɪs), *a.* [f. JOY *sb.* + -LESS.]

1. Destitute of joy; having, feeling, or manifesting no joy; sad, cheerless. †Sometimes const. *of.*

13.. *E.E. Allit. P.* A. 252, I haf ben a Ioylez Iuelere. *a* **1400–50** *Alexander* 1284 Full ioyles he rydes. Ay he gretis as he gase. **1593** SHAKS. *Lucr.* 1711 While with a joyless smile she turns away The face. **1667** MILTON *P.L.* IV. 766 Not in the bought smile Of Harlots, loveless, joyless, unindeard. **1697** DRYDEN *Virg. Georg.* III. 336 The youthful Bull..Forsakes his Food, and pining for the Lass, Is joyless of the Grove. **1732** BERKELEY *Alciphr.* II. §13 It will barely subsist, in a dull joyless insipid state. **1883** *19th Cent.* Nov. 811 The lives of the people are joyless.

2. Causing or affording no joy; cheerless, dismal, dreary.

13.. *E.E. Allit. P.* C. 146 Hit watz a ioyles gyn þat Ionas watz inne. **1588** SHAKS. *Tit. A.* IV. ii. 67 A ioylesse, dismall, blacke & sorrowfull issue, Heere is the babe as loathsome as a toad. **1740** WESLEY *Hymn*, '*Christ whose glory*' ii, Joyless is the day's return Till Thy mercy's beams I see. **1804** J. GRAHAME *Sabbath*, On other days the man of toil is doomed To eat his joyless bread, lonely. *a* **1847** ELIZA COOK *There would I be* v, The crowd and the city are joyless to me.

Hence ˈ**joylessly** *adv.*; ˈ**joylessness**.

1625 DONNE *Serm. Ps.* lxiii. 7 A faintnesse of heart, a chearlesnesse, a joylesnesse of spirit. **1766** G. CANNING *Anti-Lucretius* v. 402 The lazy blood moves joylessly. **1881** MARY C. HAY *Missing* III. 240 Gravely and joylessly looking up into Alfred's face. **1884** *Spectator* 4 Oct. 1307/2 The general joylessness of the lives of the poor.

joylile, joyly(e, obs. ff. JOLLILY, JOLLY.

joylite, joylity, etc., obs. forms of JOLLITY.

joyne, obs. form of JOIN, JUNE *sb.*

joynter, obs. form of JOINTER, JOINTURE.

joyous (ˈdʒɔɪəs), *a.* Forms: 4–7 ioyous, (5 -uss, -eos, -eus, -eux, -ouse), 5–6 ioyus, -ouse, (6 -ws, -eous), 7– joyous. [ME. a. AF. *joyous* = OF. *joios, -eus*, F. *joyeux*, f. *joie* JOY *sb.*]

1. Having a joyful nature or mood; full of glad feeling; blithe, gladsome, buoyant; also, expressive of, or characterized by, joy; = JOYFUL 1, 2.

c **1315** SHOREHAM 120 More encheyson hadde oure levedy Ioyous and blythe for to be. **1422** tr. *Secreta Secret., Priv. Priv.* 240 The good odure..makyth the herte oppyn and [io]youse. *c* **1485** *Digby Myst.* IV. 1028 Be Ioyeos now of mynd! **1560** BIBLE (Genev.) *Isa.* xxii. 2 A citie full of bruit, a ioyous citie. **1667** MILTON *P.L.* VIII. 515 The Earth Gave sign of gratulation, and each Hill; Joyous the Birds. **1711** ADDISON *Spect.* No. 128 ¶1 Women in their Nature are much more gay and joyous than Men. **1753** HAWKESWORTH *Adventurer* 20 Oct. 177, I had now ascended another scale in the climax; and was acknowledged..to be a *Joyous Spirit* [see also JESSAMY *sb.* 4]. **1827** HARE *Guesses* (1859) 241 A laugh, to be joyous, must flow from a joyous heart. **1848** C. BRONTE *J. Eyre* xvii. 168 A joyous stir was now audible in the hall.

†**b.** Const. *of* or with clause. *Obs.*

c **1305** *St. Swithin* 36 in *E.E.P.* (1862) 44 Alle men þat him iknewe ioyous þerof were. *c* **1477** CAXTON *Jason* 50 b, I am right ioyous of thy wele and worship. *a* **1548** HALL *Chron., Hen. VI* 84 He was ioyous that power and princely estate was now to him happened. **1596** SHAKS. *Tam. Shr.* IV. v. 70 Wander we to see thy honest sonne, Who will of thy arriuall be full ioyous. **1599** —— *Hen. V*, v. ii. 9 Right ioyous are we to behold your face.

2. Of things, events, etc.: Inspiring or productive of joy; gladdening, cheerful; = JOYFUL 3.

c **1450** HOLLAND *Howlat* 753 Thow ioyuss fleiss of Gedion. **1475** *Bk. Noblesse* (Roxb.) 70 It was the ioieust and plesaunt sighte that ever..Lisander had see. **1526** TINDALE *Heb.* xii. 11 No manner learnynge for the present tyme semeth to be ioyeous but greveous. *c* **1630** MILTON *Passion* 3 Of..joyous news of heavenly Infant's birth, My muse with Angels did divide to sing. **1796** H. HUNTER tr. *St.-Pierre's Stud. Nat.* (1799) II. 43 Every return of that joyous season [harvest]. **1864** KIRK *Chas. Bold* I. II. i. 450 A new sovereign, on the occasion of his 'joyous entry', as his first visit to a place after his accession was called.

3. *Comb.*

1820 SHELLEY *Hymn to Mercury* xxi, Joyous-minded Hermes from the glen Drew the fat spoils.

†**joˈyousitie, joˈyeusity.** *Obs.* Also 5 ioyous(e)te, ioyeusete. [a. F. *joyeuseté* (14–15th c. in Hatz.-Darm.), f. *joios, joyeux* JOYOUS: see -TY, -ITY.] The quality or state of being joyous; joyous or mirthful behaviour; mirth, disport.

a **1450** *Knt. de la Tour* (1868) 128 To eschewe diuerse plesauncez, disportes, and other Ioyeusete [*printed* Ioyeuseie]. **1483** CAXTON *Gold. Leg.* 112/1 Hylaire is said of Ioyouste for he was ioyous in the seruyce of god. **1491** —— *Vitas Patr.* (W. de W. 1495) I. xl. 61 b/1 She sawe alle Ioyousete and gladnesse. *a* **1572** KNOX *Hist. Ref.* IV. Wks. 1846 II. 319 Such pastyme to thame is but joyousitie, whairin our Queyn was brocht up. **1819** W. TENNANT *Papistry Storm'd* (1827) 10 'Mid sic joyeusitie, I wot Th' east neuk o' Fife was nae forgot.

ˈ**joyously**, *adv.* [f. JOYOUS + -LY².] In a joyous manner, joyfully, gladsomely.

1474 CAXTON *Chesse* 98 And went his way right ioyously. *a* **1548** HALL *Chron., Hen. VI* 136 A greate nombre of horsses..whiche thei ioyously brought with them to Roan. **1596** SPENSER *F.Q.* v. xi. 33 Whom when she saw so ioyously come forth, She gan reioyce. **1818** SHELLEY *Rosalind & Helen* 525 Nor noticed I where joyously Sate my two younger babes at play. **1856** KANE *Arct. Expl.* I. xvii. 214 He is singing in his bunk, as joyously as ever.

ˈ**joyousness.** [f. as prec. + -NESS.] The state or quality of being joyous.

1549 COVERDALE, etc. *Erasm. Par. Jas.* iv. 1 Let outragious ioyousnes be chaunged in to holsome sadnes. **1821** LAMB *Elia* Ser. I. *St. Valentine*, She was all joyousness and innocence. **1874** SYMONDS *Sk. Italy & Greece* (1898) I. viii. 166 In his work..life is toned to a religious joyousness.

joy-ride (ˈdʒɔɪraɪd), *sb. colloq.* (orig. *U.S.*). [f. JOY *sb.* + RIDE *sb.*¹] A pleasure trip in a motor car, aeroplane, etc., often without the permission of the owner of the vehicle. Also *transf.* and *fig.* Hence ˈ**joy-ride** *v. intr.*, to go for a joy-ride; *trans.*, to convey (as) on a joy-ride; ˈ**joy-rider**, one who goes on a joy-ride; ˈ**joy-riding** *vbl. sb.*; also *attrib.*

1908 W. S. BLUNT *Diary* 5 Aug. (1920) II. 217 Joy-riders..light-hearted Londoner folk concerned with nothing but their own pleasure. **1909** *N.Y. Even. Post* (Semi-weekly ed.) 15 July 2 [The] Acting Mayor vetoed the ordinance passed last week to prevent city officers from taking 'joy rides'. *Ibid.* 2 Sept. 8 'This was no haphazard expedition,' he said, 'no intensified Arctic joy ride, undertaken on nerve.' **1910** *National Police Gaz.* 2 July 3/4 As a rule there isn't much chance of joy riding in a taxi. **1913** *Aeroplane* 17 Apr. 455/2 The pilots of machines already qualified naturally took no risks of damaging their mounts by 'joy riding'. **1913** *Collier's* 27 Dec. 9 (*heading*) With the joy-riding fleet. **1915** D. O. BARNETT *Let.* 6 July 206 We joined forces and captured a motor-ambulance which joy-rided us back here. **1915** *Amer. Mag.* Oct. 28/2 You take your dago friend 'n' joy-ride with the gang all night. **1918** H. HAYENS *Lords of Air* 41 Unfortunately I was not joy-riding, but bent on serious business. **1919** *Aeroplane* 5 Feb. 555/1 There are two million people in this country who wish for what is vulgarly called a joy-ride in an aeroplane. *Ibid.* 555/2 Joy-riders will not be taken aloft one at a time but in half-dozens and dozens, in big flying boats..and multiple-engined land machines. **1922** F. HARRIS *My Life & Loves* I. ix. 187 'Aren't you tired?'..'No,' I replied, 'I feel no fatigue, indeed, I feel the better for our joy ride!' **1922** JOYCE *Ulysses* 497 You once nobble that, congregation, and a buck joy ride to heaven becomes a back number. **1925** *Flynn's* 14 Feb. 664/2 *Joy-ride*, intoxication resulting from use of drugs. **1925** *Times* 26 Sept., For the third year..no fatal accident involving passengers in other flying for hire, mainly 'joy ride' flights. **1930** E. POUND *XXX Cantos* ix. 36 With three pages of secret instructions To the effect: 'Did he think the campaign was a joy-ride?' **1952** C. DAY LEWIS tr. *Virgil's Aeneid* XII. 280 Around them..The hostile formations are pressing..While you're joy-riding over these empty fields. **1972** J. BROWN *Chancer* xii. 161 That's what you need now, he says—need a joy-ride, man... No danger neither, he says, on the joy-pop. **1972** *N.Y. Law Jrnl.* 10 Oct. 20/6 The annotation..dealing with elements of the offense defined in 'joyriding' statutes fails to disclose any case in which the person using a rented vehicle with the consent of the custodian has been held guilty of unauthorized use. **1973** *Scottish Sunday Express* 5 Aug. 7/8 A man who drove away two cars for a 'joy ride' was fined £75.

joyse, joyst(e, joys(e, obs. ff. JOIST, JUICE.

ˈ**joysome**, *a. rare.* [f. JOY *sb.* + -SOME.] Fraught with joy, joyous, gladsome.

1613–16 W. BROWNE *Brit. Past.* II. iii, Neere to the end of this all-joysome Grove. **1855** SINGLETON *Virgil* II. 103 Thee by heaven's joysome light And breezes..I entreat.

joys(s)ance, variant of JOUISANCE *Obs.*

joyssement, var. GISTMENT *Obs.*, agistment.

joyt, obs. Sc. form of JOT *sb.*¹

joywell, obs. form of JEWEL.

J.P., abbreviation of *Justice of the Peace.*

Jr., jr., abbreviation of JUNIOR.

J-shaped (ˈdʒeɪʃeɪpt), *a.* Having the shape of the letter J; used *esp.* of a graph or of a variable expressed by it. Also **J-curve**, a J-shaped curve.

1911 G. U. YULE *Introd. Theory Statistics* II. vi. 98 The extremely asymmetrical, or 'J-shaped', distribution, the class-frequencies running up to a maximum at one end of the range. **1916** *Phil. Trans. R. Soc.* A. CCXVI. 432 The area of J-curves. **1927** H. L. RIETZ *Math. Statistics* iii. 57 Type III would be J-shaped if *γa* were negative. **1939** *Amer. Jrnl. Sociol.* XLIV. 975 He [*sc.* Professor Allport] advances the 'J-curve hypothesis of conforming behavior'. **1950** S. A. STOUFFER *Measurement & Prediction* i. 41 In general, as predicted, a *J*-shaped or *U*-shaped curve was obtained with attitude data. **1968** P. MCKELLAR *Experience & Behaviour* xi. 304 If..the situation is changed by the introduction of a traffic light we have J-curve behaviour. **1973** *Times* 7 May 16/4 The notion of the post-devaluation 'J-curve', according to which an initial deterioration in the balance of payments is followed by a more-than-offsetting improvement as the volume of exports responds over time to the gain in price competitiveness.

Ju (dʒuː). [ad. *Ju Chou*, the name of a town in Honan, China.] Used to designate pottery with buff body and blue-green glaze produced in Ju Chou in the 12th century.

1906 W. BURTON *Porcelain* vi. 57 Dr. Bushell mentions a fine piece of *Ju-Yao* in his possession, which, however, has a delicate greenish glaze with no trace of blue. **1936** *Burlington Mag.* 4/1 The original Ju ware was made at the potteries at Ju Chou. **1949** G. SAVAGE *Ceramics for Collector* ii. 44 The kiln was in operation only for about twenty years, and at one time the '*ying ch'ing*' type was identified with Ju ware. **1969** *Times* 9 Dec. (Taiwan Suppl.) p. vii/2 The 24 items of Ju ware are the best of the porcelain. **1972** *Collector's Guide* June 95 Ju ware, only identified as recently as 1936 by Sir Percival David, is much rarer than Ting.

Ju, juall, obs. forms of JEW, JEWEL.

†**jub**¹, **jube.** *Obs. rare.* [a. F. *jube, jubbe*, obs. ff. *jupe* JUPE.] A short coat or jerkin.

1611 FLORIO, *Giubba*, a iub, a trusse, a sleuelesse doublet, ierkin, iacket or mandillion. **1621** *Naworth Househ. Bks.* (Surtees) 160 Making a pair of drawers and a jube.

†**jub**². *Obs.* or *dial.* [app. onomatopœic.] A thrust or knock with something blunt, a jog; the jog of a trotting horse.

1688 R. HOLME *Armoury* III. 401, I am likely to run the Risque of Rubs and Jubs. *a* **1825** FORBY *Voc. E. Anglia, Jub*, the slow heavy trot of a sluggish horse.

jub: see JUBBE.

‖**juba**^{1} ('dʒuːbə). [L. *juba* mane, foliage of trees: see JUBE^{2}.] (See quot. 1880.)

1688 R. HOLME *Armoury* II. 100/1 Rice.. beareth a seed in a sparsed juba, or tuft. **1706** PHILLIPS, *Juba*, the Main of a Horse..; among Herbalists a soft loose Beard which hangs at the end of the Husks of some Plants that are of the nature of Corn particularly in Millet. **1880** GRAY *Struct. Bot.* (ed. 6) 417/2 *Juba*, a loose panicle, with axis deliquescent.

juba^{2} ('dʒuːbə). *U.S.* Also **juber, jouba**. [Negro.] A species of dance or breakdown practised by the plantation-negroes of the southern United States, accompanied by clapping of the hands, patting of the knees and thighs, striking of the feet on the floor, and a refrain in which the word *juba* is frequently repeated. Also in *Comb.*, as ***juba-dance, -patting, -shuffle***.

18.. *Southern Sketches* 98 (Bartlett) Here were Virginia slaves, dancing jigs and clapping Juber, over a barrel of persimmon beer. **1885** *Libr. Mag.* July 1 On the rude floor of the forecastle, they danced their vigorous hoe-downs, jigs and jubah-shuffles. **1888** *Century Mag.* XXXVI. 770/1 The juba-dance and the corn-shucking were equally invested with elements of the unreal and the grotesque.

juba, obs. form of JUBE *sb.*^{1}

†**jubarb** ('dʒuːbɑːb). *Obs.* [a. F. *joubarbe*:—*jousbarbe* (= Sp. *jusbarba*):—L. *Jovis barba* Jove's beard.] The houseleek.

[*c* **1265** *Voc.* in Wr.-Wülcker 558/26 *Iouis barba*, i. iubarbe, i. singrene.] *c* **1450** *Bk. Hawkyng* in *Rel. Ant.* I. 301 Yeve here jus of rasne and jubarde. **1524** *Gt. Herbal* ccclxxxi. xij, An herbe that is called also Iobarde. **1601** HOLLAND *Pliny* II. 237 The lesse Sengreen or Iubarb groweth vpon walls.. likewise vpon the tiles of house-roofs. **1725** BRADLEY *Fam. Dict.* s.v., The Great Jubarb is a Plant that has great Pulpy and thick Leaves,.. sharp at the Ends like a Tongue.

jubarde, -die, obs. forms of JEOPARD, -DY.

†**ju'bartes**. *Obs.* Also 7 **jubertas, -artus, dubartas**, 8 **dubartus**. [mod.L. *jubartēs*, F. *jubarte*; also called *Jupiter*, or *Jupiter-fisch* (Anderson *Nachrichten von Island*, Hamburg, 1748) and GIBBERT, F. *gibbar* in Cotgr.

As to the origin of the word, J. H. Trumbull in *Fisheries & Fish. Indust. U.S.* (1884) I. 29, says: 'Rondelet.. gives a figure of a "Balæna Vera".. which the whale-fishers of Saintonge call *Gibbar* or *Gibbero Dorso*, that is "raised in a hump on which is the fin." From this provincial name came Gibbartas, Gubartas, Jubart, Jubartes, Jupiter, and half a dozen other corruptions, introduced first among mariners.' (Anderson calls *gibbar* a Basque word.)]

A name given in 17–18th c. to species of Rorqual, Fin-whale, or Finner, esp. that found near the coast of New England. (Sometimes applied erroneously, e.g. in quot. 1701 to the Cachalot.)

It figures in various works on Natural History, from Klein 1740 to Cuvier 1836, as *Balænoptera jubartes, Baleinoptère Jubarte, Rorqual Jubarte*, but the name has disappeared from more recent works.

1616 CAPT. SMITH *Descr. New Eng.* 1 We saw many [whales].. a kinde of Iubartes, and not the Whale that yeeldes Finnes and Oyle as wee expected. *c* **1640** J. SMYTH *Hundred of Berkeley* (1885) 319 The Sturgeon, Porpoise, Thornpole, Jubertas or a yonge whale. **1663** *Charter of Rhode Isl.* (in *U.S. Fisheries* 1884 Sect. I. 28), Itt shall bee laweful for them, or any of them, having struck whale, dubertus, or other greate ffish, itt or them to pursue unto any parte of that coaste. **1671** NARBOROUGH *Jrnl.* in *Acc. Sev. Late Voy.* I. (1694) 160 Saw many Sea Fowles.. with many Jubartesses. **1682** J. COLLINS *Making of Salt* 83 The Dutch ..have the Priviledge to Fish.. for Grampusses, and Dubartas, which is a bastard kind of Whale. **1701** C. WOLLEY *Jrnl. New York* (1860) 39 A Dubartus is a Fish of the shape of a Whale, which have teeth where the Whale has Bone.

juba's bush. A tall annual, *Iresine celosioides* (N.O. *Amarantaceæ*), growing in the southern United States and bearing panicles of small white flowers. Also called ***juba's brush***.

jubate ('dʒuːbət), *a. Zool.* [ad. L. *jubāt-us* maned, f. *juba* mane.] Having a mane, or a fringe of hair like a mane.

1826 KIRBY & SP. *Entomol.* IV. 278 *Jubate*,.. having long pendent hairs in a continued series.

‖**jubbah** ('dʒʌbə, 'dʒʊbbə). Also 6 **iubbe**, 9 **jubbee, jubbeh, juba, jhuba, joobey, djubba**. [ad. Arab. *jubbah*, whence also Sp. (with Arab. article) *aljuba*, It. *giubba, giuppa*, Prov. *jupa*, F. *jube, jupe* (cf. JUB^{1}); derivative F. *jupon*. Another pronunciation of the Arabic is JIBBAH.]

An outer garment worn by Muslims and Parsees, consisting of a long cloth coat, open in front, with sleeves reaching nearly to the wrists.

a **1548** HALL *Chron., Hen. VIII* 83 Thre were apparelled for Hector, Alexandre, and Iulius Cæsar, in Turkay Iubbes of grene cloth of gold wrought like Chamlet very richely. **1818** E. BLAQUIERE tr. *Pananti's Resid. Algiers* x. (1830) 201 Their robes, called *jubas*, are made like tunics. **1819** T. HOPE *Anastasius* (1820) I. i. 1 [He] saw no reason why he should not.. swing his jubbee, like a pendulum, from side to side. **1828** J. B. FRASER *Kuzzilbash* I. xii. 165, I had.. given him my Toorkoman jubbah and cap. **1831** *Literary Souvenir* 152 Over these hung a brown *joobba*, or cloak of camel's hair. **1896** *Strand Mag.* Jan. 88 He wore a crimson turban, yellow haik, brown djubba and saffron slippers.

†**jubbe**. *Obs.* Also 4–6 **iobbe**, 6 **iobb**, 7 **jub**. [Origin unascertained.] A large vessel for liquor.

c **1386** CHAUCER *Miller's T.* 442 With breed and chese and good Ale in a Iubbe. —— *Shipman's T.* 70 With hym broghte he a Iubbe of Maluesye. **1392** *Earl Derby's Exp.* (Camden) 154 Et pro j pare jobbes de iiij galonibus, iiij paribus potel botels, xij pottes galoners. **1570** LEVINS *Manip.* 181/30 Iubbe, *cantharus, scyphus*. [In BULLOKAR, COCKERAM, PHILLIPS as obsolete word, *Jub*.]

jub(b)et(t, obs. forms of GIBBET.

‖**jube**^{1} ('dʒuːbiː). Also 8 **juba**. [a. L. *jubē* 'bid' or 'order thou'; said to be from the words *Jube, domine, benedīcere*, pronounced from it by the deacon before the reading of the Gospel. (See *Myrroure of Our Ladye* (1873) 102.)]

1. A rood-loft or screen and gallery dividing the choir from the nave.

1767 DUCAREL *Anglo-Norm. Antiq.* 87 The *jube* or screen at the west end of the choir is a beautiful piece of architecture. **1838** JAMES *Richelieu* xxxv, Cross the jube, through the monks' gallery round the choir. **1861** BERESF. HOPE *Eng. Cathedr. 19th C.* 174 A feature.. reduced to its subsequent form in the 11th or 12th century.. the *jube* having been then substituted for the primitive ambo.

†**2.** See quot. (erron. *juba*). *Obs.*

1725 tr. *Dupin's Eccl. Hist. 17th C.* I. v. 68/2 The Preacher was plac'd in a Chair lifted up, which the Ancients call'd *Chair, Throne, Tribunal, Juba, Exedra*; which was ordinarily plac'd within the Enclosure of the Choir. The Bishops.. sometimes mounted the *Ambon* or *Juba*, which was betwixt the Choir and the Nave.

†**jube**^{2} (dʒuːb). *Obs. rare*$^{-0}$. [a. F. *jube* (Cotgr. 1611), L. *juba*.] A mane.

1659 TORRIANO, *Giúba*, the long Jube or fleece that hangs down from beasts necks, namely of a Lion.

jube^{3} (dʒuːb), abbrev. of JUJUBE 2.

1937 PARTRIDGE *Dict. Slang* 445/2 *Jube*, a coll. abbrev. of *jujube* (the lozenge). **1967** E. & M. A. RADFORD *No Reason for Murder* iii. 16 He bought.. bars of chocolate and jubes. **1970** J. CLEARY *Helga's Web.* vii. 118 Do you have any menthol jubes?

jube^{4} (dʒuːb). [Persian.] An open watercourse in Iranian cities.

1948 in *Punch's Almanack* 2. **1953** A. SMITH *Blind White Fish in Persia* iii. 48 By every pavement ran the jube, a stream of water which had doubtless been clean at the top of the town but did not remain so for long. **1959** T. GRIFFITH *Waist-High Culture* (1960) ix. 115 Tehran, its streets vivid with sidewalk hawkers, the flow of filth in the jubes.

jube, variant of JUB^{1}.

†'**jubeb**, an obs. variant of JUJUBE.

1598 FLORIO, *Giubebba*, a drug called iubebes [1611 Iubebs]. **1658** PHILLIPS, *Jubeb*, fruit.. a kind of Pruan, used much in Physick. **1727** BRADLEY *Fam. Dict.* s.v. *Gourd*, To steep it.. in the Juice of Jubebs. **1736** BAILEY *Househ. Dict.* 334 Take syrup of Althea and Jubebs.

jubeling, jubeting: see JUBIL *v.*

juberdy, -erte, obs. forms of JEOPARDY.

†**jubil, jubel**, *v. Obs. rare.* [ad. L. *jūbilāre*, orig. to halloo or call to any one ('jubilare est rustica voce inclamare' Festus), to shout, huzza; in Christian writers, esp. to shout for joy; cf. OF. *jubler*, F. *jubiler*, Ger. *jubeln*, Du. *jubelen*, to jubilate.]

1. *intr.* To halloo, shout (to dogs or the like).

1603 FLORIO *Montaigne* II. xi. 248 The earnestnes of showting, jubeling [*printed* jubeting] and hallowing.

2. To jubilate. Hence **jubiling, jubeling** *vbl. sb.*

c **1450** *Mirour Saluacioun* 4408 There, shal be gladnesse eterne and iubilyng bisyly. *Ibid.* 4954 Thi sawle alder-swettest [made] a magnyfy iubylyng.

jubil, *sb.*: see JUBILEE, JUBIL-TRUMPET.

jubilance ('dʒuːbɪləns). [f. JUBILANT: see -ANCE.] The fact of being jubilant; jubilation, exultation, gladness.

1864 NEALE *Seaton. Poems* 234 This jubilance of praise. **1868** J. T. NETTLESHIP *Ess. Browning* vii. 241 Passionate wail that rises to triumphant jubilance. **1874** L. MORRIS *Evensong* liv, Then came a sudden hush, and the jubilance faded away.

jubilancy ('dʒuːbɪlənsɪ). [f. as prec.: see -ANCY.] The quality or fact of being jubilant.

1894 *Forum* (N.Y.) July 592 A note of jubilancy unmistakably spontaneous.

jubilant ('dʒuːbɪlənt), *a.* [ad. L. *jūbilānt-em*, pr. pple. of *jūbilāre* to shout, raise a shout of joy: see JUBIL *v.*] Making a joyful noise, rejoicing with songs and acclamations; now generally, Making demonstrations of joy, exultingly glad.

1667 MILTON *P. L.* VII. 564 The Planets in their station list'ning stood, While the bright Pomp ascended Jubilant. *c* **1798** COLERIDGE *Sibyl Leaves, To Wordsworth* 35 Amid a mighty nation jubilant. **1811** W. R. SPENCER *Poems* 39 All nature jubilant resounds thy praise. **1887** *Spectator* 25 June 859/2 At this Jubilee-time.. by busy and jubilant England.

b. Expressing or manifesting joy.

1784 BP. HORNE *Disc. Ch. Mus.* Wks. 1818 IV. 16 Notes of joy, exulting and jubilant. **1859** KINGSLEY *Misc.* (1860) I. 152 Bursting into a jubilant canter.

jubilantly ('dʒuːbɪləntlɪ), *adv.* [f. prec. + -LY^{2}.] In a jubilant manner, with demonstrations of joy, exultantly, gladly.

1868 HOLME LEE *B. Godfrey* xlix. 272 She was welcomed ..by the children jubilantly. **1884** *Harper's Mag.* Aug. 472/1 The shout is jubilantly renewed.

†'**jubilar**, *a. Obs. rare*$^{-1}$. [In form, f. L. *jūbil-um* wild cry, shout, halloo, huzza, but in sense associated with *jūbilæus* JUBILEE + -AR: cf. F. *jubilaire* of or pertaining to a jubilee.] Of the nature or character of a jubilee.

1613 BP. HALL *Holy Panegyr.* 3 The tenth complete yeere of our Constantine deserues to be solemne and Iubilar.

jubilarian (dʒuːbɪ'lɛərɪən). [f. med.L. *jūbilāri-us* JUBILARY + -AN.] One who celebrates his or her jubilee; *spec.* in *R.C. Ch.*, a priest, monk, or nun who has been such for fifty years.

1782 in A. Mary Sharp *Hist. Ufton Court* (1892) 233 May 13th 1782 died age 79 the Rev. F. Saward Madew, O.S.F. a jubilarian, many years missionary at Ufton Court. **1882** H. FOLEY *Rec. Eng. Soc. Jesus* VII. 106 A jubilarian in religion, in the priesthood and in the mission. **1890** *Cath. News* 3 May 7/3 We have now three 'jubilarians' who have completed 50 years and over as professed nuns.

†'**jubilary**, *a.* (*sb.*) *Obs. rare.* [ad. med.L. *jūbilāri-us* one that has continued 50 years in the same state; in form f. *jūbil-um* wild cry, shout, but in sense associated with *jūbilæus* JUBILEE. Cf. F. *jubilaire*.] Of or pertaining to a jubilee, jubilar: in quot. *absol.* as *sb.*

1537 LATIMER *Serm. bef. Convoc.* Dj, How some brought forth Canonizations.. some pardons, and these of wonderful varietie, some Stationaries, some Iubilaryes, some Pocularyes for drinkers.

‖**jubilate** (dʒuːbɪ'leɪtiː, juːbiː'lɑːteɪ), *sb.*^{1} [L. *jūbilāte* shout ye, the first word of the psalm.]

1. The hundredth psalm (ninety-ninth in the Vulgate), used as a canticle in the Anglican service; also, the music to which this is set.

1706 A. BEDFORD *Temple Mus.* xi. 228 The Antient Tunes of the Te Deum, Jubilate [etc.]. **1857** F. PROCTER *Hist. Bk. Com. Prayer* 226 *Jubilate*.. ordered, together with the *Te Deum*, on the occasion of a solemn thanksgiving.

2. *transf.* A call to rejoice; an outburst of joyous triumph.

1767 H. BROOKE *Fool of Qual.* (1859) II. 244 They would speedily be with us in a joint jubilate on the banks of the Avon. **1856** VAUGHAN *Mystics* (1860) I. 179 My heart sings *jubilate* thereat. **1877** *Tinsley's Mag.* XXI. 422 Heaven's grand courts with jubilates rang.

3. *R.C. Ch.* The third Sunday after Easter, so called because Ps. 66 (65 in Vulgate), which begins with *Jubilate*, is used as the introit on that day.

†**jubilate** ('dʒuːbɪleɪt), *sb.*^{2} *Obs. rare*$^{-0}$. [ad. L. *jūbilātus*, perf. pple. of *jubilāre* to JUBILATE, taken as sb.] = JUBILARIAN.

1706 PHILLIPS, *Jubilate* (a Term us'd in the Roman Church), a Monk, Canon, or Doctor, that has been Fifty Years a Professor.

jubilate ('dʒuːbɪleɪt), *v.* [f. ppl. stem of L. *jūbilāre*: see JUBIL *v.*]

†**1.** *trans.* To make glad, to rejoice. *Obs.*

1604 T. WRIGHT *Passions* v. § 2. 168 Musicke.. iubilating the heart with pleasure.

2. *intr.* To utter sounds of joy or exultation; to make demonstrations of joy; to rejoice, exult. In recent newspaper use, sometimes, To celebrate a jubilee or other joyful occasion.

a **1641** BP. MOUNTAGU *Acts & Mon.* (1642) 205 Such as Almighty God did.. replenish.. could not but jubilate. **1659** HAMMOND *On Ps.* lxxxiv. 3 To cry aloud, vociferate or jubilate. **1721** R. KEITH tr. *à Kempis' Vall. Lilies* xxvii. 83 O ye Cherubim and Seraphim.. how fervently, and how excellently do ye sing and jubilate aloud before God. **1837** CARLYLE *Fr. Rev.* I. v. i, Hope, jubilating, cries aloud that it will prove a miraculous Brazen Serpent in the Wilderness. **1851** S. JUDD *Margaret* III. (1871) 358 The birds are jubilating in the woods.

Hence '**jubilating** *vbl. sb.* and *ppl. a.*

1853 DE QUINCEY *Autobiog. Sk.* ii. Wks. I. 55 The hurrahs were yet ascending from our jubilating lips. **1897** *Westm. Gaz.* 4 Feb. 2/3 In this morning of glad jubilating.

jubilated ('dʒuːbɪleɪtɪd), *a. R.C. Ch.* [f. as JUBILATE *sb.*^{2} + -ED.] That has completed his fiftieth year in orders.

1772 NUGENT tr. *Hist. Friar Gerund* IV. ii. 21 There had died lately in the convent a jubilated father preacher, a man of great consideration in the order.

jubilation (dʒuːbɪ'leɪʃən). [ad. L. *jūbilātiōn-em*, n. of action from *jūbilāre* to JUBILATE.] The action of jubilating, loud utterance of joy; exultation, rejoicing, gladness; public rejoicing. With *a* and *pl.* An expression of exultant joy.

1388 WYCLIF *Ps.* cl. 5 Herie ȝe him in cymbalis sownynge wel! herye ȝe him in cymbalis of iubilacioun! ech spirit, herye þe lord! *c* **1485** *Digby Myst.* (1882) II. 292 Be of good chere and perfyte Iubylacion. **1526** *Pilgr. Perf.* (W. de W.

1531) 184 b, In our hertes all solace, ioye & iubilacyon. **1634** W. TIRWHYT tr. *Balzac's Lett.* (vol. I) 133, I should remaine disconsolate amidst the publique Iubilations. **1657** SPARROW *Bk. Com. Prayer* (1661) 58 The Te Deum, Benedictus..being the most Expressive Jubilations..for the Redemption of the world. **1789** BURNEY *Hist. Mus.* (ed. 2) III. i. 8 In Church Music whether jubilation, humility, sorrow, or contrition are to be expressed. **1837** CARLYLE *Fr. Rev.* III. VII. vi, Sansculottism is dead..and is buried with ..deafening jubilation. **1879** Low *Afghan War* iii. 288 The jubilations of the garrison were short-lived.

jubilatory (ˈdʒuːbɪlətərɪ), *a.* [f. L. *jūbilāt-*, ppl. stem of *jūbilāre* to JUBILATE: see -ORY.] Expressive of jubilation.

1872 J. HATTON *Vall. Poppies* II. i. 9 The jubilatory clashing and hammering and clanging and joyful turbulence of a grand marriage peal.

jubile, *sb.*: see JUBILEE.

jubilean (dʒuːbɪˈliːən), *a.* [f. L. *jūbilæ-us* (see JUBILEE) + -AN.] Of or belonging to a jubilee.

1624 J. GEE *Hold fast* 41 To visit the holy Fathers Iubilean pompe. **1704** HEARNE *Duct. Hist.* (1714) I. 10 The Sabbatical and Jubilean Years. **1836** *Fraser's Mag.* XIII. 583 The jubilean period of forty-nine years will be complete.

jubilee (ˈdʒuːbɪliː), *sb.* Forms: 4–7 iubile, -lee, 6 iubely(e, 7 jubily, jubylee, (gubilie), 7–9 jubile, 7– jubilee. [a. F. *jubilé* (14th c. in Hatz.-Darm.), in Sp. *jubileo*, It. *giubbileo*, ad. late L. *jūbilæus* (Vulgate, etc.), used as sb. 'jubilee', but properly an adj. form (sc. *annus*), after Gr. ἰωβηλαῖος adj. (Origen, Epiphanius, etc.), f. ἰώβηλος 'jubilee' (Josephus *Antiq.* III. xii. 3), ad. Heb. *yōbēl*, 'jubilee', orig., it seems, 'ram', hence 'ram's horn used as a trumpet', with which the jubilee year was proclaimed. The Latin form *jūbilæus* instead of *jōbēlæus* shows association of the O.T. word with the native L. *jūbilum* wild cry, shout, and *jūbilāre* to shout to, shout, halloo, huzza (see JUBIL *v.*); and in Christian L. there was established an association of sense between these words and the Hebrew 'jubilee', which has extended to the modern langs. of Western Christendom. In Eng. the word was often, as in the Bible versions, spelt *jubile*; this was usually, like the F. *jubilé*, of 3 syllables; but it was sometimes a disyllable, and referred directly to L. *jūbilum* or med.L. *jūbilus*, in the sense of an exultant shout. Cf. also *jubil* in *jubil-trumpet*.]

1. a. *Jewish Hist.* (More fully ***year of jubilee***). A year of emancipation and restoration, which according to the institution in Lev. xxv was to be kept every fifty years, and to be proclaimed by the blast of trumpets throughout the land; during it the fields were to be left uncultivated, Hebrew slaves were to be set free, and lands and houses in the open country or unwalled towns that had been sold were to revert to their former owners or their heirs.

1382 WYCLIF *Lev.* xxv. 10 Thow shalt halowe the fyftith ȝeer..he is forsothe the iubilee [*ipse est enim jubilæus*; **1535** COVERD. Iubilye, **1560** (Geneva) Iubile, **1569** (Bps.) Iubilee, **1611** Iubile]. *Ibid.* 13 The ȝeer of iubilee [*anno jubilæi*]. **1382** —— *Josh.* vi. 4 The prestis shulen taak seuen trompes, whos vse is in the iubile [*buccinas, quarum usus est in jubileo*]. **1581** MARBECK *Bk. of Notes* 562 Iubely is of this Hebrew word *Iobel*, which in English, signifieth a Trumpet: a yeare of singuler mirth and ioy, and of much rest. **1613** PURCHAS *Pilgrimage* (1614) 126 Touching this yeare of Iubilee is much controversie. *Ibid.*, Scaliger..proving that the Iubilee was but fortie nine yeares complete, and that the fiftieth yeare was the first onwards of another Iubilee or Sabbath of yeares. **1845** S. AUSTIN *Ranke's Hist. Ref.* II. 205 In Würtemberg, too, the Israelitish year of jubilee was preached to the peasants. **1897** DRIVER *Introd. Lit. O.T.* (ed. 6) 57 It is impossible to think that..the institution of Jubile is a mere paper-law... At least so far as concerns the land.. it must date from ancient times in Israel.

b. *fig.* or *transf.* A time of restitution, remission, or release.

c **1584** in Gasquet & Bishop *Edw. VI & Bk. Com. Prayer* (1890) 10 Days of licence which are called days of jubilee. **1602** MARSTON *Antonio's Rev.* I. iii, You arrive in jubilee, And firme attonement of all boystrous rage. **1611** R. FENTON *Usury* II. xiii. 95 The land if it want a Iubile will in time grew hartlesse. **1614** EARL STIRLING *Domes Day* IV. xcv, All prisoners at last, death must enlarge, At that great iubily. **1621** in Elsing *Lords' Deb.* (1870) 110 Moved, whether a generall jubelee shalbe for the debtes, or whether a moderacion? **1643** SIR T. BROWNE *Relig. Med.* I. §44 The first day of our Jubilee is Death. **1711** *Light to Blind* in *10th Rep. Hist. MSS. Comm.* App. v. 116 Noe one had.. apprehension to be punished for his religion thro-out the Brittish empyre, which was a general jubily to those nations.

2. *R.C. Ch.* A year instituted by Boniface VIII in 1300 as a year of remission from the penal consequences of sin, during which plenary indulgence might be obtained by a pilgrimage to Rome, the visiting of certain churches there, the giving of alms, fasting three days, and the performance of other pious works.

It was at first appointed to take place every hundred years, but the period was afterwards shortened to fifty, thirty-three, and twenty-five years, and now 'an extraordinary jubilee is granted at any time either to the whole Church or to particular countries or cities, and not necessarily or even usually for a whole year' (*Cath. Dict.* 1885).

1432–50 tr. *Higden* (Rolls) VIII. 285 Bonefacius the viij^{the} ..grawntede grete indulgences in v^{the} yere of his governayle [1300], whiche was þe yere iubile to men visitynge the apostles Petyr and Paule. *Ibid.*, *Harl. Contin.* 491 Pope Urban the vj^{te} consideringe this tyme the age of men to decrease, ordeynede this yere to be the yere of iubile willynge that hit scholde contynue in every xxx^{ti} yere folowynge. **1477** EARL RIVERS (Caxton) *Dictes* 1, I vnderstode the Iubylee and pardon to be at..Seynt Iames in Spayne. **1534** in Peacock *Eng. Ch. Furniture* (1866) 206 Item vij tables with scriptures uppon them to hange on the altars in the tyme of the Jubyle. **1556** *Chron. Gr. Friars* (Camden) 28 Thys yere was the gret jubele at Powlles. **1560** DAUS tr. *Sleidane's Comm.* 7 b, Clemente appoynteth the yere of Iubile, which Boniface the eight had ordained every hundreth yeare, to be nowe everye fiftithe yeare. **1635** PAGITT *Christianogr.* III. (1636) 85 Leo the tenth..sent a Iubile with his pardons abroad. **1682** *Lond. Gaz.* No. 1702/2 This week was published here a Bull for an Universal Jubily, Granted by the Pope. **1749** H. WALPOLE *Lett.* (1846) II. 286 Here..we imagine that a jubilee is a season of pageants, not of devotion. **1841** W. SPALDING *Italy & It. Isl.* II. 146 Bernardino da Polenta, lord of Ravenna..in the jubilee of 1350, beset the roads with his men-at-arms, robbed the male pilgrims, and..dishonoured many of the females. **1900** *Cathol. Directory* 184 The conditions of the Great and Universal Jubilee of the Holy Year 1900.

3. a. The fiftieth anniversary of an event; the celebration of the completion of fifty years of reign, of activity, or continuance in any business, occupation, rank or condition. ***silver jubilee*** (after *silver wedding*), a name for the celebration for the twenty-fifth anniversary; so ***diamond jubilee***, applied to the celebration of the sixtieth year of the reign of Queen Victoria.

c **1386** CHAUCER *Sompn. T.* 154 Our Sexteyn and oure ffermerer That han been trewe freres fifty yeer, They may now, god be thanked of his looue, Maken hir Iubilee and walke allone. **1548** LATIMER *Ploughers* (Arb.) 26 Pamperynge of their panches lyke a monke that maketh his Jubilie. **1809** (*title*) Address to the Inhabitants of Great Britain and Ireland on the Jubilee. *c* **1830** DE QUINCEY *Autobiog. Sk.* iv. Wks. 1862 XIV. 131 In Germany..a married couple, when celebrating the fiftieth anniversary of their marriage day, are said to keep their golden jubilee; but on the twenty-fifth anniversary they have credit only for a silver jubilee. **1845** GRAVES *Rom. Law* in *Encycl. Metrop.* II. 753/1 In 1838, Huschke published..an offering on the occasion of Hugo's jubilee from the faculty of law at Breslau. **1861** C. KNIGHT *Pop. Hist. Eng.* VII. xxix. 526 The 25th of October [1809] was celebrated throughout the Kingdom as 'The Jubilee'—the fiftieth anniversary of the accession to the throne of George the Third. **1887** *Whitaker's Almanack* 551/1 Henry III completed his year of Jubilee Oct. 27, 1266; his great grandson, Edward III, Jan. 24th, 1377; and George III, Oct. 24th, 1810. **1887** TENNYSON (*title*) The Jubilee of Queen Victoria. **1887** Q. VICTORIA in *Suppl.* to *Lond. Gaz.* 25 June, The enthusiastic reception I met with..on the occasion of my Jubilee, has touched me most deeply. **1890** *Post Card* 16 May, 'Penny Postage Jubilee—1890. Guildhall, London'. **1897** G. B. SMITH *Life Q. Victoria* xii. (Rtldg.) 169 The Royal Jubilee of 1887, and the Diamond Jubilee of 1897, will recall the memorable events of a memorable period in British history. **1898** *Daily Tel.* 19 July, The Rev. Arthur Robins, rector of Holy Trinity, Windsor..celebrates his 'silver jubilee' in the Royal Borough to-day. *Ibid.* 20 July, The Sports Club are entertaining W. G. Grace on the occasion of his jubilee [50th birthday].

†**b.** A fiftieth year. *Obs. rare*$^{-1}$.

c **1618** FLETCHER *Q. Corinth* III. i, He is 50, man, in's Jubile, I warrant.

†**c.** A period of fifty years, half a century. *Obs.*

1643 SIR T. BROWNE *Relig. Med.* I. §41 If there bee any truth in Astrology, I may outlive a Jubilee. **1645** PAGITT *Heresiogr.* Ep. Ded., I have lived among you almost a Jubilee. **1655** FULLER *Ch. Hist.* IV. i. §12 Edward the third ..having reigned a jubilee, full fifty years. **1726** tr. *Gregory's Astron.* I. 249 A Jubilee, of 49 or 50 Years; a Seculum, or an Age, of 100 Years.

4. A season or occasion of joyful celebration or general rejoicing.

1592 WARNER *Alb. Eng.* v. xxv, Then loue me, for beleeue me, so will proue a Iubilie. **1619** *Pasquil's Palin.* (1877) 152 It was the day when every Kitchen reekes, And hungry bellies keep a Iubile. **1634** HEYWOOD *Maidenh. lost* III. Wks. 1874 IV. 137 Prepare we for this great solemnity, Of Hymeneall Iubilies. *a* **1711** KEN *Hymnar.* Poet. Wks. 1721 II. 99 In Heav'n they keep a Jubilee that day, When the good Shepherd brings a weeping Stray. **1804** M. CUTLER in *Life, Jrnls. & Corr.* (1888) II. 161 The Democrats are all engaged in the celebration of the Jubilee, on the possession of Louisiana. **1899** *Daily News* 27 Oct. 2/5 Witness said..he was an old sailor, and had a 'jubilee' once in three months.

5. a. Exultant joy, general or public rejoicing, jubilation.

In this and next sense often written *jubile* and in some cases pronounced *jubil*, after L. *jūbilum*.

1526 *Pilgr. Perf.* (W. de W.) 266 b, Fedeth them with ioye and iubile vnspekable. **1635** SHIRLEY *Coronat.* II, The people's joy to know us reconcil'd, Is added to the jubile of the day. **1657** G. STARKEY *Helmont's Vind.* 293 The Archeus..with the joy and jubile conceived upon its speedy help found..cheers up all its parts. **1823** SCOTT *Peveril* iii, Was it for Peveril of the Peak, in the jubilee of his spirits, to consider how his wife was to find beef and mutton to feast his neighbours? **1843** PRESCOTT *Mexico* VI. viii. (1864) 406 They..only thought of their triumph, and abandoned themselves to jubilee. **1899** E. J. CHAPMAN *Snake Witch, Drama 2 Lives* 29 Only the toad, on night like this..Comes forth in fearless jubilee.

b. Shouting; joyful shouting; sound of jubilation.

1526 *Pilgr. Perf.* (W. de W. 1531) 211 b, God ascended.. in great iubylee & glory [*Vulg.* Ps. xlvi. 6 *ascendit Deus in jubilo*]. **1667** MILTON *P.L.* III. 348 Heav'n rung With Jubilee, and loud Hosanna's fill'd Th' eternal Regions. **1810** SCOTT *Lady of L.* v. xxi, All along the crowded way Was jubilee and loud huzza. **1860** PUSEY *Min. Proph.* 481 (Zeph. iii.) Singing or the unuttered unutterable jubilee of the heart.

c. A Negro folk-song of an optimistic and joyful kind, often having a religious basis; freq. *attrib.*, esp. ***jubilee singer, song***.

1872 *N.Y. Tribune* 17 Feb. 3/6 Unique Vocal Concert by the Jubilee Singers. *c* **1872** T. F. SEWARD (*title*) Jubilee songs as sung by the Jubilee Singers, of Fisk University. **1873** G. D. PIKE *Jubilee Singers* 163 The excellent rendering of the Jubilee Band is made more effective..by the comparison of their former state of slavery..with the present prospects and hopes of their race. **1922** *Jrnl. Amer. Folk-Lore* XXXV. 248 Every Time I Feel the Spirit. This is one of the most thrilling of the later jubilee songs. **1946** S. H. HOLBROOK *Lost Men Amer. Hist.* 133 The Chautauqua offered no such strong meat as the Lyceum, but went in for bell ringers, jubilee singers, preachers..and assorted stuffed shirts. **1949** B. A. BOTKIN *Treas. S. Folklore* v. i. 701 Besides his 'jubilee' and 'sorrow songs', the Negro has his 'sinful' songs. **1956** M. STEARNS *Story of Jazz* (1957) xii. 133 The next step in this blending, which produced both ring-shout and spiritual, is the jubilee. Jubilees are both cheerful and rhythmic, usually announcing some sort of good news. **1961** J. JAHN in A. Dundes *Mother Wit* (1973) 99/1 The hymns of Christian European origin used by the missions are Africanized, producing jubilees. **1968** P. OLIVER *Screening Blues* Introd. 7 Blues recordings accounted for nearly half the total output in the 'twenties whereas religious issues, including those by solo evangelists and jubilee groups, totalled only a fraction over a sixth of the number. *Ibid.* ii. 81 The gospel, or jubilee, quartets performed all their songs in harmonized style which smoothed out the differences between the blues, popular and gospel song forms.

6. *attrib.* and *Comb.*, *as* ***jubilee-bonfire, -coin, -issue, -masquerade, -post-card, -procession, -tree, -trumpet, -type, -year***, etc. (Often with special reference to sense 1, 2, or 3; in the last case esp. frequent in the last two decades of the 19th c. in reference to the two 'Jubilees' of the reign of Queen Victoria in 1887 and 1897, the Jubilee of Penny Postage in 1890, the Swiss (25 years') Jubilee of the Postal Union in 1900, and other celebrations.)

1382 WYCLIF *Lev.* xxv. 28 The bigger shal haue that he bouȝte, vnto the iubilee ȝeer. **1647** FULLER *Good Th. in Worse T.* (1841) 92 Few [popes] had the happiness to fill their coffers with jubilee-coin. **1749** H. WALPOLE *Lett.* (1846) II. 267 The next day was what was called 'a jubilee-masquerade in the Venetian manner' at Ranelagh. **1858** DORAN *Crt. Fools* 59 The year 1480 was..the very jubilee year of German fools. **1887** *Times* 31 Dec. 9/1 The pleasant associations of the Jubilee year. **1891** *Philat. Penny Postage Jubilee* 117 The Jubilee celebrations..at the Guildhall..on May 16, 17 and 19 (1890). *Ibid.* 118 The Jubilee Post Office was more patronised than any other part of the Jubilee exhibition. **1893** SIR W. HARCOURT in *Daily News* 15 Mar. 2/2 The designs for the new coins..were better than the Jubilee issue... Eighteen millions of the new gold coins issued were..of the Jubilee type. **1897** (*title*) Illustrated Programme of the Royal Jubilee Procession.

ˈjubilee, *v. nonce wd.* [f. prec. sb.]

1. *intr.* To celebrate a jubilee.

1887 *Scot. Leader* 4 July 4 Why did Irishmen not Jubilee?

2. *trans.* To celebrate the jubilee of (a person).

1887 *Pall Mall G.* 22 Jan. 3/1 Some officials who 'jubileed' their colleagues at a banquet.

jubilist (ˈdʒuːbɪlɪst). [f. L. *jūbil-um* shout, (later) joyful shout, or Eng. *jubile*, JUBILEE + -IST.]

†**1.** One who jubilates, one who sings in praise or exultation. *Obs. rare*$^{-1}$.

1471 RIPLEY *Comp. Alch.* in Ashm. *Theatr.* Pref. (1652) 121 Of Hierarchycall Jubylestes the gratulant gloryfycation.

2. One who celebrates a jubilee. *rare*.

1889 *Harper's Mag.* June 108/1 Her lecturer described the feeling the Jubilists entertained toward their sovereign as 'chivalrous'.

jubilize (ˈdʒuːbɪlaɪz), *v.* [f. as prec. + -IZE.]

intr. **a.** To jubilate. **b.** To celebrate a jubilee. Hence **ˈjubilizing** *ppl. a.*

1649 *Test. conc. I. Beme* ii. 8 Jubelizing Tryumphant melodies of heart. **1650** HOWELL *Giraffi's Rev. Naples* I. (1664) 87 Let us jubilize for so high and signall a blessing. **1652** ASHMOLE *Theat. Chem.* Introd. 5 Then shall the People Jubilize In mutuall love. **1814** L. HUNT in *Haydon's Corr. & Table-t.* (1876) I. 270 Come, then, as soon as you can, and let us *jubilize* with you.

†**jubiˈlose**, *a. Obs. rare*$^{-1}$. [f. L. type **jūbilōs-us*, f. *jūbil-um*: see JUBILATE *v.*, and -OSE.] = JUBILANT.

c **1450** tr. *De Imitatione* III. xxxix. 110 Quikyn my spirit.. to cleue to þe in iubilose excesses.

jubil-trumpet. = *jubilee-trumpet*.

1714 tr. *à Kempis' Chr. Exerc.* IV. 234 Angels..In Heav'n the Jubil-Trumpet blow.

jubjub (ˈdʒʌbdʒʌb). [Invented by 'Lewis Carroll' (C. L. Dodgson); perh. a portmanteau word or formed after such representations of bird-cry as *jug-jug* (JUG *sb.*^{3}).] An imaginary bird of a ferocious, desperate and occasionally charitable nature, noted for its excellence when cooked.

1871 'L. CARROLL' *Through Looking-Glass* i. 22 Beware the Jubjub bird, and shun The frumious Bandersnatch.

1876 —— *Hunting of Snark* 44 Should we meet with a Jubjub, that desperate bird, We shall need all our strength for the job! *Ibid.* 58 The song of the Jubjub recurred to their minds, And cemented their friendship for ever! **1962** M. GARDNER in 'L. Carroll' *Annotated Snark* 104 Their common fear of the *Jubjub Bird* is interesting. Philologically . . Jubjub is a 'portmanteau bird', compounded of *jabber* and *jujube*. . . It flashed across me that the Jubjub was Society itself.

jubon, variant of JUPON.

jucal, var. JACAL.

jucca, juce, obs. forms of YUCCA, JUICE.

†**juck**, *sb. Obs.* Forms: 6 iuk, 6–7 iouk, 7 iucke. [Origin, form, and meaning uncertain.] ? A joint of a bird's wing.

1575 TURBERV. *Faulconrie* 106 Giue hir but a little meate . . that when she is therewith accustomed, you maye giue hir plumage and a Iuk [ed. 1611 iucke] of a ioynt. *Ibid.* 217 They giue them [sparrowhawks] ioukes [so 1611] of wings of small birdes, & Quailes, when they haue fedde them, skaring them out with their teeth, and plucking away the longest feathers, and so giue it.

juck, juke (dʒʌk, dʒuːk), *v.* Forms: 7 iouk, iuke, juke, 8– juck. [Echoic: cf. CHUCK *v.*[1]

But perh. orig. a transferred sense of JOUK *v.*[1], due to the accidental similarity to this of the sound uttered by the partridge when *jouking, jugging*, or settling down for the night. Quots. 1621, 1669, might refer to this act, rather than the call. Cf. also JUG *v.*[3]]

intr. To make a sound or call imitated by this word, as a partridge. Hence '**jucking** *vbl. sb.*

1611 COTGR., *Cabab*, the chucking, churring, or iouking of a Partridge. **1621** MARKHAM *Prev. Hunger* (1655) 241 The place where you heard them iuke. **1669** WORLIDGE *Syst. Agric.* (1681) 252 Imitating their Notes at their Juking-time, which is usually in the Morning and in the Evening. **1725** BRADLEY *Fam. Dict.* s.v. *Spread Net*, You will soon know if there be any of the Birds by their Calling and Jucking. **1870** BLAINE *Encycl. Rur. Sports* §2619 They [partridges] have several calls. . . One very important one, and to the practised sportsman readily recognised, is their jucking, when they settle down together for the night.

¶ Used in sense of JUG *v.*[3]; cf. also JOUK *v.*[1]

1828 *Sporting Mag.* XXII. 430 Bushing the fields where they are likely to *juck* or sleep.

juck, variant of JOUK *v.*[2]

†**ju'cund**, *a. Obs. rare*$^{-1}$. [ad. L. *jūcund-us* (in late L. *jocundus* JOCUND), f. *juvāre* to aid, help, delight, please: cf. also OF. *jucond, -cund*, beside *joconde*.] A by-form of JOCUND.

1596 DALRYMPLE tr. *Leslie's Hist. Scot.* VII. 2 In aduersitie faithfull, in prosperitie iucund and joyfull. **1721** BAILEY, *Jucund*, jocund, merry, pleasant.

jucundity (dʒuː'kʌndɪtɪ). ? *Obs.* [ad. L. *jūcunditās*, f. *jūcundus*: see prec. Cf. also obs. F. *jucundité*, beside *jocondité*. In Eng. *jucundity* appears as an effort to restore the original L. form; it is used not only in the subjective senses of JOCUNDITY, but in the objective sense of L. *jūcunditās* (sense 1 below).]

1. The quality of being pleasant to the senses or feelings; pleasantness, enjoyableness. With *pl.*, an enjoyable or amusing circumstance.

1620 VENNER *Via Recta* iv. 74 That the jucundity of it [food] entice them not to a perilous and nauseatiue fulnesse. **1646** SIR T. BROWNE *Pseud. Ep.* VII. xvi. 372 The new unusuall or unexpected jucundities, which present themselves to any man in his life.

2. Pleasure, delight, happiness: = JOCUNDITY 2.

1536 *Primer Hen. VIII* 148 Iesu, the most highest benignitie, Of all hearts the great iucunditie. **1822** T. TAYLOR tr. *Apuleius, Philos. Plato* II. 265 The wise man . . is the only man who always enjoys jucundity and security.

3. Enjoyment, merriment, glee: = JOCUNDITY 1.

1560 ROLLAND *Crt. Venus* I. 510 To spend their time in sum Iucunditie. *a* **1678** WOODHEAD *Holy Living* (1688) 64 Health only is the true cause of eating . . yet there accompanies it . . a perilous jucundity, and goust, which mostwhat endeavours also to step before it. **1794** MATHIAS *Purs. Lit.* (1798) 28 His modesty would attempt some jucundity from the Lusus Priapi.

jud, judd (dʒʌd). *local.* [Origin unknown: cf. JAD.]

1. *Coal-mining.* (*north.*) 'A block of coal about four yards square kirved and nicked ready for breaking down' (Gresley *Gloss. Coal Mining*); also, a portion of a 'pillar' still unremoved.

1844 FARADAY in Bence Jones *Life* (1870) II. 181 Near Williamson judd were in some danger from a fall that fell in the midst of us. **1884** *Imp. & Mach. Rev.* 1 Dec. 6726/2 A jud of this strong coal, weighing about seven tons was brought down . . in good condition. **1885** *Newcastle Daily Chron.* 25 May, Killed in the Low Main seam, Alexandrina Pit, . . whilst 'drawing a jud'.

2. (*Somerset.*) = JAD. (Gresley.)

Judæan, Judean (dʒuː'diːən), *a.* and *sb.* [f. L. *Jūdæus*, a. Gr. Ἰουδαῖος, f. Ἰουδαία, f. Ἰούδας, ad. Heb. *Jehūdah* Judah, name of a son of Jacob.]

A. *adj.* Of or pertaining to Judæa or southern Palestine. **B.** *sb.* A native or inhabitant of this region.

In Shakes. *Oth.* v. ii. 347 the first Folio has the doubtful reading *Iudean*; the other Folios and the Quartos have *Indian*.

1652 HEYLIN *Cosmogr.* III. 89 Accaron, on the South of Gath, of great wealth and power, and one that held out notably against the Danites and Judæans. **1832** J. BELL *Syst. Geogr.* IV. 206 Judean Mountains. **1852** H. W. DULCKEN tr. *Pfeiffer's Visit Holy Land* 103 The foreground of the picture is formed by the Judæan mountains. **1880** *Encycl. Brit.* XIII. 410/1 A Judæan, Amos of Tekoa. **1922** A. E. GARVIE *Beloved Disciple* x. 210 The Synoptic record is incomplete as regards the Judaean ministry. **1931** *Times Lit. Suppl.* 5 Nov. 853/1 A preliminary survey of Judaean sites. **1955** R. W. MILLAR tr. *Daniel-Rops's Jesus in his Time* 57 Eleven of the disciples were Galileans, the one Judean was Judas. **1965** M. SPARK *Mandelbaum Gate* ii. 22 She . . had driven northward through the Judean hills to Galilee. **1973** *Times* 3 Dec. 17/6 David Ben-Gurion . . took a leading part . . in recruiting for the Judaean battalions of the Royal Fusiliers.

Judæo-, Judeo- (dʒuː'diːəʊ), used as comb. form of L. *Jūdæus* JUDÆAN, JUDŒAN *a.* and *sb.*, designating persons or things pertaining to Judæa and hence (more widely) to the Jews; often = Jewish (and); **Judaeo-German**, Yiddish.

1823 *Christian Observer* App. 828/1 The New Testament in German-Hebrew, and Judeo-Polish. **1851** *Illustr. Catal. Gt. Exhib.* III. 552/1 Judæo Spanish, Old Testament. *Ibid.* 552/2 Judæo Arabic, four books of New Testament. **1863** *Chambers's Encycl.* V. 712/2 The number of Judæo-Greek fragments . . which have survived. *Ibid.* 721/2 Numerous authors wrote in Hebrew, . . and Judæo-German. **1899** *Lit. Guide* 1 Oct. 146/1 The total abandonment of the Judæo-Christian 'continuity' theory. **1900** tr. *J. Deniker's Races of Man* 424 Particular kinds of jargon, the most common of which is the Judeo-German. **1906** *Westm. Gaz.* 17 Aug. 10/2 The Judæo-Spanish world of the Levant. **1910** *Ibid.* 12 Mar. 2/1 'The Judæo-Masonic and Protestant coalition' which now governs France. **1910** *Encycl. Brit.* VI. 494/1 The Clementine literature throws light upon a very obscure phase of Christian development, that of Judaeo-Christianity. **1937** *Times Lit. Suppl.* 16 Jan. 37/2 Irrelevances about the world hegemony of Judaeo-Masonry. **1939** *New English Weekly* 27 July 237/2 The Judaeo-Christian scheme of morals. **1939** L. H. GRAY *Foundations of Language* 349 The two chief forms of creolised languages of the Teutonic group, in addition to those already noted for English . ., are *Afrikaans* . .; and *Yiddish*, or *Judaeo-German*, based upon a Franconian German dialect of the fourteenth century with many Hebrew words, and spoken by Jewish communities in Lithuania, Poland, Russia, and parts of Rumania as well as by Jewish emigrants from those areas. **1948** D. DIRINGER *Alphabet* II. iv. 267 Judezmo or Judæo-Spanish, called also Ladino, contains many Hebrew words, but is principally based on Old Spanish or Castilian. **1952** KOESTLER *Arrow in Blue* xxv. 234 Immune against German chauvinism through a hereditary judeo-cosmopolitan touch. **1957** N. FRYE *Anat. Criticism* 145 The appearance of the Judaeo-Christian deity in fire. **1960** *Encounter* Mar. 34/2 The religious zeal of Judeo-Christianity. **1964** *Language* XL. 282 Mediaeval Judaeo-French. **1974** R. A. HALL *External Hist. Romance Languages* 24 Judaeo-Spanish or 'Ladino'. *Ibid.* 30 Judaeo-Italian, now dying out, has been attested in some medieval documents, and in scattered remnants in modern Italian dialects.

Judæophobe (dʒuː'diːəʊfəʊb). [f. Gr. Ἰουδαῖος, L. *Jūdæus* JEW + Gr. -φοβος fearing.] One who has a dread or strong dislike of the Jews. So **Judæo'phobia**, dread of Jews.

1882 H. ADLER in *Eclectic Mag.* XXXV. 196 Recent Phases of Judaeophobia. *Ibid.* 205 The most rabid Judaeophobe.

Judahite ('dʒuːdəaɪt), *a.* and *sb.* [f. *Judah* name of an ancient Hebrew tribe and kingdom + -ITE[1].] **A.** *adj.* Of or pertaining to the tribe or the kingdom of Judah. **B.** *sb.* A member of the tribe, or an inhabitant of the kingdom, of Judah.

1899 J. HASTINGS *Dict. Bible* II. 792/2 Five Judahite clans were in the course of time formed. **1901** R. L. OTTLEY *Short Hist. Hebrews* vi. 137 In the early stages of the conquest we find the Kenites coalescing with the Judahites. **1932** T. H. ROBINSON *Hist. Israel* I. II. viii. 170 In Judges xv. . . Judahites are introduced into the story of Samson. *Ibid.*, An old Judahite tradition of the capture of Hebron . . is transferred to Caleb. **1950** H. H. ROWLEY *From Joseph to Joshua* i. 5 We find a Levite . . who regarded Benjamites equally with Judahites as associated peoples. **1971** *Catholic Biblical Q.* July 394, 5 and 8 a describe a Judahite defeat.

Judaic (dʒuː'deɪɪk), *a.* [ad. L. *Jūdaic-us*, a. Gr. Ἰουδαϊκός Jewish, f. Ἰουδαῖ-ος JEW.] Of or pertaining to the Jews, Jewish; of a Jewish character, or characteristic of the Jews.

1611 H. BROUGHTON *Require Agreem.* 17 For you Iewes I wil cite Iudaique matters. **1684** N. S. *Crit. Enq. Edit. Bible* xix. 190 He was not inspired with a Prophetic but a Judaic Spirit. **1882** FARRAR *Early Chr.* I. 93 The same stern, Judaic character . . marks every page of the Epistle of St. James.

Judaical (dʒuː'deɪɪkəl), *a.* Also 5 Iudeicall, 6 Iewdaical. [f. as prec. + -AL[1]: see -ICAL. (Formerly much commoner than *Judaic*: now somewhat rare.)] = prec.

c **1470** HARDING *Chron.* xcv. *heading*, Easter . . was celebrated accordyng to the Iudeicall Custome. **1546** *Supplic. Poore Comm.* (E.E.T.S.) 90 This more then Iewdaical superstition. *a* **1602** W. PERKINS *Cases Consc.* (1619) 284 In the Iudaicall law. *a* **1769** RICCALTOUN *Notes Galatians* (1772) 115 The Judaical law, as given by Moses. **1875** ROGERS *Orig. Bible* vi. (ed. 3) 220 The Gentiles were not to be trammelled with Judaical restrictions.

Ju'daically, *adv.* [f. prec. + -LY[2].] In a Judaical manner; in Jewish fashion.

1582 N.T. (Rhem.) *Gal.* ii. 14 If thou . . livest Gentile-like and not Iudaically. **1641** MILTON *Prel. Episc.* 8 Who . . Excommunicated . . all the Asian Churches for celebrating their Easter judaically. *a* **1714** BURNET *Hist. Ref.* (1715) III. 177 Vargas said, it was not to be understood Literally; (in the Original it is *Judaically*).

Ju'daico-, combining adverbial form of JUDAIC, as in ***Judaico-Christian***, Christian modified by Jewish, Jewish Christian.

1880 M. PATTISON *Milton* xiii. 177 The whole scheme of Judaico-Christian anthropology.

Judaism ('dʒuːdeɪɪz(ə)m). [ad. L. *jūdaism-us* (Tertull.), a. Gr. ἰουδαϊσμός (2 Macc. ii. 21): see -ISM. Cf. F. *Judaïsme* (16th c. in Littré).]

1. The profession or practice of the Jewish religion; the religious system or polity of the Jews.

1494 FABYAN *Chron.* VII. 334 He anon renouncyd his Iudaisme or Moysen lawe, and was cristenyd, and lyued after as a cristen man. **1611** BIBLE *2 Macc.* ii. 21 Those that behaued themselues manfully to their honour for Iudaisme. **1613** PURCHAS *Pilgrimage* (1614) 150 They being baptised, revolted to their former Iudaisme. **1725** *Lond. Gaz.* No. 6437/1 Five [were found guilty] for Judaism. **1877** J. E. CARPENTER tr. *Tiele's Hist. Relig.* 93 Judaism and Christianity had given currency to the doctrines of one God.

2. The act of Judaizing; adoption of Jewish practices on the part of Christians; a practice or style of thought like that of the Jews.

1641 MILTON *Ch. Govt.* II. iii. Wks. (1851) 168 As if the touch of a lay Christian . . could profane dead judaisms. **1641** I. H. *Petit. agst. Pocklington* 21 The Lords day may be so termed [sabbath] without any danger of Judaisme. *a* **1831** A. KNOX *Rem.* (1844) I. 97 What I have already called the Judaism of his distinct party. **1833** J. H. NEWMAN *Arians* I. i, His ceremonial Judaism was so notorious that one author even affirms that he observed the rite of circumcision.

3. *Hist.* As a rendering of med.L. *Judaismus* = JEWRY 2; applied also in official documents to the revenue derived by the Crown from the Jews, and to the treasury which received the money.

[**1251** *Close Roll, 35 Hen. III*, m. 10 Mandatum est Edwardo de Westm. quod Judaismum regis apud Westm. et magnum cellarium vinorum regis lambruscari . . faciat. [Cf. WALPOLE *Vertue's Anecd. Paint.* (1782) I. 17 *note*, This Judaism or Jewry, was probably an exchequer or treasury . . for receiving the sums levied on the Jews.] **1290** *Rolls Parlt.* I. 49/1 Quandem portionem de Judaismo suo sibi faciat assignari.] **1861** MAYHEW *Lond. Labour* II. 116 The Jews had also their Jewerie, or Judaisme, not for a 'corporation' merely, but also for the requirements of their faith and worship, and for their living together. **1884** S. DOWELL *Taxes Eng.* I. IV. vi. 90 The revenue of the Judaism, as it was termed, was managed by a separate branch of the exchequer, termed the exchequer of the Jews.

Judaist ('dʒuːdeɪɪst). [f. prec.: see -IST: cf. JUDAIZE.] One who follows or favours Jewish practice or ritual; a Judaizer; esp. in *Eccl. Hist.* used of Jewish Christians of the apostolic age.

1846 in WORCESTER citing *Eclectic Rev.* **1866** *Contemp. Rev.* I. 482 All the original apostles were Judaists. **1882** FARRAR *Early Chr.* I. 92 Christians who wished to stand aloof alike from Paulinists and Judaists.

So **Juda'istic** *a.*, of, pertaining to, or characteristic of, Judaists.

1833 J. H. NEWMAN *Arians* I. i. (1876) 14 There was nothing Judaistic in this conduct. **1880** *Academy* 10 Jan. 19/2 It is clear that the Judaistic party claimed to be thought loyal adherents of James.

Judaization (ˌdʒuːdeɪaɪ'zeɪʃən). [f. next + -ATION.] The action of Judaizing; a becoming or making Jewish in character.

1814 SOUTHEY *Poet. Ep. to A. Cunningham*, Poor Smouch endured a worse judaization Under another hand. **1872** *Spectator* 5 Oct. 1258 How could anything be feared in the direction of the Judaisation of the State from the Jews?

Judaize ('dʒuːdeɪaɪz), *v.* [ad. late L. *jūdaizāre* (Vulg.), a. Gr. ἰουδαΐζειν (Galat. ii. 14): see -IZE.]

1. *intr.* To play the Jew; to follow Jewish customs or religious rites; to follow Jewish practice.

1582 N.T. (Rhem.) *Gal.* ii. 14 How doest thou compel the Gentils to Iudaize? **1598** SYLVESTER *Du Bartas* II. ii. III. *Colonies* 378 Where Prester Iohn (though part he Iudaize) Doth in some sort devoutly Christianize. **1625** BACON *Ess.*, *Usury* (Arb.) 541 That Vsurers should haue Orange-tawney Bonnets, because they doe Iudaize. **1752** J. MACSPARRAN *America Dissected* (1753) 18 Sabbatarian Baptists . . in a Sort, judaize in their . . Manner of keeping the Sabbath. **1782** PRIESTLEY *Corrupt. Chr.* II. VIII. **1831-3** E. BURTON *Eccl. Hist.* xvi. (1845) 356 It is probable that the church at Jerusalem contained some persons, who in some points Judaized.

2. *trans.* To make Jewish; to imbue with Jewish doctrines or principles.

1653 MILTON *Hirelings* Wks. (1851) 355 Error . . in many other Points of Religion had miserably judaiz'd the Church. **1876** LOWELL *Among my Bks.* Ser. II. 273 The English translation of the Bible had had to a very great degree Judaized, not the English mind, but the Puritan temper. **1879** FARRAR *St. Paul* (1883) 86 Judaism was more Hellenised by the contact than Hellenism was Judaised.

Hence '**Judaized** *ppl. a.*, **-ing** *vbl. sb.* and *ppl. a.*

1626 JACKSON *Creed* VIII. xviii. §4 The Lutheran .. charges that translation .. with Judaizing. **1641** MILTON *Reform.* I. Wks. (1851) 30 The Apostat Aquila, the Heretical Theodotion, the Judaiz'd Symmachus. **1704** NELSON *Fest. & Fasts* xxvii. (1739) 347 He confirmed the Judaizing Christians in their errors. **1884** *Athenæum* 19 July 73/2 Not an opponent .. of Judaizing Christians like St. Barnabas.

Judaizer ('dʒuːdeɪaɪzə(r)). [f. prec. + -ER[1].] One who Judaizes; one who adheres to, or insists on adherence to, Jewish practice or ritual.

1631 R. BYFIELD *Doctr. Sabb.* 155 They can do it as Christians, not as Iudaizers. **1709** STANHOPE *Paraphr.* IV. 210 St. Peter's behaviour among the Judaizers at Antioch. **1853** J. H. NEWMAN *Hist. Sk.* (1873) II. I. iv. 201 According to the Judaizers, their nation .. was ever to be dominant.

Judas ('dʒuːdəs). Also 6 **-ace**. [a. L. *Jūdas*, a. Gr. *'Ιούδας*, ad. Heb. *y'hūdāh* Judah, name of one of the sons of Jacob, whence a common name among the later Jews, e.g. of Judas Maccabæus, and two of the disciples of Christ, of whom one is in Eng. commonly called (St.) Jude, Judas being retained for Judas Iscariot. Cf. F. *Judas*, with transferred uses as in Eng.]

1. The name of the disciple who betrayed Jesus Christ; hence allusively (cf. ISCARIOT): One who treacherously betrays under the semblance of friendship; a traitor or betrayer of the worst kind.

c **1489** CAXTON *Sonnes of Aymon* ix. 209, I .. shall be therfore taken all my lyffe as a Iudas [for betraying the sons of Aymon]. **1539** TAVERNER *Erasm. Prov.* (1545) 150 Inwardly very Iudasses. **1593** SHAKS. *Rich. II*, III. ii. 132 Three Iudasses, each one thrice worse then Iudas. **1643** PRYNNE *Sov. Power Parl.* App. 216 Such unnaturall monsters, such trayterous Judasses, such execrable infamous Apostates as these. **1898** J. ARCH *Story of Life* xvi. 385 Those who were no better than Judases.

2. (More fully ***Judas of the Paschal***): see quot. 1877. Now *Hist.*

[**1402–3** *Mem. Ripon* (Surtees) III. 212 Et in j Judas de novo facto ad serviendum in choro per iij dies .. 3*s.* 4*d.*] **1453** *Acc.* in Sharp *Cov. Myst.* (1825) 190, iiij newe torches & iiij judasses. **1476** *Ibid.* 189 A new bolle to the Judas ij^{d}. **1511** *Churchw. Acc. St. Mary at Hill* (Nichols 1797) 107 Mem. that the judas of the pascal [*printed* pastal], i.e. the tymbre that the wax of the pascal [*pr.* pastel] is driuen upon weigheth 7 lb. **1520** *Churchw. Acc. St. Giles, Reading* 10 For makyng a Judas for the Pascale 1^{d}. **1566** in Peacock *Eng. Ch. Furn.* (1866) 77 Item albes paxes Iudaces with suche trifelinge tromperey—made awaie wee knowe not howe. **1877** *Acc. Ld. H. Treas. Scot.* I. Gloss. 421 The paschal candlestick in churches, which was usually of brass, had seven branches, from the seventh or middle one of which a tall thick piece of wood, painted like a candle, and called the Judas of the Paschal, rose nearly to the roof, and on the top of this was placed at Eastertide the paschal candle of wax.

3. A small lattice or aperture in a door (in some old houses, or in prison cells), through which a person can look without being noticed from the other side; a peep-hole.

1865 [see *Judas-hole* in 4]. **1883** *Century Mag.* Nov. 74/2 A thick oaken door with a judas. **1888** *Ibid.* Feb. 523/2 This contrivance .. known to the .. prisoners as the 'Judas', enables the guard to look into the cell at any time without attracting the attention of the occupant. *Ibid.* 527/2 The .. guard peeped through the 'Judas' and discovered what the prisoner was doing.

4. *attrib.* and *Comb.* **a.** Like Judas Iscariot or his character or conduct, traitorous, as ***Judas attack***, ***Jew***, ***kiss***, ***trick***, etc. **b.** Special Combs.: **Judas-blossom**, the blossom of the JUDAS-TREE (q.v.); † **Judas candlestick** (see 2); **Judas-colour**, **Judas-coloured** *a.* (of the hair or beard) red (from the mediæval belief that Judas Iscariot had red hair and beard); † **Judas cup**, an ornamental cup used in mediæval times on Maundy Thursday; **Judas goat**, an animal used to lead others to destruction; also *transf.*; **Judas-hole** = sense 3; **Judas-like** *a.* and *adv.*, like Judas, treacherous, treacherously; **Judas priest** *int.*, a euphemism for *Jesus Christ* in an oath; **Judas-trap** = sense 3 above.

a. *c* **1400** R. LAVYNHAM *Litil Tretys* (1956) 11 Hate of herte is whan a man spekyth litil & menyth moche malyce .. & at þe laste w^{t} a iudas kesse schewith a love y fayned. *c* **1590** *Robin Conscience* 134 in Hazl. *E.P.P.* III. 235 That yov haue giuen him many a Jvdas kisse. **1655** H. VAUGHAN *Silex Scint., Rules & Lessons* 45 Who sels Religion, is a Judas Jew. **1860** GEO. ELIOT *Mill on Floss* III. VI. i. 15 A woman who was loving and thoughtful for other women, not giving them Judas-kisses with eyes askance. **1875** *Dental Cosmos* (U.S.) XVII. 533 The convention .. had outlived all the Judas attacks which had been made upon it. **1942** 'G. ORWELL' *Diary* 28 Sept. in *Coll. Ess.* (1968) II. 449 A special prayer 'for the people of Stalingrad'—the Judas kiss. **1947** E. SITWELL *Shadow of Cain* 18 When the last Judas-kiss Has died upon the cheek of the Starved Man Christ. **1973** R. LEWIS *Blood Money* ix. 146 Candour shone from his eyes, as insincere as a Judas kiss.

b. **1566** in Peacock *Eng. Ch. Furniture* (1866) 118 Item one sepulcre and one *Judas candlestick—sold. [*c* **1594** KYD *Sp. Trag.* in Hazl. *Dodsley* V. 121 And let their beards be of *Judas his own colour.] **1695** MOTTEUX *St. Olon's Morocco* 124 Observations on the Judas-colour of his Beard and Hair. **1673** DRYDEN *Amboyna* I. i, There's treachery in that *Judas-coloured beard. **1879** DOWDEN *Southey* iv. 97 An ugly specimen of the streaked-carroty or Judas-coloured kind. **1593** *Anc. Mon. Durham* (Surtees) 68 A goodly great Mazer, called *Judas cup .. used but on Maunday Thursday at night in the Frater House. **1941** *Amer. Speech* XVI. 236/1 Sheep are led to the shackling pen by a Tony or Judas goat. **1964** *Punch* 19 Feb. 283/2 Irene only used Billy as a '*judas goat' to catch Des. **1972** D. ANTHONY *Blood on Harvest Moon* xxv. 220 Not dead. Not me as the Judas goat. **1865** *Daily Tel.* 9 Nov. 6/6 The man .. you may see through the *Judas-hole when you make a round of the Model Prison with the visiting magistrates. **1914** 'HIGH JINKS, JR.' *Choice Slang* 13 **Judas Priest*, an exclamation of surprise. **1922** S. LEWIS *Babbitt* ix. 126 Judas Priest, I could write poetry myself if I had a whole year for it. **1972** J. D. BUCHANAN *Professional* xi. 123 Judas Priest! What the hell are you saying? *c* **1675** *Roxb. Ball.* (1891) VII. 353 He gave me a *Judas-like kiss. **1677** HORNECK *Gt. Law Consid.* vi. (1704) 318 Shall I, (Judas-like), kiss thee and betray thee? **1886** *Illustr. Lond. News* 4 Dec. 598/3 The small *Judas-trap in a window.

Hence (*nonce-wds.*) **Ju'dasian** *a.*, of the character of Judas; **'Judasite**, a follower of Judas (opprobriously used for 'Jesuit').

1605 WILLET *Hexapla Gen.* 184 Some rebellious and traiterous popish preists and Judasites. **1877** RUSKIN *Fors Clav.* VII. 326 Learn what these mean, Judasian Dives, if it may be.

† **'Judasly**, *a. Obs.* [f. prec. + -LY[1].] Like or characteristic of Judas; traitorous.

a **1626** BP. ANDREWES *Serm.* (1641) 8 Shall any of them .. ever have to do with any devilish or Judasly fact.

† **'Judasly**, *adv. Obs.* [f. as prec. + -LY[2].] In the manner of Judas; with abominable treachery or betrayal; traitorously.

1508 FISHER *7 Penit. Ps.* cxxx. Wks. (1876) 203 To thentent he myght Iudasly flee from the face of our lorde god. **1659** GAUDEN *Tears Ch.* IV. xvii. 519 It must needs be barbarously covetous and Judasly sacriligious.

'Judas-tree. [From a popular notion that Judas hanged himself on a tree of this kind. So Ger. *Judasbaum*; F. *arbre de Judée.*]

1. The common name of *Cercis Siliquastrum*, a leguminous tree of Southern Europe and parts of Asia, with abundant purple flowers which appear in spring before the leaves. Hence extended to other trees of the same genus.

1668 WILKINS *Real Char.* II. iv. §7. 118 Bearing elegant purple blossoms, and a thin Pod. 3. Judas tree. **1760** J. LEE *Introd. Bot.* App. 316 Judas-tree, *Cercis.* **1861** MISS BEAUFORT *Egypt. Sepul.* I. vii. 136 The Judas-tree, with its tall spikes of bright and lovely lilac flowers on the leafless branches. **1884** MILLER *Plant-n.*, Judas-tree, *Cercis Siliquastrum.* ——, American, *Cercis canadensis.* ——, Californian, *Cercis occidentalis.* **1886** *Academy* 16 Oct. 262/1 Threading our way .. through lanes gay with the blossoms of the judas-tree.

2. A local name for the Elder (*Sambucus nigra*); see under JEW'S-EAR. (Britten & Holl. *Plant-n.*)

judcock ('dʒʌdkɒk). Also 7 **iude-**, **iuge-**, **iug-**, 9 **jedcock**. [app. for *judge-cock* from its black crown compared to the judge's black cap.] A name for the Jack Snipe.

1621 *Naworth Househ. Bks.* (Surtees) 168–9 Snipes and iude-cocks .. 6 iuge-cocks .. Iugcocks. **1678** RAY *Willughby's Ornith.* 291 The Gid or Jack-Snipe or Judcock. **1839** STONEHOUSE *Axholme* 65 There were .. judcocks, snipes, ruffs, and godwits. **1885** SWAINSON *Prov. Names Birds* 193 Jack Snipe .. Also called Jedcock, Jid, or Judcock.

judd: see JUD.

judder ('dʒʌdə(r)), *v.* [Imit.; cf. SHUDDER *v.*] *intr.* To shake violently, esp. of the mechanism in cars, cameras, etc.; also of the voice in singing, to oscillate between greater and less intensity. Hence **'juddering** *vbl. sb.* and *ppl. a.*

1931 A. J. CRONIN *Hatter's Castle* I. xii. 213 The train entered this tunnel. It entered slowly, .. juddering in every bolt and rivet of its frame as the hurricane assaulted [it]. **1933** AUDEN in M. Roberts *New Country* 197 His [*sc.* a motorcyclist's] back wheel juddered; he was off with a roar. **1958** 'P. BRYANT' *Two Hours to Doom* 122 He felt the onset of compressibility vibration... The juddering stopped. **1960** *New Scientist* 21 Apr. 1015/2 The drum must run perfectly true and not 'judder' at its circumference more than 1/1,000 inch. **1962** *Times* 28 Feb. 14/6 All day long the school has been juddering and shuddering in the hysterical blasts of north-west wind. **1965** *Punch* 3 Feb. 175/1 As the train juddered a few yards back towards Westminster, he flung a huge arm round my shoulder to steady himself. **1970** *Times* 1 May 2/7 Driver Gwynn started the engine .. with much .. cranking and juddering. **1970** *Motoring Which?* July 85/1 During our track tests the front brakes vibrated and juddered when used hard. **1971** B. W. ALDISS *Soldier Erect* 120 Beggars with heroic deformities lay juddering in the gutter. **1973** *Weekly News* (Glasgow) 11 Aug. 3/3 A sustained campaign has been under way on behalf of crippled people who are provided with those juddering little three-wheeled cars to get about in.

judder ('dʒʌdə(r)), *sb.* [f. prec.] An instance or state of juddering.

1935 *Practical Motorist* 26 Oct. 993/1 (*heading*) Curing clutch judder. **1946** F. C. FIELD-HYDE *Vocal Vibrato, Tremolo & Judder* iii. 10 Judder consists of marked, rapid changes in intensity during the emission of tone, due to involuntary variations .. of the vocal tension. **1952** *Times* 18 Dec., A pronounced judder was felt .. and in spite of two corrective movements of the control column [of the aircraft] the judder continued. **1956** *Sunday Times* 28 Oct. 13/3 There is a little 'judder' from the steering wheel at speed, but it is not worrying. **1958** *Times Rev. Industry* May 31/1 The coupling operates with the smoothness and absence of jerk or judder found in hydraulic devices. **1960** O. SKILBECK *ABC of Film & TV*, *Judder*, violent vertical unsteadiness of picture due to faulty camera motion. **1972** *Daily Tel.* 12 Apr. 13/5 It is not difficult to get a touch of wheelspin and axle judder by fierce acceleration in the lower gears.

juddite ('dʒʌdaɪt). *Min.* [f. the name of John Wesley *Judd* (1840–1916), English geologist: see -ITE[1].] A mineral of the amphibole group (see quots.).

1908 L. L. FERMOR in *Rec. Geol. Survey India* XXXVII. 212 The optical characters of the mineral leave no doubt that it is a new variety of the amphibole group; I propose to name it juddite in honour of Professor J. W. Judd, F.R.S., and as a respectful tribute from a former student. **1963** W. A. DEER et al. *Rock-Forming Min.* II. 369 Although Bilgrami (1955) considered it appropriate to classify the manganese-rich alkali amphibole juddite .. with the richterite group, it has been included here in the eckermannite-arfvedsonite series. The mineral has a high content of Na .. and high Fe^{+3}, as well as high Mn, and the formula $(Na_{2\cdot5}Ca_{0\cdot5})(Mg_{2\cdot5}Mn_{1\cdot0}Fe^{+3}_{1\cdot0})Si_{7\cdot5}Al_{0\cdot5}O_{22}(OH)_2$ is typical of the eckermannite-arfvedsonite group: it is suggested that the mineral may be adequately characterized by the name manganarfvedsonite. **1970** *Mineral. Mag.* XXXVII. 708 It may thus be concluded that the juddites generally refer to (manganoan) magnesioriebeckite compositions.

† **Judeish, Judish**, *a. Obs.* Forms: α. 1–2 **Iudeisc**. β. 3 **Iudaysse**. γ. 2–3 (*Orm.*) **Iudissken**. [These are more or less distinct formations. The OE. adj. was *Iudéisc* (f. *Iudéa* Judea, *Iudéas* Jews) = OHG. *Iudeisc*; hence early ME. *Iudeisc*, and prob. *Iudaysse* (in which *I* prob. meant *J*). Ormin had (beside *Iudewisshe*) the distinct form *Iudissk* (always *Iudisskenn*, inflected form, ? gen. pl.), with which cf. OHG. *judisk*, MHG. *judisch*, Ger. *jüdisch.*] = JEWISH.

α. *c* **1000** *Ags. Gosp.* John xviii. 35 Cwyst þu, eom ic iudeisc? *c* **1000** *Gosp. Nicod.* xi. (Thwaite) 5 Ða stod þar toforan þam deman an Iudeisc wer. *c* **1175** *Lamb. Hom.* 89 þa seiden þa iudeiscen men.

β. *c* **1275** *Wom. Samaria* 54 in *O.E. Misc.* 85 Heo wyten myd iwisse þt hele is icume to monne of folke iudaysse.

γ. *c* **1200** ORMIN 263 Godess follc, Iudisskenn follc, þatt Godess laȝhess heldenn. *Ibid.* 7127 King off Iudisskenn þede. *Ibid.* 8751 Inntill Iudisskenn follkess land.

‖ **Judenhetze** ('juːdənhɛtsə). [G., = Jew-baiting.] Systematic persecution of the Jews.

1882 *19th Cent.* Aug. 254 Those forces which Europe has confessed are too powerful for it to deal with, and which have led to persecution in Russia and to *Judenhetze* in Germany.

‖ **Judenrat** ('juːdənrat). [G., = Jewish council.] A council representing a Jewish community in a locality controlled by the Germans during the war of 1939–45.

1950 J. HERSEY *Wall* I. i. 20 The *Judenrat* had been formed a month earlier, to the day. The Germans told us then that the *Kehilla*, or Community Council, would henceforth become the *Judenrat* and would be the instrument of German authority over the Jews. **1959** M. LEVIN *Eva* 20 In the very first days after the Germans came, they had ordered the Jews to select a Judenrat. **1960** H. AGAR *Saving Remnant* v. 146 In the Ghettos of Eastern Europe the Germans invariably set up a *Judenrat*: a Council of Jews to transmit orders to the community. **1967** *Sat. Rev.* (U.S.) 15 Apr. 20/2 Krüger sent his blood-spattered uniform and boots to the *Judenrat*, the community council.

‖ **judenrein** ('juːdənraɪn), *a.* [G., = free of Jews.] Of a society or organization: without Jewish members, out of which Jews have been expelled.

1942 *New Republic* 21 Dec. 817 It is not merely central and eastern Europe which are being 'purged', or rendered 'Judenrein', as the Nazis like to say. **1951** H. ARENDT *Origins of Totalitarianism* i. 4 When Hitler came to power, the German banks were already almost *judenrein.* **1960** H. AGAR *Saving Remnant* vii. 188 A country which was becoming almost Hitlerianly *Judenrein.* **1969** C. ROTH *Short Hist. Jewish People* (rev. ed.) VI. xxxi. 444 The survivors .. were rounded up and sent to the death camps, Warsaw being now *judenrein.*

† **Judew, Judeow.** *Obs. rare.* [= OHG. *judeo* (beside *judo*), OS. *judeo*, *giudeo*, *juđeo*, ad. L. *Jūdēu-s* (*Jūdæu-s*). Ormin regularly has *-ew*, *-eow*, repr. L. *-ēus*, *-æus* in proper names: cf. *Andrew*, *Bartholomew*, *Hebrew*, *Jew*, *Matthew*; F. *dieu*, *Hébreu*, OF. *Jueu*; also Goth. *judaiw-isk* Jewish.] = JEW.

c **1200** ORMIN 2245 3a þurrh Iacob, ȝa þurh Iudeow, Affterr gastlike lare. *Ibid.* 13628, & Iudew tacneþþ uss þatt mann, þatt witt tu wel to soþe.

Hence † **'Judewish** (Orm. **-isshe**), *a.* Jewish.

c **1200** ORMIN 1324 þe Iudewisshe follkess boc. *Ibid.* 1674 Amang þe Iudewisshe follc.

judge (dʒʌdʒ), *sb.* Forms: 4–6 **iuge**, 4–5 **iugge**, (4 **iug**, 5 **iewge**, **ioge**), 6–7 **iudge**, (7–8 **judg**), 7– **judge**. [ME. a. OF. *juge* = Pr. *jutge*; cf. Sp. *juez*, It. *judice*:—L. *jūdicem* (nom. *jūdex*), f. *jū-s* right, law + *-dic-us* speaking, speaker.

The F. and Pr. forms do not phonetically represent L. *jūdicem*, of which the F. repr. would be *juze* (cf. *onze*, *douze*, *treize*); they are usually referred to a by-form *judic-us*, *-um*; though some explain them as conformed to the vb. *juger*:—*jūdicāre*.]

1. a. A public officer appointed to administer the law; one who has authority to hear and try causes in a court of justice.

As a generic or descriptive term, *judge* is applicable to any person occupying such an official position, but by usage, it

has, in the United Kingdom, become much restricted as a particular designation. Collectively, the members of the Supreme Court of Judicature are 'His Majesty's Judges'; so we say 'the Judges of the Supreme Court', 'Common Law Judges', 'Chancery Judges', 'Equity Judges', 'Judges of Assize or of the Circuit Courts'; but individually these are mostly styled (Lord, or Mr.) JUSTICE (q.v.). In Scotland, the Judges of the Court of Session and High Court of Justiciary are individually styled LORD. Certain judges have other special designations, as 'President', 'Recorder', etc. But the name is regularly given in England to the presiding officer of a County Court, who is officially styled 'His Honour Judge A——'. The persons presiding judicially, in inferior courts are usually called 'justices' or 'magistrates'. In the United States 'Judge' is more widely applied to the presiding officer of any judicial court below the Supreme Court, in which the official name is 'Justice' (see b below); 'Judge' has also been more used as a designation in some British colonies or dependencies. Historically, the name cleaves to certain noted persons as 'Judge Gascoigne', 'Judge Jeffreys'.

1303 R. BRUNNE *Handl. Synne* 5639 Before þe Iuge was he broghte. **1362** LANGL. *P. Pl.* A. VIII. 171 3e Meires and 3e Maister Iuges..for wyse men ben holden. **1382** WYCLIF *Luke* xviii. 2 Sum iuge was in sum citee, which dredde not God, nether schamede of men. ?*a***1400** *Morte Arth.* 662 Bathe, jureez, and juggez, and justicez of landes. *a***1450** *Cov. Myst.* xxv. (Shaks. Soc.) 246 They arn temperal jewgys. **1530** PALSGR. 235/1 Judge of a towne, *escheuin*. **1596** SHAKS. *Merch. V.* IV. i. 224 A Daniel come to iudgement, yea a Daniel. O wise young Iudge, how do I honour thee. **1612** BACON *Ess., Judicature* (Arb.) 450 Ivdges ought to remember, that their office is *Ius dicere*, and not *Jus dare*; to interprete law, and not to make law, or giue Law. **1823** MRS. MARKHAM [Eliz. Penrose] *Hist. Eng.* (1872) 365 The cruelties perpetrated in the king's name by Judge Jeffreys and Colonel Kirk in the West of England have left a stain on their memories. **1844** LD. BROUGHAM *Brit. Const.* xvii. (1862) 273 The analogy of the Common Law Bench has been followed in the case of all the other Equity Judges. **1849** MACAULAY *Hist. Eng.* viii. (1871) I. 518 Not a single Judge had ventured to declare that the Declaration of Indulgence was legal. **1855** *Ibid.* xxi. II. 566 The chiefs of the three Courts of Common Law and several other Judges were on the bench. **1874** GREEN *Short Hist.* II. vi. 93 The judicial visitations, the 'judges' circuits', which still form so marked a feature in our legal system. **1885** MISS YONGE *Eng. Hist. Reading-bk.* III. 142 One story says that one of the Prince's friends was carried before Judge Gascoigne.

b. With qualification, as ***circuit-judge***, a judge of a circuit court; *spec.* in U.S. the judge appointed to preside alone, or with the district j., or a justice of the Supreme Court, over one of the nine circuits into which the country is divided; ***city*** (or ***municipal***), ***county***, ***district judge***, local magistrates in U.S.; ***judge ordinary***, *spec.* the judge of the Court of Probate and Divorce, previous to 1875; ***judge-advocate***, ***judge-arbitral***, ***judge in eyre***, ***puisne judge***, etc.: see ADVOCATE, etc.

1469 *Sc. Acts Jas. III* (1597) §26 Schireffes and vther Iudges Ordinar, quhilkis will not execute their office, and minister Iustice to the puir people. **1536** BELLENDEN *Cron. Scot.* (1821) I. 29 He was chosin ane juge-arbitrall to discus certane hie debates falling amang his freindis of Ireland. **1748** J. LIND *Lett. Navy* (1757) II. 81 The witnesses..give their evidences to the judge advocate. **1748** *Earthquake Peru* i. 62 With the Assistance of a Judge-Conservator. **1752** J. LOUTHIAN *Form of Process* (ed. 2) 63 The Prisoner may apply to any of the Lords of Justiciary, or Judge-competent. **1815** WELLINGTON *Let. to Earl Bathurst* 2 June in Gurw. *Desp.* XII. 439, I find it scarcely possible to get on without some legal person in the situation of Judge Advocate. **1862** LATHAM *Channel Isl.* III. xv. (ed. 2) 356 The absolute cessation of the Judges-in-Eyre of Normandy visiting the island. **1863** H. COX *Instit.* II. xi. 572 The Judge Ordinary of the Court of Probate is constituted Judge Ordinary of the Divorce Court. **1875** STUBBS *Const. Hist.* III. xix. 351 The pope had..appointed judges-delegate to hear the parties in England. **1889** BRYCE *Amer. Commw.* (ed. 2) xxii. I. 227 The Circuit court may be held either by the Circuit Judge alone, or by the Supreme court Circuit justice alone, or by both together, or by either sitting alone with the District judge. *Ibid.* I. 597 The city judges are..in most of the larger cities ..elected by the citizens... There are usually several superior judges..and a larger number of police judges or justices.

c. Phrases, ***as grave, sober, as a judge***.

1650 COWLEY *Guardian* II. ii. sig. B3/2 If I look not as grave as a Judge upon the bench, let me be hanged for't. **1734** FIELDING *Don Quixote in England* III. xiv. 57, I am as sober as a Judge. **1842** DICKENS *Let.* 28 Mar. (1938) I. 423, I remained as grave as a judge. **1856** READE *Never too late* lii, It was revealed to me..says he, as grave as a judge. **1866** MAYNE REID *Headless Horseman* xliv. 210 I'm as sober as a judge. **1889** [see GRAVE *a.*[1] 3].

d. ***Judges' Rules***: (see quot. 1965[2]).

1925 *Criminal Appeal Rep.* XVIII. 47 The Judges' Rules for the guidance of the Police discussed. **1931** D. L. SAYERS *Five Red Herrings* vii. 80 Between the Judges' Rules..and his anxiety to pull off a coup, he felt his position to be a difficult one. **1965** J. PORTER *Dover Two* iv. 54 And don't start quoting the Judges' Rules to me... The only time you need bother about the Judges' Rules is when the accused person's likely to know more about 'em than you do. **1965** *Stone's Justices' Manual* (ed. 97) I. 368 The Judges' Rules, made by Her Majesty's judges of the Queen's Bench Division, are concerned with the admissibility in evidence against a person of answers, oral or written, given by that person to questions asked by police officers and of statements made by that person. **1973** 'M. INNES' *Appleby's Answer* xix. 167 Miss Pringle wondered whether..she would..perhaps receive some caution required by what are called Judges' Rules.

2. Used of God or Christ, as supreme arbiter, pronouncing sentence on men and moral beings. Cf. JUDGEMENT 4.

*a***1340** HAMPOLE *Psalter* vii. 12 God rightwis iuge stalworth and suffrand. *c***1375** *Sc. Leg. Saints* xxii. (*Laurentius*) 662 þat þai come to þe Iug in hy. *c***1400** MAUNDEV. (Roxb.) xiii. 56 Before Godd þe souerayne Iugge. **1548–9** (Mar.) *Bk. Com. Prayer, Te Deum*, We beleue that thou shalt come to be our iudge. **1611** BIBLE *Gen.* xviii. 25 Shall not the Iudge of all the earth doe right? *a***1769** RICCALTOUN *Notes Galatians* (1772) 46 God the creator, Sovereign and judge. **1811** HEBER *Hymn 'Lord of mercy & of might'* v, Soon to come to earth again, Judge of angels and of men. **1880** PUSEY *Min. Proph.* 119 (Joel ii. 12) The strict Judge cannot be overcome, for He is omnipotent.

3. a. *Hebrew Hist.* An officer (usually a leader in war) invested with temporary authority, in ancient Israel in the period between Joshua and the kings. **b.** *pl.* (in full, ***the Book of Judges***): the seventh book of the Old Testament, containing the history of this period. [After L. *jūdex* as transl. Heb. *shōphēt*. The *Book of Judges* represents *Liber Judicum, Hebraice Sophetim* (i.e. *Shōph'tīm*) of the Vulgate.]

1382 WYCLIF *Judg.* ii. 16 The Lord areride iugis, that shulden delyuer him fro the hoondis of wasters. —— *Ruth* i. 1 In the days of oon iuge, whanne the iugis weren before in power. *c***1460** FORTESCUE *Abs. & Lim. Mon.* i. 1 The childeryn of Israell..were ruled bi hym [God] vndir Juges *regaliter et politice*. **1579** FULKE *Ref. Rastel* 756 In the Iudges, Manoah saide to the Angell..wee may offer to thee a kidde. **1602** SHAKS. *Ham.* II. ii. 422 O Iephta Iudge of Israel, what a Treasure had'st thou? *Mod.* The Song of Deborah and Barak is given in the fifth chapter of Judges.

4. A person appointed to decide in any contest, competition, or dispute; an arbiter, umpire.

*c***1386** CHAUCER *Knt.'s T.* 1779, I wol be trewe Iuge and no partie. *a***1548** HALL *Chron., Hen. IV* 12 That he woulde.. be the discoverer and indifferente iudge..of their couragious actes. **1697** DRYDEN *Virg. Past.* v. 136 The same that sung Neæra's conqu'ring Eyes; And, had the Judge been just, had won the Prize. **1728** POPE *Dunc.* II. 376 To him we grant our amplest pow'rs to sit Judge of all present, past, and future wit. **1882** J. PARKER *Apost. Life* I. 140 No blind man will be appointed as a judge of pictures in the Academy. *Mod.* He was one of the judges at a flower-show.

5. a. One who or that which judges of, determines, or decides anything in question. Often in phr. ***to be judge*** = to judge, determine, form an opinion, give a decision.

*c***1470** HENRY *Wallace* VIII. 54 Now God be juge, the rycht he kennys best. **1490** CAXTON *Eneydos* xxvii. 104 The swete balle of the eye, which is the veraye receptacle interyor of lyght visible, and Iuge of the colours by reflection obgectyf. **1591** SHAKS. *Two Gent.* v. iv. 36 Oh Heauen be iudge how I loue Valentine. **1596** —— *Merch. V.* II. v. 1 Well, thou shalt see: thy eyes shall be thy iudge. **1642** FULLER *Holy & Prof. St.* III. vi. 165 The received custome in the place where we live is the most competent judge of decency. **1711** SHAFTESB. *Charac.* (1737) I. 322 If Fancy be left judg of any thing, she must be judg of all. **1858** CARLYLE *Fredk. Gt.* II. IX. ii. 403 Approvable as a practical officer and soldier by the strictest judge then living.

†**b.** *transf.* A criterion. *Obs. rare.*

1662 STILLINGFL. *Orig. Sacr.* I. vi. §8 How could such a coppy be the Judge of all others, which could not be read or understood by those who appealed to it?

6. A person qualified to form or pronounce an opinion; one capable of judging or estimating.

1560 DAUS tr. *Sleidane's Comm.* 3 That the understanding of all Scripture must be fetched at his hande, as of a mooste certen iudge. **1653** WALTON *Angler* To Rdr. 2, I here disallow thee to be a competent judge. **1713** STEELE *Englishm.* No. 46. 302, I think my self a pretty good Judg of Mens Mien and Air. **1796** R. BAGE *Hermsprong* xxv, I am no judge of the very handsome in men. **1836–9** DICKENS *Sk. Boz, Parlour Orator*, You, gentlemen, are the best judges on that point. **1891** E. PEACOCK *N. Brendon* I. 308 You are certainly not a good judge of character.

†**7.** Applied to the rook or castle in chess. *Obs. rare.*

Judge is here Fitzherbert's rendering of *justitiarius*, the name applied to the rook in the 13–14th c. Latin treatise *Moralitas de Scaccario secundum Innocentium tertium papam*, which is the source of Fitzherbert's chess-lore.

1523 FITZHERB. *Husb.* Prol., The boke of the moralytes of the cheesse..deuyded in vi. degrees, that is to saye, the kynge, the quene, the byshops, the knightes, the iudges, and the yomenne.

8. *Angling.* Name for a kind of artificial fly.

1867 F. FRANCIS *Angling* xi. (1880) 430 The Judge..A very tasty fly.

9. *Mining.* 'A staff used for gauging the depth of the holing' (Gresley *Gloss.* 1883).

1875 J. H. COLLINS *Metal Mining* Gloss., *Judge*, a staff used for underground measurements. **1881** RAYMOND *Mining Gloss.*, *Judge*, a measuring-stick to measure coal-work under ground.

10. *Comb.*, as ***judge-like*** adj. and adv.; **judge-made** *a.* (of law), constituted by judicial decisions; †**judge-man**, a judge.

1818 SCOTT *Hrt. Midl.* xxv, I heard the *Judge-carle say it with my ain ears. **1670** DRYDEN *1st Pt. Conq. Granada* I. i. Wks. 1883 IV. 35 *Judge-like thou sit'st, to praise, or to arraign. **1824** J. S. MILL in *Westm. Rev.* I. 510 The common judge-made definition of a public libel, is, any thing which tends to bring the constituted authorities into hatred and contempt. **1832** AUSTIN *Jurispr.* (1873) II. xxix. 549 The term 'Judge-made law' would seem to denote law made by subject judges, as opposed to law made by the sovereign Legislature. **1863** H. COX *Instit.* II. iii. 328 With respect to all judicial or judge-made law. **1965** *Mod. Law Rev.* XXVIII. v. 510 The clash between democracy and judge-made law. *a***1400–50** *Alexander* 3402 þe Iustis & þe gentils & *Iugemen of lawe. *c***1440** *York Myst.* xxix. 1 Full arely the juggemen demed hym to dye. **1672** WYCHERLEY *Love in a Wood* II. i, Your chamber-wit, or scribble-wit, and last of all your *judge-wit, or critic.

judge (dʒʌdʒ), *v.* Forms: 3–5 iugge, 3–6 iuge, (5 iewge, 6 guge), 6–7 iudge, (7–8 judg), 7– judge. [ME. a. OF. *jugier*, AF. *juger* = Pr. *jutjar*, *jutgar*, Sp. *juzgar*, It. *giudicare*:—L. *jūdicāre*, f. *jūdex*, *jūdicem* JUDGE.]

I. Transitive senses.

1. To try, or pronounce sentence upon (a person) in a court of justice; to sit in judgement upon. (Also said of God or Christ: cf. prec. 2.)

*c***1290** *S.E. Leg.* I. 183/89 Heo stoden and Iuggeden hire a-mong heom alle. **1382** WYCLIF *John* xii. 48 He that dispisith me..hath him that schal iuge him. **1483** CAXTON *Cato* G iij, Whan tho seest somme persone euyl fortunate or accused or iuged of somme vyce. **1567** *Gude & Godlie B.* (S.T.S.) 11 Our Mediator and our remeid, Sall cum to Juge baith quick and deide. **1667** MILTON *P.L.* III. 330 Then all thy Saints asembl'd, thou shalt judge Bad men and Angels. **1875** JOWETT *Plato* (ed. 2) I. 408 The dead are first of all judged according to their deeds.

†**2.** *spec.* To pronounce sentence against (a person); to sentence, condemn. Const. *to* (the penalty), or *to do* or *suffer* (something). *Obs.*

*c***1310** *Flemish Insurr.* in *Pol. Songs* (Camden) 190 The barouns of Fraunce a thider conne gon..To jugge the Flemmisshe to bernen and to slon. *c***1380** WYCLIF *Sel. Wks.* III. 116 (Apostles' Creed) At þe laste he schal come doun here to man, and jugge sum to blysse and oþer to helle. **1432–50** tr. *Higden* (Rolls) III. 291 He [Socrates] was iuggede to prison, and poysonede in prison. *c***1450** *Merlin* 15 Ye shull neuer be Iuged to deth for my cause. *a***1533** LD. BERNERS *Huon* lxxxii. 252 The kynge iuged Huon to dye. *a***1626** BACON *Max. & Uses Com. Law* (1635) 17 Some whose offences are pilfring..they judge to be whipped. **1675** BROOKS *Gold. Key* Wks. 1867 V. 129 To call the souls to an account, and judge them to their state.

3. To give sentence concerning (a matter); to try (a cause); to determine, decide (a question).

1513 MORE in Grafton *Chron.* (1568) II. 766 To remaine ..till the matter were..examined..and either iudged or appeased. **1568** GRAFTON *Chron.* II. 142 It was agreed, that all matters concernyng the aforesayde articles or statutes.. should be dēmed and iudged by the French king. **1617** MORYSON *Itin.* III. 248 The Consul of the City there..is vulgarly called Burgomaster, and he judgeth all civill and criminal causes. **1690** TATE & BRADY *Ps.* xxxv. 1 Judge and defend my cause, O Lord.

4. To decide by judicial authority that something is to be done, or is the fact; to decree, order. (With *obj.* and *inf.*, or *obj. cl.*)

*c***1330** *Arth. & Merl.* 2609 Bi heighe mennes conseyl The king was iugged Ygerne to spouse. **1362** LANGL. *P. Pl.* A. II. 106 3if þe Iustise wol Iugge hire to be Ioynet with Fals. 3it be-war of þe weddyng, for witti is treuþe. *a***1450** *Knt. de la Tour* (1868) 101 Thenne the kyng iuged that the child shold be gyuen to her that wold haue hym to be saued. **1600** E. BLOUNT tr. *Conestaggio* 77 But the pretendents being heard, the King shoulde iudge to whom the Realme belonged.

5. To assign or award by judgement; to adjudge; to decree. Now *rare* or *Obs.*

1387 TREVISA *Higden* (Rolls) IV. 181 Cesar is i-made consul, and Gallia was iuged [*decreta*] to him. *c***1400** *Destr. Troy* 2407 Yf þou luge it to Iono, this ioye shall þou haue. *a***1533** LD. BERNERS *Huon* ci. 332 Ye false traytours, youre dethes is Iuged. **1595** [see JUDGED]. **1634** MILTON *L'Allegro* 122 Ladies whose bright eyes Rain influence and judge the prize Of wit or arms. **1817** W. SELWYN *Law Nisi Prius* (ed. 4) II. 704 Where two persons are in possession, the possession is judged in him who hath right.

†**6.** To administer (law) as a judge. *Obs.*

*c***1380** *Antecrist* in Todd *Three Treat. Wyclif* (1851) 144 þei syten in þe trones wiþ gloriouse myters jugyng & demyng her owne made lawes. **1390** GOWER *Conf.* III. 180 To deme and jugge commun lawe.

7. To have jurisdiction over, to govern or rule as an Israelitish judge (cf. prec. 3). Also *absol.* To hold the office of a judge.

*a***1300** *Cursor M.* 7018 Barach, and wit him Delbora, þai iuged fourti yeir or ma. *c***1450** *Cov. Myst.* xxx. (Shaks. Soc.) 303 Herowde is kyng of that countre, To jewge that regyon in lenth and in brede. **1558** KNOX *First Blast* (Arb.) 40 The example of Debora..when she iudged Israel. **1611** BIBLE *Judg.* xii. 13 After him, Abdon, the sonne of Hillel a Pirathonite iudged Israel.

8. To declare or pronounce authoritatively (a person) to be (so-and-so). Const. *for*, or with *inf.*, or simple complement. ? *Obs.* or merged in 11 b.

*c***1400** *Rom. Rose* 6311 God iugged me for a theef trichour. **1553** T. WILSON *Rhet.* (1580) 50 Beyng..suche a one (as Appollo iudged hym by his Oracle to bee wise). **1617** MORYSON *Itin.* III. 4 Hee was judged an unprofitable servant. **1721** *St. German's Doctor & Stud.* 219 That he should be taken for heir, that should be judged for heir by the law.

†**b.** with *obj. cl.* To pronounce as an opinion or authoritative statement; to declare. *Obs.*

1377 LANGL. *P. Pl.* B. I. 183 For Iames þe gentil iugged in his bokes, That faith with-oute þe faite is ri3te no þinge worthi.

9. To form an opinion about; to exercise the mind upon (something) so as to arrive at a correct or sound notion of it; to estimate; to appraise.

*a***1225** *Ancr. R.* 118 No mon ne mei juggen blod wel er hit beo cold. **13..** *E.E. Allit. P.* A. 7 Quere-so-euer I Iugged gemmez gaye, I sette hyr sengeley in synglure. **1486** *Bk. St. Albans* E j b, The .vi. yere euermoore at the leest Thow shalt well Iuge the perche of thessame beest. **1535** COVERDALE *1 Cor.* x. 15, I speake vnto them which haue discrecioun: iudge ye what I say. **1593** SHAKS. *Rich. II*, III. ii. 194 Men iudge by the complexion of the Skie The state and inclination of the day. **1671** TEMPLE *Orig. Govt.* §6 The safety and firmness of any frame of government may be best

judged by the rules of architecture. **1709** POPE *Ess. Crit.* 337 But most by Numbers judge a Poet's song. **1864** BRYCE *Holy Rom. Emp.* xxi. (1875) 378 Institutions, like men, should be judged by their prime.

†**b.** *transf.* To be a test or criterion of. *rare.*

1586 MARLOWE *1st Pt. Tamburl.* I. ii, If outward habit judge the inward man.

10. To pronounce an opinion upon, to criticize; *esp.* to pronounce an adverse opinion upon, to condemn, censure. Also *absol.* (In quot. 1377, To express or pronounce one's opinion about.)

1377 LANGL. *P. Pl.* B. II. 94 To drynke at dyuerse tauernes, And there to iangle and to iape, and iugge here euene cristene. *Ibid.* VII. 161 Þanne Iacob iugged iosephes sweuene. **1526** TINDALE *Matt.* vii. 1, 2 Iudge not lest ye be iudged. For as ye iudge so shal ye be iudged. **1599** SHAKS. *Hen. V*, Prol. 34 Who Prologue-like, your humble patience pray, Gently to heare, kindly to iudge our Play. **1782** COWPER *Progr. Err.* 611 But if the wanderer his mistake discern, Judge his own ways, and sigh for a return. **1884** *Contemp. Rev.* XLVI. 99 Every workman was thus known and judged by those who could judge him best.

11. with *obj. cl.* To form the opinion, or hold as an opinion; to come to a conclusion, infer; to apprehend, think, consider, suppose.

1297 R. GLOUC. (Rolls) 4154 Ac þe king ne Iugede noȝt þat it ssolde be so ydo. *Ibid.* 9354 Me Iuggede wat it ssolde be to tokni þis cas. *c* **1374** CHAUCER *Troylus* v. 1203 He nyste what he Iuggen of it myghte. **1508** *Dunbar's Flyting* 48** Iuge in the nixt quha got the war. **1553** T. WILSON *Rhet.* (1580) 177 As by an Ivie garland, we iudge there is wine to sell. **1591** SHAKS. *Two Gent.* I. ii. 139, I see things too, although you iudge I winke. **1615** G. SANDYS *Trav.* 224 Small townes I judge they were. **1796** ELIZA HAMILTON *Lett. Hindoo Rajah* I. 206 Judge how this shocked and offended me? **1850** SCORESBY *Cheever's Whalem. Adv.* vii. (1859) 97 Some whalemen judge it does not attain its full size until twenty-five years.

b. with *obj.* and *inf.* or simple complement (rarely with *to* or *for*): To infer, conclude, or suppose to be.

1340-70 *Alex. & Dind.* 697 Iuno þe ioilese ȝe iuggen for noble. **1377** LANGL. *P. Pl.* B. IX. 84 Iuwes þat we iugge Iudas felawes. *c* **1400** *Lanfranc's Cirurg.* 169 Þanne þe wounde is iugid mortal. *c* **1477** CAXTON *Jason* 13 Iuging in him grete corage. **1538** STARKEY *England* I. ii. 58 The sanguyn complexyon ys gugyd of other chefe and best for the mayntenance of helthe of the body. **1591** SHAKS. *Two Gent.* III. i. 25 When they haue iudg'd me fast asleepe. **1653** WALTON *Angler* i. 13, I hope you will not judge my earnestness to be impatience. **1727** GAY *Fables* I. xxiii, Who friendship with a knave hath made, Is judg'd a partner in the trade. **1755** B. MARTIN *Mag. Arts & Sc.* I. II. 119 They judge the Moon to be a Globe like our Earth. **1871** FREEMAN *Norm. Conq.* IV. xviii. 115 It was..judged better to begin the attack at once.

12. with *cognate obj.* (esp. with qualification).

1526 TINDALE *John* vii. 24 Judge not after the vtter aperaunce: but iudge rightewes iudgement. **1560** [see JUDGEMENT 3].

†**13.** *refl.* ? To submit oneself to the judgement of; to commit oneself *to*. *Obs. rare.*

c **1485** *Digby Myst.* (1882) III. 308 Yf þe trewth be sowth ..& that I Iugge me to skryptur.

II. Intransitive senses.

14. To act as judge; to try causes and pronounce sentences in a court of justice; to sit in judgement.

c **1380** WYCLIF *Sel. Wks.* III. 54 (Te Deum) Þou art bileeved to come for to juge at þe laste day. **1393** LANGL. *P. Pl.* C. XXIII. 19 And *spiritus iusticie* shal Iugen, wol he, nul he, After þe kynges counsaile and þe comune lyke. **1585** T. WASHINGTON tr. *Nicholay's Voy.* II. viii. 41, 2. other officers, which..may iudge of small matters being under the value of twenty crownes. **1639** S. DU VERGER tr. *Camus' Admir. Events* 83 As for Civill matters they may judge without appeale. **1756-7** tr. *Keysler's Trav.* (1760) III. 312 It was not so with the Italian princes, who judged without appeal. **1865** SEELEY *Ecce Homo* iii. (ed. 8) 25 A warrior-king, judging in the gate of Jerusalem.

15. To give a decision or opinion on any matter, esp. between contending parties; to arbitrate.

c **1380** WYCLIF *Serm.* Sel. Wks. I. 304 Crist forsook to juge in temporal goodis. **1470-85** MALORY *Arthur* IV. xii, Yet wylle I [Arthur] Iuge..I wylle that ye gyue vnto your broder alle the hole manoir with the appertenaunce. **1535** COVERDALE *Isa.* v. 3 Judge I praye you betwixte me and my wyne gardinge. **1591** SHAKS. *1 Hen. VI*, II. iv. 10 Judge you, my Lord of Warwicke, then betweene vs. **1694** DRYDEN *Love Triumph.* Prol. 18 If you continue judging, as you do, Every bad play will hope for damning too. **1878** BROWNING *La Saisiaz* 278 God must judge 'twixt man and me.

16. To form an opinion; to arrive at a notion, esp. a sound or correct notion, about something; to make up one's mind as to the truth of a matter; in *Logic*, To apprehend mentally the relation of two objects; to make a mental assertion or statement. Const. *of*.

c **1374** CHAUCER *Troylus* II. Proem 21 A blynd man ne kan luggen wel yn hewys. *c* **1400** *Lanfranc's Cirurg.* 282 Of þis ydropesie summen iugiþ liȝtli, and seien [etc.]. **1598** SHAKS. *Merry W.* III. v. 52 Let her consider his frailety, and then iudge of my merit. *a* **1679** HOBBES *Rhet.* iii. (1681) 4 If he judg, he must judg either of that which is to come or of that which is past. **1711** SHAFTESB. *Charac.* (1737) II. 102 To be able to judg of both, 'tis necessary to have a sense of each. **1774** GOLDSM. *Nat. Hist.* (1776) III. 141 If we were to judge of its size by the horns. **1843** MILL *Logic* I. v. §1 When the mind assents to a proposition it judges. **1860** TYNDALL *Glac.* I. xvi. 117 From its form and colour he could..judge of its condition. **1885** J. MARTINEAU *Types Eth. The.* I. I. II. ii. §2. 157 Understanding never judges... It is the Will that really judges and decides on what is presented to it by the Understanding.

judgeable ('dʒʌdʒəb(ə)l), *a. rare*⁻⁰. [f. prec. vb. + -ABLE.] Capable of being judged or judged of.

1570 LEVINS *Manip.* 3/5 Iudgeable, *estimabilis.*

'judge-and-'jury, *v. nonce-wd.* [A phrase used as a vb.] *trans.* To try by, or as by, a judge and jury; to try and pass sentence upon.

1874 T. HARDY *Far fr. Madding Crowd* xli, Now that 'tis put to me to judge-and-jury like, I can't call to mind. **1879** BROWNING *Ned Bratts* 249 There wants no earthly judge-and-jurying: here we stand—Sentence our guilty selves. **1887** HALL CAINE *Deemster* xxxiv. 224 We're going to judge and jury you, but all fair and square.

judged (dʒʌdʒd), *ppl. a.* [f. JUDGE *v.* + -ED¹.] Tried or sentenced in court, decided, awarded, estimated, etc.: see the verb.

Rare exc. in the compounds ILL-JUDGED, WELL-JUDGED.

1537 STARKEY *Let. to Pole* in Strype *Eccl. Mem.* (1721) I. II. App. lxxx. 190 If case be that you reach to the judged truth, you need not to fear. **1595** DANIEL *Civ. Wares* (1609) v. ci, As he to his iudged exile went. **1710** PRIDEAUX *Orig. Tithes* ii. 42 Precedents and judged cases have ever had the like authority.

absol. **1667** MILTON *P.L.* x. 81 Where none Are to behold the Judgement, but the judg'd.

judgement, judgment ('dʒʌdʒmənt). Forms: 3-5 iuggement, 3-6 iugement, (3 gugement, 4 iuiement, iugumen, 5 iugemente, iewge-, iugis-, yuge-, iugment), 6-7 iudge-, iudgment, (-e), 7- judge-, judgment. [a. F. *jugement* (11th c.), f. *juger* to JUDGE + -MENT: cf. Pr. *jutgamen*, med.L. *jūdicāmentum*.]

1. a. The action of trying a cause in a court of justice; trial. (Now *rare* or merged in 3.) Also applied to trial by battle (quot. 1377: see BATTLE *sb.* 2) or ordeal (***Judgement of God***).

1297 R. GLOUC. (Rolls) 1236 To bringe is neueu mid strengþe to stonde to Iugement. **1377** LANGL. *P. Pl.* B. XVI. 95 Þanne shulde Ihesus iuste þere-fore bi iuggement of armes, Whether shulde [fonge] þe fruit, þe fende or hymselue. **1390** GOWER *Conf.* III. 340 Unto the town this he besoghte, To don him riht in juggement. *c* **1470** HENRY *Wallace* II. 248 To..bryng him wp out of that vgly sell To iugisment. *a* **1548** HALL *Chron.*, *Edw. V* 6 b, They all foure were beheaded without iudgement. **1596** SHAKS. *Merch. V.* IV. i. 223 A Daniel come to iudgement, yea a Daniel. **1617** MORYSON *Itin.* III. 270 The Canton of Bern hath three Courts of Judgement. **1652** NEEDHAM tr. *Selden's Mare Cl.* 5 This caus could not by any pretens bee brought into judgment. **1672** COWELL *Interpr.*, *Judicium Dei*, the Judgment of God, so our ancestors call'd those now prohibited Tryals of Ordeal, and its several kinds.

b. Phr. ***to sit in judgement***: (*a*) *lit.* to sit as judge, to preside as a judge at a trial; (*b*) *fig.* to pass judgement *upon* (see 6), to judge, criticize (with an assumption of superiority).

c **1440** *Gesta Rom.* I. vii. 18 (Harl. MS.) Whanne the Iuge was come down..for to sitte in iugement, he sawe þis siȝt. *a* **1548** HALL *Chron.*, *Hen. VI* 161 The kyng hymself came into Kent, and there sat in iudgement upon the offendors. **1824** SCOTT *Redgauntlet* Let. v, We shall all of us have enough to do, without sitting in judgment upon other folks.

2. The trial of moral beings by God (or Christ) as Judge; *spec.* (in full, ***the Last Judgement***), the final trial of the subjects of God's moral government at the end of the world: = DOOM *sb.* 6. Often in ***day of judgement***: = DOOMSDAY.

1340 HAMPOLE *Pr. Consc.* 2802 Þan sal þai come til þe last iugement. **1382** WYCLIF *Matt.* x. 15 It shall be more suffreable to the lond of men of Sodom and Gomor in the day of iugement than to that citee. [Cf. xi. 22, in the day of dome.] *c* **1450** tr. *De Imitatione* I. iii. 4 Derke þinges, for þe whiche we shul not be blamed in þe iuggement. *c* **1511** *1st Eng. Bk. Amer.* (Arb.) Introd. 33/1 Of this people shalbe no iugement at the dredefull day of dome. **1615** G. SANDYS *Trav.* 188 The valley of Cedron..where the generall Iudgement shall be, if the Iews..may be beleeved. **1794** SULLIVAN *View Nat.* I. 39 The saints and spirits of the blessed shall take possession of it, and there remain till the general judgment. **1855** MILMAN *Lat. Chr.* IV. i. (1864) II. 173 In the Resurrection and Day of Judgement.

3. a. The sentence of a court of justice; a judicial decision or order in court.

c **1290** *S. Eng. Leg.* I. 98/205 Is þis a guod Ivggement? *a* **1300** *Cursor M.* 6776 (Cott.) Þou sal it quit wit iuiement [*v.r.* iuggement]. *c* **1450** *Cov. Myst.* xxv. 249 A wondyr case ..On wiche we must gyf iewgement. *a* **1548** HALL *Chron.*, *Hen. VIII* 244 b, He confessed the Inditement, and so had Iudgement to bee hanged. **1560** BIBLE (Genev.) *1 Kings* iii. 28 All Israel heard yᵉ iudgement, which the King had iudged. **1647-8** COTTERELL *Davila's Hist. Fr.* (1678) 5 If he caused judgment to be given in favour of his mother. *a* **1718** PENN *Tracts* Wks. 1726 I. 501 Judgment is the Determination and Result of Law. **1818** CRUISE *Digest* (ed. 2) VI. 342 Judgment that the daughters of Richard and Mathew took only estates for life. **1856** FROUDE *Hist. Eng.* (1858) I. ii. 160 She appealed from the judgment of the legates to that of the pope.

b. *Law.* (*ellipt.*) An assignment of chattels or chattel-interests made by judgement or decree of court; the certificate of such judgement as a security or form of property. Cf. *judgement-debt* in 13.

'A Judgment, in consequence of some suit or action in a court of justice, is frequently the means of vesting the right and property of chattel interests in the prevailing party' (Blackstone *Comm.* (1767) II. 436).

1677 YARRANTON *Eng. Improv.* 36 Bonds given to the King, although..never Recorded in the Exchequer, nor in any Court else; yet these Bonds are a Judgment in Law, and by virtue thereof will be first served. *a* **1718** PENN *Maxims* Wks. 1726 I. 845 As Judgments are paid before Bonds, and Bonds before Bills or Book-debts. **1745** *De Foe's Eng. Tradesman* i. 6 A judgment in goods, taken in early, is never lost. **1858** LD. ST. LEONARDS *Handy Bk. Prop. Law* xxi. 167 Upon a marriage, a mother assigned an unregistered judgment to a trustee for her daughter for life.

4. Divine sentence or decision; *spec.* a misfortune or calamity regarded as a divine visitation or punishment, or as a token of divine displeasure.

a **1300** *Cursor M.* 1591 (Gött.) In form of iugement a neu vengans on þaim god sent. *c* **1380** WYCLIF *Sel. Wks.* III. 444 If he discorde from juggement of his God. **1470-85** MALORY *Arthur* IV. xxiii, That is the ryghtwys Iugement of god sayd the damoysel. **1560** BIBLE (Genev.) *Ezek.* xiv. 21 When I send my foure sore iudgements vpon Ierusalem. **1613** SHAKS. *Hen. VIII*, II, iv. 194 Hence I tooke a thought, This was a Iudgement on me. **1703** *Lond. Gaz.* No. 3899/1 An Anniversary Thanksgiving..for our Deliverance from the Terrours of that dreadful Judgment [earthquake]. **1797** MRS. RADCLIFFE *Italian* xxii. (1824) 648 Some people said it was a judgement on him. **1816** J. WILSON *City of Plague* II. iii. 301 My sins have brought this judgment on the city.

5. a. Any formal or authoritative decision, as of an umpire or arbiter. (Now *rare.*)

c **1330** R. BRUNNE *Chron.* (1810) 303 To whils þat oure trewe duellis on jugement. *c* **1386** CHAUCER *C.T.* Prol. 833 Who so be rebel to my Iuggement Shal paye for al þat by the wey is spent. *c* **1450** *Guy Warw.* (C.) 672 And all þey seyde wyth oon assente: We graunt wele to yowre yugement. **1560** DAUS tr. *Sleidane's Comm.* 14, I will conforme my wyll vnto your iudgemente. **1602** SHAKS. *Ham.* v. ii. 291. **1619** SANDERSON *Serm. Rom.* xiv. 3. §3 This third Verse: wherein is contained..Saint Pauls judgement; or his counsell rather, and advice. **1878** BROWNING *La Saisiaz* 292 The show of things unfurled For thy summing-up and judgement.

†**b.** *Astrol.* A decision or conclusion as to a future event, deduced from the positions of the heavenly bodies: cf. *judicial astrology*. *Obs.*

1390 GOWER *Conf.* III. 2 He can al the lawe deme, And yiven every juggement Which longeth to the firmament. *Ibid.* 107 [Astrology] The which in juggementz acompteth Theffect, what every sterre amonteth.

6. The pronouncing of a deliberate opinion upon a person or thing, or the opinion pronounced; criticism; censure.

a **1225** *Ancr. R.* 118 Þeo hwule þet te heorte walleð wiðinnen of ureððe, nis þer no riht dom, ne no riht gugement. **1340-70** *Alex. & Dind.* 462 Þere nis no iargoun no iangle ne iuggeme[n]tis falce..*c* **1477** CAXTON *Jason* 14 After the Iugement of the men ye are the very myrrour of al vertues. **1560** DAUS tr. *Sleidane's Comm.* Ded. A ij b, The place and dignity, to the which (by the iudgement of al men) you are most worthely called. **1659** RAY *Corr.* (1848) 2 You have my designs, and I desire your judgment of them. **1671** TEMPLE *Lett.*, *to Sir J. Temple* Wks. 1731 II. 247 Upon all these Passages..I have fixed my Judgment of the Affairs and Counsels at present in Design. **1841** MYERS *Cath. Th.* III. viii. 31 Scripture..with its selection of facts and moral judgements of them, has been ordained of God to be written thus rather than otherwise. **1865** DICKENS *Mut. Fr.* I. vi, We'll pass no judgement upon that.

7. a. The formation of an opinion or notion concerning something by exercising the mind upon it; an opinion, estimate.

c **1380** WYCLIF *Sel. Wks.* III. 345 Wher men of worse liif mai sunner erre in þer jugement. **1390** GOWER *Conf.* III. 45 Ek also Aeremance in juggement To love he bringth of his assent. **1559** W. CUNNINGHAM *Cosmogr. Glasse* 86 This wayе in my iudgement doeth excell all the rest. **1594** SHAKS. *Rich. III*, III. iv. 45 To morrow, in my iudgement, is too sudden. **1671** R. BOHUN *Wind* 113 Wee may better make judgement of these Winds. **1741** WATTS *Improv. Mind* I. v. §1 If we would form a judgment of a book. **1799** MACKINTOSH *Stud. Law Nature & Nations* Wks. 1846 I. 385 To form a sound judgment on political measures. **1884** *Times* (weekly ed.) 5 Sept. 3/1 In his judgment they..had no occasion to bow down to any one.

†**b.** A form of religious opinion or belief; a 'persuasion'. *Obs.*

1653 CROMWELL *Sp.* in *Select. fr. Harl. Misc.* (1793) 376 If I did seem to speak any thing, that might seem to reflect upon those of the Presbyterian judgment. *c* **1665** MRS. HUTCHINSON *Mem. Col. Hutchinson* (1863) 66 Having been before of the Arminian judgement. **1687** *Assur. Abb. Lands* 90, I do not herein aim at reflecting upon the Conformists in general; for..there are many sober, vertuous and religeous Persons of that Judgment.

c. ***private judgement***: the formation of personal or individual opinion (esp. in religious matters), as opposed to the acceptance of a statement or doctrine on authority.

1718 T. HERNE (*title*) Defense of Private Judgment. **1840** CARLYLE *Heroes, Priest* (1872) 115 Liberty of private judgment, if we will consider it, must at all times have existed in the world.

8. a. The faculty of judging; ability to form an opinion; that function of the mind whereby it arrives at a notion of anything; the critical faculty; discernment.

1535 JOYE *Apol. Tindale* (Arb.) 11 Men of greter knowleg ..and more excellent iugement in holy scripture. **1599** SHAKS. *Hen. V*, III. vii. 58 You haue good iudgement in Horsemanship. **1667** MILTON *P.L.* VIII. 636 Take heed lest Passion sway Thy Judgement. **1709** POPE *Ess. Crit.* I. 9 'Tis with our judgments as our watches, none Go just alike, yet each believes his own. *a* **1832** MACKINTOSH *Revol.* 1688, Wks. 1846 II. 264 Clarendon was zealous, but of small judgment. **1870** J. H. NEWMAN *Gram. Assent* II. ix. 347 Aristotle calls the faculty which guides the mind in matters of conduct, by the name of *phronesis*, or judgment.

b. Good or sound judgement; discernment, discretion, wisdom, understanding, good sense.

1576 FLEMING *Panopl. Epist.* To Rdr. ¶v, Whose minde is beautified with the amiable iuelles of knowledge, and iudgement. **1612** ROWLANDS *Knave Harts* 20 Boy, bring good wine, when men of iudgement cals. **1784** COWPER *Task* VI. 657 A deed..owing more To want of judgment than to wrong design.

†**c.** *transf.* A person having good judgement; a competent critic; a 'judge'. (Cf. *genius, wit.*)

1606 SHAKS. *Tr. & Cr.* I. ii. 208 Hee's a man good inough, hee's one o' th' soundest iudgement[s] in Troy whosoeuer. **1668** DRYDEN *Even. Love* Epil. 3 Looking for a judgment or a wit, Like Jews, I saw them scattered through the pit. **1682** SIR T. BROWNE *Chr. Mor.* II. §4 To undervalue a solid Judgment, because he knows not the genealogy of Hector.

d. *Sc.* Reason, senses, wits.

1800 *Monthly Mag.* I. 239 The poor man has lost his judgement. *Mod.* He has gone out of his judgement. You nearly fricht me out o' my juidgements.

9. *Logic.* †**a.** = DISPOSITION 1 c. *Obs.*

1628 T. SPENCER *Logick* 149 Hitherto wee haue handled the first part of Logicke; called Invention. Wee come now to the second, termed Iudgement. **1678** PHILLIPS (ed. 4), *Judgment*, the second part of Logick which Disposes of Arguments for Disputation.

b. The action of mentally apprehending the relation between two objects of thought; predication, as an act of the mind. With *pl.* A mental assertion or statement; a proposition, as formed in the mind.

1704 NORRIS *Ideal World* II. iii. 125 The old Philosophy.. meaning by judgment the union or separation of things by affirmation or negation. **1725** WATTS *Logic* II. Introd., The foregoing sentences which are examples of the act of judgment, are properly called propositions: Plato is a philosopher, &c. **1827** WHATELY *Logic* 59 Judgement is the comparing together in the mind two of the notions or ideas which are the objects of apprehension. **1860** ABP. THOMSON *Laws. Th.* II. §67. 108 A Judgment, then, is an expression that two notions can or cannot be reconciled. **1864** BOWEN *Logic* v. 105 Judgment is that act of mind whereby the relation of one Concept to another..is determined.

10. In various biblical uses, chiefly as rendering of Heb. *mishpāt*, in its different uses.

a. Justice, righteousness, equity. (= DOOM *sb.* 8.)

a **1325** *Prose Psalter* xlix. 22 [l.21] Y shal stablis iugumen oȝayn þy face. **1526** TINDALE *Matt.* xxiii. 23 The waygthtyer mattres of the lawe..iudgement, mercy, and fayth. **1611** BIBLE *Isa.* lxi. 8 For I the Lord loue Iudgement, I hate robbery for burnt offering.

b. A (divine) decree, ordinance, law, statute.

a **1420** HOCCLEVE *De Reg. Princ.* 1343 The iugementz of god ben to vs hid. **1526** TINDALE *Rom.* xi. 33 Howe incomprehensible are his iudgementes, and hys wayes vnserchable. **1535** COVERDALE *Ps.* cxix. 30, I haue chosen the way of treuth, thy iudgmentes haue I layed before me. **1611** BIBLE *Exod.* xxi. 1 Now these are the Iudgements which thou shalt set before them [COVERD., *Genev.*, *Bps.' Bible*, lawes].

c. Sentence or decision in a person's favour; (one's) right.

1611 BIBLE *Deut.* x. 18 He doth execute the iudgement of [COVERD. etc., He doeth right vnto] the fatherlesse and widow. —— *Job* xxvii. 2 As God liueth, who hath taken away my iudgment [COVERD., my power: *R.V.* my right].

†**11.** The function of a 'judge' or ruler (in the ancient Hebrew state: see JUDGE *sb.* 3). *Obs. rare.*

1558 KNOX *First Blast* (Arb.) 41 It is euident, that her [Deborah's] iudgement or gouernement in Israel was no such vsurped power.

†**12.** A district under a jurisdiction. *Obs. rare.*

1617 MORYSON *Itin.* III. 251 The third league called the tenne judgments, (or jurisdictions) and consisting of tenne communities joined in the league..1498.

13. *attrib.* and *Comb.*, as ***judgement bar, book, call, hour, house, -monger, peal, place, throne***; **judgement-cap** = BLACK CAP 1; **judgement creditor**, a creditor in whose favour a judgement has been given ordering the payment of the debt due to him; **judgement debt**, a debt for the payment of which a judgement has been given; so **judgement debtor**, a debtor against whom such a judgement has been given; **judgement-like** *a.* (*Sc.*), 'applied to what is supposed to be like a token of divine displeasure' (Jam.); **judgement note** (*U.S.*), a promissory note containing a power of attorney to appear and confess judgement for the sum therein named (Bouvier); **judgement sample** *Statistics* (see quot.); **judgement summons**, a summons issued in a County Court against a *judgement debtor*, to show cause why he should not be imprisoned for default in payment; **judgement weather** (*Sc.*) = 'judgement-like' weather (see above).

1613 T. MILLES tr. *Mexia's etc. Treas. Anc. & Mod. T.* 713/2 They would presume so farre as the *iudgement Bars, and there spread a Gowne on the ground before the Magistrate. **1660** R. COKE *Power & Subj.* 159 He which will not celebrate it, let him undergo the penalty in the *Judgment-book. **1847** MARY HOWITT *Ballads* 207 The last great *judgment-call. **1838** *Act 1 & 2 Vict.* c. 110 §11 Providing adequate means for enabling *judgment creditors to obtain satisfaction from the property of their debtors. *Ibid.* §17 Every *judgment debt shall carry interest at the rate of four pounds per centum per annum. **1875** POSTE *Gaius* III. (ed. 2) 414. **1881** *Jrnl. Inst. Bankers* Nov. 563 Every debt proved was made a judgement debt. **1838** *Act 1 & 2 Vict.* c. 110 §15 No disposition of the *judgment debtor in the meantime shall be valid..as against the judgment creditor. **1883** *Wharton's Law-Lex.* (ed. 7), *Judgment-debtor*, one against whom a judgment ordering him to pay a sum of money stands unsatisfied. **1526** *Iudgement housse [see JUDGEMENT-HALL 1534]. **1708** M. BRUCE *Good News in Evil T.* 11 It was *Judgment-like and a token of it to that poor Land, when Godly Baruch..fell into that fault. **1659** D. PELL *Impr. Sea* 475 God..likes not such a *judgement-out-braving temper. **1830** SCOTT *Doom Devorgoil* II. ii, That sounded like the *judgment-peal. **1592** SHAKS. *Rom. & Jul.* I. i. 109 To old Free-towne, our common *iudgement place. **1947** W. E. DEMING in *Jrnl. Marketing* Oct. 145/1 **Judgment-samples*, wherein the biases and sampling errors cannot be calculated from the sample, but instead must be settled by judgment. **1888** *Pall Mall G.* 1 Sept. 11/2 A man marries on credit, and repents on *judgment summonses. **1561** T. NORTON *Calvin's Inst.* I. 33 Why should Paul feare to set Christ in the *iudgement throne of God? **1776** TOPLADY *Hymn, Rock of Ages* iv, When I..See Thee on Thy judgment-throne. **1822** SCOTT *Pirate* vi, It's no that I wad shut the door against decent folk, more especially in such *judgment-weather.

Hence **'judgemented** *a.* [see -ED²], having judgement or discernment (of a specified kind). (In comb. or with preceding adv.)

1548 GESTE *Pr. Masse* in H. G. Dugdale *Life* App. i. (1840) 95 Wel learned and godly judgemented. **1654** FULLER *Two Serm.* 68 To make them Charitably judgemented of the finall Estate of all such Infants. **1821** *New Monthly Mag.* II. 322 Boys..supreme-judgmented in taws, blood-alleys, and peg-tops.

judgemental, judgmental (dʒʌdʒ'mɛntəl), *a.* [f. JUDGEMENT, JUDGMENT + -AL.] Involving the exercise of judgement; inclined to make moral judgements.

1909 W. M. URBAN *Valuation* ii. 40 Whether exclusively judgmental or not is a question to be determined. **1952** S. KAUFFMANN *Philanderer* (1953) ix. 154 'Russell,' she said with a queer grin that was friendly and yet vaguely judgemental, 'you puzzle me.' **1964** *Philos. Rev.* LXXIII. 373 There is also..a 'judgmental' constituent of perceptual experience. **1965** HALL & HOWES *Church in Social Work* xv. 246 A criticism sometimes made of moral welfare workers.. is that they are 'judgmental' in the approach to clients. **1969** *Sci. Jrnl.* Feb. 64/1 Jenny was described rather well and the more quantitative structure analysis (versus content analysis by judgmental methods) yielded greater amounts of information about this woman. **1972** *Jrnl. Social Psychol.* LXXXVI. 13 Conforming behavior was produced..with the use of a two-choice judgmental task. **1973** *Times* 16 July 13/4 As one who is entirely unconvinced about the usefulness of boycotts—of any kind—and a little suspicious of judgmental attitudes to South Africa [etc.].

So **judg(e)'mentally** *adv.*

1971 J. B. CARROLL et al. *Word Frequency Bk.* p. xli, If the citations..are gathered in a number of separate judgmentally biased ways, the significance of each..must be assessed individually.

'judgement-day. [= *day of judgement*: see prec. 2. Cf. DOOMSDAY.] The day of God's final judgement; the last day; doomsday.

1591 SHAKS. *1 Hen. VI*, I. i. 29 Vnto the French, the dreadfull Iudgement-Day So dreadfull will not be, as was his sight. **1642** MILTON *Apol. Smect.* ad fin., Between this and the judgment day do not look for any arch deceivers. **1808** SCOTT *Marm.* VI. xi, From the tombs and around Rising at judgment-day. **1878** *N. Amer. Rev.* CXXVII. 87 The divine existence and a judgement-day.

'judgement-hall. A hall or public building in which judgements or trials at law are held; a court of justice; a tribunal. (Chiefly *Hist.*)

1534 TINDALE *John* xviii. 33 Then Pylate entred into the iudgement hall [**1526** iudgement housse; WYCLIF, mote hall; *Rhem.* palace] agayne, and called Iesus. **1600** J. PORY tr. *Leo's Africa* II. 53 They have a kinde of tribunall or iudgement-hall, wherein all contentions..are presently decided. **1872** J. H. INGRAHAM *Pillar of Fire* 232 A scene depicted in the judgment-hall of Osiris.

'judgement-seat. The seat on which a judge sits when trying a cause or pronouncing judgement; a seat of judgement; a tribunal.

1526 TINDALE *Rom.* xiv. 10 We shall all be brought before the iudgement seate [WYCLIF, trone] of Christ. **1596** DALRYMPLE tr. *Leslie's Hist. Scot.* I. 53 Forfare..quhair is ane Jugement sait and Justice courte haldne. **1604** DRAYTON *Owl* 341 Th' ambitious judgment seat I never sought, Where God is sold for coin, the poor for nought. **1819** SHELLEY *Cenci* III. ii. 24 The soul..which now stands Naked before Heaven's judgment seat. **1871** FREEMAN *Norm. Conq.* IV. xviii. 105 He was driven from the judgement-seat with scorn.

judger ('dʒʌdʒə(r)). [f. JUDGE *v.* + -ER¹. Cf. AF. *juggeour.*] One who or that which judges (in various senses), a judge; usually, one who forms, or who is (well or ill) qualified to form, an opinion.

c **1449** PECOCK *Repr.* 414 Such a iuger schulde iuge ouer presumptuoseli. **1556** J. HEYWOOD *Spider & F.* xcii. 51 Wrong iudgers, wrong iudgements. **1630** LENNARD tr. *Charron's Wisd.* (1658) 15 The eares..the Receivers and Judgers of sounds. **1859** TENNYSON *Enid* 1282 That..which a wanton fool, Or hasty judger would have called her guilt.

judgeship ('dʒʌdʒʃɪp). [f. JUDGE *sb.* + -SHIP.] The office or function of a judge.

a **1677** BARROW *Pope's Suprem.* (R.), Concerning the Pope, his universal pastourship, judgship in controversies, power to call councils. **1679** PENN *Addr. to Prot.* 180 The Umpiridge and Judgship of their Meaning. **1836–9** DICKENS *Sk. Boz, Steam Excurs.*, In the event of his not being previously appointed to a judgeship, it is probable that he will practise as a barrister. **1891** *Law Times* XC. 419/2 To fill up two High Court judgeships, a County Court judgeship..and a registrarship in bankruptcy. **1898** *Expositor* Nov. 356 The period of Samuel's judgeship.

b. *humorously* with *poss. adj.* as title for a judge.

1820 *Examiner* No. 640. 463/1 So peremptory is your Judgeship against an unfortunate Radical Reformer! **1821** *Ibid.* 467/1 His Judgeship must be in a very comfortable state of ignorance.

judgess ('dʒʌdʒɪs). Now *rare.* [f. as prec. + -ESS.] A female judge; a woman who judges.

1535 COVERDALE *Judg.* iv. 4 At ye same tyme was Iudgesse in Israel the prophetisse Debbora, the wyfe of Lapidoth. **1632** HEYWOOD *1st Part Iron Age* I. Wks. 1874 III. 279, I make you Iudgesse..You needes must say I am the properer man. **1776** J. ADAMS in *Fam. Lett.* (1876) 172 You are now ..elected into an important office, that of judgess of the Tory ladies. **1889** E. EDWARDES *Sardinia* 304 Eleonora, the judgess.

judging ('dʒʌdʒɪŋ), *vbl. sb.* [f. JUDGE *v.* + -ING¹.] The action of JUDGE *vb.*; judgement.

1303 R. BRUNNE *Handl. Synne* 5403 To consente to a fals juggyng. **1495** CAXTON *Eneydos* xxvii. 104 Her lyght empesched from the veraye Iugyng in parfyt knowlege. **1500–20** DUNBAR *Poems* ix. 131, I me confess..Of parciall jugeing and pervess wilfulness. **1631** SANDERSON *Serm.* (1681) II. 8 In all our private judgings of other mens speeches and actions. **1845** MRS. S. C. HALL *Whiteboy* viii. 63 It involved them in entanglements of false reasonings, false judgings, and crimes.

b. *attrib.*, as ***judging chair, court, place***; **judging-day** = judicial day: see JUDICIAL *a.* 4 c.

1541 BECON *News Heaven* Wks. (1564) I. 12 Al shall be present before the iudging-place of Christ. *c* **1550** LLOYD *Treas. Health* (1585) C ij, An apostem which doth not breake at the fyrst iudginge daye in a Feuer. **1603** B. JONSON *K. James' Entertainm.* Wks. (Rtldg.) 534/2 This place [Westminster]..the cabinet To all thy counsels, and the judging chair To this thy special kingdom. **1633** P. FLETCHER *Purple Isl.* v. li, Where twixt two little hils he keeps his judging court. **1896** *Daily News* 13 Feb. 2/5 (*Dog Show*) There were sixteen judging rings simultaneously in action.

'judging, *ppl. a.* [f. as prec. + -ING².] That judges; having the function of judging, judicial; *spec.* Having good judgement, able to judge, judicious, discerning; also, Censorious.

1581 SIDNEY *Apol. Poetrie* (Arb.) 33 The imaginatiue and iudging powre. **1647** CLARENDON *Hist. Reb.* III. §225 In so Grave and Judging an Assembly. **1735** POPE *Prol. Sat.* 246 Dryden alone escap'd this judging eye. **1856** MISS WINKWORTH *Tauler* Serm. xi. (1857) 267 Full of judging thoughts of other men who do not observe or approve of their ways.

Hence **'judgingly** *adv.*, with judgement, judiciously, discerningly; censoriously.

1659 MILTON *Civ. Power* Wks. (1851) 309 This work neither has own ministers nor any els can discerningly anough or judgingly perform. **1847–85** *D. P. Page's The. & Pract. Teach.* (ed. Payne) 261 One should never judgingly declare..'You are a liar'.

judgmatic (dʒʌdʒ'mætɪk), *a. colloq.* [irreg. f. JUDGE *sb.* or *v.* + *-matic*, in imitation or parody of *dogmatic*, *pragmatic*, etc.] = next.

1835 *Tait's Mag.* II. 575 Sufficiently enlightened, so as to make a judgmatic choice. **1898** R. KIPLING in *Morn. Post* 10 Nov. 5/3 A man of twenty-five years' sea-experience—cool, temperate, and judgmatic, such an one as the ordinary Warrant Officer.

judgmatical (dʒʌdʒ'mætɪkəl), *a. colloq.* [f. as prec. + -AL¹.] Characterized by good practical judgement; judicious, discerning; judicial.

1826 J. F. COOPER *Mohicans* xxv, A judgmatical rap on the head stiffened the lying impostor for a time. **1834** W. MAGINN *Bob Burke's Duel* in *Blackw. Mag.* XXXV. 751 What we call in Ireland a *judgmatical* sort of man—a word which, I think, might be introduced with advantage into the English vocabulary. **1888** *Spectator* 13 Oct. 1411/1 The tone is moderate and judgmatical throughout.

Hence **judg'matically** *adv.*, in the manner, or with the air, of a judge.

1814 COL. HAWKER *Diary* (1893) I. 113 Ably described and judgmatically criticised in almost every newspaper. **1855** LD. HOUGHTON in W. Reid *Life* (1891) I. xi. 525 Gladstone shakes his head most judgmatically over the notion.

judgment, variant of JUDGEMENT.

judicable ('dʒu:dɪkəb(ə)l), *a.* Now *rare.* [ad. late L. *jūdicābil-is*, f. *jūdicāre* to judge: see -ABLE.] Capable of being judged; liable to judgement.

1647 JER. TAYLOR *Lib. Proph.* ii. 32 They were Hereticks both in matter and form and judicable in both tribunals. **1688** H. CARE *King's Right Indulgence* 39 No Opinion is Judicable, nor no Person Punishable but for a sin.

†**judicant.** *Obs.* [ad. L. *jūdicānt-em*, pr. pple. of *jūdicāre* to judge: see -ANT.] One who judges, or passes sentence.

1570 FOXE *A. & M.* I. 225/2 That no bishop nor abbot, nor any of yᵉ clergy should be at the iudgement of any mans death or dismembring, neyther shoulde be any fautor of the sayd iudicantes [**1596** -ants].

†**judicate,** *v. Obs. rare.* [f. L. *jūdicāt-*, ppl. stem of *jūdicāre* to judge.] *trans.* To judge, decide.

1638 T. WHITAKER *Blood of Grape* 5 But the degree whether more or less intense is judicated by nature.

†**judicate**, *sb. Obs. rare.* [? ad. med.L. *jūdicātus* district under a judge, jurisdiction, f. L. *jūdex*, *jūdic-em* judge: see -ATE².] ? Jurisdiction. In quot. *attrib.*

1526 in Dillon *Customs Pale* (1892) 85 All the kings iudicate officers of the towne and marches of Callis.

judi'cation. [ad. L. *jūdicātiōn-em*, n. of action from *jūdicāre* to judge.] The action of judging, judgement (in various senses).

1625 HART *Anat. Ur.* I. i. 9 Yet may many other circumstances crosse this iudication in any indiuiduall person. **1655** STANLEY *Hist. Philos.* (1701) 22/1 There is no certain note of Judication and Assent. **1825** BENTHAM *Wks.* (1843) V. 382/1 That all-pervading and all-ruling principle, the self-judication principle.

judicative ('dʒuːdɪkətɪv), *a.* [f. L. *jūdicāt-*, ppl. stem of *jūdicāre* to judge + -IVE: see -ATIVE.] Having the function of judging.

1. Having the function of trying causes or passing sentences; judicial, juridical.

1641 LD. BROOKE *Eng. Episc.* I. vi. 31 It hath a power Judicative, (or if you will Juridicall,) but not Legislative. **1752** HUME *Ess. & Treat., Perf. Commw.* (1817) I. 499 The senate possesses all the judicative authority of the House of Lords. **1818** JAS. MILL *Brit. India* IV. v. II. 200 They were thus exclusively vested with the judicative power.

2. Having the function of forming opinions.

1647 FARINGDON *Serm.* 120 It arises from some defect in the judicative faculty. **1678** *Lively Orac.* III. §16 They.. make solemn appeals to their judicative faculties.

judicator ('dʒuːdɪkeɪtə(r)). [a. late L. *jūdicātor*, agent-n. from *jūdicāre* to judge.] One who judges, or acts as a judge.

1759 ROBERTSON *Hist. Scot.* VI. Wks. 1813 I. 463 In this perilous position stood the Church, the authority of its judicators called in question. **1786** *State Papers* in *Ann. Reg.* 262/1 Until their legality shall have been decided..by the judicators of the place into which the prize shall have been conducted. *c* **1831** CHALMERS in Jean Watson *Life And. Thomson* iv. (1882) 51 The very presence of such would have resistless effect on the divisions of our judicators.

judicatorial (ˌdʒuːdɪkə'tɔərɪəl), *a.* [f. late L. *jūdicātōri-us* JUDICATORY + -AL¹.] Of or pertaining to a judicator or judge; judicial.

1818 JAS. MILL *Brit. India* III. ii. 80 That very assembly ..which had already decreed, in its legislative capacity, that such evidence was useful, now, in its judicatorial capacity, decreed that it was the reverse.

judicatory ('dʒuːdɪkətərɪ, -'dɪkətərɪ), *sb.* [ad. late L. *jūdicātōri-um*, neuter of *jūdicātōri-us* adj.: see next.]

1. A court of judicature; a body having judicial authority; a tribunal. Now chiefly *Sc.*

1606-7 *Act of Counsell of Scot.* 4 Feb., The Writers and Clerkes of all Iudicatories within this Realme. **1676** OWEN *Worship of God* 83 From the highest Court of their Sanhedrim, to the meanest Judicatory in their Synagogues. **1707** ATTERBURY *Serm.* (1723) II. 172 Human Judicatories ..give sentence only on matters of right and wrong. **1765** *Act 5 Geo. III*, c. 49 §4 A protest..shall be registerable in the Courts of Session or other competent judicatories. **1801** A. HAMILTON *Wks.* (1886) VII. 226 The treaties of the United States had been infracted by State laws, put in execution by State judicatories. **1850** HT. MARTINEAU *Hist. Peace* II. v. vii. 318 The Scotch Church..whose four judicatories..were still all elective.

b. *transf.* and *fig.*

1656 STANLEY *Hist. Philos.* IV. (1701) 134/2 They assert that passions or affections are the Judges [κριτηρ ια]..To these assertions..concerning the Judicatories, agreeth what they assert concerning Ends. **1674** *Govt. Tongue* VI. §10 These are arraigned at every table, in every tavern; and at such variety of judicatories, there will be as great variety of sentences. **1850** MᶜCOSH *Div. Govt.* (1852) 290 It [conscience] is the highest judicatory in the human mind, judging all and being judged of none.

2. Judicature; a system of judicature.

c **1575** *Balfour's Practicks* (1754) 265 Anent the college of justice, institutioun and judicatorie thairof. **1647** CLARENDON *Hist. Reb.* VIII. §206 The Lords, as the Supreme Court of Judicatory. **1647** N. BACON *Disc. Govt. Eng.* I. xxxvii. (1739) 55 Evidence..in the Saxon Judicatory, sometimes consisted in the pregnant testimony of the fact itself. **1884** *Law Times* LXXVI. 342/1 The judicatories of Scotland and England were as independent of each other, within their respective territories, as if they were the judicatories of two foreign states.

†**3.** A judicatory or critical stage, a crisis. *Obs.*

1684 tr. *Bonet's Merc. Compit.* XIX. 810 Judicatories (or Crises) which do not terminate the disease, are signs of a predominant and perverse humour.

'**judicatory**, *a.* ? *Obs.* [ad. late L. *jūdicātōri-us* of or pertaining to judging, f. ppl. stem of L. *jūdicāre* to judge: see -ORY.]

1. Having the function of judging or passing sentence; of or pertaining to judgement.

1647 N. BACON *Disc. Govt. Eng.* I. xlix. (1739) 84 An influence upon that Judicatory power that must apply that Law. **1659** PEARSON *Creed* VII. 602 The Son of man is thus constantly represented as making..the last judicatory distinction between man and man. *a* **1718** PENN *Tracts* Wks. 1726 I. 679 A great Share in the judicatory Power. **1782** T. WARTON *Hist. Kiddington* 61 Druidical shrines, thrones of royal inauguration..and judicatory tribunals.

2. By which a judgement may be made; giving a decisive indication, critical.

1603 FLORIO *Montaigne* II. xii, To judge of the apparences ..we had need have a iudicatorie instrument. **1624** [see INDICATORY *a.* 1]. **1625** HART *Anat. Ur.* I. ii. 21 Amongst such signes some are called Decretorie, or Iudicatorie.

‖**judicatum** (dʒuːdɪ'keɪtəm, -ɑːtəm). *Philos. rare.* Pl. **-ata.** [L. *jūdicātum* judgement, pa.pple. of *jūdicāre* to judge.] (See quots.)

1913 *Mind* XXII. 15 As I use the term, the proposition is what the logicians call the import of the judgment or proposition. It is the *propositum* or *judicatum*. I do not use it as equivalent either to the act of judging or the verbal sentence. **1935** *Mind* XLIV. 365 A judgement *to the effect that* A is B seems to be just a judgement (act of judging) whose *object* or *judicatum* is that A is B. **1936** H. H. PRICE *Truth & Corrigibility* 17 The relation is between *judicata* or *judicabilia*, or—as some call them—'propositions'.

judicature ('dʒuːdɪkətjʊə(r), -eɪtjʊə(r)). Also 6 -oure. [f. med.L. *jūdicātūra*, f. ppl. stem *jūdicāt-*, of L. *jūdicāre* to judge: see -URE. Cf. F. *judicature* (1426 in Godef. *Compl.*).]

1. The action of judging; administration of justice by duly constituted courts; judicial process. Often in phr. ***court of judicature***.

Supreme Court of Judicature in England, that constituted by Acts of Parliament in 1873 and 1875, in which were united the former separate Courts of Chancery, King's Bench, Common Pleas, Exchequer, Admiralty, etc.

1530 PALSGR. 235/1 Judycature, *jugement; sentence.* *c* **1616** BACON *Adv. Dk. Buckhm.* ii. §4 Sir, the honour of Iudges in their Iudicature is the King's honour, whose person they represent. **1628** LE GRYS tr. *Barclay's Argenis* 259 Let those which hold places of Iudicature, have as many Colleagues appointed to them. **1651** HOBBES *Govt. & Soc.* xv. §17. 254 We have demonstratively shewed..that all Judicature belongs to the City, and that Judicature is nothing else but an Interpretation of the Laws. **1660** *Trial Regic.* 52 It hath not power of Judicature of Life, and Death. **1735** *Col. Rec. Pennsylv.* IV. 31 As well in the Court of Chancery as in the other Courts of Judicature. **1799** MACKINTOSH *Study Law Nature & Nations* Wks. 1846 I. 372 All the improvements of mankind in police, in judicature, and in legislation. **1819** J. MARSHALL *Const. Opin.* (1839) 189 The superior court of judicature of New Hampshire rendered a judgment upon this verdict. **1846** MᶜCULLOCH *Acc. Brit. Empire* (1854) II. 251 The system of judicature in Ireland rests on the same principles as that of England, whence it was introduced by King John. **1873** *Act 36 & 37 Vict.* c. 66 §3 The several Courts hereinafter mentioned..shall be consolidated together, and shall constitute one Supreme Court of Judicature in England.

2. The office, function, or authority of a judge; in quot. 1635–56, a judge's term of office.

1530 PALSGR. 34 A mynister of theyr common welth, outher as a capitayne, or in offyce of iudicatoure. **1621** LD. KEEPER WILLIAMS in *Fortescue Papers* (Camden) 166 Whose reversions (even of places under my judicature) I use to seale dayly. **1635-56** COWLEY *Davideis* IV. Note 13 Granted, that the 40 years assigned by S. Paul (Acts 13. 20) to Saul, are to include Samuels Judicature. **1706** PHILLIPS, *Judicature*, a Judge's Place, or Office. **1875** MAINE *Hist. Inst.* iv. 111 If the property be acquired by judicature or poetry, or any profession whatever.

b. (See quot.)

1847 CRAIG, *Judicature*..also, the extent of the jurisdiction of the judge, and of the court in which he sits to render justice. **1864** WEBSTER cites BOUVIER.

3. A body of judges or persons having judicial power; a court of justice; a legal tribunal, or such tribunals collectively.

1593 *Sc. Acts Jas. VI* (1597) §160 The saidis Assemblies and judicatoures [of the Kirk] sall direct their Bedle to the persone or personnes disobedient. **1651** EVELYN *Char. Eng.* in *Misc. Writ.* (1805) 167, I was curious before my return.. to visite their judicatures. **1677** *Lond. Gaz.* No. 1191/4 An Act for erecting a Judicature to determine differences touching Houses burnt and demolished by the late dreadful Fire. **1796** BP. WATSON *Apol. Bible* 257 If the witnesses of the resurrection had been examined before any judicature. **1863** H. COX *Instit.* II. ii. 299 The essential attribute of the judicature is the power of authoritatively interpreting the laws.

†**4.** *fig.* Mental judgement; formation or authoritative expression of opinion; criticism. *Obs.*

a **1631** DONNE in *Select.* (1840) 205, I proceed the right way in judicature, I judge according to my evidence. **1758** JOHNSON *Idler* No. 18 ⁋2 If he seats himself uncalled in the chair of judicature.

†**5.** The quality of being judicial (as opposed to moral): see JUDICIAL A. 1 b. *Obs. rare*⁻¹.

1643 MILTON *Divorce* II. xii, Our Saviour disputes not here the Judicature, for that was not his Office, but the morality of Divorce, whether it be Adultery or no.

6. *attrib.*

Judicature Acts, a name given to the statutes establishing the Supreme Court of Judicature, and regulating its practice. These include esp. Act 36 & 37 Vict. c. 66 (1873), 38 & 39 Vict. c. 77 (1875); see also 59 & 60 Vict. c. 14, Sch. 11 (Short Titles Act, 1896).

1873 *Sat. Rev.* 9 Aug. 163 The Queen confidently expects that we shall thank God..for the Budget, the Judicature Act, the Education and Endowed Schools Amendment Acts. **1880** *Manch. Guard.* 20 Dec., The Judicature Acts placed a great deal of power in the hands of the Judges. **1883** *Wharton's Law-Lex.* (ed. 7) 53/2 Court of Appeal..is constituted under the Judicature Act, 1873, the Appellate Jurisdiction Act, 1876, and the Judicature Act, 1881. *Ibid.* 801/2 The Supreme Court of Judicature Acts, 1873 and 1875..are commonly referred to as 'The Judicature Acts'.

judicial (dʒuː'dɪʃəl), *a.* and *sb.* [ad. L. *jūdiciāl-is*, f. *jūdici-um* judgement: see -AL¹. Cf. OF. *judicial* (in Gower), later *-iel.*] **A.** *adj.*

1. Of or belonging to judgement in a court of law, or to a judge in relation to this function; pertaining to the administration of justice; proper to a court of law or a legal tribunal; resulting from or fixed by a judgement in court. (Also *fig.* in reference to God, conscience, etc.)

judicial murder, murder (or what is asserted to be such) wrought by process of law; an unjust though legal death sentence.

1382 WYCLIF *Neh.* iii. 30 Unto the hous of sodeknys, and of the men sellende sheldis aȝen the judicial ȝate. *a* **1420** HOCCLEVE *De Reg. Princ.* 2683 He bad men fla hym quyk out of his skynne, And þer-with keuyr þe iudicial see. *c* **1530** L. COX *Rhet.* (1899) 71 Oracyons iudiciall be, that longe to controuersies in the lawe, and plees. **1580** HOLLYBAND *Treas. Fr. Tong*, *On se sied en iugement*, they sit at the Iudiciall seat. **1615** G. SANDYS *Trav.* 6 Where all causes are adjudged, both criminall and iudiciall. **1675** BAXTER *Cath. Theol.* II. 239 Most Protestant Divines..say that Justification is a Judicial Sentence of God as Judge. **1767** BLACKSTONE *Comm.* II. xxx. 461 A series of judicial decisions, which have now established the law in such a variety of cases. **1844** H. H. WILSON *Brit. India* III. 290 The association of the legislative and judicial power was open to obvious objection. **1858** LD. ST. LEONARDS *Handy-bk. Prop. Law* xii. 73 Judicial separation is a new term introduced for the old divorce *a mensâ et thoro.* **1861** J. PAGET *Puzzles & Par.* (1874) 147 The many judicial murders which disgraced that period of our history. **1881** GLADSTONE *Sp. in Ho. Comm.* 22 July, A judicial rent was a rent fixed according to the judgment of a judicial body, a dispassionate and impartial body between man and man.

b. Enforced by secular judges and tribunals: in ***judicial law***, opp. to ***moral*** and ***ceremonial***.

1551 T. WILSON *Logike* (1580) 15 b, The Morall Lawe standeth forever,..The Iudiciall lawe is next, the whiche.. we be not bound to observe as the Israelites were. **1650** HOBBES *De Corp. Pol.* 190 *Thou shalt not steal*, is simply a Law; but this, *He that stealeth an Ox, shall restore four-fold*, is a Penal, or as other call it, A Judicial Law. **1651** BAXTER *Inf. Bapt.* 102 A meer Judiciall Law proper to the Jewish Common-Wealth. **1819** R. HALL *Wks.* (1841) V. 327 The laws given to the Israelites were of three kinds—ceremonial, judicial, and moral.

c. *Theol.* Inflicted by God as a judgement or punishment; of the nature of a divine judgement.

1613 PURCHAS *Pilgrimage* (1614) 151 That first Anathema and iudiciall curse..denounced against the Samaritans for hindering the worke of the Temple. **1792** BURKE *Pres. St. Aff.* Wks. VII. 113 What is called a judicial blindness, the certain forerunner of the destruction of all crowns and Kingdoms. **1815** SOUTHEY in *Q. Rev.* XIII. 275 Almost it seems as if he, and the flagitious army by which he is supported,..were stricken with judicial blindness. **1849** MACAULAY *Hist. Eng.* viii. II. 277 An infatuation such as, in a more simple age, would have been called judicial.

d. ***judicial factor*** (*Sc. Law*): 'a factor or administrator appointed by the Court of Session on special application by petition, setting forth the circumstances which render the appointment necessary' (W. Bell *Dict. Law Scot.* 1861) see FACTOR *sb.* 5.

1849 *Act 12 & 13 Vict.* c. 51 §1 The Expression 'Judicial Factor'..shall mean Factor loco tutoris, Factor loco absentis, and Curator bonis. **1861** W. BELL *Dict. Law Scot.* 484/1 Before a judicial factor can obtain his discharge, the Court must be satisfied that he has faithfully performed his duty. **1894** *Daily News* 6 June 8/6 Charged.. with stealing 1,100*l.* from two estates on which he was judicial factor.

2. Having the function of judgement; invested with authority to judge causes.

1561 T. NORTON *Calvin's Inst.* III. xii. §1 We purpose not to speake of the righteousnesse of a worldly iudiciall courte, but of the heauenlye iudgement seat. **1601** SIR W. CORNWALLIS *Disc. Seneca* (1631) 4 Yet cannot these present their griefes to judiciall men. **1769** *Junius Lett.* xxii. 103 The returning officer is not a judicial, but a purely ministerial officer. **1863** H. COX *Instit.* I. iii. 15 Parliaments were originally judicial as well as legislative assemblies.

b. ***judicial combat*** (***duel***), one engaged in for formal decision of a controversy.

1820 SCOTT *Ivanhoe* xliv. **1828** —— *F.M. Perth* xxv, That the pretended judicial combat was a mockery of the divine will, and of human laws. **1834** L. RITCHIE *Wand. by Seine* 56 The practice of private duels grew naturally out of judicial combats. **1882** H. SPENCER *Princ. Sociol.* §522 Judicial duels ..continued in France down to the close of the 14th century.

c. ***Judicial Committee of the Privy Council***: one of the two Appellate Tribunals in Great Britain, established in 1832 for the disposal of appeals made to the King in Council.

These are chiefly appeals from the Colonial and Ecclesiastical Courts. Other appeals formerly made to the King in Council now come before the Court of Appeal as constituted by the Judicature Acts.

1841 *Penny Cycl.* XIX. 24 By 3 and 4 Wm. IV., c. 41, the jurisdiction of the privy council is further enlarged, and there is added to it a body entitled 'the judicial committee of the privy council'. **1863** H. COX *Instit.* I. vii. 485 Besides the House of Lords, there is another supreme tribunal of appeal —the Queen in Council, whose judicial functions are delegated to the Judicial Committee of the Privy Council. The jurisdiction of the Committee is exercised principally to review judgments of the Colonial, the Ecclesiastical, and the Admiralty Courts. **1872** J. IRVING *Ann. Time* 985/2 (23 Feb. 1871) The Judicial Committee of the Privy Council give judgment in the appeal of the Rev. Mr. Purchas, known as the 'Brighton Ritual Case'.

3. Of a judge; proper to a judge.

1800 *Asiat. Ann. Reg., Proc. E. Ind. Ho.* 58/2 [These men] somewhat similar to aldermen in London..did lately send a memorial desiring judicial salaries. *a* **1832** MACKINTOSH *Life More* Wks. 1846 I. 409 That concentration of authority in the hands of the superior courts at Westminster, which contributed indeed to the purity and dignity of the judicial character. **1856** FROUDE *Hist. Eng.* (1858) I. ii. 135 A political difficulty..was laid before the pope in his judicial

capacity, in the name of the nation. **1888** Bryce *Amer. Commw.* II. ii. xlii. 120 What is called, even in America where robes are not worn, the 'purity of the judicial ermine'.

4. Giving judgement or decision upon any matter; forming or expressing a judgement; disposed to pass judgement; relative to judgement; critical.

1589 Nashe *Pref. Greene's Menaphon* (Arb.) 8 More iudiciall in matters of conceit, than our quadrant crepundios, that spit *ergo* in the mouth of euerie one they meete. **1632** Deloney *Thomas of Reading* in Thoms *E.E. Prose Rom.* (1858) I. 135 It becommeth not me to controule your iudiciall thoughts. **1841–4** Emerson *Ess., Over-Soul* Wks. (Bohn) I. 119 The intercourse of society..is one wide, judicial investigation of character. **1846** Sumner *Pickering* in *Orat. & Sp.* (1850) II. 459 His mind was rather judicial than forensic in its cast. **1896** *N. & Q.* 8th Ser. IX. 160/2 The *Quarterly Review* has for many years been distinguished for its judicial fairness.

b. Pertaining to the judgement of the reputed influence of the heavenly bodies upon human affairs. ***judicial astrology***: see astrology 1 b.

c **1391** Chaucer *Astrol.* ii. §4 Theise ben obseruaunces of iudicial matiere & rytes of paiens, in which my spirit ne hath no feith, ne no knowyng of hir *horoscopum*. **1475** *Bk. Noblesse* (Roxb.) 60 The noble science of suche judicielle mater in causis naturelle concernyng the influence of the bodies of hevyn. **1560** [see astrology 1 b]. **1642** Fuller *Holy & Prof. St.* ii. vii. 74 As for judiciall Astrology (which hath the least judgement in it) this vagrant hath been whipt out of all learned corporations. **1728** Pemberton *Newton's Philos.* 7 Addicted to judicial astrology..and to such-like superstitions. **1827** Bentham *Ration. Evid.* Wks. 1843 VII. 210 Among alchymists and judicial astrologers there have been those who have been dupes to the impostures by which they profited.

†**c.** *Med.* That determines the issue, or belongs to the crisis, of a disease: = critical 4. (Sometimes with combination of prec. sense.) *Obs.*

1544 Phaer *Regim. Lyfe* (1553) Gj b, If the iaundis.. appeare in the vj day, beyng a day iudicial or cretike of the ague,..it is a very good sygne. **1651** Culpepper *Astrol. Judgem. Dis.* (1658) 32 The time or houses noted betwixt the Crisis, are called the judicial times, or such times wherein a man may judge what the disease is, or what it will be.

†**d.** *Rhet.* Critical. *Obs.*

1576 Fleming *Panopl. Epist.* Ep. A, Of Epistles, some be demonstrative, some suasorie, and other some iudiciall. **1586** A. Day *Eng. Secretary* i. (1625) 20, 4. speciall heads, that is to say; Demonstrative, Deliberative, Judicial, and Familiar Letters. **1620** T. Granger *Div. Logike* 3 Every proposite or matter conceived..is reduced to three heads, or kinds, Demonstrative, Deliberative, Judiciall.

†**5.** That has or shows sound judgement; judicious. *Obs.*

1581 Sidney *Apol. Poetrie* (Arb.) 33 The same man.. should..grow..to a iudicial comprehending of them. **1616** Bullokar, *Iudiciall*,..also wise; graue, of great iudgement. **1624** Capt. Smith *Virginia* v. 200 He shewed himselfe so iudiciall and industrious as gaue great satisfaction.

B. *sb.* [Elliptical uses of the adj.]

†**1.** A judicial law or ordinance: see A. 1 b. *Obs.*

c **1380** Wyclif *Wks.* (1880) 285 Sermonyalis of þe oolde lawe & summe iudycialis bynden nouȝt now. *c* **1449** Pecock *Repr.* 18–19 The posityf lawe of the ceremonyes iudicialis & sacramentalis. **1577** tr. *Bullinger's Decades* (1592) 404 The Iudicials teach the gouernment of an house or a common weale. **1652** Sparke *Prim. Devot.* (1663) 417 In all the judicials and ceremonials..there was ever somewhat moral wrapped up in them. **1721** *St. German's Doctor & Stud.* 344 By the law of God in the Old Testament, called the Judicials.

†**2.** Determination, decision, judgement. *Obs.*

1447 Bokenham *Seyntys* (Roxb.) 158 Aftyr the judycyal of very resoun To lovyn hys credytour most holdyn was he Wych of hys dette had most pardoun. **1589** Nashe *Anat. Absurd.* Epist. ¶iij, Whose effectuall iudiciall of your vertues made such deepe impression in my attentive imagination. **1631** T. Powell *Tom All Trades* 32 There is no true judiciall of the falling and rising of commodities.

†**b.** *Astrol.* A determination or conclusion as to a future event from the positions of the heavenly bodies; the system of such determinations. *Obs.*

1496 *Dives & Paup.* (W. de W.) i. xxxiv. 73 They that.. take hede to the Iudycyall of astronomye or to dyuynacyons. **1561** Eden *Arte Nauig.* Pref., The..phantasticall obseruations of the iudicials of astrologie. **1652** Gaule *Magastrom.* 23 Where is obliquity but in the judicials of astrologie?

†**c.** *Med.* Determination of the nature of a disease; diagnosis. *Obs.*

1512 *(title)* Iudycyall of Uryns. **1548** Udall *Erasm. Par. Luke* Pref. 10 The corporall physicians doo often tymes varie..in their iudicials of the diseases.

†**3.** A legal judgement. *Obs.*

1534 Barnes *Supplic. King* ii. Wks. (1572) 209 It is to your condemnation, and to your ignomynie, that you doe exercise iudicials among you. **1660** Burney *Κέρδ. δῶρον* 99 Our Saviours own argument concerning the Iudicials of an Infidel, He can but kill the body.

†**b.** An instrument of legal punishment. *Obs.*

c **1640** J. Smyth *Lives Berkeleys* (1883) I. 201 Stocks, cage, tumbrell, pillory, Cucking-stoole and other Juditialls and castigatories.

Hence **judici'ality, ju'dicialness**, the quality or character of being judicial; **judicialize** (dʒuːˈdɪʃəlaɪz) *v. trans.*, to treat judicially, arrive at a judgement or decision upon.

1727 Bailey vol. II., *Judicialness*, judicial Quality, State or Condition. **1867** *Pall Mall G.* 5 Jan. 1 His mind..has something different, in its kind of judiciality, from what is usually meant by impartial intellectual judgment. **1877** T. Sinclair *Mount* 6 Must one..judicialise the problem whether Shakespeare died from a debauch, before one can have soul-liftings with [him] on the divine spirit's wings.

judicially (dʒuːˈdɪʃəlɪ), *adv.* [f. prec. + -ly².] In a judicial manner.

1. In the way of legal judgement, or in the office or capacity of judge; in, by, or in relation to, the administration of justice; by legal process; by sentence of a court of justice.

1465 *Paston Lett.* II. 223 Judicialy syttyng the seyde M. R. **1542** Hen. VIII *Declar. Scots* B iv b, Regesters and Recordes iudicially and autentiquely made. **1617** Moryson *Itin.* ii. 16 Indited, though absent, and condemned judicially of Treason. **1783** *Ainsworth's Lat. Dict.* (Morell) iv. s.v. *Ulysses*, For which reason, the armour of Achilles was judicially given to him, rather than to Ajax. **1863** H. Cox *Instit.* iii. vii. 695 As late as 1735, Sir Robert Walpole sat judicially in the Exchequer. **1865** Lecky *Ration.* I. i. 132 The last who perished judicially in England.

b. *Theol.* In the way of a divine judgement or punishment.

1654 Fuller *Two Serm.* 66 God..may judicially harden those from whom his grace is withdrawne, for making no better use thereof. **1782** Cowper *Lett.* Wks. 1837 XV. 122 Though I love my country, I hate its follies and its sins, and had rather see it scourged in mercy, than judicially hardened by prosperity. **1835** J. H. Newman *Par. Serm.* (1836) II. x. 123 The multitude of sinners judicially blinded.

2. After the manner of a judge; with judicial knowledge and skill; critically.

1577–87 Holinshed *Chron.* III. 1402/2 A noble mind iudiciallie grounded vpon the truth of diuine philosophie. **1617** Moryson *Itin.* iii. 37, I would have a Traveller.. speake of those things, whereof he could discourse most eloquently and judicially. **1868** Freeman *Norm. Conq.* II. viii. 165 He judicially sums up what was good and what was evil in him.

†**b.** So as to determine something; determinatively. *Obs.*

1609 Douland *Ornith. Microl.* 51 Rests are placed in Songs..Essentially, when they betoken silence. Iudicially, when they betoken not silence but the perfect Moode: and then their place is before the signe of Time.

†**3.** With sound judgement, judiciously. *Obs.*

1600 E. Blount tr. *Conestaggio* 81 All agreed that the King..had not dealt therein iudicially, saying it was a meane to breed contention. **1653** Walton *Angler* iv. 108, I find Mr. Thomas Barker..deal so judicially and freely in a little book of his of Angling.

ju'diciarily, *adv. rare.* [f. next + -ly².] In a judiciary manner or sense; judicially.

1611 Cotgr., *Iudiciairement*, iudiciarily, iudicially. *c* **1619** R. Jones in *Phenix* (1708) II. 480 The words..may easily be taken judiciarily..or they may be taken popularly.

judiciary (dʒuːˈdɪʃ(ɪ)ərɪ), *a.* and *sb.* Now *rare.* [ad. L. *jūdiciāri-us*, f. *jūdici-um* judgement: see -ary, and cf. F. *judiciaire* (14–15th c. in Hatz.-Darm.).] = judicial. **A.** *adj.*

1. Of or belonging to legal or formal judgement, or to a judge in his capacity of giving such judgement; pertaining to judicature or to courts of law. = judicial A. 1.

1611 Cotgr., *Iudiciaire*,..iudiciarie, iudiciall, done in Court. **1612** T. Taylor *Comm. Titus* ii. 13 Although he shall exercise his iudiciarie power. **1670** Blount *Law Dict.* Ded., Persons, Dignified with the Judiciary Scarlet Robe. **1787** Jefferson *Writ.* (1894) IV. 475, I like the organization of the government into Legislative, Judiciary and Executive. **1876** Digby *Real Prop.* ii. 64 Laws..are made indirectly by the tribunals in deciding upon particular cases. .. [These] are sometimes called judge-made, or judiciary laws.

†**b.** = judicial A. 1 b. *Obs.*

1699 Burnet *39 Art.* vii. (1700) 101 The Judiciary Parts of the Law were those that related to them as they were a Society of Men.

†**c.** = judicial A. 1 c. *Obs.*

1656 R. Robinson *Christ all* 425 It is a judiciary hand of God upon the Papists. **1677** Gale *Crt. Gentiles* iii. 24 Judiciarie Hardnesse of heart and Blindnesse of Minde.

†**2.** Having the function of judging; deciding as a judge or arbiter: = judicial A. 2. *Obs.*

1690 Child *Disc. Trade* (1694) 146 So many of the said Judiciary Merchants as heard the said Cause and Causes, and signed the Judgments or final Decrees in them.

b. = judicial A. 2 b.

1768 Blackstone *Comm.* III. xxii. (1809) 337 The first written injunction of judiciary combats that we meet with, is in the laws of Gundebald, a.d. 501. **1826** Digby *Broadst. Hon.* (1829) I. *Godefridus* 273 The Clergy of Spain..instead of compurgatory oaths and judiciary combats, ordained the proofs by witnesses and regular examination.

†**3.** Forming a judgement or opinion, discerning: = judicial A. 4. *Obs.*

a **1631** Donne *2nd Serm. Gen.* i. 26, I have a power to judge, a judiciarie, a discretive power. **1656** Stanley *Hist. Philos.* v. (1701) 180/2 This Judgment may not unfitly be termed Judiciary.

†**b.** Of, or in reference to, astrology: = judicial A. 4 b. Also, Pertaining to the giving of judgements or decisions by any kind of divination, as 'physiognomy'. *Obs.*

1604 T. Wright *Passions* vi. 315 What vaine studies exercise..our iudiciarie Astronomers, by calculating nativitees telling events. **1640** Bp. Reynolds *Passions* ix. 78 All which..I include under the name of Iudiciarie Physiognomie. **1734** tr. *Rollin's Anc. Hist.* (1827) III. vii. vii. 327 The wild chimeras of judiciary astrology.

†**c.** *Rhet.* = judicial A. 4 d. *Obs.*

1776 G. Campbell *Philos. Rhet.* I. 17 Three sorts of orations, the deliberative, the judiciary and the demonstrative.

B. *sb.* [Cf. med.L. *jūdiciāria, jūdiciārius* sbs.]

†**1.** An art of divination: see A. 3 b. *Obs.*

1587 Golding *De Mornay* xxv. 382 What Art mooued Iacob to say it?.. If yee say Phiznomie or Iudiciarie, the good old man was blind. **1594** Carew *Huarte's Exam. Wits* (1616) 183 All the sciences belonging to the imagination..as the Mathematickes, Astrologie, Arithmeticke, Perspectiue, Iudiciarie, and the rest.

†**b.** A judicial astrologer. *Obs.*

1652 Gaule *Magastrom.* 136 May not the morose judiciaries be thus urged?

2. †**a.** A place or court of judicature. *rare.*

1681 W. Robertson *Phraseol. Gen.* (1693) 780 A Judiciary or place of Judgment.

b. = judicature 3.

1802 M. Cutler in *Life, Jrnls. & Corr.* (1888) II. 81 He at length pointed out..the impossibility of a government being supported without an independent judiciary. **1875** Gladstone *Glean.* VI. lxxxiii. 185 That strength depends on the magistracy, the police, the judiciary, the standing army. **1885** *Law Times* LXXIX. 83/1 Head of the Irish magistracy and chief of the judiciary.

judicious (dʒuːˈdɪʃəs), *a.* Also 7 *erron.* **-itious.** [ad. F. *judicieux*, *-euse* (Montaigne, 16th c.) = It. *giudizioso*, f. L. *jūdici-um* judgement: see -ous.]

1. Of persons (or their faculties, etc.): Having or exercising sound judgement; discreet, wise, sensible. **a.** in relation to intellectual matters: Forming correct opinions or notions; sound in discernment; wisely critical.

1598 Florio, *Giudicioso*, iudicious, learned, wise, discreet. **1602** Shaks. *Ham.* iii. ii. 29 Now this ouer-done.. though it make the vnskilfull laugh, cannot but make the Iudicious greeue. **1626** Jackson *Creed* viii. xxii. §2 It hath beene long agoe observed by the learned and judicious Hooker. **1669** Gale *Crt. Gentiles* i. Introd. 4 Thus also Judicious Chillingworth. **1685** Boyle *Enq. Notion Nat.* iv. 95 The famousest and judiciousest of the ancienter Rabbins. **1724** A. Collins *Gr. Chr. Relig.* 42 One of the most Judicious of Interpreters, the great Grotius. **1818** Hallam *Mid. Ages* ix. i. (1819) III. 305 There were men who made the age famous, grave lawyers, judicious historians, wise philosophers.

b. in relation to practical matters: Wise in adapting means to ends; capable and careful in action; prudent. (Now the more frequent use.)

1600 E. Blount tr. *Conestaggio* 82 Being accounted.. confident, iudicious, and diligent, although of no great experience. **1605** Shaks. *Macb.* iv. ii. 16. **1658** W. Sanderson *Graphice* 20 To give honour to this Art of Painting many worthy Gentlemen..are become Iuditious practitioners herein. *a* **1704** T. Brown *Praise Pov.* Wks. 1730 I. 92 A judicious pilot. **1819** Scott *Leg. Montrose* vi, No judicious commander allows either flags of truce or neutrals to remain in his camp longer than is prudent.

2. Of action, thought, etc.: Proceeding from or showing sound judgement; marked by discretion, wisdom, or good sense. **a.** in relation to intellectual matters.

1602 Marston *Antonio's Rev.* Prol., That..We might waigh massy in judicious scale. **1621** Burton *Anat. Mel.* i. ii. iii. xv. (1651) 137, I would that all..would read those judicious tracts of Dr. Henry Spelman. **1781** Cowper *Conversat.* 235 A tale should be judicious, clear, succinct. **1861** Geo. Eliot *Silas M.* xi, As she concluded this judicious remark, she turned to the Miss Gunns.

b. in relation to practical matters. (Now the more frequent use.)

1600 E. Blount tr. *Conestaggio* 201 This retraite..yet was ..iudicious, the place being strong by nature. **1695** Temple *Introd. Hist. Eng.* 279 To surmount all Dangers..by brave Actions and judicious Councils. **1781** Gibbon *Decl. & F.* (1869) I. xix. 530 A very judicious plan of operations was adopted. **1833** Ht. Martineau *Vanderput & S.* vi. 95 Selling again the judicious purchases they were enabled to make. **1853** Sir H. Douglas *Milit. Bridges* 143 A splendid and very instructive example of what may be effected by judicious combinations and arrangements.

†**3.** = judicial A. 1. *Obs.*

(But in the two Shaks. quots. the actual sense is doubtful. *Judicial* does not occur in Shaks.)

1605 Shaks. *Lear* iii. iv. 76 Iudicious punishment, 'twas this flesh begot Those Pelicane Daughters. **1607** —— *Cor.* v. vi. 128 His last offences to vs Shall haue Iudicious hearing. **1611** Coryat *Crudities* 279 Their courts of justice, their judicious proceedings. **1632** J. Hayward tr. *Biondi's Eromena* 178 To proceede against him by a judicious way.

ju'diciously, *adv.* [f. prec. + -ly².]

1. In a judicious manner; with sound or correct judgement; discreetly, wisely, prudently.

1601–2 Fulbecke *1st Pt. Parall.* Introd. 1 To excite.. some other..farre more fully, iudiciously, and learnedly to accomplish this busines. **1688** Boyle *Final Causes Nat. Things* iii. 91 Opium..is now imployed as a noble remedy, as indeed it is, if skilfully prepared and judiciously exhibited. **1756** Dr. Delany in *Life & Lett. Mrs. Delany* (1861) III. 388 She read and wrote two languages correctly and judiciously. **1839** James *Louis XIV*, II. 325 [There are] few examples of remote dependencies upon great empires being well or judiciously governed. **1879** Froude *Cæsar* vi. 56 Money judiciously distributed among the leading politicians had secured the Senate's connivance.

†**2.** By a legal or formal judgement; judicially.

a **1634** Coke & Davies *(title)* England's Independency upon the Papal Power, Historically and Judiciously stated. **1737** Whiston *Josephus, Antiq.* iii. xv. §2 God..had judiciously condemned them to that punishment.

†**b.** With the air of a judge 'laying down the law'; dogmatically. *Obs.*

1728 MORGAN *Algiers* Pref. 7 How many [Englishmen] have I met with..most judiciously terming the best of them [Moors and Arabs] 'savages'.

ju'diciousness. [f. as prec. + -NESS.] The quality of being judicious; soundness of judgement; discretion, wisdom, prudence, good sense.

1651 *Fuller's Abel Rediv.* (1867) II. 121 He had not met with the like before for..judiciousness. **1655** FULLER *Ch. Hist.* v. iv. §16 Such the soil of this Sir Thomas More, in which facetiousnesse and judiciousnesse were excellently tempered together. **1751-73** JORTIN *Eccl. Hist.* (R.), The examination..requires, in due proportion, judiciousness and precaution. **1886** *Law Times* LXXX. 191/2 L. J. Bowen points out, with judiciousness and precision, some of the chief results of the great changes initiated in 1873.

judo ('dʒuːdəʊ). Also formerly **jiudo, ju-do.** [Jap., f. *ju* gentleness, ad. Chinese *jou* soft, gentle + Jap. *dō*, ad. Chinese *tao* way.] A refined form of ju-jitsu introduced in 1882 by Dr. Jigoro Kano, using principles of movement and balance, and practised as a sport or form of physical exercise. Also *attrib.*

1889 *Trans. Asiatic Soc. Japan* XVI. 192 The art of Jiujutsu, from which the present Jiudo..has sprung up. *Ibid.* 204 In Judo, which is an investigation of the laws by which one may gain by yielding, *practice* is made subservient to the *theory*. **1892** *Trans. & Proc. Japan Soc.* I. 9 It is due to the study of *Jū-do* that the Japanese police..are so skilful in seizing malefactors. **1905** HANCOCK & HIGASHI *Compl. Kano Jiu-Jitsu* p. xi, *Jiudo* is the term selected by Professor Kano as describing his system more accurately than *jiu-jitsu* does. **1921** *Glasgow Herald* 1 Jan. 9/1 This 'Judo' is practised all over Japan. **1931** E. V. GATENBY in *Studies in Eng. Lit.* (Tokyo) XI. 515 There is at least one jûdô society in London. **1953** *Encounter* Oct. 24/1 She ties it in front like a judo jacket. **1958** *Radio Times* 7 Feb. 9/4 A judo club. **1971** R. BUSBY *Deadlock* xiii. 193 A pair of judo pyjamas. **1972** *Oxford Mail* 1 Aug. 10/4 Judo is a way of learning to control yourself and your opponent. *Ibid.*, The first judo club in England was founded in 1918 in London.

Hence **'judogi**, the costume worn for judo; **'judoka**, one who practises, or is expert in, judo.

1952 *Time* 22 Dec. 40/2 France, center of the European cult, now has 150,000 judo wrestlers (called judoka). **1954** E. DOMINY *Teach yourself Judo* 190 *Judogi*,..Judo costume. **1961** *New Statesman* 22 Sept. 402/2 The thrower's..right hand lifts the lapels of the Uke's judogi—his canvas wrestling-jacket. **1964** *Sunday Mail Mag.* (Brisbane) 1 Mar. 7 The only major expense in Judo is £3 for the uniform, which is known as a judogi. *Ibid.*, The examiners..award various gradings to the different judoka. **1974** *Times* 9 Jan. 14/5 With tough agility, however, the British *judoka* emerged from a tight corner.

judoist ('dʒuːdəʊɪst). [f. prec. + -IST.] An expert in judo; one who practises judo.

1950 *Chamber's Encycl.* XIV. 757/1 Whatever the attacker's movement the judoist yields to it in order to lure him into a weakened stance or position. **1966** *Times* 29 Nov. 4 Mr. Gleeson [is] one of the most experienced judoists in this country, and national coach to the British Judo Association. **1969** S. GREENLEE *Spook who sat by Door* iii. 26 Soo thinks him one of the finest natural judoists of his experience.

Judy ('dʒuːdɪ). [A familiar pet-form of the female name *Judith*.] Name of the wife of Punch in the puppet-show of 'Punch and Judy'; hence (*slang*) applied disparagingly or contemptuously, *esp.* to a woman of ridiculous appearance. Later used *colloq.* without the implication of disparagement, often simply to mean 'a girl, woman'.

1812 J. H. VAUX *Flash Dict.*, *Judy*, a blowen; but sometimes used when speaking familiarly of any woman. **1825** C. M. WESTMACOTT *Eng. Spy* II. 65 Old Punch with his Judy. **1885** RUNCIMAN *Skippers & Sh.* 3 You get caught speaking to any of them steerage judies. *a* **1901** Doesn't she look a Judy? **1929** *Papers Mich. Acad. Sci. Arts & Lett.* X. 303/1 *Judies*, girls. **1932** KIPLING *Limits & Renewals* 244 'We began to bustle our people over the bows before she went to pieces. You'll admit Paul was a help there, Red?' 'I dare say he herded the old judies well enough.' **1934** G. B. SHAW *Too True to be Good* III. 83 *The Sergeant*... [*He kisses her*] How does that feel, Judy? **1938** J. MASEFIELD *Dead Ned* 284 You'd ought to be careful with the judy. It's best to keep in her good books. **1944** *Penguin New Writing* XIX. 105 I'm off the beer, but I could use a judy for a battering-ram against any wall in creation. **1963** [see GEAR *sb.* 5 e]. **1966** F. SHAW et al. *Lern Yerself Scouse* 25 Me judy, me tart, me gerl. My lady-friend; my fiancée; my wife. **1973** *Guardian* 31 May 13/7 During a strike a man whose judy is working is obviously better off than the man with a wife and three kids about the house.

b. *Comb.*, as ***Judy-puppet***; **Judy-cow**, a local name for the lady-bird (cf. *lady-cow*).

1855 ROBINSON *Whitby Gloss.*, *Judy-cow*. **1897** *Q. Rev.* Oct. 331 They are simply Judy-puppets in the Policinello of conventionality.

Jue, obs. form of JEW.

juel, jueler, etc., obs. ff. JEWEL, -ER, etc.

†**'juelet.** *Obs. rare.* Pl. 4 **iueles.** [a. OF. *joelet, jouelet* (pl. *-ez, -etz, -es*), dim. of *joel* JEWEL.] A plaything, a toy.

1340 *Ayenb.* 77 Þe conioun his bayþ [i.e. buyeth them] uor rubys, uor safyrs, oþer uor emeroydes, þet byeþ as iueles to childeren. [*orig.* (Cotton Cleop. A v. lf. 63) ce sont come ioueles (*v.r.* in Godef., iuweletz) a enfans.]

†**'juffer.** *Obs.* [cf. Du. *juffer* maiden, young lady, miss; also, spar, beam, joint; worn-down form of *jufvrouw, jonkvrouw*; so Ger. *jungfer* (from *jungfrau*), also, in shipbuilding, *juffer*.] A piece of timber four or five inches square.

1677-83 MOXON *Mech. Exerc.* (1703) 162 *Juffers*, Stuff, about 4 or 5 inches square, and of several Lengths. Hence, **1688** in R. HOLME, **1823** in NICHOLSON *Pract. Builder.*

†**'juffle**, *v.* *Sc. Obs.* [Origin and meaning obscure; perh. related to SHUFFLE, but app. of earlier appearance.] *intr.* (?) To shuffle; to fumble ineptly, to bungle, to 'maffle'. Hence †**'juffling** *ppl. a.*; also †**'juffler.**

1500-20 DUNBAR *Poems* liii. 16 Ane hommilty jommeltye juffler, Lyk a stirk stackarand in the ry. **1535** LYNDESAY *Satyre, Interl. Auld Man* 218 Scho may call me ane iufflane iok. **15..** *Rowll's Cursing* (Bann. MS.) 251 Than Iuflar Tasy with his iaggis, And Belly Bassy with his baggis, At hellis ȝettis sall mak sic reirding.

jug (dʒʌg), *sb.*[1]

1. A pet name or familiar substitute for the feminine name Joan, or Joanna; applied as a common noun to a homely woman, maid-servant, sweetheart, or mistress; or as a term of disparagement. Now *rare.*

[Like *Suke, Suky* = *Susan* (*Sue*), *Jack, Jacky* = *John*, and other similar formations, this was prob. partly phonetic, partly a playful perversion. Forms app. related or parallel are the masculine *Jagge, Jegge* = *Jack*; *Juggin*, beside *Jankin, Jenkin, Junkin, Jackin*; *Juck* in *Juckson, Juxon*; all ultimately from *John*. (See E. W. B. Nicholson *Pedigree of Jack*, 1892.)]

1569 PRESTON *Cambyses* in Hazl. *Dodsley* IV. 183 *Ruff.* I will give thee sixpence to lie one night with thee. *Mer.* Gogs heart, slave, dost thou think I am a sixpenny jug? **1594** *Knack to know a knave* ibid. VI. 511 Then comes a soldier counterfeit, and with him was his jug. **1605** SHAKS. *Lear* I. iv. 245 *Foole*..Whoop Iugge I loue thee. **1611** COTGR., *Iannette*, Iug, Iinnie (a woman's name). *Ibid.*, *Iehannette*, Iug, or Iinnie. **1631** BRATHWAIT *Whimzies, Launderer* 59 She..will not wet her hand lest shee spoyle the graine of her skinne: Mistris Joan ha's quite forgot that shee was once jugge. **1632** ROWLEY *Woman never vexed* I. in Hazl. *Dodsley* XII. 115 *Clown* [to *Joan*] Bring him away, Jug. **1707** MRS. CENTLIVRE *Platon. Lady* 111, But hark ye, don't you marry that ill-manner'd Jug, the Relict of a cheating old rogue. **1830** MONK *Bentley* xv. 424 Joanna..was his favourite child:..having received from him the fondling appellation of Jug in her infancy, she continued to be called Jug Bentley, as long as she remained unmarried.

2. As the second element in local names of various small birds, as ***bank-jug***, the chiffchaff, also the willow warbler; ***hedge-jug***, the long-tailed titmouse. [But cf. JUG *sb.*[3]]

1881 *Leicestersh. Gloss.*, *Jugg*, and *Juggy*, a diminutive of Joan or Jane... It is now, I believe, exclusively applied to sundry small birds. **1885** SWAINSON *Prov. Names Birds* 26 Chiffchaff..Bank-bottle or -jug (Bedfordshire). From the shape and situation of its nest. *Ibid.* 32 British Long-tailed Titmouse... The penduline form of the nest, and the feathers which compose the lining, have obtained for the bird the names of Jack in a bottle..Hedge jug.

jug (dʒʌg), *sb.*[2] [Origin uncertain: possibly, as suggested by Wedgwood, a transferred use of JUG *sb.*[1], the feminine name, for which there are analogies. But no actual evidence connecting the words has yet been found. (Cf. Skeat *Etymol. Dict.* s.v.)]

1. a. A deep vessel, of varying shape and size, for holding liquids, usually with a cylindrical or swelling body, or one that tapers upward, having a handle on one side, and often a spout. Frequently with qualification denoting use or kind, as ***brown-, claret-, cream-, milk-, water-jug***, etc.

The name is applied locally with various extensions or restrictions to vessels, commonly of earthenware, also of glass or metal, sometimes even of wood or leather, occasionally, as in a *hot-water jug*, furnished with a lid; in U.S. having 'a narrow neck or orifice, usually stopped by a cork' (*Cent. Dict.*).

1538 ELYOT *Dict.*, *Cantharus*, a pot or a iugge. **1555** EDEN *Decades* 38 They haue sundry kyndes of water pottes, iugges, and drinckinge cuppes, made of earthe. **1596** SHAKS. *Tam. Shr.* Induct. ii. 90 You would presente her at the Leete, Because she brought stone-Iugs, and no seal'd quarts. **1678** MRS. BEHN *Sir P. Fancy* v. i, You're a Dutch Butter-ferkin, a Kilderkin, a double Jugg. **1756** NUGENT *Gr. Tour, Germany* II. 403 There is a great sale of stone juggs and pitchers at Andernach. **1783** O'KEEFE *Poor Soldier*, Song '*The Brown Jug*' i, This brown jug that now foams with mild ale..Was once Toby Filpot. **1824** SCOTT *Redgauntlet* Let. iv, A small jug, which he replenished with ale from a large black-jack. **1828** P. CUNNINGHAM *N.S. Wales* (ed. 3) II. 107 Common brown Toby Philpot jugs. **1885** J. MARTINEAU *Types Eth. The.* I. 131 A jug is said to be empty when it has no water. **1886** *S.W. Linc. Gloss.*, *Jug*, a stone bottle, such as is used for wine or spirits, not such as a Milk-Jug, which is called a Pitcher. *Ibid.*, *Pitcher*,..the term Jug is applied to large stoneware jars.

b. A jug with its contents; the liquid in a jug; *esp.* beer, as distinguished from the contents of a bottle, i.e. wine. Also, locally, A measure of capacity for ale or beer, usually about a pint.

1635 D. DICKSON *Pract. Wks.* (1845) I. 92 Carry out the refuse and jugs of the house. *a* **1716** SOUTH *Serm.* I. iv. (R.), The sordid temptations of the jug and the bottle. **1765** COWPER *Let. to Lady Hesketh* 14 Sept., He gave me..a black jug of ale of his own brewing. **1848** DICKENS *Dombey* v, He came up with a jug of warm water.

c. A jug used as an instrument in a jazz band. So ***jug-blower***, etc. See *jug band* (sense 3 below).

1946 R. BLESH *Shining Trumpets* (1949) v. 104 Exotic instruments may be utilized as well, such as harmonica, kazoo, jug, washboard, wood blocks and musical saw. **1956** M. STEARNS *Story of Jazz* (1957) xiv. 157 He didn't even get a chance to team up with washboard beaters, jug blowers, kazoo players, tub thumpers, or alley fiddlers. **1960** *20th Cent.* Dec. 556 The hillbilly form..is played on..the twelve-string guitar, the jug, the jew's harp. **1964** *Amer. Folk Music Occasional* I. 95 Horses of many different colors run loose in this album, the common denominator being the use by all of a jug, which (blown like a coke bottle) produces rich, booming sound, able to take the bass part. **1968** *Blues Unlimited* Nov. 8 In Memphis, we recorded Dewey Corley, who used to blow jug with the Memphis Jug Band.

2. *slang* **a.** A prison, jail; more fully STONE-JUG. orig. *U.S.*

1815-16 *Niles' Reg.* IX. Suppl. 190/1 A full grown villain, who with an accomplice, were shortly after safely lodged in the jug. **1834** H. AINSWORTH *Rookwood* III. v, In a box of the stone-jug I was born. *Ibid.*, Thus was I bowl'd out at last, And into the jug for a lag was cast. **1861** LOWELL *Biglow P.* II. i. Poems 1890 II. 229 They sentenced me..to ten years in the Jug. **1890** BOLDREWOOD *Robbery under Arms* 144 Men just out of the jug..with their close-shaved faces, cropped heads, and prison-clothes. **1899** BESANT *Orange Girl* Prol., That hospitable place..the Black Jug—where before long you will pass a few pleasant days.

b. A bank.

1845 *National Police Gaz.* 15 Nov. 97/3 Jim Morgan..disdained no branch of business, from 'craking a jug' (entering a bank) to picking a pocket. **1862** *Cornh. Mag.* Nov. 648 It is all in single pennifs on the England jug... It is in 5*l* notes on the Bank of England. **1904** [see BOX *sb.*[2] 3 i]. **1935** G. INGRAM *Cockney Cavalcade* viii. 121 Give me time to go to the 'jug'. **1960** *Observer* 24 Jan. 5/1 If a villain had seriously suggested screwing a jug (breaking into a bank).

3. *Comb.*, as ***jug-metal, -pot; jug-broke*** adj.; **jug and bottle**, used *attrib.* of the bar of a public house at which alcoholic liquors are sold for consumption off the premises; **jug band**, a jazz band in which jugs (sense 1 c above) are used; **jug-bitten** *a.* (*slang*), intoxicated; **jug-fishing** *U.S.*, a mode of fishing with the line and bait tied to a floating 'jug' or bottle (*Cent. Dict.*); **jug handle**, the handle of a jug; also *attrib.* and *fig.*, shaped like a jug handle; hence **jug-handled** *a.*, (*a*) *lit.* placed on one side, as the handle of a jug; (*b*) *fig.* (*U.S.*) unilateral, one-sided, unbalanced.

1894 G. MOORE *Esther Waters* xxx. 236 The public entrance and the *jug and bottle entrance were in a side street. *Ibid.* xlii. 327 Journeyman was surprised to see Ketley sitting quite composedly in the jug and bottle bar. **1909** *Daily Chron.* 31 Mar. 1/3 A 'jug and bottle' department ..does not come within the definition of an open bar. **1932** L. GOLDING *Magnolia St.* I. ix. 144 She got her pint from the Jug and Bottle Department. **1953** *Word for Word: Encycl. Beer* (Whitbread & Co.) 11/2 *Jug-and-bottle bar*, specially reserved for the purchase of drinks for consumption off the premises; only to be found in older pubs. **1946** R. BLESH *Shining Trumpets* (1949) xi. 253 The southern '*jug' band typical of Tennessee and Mississippi. **1970** P. OLIVER *Savannah Syncopators* The recordings of some of the jug bands. **1970** *Western Folklore* XXIX. 229 The..'gutbucket' ..is generally played in ensembles such as jug and skiffle bands. **1630** J. TAYLOR (Water P.) *Wks.* (N.), When any of them are wounded, pot-shot, *jug-bitten, or cup-shaken, so that they have lost all reasonable faculties of the minde. *a* **1658** CLEVELAND *Poems, Against Ale* ii, The *Jug-broke Pate doth owe to thee Its bloody Line and Pedigree. **1846** S. F. SMITH *Theatr. Apprenticeship* 118 Not perceiving the entire justice of this arrangement, it being somewhat on the *jug-handle principle, all on one side. **1900** E. GLYN *Visits of Elizabeth* 245 She has a jug-handle chignon. **1955** M. E. B. BANKS *Commando Climber* iii. 38 A final wall, almost vertical but amply provided with the largest of jug-handles, remained. **1961** L. MUMFORD *City in Hist.* xvi. 506 To ensure the continuous flow of traffic,..immense clover leaves and jug handles are designed. **1967** R. J. SERLING *President's Plane is Missing* (1968) ii. 27 He was one of those homely men whose virile masculinity masked such features as a big nose and jug-handle ears. **1970** A. BLACKSHAW *Mountaineering* (rev. ed.) vi. 163 A large incut hold (a 'jug-handle') in good rock is the most secure of all holds. **1881** *Congress. Rec.* 8 Dec. 60/2 English reciprocity in pleasure travel,..like their often proposed commercial reciprocity, is comparatively *jug-handled. **1904** *Boston Herald* 28 Sept. 6 The trade between Canada and the United States is..jug-handled. **1641** FRENCH *Distill.* i. (1651) 4 They may be of Copper..or of *Jug-metall, or Potters-metall glazed. **1654** GAYTON *Pleas. Notes* IV. xxii. 276 It may as well be denyed, that Duke D'Alva's face is not to be seen on *Jugge-pots in Holland.

jug (dʒʌg), *sb.*[3] Also **joug.** An imitative representation of one of the notes of the nightingale, and some other birds, usually repeated as ***jug, jug***; hence, used as a name for this note.

1523 SKELTON *Garl. Laurel* Wks. 1843 I. 401 To here this nightingale,..Warbelynge in the vale, Dug, dug, Iug, iug, ..With chuk, chuk, chuk, chuk! **1576** GASCOIGNE *Philomene* (Arb.) 113 The next note to hir phy Is Iug, Iug, Iug, I gesse. **1773** BARRINGTON in *Phil. Trans.* LXIII. 261 Nothing, however, can be more marked than the note of a nightingale called its *jug*. **1864-5** WOOD *Homes without H.* xxxi. (1868) 624 The 'jug-jug' of one Nightingale is sure to set singing all others within hearing.

jug, *sb.*[4] *rare*⁻¹. Also jugg. [f. JUG *v.*[3]] The sleeping place of partridges, where they 'jug' or nestle together.

1834 MUDIE *Brit. Birds* (1841) I. 43 The night worms and other small animals..have mostly retired into the earth before the partridges leave their 'jugg' or sleeping place.

jug (dʒʌg), *sb.*[5] Slang abbrev. of JUGGINS.

1914 D. H. LAWRENCE *Let.* 18 Dec. (1962) I. 299 But he is a jug... Don't bother anymore. **1956** H. GOLD *Man who was not with It* (1965) xi. 96 It was nice to find the born jug of the continent and to decide even about him: he knows what he wants.

Jug (dʒu:g, ju:g), *a.* and *sb.*[6] Abbrev. of *Jugoslav(ian*: see YUGOSLAV, etc.

1949 V. GIELGUD *Fall of Sparrow* xvii. 168 I've been down among the Jugs during this last week or two. **1958** P. KEMP *No Colours or Crest* x. 218 If Cairo's relations with the Jug Partisans are really so important,..why the hell didn't they warn us off before? **1961** R. B. AMOS *Wasp in Web* vii. 74 A Jug friend of mine was standing next to me. **1967** L. FORRESTER *Girl called Fathom* iv. 33 Most..are based here all the time..the nursing sister, Radik the Jug.

jug (dʒʌg), *sb.*[7] *West Indies.* Also jug-jug. [Origin unkn.] A savoury Barbadian dish served esp. at Christmas (see quots.).

1945 E. P. CLARK *West Indian Cookery* xix. 80 *Jug Jug*... Clean, cut up, and season the beef and pork... Stew the pork.., then add beef and peas and stew..until peas are soft. **1957** F. A. COLLYMORE *Notes for Gloss. Barbadian Dial.* (ed. 2) 49 *Jug, jug-jug*, a famous Christmas dish. **1958** B. HAMILTON *Too Much of Water* iv. 74 A real Barbadian breakfast.., sweet potatoes, an' jug-jug, an' okras. **1970** M. SLATER *Caribbean Cooking* 142 'Jug' is a Bajan Christmas speciality, served with turkey. Jug-Jug came to Barbados.. via the Scottish 17th Century exiles, in an attempt to produce something resembling haggis. **1973** *Advocate-News* (Barbados) 25 Dec. 4/6 The specialities of the Yuletide dinner—the turkey, the ham, the plum pudding; the pudding and souse; the peas and rice; the jug-jug; and even caviar.

[**jug**, an error for ING, meadow, in 17-18th c. Dicts., Halliwell, etc.]

jug, *v.*[1] [f. JUG *sb.*[2]]

†**1.** *intr.* To use a jug; to drink. *Obs.*

1681 W. ROBERTSON *Phraseol. Gen.* (1693) 781 Be jugging or jogging: *Aut bibe, aut abi.*

2. *trans.* (*Cookery.*) To stew or boil in a jug or jar (esp. a hare or rabbit).

1747 [see JUGGED below]. **1769** MRS. RAFFALD *Eng. Housekpr.* (1778) 135 To jug a Hare. **1868** BROWNING *Ring & Bk.* VIII. 1386 Gigia can jug a rabbit well enough. **1898** J. ARCH *Story of Life* vii. 160 If I could catch that hare..I would carry him home and jug him.

3. *slang.* To shut up in jail; to imprison. (Cf. JUG *sb.*[2] 2.) Also *transf.* To confine.

1841 CATLIN *N. Amer. Ind.* (1844) II. xxxv. 36 The poor fellow was soon jugged up. **1877** LOWELL *Lett.* II. viii. 230, I have been there every day except when I was jugged with the gout. **1890** BOLDREWOOD *Robbery under Arms* 166 I'm not going to be jugged again, not if I know it.

4. *intr.* To fish with a bait attached to a floating jug (see *jug-fishing* s.v. JUG *sb.*[2] 3). *U.S.*

1872 *Kansas Mag.* Feb. 178 Jugging for catfish in the chutes of the Missouri and the Kaw. **1947** *Life* 15 Sept. 155 The boys go jugging for catfish. They tie their fishing lines to jugs and haul them in when the jug bobs in the water.

Hence **jugged** (dʒʌgd) *ppl. a.*, esp. in ***jugged hare***; **'jugging** *vbl. sb.*

1747 MRS. GLASSE *Cookery* 50 A jugged Hare. Cut it in little pieces,..put them into a earthen Jugg,..cover the Jugg or Jar you do it in, so close that nothing can get in, then set it in a Pot of boiling water. **1809** MALKIN *Gil Blas* x. iii. ⁋ 10 The second course consisted of pigs' ears, jugged game, and chocolate cream. *a* **1834** LAMB *Lett.* xviii. Th. Pres. Game 176 A hare to be truly palated must be roasted. Jugging sophisticates her. **1893** *Chicago Advance* 31 Aug., A little discreet gagging, followed by jugging if necessary.

jug, *v.*[2] Also joug. [Echoic: cf. JUG *sb.*[3]] *intr.* Of the nightingale or other bird: To utter a sound like 'jug'. Hence **'jugging** *ppl. a.*

1598 YONG *Diana* 427 Iugging nightingales are sweetely singing. **1657** THORNLEY tr. *Longus' Daphnis & Chloe* 124 The Nightingales began to jug and warble. **1783** *Ainsworth's Lat. Dict.* (Morell) v, *Gurio*,..to jug, or jouk, as a nightingale doth. **1898** *Daily News* 7 May 10/2 The blithe lark, the jugging nightingale.

jug, *v.*[3] Also 7 jugg. [app. an altered by-form of JOUK *v.*[1] (*juke, joke*, etc.) with specialized application; cf. also JUCK *v.*, used of the call of partridges when they *jouk* or *jug.*] *intr.* Of partridges, etc.: To crowd or nestle together on the ground; to collect in a covey. Also *transf.* Hence **'jugging** *vbl. sb.*

c **1600** DRAYTON *Miseries Q. Margaret* cxlvi, Like as you see when partridges are flown,..They in the evening get together all, With pretty jugging, and each other greet. **1654** VILVAIN *Theol. Treat.* iii. 106 Jugging together like Partridges in smal Covies. **1660** HEXHAM, *Roesten*, to Jugge, or goe to Roest, as Hens, Partridges. **1672** [see JOUK *v.*[1] 1]. *a* **1825** FORBY *Voc. E. Anglia, Jug*, to squat, and nestle close together, as partridges at night. **1878** *Daily News* 12 Sept. 3/1 At night partridges roost and nestle close together on the ground in a cluster... When..thus resting they are said to *jug*.

b. *trans.* To collect close together.

1653 GAUDEN *Hierasp.* 292 Some have taken [liberty] in these times, to separate themselves from the ordinary Ministry of this Church, and by a mutuall call of one an other to jugg themselves, like Partridges, into small coveys. **1674** N. FAIRFAX *Bulk & Selv.* To Rdr., Should they [kinreds of men] have liv'd and jugg'd together to this day.

†**jug**, *v.*[4] *Obs.* Also 4-5 iag(ge, iog(ge. A variant of JAG *v.*, to 'prick'; to spur (a horse).

(The language of the whole quotation is *fig., justed, jugged*, and *overtilte*, being taken from the tilt or tournament.)

1377 LANGL. *P. Pl.* B. xx. 133 He iugged [*v.r.* iogged, **1393** C. XXIII. 134 iogged, *v. rr.* iagged, iuggede] til a iustice, and iusted in his ere, And ouertilte al his treuthe.

jugal ('dʒu:gəl), *a.* (*sb.*) [ad. L. *jugāl-is*, f. *jugum* yoke: cf. F. *jugal* (16th c. in Littré).]

†**1.** Of or relating to a yoke, esp. the matrimonial yoke or bond; conjugal. *Obs.*

1617 MIDDLETON & ROWLEY *Fair Quarrel* II. ii, When heaven had witness to the jugal knot. **1624** HEYWOOD *Gunaik.* VIII. 385 O those soft fifteene yeeres so sweetly past Which thou Calenus with Sulpitia hast In jugal consocietie. **1656** BLOUNT *Glossogr.*, *Jugal*, that is yoaked, or pertaining to..Matrimony or Wedlock.

2. *Anat.* Of or pertaining to the zygoma or bony arch of the cheek; malar, zygomatic.

1598 FLORIO, *Giugale osso*, the iugall bone, which is a portion of the bones of the head and of the vpper iawe. **1668** CULPEPPER & COLE *Barthol. Anat.* III. xi. 153 Arises outwardly from the Jugal process, and descending obliquely through the Cheeks, it is terminated in the space between the two Lips. **1766** PARSONS in *Phil. Trans.* LVI. 207 A strong membrane..inserted all along the jugal bone on each side. **1864** HUXLEY in *Reader* 5 Mar., The jugal arch is much developed in proportion to the cranium.

B. *sb. Anat.* The jugal or malar bone.

1854 OWEN *Skel. & Teeth* in *Circ. Sc., Organ. Nat.* I. 219 The jugal and squamosal are also confluent. **1883** MARTIN & MOALE *Vertebr. Dissect.* 106 The jugal forms part of the middle of the suborbital bony bar.

jugate ('dʒu:gət), *a.* [ad. L. *jugāt-us*, pa. pple. of *jugāre* to join together: see -ATE[2].]

1. *Bot.* Of a pinnate leaf: Having leaflets in pairs; usually in combination (see BI-, MULTI-, TRI-, UNIJUGATE). Also of the leaflets: Paired.

[**1857** HENFREY *Elem. Bot.* 59 The pairs of leaflets are sometimes called juga, and if only one pair exists, the leaf is unijugate.., if more pairs, multijugate.] **1887** *Syd. Soc. Lex.*, *Jugate*, coupled together, as the pairs of leaflets in compound leaves.

2. *Numism.* Placed side by side: = ACCOLLED 3.

1887 B. V. HEAD *Hist. Numorum* 579 Jugate busts of Ptolemy IV. and Arsinoe (?). **1897** W. C. HAZLITT *Suppl. Coinage Continent* 7 The jugate busts of Maximilian I., Charles V., and Ferdinand.

'jugate, *v. rare*⁻⁰. [f. L. *jugāt-*, ppl. stem of *jugāre* to yoke together: see -ATE[3].] *trans.* To yoke or couple together. So **'jugated** *ppl. a.* yoked together; in *Bot.* = JUGATE *a.* 1.

1623 COCKERAM, *Iugate*, to binde, to yoake. **1721** BAILEY, *Jugate*, to yoak or couple together. **1727** BAILEY II, *Jugated*, yoked or coupled together. **1856** WEBSTER, *Jugated.*

‖**juge** (ʒyʒ). [Fr.] A judge. ***juge d'instruction***, an examining magistrate, a police magistrate.

1882 *Standard* 25 Dec. 3/2 After giving their names and addresses they were permitted to retire, but were informed that they would be called up for examination by a *juge d'instruction.* **1911** CHESTERTON *Innocence of Father Brown* i. 2 How he turned the *juge d'instruction* upside down and stood him on his head, 'to clear his mind'. **1964** *Ann. Reg. 1963* 51 One of Lord Shawcross's solutions was recourse to an examining magistrate, on the lines of a continental *juge d'instruction.* **1973** M. CATTO *Sam Casanova* ii. 22 You're going to have a *juge d'instruction* on your back.

juge, etc., obs. forms of JUDGE, etc.

jugelour, obs. form of JUGGLER.

‖**Jugendstil** ('ju:gənt-ʃtil). [G., f. *jugend* youth (the name of a German magazine started in 1896) + *stil* style.] The German equivalent of *art nouveau*. Also *attrib.* (occas. with lower-case initial).

1928 *Minutes of G. & C. Merriam Co. Editorial Board* III. 707 Note the expression *Jugend Stil*, meaning nouveau art. **1950** B. S. MYERS *Mod. Art in Making* 254 In the works of the *Jugendstil* painters in Germany.., those ideas found their expression. **1958** M. L. WOLF *Dict. Painting* 148 *Jugendstil*, in Germany, the name applied to the *art nouveau* movement, popular from 1890 to 1905, and affecting all of the visual arts. **1960** *Times* 4 May 16/6 The individual stature of the two leading figures of the *jugendstil* period represented in this exhibition. **1963** *Listener* 24 Jan. 160/2 The Jugendstil was much more exuberant, much more demonstratively independent of any past style, and much more violent. **1967** A. WILSON *No Laughing Matter* III. 369 'Not our happiest sort of architecture, I'm afraid.' 'No? I suppose it's the usual Jugendstil of its period.' **1972** *Guardian* 16 Mar. 14/4 In Cracow there's a political cabaret 80 years old, with hair-raising original *Jugendstil* décor. **1974** *Times Lit. Suppl.* 11 Oct. 1116/2 Sheer frustration may have thrown up a Jugendstil *Parsifal*.

juger ('dʒu:dʒə(r)). [ad. L. *juger-um.* (Formerly used in Lat. form, with pl. *jugera.*)] An ancient Roman measure of land, containing 28,800 (Roman) square feet, or 240 by 120 (Roman) feet, i.e. about three-fifths of an acre.

1398 TREVISA *Barth. De P.R.* XIX. cxxix. (1495) 937 Iugerum is two hundryd fote and fourty in length and syxe score fete in brede, and two Actus makyth Iugerum. **1579-80** NORTH *Plutarch* (1612) 594 (Stanf.), [20,000] Iugera of land. **1600** HOLLAND *Livy* (*Summ. Mar.* I. i.) 1348 A valley..in breadth foure jugera. **1853** MERIVALE *Rom. Rep.* i. (1867) 10 He allowed these claimants to retain in possession five hundred *jugers* each. **1881** BLACKIE *Lay Serm.* v. 169 Two jugers of land were allotted to each [Roman] citizen.

jugful ('dʒʌgfʊl). [f. JUG *sb.*[2] + -FUL.] As much as fills a jug. ***by a jugful*** (*U.S. slang*), by a great deal, 'by a long chalk'.

1831 *Boston Transcript* 14 Nov. 2/1 'Vote on your side!' says another: 'Not by a jug full.' **1834** DOWNING *Mayday in N.Y.* (Bartlett), Downingville is as sweet as a rose. But 'tain't so in New-York, not by a jug-full. **1840** HALIBURTON *Clockm.* Ser. III. xviii. (Farmer), The last mile..took the longest [time] to do it by a jugfull. **1865** DICKENS *Mut. Fr.* II. IV. vii. 217 Mr. Riderhood..fetched his jug-full of water. **1893** *Family Herald* 25 Mar. 335/2 She overturned a jugful [of milk] upon the large black pool [of ink]. **1967** WODEHOUSE *Company for Henry* xii. 220 Did your heart melt? Not by a jugful. You gave him the sleeve across the windpipe and kicked him out. **1971** —— *Much Obliged, Jeeves* vi. 57 'Then why is Tuppy short of cash? Didn't he inherit them?' 'Not by a jugful.'

jugge, obs. form of JUDGE, JUG.

juggeler, -ellur, etc., obs. forms of JUGGLER.

‖**jugger** ('dʒʌgə(r)). Also -ar, -ur. [Hindī *jaggar.*] The common falcon of India (*Falco juggur*).

Juggernaut, ‖**Jagannāth** ('dʒʌgənɔ:t). Also 7 Jaggarnat, Jagannat, -ernot, 8 Jagernaut, (-arynat), 8-9 Jaganaut, 9 Jaggernaut, Jaga-Naut, (Jaghernaut, Jugunnath); and with lower-case initial. [a. Hindī *Jagannāth*:—Skr. *Jagannātha* 'lord of the world', f. *jagat* world + *nātha* lord, protector. (The short *a* in Hindī is = (ʌ), whence the Eng. spelling *Jugger-*, with *u* and *er.*)]

1. *Hindu Myth.* A title of Kṛishṇa, the eighth avatar of Vishṇu; *spec.*, the uncouth idol of this deity at Pūrī in Orissa, annually dragged in procession on an enormous car, under the wheels of which many devotees are said to have formerly thrown themselves to be crushed. Also *attrib.*

The first European account of the Juggernaut festival, and its attendant immolations, is that by Friar Odoric, *c* 1321. See Yule, *Cathay and the Way thither* 28.

1638 W. BRUTON in Hakluyt *Voy.* (1812) V. 56-7 Vnto this Pagod..doe belong 9,000 Brammines or Priests, which doe dayly offer Sacrifice vnto their great God Iaggarnat... And when it [the chariot] is going along the City, there are many that will offer themselves a sacrifice to this Idoll. **1682** HEDGES *Diary* 16 July I. 30 We lay by all last night till 10 o'clock this morning, yᵉ Captain being desirous to see yᵉ Jagernot Pagodas. **1727** A. HAMILTON *New Acc. E. Ind.* I. 384 *Jagarynat*..his Effigie is often carried abroad in Procession, mounted on a Coach four Stories high. **1796** MORSE *Amer. Geog.* II. 555 In this province stands the idolatrous temple of Jaganaut. **1814** *Asiat. Jrnl.* (Y.), Juggernaut made some progress on the 19th, and has travelled daily ever since. **1825** A. STIRLING in *Asiat. Res.* XV. 324 That excess of fanaticism which formerly prompted the pilgrims to court death by throwing themselves in crowds under the wheels of the car of Jagannáth, has happily long ceased. **1827** POYNDER in *Asiat. Jrnl.* XXIII. 702/1 About the year 1790, no fewer than twenty-eight Hindoos were crushed to death..under the wheels of Juggernaut. **1878** *N. Amer. Rev.* CXXVII. 342 The temple and worship of Jagannath.

2. *fig.* An institution, practice, or notion to which persons blindly devote themselves, or are ruthlessly sacrificed. Also ***Juggernaut car*** in same sense.

1854 J. W. WARTER *Last Old Squires* iv. 32 A neighbouring people were crushed beneath the worse than Jaggernaut car of wild and fierce democracy. **1865** LONGF. in *Life* (1891) III. 66 The locomotive is the American Juggernaut. **1865** OUIDA *Strathmore* I. vi. 89 Society falls down before the Juggernaut of a Triumph. **1873** J. FORSTER *Dickens* II. xix. 415 Poor Johnny Tetterby staggering under his Moloch of an infant, the Juggernaut that crushes all his enjoyments. **1878** EDISON in *N. Amer. Rev.* CXXVI. 536 Details..will wholly disappear before that remorseless Juggernaut—'the needs of man'. **1883** *Standard* 3 Sept. 4/6 (Stanf.) Practical politics, that Revolutionary Juggernaut that grinds us all under its car.

3. (Now with lower-case initial.) A large heavy vehicle; *spec.* a heavy lorry.

In quot. 1927 prob. just an ordinary motor car.

1841 THACKERAY *Second Funeral of Napoleon* iii. 58 Fancy, then,..the body landed at day-break..and transferred to the car; and fancy the car, a huge Juggernaut of a machine. **1927** W. G. M. DOBIE *Game-Bag & Creel* 20 How gladly would I have him killed or shot, That blind, fat fool who drove the Juggernaut! **1946** G. TYRWHITT-DRAKE *Eng. Circus & Fair Ground* xvii. 198 In 1919 I bid £900 for one of these juggernauts [*sc.* a traction engine] to use for hauling my circus equipment. **1969** *Evening Star* (Ipswich) 28 Apr. 16/2 Experienced colleagues of mine are concerned about container lorries—the 30-ton juggernauts—which are completely disregarding speed limits. **1972** *Guardian* 30 Nov. 32/6 (*headline*) No entry for juggernauts. *Ibid.*, The juggernaut lorry will be kept out. **1972** *Oxford Mail* 11 Dec. 3/3 A plan to banish the juggernaut lorry from many Oxfordshire village roads is being prepared. **1973** *Press & Jrnl.* (Aberdeen) 7 Aug. 8/6 (*caption*) Sunshine and shade in the Church Square, Ballater. Continental juggernauts, on their way to the west coast, would certainly change this peaceful scene. **1973** *Daily Tel.* 10 Aug. 3, French police were last night interviewing 27 Asians—17 Pakistanis and 10

Indians found in Calais under a false floor in a juggernaut bound for Britain.

Hence **'Juggernaut** *v. trans.*, to crush to death as a victim; **'Juggernautish, 'Juggernautal** *adjs.*, of the nature or character of Juggernaut.

1819 *Abeillard & Heloisa* 340 Glad should we be to put the bridle On ev'ry Jaggernautish idol. **1830** *Examiner* 651/1 After Mr. Huskisson had been Juggernauted. **1860** *All Year Round* No. 47. 492, I escape with difficulty being Juggernauted to death by the ponderous wheels of the ox-waggons. **1888** *Harper's Mag.* Jan. 190/1 An asthmatic pug sought a Juggernautal fate between the ponderous wagon wheels.

jugging, *vbl. sb.* and *ppl. a.*: see JUG *v.*[1-3]

juggins ('dʒʌgɪnz). *slang.* [Origin uncertain. As a surname of plebeian origin (app. from *Jug*; cf. *Jenkins, Tomkins, Dickens*, etc.), *Juggins* is known in 1604 (Worcestersh.); it is given to a Lancashire collier in Disraeli's *Sybil*. But it does not appear whether or how far this is the source of the slang term; some take the latter as a fantastically perverted derivative of *mug* 'greenhorn', found 1861 in Mayhew *London Lab.* III. 203, and having also a derivative *muggins* (but this not certainly earlier than *juggins*).]

A simpleton, one easily 'taken in' or imposed upon.

[**1845** DISRAELI *Sybil* III. i, 'Juggins has got his rent to pay, and is afraid of the bums' said Nixon, 'and he has got two waistcoats'.] **1882** *Punch* 7 Jan., 3 'Arry. 'The openin' of a new era. What's that?' *Second 'Arry.* 'Openin' of a new 'earer? Why a telephone of course, you Juggins!' —— *Ibid.* 23 Dec. 292. **1884** JAS. GREENWOOD in *Daily Tel.* 25 Aug. 'A Lucky Shilling.' Well, here's good luck to him as a soft-hearted juggins, and may we soon come across another! **1889** BESANT *Bell St. Paul's* I. 292 The pigeon..exists no longer. In his place is the Juggins. **1894** DOYLE *Round the red Lamp* 19 Why, you juggins..there never was an operation at all. **1894** STEVENSON & L. OSBOURNE *Ebb-tide* 211 Well, you are a juggins!

juggle ('dʒʌg(ə)l), *v.* Forms: 4-5 iogly(n, 4-6 iogel, 5 iugille, 6 iogyl(l, iuggel, -yll, iugle, iugul, 6-7 iuggle, 7 jugle, 7- juggle. [ME. a. OF. *jogler, jugler* (later *jougler*) = It. *giocolare*:—late L. *joculāre* for L. *joculārī* to jest.]

†**1.** *intr.* To act as a JUGGLER (sense 1); to amuse or entertain people with jesting, buffoonery, tricks, etc. *Obs.*

1377 LANGL. *P. Pl.* B. XIII. 232, I can noither..Iape ne iogly [1393 C. XVI. 207 Iapen ne Iogelen] ne gentlych pype. **1483** *Cath. Angl.* 199/1 To Iugille, *ioculari.* **1608** ARMIN *Nest Ninn.* 47 Will Sommers watcht to disgrace him, when he was jugling and jesting before the king.

2. To practise the skill or art of a JUGGLER (sense 2) in magic or legerdemain; to play conjuring tricks; to conjure.

c **1440** *Promp. Parv.* 263/2 Ioglyn (*K., P.* iogelyn), *prestigior.* **1530** PALSGR. 592/2 Mathewe iogyled the cleanest of any man in our dayes. **1727** DE FOE *Hist. Appar.* ix. 187 He [the Devil] can juggle and play scurvy tricks. **1883** *Standard* 21 June 2/2 He..painted, acted, juggled and mesmerised. **1885** R. L. STEVENSON in *Contemp. Rev.* Apr. 550 The conjurer juggles with two oranges.

3. *transf.* and *fig.* To play tricks so as to cheat or deceive; to practise artifice or deceit *with*.

1528 TINDALE *Obed. Chr. Man* To Rdr., Why shall I not se the scripture..that I maye know whether thyne interpretacion be the right sence, or whether thou iuglest and drawest the scripture violently vnto thy carnall and fleshly purpose? **1533** FRITH *Another Bk. agst. Rastell* Wks. (1572) 63 Here he iuggeleth wyth me and would make me beleue that he tossed me mine own ball agayne, but when I beholde it, I perceaue it to be none of mine. **1632** LITHGOW *Trav.* x. 437 A grievous thing to see incapable men, to jugle with the high mysteries of mans salvation. **1660** MILTON *Griffith's Serm.* Wks. (1851) 394 Prime Teachers, who to thir credulous Audience dare thus juggle with Scripture. **1821** LAMB *Elia* Ser. I. *Mackery End*, She never juggles or plays tricks with her understanding.

4. *trans.* To deceive by jugglery; to deceive, trick, cheat, beguile; to cheat *out of* something.

1531 TINDALE *Exp. 1 John* ii. 33 God can not but let the deuell..iuggle oure eyes to confirme us in blyndnesse. **1533** —— *Lord's Sup.* 26 He neuer thus iugled nor mocked hys so dearely beloued discyples. *a* **1654** SELDEN *Table-t.* (Arb.) 29 If Men at first were juggled out of their Estates, yet they are rightly their Successours. *a* **1764** LLOYD *The Poet* Poet. Wks. 1774 II. 19 When near his latest breath The patient fain would juggle death. **1850** BLACKIE *Æschylus* I. Pref. 21 The Spirit of Error..juggles the plain understandings of men that they become the sport of every quibble. **1866** BRIGHT *Sp., Reform* 13 Mar. (1876) 344 They have no system of compounding which would juggle men out of their franchise.

b. To bring, get, convey, or change (*away, into*, etc.) by, or as by, magic or conjuring, or by trickery or deceit.

c **1590** GREENE *Fr. Bacon* I. 99 He can make women of devils and he can juggle cats into costermongers. **1618** BOLTON *Florus* III. xix. (1636) 233 He juggled a nut into his mouth, filled with brimstone, and fire, and..spat fire as he spake. **1813** JEFFERSON *Writ.* (1830) IV. 216 Our debt was juggled from forty-three up to eighty millions. **18..** G. MEREDITH *Poems, Juggling Jerry* viii, Now from his old girl he's juggled away.

Hence **'juggled** *ppl. a.*, done by jugglery.

1536 *Protest. Lower Ho. Convoc.* in Strype *Eccl. Mem.* (1721) I. App. lxxiii. 179 *Item*, That halowed water is but iogelled water. **1618** GAINSFORD *P. Warbeck* in *Select. fr. Harl. Misc.* (1793) 71 The fame of this juggled miracle was ..blown over Flanders.

juggle ('dʒʌg(ə)l), *sb.*[1] [f. JUGGLE *v.*] A piece of juggling; a trick or act of skill performed by legerdemain; a conjurer's trick, *esp.* one claiming to be done by magic or occult influence; hence, an act of deception, an imposture, cheat, fraud.

1664 H. MORE *Myst. Iniq.* II. I. xvii. 327 Whether by the juggle of their Priests or the assistence of some officious Dæmons, there were several Miracles and strange Cures conceived to be done in the Temples. **1669** W. SIMPSON *Hydrol. Chym.* 168 It's a meer juggle upon the senses. **1686** tr. *Claude's Persec. Fr. Protest.* 3 Juggles and amusing Tricks. **1691** WOOD *Ath. Oxon.* I. 16 The Money he had got by imposing on the Vulgar with his Juggles. **1727** DE FOE *Syst. Magic* I. iii. (1840) 62 At first the Magicians satisfied the curiosity of the people by juggle and trick. **1808** SCOTT *Marm.* VI. viii, Or featly was some juggle played. **1871** FREEMAN *Hist. Ess.* Ser. I. vii. 200 By one of the most disreputable of juggles, France obtained the Italian Island of Corsica. **1882** T. A. GUTHRIE *Vice Versa* iii. (ed. 4) 41 As if he were actually the schoolboy some hideous juggle had made him appear.

'juggle, *sb.*[2] [Cf. JOGGLE.] (See quot.)

1875 KNIGHT *Dict. Mech., Juggle*, a block of timber cut to a length, either in the round or split.

'jugglement. *rare*⁻¹. [f. JUGGLE *v.* + -MENT: cf. OF. *juglement* (Godef.).] The process of juggling; a piece of juggling; a juggler's trick.

a **1708** BEVERIDGE *Priv. Th.* I. (1730) 26 The Miracles, which Jesus did, were not the Delusions and Jugglements of the Devil, but real Miracles.

juggler ('dʒʌglə(r)). Forms: α. 1 iugelere, ȝeogelere, 2 iugulere, 3-4 iugelour, (4 -elur, -ellur), 3-6 iogeler, 4-5 ioguler, -or, -ur, -our, -owre, iogoler, -our(e, -ur, iuguler, -or, iugoler, iugillure, -our, 4-6 iogelour, (5 -owre), 6-7 iuggeler. β. 3-4 iuglur, 4 joglere, 5 ioglour(e, 5-6 iuglour, 6 iogler, iougler, iuglar, 6-7 iugler, iuggler, 7 juglar, (jugleur), 7-9 jugler, 7- juggler. [ad. OF. nom. *jog-, jug-, jouglere*, acc. *jogleor, jog-, jougelour*, later *jougleur* = It. *giocolatore*:—L. *joculātor, -ātōrem*, agent-n. from *joculārī* to jest. Some of the ME. forms may represent the OF. synonym *jogeler, jougler* = Sp. *juglar*, It. *giocogliere*:—L. *juculāris* jocular, droll, in med.L. as sb. = 'mimus, scurra'; but already in the late OE. *iugelere* we see the suffix levelled under the native *-ere*, later -ER[1]. The trisyllabic *iuguler, ioguler*, etc. were app. influenced by the Latin form. See also JONGLEUR.]

†**1.** One who entertains or amuses people by stories, songs, buffoonery, tricks, etc.; a jester, buffoon. (Often used with implied contempt or reprobation.) *Obs.*

α. *c* **1175** *Lamb. Hom.* 29 Þa liȝeres and þa wohdemeres and þa iuguleres, and þa oðer sottes. *c* **1290** *S. Eng. Leg.* I. 271/19 Is Iugelour a day bi-fore him pleide faste, And nemde in his ryme and in is song þene deuel atþe laste. *a* **1300** *K. Horn* 1494 (Ritson) Men seide hit were harperis, Jogelers, ant fythelers. *c* **1420** *Chron. Vilod.* 138 In a Iogulers lykenesse y wys He went to aspye what dede his fone. **1483** CAXTON *Cato* B v, Them that can kepe no thynge secretelyas iogelers, mynstrellys, foles..and yonge chyldren. **1591** SPENSER *M. Hubbard* 86, I meane me to disguize In some straunge habit ..like a Gipsen, or a Iuggeler.

β. *a* **1225** *Ancr. R.* 210 Summe iuglurs beoð þet ne kunnen seruen of non oðer gleo, buten makien cheres, & wrenchen his muð, & schulen mid hore eien. *a* **1300** *Cursor M.* 28382 Oure fele..sith haf i..to gleumen cald and to ioglere, in tent þai suld me luueworde bere. **1557** PAYNELL *Barclay's Jugurth* I. 91, I haue no iougler nor dyzar with me to moue sportes and dissolute laughynge.

2. One who works marvels by the aid of magic or witchcraft, a magician, wizard, sorcerer (*obs.*); one who plays tricks by sleight of hand; a performer of legerdemain; a conjurer.

α. *a* **1100** *Aldhelm Glosses* 4020 (Napier 106/2) *Aruspicum*, iugelera. *Ibid.* 4476 *Marsi*, dryas, iugeleras [*Brussels MS.* ȝeogelere]. *a* **1300** *Cursor M.* 5898 Þan cald þe king his enchaunturs, Þe craftes of his iogulurs, Dun þai kest a wand iiban, And þai wex dragons son onan. *Ibid.* 20891 Symon magus, þat iugelur [*v.rr.* iuglur, iugillure, Iogelour]..ledd þe folk wit grett errur. *c* **1384** CHAUCER *H. Fame* III. 169 Ther saugh I pley Iugelours Magiciens and tregetours. **1509** *Gosp. Nicodemus* (W. de W. 1518) 12 Iames and Zambres the whiche were iogelers and wytches. **1555** EDEN *Decades* 46 He conueygheth the piece of fleshe owte of his owne mouth like a iuggeler. **1601-2** FULBECKE *1st Pt. Parall.* 97 This is many waies done, and iuggelers and professors of feates can performe it.

β. *a* **1300** [see α above]. *a* **1400-50** *Alexander* 410 Þe Iuse for his gemetry þat Iogloure takis. *c* **1450** HOLLAND *Howlat* 770 In com iapand the Ia as a iuglour. **1529** MORE *Dyaloge* II. Wks. 200/2 The serpent of Moises deuoured all the serpentes..of the Egipcyan ioglers. *a* **1548** HALL *Chron., Hen. VII* 5 No lesse deceytfull then ligier de meyne in the hand of a iuggler. **1662** PEPYS *Diary* 15 Aug., After dinner comes in a jugleur, which showed us very pretty tricks. **1761** CHURCHILL *Apol.* 122 It flies,—hey!—presto!—like a jugler's ball. **1808** A. PARSONS *Trav.* xiv. 308 Buffoons and juglers, who come in groupes with music into the channel, and play their tricks. **1875** E. WHITE *Life in Christ* III. xxi. (1878) 310 Phenomena travestied by the jugglers of the Egyptian Hall.

3. *transf.* and *fig.* One who deceives by trickery; a trickster; one who plays fast and loose (*with*).

a **1340** HAMPOLE *Psalter* xxx. 16 Þai ere all faitors & ypocrites & iogulors þat dessayues man. *c* **1380** WYCLIF *Wks.* (1880) 99 Þei [Prelatis] bicomen þe deuelis iogelours to blynde mennus gostly eiȝ en. *a* **1400-50** *Alexander* 4526 Iupitir þat Ioglour sum Iape bos haue. **1567** MAPLET *Gr. Forest* 7 This [gem] is a maruellous Iugler, for it wil cause things obiect to be presented to our eies as it listeth. **1590** SHAKS. *Mids. N.* III. ii. 282 O me, you iugler, you canker blossome, You theefe of loue. **1651** SIR E. NICHOLAS in *N. Papers* (Camden) 226 The two great Jugglers..in Scotland, viz. Hamilton and Argyle. **1769** BURKE *Late St. Nat.* Wks. 1842 I. 85 All the little tricks of finance which the expertest juggler of the treasury can practise. **1875** JOWETT *Plato* (ed. 2) IV. 376 The Sophist..is proved to be a dissembler and juggler with words.

4. *Comb.*, as ***juggler-like*** adj. or adv.

1639 HABINGTON *Castara* II. (Arb.) 97 Honour doth appeare To statesmen like a vision in the night, And jugler-like workes oth' deluded sight.

'juggleress. [a. OF. *jug-, jougleresse*, fem. of *juglere*: see prec. and -ESS.] A female juggler.

c **1430** *Pilgr. Lyf Manhode* II. cxxvi. (1869) 123 Ther is neither jogelour ne jogelouresse that maketh grettere solas there than j doo. *Ibid.* IV. xxxvi. 194 Jowgleresse. **1491** CAXTON *Vitas Patr.* (W. de W. 1495) I. xli. 62 b/1 He sawe ..the moost excellent Iougleresse or Daunceresse that was in the cytee of Anthyoche. **1824** PRICE in *Warton's Hist. Poetry* II. (1840) I. 46 *note*, A jugleress, whose pantomimic exhibitions were accompanied by her husband's harp.

jugglery ('dʒʌglərɪ). Forms: 4 iugolori, iugulori, iogelery, iugelri, iugilrie, iogelrye, 4-5 iogolori, -ry, 5 iogelorye, iogulyrye, iogulrye, ioglerie, 6 iouglarie, iuglarie, -ry, 7 juglary, 9 jugglery. [ME. a. OF. *jogle-, juglerie* (12th c.), also *jogelerie*, later *jouglerie*, f. *jogler*: see JUGGLER and -ERY.]

1. The art or practice of a juggler; †minstrelsy, play; pretended magic or witchcraft; conjuring, legerdemain.

a **1300** *Cursor M.* 19522 He wroght be-for þam gret ferli, And al was wit his Iugolori [*v.r.* iugelri]. *c* **1386** CHAUCER *Frankl. T.* 537 To maken illusion By swich an apparence or Iogelrye. *c* **1430** *Pilgr. Lyf Manhode* IV. xlvii. (1869) 198 Michel he loueth swich organe and swich song and swich jogelorye. **1552** ABP. HAMILTON *Catech.* (1884) 49 Quhasaevir usis wichecraft, Nicromansie, Enchantment, Juglarie. **1830** SCOTT *Demonol.* 81 Possessed.. professionally of some skill in jugglery. **1856** KANE *Arct. Expl.* II. xii. 126, I could not detect them in any resort to jugglery or natural magic. **1858** J. MARTINEAU *Stud. Chr.* 50 The service appears little better than a profane sacerdotal jugglery.

2. *transf.* The playing of tricks likened to those of a juggler; trickery, deception.

1699 BURNET *39 Art.* iv. (1700) 63 They could [not].. pretend that there was any Deceit or Juglary in them. **1816** SCOTT *Antiq.* xvii, This is a mere trick..the rascal had made himself sure of the existence of this old well..before he played off this mystical piece of jugglery. **1828** J. BALLANTYNE *Exam. Hum. Mind* III. x, Neither by these denominations, nor by any other jugglery of words can he alter the nature of the case. **1838** PRESCOTT *Ferd. & Is.* (1846) III. xiii. 85 As gross an example of political jugglery and falsehood.

3. *attrib.*

1563 WIN3ET *Four Scoir Thre Quest.* Wks. 1888 I. 87 [If he] did thir thingis veralie and indeid, or be ane certane jouglarie craft. **1883** G. H. BOUGHTON in *Harper's Mag.* Apr. 690/2 It looked like some insane jugglery practice.

juggling ('dʒʌglɪŋ), *vbl. sb.* [f. JUGGLE *v.* + -ING[1].] The action of the verb JUGGLE: **a.** the practice of magic or of legerdemain, conjuring; **b.** the practice of trickery or deception.

c **1380** WYCLIF *Serm.* Sel. Wks. II. 137 No jogelyng ne falsheed was ony tyme in Crist. **1483** *Cath. Angl.* 199/1 A Iugulynge, *gesticulacio.* **1528** TINDALE *Obed. Chr. Man* To Rdr., The worke of Antychrist and iugulynge of ypocrites. **1577** tr. *Bullinger's Decades* (1592) 128 Let vs not..abuse the name or worde of God, in coniuring, iugling, or sorcerie. **1667** DUCHESS NEWCASTLE *Life Duke of N.* III. (1886) 170 There was such juggling, treachery, and falsehood in his own army. **1727** DE FOE *Syst. Magic* I. ii. (1840) 47 Innocent art, secret and cunning contrivances to delude the sight; this we call juggling, legerdemain or philosophical delusion. **1788** H. WALPOLE in *Walpoliana* cxiv. 48 Ireland, by the infamous juggling of the 'Propositions' has lost all confidence in this country. **1900** *Speaker* 23 June 328/2 This disingenuous juggling with noble ideals.

c. *attrib.*

1530 PALSGR. 234/2 Iogelyng caste, *passe passe.* **1573** G. HARVEY *Letter-bk.* (Camden) 28 He plais me a pretti iugling kast of leger de main. **1589** *Pasquil's Ret.* D iv, You haue lost your iugling stick. **1727** DE FOE *Syst. Magic* I. iii. (1840) 68 The juggling trade grew stale and dull. **1750** tr. *Leonardus' Mirr. Stones* 142 (222) Quirinus is a juggling stone found in the nest of the hoopoop.

'juggling, *ppl. a.* [f. as prec. + -ING[2].] That juggles; playing tricks of magic or legerdemain; playing tricks, cheating, deceptive.

a **1533** FRITH *Disput. Purgat.* To Rdr., Sith we..will..not conferre and examine these iuggling mistes with the light of Gods word, our ignoraunce is wilfull. **1595** SHAKS. *John* III. i. 169 Though you..This iugling witchcraft with reuennue cherish, Yet I alone, alone doe me oppose Against the Pope. **1652** SIR E. NICHOLAS in *N. Papers* (Camden) 312 That juggling Cardinal will not suffer the K. of France to do any good for the K. **1756** BURKE *Vind. Nat. Soc.* Wks. I. 58 The government is..a juggling confederacy of a few to cheat the prince and enslave the people. **1814** SOUTHEY *Roderick* xx. 208 Fabling creeds, and juggling priests.

Hence **'jugglingly** *adv.*, in a juggling or deceptive manner; beguilingly.

1647 *Myst. Two Juntos* 5 It is known how malignantly and how juglingly writs for new elections were granted and executed. **1653** H. MORE *Antid. Ath.* III. xvi. (1712) 138

Who cunningly and jugglingly endeavours to infuse the poyson of Atheism into the mind of his Reader.

'jughead. *slang* (chiefly *U.S.*). [f. JUG *sb.*² + HEAD *sb.*¹] **a.** A mule; also, a stubborn horse. **b.** A foolish or stupid person; also, as a mere term of abuse.

1926 L. H. NASON *Chevrons* iii. 86 'Unload everything,' he says. Hear that, you jugheads? At four-thirty! **1936** D. MCCARTHY *Lang. Mosshorn, Jughead*, a horse which seemingly has no brains. **1942** *Sat. Even. Post* 3 Oct. 36/1 Unloose dat jughead jaw! **1966** *Publ. Amer. Dial. Soc. 1964* XLII. 18 Hardtail, a derogatory name for a mule. Others were *jarhead* and *jughead*. **1971** *Illustr. Weekly India* 25 Apr. 67/5 Jughead, what took you so long?

† **'jugial,** *a. Obs. rare.* [f. L. *jūgi-s* perpetual + -AL¹.] Continual, perpetual. Hence † **'jugially** *adv.*

1654 VILVAIN *Theol. Treat.* i. 13 This is no plain evidence for jugial creation of every particular Soul. —— *Epit. Ess.* v. lv. 109 They bring most harms to men jugialy.

jugillure, -our, obs. forms of JUGGLER.

† **jugland,** *Obs. rare*⁻¹. [ad. L. *jūglans, jūglandem* walnut, f. *jū-:—Jovi-* Jupiter + *glans* acorn.] A walnut tree.

c **1420** *Pallad. on Husb.* III. 1048 Iuglande in lond now sprynge; Ek graffe hym now.

juglandaceous (dʒuːglæn'deɪʃəs), *a. Bot. rare*⁻⁰. [f. mod.L. *Jūglandāce-æ* the walnut family (f. *jūglans*: see prec.) + -OUS.] Of or pertaining to the walnut family.

juglar, -er, -our, etc., obs. ff. JUGGLER.

† **'jugle,** *v. Obs. rare*⁻¹. [f. JUG *sb.*² + freq. suffix -LE.] To repeat the sound 'jug'.

1576 GASCOIGNE *Philomene* (Arb.) 113 Some thinke that Iugum is The Iug, she iugleth so.

juglet ('dʒʌglɪt). *Archæol.* [f. JUG *sb.*² + -LET.] A small vessel of jug shape.

1932 *Discovery* Sept. 305/1 The small juglets were commonly made in two halves and imperfectly joined together, though no mark was visible on the outer surface. **1942** *Antiquity* XVI. 187 The juglet with elongated stump base is not among the earliest types of Bronze Age pottery. **1957** K. KENYON *Digging up Jericho* 98 Out of a total of 251 vessels..111 are juglets with a round base, a wide mouth and a rather high loop-handle.

juglone ('dʒuː-, 'dʒʌgləʊn). *Chem.* Also †**juglon.** [ad. G. *juglon* (C. Reischauer 1877, in *Ber. d. Deut. Chem. Ges.* X. 1542), f. L. *iūglans* walnut: see -ONE.] 5-Hydroxy-1,4-naphthoquinone, $C_{10}H_6O_3$, a reddish-yellow crystalline compound obtained from the green shells of walnuts and having fungicidal properties.

1878 *Jrnl. Chem. Soc.* XXXIV. 233 Juglone (Nucin)... This body, prepared from the green shells of walnuts (*Juglans regia*), has been analysed by the author, who assigns to it the empirical formula, $C_{36}H_{12}O_{10}$. **1887** *Chem. News* 9 Nov. 214/1 'Juglon'. An extended series of analytical results with regard to this body. **1892** ROSCOE & SCHORLEMMER *Treat. Chem.* III. VI. 138 About 150 grms. of juglone are thus obtained from rather more than 100 kilos. of walnut-shells. **1925** *Phytopathology* XV. 783 Juglone..is an irritant causing violent sneezing and has been found..to be especially valuable as a medicant for skin diseases. **1949** E. P. ABRAHAM in H. W. Florey et al. *Antibiotics* I. xiv. 619 Brissemoret and Michaud (1917) reported the use of juglone in clinical cases of eczema, impetigo, and other skin diseases. **1971** R. H. THOMSON *Naturally Occurring Quinones* (ed. 2) iv. 222 Finely powdered juglone is an effective sternutator and like many other quinones has weak fungicidal and bactericidal properties.

jugoler, obs. form of JUGGLER.

jugo-ma'xillary, *a. Anat.* [f. *jugo-*, taken as combining form of L. *jugum* yoke + MAXILLARY.] Of or pertaining to the jugal or zygomatic arch and the jaw.

1855 in MAYNE *Expos. Lex.* **1887** in *Syd. Soc. Lex.*

Jugoslav, Jugoslavian: see YUGOSLAV, etc.

jugular ('dʒʌgjʊlə(r), 'dʒuːgjʊlə(r)), *a.* and *sb.* [ad. med. or mod.L. *jugulār-is*, f. L. *jugul-um* collar-bone, neck, throat: see -AR.]

A. *adj.* **1.** *Anat.* Of, pertaining to, or situated in the neck or throat; *esp.* an epithet of the great veins of the neck, as the ***external jugular vein***, which conveys the blood from the superficial parts of the head, and the ***internal jugular vein***, which conveys it from the inside of the skull.

1597 A. M. tr. *Guillemeau's Fr. Chirurg.* xij b/2 The Iugulare or organicke vayne. **1643** J. STEER tr. *Exp. Chyrurg.* xiii. 52 Apply Leeches..unto the jugular veynes in the necke. **1655** STANLEY *Hist. Philos.* III. (1701) 95/2 A Physiognomist..said he was stupid, because there were obstructions in his jugular parts. **1767** GOOCH *Treat. Wounds* I. 335 Neither of the carotid arteries, or internal jugular veins were opened. **1831** R. KNOX *Cloquet's Anat.* 51 Behind this, is a square eminence, covered with cartilage, which is articulated to the temporal bone, and is named the Jugular process. **1855** HOLDEN *Hum. Osteol.* (1878) 58 Immediately external to the condyles, the bone forms on each side a projection, termed the jugular eminence.

2. *Ichthyol.* Of a fish: Having the ventral fins situated in front of the pectoral, i.e. in the region of the throat; said also of a ventral fin so situated.

1766 PENNANT *Zool.* (1769) III. 31, I have copied the great sections of the Bony Fish into Apodal, Jugular [etc.]. **1774** GOLDSM. *Nat. Hist.* (1862) II. III. i. 294 The ventral fins placed more forward than the pectoral fins, as in the haddock, and then the animal is a Jugular-fish. **1875** BLAKE *Zool.* 185 In some fishes their relative position is in front of the pectorals, when they obtain technically the name of jugular fins.

B. *sb.* **1.** *Anat.* Short for *jugular vein.*

1615 CROOKE *Body of Man* 435 Veines from the outward braunch of the external iugulars. **1707** FLOYER *Physic. Pulse-Watch* 23, I cut the Jugular of a Dog. **1873** MIVART *Elem. Anat.* x. 422 A great trunk, the innominate, is formed by the union of the two jugulars and the subclavian.

2. *Ichthyol.* A jugular fish: see A. 2.

1835 KIRBY *Hab. & Inst. Anim.* I. ii. 110 The tribe of *Jugulars*..whose ventral fins are nearer the mouth than the pectoral.

† **'jugulary,** *a. Obs. rare*⁻⁰. [f. as prec. + -ARY.] = JUGULAR *a.* 1.

1626 MINSHEU *Duct. Ling.* (ed. 2), *Iugularie*, of or belonging to the throat. **1658** PHILLIPS, *Jugular*, or *Jugularie.*

jugulate ('dʒuːgjʊleɪt), *v.* [f. L. *jugulāt-*, ppl. stem of *jugulāre* to cut the throat of, to slay; f. *jugulum*: see JUGULAR and -ATE³.]

1. *trans.* To kill by cutting the throat; to kill, slay, put to death.

1623 COCKERAM, *Iugulate*, to slay or kill. **1657** TOMLINSON *Renou's Disp.* 46 That were to jugulate, not to purge men. **1660** tr. *Amyraldus' Treat. conc. Relig.* III. vi. 421 They must have been too like the victimes which they jugulated. **1834-43** SOUTHEY *Doctor* xxiii (1862) 55 And then for Death to summon the Pope and jugulate him.

2. *fig.* To 'strangle'; *spec.* to stop the course of (a disease) by a powerful remedy.

1876 BARTHOLOW *Mat. Med.* (1879) 313 It..so compresses the vessels as to jugulate the inflammatory process. **1894** *Columbus* (O.) *Disp.* 2 Jan., It is bad policy..to attempt to jugulate advertising. **1898** *Allbutt's Syst. Med.* V. 123 Misplaced attempts to 'jugulate' the disease [pneumonia].

So **jugu'lation; 'jugulator.** *rare*⁻⁰.

1623 COCKERAM, *Iugulation*, a cutting of ones throat. **1882** OGILVIE, *Jugulator*, a cut-throat or murderer. **1887** *Syd. Soc. Lex., Jugulation*, the sudden arrest of a disease by a powerful remedy.

juguler, -ur, obs. form of JUGGLER.

jugulo- ('dʒuː-, 'dʒʌgjʊləʊ), combining form of JUGULAR *a.* and *sb.*, JUGULUM, in a few anatomical terms, as **jugulo-ce'phalic** *a.*, of or pertaining to the head and throat; in ***jugulo-cephalic vein***, 'an occasional vein which connects the cephalic and the external jugular veins' (*Syd. Soc. Lex.* 1887); **jugulodi'gastric** *a.*, designating a pair of lymph nodes (sometimes also including several smaller associated nodes) in the neck (see quots.); **jugulo-omo'hyoid** *a.*, designating either of a pair of lymph nodes in the neck (see quots.).

1920 JAMIESON & DOBSON in *Brit. Jrnl. Surg.* VIII. 80 Examined from in front, certain members are particularly conspicuous..., and merit special mention: these are a large gland and a variable number of smaller nodes lying in a triangle formed by the posterior belly of the digastric, common facial vein, and internal jugular vein. These may be called the jugulodigastric glands. **1967** G. M. WYBURN et al. *Conc. Anat.* iv. 120/1 The lymph node at the angle of the jaw, the jugulodigastric, drains the tonsil. **1972** C. R. & T. S. LEESON *Human Struct.* xxix. 151/1 Jugulo-digastric. This node (or nodes) lies where the deep chain is crossed by the posterior belly of the digastric muscle. **1920** JAMIESON & DOBSON in *Brit. Jrnl. Surg.* VIII. 80 One gland..situated on or just above the omohyoid, frequently presents at the anterior border of the sternomastoid... From its connection with all parts of the tongue we have to refer to it frequently, and suggest the name jugulo-omohyoid gland. **1963** TOBIAS & ARNOLD *Man's Anat.* II. xv. 120 The jugulo-omohyoid node lies on the internal jugular vein just above the tendon of the omohyoid.

‖**jugulum** ('dʒuːgjʊləm). *Anat.* and *Zool.* [L. *jugulum* collar-bone, also neck, throat, dim. formation from *jug-*, stem of *jungĕre* to join.] A name for the collar-bone; also for the throat, or the lower front part of the neck, esp. in birds; in *Entom.* applied to corresponding parts in insects.

1706 PHILLIPS, *Jugulum*, the fore-part of the Neck, where the Wind-pipe is; the Neck-bone, Throat-bone, or Channel-bone: Also, the upper Breast-bone. **1826** KIRBY & SP. *Entomol.* III. 526 *Jugulum*. This part, which may be regarded as analogous to the throat in vertebrate animals, lies between the cheeks... It is particularly conspicuous and elevated in the Lamellicorn beetles. **1828** STARK *Elem. Nat. Hist.* I. 215 Plumage brown above, fulvous beneath; throat and jugulum black.

‖**jugum** ('dʒuːgəm). *Bot.* Pl. **juga.** [L. *jugum* yoke.] **1. a.** A pair of leaflets in a pinnate leaf. **b.** Each of the ridges on the carpels of *Umbelliferæ.*

1857 HENFREY *Elem. Bot.* 59 The pairs of leaflets [in pinnate leaves] are sometimes called *juga*, and if only one pair exists, the leaf is unijugate. **1880** GRAY *Struct. Bot.* (ed. 6) 417/2 The ridges in the fruit of Umbelliferae are termed *juga.*

2. a. *Zool.* In certain brachiopods with hinged shells, a process of the dorsal valve. **b.** *Ent.* In certain Lepidoptera, a lobe on the fore wing which is able to link it to the hind wing. Hence **'jugal, 'jugate** *adjs.*

1888 ROLLESTON & JACKSON *Forms Animal Life* (ed. 2) 693 One valve may have depression or sinuses to which correspond elevations or juga on the other. **1893** J. H. COMSTOCK in *Wilder Quarter-Century Bk.* 43 There are two distinct ways of uniting the two wings of each side in the Lepidoptera; they may be united by a frenulum or..by a jugum. *Ibid.* 84 In this genus [sc. *Hepialis*]..they [sc. the wings] are joined by a membranous lobe extending back from near the base of the inner margin of the fore wing. To this lobe I have applied the name jugum. **1895** J. H. & A. COMSTOCK *Man. Study Insects* xviii. 215 This projecting lobe is named the jugum or yoke; and the moths possessing this organ are termed the Jugatæ or the Jugate Lepidoptera. **1952** R. C. MOORE et al. *Invertebr. Fossils* vi. 213/1 A variously shaped crossbar between the spiralia is called [the] jugum; it has considerable importance in classifying some groups of spine-bearing brachiopods. **1957** RICHARDS & DAVIES *Imms's Gen. Textbk. Ent.* (ed. 9) 538 Wing-coupling apparatus of jugate type, the jugal lobe elongate and resting upon the hind wing. **1969** R. F. CHAPMAN *Insects* x. 175 The Hepialidae have a strong jugal lobe which lies beneath the costal margin of the hind wing so that this is held between the jugum and the rest of the fore wing.

† **'jugyl,** *v. Obs. rare*⁻¹. [for **jugul*, ad. L. *jugulāre*: see JUGULATE.] *trans.* To kill, slay.

c **1440** *Gesta Rom.* xxxiv. 135 (Harl. MS.) Dethe, þe whiche iugylithe and sleithe vs alle.

juice (dʒuːs), *sb.* Forms: *α.* 3-5 iuys, (4 iuyshe, iwisch, iwissh, wisch), 5 iuwys, yuis, 6-7 iuyce, iuice, 7 juyce, 7- juice. *β.* 4-6 ius, iuse, (5 iwce), 5-6 iuce, iwse, (6 ieuse). *γ.* 5 ious, iows, iowce, 5-6 iowse. *δ.* 5 ioys, (ioissh), 6 ioyse, 6-7 ioyce, 7 joice. [a. F. *jus*, ad. L. *jūs* broth, sauce, juice of animal or plant. The *β* forms are normal from F.; with the others cf. those of *duke, flute, jupe*, and *bruit, fruit.*]

1. a. The watery or liquid part of vegetables or fruits, which can be expressed or extracted; commonly containing the characteristic flavour and other properties.

α. *c* **1290** *S. Eng. Leg.* I. 360/52 Iuys of smal-Ache do þar-to. *c* **1400** tr. *Secreta Secret., Gov. Lordsh.* 83 Oynement maad of myrre, and of þe iuwys of þe herbe þat ys clepyd bletes. **1460-70** *Bk. Quintessence* 20 þe yuis of þe eerbe þat is callid morsus galline rubri. **1533** ELYOT *Cast. Helthe* II. xiv, The iuyce of theym [oranges] is colde in the second degree. **1596** SPENSER *F.Q.* IV. i. 31 Like withered tree that wanteth iuyce [*rime* flowre-deluce]. *a* **1626** BACON *New Atl.* (1900) 38 Wines we have of Grapes; and Drinkes of other Iuyce. —— *Sylva* §633 The juices of fruits are either watery or oily..Those that have oily juices, are olives, almonds, nuts of all sorts..etc., and their juices are all inflammable. **1673** RAY *Journ. Low C., Venice* 204 They take the juyce of Beet. **1884** BOWER *De Bary's Phaner.* 192 The peculiar juice which flows from milky plants.

β. **1390** GOWER *Conf.* II. 266 And tho sche tok vnto his vs Of herbes al the beste ius. *c* **1420** *Pallad. on Husb.* II. 206 Vche herbe in his colour, odour, & Iuce [*rime* letuce]. *c* **1490** Iwse [see quot. *c* **1440** in *γ*]. **1513** DOUGLAS *Æneis* XII. vii. 90 The hailsum ius of herb ambrosyane. **1528** PAYNEL *Salerne's Regim.* aj b, Celendine, whose ieuse is citrine. **1553** BRENDE *Q. Curtius* S iv, A iuse which they wringe out of Sesama. **1570** LEVINS *Manip.* 182/15 Iuce of herbes, *succus.*

γ. *c* **1400** tr. *Secreta Secret., Gov. Lordsh.* 84 Take þe iowse of þe poume-garnet swete, xxv Rotes, and of þe Iowse of swet appelys, x Rotes. *a* **1400-50** *Alexander* 339 þe ious out he wrengis. *c* **1440** *Promp. Parv.* 265/2 Iows of frutys, or herbys..[*MS. K.* (*c* **1490**) iowse or iwse], *ius, succus.* **1530** PALSGR. 235/1 Iowse of an herbe, *jus.*

δ. **14..** *Voc.* in Wr.-Wülcker 564/40 *Aporima*, ioys of gras. *c* **1450** *Two Cookery-bks.* 116 Ioissh of persely or malves. **1553** EDEN *Treat. Newe Ind.* (Arb.) 34 The humoure or ioyse which droppeth out of the braunches of the date trees. **1565-73** COOPER *Thesaurus* s.v. *Dens*, The ioyse anointed healeth the toothache. *Mod. Sc.* (Edinb., Peebles, Roxb., etc.) Joice, as 'bacca joice, the joice o' reid currans.

b. *spec.* that of the grape, made into wine. Also more generally, alcoholic liquor (*U.S. slang*).

1387 TREVISA *Higden* (Rolls) IV. 121 And schewede hem þe juse of grapes and of buries. **1606** SHAKS. *Ant. & Cl.* v. ii. 285 No more The iuyce of Egypts Grape shall moyst this lip. **1732** POPE *Ess. Man* I. 136 Annual for me, the grape, the rose renew The juice nectareous, and the balmy dew. **1813** SCOTT *Trierm.* II. ix. **1828** P. CUNNINGHAM *N.S. Wales* (ed. 3) II. 206 An over-dose of the juice. **1932** *Evening Sun* (Baltimore) 9 Dec. 31/4 *Juice*, whisky. **1940** D. ELLINGTON in *Swing* May 10/3 Everybody in our band at that time was a juice-hound, juice meaning any kind of firewater. **1956** B. HOLIDAY *Lady sings Blues* (1973) xix. 157 There was no place I could work in New York—not if they sold juice there. **1961** R. RUSSELL *Sound* 22 'Nuthin' at all like juice, either,' Hassan said. 'No hangover.' **1971** *Harper's Mag.* May 83 But they need their juice, for their kind of tension would not be relieved by the head-lightening stuff, they need the down-deep sleep of the intelligence that comes with liquor.

c. (*a*) The liquor from the sugar cane; (*b*) this made ready for evaporation.

(*a*) **1697** *Phil. Trans. R. Soc.* XIX. 381 The Juice of the Cane. **1784** P. H. MATY in *New Rev.* Sept. 194 To..cut the cane,..to have the juice expressed, and boiled into sugar. **1812** J. TAYLOR *Arbores Mirabiles* 39 The season continues ..about six weeks, when the juice is found to be too thin and poor to make sugar. **1830** G. R. PORTER *Nature & Properties Sugar Cane* 17 The cane contains three sorts of juice, one aqueous, another saccharine, and the third mucous.

(*b*) **1839** URE *Dict. Arts* 1202 Where canes grow on a calcareous marly soil, in a favourable season the saccharine matter gets so thoroughly elaborated, and the glutinous mucilage so completely condensed, that a clear juice and a

fine sugar may be obtained without the use of lime. 1887 Encycl. Brit. XXII. 626/1 Wetzel's pan,..and similar devices for the efficient evaporation of juice..are also in use.

d. Electricity, electric current. *slang.*

1896 Boston Herald 25 Dec. 4/5 Now we know what a blessing the trolley is—when the juice isn't turned off. 1903 Electrical Engineer 28 Aug. 327/2 The first he asked, a councillor Whose town had got the juice. 1916 'Taffrail' Pincher Martin xiii. 238 Call her up by wireless... Don't make our name, but use all the juice you can, so that they'll think we're very close. 1928 U. Sinclair Boston (1929) xxiv. 724 The juice was turned off, and Vanzetti was officially pronounced dead. 1934 J. M. Cain Postman always rings Twice ii. 18 They got neon signs, they show up better, and they don't burn as much juice. 1966 H. Sheppard Dict. Railway Slang (ed. 2) 9 On the juice, running on electrified lines—particularly LTE.

e. Petrol. *slang.*

1909 Installation News III. 52/2 We are not faced with a threepenny tax on each gallon of 'juice'. 1918 E. M. Roberts Flying Fighter 281 Then I discovered that the tank was nearly empty. That meant that I would have to go in search of 'juice'. 1959 N.Z. Listener 12 June 20/4 'Turn the juice on!' He felt sheepish as he twisted the key. 1968 K. Weatherly Roo Shooter 56 The Rover had him worried. If she ran out of juice..he had to walk in. 1973 Nation Rev. (Melbourne) 24–30 Aug. 1399/6 'Tis cheaper to slow down—you use less juice then, be it petroleum or gastric.

f. A drug or drugs. *slang.*

1957 [see gang-bang s.v. GANG sb.[1] 12]. 1972 H. C. Rae Shooting Gallery iii. 187, I wasn't interested in him. I mean, when you shoot juice, you lose the other thing.

2. The fluid part or moisture of an animal body or substance; now usually in *pl.* the various liquid constituents of the body, the bodily 'humours'; also used in *sing.* in the names of the digestive secretions (***gastric j.***, ***intestinal j.***, ***pancreatic j.***).

1398 Trevisa Barth. De P.R. v. xxxviii. (Bodl. MS.), þe lyuour..fongiþ Ious [W. de W. Ius], woos, and humour wherof blood is bred. 1533 Elyot Cast. Helthe i. (1541) 14 Somme [meat and drink] is good, whiche maketh good iuyce, and good bloudde: some is ylle and ingendreth yll iuyce and yll bloudde. 1675 Traherne Chr. Ethics 325 The four humors of choler, melancholy, flegm, and blood are generally known: but there are many other juyces talkt of besides. 1692 Bentley Boyle Lect. iii. 82 Marrow and Fat and Blood, and other Nutritious Juices. 1774 Goldsm. Nat. Hist. (1776) II. 128 The man who dies of hunger, may be said to be poisoned by the juices of his own body. 1899 Cagney tr. Jaksch's Clin. Diagn. v. (ed. 4) 171 The intestinal juice is a mixed secretion derived from several glands.

3. More generally, The moisture or liquid naturally contained in or coming from anything.

c 1420 Pallad. on Husb. i. 240 Lette hem drie unslayn, and vp they drinke The londes iuce. 1503 in Surtees Misc. (1888) 30 The fylthe and juse that discendes..frome the sade stye. c 1586 C'tess Pembroke Ps. civ. vii, Oile, whose iuyce unplaites the folded brow. c 1645 Howell Lett. (1688) IV. 489 It is the pure juyce of the Bee. 1695 Woodward Nat. Hist. Earth iv. (1723) 239 An Account of the mineral Juyces in the Earth. 1842 J. Aiton Dom. Econ. (1857) 171 So that the juice may run from the pig-sty down upon the dry coal ashes.

4. a. In figurative uses: usually denoting the essence or 'spirit' of something, in which its characteristic qualities are found, or which renders it useful, agreeable, or interesting.

c 1380 Wyclif Serm. Sel. Wks. II. 67 þo prestis þat geten out juys of Goddis word. 1553 T. Wilson Rhet. (1580) 172 An oration is made to seme right excellent by the kinde self, by the colour and iuice of speeche. 1642 Rogers Naaman 127 The very spirit and roote of bitternesse, which giveth joice and nourishment to all branches. 1790 Burke Fr. Rev. 18 A theory, pickled in the preserving juices of pulpit eloquence. 1895 Gladstone in Evang. Mag. Jan., The juice and sap of the Evangelical teaching..I mean by its juice and sap, the positive and not the negative part of its teaching.

†**b.** The emoluments or profits of a profession or office. *Obs. colloq.*

c 1523 Latimer Let. to Baynton in Foxe A. & M. (1583) 1740 If I would..gather up my ioyse, as wee call it, warely and narrowly, and yet neyther preache for it in mine owne Cure nor yet otherwhere. 1609 Sir E. Hoby Let. to Mr. T. H. 23 That the parochial endowments..are..too little, to afford sufficient ioyce to those infinite superficiall students.

c. Political influence (exercised by or on behalf of criminals); money paid to obtain immunity from prosecution, or lent at a usurious rate of interest, or the interest thus extorted; money acquired by corruption, gambling, or threats. Also *attrib. U.S.*

1935 A. J. Pollock Underworld Speaks 65/1 Juice, corrupt influence (shake-down) for protection to operate unlawfully. 1951 [see ice sb. 4 e]. 1961 Chicago Daily Tribune 12 Aug. 1 William ('Action') Jackson..a 'juice man' (loan collector) for syndicate hoodlum bosses. 1962 A. Buchwald How Much is that in Dollars? 75 'Well, use some juice,' Mr. Cahn said. 'Juice' is a Hollywood expression which means influence. 1963 P. Wyden Hired Killers xii. 196 'Juice'—usurious interest of up to twenty per cent—was known to fester at the root of some of these assassinations. The juice racket has been flourishing for decades. 1964 [see Cosa Nostra]. 1968 N.Y. Times 9 June 1, 29 At least two murders and perhaps more have been connected to the loan shark, or 'juice' racket, as it is called here, as well as beatings and threats. 1969 Time 11 July 24 This Las Vegas is..a venal demi-monde in which the greatest compliment that can be paid a man is to say that he has 'juice' (influence in the right places). 1970 E. R. Johnson God Keepers (1971) xiv. 146 Vito Lucchese was involved in the case and..he had a certain amount of juice around the city. 1971 Ink 12 June 14/2 His high-paid whizkid managers weren't whizzing too well so he went after some extra juice.

†**5.** Broth. [rendering L. *jūs.*] *Obs. rare.*

1388 Wyclif Isa. lxv. 4 It is a puple..which eten swynes fleisch, and vnhooli iwisch [v.rr. iwce, iuyshe, iwissh, wisch; 1382 broth].

6. *attrib.* and *Comb.*, as ***juice-drop***; ***juice-drained***, ***-squirting*** adjs.; ***juice-head*** *slang*, an alcoholic; ***juice-joint*** *N. Amer. slang*, a bar, club, or stall serving either alcoholic or non-alcoholic liquor.

1800 Lamb Let. to Manning in Talfourd Lett. (1837) I. 190 The 'Falstaff's Letters' are a bundle of the sharpest, queerest, profoundest humours, of any these *juice-drained latter times have spawned. a 1847 Eliza Cook Harvest Song iv, Rich and bursting *juice-drops run On the vineyard earth in streams. 1955 S. Whitmore Solo 247 The *juiceheads..got so fractured [i.e. drunk] that they wouldn't show up for a date. 1967 New Yorker 9 Sept. 41 If anybody wanted to get stoned the guy who owned the pad made them go up on the roof. Juice-heads drank Red Mountain. 1969 A. H. Cain Young People & Drugs 159 Juice head, one whose hang-up is booze; an alcoholic. 1927 K. Nicholson Barker 149 *Juice joint, soft drink stand. 1932 Evening Sun (Baltimore) 9 Dec. 31/4 Juice-joint, speakeasy. 1958 G. Lea Somewhere there's Music iv. 35 Six lonely nights a week in a juice joint. 1960 Wentworth & Flexner Dict. Amer. Slang 298/2 Juice-joint. 1. A soft-drink tent, stand, booth, or concession. Carnival and circus use. 2. A speakeasy; a bar or nightclub. Orig. 1920 use. 1970 C. Major Dict. Afro-Amer. Slang 72 Juice joint, tavern, bar, cabaret. 1895 Daily News 21 Sept. 6/1 A..tobacco-chewing, *juice-squirting, tippling Westerner.

juice, *v.* [f. prec. sb.] **1.** *trans.* To moisten or suffuse with juice. *rare.*

1639 Fuller Holy War iii. xxxi. 164 Some gallants..count all conquests drie meat which are not juyced with bloud. 1884 Q. Victoria More Leaves 109, I drove off..to see them 'juice the sheep'. Ibid., 'Juicing the sheep'..a large sort of trough filled with liquid tobacco and soap, and into this the sheep were dipped one after the other.

2. To animate, liven *up*, inspire. *slang.*

1964 Time 23 Oct. 61 A thing like that can really juice you up. 1972 J. Mills Report to Commissioner 259 The departmental surgeon asked Jackson if he wanted him to give Lockley a shot of something, he meant juice him up a little, keep him from passing out.

juice, obs. var. GISE *v.*; obs. f. JOIST.

juiced (dʒuːst), *a.* [f. JUICE *sb.* + -ED[2].]

1. In combination: Having juice (of a specified quality).

1592 Shaks. Rom. & Jul. ii. iii. 8 With balefull weedes, and precious Iuiced flowers. 1626 Bacon Sylva §508 The Coloured [Berries] are more juyced and courser juyced. 1832 Tennyson Lotos-Eaters 78 The full-juiced apple, waxing over-mellow.

2. Drunk. Also const. *up. slang.*

1946 C. Himes Black on Black 260 She was an old wino used to come there every night and get juiced up. 1955 D. W. Maurer in Publ. Amer. Dial. Soc. xxiv. x. 170 Men sufficiently juiced up to be robbed without much interference. 1956 B. Holiday Lady sings Blues (1973) ii. 17 The doctor said if her man had even come to enough to raise the window and let in some air he could have saved her. But he was too juiced even for that. 1968 A. Young in A. Chapman New Black Voices (1972) 149 Chicken Hawk and Wine, well-juiced, eased quietly up the back steps. 1969 Time 24 Oct. 70 Later Marvin apologized: 'I'm sorry I was so rotten this afternoon. I was a little juiced.' 1971 'S. Ransome' Trap 6 (1972) xiii. 147 He was sitting at the bar brooding over a drink—not making any trouble, not getting juiced up.

juiceful ('dʒuːsfʊl), *a. rare.* [f. JUICE *sb.* + -FUL.] Full of juice; juicy; succulent.

1619 W. Whately God's Husb. i. (1622) 139 A most sappy and iuycefull Vine. 1630 Drayton Noah's Flood 49 Simples had that power,..they so juiceful were. 1647 Trapp Comm. Matt. xxi. 20.

juice-harp. Corrupted form of JEWS' HARP.

1942 Berrey & Van den Bark Amer. Thes. Slang §577/22 Jews'-harp, jaw-harp, juice-harp. 1950 Blesh & Janis They all played Ragtime (1958) vi. 109 The childhood band he led, consisting of two tin whistles, jew's-harp ('juice-harp'), and triangle, was a country rag band. 1959 M. Stearns in M. T. Williams Art of Jazz (1960) ii. 9 Sonny Terry listened to his father's harmonica and 'juice' harp. 1968 Publ. Amer. Dial. Soc. xlix. 15 The decline of juice harp and jew's harp and the students' use of mouth harp.

juiceless ('dʒuːslɪs), *a.* [f. + -LESS.] Devoid or deprived of juice; dry; dried up.

1602 Marston Antonio's Rev. Prol., Snarling gusts nibble the juyceles leaves. 1684 T. Burnet The. Earth i. 190 The earth..by that time was more barren and juiceless..than ours is now. 1746 R. James Introd. Moufet's Health's Improv. 8 To render juiceless the Membranes, Tendons, Cartilages, and Bones of Animals. 1830 Lindley Nat. Syst. Bot. 235 Fruit drupaceous, juiceless, with several cells.

b. *fig.* Devoid of interest; insipid, 'dry'.

1620 E. Blount Horae Subs. 204 The Epitome, which is for the most part a iuycelesse Narration. 1883 American VI. 29 The juiceless remarks of these good men. 1889 Home Missionary (N.Y.) Nov. 316 Those who suppose that life on the frontier is juiceless.

juicer ('dʒuːsə(r)). [f. JUICE *sb.* + -ER[1].]

1. An electrician. *slang.* (Cf. JUICE *sb.* 1 d.)

1928 Amer. Speech III. 366 'Juicers' have a most juicy vocabulary of their own. Thanks to them Hollywood has 'kliegs' (klieg lights). 1934 Tit-Bits 31 Mar. 12/2 Here are some more studio terms. 'Juicers' are electricians. 1950 B. Schulberg Disenchanted (1951) i. 11 Assistant directors, cutters, bit players, second cameramen, sound men, juicers, grips, special effects men, Hollywood's exclusive proletariat. 1957 V. J. Kehoe Technique Film & Television Make-up i. 18 He directs the..juicers to place the lights in the most effective positions.

2. An appliance used to extract juice from fruit and vegetables.

1938 Cooperative Distributors Catal. in Amer. Speech (1942) XVII. 272/1 A well constructed juicer for oranges. 1945 Archit. Rev. XCVII. 152 (caption) The 'Dazey' super juicer..in aluminium. 1961 Listener 31 Aug. 331/2 Self-contained grinders, liquidizers, juicers and meat mincers are also made. 1972 New York 1 May 27/2 Juicers—used to extract the juice of fresh vegetables and fruits.

3. An alcoholic. *U.S. slang.*

1967 New Yorker 13 May 40 The difference between the juicers and the heads is that the juicers sometimes get a little obstreperous but the heads go sit quietly in a corner someplace. 1970 Ibid. 28 Feb. 31/1 'Forget him, he's catatonic.' 'Forget him, he's a juicer.'

juicily ('dʒuːsɪlɪ), *adv. slang.* [f. JUICY *a.* + -LY[2].] **a.** Excellently, vigorously, well. **b.** Suggestively.

1916 E. F. Benson David Blaize vi. 118 [He] hit it juicily to square leg. 1927 Wodehouse in Sunday Express 18 Oct. 9 Abstemious cove though I am as a general thing..on this occasion..I had been doing myself rather juicily. 1969 Daily Tel. 3 Dec. 13/8 The hand-outs asked juicily whether the girls who took on these jobs were really on the first step to the harem and white slavery.

juiciness ('dʒuːsɪnɪs). [f. JUICY *a.* + -NESS.] The quality of being juicy; succulence. Also *fig.*

1611 Cotgr., Humidité,..sappinesse, iuycinesse, wetnesse, waterishnesse. 1643 T. Goodwin Trial Christian's Growth 16 Christ begins to shoot some sap of his Spirit into their hearts..stirring up some juicenesse of affections. 1801 W. Taylor in Monthly Mag. XI. 648 Herder [is remarked] for the many-flavoured juiciness of his style. 1858 Hawthorne Fr. & It. Jrnls. I. 260 A fossilized city..without enough life or juiciness in it to be susceptible of decay.

juicy ('dʒuːsɪ), *a.* [f. JUICE *sb.* + -Y.]

1. a. Full of or abounding in juice; succulent.

c 1430 Lydg. Min. Poems (Percy Soc.) 54 Now wesseil N. unto thi Iousy pate, Unthrift and thou to-gidre be mett. 1552 Huloet, Iuycy, or full of iuyce,..succulentus. 1620 Venner Via Recta vii. 113 The iuycie substance of the Pomegranet is wholsome. 1641 Milton Animadv. i. Wks. (1851) 195 Those hydropick humours not discernable at first from a fair and juicy fleshinesse of body. 1697 Dryden Virg. Past. vii. 80 Nor with'ring Vines their juicy Vintage yield. 1714 Gay Trivia ii. 434 Blue plumbs and juicy pears augment his gain. 1860 Tyndall Glac. 86 The mutton..became more tender and juicy.

b. Of weather: Rainy, wet, soaking. *colloq.*

1837–40 Haliburton Clockm. (1862) 497 The weather..has been considerable juicy here lately. 1868 Helps Realmah xvii. (1876) 497 It rained incessantly..A juicy day in the country promotes meditation of the most serious kind. 1893 Outing (U.S.) XXII. 139/1 We began the juiciest ride on record. How it rained!

2. *fig.* **a.** Rich in wealth, fit to be 'sucked' (quot. 1621); of rich intellectual quality, full of interest (the opposite of 'dry'). *colloq.*

1621 Sanderson Serm. 1 Cor. vii. 24 ¶28 Those parcel-gallants that have..no other use of their wits, but to distil a kind of maintenance from juycy heirs and flush novices by play. 1838 Darwin Let. to Lyell in Life & Lett. (1887) I. 292 You have contrived to make it quite 'juicy', as we used to say as children of a good story. 1870 Lowell Among my Bks. Ser. i. (1873) 30 His own style, juicy with proverbial phrases. 1894 Academy 85/3 His 'juicy' way of teaching (if we may be pardoned for a convenient Americanism).

b. In the slang of art criticism: Having a rich colouring suggestive of a moist surface.

1897 Daily News 24 Mar. 3/2 A fine bit of juicy landscape and rich colour. 1898 Mag. Art Feb. 196 The colouring is warm, rich, and juicy; the handling very rapid.

c. Suggestive, esp. in a sexual way; piquant, racy, sensational. *colloq.*

1883 J. Greenwood Odd People 59 'Let me play you a tune, then,' said the frightened lad... 'All right, then. Play us something juicy,' exclaimed the ruffian. 1908 Kipling Lett. of Travel (1920) 153 They interpolated no juicy anecdotes of murder or theft among their acquaintance. 1920 S. Lewis Main St. ix. 102 The gang..gathered in a snickering knot to listen to the 'juicy stories'. 1923 A. Bennett Riceyman Steps i. ii. 4 Accounts of bloody crimes and juicy sexual irregularities. 1929 [see duck soup s.v. DUCK sb.[1] 12]. 1953 [see gang-bang s.v. GANG sb.[1] 12]. 1958 B. Nichols Sweet & Twenties 106 Extracting what he was pleased to call 'the juicy bits'. 1965 'O. Mills' Dusty Death xix. 177 'Aren't you going to give us a look at it?' 'Not this one, no. Far, far too juicy.' 1972 J. McClure Caterpillar Cop xiii. 218 His parents sound the sort who'd run a mile before they'd say the word 'sex'. They wouldn't have any juicy books in the house either.

d. Excellent, vigorous, first-rate; serious; profitable.

1916 E. F. Benson David Blaize vi. 119 It didn't often happen that the first ball of an innings was slogged for six. Juicy hit, too! 1922 G. Ade Let. 8 Mar. (1973) 80 The author who has only a few stories ready to market can see no prospect of juicy returns. 1934 Time & Tide 8 Sept. 1122/2 But still, with this juicy price in prospect, the shrewd professionals are hesitant. 1948 Partridge Dict. Forces' Slang 104 Juicy, (of targets) easy, or well worth the trouble of destroying. 1962 Times 18 Oct. 6/3, I have been thinking of some very juicy ways of how we can use the South Carriage Drive in one of the royal parks.

juik(e, **Juil**, **juip(e**, obs. ff. JOUK, JULY, JUPE.

juis, obs. form of JUICE; variant of JUISE *Obs.*

†**juise.** *Obs.* Forms: α. 4 iuise, iuwise, -yse, 4–5 iuyse, iewise, -yse, 5 iewesse, iuwesse, iwyse. β. 4

iuis, iuwys, iewis, 5 iewys, iewes. [a. OF. *juise*, by suffix-exchange for *juice*, ad. L. *jūdicium* judgement; a later and further analogically altered OF. form was *juis*. (See -ISE, and Schwan *Gramm. Altfranz.* (1893) §72. 1, and Anm. 2.)] Judgement, doom; a judicial sentence, or its execution; penalty.

α. [1292 BRITTON I. xx. §1 Quels del counte cleyment.. juyse de pillori ou de tumberel.] 1303 R. BRUNNE *Handl. Synne* 7795 Satan comaundede for hys seruyse He shulde be put to hys Iuwyse. *c* 1350 *Usages Winchester* in *Eng. Gilds* 355 Whanne þe ferþyng-lof is in defawte of wyȝte ouer þre shyllynges, þe bakere shal bere þe juwyse of þe town. 1390 GOWER *Conf.* I. 38 Every man schal thanne arise To Joie or elles to Juise. *c* 1425 *St. Christina* viii. in *Anglia* VIII. 122/41 Whelis in þe whiche þeues were wonte to haue her iewesse. *c* 1460 SIR R. ROS *La Belle Dame sans Merci* 622 And be nat deed, ne put to no Iuyse. [1626 COCKERAM (ed. 2), *Iewise*, .. also reward by reuenge.]

β. 1303 R. BRUNNE *Handl. Synne* 6777 Noȝt for þy þe leste of þys, Myȝt brynge a man to iuwys. 1340 HAMPOLE *Pr. Consc.* 6106 Þe day of iugements and of Iuwys. 13.. *E.E. Allit. P.* C. 224 Þenne nas.. counsel non oþer, Bot Ionas into his Iuis Iugge bylyue. 1399 LANGL. *Rich. Redeles* III. 341 Þer nas.. ne Iuge, ne Iustice þat Iewis durste hem deme. 1480 CAXTON *Chron. Eng.* cxcviii, Ye shull be honged by reson, but the kyng hath foryeue you that Iewes.

b. *transf.* The instrument of penalty; the gibbet, the cross.

c 1320 R. BRUNNE *Medit* 577 For cryste bereþ hys owne Iuwyse, Y fynde nat þat þe þeues ded þe same wyse. [1623 COCKERAM, *Iewise*, a gallowes or Gibbet.]

ju-jitsu (ˌdʒuːˈdʒɪtsuː). Also formerly jiu-jitsu, -jutsu, ju-jitzu, -jutsu; and as one unhyphenated word. [ad. Jap. *jūjutsu*, f. *jū* (Chinese *jou*: see JUDO) + *jutsu* (Chinese *shu*, *shut* art, science).] A Japanese system of wrestling and physical training, characterized by the use of certain techniques and holds to overcome an adversary. Cf. JUDO. Also *attrib.*

1875 *Japan Mail* 10 Mar. 133/1 *Jiu-jitsu* (wrestling) is also taught, but not much practised by gentlemen. 1889 [see JUDO]. 1891 L. HEARN *Let.* Nov. in E. Bisland *Life & Lett. L. Hearn* (1906) II. 70 A building in which jū-jutsu is taught by Mr. Kano. 1893 —— *Let.* 13 Oct. (1910) 183, I am working out an essay—a philosophical essay on 'Jiujutsu'. 1895 J. INOUYE *Wrestlers & Wrestling* 3 These methods were adopted and extensively practised by *Samurai*, and were finally developed into what is now known as *Jujitsu*. 1905 *Daily Chron.* 21 Feb. 7/4 Their gymnasium is often visited by ju-jitsu wrestlers. 1910 H. G. WELLS *Hist. Mr. Polly* vii. 238 A combination of something romantic called 'Ju-jitsu' and.. the 'Police Grip'. 1925 N. VENNER *Imperfect Impostor* xvi, Jos Polkins.. enwrapped him in a benevolent jiu jitsu grip that left him powerless to move. 1946 R. BENEDICT *Chrysanthemum & Sword* (1947) xii. 277 He perfects himself in jujitsu or sword play.

fig. 1906 R. WHITEING *Ring in New* xxix. 206 To lay him flat on his back by a sort of intellectual jiu-jitsu. 1928 F. ROMER *Numbers Up!* 11 'Revenge?'.. 'nothing of the kind. I shall merely practise Moral Jiu-jitsu.' 1942 WYNDHAM LEWIS *Let.* 15 July (1963) 334 There are omens of promise —in much that Mr. Roosevelt has done, or in the splendid massive jujitzu of the Russians. 1965 K. BRIGGS in Battiscombe & Laski *Chapelet for C. Yonge* 25 Practising a kind of spiritual ju-jitsu, in which by falling with the misfortune you overcome it.

Hence **ju-ˈjitsu** *v. trans.*, to overcome by means of ju-jitsu; **ju-ˈjitsian**, **ju-ˈjitsuist**, one who teaches or practises ju-jitsu.

1905 D. SLADEN *Playing Game* II. iv. 202 The wiry little Japanese having Jujitsu'd the three biggest men on the Russian flag-ship. 1905 HANCOCK & HIGASHI *Compl. Kano Jiu-Jitsu* p. v, Those famous *jiu-jitsians*, Hoshino and Tsutsumi. 1905 *Westm. Gaz.* 23 Nov. 4/2 He.. issued.. a challenge to all jiu-jitsuists of the world. 1928 *Observer* 4 Mar. 15/2 They seem to me to put up no fight at all, and to be very easily ju-jitsued by the Japanese servants.

‖**ju-ju**[1], **juju** (ˈdʒuːdʒuː). [W. African; generally thought to be a. F. *joujou* toy, plaything.] An object of any kind superstitiously venerated by West African native peoples, and used as a charm, amulet, or means of protection; a fetish. Also, the supernatural or magical power attributed to such objects, or the system of observances connected therewith; also, a ban or interdiction effected by means of such an object (corresponding to the Polynesian *taboo*).

1894 AMANDA SMITH *Autobiog.* xxvii. 215 The first thing we saw on entering was.. a large ju-ju, the head of an elephant. 1897 MARY KINGSLEY *W. Africa* ii. 38, I shall never forget one tribe I was once among, who, whenever I sat down on one of their benches, used to smash eggs round me for ju-ju. *Ibid.* xi. 239 The extinguisher-shaped juju filled with medicine and made of iron is against drowning —the red juju is 'for keep foot in path'. *Ibid.* 396 There is always a fire-doctor, who by means of ju-ju, backed as ju-ju often is by sound common sense and local knowledge, decides which is the proper day. 1897 A. BOISRAGON *The Benin Massacre* ii. 29 The Niger Coast.. is still the land of Juju. Juju here is everything, religion, superstition, custom, anything. 1900 H. BINDLOSS *Ainslie's Ju-Ju* i. 10 The black head-men have got the fetish priests to put a 'Ju-Ju' or taboo on the water-ways.

b. *attrib.*

1897 MARY KINGSLEY *W. Africa* 19 These other charms are supplied by the ju-ju priests. *Ibid.* 278 They desired to collect the head of a gentleman for their Ju Ju house. 1897 REAR-ADM. RAWSON *Disp.* in *Daily News* 8 May 7/3 In the main ju-ju compound the smell of human blood was indescribably sickening. 1897 A. BOISRAGON *The Benin Massacre* ii. 30 Nothing seemed to be celebrated properly in this Juju land unless it was accompanied by the death of some unfortunates.

Hence **ˈjujuism**, the system of beliefs and observances connected with jujus, juju religion; **ˈjujuist**, an observer of or believer in this.

1897 MARY KINGSLEY *W. Africa* 455 He is regarded by good sound jujuists as leading an irregular and dissipated life. 1899 —— *W. Afr. Stud.* App. i. 559 Not only is the teaching of Christianity opposed to Ju-Juism, but it is also opposed to the whole fabric of native customs other than Ju-Juism.

ju-ju[2] (ˈdʒuːdʒuː). *slang.* [redupl. form of MARI)JU(ANA.] A marijuana cigarette. Also *attrib.*

1940 R. CHANDLER *Farewell, my Lovely* xi. 83 'I knew a guy once who smoked ju-jus,' she said. 'Three high balls and three sticks of tea and it took a pipe wrench to get him off the chandelier.' 1963 N. FREELING *Because of Cats* x. 163 'He had juju cigarettes too; like Russians, with a big mouth piece and pretty loose...' 'The jujus are—you feel very clever.'

jujube (ˈdʒuːdʒuːb). Also 7 jejub, 7-8 jujub, 8 jujeb. Also 4-8 in L. form jujuba. [a. F. *jujube*, or med.L. (and Sp.) *jujuba*, a much altered form of Gr. ζίζυφον. In cl.Latin, this was duly reproduced in Columella and Palladius by *zizyphum* (the fruit), *zizyphus* (the tree); these appear to have passed in late pop. L. and Romanic through *zizipum*, *-us*, *zizupum*, *-us* (cf. *Appendix Probi*, ed. Heræus, 1899, '*zizipus* non *zizupus*'), **zizubum*, *-us*, to **zuzubo*, *zuzibo*, whence (with the frequent change of *z* to *j*, and use of the neuter-pl. in *-a* in fruit-names as a fem. sing.) Old Aretine dial. of It. *giuggebo* (= *jujebo*) the tree, *giuggeba* the fruit, and med.L. *jujuba*, F. *jujube*. The forms *jujeb* and *jejub* come nearer to Old Aretine *giuggeba* and vulgar L. *zizubum*.]

1. An edible berry-like drupe, the fruit of various species of *Zizyphus* (N.O. *Rhamnaceæ*).

c 1400 *Lanfranc's Cirurg.* 74 Take a potel of water of barly clensid iiij. ȝ. Iuiube, sebesten ana .ȝ. fs. [etc.]. *Ibid.* 182 Colre schal be purgid in þis maner.. sebesten .xv. in noumbre, iuiubas .xx. [etc.]. *c* 1550 LLOYD *Treas. Health* lxxxiii. (1585) Y ij b, Take of Violettes .ȝiii, of iuiubes, and of the iiii. cold sedes before namyd. 1586 BAKER *Traheron's Vigo* 441 Iuiube are fruits, which the Latines call *zizipha*. 1600 J. PORY tr. *Leo's Africa* I. 22 Damson-trees, sallowes by the waters side, and trees of Iuiubas. 1605 TIMME *Quersit.* III. 181 Take.. of alkakeng berries, twenty in number; of iuiubes six couple. 1641 FRENCH *Distill.* ii. (1651) 57 Adde .. the best Jujubs, the kernels taken out, half a pound. 1664 POWER *Exp. Philos.* I. 18 The Mites, in Jujubes and Sebesten's. *Ibid.* 19 Jejub's and Sebesten's. 1712 tr. *Pomet's Hist. Drugs* I. 134 The Jujubs are the Fruit of a Tree which grows commonly in Provence. 1718 QUINCY *Compl. Disp.* 134 Jujebs are an Italian Fruit. 1835 THIRLWALL *Greece* I. vi. 212 The Lotus-eaters—whose favourite fruit still grows, under the name of the jujube, on the same coast. 1858 CARPENTER *Veg. Phys.* §557 This.. known under the name of the jujube, is a favorite dessert in Italy and Spain.

b. Any of the species of *Zizyphus* which produce this fruit, as *Z. vulgaris* of the Mediterranean countries, *Z. Jujuba* of China, *Z. Lotus* of N. Africa.

1562 TURNER *Herbal* II. 37 a, Cypros is a tre in Egypt wyth leaues of iuiuba. 1682 WHELER *Journ. Greece* I. 73 A kind of Juiuba, whose leaves shine like silver. 1759 tr. *Adanson's Voy. Senegal* 49 He was sitting on the sand, under the shade of a jujube. 1885 LADY BRASSEY *The Trades* 99 Over our heads waved.. cocoanuts, breadfruits, jujubes, and hundreds of others.

2. A lozenge, made of gum-arabic, gelatin, etc., flavoured with, or in imitation of, the fruit (sense 1).

1835 [Remembered by Rev. C. B. Mount]. 1858 SIMMONDS *Dict. Trade* 210/2 The term jujube is.. very generally applied by chemists and confectioners to a thickened mucilaginous lozenge. 1866 *Treas. Bot.* 1251/2 The dried fruits.. are given to allay cough. The lozenges sold as Jujubes are commonly but erroneously said to be flavoured with them.

3. *attrib.* and *Comb.*, as **jujube paste**, a jelly made from jujubes, or a confection flavoured with, or in imitation of, them; **jujube-plum** = sense 1; **jujube-tree** = sense 1 b.

1858 HOGG *Veget. Kingd.* 235 *Jujube paste.. should consist of gum arabic and sugar dissolved in a decoction of this fruit.. but as made in this country the fruit forms no part of the ingredient. 1884 J. PAYNE *1001 Nights* VIII. 70 *Jujube-plums of various colours. 1548 TURNER *Names of Herbes* 82 Zizypha.. maye be called in english *Iuiuba tree. 1578 LYTE *Dodoens* VI. xlix. 722 This tree is called.. in English, the Iuiub tree. 1879 SIR E. ARNOLD *Lt. Asia* v. (1881) 110 Under dark mangoes and the jujube-trees. 1887 MOLONEY *Foresty W. Afr.* 299 Jujube or Ber Tree.. A loosely-branched tree or shrub, ten to forty feet high.

juke (dʒuːk), *sb. slang* (orig. *U.S.*). Also jook, jouk. [Prob. f. Gullah *juke*, *joog* disorderly, wicked, of W. Afr. origin; cf. Wolof *dzug* to live wickedly.] **1.** A roadhouse or brothel; *spec.* a cheap roadside establishment providing food and drinks, and music for dancing. In full *juke-house*, *juke-joint*.

1935 Z. N. HURSTON *Mules & Men* I. iii. 82 They talked and told strong stories of Ella, Wall, East Coast Mary,.. and lesser jook lights around whom the glory of Polk County surged. 1936 *Scribner's Mag.* Dec. 27/2 Jim's daddy owned the General Store and a nigger jook. 1937 in *Florida Rev.* (1938) Spring 28/1 Back yonder a 'juke' was a place, usually a shack somewhere off the road, where a field negro could go for a snort of moonshine. *Ibid.*, There were negro juke-joints as far back as I can remember. 1941 J. FAULKNER *Men Working* ii. 39 The glow from the lights of the jook house at the lake appeared above the trees. 1956 S. LONGSTREET *Real Jazz* xviii. 151 *Juke* from juke box came from juke house —which was once a whorehouse. 1958 P. OLIVER in P. Gammond *Decca Bk. Jazz* i. 23 The crude, wood-frame dance-halls called 'jooks' (or jukes). 1964 *Amer. Folk Music Occasional* I. 93 You go into the bars and the juke joints and you ask around. 1968 *Blues Unlimited* Nov. 6 Now Ike told Dave that he cut Elmore's 'Dust my broom' at a Canton juke-joint. 1971 *Black World* June 72/2 Had done sent Lueta and Carol Ann to every juke joint in Greenwood askin bout you.

2. juke-box (occas. **juke-organ**), a machine that automatically plays selected gramophone records when a coin is inserted; also *ellipt.* as *juke*. Also *attrib.*, *transf.*, and *fig.*

1937 in *Florida Rev.* (1938) Spring 25/3 The screeching of the 'jook' organ. 1939 *Time* 27 Nov. 56/2 Glenn Miller attributes his crescendo to the 'juke-box', which retails recorded music at 5¢ a shot in bars, restaurants and small roadside dance joints. *Ibid.* 25 Dec. 3/1 To the Florida Man such an instrument is a jook organ. 1942 D. POWELL *Time to be Born* (1943) x. 241 Corinne put a quarter in the juke-box to play 'Let's Be Buddies' five times. 1944 AUDEN *For Time Being* (1945) 65 War has become Like a juke-box tune that we dare not stop. 1947 *Gramophone* Dec. 95/1 It is the Petrillo thesis that records which are played in juke-boxes and broadcast over the radio.. are monsters which have threatened the musicians' very existence. 1947 [see JIVE *v.* 2 a]. 1954 *Archit. Rev.* CXVI. 92/2 The stupefying juke-box façade of the Wertheim project. 1959 C. MACINNES *Absolute Beginners* 83 See all the kids jam-packed in there beside the jukes? 1961 L. MUMFORD *City in Hist.* viii. 224 Pennsylvania Station in New York retains this noble quality —or did until that structure was converted.. into a vast jukebox. 1968 J. WINEARLS *Mod. Dance* (ed. 2) vi. 143 There emerges a constant from which the immediate must not depart. Our teenage Juke Box Juries demonstrate this ably. 1973 C. BONINGTON *Next Horizon* xvii. 244 A coffee bar for teenagers, complete with juke box. 1973 *Nation Rev.* (Melbourne) 31 Aug. 1453/4 The America they traverse, of fibro suburbs and prison farms and jukebox bars, is.. correctly and compassionately observed.

juke (dʒuːk), *v. slang* (orig. *U.S.*). Also jook, jouk. [Cf. prec.] *intr.* To dance, esp. at a juke-joint or to the music of a juke-box (see also quot. 1958). So ˈ**juking** *vbl. sb.*

1933 W. ROLAND (*title of disc*) Jookit Jookit. 1937 C. R. COOPER *Here's to Crime* ix. 190 In the 'jukin' joints' there is, of course, the prime requisite of liquor. 1941 *Amer. Speech* XVI. 319/2 'Let's jouk' is an invitation to dance, but 'let's go joukin'' is a request for a date. 1958 T. WILLIAMS *Orpheus Descending* I. 28 I'd like to go out jooking with you tonight. .. That's where you get in a car and drink a little and drive a little and stop and dance a little to a juke box. 1960 *20th Cent.* Aug. 144 But living, in these terms, is reduced to jooking. 1967 *Daily Tel.* 15 May 12/8 To juke also came to mean to dance and to go pub-crawling.

juke, obs. form of JOUK; variant of JUCK.

jukskei (ˈjœːkskeɪ). *S. Afr.* Also jeuk skei, jukschei. Pl. jukskeie, jukskeis. [Afrikaans, f. *juk* yoke + *skei* pin, SKEY *sb.*[2]; cf. *yoke-skey*.]

1. A yoke-skey.

1822 W. J. BURCHELL *Trav. S. Afr.* I. viii. 151 The yokes are straight, and pierced with two pair of mortices to receive the *jukschei* which fits in loosely, and answer to what in English husbandry are called the *bows*. 1871 LORD & BAINES *Shifts & Expedients Camp Life* ix. 452 Near each end are two mortices.. through which to pass the 'jeuk skeis', or yoke keys, which keep it in place on the neck of the ox. 1971 *Evening Post Mag.* (Port Elizabeth) 27 Feb. 2 A stinkwood yoke, with 'jukskeis', serves as a hatstand.

2. A quoits-like game; the bottle-shaped 'quoit' used in this game.

[1934 C. P. SWART *Africanderisms* (M.A. Thesis, S. Afr.), *Jukskeigooi*, a game, very similar to quoits, played by the Boers, a skey being used instead of the customary circular ring.] 1942 *Cape Times* 10 Nov. 4/2 Saturday's Jukskei results were as expected. 1947 *Ibid.* 21 Apr. 7 The jukskeis were brought.. by Mr. Tom Naude. 1950 S. DE WET *Hour of Breath* ix. 69 In the late afternoon we used to play Jukskei on the river bank below our houses. 1956 *Cape Times* 26 Jan. 1/1 A few minutes after throwing about six practice *jukskeie* at the Newlands circus grounds.. Mr. P. A. Meiring.. dropped dead. 1971 *Progress* (Cape Town) May 2/4 No one has challenged us at jukskei.

†**jul.** *Obs. rare.* [ad. L. *iūlus* IULUS, formerly sometimes written *jūlus*.] A catkin.

1725 BRADLEY *Fam. Dict.* s.v. *Ozier*, Seeds contained in their Juls or Catkins.

julaceous (dʒuːˈleɪʃəs), *a. Bot. rare.* [f. L. *jūl-us* (see prec.) + -ACEOUS.]

1880 GRAY *Struct. Bot.* (ed. 6) 417/2 *Julaceous*, catkinlike, amentaceous.

juldie, var. JILDI.

Jule, obs. form of JULY.

julep (ˈdʒuːlɛp). Forms: 5-7 iulep, -lip, 6 iulepe, -lepp, 6-7 -leb, -lap, 7 jewlep, -lip, julipe, -loup, 7-8 julip, -lap, 7- julep. [a. F. *julep* (14th c. in Hatz.-Darm.), in Pr. *julep*, Sp. and Pg. *julepe*, It. *giulebbe*, *giulebbo*, med.L. *julapium*, ad. Arab.

julāb, a. Pers. *gul-āb* rose-water, f. *gul* rose + *āb* water.]

1. A sweet drink prepared in different ways; often, simply a liquid sweetened with syrup or sugar, and used as a vehicle for medicine; sometimes, a medicated drink used as a demulcent, 'comforting', or gently stimulating mixture.

c **1400** *Lanfranc's Cirurg.* 76 To ȝeue him in þe bigynnynge Iulep—þat is a sirup maad oonly of water & of sugre. **1543** TRAHERON *Vigo's Chirurg.* v. ii. 163 Vse them with a iuleb of vyolettes. *c* **1550** LLOYD *Treas. Health* (1585) F ij, Iuleb is a cleare potyon made of dyuerse waters and suger. **1597–8** BP. HALL *Sat.* II. iv. 27 The wholesome julap, whose receat Might his diseases lingring force defeat. **1619** S. JEROME *Origen's Repent.* in Farr *S.P. Jas. I* (1848) 245 It surmounts all juloups. *a* **1625** FLETCHER *Hum. Lieut.* II. ii, The gentleman no doubt will fall to his jewlips. **1673** E. BROWN *Trav. Germ.*, etc. (1677) 152 We drank frozen Julebs. **1710** STEELE *Tatler* No. 174 ¶3 Gruels and Julps. **1754–64** SMELLIE *Midwif.* II. 180 By this julap a slight fever was produced. **1789** W. BUCHAN *Dom. Med.* (1790) 679 Cordial Julep..Expectorating Julep..Musk Julep. **1859** W. S. COLEMAN *Woodlands* (1866) 62 A very soft well-flavoured pleasant saccharine julep.

b. *transf.* and *fig.* Something to cool or assuage the heat of passion, etc.

1624 MASSINGER *Parl. Love* III. i, She is no fit electuary for a doctor: A coarser julap may well cool his worship. **1652** T. PHILPOT *Commend. Verses Benlowes' Theoph.*, These pages do dispence A Julep, which so charms the Itch of sense That [etc.]. **1659** CHAMBERLAYNE *Pharonnida* (N.), Whose heat, not all The jewleps of their tears [could quench].

2. *U.S.* A mixture of brandy, whisky, or other spirit, with sugar and ice and some flavouring, usually mint.

1804 *Europ. Mag.* XLV. 18/1 The first thing he did on getting out of bed was to call for a Julep; and I..date my own love of whiskey from mixing and tasting my young master's juleps. **1845** DE QUINCEY *Nat. Temper. Movem.* Wks. 1862 XI. 172 An appetite for brandy, for slings, for juleps. **1891** B. HARTE *Family Tasajara* II. 48 A dusty drive with a julep at the end of it.

Comb. **1859** CORNWALLIS *New World* I. 76 San Francisco was all bustle and illumination, with glittering bars filled with julep-drinkers.

†**julet.** *Obs. rare.* A coin; = JULIO.

1632 LITHGOW *Trav.* I. 38 A Crowne the dyet for each of us, being ten Julets or five shillings starling.

Julian ('dʒuːlɪən), *a.* [ad. L. *Jūliān-us* of or pertaining to *Julius*; in mod.F. *julien.*] Pertaining to Julius Cæsar: used in *Chronol.* in connexion with the reform of the calendar instituted by him in the year 46 B.C.

Julian account, = 'old style' (see STYLE); ***Julian calendar*** (see CALENDAR *sb.* 1); ***Julian epoch, era***, the time from which the Julian calendar date (46 B.C.); ***Julian period***, a period of 7980 Julian years, proposed by Joseph Scaliger in 1582 as a universal standard of comparison of chronology, consisting of the product of the numbers of years in the solar and lunar cycles and the cycle of the indiction (28 × 19 × 15); ***Julian year***, a year of the Julian calendar, or the average year (= 365¼ days) of that calendar.

1592 DEE *Compend. Rehears.* (Chetham Soc.) 22 Upon the Gregorian publishing of a Reformation of the vulgar Julian yeare. **1594** BLUNDEVIL *Exerc.* III. I. xli. (1636) 355 The Julian yeere is that which wee use at this present day. **1613** PURCHAS *Pilgrimage* (1614) 168 After Scaliger..this yeare 1612 is the 1614 of Christ, of the world 5461..of the Iulian Period 6325. **1677** W. HUBBARD *Narrative* (1865) I. 179 This 26 of March being the first Day of the Week, as the first of the Year after our Julian account. **1709** STEELE *Tatler* No. 39 ¶2 The Gregorian Computation was the most regular, as being Eleven Days before the Julian. **1816** PLAYFAIR *Nat. Phil.* II. 110 In the year 1582, the Julian year had fallen nearly 10 days..behind the sun. **1899** W. M. RAMSAY in *Expositor* Nov. 433 The Julian reform of the calendar had come into force in the beginning of 45 B.C.

'Julianist. *Ch. Hist.* [See -IST.] One of a sect of Monophysites, named after their leader Julian, bishop of Halicarnassus early in the 6th century.

1698 FRYER *Acc. E. India & P.* 272 Preposterous Julian birth, from whom came the Julianists. **1874** J. H. BLUNT *Dict. Sects* (1886) 38/2 Called, in Armenia and its neighbourhood, Julianists.

julienite ('dʒuːlɪənaɪt, juːlɪ'eɪnaɪt). *Min.* [ad. Flemish *juliëniet* (A. Schoep 1928, in *Natuurwet. Tijdschr.* X. 58), f. the name of Henri *Julien* (d. 1920), Belgian geologist: see -ITE[1].] A hydrous thiocyanate of sodium and cobalt, $Na_2Co(SCN)_4.8H_2O$, that occurs as minute blue needles and has been made artificially; orig. wrongly regarded as a cobalt chloro-nitrate.

1928 *Mineral. Mag.* XXI. 567 Julienite... Hydrated chloro-nitrate of cobalt as minute blue needles, presumably hexagonal and isomorphous with buttgenbachite: from Katanga. **1954** *Mineral Abstr.* XII. 337 Needles of julienite .., prepared by digesting Na-Co nitrite with an aqueous solution of Na sulphocyanide, are tetragonal. **1969** I. KOSTOV *Mineral.* 117 The interesting mineral julienite..is obtained during the exogenetic decomposition of primary cobalt sulphides.

‖**julienne** (ʒyljɛn). [F. (1722 in Hatz.-Darm.), f. *Jules* or *Julien* the proper name.]

1. A soup made of various vegetables, esp. carrots, chopped and cooked in meat broth. Also *attrib.*

1841 THACKERAY *Mem. Gormandizing* Misc. Ess., etc. (1885) 390 The best part of a pint of julienne..is very well for a man who has only one dish besides to devour. **1883** *Fisheries Exhib. Catal.* 63 Uncompressed Julienne Vegetables..Samples of Compressed Mixed Vegetables and Julienne as..food for fishermen.

2. Applied *attrib.* or as *adj.* to vegetables cut into small thin strips.

1889 A. B. MARSHALL *Cookery Bk.* ii. 31 *Julienne Garnish.*—Peel and cut the vegetables, such as carrots, turnips, etc., into strips about an inch long. **1906** A. FILIPPINI *Internat. Cook Bk.* 228 Cut with a sharp knife—if no julienne-shaped potato cutter is at hand—into even julienne, match-like strips. **1920** [see *cornflakes* sb. pl. s.v. CORN *sb.*[1] 11]. **1971** *Salads* (Cordon Bleu Cookery School) 100/2 Wash, peel and slice celeriac, cut across into julienne strips (about 1½–2 inches long).

Juliet ('dʒuːlɪət, -ɛt). [Female personal name (F. *Juliette*, It. *Giulietta*), dim. of *Julia.*] ***Juliet cap*** (see quot. 1957).

1909 *Westm. Gaz.* 9 Feb. 8/3 Their Juliet caps were composed of violets. **1930** *Daily Tel.* 7 Apr. 7/6 The 'Juliet' cap idea is to be found in the little theatre hats worn abroad. **1957** M. B. PICKEN *Fashion Dict.* 49/2 *Juliet cap*, small, round cap of wide, open mesh, usually decorated with pearls or other jewels, similar to that worn on the stage by Shakespeare's Juliet. Worn chiefly for evening. **1973** *Times* 15 Nov. 6/3 The bridesmaid..wore a pinafore dress and a jewelled Juliet cap.

†**ju'liferous,** *a. Obs.* [f. L. *jūlus* (prop. *iūlus*) catkin (see IULUS) + -FEROUS.] Bearing catkins, amentiferous.

1668 WILKINS *Real Char.* II. iv. 118 Whether such Pods are Catkins; called Juliferous trees. **1769** J. WALLIS *Nat. Hist. Northumbld.* I. ix. 282 The short juliferous spikes are of a straw-colour.

So **'juliform** *a.*, having the form of a catkin or of the millipedes of the genus *Iulus*.

1882 in OGILVIE (Annandale), and in other mod. Dicts.

†**julio.** *Obs.* Also 6 in anglicized form **Iuly,** 7 (Italian) **giulio,** pl. **-ii,** 9 (Latin) **julius.** [a. It. *giulio* Julius.] A silver coin worth about sixpence, struck by Pope Julius II (1503–13), formerly current in Italy.

1547 BOORDE *Introd. Knowl.* xxiii. (1870) 179 In syluer they [Italians] haue Iulys,—a Iuly is worthe .v.d. sterlynge. **1592** WOTTON *Let. to Ld. Zouch* 8 May in *Reliq.* (1685) 657 The *Julios* of Bolognia are disvalued two *quatrini*. **1612** WEBSTER *White Devil* Wks. (Rtldg.) 23/1 He..(to my acquaintance) Receiv'd in dowry with you not one julio. **1696** tr. *Du Mont's Voy. Levant* IX. 109 The Expence of his Table was fix'd at Two Julio's a Day. **1718** BERKELEY *Jrnl. Tour Italy* 13 Apr., Wks. 1871 IV. 593 A fellow extorted a Julio with his gun. **1852** W. ANDERSON *Expos. Popery* (1878) 136 The theft of a julius—less than sixpence.

julip(e, -loup, obs. forms of JULEP.

July (dʒuː'laɪ). Forms: α. 3 **Iul,** 3–5 **Iule,** 4–5 **Iuil, Iuyl,** 5–6 **Iuyll(e.** β. (2 *gen.* **Iulies**), 3, 6–7 **Iulie,** 6 **Iulii,** 5–7 **Iuly,** 7– **July.** [In OE. in L. form. In ME. *Jule, Juil,* a. OF. *Jule, Juil, Julle*:—L. *Jūlium* acc. of *Jūlius*; also *Julie*, a. AF. *Julie*, ad. L. *Jūlius*. The latter form was accented '*July* as late as Dr. Johnson's time; it is still ('dʒølɪ) in Southern Sc.; the modern Eng. pronunciation is abnormal and unexplained.]

The seventh month of the year, so named after Julius Cæsar.

[*c* **1050** *Byrhtferth's Handboc* in *Anglia* (1885) VIII. 316 Iulius on þam forman dæge anre nihte eald. *a* **1100** *Gerefa* ibid. (1886) IX. 261 Me mæiȝ in Maio and Junio and Julio on sumera fealȝian.]

α. **1297** R. GLOUC. (Rolls) 8221 In þe bigininge of Iul þis bataile was ido. *c* **1386** CHAUCER *Merch. T.* 889 Er þat dayes eighte Were passed er the Monthe of Iuyl bifille. **1398** TREVISA *Barth. De P.R.* XIX. lxxix. (1495) 910 Out take two monthes Iule and Decembre. **1480** CAXTON *Chron. Eng.* ccxxiv. 229 In the monethes of Iuyn and Iuyll next folowyng. **1502** *Bill* in *Exch. Acc.*, *Q.R.* Bundle 415 No. 7 (1) Made yͤ xixth day of Iuylle the xvijth yeare [etc.].

β. [*a* **1154** *O.E. Chron.* an. 1115 (Laud MS.) Æfter þan syððan innon Iulies monðe hider into lande com.] *c* **1290** *Beket* 2441 in *S. Eng. Leg.* I. 176 It was in þe monþe of Iulie. **1483** *Cath. Angl.* 199/1 Iuly (*A.* Iule), *julius, quidam mensis.* *a* **1548** HALL *Chron., Hen. VI* 166 The xiij. day of Iulij. *a* **1599** SPENSER *F.Q.* VII. vii. 36 Then came hot Iuly boyling like to fire, That all his garments he had cast away. **1606** HOLLAND *Sueton.* Suppl. Begin. Cæsar ¶iv b, Cæsar..was borne..vpon the fourth day before the Ides of Quintilis, which moneth, after his death, was by virtue of the Law Antonia called for that cause, Iulie. *c* **1689** *Popish Pol. Unmaskt* 112 in *3rd Coll. Poems* 23/2 In May some odd Intelligence come newly Won't suffer you to hold them until July. **1755–73** JOHNSON *Dict.*, Ju'ly. **1888** MRS. M'CANN *Poet. Wks.* 235 Scarce has July with frigid visage flown [in Australia]. **1895** *Daily News* 1 Aug. 5/4 There have been..only two Julys with a larger aggregate of sunshine.

julyflower, perversion of GILLYFLOWER.

jum, júm: see JOOM.

jumar ('dʒuːmə(r)). *Mountaineering.* [Swiss name.] A clip which when attached to a fixed rope automatically tightens when weight is applied and relaxes when it is removed, thus facilitating the climbing of the rope; also, a climb using jumars. Hence as *v. intr.*, to climb with the aid of jumars; **'jumaring** *vbl. sb.*, the action of so doing.

1966 *Climbers' Club Jrnl.* 77 Somebody spotted him dangling from his Jumars, half-way down one of the fixed ropes. **1968** P. CREW *Encycl. Dict. Mountaineering* 73/1 Jumars are the most effective device for prusiking, but they have the disadvantage of not working well on iced ropes. **1969** *Sunday Times* (Colour Suppl.) 16 Feb. 38/3, I dreamed that I was on the ropes setting off for the summit by myself and I was jumaring all night without getting anywhere. **1971** C. BONINGTON *Annapurna South Face* viii. 90 Once the ropes are in place, the climbers no longer move roped together, but simply clip onto the rope, using on the upward sections a device called a jumar clamp. This is a metal handle, with a knurled lever which is fitted over the rope. It works on a ratchet principle, sliding easily up the rope, but biting into it when put under tension. *Ibid.* xi. 125 This was the first time that this type of free jumaring had ever been necessary at this altitude in the Himalayas. **1971** D. HASTON in *Ibid.* xvii. 214 The sun was two hours away from the gully when we started the upward jumar. **1972** —— *In High Places* 2 Onward, outward, creeping on jumars and rimed ropes. It is cold... Dachstein-mitted hands freeze in jumar clutch. *Ibid.* ix. 104 The hook fitted, a quick move, and I was up. Mick jumared and I pushed on again. **1973** C. BONINGTON *Next Horizon* ix. 141 Later, I learned that an essential precaution for any jumaring is to tie a knot in the rope, so that if the jumars do slip on the rope, you don't slide straight off the end.

jumart ('dʒuːmɑːt). Also 7 **gimar.** [a. F. *jumart*, formerly *jumare*, ad. mod.Pr. *gemerre, gemarre*, of uncertain origin.] A hybrid animal, erroneously believed to be the offspring of a bull and a mare or she-ass, or of a horse or ass and a cow.

1690 LOCKE *Hum. Und.* III. v. §23 We have Reason to think this not impossible, since Mules, and Gimars [Wks. 1714 I. 206 jumarts], the one from the mixture of an Horse, and an Ass, the other from the mixture of a Bull, and a Mare, are so frequent in the World. **1809** *Phil. Trans.* XCIX. 397 A jumart..the pretended offspring of the mare and the bull.

jumbal, jumble ('dʒʌmb(ə)l). Also 7–8 **jumball.** [perh. orig. the same as GIMBAL 1, GIMMAL 1.] A kind of fine sweet cake or biscuit, formerly often made up in the form of rings or rolls; now in U.S. 'a thin crisp cake, composed of flour, sugar, butter, and eggs, flavored with lemon-peel or sweet almonds' (*Cent. Dict.*).

1615 MARKHAM *Eng. Housew.* II. ii. (1660) 97 To make the best Jumbals, take the whites of three Eggs..a little milke and a pound of fine wheat flowre and suger together finely sifted, and a few Anniseeds..make them in what forms you please, and bake them in a soft oven upon white papers. **1678** PHILLIPS (ed. 4), *Jumbals*, a sort of Sugared past, wreathed into knots. **1694** MOTTEUX *Rabelais* v. xxvii, O' Tuesdays, they us'd to twist store of Holy-bread..Jumbals and Biscuits. **1769** MRS. RAFFALD *Eng. Housekpr.* (1778) 274 To make Barbadoes Jumballs. **1860** O. W. HOLMES *Elsie V.* vii. (1891) 110 There were..hearts and rounds, and jumbles, which playful youth slip over the forefinger before spoiling their annular outline. **1892** *Mrs. Beeton's Bk. Househ. Managem.* xl. 1125 California jumbles... sugar,.. butter,..flour,..grated lemon-peel..whites of 4 eggs. **1923** CHESTERTON *Fancies versus Fads* ii. 21 It involved eating jumbles (a brown flexible cake now almost gone from us). **1974** *Daily Tel.* 29 Apr. 16/7 Miss Lane mentions the absence from the glossary of such terms as cracknells, jumbells, trencher-bread, etc.

jumbee, variant of JAMBEE.

jumbee, jumbi, jumbie, varr. JUMBY.

jumble ('dʒʌmb(ə)l), *v.* Also 6 **iomble, -byll, ioomble, iumbyll, (gomble),** (*Sc.* 5–6 **iummil,** *pa. t.* **iwmlit;** 9 **jummle,** *pa. t.* **jummilt**). [Known only from 16th c., and without cognate words. Prob. onomatopœic: cf. *bumble, fumble, mumble, rumble, stumble, tumble.*]

1. *intr.* To move about in mingled disorder; to flounder about in tumultuous confusion.

a **1529** SKELTON *Sp. Parrot* 419 To iumbyll, to stombyll, to tumbyll down like folys. **1532** MORE *Confut. Tindale* Wks. 604/2 If..Tindalles horse..falle downe in the myre.. and his maister and he lye together and iumble..till some good felowe helpe them vp. **1598** SYLVESTER *Du Bartas* II. i. III. *Furies* 271 In that fearfull Cave They [Furies] jumble, tumble, rumble, rage and rave. **1628** FORD *Lover's Mel.* III. iii, Now! my braines are a Iumbling. **1858** CARLYLE *Fredk. Gt.* II. xiv, His Germans..left Wenzel to jumble about in his native Bohemian element, as King there.

†**b.** *fig.* To be or become mixed up or confounded; to come *together* as by shaking up. *Obs.*

a **1550** *Christis Kirke Gr.* xvi, He wes nocht wyss With sic jangleurs to jummil. **1785** COWPER *Lett.* 15 Jan., But we shall jumble together again.

2. *trans.* To mingle *together* or mix *up* in confusion or disorder; to muddle, confuse.

1542 BOORDE *Dyetary* xii. (1870) 266 If they dyd knowe what they dyd gomble togyther without trewe compoundynge. *a* **1556** CRANMER *Wks.* (Parker Soc.) I. 19 You confound and jumble so together the natural members of Christ's body in the sacrament. **1600** HOLLAND *Livy* XXXVII. xxiii. 957 Now the reereward had no roume left them toward the land: and thus..they hastily were jumbled together. **1665** GLANVILL *Def. Vain Dogm.* 39 That the divided Letters of an Alphabet should be accidentally jumbled into an elegant and polite Discourse. **1779** WESLEY *Hymns* Pref. 4 The hymns are not carelessly jumbled together. **1793** BURKE *Rem. Policy Allies* Wks. 1842 I. 605 To jumble the innocent and guilty into one mass, by a general indemnity. **1855** SINGLETON *Virgil* I. Pref. 6

Jumbling up one with the other. **1868** FREEMAN *Norm. Conq.* II. App. 562 William so jumbles together the events of 1051 and of 1055.

b. with *compl.* To put, bring, cast (*in*, *out*, *down*, etc.) in clumsy confusion or disorder. ? *Obs.*

c **1555** HARPSFIELD *Divorce Hen. VIII* (Camden) 168 Therefore he jumbleth in a blind false reason. *a* **1652** J. SMITH *Sel. Disc.* iv. 72 Having once jumbled and crouded in a new kind of being. **1670–98** LASSELS *Italy* I. 47 Making a man go before each horse, lest they should jumble one-another down. **1743** H. WALPOLE *Lett. H. Mann* (1834) I. 235, I should not like having my things jumbled out of one ship into another.

c. To make *up* in a confused or random manner.

1572 BUCHANAN *Detect. Marie* in *Collect. Mary Q. Scots* (1727) II. 84 Then that all Men micht understand quhat it was that thay socht.. thay jumbil up mariages. **1673** BLOUNT *World Errors* To Rdr., A Bookseller.. employs some mercenary to jumble up another like book out of this. **1769** BURKE *Late St. Nation* Wks. II. 14 Some strange disposition of the mind jumbled up of presumption and despair. **1812** H. & J. SMITH *Rej. Addr.* xiv, Call'd by a Frenchified word.. that's jumbled of antique and new.

3. To stir up (a liquid, etc.) so as to mix the ingredients, or render turbid; to agitate, shake up, give a shaking or jolting to; hence *colloq.* to take for a drive. ? *Obs.*

1616 SURFL. & MARKH. *Country Farme* 63 The Horse.. [would have] that which is puddly and troubled.. if so be he iumble the water with his foote before he drinke. **1667** PEPYS *Diary* 24 Oct., That I might go abroad with my wife, who was not well, only to jumble her. **1693** SIR T. P. BLOUNT *Nat. Hist.* 82 They bruise and jumble it [Indigo] in the Water, till the Leaf.. becomes like a Kind of thick Mud. **1743–4** MRS. DELANY *Autobiog. & Corr.* 6 Mar. (1861) II. 275 You should give the child meat now:—and make him to be jumbled about a good deal. **1799** M. UNDERWOOD *Diseases Childr.* (ed. 4) III. 160 As though infants must necessarily be jumbled in a cradle like travellers in a mail-coach. **1813** SHELLEY in Dowden *Life* (1887) I. 317 You will.. be better able to see the country than when jumbled in a chaise.

absol. *a* **1568** *Wyf of Auchtirmwchty* 67 Than to the kyrn that he did stoure, And jwmlit at it quhill he swatt.

b. *intr.* To travel with shaking or jolting.

1748 LADY LUXBOROUGH *Lett. to Shenstone* (1775) 36, I don't love to jumble in a post-chaise alone. **1824** SCOTT *St. Ronan's* v, Trotting Nelly.. jumbled off with her cart. **1843** LEFEVRE *Life Trav. Phys.* I. I. x. 233 Little four-wheeled narrow carts in which they jumble to the fair.

4. *trans.* To put into mental confusion; to confuse, bewilder, 'muddle'.

1668 H. MORE *Div. Dial.* III. xl. (1713) 288 My mind has been so jumbled betwixt Time and Eternity, that I think I can speak sense in neither. **1724** RAMSAY *Vision* x, Oppression dois the judgment jumble. **1858–61** RAMSAY *Remin.* vi. (1870) 233, I like thae sermons best that jumbles the joodgment and confoonds the sense.

†**5.** *intr.* To make a confused or rumbling noise; to play discordantly or noisily on an instrument, to strum. Cf. JAMBLE, JANGLE. *Obs.*

1530 PALSGR. 595/2, I iumbyll, I make a noyse by removyng of heavy thynges. *Ibid.*, They have iombled so ouer my heed to nyght, I could nat slepe. *Ibid.*, To here him iombyll on a lute. **1566** DRANT *Horace, Sat.* III. Biij, A boysterous basse he bounsed out, and jumbled on his stringes. **1658** WILLSFORD *Secrets Nat.* 131 If their guts jumble.. very much. **1741** W. GOSTLING in *Phil. Trans.* XLI. 873 Like the Reports of Cannon (which the Jumbling of my Sashes prevented my distinguishing). **1805** A. WILSON in *Poems & Lit. Prose* (1876) II. 141 Jumbling cowbells speak some cottage near.

†**6. a.** *intr.* To have carnal intercourse. **b.** *trans.* To know carnally. *Obs.*

1582 STANYHURST *Æneis* IV. (Arb.) 100 Dido and thee Troian captayne doo iumble in one den. **1611** COTGR., *Toquer*,.. to iumble a woman. *a* **1693** URQUHART *Rabelais* III. xxv. 202 The Lackeys.. jumbled.. his Wife.

jumble ('dʒʌmb(ə)l), *sb.*[1] [f. JUMBLE *v.*]

1. a. A confused or disorderly mixture or assemblage, a medley; also, disorder, muddle.

1661 GLANVILL *Van. Dogm.* xviii, Had the world been coagmented from that supposed fortuitous jumble. **1678** CUDWORTH *Intell. Syst.* I. iv. §36. 551 There is a confused Jumble of Created, and Vncreated Beings together. **1711** LADY M. W. MONTAGU *Lett., to Mrs. Hewet* (1887) I. 33, I have the oddest jumble of disagreeable things in my head that ever plagued poor mortals. **1751** CAMBRIDGE *Scribleriad* II. 184 *note*, The Macaronian is.. a jumble of words of different languages, with words of the vulgar tongue latinized, and latin words modernized. **1882** FLOYER *Baluchistan* 60 The scenery.. is.. a reckless jumble of hills and rocks of every imaginable shape, size, and colour.

b. *collect. sing.* Articles for a jumble-sale; also, a jumble-sale or sales. *colloq.*

1931 *Times* 16 Mar. 1/3 Maternity Hospital, holding annual Jumble Sale.—Please deluge us with jumble. **1932** *Daily Tel.* 17 Mar. 1/2 Do please help us with our Easter Jumble on March 18th by sending anything saleable, old or new. **1962** [see FÊTE *sb.* 1 b]. **1966** *Listener* 20 Oct. 570/1 This feat of administration, this orgy of jumble and whist. **1973** J. BURROWS *Like Evening Gone* ii. 27 When did the scouts have their jumble? I'd have thought every gloryhole.. was empty.

2. A shock, shaking, or jolting; *colloq.*, a ride in a carriage (with reference to the shaking experienced).

1674 N. FAIRFAX *Bulk & Selv.* 151 The Shows or Phænomena of the world.. even the worst of its shocks and jumbles. **1800** MRS. HERVEY *Mourtray Fam.* II. 139 Mamma has lent me her carriage to go a shopping, so I wish you would take a jumble with me. **1823** MAD. D'ARBLAY *Lett.* 29 Feb., Going out.. either in brisk walks.. or in brisk jumbles in the carriage. **1851** J. COLQUHOUN *Moor & Loch* (1880) I. 262 The jumble of the sea made shooting uncertain. **1855** CHAMIER *My Travels* I. x. 56 The carriage ought to be strong to bear the jolts and jumbles to which it is subjected.

3. *Comb.*, as **jumble-letters**, letters of a word thrown into disorder in order to exercise ingenuity in their proper re-arrangement; **jumble-sale**, a sale of miscellaneous cheap or second-hand articles at a charitable bazaar or the like; **jumble-shop**, a shop where very miscellaneous goods are sold.

1893 Q. [COUCH] *Delect. Duchy* 287 Trudgeon that used to keep the jumble-shop across the water. **1898** *Westm. Gaz.* 12 Nov. 2/3 Some cheap articles for a jumble sale. **1899** *Daily News* 19 July 7/5 Competitions for money prizes for properly placing jumble letters.

Jumble ('dʒʌmb(ə)l), *sb.*[2] *slang.* [Corruption of JOHN BULL.] A Black man's nickname for a white man. Also *attrib.* or as *adj.*

1957 C. MACINNES *City of Spades* I. iii. 17 'You're a Jumble, man... That's what we call you... It's cheeky, perhaps, but not so very insulting.' 'May I enquire how it is spelt?' 'J-o-h-n-b-u-l-l.' '.. But pronounced as you pronounce it?' 'Yes: Jumble.' **1957** *Listener* 12 Sept. 402/1 Jumble, a happy corruption of John Bull, is the Englishman's nickname in the mouths of the thousands of Africans and West Indians who have flocked to London since the war. *Ibid.*, The Jumble capital. *Ibid.*, An alien and uncomprehending Jumble world. **1961** M. DICKENS *Heart of London* II. 190 Get all you can out of the Jumbles. *Ibid.* III. 294 He feeling his way about the Jumbles, he got no time to worry about Trinidad.

jumble, variant of JUMBAL.

'**jumble-bead.** [Alteration of *jumby-bead* (see JUMBY b), prob. after *mumble.*] The parti-coloured seed of the jequirity.

1855 R. G. MAYNE *Expos. Lex. Med. Sci.* (1860) 554/2 *Jumble beads*, an irreverent name for the seeds of the *Abrus precatorius*, from the purpose they are applied to in forming rosaries. **1887** [see JEQUIRITY]. **1951** A. NELSON *Medical Bot.* xxiii. 456 The seeds [of *Abrus precatorius*] may be referred to as Abrus, Jequirity, Jumble beads or Prayer beads, and are known to contain two poisonous principles.

jumbled ('dʒʌmb(ə)ld), *ppl. a.* [f. JUMBLE *v.* + -ED[1].] Mixed up in disorder, confused, muddled up, etc.: see the verb. (In quot. 1611, strummed.)

1611 *Coryat's Crudities* Panegyr. Verses, Like to the lacks of iumbled virginall. **1689** PRIOR *Ep. to F. Shepherd* 73 That jumbled words, if Fortune throw 'em, Shall well as Dryden form a poem. **1739** CIBBER *Apol.* (1756) II. 119 These jumbled ideas had some shadow of meaning. **1859** TENNYSON *Vivien* 345 The jumbled rubbish of a dream.

jumblement ('dʒʌmb(ə)lmənt). [f. as prec. + -MENT.] The action of jumbling or fact of being jumbled; confused mixture.

1706 J. HANCOCK in *Boyle Lect.* (1739) II. 210 Shall we think this noble frame.. was made by a casual jumblement of atoms? **1767** H. BROOKE *Fool of Qual.* (1792) IV. xvii. 75 A jumblement of intention. **1843** MRS. CARLYLE *Lett.* I. 271 Solitude has such a power of blending, past, present, and future,.. all into one confused jumblement.

'**jumbler.** *rare.* [f. as prec. + -ER.] One who jumbles; in quot. 1618, A strumpet.

1611 COTGR., *Barbouilleur*, a disorderly iumbler, hudler, mingler. **1618** FIELD *Amends for Ladies* II. i. in Hazl. *Dodsley* X. 111 She has been as sound a jumbler as e'er paid for't.

jumbling ('dʒʌmblɪŋ), *vbl. sb.* [f. as prec. + -ING[1].] The action of the verb JUMBLE, q.v.

1562 J. HEYWOOD *Epigr.* (1867) 217 Such rollyng, such rumblyng, ioysting and iumbling. **1600** SURFLET *Countrie Farme* I. iv. 10 The iumbling and stirring of the water will rectifie it. **1852** B. THACKRAH *Art Change-ringing* 7–8 As a true compass makes the ringing pleasant and harmonious, so.. the want of it produces those 'jumblings'.. that destroy all music. **1871** DIXON *Tower* IV. xviii. 190 A masterpiece of jumbling and confusion.

'**jumbling,** *ppl. a.* [f. as prec. + -ING[2].] That jumbles, in senses of the verb.

1678 NORRIS *Coll. Misc.* (1687) 172 As ridiculous.. as to think to write streight in a jumbling Coach. **1748** MRS. DELANY *Autobiog. & Corr.* (1861) II. 489 Very jumbling roads. **1845** R. BROWN in *Mem.* iii. (1866) 56 A rumbling, tumbling, jumbling sea.

Hence '**jumblingly**, *adv.*

1820 WAINWRIGHT *Ess. & Crit.* (1880) 71 And Jarvey jolts Janus jumblingly over the stones.

jumbly ('dʒʌmblɪ), *a.* Also *Sc.* **jumly**. [f. JUMBLE *sb.*[1] + -Y.]

1. Confused, chaotic, in a jumble.

1865 CARLYLE *Fredk. Gt.* xv. x. (1872) VI. 67 Gessler, noticing the jumbly condition of those Austrian battalions.. dashes through. **1896** B. SPENCER in *Rep. Horn Exped.* I. 103 A series of low jumbly hills.

2. Turbid, 'drumly'. *Sc.*

? **18..** *The Water o Gamery* ix. in Child *Ballads* VII. ccxv F. (1890) 182/2 [A stream] That was baith black and jumly. **1896** J. LUMSDEN *Poems* 13 Jumly broo Of melted ice.

jumbo ('dʒʌmbəʊ). [Of uncertain origin: possibly the second element in Mumbo Jumbo, a name applied (in English since the 18th c.) to a West African divinity or bogy.]

1. a. A big clumsy person, animal, or thing; popularized, esp., as the individual name of an elephant, famous for its size, in the London Zoological Gardens, subsequently sold in Feb. 1882 to Barnum; whence applied to an individual that is big of its kind or to a person of great skill or success.

1823 J. BADCOCK (J. Bee) *Dict. Turf*, *Jumbo*, a clumsy or unwieldy fellow. **1883** *Harper's Mag.* Oct. 705/2 It is the Jumbo of crickets, and just as black. **18..** *Music & Drama* X. ii. 9 (Cent.) The combined successes of that jumbo of successful business men. **1892** KIPLING & BALESTIER *Naulahka* 212 She's a Jumbo at theory, but weak in practice.

b. *attrib.* used to distinguish things of very large size, as ***jumbo straw-plait***, a plait of an inch wide. Also *Comb.*, as **jumboburger** *U.S.*, a large hamburger; **jumbo jet**, a large jet aeroplane with a seating capacity of several hundred passengers; **jumbo-size(d)** *a.*, of a large size.

1897 *Sears, Roebuck Catal.* 12/2 Peaches, Jumbo California, halves. **1900** *Westm. Gaz.* 27 Nov. 7/2 Near 250 yards of dark blue and white 'jumbo' plait were used. **1916** *Amer. City* Apr. 373/1 Large jumbo peanuts were bought, instead of culls. **1940** S. LEWIS *Bethel Merriday* i. 19 The three children.. supped on a jumbo malted milk. **1949** *Sat. Even. Post* 2 Apr. 116/3 Davis.. is a jumbo-sized (six feet two, 202 pounds) man of forty-six. **1958** *Daily Express* 1 Apr. 1/4 You and your jumbo Martinis!! **1959** *Observer* 8 Nov. 3/5 We can expect the kind of hamburger proliferation that exists in America, with beefburgers, eggburgers, cheeseburgers, jumbo burgers, superior 'Hamburger Heavens'. **1960** *Guardian* 9 Sept. 8/4 The jumbo-sized plastic bone. **1964** *Punch* 15 July 79/3 The silly girl spends most of her time eating jumboburgers. **1964** *Economist* 19 Dec. 1317/2 Some.. airlines do not expect.. an American supersonic airliner ever to go into production. Jumbo-jets, with 500 seats and two decks,.. look much cheaper to fly. **1965** *Teacher's World* 18 June 5/4 The shelves of the local supermarket are full of 'king-sized', 'giant economy' and 'jumbo' packages. **1965** *Business Weekly* 25 Dec. 31 Nosing into the Jumbo jet race: Lockheed, Boeing and Douglas. **1968** 'R. RAINE' *Night of Hawk* xxvii. 126 The meal was avocado salad, a jumbo-size steak, and a mountain of ice cream. **1969** *Listener* 13 Nov. 683/3 They can replace two flights on conventional aircraft with a single jumbo jet flight. **1970** *Drum* (E. Afr. ed.) Feb. 31/3 This airport will be capable of handling jumbo jets and is ideally situated in the heart of the safari country. **1972** J. ROSSITER *Rope for General Dietz* iii. 34 The shrill rasping of a jumbo-size cicada.. woke me. **1973** *Sun* 18 Jan. 6 The Prime Minister handled his jumbo Press conference amid the splendour of Lancaster House with poise and style.

c. *Engin.* Any of various large types of equipment used in drilling, lifting, dumping, etc.

1908 *Sat. Even. Post* 7 Nov. 11/3 Nearest the portal was the 'jumbo', a great, movable platform through which the 'muckers' dumped their barrow-loads to cars beneath. **1909** WEBSTER, *Jumbo*,.. a large traveling carriage for transporting excavated material, as in tunnel driving. **1950** *Engineering* 10 Mar. 264/3 The method is well illustrated in the Stockholm tunnel, using a truck-mounted jumbo. **1951** *Ibid.* 12 Jan. 34/2 The concrete was placed from a travelling frame or 'jumbo', as it is termed in American practice. This straddled the pipe and travelled on rails laid in an excavated trench.

d. (See quot. 1948.)

1912 *Outing* Aug. 629/2 The pilot schooners when lying at their stations, the sail carried being jumbo or forestaysail, foresail, and reefed mainsail. **1916** F. W. WALLACE *Shack Locker* (1922) i. 22 Slack off that jumbo an' the foresheet! **1927** *Canad. Fisherman* 141/2 A gigantic sea boarded the vessel and broke about fifteen feet up the jumbo stay. **1932** J. BARBOUR *48 Days Adrift* vii. 94 'Hard, down hard,' I cried; 'haul over the jumbo sheet. If we are not careful we will all be lost this time.' **1948** R. DE KERCHOVE *Internat. Maritime Dict.* 377/1 *Jumbo* (U.S.). 1. The forestaysail on fore-and-aft-rigged vessels. 2. A triangular sail which sets, point downward, on the foreyard of a square-rigged vessel or a topsail schooner in place of the regular foresail. **1956** A. F. LOOMIS '*Hotspur' Story* x. 117 The weather looked a little threatening and I set the jumbo and storm jib.

e. Short for *jumbo jet*.

1966 *New Statesman* 22 Apr. 591/2 The competitors.. need only a small handful of jumbos.. on the popular long-distance routes. *Ibid.*, A rival jumbo designed by Douglas. **1971** *Daily Tel.* (Colour Suppl.) 8 Jan. 15/4 A collision between two jumbos on the approaches to Heathrow could produce a deathroll of thousands. **1972** H. OSBORNE *Pay-Day* III. xiii. 154 They can't get him on a plane before tonight. They want someone to go down on the Jumbo today. **1973** *Guardian* 12 Mar. 10/4 Jumbo-loads of Soviet immigrants. **1974** *Observer* (Colour Suppl.) 29 Sept. 65/1 The visitors who disembarked from our jumbo at Kai Tak Airport.

2. Trade-name for a shade of grey, like that of an elephant.

1882 *Philadelphia Even. Star* 2 May, 'Jumbo' is a new gray hue.

3. A board for raising cockles, etc. out of the sand.

1886 *Westmld. Gaz.* 18 Dec., A 'jumbo' was a piece of wood used for the purpose of raising cockles and other similar fish out of the sand.

Hence (from sense 1) **jumbo'esque** (whence **jumbo'esqueness**), '**jumboism**, **jumbo'mania**. *nonce-wds.*

1893 *Westm. Gaz.* 18 Mar. 4/1 A 'Jumboesque monster'—a machine 'in which the beauty of outline has been swallowed up in ponderosity. **1882** *Punch* 11 Mar. 113 If Nature to one of my stature Gave such.. Jumboesqueness.

1900 *Westm. Gaz.* 16 Aug. 7/1 Those who have a dislike of 'jumboism', whether in finance or otherwise. **1891** *Rev. of Rev.* 15 Sept. 289/2 The Musical Times' article on 'Jumbomania'. **1899** *Spectator* 21 Oct. 569/2 'Jumbomania', ..the worship of mammoth dimensions.

jumboize ('dʒʌmbəʊaɪz), *v.* [f. JUMBO + -IZE.] *trans.* To enlarge a ship, esp. a tanker, by inserting a new middle section between the bow and stern. So **'jumboized** *ppl. a.*; **'jumboizer**; **'jumboizing** *vbl. sb.*

1956 *N.Y. Times* 23 Dec. S11/7 (*heading*) Concern to build ten and 'jumboize' nine. *Ibid.*, 'Jumboizing' consists of building an entire new center section for a tanker. The existing vessel is then cut off at the bow and stern which are later joined to the new section. **1957** *Sun* (Baltimore) 4 Apr. 16 We're 'jumboizing' present tankers. *Ibid.*, First completed 'jumboized' oil tanker. **1957** *New Yorker* 14 Sept. 33/3 In language controls, the trend is toward bastardization, if you ask us, and we wish the National Association of Manufacturers would call in all the jumboizers and miniaturizationists and bang their heads together. **1961** *Economist* 28 Jan. 366/1 Conversions and jumboizing within 56 days. *Ibid.*, The Schlieker yard had 'jumboized' on the spot the T2 tanker *Kaposia*. **1973** *Daily Colonist* (Victoria, B.C.) 10 Feb. 25/2 Ferries on this route currently do not have the double kitchens of the jumboized ships on the Shwartz Bay–Tsawassen service.

jumboo, variant of JAMBO.

jumbuck ('dʒʌmbʌk). *Austral.* and *N.Z.* [Native Australian, with the forms *jimba*, *jombok*, *dombock*, *dumbog*; said to have meant orig. 'the white mist preceding a shower', to which a distant flock of sheep was likened by the natives: see Morris *Austral Eng.* s.v.] A name given by Australian and New Zealand aborigines to sheep; in frequent colloquial use among stock-keepers in the Bush.

1824 W. WALKER *Let.* 26 Jan. in W. S. Ramson *Austral. Eng.* (1966) vi. 107 They smacked their lips and stroked their breasts, 'boodjerry patta! murry boodjerry!—fat as jimbuck!!' i.e. good food, very good, fat as mutton. **1845** C. GRIFFITH *Pres. St. Pt. Phillip Distr. N.S.W.* 162 (Morris). **1855** W. RIDLEY in *Trans. Philol. Soc.* 77 (Morris) *Jimbugg*, a slang name for sheep, they sound *jimbŭ*. **1871** C. L. MONEY *Knocking about in N.Z.* i. 7 A pivot..shot the unsuspecting 'jumbucks' into the water below. **1889** *Pall Mall G.* 18 Feb., The process by which the 'jumbucks' are shorn. **1896** H. TICHBORNE *Noqu Talanoa: Stories S. Seas* 95 Our girls very often possess fathers who own considerable stretches of 'jumbuck' property. **1898** M. ROBERTS *Keeper of Waters* 136, I see this all white with cotton-bush, and it shall be white with jumbucks to eat it down. **1933** L. ACLAND in *Press* (Christchurch, N.Z.) 28 Oct. 17/7 *Jumbuck*, slang for sheep..has always been in common use here. **1934** [see GUTS *v.*]. **1967** *Sunday Mail Mag.* (Brisbane) 16 Apr. 2 The swagman who shoved a jumbuck in his tucker bag was stealing a sheep.

jumby ('dʒʌmbɪ). Chiefly *West Indies.* Also **jumbee, jumbi, jumbie, zumbi.** [ad. Kongo *zumbi* fetish.] A ghost or evil spirit among American and West Indian Blacks. Cf. ZOMBIE.

1871 C. KINGSLEY *At Last* II. x. 56 Out of the mud comes up—not jumbies, but—a multitude of small stones. **1876** R. F. BURTON *Two Trips Gorilla Land* II. 124 There was no danger of the Zumbi, or ghost. **1887** W. H. BENTLEY *Dict. & Gram. Kongo Lang.* 505 The fetish Zumbi is supposed to bring good luck with it. It sometimes consists of a bundle of charms, at others it is an image, or even an animal. **1891** 'J. EVELYN' *Baffled Vengeance* iv. 60 The 'jumbies' (evil spirits) that haunted the ill-omened spot. **1894** 'A. SPINNER' *Study in Colour* iv. 47 To tremble over the terrible tales of the Jumbi and Duppies, that..terrify belated travellers. **1918** C. W. BEEBE *Jungle Peace* (1919) vii. 138 Sam had formerly been a warden in the Georgetown jail, and rumour had it that he left because he saw 'jumbies' in the court where one hundred and nine men had been hanged. **1951** E. A. MITTELHOLZER *Shadows move among Them* I. ii. 18 A pencil drawing of an ugly face—the face of a jumbie as imagined by Berton. *Ibid.* II. ix. 239 Believe in fairies and ghosts and jumbies and goblins. **1955** *Caribbean Q.* IV. I. 32 Caribs.. delight in telling as a matter of fact how they met a certain 'jumby' in the road after dark. **1973** *Daily Tel.* (Colour Suppl.) 21 Sept. 25/3 To comb your hair at night is an open invitation for the Jumbies to call. (Jumbies are West Indian ghosts.)

b. *attrib.*, as **jumby-bead**, the hard seed of any of several West Indian plants; **jumby-bean** = *jumby-tree*; **jumby-bird**, a bird of ill omen, esp. an owl; **jumby-tree**, any of several West Indian trees, esp. the lead tree, *Leucæna glauca*.

1802 H. SWINBURNE *Let.* 17 Feb. in *Courts of Europe* (1841) II. 339, I gathered to-day, a handful of Jumbee beads. **1871** C. KINGSLEY *At Last* II. xiii. 197 Hedges of dwarf Erythrina, dotted with red jumby beads. *Ibid.* xvi. 276 The scarlet flowers of the Jumby-bead bush. **1934** J. RHYS *Voy. in Dark* I. vi. 66 The niggers say that jumbie-beads are lucky, don't they? **1956** *Caribbean Q.* IV. III. 198 They also sold charms made of 'Jumby beads' (*abrus precatorius* and allied species). **1920** BRITTON & MILLSPAUGH *Bahama Flora* 162 *Leucaena glauca*... Probably native of continental tropical America. Jumbie Bean. **1871** C. KINGSLEY *At Last* II. xiii. 206 The obnoxious bird was not an owl, but a large goat-sucker, a Nycteribius, I believe, who goes by the name of jumby-bird among the English Negros. **1893** A. NEWTON *Dict. Birds* II. 471 Jumby-bird, a Negro name for almost any kind that is of bad omen, but especially for an Owl. **1923** E. INGERSOLL *Birds in Legend* 168 The 'jumbie-bird', or 'big witch', of the West Indian region..is the dead-black ani, a kind of cuckoo. **1960** J. BOND *Birds W. Indies* 120 Barn Owl *Tyto alba.* Local names: Owl; Screech Owl; Night Owl; Death Owl; Death Bird; Jumbie Bird. **1928** M. SUMMERS *Vampire* 265 The occult silk-cotton tree (*bombax ceiba*, often known as the Devil's tree or Jumbie tree).

‖**jume** (dʒuːm). [Native name *jume*, *gume*.] A species of glasswort (*Salicornia*) found on the seacoast of South America, which on being burnt yields a large amount of carbonate of soda.

18.. J. BALL in *Jrnl. Linn. Soc.* XXI. 233 Gume. **1877** SCHNYDER *Contrib. Fl. Argent.* 28 *Jume*, native name for many Chenopodiaceous species growing in salt-marshes in Argentina. **1879** BEERBOHM *Patagonia* ii. 18 A straggling, stunted bush, the jume, which grows here in considerable quantities.

Jumeau ('dʒuːməʊ). [Proprietary name.] The name of Pierre François and Émile *Jumeau*, 19th-century French doll-makers, used to designate a doll manufactured at their establishment; freq. *attrib.*

[**1888** *Official Gaz.* (U.S. Patent Off.) 27 Nov. 950/2 Dolls. Emile Jumeau, Paris, France. Application filed Oct. 8, 1888. Used since 1840. 'The words "Bébé Jumeau".'.] **1897** *Pearson's Mag.* July 60/1 The Bébé Jumeau is known all over the world. *Ibid.* 65/1 The Jumeau dolls serve two purposes, the one being to amuse children and the other to instruct ladies..in the latest phases of Parisian fashion. **1951** E. ST. GEORGE *Dolls of Three Centuries* iii. 27 The Jumeau doll is still being made... The present day Jumeau bears little or no resemblance to the old, collector's Jumeau. **1962** G. WHITE *Dolls of World* 192 By 1862, the Jumeau dolls were quite famous; their well-modelled heads, waxen complexions, life-like eyes and movable joints attracted much attention. **1972** *National Observer* (U.S.) 27 May 9/4 (Advt.), Antique dolls, mint condition dressed and wigged. Guaranteed no reproductions. German or French, many rare French dolls, Jumeaus all sizes. **1973** *Times* 31 July 23/3 (*caption*) A late 19th century Jumeau doll, papier mâché with bisque head, height 20½ inches.

‖**jumelle** (dʒuː'mɛl, Fr. ʒymɛl), *a.* and *sb.* [a. F. sb. and adj. fem. (masc. *jumeau*), doublet of *gemeau*, *-elle*:—L. *gemellus*, dim. of *geminus* twin. Formerly naturalized; now an alien French word.]

†**A.** *adj.* Twinned or paired; made or shaped in couples or pairs, double. *Obs.*

c **1475** *Partenay* 1182 The yates Iumelles, mighty and strong. **1484** CAXTON *Fables of Poge* v, The whiche parte was iumelle that is to wete double. **1882** CUSSANS *Hand-bk. Her.* vii. (ed. 3) 116 A Gimmal or Jumelle Ring was formed of two flat hoops of gold, which fitted accurately within each other, and constituted but one ring.

B. *sb.* Applied to something which consists of a pair of things joined. **a.** A pair of opera-glasses. **b.** 'The side pieces of a loom in which the cylinders are fitted' (*Cent. Dict.* 1890).

1865 W. CORY *Lett. & Jrnls.* (1897) 163 My jumelles box made a pillow.

†**'jument.** *Obs.* [ad. L. *jūment-um* (contraction of *jugimentum*) yoke-beast, f. stem *jug-*, of *jungĕre* to join, *jugum* yoke. Cf. F. *jument*, in OF. beast of burden; now, mare.] A beast of burden, also a beast in general.

1382 WYCLIF *Gen.* i. 25 And God made beestis of the erthe aftir ther special kyndes, iumentis [Vulg. *jumenta*], and al the crepynge thing. —— *Acts* xxiii. 24 Make ȝe redy iumentis [*gloss* or hors]. **1491** CAXTON *Vitas Patr.* (W. de W. 1495) I. xxviii. 24 b/2 A yonge damoysell, the whiche bi arte magyk was conuerted in to a Iument or a mare. *c* **1510** BARCLAY *Mirr. Gd. Manners* (1570) D vj, Thy soule..hath shape and ymage of God omnipotent Thy body is mortall as beast or vile iument. **1621** BURTON *Anat. Mel.* I. ii. II. i, That men should feed on such a kinde of meat, Which very iuments would refuse to eat. **1638–48** G. DANIEL *Eclog.* i. 42 You can forsake the Citye to Converse With Earth and Iuments. *a* **1682** SIR T. BROWNE *Misc. Tracts* 32 Fit to fasten their Juments, and Beasts of labour unto them. **1816** *Gentl. Mag.* LXXXVI. I. 420 A jackass may be properly and lineally descended from Balaam's jument. **1820** *Ibid.* Apr. 311 *Jument.* This word..is in danger of being wholly lost. It means a beast of burden.

†**jumen'tarious,** *a.* *Obs. rare*⁻⁰. [f. L. *jūmentari-us*, f. *jūmentum*: see -ARIOUS.] Of or pertaining to juments (Blount *Glossogr.* 1656).

jumentous (dʒuː'mɛntəs), *a.* [f. L. *jūmentum* JUMENT + -OUS.] Resembling that of a horse, said of urine.

1846 G. E. DAY tr. *Simon's Anim. Chem.* II. 239 The urine presented this jumentous appearance for six days. **1887** *Syd. Soc. Lex.*, *Jumentous*, a term applied to urine which is high coloured, strong smelling, and turbid, like that of the horse.

jumma ('dʒʌmə). Also **jama, jummah.** [ad. Hind. *jama* collection, amount, account, a. Arab. *jama'* total, aggregate.] During British rule in India, the assessment for land revenue from an estate or division of country. So **jumma'bundi** [Pers.-Arab. *jama'bandī* (Hind. *bandī*, a. Pers. *bandi* a tie, band; Skr. *bandh* bind)], the settlement of the revenues; the document recording this settlement.

1772 H. VERELST *View of Bengal* 214 The rents of the province, according to the Jummabundy, or rent-roll... The amount..was taken at a considerable discount from the former Jumma or valuation. **1800** *Asiatic Ann. Reg., Proc. Parl.* 38/1 The collections on the current jumma have fallen short 16,875l. **1845** *Encycl. Metrop.* XXI. 672/1 Jumma-bundee Customs. **1851** *Illustr. Catal. Gt. Exhib.* IV. 926/2 Model of a Jamma Bundi. Collector making the annual jambundi. **1858** J. B. NORTON *Topics for Indian Statesmen* 269 When he reached the station he found the magistrate absent on jumabundy. **1892** B. H. BADEN-POWELL *Land-Syst. Brit. India* I. I. i. 24 To say that the 'jama' of village A. is Rs. 300 means that the Government Land Revenue demand on the village as a whole is Rs. 300 each year. *Ibid.* II. IV. i. 563 The 'jamabandi' is perhaps the most generally useful of all the papers.

jumme, obs. form of YAM.

jump (dʒʌmp), *sb.*[1] [f. JUMP *v.*: cf. F. *saut* and *sauter*.]

1. a. An act of jumping; a spring from the ground or other base; a leap, a bound: properly said of men or animals springing with the muscular action of the limbs. Sometimes with adv., as ***jump-up***.

1552 HULOET, Iumpe, *subsultus.* Iumpe by Iumpe, *subsultim.* **1589** R. ROBINSON *Gold Mirr.* etc. (Chetham Soc.) 59 Began with speed, for to plucke up my feete, Because the place did put me to my jumps. **1599** MARSTON *Sco. Villanie* xi, The orbs celestiall Will daunce Kemps iigge: they'le revel with neate iumps. **1607** TOPSELL *Four-f. Beasts* 265 The hare..sildome looketh forward, because it goeth by iumpes. **1774** GOLDSM. *Nat. Hist.* (1776) III. 205 The cat..then seized it with a jump. **1851** MAYNE REID *Scalp Hunt.* ix. 69 We will be back in a squirrel's jump. **1890** *Spectator* 15 Mar., The god comes out of the car with a jump-up like a Jack-in-the-box.

b. esp. in reference to the distance cleared (***long*** or ***broad jump***), or height jumped (***high jump***), as an athletic performance; also, a place to be jumped across, an obstacle to be cleared by jumping, in hurdle-racing, hunting, etc.

1858 R. S. SURTEES *Ask Mamma* xl, Hoping he was..able to sit at the jumps. **1870** BLAINE *Encycl. Rur. Sports* (ed. 3) §1648 This leap..was found to be twenty-four feet clear, which..was, it must be allowed, no small jump. **1872** *Graphic* 6 Apr. 314/1 (Oxf. & Cambr. Athletic Sports) After ..the Broad Jump, and the spin for a quarter of a mile.. came the hammer-throwing. **1881** [see ATHLETE 2]. **1889** R. S. S. BADEN-POWELL *Pigsticking* 123 To educate them [horses]..it is well worth while to keep up a small line of natural jumps somewhere in the neighbourhood. **1895** *Outing* (U.S.) XXVI. 455/1 Oxford won all the runs, the high hurdle, and tied in the high jump with Yale, losing only the weights and broad jump.

c. A descent on a parachute.

1922 *Encycl. Brit.* XXX. 14/2 The parachute..is of little use unless the jump is made over 200 ft. from the ground. **1935** C. G. BURGE *Compl. Bk. Aviation* 490/1 Jumps have been made from heights up to 30,000 ft., the descent taking about 40 min. **1970** *Times* 9 Dec. 16/1 The man..made his astonishing parachute jump into allied territory.

d. A journey, trip. *slang* (orig. *U.S.*).

1923 N. ANDERSON *Hobo* v. 83 He likes to tell of making 'big jumps' on passenger trains as from the coast to Chicago in five days, or from Chicago to Kansas City or Omaha in one day. **1932** E. SMITH *Satan's Circus* 17 The performers ..amused themselves, during the tedium of long 'jumps', by making him sing to them. **1956** B. HOLIDAY *Lady sings Blues* (1973) viii. 77 We were playing big towns and little towns, proms and fairs. A six-hundred-mile jump overnight was standard. **1967** C. O. SKINNER *Madame Sarah* xii. 268 On sleeper jumps after the star had got to bed, it was Pitou's nightly duty to hear her read the lines of a role.

e. Jazz music with a strong beat; a jazz tune with a strong rhythm. Freq. *attrib.* orig. *U.S.*

1937 *Metronome* Sept. 32/2 Count Basie. *John's Idea*; *One O'Clock Jump.* **1943** R. BLESH *This is Jazz* 30 You have left only the intolerable monotony of 'jump' (riff) phrases played over and over. **1946** MEZZROW & WOLFE *Really Blues* xvii. 325 This mechanical swing-band age of jump, organ-grinder riffs, mop-mop and rip-bop. **1946** R. BLESH *Shining Trumpets* (1949) xii. 279 Jump-swing, that aptly named music which cannot be danced to but must be jumped to. *Ibid.* 282 The small jump bands that are constantly forming and disbanding. *Ibid.*, Exploiting jump rhythms. **1955** C. Fox in A. J. McCarthy *Jazzbook 1955* 6 Ellington.. produced jazz in the 'twenties, 'swing' during the 'thirties, 'jump' in the early 'forties. **1971** *Melody Maker* 9 Oct. 17/4 In a way, his band was a 1940's jump band with amplifiers. **1972** *Jazz & Blues* Sept. 10/3 The West Coast 'jump' style adopted by artists like Roy Milton and Joe Liggins. *Ibid.* 11/3 'Jump' instrumentals.

f. An act of copulation; sexual intercourse. *slang.*

1934 J. O'HARA *Appointment in Samarra* (1935) vii. 212 Then you get cockeyed and take her out for a quick jump and ruin the whole works. **1970** G. GREER *Female Eunuch* 249 A wank was as good as a jump in those days.

2. A sudden involuntary movement caused by a shock or excitement; a start. In *pl.* nervous starts; an affection characterized by such, *spec.* (*a*) chorea, (*b*) delirium tremens (*slang*).

1879 PAYN *High Spirits, Capt. Cole's Passenger* II. 204, I thought he had been drinking, and in fact was on the verge of 'the jumps'. **1881** W. E. NORRIS *Matrim.* I. i. 17 Pilkington saw it..and..it gave him the jumps to that extent that he couldn't eat a thing afterwards. **1886** MAXWELL GRAY *Silence Dean Maitland* I. x. 272 It gives me the most fearful jumps to think of. **1890** BOLDREWOOD *Miner's Right* xxviii. (1899) 126/2 'I'm afraid he's got the jumps coming on'... 'Delirium tremens', I returned; 'very likely, indeed'. **1890** ANNIE EDWARDS *Pearl-powder* vii, At Philippa's sudden apostrophe she gave a jump.

3. Of things: A movement in which a thing is suddenly and abruptly thrown up or forward. *spec.* in *Gunnery*: The vertical movement of the muzzle of a gun at the moment of discharge; the angle which measures this.

1611 COTGR., *Cahot*, the iumpe, hop, or iog of a coach, &c., in a rugged, or vneuen, way. **1879** *Man. Artillery Exer.* I. 3 When a gun is fired, the whole system has a tendency to revolve in a vertical plane round the point of the trail or rear

trucks; this lifting in front gives rise to the 'jump'. **1897** *Text-Bk. Gunnery, Jump*, is the angle between the line of departure and the axis of the piece before firing.

4. *fig.* A sudden abrupt rise in position, amount, price, value, or the like; an abrupt change of level either upward or downward; an abrupt rise of level in building; a fault in stratification.

1657 *North's Plutarch, Add. Lives* (1676) 8 He did much admire, men should quarrel and kill themselves for the honour of a jump or precedency, or some such toy. **1842** FRANCIS *Dict. Arts, Jump*, one of the numerous appellations given by miners to a fault or dislocation of different mineral strata. **1842–76** GWILT *Archit.* (ed. 7) Gloss., *Jump*, an abrupt rise in a level course of brickwork or masonry to accommodate the work to the inequality of the ground. **1883** GRESLEY *Gloss. Coal Mining, Jump* (Jump-up, Jump-down), an up-throw or a down-throw, fault. **1883** *Stubbs' Mercantile Circular* 8 Nov. 982/2 The jump in the import of raw cotton, which has more than quadrupled itself in two years. **1887** *Spectator* 3 Sept. 1173 The little barometrical jumps which have recently been observed. **1891** *Daily News* 12 Nov. 2/1 Canary seed exhibits a sudden upward jump of several shillings. **1896** *Ibid.* 18 June 3/1 Negatived by 293 votes against 118, a jump up of 100 in the majority.

5. *fig.* **a.** A sudden and abrupt transition from one thing or point to another, with omission of intermediate points; an interval, gap, chasm, involving such sudden transition, *e.g.* in argument.

1678 CUDWORTH *Intell. Syst.* I. iv. §36. 587 By this means, there will not be so vast a Chasm and Hiatus..or so Great a Leap and Jump in the Creation. **1781** COWPER *Conversation* 154 Their nimble nonsense..gains remote conclusions at a jump. **1871** BLACKIE *Four Phases* i. 62 Every one sees that there is a jump in the logic here.

b. *Contract Bridge.* A bid higher than is necessary in the suit concerned. Also *attrib.*

1927 M. C. WORK *Contract Bridge* (1928) 24 One more trick than would be required in Bridge to justify a raise or jump. *Ibid.* 56 With Ace-King-Queen..make a jump denial by bidding three. **1931** E. CULBERTSON *Contract Bridge at Glance* 11 A jump bid in a new suit by Opening bidder, after a minimum response by partner, is a Forcing Re-bid. **1933, 1959, 1970** [see FORCING *ppl. a.*]. **1970** *Globe & Mail* (Toronto) 26 Sept. 51/4 The jump to three diamonds shows 13 to 16 points. **1973** *Country Life* 27 Dec. 2184/1 The jump bid in the opponents' suit is to show that he really has them.

†**6.** *fig.* **a.** The decisive moment of plunging into action of doubtful issue; dangerous critical moment, critical point, crisis. (L. *discrimen.*) *Obs.*

[The notion is evidently that of making a jump or taking a plunge into the unknown or untried.]

1598 GRENEWEY *Tacitus Ann.* II. iii. (1622) 36 Being therefore at a iumpe to hazard all [*igitur propinquo summæ rei discrimine*], thinking it conuenient to sound the souldiers minde. **1607** *Drewill's Arraignm.* in *Harl. Misc.* (Malh.) III. 62 Being come to the very iumpe of giuing iudgement. **1622** MABBE tr. *Aleman's Guzman d'Alf.* I. 212 Seeing..that he now stood upon the iumpe of his Salvation or Condemnation. *a* **1641** BP. MOUNTAGU *Acts of Mon.* (1642) 215 This testimony of Clemens..must needs put our Imputers upon this jump, that if Sibyls Oracles were counterfaited by Christians, it was done in the Apostles times.

†**b.** Venture, hazard, risk. *Obs.*

1600 HOLLAND *Livy* VI. xxxviii. 243 Presently..they put it to the verie iumpe and finall triall what should become of those lawes. **1601** —— *Pliny* II. 219 It [hellebore] putteth the Patient to a iumpe or great hazzard. **1606** SHAKS. *Ant. & Cl.* III. viii. 6 Our fortune lyes Vpon this iumpe.

7. *Phrases. all of a jump* (orig. *U.S.*), in a jumpy or nervous state; *(at a) full jump* (*U.S.*), at full speed; *at one jump* (*U.S.*), in one go; *at the jump = at the first jump*; † *at the first jump*, at the very start (of proceedings); *for* (or *on*) *the* (*high*) *jump*, *for the jumps*, up for trial, on a charge for misdemeanour; due for punishment, *spec.* hanging; *from the jump*, from the start or commencement; *to get* (or *have*) *the jump on* (orig. *U.S.*), to gain a lead on, get an advantage over (someone); *on the jump*, (*a*) on the move; (*b*) abruptly; swiftly; (*c*) in a nervous condition; *one jump ahead*, one step in front *of* (someone or something); just avoiding a pursuer or the like (*lit.* and *fig.*).

1577 HANMER *Anc. Eccl. Hist.* (1619) 158 Procopius, stepping forth at the first iumpe [εὐθὺς ἀπὸ πρώτης εἰσόδου] before the tribunall seate of the presidents. **1825** J. NEAL *Bro. Jonathan* II. 291 What's the matter with you,—all of a jump! **1848** *New York Tribune* 11 Nov. (Bartlett), A whole string of Democrats, all of whom had been going the whole hog for Cass from the jump. **1854** M. J. HOLMES *Tempest & Sunshine* i. 12 What you ridin' Prince full jump down the pike for? **1859** *Southern Lit. Messenger* XXVIII. 143, I run down stream, an I meets Bill on the jump. **1870** DE B. R. KEIM *Sheridan's Troopers* vi. 39 The irate quadruped made for our party, coming at a 'full jump'. **1884** 'MARK TWAIN' *Huck. Finn* xviii. 162 My nigger had a monstrous easy time ..but Buck's was on the jump most of the time. **1888** *Daily Inter-ocean* 3 Feb. (Farmer), He can depend on a big crowd and fair play from the jump. **1896** ADE *Artie* xvi. 147, I put up a holler right at the jump. **1899** 'MARK TWAIN' in *Century Mag.* Nov. 76/1 It was my idea to spread [a name] all over the world, now, at this one jump. **1900** *Daily News* 4 May 3/2 Keeping the foe on the jump. **1905** J. C. LINCOLN *Partners of Tide* vi. 106 When one of us three says, 'Nickerson, do thus and so,' you *do* it, and do it on the jump. Don't stop to think 'bout it. **1912** ADE *Knocking Neighbors* 123 Rufus was sinfully Rich, but nevertheless Detestable, because his Family had drilled into him the low-down Habit of getting the Jump on the Other Fellow. **1912** F. M. HUEFFER *Panel* III. i. 289 That elderly gentleman was exceedingly 'on the jump', as nervous as a man well could be. **1914** 'HIGH JINKS JR.' *Choice Slang* 21 Only about three jumps ahead of a young conniption. **1919** *Athenæum* 1 Aug. 695/2 'He's for the high jump' is a favourite expression meaning that someone is to be charged before his company or commanding officer. *Ibid.* 8 Aug. 727/2 'For the jumps' (up for trial). **1921** C. MULFORD *Bar-20 Three* xviii. 230 Hurrying men pulled thick planks from the pile..and hauled them, on the jump, to windows and doors. **1922** E. O'NEILL *Anna Christie* (1923) 29, I didn't go wrong all at one jump. **1925** FRASER & GIBBONS *Soldier & Sailor Words* 119 *High jump, on the*, a term used of a man entered on a 'Crime sheet', and for trial for a military offence; the suggestion being that the accused would need to jump very high to get over the trouble. **1936** E. AMBLER *Dark Frontier* xi. 173 If we fall down on this job..it's me for the high jump. **1936** G. GREENE *Gun for Sale* i. 23 He sounded all of a jump. **1940** WODEHOUSE *Eggs, Beans & Crumpets* 103 If ever I saw a baby that looked like something that was one jump ahead of the police..it is this baby of Bingo's. Definitely the criminal type. **1942** 'N. SHUTE' *Pied Piper* 247 I'm for the high jump. They got the goods on me all right. **1956** 'A. GILBERT' *And Death came Too* xiv. 145, I can't afford to act for someone who's going to be found guilty. And..it looks to me remarkably likely Mrs. Appleyard is going to find herself for the high jump. **1960** D. LYTTON *Goddam White Man* xi. 183 He thinks he has the jump on us. **1963** J. PRESCOT *Case for Hearing* viii. 123 All of the accused are for the high jump. **1971** M. SINCLAIR *Sonntag* ii. 14 Someone is for the jump, I can tell you. Misinformed, that's what I was. **1972** *Real Estate Rev.* Winter 22/1 Each of these new developers hopes to get the jump on the other by adding more square footage to the units and giving more in amenities. **1972** J. PHILIPS *Vanishing Senator* (1973) I. iv. 37 Get over here on the jump... Step on it, will you? **1973** *Sun* 18 Jan. 6 That would allow the Government to permit wage rises to keep one jump ahead of prices.

8. A robbery (see quots.). *slang.*

1777 in Partridge *Dict. Underworld* (1949) 374/1 *The jump*... The dusk of the evening is the time allotted for this, as it prevents any one at a distance from observing what passes; a great number of rogues then gets lurking about, taking advantage of the unpardonable neglect of others; every window they come near that has no light in, they open, if it happens not to be fastened; they then take what is most valuable out of that room, and very often go into others in the same house. **1781** G. PARKER *View of Soc.* II. i. 140 As soon as they have completed this robbery, the *Jumper* descends... The *Jump* being thus completed, they sheer off immediately. **1788** GROSE *Dict. Vulgar T.* (ed. 2), The jump, or dining room jump; a species of robbery effected by ascending a ladder placed by a sham lamp-lighter, against the house intended to be robbed. It is so called, because, should the lamp-lighter be put to flight, the thief who ascended the ladder has no means of escape but that of jumping down. **1901** 'LINESMAN' *Words by Eyewitness* (1902) 293 They are sure to see a 'jump' in everything, even in concessions. *Note*: South African euphemism for a robbery.

9. *Comb.* (sense 1 c), as **jump boot**, a parachutist's boot; **jump-master**, a man in charge of parachutists; **jump-sack** *slang*, a parachute; **jump-suit, jump suit** orig. *U.S.*, a parachutist's one-piece garment; also, a similar garment worn by other people.

1948 *Amer. Speech* XXIII. 319 *Jump boots*, paratroopers' shoes. **1972** *Daily Colonist* (Victoria, B.C.) 4 Aug. 1/6 She ran to her husband's prostrate body, unlaced his jump boots and pulled them off. **1942** *Look* 3 Nov. 43/2 (*caption*) The jumpmaster..cries, 'Stand in the door!' and the men crowd forward, waiting for the electrifying order: 'Jump!' **1970** N. ARMSTRONG et al. *First on Moon* xiv. 353 It's like riding an airplane, getting ready to jump. Anything could go wrong. Something could happen to the airplane.., the jumpmaster. **1973** *Daily Colonist* (Victoria, B.C.) 20 May 30/5 She was standing on the wing of the airplane hanging on and waiting for the jumpmaster to say 'go'. **1942** 'B. J. ELLAN' *Spitfire!* p. x, A parachute is called a *brolly* or a *jumpsack*. **1948** *Amer. Speech* XXIII. 319 *Jump suit*, uniform worn when jumping from airplane. **1965** *Guardian* 7 May 10/1 Rayon linen jump-suit with turn-up trousers and Orlon fish-net midriff. **1965** H. KANE *Devil to Pay* (1966) xxii. 129 Nora was slender and graceful in a crisp white narrow-legged jump suit. **1969** *New Yorker* 30 Aug. 73/1 Three parachutists in jump suits. **1971** *Black World* Apr. 38/2 We worry over horsepower (no pun intended) and power steering, fashionable jump suits and Afro haircuts. **1972** *Time* 17 Apr. 58/2 He..sews conservation patches all over his jumpsuit.

jump, *sb.*[2] *Obs.* exc. *dial.* [perh. a corruption of F. *juppe* JUP, assimilated by popular etymology to JUMP *v.* and *sb.*[1]]

1. A kind of short coat worn by men in the seventeenth and eighteenth centuries: see description in quot. 1688.

1654 GAYTON *Pleas. Notes* IV. xv. 252 Even the Bedel.. without his blew Jump, and silver head tipstaffe loses reputation among the boyes and vagrants. **1665** J. COSIN *Mem. Answ. Prebends Durham* in *Surtees Misc.* (1858) 267 Wearing long rapiers, great skirted jumpes and short daggers. **1688** R. HOLME *Armoury* III. 96/2 *Iumpe*.. extendeth to the Thighs is open or buttoned down before, open or slit up behind half way: the Sleeves reach to the Wrist. **1703** *Country Farmers Catech.* (N.), By'r lady, nothing but a drugget jump and a caster, a russet gown for my wife Susan. *c* **1746** COLLIER (Tim Bobbin) *View Lancash. Dial.* Wks. (1862) 41, I donn'd meh Sunday Jump o top o meh Singlet. **1828** *Craven Dial., Jump*, a child's leathern frock. [**1887** *South Chesh. Gloss., Jumps*, clothes. Chiefly in the phrase 'Sunday jumps' = Sunday best.]

†**b.** *spec.* Applied in 17th c. to the short coat worn by Presbyterian ministers. *Obs.*

1653 *Pol. Ballads* (1860) I. 114 Here's the trunk-hose of the Rump..And a Presbyterian jump, With an Independent smock. **1656** *Artificial Handsom.* 119 What enemies were some Ministers..to long cassocks, since the Scotch jump is looked upon as the more military fashion, and a badge of a Northern and cold reformation? **1680** HICKERINGILL *Meroz* 12 The Jesuits, and the Fanaticks, especially the rigid Presbyterian... One wears a Fryars weed, the other a short synodical Jump.

2. A kind of under (or undress) bodice worn by women, esp. during the 18th century, and in rural use in the 19th; usually fitted to the bust, and often used instead of stays. From *c* 1740 usually as plural *jumps* (*a pair of jumps*).

1666 *New Eng. Hist. & Gen. Register* (1864) XVIII. 329, I give to my sonn Williams wife, ye jump which was my sister Sarah Caps. **1706** T. BAKER *Tunbr. Walks* v. i, I'll be sure to send for you when I have occasion for a new jump. **1740** in *Mrs. Delany's Life* II. 113 Her jumps will go next Sunday, and I daresay she'll put them on. **1755** JOHNSON, *Jump*, a waistcoat; a kind of loose or limber stays worn by sickly ladies. **1762** *Songs Costume* (Percy Soc.) 240 Now a shape in neat stays, now a slattern in jumps. **1784** *Specif. Jean Phillipe's Patent* No. 1444 These springs are for ladies' jumps who do not choose to wear hard incommodious stays. **1825–80** JAMIESON, *Jumps*, a kind of easy stays, open before, worn by nurses.

3. *attrib.*, as *jump-coat* = sense 1, 1 b.

1660 BLOUNT *Boscobel* I. (1680) 61 A leather-doublet..a pair of old green breeches and a Jump-coat (as the Country calls it). **1703** *Cupid Stripp'd* (N.), What long-winded brother in a short jump coat did preach to day. **1755** CARTE *Hist. Eng.* IV. 642 The habit he came in, was..a green cloth jump coat threadbare, the threads being white.

jump, *sb.*[3] Also 9 *Sc.* **jimp.** (See quots.)

1709 BLAIR in *Phil. Trans.* XXVII. 146 After this I provided some Jumps, or Leather, such as Shoemakers use for the Heels of Shoes. **1825–80** JAMIESON, *Jimp*, thin slips of leather, put between the outer and inner soles of a shoe, to give the appearance of thickness.

†**jump**, *a.*, *adv.* [Connected with JUMP *v.* 5.]

A. *adj.* Coinciding, exactly agreeing; even; exact, precise.

1581 MULCASTER *Positions* xxx. (1887) 110 When..some parte therof wanteth his due forme, his iumpe quantitie, his iust number, his naturall seat. **1584** LYLY *Campaspe* I. iii, *Cris.* Thou thinkest it a grace to be opposite against Alexander. *Diog.* And thou to be jump with Alexander. *c* **1586** SIDNEY *Arcadia* III. Wks. 1724 II. 714 Jump concord between our wit and will. **1622** FLETCHER *Prophetess* I. iii, They are as jump and squar'd out to his nature. *a* **1637** B. JONSON *Underwoods, Execr., Vulcan*, Acrostichs, and Telestichs, on jump Names. **1828** *Craven Dial., Jump*, short, compact.

†**B.** *adv.* With exact coincidence or agreement; exactly, precisely. *Obs.*

1539 TAVERNER *Erasm. Prov.* (1545) 36 Sure I am, that men of oure tyme kepe this sayenge so iompe. **1570** B. GOOGE *Pop. Kingd.* II. 20 b, In this they all do iumpe agree. **1574** STUDLEY tr. *Bale's Pageant Popes* III. 43 Ye shall finde it also make iump six hundred sixty sixe. **1579** TWYNE *Phisicke agst. Fort.* I. xxiv. 33 a, Thou art iumpe of mine opinion. **1589** R. HARVEY *Pl. Perc.* (1590) 21 Meete halfe way, and I standing iump in the middle will crie aime to you both. **1602** SHAKS. *Ham.* v. ii. 386 But since so iumpe vpon this bloodie question, You from the Polake warres, and you from England Are heere arriued. **1615** W. LAWSON *Orch. & Gard.* III. x. (1668) 29 Make your graft agree jump with the cyon. *a* **1656** USSHER *Ann.* III. (1658) 13 The time of this Belus..falls in jump with the age of this Amenophis.

Hence †'**jumply** *adv.*, coincidently, accordantly; exactly, precisely. †'**jumpness**, evenness, fitness.

a **1586** SIDNEY *Arcadia* v. (1622) 450 My meeting so iumply with them, make mee abashed. **1604** PRICKET *Honors Fame* (1881) 12 Then in that time an vndermining wit, Did closly frame all actions iumply fit. *c* **1640** J. SMYTH *Lives Berkeleys* (1883) I. 64 Age, time, place,..and other circumstances so iumply occurre. **1611** COTGR., *Justesse*, iustnesse, iumpnesse, euennesse.

jump (dʒʌmp), *v.* [A word of mod. Eng., known only from *c* 1500; app. of onomatopœic origin: cf. *bump*, etc.

Words app. parallel are MHG. and dial. Ger. *gumpen* to jump, hop, Da. *gumpe*, Sw. dial. *gumpa*, Sw. *guppa* to move up and down, Icel. *goppa* to skip; but it does not appear how the 16th c. Eng. *jump* could be historically or phonetically related to these.]

I. Intransitive senses.

1. a. To make a spring from the ground or other base by flexion and sudden muscular extension of the legs (or, in the case of some animals, as fish, of the tail, or other part); to throw oneself upward, forward, backward, or downward, from the ground or point of support; to leap, spring, bound; *spec.* to leap with the feet together, as opposed to *hopping* on one leg.

1530 PALSGR. 596/1, I jumpe, as one dothe that holdeth bothe his fete togyther, and leape upon a thyng. **1611** SHAKS. *Wint. T.* IV. iv. 347 Not the worst of the three, but iumpes twelue foote and a halfe by th' squire. **1676** HOBBES *Iliad* I. 504 And Thetis from it jumpt'd into the Brine. **1711** STEELE *Spect.* No. 118 ¶2 He jumped across the Fountain. **1719** DE FOE *Crusoe* I. (1850) 259 Friday..laughed, halloed, jumped about, danced, sung. **1797** MRS. BENNETT *Beggar Girl* (1813) III. 35 Jumping down half a dozen steps at once. **1863** GEO. ELIOT *Romola* lxviii, She jumped on to the beach and walked many paces. **1867** FRANCIS *Angling* i. (1880) 52 He should..mark where he sees a barbel jump. **1875** BUCKLAND *Log-Book* 88, I have never seen a salmon jump at sea.

b. To move suddenly with a leap, bound, or the like movement; to 'spring', 'dart', 'shoot'.

1724 DE FOE *Mem. Cavalier* (1840) 15, I jumpt out of bed. **18..** L. HUNT *Rondeau*, Jenny kissed me when we met, Jumping from the chair she sat in. **1856** KANE *Arct. Expl.* II. viii. 89, I jumped at once to the gun-stand. **1882** B. D. W.

RAMSAY *Recoll. Mil. Serv.* I. v. 90 He jumped up with apparent indignation. **1884** PAYN *Lit. Recoll.* 181 To ambush in the wooded pass..and jump out upon me where it was darkest.

c. To move with a sudden involuntary jerk as the result of excitement or of a nervous shock; to start. ***to jump for joy***, said *lit.* of children, etc., also *fig.* to be joyfully excited. ***to jump out of one's skin***: see SKIN *sb.* 6 f.

1715 DE FOE *Fam. Instruct.* I. i. (1841) I. 8 I'll thank him for it, for my heart jumps within me. **1775** MAD. D'ARBLAY *Early Diary* (1889) II. 69, I could almost have jumped for joy when he was gone, to think the affair was thus finally over. **1861** THACKERAY *Four Georges* iii. (1880) 137 So she jumped for joy; and went upstairs and packed all her little trunks. **1865** DICKENS *Mut. Fr.* I. vi, You made me jump, Charley. **1900** *Speaker* 19 May 190/1 A harsh penetrating voice that made me jump.

d. Colloq. phr. ***to jump*** (or ***go*** (***and***) ***jump***) ***in the lake***: to go away and cease being a nuisance; usu. *imp.* as a contemptuous dismissal.

1912 [see GO *v.* 32 a]. **1937** E. S. GARDNER *Case of Lame Canary* vii. 67 Suppose she tells us to go jump in the lake? **1946** H. CROOME *Faithless Mirror* ix. 97 'I'm here to stop that particular change.' 'You and what ten other fellows? Go jump in the lake.' **1966** M. WOODHOUSE *Tree Frog* xviii. 129 There was no real reason why I shouldn't have told Andy to jump in the lake as soon as he'd got us through Customs at Heathrow. **1968** [see FRUIT *sb.* 2 e]. **1974** D. GRAY *Dead Give Away* xxii. 202 She smelt pot in his room. .. He destroyed the evidence, and told her to jump in the lake.

e. ***to jump to the eye***(***s***) [tr. F. *sauter aux yeux*]: to be noticed; to be obvious or prominent.

1926 FOWLER *Mod. Eng. Usage* 311/1 *Jump to the eye(s)* is a bad Gallicism. **1929** G. GOODWIN *Conversations with G. Moore* xxvii. 174 The fact that the Banquo scene in 'Macbeth'—a scene which jumps to the eye—was overlooked, encourages me, obliges me, to think that no one reads Shakespeare. **1931** M. D. GEORGE *England in Transition* iii. 59 Things jump to the eyes of the reader of this passage which have yet been ignored.

f. ***to jump rope***: to skip with a skipping-rope. Cf. *jump-rope* s.v. JUMP-. *N. Amer.*

1934 in WEBSTER. **1961** *Western Folklore* July 179 If only two children are jumping rope, one end of the rope may be tied to a tree, the other end being turned by one of the children. *Ibid.* 193/1 When she died she told me this, When I jump rope I always miss. **1972** *Nat. Geogr.* Sept. 414 When they aren't shooting marbles or jumping rope, the youngsters lurch about on..stilts.

g. Of a parachutist: to jump out of an aeroplane.

1935 C. G. BURGE *Compl. Bk. Aviation* 490/1 After jumping and pulling the release cord the parachutist finds that the parachute opens fully in about $1\frac{1}{2}$ sec. **1942** [see *jump-master* s.v. JUMP *sb.*[1] 9]. **1969** A. WHITE *Long Drop* 220 Ben jumped. His parachute failed to open.

h. Of jazz or similar music: to have a strong or exciting rhythm; to 'swing'; so of a place, esp. a place of entertainment: to pulsate with activity; to be full of excitement or enjoyment. *colloq.* (orig. *U.S.*).

c **1938** N. E. WILLIAMS *His Hi de Highness of Ho de Ho* 16 *The joint is jumping*, the place is lively, the club is leaping with fun. **1943** H. A. SMITH *Life in Putty Knife Factory* vi. 89 He then called up a couple of his friends..and they came, and before long the joint was jumpin'. **1944** *Needle* July 23/2 The jumping-jive Harlem musicians who think that to obtain any semblance to rhythmic excitement they must leave the theme and become lost altogether. **1946** MEZZROW & WOLFE *Really Blues* (1957) vi. 71 Indiana Harbor was small but it jumped like mad. **1946** F. STACY in Rosenthal & Zachary *Jazzways* 49/2 The meaning of a 'jump tune' should be clear enough from the term itself; literally, it jumps. **1959** 'F. NEWTON' *Jazz Scene* v. 86 Nobody minded what was played so long as it 'jumped'. **1968** J. SANGSTER *Foreign Exchange* i. 31 The place was really jumping. It took me three minutes to locate the bar through the smoke haze. **1972** *Jazz & Blues* Sept. 12/1 We should give some mention to the jumping instrumentals which Fats and the band were committing to wax during the early 50's.

i. ***to jump up.*** To dance the 'jump-up' (JUMP-UP 2). *West Indies.*

1959 'M. UNDERWOOD' *Arm of Law* xiv. 165 Glad to see you enjoying carnival. But why aren't you jumping up? **1968** C. NICOLE *Self Lovers* v. 71 'Alex!..I don't suppose you'd care to jump up.'..'I'd love to.' He took her in his arms. The tempo changed to a calypso beat. **1973** *Sunday Advocate-News* (Barbados) 21 Jan. 6/6 Barbadians will have the opportunity to 'jump up' in real carnival fashion at the Barbados Cruising Club's annual carnival dance which will take place at Culloden Farm on Saturday, March 3.

2. *transf.* Of inanimate things: To be moved or thrown up with a sudden jerk like the jump of a man or beast. With quot. 1511 cf. *bump.*

1511 GUYLFORDE *Pilgr.* 60 The sayde ancre helde vs frome jumppynge and betynge vpon the sayde rok. **1568** [see JUMPING *vbl. sb.*]. **1611** COTGR., *Cahoter*, to iumpe, iog, or hop, as a coach in vneuen way. **1674** N. FAIRFAX *Bulk & Selv.* 128 Such as jump in, die wise or cubically. **1833** J. HOLLAND *Manuf. Metal* II. 134 It should..be set.. accurately, so as not to jump or sway in any part when made to revolve. **1860** TYNDALL *Glac.* I. viii. 58, I..could see the stream..flashing as it jumped over the ledges. **1894** HALL CAINE *Manxman* v. iii. 287 The sea was beginning to jump.

3. *fig.* **a.** To pass abruptly from one thing or state to another, with omission of intermediate stages; to spring up or rise suddenly in amount, price, etc.

1579 TOMSON *Calvin's Serm., 2 Tim.* 856/1 If we goe about to bring them to some instruction, they iumpe from the cocke to the asse [*ils sauteront du coq à l'asne*]. **1727** DE FOE *Syst. Magic* I. i. (1840) 36 To jump at once from the beginning of things to the present times. **1748** *Anson's Voy.* III. vi. 347 Our soundings gradually decreased..to twenty-five fathom; but soon after..they jumped back again to thirty fathom. **1886** C. SCOTT *Sheep-Farming* 189 Another upward bound was experienced, when wool jumped up suddenly to 46*s.* per tod.

b. To come *to* (†*into*), or arrive *at* (a conclusion, etc.) precipitately and without examination of the premisses.

a **1704** LOCKE in *Spect.* (1714) No. 626 ¶6 We see a little, presume a great deal, and so jump to the Conclusion. **1809** MALKIN *Gil Blas* v. i. ¶62 [He] jumped to the conclusion that there was not a more ancient house in Spain. *c* **1865** J. WYLDE in *Circ. Sc.* I. 302/2 The rigid system of philosophy cannot allow us to jump at conclusions. **1884** RIDER HAGGARD *Dawn* xlvi, So ill-natured—or rather, so given to jumping to conclusions—is society. **1897** *Allbutt's Syst. Med.* II. 1044 The diagnosis..must not be jumped at without a careful consideration of the entire circumstances of the case.

4. With prepositions in special uses. **a.** ***to jump at*** (rarely ***for***): To spring as a beast at its prey; *fig.* to accept or take advantage of eagerly. *colloq.*

1769 GRAY *Jrnl., Let. to Wharton* 3 Oct., Butter that Siserah would have jumped at, though not in a lordly dish. **1844** ALB. SMITH *Mr. Ledbury* vii. (1886) 21 The guests..all jumped at the invitation. **1873** BLACK *Pr. Thule* xxvi. 443 Lavender jumped at that notion directly. **1894** R. BRIDGES *Feast of Bacchus* III. 988 She jumped at the bargain.

b. ***to jump upon***: To spring or pounce upon as a beast upon its victim, or a victor upon the prostrate body of a foe; hence (*colloq.*), to 'come down' crushingly with word or act upon one who exposes himself to severe handling or insult. Also ***to jump on.***

1868 MISS BRADDON *Dead Sea Fruit* v. I. 78 When a wretched scribbler was, in vulgar phraseology, to be 'jumped upon'. **1887** *Lantern* (New Orleans) 1 Oct. 2/1 The idea of two big chaps jumping on one man. **1891** CHURCH *Oxford Movem.* xvi. 274 Like a general jumping on his antagonist whom he has caught in the act of a false move. **1917** D. CANFIELD *Understood Betsy* (1922) viii. 153 If you had to live the way he does, you'd be dirty!..And then you go and jump on him! **1939** I. BAIRD *Waste Heritage* xxi. 292 I'm sorry, Eddy, I didn't mean to jump on you that way. **1973** 'M. INNES' *Appleby's Answer* xvi. 138 She jumped on the butler for misunderstanding something about the drinks.

c. ***to jump down one's throat***: see THROAT *sb.* 3 a.

d. ***to jump to it***: to make an energetic start upon something; to take prompt action; usu. *imp.* Also occas. ***to jump to*** = to obey readily. *colloq.* (orig. *Mil.*).

[**1886** F. T. ELWORTHY *West Somerset Word-Bk.* 390 *Jump*, to readily accept an offer. 'Not her hab'm? Let-n ax o' her, that's all; I tell ee her'd jump to un.'] **1917** W. OWEN *Let.* 12 Feb. (1967) 434 He does nothing off his own bat, and doesn't always 'jump to' my orders! **1919** [see JERK *sb.*[1] 2 e]. **1929** *Morning Post* 13 July 16 He does not know whether the service will come to his fore- or his back-hand; but he is ready to 'jump to it', whatever happens. **1956** J. MASTERS *Bugles & Tiger* xiv. 178 A P. & O. run like a warship, where the passengers would do as they were told and jump to it, and like it. **1974** M. BABSON *Stalking Lamb* xvi. 121 When you hear my signal—jump to it!

5. a. To act or come exactly *together*; to agree completely, to coincide, tally. Const. *with.*

1567 [implied in JUMPINGLY]. **1573** G. HARVEY *Letter-bk.* (Camden) 27 Al this iumpid wel together. **1588** J. UDALL *Demonstr. Discip.* To Rdr. (Arb.) 10 The iudgments..so iumping with mine. **1590** R. SIDNEY *Madrigal* in Greene *Never too late*, How love and folly jump in every part. **1592** R. D. *Hypnerotomachia* 70 b, The corners of which triangle did iumpe with the sides, and lymbus of the subjacent plynth. **1607** WALKINGTON *Opt. Glass* 39 Wisedome and vertue iumpe in one with beauty. *a* **1658** CLEVELAND *Poems, Britannicus's Leap* 18 Good Wits may jump. **1663** BUTLER *Hud.* I. iii. 1240 For all Men live and judge amiss Whose Talents jump not just with his. **1702** S. SEWALL *Diary* 21 Feb. (1879) II. 53 Our Thoughts being thus confer'd, and found to jump, makes it to me remarkable. **1768** GOLDSM. *Good-n. Man* v, Resolutions are well kept when they jump with inclinations. **1853** W. IRVING in *Life & Lett.* (1864) IV. 125 Our humors jump together completely. **1891** *Guardian* 5 Aug. 1273/2 One passage in Mr. Morley's speech jumps with a letter we print to day.

b. ***to jump awry***, to disagree.

1762 STERNE *Tr. Shandy* V. xxviii, The trine and sextile aspects have jumped awry.

II. Transitive senses.

6. a. To pass clear over by a leap; to leap or spring over; to clear. In the game of draughts, To jump over in moving, to take (an opposing man). *U.S.*

c **1600** SHAKS. *Sonn.* xliv, For nimble thought can iumpe both sea and land. **1853** KANE *Grinnell Exp.* xxii. (1856) 176 Alternately jumping these crevices and clambering up the hummocks between them. **1860** TYNDALL *Glac.* I. ix. 64 Jumping the adjacent fissures.

fig. **1899** *Boston* (U.S.) *Transcr.* 24 Feb. 6/1 The appointee has received a promotion..by influence, and in doing it has jumped many of his fellow-officers quite as good or better than he.

b. To get on or off (a ship, train, etc.) by jumping (*U.S.*). Also, to leave (a place or thing) suddenly; *spec.* of a seaman: to desert (his ship) before his contract expires. orig. *U.S.*

1875 J. MILLER *First Fam'lies Sierras* vii. 47 Even the head man of the company..jumped a first-class poker game..to come in and weigh out dust. **1883** *American* VI. 40 This evasion of imperative duty affords impunity to the men, if they jump the boat on the route. **1891** C. ROBERTS *Adrift Amer.* v. 81, I managed to jump a freight [train] the same night and got right up to Topeka. **1899** *Westm. Gaz.* 29 Nov. 2/1 He was too old a sailor to give them a chance of 'jumping' her. **1921** C. E. MULFORD *Bar-20 Three* vii. 88 I'm admittin' I'm walkin' soft, an' ready to jump th' country right quick. **1923** R. D. PAINE *Comrades of Rolling Ocean* xiv. 260, I told you about jumping the town because I had stove up a limousine. **1939** G. GREENE *Lawless Roads* 302 He thought perhaps he'd jump the ship at Lisbon—but..he was carried remorselessly on. **1957** 'N. SHUTE' *On Beach* iv. 131 Most of them would probably jump ship.

c. Of things: To spring off, to leave (the rails).

1883 *Leisure Ho.* 282/1 The cars had 'jumped the track'. **1898** *Westm. Gaz.* 20 Jan. 7/2 The near van jumped the metals and fouled the line just as the north-bound passenger train was approaching.

d. ***to jump the bite*** (Dentistry): to correct a faulty occlusion or 'bite', esp. one due to a retracted mandible, by bringing the mandible forward as a whole.

1880 [see BITE *sb.* 1 f]. **1901** SMALE & COLYER *Dis. & Injuries Teeth* (ed. 2) iv. 158 If..the patient can be made to acquire the permanent habit of bringing the mandible forward so as to make the teeth articulate normally, the bite will have been 'jumped'. **1951** J. M. SCHWEITZER *Oral Rehabilitation* xxxv. 830 Nearly 80 years ago Class II, Division 1 (Angle), cases were treated by 'jumping the bite'. .. An attempt was made to reposition the mandible in an anteroposterior as well as a vertical and lateral direction.

e. *Contract Bridge.* To raise (a bid) higher than necessary in the suit concerned. Also *intr.*

1927 M. C. WORK *Contract Bridge* (1928) 33 If the partner jump, it must be with three cards of a suit. *Ibid.* 55 Cases of one No Trump jumped to two, and two of a Major jumped to three. **1929** —— *Complete Contract Bridge* i. 7 His proper procedure may be to shift to another declaration, or it may be to jump the original bid. **1963** G. F. HERVEY *Handbk. Card Games* 142 If responder has a count of 12 points he can jump straight to three No-Trumps.

†**7.** To effect or do as with a jump. *Obs.*

1611 SHAKS. *Wint. T.* IV. iv. 195 Loue-songs for Maids.. Iump-her, and thump-her. **1616** B. JONSON *Devil an Ass* IV. i, Why, there was Sr Iohn Monie-man could iump A Businesse quickely. **1633** W. R. *Match Midnight* III. in Hazl. *Dodsley* XIII. 63 My father..swears, if I pleased him well, it should serve to jump out my portion. **1684** N. S. *Crit. Enq. Edit. Bible* xxv. 230 The latter..jump't up new Translations of the Bible.

8. a. To cause to jump; to give a jumping motion to; to drive forward with a bound; to startle. Also *fig.*

c **1815** JANE AUSTEN *Persuas.* (1833) I. xii. 310 She..ran up the steps to be jumped down again. **1849** *Jrnl. R. Agric. Soc.* X. I. 177 The gleans must then be jumped on the ground to level the roots. **1875** BLAKE-HUMFREY *Eton Boating Bk.* 45 With a dashing stroke the Westminsters jumped their boat up to their opponents. **1883** GRESLEY *Gloss. Coal Mining, Jump*..2. To raise boring-rods in a bore-hole, and allow them to fall of their own weight. **1883** *American* VI. 40 Constructed with a view to 'jumping her' over the bars at low water. **1890** BOLDREWOOD *Col. Reformer* (1891) 222 He nearly jumped his horse on to that last bullock's back. **1893** F. ADAMS *New Egypt* 151 It is some time since I have felt so uncomfortable as I felt then, with.. this question jumped upon me like a flash of lightning. **1898** *Westm. Gaz.* 7 Apr. 2/3 People..whose nerves have been jumped by scorchers.

b. To cook in a frying-pan, shaking (them) up from time to time. Cf. JUMPED *ppl. a.*

1877 OUIDA *Puck* xxiii. 265 The cook sent me word that he's invented a new style of jumping mushrooms in wine.

c. *Sporting.* To cause (game) to start; to 'spring'.

1836 *Southern Rose* 10 Dec. 57/3 The boys were ordered to stick close to the dogs, and if they jumped the buck to catch him. **1839** *Southern Lit. Messenger* V. 377/1, I would go, but I am a going to jump mullet to-night. **1874** J. W. LONG *Amer. Wild-Fowl Shooting* 205 The most successful method of hunting ducks is identical with..'jumping them up' along the creeks. **1885** T. ROOSEVELT *Hunting Trips* 59 We had half an hour's good sport in 'jumping' these little ducks. **1894** *Harper's Mag.* Feb. 352 A bunch of antelopes which we had 'jumped' the day before.

9. a. To pounce upon, come down upon with violence or unawares; to rob, to cheat; to seize upon by sudden unexpected action; to 'steal a march' upon.

1789 GEO. PARKER *Life's Painter* 160 (Farmer) They.. pick him up and take him to the above alehouse to jump him, or do him upon the broads, which means cards. **1870** B. HARTE *Roaring Camp* 134 (Farmer) The old proprietor.. was green, and let the boys about here jump him. **1879** A. FORBES in *Daily News* 28 June 5/6 Some fellows..prowl around habitually with a single eye to 'jumping' anything conveniently portable. **1882** *St. James's Gaz.* 11 Feb., The violent manner in which the office of Prime Minister was 'jumped'. **1889** C. KING *Queen of Bedlam* 106 The Cheyenne stage, they said, was 'jumped', the driver killed, and the..passengers burned alive. **1899** *Westm. Gaz.* 17 May 1/2 To try to jump the Transvaal after the experience of three years ago..would indeed be worse than folly.

b. ***to jump a claim***, etc.: To take summary possession of a piece of land called a 'claim', on the ground that the former occupant has abandoned it, or has failed to comply with the legal requirements. Chiefly *U.S.* and *Colonial.* Also *transf.*

1854 in *Melbourne Argus* 21 Mar., Claims are being jumped daily. **1855** *Ibid.* 6 Jan., The meeting [of diggers] unanimously resolved to 'jump' all deserted holes. **1879** *Daily News* 22 Mar. 6/2 There was a word coined and current at the mines of California..which exactly suits the transaction—'jumping'... We 'jumped' the Diamond Fields, we 'jumped' the Transvaal, and we intend to 'jump' Zululand if we can. **1890** BOLDREWOOD *Miner's Right* iv. 37 If such work were not commenced within three days, any

other miners might summarily take possession of or 'jump' the claim. **1893** *Westm. Gaz.* 7 July 3/1.

10. a. To skip over, skip, pass by, evade.

to jump (*one's*) *bail*, *one's bill*, to abscond, leaving one's sureties liable or one's bill unpaid. *slang* (orig. *U.S.*).

1749 Fielding *Tom Jones* xii. iii, We have ourselves been very often.. given to jumping, as we have run through the pages of voluminous historians. **1844** Emerson *Lect. New Eng. Reformers* Wks. (Bohn) I. 262 So they jumped the Greek and Latin, and read law, medicine, or sermons, without it. **1859** G. W. Matsell *Vocabulum* 47 *Jumped his bail*, run away from his bail. **1872** G. P. Burnham *Memoirs U.S. Secret Service* 55 Pete's friend Fred Biebusch had hid himself, after jumping his bail. **1888** *Chicago Herald* (Farmer *Americanisms*), He arose at early dawn and jumped his bill. **1911** L. J. Vance *Cynthia* 177 He's jumped bail on a bigamy indictment. **1973** M. Russell *Double Hit* xxii. 165, I shan't jump bail. They'll see me.. back in court. **1974** *Guardian* 25 Jan. 24/1 [He] was given a three years' sentence in his absence, after he had jumped bail.

b. To drive past (traffic lights) when they indicate that one should stop. Also *transf.* orig. *U.S.*

1938 *Words* Mar. 44/2 *Jump*, v.t., to anticipate (the *go* signal of a traffic director). **1958** *Listener* 6 Nov. 731/1 Cutting in, jumping the lights, blind corners at sixty,.. they're things I'd never dream of doing. **1961** J. Barlow *Term of Trial* ii. ii. 160 She stared at the conflict of traffic. 'Good God!' she protested... 'They jump the lights!' **1970** J. Porter *Rather Common Sort of Crime* iv. 42 She jumped a red light.. it was a damned silly place to have traffic lights. **1973** *Daily Tel.* 5 Jan. 2/7 The driver of the local train.. said he had jumped a red signal light.

c. *to jump the gun*: see gun *sb.* 6 e; *to jump the queue*: to go unfairly to or near the front of a queue of people; to push forward out of one's turn; also *fig.*, to gain an unfair advantage or preferential treatment.

1947 *Hansard Commons* 9 Dec. 951 There is no local authority who can clear these camps by allowing the people in them to jump the queues. **1955** L. P. Hartley *Perfect Woman* viii. 82 He distrusted the quality of imagination; it was a rogue quality that jumped the queue. **1955** *Times* 27 June 8/2 The Port of London Authority gave permission for the ship to 'jump the queue' of other vessels waiting in the river for berths. **1958** Hayward & Harari tr. *Pasternak's Dr. Zhivago* ii. ix. 273 There was always a queue in the street... Of course I didn't try to jump the queue, I didn't say I was his wife. **1958** P. Townsend in N. Mackenzie *Conviction* 118 Choosing whether to dodge some taxes.. or jump the queue at the hospital. **1973** 'M. Innes' *Appleby's Answer* v. 49 One of the women makes a gesture, indicating that you should jump the queue.

†**11.** To hazard. *Obs.*

1605 Shaks. *Macb.* i. vii. 7 But heere, vpon this Banke and Schoole of time, Wee'ld iumpe the life to come. **1611** —— *Cymb.* v. iv. 188 You must.. iump the after-enquiry on your owne perill.

†**12.** To agree upon or make up hastily (a marriage, a match). *Obs.*

1589 Greene *Menaphon* (Arb.) 92 Doron smudgde himselfe vp, and iumpde a marriage with his old friend Carmela. **1590** —— *Never too late* (1600) 103 She counts the man worthy to iumpe a match with her. **1615** Swetnam *Arraignm. Wom.* (1880) p. xxvi, I aduise thee.. to haue a speciall regard to her quallities and conditions before thou shake hands or iumpe a match with her.

13. a. *Iron-forging.* To flatten, 'upset', or shorten and thicken the end of a rail or bar by endwise blows. Also *transf.*

1851 *Illustr. Catal. Gt. Exhib.* 249 The ends of the rails will not be jumped up or flattened by the wheels coming in contact with them, which is now the case. **1858** Greener *Gunnery* 434 Fine powder will not do it, but, on the contrary, would jump up the end of the harpoon, or bend it. **1874** Thearle *Naval Archit.* 99 Sometimes the butts.. are fitted by chipping and 'jumping' them; that is, by hammering the butt of the plate until it fits against the butt of the next plate. **1883** Crane *Smithy & Forge* 43 The extreme end is made white hot, and instantly thrust down or 'jumped' several times upon the anvil.

b. To join by welding the flattened ends (cf. *jump-weld* in jump-). **c.** To join (rails, etc.) end on end (cf. *jump-joint* ibid.).

1864 Webster, *Jump*... 3. (*Smith Work*) To join by a butt-weld. **1884** *Cheshire Gloss.* s.v., When a joiner, in putting up rails, nails them to the stumps exactly end to end.. he calls it 'jumping' the rails.

14. *Quarrying.* To drill by means of a jumper.

1851 Greenwell *Coal-trade Terms Northumb. & Durh.* 32 *Jump*.—To drill a hole for the purpose of blasting;.. the drill is made of a greater length, and the opposite end from the chisel end swelled out to make it heavy, and the drill driven by hand. **1865** J. T. F. Turner *Slate Quarries* 13 A hole is jumped in the block [of slate], near the edge.

jump-, the verb-stem used in *Comb.*: **jump-ball, jump ball** *Basketball*, a ball thrown between two opposing players by the referee; **jump-cord**, a cord to be jumped over; **jump-coupling**, a coupling of which the box consists of a collar of metal bored to fit the two connected ends of the shafts = *thimble-coupling*; **jump-cut, jump cut** *Cinemat.* and *Television* (see quot. 1953); also *transf.*, *attrib.* and as *v. trans.* and *intr.*; **jump-jet, jump jet**, a vertical take-off/landing jet aircraft; **jump jockey** *Horse-racing*, a jockey who rides in steeplechases; **jump-joint**, (*a*) a joint in which the parts are welded end to end together, a butt-joint (see butt *sb.*[7] 2); (*b*) a flush-joint in which the edges of the plates or planking are laid close together and make a smooth surface; hence **jump-jointed** *a.*; **jump-lead**, each of a pair of leads for conveying electric charge from one car battery to another during a jump start; **jump-ring**, a wire ring made by bringing the two ends together without welding; **jump-rocks**, a catostomoid fish, *Moxostoma cervinum*, of southern U.S.; **jump-rope, jump rope** (chiefly *N. Amer.*), a skipping-rope; **jump-seat**, (*a*) a movable carriage-seat; also *adj.* and *sb.* (ellipt.) (a carriage) provided with such a seat which can be brought into use when required; (*b*) a folding seat in a motor car; also *transf.*; **jump-shot, jump shot**, (*a*) *Billiards*, etc., a shot which causes the ball to jump; (*b*) *Basketball* (see quot. 1961); **jump-spark, jump spark**, a spark produced by the application of a potential difference to two electrical conductors separated by a narrow gap; usu. *attrib.*, designating devices or methods employing this; **jump-start** *v. trans.*, to start (a vehicle) using the charge from another vehicle's battery, by means of jump-leads; hence also as *sb.*, the starting of a vehicle in this way; **jump-stroke** (*Croquet*): see quot.; **jump take-off** *Aeronaut.*, a vertical take-off; **jump-turn, jump turn**, a turn made while jumping; *spec.* in *Skiing*; **jump-weld**, a weld effected by hammering together the heated ends of two pieces of metal; a butt-weld; hence **jump-weld** *v.*

1924 W. E. Meanwell *Sci. of Basket Ball* 62 During scrimmage watch the tip-off formations and also those for *jump ball and from out of bounds. **1939** Jourdet & Hashagen *Mod. Basketball* xi. 63 Cover your man well on all jump balls. If you are jumping someone else's man, make sure he covers yours. **1969** *Eugene* (Oregon) *Register-Guard* 3 Dec. 3D/1 The game had started on a technical foul when the Beavers were awarded a free throw instead of the usual jump ball. **1953** K. Reisz *Technique Film Editing* 280 **Jump cut*, cut which breaks continuity of time by jumping forward from one part of an action to another obviously separated from the first by an interval of time. **1962** *Listener* 9 Aug. 223/1 The eye-jerking, ear-jarring jump cuts which result when the commercials are removed from imported American programmes. **1962** *Punch* 19 Sept. 428/1 Harsh jump-cuts that might almost be breaks in the film. **1964** *Observer* 12 July 25/5 A jump-cut speeded-up sequence mostly shot from a helicopter. **1965** *Time* 18 June 80 He recklessly jump-cuts from scene to scene, using gimmicky transitions. **1968** P. Dickinson *Skin Deep* vii. 130 The soft lines of the black visage jump-cut into wary maturity. **1966** *Punch* 6 July 26/2 The restless, *jump-cutting style is sometimes disconcerting—one takes a second or two to realise that an expected bridging passage has been waived. **1972** *Times Lit. Suppl.* 9 June 649/4 A series of frenzied incidents.. a matter of jump-cuts and unfinished sentences suggestive of a painful collaboration between Ken Kesey and Ford Madox Ford. **1974** *Ibid.* 14 June 629/4 The reader adjusts soon enough to the breakneck jump-cuts of the first few pages. **1975** *New Yorker* 20 Jan. 79/1 Once Trintignant takes over as the filmmaker, the movie loses its playful movie-within-a-movie spirit, and the technique, which had been a sprinting, jump-cutting shorthand that didn't take itself too seriously, turns glassy smooth. **1964** *Sunday Times* 12 Jan. 1/4 The Ministry of Defence delays ordering the revolutionary Hawker P. 1154 '*jump jet' fighter. **1970** *New Scientist* 19 Feb. 362/1 The trials that the RAF and RN are now conducting on the employment at sea of the Harrier 'jump-jet'. **1973** *Guardian* 18 Apr. 24/5 A command cruiser designed to carry jump-jet aircraft. **1970** J. Leach *Rider on Stand* ix. 89 *Jump jockeys are a devil-may-care bunch. They accept the hazards of their profession in a happy-go-lucky manner. **1972** *Times* 29 Nov. 1/1 Michael Eddery, the jump jockey,.. had his right leg amputated. **1973** *Scotsman* 7 Aug. 15/6 Barry Brogan's dispute with the Jockey Club over renewal of his jump jockey's licence ended amicably. **1874** Thearle *Naval Archit.* 95 Among these early systems [of combining the bottom plates] was that of flush or *jump joints and butts connected by edge strips and butt straps on the inside surface. **1867** Smyth *Sailor's Word-bk.*, **Jump-jointed*, when the plates of an iron vessel are flush, as in those that are carvel-built. **1969** *Motor* 15 Nov. 85 (*caption*) KL Automotive products Ltd. have introduced two new battery booster cables (*jump leads in garage jargon). **1976** *Drive* Nov.–Dec. 40/2 Battery jump-leads... Hitch up your car to theirs with these thick, high-current-carrying leads. **1980** *Know about your Car* (A.A.) 284/1 On an automatic car with a flat battery use jump leads. [**1805** G. McIndoe *Poems & Songs* 40 At three year auld he crys for whips,.. And guns, and girrs, and jumpin'-rapes.] **1834** Emerson *Jrnl.* (1964) IV. 359 Thus is one reminded of the children's prayers who in confessing their sins, say, 'Yes, I did take the *jumprope from Mary.' **1869** L. M. Alcott *Little Women* II. x. 147 Mr. Bhaer down on his hands and knees.. Kitty leading him with a jump-rope. **1969** R. D. Abrahams (*title*) Jump-rope rhymes. **1973** *Islander* (Victoria, B.C.) 8 Apr. 8/1 Spring brings activity—jacks and jump ropes pop up with the flowers. **1864** Webster, **Jump-seat*, a carriage constructed with a movable seat;.. a movable carriage-seat. *Ibid.*, *Jump-seat, a.*, having a movable seat; as, a jump-seat rock-away. **1875** Knight *Dict. Mech.*, *Jump-seat*,.. a kind of open buggy which has a shifting seat or seats... It may be arranged as a double or single seat vehicle. **1931** *Automotive Abstr.* Aug. 238/2 Treatment of the jump-seat explains unique problems presented by this accessory. **1963** Mrs. L. B. Johnson *White House Diary* 24 Nov. (1970) 8 We all got into the same limousine—Mrs. Kennedy and Lyndon in the back seat, the Attorney General and I in the jump seats. **1972** *Guardian* 18 Sept. 14/1, I was sitting in the jump seat... We were racing through the city. **1973** *Black Panther* 6 Oct. 10/1 Only the jump seat for stewardesses was behind him. **1909** P. A. Vaile *Mod. Golf* 92 This shot has its exact counterpart on the billiard table in the useful *jump-shot. **1961** J. S. Salak *Dict. Amer. Sports* 250 *Jump shot* (basketball), a shot taken with both feet off the floor. It can be made with one or two hands with the one-handed shot in general use in the National Basketball Association. **1966** Miller & Thorp *Croquet* 174 *Jump shot*, a shot in which the ball is struck so that it leaves the ground. **1969** *New Yorker* 14 June 79/1 You go through Harlem and you'll see kids less than five feet tall with pretty good jump shots and hook shots. **1974** *Anderson* (S. Carolina) *Independent* 20 Apr. 8A/1 New York's Julius Erving, known as Dr. J., drilled the 20-foot jump shot that gave the Nets their 3–0 margin in the series with an 89–87 victory at Louisville on Wednesday. **1908** J. H. Adams in Onker & Baker *Harper's How to understand Electr. Work* 340/2 **Jump-spark*, a disruptive spark excited between two conducting surfaces in distinction from a spark excited by a rubbing contact. **1911** *Daily Colonist* (Victoria, B.C.) 20 Apr. 8/1 A regal Marine Engine... Jump spark or make-and-break ignition. **1922** A. F. Collins *Bk. Wireless Telegraph & Telephone* i. 6 The spark-coil, or induction coil,.. is used to change the battery current into a current of high pressure to make jump sparks. **1938** A. W. Judge *Automobile Electr. Maintenance* ii. 27 A brass plate at the end of the arm.. passes very close to the brass contacts.. as it rotates, so that a spark leaps across the small air gap. This is known as the jump spark method. **1963** Bird & Hutton-Stott *Veteran Motor Car* 8 'Jump-spark' ignition in American usage generally, though not always, referred to high tension coil and battery apparatus with a mechanical contact-breaker and non-trembling coil, but in English usage, at one time, 'jump-spark ignition' meant any form of H.T. ignition with spark-gaps or 'intensifiers' included in the circuit. [**1973** *Motor* 10 Nov. 22/3 (*heading*) Jump-a-start.] **1976** J. Webster *Automotive Fund. for Consumer* viii. 176 To *jump-start a car, another car with a good battery and a set of jumper cables is needed. **1977** *Washington Post* 9 Nov. B8/2 Another car, also with its hood up and facing the stalled car, was trying to give it a jump start. **1985** *New Yorker* 21 Oct. 38/2, I jump-start her car when her battery is dead, she gives me basil from her garden. **1874** J. D. Heath *Croquet Player* 41 The leapfrog or *jump stroke has lately been used.. with great success, for getting through narrow hoops at a very oblique angle... The effect of this stroke is to make the ball jump up when it strikes the further wire of the hoop. **1939** *Jrnl. R. Aeronaut. Soc.* XLIII. 62 A sustaining rotor for a gyroplane of the '*jump take-off' type. **1924** *Tourist* Winter Sports No. 12/1 **Jump turn*, a method of changing direction or stopping. **1949** Shurr & Yocom *Mod. Dance* v. 147 Add a jump in place after each landing, before executing jump-turn movement in air. **1972** M. Yorke *Silent Witness* ii. 13 He did a quick jump turn and took the narrow track, running fast along the twisting *piste*. **1864** Webster s.v. *Weld*, Butt-weld, or *jump-weld.

jumpable ('dʒʌmpəb(ə)l), *a.* [f. jump *v.* + -able.] Capable of being jumped: **a.** of being leapt over; **b.** of being taken summary possession of, as a claim.

1829 *Sporting Mag.* XXIV. 51 One of the widest brooks.. and not jumpable in all parts. **1883** E. Pennell-Elmhirst *Cream Leicestersh.* 170 Every fence has a jumpable place in it. **1884** Boldrewood *Melbourne Mem.* xvi. 114 The Heifer Station was.. 'an abandoned claim' and possibly 'jumpable'. **1885** *Milnor* (Dakota) *Teller* 12 June 5/3 There is considerable land in this neighborhood that is jumpable.

jump-about. Local name for Goutweed, *Ægopodium Podagraria* (also *Jack-jump-about*).

1656 W. Coles *Art of Simpling* xvi. 49 Ashweed, which some call Jump about. **1879** Britten & Holland *Plant-n.*, Jump-about. *Ægopodium Podagraria... Warw., Oxf.*

jumped (dʒʌmpt), *ppl. a.* [f. jump *v.* + -ed[1].]

a. Made to jump; cooked (as potatoes, etc.) in a frying-pan in which they are shaken from time to time (= F. *sauté*).

1871 *Standard* 24 Jan., I dined this evening on jumped liver. **1895** G. F. Browne *Off the Mill* 131 We regaled ourselves on larded beef, jumped potatoes, rum and cherries.

b. *jumped-up*: that has newly or suddenly risen in status or importance (often with an implication of conceit or arrogance). Also *transf.*

1835 'T. Treddlehoyle' *Bairnsla Ann.* 35 (E.D.D.), A bit ov a jumpt up dress-macker, wot reckans ta be t' biggest beauty it taan. **1867** E. Waugh *Tufts of Heather* 23 What a stark, starin', jumped-up kay-wur to send tho up theer! **1895** *Punch* 24 Aug. 93 You jumped-up, cheap, Coventry bagman. **1919** J. C. Snaith *Love Lane* xxxiv. 189 Democracy. Between you and me, Gert, it's mainly a name for a lot of jumped-up ignoramuses. **1934** J. B. Priestley *Eng. Journey* 380 It has flourished as the big city in the minds of men for generations. It is no mere jumped-up conglomeration of factories, warehouses and dormitories. **1942** L. A. G. Strong *Slocombe Dies* xxvii. 127 The better class despise me as a jumped-up chap with too good a conceit of himself. **1972** J. Wilson *Hide & Seek* i. 19 That jumped-up tarty little madam who couldn't even keep her own husband. **1973** J. Wainwright *Pride of Pigs* 177 He didn't like being talked to.. as if he was some moss-green recruit.. by a jumped-up C.I.D. clown from headquarters.

jumper ('dʒʌmpə(r)), *sb.*[1] [f. jump *v.* + -er[1].] One who or that which jumps.

1. a. A man or animal that jumps or leaps.

1611 Cotgr., *Sautier*, a leaper, iumper, skipper. **1812** *Sporting Mag.* XXXIX. 15 Almost as great a jumper as himself. **1886** Coventry & Watson *Steeple-chasing* iv, However much a horse may answer to the description of a natural jumper, he has to learn to be clever.

b. A ticket-inspector or ticket-collector. *slang.*

1900 *Westm. Gaz.* 4 May 8/2 The.. duties of the "bus-jumper"—the ghostlike functionary who appears on the top of a 'bus and demands a sight of your ticket. **1906** *Daily Chron.* 24 July 3/7 It was not a fact that unless the 'jumpers'—travelling ticket inspectors—made a certain number of reports they were discharged. **1931** *Evening Express* (Aberdeen) 4 Apr., It is not at all uncommon for a 'jumper'

to find that fifty per cent. of the occupants of a second class compartment have only third class tickets. **1937** *Daily Express* 21 Jan. 3/4 If you use a second [class carriage] with a 'third' ticket, watch for the 'jumpers', ready to pounce and demand excess. **1966** H. SHEPPARD *Dict. Railway Slang* (ed. 2) 7 *Jumper*, travelling ticket collector.

c. *Basketball.* A jump-ball or jump-shot; a player of such a ball or shot.

1937 F. C. ALLEN *Better Basketball* II. xiii. 182 Any jumper must keep his eyes fixed upon the ball until it is tapped. He must always play the ball and not the other jumper. *Ibid.* 188 Many jumpers are taught illegally to jump sooner than their opponent in order to get above him. **1958** F. MCGUIRE *Offensive Basketball* ii. 75 Getting possession of the ball depends upon a number of items which are more or less related. First comes the leaping and timing ability of the jumper. *Ibid.* 112 The two-hand overhead jump shot is made in the same manner as the one-hand jumper except that the ball is carried above the head instead of over the shoulder. **1969** Z. HOLLANDER *Mod. Encycl. Basketball* 121/2 Lucus..could also score on jumpers from the corner. **1969** *Eugene* (Oregon) *Register-Guard* 3 Dec. 3D/4 The Vikings took the lead on Snider's free throw with 46 seconds left, but Steve Halberg hit a 15-foot jumper to put the Irish back on top and North couldn't come up with an equalizer.

2. A name applied to the members of a body of Methodists which arose in Wales about the middle of the eighteenth century, who used to jump and dance as a part of religious worship; applied also to more recent sects following similar practices.

1774 in Sidney *Rowl. Hill* (1834) 101 Nothing..made him so angry as the enthusiasm of the jumpers, whom he called the caricaturists of religion. **1802** *Public Characters* 552 The Jumpers in Wales have started up as a sect within the last half century. **1852** M. W. SAVAGE *R. Medlicott* III. xii. (D.), Jenny [was] a Welshwoman; her rude forefathers were goat-herds on week-days, and Jumpers on Sundays. **1876** C. M. DAVIES *Unorth. Lond.*, The Walworth Jumpers.

3. a. An animal, esp. an insect (as a flea) or insect-larva, characterized by jumping: cf. HOPPER[1] 2.

1785 *Gentl. Mag.* LV. I. 265 A very remarkable little animal... It is the *Mus Jaculus* or *Sauteur*; and in English may be called the Jumper. **1789** G. WHITE *Selborne* xxxiv. 90 These eggs produce maggots called jumpers. **1834** M'MURTRIE *Cuvier's Anim. Kingd.* 391 The Jumpers or the Anisopoda.

b. In full, ***jumper ant.*** An Australian ant of the genus *Myrmecia.*

1907 W. W. FROGGATT *Austral. Insects* 92 The 'Jumper', *Myrmecia albo-cincta*..is one of the smaller species, about ½ an inch in length. *Ibid.* 436/2 *(index)* Jumper ant. **1926** R. J. TILLYARD *Insects Austral. & N.Z.* xxii. 287 The genus *Myrmecia*..contains the huge Bull-dog Ants and the smaller Jumpers..which swarm out of their nests and advance to the attack in a series of jumps or springs. **1970** E. F. REEK in *Insects of Australia* (Commonwealth Sci. & Industr. Res. Organization) xxxvii. 956/1 Forms such as the bulldog or jumper ants..feed largely on nectar and honey-dew as adults.

4. One who jumps a claim. See JUMP *v.* 9 b.

1855 F. S. MARRYAT *Mountains & Molehills* 240 My claim being carefully measured..and found to be correct, the 'jumper' would be ordered to confine himself to his own territory. **1890** GUNTER *Miss Nobody* vii. 86 Bob, the hero who saved the Baby Mine from the jumpers for us.

5. One who causes to jump, in quot., a flogger.

1842 ORDERSON *Creol.* ix. 96 This..brute..ordered the unhappy Rachael into the hands of the 'Jumper'.

6. Applied to various tools or contrivances having a jumping motion. **a.** *Quarrying.* A heavy drill worked either by hand or by means of a hammer, used in making blasting-holes in rock, etc. Also *attrib.* **b.** A spring or click controlling the starwheel of a repeating clock. **c.** A form of plough-share for rough soil, or for soil filled with roots (*U.S.*). **d.** *Electr.* A wire used to cut out an instrument or part of a circuit, or to close temporarily a gap in a circuit.

a. 1769 SMEATON in Brand *Hist. Newcastle* (1789) II. 586 Eye-bolts fixed in holes bored [in stones] with a jumper. **1828** *Craven Dial.*, *Jumper*, a miner's augur, used in making holes for the reception of gun-powder, for blasting or blowing up rocks. **1839–47** J. S. MACAULAY *Field Fortif.* (1851) 213 The miner holds the jumper in both hands, raises it, and lets it fall in the hole, turning it continually. *Ibid.*, When the stone is of a very hard description, it is usual to pour water occasionally into the jumper-hole.

b. 1850 E. B. DENISON *Clock & Watch Making* §92. 125 The thing called the jumper..will..drive the ray still farther forward..The jumper also acts as a click to keep the star wheel steady. **1884** F. J. BRITTEN *Watch & Clockm.* 251 The pin in moving the star wheel presses back the click or 'jumper'.

d. *a* **1901** in *N.E.D.* **1906** T. E. HERBERT *Telegraphy* xviii. 586 When any cross is necessary, the cross-connecting or 'jumper' wires between the vertical and horizontal sides of the frame are altered, so avoiding the necessity for disturbing the cabling. **1931** MOYER & WOSTREL *Radio Handbk.* xi. 560 A temporary jumper may be used to close the circuit. **1948** *Aircraft Power Plants* (Northrop Aeronaut. Inst.) ix. 216/2 Test the switch by placing heavy jumpers across the terminals. In other words, close the circuit through the switch with temporary conductors. **1967** *Electronics* 6 Mar. 282/3 The mode selector..includes a 'battery' position that enables checking the condition of the battery without removing it or connecting jumpers. **1972** G. H. REED *Refrigeration* xiii. 120 A single wire 'jumper' lead.. is useful both for by-passing faulty controls or for incorporating a capacitor in the test cord.

7. *N. Amer.* A rough kind of sledge: see quot. 1893.

1823 J. F. COOPER *Pioneers* xxix. (1869) 126/1 They frequently make these jumpers to convey their game home. **1834** J. LANGTON *Let.* 2 Feb. in *Early Days Upper Canada* (1926) 81 A jumper..is a most admirable conveyance and most properly called a jumper... It sticks at nothing; wherever the horses can scramble the jumper can leap after them. **1893** C. G. LELAND *Mem.* II. 81 A jumper,..the roughest form of a sledge, consisting of two saplings with the ends turned up, fastened by cross-pieces. **1898** R. A. GUILD in *New Eng. Mag.* June 455/1 My pulse quickens as I recall the glorious times with our 'jumper', and the hair-breadth escapes from posts and barberry bushes, in our swift descent upon the ice. **1902** A. C. LAUT *Story of Trapper* xv. 221 The rutted marks of a 'jumper' sleigh cut the hard crust. **1903** B. W. CARR-HARRIS *White Chief of Ottawa* 119 They had not gone far when the Indian drew their attention to the tracks of a jumper in the snow. **1941** *Beaver* June 28 We loaded twelve hundred pounds of freight into a canoe, besides the dogs and a jumper sleigh. **1964** E. C. GUILLET *Pioneer Days Upper Canada* 74 Early settlers from the vicinity of Meaford and Owen Sound brought their grists in home-made sleighs called jumpers, which were hauled by oxen. **1971** J. MCDOUGALL *Parsons on Plains* i. 5 Then, in winter, with our little white pony and jumper, we would make the same trips.

8. *Naut.* **a.** A preventer-rope made fast so as to prevent a yard, mast, etc. from jumping or springing up in rough weather. Also *attrib.* **b.** ***jolly jumpers***, sails above the moon-rakers (Smyth *Sailor's Word-bk.* 1867).

1856 KANE *Arct. Expl.* I. viii. 87 By a complication of purchases, jumpers, and shoves, we started the brig. **1882** NARES *Seamanship* (ed. 6) 30 Topping lift for spritsail gaff and jumper. *Ibid.* 51 The jumper is rove through a clump block on the cutwater, and is set up with a purchase in the head. **1900** *Westm. Gaz.* 14 Feb. 10/2 These enable it [the compass] to be hoisted aloft on to the jumper stay, and it is in this way removed from all influences of the magnetism.. caused by the ship's iron.

Hence **'jumperism**, the principles of the Jumpers. **'jumpery**, practice or action of jumping; humorously applied to a dance.

1800 J. WHITAKER *Let.* in Polwhele *Trad. & Recoll.* (1826) II. 524 On Methodistical Jumpers or Jumperism. **1876** C. M. DAVIES *Unorth. Lond.* 64 Whether Jumperism is ceasing to merit its distinctive appellation, I cannot..say. **1882** BESANT *All Sorts* vi. 53 Such dances as the *bolero*, the *tarantellà*, and other national jumperies.

'jumper, *sb.*[2] [prob. f. JUMP *sb.*[2]]

1. a. A kind of loose outer jacket or shirt reaching to the hips, made of canvas, serge, coarse linen, etc., and worn by sailors, truckmen, etc.; also applied to any upper garment of similar shape, e.g. a hooded fur jacket worn by Eskimos.

1853 KANE *Grinnell Exp.* vi. (1856) 45 A 'jumper' or close jacket, slipping on like a shirt, and hooded like the cowl of a Franciscan monk. *c* **1860** H. STUART *Seaman's Catech.* 80, I set of jumper and trousers for dirty work. **1860–1** GOSSE *Rom. Nat. Hist.* (1866) 255 A loose coarse canvas frock, which, in colonial phrase, is called a 'jumper'. **1879** *Unif. Reg.* in *Navy List* (1882) July 496/2 On the blue frock or jumper the badge is to be of red cloth. **1893** SELOUS *S.E. Africa* 87, I had a warm jumper over my cotton shirt.

b. *Comb.*, as ***jumper-clad*** adj.

1865 F. H. NIXON *Peter Perfume* 172 The jumper-clad diggers so rowdy and free.

2. (See quot.)

1894 *Daily Tel.* 13 Apr. 5/6 Witnesses..deposed that the 'jumper', a sort of sack used for purposes similar to that of the strait waistcoat, was in constant use in the workhouse.

3. a. = JERSEY[1] 3 a; also, a loose-fitting blouse worn over a skirt; (see also quot. 1968).

1908 *Sears, Roebuck Catal.* 1149/4 The jumper is made in surplice effect. **1908** *Dialect Notes* III. 326 *Jumpers*, a one-piece garment for children to play in, 'rompers'. **1909** *Public Ledger* (Philadelphia) 24 June 7/6 One-piece & jumper styles. **1909** *Westm. Gaz.* 7 Aug. 15/2 For smaller girls the jumper still holds its own. **1925** W. DEEPING *Sorrell & Son* i. 13 The modiste had received a consignment of silk 'jumpers'. She was unpacking them and hanging them up on the stands in her showroom where they glowed brilliantly like jewels in a case. **1928** GALSWORTHY *Swan Song* II. ix. 181 He came on Anne herself, without a hat, sitting on a gate, her hands in the pockets of her jumper. **1930** *N. & Q.* 14 June 431/1 Some five years ago the fashion-mongers gave the name of jumper to the knitted blouses ladies had been wearing under the name of sports coats. **1945** *Wales* IV. vi. 44 He turned up the cuff of his jumper and showed her the word 'Sue' tattooed with a border of foliage on his forearm. **1965** *Australian* 13 Apr. 5 She also prefers casual clothes like the jumper and skirt she is wearing here. **1968** J. IRONSIDE *Fashion Alphabet* 61 *Jump-suit.* This is an abbreviation of 'jumpers', another name for rompers (i.e. top and bloomers in one) worn by children.

b. *U.S.* A pinafore dress. Also ***jumper dress.***

1939 M. B. PICKEN *Lang. Fashion* 84/3 *Jumper-dress*, sleeveless, one-piece garment worn with guimpe. **1967** *Boston Sunday Herald* (Mag.) 16 Apr. 6/1 (Advt.), Wear as a jumper over blouses. **1971** *New Yorker* 11 Dec. 3 (Advt.), Wear a jumper to dinner!

c. *Comb.*, as **jumper suit**, (*a*) a pinafore dress; (*b*) a woman's suit consisting of a jumper and skirt made of the same material, freq. wool.

1908 *Sears, Roebuck Catal.* 1149/1 An unusually pretty jumper suit made of soft striped taffeta silk. **1925** *Times* 29 Dec. 7/6 Sports stockinette jumper suits. **1931** E. RAYMOND *Mary Leith* III. ii. 225 Mary was in a jumper suit of primrose silk. **1973** *Country Life* 2 Aug. 335/2 Soft jumper-suits in fine printed wools.

†**'jumper**, *v.*[1] *Obs.* In 4–5 iompre, 5–6 iumpere. [Origin obscure.] *trans.* To introduce incongruously or discordantly; to jumble together.

c **1374** CHAUCER *Troylus* II. 988 (1037) Ne Iompre [*v.r.* iumpere] ek no discordaunt þing y-fere, As þus to vsen termes of Phisyk. **1387–8** T. USK *Test. Love* Prol. (Skeat) I. 30 How should than a frenche man borne soche termes conne iumpere in his matter, but as the Iay chatereth Englishe.

jumper, *v.*[2] [f. JUMPER *sb.*[1]]

1. *trans.* To bore (a hole) with a jumper (see JUMPER *sb.*[1] 6 a).

1825 *Blackw. Mag.* XVII. 339 A hole..is jumpered in the rock.

2. *Electr.* To connect by means of a jumper (sense 6 d).

1929 *Post Office Electr. Engineers' Jrnl.* XXII. 79/1 From the cable terminal tag blocks all lines are jumpered *via* protecting apparatus to the 'line' tag blocks of the test boards. **1968** T. HOWARD *Black Light* xxi. 183 He made no attempt to force the locked ignition, but simply 'jumpered' the ignition wiring so that it by-passed the locked switch.

jumper *v.*[2], **jumperism**: see JUMPER *sb.*[1]

jumping ('dʒʌmpɪŋ), *vbl. sb.* [f. JUMP *v.* + -ING[1].] **a.** The action of JUMP *v.*, in various senses.

1565 COOPER *Thesaurus*, *Saltatio*, daunsyng, iumpyng. **1568** BIBLE (Bishops') *Nahum* iii. 2 The praunsing of horses and the iumping of charrets. **1699** BENTLEY *Phal.* (1836) I. 242 There was either a strange jumping of good wits, or Democritus was a sorry plagiary. **1889** *Boston* (Mass.) *Jrnl.* 25 Apr. 73 An organized and systematic 'jumping' of the claims of the men whose title rests on this fraud. *Mod. Newsp.* The jumping was exceptionally good.

b. *attrib.*, as **jumping-board**, a spring-board; also *fig.*; **jumping jockey** = *jump jockey* s.v. JUMP-; **jumping-off board** = *jumping-board*; **jumping-off ground, jumping-off place**, (*a*) a place at which one jumps off from a conveyance or alights at the end of a journey, or from which one jumps off into the region beyond; also *transf.* and *fig.*; (*b*) *N. Amer.*, a place regarded as being the farthest limit of civilization or settlement; a very remote place; the extreme limit of the earth; also *fig.*; (*c*) a starting-point for aircraft or the like; so ***jumping-off point, spot***; **jumping-pole**, a long pole used in jumping long distances or in making pole-vaults; **jumping-powder**, a slang name for a stimulant taken by a rider to nerve him for jumping; **jumping-sheet**, a stout sheet into which persons may jump from a burning building; **jumping-wire**, on a submarine: see quot. 1974.

1878 H. H. JACKSON *Bits Trav. at Home* 53 There are public gardens..with little ponds, and boats, and targets, and *jumping-boards. **1909** *Athenæum* 21 Aug. 218/2 A jumping-board for the imagination to spring from. **1947** W. BEBBINGTON *Rogues go Racing* xviii. 115 There are some [jockeys] who are known to me as habitual gamblers. Particularly is this so with certain of our '*jumping' jockeys. **1914** *Eng. Rev.* Sept. 237 Salonika..was to be the German *jumping-off board to Asia Minor. **1931** *Musical Times* 1 June 497/2 His studies abroad had given him a stock of admirably nurtured gifts, but no jumping-off board such as that offered by a career in an English institution. **1897** *Daily News* 24 Feb. 5/5 The strip of territory on the Transvaal border, which Mr. Stead called..the '*jumping-off ground'. **1900** *Ibid.* 21 May 3/1 To achieve the independence of the Republics, and from that jumping-ground begin anew. **1934** R. MACAULAY *Going Abroad* xi. 82 That's abso*lute*ly the best *jumping-off ground for the new life. **1959** P. MOYES *Dead Men don't Ski* vi. 74 Tangiers is a convenient jumping-off ground. **1826** T. FLINT *Recoll.* 366 Being, as they phrase it, the '*jumping off place', it is necessarily the resort of desperate, wicked, and strange creatures who wish to fly away from poverty, infamy, and the laws. **1834** S. E. DAWSON *Handbk. Canada* 68 Yarmouth, the jumping-off place of Nova Scotia. **1834** H. M. BRACKENRIDGE *Recoll.* x. 111, I had no jumping off or jumping up place, like those who prepare their exordium and perorations, and leave the body of the speech to take care of itself. **1847** W. I. PAULDING in J. K. & W. I. Paulding *Amer. Comedies* 197, I *have* hunted all over them parts, almost clean out to the jumping off place of creation. **1853** KANE *Grinnell Exp.* x. (1856) 70 It is the jumping-off place of Arctic navigators—our last point of communication with the outside world. **1899** B. TARKINGTON *Gentleman from Indiana* xv. 266 He had come to a jumping-off place in his life—why had they not let him jump? **1900** *Daily News* 16 Feb. 6/2 If we may borrow a figure from South African politics, the Pamirs are a 'jumping off place' for the Russian invaders of Afghanistan and India. **1909** F. ASH *Trip to Mars* xvii. 131 A narrow platform which had been erected as a 'jumping-off place' for fliers. **1922** *Encycl. Brit.* XXX. 14/2 The Governments demanded that their aeroplanes should be transported in crates, or towed with folded wings to their jumping-off places. **1930** G. B. SHAW *Apple Cart* I. 37 Today the nation would be equally amazed if a man of his ability thought it worth his while to prefer the woolsack even to the stool of an office boy as a jumping-off place for his ambition. **1953** F. STARK *Coast of Incense* 242 The way to carry out an adventure is to organize the jumping-off place as near to its borders as possible. **1964** D. JENNESS *Eskimo Admin.* II. 14 Archdeacon Stuck described Herschel Island during the whaling period as 'the world's last jumping-off place, where no law existed and no writs ran'. **1927** R. H. WILENSKI *Mod. Movement in Art* I. 13 An emotional reaction as the sole *jumping-off point. **1958** G. LASCELLES in P. Gammond *Decca Bk. Jazz* viii. 100 It is not unnatural ..for New York to have been the proving ground and the jumping-off point for a new sort of music. **1909** *Daily Chron.* 8 Sept. 1/4 To reach the neighbourhood of Cape Columbia.., his elected *jumping-off spot for the Pole. **1966** *Beautiful Brit. Columbia* Spring 23/1 Prince Rupert.. is a jumping-off spot for the Queen Charlotte Islands. **1873** L. TROUBRIDGE *Life amongst Troubridges* (1966) vi. 47 We..

jumped loads of ditches, and when we came to a very large one we made a bridge of our *jumping poles. **1972** *Listener* 31 Aug. 274/2 We had jumping-poles and we jumped from one rock to another. **1826** *Sporting Mag.* XVII. 374 The fences come very quick in Shropshire, and a little *jumping-powder is often found useful. **1858** 'SCRUTATOR' [HORLOCK] *Master of Hounds* (1864) 91, I have not yet had my glass of jumping powder. **1846** *Mechanics' Mag.* XLIV. 228 The canvass escape alluded to..is the '*jumping sheet' of the philanthropic Captain Manby. **1919** *Jane's Fighting Ships* 318 *Jumping wires were added to French submarines. **1940** 'N. SHUTE' *Landfall* iii. 73 'Did you notice how many jumping-wires she had?' 'That's the wire that runs from bow to stern over the conning-tower, isn't it?' 'That's right. Did she have one or two?' **1974** G. JENKINS *Bridge of Magpies* xv. 223 Her jumping-wire—the thick cable designed to slice through undersea objects like mine moorings—which runs from bow to stern via the conning-tower.

jumping ('dʒʌmpɪŋ), *ppl. a.* [f. as prec. + -ING[2].] **a.** That jumps, in various senses of the verb. ***jumping cat***: see CAT *sb.*[1] 13 e.

1567 [implied in JUMPINGLY below]. **1611** BIBLE *Nahum* iii. 2 The noise of..the praunsing horses, and of the iumping charets. **1659** D. PELL *Impr. Sea* 416 They can very well..abide the jumping waves of the Seas. **1844** W. H. MAXWELL *Sport & Adv. Scotl.* xiii. (1855) 118 There is..what seamen call a jumping sea. **1899** *19th Cent.* Oct. 692 The worship of the Jumping Cat, and the appeal to the man in the street.

b. In names of animals characterized by their jumping or springing movement: **jumping-beetle**, an insect destructive to turnips, etc.; **jumping-bug**, an insect of the family *Halticoridæ*; **jumping deer**, either of two North American animals, the pronghorn, *Antilocapra americana*, or the mule deer, *Odocoileus hemionus*; **jumping-hare**, a rodent quadruped of S. Africa, *Pedetes caffer* or *Helamys capensis*, resembling the jerboa; **jumping-louse**, a flea-louse, a jumping plant-louse; **jumping-mouse**, (*a*) the American deermouse, *Zapus hudsonius*; (*b*) = *jumping-rat*; **jumping-mullet**, a catostomoid fish of North America, *Moxostoma cervinum*; also a gray mullet, *Mugil albula*; **jumping-rat**, a rodent of the family *Dipodidæ*; **jumping-shrew**, the elephant-shrew of Africa, an insectivorous quadruped of the family *Macroscelididæ*; **jumping-spider**, one of the group of spiders which leap upon their prey, instead of spinning a web to catch it.

1817 *Blackw. Mag.* II. 235 His turnips are devoured by the *jumping beetle. **1806** A. HENRY *Jrnl.* 14 July in E. Coues *New Light Hist. Greater Northwest* (1897) I. ix. 305 Herds of cabbrie or *jumping deer were always in sight. **1831** R. COX *Adv. Columbia River* II. 364 The jumping-deer, or chevreuil,..frequent the vicinity of the mountains in considerable numbers. **1908** J. W. TYRRELL *Across Sub-Arctics of Canada* (ed. 3) xxi. 243 Jumping Deer are found in more or less abundance throughout the timbered country about southern parts of the [Hudson] Bay. **1936** D. MCCOWAN *Animals Canad. Rockies* xxxi. 265 The Mule deer is most common... In some parts of Canada the animal is called Jumping deer, this from its well known habit of progressing when alarmed in a series of immense leaps and bounds. **1961** R. P. HOBSON *Rancher takes Wife* vii. 108 There were the tiny little white-tailed jumping deer that would make about four meals for one man. **1839** *Penny Cycl.* XIX. 513/2 This is the..Spring-Has or *Jumping Hare of the Dutch. *Ibid.* 509/2 *Jumping Mice. **1849** *Sk. Nat. Hist., Mammalia* IV. 41 The Labrador Jumping Mouse..is very common in the fur countries of North America. **1766** J. BARTRAM *Jrnl.* 14 Jan. in Stark *Acc. E. Florida* 35 Saw a mullet jump three times in a minute or two, which they generally do before they rest, so are called *jumping-mullets. **1900** H. A. BRYDEN *Animals Afr.* ii. 16 The typical Cape *jumping shrew has a long, proboscis-like nose, large ears, long, thin hind legs, which enable him to take enormous leaps for his size, and a long, rat-like tail. **1920** F. W. FITZSIMONS *Nat. Hist. S. Afr. Mammals* IV. 2 There are several species or kinds of Jumping or Elephant Shrews inhabiting South Africa. **1971** D. J. POTGIETER et al. *Animal Life S. Afr.* 346/2 The elephant-shrews or jumping shrews (*Macroscelidea*) are insect-eaters, and the whole order is confined to Africa. **1813** BINGLEY *Anim. Biog.* (ed. 4) III. 363 The *Jumping Spider..does not, like many others, take its prey by means of a net, but is constrained to seize them only by its own activity.

c. jumping-bean, (*a*) the seed of a Mexican euphorbiaceous plant, which jumps about by reason of the movements of the larva of a tortricid moth (*Carpocapsa saltitans*) enclosed within it (*Cent. Dict.*); (*b*) a toy consisting of a small bean-shaped capsule containing a weight such as a lead ball which causes it to move unaided down a sloping surface; **jumping-betty**, a popular name of the Garden Balsam, *Impatiens Balsamina*, the seeds of which jump out of the elastic capsules when these are touched (Parish *Sussex Gloss.* 1875); **jumping-jack**, a child's toy made out of the merry-thought of a fowl; a toy figure of a man, which is made to jump by being pulled with strings; also *transf.*: see quots.; **jumping-Johnny** (see quot.); **jumping-seed** = *jumping-bean* (a).

1889 *Cent. Dict.*, *Jumping-bean. **1896** *Chambers's Jrnl.* 18 Apr. 249 A new botanical curiosity..has lately been brought into notice in England under the name of 'A Jumping Bean'. **1910** *Boy's Own Paper* 15 Jan. 256 *Tommy* (who has been watching the jumping beans for some time): 'Oi'm waitin' to see them sticks walk.' **1972** F. WARNER *Maquettes* 14 Along they go, like jumping beans from a toy factory. **1972** SWAN & PAPP *Common Insects N. Amer.* 312 The wriggling larva of an olethreutid moth, *Laspeyresia saltitans*, is the activator of the Mexican 'jumping bean', the seed of a species of *Croton*. **1883** E. E. HALE in *Harper's Mag.* Jan. 277/1 Barley-candy statuettes, *jumping-jacks, and other..toys. **1884** HENLEY & STEVENSON *Deacon Brodie* II. v. (1892) 50 He was my butt, my ape, my jumping-jack. **1899** *Westm. Gaz.* 26 May 3/2 By sailors the crested penguin is known by the name of the 'jumping jack', from its habit of jumping from the water. **1865** *Reader* No. 140. 264/1 The plate-sawing machine called a *Jumping Johnny. **1876** *Field & Forest* II. 53 These so-called *jumping seeds received from California. **1889** *Wesley Naturalist* III. 22 Those are the only 'jumping seeds' of which I had even heard until I met with these of Natal.

Hence '**jumpingly** *adv.*, in a jumping manner.

1567 DRANT *Horace, Arte Poetrye* A iv b, Do not imitate So iumpingly, so precyselie And step, for step so strayte. **1855** *Chamb. Jrnl.* III. 388 This amphitheatre slopes roughly, jumpingly down to a river.

['**jumpish**, error for *lumpish* in Nares.]

jumply, jumpness: see at end of JUMP *a.*

jump-off ('dʒʌmpɒf, -ɔːf). [f. *to jump off.*]

1. A precipitous descent; a place from which a person must jump. *U.S. colloq.*

1873 [see BED *sb.* 12 f]. **1884** C. PHILLIPPS-WOLLEY *Trottings of Tenderfoot* v. 129 The broad stem of a fallen giant gives you 150 feet of splendid wooden road; but..you find you have been gradually ascending, and now stand on what the Americans would call a 'jump off'. **1909** R. A. WASON *Happy Hawkins* ii. 26 The lantern shed a splash o' light on the shelf, but the jump-off looked like the mouth o' the pit.

b. The start of a military operation or campaign. *U.S. slang.*

1918 [see *H-Hour* s.v. H. III]. **1944** *Daily Progress* (Charlottesville, Va.) 12 May 1/8 The Fifth and Eighth armies have launched the greatest drive in Mediterranean warfare in the jump-off of Allied spring offensives. **1945** *Sun* (Baltimore) 23 Feb. 1/6 (*heading*) Canadians find going toughest since jumpoff.

2. *Aeronaut.* A vertical take-off.

In quot. 1969 'jump off point' = *jumping-off point.*

1939 *Jrnl. R. Aeronaut. Soc.* XLIII. 110 (*heading*) Possibilities of the jump-off autogyro. *Ibid.*, The available kinetic energy in the rotor system for 'jump-off' is directly proportional to the weight of the blades and to the square of the rotational speed of the rotor. **1969** *Daily Tel.* 16 Jan. 1/6 A space station in permanent orbit round the earth..could ..be used as a 'jump off' point for travel to the moon.

3. *Show-jumping.* An additional round to resolve or determine a tie.

1947 H. DISSTON *Equestionnaire* (rev. ed.) 77 In the event of a jump off over triple bars, how is the obstacle altered? **1954** P. SMYTHE *Jump for Joy* vii. 113 The final jump-off included a high wall with a pole on top. **1969** *Times* 10 May 6/5 Alan Oliver..justified..the odds laid on him in the..competition yesterday. Riding Pitz Palu, who was made favourite at 7-2 and shortened to 2-1 for the jumpoff, he..made the running from start to finish.

jump-up ('dʒʌmpʌp). *colloq.* [f. *to jump up.*]

1. An escarpment. *local Austral.*

1927 M. TERRY *Through Land of Promise* 85 We had been looking at the 'jump-up' marking the extremity of the Barkly Tableland. **1969** 'A. GARVE' *Boomerang* i. 32 There's a sharpish rise from the plain to the tableland, with a steep edge—what we call the 'jump-up'.

2. An informal West Indian dance.

1955 *Caribbean Q.* IV. ii. 102 Children and adults dancing in the shuffling manner of the Trinidad Carnival 'jump-up'. **1959** 'M. UNDERWOOD' *Arm of Law* xiv. 164 Some might be found doing a traditional mid-day jump-up. **1965** 'LAUCHMONEN' *Old Thom's Harvest* vii. 96 A few people..gathered around the calypsonian... Saul was doing a real jump-up in the centre. **1971** *Sunday Times* 13 June 9 You have some rum and a bloody good lunch, then you have a jump-up, and a proper shindig. **1973** *Advocate-News* (Barbados) 17 Feb. 6/1 With the carnival fever in the air, the students at the Cave Hill campus will stage their pre-carnival jump-up and calypso tent at the campus tomorrow, beginning at 5 p.m.

jumpy ('dʒʌmpɪ), *a.* [f. JUMP *sb.* + -Y.]

1. Characterized by jumps or sudden movements from one thing or state to another.

1869 *Daily News* 25 Nov., 'O Paradise' was thus sung to a jumpy measure in six-eight time. **1893** *Scot. Leader* 15 July 3 The stock markets were in that condition best described as 'jumpy', though the jumps were generally in the downward direction.

2. a. Characterized by sudden involuntary movements caused by nervous excitement; nervous, apprehensive.

1879 A. FORBES in *Daily News* 21 Aug. 5/3 Nothing..makes a man so jumpy and nervous as a good steady rain of shell-fire. **1894** DOYLE *Round Red Lamp* 11 It made me jumpy to watch him. **1918** *Wine, Women & War* (1926) 10 No trip for anybody with jumpy nerves. **1935** [see GOOEY *a.*]. **1957** *Sat. Even. Post* 21 Sept. 94 One of our pals in the nightclub business is jumpy and he needs a bodyguard tonight. **1974** G. MARKSTEIN *Cooler* xlvi. 167 She was jumpy about the blackout too... She *is* on edge, he decided.

b. Producing nervous excitement.

1883 BURTON & CAMERON *Gold Coast* I. iii. 75 The people seem to delight in standing, like wild goats, upon the dizziest of 'jumpy' peaks. **1896** *Westm. Gaz.* 11 Jan. 3/1 The adventure which might be called the most 'jumpy'.

Hence '**jumpiness**, the state or condition of being jumpy.

1897 *Allbutt's Syst. Med.* II. 854 There is, indeed, a general condition of jumpiness and nervousness.

jun., abbreviation of JUNIOR.

1708 [see JUNIOR *a.* 1]. **1837** DICKENS *Sk. Boz* 2nd Ser. 222 Mr. Green, sen., and his noble companion entered one car, and Mr. Green, jun., and *his* companion the other. **1922** JOYCE *Ulysses* 391 Dixon jun., scholar of my lady of Mercy. **1955** *Times* 8 July 6/7 On June 8, continued counsel, Thomas Foote, jun., saw a bank official carrying out two bags of silver to a car. **1974** *Country Life* 11 Apr. (Suppl.) 66 John Frederick Herring Jun. A farmyard scene.

juncaceous (dʒʌŋ'keɪʃəs), *a. Bot.* [f. mod.L. *Juncāce-æ* (f. *juncus* rush) + -OUS: see -ACEOUS.] Belonging to N.O. *Juncaceæ* (the rush family).

1855 in MAYNE *Expos. Lex.* **1864** WEBSTER, *Juncaceous* (*Bot.*), of, pertaining to, or resembling rushes.

†**jun'cade.** *Obs. rare*[−1]. [app. a. obs. F. *joncade* (in Rabelais), 'a certaine spoone-meat made of creame, Rose-water, and Sugar' (Cotgr.), a. Pr. *joncada*, cheese-curd, fresh cheese.] = JUNKET 2.

14.. *Voc.* in Wr.-Wülcker 590/44 *Juncata*, Juncade, *sive* a crudde ymade yn ryshes.

juncagineous (dʒʌŋkə'dʒɪniːəs), *a. Bot.* [f. mod.L. *Juncagine-æ*, f. *Juncāgo* (f. *juncus* rush), Tournefort's name for the genus *Triglochin* + -OUS.] Belonging to the Natural Order of *Juncagineæ* (or *Juncaginaceæ*), comprising certain rush-like plants, by some included in *Naiadaceæ*.

1855 in MAYNE *Expos. Lex.* **1887** in *Syd. Soc. Lex.* **1893** in *Funk's Stand. Dict.*

juncal ('dʒʌŋkəl), *a. Bot.* [f. L. *junc-us* rush + -AL[1].] Belonging to the genus *Juncus*, or to Lindley's 'alliance' *Juncāles*, comprising the orders *Juncaceæ* and (according to some) *Orontiaceæ*.

†'**juncary.** *Obs. rare.* [? ad. med.L. *juncāria*, f. *junc-us* rush: see -ARY. Cf. NFr. *jonquere, -quière*. F. *jonchère*.] Land overgrown with rushes.

1613 SIR H. FINCH *Law* (1636) 24 In a Writ the generall shall be put in demand, and in plaint before the speciall: as land before pree, pasture, wood, iuncary, marish, &c.

juncat, -cate, obs. forms of JUNKET.

junciform ('dʒʌnsɪfɔːm), *a.* [f. L. type **junciformis*, f. *juncus* rush: see -FORM.] Of the form of a rush; long and slender like a rush.

1855 in MAYNE *Expos. Lex.* **1887** in *Syd. Soc. Lex.*

junck, obs. form of JUNK.

junckerite ('dʒʌŋkəraɪt, 'jʊŋ-). *Min.* [Named 1834, after Juncker, director of the mine where it was found: see -ITE.] A synonym of SIDERITE.

1865–72 WATTS *Dict. Chem.* III. 444 *Junkerite*, spathic iron ore. **1868** DANA *Min.* (ed. 5) §725 Junckerite..proved to be only common spathic iron.

juncket, obs. form of JUNKET.

junco ('dʒʌŋkəʊ). [a. Sp. *junco*, ad. L. *junc-us* rush; cf. Sp. *junco ave* 'a bird in the Indies with a very long and narrow taile' (Minsheu, 1599).]

†**a.** A name formerly given to the Reed-sparrow or Reed-bunting (*Emberiza schœniclus*). *Obs.* **b.** Name of a North American genus of Finches, the Snow-birds; a bird of this genus.

1706 PHILLIPS, *Junco*, the Reed-Sparrow; a Bird. **1898** *Atlantic Monthly* LXXXII. 492/2 Birds which had been isolated..might be presumed to have acquired some slight but real idiosyncrasy of voice and language. But if this is true of the Carolina junco, I failed to satisfy myself of the fact. *Ibid.* 493/1 This is not to assert that the Alleghanian junco has not developed a voice in some measure its own.

juncous ('dʒʌŋkəs), *a. rare.* [ad. L. *juncōs-us*, f. *junc-us* rush: see -OUS.] Rushy.

[**1727** BAILEY vol. II, *Juncose*, full of Bulrushes.] **1755** JOHNSON, *Juncous*, full of bulrushes. **1819** H. BUSK *Vestriad* III. 565 Far as the juncous Van or wide Euphrates.

†**junct**, *a. Obs.* [ad. L. *junct-us*, pa. pple. of *jungĕre* to join.] Joined, conjunct, joint.

1475 *Waterford Arch.* in *10th Rep. Hist. MSS. Comm.* App. v. 312 The payne..to be levid by thofficers and by every of them, juncte and severall. **1513** DOUGLAS *Æneis* x. xi. 151 With handis iunct vphevit towart hevin. **1695** J. SAGE Wks. 1844 I. 141 The principal of four junct Regents.

junction ('dʒʌŋkʃən), *sb.* [ad. L. *junctiōn-em*, n. of action f. *jungĕre* to join: cf. F. *jonction.*]

1. The action of joining or fact of being joined; union, combination. **a.** physical, of material things, bodies of men, etc.

1711 ADDISON *Spect.* No. 165 ¶5 Upon the Junction of the French and Bavarian Armies. **1789** JEFFERSON *Writ.* (1859) III. 92 The latter effected a junction soon after with another part of their fleet. **1840** THIRLWALL *Greece* liii. VII. 27 The stream formed by the junction of the Hyphasis..with the Hesudrus. **1846** *Penny Cycl.* 1st Suppl. II. 669/2 Wherever ..the junction of different railways renders such distinction necessary. **1898** J. T. FOWLER *Durham Cathedr.* 51 The junction of the Nine Altars (eastern transept) with the Norman choir has been effected in a most skilful manner.

b. of abstract things, or of persons in reference to action, interest, etc.: Association, coalition.

1783 BLAIR *Rhet.* xlv, A very unseasonable junction of gallantry, with the high sentiments and public-spirited passions which predominate in other parts [of the play]. **1792** JEFFERSON *Writ.* (1859) III. 459 The public interest certainly called for his junction with Mr. Short. **1873** M. ARNOLD *Lit. & Dogma* (1876) 187 The junction of a talent for abstruse reasoning with much literary inexperience.

c. *Grammar.* In Jespersen's terminology, a group of words consisting of a primary word and an adjunct (ADJUNCT *sb.* 5 b).

1924 O. JESPERSEN *Philos. Gram.* vii. 97 If..we compare the combination *a furiously barking dog*..with *the dog barks furiously*..there is a fundamental difference between them, which calls for separate terms for the two kinds of combination: we shall call the former kind *junction*, and the latter *nexus*. *Ibid.* viii. 115 In a junction a secondary element (an adjunct) is joined to a primary word as a label or distinguishing mark. **1935** *Jrnl. Eng. & Germ. Philol.* XXXIV. 415 Two entirely different classifications are involved: (1) an assignment of importance within the frame of a sentence..(2) a scrutiny of subordination within a group ('junction'). **1966** M. PEI *Gloss. Ling. Terminol.* 136 *Junction*, a grammatical unit formed by qualified and qualifying terms (*the red barn*).

2. a. The point or place at which two things join or are joined; a joint, meeting-place; *spec.* the place or station on a railway where lines meet and unite; often in proper names, as *Clapham Junction*, *Didcot Junction*, *Carstairs Junction*.

1841 *Penny Cycl.* XIX. 258/1 A crossing on a railway with two tracks, switches being placed at both junctions. **1846** *Ibid.* 1st Suppl. II. 669/1 The engine-driver of every train, on approaching the junction indicates by..a signal light in what direction he wishes to proceed. **1860** W. COLLINS *Wom. White* xiii. (1861) 75 Situated in a solitary sheltered spot, inland at the junction of two hills. **1876** *The World* No. 116. 10 They can only book to the junction. **1899** *Daily News* 14 Sept. 7/5 Worting Junction is what is known as a 'flying junction', that is, the up Bournemouth line is carried on a bridge over the West of England tracks, and then trails down on the Basingstoke side.

b. *Electronics.* A transition zone in a semiconductor between two regions of different conductivity type (usually *n*-type and *p*-type).

1949 W. SHOCKLEY in *Bell Syst. Techn. Jrnl.* XXVIII. 435 Silicon and germanium may be either *n*-type or *p*-type semiconductors... If, in a single sample, there is a transition from one type to the other, a rectifying photosensitive *p-n* junction is formed. *Ibid.* 436 We shall use the word *junction* to include all the material near the transition region in which significant contributions to the rectification process occur. **1959** R. A. SMITH *Semiconductors* xii. 444 *p-n* junctions are generally much more stable mechanically than fine metal point contacts and the modern tendency is to use them whenever possible. **1962** SIMPSON & RICHARDS *Physical Princ. Junction Transistors* iii. 43 If the change from n^+-type to *n*-type is sufficiently gradual, electrons diffusing from the n^+-type material will recombine with holes before reaching the *n*-type material and the n^+-*n* junction will be non-rectifying. **1965** BURFORD & VERNER *Semiconductor Junctions & Devices* vii. 91 All junctions in semiconductors are inherently rectifying. To make such a *p-n* junction into an operable rectifier, we merely attach leads to the *p* and *n* regions and protect the active element..by suitable encapsulation.

3. (In full, ***junction canal***, ***j. line***, ***j. railway***.) A canal or railway forming a connexion between two other lines or with a centre of commerce.

Chiefly in proper names of canals and railways (now rare), as *Lancaster and Preston Junction*, *Grand Junction*, *Midland and South Western Junction Railway*, etc., *Grand Junction Canal*, etc.

1796 G. M. WOODWARD *Eccent. Excurs.* (1807) 161 Leicester has been much afflicted with the Junction Mania or Canal Madness. **1839** *Encycl. Brit.* (ed. 7) XIX. 17/1 On the Grand Junction railway, for 6 months, it [the ratio of revenue to profit] is 1:48. **1841** *Ibid.* XXI. 782/2 These canals are the Birmingham Old Canal..and, above all, the Grand Junction. **1841** *Penny Cycl.* XIX. 257/1 The station of the Brandling Junction railway at Gateshead.

4. *attrib.* and *Comb.*, as ***junction canal***, ***line***, ***railway*** (see 3); ***junction-box***, ***-point***, ***-rail***, ***-signal***, ***-socket***; also **junction-box**, a closed, rigid box or casing used to enclose and protect the junctions of electric wires or cables; **junction diode** *Electronics*, a diode consisting essentially of a piece of semiconductor containing a rectifying *p-n* junction; **junction-inkstand** (see quot. 1851); **junction-plate**, 'a break-joint plate riveted over the edges of boiler-plates, which make a butt-joint' (Knight *Dict. Mech.* 1875); **junction rectifier** *Electronics* = *junction diode*; **junction transistor** *Electronics*, a transistor consisting essentially of a piece of semiconductor containing two (or more) junctions that divide it into three (or more) regions.

1885 E. S. FARROW *Mil. Encycl.* II. 147/1 In submarine mining, when it is necessary to employ a multiple cable, a *junction-box is used to facilitate the connection of the several separate wires diverging from the extremities of such a cable. **1934** *Archit. Rev.* LXXV. 141/3 Junction boxes are arranged at close intervals all over the floor before the blocks or floorboards are put down. **1958** M. DICKENS *Man Overboard* ii. 28 He tripped over a large metal junction-box, where several thick cables met in a writhing tangle. **1972** *Police Rev.* 10 Nov. 1453/3 A security van..crashes into an electric junction box at the side of the road. **1952** *Proc. IRE* XL. 1348/1 This paper describes..a new type of silicon diode, namely, the *p-n* *junction diode prepared by alloying. **1970** J. EARL *Tuners & Amplifiers* ii. 28 Very few tuners are now being made with valves. The vast majority employ semiconductor devices, and of these many use transistors and junction diodes, but the trend is also towards the use of ICs. **1851** *Illustr. Catal. Gt. Exhib.* 634 *Junction inkstand, containing black and red ink in one vessel. **1839** URE *Dict. Arts*, etc. 96 (*Beer*) *ll*, *junction-pieces to connect the pipes *rr* with the kiln. **1951** *Physical Rev.* LXXXI. 475/1 The holes move mainly under the influence of diffusion in a manner similar to that discussed in connection with carriers injected across the junction in a *p-n* *junction rectifier. **1962** SIMPSON & RICHARDS *Physical Princ. Junction Transistors* iii. 35 While it is possible to produce junction rectifiers and transistors from many different semiconductors, the devices in successful commercial production are..made from either germanium or silicon. **1889** G. FINDLAY *Eng. Railway* 83 *Junction signals are not in any cases to be placed on the same post one above another. **1881** YOUNG *Every man his own Mechanic* §1101 Lateral drains..entering the main drain and connected with it by *junction-sockets and elbow-joints. **1949** W. SHOCKLEY in *Bell Syst. Techn. Jrnl.* XXVIII. 435 (*heading*) The theory of *p-n* junctions in semiconductors and *p-n* *junction transistors. **1959** R. A. SMITH *Semiconductors* xii. 449 The first type of transistor to be used was the point-contact transistor, but this has been almost entirely replaced by the junction transistor. **1962** SIMPSON & RICHARDS *Physical Princ. Junction Transistors* i. 1 The extraordinary technological growth that has taken place since that time [*sc.* 1948] has established the junction transistor as a device of major engineering and economic importance.

Hence **'junctional** *a.*, pertaining to a junction.

1875 O. P. CAMBRIDGE in *Encycl. Brit.* II. 289/1 (*Arachnida*) Showing the..soldered up, junctional lines of the caput and thorax, and thoracic segments.

junction ('dʒʌŋkʃən), *v.* [f. the sb.] *intr.* To form a junction; to join *with* or *on to*.

1904 *Electrical Investments* IV. 771/2 Railway companies whose lines junctioned with each other did not always give either the passenger or goods traffic the advantages that the physical junctions rendered possible. **1909** R. A. WASON *Happy Hawkins* xxvii, Deuced if I ever could see where your trail could have junctioned onto the Clarendon family. **1936** I. L. IDRIESS *Cattle King* xii. 105 This line..gradually draws in towards the Diamantina until it junctions with it here, just above the South Australian border. **1959** *Tararua* XIII. 47 New Zealanders and Australians occasionally use the verb *junction with* of rivers, though why this is necessary when there is the verb *join* is hard to day.

junctive ('dʒʌŋktɪv), *a.* *poet. rare.* [ad. L. *junctīv-us*, f. *junct-*, pa. ppl. stem of *jungĕre* to join.] Having the quality of joining.

1898 HARDY *Wessex Poems* 28 So may I live no junctive law fulfilling, And my heart's table bear no woman's name.

†**'junctly**, *adv.* *Obs.* [f. JUNCT *a.* + -LY².] In a conjoined way; jointly, conjunctly; closely.

[**1375** BARBOUR *Bruce* XVII. 689 (MS. C) Thai pressit the sow toward the wall, And has hir set thar to Iuntly [*MS. E* gentilly, *ed. H.* cunningly].] *c* **1470** HENRY *Wallace* VII. 1148 The bryg..Off gud playne burd was weill and iunctly maid. **1517** in Leadam *Domesday Inclos.* (1897) I. 260 Henry Salter ..and Iohn lound..have Iunctely inclosed..xvj acres. **1600** TOURNEUR *Transf. Metamorph.* lix, A steeled coate So iunctly ioynted.

juncture ('dʒʌŋktjʊə(r), -tʃə(r)). Also 5 -tur, 7 *Sc.* -tor, 8 joncture. [ad. L. *junctūra* joining, joint, f. *junct-*, ppl. stem of *jungĕre* to join: see -URE.]

1. The action of joining together; the condition of being joined together; joining, junction.

1589 WARNER *Alb. Eng.* v. xxvii, Signes workings, planets iunctures, and The eleuated poule. **1643** NETHERSOLE *Parables on Times* 14 The juncture and contignation those parts had with the whole frame. *a* **1657** SIR W. MURE *Historie* Wks. II. 239 The match and junctor of both families in one. **1703** ROWE *Fair Penit.* I. i. 218 Perhaps she means To treat in Juncture with her new Ally. **1768–74** TUCKER *Lt. Nat.* (1834) I. 282 Making arbitrary junctures for which she has given no foundation. **1821** FOSTER in *Life & Corr.* (1846) II. 41 The juncture with what precedes and follows. **1893** F. ADAMS *New Egypt* 8 This Arabian Khalif, who anticipated the Suez Canal by his juncture of the Nile and the Red Sea.

2. a. The place at which, or structure by which, two things are joined; a joint, jointing, junction.

1382 WYCLIF *1 Kings* vi. 18 Hauynge his turnours, and his iuncturis forgid, and grauyngis ouerbeynge. **1519** HORMAN *Vulg.* 339 Thou canst nat spy the iuncture though thou loke nie. **1609** BIBLE (Douay) *Hab.* ii. 11 The timber, that is betwen the junctures of the buildings. **1707** *Curios. in Husb. & Gard.* 39 The place where the Stem and the Root join, is called the Juncture. **1763** *Hist. Eur.* in *Ann. Reg.* 27/1 It stands at the juncture of that great river with another. **1858** HAWTHORNE *Fr. & It. Jrnls.* I. 153 The junctures of the marble slabs being so close.

†**b.** A joint of the body; = JOINT *sb.* 1. *Obs.*

c **1475** *Pict. Voc.* in Wr.-Wülcker 749/25 *Hic* [*sic*] *junctura*, junctur. **1513** DOUGLAS *Æneis* IV. xii. 103 The iuncturis and lethis of hir cors. **1609** BIBLE (Douay) *Ezek.* xxxvii. 7 And bones came to bones, everie one to his iuncture. **1657** TOMLINSON *Renou's Disp.* 584 Cold diseases of the..nerves and junctures. **1717** J. KEILL *Anim. Oecon.* Pref. (1738) 10 The different Junctures of the Bones.

c. *Linguistics.* The transition between two linguistic segments or between an utterance and preceding or following silence; the phonetic feature that marks such a transition. Also *attrib.*

[**1934** PRIEBSCH & COLLINSON *German Lang.* iii. 210 When a stem-vowel or declensional suffix in its crude form occurs in the first components of compound substantives and adjectives, it is called the 'Fugenvokal', i.e. juncture vowel.] **1941** *Language* XVII. 224 Those [phonemes] that relate to the way in which utterances begin and end..we call juncture phonemes... A logical order of exposition..will begin with the juncture phenomena... The present study.. will deal with junctures, stresses, [etc.]. *Ibid.* 225 The transition from a pause preceding an isolated utterance to the first segmental phoneme, and from the last segmental phoneme to the following pause, we call open juncture. **1942** BLOCH & TRAGER *Outl. Ling. Analysis* ii. 35 Phenomena relating to the way in which sounds are joined together are summarized under the term *juncture*. **1946** E. A. NIDA *Morphol.* 94 When two items are combined, there are potentially several different types of junctures, or seams, at the point of contact. **1957** S. POTTER *Mod. Ling.* iii. 73 No less elusive than intonation..are the related features of *juncture* and *pause*. Where precisely does one syllable end and another begin? **1969** *English Studies* L. 292 They regard juncture as a special type of phoneme, neither segmental nor prosodic, causing sub-signemic changes in the environment. **1972** R. WARDHAUGH *Introd. Linguistics* 64 We can say that such words as *nitrate*, *night rate*, and *Nye trait* require the postulation of a juncture phoneme to show the difference.

3. Something that connects two things; a connecting link; a means of connexion or union. *rare.*

a **1677** HALE *Prim. Orig. Man.* II. vii. 203 Since the Flood there have been some such Junctures or Land-passages between the Northern parts of Asia or Europe, and some Northern parts of the Continent of America. **1841** MYERS *Cath. Th.* IV. §32. 332 The Epistle to the Hebrews..seems to stand as the uniting and harmonising juncture of the Pauline and the Petrine preaching. **1880** J. MARTINEAU *Hours Th.* II. 23 The ascending juncture that reaches from nothingness to God.

4. A convergence or concurrence of events or circumstances; a particular or critical posture of affairs or point of time; a crisis, conjuncture.

1656 BEN ISRAEL *Vindiciæ Jud.* in *Phenix* (1708) II. 423 But at that juncture of time my coming was not presently perform'd. **1658** PHILLIPS, s.v., Juncture of time, the very nick or moment of time. **1662** PEPYS *Diary* 30 June, This I take to be as bad a juncture as ever I observed. The King and his new Queene minding their pleasures at Hampton Court. All people discontented. **1704** ADDISON *Italy* (1733) 58 As different Junctures and Emergencies arise. **1838** THIRLWALL *Greece* xv. II. 266 The course of action required by new situations, and sudden junctures. **1853** BRIGHT *Sp., India* (1876) 11 In the present critical juncture of things. **1874** GREEN *Short Hist.* v. §4. 241 The most terrible plague which the world ever witnessed advanced at this juncture from the East.

†**5.** Joint-tenancy; = JOINTURE 3. *Obs.*

1533-4 [see JOINTURE 3].

Hence **'junctural** *a.*, **'juncturally** *adv.*

1942 *Language* XVIII. 14 A suprasegmental phoneme is junctural if each member phone has a determining starting-point (or a determining end-point). **1964** [see DEMARCATIVE *a.*]. **1965** *Language* XLI. 499 A separate phoneme..(which is subject to frequent loss, mainly but not wholly juncturally conditioned). **1966** W. S. ALLEN in C. E. Bazell *In Memory of J. R. Firth* 11 This..would have been contrary to Greek junctural principles (being characteristic of close and not open juncture).

jundy ('dʒʌndɪ), *sb.* *Sc.* [Deriv. obscure.]

1. A push with the elbow; a jog, jostle, shove.

1737 RAMSAY *Sc. Prov.* (1750) 53 If a man's gawn down the brae ilk ane gie's him a jundie. **1824** MACTAGGART *Gallovid. Encycl.*, *Jundie*, a blow.

2. *fig.* Ordinary or steady course, 'jog-trot'.

1894 'IAN MACLAREN' *Bonnie Brier Bush*, *Wise Wom.* i. 206 He's aff on the jundy (trot) again. **1895** —— *Auld Lang Syne*, *Drumsheugh's Love Story* 139 It wad tak a chairge o' gunpooder tae pit Leezbeth aff her jundy.

'jundy, *v.* *Sc.* Also 8 **jundie**, **joundy**, 9 **junnie**. [Cf. the sb.] To push with the elbow or shoulder; to jog; to jostle. (*trans.* and *absol.*)

1785 BURNS *Ep. to W. Simpson* xvi, The war'ly race may drudge and drive, Hog-shouther, jundie, stretch and strive. **1804** TARRAS *Poems, Ep. to Friend* 31 Sae junnied on frae day to day, Wi' ne'er a blink o' fortune's ray. **1819** W. TENNANT *Papistry Storm'd* (1827) 98 They pous'd, they jundy'd ane anither.

June (dʒuːn), *sb.* Forms: 4–6 **Iuyn**, 5 **Iuyne**, **Ioyne**, 6 **Iung**, **Iuyng**; (2 *gen.* **Iunies**), 3 **Iun**, 4–7 **Iune**, (4 **Iunye**, 5 **Ione**), 7– **June**. [In OE. and sometimes in ME. in L. form *Jūnius*, also *Juni*; in ME. a. F. *juin*, †*juing* (= Pr. *junh*, Cat. *juny*, Sp. *junio*, It. *giugno*):—L. *Jūnius*; from 14th c. refashioned after L. as *June*.]

1. The sixth month of the year, in which the summer solstice occurs in the northern hemisphere.

α. [*c* **1050** *Byrhtferth's Handboc*, *Anglia* (1885) VIII. 312 Aprelis, iunius, september, and november. *a* **1100** *Gerefa* ibid. (1886) IX. 261 In Maio and Junio and Julio. *a* **1123** *O.E. Chron.* an. 1110 On Iunies monðe ætywde an steorra norðan eastan. **1432-50** tr. *Higden* (Rolls) I. 245 In the honor of whom he ordeynede the monethe of Iunius, that is to saye, of yonger men.]

β. **1387** TREVISA *Higden* (Rolls) III. 295 Þe firste day of Iuyn. *c* **1450** *Merlin* 54 The xj day of Iuyne. **1480** CAXTON *Chron. Eng.* ccxxiv. 229 In the monethes of Iuyn and Iuyll next folowyng. *c* **1500** *Melusine* 16 Theuen..of saint johan baptiste, whiche is on the xx. day of Iung [F. *juing*]. **1503** *Kalender of Sheph.* (colophon), Prentyt in parys the .xxiii. day of iuyng, oon thowsand cccc & III. *a* **1548** HALL *Chron.*, *Hen. VII* 37 The .xxv. daie of Iuyn.

γ. **1297** R. GLOUC. (Rolls) 8310 Þus was þe þridde day of Iun antioche inome. **13..** *K. Alis.* 1844 (Bodley MS.) Mery it is in june and hoot firmament. **1398** TREVISA *Barth. De P.R.* IX. xiv. (Bodl. MS.), Þe monþe of Iune is þe ende of springing tyme. *Ibid.* (ed. 1495) The month of Iune is begynnynge of Somer. *c* **1400** *Destr. Troy* 10822 With the

monith of May, & the mery Ione. *a* **1548** Hall *Chron., Hen. VIII* 84 The sayd .xxiiii. day of Iune, whiche was sonday and Midsomerday. **1596** Shaks. *1 Hen. IV*, iii. ii. 75 He was but as the Cuckow is in Iune, Heard, not regarded. **1749** Fielding *Tom Jones* v. x, It was now a pleasant evening in the latter end of June. **1798** Coleridge *Anc. Mar.* v. xviii, A noise like of a hidden brook In the leafy month of June. **1848** Lowell *Vis. Sir Launfal* i. Prelude iii, And what is so rare as a day in June? Then, if ever, come perfect days. *a* **1882** Kendall *Poems* (1886) 132 Twenty white-haired Junes have left us—gray with frost and bleak with gale [in Australia].

2. *Comb.*, as ***June-like*** adj.; **June-apple** = jenneting (Fallows *Suppl. Dict.* 1886); **June-berry**, the fruit (also called *service-berry*) of a small N. American tree, the shad-bush (*Amelanchier canadensis*, N.O. *Rosaceæ*); also the tree; also used for other trees or shrubs of the genus *Amelanchier*, or their fruit; **June-bug**, a name for various beetles which appear in June: (*a*) of the European genus *Rhinotrogus*; (*b*) of the genus *Lachnosterna* of the northern U.S.; (*c*) *Allorhina nitida*, of the southern U.S.; **June grass** (*U.S.*), the Kentucky blue-grass, *Poa pratensis*; **June Week**, at Durham University, the last week of the summer term, Commemoration week.

1832 D. J. Browne *Sylva Amer.* 217 The wood of the *June berry is of a pure white. **1854** Mayne Reid *Young Voyageurs* 356 The berries..are known as..'June-berries' [or] 'service-berries'. **1864** Webster, *June-berry.* **1866** *Treas. Bot.* 641/2 *June-berry*, an American name for *Amelanchier.* **1914** I. Cowie *Company of Adventurers* 327 A grizzly bear [was] found among the saskatoon (Juneberry) bushes. **1928** J. E. LeRossignol *Beauport Road* 274 The chief attraction..was along the fences and hedgerows where, in season, were strawberries, June berries..dew berries. **1969** R. C. Hosie *Native Trees Canada* (ed. 7) 234/1 Mountain Juneberry..and Saskatoon-berry..occasionally become trees. **1829** in *Amer. Speech* (1965) XL. 132 *Jim Crow*... Dere's possum up de gumtree, An Raccoon in de hollow, Wake Shakes for *June Bugs Stole my half a dollar. **1836** *Congress. Globe* 5 May 349/2 They hopped upon it, to use a homely phrase, like a duck on a June-bug. **1862** *Standard* 12 Dec., He has lighted upon [General] Scott as a hawk lights upon a June bug. **1906** W. Churchill *Coniston* xv. 189 June-bugs hummed in at the high windows. **1972** L. E. Chadwick tr. *Linsenmaier's Insects of World* 162/3 (*caption*) An American June beetle, the June bug, having completed development but still in its underground cavity. **1855** *Trans. Mich. Agric. Soc.* VI. 160 A stiff *June grass sod plat. **1919** *Maine, my State* (Maine Writers Research Club) 336 How fair her fields when June-grass waves! **1970** *Alberta Hist. Rev.* Winter 1/2 Prairie wool, a nutritious blend of..June grass..and other grasses. **1897** *Daily News* 14 May 6/5 The weather..was anything but *June-like. **1897** *Outing* (U.S.) XXIX. 316/1 It was early *June-time. **1889** *Durham Univ. Jrnl.* IX. 1 The end of last term was signalised by what was called by some 'Commemoration' and by others 'the *June Week'. **1900** *Ibid.* XIV. 229 Those who have visited the race-course during the June Week.

june (dʒuːn), *v. U.S. colloq.* and *dial.* [? f. the sb.] **a.** *intr.* To move in a lively fashion, hurry; to be restless or aimless; to wander *around.* **b.** *trans.* To drive briskly. *rare.*

1869 *Overland Monthly* III. 127 A trig, smirk little horse is a 'lace-horse', and he often has to 'june' or 'quill'. **1892** *Dialect Notes* I. 230 *June-in'*, running fast. 'She came a-june-in'.' **1895** W. C. Gore in *Inlander* Nov. 61 *June around*, to be busy but not accomplish anything. **1903** A. Adams *Log of Cowboy* xiv. 228 To june a herd of cattle across in this manner would have been shameful. **1948** *Amer. Speech* XXIII. 305/1 You stay here and I'll go down and june around awhile.

june, obs. form of Join.

juneating, junetin, perverted ff. Jenneting.

†**ju'nesse.** *Obs.* [a. F. *jeunesse*, in OF. also *jounesce*, f. *jeune* young.] Youth.

c **1430** Lydg. *Min. Poems* (Percy Soc.) 32 Thouhe she be yong, yet wol she wele abide, Vncoupled to a fresshe man of Iunesse, & take a buffard, riche of gret vilesse.

jungada, variant of Jangada, a raft.

jungar, var. Jangar.

jungermanniaceous (ˌdʒʌndʒəmænɪˈeɪʃəs), *a. Bot.* [f. mod.L. *Jungermanniace-æ* (f. *Jungermannia*, the typical genus, named by Linnæus after the German botanist Jungermann) + -ous.] Belonging to the Natural Order *Jungermanniaceæ*, the Scale-mosses, the largest order of *Hepaticæ*.

1855 in Mayne *Expos. Lex.*

‖**Junggrammatiker** (ˈjʊŋgræˌmɑːtɪkə(r)), *sb. pl. Philol.* [G.] A name given to members of a late 19th-century school of historical linguists who held that phonetic changes (sound laws) operated without exceptions. The name was accepted by the persons concerned and by others, and has been anglicized as 'neogrammarians'. Hence **junggrammatisch** *a.*

1922 O. Jespersen *Language* iv. 93 The 'blind' operation of phonetic laws became the chief tenet of a new school of 'young-grammarians' or 'junggrammatiker' (Brugmann, Delbrück, Osthoff, Paul, and others). **1936** J. R. Kantor *Objective Psychol. Gram.* viii. 108 The *Junggrammatiker*.. believed themselves to have discovered absolute phonetic laws. **1936** *Language* XII. 58 There is another point of view, ..an organic development..of the essential core of truth in the Junggrammatiker doctrine. **1938** *Year's Work Eng. Stud.* 1936 30 Wilhelm Havers..well summarizes the history of the changing attitude towards 'sound-laws' since the first confident days of the *Ausnahmslosigkeit* of the *Junggrammatiker*. **1953** J. B. Carroll *Study of Lang.* ii. 50 In opposition to the neo-grammarians (*Junggrammatiker*), as Leskien, Osthoff, and Brugmann came to be called, Schuchardt (1885), Curtius, and Ascoli pointed to what seemed to be exceptions to phonetic laws. **1958** A. S. C. Ross *Etym.* 8 It is certainly quite impossible for anyone to understand Laryngeal Theory without being thoroughly familiar with junggrammatisch Ablaut. **1965** *Language* XLI. 187 Brugmann..accepted the originally humorous epithet *Junggrammatiker* and used it as a rallying cry.

Jungian (ˈjʊŋɪən), *a.* and *sb.* [See -ian.] Of or pertaining to Dr. Carl Gustav *Jung* (1875–1961), the Swiss leader of the school of analytic psychology, or his teaching. Also *sb.*, a follower or adherent of Jung. Hence **ˈJungianism**, the teaching or system of Jung; a characteristic specimen of this.

1933 D. C. Daking (*title*) Jungian psychology and modern spiritual thought. **1942** K. W. Bash tr. *Jacobi's Psychol. C. G. Jung* iii. 59 Jungian psychotherapy is no analytical procedure... It is..a 'way of healing'. **1947** *Downside Rev.* 35 For the Jungian the whole position is altered... The historical causality of complexes is not denied, and the methods of releasing these complexes, as discovered by Freud, are recognized. **1956** *Essays in Crit.* VI. 417 How we can now avoid Jungianism is a difficult problem. **1958** *Times Lit. Suppl.* 1 Aug. 438/5 The church has a resident Jungian psychiatrist. **1959** *Ibid.* 20 Mar. 164/5 To non-Jungians..this will seem merely another Jungian book. **1964** M. McLuhan *Understanding Media* (1967) II. xx. 207 Myth and Jungian archetypes.

ˈjungible, *a. rare*⁻⁰. [ad. L. *jungibilis*, f. *jungĕre* to join.]

1656 Blount *Glossogr.*, *Jungible*, that may be joined.

jungle (ˈdʒʌŋg(ə)l), *sb.* Also 9 **jangal, jingle, jungul.** [a. Hindī and Marāṭhī *jangal* desert, waste, forest, Skr. *jangala* dry, dry ground, desert.

The change in Anglo-Indian use may be compared to that in the historical meaning of the word *forest* in its passage from a waste or unenclosed tract to one covered with wild wood. In the transferred sense of *jungle* there is app. a tendency to associate it with *tangle*.]

1. In India, originally, as a native word, Waste or uncultivated ground (= 'forest' in the original sense); then, such land overgrown with brushwood, long grass, etc.; hence, in Anglo-Indian use, **a.** Land overgrown with underwood, long grass, or tangled vegetation; also, the luxuriant and often almost impenetrable growth of vegetation covering such a tract. **b.** with *a* and *pl.* A particular tract or piece of land so covered; esp. as the dwelling-place of wild beasts.

a. **1776** Halhed *Gentoo Code* xiii. 190 Land Waste for Five Years..is called Jungle. *c* **1813** Mrs. Sherwood *Ayah & Lady* ix. 52 The banks were covered with thick jungle down to the very brink of the water. *Ibid.* Gloss., *Jungle*, brushwood, or very high grass. **1853** Sir H. Douglas *Milit. Bridges* 128 In loading and unloading, in moving through jungle. **1900** *Blackw. Mag.* May 640/1 [My] concealment for safety in the fields of jhow and jangal.

b. **1783** Burke *Sp. India Bill* Wks. IV. 24 That land..is now almost throughout a dreary desart, covered with rushes, and briers, and jungles full of wild beasts. **1804** W. Austin *Lett. fr. Eng.* 167 *note*, Lord Cornwallis writes that 3/5 of the territory has become a Jingle, that is deserted by the natives and possessed by wild beasts. **1858** J. B. Norton *Topics* 275 Transforming uninhabitable jungles into well cultivated plantations. **1889** R. S. S. Baden-Powell *Pigsticking* 45 A somewhat similar manner of beating is employed in the case of canal bank jungles.

c. Extended to similar tracts in other lands, especially tropical.

1849 Macaulay *Hist. Eng.* v. I. 603 It [Sedgemoor] was a vast pool, wherein were scattered many islets of shifting and treacherous soil, overhung with rank jungle. **1851** Layard *Pop. Acc. Discov. Nineveh* i. 4 We passed the night in the jungle which clothes the banks of the river. **1856** Stanley *Sinai & Pal.* vii. 282 The Jordan..threading its tortuous way through its tropical jungle. **1865** Livingstone *Zambesi* x. 214 Our course passed though a dense thorn jungle.

2. *transf.* and *fig.* **a.** A wild, tangled mass. Also, a place of bewildering complexity or confusion; a place where the 'law of the jungle' prevails; a scene of ruthless competition, struggle, or exploitation; esp. with qualification, as ***blackboard jungle*** in schools, ***asphalt jungle***, ***concrete jungle*** in cities.

1850 Carlyle *Latter-d. Pamph.* iii. (1872) 74 What a world-wide jungle of redtape. **1853** Kane *Grinnell Exp.* xlvii. (1856) 433 We could see the perfect jungle of sea-weed that was growing under us. **1879** *Academy* 10 May 412/2 In that tangled jungle of disconnected precedents [Digest of Justinian]. **1897** Mary Kingsley *W. Africa* xxi. 493 Out of the luxuriant jungle of information that followed I gathered that no man's soul dallies below long. **1906** U. Sinclair (*title*) The Jungle. **1920** Ade *Hand-Made Fables* 83 After the newly arrived Delegate from the Asphalt Jungles had read a Telegram..he..sauntered back to the Bureau of Information. **1924** A. D. Sedgwick *Little French Girl* ii. vi. 150 The jungle itself was part of the order, since the *demimondaine* was taken as much for granted as the *femme du monde.* **1949** W. R. Burnett (*title*) The asphalt jungle. **1954** [see blackboard]. **1956** 'E. McBain' *Cop Hater* (1958) viii. 70 Their front page..shouted 'The Police Jungle—What Goes On In Our Precincts.' **1958** [see blackboard]. **1969** D. Morris *Human Zoo* 8 The city is not a concrete jungle, it is a human zoo. **1971** *Sunday Times* 30 May 31/5 Namier ..fitted especially ill in the academic jungle. **1971** *Times* 17 July 5/2 New York seemed to me infernal... By night the streets become concrete jungles, their occupants hysteric, terrified of predators. **1972** *Guardian* 14 Feb. 10/5 The Minister lit up some lurid corners of the taxation jungle. **1974** *Black World* Jan. 38 The Waikiki jungle is kind of a —you might call it a ghetto surrounded by high-rise buildings in Waikiki.

b. ***the jungle*** (*Stock Exch. slang*): the West African share market: cf. *jungle-market* in 3 b. *pl.* Shares in West African concerns. Also *attrib.* ? *Obs.*

a **1901** *Mod. Newspr.* Signs of renewed activity in the jungle. **1904** *Daily Chron.* 2 Dec. 1/7 Kaffirs weakened, but Jungles moved upward. **1906** *Ibid.* 9 Feb. 2/3 Jungle shares were..firm. **1908** *Westm. Gaz.* 10 Dec. 15/4 A Jungle Dividend.

c. A camp for hoboes, tramps, or the like. Also *attrib. slang* (orig. *U.S.*).

[**1908** C. Johnson *Highways & Byways Pacific Coast* 215 My companions spoke of the grove they were in as the 'Hoboes Jungle'.] **1914** *Sat. Even. Post* 4 Apr. 10/3 It followed the two along the tracks and into the jungle. *Ibid.* 11/3 Frisco Red slouched into the jungle. **1915** *N.Y. World Mag.* 9 May 14 *Jungle buzzard*, a tramp who sneaks around hobo or tramp camps to get a free meal. *Ibid.*, *Jungle court*, a make-believe court held in woods by hoboes. **1923** N. Anderson *Hobo* ii. 21 Most 'jungle buzzards', men who linger in the jungles from season to season, take an interest in the running of things. **1926** J. Black *You can't Win* vi. 65 'This is a pretty snide jungle,' he said, 'no cans.' *Ibid.* 82 There was a grand jungle by a small, clean river where they boiled up their verminous clothes. **1971** *Islander* (Victoria, B.C.) 4 Apr. 12/1 During the depression in the 1930s gangs of youths ranged across the country, riding the rails and sleeping in jungles, and caused us concern.

3. a. *attrib.* and *Comb.*: simple attrib., as ***jungle-bush, -craft, -fire, -folk, -grass, -growth, -land, -life, -people, -side, -tale, -tribe***; instrumental, as ***jungle-clad, -covered, -worn***, adjs.; locative, as ***jungle-travelling, -trudging, -walking***.

1884 *Sunday at Home* June 398/2 We crept under the shade of a thick crop of *jungle-bush. **1900** *Daily News* 30 July 6/3 Mr. H. C. P. Bell has done much in excavating the *jungle-clad remains of Anuradhapura. **1886** *Pall Mall G.* 14 Dec. 13/2 *Jungle-covered wastes of abandoned cornfields. **1942** *R.A.F. Jrnl.* 27 June 24 Even an expert can make mistakes in *jungle craft. **1946** W. S. Churchill *Secret Session Speeches* 59 The Japanese armies..having added their jungle-craft..have established themselves..in the whole of these wide regions. **1889** R. S. S. Baden-Powell *Pigsticking* 37 The destruction of his home by *jungle-fire or flood. **1810** Southey *Kehama* xiii. vii, The tall *jungle-grass fit roofing gave Beneath that genial sky. **1897** Mary Kingsley *W. Africa* 573 We clamber up into the long jungle-grass region. **1894** *Athenæum* 5 May 572/1 The *jungle-growth of seventeenth and eighteenth century dreaming has been..cleared away. **1889** R. S. S. Baden-Powell *Pigsticking* 14 To..foster the sport by the grant of waste *jungle lands to serve as preserves. **1894** R. Kipling *2nd Jungle Book* (1895) 14 He made the First of the Tigers ..the judge of the Jungle, to whom the *Jungle People should bring their disputes. **1845** Stocqueler *Handbk. Brit. India* (1854) 322 Nags unworthy to contest the glories of either the turf or the '*jungle-side'. **1866** C. Brooke *Saráwak* I. 30, I did not admire Bornean *jungletrudging. **1889** R. Kipling *Fr. Sea to Sea* (1900) I. 229 Old friends, now *jungle-worn men of war.

b. Special comb.: esp. in specific names of animals inhabiting the jungles of India, as ***jungle-hog, jungle-peacock***; **jungle-bashing** *slang* [bashing *vbl. sb.* 3], movement through a jungle, esp. by soldiers; so ***jungle-basher***; **jungle-bear**, the Sloth-bear of India, *Prochilus labiatus*; **jungle bunny**, a derogatory term used by some white people to designate Blacks, Australian Aborigines, etc.; **jungle-cat**, the Marsh-lynx, *Felis chaus*; **jungle-cock**, the male jungle-fowl; **jungle-fever**, a form of remittent fever caused by the miasma of a jungle; the hill-fever of India; **jungle-fowl**, (*a*) an East Indian bird of the genus *Gallus*, esp. *G. ferrugineus* (*G. bankiva*); (*b*) a mound-bird of Australia, as *Megapodius tumulus*; **jungle green**, a dark green colour; clothes of this colour; also *attrib.*; **jungle gym** (formerly a registered trade mark in the U.S.), a type of climbing frame; **jungle-hen**, the female *jungle-fowl* (b); **jungle juice** *slang*, alcoholic liquor, esp. liquor that is either very powerful or that has been prepared illicitly or amateurishly; also *transf.*; **jungle law**, the 'law of the jungle' (see law *sb.*¹ 16 c); **jungle-market** (*Stock Exchange*), the market in shares of West African Companies; **jungle-nail**, an East Indian tree, *Acacia tomentosa* (*Treas. Bot.* 1866); **jungle-ox**, the gayal, *Bibos sylhetanus*; **jungle poultry**, jungle-fowls; **jungle-rice**, the millet-rice, *Panicum colonum*; **jungle rot** *slang*, name given to a tropical skin disease; **jungle-sheep**, an Indian ruminant, *Kemas hypocrinus*; **jungle war**, a war fought in jungle, also *fig.*; so ***jungle warfare***; **jungle-wood** (see quot.).

1963 *Times* 24 May 14/6 All the poor '*jungle-bashers' could offer by way of city reminiscence was the egregious

Calcutta. **1954** V. Bartlett *Rep. from Malaya* iii. 46 A man does an average of 700 hours '*jungle-bashing' before he kills a Communist. **1969** J. M. Gullick *Malaysia* ii. 113 British, Malay and other Commonwealth troops spent many weary hours on patrol, 'jungle-bashing' as they called it, with the object of contacting terrorists. **1966** *Publ. Amer. Dial. Soc. 1964* XLII. 27 Both middle-aged informants giving *jungle bunny*..work with adolescents. **1968–70** *Current Slang* (Univ. S. Dakota) III–IV. 76 *Junglebunny, n.* Negro (derogatory). **1973** *Sunday Times* (Colour Suppl.) 10 June 51/3 Australians in the Territory can be grossly insensitive to the pride of the local people, using terms like 'jungle bunnies'. **1974** *New Society* 14 Mar. 627/2 White South Africans who wanted to gamble, buy *Playboy*..and go to bed with a 'jungle bunny'. **1895** I. Petrie in *Life* ix. (1900) 199 A huge *jungle-cat, who had discovered the milk-jug. **1803** Syd. Smith *Ceylon* Wks. 1867 I. 43 A low and malignant fever, known to Europeans by the name of the *jungle-fever. **1894** Fenn *In Alpine Valley* I. 24 I'm burnt up with the cursed old jungle fever. **1824–5** Heber *Narr. Journey* (1828) I. xviii. 508 A small flock or covey of *jungle fowl..crowing and cackling. My companions were not able to tell me whether the jungle poultry had ever been tamed. **1871** Mateer *Travancore* 2 The jungle fowl, a small bird with brilliant plumage, is perhaps the original of the common domestic fowl. **1893** Newton *Dict. Birds* 289 Of the genus *Gallus*..four well-marked species are known. The first of these is the Red Jungle-Fowl of the greater part of India, *G. ferrugineus*..which is almost undoubtedly the parent stock of all the domestic races. **1946** *Nature* 14 Sept. 386/2 Land Army hose, sea-boot stockings, R.A.F. socks and *jungle-green pullovers also came under the scheme. **1947** Jungle green [see cobber *sb.*²]. **1973** D. Lees *Rape of Quiet Town* iii. 53 A commanding figure in jungle green with a Lüger pistol in his hand. **1923** *Official Gaz.* (U.S. Patent Off.) 30 Jan. 844/2 *Junglegym, Inc., Chicago, Ill. Filed Nov. 14, 1921. Junglegym... Playground Apparatus, in Particular Climbing Frames. **1925** *Playground* Mar. 721 (Advt.), 22 Units—Now in the New York City Playgrounds. .. Junglegym is six years old this spring. **1929** L. F. Zwarg *Study of Hist. Apparatus Physical Educ.* i. 81 Many odd contrivances [of physical education apparatus] of former years have disappeared entirely, others have from time to time been rediscovered or reinvented. The climbing tower (jungle gym) and the teeter ladder, are examples of this. **1931** *Recreation* May 97 The low climbing device (which is known as the Junglegym). **1951** W. van Hagen et al. *Physical Educ. Elem. Sch.* v. 93 Monkey rings... Manufactured under various names, such as climbing trees, junglegyms, climbing towers, castle towers, and climbing maze. **1963** Barnard & Lauwerys *Hanbk. Brit. Educ. Terms* 115 *Jungle gym*, a simple gymnastic apparatus on which children in an infant school can climb or swing as part of their free activity curriculum. **1967** J. Redgate *Killing Season* (1968) II. vii. 104 Through the kitchen window he could see the children laughing and wrestling with each other inside their jungle gym. **1973** *Washington Post* 3 Oct. B1/4 (*heading*) Recreation 1973: Everything from jungle gyms to the Bataca bromb. **1890** Lumholtz *Cannibals* 97 The *jungle-hens (mound builders)..The bird is of a brownish hue, with yellow legs and immensely large feet; hence its name *Megapodius*. **1845** Stocqueler *Handbk. Brit. India* (1854) 292 Deer of the largest kind, bisons, bears, *jungle hog. **1945** Baker *Austral. Lang.* viii. 157 **Jungle juice*, any alcoholic beverage concocted by servicemen in the tropics. *Ibid.* 158 *Jungle juice*, poor quality petrol. **1958** R. Stow *To Islands* i. 19 The cartoons..about going troppo and drinking jungle juice. **1960** *News Chron.* 9 Mar. 7/4 The draught cider and gin they drink in the West of England and call 'jungle juice'. **1967** O. Norton *Now lying Dead* vi. 99 Oh, I know what our ale can do! Jungle-juice, as the lads call it. **1894** Kipling *Jungle Bk.* 63 One of the beauties of *Jungle Law is that punishment settles all scores. **1957** M. Kennedy *Heroes of Clone* III. vi. 204 It was awkward having to explain jungle law to someone who had never..emerged from a well-kept shrubbery. **1971** *Daily Nation* (Nairobi) 10 Apr. 13/2 The Obote regime had turned the country into 'a political jungle ruled by jungle law' whereby some people earned their living by putting others into prison. **1900** *Westm. Gaz.* 12 Oct. 9/1 The new *Jungle Market, or Assis Market, as it has been called because of the number of companies whose names bear the affix assis. *Ibid.* 16 Oct. 9/1 With all its prospectusless companies the Jungle Market is a regular Monte Carlo. **1837** *Lett. fr. Madras* xiii. (1843) 118, I am taming some fine *jungle peacocks. **1886** A. H. Church *Food Grains Ind.* 50 This millet [Shama] sometimes called 'Wild Rice' or '*Jungle Rice', is a poor food. **1944** *Amer. N. & Q.* Mar. 183/1 Can somebody identify a tropical disease called '*jungle rot'? Is it a new name for an old illness? **1945** Jungle rot [see crud 2 b]. **1958** *Times* 28 Oct. 4/5 (*headline*) N.A.L.G.O. fear 'jungle war'—arbitration move opposed. **1955** E. Waugh *Officers & Gentlemen* I. vi. 70 They put me in charge of a *jungle warfare school. **1972** D. Bloodworth *Any Number can Play* viii. 61 He had forgotten more about jungle warfare than a fellow like that would learn in a lifetime. *Ibid.* xix. 194 It has..a big tangle of forest and swamp for jungle-warfare training. **1880** C. R. Markham *Peruv. Bark* 357 The *karamarda* (*Terminalia coriacea*), called '*jungle-wood', with bark very rough and cracked in squares, like a tortoise's back.

c. Passing into *adj.* = characteristic of the jungle; savage, untamed; *spec.* designating a style of jazz music characterized by primitive sounds redolent of the jungle.

1908 A. Noyes *William Morris* 118 Torn by the savage jungle-cries of the elemental passions. **1909** *Daily Chron.* 22 Jan. 3/3 These wild poems of fierce jungle-passion and horror. **1935** *Vanity Fair* (N.Y.) Nov. 71/3 The savagery of their rhythm calls forth the terms '*shake music*' and '*jungle music*'. **1955** Keepnews & Grauer *Pict. Hist. Jazz* xiii. 141 Cootie Williams..produced a fine, muted 'jungle' sound. **1955** L. Feather *Encycl. Jazz* vii. 133 Early Ellington orchestral characteristics included the use of what he originally called 'jungle style' effects, through the use of plunger mutes. **1957** *Times Lit. Suppl.* 25 Oct. 637/2 A clearly truthful account of the lives and jungle-fights of those cold-hearted career-women who make fortunes from knocking pounds of unnecessary weight off sad fat ladies without love. **1972** *Jazz & Blues* Feb. 20/2 Duke's 'jungle' sounds.

jungle (ˈdʒʌŋg(ə)l), *v.* [f. jungle *sb.* 2 c.] *intr.* To prepare a meal at a hoboes' camp; to form such a camp; to join forces with another person. Usu. with *up*.

1922 J. Tully *Emmett Lawler* 252 The fire was built in the improvised furnace, and water was carried from the brook. They returned laden with meat and eggs, potatoes, and coffee... The method is called 'jungling up' by tramps. **1924** 'Digit' *Confessions 20th Cent. Hobo* 12 *Jungle up*, bivouac in the weeds and clean up generally. **1926** J. Black *You can't Win* vi. 70 You're welcome to travel with me, kid, if you want to jungle-up for a month or two. **1931** U. Ledoux *Mr. Zero's Scrapbk.: Ho-bo-ho Medley No. 1* 11 Hoboes and Yeggs never mix and jungle in separate camps. **1937** J. Steinbeck *Of Mice & Men* i. 8 Tramps who come wearily down from the highway in the evening to jungle-up near water.

jungled (ˈdʒʌŋg(ə)ld), *a.* [f. jungle *sb.* + -ed².] Covered with jungle or wild undergrowth.

1842 Dickens *Amer. Notes* (1868) 96 Primeval forests.. where the jungled ground was never trodden by a human foot. **18..** Eliza Cook *Song Red Indian* vii, The jungled hunting-ground. —— *Old Man's Marvel* xii, The snake in the jungled brake. **1878** *N. Amer. Rev.* CXXVI. 85 The savages were posted on a thickly-jungled island in the lake.

ˈ**junglery.** *nonce-wd.* [See -ry.] A complication like that of a jungle.

1864 Carlyle *Fredk. Gt.* xv. v. IV. 68 Austrian wild junglery..rolls homeward simultaneously.

jungli (ˈdʒʌŋglɪ), *a.* and *sb.* [f. jungle + *-i*, adj. suffix as in *Hindi*, etc.] **A.** *adj.* = jungly *a.* 2; (see also quot. 1927¹). **B.** *sb.* An inhabitant of the jungle.

1920 *Blackw. Mag.* Oct. 463/1 Just oneself with half a dozen of one's men and some jungli villagers. **1927** *Chambers's Jrnl.* 29 Jan. 138/2 Already he ceases to be jungli. *Note*, Wild and boorish, a clodhopper or uneducated peasant. **1927** *Blackw. Mag.* Mar. 290/1 His crew of two junglis managed to make him understand. **1928** *Ibid.* Jan. 1/2 A system of small flying columns kept the junglis from the inertia which breeds mischief.

jungly (ˈdʒʌŋglɪ), *a.* [f. jungle *sb.* + -y¹.]

1. Of the nature of or characterized by jungle; abounding in jungle; jungle-like.

1800 Wellington *Let. to Lt.-Col. Close* 22 May in Gurw. *Desp.* (1837) I. 119 The country is so jungly that they could not act when they should arrive there. **1838** *Chamb. Edin. Jrnl.* 3 Mar. 47/3 The spot on which the cow was lying was exceedingly jungley. **1859** R. F. Burton *Centr. Afr.* in *Jrnl. Geog. Soc.* XXIX. 109 A stream..flowing under high banks bearing a dense jungly bush in a bed of mire and grass. **1866** *Daily Tel.* 22 Feb. 5/5 An undulating expanse of stony, jungly, incult desert—a mere blasted heath.

2. Inhabiting a jungle.

1880 *Sat. Rev.* 28 Feb. 285/2 The spirit of the jungly tribes was anything but divine.

ˈ**Junian,** *a.* [f. the proper name *Junius* + -an.]

1. Of or pertaining to the 'Letters of Junius', a series of letters which appeared in the *Public Advertiser*, 1768–1772, the authorship of which is one of the problems of history.

1888 W. F. Rae in *Athenæum* 11 Aug. 192/3 The peculiarity of the Junian handwriting is its dissimilarity to that of Francis. **1963** *Times Lit. Suppl.* 25 Jan. 67/1 Candidates for the Junian crown of laurels. **1964** *Language* XL. 87 A word count of the Junian material.

2. Of or pertaining to Francis Junius (1589–1677), philologist and antiquary.

1826 J. J. Conybeare in W. D. Conybeare *Illustr. Anglo-Saxon Poetry* 197 The Junian Cædmon. **1840** J. Petheram *Hist. Sk. Progress Anglo-Saxon Lit. in England* 73 The copy used was the Junian transcript in the Bodleian. **1892** S. A. Brooke *Hist. Early Eng. Lit.* II. 67 Archbishop Ussher.. found this manuscript and gave it to Francis Dujon, a scholar of Leyden, who is known in literature as Junius, and from whom the manuscript derives its name of the *Junian Caedmon*. **1897** F. A. Blackburn in *Anglia* XIX. 91 The same device is found in other manuscripts, for example in the Genesis and the Exodus of the Junian MS. in the Bodleian. **1914** *PMLA* XXIX. 146 This book was printed at Dort from the famous and beautiful Junian types representing the Gothic and Anglo-Saxon alphabets, which Junius later presented to the University of Oxford.

junior (ˈdʒuːnɪə(r)), *a.* and *sb.* [a. L. *jūnior* (for *juvenior*), compar. of *juvenis* young.]

A. *adj.* **1.** The younger: used after a person's name (†or title) to denote the younger of two bearing the same name in a family, esp. a son of the same name as his father; also (after a simple surname) the younger of two boys of the same surname in a school. Abbreviated *jun.*, *junr.*, or *jr.*

[**1409** *Durham Acc. Roll* in *Eng. Hist. Rev.* XIV. 528 Per manus Johannis Falderle Junioris.] **1623** in Cockeram. **1691** *Lond. Gaz.* No. 2669/4 Lost, a Note of Mr. Tho. Symonds junior's Hand for Mr. Tho. Symonds senior,..for 50*l.* **1698** Fryer *Acc. E. India & P.* Table 19 King of Bantam, Junior, espouses the Dutch Interest. **1708** *Lond. Gaz.* No. 4475/4 Tho. Crabb, Sen. and Tho. Crabb, Jun. of Malborrow..Wooll-men. **1838** Dickens *Nich. Nick.* v, Snawley junior, if you don't leave off..shaking with the cold, I'll warm you with a severe thrashing. **1851** *Illustr. Catal. Gt. Exhib.* 259 The whole..are from the designs of James Rock, jun.

2. Of less standing or more recent appointment; of lower position, in a class, rank, profession, etc.

In American colleges and schools. Belonging to the third year of the course, next below the *senior* or last year, or to the first or second year of a three-year course, or the first of a two-year course.

1766 in B. Peirce *Hist. Harvard* (1833) 246 That the Senior Sophisters shall attend the Tutor *A* on Mondays... That the Junior Sophisters shall attend *B* on Mondays. **1810** *Naval Chron.* XXIV. 41 His Majesty's ship *Pompée* (junior flag-ship). **1849** Macaulay *Hist. Eng.* iii. I. 309 The lord treasurer..had eight thousand a year, and..the junior lords had sixteen hundred a year each. **1870** Miss Bridgman *R. Lynne* I. ii. 12 From junior clerk, he worked his way up. **1871** M. Collins *Mrq. & Merch.* I. ii. 56 The chief of the firm went on what is called the 'junior partner' principle. His clerks became in time his partners.

3. †**a.** Belonging to youth or earlier life; youthful, juvenile. *Obs.*

1606 Sylvester *Du Bartas* II. iv. I. *Trophies* 485 So shall his owne Ambitious Courage bring For Crown a Coffin to our Iunior King. **1643** Sir T. Browne *Relig. Med.* II. §8 Our first studies and *junior* endeavours may style us Peripateticks, Stoicks, or Academicks. **1706** *Wooden World Dissected* (1708) 37 One that in his Junior Days was brought up in the Fear of the Lord.

b. Designating something intended for children or young people; also applied to a product, device, etc., that is smaller than the normal size.

1860 (*title*) The junior atlas, for schools; fourteen maps selected from the college atlas. **1884** *Chambers's Hist. Readers* (*title*) Junior English history. **1941** *Tennessean* (Nashville) 12 Aug. 9 (Advt.), Handyhot junior electric washer. **1948** (*title*) Oxford junior encyclopaedia. **1948** *Tennessean Mag.* (Nashville) 7 Nov. 23 The idea that 'Junior is a size, not an age', has been plugged with rather half-hearted vigor for several years..in clothes in the 9 to 17 size range. **1967** L. B. Archer in Wills & Yearsley *Handbk. Managem. Technol.* 125 It will be an important design consideration to know whether the product is to be presented as one of a family of different products..and/or one of a family of similar products (standard, de luxe, junior, and portable models?). **1967** M. Drabble *Jerusalem the Golden* vii. 172 She had been in the afternoon to the chemist's to buy some Junior Aspirin. **1972** *Practical Motorist* Oct. 212/1 A full-size hacksaw won't fit into the average tool box, nor will it work in tight corners. A 'junior' frame saw is a useful back-up, since it's small enough to travel with any tool kit.

4. Of later rise or appearance in history, of later date; more modern. Now rarely said of persons.

1621 Burton *Anat. Mel.* II. iv. II. ii, [Hellebor] is still oppugned..by Crato and some junior physitians. **1678** Cudworth *Intell. Syst.* Pref. 34 There is yet a Fourth Atheistick Form taken notice of..though perhaps Junior to the rest, it seeming to be but the Corruption and Degeneration of Stoicism. **1699** Bentley *Phal.* 85 Archestratus the Syracusian was junior to Plato. *Mod.* The Cretan civilization was apparently junior to that of the Nile valley.

5. Special collocations: ***junior college*** (in *U.S.*), 'a college, operating as a separate institution or as part of a standard college, which does not offer courses more advanced than those of the sophomore year' (D.A.E.); also, a similar institution in Britain and elsewhere; ***junior high*** (***school***) (*N. Amer.*), a school intermediate between elementary school and high school; ***junior miss*** (orig. *U.S.*), a young teen-aged girl; = miss *sb.*² 4; also *attrib.*; ***junior school***, (*a*) in the state educational system, a school for children aged roughly between 7 and 11; a primary school; (*b*) the lower forms of some fee-paying schools; ***junior service***, the Army; ***junior stock*** (see quot. 1914); ***junior technical school***, a school providing a technical and secondary education for boys.

1899 *Univ. Chicago Reg. 1898–99* 37/1 The Faculties of the Schools of Arts, Literature, and Science have been organized as follows; (1) The Faculty of the *Junior Colleges; [etc.]. **1949** *Manch. Guardian Weekly* 7 Apr. 8 You will not learn what are the ambitions of the students at a junior college. **1957** *Encycl. Brit.* XX. 258/1 Some schools extended secondary education upward by offering two years of additional work of 'junior college' type. **1963** *Higher Educ.: Rep. Comm. under Ld. Robbins 1961–3* 148 in *Parl. Papers 1962–3* (Cmnd. 2154) XI. 639 Other witnesses.. advocated the creation of separate junior or preparatory colleges to undertake the later stages of sixth form work and the first year of university work. **1971** *English Studies* LII. 569 The action..takes place in a classroom of a Southern Californian junior college. **1909** *Ann. Rep. Bd. Educ.* (Columbus, Ohio) 168 The Board has declared itself in favour of the *Junior High School System. **1929** *Encycl. Brit.* XX. 258/1 The junior high school has also been a vehicle for innovations in teaching methods. **1948** *Daily Ardmoreite* (Ardmore, Okla.) 12 Oct. 10/1 They met in the ninth grade in junior high. **1968** *Globe & Mail* (Toronto) 13 Feb. 30/2 (Advt.), Convenient to public, junior high and separate schools. *Ibid.* 33/6 (Advt.), Experienced Junior High, social studies and science teacher required. **1927** *Vogue* 15 Jan. 106/2 *Junior Misses' Frock. **1950** M. Allingham *Take Two at Bedtime* 17, I was still wearing the junior-miss dresses I had had at school. **1965** *Harper's Bazaar* May 75 Both dresses £1 19s. 11d. by Marks & Spencer Junior Miss. **1871** *Minutes of School Board for London* I. 156 Public elementary day schools are conveniently classfied into infant schools, for children below seven years of age; *junior schools, for children between seven and ten years of age; and senior schools, for older children. **1902** *Captain* VII. 221/1 Workington passed out of the Junior school. **1971** *Times Educ. Suppl.* 5 Feb. 41/4 (Advt.), Small groups of immigrant pupils in Junior Schools, who need additional language instruction. **1915** E. Wallace *Man who bought London* viii. 81 She had a son in

the army, and she bore the *junior service a grudge in consequence. **1914** H. HALFORD *Dict. Stock Market Terms* 50 **Junior stocks*, ordinary and deferred stocks ranking for dividend after debentures and preference stocks. **1932** *Daily Tel.* 8 Oct. 2/4 The current quotations of the junior stocks remove the likelihood of an issue in that form. **1929** *Encycl. Brit.* VII. 988/2 Its lower grades have shown a considerable increase, whether in *junior technical schools, art schools or evening classes. **1931** *Education Outlook* June 183/1 Its pupils [*sc.* of the new senior school] are distinguished from their contemporaries in grammar schools, modern schools, and junior technical schools.

B. *sb.* **1. a.** (the adj. used *absol.*) A person who is younger than another, or of more recent entrance or lower standing in a class, profession, etc.: see A. More generally (chiefly *U.S.*), a child, esp. a young boy: freq. with capital initial.

1526 *Pilgr. Perf.* (W. de W. 1531) 206 Of bysshops, doctours of the lawe & lerned men, of senyours and iunyours, of iewes and gentyles. **1678** CUDWORTH *Intell. Syst.* I. i. §37. 45 Our Continual Creation of new Souls, by means whereof they become Juniours both to the matter of the World and of their own Bodies. **1722** *Lond. Gaz.* No. 6102/4 The Juniors went first. **1797** MRS. RADCLIFFE *Italian* xx, He was pointed out by the fathers of the convent to the juniors as a great example. **1820** BYRON *Mar. Fal.* I. ii. 34 At least in some, the juniors of the number. **1888** BRYCE *Amer. Commw.* III. VI. cii. 453 In an American college the students are classed by years, those of the first year being called freshmen, of the second year sophomores, of the third year juniors. **1946** *Sun* (Baltimore) 14 Dec., Lest the joy of Christmas be marred by..Junior's nipping his pal's arm with an arrow from his archery set, [etc.]. **1951** O. NASH *Family Reunion* 31 But you take ingenuous Junior, and it's just a radio to him. **1968** *Globe & Mail* (Toronto) 13 Jan. 25/6 (Advt.), Enclosed is cheque..for..adults..and..juniors. **1970** G. GREER *Female Eunuch* 230 If junior finds out that his parents are going out, he'll scream.

b. Preceded by possessive; cf. *better*, *elder*, *inferior*, *superior*.

1548 UDALL *Erasm. Par. Luke* xiv. 7 Doctours in any vniuersitie..Not one of them but he thynketh hymself to haue had a great iniurie doen vnto hym yf he go on the left hand of an other that semeth to be his iuniour or inferiour. **1676** *Prideaux Lett.* (Camden) 55 Christ Church is now altogether becom a stranger to you, we beeing al almost your juniors. **1699** BENTLEY *Phal.* 413 Persons of Age and Authority spoke kindly to their Juniors. **1797** JEFFERSON *Writ.* (1859) IV. 155, I am his junior in life, I was his junior in Congress, his junior in the diplomatic line, and lately his junior in our civil government. **1818** BYRON *Mazeppa* iv, His wife was not of his opinion; His junior she by thirty years.

c. *Comb.*, as **junior-right**, Borough-English.

1882 C. ELTON *Orig. Eng. Hist.* viii. 185 Junior-right..has flourished not only in England..but also in some remote and disconnected regions. *Ibid.* [see JUNIORITY b].

2. A barrister who has not taken silk; a junior barrister.

1837 DICKENS *Pickw.* xxxiv, Mr. Serjeant Buzfuz..leads on the other side. That gentleman behind him is Mr. Skimpin, his junior. **1842** DICKENS *Amer. Notes* I. iii. 127 The counsel who interrogated the witness..was alone and had no 'junior'. **1872** G. H. LEWES *Let.* 5 Jan. in Geo. Eliot *Lett.* (1956) V. 234 We had..Bowen (the junior in the Tichborne case on whom Coleridge mainly relies),..and had..lots of fun. **1958** S. HYLAND *Who goes Hang?* xlix. 260 Oliver Passmore K.C., M.P. And there was a 'junior' with him called Mortimer. **1972** 'W. HAGGARD' *Protectors* iii. 26 This barrister was..a strong Junior at the criminal bar, and he'd defended Martiny's friend.

juniorate ('dʒuːnɪəreɪt). *R. C. Ch.* [See JUNIOR and -ATE[1]. Cf. med.L. *jūniōrātus* benefice or revenues given to junior clerics.] In the Society of Jesus, a two-years' course of instruction attended by junior members preparatory to entering the priesthood; a seminary for those taking this course.

1845 G. OLIVER *Coll. Biog. Soc. Jesus* 70 He was in the Juniorate, i.e. a candidate for the Ecclesiastical State. **1882** H. FOLEY *Rec. Eng. Prov. Soc. Jesus* VII. 71 He became Superior of the Seminary or Juniorate adjoining Stonyhurst College. **1891** *Tablet* 19 Sept. 467 A Juniorate for pupil teachers was established.

juniority (dʒuːnɪ'ɒrɪtɪ). [f. JUNIOR + -ITY.] The state or condition of being junior (in age, appointment, or rank); youthfulness; lower position; later standing.

1597 A. M. tr. *Guillemeau's Fr. Chirurg.* 54/2 Iunioritye or youth, and good temperature are profitable vnto the resanation of woundes. **1612** HEYWOOD *Apol. Actors* I. 30 It becomes my juniority rather to be pupil'd my selfe then to instruct others. **1668** in *3rd Rep. Hist. MSS. Comm.* (1872) 327/1 All the Aldermen went into the Hall, and there with them, according to my juniority I took my place uppon the bench. **1846** GROTE *Greece* I. xxi. II. 270 Presuming a difference of authorship between the two poems, I feel less convinced about the supposed juniority of the Odyssey.

b. A name proposed for Borough-English.

1882 C. ELTON *Orig. Eng. Hist.* viii. 185 We have a choice between 'ultimogeniture'..or one must coin a new phrase, like juniority or junior-right.

'juniorship. [f. as prec. + -SHIP.] **a.** The condition of a junior, juniority. **b.** *R.C.Ch.* Juniorate, juvenate.

1794 CHARLOTTE SMITH *Wandgs. Warwick* iii. 67 The boys who had..been the worst treated in their juniorships..were almost always the greatest tyrants in their turn. **1881** MARY C. HAY *Missing* I. 276 There would have been some excuse for Drury to resent his juniorship.

juniper ('dʒuːnɪpə(r)). Forms: α. 4–7 iunipere, (4 iuny-, 5 -pre, -pur, iwnipre), 5–6 iunyper, (5 -pyr), 6–7 iuniper, (6 -peer), 7– juniper. β. 5 ieneper(e, ienyper, 6 ieni-, ieno-, iyneper; 5 gynypre, genopir, 5–7 geneper, (6 -par, -pre), 6 genne-, giniper, 7 ginnuper. [ad. L. *jūniper-us*, repr. in Romanic by F. *genièvre* (OF. *-evre*, *-eivre*, etc.), Prov. *genibre*, *-ebre*, Sp. *enebro*, Pg. *zimbro*, It. *ginepro*. The β-forms follow OF. in substituting *e* or *i* for the *ū*, but retain the *p* of the Latin. OF. *genevre* was adopted in MDu. as *genever* (Du. *jenever*): see GENEVA[1], JENIVER.]

1. A genus of coniferous evergreen shrubs and trees, of which about thirty species are found in different parts of the northern hemisphere; specifically and originally, the common European species *Juniperus communis*, a hardy spreading shrub or low tree, having awl-shaped prickly leaves and bluish-black or purple berries, with a pungent taste, yielding a volatile oil (*oil of juniper*) used in medicine as a stimulant and diuretic, also in the manufacture of gin. The common N. American species is *J. virginiana*.

The wood is occasionally used in joinery; the seeds and wood were formerly burnt as purifiers of the air. The coal of juniper wood was fabled to have a wonderful power of remaining glowing.

a **1400** *Pistel of Susan* 71 (Vernon MS.) Þe Iunipere ientel, Ionyng be-twene. *c* **1400** MAUNDEV. (1839) xxviii. 289 That Tre hathe many Leues as the Gynypre hathe. *c* **1420** *Pallad. on Husb.* I. 397 (E.E.T.S.) Bordis of cipresse Playn and direct, vpsette hem in their kynde A foote atwyn, and hem to gedir dresse Wit iunipur [*v.r.* ienyper], box, oliue, or cupresse, So worchyng up thy wowis by and by. **1523** LD. BERNERS *Froiss.* I. ccccxix. 734 A great large dyke full of busshes of genepar, and other small busshes. *c* **1550** LLOYD *Treas. Health* (1585) S v, Give vnto the pacient..a litle oyle of Ienoper. **1578** LYTE *Dodoens* VI. lxxxii. 763 Iuniper or the beries thereof burned driueth away..all infection and corruption of the ayre. **1582** *Nottingham Rec.* IV. 199 Paid for iyneper to swetten the Hall jd. **1594** SPENSER *Amoretti* xxvi, Sweet is the Iunipere, but sharpe his bough. **1607** TOPSELL *Four-f. Beasts* (1658) 301 Anoint all his breast over with the Oyl of Ginnuper and Pepper mixt together. *a* **1682** SIR T. BROWNE *Tracts* 58 The coals of Juniper raked up will keep a glowing Fire for the space of a year. **1794** MARTYN *Rousseau's Bot.* xxix. 459 Common Juniper has three spreading, pointed leaves, coming out together, that are longer than the berry. **1823** BYRON *Juan* x. lxiii, Holland..That water-land of Dutchmen and of ditches Where juniper expresses its best juice. **1857** WHITTIER *Last Walk Autumn* ii, On a ground of sombre fir And azure-studded juniper. **1871** H. MACMILLAN *True Vine* vii. (1872) 285.

b. Loosely applied to coniferous trees of other genera, as the American Larch or Hackmatack (*Larix Americana*), and the White Cedar (*Chamæcyparis sphæroidea*) of the Southern U.S.

1748 H. ELLIS *Hudson's Bay* 138 They are commonly of Fir, or Larch, which the English there call Juniper. **1866** *Treas. Bot.* 642/1 *Juniper*,..also applied in Nova Scotia to the Hackmatack, Tamarack.

c. In the translations of the Bible, used, after the Vulgate, to render Heb. *rethem* or *rōthem*, a white-flowered species of *Retama*, *R. Rætam*, a shrub with rush-like branches, which are leafless or bear a few unifoliate leaves.

1388 WYCLIF *Job* xxx. 4 The roote of iunyperis [**1382** iunypere trees] was her mete. **1560** BIBLE (Genev.) *Ps.* cxx. 4 It is as the sharpe arrowes of a mightie man, and as the coales of Iuniper. **1608** HIERON *Wks.* I. 711 These mine aduersaries, whose tongues are as the coales of iuniper. **1671** MILTON *P.R.* II. 272 He saw the Prophet also, how he fled Into the Desert, and how there he slept Under a juniper.

2. *slang.* Gin (cf. *juniper-brandy* below).

1857 J. E. RITCHIE *Nt. Side Lond.* 195 The pots of heavy and the quarterns of juniper are freely quaffed.

†**3.** A name for the Fieldfare. *Obs.*

[**1562** TURNER *Herbal* II. 25 People eate the feldefares vndrawen..because they are full of the berries of Iuniper.] **1598** FLORIO, *Collurione*, a bird called a Fieldfare or Iuniper.

4. *attrib.* and *Comb.*, as ***juniper-berry***, *-leaf*, *-root*, *-shrub*, *-top*, *-tree*, *-wood*; †**juniper-beads**, (?) beads of juniper wood; **juniper-brandy**, a name for gin; † **juniper lecture** (*obs. colloq.*), a severe pungent 'lecture' or reprimand; so †**juniper letter**; **juniper-oil** = *oil of juniper* (see 1); **juniper pug**, a species of pug-moth (*Eupithecia sobrinota*), the larva of which feeds only on juniper; **juniper-resin** = *gum juniper*: see GUM *sb.*[2] 3 a (*Syd. Soc. Lex.* 1887); **juniper-water**, a cordial drink made from or flavoured with juniper; **juniper-worm**, the larva of a N. American geometrid moth (*Drepanodes varus*), which feeds upon juniper-leaves.

1486 *Plumpton Corr.* 51 The first gift that my lady of Syon gave to me was a par of *Jeneper beads pardonet. **1706** HEARNE *Collect.* 10 June (O.H.S.) I, The Quaker read him a *Juniper [*mispr.* Jumper] Lecture agt. Lewdness. **1744–50** ELLIS *Mod. Husbandm.* VII. II. 142 (D.) When women chide their husbands for a long while together, it is commonly said, they give them a juniper lecture; which, I am informed, is a comparison taken from the long lasting of the live coals of that wood. **1655** FULLER *Ch. Hist.* III. v. §29 Bishop Grouthead, offended thereat, wrote Pope Innocent the fourth such a *Juniper Letter taxing him with extortion. **1382** WYCLIF *Job* xxx. 4 The roote of *iunypere trees was the mete of hem. **1480** CAXTON *Ovid's Met.* x. iv, Okes, Planes, Elmes, Beches, Geneper trees. **1756–7** tr. *Keysler's Trav.* (1760) I. 41 A valley in Tirol remarkable for the height of its juniper trees. **1666** TEMPLE *Lett., to Godolphin* Wks. 1731 II. 24 A little Bottle of *Juniper Water, which is the common Cordial in that Country.

Hence † **'juniperate** *v. trans.*, to impregnate or flavour with juniper; **'junipery** *a.*, abounding in junipers.

1605 TIMME *Quersit.* III. 181 Drinke..a little wine juniperated. **1882** *Three in Norway* viii. 61 The rockiest, brookiest, juniperiest country in the world.

†**juniperine.** *Obs. rare.* In 5 -yn. [ad. L. type **juniperin-us* of or pertaining to juniper: see -INE[1].] A juniper-tree.

c **1430** *Pilgr. Lyf Manhode* II. xc. 108 This ax which men clepen annoye of lyf..with whiche j dullede sum time Helye vnder the juniperyn.

juniperite ('dʒuːnɪpəraɪt). [ad. mod.L. *Juniperītēs*, f. *juniper-us*: see -ITE[1] 2 a.] A fossil plant allied to the juniper.

1890 in *Cent. Dict.*

junk (dʒʌŋk), *sb.*[1] Forms: 5 ion(c)ke, 5–7 iunke, 7 junke, jonk, junck, 7– junk. [a. OF. *jonc*, *jounc*, *junc* = Sp., Pg. *junco*, It. *giunco*:—L. *juncus* rush.]

†**1.** A rush. *Obs.*

c **1400** MAUNDEV. (1839) ii. 13 Ȝif..Men seyn that this Croune is of thornes, ȝee schulle understonde that it was of Jonkes [*Roxb.* iunkes] of the See, that is to sey, Rushes of the See, that prykken als scharpely as Thornes. **1491** CAXTON *Vitas Patr.* (W. de W. 1495) 33 a/2 His bedde was of Ionckes, and his vestyment of hayre. *Ibid.* 43 Made fyscellis woven wyth rede and Ionkes. [**1526** *Pilgr. Perf.* (W. de W. 1531) 302 b, Tough sharpe thornes, called the iunkes of ye see.]

2. *Surg.* A form of splint, originally stuffed with rushes or bents (cf. quots.).

1612 WOODALL *Surg. Mate* Wks. (1653) 150, I appoint him juncks, as some terme them, namely bents rowled up in canvas. **1634** T. JOHNSON *Parey's Chirurg.* 559 Junkes are made of stickes the bignesse of a man's finger, wrapped about with rushes, and then with linnen cloth. **1650** tr. *Glisson's Dis. Childr., Rickets* (1742) 226 Bandages, Jonks, and clasped Boots every Body knows to be very useful in the Rickets. **1887** *Syd. Soc. Lex.*, *Junk*,..in Surgery, a thin cushion stuffed with horse-hair and strengthened or not by strips of wood or cane, used to support a broken or sprained limb... The original junk, which is still employed, consisted of reeds or stiff straw quilted between two pieces of stout calico.

junk (dʒʌŋk), *sb.*[2] Forms: 5 ionke, 7 iunke, junke, 8 junck, 8– junk. [Of obscure origin: though identical in form with prec., there is no evidence of connexion.]

1. † **a.** *Naut.* An old or inferior cable or rope; usually ***old junk***. *Obs.*

1485 *Naval Acc. Hen. VII* (1896) 49 Hausers grete and small..iij, Jonkes..iiij. *Ibid.* 55 Olde Jonkes..iiij. **1600** HAKLUYT *Voy.* (1810) III, We only roade by an old iunke. **1622** SIR R. HAWKINS *Voy. S. Sea* (1847) 155 Peeces of a Junke or rope chopped very small. **1626** CAPT. SMITH *Accid. Yng. Seamen* 16 Cables, hawsers or streame cables when that way vnseruiceable, they serue for Iunkes, fendors and braded plackets for brests of defence. **1627** —— *Seaman's Gram.* vii. 30 Fenders are peeces of old Hawsers called Iunkes. **1769** NEWLAND in *Phil. Trans.* LXII. 86 You may make your ship fast with any old junk.

†**b.** A piece of old cable used in making a fender, etc. *Obs.*

[**1626–7**: see 1.] *a* **1642** SIR W. MONSON *Naval Tracts* (1704) III. 374/1, I advise, that..the uppermost part of the Ship be arm'd with Junks of Cables. **1716** *Glossogr. Nova*, *Bongrace*, to Mariners is a Frame of old Ropes or Juncks of Cables, laid out at the Bows, Stems, and Sides of Ships..to preserve them from Damage of great Flakes of Ice.

c. Old cable or rope material, cut up into short lengths and used for making fenders, reef-points, gaskets, oakum, etc.

1666 PEPYS *Diary* 14 July, Four or five tons of corke, to send..to the fleet; being a new device to make barricados with, instead of junke. **1704** *New Hampsh. Prov. Papers* (1868) II. 440 Ordered, that Mr. Treasurer, provide..Junk for Wadding, Tar, Blacking &c. for the great Guns. **1748** *Anson's Voy.* II. ii. 133 We had not a sufficient quantity of junk to make spun-yarn. **1840** R. H. DANA *Bef. Mast* ii. 2 The steerage..was filled with coils of rigging, spare sails, old junk, and ship stores. **1882** 5 *Yrs. Penal Servit.* i. 23 Every morning the quantum of junk was served out.

d. *transf.* Any discarded or waste material that can be put to some use: cf. *junk-dealer* in 5. Also, second-hand or discarded articles of little or no use or value; rubbish.

1842 *Congress. Globe* 23 Feb. 261 Champagne was charged for under the head of 'old junk'. **1884** H. FREDERIC in *Pall Mall G.* 6 Aug. 11/1 Many..[shops] devoted to the sale of rags, and the sweepings of a city, bones, junk—a collection of pestilence-breeding filth. **1913** V. STEER *Romance of Cinema* 30 The life of a film is very short. It is 'first run' to-day and 'junk' a few short weeks hence. **1924** GALSWORTHY *White Monkey* I. v. 33 His 'junk', however, was not devoid of the taste and luxury which overflows from the greater houses of England. **1935** A. CHRISTIE *Death in Clouds* xi. 118, I have my collection..that all connoisseurs know—and also I have—well, frankly, Messieurs, let us call it junk! **1940** *Punch* 3 Apr. 386/2 A great deal of ecclesiastical junk which the Vatican..would have obvious difficulty in dispersing. **1952** R. FINLAYSON *Schooner came to Atia* 112 The boat was found battered to junk in a pool. **1974** *Woman* 4 May 5/1 Collecting junk for creative work is a way of life at school.

e. Any narcotic drug, esp. heroin; also, such drugs collectively. Also *attrib.* *slang* (orig. *U.S.*).

1925 *Writer's Monthly* June 487/1 *Junk*, dope. 1930 *Liberty* 5 July 24/1 When he has the junk in him there is no telling what he'll do. 1933 'J. Spenser' *Limey* iii. 37 You shoulda seen him when he was only half light with a shot o' the junk (dope) he used. 1937 B. Reitman *Sister of Road* (1941) vii. 74 She was full of junk, which she had received in her mail. 1938 [see connect *v.* 5 b]. 1953 W. Burroughs *Junkie* (1972) vii. 66 It doesn't take the manager long to spot a bookie or a junk-pusher. *Ibid.* x. 108 You cannot escape from junk-sickness any more than you can escape from junk-kick after a shot. *Ibid.* xii. 120 Lupita got her start with one gram of junk and built up from there to a monopoly of the junk business in Mexico City. 1957 P. Frank *Seven Days to Never* vii. 204 Pretty slick way to carry your junk... You're a junkie, aren't you? 1960 J. Gelber *Connection* I. 25 You cats ought to smoke pot instead of using junk. It would make you more agreeable. 1963 A. Trocchi *Cain's Book* 73 One must go where the junk is and one is never certain where the junk is, never sure that where the junk is is not the anteroom of the penitentiary. 1966 *Listener* 17 Mar. 401/2 Burroughs's position is explicit: junk—*i.e.*, all narcotic drugs, as opposed to hallucinogenic ones like hashish and mescalin—are purely evil. 1972 J. Brown *Chancer* ix. 85 You do anything for junk... Cheat. Lie. Steal.

f. = *junk food* (sense 5 below). orig. *U.S.*

1972 *Time* 18 Dec. 69/1 Eating is a spiritual movement... It upsets me to see people eating junk. 1973 *Jrnl. Nutrition Educ.* Apr.-June 117/2 Students eat what they..refer to as 'junk'—French fries, pretzels, chips, ice cream, candy, hot dogs.

2. *transf.* A piece or lump of anything; a chunk.

[*Chunk* may have originated under the joint influence of *chuck* and *junk*.]

1726 G. Roberts *4 Years Voy.* 155, I..gave to each of them a short Junk of Pipe. 1764 Grainger *Sugar Cane* I. Note 41 The stem is knotty, and, being cut into small junks and planted, young sprouts shoot up from each knob. *Ibid.* III. 127 The Cane..Cut into junks a yard in length. 1833 M. Scott *Tom Cringle* i. (1859) 8 A large knot in his cheek from a junk of tobacco therein stowed. 1843 Mrs. Carlyle *Lett.* I. 270 [He] snatched up a large pound-cake, cut it into junks. 1876 Miss Braddon *J. Haggard's Dau.* xxiii. 243 The huge junk of single Gloucester.

3. *transf.* orig. *Naut.* The salt meat used as food on long voyages, compared to pieces of rope; usually with epithet, as *old*, *salt*, *tough junk*.

1762 Smollett *Sir L. Greaves* xiii, Your mistress Aurelia, whom I value no more than old junk, pork-slush, or stinking stock-fish. 1792 M. Cutler in *Life, Jrnls. & Corr.* (1888) I. 486, I had infinitely rather sit down with you to a piece of salt junk at one o'clock than be tormented with the parade..of Philadelphia entertainments. 1862 Carlyle *Fredk. Gt.* x. v. (1872) III. 263 Steadfastly eating tough junk with a wetting of rum.

4. *Whale-fishery.* The lump or mass of thick oily cellular tissue beneath the case and nostrils of a sperm-whale, containing spermaceti.

1850 Scoresby *Cheever's Whalem. Adv.* x. (1859) 135 What whalers call the junk, or mighty mass of blubber, was separated from the case. *c* 1865 Letheby in *Circ. Sc.* I. 97/2 The dense mass of cellular tissue, called junk.

5. *attrib.* and *Comb.*, as *junk-mat*, etc.; (sense 1 d) *junk car*, *cart*, *collector*, *-heap*, *merchant*, *-pile*, *-room*, *-stall*, *store*, *-yard*; **junk art** (see quot.); so *junk artist*; **junk-dealer**, *U.S.*, a marine-store dealer; **junk food** orig. *U.S.*, food that appeals to popular (esp. juvenile) taste but has little nutritional value; also *fig.*; **junk-hook**, a hook used in handling the junk of a whale; **junk jewellery** = *costume jewellery*; **junk mail** *N. Amer.*, circulars, advertisements, etc., sent by post to a large number of addresses; **junk-playground** = *adventure playground*; **junk-ring**, (*a*) a metal ring confining the hemp packing of a piston; (*b*) a steam-tight metal packing round a piston; **junk sculpture** = *junk art*; so *junk sculptor*; **junk-shop**, a marine store, the shop of a junk-dealer; **junk-strap**, a chain for hoisting the junk of a whale to the deck of a vessel; **junk-vat**, in tanning, a large vat for holding weakened vat-liquor; **junk-wad**, a wad for a gun made of junk or oakum bound with spun-yarn. Also junkman[2].

1966 *Britannica Bk. of Year* (U.S.) 807/1 **Junk art*, three-dimensional art made from discarded material (as of metal, mortar, glass, or wood); junk artist, *n.* 1954 *Amer. Speech* XXIX. 99 **Junk car* or *junker*, a car in poor condition that has been made to look like a hot rod. Usually used sarcastically of any car ready for the junk yard. 1967 *Boston Sunday Herald* 26 Mar. II. 9/2 Thirty-five junk cars hauled away. 1879 *Scribner's Monthly* May 34/1 These piers..are too narrow even for the circulation of a *junk-cart. 1934 Webster, Junk collector. 1956 J. M. Mogey *Family & Neighbourhood* 10 Junk-collectors' yards. 1882 Sala *Amer. Revis.* v. (1885) 70 The marine store or '*junk' dealer, as he is styled in New-York. 1892 *Pall Mall G.* 23 May 7/2 These 'exchanges' are bought by the pound from an old junk-dealer [in New York]. 1973 *Washington Post* 9 Mar. A27/5 How many children are going to fill up on *junk foods and be too full to eat a nutritious lunch now? 1974 *Ottawa Citizen* 24 July 52/3 Canadians' consumption of..junk food is alarming. 1982 *Times* 12 Aug. 6/6 Blyton may be junk food but it's not addictive. 1986 *Times* 4 Mar. 10/5 The eastern cult for junk food may be having a remarkable effect on the health and appearance of Japan's youngsters. 1906 *Westm. Gaz.* 26 Oct. 2/1 He [*sc.* Hearst]..took hold of a *junk-heap relic of Pacific-coast journalism called the *Examiner*. 1917 R. L. Alsaker *Eating for Health* II. xiii. 195 You and I..have to conform to the laws of nature, or else we are thrown into the junk heap. 1953 C. Day Lewis *Italian Visit* iii. 34 It would take three life-times to cover The glorious junk-heap. 1973 *Guardian* 23 Mar. 12/4 In Plymouth once they raided the local junk-heap to supplement the props which they had brought with them. 1939 *Sun* (Baltimore) 8 May 17 The Duchess of Kent..envies American women their smart '*junk jewelry' (costume stuff). 1960 *Sunday Express* 21 Feb. 14/3 American women have..loaded themselves with so much 'junk' jewellery they jangle as they walk. 1954 *Reader's Digest* Oct. 37/1 The argument for *junk mail is that sorting requires little time—the postman simply delivers one throwaway to each home. 1967 *Economist* 23 Dec. 1227/1 These high charges are necessary to subsidise third class bulk mail, often called 'junk' mail, which includes millions of unsolicited advertisements sent out to lists of names as well as mail order catalogues. 1972 *Edmonton* (Alberta) *Jrnl.* 26 June 5/5 Within the first few months of their baby's life, the Duncans had received more than 1,000 pieces of junk mail. 1851 *Illustr. Catal. Gt. Exhib.* 1416 *Junk mats. 1901 *Westm. Gaz.* 8 July 3/2 Twenty tons of unsold copies of a well-known cheap magazine were sold for waste-paper to *junk merchants. 1880 *Harper's Mag.* June 67/1 The junk pile in the barn is invaded, and the rusty plough abstracted. 1912 J. H. Moore *Ethics & Educ.* 10 They should be sent without sighs or lamentations to the junk-pile. 1957 *Economist* 5 Oct. 28/2 That lively social experiment the Grimsby 'shanty town', a *junk-playground which has evolved into a children's community. 1839 R. S. Robinson *Naut. Steam Eng.* 41 On the top of the packing rings comes the *junk ring, which occupies the whole space from the boss of the piston to the sides. 1887 D. A. Low *Machine Draw.* (1892) 61 The piston rod and nut are of wrought iron, so also are the junk ring bolts. 1936 M. Allingham *Flowers for Judge* xiv. 207 They didn't keep anything valuable there. It's a sort of *junk-room. 1966 *Time* 14 Jan. E1 Long before the *tachiste* painter or the *junk sculptor, the American Indian shaped art from sand, bone, feathers—whatever he had at hand. 1969 *Harper's Mag.* Sept. 14 Students interested in musicology, junk sculpture, the Theater of the Absurd. 1970 *Times* 7 Mar. p. iv/6 He [*sc.* Brion Gysin] had time on his hands and became one of the pioneers of junk sculpture. 1800 Colquhoun *Comm. Thames* ii. 50 Receivers ..who kept Old Iron and *Junk Shops in places adjacent to the River. 1841 'Dow, Jr.' *Short Patent Sermons* 77 Trash, that wouldn't fetch two cents in the market of heaven, and but a trifle more in the junk-shops of hell. 1879 *Scribner's Monthly* May 33/2 New York is bordered with rat-holes and rotten cribs, gin-mills and junk-shops. 1881 C. C. Harrison *Woman's Handiwork* III. 171 She confessed to having purchased from a junk-shop the charming little gilt-framed oblong mirror. 1883 *Millionaire* v. xvii, Jeremiah Flint, who keeps the junk-shop down there close to the London Docks. 1939 C. Day Lewis *Child of Misfortune* I. v. 70 Lady Gresham's mind was dark, dusty and furtive as a junk-shop. 1951 M. Kennedy *Lucy Carmichael* III. i. 157, I saw it..in a tray in a junk shop. 1969 *Listener* 17 Apr. 533/1 The Metropolitan Museum in New York was a really dismal junk shop 40 years ago. 1962 *John o' London's* 11 Jan. 40/3 Oddities off *junk-stalls. 1882 J. D. McCabe *New York* 583 They..sell it to the *junk and rag stores. 1908 Kipling *Lett. of Travel* (1920) 197 We went to look at a marine junk-store. 1875 Knight *Dict. Mech.*, **Junk-wad*. 1879 *Man. Artillery Exerc.* 323 When junk or grummet wads are used they are supplied by 5. 1880 G. W. Cable *Grandissimes* 192 You may still..see one [*sc.* a villa] standing..among ..*junk-yards, and longshoremen's hovels. 1952 W. R. Burnett *Vanity Row* (1953) vi. 50 All about loomed gas tanks, warehouses, junk yards. 1953 *Manch. Guardian Weekly* 27 Aug. 7 Suffocating in a junkyard of chairs. 1966 T. Pynchon *Crying of Lot 49* i. 14 If it had been an outright junkyard, probably he could have stuck things out, made a career. 1974 M. Hastings *Dragon Island* ix. 77 The only reason this floating junkyard's still in service is that the Chinese perishers that own her can't even give her away.

junk (dʒʌŋk), *sb.*[3] Forms: (6 giunco, iunco), 7 junke, iunck(e, jounck, junc, yonk, 7–9 jonk, 8 joncke, 7– junk. [A word of Oriental origin, now adapted in most European langs.: Pg. *junco* (in 16th c. *jungo*, Barbosa), Sp. *junco*, It. *giunco* (16th c. *giunca*, Pigafetta), F. *joncque*, Du. *jonk*. App. ad. Javanese *djong* (occurring in compositions of 13th c. or earlier), 'ship, large vessel,' Malay *adjong*. The earlier Eng. forms are from other European langs.

Some have sought the origin of the word in the Chinese *ch'wan* 'ship or sailing vessel'; but the Portuguese and Dutch were established in Java and the Malay Archipelago before they visited China, and found the Javanese and Malay word (which has no connexion with the Chinese) applied to all large native vessels as well as to the Chinese ships which visited those shores.]

A name for the common type of native sailing vessel in the Chinese seas. It is flat-bottomed, has a square prow, prominent stem, full stern, the rudder suspended, and carries lug-sails.

The name is now applied to Chinese, Japanese, Loochoo, Siamese, and other vessels of this type; early writers applied it still more widely to Malay, Javan, and even South Indian native vessels.

[1555 Eden *Decades* 215 [from It. of Pigafetta] From the whiche Ilandes [Moluccas] they are brought [to India] in shyps or barkes made withowt any iren tooles... These barkes they caule *Giunche*. 1588 Parke tr. *Mendoza's Hist. China* I. III. xxi. 115 Such ships as they haue to saile long voiages be called *Iuncos*.] 1613 Purchas *Pilgrimage, Descr. India* (1864) 54 The viceroy having two ships sent him for supply, two Iunkes, eight or ten boates. 1634 Sir T. Herbert *Trav.* 184 We espied a Malabar Juncke of seventie Tunnes, bound for Acheen in Sumatra. 1697 Dampier *Voy.* (1729) I. 396 The Chinese..have always hideous Idols on board their Jonks or Ships. 1720 De Foe *Capt. Singleton* xiv. (1840) 237 A Dutch junk, or vessel, going to Amboyna. 1773 *Gentl. Mag.* XLIII. 332 The Chinese junks and boats ..were most of them sunk. 1813 J. Burney *Discov. S. Sea* III. x. 255 The unwieldiness of the Chinese jonks. 1853 Hawthorne *Eng. Note-Bks.* (1883) I. 442 All manner of odd-looking craft, but none so odd as the Chinese junk.

attrib. 1634 Sir T. Herbert *Trav.* 27 A Junck-man of Warre full of desperate Malabars. 1880 Miss Bird *Japan* II. 320 The total junk navy is 468,750 tons.

junk, *sb.*[4] A local name for a joint in the bedding of slate or other rock.

1662 Ray *Itin.* III. in Lankester *Mem. Ray* (1846) 185 At Denbyboul, about two miles from Tintagel, is the best quarry of slate in the country... It is divided..both longways and broadways, by cracks or rifts, which they call junks.

junk (dʒʌŋk), *v.* [f. junk *sb.*[2]] **1.** *trans.* **a.** To cut *off* in a lump; **b.** To cut or divide into junks or chunks. Hence **junked** (dʒʌŋkt) *ppl. a.*, chopped in pieces.

1803 *Ann. Reg.* 802 Six feet junked off the smaller part of the root..will yield several gallons of water. 1833 M. Scott *Tom Cringle* ii. (1859) 42 To produce a two-inch rope and junk it into three lengths..was the work of an instant. 1847 R. Hill in Gosse *Birds Jamaica* 392 They trod and stirred the mashed biscuits and junked fish, with which we fed them.

2. To treat as junk or rubbish; to discard, abandon; to 'scrap'.

1916 B. Hall *Diary* 11 Oct. in Hall & Niles *One Man's War* (1929) 196 When he got home his ship was a complete wreck. It will be junked. 1922 H. Titus *Timber* xxxii. 281 Perhaps he had friends..who are junking their mills now and getting ready to move. 1930 *Time & Tide* 20 Sept. 1164 Jugo-Slavia will not disband a soldier, scrap a gunboat, or junk a gun while Italy menaces her. 1945 [see *cow-country* s.v. cow *sb.*[1] 7]. *a* 1963 S. Plath *Crossing Water* (1971) 33 The roses in the Toby jug Gave up the ghost last night... You should have junked them before they died. 1972 *Listener* 21 Dec. 860/2 The free-wheeling teams..might have to junk their wagons and stumble on foot down the western slopes of the Sierra. 1973 K. Giles *File on Death* vi. 149, I dare say you can pick up junked bits of weapons. 1973 *Times* 21 Mar. 9/4 The story of a man who junked his education and went after the short-term riches of sport.

junkanoo, junkonoo: see John Canoe.

junk-bottle. *U.S.* A thick strong bottle made of green or black glass, 'the ordinary black glass porter bottle' (Bartlett *Dict. Amer.* 1860).

1805 *Naval Chron.* XIV. 65 The following article was found in a junk-bottle. 1809 W. Irving *Knickerb.* VII. vii. (1820) 490 Stopping to take a lusty dinner, and bracing to his side his junk-bottle, well charged with heart-inspiring Hollands. 1881 E. H. Elwell in *Collect. Maine Hist. Soc.* IX. 217 Sawyer drank the last drop of rum from his junk bottle.

‖**junker**[1] ('jʊŋkər). [G., from earlier *junkher*, *-herr(e*, f. MHG. *junc* (G. *jung*) young + *herre*: see her *sb.*, and cf. younker.]

A young German noble; as a term of reproach, a narrow-minded, overbearing (younger) member of the aristocracy of Prussia, etc.; *spec.* a member of the reactionary party of the aristocracy whose aim it is to maintain the exclusive social and political privileges of their class. Also *attrib.* or *transf.*

1554 *Admon. Cert. Trewe Pastor & Prophet* Pref. A v b, And herewith let my Iunker papistes which now are in their ruff and tryumph..take their aduertisement. 1845 S. Austin *Ranke's Hist. Ref.* II. 499 Luther said, the papist Junkers were in this respect more Lutheran than the Lutherans themselves. 1865 *Spectator* 11 Feb. 151 There is in Count Orloff's speech a trace of 'junker' feeling. 1891 *Blackw. Mag.* Oct. 462 Bismarck is by instinct a Junker. 1914 G. B. Shaw *What I really wrote about War* (1931) 25 The Junker is by no means peculiar to Prussia... Lord Cromer is a Junker. 1916 *Ibid.* 159 British Junker stupidity. 1919 W. H. Downing *Digger Dial.* 30 *Junker*, a superior staff-officer. 1920 E. Antonelli *Bolshevist Russia* I. ii. 32 A delegation of 'Junkers' (pupils of the Military Schools) appeared before Kerensky. *Ibid.* 35 Some Junker and regimental delegations..received no reply.

Hence '**junkerdom**, the body or world of junkers; the condition or character of a junker; '**junkerish** *a.*, characteristic of the junker party; '**junkerism**, the policy or spirit of the junkers.

1870 *Daily Tel.* 4 Oct., It may be that some of the younger German officers are somewhat imperious..I myself have had disagreeable experience of Junkerdom more than once. 1890 *New Review* Apr. 290 These were his [Bismarck's] days of Junkerdom. 1878 Seeley *Stein* II. 522 These views of Münster were branded by Stein to myself as paltry and Junkerish. 1866 *Daily Tel.* 18 Jan. 5/3 Many professors and journalists, presumably most opposed to Junkerism.

junker[2] ('dʒʌŋkə(r)). *Austral.* and *N.Z.* = jinker[2].

1888 P. W. Barlow *Kaipara* xiii. 94 He mounted the 'junker'... The unhappy [horse] gave a feeble shake with one hind leg. 1924 Lawrence & Skinner *Boy in Bush* 236 'What's a junker, Tom?' 'A low, four-wheeled log hauler, with a long pole.'

junker[3] ('dʒʌŋkə(r)). *U.S. slang.* [f. junk *sb.*[2] 1 e + -er[1].] A drug-addict; a drug-peddler.

1922 E. F. Murphy *Black Candle* II. xvii. 276 One must ..be known as a 'junker' or addict to make the purchase. 1930 *Detective Fiction Weekly* 15 Nov. 473/2 He got the poppy gum from the smugglers and turned it over to the chemists at a good profit, getting back half in cash and half in drugs, which his junkers peddled. 1930 C. R. Shaw *Jack Roller* xii. 161 Next to me in the hospital was Herbie, a junker, who was taking the cure. 1949 'J. Evans' *Halo in Brass* (1951) iv. 29 No slim-waisted junker with a snapbrim hat and a deck of nose candy for sale to the right guy.

junkerite, variant of JUNCKERITE.

† **'junkery.** *Obs.* Forms: 5 iunkerye, 6 ioncrye, ionkry, iunkerie. [Of obscure origin: agrees in sense with JUNKET *sb.* 3 and 4, but appears much earlier.] **a.** A banquet or feast. **b.** A dainty dish or sweetmeat.

1449 *Paston Lett.* (1901) IV. 24 Pertrych and his felaw bere gret visage and kepe gret junkeryes and dyneres. *a* **1500** MEDWALL *Nature* (Brandl) II. 210 There shall no gentylman ..Be better serued..For a banket or a ionkry, For a dyshe two or thre. **1509** FISHER *Fun. Serm. C'tess Richmond* Wks. (1876) 294 Eschewynge bankettes, reresoupers, ioncryes betwyxe meales. **1542** UDALL *Erasm. Apoph.* I. §81. 104 Marchepaines or wafers w[t] other like iunkerie.

junket ('dʒʌŋkɪt), *sb.* Forms: α. 4–7 ionket, (5 -ett, 6 -et(t)e), 6 ionckette, 6–7 iuncket, (6 -ete, 7 -ette), iunquet, iunket, 7–9 juncket, junkett, 7- junket. β. 6 ioncat, 6 iouncat, 6–7 iuncat, -cate, 7 iunkat, -kate, 7–8 juncate. See also JUNCADE. [Of somewhat obscure history, in respect both of forms and senses, but app. a. ONF. *jonket, *jonquet or *jonquette*, rush-basket, f. *jonc* rush, JUNK *sb.*[1] Norman patois has '*jonquette* espèce de crême faite avec du lait bouilli, additionné de jaunes d'œuf, de sucre et de caramel' (Moisy), and the related forms *jonchée* (= med.L. *juncata*, It. *giuncata*) and *jonchiere, jonquiere* (:—**juncāria*) are common in senses 1 and 2 of our word (see Littré and Godef.).

The β-forms in sense 2 may be directly from med.L. *juncata* (cf. JUNCADE); but their late occurrence in sense 3 is notable. The history of sense 2 is not quite clear; and the relationship of 3 to 4 is complicated by the earlier JUNKERY.]

1. A basket (orig. made of rushes); *esp.* a basket in which fish are caught or carried. Now *dial.*

1382 WYCLIF *Exod.* ii. 3 Whanne he myȝte hide hym no lenger, he tok a ionket of resshen..and putte the litil faunt with ynne. —— *Job* 2nd Prol. (1850) II. 671 If forsothe a iunket with resshe I shudde make. **1483** *Cath. Angl.* 198/1 A Ionkett for fysche. **1565–73** COOPER *Thesaurus, Caudecæ*, little coffers of wickers: iunkets wherein yeeles are taken. **1703** THORESBY *Let. to Ray* (E.D.S.), *Junket*, a wicker long wisket to catch fish. **1829** in HUNTER *Hallamsh. Gloss.* **1883** *Fisheries Exhib. Catal.* 366 Junkets..hand Junkets. **1893** *Northumbld. Gloss.*, *Junket*, a basket for catching fish.

2. A cream-cheese or other preparation of cream (originally made in a rush-basket or served on a rush-mat: see JUNCADE); now, a dish consisting of curds sweetened and flavoured, served with a layer of scalded cream on the top. (Popularly associated with Devonshire, but answering to the 'curds and cream' of other districts.)

c **1460** J. RUSSELL *Bk. Nurture* 93 Milke, crayme, and cruddes, and eke the Ioncate, þey close a mannes stomak ..þerfore ete hard chese aftir. **1513** *Bk. Kernynge* in *Babees Bk.* 266 Be ware of cowe creme, &..Iouncat, for these wyll make your soueraygne seke but he ete harde chese. **1620** VENNER *Via Recta* v. 91 There are also certaine Iunkets vsually made of milke..as of the best of the milke coagulated, there is made a kinde of Iuncket, called in most places a Fresh-Cheese. *a* **1693** URQUHART *Rabelais* III. xxxiii, No artificers are then [August] held in greater Request than the Afforders of refrigerating Inventions, Makers of Junkets [F. *joncades*]. **1825** HONE *Every-day Bk.* I. 561 Junket, made of raw milk and rennet..sweetened with sugar, and a little cream added [at Penzance]. **1826** POLWHELE *Trad. & Recoll.* II. 533 Cornwall produced nothing good but junket and the 'Weekly Entertainer'. **1881** *Cornh. Mag.* Nov. 609 Junkets identical with those for which Devonshire is famous, but made of ewe's instead of cow's milk.

† **3.** Any dainty sweetmeat, cake, or confection; a sweet dish; a delicacy; a kickshaw. *Obs.*

α. **1547–64** BAULDWIN *Mor. Philos.* (Palfr.) 137 To behold the furnished table..with variety of the most dainty iunkets, costly and delicate dishes. **1566** ADLINGTON *Apuleius, Gold. Ass* x. xlv, Bread pasties, tartes, custardes and other delicate ionckettes dipped in honie. **1629** PARKINSON *Parad., Orchard* xviii. 586 [Orange peel] Candied with Sugar to serve with other dryed Junquets. **1694** WESTMACOTT *Script. Herb.* 85 Fillberds..being an excellent Junket instead of Tobacco in their compotating humours. **1715** tr. *Pancirollus' Rerum Mem.* I. IV. x. 184 Junkets or Sweetmeats, were pompously brought in with the Solemnity of a Flute.

β. **1586** T. B. *La Primaud. Fr. Acad.* I. 194 It agreeth not with them that make profession of manlie fortitude..to take such iuncates. **1608** TOPSELL *Serpents* (1658) 815 The people..do make of these Worms divers juncats, as we do Tarts, Marchpanes, Wafers, and Cheese-cakes. **1658** ROWLAND *Moufet's Theat. Ins.* 914 Juncates or honey-meats, and wafers, they have divers names as the thing is made. **1764** HARMER *Observ.* III. iv. 134 A cake seems to be used for all juncates or dainty meats.

4. A feast or banquet; a merrymaking accompanied with feasting; also in mod. use (chiefly *U.S.*), a pleasure expedition or outing at which eating and drinking are prominent; a picnic-party. Also *transf.* and *fig.*; *spec.* (see quot. 1886).

1530 PALSGR. 235 Ionkette, *banquet*. **1540** MORYSINE *Vives Introd. Wysd.* C j b, Spendynge his patrimonie vppon ionkettes [L. *comessationes*], mynstreles, and scoffers. *a* **1655** VINES *Lord's Supp.* (1677) 30 With these junkets and feasts they joyned the celebration of the Lords Supper. **1712** STEELE *Spect.* No. 298 ¶5 At a late Junket which he was invited to. **1751** JOHNSON *Rambler* No. 142 ¶6 She taught him..to catch the servants at a junket. **1814** MAD. D'ARBLAY *Wanderer* III. 73, I come..to ask the favor of your company..to a little junket at our farm. **1848** THACKERAY *Van. Fair* xxviii. **1873** DIXON *Two Queens* I. IV. viii. 229 Amidst his bridal junkets, Charles was told [etc.]. **1886** *Detroit Free Press* 4 Sept. 4/2 The term 'junket' in America is generally applied to a trip taken by an American official at the expense of the government. **1946** R. BLESH *Shining Trumpets* (1949) vii. 162 The first recording junket of modern times. **1954** KOESTLER *Invis. Writing* xxxi. 326 Bloomsbury and Greenwich Village went on a revolutionary junket. **1966** *Telegraph* (Brisbane) 13 Apr. 51/1 United States delegates to the Inter-Parliamentary Union conference in Canberra are upset that their trip has been described as a junket. **1966** *Sunday Times* 11 Dec. 3/2 A week here as a member of a gambling junket. **1973** *Black World* Apr. 96 On a junket to L.A. and New York looking for scripts. **1973** *Times* 18 Aug. 14/1 The only way I could get to see the countries about whose politics I would write so knowledgeably was to get myself attached to groups of travel writers on facility trips, or what the Americans call junkets.

5. *Comb.*, as ***junket-basket*** (= picnic-basket).

1825 HONE *Every-day Bk.* I. 439 Well-stored junket-baskets.

Hence **junke'taceous, 'junketous** *adjs.*, given to junketing. *nonce-wds.*

1760 H. WALPOLE *Corr.* (1837) II. 16 You are as junkettaceous as my lady Northumberland. **1830** LADY GRANVILLE *Lett.* (1894) II. 66 She rather likes the thought, having a more junketous soul than me.

junket ('dʒʌŋkɪt), *v.* Also 7 -cat. [f. prec. sb.]

1. *intr.* To hold a banquet or feast; to make merry with good cheer; also (chiefly *U.S.*) to join in a picnic; to go on a pleasure excursion.

1555 [see JUNKETING *vbl. sb.*]. **1613** PURCHAS *Pilgrimage* II. xiv. 192 If a female child be borne there is small solemnitie only..some yong wenches stand about the cradle, and lift it vp with the child in it, and name it..and after this they iunket together. **1638** SIR T. HERBERT *Trav.* (ed. 2) 350 A creature..rather made to wonder at, than to juncket on. **1657** REEVE *God's Plea* 86 A sad thing it is, that..when some are fasting, others should be juncating. **1715** tr. *Pancirollus' Rerum Mem.* I. II. vi. 80 The Fire was in the middle of the Room, about which the Family did make Merry and Junket. *a* **1745** SWIFT *Direct. Servants* i. *General*, Whatever good bits you can pilfer in the day, save them to junket with your fellow-servants at night. **1821** LADY GRANVILLE *Lett.* (1894) I. 205 The same party junket on Friday to Chiswick. **1874** GREVILLE *Mem. Geo. IV* (1875) III. xxiv. 122 The Chancellor had intended to go junketting on the Rhine.

2. *trans.* To entertain, feast. *rare.*

1745 H. WALPOLE *Lett.* (1846) II. 64 The good woman.. was in such a hurry to junket her neighbours.

junketeer (ˌdʒʌŋkɪ'tɪə(r)). orig. *U.S.* [f. JUNKET *sb.* + -EER.] = JUNKETER.

1939 *Amer. Speech* XIV. 237/1 Junketeer is a term used in the press in these days. **1963** *Economist* 1 June 902/2 The 'junketeers' need not submit any receipts or documents. **1969** *Daily Tel.* 21 Feb. 19/6 Most of the junketeers have been Americans with personal credit ratings of 2,000 dollars upwards.

'junketer. [f. JUNKET *v.* + -ER[1].] One who junkets or feasts; one who takes part in a junketing.

1825 SCOTT *Fam. Lett.* 29 Nov. (1894) II. 381, I have been asked to meet Lord Melville at several parties, which has made me more of a junketter than usual. **1868** *Pall Mall G.* 5 Aug., Steamboat companies, which..are sadly prone to carry excursionists and junketers about on Sundays. **1873** MISS BRADDON *Str. & Pilgr.* III. xii. 353 The junketers dispersed more or less unwillingly to their several chambers.

'junketing, *vbl. sb.* [f. as prec. + -ING[1].] The action of the verb JUNKET; feasting, banqueting, merrymaking; also (chiefly *U.S.*), a going on a pleasure excursion, picnicking; with *a* and *pl.*: A feast, banquet, picnic, etc.

1555 W. WATREMAN *Fardle Facions* II. x. 235 Their Spiritualtie vsed Iunckettyng [L. *potationibus*] oftener then the Laietie. **1577** HARRISON *England* II. vi. (1877) I. 151 In these iunkettings. **1667** SOUTH *Serm. Ps.* lxxxvii. 2 The apostle would have no revelling, or junketting upon the altar. **1712** STEELE *Spect.* No. 466 ¶3 In my Absence our Maid has let in the spruce Servants in the Neighbourhood to Junketings. **1731** *Gentl. Mag.* I. 103 Depredations by guttling and tippling, junketting, gossiping, gaming, etc. are to be all item'd to the government. **1876** GREEN *Stray Stud.* 47 To the priest, of course, Carnival is simply a farewell to worldly junketings. **1877** A. B. EDWARDS *Up Nile* xxi. 646 The fishing and fowling and feasting and junketting that we saw.

b. *attrib.*, as ***junketing dish, house, party, trip.***

1597 GERARDE *Herbal* II. lxviii. 298 The seede..is often vsed in comfits, or serued at the table with other iunketting dishes. **1620** VENNER *Via Recta* vii. 148 The same being put into iunketting dishes..giueth vnto them a delectable.. taste. **1820** W. IRVING *Sketch Bk.* II. 158 Snug junketting parties at which I have been present. **1893** Q. [COUCH] *Delect. Duchy* 67 The morals of the junketing houses underwent change.

† **'junketry.** *Obs. rare*[-1]. In 6 iunquetry. [f. JUNKET *sb.* + -RY, perh. a refashioning of JUNKERY.] A confection; a sweetmeat; = JUNKET 3.

1599 NASHE *Lenten Stuffe* 23 Galingale, which Chaucer preheminentest encomionizeth aboue all iunquetries or confectionaries whatsoeuer.

junkie ('dʒʌŋkɪ). *slang* (orig. *U.S.*). Also junkey, junky. [f. JUNK *sb.*[2] 1 e + -IE.] A drug-addict; also occas., a drug-peddler. Also *attrib.* or as *adj.* (chiefly in form *junky*).

1923 [see GUN *sb.* 3 e]. **1929** *Flynn's* 2 Feb. 125/2 He's a confirmed 'junkie' and, of course, he'll get hold of it if he can. **1930** *Time & Tide* 20 Sept. 1181 He became a recognised junky and earned his living as a useful subordinate member of a drug-traffic gang. **1930** *Detective Fiction Weekly* 20 Dec. 362 (*heading*) Undercover man Murray follows the junkey trail into the greatest city's street of evil. **1949** N. ALGREN *Man with Golden Arm* 25 You're not a student any more... Junkie—you're *hooked*. **1951** *N.Y. Times* (City ed.) 27 June 19/5 An addict who sells narcotics, for which he usually gets his own daily supply, is called a 'junkie', he explained, and they hang out in taverns and cafes until the police raid them. **1959** W. BURROUGHS *Naked Lunch* 13 He would suck the juice right out of every junky he ran down. *Ibid.* 53 He spoke in his dead, junky whisper. **1959** C. MACINNES *Absolute Beginners* 68 If you have a friend who's a junkie..you soon discover there's no point whatever discussing his addiction. **1969** *Daily Tel.* (Colour Suppl.) 16 May 33/2 Combined with my appetite-killing pills and my tranquillisers I was possibly the junkiest man on the [ski] slopes. **1970** *Times* 22 Sept. 10/4 Over-prescribing by the notorious junkie doctors. **1971** *Daily Tel.* 18 June 17/3 They plan to tour villages showing a film about 'junkies' and giving lectures to youngsters about the dangers of drugs. **1972** J. BROWN *Chancer* iv. 59 Lacerated hands, the hands of junkies, scarred where needles had searched for veins. **1973** *Black World* May 47 Talk about how to get more money, how to get educated, how to have scientists for children rather than junkies.

'junkman[1]. [f. JUNK *sb.*[3]] A man belonging to the crew of a junk.

1862 J. HENDERSON in *Mem.* iii. (1867) 103 (Shanghai) A large number of junkmen come from all parts of the country. **1880** MISS BIRD *Japan* I. 382 The many ghosts in which junkmen believe.

'junkman[2]. orig. *U.S.* [f. JUNK *sb.*[2]] A dealer in junk or marine stores.

1872 E. CRAPSEY *Nether Side N.Y.* 39 The shop of a junkman selected..as the purchaser of the plunder. **1879** *Scribner's Mag.* May 37/2 He is a licensed junkman; he holds a license for running a boat and buying and selling old refuse articles of any kind—a kind of water-ragman. **1895** *Outlook* (N.Y.) 24 Aug. 304/2 What the Sheriff could get for the goods sold in a lump for cash..with possibly only a junkman for a bidder. **1963** H. GARNER in R. Weaver *Canad. Short Stories* (1968) 2nd Ser. 38 The two of them helped the junkman load his truck. **1972** R. K. SMITH *Ransom* IV. 150 The old pawnbroker watched the junkman.

junky ('dʒʌŋkɪ), *a.* [f. JUNK *sb.*[2] + -Y[1].]

1. Worthless, valueless, rubbishy.

1946 'G. ORWELL' *Coll. Ess.* (1968) IV. 92 The kind of junky books..that accumulate in the bottoms of cupboards. **1966** *Punch* 27 July p. vii, Dealing in junky but odd bric-à-brac and more expensive furniture. **1972** *N.Y. Times* 3 Nov. 16/8 'Those are junky schools,' she declared. 'They have riots up there every day.' **1974** *New Yorker* 25 Feb. 62/3 Not necessarily cheap junk, however. In the past couple of years, an extraordinary demand for junky furniture seems to have arisen in London.

2. See JUNKIE.

Juno ('dʒuːnəʊ). [L. *Jūno* (acc. *Jūnōnem*), in Latin mythology the wife of Jupiter; the goddess of marriage and child-birth.]

1. A woman resembling the goddess Juno in qualities ascribed to her; a woman of stately beauty; a jealous wife, etc.

1606 SYLVESTER *Du Bartas* II. iv. II. *Magnificence* 858 Here, many a Iuno, many a Pallas here..Catch many a gallant Lord. **1621** BURTON *Anat. Mel.* III. iii. II. i. (1676) 371 It is an ordinary thing for women in such cases to scratch the faces..of such as they suspect; as Henry the seconds importune Juno did by Rosamond at Woodstock. **1641** MILTON *Areop.* (Arb.) 41. No envious Juno sate cross-leg'd over the nativity of any mans intellectual off-spring. **1728** POPE *Dunc.* II. 163 His be yon Juno of majestic size. **1859** READE *Love me little* II. i. 40 These Junones, severe in youthful beauty.

2. *Astron.* Name of the third of the asteroids.

1834 *Penny Cycl.* II. 537/1, 1804. Harding discovers the planet Juno. **1868** LOCKYER *Guillemin's Heavens* (ed. 3) 214 The third planet discovered, Juno, which was supposed to be a third fragment of the hypothetical planet.

3. In plant-names: **Juno's rose,** the white Lily (*Lilium candidum*); **Juno's tears,** Vervain.

1597 GERARDE *Herbal* II. ccxxxv. §2. 581 Veruain is called ..in English Iunos teares. **1706** PHILLIPS (ed. Kersey), *Juno's Rose*, the Lilly.

4. *Comb.*, as ***Juno-like*** adj. and adv.

1607 SHAKS. *Cor.* IV. ii. 53 Come, let's go..and lament as I do, In Anger, Iuno-like. **1896** MRS. CROKER *Village Tales* 101 Durali was tall, erect, and Juno-like.

Hence **Junoesque** (dʒuːnəʊ'ɛsk) *a.*, resembling Juno in stately beauty.

1888 F. HUME *Mad. Midas* I. iii, A tall voluptuous-looking woman of what is called a Junoesque type. **1894** *Q. Rev.* Jan. 143 Her beauty was of that Junoesque type which..requires time..to expand to its full flower.

Junonian (dʒuː'nəʊnɪən), *a.* [f. L. *Jūnōni-us* + -AN.] Of or pertaining to Juno.

1794 T. TAYLOR *Pausanias* v. xvi. (1824) II. 41 Sixteen women..every fifth year weave a veil for Juno, and establish Junonian games. **1813** A. BRUCE *Life Alex. Morris* iii. 70 Her Junonian or rather Sinonian arts.

Also † **Ju'nonical** *a. Obs.*

1582 STANYHURST *Æneis* I. (Arb.) 39 Yeet do I stil feare me theese fayre Iunonical harbours. In straw thear lurcketh soom pad.

junour, junquet, obs. ff. JOINER, JUNKET.

Junr., abbreviation of JUNIOR.
1813 JANE AUSTEN *Let.* 16 Sept. (1952) 326 The Letter you forwarded from Edwd Junr has been duly received. **1819** M. EDGEWORTH *Let.* c 1 Jan. (1971) 154 Mr. Brooke Boothby (Junr.) and Mr. Henry Vernon dined here.

‖**junshi** (ˈdʒunʃi). *Hist.* [Jap.] In Japan, suicide at the death of one's lord, self-immolation.
1871 A. B. MITFORD *Tales Old Japan* II. 57 The ancient Japanese custom of *Junshi*; that is to say 'dying with the master'. **1904** L. HEARN *Japan: Attempt at Interpretation* iv. 47 With the rise of the military power there gradually came into existence another custom of *junshi*, or following one's lord in death,—suicide by the sword.

†**junt**¹. *Obs.* [app. ad. It. *giunta*, *gionta* 'a coosening, cheating, or conycatching tricke' (Florio, 1598), whence *giuntare* to trick.] A trick, cheat.
1608 MIDDLETON *Trick to catch the old one* v. ii, *H.* Daintily abus'd, you've put a junt upon me! *L.* Ha, ha, ha! *H.* A common Strumpet.

junt² (dʒʌnt). *Sc.* [Of obscure origin: cf. JUNK *sb.*² 1 d, and Sc. *dunt* a piece or lump.]
a. A lump or large piece, esp. of meat or bread; a chunk; also, a large quantity of a liquid. **b.** *transf.* A squat, chunky person.
a. 1715 RAMSAY *Christ's Kirk Gr.* II. xx, Twa good junts of beef, Wi' hind and fore spoul of a sheep. **1797** A. DOUGLAS *New Year's Wish* Poems (1806) 67 A junt o' beef, baith fat an' fresh..in your pat. **1824** MACTAGGART *Gallovid. Encycl.*, *Junt*, a large quantity of liquid of any kind ..Gowdie, the cow, gives a junt of milk.
b. 1787 W. TAYLOR *Sc. Poems* 26 Brave Jess, the fodgel junt, Did ha[u]d Dad's hands.

junta (ˈdʒʌntə, *U.S.* ˈhʊ-). Also 8 **juncta**. [a. Sp. (and Pg.) *junta* = It. *giunta*:—L. *juncta*, fem. pass. part. of *jungĕre* to JOIN, in Romanic used as a sb. The equivalent F. form is *jointe* JOINT; mod.F. *junte* junta, is from Sp.]
1. With reference to Spain or Italy: A deliberative or administrative council or committee.
In mod. hist. the term is best known as the name of the local councils established in different districts of Spain to conduct the war against Napoleon in the summer of 1808; the Central Junta was formed in Sept. of the same year.
1623 J. MEADE in Ellis *Orig. Lett.* Ser. I. III. 162 At length the Junta of Divines [at Madrid] coming to agreement the marriage was declared. *c* **1645** HOWELL *Lett.* III. x. (1650) 52 A particular *Junta* of some of the Counsell of State and War, might be appointed to determin the business. **1754** A. DRUMMOND *Trav.* II. 61 The senate [at Venice] consists of a hundred and twenty nobles, one half of whom are ordinary, and the other distinguished by the appellation of the junta. **1809** *Hist. Eur.* in *Ann. Reg.* 6/1 Details of the weakness and tardiness of the Spanish Junta. **1887** DOWDEN *Life Shelley* II. viii. 342 Here the troops were on the side of the viceroy and his junta.
2. In general sense: = JUNTO 1.
1714 SWIFT *Pres. St. Aff.* Wks. 1755 II. I. 214 Ready for any acts of violence, that a Junta composed of the greatest enemies to the constitution shall think fit to enjoin them. *a* **1715** BURNET *Own Time* (1766) I. 85 Some of the English Juncta moved that pains should be taken to unite the two parties. **1867** GOLDW. SMITH *Three Eng. Statesmen* (1882) 77 A junta of fanatics, who wanted to sweep away law, learning, and civil society.

junte, juntee, obs. ff. JOINT *sb.*, JAUNTY.

junto (ˈdʒʌntəʊ). Also 7–8 **juncto**. [Erroneous form of JUNTA, by assimilation to Sp. sbs. in *o* (cf. -ADO 2). The form *juncto* (after L. *junctum*) was very common down to 1700.]
1. A body of men who have joined or combined for a common purpose, especially of a political character; a self-elected committee or council; a clique, faction, or cabal; a club or coterie.
a. In politics or matters of public interest.
In English History the term has been chiefly applied to the Cabinet Council of Charles I, to the Independent and Presbyterian factions of the same period, to the Rump Parliament under Cromwell, and to the combination of prominent Whigs in the reigns of William III and Anne.
1641 LD. BROOKE *Eng. Episc.* (1642) 35 Are these men fit ..to direct and advise..in the Privie Juncto's; to sit at the Helme, to dictate Lawes. **1645** WITHER *Vox Pacif.* III. 102 This new *Junto*, doth so strong become By their conferring Offices and Places. **1657** HAWKE *Killing is M.* 5 How unworthily..doth this Impostor brand that pacifique and prudent Parliament..with the strange name of a *Junto*. **1680** LOVE in *Reflect. 'Curse-ye-Meroz'* 22 The Juncto [the Rump] at Westminster have..received more Money in one year than all the Kings of England. **1708** PENN in *Pa. Hist. Soc. Mem.* X. 289 You should form a small junto, and meet for that and other publick ends. *a* **1734** NORTH *Exam.* II. v. §32 (1740) 333 These subdivided Offices or Branches of Power, may be committed to single Persons or Junctos as Laws have provided. **1783** COWPER *Lett.* 27 Dec., Wks. (1876) 151 The patriotic junto whose efforts have staved off the expected dissolution. **1888** BRYCE *Amer. Commw.* I. xxv. 374 There was believed to be often a secret Junto which really controlled the ministry.
†**b.** In ecclesiastical affairs. *Obs.*
1641 H. P. *Quest. Div. Right Episc.* 10 If London..should arbitrate by a Junto of all her Divines. **1677** W. HUGHES *Man of Sin* II. v. 87 The Trent *Juncto* hath voted for them. *fig. a* **1716** SOUTH *Serm.* (1744) VII. iv. 70 One diocesan bishop, will better defend this enclosed garden of the church, than a juncto of five hundred shrubs, than all the quicksets of Geneva.
c. In general sense.
1659 T. PECKE *Parnassi Puerp.* 171 And did the Juncto of the Gods agree, To make you Sol? **1673** [R. LEIGH] *Transp. Reh.* 36 None were so loud, as a Junto of Wits. **1713** ADDISON *Guard.* No. 140 ¶4 As..lately settled in a junto of the sex. **1820** W. IRVING *Sketch Bk.* II. 47 At the corners are assembled juntos of village idlers and wise men.
†**2.** = JUNTA 1. *Obs.*
1701 LUTTRELL *Brief Rel.* (1857) V. 6 From Madrid, that the people seem dissatisfyed with their juncto. **1747** *Gentl. Mag.* 119 The deputation of the nobless, which they call the junto of the holy office.
3. *Comb.*, as **junto-lord**, one of the Whig combination in Anne's reign; **junto-man**, a member of a junto.
1647 SPRIGGE *Anglia Rediv.* IV. vii. (1854) 263 Lords, knights, and parliament men (otherwise juncto men). **1648** C. WALKER *Hist. Independ.* I. 21 The Junto-men..the State-Mountebanks. **1713** SWIFT *Hist. Last Sess.* Wks. 1758 IX. 28 The Juncto Lords as they were then called.
Hence **jun'tocracy** *nonce-wd.* [see -CRACY], government by a junto.
1774 BURGH *Pol. Disquis.* in *Examiner* (1831) 140/2 The British government is really a juntocracy,..or government by a minister and his crew.

junyper(e, -pyr, obs. forms of JUNIPER.

†**jup**. *Obs. rare.* Also **juppe**. [a. F. *juppe*, obs. var. of *jupe*: see JUPE and JUMP *sb.*²] A woman's jacket or bodice. Cf. JUPE 2.
1603 *Q. Eliz. Wardr.* in *Leisure Ho.* (1884) 673/2, 43 saufe-gardes and juppes. **1670** FLECKNOE *Epigr.*, *Damoiselles a la mode* 74 This Play of ours, just like some Vest or Jup, Worn twice or thrice, was carefully laid up. **1671** E. PANTON *Spec. Juventut.* v. v. 265 We had the confidence to take off her Juppe, which we have brought.

jupard, -y(e, jupart, -ye, obs. ff. JEOPARD, JEOPARDY.

jupati (ˈdʒuː-, ˈhuːpətɪ). [Pg., a. Tupi.] A Brazilian palm, *Raphia tædigera*, bearing large leaves whose long stalks are used locally as a building material.
1856 B. SEEMANN *Popular Hist. Palms* 331 *Raphia tædigera* Mart., the Jupati of the Lingoa Geral, is one of the many noble Palms which grow on the rich alluvium of the Amazon. **1863** H. W. BATES *Naturalist on River Amazons* I. v. 196 The moon now broke forth and lighted up..the leaves of monstrous Jupatí palms which arched over the creek. **1908** in R. Spruce *Notes of Botanist on Amazon & Andes* II. 521 Glossary of native names... Jupati. *Rhaphia* [sic] *tædigera*. A short-stemmed but noble palm with immense leaves. **1972** Y. LOVELOCK *Vegetable Bk.* 302 Palms are to be found spanning the equatorial belt around the world. They include..the Japanese [*sic*] jupati palm.

jupe (dʒuːp, F. ʒyp). Now only *Sc.* and *north. dial.* (exc. as F.). Forms: 3 iuype, 4 ioupe, 5 iowpe, 7 juipe, joope, 9 joup, juip, jupe. [a. F. *jupe*, in OF. also *jube*, *gipe* (see GIPE) = Prov. *jupa*, Sp. and Pg. (with Arabic article) *aljuba*; also OF. *juppe* (see JUP), *jubbe* (see JUB), *gippe* = It. *giuppa*, *giubba*, a. Arab. *jubbah*, *jibbah* JUBBAH. Derivative forms are GIPEL, GIPON, GIPPO¹, and JUPON. For the treatment of the vowel in ME., cf. the forms of *duke*, *flute*, and *juice*.]
†**1.** A loose jacket, kirtle, or tunic worn by men. *Obs.* (In later use chiefly *Sc.*)
c **1290** *S. Eng. Leg.* I. 455/215 Þe bischop eode into þe vestiarie: is cope he gan of strepe, he nadde under is vestimenz to habbe on bote is Iuype. *c* **1300** *Havelok* 1767 Also he seten, and sholde soupe, So comes a ladde in a ioupe. *c* **1440** *Promp. Parv.* 265/2 Iowpe, garment. **1635** BRERETON *Trav.* (Chetham Soc.) 188 Speech in Scotland..for a man's coat, a juipe or joope. **1802** J. SIBBALD *Chron. Sc. Poetry* Gloss., *Jupe*, a wide or great coat. **1823** CARLYLE *Let.* in Froude *Life* (1882) I. xii. 203, I put on my gray duffle sitting jupe. **1837** —— *Fr. Rev.* I. II. ii, Frightful men..clad in jupes of coarse woollen, with..girdles of leather.
2. *Sc.* A woman's jacket, kirtle, or bodice. Also *pl.* a kind of bodice or stays.
a **1810** in Cromek *Rem. Nithsdale Song* 64, I pat on my jupes sae green, An' kilted my coaties rarely. **1822** GALT *Steam-Boat* xvii. 356 The branch of a bramble bush caught her by the jupe. **1858** RAMSAY *Remin.* Ser. I. (1860) 261 A bedgown, or loose female upper garment, is still in many parts of Scotland termed a jupe. **1859** R. F. BURTON *Centr. Afr.* in *Jrnl. Geog. Soc.* XXIX. 138 The married women usually wear a jupe, in shape, behind, recalling the old swallow-tailed coat of Europe.
‖**3.** [mod. borrowing from Fr.] A woman's skirt.
1825 R. P. WARD *Tremaine* III. iii. 18 This little French girl..was dressed so piquantely in a jacket and short jupe. **1851** *Harper's Mag.* II. 288/1 The Morning Costume is a jupe of blue silk. **1883** BURTON & CAMERON *Gold Coast* I. iii. 57 Votaries prostrating themselves before a dark dwarf 'Lady' with jewelled head and spangled jupe. **1886** *Pall Mall G.* 10 July 10/2 The Princess of Wales wore a corsage of white and silver brocade over a jupe of *poult de soie*.

juperd, -dy, jupert, -tie, obs. ff. JEOPARD, JEOPARDY.

Jupiter (ˈdʒuːpɪtə(r)). Also 3–4 Iubiter, 4 Iuppiter, 6 Iupyter. [a. L. *Jūpiter*, *Juppiter*, f. *Jov-is* JOVE + *pater* father.]
1. a. The supreme deity of the ancient Romans, corresponding to the Greek Zeus; the ruler of gods and men, and the god of the heavens, whose weapon was the thunderbolt. Also in exclamations (cf. JOVE), but chiefly in literary use.
c **1205** LAY. 13905 We habbeð godes gode..þe feorðe heah Iupiter [*c* **1275** hatte Iubiter] of alle þinge he is whar. **1340–70** *Alex. & Dind.* 656 Minerua..was engendred wiþ gin of iubiterus hede. *c* **1374** CHAUCER *Troylus* II. 183 (232) By þe goddesse Mynerue And Iuppiter þat maketh þe þonder rynge..ye be the womman..That I best loue. **1600** SHAKS. *A. Y. L.* II. iv. 1 O Iupiter, how weary are my spirits? **1611** —— *Cymb.* II. iv. 121, 122 By Iupiter, I had it from her Arme. *Post.* Hearke you, he sweares; by Iupiter he sweares. **1667** MILTON *P.L.* IV. 499 [Adam] Smil'd with superior Love, as Jupiter On Juno smiles. **1781** COWPER *Conversat.* 822 Gods and goddesses discarded long..Are bringing into vogue their heathen train, And Jupiter bids fair to rule again. **1819** SHELLEY *Cyclops* 564 By Jupiter! you said that I am fair.
transf. **1576** FLEMING *Panopl. Epist.* 232 For, I [a physician] beeing Iupiter their helping Father, give life when I list. **1650** B. *Discolliminium* 26 They shall prove such Jupiters as to fall a thundring and lightning..over our heads.
b. ***Jupiter Pluvius***, Jupiter as the dispenser of rain; hence used trivially in reference to a fall or storm of rain.
1864 G. A. SALA *Quite Alone* I. ii. 39 'Take my advice, and ..borrow somebody else's umbrella.'.. 'Are you, too, ready for the wrath of Jupiter Pluvius?' **1874** G. H. WEST *Rugby Union Football Ann.* 62 But 'Jupiter Pluvius' and the Fates were against it. **1922** JOYCE *Ulysses* 598 It cleared up after the recent visitation of Jupiter Pluvius.
2. a. *Astron.* The largest of the planets in the solar system, revolving in an orbit lying between those of Mars and Saturn.
c **1290** *St. Michael* 420 in *S. Eng. Leg.* I. 311 Saturnus is al a-boue, and Iupiter seth þe next. **1398** TREVISA *Barth. De P.R.* VIII. xii. (1495) 319 Iubiter is a goodly planete hote and moyste. **1549** *Compl. Scot.* vi. 53 Nyxt saturne standis the spere & hauyn of Iupiter. **1727–41** CHAMBERS *Cycl.* s.v., Jupiter appears almost as large as Venus, but is not altogether so bright. **1854** BREWSTER *More Worlds* ii. 25 Jupiter, a world of huge magnitude, 1320 times greater in bulk than our Earth.
†**b.** *Alch.* A name for the metal tin. *Obs.*
c **1386** CHAUCER *Can. Yeom. Prol. & T.* 275 Sol gold is.. Saturnus leed and Iuppiter [*v.r.* Iupiter, Iubiter] is tyn. **1460–70** *Bk. Quintessence* 8 If it falle vpon a plate of venus or Iubiter into þis watir, it turneþ hem into lijknes of peerl. **1694** SALMON *Bate's Dispens.* (1713) 577/1 Drink with Filings of Jupiter, or Tin. **1758** REID tr. *Macquer's Chem.* I. 49 The Alchymists..bestowed on the seven Metals..the names of the seven Planets of the Ancients... Thus Gold was called *Sol*, Silver *Luna*, Copper *Venus*, Tin *Jupiter*, Lead *Saturn*, Iron *Mars*, and Quick-silver *Mercury*.
†**c.** *Her.* Name for the tincture AZURE in blazoning by the names of heavenly bodies. *Obs.*
1572 BOSSEWELL *Armorie* II. 58 b, The fielde is parted per fesse, Iupiter and Saturne, a goate saliant, of the moone. **1725** COATS *Dict. Her.*, *Jupiter*, has been by such Heralds as have thought fit to blazon the Arms of Princes by Planets instead of Metals and Colours, apply'd to stand in the Place of Azure. **1766** PORNY *Heraldry* iii. (1787) 21 Azure..Its Precious Stone is Sapphire, and the Planet Jupiter.
3. In names of plants, as †**Jupiter's distaff**, (*a*) a kind of yellow-flowered sage, perh. *Salvia glutinosa* or *Phlomis fruticosa*; (*b*) ? = *Jupiter's staff*; **Jupiter's eye**, Houseleek, *Sempervivum tectorum*; †**Jupiter's flower**, a rendering of Gr. *Διὸς ἄνθος* or L. *Jovis flos*, formerly identified with columbine; **Jupiter's nut**, rendering of L. *jūglans* (= *Jovis glans*), walnut; **Jupiter's staff**, name for Mullein, *Verbascum Thapsus*, from its tall upright stem. See also JUPITER'S BEARD.
1597 GERARDE *Herbal* II. ccliv. §3. 627 *Colus Iouis.* Iupiters *distaffe. **1657** W. COLES *Adam in Eden* xxiii. 48 Yellow Clary, or Jupiters Distaffe is hot and drying. **1678** PHILLIPS (ed. 4), *Jupiter's Distaffe*, a kind of Clary with a Yellow flower; it is otherwise called Mullein. **1597** GERARDE *Herbal* II. cxxxv. §2. 412 Housleeke, and Sengreene..of some [called] Iupiters *eie. **1861** [see JUPITER'S BEARD]. **1601** HOLLAND *Pliny* II. 92 The summer floures, to wit, Lychnis, Iupiters *flower or Columbine, and a second kind of Lilly. **1866** *Treas. Bot.* 640/1 In the golden age..the gods lived upon Walnuts, and hence the name *Juglans*, *Jovis glans*, or Jupiter's *nuts. **1664** R. TURNER *Botanologia* 216 Jupiters *Staff.

Jupiter's beard. [tr. L. *Barba Jovis.*] A name for various plants.
†**a.** *Chrysocoma Linosyris* (*L. vulgaris*), a South European plant with yellow composite flowers. *Obs.* **b.** *Anthyllis Barba-Jovis*, the Silverbush, a South European evergreen leguminous shrub, having leaves covered with silvery down; also applied to *A. vulneraria*, and the allied American genus *Amorpha*. **c.** The common houseleek, *Sempervivum tectorum* = JUBARB. **d.** *Hydnum Barba-Jovis*, a hymenomycetous fungus with a white fibrous margin.
1567 MAPLET *Gr. Forest* 47 Ivpiters Beard, called of the Greekes *Chrysokome*, as you would say Goldilocks. It is hairie like Isope. *Ibid.* 56 Penroyall, of some Chrusitis, of others Iupiters beard. **1760** J. LEE *Introd. Bot.* App. 316 Jupiter's Beard, *Anthyllis*. *Ibid.*, Jupiter's Beard, American, *Amorpha*. **1794** MARTYN *Rousseau's Bot.* xxv. 353 That which is generally called Jupiter's Beard or Silver-bush, from the splendid whiteness of the leaves which is owing to a fine nap or down that covers them. **1861** MRS. LANKESTER *Wild Fl.* 57 House-leek..is frequently called Jupiter's Eye, Bullock's Eye, or Jupiter's Beard. **1879** PRIOR *Plant-n.* 127 *Jupiter's beard*,..the house-leek, so called from its massive inflorescence, like the sculptured beard of Jupiter.

jupon (ˈdʒuːpɒn, dʒuːˈpɒn, F. ʒypɔ̃). Forms: 5 iopon, -en, -oun, iupone, 6 iuppin, *Sc.* iowpoun, (7 juppon), 9 jupon. See also GIPON. [a. F. *jupon*,

OF. also *juppon*, *gip(p)on* (= Sp. *jubon*, Pg. *jubão*, *gibão*, It. *giubbone*, *giuppone*), deriv. of *jupe*, etc. JUPE.]

1. A close-fitting tunic or doublet; esp. one worn by knights under the hauberk, sometimes of thick stuff and padded; later, a sleeveless surcoat worn outside the armour, of rich materials and emblazoned with arms. *Obs.* exc. *Hist.*

c **1400** CHAUCER *Knt.'s T.* 1262 (Camb. MS.) In a brest plate & in a ly3t Iopoun [*other MSS.* gypon, Iepon, gippon]. *c* **1440** *Morte Arth.* 905 Aboven þat a iesseraunt of ientylle maylez, A iupone of Ierodyne iaggede in schredez. *c* **1450** *Alexander* 2450 Sum in Iopons, sum in Iesserantis. *Ibid.* 4722 3it wont men in þa woddis..in Iopons of hidis. **1480** CAXTON *Descr. Brit.* 39 Without iopen [*Rolls ed.* gipoun] tabard clok or bell. [**1700** DRYDEN *Palamon & Arc.* 1304 Some wore a breastplate, and a light juppon.] **1826** W. ELLIOTT *Nun* 13 A jupon shone Over his armour. **1864** BOUTELL *Her. Hist. & Pop.* xv. (ed. 3) 183 The shield and jupon of the effigy in Bristol Cath[edral].

†**2.** A short kirtle worn by women. Cf. JUP, JUPE 2. *Obs.*

1542 *Inv. R. Wardr.* (1815) 84 Item ane jowpoun of blak velvott lynit with gray. **1595** R. WHYTE *Let. to Sir R. Sydney* 13 Dec. in Collins *State Lett.* (1746) I. 376 In her Bed Chamber, [Sir John Packering] presented her with a fine Gown and a Juppin, which things were pleasing to her Highnes.

‖**3.** A woman's skirt or petticoat. (Only as Fr.)

1851 *Harper's Mag.* II. 576 (Stanf.) Jupon of plain, white cambric muslin.

juppe, variant of JUP, *Obs.*

juppertie, jupurdy, obs. ff. JEOPARDY.

†**jur**, *v. Obs.* Also 7 jurre. [Echoic: cf. JAR *v.*[1] and CHURR *v.*] *intr.* To butt with (or as with) the horns or head. Said of a ram, a battering-ram, etc. Hence '**jurring** *vbl. sb.*

1600 HOLLAND *Livy* XXXVII. xxxii. 963 By that time..the [battering] ramme was jurring also at the other part. **1601** —— *Pliny* IX. xxxi. (1634) I. 253 Crabs..will fight one with another, and then ye shall see them jur and butt with their horns like rams. **1668** G. C. in H. More *Div. Dial.* Pref. 1 (1713) 12 The Arietations or Jurrings of the Spirits in the Ventricles of the Brain. **1828** *Craven Dial.*, *Jur*, to hit, to strike, to push with the head.

†**jur**, *sb. Obs. rare.* In 7 jurre. [f. prec.] A butt or push made by a ram or battering-ram.

1600 HOLLAND *Livy* XXXVI. xxiii. 932 When as the walls should be shaken with the rammes, they caught not hold of them..and by plucking them aside, avoided their jurres. **1609** —— *Amm. Marcell.* XXIII. iv. 222 To breake whatsoever standeth against it, with mightie strokes and maine jurres.

Jura ('dʒʊərə, ‖ʒyra). *Geol.* [Name of the range of mountains on the borders of France and Switzerland that gave its name to the Jurassic system; in this use prob. a. Ger. *Jura*, *Jura-* Jurassic (sb. and adj.).] Jurassic rocks or strata; the Jurassic system. Also *attrib.*, = JURASSIC *a.*

Jura-trias = TRIASSIC; *lower* or *black Jura* = LIAS 2; *middle* or *brown Jura* = DOGGER[3] 2; *upper* or *white Jura* = MALM *sb.* 1 a.

1829 *Proc. Geol. Soc.* I. 94 On the descent to Sospello [near Nice] are found, in a regular descending series, greensand, Jura, oolitic (or younger Alpine) limestone, lias, redmarl, and older Alpine limestone or dolomite. **1851** *Q. Jrnl. Geol. Soc.* VII. II. 42 (*heading*) On the comparison of the German Jura formation with those of France and England. *Ibid.* 46 In the Jura, or in the lower land of Berne, where the 'black Jura' is developed, there is no great extension in width. *Ibid.* 47 The Marne, Seine,..Indre, &c., all of which flow westward, descend from the Lias to the 'brown Jura', and thence to the 'white'; whilst in the German 'Jura' the rivers flow from the heights of the 'white Jura' through the 'brown' and the 'black'. *Ibid.* 85 The 'Jura'-formations in northern Asia. **1893** P. LAKE tr. *E. Kayer's Text Bk. Compar. Geol.* 241 In England the Jura forms a broad zone striking N.N.E. **1895** *Jrnl. Geol.* III. 380 During all this time the Upper Jura of South America..retained its central European character. **1900** *Jrnl. Geol.* VIII. 216 The rocks of the region represent..remnants of formations belonging to the Algonkian, Cambrian, Silurian, Carboniferous, Juratrias, Cretaceous, and Eocene periods. **1929** *Bull. Geol. Soc. Amer.* XL. 176 (*heading*) Delimitation of Jura and Trias in British Columbia. **1955** G. G. WOODFORD tr. *M. Gignoux's Stratigr. Geol.* vii. 314 In describing the Swabian Jura, Quenstedt and Leopold von Buch distinguished three successive groups of rocks, to which they gave the names Black Jura, Brown Jura, and White Jura, in accordance with their appearance in outcrops. These three groups correspond approximately to what we now call the Lower Jurassic or Lias, the Middle Jurassic or Dogger and the Upper Jurassic or Malm.

jural ('dʒʊərəl), *a.* [f. L. *jūr-*, stem of *jūs* law, right + -AL[1].]

1. Of or relating to law or its administration; legal; juristic.

1635 HEYWOOD *Lond. Sinus Salutis* Wks. 1874 IV. 289 Iuno..to your Iurall seat Brings State and Power. **1676** R. DIXON *Nat. Two Test.* To Rdr., I prefer the Jural sense.. and make use of Jural Terms borrowed from Laws Ecclesiastical and Civil. **1783** E. STILES *United States elevated* 24 The jural systems of Europe where reigns a mixture of Roman, Gothic..and other local or municipal law. **1861** MAINE *Anc. Law* i. 2 Many jural phenomena lie behind these codes. **1880** MUIRHEAD *Gaius* IV. §134 The question is as to facts, which ought to be stated according to their natural rather than their jural meaning.

2. *Moral Philos.* Of or pertaining to rights and obligations.

18.. WHEWELL (Webster, 1864) By the adjective jural we shall denote that which has reference to the doctrine of rights and obligations. **1845** —— *Elem. Mor.* II. xviii, That balanced *jural* condition of Society, in which Rights are necessary. **1865** J. GROTE *Treat. Moral Ideas* vii. (1876) 96 *marg.*, Distinction between jural and non-jural views of morality.

Hence '**jurally** *adv.*, with reference to law, or to rights and obligations.

1874 H. SIDGWICK *Meth. Ethics* III. vi. 274 Sometimes there occurs a clear rupture of order in a society..and then a new order, springing out of and jurally rooted in disorder.

jurament ('dʒʊərəmənt). *Obs.* exc. *Hist.* [ad. L. (post-cl.) *jūrāment-um*, f. *jūrāre* to swear: see -MENT.] An oath. *to do juraments* (*Univ. slang*): see quot. 1877.

1575 *Galway Arch.* in *10th Rep. Hist. MSS. Comm.* App. v. 441 The parties have plighted their juramentes and put herunto their signes and seales. **1594** *Zepheria* xxxi, Ioue.. smiles at louers iurament. **1708** HEARNE *Collect.* 10 July (O.H.S.) II. 118 Mr. Covert of Hart Hall..having been deny'd three times [for his Degree of B.A.] the reasons were given into the Vice-Chanc. —1. That he had not done Juraments. **1877** CHR. WORDSWORTH *Scholæ Academ.* 217 When a student was once senior Soph, he merely went into the Schools every term, and proposed one Syllogism *juramenti gratiâ*, and was said to be 'doing juraments'.

†**jura'mental**, *a. Obs. rare.* [f. prec. + -AL[1]. Cf. med.L. *jūrāmentālis* one who takes an oath.] Of or pertaining to an oath. Hence †**jura'mentally** *adv.*, with an oath.

1651 HOWELL *Venice* Proeme 2 Ecclesiastics..in regard they have a dependance and juramentall obligation, in divers things, to another Prince, *viz.* the Pope. *a* **1693** URQUHART *Rabelais* III. xix. 156 A Promise juramentally confirmed.

‖**Jurançon** (ʒyrɑ̃sɔ̃). [Name of a commune in the Basses Pyrénées.] The white wine produced in Jurançon.

[**1833** C. REDDING *Hist. Mod. Wines* v. 138 The first growths of Jurançon and Gan bring two hundred francs the hectolitre.] **1920** A. L. SIMON *Blood of Grape* ix. 243 Fine wines..from the Mediterranean Coast and the Pyrénées (..*Rivesaltes*, *Jurancon*, etc., etc.). **1926** P. M. SHAND *Bk. Wines* v. 64 Like all fine wines, Jurançon owes its quality to one supreme and informing vine. **1969** L. ORIZET *Wine Bk.* 144 The production seldom exceeds 400,000 gallons of genuine white Jurançon a year, and a few gallons of red wine.

jurant ('dʒʊərənt), *a.* and *sb.* [ad. L. *jūrānt-em*, pr. pple. of *jūrāre* to swear.]

A. *adj.* Taking an oath; swearing. In *Sc. Hist.* opposed to *non-jurant*, *non-juring* (q.v.).

1715 *Wodrow Corr.* (1843) II. 23 Some judicious Nonjurors, who are firmly of opinion that the spring of this is from some Jurant brethren. **1720** *Ibid.* 535 He had charged all his Jurant brethren as perjured, and yet came in afterwards and took the oath. **1837** CARLYLE *Fr. Rev.* II. I. vii, Such universally prevalent, universally jurant, feeling of Hope.

B. *sb.* One who takes an oath. In *Sc. Hist.* opposed to *non-jurant*, *non-juror* (q.v.).

1585 T. WASHINGTON tr. *Nicholay's Voy.* IV. xii. 125 Whensoever they wulde sweare amitie and confederation.. betweene both the Iurants. **1770** BP. FORBES *Jrnls.* (1886) 295 The fruit of my labours at Inverness may, perhaps, fall into the hands of a Jurant. **1849** *Life Rev. James Fisher* iii. 53 A religious clause declaring the jurant's profession and allowance..of the true religion as presently professed.

Jurassic (dʒuː'ræsɪk), *a.* and *sb. Geol.* [ad. F. *Jurassique*, f. *Jura* (see def.) after *Liassic*, *Triassic*.] **a.** Of or pertaining to the Jura mountains: applied to geological formations belonging to the period between the Triassic and the Cretaceous, characterized by the prevalence of oolitic limestone, of which the Jura mountains between France and Switzerland are chiefly formed. Also applied to the period itself and to flora and fauna found in Jurassic formations.

1831 *Proc. Geol. Soc.* I. 241 The Jurassic and Alpine limestones. **1833** LYELL *Princ. Geol.* III. 372 Sedimentary formations..as modern as the jurassic or oolite formations. **1847** *Q. Jrnl. Geol. Soc.* III. 117 A succession of deposits.. formed during the Jurassic period. **1851** *Ibid.* VII. 179 But for the 'plant-beds' at Gristhorpe, Cloughton, Kiburn, and Whitby, we should know little of the ancient vegetation of the Jurassic period. These localities have supplied, in fact, the types of the Jurassic Flora. **1865** LUBBOCK *Preh. Times* 290 The Aube runs through cretaceous and Jurassic strata. **1909** CHAMBERLIN & SALISBURY *Geol.: Shorter Course* xxiv. 712 (*caption*) A group of Jurassic ammonites. **1938** L. D. STAMP *Physical Geogr. & Geol.* xiii. 207 At the close of the Jurassic period the sea retreated and left a great lake in south-eastern England. **1968** D. A. ROBSON *Sci. Geol.* ix. 242 The succession is reminiscent of that of the Carboniferous Coal Measures, except for its distinctive Jurassic flora.

b. *absol.* as *sb.* The Jurassic system or the Jurassic period.

1831 *Proc. Geol. Soc.* I. 241 Chalk does not exist in the Carpathians, nor could the author recognise it at Cracow, the limestone of which he refers to the Upper Jurassic. **1873** DAWSON *Earth & Man* viii. 189 The Trias is succeeded by a great and complex system of formations, usually known as the Jurassic. **1902** A. J. JUKES-BROWNE *Student's Handbk. Stratigr. Geol.* xiv. 331 The Upper Jurassic, again, is an argillaceous series. **1938** A. K. WELLS *Outl. Hist. Geol.* xv. 153 The Lower Jurassic is co-extensive with the Lias, a formation..splendidly exposed in parts of the English coast that enjoy a measure of popularity as sea-side resorts. **1956** W. J. ARKELL *Jurassic Geol. of World* i. 3 In the popular imagination the Jurassic is the period of great marine reptiles and flying dragons. **1973** *Nature* 13 July 92/1 Rifting probably started in the Triassic and by the Jurassic a reasonably large Tethyan Ocean was in existence.

jurat[1] ('dʒʊəræt, F. ʒyra). Also 6 iurate, -att(e, 7–8 jurate. [ad. med.L. *jūrāt-us*, lit. 'sworn man', sb. use of the pa. pple. of *jūrāre* to swear. In sense 4 a. the equivalent of F. *jurat* (orig. a Prov. form = F. *juré*).]

1. One who has taken an oath; a person who performs some duty on oath; *spec.* one sworn to give information about the crimes committed in his neighbourhood, and in other ways to assist the administration of justice; a juror. *Obs.* exc. *Hist.*

1531 ELYOT *Gov.* III. vii, In iudiciall causes..witnesses and iurates which shall procede in the triall, doo make no lasse othe. *a* **1548** HALL *Chron.*, *Hen. VII* 7 They were thought to have been confederates and Iurates of this newe conspiracy. **1564** in Strype *Ann. Ref.* (1709) I. xli. 420 To every parish belongeth..Four or eight jurats for offences given and taken. **1660** R. COKE *Power & Subj.* 104 Aldred the Archbishop..and Hugh the Bishop of London..wrote that which the jurats had delivered. **1861** PEARSON *Early & Mid. Ages Eng.* 415 The first step the justices in eyre took.. was to impanel four jurats from every township, and twelve from every hundred.

2. A municipal officer (esp. of the Cinque Ports) holding a position similar to that of an alderman.

1464 *Rolls Parlt.* V. 515/2 Provost and Baillif, Jurates men and Burgeis men and their Successours. **1485** *Ibid.* 338/1 Bailiff and Jurates..of all and every the said v Portes. **1584** R. SCOT *Discov. Witchcr.* XII. xvi. (1886) 209 M. L. Stuppenie, late Jurat of the same towne [New Romney]. **1660** PEPYS *Diary* 7 May, Here were also all the Jurates of the towne of Dover. **1701** in *Gentl. Mag.* (1818) LXXXVIII. II. 402 Went to Church [at Gravesend] to which he had seen the Mayor go in procession..attended by his brethren the Jurats, twelve in number. **1768** BLACKSTONE *Comm.* III. vi. 79 A writ of error lies from the mayor and jurats of each port to the lord warden of the cinque ports, in his court of Shepway. **1778** *Eng. Gazetteer* (ed. 2) s.v. *Rye*, The corporation..consists of a mayor, 12 jurats, and the freemen. **1875** STUBBS *Const. Hist.* III. xxi. 561 If these twenty-five jurats are the predecessors of the twenty-five aldermen of the wards.

3. In the Channel Islands, one of a body of magistrates, chosen for life, who in conjunction with the Bailiff form the Royal Court for administration of justice; they are ex officio members of the States.

Their number is twelve for each of the islands of Guernsey and Jersey, and six for Alderney.

[**1339** *Rolls Parlt.* II. 109/2 William Payn, un des Jurez de l'Isle de Gereseye.] **1537** T. CUMPTUN in Ellis *Orig. Lett.* Ser. II. III. 92 [An] Inventory..made in the presence of the Deane and of too Jurattes of this Isle. **1694** FALLE *Jersey* Pref. B iij b, A Gentleman of Iersey..one of the Iurats of the Royal Court of that Island. **1765** BLACKSTONE *Comm.* I. Introd. §4. 106 All causes are originally determined by their own officers, the bailiffs and jurats of the islands. **1873** J. LEWES *Census* 1871. 204 Twelve jurats chosen by the members of the 'States'.

4. With reference to France, etc.: **a.** A municipal magistrate in certain towns, as Bordeaux. **b.** A member of a company or corporation, sworn to see that nothing is done against its statutes.

1432 *Rolls Parlt.* IV. 406/1 The Mair and Juratz of the Toune of Burdeux. **1523** LD. BERNERS *Froiss.* I. lxiii. 85 They of Tourney..made newe prouost, and iurates, acordynge to their auncyent vsages. **1670** COTTON *Espernon* III. IX. 420 Upon the Banks of the River Garonne; where the Jurats of Bordeaux came to receive him. **1714** *Fr. Bk. Rates* 123 The Jurats of the Merchants, wholesale Mercers, and Haberdashers of the City of Paris. **1804** *Med. Jrnl.* XII. 542, I informed the Jurats, that..my colleague or myself would return to the isle [Malta].

jurat[2] ('dʒʊəræt). *Law.* [ad. L. *jūrātum* that which is sworn, neut. pa. pple. of *jūrāre* to swear.] A memorandum as to when, where, and before whom an affidavit is sworn.

1796 *Reg. Gen., Mich. 37 Geo. III* in *Term Reports* (1802) VII. 82 No affidavit shall be..made use of..in the jurat of which there shall be any interlineation or erasure. **1833** *Penny Cycl.* I. 164/2. **1896** *Daily News* 4 Aug. 2/6 The proof of the trustees..was not admitted, the jurat being informal.

†'**jurate**, *pa. pple. Obs. rare*[−1]. [ad. L. *jūrāt-us* sworn: see JURAT[1].] Sworn, bound by oath.

1433 *Waterf. Arch.* in *10th Rep. Hist. MSS. Comm.* App. v. 295 Ony man jurate in an enqueste.

juration[1] (dʒʊ'reɪʃən). *rare.* [ad. late L. *jūrātiōn-em*, n. of action from *jūrāre* to swear.] The action of swearing; an oath.

1656 BLOUNT *Glossogr.*, *Juration*, an Oath. **1854** MRS. AUSTIN in J. Ross *3 Generat. Englishw.* (1888) II. ii. 13 'Two oaths', or to speak more accurately (for there is no juration in the case), two 'd—ns'.

juration[2], aphetic form of ADJURATION.

c **1425** *St. Christina* xxii. in *Anglia* VIII. 127/40 þen Cristyn was preyed and adiurid of the wife..Whos iuracyone Cristyn took at grefe.

ˈ**jurative**, *a. rare.* [ad. late L. *jūrātivus*, f. ppl. stem of *jūrāre* to swear.] = JURATORY.
In mod. Dicts.

jurator (dʒʊˈreɪtə(r)). *rare.* [a. L. *jūrātor*, agent-n. from *jūrāre* to swear; in med.(Anglo)L., a juror, a juryman.] = JURAT[1] 1.
1622 CALLIS *Stat. Sewers* (1647) 97 The Four and twenty Iurators in Kent in Rumney Marsh, who always upon their Oaths set down every particular mans ground in certain.. and accordingly were the parties severally taxed. **1872** O. SHIPLEY *Gloss. Eccl. Terms* s.v. *Compurgator*, A jurator who ..swore to his innocence.

juratorial (dʒʊərəˈtɔərɪəl), *a.* [f. as next + -AL[1].] Of or belonging to a jury.
1865 *Pall Mall G.* 4 Oct. 2 The most flagrant instances of juratorial perversity.

juratory (ˈdʒʊərətərɪ), *a.* [ad. late L. *jūrātōri-us* confirmed by oath: see JURAT[1] and -ORY.] Of or pertaining to an oath or oaths; expressed or contained in an oath.
1553 in Picton *L'pool Munic. Rec.* (1883) I. 32 Thos. More ..tooke the oathe of a Burgesse to doe all thynges according to the vertue of the burgesses oathe..and also the laudable uses and customs of the sayd towne and not juratory. **1647** R. STEWART *Answ. Lett. Dr. Turner* 51 Freed from his juratory obligation. *a* **1734** NORTH *Exam.* I. iii. §136 (1740) 211 The juratory, dying Denials, of the whole criminal Charge of the Plot, made by every individual suffering Person at his Execution. **1806** W. TAYLOR in *Ann. Rev.* IV. 260 Affirmative or Juratory declarations of opinion.

jurdan, -en, obs. forms of JORDAN.

†**jure**, *sb.* Chiefly *Sc. Obs.* [ad. L. *jūr-*, stem of *jūs* law, right: 'in jure' answers to L. *in jūre.*]
1. The science of law, jurisprudence.
1496 *Sc. Acts Jas. IV* (1814) 238/1 To remane thre ȝeris at þe sculis of art and Iure, sua þat þai may haue knawlege..of þe lawis. **1500–20** DUNBAR *Poems* lxiii. 4 Doctouris in jure and medicyne. *Ibid.* lxv. 3 To speik of science..Off jure, of wisdome, or intelligence. **1556** LAUDER *Tractate* 448 Thay suld haue knawlage of boith the Iuris, Als weill the Canone as Ciuile law.
2. A just privilege, a right.
1533 BELLENDEN *Livy* IV. (1822) 314 Gif the tribunis has ..tane fra the Faderis thare majesties and juris. *c* **1745** in *Gentl. Mag.* (1773) XLIII. 498 Sherlock the Elder, with his jure divine, Did not comply till the battle of Boyne.

‖ˈ**jure**, L., abl. of *jūs* right; in phr. ˈ**jure diˈvino** by divine right (see DIVINE *a.* 2); hence **juredivinist**, a believer in the divine right of kings; **jure-divinoship** (*nonce-wd.*).
1663 SIR G. MACKENZIE *Relig. Stoic* vi. (1685) 51 The sole jure-divinoship of all Ecclesiastical Rites. **1681** [T. FLATMAN] *Heraclitus Ridens* (1713) I. 237 All your Bishops, and Tantivy Clergymen,..your *Jure Divinists*, who have renounced the Covenant. **1749** FIELDING *Tom Jones* II. i, A *jure divino* tyrant.

jure, *v. nonce-wd.*
1. Used contextually with reference to *juror*, as if = make jurors of you.
1596 SHAKS. *1 Hen. IV*, II. ii. 97 You are Grand Iurers, are ye? Wee'l iure ye ifaith.
2. *nonce*-adaptation of L. *jurare* to swear (with allusion to Horace *Ep.* I. i. 14, *Nullius addictus jurare in verba magistri*).
1818 KEBLE in Sir J. Coleridge *Mem.* iii. (1869) 24 If I must *jure* into any man's *Verbs* I think on the whole it would be his.

‖**jurel** (ˈdʒʊərəl). [Sp.-American.] A fish of the genus *Caranx*, found along the southern coast of the United States.
1760–72 tr. *Juan & Ulloa's Voy.* (ed. 3) II. 226 The chief kinds are cod, berrugates, the spur fish, sole, turbet, jureles, and lobsters. **1890** in *Cent. Dict.*

†**jurenay**, var. of JORNAY. *Obs.*
1495 in *Ld. Treas. Acc. Scot.* I. 226, ij ellis of crammesy vellous, to be a jurenay aboue his harnes.

jurgon, obs. form of JARGON *sb.*[1]

juriballi (jʊərɪˈbælɪ). Also **euri-**, **youraballi.** [Arawak (Makuchi).] Any of several trees belonging to the family Meliaceæ, especially a species of *Trichilia*, the bark of which was formerly used as a febrifuge; also, the bark itself.
1834 J. HANCOCK in *Trans. Medico-Botanical Soc. 1832–33* 36 (*title*) Remarks on the Juribali, or Euribali. **1846** J. LINDLEY *Veget. Kingd.* 462 Juriballi bark, a Demerara product..is described as being a potent bitter and astringent, far superior to Peruvian bark in fevers of a typhoid and malignant nature. **1851** *Illustr. Catal. Gt. Exhib.* IV. 982/1 Youraballi. **1903** *Imperial Inst. Techn. Rep.* 285 The Crabwood and Euriballi would have shown fair results.

juridic (dʒʊˈrɪdɪk), *a.* [ad. L. *jūridicus*, f. *jūs*, *jūr-* law + *-dicus* saying, f. root of *dīcĕre* to say. Cf. F. *juridique* (1453 in Godef.).]
1. Of or pertaining to law, legal: = next 1.
1553 T. WILSON *Rhet.* (1580) Table Q ij b, Division of causes of iuridic. **1691** WOOD *Ath. Oxon.* I. 7 It is penned in a Juridic Stile. **1894** *Thinker* V. 439 This relationship was essentially juridic in character.
2. = JURIDICAL 2.
1892 *Monist* II. 298 The revolution of the last century.. forgot the rights of juridic persons, of corporations, and law became an..individualiser.

juridical (dʒʊˈrɪdɪkəl), *a.* Also 6 **iurysdycall.** [f. as prec. + -AL[1]. With the early form *jurisdical* (like *jurisdiction*), cf. OF. *jurisdiciable* (Godef.).]
1. Of, relating to, or connected with the administration of law or judicial proceedings; sometimes in more general sense = legal.
juridical styles (Sc.), set forms of legal documents, = the 'common forms' of English lawyers.
1502 *Ord. Crysten Men* (W. de W. 1506) IV. xxi. 250 Without lycence of the pope & concessyon Iurysdycall. **1584** BURLEIGH *Let. to Whitgift* in Fuller *Ch. Hist.* IX. v. §9 (1655) 155 This Juridicall and Canonicall siftner of poor Ministers, is not to edifie and reform. **1611** in Gutch *Coll. Cur.* I. 101 Ceremonial and juridical assemblies of magistracy. **1759** JOHNSON *Idler* No. 54 ¶1, I..present you with the case..in as juridical a manner as I am capable. **1839** JAMES *Louis XIV*, II. 51 That trial..as far as Juridical decision went, was a mere farce. **1884** SIR C. BOWEN in *Law Times Rep.* LI. 531/2 The various uses that have been made by judges or juridical writers of the terms.
2. Assumed by law to exist; juristic.
1900 *Daily News* 20 Apr. 7/5 A Bill..extending to juridical persons, that is, duly registered corporations or partnerships, the right to engage in mining.

juridically (dʒuːˈrɪdɪkəlɪ), *adv.* [f. prec. + -LY[2].] In a juridical manner; with reference to the administration of law; with legal authority; legally; in the view of the law.
1602 T. FITZHERBERT *Apol.* 10 To proue it iuridically, in a matter of lyfe and death. **1642** *Remonst. Div. Passages conc. Ch. & Kingd. Irel.* 24 Being called upon and examined juridically, upon oath he deposed these words. **1795** BURKE *Tracts Popery Laws* Wks. 1842 II. 434 The received opinion, though not juridically delivered, has been [etc.]. **1823** LINGARD *Hist. Eng.* VI. 321 He had examined that marriage juridically; had pronounced it good and valid.

†**juriˈdicial**, *a. Obs.* [ad. L. *jūridiciāl-is*: see JURIDIC and -IAL. Cf. obs. F. *juridicial* (*a* 1521 in Godef.).] **a.** Relating to the legality of an action. **b.** = JURIDICAL 1.
The two earlier quots. refer to the different classes of legal questions enumerated in Cicero's *De Invent.* II. xxiii. 69.
c **1530** L. COX *Rhet.* (1899) 79 Whan there is no dout but that the dede is done, and who dyd it, many tymes controuersy is had, whether it hathe bene done laufully or not. And this state is negociall or iuridiciall. **1553** T. WILSON *Rhet.* (1580) 90 The State I. Coniecturall. II. Legall. III. Iuridiciall. **1610** W. FOLKINGHAM *Art of Survey* I. i. 2 The Legall part prescribes Methodicall & Juridiciall confines to the whole course of Survey.

juried (ˈdʒʊərɪd), *a.* [f. JURY *sb.* + -ED[2].] Formed into a jury; hence *fig.* formed into a company of twelve.
1839 BAILEY *Festus* viii. 92 You too, ye juried signs,..farewell!

†ˈ**jurier.** *Obs. rare.* Forms: 5 iuryour, 6 iuryer, 7 juriar. [App. an alteration of *jurour* JUROR, after *jury*: but cf. *clothier*, *furrier*, etc.] One who has taken an oath; a juror or juryman.
1496 *Bk. St. Albans* E v, A sentence of Iuges, A dampnyng of Iuryours. **1534** WHITINTON *Tullyes Offices* III. (1540) 132 Whan sentence is to be gyue to [= by] him that hath sworne or made an othe, let the iuryer remember that he taketh god to be wytnesse. **1687** WINSTANLEY *Lives Poets* 55 He was found guilty by twelve common juriars.

jurimetrics (dʒʊərɪˈmɛtrɪks). [f. L. *juris*, gen. of *jūs* law + *-metrics*, as in *biometrics*, *econometrics*.] The use of scientific methods in the study of legal matters. So **jurimeˈtrician**, **juriˈmetricist**, a student of, or expert in, jurimetrics.
1949 L. LOEVINGER in *Minnesota Law Rev.* XXXIII. 483 The next step forward in the long path of man's progress must be from jurisprudence (which is mere speculation about law) to *jurimetrics*—which is the scientific investigation of legal problems. **1964** *Jrnl. Politics* XXVI. 915 Professor Spaeth's view of what jurimetrics may hope to accomplish. **1966** *Sci. Amer.* Sept. 296 Being, in this enterprise, jurimetricists and not legal historians, they chose the molds of analytic rather than historical jurisprudence for the ordering of their materials. *Ibid.* 295 The fruit of the union of jurisprudence and social science has inevitably been christened 'jurimetrics'. **1970** *Encycl. Sci. Suppl.* (Grolier) 287 Polimetricians, psychometricians, jurimetricians are all rapidly proliferating species of a genus of mathematically minded scholars.

juring (ˈdʒʊərɪŋ), *ppl. a. rare.* [f. **jure* vb. (as ad. L. *jūrāre*) + -ING[2].] Taking the oath; jurant. (Opp. to *non-juring*.)
1710 *Managers' Pro & Con* 43 Juring, Non-juring, and.. abjuring Clergy. **1870** *Union Rev.* 32 The number of juring clergy began to fail.

jurisconsult (ˌdʒʊərɪskənˈsʌlt). [ad. L. *jūrisconsultus*, f. *jūris*, gen. of *jūs* law + *consultus* skilled: see CONSULT *sb.*[2] Cf. F. *jurisconsulte* (15th c. in Hatz.-Darm.).] One learned in law, esp. in civil or international law; a jurist; a master of jurisprudence.
1605 BACON *Adv. Learn.* II. i. §2 In divers particular sciences, as of the jurisconsults. **1676** W. ROW *Contn. Blair's Autobiog.* xi. (1848) 365 Proper for jurisconsults, lawyers, and politicians. **1803** *Edin. Rev.* I. 367 More interesting than a municipal judge or juris consult. **1871** MORLEY *Condorcet* in *Crit. Misc.* Ser. I. (1878) 60 It was to Condorcet's honour as a jurisconsult that he should have had so many scruples.
attrib. **1870** LOWELL *Among my Bks.* Ser. I. (1873) 115 We must give his argument in the..splendor of its jurisconsult latinity.

†**jurisconˈsultor.** *Obs. rare*[−1]. = prec.
1549 *Compl. Scot.* xvii. 144 The philosophovrs ande iurisconsultours in the anciant dais, hes familiarly discriuit one thing be the contrar thyng.

jurisdiction (dʒʊərɪsˈdɪkʃən). Forms: 4–6 iure-, (4 iuri-, iurdiccion), 4–7 iurisdiccion, etc. (with usual interchange of *i* and *y*, *cc* and *ct*, *on* and *oun*), 5 iurisdycion, 7– jurisdiction. [orig. a. OF. *jure-*, *juri-*, *jurdiction*, *-dicion* (F. *juridiction*), ad. L. *jūrisdictiōn-em*, f. *jūris*, gen. of *jūs* law + *dictio*, n. of action f. *dīcere* to say, declare. Subsequently assimilated to the L. form, which was also used in F. in the 17–18th cents.]
1. Administration of justice; exercise of judicial authority, or of the functions of a judge or legal tribunal; power of declaring and administering law or justice; legal authority or power.
[**1267** *Act 52 Hen. III*, c. 2 (Stat. Marleberge) Qui non sit de feodo suo, aut super ipsum habeat jurisdictionem per Hundredam vel ballivam que sua sit.] *a* **1300** *Cursor M.* 26324 He [a priest] has his iuredic̄tion tint o þis man al wit resun. *c* **1380** WYCLIF *Sel. Wks.* III. 265 Þes wordis of Crist meneþ two juridicciouns, as spiritual and seculer. *c* **1386** CHAUCER *Friar's T.* 21 Thanne hadde he thurgh his Iurisdiccion [*MS. Petw.* -diction, *Harl.* iurediccioun, *Camb., Corp., Lansd.* iurdiccion, -diction, -e] Power to doon on hem correccion. **1395** PURVEY *Remonstr.* (1851) 30 Neithir the king, neithir his justisis han jurisdicciuoun on clerkis, trespace thei nevere so moche. **1490** CAXTON *Eneydos* xxix. 111 Whan som body hathe submytted hymself ..to the iurisdicyon of some Iuge [etc.]. **1509** HAWES *Conv. Swearers* 10 By pryncely preemynence and Iuredyccyon. **1538** STARKEY *England* II. i. 170 In admynystratyon of justyce..in such thyngys as they had jurysdycyon of. *a* **1548** HALL *Chron.*, *Hen. VIII* 246 Ecclesiasticall persones, should not..exercise iurisdiccion, or any kynd of aucthoritie in temporall matters. *c* **1670** HOBBES *Dial. Comm. Laws* (1677) 153 To declare the Law, which is not Judgment, but Jurisdiction. **1756–7** tr. *Keysler's Trav.* (1760) III. 431 The nobility of the district of Padua had formerly the criminal jurisdiction, as it is called, over their vassals. **1844** H. H. WILSON *Brit. India* II. 129 The districts ..were not intended to be exempted from the jurisdiction of the Company's officers. **1863** H. COX *Instit.* III. iv. 640 The Chief Justiciar..had general jurisdiction of pleas civil and criminal. **1864** BRYCE *Holy Rom. Emp.* xix. (1875) 343 Free from all jurisdiction of the Pope or any Catholic prelate. **1892** F. T. PIGOTT (*title*) Exterritoriality: the law relating to Consular Jurisdiction. **1896** *Law Times Rep.* LXXIII. 690/1 This court has no jurisdiction over the property in America.
fig. **1594** CAREW *Huarte's Exam. Wits* (1616) 128 If wee will faine a perfect Logician..all the Sciences..appertaine to his iurisdiction.
2. Power or authority in general; administration, rule, control.
c **1425** LYDG. *Assembly of Gods* 480 Euery other thyng in whom Dame Nature Hath any iurysdiccion. **1433** —— *St. Edmund* II. 929 For God hath power and Iurysdiccioun Make tongis speke of bodies that be ded. **1667** MILTON *P.L.* II. 319 To live exempt From Heav'n's high jurisdiction. **1756–82** J. WARTON *Ess. Pope* II. IX. 113 The tranquillity and ease of the mind, depend upon a thousand things that are not under our jurisdiction. **1860** MARSH *Eng. Lang.* xii. 261 Man's language is higher than himself..and still less subject than he to the jurisdiction of the laws of material nature.
3. The extent or range of judicial or administrative power; the territory over which such power extends.
c **1380** WYCLIF *Wks.* (1880) 57 Prelatis letten & forbeden prestis to preche þe gospel in here iurdiccion or bischoperiche, but ȝif þei han leue & letteris of hem. **1474** CAXTON *Chesse* IV. iv. K viij, The Iuge ought to deffende and kepe the labourers and possessyons which ben in his Iurisdyccion by al right and lawe. **1555** EDEN *Decades* 23 In al this tracte, they passed throwgh the Iurisdiction of other princes. **1632** LITHGOW *Trav.* 25 The other sequestrate Tuscan jurisdiction, is the little comonwealth of Luca. **1770** *Connect. Col. Rec.* (1885) XIII. 399 Resolved that the said lines..shall be the jurisdictions..between the said towns. **1833** HT. MARTINEAU *Charmed Sea* ii. 15 Whether he should not send on this procession, and keep the next that might arrive within his jurisdiction. **1833** J. H. NEWMAN *Hist. Sk.* (1873) II. [III.] I. i. 4 Basil's care of the churches ..extended far beyond the limits of his own jurisdiction.
fig. **1635** N. CARPENTER *Geog. Del.* II. xii. 191 God hath.. permitted the sea sometimes to breake his appointed limits, and inuade the Iurisdiction of the land. **1671** R. BOHUN *Wind* 91 They [winds] never cease blowing within their own jurisdiction.
4. A judicial organization; a judicature; a court, or series of courts, of justice.
1765 BLACKSTONE *Comm.* I. Introd. §3. 79 Peculiar laws.. adopted and used only in certain peculiar courts and jurisdictions. *Ibid.* I. vii. 242 No jurisdiction upon earth has power to try him in a criminal way. **1821** J. Q. ADAMS in Davies *Metric Syst.* III. (1871) 269 The jurisdictions to which resort must be had..are those of municipal police. **1878** LECKY *Eng. in 18th C.* II. v. 67 The abolition of hereditary jurisdictions.

jurisdictional (dʒʊərɪsˈdɪkʃənəl), *a.* [f. prec. + -AL[1]: cf. F. *juridictionnel.*] Of or pertaining to jurisdiction.
1644 JESSOP *Angel of Eph.* 25 The Jurisdictionall Preeminence of a Bishop over the Presbyters. **1780** in I. Allen *Hist. Vermont* (1798) 149 The Legislature of this State do lay a jurisdictional claim to all the lands whatever, east of

Connecticut river. **1811** *Gen. Hist.* in *Ann. Reg.* 124 All jurisdictional seigniories are thereby abolished, and are declared incorporated with the nation. **1897** *Eng. Hist. Rev.* Jan. 152 To avert the hostility of the canonists by.. conceding some of their jurisdictional claims.

Hence **juris'dictionally** *adv.*, in the way of a judicial decision; with regard to jurisdiction.

1674 P. Walsh *Quest. Oath Alleg.* (1677) 13 A Formal and Authoritative Tribunal to decide Jurisdictionally who shall be Pope or King. **1881** *Ch. Q. Rev.* Apr. 196 In the East the patriarchates were of very wide extent, geographically and jurisdictionally.

jurisdictive (dʒʊərɪs'dɪktɪv), *a. rare.* [f. *jurisdiction*, on analogy of *administration, administrative*, and the like (but adjs. in *-ive* are properly formed on vbs., and there is no L. **jūrisdīcĕre*).] Of or pertaining to jurisdiction.

1640 Bp. Hall *Episc.* II. vii. 47 Probabilities of a Supereminent, and Jurisdictive power, in these speciall Angels. **1641** Milton *Ch. Govt.* II. iii, That jurisdictive power in the Church there ought to be none at all. **1649** Prynne *Vind. Liberty Eng.* 34. **1763–83** Cath. Macaulay *Hist. Eng.* V. 174 (Jod.) Who were to exercise jurisdictive power. **1862** Beveridge *Hist. India* II. v. v. 379 The jurisdictive powers and authorities of the supreme court.

jurisprudence (dʒʊərɪs'pruːdəns). [ad. L. *jūrisprūdentia* (also *prūdentia jūris*): cf. It. *giurisprudenza*, F. *jurisprudence* 'the skille or knowledge of laws' (Cotgr. 1611): perh. the immed. source.]

1. a. Knowledge of or skill in law.

1628 Coke *On Litt.* Epil., For a farewell to our jurisprudent, I wish vnto him the gladsome light of jurisprudence. **1758** Blackstone *Study of Law* in *Comm.* (1809) I. 27 Aristotle himself has said.. that jurisprudence, or the knowledge of those laws, is the principal, and most perfect branch of ethics. **1795** Wythe *Decis. Virginia* 15 Being supposed to be known by men of jurisprudence.

b. The science which treats of human laws (written or unwritten) in general; the philosophy of law.

1756 J. Warton *Ess. Pope* I. vi. 300 The talents of Abelard were not confined to theology, jurisprudence, philosophy. **1781** Gibbon *Decl. & F.* xvii. II. 40 The youth.. who had devoted themselves to the study of Roman jurisprudence. **1799** Mackintosh *Stud. Law Nature & Nations* Wks. 1846 I. 345 Writers on general jurisprudence have considered states as moral persons. **1832** Austin *Jurispr.* (1879) I. Prelim. Explan. 32, I shall distinguish general jurisprudence or the philosophy of positive law, from what may be styled particular jurisprudence, or the science of particular law. **1861** *Q. Rev.* CX. 115 The domain of Comparative Jurisprudence, of which English Law forms a small province.

2. A system or body of law; a legal system.

1656 Blount *Glossogr.*, *Jurisprudence*... the stile or form of the Law. **1781** Gibbon *Decl. & F.* xliv, Under his reign ..the civil jurisprudence was digested in the immortal works of the *Code*, the *Pandects*, and the *Institutes*. **1818** Hallam *Mid. Ages* viii. II. (1819) II. 467 The difference between our Saxon and Norman jurisprudence. **1839** Ld. Brougham *Statesm. Geo. III, Ld. Mansfield* (ed. 2) 58 Heads peculiar to Scottish jurisprudence, to which the English law affords no parallel. *a* **1859** Macaulay *Hist. Eng.* xxv. V. 235 The history of our medical jurisprudence. *a* **1862** Buckle *Misc. Wks.* (1872) I. 1 The noblest gift Rome has bequeathed to posterity, is her jurisprudence.

juris'prudent, *sb.* and *a.* [a. obs. F. *jurisprudent*, back-formation from *jurisprudence*: cf. *prudence, prudent*. The L. expression was *jūris-perītus*, or *jūre-perītus*.]

A. *sb.* One versed in, or treating of, jurisprudence; a man learned in the law; a jurist.

1628 [see prec. 1]. **1659** T. Pecke *Parnassi Puerp.* 12 Lawyers by Law, are Jurisprudents named. *a* **1859** De Quincey *Klosterheim* v. Wks. 1890 XII. 46 Klosterheim.. had been pronounced by some of the first jurisprudents a female appanage. **1892** *Q. Rev.* Apr. 363 Monogamy, as admirably defined by the great Roman jurisprudent.

B. *adj.* Versed or skilled in jurisprudence; having knowledge of the principles of law.

1737 R. West *Let.* 2 Dec. in *Gray's Corr.*, Adieu! I am going to my tutor's lectures on one Puffendorff, a very jurisprudent author. **1837–9** Hallam *Hist. Lit.* I. vii. §50 The eulogy of Cicero on Scævola, that he was the most jurisprudent of orators, and the most eloquent of lawyers.

jurisprudential (-'dɛnʃəl), *a.* [f. L. *jūrisprūdentia* + -al[1].] Of or pertaining to jurisprudence; rarely of persons: jurisprudent B.

1775 C. Johnston *Pilgrim* II. x. 255 Three civil professions called liberal..the sacerdotal, the jurisprudential, and the medical; or, as they are called here, the Gown, the Long-robe, and the Faculty. **1819** *Blackw. Mag.* IV. 750/1 The doctor cannot be suspected of having any jurisprudential learning himself. **1852** S. Bailey *Disc. Var. Subj.* 100 It [relevant] had long been a jurisprudential word in Scotland. **1884** W. S. Lilly in *Contemp. Rev.* Feb. 251 The great jurisprudential ideas which we find in the literature of the decadent Empire.

Hence **jurispru'dentialist**, a writer on jurisprudence, a legal practitioner. **jurispru'dentially** *adv.*, in relation to jurisprudence.

1802–12 Bentham *Ration. Judic. Evid.* IX. III. vii, As to the jurisprudentialist, his most common state is, perhaps, a sort of middle state between the two [impostor and dupe]. **1828** *Examiner* 737/1 Viewing it jurisprudentially.

juris'prudist. [irreg. f. jurisprud-ence + -ist.] = jurisprudent *sb.*

1793 *State Papers* in *Ann. Reg.* 213, I have forgotten what these mercenary jurisprudists have written upon the rights of nations. **1871** Lytton *Coming Race* xxvi, It is allowed by jurisprudists that it is idle to talk of rights when there are not corresponding powers to enforce them.

jurist ('dʒʊərɪst). [a. F. *juriste*, ad. med.L. *jūrista* f. *jūs, jūr-* law, right: see -ist.]

1. One who practises in law; a lawyer (*obs.* exc. *U.S.*). Also, a judge (*obs.*).

1481 Caxton *Myrr.* I. v. 26 They.. become aduocates and iuristes for to amasse and gadre alway money. **1489** Caxton *Faytes of A.* I. i. 7 As wel auncyent nobles as iuristes and other. **1653** Urquhart *Rabelais* I. xvii, The Parisians.. are by nature both good jurers and good jurists. **1849** Macaulay *Hist. Eng.* vii. II. 375 All the ablest jurists and advocates of the Tory party had, one after another, refused to comply. **1905** E. B. Holt tr. *H. Münsterberg's Americans* iv. 88 Sixty-one of them [*sc.* members of the Senate] were jurists... As to the jurists, they are not men who are still active as attorneys or judges. **1931** W. G. McAdoo *Crowded Years* iii. 41 A well-known jurist at that time was Judge Trewhitt. **1936** *S. P. E. Tract* XLV. 188 Even more important is the divergence between the English and American uses of *jurist*, which is not restricted in the United States to the meaning of an expert in the science of law. It is commonly applied to any one who has obtained the qualifications required for legal practice. **1973** N. W. Schur *British Self-Taught* 211 In America *jurist* is synonymous with *judge*. Unfortunately not all *jurists* (in the American sense) are *jurists* (in the English sense).

2. One who professes or treats of law; one versed in the science of law; a legal writer.

a **1626** Bacon (J.), This is not to be measured by the principles of jurists. **1765** Blackstone *Comm.* I. vii. 254 In respect to civil suits, all the foreign jurists agree. **1844** H. H. Wilson *Brit. India* I. 415 The doctrines of the Mohammedan jurists are somewhat at variance on this matter. **1879** Froude *Cæsar* xiii. 177 The body of admirable laws which are known to jurists as the 'Leges Juliæ'.

3. In the Universities: A student of law, or one who takes a degree in law.

1691 A. Wood *Ath. Oxon.* I. 514 This person [John Jones] being entred and settled in a jurists place, he applyed himself to the study of the civil law. **1758** Blackstone *Study of Law* in *Comm.* (1809) I. 15 One of the three questions to be annually discussed at the act by the jurist-inceptors shall relate to the common law. **1898** *Westm. Gaz.* 17 Oct. 1/3 Downing provided the Senior Jurist in the years 1882, 1883, and 1884.

juristic (dʒʊ'rɪstɪk), *a.* [f. med.L. *jūrista* jurist + -ic: see -istic.] Of or belonging to a jurist; pertaining or relating to the subject or study of law; legal; created by law.

1831 Carlyle *Early Germ. Lit.* in *Misc. Ess.* (1872) III. 198 Men as brave as they of the Robber-Towers,.. who in many a stout fight taught them a juristic doctrine. **1837** —— *Fr. Rev.* III. II. vi, In the Convention Tribune, it drones continually, mere Juristic Eloquence. **1875** Poste *Gaius* I. 153 A University of persons in the private code is a fictitious or juristic person [cf. Ger. *juristische Person*].

So **ju'ristics** *sb.*, the study or theory of law.

1837 Carlyle *Fr. Rev.* III. II. v, The rest.. welter amid Law of Nations, Social Contract, Juristics, Syllogistics.

ju'ristical, *a.* [f. as prec. + -al[1].] = prec.

1854 *Fraser's Mag.* XLIX. 483 The juristical training of his mind and the legal discipline of his intellect. **1871** Markby *Elem. Law* (1874) §123 There is a fictitious person, or, as I prefer to call it, a juristical person.. to which all the rights are supposed to belong.

Hence **ju'ristically** *adv.*, in relation to law, from a legal point of view.

1878 F. Harrison *Eng. Sch. Jurispr.* I. in *Fortn. Rev.* Oct. 489 Politically and socially speaking, law rests on something more than force. Juristically speaking, it rests on force, and force alone. **1881** *Blackw. Mag.* Apr. 540 Possession is morally as well as juristically nine points of the law.

jurnalle, jurney, obs. ff. journal, journey.

jurnut, obs. variant of gernut.

1674–91 Ray *N.C. Words* 39 *Jurnut*, Earth Nut, *Bulbocastanum*.

juror ('dʒʊərə(r)). Forms: 4–6 iurrour(e, 4–7 iurour, (4 ? ieror, 4–5 iuroure, -owre, 5 iorour, -owre, iorrour, 6 iourer, iewror), 6–7 iuror, (7 iurer, jurer), 7– juror. [a. AF. *jurour* = OF. *jureor* (later *jureur*, 12th c.) = Pr. *jurador*, It. *giuratore*:—L. *jūrātōr-em*, agent-n. from *jūrāre* to swear. The L. *jūrātor* and AF. *jurour* occur in Eng. records long before the vernacular word.]

1. One of a company of persons (orig. men) sworn to deliver a verdict on a matter officially referred to them; a member of a jury; a juryman or jury-woman.

The word has the same historical development as is seen in jury, but has now a wider range of application than *juryman* and *jury-woman*, being freely used historically of members of the ancient inquests out of which the jury system arose, as well as of members of a jury chosen to adjudicate between competitors, and award prizes, to whom 'juryman' is seldom applied.

[**1188** Glanvill II. xvii, Aut bene notum est ius ipsum ipsis iuratoribus omnibus aut quidam sciunt.. aut omnes ignorant. **1290** *Rolls Parlt.* I. 19/2 In cujus rei testimonium predicti Juratores Sigilla sua apposuerunt. Et dicunt.. quod dampna illa se extendunt ad Viginti Libras. **1292** Britton I. i. §11 Et volums qe.. nos Justices.. ne pasent mie les pointz de nos brefs, ne des presentementz de jurours. *Ibid.* I. v. §8 Cum.. les jurours soint venuz en court, si porunt il estre chalengez.] **1377** Langl. *P. Pl.* B. vii. 44 Ac many a iustice an[d] iuroure wolde for Iohan do more. *c* **1380** Wyclif *Wks.* (1880) 183 ȝit iurrouris in questis wolen forsweren hem wittyngly for here dyner and a noble. ? *c* **1400** Lydg. *Æsop's Fab.* iii. 133 Al suche raveyne.. Beganne at false jurrours and at false witnesse. **1530–1** *Act 22 Hen. VIII*, c. 14 It shall be forthwith tried.. by the same iurours of the same countie. **1579** Fulke *Heskins Parl.* 389 We haue excepted against many of the Iewrors. **1602** T. Fitzherbert *Apol.* 12 Our Iurers are not to Iudge de Iure, but de facto, not of matter of Lawes, or right it self, but of matter of fact only. **1613** Shaks. *Hen. VIII*, v. iii. 60, I shall both finde your Lordship, Iudge and Iuror, You are so mercifull. **1769** Blackstone *Comm.* IV. x. 140 The false verdict of jurors, whether occasioned by embracery or not, was antiently considered as criminal. **1821** J. Q. Adams in C. Davies *Metr. Syst.* III. (1871) 126 The attorney-general.. agreed to withdraw a juror and advised to leave the remedy to parliament. **1877** Ld. Cairns in *Law Rep.* 3 App. Cases 197 The judge has a certain duty to discharge, and the jurors have another and a different duty.

b. With qualification, as ***grand juror, common*** or ***petty juror, special juror***. (Cf. jury *sb.* 2.)

1596 Shaks. *1 Hen. IV*, II. ii. 96 You are Grand Iurers, are ye? Wee'l iure ye ifaith. **1681** *Lond. Gaz.* No. 1667/3 The humble and joynt Addresse of.. the Grand Jurors of Your Majesties County of Montgomery. **1809** Tomlins *Law Dict.* s.v. *Jury* i, The Jurors contained in the panel are either *special* or *common* Jurors. **1823** J. F. Cooper *Pioneers* xxxiii. (1869) 141/2 On his way to hear and to decide the disputes of his neighbours, as a petit juror. **1883** *Wharton's Law Lex.* (ed. 7) s.v. *Jury*, There is no remuneration for common jurors.. Special jurors get a guinea a cause by s. 34 of 6 Geo. IV. c. 50. **1891** *Law Times* XCI. 205/2 The functions of a grand juror are too often those of the fifth wheel in the coach.

†**2.** (From the corrupt conduct formerly attributed to jurors.) One who brings false witness or a false presentment (against the innocent, or in favour of the guilty); a slanderer, backbiter; an oppressor; a covetous man. *Obs.*

c **1380** Wyclif *Wks.* (1880) 63 þei.. hiren also iurrouris & oþere gentil men of contre to forswere hem wyttyngly on þe bok. *c* **1380** —— *Sel. Wks.* III. 394 If þer be any cursid jurour extorsioner or avoutrer, he wil not be schryven at his owne curat, bot go to a flatryng frere, þat wil asoyle hym falsely for a litel money by ȝeere. *c* **1440** *Gesta Rom.* II. lii. 372 (Add. MS.) Bi the foxe are vndirstondyn vokettes.. courteers, Iurrours, and wily men. **1509** Barclay *Shyp of Folys* (1570) 151 Sclaunderers, lyers, and iurours of the syse. **1538** Bale *Johan Baptiste* 85 in *Harl. Misc.* I. 104 The covetouse iourer shall now be lyberall. **1550** —— *Image both Ch.* (*Rev.* xiv. 18) Sodainly as a snare shall that terrible day light vpon them vnbewares, as did death on the couetous iourer.

3. One of a body of persons appointed to award prizes in a competition.

1851 *Illustr. Catal. Gt. Exhib.* 34 If exhibitors accepted the office of jurors, they ceased to be competitors for prizes in the class to which they were appointed.

4. One who takes or has taken an oath; one who swears allegiance to some body or cause. (Cf. non-juror.)

c **1592** Marlowe *Massacre Paris* II. vi, I am a juror in the holy league. **1623** Cockeram, *Iuror*, a swearer. *c* **1700** Ken in Anderdon *Life* xxiv. (1854) 691 [Frampton had] never interrupted communion with the jurors, [and would concur in anything which tended to peace]. **1881** Agnew *Theol. Consol.* 287 The Presbyterian ministers who were jurors, were regarded as lukewarm servants of their Church and country.

b. A profane swearer. *nonce-word.*

1653 Urquhart *Rabelais* I. xvii, The Parisians.. are by nature both good Jurers and good Jurists, and somewhat overweening. **1709** Steele *Tatler* No. 137 ¶3 (Were there no Crime in it) nothing could be more diverting than the Impertinence of the High Juror.

†**'jurory.** *Obs.* In 5 iorory, iorowrye, iurrowry, iorourry. [f. juror 2 + -y: cf. OF. *jurerie* 'fonction du juré' (Godef.).] Bearing of false witness or false presentments; slander, defamation. (Cf. juror 2.)

c **1440** *Promp. Parv.* 265/1 Iorowrye (*P.* iorory), *susurrium.* *c* **1485** *Digby Myst.* v. 639 And I vse Iorourry, Enbrace questes of periury.

jurr. *Sc.* A low or worthless woman.

1786 Burns *A. Armour's Prayer* vii, As for the jurr, poor worthless body, She's got mischief enough already. **1885** Edgar *Old Ch. Life Scotl.* 337 The scandalous conduct of this 'jurr' led to a public demonstration of feeling.

jurram, variant of jorram.

jury ('dʒʊərɪ), *sb.* Forms: 4 iuree, 4–5 iure, 5 iurye, 6–7 iurie, 7 jurie, (6 iewrie, 7 jewry), 6–7 iury, 7– jury. [a. AF. *juree, jure* (as in senses 1, 2) = OF. *jurée* oath, juridical inquiry, inquest; med.L. *jūrāta*, sb. from fem. pa. pple. of *jūrāre* to swear (see -ade suffix).]

I. In legal use.

1. A company of persons (orig. men) sworn to render a 'verdict' or true answer upon some question or questions officially submitted to them; in modern times, in a court of justice, usually upon evidence delivered to them touching the issue; but in the earliest times usually upon facts or matters within their own knowledge, for which reason they were summoned from the neighbourhood to which the question submitted to them related, or in which the person or persons lived as to whose

conduct or death an 'inquest' or investigation was held.

Originally, 'The question to be addressed to them may take many different forms: it may or may not be one which has arisen in the course of litigation; it may be a question of fact or a question of law, or again what we should now-a-days call a question of mixed fact and law. What are the customs of your district? What rights has the king in your district? Name all the land-owners of your district and say how much land each of them has. Name all the persons in your district whom you suspect of murder, robbery or rape. Is Roger guilty of having murdered Ralph? Whether of the two has the greatest right to Blackacre, William or Hugh? Did Henry disseise Richard of his free tenement in Dale? The jury of trial, the jury of accusation, the jury which is summoned where there is no litigation merely in order that the king may obtain information, these all spring from a common root' (Pollock & Maitland *Hist. Eng. Law* I. 118).

Concerning the origin of the jury system in its various applications, and esp. of trial by jury, much has been written; but the name, in its English form, is not known to us till a *jury* had practically become what it is now, as a grand jury at an assize or at quarter sessions, a common or special jury in a criminal or civil trial, or a coroner's jury at an inquest (see CORONER and INQUEST).

In England, juries in all criminal trials, in civil trials in the superior courts, and in writs of inquiry, consist of 12 people, who must usually be unanimous in their verdict except by agreement of the parties. A coroner's jury may consist of any number from 7 to 11; and in this, a majority verdict is sufficient. Juries in county courts consist of 8. In Scotland, the number of a jury in a criminal trial is 15, and the verdict of a majority is accepted; in a civil trial, the number is 12, as in England.

[**1188** GLANVILL IX. xi, Inquirentur autem huiusmodi purpresture..per iuratam patrie siue visineti. **1290** *Rolls Parlt.* I. 20/1 Cum jur[atores] illius Inquis[itionis] calumpniavit qui per calumpniam suam amoti fuerunt de Jur[ata] illa. **1292** BRITTON I. xxii. §10 Des viscountes et des bailliffs qi ount plus de gentz somouns qe mester ne serroit en jureez et en enquests. *Ibid.*, Et de ceux ausi qi ount mis en jureez et en enquestes gentz malades. **1328** *Rolls Parlt.* II. 19/2 Il ne doit estre en Jurrez et Assises, si est il mys en un Jure de graunt Assise..devant les Justices du Baunk.] ? *a* **1400** *Morte Arth.* 662 Ordayne thy selvene bathe jureez, and juggez, and justicez of landes. **1467** *Waterf. Arch.* in *10th Rep. Hist. MSS. Comm.* App. v. 305 There shal none of the saide counsaile..passe in no jure betwene party and party. **1494** FABYAN *Chron.* 351 A quest of .xii. Knyghtes of Myddlessex, sworne vpon a iurye, atwene the abbot of Westmynster and the cyte, for certayne pryuyleges that the cytezens of London claymed within Westmester. **1533** MORE *Debell. Salem* Wks. 988, I durst as wel trust ye truth of one iudge as of two iuries. **1603** SHAKS. *Meas. for M.* II. i. 19 The Iury passing on the Prisoners life May in the sworne-twelue haue a thiefe or two. **1607** COWELL *Interpr.* s.v. *Homage*, Homage is sometime vsed for the Iurie in the Courte Baron..because it consisteth most commonly of such, as owe homage vnto the Lord of the fee. **1632** *Star Chamb. Cases* (Camden) 178 None are excused from tryalls of jurie and serving in juries under the degree of a noble man. **1709** STEELE *Tatler* No. 50 ¶12 Submitting my self to be try'd by my Country, and allowing any Jury of 12 good Men, and true, to be that Country. **1769** BLACKSTONE *Comm.* IV. xxiii. 301 An inquisition of office is the act of a jury summoned by the proper officer to enquire of matters relating to the crown, upon evidence laid before them. **1852** FORSYTH *Trial by Jury* 206 It is quite clear that the separation of the accusing from the trying jury existed in the reign of Edw. III. **1859** DICKENS *T. Two Cities* II. xii, The jury did not even turn to consider. **1895** POLLOCK & MAITLAND *Hist. Eng. Law* I. 122 The great fiscal record known to us as Domesday Book was compiled out of the verdicts of juries.

2. With particularizing additions:

a. ***coroner's jury***: see CORONER and INQUEST.

a **1548** HALL *Chron., Hen. VIII* 55 The sentence of the quest, subscribed by the crowner..and so the sayd Iury hathe sworne. **1667** PEPYS *Diary* 22 Jan., Find the Crowner's jury sitting. **1762** GOLDSM. *Nash* 96 The coroner's jury being impanelled, brought in their verdict lunacy. **1883** *Wharton's Law-Lex.* (ed. 7) s.v., Unanimity is not required from a grand jury or a coroner's jury.

b. ***grand jury***: a jury of inquiry, accusation, or presentment (as distinguished from a petty jury or jury of trial), consisting of from twelve to twenty-three 'good and lawful men of a county', who were returned by the sheriff to every session of the peace, and of the assizes, to receive and inquire into indictments, before these were submitted to a trial jury, and to perform such other duties as were committed to them. *Hist.* exc. *U.S.*

This body represents the *grand* INQUEST (q.v.) of earlier times. In England its action by statute and usage became greatly restricted; its principal duty before its abolition in 1933 was 'to examine into accusations against persons charged with crime, and if it see just cause, then to find bills of indictment against them, to be presented to the court'; besides which, however, it could express opinions on changes in judicial procedure, make recommendations on this and kindred subjects, make presentments of nuisances, etc. Formerly, a Grand Jury of twenty-four was summoned also upon a writ of attaint, to inquire whether a petty jury had given a false or corrupt verdict (abolished by 6 Geo. IV, c. 50). In Ireland the Grand Jury had, down to 1898, very extensive powers in reference to the general administration of the country. In Scotland *grand juries* have never existed.

[**1433** *Rolls Parlt.* IV. 448/2 Pleder tiel feint & faux plee & delaier le graund Jurre, quant il fuist prest de passer.] **1495** *Act 11 Hen. VII*, c. 21 If it be founden by the graunde Iurie in the same Atteynt that the petite Iury haven geven a true Verdite, that then the graunde Iurie shall have auctoritie and power to enquire if any of the petit Iury toke or perceyved any Somme of Money, or other rewarde [etc.]. **1523** FITZHERB. *Surv.* 22b, Euery man of the graunt iury, must haue landes to the value of .xx. li. of freholde. **1607** COWEL *Interpr.* s.v., The Grand Iurie consisteth ordinarily of 24 graue and substantiall gentlemen..to consider of all bils of Inditement preferred to the court. **1635** *Irish Acts 10 Chas. I*, c. 26 §3 The said Iustices..with the assent of the Grand-Iury, shall have power..to taxe..every Inhabitant ..for the new building, repayring [etc.]..of such Bridges, Causeyes and Toghers. **1714** MANDEVILLE *Fab. Bees* (1725) I. Pref. 12 The book..has been presented by the grand-jury, and condemn'd by thousands who never saw a word of it. **1769** BLACKSTONE *Comm.* IV. xxiii. 301 As many as appear upon this panel are sworn upon the grand jury, to the amount of twelve at the least, and not more than twenty-three; that twelve may be a majority. **1817** *Parl. Deb.* (*Ho. Lords*) 1825 Irish Grand Jury Presentment Bill... The Earl of Donoughmore opposed the measure..because..it deprived grand juries of the power of appointing their own officers. **1827** HALLAM *Const. Hist.* (1876) III. xvi. 271 The grand jury of Kent..presented accordingly a petition on the 8th of May 1701. **1881** HENDERSON in *Encycl. Brit.* XIII. 240/1 The power of imposing county rates [in Ireland] is, except in the case of the county of Dublin, exercised by the grand juries..at the assizes.

c. ***petty*** (or ***petit***) ***jury*** (in contradistinction to *grand jury*), ***trial jury***, ***traverse jury***, or ***common jury*** (in contradistinction to *special jury*): a jury which tries the final issue of fact in civil or criminal proceedings, and pronounces its decision in a 'verdict' upon which the court gives judgement.

1495 [see prec.]. **1533** MORE *Debell. Salem* Wks. 998/2 Yf it apere vnto the graund iurye in theyr conscience, that the petyt iury wylfully of som corrupt mynde regarded not the wytnesses. **1607** in COWEL. **1711** ADDISON *Spect.* No. 122 ¶3 He..has been several times Foreman of the Petty-Jury. **1768** BLACKSTONE *Comm.* III. xxiii. 358 A common jury is one returned by the sheriff according to the directions of the statute 3 Geo. II. c. 25. which appoints that the sheriff.. shall not return a separate panel for every separate cause, as formerly. **1863** H. COX *Instit.* II. ix. 517 Where an information is filed..it must be tried by a special or petit jury.

d. ***special jury***: a jury consisting of persons who (being on the Jurors' book) are of a certain station in society, as esquires, bankers, or merchants, or occupy a house or other premises of a certain rateable value. ***good jury***: see quot. 1898.

a **1726** GILBERT *Cas. Law & Eq.* (1760) 130 The Court granted a rule for a good jury in Middlesex. **1730** *Act 3 Geo. II*, c. 25 §15 In such manner as special Juries have been and are usually struck. **1768** BLACKSTONE *Comm.* III. xxiii. 357 Special juries were originally introduced in trials at bar, when the causes were of too great nicety for the discussion of ordinary freeholders; or where the sheriff was suspected of partiality. **1844** LD. BROUGHAM *Brit. Const.* xix. §6 (1862) 351 Tried by a special jury—that is, by persons of a superior rank. **1870** SIR W. BOVILL in *Law Rep.* 5 C.P. 167 The practice of ordering a good jury existed long before the passing of the Acts which regulate special juries. **1898** THAYER *Evid. Com. Law* 419 The development of the mercantile law by the use of special juries. **1898** A. W. DONALD in *Encycl. Laws Eng.* (Renton) VII. 154 *A Good Jury*—a jury obtained by a judge's order for the purposes of a writ of inquiry. In London since the passing of the Juries Act of 1825, the sheriffs on receiving an order for a good jury have treated it as an order for a special jury.

e. ***jury de medietate*** [med.L., = of halfness or moiety], a jury composed equally of two classes of men, a half-and-half jury; esp. (***j. de medietate linguæ***) one composed half of Englishmen and half of foreigners.

1768 BLACKSTONE *Comm.* III. xxiii. 360 Motion to the court for a jury *de medietate linguæ*. **1769** *Ibid.* IV. x. 128 Imbezzling or vacating records..may be tried either in the king's bench or common pleas, by a jury *de medietate*: half officers of any of the superior courts, and the other half common jurors. *Ibid.* IV. xix. 278 By a jury formed *de medietate*, half of freeholders and half of matriculated persons, is the indictment to be tried [at Oxford]. **1870** *Act 33 Vict.* c. 14 §5 From and after the passing of this Act, an alien shall not be entitled to be tried by a jury *de medietate linguæ*.

f. ***jury of matrons***: a jury of discreet women impanelled to inquire into a case of alleged pregnancy.

1710–11 ADDISON *Tatler* No. 116 ¶1, I desired the Jury of Matrons, who stood at my Right Hand, to inform themselves of her Condition. **1769** BLACKSTONE *Comm.* IV. 395 In case this plea be made in stay of execution, the judge must direct a jury of twelve matrons or discreet women to inquire the fact. **1845** *Encycl. Brit.* (ed. 8) s.v., A jury of matrons is resorted to, in a writ *de ventre inspiciendo*, or when a feminine prisoner condemned to death pleads pregnancy in stay of execution.

II. *transf.*

3. Applied historically to the body of DICASTS (δικασταί) of ancient Athens, or the *judices* of ancient Rome, whose functions corresponded in part to those of an English jury.

1856 C. R. KENNEDY tr. *Demosthenes* Midias 63 The rudeness and the insolence, men of the jury, with which Midias uniformly behaves to all, are pretty well known, I imagine, both to you and to the rest of my fellow-countrymen. **1881** S. H. BUTCHER *Demosthenes* i. (1893) 10 In the time of Lysias corrupt officials often told the jury point-blank that unless they gave an adverse verdict there would be no funds to pay their salaries. *Ibid.* 12 It is not easy to see how juries consisting of five hundred members or more could be effectively bribed.

4. A body of persons selected to award prizes in an exhibition or competition.

1851 *Illustr. Catal. Gt. Exhib.* 30 In announcing the Prizes, the Commissioners laid down certain general principles for the guidance of the Juries. **1900** *Westm. Gaz.* 8 May 10/1 The prize-jury..examined the merits of no fewer than 990 competitive stories.

†5. (from the usual number of persons in a jury in sense 1.) A company of twelve; a dozen. *Obs.*

1592 WARNER *Alb. Eng.* VII. xxxvi. (1612) 172 Three-headed Cerberus in chaines should make the Iurie full. **1649** FULLER *Just Man's Fun.* 27 All the Jurie of the Apostles. **1650** —— *Pisgah* Ezek. Vis. i, A compleate square..with a just Jury of gates, three on each side.

III. 6. *attrib.* and *Comb.*, as ***jury-packing***, ***-panel***, ***-roll***, ***-room***, ***service***, ***system***, ***-trial***; **jury-book**, a book containing the names of persons liable to serve on juries; **jury-box**, an enclosed space in which the jury sit in court; **jury chancellor**, the foreman of a jury (in Scotland): = CHANCELLOR 8; **jury-fixer** *U.S.*, one who bribes or otherwise illegally influences a jury or juror; so ***jury-fixing***; **jury-list**, a list of persons liable to be summoned to act as jurymen; †**jury-process**, a writ formerly issued for the summoning of a jury; **jury-trial**, trial by jury; **jury-woman**, (*a*) one of a jury of matrons; (*b*) a female juror.

1870 *Act 33 & 34 Vict.* c. 77 §12 No person whose name shall be in the *jury book as a juror shall be entitled to be excused from attendance. **1826** SYD. SMITH *Wks.* (1859) II. 112/2 He does not conjure the farmers in the *jury-box, by the love which they bear to their children. **1867** TROLLOPE *Chron. Barset* xli, The men in the jury-box may decide it how they will. **1867** CARLYLE *Remin.* II. 10 The *jury chancellor..smote his now dry brow with a gesture of despair. **1882** *Washington Post* 18 Mar. (Th.), There might be some scope in the proceedings before the Grand Jury for a '*jury fixer'. **1931** *Blue Valley Farmer* (Okla. City) 24 Dec. 1/6 Fill the town with secret service men to catch the jury fixers. **1887** *Library Mag.* Apr. 531/2 Bribery and *jury-fixing would speedily disappear. **1946** C. MCWILLIAMS *Southern California Country* 245 The long and sordid aftermath, involving jury-fixing, bribery, and murder. **1825** *Act 6 Geo. IV*, c. 50 §6 *marg.*, High Constables to issue Precepts to Churchwardens, etc...to make out *Jury Lists. **1887** *Westm. Rev.* June, An address, in which they complain ..of *jury-packing; of the land tenure; of trade regulations confining them to certain markets. **1888** *Times* (weekly ed.) 21 Dec. 2/4 The usual charge against the Executive of jury packing. **1891** T. E. BRIDGETT *Life Sir T. More* 416 A *jury-panel was formed. **1828** P. CUNNINGHAM *N.S. Wales* (ed. 3) II. 127 A chance would thus be afforded of having an honest man on the *jury-roll. *a* **1832** MACKINTOSH *Revol.* 1688 Wks. 1846 II. 296 The friends of the Bishops watched at the door of the *jury-room, and heard loud voices at midnight. **1955** *Radio Times* 22 Apr. 28/3 *Jury Service is often regarded as a tiresome duty. **1973** E. MCGIRR *Bardel's Murder* i. 26, I got caught for jury service, six horrible days of it. **1875** W. STUBBS *Constitutional Hist. Eng.* I. xiii. 611 Many writers of authority have maintained that the entire *jury system is indigenous in England. **1974** *Times* 2 May 18/6 The acquittals..demonstrate the strength of a jury system which acquits when there is reasonable doubt. **1810** BENTHAM *Packing* (1821) 91 When a political libel is the offence, the form of *jury trial is but a melancholy farce. **1844** LD. BROUGHAM *Brit. Const.* ix. §3 (1862) 126 The use of Jury-trial is admirable..where a question of conflicting evidence arises. **1805** EUGENIA DE ACTON *Nuns of Desert* I. 236 We wish to bribe her *Jury-women, but they are inflexible. **1883** *Wharton's Law-Lex.* (ed. 7), *Jury-woman*, or *Jury of Matrons*. **1927** *Daily Tel.* 24 May 17/6 The manner in which the recalcitrant jurywoman is eventually brought round is not altogether convincing. **1962** *Punch* 21 Nov. 733/2 One of the two jury-women who made up our twelve disappeared completely during the last day's hearing.

Hence ˈ**juryless** *a.*, without a jury.

1808 BENTHAM *Sc. Reform* 29 By a wicked and jury-less Court of Conscience act. **1810** —— *Packing* (1821) 115 A Juryless Judge preferable to a covertly pensioned Jury.

jury-, jury *a.* (*Naut.*): see under JURY-MAST.

juryer, juryour: see JURIER.

juryman (ˈdʒʊərɪmən). [f. JURY + MAN.] A man serving on a jury; a member of a jury: = JUROR 1.

1579 FULKE *Heskins' Parl.* 389 To make him a lawfull Iewrie man. **1652** W. LEACH (*title*) The Bribe-Takers of Jurymen discovered. **1712–14** POPE *Rape Lock* III. 22 The hungry Judges soon the sentence sign, And wretches hang that jury-men may dine. **1768** BLACKSTONE *Comm.* III. xxiii. 380 Here therefore a competent number of sensible and upright jurymen..will be found the best investigators of truth. **1861** PEARSON *Early & Mid. Ages Eng.* 24 The distinction of the judge of law from the judge of fact or juryman was derived from Italian sources many hundred years later.

b. As rendering of Gr. δικαστής DICAST or of L. *judex*.

1879 FROUDE *Cæsar* iii. 26 All cases of importance, civil or criminal, came before courts of sixty or seventy jurymen. **1881** S. H. BUTCHER *Demosthenes* i. (1893) 10 There were still jurymen eager to serve and litigants ready to supply cases.

c. With qualification, as ***grand-juryman***, a member of a grand jury.

1599 NASHE *Lenten Stuffe* 3 I'le be sworne hee was a grande iurie man, in respect of me. **1601** SHAKS. *Twel. N.* III. ii. 17 They haue beene grand Iurie men, since before Noah was a Saylor. **1752** J. LOUTHIAN *Form of Process* (ed. 2) 196 Naming all the Grand Jury-mens Names without their Additions. **1881** E. ROBERTSON in *Encycl. Brit.* XIII. 786/1 The qualification of the grand jurymen is that they should be freeholders of the county,—to what amount appears to be uncertain.

'jury-,mast. [Origin unknown.
App. either a corruption of some earlier name, or a jocular appellation invented by sailors. For the suggestion that it may have been short for *injury-mast*, no supporting evidence has been found.]

1. *Naut.* A temporary mast put up in place of one that has been broken or carried away.

1616 CAPT. SMITH *Descr. New Eng.* 50 We had reaccommodated her a Iury mast, and the rest, to returne for Plimouth. **1627** —— *Seaman's Gram.* iv. 18 A Iury Mast, that is, when a Mast is borne by the boord, with Yards, Roofes, Trees, or what they can, spliced or fished together they make a Iury-mast. **1750** BLANCKLEY *Naval Expos.* 84 *Jury Mast.* Whatever is set up in the Room of a Mast lost in a Fight, or by a Storm, and fastened into the Partners, and fitted with a lesser Yard, Sails, and Ropes, is called a Jury Mast. **1782** in Nicolas *Disp. Nelson* (1845) I. 55 We have been employed since in getting jury-masts yards and bowsprit, and stopping the holes in our sides. **1847** LD. G. BENTINCK in *Croker Papers* (1884) III. xxv. 144 To keep the dismantled ship floating and fighting under jury-masts.

b. So *jury foremast, jury mainmast*, etc.

1719 DE FOE *Crusoe* II. ii, Having no sails..but a main course, and a kind of square sail upon a jury fore-mast. **1748** *Anson's Voy.* III. i. 297 We saw her main-top mast, which had hitherto served as a jury main-mast, share the same fate. **1836** MARRYAT *Midsh. Easy* (1863) 190 Before the day was over, a jury-foremast had been got up.

c. *transf.* An apparatus employed in the treatment of Pott's disease, to keep the spinal column straight, and prevent lateral curvature.

1883 HOLMES & HULKE *Syst. Surgery* (ed. 3) II. 413 In Professor Sayre's Plaster of Paris Corset and Jury-mast..we have a much better appliance. **1894** *Lancet* 3 Nov. 1029.

2. Hence *jury-* is used in comb. to designate other parts of a ship put together or contrived for temporary use, as **jury-rig, jury-rigging** (whence **jury-rig** *v.*, **jury-rigged** *ppl. a.*), **jury-rudder, jury-tiller**; and humorously of other things as **jury-buttocks; jury-leg**, a wooden leg, or any contrivance to supply the place of a disabled leg (whence **jury-legged** *a.*); **jury meal**.

1666 DENHAM *Direct. Painter* II. (1667) 25 Guard thy Posterior least all be gone; Though Jury-Masts, tho'hast Jury-buttocks none. **1751** SMOLLETT *Per. Pic.* I. vi, You jury-legged dog. **1788** NEWTE *Tour Eng. & Scot.* 116 The ships to be jury rigged: that is, to have smaller masts, yards, and rigging, than would be required for actual service. **1840** MARRYAT *Poor Jack* xxiii, Having jury-rigged her aft, we steered our course. **1844** MACAULAY *Misc., Barère* (1860) II. 127 She may come safe into port under jury rigging. **1850** *Tait's Mag.* XVII. 422/2 To rig him out with a sort of jury-leg, manufactured for the nonce from a young tree. **1867** SMYTH *Sailor's Word-bk., Jury-rudder*, a contrivance..for supplying a vessel with the means of steering when an accident has befallen the rudder. **1883** *Century Mag.* Oct. 944/1 The steward..had a jury-meal rigged up in presentable shape.

b. Hence *jury* is also taken independently as an *adj.* = temporary, makeshift.

1821 BYRON *Let. to Rogers* 21 Oct., I have..some jury chairs and tables. **1833** MARRYAT *P. Simple* xlvi, Rig something jury forward, and follow me. **1835** SIR J. ROSS *Narr. 2nd Voy.* iii. 38 We..set up the new topmast in place of the jury one.

jurysdycall, obs. variant of JURIDICAL.

jus, juse, obs. form of JUICE.

jus, jus', colloq. and dial. shortening of JUST *adv.*

1801 T. TENNEY *Female Quixotism* II. xiv. 145 He kill us all, one after toder, jus as easy as we kill chickens. **1884** J. C. EGERTON *Sussex Folk* iii. 33, I jus should be glad if you could get rid an 'em for me. **1935** Z. N. HURSTON *Mules & Men* (1970) I. i. 28 Jus' go wid Gabriel. **1973** *Black World* July 56/2 We jus' laid on the corner and watched. *Ibid.* Aug. 55/1 He walked over to the Village an' dug a backdoor with a lock jus' beggin' to be picked.

‖**jus cogens** (dʒʌs 'kəʊgɛnz). [L., compelling law.] A principle of international law which cannot be set aside by agreement or acquiescence. So, in modern use, as laid down by the Vienna Convention on the Law of Treaties (1969), 'a peremptory norm of general international law'. (See quots.)

1895 W. H. RATTIGAN *Private Internat. Law* vi. 163 A *jus cogens* regulating rights of this description is a product of modern commercial and intellectual activity, and finds no place, for instance, in the jurisprudence of the Roman Empire. **1937** *Amer. Jrnl. Internat. Law* XXXI. 571 The answer to this question depends on the preliminary question, whether general international law contains rules which have the character of *jus cogens.* **1945** M. WOLFF *Private Internat. Law* III. 168 Savigny..clearly showed that the rules of an absolute, imperative character (the *ius cogens*) to be found in any legal system are of two kinds. There are first of all those rules 'that are enacted merely for the sake of persons who are the possessors of rights', such as the laws limiting the capacity to act on account of age or sex, or laws concerning the transfer of property; and secondly the rules that are not made solely for the benefit of single individuals but rest on moral grounds, or on the 'public interest'... *ius cogens privatorum pactis mutari non potest.* **1957** G. SCHWARZENBERGER *Internat. Law* (ed. 3) I. xx. 352 In this respect, the rules governing the principle of the freedom of the seas are not *jus cogens* which as such is unalterable, but as much *jus dispositivum* as any of the other rules of international law. **1960** F. A. MANN in *Brit. Year Bk. Internat. Law 1959* 45 Lord McNair must allow the *jus cogens* of the proper law to override the general principles which are merely incorporated into it. **1965** *Texas Law Rev.* XLIII. 455 The problem of international *jus cogens* can be stated in a simple question: Are there rules of international law which, by consent, individual subjects of international law may not modify? **1969** *Vienna Convention on Law of Treaties* 18 in *Parl. Papers 1968–9* (Cmnd. 4140) LV. 395 Treaties conflicting with a peremptory norm of general international law (jus cogens). A treaty is void if, at the time of its conclusion, it conflicts with a peremptory norm of general international law. For the purposes of the present Convention, a peremptory norm of general international law is a norm accepted and recognized by the international community of States as a whole as a norm from which no derogation is permitted and which can be modified only by a subsequent norm of general international law having the same character. **1971** M. AKEHURST *Mod. Introd. Internat. Law* (ed. 2) iii. 60 The technical name now given to the basic principles of international law, which states are not allowed to contract out of, is 'peremptory norms of general international law', otherwise known as *jus cogens.*

‖**jus gentium** (dʒʌs 'dʒɛnʃɪəm). [L.] = *law of nations* (see LAW *sb.*[1] 4 c).

1548 HOOPER *Declar. Commandm.* iii. 31 They shuld observe the commune lawes vsyd among all people whiche is callid ius gentium. **1682** EVELYN *Let.* 19 Sept. in *Diary & Corresp.* (1906) 666 The right of passes, and petitions thereupon, were formed upon another part of the *Jus Gentium*, than our pretended dominion of the seas. **1771** 'JUNIUS' *Lett.* (1772) II. lxi. 285 Any law that contradicts or excludes the common law of England; whether it be *canon, civil, jus gentium*, or *levitical.* **1839** *Penny Cycl.* XIII. 361/2 According to their [*sc.* Roman lawyers'] phraseology,..*jus gentium* consists of those rules of law which are common to all nations. **1856** BOUVIER *Law Dict.* (ed. 6) I. 685 Among the Romans by *jus civile* was understood the civil law, in contradistinction to the public law, or *jus gentium.* **1880** *Encycl. Brit.* XIII. 191/1 The ambiguity of the phrase *jus gentium* enabled the early founders of international law to apply the principles of the *jus naturæ* to the conduct of states *inter se* in a way of which there is no example in the Roman law-books. **1959** JOWITT *Dict. Eng. Law* II. 1035/1 *Jus gentium*, the law of nations.

jusi ('huːsiː). Also **husi, jussi.** [a. Sp. *jusi*, ad. Tagalog *husi.*] A delicate fibrous fabric woven in the Philippine Islands.

1851 *Illustr. Catal. Gt. Exhib.* IV. 1344/1 Piece of 'jusi', and a shawl of 'jusi'. *Ibid.*, Pieces of striped jusi dresses. **1902** *Encycl. Brit.* XXXI. 667/1 Beautiful fabrics called 'piña' and 'jusi', the former woven of pineapple-leaf fibre and the latter of this fibre mixed with silk.

‖**jus primæ noctis** (dʒʌs 'praɪmiː 'nɒktɪs). [L., right of the first night.] = *droit du seigneur* (see DROIT[1] 1 b).

1887 F. K. WISCHNEWETZKY tr. *Engels's Condition of Working-Class in England in 1844* 99 Factory servitude.. confers the *jus primæ noctis* upon the master... If the master is mean enough,..his mill is also his harem. **1911** *Encycl. Brit.* XV. 593/1 *Jus primae noctis* or *droit du seigneur*, a custom alleged to have existed in medieval Europe, giving the overlord a right to the virginity of his vassals' daughters on their wedding-night... The *jus*, it seems, is a myth, invented no earlier than the 16th or 17th century. **1923** A. HUXLEY *Antic Hay* xviii. 250 It was on a splendid subject —the 'Jus Primæ Noctis, or Droit du Seigneur'. **1933** 'G. ORWELL' *Down & Out* xxxiv. 256 He had heard..of..the *jus primae noctis* (he believed it had really existed). **1970** G. GREER *Female Eunuch* 228 No serf, writhing under the law of *jus primae noctis*,..ever had it worse. **1971** *Black Scholar* Dec. 13/1 The integration of rape into the sparsely furnished legitimate social life of the slaves harks back to the feudal 'right of the first night', the *jus primae noctis.*

jus'publicist. *nonce-wd.* [f. L. *jūs public-um* public law: see -IST.] One who has to do with public law or rights.

1809–10 COLERIDGE *Friend* (1865) 188 This..it is the province of the philosophical juspublicist to discover and display.

‖**jusqu'au bout** (ʒysko bu), *adv. phr.* [Fr.] To the end, to the conclusion, to completion; to the bitter end; *spec.* in the war of 1914–18, used in the context of carrying on fighting until a conclusive victory has been gained. Hence **jusqu'auboutisme**, the policy of carrying on to the bitter end; **jusqu'auboutist(e** (also without apostrophe), an advocate of *jusqu'auboutisme.*

1917 A. HUXLEY *Let.* 30 Sept. (1969) 134 Are the French socialists going to make much fuss at Bordeaux? I think and hope we are all Jusquauboutistes here. **1918** G. B. SHAW *What I really wrote about War* (1931) 280 In Constantinople it will be a matter of fighting *jusqu'au bout. Ibid.* 282, I am a Jusqu'auboutist. I do not want this war to be compromised as long as it will be possible for any of the belligerent Powers afterwards to pretend that if it had only gone on for another year it would have won. **1933** A. HUXLEY *Let.* 13 Aug. (1969) 372, I have never more passionately felt the need of using reason jusqu'au bout. **1968** *Listener* 4 July 12/1 The rhetoric of the klieg-lit European student leaders spouting mocking *jusqu'auboutisme* like post-Marxist Beatles.

†**jusquiam.** *Obs.* [= F. *jusquiame* (13th c. in Hatz.-Darm.), ad. late L. *iusquiamus* (Palladius).] = HYOSCYAMUS.

[*c* **1000** *Sax. Leechd.* I. 94 Ðeos wyrt þe man..iusquianum nemneð, & oðrum naman belone, & eac sume men henne belle hatað. *c* **1400** *Lanfranc's Cirurg.* 264. **1527** ANDREW *Brunswyke's Distyll. Waters* II. ccIxxv. T ij b/1 The venims of Opium and Iusquiamus. **1565** J. HALLE *Hist. Expost.* Table 52 *Hyosciamus*, henbane is called in Greeke 'Ὑοσκυαμος': in Latin: Hiosciamus..of the Apothecaries Iusquiamus.] **1727** BRADLEY *Fam. Dict.* s.v. *Goose*, Henbane, or Jusquiam, call'd the Death of young Geese. **1736** BAILEY *Househ. Dict.* 318 Take half an ounce of..the ointment of jusquiam.

†**jussel.** *Obs.* Forms: 4–5 iusshell(e, 5 gusschelle, guissell, iuschel(le, iuselle, 5–6 iussell(e, 5–7 iussel, iussall, 7 jussel, 8–9 *dial.* jossel, jossle. [a. OF. *jussel* juice, broth (Godef.), ad. L. *juscellum*, dim. of *jusculum*, dim. of *jūs* broth, soup.] In ancient cookery, a name including various forms of mince or hotch-potch.

? *c* **1390** *Forme of Cury* in Warner *Antiq. Culin.* (1791) 11 Jusshell... Jushell enforced. **14..** *Tourn. Tottenham, Feest* vii. in Hazl. *E.P.P.* III. 95 Ther come in iordans in iussall. *c* **1420** *Liber Cocorum* (1862) 11 Iusselle. Take myud bred, and eyren þou swynge; Do hom togeder with out lettyng, Take fresshe broth of gode befe, Coloure hit with safron, þat is me lefe, Boyle hit softly, and in þo boylyng, Do þer to sage and persely ȝoyng. *c* **1430** *Two Cookery-bks.* 16 Iuschelle of Fysshe. Take fayre Frye of Pyke, and caste it raw on a morter, an caste þer-to gratid brede [etc.]. *c* **1440** *Promp. Parv.* 268/1 Iusselle, or dyschelle, dyshemete.., *jussellum.* *c* **1450** *Two Cookery-bks.* 87 Guissell. **1513** *Bk. Keruynge* in *Babees Bk.* 273 Blaunche manger, Iussell, and charlet. **1552** HULOET, Iussell, a meat made of chopped herbes, *minutal.* **1781** J. HUTTON *Tour to Caves* Gloss. (E.D.S.), *Jossel*, an hodge-podge. **1828** *Craven Dial., Jossle*, hodge podge, a dish composed of a variety of meat.

Jussiæan (dʒʌsɪ'iːən), **Jussieu(e)an** (dʒʌsɪ'juːən), *a.* Also **Jussiean.** [f. mod.L. *Jussiæus*, or its origin, the French surname *Jussieu* + -AN.] Of or pertaining to Bernard de Jussieu (1699–1777) and his nephew Antoine Laurent de Jussieu (1748–1836), or to the natural system of botanical classification devised by them.

1824 J. C. LOUDON *Encycl. Gardening* (ed. 2) 47 All the hardy plants..arranged in groups, according to the Jussieuean system. **1857** A. HENFREY *Elem. Bot.* §392 The Jussieuan System. **1865** G. BENTHAM *Handbk. Brit. Flora* p. viii, The so-called Linnæan or Jussiæan systems. **1876** *Encycl. Brit.* IV. 81/1 It [*sc.* the Linnæan method] was superseded by the Jussiean method.

jussion ('dʒʌʃɛn). *rare.* [a. F. *jussion*, ad. L. *jussiōn-em* order, command, f. *juss-*: see next.] Order, command. ***letters of jussion*** [F. *lettres de jussion*], letters by which the French king ordered the parliament to register an ordinance.

1772 *Ann. Reg.* 90*/1 The King sent a message to the parliament, that if they did not obey his letters of jussion, and resume their functions, he would remove the magistrates from their employments. **1830** BENTHAM *Official Aptitude Maximized* Pref., Wks. 1843 V. 270/2 *note*, Imperation, in its two shapes—positive command, or say jussion, on the one hand, and prohibition, or say inhibition, on the other.

jussive ('dʒʌsɪv), *a.* (*sb.*) [f. L. *juss-*, ppl. stem of *jubēre* to command: see -IVE.] Expressing a command or order: esp. in Grammar, applied to forms of the verb.

1846 T. H. KEY *Lat. Gram.* 58 The imperative mood commands..The jussive mood directs. **1850** B. DAVIES tr. *Gesenius' Heb. Gram.* xlviii, We must distinguish..between the common form of the Future and..a shortened form (with a Jussive force). **1870** tr. *Lange's Comm., Song Sol.* vii. 166 The following voluntative or jussive future. **1881** *Athenæum* 27 Aug. 274/2 We do not believe in the jussive pluperfect subjunctive. **1899** A. N. JANNARIS in *Expositor* Apr. 299 The above jussive, or hortative and desiderative function of this infinitive.

B. *sb.* A verbal form expressing command.

1900 R. C. THOMPSON *Rep. Magic. Nineveh* II. p. xxxv, *Lillik-limur* are the equivalents of the Hebrew jussive.

†**'jussory,** *a. Obs. rare.* [f. as prec.: see -ORY.] Of or pertaining to command.

1613 PURCHAS *Pilgrimage* (1614) 183 Every of his members also doe provoke him to performe those iussorie inventions.

†**'jussulent,** *a. Obs. rare*⁻⁰. [ad. L. *jussulentus* having broth, f. *jūs* broth.] (See quots.)

1656 BLOUNT *Glossogr., Iussulent* (*jussulentus*), that which is sod or stewed in pottage or broth. **1658** PHILLIPS, *Jussulent*, full of broth or pottage.

just, *sb.*[1] Older form of JOUST *sb.*

†**just,** *sb.*[2] *Obs.* Also **iuste, iuyste, ioust.** [a. OF. *juste, juiste, juyste*, ad. med.L. *justa* (sc. *mensūra*) right measure (of drink); the vessel holding this (Du Cange).] A large-bellied pot with handles, used for holding wine or beer.

1387 TREVISA *Higden* (Rolls) VII. 121 Hym was ȝoven a iuste [*printed* viste, *MS. Harl.* 1900 (ibid. 513) iust, L. *iusta*] of gold, honoured wonderfully wiþ precious stones. **14..** *Voc.* in Wr.-Wülcker 598/16 *Obba*,..a Juyste. *c* **1440** *Promp. Parv.* 268/2 Iuste, potte. *a* **1529** SKELTON *Elynour Rummyng* 192 For they go to roust Streyght over the ale-ioust.

attrib. **1377** LANGL. *P. Pl.* B. XIII. 83, I shal iangle to þis Iurdan with his iust wombe.

just (dʒʌst), *a.* [a. F. *juste* (= Pr. *just*, Sp., Pg. *justo*, It. *giusto*) or immed. ad. L. *jūstus* righteous, equitable, rightful, f. *jūs* right, law, justice.]

1. That does what is morally right, righteous. ***just before (with) God*** or, simply, *just*: Righteous in the sight of God; justified. Now chiefly as a Biblical archaism.

1382 Wyclif Ezek. xxxiii. 12 The riȝtwijsnesse of a iust man [Vulg. justitia justi; 1388 The riȝtfulnesse of a riȝtful man]. —— Luke i. 6 Sothli thei bothe weren iuste [so 1388: Vulg. justi] bifore God. —— Rom. iii. 26 That he be iust [so 1388: Vulg. justus], and iustifyinge him that is of the feith of Ihesu Crist. 1526 Tindale Matt. v. 45 He..sendeth his reyne on the iuste and on the iniuste [Vulg. bonos et malos]. 1560 Daus tr. Sleidane's Comm. 6 Scripture, declareth playnly, howe it is faith that maketh us iust before God. 1561 T. Norton Calvin's Inst. iii. iv. §28. 211 The iustest man passeth no one day wherein he falleth not many times. 1659 Shirley Ajax & Ulysses iii, Only the actions of the just Smell sweet and blossom in the dust. 1719 Watts Hymn, 'Not to the terrors' iii, Behold the spirits of the just, Whose faith is turn'd to sight! 1824 R. Hall Wks. (1832) VI. 355 God can be at once the just and the justifier.

†b. absol. in singular. Obs. or arch.

1382 Wyclif Acts vii. 52 The prophetis..that bifore teelden of the comynge of the iust [1611 the Iust one]. 1526 Tindale Acts vii. 52 That iust whom ye haue betrayed. 1535 Coverdale Ps. xxxvi[i]. 12 The vngodly layeth wayte for the iust, & gnasȝsheth vpon him with his tethe [so 1611 and R.V.].

2. Upright and impartial in one's dealings; rendering every one his due; equitable.

1382 Wyclif 1 John i. 9 If we knowlechen oure synnes, he is feithful and iust [Vulg. justus] that he forȝiue to us our synnes. 1484 Caxton Fables of Æsop ii. Proem, The good ond Iuste be not subget to the lawe as we fynde and rede of alle the Athenyens. 1503 Dunbar Thistle & Rose 122 Scho ..bawd him be als just to awppis and owlis, As vnto pacokkis. 1553 T. Wilson Rhet. (1580) 209, I mistrust not the Iudges, because thei are iuste. 1605 Shaks. Lear v. iii. 170 The Gods are iust, and of our pleasant vices Make instruments to plagve vs. 1725 Pope Odyss. xiii. 249 Some juster prince perhaps had entertained, And safe restored me to my native land. 1771 Junius Lett. lvi. 294 How much easier it is to be generous than just. 1850 Tennyson In Mem. Prol., Thou madest man, he knows not why..And Thou hast made him: Thou art just. 1853 Lytton My Novel v. iii, He was just, but as a matter of business. He made no allowances. 1860 Ruskin Mod. Paint. V. ix. i. §13. 204 Just! What is that?..dealing equitably or equally.

†b. Faithful or honourable in one's social relations. Const. of, to. Obs.

1601 Shaks. Jul. C. iii. ii. 90 He was my Friend, faithfull, and iust to me. 1624 Capt. Smith Virginia i. 3 He was very iust of his promise. 1727 Pope Epit. R. Digby, Just of thy word, in ev'ry thought sincere. 1809 Campbell Gert. Wyom. iii. xxix, Friend to more than human friendship just.

3. a. Consonant with the principles of moral right or of equity; righteous; equitable; fair. Of rewards, punishments, etc.: Deserved, merited.

c1400 Destr. Troy 214 More it Ioyes me, Iason, of þi iust werkes. c1430 Hymns Virg. 114 The hiȝest lessoun þat man may lere Is to lyue iust lijf. 1553 Eden Treat. Newe Ind. (Arb.) 5 If honest commendacions be a iust reward dew to noble enterprises. 1590 R. Hitchcock Quintess. Wit 5 That warre is iust, that is necessarye. 1632 J. Hayward tr. Biondi's Eromena 33, I will never rest, till I have executed just vengeance on him that unjustly slew thee. 1766 Goldsm. Vic. W. viii, You'll think it just that I should give them an opportunity to retaliate. 1840 Dickens Barn. Rudge vi, Is this fair, or reasonable, or just to yourself?

quasi-sb. 1667 Milton P.L. vi. 381 Strength from Truth divided and from Just..naught merits but dispraise.

b. Constituted by law or by equity, grounded on right, lawful, rightful; that is such legally; †legally valid (obs.).

c1430 Lydg. Min. Poems (Percy Soc.) 17 The degre be just successioune..Unto the kyng is now descended doune. 1542 in Marsden Sel. Pl. Crt. Adm. (1894) I. 116 Being in his lyfetyme juste owner and possessor of a certayne waterboote. 1642 Perkins' Prof. Bk. ix. §581. 253 Where a just grant or other thing cannot take effect without a deed. 1667 Milton P.L. ii. 38 We now return To claim our just inheritance of old. 1712–14 Pope Rape Lock iii. 60 The rebel Knave, who dares his prince engage, Proves the just victim of his royal rage. 1726–31 Tindal Rapin's Hist. Eng. (1743) II. xvii. 100 Another Person has a juster title than she to the Crown. 1849 Macaulay Hist. Eng. iv. I. 443 He [James II] would still go as far as any man in support of her [his country's] just liberties.

4. Having reasonable or adequate grounds; well-founded.

c1374 Chaucer Troylus iii. 1178 (1227) Al quyt from euery drede and teene As she þat Iuste cause hadde hym to triste. 1553 T. Wilson Rhet. (1580) 217 Images we maie chaunge, as the matter shall give iuste cause. 1633 P. Fletcher Purple Isl. xi. xii, A simple maid, With justest grief and wrong so ill apaid. 1792 Anecd. W. Pitt II. xxix. 130 The excuse is a valid one if it is a just one. 1796 Eliza Hamilton Lett. Hindoo Rajah I. 45 Alas! my fears were just. The pure spirit had fled. 1858 Gen. P. Thompson Audi Alt. II. lxxiv. 23 The justest object of jealousy to wise men in all ages.

5. Conformable to the standard, or to what is fitting or requisite; right in amount, proportion, æsthetic quality, etc.; proper; correct.

c1430 Lydg. Min. Poems (Percy Soc.) 60 Iuste weight halte justly the balaunce. 1588 W. Smith Brief Descr. Lond. (Harl. MS. 6363 lf. 13) If they ffynd [the weights] not Iust: they breake them. 1598 Yong Diana 491 A maruellous sweete concent keeping iust time and measure. 1671 R. Bohun Wind 67 So that a just and moderate condensation is necessary to the constitution of Winds. 1734 J. Ward Introd. Math. ii. xi. (ed. 6) 139 The First Root is 300 being less than Just. 1750 Johnson Rambler No. 23 ¶9 Rules for the just opposition of colours, and the proper dimensions of ruffles and pinners. 1821 J. Q. Adams in C. Davies Metr. Syst. iii. (1871) 74 The first of these injunctions.. commands that the standards should be just. 1877 E. R. Conder Bas. Faith v. 203 The just balance between the moral and intellectual sides of his nature is often destroyed.

b. Mus. in just interval, intonation, etc.: Harmonically pure; sounding perfectly in tune.

1850 Gen. P. Thompson (title) Theory and Practice of Just Intonation. 1878 W. H. Stone Sci. Basis Music v. §90 The differences of the old [mean-tone] and equal systems [of temperament], and their respective departures from just intonation. 1881 Broadhouse Mus. Acoustics 353 Just Intonation, where all the Fifths and Thirds are perfect, used only by singers and theorists.

6. Of speech, ideas, opinions, arguments, etc.: In accordance with reason, truth, or fact; right; true; correct. Often with mixture of sense 3.

1490 Caxton Eneydos xxi. 77 He refuseth to lene his eeres for to vnderstande my wordes that ben soo iuste and resonable. a1610 Healey Theophrastus (1636) 20 He maintaineth, that strangers speake wiser and juster things than his own fellow-citizens. 1725 Pope Odyss. iii. 306 Much he knows, and just conclusions draws From various precedents, and various laws. 1774 Goldsm. Nat. Hist. (1776) V. 136 A single glance of a good plate or a picture imprints a juster idea that a volume could convey. 1888 Bryce Amer. Commw. II. lxxv. 618 To present a just picture of American public opinion one must cut deeper.

†b. Of a copy, description, calculation, etc.: Exact, accurate. [So F. juste.] Said also of personal agents. Obs.

1563 Winȝet Four Scoir Thre Quest. To Rdr., Wks. 1888 I. 60 We sett furth this iust copie without altering or eiking ony thing. 1657 R. Ligon Barbadoes (1673) 33 Having given you a just account..of the bread and drink of this Island. 1691 Swift Athen. Soc., Like a just map. 1704 J. Pitts Acc. Mahometans Pref. (1738) 7, I have since procured a just Translation. 1727 Swift What passed in London, I am apt to think his calculation just to a minute. 1798 G. Forster Journ. Bengal to Eng. I. 80 The Hindoos of this day are just imitators, and correct workmen; but they possess merely the glimmerings of genius.

†7. Adapted to something else, or to an end or purpose; appropriate; suitable. Obs.

c1384 Chaucer H. Fame ii. 211 [It] stant eke in so Iuste a place That euery sovne mot to hyt pace. 1664 Evelyn Kal. Hort. Introd. (1729) 187 How many Things to be done in their just Season. c1665 Mrs. Hutchinson Mem. Col. Hutchinson (1846) 32 He was very liberal to them, but ever chose just times and occasions to exercise it. 1684 R. Waller Nat. Exper. 10 Our Instrument remains still unalterably just to every place where 'tis made use of.

†8. Of clothing, armour, etc.: Well adjusted, fitting exactly. Hence, Fitting too closely, tight. [So F. juste.] Obs.

a1400 Sir Perc. 273 His hode was iuste to his chynne. c1400 Destr. Troy 9505 Mekull iust armur. a1450 Knt. de la Tour (1868) 38 Streite and welle sittinge and iuste, that sum tyme the fruite that was in me suffered payne and was in perelle. 1649 Lovelace Poems, Aramantha, It [a robe] sate close and free, As the just bark unto the Tree.

†9. Of a calculated result, measure, amount, number, date, etc.: Exact, as opposed to approximate. Also with defining word: That is exactly what is designated; = '(the) exact..'. Obs.

c1391 Chaucer Astrol. ii. §3 To haue take a Iust Ascendent by their Astrilabie. 1551 Recorde Pathw. Knowl. i. iv, Open your compasse to the iust length of y^{e} line. 1594 Acc.-Bk. W. Wray in Antiquary XXXII. 118 [He] owes me ..the just some of iiijli. xixs. id. 1596 Shaks. Merch. V. iv. i. 327 If thou tak'st more Or lesse then a iust pound. 1608 Willet Hexapla Exod. 875 The forepart of the court was a iust square. 1655 Fuller Ch. Hist. ix. iv. §3 We cannot exactly tell the just time thereof. 1723–4 Chambers tr. Le Clerc's Treat. Archit. I. 105 It should be rais'd to the just height of the Windows. 1759 B. Martin Nat. Hist. Eng. I. Cornwall 4 Its Height and just Balance.

†b. Of an instrument, natural action, etc.: Exact or uniform in operation, regular, even. Obs.

c1386 Chaucer Sompn. T. 382 Thou shalt me fynde as Iust as is a squyre. 1579 Gosson Sch. Abuse (Arb.) 26 The vnfallible motion of the Planets, the iuste course of the yeere. 1665–6 Phil Trans. I. 61 An instrument composed of two Rulers..will be no longer just at all. 1721 Bailey, Just Divisors are such Numbers or Quantities which will divide a given Number or Quantity, so as to leave no Remainder. 1769 Sir W. Jones Pal. Fortune in Poems, etc. (1777) 23 Mark'd the just progress of each rolling sphere.

†10. Corresponding exactly in amount, duration, position, etc.; equal; even, level. Obs.

1551 Robinson tr. More's Utop. ii. iv. (1895) 141 Dyuydynge the daye and the nyghte into xxiiii iust houres. 1594 Blundevil Exerc. iii. i. xxxiii. (1636) 343 Untill the last degree of the said Signe do appeare just with the upper edge of the Horizon. c1630 Risdon Surv. Devon §46 (1810) 52 That..well in Derbyshire, which ebbeth and floweth by just tides. 1725 Pope Odyss. xiv. 483 The destin'd victim to dis-part In sev'n just portions.

†b. Characterized by or involving exact correspondence. Obs.

1753 Hogarth Anal. Beauty xi. 83 They meet in just similitude. 1802 Paley Nat. Theol. xvi. (1819) 258 In consequence of the just collocation, and by means of the joint action of longitudinal and annular fibres.

†11. That is such properly, fully, or in all respects; complete in amount or in character; full; proper, 'regular'. just battle, in quot. 1603, a regular (pitched) battle [= OF. juste bataille]. just age (years), full age or age of discretion. Obs.

1588 H. G. tr. Cataneo (title) Briefe Tables to know redily how manie ranckes of footemen..go to the making of a iust battaile. 1588 D. Rogers in Ellis Orig. Lett. Ser. ii. III. 148 They are not minded to Crowne the yonge kinge, before he come to just yeares. 1603 Knolles Hist. Turks (1621) 663 The skirmish was like to have come to a just battell. a1618 Sylvester Judith To Rdr., I am the first in Fraunce who in a just Poem hath treated in our tongue of sacred things. 1622 Bacon Hen. VII 42 This warre was rather a suppression of Rebels, then a warre with a iust Enemie. 1624 Bedell Lett. x. 136 It would require a iust volume to shew it. 1668 Culpepper & Cole Barthol. Anat. iii. i. 128 When a man comes to a just age. 1732 Berkeley Alciphr. i. §12 Published ..sometimes in just volumes, but often in pamphlets and loose papers. 1778 Bp. Lowth Transl. Isaiah ix. 7 note, A just poem, remarkable for the regularity of its disposition, and the elegance of its plan.

12. nonce-use. That just is or takes place: cf. just adv. 5.

1884 Browning Ferishtah, Two Camels 117 A lip's mere tremble, Look's half hesitation, cheek's just change of colour.

13. Comb. a. with a pple. (or another adj.), where just is adverbial in sense, = justly: as just-borne, -conceived, -consuming, -dooming, -judging, -kindled, -tempered, -thinking; just gentle. b. parasynthetic, as just-minded (whence just-mindedness).

1595 Shaks. John ii. i. 345 Before we will lay downe our *iust-borne Armes. 1633 Ford Love's Sacr. v. i, The boundless spleen Of *just-consuming wrath. 1598 Sylvester Du Bartas ii. ii. i. Noah 94 The deeds of Heav'ns *just-gentle king. Ibid. 350 In my *just-kindled ire. 1848 Buckley Iliad 110 *Just-minded, wise-reflecting Bellerophon. 1887 Pall Mall G. 20 Aug. 2/2 Confidence in the *just-mindedness of their employers. 1829 E. S. Swaine in Bischoff Woollen Manuf. (1842) II. 238 At the very name of a drawback or bounty..the *just-thinking legislator must shrink with an instinctive distrust.

just, v.[1] Older form of joust v.

just (dʒʌst), v.[2] [Aphetic f. adjust.] trans. To adjust. Hence 'justing vbl. sb.

1628 in G. Barry Orkney Isl. App. (1805) 473 That every pundlar be justed and made equal with the King's pundlar. 1883 Pall Mall G. 28 Sept. 14/1 Thoroughly understands gauging, justing, and every branch of the business to the minutest details.

just (dʒʌst), adv. [f. just a.: cf. adverbial use of F. juste.]

1. Exactly, precisely; verily, actually; closely: cf. even adv. 6. Formerly often even just. Qualifying a prep., adv., or advb. phrase; or (in e, f, g) an adj., pron., or sb.

a. Of place or position. just at, in, over (etc.) the = at, in, over (etc.) the very. †just to, right up to, even to, as far as to; just to the, to the very.

?a1400 Morte Arth. 1123 The gyaunt he hyttez, Iust to the genitales; and iaggede thame in sondre. 1463 Bury Wills (Camden) 39 That ymage to be set just ageyn the peleer. a1533 Ld. Berners Huon lxxxiii. 259 He passyd iust by kyng Charlemayn. 1560 Daus tr. Sleidane's Comm. 287 There was also a chapel iust by, wherin were burning innumerable Tapers. 1568 Grafton Chron. II. 267 The Englishe Marshalles ranne abroade even iust to Parys, and brent Saint Germayns. 1616 Surfl. & Markh. Country Farme 2 Euen iust in the place whereupon the Sunne riseth. 1617 Moryson Itin. 160 You have now hit me just where my paine lies. 1665 R. Hooke Microgr. v. 9 They double all the Stuff that is to be water'd, that is, they crease it just through the middle of it. 1711 Steele Spect. No. 254 ¶6 A beautiful young Creature who sat just before me. 1745 De Foe's Eng. Tradesman xxv. (1841) I. 248 We are butted and bounded just where we were in queen Elizabeth's time. 1749 Fielding Tom Jones vii. x, Here is a very creditable, good house just by. 1884 Sir N. Lindley in Law Rep. 25 Chanc Div. 319 The case..appears to me to break down just at the critical point. Mod. You know where the path crosses a small stream: I met him just there; yes, just at that spot.

b. Of time.

1574 Bourne Regim. for Sea Introd. (1577) C iij, Then ryseth the Sunne at fiue of the clocke iust, and setteth at seuen of the clocke iust. 1599 Shaks. Hen. V, ii. iii. 13 A parted eu'n iust betweene Twelue and One. 1672 C. Manners in 12th Rep. Hist. MSS. Comm. App. v. 25 Mr. Cooper..actually began it, but just then fell dangerously sicke. 1698 Fryer Acc. E. India & P. 59 Just that Day Twelvemonth you left me Aboard Ship at Gravesend. 1777 Johnson Lett. to Mrs. Thrale 6 Oct., I purpose soon to be at Lichfield, but know not just when. 1853 Lytton My Novel iii. iv, Just at that precise moment, who should appear but Mr. Stirn! 1895 Bookman Oct. 18/1 New Guinea was filling a good deal of colonial thoughts just then.

c. Of manner. just as = precisely in the way that, in the very way that. just so, (a) precisely in that way; exactly as has been said; (b) in the required or appropriate manner; (c) very close or friendly; (d) neatly and tidily; also as adj.; just-so story, a story which purports to explain the origin of something; a myth.

1607–12 Bacon Ess., Custom & Educ. (Arb.) 368 To heare Men professe,..give great wordes, and then doe iust as they have done before. 1665 R. Hooke Microgr. lx. 57 A Sphere, which will..grow bigger, just after the same manner..as the waves or rings on the surface of the water. 1735 Pope Ep. Lady 161 She speaks, behaves, and acts just as she ought. 1751 Richardson in Johnson Rambler No. 97. ¶24 When I courted and married my Lætitia, then a blooming Beauty, every Thing passed just so! 1794 Massachusetts Spy 3 Sept. (Th.), A few years ago, every body supposed that if people did not behave just so, they ought to be punished. 1819 Byron Juan ii. clxvii, He was in love..so was she Just in the way we very often see. 1824 'A. Singleton' Lett. 18 Their just so garb, which, when adopted, was the court costume of the time, makes them [sc. Quakers] appear like antediluvians. 1831 J. Constable Let. 4 Dec. (1966) IV. 361 Was it now in its first state, I would rejoice to publish it just so. 1836 Charlotte Elliott Hymn, Just as I am, without one plea. 1881 Grant White England xvi. 388 Just so, just so, is the most common phrase of general assent. 1886 Lantern (New Orleans) 15 Sept. 4/2 It looks as though the contractors and the aldermen are just so, and fully

understand each other. **1887** Parish & Shaw *Dict. Kentish Dial.* 85 He's got a bad master, but he will have everything done just-so; and you wunt please him without everything is just-so. **1891** E. Peacock *N. Brendon* I. 117, I will do just as you advise. **1902** Kipling (*title*) Just so stories. **1922** J. Strachey tr. *Freud's Group Psychol.* x. 90 This is only a hypothesis..a 'Just-So Story'. **1930** *Times Lit. Suppl.* 27 Feb. 155/2 The charm of an album of Just-so stories, such as proves that even the humblest members of the human race possess..the saving grace of vision. **1952** L. MacNeice *Ten Burnt Offerings* 76 Reposed on a Sunday lap in the just-so room. **1960** R. Pound *Selfridge* i. 8 He always looked as if he had just come out of the bandbox. His mother..kept him just so. **1969** E. Bishop *Compl. Poems* 198 A raccoon.. was the executioner. He was very fastidious and did everything just so. **1969** R. A. Noblett *Stavin' Chain* 5 Now Stavin' Chain wuz a man just so: When he got good whiskey, he would gurgle it slow. **1973** *Times Lit. Suppl.* 25 May 576/2 At first sight *My Country* is another of these just-so stories.

d. Of degree. ***just as, just so***, to the same degree as.

1551 Recorde *Pathw. Knowl.* I. xix, Then shall you make one right line iuste as long as two of those vnequall sides. **1688** J. Smith *Baroscope* 51 So much of it as may sink it down just so low as the End of the Gage. **1766** Goldsm. *Vic. W.* xx, Finding that my expectations were just as great as my purse. **1849** Macaulay *Hist. Eng.* vii. II. 209 His object was to grant just so much favour to them as might suffice to frighten the Churchmen into submission. **1889** R. S. S. Baden-Powell *Pigsticking* 146 All other articles can be obtained just as well on the spot.

e. Of amount, number, or quantity: with a sb. or adj.

1583 Stubbes *Anat. Abus.* II. (1882) 38 Such as..haue either iust nothing, or else very little at all. **1590** Shaks. *Com. Err.* IV. i. 7 Euen iust the sum that I do owe to you. **1596** —— *Merch. V.* IV. i. 326 Nor cut thou lesse nor more But iust a pound of flesh. **1653** H. More *Antid. Ath.* I. vii. (1712) 20 There are just five regular Bodies. *c* **1717** Prior *Epitaph* 12 They did just Nothing all the Day. **1821** J. Q. Adams in C. Davies *Metr. Syst.* III. (1871) 229 The troy weights..had then been just one century in use. **1883** *Daily News* 22 Sept. 4/5 It is just a fortnight since Mr. Gladstone embarked.

f. Of likeness, sameness, identity, or the contrary, with a sb. or adj. ***just it***, precisely the very thing or point in question.

1594 Hooker *Eccl. Pol.* IV. iv. §1 They go about to make us belieue that they are just of the same opinion. **1600** Shaks. *A.Y.L.* II. i. 56 'Tis iust the fashion. **1657** R. Ligon *Barbadoes* (1673) 39 As dry as Stock-fish, and just such meat for flesh, as that is for fish. **1796** Jane Austen *Pride & Prej.* ii, The astonishment of the ladies was just what he wished. **1809** Malkin *Gil Blas* VII. ii. ¶3 You seem to be just the thing for him. **1851** Mayne Reid *Scalp Hunt.* ii. 19 St Vrain said I was just the man for their life. **1862** Mrs. H. Wood *Mrs. Hallib.* II. iii, 'You have eaten it all the season'. 'That's just it', answered Herbert. 'I have eaten so much of it that I am sick of it'. **1865** Mrs. Carlyle *Lett. III.* 252 One cannot do just what one likes best.

g. Used freely before a demonstrative, an interrogative introducing a subject-clause, etc. orig. *U.S.*

1884 G. B. Goode *Fisheries U.S.* Sect. v. II. 543 Just what makes the best lodgement for oyster spawn..has been greatly discussed. *Ibid.* 544 Just how many bushels a man will place on an acre depends upon both his means and his judgment. **1900** Hempl in *School Rev.* (U.S.) June 322 Just this happened in Latin. **1960** R. A. Knox *Occasional Sermons* 227 Many who value the name of Christian still find it reasonable to believe that he did just that. **1971** *You* Sept. 24/1 Doctors and researchers are spending their energies and our money on finding out just how the female body ticks. **1974** *Times Lit. Suppl.* 8 Mar. 243/5 One wonders just how biased a view we develop of the human ecology of tropical Africa.

h. ***not just***: not exactly, not quite.

1719 De Foe *Crusoe* I. xix, Our guide being something before us, and not just in sight. **1816** Chalmers *Let.* in *Life* (1851) II. 59, I told you..that I was not just so well.

†**2. a.** In an exact or accurate manner; so as to correspond exactly; with precision; accurately; punctually; correctly. *Obs.*

1549–62 Sternhold & H. *Ps.* ciii. 14 The Lord that made vs knoweth our shape, Our mould and fashion iust. **1575** *Gamm. Gurton* II. ii, Her cock..y^t nightly crowed so iust. **1590** Swinburne *Testaments* 19 b, Borrowing that definition, which agreeth so iust with their testamentes. *c* **1600** Shaks. *Sonn.* cix, I returne againe Iust to the time. **1667** Pepys *Diary* 1 Oct., The instrumental musick he had brought by practice to play very just. **1743** T. Jones in *Buccleuch MSS.* (Hist. MSS. Comm.) I. 405, I..send the enclosed plan, which describes the ground very near just.

†**b.** So as to fit exactly; in a close-fitting way: cf. Just *a.* 8. *Obs.*

1561 Daus tr. *Bullinger on Apoc.* (1573) 16 b, This [coat] cleaueth iust to the body. **1607** Topsell *Four-f. Beasts* (1658) 310 The first pin would be somewhat flat in the midst, to the intent that the other, being round, may..close the juster together. **1676** Etheredge *Man of Mode* I. i, You love to have your clothes hang just, sir.

†**3.** In replies and expressions of assent; = 'Exactly so', 'just so', 'right'. Also ***even just***. *Obs.*

a **1533** Frith *Answ. Rastel* Wks. (1573) 14 Euen iust, if heauen fell we should catche larkes. **1588** Shaks. *Tit. A.* IV. ii. 24 O 'tis a verse in Horace, I know it well... *Moore.* I iust, a verse in Horace. **1600** —— *A.Y.L.* III. ii. 281 *Iaq.* Rosalinde is your loues name? *Orl.* Yes, Iust. **1694** Congreve *Double Dealer* III. ii, *F.* You know laughing without a jest is as impertinent; hee! as,—*C.* As dancing without a fiddle. *F.* Just, i' faith! **1698** Vanbrugh *Prov. Wife* II. ii, *T.* I guess the dialogue, madam, is supposed to be between your majesty and your first minister. *Lady F.* Just.

4. *absol.* of time: Exactly at the moment spoken of; precisely now (or then). **a.** with retrospective reference: Not before this (or that) moment; hence loosely, A very little before; with little preceding interval; within a brief preceding period; very recently. **b.** with prospective reference: Not after this (or that) moment; hence loosely, A very little after, 'directly', 'in a moment', very soon; also, of state or condition, On the point of being.., all but, very nearly. (See also *just now* in 7.)

1667 Milton *P.L.* IV. 863 The western point, where those half-rounding guards Just met, and closing stood in squadron joind. **1671** R. Bohun *Wind* 177 Winds..where they come just off from the Burning Sands. **1681–6** J. Scott *Chr. Life* (1747) III. 548 With what a stern and terrible Majesty he sits upon yonder flaming Throne, from whence he is now just ready to exact of ye a dreadful Account. **1697** Dryden *Virg. Georg.* IV. 430 Broken Boughs and Thyme, And pleasing Casia just renew'd in prime. **1719** De Foe *Crusoe* I. xviii, Presently the captain replied, 'Tell his excellency I am just a coming'. **1758** S. Hayward *Serm.* v. 145 The apostle had just been speaking of Jesus Christ. **1768** Sterne *Sent. Journ.* (1778) II. 10 (*Fille de Chambre*), I was just bidding her—but she did it of herself. **1818** Cruise *Digest* (ed. 2) VI. 492 His only child was just dead. **1884** *Daily News* 23 May 5 The writer adds that he 'saw a man just dead, and he was crawling towards us'. [*Eng. Dial. Dict.* s.v., *Pembrokesh.* 'He's just dead' = likely to die soon.] *Mod.* I have just seen him cross the street.

5. No more than; only, merely; barely. Often preceded by *but* or *only*. **a.** qualifying a vb. or adj.

1665 R. Hooke *Microgr.* vii. 38 Distilled water, that is so cold that it just begins to freeze. **1693** Dryden *Juvenal* (1697) p. lxxv, Let Horace, who is the Second, and but just the Second, carry off the Quivers and the Arrows. **1735** Pope *Ep. Lady* 50 She..was just not ugly, and was just not mad. **1739** Chesterf. *Lett.* (1774) I. xxxvi. 125 He can just be said to live, and that is all. **1810** Scott *Lady of L.* III. ii, The Western breeze Just kissed the lake, just stirred the trees. **1826** —— *Woodst.* xiii, Everard had but just time to bid Wildrake hold the horses. **1849** Macaulay *Hist. Eng.* ii. I. 157 Men who..seemed to think that they had given an illustrious proof of loyalty by just stopping short of regicide. **1889** R. S. S. Baden-Powell *Pigsticking* 98 Fissures just wide enough to admit a horse's leg.

b. with a *sb.*

1785 Burns *1st Ep. Lapraik* ix, I am nae Poet, in a sense, But just a Rhymer, like, by chance. **1865** Mrs. Carlyle *Lett.* III. 279 Just a line to say that all goes well. **1884** W. C. Smith *Kildrostan* 92 Doris is not a Cleopatra..she's just a Highland lady Touched with an Eastern strain.

c. Used to extenuate the action expressed by a verb, and so to represent it as a small thing.

1815 Scott *Wav.* lxiii, As it's near the darkening, sir, wad ye just step in by to our house? **1826** Disraeli *Viv. Grey* II. xvi, I will just walk on till I am beneath her window. **1862** G. Macdonald *D. Elginbrod* vii. 129 Just tell my maid to bring me an old pair of gloves. **1884** F. M. Crawford *Rom. Singer* I. 4 Just imagine whether you are not quite as able to feed him as Gigi is. **1898** Flor. Montgomery *Tony* 13 Mother! do just get in with me for a few minutes till the train starts.

6. a. No less than; absolutely; actually, positively; really; quite; neither more nor less than, simply.

1726 J. M. *Trag. Hist. Chev.* 84 When I heard this melancholy News, I was just ready to expire with Grief. **1768** Ross *Helenore* I. 11 They were a' just like to eat their thumb That he with Nory sae far ben should come. *Ibid.* 30 Her stinking breath Was just enough to sconfise ane to death. **1838** Jas. Grant *Sk. Lond.* 209 She jost did, Sir. **1863** Mrs. H. Wood *Mrs. Hallib.* xix, If anybody asked you for your head, ma'am, you'd just cut it off and give it. **1866** Ruskin *Crown of Olives* (1873) 75 'But what has all this to do with our Exchange?'..My dear friends, it has just everything to do with it. *a* **1901** *Mod. colloq.* He's got a double first, isn't it just splendid? **1937** A. Huxley *Ends & Means* xii. 199 In the abstract this scheme seems good enough; but in practice it just doesn't work. **1962** *Listener* 18 Jan. 135/1 The functionalist revolution just doesn't seem to have reached architectural photography. *Ibid.* 25 Oct. 694/2 It is just not true that cultivated people are able to pronounce equally on films, books, paintings, the theatre. **1972** *Newsweek* 10 Jan. 34/1 Now most businessmen think they just have to have a guard.

b. As an emphatic expletive, strengthening an assertion: Truly, indeed.

1855 Smedley *H. Coverdale* v. 26 Won't they be surprised to see us, just? *c* **1863** T. Taylor in M. R. Booth *Eng. Plays of 19th Cent.* (1909) II. 119 Ain't it a bore, just! *c* **1875** 'Brenda' *Froggy's Little Brother* (new ed.) iv. 41 'Now, haven't we 'ad a supper *just*?' exclaimed Froggy with satisfaction. **1891** *Newcastle Even. Chron.* 19 Mar. 3/4 *Mr. Williamson.* Was it a ferocious dog? *Witness.* It was, just. **1894** Kipling *Let.* 28 July in C. E. Carrington *Rudyard Kipling* (1955) ix. 217 Won't New York be hot—just! *a* **1901** *Mod. Sc. A.* I did not take it! *B.* You did just. **1903** A. Bennett *Leonora* viii. 228 'He's a good dancer.' 'I should think he was!..Isn't he just, mother?' **1904** E. Nesbit *Phoenix & Carpet* v. 94 'Luv us!' said Ike, 'ain't it been taught its schoolin', just!' **1930** J. B. Priestley *Angel Pavement* i. 16 She let herself go all right, didn't she just! **1943** K. Tennant *Ride on Stranger* (1968) iv. 36 'I don't believe you'd do that anyway yourself. Just grab money.' 'Wouldn't I just,' her mentor said exultantly.

c. ***just too bad***, unfortunate but inevitable.

1935 H. L. Ickes *Secret Diary* (1953) I. 270 If, in the course of his investigation, Glavis runs across your brother or my son, that will be just too bad, but it will be in the line of his duty. **1938** Auden & Isherwood *On Frontier* II. 75 If some one's mistaken or lying or mad, Or if we're defeated, it will be just too bad. **1962** J. F. Powers *Morte d'Urban* ix. 199 Well, isn't that just too bad? **1962** 'S. Woods' *Bloody Instructions* viii. 87, I admit you'll come in for some rough handling, and that's just too bad.

7. ***just now***. **a.** Exactly at this point of time; at this exact moment; precisely at present.

1681–6 J. Scott *Chr. Life* (1747) III. 324 The Prince of Devils is just now mustering up all his Legions against me. **1860** Mrs. Carlyle *Lett.* III. 43 Just now I am too vexed for making a good story. **1867** Freeman *Norm. Conq.* I. v. 394 Just now he did nothing to check the panic. *Mod.* That is his residence; but he is not there just now.

b. But now; only a very short time ago.

1633 Ford *'Tis Pity* I. iv, My barber told me just now, that there is a fellow come to town [etc.]. **1711** Addison *Spect.* No. 106 ¶6 The good Man whom I have just now mentioned. **1875** Jowett *Plato* (ed. 2) III. 296 As you were saying just now.

c. Directly, immediately, very soon, presently. Also *S. Afr.* [tr. Afrikaans *netnou*].

1682 D'Urfey *Butler's Ghost* I. 75 That I will, Cries he. But (quoth the Squire) just now T'must be. **1879** Trollope *Thackeray* ix. 187, I will give one or two instances just now. **1901** *Eng. Dial. Dict.* s.v., *Cumberl.* I'll come just now. [So in most local dialects.] **1939** 'D. Rame' *Wine of Good Hope* I. iii. 40 'Well, eat then,' said Lowell. 'I'll come just now.' **1953** N. Gordimer *Lying Days* II. ix. 92 'Well,' I said, 'I'll open it just now—.' **1966** A. Sachs *Jail Diary* xvi. 143 'Would you mind switching off the light after you lock up.' 'The men on cell duty will do that just now.'

8. *Comb.* with pples., and with adjs.

1605 Sylvester *Du Bartas* II. iii. IV. *Captaines*, Just-Duked Josuah cheers the Abramides To Canaans Conquest. **1818** Bentham *Ch. Eng.* 55 An infant? Yea, a just-born infant. **1847** L. Hunt *Men, Women, & B.* (1876) 297 A just-bearable specimen of the way in which ladies of quality could write. **1876** Geo. Eliot *Dan. Der.* lxiii, Her curls in as much disorder as a just-awakened child's. **1884** F. H. Myers in *Fortn. Rev.* 613 The companionship of the just-elder sister. **1885** J. K. Jerome *On the Stage* 27 There being a dismal, just-got-up sort of look about him.

‖**justaucorps** ('ʒystokɔr). Also 7 justacorps. -acor, -icore, -icord, -ico, 9 justiecor; justi-, justycoat: see also chesticore and jeistiecor. [F., f. *juste* close-fitting + *au corps* to the body. The anglicized forms *justicore*, etc. now survive only as archaisms.]

A close-fitting garment: *spec.* **a.** A body-coat reaching to the knees, worn in the latter half of the 17th and part of the 18th cent. **b.** An outer garment worn by women in the latter part of the 17th c. **c.** *Sc.* A jacket or waistcoat with sleeves.

1656 Blount *Glossogr.* To Rdr., In London many of the Tradesmen have new Dialects..The Taylor is ready to mode you into a..Justacor, Capouch [etc.]. **1667** Pepys *Diary* 26 Apr., With her velvet-cap..and a black just-au-corps. **1672** *Acc.-Bk. Sir J. Foulis* Mar. (1894) 4 For silk and threid..to make my justicord. **1678** Dryden *Limberham* IV. i, Give her out the flower'd Justacorps, with the Petticoat belong to't. **1705** Elstob in Hearne *Collect.* 30 Nov. (O.H.S.) I. 107 His justaucorps brac't to his body tight. *a* **1825** *MS. Poems* (Jam.), The justicoat syne on he flung. **1854** Mrs. Oliphant *Magd. Hepburn* I. 154 I'll buy him a bonnie justiecor. **1887** *Diary W. Cunningham* Introd. 28 He had also a Justycoat, or tightly-fitting body coat. **1896** *Westm. Gaz.* 28 July 1/3 The scene..is laid in the Pyrenees ..the women look gorgeous in red justaucorps.

‖**juste milieu** (ʒyst miljø). [Fr., lit. 'the right mean'.] The happy medium, the golden mean; judicious moderation, esp. in politics.

1833 Mill *Lett.* (1910) I. 76 The Enfantin portion..have become *juste milieu* men in politics. **1866** Mrs. Gaskell *Wives & Daughters* II. xxvii. 279 Now I hope that man in the garden is the *juste milieu*,—I'm that myself, for I don't think I'm vicious, and I know I'm not virtuous. **1875** J. G. Saxe *Leisure-Day Rhymes* 261 For me, the *juste milieu* I seek; I fain would leave alone The girl who rudely slaps my cheek Or volunteers her own! **1882** E. W. Hamilton *Diary* 13 June (1972) I. 289, I suppose between the extremes there must be a *juste milieu*, but as to where it is I am at sea. **1936** E. Sitwell *Victoria of Eng.* iii. 48 It was the *juste milieu* that ruled her life. **1945** A. J. P. Taylor *Course of German Hist.* 13 One looks in vain in their history for a *juste milieu*, for common sense.

†'**justen**, *v.* *Obs.* [f. Just *a.*, after *fasten*, *hasten*, etc.] *trans.* To adjust, regulate.

1659 Leak *Waterwks.* 20 When the said Dyal shall be well justned, it shall continue a long time without alteration. *Ibid.* 23 To justen the course of the Hours, you must lengthen or shorten the Syphon. **1665** R. Hooke *Microgr.* Pref. cij, Having thus justned and divided it.

†**justening, justninge**, an erroneous form, app. confounding justing, *jousting*, and gestening.

c **1330** *Florice & Bl.* (1857) 215 Th' Ameral hath to his iustening [*v.rr.* iustninge, Iustinges, gestninge] Other half hondred of riche king [*v.r.* kinges]. *c* **1375** *Sir Beues* 3766 (MS. Caius Coll.) Sere wost þou no þyng Off þis ylke grete iustenyng [*v.r.* iustyng].

juster, older var. of jouster.

'**justful**, *a.* *Obs.* exc. *dial.* [irreg. f. Just *a.* + -ful.] Just, rightful, righteous.

1534 Whitinton *Tullyes Offices* I. (1540) 14 Not to make promesse to a madde man..may be ryght and iustfull. *a* **1634** Chapman *Alphonsus* (1654) 64 The rightfull Gods have pour'd their justfull wrath Upon thy Tyrants head. [**1882** Jas. Walker *Jaunt to Auld Reekie* 221 Aye hae justfu' dealins wi'them.]

justice ('dʒʌstɪs), *sb.* Forms: 2–4 iustise, (3 -ize), 3–6 -is, -ys, (4 iostyse), 3–7 iustice, 4–6 -yce, 5 -yse, (6 -es), 7– justice. [a. OF. *justise*, *-ice*

(*jostise*) uprightness, equity, vindication of right, administration of law, jurisdiction, court of justice, infliction of punishment, gallows, judge, etc. (= Pr., Sp. *justicia*, Pg. *justiça*, It. *giustizia*), ad. L. *jūstitia* righteousness, uprightness, equity, f. *jūstus* JUST. Sense 4 was the first to be adopted from Norman Fr.]

I. The quality of being just.

1. The quality of being (morally) just or righteous; the principle of just dealing; the exhibition of this quality or principle in action; just conduct; integrity, rectitude. (One of the four cardinal virtues.)

COMMUTATIVE, DISTRIBUTIVE *justice* : see these words.

c **1340** *Cursor M.* 8748 (Fairf.) Alle loued salamon for his Iustise. **1387** T. USK *Test. Love* III. i. (Skeat) l. 73 Vertues of soule.. whiche been Prudence, Justice, Temperaunce, and Strength. **1470–85** MALORY *Arthur* I. vii, Ther was he sworne vnto his lordes & the comyns for to be a true kyng, to stand with true Iustyce fro thensforth the dayes of his lyf. **1531** ELYOT *Gov.* III. i, The auncient Ciuilians do saye iustice is a wille perpetuall and constaunt, whiche gyueth to euery man his right. **1600** E. BLOUNT tr. *Conestaggio* 265 A certaine person.. said that in iustice they should burne these priests. **1613** SHAKS. *Hen. VIII*, III. i. 116 If you haue any Iustice, any Pitty. **1733** POPE *Ess. Man* III. 280 Forc'd into virtue thus by Self-defence, Ev'n kings learn'd justice and benevolence. **1769** *Junius Lett.* v. 27 In justice to our friends. **1848** W. J. O'N. DAUNT *Recoll. O'Connell* I. i. 10 The most important ingredient in 'justice to Ireland' is the restoration of the Irish Parliament. **1855** MACAULAY *Hist. Eng.* xii. III. 212 It would be found that the path of justice was the path of wisdom.

†**2.** *Theol.* Observance of the divine law; righteousness; the state of being righteous or 'just before God'. *Obs.*

1534 MORE *Treat. Passion* Wks. 1281/1 By the fall of Adam, the whole kynde of man.. lost original iustice. **1563** MAN *Musculus Commonpl.* 117 b, Regenerate into new men, so that suppressyng the raygne of synne, we may serve justice. **1581** MARBECK *Bk. of Notes* 187 Christ hauing fulfilled it [the law] for vs, is made our iustice, sanctification, &c. **1622** H. SYDENHAM *Serm. Sol. Occ.* (1637) 70 Whence I gather.. that that justice which is conferred on them consists rather in the participation of Christs merits.. than in any perfection of vertues or qualities infused.

3. Conformity (of an action or thing) to moral right, or to reason, truth, or fact; rightfulness; fairness; correctness; propriety; = JUSTNESS 2, 3.

1588 SHAKS. *Tit. A.* I. i. 2 Defend the iustice of my Cause with Armes. **1591** —— *Two Gent.* IV. iii. 29 Thinke.. on the iustice of my flying hence, To keepe me from a most vnholy match. **1608** —— *Per.* IV. iii. 9 A Princes To equall any single Crowne a'th'earth, Ith iustice of compare. **1746** MORELL *Judas Maccabeus*, '*Sound an alarm*', Justice with courage is a thousand men. *a* **1769** RICCALTOUN *Notes Galatians* 148 With great justice does he bear the title of truth. **1885** *Law Times* LXXIX. 130/1 Every lawyer.. will appreciate the justice of these observations.

†**b.** Just claim, right (*to* something). *Obs.*

1621 FLETCHER *Isl. Princess* II. viii, What justice have you now vnto this lady?

II. Judicial administration of law or equity.

4. Exercise of authority or power in maintenance of right; vindication of right by assignment of reward or punishment; requital of desert.

poetical justice: the ideal justice in distribution of rewards and punishments supposed to befit a poem or other work of imagination.

1137–54 *O.E. Chron.* an. 1137 Þa the suikes under gæton ð[at] he [Stephen] milde man was.. & na iustise ne dide. *Ibid.* an. 1140 He dide god iustise and makede pais. *a* **1300** *Cursor M.* 150 Sal be sythen tald.. o salomon þe wis How craftilik he did iustis. *c* **1460** FORTESCUE *Abs. & Lim. Mon.* xix. (1885) 156 We shul nowe mowe enjoye oure owne goode, and live vndir justice. *a* **1548** HALL *Chron., Hen. V*, 73 b, I am.. an anoynted kyng, to whom.. it apperteineth.. to minister to them indifferent iustice. **1670** CLARENDON *Contempl. Ps.* Tracts (1727) 601 Where justice is not, the fertilest land becomes barren. **1679** DRYDEN *Troilus & Cr.* Pref., We are glad when we behold his Crimes are punish'd, and that Poetical Justice is done upon him. **1751** JOHNSON *Rambler* No. 93 ¶6 Addison is suspected to have denied the expediency of poetical justice because his own Cato was condemned to perish in a good cause [cf. *Spect.* No. 40]. **1873** HAMERTON *Intell. Life* II. ii. (1876) 405 This rough justice of the world.

5. The administration of law, or the forms and processes attending it; judicial proceedings; †in early use, Legal proceedings of any kind (*obs.*).

bed of j., college of j., court of j.: see BED 7, COLLEGE 1 c, COURT 11. ***High Court of Justice***: see quot. 1873.

1303 R. BRUNNE *Handl. Synne* 1310 Þe fyfþe.. ys sle no man wyþ þyn honde Wyþ outyn iustyce, for felonye. *c* **1330** —— *Chron.* (1810) 315 Þo ilk men.. suld.. enforme ȝour kynges, Withouten mo justise or trauaile of oþer lordynges. **1484** CAXTON *Fables of Æsop* v. x, My fader was no legist.. ne also man of Iustyce. **1591** LAMBARDE *Archeion* (1635) 16, I gather.. that the King himselfe had a High Court of Justice. **1612** BACON *Ess., Judicature* (Arb.) 456 The place of Iustice is an hallowed place. **1615** G. SANDYS *Trav.* 62 Here the Vizier Bassas of the Port.. do sit in iustice. *a* **1715** BURNET *Own Time* (1823) I. 300 The Lord Clarendon put the justice of the nation in very good hands. **1727** A. HAMILTON *New Acc. E. Ind.* I. v. 48 In no Part of the World is Justice bought and sold more publickly than here. **1859** TENNYSON *Enid* 37 Assassins, and all flyers from the hand Of Justice. **1873** *Act 36 & 37 Vict.* c. 66 §4 The said Supreme Court shall consist of two permanent Divisions, one of which, under the name of 'Her Majesty's High Court of Justice', shall have and exercise original jurisdiction.

†**b.** The persons administering the law; a judicial assembly, court of justice. *Obs.* (In early quots. difficult to separate from pl. of sense 8.)

a **1300** *Cursor M.* 14855 If ani man war tan for oght He suld before iustijs [*v.rr.* iustice, iustis] be broght. *c* **1330** R. BRUNNE *Chron.* (1810) 58 Þerfor was þe dome gyuen þorgh þe Iustise, To exile þe erle Godwyn. *c* **1400** *Ywaine & Gaw.* 3446 It es the assyse, Whils sityng es of the iustise. **1529** RASTELL *Pastyme, Hist. Brit.* (1811) 222 There was a solempne justyce in Smythfylde where were present ye kynge of Englande [etc.]. **1654** SIR E. NICHOLAS in *N. Papers* (Camden) II. 85 Touching the proceedings against the Brasilians and particularly such as were of the high justice there.

†**c.** Judicial authority, jurisdiction. *Obs.*

c **1450** *Merlin* 575 The xix kynges.. comaunded alle hem that were vnther theire Iustice. **1617** MORYSON *Itin.* III. 205 Not onely the free Cities of the Empire have the priviledge of the Sword, or capitall Iustice granted to them.

d. In colloq. phrases, as ***Jedwood*** or ***Jeddart*** (= Jedburgh) ***justice***, trial after execution. Similarly † ***Cupar justice***. ***justices' justice***, an ironical expression for the kind of justice administered by petty magistrates, esp. when marked by disproportionate severity.

1706 A. SHIELDS *Enq. Ch. Commun.* Pref. 8 Guilty of Couper Justice and Jedburgh Law as the proverb is. **1802** SCOTT *Minstr. Scot. Border* Pref. (1869) 27 The memory of Dunbar's legal proceedings at Jedburgh, are preserved in the proverbial phrase, 'Jeddart Justice' which signifies trial after execution. **1828** —— *F.M. Perth* xxxii, We will have Jedwood justice—hang in haste and try at leisure. **1831** *Examiner* 802/2 [An example of] Justices' Justice. **1867** MISS BRADDON *Aur. Floyd* xvi, Servants'-hall justice all the world over. **1879** FARRAR *St. Paul* (1883) 357 The 'justice's justice' of the Vibiuses and Floruses.

†**6.** Infliction of punishment, legal vengeance on an offender; *esp.* capital punishment; execution. ***to do justice on*** or ***upon*** (***of***), to punish, esp. by death. *Obs.*

[**1137–54**: see 4.] *c* **1400** *Rom. Rose* 7036 Blamed of any vyce, Of whiche men shulden doon Iustyce. *c* **1477** CAXTON *Jason* 78 He sente to Zethephius that he sholde do iustice on his seruauntes. **1489** —— *Sonnes of Aymon* 584 Lete ys be drowned, hanged, or drawen, or what iustyse ye wylle. **1523** LD. BERNERS *Froiss.* I. ccxxx. 310 Bycause of the marueylous cruell iustyece that he had done. *a* **1625** FLETCHER *Bloody Brother* III. i, *Rob.* Take his head Off with a Sword. *Bel.*.. 'Tis the best Of all thy damned justices. [**1876** FREEMAN *Norm. Conq.* V. xxiv. 520 Justice.. in the special sense of heavy and speedy vengeance on offenders.. was.. far more on men's lips than it had been in the elder day.]

†**b.** A place or instrument of execution; a gallows. *Obs.*

c **1470** HENRY *Wallace* VII. 30 Thar ordand thai thir lordis suld be slayne: A iustice maid, quhilk wes of mekill mayne. **1484** CAXTON *Fables of Æsop* VI. xiv, As men ledde hym to the Iustyce, his moder folowed hym and wepte sore.

7. Personified, esp. in sense 4: often represented in art as a goddess holding balanced scales or a sword, sometimes also with veiled eyes, betokening impartiality. (= L. *Justitia*.)

1599 SHAKS. *2 Hen. IV*, V. ii. 102 You are right Iustice, and you weigh this well: Therefore still beare the Ballance, and the Sword. **1629** MILTON *Morn. Nativity* 141 Yea, Truth and Justice then Will down return to men, Orbed in a rainbow. **1784** COWPER *Task* IV. 683 Conducting trade At the sword's point, and dyeing the white robe Of innocent commercial justice red. **1872** SWINBURNE *Ess. & Stud.* (1875) 28 He called upon justice by her other name of mercy; he claimed for all alike the equity of compassion.

III. An administrator of justice.

The name *Justitia* was applied (in the 11th cent.) in a general way to persons charged with the administration of the law, esp. to the sheriffs; it was subsequently limited to the president or one of the members of the Curia Regis, out of which the courts of King's Bench, Common Pleas, and Exchequer were developed. These judges were specifically denominated *justices itinerant, in eyre, of assize, of oyer and terminer, of jail delivery*, etc.: see these words. In the Court of Exchequer (which had a peculiar history) they were termed *barons*.

8. *generally.* A judicial officer; a judge; a magistrate.

[*c* **1172** *Vie de St. Thom.* 46 Et quant il s'en parte de la cambre de rei Justices et baruns, tel que numer ne dei, L'escrierent en haut a hu et a desrei. **1188** GLANVILL VI. vii, Pone coram me vel iusticiis meis.. loquelam quae est in comitatu tuo inter A. et N.]

c **1200** *Vices & Virtues* 105 Iusticia þat is rihtwisnesse... Hie awh wel to bene iustise inne godes temple. *c* **1290** *S. Eng. Leg.* I. 37/111 Abiatar þat þo was Iustise, luþur inovȝ. **1297** R. GLOUC. (Rolls) 1416 Pilatus he sende þuder hor Iustise to be þere Vorto holde hom harde inou. *a* **1300** *Cursor M.* 4617 Stiward of al mi kingrik Sal þou be made and hei iustis. **13..** *E.E. Allit. P.* B. 877 Who Ioyned þe be Iostyse our iapez to blame. *c* **1380** *Sir Ferumb.* 3817 Alle.. prayede god, þe heȝe iustys, Scholde scheld him fram ys enymys. *c* **1485** *E. Eng. Misc.* (Warton Club) 29 To ȝeyf aconthis at the laste, Befor the most feyrful Justyse. **1611** BIBLE *1 Esdras* viii. 23 Thou, Esdras.. ordaine iudges, and iustices, that they may iudge in all Syria and Phenice. **1685** BAXTER *Paraphr. N.T., Acts* xiii. 15 Thus were their Rulers like Church Justices.

9. *spec.* In Great Britain and the United States: A member of the judicature. **a.** A judge presiding over or belonging to one of the superior courts, *spec.*, in England, one of the courts of King's Bench, Common Pleas, and Exchequer; since the consolidation of the courts in 1875, a member of the Supreme Court of Judicature; formerly applied also to various officers exercising special judicial functions, as the commissioners who governed Ireland during the absence of the Lord Lieutenant or the vacancy of that office.

High Justice (in quot.[2] 1297) = JUSTICIAR 1. ***Chief Justice*** or ***Lord Chief Justice***, formerly, the title of the judges presiding over each of the courts of King's Bench and of Common Pleas; both offices are now merged under the title of ***Lord Chief Justice of England***. The judges of the Court of Appeal are called ***Lords Justices***, and have the style of *Right Honourable*; a judge of the High Court of Justice is called ***Mr. Justice***, and has the style of *Honourable*. In the United States ***Chief Justice*** is the designation of the presiding judge in the U.S. Supreme Court, and in the supreme court of each state. So elsewhere in places formerly or still under British influence. See also JUSTICE-CLERK, JUSTICE-GENERAL.

[**1276** *Act 4 Edw. I*, Acorde est.. que Iustices ailent parmi la terre, a enquere e oier et terminer les pleintes e les quereles de trespas.] **1297** R. GLOUC. (Rolls) 10201 Þe bissopes.. amansede vaste Alle þat suich dede dude, king & quene boþe, & hor Iustizes ek. *Ibid.* 10754 Sire steuene of segraue was imad þo hei iustise In sire hubertes stude de boru. **1377** LANGL. *P. Pl.* B. III. 319 Al shal be but one courte, And one baroun be iustice. *a* **1400** in *Eng. Gilds* (1870) 361 Þe wryt þat me pledeth in þe citee by-fore Justyces. **1556** *Chron. Gr. Friars* (Camden) 81 That same nyght was browte in sir Roger Chamle cheffe justes of the kynges bench, sir Edwarde Montageu cheffe justys of the comyn place. **1586** A. DAY *Eng. Secretary* I. (1625) 33 The Lord chiefe Justice of England in the time of King Henry the fourth, who was so strictly bent to the observation of justice. **1681** LUTTRELL *Brief Rel.* 11 May, The lord chief justice Pemberton told him, That.. there were three of them, (Mr. justice Jones, Mr. justice Raymond, and my self) of opinion that his plea should be over-ruled. *a* **1734** NORTH *Life Ld. Guildford* (1825) I. 196 He was advanced to the post of Lord Chief Justice of the Common Pleas. *Ibid.* 312 This Sir William Scroggs was made Lord Chief Justice of the King's Bench, while his Lordship sat in the Common Pleas. **1873** *Act 36 & 37 Vict.* c. 66 §5 The several Puisne Justices of the Courts of Queen's Bench and Common Pleas respectively. *Ibid.* §6 The ordinary and additional Judges of the Court of Appeal shall be styled Lord Justices of Appeal. **1883** *Wharton's Law-Lex.* (ed. 7) 146/1 In 1881, after the promotion of Lord Chief Justice Coleridge to the office of Lord Chief Justice of England, the office [of Chief Justice of the Common Pleas] was abolished.. under s. 31 of the Jud. Act 1873, and merged in that of Lord Chief Justice of England. **1890** GROSS *Gild Merch.* II. 16 The burgesses of Beaumaris were summoned before the Justices Itinerant.

fig. **1622** BP. HALL *Serm.* v. 129 Every man makes him-self a Justice Itinerant, and passeth sentence of all that comes before him. **1633** EARL MANCH. *Al Mondo* (1636) 79 Thy conscience is a Justice Itinerant with thee.

b. A justice of the peace (see next) or other inferior magistrate; esp. in pl. ***the Justices***.

1586 A. DAY *Eng. Secretary* II. (1625) 10 Being.. brought before a Justice upon suspition of his wretched living. **1598** SHAKS. *Merry W.* II. iii. 49 Though wee are Iustices, and Doctors, and Church-men.. wee haue some salt of our youth in vs. **1599** B. JONSON *Ev. Man out of Hum.* v. ii, A Kins-man of Iustice Silence. **1749** FIELDING *Tom Jones* II. vi, Much less would have satisfied a bench of justices on an order of bastardy. **1771** SMOLLETT *Humph. Cl.* 12 June, The house was visited by a constable.. with a warrant from Justice Buzzard to search the box of Humphry Clinker. **1867** *Act 29 & 30 Vict.* c. 118 §15 Where a child apparently under the age of twelve years is charged before two Justices or a Magistrate.

10. Justice of the peace († **Justice of peace**): an inferior magistrate appointed to preserve the peace in a county, town, or other district, and discharge other local magisterial functions. Abbreviated J.P. Hence †***Justice-of-peaceship***.

Justices of the peace were instituted in England in 1327, and are appointed by the sovereign's special commission, directing them, jointly and severally, to keep the peace in the area named. Their principal duties consist in committing offenders to trial before a judge and jury when satisfied that there is a *primâ facie* case against them, convicting and punishing summarily in minor causes, granting licenses, and acting, if County Justices, as judges at Quarter Sessions. See also QUORUM.

[**1320** *Rolls Parlt.* I. 379/1 Loco Thome Yngglesthorp nuper assignati Justic. Pacis. **1363** *Act 37 Edw. III*, c. 12 En les commissionz des iustices de le peace.] **1439** *Rolls Parlt.* V. 33/1 Yat Justicez of yee Pees haue power to enquer therof. **1583** STUBBES *Anat. Abus.* II. (1882) 106 Maye they bee Iustices of peace, Iustices of Quoram, Iustices of Assises. **1597** SHAKS. *2 Hen. IV*, III. ii. 64, I am Robert Shallow.. a poore Esquire of this Countie, and one of the Kings Iustices of the Peace. *a* **1613** OVERBURY *Characters, Meere Common Lawyer* Wks. (1856) 86 The stating him in a Justice of peace-ship. **1662–3** PEPYS *Diary* 17 Mar., Our patent to be Justices of the Peace in the City. **1752** FIELDING *Amelia* I. ii, The clerk.. doubted whether a justice of peace had any such power. **1824** SCOTT *St. Ronan's* xxxii, You will answer the purpose a great deal better.. provided you are a justice of peace. **1898** J. K. JEROME *Sec. Thoughts* 266 The local J.P. of the period.

IV. Phrases and combinations.

11. Phrase. ***to do justice to*** (a person or thing): **a.** to render (one) what is his due, or vindicate his just claims; to treat (one) fairly by acknowledging his merits or the like; hence, To treat (a subject or thing) in a manner showing due appreciation, to deal with (it) as is right or fitting. ***to do oneself justice***, to perform something one has to do in a manner worthy of one's abilities.

1679 DRYDEN *Troilus & Cr.* Pref., I cannot leave this subject before I do justice to that Divine Poet by giving you one of his passionate descriptions. **1715** DE FOE *Fam. Instruct.* II. i. (1841) I. 171 You must do your Master justice now: for, if I mistake not, you wrong him very much by your own account. **1792** *Aneed. W. Pitt* III. xxxix. 44 Let me do justice to a man, whose character and conduct have been

infamously traduced. **1849** MACAULAY *Hist. Eng.* iv. I. 463 James, to do him justice, would gladly have found out a third way. **1855** PRESCOTT *Philip II*, II. vii. I. 216 The abstract here given does no justice to the document. **1870** E. PEACOCK *Ralf Skirl.* II. 114 To the food he did ample justice. *Mod.* Being nervous in the course of his speech, he did not do himself justice.

†**b.** To pledge in drinking. *Obs.*

1604 SHAKS. *Oth.* II. iii. 90 *Cas.* To the health of our Generall. *Mon.* I am for it Lieutenant: and Ile do you Iustice. *a* **1700** B. E. *Dict. Cant. Crew* s.v., *I'll do you Justice Sir*, I will Pledge you.

12. *attrib.* and *Comb.*: attrib., as ***justice-box***, ***-business***, ***-day***, ***-hall***, ***-height***, ***-hill***, ***-parson***, ***-room***; objective, etc., as ***justice-maker***, ***justice-dealing***, ***-like***, ***-loving***, ***-proof***, ***-slighting*** adjs.; **justice-broker**, a magistrate who 'sells' justice; †**justice-court**, a court of justice; *spec.* the Court of Justiciary; **justice-eyre (-air)**: see EYRE; **justice-seat**, seat of justice, judgement-seat; *spec.* (see quot. 1641).

1820 T. MITCHELL *Aristoph.* I. 53 Their whole soul lodged In the *justice-box, and ne'er so pleased.. As when they give some criminal a gripe. **1691** DRYDEN *Amphitryon* IV. i. 42 The Devil take all *Justice-brokers. **1848** THACKERAY *Van. Fair* xlv, Plunged in *justice-business. **1528** *Sc. Acts Jas. V* (1597) §7 In the justice aires, or *justice courts. **1596** DALRYMPLE tr *Leslie's Hist. Scot.* I. 53 The toune of Brichine.. quhair is ane.. Justice court haldne. *a* **1649** DRUMM. OF HAWTH. *Hist. Jas. V* Wks. (1711) 86 Warden of the east marches, keeping the days of truce and justice-courts. **1616** J. LANE *Contn. Sqr.'s T.* VIII. 348 As if your last howl weare not *justice day. **1835** THIRLWALL *Greece* I. iv. 80 The *justice-dealing kings, Dorus and Xuthus. *c* **1500** *Adam Bel* 65 She went vnto the *iustice hall. *a* **1613** OVERBURY *Characters, Elder Brother* Wks. (1856) 67 His ambition flies *justice-height. **1597** SHAKS. *2 Hen. IV*, v. i. 76 Turn'd into a *Iustice-like Seruingman. **1845** MIALL in *Nonconf.* V. 197 Impartial and *justice-loving men. **1678** CUDWORTH *Intell. Syst.* I. v. 893 (Contents) These *Justice-makers.. pretend to derive their factitious Justice from Pacts and Covenants. **1824** SYD. SMITH *Wks.* (1859) II. 48/2 The settlers take the law into their own hands, and give notice to a *justice-proof delinquent to quit the territory. **1809** *Sporting Mag.* XXXIII. 92 The *justice-room in the Bail of Lincoln. **1548** R. HUTTEN *Sum of Diuinitie* R viij b, We must al appeare before the *iustice seate of Christe. **1641** *Termes de la Ley* 193 b, *Iustice seat* is the highest Court that is held in a Forest, and it is alwayes held before the Lord chiefe Iustice in Eyre of the Forest. **1848** WHARTON *Law Lex.* s.v. *Forest Courts*, The court of justice-seat.. was a court of record; but since the Revolution in 1688, the forest laws have fallen into total disuse. **1856** KANE *Arct. Expl.* II. xii. 128 The idlers.. gather about the justice-seat.

justice ('dʒʌstɪs), *v.* Forms: 3–6 **-ise(n**, 4–7 **-ice**, 6 **-yce**, 7– **justice**. [a. AF. *justice-r* = OF. *justicier*, *-cer*, *-ser* (Pr. *justiziar*, Pg. *justiçar*, It. *giustiziare*), ad. med.L. *justitiāre* to exercise justice over, bring to trial, punish, *refl.* to submit to justice, f. L. *justitia* JUSTICE.]

†**1.** *trans.* To administer justice to; to rule, govern. *Obs.*

c **1320** *Cast. Love* 298 Wiþ oute whom he ne mai His kindom wiþ pees wysen, Ne wiþ rihte hit iustisen. *c* **1330** R. BRUNNE *Chron. Wace* (Rolls) 2230 Regned Rehudybras.. To iustice þe folk fol wys he was. **1481** CAXTON *Godfrey* 289 [They] made an hye noble man.. named Raoul, for to be kynge, vpon them, by whom they wold be Iustised and gouerned.

†**2.** To try in a court of law; to bring to trial; to punish judicially. *Obs.*

c **1330** R. BRUNNE *Chron.* (1810) 100 þe kyng in þe courte of þe lay þe clerkes wild justise. **1581** LAMBARDE *Eiren.* I. ix. (1602) 39 The names of such, as (being indited) did flie, and did refuse to be Iustised. *a* **1586** SIDNEY *Arcadia* II. xxix. ¶5 Perswading the iusticing her. **1732** NEAL *Hist. Purit.* I. 415 The body of a subject is to be justiced *secundum legem terrae*, as Magna Charta.. saith.

3. *intr.* To administer justice (as a justice of the peace); see JUSTICING *vbl. sb.*

†'**justiceable**, *a. Obs. rare*⁻¹. [f. JUSTICE *v.* (or ? misprint for *justiciable*).] = JUSTICIABLE.

1603 HAYWARD *Answ. Doleman* iii. H ij, Many pettie kings .. were subiect to their Nobilitie, and iusticeable by them.

Justice-Clerk. *Sc. Law.* [For *Justice's Clerk.*] (Since 1681, ***Lord Justice-Clerk.***) The vice-president of the Scotch Court of Justiciary, presiding also over the Outer House or Second Division of the Court of Session. Hence **Justice-Clerkship.**

His title is derived from the fact that he was originally the Clerk of the JUSTICE-GENERAL, whose legal duties he eventually entirely performed.

1424 *Sc. Acts Jas. I* (1597) §20 The Iustice Clerk be the inditement, sall gar sik trespassoures be corrected before the Iustice, and punished as said is. *c* **1575** *Balfour's Practicks* (1754) 565 Item, The Justice-clerk sall have for ilk persoun that is clengit be ane assise.. iiij.d. **1737** J. CHAMBERLAYNE *St. Gt. Brit.* II. II. iv. 376 Lord Justice-Clerk.. he is the Second Person in the Justice-Court, being next to the Justice-General; but now he is one of the Officers of State, though the Justice-General be none. **1861** W. BELL *Dict. Law Scot.* 541 The Lord-Justice-Clerk in absence of the Lord-Justice-General, is the presiding judge in the Court of Justiciary... Prior to 1641 the Justice-Clerk was not one of the judges.. but merely the clerk and assessor of Court.

Justice-General. *Sc. Law.* [f. JUSTICE *sb.* 9 + GENERAL *a.*: cf. *Attorney-General.*] (Now ***Lord Justice-General.***) The president of the Scotch Court of Justiciary: an office which, having become a sinecure usually held by a nobleman (the actual duties being discharged by the Justice-Clerk), was by 1 Will. IV. c. 69. §18 merged in that of Lord President of the Court of Session.

c **1575** *Balfour's Practicks* (1754) 565 It is statute and ordanit, that the Justice general sall have.. for ilk day of the air, five pundis. **1737** [see JUSTICE-CLERK]. **1752** LOUTHIAN *Form of Process* (ed. 2) 3 The Justice-court had then for its Members, the Justice-General, the Justice-Clerk, the Justice-Deputes, the Clerk-Depute, the Dempster, the Officers and Macers. **1830** *Act 1 Will IV*, c. 69 §18 *margin*, Office of lord justice general on next vacancy to devolve on lord president.

Hence **Justice-Generalship.**

1804 G. ROSE *Diaries* (1860) II. 175 The Justice-Generalship of Scotland.

†'**justicehood.** *Obs. rare*⁻¹. [see -HOOD.] The office or dignity of a justice; justiceship.

a **1637** B. JONSON *Expost. Inigo Jones* 77 Should but the king his justice-hood employ, In setting forth of such a solemn toy?

'**justiceless**, *a. rare.* [f. JUSTICE *sb.* + -LESS.] Without administration of justice.

c **1330** R. BRUNNE *Chron.* (1810) 245 þider bihoued him nedes to set þat lond in pes, For foles haf no drede, þat long is justiseles.

†'**justicely**, *a. Obs.* In 5 **iustisly**. [f. JUSTICE *sb.* + -LY¹.] Pertaining to a justice or judge.

1434 MISYN *Mend. Life* 111 To þame þat all þinge for hym forsakes hy worschip he has behest, & Iustisly power.

†'**justicement.** *Obs.* [a. AF. and OF. *justicement* administration of justice, f. *justicer* vb., to JUSTICE + -MENT.] Administration of justice.

[**1275** *Act 3 Edw. I*, c. 33 Qe nul Visconte ne seoffre.. Seneschaus de grant Seygnurs, ne autre sil ne seit attorne son Seygnur a suite fere, ne rendre les Iugemenz des Contez [*Laud MS. substitutes* a fer Iusticement del conte] ne pronuncier les Iugemenz. **1642** COKE reads 'justicements', and glosses 'That is, all things belonging to Iustice'.] **1670** BLOUNT *Law Dict.* **1755** JOHNSON, *Justicement*, procedure in courts. **1848** WHARTON *Law Lex.*

justicer ('dʒʌstɪsə(r)). Forms: 4–5 **iustyser**, 5 **-icer**, **-ycer**, 5–6 **-iser**, **-icere**, 5–7 **-icier**, 7– **justicer**. [prob. orig. AF. form of OF. *justicier* (12th c. in Hatz.-Darm.), = med.L. *jūstitiārius*, and thus orig. the etymological equivalent of JUSTICIAR, JUSTICIARY; but commonly used in a less technical sense as agent-noun from JUSTICE *v.*: cf. OF. *justiceor*, *-eur* (in nom. case *justiciere*), agent-n. of *justicier* vb., of which also the Eng. form would be at length *justicer.*]

1. One who maintains or executes justice; a supporter or vindicator of right. *arch.*

c **1330** R. BRUNNE *Chron. Wace* (Rolls) 2221 Ne he couþe be no iustyser. **1474** CAXTON *Chesse* 14 That afterward was a good prynce and a good iusticier. *c* **1500** *Melusine* 97 They said that the kyng had doo right wel as a valyaunt & lawfull iustiser shuld doo. **1585** FOXE *Serm. 2 Cor.* v. 72 So it pleased the gracious goodnesse of our mercifull God.. to become now of a terrible Iusticer, a tender father toward us. **1624** HEYWOOD *Gunaik.* IV. 179 That inhumane rashnesse.. by which men have undertooke to be their owne justicers. **1848** KINGSLEY *Saint's Trag.* v. iii, We are Heaven's justicers! Our woes anoint us kings! **1869** LD. LYTTON *Orval* 79 (*Draws his dagger*) Out, thou sharp Straightforward justicer!

2. An administrator of justice. †**a.** In general sense: A ruler or governor invested with judicial authority. *Obs.* **b.** One who administers justice in a court of law; a judge, magistrate. *arch.*

1481 CAXTON *Godfrey* 29 They made in euery kynred or lygnage a prince whiche was theyr Iusticer. **1598** BARRET *Theor. Warres* v. i. 145 As high and supreame Iusticer of all the Army. **1605** SHAKS. *Lear* III. vi. 25 Come sit thou here, most learned Iusticer. **1653** H. COGAN tr. *Pinto's Trav.* vi. 17 As it were chief Justicer amongst the Mahometans. **1799** W. TAYLOR in *Monthly Rev.* XXVIII. 513 The Corsican barristers claim that all the justicers.. shall be native and resident Corsicans. **1803** —— in *Ann. Rev.* I. 438 His subdivided schedules of contents.. trace the bounds of their parish sovereignties, and note whether the presiding justicer be entitled a prince, a baronet, or an esquire. **1871** ROSSETTI *Poems, Dante at Verona* liii, They named him Justicer-at-Law.

†**c.** *transf.* A judge, critic. *Obs.*

1609 HOLLAND *Amm. Marcell.* XXV. v. 271 If some severe Censor and precise Iusticer blame this act. **1612–15** BP. HALL *Contempl.*, *O.T.* XV. v, How severe Justicers wee can bee to our very owne crimes in others persons?

3. *spec.* = JUSTICE 9, JUSTICIARY *sb.*¹ 1, 2. *arch.*

1535 *Act 27 Hen. VIII*, c. v. §1 The said Iusticers.. shal be sworne astricted and obliged to the kepinge of their sessions of the peace. **1567** HARMAN *Caveat* 21 Thereby the Justicers.. may in their circutes be more vygelant to punish these malefactores. **1655** FULLER *Ch. Hist.* III. vi. §34 As for the civil government of Jews in England, the King set over them one principal Officer, called the Justicer of the Jews. **1700** TYRRELL *Hist. Eng.* II. 1113 The chief Justicers, or Justicers in Eyre in their Circuits. **1880** *Daily Tel.* 22 Nov., John Fineux, Chief Justicer to King Henry VIII.

justiceship ('dʒʌstɪsʃɪp). [f. JUSTICE *sb.* + -SHIP.] The office or dignity of a justice or judge; the functions of a justice, or their discharge. Similarly ***Chief Justiceship.***

1542–3 *Act 34 & 35 Hen. VIII*, c. 26 §13 Any office of Stewardeshipps Chamberlaineshipps Chancellourshipps or Iusticeshipps. *a* **1645** HABINGTON *Surv. Worc.* in *Worc. Hist. Soc. Proc.* III. 428 His offyce of Cheyfe-Justiceshyp of the Marches of Wales. **1749** FIELDING *Tom Jones* VII. ix, Desiring her brother to execute justiceship (for it was indeed a syllable more than justice) on the wench. **1793** G. READ in *Life & Corr.* (1870) 547, I have at length determined to accept of the chief justiceship of the supreme court [of Delaware]. **1897** *Westm. Gaz.* 30 Sept. 8/1 The *doyen* of English judges.. who retired from a Justiceship of the Queen's Bench in 1890.

b. With *poss. adj.* as a title for a justice.

1692 *Vindication* 12 Can any one.. believe that His Justiceship.. was never so imposed on? **1736** LEDIARD *Life Marlborough* I. 58 His exquisite Justice-ship employ'd.. the whole Wisdom of the Nation, to undo his vile Undoings.

justiciable (dʒʌ'stɪʃɪəb(ə)l), *a.* (*sb.*) [a. AF. and OF. (F.) *justiciable* amenable to a jurisdiction, used also as sb., f. *justicier* to JUSTICE: cf. med.L. *justitiābilis.*] Liable to be tried in a court of justice; subject to jurisdiction.

[**1370** *Rolls Parlt.*, Queux ne sont mye justiciables en touz cas.] **1656** BLOUNT *Glossogr.*, *Justiciable* (Fr.), under jurisdiction, subject to suit or Laws, that is to do his suit to the court of another. **1755** JOHNSON, *Justiciable*, proper to be examined in courts of justice. **1836** WHEATON *Elem. Internat. Law* II. ii. (1855) 175 Criminal offences.. are justiciable only by the courts of that country where the offence is committed. **1888** BRYCE *Amer. Commw.* I. 323 Offences against Federal statutes are justiciable in Federal courts.

B. *sb.* One who is subject to the jurisdiction (of another).

1897 MAITLAND *Domesday & Beyond* 125 He can prevent the king's officers from entering his precinct and meddling with his justiciables. **1900** *Athenæum* 5 May 556/3 Remedies which shall satisfy his justiciables that their position is.. positively enviable.

Hence **justicia'bility**, the quality or fact of being justiciable.

1802 BENTHAM *Judicial Procedure* i. Wks. 1843 II. 9/1 Under the name of security for eventual justiciability. **1888** TRAILL *William III* 97 Exclusive privileges in the matter of justiciability which were possessed by the Peers.

ju'sticial, *a. rare.* [ad. med.L. *jūstitiāl-is*, f. *jūstitia* JUSTICE.] Of or pertaining to justice or its administration.

c **1425** LYDG. *Assembly of Gods* 904 Pesyble prelates, iustyciall gouernours. **1600** DYMMOK *Ireland* (1843) 10 The present gouerment.. is devided into three partes, Ecclesiasticall, Martiall and Cyuill or Justiciall. **1826** BENTHAM in *Westm. Rev.* VI. 485 In argument, the difference,.. is, of course, made use of as a ground for difference in judicial decision.

Justicialism (dʒʌ'stɪʃəlɪz(ə)m). Also in Sp. form **Justicialismo** (xustiθja'lismo), and with small initial. [f. Sp. *justicia* justice + -AL + *-ismo* -ISM.] The name given by Juan Domingo Perón (1895–1974), President of Argentina (1946–55 and 1973–4), to his political doctrine: a combination of Fascism and socialism. Cf. PERONISM. So **Ju'sticialist**(a *a.*

1949 tr. *J. Perón's Speech at Opening 83rd Parl. Session Nat. Congr.* 7 The year that has gone by will be recorded in the Argentine history as the year of the 'justicialist' Constitution. [**1950** R. A. MENDE (*title*) El Justicialismo.] **1952** *Time* 12 May 28/3 If we take advantage of this historic moment, we shall impose Justicialism on the world and the coming century will be Justicialist. **1953** G. I. BLANKSTEN *Perón's Argentina* xii. 276 The current label [for Perón's system] is *Justicialismo*. **1955** G. PENDLE *Argentina* vi. 107 The basis of 'justicialist philosophy' was never more clearly expressed, perhaps, than in the following presidential assertion: 'For us there is nothing fixed and nothing to deny. We are anti-Communist because Communists are sectarians, and anti-capitalist because capitalists are sectarians. Our Third Position is not a central position. It is an ideological position which is in the centre, on the right or on the left, according to specific circumstances.' **1971** A. HENNESSY in A. Bullock *20th Cent.* 120/2 In spite of.. exaggerated claims for the ideology of 'justicialism' as a Third Position—neither capitalism nor communism—Peronism's impact outside Argentina was limited. **1972** *Buenos Aires Herald* 3 Feb. 9/2 A Justicialista Party executive committee member. **1972** *Times* 17 Nov. 16/2 Justicialismo, a vague word described as a middle way between communism and capitalism. *Ibid.* 16 Dec. 4/5 The candidate will be a Justicialist civilian.

justiciar (dʒʌ'stɪʃɪə(r)). Also **justitiar**, **-cier**. [ad. med.L. *jūstitiārius*: cf. next. *Justiciar* and *justiciary* are not contemporary names, but appear in the 15th and the 16th c. respectively, as adaptations of the med.L. See also JUSTICER.]

1. *Eng. Hist.* The chief political and judicial officer under the Norman and early Plantagenet kings, who represented the king in all relations of state, acting as regent in his absence and as royal deputy in his presence, and presiding over the Curia Regis. Called more fully ***Capital*** or ***Chief Justiciar***: = JUSTICIARY *sb.*¹ 1.

The office of justiciar came to an end in the 13th cent., his judicial functions passing to the Lord Chief Justice.

[*a* **1135** in Rymer *Fœdera* I. 12 Coram me vel capitali Justiciario meo. **1214** *Ibid.* 181 Sciatis quod constituimus Justiciarium nostrum angliæ Venerabilem patrem nostrum Dominum P. Winton. Episcopum.] **1579–80** NORTH

Plutarch (1656) 449 *note*, The Greek hath it only thus, 'are called Victory', as it were in the abstract, as we call Our Lord Chief Justice, who is but a Justiciar. **1598** STOW *Surv.* xxxii. (1603) 288 Hubert, ArchBishop of Canterburie, and Iusticier of England [in the year 1197]. **1611** SPEED *Hist. Gt. Brit.* IX. vi. §3 Robert Earle of Leicester, Chiefe Iusticiar of England. **1876** FREEMAN *Norm. Conq.* V. xxiv. 432 The Justiciar, chief administrator of the law,..was, while his office lasted, the most powerful subject in the realm.

2. A judge presiding over, or belonging to, one of the king's superior courts, or exercising special judicial functions: = JUSTICE 9a. *Obs.* exc. *Hist.*

[**1215** *Magna Charta* c. 18 Mittemus duos Justiciarios per unumquemque comitatum per quattuor vices in anno. *c* **1220** JOCELIN *Chron.* (Camden) 71 Venit tamen in questionem coram justitiariis ad scaccarium. *c* **1250** BRACTON II. I. vii. §2 Habet etiam [rex] curiam et iustitiarios in banco residentes..Habet etiam iustitiarios itinerantes de comitatu in comitatum.] **1485** *Rolls Parlt.* VI. 348 The offices of Lieutenauntshipp, Justiciar and Chamberlaynshipp, of Carmardeynshire and Cardeganshire. *c* **1575** *Balfour's Practicks* (1754) 140 Without speciall command of the King, or of the Justiciar of the forest. **1611** SPEED *Hist. Gt. Brit.* IX. ix. (1623) 626 Another of the Kings Justiciars..was so confidently greedy that in one circuit he appropriated to himselfe aboue two hundreth pound lands. **1640** YORKE *Union Hon.* 14 Roger de Clifford..whom the King had despatched into those parts, as Justiciar of all Wales. **1897** MAITLAND *Domesday & Beyond* 101 French justiciars and French clerks have become the exponents of English law.

b. In Scotland, under the early kings, the title of two supreme judges, having jurisdiction north and south of Forth respectively. *Obs.* exc. *Hist.*

[**1318** *Sc. Acts 13 Robt. I*, c. 4 §2 Ballivus in cuius ballia talis malefactor moratur habeat mandatum iusticiarii infra cuius iusticiariam transgressio facta fuit.] **1609** SKENE *Reg. Maj.* 21 [transl. prec.] The Ballie or Judge, within quhais jurisdiction the malefactor dwelis, sall haue ane command of the Justitiar, within quhais Justitiarie the crime is committed. *Ibid.* 58 It is statute, that Justitiars salbe beath vpon the southside, and the northside of the water of Forth. **1828–40** TYTLER *Hist. Scot.* (1864) I. 248 William the Lion ..appears to have changed or new modelled these offices, by the creation of two great judges named Justiciars.

3. *gen.* An administrator of justice; one who maintains or executes justice: = JUSTICER 1, 2.

1623 *Kings of Scot.* in *Harl. Misc.* (Malh.) III. 462 He was a good justiciar, in whose time there was a law made, that [etc.]. *a* **1649** DRUMM. OF HAWTH. *Poems* 195 Ah spare this Monument, great Guests it keeps, Three grave Justiciars. **1651** N. BACON *Disc. Govt. Eng.* II. xxvi. (1739) 115 The Duke of Suffolk..he suffered to be tried..for a Murder done upon a mean person, and by such means obtained the repute of a zealous Justiciar. *a* **1734** NORTH *Life Ld. Guildford* (1808) I. 2 Considering the value of this great justitiar [Lord Keeper North].

4. Used to designate various foreign officials and functionaries.

1851 SIR F. PALGRAVE *Norm. & Eng.* I. 86 He was one of the Commissioners or Justiciars deputed to England as soon as Richard died. **1898** *Daily News* 25 Oct. 3/3 The narrative is put into the mouth of Hugo Gottfried, only son of the hereditary Executioner. For fourteen generations the Gottfrieds have held the office of Justiciar.

†**5.** *Theol.* = JUSTICIARY 5. *Obs.*

1772 FLETCHER *Logica Genev.* 120 Against whom have you employed your pen..Is it only against the proud justiciars?

Hence **ju'sticiarship**, the office of justiciar.

1677 *Spottiswood's Hist. Ch. Scot.* App. 36 King Charles ..gave him the hereditary Justiciarship. **1867** PEARSON *Hist. Eng.* II. 2 The intrusion of foreign favourites into bishoprics and Justiciarships.

justiciary (dʒʌ'stɪʃɪərɪ), *sb.*[1] Also **justitiary**. [ad. med.L. *jūstitiāri-us*, *-ciāri-us* judge, f. *jūstitia* JUSTICE: see -ARY[1] B. 1. A doublet of JUSTICIAR.]

1. *Eng. Hist.* The chief political and judicial officer under the Norman and early Plantagenet kings; more fully, ***Chief Justiciary***: = JUSTICIAR 1.

Found only in modern historians, as a rendering of med.L. *justiciarius*: the form JUSTICIAR was in use a century earlier.

1700 TYRRELL *Hist. Eng.* II. 848 Hubert de Burgh the Justitiary. **1769** BLACKSTONE *Comm.* IV. xxxiii. 416 [After the Conquest] the *aula regis*..was erected: and a capital justiciary appointed. **1818** HALLAM *Mid. Ages* viii. II. (1819) II. 461 The King's Court..was composed of the great officers; the chief justiciary, the chancellor, the constable, marshall, chamberlain, steward, and treasurer, with any others whom the king might appoint. **1863** H. COX *Instit.* II. viii. 506 In the time of William I. the Chief Justiciary was, after the King, the principal political person in the kingdom.

2. = JUSTICE 9a, JUSTICIAR 2. *Obs.* exc. *Hist.*

1761 *London* IV. 10 The citizens..had..the county of Middlesex added to their jurisdiction..with a power of appointing..a Justiciary from among themselves. **1827** *Gentl. Mag.* XCVII. II. 495 On the 12th of February, 1267, Alexander III. issued a patent..witnessed by the Earl of Buchan, Justiciary. **1868** MILMAN *St. Paul's* 36 He had been a travelling justiciary in 1179. **1874** GREEN *Short Hist.* ii. §5. 83 A royal justiciary secured law to the Jewish merchant.

3. One who maintains or executes justice; an administrator of justice; = JUSTICER 1, 2.

a **1548** HALL *Chron. 10 Henry V*, This sheperd was such a iusticiary that no offence was vnpunished, no frend-ship vnrewarded. **1590** GREENE *Royal Exch.* Wks. 1882 VII. 240 Ariscides, the perfect Justiciarie of his time. **1675** CAVE *Antiq. Apost.* (1702) 14 The supream ruler and justiciary of the world. **1855** MILMAN *Lat. Chr.* v. ii. II. 313 The Emperor is..the supreme justiciary in his Gallic and German realm. **1895** *Daily News* 16 Sept. 6/5 The Right, in this instance, was the justiciary of the Republic.

4. Used to designate various foreign officers of state and judicial functionaries, esp. F. *justicier*, Sp. *justiciero*, It. *sindaco*, etc.

1763 GIBBON *Misc. Wks.* (1814) III. 36 The justiciary of Arragon, a name dreadful to royal ears. **1768** STERNE *Sent. Journ., Passport, Versailles* iv, The passport was directed to all..generals of armies, justiciaries and all officers of justices. **1854** MILMAN *Lat. Chr.* x. iv. IV. 378 The Senate and people of Rome..had sent justiciaries into Tuscany..to receive oaths of allegiance..and to exact tribute.

†**5.** *Theol.* One who holds that man can of himself attain to righteousness. Cf. JUSTICE 2. *Obs.*

1532 BECON *Pomander Prayer* Wks. 1843–4 II. 89 Suffer me not therefore, O Lord, to be in the number of those justiciaries which, boasting their own righteousness.. despise that righteousness that cometh by faith. **1550** —— *Govern. Virtue* ibid. I. 423 Christ 'came not to call the justiciaries, but sinners to repentance.' **1563** *Homilies* II. *Rogation Week* I. ¶6 Iusticiaries and hipocrites, which rob Almighty God of this honour, and ascribe it to themselues. *a* **1625** BOYS *Wks.* (1630) 456 The Pharisee..is a type of all Iustitiaries hoping to be saued by the righteousness of the law. *a* **1716** SOUTH *Serm.* (1744) IX. 146 The pompous austerities and fastings of many religious operators, and splendid justiciaries.

Hence **ju'sticiaryship**, the office of justiciary.

1700 TYRRELL *Hist. Eng.* II. 890 He required Him..to give an Account of his Justitiaryship. **1870** *Pall Mall G.* 10 Aug. 11 De Olifard found his reward in a grant of lands in Roxburghshire and the justiciaryship of Lothian.

justiciary (dʒʌ'stɪʃɪərɪ), *sb.*[2] Also **justitiary**. [ad. med.L. *jūstitiāria*, *-ciāria*, f. *jūstitia* JUSTICE: see -ARY[1] B. 3.]

1. *Sc.* The jurisdiction of a justiciar or justiciary: see JUSTICIAR 2 b.

High Court of Justiciary, the supreme criminal tribunal of Scotland. ***circuit court of justiciary***, ***justiciary court***, a circuit court held by judges of the High Court. ***commissioners of justiciary***: see quot. 1846.

[**1318**: see JUSTICIAR 2 b.] **1473** in *Acc. Ld. High Treas. Scot.* (1877) I. 68 Item gevin to the Justice Schire Dauid Guthere of that Ilk, knycht, for his fee of this ȝere of his office of Justiciary..j^c ti. **1491** *Sc. Acts Jas. IV* (1597) §43 The Clerke of the Iusticiarie sall take dittay there-vpon, and they to be punished as oppressoures. **1579** *Sc. Acts Jas. VI* (1597) §86 To that effect [our soueraine Lord]..grantis and givis to them power and commission of Iusticiarie. **1746–7** *Act 20 Geo. II*, c. 43 §1 That all Heretable Jurisdictions of Justiciary.. within that part of Great Britain called Scotland..shall be..abrogated. **1752** *Scots Mag.* (1753) Oct. 493/1 The circuit-courts of justiciary. **1752** J. LOUTHIAN *Form of Process* (ed. 2) 6 The five Lords..are called Commissioners of Justiciary, and are invested with an equal Power and Jurisdiction in all Criminal Causes. **1846** MᶜCULLOCH *Acc. Brit. Empire* (1854) II. 223 The Court of Justiciary..consists of five judges, who are also judges of the Court of Session, specially commissioned by the sovereign, together with the justice-general and justice-clerk.

attrib. **1819** R. CHAPMAN *Jas. V* 128 To put an end to those disorders, the king established a justiciary court at Jedburgh. **1844** LD. BROUGHAM *Brit. Const.* xix. §6. (1862) 367 The distinction of justiciary, session, and jury judges is done away.

2. Judicature.

1869 DRAPER *Amer. Civ. War* I. xxvi. §6. 445 Already has that [non-slaveholding] power reduced the supreme justiciary to a mere temporary bulwark.

justiciary (dʒʌ'stɪʃɪərɪ), *a.* [ad. med. or mod.L. *jūstitiāri-us*, F. *justiciaire* 'of or belonging unto Justice' (Cotgr. 1611).]

1. Pertaining to, or connected with, the administration of justice, or the office of a justice. (See also JUSTICIARY *sb.*[2] 1 *attrib.*)

1581 MULCASTER *Positions* xxxix. (1887) 207 They may spare number enough..to all martiall and militare affaires to all iusticiarie functions. **1632** BROME *North. Lasse* III. ii. Wks. 1873 III. 57 You have alwayes been so strict and terrible in your Iustitiarie courses. **1711** E. WARD *Vulg. Brit.* VI. 77 Those Justitiary Fools Old Headboroughs and Constables. **1897** MAITLAND *Domesday & Beyond* 102 The demarcation of justiciary areas.

†**2.** *Theol.* Pertaining to, or believing in, 'the righteousness which is of the law'; self-righteous: see JUSTICIARY *sb.*[1] 5. *Obs.*

1615 T. ADAMS *Blacke Devill* 3 A justiciary, imaginary, self-conceited righteousnesse. **1630** SYMMER *Rest Weary* v. B iij b, The proud Pharisee and Iusticiarie Hypocrite. *a* **1665** J. GOODWIN *Filled w. the Spirit* (1867) 114 Such a kind of Christian or believer who savours much of the justiciary and legal spirit.

‖**justicies** (dʒʌ'stɪʃiːz). *Law.* [med.L., 2nd pers. sing. pres. subj. of *jūsticiāre* to JUSTICE.] A writ, now abolished, directed to a sheriff, empowering him to hold plea of debt in his county court for sums exceeding forty shillings; so called from the opening words: see quot. 1284.

[**1284** *Stat. Wallie* 12 Edw. I, c. 6 Precepimus tibi quod justicies A. quod..sine dilatione reddat B. centum solidos.] **1534** FITZHERB. *Nat. Brevium* lv. (1598) 117 Et le brief daccompt que serra sue en le county est un Iusticies direct al vicomte.] **1607** COWELL *Interpr.* s.v., By this Writ called Iusticies, the Shyreeue may hold plee of a greate summe, whereas of his ordinary authoritie he cannot hold plees but of summes vnder 40 shillings. **1768** BLACKSTONE *Comm.* III. iv. 36 The county court may also hold plea of..personal actions to any amount, by virtue of a special writ called a *justicies*. **1846** *Act 9 & 10 Vict.* c. 95 *Preamb.*, The County Court..having Cognizance..by virtue of a Writ of Justicies.

justicing ('dʒʌstɪsɪŋ), *vbl. sb.* [f. JUSTICE *v.* + -ING[1].] The administration of justice. Chiefly *attrib.*, esp. in ***justicing-room***, e.g. in the house of a justice of the peace.

1606 B. BARNES *4 Bks. Offices* 145 That kinde of iustecying which is said to be common amongst the Turkes. **1611** SPEED *Hist. Gt. Brit.* IX. xx. (1623) 965 In this progresse, or rather itinirary Iusticing. **1820** MISS MITFORD in L'Estrange *Life* (1870) II. 97 He is not the author of the book on justicing. **1866** READE *Griffith Gaunt* (1887) 39 Justicing-day brought him many visits. **1873** MISS BROUGHTON *Nancy* I. 19 Prayers are held in the justicing room.

justico, -coat, -core, forms of JUSTAUCORPS.

justifiability (ˌdʒʌstɪfaɪə'bɪlɪtɪ). [f. next: see -ITY.] = JUSTIFIABLENESS.

1884 *Law Times* 6 Sept. 320/2 The justifiability of hostile acts unpreceded by declaration of war. **1897** *Allbutt's Syst. Med.* III. 921 Attacks..so slight as to make the justifiability of any operation a matter of question.

justifiable ('dʒʌstɪfaɪəb(ə)l), *a.* [a. F. *justifiable* (13–14th c.), f. *justifier* to JUSTIFY.]

†**1.** = JUSTICIABLE. *Obs.*

1523 FITZHERB. *Surv.* xviii. 33 b, Here you my lorde R. that I W. de C. fro thus day forthe to you shalbe faythfull and lowly..and I shall be iustyfyable of body and of goodes. **1643** PRYNNE *Sov. Power Parlt.* App. 17 Whom Cæsar.. calleth *Reguli*, little Kings, being themselves subjects and justifiable to the Nobility, who had all the Soveraignty.

2. Capable of being legally or morally justified, or shown to be just, righteous, or innocent; defensible.

justifiable homicide: see HOMICIDE *sb.*[2]

1561 T. NORTON *Calvin's Inst.* IV. xiii. (1634) 628 *marg.*, Departure from Monkerie to some other honest kind of life [is] justifiable. **1586** A. DAY *Eng. Secretary* II. (1625) 39 May it not sometimes be justifiable to breake a mans head? **1624** CAPT. SMITH *Virginia* Pref. §4 The stile of a Souldier is not eloquent, but honest and iustifiable. **1717** J. KEILL *Anim. Oecon.* (1738) 8 In no Case..is the drawing off a large Quantity of Blood at a time justifiable. **1802** MAR. EDGEWORTH *Moral T.* (1816) I. xiii. 104 Little artifices which a tradesman thinks himself justifiable in practising. **1859** J. CUMMING *Ruth* ii. 15 Emigration from one's own land seems hardly justifiable.

†**b.** Of an assertion, etc.: Capable of being maintained, defended, or made good. *Obs.*

1612 SELDEN *Illustr. to Drayton's Poly-olb.* viii. 127 It is iustifiable by Cæsar, that they vs'd to shaue all except their head and vpper lip..but in their old Coynes I see no such thing warranted. **1646** SIR T. BROWNE *Pseud. Ep.* III. xxiv. 170 Some in the water doe carry a justifiable resemblance to some at the Land. **1651** *Raleigh's Ghost* 201 That so much raine could cause so great an inundation..may be made justifyable partly by reason, and partly by experience.

†**3.** Fitted to justify a claim or the like. *Obs.*

1755 MAGENS *Insurances* II. 417 The justifiable Instruments of the Cargo and Loss of the Goods insured and abandoned, the Assured ought to manifest and present to the Assurers.

justifiableness ('dʒʌstɪfaɪəb(ə)lnɪs). [f. prec. + -NESS.] The quality of being justifiable.

1640 BP. HALL *Humble Remonstr.* 30 Our position is onely affirmative; implying the justifiablenesse, and holynesse of an Episcopall calling. **1684** N. RESBURY *Case Cross Baptism* 7, I will not stand accountable for the Justifiableness of these passages. **1885** *L'pool Daily Post* 11 Apr. 4/7 The nation was ..divided in opinion as to the justifiableness of hostilities.

justifiably ('dʒʌstɪfaɪəblɪ), *adv.* [f. as prec. + -LY[2].] In a justifiable manner; so as to admit of justification.

1672 SOUTH *Serm. 1 Cor.* viii. 12 No man amongst us can justifiably plead weakness of conscience in that sense. **1734** FIELDING *Univ. Gallant* III. i, Anything which this lady may not justifiably suffer. **1856** RUSKIN *Mod. Paint.* IV. v. v. §1 An English painter justifiably loves fog, because he is born in a foggy country.

†'**justificable**, *a.* *Obs. rare.* [ad. med.L. *jūstificābil-is*, f. *jūstificāre* to JUSTIFY: see -ABLE.] Capable of being justified, justifiable.

1655 DIGGES *Compl. Ambass.* 57 We have thought..this so plain and justificable a case. **1671** *True Nonconf.* 400 Let it be so, that much of their way was justificable upon the account of these motives.

†**ju'stifical**, *a.* *Obs. rare.* [f. L. type **jūstific-us* (see -FIC) + -AL[1].]

a. Justificatory, justificative. **b.** Executing justice.

1646 SIR J. TEMPLE *Irish Rebell.* Pref. 8 For the justificall reasons of their rising in arms. **1656** BLOUNT *Glossogr.*, *Justifical*, that executes or doth Justice.

justification (ˌdʒʌstɪfɪ'keɪʃən). [ad. late L. *jūstificātiōn-em* (Augustine, etc.), n. of action f. *jūstificāre* to JUSTIFY. Cf. F. *justification* (12th c. in Godef.), perh. the immediate source.]

†**1.** Administration of justice or the law; execution of sentence; capital punishment. *Obs.*

1387–8 T. USK *Test. Love* II. xiii. (Skeat) l. 88 How should mercie been proued, and no trespasse were, by due iustification to be punished? **1422** tr. *Secreta Secret., Priv. Priv.* 211 Whan he shall Iustificacion done, he sholde noone dyuersite of Persones make. **1450–80** tr. *Secreta Secret.* 18 Vnto the tyme that god hath herde hem and done his iustificacioun in vengeaunce doyng. [**1878** VEITCH *Border Hist. & Poetry* ix. 286 A not less memorable case of 'justification', that of Adam Scott.]

†**2.** An ordinance; an ordained form. *Obs.*

c **1450** tr. *De Imitatione* III. lv. 131 Goode it is to me, lorde, þat þou hast mekid me, þat I mowe lerne þi iustificacions. **1582** N.T. (Rhem.) *Luke* i. 6 Walking in al the commaundements and iustifications of our Lord without blame. **1609** BIBLE (Douay) *Num.* ix. 3 Let the children of Israel make the Pasch in his time..according to al the ceremonies and iustifications therof.

3. The action of justifying or showing something to be just, right, or proper; vindication of oneself or another; exculpation; †verification, proof (*obs.*). **b.** That which justifies; a justifying circumstance; an apology, a defence.

1494 FABYAN *Chron.* VII. 507 With many couert wordys to the..iustyfycacion of hymselfe and excusynge of his owne dedys. **1555** EDEN *Decades* 240 Yet was he gladde to haue it tryed by iustice for the better iustification of his cause. **1635** NAUNTON *Fragm. Reg.* (Arb.) 39 Neither was she unmindfull of this Lord Norris, whose Father..in the business of her Mother, dyed in a Noble cause, and in the justification of her innocencie. **1729** BUTLER *Serm. Forgiveness* Wks. 1874 II. 109 Nothing can with reason be urged in justification of revenge. **1823** DE QUINCEY *Lett. Educ.* ii. (1860) 32 The metre, and the style..would immediately have lost their justification. **1870** MRS. RIDDELL *Austin Friars* iii, She could plead so much in her own justification.

4. *Theol.* The action whereby man is justified, or freed from the penalty of sin, and accounted or made righteous by God; the fact or condition of being so justified.

Protestant theologians regard justification as an act of grace in which God accounts man righteous, not owing to any merit of his own, but through imputation of Christ's righteousness, as apprehended and received by faith. Roman Catholic theologians hold that it consists in man's being made really righteous by infusion of grace, such justification being a work continuous and progressive from its initiation.

[**1382** WYCLIF *Rom.* v. 16 Sothli dom of oon in to condempnacioun, grace forsothe of manye giltis in to iustificacioun.] **1526** *Pilgr. Perf.* (W. de W. 1531) 31 This grace is called the grace of iustificacyon, or grace iustifyenge, for it iustifyeth our soules before god. **1565** T. NORTON *Calvin's Inst.* III. xi. §2 (1632), We simply expound justification to be an acceptation, whereby God receiving us into favour, taketh us for righteous, and we say that the same consisteth in forgivenesse of sinnes, and imputation of the righteousnesse of Christ. **1571** *39 Articles Ch. Eng.* xi, Of the iustification of man... That we are iustified by fayth onely, is a most wholesome doctrine, and very full of comfort. *Ibid.* xii, Good workes, which are the fruites of fayth, and folowe after iustification. **1585** HOOKER *Serm. Justification* §5 The first receipt of grace in their [Papists'] divinity is the first iustification: the increase thereof, the second iustification. **1675** BROOKS *Gold. Key* Wks. 1867 V. 61 Justification doth not increase or decrease, but all sin is pardoned at the first act of believing. **1771** WESLEY *Wks.* (1872) V. 57 The plain Scriptural notion of justification is pardon, the forgiveness of sins. **1837** HALLAM *Hist. Lit.* (1855) I. I. vi. 381 The tenet of justification or salvation by faith alone, called, in the barbarous jargon of polemics, solifidianism. **1871** R. H. HUTTON *Ess.* I. 6 They have seen so much goodness without faith,..that they begin to preach justification by sincerity as a more human, if not a more divine formula than justification by faith. **1885** *Catholic Dict.* 495/2 To the Catholic, sanctification and justification are the same thing, or at most two aspects of the same thing—viz. of the act by which God makes a soul just and holy in his sight.

5. *Law.* **a.** The showing or maintaining in court that one had sufficient reason for doing that which he is called to answer; a circumstance affording grounds for such a plea. **b.** The justifying of bail: see JUSTIFY 7 b.

1529 [see JUSTIFY 7 a]. **1660** *Trial Regic.* 19 If you have any thing of Justification, plead Not guilty. **1781** W. BLACKSTONE *Rep.* II. 1179 After many nugatory notices of justification, the defendant's bail appeared in Court to justify. **1809** TOMLINS *Law Dict.* s.v., If the action concern a local thing, a Justification in one place is not a Justification in another place. **1883** *Wharton's Law-Lex.* (ed. 7) s.v., A defence of justification is a defence showing the libel to be true, or in an action of assault showing the violence to have been necessary. **1886** *Philadelphia Times* 10 Apr. (Cent.), Mr. M—— said that Recorder S—— had fixed bail at $25,000, and justification in $50,000 would be enough.

6. The action of adjusting or arranging exactly; *spec.* in *Type-founding* and *Printing*: see JUSTIFY *v.* 9.

1672 T. MARSHALL *Let. to Dr. Fell* 19 Jan. (in H. Hart *Cent. Typogr. Oxford* 165/2) To expedite y^e justification of Matrices. **1727–41** CHAMBERS *Cycl.* s.v. *Foundery*, The justification, as to thickness, is made on a piece of marble; and for the height on an iron compository. The justification of the height is guided by the *m* of some body of characters already justified. **1824** J. JOHNSON *Typogr.* II. 132 Where a line is even spaced, and yet requires justification. *Ibid.* 133 No reasonable excuse either for bad justification or improper spacing. **1875** *Ure's Dict. Arts* III. 644 When he comes to the end of his line, and finds that he has a syllable or word which will not fill out the measure, he has to perform a task which requires considerable care and taste. This is called justification.

justificative (ˈdʒʌstɪfɪkeɪtɪv), *a.* [f. late L. *jūstificāt-*, ppl. stem of *jūstificāre* to JUSTIFY + -IVE. Cf. F. *justificatif* (16th c. in Godef. *Compl.*).] Serving to justify; justificatory; of the nature of supporting evidence.

1611 COTGR., *Iustificatif*, iustificatiue, iustifying, righting. **1622** MABBE tr. *Aleman's Guzman D'Alf.* II. 242. **1827** BENTHAM *Ration. Evid.* Wks. 1843 VII. 15 Some justificative, or extenuative, or exemptive, circumstance. **1890** SAINTSBURY *Ess.* 245 With justificative selections from Buffon..and other authorities.

ˈ**justificator.** [ad. late L. *jūstificātor*, agent-n. f. *jūstificāre* to JUSTIFY.] One who justifies.

The L. word occurs in a document of William Rufus (see first quot.), whence it has passed into the law dicts. as an English word.

[**11..** *Writ* in *Liber Ramesiæ* §188 Will. Rex Angl. H. Camerario & Justificatoribus suis, omnibusque suis fidelibus Norff., salutem.] **1670** BLOUNT *Law Dict.*, *Iustificators* [in prec. quot.] seem to signify Compurgators. **1755** JOHNSON, *Justificator*, one who supports, defends, vindicates, or justifies. **1799** MAR. EDGEWORTH *Ess. Self-Justif.* in *Lett. Lit. Ladies* (1805) 225 To one of your class of justificators, this is the highest offence. **1809** TOMLINS *Law Dict.*, *Justificators*, a kind of compurgators, or those that by oath justified the innocence, or oaths of others.

justificatory (ˈdʒʌstɪfɪkeɪtərɪ), *a.* [f. late L. *jūstificāt-*, ppl. stem of *jūstificāre* to JUSTIFY + -ORY.] Tending to justify; having the effect or purpose of justifying.

1579 FENTON *Guicciard.* VIII. (1599) 314 To hold fast that that hath bin gotten, is a colour iustificatorie to enable the title and interest of the thing. **1691** WOOD *Ath. Oxon.* II. 355 Printed at Amsterdam, with a justificatory preface. **1860** A. L. WINDSOR *Ethica* vii. 344 A man..almost sarcastically justificatory of the claims of self-interest. **1876** BANCROFT *Hist. U.S.* III. vii. 109 The Newcastle administration..summarily condemned the colony by rejecting its loyal justificatory address to the king.

b. Serving or intended to support a statement.

1779 GIBBON *Misc. Wks.* (1814) IV. 576 Mr. Davis has..suppressed one of the justificatory Notes on this passage. **1836** *Penny Cycl.* V. 269/1 In 1752 followed a justificatory tract on several disputed points.

justified (ˈdʒʌstɪfaɪd), *ppl. a.* [f. JUSTIFY + -ED¹.] Made just or right; made or accounted righteous; warranted; supported by evidence; in *Printing*: see JUSTIFY *v.* 9.

a **1586** SIDNEY *Arcadia* II. (1590) 128 That bad officer..gave him leave..to bear his sword prepared for the justified murther. **1671–2** T. MARSHALL *Let. to Dr. Fell* 9 Feb. (in H. Hart *Cent. Typogr. Oxford* 169/1) A large Collection of Proofes from Jæques Vallet, wch shew ye various Sorts of justifyed Matrices he is willing to sell. **1738** WESLEY *Ps.* CXVIII. vi, The Voice of Joy, and Love, and Praise..Among the Justified is found. **1820** R. HALL *Wks.* (1832) VI. 306 Either impenitent sinners or justified believers. **1891** J. WINSOR *Columbus* II. 55 A scholarly and justified narrative.

justifier (ˈdʒʌstɪfaɪə(r)). [f. as prec. + -ER¹.]

1. One who justifies: see JUSTIFY *v.*

1526 TINDALE *Rom.* iii. 26 That he myght be counted iuste, and a iustifiar of hym which belevith on Iesus. **1528** FRITH *Answ. Rastel* Wks. (1573) 16 You must graunt, that we haue a Christ or no Christ..a iustifier or no iustifier. **1629** H. BURTON *Babel no Bethel* 32 That I leaue to you, her justifier. **1711** STRYPE *Parker* III. xiv. 236 Justifiers of themselves and Hypocrites. **1838** J. H. NEWMAN *Justification* x. §2 Faith is the sole justifier.

2. *Type-founding* and *Printing.* **a.** A workman who justifies: see JUSTIFY 9; hence, in a typesetting machine: see quot. 1888. **b.** A wedge or the like for fixing an adjusted part of a printing-press, as the stone in the coffin, etc.

1683 MOXON *Mech. Exerc.*, *Printing* xi. ¶17 Justifiers of Wood, the length of every side,..must be thrust between the insides of the Coffin and the outsides of the Stone, to Wedge it tight..after the Press-man has Bedded it. **1824** J. JOHNSON *Typogr.* II. 512 To admit of justifiers between the stone and coffin, which are put to keep the stone steady after it is bedded. **1890** *Cent. Dict.* s.v. *Justifier*, in type-founding, the workman who fits up a suite of strikes or unjustified matrices for use on one mold. **1888** *Pall Mall G.* 10 Sept. 11/2 Even more ingenious is the second machine, or 'justifier', to which the type set up by the typotheter is taken. The 'justifier'..spaces out the lines with great regularity and in so short a time that 20,000 ens per hour is about the average output.

justify (ˈdʒʌstɪfaɪ), *v.* [a. F. *justifier* (12th c. in Godef. *Compl.*), ad. late (chiefly eccl.) L. *jūstificāre* to act justly towards, do justice to, make just, pardon, vindicate, f. *jūst-us* JUST: see -FY.]

†**1.** *trans.* To administer justice to; to try as a judge, to judge; to have jurisdiction over, rule, control, keep in order; to do justice to, treat justly. **b.** *absol.* To administer justice, to judge. *Obs.*

a **1300** *Cursor M.* 150 (Gött.) Of salomon þe wise, Hou craftili he did iustifie. **13..** *St. Erkenwolde* 229 in Horstm. *Altengl. Leg.* (1881) 271, I iustifiet þis ioly toun..more þene fourty wynter. **1377** LANGL. *P. Pl.* B. XIX. 44 Þe iewes he iustified & tauȝte hem þe lawe of lyf. **1390** GOWER *Conf.* III. 379 Hem [i.e. Clergy] oughte wel to justefie Thing, which belongith to here cure, As forto praie. **1449** *Sc. Acts Jas. II* (1814) 36/2 Þat al Regaliteis..be..iustifiit be the kingis Justice, quhil þai remayn in þe kingis handis. *c* **1460** FORTESCUE *Abs. & Lim. Mon.* ii. (1885) 112 Thai..ordenyd the same reaume to be ruled and justified by suche lawes as thai all wolde assent vnto. **1581** LAMBARDE *Eiren.* III. ii. (1588) 338 Them that undertake for the partie, that he shall abide to be justified by law. **1620** J. WILKINSON *Coroners & Sherifes* 12 [The Statute] giveth power to Forresters, Parkers, and Warreners to kill the offendors if they will not be justified.

†**2.** *trans.* To execute justice upon (a malefactor); to condemn to punishment; to punish, *esp.* (*Sc.*) to punish with death, execute. *Obs.*

1340 HAMPOLE *Pr. Consc.* 5987 Fadirs and modirs sal rekken þat tyde..And loverdes alswa of þair men..Þe whilk þai wald noght iustify. *c* **1450** LONELICH *Grail* xvi. 318 Thanne Axede him Nasciens..Whi that so sore Iustefyed he were. **1568** GRAFTON *Chron.* II. 353 To iustefie and punishe them for their offenses. *c* **1575** *Balfour's Practicks* (1754) 596 Thay beand swa convict, sall be justifyit to the deid thairfoir. **1700** COLLIER *2nd Def. Short View* (1738) 399 In Scotland they say when a Man is hanged he's justified. **1820** BYRON *Mar. Fal.* V. i. 94 Let them be justified; and leave exposed Their wavering relics in the place of judgment. **1860** C. INNES *Scot. in Mid. Ages* vi. 182 The murderer taken red-hand..was 'justified'..without any unnecessary or inconvenient delays of process.

3. To show (a person or action) to be just or in the right; to prove or maintain the righteousness or innocence of; to vindicate (†*from* a charge).

13.. *E.E. Allit. P.* A. 699 Non lyuyande to þe is Iustyfyet. **1382** WYCLIF *Ps.* l. 6 [li. 4] That thou be iustefied in thi woordis, and ouercome whan thou art demed. *c* **1450** tr. *De Imitatione* III. xxix. 99 Þou..iustifiest me in all my disposicions. **1535** COVERDALE *Ecclus.* vii. 5 Iustifie not thy self before God. **1600** E. BLOUNT tr. *Conestaggio* 224 Some of his friendes, laboured to iustifie him. **1707** *Curios. in Husb. & Gard.* 119 Justifying them from any Objections that might be made against them. **1868** M. PATTISON *Acad. Org.* v. 148 We have no longer the difficult task of justifying science in the eyes of the nation.

absol. **1647** N. BACON *Disc. Govt. Eng.* I. xxxvi. (1739) 53 Neither Monk, Woman, nor Clerk was by Law to justify by Battle in their own person.

b. Of a state of things, circumstance, or motive: To afford a justification of. (Often in passive.)

1635 A. STAFFORD *Fem. Glory* (1869) 82 The profane Idolatrizing of this Superlative Saint, will iustifie me in all eyes. **1709** ATTERBURY *Spittal Serm.*, *Luke* x. 32 The publick burthens..will not justify us in giving nothing. **1775** BURKE *Sp. Concil. Amer.* Wks. III. 102, I think then I am..justified in the sixth and last resolution. **1860** DICKENS *Uncomm. Trav.* xvi, The pair have a dejected consciousness that they are not justified in appearing on the surface of the earth.

4. To absolve, acquit, exculpate; *spec.* in *Theol.* to declare free from the penalty of sin on the ground of Christ's righteousness, or to make inherently righteous by the infusion of grace: see JUSTIFICATION 4. Also *absol.*

1382 WYCLIF *Isa.* v. 23 Wo..that iustefien the vnpitous for ȝiftes. —— *Rom.* iii. 26 That he be iust, and iustifyinge him that is of the feith of Ihesu Crist. *Ibid.* 28 Forsothe we demen a man for to be iustifyed by feith, withouten workis of lawe. **1526** TINDALE *Rom.* iv. 25 Jesus..Which was delivered for oure synnes, and rose agayne forto iustifye vs. **1535** COVERDALE *Exod.* xxiii. 7 The innocent and righteous shalt thou not sley, for I iustifie not ye vngodly. **1550** VERON *Godly Sayings* (1846) 15 For say they..if the Sacramente dothe not iustyfye, & brynge grace of itselfe, then it is but bare breade & wyne. *a* **1620** DONNE *2nd Serm. John* xvi. 8 Only thy good life can assure thy conscience and the world, that thou art justified. *a* **1740** WATERLAND *Doctr. Justification* iv, God..has made no promise or covenant to justify any one without the use of Baptism. **1859** J. CUMMING *Ruth* viii. 138 It is the office of Jesus to pardon, to justify, to welcome.

5. To make good (an argument, statement, or opinion); to confirm or support by attestation or evidence; to corroborate, prove, verify. †Formerly with *complementary obj.*, *obj.* and *inf.*, or *subord. clause.* (Now coloured by 6.)

1390 GOWER *Conf.* III. 140 Rethoriqes eloquences..Wherof a man schal justifie Hise wordes in disputeisoun. **1494** FABYAN *Chron.* v. civ. 79 So that I myght somwhat iustifie my reporte by some Auctour of Auctorite. **1559** in Strype *Ann. Ref.* (1824) I. II. App. xi. 34 This shalbe justified owt of Irenæus. **1600** SHAKS. *Temp.* v. i. 128 Were I so minded, I heere could..iustifie you Traitors. *a* **1680** BUTLER *Rem.* (1759) I. 41 For who can justify, that Nature there Is ty'd to the same Laws, she acts by here? **1732** BERKELEY *Alciphr.* v. §33 He justified the notion to be innocent. **1781** GIBBON *Decl. & F.* xxvi. (1869) II. 11 The narratives of antiquity are justified by the experience of modern times. **1884** *Manch. Exam.* 6 May 5/3 It would be hard to justify this particular assertion by an appeal to facts.

†**b.** To maintain as true, affirm, aver. *Obs.*

1579–80 NORTH *Plutarch, Marius* (1676) 353 The which would not be beleeved..for the uncredible force and Power of the Armies which was justified to come. **1658** OSBORN *Q. Eliz.* (1673) 461 An Inquisition..which a Cursiter did about that time justifie he had inrolled. **1781** W. BLANE *Ess. Hunting* (1788) 71 The Doctor..to this day relates and justifies the truth of every circumstance I have mentioned.

†**c.** To acknowledge as true or genuine. *Obs.*

1608 SHAKS. *Per.* v. i. 219 She shall tell thee all; When thou shalt kneele, and justifie in knowledge, She is thy verie Princes. *c* **1611** CHAPMAN *Iliad* xv. 110 The great God had a son, Whom he himself yet justifies.

6. To show or maintain the justice or reasonableness of (an action, claim, etc.); to adduce adequate grounds for; to defend as right or proper.

1560 DAUS tr. *Sleidane's Comm.* 7 He aunswered, that he woulde iustifye that, that he had done, eyther in present disputation, or by writinge. **1641** MILTON *Ch. Govt.* II. iii, How can they justify to have turned their domestic privileges into the bar of a proud judicial court? **1667** —— *P.L.* I. 26 That..I may assert th' eternal Providence, And justifie the wayes of God to men. **1704** PENN in *Pa. Hist. Soc. Mem.* IX. 357, I justify not my son's folly. **1884** F. TEMPLE *Relat. Relig. & Sc.* v. (1885) 155 All who thus claim super-natural authority must, of course, justify their claim.

b. To make right, proper, or reasonable; to furnish adequate grounds for, warrant.

1658 BRAMHALL *Consecr. Bps.* iii. 48 This very necessity had..justified the Act. **1718** PRIOR *Hans Carvel* 67 The end must justifie the means; He only sins who ill intends. **1732** ARBUTHNOT *Rules of Diet* 419 Those Reasons seem to justify Bleeding. **1742** YOUNG *Nt. Th.* IV. 309 'Tis guilt alone can justify his death. **1813** SCOTT *Rokeby* I. viii, Much in the

stranger's mien appears, To justify suspicious fears. **1891** *Speaker* 2 May 526/2 The vast circle of his readers justified his complacency by their applause.

†**c.** To render lawful or legitimate. *Obs.*

1651 HOBBES *Leviath.* II. xxii. 117 Whatsoever is commanded by the Soveraign Power, is as to the Subject.. justified by the Command. **1725** POPE *Odyss.* VI. 346 Till.. public nuptials justify the bride.

7. *Law. intr.* and *trans.* **a.** To show or maintain sufficient reason in court for doing that which one is called upon to answer for; to show adequate grounds for (that with which one is charged).

1529 *Act 21 Hen. VIII*, c. 19 §2 The Lorde.. may avowe or his Baylyffe or servaunt make conysaunce or justifye for takyng of the said dystresses upon the same landes.. alegyng in the said avourie conysaunce and iustificacyon the same Maners Landes and Tenementes to be holdin of hym. **1591** *Child Marriages* 150 The said Smith.. did arreste the said Roger Dod.. and beinge charged to be a wronge, and contrary to the liberties and charters of this citie, iustifieth to be lawfull. **1765** BLACKSTONE *Comm.* I. xiv, 429 A master like-wise may justify an assault in defence of his servant, and a servant in defence of his master. **1768–74** TUCKER *Lt. Nat.* (1834) II. 258 If a man be impeached for beating an-other, he may justify by showing it was done in his own necessary defence: if for false imprisonment, he may justify under the warrant of a lawful magistrate. **1893** *Weekly Notes* 67/2 The appellant could not justify his attempt to force an entrance, and was rightly convicted of an assault.

b. *to justify* (†*oneself*) *as bail, to justify bail*: to show, by the oath of a person furnishing bail or other surety, that after the payment of his debts he is of adequate pecuniary ability.

1692 *Act 4 Will. & M.* c. 5. §2 The Justices.. shall make such Rules.. for the justifying of such Bails.. as to them shall seem meet. **1766–80** BURROW *Reports* IV. 2527 The sum he was required to justify in, was £9000. **1768** BLACKSTONE *Comm.* III. xix. 291 The bail.. must justify them-selves in court.. by swearing themselves house-keepers, and each of them to be worth double the sum for which they are bail, after payment of all their debts. **1780** *Newgate Cal.* V. 49 They.. justified bail for sums to a considerable amount, though they were not possessed of property to the value of twenty shillings. **1880** *Standard* 9 Apr. 6/1 Bail for the husband was put in and justified. **1883** *Wharton's Law-Lex.* (ed. 7), *Justifying security.* Administrators in certain cases are required by the Court of Probate to give justifying security.

†**8.** To account just or reasonable; to approve of; to ratify. *Obs.*

1682 GREW *Anat. Plants* Pref., I was glad to see it [a book] so far justify'd by that Illustrious Society. **1729** BUTLER *Serm., Love Neighbour* Wks. 1874 II. 146 God him-self will in the end justify their taste, and support their cause.

9. To make exact; to fit or arrange exactly; to adjust to exact shape, size, or position. Now only in technical use; esp. (*Type-founding*), To adjust a 'strike' or 'drive' by making the sides level and square, and keeping the impression at the proper depth, so as to form a correct matrix; (*Printing*) To adjust types of smaller and larger bodies together, so that they will exactly fill up the forme; to space out the line of type in the composing stick properly; also *intr.* of type.

1551 RECORDE *Cast. Knowl.* (1556) 35 By true woorkinge to iustifie your Globe, which fyrste maye bee made as rounde, as any Turner can doo it, and then shall your instrument.. correct it exactlye if it be amysse. **1671–2** T. MARSHALL *Let. to Dr. Fell* 9 Feb. (in H. Hart *Cent. Typogr. Oxford* 167/1) He undertakes to justify Matrices, but not cut Punctions... I suspend ye urging of ye Matrices to be justifyed by Mr. Van Dijke. **1683** MOXON *Mech. Exerc., Printing* xvi. ¶2 Justifying of Matrices is, 1. to make the Face of the Sunken Letter, lie an exact designed depth below the Face of the Matrice, and on all its sides equally deep from the Face of the Matrice. 2. It is to set or Justifie the Foot-line of the Letter exactly in Line. 3. It is to Justifie both the sides, viz. the Right and left-sides of a Matrice to an exact thickness. *Ibid.* xxii. ¶4 Justifying (in Compositers Language) is the stiff or loose filling of his Stick, for if it be fill'd very stiff with Letters or Spaces, they say it is hard Justified, if loosly, they say it is loose Justified. *Ibid.* xxiv. ¶5 Justifying the Head is to put into the Mortesses in the Cheeks.. an equal and convenient thickness of.. square pieces of Felt, Pastboards, or Scaboards.. that when the Press-man Pulls, the Tennants of the Head shall have an equal Horizontal level Check. **1824** J. JOHNSON *Typogr.* II. 124 Taking care to space and to justify our matter. **1828** WEBSTER s.v., Types of different sizes will not justify with each other. **1892** *Brit. Printer* V. No. 26. 19 Ample knowledge of how to justify is not yet the common property of printers. **1900** H. HART *Cent. Typogr. Oxford* Pref. p. viii, Nowadays a type-founder desiring to enlarge the number of his founts, would be able.. to buy 'strikes', which when justified would become matrices.

justifying ('dʒʌstɪfaɪɪŋ), *vbl. sb.* [f. JUSTIFY *v.* + -ING[1].]

1. The action of the vb. JUSTIFY. **a.** The action of making, proving, or accounting just; justification.

1382 WYCLIF *Rom.* iv. 25 The which is bitakun for oure synnes, and roos ȝen for oure iustifiynge. **1615** G. SANDYS *Trav.* 59 This excuse is so.. large, that it may extend as well to the iustifying of the absurdest errours. *a* **1769** R. RICCALTOUN *Notes Galatians* 109 Justifying implies more than bare pardon. It supposes a judicial procedure.

†**b.** Condemnation; execution. *Sc. Obs.*

a **1578** LINDESAY (Pitscottie) *Chron. Scot.* (1899) I. 183 To saif the lordis from iustifieing in the Kingis furie.

†**2.** An ordinance; = JUSTIFICATION 2. *Obs.*

1382 WYCLIF *Ps.* cxviii. [cxix.] 5 Wolde God weren dressid my weies; to be kept thi iustifiyngus. **1395** PURVEY *Remonstr.* 32 That thei kepe the iustifyingis of God, and seken out his comaundementis. **1526** TINDALE *Heb.* ix. 1 That fyrst tabernacle verely had iustifyinges and servynges off God.

3. In *Type-founding* and *Printing*: see JUSTIFY *v.* 9. *justifying-stick*, an attachment to a typesetting machine for justifying the lines.

1671–2 T. MARSHALL *Let. to Dr. Fell* 19 Jan. (in H. Hart *Cent. Typogr. Oxford* 166/2) Y^e^ Founders.. have no regard to cutting and justifying, unless perhaps to supply a Defect, or two. **1683** [see JUSTIFY *v.* 9].

'**justifying**, *ppl. a.* [f. as prec. + -ING[2].] That justifies (in senses of the verb).

1526 *Pilgr. Perf.* (W. de W. 1531) 31 The grace of iustificacyon, or grace iustifyenge. **1585** HOOKER *Serm. Justif.* §3 There is a iustifying and sanctifying righteousnes here. **1701** NORRIS *Ideal World* II. ii. 64 This is no warrantable or justifying reason. **1865** PUSEY *Truth Eng. Ch.* 5 The Lutheran doctrine.. that 'justifying faith is that whereby a person believes himself to be justified'.

Hence '**justifyingly** *adv.*, in a justifying manner.

1711 *Peace in Divinity* 3 The unregenerate Man believes historically, though not justifyingly.

†**justily, justislich**, *adv. Obs.* = JUSTLY 5.

c **1350** *Will. Palerne* 1724 No man vpon mold miȝt oþer perceyue Buy sche a bere were to baite at a stake; So iustislich eche liþ ioyned by ihesu of heuen. *Ibid.* 2596 So iustili on eþer of hem were ioyned þe skinnes.

justing, older var. of JOUSTING *vbl. sb.*

Justinianian (dʒʌstɪnɪ'eɪnɪən), *a.* Also **-ean.** [f. *Justinian*, proper name + -IAN; *Justinianean* is f. late L. *Jūstiniāne-us* + -AN.] Of or pertaining to Justinian, Emperor of the East 527–565.

Justinianian code, a compilation of the best Roman laws made by order of Justinian, published in 529 and, in a revised form, in 534; also used as a general name for all the compilations of Roman law made by Justinian's command, including the *pandectæ, institutiones*, and *novellæ*: see DIGEST, INSTITUTE, NOVEL.

1826 C. BUTLER *Grotius* Introd. 32 The language and spirit of the Justinianean code. **1880** MUIRHEAD *Gaius* Introd. 9 Comparison of the Justinianian Institutes with passages in the Digest.. showed.. that in several places the later work was a literal transcript of the earlier. *Ibid.*, The authors of the Justinianian compilation.

Justinianist (dʒʌ'stɪnɪənɪst). [f. as prec. + -IST.] One who is learned in the Institutes of Justinian; a student of the civil law, a 'civilian'.

1658 PHILLIPS, Students of the Civil Law are called *Justinianists.* **1848** WHARTON *Law Lex.*, *Justinianist*, a civilian; one who studies the civil law.

‖**justitium** (dʒʌ'stɪʃɪəm). [L., cessation from business in the courts of justice, legal vacation, f. *jūs* law, right + *-stitium*, f. ppl. stem of *sistĕre* to stand, stop.] A legal vacation.

1646 SIR T. BROWNE *Pseud. Ep.* IV. xiii. 222 As though there were any seriation in nature or justitiums imaginable in professions, whose subject is naturall. **1691** BLOUNT *Law. Dict.*, *Justitium*, a ceasing from the Prosecution of Law and exercising Justice, in places Judicial: The Vacation. **1721** in BAILEY; and in later Dicts.

justle, another form of JOSTLE *v.*

†'**justless**, *a. Obs. rare*$^{-1}$. [irreg. f. JUST *a.* + -LESS.] Devoid of justice.

1578 T. PROCTER *Gorg. Gallery* in *Heliconia* (1815) I. 89 The Heavens Justles I will say to bee In case they shew the Just revenge of mee.

justly ('dʒʌstlɪ), *adv.* [f. JUST *a.* + -LY[2].]

1. Uprightly; righteously. *Obs.* or *arch.*

1382 WYCLIF *Esther* Prol., God helpith hem that.. lyuen iustli in the drede of him. —— *Titus* ii. 12 That we.. lyue sobreli, and iustli, and piteuously in this world. **1484** CAXTON *Fables of Æsop* II. i, No thyng is so good as to lyue Iustly and at lyberte. **1611** BIBLE *Micah* vi. 8 What doeth the Lord require of thee, but to do iustly, and to loue mercy, and to walke humbly with thy God?

2. In accordance with justice or equity; with justice; rightfully, rightly; deservedly.

1382 WYCLIF *Luke* xxiii. 40 Nethir thou dredist God, that thou art in the same dampnacioun? And treuly we iustly. *c* **1425** LYDG. *Assembly of Gods* 1222 Iustly vnto that ye shall me pryuy make. **1555** in Strype *Eccl. Mem.* (1721) III. App. xliv. 126 How few are they that can justly excuse themselves. **1600** E. BLOUNT tr. *Conestaggio* 31 Without any pretext or iudgement to whom of them the estate did iustly appertaine. **1636** MASSINGER *Bashf. Lover* v. iii, There lives no prince that justlier can Challenge the princess' favour. **1711** BUDGELL *Spect.* No. 150 ¶10 The old Gentleman was in some measure justly served for walking in Masquerade. **1849** MACAULAY *Hist. Eng.* v. I. 589 His eldest daughter was justly popular.

3. With a proper use of reasoning or of language; with good reason or truth; rightly, properly.

14.. *Ephyphanye* in *Tundale's Vis.* 120 Therfor.. Ye may justly Phagyphanye hit call. **1538** STARKEY *England* I. ii. 49 Thes are the most general partys of thys polytyke body, wych may justely be resemblyd.. to thos chefe partys in mannys body. **1617** MORYSON *Itin.* III. 267 They retired in a close body and good array.. so as they could not be justly said to flie. **1679** PENN *Addr. Prot.* I. i. (1692) 3 This I justly fear and take to be our case. **1747** WESLEY *Prim. Physick* (1762) p. xxv, These Physicians have justly termed edged Tools. **1849** MACAULAY *Hist. Eng.* iv. I. 510 James justly regarded these renegades as the most serviceable tools that he could employ.

†**4.** In the way which the nature and purpose of a thing makes right; properly, rightly, correctly.

1551 RECORDE *Pathw. Knowl.* To Rdr., Neither is mi wit so finelie filed.. that I maie perform iustlie so learned a laboure. **1644** EVELYN *Diary* Apr., The walkes are.. so justly planted with limes, elms, and other trees. **1774** GOLDSM. *Nat. Hist.* (1776) IV. 286 The tiger will more willingly attack any other animal.. than one whose strength is so justly employed.

5. With exactness, exactly, precisely, accurately; with accurate fitting, closely. *Obs.* exc. *dial.*

c **1330** R. BRUNNE *Chron.* (1810) 241 Þei fleked þam ouer-thuert, justely forto ligge. *c* **1350** *Will. Palerne* 751 Þat preui pleyng place.. Ioyned wel iustly to meliors chamber. *c* **1391** CHAUCER *Astrol.* II. §29 To knowe Iustly the 4 quarters of the world. *c* **1450** LONELICH *Grail* lii. 592 Piers.. Made his hors Al Redy, & his helm gan lasen ful Iostly. **1563** SHUTE *Archit.* D iij b, The Proiecture.. doth answer iustly with the thicknes of the pillor. **1613** PURCHAS *Pilgrimage* (1614) 449 The former part of this report agreeth justly with that.. touching Cathay. **1692** *Capt. Smith's Seaman's Gram.* II. xxxi. 143 Let them.. justly fit the bore. **1737** BRACKEN *Farriery Impr.* (1757) II. 28 The Pillion cannot sit justly upon the Spine. *Mod. dial.* I doänt justly know when my father died.

b. qualifying an adv., adj., or prep. = Exactly.

c **1400** *Destr. Troy* 512 Sho.. Ioynet by Iason iustly to sit. *a* **1563** BALE *Sel. Wks.* (Parker Soc.) 602 It is six times so much, which cometh to nine foot justly. **1591** SYLVESTER *Du Bartas* I. ii. 784 If the Cloud side-long sit.. or justly opposite To Sun and Moon. **1793** SMEATON *Edystone L.* §97 It could be brought justly horizontal by means of a pocket Spirit-Level.

†'**justment**[1]. *Obs. rare*$^{-1}$. [irreg. f. JUST *a.* + -MENT: after L. *jūsta* due ceremonies.] In *pl.* Due ceremonies or formalities, *esp.* funeral rites, obsequies (= L. *jūsta*).

1648 HERRICK *Hesper, To Shade of Father*, Neither haire was cut, or true teares shed By me, o'r thee (as justments to the dead).

'**justment**[2]. *local.* A variant of GISTMENT, AGISTMENT, in the senses: **a.** The pasturing of a stranger's cattle; the payment made or received for this. **b.** A piece of land of which the pasture or grazing is let.

1630 T. WESTCOTE *Devon* (1845) 323 The farm then let at justment for £4. 13*s.* **1715** *Exeter Merc.* 16 Sept. 5 To rent from Michaelmas next, a Justment of between Thirty and Forty Pounds a Year.. haveing a large Orchard now in its Prime. **1900** [Still in use in North Devon (J. Groves Cooper, Bideford).]

justness ('dʒʌstnɪs). [f. JUST *a.* + -NESS.] The quality of being just: = JUSTICE in its non-legal senses: cf. F. *justesse* beside *justice.*

†**1.** The quality of being just or upright; righteousness; uprightness. *Obs.*

c **1430** *Pilgr. Lyf Manhode* I. cxxv. (1869) 66 Thilke scauberk is cleped humilitee.. jn whiche thow shuldest thi swerd herberwe, and thi justnesse hide. **1561** DAUS tr. *Bullinger on Apoc.* (1573) 40 Fayth seemeth here.. to be taken.. for faythfulnes and trustines, that is to wit, for iustnes, vpright dealing, and trueth. **1658** CLEVELAND *Rustic Rampant* Wks. (1687) 391 Good Men if they miscarry, do not only lose themselves but their Integrity, their Iustness, their Honesty. **1726** G. ROBERTS *Four Years Voy.* 346, I should not question his Iustness, were it a Cargo of twice the Value.

2. The quality or fact of being morally right or equitable, or of having valid or reasonable grounds; rightfulness; fairness; validity, soundness.

1559 KNOX *Let. to Cecil* in Strype *Ann. Ref.* (1709) I. ix. 123 If.. she grounded the justness of her title upon consuetude, laws, and ordinances of men. *a* **1680** BUTLER *Rem.* (1759) II. 479 The Justice that is said to establish the Throne of a Prince, consists no less in the Justness of his Title, than the just Administration of his Government. **1759** ROBERTSON *Hist. Scot.* I. Wks. 1813 I. 10 Neither Edward nor the Scots seemed to distrust the justness of their cause. **1809** T. PAINE in *Naval Chron.* XXI. 117 Men are led away by the greatness of an idea, and not by the justness of it. **1884** *Chr. Commw.* 11 Dec. 119/2 We are not.. concerned about the justness of what Lord Lytton says.

3. The quality or state of being right, proper, or correct; conformity to truth or to a standard; correctness; propriety; †exactness, accuracy (*obs.*).

1666–7 PEPYS *Diary* 16 Feb., Very good musique they made... Their justness in keeping time by practice much before any that we have. **1684** R. WALLER *Nat. Exper.* 10 The Justness of the most Acurate Clocks cannot discover it. **1757** PRINGLE in *Phil. Trans.* L. 383 Some doubts he had then about the justness of Dr. Springsfeld's experiments with lime-water. **1796** MORSE *Amer. Geog.* II. 102 The horned cattle have been brought to the largest size and greatest justness of shape. **1873** M. ARNOLD *Lit. & Dogma* p. xxiv, After we have got all the facts of our special study, justness of perception to deal with the facts is still required.

justninge: see JUSTENING.

†'**justry.** *Sc. Obs.* [f. JUST *a.* + -RY: the formation from an adj. is unusual.] **a.** Justice. **b.** Jurisdiction (of a sheriff, etc.). **c.** The circuit court of an itinerant judge, a justice eyre.

c **1425** WYNTOUN *Cron.* VII. ix. 249 This Alysandyr.. Wes throwcht the kynryk traveland, Haldand Courtis and Justrys. *c* **1470** HENRY *Wallace* VI. 103 The Makar above [*MS.* abow], Quilk has in hand off justry the ballance. **1503**

Sc. Acts Jas. IV (1814) 241 The part of Coule that is not within the bondis of my Erle of Ergilis Justry.

jut (dʒʌt), *sb.*[1] *Obs.* or *dial.* [Of same origin as JUT *v.*[1]] The act of striking or knocking against an obstacle; the shock of collision; a push, thrust, or shove against a resisting body. Also *fig.*

a **1553** Udall *Royster D.* III. iii. (Arb.) 43, Yond commeth Roister Doister.. I will not see him, but giue him a iutte in deede. **1569** Sir J. Hawkins *Voy. Guinea* in Arb. *Garner* V. 220, I thought it rather better to abide the jutt of the uncertainty, than the certainty. **1607** *Schol. Disc. agst. Antichr.* II. vi. 59 The least iutt that is [being able] to put out of ioynt the foote that hanged loose before. **1782** Miss Burney *Cecilia* II. iii, The fiend, with a jut of his foot may keep off the old from a dread of the future.

jut (dʒʌt), *sb.*[2] [var. of JET *sb.*[3]: cf. JUT *v.*[2]]

1. A jutting out; that which juts or projects; a projection or protruding point. Cf. JET *sb.*[3] 1.

1786 Burns *Brigs of Ayr* 132 Gaunt, ghastly, ghaist-alluring edifices, Hanging with threat'ning jut, like precipices. **18..** Moir *Poems, The Fowler,* The land's extremest point, a sandy jut. **1842** Tennyson *Morte d'Arthur* 50 Stepping down By zig-zag paths, and juts of pointed rock. **1893** M. Gray *Last Sent.* II. vii. II. 98 The jut of the porch sheltered this window.

†2. A jerking movement or swagger of the body; = JET *sb.*[3] 3. *Obs. rare.*

1709 Congreve tr. *Ovid's Art Love* III. Wks. 1773 III. 272 One has an artful swing and jut behind.

3. *Comb.*, as **jut-jawed** *a.*, having a jutting jaw.

1943 *Commonweal* (N.Y.) 11 June 195 The company sergeant-major, a tough, jut-jawed, red-faced, bull-necked veteran of the last war. **1952** T. Pyles *Words & Ways Amer. Eng.* v. 94 The dour, thin-lipped, jut-jawed righteousness of his [*sc.* N. Webster's] later portraits. **1959** *Daily Mail* 21 Mar. 6/4 That jut-jawed Marshal of the R.A.F.

jut, *sb.*[3], variant of JET *sb.*[4] = GIST *sb.*[3]

jut (dʒʌt), *v.*[1] *Obs.* or *dial.* Also 6–7 iutt(e. [app. onomatopœic; expressing both in sound and feeling the obstructed action in question.]

†1. *intr.* To strike, knock, or push *against* something. *Obs.*

1548 Udall *Erasm. Par. Luke* xi. 110 It shal no where stumble nor iutte against any thyng. **1565–73** Cooper *Thesaurus* s.v. *Incurro,* To runne & iutte or hitte against a thing in the darke. **1628** Earle *Microcosm., Plausible man* (Arb.) 59 One that would faine run an euen path.. and iutt against no man.

2. *trans.* To push, thrust, shove, jolt; to knock against something. *Obs.* exc. *dial.*

1565 Jewel *Def. Apol.* II. xiv. (1611) 267 These two propositions.. may well stand together without iutting the one the other out of place. **1607** *Schol. Disc. agst. Antichr.* II. vi. 59 C. Aufidius [dyed] by iutting his foot, when he was entring into Senat. **1863** Barnes *Dorset Gloss., Jut,* to give one a sudden blow or concussion when still, particularly when writing. **1886** *S.W. Linc. Gloss.* s.v., The waggons did jut us.

jut (dʒʌt), *v.*[2] [Phonetic var. of JET *v.*[2]] *intr.* To project or protrude (prop. as a prominence beyond the main line). Often with *out* or *forth.*

1565–73 Cooper *Thesaurus, Meniana,*.. Buildings of pleasure hanging and jutting out. **1578** Banister *Hist. Man* I. 24 This Processe iuttyng forth like a knot in a peece of wood. **1698** Tyson in *Phil. Trans.* XX. 112 In a Snake's Skin part of one Scale juts over another. **1741** Richardson *Pamela* I. 223 A little summer-parlour that juts out towards the garden. **1819** W. Erskine in Welsh *Life Dr. T. Brown* iv. (1825) 152 The island of Salsette juts out into the noble bay of Bombay. **1847** J. Wilson *Chr. North* (1857) I. 250 The points and promontories jutting into the lake. **1886** Sheldon tr. *Flaubert's Salammbô* 22 Palm trees here and there jutting beyond the walls did not stir.

†**b.** *transf.* To encroach *upon.* *Obs.*

1623 [see JET *v.*[2] 1 b, quot. 1594].

jut, *v.*[3], jutting, = JET *v.*[1], JETTING *ppl. a.*[1]

1761 Churchill *Rosciad* I. 161 Then, with a self-complacent jutting air, It smil'd, It smirk'd, It wriggl'd to the chair. **1823** Mrs. Shelley *Valperga* I. 286 Thus they jutted up and down before their master, fancying that he would admire them.

jute[1] (dʒuːt). [ad. Bengālī *jhōṭo, jhuto*:—Skr. *jūṭa,* less usual form of *jaṭā* braid of hair.]

1. The fibre obtained from the bark of the plants *Corchorus capsularis* and *C. olitorius* (N.O. *Tiliaceæ*), imported chiefly from Bengal, and used in the manufacture of gunny, canvas, bagging, cordage, etc.

1746 *Log of Ship 'Wake'* 22 Sept. (R. C. Temple, in *Indian Antiq.* 1901) 8 (a.m.) Sent on shore 60 Bales of Gunney belonging to the Company wth all the Jute Rope.. 20 Ropes in all, 116 Bundles. **1801** *Trans. Soc. Arts* XIX. 240 Paut is known in India and has been sent to Europe, by the name of jute. **1851** *Illustr. Catal. Gt. Exhib.* 202 Samples of hemp, jute, and the fibrous substances prepared. **1879** *Daily News* 23 Aug. 6/2 The oil.. is used.. for giving a silk-like appearance to jute. **1879** *Cassell's Techn. Educ.* VI. 337 Jute, or Gunny Fibre, is the produce of *Corchoris capsularis.*

b. The plant which furnishes this fibre, or any plant of the genus *Corchorus.*

bastard jute, a name of *Hibiscus cannabinus,* the fibre of which is used to adulterate jute. *American jute*: see VELVETLEAF.

1861 Swinhoe *N. China Camp.* 373 Jute of large growth is sown in March and gathered in October.

2. *attrib.*, as ***jute-bagging, -cloth, -fibre, -rope, -wood, -yarn***; **jute-butts** or **-cuttings**, the stump of the jute plant, the fibre of which is employed for inferior purposes.

1746 [see 1]. **1851** *Illustr. Catal. Gt. Exhib.* 513, 4 pieces of jute stair carpeting. **1870** *Daily News* 14 Feb., The girls in these jute works are employed.. in parties of four or five each. **1870** J. Yeats *Nat. Hist. Comm.* 201 When wet, jute fibre quickly rots. **1888** *Pall Mall G.* 13 Sept. 1/1 The American cotton-growers require about 45 million yards of jute bagging every year in which to pack their cotton.

Jute[2] (dʒuːt). [In pl. *Jutes,* a mod. rendering of Bæda's *Jutæ* and *Juti,* in OE. *Eotas, Iótas, ?Iútan* (gen. pl. *Iútna*), also *Geátas*; = Icel. *Iótar* people of Jutland on the mainland of Denmark.]

In *pl.* One of the three Low German tribes which, according to the account preserved by Bæda, invaded and settled in Britain in the fifth and sixth centuries; they are said to have occupied districts now included in Kent and Hampshire.

[*c* **731** Bæda *Hist. Angl.* I. xv, Advenerant autem de tribus Germaniæ populis fortioribus, id est Saxonibus, Anglis, Jutis. De Jutarum origine sunt Cantuari et Victuari.] *c* **900** tr. *Bæda's Hist.* I. xv. (1890) 52 Comon hi of þrim folcum ðam strangestan Germanie, þæt [is] of Seaxum, of Angle, & of Geatum. Of Geata fruman syndon Cantware & Wihtsætan. (Cf. *O. E. Chron.* an. 449 Of Ald Seaxum, of Anglum, of Iotum. Of Iotum comon Cantwara, and Wihtwara.. & þæt cyn on West Sexum þe man nu ȝit hæt Iutna cynn.) [*c* **731** Bæda *H.A.* IV. xvi, Fuga lapsi sunt de insula [Vecte] et in proximam Jutorum provinciam translati.] *c* **900** tr. *Bæda's Hist.* IV. xvi[ii]. (1890) 308 þa fluȝon þa cneohtas ut of [Wiht] þæm ealonde, & wæron ȝelædde in þa neah-mæȝðe, seo is ȝeceȝd Eota lond. **1387** Trevisa *Higden* (Rolls) V. 265 Of þe Iutes com þe Kentiche men, and þe men of the yle of Wight. **1670** Milton *Hist. Eng.* III. Wks. (1847) 507/2 The Saxons.. and.. two other tribes.. Jutes and Angles. **1839** *Penny Cycl.* XIII. 167/2 The first Germanic invaders of Britain after the departure of the Romans were Jutes. **1874** Green *Short Hist.* i. 1 To the north of the English [in Sleswick] lay the tribe of the Jutes, whose name is still preserved in their district of Jutland.

jute, variant of JOUTE *Obs.*, pottage.

[**juter**, prob. a misreading of *niter,* NITRE.

1668 Worlidge *Dict. Rust.* in *Syst. Agric.* 272 *Juter,* a term, by some used for the fertile coagulating saltish nature of the Earth. Hence in Kersey's *Phillips,* Bailey, etc.]

jutia, var. HUTIA.

Jutish ('dʒuːtɪʃ), *a.* [f. JUTE[2] + -ISH[1].] Of or pertaining to the Jutes.

1839 Yeowell *Anc. Brit. Ch.* xiii. (1847) 141 Two Jutish chieftains, Hengist and Horsa, arrived in the Isle of Thanet. **1865** T. Wright in *Intell. Observ.* No. 37. 70 The same Jutish race.

jutka ('dʒʌtkə). [f. Hindi *jhaṭka* a jerk, jolt, lurch.] In southern India, a light two-wheeled vehicle drawn by a horse.

1886 Yule & Burnell *Hobson-Jobson* 362/2 *Jutka,*.. the native cab of Madras, and of Mofussil towns in that Presidency; a conveyance only to be characterised by the epithet *ramshackle*... It consists of a sort of box with venetian windows, on two wheels, and drawn by a miserable pony. It is entered by a door at the back. **1907** B. M. Croker *Company's Servant* xxxi. 318 She.. got her baggage on a jutka and drove away. **1927** *Scots Observer* 16 Apr. 3/2 All afternoon jutkas and carts.. are arriving. **1947** R. K. Narayan *Astrologer's Day* 4 *Jutka* drivers swore at their horses. **1961** K. Nagarajan *Chron. Kedaram* 117 It was so reminiscent of a *jutka* pony.

jutting ('dʒʌtɪŋ), *vbl. sb.* [f. JUT *v.*[2] + -ING[1].] The action of JUT *v.*[2]; *concr.* a projection or protruding part; = JETTING *vbl. sb.*[2] 1, JUT *sb.*[2] 1.

1565–73 Cooper *Thesaurus, Proiectus,* the iutting or leaning out of a building. *Ibid., Proiectura,* the iutting or leaning out in pillers or other building. **1644** Evelyn *Diary* 17 Nov., On the battlements of the Church.. you would imagine yourself in a town, so many are the cupolas, pinnacles, towers, juttings. **1774** Goldsm. *Nat. Hist.* I. 233 There is scarce a strait.. or the jutting of a promontory, that has not been minutely described. **1859** J. R. Edkins *Chinese Scenes* (1863) 54 A time-worn pagoda, its numberless corners and juttings, edged with bronze and brass.

'**jutting**, *ppl. a.*[1] [f. JUT *v.*[1] + -ING[2].] That juts, knocks, or strikes.

1772 W. Mason *Eng. Gard.* II. 344 Oft the ram And jutting steer drive their entangling horns Through the frail meshes.

jutting ('dʒʌtɪŋ), *ppl. a.*[2] [f. JUT *v.*[2] + -ING[2].] That juts; projecting, standing out beyond the main body.

1624 Wotton *Archit.* in *Reliq.* (1651) 236 All the projected or jutting parts. **1715** tr. *Pancirollus' Rerum Mem.* I. II. iii. 64 Outwardly extended or jutting Buildings. **1849** Ruskin *Sev. Lamps* iii. §23. 91 Sloping roof, jutting porch, projecting balcony. **1870** Bryant *Iliad* XVI. II. 134 An angler sits Upon a jutting rock.

Hence '**juttingly** *adv.*, projectingly.

1856 in Webster.

†**jutty**, *sb. Obs.* Also 5 iutte, 6 iotye, iuttey, iuttie. [A phonetic variant of JETTY *sb.*, a. F. *jetée* the action of throwing or casting, something thrown out, etc. The *u* for *e* as in JUT *v.*[2]]

1. A pier, breakwater, or embankment; = JETTY 1.

1486 *Bk. St. Albans* D j, I haue seen them made sum to sle the pie sum to sle the Tele vppon the Reuer: at the Iutte. *Ibid.* D j b, Iff youre hawke nym the fowle at the fer side of the Ryuer or of the pitt from you Then she sleeth the fowle at the fer Iutty. **1547** *Act 1 Edw. VI,* c. 14 §8 For the mayntenaunce of Piers, Iutties, walles or banckes against the rages of the sea. **1547** Ld. Grey, etc. *Let. to Protector* 18 Apr. (*S.P.*, P.R.O., *Foreign* XIV. No. 121) 'No fort', said we, 'but a Iutty to amende the havon to save both your shippes and ours'. *a* **1653** G. Daniel *Idyll.* ii. 21 The Iutty of Discretion.. drowned in the Tide. **1804** *Trans. Soc. Arts* XXII. 248 By a pier-head on the East and jutties on the West side.

b. **jutty-head** = *jetty-head* (JETTY *sb.* 4): see quot. 1750.

1559 in Boys *Sandwich* (1792) 739 There must be two juttie heddes towards the sea. **1587** Fleming *Contn. Holinshed* III. 1547/1 When the two iuttie heads are once finished.. so as the hauens mouth be perfected. **1750** Blanckley *Naval Expos.* 84 *Jutty heads,* Platforms standing on Piles which are made near the Docks, and project without the Wharfs for the more convenient docking and undocking Ships.

2. A projecting part of a wall or building; = JETTY *sb.* 2.

1519 Horman *Vulg.* xxix. R vj, Buyldynge chargydde with iotyes is parellous when it is very olde, *Mœniana ædificia vetustate corrupta periculo sunt obnoxia.* **1591** Percivall *Sp. Dict., Salidizo,* the iuttie of an house, the bearing out of a wall. **1605** Shaks. *Macb.* I. vi. 6 No Iutty frieze, Buttrice, nor Coigne of Vantage, but this Bird Hath made his pendant Bed. **1703** T. N. *City & C. Purchaser* 285 Leaving that Ledge, or Jutty.. call'd a Water-table.

fig. **1602** Carew *Cornwall* 36 b, To salue himselfe of a desperate debt, prosecuted the same so far forth, as he brought it to the iutty of a *Nisi prius.*

'**jutty**, *a.* [f. JUT *sb.*[2] + -Y.] Characterized by jutting out.

1827 Hood *Hero & L.* xlii, Hard by some jutty cape. **1868** G. M. Hopkins *Jrnl.* 19 July (1959) 178 Lying in jutty bends. **1922** A. S. M. Hutchinson *This Freedom* ii. 23 He swung round and pushed his dark face and jutty nose into the face of Bolas. **1937** G. M. Young *Daylight & Champaign* 93 Driving away the birds who nest in the jutty frieze.

jutty ('dʒʌtɪ), *v. Obs.* or *arch.* Forms: 5 iutteye, 7 iuttie, 7– jutty. [Related to JUTTY *sb.*: cf. also JETTY *v.*[1]]

1. *intr.* To project, jut, esp. as part of a building, or as a pier or breakwater. *arch.*

14.. *Voc.* in Wr.-Wülcker 591/6 *Jutto,* to Iutteye. **1600** J. Pory tr. *Leo's Africa* I. 34 Where it beginneth to iuttie forth into the sea. **1649** G. Daniel *Trinarch., Hen. IV,* xxvi, Some Common Principles may Iutty out And stand as Peirs, the lesser Barks to shroud. **1855** Singleton *Virgil* I. 232 On this side and on that, prodigious rocks And twin(-like) cliffs jutty into the heaven.

†2. *trans.* To project, beyond, overhang. *Obs.*

1599 Shaks. *Hen. V,* III. i. 13 As fearefully, as doth a galled Rocke O're-hang and iutty his confounded Base.

†3. To cause to project or overhang; to build out; = JET *v.*[2] 2. *Obs.*

1611 Cotgr., *Voyer,* a Surueyer.. who.. limits, vnto those that build in a street, their ground and scope of iuttying. *Ibid., Souspendu,*.. hung ouer: iuttied, or set out beyond.

Hence '**juttying** *vbl. sb.*, the action of the vb., also, a projection; '**juttying** *ppl. a.*, projecting.

1609 Holland *Amm. Marcell.* XXVII. ix. 318 He tooke away all those juttying galleries of pleasure called Meniana. **1611** Cotgr., *Soupenduë,* a penthouse; iuttie.. a iuttying, or a leaning out or beyond.

†'**jut-'window**. *Obs. rare*$^{-1}$. [f. JUT *v.*[2] or *sb.*[2] + WINDOW.] A jutting or projecting window; a bay-window.

1687 Congreve *Old Bach.* IV. viii, Her eyes were the two jut-windows, and her mouth the great door.

Juu, obs. form of JEW.

†'**juvament**. *Obs. rare.* [ad. late L. *juvāmentum,* f. *juvāre* to help: see -MENT.] Help, aid, assistance.

c **1400** *Lanfranc's Cirurg.* 27 þe secunde Iuuament is: þat þei hangen & bynden summe membris wiþ oþere. *Ibid.* 109 þis ioynynge togidere of oon boon wiþ anoþir was maad bicause of iuvamentis þat I haue told to forn.

†**juvate**, *v. Obs. rare.* [irreg. f. L. *juvāre* to help: see -ATE[3].] *trans.* To help, aid.

1708 Motteux *Rabelais* (1737) V. 232 Juvated by the Town's Proximity.

juve (dʒuːv). Colloq. abbrev. of *juvenile lead.* Also *attrib.*

1935 *Variety* 17 Apr., Jones is a good-looking juve and possesses a corking tenor. **1968** P. Loraine *Dead Men of Sestos* viii. 115 I'm the young tenor, the juve, the one with the tennis racket. **1974** *Observer* 25 Aug. 22/3 The cherished tradition which demands that the worst thing about the Hammer horror [film]s shall be their juve leads.

†'**juvenal**, *a.* and *sb.*[1] *Obs.* Also 6–7 -all, 7 iuvinal. [ad. L. *juvenāl-is* (= *juvenīl-is*) of or belonging to youth, f. *juvenis* a young person.]

A. *adj.* Juvenile.

1638 T. WHITAKER *Blood of Grape* 43 More hot then ripe and juvenall age. **1733** [see JUVENILE B. 1]. **1821** *Blackw. Mag.* X. 33/1 A classical book of juvenal sports.

B. *sb.* A youth; a 'juvenile'.

1588 SHAKS. *L.L.L.* I. ii. 8 How canst thou part sadnesse and melancholy my tender Iuuenall? **1607** DEKKER & WEBSTER *Westw. Hoe* III. i. D.'s Wks. 1873 II. 320, I am one of his Iuvinals. **1664** COTTON *Scarron.* IV. (1741) 72 She the small Ascanius takes, Troy's Juvenal. [**1820** SCOTT *Monast.* xiv, (*Sir Piercie Shafton is represented as saying*) Touching this juvenal, he hath that about him which belongeth to higher birth.]

Juvenal ('dʒuːvənəl), *sb.*[2] Anglicized form of the cognomen of the Roman satirist Decimus Junius *Juvenalis*, used gen. to designate a satirist.

1592 GREENE *Groats W. Wit* sig. F1, With thee I ioyne yong Iuuenall [*sc.* Nashe], that byting Satirist. **1693** DRYDEN tr. *Juvenal's Satires* p. vii, I might find in France, a living Horace and a Juvenal, in the person of the admirable Boileau. **1841** I. D'ISRAELI *Amenities of Lit.* III. 132 Jonson, the Juvenal of our drama. **1885** *Brewer's Dict. Phrase & Fable* (ed. 17) 469/1 The English Juvenal. John Oldham... The Juvenal of Painters. William Hogarth. **1902** *Daily Chron.* 20 Feb. 3/2 The art of satire is dead in England... The Juvenals of Fleet-street are no more.

Juvenalian (dʒuːvɪˈneɪlɪən), *a.* [f. L. *Juvenālis* Juvenal + -AN.] Characteristic of Juvenal, the Roman satirist.

1839 HALLAM *Hist. Lit.* II. v. §71 Hall has more of the direct Juvenalian invective. **1892** DOBSON *18th Cent. Vignettes* 208 The Juvenalian manner of that great graphic satirist.

juvenate ('dʒuːvɪnət). *R.C. Ch.* [f. L. *juvenis* young man + -ATE[1].] = JUNIORATE.

1889 in WORCESTER *Suppl.*

†**ju'vencle.** *Obs.* [ad. L. *juvencula* (*Vulg.* Ps. lxviii. 26, 1 Tim. v. 2). Cf. JOVENCEL.] A young woman, a girl.

c **1430** LYDG. *Min. Poems* (Percy Soc.) 30 And no iuvencle, for if thou say thus loo, Yong womman may do more than fyere heet, She thynketh thi colde for hir is nothing meet.

†**juvenency.** *Obs. rare.* [irreg. f. L. *juvenis* a young person: see -CY.] Youth.

1656 RUTHVEN in *N. & Q.* 3rd Ser. III. 3 The Infancy and Juvenency of the Petitioner's father suffered 19 years Imprisonment in the Tower.

juvenescence (dʒuːvɪˈnɛsəns). [f. as next: see -ENCE.] The state of becoming young or youthful; youthful state or condition, youth.

1800 ANNA SEWARD *Lett.* (1811) V. 275 Two impossible attainments, that of making gold by transmutation, and of renewing juvenescence by an elixir. **1832** *Fraser's Mag.* VI. 255 The days of Ebony's juvenescence. **1851** J. HAMILTON *Royal Preacher* iv. (1858) 49 The renewed soul's perpetual juvenescence. **1862** R. H. PATTERSON *Ess. Hist. & Art* 512 When his mind was scarcely out of its juvenescence.

juvenescent (dʒuːvɪˈnɛsənt), *a.* [ad. L. *juvenēscent-em*, pr. pple. of *juvenēscĕre* to reach the age of youth.]

1. Becoming young or youthful.

1821 LAMB *Elia* Ser. I. *Old Benchers Inner Temple*, Reductive of juvenescent emotions. **1876** J. ELLIS *Cæsar in Egypt* 192 Thy ecstatic influence To life renews.. The juvenescent soul and sense.

2. *nonce-use.* Immature, undeveloped.

1875 tr. *Schmidt's Desc. & Darw.* 223 The lama is a juvenescent and feeble copy of the camel.

juvenile ('dʒuːvɪnaɪl), *a.* and *sb.* [ad. L. *juvenīlis* of or belonging to youth, f. *juvenis* a young person. Cf. F. *juvénile* (15th c.).

(L. *juvenīlis* referred to a more advanced age than its Eng. repr.; *juvenis* being a young man or woman, beyond the stage of adolescence, i.e. between 21 or 25 and 40.)]

A. *adj.* 1. a. Young, youthful. *spec.* Designating young offenders against the law, or the offences committed by them; esp. in *juvenile delinquency*, *delinquent*; also *juvenile adult*, a person below the legal age of responsibility and above a certain minimum age, who is held to be punishable for breaking the law (the term was discontinued by the Family Law Reform Act of 1969).

1625 BACON *Ess.*, *Viciss. Things* (Arb.) 576 Learning hath his Infancy, when it is.. almost childish; Then his Youth, when it is Luxuriant and Iuuenile. **1671** GREW *Anat. Plants* vii. §11 In its first and juvenile Constitution, it is a very Spongy and Sappy body. **1782** V. KNOX *Ess.* (1819) I. xvii. 101 Man at every age seeks to be pleased, but more particularly at the juvenile age. **1796** JANE AUSTEN *Sense & Sens.* I. vii, He was a blessing to all the juvenile part of the neighbourhood. **1816** *Rep. Soc. investigating Causes Increase in Juvenile Delinquency* 5 It was found that Juvenile Delinquency existed in the metropolis to a very alarming extent. **1817** *Observer* 14 Sept. 1/3 Your Committee have anxiously sought for information as to the number of juvenile delinquents who are annually committed to the different prisons in the metropolis;.. the greater part of these Juvenile Offenders.. are mixed indiscriminately with old offenders of all ages. **1837** DICKENS *Let.* *c* 2 Oct. (1965) I. 315 Many thanks for your statistical Magazine, which contains some tables concerning juvenile delinquency. **1837** —— *O. Twist* (1838) I. xix. 321 Then the Juvenile Delinquent Society comes, and takes the boy away. **1852** MRS. STOWE *Uncle Tom's C.* vii, Although the order was.. carried to Aunt Chloe by at least half a dozen juvenile messengers. **1847**, **1854** [see OFFENDER]. **1902** [see BORSTAL]. **1916** *Lancet* 2 Feb. 365/1 (*title*) Juvenile crime. **1917** C. LEESON (*title*) The child and the war, being notes on juvenile delinquency. **1926** *Encycl. Brit.* I. 411/1 In 1894 two public inquiries into the administration of prisons and of Home Office schools arrived.. at the same.. conclusion, viz: 'that the age 16–21 was the dangerous age; that we must concentrate on that; on the incipient criminal' or, as he was officially christened, the juvenile adult. **1958** *New Statesman* 25 Oct. 551/1 Some years ago when the current crop of juvenile delinquents were being labelled in the press as cosh-boys, I had written an article that contained interviews with some live specimens, hand-picked for me by an underworld acquaintance. **1959** JOWITT *Dict. Eng. Law* II. 1041/1 *Juvenile adult*, a person not less than sixteen and not more than twenty-one. **1964** M. ARGYLE *Psychol. & Social Probl.* v. 59 Juvenile delinquency is one of our most pressing social problems. *Ibid.* xv. 187 The rate of juvenile crime has risen rapidly during the decade, particularly since 1955.

b. *juvenile lead* = JUVENILE *sb.* 2; *spec.* an actor who plays the leading youthful part in a play, etc.; the rôle so played. So *juvenile leading*.

1870 [see HEAVY *a.*[1] 21]. **1885** J. K. JEROME *On Stage* (1891) xi. 102 Juvenile Lead's opinion is that the stage manager is a fool. **1897** G. B. SHAW *Our Theatres in Nineties* (1932) III. 210 This is not human nature or dramatic character; it is juvenile lead, first old man, heavy lead, heavy father. **1910** M. BEERBOHM *Around Theatres* (1924) II. 460 The 'ingénue' and 'juvenile lead' of old-fashioned commercial drama. **1946** G. MILLAR *Horned Pigeon* i. 7 The part.. might lead to great things, even to juvenile leads. **1973** J. PORTER *It's Murder with Dover* xvi. 160 MacGregor flashed his juvenile lead smile.

2. Belonging to, characteristic of, suited to, or intended for youth. *juvenile court*, a court of law for the trial of young offenders.

1661 GLANVILL *Van. Dogmatizing* Ep. Ded. A iij, I hope you'l consider, that Scepticism is.. no crime in a Juvenile exercitation. **1790** BURKE *Fr. Rev.* 96 This inspires a juvenile warmth through his whole frame. **1844** (*title*) Juvenile Missionary Magazine of the London Missionary Society. **1848** DICKENS *Dombey* i, Dressed in a very juvenile manner. **1882** HINSDALE *Garfield & Educ.* II. 381 At that period, few juvenile books were published. **1899** *Illinois Laws* 132 A special court room, to be designated as the juvenile court room, shall be provided.. and the court may, for convenience, be called the 'Juvenile Court'. **1908** *Act 8 Edw. VII* c. 67 §111 A court of summary jurisdiction when hearing charges against children.. shall.. sit either in a different building.. or on different days.., and a court of summary jurisdiction so sitting is in this Act referred to as a juvenile court. **1944** *Ann. Reg. 1943* 381 More attention than usual was focussed on the work of the Juvenile Courts. **1972** *Daily Tel.* 5 May 13/1 The Scots.. abolished juvenile courts and replaced them with a system of children's panels.

3. *Geol.* [tr. G. *juvenil* (E. Suess 1902, in *Verh. d. Ges. deutsch. Naturf. u. Ärzte* 141).] Originating within the earth (or another planet) and brought to the surface for the first time.

1907 *Econ. Geol.* II. 266 Many mineral springs may be of magmatic origin, but since their starting points are inaccessible they can be proved to be juvenile only by showing that they cannot be meteoric. **1909** H. B. C. & W. J. SOLLAS tr. *Suess's Face of Earth* IV. xv. 549 [The hot springs] of Carlsbad.. bring yearly to surface a million kilogrammes of juvenile salt. *Ibid.* 559 We must assume that the juvenile gases are originally liberated beneath the Sal mantle. **1944** *Bull. Geol. Soc. Amer.* LV. 1375 Clearly one cannot hold that the volcano was kept alive merely by free juvenile gas rising from an abyssolithic injection. **1955** [see CONNATE *a.* 5]. **1973** *Sci. Amer.* Jan. 56/2 One speculation is that deep permafrost is involved, associated perhaps with the arrival near the surface of juvenile water preceding and accompanying the rise of molten rock near the surface of the planet during the volcanic episode apparent to the west.

4. Special collocations: **juvenile foliage**, **leaf**, a type of foliage characteristic of the immature stages of certain trees, shrubs, or woody climbers, differing in shape, colour, etc., from the adult form; **juvenile hormone** *Ent.*, the hormone that controls the development of larval characteristics in insects; **juvenile wood**, an inner core of wood in a tree, distinguished by particularly small cells.

1957 M. HADFIELD *Brit. Trees* 96 The *juvenile foliage [of *Cryptomeria*] is spreading, with flatter and softer leaves than the adult. **1971** T. T. KOZLOWSKI *Growth & Devel. Trees* I. iii. 95 Plants derived from needle-leaved cuttings [of *Chamæcyparis pisifera*] retained juvenile foliage if the source tree did so. **1940** V. B. WIGGLESWORTH in *Jrnl. Exper. Biol.* XVII. 221 In previous papers the 'inhibitory hormone' was so called because in its presence the production of imaginal characters at moulting is suppressed. But in view of its probable mode of action through the activation of the nymphal system at the expense of the imaginal, it might be preferable to refer to this hormone as the 'nymphal' or '*juvenile' hormone. **1965** LEE & KNOWLES *Animal Hormones* xiii. 161 Normal development depends on changes in the relative amounts of ecdysone and the juvenile hormone which are available to the tissues. **1967** *New Scientist* 20 Apr. 154/1 Juvenile hormone.. is necessary for the normal growth of immature insects—caterpillars and grubs, for example. **1970** *Daily Tel.* 16 Nov. 6/1 Many South American plants contain similar substances to insect juvenile hormone. **1910** L. COCKAYNE *N.Z. Plants* iv. 60 After a few weeks its [*sc.* a veronica's] new growth will be of the juvenile form, and *juvenile and adult leaves will be on the plant at the same time. **1946** A. B. JACKSON *Identification of Conifers* 2 In many cases the juvenile leaves differ in form, attachment or arrangement from those on the adult tree. **1956** F. W. JANE *Struct. Wood* ix. 191 *Juvenile wood often has cells of smaller dimensions, often much smaller, than those of the trunk. **1971** T. T. KOZLOWSKI *Growth & Devel. Trees* I. iii. 109 The wood in the region of the pith, which is formed early.. is termed juvenile (sometimes called core or pith) wood.

B. *sb.* 1. A young person; a youth.

1733 P. ARAM in Gent *Rippon* 12 Thus angry speaks, and yet deceitful smiles, With Juv'nal Air, on tender Juveniles. **1847** C. BRONTE *J. Eyre* xviii. II. 83 'Yes—yes—yes!' cried the juveniles, both ladies and gentlemen. 'Let her come—it will be excellent sport!' **1871** LONGF. in *Life* (1891) III. 172 Some bashful juvenile is even now timidly applying his hand to it.

2. *Theatr.* An actor who plays a youthful part.

1890 in *Cent. Dict.* **1898** G. B. SHAW *Our Theatres in Nineties* (1932) III. 307 Ferdinand Gadd, the leading juvenile of The Wells. **1933** P. GODFREY *Back-Stage* iv. 46 His legs are too short or too long.. for him to be a successful male juvenile. *Ibid.* vi. 72 Dramatists, like stage juveniles, are considered young until they are past the age of forty. **1973** *Times* 17 Nov. 11/5 I'm going to be your juvenile next season.

3. A book written for children. Freq. *pl.* Also *attrib.*

1849 *Mother Goose in Hieroglyphics* (1963) (Advt.), Pictures from the history of the Swiss... A very instructive and entertaining Juvenile, designed for children from ten to fifteen years of age. **1908** *Daily Chron.* 27 Nov. 3/5 What would John Newbery say if he were to.. see his old shop.. filled with this season's 'juveniles'? **1930** *Publishers' Weekly* 5 July 28 We announce 10 juveniles. **1947** *Times Lit. Suppl.* 15 Nov. 593/2 (Advt.), The exacting and critical Juvenile public in this country.

Hence **'juvenilely** *adv.*, in a juvenile or youthful way; **'juvenileness**, youthfulness; **juve'nilify**, **'juvenilize** *vbs. trans.*, to make young or youthful.

1727 BAILEY vol. II, *Juvenilely*, *Juvenileness*. **1833** *Blackw. Mag.* XXXIII. 848/1 Our system is juvenilized by all matin rural influences. **1833** M. SCOTT *Tom Cringle* xii. (1859) 279 Our old friend.. quite juvenilified by the laughing scene. **1889** J. M. ROBERTSON *Ess. Crit. Meth.* 246 Juvenilely facetious.

juvenilia (dʒuːvɪˈnɪlɪə), *sb. pl.* [L., neut. pl. of *juvenilis* JUVENILE *a.*] Literary or artistic works produced in the author's youth (freq. as a title of such works collected). Also *transf.*

1622 G. WITHER (*title*) Ivvenilia: a collection of those poemes which were heretofore imprinted and written by George Wither. **1633** DONNE (*title*) Iuuenilia: or certaine paradoxes and problemes. **1693** DRYDEN tr. *Juvenal's Satires* p. ix, His *Juvenilia*, or Verses written in his Youth. *a* **1849** H. COLERIDGE *Ess. & Marginalia* (1851) II. 265 Whatever effect these juvenilia may have produced at the time, they are quite worthless now. **1896** in Tennyson *Works* 2 Juvenilia. **1929** *Sunday Dispatch* 13 Jan. 10/5 Not that I belong to the school which would trace, in these innocent juvenilia of our nation, an anthropological or historical origin. **1952** *Brontë Soc. Trans.* XII. 126 Prose and verse by Charlotte and Branwell [in M. Christian's 'Census of Brontë Manuscripts in the United States'] classified as unpublished are mostly in the *Juvenilia* category. **1971** W. GÉRIN in C. Brontë *Five Novelettes* 7 Charlotte Brontë wrote the following novelettes between the years 1836 and 1839, from the time when she had just turned twenty until her twenty-third year. They cannot, therefore, be technically reckoned as belonging to her juvenilia. **1973** *Times Lit. Suppl.* 23 Nov. 1453/1 It is always difficult to judge the literary merit of juvenilia.

juvenility (dʒuːvɪˈnɪlɪtɪ). [ad. L. *juvenīlitās* youth, juvenility, f. *juvenīlis* JUVENILE: see -ITY. Cf. mod.F. *juvénilité* (1866 in Littré).]

1. Juvenile condition; youthfulness; youthful manner, quality, character, or vigour.

1623 COCKERAM, *Iuuenilitie*, youth. **1629** PRYNNE *Old Antith.* Pref. 8 If it stand with my juvinility and your venerable and hoary gravity. **1651** N. BACON *Disc. Govt. Eng.* II. xxvi. (1739) 118 He was in the nature or condition of a Pro-Rex, during the King's Juvenility. **1753** FOOTE *Eng. in Paris* I. (1780) 15 Allowing for the Sallies of Juvenility. **1815** J. ADAMS *Wks.* (1856) X. 141 Declining the engagement on account of the juvenility of our nation, the infancy of our government. **1885** *Leeds Merc.* 12 Sept. 6/5 The juvenility of his ideas is made manifest whenever he opens his mouth.

2. *concr.* Juveniles collectively; 'youth'.

1823 J. BADCOCK *Dom. Amusem.* p. v., Trifles which were intended to attract juvenility. **1849** J. HAMILTON *Mem. Lady Colquhoun* iii. 93 The juvenility of the district all mustered at the same seat of learning.

3. *pl.* Juvenile characteristics, acts, or ideas.

1661 GLANVILL *Van. Dogmatizing* Ep. Ded. (R.), Customary strains and abstracted juvenilities have made it difficult to commend and speak credibly in dedications. **1706** *Reflex. upon Ridicule* 380 Juvenilities unbecoming the character of old age. **1872** MORLEY *Voltaire* ii. 65 There was no question of the sentimental juvenilities of children crying for light.

†**juvent.** *Obs.* Also 4-6 iuvente. [a. OF. *juvent* (12th c.):—L. *juventūs*; and *juvente* (11th c.):—L. *juventa* youth.] Youth.

1377 LANGL., *P. Pl.* B. XIX. 104 In his iuuente [*v.r.* Iuuentee] þis ihesus atte iuwen feste Water in-to wyn tourned. **1390** GOWER *Conf.* II. 262 Of which an Alter mad ther was.. And efte an other to Iuvente, As sche which dede hir hole entente. *c* **1470** HARDING *Chron.* XCVI. i, Both young and fayre in florishyng iuuent. *c* **1510** BARCLAY *Mirr. Gd. Manners* (1570) Bvj, Wherefore ought our iuuent be prudently conuayde. **1524** EARL ARREN in *St. Papers Hen. VIII*, IV. 158 Not as ane pupill in juvente and lese aige.

[**juventate**, error for JUVENTUTE.

In ASH 1775; whence in WORCESTER 1859, followed by later Dicts.]

'juventude. *rare.* [f. assumed L. type **juventūdo* for *juventūs*, *-tūtem*: cf. med.L. *juventitudo* (8th c. in Du Cange).] Youth.
c **1470** HARDING *Chron.* XXXV. v, Sicilius..crowned was, and dyed in iuuentude. **1890** *Pall Mall G.* 13 May 2/3 Since the earliest days of our dramatic juventude.

† **'juventute.** *Obs. rare.* [ad. L. *juventūs*, *-tūt-em* the age of youth, f. *juvenis* a young person. Cf. obs. F. *juventute* (Godef.).] Youth; the age of youthful vigour or early manhood.
1533 ELYOT *Cast. Helthe* (1541) 13 a, Ages be foure: Adolescency to xxv yeres..Iuventute into xl yeres, hotte and drye, wherin the body is in perfyte growthe. **1542** [see JUVENTY, quot. *c* 1407]. **1742** in BAILEY (ed. 10).

† **'juventy.** *Obs.* In 4–5 iuuente(e. [ad. OF. *joveneté*, ad. L. *juventās*, *-tātem* youth: cf. *bonitātem*, *bonté*, *bounty*, etc.: see -TY.] Youth; = JUVENT, JUVENTUTE.
1377 [see JUVENT]. *c* **1407** SCOGAN *Moral Balade* 11 More I complayn my mispent juventè [*rime* me; *Chaucer's Wks.*, *ed. Thynne* 1542, *Stowe* 1561, iuuentute]. *c* **1470** HARDING *Chron.* LXXXII. iii, The virgyns then, of pure virgynitee, And then thynnocentes of tender iuuentee.

juvescence (dʒuː'vɛsəns). *rare.* [irreg. f. JUVE(NILE *a.* and *sb.*: see ADOLESCENCE.] The state of becoming young, juvenescence.
1920 T. S. ELIOT *Ara Vos Prec* 11 In the juvescence of the year Came Christ the tiger. **1948** S. SPENDER in *Time & Tide* 10 Jan. 33/1 That kissing of steel furies Preparing a world's childless juvescence.

juvey, var. JUVIE.

juvia ('dʒuː-, 'huːvɪə). [Amer. Sp.] The Brazil-nut. Also *attrib.*
c **1840** W. RHIND *Hist. Vegetable Kingdom* xxxix. 387 The triangular grains which the shell of the juvia incloses, are known in commerce under the name of Brazil nuts. **1852** T. ROSS tr. *A. von Humboldt's Personal Narr. Trav. Amer.* II. xxiii. 390 Juvia-trees, which furnish the triangular nuts called in Europe the almonds of the Amazon, or Brazil-nuts. **1858** W. BAIRD *Cycl. Nat. Sci.* 69/1 The natives are very fond of this nut, and celebrate the harvest of the *Juvia* with great rejoicings. **1860** MAYNE REID *Odd People* 142 The splendid fruits of the *Bertholetia excelsa*, or juvia-tree, known in Europe as 'Brazil nuts'.

juvie ('dʒuːvɪ). *U.S. slang.* Also **juvey.** [Colloq. shortening of JUVENILE *a.* and *sb.*] A juvenile or juvenile delinquent; also, a detention centre or a court for juvenile delinquents.
1941 J. SMILEY *Hash House Lingo* 34 *Juvie*, child. **1966** *Time* 2 Dec. 52/3 Los Angeles County police went after the 'juvies' (minors under 18), began carting them off by the busload. **1967** *New Yorker* 25 Feb. 128/3 But the teacher at juvey said, 'You have to finish it.' **1967** E. B. NICKERSON *Kayaks to Arctic* vii. 58, I wondered..if we would have to bail them out of the Canadian equivalent of 'Juvies'. **1970** P. STADLEY *Autumn of Hunter* (1971) viii. 115 Just where would you take me, little juvie? To a drive-in movie?

† **juvyn,** *a. Obs. rare*$^{-1}$. [ad. L. *juvenis* young.] Young, youthful.
(But perhaps we ought to read *juvynage* as one word.)
c **1450** in *Archiv. Stud. Neu. Spr.* (1900) CIV. 308 And other rehersith, that this juvyn age..To parfitnesse shuld sette yongly corage.

Juw(e, obs. form of JEW.

juwel(e, juweler, obs. ff. JEWEL, JEWELLER.

juwise, juwys(e, var. JUISE *Obs.*, judgement.

† **juxt,** *adv. Obs. rare.* [ad. L. *juxtā* near, by the side of.] Next, in the next place.
1614 P. FORBES *Defence* 29 It is, first, a vicious argumentation, and, iuxt, a contumelious blasphemie against the truth of God.

juxta, *a. rare.* [The prefix JUXTA- used as a separate word.] Next-lying, immediately adjacent.
1860 MAURY *Phys. Geog. Sea* (Low) iv. §232 The juxta air comes in to occupy the space which that carried up by the vapour leaves behind it.

juxta- (dʒʌkstə), *prefix*, repr. L. *juxtā* adv. and prep. 'near, by the side of, according to', used in recent formations, in which it stands in prepositional relation to the sb. represented in the second element. **juxta-am'pullary** *a.*, situated by the side of an ampulla; **juxta-ar'ticular** *a. Anat.*, situated near a joint; **juxta-ma'rine** *a.*, situated by the sea; **juxta-'spinal** *a.*, situated by the side of the (or a) spine; **juxta-'tabular** *a.*, *Rom. Law*, according to a testament or written document.
1897 *Allbutt's Syst. Med.* III. 721 *Juxta-ampullary or peri-ampullary carcinoma. **1900** *Juxta-articular in DORLAND *Med. Dict.* **1910** CASTELLANI & CHALMERS *Man. Trop. Med.* lviii. 1137 (*heading*) Juxta-articular nodules. **1940** *Q. Bull. Northwestern Univ. Med. Sch.* XIV. 270/1 Juxta-articular nodes are non-inflammatory, painless, fibrous, subcutaneous growths. **1899** *Westm. Gaz.* 14 Mar. 3/3 Caves that are subterranean and *juxta-marine. **1876** *Trans. Clin. Soc.* IX. 190 There was no loss of lung-note between the scapulæ nor in the *juxta-spinal regions. **1875** POSTE *Gaius* II. (ed. 2) §148 *Juxta-tabular [= *secundum tabulas*] possession..if defeasible by an adverse claimant, is ineffective.

juxtaglomerular (ˌdʒʌkstəglɒ'mɛrjələ(r)), *a. Anat.* [f. JUXTA- + GLOMERULAR *a.*] Situated next to a glomerulus of the kidney; ***juxtaglomerular apparatus***, a structure variously considered to comprise (i) a juxtaglomerular body alone, (ii) one of these bodies and a *macula densa*, or (iii) (also ***juxtaglomerular complex***) one of each of these, together with lacis cells and the afferent and efferent arterioles of a glomerulus; ***juxtaglomerular body***, a mass of tissue scattered along the wall of the afferent arteriole of a glomerulus, composed of cells (***juxtaglomerular cells***) with conspicuous cytoplasmic granules, believed to be the site of renin secretion.
1935 *Biol. Abstr.* IX. 2181/2 The neuro-myo-arterial juxtaglomerular segments of the kidney. **1939** *Proc. Soc. Exper. Biol. & Med.* XLII. 227 The media of these vessels [*sc.* the interlobular and glomerular arteries] is composed not only of ordinary smooth muscle cells but also of larger, more afibrillar and probably less contractile cells. In the kidney these cells are found all along the arterial vascular tree and accumulate in groups at the vascular poles of the glomeruli to form the 'juxta glomerular apparatus' or 'polkissen'. **1942** J. F. A. MCMANUS in *Lancet* 3 Oct. 394/2 (*heading*) The juxtaglomerular complex. *Ibid.*, There are an increasing number of references..to a structure termed the 'juxtaglomerular apparatus'. By this term we mean a group of apparently specialised structures in relation to, and including, the afferent and efferent arterioles of the glomerulus. The term 'complex' is used here in preference to Goormaghtigh's term 'apparatus', since he restricts the meaning to the vascular and perivascular arteriolar structures. *Ibid.* 395/1 Ruyter in 1925 saw granular, afibrillar cells in the juxtaglomerular portion of the afferent arteriole in the mouse. **1952** A. C. ALLEN *Kidney* ii. 32/2 The macula densa in combination with the juxtaglomerular body is referred to as the juxtaglomerular apparatus. **1958** *Amer. Jrnl. Path.* XXXIV. 863 (*heading*) The juxtaglomerular cells in man. **1968** PAGE & MCCUBBIN *Renal Hypertension* i. 40 (*heading*) Structure of the juxtaglomerular complex. **1968** E. L. BECKER *Struct. Basis Renal Dis.* i. 34 The juxtaglomerular apparatus..is considered to consist of four portions: the specialized portion of the afferent arteriole containing characteristic granules; the first portion of the distal convoluted tubule, or macula densa; the cushion of cells at the vascular pole, continuous with the mesangium, termed the polkissen 'lacis' cells; and the efferent arteriole.

juxtapose (dʒʌkstə'pəʊz), *v.* [a. mod.F. *juxtapose-r* (1835 in Hatz.-Darm.), f. L. *juxtā* + F. *poser*: see COMPOSE *v.*] *trans.* To place (two or more things) side by side, or close to one another, or (one thing) by the side of another. Hence **juxtaposed** (-'pəʊzd), *ppl. a.*
1851 H. TORRENS in *Jrnl. Asiat. Soc. Bengal* 2 A people whom chronology helps up to juxta-pose. **1855** H. SPENCER *Princ. Psychol.* II. ii. (1872) I. 191 They are juxtaposed and contrasted. **1862** R. H. PATTERSON *Ess. Hist. & Art* 20 If the colours of the juxtaposed objects are not of the same tone. **1879** *Cassell's Techn. Educ.* III. 191/2 When colours are juxtaposed, they become influenced as to their hue.

juxtaposit (dʒʌkstə'pɒzɪt), *v. rare.* [f. L. *juxtā* by the side of + *posit-*, ppl. stem of *pōnĕre* to put, place.] = JUXTAPOSE.
1681 GLANVILL *Sadducismus* 171 So far from unity of Essence, that it consists of juxtaposited parts. **1758** BATTIE *Madness* iv. 25 Those particles are by such pressure differently juxtaposited. **1894** J. OWEN in *Academy* 3 Feb. 93/3 Parallel passages in which phrases of Enoch are juxtaposited by texts of the New Testament.

juxtaposition (ˌdʒʌkstəpəʊ'zɪʃən). [a. F. *juxtaposition* (1690 in Hatz.-Darm.), f. L. *juxtā* + F. *position.*] **a.** The action of placing two or more things close together or side by side, or one thing with or beside another; the condition of being so placed.
1665 GLANVILL *Scepsis Sci.* vii. 37 Parts that are united by a meer juxta-position. **1680** BOYLE *Scept. Chem.* II. 140 There is but a Juxta-position of separable Corpuscles. **1690** LOCKE *Hum. Und.* IV. ii. §2 When the Mind cannot so bring its Ideas together, as by their..Juxta-position or Application one to another, to perceive their Agreement or Disagreement. **1707** *Curios. in Husb. & Gard.* 29 Plants.. receive their Nourishment by Intus-susception, and..grow not like Stones, by Juxta-Position. **1840** MRS. F. TROLLOPE *Widow Married* xxv, The ineffable two hours of their juxta-position at the dinner-table. **1868** FREEMAN *Norm. Conq.* II. App. 597 The juxtaposition of the words which follow is remarkable.

† **b.** *spec.* in *Cryst.* Contactual union between twinned crystals; ***juxtaposition twin***, a composite crystal of two (or more) crystals joined along a plane; a contact twin. *Obs.*
1883 *Encycl. Brit.* XVI. 366/1 In aragonite the crystals are partly interpenetrating, and partly merely in juxtaposition. **1890** G. H. WILLIAMS *Elem. Crystallogr.* ix. 185 Two individual crystals in twinning position are usually, though by no means always, united in a plane, which may or may not coincide with the twinning plane. Twins of this sort are called contact or juxtaposition twins. **1911** A. E. H. TUTTON *Crystallogr.* xxvi. 420 In the case of 'juxtaposition twins' the plane of union, whether the twin plane or not, is known as the 'plane of composition'. **1917** F. M. JAEGER *Lect. Princ. Symmetry* vii. 171 The classification of twins into such as are produced by juxtaposition or by penetration, may have certain advantages from a practical standpoint.

Hence **juxtapo'sitional** *a.*, relating to or characterized by juxtaposition.
1863 *Smith's Dict. Bible* III. 539/2 Our own language, though classed as inflectional..is in many respects as isolating and juxtapositional as any language of that class. **1868** MAX MÜLLER *Rede Lect.* II. in *Sel. Ess.* (1881) I. 84 The three stages in the history of the Aryan languages, the juxtapositional, the combinatory and the inflectional.

juxtapositive (dʒʌkstə'pɒzɪtɪv), *a. Gram.* [f. JUXTAPOSIT(ION + -IVE.] The designation of a case expressing juxtaposition.
1880 A. H. SAYCE *Introd. Sci. Lang.* I. v. 370 Steinthal, however, goes on to divide his formless languages into 'juxta-positive' and 'compositive'. **1890** A. S. GATSCHET *Klamath Indians* I. 490 Juxtapositive case in -tana.

juyce, juys, obs. forms of JUICE.

Juyll, Juyn, etc., obs. forms of JULY, JUNE *sb.*

juyse, variant of JUISE *Obs.*, judgement.

juyste, obs. form of JUST.

juzail, variant of JEZAIL.

† **jyane,** obs. Sc. form of GIANT.
a **1568** CLERK in *Bann. P.* 297/36 My vnspaynd jyane.

† **jybbet,** var. of GIBBET *sb.*², a note on the horn.
1649 G. DANIEL *Trinarch., Hen. IV*, cclxix, Hee calls 'em in With Jybbet, which the Kennel now enflames.

jybe, jyce: see GIBE, JOIST.

jymiam, jymold: see JIM-JAM, GIMMALED.

jyneper, obs. form of JUNIPER.

jynx (dʒɪŋks). Also 7 jyng. Pl. **jynges** ('dʒɪndʒiz). [a. mod.L. *jynx*, pl. *jynges*, = L. *iynx*, a. Gr. ἴυγξ, pl. ἴυγγες the wryneck, a bird made use of in witchcraft; hence, a charm, a spell.]

1. A bird, the wryneck (*Jynx* or *Iynx torquilla*); also called YUNX.
1649 G. DANIEL *Trinarch., Hen. V*, ccxcv, Where not a Silver Iyng, or Pigeon, fell To Pay the Markman. **1706** PHILLIPS, *Jynx*, the Wry-neck, or Emmet-hunter, or as some say, the Wag-tail. **1708** *Phil. Trans.* XXVI. 123 The Jynx or Wryneck..I first heard this year on March 29. [**1845** *Zoologist* III. 1107 Its sharp and harsh cry, resembling a repetition of Jynx, Jynx, Jynx.] **1857** BIRCH *Anc. Pottery* (1858) I. 297 A youth or females hold a bird, supposed to be the iynx, in their hands.

2. *transf.* A charm or spell.
a **1693** URQUHART *Rabelais* III. i. 23 These are the Philtres, Allurements, Jynges, Inveiglements [*les philtres, iynges, et attraictz*], Baits, and Enticements of Love.

3. Name of an order of spiritual intelligences in ancient 'Chaldaic' philosophy.
1655 STANLEY *Hist. Philos.* (1701) 17/2 [tr.] Then is the Intelligible Jynx; next which are the Synoches, the Empyreal, the Ætherial and the Material; after the Synoches are the Teletarchs..Intelligent Jynges do themselves also under-stand from the Father By unspeakable Counsels being moved so as to understand.

jys(se, jyst, jywel, obs. ff. GIS, JOIST, JEWEL.

K

K (keɪ), the eleventh letter of the alphabet in English and other modern languages, was an original letter of the Roman alphabet, taken from the Greek *Kappa* K, originally ꓘ, from Phœnician and general Semitic *Kaph* ꓘ. Its sound in Greek and Latin was, as in English, that of the back voiceless stop consonant, or guttural *tenuis*. But at an early period of Latin orthography, the letter C (originally representing Greek *Gamma*) was employed for the k sound, and the letter K itself fell into disuse, except in a few words, notably the term *Kalendæ* and the prænomen *Kæso*, where the traditional abbreviations Kal. and K. kept up the memory of the archaic spelling. But, with the exception of such archaisms, C became the regular Latin symbol of the k sound, and, as such, was substituted for Greek Kappa when Greek words were latinized, as in *Κίμων, Κῦρος, κόμμα, Cīmōn, Cȳrus, comma*. In late Latin, when the sound of C before a front vowel had become palatalized, or passed over to (tʃ), as in Italian *cento, città*, the same fate befell the C of latinized Greek words, such as *Cyrus*; but later Greek words in living (esp. Christian) use such as *kȳrie eleïson* (*κύριε ἐλέησον*), which retained the Greek pronunciation, continued to be written with K. To Latin scribes of the sixth, seventh, and eighth centuries, K was thus known as a supplementary letter to C, of use in Greek or other foreign words which had the 'hard' or k sound of C before *e, i*, or *y*. Hence it was naturally put to use in the writing of Old High German, Old Saxon, Old Frankish, Early Italian, and some dialects of Old French, in which a k sound came before *e, i*, or *y*. In writing these languages, C was usually employed, as in Latin, before *a, o, u*, or finally; but in practice there was considerable overlapping, with the final result that, in German, K ousted C, and is now the proper letter for this sound in that language, as well as in Dutch and all the Scandinavian tongues; while, in French, K was ousted partly by C, partly by Qu, according to derivation. (Thus Old Northern French ***kanon, karole, katre, ke, ki, kel***, became later ***canon, carole, quatre, que, qui, quel***.) So 13th c. It. ***ke, ki, perké***, became later ***che, chi, perchè***.

In the Romano-British alphabet, K was, as in Latin, of rare use, and was not adopted as a regular letter in Welsh or Irish; though, as being quite familiar to Latin scribes, it was occasionally written as a casual variant of C. In Old English, the original Teutonic k-sound was already in the earliest times fronted or palatalized before original front vowels (not the umlauts of back vowels), and for this variety of sound (c) a distinct symbol was provided in the Runic alphabet. Yet, in the OE. use of the Roman alphabet, both the guttural and the palatal sound were represented by C, although in the practice of individual scribes K was by no means infrequent for the guttural, especially in positions where C would have been liable to be taken as palatal, or would at least have been ambiguous, as in such words as ***Kent, kéne, kennan, akenned, kynn, kyning, kyðed, folkes, céak, picke***. But, even in these cases, C was much more usual down to the 11th century; and K can be regarded only as a supplemental symbol occasionally used instead of C for the guttural sound. After the Conquest, however, the Norman usage gradually prevailed, in accordance with which C was retained for the original guttural only before *a, o, u, l, r*, and K was substituted for the same sound before *e, i, y*, and (later) *n*; while the palatalized OE. *c*, now advanced to (tʃ), was written Ch. Hence, in native words, initial K now appears only before *e, i, y* (*y* being moreover usually merged in *i*), and before *n* (:—OE. *cn-*), where it is no longer pronounced in Standard English, though retained in some dialects. Medially and finally, *k* is used after a consonant (*ask, dark, twinkle*), or long vowel (*make, hawk, like, speak, week*); after a short vowel, *ck* is used instead of *cc* or *kk*, but the unstressed suffix, formerly *-ick* (*musick*), is now *ic*, though, when a suffix in *e* or *i* follows, *k* reappears (*traffic, trafficker, trafficking*).

The native K words, being thus confined to ke-, ki-, kn- (with one or two from the dialects in ka-, ky-), are a small company. But their number is greatly reinforced by the foreign words of recent adoption, many of them very imperfectly naturalized, with which this letter is crowded. These include a few modern European words, Germanic or Slavonic; but they consist mainly of names of animals, plants, trade products, and native offices, from Oriental, African, American, Australian, and Oceanic languages. The number of these words is augmented by reason of the fact that some of those languages have two, or even three, distinct gutturals, for which, in ordinary English spelling, K has to stand; the combination kh is similarly put for several fricative and aspirated sounds in Arabic, Turkish, Persian, Hindī, and other tongues. (See the individual words, in the etymology of which the actual origin of the letter is stated.) In giving these words English hospitality, it was formerly usual to follow English analogies and write C before *a, o, u, l, r, h*; but the more recent tendency has been to favour the use of K in these positions also; giving the non-English initial combinations ka-, kh-, kl-, ko-, kr-, ku-, by which the uncouth or barbarous character of the words is more strongly suggested. Thus *cadi, Calmuck, Can* (*Chan, Cham*), *cloof, Coran, creese*, now more frequently appear as ***kadi, Kalmuk, Khan, kloof, Koran, kris***.

In words from Greek also, many prefer to retain K, instead of latinizing it to C; and this spelling is generally accepted in some words of recent formation, as ***kaleidoscope, kamptulicon, katabolism, kinetic, kudos***, while in others, as ***kainozoic, kakodyle, krasis***, C and K still struggle for predominance. In a very few words (not of English formation), K represents Greek χ, esp. in the words in ***kilo-***, as ***kilogram(me), kilometre***, etc.

1. The letter. The plural appears as *K*s, K's, *k*s, k's. (Although now generally pronounced (keɪ), the pronunciation (kiː) was formerly also current.)

*c*1000 ÆLFRIC *Gram.* iii. (Z.) 6, *B, c, d, g, p, t* ʒeendiað on *e. h* and *k* ʒeendiað on *a* æfter rihte. *q* ʒeendað on *u*. **1552** HULOET s.v., Latin wordes begynninge with K be verye rare. **1573–80** BARET *Alv.*, K Is borrowed of the Greekes: and in writing of our English standeth vs in verie much stead. *c*1620 HUME *Brit. Tongue* 14 Behind the voual, if a consonant kep it, we sound it [c] alwayes as a k. **1674** RAY *Coll. Words* Err. Alphab. (E.D.S.) 25 C..if we use it in its proper power..differs not at all from k. **1899** *Westm. Gaz.* 17 Aug. 6/2 She says women have no business to interfere with anything outside the four K's..The four K's are—'Kinder, Kirche, Küche, and Kleider—children, church, kitchen, and dress.'

attrib. **1887** SKEAT *Princ. Etymol.* I. 354 The substantive *Care* preserves the *k*-sound. **1900** *Contemp. Rev.* Feb. 270 All the k-languages are spoken by peoples living either in the East of Europe or in Asia. *Ibid.* 272 The distribution of the k-peoples does not concern us.

2. Used, like the other letters of the alphabet, to express serial order, as in numbering the sheets or quires of a book, lettering parts of a figure, enumerating items of a list, etc.; the successive groups or sections of a classification; the companies of a military force; the batteries of the Royal Artillery; the different MSS. of a work, etc.

In serial order K is the 11th or 10th member, according as J is or is not reckoned as a member of the series (see J).

3. a. In *Chem.* K is the symbol for Potassium (mod.L. *kalium*). It was formerly used to designate a compound of gold (*Syd. Soc. Lex.*). In *Meteorol.* K = cumulus. In *Assaying*, etc. K = carat. In *Astron. k* designates Gauss's Constant, the square of which is a measure of the mass of the sun. For *k* in Quaternions, see I (the letter) 6; in *Cryst.* see H 7.

1853 SIR W. R. HAMILTON *Lect. Quaternions* 59 Let i, j, k, denote three straight lines equally long, but differently directed [etc.]. **1886** *Encycl. Brit.* XX. 161/2 The fundamental i, j, k of quaternions.

b. In *Physics k* (or *K*) is the symbol of thermal conductivity. [Introduced by J. B. J. Fourier, 1822.]

[**1822** J. B. J. FOURIER *Théorie anal. de la Chaleur* i. 54 Nous avons choisi ce même coëfficient K, qui entre dans la seconde équation, pour la mesure de la conducibilité spécifique de chaque substance.] **1850** in *Trans. R. Soc. Edin.* (1864) XXIII. 137 The specific heat of the metal being known, we can convert this amount of heat or flux across *x* into absolute measure; for the Flux is = − K *dv*/*dx* and *dv*/*dx* is known... Thus every experiment becomes an independent means of finding K. **1880** *Encycl. Brit.* XI. 579/2 Let *k* be the thermal conductivity of the substance and *c* its thermal capacity per unit bulk. **1947** *Sci. News* IV. 147 With glass..the heat conductivity (*k*) is 0·002. *Ibid.* 148 Steel (*k* = 0·10). **1969** *Jane's Freight Containers 1968–69* 239/1 The k-value according to choice of insulating material is about 0·4 to 0·5 kcal/m² h°C.

c. *Physics.* The designation of one of the strongest Fraunhofer lines, situated in the extreme violet at a wavelength of 3934 Å and due to absorption by calcium ions.

1879 *Proc. R. Soc.* XXVIII. 367 The calcium line with wave-length 4226..appears more or less expanded with a dark line in the middle..; the remaining bright lines of calcium are also frequently seen in the like condition, but sometimes the dark line appears in the middle of K (the more refrangible of Fraunhofer's lines H), when there is none in the middle of H. **1897** *Ibid.* LXI. 437 The H and K lines have become thin and defined. **1967** R. G. GIOVANELLI in J. N. Xanthakis *Solar Physics* xii. 353 The Balmer lines and the *H* and *K* lines of ionized calcium are..strong Fraunhofer absorption lines.

d. In *Physics* and *Chem. k* is the symbol of Boltzmann's constant.

1901 *Sci. Abstr.* IV. 230 For a comparison of his own reasoning with that of Boltzmann on gas molecules, the author deduces from *k* an estimate (6·175 × 10²³) for the number of molecules in the gramme molecule of any element. **1915**, etc. [see BOLTZMANN]. **1962** W. B. THOMPSON *Introd. Plasma Physics* ii. 17 A temperature of 11,600°K is needed to give an energy *kT* of 1 eV so that the mean kinetic energy of a molecule, $\frac{3}{2}kT$, reaches 1 eV only when *T* = 7,730°K.

e. In *Physics K* is used to designate the series of X-ray emission lines of shorter wavelength obtained by exciting the atoms of any particular element (cf. L 7a); these arise from electron transitions to the innermost, lowest-energy atomic orbit, of principal quantum number 1, which is thus termed the ***K-shell***, and electrons in this shell ***K-electrons***. **K(-electron) capture**, the capture by an atomic nucleus of one of the *K*-electrons.

1911 C. G. BARKLA in *Phil. Mag.* XXII. 406 It is seen that the radiations fall into two distinct series, here denoted by the letters K and L. [*Note*] Previously denoted by letters B and A... The letters K and L are, however, preferable, as it is highly probable that series of radiations both more absorbable and more penetrating exist. **1923** H. L. BROSE tr. *Sommerfeld's Atomic Struct. & Spectral Lines* iii. 144 If the excitation occurs through the agency of cathode rays, it is easy to imagine that the tearing-off of the 'K-electron' is effected by the impact of a cathode-ray particle that has penetrated into the atom. **1923** E. N. DA C. ANDRADE *Struct. Atom* vi. 100 Moseley identified in the *K* series the two lines which he called α and β... In the *L* series he identified five lines. **1938** L. B. LOEB *Atomic Struct.* iii. 83 A tube with 1,470 volt electrons may excite *K* x-rays of Al, while it takes 60,600 volt electrons to excite the *K* x-rays of tungsten. **1946** H. SEMAT *Introd. Atomic Physics* (ed. 2) viii. 342 Probably the most clearcut example of *K*-electron capture is the radioactive disintegration of vanadium, $_{23}V^{49}$, into titanium, $_{22}Ti^{49}$, with the capture of a *K* electron by the vanadium nucleus to form a titanium atom in the *K* state. **1951** J. DOUGALL tr. *Born's Atomic Physics* (ed. 5) vii. 220 *K*-capture should therefore compete with β-decay. **1970** HURST & TURNER *Elem. Radiation Physics* ii. 24 A few nuclei.. capture an atomic electron from outside the nucleus, most often from the K-shell, and emit a neutrino.

f. *Physics* and *Chem.* In the old quantum theory *k* is the azimuthal or subordinate quantum number (introduced by N. Bohr 1920, in *Zeitschr. f. Physik* II. 445), which determines the shape of electronic orbits of the same *n*; (now superseded by the quantum number *l*). In molecular spectroscopy *K* is a quantum number which in diatomic and linear molecules represents the total angular momentum apart from electronic spin (now usu. replaced by *N*), and in polyatomic molecules represents the component of the total momentum about an axis of symmetry.

1922 A. D. UDDEN tr. *Bohr's Theory of Spectra* II. iii. 44 The perturbations are periodic, so that we may assume that to each energy value of a stationary state of the unperturbed system there belongs a series of discrete energy values of a whole number *k*. *Ibid.* III. iii. 85 Where it is necessary to differentiate between orbits corresponding to various values of the quantum number *k*, a central orbit, characterized by given values of the quantum numbers *n* and *k*, will be referred to as an n_k orbit. **1930** R. S. MULLIKEN in *Physical*

Rev. XXXVI. 613 In [Hund's] case *b*, $\Lambda h/2\pi$ and the nuclear angular momentum combine to give a quantised resultant. .. For the corresponding quantum number..the designation *K* is now recommended. The possible values of *K* are Λ, $\Lambda + 1$, $\Lambda + 2$... There is usually a small magnetic field in the molecule parallel to *K*, so that *K* and *S* form a resultant *J*. **1934** H. L. Brose tr. *Sommerfeld's Atomic Struct. & Spectral Lines* (ed. 3) ii. 115 In wave mechanics the azimuthal quantum number, our n_k or Bohr's *k*.., becomes replaced by the quantity $l = n_k - 1$, $l = 0, 1, 2$... **1961** Powell & Crasemann *Quantum Mech.* i. 24 A perturbation of the force, such as might be produced by the presence of other electrons, has the effect of removing the degeneracy, so that states with the same value of *n* but different values of *k* have different energies. **1962** P. J. & B. Durrant *Introd. Adv. Inorg. Chem.* vii. 226 Paschen-Back effect [for diatomic molecules] (strong magnetic field)... **K** and S are not coupled together but are coupled directly to the field. **1966** C. N. Banwell *Fund. Molecular Spectroscopy* iii. 94 Parallel Vibrations [of Symmetric Top Molecules]. Here the selection rule is: $\Delta v = \pm 1$, $\Delta J = 0, \pm 1$, $\Delta K = 0$.

g. *Psychol.* The letter chosen to represent the spatial factor, or aptitude for remembering form and structure, in some ability-tests.

1935 *Brit. Jrnl. Psychol.* Monogr. Suppl. xx. vii. 65 In order to distinguish these eight tests from the rest of the table they may for convenience be called the *K* tests. *Ibid.* 75 Therefore there is in them [*sc.* specific correlations], over and above '*g*', *one group factor*; this we name the K factor. **1944** L. L. Thurstone *Factorial Study Perception* iii. 117 It is quite likely that the factor *K* is determined by experimental dependence. **1950** Spearman & Jones *Human Ability* xii. 132 For the first time, the spatial test does, in some degree, measure K. **1969** P. E. Vernon *Intelligence & Cultural Environment* ix. 59 Embedded Figures and the Kohs Block test are good measures of the *k* factor of British psychologists..and this is much the same as Thurstone's original *S* (spatial) factor.

h. [From its use as an abbrev. for *kilo-*.] In connection with *Computers* K or k is used to represent 1,000 (or 1,024: see quot. 1970). Also used transf. to represent 1,000 (pounds, etc.), esp. of salaries offered in job advertisements.

1966 P. D. Reynolds *Computer ABC* 54 The internal storage of computers is commonly arranged..to hold a quantity of data which is some power of 2, for example, 4096 characters, bytes or words, which is 2^{12}. The convention is to refer to this number as 4K. 64K..amounts to 65,536(2^{16}). **1967** Cox & Grose *Organiz. Bibliogr. Rec. by Computer* ii. 2 It seemed desirable..wherever possible to ignore the limitations of the computer available to us (a KDF 9 with a store size of 16 K 48-bit words). **1968** *Data Communications* Sept. 143/3 (Advt.), Engineers, Mini-Micro Programmers, Analysts.. Salaries $15–45K. **1970** O. Dopping *Computers & Data Processing* ii. 35 Sometimes, a 'K' is used for a number which is either 1,000 or 1,024, depending on whether the context calls for integral powers of 10 or 2. If we say that a certain computer has a memory capacity of 4 K words, then, this means either 4,000 or 4,096 words, depending on whether the computer in question has a decimal or binary address system. However, the usage is a little loose: the number $2^{16} = 65{,}536$ is written either as 64 K or 65 K. **1970** *Daily Tel.* 3 Dec. 21/3 (Advt.), All progs. PL1-COBOL Ass. plan rpg. for IBM/ICL/Hyl. to £3k. **1971** *Daily Tel.* 21 July 20 (Advt.), I.B.M. programmers... Sal. from £1,600 to £2·4k. **1971** *New Scientist* 9 Sept. 569/1 Typically, a minicomputer has a minimum memory of between one and eight K words. **1985** G. V. Higgins *Penance for Jerry Kennedy* viii. 65, I got that property for eighteen grand, net... I had eighteen K then. **1986** *Daily Tel.* 26 Feb. 25 (Advt.), Financial administrator, Thames Valley, from £12k. **1986** *Washington Post* 31 Aug. B15 (Advt.), Computer systems programmer, $35–$40k, downtown. *Ibid.* K24 (Advt.), Alfa Romeo—'84... Perf. cond. 23k ml.

4. K. is an abbreviation, **a.** for some Christian names, as *Kate, Katherine, Kenneth*. **b.** for *King*: formerly used alone; now usually in comb., as **K.B.**, King's Bench; **K.C.**, King's Counsel, King's College; **K.H.B.** *colloq.* (see quot. 1925); **K.O.S.B.**, King's Own Scottish Borderers; **K.Q.**, 'King and queen' iron. **c.** for *Knight* (standing alone **Kt.**) also used *colloq.* for *knighthood*; in **K.B.**, Knight Bachelor; **K.B.E.**, Knight Commander of the Order of the British Empire; **K.B.S.**, Knight of the Blessed Sacrament; **K.C.B.**, Knight Commander of the Bath; **K.C.S.I.**, Knight Commander of the Star of India; **K.C.M.G.**, Knight Commander of the Order of St. Michael and St. George; **K.C.V.O.**, Knight Commander of the Victorian Order; **K.G.**, Knight of the Garter; **K.G.C.B.**, Knight Grand Cross of the Bath; **K.H.**, Knight of Hanover (*Obs.*); **K.P.**, Knight of the Order of St. Patrick; **K.S.G.**, Knight of the Order of St. Gregory the Great; **K.T.**, Knight of the Order of the Thistle, etc. **d.** *Electro-physiol.* = *kathode* (also **ka.**), *kathodic* (see cathode, etc.), in **K.C.C.**, kathodic closure contraction; **K.C.Te.**, kathodic closure tetanus; **K.D.T.**, kathodic duration tetanus; **K.O.C.**, kathodic opening contraction (*Syd. Soc. Lex.*). **e.** for *kilo-*, as **kcal.**, **kcal**, kilocalorie(s); **kg.**, kilogram; **kHz**, kilohertz; **km.**, kilometre; **kVA** (also **kv.-a.**, etc.), kilovolt-ampere(s); **kW** (also **K.W.**, **kw.**, etc.), kilowatt(s); **kWh**, kilowatt-hour(s). **f.** In miscellaneous abbreviations, as °K, K, (degree) Kelvin (see Kelvin, kelvin 3 b); **K.E.**, **k.e.**, kinetic energy; **K.G.B.** [Komitet Gosudarstvennoĭ Bezopasnosti] = Committee of State Security (U.S.S.R.); **K.i.H.**, **K.I.H.**, Kaisar-i-Hind; **K.K.K.**, Ku Klux Klan; **K.L.**, Kuala Lumpur; **K.L.M.** [Koninklijke Luchtvaart Maatschappij], Royal Dutch Airlines; **K.M.T.**, Kuomintang; **K.O.**, **k.o.**, knock(ed) out (cf. kayo *v.* and *sb.*); **K.P.** (*U.S.*), kitchen police(man); **K.P.D.** [Kommunistische Partei Deutschlands], German Communist Party; **k.p.h.**, kilometres per hour; **K ration** [f. the initial letter of the surname of Ancel *K*eys (1904–), American physiologist], a package of concentrated food; **KWIC** = *key-word-in-context* (key *sb.*[1] 18).

1614 Selden *Titles Hon.* 5 Where Moses speaks of Amraphel *K. of Sinaghr, the Paraphrase of Onkelos hath expresly K. of Babel. **1623** *Shakspere's 2 Hen. IV*, i. ii. 86 Doth not the K. lack subiects? Do not the Rebels want Soldiers? **1910** *Lett. Lord Kilbracken & Gen. Godley* (*c* 1932) 13 Long may you live to wear your honours, and I hope that 'the coming *K' will not be long deferred. **1966** J. Betjeman *High & Low* 70 That very near miss for an All Souls' Fellowship, The recent compensation of a 'K'. **1968** *Listener* 13 June 770/3 A 'K' isn't certain any more, even if you're a civil servant. **1973** *Times* 24 Aug. 12/8 There might not have been much merit in a political knighthood, but there was no harm in it... The 'K', when it came, was a boon to the Member's wife, and a blessing to the Member himself. **1911** *Physical Rev.* XXXIII. 226 The value of the ice point..was taken as *273·2°K. **1937** M. W. Zemansky *Heat & Thermodynamics* xiii. 232 The isothermal compressibility of copper is plotted against the Kelvin temperature in Fig. 72. Above about 100°K the rise..is approximately linear. **1959** *Sci. News* LI. 11 The lowest temperature that can conveniently be obtained by evaporating helium under reduced pressure is about 1°K. **1970** *Nature* 10 Oct. 144/2 The coolest spectrum recorded over the Antarctic plateau indicates a surface temperature of 190 K (– 83°C). **1972** *Amat. Photographer* 12 Jan. 38 Household Bulbs... 150 watts is usually the maximum, with a colour temperature of around 2,700 to 2,900°K. **1818** Cruise *Digest* (ed. 2) V. 213 It was resolved by the Court of *K.B. **1833** *Byron's Wks.* (1846) 584/2 Any list of K.B.'s or K.H.'s. **1952** 'W. Cooper' *Struggles of Albert Woods* iv. i. 206 They tell me your Principal got a plain K and was hoping for *K.B.E. **1968** *Listener* 12 Dec. 787/3 He was given a KBE for his efforts. **1916** *Let.* 12 June in *Knights of Blessed Sacrament* (Catholic Truth Soc.) (1918) 14, I have started the *K.B.S. among my men here. **1923** A. O'Connor *Knight in Palestine* ii. 11 The K.B.S. and another Catholic made ready the altar. **1898** Besant *Orange Girl* ii. xi, Mr. Caterham, *K.C., our senior counsel. **1954** R. T. Sanderson *Introd. Chem.* iv. 43 Larger quantities of heat are measured in kilocalories, which are 1000 calories each. They are sometimes abbreviated as Cal with a capital C; more commonly they are simply *kcal. **1964** N. G. Clark *Mod. Org. Chem.* iii. 29 The energy required to bring about this rotation is seen to be 5 kcal, a relatively trivial amount capable of being supplied by the thermal motion of neighbouring molecules. **1849** Thackeray *Three Sailors* in S. Bevan *Sand & Canvas* xxv. 341 There's the British fleet a riding at anchor, With Admiral Napier, *K.C.B. **1880** E. W. Hamilton *Diary* 29 Aug. (1972) I. 40 Loch, the Governor of the Isle of Man, is to be a KCB. **1904** *Westm. Gaz.* 8 Jan. 6/2 Lord Lawrence used to speak of England's aggressive policy in India as the 'K.C.B.' mania. **1972** *Times* 6 May 1/4 Sir James..was appointed KCB in the New Year Honours. **1897** *Whitaker's Almanack* 108 The Royal Victorian Order. Instituted 21st April, 1896... Knights Grand Cross. G.C.V.O... Knights Commanders. *K.C.V.O. **1968** *Listener* 29 Aug. 278/1 His sufferings.. were not assuaged by a KCVO. **1888** A. Aveling *Mech. & Exper. Sci.: Mech.* xiii. 137, *k.e. of the two masses after collision = $mv^2/2$. **1909** Jackson & Roberts *First Dynamics* 88 The gain of K.E. equals arithmetically the work done by the forces. **1965** Van Wylen & Sonntag *Fund. Classical Thermodynamics* v. 84 E = Internal energy + Kinetic energy + Potential energy or $E = U + \text{KE} + \text{PE}$. **1892** *Pall Mall G.* 21 Mar. 7/1 A movable drum weighing $2\frac{1}{2}$ *kg... a line of 23 km. length. **1876** Trollope *Prime Minister* IV. iv. 52 (*heading*) The new *K.G. **1880** E. W. Hamilton *Diary* 23 Aug. (1972) I. 37 A Garter is vacant by death of Lord Stratford de Redcliffe.. Lord Palmerston is a precedent for a commoner receiving a KG. **1904** K. G. [see gunner 1 c]. **1972** *Whitaker's Almanack 1973* 463 The Viscount Montgomery of Alamein K.G., G.C.B., D.S.O. **1960** *Analog Science Fact/Fiction* Oct. 122/2 The *KGB was once again checking on every foreigner. **1966** J. Porter *Sour Cream* v. 58 The K.G.B. is willing to shell out a small fortune in roubles for me, dead or alive. **1972** K. Benton *Spy in Chancery* i. 8 The Russian who's made the approach ..isn't the type of KGB operative one would expect to make a run for it. **1833** *K.H. [see *K.B.* above]. **1899** Miss G. Palgrave *F. T. Palgrave* 1 Sir Francis Palgrave, K.H., Deputy Keeper of Her Majesty's Records. **1916** 'Taffrail' *Pincher Martin* iv. 62 He was a *K.H.B., and they were not sorry to be rid of his presence. **1925** Fraser & Gibbons *Soldier & Sailor Words* 134 *A K.H.B.*: a King's Hard Bargain. A worthless or incorrigible fellow. (Old Service term.) **1955** *Proc. IRE* XLIII. 880/3 A happy solution would be more widespread use of the term 'hertz', meaning cycle-per-second. Thus the units of frequency would be hertz (or hz), *khz, and Mhz. **1974** *Electronics* 26 Dec. 48 E A portable a-m signal generator..covers 85 kHz to 100 MHz. *a* **1912** W. T. Rogers *Dict. Abbrev.* (1913) 108/2 *K.I.H., Kaiser-i-Hind (Emperor of India). **1942** Partridge *Dict. Abbrev.* K.i.H. or K.I.H., the Kaisar-i-Hind Medal; for useful service in India. **1973** *Daily Tel.* 20 Sept. 36/7 Alice Headwards-Hunter, K.I.H., F.R.C.S.E., D.C.H., formerly of Calcutta. **1872** in W. L. Fleming *Documentary Hist. Reconstruction* (1907) II. 132 We advanced upon the supposed *K.K.K.'s. **1877** J. M. Beard *K.K.K. Sk.* 35 The horses of the raid were.. furnished with all those *cap-a-pie* appointments of K.K.K. regalia. **1952** *N.Y. Times* 1 Aug. 16/2 For conspiracy to flog a Negro woman, the so-called 'Imperial Wizard' of the local KKK has been given..four years. **1970** G. Jackson *Let.* Apr. in *Soledad Brother* (1971) 48 I've already mentioned that most of them are K.K.K. types. **1961** 'G. Black' *Suddenly, at Singapore* ix. 129 From there we could have been going to *K.L. or anywhere in Malaya. **1973** *Observer* 7 Oct. 36/6 Here is the capital, Kuala Lumpur, which the old Malay hands called KL and now everybody does. **1933** *Meccano Mag.* Mar. 193/1 A pilot flying on the *K.L.M. route to Batavia. **1968** *Listener* 28 Nov. 704/3 KLM suggest you come to Amsterdam just to see the airport. **1892** *km. [see *kg.* above]. **1959** *Times Lit. Suppl.* 8 May 270/4 Two months later Chiang struck again by excluding Communists from any higher posts in the *K.M.T. **1969** J. M. Gullick *Malaysia* ii. 85 At one time the Chinese middle class gave its support to the Kuomintang, an effective if externally orientated nationalist movement, but the KMT was ground between .. British restrictions .. and .. communist penetration of the Chinese working class. **1972** 'M. Hebden' *Killer for Chairman* i. ix. 115, I last saw you in Canton... There was one of the K.M.T. generals still hiding there. **1922** T. Burke *London Spy* 209 As a youth the ring attracted him... A few *k.o.'s put an end to that. **1923** H. Cox *Dogs & I* xxii. 209 The Field Spaniel has received the 'K.O.' and taken the count! **1927** *Observer* 25 Dec. 12/6 His record.. includes a k.o. victory over Paul Berlenbach. *Ibid.*, Knut Hansen, who k.o. Phil Scott in the first round. **1928** *Daily Express* 25 June 17/7 Young Stanley..was then k.o. by a right swing to the jaw. **1951** 'J. Wyndham' *Day of Triffids* viii. 142 Coker an' another chap was giving them the k.o. as they tripped. **1971** *Weekend World* (Johannesburg) 9 May 1/2 Morodi said he was not upset by the defeat—the first k.o. he has suffered in 70 fights. **1909** *Who's Who* p. xi/1 *K.O.S.B. King's Own Scottish Borderers. **1914** F. W. Spicer *Diary* in P. Young *Brit. Army* (1967) xv. 203 On our right was the 13th Infantry Brigade, with the 2/K.O.S.Bs. joining up with our right Company. **1924** *Cricketer Ann. 1923–4* 82 The band and pipers of the K.O.S.B.'s. **1964** 'T. Carew' *Vanished Army* ii. 128 The K.O.Y.L.I. saw strange faces in their depleted ranks—men of the Suffolks, K.O.S.B. and Manchesters. **1917** D. C. Falls *Army & Navy Information* 84 *K.P., Kitchen Police. A mild form of punishment. **1921** J. Dos Passos *3 Soldiers* i. 10 The men.. filed by the great tin buckets at the door, out of which meat and potatoes were splashed into each plate by a sweating K.P. in blue denims. **1929** [see *kitchen police* s.v. kitchen *sb.* 7]. **1956** B. Holiday *Lady sings Blues* (1973) xviii. 143 After all the big personnel experts got together to figure out a job that was right for a city girl like me, I was cast for the part of Cinderella of Cottage No. 6. This was nothing but a fairytale name for permanent K.P. **1973** *Publishers Weekly* 25 June 70/2 For an uncertain spell he struggles through the miserable childhood of 'Norma Jean' in a welter of secondhand conjectures—Mailer doing biographical KP. **1922** *Encycl. Brit.* XXXI. 280/2 The violent agitation conducted by the central committee of the *K.P.D. in Berlin. **1935** C. Isherwood *Mr Norris changes Trains* vi. 98, I am not a member of the Communist Party..I merely sympathize with the attitude of the K.P.D. to certain non-political problems. **1964** *New Statesman* 28 Feb. 332/1 Relations with Germany—and with the German Communist Party, the KPD—stood at the centre of the picture. **1966** G. B. Mair *Kisses from Satan* ix. 106 They were doing over a hundred *k.p.h. on a snaky road. **1972** W. Garner *Ditto, Brother Rat!* xxiii. 172 The speedo needle crept past the 150 kph mark. **1826** *Sporting Mag.* XVIII. 391 They are manufactured from scrap iron (the best *K.Q., or King and Queen as it is called). **1851** Nimrod *The Road* 11 Axle trees of the best K.Q. iron. **1944** *R.A.F. Jrnl.* Aug. 283 We get American '*K' rations, with a few extras. **1967** 'T. Carew' *Korea* ii. 19 A K ration consisted of a tin of compressed meat hash, coffee, powdered milk, a fruit bar, cigarettes, chewing gum, and toilet paper. **1909** Webster, *K.S.G. **1905** S. P. Thompson *Dynamo-Electr. Machinery* (ed. 7) II. iii. 173 An 8-pole, 60 *KVA three-phase generator. **1930** *Engineering* 14 Mar. 355/1 Supplies to the villages will be..through pole transformers with capacities of 50, 20 and 10 kv.-a. **1959** *B.S.I. News* June 9/1 The standard applies to power transformers, reactors and earthing transformers having windings insulated with four different classes of insulating material, with single-phase ratings of 1kVA and above or polyphase ratings of 2kVA or above. **1905** A. H. Bate *Princ. Electr. Power* iii. 34 Electrical power can thus be expressed in either of three units, namely:—The watt, equal to 1 volt multiplied by 1 ampere. The kilowatt (*K.W.), equal to 1000 watts. And the electrical horse-power. **1930** *Engineering* 23 May 667/1 The maximum load in the area during 1928–29 was 26,059 kw., [etc.]. **1959** *Chambers's Encycl.* V. 93/2 Central power stations for public electricity supply may range in capacity from the comparatively small size of 40,000 kW to the very large capacity of 500,000 kW or more. **1930** *Engineering* 28 Feb. 299/2 The best yearly record has been reduced to as low as 12,500 B.Th.U. per *kw.-h. sent out. **1963** *Times* 3 June 12/1 The Minister expressed his belief that in 1968–70 30,000m. kWh of a total electricity production of 260,000m. kWh will be produced by France's atomic plants. **1959** H. P. Luhn in *IBM Corporation ASDD Rep.* RC-127 (*title*) Keyword-in-context index for technical literature (*KWIC index). **1967** Cox & Grose *Organiz. Bibliogr. Rec. by Computer* vi. 154 It has been decided not to produce a KWIC index at this stage. **1969** *Computers & Humanities* III. 166 An obvious prerequisite for this kind of dictionary construction is large key-word-in-context (KWIC) lists drawing on large samples of the language.

Hence **K.C.B.-ship**, and the like; **K.C.B.** *v. nonce-wd.*, to invest with the order of K.C.B.

1881 Black *Beaut. Wretch* I. 24 [He] had got his K.C.B.-ship for long service in India. **1886** *Athenæum* 3 Apr. 456/3 In 1869 [he] accepted a K.C.M.G. ship in lieu of the peerage he had hoped for. **1892** *Temple Bar Mag.* Sept. 127 He was K.C.B.'d the other day.

†**ka**, *v.*[1] *Obs.* exc. *dial.* Forms: 6–7 **ka**, 6 **kawe**, 6–7 **kaw**, **kay**, **k**, 7–8 **kae**, 9 **kaa**. [Of obscure origin: the synonymous *claw me*, *claw thee* is found earlier (see claw 5 b).

The various forms agree curiously with the various names of the letter K, which is itself used in quot. 1605, where there is also a pun on *key* (then pronounced (ke:).)]

A word found only in the phrases ***ka me***, ***ka thee*** or ***ka me and I'll ka*** (also ***kob***) ***thee***, which imply mutual help, service, flattery, or the like.

1546 J. Heywood *Prov.* (1867) 34 Ka me, ka the, one good tourne askth an other. **1595** Lodge *Fig for Momus* Sat. i. B ij b, To keepe this rule, kaw me and I kaw thee. **1603** Florio *Montaigne* (1634) 488 Now nature stood ever on this point, Kae mee, Ile kae thee. **1605** Chapman, etc. *Eastw. Hoe* II. i, K me, k thee, runs through court and country. *Secur.* Well said.. Those Ks ope the doors to all this world's felicity. **1608** Armin *Nest Ninn.* (1842) 34 But kay me Ile kay thee, giue me an inch to-day; Ile giue thee an ell tomorrow. *a* **1658** Ford, etc. *Witch Edmonton* II. i, If you'll be so kind to ka me one good turn, I'll be so courteous to kob you another. **1676** Marvell *Mr. Smirke* 42 Turn'd into Jackdaw, and grew as black as a Crow, Filching, and Kaw me and Ile Kaw thee, ever after. **1721** Kelly *Sc. Prov.* 227 Kae me, and I'll kae thee; Spoken when great People invite and feast one another, and neglect the Poor. **1893** *Northumbld. Gloss.* s.v., 'Kaa me, kaa thee', or 'Kaa mee an' aa'll kaa thee', a common saying.

† **ka** (kə), *v.*² Var. *quo*': see quoth, quotha.

a **1553** Udall *Royster D.* I. ii. (Arb.) 17 Enamoured quod you?.. Enamoured ka? mary sir say that agaiene. **1588** *Marprel. Epist.* 20 That is my meaning, ka dumb Iohn.

ka (kɑː), *sb.* Also **kaa**. The name given by the ancient Egyptians to a spiritual part of a human being or a god which survived after death and could reside in a statue of the dead person.

a **1892** Tennyson in A. G. Weld *Glimpses Tennyson* (1903) 119, I believe that beside our material body we possess an immaterial body, something like what the ancient Egyptians called the Ka. **1905** E. F. Benson *Image in Sand* i. 11 Somebody's Ka—his ghost, you know, or his astral body. **1923** *Glasgow Herald* 22 Feb. 4 The Princess has a Ka, or better self. **1952** J. M. White *Anc. Egypt* 40 The Ka lived in the tomb with the mummy. **1968** V. Ions *Egyptian Mythol.* 123 The *ka*, the vital principle of a man or of a god. **1972** *Daily Tel.* (Colour Suppl.) 3 Mar. 29/4 The Ancient Egyptians, whose civilisation goes back earlier than 3,000 BC, believed that the *ka* or spirit of a man could only survive if his body was preserved.

ka, obs. variant of kae, jackdaw; of caw, cry of a crow; Sc. f. call, drive.

ka-, frequent variant of ca-, in ME., and in modern representation of alien words from oriental and other languages; e.g. *kaaba, kabaye, kabane, kackle, kadi, kaffeine, kage, kalme, kamel, kandle.*

Kaaba, Kaabeh, varr. Caaba.

† **kaak**, *v. Obs.* [Imitative: cf. cawk *sb.*² and *v.*] *intr.* Of a crow: to caw.

1605 Sylvester *Du Bartas* II. iii. I. *Vocation* 1276 As thick as Crowes in hungry shoals do light On new-sow'n lands,.. Kaaking so loud.

kaak, obs. form of cake.

‖ **kaama** (ˈkɑːmə). Also **caama, kama, khama (kgama)**. [Given by Burchell as the Hottentot name, but app. now current in Sechuana (Lloyd *Three Great African Chiefs* 18).] The hartebeest, a South African antelope (*Alcelaphus caama*).

1824 Burchell *Trav.* II. 81 The Hartebeest of the Cape Colony is called Caama or Kaama by the Hottentots. **1834** *Penny Cycl.* II. 90/1 The caama.. inhabits the plains of South Africa. **1866** Livingstone *Last Jrnls.* (1873) I. vi. 157 Much spoor of elands, zebras, gnus, kamas. **1883** J. Mackenzie *Day-dawn* 48 In the distance we sometimes descried the sly khama.

kaan, kaava, kab: see khan¹, kava, cab *sb.*¹

Kababish (kəˈbɑːbɪʃ). Also 8 **Cubbabeesh**, 9 **Kobabeish**. [Arab. *kabābīš*, pl. of *kabbāšī*.] A nomadic Arab people of the northern Kordofan and Dongola provinces of the Sudan. Also *attrib.*

1790 J. Bruce *Trav.* IV. viii. x. 515 Lately the Beni Gerar, Beni Faisara, and Cubba-beesh, have expelled the ancient Arabs of Bahiouda. *a* **1817** J. L. Burckhardt *Trav. Nubia* (1822) 438 The Djerar, Kobabeish, and Feysara live to the north and north-east. **1861** J. Petherick *Egypt, Soudan & Cent. Afr.* xvii. 282 The entire Kababish nomade tribe inhabiting the northern confines of the province emigrated to Darfour. **1891** F. R. Wingate *Mahdiism & Egyptian Sudan* ix. 288 The Kababish, who lived in the desert west of Dongolee. **1898** Alford & Sword *Egyptian Soudan* I. ii. 26 The earliest and most important revolt against the Khalifa was the rising of the Kababish Arabs. **1918** C. G. & B. Z. Seligman in *Harvard Afr. Stud.* II. 105 The Kabâbîsh constitute the richest and most powerful of the Arab tribes of the Anglo-Egyptian Sudan. **1954** H. A. MacMichael *Sudan* vii. 74 Little tribal authority survived except among those nomadic tribes, such as the Kababish. **1960** A. Tibble *With Gordon in Sudan* ii. 48 Those camel-owning nomads whom Gordon would meet between Dongola and Metemma were the Kababish.

kabad(d)i (kəˈbɑːdɪ). [Tamil.] A game popular in northern India and Pakistan played between two teams of nine boys or young men (see quot. 1935). Also *attrib.*

1935 W. M. Ryburn *School Organization* 278–80 Kabaddi... 3. Each team consists of nine players... 5. The members of each team remain in their respective semi-circles... 10. A player scores a point for his team if he succeeds in getting back to his semicircle after touching some opponent (with the hand only) or after pushing some opponent out of his semicircle provided that he holds his breath all the time. He will say that word 'kabaddi' over and over to show that he is holding his breath... An attempt by a player to touch an opponent is known as a kabaddi. **1943** Moraes & Stimson *Introd. India* (ed. 3) 171 Among Indian games *kabadi (hu-tu-tu)* and *kho-kho* are prominent (they are too complicated to describe here). **1965** E. Linton *World in Grain of Sand* x. 172 There was volley ball, tug of war and 'kabadi'. Kabadi, the Indian wrestling game, is fascinating to watch. **1969** *Femina* (Bombay) 26 Dec. 45/1 The versatile collegians of Bombay lifted the Inter-Varsity table tennis, kabaddi and swimming titles. *Ibid.* 45/4 (*caption*) Rajkumari Jain.. during the inter-varsity kabaddi tourney. **1971** *Illustr. Weekly India* 11 Apr. 51/1 (*caption*) A variety of Indian games (like *khokho* and *kabaddi*) find play here. **1974** *Dawn* 17 Apr. 4/3 Special attention was being paid to the popularization of indigenous games like Kabaddi and even a National Kabaddi Federation had been formed.

Kabaka (kəˈbɑːkə). The Bantu title which was given to the ruler of the province of Buganda in Uganda. Hence **Kaˈbakaship**, the office of Kabaka.

1878 H. M. Stanley *Through Dark Continent* I. 189 General jack-of-all-trades for the *Kabaka*. **1925** J. W. Mackail *J. L. Strachan-Davidson* 90 The choice of an English tutor for the eight-year-old Kabaka of Uganda. **1954** *Ann. Reg. 1953* 123 The U.K. Government had withdrawn recognition from the Kabaka of Buganda. **1960** *Economist* 8 Oct. 136/2 The public esteem for the institution of the Kabakaship in Buganda. **1966** *Ibid.* 9 July 139/1 Mr Obote seems to intend to maintain the Kabakaship. *Ibid.* 139/2 Any descendant of Mutesa I is eligible for selection as Kabaka. **1971** *Sunday Nation* (Nairobi) 11 Apr. 6/2 Mutesa was their last Kabaka and.. Uganda is to stay a Republic.

‖ **kabalassou** (kæbəˈlæsuː). Also **cab-**. [? Altered from kabassou.] The giant armadillo, *Priodontes gigas.*

1884 *Stand. Nat. Hist.* V. 50 The Kabalassous, or Priodontines, exhibit a still further deviation.. in the structure of the fore feet.

kabane (kəˈbɑːneɪ). Also **kabané**. [Jap.] In ancient Japan, a series or system of titles of rank.

1890 B. H. Chamberlain *Things Japanese* 252 The *kabane* or *sei*, a very ancient and aristocratic sort of family name, but now so widely diffused as to include several surnames in the narrower sense of the word. **1904** L. Hearn *Japan: Attempt at Interpretation* xii. 260 Caste would not seem to have developed any very rigid structure in Japan; and there were early tendencies to a confusion of the kabané. **1931** G. B. Sansom *Japan* I. ii. 39 An integral part of the clan system.. was the system of titles, or *kabane*. **1970** J. W. Hall *Japan from Prehist. to Mod. Times* v. 36 A more precise set of titles of rank (*kabane*) had also been evolved.

kabaragoya (kəbɑːrəˈgəʊjə). Also **kabragoya**. [Etym. unknown.] The watermonitor, *Varanus salvator*, a large lizard found in south-eastern Asia.

1681 R. Knox *Ceylon* I. vii. 30 There is a Creature here called *Kobberaguion*, resembling an Alligator. The biggest may be five or six foot long, speckled black and white. **1892** C. F. G. Cumming *Two Happy Years in Ceylon* (ed. 4) II. xx. 176 A gigantic lizard, or rather iguana, of a greenish-grey colour, with yellow stripes and spots, called by the natives kabragoya, awoke from its midday sleep... The kabragoya is amphibious. **1960** H. W. Parker tr. *Mertens's World of Amphibians & Reptiles* x. 181 In south-eastern Asia the large Kabara Goya (*Varanus salvator*), despite its timidity, prefers to be associated with man.

Kabardian (kəˈbɑːdɪən), *sb.* and *a.* Also **Kabard, Kabardan, Kabardin(e), Kabardinian**. [f. Russ. *Kabarda* (place-name) + -ian.]

A. *sb.* **a.** A member of one of the peoples inhabiting the Kabardino-Balkarian Republic in the northern Caucasus, related ethnically to the Circassians, of Caucasian race but non-Indo-European in language. **b.** The north-western Caucasian language of this people.

1824 *Encycl. Brit.* III. 166/2 The most remarkable are the Kabardines,.. the Kisti, the Ossetes. **1888** *Ibid.* XXIII. 514/2 Kabards, Circassians, Osses, and Karapapakhs. **1931** G. C. Wheeler tr. *Nansen's Through Caucasus* 43 The Kabardians live on the north side of the Caucasus along the Terek. **1956** J. Lotz in Saporta & Bastian *Psycholinguistics* (1961) 10/1 In Kabardian, also of the Caucasus. **1960** A. H. Kuipers *Phoneme & Morpheme in Kabardian* 8 The Kabardians differed from their Western relatives in that they formed a well-developed feudal ceremony. **1965** D. Fidlon tr. *Trunov's Trip N. Caucasus* 11 'The place swarms with birds,' the Kabardinian continued.

B. *adj.* Of, pertaining to, or characteristic of the Kabardians or their language.

1902 [see Ingush]. **1940** J. F. Baddeley *Rugged Flanks Caucasus* II. xxii. 220 This ceremonial observance is.. a point of honour with the Kabardān nobility. **1950** D. Jones *Phoneme* 222 The Kabardian language of the Caucasus. **1965** D. Fidlon tr. *Trunov's Trip N. Caucasus* 14 She was a graceful Kabardinian girl with a healthy suntan.

‖ **kabassou** (kəˈbæsuː). [F. (Buffon) a. Galibi *capaçou* (Sauvage *Dict.* 1763).] An armadillo of the genus *Xenurus*.

1774 Goldsm. *Nat. Hist.* (1862) I. vi. iii. 471 The fifth kind of Armadillo is the Kabassou or Cataphractus, with twelve bands. **1834** *Penny Cycl.* II. 354/2 The Kabassous, or fourth division of Baron Cuvier, have.. five toes.

kabaya, var. kebaya.

kabbala(h, -ism, -ize, var. cabbala, etc.

kabbelow, kabeliau, var. cabilliau, cod-fish.

kabber, obs. form of caber.

kabeljou (ˈkɑːbəljaʊ, ˈkɒbəljaʊ, ‖ˈkabəljou). *S. Afr.* Also **cabaljao, cabeliau, kabbeljou, kabeljaauw, -jauw, -jouw, kobeljauw, -jouw** and, abbreviated, **kob**². [Afrikaans, = Du. *kabeljauw* (see cabilliau).] A large marine food fish, *Johnius hololepidotus*, of the family Sciænidæ.

1731 [see cabilliau]. **1838** J. E. Alexander *Expedition Interior Afr.* II. iv. 83 We got a great prize in a stranded cabaljao, fifty pounds weight, like a huge salmon. **1912** J. T. Cunningham *Reptiles, Amphibia, Fishes* 277 The name kabeljaauw [= cod].. in South Africa has been transferred to a fish of a very different species,.. the maigre, *Sciaena aquila*. **1913** C. Pettman *Africanderisms* 271 Kobeljauw or Kabeljauw. **1930** C. L. Biden *Sea-Angling Fishes of Cape* 109 The kabeljou is often mistaken for the geelbek. **1950** *Cape Times* 17 Nov. 13/8 Last week-end kobeljouw catches were kept down by the difficulty of casting into the teeth of the wind. **1952** *Ibid.* 7 Nov. 3/5 Fishing-boats brought home the first few kabbeljou of the season. **1959** *Ibid.* 16 Nov. 2/5 A.. visitor.. landed a 94-pound Kabeljouw in the Klein Rivier lagoon. **1973** *Farmer's Weekly* (S. Afr.) 13 June 102 The species being tagged include grunter and white steenbras, elf (shad), kob (kabeljauw or Cape Salmon in Natal) haarders (mullet) and leervis (garrick).

Kabistan (kæbɪˈstɑːn). Also **Cabistan**. Erron. for *Kubistan* after the district of Kuba in Azerbaijan, used *attrib.* or *absol.* to designate a finely woven, short napped rug or carpet with intricate geometric design made in that area; also called Kuba.

1900 J. K. Mumford *Oriental Rugs* ix. 111 In the Kabistans the weft and sometimes the warp is of cotton cord. **1904** M. B. Langton *How to know Oriental Rugs* iii. 117 The Cabistan rug is a most desirable, moderate-priced rug, of artistic worth. **1913** G. G. Lewis *Pract. Bk. Oriental Rugs* (rev. ed.) x. 128 S Forms.. are very common in the Caucasian fabrics, especially in the Kabistans and Shirvans. **1931** A. U. Dilley *Oriental Rugs & Carpets* Pl. 52 (*caption*) Kabistan or Hila, Geometric adaptation of Persian pattern. **1964** *Sunday Times* (Colour Suppl.) 19 Jan. 24 Cabistan. Similar to Shirvan rugs in weave and colour. **1970** J. Franses *European & Oriental Rugs* 44 (*caption*) Antique Kabistan rug. **1972** [see Kuba].

kabitka, kabob, var. kibitka, cabob.

1798 T. Morton *Secr. worth knowing* I. i, One of your fine kabobbed fricasees. **1883** H. W. V. Stuart *Egypt* 296 Kabobs or little disks of various meats impaled upon wooden skewers,.. and brought up hissing hot.

kabouri (kəˈbʊrɪ). *Guyana.* Also **kaboura, kaburi**. [Origin unknown.] A fly of the genus *Simulium*.

1899 J. Rodway *In Guiana Wilds* xi. 161 The great pest was the kaburi, which raised a blister in every spot where its venomous proboscis was inserted. **1917** W. G. White in C. W. Beebe et al. *Trop. Wild Life Brit. Guiana* I. xxxiv. 486 No one can know the district without knowing the kabouri fly... It is a blood-sucker, which marks one as with fine pocks... I am told that there are two species of kabourie; *Simulium guianense*, and *Simulium amazonicum*. **1954** G. Durrell *Three Singles to Adventure* iv. 92 We were fiercely attacked by great numbers of tiny black flies a little larger than a pin-head but with a bite that was out of all proportion to their size... 'They're kaboura flies...' The kabouras continued their assault on us.

‖ **kabouter** (kəˈbaʊtə(r)). [Du.] A gnome, goblin, or dwarf; *transf.*, used for a member of an anti-establishment political movement in Holland.

1961 T. Henrot *Belgium* 182 Each region has its familiar spirits.. the dwarves kindly and quarrelsome—*Nûtons* in the grottoes of Namur, *Kabouters* on Campine's heaths, *Sotâis* of the Amblève. **1970** *Guardian* 6 June 11/4 Remember the Provos, Amsterdam's pacifist rebels..? Their successors, the Kaboute [*sic*] or Elves, have gone one better. They campaigned in the nude for this week's city council elections. **1970** *Daily Tel.* 30 June 16 *World in Action* (ITV) introduced the Kabouter, the gnomes of Amsterdam, an anti-establishment movement who wear pointed hats.. and, to general astonishment, have won five seats on the city council. **1971** *Guardian* 13 Apr. 11/4 The Kabouters—the Dutch street action group. **1973** *Reader's Digest* Apr. 97/1 What city would have a political movement called the *kabouters*, or pixies?

Kabuki (kəˈbuːkɪ, ‖kabuki). Also with small initial. [Jap., f. *ka* song + *bu* dance + *ki* art, skill.] A traditional and popular form of Japanese drama which employs highly stylized singing, miming, and dancing in addition to acting, and in which (since *c* 1650) all the parts are played by males. Also *attrib.* Hence **Kabukiˈesque** *a.*, in the style or manner of the Kabuki theatre.

1899 W. G. Aston *Hist. Jap. Lit.* VI. iii. 288 Kabuki theatres, which had men for actors, had been established there before the middle of the seventeenth century. **1928** *Daily Tel.* 4 Dec. 8/4 The Kabuki affords freedom for old and favourite plays, for new ones on Western lines, and for adaptations of Western drama. **1951** *Oxf. Compan. Theatre* 411 The present day Japanese theatre takes three distinct, although related forms, the *Nō* or lyrical drama, *Ningyō-shibai* or marionettes, and *Kabuki*, the popular theatre. **1954** F. Bowers *Jap. Theatre* vii. 224 Another woman who lies down to offer herself as a substitute for the married woman—a postwar Kabukiesque 'substitution'. **1960** B. Leach *Potter in Japan* viii. 190 The merchant class with its popular arts of the Kabuki theatre and the colour print. **1970** *Oxf. Compan. Art* 1171 Favourite subjects were theatre scenes, which began to appear along with the development of the popular *Kabuki* theatre in the 17th. c. **1972** *Nat. Geographic* Sept. 378 Man in maiden's guise

charms theater-goers in the classical drama known as Kabuki. **1972** *Mainichi Daily News* (Japan) 6 Nov. 3/5 Collection and sale of kabuki dolls.

Kabuli (kə'buːlɪ), *a.* and *sb.* Also **Cabuli, Kabulian.** **A.** *adj.* Of, pertaining to, or characteristic of the city or province of Kabul in Afghanistan.

1887 KIPLING *Plain Tales from Hills* (1888) 173 Baskets of fruit and pistachio nuts and Cabuli grapes. **1893** —— *Day's Work* (1898) 3 A little switch-tailed Kabuli pony. **1909** *Westm. Gaz.* 2 Feb. 5/1 These Cabuli rooks do not visit us every winter. **1966** P. KING *Afghanistan* 64 (*caption*) Kabuli carpet seller.

B. *sb.* A person or animal from Kabul; also, the Iranian language of some of the people of this area or its script.

1895 KIPLING *Day's Work* (1898) 188 You're to take one of Sir Jim's horses. There's a gray Cabuli here. **1909** M. DIVER *Candles in Wind* xi. 112 He urged the Kabuli forward. **1948** D. DIRINGER *Alphabet* 301 The Kharoshthi, which is called also Bactrian..Kabulian..and so forth. **1964** H. H. PAPER tr. *Shafeev's Short Gram. Outl. Pashto* 1 Until 1936 the official language of Afghanistan was Kabuli, one of the dialects of Tajik.

kaburi, var. KABOURI.

Kabyle (kə'baɪl). Also **Kabail, Kabile, Kabyl.** [Arab. *ḳabā'il*, pl. of *ḳabīla* tribe.] A member of a group of Berber peoples inhabiting northern Algeria and Tunisia; these peoples collectively; also, the Berber (Hamitic) language of these peoples. Also *attrib.* ***Kabyle dog*** (see quot. 1945).

1738 T. SHAW *Trav. Barbary* i. 8 The several Portions and Districts..are chiefly known and distinguished by the particular Names of the Kabyles..or African Families, who respectively possess them. **1818** E. BLAQUIÈRE tr. *Pananti's Narr. Residence Algiers* 181 The Bedouins are divided into many scattered tribes, called *Kabiles*, and vulgarly *Nege*. **1861** *Chambers's Encycl.* II. 44/1 In Algeria, where they [*sc.* Berbers] usually are termed Kabyles, they are yet unconquered by the French. **1868** L. WINGFIELD *Under Palms in Algeria & Tunis* I. iv. 84 He told us many things about the 'interieur' of Kabyle life. **1882** F. W. NEWMAN *Libyan Vocab.* 3 The Libyan language..was but one, according to St. Augustine. Now there are at least four, the Kabail in Algeria, the Shilha in the mountains of Morocco, the Tuarik..beyond the Atlas, and the Ghadamsi at Ghadames. *Ibid.* 38 Kabail verbs and verbals, including adjectives. **1900** A. WILKIN *Among Berbers of Algeria* 178 Cheek by jowl the villages of Frenchmen and Kabyles stand. **1900** *Knowledge* 1 Aug. 173/2 The various Kabyle tribes. **1924** *Glasgow Herald* 14 Aug. 7 The Kabyles are agricultural Berbers living in the uplands of Morocco and Algeria. **1945** C. L. B. HUBBARD *Observer's Bk. Dogs* 176 Kabyle Dog..a sheepdog native to the Kabyle Mountains. **1963** *Guardian* 9 Oct. 11/1 President Ben Bella..does not speak Kabyle and many Kabyles do not understand Arabic. **1969** E. GELLNER *Saints of Atlas* i. 14 A Kabyle worker in France..has also kept his Berber speech. **1974** *Times* 30 May 10/5 Sons are what Kabyl husbands demand... Sterility and daughters alike are no good, and Kabyl women know it.

kac(c)he, kacchere, kace, obs. ff. CATCH, CATCHER, CASE.

kach(ch)eri, var. CUTCHERRY, CUTCHERY.

kacheree, var. CUTCHERRY.

kach(h)a, var. CUTCHA *a.*

Kachin (kə'tʃɪn). [Burmese.] A member of a Tibeto-Burman ethnic group inhabiting the mountainous regions of north-east Burma; its language group, which includes Chingpaw, Atsi, Maru, etc. Also *attrib.*

1892 W. R. WINSTON *Four Yrs. Upper Burma* 102 In the north of Burma..are found the Kachins, a warlike hill people. **1903** G. A. GRIERSON *Linguistic Survey of India* III. II. (*title*) Specimens of the Bodo, Nāgā, and Kachin groups. **1906** O. HANSON (*title*) A dictionary of the Kachin language. **1925** *Blackw. Mag.* Dec. 864/1 The reiterated word accented in Kachin is most descriptive. **1934** 'G. ORWELL' *Burmese Days* xiv. 211 Producing two green pigeons from his Kachin bag. **1962** [see CHIN *sb.*[2]]. **1963** C. MAXWELL-LEFROY *Land & People of Burma* vii. 47 Warm green tea,..shyly handed to us by a pretty Kachin girl. **1970** F. S. V. DONNISON *Burma* ii. 47 The Kachins are nine-tenths Animists and the rest Christians.

kachina (kə'tʃiːnə). Also **cachina, katc(h)ina**, and with capital initial. [Hopi *qacina* supernatural.] In North American Pueblo Indian mythology, one of the deified ancestral spirits which periodically visit the pueblos, to bring rain, etc. Also in *Comb.*, as ***kachina dance***, a dance performed at annual ceremonies by masked and elaborately costumed men impersonating the kachinas whom they seek to invoke; ***kachina doll***, a doll representing a kachina, given to children at the annual ceremonies by the kachina dancers.

1888 S. WALLACE *Land of Pueblos* 47 The *cachina* dance, which they celebrate at certain seasons of the year. **1907** F. W. HODGE *Handbk. Amer. Indians* I. 638/1 Kachina. A term applied by the Hopi to 'supernatural beings impersonated by men wearing masks'. **1910** G. W. JAMES *Grand Canyon* 122 For use in the katchina dances, katchina baskets are made. **1948** *Seattle Sunday Times* (Mag.) 26 Sept. 3/4 The masked dancers who impersonate deities, or katchinas, in the great rain rites and rituals. **1959** E. TUNIS *Indians* 126/2 He saw the sacred kachinas, and he was given dolls dressed like them to play with. **1968** N. BENCHLEY *Welcome to Xanadu* ii. 29 Harry was a Hopi Indian, and..he sold silverware and pottery and kachina dolls. **1972** *Sat. Rev.* (U.S.) 3 June 33/2 The high-voltage transmission towers..march across the desert like giant skeletal Kachinas—Hopi ceremonial figures—carrying the white man's electricity.

kack-handed, var. CACK-HANDED *a.*

kackle, var. CACKLE *v.*[2] *Naut.*

kad-: see also CAD-.

Kadarite ('kædəraɪt). Also **Kaderite.** [f. Arab. *qadar* predestination + -ITE.] A member of a Muslim sect, *alqadariyah*, which denies predestination and maintains the doctrine of free will.

1727-41 CHAMBERS *Cycl.*, *Kadari* or *Kadarites.* **1860** GARDNER *Faiths World* II. 465/2 Kaderites.

‖**Kaddish** ('kædɪʃ). Also 7 **kaddesch, kiddisch.** [Aram. *qaddīsh* holy, holy one.] A portion of the daily ritual of the synagogue, composed of thanksgiving and praise, concluding with a prayer for the advent of universal peace; specially recited also by orphan mourners.

1613 PURCHAS *Pilgrimage* (1614) 181 The son of a deceased Iew is bound to say, for the space of one yeare, a prayer called *Kiddisch*. *Ibid.* 200 Then the..Chanter, singeth halfe their prayer called *Kaddesch*. **1876** GEO. ELIOT *Dan. Der.* liii, If you think *Kaddish* will help me—say it, say it. You will come between me and the dead. **1892** ZANGWILL *Childr. Ghetto* xxii, Moses bore the loss with resignation, his emotions discharging themselves in the daily *Kaddish*.

Kadet, var. CADET[2].

‖**kadi, kadee**, variants of CADI. Hence '**kadilik**, the jurisdiction of a cadi.

1704 J. PITTS *Acc. Mahometans* 27 The Man to be married ..goes to the *Kadee*, i.e. Judge, or Magistrate. **1802-3** tr. *Pallas' Trav.* (1812) II. 368 Villages..added to the Kadilik of Mankup. **1847** MRS. A. KERR *Hist. Servia* 48 These three offices, of Pacha, Kadi, and Bishop,..might all be obtained for money.

Kadiak, var. KODIAK.

‖**kadin** ('kɑːdɪn). Also **kadine.** [Turk.; the form *kadine* is prob. through Fr.] A lady of the Sultan's harem.

1843 *Penny Cycl.* XXV. 394/2 The women of the harem are divided into five classes:—1, 'Kádin', or 'wives of the Sultan', in number from four to seven. **1896** *Westm. Gaz.* 16 Sept. 1/3 He seldom notices any woman in his harem except the chief kadine. **1937** *Times Lit. Suppl.* 16 Jan. 36/2 He [*sc.* the Sultan] was content with four *kadins*.

kadir, var. KHADAR.

kadish ('kɑːdɪʃ). Also 9 **gedish.** [Arab. *kadīš*, f. O.Turk. *igdiş* a cross-breed, f. *igid-* to feed, rear; cf. Turk. *idiş* gelding.] An Arabian horse that is not a thoroughbred; a cross-bred horse, a nag; a gelding.

a **1817** J. L. BURCKHARDT *Trav. Syria & Holy Land* (1822) 295 A man with two or three is esteemed wealthy; and such a one has probably two camels, perhaps a mare, or at least a Gedish (a gelding), or a couple of asses. **1879** A. BLUNT *Let.* 6 May in Lady Wentworth *Authentic Arabian Horse* (1945) 26 They have made my horses vulgar 'Kadishes'. **1924** *Blackw. Mag.* Mar. 346/2 Others less generous or more cautious sent *kadish* horses, only fit for the plough. **1945** LADY WENTWORTH *Authentic Arabian Horse* i. 34 All Oriental potentates regarded the Arabian as the only Horse and the rest as 'Kadishes', a word which exactly corresponds to the word 'cur' in English. It was the excellence of these Arabians..whose fame earned for the country-bred Kadishes a reflected radiance. **1970** A. DENT tr. *Schiele's Arab Horse in Europe* 24 If there were the tiniest lacuna or unknown quantity in its ancestry, it was no longer regarded as 'asil' and was demoted to the status of 'kadish'.

‖**kadkhoda** (kad'koːda). Also **kadkhuda**, and with capital initial. [Pers. *kadkhudá*.] The head man of an Iranian village.

1934 F. STARK *Valleys of Assassins* 56 We..were welcomed by the *kadkhuda* and a dozen tribesmen or so. **1953** A. SMITH *Blind White Fish in Persia* v. 80 The Kadkhoda, the bailiff of the village, blows out his lamp and retires to bed. **1963** *Times* 6 Feb. 12/6 The *kadkhoda*, or head man.

KADU, Kadu ('kɑːduː). [f. the initials of the words *K*enya *A*frican *D*emocratic *U*nion.] The name of a Kenyan political party.

1962 *Listener* 12 Apr. 643/3 The two main African parties, Kadu and Kanu. **1964** *Ann. Reg. 1963* 107 During the campaign rifts appeared in KADU.

kae (ke), *sb.*[1] *north. dial.* and *Sc.* Forms: 4-6 **ka**, 5 **kaa**, 6 **ca, kay, ke**, 5, 8- **kae**. [Northern form of ME. Co, corresponding to MDu. *ca, ka(e* (Du. *ka*), OHG. *chaha, châ* (MHG. *kâ*), Da. *kaa*, Norw. *kaae.* The direct source may have been an ON. **ká, kǫ́.* Cf. CHOUGH.] A jackdaw. Also *fig.*

1340 HAMPOLE *Pr. Consc.* 1539 Some gas hypand als a ka. *c* **1450** HOLLAND *Howlat* 191 Crawis and Cais, that cravis the corne. **1483** *Cath. Angl.* 200/1 Ka (*A.* Kae), *monedula.* **1535** LYNDESAY *Satyre* 5241 *direct.*, An Crow or ane Ke salbe castin vp, as it war his saull. **1536** BELLENDEN *Cron. Scot.* (1821) II. 450 Kayis and piottis, clekit thair birdis in winter. **1786** BURNS *Earnest Cry & Prayer* xxiv, In spite o' a' the thievish kaes That haunt St. Jamie's! **1876** SMILES *Sc. Natur.* ii. (ed. 4) 25 At last he brought with him..a Kae, or jackdaw.

b. *Comb.*, as **kae-witted** *a.*

1837 R. NICOLL *Poems* (1843) 104 He maun been but a kae-witted bodie!

kae, *sb.*[2] [Imitative.] The cry of a jackdaw.

1850 *Zoologist* VIII. 2913 The well known kae of the jackdaw.

kae, variant of KA *v. Obs.*

kæmmererite, obs. var. KÄMMERERITE.

kaempferol ('kæ-, 'kɛmpfərɒl). *Chem.* Also **kampherol** ('kæmfərɒl). [f. mod.L. *Kaempferia*, generic name of the plant (*K. galanga*) from which it was first obtained, f. the name of Engelbert *Kaempfer* (1651-1716), German physician and traveller: see -OL.] A yellow crystalline flavonoid, $C_{15}H_{10}O_6$, that occurs alone and in glycosides in various plants; 3,4′,5,7-tetrahydroxyflavone.

1897 H. M. GORDIN *On Crystallised Substances contained in Galangal Root* (Dissertation, Univ. of Berne) 37 Demethylised kampherid or kampherol as we agreed to call it crystallises from alcohol in light yellow needles. It contains one molecule of water of crystallisation. **1900** *Proc. Chem. Soc.* XVI. 183 The colouring matter has properties resembling those assigned to kampherol. **1923** *Nature* 17 Nov. 747/2 Four different species of Acacia..have been examined... The water soluble yellow pigment was a glucoside of kæmpferol. **1963** *Brit. Pharmaceutical Codex* 718 The drug [*sc.* senna leaf] also contains rhein, aloe-emodin, kæmpferol and isorhamnetin in the free state and combined as glycosides. **1969** KIRK & OTHMER *Encycl. Chem. Technol.* (ed. 2) XIX. 743 China tea, *C. sinensis*, contains relatively large amounts of triglycosides of quercetin and kaempferol.

kaersutite (kɛə'sʊtaɪt). *Min.* [ad. Da. *kaersutit* (J. Lorenzen 1884, in *Meddelelser om Grønland* VII. 27), f. *Kaersut*, name of the locality (on the shore of Umanak Fiord on the west coast of Greenland) where it was first found: see -ITE[1].] A dark brown or black kind of hornblende characterized by a high titanium content and occuring as a constituent of many volcanic rocks.

1886 *Jrnl. Chem. Soc.* L. 519 Analyses of minerals from Greenland... Kærsutite, colour black, streak brown. **1939** *Trans. & Proc. R. Soc. N.Z.* LXIX. 305 It appears that in the Dunedin district brown monoclinic amphiboles occur very generally in the only slightly alkaline basalts and trachybasalts of the first and second volcanic phases, and prove to be basaltic hornblendes which in the two samples analysed have just sufficient content of TiO_2 to permit their being classed as kaersutite. **1966** W. A. DEER et al. *Introd. Rock-Forming Min.* II. 177 Kaersutite is a typical constituent of alkaline volcanic rocks, and occurs as phenocrysts in trachybasalts, trachyandesites, trachytes.. and alkali rhyolites; in the more silica-rich rocks it occurs also as a groundmass constituent. **1968** *Mineral. Mag.* XXXVI. 1001 Aoki (1963) considered an amphibole from a trachyte with 4·36% TiO_2 (0·49 Ti) as not a typical kaersutite... It is clear that any lower limit of titanium for kaersutite must be an arbitrary one.

Hence **kaersu'titic** *a.*, of the nature of or resembling kaersutite.

1968 *Mineral. Mag.* XXXVI. 1001 The data..strongly suggest that upper mantle amphibole is probably a kaersutitic hornblende.

kaf, variant of COF *a. Obs.*, quick, fierce.

kaf(e, kaff, north. dial. forms of CHAFF *sb.*[1]

‖**kafenion** (kæfə'niːɒn). [Gr. *καφενεῖον*.] A Greek coffee-house or café.

In the Greek word the final *-n* is often dropped in the spoken form (thus quot. 1939). The Gr. pl. form is *καφενεῖα*.

1939 E. AMBLER *Mask of Dimitrios* iv. 63 It took another week, a week of waiting, of sitting in *kafenios*, of being introduced to thirsty gentlemen with connections in the municipal offices. **1964** *Punch* 24 June 925/2 They overflowed the local kafenion. **1967** J. EASTWOOD *Little Dragon from Peking* xiii. 130 The kind of reception accorded to a woman unaccompanied in, say, a male-dominated, male-preserve Kafenion in rural Greece. **1974** 'M. YORKE' *Mortal Remains* I. vii. 24 There was a Kafenion on the water-front, so he sat at a table..and ordered coffee.

†**kafer.** *Obs. rare*[−1]. [? a. G. *käfer.*] = CHAFER[1].

1599 T. M[OUFET] *Silkwormes* 53 Nor eate they all, as greedy Kafers do.

kafeyah, kaffiyeh, variants of KEFFIYEH.

‖**kaffeeklat(s)ch** ('kafeːklatʃ). Also with hyphen or as two words, and with capital initial(s). [G., f. *kaffee* coffee + *klatsch* gossip.] Gossip over coffee cups; a coffee party; cf. *coffee klatsch* (s.v. COFFEE *sb.* 5 b). Hence **kaffeeklatscher** *sb.*, **kaffeeklatsching** *vbl. sb.* Cf. KLATSCH.

1888 in A. RANDALL-DIEHL *2000 Words & Definitions.* **1903** *Current Opinion* Aug. 205/2 She usually operates as an amateur, appearing at *Kaffeeklatsches.* **1906** S. FORD *Shorty McCabe* 111 He let it out one day after we'd had our little kaffee klatch with the gloves. **1911** *International* (N.Y.) July 35/2 Theatrical *Kaffeeklatsch* has now absorbed the space where once the redoubtable Charles Edward fought his battles. **1919** F. HURST *Humoresque* 322 They're a darn sight

better than the wads of respectability I see waddlin' in here to swap *Kaffee Klatsches* with you! **1936** H. MILLER *Black Spring* 134 It's the hour of the kaffee-klatchers sitting around the family table. **1956** W. H. WHYTE *Organization Man* (1957) xxii. 286 Dot will be *Kaffee-klatsching* and sun-bathing with the girls. **1958** M. WEST *Second Victory* i. 5 They came in summer to take the waters, to sit on the terrace for *Kaffeeklatsch*. **1969** R. LOCKRIDGE *Murder in False Face* ix. 112 If [he]..wants a morning kaffee-klatch it's all right with me. **1972** J. WILLIAMS *Home Fronts* xiii. 233 The traditional friendly *Kaffeeklatsch*—the afternoon coffee party with friends.

Kaffir ('kæfə(r)); prop. **Kafir** ('kɑːfɪr), *sb.* and *a.* Also **kaffer, kaffir, kafir, kaffre**; and see CAFFRE. [a. Arab. *kāfir* infidel: see CAFFRE.]

A. *sb.* **1.** = CAFFRE 1, 'infidel', Giaour.

1790 J. BRUCE *Trav.* IV. VIII. ix. 497 Why did not you tell those black Kafrs..to stay a little longer. **1814** SOUTHEY *Roderick* v. 198 A Moor came by, and seeing him [the Goth], exclaimed Ah, Kaffer! worshipper of wood and stone. **1865** *Daily Tel.* 23 Oct. 5/1 Mecca..if the Moslems would permit ..a 'kaffir' to come there.

2. a. = CAFFRE 2; one of a South African race belonging to the Bântu family. Also *attrib.*, and as the name of their language. Also, usu. disparagingly, with reference to any Black African; *transf.*, as a term of opprobrium, a white man who associates with or is thought to favour Black Africans.

1792 E. RIOU tr. *J. van Reenen's Jrnl. Journey from Cape Good Hope* 22 We saw several Kaffers. **1801** *Monthly Rev.* XXXV. 346 The incursions of the tribe of people called Kaffers. **1834** BOYCE (*title*) Grammar of the Kaffir Language. **1852** GODLONTON & IRVING *Narr. Kaffir War* III. xv. 180 The other teachers..who could speak Kaffir. **1857** *Chambers's Inform. People* II. 294/2 The Kafirs, a race strikingly different both from Hottentots and negroes. The Kafir nation consists of numerous sections. **1890** *Pall Mall G.* 15 May 3/1, I asked questions about the Kafir voter. **1926** S. G. MILLIN *S. Africans* 209 In the old days..men, thrusting their ancestry, their traditions..completely behind them, became what people sometimes call in South Africa 'white Kafirs'. They merged themselves with the natives, stayed for ever with the wives they had bought and with their African children. **1949** [see HOTNOT]. **1949** *Cape Argus* 9 July 3/5 'Did you think he was a perfectly reliable person to give information to?'—'I would have given the statement to a Kaffir if someone had sent a Kaffir along.' **1959** *New Statesman* 2 May 62/3 How, for instance, does one describe negroid South Africans? The early missionary word 'kaffir', meaning heathen, has become a term of abuse. **1960** *Cape Times* 6 Sept. 7 A mob which swore at the police, called them 'white Kafirs', and hurled bottles at them. **1961** L. VAN DER POST *Heart of Hunter* I. iii. 62 Kaffir is the term used by Europeans to describe all black people in Africa irrespective of their race and origin. **1967** [see COOLIE, COOLY 2 b]. **1973** *Deb. Senate S. Afr.* 17 May 2777 When we ..were young people the word 'kaffir' meant nothing more than to indicate a Black man... It has deteriorated to such an extent that it offends people with a dark coloured skin and ..we try to avoid it. *Ibid.* 2798, I have heard people when I visit a farm call out 'Kaffir' and a wife appears, and he says 'my kaffir, prepare food for us'..; but, if I called my friend the hon. Senator.., 'You are a kaffir', then it has another meaning.

b. *pl.* The Stock Exchange term for South African mine shares. Also *attrib.*

1889 *Rialto* 23 Mar. (Farmer), Tintos climbed to 12½, and even Kaffirs raised their sickly heads. **1895** *Daily News* 2 Apr. 2/2 Dealers in the Kaffir market. **1895** *Nation* (N.Y.) 19 Dec. 451/2 The mines floated on the London Stock Exchange which are classed under the general head of 'Kaffirs'. **1899** H. FREDERIC *Market Place* 32 It was one of the men I've been talking about—one of those Kaffir scoundrels.

3. Usu. **Kafir.** A member of a people inhabiting the Hindu Kush mountains of north-east Afghanistan; **Kafir harp**, a primitive harp with four or five strings used by this people.

1854 LATHAM *Hum. Spec.* in *Orr's Circle Sc., Organ. Nat.* I. 336 Kafiristan, or the Land of the Kafirs..on the water-shed between the Oxus and the north-western system of the Indus. *Ibid.* 338 A Kafir, when sitting on the ground, stretches his legs like a European. **1896** SIR G. ROBERTSON (*title*) Kafirs of the Hindu Kush. **1961** A. BAINES *Mus. Instruments* 43 In the Kafir harp the lower end of the bow reappears above the skin.

4. *attrib.* and *comb.* **Kaffir beer**, an alcoholic beverage brewed from Kaffir corn by the Black inhabitants of S. Africa; **Kaffirboetie** ('kæfəbuːtiː) *S. Afr.* [partial tr. Afrikaans *Kafferboetie*, f. *Kaffer* Kaffir + *boetie* little brother], an opprobrious term for a Negrophil; **Kaffir-boom** [Du. *boom* tree] = *Kaffir-tree*; **Kaffir bread**, the name of several species of South African cycads with edible pith; **Kaffir Circus** *Stock Exchange slang*, the body of brokers who operate in 'Kaffirs', or the place where they operate; **Kaffir corn**, Indian millet, *Sorghum vulgare*; **Kaffir crane**, a name formerly used for the crowned crane, *Balearica pavonina regulorum*, which is grey with a tuft of black feathers on top of its head; **Kaffir date** or **plum**, or **Kaffir's scimitar tree**, a South African tree, *Harpephyllum caffrum*, N.O. *Anacardiaceæ*; **Kaffir finch, fink**, the red bishop-bird, *Pyromelana oryx*, or a closely related bird of the sub-family Ploceinæ; **Kaffirland**, the land of the Kaffirs; **Kaffir lily**, a herb of the family Iridaceæ, *Schizostylis coccinea*, bearing spikes of gladiolus-like flowers; also = CLIVIA; **Kaffir (water-)melon**, either of two species of melon, *Citrullus caffer* or *C. vulgaris*; **Kaffir orange**, a shrub or small tree of the genus *Strychnos*, esp. *S. pungens*, or its fruit; **Kaffir piano**, a S. African marimba or xylophone; **Kaffir pot**, an iron cooking-pot usu. on three short metal legs; **Kaffir's scimitar tree** = *Kaffir date* above; **Kaffir tea**, the plant *Helichrysum nudifolium*; **Kaffir('s) tree**, a South African leguminous tree, *Erythrina caffra*; **Kaffir truck** *S. Afr.*, term applied to small miscellaneous general goods for barter or sale.

1837 R. B. HULLEY in F. Owen *Diary* (1926) 174 About a hundred pots filled with *Kaffir beer were brought and placed before the..men. **1905** *Transvaal Agric. Jrnl.* Jan. 314 Kaffir beer, which..is not..a bad drink for natives. **1952** L. MARQUARD *Peoples & Policies S. Afr.* iv. 101 Africans may..drink kaffir beer. This is a traditional African drink, brewed by African women from fermented kaffir corn and containing a maximum of 2 per cent of alcohol. **1968** M. PYKE *Food & Society* iv. 43 It is a very great error..to assume..that this Kaffir-beer is simply and solely an intoxicating drink. **1939** R. F. A. HOERNLÉ *S. Afr. Native Policy* p. vii, For a member of the White group to be concerned about the impact of white domination on the non-European population of the Union..is to earn for himself the title of 'negrophilist', **kafir-boetie*, or—most scathing of all—'liberal'. **1942** P. ABRAHAMS *Dark Testament* I. xiii. 71 One's got to live. I can't let the other fellows call me a 'Kaffir boetie'. **1947** A. KEPPEL-JONES *When Smuts Goes* ii. 20 The disgruntled factions of trade unionists and liberals, Indians and 'Kafferboeties', seemed very small fry. **1958** N. GORDIMER *World of Strangers* v. 115 You must be Communist or Anti-Communist, Nationalist or Kaffirboetie. **1965** *Punch* 24 Feb. 272/3 Multi-racialists, educationalists, Kafir-boeties. **1827** G. THOMPSON *Trav. & Adv. S. Afr.* I. I. ii. 18 The stakes of this fence, consisting chiefly of *Caffer-boom (*Erythrina Caffra*) which grows abundantly in the neighbourhood, had in numerous instances struck root. **1880** *Silver & Co.'s S. Africa* (ed. 3) 135 Kaffir-boom..wood soft and light. **1949** *Cape Argus* 15 Oct. 4/5 The Alexandria forests, red with giant kaffir-booms. **1953** J. PACKER *Apes & Ivory* xv. 160 The red flowers of the *kaffir-booms* flamed in the hard clear light. **1964** A. ROTHMANN *Elephant Shrew* 19 There was a big clump of wild bananas in this camp, and also two large, spreading kaffirbooms. **1801** J. BARROW *Acct. Trav. S. Afr.* I. iii. 189 The *zamia cycadis*, or *Kaffer's bread-tree, growing on the plains. **1882** *Garden* 10 June 410/3 Encephalartos, or Kaffir Bread, is a genus confined to South Africa. **1958** L. G. GREEN *S. Afr. Beachcomber* 14 Beyond the Buffalo River lies the Wild Coast, with the frangipane and kaffir-bread trees growing down to the beaches. **1896** M. DONOVAN *Kaffir Circus* 96 A big boom is on in the *Kaffir Circus, and Laure's shares are worth £15,000. **1901** C. DUGUID *How to read Money Article* 121 The market in which they are dealt in the Stock Exchange is often called the 'Kaffir Circus'. Term does not comprise Rhodesians. **1902** *Encycl. Brit.* XXXII. 865/1 At first..the 'Kaffre circus', as it was called, was regarded with contempt by the older *habitués* of the Stock Exchange. **1928** *Daily Chron.* 9 Aug. 8/6 Otherwise the Kaffir Circus presented a very idle appearance. **1785** G. FORSTER tr. *Sparrman's Voy. Cape Good Hope* II. x. 10 The kind of corn which they sow, is.. known to yield abundantly. The colonists call it *caffer-corn. **1792** Kaffir corn [see *black bean* (BLACK *a.* 19)]. **1836** *Encycl. Brit.* (ed. 7) XII. 659/2 The soil is fertile, and has produced three crops of Kaffre and Indian corn in the year. **1896** *N. Amer. Rev.* CLXIII. 715 Put the land into kafir corn. **1954** R. ST. JOHN *Through Malan's Afr.* i. 14 Indian millet is called Kaffir corn. **1973** *Farmer's Weekly* (S. Afr.) 13 June 3 (Advt.), Prevent fallen kaffir corn and other crops from being double cut. **1834** A. SMITH *Diary* 15 Nov. (1939) I. 137 Saw several *Caffer cranes. **1853** F. FLEMING *Kaffraria* iii. 68 The handsomest of these [birds] to be met with is the Kaffir Crane..a species of the *Anthropoides-Pavonia* or Crowned-Demoiselle. **1906** W. L. SCLATER *Birds S. Afr.* IV. 279 *Bugeranus carunculatus.* Wattled Crane..sometimes 'Kaffir Crane' of Colonists. *Ibid.* 284 *Balearica regulorum.* Crowned Crane.. 'Kaffir Crane' of some. **1822** W. J. BURCHELL *Trav. S. Afr.* I. i. 20 In the aviary I saw..the **Kaffers Fink*. **1834** [see FINK *sb.*[1]]. **1844** J. BACKHOUSE *Narr. Visit Mauritius & S. Afr.* xiv. 202 The Caffer Finch of this part of the country is *Ploceus spilonotus*. **1897, 1908** [see FINK *sb.*[1]]. **1931** Kaffir fink [see *bishop-bird*]. **1973** A. P. BRINK *Birds* 4 You're so cocky. What are you—a kaffir finch? **1821** E. BLOUNT *Notes on Cape Good Hope* 137 A poet of great respectability..was ready to invoke the muse of *Kaffer-land. **1853** *Househ. Words* 11 June 338/1 Let us..see what the noble savage does in Zulu Kaffirland. **1900** W. D. DRURY *Bk. Gardening* x. 348 *Schizostylis coccinea* (Crimson Flag; *Kaffir Lily) is a lovely iridaceous subject with bright crimson gladiolus-like spikes of flower. **1946** M. FREE *All about House Plants* xii. 94 *Clivia miniata*, Kafir Lily. Give only enough water to keep leaves from wilting. **1951** *Dict. Gardening* (R. Hort. Soc.) IV. 1904/1 *S[chizostylis] coccinea.* Crimson Flag; Kaffir Lily. **1970** M. ALLAN *Tom's Weeds* ii. 27 A feature of Number 1 greenhouse was the imantophyllum or Kaffir lily, renamed clivea by John Lindley in honour of the Duchess of Northumberland (of Syon House) who was a member of the Clive family. **1886** G. A. FARINI *Through Kalahari Desert* xii. 199 Close by were a lot of young gourds growing which Kert said were *Kaffir melons; they were quite unlike our English watermelons; nor were they like a pumpkin. **1950** *Cape Times* 1 June 7/6 The National Parks Board has authorized expenditure on kafir melons with which to feed the elephants in summer-time. **1859** R. J. MANN *Colony of Natal* viii. 159 The '*Kafir orange' of the sea-coast-bush is a 'strychnos' and has strychnine in its seeds. **1907** T. R. SIM *Forests & Forest Flora Cape Good Hope* 274 *Strychnos spinosa* (Kafir Orange..). An evergreen shrub 8–10 feet high, seldom a small tree... Fruit size of an orange, or larger, with rind green when young, yellow when ripe, hard shell, and numerous flat seeds lying in acidulous edible pulp. **1932** WATT & BREYER-BRANDWIJK *Medicinal & Poisonous Plants S. Afr.* 140 The pulp of the fruit of *Strychnos pungens* Solered., Wild orange, Kaffir orange..is acidulous from the presence of citric acid, and is very refreshing. **1952** S. CLOETE *Curve & Tusk* (1953) xiii. 112 There were patches where the marsala or kaffir orange grew, its round, hard-shelled fruit a favourite dish of the baboon and kudu. **1891** MONTEIRO *Delagoa Bay* 253 (Pettman), The song had a rapidly played accompaniment on the *Kaffir piano. **1897** J. BRYCE *Impressions S. Afr.* xiv. 251 The so-called 'Kaffir piano', made of pieces of iron of unequal length fastened side by side in a frame. **1931** J. MOCKFORD *Khama* xxiii. 157 To the throb and wail of these kafir pianos the big-bodied, lusty mine-boys dance freely in two long lines. **1948** H. V. MORTON *In Search of S. Afr.* x. 311 A native band was thrumming on 'Kaffir pianos', instruments like large xylophones. **1880** *Silver & Co.'s S. Africa* (ed. 3) 139 The *Kaffir Plum..an edible fruit about an inch long. **1896** H. A. BRYDEN *Tales of South Africa* 260 The *kaptein*.. persuaded the *vrouw* to follow his own example, and roast wild duck or a joint of springbok in a *Kaffir pot. **1922** S. G. MILLIN *Adam's Rest* III. x. 254 Over the fire stood a big black tripod Kaffir-pot. **1959** A. FULLERTON *Yellow Ford* xiii. 177, I use a kaffirpot, a three-legged thing made of cast iron. **1851** J. J. FREEMAN *Tour S. Afr.* xv. 362 One kind hearted woman..prepared a Kaffir meal for us—a pot of sour-milk, some Kaffir corn bread and some *Kaffir tea. **1899** G. RUSSELL *Hist. Old Durban* 96 An indigenous herb both nutritive and refreshing, which is known to us as *Kaffir tea*. **1949** L. G. GREEN *In Land of Afternoon* 55 Bush tea is popular in the fashionable cafes of the United States. They call it 'Kaffir tea' over there. **1792** E. RIOU tr. *J. van Reenen's Jrnl. Journey from Cape Good Hope* 38 We interred the body of our friend, under a large *kaffer-tree standing alone. **1866** *Treas. Bot.* 468/1 *Erythrina caffra*, the Kaffir-boom of the Dutch, or Kaffir's tree. **1855** G. H. MASON *Life with Zulus* 133 (Pettman), This portion of South Africa is dependent entirely on the P. M. Berg traders for..**caffre truck*. **1900** J. ROBINSON *Life Time in S. Afr.* 279 (Pettman), Glass, beads, knives, scissors, needles,..small looking-glasses—such are the chief staples of *Kaffir truck*. **1948** E. ROSENTHAL *Afr. Switzerland*: *Basutoland* vii. 83 Basuto, who crowd a quaint kiosk loaded with what is called 'Kaffir Truck' in South Africa—bangles, beads, mirrors, combs, and the like. **1951** D. LESSING *This was Old Chief's Country* ix. 198 He had gone into town and was down among the kaffir-truck shops buying a supply of aprons for his houseboys. **1832** *Graham's Town* (Cape Province) *Jrnl.* 1 June 92 All the Caffers..were dispatched forward, that they might get *Caffer water melons to make soup. **1838** W. H. HARVEY *Genera S. Afr. Plants* 105 The water-melon of which two colonial species *C. Caffer* (Kaffir-water-melon) and *C. amarus*..are described. **1932** WATT & BREYER-BRANDWIJK *Medicinal & Poisonous Plants S. Afr.* 180 *Citrullus vulgaris* Schrad is known as Water-melon, Wild water-melon, Kaffir water-melon.

B. *adj. S. Afr. slang.* Bad, unreliable.

1934 'N. GILES' *Ridge of White Waters* II. vii. 266 'Another kaffir bargain!' said Sir Alfred wearily. **1961** *Spectator* 14 July 53 'That was a real Kaffir shot.'..This.. was the first time I had come across Kaffir, *adj.*: bad, clumsy, inferior..etc.

Hence **'Kaffirhood**; **'Kaffirize** *v.*

1858 *Compend. Kafir Laws and Cust., Mount Cope, Brit. Kaffraria* 166 A Kafirized form of some tribal name given by the Hottentots. **1877** J. A. CHALMERS *Tiyo Soga* xxi. 435 He was disposed to glory in his Kafirhood.

kaffle, kafle, variants of COFFLE, caravan.

Kaffrarian, var. CAFFRARIAN *a.*

kafila, variant of CAFILA, caravan.

Kafkaesque (kæfkə'ɛsk), *a.* Also with hyphen. [See -ESQUE.] Of or relating to the Austrian writer Franz *Kafka* (1883–1924) or his writings; resembling the state of affairs or a state of mind described by Kafka. Hence **Kafka'esquely** *adv.*

1947 *New Yorker* 4 Jan. 61/1 Warned, he said, by a Kafka-esque nightmare of blind alleys. **1954** KOESTLER *Invis. Writing* x. 120 Long before the Moscow purges revealed that weird, Kafka-esque pattern to the incredulous world. **1958** *Spectator* 24 Jan. 114/2 An authentic Kafkaesque atmosphere of despair and horror. **1958** E. DUNDY *Dud Avocado* I. viii. 147 Postcards and wires to the Paris Embassy were all Kafkaesquely re-routed to that powerful Man in Charge. **1963** *Times* 23 May 6/7 Kafkaesque in its grip and pitiless in its exposition of the cruellest of tortures, that of hope. **1972** *Newsweek* 10 Jan. 51/2 The Kafkaesque self-abnegation of the infamous 'show trials' [in Russia].

Also **'Kafka** *sb.* used *attrib.*, **'Kafkan, 'Kafkaish, 'Kafkian** *adjs.* = KAFKAESQUE *a.*

1936 M. LOWRY *Let.* (1967) 11 This is the perfect Kafka situation. **1951** S. SPENDER *World within World* v. 272 They became more Kafkaish than ever. **1959** *N. & Q.* Oct. 381/1 A *re*-statement of the Kafkan anguish. **1962** tr. *J. L. Borges's Labyrinths* (1970) 234 The moving object and the arrow and Achilles are the first Kafkian characters in literature. **1962** *Guardian* 26 Sept. 8/6, I..had wondered if the whole project would turn out to be a Kafka nightmare. **1966** *New Statesman* 25 March 437/1 All the Kafkan stuff.. gone seedy and suicidal in a backstreet rooming-house. **1971** N. FREELING *Over High Side* II. 82 So little of what one did made any sense. One lived in a Kafka world.

kaftan, kaftaned, varr. CAFTAN, CAFTANED *ppl. a.*

kafuffle, var. KERFUFFLE.

kag-: see also CAG-.

kagg: see CAG *sb.*[3]

†**kaggerleȝc.** *Obs. rare.* [f. **kagger* (not recorded) + *-leȝc*, -LAIK.] Wantonness.

c **1200** ORMIN 2187 Forr kaggerrleȝȝc shall don þatt ȝho Shall dafftleȝȝc forrwerrpenn. *Ibid.* 11655 All þe flæshess kaggerrleȝȝc & alle fule lusstess.

kaght, kaȝt, obs. pa. t. and pple. of CATCH *v.*

‖**kago** (ˈkɑːgo). Also **cango**. [Jap. *kango*, of Chinese origin.] A Japanese palanquin of basketwork slung on a pole and carried on the shoulders of bearers.
1857 R. TOMES *Amer. in Japan* viii. 191 That horses, kagos, and kago-bearers, should be in readiness. **1895** *Outing* (U.S.) XXVI. 7 With the long kagos, three coolies are always used, and sometimes four. **1898** *Century Mag.* July 346 No kago, or swinging cars.

‖**kagu** (ˈkɑːguː). [Native name.] A grallatorial bird (*Rhinochetus jubatus*) of unusual type, peculiar to New Caledonia.
1862 *Lond. Rev.* Aug. 30 The little Kagu..a newly-discovered bird from New Caledonia. **1883** *Cassell's Nat. Hist.* IV. 175 Both the Kagu and the Sun Bittern..go through, even in captivity, the extraordinary antics..characteristic of the Crane family. **1893** NEWTON *Dict. Birds* 472 The Kagu..is rather a long-legged bird, about as large as an ordinary Fowl.

‖**kagura** (ˈkɑːgʊrə). [Jap.] A sacred dance performed at Shinto festivals, one of the oldest dances of Japan; also, one performed at a village shrine on a festive day.
1884 SATOW & HAWES *Handbk. for Travellers Cent. & N. Japan* (ed. 2) 63 At some temples young girls fill the office of priestess, but their duties do not appear to extend beyond the performance of the pantomimic dances known as *Kagura*, [etc.]. **1899** W. G. ASTON *Hist. Jap. Lit.* v. iii. 197 The drama in Japan was in its beginnings closely associated with religion. Its immediate parent was the Kagura, a pantomimic dance, which is performed at this day to the sound of fife and drum at Shinto festivals. **1936** K. NOHARA *True Face of Japan* v. 191 Dances and festival plays were performed in front of Shinto shrines, which were called *Kagura*, or 'Joys of the Gods'. **1946** R. BENEDICT *Chrysanthemum & Sword* (1947) v. 90 Watching wrestling matches or exorcism or *kagura* dances, which are liberally enlivened by clowns. **1966** P. S. BUCK *People of Japan* (1968) xii. 132 At special times the Shinto priests perform their own religious dance, the *kagura*.

‖**Kahal** (ˈkaːhal). [Heb. *ḳāhal* assembly, community.] One of the former localized Jewish communities in Europe; also, the governing body of such a community.
1901 *Daily Chron.* 14 June 3/4 The power of the *Kahal*—the court of the congregation. **1907** I. ZANGWILL *Ghetto Comedies* 342 The very Rabbi was petrified; the elders of the *Kahal* stood dumb. **1916** H. SACHER *Zionism & Jewish Future* 19 In every Kahal (community) many youths.. studied. *Ibid.* 20 A Kahal of fifty families. **1937** WYNDHAM LEWIS *Blasting & Bombarding* v. v. 280, I took no further interest in this cowboy songster, said to be a young sprig of the Kahal. **1971** *Encycl. Judaica* V. Gloss., *Kahal*, Jewish congregation; among Ashkenazim, *Kehillah*.

‖**kahau** (ˈkɑːhaʊ). [Malay *kāhau*, so called from its cry.] The proboscis-monkey of Borneo (*Nasalis larvatus*).
1840 *Penny Cycl.* XVI. 92/2 In the Kahau the hairs on the chin scarcely assume the appearance of a beard. **1861** WOOD *Nat. Hist.* I. 41 In size the Kahau is about equal to the hoonuman, and seems to be an active animal.

kahawai (ˈkɑːwaɪ, ‖ˈkahawai). Also **kawai**. [Maori.] A perciform, marine, food fish, *Arripis trutta*, found in shoals in New Zealand and south-eastern Australian waters.
1838 J. S. POLACK *New Zealand* I. 322 The *káháwai*, or colourless salmon. **1845** E. J. WAKEFIELD *Adventure N.Z.* I. 92 A shoal of *kawai* came into that part of the bay. The *kawai* has somewhat of the habits of the salmon. **1849** W. T. POWER *Sketches in N.Z.* ix. 76 The kawai is not unlike the salmon in size and shape, and, like it, comes up the rivers in shoals in the spring. **1870** R. TAYLOR *Te Ika a Maui* (ed. 2) 623 The Kahawai..is one of the most abundant, and is called mackerel by the settlers. **1927** *Daily Express* 26 Feb. 1 The Duchess returned to the Renown with seventeen 'schnapper' and one 'kahawai'. **1962** *Antiquity* XXXVI. 272 *Fish-hooks*..another type of lure with barbed point notched for lashing (the *kahawai* lure). **1962** G. W. JACKSON *N.Z. Beach & Boating Bk.* viii. 82 The bait is..a bundle of sprats or a whole kahawai. **1963** *Evening Post* (Wellington, N.Z.) 30 Nov., Stripping fillets of kahawai and baracouta we cut them into fish shapes and the reaction was immediate, the big fellows accepting them as readily as they had the rock cod earlier.

kahht, obs. pa. t. and pple. of CATCH *v.*

kahika (ˈkɑːɪkə). [Maori.] = KAHIKATEA.
1921 H. GUTHRIE-SMITH *Tutira* x. 71 Close to this orchard grew..three tall white pines, survivors of the kahika grove, from which the flat had probably taken its name. **1949** P. BUCK *Coming of Maori* (1950) IV. i. 450 She [*sc.* Hinewaoriki] gave birth to twins in the form of the *kahika* and *matai* trees.

‖**kahikatea** (ˈkahikatea). Also **kaikaterre**, **kakaterra**. [Maori.] A New Zealand tree, *Podocarpus dacrydioides*, N.O. *Coniferæ* (or *Taxaceæ*); called by the colonists *white pine*. Also *attrib.*
1823 CRUISE *Ten Months N. Zeal.* 145 (Morris s.v. *Kauri*) The timber purveyor of the Coromandel having given cowry a decided preference to kaikaterre. **1875** T. LASLETT *Timber* 304 (Morris) The kahikatea or kakaterra-tree. **1876** W. BLAIR in *Trans. N. Zeal. Inst.* IX. x. 160 (ibid.) This timber is known in all the provinces, except Otago, by the native name of 'Kahikatea'.

kahili (kəˈhiːlɪ). [Hawaiian.] A feather standard, mounted on a tall pole, symbolic of royalty in Hawaii and used on ceremonial occasions.
1866 'MARK TWAIN' *Lett. from Hawaii* (1967) 180 A dozen or more of these gaudy kahilis were upheld by pallbearers. **1883** C. F. G. CUMMING *Fire Fountains* I. 35 At the door of the mausoleum are placed tall *kahilis*, honorific symbols, which to irreverent foreign eyes are suggestive of gigantic feather-brushes, or rather bottle-brushes. **1915** W. A. BRYAN *Nat. Hist. Hawaii* 61 In the hand is a small kahili with ivory and tortoise shell handle. **1937** D. & H. TEILHET *Feather Cloak Murders* xv. 267 The Baron was next to find two rotted kahilis, ancient feather standards. **1948** KUYKENDALL & DAY *Hawaii* xi. 108 In the shadow of somber *kahilis* (royal standards) his ministers and his subjects marched past. *Ibid.* xvi. 166 He stood beside..the *kahili*, symbolic of Hawaiian chieftainship.

Kahn (kɑːn). *Med.* The name of Reuben Leon *Kahn* (b. 1887), Lithuanian-born U.S. bacteriologist, used *attrib.* and *absol.* to designate a diagnostic test for syphilis devised by him in 1922, in which serum or spinal fluid that has been inactivated by heating is shaken with a suspension of antigen obtained from beef heart and the mixture examined for flocculation (usually after a period of incubation).
1922 *Jrnl. Amer. Med. Assoc.* 9 Sept. 874/1 The clinical application of the Kahn precipitation test compares favorably in sensitiveness with the standard Wasserman reaction. *Ibid.* 873/1 In the serums examined from patients with late bone and joint involvement, the Kahn reaction again compares very favorably with the two Wasserman reactions. **1950** R. R. WILLCOX *Text-bk. Venereal Dis.* ix. 115 As a verification test the Kahn performed at different temperatures..has not proved entirely satisfactory. **1953** *Med. Ann.* LXXI. 7 Positive Wassermann and Kahn reactions may be given, for a time, by the serum of patients recovering from glandular fever. **1964** KING & NICOL *Venereal Diseases* vii. 95 Of the many flocculation tests available, the Kahn test has been the most widely used, but in recent years the Price precipitation test (PPR) has increased in popularity in Great Britain.

kahuna (kəˈhuːnə). [Hawaiian.] **a.** A Hawaiian priest or minister; an expert or wise man. **b.** *Surfing.* (With capital initial.) A term adopted to designate a 'god' of surfing.
1886 H. H. GOWEN *Let.* 6 Dec. in *Paradise of Pacific: Hawaii* (1892) viii. 85 The *Kahunas* advised him to stave off the calamity by getting rid of the *white power.* **1915** W. A. BRYAN *Nat. Hist. Hawaii* 54 A numerous class of more irregular priests or Kahunas, that were little more than sorcerers. **1920** *Nature* 15 July 628/1 A much longer paper ..deals with the functions of the *Kahuna* 'the priesthood called the Order of Sorcery'. The word in varying forms (*tahuna, tahunga, tauna*) is used throughout the Eastern Pacific to denote possessed of varying degrees of wisdom from priesthood to sorcery. **1948** KUYKENDALL & DAY *Hawaii* i. 8 The *kahunas* (priests, doctors, sorcerers, navigators, and experts in various other lines) comprised a class closely associated with the chief. **1962** *Austral. Women's Weekly* (Suppl.) 24 Oct. 3/2 Kahuna..the god of the Californian and Hawaiian board-riders. **1970** *Studies in English* (Univ. Cape Town) I. 25 The word 'kahuna' has been personified into *Kahuna*, the god of surfing.

kahute, kaiak, var. CAHUTE, KAYAK[1].

kai (kai). *N.Z.* [Maori.] Food, victuals.
[**1838** J. S. POLACK *New Zealand* I. 289 There is a much larger variety of this esculent [*sc.* potato] called *kai pakehá*, or white man's food.] **1845** E. J. WAKEFIELD *Adventure N.Z.* I. 265 The determination of the natives not to move till all the *kai* was exhausted. **1925** FRASER & GIBBONS *Soldier & Sailor Words* 134 *Kai*, food. (A Maori word, used among the New Zealand troops in the War.) **1927** T. E. DONNE *The Maori, Past & Present* 95, I kep in te whare for tree day, but no *kai* (food). **1952** R. FINLAYSON *Schooner came to Atia* iii. 17, I can take Tua smokes and good kai. **1970** *N.Z. Listener* 12 Oct. 12/1 Some kai would go nicely now. Empty bellies do things to people.
So (in reduplicated form) **kaikai** (kaikai), food; feasting; a feast.
[**1807** J. SAVAGE *Some Acct. N.Z.* xi. 75 *Kiki*..food.] **1845** E. J. WAKEFIELD *Adventure N.Z.* I. 29 He explained..that there would be much *kai kai* or feasting. **1894** STEVENSON & OSBOURNE *Ebb-Tide* I. iv. 60 There shall be no growling about the kaikai, which will be above allowance. **1901** A. C. HADDON *Head-Hunters* 39 One afternoon some of us went to a *kaikai*, or feast. **1941** BAKER *N.Z. Slang* 26 In early records the 'pidgin' forms kaikai or kiki are often discovered. **1969** *Coast to Coast 1967–68* 48 No, she didn't say tucker. The kanakas said kai-kai.

kai-apple, variant of KEI-APPLE.

kaichspell, kaicle: see CACHESPELL, KECKLE.

kaid, var. KED.

‖**kaïd** (kɑːˈiːd). Also **caid, kaid, kayed**. = ALCAYDE. Hence **ˈkaidship**.
1816 'ALI BEY' *Trav.* I. 5, I handed it [*sc.* my passport] to the captain, who ordered that no one should come on shore, and went away to shew my passport to the *Kaïd*, or Governor. *a* **1817** J. L. BURCKHARDT *Trav. Nubia* (1819) 364 The Shikh of the tribe is never the commander..of the armed parties, which the tribe sends out against an enemy. He may join the expedition, but the command of it is in the Kayed, or leader, a dignity which is always hereditary in the same family. **1843** *Penny Cycl.* XXV. 363/2 The kaïds administer justice in the same manner as in the interior towns. *c* **1860** WRAXALL tr. *R. Houdin* xxi. 309 A caïd who spoke French excellently. **1883** D. HANNAY in *Mag. Art* Sept. 450/1 Here sat the king or his caid. **1920** *Glasgow Herald* 23 Sept. 6 Kaid of Tangier. **1920** *Blackw. Mag.* Dec. 742/2 His half-brother was already nominated to the kaidship. **1925** *Ibid.* Nov. 622/2 Presently the Kayed will appear, walking with his chief villagers.

kaie, obs. f. KEY.

kaif, var. KEF.

kaig, obs. f. CAGE.

kaik, var. CAIQUE; obs. Sc. f. CAKE.

kaik, var. KAINGA.

kaikomako (kaikɔːˈmakɔ). *N.Z.* [Maori.] A New Zealand tree, *Pennantia corymbosa*, which bears panicles of fragrant white flowers.
1832 G. BENNETT in *London Med. Gaz.* 22 Sept. 794/2 (*heading*) Kaiko-mako tree of the natives of New Zealand... This tree..attains the elevation of twenty-five to thirty feet. .. The wood of the..Kaiko-mako, is only used by the natives for procuring fire. **1882** W. D. HAY *Brighter Britain!* II. 198 The Kaikomako..will be much cultivated as a garden ornament. **1910** L. COCKAYNE *N.Z. Plants* iii. 37 *Pennantia corymbosa* (the kaikomako) vies in its purity with any bridal flower. **1963** POOLE & ADAMS *Trees & Shrubs N.Z.* 122 *P*[*ennantia*] *corymbosa*... Kaikomako. Tree reaching 12m... Flowers small, dioecious, fragrant.

kail, variant of KALE, colewort, broth.

kails, -es, variants of KAYLES, ninepins.

ˈ**kaily**, *a. Sc. rare.* [f. *kail*, KALE + -Y.]
1. Besmeared with kail.
a **1605** POLWART *Flyting w. Montgomerie* 777 Pudding pricker..Kailly lippes.
2. *nonce-use.* Having the characteristics of the 'kailyard school': see KALE-YARD 2.
1897 *Academy* 3 Dec. 378/1 It is impossible to avoid the term 'Kailyard' in this connexion. More than a little kaily is the work.

kaim, variant of KAME, COMB, ridge.

‖**kaimakam** (kaɪməˈkɑːm). Forms: 7 **chaima-, chayma-, cayma-**, 7–9 **caima-**, 7– **kaima-**; 7 **-con**, 7–8 **-can**, 7–9 **-kan, -cham, -cam**, 8– **-kam**; 20 **qaimaqam**. [Turkish *qāimaqām*, ad. Arab. *qā'im maqām* one standing in the place (of another), f. *qā'im* standing + *maqām* place, station.]
In Turkey and regions under Turkish influence: A lieutenant, deputy, substitute; a lieutenant-colonel; a deputy-governor; *spec.* the deputy of the Grand Vizier, and governor of Constantinople.
c **1645** HOWELL *Lett.* III. xxi. (1705) 127 He desir'd him to leave a charge with the *Caimacham*, his deputy. **1682** WHELER *Journ. Greece* II. 180 All Civil and Criminal Causes are tryed by the Vizier, or his Deputy, the Chaimacham. **1718** LADY M. W. MONTAGU *Let. to C'tess Bristol* 10 Apr., I was forced to send three times to the *caimaikan* (the governor of the town). **1772** *Hartford Merc. Suppl.* 18 Sept. 1/1 The victory of Ali-Bey over the Kiaja of the new Caimacan of Egypt. **1820** T. S. HUGHES *Trav. Sicily* I. vi. 188 His caimacam or vice-roy. **1876** GLADSTONE *Bulg. Horrors* 61 The Turks..their Kaimakams and their Pashas, one and all, bag and baggage. **1961** *Times* 17 July 11/2 The then Shaikh of Kuwait, who in the following year was invested with the rank of qaimaqam. **1970** H. TREVELYAN *Middle East in Revolution* 182 When in 1899 Mubarak as Sabah of Kuwait murdered his brothers, he sought protection with the Turkish Government which gave him the honorary title of Qaimaqam or Sub-Governor of a district.
Hence ‖**kaimaˈkamlik**, the jurisdiction of a kaimakam.

kaiman, kain: see CAYMAN, CAIN.

‖**kain** (ˈkaɪn). [Malay.] Cloth, a piece of cloth. Usu. with defining word following (see quots.).
1783 W. MARSDEN *Hist. Sumatra* 44 The *cayen sarrong* is not unlike a Scots highlander's plaid..being a piece of party colored cloth about six or eight feet long, and three or four wide, sowed together at the ends. **1848** H. LOW *Sarawak* v. 143 Their dress..consists of the kain tapé, or cloth, which has been described as a wide sack open at both ends. **1910** C. W. HARRISON *Illustr. Guide Federated Malay States* II. 206 The great majority of sarongs are of cotton cloth known as *kain plekat.* **1919** P. MIJER *Batiks* i. 7 'Kains' can be bought as cheaply as a dollar each. **1947** R. O. WINSTEDT *Malays* viii. 148 The obsolescent 'lime' pattern (kain limau) ..reminds one of Indian designs. *Ibid.*, Patani, Pahang and Selangor produce cloths (*kain telepok*) gilded by a technique practised also in the Punjab. **1958** H. FORSTER *Flowering Lotus* ii. 25 Formal Javanese wear, for gentlemen as for ladies, was the *kain batik.* This was a simple length of cotton cloth, decorated with an elaborate pattern. **1963** J. KIRKUP *Tropic Temper* iv. 41 There are many ways of folding the big, starched kerchief in a form of head-dress... On the East Coast it is called kain satangan. *Ibid.* xv. 167 Round their waists they wore vivid red or purple kain songket which is a silver or gold-threaded sarong reaching down to the knees and tied on the left hip in an especially intricate knot. **1967** F. MULLALLY *Prizewinner* ii. 39 Indonesians in bosom-moulding *kabajas* and *batik kains.* **1971** *Carry Singapore in your Pocket* (Singapore Tourist Promotion Board) (ed. 3) 53 *Kain songket*, spun silk woven on cottage handlooms highly prized for its dazzling beauty of gleaming motifs in gold or silver. **1972** M. SHEPPARD *Taman Indera* 117 *Kain lepas*, unsewn sarong-length, often of gold thread silk. *Ibid.* 118 (*caption*) Part of a length of *Kain Limar*, from Kelantan. Fine silk cloth with a rose red warp and a mosaic pattern. **1972** *Sunday Times* (Kuala Lumpur) 25 June 7/4 The Queen was given a kain kebat—a dress resembling the sarong.

kainga (kɑːˈɪŋgə, ‖kɑːiŋa). *N.Z.* Also (*South Island*) **kaik.** [Maori.] A place of residence; a settlement, village.

1820 *Gram. & Vocab. Lang. N.Z.* (Church Missionary Soc.) 157 Káinga... A place of residence, a home, &c. **1838** J. S. POLACK *New Zealand* I. 66 These animals were a disgrace to the *kaingá*, or village, of which they formed part. **1879** [see *gum-digging* (GUM *sb.*[2] 9)]. **1884** *Maoriland* 84 The drive may be continued from Portobello to the Maori kaik. **1904** 'G. B. LANCASTER' *Sons o' Men* 56 He had.. fallen foul of many native kiangas [*sic*] where the pakeha was unwelcome. **1905** W. B. *Where White Man Treads* 281 And so to-day: when you see small square potato patches dot the landscape near his kaingas, this meagre husbandry is no sign of improvidential laziness. **1926** J. COWAN *Trav. N.Z.* I. 114 They are places for the artist, these out-of-the-way *kaingas*. **1938** R. D. FINLAYSON *Brown Man's Burden* 49 The Maori just sits in his kaianga and takes what comes to him. **1944** *Mod. Jun. Dict.* (Whitcombe & Tombs) 229 Kaik, kainga... A Maori village; 'kaik' in the South Island only. **1967** A. & D. REID *Paddle Wheels on Wanganui* 12 The excitement of the riverside Maoris as the ship passed their lonely kaingas.

kainite (ˈkaɪnaɪt). *Min.* Also **cænite, cenite, kainit.** [ad. Ger. *kainit*, f. Gr. καιν-ός new + -ITE: named by C. F. Zincken in 1865, with reference to its recent formation.] Hydrous chloro-sulphate of magnesium and potassium, found in Prussia and Galicia, largely used as a fertilizer.

1868 DANA *Min.* (ed. 5) 642 Kainite.. is nothing but the impure picromerite. **1877** *Daily News* 8 Oct. 2/6 Since the memorable discoveries of kainit and other mineral salts nearly twenty years ago at Stassfurth and Leopoldshall. **1882** PLAYFAIR *Indust. U.S.* in *Macm. Mag.* XLV. 335 The old exhausted soils lost their productiveness chiefly by the withdrawal of potash, but this is now found in the minerals carnallit and kainit. **1950** *Engineering* 4 Aug. 101/2 Among the interesting and unusual cargoes which had been shipped from time to time, there were some which had been described, respectively, as praff, shooks, kainit, and thiolith. **1971** *Farmers Weekly* 19 Mar. 38/3 This week we have been dressing beet ground with kainit, a cheap source of potash and salt.

kainosite (ˈkaɪ-, ˈkeɪnəsaɪt). *Min.* = CENOSITE.

1888 *Jrnl. Chem. Soc.* LIV. 234. **1925** *Mineral. Mag.* XX. 356 Unless obviously in error, species names should be accepted in as nearly as possible the same form as that given by the first author... As an example, take the two names Kainosite and Kainite, originally given in Swedish and German in the forms Kainosit and Kainit respectively, and both derived from the Greek καινός, new. The first was altered by Dana (1892) to Cenosite, which is scarcely recognizable even in English. **1968** I. KOSTOV *Mineral.* 306 Nordite and kainosite are orthorhombic.

kainozoic, var. CAINOZOIC, Tertiary (*Geol.*).

kaip, obs. form of CAPE *sb.*[1], COPE *sb.*[1]

kaipoun, kaip-stone, obs. Sc. ff. CAPON, COPESTONE.

kair, obs. Sc. form of CARE *sb.*[1]

kair, Sc. dial. form of *ca'er* for *calver*, pl. of CALF: see CAURE, KAWR.

1626 in Cramond *Ann. Banff* (1891) I. 55 Persons.. have Kye and Kair daylie going throw ther niehtbours cornes.

kairdique, Sc. var. of CARDECU *Obs.*

1645 *Sc. Acts Chas. I* (1819) VI. 197/2 The Rose Noble eleven punds. The Kairdique twentie shilling.

kairine (ˈkaɪraɪn). *Chem.* [app. f. Gr. καιρ-ός proper time, opportunity + -INE[5].] A chinoline-compound, *oxy-methyl-quinoline tetrahydride*, sometimes used in medicine as a strong antipyretic.

1883 *Times* 2 Aug. 10/1 Professor Fischer, of Munich.. found that.. a substance can be obtained, in the form of a white crystalline powder, from coal tar, which greatly resembles quinine in its action on the human organism. Fischer has given it the name of 'kairin'. **1891** THORPE *Dict. Applied Chem.* s.v., The hydrochloride.. crystallises in colourless, lustrous, monoclinic forms.. and was at one time employed as a febrifuge, under the name of kairine.

kairn, kairte, obs. ff. CAIRN *sb.*, CARTE.

kairoline (ˈkaɪrəʊlɪn, -iːn). *Chem.* [ad. G. *kaïrolin* (Hoffmann & Konigs 1883, in *Ber. d. Deut. Chem. Ges.* XVI. 740), f. *kaïrin* KAIRINE with insertion of *-ol*, -OL.]

1,2,3,4-Tetrahydro-*N*-methylquinoline: an oily liquid, $C_{10}H_{13}N$, with antipyretic properties.

1883 *Pharmaceutical Jrnl.* XIV. 384 The chinolinmethyl-hydride (kairoline) of Konigs and Hoffmann.. [was] tried and also found to have antipyretic properties. Kairoline is built up in precisely the same way as kairine, except that one atom of H is replaced by HO. **1953** *Jrnl. Amer. Chem. Soc.* LXXV. 3030 Following the procedure of Gilman and Banner kairoline was prepared from freshly distilled 1,2,3,4-tetrahydroquinoline.. and freshly distilled dimethyl sulfate.

‖**kairos** (ˈkaɪrɒs). [Gr. καιρός right or proper time.] Fullness of time; the propitious moment for the performance of an action or the coming into being of a new state.

1936 E. L. TALMEY tr. *Tillich's Interpretation of Hist.* II. ii. 129 We call this fulfilled moment, the moment of time approaching us as fate and decision, *Kairos*. In doing this we take up a word that was, to be sure, created by the Greek linguistic sense, but attained the deeper meaning of fullness of time, of decisive time, only in the thinking of early Christianity and its historical consciousness. **1939** V. A. DEMANT *Religious Prospect* viii. 220 A teaching that all man can know is how to respond to the Unconditioned at each moment of decision, which he calls the Kairos. **1948** J. L. ADAMS tr. *Tillich's Protestant Era* (1951) I. iii. 47 Every kairos is.. implicitly.. an actualization of the unique kairos, the appearance of the Christ. *Ibid.* 48 We are convinced that today a kairos, an epochal moment of history, is visible. **1963** AUDEN *Dyer's Hand* III. 140 The Greek notion of *Kairos*, the propitious moment for doing something, contained the seed of the notion of punctuality.

Kaiser (ˈkaɪzər). Now *Hist.* Forms: α. 2-4 **caisere,** 2-5 **caysere,** 3-4 **kaisere, caiser,** 3-6 **cayser,** 3, 6 **caisar,** (5 **kayssar**), 4-6 (9) **kayser,** 4-6, 9 **kaisar,** 3-4, 6, 9- **kaiser.** β. 3 **keisere,** (*Orm.* **keȝȝsere**), **kæisere,** 3, 7-9 **keiser,** 4 **keyzar,** 4-7 (9) **keysar,** 6-7 **keisar, keyser.** γ. 6-9 **kesar,** 6 **keaser,** 7-8 **kæsar,** 9 **kezar.** [Ultimately ad. L. *Cæsar* CÆSAR, which at an early period passed (perh. through Gr. καῖσαρ) into the Teutonic langs., appearing as Goth. *kaisar*, OHG. *keisar* (MHG. *keisar*, G. *kaiser*), OS. *kêsur*, *-ar* (MDu. *keiser*, *keyser*, *keser*, Du. *keizer*), OFris. *keisar*, *-er*. In OE. *cásere* and ON. *keisari* the terminal syllable was assimilated to the *-ere*, *-ari* of agent-nouns. OE. *cásere* normally gave early ME. *cāser* KASER; the usual ME. forms *kaiser*, *keiser*, and later variants, were adopted afresh from other Teutonic languages. Ormin used both *kasere*, *kaserr* from OE. and *keȝȝsere* from ON.

In 14-15th c. the word was mainly northern, and the *ai*-form prevailed. About the middle of the 16th c. *ei* (*ey*) again became usual, prob. under Dutch or German influence. The mod. form *kaiser* is directly adopted from G., in which it represents a Bavarian (and Austrian) spelling which supplanted the normal *keiser* in the 17th c. (see Grimm and Kluge, s.v.).]

1. a. The Emperor: cf. EMPEROR 1 and 2.

†(*a*) The (ancient) Roman Emperor (*obs.*); (*b*) The Emperor of the West; the head of the Holy Roman (German) Empire (now *Hist.*); (*c*) The Emperor of Austria (from 1804); (*d*) The German Emperor (from 1871). The mod. English use in sense *b*, whence *c* and *d* follow, appears to be mainly due to Carlyle.

c **1160** *Hatton Gosp.* Matt. xxii. 21 Aȝyfeð þan caysere þa þing þe þas cayseres synde. —— John xix. 12 Ne ert þu þas caiseres freond. *c* **1200** ORMIN 3519 Forrþi chæs he to wurrþen mann O þatt Keȝȝseress time. *a* **1225** *Juliana* 67 Maximien þe mihti caisere of rome. **1807** J. BARLOW *Columb.* v. 679 The Austria's keiser and the Russian czar. **1858** CARLYLE *Fredk. Gt.* I. v. (1872) I. 43 Kaiser Leopold [I].. had no end of Wars. *Ibid.* II. v. I. 70 Barbarossa himself,.. greatest of all the Kaisers. **1866** *Spectator* 1 Dec. 1326 It is rumoured that the Kaiser intends to offer the Hungarians the possession of their own army. **1888** *Times* (weekly ed.) 10 Aug. 16/3 The author's personal intercourse with the late Kaiser. **1897** W. T. STEAD in *Contemp. Rev.* April 596 The Kaiser's chief.. offence in the eyes of most Englishmen was his telegram of congratulation to President Kruger after the surrender of Dr. Jameson.

b. An emperor, as a ruler superior to kings.

Esp. in *king or kaiser*, an alliterative phr. common from 13th to 17th c.; in modern use an archaism, chiefly due to Scott.

α. *a* **1225** *Ancr. R.* 138 Hire schuppare.. þet is King and Kaiser of heouene. *a* **1300** [see β]. *c* **1300** *Havelok* 1725 þe beste mete þat king or cayser wolde ete. ? *a* **1400** *Morte Arth.* 1894 We hafe cownterede to day,.. With kyngez and kayseres. *c* **1440** *York Myst.* xvi. 15 Kayssaris in castellis grete kyndynes me kythes. **1513** DOUGLAS *Æneis* VIII. Prol. 137 Sum [wald be] capytane, sum Caisar, and sum King. **1563** GOOGE *Eglogs*, etc. (Arb.) 84 Court and Cayser to forsake, And lyue at home. *a* **1618** SYLVESTER *Mem. Mortality* xiv, This Life (indeed) is but a Comœdie, Where this, the Kaisar playes; and that, the Clown. **1818** SCOTT *Br. Lamm.* xxvi, And what signifies 't.. to king, queen, or kaiser? **1825** —— *Talism.* xi, As high as ever floated the cognizance of king or kaiser. **1843** LYTTON *Last Bar.* VIII. i, To ride by the side of king or kaisar. **1882** MRS. RIDDELL *Pr. Wales's Garden-Party* 19 Whether her husband were King or Kaiser,.. signified not a pin to the bishop's daughter.

β. *c* **1205** LAY. 7331 þu þenchest to been keisere of alle quike monne. *a* **1225** *St. Marher.* 4 Icrunet.. keiser of kinges. *a* **1300** *Cursor M.* 3359 (Cott.) Yon es þi keiser [*v.rr.* kayser, caisere] sal be þin. *c* **1375** *Ibid.* 9409 (Laud) Wytte and skylle he yaf.. Ouyr alle this world to be keyzar. **1546** J. HEYWOOD *Prov.* (1867) 39 Kyng or keyser must haue set them quight. **1620** SHELTON *Quix.* III. i. 3 To tell neither King nor Keisar, nor any earthly Man. **1640** BROME *Antip.* II. v. Wks. 1873 III. 265 No degree, from Keyser to the Clowne. **1682** MRS. BEHN *Round-heads* I. i. Wks. (1716) 396 He is our General, our Protector, our Keiser.

γ. **1539** TAVERNER *Erasm. Prov.* (1545) 64 Though he be hym selfe a prynce, a kynge, a kesar. **1567** TURBERV. in Chalmers *Eng. Poets* II. 648/1 He slayes the Keasers and the crowned Kings. **1591** SPENSER *Teares Muses* 570 Hir holie things, Which was the care of Kesars and of Kings. **1647** H. MORE *Song of Soul* II. App. civ, Which were erect to the memoriall Of Kings, and Kæsars. **1722** ATTERBURY *Let. to Pope* 6 Apr., As far from Kings and Kæsars as the space will admit of. **1832-4** DE QUINCEY *Cæsars* Wks. 1862 IX. 7 Modern kings, kesars or emperors. **1876** *Whitby Gloss.* s.v., They nowther heed for king nor kezar.

2. *Comb.* **Kaiser moustache** (also **Kaiser Bill moustache, Kaiser Wilhelm moustache**): see quot. 1966; **Kaiser's war**, the war of 1914-18.

1938 J. CARY *Castle Corner* 108 His small, reddish moustache was curled up at the ends. It was not a Kaiser moustache. **1946** G. MILLAR *Horned Pigeon* xvi. 213 The clientèle favoured cropped hair and either Hitler or Kaiser Wilhelm moustaches. **1952** 'M. INNES' *Private View* iv. 70 Absolutely trustworthy—my batman.. in the Kaiser's war. **1958** P. KEMP *No Colours or Crest* (1960) x. 205 The one appointed as our personal bodyguard was a bibulous, red-faced fellow with an enormous 'Kaiser Bill' moustache. **1963** BIRD & HUTTON-STOTT *Veteran Motor Car* 16 Before the Kaiser's war famous firms made cars in Scotland. **1966** J. S. COX *Illustr. Dict. Hairdressing* 86/1 *Kaiser Moustache*, a moustache of which the ends are turned up in the manner of William II, Emperor of Germany, the Kaiser. **1971** A. PRICE *Alamut Ambush* x. 118 The war the wheelwright was remembering was the Kaiser's, not Hitler's. **1974** A. ROSS *Bradford Business* 20 The man.. was tall.. with a shock of white hair and a Kaiser Bill moustache.

Hence **ˈKaiserate, ˈKaiserdom** = KAISERSHIP; **ˈKaiserish** *a.*; **ˈKaiserism,** absolutism as exhibited in the rule of the German emperor; **ˈKaiserist,** an adherent of the absolutist political system of the German emperor, *esp.* that of Wilhelm II (ruled 1888-1918); so **Kaiseˈristic** *a.*; **ˈKaiserling,** a minor emperor; **ˈKaisership,** the office of emperor, the rule of the Kaiser.

1848 J. R. LOWELL *Fable for Critics* 73 Two dozen of Italy's exiles who shoot us his Kaisership daily. **1852** *Tait's Mag.* XIX. 550 Let them bring us a kingling's or kaiserling's heir. **1881** R. ADAMSON *Fichte* 81 Even the shadowy bond which seemed to unite the German States had been dissolved by the Austrian emperor's renunciation of the Kaiserate. **1888** *Contemp. Rev.* LIV. 622 The 'weakening' of Wilhelm's opposition to the Kaisership. **1892** *Daily News* 27 Feb. 5/2 That party in Germany which does not find the Kaisership a perfect instrument of progress. **1905** *Westm. Gaz.* 27 Apr. 2/2 We confess to finding his speech.. distinctly Kaiserish. **1914** C. BRERETON *Who is Responsible?* 101 In order to smash and pulverize Kaiserdom and all that it stands for in the world. **1914** T. ROOSEVELT in *N.Y. Herald* 5 Sept. 8/2 The American people will countenance nothing.. that resembles.. Kaiserism. **1915** *Morning Post* 13 Feb. 6/7 The Revolutionaries, who declare that 'Kaiserism' is as deadly a form of 'Absolutism' as any that can be encountered. **1919** *New Appeal* (Girard, Kansas) 18 Jan. 4/6 The Tribune's editorials.. have generally been in a Kaiseristic vein. **1920** B. CRONIN *Timber Wolves* vii. 121 A more flagrant example of business Kaiserism never happened. **1920** *Glasgow Herald* 10 June 4 The curious relations between Kaiserists and anarchists. **1923** *Ibid.* 23 May 7 The Kaiserist system of political autocracy. **1972** *Times Lit. Suppl.* 27 Oct. 1272/5 A brilliant imperial stroke in the defence of world liberty against Kaiserism.

kaist, obs. Sc. pa. t. of CAST *v.*

1563 WINȜET *Four Scoir Thre Quest.* Wks. 1888 I. 127 Disciplis.. quha sauld thair geris.. and kaist the prices thairof at the Disciplis feit.

‖**kaitaka** (kaɪˈtɑːkə). *N.Z.* [Maori.] A flaxen cloak worn by Maoris.

1882 W. D. HAY *Brighter Britain!* II. 148 The kaitaka, a toga with a silky gloss and texture, was very highly esteemed. **1884** M. MARTIN *Our Maoris* vi. 84 The kaitaka, made of the finest flax and ornamented by a handsome border. **1949** P. BUCK *Coming of Maori* (1950) II. v. 173 The plain cloaks with *taniko* borders divide into two classes. 1. *Parawai* or *Kaitaka*... 2. *Paepaeroa*.

kaitif, kaitrine, obs. ff. CAITIFF, CATERAN.

kaivle, obs. Sc. f. CAVEL *sb.*[1], lot.

kajak, variant of KAYAK[1].

‖**kajang** (ˈkɑːdʒæŋ). Also **cajang, kadjan, kedgang.** [Malay *kājang*.] Matting made from the leaves of palms or pandanus.

1821 J. LEYDEN tr. *Malay Annals* viii. 261 Raja Ahmed.. flew a huge kite, as big as a cajang, (or tent folding screen). **1839** T. J. NEWBOLD *Pol. & Statistical Acct. Straits of Malacca* I. vi. 369 The Rhio gambier is often adulterated with sago, and rendered heavier by the Chinese purposely packing it in baskets lined with wet cajangs. **1845** J. BROOKE *Jrnl.* 1 Feb. in H. Keppel *Expedition Borneo* (1846) II. vi. 131 The number of fallen trees.. obliged us to quit our boat, and remove all the kajang covers. **1848** F. S. MARRYAT *Borneo* 63 The Malay war-boat.. is built of timber at the lower part, the upper is of bamboo, rattan, and kedgang (the dried leaf of the Nepa palm). **1901** A. C. HADDON *Head-Hunters* 299 The roof was covered with *kajangs* from the boats. **1904** E. H. GIGLIOLI tr. *Beccari's Wanderings Gt. Forests Borneo* 223 Sampans have generally a roofing of 'kadjan', a sort of matting made with palm or pandanus leaves. **1922** *Chambers's Jrnl.* 503/1 Under the *kajang* (native rush matting) covering. **1959** 'M. DERBY' *Tigress* iv. 161 The *kajang*-maker, who wove waterproof strips of matting of screw-pine leaves for roofing boats and carts.

Kajar (ˈkɑːdʒɑː(r)). Also **Kadjar, Qajar.** [Pers. *ḳājār*.] A member of a northern Iranian people of Turcoman origin, who formed the ruling dynasty of Persia from 1794 to 1925. Also *attrib.*

1883 *Encycl. Brit.* XV. 651/2 Branches of the royal Afsháre and Kájár tribes of Túrki descent. **1902** P. M. SYKES *Ten Thousand Miles in Persia* 121 Baluchis call all Persians *Gajar*, a corruption of Kájár, the reigning dynasty. **1932** A. T. WILSON *Persia* v. 103 Under the Qajars, roads and caravansarais were allowed to decay. **1968** R. SANGVHI *Aryamehr: Shah of Iran* xxiii. 232 Power sprang originally from their association with the Qajar monarchy. **1973** *Country Life* 31 May 1548/1 Those pictures are of a kind made in large numbers, mostly at Isfahan and Shiraz, throughout the Qajar period.

kajat, var. KIAAT.

kajatenhout: see KIAAT.

‖**kajawah** (kəˈdʒɑːwə, ˈkɑːdʒəwə). Forms: 7 **cajua, cajava, kedg-, cedgeway,** 9 **kedjavé, kidja-, kha-, kajawah, -weh.** [Urdū (Pers.) *kajāwah*; also Pers. *kajawah*.] A camel-litter for women; a

kind of large pannier or wooden frame, a pair of which are carried by a camel.

1634 SIR T. HERBERT *Trav.* 151 Women of note travell upon Coozelbash-Camels, each Camell loaded with two Cages (or *Cajuaes* as they call them) which hang on either side the beast. 1678 J. PHILLIPS tr. *Tavernier's Trav.* I. II. iii. (1684) 63 Fifty Camels that carry'd his women; their *Cajavas* being cover'd with Scarlet-cloth. 1698 FRYER *Acc. E. India & P.* 309 Others in Kedgways, or Wooden-Houses, one on each side of a Camel, tied like Panniers. *Ibid.* 394 Nor must they stir abroad unvailed, unless shut up in Cedge-waies, and then well attended. 1783 G. FORSTER *Journ. fr. Bengal* (1798) II. xiv. 93 This pannier, termed in the Persic, kidjahwah, is a wooden frame [etc.]. 1849 E. B. EASTWICK *Dry Leaves* 160 His left leg was heavily chained to a Kajáwah, or camel-saddle. 1894 R. KIPLING *Jungle Bk.* 196 The men piled our kajawahs..outside the square.

kajeput, kaju, var. CAJUPUT, CASHEW.

‖**kaka** ('kɑːkɑː). Also 8 **kagháá**. [Maori.] A New Zealand parrot of the genus *Nestor*, esp. the typical species *Nestor meridionalis*; its general colour is olive-brown, varied with red or yellow.

c1774 J. R. FORSTER (Newton) Kagháá. 1835 W. YATE *Acc. N. Zeal.* 54 (Morris) Kaka,—a bird of the parrot kind; much larger than any other New Zealand parrot. 1873 SIR W. BULLER *Birds N. Zeal.* (1888) I. 24 The existence..of a species of Kaka Parrot (*Nestor productus*) on Philip Island. 1884 BRACKEN *Lays Maori* 38, I heard mocking Kakas wail and cry above thy corse.

b. kaka-beak, -bill, 'a New Zealand plant, the *Clianthus*, so called from the supposed resemblance of the flower to the bill of the *Kaka*' (Morris *Austral Eng.* 1898).

1892 *Otago Witness* 24 Nov. (Morris) The *Clianthus puniceus* or scarlet glory pea of New Zealand, locally known as kaka beak.

‖**kakahi** ('kɑːkəhɪ). *N.Z.* [Maori.] The freshwater mussel, *Hyridella menziesi*.

1921 H. GUTHRIE-SMITH *Tutira* viii. 55 The shallows of the lake were paved with mussel-beds—kakahi. 1949 P. BUCK *Coming of Maori* (1950) II. viii. 235 The rake was lowered from a canoe on to the shoals with beds of the fresh-water clam termed *kakahi*. 1962 *Post-Primary School Bull.* XV. I. 19 Kakahi are to be found embedded in the muddy and sandy bottoms of rivers and lakes. 1966 *Encycl. N.Z.* II. 616/1 These bivalve shellfish are..the kakahi of the Maoris.

‖**kakaho** ('kɑːkɑːhɔː). *N.Z.* [Maori.]

a. The dry flower-stalk of the *toetoe raupo* (*Arundo conspicua*), used for thatching and the making of mats and cloaks. **b.** From its use for cloaks, a general term for clothing.

1832 A. EARLE *Narr. Residence N.Z.* (1966) 59 They were clothed in mats, called Ka-ka-hoos. 1936 *Punch* 14 Oct. 443/1 Pingao and kakaho, which are used in tuku-tuku work. 1949 P. BUCK *Coming of Maori* (1950) II. ii. 122 The walls were sometimes lined with *kakaho* reeds but without cross stitch designs. *Ibid.* v. 166 The general term for clothing is *kakahu* or *kahu* but the different types of garments have received specific names. 1974 *Nat. Geographic* Aug. 209/1 Mrs. Emily Schuster, supervisor of women's work, showed me how her girls put together a *kakahu*, the magnificent feathered cape for ceremonial occasions.

‖**kakapo** ('kɑːkɑːpɔː). [Maori, f. *kaka* parrot + *po* night.] The ground-parrot or owl-parrot of New Zealand, *Strigops habroptilus*, with green plumage, marked with dark-brown and yellow.

1843 DIEFFENBACH *Trav. N. Zeal.* II. 194 The bird called Kakapo by the natives. 1852 LYALL in *Proc. Zool. Soc. Lond.* 32 The Kakapo lives in holes under the roots of trees, and is also occasionally found under shelving rocks. 1893 NEWTON *Dict. Birds* 475 In captivity the Kakapo is said to show much intelligence, as well as an affectionate and playful disposition.

‖**kakaralli** (kɑːkə'rælɪ). Also **-ali**. [Native name.] The wood and bark of *Lecythis Ollaria*, N.O. *Myrtaceæ*, a tree found in Guyana, the timber of which is very durable in salt water.

1858 SIMMONDS *Dict. Trade.*

‖**kakariki** (kɑːkɑː'riki). [Maori, f. *kaka* parrot + (*r*)*iki* little.] A New Zealand green parrakeet of the genus *Platycercus*.

1855 R. TAYLOR *Te Ika a Maui* 404 (Morris) The Kakariki..is a pretty light green parrot with a band of red or yellow over the upper beak and under the throat. 1867 HOCHSTETTER *N. Zealand* 167 The several Platycercus species, Kakariki of the Maoris, are parrots with brilliant colours.

†**kakaroch,** obs. form of COCKROACH.

1665 SIR T. HERBERT *Trav.* (1677) 52 They..will not kill so much as a Louse..a Kakaroch.

kake, kakel, obs. ff. CAKE, COCKLE.

‖**kakemono** (kake'moːno). [Japanese, f. *kake-* to hang + *mono* thing.] A Japanese wall-picture, painted on silk or paper, and mounted on rollers, so as to be rolled up and put away when desired.

1890 *Daily News* 4 Mar. 7/1 As for the 'kakemono', or native picture, one might be acquainted with a thousand specimens and yet..be still in oblivion as to the real appearance of the Sacred Mountain. 1890 *Pall Mall G.* 25 Nov. 3/1 The 'kakemonos' are rolled and placed away with ..remarkable care. 1894 *Daily News* 22 Sept. 6/5.

kakerlak, variant of KAKKERLAK.

‖**kaki** ('kɑːki). [Japanese.] The Chinese date plum or persimmon of Japan, *Diospyros Kaki*.

1727 J. G. SCHEUCHZER tr. *Kæmpfer's Hist. Japan* I. I. 116 There are three different sorts of Fig-trees growing in Japan. One is call'd *Kaki*, if otherwise it may be called a Fig-tree, it differing from it in several particulars. 1795 tr. *C.P. Thunberg's Trav. Europe, Afr. & Asia* (ed. 2) III. 61 Another cause [of diarrhœa] supervened, viz. the excessive eating of the fruit of the Kaki (*Diospyros kaki*) which was at this time ripe. *Ibid.* IV. 38 For the desert [*sic*], they have kaki-figs. 1866 *Treas. Bot.* 411/2 The fruit of the Kaki or Chinese Date Plum, is as large as an ordinary apple, of a bright red colour. 1889 *Sci. Amer.* LX. 225 The hybridizing of the kaki and the American persimmon. 1892 F. T. PIGGOTT *Garden of Japan* 43 The golden clusters of tiny flowers of *Diospyros kaki* give promise of a rich harvest of luscious fruit in the autumn—the *Kaki* loved of the Japanese. 1920 W. POPENOE *Man. Tropical & Subtropical Fruits* xii. 353 (*heading*) The Kaki or Japanese Persimmon. *Ibid.* 354 The kaki is a deciduous tree growing up to 40 feet in height. *Ibid.* 355 From Japan the kaki has been carried around the world. 1936 K. NOHARA *True Face of Japan* v. 162 The fruiterer with apples, mandarines and *kaki* fruits. 1951 *Dict. Gardening* (R. Hort. Soc.) II. 688/1 *D*[*iospyros*] *Kaki*. Kakee or Chinese Persimmon. *Ibid.* III. 1098/1 Kaki. See *Diospyros Kaki*, Japanese name. 1965 J. OHWI *Flora Japan* 725/1 *Diospyros kaki* Thunb...—Kaki-no-ki.

Kakiemon (kɑː'kiːeɪmɔːn). [f. the name of Sakaida *Kakiemon*, a 17th-c. Japanese potter.] A Japanese porcelain first made by Kakiemon at Arita, characterized by asymmetrical designs, large areas of undecorated porcelain, and the use of iron red enamel, with blue, green, and yellow enamels as foils; also, any porcelain in the style of Kakiemon, which was widely imitated in Europe. Also *attrib.*

1890 J. L. BOWES *Jap. Pott.* 171 (*heading*), Arita wares. Kakiyemon ware... A tea bowl. 1902 T. J. LARKIN in W. G. Gulland *Chinese Porc.* II. 322 The shapes and decoration.. never were appreciated..by them with the exception of the Kakiemon porcelain. 1906 R. L. HOBSON *Porcelain* xx. 187 The enamel painting was largely in the Kakiemon style,..a pattern consisting of one or two birds..and a spray of bamboo or plum. 1932 W. A. THORPE tr. *Schmidt's Porc. as Art* 20 The decoration which best kept the equivalence of white ground and coloured design was the type known as Kakiemon. 1965 FINER & SAVAGE in J. Wedgwood *Sel. Lett.* viii. 151 The Chelsea mark rarely appears on their extremely close copies of Japanese Kakiemon porcelain. 1970 *Oxf. Compan. Art* 610 For refinement of shape, material, and decoration these *kakiemon* wares fully equal their Chinese counterparts. 1970 *Times* 11 Mar. 12/6 Ten years ago Meissen copies of Kakiemon wares fetched about ten times the Japanese originals.

kakistocracy (kækɪ'stɒkrəsɪ). [f. Gr. κάκιστο-ς worst + -κρατία rule, after *aristocracy*.] The government of a state by the worst citizens.

1829 T. L. PEACOCK *Misfort. Elphin* vi. 93 Our agrestic kakistocracy now castigates the heinous sins which were then committed with impunity. 1876 LOWELL *Lett.* II. vii. 179 Is ours a government of the people, by the people, for the people, or a Kakistocracy rather, for the benefit of knaves at the cost of fools? 1879 BARING-GOULD *Germany* II. 286 The..*régime* is at once a plutocracy and a kakistocracy.

So †**kakisto'cratical** *a.*

1641 'SMECTYMNUUS' *Vind. Answ.* vi. 82 But when the men in whose hands the government of the Church is, are bad; then it is τῶν κακίστων κράτος, or Kakistocraticall.

‖**kakke** ('kake). Also **kakké**. [Jap., f. *kyaku*, *kaku* leg + *ki*, *ke* illness, disease.] The Japanese name for beriberi.

1874 *Boston Med. & Surg. Jrnl.* XC. 361 We have received a late number of the *Japan Mail*, containing an interesting description..of a species of endemic disease, known as *kak-ke*, peculiar to the Islands of Japan. 1893 A. M. BACON *Jap. Interior* ix. 153 Had I died of kakke the year before last, there would have been no help, would there? 1906 *Practitioner* Nov. 695 In her previous wars, Japan saw her armies practically prostrate with beri-beri or kakké. 1930 A. C. REED *Trop. Med. in U.S.* vii. 311 This [belief] would relate wet or edematous beriberi..to the 'kakke' of the Labrador fisherman..and certain forms of ship beriberi. 1951 E. R. WHITMORE in R. B. H. Gradwohl *Clin. Trop. Med.* lxi. 1333 Kakké is mentioned in a Chinese pamphlet of the second century B.C...: it is recorded as occurring in Japan in the ninth century.

‖**kakkerlak** ('kakərlak). Also 8 **kackerlake**, 9 **kakerlak**, **kakkerlac**. [Du. *kakkerlak*, G. *kakerlak* cockroach, albino, believed to be of S. American origin. F. has *kakerla*(*t*, *cancrelat* in sense 1, *kakerlaque*, *chacrelas* in sense 2 (Littré).

The avoidance of light is supposed to be the connecting link between the senses.]

1. = COCKROACH, q.v.

1813 [see COCKROACH]. 1883 *Cassell's Nat. Hist.* VI. 132 This family [the *Blattidæ*] includes the numerous species of Cockroaches, or Kakerlaks.

2. An albino (the Dutch name in Java).

1777 ROBERTSON *Hist. Amer.* (1796) II. IV. 69 The Kackerlakes are a degenerate breed, not a separate class of men. 1888 in *Syd. Soc. Lex.*

Hence '**kakkerlakism** [F. *kakerlaquisme*], a synonym for albinism as existing in Java. (*Syd. Soc. Lex.*)

kako-, var. spelling of CACO-, repr. Gr. κακο- bad, evil, favoured by many recent writers, esp. in technical terms, or in such as directly represent Gr. words: e.g. *kakodaimon*, *kakodoxy*, *kakogenesis*, *kakography*, *kakotopia*, *kakotrophy*, *kakoxenite*, etc., and esp. **kakodyl(e**. Examples of these are very rare before the 19th c., and appear chiefly in its later half. See the words under C.

kako'topia. [f. KAKO- + EU)TOPIA, U)TOPIA.] = DYSTOPIA. Cf. CACOTOPIA.

1915 P. GEDDES *Cities in Evolution* ii. 74 The material alternatives of real economics, which these obsessions of money economics have been too long obfuscating, are broadly two, and each is towards realising an ideal, a Utopia. These are the paleotechnic and the neotechnic—Kakotopia and Eutopia respectively. 1970 *New Yorker* 10 Oct. 100/3, I use 'kakotopia'..as the opposite of 'utopia', to describe a misplanned and ugly urbanoid place. 1970 L. MUMFORD *Pentagon of Power* 49 This nightmarish conclusion..has been a recurrent theme of later technological kakotopias.

kakun, obs. form of CALKIN.

kakur ('kɑːkʊə(r)). Also **kakar**, **karkur**. [prob. f. Hindi *kākar*.] The muntjak or barking deer, *Muntiacus muntjak*.

1876 A. A. KINLOCK *Large Game Shooting* II. 26 The Kakur is one of the smallest Deer, not being much more than eighteen inches in height. 1887 J. M. BROWN *Shikar Sk.* 254 The harsh roar of a karkur rang out close to us. 1925 A. G. ARBUTHNOT in G. Burrard *Big Game Hunting* 141 The flesh of kakur is excellent. 1946 J. CORBETT *Man-Eaters of Kumaon* (ed. 2) 185, I..went to sleep listening to a kakar barking in the scrub jungle behind my tent. 1964 R. PERRY *World of Tiger* iv. 56 Occasionally in India, and more frequently in Burma and Malaya, the little kakar, the muntjac or barking deer, is preyed upon.

kakyl, -ylle, obs. forms of CACKLE *v.*[1]

kal, var. CAL, Cornish name of wolfram.

1758 BORLASE *Nat. Hist. Cornwall* 196 The Kal connects the metallic parts [of tin].

kal, kall, obs. forms of CALL.

Kalá, var. KULLAH.

kala azar (kɑːlə, kælə ə'zɑː(r)). *Path.* Also with hyphen. [Assamese, f. *kālā* black + *āzār* disease.] A febrile disease of tropical and subtropical regions caused by the protozoan *Leishmania donovani* and transmitted by sand flies of the genus *Phlebotomus*: usually associated with emaciation, enlargement of the spleen and liver, and often bronzing of the skin. Also known as visceral leishmaniasis.

1883 J. J. CLARKE in *Ann. Sanitary Rep. Assam 1882* 36 As far back as 1869, the attention of administrative officers in Assam became directed to a peculiar disorder (called 'Kala Azar', the 'Black Disease', from the singular bronzing of the skin so often observed with it), the ravages of which decimated..numerous villages in the district of the Gáro Hills. 1908 L. ROGERS *Fevers in Tropics* i. 31 Kala-azar is the epidemic manifestation of a fever, endemic in extensive areas of India, which has spread slowly for thirty years up the Assam valley. 1930 ROGERS & MEGAW *Trop. Med.* ii. 81 The name kala-azar..was in use in Bengal and Assam long before the nature of the disease was known. 1932 GAIGER & DAVIES *Vet. Path. & Bacteriol.* xxiii. 346 Visceral leishmaniasis is known in human beings as kala-azar, and is found frequently in dogs.., especially on the shores of the Mediterranean. 1966 'HAN SUYIN' *Mortal Flower* i. 35 The German pension..was run by Mrs Apelt, whose husband was dying of kala-azar acquired in Manchuria. 1970 PASSMORE & ROBSON *Compan. Med. Stud.* II. xix. 8 *Leishmania donovani* causes kala azar or visceral leishmaniasis in man and animals, and the disease occurs in certain parts of all continents except Australia.

‖**kaladana** (kɑːlə'dɑːnə). [Hindī, f. *kālā* black + *dānā* grain, seed.] The plant *Ipomœa Nil*, N.O. *Convolvulaceæ*. The seeds (*kaladana-seeds*) are employed as a cathartic.

1866 *Treas. Bot.* 643/2.

†**kalader, -dre,** variants of CALADRIE *Obs.*

1572 BOSSEWELL *Armorie* II. 70, D. beareth Verte, a Kaladre gardante. 1688 R. HOLME *Armoury* II. 256/1 The Kalader, or Kaladre..is..after the form and shape of a Hawk.

‖**kalan** (kə'lɑːn, 'keɪlən). [Native name.] The sea-otter of the northern Pacific (*Enhydris lutris*).

1861 WOOD *Nat. Hist.* I. 386 The fur of the Kalan is extremely beautiful..and very warm in character. 1887 *Fisheries U.S.* Sect. v. II. 487 An adult kalan is an animal not much larger than a mature and well-conditioned beaver.

kalanchoe (ˌkælən'kəʊiː). [Fr. (M. Adanson *Familles des Plantes* (1763) II. 247), ult. f. Chinese.] A sub-shrub of the genus so called, belonging to the family Crassulaceæ, native to Africa and southern Asia, and distinguished by succulent leaves and red, pink, or white flowers borne in terminal panicles; often cultivated as a house or greenhouse plant.

1830 J. C. LOUDON *Hortus Britannicus* 160 *Kalanchoe* Adan. Kalanchoe. (Chinese name). 1864 *Curtis's Bot. Mag.* XC. 5460 (*caption*) Large-flowered Kalanchoe. 1915 L. H. BAILEY *Stand. Cycl. Hort.* III. 1732/2 Any number of kalanchoës may appear in the collections of fanciers. 1942 *E. Afr. Ann. 1941–2* 44/1 Kalanchoes, with their large heads of four-petalled flowers are very showy. 1951 *Dict. Gardening* (R. Hort. Soc.) III. 1098/1 Kalanchoes require a good, well-

drained soil. **1970** M. ALLAN *Tom's Weeds* xix. 150 There were plenty of interesting plants..[including] the pretty little kalanchoe which Rochford's are now popularizing.

kalander, kalendes, etc.: see CAL-.

kalange, obs. form of CHALLENGE.

kalashi, kalashy, kalas(s)i, varr. KHALASI.

‖**kalashnikov** (kəˈlæʃnɪkɒf, kəˈlɑːʃnɪkɒf). [Russ.] The name of a type of rifle or sub-machine gun made in the U.S.S.R. Also *attrib.*

1970 *N.Y. Times* 30 Oct. 41 A ragtag group of *fedayeen* bearing *kalashnikovs*, hand grenades and often Pepsi-Cola bottles, swarms around the headquarters area. **1971** E. LUTTWAK *Dict. Mod. War* 19/2 AK-47 (Avtomat Kalashnikov). Soviet rifle (includes AKM and RPK). **1972** *Times* 12 Jan. 10 They consist of forays across the border by from 40 to 100 men armed with Russian mortars, rockets, recoilless guns and kalashnikov automatics. **1973** *Times* 11 Apr. 1/8 He ran to get his *kalashnikov* (a Russian assault weapon) but when he returned, the Israelis had burst through the door.

kalathos, kalavansa, kalculer: see CAL-.

kald, kaldhed, northern ff. COLD, -HED.

a **1300** *E.E. Psalter* lxv. 12 þou led us in kaldhed to be [Vulg. *in refrigerium*].

kale, kail (keɪl, *Sc.* kel). Forms: *α.* 3-4 **cal,** 3-9 **cale,** (5-6 *Sc.* **cail** (1, 6 **call,** 7 **cayle**), 4, 8- **kale,** (6-7 *Sc.* **kaill**), 7- *Sc.* **kail.** *β.* 5 **kelle,** 6 **kel,** 6-7 **kele, keel(e,** 7-9 **keal(e,** 8 **kell.** [Northern form of COLE, q.v. The normal north. Eng. spelling was *cale* (now rare), the Sc. *kaill, kail*; the latter still common in Sc. writers or with reference to Scotland, though *kale* is more frequent in general use. The *β*-forms are mainly southern spellings indicating the narrow Northern vowel.]

1. a. A generic name for various edible plants of the genus *Brassica*; cole, colewort, cabbage; *spec.* the variety with wrinkled leaves not forming a compact head (*B. oleracea acephala*), borecole.

a **1300** *Cursor M.* 12523 He sent him to þe yerd..for to gedir þam sum cale. *a* **1340** HAMPOLE *Psalter* xxxvi. 2 As kale of gressis soen sall þai fall. **1483** *Cath. Angl.* 51/2 Cale, *olus.* **1548** TURNER *Names of Herbes* 20 Brassica is named.. in englishe colewurtes, cole or keele. **1698** M. LISTER *Journ. Paris* (1699) 150 The Keel is to be found wild upon the Maritime Rocks. **1772-84** COOK *Voy.* (1790) I. 215 One of the sailors, who..had been sent to gather kale. **1813** Cale [see BORECOLE]. **1814** SCOTT *Wav.* viii, Gardens, or yards.. stored with gigantic plants of kale or colewort. **1860** G. H. K. in *Vac. Tour.* 148 When times were tolerably quiet, they ..cultivated their oats and kail in peace.

b. With qualifying word: ***curled, curly,*** †***frizzled, German,*** or ***green kale,*** the ordinary borecole, with green leaves, very much curled; †***great, lang, Scotch kale,*** a variety of borecole with less wrinkled leaves, of a purplish colour; ***wild kale,*** Colewort. Also ***corn-, field-, wild kale,*** Field-Mustard (*Sinapis arvensis*); ***Indian kale*** (see quot. 1890). See also BOW-, SEA-KALE.

1673 WEDDERBURN *Vocab.* 18 (Jam.) *Brassica*, great kail, unlocked. *Brassica capitata alba*, white locked kail. *Brassica crispa*, frizzled or curled kail. *Brassica minor*, smaller kail. **1731-59** MILLER *Gard. Dict.* (ed. 7), *Brassica Siberica*, Siberian Borecole, called by some Scotch Kale. **1773** HAWKESWORTH *Voy.* III. 564 The plant which in the West Indies is called Indian Kale and which served us for greens. **1855** DELAMER *Kitch. Gard.* (1861) 58 Borecole, Scotch Kale, &c. **1890** WATT *Dict. Econ. Prod. India, Indian Kale*, a name sometimes given to edible Aroids in those parts of the country where the leaves are eaten.

2. a. Broth in which Scotch kale or cabbage forms a principal ingredient; hence *Sc.* Broth or soup made with various kinds of vegetables. ***water-kale,*** broth made without meat or fat.

As kale was long the chief element of dinner in Scotland, the word was often used to denote the meal itself.

c **1470** HENRYSON *Mor. Fab.* ii. (*Town & C. Mouse*) 321, I had lever thir fourtie dayis fast, With watter caill..Than all your feist. *a* **1480** *Burlesque* in *Rel. Ant.* I. 85 Ther whas rostyd bakon, moullyde brede, nw soure alle, Whettestons and fyre-brondys choppyde in kelle. *a* **1529** SKELTON *Vox populi* 19 Nother malte nor meale,..mylke nor kele. **1567** *Gude & Godlie B.* (S.T.S.) 206 The Monkis of Melros maid gude kaill On Frydayis quhen thay fastit. **1611** COTGR. s.v. *Viande*, No man can make of ill acates good cale [*vn bon potage*]. **1642** MILTON *Apol. Smect.* i. Wks. (1851) 277 When he brings in the messe with Keale, Beef, and Brewesse, what stomach in England could forbeare to call for flanks and briskets? *c* **1730** BURT *Lett. N. Scotl.* (1818) I. 198 Your ordinary fare has been little else beside brochan, cale, etc. **1816** SCOTT *Bl. Dwarf* i, I will be back here to my kail against ane o'clock. **1858** RAMSAY *Remin.* Ser. I. v. (1860) 108 The old-fashioned easy way of asking a friend to dinner was to ask him if he would take his kail with the family. **1873** C. GIBBON *Lack of Gold* iii, We'll sup our kail out o't together.

b. *Sc.* Phrases: ***cauld kale het again,*** something stale served up again; e.g. an old sermon doing duty a second time. ***to give one his kale through the reek,*** to treat one in some unpleasant fashion, to let one 'have it'.

1660 in J. Ramsay *Scotl. & Scotsmen 18th Cent.* (1888) II. 80 We will take cold kail het again tomorrow. **1816** SCOTT *Old Mort.* xiv, When my mither and him forgathered they set till the sodgers, and I think they gae them their kale through the reek! **1823** GALT *Entail* III. xxx. 282 Theirs was a third marriage, a cauld-kail-het-again affair. **1840** C. BRONTE in Mrs. Gaskell *Life* 142 He would have given the Dissenters their kale through the reek—a Scotch proverb.

3. *N. Amer. slang.* Money.

1912 J. SANDILANDS *Western Canad. Dict.* 26 Kale, money, or wealth. **1922** [see *funfest* s.v. FUN *sb.* 3 b]. **1926** *Flynn's* 16 Jan. 638/1 The kale is cut up an th' biggest corner goes to th' brains. **1927** *Daily Express* 23 Sept. 1 Enough 'kale' (prize-fighters' name for money) has been received.. to assure the promoters a profit of approximately £100,000. **1946** B. TREADWELL *Big Bk. of Swing* 124/2 *Kale*, paper money.

4. *Comb.*, as (sense 1) ***kale-blade, -castock, -knife, -leaf, -plant, -seed, -seller;*** (sense 2) ***kale-pot:*** also **kale-bell,** the dinner-bell; **kale-brose,** oatmeal-brose made with the fat skimmings of meat-broth; **kale-gully,** a knife for cutting kale; **kale-runt, -stock,** the stout stem of a kale-plant, a castock: **kale-time,** dinner-time; **kale-turnip** = KOHLRABI (*Chambers's Encycl.* 1890); **kale-wife,** a woman who sells kale or greens; **kale-worm,** the caterpillar of the cabbage butterfly; a caterpillar in general. See also KALE-YARD and CALGARTH.

a **1776** *Watty & Madge* in Herd *Coll. Scot. Songs* II. 109 But hark!—the *kail-bell rings, and I Maun gae link aff the pot. **1849** *Sidonia Sorc.* I. 249 The sexton rung the kale-bell. This bell was a sign..to the women-folk, who were left at home..to prepare dinner. **1816** SCOTT *Antiq.* xxi, As caller as a *kail-blade. **1816** —— *Old Mort.* xxviii, When the quean threw sae muckle gude *kail-brose scalding het about my lugs. **1715** RAMSAY *Christ's Kirk Gr.* II. i, Arm'd wi a great *Kail-gully. **1612** *N. Riding Rec.* (1884) I. 263 An assault with a *Cayle knife. **1483** *Cath. Angl.* 51/2 A *Cale lefe.., *caulis.* **1535** STEWART *Cron. Scot.* III. 412 Scant worth ane kaill leif. **1578** LYTE *Dodoens* II. lxxxi. 258 The leaues of the same rosted in a Call leaffe. *c* **1425** *Langl.'s P. Pl.* B. VI. 288, I haue percil and porettes and many kole-plantes [*MS. Cambr. Dd.* I. 17 *cale-plantes]. **1787** GROSE *Prov. Gloss.*, **Kale-pot*, pottage-pot. *North.* **1862** J. GRANT *Capt. of Guard* xlv, The iron bar whereon the kail-pot swung. **1785** BURNS *Death & Dr. Horn-bk.* xvii, Fient haet o't wad hae pierc'd the heart Of a *kail-runt. **1871** C. GIBBON *Lack of Gold* v, 'Kail runts', from which the leaves had been picked clean. **1743** MAXWELL *Sel. Trans. Soc. Improv. Agric. Scot.* 269 A Description of the Method of raising *Kail-seed, from burying the Blades in the Earth. **1483** *Cath. Angl.* 51/2 A *Cale seller, *olitor.* *a* **1670** SPALDING *Troub. Chas. I* (1792) II. 241 John Calder, kail-seller there. *c* **1425** *Voc.* in Wr.-Wülcker 644/5 *Hoc magudere*, *calstok. **1522** SKELTON *Why not to Court* 350 Nat worth a soure calstocke. **1681** COLVIL *Whigs Supplic.* (1751) 58 They..rooted out our kail stocks. **1821** GALT *Ann. Parish* xxviii. (1895) 178 Among the kailstocks and cabbages in their yards. **1787** BURNS *Let. to W. Nicol* 1 June, After *kail-time. **1827** SCOTT *Jrnl.* 19 Mar., We will hear more in detail when we can meet at Kail-time. **1563** WINȜET *Four Scoir Thre Quest.* Wks. 1888 I. 114 *marg.*, Ȝea, the *cailwyfe seis ȝow heir, bund fute and hand. **1785** *Jrnl. Lond. to Portsmouth* in R. Forbes *Poems Buchan Dial.* 8 They began to misca' ane anither like kail-wives. **1483** *Cath. Angl.* 51/2 A *Cale worme, *eruca.* **1818** SCOTT *Hrt. Midl.* xii, It is but a puir crawling kail-worm after a'.

ˈkale-, ˈkail-yard. *Sc.* [f. KALE + YARD. The strictly Sc. form is *kail yaird* (kelˈjɛrd).]

1. A cabbage-garden, kitchen-garden, such as is commonly attached to a small cottage.

1725 RAMSAY *Gentle Sheph.* II. iii, A green kail-yaird. *c* **1730** BURT *Lett. N. Scotl.* (1754) I. ii. 33 A fit Enclosure for a Cale-Yard, *i.e.* a little Garden for Coleworts. **1800** A. CARLYLE *Autobiog.* 473 Trees..planted in every kail-yard, as their little gardens are called. **1816** SCOTT *Old Mort.* xxxviii, What comes o' our ain bit free house, and the kale-yard, and the cow's grass? **1894** MRS. WALFORD *Ploughed* 42 The little rough gravelled approach and kail-yard.

2. Used with reference to a class of recent fiction, affecting to describe, with much use of the vernacular, common life in Scotland; hence *attrib.* as ***Kailyard School,*** a collective term applied to the writers of such novels or sketches; ***kailyard dialect, vocabulary.*** Hence **kailˈyarder, -ism.**

[The appellation is taken from the Scottish Jacobite song 'There grows a bonnie brier bush in our kailyard', from which 'Ian Maclaren' took the title of the series of short stories 'Beside the Bonnie Brier Bush' (1894), which was an early and popular example of this school of writing.]

1895 J. H. MILLAR *Literature of Kailyard* in *New Review* Apr. 384 Mr. J. M. Barrie is fairly entitled to look upon himself as *pars magna*, if not *pars maxima*, of the Great Kailyard Movement. **1895** *Blackw. Mag.* June, Those romances in dialect, very fitly and cleverly called the Literature of the Kailyard by a recent critic. **1896** *Dundee Advertiser* 1 Aug., Having been assured by many critics that the Kailyard School is quite photographic in its reproduction of Scottish life and character. **1896** *Westm. Gaz.* 7 Nov. 3/2 Among its contributors lately has been.. one of the minor 'kailyairders'. **1899** *Academy* 7 Jan. 3/1 But Mr. Crockett is no Kailyarder in his romances. *Ibid.* 14 Jan. 50/2 A little outburst of Kailyardism. **1900** *Athenæum* 9 June 709/3 He wrote as he spoke, and his kailyard vocabulary occasionally baffles his editor.

‖**kaleege, kalij** (kəˈliːdʒ, ˈkɑːlɪdʒ). *E. Ind.* Also **kallege.** [a. Hindī *kālij* (Yule).] An Asiatic pheasant of the genus *Euplocamus* or *Gallophasis*, found in the Himalayan region. (Corruptly *college-pheasant.*)

1864 OWEN *Power of God* 43 Peacocks and kaleeges are indigenous to Southern Asia and its islands. **1886** YULE *Anglo-Ind. Gloss.*, *College-pheasant*,..the name..for the birds of the genus *Gallophasis* of Hodgson, intermediate between the Pheasants and the Jungle-fowls. **1893** NEWTON *Dict. Birds, Kallege* or *Kalij.*

kaˈleidograph. [f. as next + Gr. -γραφος writing, writer.] An apparatus for displaying on a screen or a glass disk the symmetrical patterns seen in a kaleidoscope.

kaleidophone (kəˈlaɪdəʊfəʊn). [f. as next + Gr. φωνή sound.] An instrument (invented by Prof. Wheatstone) for exhibiting the phenomena of sound-waves, by means of a vibrating rod or plate having a reflector at the end.

1827 *Q. Jrnl. Sc.* 344 Description of the Kaleidophone or phonic Kaleidoscope, a new philosophical toy. **1873** W. LEES *Acoustics* II. iv. 68 The magic disc, the thaumatrope, the kaleidophone..etc., all owe their action to this principle.

kaleidoscope (kəˈlaɪdəʊskəʊp), *sb.* [f. Gr. καλ-ός beautiful + εἶδο-ς form + -SCOPE. Named by its inventor, Sir David Brewster, in 1817.

Calidoscope in Newman, *Gramm. Assent* I. v. (1870) 107.]

An optical instrument, consisting of from two to four reflecting surfaces placed in a tube, at one end of which is a small compartment containing pieces of coloured glass: on looking through the tube, numerous reflections of these are seen, producing brightly-coloured symmetrical figures, which may be constantly altered by rotation of the instrument.

1817 *Specif. Brewster's patent* No. 4136 (*heading*) A new optical instrument called the Kaleidoscope. **1818** MURRAY *Let. to Byron* in Smiles *Mem.* (1891) I. xvi. 398, I send you a very well-constructed Kaleidoscope, a newly-invented toy. **1822** J. FLINT *Lett. Amer.* 20 The Kaleidoscope of Dr. Brewster is here fabricated in a rude style, and in quantities so great, that it is given as a plaything to children. **1878** HUXLEY *Physiogr.* 62 The beautifully symmetrical shapes seen in a common kaleidoscope.

b. *fig.* A constantly changing group of bright colours or coloured objects; anything which exhibits a succession of shifting phases.

1819 BYRON *Juan* II. xciii, This rainbow look'd like hope —Quite a celestial kaleidoscope. **1824** MACAULAY *Misc. Writ.* I. 82 The mind of Petrarch was a kaleidoscope. **1864** PUSEY *Lect. Daniel* Pref. 29 To allow truth and falsehood to be jumbled together in one ever-shifting kaleidoscope of opinions. **1878** HUTTON *Scott* i. 8 A hundred changing turns of the historical kaleidoscope.

c. *attrib.*

1834 *Edin. Rev.* LX. 69 The few kaleidoscope passages, where ambitious words and crowded figures are so richly embroidered in. **1855** BRIMLEY *Ess.*, *Noct. Ambr.* 306 A kaleidoscope quickness and variety of intellect.

kaˈleidoscope, *v.* [f. the sb.] To present the appearance of a brightly coloured and constantly changing pattern; to cause to come together or coalesce with pleasing results. Hence **kaˈleidoscoping** *ppl. a.* and *vbl. sb.*

1891 *Daily News* 5 Mar. 5/3 The spectators in the gallery cheered heartily when some particularly effective kaleidoscoping of colours happened amongst the dancers on the floor below. **1894** *Ibid.* 1 Feb. 3/1 If the ladies and gentlemen so industriously kaleidoscoping below only cared, they might do something better on these carnival nights than play at devils and clowns. **1900** *Literature* 14 July 25/1 In 'Isis'..Villiers kaleidoscoped from his memory and imagination what he had read in many Oriental and medieval books. **1933** *Discovery* July 218/2 The sitting-rooms, parlour, drawing-room, morning room, study, library, ballroom and so on have all been kaleidoscoped into the living room. **1971** *Guardian* 4 Jan. 9/2 These days of kaleidoscoping time.

kaleidoscopic (kəlaɪdəʊˈskɒpɪk), *a.* [f. KALEIDOSCOPE *sb.* + -IC.] Of or belonging to the kaleidoscope; exhibiting brightly coloured or continually varying figures like those seen in the kaleidoscope.

a. With reference to (changing) colours.

1846 in WORCESTER. **1853** FORBES & HANLEY *Hist. Brit. Mollusca* I. 9 Few bodies..exhibit such exquisite and kaleidoscopic figures as these..displayed in the combinations of the compound Ascidians. **1873** G. C. DAVIES *Mount. & Mere* viii. 56 Kaleidoscopic effects of sunshine and shade.

b. *fig.*

1855 H. SPENCER *Princ. Psychol.* (1872) I. II. ii. 182 A perpetual kaleidoscopic change of feelings. **1858** O. W. HOLMES *Aut. Breakf.-t.* (1865) 153 An array of pleasant kaleidoscopic phrases. **1884** *Pub. Opinion* 12 Sept. 318/2 One brief incident of a kaleidoscopic career.

kaleidoˈscopical, *a.* [See -ICAL.] = prec.

1858 *Times* 1 Dec. 8/3 Brilliant, and prismatic, and kaleidoscopical are the intellects. **1861** T. L. PEACOCK *Gryll Grange* xiv. 114 His imagination..is overloaded with minutiæ and kaleidoscopical colours.

Hence **kaleidoˈscopically** *adv.*, after the manner of a kaleidoscope, with continual changes.

1866 *Sat. Rev.* 7 Apr. 400 Mr. Gladstone is always in earnest..But then he is so kaleidoscopically sincere. **1891** T. HARDY *Life's Little Ironies* (1894) 91 The long plate-glass mirrors..flashed the gyrating personages and hobby-horses kaleidoscopically into his eyes.

kalend, -ar, etc.: see CAL-.

kalenge, obs. f. CHALLENGE.

kaleon, variant of KALIAN.

kalf(f, obs. forms of CALF[1].

kalgan ('kɑːlgɑːn). [f. *Kalgan*, name of the capital of Chahar Province, China.] Used *attrib.* or *absol.* to designate a fur obtained from the kalgan lamb.

[**1930** M. BACHRACH *Fur* iii. 35 Kalgan in Chihli, northern China, is a junction city on the Kiachta-Peiping route, and furs offered from that city are taken in the districts just mentioned.] **1960** *Guardian* 22 Apr. 8/3 Furs.. never.. seen in London before. Among them were.. Kalgan lamb gill. **1970** *Ibid.* 18 Nov. 13/2 A wild suede coat may be trimmed with shaggy Kalgan. **1972** *Times* 28 July 10/4 (*caption*) Tank top and battle jacket lined in white kalgan lamb.

kali[1] ('keɪlaɪ, 'kælɪ). Forms: 7 chali, 8 **kaly**, **caly**, 6- kali. [Arab. *qalī*: see ALKALI.]

1. The Prickly Saltwort or Glasswort (*Salsola Kali*); = ALKALI 2. Also applied to other species of *Salsola*, as Barilla (*Salsola Soda*).

1578 LYTE *Dodoens* I. lxxviii. 115 The herbe named of the Arabians Kali, or Alkali. **1615** G. SANDYS *Trav.* 116 A desart producing here and there.. a weed called Kali [*printed* Kall] by the Arabs. **1646** SIR T. BROWNE *Pseud. Ep.* 51 Glasse, whose materialls are fine sand, and the ashes of Chali or Fearne. **1766** W. STORK *Acc. E. Florida* 49 This herb resembles entirely our samphire in England, and is called barilla or kaly. **1884** *Evang. Mag.* 343 Here, among the softer sand.. is growing.. the Kali, or Saltwort.

b. ***Egyptian kali***, name for *Mesembryanthemum nodiflorum*.

1760 J. LEE *Introd. Bot.* App. 316. **1794** MARTYN *Rousseau's Bot.* xxi. 293 Egyptian Kali, esteemed for making the best potash, is also of this genus.

†**2.** A saline substance obtained by the calcination of saltwort; soda-ash; = ALKALI 1; hence, vegetable alkali, potash. (Latinized *kalium*, whence the chemical symbol K for potassium.)

1799 W. G. BROWNE *Trav. Africa*, etc. xxv. 397 *note*, Twenty-five pounds of kali, and five pounds of pulverized chalk. **1811** A. T. THOMSON *Lond. Disp.* (1818) 437 Take of nitrate of kali, six pounds. **1819** *Pantologia* s.v., The kali of the pharmacopeias is the vegetable alkali or potash.

Kali[2] ('kɑːliː). *Hinduism.* Also **Cali**. [Skr. *kālī* fem. of *kāla* black, dark; also taken as fem. of *Kālā* time (as destroyer), one of the names of Siva.] The name given to the Hindu mother-goddess Devi, consort of Siva, in her most terrible form as goddess of destruction and death, when she is depicted as blackskinned, smeared with blood, and wearing a necklace of skulls and a girdle of snakes.

1798 W. C. BLAQUIRE tr. in *Asiatick Researches* V. 369 Let the sacrificer say *Hrang, hrīng*. Ca'li, Ca'li, O horrid-toothed goddess; eat, cut, destroy all the malignant. **1810** E. MOOR *Hindu Pantheon* 145 Of the many names of the goddess.. those of Parvati, Bhavani, Durga, Kali, and Devi.. are the most common. **1832** C. COLEMAN *Mythol. Hindus* vii. 92 Kali is also called the goddess of cemeteries, under which form she is described dancing with the infant Siva in her arms. **1882** W. J. WILKINS *Hindu Mythol.* vii. 257 Kāli (the black woman), or, as she is more commonly called Kāli Mā, the black mother, with the aid of Chandi, slew Raktavija, the principal leader of the giant's army. **1917** A. COOMARASWAMY in Coomaraswamy & Duggirala tr. *Mirror of Gesture* 8 Kālī.. dances in the burning ground.. to signify the heart of the devotee made empty by renunciation. **1933** E. A. PAYNE *Śāktas* ii. 13 Hibiscus flowers have become a favourite present to Kālī, probably because they are the colour of blood. **1952** S. SELVON *Brighter Sun* vii. 130 Don't know Indian people haveam own god?.. To pray Kali for rain? **1971** 'G. BLACK' *Time for Pirates* i. 9 They were Moslems, which meant that there shouldn't have been a place in their faith for a worship of Kali, the Destroyer.

‖**kalian, kalioun** (kæ'ljɑːn, kæ'ljuːn). Also **kaleon, kalliyun, kalyan**. See also CALEAN. [Pers. *kaliān*, Arab. *qalyān*, *qalyūn*.] A Persian form of the hookah or narghile, a tobacco-pipe in which the smoke passes through water.

1835 *Court Mag.* VI. 65/2 Georgoory kalian, or pipe smoked through water. **1876** A. ARNOLD in *Contemp. Rev.* June 49 They sit smoking a *kaleon*. **1881** *Daily News* 15 July 5/3 We had the usual half-hour's pause.. to smoke the kalioun, or water pipe. **1890** *Times* 27 Feb. 13/2 Tobacco.. adapted to the smoking of the Persian kalian, or Turkish narghileh.

kaliborite (kælɪ'bɔəraɪt). *Min.* [f. KALI[1] + BORON + -ITE[1].] 'A hydrous borate of magnesium and potassium, found in small, white, monoclinic crystals' (Chester).

1892 in DANA *Min.* (ed. 6). **1895** THORPE *Dict. Applied Chem.*, *Kaliborite*, a mineral resembling *kieserite*, found by Felt in the salt deposits at Schmidtmannshall.

kalicine ('kælɪsiːn). *Min.* [a. F. *kalicine* (F. Pisani 1865, in *Compt. Rend.* LX. 919), irreg. f. *kali*, mod.L. *kalium* (see KALI[1] 2), old names for potassium + *c* + *-ine* -INE[5].] Potassium bicarbonate, $KHCO_3$.

1892 E. S. DANA *Dana's Syst. Min.* (ed. 6) 294 Kalicine... Potassium bicarbonate. **1922** J. W. MELLOR *Comprehensive Treat. Inorg. & Theoret. Chem.* II. xx. 774 The corresponding potassium hydrocarbonate, $KHCO_3$, was reported by F. Pisani to occur at Chypis (Canton Wallis) as a mineral which he called kalicine or kalicinite. **1965** *Chem. Abstr.* LXIII. 1514 Investigations on various blast furnaces showed the destructive effects of alkali metals, Zn, Pb, and C on the refractory shaft lining... Alkali metal and Zn compds... form a no. of minerals, such as kalicine, kalsilite,.. and zincite. **1968** I. KOSTOV *Mineral.* 530 Kalicine and teschemacherite occur as finely crystalline white masses.

kalicinite (kæ'lɪsɪnaɪt). *Min.* [f. prec. + -ITE[1].] = prec.

1922 *Mineral. Mag.* XIX. 343 Kalicinite... Variant of Kalicine.. for monosymmetric $HKCO_3$. **1971** *Mineral. Rec.* II. 130/1 Buetschliite, kalicinite, carbonaceous material, and quartz are constituents of fused wood-ash clinkers formed as a result of the burning of a dead, but still standing chestnut-oak tree near Long Shop, Montgomery County, Virginia.

‖**kalidium** (kə'lɪdɪəm). *Bot.* [mod.L. a. Gr. καλίδιον, dim. of καλιά hut.] In florideous algæ, a cystocarp containing undivided spores.

1872 MRS. HOOKER tr. *Le Maout & Decaisne's Syst. Bot.* (1876) 968 *Kalidia, capsules*, and *cystocarps* are bodies of the same form as the preceding but containing undivided spores. **1890** *Cent. Dict.* s.v. *Kallymenia*, The cystocarps or kalidia which are formed in the middle of the frond are hemispherical. **1900** JACKSON *Gloss. Bot. Terms*, *Kalidion*, *Kalidium*.. = Cystocarp.

kaliform ('kælɪfɔːm), *a.* [f. KALI[1] + -FORM.] Having the appearance of the Kali or Glasswort.

1868 in PAXTON *Bot. Dict.*

kaligenous (kæ'lɪdʒɪnəs), *a.* *Chem.* Also **-geneous**. [f. KALI[1] + -GEN + -OUS; cf. F. *kaligéneux*.] Producing an alkali: said of metals that form alkalis with oxygen. Cf. ALKALIGENOUS.

1854 J. SCOFFERN in *Orr's Circ. Sc.*, *Chem.* 438 The kaligenous metals, potassium and sodium.. readily admit of welding. *c* **1865** J. WYLDE in *Circ. Sc.* I. 371/2 We shall divide them into three classes; namely, metals proper, kaligeneous, and terrigeneous.

kalij, variant of KALEEGE.

‖**kalimba** (kə'lɪmbə). [Bantu.] A musical instrument played with the thumbs, consisting of metal strips along a small, hollow piece of wood.

1968 *Sat. Rev.* (U.S.) 26 Oct. 89 Buckley blends unusual 'noises' into the music: clinks, kalimba, calliope, gunfire, and an odd assortment of rhythm instruments. **1971** *Ink* 12 June 19/2 Toni Brown wrote most of the songs, sings lead on a couple of them, and plays keyboards.. and something called a kalimba.

kalimeter, -metry, kaline: see ALKAL-.

1890 in GOULD *Med. Dict.*

kalinite ('kælɪnaɪt). *Min.* [f. *kaline* (= alkaline) + -ITE[1].] Native potash alum.

1868 in DANA *Min.* (ed. 5) 652. **1887** MALLET *Mineral. India* 147 Kalinite occurs as an aggregate of minute crystals.

kaliophilite (kælɪ'ɒfɪlaɪt). *Min.* [Named 1886, f. mod.L. *kali-um* potassium + Gr. -φιλ-ος loving + -ITE[1].] A silicate of aluminium and potassium, found in colourless prismatic crystals.

1887 *Amer. Jrnl. Sc.* Ser. III. XXXIII. 424 Mierisch describes a mineral allied to nephelite, calling it kaliophilite.

kalioun: see KALIAN.

kalisa'ccharic, *a.* [f. KALI[1] + SACCHARIC.] A synonym of GLUCIC, q.v.

kalistrontite (kælɪ'strɒntaɪt). *Min.* [ad. Russ. *kalistrontsit* (M. L. Voronova 1962, in *Zap. Vsesoyuz. Mineral. Obshch.* XCI. 712), f. *káli-ĭ* potassium (cogn. w. KALI[1]) + *strónts-iĭ* STRONTIUM + *-it* -ITE[1].] A sulphate of potassium and strontium, $K_2Sr(SO_4)_2$, found as colourless hexagonal crystals.

1963 *Mineral. Abstr.* XVI. 183/2 A new potassium and strontium sulphate found in saline anhydrite rocks from a borehole near the village of Alshtan, Bashkir, A.S.S.R., is named kalistrontite. **1968** I. KOSTOV *Mineral.* 504 Kalistrontite is trigonal, isostructural with palmierite $K_2Pb(SO_4)_2$.

kalk(e, kalketrappe, obs. ff. CAULK, CALTROP.

kalkyn, kall, kallash, obs. ff. CALKIN, CALL, CAUL, CALASH.

kallaut, variant of KHILAT.

kalli-, a recent spelling of some words in CALLI-.

kallidin ('kælɪdɪn). *Biochem.* [a. G. *kallidin* (E. Werle 1948, in *Angew. Chem.* LX. A. 53), f. G. *kall-ikrein* KALLIKREIN + *pept-id* PEPTIDE: see -IN[1].] †**a.** A supposed hypotensive peptide, released from a globulin by the enzyme kallikrein, which stimulates the uterus and intestine; later shown to be a mixture of two such peptides, bradykinin and kallidin (sense b). *Obs.*

1950 *Chem. Abstr.* XLIV. 5476 Kallidin (previously called DK substance) is a low-mol.-wt. peptide. **1959** *New Scientist* 16 Apr. 856/1 When its properties were studied, bradykinin showed itself to be extremely similar to the peptide kallidin, whose existence was first demonstrated in Germany between the wars.

b. (Also *kallidin II*.) The peptide having the same sequence of constituent amino-acids as bradykinin except for an additional lysergic acid residue at the hydrogen end.

1961 PIERCE & WEBSTER in *Biochem. & Biophys. Research Communications* V. 353 The present report describes the isolation of two kallidins from the incubation of human urinary kallikrein with acid-treated human plasma. *Ibid.* 354 Two peaks of activity [on a chromatograph] were obtained. These were designated kallidins I and II. *Ibid.* 356 These data indicate that kallidin I is identical with bradykinin and that kallidin II is a decapeptide. **1965** *Jrnl. Physiol.* CLXXVI. 1 Bradykinin and kallidin II are respectively, a nona- and a deca-peptide, which occur in man and other species... Kallidin II (hereafter referred to as kallidin), which is converted from kallidinogen by the enzyme kallikrein, appears to be the immediate precursor of bradykinin. **1970** PASSMORE & ROBSON *Compan. Med. Stud.* II. xvii. 1 The name kallidin now refers specifically to lysyl-bradykinin.

kallikrein ('kælɪkriːɪn, -kriːn). *Biochem.* Also †**callicrein**. [a. G. *kallikrein* (H. Kraut et al. 1930, in *Zeitschr. f. physiol. Chem.* CLXXXIX. 99), f. Gr. καλλίκρε-ας sweetbread (f. καλλι-, comb. form of κάλλος beauty + κρέας flesh): see -IN[1].] **a.** An enzyme found in the human pancreas and elsewhere in the body, which releases kallidin from a plasma precursor and has been used therapeutically as a vasodilator and hypotensive agent.

1930 *Chem. Abstr.* XXIV. 4541 The name *callicrein*, taken from a Greek synonym for pancreas, is proposed for this circulatory hormone. **1956** ROBSON & KEELE *Recent Adv. Pharmacol.* (ed. 2) xiv. 480 Kallidin is formed by the proteolytic action of a widely distributed (in saliva, serum, urine, pancreas, etc.) enzyme called Kallikrein, which under the name Padutin has been used therapeutically. **1967** *Martindale's Extra Pharmacopoeia* (ed. 25) 1440 Kallikrein is a dilator of the peripheral blood-vessels... It has been used in the treatment of vasospastic circulatory disorders, including.. chilblains.

b. Any enzyme which liberates a kinin from a protein.

1966 M. E. WEBSTER in E. G. Erdös *Hypotensive Peptides* 650 A kallikrein is defined as an endogenous enzyme which rapidly and specifically liberates a kinin from kininogen... In view of the many known chemical and physical differences between the kallikreins, each kallikrein should be identified by species and source, e.g. hog pancreatic kallikrein. **1969** *Physiol. Rev.* XLIX. 510 The kallikreins (kininogenases) are a group of enzymes... They have marked actions on blood vessels and smooth muscles in vivo that.. are due to the rapid enzymatic cleavage of a specific substrate, an α_2 globulin present in plasma and lymph.

kallilite ('kælɪlaɪt). *Min.* [ad. G. *kallilith* (f. Gr. καλλι-, comb. form of κάλλος beauty + λίθος stone: see -LITE), transl. *Schönstein*, name of the place where it is found.] Sulphide of bismuth and nickel. (Dana *Min.* 1892.)

'**kallipyg.** *rare.* [Cf. CALLIPYGIAN *a.*] A person with finely developed buttocks.

a **1913** F. ROLFE *Desire & Pursuit of Whole* (1934) xvii. 178 Some bulgy kallipyg with swung skirts and cardboard waist.

kallitype ('kælɪtaɪp). *Photogr.* [f. Gr. καλλι-, comb. form of κάλλος beauty + -TYPE.] A disused photographic printing-process using either paper coated with a ferric salt and silver nitrate which is developed in a solution of borax and Rochelle salt, or paper sensitized with a ferric salt and developed in silver nitrate solution.

1890 *Brit. Jrnl. Photogr.* 23 May 335/2 We may here state that we have received.. two specimens of kallitype. **1941** *Ibid.* LXXXVIII. 445 Owing to the present scarcity of printing material it seemed worth while canvassing some of the old abandoned processes of photographic printing; the most probably useful seemed to be Kallitype. This was widely used before the days of P.O.P. and bromide. **1965** J. KOSAR *Light-Sensitive Syst.* i. 39 In the past, silver-iron printing papers were employed also for producing continuous-tone prints. This process was named 'Kallitype'; its attractive feature was the possibility of toning the prints with toning baths.

kalliver, kalliyun: see CALIVER, KALIAN.

kalloscope ('kæləʊskəʊp). *Disused.* [Irreg. f. Gr. κάλλος beauty + -SCOPE.] A type of STEREOSCOPE.

1901 *Daily Chron.* 10 Aug. 5/6 The suppression of what are known as kallascopes [*sic*], stereoscopes and similar machines. **1902** *Ibid.* 3 May 4/5 The 'Automatic Kalloscope'.. which attracted the attention of the police.

kalmia ('kælmɪə). *Bot.* Also **calmia**. [mod.L. (Linnæus *Nova Plantarum Genera* (1751) no. 1079), f. the name of Pehr *Kalm* (1716–1779), Swedish botanist + -IA[1].] An evergreen shrub of the genus so called, belonging to the family Ericaceæ, native to North America, and bearing clusters of pink or white flowers; also called mountain laurel or calico-bush.

1765 J. BARTRAM *Diary* 6 Sept. in *Trans. Amer. Philos. Soc.* (1942) XXXIII. 24/1 Here grows most northward trees here [*sic*] except.. white pine & our 3 calmias. **1776** J. LEE *Bot.* Table i. 282 *Kalmia*, dwarf American laurel. **1784** ANNA SEWARD *Lett.* (1811) I. 15 Dr. Darwin.. asked if I had seen the Calmia. **1785** H. MARSHALL *Arbustrum Americanum* 72 Narrow leaved Kalmia.. delights in moist or swampy places. **1838** *Boston Weekly Mag.* 22 Sept. 17/2 The *Rhodora* is followed in succession by the *Honeysuckles*, the

Kalmias or *Laurels*, the *Azalea*. **1841** BRYANT *Poems, Earth's Children Cling to Earth*, Yon wreath of mist that leaves the vale..Clings to the fragrant Kalmia. **1878** R. T. COOKE *Happy Dodd* 347 With..glittering clusters of Kalmia leaves..she adorned all the rooms. **1900** L. H. BAILEY *Cycl. Amer. Hort.* II. 854/1 The Kalmias thrive well in a sandy, peaty or loamy soil. **1955** *Sci. News Let.* 21 May 334/2 Kalmia, or mountain laurel, is a most attractive plant at any time, for its dark shining leaves are evergreen... Its clusters of closed starflowers, pink..are things for poets to write sonnets about.

Kalmuck (ˈkælmʌk). Also 8 **-muc**, 9 **-muk, -myk,** 7-9 **Calmuc(k**. [Russ. *kalmýk*.] **1. a.** A member of a Mongolian people living on the north-west shores of the Caspian Sea. Also *attrib.* or as *adj.*

1613 PURCHAS *Pilgrimage* IV. xiii. 358 Master Ienkinson mentioneth a Nation liuing among the Tartars, called Kings; which are also Gentiles, as are also the Kirgessen.. and the Colmackes, which worship the sunne. **1617** *Ibid.* (ed. 3) IV. xv. 482 There are some..which are not Mahumetans, nor shaue their haire of their heads after the Tartarian manner; and therefore they call them Calmuck or Pagans. **1757** J. DYER *Fleece* IV. 126 The Cossac there, The Calmuc, and Mungalian, round the bales In crouds resort. **1783** W. TOOKE tr. *Georgi's Russia* IV. 121 The dwellings of the heathenish and christian Kalmucs. *Ibid.* 125 The Kalmuc hords on the Volga. **1822** BYRON *Don Juan* VII. lviii. 273 Suwarrow, who was standing in his shirt Before a company of Calmucks. **1882** R. L. STEVENSON *New Arabian Nights* (ed. 2) II. 66 His broken nose and high cheekbones gave him somewhat the air of a Kalmuck. **1902** *Encycl. Brit.* XXX. 8/2 Kalmyk, or Kalmuck Steppe, a territory or reservation belonging to the Kalmyks. **1903** LD. R. GOWER *Rec. & Reminisc.* 430 A man..with a rather Kalmuk-featured face and white curly hair. **1963** V. NABOKOV *Gift* ii. 114 The compact, sturdy Kalmuk ponies walk in single file forming echelons. **1972** J. POYER *Chinese Agenda* (1973) xiii. 180 A caravan of Kalmuck traders. *Ibid.* 181 These Kalmucks are strictly traders.

b. The language of this people, belonging to the Ural-Altaic group.

1883 *Encycl. Brit.* XVI. 750/2 The Kalmuk and East Mongolian dialects do not differ much... In Kalmuk..the guttural can only be traced through the lengthening of the syllable. **1947** [see BURIAT].

2. (With small initial letter.) A kind of shaggy cloth, resembling bearskin (see also quot. 1940).

1860 S. JUBB *Hist. Shoddy-Trade* 40 A cloth called calmucks..has..replaced 'short ends'. **1940** *Chambers's Techn. Dict.* 128/1 *Calmuc*, a coarse type of wool, from the Khirghiz district, Central Asia.

Hence **Kalˈmuckian** *a.*

1727 J. G. SCHEUCHZER tr. *Kæmpfer's Hist. Japan* I. I. vi. 90 The Prince of the Calmuckian Tartars.

kalo-, a recent variant of CALO-.

kaloge, obs. form of GALOSH.

1373-4 *Durham Acc. Rolls* (Surtees) 578 Pro bots, kaloges empt, pro dicto d'no Priore, 2*s*.

‖**kalokagathia** (ˌkæləʊkæˈgæθɪə, ˌkeɪləʊ-). [Gr. καλοκαγαθία, f. καλοκάγαθος = καλὸς κἀγαθός for καλὸς καὶ ἀγαθός beautiful and good (the perfect character).] Nobility and goodness of character.

1921 tr. *W. Rathenau's New Soc.* x. 102 The Greeks.. adopted as their highest law..that impulse of the will which they called *Kalokagathia*. **1930** N. MITCHISON in *Time & Tide* 14 June 773/1 The formal kalokagathia of that incredible time.

‖**kalon** (ˈkælən). [Gr. καλόν, neut. of καλός beautiful, esp. in phrase τὸ καλόν, *to kalon*, 'the beautiful'.] The (morally) beautiful; the ideal good; the 'summum bonum'.

1749 FIELDING *Tom Jones* V. v, Good fame is a species of the Kalon, and it is by no means fitting to neglect it. **1817** BYRON *Manfred* III. i. 13, I should deem The golden secret, the sought 'Kalon', found. **1827** LYTTON *Pelham* lxvi. III. 37 All philosophies recommend calm as the *to kalon* of their code.

‖**kalong** (ˈkɑːlɒŋ). [Malay *kālong*.] The Malay frugivorous fox-bat (*Pteropus edulis*), the largest known bat, found in immense numbers in Java, Sumatra, and adjacent islands, where it is used for food.

1824 HORSFIELD *Zool. Res. Java, Pteropus rostratus*, The *Pteropus rostratus*..is far less abundant than the *Pteropus javanicus*, or *Kalong*. **1837** *Penny Cycl.* VII. 27/1 The flight of the Kalong is slow and steady, pursued in a straight line, and capable of long continuance. **1883** *Cassell's Nat. Hist.* I. 271.

kalotrope (ˈkæləʊtrəʊp). [f. Gr. καλός beautiful + -τροπος turning.] The name given to a kind of geometric thaumatrope.

1846 J. JOYCE *Sci. Dial.* xxii. 333 The Kalotrope is a modification of the dissolving views. *c* **1865** J. WYLDE in *Circ. Sc.* I. 77/2 Mr. Rose..has invented a very interesting instrument, which he calls the kalotrope.

kalotyˈpography. Beautiful printing.

1834 SOUTHEY *Doctor* ii. 27 Perfect therefore it [the dedication] shall be, as far as kalotypography can make it.

‖**kalpa** (ˈkælpə). [Skr. *kalpa*.] In Hindu cosmology: A great age of the world (see quot. 1834); a day of Brahma; a thousand yugas.

1794 SULLIVAN *View Nat.* II. xliv. 287 The Hindoos are taught to believe that at the end of every kalpa, or creation, all things are absorbed in the Deity. **1834** *Nat. Philos.* III. *Hist. Astron.* App. 117 The Bramins at this time chose to select a period of 4,320,000,000 years, which they called a Kalpa. **1899** A. B. BRUCE *Moral Order World* i. 20 A great Kalpa is the period beginning with the origin of a world and extending beyond its dissolution to the commencement of a new succeeding world.

kalpac(k, -pak, var. of CALPAC(K, an oriental cap. Hence **kalpacked** = CALPACKED.

1717 LADY M. W. MONTAGU *Lett., to C'tess Mar* 10 Mar. (1827) 225 Round her *kalpâc* she had four strings of pearl. **1882** E. O'DONOVAN *Merv Oasis* I. i. 15 There are kalpaked Tartars in the streets.

kalsilite (ˈkælsɪlaɪt). *Min.* [f. the letters *KAlSi* in its chemical formula + -LITE.] A rare silicate of potassium and aluminium, $KAlSiO_4$, that is chemically and physically similar to nepheline and occurs in some potassium-rich lavas.

1942 A. HOLMES in *Mineral. Mag.* XXVI. 198 Mr. Bannister's results, supplemented by micro-chemical analyses made by Dr. M. H. Hey, are recorded in the communication which follows this paper. The new data indicate that the mineral is..a hitherto unrecognized polymorph of $KAlSiO_4$ for which the appropriately mnemonic name kalsilite is proposed. **1942** BANNISTER & HEY in *Ibid.* 221 It is proposed to name the new mineral kalsilite after its composition $KAlSiO_4$. **1967** *Nature* 24 June 1322/1 Kalsilite ($KAlSiO_4$) occurs as a major constituent of a large sedimentary xenolith metamorphosed to the sanidinite facies within the gabbro of Brome Mountain, Quebec. Kalsilite is extremely rare and has previously been found only as an igneous mineral in three volcanic areas. **1972** M. H. BATTEY *Mineral. for Students* II. 292/2 The ratio of K to Na in nepheline varies and there is a series towards kalsilite $KAlSiO_4$ which is a rare mineral found in certain potassic lavas on the Uganda-Congo border.

kalsomine (ˈkælsəʊmaɪn). [Trade-name: recorded earlier than CALCIMINE.] = CALCIMINE. Also as *v. trans.* and *intr.*, to whitewash with kalsomine. Hence **ˈkalsomined** *ppl. a.*, **ˈkalsominer, ˈkalsomining** *vbl. sb.*

1840 *Athenæum* 20 June 502 Kalsomine. **1858** W. A. BUTLER *Two Millions* 42 From lowest basement up to topmost attic, The whole was gorgeous, glaring and prismatic; Pannelled and kalsomined. **1883** *Harper's Mag.* Mar. 503/2 Paint and kalsomine can not be counted upon. **1884** H. G. CARLETON *Thompson St. Poker Club* 20 An extensive kalsomining contract. **1888** *Pall Mall Gaz.* 3 Mar. 11/1 Over face, arms, neck,..and bosom she spreads a coat of liquid white... In plain words, she, as it were, kalsomines herself. **1891** H. C. BUNNER *Zadoc Pine* 166 White kalsomined bedrooms. **1893** K. A. SANBORN *Truthful Woman S. California* 81 Those who feel an unctuous joy in painting the lily, kalsomining the calla, and adding perfumes to the violet. **1904** 'O. HENRY' *Cabbages & Kings* xiv. 248 Let me kalsomine you a little mental sketch to consider. **1916** H. L. WILSON *Somewhere in Red Gap* iv. 128 He was a painter and grainer and kalsominer and paperhanger. *Ibid.* 135 He..began to paper and paint and grain and kalsomine. **1924** *Spectator* 1 Nov. 640 These walls can be whitewashed or covered with vines on the outside and kalsomined within. **1936** L. C. DOUGLAS *White Banners* iii. 57 The specifications for improvements: a new sink, repair of the hot-water machine, kalsomining in the kitchen. **1945** B. MACDONALD *Egg & I* (1946) 49 We laid new floors; put in windows; kalsomined the walls.

kalstocke, kalunder, obs. forms of CASTOCK, CALENDAR.

kaluszite (kəˈlʊsaɪt). *Min.* [ad. G. *kaluszit* (1872), f. *Kalusz* in Galicia.] = SYNGENITE.

1875 WATTS *Dict. Chem.* VII. 1142 Analyses (made on specimens originally called kaluszite).

kalver, variant of CALVER *a.*

1342-3 *Durham Acc. Rolls* 38 In 3 salmon Kalver, 3*s*.

kalyan: see KALIAN.

Kalydor (ˈkælɪdɔə(r)). Also **kalydor**. (The proprietary name of) a type of skin tonic of which almond oil forms the basis.

1824 *Advt.* in C. W. Cunnington *Feminine Attitudes 19th Cent.* (1935) 309 The Kalydor..a never-failing specific for all cutaneous deformities. **1828** tr. *L. af Holberg's Journey to World under Ground* 239 The fourth attended with a bottle of kalydor, for the improvement of the complexion. **1861** [see AMANDIN(E]. **1876** *Trade Marks Jrnl.* 13 Dec. 993 Rowland's Kalydor for improving and beautifying the complexion. Eradicates all cutaneous eruptions... Henry Edward Rowland and George William Rowland, trading as Alexander Rowland and Sons,..Hatton Gardens, Middlesex. **1901** C'TESS C. *Beauty's Aids* 242 (Advt.), Rowland's Kalydor..successfully opposes the attacks of the hot summer sun or damp chilly weather..allays all smarting irritations..removes freckles, tan, sunburn, prickly heat.. imparts a luxuriant beauty to the complexion, and arrays the neck, hands, and arms in matchless whiteness. **1907** *Yesterday's Shopping* (1969) 539/2 Rowland's Kalydor bot. 2/0. **1939-40** *Army & Navy Stores Catal.* 438/3 Rowland's Kalydor—bot. 2/6.

kam, obs. var. CHAM, KHAN[1], var. CAM *a.* and *adv.*; obs. f. *came*, pa. t. of COME *v.*

kam-: see also CAM-.

kama, kamachi, var. KAAMA, KAMICHI.

kamachili (kɑːməˈtʃiːlɪ). Also **camanchile, guamachil, kamachile, kamachilis.** [Tagalog: see quot. 1923.] A tree, *Pithecolobium dulce*, of the family Leguminosæ, native to tropical America and naturalized in the Philippines, having edible pods and bark that yields a yellow dye. Also *attrib.*

1866 LINDLEY & MOORE *Treas. Bot.* II. 898/2 *P[ithecolobium] dulce*..produces cylindrical irregularly swollen pods, curled at the top, containing a sweet edible pulp, which the Mexicans, who call the tree Guamachil, boil and eat. **1903** E. D. MERRILL *Dict. Plant Names Philippine Islands* 44 Camachilis, T[agalog]. Pithecolobium dulce Benth. **1915** *Philippine Jrnl. Sci.* A. X. 353 The price of air-dried camanchile bark has risen. **1923** E. D. MERRILL *Enumeration Philippine Flowering Plants* II. 243 *Pithecolobium dulce*... Throughout the Philippines... Introduced from Mexico; now pantropic. Local names:.. kamachili (Tag.); kamachilis (Tag.)..all corruptions or modifications of the Aztec *kwamochitl*. **1937** *Nature* 16 Oct. 687/1 Several trees growing in the Philippine Islands yield liquors suitable for tanning purposes. The betel nut, *Areca Catechu*..and kamachile, *Pithecolobium dulce*, are..the most important trees. **1954** W. H. BROWN *Useful Plants of Philippines* II. 154 Camanchile bark is used almost exclusively by Filipino tanners.

kamacite (ˈkæməsaɪt). *Min.* [ad. G. *kamacit* (Reichenbach, 1861), f. Gr. κάμαξ, καμακ-, vine-pole: see -ITE[1].] A variety of meteoric iron, exhibiting certain peculiar figures in its structure.

1890 in *Cent. Dict.* **1898** in DANA *Text-bk. Min.* 281.

kamagraph (ˈkæməgrɑːf, -æ-). [f. next.]

a. A painting reproduced by kamagraphy. **b.** A printing press which produces kamagraphs.

1967 *Time* 23 June 49 Each kamagraph looks as though the artist had painted it by hand. **1968** *Collier's Encycl. Year Book* 131 Max Ernst, the well-known dada and surrealist painter; Edouard Pignon, a French abstractionist; and the late René Magritte, the extraordinary Belgian surrealist who died this year, have all executed special work for the kamagraph.

Hence **kaˈmagrapher, kamaˈgraphic** *a.*

1970 *Britannica Bk. of Year* (U.S.) 798/2 *Kamagraphy*, a process for making multiple copies of a painting produced by an artist on a specially treated canvas in which the copies retain the texture of the brushstrokes of the original but the original is destroyed in the process; *kamagraph, kamagrapher; kamagraphic, adj.*

kamagraphy (kəˈmægrəfɪ). [ad. F. *kamagraphie*.] A process for making copies of original paintings, using a special press and treated canvas, which reproduces exactly the colour and texture of the brushstrokes.

1967 *Time* 23 June 49 Kamagraphy faithfully produces 250 perfect copies of a painting on a special press, destroying the original in the process. **1968** *Collier's Encycl. Year Book* 131 A French process called kamagraphy has been developed by engineer André Cocard, with the backing of art collector and vintner Alexis Lichine. **1970** [see prec.].

kamahi (‖ˈkɑːmahi, ˈkɑːmaɪ). *N.Z.* Also **kaamahi, karmahi, karmai.** [Maori.] A forest tree, *Weinmannia racemosa*, belonging to the family Cunoniaceæ, and bearing racemes of small, cream flowers.

1867 J. D. HOOKER *Handbk. N.Z. Flora* II. 765/2 Karmahi, *Hector*. *Weinmannia silvicola* and *racemosa*. **1868** J. HECTOR in *Trans. N.Z. Inst.* I. III. Essay 4 The flat land and low spurs are covered with the common species of Pines and Birch, such as Rimu, Totara, Weinmannia (Karmahi), and Fagus (Tawai). **1868** J. BUCHANAN in *Ibid.* Essay 37 Towai, or Karmai (*Weinmannia racemosa*). A beautiful large tree, especially when in flower. **1899** T. KIRK *Students' Flora N.Z.* 140 *W[einmannia] racemosa*, Linn. f. A shrub or large tree, often from 70 ft.-90 ft. high... *Kamahi*. **1953** *Landfall* VII. 122 He had played his violin under a kamahi tree. **1963** B. PEARSON *Coal Flat* iv. 59 In a little clearing in the kaamahi and fuchsia and young bush..was Mrs Seldom's little house. **1966** *Weekly News* (Auckland) 22 June 44 The kamahi present on this charming little hill is a hardy tree.

Kamakura (ˈkɑːməkʊərə). The name of a town in central Japan, used *attrib.* to designate the art of the period (1192-1333) during which Kamakura was the seat of government.

[**1890** B. H. CHAMBERLAIN *Things Japanese* 227 The grandest example of..colossal bronze-casting is the *Daibutsu* (literally, 'great Buddha') at Kamakura.] **1902** F. BRINKLEY *Oriental Series: Japan* VII. iii. 110 Nearly four hundred years may be regarded as the Kamakura epoch from the point of view of the sculptor's art, and may also be regarded..as the final era of vigorous originality in religious sculpture. **1912** E. F. FENOLLOSA *Epochs Chinese & Jap. Art* I. ix. 197 Several phases of Kamakura art..went on parallel to the main stream of secular makimono painting. **1952** L. WARNER *Enduring Art Japan* iv. 52 Kamakura scrolls seemed to epitomise the other changes. **1970** *Oxf. Compan. Art* 606/2 Works of the spiritual stature of the Tempyō sculptures or the Kamakura portraits were isolated incidents rarely attained.

‖**kamala** (ˈkæmələ). [Skr. *kamala*. The Hindī form *kamīlā* or *kamēlā* is recognized, with pron. (kəˈmiːlə), in some recent dicts.] A fine orange-coloured powder consisting of the glandular hairs from the fruit-capsules of an East Indian euphorbiaceous tree (*Mallotus philippinensis* or *Rottlera tinctoria*), used for dyeing silks yellow, and employed as a vermifuge. Also *attrib.*

1820-32 in W. ROXBURGH *Flora Indica*. **1858** HANBURY in *Pharmaceut. Jrnl.* Feb. **1866** *Treas. Bot.* 993/1 A red mealy powder..well known in India as Kámalá, and much used by Hindoo silk-dyers. **1876** HARLEY *Mat. Med.* (ed. 6) 444 The Kamala Tree is common in hilly districts of India.

kamarband, variant of CUMMERBUND.

Kamares (kə'mɑːriːz). Also **Kamarais**. [Gr. Καμάραις, name of a cave-sanctuary of the Minoans on Mt. Ida in Crete, where the pottery was first found.] A type of Minoan pottery from the Middle Bronze Age, characterized by the use of red, white, and yellow ornaments on a black ground, depicting abstract or stylized plant designs. Also *attrib.*

1895 *Proc. Soc. Antiquaries London* XV. 356 The red.. on very thin black-glazed ware, is exactly of the Kamárais tint, while the drawing has the Kamárais touch. *Ibid.*, We may consider that the Kamárais pottery began at least as early as 2300 B.C. **1902** *Encycl. Brit.* XXXI. 56/1 This ware, known as 'Kamáres', from a cave near a village on the south-east of Mount Ida. **1948** A. LANE *Greek Pott.* iv. 22 The 'Kamares' style named after a cave in Crete where many examples were found. **1949** W. F. ALBRIGHT *Archaeol. of Palestine* v. 93 There was nothing in Palestine like the delicate Kamares ware of Middle Bronze Crete, which was in great demand in Egypt. **1960** T. BURTON-BROWN *Early Medit. Migrations* i. 1 Certain classes of pottery.. were believed to indicate direct contacts between the peoples of Egypt and those of the Aegean area. Amongst these are sherds of polychrome painted fabrics, some of which may be either Kamares wares from Crete, or related wares. **1970** *Oxf. Compan. Art* 725/2 The 'egg-shell' Kamares ware.. bears some of the very best of Minoan decoration, with some floral motifs possibly derived from geometric forms rather than copied from nature.

kamarezite (kə'mɑːrəzaɪt). *Min.* [ad. G. *kamarezit* (K.H.E.G. Busz 1893, in *Verh. d. naturhist. Vereins* L. *Sitzungsber. d. naturwiss. Sekt.* 84) f. *Kamareza*, name of the place in Greece where it was first found: see -ITE[1].] A grass-green basic sulphate of copper, originally thought to be $Cu_3(SO_4)(OH)_4.6H_2O$, but later found to be identical with brochantite, $Cu_4SO_4(OH)_6$.

1895 *Jrnl. Chem. Soc.* LXVIII. II. 506 Kamarezite... This new mineral from Kamareza, Laurium, Greece, is grass-green and shows a crystalline structure. **1951** C. PALACHE et al. *Dana's Syst. Min.* (ed. 7) II. xxxi. 588 *Kamarezite*... Orthorhombic (?). In minute crystals. **1965** *Amer. Mineral.* L. 1456 The optical, physical, crystallographic, and chemical evidence that have been presented.. is (*sic*) strong support for the contention that the mineral described as kamarezite by Busz (1893, 1895) is brochantite. *Ibid.* 1457 We recommended that kamarezite be removed from the list of accepted mineral species; this recommendation has been accepted by.. the Commission on New Minerals and Mineral Names.

kamas, variant of CAMAS, QUAMASH.

kamassi (ka'masɪ). *S. Afr.* Also **camassie, kamasse, kamassie.** [Afrikaans *kammassie*, f. native name.] A South African evergreen tree, *Gonioma kamassi*, of the family Apocynaceæ, or its hard yellow wood. Also *attrib.*

1793 tr. *C.P. Thunberg's Trav. Europe, Afr., & Asia* II. 110 Camassie wood (Camassie-hout), is merely a shrub, and consequently produces small pieces only, which serve for veneering. **1814** R. B. FISHER *Importance of Cape Good Hope* 84 The kamasse, a sort of bark, being the rhind or shavings of the tree of that name. **1907** T. R. SIM *Forests & Forest Flora Cape Good Hope* 323 The Knysna export under the name of Boxwood was all, or mostly, Kamassi-wood, without any Boxwood. **1924** RECORD & MELL *Timbers Tropical Amer.* 506 One of the two South African woods known to the world trade is the so-called Knysna or Kamassi boxwood. **1935** L. CHALK et al. *Forest Trees & Timbers Brit. Empire* III. 15 Kamassi attains about 40 ft. in height and generally a maximum girth of 2 to 3 ft. *Ibid.* 17 Kamassi is one of the two timbers exported from South Africa regularly in small quantities. **1951** *Dict. Gardening* (R. Hort. Soc.) II. 908/2 *G[onioma] Kamassi.* Evergreen shrub... Yields the hard Kamassi wood of S. Africa. **1973** PALMER & PITMAN *Trees S. Afr.* III. 1905 Kamassi occurs in numbers in the Midland forests of the Cape. *Ibid.* 1906 It is exported in small quantities, as is Cape box for which kamassie is often mistaken.

Kama Sutra (ˌkɑːmə 'suːtrə). Also (as one word) **Kamasutra**. [Skr. *kāma* love + *sūtra* (see SUTRA).] The title of an ancient Sanskrit treatise on the art of love and sexual techniques; hence used allusively.

1883 BURTON & ARBUTHNOT *Kama Sutra of Vatsyayana* 3 In the present publication it is proposed to give a complete translation of what is considered the standard work on love in Sanscrit literature, and which is called the 'Vatsyayana Kama Sutra', or Aphorisms on Love, by Vatsyayana. *Ibid.* iii. 24 Man should study the Kama Sutra and the arts and sciences subordinate thereto... Even young maids should study this Kama Sutra. **1915** *Encycl. Relig. & Ethics* VIII. 450/1 The *Kāmasūtra* permits love matches generally. **1960** 'S. HARVESTER' *Chinese Hammer* xix. 172 A large illustration of many-armed embrace whose postures owed more to the Hindu *Kamasutra* than to a depiction of a Tibetan *Dukor* with his bejewelled *shakti*. **1961** C. WILLOCK *Death in Covert* iii. 73 Individual pillars were decorated with some rather questionable designs. Whynne.. said: 'Don't worry. We shall be building an outdoor Espresso Bar.. round the most Kama Sutra of those.' **1964** *Listener* 26 Nov. 848/3 For its delineation of the almost innumerable techniques for handling a locomotive, *The Train* must be accounted the *Kama Sutra* of the permanent way. **1970** J. BOLAND *Big Job* xii. 100 The things I've taught that girl. Proper little Kama Sutra, I am. **1972** R. QUILTY *Tenth Session* 93 He'll be bursting in any minute. Kama Sutra lips—ready for the last waltz.

Kamba ('kæmbə). [Bantu.] A Bantu-speaking people of central Kenya, related ethnically to the Kikuyu; a member of this people; their language.

1885 J. T. LAST *Gram. Kamba Lang.* 14 Probably the cardinal numbers are seldom used by the Kambas beyond *iyana*, 100. *Ibid.* 31 The simplest form of the verb is used in Kamba, as in Swahili and English, for the second person singular of the imperative. **1938** W. M. HAILEY *Afr. Survey* ii. 24 Among the Kikuyu and Kamba, a whole age-grade of boys is initiated at one time. **1959** B. BERNARDI *Mugwe* i. 2 They share this tradition with the other bordering Bantu peoples, the Kikuyu,.. the Mbere and the Kamba. **1963** *Times* 31 May 10/2 Mr. Sagini is a Kisii, Mr. Mwanyumba (Works) is a Taita and Mr. Mwendwa (Labour) is a Kamba.

Kamba, var. KHAMBA.

kambe, kambrell, obs. ff. COMB, CAMBREL.

Kamchadal ('kæmtʃədæl). Also **Kamtchat(ka)dale, Kamt(s)chadale.** [Russ.]

a. A member of a Mongoloid people inhabiting the Kamchatka peninsula on the Pacific coast of Siberia. **b.** The language of this people.

1764 J. GRIEVE tr. *Krasheninnikov's Hist. Kamtschatka* III. iii. 175 Thus it appears likely, that the Kamtschadales lived formerly in Mungalia beyond the river Amur, and made one people with the Mungals. **1790** tr. *J.B.B. de Lesseps's Trav. Kamtschatka* I. 134 It is observed.. that Kamtschadales of either sex, do not live longer than Russians. **1824** J. D. COCHRANE *Narr. Journey Russia & Siberian Tartary* (ed. 2) II. xi. 43 The number of real Kamtchatdales who retain their ancient usages is small. **1855** *Eng. Cycl.: Nat. Hist.* III. 557 The Kalan of the Kamtchatkadales. **1871** E. B. TYLOR *Primitive Culture* I. iii. 98 This spiritualistic belief among the Kamchadals is, no doubt, the key to their superstition as to rescuing drowning men. **1909** *Westm. Gaz.* 28 Aug. 10/2 The Kamchadals, one of the numerous tribes inhabiting the North of Siberia. **1933** L. BLOOMFIELD *Lang.* iv. 70 The Hyperborean family.. consists of Chukchee.. Koryak.. and Kamchadal. **1937** R. H. LOWIE *Hist. Ethnol. Theory* ii. 15 The Kamchadal cooked meat in wooden troughs filled with water into which they threw heated rocks. **1956** [see GILYAK].

Kamchatkan (kæm'tʃætkən), *sb.* and *a.* Also **Kamschatkan, Kamskatchan, Kamt(s)chatkan.** [f. *Kamchatka* (place-name); see -AN.]

A. *sb.* A person from the peninsula of Kamchatka in Siberia; often = prec. **B.** *adj.* Of or pertaining to Kamchatka.

1797 *Encycl. Brit.* IX. 429/2 The southern Kamtchatkans commonly build their villages in thick woods. **1833** W. L. MACKENZIE *Sk. Canada & U.S.* 25 Even the wild Greenlander, the grim Kamschatkan, and the desolate Siberian love their barren wastes. **1865** DICKENS *Mut. Fr.* II. IV. v. 201 [She] sometimes might have issued her directions to equal purpose in the Kamskatchan language. **1871** *Month* May-June 552 The marvellous fertility and floweriness of a Kamtchatkan summer. **1888** *Athenæum* 3 Mar. 270/3 An Eskimo offshoot, though mixed with Tuski or Kamtchatkan blood. **1890** J. G. FRAZER *Golden Bough* II. iii. 110 It was a principle with the Kamtchatkans never to kill a land or sea animal without first making excuses to it. **1917** W. M. SALTER *Nietzsche* 263 The Kamschatkans required that snow should never be scraped off with a knife. **1937** *Times* 30 Dec. 9/3 By a Convention signed in 1928 Japan was given extensive fishing rights in Russian waters off the Kamchatkan and other eastern coasts.

kame, kaim (keɪm). *North.* and *Sc.* form of COMB *sb.* (q.v.) in various senses, esp. that of a steep and sharp hill ridge; hence in *Geol.* one of the elongated mounds of post-glacial gravel, found at the lower end of the great valleys in Scotland and elsewhere throughout the world; an esker or osar.

1862 [see COMB *sb.* 6 d]. **1863** A. C. RAMSAY *Phys. Geog.* xxvi. (1878) 430 Those marine gravelly mounds, called Kames or Eskers. **1884** *Geol. Mag.* 565 He [Prof. H. Carvell Lewis] described in detail a number of marginal kames in Pennsylvania. **1894** *Jrnl. R. Agric. Soc.* June 388 The most southerly examples of true eskers or kames in this country.

kame, obs. Sc. and north. f. COMB *v.*[1]

kameel (kə'miːl). *S. Afr.* [Afrikaans, a. Du. *kameel* camel.] The giraffe, *Giraffa camelopardalis.*

1839 W. C. HARRIS *Wild Sports S. Afr.* 373 *Camelopardalis Giraffa.* The Giraffe. Kameel of the Cape Colonists. **1896** H. A. BRYDEN *Tales S. Afr.* 70 As.. we wanted meat, I rammed the spurs in and galloped headlong for the kameels. **1900** W. L. SCLATER *Fauna S. Afr.* I. 264 The name giraffe.. is practically unknown in South Africa where the term 'kameel' is always used. **1925** F. C. SLATER *Shining River* 234 Kameel—The Southern giraffe, formerly found throughout the country north of the Orange River.

kameeldoorn (kə'miːlduən). *S. Afr.* Also **kameeldoring.** [Afrikaans, ad. Du. *kameel* camel + *doorn* thorn.] = *camel-thorn* (*b*) (s.v. CAMEL *sb.* 5).

1822 W. J. BURCHELL *Trav. S. Afr.* I. xviii. 453 A large solitary tree of *Kameel-doorn* (Camel-thorn, or the tree on which, generally, the Camelopardalis browses), the first I had seen of the species, was standing here. **1896** H. A. BRYDEN *Tales S. Afr.* 44 Groves of giraffe acacia (*kameel doorn*), through which still wander freely in these pathless, waterless solitudes the tall giraffe. **1937** S. CLOETE *Turning Wheels* 53 Passing the big group of kameel-doorns that were a landmark, they turned slightly west. **1948** [see GOMPAAUW, GOMPAUW]. **1957** *Cape Times* (Mag. Section) 20 July 2/7 Ghani got out lazily.. stationing himself beneath a shady kameeldoring overlooking the hotel yard. **1972** *S. Afr. Garden & Home* Oct. 33 The striking crimson-breasted shrike.. seen perched on a *kameel-doring*.

kameez(e (kæ'miːz) [Cf. CAMISE.] In S. Asian countries, a long shirt or blouse.

1955 [see SHALWAR]. **1966** J. & R. GODDEN *Two under Indian Sun* iii. 73 A coat and trousers instead of dhoti and kameeze. **1971** *Femina* (Bombay) 2 Apr. 51/2 An off-shoot of the same idea is a two-piece unit, basically a kameez and gharara, but the kameez-sleeves being of the same material as the gharara, extra colourful, while the body of the kameez itself is a plain dark self-colour. **1972** 'E. PETERS' *Death to Landlords!* i. 21 She had taken to the *shalwar* and *kameez* of the Punjabi women.

‖**kameka**, var. CAMACA, silk, satin. *Obs.*

1338 *Durham Acc. Rolls* (Surtees) 375, j pannus novus de serico viridis coloris de Kameka.

kamel, -elle, obs. ff. CAMEL *sb.*

kamela, -eela: see KAMALA.

kamelyne, var. CAMELINE *sb.*[1] *Obs.*

kamerad ('kæmərɑːd, ‖kamə'raːt). [G., ad. F. *camarade* COMRADE.] Comrade, companion: the exclamation used as an appeal for quarter by a German-speaking soldier on surrendering. Hence jocularly as *v. intr.*, to say 'kamerad', express one's wish to surrender.

1914 *Illustr. London News* 10 Oct. 497 How the enemy surrenders, saying, 'Kamerad.. Pardon!' **1916** 'BOYD CABLE' *Action Front* 63 'Nein, nein!' answered Ainsley. 'You kamarade—sie kamarade.' The other, in somewhat voluble gutturals, insisted that Ainsley must 'kamarade', otherwise surrender. **1917** P. MACGILL *Brown Brethren* vii. 105 'Kamerad! Kamerad!' they whined, their arms shaking as if stricken with palsy. **1917** *Times Hist. War* XIV. 199/2 Then Gardener shouted to the others.. 'You're late. Everybody else has Kameraded.' **1918** *Daily News* 21 Sept. 5/2 When our men came down the steps of the dugout the card-players perfunctorily held up their hands and 'Kameraded'. **1923** *Westm. Gaz.* 3 July, Sir W. Joynson-Hicks cried 'Kamerad' at once. He tried to let himself down lightly by saying that he had expected a unanimous acceptance. **1930** KIPLING *Limits & Renewals* (1932) 259 'Kamerad, Bull! I'll come in,' said Loftie. Vaughan's hands had gone up first. **1973** C. EGLETON *Seven Days to Killing* viii. 89 He threw his weapon aside, held up his hands and yelled Kamerad.

kamester, var. KEMPSTER.

‖**kami** ('kaːmi). [Japanese, = 'superior, lord'.] **1.** A title given by the Japanese to daimios and governors, = 'lord'. Also **kami-dana** = *god-shelf* s.v. GOD *sb.* 16 *a.*

1616 R. COCKS *Diary* (1883) I. 131 Micarna Camme Samme, the Emperours sonns sonne. **1663** R. MANLEY tr. *Caron & Schouten's True Descr. Kingdoms Japan & Siam* 115 *Owarny Cammy Samma*, the old Emperors Brother. **1876** [see *god-shelf*]. **1904** L. HEARN *Japan: Attempt at Interpretation* viii. 150 The domestic god-shelf—*Kamidana.* **1931** G. B. SANSOM *Japan* I. iii. 46 At one end of the scale the Sun Goddess, that Heaven-Shining-Great-August Deity is a *kami*, and at the other mud and sand and even vermin are *kami.* **1965** W. SWAAN *Jap. Lantern* iii. 33 Mirrors are sacred objects associated with *kami* (spirits). **1970** J. W. HALL *Japan from Prehist. to Mod. Times* iv. 32 Often translated as 'god', 'deity', or 'spirit', *kami* can best be described as localized spiritual forces. **1972** *Guardian* 23 Sept. 10/3 He spends twenty minutes in personal prayer to the 'kami' of the shrine, who in this case are the Emperor Meiji, the monarch who presided over the modernisation of Japan in the late nineteenth century, and his consort, Empress Shoken.

2. In the Shinto or native religion of Japan, A divinity, a god (used by Protestant missionaries and their converts as the name of the Supreme Being, God). Also attrib., as ***kami-religion.***

1727 SCHEUCHZER tr. *Kæmpfer's Japan* I. 206 Superstition at last was carried so far, that the Mikaddo's.. are looked upon.. as true and living images of their *Kami's* or Gods, as *Kami's* themselves. **1871** TYLOR *Prim. Cult.* xvii. II. 317 The Japanese.. have.. kept up.. the religion of their former barbarism. This is the Kami-religion, Spirit-religion. **1886** HUXLEY in *19th Cent.* XIX. 494 The state-theology of China and the Kami-theology of Japan. *note*, 'Kami' is used in the sense of Elohim, but is also, like our word 'Lord', employed as a title of respect among men.

‖**kamichi** ('kamiʃi). [Brazilian, through F. *kamichi* (Buffon), *Kamichy* (1741 Barrère, cited by Hatz.-Darm.).] The horned screamer (*Palamedea cornuta*), a bird of Guiana and the Amazon.

1834 McMURTRIE *Cuvier's Anim. Kingd.* 154 The *Kamichi* resembles the Jacanas, but on a very large scale. **1840** *Penny Cycl.* XVII. 155/2 D'Azara says that both this bird and the Kamichi are provided with a cottony down at the base of the feathers.

kamik ('kæmɪk). Also **kammik.** [Eskimo.] A long boot of sealskin worn by the Eskimos.

1891 L. GIBSON *Jrnl.* 15 Aug. in R. E. Peary *Northward over Gt. Ice* (1898) I. iii. 109 The [Eskimo] woman made us a pair of Kamiks. **1900** *Scribner's Mag.* Sept. 297/1 Seal-skin kammiks, or top boots. **1910** R. E. PEARY *North Pole* xiv. 128 The *kamiks*, or boots, of sealskin, soled with the heavier skin of the square-flipper seal. **1922** *Chambers's Jrnl.* 425/1 Untying the upper part of his *kamik*, or long boot. **1933** J. BUCHAN *Prince of Captivity* iii. 106 Their reindeer-skin kamiks had been worn into holes. **1945** D. LEECHMAN *Eskimo Summer* 29 Nearly all of them [*sc.* Eskimo girls] were

wearing sealskin *kamiks*, but one or two girls actually had on silk stockings and shoes with medium high heels. **1969** *Daily Tel.* (Colour Suppl.) 18 Apr. 11/4 Eskimo wives stitching parkas and *kamiks*, or sealskin boots, which they trade at the local co-op store.

‖**kamikaze** (kæmɪˈkɑːziː). Also with capital initial. [Jap., 'divine wind', f. *kami* god, KAMI + *kaze* wind.

The word was originally used in Jap. lore with reference to the supposed divine wind which blew on a night in August 1281, destroying the navy of the invading Mongols.]

A. *sb.* **1.** 'The wind of the gods' (see small-type note above).

1896 L. HEARN *Kokoro* x. 137 That mighty wind still called *Kami-kazé*,—'the Wind of the Gods', by which the fleets of Kublai Khan were given to the abyss. *Ibid.*, But.. the Kami-kazé did not come. **1970** J. W. HALL *Japan* vii. 93 The 'divine wind' (*kamikaze*) which Japan's protective *kami* had generated against its enemies.

2. One of the Japanese airmen who in the war of 1939–45 made deliberate suicidal crashes into enemy targets (usu. ships). **b.** An aircraft, usu. loaded with explosives, used in such an attack. Also *transf.*

1945 *Newsweek* 27 Aug. 25 As a British task force was hoisting victory pennants a Kamikaze darted out of the clouds toward the ship. **1952** *Time* 22 Dec. 17/1 No land-based bomber—including the Japanese *Kamikaze*—has ever sunk a U.S. carrier while the carrier was traveling in a task group. **1954** *Time* 4 Jan. 67/1 Fleets of Kamikazes plunged out of the sky, their suicidal pilots aiming their bomb loads at the destroyers. **1959** *Sunday Times* 5 Apr. 13/5 The Kamikaze hit the bridge, killing thirty and wounding eighty-seven. **1964** *Sun-Herald* (Sydney) 21 June 28/2 Three Australian guards and more than 200 kamikazes died. **1971** *Observer* 28 Nov. 3/6 The stand of the *kamikazes* means that in any critical division the Government is assured of a working majority.

3. *Surfing.* (See quots.)

1963 *Pix* 28 Sept. 62/3 Kamikaze: riding the nose with the hands in cross across chest. **1967** J. SEVERSON *Great Surfing* Gloss., *Kamikaze*, a planned wipe-out; taken on purpose with no hope of saving the board or avoiding the swim. **1970** *Studies in English* (Univ. of Cape Town) I. 32 A *kamikaze* occurs when the surfer takes a wipe-out fair on the nose of his surfboard.

B. *adj.* **1.** Of, pertaining to, or characteristic of a *kamikaze* (sense 2, above).

1946 *Chem. & Engin. News* XXIV. 1030/2 The Army and Navy.. provided protective [smoke] screens against the Kamikaze attack of the Japanese. **1954** P. K. KEMP *Fleet Air Arm* 203 A Kamikaze, or suicide, plane dived into the base of H.M.S. *Indefatigable*'s island. **1956** A. H. COMPTON *Atomic Quest* iv. 225 Japan's one great new weapon was her 'kamikaze' planes, loaded with bombs and guided to their targets by heroic suicide pilots. **1960** *Spectator* 3 June 803 With the suicidal self confidence of kamikaze pilots ramming an aircraft-carrier. **1966** *New Scientist* 11 Aug. 305/3 After the mobilization of the bedbugs for guard duties in Vietnam comes news of *kamikaze* porpoises. **1974** *Illustr. London News* Feb. 25/3 Newspaper speculation that *kamikaze* dolphins, with explosives strapped to them, had been trained to ram and destroy enemy craft.

2. *transf.* and *fig.* Reckless, dangerous, or potentially self-destructive (*lit.* and *fig.*).

a **1963** S. PLATH *Ariel* (1965) 23, I have taken a pill to kill The thin Papery feeling. Saboteur, Kamikaze man. **1963** *Punch* 16 Jan. 81/3 One of the *Kamikaze* apes at the RAF's Central Ape School. **1964** J. H. ROBERTS *Q Document* (1965) viii. 198 The Ginza was crowded... The kamikaze cabs did not seem to be affected.. by the condition of the streets. They followed the same erratic courses through the staggered lines of more cautious drivers. **1966** L. COHEN *Beautiful Losers* (1970) I. 92 Kamikaze insects splashed against the glass. **1967** *Telegraph* (Brisbane) 5 Apr. 8/1 No one is too anxious to be a 'Kamikaze kid', and take on a seat without hopes. **1968** *Evening Standard* 29 Aug. 13/3 He developed a contempt for the kamikaze liberals who prefer glorious defeat to sensible accommodation. **1974** D. SEAMAN *Bomb that could Lip-Read* xi. 88 The Royal Army Ordnance Corps—not normally looked upon as a kamikaze outfit—supplies two such [bomb disposal] units, the only ones in the whole British Army.

kamila: see KAMALA.

Kamilaroi (kəˈmɪlərɔɪ). [Austral. Aboriginal.] A group of Australian Aboriginal peoples living between the Gwydir and Lachlan rivers in New South Wales; also, their language.

1856 W. RIDLEY (*title*) Kamilaroi and other Australian languages. **1877** L. H. MORGAN *Anc. Society* II. i. 51 The Kamilaroi are divided into six gentes, standing with reference to the right of marriage, in two divisions. **1911** J. G. FRAZER *Golden Bough*: *Magic Art* (ed. 3) I. iii. 101 The Cammeroi of whom Collins speaks are no doubt the tribe now better known as the Kamilaroi. **1952** A. G. MITCHELL in *Chambers's Shorter Eng. Dict.* Suppl., *Kamilaroi*,.. one of the New South Wales aboriginal tribes. **1972** *Talanya* I. 21 The Wiradjuri language.. met Kamilaroi on the north.

kamis, kamisado, var. CAMISE, -SADO.

‖**kamish** (kəˈmiːʃ). [ad. Russ. *kamýsh* reed.] The common reed, *Phragmites communis*.

1902 *Westm. Gaz.* 25 Jan. 3/1 As we advanced the mountainous country changed gradually into desert, and the desert again into steppes overgrown with kamish, or reeds, where good water could be dug out almost anywhere. **1964** R. PERRY *World of Tiger* i. 2 The vast beds of kamish reeds ..which stretch for miles from the slow flood of the Kuban to the Persian shore of the Caspian.

kamme, obs. form of CAM *a.* and *adv.*

kammede, kammok, kamp: see CAM-.

kämmererite (ˈkɛm-, ˈkæmərəraɪt). *Min.* Also †**kæm-**, **kam-**. [ad. Sw. *kæmmererit* (N. Nordenskiöld 1842, in *Acta Soc. Sci. Fennicæ* I. 486), f. the name of August Alexander *Kämmerer* (1789–1858), Prussian surveyor of mines: see -ITE¹.] A mineral of the chlorite group that is a chromiferous variety of pennine and occurs as soft, flaky, pale violet crystals.

1854 J. D. DANA *Syst. Min.* (ed. 4) II. 292 Kæmmererite occurs in hexagonal prisms, of a reddish violet color... Found with chromic iron at Bissersk, Siberia; also at Texas, Lancaster Co., Pennsylvania. **1926** *Amer. Jrnl. Sci.* CCXI. 284 Chlorite includes as end members..(7) $H_4Mg_2Cr_2SiO_9$ (kämmererite or Kr). **1928** *Q. Jrnl. Geol. Soc.* LXXXIII. 647 The most extensively-developed chromiferous silicate in the Shetlands is the chrome-chlorite (kämmererite). **1958** *Amer. Mineralogist* XLIII. 954 Chromium substitutes into both the octahedral and tetrahedral positions of chlorite. Above 2 per cent chromic oxide content, the former are termed kammererite, and the latter kotschubeite.

Kampa, var. KHAMBA.

kampherol, var. KAEMPFEROL.

‖**kampong** (kæmˈpɒŋ). Also **campong**, **kampung**. [Malay *kampong*, *kampung* inclosure: see COMPOUND *sb.*²] A Malay village.

1844 BROOKE *Jrnl.* in Mundy *Narrative Borneo* (1848) I. 371 His *campong* was at Singi. **1875** THOMSON *Straits Malacca* 18 There are Malay *campongs* (villages) scattered over the island. **1900** *Blackw. Mag.* Mar. 401/2 The rebel chiefs.. are hustled out of the kampongs. **1972** *Straits Times* (Malaysian ed.) 23 Nov. 13/7 A kampung worker..was sentenced to 18 months' jail today. *Ibid.* 24 Nov. 19/8 (*heading*) Elephant visits keep a whole kampung on edge.

kampseen, kamsin, variants of KHAMSIN.

kamptulicon (kæmpˈtjuːlɪkɒn). [A tradename, made up from Gr. καμπτ-ός flexible + οὖλ-ος thick + -ικόν neut. adj. suffix.] Floor-cloth composed of a mixture of india-rubber, gutta-percha, and cork, mounted on canvas.

(The material was patented by E. Galloway in 1844 (No. 10054), but the word does not appear in the specification.)

1844 G. WALTER (*title*) Description of the Patent Kamptulicon Life Boat. **1851** *Specif. L. Bunn's patent* No. 13713 Improvements in the manufacture of Kamptulicon. **1858** *Ann. Reg.* 196 The floor is covered with a carpet of Kamptulicon, an excellent non-conductor.

Kampuchean (kæmpuːˈtʃiːən), *a.* and *sb.* [f. *Kampuchea* native name of Cambodia (used officially since 1975) + -AN.] = CAMBODIAN *a.* and *sb.*

1976 *Survey People's Republic of China Press* (U.S. Consulate General, Hong Kong) Apr. 149 Pich cheang, charge d'affaires ad interim of the democratic kampuchean embassy in Peking. **1977** *Times* 20 July 14/2 The Kampucheans claim that 'only the most serious criminals' were executed after liberation. **1979** *Time* 22 Jan. 33 North Koreans attempted.. to teach the Kampucheans to fly MiG aircraft. **1979** *China Now* Jan.–Feb. 5/2 In Ho Chi Minh City many Chinese were kidnapped and press-ganged into the..'New Economic Zones' on the Kampuchean front. **1979** *Times of India* 17 Aug. 1/2 Intense fighting now going on.. between the supporters of ousted Kampuchean regime of Pol Pot and Vietnamese forces backing the new rulers in Phnom Penh. **1983** *Kampuchea* (Austral. Govt. Dept. Educ. & Youth Affairs) 5 Many Pali and Sanskrit terms used by Kampucheans are also used by Thais and Laotians.

Kamschatkan, Kamskatchan, varr. KAMCHATKAN *sb.* and *a.*

Kamtchat(ka)dale, Kamt(s)chadale, varr. KAMCHADAL.

Kamt(s)chatkan, varr. KAMCHATKAN *sb.* and *a.*

kan, obs. f. CAN *sb.* and *v.*, KHAN²; var. KHAN¹.

kana (ˈkɑːnə). Also 8 **canna**, **kanno**. [Jap.] Japanese syllabic writing, the chief varieties of which are HIRAGANA and KATAKANA.

1727 J. G. SCHEUCHZER tr. *Kæmpfer's Hist. Japan* I. I. iv. 68 The Names of the Provinces.. are only in their *Canna*, or common Writing. *Ibid.* IV. iv. 305 Publish'd in the vulgar characters, call'd *Kanno*. **1874** *Trans. Asiatic Soc. Japan* I. 104 The invention of the Japanese syllabic *kana* ten centuries ago. **1879** *Ibid.* VII. 101 It is supposed that he is responsible for the *kana* readings given by the side of the Chinese text. *Ibid.* 230 The *kana* in the Kozhiki and Nihongi are the earliest examples of the use of Chinese characters by the Japanese as phonetic symbols. **1931** H. O. YARDLEY *Amer. Black Chamber* 194 Every time I.. saw this benevolent-faced whiskered old missionary as he puzzled over Japanese words, *kana* and code groups. **1965** W. SWAAN *Jap. Lantern* vi. 74 Each of the symbols, known as *kana*, represented either a vowel or a syllable. **1968** *Encycl. Brit.* XII. 882 These syllabaries or *kana*, originally consisting of about 50 syllables, greatly stimulated the development of literature. **1973** *Physics Bull.* May 279/2 Japanese is normally written, typed or printed in a mixture of Chinese and Japanese Kana characters. The simplest set of these, the 'education set', already contains 881 Chinese characters and the 'daily use' and 'standard' sets contain 1850 and 2669 characters respectively. The dictionary set amounts to between 10 000 and 15 000 characters.

kanae (ˈkanaɪ). *N.Z.* Also **kanai**. [Maori.] A grey mullet, *Mugil cephalus*, found in New Zealand waters.

1820 *Gram. & Vocab. Lang. N.Z.* (Church Missionary Soc.) 158 *Kanáe*,.. the mullet fish. **1838** J. S. POLACK *New Zealand* I. 322 Some deep banks lie off the east coast, on which the *kanai*, or mullet.. abound. **1860** A. S. ATKINSON *Jrnl.* 25 Dec. in *Richmond-Atkinson Papers* (1960) I. 671 Magnificent breakfast of kanae & oysters. **1888** in E. E. Morris *Austral Eng.* (1898) 229/1 The months of December, January, and February in each year are here prescribed a close season for the fish of the species of the mugil known as mullet or kanae. **1966** *Encycl. N.Z.* II. 600/2 Mullet, grey (*Mugil cephalus*), or kanæ of the Maoris, is an excellent food fish, rich in fat and protein, and especially suitable for smoking.

kanaff, var. KENAF.

‖**kanaima** (kəˈnaɪmə). [Native name.] The name given by the Indians of Guyana to an evil avenging spirit.

1951 E. MITTELHOLZER *Shadows move among Them* I. i. 8 The Genie might lure you away—or a *kanaima*. *Ibid.* xiii. 115 A *kanaima* bit me... He's a terrible Indian man who stalks through the jungle looking for people to attack.

‖**kanaka** (ˈkænəkə, in Australia *improperly* kəˈnækə). Also **canaker**, **kanaker**, **kanacka**. [Hawaiian *kanaka* = Samoan, Tongan, and Maori *tangata* man.] A native of the South Sea Islands, esp. one employed in Queensland as a labourer on the sugar plantations. Also *attrib.* Also, the Hawaiian language (*obs.*).

1840 R. H. DANA *Bef. Mast* xx. 59 The Catalina had several Kanakas on board. **1857** R. TOMES *Amer. in Japan* vi. 140 The Sandwich Islanders—or Kanakas, as they are now familiarly known to the sailors and traders. **1866** 'MARK TWAIN' *Lett. from Hawaii* (1967) 68, *k* and *t* are the same in the Kanaka alphabet. *Ibid.* A white chief clerk.. handed the document to Bill Ragsdale.. who translated and clattered it off in Kanaka. **1890** BOLDREWOOD *Col. Reformer* xv. 175 You must get a Kanaka crew that can't be drowned. **1893** R. KIPLING *Banjo Song*, We've shouted on seven-ounce nuggets, We've starved on a kanaka's pay.

Hence **Kanakaland**, Queensland; also **Kanakalander**, an inhabitant of Queensland. *Obs.*

1945 BAKER *Austral. Lang.* x. 186 Kanakalanders... Used during the closing decades of the last century when many Pacific island natives were imported. *Ibid.*, 187 Queensland: *Bananaland*, *Kanakaland* (now obsolete) and *the Nigger State* (now obsolete).

Kanam (kəˈnɑːm). The name of a place in Kenya, on the south shore of the Kavirondo gulf of Lake Victoria, used *attrib.* in **Kanam jaw**, **man**, **mandible**, to designate the fossil hominid remains found there by L. S. B. Leakey in 1932.

1933 L. S. B. LEAKEY in *Man* XXXIII. 200 (*title*) The status of the Kanam mandible and the Kanjera skulls. **1935** —— *Stone Age Races Kenya* ii. 11 Further examination of the Kanam mandible has led me to separate it from the species *Homo sapiens* and to give it a new specific name *Homo kanamensis*. *Ibid.* 148/2 (*index*) Kanam Man. **1952** M. R. SAHNI *Man in Evolution* x. 246 If the evidence of the Kanam jaw from East Africa were relied upon, it would take us back to the Lower Pleistocene. **1965** M. H. DAY *Guide to Fossil Man* 145 Kanam man. *Ibid.* 147 Originally Keith thought.. that the Kanam mandible was evidence of the early development of a modern type of man... Later Keith said that the small front teeth of the Kanam jaw suggested a closer relationship to the australopithecines than to modern man. **1968** P. V. TOBIAS in G. Kurth *Evolution & Hominisation* (ed. 2) 180 A re-assessment of the morphology of the Kanam mandibular fragments convinced me that... the specimen clearly contains a number of archaic features which relate it most closely to the Upper Pleistocene mandible from Dire-Dawa, in the Harrar district of Ethiopia.

kanamycin (kænəˈmaɪsɪn). *Pharm.* [f. mod.L. *kanamyc-eticus*, specific epithet (see def.) + -IN¹; cf. -MYCIN.] (One of) a mixture of antibiotics, chemically related to neomycin, which are produced by the bacterium *Streptomyces kanamyceticus* and are effective against a wide range of bacteria.

1957 H. UMEZAWA et al. in *Jrnl. Antibiotics* (Tokyo) A. X. 188 An antibiotic was isolated from a streptomyces which was assigned to a new species *S. kanamyceticus*, *n. sp.* Okami et Umezawa... This antibiotic was named kanamycin. **1958** *Ann. N.Y. Acad. Sci.* LXXVI. 27 Paper chromatography of kanamycin preparations revealed a second antibiotic, designated kanamycin B, which has been isolated and characterized. **1958** *Observer* 3 Aug. 9/4 A new antibiotic, kanamycin, discovered and developed by Professor Umezawa and his colleagues.. of Tokyo, is now being marketed in the United States. It is active against staphylococcus... It also appears to be highly effective in acute gonorrhea in males. **1963** *Brit. Pharmaceutical Codex* 414 Toxic effects occur with sufficient frequency to make kanamycin useful only when the infecting organisms are resistant to other antibiotics. **1969** H. SMITH *Antibiotics in Clin. Pract.* vii. 97 Chemically, kanamycin is related to neomycin, consisting of two amino sugars linked to a deoxystreptamine. This polybasic water soluble antibiotic in commercial preparations consists.. of kanamycin A and B... It is a white crystalline powder dissolving easily in water. **1969** KIRK & OTHMER *Encycl. Chem. Technol.* (ed. 2) 42 The kanamycins are produced by selected strains of *Streptomyces kanamyceticus*.

Kanarese (kænəˈriːz), *a.* and *sb.* Also **Canarese**. [f. *Kanara* + -ESE.] **A.** *adj.* Of or pertaining to Kanara in western India, or its people. **B.** *sb.* **a.** A native of Kanara. **b.** The language of Kanara, belonging to the Tamulic class of the Dravidian family, closely allied to Telugu; also called

Karnata, and now generally and officially Kannada.

1838 KRISHNAMACHARYA (*title*) A grammar of the modern Canarese language. **1847** *Jrnl. Asiatic Soc. Bengal* XVI. II. 1142 The same effect is observable even in Telugu and Canarese. **1856** [see KARNATA *a.* and *sb.*]. **1875** *Encycl. Brit.* III. 513/2 Marâthi and Kanarese are both spoken. **1880** *Ibid.* XII. 428/2 In the different parts of the [Hyderabad] territory the Marathi, the Kanarese, and Telugu languages are spoken. **1920** *Publ. Opinion* 26 Nov. 521/2 Instruction in the following tongues, Hindustani, Kaffir, Kanarese. **1921** *Q. Rev.* Oct. 328 That Indian Kings were deified after death is placed beyond doubt by a Kanarese inscription. **1939** L. H. GRAY *Foundations of Lang.* 30 The languages of South India (Tamil, Telugu, Kanarese, etc.). **1969** *Enactment* (Delhi) Nov. 12/1, I do not hurl abuses and acid bulbs on my neighbours because they speak.. Kanarese and I speak Konkani. **1971** *Hindustan Times Weekly Rev.* (New Delhi) 4 Apr. p. iv/5 (Advt.), Please send me a free set of recipes in .. Malayalam/Gujarati/Marathi/Kanarese.

‖**kanari** (kə'nɑːrɪ). Also **-rie, -ry.** [Malay *kanārī*.] An East Indian tree of the genus *Canarium* (N.O. *Burseraceæ*), producing edible nuts, from which oil is extracted. Also *attrib.*

1779 FORREST *Voy. N. Guinea* 152 Got a great many Kanary nuts, the kernels of which.. are full of oil. **1800** *Asiatic Ann. Reg., Misc. Tr.* 208/1 The kanary is a remarkably fine kind of almond. **1887** ANNA FORBES *Insulinde* ii. 21 A long wide avenue of kanarie-trees.

kanaster, var. CANASTER, a kind of tobacco.

‖**kanat** (ka'nɑːt). Also **kanát, kanaut,** etc.; **qanat.** [Pers., a. Arab. *ḳanāt*.] A gently sloping underground channel or tunnel, usu. *spec.* in Persia, leading water from the interior of a hill to a village in the valley below, and provided at regular intervals with a series of vertical shafts communicating with the surface of the ground to assist in its construction and maintenance.

1855 *Q. Jrnl. Geol. Soc.* XI. I. 252 Subterraneous canals called Konáts, for irrigation derived from the river, have been cut by Persian perseverance for miles through the gravel at a great depth below the surface. Their course is traceable by the heaps of pebbles thrown out at regular intervals through walls. **1861** *Jrnl. R. Geogr. Soc.* XXXI. 37 By means of a subterranean passage—the excavated earth being thrown up, forming these cannauts..—water is brought sometimes 5 and 6 miles across the plain. **1865** *Ibid.* XXXV. 180 The Afladj is not a province of itself, but, as its name denotes, is that portion of Dowasser which is watered by kanaats, or underground waterducts. **1874** *Ibid.* XLIV. 185 For irrigation the plains and valleys depend on the mountains, and at the base of these are 'kanats', or underground channels. **1894** G. BELL *Safar Nameh Persian Pict.* 81 A kanat which is carrying water to many gardens. **1902** P. M. SYKES *Ten Thousand Miles in Persia* iv. 44 A heavy shower or a sandstorm frequently choking up the *kanát*. **1922** EARL OF RONALDSHAY *Sport & Politics under Eastern Sky* 364 Our road took us along the *karez* or *kanat* which brought water from the mountains at the head of the plain. **1944** G. C. THOMPSON *Tombs & Moon Temple of Hureidha* 10 The Persian *qanat*, for instance, is seen on the coast, and in the Yemen. **1953** A. SMITH *Blind White Fish in Persia* i. 19 Shortly after the collection of facts had begun, we learnt of the qanats. It was written that there were 100,000 miles of them in Persia, that they were artificial underground water channels and that the deepest was over 1,000 feet. *Ibid.* iii. 55 As with birds before an island, the qanat wells warned you of the approach of a town. **1958** A. J. TOYNBEE *East to West* lix. 176 One sees line upon line of qanat-made molehills. **1966** P. ENGLISH *City & Village in Iran* i. 19 By the sixth century B.C.,.. qanat technology was known on the Central Plateau. *Ibid.* iii. 50 The qanat-watered towns and villages on the slopes of the Kuhi Jupar. **1968** *Encycl. Brit.* X. 949 Teheran and Marrakesh are among the many modern cities whose water is supplied by kanats. **1976** *Apollo* Apr. 302/3 Seen from the air, the ventilating shafts of these *qanats* punctuate the buff-coloured plains like perforations in paper. **1976** *Times* 17 Aug. 11/6 If the underground water resources of a semi-arid region are so immense that they can keep the 'qanats' running for the whole year then the unexploited groundwater resources of the British Isles must be incalculable.

kanat, kanaut, var. CANAUT.

‖**kanchil** ('kɑːntʃɪl, -æ-). [Malay *kanchil, kanchīl*.] The smallest known species of chevrotain (*Tragulus Kanchil*), found in the forests of Borneo, Java, and Malacca.

1820 SIR S. RAFFLES in *Trans. Linn. Soc.* (1822) XIII. 263 It is a common Malay proverb to designate a great rogue, to be as cunning as a Kanchil. **1885** *Stand. Nat. Hist.* V. 287 The commonest species, the Kanchil of the Malays.

kancre, obs. f. CANKER.

kand, var. CAND, fluor-spar.

kandel, -dil, obs. ff. CANDLE.

Kandh, var. KHOND.

kandjar, variant of KHANJAR, dagger.

Kandyan ('kændɪən), *a.* and *sb.* Also **Kandian.** [f. *Kandy, Candy*, in Sri Lanka; see -AN.] **A.** *adj.* Of, pertaining to, or characteristic of the town or kingdom of Kandy, or of its inhabitants. **B.** *sb.* A native or inhabitant of Kandy; the language of the Kandyans.

1849 in T. Skinner *Fifty Yrs. Ceylon* (1891) 220 Robberies and bloodshed became familiar to the Kandyan. **1883** J. FERGUSON *Ceylon in 1883* 129 The Kandyan Buddhist temples. *Ibid.* 138 Of nothing is the elephant so much afraid as of fire, and with nothing will a Kandyan approach a wild elephant so readily. **1891** T. SKINNER *Fifty Yrs. Ceylon* 30 My raw untaught Kandians. **1892** C. F. G. CUMMING *Two Happy Years in Ceylon* I. 255 Most of the chiefs who attended the reception could talk more or less English, but the ladies were as deficient therein as we were in Kandyan. **1923** A. GIBSON *Cinnamon & Frangipanni* 23 Some of the real old Kandyan brass. **1933** P. FLEMING *Brazilian Adventure* ii. 20 He spent all his.. money on a fruitless search.. for the buried treasure of the Kandyan Kings. **1942** H. A. J. HULUGALLE *Ceylon* 10 The up-country Sinhalese are loosely called Kandyans. **1956** R. PIERIS *Sinhalese Social Organization* 3 The Kandyan kingdom maintained its independence under the kings of Kandy from Vimala Dharma Sūrya I (reg., A.D. 1591–1604) to the deposition of Śrī Vikrama Rājasiṃha by the British in 1815. **1969** *Femina* (Bombay) 26 Dec. 5/4 She also excels in the Kandyan dances of Ceylon. **1971** *Weekend* (Ceylon) 12 Sept. 4/1 (Advt.), Father Burgher Mother Kandyan Goigama Buddhist seek partner for their pretty educated homely daughter.

kane, variant of *kain*, CAIN, payment in kind.

kane, obs. form of CANE *sb.*[1], KHAN[1].

kanell, variant of CANEL, CANNEL *sb.*[1]

†**kaner.** *Sc. Obs. rare*⁻¹. [f. *kane*, CAIN *sb.*[1] + -ER[1].] One who collects cain or rent; a steward.

1590 in *Thanes of Cawdor* (Spald. Cl.) 193 Item to the Lairdis Kaner for keiping of the yair.. thre bollis victuell.

Kanesian (kə'niːʒən). [Irreg. f. *Kanesh*, ancient city of Asia Minor + -IAN.] The principal dialect of Hittite, also called Kaneshite.

1921 [see NESITE]. **1928** C. DAWSON *Age of Gods* xiii. 302 The official language of the [Hittite] empire has been named by its discoverers Nashili or Kanesian. **1950** H. L. LORIMER *Homer & Monuments* i. 4 Lydian, the language of the Lemnian inscription, and Etruscan are all three closely interrelated and belong, like Kanesian, to that early (though post-Luvian) stage of I.-E.

kaneuas, obs. form of CANVAS.

‖**kang** (kæŋ). Also **k'ang, khang.** [Chinese.] A kind of stove for warming rooms used by the Chinese; also, a brick or wooden erection for sleeping upon, warmed by a fire placed underneath.

1770 *Acc. of the Kang* in *Phil. Trans.* LXI. 62 The parts of a Kang are, 1. a furnace; 2. a pipe for the heat [etc.]. **1870** *Mem. W. C. Burns* 514 Mr. Burns's room with its two chairs, table and khang. **1892** T. M. MORRIS *Winter N. China* 111 The ground floor was occupied by a k'ang about fourteen feet by six feet.

kang, variant of CANG *sb.* and *a.*, CANGUE.

kanga[1] ('kɑːŋə). *N.Z.* Also **kaanga.** [Maori.] Indian corn, *Zea mays.*

1843 E. DIEFFENBACH *Trav. in N.Z.* II. III. 366 *Kanga*, corn, maize. **1905** W. B. *Where White Man Treads* 2 Plantations of.. Kaanga (Indian corn). **1949** P. BUCK *Coming of Maori* (1950) II. i. 111 Indian corn.. received the name of *Kanga*, the Maori form of the word corn... A unique method of utilizing it as food was evolved... The unhusked cobs were placed in fenced enclosures in still water where the grain became soft. **1959** *Economic Botany* XIII. 321/2 The vernacular name covering all maize is *kaanga.*

kanga[2] ('kæŋgə). *Austral. colloq.* [Shortened form of *kangaroo.*] = KANGAROO *sb.* 1.

[**1926** A. A. MILNE *Winnie-the-Pooh* vii. 91 Christopher Robin.. said that a Kanga was Generally Regarded as One of the Fiercer Animals. *Ibid.* 93 Kanga never takes her eye off Baby Roo, except when he's safely buttoned up in her pocket.] **1942** C. BARRETT *On Wallaby* iv. 73 'Leaves a kanga cold,' Tim declared after seeing a jerboa in action. **1969** *Sun* (Melbourne) 12 July 9/3 (*heading*) Kangas: all are to blame.

kanga, var. KHANGA.

‖**kangany** (kɑːn'gɑːnɪ). Also **canganeme, cangany, kangani.** [f. Tamil *kaṇkāṇi*, f. *kaṇ* eye + *kāṇ* to see.] An overseer or headman of a gang of local labourers in Sri Lanka, southern India, and Malaya.

1817 'PHILALETHES' *Hist. Ceylon* lvi. 324 *Canganeme*. This officer musters the people of the village, and calls them together when there is any work to be done. *Ibid.* 336 Canganys, corporals under the aratsches. **1886** R. W. JENKINS *Ceylon in Fifties & Eighties* 78 Kangani, head of a gang of coolies. **1903** *Westm. Gaz.* 30 May 4/3 The kanganies (head coolies).. say if their coolies are not given work they must remove them to another estate. **1923** *Glasgow Herald* 21 Apr. 4/1 When the tasks are all filled the tappers go to work.. under the native overseers or Kanganies. **1926** *Blackw. Mag.* Apr. 507/1 Several Tamil headmen—Kanganies—are sent to India with recruiting licenses. Each Kangany will go to his own village in South India. **1964** K. G. TREGONNING *Hist. Mod. Malaya* 199 As indentured labour diminished in importance.. it was replaced by the *kangany* system, whereby a foreman or senior labourer from the estate was sent back to India, empowered to recruit in his old village... The *kangany* system was abolished in 1938.

kangaroo (kæŋgə'ruː), *sb.* Also 8 **kanguru, -gooroo,** 8–9 **-guroo,** (8 **gamgarou**). [Stated to have been the name in a native Australian lang.

Cook and Banks believed it to be the name given to the animal by the natives at Endeavour River, Queensland, and there is later affirmation of its use elsewhere. On the other hand, there are express statements to the contrary (see quots. below), showing that the word, if ever current in this sense, was merely local, or had become obsolete. The common assertion that it really means 'I don't understand' (the supposed reply of the native to his questioner) seems to be of recent origin and lacks confirmation. (See Morris *Austral English* s.v.)

1770 COOK *Jrnl.* (1893) 224 (Morris) (Aug. 4) The animals which I have before mentioned, called by the Natives Kangooroo or Kanguru. **1770** J. BANKS *Jrnl.* (1896) 301 (Aug. 26) The largest [quadruped] was called by the natives *kangooroo.* **1787** ANDERSON in *Cook's Voy.* (1790) IV. 1295 We found, that the animal called kangooroo, at Endeavour River, was known under the same name here [in Tasmania]. **1792** J. HUNTER *Port Jackson* (1793) 54 The animal.. called the kangaroo (but by the natives patagorong) we found in great numbers. **1793** W. TENCH *Compl. Acc. Port Jackson* 171 The large, or grey kanguroo, to which the natives [of Port Jackson] give the name of Pat-ag-a-ran. *Note*, Kanguroo was a name unknown to them for any animal, until we introduced it. **1834** THRELKELD *Austral. Gram.* (Hunter's River) 87 (Morris) *Kóng-go-róng*, the Emu.. likely the origin of the barbarism, kangaroo, used by the English, as the name of an animal called Mo-a-ne. **1835** T. B. WILSON *Narr. Voy. World* 211 (ibid.) They [natives of the Darling Range, W.A.] distinctly pronounced 'kangaroo' without having heard any of us utter the sound. **1850** *Jrnl. Ind. Archipelago* IV. 188 (*Kangaroo.*) It is very remarkable that this word, supposed to be Australian, is not to be found as the name of this singular marsupial animal in any language of Australia.. I have this on the authority of my friend Captain King.]

1. A marsupial mammal of the family *Macropodidæ*, remarkable for the great development of the hind-quarters and the leaping-power resulting from this. The species are natives of Australia, Tasmania, Papua, and some neighbouring isles; the larger kinds being commonly known as *kangaroos*, and the smaller ones as *wallabies*. (Also used by sportsmen as a collective plural.)

The first species known in Europe was the great kangaroo (*Macropus giganteus*), discovered by Captain Cook in 1770; the male of this is about 6 feet in height when standing erect.

1773 HAWKESWORTH *Voy.* III. 578 (*1st Voy. Cook*) The next day our Kangaroo was dressed for dinner and proved most excellent meat. **1774** GOLDSM. *Nat. Hist.* VII. XVI. II. 434 The kanguroo of New Holland, where only it is to be found, is often known to weigh above 60 pounds. **1796** *Gentl. Mag.* LXVI. I. 467 The Gamgarou, or as Pennant calls it Kangaroo, is a native of New South Wales. **1845** DARWIN *Voy. Nat.* xix. (1852) 441 Now the emu is banished to a long distance and the kangaroo is become scarce. **1884** BOLDREWOOD *Melb. Mem.* iii. 23 Though kangaroo were plentiful, they were not.. overwhelming in number.

2. With qualifying words, as **antelope** or **antilopine kangaroo**, one of the larger kangaroos (*Halmaturus antilopinus*); **banded k.**, the banded wallaby (genus *Lagostrophus*); **brush k.** = WALLABY (cf. BRUSH *sb.*[1] 4); **forest k.** (cf. FOREST *sb.* 5); **giant, great** (†**sooty**) **k.**, *Macropus giganteus* (see 1); **hare-k.**, a small kangaroo, of the genus *Lagorchestes* (cf. HARE *sb.* 6); **musk k.**, a very small kangaroo (genus *Hypsiprymnodon*); **rat-k.** = KANGAROO-RAT; **rock k.**, the rock-wallaby (genus *Petrogale*); **tree k.**, an arboreal kangaroo (genus *Dendrolagus*).

1802 BARRINGTON *Hist. N.S. Wales* viii. 273 A place.. thickly inhabited by the small brush kangaroo. **1825** FIELD *N.S. Wales* Gloss., Forest-kangaroo, *Macropus major.* **1836** *Encycl. Brit.* (ed. 7) XIV. 129/1 A still larger species, called the sooty kangaroo.. inhabits the south coast of New Holland. *Ibid.*, The banded kangaroo.. inhabits the islands on the west coast of New Holland. **1839** *Penny Cycl.* XIV. 463/1 Skeleton of *Macropus major* (the Great Kangaroo). **1841** J. GOULD *Monograph Macropod.* I. Plate xii, That division of the family which includes the Rat and Jerboa Kangaroos. *Ibid.*, The name of Hare Kangaroo has been given to this species [*Lagorchestes leporoïdes*]. *Ibid.* II. Plates xi & xii, *Dendrolagus ursinus* and *D. inustus*,.. two very remarkable and highly interesting species of Tree Kangaroos. **1846** G. R. WATERHOUSE *Nat. Hist. Mamm.* I. 96 The Antilopine Kangaroo is clothed with short stiff hairs, and these lie close to the skin, as in many of the Antelope tribe. *Ibid.* 168 The specimens of the Brush-tailed or Rock Kangaroo in the British Museum were.. procured by Mr. Gould from the Liverpool Range. **1856** KNIGHT *Cycl. Nat. Hist.* III. 712 The Hare-Kangaroo is a pretty little Kangaroo, about the size of the common hare. **1863** GOULD *Mammals Austr.* II. 54 No other species of Rock Kangaroo has yet been discovered with such short and scanty hair as the *Petrogale brachyotis*. *Ibid.* 57 The Tree-Kangaroo has only in one instance been brought alive to Europe. **1881** *Encycl. Brit.* XIII. 840/2 The potoroos or rat-kangaroos are small animals, none of them exceeding a common rabbit in size.

3. *fig.* **a.** An animal which leaps like a kangaroo. **b.** One who advances by fitful jumps.

1827 P. CUNNINGHAM *N.S. Wales* I. xvi. 290 A stock-yard under six feet high, will be leaped by some of these *kangaroos* (as we term them) with the most perfect ease. **1865** *Cornh. Mag.* Feb. 213 I'm capable of a great jerk, an effort, and then a relaxation—but steady every-day goodness is beyond me. I must be a moral kangaroo!

c. *humorous.* A native of Australia.

1888 *Pall Mall G.* 12 Apr. 5/2 The 'kangaroos'—as our colonial friends are sometimes dubbed. **1897** *Globe* 9 July 1/4 Thomas Atkins.. has nicknamed the Colonial troops the 'Kangaroos'.

†**d.** A kind of chair (? named from its shape).

1834 MAR. EDGEWORTH *Helen* I. xv, It was neither a lounger, nor a dormeuse, nor a Cooper, nor a Nelson, nor a kangaroo.

e. A form of bicycle with sloping backbone, introduced in 1884: an early form of the 'safety' type.

1884 *Cyclist* 9 July 1 (*Advt.*) The 'Kangaroo'. 'Premier Safety Bicycle'. Since its introduction early in the present season [etc.]. **1884** *Wheel. World* Nov. 241/1 The long-anticipated 'Kangaroo Safety Bicycle' run duly came off. **1897** MECREDY & WILSON *Art Cycling* 28 In 1884 came the great 'Kangaroo' rage.. the 'Kangaroo's' popularity waned rapidly.

f. *pl.* In Stock Exchange slang: West Australian mining shares; also, dealers in these shares.

1896 *19th Cent.* Nov. 711 Westralian mining shares .. 'Kangaroos', as they were fondly called. **1897** *Westm. Gaz.* 10 June 8/1 Even among the lively Kangaroos, practical joking in the House seems to have come to a full stop. *Ibid.* 1 Oct. 8/1 The Kangaroos are coming on.. but other markets.. are still awaiting the public's pleasure.

g. Applied to a form of Parliamentary closure by which some amendments are selected for discussion and others excluded.

1913 *Q. Rev.* Apr. 551 The 'kangaroo' or selection by the Chairman of Committee of the amendments to be discussed. **1927** [see *guillotine resolution* s.v. GUILLOTINE *sb.* 4].

h. A system of containerized freight transportation by railway in which a loaded road trailer complete with wheels is carried on a flat rail car; also called 'piggyback'.

1967 *Guardian* 3 July 6/3 On the European continent.. there has recently been a very rapid increase in 'Kangaroo', the system of piggyback for road trailers and semi-trailers developed by French railways. **1969** *Jane's Freight Containers 1968–69* p. iii/2 Rolling stock and terminals designed for containers should be owned or operated, or.. TOFC ('piggyback' or 'kangaroo') equivalent should be owned or operated. *Ibid.* 178/1 Vehicles available: T.I.R. flat and kangaroo trailers.

4. *attrib.* and *Comb.* **a.** General combs., as ***kangaroo attitude, hunt, hunting, leather, market*** (sense 3), ***net, tail, tendon***; also ***kangaroo-like*** adj., ***-wise*** adv.

1828 P. CUNNINGHAM *N.S. Wales* (ed. 3) II. 82 Kangaroo-leather boots. **1835** *Court Mag.* VI. 11/2 The finical air and kangaroo attitude with which his kid-gloved hands hold the white reins. **1859** CORNWALLIS *New World* I. 197 Kangaroo-tail soup, which was there [Melbourne] much esteemed. **1877** E. R. CONDER *Bas. Faith* Note F 447 This kind of reasoning neither marches nor soars: it progresses kangaroo-wise—by wide leaps. **1884** *Stand. Nat. Hist.* V. 96 The.. Pocket-mice, a number of which are jerboa-like or kangaroo-like. **1894** MRS. C. PRAED *Chr. Chard* I. i. 8 They knighted him because he got up a kangaroo hunt for a prince. **1897** *Westm. Gaz.* 10 June 8/1 In the Kangaroo market.. the outlook is equally favourable.

b. Special combs.: **kangaroo-apple**, the edible fruit of the Australian plants *Solanum laciniatum* (or *aviculare*) and *Solanum vescum*; also, the plants bearing this; **kangaroo-bear**, the Australian tree-bear or koala (*Encycl. Dict.* 1885); **kangaroo-beetle**, a beetle with enlarged hind-legs, *esp.* one belonging to the genus *Sagra*; **kangaroo closure** (see 3 g); **kangaroo court** orig. *U.S.*, an improperly constituted court having no legal standing, e.g. one held by strikers, mutineers, prisoners, etc.; **kangaroo-dog**, a large dog trained to hunt the kangaroo; **kangaroo-fly**, a small Australian fly (*Cabarus*); **kangaroo('s)-foot-plant**, the Australian plant *Anigozanthus Manglesii* (*Treas. Bot.*); **kangaroo-grass**, a tall fodder-grass (*Anthistiria australis*), found in Australasia, Southern Asia, and Africa; **kangaroo-hound** = *kangaroo-dog*; **kangaroo justice**, the trying of a person by an unauthorized court, as a kangaroo court; also, the decision of such a court, taken with a disregard for normal legal procedures and criteria; **kangaroo mouse**, (*a*) the Australian pouched mouse; (*b*) a small American rodent of the genus *Perognathus*; **kangaroo paw**, an Australian herb belonging to the genus *Anigozanthos* of the family Hæmodoraceæ; **kangaroo ship** (see quot.); **kangaroo-shoot**, a hunting expedition to shoot kangaroos; hence **kangaroo-shooter, -shooting; kangaroo-skin**, the skin of the kangaroo used as leather or fur; **kangaroo-thorn**, an Australian spiny shrub (*Acacia armata*) used for hedges; **kangaroo-vine**, an evergreen climber, *Cissus antarcticus* (Craig 1848). Also KANGAROO-RAT.

1834 ROSS *Van Diemen's Land Ann.* 133 (Morris) The *kangaroo-apple, resembling the apple of a potato. **1846** G. H. HAYDON 5 *Yrs. Austral. Felix* 85 (ibid.) The kangaroo-apple.. is a fine shrub found in many parts of the country. **1839** WESTWOOD *Insects* I. 214 A South American insect, figured long since by Francillon, under the name of the *Kangaroo Beetle.. in which the size of the hind legs is still more extraordinary. **1883** *Cassell's Nat. Hist.* V. 348 The large brilliantly-metallic *Sagræ*, or Kangaroo-beetles of tropical Asia and Africa. **1930** *Times Educ. Suppl.* 22 Nov. p. i/1 It will be necessary to further restrict the rights of private members of the House of Commons by use of what is known as 'The *Kangaroo Closure'. **1853** 'P. PAXTON' *Stray Yankee in Texas* 205 By a unanimous vote, Judge G—— was elected to the bench and the 'Mestang' or '*Kangaroo Court' regularly organized. **1895** *Harper's Mag.* Apr. 718/2 The most interesting of these impromptu clubs is the one called in the vernacular the 'Kangaroo Court'. It is found almost entirely in county jails. **1931** 'DEAN STIFF' *Milk & Honey Route* 209 *Kangaroo court*, mock court held in jail for the purpose of forcing new prisoners to divide their money. **1935** A. J. POLLOCK *Underworld Speaks* 66/1 *Kangaroo Court*, a jail tribunal comprised of inmates which collects money from prisoners awaiting trial to supply the needy with tobacco, food and a few luxuries—its decision regarding disputes is final. **1966** *Times* 14 Mar. 10/1 Shop stewards at Theale are to meet tomorrow to consider paying back the sums levied by a kangaroo court. **1971** *Times* 20 Jan. 15/3 Citizens who live in the riotous areas [of N. Ireland] deserve protection from.. kangaroo courts. **1973** C. MULLARD *Black Brit.* III. vii. 81 Such practices are surely more like those of a kangaroo court than those that the Race Relations Board should encourage. **1806** *Hist. N.S. Wales* (1818) 265 (Morris) Four valuable *kangaroo-dogs. **1850** J. B. CLUTTERBUCK *Port Phillip* iii. 35 A cross of the Scotch greyhound and English bulldog, called the Kangaroo dog. **1890** R. BOLDREWOOD *Col. Ref.* (1891) 314 A brace of rough greyhounds—the kangaroo-dog of the colonists. **1833** C. STURT *S. Australia* I. ii. 71 (Morris) Our camp was infested by the *kangaroo-fly, which settled upon us in thousands. **1827** P. CUNNINGHAM *N.S. Wales* I. xii. 209 Of native grasses we possess the oat-grass, rye-grass, fiorin, *kangaroo-grass, and timothy. **1884** BOLDREWOOD *Melb. Mem.* 19, I.. feel the thick Kangaroo grass under my feet. **1865** LADY BARKER *Station Life N. Zeal.* 28 (Morris) A large dog, a *kangaroo-hound (not unlike a lurcher in appearance). **1909** *Daily Chron.* 15 Jan. 6/7 It seems to me to be something like *Kangaroo justice. **1966** *Oxford Mail* 11 Mar. 1/6 The unconstitutional strike at B.M.C. Service, Cowley, and the 'kangaroo justice' to which seven men were subjected. **1867** *Amer. Naturalist* I. 394 They are known in the vernacular as '*Kangaroo' or 'Jumping' Rats and Mice, and are entirely confined to Transmississippian regions. **1888** MACDONALD *Gum Boughs* 256 (ibid.) The tiny interesting little creature known on the plains as the 'kangaroo-mouse'. **1875** J. MILLER *First Fam'lies Sierras* (1876) xxx. 243 Wood-rats, kangaroo-mice.. had gone into winter-quarters under the great logs. **1902** *Western Austral. Year-Bk. 1900–01* I. II. ix 304 Some of the most remarkable flowers in the flora of Western Australia [are].. *Kangaroo Paws, of which there are nine species altogether. **1949** D. WALKER *We went to Austral.* 184 With the kangaroo paw it is the stalk that is scarlet and the blending of the colours peculiar. **1966** *Times* 11 Nov. (W. Austral. Suppl.) p. iv/2 The red-and-green kangaroo paw (*Anigosanthus manglesii*, the state's floral emblem) is a barbaric cluster of rich green-and-gold, paw-like flowers on a regal three-foot stem of deep scarlet, yet it is only one of nine species known to exist in the state. **1919** H. JENKINS *John Dene of Toronto* (1920) ii. 32 'A "mother",' he explained, 'is a *kangaroo-ship, a dry-dock ship for salvage and repair of submarines.' **1933** *Bulletin* (Sydney) 11 Oct. 11/3 The royal pair had been participating in a *kangaroo-shoot. **1902** J. H. M. ABBOTT *Tommy Cornstalk* i. 11 Indeed, it is doubtful whether there is any better shot in the world than the *kangaroo-shooter. **1963** A. LUBBOCK *Austral. Roundabout* 15 The kangaroo-shooters go out at night in cars, and the kangaroos.. are shot down. **1888** A. C. GUNTER *Mr. Potter* vi. 80 The Australian has been accustomed to *kangaroo-shooting. **1777** COOK in Bischoff *Van Diemen's Land* (1832) II. 41 These females wore a *kangaroo skin. **1828** P. CUNNINGHAM *N.S. Wales* (ed. 3) II. 151 A desperate-looking ruffian habited in a huge hairy cap and shaggy kangaroo-skin jacket. **1872** C. H. EDEN *In Queensland* 106 (Morris) Kangaroo-skin boots are very lasting and good.

Hence **kanga'rooer**, one who hunts kangaroos.

1909 in *Cent. Dict.* Suppl. **1936** A. RUSSELL *Gone Nomad* viii. 63 That night we hobbled out at a kangarooer's camp.

kangaroo (kæŋgə'ru:), *v.* [f. prec. sb.]

1. *intr.* To hunt the kangaroo. Chiefly in *pres. pple.* and *vbl. sb.*

1849 STURT *Centr. Austr.* I. 91 [The natives] were about to go out kangarooing.. They had their hunting spears. **1890** R. BOLDREWOOD *Robbery under Arms* 15 We were sick of kangarooing, like the dogs themselves. —— *Miner's Right* (1899) 135/2, I lent it to him to go kangarooing.

2. *intr.* To make a great jump (*lit.* and *fig.*).

1889 *Chicago Advance* 12 Dec., Those who kangaroo from the foregoing inferences.. to the conclusion that [etc.]. **1892** *Pall Mall G.* 19 Sept. 2/3 When the horses kangarooed over the 8-ft. water-jump.

kangaroo-rat.

1. A small Australian marsupial, belonging to one or other of several genera, esp. *Potorous* and *Bettongia*; a rat-kangaroo, potoroo, or bettong.

1788 PHILLIP in *Hist. Rec. N.S. Wales* I. ii. 135 (Morris) Either the squirrel, kangaroo rat, or opossum. **1828** P. CUNNINGHAM *N.S. Wales* (ed. 3) I. 289 The kangaroo rat, or more properly rabbit, is about the size of the smallest of the latter kind of animal. **1856** KNIGHT *Cycl. Nat. Hist.* III. 710 The manners of the Kangaroo-Rat are mild and timid.

2. An American pouched rodent, *Dipodomys*, common in the south-western States and in Mexico.

1891 FLOWER & LYDEKKER *Mammals* 479 *D[ipodomys] phillipsi*, the Kangaroo-Rat of the desert regions east of the Rocky Mountains.

Kang-Hai, Kang-He, Kang-Hi, erron. forms of next.

1910 *Encycl. Brit.* V. 747/1 On the finely prepared K'ang-hi wares much more striking and brilliant colour effects were obtained. **1911** in C. Schreiber *Jrnls.* II. (plate facing p. 16), Powdered blue.. bottle of the Kang-He period. **1966** S. MORROW *Moonlighters* xvi. 166 A.. game of hide-and-seek which had toppled an irreplaceable K'ang Hai pot from his mother's desk.

K'ang-Hsi (kæŋʃi:). [Royal name of Hsüan-Yeh, emperor of China 1661–1722.] Used *attrib.* with ref. to the Chinese pottery and porcelain of the latter half of the seventeenth century and the first quarter of the eighteenth, notable for very fine blue-and-white wares and the development of *famille verte* and *famille noire* enamels.

1906 S. W. BUSHELL *Chinese Art* II. viii. 33 The use of cobalt as a ground wash, foreshadowing the greater triumphs of the coming K'ang Hsi epoch. **1934** *Burlington Mag.* Mar. p. xv/1 The K'ang Hsi figures of *Kuan-yin*.. are especially remarkable. **1937** E. LINKLATER *Juan in China* xii. 213 A small flower-painted black vase. 'K'ang-hsi,' she said. **1943** D. WELCH *Maiden Voy.* xxii. 188 The K'ang-Hsi blue and white which the Dean was buying for his grey-walled room at home. **1965** D. TORR *Diplomatic Cover* vi. 103 Powder blue Chinese vases, a Sèvres biscuit group, a Nevers faience jug and the precious little Kang Hsi figures.

'kangled, *ppl. a. Obs.* exc. *dial.* [f. *kangle*, to tangle; still in midland dial.] Tangled.

1577 KENDALL *Trifles* 28 *The Combe*, Adornde with teeth on euery side.. I parte the kangled locks. **1851** STERNBERG *Dial. Northants* (E.D.D. s.v. *Cangle*), That thread be kangled.

‖**kangri** ('kaŋgri). [Hindi *kangṛī*; cf. Kashmiri *kangurü*.] A small wicker-covered clay-lined pot filled with glowing charcoal, carried esp. by Kashmiris next to the skin to warm the air beneath the clothing.

1911 *Allbutt's Syst. Med.* (ed. 2) IX. 591 Scars due to burns (compare the kangri carcinoma of Thibet). **1912** *Med. Ann.* 197 A form of cancer.. in the natives of Kashmir,.. due to their habit of carrying a portable fire-basket (kangri) beneath their clothes in contact with the abdominal skin. **1956** LD. AMULREE in A. Pryce-Jones *New Outl. Mod. Knowl.* 214 Among the Indians it has been shown that cancer of the skin is associated with the use of kangri heaters applied to the abdomen. **1968** *Daily Tel.* (Colour Suppl.) 20 Dec. 27 (*caption*) She keeps warm with a kangri, a pot filled with hot embers. **1972** *Times* 5 Aug. 11/1 If it is cold.. a Kashmiri may offer the visitor his kangri... The kangri is a small wicker basket with a metal pan filled with glowing coals.

kanhschipe, = *kangshipe* s.v. CANG.

kanickanick, etc., var. KINNIKINNIC.

†**'kaniker.** *Obs. rare*$^{-1}$. Later form of GANNEKER, a seller of ale.

1619 DALTON *Country Just.* vii. (1630) 32 In Townes which are not thorow-fare, the Iustices shall doe well to be sparing in allowing of any Alehouse.. And then Kanikers (onely to sell to the poore, and out of their doores) would suffice.

Kanjar ('kændʒɑ:(r)). A generic term for certain small gypsy communities which wander about India.

1875 *Encycl. Brit.* III. 508/1 The aboriginal tribes consist of the Bhars, Cherus, Dhāngars, Kanjhárs, Kharwárs, Kols. **1885** *Ibid.* XVIII. 72/1 The Nats and Kanjars wander like gipsies over the country. **1916** R. V. RUSSELL *Tribes & Castes Cent. Provinces India* III. 333 The Kanjars and Berias are the typical gipsy castes of India. **1924** *Chambers's Jrnl.* Aug. 497/2 Dulloc.. was nothing better than an outcast Kanjar. **1931** E. A. H. BLUNT *Caste System of N. India* 150 All Kanjars, however, are not criminals; many are poor and fairly respectable hunters and *shikaris*.

‖**kanji** ('kandʒi). [Jap., f. *kan* Chinese + *ji* letter, character.] **a.** The corpus of borrowed and adapted Chinese ideographs which forms the principal part of the Japanese writing system. Cf. KANA. **b.** Any one of these ideographs. Used esp. *attrib.*

1920 W. M. MCGOVERN *Colloq. Japanese* 7 The *Honji* or *Kanji* consist of the ideographs taken over from China. **1960** *New Scientist* 21 Apr. 1014/3 The Japanese newspaper contains roughly 50 per cent. kanji or Chinese characters, 40 per cent. kana letters or phonetic signs, and 10 per cent. Arabic figures and other signs. **1964** M. CRITCHLEY *Developmental Dyslexia* iv. 14 More difficulty was experienced in reading the syllabary Kana script than the ideographic Kanji symbols of Chinese origin. **1965** W. SWAAN *Jap. Lantern* vi. 74 The immense prestige of the *kanji* (Chinese characters) proved irresistible. **1972** *Mainichi Daily News* (Japan) 6 Nov. 17/4 (Advt.), Plastic Kanji Cards... All the 1,900 symbolic characters now used in Japanese newspapers and magazines, in Plastic Cards. *Ibid.*, An easy method to learn the 1,900 Chinese-Japanese characters (Kanji) now used.

kankar, another spelling of KUNKUR.

†**kanke'dort.** *Obs. rare.* Also 4–5 **kankerdort.** [Of unascertained etymology.] ? A state of suspense; a critical position; an awkward affair.

c **1374** CHAUCER *Troylus* II. 1703 (1752) Was Troylus nought in a kankedort [*v.r.* kankerdort, *rimes* sort, comfort] That lay and myghte whysprynge of hem here? [Cf. **1493–1500** MEDWALL *Nature* (Brandl) I. 1286 He wyll no lengar me support And that were a shrewd crank dort.]

†**kanker, -kre,** obs. forms of CANKER *sb.* and *v.*

1426 LYDG. *De Guil. Pilgr.* 4239 Thow lefftyst the rust To kankren in thy conscience. *Ibid.* 11837 Vertues.. Han dyuers extremytes, Kankres at outher ende That ffrete on hem. **1530** PALSGR. 316/2 Kankred as brasse.., *vermolu.*

kankerbos, kankerbossie ('kaŋkəbɒs, -ˌbɒsɪ). *S. Afr.* [Afrikaans.] = *cancer bush* (CANCER *sb.* 5).

1913 C. PETTMAN *Africanderisms* 248 Kanker boschje.—*Sutherlandia frutescens, R. Br.* is so named in the Riversdale district. **1931** *Farming in S. Afr.* Sept. 216 They preferred by far the 'klein kankerbos'. **1949** L. G. GREEN *In Land of Afternoon* 50 There is the kankerbos, which has failed to provide a cure for cancer. **1953** *Cape Times* 14 July 2/7 These [*sc.* existing plantings] will be followed by the

introduction of more woody species, such as bitou, blombos, kankerbossie and waxberrie.

‖**kankie** (ˈkæŋkɪ). Also 8 canky. [West African; *nkankye* in Ashantee, *kankyew* in Fantee.] Native African bread made from maize-flour.

1735 S. ATKINS *Voy. Guinea* 90 Salary sufficient to buy Canky, Palm-oil, and a little Fish, to keep them from starving. **1863** R. F. BURTON *W. Africa* II. ix. 144 Kankie is native bread; the flour..must be manipulated till it becomes snowy white; after various complicated operations ..it is boiled or roasted and packed in plantain leaves. **1887** MOLONEY *Forestry W. Afr.* 448 On the Gold Coast the natives..make it into a kind of bread resembling the kankie. *Ibid.* 451 Converted by the Fantes into kankie-cakes.

Kannada (ˈkænədə). Now the official and the more usual name for KANARESE *sb.* b.

1856 [see KARNATA *a.* and *sb.*]. **1877** A. HOVELACQUE *Sci. of Lang.* 78 The *Kanarese*, or *Kannada*, occupies the north Dravidian district. **1942** MORAES & STIMSON *Introd. India* ii. 16 Other widely spoken languages are the southern group —Tamil, Telugu, Kannada and Malayalam. **1959** *Clarendonian* June 46 New editions of the *First Aid* textbook have recently been published in Arabic, Greek, Turkish, Chinese, Gujarati, Kannada, and Bengali. **1969** *Filmfare* (Bombay) 1 Aug. 23/4 There is friction between distributors, exhibitors and the State Government regarding exhibition of Kannada films in Bangalore.

kannakin, variant of CANNIKIN.

1851 H. MELVILLE *Whale* lxxii. 359 Will you look at that kannakin, sir?

kanne, obs. form of CAN *sb.*¹, KHAN².

kannell-bone, var. CANNEL-BONE.

kannette, var. KENNET².

kanny, obs. f. CANNY *a.*

‖**kanoon** (kəˈnuːn). Also kanun, qanon, qanun. [a. Pers. or Arab. *qānūn*.] A species of dulcimer, harp, or sackbut, having fifty to sixty strings, which rest on two bridges and are played with the fingers.

1817 MOORE *Lalla R., Fire-Worshippers* (1854) 155 Singing over Some ditty to her soft Kanoon. **1864** ENGEL *Mus. Anc. Nat.* 45 Among the different species of dulcimers at present in use in the East the kanoon must be noticed. **1874** C. ENGEL *Descr. Catal. Musical Instruments S. Kensington Museum* 208 The *kanoon*, or *qânon*, an instrument especially appertaining to the Arabs and Persians, is, like the *santir*, a kind of dulcimer evidently of high antiquity in the East. **1891** HALL CAINE *Scapegoat* vii, He began to play on his Kánoon. **1931** C. S. HURGRONJE *Mekka in Latter Part of 19th Cent.* 44 Much worse is their habitual accompaniment of song with musical instruments: especially the *qabûs*, a four-stringed instrument which much resembles the *kemènjeh*, only that its strings are of gut instead of horsehair, and also the well known *qânûn* (guitar). **1957** H. G. FARMER in E. Wellesz *Anc. & Oriental Mus.* xi. 444 The psaltery was attributed to Al-Fārābī,..but the instrument is not mentioned by him under its millennium-old name of *qānūn*... As the *qānūn* it was known in Muslim Spain in the eleventh century, and in the fourteenth century it was mounted with sixty-four strings, tuned tricordally, in Persia. **1976** D. MUNROW *Instruments Middle Ages & Renaissance* 21/4 Little metal flaps fitted on the modern Arab qānūn..enable the players to alter the pitch of a course of strings with an adroit flick of the fingers. *Ibid.* 23/2 The Arabic qānūn today is a large psaltery played with great virtuosity in Middle Eastern orchestras, and is a direct descendant of the forerunner of the European psaltery.

‖**káns** (kɑːns). *India.* [a. Hindi *kans*, f. Skr. *kāśa*.] A large grass, *Saccharum spontaneum*.

1874 E. F. T. ATKINSON et al. *Statistical Acct. N.-W. Provinces India* I. 89 The very destructive weed *káns*.. yields a good coarse grass for thatching. **1884** *Encycl. Brit.* XVII. 234/2 Cultivators dare not leave their lands fallow, even for a single year, for the ground would be immediately occupied by rank *káns* grass. **1918** R. N. PARKER *Forest Flora Punjab* 535 *Saccharum spontaneum*... Vern. *káns*, *káhi*, *kán*. Throughout the plains of the Punjab.

Kansa (ˈkænzə). Also **Kansas, Kanzas**, etc. [Native name.] A Siouan Indian people formerly of Kansas and now in Oklahoma; also known as KAW; a member of this people; the name of their language. Also *attrib.* or as *adj.*

1722 D. COXE *Descr. Carolana* i. 11 The Southerly of these two Rivers, is that of the Ousoutiwy upon which dwell..the Kansæ, Mintou, Erabacha and others. **1806** WILKINSON in Z. M. Pike *Acct. Expeditions Sources Mississippi* (1810) 108 You may attach to this deputation..the same number of Kanses chiefs. **1847** D. COYNER *Lost Trappers* (1859) 41 They were informed of the trade made by Captain Williams and the chief of the Kansas village. **1848** E. BRYANT *California* 41, I asked him if he was a Kansas. **1907** F. W. HODGE *Handbk. Amer. Indians* I. 654/1 The Kansa figured but slightly in the history of the country until after the beginning of the 19th century. **1933** L. BLOOMFIELD *Lang.* iv. 72 The Siouan family includes many languages, such as ..Kansa. **1957** *Encycl. Brit.* XX. 714/1 The principal Siouan tribes were..in the west, Dakota and Assimiboin,.. tribes speaking Dhegiha, viz., Omaha, Ponca, Kansas, [etc.].

kansamah, variant of KHANSAMAH.

Kansan (ˈkænzən), *sb.* and *a.* [f. *Kansas*, the name of one of the United States: see -AN.]

A. *sb.* A native or inhabitant of the State of Kansas; = KANSIAN.

1868 J. N. HOLLOWAY *Hist. Kansas* 574 At a favorable opportunity the Kansans seized the Ruffians,..and held them for trial. **1924** M. CRETCHER (*title*) The Kansan. **1964** *Amer. Folk Music Occasional* I. 40 Now I am teamed up with another singer. He's a Kansan like myself. **1973** *Times* 9 Nov. 12/1 The editor of the *Journal* of Salina, Kansas.. suggests Kansans are longing for Mr Nixon to make a last-minute comeback.

B. *adj. Geol.* Of, pertaining to, or designating the second Pleistocene glaciation of North America, which was probably contemporary with the Mindel glaciation in the Alps. Also *absol.*, the Kansan glaciation or the deposits it produced.

1894 in J. Geikie *Gt. Ice Age* (ed. 3) xlii. 755 While the formation in Kansas is subordinately divisible, it appears to be an essential unity, and therefore the name *Kansan formation* is selected..as a convenient designation of the outermost drift sheet. **1896, 1934, 1957** [see ILLINOIAN *a.*].

Kansas City. [City in Missouri, U.S.A.] Used *attrib.* with ref. to a style of big-band jazz which evolved in Kansas City in the 1930s.

1946 *Hollywood Q.* July 449 We have..Kansas City jazz. **1955** L. FEATHER *Encycl. Jazz* i. 22 Kansas City jazz was brewing in the bands of Benny Moten and Andy Kirk. **1958** P. GAMMOND *Decca Bk. Jazz* ix. 116 A further facet of Kansas City jazz: the singularity of the beat which it evolved to underline the inspiration of its soloists, and of its principal orchestral exponent, the Count Basie band. **1959** M. T. WILLIAMS *Art of Jazz* (1960) xviii. 188 Charlie Parker is an exponent of the Kansas City style in general and Lester Young in particular.

†**Kansian** (ˈkænzɪən). *Obs.* [f. as KANSAN *sb.* + -IAN.] = KANSAN *sb.*

1855 W. WHITMAN *Leaves of Grass* 58 Not only the free Utahan, Kansian, or Arkansian. **1873** J. H. BEADLE *Undevel. West* 214 It was laid out by a town company of ambitious Kansians. **1878** —— *Western Wilds* ix. 133 Discount sixty per cent when a Kansian talks about snakes. **1879** W. WHITMAN *Specimen Days* (1882–3) 141 We found a train ready and a crowd of hospitable Kansians to take us on to Lawrence.

kant, obs. form of CANT *a.*, and of CANT *sb.*¹, esp. in sense 5; also an oblique arm of a pier.

1793 SMEATON *Edystone L.* §51 The bottom projection, which has been called the Kant, and which fills up the angle formed between the uprights and the sloping surface of the rock. **1861** SMILES *Engineers* II. VII. vii. 217 *note*, Two great piers, one..the straight part extending outwards about 154 yards, from which there were to be two kants of about 64 yards each. *Ibid.* 219 The moment the vessel gets within the outer angles of the two return arms or kants, she may be said to be in or out of the harbour, as the case may be.

‖**kantar** (kænˈtɑː(r)). Also 7 kintar, 7– cantar. [Arab. *qinṭār*, pl. *qanāṭīr*, ad. (prob. through Syriac) L. *centēnārium* CENTENARY *sb.*¹ In OF. *quantar*, *canter*, med.L. *cantār(i)um* (Du Cange), It. *cantáro*. The form *qinṭār* is represented by OF. *quintar*, Sp. and F. *quintal*, QUINTAL.

(Sp. *cántara*, *cántaro*, a wine-measure, is unconnected.)]

A weight, properly 100 (Arabic) pounds, but varying considerably in different parts of the Mediterranean; also, a vessel containing this weight of any article.

1555 EDEN *Decades* 229 One Cantar is a hundreth pounde weight. **1615** W. BEDWELL *Arab. Trudg.* N ij b, s.v. *Rethl*, Now an hundred Rethels do make a Cantar, or Kintar as some do pronounce it, that is an hundred weight. **1773** BRYDONE *Sicily* xvii. (1809) 186 Mortars to throw a hundred cantars of cannon-ball or stones. **1802–3** tr. *Pallas's Trav.* (1812) I. 488 Vessels sailing under the Turkish flag are paid about one-third less for their freight, computed per Kantar. **1894** *Times* 6 Nov. 5/6 The Egyptian cotton crop is estimated at nearly 5,500,000 kantars (the kantar = 99 lb.).

†**kantch.** *Obs. rare*⁻¹. App. the dialect word *canch* (see *E.D.D.* s.v., and KENCH¹) 'slice, small addition, pile', used for the sake of a rime.

1608 TOPSELL *Serpents* (1658) 618 Of green hogs-fennel, take the lowest branches Of Nosewort sharp, so much: then to them joyn A like proportion of Roes horn in weight and kantches.

Kantean *a.*, var. KANTIAN *a.*

kantel, obs. form of CANTLE *sb.* and *v.*

‖**kantele** (ˈkantiliː). [Finn.] A form of zither used in Finland and Karelia.

1921 *Glasgow Herald* 24 Nov. 8 Eastern Karelia, where the kantele players still survive, is the home of the most characteristic Finnish music. **1960** G. TAYLOR *Mortlake* III. ix. 272 The kantele..was a large wooden box, pentagonal and tapering at one end. The five strings were stretched the length of the instrument. **1969** *Listener* 24 July 124/1 The best bits were musical: a lovely Lapp pentatonic chant, a zither-like instrument called a *kantele*, and, of course, liberal doses of Sibelius.

kantharos: see CANTHARUS.

Kantian (ˈkæntɪən), *a.* and *sb.* Also **Kantean.** [f. the name of the celebrated German philosopher Immanuel Kant (1724–1804) + -IAN.]

A. *adj.* Of, pertaining to, or connected with Kant or his philosophy.

Kant's characteristic doctrine was that a critical analysis of our experience discloses: (*a*) in logic, that thought actively synthesizes the matter of sense under certain laws ('forms' and 'categories') which are *a priori* determinable as universally valid for and within experience; (*b*) in ethics, that an absolutely valid moral 'law' is similarly determinable, whence the reality of God, Freedom, and Immortality is deducible as 'practically necessary', even though to speculative thought the nature and very existence of the non-phenomenal or noümenal must remain 'problematic'.

Hence *Kantian* tends to connote 'apriorism' or 'transcendentalism', viz. the view that certain necessary truths are determinable as implications of our logical and moral experience. (R. R. Marett.)

1796 F. A. NITSCH *Gen. View Kant's Princ. concerning Man* 1, I venture to address the Learned and Philosophers, on the Kantean principles. **1798** A. F. M. WILLICH *Elem. Critical Philos.* 22 Plattner..has employed rational scepticism against the Kantian system. **1811** H. C. ROBINSON *Diary* 29 Mar. (1967) 3, I doubt the concurrence of this explanation of a general idea with the Kantian theory. **1817** *Edin. Rev.* XXVIII. 491 Mr. Coleridge has ever since ..been..floating or sinking in fine Kantean categories. **1858** W. R. PIRIE *Inq. Hum. Mind* II. iv. 194 A strong bias in favour of the Kantian metaphysics. **1862** H. SPENCER *First Princ.* I. iii. §15 (1875) 49 Shall we then take refuge in the Kantian doctrine? shall we say that Space and Time are forms of the intellect—*a priori* laws or conditions of the conscious mind? **1877** E. CAIRD *Philos. Kant* 666 The ultimate decision..as to the Kantian Criticism of Pure Reason must turn upon the opposition of perception and conception, as factors which reciprocally imply, and yet exclude, each other.

B. *sb.* One who holds the philosophical system of Kant.

1799 COLERIDGE *Notebooks* (1957) I. 390 Brown was no Kantian & probably held nothing but high degrees of Probability possible. **1805** J. MACKINTOSH in R. J. Mackintosh *Mem. Life Sir J. Mackintosh* (1836) I. 260, I own to you that I am not a whit more near being a Kantian than I was before. **1832** *Edin. Rev.* LVI. 164 *note*, The Kantians 'make a broad distinction between the Understanding and Reason'.

Hence **ˈKantianism**; so **ˈKantism, ˈKantist, ˈKantite** (*rare*).

1803 BEDDOES *Hygëia* IX. 205 *note*, I hate metaphysics.. that is, the school-learning of old and modern Kantianism. **1819** *Pantologia* s.v., Kantian Philosophy, Kantism, or Critical Philosophy. **1825** CARLYLE *Schiller* (1845) App. 290 He answered me like an accomplished Kantite. **1830** MACKINTOSH *Eth. Philos.* Wks. 1846 I. 214 The..professor ..has rapidly shot through Kantianism. **1839** CARLYLE *Misc., St. Germ. Lit.* (1872) I. 67 The Kantist, in direct contradiction to Locke and all his followers..commences from within. **1845** MAURICE *Mor. & Met. Philos.* in *Encycl. Metrop.* II. 667/1 Kantism, or the attempt to build upon this doctrine of a practical and speculative reason, has inevitably led to the loss of all these good consequences. **1886** SIDGWICK *Hist. Ethics* (1892) 271 Kantism in the ethical thought of modern Europe holds a place somewhat analogous to that occupied by the teaching of Price and Reid among ourselves.

‖**ˈkantikoy, canticoy, kintecoy.** *Amer. Ind.* Also 7 cantica, -co; kinticoy, 9 kentikaw, kantickie. [An Algonquin word.] A dance practised by some of the American Indians on various occasions; a dancing-match. Also *transf.*

1670 D. DENTON *Descr. New York* (1845) 11 At their Cantica's or dancing Matches, where all persons that come are freely entertain'd. **1671** *New Jersey Archives* (1880) I. 73 The Proposall..was to cause a Kinticoy to bee held. **1675** in J. Easton *Narr.* (1858) 126 Several Indyans..are in a few Dayes to have a great Kintecoy at Seaquetalke. **1683** PENN *Wks.* (1782) IV. 309 Their worship consists of two parts, sacrifice and cantico. **1701** C. WOLLEY *Jrnl. New York* (1860) 37 Their Kin-tau-Kauns, or time of sacrificing is at the beginning of winter. **1860** BARTLETT *Dict. Amer.*, *Canticoy*,..an Iroquois Indian word..It is still used by aged people in New York and on Long Island. **1866** WHITTIER *Marg. Smith's Jrnl.* Pr. Wks. 1889 I. 144 Wauwoonemeen..told us that they did still hold their Kentikaw, or Dance for the Dead.

Hence **ˈkantikoy (kintecoy,** etc.) *v.*

1649 *Broad Advice* in 2 *N.Y. Hist. Coll.* II. 258 (Cent.) The first of these Indians..wished them to let him kintekaeye—being a dance performed by them as a religious rite. **1675** in J. Easton *Narr.* (1858) 126 A Speciall Warrant ..to Demand the Indyans Armes of Rockaway and Seaquatalke, who are to Kintecoy there.

kantref, kantry, obs. ff. CANTREF.

KANU, Kanu (ˈkɑːnuː). [f. the initials of the words *Kenya African National Union*.] The name of a Kenyan political party.

1960 *Times* 6 June 6/5 Kenyatta was recently elected as President of Kanu. **1961** *Economist* 17 June 1244/1 The divisional and provincial boards..are manned by officials and trusty Africans of the old school. KANU branches have asked..to have representation on these boards. **1962** [see *KADU, KADU]. **1969** *Reporter* (Nairobi) 13 June 5/2 The KANU Government had been sustained by the faith and confidence of the people. **1971** *Daily Nation* (Nairobi) 10 Apr. 2/3 The people of Kisumu District are fully behind him, the Government and Kanu.

Kanuck, var. CANUCK.

kanuka (ˈkɑːnʊka). *N.Z.* [Maori.] A small, white-flowered, evergreen tree, *Leptospermum ericoides*; also called *white tea-tree*.

1906 T. F. CHEESEMAN *Man. N.Z. Flora* 161 *L[eptospermum] ericoides*... Abundant from the North Cape to the Bluff... Kanuka; Maru. **1929** W. MARTIN *N.Z. Nature Bk.* II. 84 The endemic Kanuka or Tea-tree..is restricted to low levels. **1963** *Weekly News* (Auckland) 26 June 28 (*caption*) Kanuka plants being lined out in rows in the outdoor section of the nursery. **1966** *Ibid.* 1 June 16/3 Smoke is drifting, blue and hazy, through the kanukas above the campfire. **1966** *Encycl. N.Z.* II. 406/2 Kanuka grows into a small tree up to 40 or more feet high.

Kanuri (kə'nu:rɪ). [Native name.] A group of Negroid peoples living in the region of Lake Chad, in north-eastern Nigeria; their language, which belongs to the Central Saharan group.
1876 *Encycl. Brit.* IV. 61/1 The leading people of the country, called Bornuese or Kanuri, present a perfect specimen of the negro form and features. **1888** *Ibid.* XXIII. 334 Barth on linguistic grounds grouped them with the Kanuri of Bornu, who are undoubtedly Negroes. **1932** W. L. GRAFF *Lang.* 434 Kanuri, of the Nilo-Chadian group. **1959** *Listener* 29 Oct. 740/1 The.. Kanuri of Nigeria. **1966** J. H. GREENBERG *Languages of Africa* (ed. 2) 132 In agreement with Eastern Sudanic Kanuri has a *tə-* prefix for the causative in a few verbs of the 'strong' conjugation.

kanvas, kanyon, etc.: see CAN-.

‖**kanzu** ('kænzu:). [Swahili.] A long white cotton or linen robe as worn by East African men.
1902 *Westm. Gaz.* 24 Nov. 2/1 Dressed in a white kanzu, or long shirt, with a tweed coat over it,.. he was an attractive little figure. **1920** *Chambers's Jrnl.* Sept. 572/2 He wears.. the white linen Kanzu or long robe rather like a nightgown. **1966** B. KIMENYE *Kalasanda Revisited* 17 He was wearing a kanzu in deference, no doubt, to the Sabbath, instead of his week-day costume. **1970** *Times* 20 May 7/1 He was wearing a kanzu (cotton robe) over his shirt.

kaoliang ('keɪəʊljæŋ). [Chinese; lit. 'high grain'.] The Indian millet, *Sorghum vulgare.*
1904 *Westm. Gaz.* 5 Sept. 7/1 The kao-ling (millet). **1909** *Official Hist. Russo-Jap. War* (ed. 2) I. vi. 56 The advanced guard.. erected screens of *kao-liang* and trees at every point. **1923** *Chambers's Jrnl.* 40/2, I found the god of rain.. glaring at me from the middle of a parched kaoliang patch. **1928** *Brit. Chem. Abstracts* B. 443 A relatively easy-bleaching soda pulp can be obtained from the stalk of 'Kaoliang'. **1945** R. HARGREAVES *Enemy at Gate* 265 The field of fire was invariably obscured by meadows of high-standing *kao-ling.* **1958** A. N. STEWARD *Man. Vasc. Plants Lower Yangtze Valley* 485 *Sorghum vulgare*..(Kao Liang; Tall Millet)... Cultivated in warm countries.

kaolin ('kɑ:əlɪn, 'keɪəlɪn). Also 8 **kaulin,** 9 **kaoline.** [a. F. *kaolin*, ad. Chinese *kao-, kau-ling*, name of a mountain (f. *kao* high + *ling* hill) northwest of the town of King-tê-chên in North China, whence the material was orig. obtained.
The '*matière appelée kao-lin*' was made known in Europe in 1712 by Father d'Entrecolles, 'Lettre sur la fabrication de la porcellaine à King-te-ching' (in *Lettres édifiantes*, &c. *des missions étrangères* III. 210). His F. spelling approximately represented the Chinese word, which would be better expressed in Eng. by *kaüling* or *kauwling* ('kɑ:ʊlɪŋ).]
A fine white clay produced by the decomposition of feldspar, used in the manufacture of porcelain; first employed by the Chinese, but subsequently obtained also in Cornwall, Saxony, France (near Limoges), United States, etc.
1727–41 CHAMBERS *Cycl.*, The first earth, called Kaulin, is beset with glittering corpuscles. **1753** *Ibid., Suppl.* s.v., Persons who have been at the China works, say, that the porcelain is made of equal quantities of *petuntse* and *kaolin.* **1807** C. W. JANSON *Stranger Amer.* 229 Different kinds of clay are found here, among which it is believed, is the real kaolin, to which the porcelain of China owes its reputation. **1813** BAKEWELL *Introd. Geol.* (1815) 404 Decomposed white felspar, or kaolin, produced from the granite rocks of Cornwall. **1876** PAGE *Adv. Text-bk. Geol.* vii. 130 Fine impalpable clay known as Kaolin or China clay.
attrib. **1875** *Ure's Dict. Arts* I. 809 Most of the kaolin-clays contain some spangles of mica.

kaolinic (kɑ:ə-, keɪə'lɪnɪk), *a.* [f. prec. + -IC. Cf. F. *kaolinique.*] Of the nature of kaolin.
1879 J. J. YOUNG *Ceram. Art* 56 Natural porcelain is made from kaolinic clay.

kaolinite ('kɑ:ə-, 'keɪəlɪnaɪt). *Min.* [f. as prec. + -ITE[1].] A general term for those porcelain clays, found in masses of minute crystalline scales, of which kaolin is the typical variety.
1867 *Amer. Jrnl. Sc.* Ser. II. XLIII. 351 We propose for it [the name] Kaolinite, in allusion to the material which furnishes it most commonly and abundantly. **1875** *Ure's Dict. Arts* I. 809. **1879** RUTLEY *Stud. Rocks* xiv. 285 By the careful levigation of some clays, Dr. John Percy has eliminated minute, but beautifully-developed, crystals of Kaolinite.

kaolinitic (keɪəlɪ'nɪtɪk), *a. Min.* [f. KAOLINIT(E + -IC.] Of the nature of or containing kaolinite.
1885 *Nature* 8 Oct. 559/1 The interstitial dusty, siliceous, and kaolinitic paste has only crystallised in part. **1940** *Mineral. Abstr.* VII. 427 The formation of kaolinitic-nontronitic clays is primarily due to the hydrothermal processes. **1965** G. J. WILLIAMS *Econ. Geol. N.Z.* xx. 364/2 Clay from well-weathered greywacke, transported and deposited in fresh water is kaolinitic and of fine grain size. **1971** *Nature* 6 Aug. 371/2 The thin, curious, kaolinitic bands called tonsteins discovered more recently in the coalfields of Western Europe.

kaolinize ('kɑ:ə-, 'keɪəlɪnaɪz), *v.* [f. KAOLIN + -IZE.] *trans.* To convert into kaolin. Hence **kaolini'zation.**
1874 RAYMOND *Statist. Mines & Mining* 339 The granite, which is uniformly decomposed to a great depth, becoming more or less perfectly kaolinized. **1878** LAWRENCE tr. *Cotta's Rocks Class.* 207 A sign of commencing decomposition (Kaolinising of the felspar). **1886** PRESTWICH *Geol.* I. 57 Some Roman mill-stones of granite.. were found to be converted throughout into a kaolinised grit. **1886** SIR J. W. DAWSON *Inaug. Addr. Brit. Assoc.*, [Not] a process of kaolinisation so perfect as to eliminate all alkaline matters.

kaon ('keɪɒn). *Nuclear Physics.* Also †**kayon.** [f. *ka(y)-* (repr. the pronunc. of the letter *K* in K(-)MESON, K(-)PARTICLE) + -ON[1].] Any of a group of mesons which have masses several times those of the pions and non-zero hypercharge, and on decaying usually produce two or three pions or else a muon and a neutrino.
1958 *Phil. Mag.* III. 330 Writing $m_K{}^+$, $m_\pi{}^+$, $m_\pi{}^0$, m_μ, for the kayon, charged pion, neutral pion, and muon masses. **1958** *Proc. 2nd U.N. Internat. Conf. Peaceful Uses Atomic Energy* XXX. 44/2 When the newly produced kaons disintegrate, only half of them should exhibit the short lifetime 10^{-10} sec. **1960** *Rev. Mod. Physics* XXXII. 479/1 Kayons were clearly observed at least as early as 1947. **1960** *McGraw-Hill Encycl. Sci. & Technol.* IV. 543 *K*-meson (kaon). **1963** K. W. FORD *World of Elem. Particles* vi. 180 The weak interactions.. act in their own leisurely fashion and bring about the kaon decay after about 10^{-10} sec. **1968** *New Scientist* 18 Jan. 144/2 It has generally been supposed that cosmic-ray muons are the product of the radioactive decay of the mesons known as pions and kaons. **1972** G. L. WICK *Elem. Particles* iv. 77 Both the lambda and the kaon decay into strongly interacting particles, but the lifetimes are very long.
Hence **ka'onic** *a.*, of or pertaining to a kaon, or an atom having a kaon orbiting the nucleus.
1965 *McGraw-Hill Yearbk. Sci. & Technol.* 181/1 (In table), Kaonic state. **1969** *Physical Rev. Lett.* XXII. 1238/1 The ultimate ability of kaonic x rays to yield information on the nuclear-size parameters requires the accurate determination of the kaon-nucleus potential. **1972** *Physics Bull.* Mar. 149/3 The study of kaonic atoms may provide us with information about the extreme surface region of the nucleus. **1972** *Sci. Amer.* Nov. 106/3 Increasing the charge of the nucleus shrinks the kaonic orbits and brings the kaons closer to the nucleus.

kap-: see CAP-.

‖**kapa,** another form of TAPA.
1909 in *Cent. Dict.* Suppl. **1913** R. BROOKE *Let.* 28 Oct. (1968) 521 Their women held up pieces of 'kapa'—which is bark beaten into a stiff cloth, and covered with a brown pattern.

‖**kapai** ('kæpaɪ), *a.* and *adv. N.Z.* Also **carpi, ka pai.** [Maori *ka pai.*] Good, fine; also as an exclamation of pleasure or approval.
1836 W. B. MARSHALL *Personal Narr. Two Visits N.Z.* II. 256 'Kapai! Good!' being the only vocable by which satisfaction at the receipt of kindness is communicable. **1840** E. HOBSON *Let.* 29 June in A. Drummond *Married & gone to N.Z.* (1960) 50 My dear husband.. is on excellent terms with the natives, who call him the Carpi (good) Governor. **1861** *Taranaki Punch* 2 Jan. 2/1 The pudding turned out *kapai* until we came to cut it. **1918** *N.Z.E.F. Chrons.* 27 Feb. 37/1 The evening was simply 'kapai'. **1933** F. E. BAUME *Half-Caste* v. 55 You're looking kapai, Ngaire. **1938** R. D. FINLAYSON *Brown Man's Burden* 30 They can do South Sea hulas... Ka pai! they're very good. **1960** N. HILLIARD *Maori Girl* II. xiii. 153 '*Kapai!*' shouted Henry.

‖**kaparrang, -ring** (kə'pɑ:rəŋ, -rɪŋ). *S. Afr.* Also **caparran, kaproen.** [ad. Jav. *gamparan.*] A wooden sandal worn by the Cape Malays.
1867 M. KOLLISCH *Mussulman Population Cape Good Hope* 23 Both sexes in some instances carefully ignoring the use of shoes, rather preferring clogs, called *kaparrans* (which is a small piece of wood with two slips joined underneath, and a wooden knob on the upper side). **1870** *Cape Monthly Mag.* Aug. 109 A Malay beauty.. clatters upon '*caparrans*' (a species of wooden buskin). **1911** *State* Dec. 596 (Pettman), The old coloured woman walking carefully in *kaproens.* **1953** *Cape Argus* (Mag. Section) 28 Feb. 3/6 Malays, with 'Kapparings' on their feet,.. were our fish vendors. **1972** I. D. DU PLESSIS *Cape Malays* (ed. 3) iii. 33 Kaparrings (probably from the Javanese gamparan: wooden sandals with a knot to push between the big and second toes) are still in use in the Mosques.

kape, obs. form of CAPE *sb.*[1], COPE *sb.*[1]

‖**kapelle** (ka'pɛlə). Also **cap-.** [Ger., ad. med.L. *capella* CHAPEL.] In Germany, a musical establishment consisting of a band or orchestra, with or without a choir, such as used to be maintained at most of the German courts. Hence ‖**kapellmeister** (ka'pɛl'maɪstər), the leader or conductor of a kapelle, chapel choir, or orchestra.
1838 *Penny Cycl.* XII. 341/2 In 1816 he became Kapellmeister to the king of Würtemberg. **1873** OUIDA *Pascarel* I. 193 He was kapellmeister in our burgh. **1880** POHL in Grove *Dict. Mus.* I. 705/1 To secure the young composer as his second Capellmeister.

‖**Kapenaar** ('kɑ:pənɑ:r). *S. Afr.* Also **Kaapenaar.** [Afrikaans *kapenaar*, f. *kaap* Cape + *-enaar* pers. suffix.] **1.** An inhabitant of Cape Town or of the Cape Peninsula and its environs.
1834 *Cape of Good Hope Lit. Gaz.* IV. 180 (Pettman), The Capenaars have.. attempted to justify the holding of human flesh in bondage by appeals to Scripture. **1902** *Dowey's Early Annals of Kobstad* 99 (Pettman), He was a Kaapenaar. **1946** *Spotlight* (Johannesburg) 13 Dec. 2 b Kapenaars.. feel that the Cabinet is really learning something of agricultural economy. **1959** *Cape Times* 9 Mar. 10/5 A statement more pleasing to.. all true Kapenaars than that the long battle for the preservation of the building has been won. **1973** *Ibid.* 22 Jan. 5 Is it the mountain which makes Kaapenaars so allergic to change?

2. A large, silver-coloured, marine, food fish, *Argyrozona* (or *Polystegamus*) *argyrozona*, of the family Denticidæ.
1902 J. D. F. GILCHRIST in *Trans. S. Afr. Philos. Soc.* XL. 223 At Port Elizabeth it is called not Silver-fish, but Kapenaar. **1913** W. W. THOMPSON *Sea Fisheries of Cape Colony* 154 *Dentex argyrozona*... Silver-fish; Kaapenaar (Port Elizabeth). **1947** K. H. BARNARD *Pictorial Guide S. Afr. Fishes* 157 Silverfish, Kapenaar (*Polystegamus argyrozona*)... Table Bay to Natal, down to 70 fathoms. One of the best known, and economically important South African fishes. As well as being sold fresh, it is cured and smoked and sold as 'haddock'. **1962** *Pretoria News* 5 Jan. 4/2 The Japanese come for what they call red bream or 'red fish', which includes the red roman, 74, kaapenaar and silver fish.

kaper, kapnite, var. CAPER, CAPNITE.

kapnography (kæp'nɒgrəfɪ). [f. Gr. καπνό-ς smoke + -γραφία writing.] Name for a mode of producing designs or pictures on a smoked surface of glass, etc. Hence **kapno'graphic** *a.*
1890 in *Cent. Dict.*

‖**kapok** ('keɪpɒk, formerly 'kɑ:pək). Also **kapoc,** CAPOC. [Malay *kāpoq.*] A large tropical tree, *Ceiba casearia*; silk cotton, the fibre produced from the soft covering of the seeds within its fruit, used to stuff mattresses, cushions, etc. Also *attrib.*
1735 T. SALMON *Mod. Hist.* XXVII. vi. 186 There is also [in Guinea] the Capot Tree, that bears a sort of Cotton. **1750** [see CAPOC]. **1795** tr. *C.P. Thunberg's Trav. Europe, Afr. & Asia* II. 284 The cotton which encloses the seed in the capsule, is called Kapock, and is not used for spinning, but for making mattrasses, bolsters, and pillows. **1858** in SIMMONDS *Dict. Trade.* **1881** WATTS *Dict. Chem.* VIII. 1144 The kapok-tree.. of Java and the Indian Archipelago bears a seed resembling.. that of the cotton plant. *Ibid.*, Kapok cake. **1887** MOLONEY *Forestry W. Afr.* 184. **1888** *Hatter's Gaz.* 1 Mar. 143/2 In Java, where it is met with abundantly, kapok has attracted considerable attention... It was first imported into Europe in 1851. **1907** *Yesterday's Shopping* (1969) 692/2 Life belts. 'Kapok' pillow belt. **1940** E. J. H. CORNER *Wayside Trees Malaya* I. 436 The Kapok is grown mainly for the wool obtained from the fruits. **1958** J. SLIMMING *Temiar Jungle* v. 77 Chabok.. raised his blow-pipe, quickly inserting a dart into the mouthpiece and packing the end with a small twist of raw kapok. **1963** J. KIRKUP *Tropic Temper* 33 It had a good firm mattress stuffed with locally-grown fresh kapok. *Ibid.* 127 The kapok tree's gaunt appearance with its thin branches stuck out at right-angles to the dead-straight trunk, has earned it the nickname of P.W.D. tree. (Because people think it resembles a telegraph pole erected by the Public Works Department.) **1966** D. FORBES *Heart of Malaya* vi. 66 The kapok tree, called the midnight horror, with its long seed pods hanging down like drooping fingers, and the fan palm were common enough. **1974** L. DEIGHTON *Spy Story* xx. 209 We stood around.. wearing kapok-lined white snow-suits.

Kaposi (kə'pəʊsɪ). *Path.* The name of M. K. *Kaposi* (1837–1902), Hungarian dermatologist, who described the condition in 1872 (*Arch. f. Dermatol. und Syphilol.* IV. 265), used (now as ***Kaposi's sarcoma***) to designate a progressive disease characterized by multiple malignant tumours esp. of the lymph nodes, or of the skin of the extremities, and occurring esp. in cases of defective immunity.
1897 *Brit. Med. Jrnl.* 2 Oct. 866/2 (*heading*) A case of idiopathic multiple pigmented sarcoma (Kaposi type). **1905** *Brit. Jrnl. Dermatol.* XVII. 138 The case is a typical but relatively early one of the so-called idiopathic multiple pigment sarcoma.. of Kaposi. **1916** *Ibid.* XXVIII. 334 Dr. S.E. Dore did not think this was a case of Kaposi's sarcoma. **1966** *Arch. Dermatol.* XCIII. 554/1 Three adults with Kaposi's sarcoma of the lymph nodes showed a clinical picture simulating a malignant lymphoma or a granulomatous disease in the absence of characteristic skin lesions. **1985** *Guardian* 22 Aug. 3/7 Many Aids patients.. develop a hitherto rare skin cancer called Kaposi's sarcoma, previously seen mainly in kidney patients.

kapp (kæp). [Named after Gisbert Kapp, a celebrated designer of dynamos, who adopted this unit for convenience in practical use. Cf. *ampere, ohm, volt.*] A workshop unit of magnetic lines of force, = 6000 times the centimetre-gramme-second unit.
1891 L. CLARK *Dict. Metr. Meas.* 50.

kappa ('kæpə). [Gr. κάππα.] **1.** The tenth letter of the Greek alphabet, *K*, *κ*.
c **1400** [see LAMBDA 1]. **1746** T. NUGENT tr. *De Port Royal's New Method of Learning Gk. Tongue* I. ii. 3 The Greeks have 24 Letters, whose Figure, Name, and Power are as followeth:.. Thêta.. Iôta.. Cappa.. Lambda [etc.]. *Ibid.* xi. 41 *Κάππα, Kappa*, from the Hebrew *Cap* or *Caph*, or rather from the ancient *Kappa.* **1791** R. P. KNIGHT *Analytical Ess. on Gk. Alphabet* i. 5 After the invention of the Kappa, the simple Gamma seems to have fallen into disuse in some dialects. *Ibid.*, The harshest and most emphatical palatial consonant.. is the Kappa. **1871** [see CHAPTER *sb.* 5 c]. **1948** D. DIRINGER *Alphabet* II. viii. 453 The *qoph*, which expresses the Semitic emphatic *k*, was adopted [*sc.* into the Greek alphabet] as *kappa*, differentiated from *koppa.*
2. *Biol.* An agent in some strains of *Paramecium aurelia* that confers on cells possessing it the property of producing a substance toxic to *Paramecium* cells lacking it, and exists as small cytoplasmic particles (***kappa***

particles) capable of reproducing independently of the cell containing them and of infecting other *Paramecium* cells; these particles collectively. Freq. *attrib.*

1945 T. M. SONNEBORN in *Amer. Naturalist* LXXIX. 319 The alternative characters, killer and non-killer, are determined by a pair of allelic genes, K and k, and a cytoplasmic factor, which may be called kappa. Clones are killers only when both the dominant gene K and the cytoplasmic factor kappa are present; they are non-killers when kappa is absent, regardless of genic constitution. *Ibid.* 332 How can the unequal division of kappa at fission be accounted for? **1947** *Genetics* XXXII. 106 Under conditions in which the concentration of kappa decreases, two methods may be used to find the number of kappa particles per original killer cell. **1951** G. H. BOURNE *Cytol. & Cell Physiol.* (ed. 2) ii. 91 The factor kappa can reproduce itself in the cytoplasm but only if the gene *K* is present in the nucleus. **1965** PEACOCKE & DRYSDALE *Molecular Basis Heredity* ii. 7 These so-called kappa particles are probably best regarded as self-determining invaders and not as part of the normal cell. **1969** J. R. PREER in *Res. Protozool.* 174 Kappa itself has been shown.. to respire and utilize glucose and sucrose *in vitro*. The presence in kappa of the biochemical apparatus required for such a sophisticated metabolism clearly eliminates the possibility that it is a virus. *Ibid.* 183 The kappas of stocks 7 and 51.

‖**kappie** (ˈkapi). *S. Afr.* Also 9 **cappie, kap(p)je.** [Afrikaans, = Du. *kapje* dim. of *kap* hood.] A sun-bonnet or coal-scuttle bonnet.

1834 A. SMITH *Diary* (1939) I. 92 All that a farmer's daughter can do or ever does is to make cappies. **1871** J. MACKENZIE *Ten Yrs. North of Orange River* iv. 62 Her taste as to colours and shapes in kapjes, handkerchiefs and dresses. **1883** 'R. Iron' *Story Afr. Farm* I. ii. 26 Em took off her big brown Kappje and began.. to fan her red face with it. **1902** *Daily Chron.* 18 Mar. 3/4 Women, in big, flapping kapjes, were at work on household business. **1939** S. CLOETE *Watch for Dawn* iii. 47 In her anger she had pulled her kappie from her head. **1966** E. PALMER *Plains of Camdeboo* xviii. 295 In burst Hannie Rafferty, her blue kappie askew, her round face red. **1974** *Africana Notes & News* Sept. 93 The strong contrast of her black kappie against the white kappie of the woman at her side.

‖**kapu** (ˈkapu), *a.* and *sb.* [Hawaiian.] = TABOO, TABU *a.* and *sb.*

1933 *Ancient Hawaiian Civilization* (Bishop Museum, Honolulu) 35 The kapu was the ancient social and religious law of Hawaii... The word itself can best be translated 'forbidden'. The king and all his family, his clothes, and his possessions, were kapu because of the ali'i's sacredness. All the rules and prohibitions established by the ali'i.. were called the 'kapu system'. *Ibid.* 71 These prayers and the feast removed the kapu on the new dwelling. **1954** J. SHERIDAN in J. Macdonald *Lethal Sex* (1959) 151 That room is *kapu*. Definitely not the background for the sort of shindig his wife throws. **1968** *Awake!* 8 May 21/1 Under this [Polynesian] pagan religious system there was a set of taboos called *kapu*,.. that controlled almost every action of every person.

kapur (ˈkæpə(r)). [Malay.] A large dipterocarp timber tree of the genus *Dryobalanops*, esp. *D. aromatica*, native to Malaya, Sumatra, and Borneo; also, the wood of a tree of this kind.

1935 I. H. BURKILL *Dict. Econ. Products Malay Peninsula* I. 863 There is probably a total of more than 500,000 acres of 'kapur' forest in the Peninsula. **1940** E. J. H. CORNER *Wayside Trees Malaya* I. 212 The *Kapur* may form almost pure forests, and it is at once distinguished by its beautiful, open, fine-leafed crown. **1956** *Handbk. Hardwoods* (Forest Prod. Res. Lab.) 125 Kapur grows to a height often exceeding 200 ft. **1963** *Engineering* 25 Oct. 525/2 Beams composed of four species, western hemlock, European redwood, jarrah and kapur. **1972** *Timber Trades Jrnl.* 13 May 39/2 Of the lesser species merbau and kapur are readily available.

kaput (kəˈpʊt), *a.* (in pred. use). *slang.* Also **kaputt.** [ad. G. *kaputt*, f. Fr. (*être*) *capot* (to be) without tricks in the card-game of piquet; see CAPOT *sb.*[1]] **a.** Finished, worn out; dead or destroyed. **b.** Rendered useless or unable to function.

1895 W. M. CONWAY *Alps from End to End* iii. 59 The thing would then go *wie's Donnerwetter* and the man would be *kaput* at once. [**1914** DUCHESS OF SUTHERLAND *Six Weeks at the War* p. xiv, When Prussian military despotism is 'Kaputt'—to use the Germans' favourite word about their foe, meaning 'done'.] **1924** *Glasgow Herald* 11 Dec. 7 The intellectual consciousness is kaput. *a* **1930** D. H. LAWRENCE *Last Poems* (1932) 286 So self-willed, self-centred, self-conscious people die The death of nothingness, worn-out machines, kaput! **1955** E. POUND *Classic Anthol.* I. 19 North gate, sorrow's edge, Purse kaput, nothing to pledge. **1959** J. BRAINE *Vodi* iv. 63 He could now see that his whole life was *kaputt*. **1972** *New Yorker* 9 Sept. 30 It's a real American tragedy—Wunderkind at twenty, Übermensch at thirty, kaputt at forty. **1975** J. SYMONS *Three Pipe Problem* xix. 220 Sherlock Holmes is finished. Finito. Kaput.

‖**kar, Kar** (kɑː(r)). *Physical Geogr.* Pl. **kare, kars;** also *erron.* **kar, karen.** [Ger.] = CIRQUE 2, CWM.

1893 *Geogr. Jrnl.* I. 352 The direct erosive action of ice in forming 'glacier-pots' (Karen) and inland lakes. **1905** *Jrnl. Geol.* XIII. 2 Above the shoulders the valley slopes are far from being regular; often they form cirque-like niches, at the bottoms of which little tarns occur. These are the *Kar* of the Alps, the 'corries' of Scotland. *Ibid.* 16 Now and then we find here mountains with a single corrie or *Kar*. *Ibid.*, There is a sharp crest line which separates the corries or *Kare* of opposite sides. **1957** G. E. HUTCHINSON *Treat. Limnol.* I. i. 59 Such amphitheaters are called *cirques* in the French-speaking parts of the Alps, *Kars* in the German-speaking regions, *cwms* in Wales, and *corries* in Scotland. All four terms have achieved some degree of international usage, but the first seems to have been the most widely employed. **1963** D. W. & E. E. HUMPHRIES tr. *Termier's Erosion & Sedimentation* v. 128 The heads of the fjords formed in this way are called *botn, dalbotn* or *saekkedaler*.. and differ from the true glacial cirque or *fjeldbotn*. They are almost the equivalent of the *trogschluss* or *kar* of the Alps.

kar, obs. form of CAR, CARE.

Karabagh (ˈkærəbɑː). Also **Carabagh.** The name of a region in the Soviet republic of Azerbaijan used *attrib.* or *ellipt.* to denote a thick knotted carpet or rug (orig.) made there, usually with a floral but occas. an animal pattern.

1900 J. K. MUMFORD *Oriental Rugs* ix. 118 The production of Karabaghs.. has of late been pushed forward without stint. **1962** C. W. JACOBSEN *Oriental Rugs* 227 Karabagh Rugs... Also spelled Carabagh... Where made: In the southern part of what used to be called Caucasia, now the Russian States of Armenia, Azerbaijan, and Nakichevan. **1973** *Country Life* 6 Dec. (Suppl.) 40g Karabagh rug... Caucasus dated 1876.

†**karabe** (ˈkɑːrabeɪ). *Obs.* [= F., It., Pg. *carabé* (also F., Pg. *karabé*), ad. Arab. *kahrubā*, a. Pers. *kāhrubā* 'attracting straws,' amber, f. *kāh* straw + *rubā* carrying off.] Yellow amber. ***karabe of Sodom***, bitumen.

1545 RAYNOLD *Byrth Mankynde* II. vi. (1634) 126 Karabe, otherwise named Amber. **1727-41** CHAMBERS *Cycl.*, *Amber*, *Succinum*, or *Karabe*. **1794** SULLIVAN *View Nat.* II. 105 The Karabe of Sodom.. is black, not very weighty and solid. **1799** G. SMITH *Laboratory* II. 443 Take one ounce of the whitest Karabe (Amber).

Hence **ka'rabic** *a.*, in ***karabic acid*** = succinic acid (*Syd. Soc. Lex.* 1887).

karabiner (kærəˈbiːnə(r)). *Mountaineering.* Also **carabiner,** *erron.* **karibiner.** [Shortened form of G. *karabiner-haken* spring-hook.] A coupling device consisting of a metal oval or D-shaped link with a gate protected against accidental opening. Cf. KRAB.

1932 *Amer. Alpine Jrnl.* 526 (*caption*) Safety snap (carabiner). **1933** G. D. ABRAHAM *Mod. Mountaineering* x. 182 Light pitons.. are used and karibiners. The latter are special oval-shaped rings with a hinge or swivel somewhat like that found on the end of a watch chain. **1942** K. A. HENDERSON *Amer. Alpine Club's Handbk. Amer. Mountaineering* vi. 124 *Snap-rings*, sometimes called by their German name, *karabiner*, are used to fasten the rope to the piton. They come in both oval and pear-shaped form. **1946** J. E. Q. BARFORD *Climbing in Brit.* ii. 25 These are called karibiners in Germany.. and consist of an oval steel ring with a spring loaded hinged link on one side. **1959** W. H. MURRAY *Five Frontiers* iv. 93 Round my waist I tied a loop of rope, clipped on a karabiner (a steel ring with a spring clip, used in rock-climbing). **1965** *New Scientist* 22 July 205/3 The karabiner is basically a hook which is closed by a pivoted arm that may or may not snap home on the latch. **1972** D. HASTON *In High Places* i. 7 Oval metal snaplinks, called carabiners. **1973** C. BONINGTON *Next Horizon* xii. 169 A jerk—you drop three inches... But you're alive! The knot in the sling attached to the karabiner in your waist harness had jammed on the gate of the karabiner, and had then freed itself, letting you drop those few inches.

‖**karaburan** (kærəˈbjʊərən). [Turk., f. *kara* black + *buran* whirlwind.] A hot dusty wind in Central Asia.

1903 J. T. BEALBY tr. *Hedin's Cent. Asia & Tibet* I. xx. 331 The first real *kara-buran*, or 'black tempest',.. came.. early... Drift-sand and dust swept down the Tarim and made the air so thick that we were unable to see the steep dune which faced us. **1931** A. A. MILLER *Climatol.* xiii. 243 Strong winds from almost any point of the compass spring up by day, carrying clouds of dust and sand... The *karaburan* is of this type, blowing strongly from the north-east in the Tarim basin. **1949** W. MOORE *Dict. Geogr.* 90 The sand blown along by the karaburan is one of the principal causes of the changes in the courses of rivers through the desert.

Karadagh, Kara Dagh (ˈkærədɑː). The name of a range of mountains in north-western Iran, used *attrib.* or *ellipt.* to denote a thick woollen carpet or rug (orig.) made there and knotted with either a geometrical or a floral pattern.

1900 J. K. MUMFORD *Oriental Rugs* xi. 180 The Kara Dagh weavings are not often seen in market. **1962** C. W. JACOBSEN *Oriental Rugs* 228 If there are any rugs coming to Ardebil or Tabriz as Karadaghs, it will be news to most buyers in Tabriz. What little information is available describes these as being very much like the Caucasian Karabaghs, thick rugs with both geometric and floral designs... The new Ardebil rugs are successors to the Karadaghs.

‖**karagan** (ˈkɑːrəgən). [Turkī, f. *kara* black: so mod.F. *karagan.*] A species of fox, *Vulpes karagan*, inhabiting Tartary.

1800 SHAW *Zool.* I. 323 Karagan Fox.. a small species, which, according to Dr. Pallas, is very common in almost all parts of the Kirghisian deserts. **1869** GRAY *Catal. Mammalia* 205 *Vulpes karagan* (Karagan). Larger than the Corsac.

Karaism (ˈkɛərəɪz(ə)m). [f. as KARAITE: see -ISM.] The religious system of the Karaites.

1882-3 SCHAFF *Encycl. Relig. Knowl.* II. 1225 The founder of Karaism was Anan, the son of David.

karait, variant of KRAIT.

Karaite (ˈkɛərəaɪt). [f. Heb. *q'rāīm* scripturalists (f. *qārā* to read) + -ITE[1].] A member of a Jewish sect (founded in the eighth cent. A.D.), which rejects rabbinical tradition and bases its tenets on a literal interpretation of the scriptures. They are found chiefly in the Crimea, and the adjacent parts of Russia and Turkey.

1727-41 CHAMBERS *Cycl.* s.v. *Caraite*, The Caraites themselves pretend to be the remains of the ten tribes led captive by Salmanassar. **1839** E. D. CLARKE *Trav. Russia*, etc. 97/1 The Karaïtes deem it an act of piety to copy the Bible. **1893** *Daily News* 3 Mar. 5/4 There are at present but few Karaites, who all live in the Crimea, speak the Tartar tongue, and dress after the Tartar fashion.

attrib. **1900** *Expositor* Sept. 238 The British Museum contains a considerable number of Karaite MSS.

Hence **ˈKaraitism** = KARAISM.

1727-41 CHAMBERS *Cycl.* s.v. *Caraite*, A contrary party, continuing to keep close to the letter, founded Caraitism.

karaji, var. KORADJI.

‖**karaka** (kaˈraka, kəˈrækə). Also **kuraka.** [Maori.] The bow-tree of New Zealand; *Corynocarpus lævigata* (N.O. *Anacardiaceæ*). Also *attrib.*, as ***karaka-berry, -fruit, -leaf, -nut, -tree.***

The fruit has an edible pulp and poisonous kernel, which however may be eaten after being roasted and steeped in a running stream of water for a considerable length of time.

1834 G. BENNETT *Wanderings New South Wales* I. xvii. 336 The Karaka tree, (*Corynocarpus lævigata*,) of New Zealand, was in thriving condition, having reached the elevation of from six to nearly fourteen feet, and borne fruit. **1845** E. J. WAKEFIELD *Adv. New Zeal.* I. 233 (Morris) The karaka-tree much resembles the laurel in its growth and foliage. **1859** A. S. THOMSON *Story New Zeal.* 157 (ibid.) The karaka fruit is about the size of an acorn. **1883** RENWICK *Betrayed* 35 Bring the heavy Karaka leaf. **1905** W. B. *Where White Man Treads* 16 And of nuts—the karaka, with its coating of soft yellow pulp. **1921** H. GUTHRIE-SMITH *Tutira* xii. 102 Single plants of karaka (*Corynocarpus lævigatus*) grew also. **1938** R. D. FINLAYSON *Brown Man's Burden* 77 Herding the cows down by the karaka trees. **1949** E. DE MAUNY *Huntsman in Career* 72 He could see the red karaka berry. **1957** J. FRAME *Owls do Cry* II. xv. 67 Green as karaka leaf.

Hence **ka'rakin** *Chem.* [-IN[1]], a substance extracted from karaka-nuts by the process of washing.

1875 WATTS *Dict. Chem.* 2nd Suppl. 710 The bitter substance, karakin,.. crystallises in beautiful radiate needles.

Karakalpak, Kara-Kalpak (ˈkærəkælˈpæk), *a.* and *sb.* [Kirghiz, f. *kara* black + *kalpak* cap.] **A.** *adj.* Of or pertaining to a Turkic people inhabiting a region south of the Aral Sea. **B.** *sb.* **a.** This Turkic people; a member of this people. **b.** (Also **Kara-Kalpaki.**) The Turkic language of the Karakalpak people.

1832 [see KAZAKH]. **1865** J. & R. MICHELL tr. *Valikhanof's Russians Cent. Asia* ii. 24 The Mission was met by four deputies... These were the Karakalpak Prince Istleu [etc.]. **1875** G. R. ABERIGH-MACKAY *Notes W. Turkistan* 79 Karakalpaks offer allegiance to Russia.. 1723. **1882** *Encycl. Brit.* XIV. 94/1 The Kipchaks, forming a connecting link between the nomad and settled Turki peoples of Ferghana and Bokhara, and the Kara-Kalpaks on the south-east side of the Aral Sea. **1888** *Encycl. Brit.* XXIII. 661/2 Tatar dialects (..Kumi, Karatchai, Kara-Kalpaki). **1959** E. H. CARR *Socialism in One Country* II. xx. 270 The Kara-Kalpak autonomous region of the Kazakh autonomous SSR. **1970** *Encycl. Brit.* XXII. 399/1 Kara-Kalpak, which is hardly more than a Kazakh dialect, is used.. by the Kara-Kalpaks living in Afghanistan.

‖**karakia** (karaˈkia). *N.Z.* Pl. **-kia, -kias.** [Maori.] An incantation (see quot. 1949).

1832 H. WILLIAMS *Jrnl.* 6 Jan. in H. Carleton *Life H. Williams* (1874) I. 111 If they should be where they cannot land, everyone immediately ceases talking, and they commence 'karakia [their incantations]. **1843** E. DIEFFENBACH *Trav. N.Z.* II. I. vii. 114 The 'Karakia' (prayers).. are most powerful when coming from a priest who is distinguished by high birth. **1862** A. S. ATKINSON *Jrnl.* 10 Sept. in *Richmond-Atkinson Papers* (1960) I. xiii. 791 We got there just after the flag had been hoisted & while the karakia were being chanted. **1874** J. C. JOHNSTONE *Maoria* 191 *Karakia*, incantations. In their use of this word the Maoris had no idea of prayer, and it is a mistake to attach that meaning to Karakia. **1905** W. B. *Where White Man Treads* 38 [The Maori's] 'karakia' (incantations) were invocations to his gods to preserve him from the Unknown. **1921** H. GUTHRIE-SMITH *Tutira* x. 70 Preparing herself.. by the recitation of proper *karakias*—incantations. **1949** P. BUCK *Coming of Maori* (1950) IV. iii, The priests established oral communication with their gods by means of *Karakia*. A *Karakia* may be defined as a formula of words which was chanted to obtain benefit or avert trouble... They cover a range which exceeds the bounds of religion. It is therefore impossible for one English word to cover adequately all the meanings of *Karakia*. All *Karakia* are chants but there are a number of chants,.. which are not *Karakia*... Probably incantation is the nearest in general meaning. **1959** TINDALE & LINDSAY *Rangatira* iv. 41 The karakia ceremony in which the canoe said farewell to the stump on which it had grown. **1968** *Landfall* XXII. 255 Underneath, Back, back The old life seeths, Sound of old chants, Of karakias In my skin.

Hence as *v. trans.*, to put a spell on (a person or object) by chanting or reciting *karakia*; also *intr.*, to chant or recite *karakia*.

1833 H. WILLIAMS *Let.* in H. Carleton *Life H. Williams* (1874) I. 134 His old superstition was too strong, though he did not submit to be *karakia'd* previous to dissolution. **1836**

J. A. WILSON *Jrnl.* in *Missionary Life & Work N.Z.* (1889) III. 42 They invited me to hold afternoon prayers..I reminded them of the cruel and bloody war they had long waged... They..again pressed me to *karakia*. **1874** H. CARLETON *Life H. Williams* I. 41 The natives said he had '*Karakia'd*' us—a term they apply to our religious worship.

Kara-Kirghiz (ˌkærəkɪə'giːz). [Native name, f. *kara* black + KIRGHIZ.] = KIRGHIZ *sb.* and *a.*

1879 *Encycl. Brit.* IX. 85/2 The nomads are mainly Kipchaks and Kara Kirghiz. **1959** E. H. CARR *Socialism in One Country* II. xx. 268 The Kirgiz (here called Kara-Kirgiz) population was to form a new autonomous region within the RSFSR. **1967** D. S. PARLETT *Short Dict. Lang.* 73 *Kirgiz* (Kara-Kirgiz).., apparently one of the oldest (or oldest attested) Turkic tribes. **1971** *Whitaker's Almanack 1972* 966 In 1924, a Kara-Kirghiz Autonomous Province was formed within the R.S.F.S.R.

karakul ('kærəkəl). Also caracul(e), carakul, karacul. [Russ., f. *Karakul*, name of a province and lake in Bokhara, where the breed originated.] **a.** A breed of sheep with coarse wiry fur; a sheep of this breed. **b.** The glossy curled coat of a young karakul lamb, valued as fur. Also *attrib.*, as ***karakul cloth***, a kind of cloth made in imitation of karakul.

1853 M. ARNOLD *Sohrab & Rustum* in *Poems* 10 And on his head he plac'd his sheep-skin cap, Black, glossy, curl'd, the fleece of Kara-Kul. **1894** *Westm. Gaz.* 20 Sept. 3/3 Here is fashion's forecast for the winter season:—Blue the leading colour... Caracule the popular fur. *Ibid.* 4 Oct. 3/3 The most striking of this season's productions is caracule-cloth, which closely resembles the fur of that name. **1894** *Queen* 27 Oct. 735/3 A 'Caracule' plush, which simulates that fashionable fur. **1895** *Army & Navy Co-op. Soc. Price List* 1095 Astrachans, &c... Black Caracul. **1898** *Daily News* 15 Oct. 6/4 A tight-fitting caracul with revers of chinchilla. **1913** *Illustr. Technical World* XIX. 700/1 The Karakul is a desert sheep native to Bokhara, Central Asia. **1929** *Daily Express* 26 Jan. 5/3 The smarter coats are generally collared with a flat fur. These include astrachan, krimma, and caracul, in black, beige, or grey. **1930** *Economist* 4 Jan. 10/2 There have also been established in the prairie provinces karakul sheep farms, from which astrakhan and broadtail are secured. **1948** L. G. GREEN *To River's End* viii. 88 On both sides of the river the karakul lamb is flourishing. *Ibid.* x. 111 Glossy black karakul skins drying on their frames. **1949** *Amer. Speech* XXIV. 95 Lambs from China or the interior of Asia possess pelts distinguished by a flat, open, wavy curl and give their name to a common variety of skin very common in the industry called *karacul*, also spelled *carakul*. **1957** V. NABOKOV *Pnin* v. 134 The warm rose-red silk lining of her karakul muff. **1960** *Times* 31 May (S. Afr. Suppl.) p. vi/7 Wool, of course, is a major export and is well supported by karakul pelts.

karakurt ('kærəkʊət). [Turki, f. *kara* black + *kurt* wolf.] A venomous, black spider, *Latrodectus tredecimguttatus*, found in southern Russia and eastern Europe; = MALMIGNATTE.

[**1909** A. PETRUNKEVITCH in *Sci. Amer.* 22 May 395/3 Like other species of *Latrodectus*, *Karakurt* does not show much inclination to attack.] **1932** E. NIELSEN *Biol. Spiders* I. i. 43 One of the most poisonous spiders is the Russian *Karakurt* (*Lathrodectus lugubris*), which causes great damage in the steppes of South Russia in the hot months of the summer.

karamat, var. KRAMAT.

Karamojo (kærə'məʊdʒəʊ). Also **Karamojong.** [Native name.] **a.** A Nilotic people of north-eastern Uganda; a member of this people. **b.** The language of this people.

1911 *Encycl. Brit.* XXVII. 559/1 (*heading*) Nile negroes (Aluru,..Turkana and Karamojo). **1959** A. MOOREHEAD *No Room in Ark* vii. 137 The Karamojong is a warrior and a herdsman of cattle. *Ibid.* 144 The Karamojong warrior wears the kind of accessories a well-dressed western woman might have, but without the clothes. **1961** WEBSTER, *Karamojong*, a Nilotic language of the Karamojong people. **1964** C. WILLOCK *Enormous Zoo* i. 3 In the north-east [of Uganda] lay the Karamoja,..a semi-desert peopled by the Karamojong, a group of nomadic, pastoralist tribes. **1966** J. H. GREENBERG *Lang. Afr.* (ed. 2) v. 86 The Eastern Sudanic family has the following..branches:..Nilotic:..Eastern: Dodoth, Karamojong, Teso. *Ibid.*, We may compare Nilo-Hamitic..Karamojong *ano*, Kakwa *an* with Nilotic Shilluk *an*, Anuak *ana*.

‖**karamu** ('karamuː, kærə'muː). [Maori.] The name of several species of *Coprosma*, a genus of Australasian trees and shrubs (N.O. *Rubiaceæ*), some of which produce edible fruits.

bush-karamu, the Otago orange-leaf, or Looking-glass bush (*C. lucida*).

1874 J. WHITE *Te Rou* 221 (Morris) Then they tied a few Karamu branches in front of them. **1876** in *Trans. New Zeal. Inst.* IX. 545 (ibid.), I have seen it stated that coffee of fine flavour has been produced from the karamu.

karana (kə'rɑːnə). *India.* [Skr. *kárana* doing, making, (hence) position, posture.] One of the 108 basic postures in Indian dance, details of which were set out in the *Natya Sastra* by the sage Bharata Muni, traditionally after instruction from the god Siva, lord of the dance.

1936 B. V. N. NAIDU et al. tr. *Bharata's Taṇḍava Lakṣaṇam* ii. 19, I shall now enumerate..the Karaṇas and Rēcakas... A Karaṇa in dance is the co-ordination of movements of the hands and feet. **1948** G. VENKATACHALAM *Dance in India* 132 *Karana*, a fundamental pose. **1956** P. BANERJI *Dance of India* (ed. 5) iv. 51 The Karanas are single postures, the special feature of them being that the left hand is generally put on the breast while the right hand follows the movements of the feet. *Ibid.* 52 A Karana is the source and origin of all the movements. **1965** E. BHAVNANI *Dance in India* iii. 17 In the Nataraja temple at Chidambaram.. there are carvings of the 108 *Karanas* or basic dance postures. **1967** SINGHA & MASSEY *Indian Dances* ii. 41 Just as in Bharata's time the basic unit of dance was the karana, so it is generally agreed that today this unit is the *adavu*, which seems to have evolved from the karana. **1969** *Weekly Mail* (Madras) 26 July 10/4 Karanas can be classified as those which are anukaranas (imitations)..and those which are abstract meant only for aesthetic (internal) pleasure.

Karankawa (kə'ræŋkəwə), *sb.* and *a.* Also **Carancahua, Carancoway, Carankoua.** [Native name.] **A.** *sb.* An Indian people of the Gulf coast of Texas; a member of this people; also, their language. **B.** *adj.* Of or pertaining to this people. Also **Ka'rankawan** *a.* and *sb.*

1806 J. SIBLEY in *Message from President of U.S., communicating Discoveries made in exploring the Missouri by Captains Lewis & Clark* 72 Carankouas, live on an island, or peninsula, in the bay of St. Bernard. **1823** W. B. DEWEES *Lett. from Early Settler Texas* (1852) 30 During their absence the Carancoway Indians attacked the vessel. **1891** *7th Ann. Rep. U.S. Bureau Amer. Ethnol. 1885–6* 82 (*heading*) Karankawan [linguistic] family. (*text*) The Karankawa formerly dwelt upon the Texan coast. **1907** F. W. HODGE *Handbk. Amer. Indians* I. 657/1 Karankawa... The signification of the name has not been ascertained. **1948** *True* May 126/2, I hear the Carancahuas been putting on war paint down south of here. **1957** *Encycl. Brit.* XII. 203 A/1 Powell classification (1891)..Language family.. Karankawan (Extinct). *Ibid.* 203 B/2 (*heading*) Sapir arrangement (1929). (*text*) Coahuiltecan *a.* Tonkawa. *b.* Coahuilteco. *c.* Karankawa. **1966** C. F. & F. M. VOEGELIN *Map N. Amer. Indian Langs.* (*caption*) Language isolates and families with undetermined phylum affiliations... Karankawa Language Isolate.

karanteen ('kærəntiːn). *S. Afr.* Also **-ine.** Either of two marine fishes of the family Sparidae, *Crenidens crenidens*, or the larger *bamboo-fish* (BAMBOO *sb.* 2), *Sarpa salpa*, also known, in Natal, as the striped karanteen.

1905 *Natal Mercury Pictorial* 334 (Pettman), The fish pictured today is a Karantine. It is a local species. **1913** [see *bamboo-fish*]. **1930** C. L. BIDEN *Sea-Angling Fishes of Cape* 62 Mackerel, mullet, sardine, and bamboo-fish (Natal karanteen) are the best lures. **1947** K. H. BARNARD *Pict. Guide S. Afr. Fishes* 152 White Karanteen (*Crenidens crenidens*)... Silvery, greenish or bluish above, narrow dark longitudinal stripes. *Ibid.* 156 Striped Karanteen (Natal) (*Sarpa salpa*)... Silvery, greenish or bluish above, yellow-orange longitudinal stripes. **1953** J. L. B. SMITH *Sea Fishes S. Afr.* (rev. ed.) 274 *Sarpa salpa*... Striped Karanteen, Bamboo Fish (Natal)..is said to occur right round Africa. *Ibid.* 275 *Crenidens crenidens*... Karanteen... Comes from Indian waters, extends to Durban. **1970** *Albany Mercury* (S. Afr.) 29 Jan. 15 Smaller fish—such as mullet and karanteen —making up his [*sc.* the leerfish's] staple diet.

karat. Var. of CARAT. *Obs.* exc. *U.S.*

1901 *Manufacturing Jeweler* 28 Feb. 244 (Advt.), Our rose gold, green gold, Roman and karat gold..are well known and universally used. **1903** 'O. HENRY' in *Ainslee's Mag.* Mar. 125/1 There stood..a first-class looking little man, with a four-karat diamond on his finger. **1945** *Jewelers' Dict.* 124/2 In U.S. usage *karat* designates the proportion of fine gold in an alloy; while *carat* is applied to the weight of a stone. **1972** *Newsweek* 10 Jan. 15/1 (Advt.), *Cross* pens and pencils are recognized as fine writing instruments. Available in lustrous chrome, sterling silver, gold filled and solid fourteen karat gold, they are purchased with pride. **1972** *Sci. Amer.* Dec. 8/1 (Advt.), Exclusive, extra-large, 18-karat gold point with etched facing assures super-smooth writing action.

‖**karatas** (kə'reɪtəs). Also 8 **karata.** [? Of Carib origin: the name is mentioned in 1667 by Du Tertre *Hist. Antilles* (Hatz.-Darm.).] A West Indian and South American plant (*Bromelia Karatas*), allied to the pine-apple, and yielding a valuable fibre; silk-grass.

1727–41 CHAMBERS *Cycl.*, *Karata*, by some called *caraguata maca*, a kind of aloe growing in America. **1768** MILLER *Gard. Dict.*, *Karatas*, the wild Ananas or Penguin. .. This plant is very common in the West Indies, where the juice of its fruit is often put into punch, being of a sharp acid flavour. **1848** in CRAIG; also in later dicts.

karate (kə'rɑːtiː), *sb.* [Jap., lit. 'empty hand'.] A Japanese system of unarmed combat in which hands and feet are used as weapons. Also *attrib.*, esp. **karate chop**, a sharp slanting blow with the hand.

1955 E. J. HARRISON *Fighting Spirit Japan* (ed. 2) vii. 74 Karate resembles both jujutsu and judo. *Ibid.*, A single karate technique..is capable of inflicting fatal injury upon its victim. **1962** *Movie* Dec. 35/3 The interest of the karate techniques employed. **1964** *Guardian* 11 Jan. 5/1 Her unsporting habit of dispatching people of both sexes with a carefully rehearsed Karate blow. **1964** I. FLEMING *You only live Twice* x. 127 Your judo and karate are special skills requiring years of practice. **1966** J. PORTER *Sour Cream* ix. 126 She probably knew the lot: unarmed combat, judo, karate. **1970** *New Yorker* 5 Dec. 49 'I'm Larry Taylor,' a breathless, sharp-featured young man said, offering a karate-chop handshake to Jay Steffy. **1971** *Ink* 12 June 17/4 He floored the guard with a karate chop.

Hence ‖**karateka** (ka'raːtikaː), an exponent or devotee of karate, a karate expert.

1966 *New Scientist* 7 July 8/1 Karatekas, those fearsome exponents of the Japanese technique of self-defence called Karate..often display their prowess by breaking..bricks with their bare hands. **1972** *Straits Times* (Malaysian ed.) 26 Sept. 3/2 Some 700 karatekas from the Police Reserve Unit ..will be attending. **1972** D. LEES *Zodiac* 122 The other guy was making like a karateka. **1973** [see KATA].

karate (kə'rɑːtiː), *v.* [f. prec.] *trans.* To strike or beat with karate blows. Also **karate-chop** *v.*, to strike with a karate chop.

1966 T. PYNCHON *Crying of Lot 49* v. 134 'I'm unarmed. You can frisk me.' 'While you karate-chop me in the spine, no thank you.' **1968** *New Yorker* 14 Sept. 129 A wolf was bugging me, so I..karated him, and called the fuzz. **1970** *Time* 11 May 62 The wife..can karate-chop hell out of her husband.

karat-tree ('kærəttriː). [f. CARAT + TREE.] The Abyssinian Coral-tree, *Erythrina abyssinica* (N.O. *Leguminosæ*), with scarlet flowers, and seeds which have been supposed to be the original of the carat-weight (Paxton *Bot. Dict.* 1868).

karausse, obs. f. CAROUSE.

karavan, -serai, obs. ff. CARAVAN *sb.*, etc.

karaya (kə'raɪə). [ad. Hind. *karāl*, *karāyal* resin.] In full, ***karaya gum***, ***gum karaya***. A gum exuded by the Indian tree *Sterculia urens* when the bark is pierced: used industrially, esp. as a substitute for gum tragacanth.

1893 G. WATT *Dict. Econ. Products of India* VI. III. 365 The gum [of *Sterculia urens*], under the name of *karai-gond*, is largely used in Bombay in the manufacture of native sweetmeats (*Dymock*). **1916** *Sci. Amer. Suppl.* 16 Dec. 393/2 (*heading*) What is karaya gum? **1918** *Jrnl. Amer. Pharmaceutical Assoc.* VII. 789 Karaya gum is used extensively in India as a substitute for tragacanth in the preparation of sweetmeats, and also locally as a demulcent in the treatment of throat affections. **1947** C. L. MANTELL *Water-Soluble Gums* iii. 50 Karaya gum has been used in the United States since the latter part of the 19th century, but the large scale use in the United States dates from World War I, when the price of tragacanth was high. Karaya is frequently sold as tragacanth. **1954** KIRK & OTHMER *Encycl. Chem. Technol.* XIII. 883 Gums derived from Irish and Iceland moss, karaya, algin, and quince seeds have received limited applications in textile finishes. **1962** M. G. DENAVARRE *Chem. & Manuf. Cosmetics* (ed. 2) II. 119 Although karaya has sometimes been used as a tragacanth adulterant, its acidity, odor, color, negative starch reaction, and ability to swell in 60% alcohol will quickly differentiate it from tragacanth. Gum karaya has found its widest cosmetic use in making finger-waving concentrates for subsequent dilution to proper consistency with water. **1974** *Daily Colonist* (Victoria, B.C.) 20 Oct. 2/3 Mrs. Wallace decided to experiment with Karaya vegetable gum powder made from the extract from a tree grown in India, in an effort to promote healing of Nunn's wound.

karbi ('kɑːbɪ). *Austral.* [Aboriginal name.] A small, dark, stingless, native bee, *Trigona carbonaria*.

1884 H. J. HOCKINGS in *Trans. Entomol. Soc. London* 149 Of these stingless bees of Australia two varieties only have come under my immediate observation... 'Karbi' or 'Keelar' and 'Kootchar' are the names given to them by the natives. *Ibid.* 150 'Karbi' gather but little honey. **1932** *Victorian Naturalist* (Melbourne) XLVIII. x. 185 The aborigines were familiar with several species, and..*Trigona cassiæ* Ckll. is known as 'Koochee', and *Trigona carbonaria* Smith, as 'Koobee', or 'Karbi'. **1948** *Bull. Amer. Mus. Nat. Hist.* XC. 22/1 The spiral staircase type of nest was recorded by Hockings..in the case of an Australian *Trigona* known as 'karbi' or 'keelar' that he believed to be *carbonaria* F. Smith.

karboy, var. CARBOY.

karcas(s)e, obs. f. CARCASE.

karcheffe, -cher, obs. ff. KERCHIEF, KERCHER.

kard(e, obs. f. CARD *sb.*¹ and *v.*¹; var. CARDE.

kardel, var. CARDEL.

† '**kardester.** *Obs. rare.* [Obs. form of **cardster*, fem. of CARDER.] A woman who cards.

1363 *Rolls Parlt.* II. 278/1 Broudesters, Kardesters, Pyneresces de Leine. **14..** *Voc.* in Wr.-Wülcker 575/40 *Corptrix*, a kardestere.

kardil, obs. f. CRADLE *sb.*

kardio-: see CARDIO-.

kare, obs. f. CARE *sb.*

‖**kareao, kareau** (karea'uː, -'ɑːɔ). [Maori.] The native name for the New Zealand creeping plant *Ripogonum parviflorum*. Also ***kareao-vine***.

1845 E. J. WAKEFIELD *Adv. New Zeal.* I. 218 (Morris) A tedious march..along a track constantly obstructed by webs of the kareau, or supple-jack. **1873** BULLER *Birds New Zeal.* (1888) II. 317 Our shins aching from repeated contact with the kareao-vines.

karect(e, var. CARACT; obs. f CARAT.

‖**karee** ('kæriː). Also **karree.** [S. Afr. Du. *karree* (*-hout*, *-boom*), from Hottentot name.] Either of two South African trees of the genus *Rhus*, *R. lancia* or *R. viminalis*, of the family Anacardiaceæ.

1815 A. PLUMPTRE tr. *Lichtenstein's Trav. S. Afr.* II. xliv. 223 Mimosas,..willows, and *karree bushes*. Among the latter the colonists include several sorts of *rhus*. [**1822** BURCHELL *Trav.* I. 179 Very large bushes of *Karreehout*, which..have a great resemblance to our common willows.] **1824** *Ibid.* II. 199 The bow itself is made not always of the same sort of wood... The karree-tree..is most generally

used for this purpose. **1834** A. G. BAIN *Let.* 18 Dec. in *Jrnls.* (1949) 151 It was actually two large karee trees with large pools of rainwater around them. **1842** MOFFAT *Miss. Tours S. Afr.* i. 6 Kharree trees and shrubs umbrageous at all seasons of the year. **1876** MISS FREWER tr. *Verne's Adv. in S. Afr.* v. 39 The karrees with dark green foliage. **1898** W. C. SCULLY *Vendetta of Desert* xviii. 177 They quickened their paces so as to reach a long, low ridge dotted with *karee* bushes. **1934** L. VAN DER POST *In a Province* viii. 110 Noon beats on tattered parasols of karee-thorn over them. **1939** S. CLOETE *Watch for Dawn* xxviii. 418 Behind a thick clump of karee boom a Kaffir squatted motionless. **1958** L. VAN DER POST *Lost World of Kalahari* i. 15 In the rivers and streams he constructed traps beautifully woven out of reeds and buttressed with young karee wood or harde-kool. **1966** E. PALMER *Plains of Camdeboo* xvii. 287 Along the river-beds across the plains are thorn trees and karees. *Ibid.* 288 The karee trees, with their round crowns of yellow-green drooping foliage, were a welcome sight to the travellers.

karela ('kʌrələ). Also **kareli, karilla.** [Hindi.] The balsam pear or bitter gourd, *Momordica charantia*, a climbing plant of the family Cucurbitaceæ, native to south-east Asia and tropical Africa, and cultivated in India for its edible, rough-skinned, yellow or white fruit, which is lemon-shaped and may be as much as eight inches long.

1839 J. W. MASTERS in *Trans. Agric. & Hort. Soc. India* III. 200 *Karilla*, annual, propagated by seeds. **1881** J. A. MURRAY *Plants & Drugs of Sind* 41 (*heading*) Momordica balsamina... The Balsam Apple. Vernacular—Karelo-Jangro, *Sind*. Fruit ovoid, smooth,..tapering at both ends. Eaten in pickle. **1893** G. WATT *Dict. Econ. Products India* V. 256 The rainy season kind, called *kareli*, has rather smaller fruits and is more esteemed than the hot-weather variety, known in some districts under the name of *karela*. **1895** KIPLING *Second Jungle Bk.* 81 The Karela, the vine that bears the bitter wild gourd. **1962** J. F. DASTUR *Medicinal Plants India & Pakistan* (ed. 2) 112 (*heading*) *Momordica charantia* Linn. Family: Cucurbitaceae. *Local names*: Karela, karvel. *English names*: African Cucumber, Bitter Gourd. **1969** *Sunday Statesman* (Calcutta) 27 July 4 Vegetable vendors have lao sag at 30 paise a bundle... Tinda, french beans and karela are all Re 1 a kg.

Karelian (kə'ri:lɪən), *sb.* and *a.* Also **Carelian.** [f. *Karelia*, name of a region in Eastern Finland and of a republic in the adjoining parts of the U.S.S.R.] **A.** *sb.* **a.** A native or inhabitant of Karelia. **b.** The Finno-Ugric language of this people.

1855 R. SEARS *Illustr. Descr. Russ. Empire* iii. 94 The district of the government traversed by this canal is inhabited by a tribe of Carelians. **1879** *Encycl. Brit.* VIII. 700/1 Finnic or Ugrian represented by (*a*) Finnish proper or Suonic, (*b*) Karelian. **1882** *Ibid.* XIV. 307/2 The Karelians were pressing on the Eastern Lapps. **1921** *Glasgow Herald* 21 Nov. 10 The Karelians want..to open..peace negotiations. **1931** K. M. STEWART-MURRAY *Conscription of a People* vii. 75 The conscription of 30,000 Karelians for lumbering early in 1931. **1935** HUXLEY & HADDON *We Europeans* vii. 220 The east [of Finland is inhabited] by Karelians. **1942** K. W. DEUTSCH in J. A. Fishman *Readings Sociol. of Lang.* (1968) 600 Seven of these [smaller nations] reached some form of statehood between 1900 and 1941: Albanians, Irish, Byelo-Russians, Karelians, Moldavians —the three last-named only as 'Union Republics' within the federal framework of the U.S.S.R., [etc.]. **1961** L. F. BROSNAHAN *Sounds of Lang.* viii. 177 In Finno-Ugrian it [*sc.* palatalisation opposition] is present in eastern dialects of Finnish and Estonian, southern Karelian, and in all the languages of this family which occur to the east. **1967** E.-L. WUORIO *Midsummer Lokki* iii. 93 Kalle Koli, Finnish war-hero, Karelian, ex-gentleman farmer, and now an evacuee.

B. *adj.* Of or relating to Karelia, the Karelians, or their language.

1879 *Encycl. Brit.* IX. 218/2 It was Torkel Knutson who conquered and connected the Karelian Finlanders in 1293. **1920** *Glasgow Herald* 29 Oct. 9/2 The Karelian population in the governments of Archangel and Olonets will enjoy the right to national self-determination. **1954** *Chambers's World Gazetteer* 357/1 The great Finnish epic *Kalevala* is of Karelian origin. **1967** E.-L. WUORIO *Midsummer Lokki* iii. 72 The heavy Karelian accent made it difficult for Luke to understand. **1969** E. H. PINTO *Treen* 331 Karelian birch cigar cases..enjoyed quite a vogue in the first 30 years of this century. **1974** *Sci. Amer.* Sept. 101/1 After World War II some 2·7 million Sudeten Germans were transferred to Germany and 415,000 Karelian Finns were moved to Finland.

karelianite (kə'ri:lɪənaɪt). *Min.* [f. prec. + -ITE[1].] An oxide of vanadium, V_2O_3.

1963 J. V. P. LONG et al. in *Amer. Mineralogist* XLVIII. 40 Electron microprobe analyses and the crystallographic data obtained suggest the existence of a new vanadium mineral, V_2O_3, isostructural with hematite, eskolaite and corundum. The name karelianite, after the region of Finland in which the Outokumpu mine is situated, is proposed for this mineral, the name to be applied to the pure end member. **1967** *Mineral. Abstr.* XVIII. 282/2 Three principal minerals compose the dominantly vanadiferous ores [at Mounana, Gabon]—karelianite, montroseite, and roscoelite. Karelianite, rarely more than 0·5 mm in size, occurs as grains in the grit cement or as blades forming 60° stars in quartz.

karelinite ('kærəlɪnaɪt). *Min.* [Named 1858, after Karelin its discoverer: see -ITE[1].] A lead-grey oxysulphide of bismuth found in the Altai.

1861 in BRISTOW *Gloss. Min.* **1868** in DANA *Min.*

karelling, obs. form of CAROLING.

†**karemon**, var. CARMAN[2] *Obs.*, man, male.

a **1400** *Pistill of Susan* 249 (Cotton MS.) Sche..karpyd to þat karemon, as she well kowthe.

Karen (kə'rɛn), *sb.* and *a.* Also †**Carayner, Carian(er), Carianner.** [f. Burmese *ka-reng* wild, dirty, low-caste man.] **A.** *sb.* **1.** One of a group of non-Burmese Mongoloid tribes scattered throughout Burma, esp. to the east; a member of one of these tribes.

c **1759** in A. Dalrymple *Oriental Repertory* (1793) I. 100 This Country contains two Nations, the Bûraghmahns, and Peguers... There is another People in this Country called Carianners, whiter than either. **1800** M. SYMES *Acct. Embassy to Kingdom of Ava* vi. 207 Carayners, or Carianers ..inhabit different parts of the country. **1833** W. TANDY tr. *Sangermano's Descr. Burmese Empire* vi. 34 The Carian, a good and peaceable people. **1833** BENNETT *Let.* 11 Nov. in F. Mason *Karen Apostle* (1847) v. 45 Four of the Karens were yesterday baptized. **1885** [see *crow-flight* s.v. CROW *sb.*[1] 11]. **1910** *Jrnl. R. Soc. Arts* LVIII. 701/2 The Karen undoubtedly had his original home in China. **1922** W. G. WHITE *Sea Gypsies of Malaya* i. 18 Upon the 'backbones' of Burma live the Karens... The Karens are..monolatrists, if not monotheists. **1937** R. H. LOWIE *Hist. Ethnological Theory* (1938) vii. 84 He [*sc.* Tylor] definitely ascribes the latter view only to Algonkians, Fijians, and Karens. **1962** [see CHIN *sb.*[2]]. **1965** B. SWEET-ESCOTT *Baker St. Irreg.* viii. 236 Hitherto we had been compelled to discourage widespread guerrilla activity among the loyal tribes such as the Karens. **1972** *Nat. Geographic* Feb. 270/1, I knew that a handful of Karens had moved into these hills about 125 years ago and now far outnumbered the native Lua.

2. The language of this people.

1861 J. WADE *Karen Vernacular Gram.* p. iii, Without this knowledge no one can determine, with confidence, what is good..Karen, and what is mere colloquial jargon. **1871** C. M. YONGE *Pioneers & Founders* vi. 161 She tried to learn Karen, but never had time, and..she could always have an interpreter. **1887** D. M. SMEATON *Loyal Karens Burma* ii. 73 Reduplication of words in Karen conveys an adverbial signification. **1961** *Dental Practitioner* XI. 369/1 Indeed, 'PAT' has now been programmed to produce phrases in English, Swedish, Polish, and Karen (a language of Burma). **1970** M. PEREIRA *Pigeon's Blood* vii. 81, I can speak ten dialects of Chinese, but not a word of Karen or Shan.

B. *adj.* Of or relating to the Karens or their language.

1839 [see FINE-TOOTH *a.*]. **1885** A. R. COLQUHOUN *Burma & Burmans* i. 11 The White Karen chief of Western Karennee. **1887** D. M. SMEATON *Loyal Karens Burma* ii. 73 The Karen language is monosyllabic. **1892** W. R. WINSTON *Four Yrs. Upper Burma* x. 99, I have..listened in Upper Burma to..glees, choruses and solos, rendered by Karen young men and maidens. **1948** D. DIRINGER *Alphabet* vii. 412 The Karen character is a modern adaptation of the Burmese script to the Karen tongue. **1959** *Listener* 30 Apr. 746/1 The Karen rebels. **1972** *Nat. Geographic* Feb. 270/1 We found our Karen neighbors bore their troubles in a cheery, resilient, and generally relaxed way.

kareyn(e, karf(e, obs. ff. CARRION, CARVE.

‖**karez** ('kɑ:rɛz). Also **kareze.** [Pers. (whence Pushtu) *kārez*.] In Afghanistan and Baluchistan: = KANAT.

1875 *Encycl. Brit.* I. 232/1 The water of the *kârez*, or subterranean canals. **1880** *Ibid.* XIII. 836/2 Irrigation by 'karez' is also largely resorted to. **1902** [see KANAT]. **1920** *Blackw. Mag.* Feb. 246/2 Then I planned a *kareze*, a subterranean water-cut. **1924** *Glasgow Herald* 29 May 9 The Persian husbandmen had even begun to repair and refit their wonderful 'karezes'. **1969** B. L. C. JOHNSON *South Asia* iv. 95/1 A karez system consists of a near horizontal tunnel driven from the level of the cultivable land near the centre of an intermontane basin to intersect the water-table in the gravelly detritus which constitutes the fans along the mountain foot... At the lower end of the tunnel emerges a small stream of water which is led to the fields. An important advantage of the karez is that the water travels most of its way underground, and so with the minimum risk of loss by evaporation.

‖**karezza** (kə'rɛtsə). Also **carezza.** [It. *carezza* caress.] Sexual union in which ejaculation or complete orgasm is avoided (see quot. 1896); = *coitus reservatus*.

1896 A. B. STOCKHAM *Karezza* ii. 22 Karezza consummates marriage in such a manner that through the power of will, and loving thoughts, the final crisis is not reached, but a complete control by both husband and wife is maintained throughout the entire relation. **1953** [see *coitus reservatus* s.v. COITUS c]. **1956** A. HUXLEY *Adonis & Alphabet* 276 He advocated Male Continence and what Dr Stockham was later to call *Karezza*. **1970** W. W. ROBSON *Mod. Eng. Lit.* v. 105 Late in his life..he [*sc.* Aldous Huxley] speculated optimistically on the benefits of a technique of sexual intercourse known as *carezza*. **1970** B. WALKER *Sex & Supernatural* ix. 83 In time 'karezza' was believed to bestow extraordinary..blessings.

kari, karibdous: see KARRI, KARYBDYS.

Karitane (kærɪ'tɑ:nɪ). *N.Z.* [f. *Karitane*, a township in the South Island of New Zealand.] Used *attrib.*, of or pertaining to the system of ante- and post-natal care for mothers and babies initiated by Sir F. Truby King (1858-1938).

1913 F. T. KING *Feeding & Care of Baby* 43 What has been achieved..on a relatively small scale at the Karitane Hospital is reflected enormously magnified in the district work. **1917** W. WRENCH *Let.* in M. King *Truby King* (1948) xxiv. 234, I am convinced that our greatest need in this country is a Training Centre on Karitane lines. **1930** *Bulletin* (Sydney) 26 Mar. 42/3 The Karitane Training Centre in Nelson-street, Woolahra, has appointed Sister May Richardson as its matron. **1945** R. M. BURDON *N.Z. Notables* 2nd Ser. iv. 62 [Truby King] had long wished to build a proper Karitane Hospital in Wellington where, as yet, there was only a mothercraft home. **1947** 'A. P. GASKELL' *Big Game* 122 Margaret had started training as a Karitane nurse. **1948** M. KING *Truby King* xv. 107 The word 'Karitane' has become famous in connection with Truby King Mothercraft work; but its origin is far removed from babies. The Huriawa or Karitane Peninsula lies at the south end of the wide Waikouaiti Bay. **1958** *N.Z. News* 11 Mar. 3/1 As an example, he [*sc.* Sir Truby King] successfully treated thirteen neglected infants in his own home, and ultimately six model 'Karitane' homes were founded throughout the Dominion. **1966** *Encycl. N.Z.* II. 222/2 A nurse was needed for the first Karitane baby.

karite, variant of KRAIT.

†**karité, kariteþ**, obs. forms of CHARITY.

c **1200** *Vices & Virtues* 37 Se ðe wuneð on karite, he wuneð on gode. *Ibid.*, Wuniȝen on karite, þat is, luue of gode and of mannen. **1706** PHILLIPS, *Karite* or *Carite*, a Name which our Monks in former times gave to the best Drink or strong Beer that was kept in their Monastery.

kark, var. CARK *sb.*

karkaise, -keis, obs. ff. CARCASS.

karkee, bad f. KHAKI.

karknett, karkynet, obs. ff. CARCANET.

karl(e, karl-hemp, obs. ff. CARL, CARL-HEMP.

karling, variant of CARLINE[1].

Karlowitz(er), varr. CARLOWITZ.

‖**karma** ('kɑ:mə). Also **karman.** [Skr. *karma*, *karman-*, action, fate.] In Buddhism, the sum of a person's actions in one of his successive states of existence, regarded as determining his fate in the next; hence, necessary fate or destiny, following as effect from cause. Also in Hinduism.

Latterly adopted by Western popular 'meditative' groups.

1827 H. T. COLEBROOKE in *Trans. R. Asiatic Soc.* I. 111 The next head in Canáde's arrangement, after quality, is action (*carme*). **1828** B. H. HODGSON in *Ibid.* (1830) II. 250. **1830** H. T. COLEBROOKE in *Ibid.* II. 38 Questions most recondite, which are agitated by theologians, have engaged the attention of the *vêdántins* likewise..such as..efficacy of works (*carman*). **1836** *Penny Cycl.* V. 531/1 The progress of the soul towards matter is therefore the effect of a succession of acts (Karma—whence the name of the school Kârmika) on the part of the soul. **1853** P. D. HARDY *Budhism* 39 As the cause of reproduction, karma, is destroyed, it is not possible for him [the rahat] to enter upon any other mode of existence. **1879** MAX MÜLLER *Sel. Ess.* (1881) II. 495 What the Buddists call by the general name of *Karman*, comprehends all influences which the past exercises on the present, whether physical or mental. **1881** A. P. SINNETT *Occult World* 132 Every thought of man upon being evolved passes into the inner world... It survives as an active intelligence.. so man is continually peopling his current in space with a world of his own... The Buddhist calls this his 'Shandba'; the Hindu gives it the name of 'Karma'. **1882** WOOD tr. *Barth's Relig. India* 112 The individual..entirely perishes. The influence of its karman alone, of its acts, survives it. **1892** *Month* Jan. 10 'Karma'..literally signifies 'action', and in Theosophic phraseology indicates the unvarying chain of cause and effect that governs the universe. **1899** L. HEARN *In Ghostly Japan* iii. 28 The destruction of Karma by virtuous effort is likened to the burning of incense by a pure flame. **1915** A. M. STEVENSON *Heart of Jainism* viii. 175 While Hindus think of karma as formless (*amūrta*), Jaina believe karma to have shape. **1948** N. MICKLEM *Relig.* ii. 45 Thus the doctrine of *karma* (*literally* 'action') or transmigration is intimately associated with the philosophy of the *Upanishads*. **1962** T. C. LETHBRIDGE *Witches* x. 133 The individual's choice of a future earthly body is limited however by what is known as the 'Law of Karma'. **1969** *Surfer* IX. VI. 38 May your destiny always be flavoured with good—good karma in this life. *Ibid.* 62 This is a bad Karma contest. **1971** *Nat. Geographic* Mar. 321/2 Officials, too, are subject to the law of karma—that sooner or later every action brings its retribution, in this existence or in one to come. **1971** *Rolling Stone* 24 June 32/2 John Sebastian's recording career has been plagued with an unusually bad karma. **1972** *Last Whole Earth Catalog* (Portola Inst.) 407/2 Because the karma is a little slower when you're not stoned, but it's the same karma and it works the same way.

Hence '**karmic** *a.*, pertaining to, relating to, or concerning *karma*.

1883 A. P. SINNETT *Esoteric Buddhism* xii. 195 Thus, on a careful examination of the matter the Karmic law..will be seen not only to reconcile itself to the sense of justice, but to constitute the only imaginable method of natural action that would do this. **1885** A. P. SINNETT *Karma* II. 110 To seek ..some comprehension of the Karmic principle in operation. **1931** L. H. MYERS *Prince Jali* vi. 63 Would not a good Buddhist see in her only a link in the long karmic chain? **1949** S. BARBANELL *Silver Birch Speaks* xiii. 142 One limit imposed, and always imposed, is what I would call the karmic debt of the patient, the relationship between mind and body determined by that individual's spiritual growth and attainment. **1974** *Publishers Weekly* 29 Apr. 47/2 Brodsky begins with an introduction to current genetic theory and proceeds to relate that to Eastern karmic understanding.

‖**karmadharaya** (kɑ:mə'dɑ:rəjə). *Linguistics.* [Skr., f. KARMA + *dhāraya* holding, bearing.] A compound in which the first member describes the second, as *highway* (adjective + noun), *steamboat* (attrib. noun + noun).

1846 M. WILLIAMS *Elem. Gram. Sanscrit Lang.* ix. 158 Native grammarians class compound nouns under five heads:... The 3d, *Karmadhâraya*, or those composed of an adjective and substantive. **1933** L. BLOOMFIELD *Lang.* xiv. 235 The Hindus found it convenient to set off..a special class of syntactic attribute-and-head compounds

(*Karmadharaya*), such as *blackbird*. **1957** S. POTTER *Mod. Ling.* iv. 92 That important type of compound called *karmadharaya* by Indian grammarians is represented by E *blackbird*, consisting of attribute + substantive.

‖**karma-marga** (ˌkɑːməˈmɑːgə). *Hinduism.* [Skr., f. KARMA + *mārga* road, path.] A strict following of Hindu precepts as a means of attaining a better life in one's next incarnation; the way of works or action (contrasted with *bhakti-marga* and *jnana-marga*).

1877 M. WILLIAMS *Hinduism* i. 11 Belief in the efficacy of works, penances, and austerities,..is the *Karma-mārga*, 'way of works'. **1883** [see JNANA b]. **1937** [see BHAKTI b]. **1945** [see JNANA b].

Kármán (ˈkɑːmɑːn, -ən). Also **Karman**. [Name of Theodore von *Kármán* (1881–1963), Hungarian-born physicist and aeronautical engineer who investigated the phenomenon.] ***Kármán* (*vortex*) *street***, or ***Kármán street of vortices***: a vortex street in which the vortices of one line are situated opposite points midway between those of the other line, an arrangement which is stable in certain conditions.

1928 *Proc. R. Soc.* A. CXX. 34 (*heading*) The characteristics of the Karman vortex street in a channel of finite breadth. **1929** *Phil. Trans. R. Soc.* A. CCXXVIII. 275 The following investigations deal with a Kármán street of vortices, or unsymmetrical double row, in a channel of finite width. **1936** *Proc. R. Soc.* A. CLIV. 68 Some very fine photographs of Kármán streets have been taken..in the water tank at the Aeronautical Research Laboratory of the Imperial College. **1949** O. G. SUTTON *Sci. of Flight* iii. 64 In certain conditions the eddies detach themselves alternately from either edge of an obstacle placed across stream and as they break away they form in the wake the pattern known as the Kármán vortex street. **1956** A. A. TOWNSEND *Struct. Turbulent Shear Flow* vii. 149 The eddies occur alternately in each half of the wake (as in a Kármán vortex street).

Karman, var. KIRMAN.

Karmathian, Car- (kɑːˈmeɪθɪən), *sb.* (*a.*) [After Karmat, the founder of the sect.] One of a sect of Muslims, founded in the 9th cent. Also as *adj.* Belonging to this sect.

1819 *Pantologia*, *Karmatians*, a sect of Mohammedans, who once occasioned great disorders in the empire of the Arabs. **1875** *Encycl. Brit.* II. 259/2 As to the special tenets professed by the Karmathians..they were, in their ultimate expression, pantheistic in theory and socialist in practice. **1883** *Ibid.* XVI. 594/1 Towards 887 A.D. an Ismailian, Hamdán, surnamed Ḳarmaṭ, founded the branch sect of the Carmathians.

‖**karma-yoga** (ˌkɑːməˈjəʊgə). *Hinduism.* [Skr., f. KARMA + YOGA.] The attainment of perfection through disinterested action. So ˌ**karma-ˈyogi**, an adherent or devotee of *karma-yoga*.

1896 'VIVEKÂNANDA' *Addresses Vedânta Philos.* I. 19 The Karma Yogî..is the man who understands that the highest ideal is non-resistance, but who also knows that it is the highest manifestation of power. *Ibid.* 55 Karma Yoga is the Yoga of work, to reach the goal of perfection by means of work. **1960** KOESTLER *Lotus & Robot* I. i. 36 Vinoba Bhave could be described as a Karma-Yogi—a person who seeks fulfilment by action. **1962** A. HUXLEY *Island* vi. 78 It's a real yoga... As good as raja yoga, or Karma yoga, or bhakti yoga. **1969** *Indo-Asian Culture* Oct. 42 Gandhiji's philosophy of action is *karmayoga*.

karmic: see KARMA.

karn, -e, var. CAIRN *sb.*; obs. f. KERN *sb.*[1]

Karnata (kɑːˈnɑːtə), *a.* and *sb.* Also **Carnataca, Carnati(c), Karnatak(a), Karnatakam, Karnatic, Kurnata.** [f. *Karnata* (Karnataka), a region of south-west India; also var. of *Carnatic* (Karnatak), the name given, under British rule, to a region of southern India in the presidency of Madras.] **A.** *adj.* Of or pertaining to Karnata or the Carnatic. **B.** *sb.* **a.** The music of southern India, purer in form and more ancient than the Hindustani music of the north. †**b.** *Obs.* The native language of Karnata and the Carnatic; = KANARESE *sb.* b.

1792 W. JONES in *Asiatick Researches* III. 82 On the formulas exhibited by Mirzakhan I have less reliance; but, since he professes to give them from *Sanscrit* authorities, it seemed proper to transcribe them: (*heading*) Dipaca: ..*Netta*:..*Cédaṛi*:..*Carnati*. **1801** H. T. COLEBROOKE *Ibid.* VII. 227 Carnáta, or Cánara, is the ancient language of Carnátaca. **1814** W. CAREY *Gram. Telinga Lang.* p. i, The languages of the south of India, i.e. The Telinga, Kurnata, Tamul, Malayala, and Cingalese. **1820** J. MCKERRELL *Gram. Carnataca Lang.* p. i, The Carnátaca Language..is nearly the universal Language of all the dominions of the late Tippoo Sultan. **1855** H. H. WILSON *Gloss. Judicial & Revenue Terms* p. ix, In Karnáta, *kul* is a payer of government revenue. **1856** R. CALDWELL *Compar. Gram. Dravidian Lang.* 6 The Kannadi or Karnâtaka..is spoken throughout the plateau of Mysore... 'Karnâtaka'..is defined to mean primarily 'a species of dramatic music', or 'comedy': it is used secondarily in Telugu as an adjective to signify 'native', 'aboriginal'..it then became the common designation of the Telugu and Canarese, or 'native' languages: and, finally, was restricted still further, and became the distinctive appellation of the Canarese alone. **1892** A. M. CHINNASWAMI MUDALIYAR *Oriental Mus. in European Notation* 9 The unfettered use of accidentals in European Music is regarded by the Karnāta musician as due to want of principle and system. *Ibid.* 12 The primary distinction is into two classes, Mārga (celestial) and Dēsi (terrestrial); the latter is now broadly divided into Hindustani and Karnāta. **1914** A. H. F. STRANGWAYS *Mus. Hindostan* 15 The Carnatic system frankly ignores the niceties..of intonation. **1920** E. CLEMENTS *Rāgas of Tanjore* 43/2 The Chaturdandi Prakāshikā..is said to be the principal treatise followed by modern Karnatic musicians. **1929** E. ROSENTHAL *Story Indian Mus.* i. 10 There is a wide diversity between the classification of *rágas* in the northern or Hindustani system, and in the southern or Carnatic system. **1948** G. VENKATACHALAM *Dance in India* x. 90 Carnatic music had its origin in the Telugu country. **1952** P. SAMBAMOORTHY *Dict. S. Indian Mus. & Musicians* p. vi, A few pictures are from the valuable collection of musical instruments in the Central College of Karnataka Music,.. Madras. **1968** *Jrnl. Musical Acad. Madras* XXXIX. 49 Is the wealth of Karnataka music preserved and handed down to posterity? **1971** *Shankar's Weekly* (Delhi) 4 Apr. 25/1 There is much more honesty..in a Jon Higgins submitting himself to the discipline of Karnatak music wholeheartedly. **1972** P. HOLROYDE *Indian Mus.* iii. 84 The Karnatakam remained uninfluenced... South Indian music, properly known as Carnatic, and South Indian dance, survived therefore in more-or-less pure form.

Karnaugh (ˈkɑːnɔː). [The name of Maurice *Karnaugh* (b. 1924), U.S. physicist, who published an account of the diagram in 1953.] ***Karnaugh map*** or ***diagram***: a diagram that consists of a rectangular array of squares each representing a different combination of the variables of a Boolean function (used, e.g., to find by inspection a simpler equivalent function).

1958 M. PHISTER *Logical Design Digital Computers* 405 (Index), Karnaugh map. **1960** W. C. IRWIN *Digital Computer Princ.* xiv. 76 The most elementary Karnaugh map represents a function of two variables. **1968** HILL & PETERSON *Introd. Switching Theory* vi. 87 The Karnaugh map is essentially a diagrammatic form of truth table, and.. the Venn diagram concepts of union and intersection of areas aid us in setting up or interpreting a Karnaugh map. **1970** O. DOPPING *Computers & Data Processing* i. 28 When the number of sets is large, the overall view is improved by using a kind of modified Venn diagrams called Karnaugh diagrams or Veitch diagrams. **1973** *Math. Teaching* Sept. 48/1 The Karnaugh map takes the place of a truth table.

karnel, obs. f. KERNEL; var. CARNEL.

karo (ˈkarɔ). *N.Z.* [Maori.] An evergreen shrub or small tree, *Pittosporum crassifolium*, which bears crimson flowers.

1853 J. D. HOOKER *Bot. Antarctic Voy.*: *Flora Novæ-Zelandiæ* I. 23 *Pittosporum cornifolium*... Nat[ive] name, 'Karo'. **1868** W. COLENSO in *Trans. N.Z. Inst.* I. III. Essay. 5 Of our shrubs and smaller timber trees, several are of strikingly beautiful growth, or blossom, or foliage; and are often seen to advantage in some clear glade..and, on the sea-coast,..the Karo, *Pittosporum crassifolium*. **1928** COCKAYNE & TURNER *Trees N.Z.* 104 *Pittosporum crassifolium*... Karo. A small tree, 15–30 ft. high, or frequently a dense shrub. **1950** *N.Z. Jrnl. Agric.* Dec. 533/1 The native karo (*Pittosporum crassifolium*) will thrive in heavy shade and will stand strong salt winds and much drier soil conditions than boxthorn, but it requires permanent double fencing to protect it from stock. **1963** J. T. SALMON *N.Z. Flowers & Plants in Colour* 53 The rich sweet scent of karo flowers fills the air of a calm evening when the tree is in flower.

karob, -e, obs. forms of CAROB.

1658–1706 in PHILLIPS.

Karok (kəˈrɒk). Also †**Cahroc, Kahruk.** [f. Karok *káruk* upstream.] **a.** An Indian people of the Klamath river valley in northwestern California. **b.** The language of this people. Also *attrib.*

1851 G. GIBBS *Jrnl.* 12 Oct. in H. R. Schoolcraft *Hist. & Stat. Information Indian Tribes* (1853) III. 151 They do not seem to have any generic appellation for themselves, but apply the terms 'Kahruk', up and 'Youruk', down, to all who live above or below themselves. **1872** *Overland Monthly* Apr. 328/2 The Cahrocs are probably the finest tribe of Indians in California. *Ibid.* 330/2 The Cahroc language, though rich in its vocabulary, is said to contain no expression for 'virtue'. **1877** *Contrib. N. Amer. Ethnol.* III. 32 The Karok language is said by those acquainted with it to be copious, sonorous, and rich in new combinations. **1903** G. W. JAMES *Indian Basketry* (ed. 3) 53 The Karoks (often spelled Cahrocs) are a fine, vigorous people. **1913** [see HOKAN]. **1921** E. SAPIR *Lang.* ix. 220 'Hokan' languages (Shasta, Karok). **1940** *Oregon Guide* 34 The southern part of Oregon was occupied by..two 'spill-overs' from California —the Shastas and Karoks. **1962** J. J. GUMPERZ in J. A. Fishman *Readings Sociol. of Lang.* (1968) 467 Certain Californian Indian tribes (the Yurok, Karok and Hupa). **1971** *Language* XLVII. 830 The Karok shift suggests consonant frequency raising in addition to palatalization.

†**karol, karolle**, etc. obs. ff. CAROL *sb.* and *v.*

Early examples of sense 5 of the sb.

1419–20 *Durham Acc. Rolls* (Surtees) 28 Et in soluc. facta pro karolles in claustro, 10s. **1483** *Cath. Angl.* 200/2 A Karalle or a wryting burde, *pluteus*.

Karolingian, variant of CAROLINGIAN.

‖**karoo, karroo** (kəˈruː). Also 8 karo, 9 karro. [Of Hottentot origin; but the precise etymology is uncertain. According to Lichtenstein (1811) and Burchell (1822), *karoo* or *karro* is a Namaqua Hottentot adj. meaning 'hard', but later authorities give for this *ˈkarusa* (Tindall 1857) or *ˈgarosa* (Kroenlein 1889), while the modern Hottentot name for the karroo is said to be *toró* (Kroenlein). *Garo* 'desert', has also been suggested as a possible source. Lichtenstein and Burchell may have wrongly identified *toró* or *garo* with the adj. meaning 'hard'. (See J. Platt, in *N. & Q.* 9th s. IV. 105; *Athenæum* 19 May, 1900.)

The earlier spellings indicate a pron. (kəˈroː); it is not clear whether (kəˈruː) is a phonetic development of this or due to the influence of Dutch orthography.]

The name given to barren tracts in South Africa, consisting of extensive elevated plateaus, with a clayey soil, which during the dry season are entirely waterless and arid.

The Great Karoo extends over an area 300 miles from West to East, and from 70 to 80 from South to North, in the centre of Cape Province.

1789 PATERSON *Narr. 4 Journeys* 44 Next day we proceeded through what the Dutch call Karo, an extensive plain. **1812** ANNE PLUMPTREE tr. *Lichtenstein's Trav. S. Afr.* 112 The Great Karroo, as it is called, a parched and arid plain. **1822** BURCHELL *Trav.* I. 207 A range of mountains.. separates the great Karro from the inhabited parts of the colony. **1845** DARWIN *Jrnl. Beagle* v. 89 Rhinoceroses and elephants [roaming] over the *Karros* of Southern Africa. **1847** *Nat. Encycl.* I. 256 The karoos in the dry season are almost as barren as the wastes of the Sahara. **1880** *S. Africa* (ed. 3) 155 Grasses and herbage found on the..Veldts and the Karroo.

b. *attrib.*, as ***karoo bush, country, desert, shrub***; also **karoo beds, formation, series**, an important South African series of rocks, of Triassic age, chiefly sandstone mixed with volcanic matter; **karoo ground**, a yellowish iron-clay.

1836 *Penny Cycl.* VI. 257/2 The Great Karroo is one of the most barren and desolate spots imaginable... The soil is a sand mixed with clay containing particles of iron, which gives it a yellowish colour: all soil of a similar colour in other parts of the Colony is called by the name of Karroo ground. **1842** MOFFAT *Miss. Tours S. Afr.* i. 17 The Karroo country ..is a parched and arid plain. **1876** *Encycl. Brit.* V. 42/1 The 'Karroo beds'..are believed from the abundance of fossil wood and fresh-water shells to be of lacustrine origin. **1885** RIDER HAGGARD *K. Solomon's Mines* v. 64 The waterless desert covered with a species of karoo shrub. **1886** H. CARVELL LEWIS *Papers on the Diamond* (1897) 7 The diamond-bearing pipes [at Kimberley] penetrate strata of Triassic age which are known as the Karoo beds. *Ibid.*, The Kimberley shales belong to the lower Karoo formation.

karoro (ˈkarɔːrɔː). *N.Z.* [Maori.] The southern black-backed gull, *Larus dominicanus*.

1861 A. S. ATKINSON *Jrnl.* 18 Jan. in *Richmond-Atkinson Papers* (1960) I. 680 Saw another noteworthy sight..a young karoro just out of the nest, running along in a curious human way all by himself. **1888** W. L. BULLER *Hist. Birds N.Z.* (ed. 2) II. 47 *Larus dominicanus*. (Southern Black-backed Gull.)..Native names. Karoro; the young bird distinguished as Ngoiro, Koiro, and Punua. **1930** W. R. B. OLIVER *N.Z. Birds* 260 Black-backed Gull. Karoro..[is] one of the most common and conspicuous birds on our coasts. **1966** R. A. FALLA et al. *Field Guide to Birds N.Z.* 154 Southern black-backed gull *Larus dominicanus*... Maori name: Karoro.

†**karos**, obs. f. CARUS, heavy sleep, torpor.

1598 SYLVESTER *Du Bartas* II. i. III. *Furies* 356 The Karos, th' Apoplexie, and Lethargie. **1623** in COCKERAM.

kaross (kəˈrɒs). Forms: α. 8 **krosse, cross,** 8–9 **kross**; β. 8– **kaross,** 9 **caross, karross.** [South African *karos*: see note below.]

A mantle (or sleeveless jacket) made of the skins of animals with the hair on, used by the Hottentots and other peoples of South Africa.

α. **1731** MEDLEY tr. *Kolben's Cape G. Hope* I. 187 Their Krosses (as the Hottentots term them) or mantles, cover the trunk of their bodies. **1775** MASSON in *Phil. Trans.* LXVI. 295 These Hottentots were all cloathed in crosses, or mantles, made of the hides of oxen. **1785** G. FORSTER tr. *Sparrman's Voy. Cape G. Hope in 1772*, etc. II. v. 187 These cloaks or Krosses, as they call them in broken Dutch. **1814** THUNBERG *Acc. Cape* in *Pinkerton's Voy.* XVI. 33 The sheepskin, which they call a Kross. **1839** MARRYAT *Phant. Ship* x, They wore not their sheepskin krosses.

β. **1785** G. FORSTER tr. *Sparrman's Voy. Cape G.H.* (1786) I. 188 The women have a long peak to their karosses. **1822** BURCHELL *Trav.* I. 267 The kaross, a genuine Hottentot dress, made of sheepskin prepared with the hair on, was pretty much used by both sexes. **1824** *Ibid.* II. 350 *Kaross* and *kobo* are but two words for the same thing: the former belongs to the Hottentot, and the latter to the Sichuana language. **1834** PRINGLE *Afr. Sk.* i. 132 Dressed in the old sheep-skin mantle or caross. **1880** SIR S. LAKEMAN *What I saw in Kaffir-Land* 58 Blankets and karosses were also left behind.

Comb. **1883** J. MACKENZIE *Day-dawn in Dark Places* 170 Disturbed..in their skin-dressing and kaross-making.

[Not a Bantu word, and app. not Hottentot. In W. Ten Rhyne's vocabulary of 1673 (in Churchill's *Voy.* IV. 845) '*Karos* colobium' (i.e. a jacket without sleeves or with arm-holes) is placed among the 'Corrupt Dutch Words', which are separated from the 'Original Hottentot Words'. In Sparrman's *Voy.* 1772–6 (see quot. 1785) it is called 'broken Dutch'. P. Kolbe (1745, in Astley's *Voyages* III. 351) gives the name of *kut-kros* to the skin-apron worn by women, and *kul-kros* to that of the men: in these the first element is Dutch. But it has not been ascertained of what Dutch word *kros* or *karos* could be a corruption. (Mr. James Platt, to whom these data for the history of the word are due, has suggested the possibility of its representing Du. *kuras*, or Pg. *couraça*, Sp. *coraza*, cuirass. (Ten Rhyne's 'Corrupt

Dutch Words' include *krallen*, kraal, really from Sp. *corral*, Pg. *curral*.) See *Notes and Queries* 9th Ser. V. 125, 236; *Athenæum* 19 May 1900.) But Hesseling, *Het Afrikaansch* (Leiden 1899) 81, thinks the word Hottentot.]

karoyne, karp(e, obs. ff. CARRION, CARP *v.*[1]

karper, var. KURPER.

karpinskyite (kɑːˈpɪnskɪaɪt). *Min.* [ad. Russ. *karpinskiit* (L. L. Shilin 1956, in *Doklady̆ Akademii Nauk SSSR* CVII. 737), f. the name of A. P. *Karpinsky* (1847–1936), Russ. geologist: see -ITE[1].] A hydrous alumino-silicate of sodium, beryllium, zinc, and magnesium, $Na_2(Be,Zn,Mg)\ Al_2Si_6O_{16}(OH)_2$, occurring as radial aggregates of white, needle-shaped crystals.

1956 *Doklady̆ Akademii Nauk SSSR* CVII. 628 (*table of contents*) Karpinskyite—a new mineral. **1958** *Mineral. Mag.* XXXI. 963 Karpinskyite. **1968** I. KOSTOV *Mineral.* 406 Leifite..is similar to cancrinite, and so also is karpinskyite.

karrat, karrawan, karre, karreine, karrek, obs. ff. CARAT, CARAVAN *sb.*, CARR[2], CARRION, CARRACK.

karree, var. KAREE.

‖**karren, Karren** (ˈkarən), *sb. pl. Geomorphol.* [Ger.] The furrows, fissures, or grikes of a *karrenfeld*; also, = *karrenfelder*.

1894 *Geogr. Jrnl.* III. 322 The chief features of such limestone regions are those known as *karren, dolinen*, blind valleys, and *poljen*. The *karren*, or surfaces composed of blocks of limestone separated by narrow fissures, are dealt with very briefly. **1898** *Ibid.* XII. 90 Karren are peculiar fissures in the rocky surface of some mountainous regions. **1902** LD. AVEBURY *Scenery of Eng.* xiii. 437 In calcareous districts the surface is sometimes quite bare and intersected by furrows... Such districts are known on the Continent as 'lapiées' or 'karren'. **1924** *Geogr. Rev.* XIV. 27 Lapiés are found at all altitudes from sea level to lofty mountain summits. They were first observed and described in the limestone Alps in Switzerland, where in the cantons of German speech they are called *Karren* or *Schratten*. **1960** B. W. SPARKS *Geomorphol.* vii. 155 The surface of the limestone..is often conspicuously furrowed and fretted (clints, grykes, lapiés, rascles, Schratten, Karren). **1971** J. N. JENNINGS *Karst* iv. 41 Very many *Karren* in central and western Europe must be regarded as stripped.

‖**karrenfeld, Karrenfeld** (ˈkarənfɛlt, -fɛld). *Geomorphol.* Pl. **-felder, -felds.** [G., f. *karren* (see prec.) + *feld* field.] An area or landscape, usu. of limestone bare of soil, which has been eroded by solution of the rock giving an extremely dissected surface with conspicuous furrows and fissures, often separated by knifelike ridges.

1885 A. GEIKIE *Text-bk. Geol.* (ed. 2) III. ii. 322 Limestones frequently assume a remarkable channelled rugose surface, with projecting knobs, ridges and pinnacles especially developed in high bare tracts of ground. (Karrenfelder.) **1922** *Geol. Mag.* LIX. 394 In Switzerland, notably in the canton Glarus, these bare surfaces known as *Karrenfelder* have been the subject of detailed studies by Heim. **1923** *Nature* 9 June 787/1 These have originated in guano, which gathered in the hollows of a 'karrenfeld', worn out of upraised coral-limestone. **1948** C. A. COTTON *Landscape* (ed. 2) xxiii. 445 It has been suggested that all karrenfelds are such surfaces stripped of soil in recent times. **1957** G. E. HUTCHINSON *Treat. Limnol.* I. i. 100 In some cases a *karrenfeld*, consisting of small pinnacles separated by crevices, may form.

‖**karri** (ˈkærɪ). Also **kari.** [Native name (W. Australia).] An Australian tree (*Eucalyptus diversicolor*, one of the 'blue gums'); also, its hard red timber, used in street-paving. Also *attrib.*

1870 W. H. KNIGHT *W. Austral.* 38 (Morris) The Karri.. is another wood very similar in many respects to the tuart. **1875** T. LASLETT *Timber* 196 (ibid.) The kari-tree is found in Western Australia. **1893** *Daily News* 21 Sept. 5/3 A 'panel' of karri wood has been laid opposite the West Strand Post Office, where the wear and tear is exceedingly heavy. **1897** *Illustr. Lond. News* 1 May 598 They..neither rot in the ground nor yield to the ravages of the white ant..it is not necessary to creosote Karri or Jarrah sleepers.

Karri-Kot: see CARRY-COT.

karroo, var. spelling of KAROO.

‖**karrozzin** (kəˈrɒtsɪn). Also **carozzi, carrozzi, karrozin.** [Maltese, f. It. *carrozza* carriage.] A horse-drawn cab used in Malta. Also *attrib.*

1926 E. SHEPHERD *Malta & Me* vii. 53, I..preferred the dreary carozzi. *Ibid.* xvi. 129 The roads leading to Valletta are black from early morning with carozzis. **1943** *Epic of Malta* 25 (*caption*) The picture above shows a 'carrozzi' (Maltese cab) at its usual.. stand. *Ibid.* 89 (*caption*) In the picture below Maltese ponies are seen sheltering beside their 'carozzis' (cabs). **1960** *Sunday Express* 6 Nov. 19/4 You can ride in a horse-drawn cab (called a *karrozin*). **1964** G. BUTLER *Coffin in Malta* iii. 66 The flower-sellers and the karrozzin drivers in the square. **1968** *Clarendonian* XXII. 269 One could get up into town by a lift up the cliff face for 2½d... or by karrozzin, the Maltese name for the colourful horse and buggy. **1972** *Daily Tel.* (Colour Suppl.) 21 Jan. 21 (Advt.), They're horse-drawn 'karrozzins', and each one is so beautifully painted you get the feeling all the owners are in earnest competition. Hire one, and go for a ride through Malta's tiny winding streets, at a good steady trot.

karrusel (kæruːˈsɛl). *Horology.* Also **karussell.** [Da., = CAROUSEL 2.] (See quot. 1962.)

1892 B. BONNIKSEN *Brit. Pat. No. 21,421* 24 Nov., The drawing accompanying this following description, is an illustration of what I have named a position-equalizing-karrusel (hereinafter termed 'karrusel'; the word 'karrusel' means the same as a 'roundabout') its purpose is to make the balance of..any..portable timepiece, turn round itself in any given time. **1929** G. H. BAILIE *Watches* xix. 347 A different type of tourbillon was invented by Bonniksen of Coventry in 1892 and called by him a Karussell. **1962** E. BRUTON *Dict. Clocks & Watches* 98 *Karrusel*, arrangement similar to the tourbillon in which the escapement revolves every 52½ minutes.

karsey, var. KARZY.

Karshuni, var. GARSHUNI.

karst, Karst (kɑːst). **1.** The name (*the Karst*, G. *der Karst* (= Serbo-Croat *Kras*)) of a high barren limestone region south of Ljubljana in N.W. Yugoslavia that has given its name to a kind of topography typified there (see 2); used *attrib.* in *Geomorphol.* (now usu. with small *k*) to designate similar regions and scenery, features, and phenomena associated with them, etc.; **karst land, karstland**, karstic land; a karstic region.

1894 *Geogr. Jrnl.* III. 321 Under the general designation *Karst-phenomena*, physical geographers in Germany include a variety of land-surface features, all characteristic of limestone regions, which, when the features in question are present, are known as 'Karst-regions'. *Ibid.* 509 A monotonous limestone plateau almost without water and vegetation, and occasionally exhibiting the very worst Karst features. **1898** Karst-land [see BLIND *a.* (and *adv.*) 11 c]. **1903** *Westm. Gaz.* 10 Feb. 3/1 The latter [*sc.* Herzegovina], although fertile in parts and well cultivated, is a Karst country, warm and southern. **1908** H. B. C. & W. J. SOLLAS tr. *Suess's Face of Earth* III. vi. 231 In the Shan states of Burma, several of the coulisses which approach from the north and north-east disappear beneath a karst-like plateau of Palaeozoic limestone. **1909** CHAMBERLIN & SALISBURY *Geol.: Shorter Course* xxiii. 689 The limestone and dolomite are much more resistant than the associated shales, and as a result, erosion has developed a distinctive topography (Karst topography) at several points in the southern Alps. **1921** *Geogr. Rev.* XI. 594 In a region where karst topography is fully developed the water circulates almost entirely underground. *Ibid.* 631 To Penck and others we owe something for their development of the idea of the karst cycle. **1922** *Geol. Mag.* LIX. 394 Karst phenomena are not infrequent in the Alpine limestone districts. **1924** *Glasgow Herald* 25 Aug. 4 Karakul sheep were also introduced..in the Austrian 'karst land', in the mountains between Croatia and the Adriatic. **1932** W. H. EMMONS et al. *Geol.* v. 80 In the United States similar topography is developed in limestone areas in central Tennessee and Kentucky and is referred to as Karst topography. **1939** BAILEY & WEIR *Introd. Geol.* xxxi. 183 Karst land is rare in Scotland. **1954** W. D. THORNBURY *Princ. Geomorphol.* xiii. 349 Whether there exists a distinct cycle of land-form evolution in limestone terrains which we may designate as a karst cycle or whether what has been so designated is better considered as the karst phase of a fluvial cycle is a disputed question. **1957** G. E. HUTCHINSON *Treat. Limnol.* I. i. 107 Along the southwestern shore of the lakes where the karst topography is best developed, there are not only many islands but also very deep holes. **1958** *Geogr. Jrnl.* CXXIV. 184 (*heading*) The karstlands of Jamaica. **1963** 'M. ALBRAND' *Call from Austria* xvii. 145 He might have fallen into one of those *karst* holes you can't spot until it's too late. **1963** D. W. & E. E. HUMPHRIES tr. *Termier's Erosion & Sedimentation* xiv. 316 A karst-eroded surface. **1971** *Guardian* 5 June 9/2 This is Italy's deep south, karst country, hot and dry, split with canyons.

2. (With small *k*.) A kind of topography of which the Yugoslavian Karst is typical, found in areas of readily dissolved rock (usually limestone) and predominantly underground drainage and marked by numerous abrupt ridges, fissures, sink-holes, and caverns; a region dominated by this kind of topography.

In quot. 1902 the Karst in Yugoslavia is referred to.

1902 *Geogr. Jrnl.* XX. 429 The uvala is a large, broad sinking in the karst with uneven floor. **1916** H. F. CLELAND *Geol.* iii. 72 Karst is used as a descriptive term for any limestone region which has been etched and eroded by water into a rough surface. **1922** *Geol. Mag.* LIX. 394 The south of France where the karst attains its greatest development in Western Europe. **1937** WOOLDRIDGE & MORGAN *Physical Basis Geogr.* xix. 289 The surface of a well-developed karst has lost all semblance of normal water-modelled forms. It is a stone desert, a chaos of pits, elongated hollows, and ridges. **1958** *Geogr. Jrnl.* CXXIV. 192 Considerable areas of degraded karst occur in northern and central Jamaica. **1963** D. W. & E. E. HUMPHRIES tr. *Termier's Erosion & Sedimentation* vi. 148 Bauxites occur very frequently on karsts. **1966** J. C. PUGH in G. H. Dury *Ess. Geomorphol.* 135 Some workers prefer to regard cockpit country and tower karst as typical of karst in general, holding that in the past too much emphasis has been placed on solution and on associated collapse of passages, and too little on surface features of solution which are not restricted to tropical regions. **1968** R. W. FAIRBRIDGE *Encycl. Geomorphol.* 682/2 The terrace surface is a deeply etched karst ('karrenfeld'), with pinnacles 15 feet high, alternating with deep crevices, partly filled with red soil. **1972** J. ROGLIĆ in Herak & Stringfield *Karst* i. 6 Following Cvijić, he considered the doline a basic feature ('Leitform') of karst.

Hence **ˈkarstic** *a.*, of or characteristic of karst; that is (a) karst.

1925 *Geogr. Rev.* XV. 72 The poljes have been formed by karstic and fluvial erosion. *Ibid.* 140 They occur in volcanic and karstic terrains. **1933** *Geogr. Jrnl.* LXXXI. 275 Karstic drainage occurs in limestone, dolomite, gypsum. **1957** G. E. HUTCHINSON *Treat. Limnol.* I. i. 19 In common with the other large lakes of the region [*sc.* the Balkans], both show some karstic features. **1963** D. W. & E. E. HUMPHRIES tr. *Termier's Erosion & Sedimentation* vi. 148 The karstic form of the limestone has thus acted as a trap for the transported sediment. **1970** R. J. SMALL *Study of Landforms* iv. 152 Enclosed depressions in karstic areas are usually attributed either to (i) slow downward development by solution processes..or to (ii) collapse of rock above an underground passage or cavern.

karstenite (ˈkɑːstənaɪt). *Min.* [ad. G. *karstenit*, named 1813, after D. L. G. Karsten: see -ITE[1].] Anhydrous sulphate of lime; now called ANHYDRITE.

1844 in DANA *Min.*

karstification (ˌkɑːstɪfɪˈkeɪʃən). *Geomorphol.* [f. KARST, KARST + -IFICATION.] Development of karst or karstic features; alteration into karst. So **ˈkarstify** *v. trans.*, to subject to karstification; **ˈkarstified, ˈkarstifying** *ppl. adjs.*

1958 *Geogr. Jrnl.* CXXIV. 186 'Karstification' of the White Limestones began..after the mid-Miocene movements. **1968** R. W. FAIRBRIDGE *Encycl. Geomorphol.* 582/2 For a karst to develop fully or for an area to become karstified, the region must possess the following set of features. **1972** *Science* 12 May 664/2 The book is a bit thin on chemistry, considering that karstification is mainly a chemical process. **1972** F. DARÁNYI in Herak & Stringfield *Karst* viii. 283 Karst surfaces in Hungary occupy an area of some 3,000 km². The contributions of the various epochs are, however, very different, being dependent on stratigraphic position, thickness, tectonic setting, and karstifying agents. *Ibid.*, On the present-day surface of the western half of the Mecsek, the 400 m thick Anisian sequence has been karstified.

karsting (ˈkɑːstɪŋ), *vbl. sb. Geomorphol.* [f. as prec. + -ING[1].] = KARSTIFICATION.

1921 *Geogr. Rev.* XI. 597 In youth, the surface of the land is still principally drained by the rivers which flow on the former surface of the land before the limestone subject to karsting was laid bare. **1956** D. L. LINTON *Sheffield* ii. 27 Our knowledge of the 'karsting' of the limestone plateau of the southern Pennines is still elementary.

karˈstology. *Geomorphol.* [f. as prec. + -OLOGY.] The study of karst.

1968 R. W. FAIRBRIDGE *Encycl. Geomorphol.* 560/2 There are furthermore several national and international organizations that promote congresses and publications in Speleology and Karstology. **1972** HERAK & STRINGFIELD *Karst* i. 2 The classical connection of karstology with the Dinaric karst was not accidental.

kart (kɑːt). Short for GO-KART. Hence **ˈkarting** *vbl. sb.*, the sport of driving or racing a kart.

1959 *Motor* 9 Sept. 111/1 The whole affair may well seem reprehensible to those who feel that an injustice has been wrought on the children or that karting is too juvenile for adults, but after trying a kart, although one must admit that they are a joke, there is no doubt that they are one of the very best jokes to come out of the U.S.A. since Thurber's dogs. After 10 minutes' karting the cynic is invariably asking where he can get one. **1961** *Sunday Express* 1 Jan. 15/3 '*Karting clothes*' the newest fad. **1964** K. WHEELER *Sport* 123 The newest motor sport is Karting. In the late 1950s the first little midget cars were seen on the tracks... Now karting is much faster, and an officially recognised sport with its own trophies and its own champions... A kart can cost as little as £80. **1968** *Times* 2 Aug. 13/2 Her tiny 100 c.c. machine is capable of 80 m.p.h. She has been driving since she was 13, the minimum age for kart racing in this country.

kart, obs. form of CART *sb.*

kart-, obs. form of CART-.

*c***1425** *Voc.* in Wr.-Wülcker 650/21 *Hic carpentarius*, kartwryght. **14..** *Ibid.* 568/16 *Bigata*, a kartlode. *Ibid.* 593/29 *Lolidolium*, a kartsadell. *Ibid.* 611/6 *Selabicalis* [? read *scala bigalis*], a kartladdere.

‖**kartel** (ˈkɑːt(ə)l). Also **cartel, cartle.** [S. African Dutch; app. ad. Pg. *catel, catle, catre* 'little bed', according to Schuchardt (*Kreol. Stud.* IX. 119), a South Indian word, Tamil *kattil* bedstead, adopted and diffused by the Portuguese.] The wooden bed or hammock, in a South African ox-wagon.

1880 P. GILLMORE *On Duty* 275 The worthy missionary had his waggon brought in front of the porch, swung a cartle in it, and made my bed there. **1883** OLIVE SCHREINER *Story Afr. Farm* II. xii. (1887) 276 Next day Gregory carried her ..to the waggon... As he laid her down on the 'kartel' she looked far out across the plain. **1885** RIDER HAGGARD *K. Solomon's Mines* iii. (1887) 42 In this after part was a hide 'cartle' or bed. **1910** J. BUCHAN *Prester John* viii. 151, I.. flung my kaross on the cartel which did duty as a bed.

karthe, erron. f. *scart*, SCRAT, hermaphrodite.

‖**karuna** (kəˈruːnə). *Buddhism.* [Skr. *karuṇā* charity, compassion.] Loving compassion, as that sought and attained by a *Bodhisattva*.

1850 R. S. HARDY *Eastern Monachism* xx. 246 When we see any object in distress, we feel kampáwíma, agitation, in the mind; and from this arises karuná, pity or compassion. **1960** A. HUXLEY *Let.* 17 July (1969) 893 Then no me any more and a kind of *sat chit ananda*, at one moment without *karuna* or charity. **1962** —— *Island* ix. 152 A fair chance.. of eventual *prajnaparamita* and *karuna*, eventual wisdom and compassion.

karval, -vel, obs. forms of CARVEL.

karve, karver, obs. ff. CARVE, CARVER[1].

kary, karyage, obs. ff. CARRY, CARRIAGE.

†**Karybdys, Karibdous,** obs. ff. CHARYBDIS. *c* **1400** *Rom. Rose* 4713 It [Love] is Karibdous perilous, Disagreable and gracious. *c* **1400** tr. *Secreta Secret., Gov. Lordsh.* 50 Sylla and karybdys.

karyn, karyun, obs. forms of CARRION.

†**karyn(e,** var. CARENE² *Obs.*, forty days' fast. **1502** ARNOLDE *Chron.* 150 Here folow' the knowelege what a Karyne ys... He that fulfilleth alle thes poyntis vij. yere duryng, dothe and wynnethe a Karyne, that ys to sey a Lenton.

karyo- (ˈkærɪəʊ), sometimes **caryo-**, combining form of Gr. κάρυον nut, kernel, employed in a number of biological terms referring to the nucleus of an animal or vegetable cell, esp. to changes which take place in its structure. The earliest of these were *karyolysis, karyolytic* (introduced by Auerbach in 1874) and *karyokinesis* (Schleicher). Those generally recognized are the following:

karyˈogamy [-GAMY], fusion of cell nuclei; **karyokinesis** (-kaɪˈniːsɪs) [Gr. κίνησις motion], the complicated series of changes observed in indirect or 'mitotic' division of a cell-nucleus; hence **karyokinetic** (-kaɪˈnɛtɪk) *a.*, pertaining to karyokinesis; **ˈkaryoˌlymph**, the more fluid portion of a cell-nucleus; **karyolysis** (kærɪˈɒlɪsɪs) [Gr. λύσις], the dissolution of a cell-nucleus (*Syd. Soc. Lex.* 1887); hence **karyolytic** (-ˈlɪtɪk) *a.*; **ˈkaryomere** [Gr. μέρος part], a vesicular chromosome enclosed in a nuclear membrane of its own, such as forms at telophase in the division of some cells; **karyomiˈtosis** [Gr. μίτος a thread], separation of the nuclear fibres in the process of cell-division; hence **karyomiˈtoic, -miˈtotic** *adjs.*; **ˈkaryoˌplasm** [Gr. πλάσμα thing moulded], the formed substance or protoplasm of the nucleus; nucleoplasm (*Syd. Soc. Lex.*); **karyo-plasˈmatic, -ˈplasmic** *adjs.*, of or pertaining to karyoplasm; **karyoˈrrhexis** [Gr. ῥῆξις breaking], bursting of a cell-nucleus; **karyosteˈnosis** [Gr. στένωσις constriction], direct or 'amitotic' division of the nucleus, by simple elongation and constriction; hence **karyosteˈnotic** *a.*; **karyoˈtheca** *rare*, the nuclear membrane.

1891 *Jrnl. R. Microsc. Soc.* 49 In *Hydatina*, as in some Hymenoptera, there is established between arrhenotoky (parthenogenetic production of males) and fecundating *karyogamy, a relation so necessary that the second is impossible without the first. **1901** G. N. CALKINS *Protozoa* iii. 97 It is quite possible that many cases of so-called conjugation are only instances of plastogamy, or fusion of the cell-body, and are not followed by union of the nuclei (karyogamy), as in fertilization. **1970** J. WEBSTER *Introd. Fungi* 187 Karyogamy (i.e. nuclear fusion) occurs within certain of the binucleate cells. **1882** VINES tr. *Sachs' Bot.* 17 In the process of division into two the nucleus usually goes through a series of changes which are designated by the term *Karyokinesis. **1894** H. DRUMMOND *Ascent Man* i. 80 The fertilised ovum has completed the complex preliminaries of Karyokinesis. **1885** SEDGWICK in *Proc. R. Soc.* XXXIX. 243 The *karyo-kinetic figures characteristic of the ectodermal nuclei. **1888** ROLLESTON & JACKSON *Anim. Life* Introd. 23 The ovular nucleus.. undergoes karyokinetic changes. **1899** *Allbutt's Syst. Med.* VI. 491 Fine fibrils.. floating in the *karyolymph. *Ibid.* 168 The leucocytes, often at an early date, undergo fatty degeneration and necrosis, their nuclei disappearing both by *karyolysis and karyorrhexis. **1883** tr. *Ziegler's Path. Anat.* I. §75 Radiating lines of granules making up the so-called *karyolytic figure. **1912** *Jrnl. Acad. Nat. Sci. Philadelphia* XV. 525 The most general results of increased temperature are:... (4) Formation of numerous *karyomeres from these scattered chromosomes; indeed by slight increase of temperature almost every chromosome may be caused to remain distinct from every other one, and to give rise to a separate chromosomal vesicle. **1934** L. W. SHARP *Introd. Cytol.* (ed. 3) x. 136 Of considerable interest are those nuclei in which every chromosome of the telophase group forms an individual vesicle, or karyomere. In some cases the karyomeres may eventually fuse partially or completely, but in others they remain separate although in contact, forming what is virtually a group of small nuclei containing one chromosome each. *Ibid.* 146 The limits of the several chromosomes remain visible through this stage [*sc.* between mitoses] in certain nuclei; in extreme cases the nucleus is virtually a group of separate elementary nuclei, or karyomeres. **1969** BROWN & BERTKE *Textbk. Cytol.* xvii. 318/2 Karyomeres are rather like micronuclei except that they are normal and become associated to form a 'compound' nucleus. **1885** SCHÄFER in *Proc. R. Soc.* XXXVIII. 91 The cells of lymphoid tissue multiply abundantly by *karyomitosis. *Ibid.*, Those peculiar changes in the nucleus which have been termed karyokinetic or *karyomitoic. **1897** *Allbutt's Syst. Med.* II. 7 These cells.. frequently show the phenomenon of karyo-mitosis, that is, a division of their nucleus with a star-shaped figure at each end. **1899** *Ibid.* VI. 491 The nucleus or *karyo-plasm, also shows a reticulum of exceedingly fine fibrils. **1920** L. DONCASTER *Introd. Study Cytol.* ii. 16 Hertwig regards a disturbance of the normal karyo-plasmatic ratio as the immediate cause of cell-division, and supposes that the unequal rate of growth of nucleus and cytoplasm brings about a condition of '*karyo-plasmatic strain' leading to cell-division and a consequent restoration of the normal ratio. **1909** *Cent. Dict.* Suppl., *Karyoplasmic. **1924** E. V. COWDRY *Gen. Cytol.* VI. 351 Hertwig's karyoplasmic relation hypothesis. **1925** E. B. WILSON *Cell* (ed. 3) iii. 237 These various facts show on how precarious a basis rest theories of senescence and rejuvenescence which refer these processes to changes in the karyoplasmic ratio. **1948** R. A. R. GRESSON *Essent. Gen. Cytol.* i. 2 It has been found that a quantitative relationship exists between nuclear mass and cytoplasmic mass; this is known as the karyoplasmic ratio. **1966** D. M. KRAMSCH tr. *Grundmann's Gen. Cytol.* ii. 66 The optical appearance of the karyoplasmic area is homogeneous and frequently seems to be empty. **1896** E. B. WILSON *Cell* 337 **Karyotheca*, the nuclear membrane. **1948** W. ANDREW tr. *E. D. P. de Robertis's Gen. Cytol.* iii. 45 Between the two parts of this heterogeneous system.., there is found the karyotheca or nuclear membrane.

karyogram (ˈkærɪəʊgræm). *Biol.* [f. KARYO- + -GRAM.] **a.** A karyotype or idiogram.

In quot. 1952 (by a Jap. writer) perh. an error for *karyotype*, which is used throughout the paper (in sense 1 a).

1952 *Cytologia* XVII. 311 (*heading*) Karyogram studies in birds. **1965** *Amer. Jrnl. Bot.* LII. 968 (*caption*) Karyogram from untreated apical and nodal cells.. showing chromosome length greater than that in pretreated antheridial filament cells. **1971** *Nature* 9 Apr. 368/1 (*caption*) A typical karyogram of Chinese hamster strain *wg* 3 *IMP-*: twenty-two chromosomes, all but one (bottom right) distinguishable from those of mouse strain *3T3 TK-*.

b. A diagram in which each chromosome of a set is represented by a point positioned with respect to a vertical and a horizontal axis, these axes corresponding to two numerical characteristics of the chromosomes.

1960 K. PATAU in *Amer. Jrnl. Human Genetics* XII. 255 A chromosome characterized by two quantities is best represented by a point in a two-dimensional co-ordinate system. The choice of these quantities—total length and arm index or two arm lengths, is in principle irrelevant... Let the percent length, l, of the longer arm serve as abscissa and the percent length, s, of the shorter arm as ordinate. The scatter diagram obtained by plotting in this manner all chromosomes of the given complement will henceforth be referred to as a 'karyogram'. **1966** STEWART & KILLEAN in Darlington & Lewis *Chromosomes Today* I. 211 In the production of karyograms the basic data are taken from a photographic enlargement of the chromosome plate to be analysed. **1969** *Nature* 22 Nov. 801/2 The results of a chromosome analysis can be displayed in several ways. The methods commonly used are the karyotype.. and the karyogram, in which each chromosome is represented by a point in a bivariate coordinate system.

karyology (kærɪˈɒlədʒɪ). *Biol.* [f. KARYO- + -LOGY.] **a.** The distinctive or characteristic features (esp. as regards chromosomes) of a particular cell nucleus, or of the nuclei of a particular species, strain, etc. **b.** The study of cell nuclei, esp. the chromosomes they contain.

1895 *Ann. Bot.* IX. 631 Wager ('89) has carefully investigated the karyology of *Peronospora parasitica*. **1932** *Symbolae Bot. Upsalienses* I. 150 The chromosomes have individuality or genetic continuity from one cell generation to another. This conception.. may be considered as the foundation of all comparative karyology. **1948** W. ANDREW tr. *E.D.P. de Robertis's Gen. Cytol.* vii. 134 There was considerable progress in karyology, which is a branch of cytology dealing with the nucleus or karyosome, to the detriment of the study of the cytoplasm or cytosome. **1965** *Jrnl. Nat. Cancer Inst.* (U.S.) XXXV. 766/1 This.. indicates a significant difference between the general karyology of the normal cell and of the tumor cell population. **1970** *Cytologia* XXXV. 294 (*heading*) Karyology of *Sequoia sempervirens*: karyotype and accessory chromosomes. **1971** *Daily Colonist* (Victoria, B.C.) 24 Dec. 4/2 Karyology, or the study of the number, shape, and size of chromosomes, is Dr. Wiens' specialty.

Hence **karyoˈlogic** (chiefly *U.S.*), **-ˈlogical** *adjs.*, of or pertaining to karyology; **karyoˈlogically** *adv.*, as regards or in relation to karyology.

1927 *Trudy̆ po Prikladnoĭ Botanike i Selektsii* XVII. III. 64 Presence, shape and size of the satellite are characters of much importance in karyological systematics. *Ibid.* 65 The plates given.. represent races which are karyologically most sharply different. **1929** *Cytologia* I. 76 (*heading*) Karyological studies in *Hemerocallis*. **1935** *Experiment Station Rec.* LXXII. 754 Karyologic and genetic studies with Fragaria. **1962** *Exper. Cell Res.* XXVI. 434 (*heading*) Karyologic studies on polyoma virus induced mouse tumors. **1962** *Lancet* 27 Jan. 219/1 Karyologically the cells with 47 chromosomes were typically mongoloid, and those with 46 chromosomes were normal. **1970** *Nature* 11 July 169/1 The karyological properties of MRC-5 cells conform to those required of a diploid cell of human origin to be used for producing viral vaccines intended for human use. **1974** *Ibid.* 5 Apr. 504/2 A unique possibility of investigating RSV production on a permanent cell line which is well defined karyologically.

ˈkaryosome. [f. KARYO- + Gr. σῶμα body; in sense 1, ad. G. *karyosoma* (M. Ogata 1883, in *Arch. f. Anat. u. Physiol.* (Physiol. Abt.) 414).]

1. a. A body of chromatin in a nucleus resembling a nucleolus but distinguished from the 'true' nucleolus or plasmosome. **b.** Any densely staining central body of a nucleus.

1889 [see *hyalosome* s.v. HYALO-]. **1890** WALDEYER in *Jrnl. Microsc. Sci.* XXX. 168 Distinguished as.. 'karyosomes', bodies that are stained blue;.. 'plasmasomes', which stain red;.. 'hyalosomes', which are not stained. **1896** E. B. WILSON *Cell* i. 24 The bodies known by this name [*sc.* nucleolus] are of at least two different kinds. The first of these, the so-called true nucleoli or plasmosomes.., are of spherical form... Those of the other form, the 'net-knots' (Netzknoten), or karyosomes, are either spherical or irregular in form, stain like the chromatin, and appear to be no more than thickened portions of the chromatic network. **1901** G. N. CALKINS *Protozoa* v. 146 In most cases they [*sc.* the nuclei of Sporozoa] consist of a firm and resisting membrane containing a single large chromatin reservoir or karyosome. **1920** L. DONCASTER *Introd. Study Cytol.* ii. 18 The karyosome or chromatic nucleolus is a mass of chromatin of varying size... It appears to serve as a reservoir of chromatin from which the chromosomes.. may draw part at least of their supply when nuclear division is approaching. **1926** G. N. CALKINS *Biol. Protozoa* ii. 60 The centrally placed intranuclear body is generally described under the name karyosome, a term which has been so widely used by students of the Protozoa and for so many obviously different structures that it is practically synonymous with endosome or Binnenkörper. **1948** W. ANDREW tr. *E.D.P. de Robertis's Gen. Cytol.* iii. 59 In the fixed nucleus one can distinguish:.. (4) in some nuclei there are found larger and denser flakes of chromatin situated in the chromonemata, the chromocenters or karyosomes, also called false nucleoli or chromatin nucleoli. **1961** MACKINNON & HAWES *Introd. Study Protozoa* i. 12 The term karyosome (the endosome of some authors) is here used descriptively as the name of any conspicuous, deeply staining body lying in the nuclear sap, without regard to its constitution. Undoubtedly some karyosomes are really nucleoli (*Trichomonas vaginalis*) and they disappear during mitosis; others play an important part in that process (*Naegleria*) and some are Feulgen positive (*Trichomonas sanguisugae*). **1969** BROWN & BERTKE *Textbk. Cytol.* xvii. 320/1 The terms 'karyosome', 'endosome', and 'central body' are applied to nucleolus-like nuclear organelles that are permanent structures... Karyosomes, etc. are probably permanent nucleoli that undergo division and are found in numerous algae, protozoa, and some fungi.

†**2.** = NUCLEUS *sb.* 7. *Obs.*

1894 S. WATASÉ in *Biol. Lect. Marine Biol. Lab. Wood's Holl 1893* 84 An animal cell may be described as composed of two sharply distinct organs: the cell body (cytosome), and the nucleus (caryosome). **1948** [see KARYOLOGY].

karyotin (ˈkærɪəʊtɪn). *Biol.* Also **-ine**. [a. G. *karyotin* (H. Lundegård 1910, in *Svensk bot. Tidskr.* IV. 177), f. *karyo-* KARYO- + *-tin* (after *chromatin*).] The stainable material of a cell nucleus; the substance of which the nuclear reticulum is composed.

1925 E. B. WILSON *Cell* (ed. 3) i. 90 Such considerations led Lundegårdh ('10) to propose that the term 'chromatin' be replaced by 'karyotin' (caryotin), the substance thus designated appearing in either a basichromatic or an oxyphilic phase. **1934** L. W. SHARP *Introd. Cytol.* (ed. 3) iii. 55 Only future research can decide whether karyotin ('chromatin' in the wide sense) is a true chemical compound. **1948** W. ANDREW tr. *E.D.P. de Robertis's Gen. Cytol.* vii. 138 Other authors admit the existence of two distinct phases: the karyolymph, which is considered as a colloid sufficiently stable to be precipitated only with acids and fixatives, and the karyotin, a more labile and complex colloid dispersed in the karyolymph, which would precipitate with great facility. **1966** D. H. KRAMSCH tr. *Grundmann's Gen. Cytol.* ii. 66 The nucleus was.. regarded as a solution, a sol in which little droplets, the so-called karyotine droplets, representing a somewhat more solid 'phase', were dispersed.

karyotype (ˈkærɪəʊtaɪp), *sb. Biol.* and *Med.* [ad. Russ. *kariotip* (L. N. Delone (Delaunay) 1922, in *Vestnik Tiflisskogo botanicheskogo Sada* 2nd Ser. I. 49): see KARYO- and -TYPE.

Orig. coined by Delaunay in sense 2, but according to quot. 1931 it was later coined independently (again in Russ.) by Lewitsky (1924), in sense 1 a.]

1. a. The chromosomal constitution of a cell (and hence of an individual, species, etc.) as determined by the number, size, shape, etc., of the chromosomes (usually, as observed at metaphase during cell division).

1929 *Amer. Jrnl. Bot.* XVI. 415 In studying the karyotypes of different varieties of *Hyacinthus orientalis* which have chromosomes with permanent secondary constrictions, del Mol (1927) found correlation between the number of chromosomes with constrictions and the number of nucleoli. **1931** G. A. LEWITSKY in *Trudy̆ po Prikladnoĭ Botanike i Selektsii* XXVII. I. 221, I have proposed myself, independently from Delaunay, the same term 'Karyotype', but merely for designation of nuclear peculiarities of a given organism or systematical unit. **1934** L. W. SHARP *Introd. Cytol.* (ed. 3) ix. 128 The diagrammatic representation of a karyotype.. is called an idiogram. *Ibid.* 129 Groups of related genera, as well as the related species of a genus, often have the same general karyotype. **1956** *Nature* 18 Feb. 336/1 In species of *Hemerocallis*, etc., different individuals of the same species differ in the karyotypes of the normal cells, even if these do not differ in chromosome number. **1957** C. P. SWANSON *Cytol. & Cytogenetics* xiii. 449 It is from a close study of related species.. that the evolution of the karyotype has been to a limited extent unravelled. **1957**, etc. [see IDIOGRAM]. **1961** *Lancet* 29 July 263/2 The mother.. and the father.. were also examined by fibroblast tissue culture and their karyotypes were apparently normal. **1964** M. HARRIS *Cell Culture & Somatic Variation* iv. 239 In these materials, normal chromosome complements were reported to predominate, with abnormal karyotypes appearing ordinarily only in tumors of large size or after transplantation. **1971** *Nature* 31 Dec. 506/3 It should now be possible, in theory at least, to eradicate Down's syndrome (mongolism) by recognizing its karyotype in foetal cells, and aborting the foetuses concerned.

b. A systematized representation of the chromosomes of a cell or cells, esp. a photographic one (cf. IDIOGRAM).

1950 in WEBSTER Add. **1960** *Lancet* 14 May 1063/1 In contemporary publications the terms, karyotype and idiogram, have often been used indiscriminately. We would recommend that the term, *karyotype*, should be applied to a systematised array of the chromosomes of a single cell prepared either by drawing or by photography, with the extension in meaning that the chromosomes of a single cell can typify the chromosomes of an individual or even a species. **1969** *Nature* 22 Nov. 801/2 The results of a chromosome analysis can be displayed in several ways. The methods commonly used are the karyotype, 'a systematized

array of the chromosomes of a single cell', and the karyogram. **1970** *Sci. Jrnl.* June 76/3 The best way we know of detecting abnormalities is to cut out each chromosome from a photomicrograph and pair them up like a jigsaw. This array, known as a karyotype, is constructed according to an international convention. **1970** J. D. BURKE *Cell Biol.* ix. 267 (*caption*) The mitotic meta-phase chromosomes of a somatic cell of a male, arranged in a karyotype. **1973** *Lancet* 24 Feb. 420/1 Strictly speaking the actual pictures are karyotypes, and an idiogram is a diagram of the chromosome state of an individual.

†**2.** [After the original meaning of the Russ.] A group of species having similar karyotypes (sense 1 a). *Obs. rare.*

1931 *Trudȳ po Prikladnoĭ Botanike i Selektsii* XXVII. i. 221 [*Referring to the work of L. N. Delaunay.*] The variations from species to species within the indicated genera, or 'karyotypes' are, as it were, quantitative. In most cases it is but the length of the arms of the chromosomes..which undergoes variation. **1932** H. G. BRUUN in *Symbolae Bot. Upsalienses* I. 111 The species [of *Primula*] can be divided according to their nuclear constitution into different cytological types..called 'karyotypes'. *Ibid.* 117 Allied species as a rule also belong to the same karyotype. *Ibid.* 195 In agreement with this [statement of Delaunay's], 'Karyotypus' has been defined as a taxonomical conception, for which reason its use is made impossible in discussing the relation between taxonomy and cytology... In this work.. the unconditional term 'cytological type' has had to be employed instead. But there exists an obvious need of a term to include all the species with nuclei of similar type, independent of taxonomical considerations, and in this sense I suggest that the term 'karyotype' be used... The karyotype should, therefore, be founded exclusively on chromosome-morphology.

karyotype ('kærɪəʊtaɪp), *v. Biol.* and *Med.* [f. prec. sb.] *trans.* To determine or investigate the karyotype of.

1963 *Lancet* 24 Aug. 417/1 The more cells examined (karyotyped) the greater the chance of encountering neoplastic cells. **1971** *Nature* 11 June 387/1 Ninety-seven of these modal cells were karyotyped according to the Denver-London system. **1972** *Lancet* 29 July 213/2 Newborn infants who were suspected of having an anomalous cytogenetic constitution of any kind have been photographed, X-rayed, and karyotyped.

Hence '**karyotyped** *ppl. a.*, '**karyotyping** *vbl. sb.*

1963 *Lancet* 24 Aug. 417/1 We have undertaken..the karyotyping of cells obained by lumbar puncture. **1966** *New Scientist* 3 Nov. 217/1 Foetal karyotyping would not, of course, reveal all genetic defects. It would show up gross chromosome abnormalities. **1971** *Nature* 2 July 25/1 In the karyotyped cells, all the normal chromosomes could be separated into pairs on the basis of their distinctive patterns of fluorescence.

karyotypic (kærɪəʊ'tɪpɪk), *a. Biol.* and *Med.* [f. as prec. + -IC.] Of or pertaining to a karyotype. Also **karyo'typical** *a.*, in the same sense.

1931 *Trudȳ po Prikladnoĭ Botanike i Selektsii* XXVII. i. 236 The lowest type of karyotypical variations are certainly the polyploid multiplication of sets. **1959** *Cytologia* XXIV. 390 No work has yet been carried out to find out how far karyotypic changes..have contributed to the origin of these varieties. **1963** *Canad. Jrnl. Genetics & Cytol.* V. 132 The idiogram can also be considered as a standard for detecting potential karyotypical alterations. **1964** M. HARRIS *Cell Culture & Somatic Variation* iv. 201 Various neoplasms among a series of related tumors were found to share these features, although individual differences were found in the detailed karyotypic patterns. **1968** *New Scientist* 2 May 219/2 Karyotypic analysis, or biochemical tests for the presence of sex-linked genes.., might be employed as alternative methods of sexing.

Hence **karyo'typically** *adv.*, as regards karyotype.

1965 *Canad. Jrnl. Genetics & Cytol.* VII. 358 Karyotypically abnormal cells. **1972** *Science* 23 June 1333/1 Differences in..chromosome lengths between two karyotypically divergent groups of *Peromyscus maniculatus* are taken as evidence for an addition-deletion mechanism of chromosomal variation. **1972** *Nature* 8 Sept. 88/2 Several HAT-resistant clones were karyotypically male.

karzy ('kɑːzɪ). *slang.* Also **carsey, carsy, karsey, karzey.** [Corruption of It. *casa* house.] = WATER-CLOSET.

1961 PARTRIDGE *Dict. Slang* Suppl. 1029/1 *Carsey*,..a w.c. **1965** *Daily Mail* 2 Oct. 5/4 Where do you spend a penny? (a) Toilet..(d) Karzy. **1966** D. FRANCIS *Flying Finish* ix. 118, I was in the cockpit most of the time... I went aft to the karzy once. **1967** J. BURKE *Till Death us do Part* v. 84 Have you seen the carsy? Just a bucket with a seat on top. **1968** T. E. B. CLARKE *Trail of Serpent* xiii. 122 You made a real thorough search? Everywhere? Outhouses, karzey, the lot? **1969** K. GILES *Death cracks Bottle* iv. 38 Apart from a working pee none of my ladies nor me got out of here. There's only one door to the carsey. **1970** G. F. NEWMAN *Sir, You Bastard* 262 Visits to the karsey.

kas-: see also CAS-.

kasbah ('kæzbɑː). Also **casbah, cashbah, cassaubah, kasba, kasbar.** [ad. F. *casbah*, f. N. Afr. Arab. dial. *ḳaṣba* fortress.] **a.** A North African castle or fortress. **b.** The Arab quarter surrounding a castle or fortress in a North African town, esp. that of Algiers.

1738 T. SHAW *Trav. Barbary & the Levant* 313 They made an unsuccessful Attempt upon the Government, by endeavouring to seize upon the *Cassaubah*. **1844** J. H. DRUMMOND HAY *Western Barbary* 113 We paced with measured steps to the *Kasba*, or citadel, wherein is situated the '*Dar-al-Kebeer*', the residence of the governor. **1857** H. BARTH *Travels* I. 147 The little kasbah, which is never wanting in any of these towns, was in tolerable condition. **1867** 'OUIDA' *Under Two Flags* II. i. 12 Singing her refrain, ..as she bounded over the picturesque desolation of the Cashbah. **1890** G. W. HARRIS *Pract. Guide Algiers* I. 41 This Casbah, in the good old days of Algerian predominance, was a magnificent palace fitted with all the luxury and refinement of the epoch. **1902** *Westm. Gaz.* 9 Dec. 3/1 Algiers.., with its quaint Kasbah, or native quarter, its Citadel,..and its interesting suburbs. **1930** E. WAUGH *Labels* viii. 189 Five Scots people..were caught by a very shady guide who took them up to the Kasbar in a taxi-cab. **1958** *Times Lit. Suppl.* 11 July 393/4 The kasbah country south of the Atlas *is* on the tourist route, and well organized. **1961** *Times* 6 May 9/7 In Algiers the Casbah is entirely without romance. **1969** R. LANDAU *Kasbas S. Morocco* 11 The first kasbas (qasbas, more precisely) were built by the Almohad dynasty in the thirteenth century; they were not simply fortresses, but were the walled-in section of the ruler's capital, a complex with palace, main mosque,..and various state offices. **1971** *Country Life* 28 Oct. 1120 The kasbahs, or mud fortresses, of the pre-Saharan oases in southern Morocco are virtually unique as a form of defensive architecture.

†'**kaser.** *Obs.* Forms: 1 caser, 1–2 (5) casere, 1–3 kasere, 3 kaserr, 5 kasar, 7 cazard. [OE. *cásere*, repr. the Comm. Teut. type *kaisar*, ad. L. *Cæsar* or Gr. *Kaîσaρ*, the *ai* giving OE. *á*, as in native words. The southern ME. form would have been *cōser*; but the word is known only in the northern form, having been early supplanted by the newer adoptions KAISER and CÆSAR.

The ending is conformed to the *-ere* of agent-nouns like *dómere, bócere*, etc.; cf. ON. *keisari*. But the *Lindisf. Gosp.* Gloss. has *caser* as dat. and acc. (dat. also *casere, -eri, -ari*), and in the genitive *cæsares, casseres, cessares*.]

The Emperor, an emperor; = KAISER.

c **888** K. ÆLFRED *Boeth.* xxxviii. §1 þæs kaseres nama wæs Agamenon. *a* **900** *Martyrol. Fragm.* in *O.E. Texts* 178 Datianus se casere. *c* **950** *Lindisf. Gosp.* John xix. 15 Nabbo we cyning buta ðone caser. *a* **1154** *O.E. Chron.* an. 1106 ȝewinn betwux þam Casere of Sexlande and his sunu. *c* **1200** ORMIN 8329 þe Romanisshe king..þatt ta wass Kaserr oferr hemm. *Ibid.* 9172 He wass sett to been Kasere i Rome riche. *c* **1425** WYNTOUN *Cron.* v. ix. 2742 Casere, kyng, na empriowre. *c* **1460** *Towneley Myst.* xiv. 220 That prynce that shalle ouer com in hy kasar and kyng. *a* **1605** MONTGOMERIE *Misc. Poems* iii. 40 Sho [Fortune] counts not kings nor cazards mair nor cuiks. *Ibid.* xiv. 43.

Comb. *c* **1200** ORMIN 3270 An Romanisshe Kaserrking Wass Augusstuss ȝehatenn. *Ibid.* 3294, etc.

‖**kasha**[1] ('kæʃə). Also **casha.** [Russ.] **1.** A gruel or porridge made from cooked buckwheat or other meals or cereals.

1808 M. WILMOT *Jrnl.* 5 July in *Russ. Jrnls.* (1934) III. 356 Their Casha is very like *Stirabout*, & this is a favourite dish. **1903** [see BLINTZE]. **1958** HAYWARD & HARARI tr. *Pasternak's Dr. Zhivago* II. ix. 270 I'll get Uncle Yury to stay to dinner and take the kasha out of the oven. **1961** N. FROUD et al. tr. *Montagné's Larousse Gastronomique* 554 Kasha is the Russian for cooked buckwheat. **1966** N. BEHN *Kremlin Let.* xiv. 141 Breakfast..consisted of one small bowl of kasha.. the [Russian] equivalent to American hot cereals. **1971** *New Statesman* 1 Jan. 8/3 Rents are low in Russia..and the basic necessities—bread, potatoes and *kasha* flour—are not dear. **1973** *Times* 3 Feb. 13/5 You can try the kneidlach soup (with matzo-meal dumplings), the kasha (buckwheat) and the tzimmes.

2. A beige colour resembling that of buckwheat groats.

1957 M. MCCARTHY *Memories Catholic Girlhood* viii. 200 She had an outfit made..in a new colour called 'kashha'. **1971** *Guardian* 19 Jan. 9/3 Principal colours are navy, 'Kasha' (a Russian buckwheat porridge beige), and 'smoke'.

Kasha[2] ('kæʃə). Also **kasha.** The proprietary name, originated by Rodier, a French textile manufacturer, of a soft napped fabric made from wool and hair. Also in various *Combs.* (see quots.). Also applied to a cotton lining material.

1920 *Queen* 10 Apr. 466 Dress with very wide skirt in pale green kasha. **1923** *Daily Mail* 12 Feb. 15 White Kasha cloth. **1926** *Queen* 17 Feb. 10 A modified Inverness coat made by Lelong in the new kasha with the slightly spongy surface —kashatoile. **1926** G. G. DENNY *Fabrics* (ed. 2) II. 53 *Kasha*, (a) fine, soft, napped wool dress fabric originated with Rodier Freres, Paris. (b) Cotton plain weave napped on reverse side, for linings. **1928** *Observer* 4 Mar. 20/4 The couturiers..give prominence to jersey, crêpella, Kashatoil, Kashangora, and a host of other materials. **1941** R. STOUT *Red Threads* i. 6 He must have the natural kasha, the one with nubs, by tomorrow. **1942** G. G. DENNY *Fabrics* (ed. 5) I. 37 *Kasha*, fine, soft napped wool dress fabric with crosswise streaked effect in dark hairs... Similar textures in wool and cotton now made in United States called Kasha. **1967** *Boston Sunday Globe* 23 Apr. (Advt. Suppl.), Roomy enough to sleep 2 or separate into two single full size sleeping bags. Top, bottom and snap-on canopy made of cotton duck, with kasha flannel lining. **1968** J. IRONSIDE *Fashion Alphabet* 234 *Kasha*, very soft pale beige fabric made from goat-hair and wool.

Kashan (kə'ʃɑːn). Also **Keshan.** The name of a province and town in central Iran, used (freq. *attrib.*) to designate a finely woven rug, usu. of wool or silk, made there.

1905 M. C. RIPLEY *Oriental Rug Bk.* 305 Kashan rugs. **1920** C. J. D. MAY *How to identify Persian Rugs* v. 61 *Sarouks*... The student may regard these merely as a slightly inferior grade of Kashan. **1931** A. U. DILLEY *Oriental Rugs & Carpets* iv. 122 Kashan rugs, always important, were so far unrecognized as a separate weaving thirty years ago that no mention of them was made in the first modern rug books. **1960** H. HAYWARD *Antique Collecting* 157/1 *Kashan carpets*, Persian carpets in which medallion and prayer designs predominate, woven in wool or silk. **1962** *Times* 12 June 20/1 (Advt.), A beautiful and rare carved silk Keshan rug...a superb natural Keshan carpet. **1962** C. W. JACOBSEN *Oriental Rugs* II. 230 In the 20 nearby villages..Kashans are woven which are equal to those made in the city itself. **1963** L. DEIGHTON *Horse under Water* xxxviii. 150 I'm leaving before I vomit over your beautiful Kashan carpet. **1967** J. MORGAN *Involved* 126 Thomas looked up from an all-silk Kashan rug he was lying on.

Kashgai ('kæʃgaɪ). Also **Kashkai, Qashgai, Qashqai.** A Turkic-speaking people living around Shiraz in Persia; a member of this people. Also *attrib.*

1885 *Encycl. Brit.* XVIII. 625/1 The Kashgais, or those wandering semi-Turkish tribes brought down from Turkestan to the neighbourhood of Shiráz, have the credit of possessing good steeds. **1921** *Glasgow Herald* 19 April 5 Among the most important questions were the relations with the Kashgais and other nomad tribes. The Kashgais were about 135,000 strong. **1937** *Sunday Times* 29 Aug. 7/5 The region is occupied by scattered and turbulent Qashgais upon whom the Tehran Government has only very recently imposed its authority. **1957** H. H. VREELAND *Iran* ix. 105 The Qashqa'i tribesmen are important in this area. *Ibid.* x. 128 The Qashqa'i have firmly resisted conscription, and no tribal members have yet been taken into the army.

b. Used *attrib.* or *absol.* to designate a type of nomad rug made by them.

1922 KENDRICK & TATTERSALL *Hand-Woven Carpets* 196 Kashkai carpets. **1931** A. U. DILLEY *Oriental Rugs & Carpets* iv. 95 Both Afshar and Kashgai rugs are Caucasian nomad transplants. **1962** C. W. JACOBSEN *Oriental Rugs* II. 257 Plate 104 is a typical design found in many Qashqai (Mecca Shiraz) but no two designs are exactly alike. *Ibid.* III. 403 The correct technical name is 'Qashqai Prayer Rug'.

Kashgar ('kɑːʃgɑː(r)). [See sense 2.] **1.** A language or dialect of the central Turkic or Turco-Tatar group of Altaic languages, spoken in Kashgar. Also *attrib.* or as *adj.*

1875 R. B. SHAW *Sk. Turki Lang.* p. xv, An examination of the Yarkánd and Káshghar dialect accounts for them in another way. **1918** G. W. HUNTER *Examples Turki Dial.* III. 1 Under this section is included Kashgar Turki and Kirghese Turki as they have much in common... Kashgar Turki is spoken by the Sart..people of Chinese Turkestan. **1948** D. DIRINGER *Alphabet* 568 Kashgar Turkish, spoken between the T'ien Shan mountains and northern Tibet. **1954** PEI & GAYNOR *Dict. Ling.* 113 *Kashgar*, an Asiatic language; member of the Central Turkic group of the Altaic sub-family of the Ural-Altaic family of languages.

2. The name of a city and district of Sinkiang-Uighur (formerly East Turkestan), used *attrib.* or *absol.* to designate a type of Turkoman carpet.

1900 J. K. MUMFORD *Oriental Rugs* (1901) 273 Kashgar rugs. **1931** A. U. DILLEY *Oriental Rugs & Carpets* x. 224 Kashgar and Yarkand rugs..are attributed more or less arbitrarily. *Ibid.* pl. 69 (*caption*) Kashgar, Disc-Star-Seal Pattern. **1962** C. W. JACOBSEN *Oriental Rugs* II. 232 Kashgars are more like a Chinese rug than a Bokhara. None are available, and I have seen a few rugs that were called Kashgar but there is not enough definite information on these rugs... We seldom come across the name.

Kashmir ('kæʃmɪə(r), kæʃ'mɪə(r)). [Var. of CASHMERE.] **1.** A native or inhabitant of Kashmir. Freq. *attrib.*, of or pertaining to Kashmir.

1882 F. M. CRAWFORD *Let.* 21 July in M. H. Elliott *My Cousin F. M. Crawford* (1934) vi. 136 The Tibetans have no postage stamps, but the Kashmirs have. **1887** J. M. BROWN *Shikar Sk.* 237 The Kashmir stag—cervus Cashmeriensis. **1925** A. G. ARBUTHNOT in G. Burrard *Big Game Hunting* 126 A very old Kashmir shikari. **1971** R. RUSSELL tr. *Ahmad's Shore & Wave* i. 15 Courtiers..who had been.. patiently gazing at the Kashmir carvings on the wooden columns.

2. Also **Cashmere.** Used *attrib.* of a Caucasian pileless carpet, characterized by the many loose yarn ends on the back resembling a Cashmere shawl. Also *ellipt.*

1900 J. K. MUMFORD *Oriental Rugs* (1901) ix. 119 It is the shaggy ends of the colored nap-yards, left loose at the back of these rugs, which has given them the name of 'Kashmir'. .. The true name of the so-called 'Kashmir' rugs is Shemakha, derived from the city where they are marketed. **1904** M. B. LANGTON *How to know Oriental Rugs* iii. 127 The Cashmere or Soumak rugs are not from the Vale of Cashmere, in India,..but are made by the nomad tribes in and about Shemakha, the old capital of Shirvan. **1931** A. U. DILLEY *Oriental Rugs & Carpets* vii. 179 Soumak rugs, formerly called Kashmir,..derive their true name from the town of Shemakha. **1962** C. W. JACOBSEN *Oriental Rugs* II. 297 Rugs are generally called Soumak or Kashmirs... The distinguishing feature of this rug is the loose ends of stitch yarn at the back of the rug, about the same effect as we find in the Cashmere shawl.

Hence **Kash'mirian**, a native or inhabitant of Kashmir.

1876 C. F. G. CUMMING *From Hebrides to Himalayas* II. 309 Kashmerians, Persians, Paharis, Hindus of every possible sect.

Kashmiri (kæʃ'mɪərɪ), *a.* and *sb.* Also **Kashmiree.** [f. prec. + -I.] **A.** *adj.* Of or pertaining to Kashmir, a state in the western Himalayas. **B.** *sb.* **a.** A native or inhabitant of Kashmir. **b.** The Dardic language spoken in Kashmir.

1880 *Encycl. Brit.* XIII. 821/2 The language distinct from Turki, Persian, Hindi, and Kashmiri. **1884** KIPLING *Let.* in C. E. Carrington *Rudyard Kipling* (1955) iv. 56 There came out a Cashmiri girl that Moore might have raved over. **1891**

'L. MALET' *Wages of Sin* III. v. vii. 56 The Kashmiree beauties. **1901** KIPLING *Kim* i. 33 A smooth-faced Kashmiri pundit. **1936** P. FLEMING *News from Tartary* VII. xi. 375 Kashmiri herdsmen camped in grubby tents. **1953** R. GODDEN *Kingfishers catch Fire* xiii. 159 She had to speak to them in Urdu and they probably only knew Kashmiri. **1955** *Times* 27 June 6/3 It is therefore surprising that so little attention is given to the political welfare of the four million Kashmiris. **1971** *Shankar's Weekly* (Delhi) 4 Apr. 5/3 He was taken for a Kashmiri priest. **1974** 'S. HARVESTER' *Forgotten Road* i. 11 He spoke.. Hindi and Kashmiri, Tamil and Gujerati and Konkani among the many tongues of India.

Kashrut (kɑːʃ'ruːt). Also **Kashres, Kashrus, Kashruth**, and with lower-case initial. [Heb., = fitness, legitimacy (in religion), f. *kāshēr* KOSHER *a.*] The body of Jewish religious laws relating to the fitness of food, and also of persons and objects; the observance of these laws. Also *attrib.*

1907 *Daily Chron.* 7 Dec. 4/7 The word 'Kashruth'.. denotes the dietary laws as laid down by Moses, together with.. commentaries and explanations thereof made by the Rabbis in the intervening centuries... 'Questions of Kashruth' concern themselves even with the utensils used in the preparation and serving of the food... [They] can only be decided by the Rabbi. **1953** *Jewish Chron. Trav. Guide* 12 In this group come those establishments in regard to the kashrut of which no information is to hand, or which, while not insisting on strict observance of kashrut, have a special interest for Jewish clients. *Ibid.* 43 The following.. are under the official supervision of the Beth Din and Kashrus Commission. **1962** *New Jewish Encycl.* 264 Most Jewish communities the world over set up Kashrut regulations and provide.. for the supervision of the slaughtering and distribution of meat. **1970** L. M. FEINSILVER *Taste of Yiddish* 242 *Kashres*, the system of kashruth observance, or 'keeping kosher'... Though the Reform movement originally rejected the binding force of kashruth, some Reform Jews today 'keep kosher'. **1973** *Jewish Chron.* 19 Jan. 8/1 The freedom and the high standards of kashrut which we in Britain enjoy should be shared equally by the Jewish communities in the rest of the EEC. **1973** *Times* 3 Feb. 13/4 The laws of Kashrus, which govern Jewish cooking and give us the label 'Kosher Food'.

Kashube (kə'ʃuːb). Also **Kashub, Kaszube.** [f. *Kashubia* (Pol. *Kaszuby*), a region of Poland west and north-west of Gdansk.] **a.** A member of the Slavonic people inhabiting Kashubia. **b.** The Slavonic language spoken in this region. Also *attrib.* or as *adj.* So **Ca'ssubian, Ka'shubian, Ka'shubish, Ka'ssubian** *sbs.* and *adjs.*

1893 W. R. MORFILL *Poland* i. 13 The language of the Kashubes differs in some interesting points from the Polish, having a fluctuating accent.. and more nasal sounds. **1919** A. B. BOSWELL *Poland & the Poles* 14 The original Pomeranians were absorbed by German colonists. But in the region west of the Vistula there still dwells a tribe called the Kaszubes who are descended from them... This region of Pomerania.. is known to the Poles as the Kaszubian Switzerland. *Ibid.* 26 Lower Polish dialects.. Kaszubian. **1934** PRIEBSCH & COLLINSON *German Lang.* I. i. 11 The Cassubian and almost extinct Slovinzian (brought by Lorentz under the collective name Pomoranian). **1935** *Times Lit. Suppl.* 15 Aug. 506/2 A Slav language, called sometimes Slovincian and sometimes Cassubian. **1936** *Discovery* Mar. 95/1 The Cassubians are an ancient and peculiar tribe who live on the seashore on both sides of the German-Polish frontier line. **1950** A. P. GOUDY in *Cambr. Hist. Poland* i. 9 From the linguistic point of view Slovinzish and Kashubish belong to the Polish group. **1950** [see LECHITIC *sb.* and *a.*]. **1955** *Archivum Linguisticum* VII. 133 The accent is free in North Kashubian. **1957** *Encycl. Brit.* XIII. 293 *Kashubes*, a Slavonic people living in the northwest of Poland. *Ibid*, In Kashube, as against Polish, all vowels can be nasal instead of *a* and *e* only. *Ibid.* XVIII. 152/1 Linguistically.. two local Pomeranian dialects remained until the 20th century, the Slovince (Slowinski) and the Cassubian (Kaszubski). **1972** W. B. LOCKWOOD *Panorama Indo-Europ. Lang.* 158 The present territory of these Pomeranian Slavs, Kashubs as they call themselves, comprises no more than the north-eastern tip from Lake Leba to the southern outskirts of Gdynja (Gdingen). Its southern border is ill-defined, being followed by a broad band of transitional dialects, basically Kashubian, but already highly polonised.

†**kasi, kasik,** obs. forms of KAZI, CACIQUE.

1748 *Earthquake Peru* iii. 226 The Kasik of Pisco coming to Lima to demand some goods.

kasidah, var. QASIDA.

†**kask,** *a. Obs. rare*⁻¹. [a. ON. *karsk-r* (Sw., Da. *karsk*, Norw. dial. *kask* brisk, bold = LG. *karsch, kasch, kask*).] Active, vigorous.

c **1300** *Havelok* 1841 Þe laddes were kaske and teyte, And vn-bi-yeden him ilkon.

kas-kas (KASKAS). *Jamaican.* Also **cuss-cuss, kass-kass, kos-kos, kus-kus.** [f. Twi *kasákàsa* to dispute.] In folk usage: a dispute, quarrel.

Pronunciation perh. influenced by Eng. *cuss* var. *curse.*

1873 C. J. G. RAMPINI *Lett. from Jamaica* 176 Cuss-cuss (calling names) no bore hole in my skin. **1943** L. BENNETT *Jamaican Humour in Dial.* 15 Dat marga gal Wingy Want put me eena kus-kus An big lian story. **1950** —— et al. *Anancy Stories & Dial. Verse* 33 Anancy never like fe se' two people live neutral, so him start fe carry lie and story between dem, and start big kaskas. **1961** F. G. CASSIDY *Jamaica Talk* iii. 29 When Jamaicans become angry and indulge in a *kas-kas*, the lilt is quite lost and the imprecations come pelting in a high-pitched volley. **1971** *Jamaican Weekly Gleaner* 3 Nov. 5/1 She's.. fed up of kass-kass with customers.

kasolite ('kæsəʊ-, 'keɪzəʊlaɪt). *Min.* [a. F. *kasolite* (A. Schoep 1921, in *Compt. Rend.* CLXXIII. 1476), f. *Kasolo*, the name of a locality (prob. near Shinkolobwe, west of Likasi) in Katanga province, Zaïre: see -ITE¹.] A yellow, rather soft, hydrous silicate of lead and uranium, Pb (UO_2) (SiO_4). H_2O.

1922 *Mineral. Mag.* XIX. 343 Kasolite... Hydrated silicate of uranium and lead, $3PbO.3UO_3.3SiO_2.4H_2O$, forming ochre-yellow, monoclinic crystals. **1958** E. W. HEINRICH *Mineral. & Geol. Radioactive Raw Materials* viii. 294 Kasolite occurs preferentially in dolomitic-graphitic shale.

kassidar, var. KHASSADAR.

Kassite ('kæsaɪt), *sb.* and *a.* Also **Cossæan, Kasshi, Kossæan.** [Native name.] **A.** *sb.* A member of an Elamite people from the central range of the Zagros mountains, who ruled Babylon from the 18th to the 12th century B.C.; also, their language. **B.** *adj.* Of or pertaining to the Kassites.

1888 Z. A. RAGOZIN *Assyria* (ed. 2) ix. 300 The next.. expedition, against the very warlike and turbulent mountain tribes of the *Kasshi* (*Cossæans* of classical writers), is of some interest because of the details we are given concerning that most rugged region of the Zagros range. **1894** A. H. SAYCE *Primer of Assyriology* iii. 47 Babylonia was conquered by Kassite princes who ruled over it for 576 years and nine months (B.C. 1806–1229). **1898** C. R. CONDER *Hittites & their Lang.* ii. 41 The Kassites thus became dependent on Assyria. **1902** *Encycl. Brit.* XXVI. 43/1 Babylonia was conquered by Kassites or Kossæans from the mountain of Elam, under Kandis or Gaddas (in 1800 B.C.), who established a dynasty which lasted for 576 years and nine months. **1909** *Daily Chron.* 14 Jan. 4/4 There is a letter to Kadashman-Targu, the Kassite King of Babylon, as to the appointment of a successor. **1928** [see GUTIAN *sb.* and *a.*]. **1934** A. TOYNBEE *Study of Hist.* I. 116 The Kingdom of the Sea-Land.. had been annexed to the barbarian 'successor-state', subsequently established by the Kassites at Babylon, at the turn of the eighteenth and seventeenth centuries B.C. **1938** T. FISH in E. I. J. Rosenthal *Judaism & Christianity* III. ii. 31 In the second millennium Babylonia was Semitic, though the rulers and the court at Babylon were non-Semitic (Kassite) for several centuries. **1939** L. H. GRAY *Found. Lang.* xii. 380 Attempts have been made to connect the language [*sc.* Elamite] with Altaic,.. with Kassite, and with Carian... The language of the *Kassites* (or *Cossaeans*) .. is known only from a scanty glossary. **1964** G. ROUX *Ancient Iraq* vi. 79 The Sumerians.. and.. the Amorites, Kassites, Assyrians and Chaldaeans who, after them, ruled in succession over Mesopotamia.

‖**kassu** ('kæsuː). [var. of CACHOU, CATECHU.] The kind of catechu obtained from the nuts of the Areca palm (*Areca Catechu*); used as a masticatory and in tanning leather and dyeing.

1862 BIRDWOOD *Catal. Econ. Prod. Bombay.*

Kassubian: see KASHUBE.

kast, -e, obs. forms of CAST *sb.* and *v.*

†**kastainy, -and, -eyne,** variants of CASTANE *Obs.*, chestnut. In quot. *attrib.*

a **1400–50** *Alexander* 1537 He castis on a Cape of kastand [*Dublin MS.* castans] hewes.

†**kasté.** *Obs. rare*⁻¹. [a. ONF. *casteé* = OF. *chasteé*: see CHASTITY.] Chastity.

13.. in *Pol., Rel. & L. Poems* (1866) 241 Vs preyen bileue, god wille, & pite, Vs kepen god hope, Mekenesse, & kaste.

†**kastin,** var. *casten*, CASTE *v. Obs.*, to chasten.

c **1200** *Vices & Virtues* 143 He besohte at gode þat naht ne scolde reinin, for ðe folke to kastin.

kastril, obs. f. KESTREL.

kastura (ka'stuːrə). Also **kasturi, kustoorah.** [Hindi *kastūrī.*] The Himalayan musk deer, *Moschus moschiferus.*

1837 T. HUTTON in *Jrnl. Asiatic Soc. Bengal* VI. 936 The Kastúra, or musk deer of these hills is to be found in the deep forest shades of Mahássú throughout the year. **1867** T. C. JERDON *Mammals India* 267 *Moschus moschiferus*... *Kastúrá*, H.— *Rous* or *Roos* and *Kasturé*, Kashmir. **1884** R. A. STERNDALE *Nat. Hist. Mammalia India & Ceylon* 494 The Musk Deer. Native names—*Kastura*, Hindi; ..*Kasturé*, in Kashmir. **1893** [see MUSK-DEER]. **1904** F. G. AFLALO *Sportsman's Bk. India* 186 Local Names of various Game... Musk deer. Kustoorah. **1951** ELLERMAN & MORRISON-SCOTT *Checklist Palaearctic & Indian Mammals* 353 *Moschus moschiferus* Linnaeus, 1758. Musk Deer (Kastura). **1955** P. BAUER *Kanchenjunga Challenge* IV. ii. 184 The Kasturi is a [Himalayan] musk deer and on this account it has been almost exterminated.

kastyn, obs. inf. of CAST *v.*

‖**kat** (kat). Also **khat, qat, quatt.** [Arab. *qat.*] A shrub, *Catha edulis*, N.O. *Celastraceæ*, a native of Arabia, where it is extensively cultivated for its leaves, which have properties similar to those of tea and coffee; the narcotic drug obtained from the leaves of this plant. Also *attrib.*

1858 *Penny Cycl.* 2nd Suppl. 107/1 *C*[*atha*] *edulis* is the Kat or Khât of the Arabs. **1866** *Treas. Bot.* 239 The use of Kât in Arabia is said.. to have preceded that of coffee. **1932** E. WAUGH *Black Mischief* iv. 119 Mahmud el Khali bin Sai'ud.. sat among his kinsmen, moodily browsing over his lapful of khat. **1958** *Times* 16 May 7/2 Lifting the ban on the importation into Aden Colony of qat, the narcotic leaf, was recommended by the qat commission of enquiry. **1960** A. WAUGH *Foxglove Saga* vi. 107 The standard British Pig, the very mention of whose name was said to make distant sheikhs and rebellious tribesmen in savage areas of the Empire drop their weapons and chew khat with a renewed vigour. **1963** *Times* 12 Mar. 12/7 Qat-chewing is not designed for the promotion of conversation. **1966** 'S. HARVESTER' *Treacherous Road* xi. 104 Ledgers and records .. gave details of his exports of coffee, *qat*, fruit. **1968** *Daily Colonist* (Victoria, B.C.) 17 Dec. 5/2 A new product.. is chewing gum containing.. 'Quatt', a mild narcotic produced from the tender leaves of a tea-like bush growing in profusion throughout the Middle East. **1969** VERDCOURT & TRUMP *Common Poisonous Plants E. Afr.* 98 Khat is a narcotic drug well-known to Arabs and Somalis. *Ibid.*, If khat-eating is accepted as less harmful than some have supposed, then a very profitable native local industry could be properly controlled. **1971** [see *gobstopper* s.v. GOB *sb.*²]. **1978** *Guardian Weekly* 17 Sept. 9/1 Normally, the day's qat session begins in the afternoon but during Ramadan it is chewed through most of the night.

kat: see KETE *v.*

kat-: see also CAT-.

‖**kata** ('kata). [Jap.] A system of basic exercises or formal practice used to teach and improve the execution of Judo techniques, devised by Prof. Jigoro Kano (1860–1938).

1954 E. DOMINY *Teach Yourself Judo* 190 *Kata*, a prearranged series of movements performed for the purpose of demonstration. **1956** C. YERKOW *Judo Katas* i. 14 This training is called *kata* and means form-practice, both for stand-up techniques and in mat-work. **1961** *New Statesman* 22 Sept. 402/2 Kata is the general technique of posture and balance. **1970** G. JACKSON *Let.* in *Soledad Brother* (1971) 247 It's never bothered me too much before, the sex thing. I would do my exercises and the hundreds of katas, stay busy with something. **1973** *Express* (Trinidad & Tobago) 27 Apr. 31/3 Over 500 karatekas will be competing for titles in.. katas (imaginary combat).

kata, shortened f. KATATHERMOMETER.

kata-, *pref.* a direct adoption of Gr. κατα-, employed in some recent scientific formations in preference to the Latinized spelling CATA- (q.v.). See Introductory Note on letter K.

‖**katabasis** (kə'tæbəsɪs). [a. Gr. κατάβασις a going down, descent, f. καταβαίνειν to go down; cf. ANABASIS.] A going down; a military retreat, in allusion to that of the ten thousand Greeks under Xenophon, related by him in his Anabasis.

1837 DE QUINCEY *Revolt Tartars* Wks. 1862 IV. 112 The Russian anabasis and katabasis of Napoleon. **1899** *Westm. Gaz.* 17 May 4/1 Little space is devoted to the *Anabasis*; it is, as in the story of Xenophon, the *Katabasis* which fills the larger part.

katabatic (kætə'bætɪk), *a. Meteorol.* [f. Gr. καταβατ-ός descending (f. καταβαίνειν to go down) + -IC (or ad. Gr. καταβατικ-ός affording a means of descent).] Of a wind: blowing down a slope, or from an elevated region to a lower one, esp. when caused by the effect of gravity on air cooled by the underlying ground. Cf. ANABATIC *a.* 2.

1918 *Meteorol. Gloss.* (Meteorol. Office) 182 A local cold wind is called Katabatic if it is caused by the gravitation of cold air off high ground. **1920** W. J. HUMPHREYS *Physics of Air* vii. 111 Where the valley is long and rather steep.. the down-flowing air current may attain the velocity of a gale and become a veritable aerial torrent. This drainage flow is known.. as the mountain breeze, or mountain wind; also canyon wind, katabatic wind, and gravity wind. **1936** *Geogr. Jrnl.* LXXXVII. 433 The extremely cold katabatic winds blowing off the high Greenland ice-cap.. lowered the temperature. **1954** W. D. THORNBURY *Princ. Geomorphol.* xiv. 362 The radially outflowing winds which Hobbs took as evidence of the existence of a permanent anticyclone over the interior of the Greenland ice cap are really katabatic winds or cold air draining down-slope under the influence of gravity. **1967** R. W. FAIRBRIDGE *Encycl. Atmospheric Sci.* 1153/1 Foehn... This is a gusty katabatic wind which crosses the Alps.. and is characterized by dryness and warmth.

Hence **kata'batically** *adv.*, as a result of downward motion.

1967 R. W. FAIRBRIDGE *Encycl. Atmospheric Sci.* 1152/2 They consist of more or less cool, dry, continental air, nearly always of anticyclonic source, at times katabatically warmed.

katabolic, katabolism: varr. of CATABOLIC *a.*, CATABOLISM.

katabothron, var. KATAVOTHRON.

katadicrotism (kætə'daɪkrətɪz(ə)m). [f. Gr. κατά down + DICROTISM.] 'The occurrence of dicrotism in the downward stroke of a sphygmographic tracing' (*Syd. Soc. Lex.* 1887).

Commonly expressed by *dicrotism* without prefix (see DICROTIC *a.*), the opposite being *anacrotism.*

katakana (kætə'kɑːnə). Also 8 **kattakanna**, 9 **katagana.** [Jap., f. *kata* side + *kana* KANA.] One of the two varieties of the Japanese syllabic writing, the characters of which are more angular than the hiragana, derived from abbreviated forms of Chinese ideographs of the

corresponding sounds, and used chiefly in scientific and official documents and in spelling out foreign words adopted into the Japanese language. Cf. HIRAGANA.

1727 J. G. SCHEUCHZER tr. *Kæmpfer's Hist. Japan* II. v. xiv. 590 The other was a map of the whole world, of their own making, in an oval form, and mark'd with the Japanese *Kattakanna* characters. **1822** F. SHOBERL tr. *Titsingh's Illustr. Japan* 194 These works, published in the learned language, *Gago*, with the *kata-kana*, or women's letters, have been re-printed expressly for them. **1859** A. STEINMETZ *Japan & her People* I. vii. 305 *Katagana* is very simple, each sound having one invariable representative. **1861** G. SMITH *Ten Weeks in Japan* xi. 173 A copy of St. Luke's gospel in the Katagana Japanese character published at Hong-kong. **1880, 1928** [see HIRAGANA]. **1970** *Jrnl. Gen. Psychol.* LXXXII. 40 The transmission of the Katakana syllabary by electrical signals applied to the skin. **1973** *Physics Bull.* May 280/3 We have also extended the process by including in addition to the 881 Chinese characters, the 50 Japanese Kata-Kana and 50 Hira-Gana characters and 10 numerals.

katalase, var. CATALASE.

katamorphism (kætəˈmɔːfɪz(ə)m). *Petrol.* [f. Gr. κατά down + μορφή form: see -ISM.] Alteration of rocks (usually at or near the earth's surface) characterized by the formation of chemically simpler minerals from more complex ones. Hence **kataˈmorphic** *a.*

1904 C. R. VAN HISE in *Monogr. U.S. Geol. Survey* XLVII. 43 The geological factor which in this treatise will serve as the primary basis for a classification of metamorphism is the dominant factor of depth. On this basis metamorphism will be classified into (1) alterations in the zone of katamorphism and (2) alterations in the zone of anamorphism... The zone of katamorphism may be defined as the zone in which the alterations of rocks result in the production of simple compounds from more complex ones. *Ibid.* 162 Katamorphic zone. **1916** F. H. LAHEE *Field Geol.* ix. 230 Any kind of alteration that any rock has undergone, whether katamorphic or anamorphic, comes under the head of metamorphism, but there are many geologists who prefer to restrict the meaning of the more general term so that it does not include weathering. **1946** *Amer. Mineralogist* XXXI. 288 It is very well known that oxidation is one of the important chemical processes of katamorphism, especially of weathering.

‖**katana** (kəˈtɑːnə). Also 7 **cattan**. [Jap.] A long single-edged sword of the Japanese samurai.

1613 J. SARIS *Jrnl.* 11 June in *Voy. Japan* (1900) 79 Either of them had two Cattans or swords of that Countrey by his side. **1615** R. COCKS *Diary* 17 June (1883) I. 10, I delivered Mr. Richard Wickham the rich *cattan* he left in my custody at his departure towardes Siam. **1874** *Trans. Asiatic Soc. Japan* 57 The word 'sword' is invariably rendered by the Japanese word '*ken*', which signifies a long, straight, double-edged sword, as opposed to the '*katana*', of modern times, which has but a single edge, and is slightly curved towards the point. **1890** B. H. CHAMBERLAIN *Things Japanese* 328 The Japanese sword of ancient days (the *tsurugi*) was a straight double-edged heavy weapon some three feet long... That of medieval and modern times (the *katana*) is lighter, shorter, has but a single edge, and is slightly curved towards the point. **1906** *Macm. Mag.* Apr. 457 An escort of sturdy little Japanese armed with service rifles and the keen-bladed *katana*. **1959** R. KIRKBRIDE *Tamiko* xvii. 138 He'd cut both our heads off with honourable katana. **1963** *Art of Armourer: Exhib. Armour, Swords & Firearms* (V. & A. Mus.) 97 Blade of the long sword (*katana*) signed.., and dated in the 6th year of the period Yeishō (1509).

kataphoric: var. of CATAPHORIC *a.*

kataplectic, -pleiite, -plexy: see CATA-.

katastate (kəˈtæstət). *Biol.* [f. Gr. κατά down + στατ-ός placed.] One of the simpler products resulting from katabolism in a living organism.

1889 GEDDES & THOMSON *Evol. Sex* xii. 162 The essentially katabolic male cell.. brings to the ovum a supply of characteristic waste products or katastates, which stimulate the latter to division. **1893** J. R. DAVIS *Biol.* (ed. 2) I. 13 Katabolism.. involves the degradation of protoplasm into simpler and simpler compounds (katastates).

katatherˈmometer (ˌkætə-). Also **kata thermometer, kata-thermometer.** [f. KATA- + THERMOMETER.] An alcohol-in-glass thermometer with an enlarged bulb and restricted scale, used for determining the cooling power of ambient air by measuring the time taken for its temperature to fall from one fixed value to another. Also shortened to **ˈkata**.

1914 *Rep. Brit. Assoc. Adv. Sci. 1913* 673 (*heading*) The katathermometer. By Professor Leonard Hill. **1915** L. HILL et al. in *Phil. Trans. R. Soc.* B. CCVII. 185 The kata-thermometer.. is an instrument designed primarily for the measurement of its own rate of cooling when its temperature approximates to that of the human body. **1915** *Ibid.* 191 The heat lost from the kata at body temperature. **1930** W. G. KENDREW *Climate* xxx. 189 The conditions of a perspiring body may be imitated by surrounding the bulb of the kata-thermometer with wet muslin. **1936** *Discovery* Sept. 280/1 When the air conditions of the bakery were tested, the 'Katathermometer' revealed most unsuitable conditions. **1938** *Jrnl. Amer. Med. Assoc.* 18 Nov. 1649/2 The time required for the alcohol meniscus to fall from the 100 to the 95 degree mark is then observed, and the 'kata factor' marked on the stem.. is divided by this time in seconds, giving the 'cooling power' of the air. **1948** W. N. WITHERIDGE in F. A. Patty *Industr. Hygiene & Toxicol.* I. x. 346 The kata thermometer has been calibrated as an air-velocity instrument. **1963** HERTIG & BELDING in C. M. Herzfeld *Temperature* III. III. xxxii. 348 The thermoanemometer.. and the katathermometer are representative of instruments whose readings are proportional to the rate of heat loss.

Hence ˌ**katathermoˈmetric** *a.*

1923 *Med. Res. Council Special Rep. Ser.* No. 73. 90 (*heading*) A kata-thermometric comparison of methods of heating and ventilation.

katatonia: var. of CATATONIA.

‖**katavothron** (kætəˈvɒθrən). Also **catabothron, kaˈtabothron.** Pl. **-a** (**-ons**). Forms with initial *k* and medial *v* are most usual (with varying endings: see note below). [a. mod.Gr. καταβόθρα swallow-hole, f. κατά down + βόθρος hole.

Katavothra (or *-bothra*) is the correct sing. form, with plurals *-ai* (*-æ*) and *-es* (corresponding respectively to the mod.Gr. pl. forms καταβόθραι and καταβόθρες). *Katavothre* is an erron. sing. formation from *katavothres*; the sing. ending *-on* (pl. *-a, -ons*) corresponds to nothing in mod. or ancient Gr. and prob. arose as a result of mistaking καταβόθρα for a neut. pl.]

A subterranean channel or deep chasm formed by the action of water.

1820 T. S. HUGHES *Trav. Sicily* II. xii. 311 A lake whose superfluous waters are carried off by a catabothron or subterranean channel. **1833** LYELL *Princ. Geol.* III. 144 The gulphs (katavothrons) of the plain of Tripolitza have swallowed up of late years thousands of human bones. **1846** GROTE *Greece* II. viii. II. 596 Tegea and Mantineia—conterminous towns.. separated by one of those capricious torrents which only escapes through katabothra. **1869** H. F. TOZER *Highl. Turkey* I. vii. 160 The Mediævals.. had the idea of there being a catavothra from the lake. **1878** *Encycl. Brit.* VIII. 685/2 The subterranean course of the streams is frequently indicated by peculiar vents or pits caused by the subsidence of the soil; they are popularly known in Greece as *catavothra*. **1892** A. J. JUKES-BROWNE *Student's Handbk. Physical Geol.* (ed. 2) xi. 197 The torrents of the Morea are usually charged with reddish mud, sand, and pebbles, when they enter the *katavothra*, but are pure and limpid when they flow out again. **1892** *Proc. R. Geogr. Soc.* XIV. 466 (*heading*) The katavothræ of the Morea. *Ibid.* 467 All these basins are drained by underground channels, to the entrance of which the name katavothra is given. **1937** *Geogr. Jrnl.* XC. 448 Since the water was drawn off, the mouths of twenty-five large katavothrai.. have appeared in the sides of the surrounding hills. **1957** G. E. HUTCHINSON *Treat. Limnol.* I. i. 107 Though these variations [in level] can in part depend on rainfall, they are largely independent of it and may be attributed to the silting of the katavothrai or sinks which drain the lake. **1970** *Water-Supply Paper U.S. Geol. Survey* No. 1899-K. 11/2 *Katavothron*, a closed depression or swallow hole. **1971** J. N. JENNINGS *Karst* v. 74 The French name *estavelle* is commonly used for these alternating orifices but they are also well known by the Greek *katavothre*.

katch, obs. form of CATCH *sb.* and *v.*

katc(h)ina, varr. KACHINA.

‖**katchung** (ˈkætʃʌŋ). Also **katjang**. [f. Malay and Javanese *katjang* 'bean', applied to species of *Lablab, Dolichos, Phaseolus, Arachis*, etc.; *katjang-mienjak, -soeoek, -tana*, are names, in different islands, of *Arachis hypogæa*.] The ground-nut, *Arachis hypogæa* (N.O. *Leguminosæ*). Hence **katchung-oil**, expressed from the seeds of this, used in warm climates as a substitute for olive oil.

1858 in SIMMONDS *Dict. Trade*, Katchung-oil. **1883** in PERCY SMITH *Gloss. Terms.*

Kate (keɪt). A pet-form of the female name Katherine; now also used as a baptismal name. Also, a dialect name for several species of finches, as the brambling, hawfinch, and goldfinch.

1773 BARRINGTON in *Phil. Trans.* LXIII. 283 *note*, The London bird-catchers also sell.. the yellow hammer, twite and brambling [*note*, They call this bird a kate] as singing birds. **1802-33** G. MONTAGU *Ornith. Dict.* (ed. Rennie) 53 Mountain Finch.. (*Provincial*) Kate. **1885** SWAINSON *Prov. Names Birds* 58 In the north, young goldfinches are called Grey Kates or Pates.

Kate Greenaway (keɪt ˈgriːnəweɪ). The name of Kate (Catherine) Greenaway (1846-1901), English artist and illustrator of children's books, used *attrib.* and *absol.* to designate the style of children's clothing modelled on her drawings.

1902 *Little Folks* 153/1 Mothers began to dress their little boys and girls in what they came to call 'Kate Greenaway dresses'. **1907** 'E. GODFREY' *Eng. Children in Olden Time* xvi. 262 The Little Female Academy is supposed to exist about 1770, so by that time the pretty little 'Kate Greeneway' [*sic*] garments prevailed. **1940** BEERBOHM *Lett. to R. Turner* (1964) App. B. 294 The Preraphaelite influence, with the Kate Greenaway influence thrown in. **1957** M. B. PICKEN *Fashion Dict.* 193 (*caption*) Kate Greenaway.. Coat, 1890's. **1959** *Times* 21 Sept. 12/3 The child bridesmaid.. wore a long Kate Greenaway dress. **1960** S. KALE *Fire Escape* v. 27 Priscilla was naturally chosen to take part in a scene calling for Kate Greenaway fashions. **1965** M. SHARP *Sun in Scorpio* III. xxv. 131 Elspet was peddling lavender-bags in her Kate Greenaway. *Ibid.* 130 'That's me being bridesmaid in Kate Greenaway,' pointed out Elspet. **1966** J. S. COX *Illustr. Dict. Hairdressing* 86 *Kate Greenaway style*, hairdresses for young children inspired by the hair fashions depicted in the coloured illustrations by Kate Greenaway published between 1879-1895. **1968** J. IRONSIDE *Fashion Alphabet* 140 *Kate Greenaway*, a child's bonnet of the style illustrated by Kate Greenaway, similar to those worn in the Empire period and with a frill round the face. Still worn by small bridesmaids sometimes.

katel(l, obs. form of CATTLE.

katelectrotonus, -tonic: see CATELECTRO-.

1878 FOSTER *Phys.* I. ii. §2. 61 The changes.. are spoken of as katelectrotonus, and the nerve is said to be in a katelectrotonic condition.

kater, var. CATER *sb.*[1]

katereme, var. QUATREME *Obs.*

katereyn, -ryn, var. QUATRIN *Obs.*

Kateryn cup: see CATHERN.

‖**kat' exochen** (kæˈtɛksɒxɛn), *adv. phr.* Now *rare.* Also 6 **catexochen, katexoken.** [ad. Gr. κατ' ἐξοχήν.] Pre-eminently, 'par excellence'.

The phrase is usually found in untransliterated Greek characters.

1588 A. FRAUNCE *Lawiers Logike* sig. ¶¶IV The Romayne Lawe, which Iustinian calleth the Cyuill law κατ'ἐξοχὴν, (as Homer is called the Poet). *a* **1625** BOYS *Wks.* (1630) 621 Infidelitie called in holy Scripture sinne catexochen. *Ibid.* 866 And this day is termed here catexochen the day. **1633** MASSINGER *Guardian* III. i, You are a lover already; Be a drunkard too, and after turn small poet; And then you are mad—*katexoken*, the madman. **1698** J. SERGEANT *Non Ultra* (in *Monist* XXXIX, 1929) 605. §21 Which Propositions being.. most fully and Properly such we do therefore, κατ'ἐξοχὴν, call Identical. **1841** MILL *Let.* 1 Mar. in *Works* (1963) XIII. 466 Poetry κατ' ἐξοχήν or poet's poetry as opposed to everybody's poetry. **1865** —— *Exam. Hamilton's Philos.* xx. 402 If any general theory of the sufficiency of Evidence and the legitimacy of Generalization be possible, this must be Logic κατ'ἐξοχήν. **1879** W. JAMES *Coll. Ess. & Rev.* (1920) 88 Schopenhauer.. says that Intuition.. 'is knowledge κατ'ἐξοχήν'. **1969** D. DAUBE *Roman Law* i. 26 The surety's promise is so striking that he is the promiser *kat' exochen.*

kathak (kəˈtɑːk). [Skr., = professional storyteller.] **a.** A North Indian caste of story-tellers and musicians; a member of this caste. **b.** A North Indian classical dance composed of passages of mime alternating with passages of dance.

1931 E. A. H. BLUNT *Caste System of N. India* 244 Kathak.—These religious troubadours carefully preserve their ancient ballads, and allow nobody to tamper with them. **1941** 'LA MERI' *Gesture Lang. Hindu Dance* 17 Pantomime is relatively unimportant in Kathak, virtuosity being entirely in the feet. **1957** G. B. L. WILSON *Dict. Ballet* 158 *Kathak*, one of the four main forms of Indian dancing. **1959** *Marg.* XII. IV. 10 Thakur Prasad, a Kathak, migrated to Lucknow about the beginning of the 19th century and became the Court Dancer of Wajid Ali Shah. *Ibid.* 12 The contribution which the Jaipur gharana has made to the preservation and spread of the Kathak dance is very considerable. To this school goes the credit of having given us some of our best Kathaks. **1967** SINGHA & MASSEY *Indian Dances* xv. 125 The word Kathak, story-teller, derives from 'katha' which means story. **1969** *Amrita Bazar Patrika* 5 Aug. 4/6 The group-dances were generally imposing based on the kathak, and soft touch of Manipuri and choreographer Namita Chatterjee intelligently introduced the various folk-dances—Rajasthani, Manipuri, Garba, Lotus to avoid the spell of monotony. **1969** *Cultural News from India* Nov. 25 To observe the sixtieth birth-day of Ustad Dabir Khan a two-hour Saraswat Veena and Surbahar recital was given... Munawar Ali Khan (vocal), Ustad Bahadur Khan (sarod), Bandana Sen (Kathak dance) and Keramatullah (tabla) were among those who took part in the programme. **1971** *E. Afr. Standard* (Nairobi) 10 Apr. 6/7 Apart from the film songs, there was a delightful Kathak group dance by three very young pupils of Uma Devi.

Kathakali (kɑːtəˈkɑːlɪ). Also **Kadhakali.** [Malayalam *kathakali* drama, f. *katha* story (Skr. *kathā*) + *kali* play.] A South Indian dance-drama based on Hindu literature, and characterized by its stylized costume and make-up, and frequent use of mime.

1900 T. K. GOPAL PANIKKAR *Malabar & its Folk* v. 74 Malabar Drama... Our drama.. assumes various forms of which Krishnattom and Ramanattom are the principal ones. The latter is usually called *Kadhakali* and constitutes our drama proper... Our drama is altogether a dumb-show in which the actors never utter a word but do everything by signs and gestures. **1933** R. K. YAJNIK *Indian Theatre* iii. 61 The 'Kathākali' of the Malabar district.. fairly gives an idea of what a country drama is like. **1967** *Spectator* 18 Aug. 193/3 At the Saville.. we are seeing Kathakali for the first time in its pure form. Dating from the sixteenth century, indigenous to Malabar, it is a dance-drama drawn from the great Indian epics. **1969** *Cultural News from India* Nov. 13 Kanak has devoted her whole heart and soul to the study of Kathakali and defied tradition in the fact that females are traditionally debarred from dancing the genre. **1969** R. SHANKAR *My Music* iii. 63/2 The noble style of the dance drama, *Kathakali.* **1974** H. R. F. KEATING *Bats fly Up* i. 10 The measured-to-a-fingersbreadth gestures of a Kathakali dancer.

katharevousa (ˌkæθəˈrɛvəsə). Also **katharevoussa, katharevusa.** [mod.Gr. καθαρεύουσα, fem. of καθαρεύων, pres. pple. of Anc.Gr. καθαρεύειν to be pure, f. καθαρός pure.] The purist form of Modern Greek; the 'official' language as opposed to the spoken and literary DEMOTIC *a.* 1 b.

1912 S. ANGUS tr. *Thumb's Handbk. Mod. Gr. Vernacular* p. xi, The term 'modern Greek'.. designates *two* forms of language—first, the living language..; and, secondly, the literary language, the καθαρεύουσα. **1956** J. PRING *Compan. Greece* 31 Katharevusa is used not only in official and technical matters, but also in public notices, shop signs and

the news columns of the press. **1959** *Times Lit. Suppl.* 15 May 288/4 The literary language was..the *katharevousa*, that artificial pseudo-antique speech. **1969** R. Browning *Med. & Mod. Gr.* 150 *Katharevousa*, the learned, archaising form of Modern Greek. **1969** 'E. Lathen' *When in Greece* vi. 63 His Greek was..a shade pedantic. He used the precise formulations of the *Katharevoussa*. **1974** C. Spencer *How the Greeks kidnapped Mrs Nixon* viii. 53 The Greek Prime Minister was..using, as was customary, the official language, *Katharevousa*.

katharometer (kæθə'rɒmɪtə(r)). [f. Gr. καθαρός pure: see -METER.] An instrument for determining the concentration of one gas in another by comparing the rate of heat loss of an electrically heated wire in the mixture with that in the second gas alone.

1917 G. A. Shakespear in *Rep. & Mem. Advisory Comm. Aeronaut.* No. 317. 3 The following is a brief account of a permeability tester..designed for the rapid testing of balloon and airship fabrics... At the centre of the lower part a katharometer (an instrument for measuring directly the percentage of hydrogen in the air) is fixed. **1945** G. R. Noakes *Text-bk. Heat* ix. 354 The conductivity of hydrogen is about seven times as great as that of air under similar conditions, and this has been made the basis of an instrument called the 'katharometer' (or purity tester) originally designed by Shakespear and Daynes for detecting the leakage of hydrogen through balloon fabrics. **1961** *Engineering* 2 June 780/1 One [detector] widely adopted is the katharometer which measures thermal conductivity... It has a zero or constant response so long as carrier gas alone is flowing, but produces a signal each time one of the components emerges from the column. **1971** D. W. Grant *Gas-Liquid Chromatogr.* vi. 116 The katharometer is normally situated in a separately heated air oven, next to the column oven.

katharophore ('kæθərəfɔə(r)). [f. Gr. καθαρός pure + φορός bearing.] An instrument for cleansing the urethra.

1890 Gould *Med. Dict.*

katharsis, kathartic: see CATHAR-.

kathenotheism (kə'θɛnəʊθiːɪz(ə)m). [f. Gr. καθ' ἕνα 'one by one' + THEISM. Cf. HENOTHEISM.] The form of polytheism characteristic of the Vedic religion, in which each god for the time is considered single and supreme.

1865 Max Müller *Sel. Ess.* (1881) II. 137 This surely is not what is commonly understood by polytheism. Yet it would be equally wrong to call it *Monotheism*. If we must have a name for it I should call it *Kathenotheism*, or simply *Henotheism*—*i.e.* a belief in single gods. **1871** Tylor *Prim. Cult.* II. 321.

katheran, obs. f. CATERAN.

kathete ('kæθiːt), anglicized f. *kathetus*, CATHETUS.

1912 G. Kapp *Electr.* viii. 210 The well-known Pythagorean axiom that the sum of the squares of the kathetes in a rectangular triangle is equal to the square of the hypotenuse.

katheter, kathetometer: see CATHET-.

1849 R. V. Dixon *Heat* I. 52 An instrument, since called a kathetometer..used in physical investigations for the purpose of measuring small differences of vertical heights.

Kathi ('kɑːðɪ). Also **kathi**. [Malay.] A judge in Islamic law, who also functions as a registrar of Muslim marriages, divorces, etc.

1947 R. O. Winstedt *Malays* 117 The Chief Kathi of Kelantan fined 14 men and 2 women $15 each, with imprisonment in default. **1963** J. Kirkup *Tropic Temper* 31 In religious matters the Kathi or Muslim religious authority exercises magisterial powers. **1967** W. R. Roff *Origins Malay Nationalism* iii. 73 In June 1884 the Council decided to appoint a State Kathi, 'to decide disputes involving Muhammadan Law and Custom', and the appointment of assistant kathis for the districts was ratified in the following year. **1972** M. Sheppard *Taman Indera* 96 He [*sc.* a *Mufti*] can, if requested, conduct a marriage, but this is normally undertaken by a minor official called *Kathi*. *Ibid.* 102 *Kathi*, A Registrar of Muslim marriages. **1972** *Straits Times* (Malaysian ed.) 25 Nov. 13/2 A former school servant, who declared before a kathi that he was a bachelor and married a second time, was jailed for a day and fined $500 or three months' jail yesterday.

kathode, -odic, kation, etc.: see CAT-.

‖**kati** ('kætɪ). *Malaysia.* Also **katti**. [Malay: see CATTY *sb.*] = CATTY *sb.*

1727 J. G. Scheuchzer tr. *Kæmpfer's Hist. Japan* I. iv. viii. 367 Camphire of Baros, a *Katti*, or 1 pound and a qr. *à* 33 *Siumome*, or *Thails*. **1820** J. Crawfurd *Hist. Indian Archipelago* I. iii. i. 273 One hundred katis make a pikul, or 133⅓ lbs. avoirdupois. **1900** W. W. Skeat *Malay Magic* v. 214 Prices varying according to the quality from $15 to $40 per *katti*. **1947** R. O. Winstedt *Malays* 126 One buffalo costing a *kati* of silver. **1969** J. M. Gullick *Malaysia* v. 232 The miners..are expected to recover 6 *katis* (8 lbs.) of tin ore from each cubic yard of soil. **1972** *Straits Times* (Malaysian ed.) 25 Nov. 13/2 Chicken cost $1.20 per kati.

kationoid, var. CATIONOID *a.*

‖**katipo** ('katipɔː, 'kætɪpəʊ). [Maori.] A large, black, venomous New Zealand spider, *Latrodectus katipo*, closely related to the Australian *jockey spider* (JOCKEY *sb.* 9) and the American *black widow* (BLACK *a.* 19).

1843 E. Dieffenbach *Trav. N.Z.* II. iii. ix. 366/2 Katipo—a black spider on the seashore, regarded as poisonous. **1852** Mundy *Our Antipodes* (1857) 178 A bite on the face by a venomous spider called by the natives Katipo. **1870** Chapman in *Trans. New Zeal. Inst.* II. 82 Proofs of the violently poisonous nature of the bite of the Katipo. **1915** *Chamber's Jrnl.* May 319/1 The katipo spider..is the Dominion's [*sc.* New Zealand's] one poisonous creature. **1934** *Bulletin* (Sydney) 4 July 21/4, I gathered katipo by the dozen on the sandhills at the entrance of the Wanganui. **1942** C. Barrett *On the Wallaby* ii. 29 The katipo or red-backed spider enjoys a very wide distribution in Australia. **1963** *Evening Post* (Wellington, N.Z.) 20 Dec., The katipo spider..is black with a red stripe on its back.

katjiepiering (ˌkatji'pirɪŋ). *S. Afr.* Also **catjepiring, katjepeering, katjiepeering.** [Afrikaans, f. Malay *katja-piring*, *kachapiring*, the Cape jasmine, *Gardenia jasminoides*.] A South African evergreen shrub of the genus *Gardenia*, esp. *G. thunbergia*, belonging to the family Rubiaceæ and bearing large, fragrant, white or yellow flowers.

1793 tr. *C. P. Thunberg's Trav. Europe, Afr. & Asia* II. 111 Wild Catjepiring (*Gardenia Thunbergia*) is a hard and strong kind of wood, and on this account used for clubs. **1869** W. G. Atherstone in R. Noble *Cape & its People* 373 The wagons..stand on a bed of wild flowers..fragrant clematis—the 'traveller's joy',—vying in sweetness with the wild 'katjepeering'. **1910** D. Fairbridge *That which hath Been* 269 Friends bring the first daphne of the year, the richest purple violets, the sweetest katjiepierings, until the house is heavy with the perfume of flowers. **1949** *Cape Argus* 3 Dec. 18/5 Gardenias (Katjiepering), flowering, 4s. 6d. each. **1972** *Stand. Encycl. S. Afr.* V. 120/1 Gardenia. Katjiepiering. Genus of evergreen shrubs..which bear sweetly scented white flowers.

katonkel (kə'tɒŋkəl). *S. Afr.* Also **katonker, katunka, katunker.** [Afrikaans, f. Malay *kentangkai* a kind of fish.] Either of two marine game fishes: (*a*) *Scomberomorus commersoni*, of the family Scomberomoridæ, which may be six feet long, occurs in the Indo-Pacific ocean, and is also called barracuda; (*b*) *Sarda sarda*, of the family Scombridæ, a much smaller fish found in the Atlantic, and also called bonito.

1853 L. Pappe *Synopsis Edible Fishes Cape Good Hope* 26 Stromateus Capensis. Mihi. N. Sp. (*Katunker*.).. A good table-fish, but not common. It is caught with the hook and net, chiefly East of Table Bay. **1893** H. A. Bryden *Gun & Camera S. Afr.* 449 Many of the Cape fish are endowed with the quaintest Dutch names. Here are a few of them: Kabeljouw,..katunka, elftvisch. **1930** C. L. Biden *Sea-Angling Fishes of Cape* vii. 144 The word 'Katonkel' has been corrupted from what was known by the Port Elizabeth Malays as 'katunker' or 'katonker' which originated from the original Malay word 'kentangkai', a kind of sea-fish. **1959** *Cape Times* 18 Feb. 2/4 This is the first time in eight years that so many barracuda (katonkels) have been caught at one time. **1974** *Eastern Province Herald* (S. Afr.) 1 Aug. 21 Katankel were a regular summer fishing feature of Port Elizabeth when the harbour breakwater was open to anglers.

katoptrite (kə'tɒptraɪt). *Min.* Also **catoptrite.** [ad. G. *katoptrit* (G. Flink 1917, in *Geol. För. Förh.* XXXIX. 432), f. Gr. κάτοπτρ-ον mirror (alluding to its brilliant lustre): see -ITE¹.] A silico-antimonate of bivalent manganese (partly replaced by magnesium and bivalent iron) and aluminium (partly replaced by trivalent iron) occurring as black, lustrous, monoclinic crystals.

1917 *Chem. Abstr.* XI. 2650 Catoptrite, a new mineral from Nordmarken. **1919** *Jrnl. Chem. Soc.* CXVI. ii. 112 Katoptrite occurs as tabular crystals and irregular lumps with magnetite in granular limestone in the Brattfors mine at Nordmark. **1951** C. Palache et al. *Dana's Syst. Min.* (ed. 7) II. 1029 Catoptrite. **1966** *Amer. Mineralogist* LI. 1495 The analysis of Flink (1917)..seems to be essentially correct, even considering the peculiar composition of catoptrite. The analysis computes to very nearly $(Mn_{.86},Mg_{.10},Fe_{.04})_{14}{}^{2+}(Al_{.83},Fe_{.17})_{4}{}^{3+}Sb_2Si_2O_{29}$. **1968** I. Kostov *Mineral.* 328 Katoptrite and parwelite are monoclinic.

katour, var. CATER *sb.*¹

katow, obs. f. KOTOW.

katri, var. KHATRI.

Kat stitch (kæt stɪtʃ). [f. *Kat*, abbrev. of Katharine, in ref. to Katharine (Catherine) of Aragon who was thought to have invented the stitch: see STITCH *sb.*¹ 9.] In lace-making, a stitch which forms a star-shaped ground net.

1919 T. Wright *Romance of Lace Pillow* ix. 84 Downton, five miles from Salisbury, produced..a lace with a net.. which is similar to Bucks Point, and the Kat Stitch finds favour with the workers. *Ibid.* xiv. 194 Catherine the Saint became confused with Katharine the Queen—that is to say, Katharine of Aragon..of Kat Stitch fame. **1931** M. Maidment *Man. Hand-Made Bobbin Lace Work* x. 158 *Bucks Kat Stitch or Wire Ground.* This stitch is used as a ground net or filling, and it is sometimes varied by the use of plaits. **1960** H. Hayward *Antique Coll.* 156/2 *Kat stitch*, a term used in lace-making to describe a *fond chant* ground but frequently found in Bedfordshire lace and given legendary association with Katherine of Aragon.

‖**katsuo** ('katswo). [Jap.] = BONITO, *Katsuwonus pelamis*, an important food fish in Japan, whether fresh or dried. So '**katsuobushi**, a dried quarter of this fish.

1727 J. G. Scheuchzer tr. *Kæmpfer's Hist. Japan* I. i. 136 The best sort of *Katsuwo* fish is caught about Gotho. **1884** tr. *J. J. Rein's Japan* i. vii. 194 Most conspicuous is the common bonito or Katsu-uwo (Thynnus pelamys), one of the most important and most valued fishes of Japan. **1891** A. M. Bacon *Jap. Girls & Women* i. 5 Sometimes a box of eggs, or a peculiar kind of dried fish, called *Katsuobushi*, is sent with this present. **1899** L. Hearn *In Ghostly Japan* xiv. 227 The Yaidzu-fishing-industry, which supplies dried *katsuo* (bonito) to all parts of the Empire. **1965** W. Swaan *Jap. Lantern* iv. 51 Sticks of *katsuobushi*, a form of *bonito*, a species of striped tunny. **1969** *Guardian* 16 July 16/4 One staple [Japanese food]..is dried bonito (*Katsuobashi*).

‖**katsura** (kat'sura). [Jap.] A type of wig worn mainly by Japanese women.

[**1894** L. Hearn *Glimpses Unfamiliar Japan* II. xviii. 421 As soon as the girl becomes old enough to go to a female public day-school, her hair is dressed in the pretty, simple style called katsurashita.] **1908** N. G. Munro *Prehistoric Japan* xiii. 567 The word *Katsura* means a vine, such as the Ainu use on certain occasions for personal decoration. In the middle ages it was applied to artificial hair, which meaning is still retained; the evidence scarcely justifies the conviction that wigs were worn by the prehistoric Yamato. **1970** J. Kirkup *Japan behind Fan* ii. 63, I watched..a display of graceful dances by girls in kimono,..*obi* (belt) and black-lacquered *katsura*, or wig.

‖**katsuramono** (katˌsura'mono). Also **kazuramono.** [Jap., f. prec. + *mono* piece, play.] One of the categories of Japanese Noh plays in which the chief character is female and the theme romantic. It is usually presented third in the sequence of five plays of different categories which makes up a performance of Noh. Also *ellipt.* **katsura.**

1916 Fenollosa & Pound *Noh* 15 Kazura, or Onnamono, 'wig-pieces', or pieces for females, come third. Many think that any Kazura will do, but it must be a 'female Kazura', for after battle comes peace. **1932** B. L. Suzuki *Nōgaku* 19 A romantic play (*jo* or *katsuramono*), in which the chief character is a woman and the chief motive love. **1948** *Introd. Classic Jap. Lit.* 141 The regular *kazuramono* contains a *jonomai*, a dance consisting of five movements and a prelude. **1964** W. G. Raffé *Dict. Dance* 353/2 They [*sc.* Noh plays] range..from romantic themes (*katsuramono*) to farce (*kyogen*). **1965** W. Swaan *Jap. Lantern* xiii. 153 *Katsuramono* or wig-plays consisting chiefly of posturing by a woman.

katt, -e, obs. ff. CAT.

kattair, obs. f. CATARRH.

kattamaran, obs. f. CATAMARAN.

†'**katted**, *ppl. a. Obs.* [For *catted*, f. dial. *cat*, a lump of clay mixed with straw. See *Eng. Dial. Dict.* s.v.] Plastered with clay.

1684 I. Mather *Remark. Provid.* (1856) 5 b, A violent flash..of lightning, which brake and shivered one of the needles of the katted or wooden chimney. [**1885** *Century Mag.* XXIX. 874/1 The chimneys were usually built of sticks of wood and well plastered on the inside with clay. These 'Katted' chimneys, as they were called in New England, often took fire.]

Kattern ('kætɜːn). Also **Cathern, Cattern.** [Corruption of Catherine, in ref. to St. Catherine of Alexandria, the patron saint of spinners, who was martyred in A.D. 307.] Used in the possessive in **Kattern's day**, 25 November, the feast day of St. Catherine, which was formerly celebrated by lace-makers in the Midlands (see also quot. 1849). Also *ellipt.* **Kattern('s).** Hence '**katterner**; '**katter(n)ing** *vbl. sb.*

[**1521** in H. Ellis *Brand's Pop. Antiq.* (1813) I. 322 Mem. that reste in the hands of the wyffe of John Kelyoke and John Atye, 4 merkes, the yere of ower Lorde God 1521, of Sent Kateryn mony.] **1730** C. Lamotte *Ess. Poetry & Painting* ii. 126 St. Catherine..is held in so much Veneration in the Church of Rome...her Holiday is observed, not in Popish Countries only, but even in many Places in this Nation, young Women meeting on the 25th of November, and making merry together, which they call Catherning. **1849** H. Ellis *Brand's Pop. Antiq.* (rev. ed.) I. 413 Until within a very recent period, it was the custom of the dean and chapter of Worcester, yearly, on St Catharine's Day,..to distribute amongst the inhabitants of the college precincts a rich compound of wine, spices, &c., which was..called the Cattern or Catharine bowl. **1862** *N. & Q.* 17 May 387/2 In Buckinghamshire, on Cattern Day..these hard-working people hold merry-makings, and eat a sort of cakes they call 'wigs'. **1865** F. B. Palliser *Hist. Lace* xxx. 352 To this very day..the lace-makers still hold 'Cattern's day', the 25th Nov., as the holiday of their craft. **1875** W. D. Parish *Dict. Sussex Dial.* 25 *Catterning*, to go catterning is to go round begging for apples and beer for a festival on St. Catherine's Day, and singing,—'Cattern' and Clemen' be here, here, here, Give us your apples and give us your beer.' **1899** A. M. Sharp *Point & Pillow Lace* vii. 171 Till well within the present century the name-day of the kind but most unhappy lady [*sc.* Catherine of Aragon], St. Catherine's Day,..was annually kept as a treat-day for young lace-makers,..and called 'Kattern's Day'. **1919** T. Wright *Romance of Lace Pillow* xiv. 194 In some parts of Northants, Bucks and Beds, the leading festival [for lace-makers] was Catterns (St. Catharine's Day), Nov. 25th—St. Catharine being the patron saint of the spinners. **1942** W. Rose *Good Neighbours* xv. 131 The mid-winter turning of the days, with its joyous celebrations, of which the visit of the 'Katterners' or 'Mummers'—as they were called—was an announcement

and a beginning. **1950** *Bedfordshire Mag.* II. xv. 254 How many Bedfordshire people have kept Kattern? Yet St. Catherine's day was once an important occasion to pillow-lace makers. **1959** *Times* 4 Dec. 19/1 English 'luck-visits'.. take their names from the Christian usage that overlies pagan observance—as souling, kattering (St. Catherine), [etc.].

katterwayng, kattesminte, obs. ff. CATERWAULING, CATMINT.

katti: see KATI.

kattie, katty, var. CATTY *sb.*

katun (ˈkɑːtuːn). [Maya.] A period of twenty years, each with 360 days, in the calendar of the Mayan Indians.

1902 *Amer. Anthropologist* Jan.–Mar. 135 Moreover, in A3 we find the Katun sign with the number 1, which may be a declaration that the date is in a first Katun or beginning Katun, for I can see no reason why the beginning Cycle, Katun, Tun, Uinal and Kin should not have been called the first. **1934** A. HUXLEY *Beyond Mexique Bay* 212 Each stela marks the close of one of the shorter of the chronological periods, in terms of which they [*sc.* the Mayas] reckoned their position in endless duration—the close of a Katun of 7200 days. **1950** *Caribbean Q.* II. II. 28 Each altar is in fact a huge day glyph marking the end of a Katun (7,200 days). *Ibid.*, The ancient inhabitants..set up beside the altars stelae bearing Long Count glyphs including the altars' Katun numbers, thus setting the Katun dates into their correct positions. **1968** D. BAGLEY *Vivero Let.* vii. 179 It's a stele—a Mayan date-stone. In a given community they erected a stele every katun—that's a period of nearly twenty years.

katwal, var. COTWAL.

†**Katy.** *Obs. rare*$^{-1}$. [dim. of the female name *Kate*: cf. KITTOCK, KITTY.] A wanton.

1535 LYNDESAY *Satyre* 267 Pray my Ladie Priores The suith till declair, Gif it be sin ta tak ane Kaity [*v.r.* Katy].

katydid (ˈkeɪtɪdɪd). *U.S.* Also **catydid, kattiedid, kittydid.** [Echoic.] A large longhorn grasshopper of the family Tettigoniidæ, of arboreal habits, which produces by stridulation a noise to which its name is due; the common or broad-winged species (*Cyrtophyllum concavum*) abounds in the central and eastern states of America.

[**1751** J. BARTRAM *Observations Pensilvania to Ontario* 70 It was fair and pleasant, and the great green grasshopper began to sing (*Catedidist*) these were the first I observed this year.] **1784** J. F. D. SMYTH *Tour U.S.A.* II. 243 They are named by the inhabitants here *katy did's*, from their note, which is loud and strong, bearing a striking resemblance to those words. **1800** A. WILSON in *Poems & Lit. Prose* (1876) II. 346 Owls, crickets, treefrogs, kittydids resound. **1805** *Ibid.* 113 October..roused the katydid in chattering wrath. **1825** PAULDING *J. Bull in Amer.* iii. 35 The frogs croaked, the caty-dids caty-didded it, the crickets chirped. **1832** MRS. F. TROLLOPE *Dom. Mann. Amer.* (1894) I. 135 Locusts, kattiedids, beetles, and hornets. **1838** E. FLAGG *Far West* II. 214 Even until the morning dawned did a concert of whippoorwills and catydids keep up their infernal oratorio. **1858** O. W. HOLMES *Aut. Breakf.-t.* (1883) 186 Voices..stridulous enough to sing duets with the katydids. **1859** A. CARY *Pict. Country Life* iv. 92 The caty-dids..were noisily welcoming the early autumn. **1886** *Outing* (U.S.) IX. 106/2 Soon the chiding katydids mingled their voices with the rush of the foaming river. **1909** *Springfield* (Mass.) *Weekly Republ.* 16 Sept. 1 All around the globe people are like katydids, saying he did and he didn't in an endless reiteration. **1935** M. MOORE *Sel. Poems* 64 The small tuft of fronds or katydid legs above each eye. **1942** E. O. ESSIG *College Entomology* viii. 95 The name 'katydid' has gradually replaced all others. It originated in the United States, having been derived from characteristic stridulatory sounds produced by the males of certain green species, notably *Pterophylla camellifolia*..whose note, the loudest of all species of the eastern states, simulates 'Katy did, Katy she did'. **1957** L. EISELEY *Immense Journey* 25 The skilled listener can distinguish man's noise from the katydid's rhythmic assertion. **1972** SWAN & PAPP *Common Insects N. Amer.* iii. 74 Katydids are predominantly green, have exceedingly long antennae, are more often heard than seen.

katy-handed, *a. Sc.* [Of doubtful origin. Both form and meaning suggest connexion with Da. *keithaandet* left-handed (f. *keithaand, keite* the left hand); but cf. also Gael. *ciotag* left hand. Cf. KAY *a.*]

Left-handed.

1822 GALT *Steam-boat* ix. 191 The spurtle-sword..was very incommodious to me on the left side, as I have been all my days Katy-handed.

Katyusha (kəˈtjuːʃə). [Russ.] A Russian rocket launcher.

1955 M. REIFER *Dict. New Words* 116/1 *Katyusha*, Soviet counterpart of the bazooka, an anti-tank weapon employing rockets. **1970** *Guardian* 28 Jan. 10/6 To talk of demilitarisation in the days of Katyushas is obsolete. *Ibid.* 2 June 2/5 Arab guerillas fired Russian-made Katyusha rockets into the Northern Israeli town of Beisan. **1972** E. AMBLER *Levanter* vi. 170, I remembered what Barlev had told me about the 120-mm. Katyusha rocket: fifty kilo warhead, range of about eleven kilometres.

katzenjammer (ˈkætsən,dʒæmə(r)). *U.S. colloq.* [G., f. *katzen* (comb. form of *katze* cat) + *jammer* distress, wailing.] **a.** A hangover, or a symptom of one.

1849 *Ex. Doc. 31st U.S. Congress 1 Sess. House* No. 5. III. 733 Some of Mr. Hale's men had kept up a drunken frolic all night, general kakenjammer [*sic*], therefore all day. **1877** R. J. BURDETTE *Rise & Fall of Mustache* 291 This 'Centennial Cordial and American Indian Aboriginal Invigorator'..has positively no equal for the cure of..katzenjammer. **1948** *Life* 5 Apr. 111/2 Attempting to drink himself to death on.. vodka and champagne... The result one of the most colossal *Katzenjammers* ever recorded. He was in bed for a week. **1965** P. DE VRIES *Let Me count the Ways* ix. 125 The symptoms classic to hangover persist. Dizziness, nausea, headache—you know that katzenjammer just above the eyes.

b. *transf.* and *fig.* An unpleasant aftermath or reaction; depression, 'blues'; clamour, uproar.

1897 W. W. COOK in *Yellow Kid* 8 May 26/2 He has a deplorable habit of constantly looking for something. Either he is the relict of some individual who was brought up in a sawmill or else he is suffering from a bad attack of katzenjammer. **1900** W. JAMES *Let.* 8 June in R. B. Perry *Tht. & Char. W. James* (1935) II. 198, I am afraid of what the French people may do during the *Katzenjammer* which will inevitably succeed the Exhibition. **1922** W. STEVENS *Let.* 24 Aug. (1967) 228 Nothing has survived the subsequent katzenjammer. **1949** I. DEUTSCHER *Stalin* x. 406 Amid the *Katzenjammer* which befell them after 1933, most leaders of the German left were only too eager to explain away their own failure. **1960** B. KEATON *Wonderful World of Slapstick* (1967) iv. 74 The Katzenjammer spirit of the other acts on the bill inspired them to contribute new plot turns.

c. ***Katzenjammer Kids*** (or ***Children***), mischievous, naughty children; *enfants terribles*. So called from the title of a comic strip, first drawn by Rudolph Dirks in 1897 for the *New York Journal*, featuring Hans and Fritz, two incorrigible children. Also *attrib.*

1897 R. DIRKS in *N.Y. Jrnl.* 12 Dec. 8 (*comic strip title*) Ach, Those Katzenjammer Kids! **1910** M. G. PEDRICK in *Good Housekeeping* (N.Y.) May 625/2 The children are engrossed with the mishaps of Happy Hooligan, Smarty, Gaston or the 'demoniacal ingenuity of the Katzenjammer Kids'. **1947** W. STEVENS *Let.* June (1967) 558 The noisy Katzenjammer children..were upstairs saying their prayers. **1962** *Times Lit. Suppl.* 13 July 511/3 He has no difficulty in matching the varied dialects of the Greek, drawing as required on such rich sources as mint-julep Southern, broad Brooklynese or Katzenjammerkids German.

kau-: see also CAU-.

kauce, obs. f. CAUSEY.

kauch, var. KIAUGH.

kaue, kauelacion, obs. ff. CAVE *sb.*^{1}, CAVILLATION.

kauersin, var. CAORSIN.

kaught, kauȝt, obs. ff. *caught*: see CATCH.

kauk, var. CAUK *sb.*; obs. f. CAULK *v.*

‖**kau kau** (kaʊ kaʊ). [Native name.] In New Guinea, the sweet potato.

1937 *Official Handbk. New Guinea* v. 435 In Morobe District, taro, sweet potatoes (*kau-kau*), sugar-cane and bananas furnish the main food, supplemented by yam, coco-nut and sago in certain areas. **1957** M. WEST *Kundu* xiv. 166 They returned laden with taro and kau-kau and sugar-cane. **1964** *Economist* 30 May 985/1 Sago and *kau kau* provide a basic if poor quality diet [in Papua].

kaul(l, obs. f. CAUL.

kaulk, var. CAWK *sb.*^{1}

kaupe, obs. f. COPE *v.*^{2}, COUP *sb.*^{1}

kauret, obs. f. COWRIE.

kauri (ˈkaʊrɪ). Also **cowry, -ie, cowdi(e, kourie, kowdie, kowrie.** [Maori *kauri*, in Lee's *New Zeal. Vocab.* (1820) written *kaudi*, *r* and *d* interchanging in Maori.]

A tall coniferous tree of New Zealand (*Agathis* or *Dammara australis*), which furnishes valuable timber and a resin known as kauri-gum.

1823 R. A. CRUISE *Ten Months New Zeal.* 145 (Morris) The banks of the river were found to abound with cowry. **1835** W. YATE *Acc. New Zeal.* 37 (ibid.) As a shrub..the kauri is not very graceful. **1852** MUNDY *Our Antipodes* (1857) 128 Thirteen fine young Kauris varying in girth from that of a quarter cask to a hogshead. **1883** RENWICK *Betrayed* 47 As some tall Kauri soars in lonely pride.

b. *attrib.* and *Comb.*, as ***kauri bush, forest, pine, spar, trade, tree, wood***; also **kauri-gum, -resin,** the fossil resin of kauri, used as a varnish (cf. DAMMAR); obtained in quantities by digging where the trees have formerly grown.

[**1851** *Illustr. Catal. Gt. Exhib.* 204 Gum kauri, or Australian copal.] **1852** MUNDY *Our Antipodes* (1857) 127 A forest of the Kauri pine, the pride of the New Zealand Sylva. *Ibid.* 185 Intending to touch in that country to get Kauri spars. **1858** SIMMONDS *Dict. Trade* 111/2 From the fossil deposits..the kowrie resin of commerce is obtained. **1867** HOCHSTETTER *New Zeal.* 148 The Kauri pine yields..a second very valuable product, the Kauri gum. **1875** URE *Dict. Arts* III. 25 Kourie wood..It is also called cowdie and kaurie wood. **1899** T. KIRK *Forest Flora N. Z.* 143 When the timber was first introduced into Britain it was termed 'cowrie' or 'kowdie-pine'.

‖**kausia** (ˈkɔːsɪə, ˈkaʊsɪə). *Gr. Antiq.* Also **causia.** [Gr. καυσία.] A low broad-brimmed felt hat worn by the ancient Macedonians.

1850 LEITCH tr. *C. O. Müller's Anc. Art* §338 (ed. 2) 402. **1856** GROTE *Greece* II. xciv. XII. 337 Himself [Alexander the Great] steering his vessel, with the kausia on his head, and the regal diadem above it. **1860** W. ALEXANDER *St. Augustine's Holiday* (1886) 217 A glittering tiar above his kausia.

‖**kava** (ˈkɑːvə). Also **cava, kaava, kawa;** also AVA. [South-western Polynesian.] An intoxicating beverage prepared from the macerated (chewed, grated, or pounded) roots of the Polynesian shrub *Piper methysticum* or *Macropiper latifolium* (N.O. *Piperaceæ*). Also, this plant, or its root.

1817 J. MARTIN *Mariner's Tonga Islands* ix, Finow.. proposed..to go into this cavern and drink cava. **1866** *Treas. Bot.* 708/1 The root called by the Polynesians Ava or Kava. *Ibid.*, It appears that Kava has, like tobacco, a calming effect rather than an intoxicating one. **1890** STEVENSON *Lett.* (1899) II. 2, I hope some day to offer you a bowl of kava there, or a slice of a pineapple.

b. *attrib.* and *Comb.*, as ***kava bowl, -drinker, -drinking, plant, root***; also **kava-ring,** a ceremonious gathering to drink kava.

1823 BYRON *Island* II. ii, Strike up the dance! the cava bowl fill high! **1866** *Treas. Bot.* 708/2 All the lower classes of whites in Feejee are Kava drinkers. **1870** MEADE *New Zeal.* 302 When a kava-ring takes place..the time for speaking terminates with the expression of the kava.

Hence ˈ**kavain, kawain** *Chem.* [Fr. *kawaïne*, Ger. *kavahin*], a crystalline resin occurring in the kava root (Morley & Muir, 1892).

1865–72 WATTS *Dict. Chem.* III. 445 *Kawain*, a crystallisable non-azotised substance, from Kawa-root. **1881** *Ibid.* 3rd Suppl. 1145 Kawain agrees in many of its properties with cubebin. **1882** *Encycl. Brit.* XIV. 18 The root [of kava] contains..a neutral crystalline principle discovered in 1844 by Mr. J. R. N. Morsori, and called *kavahine*. **1887** *Syd. Soc. Lex.*, *Kavahin*, *Kavaïn*, same as Methysticin.

‖**kavadi** (ˈkɑːvədɪ). [ad. Tamil *kāvaṭi*.] A decorated arch carried on the shoulders as an act of penance, esp. by Hindus in Malaysia.

1954 V. BARTLETT *Rep. from Malaya* ii. 27 A 'kavadi'..is a gaily-decorated but heavy wooden harness normally supported on one shoulder. **1961** *Times* 8 Mar. 14/6 [Ceylon] On their shoulders the traditional kāvadis. **1963** J. KIRKUP *Tropic Temper* 254 Blocks of pure camphor for burning..before the holy men and penitents carrying kavadis. **1966** S. WAVELL et al. *Trances* 148 Many are poor and walk long distances carrying upon their shoulders a heavy superstructure known as *kavadi* bearing flowers and fruit and peacock feathers to place before the image of Subramaniam. **1970** S. ARASARATNAM *Indians in Malaysia & Singapore* vi. 171 Popular forms of devotion..as practised in South India have persisted... Among the most significant of these is the carrying of the *kavadi*, a large wooden decorated arch, as an act of penance. **1972** *Straits Times* (Malaysian ed.) 27 Nov. 26/1 (Advt.), Devotees of Lord Subramaniam carry penitent 'kavadis'. **1973** *Observer* 7 Oct. 36/6 The penitents..climb 272 steps to the place where the Lord's image is installed, their bodies enclosed in the kavadi, a wooden frame decorated with feathers and supported by long metal rods which are hooked into their flesh.

‖**kavass** (kəˈvɑːs, -ˈvæs). Also **cavash, cavass, kawass, (kaouas, kervas).** [Turk. (Arab.) *qawwās* bow-maker, f. *qaws* bow.] An armed constable or police officer, an armed servant or courier (in Turkey).

1819 T. HOPE *Anastasius* (1828) II. 30, I..had, by way of retinue..half a dozen kawasses to clear my way of canaille. **1852** BADGER *Nestorians* I. 335 The authorities..had sent a mounted *kawass*..to demand the restoration of the plunder. **1880** KINGLAKE *Crimea* VI. x. 395 Engaging the services of a 'cavash'. **1885** *Times* 16 Dec. 5 The murderer..had been Hansal's cavass. **1897** MRS. RAMSAY *Every Day Life Turkey* ii. 65 He had been kavass at the French consulate.

kave, kaversyn, obs. ff. CAVE, CAORSIN.

kavel, kavia, obs. ff. CAVEL *sb.*^{1}, CAVIARE.

kavir (kəˈvɪə(r)). Also **kevir.** [Pers.] A salt-desert, or more rarely a saline swamp, in Persia; terrain of this type; also *spec.* (***the Kavir***), the great central salt-desert of Persia, more commonly called the Dasht-i-kavir.

1881 *Proc. R. Geogr. Soc.* III. 515 The road..across the Kavir or Great Salt Desert was very difficult. *Ibid.* 517 Soon after passing Illahabad a small piece of *kavir* or salt desert is passed. *Ibid.* 518 There are various sorts of kavir, depending upon the soil and the amount of salt. **1896** *Geogr. Jrnl.* VII. 34 These bushes grow..along the borders of the swampy part of the salt desert, which is known as the Kavir or Dasht-i-Kavir. *Ibid.* 166 The greater portion of the tract consists of *kavir*, or sandy soil strongly impregnated with salt. **1902** P. M. SYKES *Ten Thousand Miles in Persia* iii. 33 And that *Kavir* is applied to every saline swamp in the whole blighted expanse. **1963** D. W. & E. E. HUMPHRIES tr. *Termier's Erosion & Sedimentation* v. 118 As a result of evaporation, some closed basins are floored by a saline crust which is called *sebkha* in North Africa.., *solonchak* in the region of the Caspian, and *kevirs* in Transcaspia.

Kavirondo (,kɑːvɪˈrɒndəʊ). Also **Kaverond(a), Kavirond.** [Native name.] **a.** The name of two Kenyan peoples, one Nilotic (cf. LUO *sb.* and *a.*), one Bantu (also called Wa-Kavirondo); a member of these peoples; any of the Nilotic and Bantu languages spoken by these peoples. Also *attrib.*

1870 *Jrnl. R. Geogr. Soc.* XL. 308 At Kaverond..there are villages. The people of this place are called Wa-Kaverond. They are the same as the Wa-Kosóva, only a different tribe or clan. The language is one. **1873** C. NEW

Life E. Afr. xxiii. 468 Captain Speke gives only a few words of the Gani dialect.. and there are the very words which are used by the Wakavirondo for the same things. *Ibid.* 526 A Table showing the variations in the dialects and languages spoken by some of the tribes... Kisuaheli.. Masai, Kavirondo. **1882** *Proc. R. Geogr. Soc.* New Ser. IV. 743 The town of the Kavirondo chief Sendēge. *Ibid.* 744 Mr. Wakefield's vocabulary of the Kavirondo language clearly shows that this tribe does not belong to the Bantu family... Two islands lie off Kisumo... Both are cultivated by Kavirondo. **1885** J. THOMSON *Through Masai Land* (ed. 3) xi. 475 Their shields are of all shapes and sizes, though the characteristic Kavirondo form is enormous in dimensions and weight. *Ibid.* 478 We picked the bones of fat Kavirondo fowls. *Ibid.* 485 The Wa-kavirondo are apparently a homogeneous race... Yet.. there were two totally distinct languages. The inhabitants of.. Lower Kavirondo.. speak a language resembling.. that spoken by the Nile tribes, while those of Upper Kavirondo speak a Bantu dialect. **1902** C. W. HOBLEY *Eastern Uganda: Ethnol. Survey* i. 13 No Kavirondo marries in his own clan, and the degeneracy due to inbreeding is obviated. *Ibid.* vi. 88 There are many striking resemblances between the Nyamwezi language and the Bantu language of Kavirondo. **1921** *Manual on E. Afr.* (Church Missionary Soc.) 13 Leaving the coast.., we come to the Nilotic tribes—the Masai.. and Nilotic Kavirondo. The greatest tribe of all in point of numbers is the Kavirondo, of which there are about 9,000,000; but it is divided by language into two groups, Nilotic and Bantu. **1950** HUNTINGFORD & BELL *E. Afr. Background* (ed. 2) xiv. 111 *Kavirondo*, this is properly a name of the Nilotic Luo people in Kenya. According to one native explanation, it was applied by the people of one side of Kavirondo Gulf to the people of the other side as a term of abuse, derived from a Luo word *rondo* 'to deceive'... From this restricted area it has become applied to (1) The Nilotic Luo as a whole;..(3) the Bantu inhabitants of this area. **1956** *Linguistic Survey Northern Bantu Borderland* (Internat. Afr. Inst.) I. III. 129 The northern corner of the 'Bantu Kavirondo pocket'. *Ibid.* 130 A note on 'Bantu Kavirondo'. This name refers to a pocket of Bantu-speaking peoples between the..'Nilotic Kavirondo'.. and the Jopadhola and speakers of Nandi dialects.

b. Kavirondo crane = *Kaffir crane* (KAFFIR 4).

1928 *Daily Express* 31 July 4 The handsomest [bird] is the Kavirondo or golden-crested crane, kept as a pet by some native tribes in Kenya, a gorgeous stork-like bird plumaged in browns, blues, greys, and gold. **1938** F. J. JACKSON *Birds Kenya Colony* I. 317 The East African Crowned Crane, known locally as the Straw-crested, Golden-crested, and sometimes the Kavirondo crane, is found throughout Kenya colony... Why it ever became known as the Kavirondo crane is a mystery.

†**kavis**, obs. Sc. f. *calves*, pl. of CALF.

15.. *Wyf of Auchterm.* 23 in *Bann. Poems* 342 Content am I To tak the pluche.. So ȝe will rowll baith kavis and ky.

†**kavyd**, obs. f. *caved*, ppl. adj. from CAVE *v.*[1]

1426 LYDG. *De Guil. Pilgr.* p. 449 And in kavyd stones ffounde an hoole, an yrchone to have his Reffuge ther Inne.

Kaw (kɔː). *U.S.* Also **Caw, Kah.** Another name for the KANSA. Also *attrib.* or as *adj.*

1804 LEWIS & CLARK in R. G. Thwaites *Orig. Jrnls. Lewis & Clark Exped.* (1905) VI. 84 (*in list*) 3. Kanzas; Karsea; Kah. **1823** W. BECKNELL in *Missouri Intelligencer* 22 Apr. 2/5 We.. shaped our course over the high land which separates the waters of that and the Caw rivers. Among the Caw Indians we were treated hospitably. **1844** J. GREGG *Commerce Prairies* I. 41 It was either a hoax.. or else a stratagem of the Kaws (or Kansas Indians). **1930** E. FERBER *Cimarron* xviii. 280 The Oklahoma Territory and the Indian Territory, with an Indian population of.. various tribes.. Kaws, Choctaws, Seminoles. **1942** *R.A.F. Jrnl.* 16 May 28 The festivities.. were planned by Mose Bellmard, chief of the Kaw Indian tribe.

kaw, obs. form of CAW; var. KA *v. Obs.*

kaw-: see CAW-, CAU-.

kawa, kawain, var. KAVA, KAVAÏN.

kawai, var. KAHAWAI.

kawaka (ˈkɑːwəkə). *N.Z.* [Maori.] A New Zealand cedar, *Libocedrus plumosa.*

1832 G. BENNETT in *London Med. Gaz.* 7 Jan. 506/2 A tree of the Natural Family *Coniferæ*, collected without.. flower or fruit: it is named Káwaka by the natives of New Zealand, attaining the height of from 60 to 70 feet... The natives informed me that it derived the name Káwaka from the branches growing out regularly on each side of the tree. **1855** R. TAYLOR *Te Ika a Maui* 440 *Kawaka, koaka* (*dacrydium plumosum*). This tree grows in large quantities on the central plains; the wood is of a very dark red grain, and is said to be as durable as the *totara.* **1906** T. F. CHEESEMAN *Man. N.Z. Flora* 647 *Kawaka; New Zealand Arbor-vitæ.* Wood dark-red, beautifully grained, said to be durable, but on account of its scarcity little used. **1966** *Encycl. N.Z.* II. 208/2 Kawaka occurs in lowland forest from Northland to the centre of the North Island and again in the north-west tip of the South Island.

kawa-kawa[1] (ˈkawaˈkawa). [Maori.] **1.** A shrub or small tree, *Macropiper excelsum*, of the family Piperaceæ, native to New Zealand and neighbouring islands; also called pepper-tree.

1850 J. GREENWOOD *Journey to Taupo* 30 A most refreshing light beverage made from the leaves of the Kawa-kawa tree. **1910** L. COCKAYNE *N.Z. Plants* v. 80 On the Little Barrier, at the foot of the cliffs, it [*sc.* a member of the gourd family] is abundant, scrambling over the kawa-kawa. **1938** R. FINLAYSON *Brown Man's Burden* 47 The wreaths of bitter kawakawa around their heads were not more bitter than their tears of grief. **1949** P. BUCK *Coming of Maori* (1950) III. vi. 407 Hot infusions of leaves such as the *kawakawa.* **1966** *Encycl. N.Z.* II. 785/1 Numerous other berries were eaten raw, especially by children... Examples are kahikatea.. and kawakawa.

2. *N.Z.* A variety of GREENSTONE 2.

1880 *Encycl. Brit.* XIII. 540/2 The green jade-like stones which are known to the Maories as *kawa-kawa* and *tangiwai* do not appear to be either jade or jadeite. **1909** *Q. Jrnl. Geol. Soc.* LXV. 368 The variety [of greenstone], however, which is almost exclusively used by the lapidary and jeweller, is the common green kawakawa. **1965** G. J. WILLIAMS *Econ. Geol. N.Z.* x. 156/2 *Kawakawa*.. was named from its resemblance to the leaf of a shrub; the colour is dark green in various shades including spinach-green, seaweed-green, and olive-green.

kawakawa[2] (ˌkɑːvəˈkɑːvə). [Hawaiian.] The little tuna, *Euthynnus yaito.*

1887 H. H. GOWEN *Let.* in *Paradise of Pacific* (1892) xi. 130 The *kawakawa*, a large fish tasting somewhat like mackerel. **1915** W. A. BRYAN *Nat. Hist. Hawaii* xxvii. 363 The little tunny or kawakawa is at once recognized as a mackerel. **1944** S. W. TINKER *Hawaiian Fishes* 156 The kawakawa is dark blue in color above and almost silvery beneath.

†**kawdron**, obs. form of CAULDRON *sb.*

c **1483** CAXTON *Dialogues* 7/6 Pots of coppre, kawdrons.

‖**Kawi, Kavi** (ˈkɑːvɪ). [f. Skr. *kāvya* poem.] The classic or poetic language of Java and the adjacent Bali, being the ancient language mixed with a great number of words of Sanskrit origin.

1817 RAFFLES *Java* (1830) I. 411 In Bâli the Kawi is still the language of religion and law; in Java it is only that of poetry and ancient fable. **1881** *Encycl. Brit.* XIII. 608/1 The language of the old inscriptions and manuscripts.. is usually called Kawi.

kax, var. KEX.

kay, key, *a. dial. rare.* [= Da. (obs. or dial.) *kei* (in *den kei haand* the left hand); cf. Sw. dial. *kaja* left hand, *kajhandt* left-handed (Rietz).

App. limited to Cheshire and Lancashire; *keck-handed* is current in Shropshire and other midland counties.]

Left (hand or foot). Also *kay-fisted, -nieved, -pawed*, left-handed.

13.. *Gaw. & Gr. Knt.* 422 þe kay fote on þe folde he before sette. **1611** COTGR., *Gauchier*, left-handed, key-fisted. **1865** WAUGH *Besom Ben* vii. 90 He wur keigh-neighvt. **1886** *Chester Gloss.*, *Kay-fisted*, left-handed. **1887** *S. Chesh. Gloss.*, *Key-paw*, the left hand. *Key-pawed*, left-handed. **1895** in *N. & Q.* 23 Mar. 235/2 In Lancashire it is said of a man who uses his left hand.. that he is 'K-pawed'.

kay (keɪ), *int.* [Representation of the sound of the letter *K.*] = O.K. used as *int.*

1959 I. JEFFERIES *Thirteen Days* v. 66 'How about a quick half-hour *now*?' I said. 'Kay.' **1968** S. CHALLIS *Death on Quiet Beach* v. 72 Kay. We'll check her out. **1972** J. WAINWRIGHT *Night is Time to Die* 189 'And sling him in the cells,' added the D.D.I... 'Kay.'

kay, var. KA *v.*[1]; var. or obs. f. KEY.

kaya (ˈkaja). [Jap.] A Japanese evergreen tree, *Torreya nucifera*, of the family Taxaceæ, with large seeds which contain oil; also, the wood of this tree.

[**1727** J. G. SCHEUCHZER tr. *Kæmpfer's Hist. Japan* I. I. ix. 119 Of all the Oils express'd out of the seeds of these several plants, only that of the *Sesamum* and *Kai*, are made use of in the kitchen.] **1889** J. J. REIN *Industries Japan* I. iii. 157 Kaya-no-abura, Kaya-oil, is manufactured by the Japanese from the seeds of *Torreya nucifera*, S. and Z., the Kaya, which are like hazel-nuts or acorns... The Kaya resembles our yew. It is found in most cases as of underwood, scattered like brush in mountain forests; seldom as a tree. In autumn the plant is laden with nuts, which are good to eat, although having a resinous after-taste. **1894** C. S. SARGENT *Notes Forest Flora Japan* 76 The Kaya should be cultivated wherever the climate permits it to display its beauty. **1923** DALLIMORE & JACKSON *Handbk. Coniferæ* 75 *Torreya nucifera*, Siebold & Zuccarini. Kaya... Wood lustrous yellow to pale brown, durable under water, used for chests, boxes, cabinets, furniture, water-pails, and for Japanese chessmen. **1965** J. OHWI *Flora Japan* 110/1 Kaya. Glabrous tree with spreading brownish branches. **1969** R. C. BELL *Board & Table Games* II. iii. 61 The best boards are made of a species of yew, called 'Kaya' (*Torreya Nucifera*).

‖**kayak**[1] (ˈkaɪək). Also 8 **kaiak, kiack,** 8–9 **kajak,** 9 **kayac(k), kya(c)k, kaiack, kajac, cayak.** [Eskimo; the term is common to all the dialects, from Greenland to Alaska. The *k*'s have a deep guttural sound, sometimes represented by *k, rk,* or *rkr*.] **a.** The canoe of the Greenlanders and other Eskimo, made of a framework of light wood covered with sealskins sewn together; the top has an opening in the middle to admit the single kayaker, who laces the covering round him to prevent the entrance of water.

[**1662** J. DAVIES tr. *Olearius' Voy. Ambass.* 71 The Greenlanders speak.. *Kajakka*, a little Boat.] **1757** J. SCOTT *Ode Winter* 22 Their hands.. The kajak and the dart prepare. **1768** WALES in *Phil. Trans.* LX. 108 Three Eskimaux in their canoes, or, as they term them, Kiacks. **1769** FALCONER *Dict. Marine* (1789) L b, The canoe is called *kaiak*, or man's boat, to distinguish it from *umiak*, the woman's boat. **1819** SIR J. ROSS *Voy. Arct. Reg.* iv. 54 Our Eskimaux returned with seven natives in their canoes, or kajacks. **1841–71** T. R. JONES *Anim. Kingd.* (ed. 4) 597 The double-bladed oar with which the Greenlander so dexterously steers his kajac, or canoe. **1878** NARES *Polar Sea* I. ii. 20 A few of the officers became rather expert in the use of the kayak.

Comb. **1888** *Times* 16 Nov. 10/2 They hired two kajak-men to bring letters to Ivigtut.

b. Any canoe developed from the Eskimo kayak, used for touring or sport.

1936 A. R. ELLIS *Canoeing for Beginners* i. 10 Constructional plans of the British Scout Kayak... This craft is a very seaworthy little piece of work... It is about 15 feet in length. **1946** P. W. BLANDFORD *Canoeing To-Day* i. 4 It is common to refer to a folding craft as a canoe and a rigid craft as a kayak, although the latter is not built on Eskimo lines. *Ibid.* 62 *Kayak*, originally the Eskimo craft, but now generally applied to any rigid canvas-covered decked canoe. **1962** —— *Canoes & Canoeing* i. 15 What the European calls a canoe the American calls a *kayak*, and what the American calls a canoe the European usually qualifies as a *Canadian canoe*, keeping the word kayak for the special slim craft based on the Eskimo pattern. **1966** J. SAMSON in B. C. Skilling *Canoeing Complete* i. 24 About 1840 the first copies of Greenland kayaks appeared in Europe... After 1865 canoeing began to rise as a new kind of sport. The Scot, McGregor, made his sensational voyages in kayaks of his own design.

c. *attrib.* and *Comb.*

1963 *Internal Jrnl. Social Psychiatry* IX. I. 19 Kayak-angst (kayak-phobia, kayak dizziness) is well known throughout all districts of West Greenland... Kayak-angst is scarcely mentioned in English written accounts, with the exception of brief references in Freuchen, Birket-Smith and a few others. **1963** B. C. SKILLING in *Canoe Venture* 20 In the kayak world it was accepted that to have complete control the canoe and man must become as one. **1964** *Slalom & White Water Course* (Ontario Voyageurs Kayak Club) i. 4 Modern kayak-paddling technique is a combination of the classical style and of elements adopted from the Canadian canoe. **1964** N. HUNT *Adventures in Canoeing* i. 13 He feels his individual make-up is in line with these exciting aspects of kayak sport. *Ibid.* ii. 24 A lightweight, strong and water-tight hull, easy to make and no more expensive than a soft-skinned kayak kit. *Ibid.* iii. 37 Free your legs from the knee grips by pressing the thighs towards the kayak floor. *Ibid.* vii. 89 A broken kayak paddle.

Hence **ˈkayak** *v. intr.*, to travel by kayak; **ˈkayaker**, one who manages a kayak; **ˈkayaking**, the managing of a kayak; also *attrib.*; **ˈkayakist**, one who paddles a kayak.

1856 KANE *Arct. Expl.* I. xxx. 416 Almost in an instant the animal charged upon the kayackers. **1875** H. RINK *Tales & Trad. Eskimo* I. 294 Another day, when he was kayaking along the coast, he remarked some loose pieces of ice. *Ibid.* 295 His wife repeated the tale of his misfortunes to every kayaker on his return home. *Ibid.* lxii. 349 The following day the father kayaked the same way past the cape, and came in sight of the tents. **1887** *Cent. Mag.* Aug. 556/1 He had learned.. the rudiments of kayaking. **1960** *Spectator* 2 Sept. 340 She's training with the world's top kayakists. **1963** R. GEORGE in *Canoe Venture* 5 The Australian and American founders, who swore that they would never raise the status of kayak to canoe even though it was going to be a canoeing club of kayakists. *Ibid.* 21 The paddlers sat on their wickerwork seats and watched with disdain the gyratics of the new kayakers. **1964** *Slalom & White Water Course* (Ontario Voyageurs Kayak Club) v. 12 His name is probably not mentioned in Czech kayaking literature. *Ibid.* xii. 22 Slalom competitions are considered the 'matriculation' of the kayaking fraternity. **1966** B. C. SKILLING *Canoeing Complete* 11 The knowledge and experience which he and other members of his parties gained in kayaking with the Eskimos. *Ibid.* x. 176 It will be found that few kayakers can paddle with equal facility on both sides of their canoe using a single-bladed paddle stroke. **1967** *Nat. Geographic* Sept. 328/1 Halting for lunch, the kayakers beach their craft.. then join youngsters splashing in the mole-protected harbor. **1969** *Pubn. Amer. Dial. Soc.* LI. 1 The sport of whitewater kayaking was developed in the United States... Kayak slalom, the most complex form of kayaking, is a competition in which the kayakist or paddler must pass through a series of gates in the rapids. **1973** *New Earth Catalog* 17/1 A kayak outfitter with kits and.. instruction on the art of kayaking down some of Colorado's rivers.

kayak[2] (ˈkaɪæk). *Canada.* Also **kia(c)k, kyack.** [Prob. f. Algonquian.] = ALE-WIFE[2].

1849 A. GESNER *Industr. Resources Nova Scotia* 121 Sometimes a hundred men, among whom is a sprinkling of Indians, are engaged in taking the 'kiacks' from the stream. **1878** C. HALLOCK *Sportsman's Gazetteer* (ed. 4) 271 Kyack.—*Pomolobus pseudoharengus.* **1965** *Canad. Geogr. Jrnl.* June 209/1 'Alewives' is the common name used in Britian and New Zealand, while the MicMac Indians called the fish 'kayaks', and in Latin it's *Pomolobus pseudoharengus.* **1965** E. RICHARDSON *Living Island* 109 To feast upon the sweet spring clams and the running kyack-cooks (we still call alewives 'kyacks').

Kayan (ˈkaɪən). Also **Kyan.** [Native name.] The name of a people of Sarawak and Borneo, of a member of this people, and of their language. Also *attrib.* or as *adj.*

1846 C. D. BETHUNE in *Jrnl. R. Geogr. Soc.* XVI. 297 The indigenous population [of Borneo] is included under the names of Dayák, Kadáyan, Milanau, Káyan, Murút, Dusúr. *Ibid.* 299 The Káyan is the most numerous tribe... Their dialect is different from the Dayák. *Ibid.*, Hill tribes.. much oppressed by the Káyans. **1848** H. LOW *Sarawak* iv. 97 The Dyaks, the Kyans, and other aboriginal tribes. *Ibid.* x. 331 The swords of the Kyan tribes are of very peculiar construction. **1858** S. ST. JOHN *Jrnl.* 1 Sept. in *Life Forests Far East* (1862) II. iii. 45, I then made Japer hail in the Kayan and also in the Murut languages. **1873** *Proc. R. Geogr. Soc.* XVII. 133 Their [*sc.* the Pakattans'] language is quite different to Malay, Dyak, or Kyan. **1886** in F. Hatton *N. Borneo* (ed. 2) vii. 322 No European blade is more finely tempered than these Kayan weapons. *Ibid.* 329 This Kayan instrument gives forth a soft and soothing kind of music. **1914** *Sat. Rev.* 31 Jan. 147/2 The Ranee carries her love for her people to the extent of even finding excuses for the head-hunting propensities of the Dyaks and Kayans. **1938** C. H. HARTLEY in T. Harrisson *Borneo Jungle* 149 The orators spoke in Kayan, but subsequently translated their remarks into Malay. **1960** K. F. WONG *Pagan Innocence* pl. 64 (*caption*) Her baby has been given a good start in life, from

the Kayan point of view, by the acquisition of ear-rings to elongate the lobes. **1960** *Guardian* 9 Nov. 10/3 The population [of Sarawak] includes..Malays, Melanaus, Kayans..and others. **1964** T. HARRISSON in Wang Gungwu *Malaysia* III. xi. 170 A Kayan put down among Kelabits will not understand a word.

kayan, kaye, obs. forms of CAYENNE, KEY.

kayf (keɪf). Representation of a slang or jocular pronunciation of CAFÉ. Cf. CAFF.

1962 F. NORMAN *Guntz* i. 8, I had some eggs and bacon in a kayf just around the corner. **1964** *Spectator* 20 Mar. 380/1 This kayf-world follows every cool, snide and beat twist of Sixties fashion.

†**kayface**, obs. perversion of *Caiaphas*: here used allusively.

1528 ROY *Rede me* (Arb.) 115 O cruell kayface, full of crafty conspiracion. Howe durst thou geve then falce iudgement?

kaykylle, obs. form of CACKLE *v.*[1]

1483 *Cath. Angl.* 200/1 To kaykylle (*A.* kakylle), *gracillare*.

kayles (keɪlz), *sb. pl.* Now *dial.* or *Hist.* Forms: α. 4 **keyles**, 5 **caylys**, 6 **cayles**, **kayls**, **kayells**, **keiles**, 6–7 **cailes**, (7 **keils**, **kyele-**), 4– **kayles**. β. 6–7 **keeles**, 6–8 **keels**, 7 **keales**, 8 **keals**. γ. *Sc.* 5 **kilis**, 7 **kiles**, 7– **kyles**. [Corresp. to MDu. *keghel*, *kegel* (also *keyl-* in *keylbane* skittle-alley; Du. *kegel*, pl. *kegels* and *kegelen*) = OHG. *chegil* (MHG. and G. *kegel*) tapering stick, ninepin, cone, etc. Da. *kegle* and Sw. *kegla*, *kägla* are from LG.; F. *quille* (known from 1320) is commonly supposed to be an adoption of the Teutonic word; Welsh has *ceilys* from English. The phonology of the Eng. forms presents difficulties: ME. *ei* (*ai*) does not normally give *ea*, *ee* in later English. The Scotch form was prob. from Fr.]

1. *pl.* The set of pins of wood or bone used in a kind of ninepins or skittles; more frequently, the game played with these.

α. *c* **1325** *Song* in *Rel. Ant.* I. 292 Ther-fore has ure mayster ofte horled mi kayles. **1388** *Act 12 Rich. II*, c. 6 §1 Les..jeues appellez Coytes dyces gettre de pere keyles & autres tielx jeues importunes. *c* **1450** *Advice to Apprentices* in *Rel. Ant.* II. 224 Exchewe allewey..Caylys, cardyng, and haserdy. **1540** *Order* in Rymer *Fœdera* (1710) XIV. 707 The Playes of Handeoute and Keiles. **1602** CAREW *Cornwall* (1769) 10 The residue of the time they weare out at Coytes, Kayles or like idle exercises. **1633** B. JONSON *Chloridia*, All the furies are at a game called nine-pins or keils. **1737** PEGGE *Kenticisms* (E.D.S.), *Cales*, skittles, ninepins. So they call them at Canterbury. **1838** MRS. BRAY *Trad. Devonsh.* II. 170 Kales..This is our provincial name, for..nine-pins or skittles. **1887** *Kentish Gloss.*, *Cailes*, skittles, ninepins.

β. *a* **1586** SIDNEY *Arcadia* I. (1622) 83 And now at keels they try a harmelesse chaunce. **1598** FLORIO, *Aliossi*, a play called Nine pins or keeles, or skailes. **1642** CHAS. I *Let. both Houses Parlt.*, You..will quickly resolve all their debates and all their actions, into keales. **1721** B. LYNDE *Diary* 15 June (1880) 131 Playing keels. *Ibid.* 7 July 132 Played keels with Icha. **1887** *Kentish Gloss.*, *Keals*.

γ. **1496** *Acc. Ld. High Treas. Scot.* I. 275 Item, that samyn nycht in Drummyn, to the King to play at the kilis, xxviij s. **1617** MINSHEU *Ductor*, Kiles, or nine pinnes. **1653** URQUHART *Rabelais* I. i, They found nine Flaggons set in such order, as they use to ranke their kyles in Gasconie. **1715** *Sherrifmuir* in *Jacob. Songs & Ball.* (1887) 96 They houghed the clans like ninepin kyles. [*Kyles* or *kiles* were played in Hawick in early part of 19th c.]

b. *sing.* One of the pins used in the game. *rare.*

1652 URQUHART *Jewel* Wks. (1834) 278 To use their king as the players at nine-pins do the middle kyle, which they call the king, at whose fall alone they aim.

¶Johnson has the following, apparently through confusion with another game: '*Kayle*, a kind of play still retained in Scotland, in which nine holes ranged in three's are made in the ground, and an iron bullet rolled in among them.'

2. *Comb.* (of the sing. *kayle-*, *keel-*, etc.), as ***kayle-alley***, ***-bone***, ***-pin***, ***play***.

1621 BURTON *Anat. Mel.* II. ii. IV, Keelpins, tronkes, coits, ..and many such, which are the common recreations of country folkes. **1634** BRERETON *Trav.* (Chetham Soc.) 51 Keale-bones and checke-stones to play with children. **1664** EVELYN *Sylva* (1776) 261 Osiers good for hurdles, sieves.. kyele-pins [etc.]. *c* **1702** in Rogers *Soc. Life Scotl.* (1884) II. xii. 252 Bowling-greens, kyle-alleys. **1726** *Brice's Weekly Jrnl.* 11 Feb. 3 A very spacious Yard, for both Keal and Tennis-Play. **1801** STRUTT *Sports & Past.* III. vii. 238 Primitively the kale-pins do not appear to have been confined to any certain number.

kaylied ('keɪlɪd, -laɪd), *a. dial.* and *slang.* Also **kailed, kalied**. [Origin unkn.] Extremely drunk. Also with *up*.

1937 PARTRIDGE *Dict. Slang* Add. 986/1 *Kalied up, get*, to become drunk: from ca. 1927. **1966** 'L. LANE' *ABZ of Scouse* 58 'Kaylied' means drunk. **1978** 'J. GASH' *Gold from Gemini* vi. 53 He offered to brew up but my stomach turned. That left him free to slosh out a gill of gin. Dandy was permanently kaylied.

kaylong, var. KELONG.

kaynard, var. CAYNARD *Obs.*, sluggard.

kayo ('keɪəʊ), *a. slang* (orig. *U.S.*). [Reversal of the pronunc. of O.K. under the influence of next (see K 4 b).] = O.K. *a.*

1923 H. C. WITWER in *Cosmopolitan* Apr. 128/2 Anything you say is kayo with me, kid, unless you tell me good bye! **1928** WODEHOUSE *Money for Nothing* v. 103 If you think it's kayo, then it's all right by me. **1946** *Amer. Speech* XXI. 138 How these new speech forms [*sc.* abbreviations] in turn may be translated back into the written word is shown by *kayo*, [etc.].

kayo ('keɪəʊ), *v.* and *sb. colloq.* (orig. *U.S.*). [Representation of the pronunc. of *K.O.* (*s.v.* K 4).] **A.** *v. trans.* = KNOCK *v.* 14 a. **B.** *sb.* = KNOCK-OUT *sb.* 2.

1923 H. C. WITWER *Fighting Blood* 324 You never been knocked cold in your life—why go out of your way to get kayoed? **1932** J. T. FARRELL *Young Lonigan* iii. 112 He sat down, saying to himself that he was Young Studs Lonigan ..now in training for the bout when he would kayo Jess Willard for the title. **1933** *Amer. Speech* VIII. III. 39/1 The knockout blow or kayo itself is variously called kay,..K.O. **1939** WODEHOUSE *Uncle Fred in Springtime* xx. 303, I still don't see..why he should have slipped kayo drops in. **1968** *Globe & Mail* (Toronto) 3 Feb. 40/4 Quarry with 14 kayos in a 25-1-4 record is known as a stopper. **1972** *Times* 10 Nov. 14/6 There was..the kayoing of the prop forward by a deliberate punch. **1975** *Cleveland* (Ohio) *Plain Dealer* 23 Mar. 2-C/2 Rademacher, who was kayoed by Patterson in the sixth round in 1957, won a gold medal in the 1956 Olympic Games for boxing.

kayre(e, kayrd, kaytefe (-yf), kaythur, obs. ff. or var. CAIR *v.*, CARD, CAITIFF, CATHER.

kayser ('kaɪzə(r)). *Physics.* [Name of J. H. G. *Kayser* (1853–1940), German spectroscopist.] A name proposed for the unit of wave number, cm^{-1}.

1951 W. F. MEGGERS in *Jrnl. Optical Soc. Amer.* XLI. 1064 Because H. Kayser first founded the correct procedure in determining spectroscopic wave numbers..I think it appropriate to propose that the name of the unit, hitherto called cm^{-1}, be Kayser, with *K* as the natural abbreviation. **1953** *Ibid.* XLIII. 411 The Joint Commission for Spectroscopy recommends that the unit of wave number hitherto designated as cm^{-1} be named kayser. **1968** HILL & DAY *Physical Methods Adv. Inorg. Chem.* iv. 112 The units of wave numbers are cm^{-1} or kayser (K) with 1000 kayser = 1 kilokayser (kK).

Kayser-Fleischer ring ('kaɪzəflaɪʃə rɪŋ). *Path.* [f. the names of Bernhard *Kayser* (1869–1954) and Bruno *Fleischer* (b. 1874), German ophthalmologists.] A pigmented ring around the cornea of a variable orange, green, or brown colour, diagnostic of Wilson's disease.

1930 *Amer. Jrnl. Ophthalm.* XIII. 1049/2 We must rely to a great extent upon the presence of a Kayser-Fleischer ring for a differential diagnosis [of Wilson's disease]. **1948** *Amer. Jrnl. Med. Sci.* CCXV. 601/2 Both brothers present an unusually well developed orange-green Kayser-Fleischer ring. **1970** PASSMORE & ROBSON *Compan. Med. Stud.* II. xxv. 38 A characteristic brown ring sometimes visible in the outer cornea, the Kayser-Fleischer ring.

kaza ('kaza). Also **caza**. [Turkish *kaza*, related to *kadi* CADI.] A district in Turkey subject to a judge's jurisdiction.

1885 *Encycl. Dict.* IV. 468/3 *Kā́z´-a*,..a district or subdivision of sandjak, marked out for administrative purposes. **1903** *Westm. Gaz.* 20 Aug. 7/2 In the Caza of Lerin. **1920** *Glasgow Herald* 9 Aug. 7 The reincorporation with Lebanon of the four cazas of Baalbek, Bekkam, Rachaya, and Hasbaya. **1920** *Glasgow Herald* 27 Aug. 9 General Gouraud has arrived at Zableh, where he announced the reunion with the Lebanon of the four kazas of Baalbek, Bekoa, Ruchaya, and Hasbaya. **1922** *Contemp. Rev.* Dec. 705 The local bishop, vicar or priest has been an ex-officio member of the governmental Council of the *vilayet*, *sanjak* or *caza* in which he resided. **1972** D. DAKIN *Unification of Greece* xii. 162 A broad band of territory composed of the *kazas* (districts) of Monastir and Florina in the west; of Gevgeli, Vodena.., and Yanitsa in the central region; and Serres and Zihna in the east.

kazachoc (kæzə'tʃɒk). Also **kozatchok** and other forms repr. the acc. or pl. of the Russ. word. [Russ., dim. of *kazák* Cossack.] A Slavic, mainly Ukrainian, dance with a fast and usu. quickening tempo. Sometimes used erron. for a step of this dance, properly called the *prisiadka*, in which the male dancer squats on his heels and kicks out each leg alternately to the front.

1928 C. GARNETT tr. *Gogol's Mirgorod* 65 No-one could have watched without inner emotion how all danced that most free, most furious dance the world has ever seen, called from its mighty originators the Kozatchok. **1960** B. KEATON *Wonderful World of Slapstick* (1967) ii. 45 He couldn't walk straight because of the dense smoke, he couldn't bend down or even do a Russian Kazatsky. **1962** *Listener* 11 Jan. 71/1 He played Polish and Russian dances like the mazurka, the polka, and the Kozochka. **1966** K. GILES *Provenance of Death* iii. 78 She switched on the player and danced the *Kazachka*, mainly to spite Harry who invariably fell over when he tried.

Kazak (kə'zɑːk). [ad. *Kazakh*, name of a town in Azerbaijan.] A type of Caucasian wool rug, characterized by large geometric designs in striking colours, and a thick durable quality.

1900 J. K. MUMFORD *Oriental Rugs* (1901) ix. 107 The regulation rug of the Derbend variety..partakes of the character of the Kazak. **1954** I. MURDOCH *Under Net* vi. 90 An exquisitely golden yellow and midnight blue striped Kazak rug. *Ibid.* 102, I took a last..look at the Afghans and Kazaks. **1962** C. W. JACOBSEN *Oriental Rugs* 233 Kazaks and Karabaghs are thick piled Caucasian rugs. The Kazaks are geometric in design. **1973** *Times* 2 Apr. 6 (Advt.), A fascinating Royal Pakistani Kazak.

Kazakh (kə'zɑːk). Also **K(h)asa(c)k, Kazak, Qazaq.** Pl. **Kazakhi, Kazakhs.** [Russ.] One of a Turkic people of central Asia, forming the basic population of the Kazakh S.S.R. (Kazakhstan); the language spoken by this people. Also *attrib.* or as *adj.*

1832 J. BELL *Syst. Geogr.* IV. 396 Amongst the names of tribes noticed..are: the *Kuthai Kipchaucks, Kuzzauks*,.. and *Kara Kalpaks*. **1886** R. N. CUST *Lang. as Illustr. by Bible-Translation* 32 The Túrki Branch [of Ural-Altaic], containing Chuvásh, Kazáni, Nogái..and Kirghiz in the Kazák Dialect. **1907** G. W. HUNTER in M. Broomhall *Chinese Empire* 296 There are large numbers of Kirghiz—Khasack tribes—here in the district of Urumchi. They are mostly wandering nomadic tribes, though some have farms and settled abodes. **1918** G. W. HUNTER *Examples Turki Dial.* Pref., Whilst doing some Qazaq Turki translation work we found it necessary to read some native Qazaq books. And we thought it might be useful to keep a record of our studies in Qazaq, and in the various other Turkish dialects... Much still requires to be done in Qazaq, Tartar and the Kirghese dialects. **1945** *Dairy Sci. Abstr.* VII. 3 Crossbred cows..gave an average milk yield..39·2 per cent. more than Kazakh cows... Crossbreeding Kazakh and Schwyz cattle. **1948** D. DIRINGER *Alphabet* 568 Eastern or Altai-Kirghiz Turkish or Kazakh Turkish, spoken by several hundred thousand nomads in the Altai and T'ien Shan mountains. **1949** N. JASNY *Socialized Agric. USSR* III. xiv. 330 On the price paid by the Kazakhi for collectivization see the end of the preceding chapter. *Ibid.* III. xiii. 323 The Kazakhi, a Mongol pastoral tribe inhabiting mainly Kazakhstan... The Kazakhi should have numbered 4·6 million in 1939. **1957** *Chambers's World Gazetteer* (rev. ed.) 359/2 Kazakh SSR, or Kazakhstan... Kazakhs..constitute 60% of the total pop... The written Kazakh language has existed only since the revolution. **1968** BETHELL & BURG tr. *Solzhenitsyn's Cancer Ward* I. iv. 49 Next to him Egenberdiev, a middle-aged Kazakh shepherd, was not lying but sitting on his bed, legs crossed as though he was sitting on a rug at home. **1969** *Guardian* 21 June 9/5 The Russians have broadcast propaganda in the Kazakh language from Alma Ata. **1972** *Times* 11 Dec. 1/7 An 800-mile border with China. It crosses mountainous areas which provide pasture land used by Kazakh and other hill shepherds.

‖**kazi** ('kɑːziː). Also 7 **kasi, casi, cazee, cazy**, 9 **cauzee, cauzy, kází**. [a. Arab. *qāḍī* CADI. In Persia and India, Arabic *ḍ* is pronounced as *z*.] A civil judge; = CADI.

1625 PURCHAS *Pilgrims* I. 439 Ouer against the great gate [sc. at Agra] is the *Casi*, his seat of Chiefe-Iustice in matters of law. **1662** J. DAVIES tr. *Olearius' Voy. Ambass.* 367 At the judgement of Criminal causes, joyntly with the Seder and the *Kasi*, and the other..Judges. **1698** FRYER *Acc. E. India & P.* 94 The Cazy or Judge..marries them. **1815** ELPHINSTONE *Acc. Caubul* (1842) I. 235 The Cauzees appointed by the King. **1880** *Bill introd. Council of Gov. Gen.* 30 Jan. (Y.) The presence of Kazis..is required at the celebration of marriages.

kazoo (kə'zuː). Also **gazoo, gazooka**. [Of U.S. origin; app. with some reference to the sound.] (See quot. 1938.) Now also made of plastic or metal and played as a jazz instrument.

1884 in *Lisbon* (Dak.) *Star* 31 Oct., A kazoo is an instrument invented to give pleasure and satisfaction to the small boy. **1895** *Montgomery Ward Catal.* 245/3 Kazoos, the great musical wonder,..anyone can play it; imitates fowls, animals, bagpipes, etc. **1926** *Daily Colonist* (Victoria, B.C.) 24 Jan. 9/3 There will be an abundance of paper hats, balloons, kazoos and other novelties. **1926** WHITEMAN & MCBRIDE *Jazz* ix. 201 Did you ever see a kazoo? Of course you must have—a small worthless-looking piece of tin. A kazoo stuck into a mute will give a buzzy sound that comes handy in certain pieces. **1927** *Bulletin* 24 Aug., A new musical atrocity is reported to be coming to Scotland. It is the Gazoo. This instrument of ear-torture is simply an adaptation of the primitive 'comb and tissue paper'. **1938** *Oxf. Compan. Mus.* 583/2 *Mirliton*, the French name for what English children call (or used to call) 'Tommy Talker', or 'kazoo'. It is a tube with a membrane at each end and two holes in the side, near the two ends, into one of which holes one sings in one's natural voice, the tone issuing in a caricatural fashion. **1938** 'R. HYDE' *Nor Years Condemn* x. 195 The Maoris could make the dish-like gazookas of tin and wire sound like guitars. **1940** *Amer. Speech* XV. 125 George Gershwin's..'Blue Monday' has..*Kazoo Mutes* (to cornets). **1956** J. LATIMER *Sinners & Shrouds* ix. 83 'A neglected instrument, the kazoo,' he was saying. 'A cock's challenge in Red McKenzie's hands, raucous and lewd, a braggart, a bully, a flap-wing lover.' **1956** M. STEARNS *Story of Jazz* (1957) xv. 171 Jack Bland, Dick Sliven, and Red McKenzie played a banjo, a comb wrapped in tissue paper, and a kazoo (a toy horn with tissue paper that vibrates with humming). **1959** *Manch. Guardian* 26 Aug. 5/2 There is.. a new outbreak of kazooing in South Wales... On the history of gazooka (as it is called in South Wales) Mr. Gwyn Thomas..is an expert. *Ibid.*, One hears that there is..a new outbreak of kazooing in South Wales and Bootle. **1965** G. MELLY *Owning-Up* xi. 135 A kind of sub-jazz in which kazoos, tea-chest and broom-handle basses..and empty suitcases replaced the more conventional musical instruments. **1966** T. PYNCHON *Crying of Lot 49* i. 10 The Fort Wayne Settecento Ensemble's variorum recording of the Vivaldi Kazoo Concerto. **1968** *Blues Unlimited* Nov. 8 Dewey Corley..now plays kazoo and washtub bass. **1970** *Peace News* 8 May 8/4, I think the time has come for us to make our own music... To beat on pots and pans, blow kazoos and our combs wrapped in wax paper. **1972** *Guardian* 29 May 5/5 The unusual cigar-shaped instrument, the kazoo—a cheap toy which makes a vibrant noise when blown—can help unmusical children to sing in

tune. 1973 *Ibid.* 19 Feb. 8/4 A Kazoo will give out a sort of buzzing noise... As one of the 120 Kazooing members of the audience I found it fun.

Also **ka'zoo** *v.*, to make a sound like that of a kazoo; **ka'zooer**, **ka'zooist**, one who plays the kazoo; **ka'zooing** *vbl. sb.* and *ppl. a.*

1909 R. A. WASON *Happy Hawkins* (1912) xxvi. 301 The storm that was presently kazooin' along was fierce an' horrible. 1959 *Guardian* 26 Aug. 5/2 The kazooers' parents give tremendous support. 1970 *Guardian Weekly* 14 Mar. 16/1 Running the gauntlet of a battalion of kazooists.

‖**kea** ('kea, 'kɪə). [Maori: from the cry of the bird.] The Green Alpine Parrot of New Zealand (*Nestor notabilis*), which destroys sheep in order to prey upon their kidney-fat.

It was originally frugivorous, but had become before 1881 a pest to sheep-farmers in the Southern Alps of N.Z.

1862 J. VON HAAST *Explor. Head Waters Waitaki* in *Geol. Westland* (1879) 36 (Morris) A number of large green alpine parrots.. the kea of the natives. 1871 *Nature* IV. 489/1 The Kea.. may be seen and heard in certain localities amidst the wild scenery of the Southern Alps in the middle island of New Zealand. 1883 *Standard* 7 Sept. 5/2 The rabbit, the sparrow, and the kea are getting so numerous that.. the squatters are almost in despair. 1895 *Times* 20 Dec. 13/1 The Kea of New Zealand.. a mountain parrot naturally frugivorous, which has developed a fatal taste for mutton.

kea-, a frequent dial. (Sc. and N. Eng.) representative of *ca-*, *ka-*, as in *keake*, *keale*, etc.

keach (kiːtʃ), *v. Obs.* exc. *dial.* Forms: 4 **keche, kecche, kyche,** 6 **kiche,** 6–7 **keech,** 7 **keatch, ketch,** 7– **keach.** [Of obscure origin: cf. CLEACH *v.* (sense 3).] *trans.* To take up (water, etc.) with a shallow vessel; to scoop up, ladle out: = CLEACH *v.* 3.

1387 TREVISA *Higden* (Rolls) VIII. 235 Ye schal kecche up water [*v.rr.* kyche, cleche]. 1598 FLORIO, *Intingere*, to dip in, to kiche up [1611 to keech up]. 1611 *Ibid.*, *Attingere*,.. to draw or keach water. *c* 1682 J. COLLINS *Salt & Fishery* 89 The Oyle will swim at top, from whence it may be keeched with a pot. 1881 *Oxfordsh. Gloss.* Suppl., *Keach up*, to take up water by ladling.

Hence **'keaching** *vbl. sb.*, in *Comb.* **keaching-ladle; keaching-net** = CLEACHING-NET.

1624–5 *Althorp MS.* in Simpkinson *The Washingtons* (1860) App. p. lix, For mending the drag nett & for 2 new keatching netts. 1633–4 *Ibid.* p. lxiii, To the tinker for mending the keeching ladle in the kitching.

keach, keagh, variants of KIAUGH, *Sc.*

†**keach-cup.** *Obs. rare*⁻¹. [f. *keach* vb. *dial.* to toss + CUP.] A toss-pot, drunkard.

a 1225 *Ancr. R.* 216 Gif þe gulchecuppe [*C.* keache cuppe, *T.* kelche cuppe] weallinde bres to drincken.

†**kead,** obs. form of CADE *sb.*²

1688 R. HOLME *Armoury* II. 176/2 Kead Lamb, when brought up without the help, or sucking of the Ewe.

†**keak** (keːk), *v. Obs. rare.* Also 6 **keke,** 7 **keake, keek.** [Imitative.] *intr.* To cackle.

1545 ASCHAM *Toxoph.* II. (Arb.) 130 Theues on a night had stolne Iupiter, had a gouse not a kekede. 1598 *Herrings Tayle* A ij, Helpe sportfull Muse to tune my gander-keaking quill. 1621 J. TAYLOR (Water P.) *Taylor's Goose* Wks. (1630) I. 104/1 The sober Goose.. did harshly keake and hisse. 1634 T. JOHNSON *Parcy's Chirurg.* II. (1678) 42 The Geese .. take care, that by their keeking and their noise, they do not expose themselves to the rapacity of Birds of prey.

†**keak,** *sb. Obs. rare*⁻¹. In 7 **keake.** [f. prec. vb.] A cackle, cackling.

1600 BRETON *Pasquils Mad-cappe* (1626) B, He.. Must be attentiue to the Ganders keake, Or giue a plaudite, when the Goose doth speake. [1878 *Cumbld. Gloss.* Suppl., *Kayk*, the cry of a goose.]

keal, -e, keallach, keame, keap, var. KEEL, KELLACH, KEMB, KEP.

keap-, kep-, keaping-stane, Sc. forms of COPE-, COPING-STONE.

1610 *Burgh Rec. Aberdeen* (Spalding Club) II. 300 The keaping stane to be of outlairis, frie wark, and boulted with irne. 1667 J. LAMONT *Diary* (1810) 246 By the fall of a keap-stone.. his head was bruised into pieces.

keare, kearl, kearmas, kearn(e, kearnach, keatch, keather, obs. or var. ff. KIER, CARL, KERMIS, CAIRN, KERN, KERNAUGH, KEACH, CATHER.

Keating ('kiːtɪŋ). The name of Thomas *Keating*, a 19th-century chemist, used (usu. *attrib.* or in the possessive) as the proprietary name of an insect powder first manufactured by him.

1876 *Trade Marks Jrnl.* 11 Oct. 576/2 Keating's Persian insect destroying powder.. Thomas Keating. 1886 B. POTTER *Jrnl.* Dec. (1966) 193 The little room above the saddle room was sprayed with Keatings powder and shut up. 1893 E. F. BENSON *Dodo* II. xviii. 378, I am in England. .. I shall sleep in a clean white bed, and I shall not have to use Keating. 1909 *Trade Marks Jrnl.* 24 Mar. 487 Keating's Powder... Insect Destroying Powder. Thomas Keating.. Wholesale Chemists. 1915 A. D. GILLESPIE *Lett. from Flanders* (1916) 218, I have plenty of Keating's powder left. 1920 D. H. LAWRENCE *Touch & Go* III. ii. 84 And are you going to comb 'em out, or do you propose to use Keating's? 1926 A. HUXLEY *Let.* 10 Aug. (1969) 271 The typhoid is said to be very bad... be fore-armed and take a lot of Keatings. 1928 F. STARK *Lett. from Syria* (1942) iv. 136 As for fleas, Keating's has succumbed to numbers. 1941 G. GREENE in *Spectator* 4 July 8/2 Keating's Powder has taken the place of the military escort.

keatite ('kiːtaɪt). *Min.* [f. the name of P. P. *Keat* (born 1923), U.S. chemist who first synthesized it + -ITE¹.] An artificial modification of silica produced at high pressures as tetragonal crystals.

1954 [see COESITE]. 1955 *Trans. Brit. Ceramic Soc.* LIV. 665 The polymerized silicic acid now crystallizes.. to the crystalline tetragonal phase, keatite. 1959 *Zeitschr. für Kristallogr.* CXII. 410 The density of keatite (50 /gr·cm³) is intermediate to that of cristobalite.. and quartz. 1962 C. FRONDEL *Dana's Syst. Min.* (ed. 7) III. 308 Keatite has been synthesized by heating commercial dried silica.. in water containing an alkali.

Keatsian ('kiːtsɪən), *a.* and *sb.* [f. the name of the English poet John *Keats* (1795–1821) + -IAN.] **A.** *adj.* Of, pertaining to, or characteristic of Keats or his poetry. **B.** *sb.* A student or admirer of Keats or his poetry.

1845 T. WADE *Let.* 26 May in H. E. Rollins *Keats Circle* (1948) II. 119 A Keats-ian poem. 1891 *Athenæum* 23 May 667/3 A little manuscript book.. of some interest to Keatsians. 1901 H. B. FORMAN in Keats *Compl. Works* III. 112 He [*sc.* Woodhouse] opens with a Keatsian enough punctuation of the first four lines. 1910 H. WALKER *Lit. Victorian Era* II. ii. 299 A Keatsian worship of beauty.. is his [*sc.* Tennyson's] characteristic. 1934 F. L. & P. LUCAS *From Olympus to Styx* vi. 69 In spite of its Keatsian name, Lamia has little romance or even history. 1968 *Guardian* 22 Mar. 9/3 The kind of detail, immensely rewarding to Keatsians, with which Mr Gittings's biography swarms, is well exemplified by his suggestion about the authorship of the essay for 'The Indicator' which Leigh Hunt was composing extempore.. while Keats.. lay listening on a sofa. 1970 *Daily Tel.* 19 Sept. 9/6 The day.. beginning as a mist wherein the Keatsian 'mellow fruitfullness' lay wrapped in its own swaddling clothes.

So **Keatsi'ana** (see ANA *suff.*, -IANA).

1818 R. WOODHOUSE *Let.* Nov. in H. E. Rollins *Keats Circle* (1948) I. 66, I shod like to add that to my collection of 'Keatsiana'. 1898 [see -IANA]. 1962 *Daily Tel.* 21 Mar. 17/5 (*heading*) Keatsiana... I have been commissioned to write a book on Keats [etc.].

keave, dial. form of CAVE *sb.* and *v.*

keaver, obs. f. KIVER.

keavle, Sc. dial. f. CAVEL *sb.*¹

keb (kɛb), *sb.*¹ *local.* Also 6 **kebbe,** 9 **kebb.** [Etymology uncertain; cf. G. *kibbe*, *kippe*, ewe.] A ewe that has lost her lamb, or whose lamb is still-born. Also ***keb-ewe.***

1470–73 in *Rec. Andover* 20 Recᵈ pro viij ovibus ecclie vocat[is] Kebbys viijˢ. 1549 *Compl. Scot.* vi. 66 Baytht ȝouis and lammis, kebbis and dailis. 1581 J. BELL *Haddon's Answ. Osor.* 431 b, Full of sicknesse, and like an olde kebbe full of wrinckles. 1822 W. J. NAPIER *Pract. Store-farm.* 60 Of lambs, the superabundance of twins has far exceeded the loss by kebbs. 1824 *Gallovid. Encycl.*, *Keb-Ewes.*

b. *Comb.*, as **keb-house** (see quot.).

1886 C. SCOTT *Sheep-Farming* 118 Such a shed.. is termed a keb-house,—a 'keb' being a ewe that has lost her lamb, and the house the place where she may be confined while being made to adopt another.

†**keb, kebb,** *sb.*², var. CAB *sb.*² *Obs.*, Cavalier.

c 1645 T. TULLY *Siege Carlisle* (1840) 45 Yᵉ whole body charging, the Kebs were put to a second retreat. 1664 *Depos. Cast. York* (Surtees) 118 Hee would banish both the informer and all his like, kebbs as they were.

†**keb,** *v.*¹ *Obs. rare.* [Perh. from root of MDu. *kebbelen*, E.Fris. *kabbeln* to chatter, babble; MDu. *kabbelen* (Du. *kibbelen*), LG. *kabbeln* to quarrel, dispute.] *intr.* To boast, brag.

c 1315 SHOREHAM 96 Wanne he aldey swereth ydelleche, In kebbynge and in caute. *Ibid.* 111 ȝef that kebbede eny of ous, Ich woȝt wel that he leȝ. *Ibid.*, Wyth kebbynges aperte.

keb (kɛb), *v.*² *dial.* [Cf. KEB *sb.*¹]

intr. Of a ewe: **a.** To cast a lamb prematurely, or dead. **b.** *to keb at*, to refuse to suckle (a lamb).

1816 SCOTT *Bl. Dwarf* ii, Bewitching the sheep, causing the ewes to 'keb'. 1883 GRAHAM *Writings* II. 36 (E.D.D.) She wad keb at it, as the black ew did at the white ew's lamb. 1893 *Northumbld. Gloss.*, *Keb*, to drop a dead lamb.

Hence **kebbed** (kɛbd), *ppl a.*

1824 *Blackw. Mag.* XV. 181 A kebbed ewe is one whose lamb dies. 1893 *Northumbld. Gloss.* s.v., When a lamb dies in birth it is called a kebbed lamb and the mother a kebbed yow.

kebab (kɪ'bæb, -'bɑːb). Also **keebaub, khubab, kibab, kibaub, qabab.** [Var. of CABOB.] = CABOB 1; pieces of meat roasted on a skewer (see also quot. 1970). Cf. DONER KEBAB, SHISH KEBAB.

1813 J. FORBES *Oriental Mem.* II. xvi. 12 A superb dinner of fifty covers, cooked in the Mogul taste.. pilaurs, keb-abs, curries, and other savoury dishes. 1839 C. M. KIRKLAND *New Home* xiv. 87 She would have made out nobly on kibaubs. *a* 1861 T. WINTHROP *John Brent* (1883) xii. 105 Mr. Clitheroe was like a lamb whom the shepherd intends first to shear close.. and at last to cut up into keebaubs. 1902 *Daily Chron.* 19 Nov. 8/4, I leave these, and press on past rows of animals, heaps of fodder, dealers and kibab sellers and market women. 1932 *Times Lit. Suppl.* 10 Nov. 836/4 A learned disquisition on skewer-cooking, of Eastern origin, leading to various kinds of *kebabs*. 1954 *Gd. Housek. Cookery Bk.* 450/2 The Muslims who gave the dish its name (which can also appear in such forms as khubab, kibbab and qabab) used their swords to impale the food. 1955 G. BAND *Road to Rakaposhi* viii. 100 The evening meal was preceded by a *kebab*. Beef liver and kidney sliced in small chunks was skewered on to long thin sticks and roasted over an open fire. 1963 R. CARRIER *Great Dishes of World* 139 If the weather is too cool for outdoor cookery, *kebabs* can be grilled indoors with ease. 1970 SIMON & HOWE *Dict. Gastron.* 234/1 Cubes of vegetables are also called kebabs; there are kebab ragoûts. .. There are also fish kebabs. 1973 *Times* 9 Nov. 14/4, I then bought some kebab skewers. 1974 *Times* 4 May 11/6 The Open Space in Tottenham Court Road.. is within easy reach of.. the kebab houses around Charlotte Street. The least frantic at lunchtime seem to be the Cypriana Kebab House.. and the Venus Kebab House.

kebar, kebir, var. CABER, pole, spar. *Sc.*

‖**kebaya** (kə'bɑːjə). Also 6 **cabie, cabaia,** 7 **cabbay, cabay(e, -ya;** 9 **kabaya.** [Ultimately of Pers. or Arab. origin. The forms *cabie*, *cabbay* are perh. directly a. Pers. *qabāy*; *cabaia*, *cabaya* are from Pg., whence also F. *cabaye*. *Kabaya* and *kebaya* are immed. from Malay, whence also Du. *kabaaj*.] A light loose tunic such as is commonly worn in the East; now *spec.* that worn in Malay countries by native women and by Europeans in dishabille.

1585 R. FITCH in *Hakluyt's Voy.* (1810) II. 386 The King is apparelled with a Cabie made like a shirt tied with strings on one side. 1598 tr. *Linschoten's Voy.* 70 They wear sometimes when they go abroad a thinne cotton [? or] linnen gowne called *Cabaia*. 1634 SIR T. HERBERT *Trav.* 81 Attiring himselfe in red, his Tulipant, Cabbay, Boots, Scabberd. 1662 J. DAVIES tr. *Maudelslo's Trav. E.I.* 64. 1883 MRS. BISHOP *Sk. Malay Penins.* iii. in *Leisure Ho.* 81/1 Their lower garment, or *sarong*, reaching from the waist to the ankles.. above which is worn a loose-sleeved garment, called a kabaya, reaching to the knees. 1909 R. O. WINSTEDT *Papers on Malay Subjects*: *Life & Customs* II. 40 The long, shapeless *kĕbaya*.. [is] now universally worn by women. 1939 A. KEITH *Land below Wind* vi. 92 The *kebaya*, a short Malay blouse, was purchased, and Kuta.. fastened it with one insecure brooch. 1958 H. FORSTER *Flowering Lotus* ii. 25 My eye was often disappointed by chromatic discords between the ladies' skirts and their *kebayas*, long-sleeved jackets for which they favoured brightly variegated flower patterns. 1963 *N.Z. Woman's Weekly* 17 June 21/2 For sheer glamour, Nancy's sarong kebaya (the Malayan dress) stole the day. This was a closely fitting skirt in a royal blue with a pleated panel in the front worn with an overblouse of lace in a paler shade of blue. 1966 D. FORBES *Heart of Malaya* iv. 52 He dressed her up in beautiful clothes—sometimes cheongsams, sometimes saris, sometimes sarong kebayas. 1972 *Guardian* 13 Jan. 5/3 Our beautiful M[alaysia] S[ingapore] A[irlines] hostesses in their sarong kebayas are dedicated to superb in-flight service.

†**'kebber.** *Obs.* Also 8 **kebbar.** [? Related to KEB *sb.*¹] An old or diseased sheep which is removed from the flock; a crone.

1538 ELYOT *Bibl.*, *Reieculæ uel reijculæ oues*, sheepe drawen out of the folde for aege or syckenesse, kebbers, crones, or cullyars. 1611 COTGR. s.v. *Rebut*, *Brebis de rebut*, Drapes, Cullings, or Kebbers; old, or diseased sheepe which be not worth keeping. 1726 *Dict. Rust.* (ed. 3) s.v., Kebbers or Cullers, refuse Sheep taken out of the Flock.

'kebbie, 'kebby. *north.* and *Sc.* [cf. KIBBLE, KIBBO.] A staff or stick with a hooked head.

1816 SCOTT *Old Mort.* xiv, Ane o' them was gaun to strike my mither wi' the side o' his broadsword—So I got up my kebbie at them, and said I wad gie them as gude. 1899 *Cumbld. Gloss.* 182/2 *Kebby stick*,.. a hook-headed walking-stick; shepherd's crook. [Also *kebby*.]

kebbuck ('kɛbək). *Sc.* Forms: 5–6 **cabok,** 7 **kebeck,** 8 **cabbac(k,** 9 **kebbock, kibbock, (kebec),** 8– **kebbuck.** [Of obscure origin: Gael. *càbag* cheese, not in Irish, may be from Sc.] A cheese: sometimes denoting a special kind (see quot. 1816). Formerly also ***a kebbuck of cheese.***

c 1470 HENRYSON *Mor. Fab.* x. (*Fox & Wolf*) xviii, Ye sall ane cabok haif in to your hand. *Ibid.* xxiv. 1493 *Acta Audit.* (1839) 176/2 A cabok of cheiss takin for a halfpenny. 1565 *Prestwick Burgh Rec.* (1834) 68 Ane cabok of cheys. 1715 RAMSAY *Christ's Kirk Gr.* II. xx, A kebbuck.. that maist could creep. 1785 BURNS *Cotter's Saturday Nt.* xi, The dame brings forth.. To grace the lad, her weel-hained kebbuck. 1816 SCOTT *Old Mort.* viii, A huge kebbock—a cheese, that is, made with ewe-milk mixed with cow's milk. 1893 CROCKETT *Stickit Minister* 276 A little round kebbuck.

attrib. 1787 BURNS *Holy Fair* xxv, An' dinna, for a kebbuck-heel, Let lasses by affronted.

kebla, keblock, kebob, kecche, keche, var. or obs. ff. KIBLAH, KEDLOCK, CABOB, CATCH *v.*, KEACH *v.*

kebla(h, kebleh, varr. KIBLAH.

†**'kechel.** *Obs. rare.* [OE. *cœcil*, prob. *cœ́cil* = MHG. *chüechel* (G. dial. *küchel*):—**kōkilo-* related to OHG. *chuoche* (MHG. *kuoche*, G. *kuchen*), MLG. *kôke*:—**kōkon-*; f. **kōk-*, ablaut-variant of **kak-*, whence CAKE, q.v. See also KICHEL.] A little cake. ***a God's kechel***: a cake given as alms in the name, or for the sake, of God (cf. GOD 16 c).

a 700 *Epinal Gloss.* 993 *Tortum* coecil. *c* 1200 ORMIN 8662 Acc allre firrst macc þu to me þærofe an litell kechell. *c* 1386 CHAUCER *Sompn. T.* 39 Yif vs a busshel whete malt or reye, A goddes kechyl [*v.rr.* -el, -il] or a trype of cheese.

kechen(e, -in(e, -ing, etc., obs. ff. KITCHEN.

Kechua, var. QUECHUA.

keck (kɛk), *sb.* Now *dial.* [A sing. of *kex*, *kecks*, mistaken as a pl. form.] Any of the large Umbelliferæ, or their hollow stems: = KEX. ***broad-leaved keck***, the Cow Parsnip (*Heracleum Sphondylium*); ***trumpet-keck***, ? Wild Angelica.

a **1624** BP. M. SMITH *Serm.* (1632) 234 The old man threw a dart; it had been as good he had thrown a kecke or a straw. **1706** PHILLIPS, *Kecks*, dry Stalks. **1821** CLARE *Vill. Minstr.* II. 100 Half hid in meadow-sweet and keck's high flowers. **1827** —— *Sheph. Cal.*, etc. *Last of Autumn* xi, Trumpet-kecks.. Whose hollow stalks inspired such eager joy. **1887** *S. Chesh. Gloss.* s.v., As dry as a keck.

b. *Comb.*, as ***keck-stalk***; † **keck-bugloss**, some medicinal herb.

a **1693** URQUHART *Rabelais* III. xxxi, The Fervency of Lust is abated by.. Chastree, Mandrake, Bennet, Keck-buglosse [F. *orchis le petit*]. **1821** CLARE *Sonn. Night* in *Vill. Minstr.* II. 179 From keck-stalk cavity, or hollow bean.

keck (kɛk), *v.* [Echoic.

Cf. **1575** *Gamm. Gurton* IV. ii, Till I made her olde wesen to answere again, kecke.]

1. *intr.* To make a sound as if about to vomit; to retch; to feel an inclination to vomit; hence ***to keck at***, to reject (food, medicine, etc.) with loathing. Also *fig.* expressing strong dislike or disgust.

1601 HOLLAND *Pliny* II. 148 Their pouder is.. ordained for them who.. are ready to keck and heaue at euery little thing. **1642** MILTON *Apol. Smect.* Introd. Wks. (1851) 265 The worser stuffe she strongly keeps in her stomach, but the better she is ever kecking at, and is queasie. **1681** TEMPLE *Mem.* III. Wks. 1731 I. 335, I had propos'd Lord Hallifax as one of the Lords, whom the King had indeed keck'd at.. more than any of the rest. **1710** SWIFT *Lett.* (1767) III. 61, I have taken a whole box of pills, and keckt at them every night. **1821** LAMB *Elia* Ser. I. *Imperf. Symp.*, If they can sit with us at table, why do they keck at our cookery?

b. = KINK *v.*[1] (Cf. Norw. *kikje.*)

1721 BAILEY, *To Keck, Keckle*, to make a Noise in the Throat, by reason of Difficulty in Breathing.

2. *intr.* Of a bird: To utter a sound like *keck*.

1844 in Whitelaw *Bk. Scot. Song* (1875) 347/2 Our grey clocking hen she gaed Kecking her lone. **1878** P. ROBINSON *Indian Garden* I. *Green Parrots*, The hawk now and again affords healthy excitement to a score of crows who keck at him as he flaps unconcerned.. through the air.

Hence **'kecking** *vbl. sb.*

1709 *Rambling Fuddle-Caps* 12 B'ing ready to spew, I suppose, by his kecking. **1751** STACK in *Phil. Trans.* XLVII. 275 When this medicine produces nothing more than keckings at stomach.

keck-handed *a.*, var. CACK-HANDED *a.*

† **'keckish**, *a. Obs. rare.* [f. KECK *v.* + -ISH[1].] Inclined to keck; squeamish.

1603 HOLLAND *Plutarch's Mor.* 781, Inordinate passion of vomiting, called Cholera, is nothing different from a keckish stomacke and a desire to cast.

keckle ('kɛk(ə)l), *v.*[1] Forms: 6 kekell, kekkyl, 6–7 kekle, 7– keckle. [var. (chiefly Sc.) of CACKLE *v.*[1], and in sense 2 of CHECKLE *v.*]

1. *intr.* Of a hen or other bird: To cackle.

1513 DOUGLAS *Æneis* VII. Prol. 118 And kais keklis on the ruiff abone. **1549** *Compl. Scot.* vi. 39 Quhilk gart the hennis kekkyl. **1635** BARRIFFE *Mil. Discip.* (1643) 351 That will not take the liberty of a Hen to keckle over her owne egge. **1883** GRAHAM *Writings* II. 31 (E.D.D.) Whan the hens begin to keckle.

2. Of a person: To chuckle, laugh, giggle, CHECKLE.

1513 DOUGLAS *Æneis* V. iv. 40 The Troianis lauchis fast seand hym fall, And, hym behaldand swym, thai keklit all. **1728** RAMSAY *Bob of Dunblane* i, For fainness, deary, I'll gar ye keckle. **1833** M. SCOTT *Tom Cringle* xi. (1859) 246 He keckled at his small joke very complacently.

b. *trans.* To utter with or express by chuckling.

1857 KINGSLEY *Two Y. Ago* iv. I. 104 'Ah, you're a wag, Sir', keckled the old man. **1874** LISLE CARR *Jud. Gwynne* I. ii. 58 Then she keckled a tiny laugh of supreme derision.

Hence **'keckling** *vbl. sb.* and *ppl. a.*

1719 RAMSAY *3rd. Answ. Hamilton* xv, Gin ony.. Ca' me conceited keckling chucky. **1790** *Scots Songs* II. 51 A keckling hen To lay her eggs in plenty. **1834** M. SCOTT *Cruise Midge* xxi, The laughing, and fistling, and keckling we heard.

keckle ('kɛk(ə)l), *v.*[2] *Naut.* See also CACKLE *v.*[2] [Etym. unknown.] *trans.* To case a cable or hawser with rope in order to prevent chafing.

1627 CAPT. SMITH *Seaman's Gram.* vii. 30 To keckell or sarue the Cable, as is said, is.. to bind some old clouts to keepe it from galling in the Hawse or Ring. **1678** PHILLIPS (ed. 4), *Keckle* (in Navigation), to turn a small Rope about the Cable or Bolt-rope, when we fear the galling of the Cable in the Hawse. **1882** NARES *Seamanship* (ed. 6) 24 *Keckling a hawser* [is] serving it over with rope, which keeps it from being chafed.

Hence **'keckling** *vbl. sb.*; also *concr.* (see quot.).

1753 CHAMBERS *Cycl. Supp.* s.v., When the cables gaul in the hawse.. the seamen wind some small ropes about them; and this is called *keckling*. **1769** FALCONER *Dict. Marine* (1789), *Kaicling*, or *Kecling*, a name given to any old ropes, which are wound about a cable.

'keckle, *v.*[3] *dial.* [freq. of KECK.] = KECK *v.* I.

1619 W. WHATELY *God's Husb.* I. (1622) 72 The hypocrite .. can swallow a Cammell with the same throat, which did euen keckle at a Gnat. **1893** *Northumbld. Gloss.*, *Keckle*,.. to make a noise in the throat when swallowing.

keckle ('kɛk(ə)l), *sb. Sc.* [f. KECKLE *v.*[1]] **a.** A short spasmodic laugh; a chuckle. **b.** Cackling, chattering, etc. (Cf. CACKLE *sb.* 3 b.)

1820 *Blackw. Mag.* VIII. 260 Miss Becky Glibbans gave a satirical keckle at this. **1822** GALT *Provost* xii. (1842) 38 'I' gude faith', cried the bailie, with a keckle of exultation, 'here's proof enough now'. **1871** W. ALEXANDER *Johnny Gibb* xlvi. (1873) 257 A bit keckle o' a lauch.

keckle-meckle. *Mining.* ? *Obs.* (See quot.)

1747 HOOSON *Miner's Dict.* K iv b, *Keckle-Meckle*. The poorest kind of mines that yields Ore, and the Ore is of the poorest sort... *Keckle-Meckle* Stuff has the Ore run with it in small Strings and Races, or spotted with it much like Birds Eyes.

† **'kecklish**, *a. Obs. rare.* [f. KECKLE *v.*[3] + -ISH[1].] = KECKISH.

1601 HOLLAND *Pliny* XX. xiv, The female Penyroiall.. staieth a kecklish stomack. *Ibid.* XXIII. Proeme.

kecks, kecksie, variants of KEX, KEXY.

keck-shoes, -shose, obs. variant of KICKSHAW.

kecksy ('kɛksɪ). Chiefly *dial.* Also 7 **keksy**, 9 **kicksey, kexy, gicksy**. [f. *kecks*, KEX, prob. by taking the pl. *kexes* as = *kexies*.] = KEX, a hollow plant-stem.

1599 SHAKS. *Hen. V*, V. ii. 52 Hatefull Docks, rough Thistles, Keksyes, Burres. **1800** HURDIS *Fav. Village* 109 Thou.. frost, that in a night.. covers the lake, E'en to the kicksey vulnerable. **1816** COLERIDGE *Lay Serm.* in *Biog. Lit.* (1882) 326 Among other odd burrs and kecksies. **1825** BRITTON *Beauties Wilts.* III. (E.D.S.), *Kecks, Kecksy*. **1886** *S.W. Linc. Gloss.* s.v. *Kex*, As dry as an old kecksy.

† **'kecky**, *a. Obs. rare*[−1]. [f. KECK *sb.* + -Y.] Of the nature of a keck or kex; = KEXY.

a **1711** GREW (J.), A sort of cane.. [which] consisteth of hard and blackish cylinders, mixed with a soft kecky body.

ked, kade (kɛd, keɪd), *sb.*[1] Also 6 **cade**, 7 (? **kidde**), **kaid**, 8–9 **kead**. [Of unknown derivation; the phonology points to *cāde* as the etymological form; this would give north.Eng. and south.Sc. *keäd*, *keäde*, which, on the analogy of *heäd* head, would be anglicized as *kead*, *ked* (kɛd).] A sheep-tick or sheep-louse (*Melophagus ovinus*).

1570 LEVINS *Manip.* 8 A cade, sheepe louse. *a* **1605** MONTGOMERIE *Flyting w. Polwart* 492 Some, luikand lyce, in the crowne of it keeks; Some choppes the kiddes into their cheeks. **1653** W. LAWSON *Comm. Secr. Angling* in Arb. *Garner* I. 196, I rather think the kades and other filth that fall from sheep do so glut the fish that they will not take any artificial bait. **1697** CLELAND *Poems* 34 (Jam.) Their swarms of vermine, and sheep kaids Delights to lodge, beneath the plaids. **1781** J. HUTTON *Tour to Caves* Gloss. (E.D.S.), *Kead*, a sheep's louse. **1811** *Mann. & Cust.* in *Ann. Reg.* 443/2 The sheep are very much infested by vermin known in England by the name of ticks or keds. **1842–51** H. STEPHENS *Bk. of Farm* (1891) III. 140 Keds become most numerous when sheep get from a lean to a better condition.

Ked (kɛd), *sb.*[2] orig. *U.S.* [See quot. 1967.] Proprietary name of a soft-soled canvas shoe.

1917 *Trade Marks Jrnl.* 14 Nov. 1092 Keds.. Rubber, Leather, and Fabric Footwear. United States Rubber Company.. New York,.. Manufacturers of Rubber Goods. **1961** *Encounter* Apr. 23/2, I am wearing Keds, and feel light on the foam rubber soles. **1966** B. H. DEAL *Fancy's Knell* (1967) i. 15 He found the Ked. He picked it up.. reluctant to think beyond the small canvas shoe in his hand. **1967** L. J. HEALEY in R. L. Cohen *Footwear Industry* x. 93 We [*sc.* U.S. Rubber Co.] wanted to call it Peds, but.. it came too close to.. other brand names. So we batted it around for awhile and decided on the hardest-sounding letter in the alphabet, K, and called it Keds, that was in 1916. **1968** H. C. RAE *Few Small Bones* II. viii. 138 He dug a hole in the junk on the couch, tossing a track-suit and a pair of Keds.. on to the floor.

ked, kedde, var. *kidde*, pa. t. and pa. pple. of KITHE *v.*

keddah, var. KHEDA.

keddie, keddle, kedel(l, kede, obs. ff. KIDDY *sb.*[1], KIDDLE, KID *sb.*[1]

kedge (kɛdʒ), *sb.* [? short for KEDGE-ANCHOR. Also *catch*: see CATCH *sb.*[3]] = KEDGE-ANCHOR.

1769 FALCONER *Dict. Marine* (1789), *Kedge*, a small anchor used to keep a ship steady whilst she rides in a harbour or river, particularly at the turn of the tide... The kedges are also.. useful in transporting a ship, *i.e.* removing her from one part of the harbour to another, by means of ropes. **1833** M. SCOTT *Tom Cringle* ix. (1859) 197 The schooner every now and then taking the ground, but she was always quickly warped off again by a kedge. **1854** H. MILLER *Sch. & Schm.* (1858) 22 The other moiety of the men, tugging hard on kedge and haulser, drew the vessel off.

Comb. **1836** *Encycl. Brit.* (ed. 7) XII. 684/1 This is.. prevented by a kedge-rope that hinders her from approaching it.

kedge, *a. E. Angl. dial.* Also 5 **kygge, kydge** (? **kyde**), 9 **kidge**. [Of unknown etym.; cf. KEDGY, CADGY.] Brisk, lively; in good spirits.

c **1440** *Promp. Parv.* 274/2 Kygge, or ioly (*H.* kydge, *P.* kyde), *jocundus, hillaris, vernosus*. **1674** RAY *S. & E. Countrey Words* 69 *Kedge*, brisk, budge, lively, *Suff.* **1801** BLOOMFIELD *Rural T.*, *Rich. & Kate* xxiv, I'm surely growing young again; I feel myself so kedge and plump. **1829** H. MURRAY *North America* II. III. iii. 367 Are his spirits kedge? **1856** in *W. S. Simpson's Life* (1899) 30, I ain't so well to-day as I was yesterday: I was quite kidge then.

kedge (kɛdʒ), *v. Naut.* Also 7 **kedg**. [Perh. a specialized variant of CADGE *v.* For the change from *a* to *e*, cf. *keg*, *ketch*, from *cag*, *catch*, etc.

The earliest forms evidenced are those of the vbl. sb. *kedging* in the comb. *cagging-anchor*, *-cable*, and the agent-n. *kedger* (*cagger*) which are perh. to be referred to CADGE *v.* in the sense 'tie, fasten'. The vb. may be a back-formation from this, after the special sense was developed.]

intr. **a.** To warp a ship, or move it from one position to another by winding in a hawser attached to a small anchor dropped at some distance; also *trans.* to warp. **b.** Of a ship: To move by means of kedging.

1627 CAPT. SMITH *Seaman's Gram.* vii. 29 The least are called Kedgers, to use in calme weather.., or to kedg vp and downe a narrow Riuer. **1678** PHILLIPS (ed. 4), *To Kedge*, to set up the Foresail or Foretopsail and Missen, and set a Ship to drive with the Tide [1706 letting fall, and lifting up the Kedge-Anchor, as often as Occasion serves] when in a narrow River we would bring her up or down, the Wind being contrary to the Tide. **1840** R. H. DANA *Bef. Mast* xxiv. 75 She went to windward as though she were kedging. **1897** tr. *Nansen's Farthest North* I. 166 We 'kedged' the Fram with her anchor just clear of the bottom.

So **kedging** ('kɛdʒɪŋ) *vbl. sb.* (also 5 **caggering** (?), **cagg(e)-, kaggyng**), warping with a kedge-anchor; also *attrib.*

1485 *Naval Acc. Hen. VII* (1896) 52 Cables.. vj, Caggering [sic] cables.. j. **1486** *Ibid.* 12 A caggeyng cable weying M[l]c iij quarterons. *Ibid.* 18 Caggyng cable.. j. **1495** *Ibid.* 192 Kaggyng Ankers.. ij. **1497** *Ibid.* 290 Ankers of diuerse sortes.. Caggyng Ankers j, Warpyng Ankers j. **1627** CAPT. SMITH *Seaman's Gram.* vii. 29 They row by her with an Anchor in a boat, and.. so by a Hawser winde her head about,.. and this is kedging. **1704** J. HARRIS *Lex. Techn.* s.v., They.. let fall [a small anchor] in the middle of the Stream, and so wend or turn her Head about, lifting the Anchor up again... This work is called Kedging,.. and the Anchor.. the Kedger, or Kedge-Anchor. **1830** MARRYAT *King's Own* xlii. **1891** *Times* 24 Oct. 6/6 That he had, during a calm, propelled the Minnow by means of kedging.

kedge-anchor. Now *rare.* [f. KEDGE *v.* Rarely *catch-anchor*: see CATCH *sb.*[3]] A small anchor with an iron stock used in mooring or warping; = KEDGE *sb.*

1704 [see prec.]. **1706** PHILLIPS, *Kedge-Anchors*, are small Anchor[s] us'd in calm Weather, and in a slow stream. **1712** E. COOKE *Voy. S. Sea* 2 Came to with our Kedge-Anchor. **1899** F. T. BULLEN *Log Sea-waif* 110 The miserably slow method of warping out by a kedge-anchor.

† **kedgell**, obs. form of CUDGEL.

1578 *Wills & Inv. N.C.* (Surtees, 1860) 19 To John Hedworthe,.. my browne kedgell stafe for a token.

† **'kedger**[1]. *Obs.* [f. KEDGE *v.* + -ER[1].] A small anchor or grapnel; = KEDGE *sb.*

1497 *Naval Acc. Hen. VII* (1896) 281 Ankers called Caggers. **1626** CAPT. SMITH *Accid. Yng. Seamen* 16 The streame Anchor, graplings or kedgers. **1630** —— *Trav. & Adv.* 40 They boorded him againe as before; and threw foure kedgers or grapnalls in iron chaines. **1704** [see *kedging* above]. **1727–51** in CHAMBERS *Cycl.* s.v. *Kedging*.

kedger[2], dial. form of CADGER.

1696 *Phil. Trans.* XIX. 343 The Decoy-men Contract for them all at a certain Rate per Dozen, which the Carryers (Kedgers) are obliged to take off their Hands. [Still dial., Yorksh., Norfolk, etc.; see E.D.D.]

‖**kedgeree** ('kɛdʒəriː). Forms: 7 **kits-, ketch-, quiche-, kichery, cutcherry**, 8 **kitcheree, -aree**, 9 **kedjerie; keg-, kedg-, kidgeree, khichri**. [Hindī *khichrī*, Skr. *k'rsara* 'dish of rice and sesamum'.]

a. An Indian dish of rice boiled with split pulse, onions, eggs, butter, and condiments; also, in European cookery, a dish made of cold fish, boiled rice, eggs, and condiments, served hot. Also *transf.* and *fig.*

1662 J. DAVIES tr. *Mandelslo's Trav.* 81 Their ordinary Diet being onely *Kitsery*, which they make of Beans pounded, and Rice, which they boile together... Then they put thereto a little Butter melted. **1698** FRYER *Acc. E. India & P.* 81 Their delightfullest Food being only *Cutchery*, a sort of Pulse and Rice mixed together. *Ibid.* 320 Here is a great Plenty of what they call *Ketchery*. **1727** A. HAMILTON *New Acc. E. Ind.* I. xiv. 161 Some Doll and Rice, being mingled together and boyled, make Kitcheree. **1816** 'QUIZ' *Grand Master* 51 The servant enters with a dish, Containing kedgeree and fish. **1867** BP. FRASER in Hughes *Life* (1887) 143 Kedgeree is a capital thing for breakfast. **1879** MRS. JAMES *Ind. Househ. Managem.* 88 Kegeree is composed of the remains of cold fish, and is usually a breakfast dish. **18..** MRS. BEATON *Househ. Managemt.* 140 Kegeree.

fig. **1909** in WEBSTER. **1928** R. CAMPBELL *Wayzgoose* ii. 48 English, art, music, vegetables, and song, All to the same consistency you mash. Your life—a Kedgeree! Your mind—a hash! **1938** *Archit. Rev.* LXXXIII. 3/1 Winstanley's Eddystone was a remarkable kedgeree of bits and pieces—its builder had previously been known chiefly for some remarkable waterworks in Hyde Park. **1968** R. WEST *Sk. Vietnam* ii. 65 Furniture, clothes, shrines.. were heaped on to the lorry in a gigantic kedgeree.

b. *Comb.*, as **kedgeree-pot**, a large earthenware pipkin, used for holding water and cooking.

a **1826** HEBER *Jrnl.* (1828) I. 123 On the Hoogly very large nets.. are used, with Kedgeree pots for floats. **1830** MOUNTAIN in *Mem.* (1857) vi. 117 A small raft of Kedgeree pots. **1839** THACKERAY *Major G.* i, To boil them in kedgeree pots.

kedging: see KEDGE *v.*

kedgway, obs. form of KAJAWAH.

kedgy, dial. f. CADGY, brisk, sprightly.
1719 RAMSAY *Ep. to Arbuckle* 132 When we're kedgy o'er our claret. **17..** —— *Ep. to Hamilton* ii, Kedgy carles think nae lang, When stoups and trunchers gingle.

kedjavé, kedle, var. KAJAWAH, KIDDLE *sb.*

kedlock ('kɛdlək). *Obs.* exc. *dial.* Forms: (? 1 cedelc), 4 **ketelok**, 6 **kedlok**, 7- **ketlock**, 7-8 **cadlock**, 9 **keblock**, **kellock**, 6- **kedlock**. *β.* 6-8 **chadlock**, 9 **chedlock**. [app. repr. OE. *cedelc* 'herb mercury', of unknown etym.; the difficulties as to form and orig. meaning are the same as in the case of the synonymous CHARLOCK, q.v. Connexion with the synon. G. *kettich*, LG. *köddich*, Da. dial. *kiddik*, has been suggested.]

1. A popular name of Field Mustard (*Sinapis arvensis*) and other yellow-flowered cruciferous plants common as field-weeds; = CHARLOCK.
[*a* **1000** *Ags. Voc.* in Wr.-Wülcker 297/30 *Mercurialis*, cedelc, cyrlic. *c* **1000** *Sax. Leechd.* I. 34 *Herba mercurialis* þæt is cedelc.] **13..** HAMPOLE *Psalter* xxxvi. 2 (MS.S.) Gressis þat grouys bi þaim ane in þe feld, as brisokis, or ketelokes. **1523** FITZHERB. *Husb.* §20 Kedlokes hath a leafe lyke rapes, and beareth a yelowe floure, and is an yll wede. **1620** MARKHAM *Farew. Husb.* (1625) 34 Darnell, ketlocks, docks, rape, and such like herball stuffe. **1794** MARTYN *Flora Rust.* III. 101 It [*Sinapis arvensis*] is known among husbandmen by the names of Charlock, Carlock, Garlock, Chadlock, Cadlock, and Kedlock. **1876** *Whitby Gloss.*, *Runch, Cherlock, Chedlock*, or *Kedlock*. **1890** *Gloucester Gloss.*, *Kedlocks, kellocks, kellock*, or *ketlock*.

2. Identified with KEX.
1694 WESTMACOTT *Script. Herb.* (1695) 86 Hemlock..'tis known to most, being called also Kex, or Kedlock. **1887** *S. Chesh. Gloss.*, *Kedlock* (ky'ed-lŭk), an umbelliferous plant.

kee, s.w. dial. f. *kye*, pl. of COW: cf. KEY *sb.*[4]
1714 GAY *Sheph. Week* II. 21 Cic'ly the Western Lass that tends the Kee, The Rival of the Parson's Maid was She. [*Note:—Kee*, a West-Country Word for Kine or Cows.] *a* **1746** *Exmoor Scolding* (E.D.S.) 202 Whan tha goast to tha melking o' tha Kee.

†**kee**, weakened form of *quo(th*: cf. KA *v.*[2]
1602 *Narcissus* (1893) 575 Ile bee at hand, kee pickpurse.

kee, keeble, obs. ff. KEY *sb.*[1], KIBBLE *sb.*[3]

keebaub: see KEBAB.

keech (kiːtʃ), *sb. Obs.* exc. *dial.* Also **keach**. [Of obscure origin. Some mod. dialects (Wilts, Hants) have a vb. *keech* to congeal, consolidate (as fat). Sense 2 appears to be related to the root of KECHEL; but cf. quot. 1879 in 1.]

1. A lump of congealed fat; the fat of a slaughtered animal rolled up into a lump. Also *dial.* with other allied meanings.
In quot. 1613 referring to Cardinal Wolsey, as the son of a butcher. *Tallow catch* in *1 Hen. IV*, II. iv. 252 is explained by some editors as *tallow keech*.
[**1597** SHAKS. *2 Hen. IV*, II. i. 101 Did not goodwife Keech the Butchers wife come in then?] **1613** —— *Hen. VIII*, I. i. 55, I wonder, That such a Keech can with his very bulke Take vp the Rayes o' th' beneficiall Sun, And keepe it from the Earth. [Cf. STEEVENS *note* (1778).] **1773** JOHNSON in *J. & Steevens' Shaks., Hen. VIII*, II. i, A *keech* is a solid lump or mass. A cake of wax or tallow formed into a mould is called yet in some places a *keech*. **1879** MISS JACKSON *Shropsh. Word-bk.*, *Keech*, a cake of consolidated fat, wax, or tallow. **1886** ELWORTHY *W. Som. Word-bk.*, *Keech*, the fat from the intestines of slaughtered animals; the caul. It is usually rolled up while warm into a solid lump.

2. (See quot. Cf. *N. & Q.* 9th s. VII. 94/2.)
1677 LITTLETON *Lat. Dict.*, *Keech*, a kind of Cake, *collyra, libum*. **1854** MISS BAKER *Northampt. Gloss.*, *Keech*, a large oblong or triangular pasty, made at Christmas of raisins and apples chopped together.

Hence **keech** *v. dial.* (see quots.).
1863 BARNES *Dorset Gloss.*, *Ketch, Keach*, to set hard, as melted fat cooling. **1879** MISS JACKSON *Shropsh. Word-bk.*, *Keech*, to consolidate, as warm fat, wax, etc. does in cooling. **1893** *Wilts. Gloss.* s.v. *Catch. Keach, Keatch*, to grow thick, as melted fat when setting again.

keech, keed, obs. ff. KEACH *v.*, KID *sb.*[1]

keef, keejang: see KEF, KIDANG.

keek (kiːk), *v.* Now only *Sc.* and *north. dial.* Forms: 4 **kike, kyke, keke**, 5 **keky(y)n, kek**, 5-6 *Sc.* **keik**, 7- **keek**. [Not known in OE., but has LG. cognates: MDu. *kîken, kieken* (Du. *kijken*), LG. *kîken* (formerly sometimes used in HG.); Da. *kige*, Sw. and Norw. *kika* (prob. from LG.). MDu. and LG. had also *kicken* (employed by Luther).
It is not clear whether the original ME. form was *kīken* or *kĭken*; the former would agree with the continental forms, but the latter would better explain the variant *kēken*, from which the mod. *keek* has come down. It is noticeable that the vowel of *keek* corresponds with that of other words of similar meaning, as *peek, peep, peer*, Sc. *teet*, and may be due to analogy or feeling of appropriateness.]

1. *intr.* To peep; to look privily, as through a narrow aperture, or round a corner; †to glance, gaze (*obs.*).
c **1386** CHAUCER *Miller's T.* 259 This Nicholas sat capyng euere vp-righte As he had kiked [*v.rr.* kykyd, keked] on the newe moone. *Ibid.* 655 Into the roof they kiken [*so best MSS.*; *also* kyken, keken, kepen, loken], and they cape. *c* **1400** *Beryn* 900 All that he set his eye on, or aftir list to keke Anoon he shuld it have. *c* **1440** *Promp. Parv.* 269/2 Kekyyn, or priuely waytyn (*K., H., S., P.* kekyn), *intuor, observo*. **1572** *Satir. Poems Reform.* xxxii. 47 In hoill and boir we byde..Dar not keik out for Rebellis that dois ryde. *a* **1605** MONTGOMERIE *Flyting w. Polwart* 491 Some..in the crowne of it keeks. *a* **1724** in Ramsay *Tea-t. Misc.* (1733) I. 60 Keek into the draw-well, Janet. **1802** in Anderson *Cumbid. Ball.* 28, I keek by the hay-stack, and lissen, For fain wad I see Sally Gray. **1889** BARRIE *Window Thrums* xvi. 146 Up you'll be, keekin'..through the blind to see if the post's comin'.

b. *fig.* Of things.
c **1470** HENRYSON *Mor. Fab.* viii. (*Preach. Swallow*), Quhen columbine up keikis throw the clay. **1723** RAMSAY *Fair Assembly* xxiv, Where they appear, nae vice dare keek. **1790** A. WILSON *Discons. Wren* Poet. Wks. (1846) 95 The morn was keeking frae the east. **18..** H. S. RIDDELL *Poet. Wks.* (1871) I. 36 (E.D.D.) The nest o' the birds keeking out between The leaves and the roots.

2. In verbal phrases used as sbs., as ***keek-in-the-stoup, keek-round-corners***.
1721 KELLY *Scot. Prov.* 226 Keek in the Stoup was ne'er a good Fellow. **1894** CROCKETT *Raiders* 307, I want nae spies and keek-roon-corners in my hoose!

3. *Comb.* **keek-bo**, peep-bo! bo-peep; **keek-bogle** (*Sc.*), hide-and-seek.
[**1791** J. LEARMONT *Poems* 168 Those who now his favour seek Wad stand afar, An' ne'er play at him bogle keik.] **1835** WEBSTER *Rhymes* 11 (E.D.D.) The sun..seem'd as if playing keekbo wi' the moon.

keek (kiːk), *sb. Sc.* and *north. dial.* [f. KEEK *v.*] A peep; see the verb.
1773 FERGUSSON *Poems* (1785) 215 (E.D.D.) So glowr the saints when first is given A fav'rite keek o' glore and heaven. **1785** BURNS *Halloween* xix, He by his shouther gae a keek. **1824** SCOTT *Redgauntlet* ch. xii, Take a keek into Pate's letter. **1863** in Robson *Bards of Tyne* 231 From it down every Quayside-chare there's such a glorious keek. **1886** STEVENSON *Kidnapped* xviii. 174 Let's take another keek at the red-coats.

b. *Comb.*, as **keek-hole**, a peep-hole; **keek-show**, a peep-show.
1883 *Sunday Mag.* Sept. 574/2 A rich assortment of merry-go-rounds, keek-shows, and jugglers. **1891** R. FORD *Thistledown* 87 (E.D.D.) Keek-holes through which fitful glances are obtained.

keek, variant of KEAK *v. Obs.*, to cackle.

kee-kee, variant of KIE-KIE.

keeker ('kiːkə(r)). *north. dial.* [f. KEEK *v.* + -ER[1].] A peeper, a gazer; in *pl.* the eyes, 'peepers'; *spec.* an overlooker or inspector in a coal-pit, who sees that the coal is sent up in a proper state.
1808-18 JAMIESON, *Keekers*, a cant term for eyes. *Ibid.*, *Starn-keeker*, a star-gazer. **1863** in Robson *Bards of Tyne* 92 Tell wor keeker aw deed..Tell wor owners an viewers aw'l howk ne mair coal. **1893** *Durham Direct.* 90 Bennett, J., keeker.

keeking-glass. *Sc.* and *north. dial.* [See KEEK *v.*] A looking-glass.
a **1724** in Ramsay *Tea-t. Misc.* (1733) I. 60 For the love ye bear to me Buy me a keeking-glass. *a* **1796** BURNS *Impromptu* 3 My face was but the keekin' glass, An' there ye saw your picture. **1820** SCOTT *Monast.* xiv, A breast-plate you might see to dress your hair in, as well as in that keeking-glass. **1882** J. WALKER *Jaunt & other Poems* 12 A bonnie lass That plaits her ringlets at the keeking glass.

keek-keek, *int. Sc.* and *north. dial.* Also 6 *Sc.* **keik, keik**. [f. KEEK *v.*] A call used by children in the game of hide-and-seek.
a **1568** *Jok & Jynny* 13 in Laing *Anc. Poet. Scot.* 358 'Te he', quod Jynny, 'keik, keik, I se ȝow'. **1893** *Northumbla. Gloss.*, *Keek-keek*, the word used by children in playing hide-and-seek.

keel (kiːl), *sb.*[1] Forms: 4-6 **kele**, (4 **kelle**, 5 **keole**, 6 **kyele, kile**), 6-7 **keele**, *Sc.* **keill**, 7- **keel**. [prob. a. ON. *kjǫl-r* (Da. *kjøl*, Sw. *köl*):—**kelu-z*; not connected with Du. and G. *kiel* (KEEL *sb.*[2]). F. *quille*, in a Rouen document of 1382 (Hartz.-Darm.) was prob. also from ON.; Sp. *quilla*, It. *chiglia* may be from French. The sense-development of the English word has been influenced by its use to translate L. *carina* keel, hull, ship.
ON. *kjǫlr* is not parallel, either in sense or form, with the OE. (*scipes*) *celae*, which in the earliest glossaries renders L. *rostrum* beak.]

1. a. The lowest longitudinal timber of a ship or boat, on which the framework of the whole is built up; in boats and small vessels forming a prominent central ridge on the under surface; in iron vessels, a combination of iron plates taking the place and serving the purpose of the keel of a wooden vessel.
1352 [see *keel-rope* in 7 b]. **1387** TREVISA *Higden* (Rolls) II. 233 þe schippe was..þritty cubite high from þe cule [*v.r.* kele] to þe hacches. **1398** —— *Barth. De P.R.* v. xxxii. (MS. Bodl.) lf. 17 b/1 Alle þe bones in þe body beþ ifounded in þe rigge, as a schippe of þe keole. **1496** *Naval Acc. Hen. VII* (1896) 181 For Reparacion..of the Soueraignes grete Bote & Jolywat..for the Kele & Belge of the same. **1551** ROBINSON tr. *More's Utop.* I. (1895) 31 Afterwarde thei founde shyppes wyth rydged kyeles. **1555** EDEN *Decades* 2 The keele or bottome of the biggeste vessell ranne vpon a blynde rocke. **1611** FLORIO, *Dare carena*, to giue the keele, to carene as Mariners say. **1622** MALYNES *Anc. Law Merch.* 152 Then shall he [unfit pilot]..lose his hire,..or else (by the Law of Denmarke) passe thrice vnder the Ships Keele. **1665** *Lond. Gaz.* No. 5/1 A Vessel you have heard so much of with a double Keel. **1725** POPE *Odyss.* II. 468 The crooked keel the parting surge divides. **1804** *Naval Chron.* XI. 212 A boat oversets and lies keel up. **1849** LONGF. *Build. Ship* 136 The keel of oak for a noble ship, Scarfed and bolted, straight and strong. **1869** SIR E. REED *Shipbuild.* ii. 18 The keels of iron ships were originally external, and not unfrequently of wood. **1871** R. ELLIS *Catullus* lxiv. 10 Texture of upright pine with a keel's curved rondure uniting.
fig. **1642** FULLER *Holy & Prof. St.* I. i. 2 Our good wife sets up a sail according to the keel of her husbands estate. **1898** *Lit. World* 20 May 453 The keel of his education was laid at Dummer House, near Basingstoke.

b. With qualifying terms: **bar-keel**, a projecting keel formed by a bar or plate; **box-keel**, a composite iron keel whose section is that of a box; **dish-keel**, a keel formed of iron-plates with dish-shaped section; **drop-keel**, (*a*) a centre-board; (*b*) a projecting keel, as distinguished from a flat plate-keel; **false keel**, (*a*) an additional keel attached to the bottom of the true keel to protect it and increase the stability of the vessel; (*b*) an external keel subsequently added to a vessel; **inner keel**, the kelson of an iron vessel; **outer keel**, the plate-keel in the hull of an iron vessel; **plate-keel**, a keel formed by a line of iron plates, which do not project below the hull; **rank-keel**, a very deep keel; **sliding keel**, a centre-board; **vertical keel** (see quots. 1883 and 1890); etc. See also BILGE-KEEL, *fin-keel* (FIN *sb.*[1] 6).
1627 False keel [see FALSE *a.* 17 b]. **1691** T. H[ALE] *Acc. New Invent.* 49 New Stirrups put to secure the false Keel. **1706** PHILLIPS, *Rank-keel* is a deep Keel, which keeps a Ship well from rolling. **1792** LD. CHATHAM in *Naval Chron.* XIII. 203 His Majesty's armed Vessel built with sliding Keels. **1805** *Ibid.* 201 In the year 1774, that gentle-man [Capt. J. Schank, R.N.] first constructed a Boat with sliding keels. **1825** CLARK, etc. *Shipwrights Scale Prices* 4 To chisel up the under side of the main or false keel. **1874** THEARLE *Naval Archit.* 69 There are three principal forms of keel in vogue, viz:—bar, flat plate, and centre plate or side bar keels. Of these the former is the commonest. **1883** NARES *Constr. Ironclad* 4 The vertical keel..is placed upright on its edge on the outer keel... It is about 3½ feet high, and on it, parallel to the outer keel, is fastened the inner keel. **1890** W. J. GORDON *Foundry* 65 On the blocks is laid the flat keel, which is practically the centre-line of plating; on this is placed the vertical keel, and on this come the keelsons.

c. Phr. † ***in keel***, in the hull. ***on*** (or ***with***) ***even keel***, with the keel level: see EVEN *a.* 1 c.
1568 SEMPILL *Marg. Fleming* 9 in *Satir. Poems Reform.* xlvi, With evin keill befoir the wind Scho is richt fairdy with a saill. **1627** CAPT. SMITH *Seaman's Gram.* xi. 54 Trying her sailing..upon an euen Keele. **1643** PRYNNE *Sov. Power Parl.* App. 209 Those who are in keel [are] as safe as those in the shrouds, if the storme rage. **1867** F. FRANCIS *Angling* ix, A steady draw and an even keel.

2. a. A ship, vessel. (*poetic*, after L. *carīna*.)
a **1547** EARL SURREY *Æneid* II. 229 The God that they by sea had brought In warped keeles. **1697** DRYDEN *Virg. Past.* IV. 47 No Keel shall cut the Waves for foreign Ware. **1870** MORRIS *Earthly Par.* I. I. 16 To buy a new keel with my gold, And fill her with such things as she may hold.

b. A yacht built with a permanent keel instead of a centre-board.
1883 *Harper's Mag.* Aug. 453/1 Many keels are afloat.

3. a. That part of anything which corresponds in position, form, or otherwise to a ship's keel; the bottom or under surface; a keel-like lower part.
1726 LEONI *Alberti's Archit.* II. 10/1 The keel or bottom of any weight, that is to be drawn along, shou'd be even and solid. **1815** *Sporting Mag.* XLVI. 131 Tom knock'd his friend keel upwards on the floor. **1826** J. ADAMSON *Sk. Inform. Rail-Roads* 6 To the part projecting downwards..we may apply the..designation of the keel of the rail.

b. A longitudinal member or assembly of members running the length of a rigid or semi-rigid airship at the bottom of the envelope.
In quot. 1877, and perh. also 1888, *keel* has not acquired this specific sense.
[**1877** *Design & Work* 1 Dec. 602/2, I arrived at this principle [of propelling the air boat]:..that though the car must contain the weight of passengers, cargo, and machinery, even to do duty as the weighted keel or plummet, yet it is only in that character it can serve the navigation in aid of propulsion.] **1888** *Peel City Guardian* 22 Sept. 3/3 Connecting the balloon with the arrow-like rod beneath is a keel of the same material as that composing the body of the balloon. **1893** *Eng. Illustr. Mag.* July 746/2 From the outer gallery the [airship] *Attila* looks as if her bottom was gently curved, terminating in the customary orthodox keel... But three feet below the level at which we stand lies a flat projecting bottom. **1910** A. WILLIAMS *Engin. Wonders of World* III. 48/2 The distribution of the load over the gas holder in such a way as not to strain any part unduly is, in the case of a Zeppelin airship, simplified by the employment of a girder keel. **1929** E. F. SPANNER *About Airships* iii. 28 Throughout the length of the keel there is a more or less uniform lift, varying according to the size of the gasbags. **1955** *Oxford Jun. Encycl.* IV. 20/2 The semi-rigid type, in which a long rigid keel supports the passenger and engine-cars, has been developed mainly by the Italians. *Ibid.*, Keels running through the hull [of a rigid airship] add strength and provide access to various parts of the ship. **1974** J. B. COLLIER *Airship* 12/1 The distinction between these two types [*sc.* non-rigid and semi-rigid airships] is

sometimes hard to draw, but 'semi-rigid' implies..that the airship in question has a rigid keel.

†**c.** In some early aeroplanes and kites, a vertical fin fixed towards the rear of the fuselage and parallel to it, and intended to give lateral stability. *Obs.*

1894 O. CHANUTE *Progress in Flying Machines* 184 Very good results with central keels have been obtained by M. Boynton with his various forms of 'Fin' kites. *Ibid.* 185 Keels have been frequently proposed for aeroplanes, in which they will produce less resistance to forward motion than obtains with other arrangements. **1907** C. DIENSTBACH in *Navigating the Air* (Aero Club Amer.) p. xxxix, A multiplicity of 'keels', which might be called 'barbarian' if compared to American moderation. **1910** R. W. A. BREWER *Art of Aviation* xvii. 230 The Antoinette machine has a smaller keel, but some of the monoplanes dispense with this surface altogether. **1911** G. C. LOENING *Monoplanes & Biplanes* xii. 255 In the old Voisin type use was made of several vertical keels, partitions, placed not only at the rear, but also between the main surfaces themselves. **1919** H. SHAW *Text-bk. Aeronaut.* vii. 97 The dihedral planes give rise to a greater righting moment, when tilted at a similar angle, than the keel, and so are more efficient.

d. A longitudinal member running along the centre of the bottom of the hull of a flying boat (or the float of a seaplane), or the fuselage of a landplane from one end to the other.

1920 *Flight* 23 Sept. 1019/2 The hull lines are somewhat unusual, the downward sweep of keel and chines in front of the rear step being rather more pronounced than usual. **1930** P. H. SUMNER *Marine Aircraft* vi. 164 The type of keel used in the flexible circular flying boat hull is that which is built up as a light girder, comprising a keel proper, keelson and rider piece. The keel proper..is rabbeted on its upper face and receives the vertical keelson. **1933** W. MUNRO *Marine Aircraft Design* iv. 58 The detail design of frames, bulkheads, stringers, keel, etc., is very definitely affected by the heat treatment and anodic treatment of the material. **1968** *Flight International* 12 Dec. 983/1 Because of the four-leg main under-carriage [of the Boeing 747]..a centre-line keel links the lower part of the forward and rear fuselage. **1969** *Jane's 100 Significant Aircraft* 81/1 Four-engined commercial flying-boat... Structure composed of deep keel, widely spaced transverse frames and heavy stringers.

4. A central ridge along the back or convex surface of any organ or structure, as a leaf, a petal, a glume of grass, the lower mandible of a bird, etc. In dogs, the sternum or breast-bone, esp. in the dachshund and other breeds in which it is a prominent feature.

1597 GERARDE *Herbal* I. lxxxvi. 138 The blades of the Leeke be long..hauing a keele or crest in the backside. **1807** VANCOUVER *Agric. Devon* (1813) 327 The full-sized North Devon cow,..open bosom, with a deep chest or keel preceding and between its legs. **1851–6** WOODWARD *Mollusca* 45 The discoidal ammonites sometimes..have the keel on one side, instead of in the middle. **1852** DANA *Crust.* I. 595 The beak is rather short..with a keel above. **1870** HOOKER *Stud. Flora* 214 Leaves with the keel usually setose. **1950** C. L. B. HUBBARD *Dachshund Handbk.* iv. 50 Chest oval, well let down between the forelegs, with the deepest point of the keel level with the wrist joints. **1962** R. H. SMYTHE *Anat. Dog Breeding* i. 19 Dachshunds possess an over-lengthy body and an over-developed sternum, the 'keel'. **1971** F. HAMILTON *World Encycl. Dogs* 344 The Standards [for dachshunds] require that the height at the shoulder should be half the length of the body..the lowest point of the keel being on a level with the wrist joint.

5. *spec.* in *Bot.* and *Zool.*

a. The two lowest petals of a papilionaceous corolla, more or less united and shaped like the prow of a boat; the carina; also any analogous structure in other orders, as the lower petal in *Polygala*, etc. **b.** A prominent ridge along the breastbone of birds of the class *Carinatæ*, at first cartilaginous but afterwards becoming ossified. †**c.** A name for the notochord which appears in an egg during incubation (*obs.*).

1674 N. FAIRFAX *Bulk & Selv.* 35 The shaplings or tiny keoles of the great Malpighiuses eggs. **1766** PARSONS in *Phil. Trans.* LVI. 208 The crane is the next..which has such a turning of the aspera arteria in the keel of the sternum. **1770–4** A. HUNTER *Georg. Ess.* (1803) III. 116 The medullary substance, with what Malpighi calls the keel (*carina*) and the nervous system, are latent in the egg. **1776** J. LEE *Introd. Bot.* Explan. Terms 396 *Carina*, the Keel, the lower Petal often in Form of a Boat. **1845** LINDLEY *Sch. Bot.* iv. (1858) 39 (*Polygala*) Petals hypogynous, 3; of which one is anterior and larger than the rest (the *keel*). **1870** ROLLESTON *Anim. Life.* Introd. 55 Birds are divided into two orders, the *Ratitæ*, in which the sternum has no crest..and the *Carinatæ*, in which the sternum has a crest or keel.

6. a. *Arch.* A ridge or edge on a rounded moulding.

1879 SIR G. SCOTT *Lect. Archit.* I. 248 The heaviness of large roll mouldings was often relieved by..raised edges or 'keels'. **1886** WILLIS & CLARK *Cambridge* II. 133 The large rounds have both narrow fillets or wings, and sharp edges or keels, worked on them.

b. [Norw. *kjøl.*] The spinal ridge of mountains stretching down the centre of Norway.

1856 LD. DUFFERIN *Lett. High Latitudes* (1857) xii. 381 The back-bone, or *keel*, as the sea-faring population soon learnt to call the flat snow-capped ridge that runs down the centre of Norway. **1968** G. JONES *Hist. Vikings* II. i. 59 The upturned keel of mountains running south from Finnmark almost to Stavanger and Värmland. *Ibid.* 69 The mountain wildernesses of the Keel.

7. *Comb.* **a.** General, as ***keel-rib, -timber; keel-billed, -compelling, -shaped, -spanning*** adjs.

1669 STURMY *Mariner's Mag.* v. 43 Having the Proportion of any one Ship..with the length of her Keel-Timbers. **1787** *Fam. Plants* I. 33 Per[ianth]..the valvelets keel-compressed. **1812** BYRON *Ch. Har.* II. xx, Blow, swiftly blow, thou keel-compelling gale. **1851–6** WOODWARD *Mollusca* 241 Their keel-shaped foot is adapted for ploughing through sand or mud. **1854** GOULD *Toucans* 2, *Ramphastos carinatus*, Keel-billed Toucan. **1871** MORRIS in Mackail *Life* (1899) I. 245 The boats are built high stem and stern, with the keel-rib running up into an ornament at each end.

b. Special combs.: **keel-band**, a strip of iron fastened along the keel of a boat; **keel-bill, keel-bird**, a West Indian bird, *Crotophaga minor*, of the cuckoo family; **keel-block**, one of the short pieces of timber on which the keel of a vessel rests in building or a dry dock (Hamersly *Naval Encycl.* 1881); †**keel-drawing** = KEELHAULING; **keel-line**, (*a*) the line of timber forming the keel; (*b*) a small rope used in lacing a bonnet or additional sail to the foot of another sail; **keel-moulding**, a roll-moulding having a keel (sense 6) worked on it, frequent in mediæval architecture; **keel-petal**: see 5 a; **keel-piece**, one of the timbers or sections composing the keel (Hamersly *Nav. Encycl.*); **keel-plate**, one of the iron plates forming the keel in iron vessels; **keel-raking** = KEELHAULING; **keel-riveter**, a machine for riveting the keels of iron vessels on the stock; †**keel-rope**, 'a coarse rope formerly used for clearing the limber holes' by drawing it backwards and forwards (Smyth *Sailor's Word-bk.*); **keel-staple**, a staple used in fastening the false keel to the main keel (*ibid*). Also KEEL-BOAT, KEELHAUL *v.*

1857 P. COLQUHOUN *Comp. Oarsman's Guide* 28 The *keel-band, a thin strong piece of iron coming up over the nose, and up to the transom. **1811** G. SHAW *Gen. Zool.* VIII. 382 The *Keel-Bill is a bird of a tame and gentle nature. **1700** S. L. tr. *Fryke's Voy. E. Ind.* 10 This Punishment is call'd *Keel-halen*, which may be call'd in English *Keel-drawing. **1829** *Sporting Mag.* XXIV. 125 Prior to the *keel-line being placed on the stocks. **1851** KIPPING *Sailmaking* (ed. 2) 37 Bonnets have a head tabling, 2½ inches broad, on which a line of 12-thread, named Keel-line, for forming the latchings, is sewed in bights. **1876** DARWIN *Cross-Fertil.* 155 They did not depress the *keel-petals so as to expose the anthers and stigma. **1874** THEARLE *Naval Archit.* 75 A vertical *keel plate, extending from the inner surface of the flat keel plates to the inner bottom plates. **1706** PHILLIPS s.v. *Ducking*, If the Offence be great, he is also drawn under the Ships-Keel; which is termed *Keel-raking. **1352** *Exch. Acc. Q.R.* Bundle 20 No. 27 (P.R.O.) Et de iis. solutis pro quadam corda de crine, vocata *Kellerope posit um (*sic*) in fundo navis ad faciendum per navem bonum exitum aque. **1626** CAPT. SMITH *Accid. Yng. Seamen* 14. **1627** —— *Seaman's Gram.* vi. 28 The Keele rope..is of haire in the Keele to scower the Limber holes.

keel (kiːl), *sb.*[2] Forms: 5 kele, 5–7 keil(l, (6 keile, keyle), 6–7 keele, (8 kiell), 7– keel. [app. a. MDu. *kiel* (= MLG. *kêl, kîl*, MHG. *kiel*), ship, boat, repr. a Com. Teut. word (**keuloz*) which appears (chiefly in poetry) as OE. *céol*, OS. *kiol*, OHG. *chiol, cheol, chiel*, ON. *kjóll*. These forms cannot be connected with ON. *kjǫl-r* keel (see KEEL *sb.*[1]); but under the influence of Scandinavian, English, or French, or of all combined, the Du. and G. *kiel* has since the 16th c. lost its original sense of 'ship' and acquired that of 'keel' (KEEL *sb.*[1]): see Grimm, Kluge.

OE. *céol* would have given **cheel* in modern Eng.]

1. A flat-bottomed vessel, esp. of the kind used on the Tyne and Wear for the loading of colliers; a lighter.

The name is or has been in local use in the east of England from the Tyne to the Norfolk Broads; it has also been used in U.S. locally both for a river and a coasting vessel. The old keel which brought coal from the upper Tyne to ships in the harbour at Tynemouth was carvel-built and had a square sail, as well as a heavy oar worked by three keel-bullies. The existing keel is clinker-built and used only for riverside traffic. See R. Oliver Heslop in *N. & Q.* 9th Ser. VII. 65–6.

1322 [implied in KEELER[1]]. **1421** *Act 9 Hen. V*, c. 10 Certeinz vesselx appellez Keles, par les queux tielx charbons sont caries de la terre jesques a les naefs en le dit port. **1531–2** *Act 23 Hen. VIII*, c. 18 Many shippes, keiles, cogges, and botes..haue heretofore had their franke passages..vpon the saide riuer. **1546** LANGLEY *Pol. Verg. de Invent.* III. xi. 78 Pheniciens [invented] the Keele or demye barke. **1600** HOLLAND *Livy* XXI. lvii. 426 Convoy of victuals ..which came by the Po, in Keeles and such like vessels. **1669** *Lond. Gaz.* No. 342/4 Two Wisbidge Keels were forced upon the shoar in this Bay. **1708** J. C. *Compl. Collier* (1845) 48 Those Persons who live at the Ports and have Keels (which are much like to Lighters Built) to load the Ships. **1808** PIKE *Sources Mississ.* III. App. 31 It..is 300 yards wide and navigable for large keels. **1833** HT. MARTINEAU *Tale Tyne* ii. 41 A waggon was at the moment being emptied into a keel. **1863** in *Tyneside Songs* 16 Weel may the keel row, that my laddie's in. **1869** FREEMAN *Norm. Conq.* III. xiv. 362 [The Wharfe] still navigable as high as Tadcaster for the small craft of the river, whose local name of keels suggests the memory of the first vessels which landed our fathers in the Isle of Britain. **1876** in Ruskin *Fors Clav.* VI. 395 Humber Keels are..house and home to the Keel family. **1883** G. C. DAVIES *Norfolk Broads* iv. (1884) 32 There was another class of vessels called 'Keels', which were fitted with huge square lug-sails, and were chiefly used for carrying timber. These are now unknown.

b. The quantity of coals carried in a keel, now = 8 Newcastle chaldrons or 21 tons 4 cwt.

The statute of 1421 shows that a keel was then supposed to carry 20 chalders, but the weight of the chalder is not given (cf. quot. 1529 below).

[**1421** *Act 9 Hen. V*, c. 10 Tieles Keles del portage..de xx chaldrez. **1529** W. FRANKELEYN in Fiddes *Wolsey* (1726) II. 165 A great substance of colis to the nombre of 25 score kele, every kele contayning 20. chald'.] **1750** CLEPHONE *Jrnl.* in C. Innes *Sk. Early Sc. Hist.* App. (1861) 550 A Kiell is 8 chalder. **1763** SIR S. JANSSEN *Smuggling* 112 An ordinary Ship-Load [of coals] is about fifteen Keel, every Keel is about eight Newcastle Chaldron, and each of those Chaldrons are seventy two Bushels. **1815** *Chron.* in *Ann. Reg.* 82 Scale for manning the ships..ships of six keels, four men two boys. **1851** KIPPING *Sail-making* (ed. 2) 92 *note*, A collier is said to carry so many 'keels of coals'.

2. Used to render OE. *céol* in the passage of the O.E. Chron. relating to the first coming of the Angles to Britain. (Cf. CHIULE, CYULE.)

In this use often erroneously identified with KEEL *sb.*[1], on the analogy of L. *carina* keel and ship.

[*c* **525** GILDAS *De Excidio Brit.* xxiii, Tribus, ut lingua ejus [gentis] exprimitur, cyulis, nostra lingual ongis navibus. *a* **1000** *O.E. Chron.* an. 449 (Laud MS.) Hi þa coman on þrim ceolum hider to Brytene.] **1605** VERSTEGAN *Dec. Intell.* xv, Hingistus and Horsus..had the conduction of these forces over into Brittains in three great and long shippes, then called keeles. **1685** STILLINGFL. *Orig. Brit.* v. 313 The Angles or Saxons..came hither in three Keels or long Boats at first. **1881** GREEN *Making Eng.* i. 28 In three 'keels'.. these Jutes landed at Ebbsfleet in the Isle of Thanet.

3. *Comb.*, as ***keel-holder, -owner***; **keel-deeter** (**-dighter**), *dial.* (see quot. 1789 and DIGHT *v.* 14 f). See also KEEL-BOAT, -BULLY, -MAN[1].

1789 BRAND *Hist. Newcastle* II. 262 *note*, The wives and daughters..who sweep the keels, and have the sweepings for their pains, are called Keeldeeters. **1891** *Pall Mall G.* 14 Feb. 4/2 A small keelholder in Hull. *Ibid.* 1 June 1/3 The son of a small keelowner.

keel (kiːl), *sb.*[3] Chiefly *Sc.* Also 5 keyle, 6 keyll, keil, 9 keal. [Of uncertain origin. Gael. and Ir. *cìl* may be from Sc.]

1. A variety of red ochreous iron-ore used for marking sheep, stone, timber, etc.; ruddle. Also, the red mark made with this on sheep, etc.

1480 *Acta Dom. Conc.* (1839) 57/2 To prufe þat þe gudis ..war one þe lard of fernyis avne landis, & had his keyle & his mark. **1513** DOUGLAS *Æneis* x. vii. 82 At this time has Pallas..Markyt ȝou swa..That by hys keyll ȝe may be knaw fra thens. **1596** *Compt Buik D. Wedderburn* (S.H.S.) 46 Twa furris hard Keill. **1728** RAMSAY *Betty & Kate* iii, With a piece cawk and keel..He can the picture draw Of you or me. **1789** BURNS *Captain Grose's Peregrin.* ii, He has an unco sleight O' cauk and keel. **1817** *Blackw. Mag.* II. 85/1 The ewes were..half covered with a new keel, with which Millar had himself marked them. **1882** J. HARDY in *Proc. Berw. Nat. Club* IX. No. 3. 430 A band of 'keel' or ruddle occurs in a quarry. **1894** CROCKETT *Raiders* 382, I took..to the trade of selling..red keel for the sheep.

2. *Weaving.* A mark made (with keel or other substance) by the warper at each end of a warp of yarn before it is delivered to the weaver, to ensure his weaving and returning the full length of the yarn given out to him.

a **1813** A. WILSON *Poems, Hollander*, Anither's been upo' the push, To get his keel in claith. **1866** T. BRUCE *Summer Queen* 323 The pattern weel might stan' the light Fair woven to the keel. *a* **1885** W. SIM in *Poets Clackmannan.* 139 Tramp your treadles tell ye see Your hinmost keel and thrum in.

†**keel**, *sb.*[4] *Obs. rare.* [? a. LG. *keele, keelle, kelle* = G. *kelle* (OHG. *chella*), ladle, vessel, tub: in quots. 1617 and 1730–6 app. erron. associated with KEEL *v.*[1], KEELER[2].] A tub or vat for holding liquor.

1485 *Naval Acc. Hen. VII* (1896) 72 Keeles..iij, Spittes of Iren..j, Gridirnes..ij. **1617** MINSHEU *Ductor* 259/1 Keele, a vessell to coole wort or new brewed Ale and Beere. **1648** HEXHAM, A Keel for wine or beer, *een vat ofte kuype* [etc.]. **1730–6** BAILEY (fol.), *Keel*, a vessel for liquors to stand and cool in.

keel (kiːl), *v.*[1] *Obs.* exc. *dial.* Forms: 1 cǿlan, célan, 2–4 kelen, 4 keelen, 4–6 kele, 5 keyle, keille, 6 kiele, keale, 5–7 keele, 6– keel. [Com. Teut.: OE. *cǿlan, célan* = Du. *koelen*, LG. *kölen*, OHG. *chuolen, kualen* (MHG. *küelen*, G. *kühlen*), ON. *kǿla* (Da. *køle*, Sw. *kyla*):—**kōljan* f. **kōl-*: see COOL *a.* and *v.*, and cf. AKELE.]

1. *trans.* To cool; to cause to lose heat; to refresh by cooling.

c **825** *Vesp. Psalter* xxxviii. [xxxix.] 14 Ðæt ic sie ȝecoeled [L. *ut refrigerer*]. *a* **900** *O.E. Martyrol.* 18 Mar. 40 Se uplica sæ..celeð þæra tungla hæto. *a* **1300** *Cursor M.* 12541 He.. hent his hand and bleu þar-in Keland he made al hale his hand. **1382** WYCLIF *Luke* xvi. 24 Send Lazarus, that he dippe the laste part of his fyngur in watir, and kele my tunge. *c* **1470** HARDING *Chron.* XCIV. ii, In water [he] was cast, his fleshe to keele and lisse. **1502** ARNOLDE *Chron.* (1811) 168 And the North Weeste wynde haue kynde to kiele and drye too mych trees that be newe sett. **1581** J. BELL *Haddon's Answ. Osor.* 483 b, You..may keepe your breath to keale your potage. **1828** *Craven Dial.*, *Keel*, to cool. **1883** *Almondb. & Huddersf. Gloss.* s.v., A person may keel himself, or let his tea keel.

b. *spec.* To cool (a hot or boiling liquid) by stirring, skimming, or pouring in something cold, in order to prevent it from boiling over; hence freq. in phr. *to keel the pot.* Also *fig.*

1393 LANGL. *P. Pl.* C. XXII. 280 And lerede men a ladel bygge with a long stele, That cast for to kele [B.-*text* XIX. 275 kepe] a crokke and saue þe fatte aboue. *c* **1420** *Liber Cocorum* 11 Whenne hit welles up, thou schalt hit kele With a litel ale. **1536** *Remedy Sedition* 21 a. **1588** SHAKS. *L.L.L.* v. ii. 930 While greasie Ione doth keele the pot. **1602** MARSTON *Ant.*

& *Mel.* v. Wks. 1856 I. 56 Boy, keele your mouth, it runnes over. **1607** —— *What you will* in *Anc. Drama* II. 199 Faith Doricus, thy brain boils, keel it, keel it, or all the fat's in the fire. **1781** HUTTON *Tour Caves* (ed. 2) Gloss. (E.D.S.), *Keel*, to keep the pot from boiling over. **1846** BROCKETT *N.C. Gloss.* (ed. 3) I. 243 There is a local game called 'Keeling the pot', in which a girl says, 'Mother, the pot's boiling over'; and the answer is, 'Get a ladle and keel it'.

†**2.** *fig.* To make less violent, eager, or ardent; to assuage, mitigate, lessen. *Obs.*

c **1175** *Lamb. Hom.* 141 þa twelf kunreden sculden þer mide heore þurst kelen. *c* **1230** *Hali Meid.* 25 To kele þi lust wiþ fulþe of þi licome. *c* **1375** *Sc. Leg. Saints* xxi. (*Clement*) 102 þai cuth nocht keyle hyre care. *c* **1400** *Destr. Troy* 11464 His corage was kelit with age. **1508** FISHER *7 Penit. Ps.* cii. Wks. (1876) 158 To slake and kele the hete of vnlawfull desyre. **1641** MILTON *Reform.* II. Wks. (1851) 44 Likely to lessen and keel the affections of the Subject.

†**b.** With personal object and const. *of, from.*

c **1420** *Anturs of Arth.* iv, Thay..Cumfordun hor kenettes, to kele hom of care. *c* **1450** *Merlin* 214 The kynge yet was not keled of the love of the stiwardes wif. *c* **1460** *Towneley Myst.* iii. 118, I thee command, from cares the to keyle.

3. *intr.* To become cool or cold.

c **1420** *Liber Cocorum* 19 Take a pownde of ryse, and sethe hom wele, Tyl that thay brostene; and let hom kele. **1450–80** tr. *Secreta Secret.* 26 If thou ete and haue noon appetite, þe hete of thi stomak shalle kele. *c* **1485** *E.E. Misc.* (Warton Club) 78 Than let hit kele to hit be lewke-warme. **1502** ARNOLDE *Chron.* (1811) 188 Set it ouer the fire..and then let it keele awhile. **1883** [see sense 1].

4. *fig.* To grow cold, in feeling, etc.; to become less violent, fervid, or ardent, to 'cool down'; to diminish in intensity. Const. *of, from.*

c **1325** *Metr. Hom.* 32 Mi soru sal son kele. *Ibid.* 67 O pryde comes all his unsell, That neuer may slake ne kell. *a* **1340** HAMPOLE *Psalter* xli. 13 He gars sa many kele fra godis luf. ? *c* **1460** *How a Marchande dyd hys Wyfe betray* 265 in Hazl. *E.P.P.* (1864) I. 208 The marchandys care be gan to kele. **1504** C'TESS RICHMOND tr. *De Imitatione* IV. (E.E.T.S.) 265 Vnto me..that so often synnes, and so soon keles. **1818** TODD s.v., 'He keals', that is, he is cowardly; his courage cools. *Lanc.* **1891** *Sheffield Gloss.* Suppl. s.v., 'The door never keels of beggars'.

keel (kiːl), *v.*[2] [f. KEEL *sb.*[1]]

1. *trans.* To plough (the sea) with a keel. (*nonce-use.*)

1808 J. BARLOW *Columb.* IX. 534 The Lombards keel their Adriatic main.

2. *intr.* Of a ship: To roll on her keel.

1867 SMYTH *Sailor's Word-bk.* s.v. *Keeling.*

3. *trans.* To turn up the keel of, show the bottom of. ***to keel over***, to turn over, 'turn wrong side uppermost', turn (a man or beast) upon his back; to upset, capsize. (*lit.* and *fig.*) orig. *U.S.*

1828 WEBSTER, *Keel*, to turn up the keel; to show the bottom. **1856** MRS. STOWE *Dred* I. 116 (Bartlett) When we get keeled up, that will be the last of us. **1876** BESANT & RICE *Gold. Butterfly* (1877) 148 He was keeled back..on a strong chair, with his feet on the front of the table. **1894** STOCKTON in Mrs. Clifford *Grey Romance*, etc. 175 We now all set to work to keel over the yacht. **1897** R. KIPLING *Captains Courageous* i. 6 It would take more than this to keel me over.

b. *intr.* To turn or be turned over; to be upset; to fall over or be felled as if by a shock. orig. *U.S.*

a **1860** *N.Y. Despatch* (Bartlett), Keel over they must, and a gradual careen would be much better than a sudden capsize. **1895** CROCKETT *Men of Moss-Hags* xli. 296 They keeled ower on their backs. **1897** OLIVE SCHREINER *Trooper Pet. Halkett* II. 209 The third man keeled round on to his stomach again.

†**keel**, *v.*[3] *Obs. rare.* [f. KEEL *sb.*[2]] *trans.* To convey in a keel. Hence '**keeling** *vbl. sb.*

1591 R. HITCHCOCK in *Garrard's Art Warre* 355 Where they sende it downe in keeles, to giue for keeling of a quarter iiij. d. **1599** NASHE *Lenten Stuffe* (1871) 27 Their goods and merchandise, from beyond seas, are keeled up..to their very thresholds [in Norwich].

keel (kiːl), *v.*[4] *Sc.* [f. KEEL *sb.*[3]] *trans.* To mark with ruddle. Hence '**keeling** *vbl. sb.*

1508 KENNEDIE *Flyting w. Dunbar* 431 Thow has thy clamschellis, and thy burdoun kelde [*Bann. MS.* keild]. **1562** WINȜET *Cert. Tractates* Wks. 1888 I. 33 Be war to moue ..seditioun in this nobyll town be ȝoure calking and keling. *c* **1817** HOGG *Tales & Sk.* I. 142 Sheep..all..smeared and keeled. **1886** C. SCOTT *Sheep Farming* 151 The sale ewe lambs in hill flocks are also keeled on the neck to distinguish them from the wether lambs.

keel, obs. variant of KILN.

keelage ('kiːlɪdʒ). *rare.* [f. KEEL *sb.*[1] + -AGE; in med.L. *killagium.*] A toll or due payable by a ship on entering or anchoring in a harbour.

[**1409** in Rymer *Fœdera* VIII. 573 Capit ibi Killagium, scilicet de qualibet Navi cum Batello applicante ibi, Octo Denarios [etc.].] **1679** BLOUNT *Anc. Tenures* 146 Keelage, whereby he had by custom what is here expressed for the Keel of every ship, that came into his sea-port with a boat. **1685** *Termes de la Ley*, *Keelage*..is a Custom paid at Hartlepool in Durham, for every Ship coming into that Port. **1825** BROCKETT, *Keelage*, keel dues in port.

keelavine, variant of KEELIVINE.

keel-boat ('kiːlbəʊt). [f. KEEL *sb.*[1] and [2].]

†**a.** ? A small keel: cf. KEEL *sb.*[2] *Obs.* **b.** A large flat boat used on American rivers. *U.S.* **c.** A yacht having a keel instead of a centre-board.

a. 1695 *Lond. Gaz.* No. 2073/1 An Act for the better Admeasurement of Keels and Keel-Boats, in the Port of New-Castle. **1746** *Act 19 Geo. II*, c. 22 Any Ship, Pink, Crayer, Lighter, Keil-boat, or other Vessel whatsoever.

b. 1786 in *Mag. Amer. Hist.* (1877) I. 176 Great numbers of Kentucke and keel boats passing every day; some to the Falls, others to Post Vincent—Illinois Country. **1822** J. FLINT *Lett. Amer.* 85 Keel boats are large shallow vessels, varying from thirty to seventy tons burden. They are built on a keel with ribs, and covered with plank, as ships are. **1837** W. IRVING *Capt. Bonneville* III. 119 Captain Sublette was ascending the Yellowstone with a keel boat, laden with supplies. **1874** E. EGGLESTON *Circuit Rider* xxvii. 266 A stranger..reported that he had seen such a man on a keel-boat. **1949** *Indiana Mag. of Hist.* June 147 The first keelboat on the St. Joseph River, the 'Fair Play', arrived at South Bend July 1, 1832.

c. 1893 *Westm. Gaz.* 17 Oct. 5/3 On the other side of the Atlantic the most famous contemporary yachts have also been keel-boats. *Ibid.*, It has been a matter of general opinion that, other things being equal, a keel boat can run a centreboard.

Hence **keel-boater, -boatman.**

1839 *Knickerbocker* XIII. 344 A..keel-boatman..saw a steam-boat gallantly paddling up against the centre current of that 'Father of Rivers'. **1883** 'MARK TWAIN' *Life on Mississippi* iii. 41 The keelboatman became a deck hand, or a mate. **1912** I. S. COBB *Back Home* 296 [He was] the roughest of them all..rougher even than the keel-boaters and the trappers. **1941** F. L. DORSEY *Master of Mississippi* 129 Keelboatmen and 'broadhorn' pushers eyed it with suspicion. **1949** B. A. BOTKIN *Treas. S. Folklore* II. ii. 191 Besides madmen and devils the Mississippi River also bred giants—the keelboatmen whose acknowledged king was Mike Fink.

keel-bully. [f. KEEL *sb.*[2] + BULLY *sb.*[1] 2.] One of the crew of a keel; a Tyneside lighterman.

a **1700** B. E. *Dict. Cant. Crew, Keel-bullies*, Lightermen that carry Coals to and from the Ships, so called in Derision. **1789** BRAND *Hist. Newcastle* II. 261 *note.* **1860** [see BULLY *sb.*[1] 2]. **1863** in Robson *Bards Tyne* 73 The keelbullies a', Byeth greet an' sma'.

keele, obs. variant of KILN *sb.*

keeled (kiːld), *a.* [f. KEEL *sb.*[1] + -ED[2].]

a. Of a boat: Having a keel; furnished with a keel.

1847 MEDWIN *Shelley* I. 239 The boat was..keeled and clinker-built. **1853** SIR H. DOUGLAS *Milit. Bridges* 100 As is often the case with keeled boats, the sides and timbers are slight.

b. Having a central dorsal ridge; carinate.

1787 *Fam. Plants* I. 99 Perianth five-parted..the divisions, awl'd, keel'd. *Ibid.* 375 Seeds..keel'd, annexed to the gaping suture. **1828** STARK *Elem. Nat. Hist.* II. 85 Shell oblong,..flattish on the posterior, and somewhat angulated and keeled on the anterior side. **1848** R. TYAS *Favourite Field Flowers* I. 3 Two strap-shaped, keeled, and blunt leaves. **1865** *Reader* 29 Apr. 486/2 The keeled sternum, the grand feature of the skeleton of birds, is very fully developed. **1879** SIR G. SCOTT *Lect. Archit.* II. xiii. 148 Their edges often filleted, or 'keeled', that is, decorated by an arris or edge projecting from their round surface.

c. keeled scale, in certain reptiles, a scale with a central ridge.

1870 A. R. WALLACE *Contrib. Theory Nat. Selection* iii. 99 The large caterpillar..startled him by its resemblance to a small snake... It resembled a poisonous viper, not a harmless species of snake, as was proved by the imitation of keeled scales on the crown produced by the recumbent feet, as the caterpillar threw itself backward! **1907** R. L. DITMARS *Reptile Bk.* xviii. 160 With most of the species [of plated lizard], the scales of the middle portion of the back are strongly keeled. **1970** *New Yorker* 19 Sept. 30/3 It [*sc.* DeKay's snake, *Storeria dekayi*] has keeled scales—a keeled scale is one with a ridge down its middle—which give it a smooth, unshiny appearance.

d. keeled scraper (F. *grattoir caréné*) *Archæol.*, a form of prehistoric flint-tool.

1911 W. J. SOLLAS *Anc. Hunters* viii. 218 Carefully flaked like the snout of the keeled scraper. **1921** M. C. BURKITT *Prehistory* iv. 75 *Keeled scrapers.* This tool..is very common in Middle Aurignacian times. It has a flat under surface, from which the flakes on the upper surface are struck off in a fan-shaped manner. **1927** PEAKE & FLEURE *Hunters & Artists* iv. 46 Here [*sc.* at La Ferrassie etc.] we find keeled scrapers, of a massive form but carelessly made, and more rarely gravers trimmed obliquely. **1968** *Encycl. Brit.* IX. 448/1 Core scrapers were made on small blocks or were actual cores reutilized as scrapers. Keeled scrapers present a systematic and symmetric removal of tiny blades to form a thick, fluted scraper extremity.

keeledar, keeleg, var. KILLADAR, KILLICK.

keeler[1] ('kiːlə(r)). *rare.* Also 4 **keler.** [f. KEEL *sb.*[2] + -ER[1].] †**a.** A keelman. **b.** (See quot. 1875).

1322 *Tynemouth Chartulary* (MS.) lf. 68 [cf Gibson *Monast. Tynemouth* I. 139] Et omnes..seruientes in bargiâ qui dicuntur kelers..venient quolibet anno ad Natale domini in festo sanctorum Innocentium apud Whiteley. **1875** *Ure's Dict. Arts, Keeler*, a manager of coal-barges and colliers in the Durham and Northumberland districts.

keeler[2]. *Obs.* exc. *dial.* Forms: 5 **kelare, kyler,** 6 **kieler, kealer, -or,** 7 **keellar,** 7– **keeler,** (8–9 **killer**). [f. KEEL *v.*[1] + -ER[1].]

1. A vessel for cooling liquids; a shallow tub used for household purposes.

c **1440** *Promp. Parv.* 269/2 Kelare, vesselle, *frigidarium.* **1465** in *Paston Lett.* III. 435, vj kylers, ij clensyng sates. **1567** *Richmond Wills* (Surtees) 211 In the brewhouse, iiij leades for kealors. **1601** HOLLAND *Pliny* II. 510 They vsed to seeth the same..and poure it into certaine troughs or broad keelers of wood. **1758** FRANKLIN *Lett.*, etc. Wks. 1840 VI. 536 A shallow tray, or keeler, should be under the frame to receive any water that might drip from the wetted cloths. **1825** *Ann. Reg.* 72 A milk-tub, which they call a keeler. **1854** *Househ. Words* 2 Sept. 54/2 They are pressed into keelers—tubs made of substantial oak, lessening in size to suit the lessening bulk of the cheese as it dries. **1895** *Montgomery Ward Catal.* 578/3 Indurated Wood Fibre Ware... Keelers ..Diam. 20 in. *a* **1901** *Mod. dial.* (*Kent*), Put the water in that keeler and set it outside, it will soon cool then. **1909** E. I. DENNY *Blazing the Way* III. i. 393 A distracted grey-haired lum-e-i, his mother, came to our house to beg for a keeler of water.

2. A shallow wooden box used in dressing mackerel (*Cent. Dict.* 1890).

3. *Comb.*, as ***keeler-tub.***

1866 LOWELL *Biglow Papers* Introd., *Keeler-tub*, one in which dishes are washed.

keeles, keel-fat, var. KAYLES, KEEL-VAT.

'**keelful.** [f. KEEL *sb.*[2] + -FUL.] As much as a keel will hold.

1478–9 *Acc. Rolls Durham* (Surtees) 647, 2 keylfulis lapidum.

keelhaul ('kiːlhɔːl), *v.* Also 7–9 **-hale,** 8–9 **-hawl.** [ad. Du. *kielhalen* (with the elements englished as *keel, haul*); cf. also G. *kielholen*, Da. *kjølhale*, Sw. *kölhala*, app. all from Du.

Du. *kielhalen* occurs in an ordinance of 1629; the punishment itself is mentioned, in an ordinance of 1560, as *onder den kiele deurstricken*; abolished in Holland in 1853.]

trans. To haul (a person) under the keel of a ship, either by lowering him on one side and hauling him across to the other side, or, in the case of smaller vessels, lowering him at the bows and drawing him along under the keel to the stern.

[**1626** CAPT. SMITH *Accid. Yng. Seamen* 4 To punish offenders..as ducking at Yards arme, hawling vnder the Keele.] **1666** *Lond. Gaz.* No. 112/3 He..caused Blake to be loaded with Chains..and..ordered him to be three times Keel-haled (as they [the Dutch] call it). **1751** SMOLLETT *Per. Pic.* (1779) I. xxv. 231 He ought to be keel-hawled for his presumption. **1769** FALCONER *Dict. Marine* (1789), *Donner la grand Cale*, to keel-haul; a punishment peculiar to the Dutch. **1831** TRELAWNEY *Adv. Younger Son* I. 203 If I catch any more on board, I'll keelhale them. **1882** *Standard* 11 Sept. 5/5 Two officers of Arabi's army..had been keel-hauled.

Hence '**keelhauling** *vbl. sb.*, the action of drawing under the keel; the fact of being keelhauled; also '**keelhaul** *sb.*, an act of keelhauling.

1753 MISS COLLIER *Art Torment.* 15 Some sorts of curious marine discipline, as the cat-of-nine-tails, keel-hawling, and the like. **1821** *Blackw. Mag.* X. 366 Even previous to 1797 the old punishment of 'keel-hauling', for slight offences, had entirely gone out. **1831** TRELAWNEY *Adv. Younger Son* (1890) 450, I was about to treat him with a keelhale.

keelie ('kiːlɪ). *north. dial.* and *Sc.* [Imitative of the bird's cry.]

1. A local name for the sparrow-hawk or kestrel.

1808 JAMIESON, *Keelie*, a hawk, chiefly applied to a young one. *Loth., Teviotd.* **1893** *Northumbld. Gloss., Keely-haak*, the kestrel... Its note 'keely-keely' gives it the name. **1898** J. COLVILLE *Scott. Vernacular* (1899) 11 Sclim the branchless stem of the fir for the keelie's nest.

2. A low or vulgar boy; a street-loafer or rough. *Sc.*

[*a* **1825** SCOTT (Jam.), A combination of young blackguards in Edinburgh hence termed themselves the Keelie Gang.] **1863** *N.B. Daily Mail* 18 Aug., The defender ..said that I was a Saltmarket keelie, a fighting man, a thief. **1909** *Athenæum* 1 May 528/2 Most people will..appreciate the sterling..character..of the Glasgow 'keelie' of twelve. **1937** *Times Lit. Suppl.* 13 Nov. 870/3 Wondering..whether the rascally little Glasgow 'keelie'..will succeed in betraying both sides for pay. **1962** 'H. CALVIN' *System* ii. 31 A Glasgow keelie who had grown up in a two-roomed slum. **1969** I. & P. OPIE *Children's Games* iv. 155 'It has to be played in the dark', remarks a keelie. **1973** *Times* 18 May (Glasgow Suppl.) p. iv/2 The archetypal Glasgow keelie is a gallus man.

keeling ('kiːlɪŋ), *sb.*[1] *Sc.* and *north. dial.* Forms: 3–9 **keling,** (4 **kyling,** 5 **chelynge,** 5–6 **kelyng(e,** 6 **kieling,** *Sc.* **keyling, killine,** 6–7 **killing,** 7 **killin,** 7–8 *Sc.* **keilling,** 8 **kiling),** 7– **keeling.** [Origin uncertain: the name, like COD, seems to be confined to English, but may be ultimately related to Icel. *keila* 'gadus longus', or to Da. *kolle, kuller*, Sw. *kolja* haddock. Ir. *ceilliuin*, Gael. *cílean* are no doubt from English. The form *cheling* is difficult.] A cod-fish.

The exact sense seems to have varied, in different localities, from 'large cod' to 'small cod' or 'codling'.

c **1300** *Havelok* 757 Keling he tok, and tumberel Hering, and þe makerel. **1323–4** *Acc. Rolls Durham* (Surtees) 13 In 13 Kelinges. **1340** *Ibid.* 37 In..4 kyling. *c* **1440** *Promp. Parv.* 72/1 Chelynge, fysche. *c* **1450** *Two Cookery-bks.* 94 Take paunches and lyuers of a codlyng, or haddok, or elles kelyng. **1596** DALRYMPLE tr. *Leslie's Hist. Scot.* I. 13 Sindrie fresche water lochis..that abundes in mony kyndes of fische, cheiflie..Killine, Skait, and Makrell. *c* **1620** Z. BOYD *Zion's Flowers* (1855) 72 The Killings, Herrings, Castocks. **1710** SIBBALD *Hist. Fife* 51 *Asellus major vulgaris*, the Cod; our Fishers call it Keeling, and the young Ones Codlings. **1793** *Statist. Acc. Scot.* VII. 205 Large cod called Keilling are also got in Spring and Summer. **1860** C. INNES *Scot. Mid. Ages* viii. 237 Our common sea fish..Keling, ling, haddock.

keeling ('ki:lɪŋ), *sb.*² [f. KEEL *sb.*¹ + -ING¹.] The material or make of a ship's keel.

1884 *Lake's Falmouth Packet* 13 Sept. 5/5 The 'Mignonette'..was really half cutter, her keeling and timbers being those of a 40 ton vessel.

keeling, *vbl. sb.*¹ *Obs.* exc. *dial.* [f. KEEL *v.*¹ + -ING¹.] The action of the vb. KEEL; cooling.

1382 WYCLIF *Acts* iii. 20 Whanne the tymes of kelynge [*gloss* or refreischinge]..schulen come. **1398** TREVISA *Barth. De P.R.* v. xix. (MS. Bodl.) lf. 10/1 Wiþoute keling þerof þe hert schuld be brende. **1573** *Art Limning* (1588) 106 Stirre it [Vermilion] well together in the keeling. **1657** R. LIGON *Barbadoes* (1673) 90 After much keeling, they take it out of the tach.

keeling, *vbl. sbs.*² and ³: see KEEL *vbs.*³ and ⁴.

'keelivine, keelie vine. *Sc.* and *north. dial.* Also (8 kilie vine), 9 kyle-, keela-, keely-, guilli-, cala-, -vine. [Of uncertain origin.

In South of Scotl. and Northumberland pronounced as two (or three) words *keelie vine* (or *keel i' vine*), (contracted in Scotl. *keelie*, in Northumb. *vine*), and commonly explained as from KEEL *sb.* + *vine* (referring to the pencil 'vine' or cedar), the name being only applied to a pencil enclosed in wood. But in other districts the name is pronounced as one word, and applied to the substance black-lead itself: cf. KILLOW, another name of this. See other suggestions in Jamieson. If quot. 1720 belongs here, the correct etymology ought also to explain *kilie vert* there mentioned.]

A black-lead pencil, or more generally, any coloured pencil enclosed in wood (as a *red keelie-vine*); also, in some places, black-lead, plumbago.

[**1720** DR. MITCHELL *Let.* (Jam.), If Gods Providence were not wonderful, I would long since been crying Kilie vine, and Kilie vert, considering I began upon a crown, and a poor trade.] **1808–18** JAMIESON, *Keelivine*, a black-lead pencil. **1826** J. WILSON *Noct. Ambr.* Wks. 1855 I. 146 With the verra mere, naked unassisted keelivine (that day fortunately it was a red ane) I caught the character o' the apparition. **1884** *Scot. Ch. Rev.* I. 5 His appliances as yet are a keelyvine and a Balaam-box. **1893** *Northumbld. Gloss., Keely-vine*, a pencil, originally a pencil made from keel, but applied generally to 'vines' or pencils. **1899** *Cumbld. Gloss., Calavine*, a black-lead pencil.

b. *attrib.*, as ***keelivine pen***, a pencil.

1782 SIR J. SINCLAIR *Obs. Sc. Dial.* 120 Black-lead is called killow, or collow, in Cumberland; and a guillivine-pen, is probably a corruption of a fine killow pencil. **1816** SCOTT *Antiq.* xxxviii, Put up your pocket-book and your keelyvine pen. **1833** *Fraser's Mag.* Oct. 398 In a hole he had ..jock-to-legs, keelavine pens.

Hence **'keelivined** *a.*, marked with pencil.

c **1818** SCOTT in *Lockhart* xlii, I thought it had been well known that the keelavined egg must be a soft one for the Sherra.

keelless ('ki:llɪs), *a.* [f. KEEL *sb.*¹ + -LESS.]

1. Of a boat: Having no keel.

1879 *Daily News* 7 Apr. 3/3 The worst crew that either University has sent to Putney since the days when keelless boats first came into use, just 22 years ago. **1896** *Westm. Gaz.* 20 June 5/2, I was out since six o'clock in my shallow keelless boat.

2. *Zool.* Having no keel along the breast-bone.

1884 G. ALLEN in *Longm. Mag.* Jan. 293 Keelless and often almost wingless birds. **1886** *Century Mag.* XXXI. 358 This great order of the Ratitæ, or keelless birds. **1895** *Pop. Sci. Monthly* Apr. 762 All had keelless sterna.

keelman¹ ('ki:lmən). [KEEL *sb.*²] One who works on a keel or barge.

1516 *Patent Roll 8 Hen. VIII*, Pt. 1, m. 15–16 (P.R.O.) The craftes of..Porters, Kelemen, Sclatters. **1592** *Wills & Inv. N.C.* (Surtees 1860) 251 Henrie Robinsone of the towne of Newcastell-upon-Tyne, keillman. **1695** *Lond. Gaz.* No. 3193/3 Newcastle, June 12... The Keel Men are gone to work again. **1774** WESLEY *Wks.* (1872) IV. 21 In the morning I preached at the Ballast-Hills among the glassmen, keelmen, and sailors. **1829** SOUTHEY *Sir T. More* (1831) II. 56 It has become a place of colliers and keelmen.

'keelman². *Sc.* [KEEL *sb.*³]

1. A dealer in keel or ruddle.

1796 *Acc.* in Scott *Old Mort.* Introd. (1862) 8 To 3 Chappins of Yell with Sandy the Keelman, 0 0 9.

2. One of a class of Irish linen-dealers (see quot.).

1821 BRENNER *Irish Linen Trade* in *Cassell's Gt. Indust. Gt. Brit.* (1878–80) II. xvi. 196 The 'Keelmen' were so-called from the first persons who got into the trade being very illiterate, and, unable to write in ordinary characters, they marked on each piece of linen the price at which it was bought with 'keel'.

keels, variant of KAYLES.

keelson (also **keelsale**), var. KELSON.

†**keel-toll.** *Obs.* [f. KEEL *sb.*¹ (or ? *sb.*²) + TOLL.] = KEELAGE.

?**1499** in Gross *Gild Merch.* II. 44 (Chester) De qualibet Naue intrante libertatem predictam cum quibuscunque marcandisis seu victualibus vocatum Keyltoll iiii.*d.* et Clerico 1.*d.*

keel-vat. *rare.* Also -fat. [KEEL *sb.*⁴ or KEEL *v.*¹] A wooden tub; a keeler.

1552 HULOET, Keelerue [?] or keele vat, for ale, wyne or beere, *labrum*. **1755** JOHNSON, *Keel-fat*, cooler; tub in which liquor is let to cool. **1886** *S.W. Linc. Gloss., Keal*, a cold.. almost out of use in this part of Lincolnshire, as is its compound, 'Keal-fat', a cooling-vat used in brewing.

'keely, *a. rare.* Also **kealy**. [f. KEEL *sb.*³ + -Y¹.] Abounding in keel; of the nature of keel.

1712 J. MORTON *Nat. Hist. Northampt.* i. §38. 41 Our ordinary Sort of kealy Land is a Red-land, with a large Inter-mixture of Reddish Stones, which every one here calls Keale. **1753** CHAMBERS *Cycl. Supp., Kealy soil*, in agriculture, is used by the husbandmen for a sort of land, plentifully strewed with keale or kale.

keelyvine, variant of KEELIVINE.

keem, obs. f. KEMB *v.*

Keemun ('ki:mu:n). Also **Kee-Moon, Kee Mun, Kee-mun.** The name of a district in China used to describe a black tea grown there. Also *attrib.*

1892 J. M. WALSH *Tea* v. 85 Kee-mun..is another of the newest descriptions of China Congou teas... The dried leaf varies considerably in style and appearance, some lots having an evenly-curled and handsome leaf, while others again are brownish and irregular. **1907** *Yesterday's Shopping* (1969) 1 Finest China, Plain (Keemun)—lb. 3/2. **1935** W. STEVENS *Let.* 20 Dec. (1967) 303 This morning for breakfast I had some of the best Kee-Moon, and found it to be a delightful tea. **1958** *Catal. County Stores* (Taunton) June 18 A Blend of Pure China Keemun and Finest Formosan Oolong Teas. **1967** V. C. CLINTON-BADDELEY *Death's Bright Dart* 64 Neither Lapsang, nor Kee Mun, nor Oolong, nor Jasmine..and certainly not Earl Grey. He brewed a pot of Darjeeling.

keen (ki:n), *sb.* [a. Ir. *caoine* ('ki:nə), f. *caoinim* (OIr. *cáinim, cóinim*) I weep, wail, lament; cf. KEEN *v.*²] An Irish funeral song accompanied with wailing in lamentation for the dead.

1830 CROFTON CROKER in *Fraser's Mag.* I. 191 The following Keens..I have translated from the Irish. **1841** S. C. HALL *Ireland* I. 226 The keener having finished a stanza of the keen, sets up the wail. **1895** *Q. Rev.* Oct. 319 His mother was famed..for her skill in giving the keen.

keen (ki:n), *a.* (*adv.*) Forms: 1 céne, 2–6 kene, 3–4 ken, 4–7 keene, (5 *Sc.* keyne, 6 kein(e), 7– keen. [Com. Teut.: OE. *céne* = OS. **kôni* (MDu. *coene*, Du. *koen*), MLG. *kône, kœne*, OHG. *chôni, chuoni* (MHG. *küene*, G. *kühn*), ON. *kœnn*:—OTeut. **kōnjo-*. There are no cognates outside of Teutonic.

The original meaning is somewhat obscure. The prominent sense in OE., as in Low and High German, was that of 'bold, brave,' but ON. *kœnn* meant only 'expert, skilful, clever', a sense also represented in OE. (ODa. *kiön, kön*, OSw. *kön, kyn*, 'bold', are app. from LG., the original Scand. sense being found in ODa. *lovkiön* 'learned in the law'.) It has been suggested that the ON. sense is the original one, the connecting link with the other being the idea of 'skilled in war', 'expert in battle' (= ON. *vígkœnn*), but there is no clear evidence of this. The development of the specifically English sense 'sharp' is also obscure.]

A. *adj.* †**1.** Wise, learned, clever. *Obs.* (Cf. 7 b.)

a **1000** *Boeth. Metr.* x. 51 Se wæs uðwita ælces þinges cene and cræftiȝ, þæm wæs Caton nama. *c* **1205** LAY. 4989 Þa alde quene, a wifmon wis and kene. *a* **1225** *Leg. Kath.* 2070 Beo nu ken & cnawes..hu heh & hu hali is þes cristenes godd. **13..** *E.E. Allit. P.* B. 1575 Þer comen mony Clerkes out of Caldye þat kennest wer knauen.

†**2. a.** Brave, bold, valiant, daring. *Obs.*

c **897** K. ÆLFRED *Gregory's Past.* xxxiii. 218 Betra bið se ȝeðyldeȝa wer ðonne se stronga & se kena. *c* **993** *Battle of Maldon* 215 Nu mæȝ cunnian hwa cene sy. *c* **1200** ORMIN 19962 Godess bodeword..to kiþenn forþ Biforenn kafe & kene. *c* **1205** LAY. 520 He nom his kene men þa to compe weren gode. *a* **1300** *K. Horn* 164 Whannes beo ȝe, faire gumes,..Of bodie swiþe kene. *c* **1386** CHAUCER *Monk's T.* 259 Cenobia..So worthy was in Armes and so keene That no wight passed hire in hardynesse. *c* **1420** *Anturs of Arth.* xlvii, The knyȝte that was curtase cruail and kene. **1508** DUNBAR *Gold. Targe* 137 Scho bad hir archearis kene Go me arrest. *a* **1605** MONTGOMERIE *Misc. Poems* xiii. 29 Love maks a couard kene.

†**b.** As an alliterative epithet of kings or other rulers; hence, Mighty, powerful, strong. *Obs.*

a **1000** *Ps.* l. (Cott. Vesp. D. vi.) 3 David wæs..cyninga cynost, Criste liofost. *a* **1225** *Leg. Kath.* 181 Aȝein se kene keisere & al his kineriche. *a* **1300** *K. Horn* 507 'King,' he sede, 'so kene Grante me a bene'. **13..** *E.E. Allit. P.* B. 1593 'Kene kyng,' quoth þe quene, 'kayser of vrþe'. *c* **1400** *Destr. Troy* 1467 To cache a castell þat was kene holdyn. *a* **1510** DOUGLAS *K. Hart* I. xviii, Harde by this castell of this King so kene.

†**c.** Fierce, savage (chiefly of beasts); cruel; harsh (*to* a person). *Obs.*

a **1000** *Cædmon's Exod.* 322 (Gr.) Hæfdon him to seȝne.. gyldene leon..deora cenost. *c* **1000** *Sax. Leechd.* I. 372 Se þe hafað hundes heortan mid him, ne beoð onȝean hine hundas cene. *a* **1300** *Cursor M.* 6715 If his lauerd kneu him kene o horn..Þis ox þan sal be taght to slan. **1340** HAMPOLE *Pr. Consc.* 1228 Wild bestes..Als lyons, libardes and wolwes kene. *c* **1375** *Sc. Leg. Saints* ii. (*Paulus*) 647 Nero, þat tyran kene. *c* **1398** CHAUCER *Fortune* 27 Whi seysthow thanne y am [to] the so kene þat hast thy self owt of my gouernaunce. **1500–20** DUNBAR *Poems* xxxviii. 11 The cruell serpent.. The auld kene tegir, with his teith on char. **1622** FLETCHER *Sea Voy.* III. i, I'll make ye..warry one another like keen bandoggs.

†**d.** Bold, proud, forward, insolent, heinous.

1297 R. GLOUC. (Rolls) 6471 Me ne dar noȝt esse [= ask] weþer he were kene þo & prout. *a* **1400–50** *Alexander* 748 For þi kene carpyng cache now a shame. *c* **1450** *St. Cuthbert* (Surtees) 2404 Gude ensampill, men to mene Meke to be, noȝt proude na kene. **1508** KENNEDIE *Flyting w. Dunbar* 322 And knaw, kene skald, I hald of Alathya. **1567** *Satir. Poems Reform.* v. 42 For to defend the tratoure kene. **1594** MARLOW & NASHE *Dido* v. ii, Trait'ress too keend and cursed sorceress!

3. a. Of weapons, cutting instruments, and the like: Having a very sharp edge or point; able to cut or pierce with ease. Also of an edge or point: Extremely sharp. (Now somewhat rhetorical, exc. in ***keen edge***, the ordinary word being *sharp*.)

a **1225** *Juliana* 57 Irnene gadien kene to keoruen. *a* **1225** *Leg. Kath.* 1952 Þe hweoles beon þurhspitet mid kenre pikes þen eni cnif. *c* **1385** CHAUCER *L.G.W.* 2654 *Hypermn.*, Out he caught a knyfe as A rasour kene. *a* **1541** WYATT *Poems* (1831) 172 He drew his bow with arrowes sharpe and kene. **1588** SHAKS. *L.L.L.* I. i. 6 His sythes keene edge. *c* **1600** —— *Sonn.* xix, Plucke the keene teeth from the fierce Tygers jawes. **1732** BERKELEY *Alciphr.* VI. §8 The keen edge of a razor. **1752** YOUNG *Brothers* IV. i, Like that poor wretch.. Who, while in sleep..Draws his keen sword. **1875** JOWETT *Plato* (ed. 2) III. 374 The keen edge will not be blunted. *fig.* *a* **1380** *Virgin Antioch* 24 in Horstm. *Altengl. Leg.* (1878) 26 Stured on..Wiþ twey kene prikkes of couetise. **1603** SHAKS. *Meas. for M.* II. i. 5 Let vs be keene, and rather cut a little Then fall, and bruise to death. **1713** YOUNG *Last Day* I. 186 Thou..Hast felt the keenest edge of mortal pain. **1784** COWPER *Task* IV. 164 Set a keener edge On female industry. **1819** SHELLEY *Masque Anarchy* lxxiv, Words Keen to wound as sharpened swords.

b. Of prices: competitive. Cf. quot. 1862, sense 6 below, and KEENLY *adv.* 6.

1964 A. FIBER *Independent Retailer* v. 55 (*heading*) Mail order has grown rapidly in recent years... As warehouses and offices are situated in low-rent areas and there is no need of a sales staff, overheads are low. Prices, therefore, are often very keen. **1975** *Evening Herald* (Dublin) 8 May 13/3 (Advt.), Dennis Rent a Car. Keenest rates. New Street, Dublin 8.

4. *transf.* Of things, substances, or agencies that affect the senses: **a.** Operating on the touch or taste like a sharp instrument; causing pain or smarting; acrid, pungent, stinging. (Now unusual.)

1398 TREVISA *Barth. De P.R.* XVII. clv. (MS. Bodl.) lf. 229 b/2 Þouȝe al þe herbe in substaunce be kene and feruente. **1486** *Bk. St. Alban's* C vj a, Take hony..and a kene nettyll. **1523** FITZHERB. *Husb.* §43 For terre of hym selfe is to kene, and is a fretter, and no healer. **1618** LATHAM *2nd Bk. Falconry* (1633) 138 Take some of the keenest onions you can possibly get. **1658** in *12th Rep. Hist. MSS. Comm.* App. v. 6 The keenest mustard. **1796** MORSE *Amer. Geog.* I. 192 Its fruit small, possessing, perhaps of all vegetables, the keenest acid. **1819** SHELLEY *Prometh. Unb.* I. 43 The genii of the storm..afflict me with keen hail.

b. Of cold (†or heat): Piercing, intense. Of wind, air, etc.: Very sharp, biting, piercing.

1340 HAMPOLE *Pr. Consc.* 3094 Þat fire is hatter and mare kene, þan al þe fire that here es sene. *c* **1350** *Will. Palerne* 908 But quicliche so kene a cold comes þer-after. **1567** *Gude & Godlie B.* (S.T.S.) 190 This wind sa keine. **1667** MILTON *P.L.* x. 1066 While the Winds Blow moist and keen. **1780** COWPER *Table-t.* 294 Place me where Winter breathes his keenest air. **1860** TYNDALL *Glac.* I. iii. 27 The breeze at the summit was exceedingly keen.

c. Of sound, light, scent: Sharp, piercing, penetrating; shrill; vivid; clear; strong.

c **1400** *Destr. Troy* 1206 Þe crie wax kene, crusshyng of wepyns. *a* **1400–50** *Alexander* 1604 Lordis & ladis..Kest vp a kene crie. **1602** MARSTON *Ant. & Mel.* I. Wks. 1856 I. 16 Keen lightning shot Through the black bowels of the quaking ayre. **1819** SHELLEY *Prometh. Unb.* II. iv. 27 Pain, whose unheeded and familiar speech Is howling, and keen shrieks. **1822** —— *Hellas* 344 One star..with keen beams, Like arrows through a fainting antelope. **1891** *Daily News* 6 Nov. 2/6 The scent was so wonderfully keen that they raced two consecutive foxes down.

d. Jolly good, very nice, splendid. *colloq.* (orig. *U.S.*).

1914 'HIGH JINKS, JR.' *Choice Slang* 14 *Keen*, excellent... 'A keen day.' 'A keen time.' **1925** *College Humor* Aug. 76/1 *Keen*, fine, attractive, splendid. **1940** *New Yorker* 16 Nov. 19/3 'My mother's going to buy me four new dresses.' ..'That's keen.' **1948** *Hearst's International* Dec. 162/3 'What are you studying at school?' 'Journalism.' 'That sounds keen,' said Sally. **1964** *Punch* 8 July 38/1 It's fab, Henchcliffe, it's gear, moody, groovy, keen and withitly gogo. **1968** N. FLEMING *Counter Paradise* vi. 87 He slowed to a standstill beside the second flag. 'Keen,' he said.

5. Of agencies that affect the mind: **a.** Of circumstances, thoughts, feelings, etc.: Causing acute pain or deep distress. Also, of pain, grief, etc.: Acute, intense, bitter.

a **1300** *Cursor M.* 4724 Þe folk mon dei,..þis hunger es sa ken. *Ibid.* 21492 Þis dome þat was sa kene. *c* **1350** *Will. Palerne* 616 It komses of a kene þouȝt þat ich haue in hert. *c* **1470** HENRY *Wallace* II. 298 This cairfull cas so kene. **1647** CLARENDON *Hist. Reb.* I. §191 It may be he retained too keen a memory of Those who had..Persecuted him. **1742** GRAY *Dist. Prosp. Eton* viii, Keen Remorse with blood defil'd. **1865** DICKENS *Mut. Fr.* III. xiii, Mr. Tremlow..had betrayed the keenest mental terrors.

b. Of language: Sharp, severe, incisive, cutting.

a **1400** *Pistill of Susan* 199 Þe renkes reneyed þis comeliche accused with wordes wel kene. **1595** SHAKS. *John* III. i. 182 Good Father Cardinall, cry thou Amen To my keene curses. **1670** EVELYN *Diary* 28 Aug., Enjoyning me to make it a little keene, for that the Hollanders had very unhandsomely abus'd him. **1788** GIBBON *Decl. & F.* l, They pointed their keenest satire against a despicable race. **1855** MACAULAY *Hist. Eng.* xviii. IV. 120 Keen speeches had been made,..but nothing had been done.

6. a. Of persons: Eager, ardent, fervid; full of, or manifesting, intense desire, interest, excitement, etc. Also, of desire, feeling, etc.: Intense.

c **1350** *Will. Palerne* 1011 Þan eiþer hent oþer hastely in armes, & wiþ kene kosses kuþþed hem to-gidere. **1377**

LANGL. *P. Pl.* B. XII. 252 þough he crye to cryst þanne with kene wille. **1570** LEVINS *Manip.* 69/35 Keene, *feruidus.* **1596** SHAKS. *1 Hen. IV*, IV. ii. 86 A dull fighter, and a keene Guest. **1715** *Lond. Gaz.* No. 5383/3 The Courage of the.. Troops was never Keener. **1776** ADAM SMITH *W.N.* I. i. (1869) I. 10 When he first begins the new work he is seldom very keen and hearty. **1827** D. JOHNSON *Ind. Field Sports* 51 The keenest native sportsman I ever met with. **1862** SIR B. BRODIE *Psychol. Inq.* II. ii. 38 In this age of keen competition. **1865** TYLOR *Early Hist. Man.* i. 10 They were listened to by high and low with the keenest enjoyment. **1880** McCARTHY *Own Times* III. xlv. 346 He had a keen interest in some branches of science.

b. Const. *about, against, at, for, †of*, or with inf.; also colloq. *on* (*upon*): interested in; also, sweet on, in love with.

a **1400-50** *Alexander* 1892 Corageous & kene ȝoure clere gold to wyn. **1523** FITZHERB. *Husb.* §68 She wyl not holde to it, excepte she be kene of horsyng. **1711** BUDGELL *Spect.* No. 116 ¶4 Sir Roger is so keen at this Sport. **1714** SWIFT *Pres. St. Aff.* Wks. 1755 II. I. 208 Men were not so keen upon coming in themselves. **1768** BEATTIE *Minstr.* I. lviii, Still keen to listen and to pry. **1855** KINGSLEY *Serm. Times* xiii. 217 Religious professors.. are just as keen about money. **1874** S. COX *Pilgr. Ps.* iii. 67 Who is more keen for gain than the modern Jew? **1889** E. DOWSON *Let.* 15 May (1967) 78 Is there anything you are particularly keen on? **1893** STEVENSON *Catriona* ix. 97 He was keen to say good-bye to ye. **1897** MARY KINGSLEY *W. Africa* 653 They'll let nature take its course if they don't feel keen on a man surviving. **1936** R. LEHMANN *Weather in Streets* IV. iii. 418 She's attractive, intelligent, amusing—and obviously pretty keen on me, my dear. **1943** C. BAX *Time with Gift of Tears* xxxix. 226 Maxine urged Guinivere to take Buster Graham more seriously. 'He's frightfully keen,' she said, 'on *you*.'

7. a. Of the eyes or eyesight: Sharp, penetrating. Hence, of hearing, smell, or other sense: Acute, highly sensitive. Also of persons or animals: Sharp *of* (sight, smell, etc.).

c **1720** GAY *Songs & Ball., New Song New Similies*, Her glance is as the razor keen. **1789** WOLCOTT (P. Pindar) *Expost. Odes* i. Wks. 1812 II. 217 Hunting, like Bloodhounds, with the keenest noses. **1822** HAZLITT *Table-t.* I. ii. 30 Looking through those he saw, till you turned away from the keen glance. **1841** JAMES *Brigand* xxvi, I for one have keener perceptions when an enemy is near. **1866** G. MACDONALD *Ann. Q. Neighb.* xxvi. (1878) 448 She looked hard at me with her keen gray eyes. **1875** JOWETT *Plato* (ed. 2) III. 28 Dogs keen of scent and swift of foot.

b. Of persons: Intellectually acute, sharpwitted, shrewd: often with mixture of sense 6. Also of the mind or mental operations: Endowed or conducted with great acuteness.

1704 J. LOGAN in *Pa. Hist. Soc. Mem.* IX. 324 He seems to me one of the keenest men living. **1794** SULLIVAN *View Nat.* II. 75 When the keenest researches are.. proceeding in the different parts of the European world. **1807** CRABBE *Par. Reg.* III. 521 To this poor swain a keen attorney came. **1849** MACAULAY *Hist. Eng.* ii. I. 246 Nature had given him a keen understanding. **1880** L. STEPHEN *Pope* iv. 102 Her letters are characteristic of the keen woman of the world.

c. Of the face or looks: Suggestive of mental acuteness or sharpness.

1798 WORDSW. *Peter Bell* I. xxiii, His face was keen as is the wind That cuts along the hawthorn-fence. **1894** *Punch* CVI. 109 Her hair which so cunningly curled About her keen face.

†**B.** *adv.* = KEENLY. *Obs.*

a **1400** CHAUCER *Merciles Beaute* 3 So woundeth hit through-out my herte kene. *c* **1475** *Rauf Coilȝear* 872 Thou art ane sarazine.. that counteris sa kene. **1560** ROLLAND *Crt. Venus* I. 636 Outthrow the hart thay thirll me sa kene. **1667** MILTON *P.L.* IX. 588 Hunger and thirst.. quick'nd at the scent Of that alluring fruit, urg'd me so keene.

C. *Comb.* **a.** Parasynthetic, etc., as ***keen-aired, -bladed, -eared, †-edge, -edged, -eyed, -faced, -fanged, -nosed, -scented, -sighted*** (hence ***keensightedness***), ***-visioned, -witted***, etc.

1730-46 THOMSON *Autumn* 434 The winds Blown o'er the *keen-air'd mountain by the North. **1906** *Macm. Mag.* Apr. 457 An escort of sturdy little Japanese armed with service rifles and the *keen-bladed *katana*. **1908** E. WHARTON *Hermit* iv. 25 She was a light sleeper, and *keen-eared. **1629** MASSINGER *Picture* II. i. Wks. (Rtldg.) 219/2 With his *keene-edge spear He cut and carbonaded them. **1591** SHAKS. *1 Hen. VI*, I. ii. 98 Here is my *keene-edg'd Sword. **1829** T. HOOK *Bank to Barnes* 128 Unrivalled in.. keen-edged satire. **1781** COWPER *Expost.* 631 The *keen-eyed eagle. **1921** Keen-eyed [see *firm-lipped*]. **1797** T. PARK *Sonn.* 72 *Keen-nos'd Sancho.. foretells a Partridge nigh. **1952** C. DAY LEWIS tr. *Virgil's Aeneid* IV. 76 Massylian riders galloped behind a keen-nosed pack. **1887** BOWEN *Virg. Æneid* IV. 132 Hounds *keen-scented of race. **1862** BAGEHOT in *National Rev.* Jan. 214 If you place the most *keen-sighted lady in the midst of the pure futilities.. of an aristocracy, she will sink to the level of those elements. **1813** L. HUNT in *Examiner* 3 May 278/2 His strength, his *keensightedness, and his ferocity. **1836** J. H. NEWMAN in *Lyra Apost.* (1849) 121 *Keen-visioned seer, alone. **1855** MACAULAY *Hist. Eng.* xvii. IV. 21 Sarcasms.. dropped but too easily from the lips of the *keenwitted Dorset.

b. Adverbial, with active and passive pples., as ***keen-bent, -biting, -bitten, -cut, -judging, -piercing, -set***; also with adj., as †***keen-cold***.

a **1758** DYER *Fleece* II. 158 Rough winds *Keen-biting on tempestuous hills. **1591** SYLVESTER *Du Bartas* I. ii. 698 The ..*keen-cold thicknes of that dampish Cloud. **1871** PALGRAVE *Lyr. Poems* 114 One *keen-cut group.. Sophocles could show. **1819** SHELLEY *Cenci* IV. iv. 115 Your gentleness and patience are no shield For this *keen-judging world. **1863** MRS. GASKELL *Sylvia's L.* iv. (1877) 34 I'm just *keen-set for my supper.

†**keen**, *v.*[1] *Obs. rare.* [f. KEEN *a.*] *trans.* To render keen; to sharpen.

1599 H. BUTTES *Dyets drie Dinner* Aa iij b, Now, lest thou keen thy blunted appetence. *c* **1689** *Popish Pol. Unmaskt* 35 in *3rd Coll. Poems* (1689) 23/1 You Cow the Bold, and Keen the Cowards heart. **1727-46** THOMSON *Summer* 1259 When cold Winter keens the brightening flood.

keen (kiːn), *v.*[2] [f. Ir. *caoin-* (kiːn), stem of *caoinim* I wail: see KEEN *sb.*]

1. *intr.* To utter the keen, or Irish lamentation for the dead; to wail or lament bitterly.

1811 [implied in KEENER[1]]. **1845** MRS. S. C. HALL *Whiteboy* vi. 55 The men.. in general suffer the women to 'keen' as long as they please. **1853** C. BRONTE *Villette* xlii. (1890) 518 Peace, peace, Banshee—'keening' at every window! **1857** G. LAWRENCE *Guy Liv.* xvii. (1866) 165 It is the wild Irish women keening over their dead.

2. *trans.* To bewail with Irish wailing.

1830 CROFTON CROKER in *Fraser's Mag* I. 200 Suppose that I am dead, and you were sent for to keen me.. No one would keen you as I would.

3. To utter in a shrill wailing tone.

1893 W. R. LE FANU *70 Yrs. Irish Life* 278 The wild, wailing Irish cry, 'keened' by many women. **1897** *Cornh. Mag.* Mar. 339 His witch-like voice keened out, 'Good God!' [etc.]

Hence **'keening** *vbl. sb.*

1876 STAINER & BARRETT *Dict. Mus. Terms* 248 When the body was laid down.. the keening was suspended. **1892** STEVENSON *Across the Plains* 264 The high voice of keening .. strikes in the face of sorrow like a buffet.

keen, var. KIN *sb.*[2]; obs. dial. var. *kine*, pl. of cow; obs. f. KEN *v.*[1]

keend, obs. var. KEEN *a.*; obs. f. KIND *a.*

Keene (kiːn). [Name of Richard Wynn *Keene*, who patented the plaster in England in 1838.] ***Keene's cement***: a plaster which sets to a very hard white finish and consists of gypsum that contains added alum (or another salt) and has been thoroughly calcined at a high temperature.

1869 J. RUST *Brit. Pat. 621* 2, I would prepare a slab of the required size in cement, by preference Keene's cement. **1917** E. A. DONCASTER in G. Martin *Industr. & Manuf. Chem.: Inorg.* II. lix. 117 Keene's cement is now the general name for a number of different plasters prepared by various manufacturers, the original patent having expired. **1947** J. C. RICH *Materials & Methods Sculpture* iv. 60 Dry, powdered mineral colors can be added to Keene's cement, which is occasionally used sculpturally as a casting material.

keener[1] ('kiːnə(r)). [f. KEEN *v.*[2] + -ER[1].] One who keens or laments; a professional mourner at Irish wakes and funerals who utters the keen.

1811 BUSBY *Dict. Mus.* (ed. 3), *Keeners*, the name of the Irish Singing Mourners. **1845** MRS. S. C. HALL *Whiteboy* vi. 55 The *ban caointhe*, or chief keener, had assumed her place beside the head of the bed. **1894** W. B. YEATS *Celtic Twilight* 101 As he drew near came to him the cry of the keeners.

keener[2] ('kiːnə(r)). *U.S.* [f. KEEN *a.* + -ER[1].] One who drives a hard bargain; also, a person or thing in some way superior.

1839 [see FIX *sb.* 1]. **1860** BARTLETT *Dict. Amer.* (ed. 3), *Keener*, a very shrewd person, one sharp at a bargain, what in England would be called 'a keen hand'. Western. **1872** SCHELE DE VERE *Americanisms* 496 *Keener*, a noun made from the adjective, is a Western term for a sharp man. 'I tell you he is a keener, you can't get on his blind side.' **1942** BERREY & VAN DEN BARK *Amer. Thes. Slang* §436/2 *Cheat*, keener. *Ibid.* §461/18 *Swindler*, keener. *Ibid.* §542/22 *Bargainer*, keener. *Ibid.* §743/2 *Cardsharp*, keener.

†**'keenly**, *a. Obs. rare.* [ME. **kēnlīch* (superl. *kenlokeste*) = MHG. *küenlîch* (G. *kühnlich*): see KEEN *a.* and -LY[1].] Bold, courageous.

c **1205** LAY. 25429 Ah hit weoren men þa kenlukeste [*c* **1275** þe kenlokeste men] þa æi mon ikende. **1570** *Satir. Poems Reform.* xxiii. 2 O kenely knicht, in martiall deidis most ding.

keenly ('kiːnlɪ), *adv.* Forms: 1 cénlíce, 2-3 ken(e)liche, 3-4 ken(e)li, 4-5 -ly, 6- **keenly**. [OE. *cénlíce* = MDu. *cœnlijc, -like*, MLG. *kônlîken*, MHG. *küenlîche* (G. *kühnlich*): see KEEN *a.* and -LY[2].] In a keen manner.

†**1.** Fiercely, boldly. *Obs.*

c **1000** ÆLFRIC *Saints' Lives, Oswald* (1890) II. 126 Oswold him com to, and him cenlice wiðfeaht. *c* **1175** *Lamb. Hom.* 107 Ʒif we kenliche fehtað. *c* **1300** *Cursor M.* 24769 (Edin.) Selcuþe kenli cuþe he fiht. *c* **1400** *Destr. Troy* 7231 He keppit hym kenely, and coupid to-gedur.

2. a. Eagerly, ardently.

c **1350** *Will. Palerne* 859 Fayn sche wold.. haue him clipped and kest kenely þat tide. *c* **1400** *Destr. Troy* 5270 What causes ye.. so kenly to pray, This syre for to saue. *c* **1400** *Melayne* 1286 With dartis kenely owte thay caste. **1513** DOUGLAS *Æneis* IX. xi. 3 Thayr bustuus bowys keynly do thai bend.

†**b.** Sharply, quickly, in haste. *Obs.*

13.. *Gaw. & Gr. Knt.* 1048 Then frayned þe freke.. Quhat derne dede had hym dryuen.. So kenly fro þe kyngez kourt to kayre al his one. **13..** *E.E. Allit. P.* B. 945 Þise aungeles.. beden hem passe fast & þay kayrene con & kenely flowen. *a* **1400-50** *Alexander* 1353 Þe kynge callez a clerke kenely on þe morne, As radly as euer he rose.

3. With, or as with, a sharp edge or instrument; sharply: cuttingly, piercingly.

c **1592** MARLOWE *Massacre Paris* III. iv, Whet thy sword on Sextus' bones, That it may keenly slice the Catholics. **1645** MILTON *Tetrach.* To Parlt., To smite so keenly with a reviling tongue. *a* **1794** SIR W. JONES *1st Nem. Ode Pindar* III. iii, For private woes most keenly bite Self-loving man. **1837** MARRYAT *Dog-fiend* i, The wind was from the northward and blew keenly.

4. *transf.* Sharply, piercingly, incisively. **a.** Of sensuous impressions: Acutely.

c **1205** LAY. 21296 þa clupede þe king, kenliche lude. *c* **1384** CHAUCER *H. Fame* III. 635 Thrugh the worlde wente the soun, Also kenely, and eke softe. *a* **1400-50** *Alexander* 2154 Knyghtez kest vp a cry & kenely þaim mene. **1810** SCOTT *Lady of L.* III. i, The warning note was keenly wound. **1821** JOANNA BAILLIE *Metr. Leg.* 154 His brightest hour.. More keenly bright than Summer's settled sheen.

b. Of expression of (critical) opinion, etc.

a **1300** *Cursor M.* 14621 Allan iesus þaim stod emid, Keneli to him þai resun did. *a* **1400** *Pistill of Susan* 214 Heo ..comaunded hem kenely þe ȝates to close. *c* **1440** *York Myst.* xxiv. 64 Woman! wher are þo wighte men went That kenely here accused þe? **1841** W. SPALDING *Italy & It. Isl.* II. 36 The origin of these.. monuments has been keenly disputed. **1879** McCARTHY *Own Times* II. xxviii. 350 Every detail was keenly criticised.

c. Of the exercise of the organs of sense, the attention, or the intellect.

1824 R. STUART *Hist. Steam Engine* 29 The attention of mechanics, thus keenly directed to the subject. **1845** DISRAELI *Sybil* (1863) 201 'You are right', said Morley looking at her rather keenly. **1876** LOWELL *Among my Bks.* Ser. II. 323 Byron the most keenly intellectual of the three.

5. With reference to feeling: Acutely, intensely, deeply, strongly.

a **1400-50** *Alexander* 4151 þan was kniȝtis of þe case kenely affraid. **1792** *Anecd. W. Pitt* II. xxviii. 119 Perhaps no gentleman ever felt the poignant sting of ingratitude so keenly. **1849** RUSKIN *Sev. Lamps* p. v, There are.. cases in which men feel too keenly to be silent. **1876** GREEN *Stray Stud.* 18 No one enjoyed more keenly the pleasures of life and society. **1881** LADY HERBERT *Edith* 5 Gordon was keenly interested in the questions of the day.

6. *Comm.* At a keen price, cheaply.

1928 *Daily Express* 28 Aug. 7 With advantages like this we can quote more keenly.

keenness ('kiːnnɪs). [f. KEEN *a.* + -NESS.] The quality of being keen; sharpness, acuteness.

1. Sharpness of edge or point.

1530 PALSGR. 235/2 Kenesse, sharpnesse, *aspreté*. **1697** DRYDEN *Æneid* XII. 143 The God of fire.. Immortal keenness on the blade bestowed. **1833** J. HOLLAND *Manuf. Metal* II. 19 A blade.. with the greatest keenness of edge.

2. Piercing severity, intensity (of heat, cold, etc.).

1605 DRAYTON *Eclogues* X. i, The poor herds.. Shudder'd with keenness of the winter's cold. **1694** SALMON *Bates' Dispens.* (1713) 509/1 It is good for any Disease proceeding from sharp Humours, because it.. asswages them, taking away their Keenness. **1828** SCOTT *F.M. Perth* xii, Exposed to the keenness of a Scottish blast in February. *a* **1848** R. W. HAMILTON *Rew. & Punishm.* viii. (1853) 345 What could soften the keenness of that flame?

3. Intensity of feeling or action; eagerness, incisiveness.

1596 SHAKS. *Merch. V.* IV. i. 125 No mettall can.. beare halfe the keennesse Of thy sharpe enuy. **1695** J. EDWARDS *Perfect. Script.* 424 This.. makes him with an unwonted keenness and severity cry out against them. **1723** *Wodrow Corr.* (1843) III. 11 Free from severity and keenness, that is ready to mix in with debates of this nature. **1875** McLAREN *Serm.* Ser. II. ii. 199 Youth has mostly a certain keenness of relish for life. **1878** LECKY *Eng. 18th Cent.* II. vii. 417 Abundant evidence of the keenness of the antagonism.

4. Intellectual sharpness; acuteness: shrewdness.

1707 WYCHERLEY *Pope's Lett.* (1735) I. 27 The Keenness of the Mind soonest wears out the Body. **1828** CARLYLE *Misc.* (1857) I. 211 In the Poetry of Burns, keenness of insight keeps pace with keenness of feeling. **1849** MACAULAY *Hist. Eng.* viii. II. 407 His meagre and wrinkled ..face strongly expressed.. the keenness of his parts. **1885** *Manch. Exam.* 4 Feb. 3/5 Severity in selection and.. keenness in criticism.

5. Acuteness of the senses or organs of sense.

1859 GEO. ELIOT *A. Bede* ii, There was no keenness in the eyes; they seemed rather to be shedding love than making observations. *Mod.* Their keenness of sight is remarkable.

keeno, var. KENO *sb.* (and *int.*).

†**'keenship.** *Obs. rare.* In 3 kenschipe, -s(c)ipe. [f. KEEN *a.* + -SHIP.] Keenness, boldness, fierceness.

c **1205** LAY. 6364 þes biȝet þesne kinedom þurh kenschipe muchele. *a* **1225** *St. Marher.* 11 Ich habbe adun the drake idust. ant his kenschipe akast.

keep (kiːp), *v.* Pa. t. and pa. pple. **kept**. Forms: *Infin.* 1 (2) cépan, 2-3 kepan, 2-4 -en, (4 -in, 5 -yn), 3-5 kep, 3-6 kepe, 5-7 keepe, (6 keype, *Sc.* keip(e)), 6- keep. *Pa. t.* 1 cépte, 3-5 kepte, (3-4 kipte), 3- kept; 4-5 keped(e, 5 -id, -yd, 5-6 *Sc.* -it, -yt. *Pa. pple.* 4 i-kept, 4- kept; 6 *Sc.* kepit. [Late OE. *cépan*: no related words known in the cognate langs.; ulterior etymology unknown. The primary sense in OE. is also difficult to ascertain; the verb appears to have been orig. construed with a genitive.

The word prob. belonged primarily to the vulgar and non-literary stratum of the language; but it comes up suddenly into literary use *c*1000, and that in many senses, indicating considerable previous development. The original sense may have been 'to lay hold' with the hands, and hence with the attention, 'to keep an eye upon, watch'. About 1000, it was taken to render L. *observāre* (orig. 'to watch, keep an eye upon, take note of'), and its subsequent development seems

to have been largely influenced by the senses of this L. word, nearly all of which it has been used to render. It also renders the simple L. *servāre* (orig. 'to watch, observe'), and the compounds *conservāre*, *præservāre*, *reservāre*. In sense there is also close affinity between *keep* and HOLD (orig. 'to keep watch over', 'keep in charge'): in many uses they are still synonymous, and many phrases which have now the one verb formerly had the other; but in later usage, at least, *keep* implies the exercise of stronger effort to retain, so that *have*, *hold*, *keep*, form a series, the members of which pass into each other with progressive intensity of action. *Hold* has moreover often a sense of 'sustain, support, keep from falling', not belonging to *keep*.

If *cēpan* was an old word, it would go back to an OTeut. **kōpjan*; but no trace of this vb. is found elsewhere. Some compare OE. *copián* (found only once) = L. 'compilare', and ME. *copnien* to watch or wait for; but uncertainty as to the length of the *o* in these words makes it doubtful whether they belong to the root *kôp-*. Kluge (Beiträge VIII. 537) has suggested radical connexion with OHG. *chuofa*, OLG. *kôpa* cask, coop (as a thing for holding or keeping). The alleged Flem. *kepen* in Kilian is an error.

Uncertainty as to the original sense makes a historical scheme of the sense-development difficult. In the following, some early (and obsolete) senses are placed first under branch I; branch II has the chief trans. senses, *= 'pay attention, observe', **= 'guard, preserve', ***= 'hold in custody', ****= 'conduct, carry on'; III the intrans. senses derived from these; IV the combinations with adverbs. Although the four groups under II are distinct enough in the primary and literal senses, the distinction tends to melt away in the fig. uses, and esp. in the innumerable phraseological expressions into which *keep* enters; in several cases these combine the notions of two or more groups. In many phrases, also, the sense of *keep* is so indefinite and so dependent upon that of the object or complement, as to be scarcely capable of separate analysis; such phrases are treated under the sb. or adj. in question: e.g. *keep* COMPANY, *keep* WATCH, *keep* CLOSE.]

I. Early senses (with *genitive* in OE., afterwards with *simple object*).

1. To seize, lay hold of; to snatch, take. *Obs.*

c **1000** ÆLFRIC *Hom.* II. 246 Swa hwilcne swa ic cysse, cepað his sona. *a* **1175** *Cott. Hom.* 243 Gif hi us ofercumeð ne cepeð hi of hus gold ne selfer bute ure bane. **1297** R. GLOUC. (Rolls) 2950 Eldol, erl of gloucestre..Barnde & kepte her & þer, & slou aboute wyde. *c* **1330** R. BRUNNE *Chron.* (1810) 166 Fulle broþely & brim he kept vp a trencheour.

†**2.** To try to catch or get; to seek after. *Obs.*

c **1000** ÆLFRIC *Hom.* II. 522 Se ðe oðerne lufað..nele he him hearmes cepan. *c* **1000** *St. Basil's Admon.* v. (1849) 46 Ne kep ðu..ðinum nextan facnes. *c* **1175** *Lamb. Hom.* 107 Þet weo on gode weorcas godes luue kepan, and naut idel-ȝelp. *c* **1200** ORMIN 1277 Fra þatt hire make iss dæd Ne kepeþþ ȝho nan oþerr.

†**3.** To take in, receive, contain, hold. *Obs.*

c **1020** *Rule St. Benet* xxxvi. (Logeman) 67 Ah þa sylfan untruman..ȝeþyldelice sind to cepanne [L. *patienter portandi sunt*]. *a* **1225** *Leg. Kath.* 399 Tu schalt..to curt cumen seoðen, & kinemede ikepen. *c* **1325** *Body & Soul* in *Map's Poems* (Camden) 344/1 Ʒit schalt thou come..to court, and ich the with, For to kepen ure rihte pay. **1340** HAMPOLE *Pr. Consc.* 5408 Helle bynethen þat es wyde and depe, Sal þan be open þam to kepe. *Ibid.* 7371 Helle yhit es swa depe, And swa wyde and large..that it moght kepe Alle the creatures..Of alle the world.

†**4.** To take in with the eyes, ears, or mind; to take note of, mark, behold, observe. *Obs.*

c **1000** ÆLFRIC *Hom.* I. 580 Zacheus..cepte þæs Hælendes fær, and wolde ȝeseon hwilc he wære. *c* **1000** *Sax. Leechd.* III. 268 Menn maȝon..cepan be his bleo..hwylc weder toweard byð. *c* **1127** *O.E. Chron.* an. 1127 Soðfeste men heom kepten on nihtes. *a* **1325** *Prose Psalter* cxxix. [cxxx.] 3 Lord, ȝif þou hast kept [Vulg. *si observaveris*] wickednes, Lord, who shal holde hem vp? *c* **1400** *Prymer* (1895) 53 Lord! if þou kepist wickidnessis, lord! who schal susteyne?

†**b.** To watch. *Obs.*

c **1000** *Lambeth Ps.* lv. 7 [lvi. 6] (Bosw.) Hiȝ minne ho oððe hohfot cepaþ oððe beȝemaþ. **1697** DRYDEN *Æneid* VI. 476 While the stars and course of heaven I keep, My wearied eyes were seiz'd with fatal sleep.

†**5.** To watch for, wait for, await (a coming event or person). *Obs.*

c **1000** ÆLFRIC *Hom.* II. 172 Ða munecas..ȝeorne ðæs andaȝan cepton. *a* **1225** *Leg. Kath.* 2457 Þe wununge of euch wunne kepeð and copneð þi cume. *c* **1290** *Magdalena* 595 in Horstm. *Altengl. Leg.* (1878) 161 Seiȝe heom þat huy kepen me aftur þe midniȝhte, For þare ich hopie for to beo. **1470-85** MALORY *Arthur* VIII. x, Syre Trystram rode pryuely vnto the posterne where kepte hym la beale Isoud.

†**6.** To lie in wait for, watch for stealthily with hostile purpose; to intercept on the way. *Obs.*

c **1000** ÆLFRIC *Hom.* II. 506 Þa ferde Martinus, and þæt folc his cepte, and hine ȝelæhton. *a* **1100** *O.E. Chron.* (MS. D.) an. 1052 Þa sceoldon cepan Godwines eorles ðe on Brycge wæs. *c* **1205** LAY. 26887 Whar me heom kepen mihte in ane slade deopen. **1297** R. GLOUC. (Rolls) 1964 A gret erl him kepte þer in a wod bi syde. *c* **1330** R. BRUNNE *Chron.* (1810) 10 Kebriht he kept at Humber, & on him he ran.

†**b.** *intr.* or *absol.* To lie in ambush. *Obs. rare.*

c **1205** LAY. 26937 Heo comen in ænne wude..sweoren heom bitwænen þat þer heo wolden kepen.

†**c.** *trans.* To intercept (a missile); to ward off (a stroke). See KEP *v. Obs.*

c **1175** *Lamb. Hom.* 153 Þe duntes boð uuel to kepen, þet mon nat nefre on hwilche halue ho wilen falle. *c* **1450** *Merlin* 223 Frelent raised the axe..And he kepte the stroke upon his shelde.

†**7.** To meet in resistance or opposition; to encounter. *Obs.*

c **1205** LAY. 23939 Frolle..igræp his spere longe, and kept Arður anan alse he aneoust com. **13..** *Gaw. & Gr. Knt.* 307 When non wolde kepe hym with carp he coȝed ful hyȝe. **1375** BARBOUR *Bruce* XIV. 197 Soyn with thair fayis assemblit thai, That kepit thame richt hardely. *c* **1400** *Destr. Troy* 8332 The knight hym kept, caupit with hym so, That bothe the hathell and his horse hurlit to ground.

†**8.** To intercept or meet in a friendly way; to greet, welcome. *Obs.*

1340 HAMPOLE *Pr. Consc.* 5028 Againe þe comyng of Ihesu Criste, To kepe him when he doun sal come [cf. 5051 to mete Criste]. *c* **1400** *Ywaine & Gaw.* 1387 Thai..dight tham in thair best aray, To kepe the King that ilk day. *c* **1450** *St. Cuthbert* (Surtees) 2004 Þe woman rase..And come Cuthbert for to kepe. *c* **1460** *Towneley Myst.* xxxi. 48 There mon ye kepe hym at his come.

II. Transitive uses (in early use also *intr.*).

* *To have regard, pay attention to, observe.*

†**9.** To have regard, to care, to reck; in ME. only with negative: To care nothing, to 'reck nought'. **a.** Const. with *genitive*, or *of*. *Obs.*

a **1050** *O.E. Chron.* an. 1013 (MSS. C, E.) Hi nanre brycge ne cepton. *c* **1200** ORMIN 4408 Ʒiff þatt tu nohht ne kepesst her Noff Crist, noff Cristess moderr. *c* **1290** *Beket* 998 Go hunnes, of þe ne kepe y noȝt. **1297** R. GLOUC. (Rolls) 11359 He ne kepte noþing of hor seruise. *c* **1350** *Will. Palerne* 4738, I kepe nouȝt of þi kingdom..ne of þi loueli lemman.

†**b.** With *inf.* or *obj. cl.* To care. *Obs.*

c **1175** *Lamb. Hom.* 55 Bute we bileuen ure ufele iwune, Ne kepeð he noht þet we beon sune. *c* **1200** ORMIN 7191 Ʒiff þatt teȝȝ..griþþ Ne kepenn nohht to follȝhenn. *a* **1250** *Owl & Night.* 154 Ne kepe ich noht þat þu me clawe. *c* **1386** CHAUCER *Knt.'s T.* 2102 Ne how the grekes pleye The wake pleyes ne kepe I nat to seye. —— *Can. Yeom. Prol. & T.* 815, I kepe han [*v. rr.* to han, haue, to haue, for haue, for to haue] no loos Of my craft. **1477** SIR J. PASTON in *P. Lett.* III. 188 To any suche bargayne I kepe never to be condescentyng. *c* **1530** *Hickscorner* in Hazl. *Dodsley* I. 192 Yet I keepe nat to climbe so hye. **1589** PUTTENHAM *Eng. Poesie* I. viii. (Arb.) 36, I kept not to sit sleeping..till a Queene came.

†**c.** With *simple obj.* To care for, to reck of; to regard, desire. *Obs.*

1297 R. GLOUC. (Rolls) 746 He ansuerede..þat he ne kepte bote hire [Cordelia] one wiþ oute alle oþer þinge. **1362** LANGL. *P. Pl.* A. IV. 156 So þat Concience beo vr counseiler, kepe I no betere. *c* **1420** *Pallad. on Husb.* XII. 270 But as of grauel lond no thing they kepe. **1423** JAS. I *Kingis Q.* cxli, More Ioy in erth kepe I noght bot ȝour grace. **1470-85** MALORY *Arthur* VI. xv, I had kepte no more ioye in this world but to haue thy body dede.

†**10.** *intr.* To have care, take care; to give heed, attend, look *to*. *Obs.*

a **1300** *Cursor M.* 26170 (Cott.) Es na herd set for to kepe Wit right bot til his aun scepe. *c* **1340** *Ibid.* 20099 (Trin.) I shal biteche þe a fere þat trewely shal kepe [*Gött.* take kepe] to þe. **1382** WYCLIF *Zech.* xi. 11 The pore of the floc that kepen to me, knewen thus, for it is the word of the Lord. *a* **1400-50** *Alexander* 821 Comand kenely hys knyghtez to kepe to hys blonkez.

11. *trans.* To pay attention or regard to; to observe, stand to, or dutifully abide by (an ordinance, law, custom, practice, covenant, promise, faith, a thing prescribed or fixed, as a treaty, truce, peace, a set time or day; see further under the sbs.).

In some of these the sense appears to blend with that of 'maintain, preserve intact'. In this sense it is usually the opposite of *disregard*, *violate*, *break*.

c **1000** ÆLFRIC *Hom.* II. 324 Swa swa ða clænan nytenu cepað heora timan. *Ibid.* I. 102 Nu ȝe cepað daȝas and monðas mid ydelum wiȝlungum [cf. **1382** WYCLIF *Gal.* iv. 10 Ʒe kepen [*MS. Q gloss* or weyten] dayes [Vulg. *dies observatis*] and monethis, and tymes]. *a* **1380** *St. Ambrose* 1119 in Horstm. *Altengl. Leg.* (1878) 25 Whon I come at Rome I kepe þe maner of þat fay..To what churche so euer þou cum þer of kep þou þe custum. **1387** TREVISA *Higden* (Rolls) VIII. 19 He bitook his breþeren þre poyntes to kepe, and seide þat he hadde kepte hem..al his lyf tyme. **1485** CAXTON *Chas. Gt.* 195 Obeye and kepe hys comandementes. *a* **1533** LD. BERNERS *Huon* xlv. 151, I know you wyll kepe couenaunt with me in that ye haue promysyd me. **1549** LATIMER *3rd Serm. bef. Edw. VI* (Arb.) 87 Thy Iudges are vnfaythefull, they kepe no touche..they wil pretende this and that, but thei kepe no promise. **1563** WINȜET *Four Scoir Thre Quest.* Wks. 1888 I. 115 St. Paull commandit..his traditionis to be keipit. **1668** R. STEELE *Husbandman's Calling* x. (1672) 273 As breaking rules turn'd the first husbandman out of Paradise, so keeping rules will bring you into Paradise again. **1711** STEELE *Spect.* No. 41 ¶7 It is certain no Faith ought to be kept with Cheats. **1867** TROLLOPE *Chron. Barset* II. lxxx. 346 A gentleman should always keep his word to a lady. **1869** FREEMAN *Norm. Conq.* III. xii. 246 Such an oath was one which he certainly had no thought of keeping. **1891** G. MEREDITH *One of our Conq.* III. xii. 252 He rose; he had to keep an appointment.

12. To observe with due formality and in the prescribed manner (any religious rite, ceremony, service, feast, fast, or other occasion); to celebrate, solemnize.

1432-50 tr. *Higden* (Rolls) VI. 53 Ordeynenge þe faste of Lente to be kepede in his realme. **1463** *Bury Wills* (Camden) 17 The wiche messe of our lady I wille the Seynt Marie preest kepe in a whith vestement. **1535** COVERDALE *1 Sam.* xxx. 16 They were scatred vpon all yᵉ grounde, eatinge and drynkynge, and kepynge holy daye. *a* **1548** HALL *Chron.*, *Hen. VI*, 167b, Sent to the towre of London, where he without great solempnitie, kept a dolefull Christmas. **1560** DAUS tr. *Sleidane's Comm.* 224 But what tyme the maryage was in maner appointed to be kept, he died. *Ibid.* 451b, Kyng Ferdinando kept her funerall at Auspurge. **1687** W. SHERWIN in *Magd. Coll.* (O.H.S.) 216 They..keep disputations and other exercises. **1774** J. HAWLEY in *J. Adams' Wks.* (1854) IX. 344 He keeps Sabbath at Boston. **1801** STRUTT *Sports & Past.* III. i. 133 To keep the justs in a place appointed. **1877** MISS YONGE *Cameos* Ser. III. I. 4 The King was keeping the feast of Easter. **1887** BOWEN *Virg. Eclogues* III. 76 To-day my birthday is kept.

13. To observe by attendance, presence, residence, performance of duty, or in some prescribed or regular way.

Formerly in to ***keep church***, ***evensong***, ***market***, etc.; now chiefly in to ***keep chapels***, ***halls***, ***roll-call*** (at college or school), *to **keep*** (prescribed) ***terms***, ***residence***, etc. Also, in weakened sense, to ***keep regular*** or ***proper*** (and so ***irregular***, ***late***, ***early***) ***hours***. See the sbs.

1450-1530 *Myrr. our Ladye* 29 They that kepe the Chyrch ar parteners of theyr mynistracion. **1479** in *Eng. Gilds* (1870) 426 The Maire & Shiref shall..kepe theire Aduent sermondes. **15..** in *Pref. to Ld. Berners' Froiss.* (1812) 13 The King hymselfe..kepte euensong of saynt george in his robe of the garters. **1608** BP. HALL *Virtues & V.* II. 83 Hee ..asks what fare is usuall at home, what houres are kept. *a* **1653** BINNING *Serm.* (1845) 607 They know not how to be saved, unless their prayers do it, or their keeping the kirk. *a* **1713** ELLWOOD *Autobiog.* (1714) 81 A Dyer of Oxford, who constantly kept Thame Market. **1738** SWIFT *Pol. Conversat.* 125 What! you keep Court-Hours I see. **1746** WESLEY *Wks.* (1872) XII. 76, I keep my church as well as any man. **1821** SHELLEY *Ginevra* 102 And left her at her own request to keep An hour of quiet and rest. **1824** SCOTT *Redgauntlet* ch. x, I keep the kirk, and I abhor Popery—I have stood up for the House of Hanover. **1852** THACKERAY *Esmond* I. x, So long as he kept his chapels, and did the college exercises required of him. **1894** LD. WOLSELEY *Life Marlborough* I. 229 Early hours were generally kept.

** *To guard (from external violence or injury), to preserve, maintain.*

14. To guard, defend, protect, preserve, save. (Const. *from*, †*of*.) **a.** a person.

c **1175** *Lamb. Hom.* 71 Þu..kep us from his waning, þat laþe gast, þet laþe þing. *a* **1300** *Cursor M.* 14075, I sal þe kepe forth fra þis dai. *c* **1330** *Spec. Gy Warw.* 48 To kepen his soule from þe qued. **1377** LANGL. *P. Pl.* B. Prol. 125 Crist kepe þe, sire kyng. *c* **1440** *Promp. Parv.* 272/2 Kepyn, *custodio*, *servo*, *conservo*. *c* **1489** CAXTON *Blanchardyn* xiv. 48 His goode shelde kept hym. **1593** T. WATSON *Tears Fancie* xxii. Poems (Arb.) 189 My Mistres slept: And with a garland ..Her daintie forehead from the sunne ykept. **1599** SHAKS. *Hen. V*, v. i. 71 God bu'y you, and keepe you, and heale your pate. **1669** BUNYAN *Holy Citie* 18 It is called a City..to shew us how strong and securely it will keep its Inhabitants at that day. **1697** KEN *Evening Hymn* i, Keep me, O keep me, King of kings, Beneath Thine own Almightly wings. **1719** HAMILTON *3rd Ep. to Ramsay* xiii, May thou..Be keeped frae the wirricow, After thou's dead. **1887** SWINBURNE *Locrine* IV. i. 234 God keep my lord!

b. a thing.

c **1250** *Gen. & Ex.* 3378 He let bi-aften ðe more del, To kepen here ðing al wel. *a* **1300** *Cursor M.* 10035 (Gött.) Þer standis thre baylis widvte, þat wele kepis þat castel For [*vr.* from] arw, schott and quarel. *c* **1330** R. BRUNNE *Chron.* (1810) 161 Bernard of Bayoun, þat was kepand þe se. *c* **1380** *Antecrist* in Todd *Three Treat. Wyclif* (1851) 129 To kepe þe chaumbur and halle of noyse and dyn. *c* **1470** *Gaw. & Gol.* 44 The yettis war clenely kepit with ane castell. *a* **1533** LD. BERNERS *Huon* lii. 177 It were better for the to..helpe to kepe a towne or a castell. **1560** DAUS tr. *Sleidane's Comm.* 400b, The horsemen were left..to defende and kepe the passage. **1672** R. MONTAGU in *Buccleuch MSS.* (Hist. MSS. Comm) I. 519 To help in keeping my corner against your enemies and mine. **1683** *Plymouth Col. Rec.* (1856) VI. 114 Keeping the dores and not opening them to the said John Irish when hee come. **1842** MACAULAY *Horatius* xxix, Now who will stand on either hand, And keep the bridge with me? **1892** *St. Nicholas Mag.* XIV. 541/2 They're not keeping our goal as they ought to.

c. *from* some injurious operation or accident.

1375 BARBOUR *Bruce* XVII. 177 Thai kepit that fra distroying. **1398** TREVISA *Barth. De P.R.* XVI. xciv. (MS. Bodl.) lf. 183/2 Salte..kepeþ and saueþ dede bodies fro rotinge. **1579** GOSSON *Sch. Abuse* (Arb.) 61 Keepe your sweete faces from scorching. **1596** SHAKS. *Tam. Shr.* III. ii. 59 To keepe him from stumbling. **1631** GOUGE *God's Arrows* III. §65. 304 They were wont..to annoint their rolles ..with a liquour..which kept them from rotting.

†**d.** *refl.* To defend oneself; to be on one's guard. *Obs.*

c **1175** *Lamb. Hom.* 59 To blecen..his nome and kepen us from hearm and scome. *c* **1375** *Cursor M.* 10071 (Laud) Was no man..Might kepe hym from that fend felle. *c* **1400** *Destr. Troy* 7860 We are folke full fele..Assemblit in this Cite oure seluyn to kepe. **1470-85** MALORY *Arthur* IX. xvii, Sir Tristram drewe oute his swerd, and said, sire Kehydius, kepe the. **1535** COVERDALE *Jer.* ix. 4 One must kepe him-self from another. **1634** W. TIRWHYT tr. *Balzac's Lett.* (vol. I.) 15, I keepe my selfe as carefully as though I were composed of christall.

†**15.** To be on one's guard against some action or occurrence; to take care, beware (that...).

a. *refl. Obs.*

c **1340** *Cursor M.* 8389 (Trin.), I haue me kept þat neuer oþer wiþ me siþen slept. **13..** *Gaw. & Gr. Knt.* 372 'Kepe þe, cosyn', quoth þe kyng, 'þat þou on kyrf sette'. **1483** CAXTON *Gold. Leg.* 179/1 Kepe yᵉ wel that thou telle thys vysyon to no man.

†**b.** *intr.* or with *obj. cl. Obs.*

c **1375** *Sc. Leg. Saints* iii. (*Andrew*) 216 Þe Iuge..dange hym in a dongeone depe, þat he na schapit bad to kepe [= bade to take care that he escaped not]. *c* **1386** CHAUCER *Prol.* 130 Wel koude she carie a morsel and wel kepe That no drope ne fille vp on hire brist. *c* **1400** MAUNDEV. (Roxb.) xxiii. 108 Before þe dure standez certayne lordes..for to kepe þat nane entre in at þe dure. *c* **1500** *Melusine* 112 Kepe wel ye borow nothing but that ye may yeld it ayen. **1526** TINDALE *Pathw. Script.* Wks. (Parker Soc.) I. 23 We tame the flesh therewith..and keep that the lusts choke not the word of God.

16. To take care of, look to the well-being of; to look after, watch over, tend, have charge of.

a. a person.

c **1250** *Gen. & Ex.* 2625 Ghe kepte it wel in fostre wune, Ghe knew it for hire owen sune. *a* **1300** *Cursor M.* 16761 Als for his moder Iohn hir keped, And in his ward hir toke. *c* **1350** *Will. Palerne* 66 Wiȝtliche wiþ þe child he went to his house, and bitok it to his wif tiȝtly to kepe. **1420** in *E.E. Wills* (1882) 54, I will þat þᵉ Nonne þat kepid me in my seknes haue ij nobles. **1513** MORE *Rich. III* (1883) 38 Mans law serueth the gardain to kepe the infant. The law of nature wyll the mother kepe her childe. **1599** SHAKS. *Hen. V*, II. i.

33 Cal'st thou mee Hoste .. I sweare I scorne the terme: nor shall my Nel keep Lodgers.

b. cattle or the like.

c 1250 *Gen. & Ex.* 2772 Moyses was numen .. for te loken hirdnesse fare; Riche men ðo kepten swilc ware. c 1350 *Will. Palerne* 8 þis cowherd comes .. to kepen is bestes Fast by-side þe borwȝ. c 1400 *Three Kings Cologne* 29 þe schepherdes of þat contrey .. be wonte to kepe her flok of schepe in þe nyȝt. 1526 TINDALE *Luke* xv. 15 A citesyn .. sent hym to the felde to kepe [1611 feed] his swyne. 1535 COVERDALE *1 Sam.* xvi. 11 There is yet one .. and beholde, he kepeth [so 1611 and *R.V.*] the shepe. 1600 SHAKS. *A.Y.L.* I. i. 40 Shall I keepe your hogs, and eat huskes with them? 1632 LITHGOW *Trav.* III. 93 Flockes of them feeding in the fields, and usually kept by children. 1697 DRYDEN *Virg. Georg.* IV. 567 This Neptune gave him, when he gave to keep His scaly Flocks. 1801 STRUTT *Sports & Past.* II. ii. 65 David, who kept his father's sheep.

c. a thing.

a 1300 *Cursor M.* 5292 þe lordshipe of al þis lond To reule & kepe is in myn hond. a 1325 *Maudelein* 1 in Horstm. *Altengl. Leg.* (1878) 163 Martha keped swiþe wel Hir londes. 1377 LANGL. *P. Pl.* B. XII. 115 *Archa dei* in þe olde lawe leuites it kepten. c 1386 CHAUCER *Doctor's T.* 85 A theef of venysoun, that hath forlaft .. his olde craft, Kan kepe a fforest best of any man. 1500–20 DUNBAR *Poems* lii. 10 Ȝour Hienes can nocht gett ane meter To keip ȝour wardrope. 1535 COVERDALE *Exod.* xxii. 7 Yf a man delyuer his neghboure money or vessels to kepe, and it be stollen from him out of his house [etc.]. 1585 T. WASHINGTON tr. *Nicholay's Voy.* I. xi. 13 b, The Caddy, which keepeth the town upon tribute under the king of Alger. 1712–14 POPE *Rape Lock* V. 115 There Hero's wits are kept in pond'rous vases. 1850 TENNYSON *In Mem.* xxiii, The shadow cloak'd from head to foot, Who keeps the keys of all the creeds.

d. *to keep wicket*: see WICKET 3. Also *absol.*, to act as wicket-keeper.

1862 *Baily's Monthly Mag.* Aug. 85 The Surrey people .. selecting .. a John Walker to keep. 1920 P. F. WARNER *Cricket Reminisc.* 161 Lockyer 'kept' for the Players on and off between 1854 and 1866. 1931 *N. & Q.* 14 Feb. 121/2 Alfred [Lyttelton], of course, 'kept' for England. 1959 *Times* 29 June 11/4 One of Somerset's clerical wearers of the gloves .. who, after 'keeping' to W. G. .. recorded that not a single ball had passed the bat.

17. To maintain or preserve in proper order.

1382 WYCLIF *Ecclus.* xliii. 4 Kepende the furneys in the werkis of brennyng. c 1386 CHAUCER *Merch. T.* 138 Wel may the sike man biwaille and wepe Ther as ther nys no wyf the hous to kepe. 1463 *Bury Wills* (Camden) 28 Yeerly to the Sexteyn .. viijs. to kepe the clokke. 1667 MILTON *P.L.* VIII. 320 This Paradise I give thee, count it thine To Till and keep. 1699 LISTER *Journ. Paris* 188 This is the only House in Paris I saw kept .. with the most exact cleanliness and neatness, Gardens and all. 1827 STEUART *Planter's G.* (1828) 352 This space is kept with the scythe. 1862 *Temple Bar Mag.* IV. 259 His rooms were as neatly kept as those of a woman.

18. To maintain continuously in proper form and order (a record, diary, journal, accounts of money received and paid, etc.). *to keep books*, to make the requisite entries in a merchant's books so that these shall always represent the state of his commercial relations: see BOOK-KEEPING.

1552 *Ordre Hosp. St. Barthol.* B v b (Treasurer) Ye shal also kepe one seueral accompte betweene the Renter & you. *Ibid.* C j (Almoner) Keping one entier and perfecte Inuentarie .. in a boke. 1560 DAUS tr. *Sleidane's Comm.* 175 Notaryes and scribes .. whyche shoulde penne, and kepe althynges diligentelye. 1604 E. G[RIMSTONE] *D'Acosta's Hist. Indies* IV. vii. 226 The first Registers of Entries are not so exactly kept as at this day. 1633 MASSINGER *Guardian* I. i, A hopeful youth, to keep A merchant's book. 1751 LABELYE *Westm. Br.* 66 The keeping proper Accounts of these was .. allotted to Richard Graham. 1803 *Pic Nic* No. 14 (1806) II. 251 He had kept a diary of all his transactions. 1869 W. LONGMAN *Hist. Edw. III*, I. xiv. 262 No record was kept of the losses of the English. 1891 *Speaker* 2 May 531/1 The useful habit of keeping commonplace books.

19. To provide for the sustenance of; to provide with food and clothing and other requisites of life; to maintain, support. Also *refl.*

1377 LANGL. *P. Pl.* B. Prol. 76 Thus þey geuen here golde glotones to kepe [A. Prol. 73 Glotonye to helpen]. c 1475 *Rauf Coilȝear* 960 Than Schir Rauf gat rewaird to keip his Knichtheid. 15.. in *Dunbar's Poems* (S.T.S.) 306/44 Spend pairt of the gude thow wan, And keip the ay with honestie. 1616 BEAUM. & FL. *Scornf. Lady* III. ii, What shall become of my poor family? They .. must keep themselves. 1668 R. STEELE *Husbandman's Calling* ii. (1672) 16 A husbandman is a man .. that makes the ground that bred him keep him. 1858 *Jrnl. R. Agric. Soc.* XIX. I. 207 The land would barely keep the cows. 1889 MRS. LYNN LINTON *Thro' the Long Night* I. I. viii. 131 Should he ever be able to keep a wife? *Mod.* He cannot keep himself yet, but is dependent on his parents.

b. Const. *in* (the particular item provided).

1888 MISS TYTLER *Blackhall Ghosts* II. xix. 117 Jem has to keep us in everything, in clothes as well as the rest. 1890 MRS. H. WOOD *House of Halliwell* I. xii. 323 He kept the younger ladies in gloves.

20. To maintain, employ, entertain in one's service, or for one's use or enjoyment: in reference to animals or things, there is a mingling of the sense of possession.

a 1548 HALL *Chron., Edw. IV*, 233 b, [He] caused .iij. C. men of armes to be kept secretly in their capitaynes houses. 1598 SHAKS. *Merry W.* I. i. 284, I keepe but three Men, and a Boy yet, till my Mother be dead. 1607 —— *Timon* IV. iii. 200 Because thou dost not keepe a dogge. 1637 *Star Chamb. Decree* §28 No Master-Founder .. shall keepe aboue two Apprentices. 1789 BRAND *Hist. Newcastle* II. 237 November 24th 1697, there is an order of this society forbidding the apprentices .. to keep horses, dogs for hunting, or fighting cocks. 1833 H. MARTINEAU *Briery Creek* iii. 63 This morning, you thought of no such thing as keeping pigs. 1853 LYNCH *Self-Improv.* v. 104 A man .. who 'keeps a gig', but cannot 'afford to keep a conscience'. 1860 *Temple Bar Mag.* I. 42 Rich men kept a newsmonger, as they kept a valet. 1893 *National Observer* 6 May 619/2 He need not himself keep chickens.

b. *to keep a woman* as mistress: *to keep a newspaper* as a hired organ: cf. KEPT 1.

1560 DAUS tr. *Sleidane's Comm.* 49 Others kept harlots, and lived dishonestly. 1606 SHAKS. *Tr. & Cr.* V. i. 104 They say, he keepes a Troyan Drab. 1660 F. BROOKE tr. *Le Blanc's Trav.* 36 Giving a box on the ear to a Lord that kept her for a time. 1712 STEELE *Spect.* No. 276 ¶3, I am kept by an old Batchelor. 1728 YOUNG *Love Fame* III. 196 Philander .. In secret loves his wife, but keeps her maid. 1895 MISS DOWIE *Gallia* 114 It was habitual for women to disapprove of a man who kept a mistress.

21. To have habitually in stock or on sale.

1706 *Wooden World Dissected* (1708) 57 The worser Liquor he keeps, the more he brews his own Profit. 1851 HAWTHORNE *Ho. Sev. Gables* iii. 41 [She] gave her hot customer to understand that she did not keep the article.

†**22.** *refl.* To conduct or comport oneself, behave. *Obs.*

1362 LANGL. *P. Pl.* A. I. 92 Kynges and knihtes scholde kepen hem bi Reson. c 1386 CHAUCER *Doctor's T.* 106 This mayde .. So kept hir self, hir neded no maistresse. c 1400 *Lanfranc's Cirurg.* 272, I tauȝte him how he schulde kepe him-silf, and how he schulde diete him-silf.

23. To preserve in being or operation; to maintain, retain, or continue to hold (a quality, state, or condition) or to practise or exercise (a habit or action). Cf. *keep up* in 57 d, e.

Hence in many phrases, as *to keep silence*; *to keep affinity, companionship, company, consort, converse, correspondence*; *to keep compass, measure, pace, step, time, tune, wing* (with); *to keep guard, a look out, sentinel, ward, watch*: for which when the sense is specialized, see the sbs.

c 1315 SHOREHAM 11 The prestes so thries duppeth .. gode ȝeme kepeth The ned. c 1375 *Sc. Leg. Saints* xxvii. (*Machor*) 343 He kepyt ay his innocens. c 1380 WYCLIF *Wks.* (1880) 21 So þat þei kepen pacience and charite. c 1400 *Apol. Loll.* 42 Crist kepid ai þat state. c 1470 HENRY *Wallace* XI. 316 That king till him kepit kyndnes and luff. a 1480 in *Babees Bk.* 20/52 Honoure and curtesy loke þou kepe. 1500–20 DUNBAR *Poems* xxix. 18 Than mon I keip ane grauetie. 1530 PALSGR. 596/2, I kepe abstynence, I forbeare meate and drinke. a 1548 HALL *Chron., Hen. VIII*, 261 b, Charitie is not kept amongest you. 1552 HULOET, To kepe bawdrye or whoredome. 1568 GRAFTON *Chron.* II. 32 Now almost no countrie kepeth either weight or measure one with the other to the great hurt of the Realme. 1597 SHAKS. *1 Hen. IV*, V. iv. 65 Two Starres keepe not their motion in one Sphere. 1603 —— *Meas. for M.* II. i. 5 Let it keepe one shape. 1632 B. JONSON *Magn. Lady* II. i. Wks. (Rtldg.) 447/1 You, that will keep consort with such fidlers. 1651 WITTIE tr. *Primrose's Pop. Err.* III. ii. 138 The Ancients .. did keep a fequent use of baths and frictions. 1698 FRYER *Acc. E. India & P.* 331 To make them [Lamb-skins] keep their Curl. a 1715 BURNET *Own Time* (1823) II. III. 51 To keep no farther correspondence with duke Hamilton. 1750 GRAY *Elegy* xix, Along the cool sequester'd vale of life They kept the noiseless tenour of their way. 1818 SHELLEY *Rev. Islam* II. xviii, Did Laon and his friend .. a lofty converse keep. 1822 —— *Hellas* 18 Who now keep That calm sleep. 1890 F. M. CRAWFORD *Cigarette-maker's Rom.* I. iii. 99 The Count himself kept his composure admirably.

24. With complement: To preserve, maintain, retain, or cause to continue, in some specified condition, state, place, position, action, or course.

The complement may be an adj., sb., pple., adv., or prep. phrase, e.g. *to keep alive, clean, close, dark, dry, fast, holy, open, secret, still, sweet, warm*; *to keep a prisoner, a secret*; *to keep going, shut*; *to keep at arm's length, at bay, at it, at work, in countenance, in readiness, in repair, in suspense, in touch, out of mischief, to time*, etc. For these in specialized senses, and for phrases, such as *to keep the ball rolling, the pot boiling, one's hair on, one's eye upon, one's eyes about one, one's head above water*, etc., see the adjs. or sbs.

c 1340 HAMPOLE *Prose Tr.* 8 Scho [the bee] kepes clene and bryghte hire winges. 1377 LANGL. *P. Pl.* B. v. 623 þe dore closed Kayed and cliketted to kepe þe with-outen. 1414 BRAMPTON *Penit. Ps.* xix. (Percy Soc.) 8 My synne[s], that I in schryfte schulde schewe, I kepe hem clos for schame or fere. a 1500 in *Babees Bk.* 19/42 Yt kepys hym out offe synne & blame. *Ibid.* 21/66 Hande, fote, & fynger kepe þou styll. 1500–20 DUNBAR *Poems* xlviii. 70 Scho bad eik Juno .. That scho the hevin suld keip amene and dry. 1585 T. WASHINGTON tr. *Nicholay's Voy.* III. xxii. 112 To keepe the Arabians .. in greater sobriety. *Ibid.* IV. xv. 130 They .. kept the portes and passages so shutte, that they kept away the corne. 1593 SHAKS. *Rich. II*, III. ii. 28 That Power that made you King Hath power to keepe you King. 1607 TOPSELL *Four-f. Beasts* (1658) 119 It is necessary that their kennel be kept sweet and dry. 1657 R. LIGON *Barbadoes* (1673) 102 To keep it continually in the shade. 1698 FRYER *Acc. E. India & P.* 125, I kept the Coolies to their Watch. 1712 STEELE *Spect.* No. 263 ¶4 It is [thus] .. that Hatreds are kept alive. *Ibid.* No. 264 ¶2 While he could keep his Poverty a Secret. 1774 GOLDSM. *Nat. Hist.* (1776) V. 126 He is .. still kept fast by a string. 1840 *Jrnl. R. Agric. Soc.* I. III. 225 The ploughmen could scarcely keep their ploughs in the ground. 1845 FORD *Handbk. Spain* I. 66 Keep the door shut and the devil passes by. 1854 DICKENS *Hard Times* I. xiv, In the daytime old Bounderby has been keeping me at it rather. 1883 G. M. FENN *Middy & Ensign* xxxi, I'll keep him to his promise. 1890 T. F. TOUT *Hist. Eng. fr.* 1689. 48 He kept the merchants and tradesmen Whigs by his sound commercial .. measures. 1891 *Temple Bar Mag.* Feb. 281 There was the steam-kettle to keep on the boil. 1892 *National Observer* 17 Dec. 100/1 It promises help .. to keep him in funds when he is out on strike.

b. *refl.* To preserve or maintain oneself, or continue, in such condition, etc. (Hence the intrans. use in 39.)

1362 LANGL. *P. Pl.* A. I. 169 Curatours þat schulden kepe hem clene of heore bodies. a 1380 *Virg. Antioch* 137 in Horstm. *Altengl. Leg.* (1878) 27, I may me kepe chast eueridel. c 1400 *Destr. Troy* 10513 Kepis you in couer, cleane out of sight! c 1430 *Syr Gener.* (Roxb.) 2835 This traitour kept him close that night. c 1489 CAXTON *Sonnes of Aymon* xxiv. 512 Baron, kepe you by reynawde. a 1533 LD. BERNERS *Huon* xxi. 64 Yf ye can kepe your selfe without spekynge to hym, ye maye than well skape. 1549 (Mar.) *Bk. Com. Prayer, Matrimony*, Wilt thou .. forsaking all other kepe thee only to her, so long as you both shall liue? 1585 T. WASHINGTON tr. *Nicholay's Voy.* I. iv. 3 b, Theyr watches keepe themselves in an ambush neare unto a wood. 1788 W. BLANE *Hunt. Excurs.* 15 The Prince, by laying hold of the Howdah, kept himself in his seat. 1879 BROWNING *Martin Relph* 32 The many and loyal should keep themselves unmixed with the few perverse.

*** *To detain or hold in custody, restraint, concealment, etc.; to prevent from escaping or being taken from one.*

25. To hold as a captive or prisoner; to hold in custody or in restraint of personal liberty; to prevent from escaping.

c 1330 R. BRUNNE *Chron.* (1810) 219 þat kept him in prisoun, Edward did him calle. 1375 BARBOUR *Bruce* XVIII. 512 He .. bad haf him avay in hy, And luk he kepit war stratly. 1382 WYCLIF *Acts* xvi. 23 Thei senten hem into prisoun, commaundinge to the kepere that he diligentli schulde kepe hem. c 1400 *Destr. Troy* 12084 þat commly be keppet, ne in cloese haldyn. 1526 TINDALE *Acts* xxviii. 16 Paul was suffered to dwell alone with wone soudier that kept hym. 1585 T. WASHINGTON tr. *Nicholay's Voy.* I. vii. 6 They kept me as prisoner. 1892 *Law Times* XCIII. 414/2 He did not think that the defendant ought to be kept in prison any longer.

26. To retain in a place or position by moral constraint; to restrain from going away; to cause or induce to remain; to detain. Also *fig.*

1653 MIDDLETON & ROWLEY *Changeling* V. iii, Keep life in him for further tortures. 1782 COWPER *Progr. Err.* 416 A dunce that has been kept at home. 1801 PITT in *G. Rose's Diaries* (1860) I. 291, I have been kept till this instant. 1877 MISS YONGE *Cameos* Ser. III. xxix. 291 Colet would fain have kept Erasmus to lecture at Oxford. 1885 E. F. BYRRNE *Entangled* II. xviii. 29 Don't let me keep you. 1890 CLARK RUSSELL *Ocean Trag.* I. ii. 31 There was nothing to keep me in England.

27. To hold back, prevent, withhold; to restrain, control. Const. *from* (*off, out of*).

c 1340 *Cursor M.* 2893 (Fairf.) Ihesu criste ȝou kepe fra syn. c 1460 *Urbanitas* 74 in *Babees Bk.* 15 In chambur among ladyes bryȝth Kepe thy tonge and spende thy syȝth. 1539 BIBLE (Great) *Ps.* xxxiv. 13 Kepe thy tonge from euell. 1560 DAUS tr. *Sleidane's Comm.* 355 Yea they .. have not kept their handes also from yonge babes and children. 1591 SHAKS. *1 Hen. VI*, I. i. 160 The Earle of Salisbury .. hardly keepes his men from mutinie. 1642 MILTON *Apol. Smect.* viii, How hard is it when a man meets with a Foole to keepe his tongue from folly! 1650 WELDON *Crt. Jas. I* 139 The Bishops might have done better to have kept their voyces. 1729 BUTLER *Serm. Balaam* Wks. 1874 II. 87 Those partial regards to his duty .. might keep him from perfect despair. 1858 *Jrnl. R. Agric. Soc.* XIX. I. 184 A cold, dry spring may keep the seed from germinating.

b. *refl.* To restrain oneself, refrain, hold back; to abstain. (Hence *intr.*, sense 43.)

1340 HAMPOLE *Pr. Consc.* 954 Gude it es þat a man him kepe Fra worldisshe luf and vany worshepe. c 1460 in *Babees Bk.* 13/19 Fro spettyng & snetyng kepe þe also. 1483 CAXTON *G. de la Tour* D v b, This is a good ensample to awarraunt and kepe hymself of fals beholdynge. c 1500 *Melusine* xxxvi. 295 Hys brother coude not kepe hym, but he asked after Melusyne. a 1533 LD. BERNERS *Huon* lix. 205 He .. coude not a kept hym selfe fro lawghynge. 1601 SHAKS. *Two Gent.* IV. iv. 11 'Tis a foule thing, when a cur cannot keepe himselfe in all companies. 1892 *Black & White* 26 Nov. 610/1, I shall not be able to keep myself from strangling her.

28. To withold from present use, to reserve; to lay up, store up. *refl.* To reserve oneself.

c 1340 *Cursor M.* 970 (Fairf.) Of alkyn frute þat ys þine Kepe me þe teynde for þat ys myne. c 1400 MAUNDEV. (1839) v. 52 The Gerneres .. to kepe the greynes for the perile of the dere ȝeres. 1535 COVERDALE *2 Esdras* ix. 21, I .. haue kepte me a wynebery of the grapes. 1579 GOSSON *Sch. Abuse* (Arb.) 17 Philip .. exhorted his friends to keepe their stomackes for the seconde course. 1632 LITHGOW *Trav.* VI. 258 The water of Jordan .. the longer it is kept, it is the more fresher. 1822 SHELLEY *Hellas* 879 The Anarchs .. keep A throne for thee. 1868 FREEMAN *Norm. Conq.* II. x. 428 The .. Chronicler .. seems rather to keep himself for great occasions. 1875 *Ibid.* (ed. 2) III. xii. 77, I have purposely kept that question for this stage of my history.

29. Actively to hold in possession; to retain in one's power or control; to continue to have, hold, or possess. Also *absol.* (The opposite of *to lose*: now a leading sense.)

c 1400 MAUNDEV. xxiii. (1839) 252 Thei con wel wynnen lond of Straungeres, but thei con not kepen it. c 1460 FORTESCUE *Abs. & Lim. Mon.* vi. (1885) 121 It is power to mowe haue and kepe to hym self. c 1470 HENRY *Wallace* IX. 1935 Off ryches he kepyt no propyr thing; Gaiff as he wan. 1559 *Mirr. Mag., Dk. Suffolk* viii, To get and kepe not is but losse of payne. 1596 SHAKS. *1 Hen. IV*, I. iii. 213 Ile keepe them all. By heauen, he shall not haue a Scot of them. 1662 STILLINGFL. *Orig. Sacr.* III. iii. §8 With what care they are got, with what fear they are kept, and with what certainty they must be lost. a 1715 BURNET *Own Time* (1823) I. II. 159 The great art of keeping him long was, the being easy, and the making everything easy to him. 1803 *Pic Nic* No. 8 (1806) II. 41 These poets now keep but a feeble hold of the stage. 1861 *Temple Bar Mag.* III. 336 The variety keeps the children's attention. 1890 *Lippincott's Mag.* May 632 His slim forefinger between its leaves to keep the place. *Mod.* The difficulty now is not to *make* money, but *keep* it; you make it and *lose* it.

†**b.** *to keep one's own* = to hold one's own (HOLD *v.* 31). *keep your luff, offing, wind*: see the sbs.

1627 Capt. Smith *Seaman's Gram.* ix. 39 If you would.. keepe your owne, that is, not.. fall to lee-ward.

c. *fig.* in phrases, as *to keep one's temper* (i.e. not to *lose* it): see the sbs.

†**d.** *ellipt.* To retain in the memory, remember.

1573 Baret *Alv.* I 27 We keepe those thinges most surely, that we learne in youth. **1612** Brinsley *Lud. Lit.* 141 Thus they shall keepe their Authours, which they haue learned.

e. Colloq. phr. *you* (etc.) *can keep* (something): it arouses no desire, envy, or interest in me; I am not interested in (it), I do not like (it).

1956 J. Popplewell in *Plays of Year 1955* XIII. 335 *Robert.* My hobby's writing plays. *Tom.* You can keep it. **1962** M. Drabble *Summer Bird-Cage* i. 8 The reviews.. talk about his delicate perception and keen wit, but for me they can keep them. **1967** R. Wilkinson *Pressure Men* viii. 72, I felt better here. They could keep London. **1971** *Guardian* 11 Dec. 5/1 They're a miserable lot of sods. If that is an example of the spirit of the people of Windsor, they can keep it. **1973** *Ibid.* 12 Apr. 13/3 It makes me a bit sick actually and they can keep their mag as far as I am concerned.

30. To withhold (*from*): implying exertion or effort to prevent a thing from going or getting to another.

c **1461** *Paston Lett.* II. 73 It is a comon proverbe, 'A man xuld kepe fro the blynde and gevyt to is kyn'. **1568** Grafton *Chron.* II. 282 Mine adversary, who kepeth wrongfully from me mine heritage. **1585** T. Washington tr. *Nicholay's Voy.* iv. xvi. 131 Where they would not receive his salvation, the same for ever shalbe kept from them. **1667** Milton *P.L.* ix. 746 Great are thy Vertues, doubtless, best of Fruits, Though kept from Man.

31. To hide, conceal; not to divulge. Chiefly in phr., as *to keep* counsel, *a* secret: see the sbs.

1382 Wyclif *Isa.* xlviii. 6 Thingus.. kept ben that thou knowist not. *c* **1400** *Rom. Rose* 2858 A felowe that can welle concele, And kepe thi counselle, and welle hele. **1560** Daus tr. *Sleidane's Comm.* 321 b, To the promotours they promise a reward and to kepe their counsel. **1781** D. Williams tr. *Voltaire's Dram. Wks.* II. 233 Take the money and keep the secret. **1847** Marryat *Childr. N. Forest* xvii, 'You must keep our secret, Oswald'. **1859** Thackeray *Virgin.* xxi, There is no keeping any thing from you. **1888** G. Gissing *Life's Morn.* II. xiv. 227 For a week he kept his counsel, and behaved as if nothing unusual had happened.

32. To continue to follow (a way, path, course, etc.), so as not to lose it or get out of it.

c **1425** Lydg. *Assembly of Gods* 256 Thowgh ye wepe yet shal ye before me Ay kepe your course. **1553** S. Cabot in Hakluyt *Voy.* (1589) 259 All courses in Navigation to be set and kept by the aduice of the Captain. **1595** Shaks. *John* ii. i. 339 Vnlesse thou let his siluer Water, keepe A peacefull progresse to the Ocean. **1598** —— *Merry W.* iii. ii. 1 Nay keepe your way.. you were wont to be a follower, but now you are a Leader. **1632** Lithgow *Trav.* vi. 258 The Friers and Souldiers removed; keeping their course towards Jericho. **1719** De Foe *Crusoe* ii. ix, We kept no path. **1870** E. Peacock *Ralf Skirl.* II. 98 Taking care to keep the middle of the road. **1892** *Field* 21 May 777/1 How the driver kept the track is a marvel.

33. To stay or remain in, on, or at (a place); not to leave; esp. in *to keep one's bed, one's room* (as in sickness); *to keep the house*. Cf. *keep to*, 44 b.

1413 *Pilgr. Sowle* (Caxton) i. xxii. (1859) 25 Thou kepyst now thy bed. Thyne ydlenes and slouthe hath this y bred. *c* **1430** *Syr Gener.* (Roxb.) 1526 His doghtre Clarionas She kept the chambre, as Reason was. **1523** Ld. Berners *Froiss.* I. xlix. 69 These engyns dyd cast night and day great stones.. so that they within were fayne to kepe vautes and sellars. **1534–1828** [see bed *sb.* 6 c]. **1542–1864** [see house *sb.* 17 d]. **1575** Laneham *Let.* (1871) 33 The weather being hot, her highnes kept the Castl for coolness. **1647** Trapp *Comm., Titus* II. 343 The Aegyptian women ware no shoes, that they might the better keep home. **1667** Sir E. Lyttelton in *Hatton Corr.* (Camden) 51, I have kept my chamber ever since last Tuesday. **1796** Jane Austen *Pride & Prej.* xiii, My poor mother is really ill, and keeps her room. **1885** Emily Lawless *Millionaire's Cousin* iv. 76 Am I bound to keep my own side of the partition?

b. To stay or retain one's place in or on, against opposition; as *to keep the deck, the saddle, the field, the stage, one's seat, one's ground*.

1599 Shaks. *Hen. V*, iv. vi. 2 But all's not done, yet keepe the French the field. **1632** Lithgow *Trav.* iii. 99 The tempest continuing (our Boate not being able to keepe the Seas) we were constrained to seeke into a Creeke. **1748** *Anson's Voy.* iii. i. 298 Only sixteen men, and eleven boys were capable of keeping the deck. **1823** *Blackw. Mag.* XIV. 555 Not a single tragedy of Beaumont and Fletcher's has been able to keep the stage. **1835** Thirlwall *Greece* I. iv. 113 It [the story] kept its ground in spite of the interest.. in distorting or suppressing it. **1849** Macaulay *Hist. Eng.* v. I. 579 The wonder is.. that they were able to keep their seats. **1890** *Blackw. Mag.* CXLVIII. 435/2 A first-class boat, capable of keeping the sea all the year round.

**** *To carry on, conduct, hold.*

34. To carry on, conduct, as presiding officer or a chief actor (an assembly, court, fair, market, etc.); = hold *v.* 8.

1432–50 tr. *Higden* (Rolls) V. 119 [Silvester] whiche kepede the firste grete cownsayle of Nicene. *c* **1489** Caxton *Sonnes of Aymon* 202 He wolde kepe parlyamente wyth them. **1535** Coverdale *2 Macc.* iv. 43 Of these matters therfore there was kepte a courte agaynst Menelaus. **1546** in *Eng. Gilds* (1870) 222 In the same Towne there ys a merkett, wekely kepte. **1585** T. Washington tr. *Nicholay's Voy.* iii. xvii. 102 b, There.. they kept a generall chapter or assembly. **1634** W. Wood *New Eng. Prosp.* (1865) 42 This Towne [Boston].. being the Center of the Plantations where the monthly Courts are kept. **1752** Fielding *Amelia* xi. iii, His wife soon afterwards began to keep an assembly, or, in the fashionable phrase, to be 'at home' once a week. **1877** Miss Yonge *Cameos* Ser. iii. xxi. 196 Henry was keeping court at Lincoln, where he meant to spend Easter.

35. To carry on and manage, to conduct as one's own (an establishment or business, a school, shop, etc.). *to keep house*: see house *sb.* 17 a, b.

1513 More in Grafton *Chron.* (1568) II. 761 Edward the Noble Prince.. kept his house at Ludlow in Wales. **1601** Shaks. *Twel. N.* iii. ii. 81 Like a Pedant that keepes a Schoole i' th Church. **1660** F. Brooke tr. *Le Blanc's Trav.* 29 He kept an Inn common to all passengers. **1698** Fryer *Acc. E. India & P.* 194 Barbers.. seldom keep Shop, but go about the City with a checquered Apron over their Shulders. **1711** Steele *Spect.* No. 155 ¶2, I keep a Coffee-house. **1847** *Knickerbocker* XXX. 511 A girl whose education does not qualify her for 'keeping school'. **1849** E. Chamberlain *Indiana Gazetteer* (ed. 3) 196 There are in the County.. school houses in which schools are kept, a portion of the year, in most of the school districts. **1867** 'T. Lackland' *Homespun* ii. 264 Mr. John Porringer.. 'kept' this school, and was in the way of keeping it so long as he lived and liked. **1877** W. O. Russell *Crimes & Misdem.* ii. xxviii. 427 The keeping a bawdy-house is a common nuisance. **1890** *Harper's Mag.* Oct. 747/2 They came here and kept lodgings.

36. To carry on, maintain; to continue to make, cause, or do (an action, war, disturbance, or the like). Cf. *keep up*, 57 f.

c **1425** Lydg. *Assembly of Gods* 1825 In man shall thow fynde that werre kept dayly. **1560** Daus tr. *Sleidane's Comm.* 208 b, Warre was to be kepte upon hys frontiers. **1568–1807** [see coil *sb.*[2] 4]. **1590** Shaks. *Com. Err.* iii. i. 61 Who is that at the doore y^t keepes all this noise? **1601** —— *Twel. N.* ii. iii. 76 What a catterwalling doe you keepe heere? **1602** Marston *Antonio's Rev.* iii. iv, What an idle prate thou keep'st, good nurse; goe sleepe. **1665** Glanvill *Def. Vain Dogm.* 41 'Tis strange that the Ancients should keep such ado about an easie Probleme. *a* **1784** Johnson in *Mrs. Piozzi's Anecd.* 34 The nonsense you now keep such a stir about. **1818** Shelley *Rev. Islam* vi. vii, Ships from Propontes keep A killing rain of fire.

III. Intransitive uses.

* *Arising from ellipsis of reflexive pronoun.*

37. To reside, dwell, live, lodge. (Freq. in literary use from *c* 1580 to 1650; now only *colloq.*, esp. at Cambridge University and in U.S.)

[**1402–3** *Durham Acc. Rolls* (Surtees) 217 Camera ubi pueri custodiunt.]

c **1400** Maundev. (Roxb.) xxv. 117 Þis emperour.. hase many men kepand at his courte. **1401** *Pol. Poems* (Rolls) II. 65 Sich as ben gaderid in coventis.. the whiche for worldly combraunce kepen in cloistris. **1504** *Bury Wills* (Camden) 102, I wyll y^t he or they shall keep at Cambryge at scoole. **1601** Holland *Pliny* I. 127 Among the mountaines of this tract, the Pygmæans, by report do keepe. **1633** P. Fletcher *Purple Isl.* v. xxv, Here stands the palace of the noblest sense; Here Visus keeps. **1719** in Willis & Clark *Cambridge* (1886) II. 214 In ye Room where Mr Maynard keeps there was acted.. a Pastoral. **1775** Abigail Adams in *J. Adams' Fam. Lett.* (1876) 128, I have.. been upon a visit to Mrs. Morgan, who keeps at Major Mifflin's. **1825** J. Neal *Bro. Jonathan* I. 255 A little 'Virginny gal' who was 'keepin' there. **1859** [J. Payn] *Foster Brothers* xvii. 314 Where does Mr. Hollis 'keep'? inquired he of his bedmaker. **1883** *Cambridge Staircase* viii. 137 Holtmore.. keeps out of college. **1889** *Boston* (Mass.) *Jrnl.* 8 July 3/3 Just where Mrs. Stevens kept in Boston is unknown to history.

38. a. To remain or stay for the time (in a particular place or spot).

1560 Daus tr. *Sleidane's Comm.* 214 The rest.. were driven to kepe in caves and sellars under the earth. **1597** Morley *Introd. Mus.* Pref., Being compelled to keepe at home. **1606** Shaks. *Ant. & Cl.* iii. vii. 75 Marcus Octauius.. and Celius are for Sea: But we keepe whole by Land. **1719** De Foe *Crusoe* i. iv, We had kept on board. *Ibid.* xvi, I kept.. within doors. **1863** Geo. Elliot *Romola* xxxv. He suggested that she should keep in her own room. **1890** Clark Russell *Ocean Trag.* III. xxx. 136, I told him to keep where he was. **1891** F. W. Robinson *Her Love & His Life* III. vi. ii. 112 The wind kept in the proper quarter.

b. Of a school: to be held. *U.S.*

1845 *Knickerbocker* XXVI. 277 One afternoon, when 'school didn't keep', some one got into the house. **1867** 'T. Lackland' *Homespun* i. 123 The District School has not 'kept' since the week began. **1908** M. E. Freeman *Shoulders of Atlas* 68 School ain't going to keep today.

39. To remain or continue in a specified condition, state, position, etc.

a. With adverbial or prepositional phrases: see also branch IV.

1598 Shaks. *Merry W.* iii. iii. 89 Keepe in that minde, Ile deserue it. **1660** F. Brooke tr. *Le Blanc's Trav.* 93 You must recede and keep at distance. **1670–98** Lassels *Voy. Italy* II. 234 We strangers.. must keep out of their way, and stand a loof off. **1697** Dryden *Æneid* ii. 986 Creusa kept behind. **1705** Bosman *Guinea* 114 If they have not hit the Buffel they sit still, and keep out of Danger. **1805** Nelson 20 Oct. in Nicolas *Disp.* (1846) VII. 136 To keep.. in sight of the Enemy in the night. **1823** *Douglas, or, Otterburn* II. viii. 102 Mervine kept by the side of his friend. **1883** Fenn *Middy & Ensign* xxviii. 171 The men kept in excellent health. **1890** T. F. Tout *Hist. Eng. fr. 1689*, viii. iv. 48 He kept in touch with public opinion.

b. with adj. (or equivalent substantive).

1590 Shaks. *Com. Err.* ii. i. 26 This seruitude makes you to keepe vnwed. *c* **1600** *Acc.-Bk. W. Wray* in *Antiquary* XXXII. 80 This.. will keep but one yeare good. **1699** Dampier *Voy.* II. iii. iv. 47 When these hot Winds come the better sort of People.. keep close. **1814** Doyle in W. J. Fitz-Patrick *Life* (1880) I. 66 We were constantly making efforts to keep clear of them. **1825** *New Monthly Mag.* XV. 406 It will keep sweet a very long time. **1870** Lowell *Stud. Wind.* 120 It is the part of a critic to keep cool under whatever circumstances. **1883** Fenn *Middy & Ensign* xiv. 78 We want to keep friends.

40. To continue, persevere, go on (in a specified course or action).

a **1548** Hall *Chron., Edw. IV* 211 b, The Dukes messengers.. durst not kepe on their iorney. **1568** Grafton *Chron.* II. 91 He had such comfort of the king, as he kept on his purpose. **1593** Shaks. *Rich. II*, v. ii. 10 The Duke.. With slow, but stately pace, kept on his course. **1709** Steele *Tatler* No. 48 ¶4 We kept on our Way after him till we came to Exchange-Alley. **1857** B. Taylor *North. Trav.* 48 We kept down the left bank of the river for a little distance. **1889** W. Westall *Birch Dene* III. ii. 41 Turn to the left and keep straight on. **1891** H. S. Merriman *Pris. & Capt.* III. xiv. 235 After passing Spitzbergen they would keep to the north.

b. With pres. pple. as complement.

1794 Gifford *Baviad* (1800) 27 *note*, Some contemptible vulgarity, such as 'That's your sort!'.. 'What's to pay?' 'Keep moving', etc. **1806–7** J. Beresford *Miseries Hum. Life* (1826) vi. *Miseries Stage Coaches* iv, The Monster.. keeps braying away. **1858** Hawthorne *Fr. & It. Jrnls.* I. 124 Niagara.. keeps pouring on forever and ever. **1890** T. F. Tout *Hist. Eng. fr. 1689*, 134 He kept changing his plans. **1892** *Temple Bar Mag.* Feb. 198 She kept tumbling off her horse.

41. To remain in good condition; to last without spoiling. Also *fig.* to admit of being reserved for another occasion.

a **1586** Sidney *Arcadia* (1598) 76 Doth beauties keepe which never sunne can burne Nor stormes do turne! **1626** Bacon *Sylva* §627 Grapes.. it is reported.. will keep better in a vessel half full of wine, so that the grapes touch not the wine. **1705** *Lett.* in Chr. Wordsworth *Scholæ Academ.* (1877) 291 When he is to be buried I can't tell, but they say he can't keep long. **1719** De Foe *Crusoe* i. xii, I had no hops to make it keep. **1836** Gen. P. Thompson *Exerc.* (1842) IV. 106, I will defer any observations.. till my next. And there was nothing but what will keep. **1847** Marryat *Childr. N. Forest* v, He brought home more venison than would keep in the hot weather. **1889** Doyle *Micah Clarke* xi. 92 Your story, however, can keep.

** *With prepositions in specialized senses.*

(Chiefly from 38, 39, 40.)

42. keep at ——. To work persistently at; to continue to occupy oneself with. Also *to keep at it*: see at *prep.* 16 b.

1825 *New Monthly Mag.* XVI. 490 He should have kept at the law, he would have done for that. **1846** *Jrnl. R. Agric. Soc.* VII. i. 130 By keeping at it all day he is able to get over nearly 2 acres. **1890** *Pictorial World* 9 Oct. 445/3 Who could keep at work on a morning like this? **1891** *St. Nicholas Mag.* 261 Still they keep at it, early and late.

b. Hence humorous *nonce-compounds.*

1882 *Three in Norway* v. 38 In a nice keep-at-it-all-day-if-you-like kind of manner. **1895** *Proc. 14th Conv. Amer. Instruct. Deaf* p. lxix, In school, and out of school,.. at work or play; in short, by everlasting keep-at-it-iveness.

43. keep from ——. To abstain from; to remain absent or away from.

1513 More in Grafton *Chron.* (1568) II. 767 The prosperitie whereof.. standeth.. in keeping from enemies and evill dyet. *c* **1586** C'tess Pembroke *Ps.* lxxiv. x, What is the cause.. That thy right hand far from us keepes? **1590** Shaks. *Com. Err.* iii. i. 18 You would keepe from my heeles, and beware of an asse. **1727** Gay *Beggar's Op.* i. viii, I shall soon know if you are married by Macheath's keeping from our house.

b. To restrain or contain oneself *from.*

1877 Miss Yonge *Cameos* Ser. iii. xiv. 125 Nor was Louis able to keep from turning pale. **1889** Doyle *Micah Clarke* ii. 20 We could not keep from laughter. **1890** *Lippincott's Mag.* Feb. 150, I could hardly keep from smiling.

44. keep to ——. a. To adhere to, stick to, abide by (a promise, agreement, etc.); to continue to maintain or observe. Also with *indirect passive.*

1625 Burges *Pers. Tithes* 24 He must keepe to his Rule, or hee damnably sinneth. **1697** Dampier *Voy.* (1729) I. 518 Not finding the Governour keep to his agreement with me. **1779** Sheridan *Critic* i. i, If they had kept to that, I should not have been such an enemy to the stage. **1802** Mar. Edgeworth *Moral T.* (1816) I. x. 85, I will keep to my resolution. **1825** *New Monthly Mag.* XV. 511/2 The author has kept very closely to the historical facts. *Mod.* I hope the plan will be kept to.

b. To confine or restrict oneself to. *to keep to oneself*, also (*colloq.*) *to keep oneself to oneself*, to avoid the society of others.

1698 Fryer *Acc. E. Ind. & P.* 174 He is married to Four Wives, to whom he keeps religiously. **1711** Addison *Spect.* No. 129 ¶1 Did they keep to one constant Dress they would sometimes be in the fashion. **1748** Richardson *Clarissa* IV. 27, I was resolved to keep myself to myself till I knew the issue of it. **1788** W. Blane *Hunt. Excurs.* 17 They generally keep to the thick forests where it is impossible to follow them. **1826** Disraeli *Viv. Grey* v. xv, We had much better keep to the road. **1846** *Swell's Night Guide* 45 The divil a rap but that had bin her own, if she'd bin after keeping hersilf to hersilf. **1848** J. H. Newman *Loss & Gain* iii. ix. 374 What can I have done better than keep myself to myself, go by my best reason, consult the friends whom I happened to find around me, as I have done, and wait in patience till I was sure of my convictions? **1881** G. M. Craik (Mrs. May) *Sydney* III. ii. 44 He had merely to keep to the sofa for two or three days. **1889** J. Masterman *Scotts of Bestminster* I. iv. 142 Content with each other, they kept to themselves. **1891** *Sat. Rev.* 18 Apr. 483/1 She shall keep to her room and he will keep to his. **1905** H. G. Wells *Kipps* i. i. 7 They 'kept themselves to themselves', according to the English ideal. **1960** 'H. Carmichael' *Seeds of Hate* iv. 37 My husband and I like to keep ourselves to ourselves. We haven't got many friends. **1960** D. Lessing *In Pursuit of English* iv. 158 She keeps herself to herself so much. **1973** J. Porter *It's Murder with Dover* ii. 17 Miss Marsh has always been one for keeping herself to herself.

45. keep with ——. To remain or stay with; to associate or keep company with; to keep up with.

a **1533** LD. BERNERS *Huon* liv. 181 He may as sone go to your enemyes parte as to kepe with you. **1611** SHAKS. *Wint. T.* I. ii. 344 Goe then; and..keepe with Bohemia, And with your Queene. **1817** W. SELWYN *Law Nisi Prius* (ed. 4) II. 940 To keep with convoy during the whole voyage. **1891** *Field* 19 Dec. 956/3 The very select few who were fortunate enough to keep with hounds.

IV. With adverbs.

46. keep away. a. *trans.* To cause to remain absent or afar; to prevent from coming near.

a **1548** HALL *Chron., Edw. IV* 211 Her frendes..said, that she was kept awaie..by Sorcerers and Necromanciers. **1591** SHAKS. *1 Hen. VI*, IV. 22 Let not your priuate discord keepe away The leuied succours that should lend him ayde. **1872** FREEMAN *Europ. Hist.* xvii. §3. 352 The French frontier, which first reached the Rhine in 1648, is now kept quite away from it.

b. *intr.* To remain absent or at a distance; to hold one's course at a distance; to move off.

1604 SHAKS. *Oth.* III. iv. 173 What? keepe a weeke away? Seuen dayes, and Nights? *a* **1889** W. COLLINS *Blind Love* (1890) III. liii. 130, I could not keep away from you.

c. *Naut. trans.* To cause to sail 'off the wind' or to leeward. *intr.*, to sail off the wind or to leeward.

1805 SIR E. BERRY 13 Oct. in Nicolas *Disp. Nelson* (1846) VII. 118 *note*, I was determined not to keep away, and I could not tack without the certainty of a broadside. **1867** SMYTH *Sailor's Word-bk.* s.v., *Keep her away*, alter the ship's course to leeward, by sailing further off the wind. **1875** BEDFORD *Sailor's Pocket Bk.* iv. (ed. 2) 127 If the vessel keeps away [from wind's eye] 5 points, she must steam or sail at the rate of 7·2 knots, to be in an equally good position.

47. keep back. a. *trans.* To restrain; to detain; to hold back forcibly; to retard the progress, advance, or growth of.

1535 COVERDALE *2 Kings* iv. 24 Dryue forth, and kepe me not bak with rydinge. **1560** DAUS tr. *Sleidane's Comm.* 463 b, I have kept backe no man from the true Religion. **1678** WANLEY *Wond. Lit. World* v. i. §98. 468/1 He..strongly kept back the Turk from encroachments upon his Dominions. **1698** FRYER *Acc. E. India & P.* 310 The Wheat stands, to endure a farther ripening, being kept back by the Chill Winds. **1848** *Jrnl. R. Agric. Soc.* IX. II. 556 Bine that has been kept back..by cold weather. **1890** FENN *Double Knot* I. iv. 129 She made a brave effort to keep back her tears.

b. To withhold; to retain or reserve designedly; to conceal.

1535 COVERDALE *Ps.* xxxix. [xl.] 10, I kepe not thy louynge mercy..backe from the greate congregacion. **1583** STUBBES *Anat. Abus.* II. (1882) 80 The church will keepe no part of the liuing backe from the pastor, if he doe his dutie. **1607–12** BACON *Ess., Seeming Wise* (Arb.) 216 Some are so close, and reserved, as they..seeme alwaies to keepe back somewhat. **1647** H. MORE *Song of Soul* II. I. II. vii, Long keppen back from your expecting sight. **1888** G. GISSING *Life's Morn.* II. xv. 302 It really seemed to me as if she were keeping something back.

c. *intr.* To hold oneself or remain back.

1837 DICKENS *Pickw.* iv, There was a request to 'keep back' from the front.

48. keep down. a. *trans.* To hold down; to hold in subjection or under control; to repress. *spec.* to retain (food, etc.) in one's stomach, without vomiting.

1581 PETTIE tr. *Guazzo's Civ. Conv.* I. (1586) 3 b, Sudden flames by force kept downe. **1607** TOPSELL *Four-f. Beasts* (1658) 155 They keep them low and down by substraction of their meat. **1659** D. PELL *Impr. Sea* 38 You should..keep down your spirits both in this and other cases. **1722** DE FOE *Col. Jack* (1840) 67 Will kept the man down who was under him. **1849** MACAULAY *Hist. Eng.* i. I. 34 A hundred thousand soldiers..will keep down ten millions of ploughmen and artisans. **1889** *Repent. P. Wentworth* III. xvi. 291 She had hard work to keep down her tears. **1955** 'A. GILBERT' *Is she Dead Too?* vi. 119 Think you could keep some hot tea down? Well, have a try. **1968** 'S. WOODS' *Past Praying For* II. 71 Nothing had been given to Oliver without Dr. Noyes's consent; and, anyway, he couldn't keep anything down. **1969** A. E. LINDOP *Sight Unseen* xxix. 246 He's best with his Eno's if I can get him to keep it down. **1973** 'A. YORK' *Captivator* iv. 62 'Aren't you going to eat?..' 'I don't think I could keep it down.'

b. To keep low in amount or number; to prevent from growing, increasing, or accumulating.

1818 CRUISE *Digest* (ed. 2) II. 201 The executors..ought to keep down the interest. **1840** *Jrnl. R. Agric. Soc.* I. III. 259 The Tartarian oats kept down the clover. **1851** *Beck's Florist* Jan. 21 Pick off decaying leaves, and keep down insects. **1869** W. LONGMAN *Hist. Edw. III*, I. xvi. 309 Employers.. combined to keep down wages.

c. *Painting.* (See quot. 1854.)

1768 W. GILPIN *Prints* 210 The effect..might have been better, if all the lights upon it had been kept down. **1805** E. DAYES *Works* 290 Should the objects give a sufficient quantity of Light and Shade, the sky may be kept down. **1854** FAIRHOLT *Dict. Terms Art, Kept down*, subdued in tone or tint, so that that portion of the picture thus treated is rendered subordinate to some other part.

d. *Printing.* To set in lower-case type, as a word or letter; to use capitals somewhat sparingly.

1888 JACOBI *Printer's Vocab.*

e. *intr.* To remain low or subdued.

1889 MARY E. CARTER *Mrs. Severn* III. III. ix. 219 Praying that the wind would keep down for a few hours.

49. keep in. a. *trans.* To confine within; to hold in check; to restrain; not to utter or give vent to; *spec.* to confine in school after hours.

a **1420** HOCCLEVE *De Reg. Princ.* 1015 We..keepe muste our song and wordes in. *c* **1491** *Chast. Goddes Chyld.* 18 To kepe in his chyldern that they sholde not sterte abrode fro the scole. **1601** SHAKS. *Twel. N.* I. v. 209 It is more like to be feigned; I pray you keep it in. **1690** W. WALKER *Idiomat. Anglo-Lat.* 24 He is not able to keep in his anger. **1713** ADDISON *Cato* I. iv, Your zeal becomes importunate..but learn to keep it in. **1893** *Pall Mall Mag.* I. 28 He had been 'kept in'.., and his schoolmates had all gone.

†**b.** To keep from public currency. *Obs.*

1573 BARET *Alv.* K 25 To keepe in corne, to the end to make it deere. **1671** M. BRUCE *Good News in Evil Times* (1708) 68 Thanks be to him that hath ay keeped in our Black side yet, and hath not let the World see it yet.

c. To keep (a fire) burning: cf. IN *adv.* 6 g. Also *intr.* of a fire: To continue to burn.

1659 J. ARROWSMITH *Chain Princ.* 160 As culinary fire must be kindled and kept in by external materials. **1711**, **1793** [see IN *adv.* 6 g]. **1849** *Jrnl. R. Agric. Soc.* X. I. 149 The fire..keeps in well twelve hours. **1892** *Review of Rev.* 15 Mar. 299/1 The fire can be kept in all night.

d. *Printing.* To set type closely spaced.

1683 MOXON *Mech. Exerc., Printing* Dict., *Keep in*, is a caution either given to, or resolved on, by the Compositer, where there may be doubt of Driving out his Matter beyond his Counting off. **1888** JACOBI *Printers' Vocab.*

e. *to keep one's hand in*: see HAND *sb.*[1] 53.

f. *intr.* To remain indoors, or within a retreat, place, position, etc.

c **1430** *Syr Gener.* (Roxb.) 711 Euermore she kept hir in. **1518** in W. H. Turner *Select. Rec. Oxford* 18 The inhabitants of thos howses that be..infectyd shall kepe in. **1652** GAULE *Magastrom.* 250 It still keeps in (like an owle) all the day-time. **1850** F. T. FINCH in 'Bat' *Cricket Man.* 95 Though for years we may keep *in*, we must at length go *out*.

g. To keep in line or in touch *with*.

1781 W. BLANE *Ess. Hunting* (1788) 35, I could never yet see any creature on two legs keep in with the Dogs.

h. To remain in favour or on good terms *with*. Cf. IN *adv.* 9 a. (Now *colloq.*)

1598 GRENEWEY *Tacitus, Ann.* IV. v. (1622) 96 He kept in with Cæsar in no lesse fauour then authority. **1666** PEPYS *Diary* 1 July, Though I do not love him, yet I find it necessary to keep in with him. **1720** OZELL *Vertot's Rom. Rep.* II. XIV. 333 Cæsar.. resolved to keep in equally with the Senate and Antony. **1883** BLACK *Yolande* III. v. 86 He's violent enough in the House; but that's to keep in with his constituents.

50. keep off. a. *trans.* To hinder from coming near or touching; to ward off; to avert.

a **1548** HALL *Chron., Edw. IV* 233 b, Covered with bordes, onely to kepe of the wether. **1592** SHAKS. *Rom. & Jul.* III. iii. 54 Ile giue thee Armour to keepe off that word. **1662** J. DAVIES tr. *Olearius' Voy. Ambass.* 24 Having white staves in their hands, to keep off the people. **1727** GAY *Begg. Op.* I. viii. (1729) 11 O Polly..By keeping men off, you keep them on. **1883** FENN *Middy & Ensign* xxii. 133 An umbrella held up to keep off the sun.

b. *intr.* To stay at a distance; to refrain from approaching; not to come on.

1591 SHAKS. *1 Hen. VI*, IV. iv. 21 You..Keepe off aloofe with worthlesse emulation. **1803** J. HILLYAR Aug. in Nicolas *Disp. Nelson* (1845) II. 186 *note*, The Master..told the Boats to keep off. **1861** DICKENS *Gt. Expect.* xxxix, I..put him away. 'Stay!' said I. 'Keep off!' **1891** *Field* 7 Nov. 699/2 If the frost keeps off.

c. *trans.* To avoid or stay away from; not to use; also as *attrib. phr.*; *keep off the grass*: see GRASS *sb.*[1] 9.

1949 M. MEAD *Male & Female* ii. 42 Tchamwole..placed a keep-off sign on the coconut-palm-trees. **1968** *Listener* 12 Dec. 790/3 Girls at Amman University have been instructed ..to keep off heavy make-up.

51. keep on. a. *trans.* To maintain or retain in an existing condition or relation; to continue to hold, occupy, employ, entertain, or display.

1669 R. MONTAGU in *Buccleuch MSS.* (Hist. MSS. Comm.) I. 439 Till the end of the quarter..her family should be kept on. **1847** *Jrnl. R. Agric. Soc.* VIII. I. 10 If young, they are sometimes kept on for another season, and sent to fold. **1889** ADEL. SERGEANT *E. Denison* I. I. xi. 138 Bingley asked him awkwardly whether he meant to 'keep on the house'. **1890** MRS. H. WOOD *House of Halliwell* II. viii. 213 Let me reproach him as I will, he keeps on that provoking meekness.

b. To keep (a fire, etc.) going continuously.

1891 *Review of Rev.* 15 Sept. 287/2 When a fire is needed to be kept on all night.

c. *intr.* To continue or persist in a course or action; to go on with something. Now freq. with *pres. pple.*

1589 PUTTENHAM *Eng. Poesie* II. iii. (Arb.) 83 In this manner doth the Greeke *dactilus* begin slowly and keepe on swifter till th' end. **1604** SHAKS. *Oth.* III. iii. 455 The Ponticke Sea, Whose Icie Current..keepes due on To the Proponticke. **1724** DE FOE *Mem. Cavalier* (1840) 240 We kept on all night. **1856** *Titan Mag.* Dec. 516/1 'We shall never come across each other again', she kept on saying to herself. **1889** DOYLE *Micah Clarke* xxii. 224 Strike quick, strike hard, and keep on striking.

†**d.** To keep the head covered. *Obs.*

1652–62 HEYLIN *Cosmogr.* III. (1673) 133/2 They keep on of all sides..accounting it an opprobrious thing to see any men uncover their heads.

e. To remain fixed or attached; to stay on.

1892 *Cassell's Fam. Mag.* July 469/2 [His] buttons never keep on.

52. keep out. a. *trans.* To cause to remain without; to prevent from getting in.

c **1425** LYDG. *Assembly of Gods* 770 [He] Wold kepe out that other he shuld nat esyly entre. **1560** DAUS tr. *Sleidane's Comm.* 94 The Sea brake in over the walles, that we made to kepe it out. **1681** FLAVEL *Meth. Grace* xxxiv. 575 He teaches them how to paint the glass, that he may keep out the light. **1780** COXE *Russ. Disc.* 169 In order to keep out the rain. **1821** CLARE *Vill. Minstr.* I. 84 Locks..To keep out thieves at night. **1865** DICKENS *Mut. Fr.* I. i, Keep her [a boat] out, Lizzie. Tide runs strong here.

b. *Printing.* To set type widely spaced.

1683 MOXON *Mech. Exerc., Printing Dict.* s.v., He Sets Wide, to Drive or Keep out. **1888** JACOBI *Printer's Vocab.*

53. keep over. *trans.* To reserve, hold over.

1847 *Jrnl. R. Agric. Soc.* VIII. I. 6 Some breeders keep them [lambs] over until the next spring. **1893** *Field* 4 Mar. 331/2 Keeping over old wheat stocks for a rise in price.

54. keep to. *Naut. trans.* To cause (a ship) to sail close to the wind.

1692 *Capt. Smith's Seaman's Gram.* xvi. 76 In keeping the Ship near the Wind, these terms are used..*keep her to, touch the Wind.* **1706** PHILLIPS, *Keep your loof* or *Keep her to.*

55. keep together. a. *trans.* To cause to remain in association or union. ***to keep body (†life) and soul together***: to keep (oneself) alive.

1601 SHAKS. *Twel. N.* III. i. 56 *Clo.* Would not a paire of these haue bred sir? *Vio.* Yes being kept together, and put to vse. **1693** TATE in *Dryden's Juvenal* xv. (1697) 375 The Vascons once with Man's Flesh (as 'tis sed) Kept Life and Soul together. **1841** *Jrnl. R. Agric. Soc.* II. I. 43 It is a poor loose sand..only kept together by the roots of the sea-bent. **1884** *Century Mag.* Nov. 54/2 How on earth they managed to keep body and soul together.

b. *intr.* To remain associated or united.

1560 DAUS tr. *Sleidane's Comm.* 435 Let them..kepe together, and in no wise scatter abrode. **1599** SHAKS. *Hen. V*, II. ii. 105 Treason, and murther, euer kept together. **1768** J. BYRON *Narr. Patagonia* (ed. 2) 13 It did not become him to desert it as long as the ship kept together. **1820** W. IRVING *Sketch Bk.* (1859) 181, I have a particular respect for three or four..chairs..which seem to me to keep together.

56. keep under. *trans.* To hold in subjection or under control; to keep down.

1486–1504 *Quinton MSS.* in Denton *Eng. in 15th cent.* Note D. (1888) 318 For mane men wyll ley owt more to kepe vnder the pore th(en) for to helpe thaym. **1579** GOSSON *Sch. Abuse* (Arb.) 37 Giue them a bitte to keepe them vnder. **1611** BIBLE *1 Cor.* ix. 27, I keepe under my body, and bring it into subiection. **1712** BERKELEY *Pass. Obed.* §13 Like all other passions, [they] must be restrained and kept under. **1843** *Jrnl. R. Agric. Soc.* IV. I. 116 The services of birds in keeping under noxious insects. **1889** J. MASTERMAN *Scotts of Bestminster* II. ix. 115 She had been accustomed to be kept under all her life.

57. keep up. a. *trans.* To keep shut up or confined.

1604 SHAKS. *Oth.* I. ii. 59 Keepe vp your bright Swords, for the dew will rust them. **1654** in Picton *L'pool Munic. Rec.* (1883) I. 191 Swyne..ought to bee kept up in their styes. **1673** WYCHERLEY *Gentl. Dancing Master* II. i, Have you kept up my daughter close in my absence? **1737** WHISTON *Josephus, Antiq.* IV. viii. §36 If his owner..having known what his nature was..hath not kept him [an ox] up. **1847** *Jrnl. R. Agric. Soc.* VIII. I..31 When sheep are kept up in sheds during the winter.

†**b.** To keep secret or undivulged. *Obs.*

1678 CUDWORTH *Intell. Syst.* I. iii. §38. 177 So long as these things are concealed and kept up in Huggermugger. *a* **1715** BURNET *Own Time* (1823) II. 115 They..had not sailed when the proclamation came down: yet it was kept up till they sailed away. **1725** RAMSAY *Gent. Sheph.* II. iii, What fowk say of me, Bauldy, let me hear; Keep naithing up.

c. To support, sustain; to prevent from sinking or falling. Also *intr.* To bear up, so as not to break down.

to keep the ball up (see BALL *sb.*[1] 18). ***to keep one's wicket up*** (*Cricket*): to remain in, to continue one's innings.

1681 FLAVEL *Meth. Grace* ix. 190 Of great use to keep up the soul above water. **1694** F. BRAGGE *Disc. Parables* xiii. 425 To keep up their spirits. **1801** H. SWINBURNE in *Crts. Europe close last Cent.* (1841) II. 299 This ridiculous folly keeps the stocks up. **1868** ROGERS *Pol. Econ.* ix. (1876) 88 The purpose of a trades-union is to keep up the price of labour. **1884** *Lillywhite's Cricket Ann.* 60 He kept up his wicket until the finish. **1889** J. MASTERMAN *Scotts of Bestminster* II. xii. 262 But for her sweetness and bravery, I never could have kept up through all this terrible trial.

d. To maintain in a worthy or effective condition; to support; to keep in repair; to keep burning.

1552 HULOET, Kepe vp by cheryshinge, *alo, foveo.* Kepe vp by maintenaunce, *sustento.* **1670** SIR S. CROW in *12th Rep. Hist. MSS. Comm.* App. v. 15 Findeing that business ..a burden..to keepe it upp in that perfection I found and made itt. **1678** LADY CHAWORTH *Ibid.* 51 The King had a mind..to keep up his army and navy till that peace was made. **1701** W. WOTTON *Hist. Rome, Marcus* vi. 106 The Athenians still kept up regular Professors for all those Sciences. **1840** R. H. DANA *Bef. Mast* xxvi. 86 We kept up a small fire, by which we cooked our mussels. **1875** FREEMAN *Norm. Conq.* III. xii. 173 A causeway which is still in being and which is kept up as a modern road.

e. To maintain, retain, preserve (a quality, state of things, accomplishment, etc.); to keep from deteriorating or disappearing.

1670 A. ROBERTS *Adv. T.S.* 51 Orders of Men..that keep up the Honour of Religion amongst them. **1705** ADDISON *Italy* Wks. II. 132 Albano keeps up its credit still for Wine. **1791** *Gentl. Mag.* 20/2 The clergy would, from the calls of their profession..keep up their classical acquirements. **1836** JAS. GRANT *Gt. Metropolis* I. ii. 44 They must maintain their dignity; they must keep up appearances. **1884** MRS. PIRKIS *Judith Wynne* I. v. 48 Oughtn't she to have a horse, and keep up her riding?

f. To maintain, continue, go on with (an action or course of action). Esp. in phr. ***keep it up***; *spec.* to prolong a party, drinking-spree, etc.; to 'live it up'.

1513 MORE in Grafton *Chron.* (1568) II. 778 For his dissimulation onely kept all that mischiefe up. **1711** STEELE *Spect.* No. 51 ¶2 The Difficulty of keeping up a sprightly Dialogue for five Acts together. **1752** J. MILLWARD *Let.* in M. M. Verney *Verney Lett.* (1930) II. II. xxxiv. 250 When

they [*sc.* the Welsh] get in liquor they are very troublesome and noisy. They kept it up all night. **1781** Hist. Eur. in Ann. Reg. 16/1 Continual firing..was kept up during the day. **1788** GROSE Dict. Vulgar T. (ed. 2), *To keep it up*, to prolong a debauch. We kept it up finely last night; metaphor drawn from the game at shuttlecock. **1801** C. KEITH Har'st Rig. & Farmer's Ha' (ed. 2) 62 Clear-blooded health..flees awa' frae *keeping 't up*, and midnight riot. **1810** M. DWIGHT Journey to Ohio (1912) 16 The men dress much better—they put on their best cloaths on sunday,..& 'keep it up' as they call it. **1837** DICKENS Pickw. lii. 565 We were keeping it up pretty tolerably at the Stump last night, and I'm rather out of sorts this morning. **1869** FREEMAN Norm. Conq. III. xiv. 367 The fight is kept up till night-fall. **1874** L. TROUBRIDGE Life amongst Troubridges (1966) 76 There were forty-six people and we kept it up till one... I had several good valses. **1890** Lippincott's Mag. Jan. 11 He and I have kept up a correspondence. **1958** A. HUXLEY Let. 11 Jan. (1969) 842 Thank you for your long and very interesting letter—written, too, in the most wonderfully black ink... Keep it up!

g. To cause to remain out of bed.

1766 GOLDSM. Vic. W. ix, Well pleased, that my little ones were kept up beyond the usual time. **1839** THACKERAY Fatal Boots xii, Keeping her up till four o'clock in the morning. **1889** ADEL. SERGEANT Luck of House II. xxxvi. 228, I will keep you up no longer, for you look terribly pale and fagged.

h. *Printing.* To keep (type or matter) standing; also, to use capitals somewhat freely.

1888 JACOBI Printers' Vocab.

i. *to keep up to*: to prevent from falling below (a level, standard, principle, etc.); to keep informed of. Also *intr.* for *refl.*

1712 STEELE Spect. No. 308 ¶2 My Lady's whole Time and Thoughts are spent in keeping up to the Mode. **1726** LEONI Alberti's Archit. I. 46/1 This Strength in the Corners is..only to keep the Wall up to its duty. **1841** Jrnl. R. Agric. Soc. II. I. 144 It keeps him better up to his work. **1889** J. MASTERMAN Scotts of Bestminster III. xv. 41 A London correspondent who kept the country-folk up to the doings of the townsfolk. **1890** Univ. Rev. Aug. 633 We should keep up to the mark in these matters.

j. *intr.* To continue alongside, keep abreast; to proceed at an equal pace *with* (*lit.* and *fig.*). Esp. (orig. *U.S.*) in phr. ***to keep up*** (often ***keeping up***) ***with the Joneses*** (or *Jones's*): to strive not to be outdone by one's neighbours; to emulate one's neighbours; also *transf.*

a **1633** G. HERBERT Country Parson ii. (1652) 5 They are not to be over-submissive and base, but to keep up with the Lord and Lady of the house. **1706** Wooden World Dissected (1708) 35 He tries every Way..to keep up with his Leader. **1890** W. F. RAE Maygrove II. vii. 272 Don't walk so fast.. I can hardly keep up with you. **1913** A. R. MOMAND in Globe (N.Y.) 1 Apr. 16/3 (*Comic-strip title*) Keeping up with the Joneses—by Pop. **1926** Amer. Speech I. 281 Today most of us live in automobilia, where the automocracy is everlastingly trying to 'keep up with the Joneses'. **1927** CHASE & SCHLINK Your Money's Worth i. 7 Certain things we buy..to keep up with the Joneses, or happily, to surpass the Joneses. **1933** E. WEEKLEY in Trans. Philol. Soc. 94 This tendency to personify by the use of a familiar name is due to the same psychology which describes the social ambitions of the suburbs as 'keeping up with the Joneses'. **1952** F. P. KEYES Larry Vincent (1953) xxi. 284 He could not be thankful enough that he did not have a nagging wife, one who insisted on making a show, on 'keeping up with the Joneses', as people were beginning to say. **1957** Observer 25 Aug. 7/3 Britain.., always wanting to keep up with the Joneses of the richer South, hankered all the time after white bread only and achieved it one hundred per cent. by the mid-nineteenth century. **1958** Times 8 Nov. 7/2 Keeping up atomically with the Joneses is precisely what the talks were supposed to prevent. **1963** [see DOOR-STEP c]. **1970** Times 25 May 7/4 We like to keep up with the Joneses and are therefore well disposed to the new definition of democracy. **1971** Times Lit. Suppl. 1393/3 The lesser funerals, of Pooters with Joneses to keep up with, increased in cost, display and competitiveness.

†**k.** To stay within doors; to put up or stop *at.*

1704 D'CHESS MARLBOROUGH in Buccleuch MSS. (Hist. MSS. Comm.) I. 353, I am very sorry to hear Lord Monthermont has had any accident to make him keep up. **1768** STERNE Sent. Journ. (1778) II. 195 (*Case Delicacy*) The Voiturin found himself obliged to keep up five miles short of his stage at a little decent kind of an inn.

l. To continue to maintain a friendship or acquaintance; to keep in touch. (Cf. 57 f.)

1903 C. COLERIDGE C. M. Yonge iv. 127 She did not seem to be able to keep in personal touch with them... She could not, as we say, 'keep up' with them. **1916** E. V. LUCAS Vermilion Box xlii. 45, I heard this morning of the death..of two of my oldest friends—Jack Cazalet, who was at school with me, and Sandford Thrale, whom I knew at Oxford. Both went straight into the army, but we had kept up. **1947** 'N. SHUTE' Chequer Board 205 We were all in it together then. We ought to have kept up. **1971** 'L. MARSHALL' Murder's just for Cops xviii. 125 We always kept up—even after I got married. **1971** 'D. SHANNON' Ringer (1972) i. 20 Mrs. Sneed had known Carolyn..before she got married, five years back, and they had 'kept up'.

V. 58. Combs., as †**keep-door** (*nonce-wd.*), a porter, door-ward; **keep-fit** *a.*, denoting exercises, etc., designed to keep people fit and healthy, and (occas.) a person who does such exercises; also *ellipt.* as *sb.*; †**keep-friend** (see quot.); **keep-left** *a.*, designating a sign, etc., directing traffic to the left of the road; †**keep-net**, ? a net for keeping fish in; †**keep-off**, a means of keeping (persons, etc.) off; also as *adj.*, serving to keep (foes) off; **keep-out** *a.*, designating a sign that prohibits entry. Also KEEPSAKE.

1682 MRS. BEHN City Heiress 45 Good Mistriss *keep-door, stand by; for I must enter. **1938** M. CARTER Living Soul in Holloway vi. 77 Gardening comes into their day's programme and '*keep fit' exercises. **1939** 'N. BLAKE' Smiler with Knife v. 88 A healthy, bouncing, Keep-Fit sort of girl. **1961** J. STROUD Touch & Go xii. 119 A Girls' Keep Fit class was in session. **1965** W. LAMB Posture & Gesture ii. 31 There could be a revolution in all physical behaviour pursuits,..including..country dancing, ballet, and 'Keep Fit'. **1967** O. NORTON Now lying Dead iii. 54 Monday he goes to his Keep Fit. Imagine him in his little black shorts! **1971** Fremdsprachen XV. 63 Women..going to 'Keep Fit' classes. **1974** H. R. F. KEATING Bats fly Up vii. 78 The OSP's well-known mania for keep-fit. **1675** Hist. Don Quix. 45 He had besides two iron rings about his neck, the one of the chain, and the other of that kind which are called A *keep-friend, or the foot of a friend; from whence descended two irons unto his middle. **1936** Discovery Nov. 359/1 Street lamps, traffic bollards, and '*keep left' signs are automatically lit. **1962** C. WATSON Hopjoy was Here iv. 38 A pair of dogs..coupled on the road's crown and performed a six-legged waltz around a keep-left bollard. **1623** WHITBOURNE Newfoundland 75 Ten *keipnet Irons..Twine to make Keipnets, &c. *c* **1611** CHAPMAN Iliad VII. 121 He fought not with a *keep-off spear, or with a far-shot bow. **1615** —— Odyss. XIV. 759 A lance..To be his keep-off both 'gainst men and dogs. **1971** J. MCCLURE Steam Pig v. 75 A deserted area surrounded by *Keep Out signs. **1974** Times 9 May 6/5 To protect your garden a 'keep out' sign is not enough. You also need a tall fence.

keep (kiːp), *sb.* Forms: 3-5 **kep**, 3-6 **kepe**, (5 **kype**), 4-6 *Sc.* **keip**, 4-7 **keepe**, (9 **keape**), 3- **keep**. [f. KEEP *v.*]

†**1.** Care, attention, heed, notice; usually in phrases ***to nim, take, give keep***, to take or give heed, take notice. (Const. *of*, *infin.*, or *clause*.)

c **1250** Gen. & Ex. 1333 Bi-aften bak, as he nam kep, faste in ðornes, he saȝ a sep. *a* **1300** Cursor M. 20128 Hir sun to serue was al hir kepe. *Ibid.* 20498 To þis ferli tas all nu kepe. *a* **1325** Prose Psalter lxix. [lxx.] 1 Ȝeue kepe, God, to my helpe. *c* **1400** MAUNDEV. (1839) v. 51 A Man ought to take gode kepe for to bye Bawme. **1509** BARCLAY Shyp of Folys (1570) 174 What God hath done for you ye take no keepe. **1602** Narcissus (1893) 712, I tooke good keepe, and saw thee eke shedd teares. **1647** H. MORE Song of Soul III. III. xxxvii, Who of nought else but sloth and growth doth taken keep. [**1886** A. LANG Lett. Dead Auth. 36 As to things old, they take no keep of them.]

2. a. Care or heed in tending, watching, or preserving; charge; orig. only in phr. †*to take keep.*

a **1300** Cursor M. 5729 (Gött.) Moyses þat time tok kepe To his elde fadris schepe. *c* **1440** Partonope 289 Partanope ys now softe falle on sleepe This fayre lady of hym takyth keepe. *c* **1475** Rauf Coilȝear 640 Tak keip to my Capill, that na man him call. **1491** CAXTON Vitas Patr. (W. de W. 1495) II. 241 a/1 Take euer a besy kepe of thy selfe. *a* **1568** ASCHAM Scholem. I. (Arb.) 49 Vnder the kepe, and by the counsell, of some graue gouernour. **1586** J. HOOKER Hist. Irel. in Holinshed II. 100/2 Your dominion in Ireland, wherevnto they haue so little keepe. **1647** H. MORE Poems 311 Of his precious soul he takes no keep. **1818** KEATS Endym. I. 68 If from shepherd's keep A lamb stray'd far.

†**b.** That which is kept; a charge. *Obs.*

1579 SPENSER Sheph. Cal. July 133 Often he vsed of hys keepe a sacrifice to bring.

3. *Hist.* The innermost and strongest structure or central tower of a mediæval castle, serving as a last defence; a tower; a stronghold, donjon.

Perhaps orig. a translation of It. *tenazza.*

a **1586** SIDNEY Arcadia (1598) 249 He who stood as watch upon the top of the keepe. **1598** BARRET Theor. Warres VI. iv. 244 The Tenaza or Keepe, which standeth without the body of the Castell. **1654** EVELYN Mem. 8 June, The Castle itself is large in circumference... The Keep, or mount, hath..a very profound well. **1796** BURKE Let. Noble Lord Wks. VIII. 49 Like the proud Keep of Windsor rising in majesty of proportion, and girt with the double belt of its kindred and coeval towers. **1813** SCOTT Trierm. I. xiii, Buttress, and rampire's circling bound, And mighty keep and tower. **1819** W. BURGH Notes Mason's Eng. Gard. IV. Note L, The Gothic castle..consisted, in every instance, of the keep or strong-hold, and the court or enclosure annexed to the keep. **1877** TENNYSON Harold II. ii, The walls oppress me, And yon huge keep that hinders half the heaven.

4. An article which serves for containing or retaining something. †**a.** A meat-safe. *Obs. rare.*

1617 MINSHEU Ductor s.v., A Keepe is..also vsed for a safe, which is a thing to keepe the meate from the flies in Sommer season. **1649** Bury Wills (Camden) 221 A..cup-bord, a keepe, two wrought chairs.

b. A stew, pond, or reservoir for fish; a weir or dam for retaining water. *rare.*

1617 MINSHEU Ductor s.v., A Keepe is also used..for a place made in waters to keep and preserve fish. **1847** J. DWYER Princ. Hydraul. Engin. 75 The motion of water over a bar or keep, such as had been calculated for the new cut.

†**c.** A clasp or similar fastening. *Obs.*

1615 CHAPMAN Odyss. XVIII. 432 Buttons..made to fairly hold The robe together, all lac'd downe before, Where Keepes and Catches both sides of it wore.

d. *Coal-mining.* One of the set of movable iron supports on which the cage rests when at the top of the shaft: = KEP *sb.*

1851 GREENWELL Coal-trade Terms Northumb. & Durh. 33 The cage rising between the keeps, and forcing them back; but when drawn above the keeps, they fall forward to their places. **1867** W. W. SMYTH Coal & Coal-mining 166 The cage is lifted..a little above the plane of the bank..and then allowed to drop on to the keeps.

e. *Mech.* In a locomotive engine: A part of the axle-box, fitted beneath the journal of the axle and serving to hold an oiled pad against it.

1881 Metal World No. 15. 227 Care should be taken in boring out the axle-box keeps, as if the keeps are not bored correctly the journals..will not work true in them.

†**5.** A keeper, a herd (in N. America). *Obs. rare.*

1641 Boston Rec. (1877) II. 60 If any goates be without a keep after the 14th day of the next moneth..the owners of them shall forfett..halfe a bushel of Corne. *Ibid.* 61 [They] shall agree with a Cowe keep for the towne for the present summer.

6. a. The act of keeping or maintaining; the fact of being kept. See KEEP *v.* 19-24.

1763 in F. B. Hough Siege Detroit (1860) 191 The Safety and Protection of Schenectady depends in a great Measure on the keep of a good Guard in the Town. **1824** MISS MITFORD Village Ser. I. (1863) 64 Our old spaniel..and the blue grey-hound..both of which fourfooted worthies were sent out to keep for the summer. **1847-78** HALLIW. s.v. *Keep, Out at keep*, said of animals in hired pastures.

b. ***in good keep***, well kept, in good condition; so ***in low keep***, etc.

1808 Trial Lieut. Gen. Whitelocke I. 215 Many of them exceedingly good horses, but in low keep. **1811** LAMB Good Clerk Misc. Wks. (1871) 384 As the owner of a fine horse is [solicitous] to have him appear in good keep.

c. The food required to keep a person or animal; provender, pasture; maintenance, support. Freq. in phr. ***to earn one's keep*** (also *fig.*).

1801 JANE AUSTEN Let. 3 Jan. (1952) 101 The keep of two will be more than of one. **1815** M. BIRKBECK Notes Journey through France (ed. 3) 21 M. Tessier hires the whole of the keep of this flock. He pays £62. 10s. sterling to the farmer for the sheep pasture... He buys Lucerne hay for four winter months..making the expense of keep £142. 10s. sterling. *a* **1825** FORBY Voc. E. Anglia s.v., I am short of keep for my cows. **1829** SOUTHEY Pilgr. Compostella Poet. Wks. VII. 264 The Corporation A fund for their keep supplied. **1848** LOWELL Biglow P. Poems 1890 II. 148 You're so darned lazy, I don't think you're hardly worth your keep. **1937** R. MACAULAY I would be Private I. xv. 137 Now he can just earn his keep digging treasure on those cays. **1963** A. ROSS Australia 63 iv. 99 The four Test stars..whose appearance cost the Tasmanian authorities £A300, again individually and in bulk failed to earn their keep. **1971** Country Life 4 Nov. 1237/2 Under favourable growing conditions this will provide late autumn keep, really valuable spring feed, or both. **1972** Accountant 19 Oct. 497/3 'All assets must earn their keep,' declared Mr Shaw.

7. Phr. ***for keeps***: to keep, for good; hence, completely, altogether; also in extended use: in deadly earnest. *colloq.* (orig. *U.S.*). In *Cricket*, defensively, in order to remain at the wicket.

1861 Ladies' Repository Oct. 627/1 Pay him! Nothing. He and I played for 'keeps', and I was the best player and won all his. **1871** Wright County Monitor (Clarion, Iowa) 29 Nov., Winter has at last come 'for keeps'. **1886** Advance 9 Dec. (Farmer), We..promise not to play marbles for keeps, nor bet nor gamble in any way. **1893** S. R. CROCKETT Stickit Minister 79 She'll even set down the black bag to play for keeps wi' the boys at the bools. **1897** R. KIPLING Captains Courageous 263 I'm coming into the business for keeps next fall. **1897** National Police Gaz. (U.S.) 26 May 3/1 He is in the business for 'keeps', as they say in America. **1899** H. FREDERIC Market Place 195 I've got something the matter with me..I've got it for keeps. **1905** Westm. Gaz. 19 Sept. 3/2 Any other batsman..would doubtless have played for 'keeps' and taken not the slightest risk. **1923** Cricketer Ann. 1922-3 90 To-day, the dominant feature of the game is the individual 'playing for keeps'. **1933** D. L. SAYERS Murder must Advertise xv. 253 Ten to one 'e'll lose 'im for keeps, now. **1949** D. G. SMITH I capture Castle III. xii. 214 Maybe when I bring you back we shall find it's gone for keeps. **1970** G. E. EVANS Where Beards wag All xix. 219 You played *for keeps* sometimes, in other words all the marbles you won became yours. **1972** D. LEES Zodiac 107 These bastards are playing for keeps... I'm in trouble. **1973** 'H. HOWARD' Highway to Murder ix. 108 Everybody belonged to the rat race where people played for keeps.

8. *Comb.*, as **keep-tower** = sense 3; **keep-worthy** *a.*, worth keeping, worthy of being kept.

1830 W. TAYLOR Hist. Germ. Poetry I. 182 Bodmer..was the editor of the Zurich charter..and of other keep-worthy documents. **1865** STREET Goth. Archit. Spain 187 The enormous Keep-tower which rises out of its western face.

keepable ('kiːpəb(ə)l), *a.* [f. KEEP *v.* + -ABLE.] That can be kept or preserved. Hence **keepa'bility**.

1891 Field 21 Nov. 774/2 Another fish..not..quite up to the size we had decided to be keepable. **1898** R. H. WALLACE Adulteration of Dairy Prod. 12 The keepability was also tested, and Swedish butter proved to be on an average more keepable than butter from other countries. **1962** Times 3 July (Agric. Suppl.) p. vii/4 The keepability of these pig meat products.

keep-alive ('kiːpəlaɪv), *a.* *Electronics.* [f. *to keep alive* (KEEP *v.* 24).] Applied to devices and phenomena in certain kinds of discharge tube which operate or occur continuously and serve to initiate an intermittent main discharge or facilitate its establishment. Also *ellipt.*, such a device or phenomenon.

1933 J. H. MORECROFT Electron Tubes viii. 182 In large bulbs a 'keep-alive' circuit is used to maintain the ionization. **1947** A. E. WHITFORD in L. N. Ridenour Radar Syst. Engin. xi. 410 To insure rapid breakdown at the beginning of each pulse, a supply of ions in the gap is maintained by a continuous auxiliary discharge inside one of the cones. This requires an extra electrode, known as the 'keep-alive' electrode. **1947** CROWTHER & WHIDDINGTON Science at War i. 47 The final form was a cavity..with a small pilot discharge or 'keep alive' to help the gas discharge to start. **1959** R. L. SHRADER Electronic Communication xxix. 842 To make the TR tube more sensitive, a d-c keep-alive voltage is

applied across it at all times. This voltage is not quite high enough to support ionization. **1965** GEWARTOWSKI & WATSON *Princ. Electron Tubes* xv. 554 Tubes in which radioactive material has been placed for the purpose of obtaining short ionizaion times are said to have a radioactive keep-alive. *Ibid.*, In some tubes a low-current discharge between auxiliary electrodes is operated continuously as a keep-alive mechanism.

keeper ('ki:pə(r)), *sb.* [f. KEEP *v.* + -ER[1].] One who or that which keeps.

I. From trans. senses of the vb.

1. a. One who has charge, care, or oversight of any person or thing; a guardian, warden, custodian.

a **1300** *Cursor M.* 1096 Quen was i keper of þi child. *c* **1330** R. BRUNNE *Chron. Wace* (Rolls) 15812 Ne God wil namore þat þey be Keperes of þat dignete. *c* **1375** *Sc. Leg. Saints* xii. (*Mathias*) 137 He hyme mad hale kepare of al þe thinge, þat he had in-to gowernynge. **1382** WYCLIF *Gen.* iv. 9, I wote neuere; whether am I the keper of my brother? [COVERD. I knowe not: Am I my brothers keper?]. —— *Acts* xvi. 27 The kepere of the prisoun..seynge the ȝatis of the prisoun openyd..wolde sle hym silf. **1388** —— *Gen.* iv. 2 Abel was a kepere of scheep, and Cayn was an erthe tilyere. *c* **1400** MAUNDEV. (Roxb.) xxiv. 110 [þai] ware made hirdmen and kepers of bestez. **1509–10** *Act 1 Hen. VIII*, c. 17 §1 The Keper of the said great Warderobe for the tyme beyng. *a* **1533** LD. BERNERS *Huon* viii. 19 Gerarde..demandyd.. whether he was kepar of that passage or not. **1570** *Satir. Poems Reform.* xviii. 37 He was keipar of ȝour commoun weill. **1631** GOUGE *God's Arrows* III. §65. 304 The Church.. is a faithful keeper and preserver of the Oracles of God. **1693** DRYDEN *Juvenal* vi. (1697) 140 Keep close your Women, under Lock and Key: But, who shall keep those Keepers? **1718** PRIOR *Knowledge* 203 Untam'd and fierce the tiger.. seeks his keeper's flesh. **1810** SCOTT *Lady of L.* III. xiv, The herds without a keeper strayed.

b. Forming the second element in many compounds; as ***alphabet-keeper, ass-keeper, beast-keeper, book-keeper, bridge-keeper, cash-keeper, chapel-keeper, cow-keeper, deer-keeper, dog-keeper, door-keeper, gamekeeper, gate-keeper, goal-keeper, green-keeper, hound-keeper, housekeeper***, etc., of which those of permanent standing will be found in their alphabetical places.

c **1440** [see HOUSEKEEPER]. **1535** [see DOOR-KEEPER]. **1555** [see BOOK-KEEPER]. **1670** [see GAMEKEEPER]. **1707** J. CHAMBERLAYNE *Pres. St. Gt. Brit.* III. 679 Officers of the Foreign [Post] Office.. Mr. James Lawrence, Alphabet-Keeper, 100*l*. **1766** ENTICK *London* IV. 295 In the foreign office, there is also a comptroller, and an alphabet keeper. **1897** *Outing* (U.S.) XXIX. 440/2 The old hound-keeper declared that [the bitch] would never come back. **1900** *Daily News* 3 July 7/5 One piece fell beside the register-keeper. **1900** *Westm. Gaz.* 14 July 2/3 The street chapel-keeper also wished to desert his post.

c. Special uses:

Keeper of the Exchange and Mint: the Master of the Mint, an office held since 1870 by the Chancellor of the Exchequer. ***Keeper of the Great (†Broad) Seal***: an officer in England and Scotland who has the custody of the Great Seal; in England the office is now held by the Lord High Chancellor. ***Keeper of the Privy Seal***: (*a*) in England an officer through whose hands pass charters, etc. before coming to the Great Seal, now called Lord Privy Seal; (*b*) a similar officer in Scotland and the Duchy of Cornwall. †***Keeper of the Touch***: see quot. 1607.

1423 *Rolls Parlt.* IV. 257/1 If..the..Keper of the touche afore seid touche ony such Hernois wyth the Liberdisheed. **1454** *Ibid.* V. 256/2 The Chaunceller of Englond, and the Keper of the prive Seale. **1467–8** *Ibid.* V. 634/1 Hugh Bryce of London, Goldsmyth, keper of the Kyngs eschaunge in London. **1477** *Act 17 Edw. IV*, c. 5 Such and as many keepers of the same Seals, as he shall think necessary. **1562–3** *Act 5 Eliz.* c. 18 (*title*) An Acte declaring thauctoritee of the L. Keeper of the Great Seale of England and the L. Chancellor to bee one. **1607** COWELL *Interpr., Keeper of the priuy Seale*..seemeth to be called Clerke of the priuy Seale. *Ibid., Keeper o' the Touch*, anno 2 H. 6. cap. 14. seemth to be that officer in the kings mint which at this day is termed the master of the assay. **1688** *Col. Rec. Pennsylv.* I. 230 Thomas Lloyd Keeper of yᵉ Broad Seal. **1863** H. COX *Instit.* I. vii. 92 The Lord Chancellor or Lord Keeper is..Prolocutor or Speaker of the House of Lords.

d. An officer who has the charge of a forest, woods, or grounds; now *esp.* = GAMEKEEPER.

1488–9 *Act 4 Hen. VII*, c. 6 Stiwards Foresters and other kepers within the Kynges Forest of Ingilwode. *a* **1530** HEYWOOD *Weather* (Brandl 1898) 413 Rangers and kepers of certayne places, As forestes, parkes, purlewes and chasys. **1602** *2nd Pt. Return fr. Parnass.* II. v. 883, I causd the Keeper to seuer the rascall Deere from the Buckes of the first head. **1648** *Bury Wills* (Camden) 218 To George Betts, my keeper, five pounds. **1763** *Brit. Mag.* IV. 108 Duke of Kingston, keeper of Sherwood Forest. **1863** KINGSLEY *Water-Bab.* i. (1889) 16 He did not know that a keeper is only a poacher turned outside in, and a poacher is a keeper turned inside out.

†e. A nurse; one who has charge of the sick.

c **1450** *St. Cuthbert* (Surtees) 3624 Walstede, he sais, entir with me, For my kepar sall' þou be. *c* **1470** HENRY *Wallace* II. 366 Quhen Wallace was ralesched off his payne..His trew kepar he send to Elrisle. **1587** FLEMING *Contn. Holinshed* III. 1376/1 In some great extremitie of sicknesse ..some honest ancient woman a keeper, may watch with anie of them. **1651** WITTIE tr. *Primrose's Pop. Err.* III. iv. 144 Such as bee sick of feavers, for whom principally keepers are provided.

f. *Cricket.* A wicket-keeper.

1744 *Laws* [of Cricket] in *New Dict. Arts & Sci.* (1755) IV. 3459/2 When the ball has been in hand by one of the keepers or stoppers. **1868** J. LILLYWHITE *Cricketers' Compan.* 49 The best 'keeper' who ever stood behind a wicket. **1926** H. STRUDWICK *25 Yrs. behind Stumps* 244 There were very few, if any, better keepers than the Notts man. **1927** [see AUNT 4b]. **1975** *Cricketer* May 9/2 A tall 'keeper's rise from his crouch is less rapid than a smaller man's.

g. *Football.* A goal-keeper.

1957 J. MILBURN *Golden Goals* 140 (*caption*) Milburn rates Ditchburn among the greatest 'keepers he has ever faced. **1974** *Oxf. Mail* 21 Aug. 16 (*caption*) Bicester's Phillip Pratt (10) heads the ball past Thame keeper Micky Taylor for his second goal.

2. One who observes or keeps a command, law, promise, etc.

1382 WYCLIF *Ezek.* xliv. 8 Ȝe han putte keepers of myn obseruances in my sayntuarie to ȝour self. **1526** *Pilgr. Perf.* (W. de W. 1531) 54 He calleth the kepers of the commaundementes his frendes. **1625** BACON *Ess., Boldness* (Arb.) 519 For Boldnesse is an ill keeper of promise. *a* **1796** BURNS *Verses to Rankine* i, I am a keeper of the law In some sma' points, altho' not a'. **1875** JOWETT *Plato* (ed. 2) III. 428 From being a keeper of the law he is converted into a breaker of it.

3. One who owns or carries on some establishment or business.

Often the second element in combs., as *alehouse-, hotel-, lodging-house keeper*; INNKEEPER, SHOPKEEPER.

c **1440** *Promp. Parv.* 272/1 Kepare of an howse, or an howse holdare, *paterfamilias*. **1495** *Act 11 Hen. VII*, c. 2 §5 To take suertie of the kepers of ale houses of their gode behavyng. **1713** *Lond. Gaz.* No. 5141/4 Isaac Beckett.. Alehouse-keeper. **1851** HAWTHORNE *Ho. Sev. Gables* iii. 39 A forlorn old maid, and keeper of a cent-shop. **1870** W. M. BAKER *New Timothy* 167 (Cent.) A weakly, aged keeper of a little shoe-store in a village.

†4. One who keeps a mistress. *Obs.*

1676 ETHEREDGE *Man of Mode* I. i, An old doting keeper cannot be more jealous of his mistress. **1712** STEELE *Spect.* No. 461 ¶11 A Man may be a very fine Gentleman, tho' he is neither a Keeper nor an Infidel. **1748** RICHARDSON *Clarissa* (1811) IV. 151 The risk of a keeper, who takes up with a low-bred girl. *c* **1810** W. HICKEY *Mem.* (1960) xviii. 291 He at that time was the professed keeper of Mrs. Cuyler, a great jack whore, without pretensions to manners. **1846** *Swell's Night Guide* 83 Keepers are the sinews of your trade.

5. One who or that which keeps or retains, in various senses of the vb. Also *keeper-back*.

a **1548** HALL *Chron., Hen. V* 81 There is no lesse praise to be geven to the keper then to the getter. **1593** SHAKS. *Rich. II*, II. ii. 70 He is a Flatterer, A Parasite, a keeper backe of death. *a* **1617** HIERON *Wks.* (1620) II. 457 Keepers from Gods ministers, that which they ought to haue. *a* **1859** MACAULAY *Hist. Eng.* xxiii. V. 105 The best keeper of secrets in Europe.

6. a. Any mechanical device for keeping something in its place; a clasp, catch, etc. *spec.* (*a*) a loop securing the end of a buckled strap; (*b*) the mousing of a hook; (*c*) a jam-nut or check-nut; (*d*) the gripper in a flint-lock, securing the flint; (*e*) the box into which the bolt of a lock projects when shot. (Knight *Dict. Mech.*, 1875.)

1575 LANEHAM *Let.* (1871) 37 A narro gorget, fastened afore with a white clasp and a keepar close vp to the chin. **1625** *Naworth Househ. Bks.* (Surtees) 214 Tape, claspes and keepers. **1667** *Vestry Bks.* (Surtees) 336 To Tho. Cooper for makeing a keeper for Mʳ Lambton's pew dore, 2*d*. **1778** *Eng. Gazetteer* (ed. 2) s.v. *Higham*, Great catch-hooks and keepers of silver. **1867** J. HOGG *Microsc.* I. ii. 84 A gilt iron bar, ledge, or keeper, serves for an object-rest. **1888** *Sci. American* LVIII. 408/1 A glove fastener has been patented. .. It has a cylindrical keeper with one lower edge struck up to form a lip. *Ibid.*, A keeper with a slot in its upper surface adapted to receive the latch and tongue [of a glove fastener].

b. A bar of soft iron placed across the poles of a horse-shoe magnet to prevent loss of power; an armature.

Also, one of the lateral projections attached to the poles of an electro-magnet to bring these into close proximity to the revolving armature; a shoe (Knight *Dict. Mech.* Suppl. 1884).

1837 BREWSTER *Magnet.* 312 The weight was carefully removed, so as not to displace the armature or keeper. *c* **1860** FARADAY *Forces Nat.* v. 133. **1868** LOCKYER *Elem. Astron.* 274 A pricker attached to the keeper of an electro-magnet.

c. A ring that keeps another (esp. the wedding-ring) on the finger; a guard-ring.

1851 MAYHEW *Lond. Labour* I. 499 (Hoppe) A gold ring, a silver ring, and a chased keeper. **1858** *Ann. Register* 7, 150 wedding rings and keepers. **1894** HALL CAINE *Manxman* IV. xiv, She..hurried every thing into it—the money, the earrings, the keeper off her finger, and then she paused at the touch of the wedding-ring.

d. A simple ring worn in the ears to keep a pierced hole open.

1960 *Woman's Realm* 2 Apr. 69/3 Pure gold keeper rings to keep the ear-piercing open, ready for the first real earrings. **1968** K. O'HARA *Bird-Cage* vii. 55, 1 pair gold keeper ear-rings.

II. From intr. senses of the verb.

7. One who continues or remains *at* a place.

1611 BIBLE *Tit.* ii. 5 To be discreet, chaste, keepers at home.

8. A fruit, or other product, that keeps (well or ill).

1843 *Jrnl. R. Agric. Soc.* IV. II. 389 An excellent apple, and good keeper. **1892** *Garden* 27 Aug. 178 The best Apple ..splendid keeper, will last until May. **1892** *Seed Catalogue*, Royal Ash-leaf kidney [potato], heavy cropper and good keeper.

Hence **'keepering**, the work of a gamekeeper.

1861 *Baily's Monthly Mag.* Jan. 185 His keepering consisted..in an amiable crusade..against 'them darned rats'. **1892** J. WILKINS *Autobiog. Gamekpr.* I. i. 13 It made me take a liking for keepering. **1963** P. MACTYRE *Fish on Hook* iii. 48 Wynramne isn't much of a hand at the keepering. **1971** *Country Life* 12 Aug. 363/3 A shepherd..deplored the increase in the depredations of the fox, since, he said, 'keepering' had gone out of fashion.

keeper ('ki:pə(r)), *v.* [f. the sb. or as a back-formation f. KEEPERING.] *trans.* To look after as a gamekeeper. So **'keepered** *ppl. a.*

1921 *Chambers's Jrnl.* Sept. 388 An estate well-preserved and well-keepered. **1958** *Times* 13 Sept. 9/3 The full benefits of hand-rearing can be enjoyed only on ground which is adequately keepered. **1961** R. JEFFERIES *Evidence of Accused* i. 9 If the estate were keepered..it would become a rattling good shoot. **1971** *Country Life* 23 Sept. 766/3 In recent years this chalk-stream water [*sc.* River Itchen] has been well keepered and only lightly fished by a maximum of three rods. **1972** *Times* 7 Aug. 22/3 (Advt.), Keepered partridge and pheasant shoot.

keeperess ('ki:pərɪs). *rare.* [f. KEEPER *sb.* + -ESS.] A female keeper or custodian. **b.** A woman who keeps a man.

1748 RICHARDSON *Clarissa* (1811) VI. 359 (D.) Hardly ever, I dare say, was there a keeper that did not make a keeperess; who lavished away on her kept-fellow what she obtained from..him who kept her. **1863** READE *Hard Cash* III. 66 The keeperesses eclipsed the keepers in cruelty to the poorer patients.

'keeperless, *a. rare.* [f. KEEPER *sb.* + -LESS.] Not having a keeper or guardian.

1836 T. HOOK *G. Gurney* (1850) I. iii. 40 People accounted sane and permitted to range the world keeperless.

keepership ('ki:pəʃɪp). [f. KEEPER *sb.* + -SHIP.] The office or position of a keeper.

1530 in W. H. Turner *Select. Rec. Oxford* 67 Richard Edys, nowe Keper of Bockardowe, to enjoy the kepershippe of Bocardowe. **1627** DK. NEWCASTLE *Let.* in *Life* (1886) 322 Since I am not repaired in the Keepership. **1825** BENTHAM *Offic. Apt. Maximized, Observ. Peel's Sp.* (1830) 37 The keepership of the prison named after his judicatory [the King's Bench]. **1880** *Antiquary* May 227/1 The keepership of the mineralogical department of the British Museum.

†'keepful, *a. Obs. rare*[−1]. [f. KEEP *sb.* 1 + -FUL.] Careful, heedful.

1489 CAXTON *Faytes of A.* I. xv. 43 He myght haue eschewid hys hurt yf he had be as kepefull.

keeping ('ki:pɪŋ), *vbl. sb.* [f. KEEP *v.* + -ING[1].] The action of the verb KEEP in various senses.

I. From trans. senses of the vb.

1. Observance of a rule, command, ordinance, institution, practice, promise, etc.

c **1380** WYCLIF *Sel. Wks.* III. 350 Keping of Goddis mandementis. **1473–4** *Act 12 & 13 Edw. IV* in *Rolls Parlt.* VI. 33/2 The kepyng of assise of Brede, Wyne, and Ale. **1573** *Reg. St. Andrews Kirk Sess.* (1889–90) 389 Be superstitius keping of ȝwill-day halyday. **1678** WANLEY *Wond. Lit. World* v. iii. §15. 474/1 The controversie about the keeping of Easter.

2. a. The action, task, or office of looking after, guarding, defending, taking care of, etc.; custody, charge, guardianship.

a **1300** *Cursor M.* 20106 þan name þe apostil..In-til his keping, þat maidan. *c* **1380** WYCLIF *Wks.* (1880) 21 God almyȝty takiþ so gret kepyng of smale briddis [etc.]. *c* **1440** *Gesta Rom.* I. xxxv. 357 (Addit. MS.) The porter said, 'have kepyng of thi self'. *a* **1533** LD. BERNERS *Huon* lx. 209 We that hath this place in kepinge are frenchemen. **1651** HOBBES *Leviath.* III. xl. 25 The Book of the Law was in their Keeping. *a* **1735** ARBUTHNOT *John Bull* III. xxi. Misc. Wks. 1751 II. 92 As upright as a new Chancellor, who has the keeping of the King's Conscience. **1860** TYNDALL *Glac.* I. xviii. 126 To hand over your impressions to the safe keeping of memory.

b. Guard, defence. ***on*** (***at, of, upon***) ***one's keeping***, on one's guard. *Obs.* exc. *dial.*

1388 WYCLIF *Jer.* li. 12 Encreese ȝe kepyng, reise ȝe keperis. *c* **1425** *Eng. Conq. Irel.* 52 Amorow þay lefte good kypynge yn the syte. **1523** LD. BERNERS *Froiss.* I. cxxxix. 167 Than she..sette good kepyng ouer them. **1571** HANMER *Chron. Irel.* (1633) 139 To be more upon their keeping, to prevent treachery. **1590** SPENSER *F.Q.* I. xi. 2 Henceforth, bee at your keeping well. **1668** *Ormonde MSS.* in *10th Rep. Hist. MSS. Comm.* App. v. 71 Some actions..put your petitioner on his keeping. **1898** KATH. TYNAN in *Westm. Gaz.* 12 Oct. 1/3 He was already, as they say in Ireland, 'on his keeping'; that is to say, a hunted man.

†c. A flock (of sheep). Cf. *herd. Obs. rare*[−1].

1641 BEST *Farm. Bks.* (Surtees) 1 A flocke, a keepinge, or a fold of sheepe.

d. *Cricket.* Wicket-keeping.

1868 in W. A. Bettesworth *Walkers of Southgate* (1900) 291 Stephenson's 'keeping' was also first-rate. **1920** P. F. WARNER *Cricket Reminisc.* 156 His [*sc.* Blackham's] keeping to Mr. Spofforth with the 1878 Australian XI. was a revelation.

3. The taking care of a thing or person; the giving of attention so as to maintain in good order or condition; the state or condition in which a thing is kept.

c **1330** R. BRUNNE *Chron. Wace* (Rolls) 14887 Giue Englische men euen kepynge, Mete & drynke, & oþer þynge. **1468** *Chron. Eng.* in Hearne *R. Glouc.* (1724) 482 His hondes ..shewethe sumwhat vnwyt and necclygence, for he vtterliche leueth the kepyng of hem. **1523** FITZHERB. *Husb.* §112 Cratches is a sorraunce that wyll cause a horse to halte, and commeth of yll kepynge. **1523** *Churchw. Acc. St. Giles, Reading* 19 Paid for kepyng of the clok iijˢ iijᵈ. **1603** OWEN *Pembrokeshire* (1891) 280 Farre exceeding anye of the companie for stature, and good keapinge. **1712** J. JAMES tr. *Le Blond's Gardening* 68 This Keeping consists in mowing the Grass often. **1880** *Ann. Rep. R. Hort. Soc.* 5 The Garden ..in the highest state of keeping which the means of the Society allowed.

4. The maintaining of a state or condition.

c **1375** *Sc. Leg. Saints* xxxvi. (*Baptist*) 14 Angele als callit wes he, fore kepyng of verginite. *c* **1430** *Life St. Kath.* (1884)

35 To lese þe name and croune of ȝoure profession by kepynge of silence. *a* **1548** HALL *Chron., Hen. VI* 170 Exhort them to yᵉ..kepyng of good order within the citie. **1596** DALRYMPLE tr. *Leslie's Hist. Scot.* v. 261 Beneuolent keiping of kyndnes, cumpanie, and freindschip.

5. a. Maintenance, sustenance with food; food, fodder; = KEEP *sb.* 6 c.

1644 *Boston Rec.* (1877) II. 80 Charity White is allowed 26*s.* for thirteene weekes keeping of John Berry. **1671** MILTON *Samson* 1260 My labours, The work of many hands, which earns my keeping. **1708** *Yorksh. Racers* 7 His stable-room and keeping are unpaid. **1876** HOLLAND *Sev. Oaks* xii. 162 Mike thought he could hire a horse for his keeping and a sled for a small sum.

b. The maintaining of a mistress or lover; the fact or condition of being so maintained.

1675 WYCHERLEY *Country-Wife* I. Wks. (Rtldg.) 73/2 But prithee..Is not keeping better than marriage? **1678** DRYDEN *Limberham* Pref., 'Twas intended for an honest Satyr against our crying Sin of Keeping. **1727** GAY *Begg. Op.* II. iv, Pray Madam were you ever in keeping? **1768** H. WALPOLE *Hist. Doubts* 49 *note*, On the death of the king she [Jane Shore] had been taken into keeping by lord Hastings. **1853** MRS. GASKELL *Ruth* III. i. 29 She beguiled a young gentleman, who took her into keeping. **1932** J. M. S. TOMPKINS *Pop. Novel in England 1770–1800* v. 193 Women of the town flaunt at the races and are taken into keeping. **1964** *Listener* 12 Mar. 444/3 There is no stigma on 'keeping' or 'living', nor on illegitimacy.

†**6.** Confinement, imprisonment; prison. *Obs.*

1382 WYCLIF *Luke* xxi. 12 Thei schulen sette hir hondis on ȝou..bitakinge in to synagogis and kepingis [*gloss* ether prisouns]. *c* **1400** *Destr. Troy* 13953 Telamoc..come out of kepyng to his kid fadur. **1513** MORE in Grafton *Chron.* II. 772 Her kepyng of the king his brother in that place.

7. The action or fact of retaining as one's own; retention; *pl.* things kept or retained.

c **1400** *Rom. Rose* 5594 In getyng he hath such woo, And in the kepyng drede also. *a* **1548** HALL *Chron., Hen. VI* 152 b, Of the gettyng of this mannes goodes..I wil not speake: but the kepinge of them [etc.]. **1634** SIR T. HERBERT *Trav.* 185 They concluded she was good prize and worth the keeping. **1857** W. SMITH *Thorndale* 573 If there is to be any keeping, there must be some limit put on the taking.

8. Reservation for future use; preservation.

1560 DAUS tr. *Sleidane's Comm.* 434 A piece of bread..so drye..with longe kepinge. **1718** *Freethinker* No. 27 ¶1 True Wit and Good Sense will bear keeping. **1730** SWIFT *Betty the Grizette*, A tawny speckled pippin Shrivel'd with a winter's keeping. **1870** L'ESTRANGE *Miss Mitford* I. vi. 181 Are not poems, like port wine, the better for keeping? **1875** JOWETT *Plato* (ed. 2) III. 696 Fruits which spoil with keeping.

9. a. In *Painting. orig.* The maintenance of the proper relation between the representations of nearer and more distant objects in a picture; hence, in more general sense, 'the proper subserviency of tone and colour in every part of a picture, so that the general effect is harmonious to the eye' (Fairholt); the maintenance of harmony of composition.

1715 J. RICHARDSON *The. Painting* 224 The Composition is not to be justifyed..the Groups are too Regularly placed, and without any Keeping in the Whole, that is, they appear too near of an Equal Strength. **1762** GOLDSM. *Cit. W.* lv, [Parodying art slang] 'What do you think, sir, of that head in the corner, done in the manner of Grisoni? There's the true keeping in it. **1768** W. GILPIN *Upon Prints* 20 *Keeping* then proportions a proper degree of strength to the near and distant parts, in respect to *each other.* **1780** JOHNSON *Let. to Mrs. Thrale* 1 May, There is contour, and keeping, and grace, and expression, and all the varieties of artificial excellence. **1792** *Resid. France* (1797) I. 87 Some mixture of splendour and clumsiness, and a want of what the painters call keeping. **1809** MAR. EDGEWORTH *Absentee* x, In Lady Clonbrony's mind, as in some bad paintings, there was no keeping; all objects, great and small, were upon the same level. **1859** GULLICK & TIMBS *Paint.* 172 The keeping and repose in this cartoon are inimitable.

b. *generally.* Agreement, congruity, harmony.

1819 HAZLITT *Eng. Com. Writers* vi. (1869) 153 There is the exquisite keeping in the character of Blifil, and the want of it in that of Tom Jones. **1870** LOWELL *Study Wind.* 406 For wit, fancy, invention, and keeping, it [the Rape of the Lock] has never been surpassed.

c. Phr. ***in*** or ***out of keeping*** (***with***): in or out of harmony or agreement (with).

c **1790** IMISON *Sch. Art* II. 59 In what respect it is out of keeping; that is, what parts are too light, and what too dark. **1806** F. HORNER *Let.* in *Life* vii. (1849) 175 They were so in keeping with the whole that the prevailing tone was..never interrupted. **1824** MISS FERRIER *Inher.* xlvii, To use an artist phrase, nothing could be more in keeping with the day than the reception Miss S. met with. **1830** *Blackw. Mag.* XXVII. 310 It is in 'fine keeping', as the phrase is. **1841** LEVER *C. O'Malley* iv. 24 His own costume of black coat, leathers and tops, was in perfect keeping. **1841** MYERS *Cath. Th.* III. v. 14 Such an utterance of Truth would..be out of keeping with our present condition in the flesh. **1878** BOSW. SMITH *Carthage* 26 Indications..in thorough keeping with the view we have taken.

II. From intr. senses of the vb.

10. Staying or remaining in a place or in a certain condition; remaining sound.

1742 *Lond. & Country Brew.* I. (ed. 4) 22 The Handful of Salt..hinders their Ale from keeping. **1776** J. HUNTER *Let. to Jenner* 22 Jan., Wks. 1835 I. 59 Their keeping into one substance would make me inclinable to believe that it is a new substance. **1785** SARAH FIELDING *Ophelia* I. xxv, I took advantage of my disorder to excuse my keeping at home.

III. 11. With adverbs, as ***keeping back***, ***down***, ***in***, ***out***, ***up***: see KEEP *v.* IV.

1552 HULOET, Kepynge backe or a part, *reseruatio, retentio.* *a* **1568** ASCHAM *Scholem.* I. (Arb.) 48 Sharpe kepinge in, and bridleinge of youth. **1667** PEPYS *Diary* 26 Apr., He says that the king's keeping in still with my Lady Castlemaine do show it. **1814** WELLINGTON 15 May in Gurw. *Desp.* (1838) XII. 12 An allowance for the purchase and keeping up of a mule in the public service. **1835** MACAULAY *Ess., Mackintosh's Hist. Rev.* (1887) 366 By resistance they meant the keeping out of James the Third. **1884** *Nonconf. & Indep.* 25 Sept. 927/3 The system of 'keeping in' [at school] is barbarous. **1897** *Allbutt's Syst. Med.* IV. 371 The keeping down of uræmic accumulation.

IV. 12. *attrib.* and *Comb.*, as ***keeping-beer***, ***ewe-lamb***, ***-ground***, ***-sheep***, etc.

1741 *Compl. Fam.-Piece* I. vi. 284 The Season for brewing Keeping-beer. **1773** *Hist. Brit. Dom. N. Amer.* II. ii. §12. 217 When whales are much disturbed, they quit their keeping-ground. **1886** SCOTT *Sheep-Farming* 115 A new system of not weaning the keeping ewe lambs at all.

'keeping, *ppl. a.* [f. as prec. + -ING².] That keeps, in various senses (see the verb). Esp. of fruit (cf. KEEP *v.* 41).

c **1430** *A B C of Aristotle* in *Babees Bk.* 12 [Be not] to kinde, ne to kepynge, & be waar of knaue tacchis. **1677** MRS. BEHN *Rover* II. ii, All this frights me not: 'tis still much better than a keeping husband. **1703** ROWE *Fair Penit.* I. i. 236 Some keeping Cardinal shall doat upon thee. **1801** WOLCOTT (P. Pindar) *Tears & Smiles* Wks. 1812 V. 30 Daughters and dead fish, we find Were never keeping wares. **1816** JANE AUSTEN *Emma* II. ix. 187 There never was such a keeping apple any where as one of his trees. **1842** HOOD *Let.* 12 Oct. in F. F. Broderip *Memorials Thomas Hood* (1860) II. iv. 140 Our gardener said they [*sc.* pears] were a *keeping* sort, and would be good at Christmas. **1963** *Times* 11 Feb. 13/5 The majority of pupils ate sandwiches and keeping-apples.

'keeping-room. *local* and *U.S.* [KEEP *v.* 37.] The room usually occupied by a person or family as a sitting-room; a parlour.

1790 MARSHAM in *G. White's Selborne* (1877) II. 257 On the 24th I found a dark butterfly in my keeping-room. **1794** A. YOUNG *Agric. Suffolk* (1797) 11 The door..opening immediately from the external air into the keeping-room. **1852** MRS. STOWE *Uncle Tom's C.* xv, In the family 'keeping-room', as it is termed [of the New England farm-house]. **1871** 'M. LEGRAND' *Cambr. Freshm.* 55 Most fortunate to get into college in your first term, sir. Yes, sir, this is your keeping-room; and..this here's your study.

keepsake ('kiːpseɪk). [f. KEEP *v.* + SAKE: cf. *namesake.*] **a.** Anything kept or given to be kept for the sake of, or in remembrance of, the giver. *spec.* the name given to certain literary annuals consisting of collections of verse, prose, and illustrations, common in the early part of the nineteenth century; so called as being designed for gifts.

1790 MAD. D'ARBLAY *Diary* Apr., She sent me a little neat pocket volume, which I accept..as just the keepsake [etc.]. **1794** MRS. RADCLIFFE *Myst. Udolpho* xxvi, A beautiful new sequin, that Ludovico gave me for a keepsake. **1861** *Sat. Rev.* 7 Dec. 587 She pulls out a pair of scissors, and cuts out a patch as a keepsake. **1862** THORNBURY *Turner* I. 249 About 1824, the frivolous keepsake mania..gave an impetus to modern art. Keepsakes are said to have originated in an idea suggested by Mr. Alaric Watts. **1885** R. BUCHANAN *Annan Water* iv, Take the money and buy yourself a keep-sake to remind you of me.

b. *attrib.*; *spec.* Having the inane prettiness of faces depicted in a keepsake volume; having the namby-pamby literary style of such books.

1839 THACKERAY in *Corsair* (N.Y.) 26 Oct. 522/1 A book on Versailles with numerous engravings in the Keepsake fashion. **1848** (*title*) Keepsake Gift Book of Tales and Poetry. **1895** HAMILTON AÏDÉ *Elizabeth's Pretenders* 199 With the faintest touch of rouge..and her keepsake air, she felt herself to be irresistible. **1898** *Daily Chron.* 8 Oct. 4/7 'Eyes raised towards heaven are always fine eyes' may have a sort of 'keepsake' prettiness, but is really not common sense.

Hence **'keepsaky** *a.*, of the style of the compositions or illustrations in a keepsake volume.

1871 GEO. ELIOT in Cross *Life* III. 145 That keepsakey, impossible face which Maclise gave him [Dickens]. **1891** *Daily News* 26 Dec. 3/1 The more smooth and keepsaky style [of illustration].

keercheef, obs. form of KERCHIEF.

keer-drag. A form of drag-net having a very small mesh towards the end, used by zoologists for collecting small fishes and other marine animals.

1836 YARRELL *Brit. Fishes* I. 211 Fishing with a small but very useful net..called a keerdrag. **1853** P. H. GOSSE in *Zoologist* II. 3993, I take it in considerable numbers in Weymouth Bay, by means of the net known as a 'keerdrag', which rakes the bottom.

keere, keerie: see KIER, KIERIE.

keertan, var. KIRTAN.

keeshond ('keɪshɒnd). Also **-hound.** Pl. **-honden.** [Du.] A grey, long-coated dog, a variety of the spitz, of medium size, with a fox-like head, pointed ears, and tail curled over the back; originally a Dutch or German breed.

1926 *Westm. Gaz.* 10 Feb., Kesshonds [*sic*] will find many admirers on account of their showy wolf-coloured coats. Some have been exhibited recently as Dutch barge dogs. **1927** *Daily Express* 15 June 15 The Keeshounds, Dutch dogs,..were shown in this country for the first time. They are about the size of a Chow, grey black in colour, exceedingly strong. **1927** E. C. ASH *Dogs: their Hist. & Devel.* I. 159 The keeshond is the well-known Dutch dog, often seen on the barges. **1950** A. C. SMITH *Dogs since 1900* 260 In 1926 the Kennel Club decided that..all previously registered as Dutch Barge Dogs should be transferred to the Keeshond registers. **1971** F. HAMILTON *World Encycl. Dogs* 596 Keeshonden were the dogs of the peasantry—living in villages and on farms as well as barges. *Ibid.* 598 The Keeshond's long coat requires special attention once a week with a stiff brush. **1972** *Country Life* 10 Feb. 328/3 Miss H. M. Loughrey..picked out a Dalmatian, a chow chow,..a keeshound.

keeslip, Sc. form of CHEESELIP¹, rennet; also a name of *Galium verum* = CHEESE-RENNET.

keessel, var. KISSEL.

keest (kiːst). *Sc.* Also **kiest, kyst.** [a. Du. *keest* marrow, kernel, best part of anything.] Marrow, sap, substance, vigour. Hence **'keestless** *a.* void of sap or substance.

1802 SIBBALD *Chron. Sc. Poetry* Gloss., *Kystless*, tasteless. **1814** CARLYLE *Early Lett.* Oct. (1886) I. 26 So cold and kiestless am I. **1825** JAMIESON, *Keest*, sap, substance. **1890** *Alison H. Dunlop* 132 The ceaseless wetting of the thread would take the substance—the very keest—out of his ward's body.

keest, obs. pa. t. of CAST *v.*

keester, var. KEISTER.

'keet (kiːt). *Austral.* Colloquial shortened form of LORIKEET or PARAKEET.

1936 A. RUSSELL *Gone Nomad* x. 83 Snow-white cockatoos flashed in flocks across the stream, green 'keets screeched among the gums. **1959** S. H. COURTIER *Death in Dream Time* iii. 27 That's where the 'keets come... They're a wonderful sight in the flame-trees..all green and gold.

keething, keetlyng: see KITHING, KITLING.

keeve, kive (kiːv, kaɪv). Forms: α. 1 **cýf**, 2 **cuf**, 3 **kiue**, 4–8 **kive**, 6 **kyve**. β. 5–6 **keve**, 8– **kieve**, 9 **keave**, 7– **keeve**. [OE. *cýf* may represent an OTeut. **kūbjā*, but has no exact equivalent in the cognate langs. The sense is that of LG. *küven*, *keuben* and G. *kübel* (MHG. also *kübbel*; cf. OHG. *milich-chubili* milk-pail), but these have short *u* as stem-vowel.

The normal repr. of OE. *cýf*, *cýfe* is *kive*, but the word is now practically obs., exc. in s.w. dial., where the form is *keeve*; cf. *fere, here, heve, kee* = *fire, hire, hive, kye.*]

1. A tub or vat; *spec.* a vat for holding liquid in brewing and bleaching; in *Mining*, a vessel in which tin or copper ore is washed.

α. *c* **1000** ÆLFRIC *Hom.* I. 58 Se het afyllan ane cyfe mid weallendum ele. *Ibid.* II. 178 Þa stod ðær an æmtiȝ cyf. *a* **1300** *Sat. People Kildare* xiv. in *E.E.P.* (1862) 155 Hail be ȝe skinners wiþ ȝure drenche kiue, Who so smilliþ þer-to wo is him aliue. **1509** *Yatton Churchw. Acc.* (Som. Rec. Soc.) 130 Payd to yᵉ hoper for hopyng of yᵉ kyve..*jd.* *a* **1661** FULLER *Worthies, Derbysh.* I. (1662) 230 They must brew every day, yea pour it out of the Kive into the Cup. **1743** *Lond. & Country Brew.* IV. (ed. 2) 266 In Winter they ferment a little first in the Kive or Tun to put to the Wort in the Barrel. **1755** SHEBBEARE *Lydia* (1769) II. 100 (E.D.D.) A brewer's kive filled with new beer.

β. **1446** *Yatton Churchw. Acc.* (Som. Rec. Soc.) 83 It. for the chetyl and the keve..vid. **1574** in Worth *Tavistock Par. Acc.* (1887) 30 For mendyng of the lyme Keve vjd. **1674** RAY *S. & E. Country Words* 69 *A Keeve* (Devon), a Fat wherein they work their beer up before they tun it. **1743** MAXWELL *Sel. Trans. Soc. Improv. Agric. Scot.* 343 As for the Bleaching-house, it ought to be furnished with..good Keeves or Tubs for Bucking. **1776** BOLTON in A. Young *Tour Irel.* (1780) II. 201 (Cider-making) As the juice is thus pressed out, let it be poured into large vessels, usually called Keeves, to undergo the fermentation. **1875** *Ure's Dict. Arts* II. 107 A large kieve of water, in which the sieve is suspended by the iron rod. **1887** R. HUNT *Brit. Mining* (ed. 2) 910/2 *Kieve*, a vat or large iron-bound tub for washing ores. **1959** *Times* 10 Nov. p. iii/5 Large mashing vessels called kieves from which the wort is drawn off leaving the grains behind. **1967** *New Scientist* 6 July 23/1 The mash is cooked up with water in mash tuns, or kieves.

2. A local name for the mill-hoop, the enclosing case of a run of stones in a flour mill (HOOP *sb.*¹ 2).

3. *attrib.* and *Comb.*, as ***keeve-net*** (Cornw.), ***keeve-work***.

1550–1600 *Customs Duties* (B.M. Add. MS. 25097), Kive or dole eles, the barrell of either, xxxs. **1776** G. SEMPLE *Building in Water* 60 *Keeve-work*, that is, making large Vessels of red Deal Boards, hooped both with Iron and strong Oak Hoops. **1883** *Leisure Hour* 697/2 These [pilchards] he catches..in his 'kieve net'—a net somewhat like an angler's landing-net.

keever, obs. form of KIVER.

Keewatin (kiː'weɪtɪn). *Geol.* The name of a district in the Northwest Territories, Canada, used *attrib.* and *absol.* to denote the oldest division of the Archæan in North America and rocks representing it, found in the Canadian Shield region.

1886 A. C. LAWSON in *Ann. Rep. Geol. Survey Canada 1885* I. 14CC, The most appropriate name for the series that suggests itself to me is 'Keewatin', the Indian name for the North-west, or the North-west wind, which has been applied to the district within which the rocks occur. *Ibid.* 19CC, The contact of the Laurentian gneiss and the Keewatin schists. **1925** *Bull. Geol. Soc. Amer.* XXXVI. 363 The Coutchiching beds pass down under the Keewatin. **1927** *Jrnl. Geol.* XXXV. 143 At present the general use of

the term Keewatin in the United States and Canada is as the name of the oldest rock series of the region. *Ibid.*, The view that the Keewatin rocks are the oldest in Canada is moreover inconsistent with much recent geological work. **1970** DORR & ESCHMAN *Geol Michigan* iv. 39/1 Nearly 3·5 billion years ago, during Keewatin time, streams from bordering highlands deposited sediments and lavas poured out on the surface of the earth in what is now the Upper Peninsula of Michigan. **1972** L. W. MINTZ *Hist. Geol.* xiii. 388 Keewatin rocks, like all other very old sediments, appear to be oceanic in origin and consist chiefly of metamorphosed lavas and turbidites.

‖**kef, keif, kief** (kɛf, kaɪf, kiːf). Also **kaif, keef, kieff, kif(f).** [Arab. *kaif*, colloquially *kef*, well-being, good-humour, enjoyment, pleasure.]

1. A state of drowsiness or dreamy intoxication, such as is produced by the use of bhang, etc. **b.** The enjoyment of idleness; 'dolce far niente'. ***to make*** (or ***do***) ***kef***, to pass the time in idleness.

1808 R. DRUMMOND *Illustr. Gram. Guzarattee*, etc. (Y.), A kind of *confectio Japonica*.. causing keif, or the first degree of intoxication. **1852** BADGER *Nestorians* I. 327 Parties of Christians were making *keif*, i.e. taking their pleasure and drinking arack. **1864** SALA in *Daily Tel.* 23 Dec., You may smoke, you may enjoy your *kef*. **1865** W. CORY *Lett. & Jrnls.* (1897) 163, I fell into *kef*, being incapable of sustained thought. **1885** MRS. H. WARD tr. *Amiel's Jrnl.* (1891) 72, I came to understand the Buddhist trance of the Soufis, the kief of the Turk. **1892** MARIANNE NORTH *Recoll. Happy Life* II. 9 All the grand people were doing 'kef' after breakfast under the trees. **1897** KEITH *Plea Simpler Faith* 137 To him [the Bedouin] the greatest enjoyment is his Kaif, his perfect idleness.

2. (In Morocco and Algeria, in form *kief, keef.*) Indian hemp or other substance smoked to produce this state. Also *attrib.*

1878 HOOKER & BALL *Morocco* 188 The habitual uses of kief prepared from Indian hemp. **1880** BENTLEY & TRIMEN *Medicinal Plants* IV. §231 In Algeria the Hemp is cultivated under the name of Kif. **1889** HALL CAINE *Scape-goat* (1891) I. 193 Men lay about holding pipes charged with keef. **1892** *Blackw. Mag.* Sept. 426 The lazy slave of Wazan lounging in the sun, kiff-pipe in mouth. **1907** *Daily Chron.* 7 Dec. 3/5 What opium is in China, Kieff (Indian hemp) is threatening to become in Morocco. **1925** *Blackw. Mag.* Nov. 621/2 The sentry.. lays down his rifle to accept the pipe of kieff from this same officer. **1938** *Mr.* (N.Y.) Dec. 117/1 In one corner two Arabs were sitting quietly smoking, and the smell of *kif* (hashish) was in the air. **1960** *Spectator* 29 July 176 He lived longest in Tangier, in a room in the Medina where he cooked hashish candy.. crouched in a Reich orgone box smoking kif. **1962** *Ibid.* 3 Aug. 165 The triumphs of various kif (hashish) smokers over their persecutors. **1963** T. TULLETT *Inside Interpol* iv. 45 Hashish.. is generally smoked in a 'kif' pipe. **1969** [see DAGGA[1]]. **1971** *Frendz* 21 May 13 Dope... Turkish... Commonly cut with Honey, earth, kief glue & boot polish to make it black.

ˈ**keffekilite.** *Min.* [f. next + -ITE[1]: named (in Ger. form *keffekilith*) by Fischer 1811.] A greyish greasy lithomarge found in the Crimea.

1868 in DANA *Min.*

‖**keffekill.** *Min. Obs. rare.* Also **kiffe-, kiefe-.** ['Said to mean the earth of Keffe or Kaffe, the town of the Crimea from which it was shipped' (Chester, *Dict. Names Min.*). Perh. repr. Pers. *kef-i-gil* 'foam of clay'; but the classical Pers. name is *kef-i-daryā* 'foam of the sea' (J. T. Platts).] = MEERSCHAUM.

[**1758** CRONSTEDT *Mineralogie* 79 states, that the *Keffekil Tartarorum* was used by the Tartars as soap.] **1784** KIRWAN *Elem. Min.* 59 Meershaum of the Germans, Keffekill. **1796** *Ibid.* (ed. 2) I. 145 Keffekill or myrsen.. is said to be when recently dug of a yellow colour, and as tenacious as cheese or wax. **1807** T. THOMSON *Chem.* (ed. 3) II. 477 To the first of these classes belongs the ruby; to the second, steatites and kiffekille.

ˈ**keffel.** *dial.* and *obs. slang.* Also 7-8 **keffal,** 8 **kefield,** 9 **kephel.** [a. Welsh *ceffyl* horse: see CAPLE.] A horse, *esp.* a sorry horse.

a **1700** B. E. *Dict. Cant. Crew*, *Keffal*, a Horse. **1706** E. WARD *Hud. Rediv.* I. XII. 26 At last a Negro Devil came On a dun Kefield, blind and lame. **1748** RICHARDSON *Clarissa* II. xx. 130 Old Robin at a distance, on his roan Keffel. *c* **1825** *Houlston Tracts* II. xlviii. 3 Thomas Shelton's kephels are so thin and weak, they can hardly lift one leg after the other. **1879** MISS JACKSON *Shropsh. Word-bk.*, *Keffel*, a sorry, worthless horse.

‖**keffiyeh** (kɛˈfiːjeɪ). Also **kefiyeh, -ia, kef(f)eyah, keffie(h), kafieh, kaff-, kufiyeh.** [Arab. *kaffīyah* or *kuffīyeh*, by some held to be ad. late Lat. *cofea, cuphia*: see COIF.] A kerchief worn as a head-dress by the Bedouin Arabs.

a **1817** J. L. BURCKHARDT *Bedouins* (1831) I. 48 All the Bedouins wear on the head.. a turban or square kerchief of cotton.. called *keffie*. *a* **1839** LADY H. STANHOPE *Mem.* (1845) I. iii. 98 (Stanf.) A silk handkerchief, commonly worn by the Bedouin Arabs, known by the Arabic name of keffeyah. **1847** DISRAELI *Tancred* III. vii, That audacious-looking Arab in a red *kefia*. **1881** L. WALLACE *Ben Hur* I. i, His face was.. hidden by a red *kufiyeh*. **1892** *Blackw. Mag.* Mar. 409 His head protected by a kefiyeh.

‖**kefir** (ˈkɛfə(r)). Also **kefyr, kephir.** [Caucasian.] An effervescent liquor resembling koumiss, prepared from milk which has been fermented; employed as a medicine or food for invalids.

1884 *Nature* 3 July 216/2 Kephir has only been generally known even in Russia for about two years. **1894** *Lancet* 3 Nov. 1072 Koumiss and kefyr and examples of sour fermented milk containing an excess of carbonic acid gas.

b. ***kefir ferment, grains,*** or ***seeds,*** a composite substance used by the Caucasians to ferment milk.

1887 in *Syd. Soc. Lex.* **1898** BLACKMAN in *Working Men's Coll. Jrnl.* V. 60 The inhabitants of the Caucasus have kephir grains. To produce kephir, about 6 parts of milk is mixed with 1 part of the grains... Kephir grains consist of 2 sorts of bacteria and a yeast.

†**keft,** *pa. pple. Obs. rare*[−1]. [? a. ON. *keypt, keyft*, pa. pple. of *kaupa* to buy: see COUP *v.*[1]] Bought, paid for: = *abought*, pa. pple. of ABY *v.*

c **1300** *Havelok* 2005 þus wolde þe theues me haue reft, But god þank, he hauen-et sure keft.

‖**keftedes** (kɛfˈtɛðiːz), *sb. pl.* Also **keftedhes, keftethes, keph-.** [Gr. κεφτές, pl. κεφτέδες meat ball, f. Turk. *köfte*.] A Greek dish of small meat balls made with herbs and onions.

1912 E. CRAIES *Recipes from East & West* 82 Mix.. some grated Parmesan cheese, as it makes the keftedes much lighter. **1958** R. LIDDELL *Morea* II. vii. 173 The pleasant young woman in charge of the children handed round *keftèdhes* and hard-boiled eggs. **1966** *Observer* (Colour Suppl.) 2 Oct. 45/4 Keftethes.. minced veal.. grated onion .. breadcrumbs. **1970** *Times* 29 Apr. 18/4 You will get.. keftedes (spiced meat balls).

Keftian (ˈkɛftɪən), *sb.* and *a.* Also **Keftiu** *sing.* and *coll.*; pl. **Caphtorim** (Heb. *Kaphtōrīm*). [Cf. *Caphtor*, Heb. *Kaphtōr*, name in O.T. for the place of origin of the Philistines.] **A.** *sb.* Name in Egyptian records of a people of the E. Mediterranean, identified by some authorities with the Cretans; a member of this people.

c **1000** ÆLFRIC *Heptateuch* Gen. x. 14 Mesraim, Cames oþer sunu, gestrynde six suna; of þam comon þa Philistei & seo mægð Capturym. **1611** BIBLE *Gen.* x. 14 And Mizraim begat.. Casluhim (out of whome came Philistiim) and Caphtorim. **1891** A. H. SAYCE *Races Old Testament* iii. 53 The Caphtorim.. were the natives of the coast-land Caphtor. **1903** H. R. HALL in *Ann. Brit. Sch. Athens 1901–1902* 164 The facial type of the Keftians.. is definitely European. *Ibid.* 165 Apparently Müller regarded the Keftiu not as themselves genuine Mycenaeans, but as mere handers on of Mycenaean objects. **1913** R. A. S. MACALISTER *Philistines* i. 14 The Egyptians were brought into direct contact with the Keftians. **1931** *Times Lit. Suppl.* 13 Aug. 623/2 G. A. Wainwright in 'Keftiu: Crete or Cilicia?' publishes further evidence in support of his thesis that the Keftiuans of the Egyptian monuments are not Cretans.. but Cilicians. **1961** C. F. PFEIFFER *Baker's Bible Atlas* (1962) iii. 41/2 The family of Mizraim had several branches: Ludim, Anamim, Lehabim,.. and Caphtorim. **1967** H. E. L. MELLERSH *Minoan Crete* v. 55 There can hardly be any doubt at all that the Keftiu were the Cretans.

B. *adj.* Belonging to or relating to this people or their language.

1903 H. R. HALL in *Ann. Brit. Sch. Athens 1901–1902* 175 A list of Keftian proper names on a writing-board and a list of words of the Keftian language on papyrus,.. are the last records of the men of Keftiu. **1913** R. A. S. MACALISTER *Philistines* i. 13 It has been suggested that it might be a nominative suffix of the Keftian language. *Ibid.* iv. 115 The sign *a*, a man running, shows the simple waist-band which forms the sole body-covering of the Keftian envoys. **1929** J. GARSTANG *Hittite Empire* ii. 42 It was left to the Keftian traders to carry on commercial intercourse that brought to Egypt the wares of Crete and Mycenae.

keg (kɛg), *sb.* [Later form of CAG *sb.*[1], q.v.]

1. a. A small barrel or cask, usually of less than 10 gallons.

1632 SHERWOOD, A kegge, *Caque. Voyez* a Cag. **1678** PHILLIPS (ed. 4) App., *Kag*, or *Keg*.. a large Vessel for the laying of Sturgeon in pickle. **1766** W. GORDON *Gen. Counting-ho.* 318, 5 kegs of barley. **1812** BYRON *Juan* II. xlvi, Two casks of biscuit and a keg of butter. **1835** MRS. CARLYLE *Lett.* I. 47 One could have a little keg of salt herrings sent.

†**b.** A portion of sturgeon sufficient to fill a keg (cf. CAG *sb.*[1] 1, quot. 1704). *Obs.*

1617 MINSHEU *Ductor*, A Kegge of Sturgion,.. *Vne piece d'esturgeon.* **1622** DRAYTON *Poly-olb.* xxv. (1748) 367 The Sturgeon cut to keggs (too big to handle whole).

c. *slang.* The stomach.

1887 F. FRANCIS *Saddle & Mocassin* 270 (Farmer) We'd been having a time and my keg was pretty full too.

d. *spec.* A barrel of beer; beer. *Austral.* and *N.Z. slang.*

1945 E. G. WEBBER *Johnny Enzed in Middle East* 15/2, I thought it was the keg. **1957** 'N. CULOTTA' *They're a Weird Mob* (1958) viii. 110 We struggled with the kegs, and got them set up on the bench. **1959** M. SHADBOLT *New Zealanders* 108 Wild proletarian parties, in slummy Freeman's Bay, where kegs flowed and fights flared. **1965** J. O'GRADY *Aussie English* 16 Containers run from five-ounce glasses to eighteen-gallon kegs.

e. In full ***keg ale, beer, bitter.*** Ale, beer, etc., from a keg (see quot. 1972).

1949 M. WEEKS *Beer & Brewing in Amer.* 25 Keg (draught) beer is kept at low temperatures. **1961** *Brewers' Jrnl.* XCVII. 373/2 Mr. G. Dent drew attention to increased beer sales, and in particular a large increase in Keg beers. **1963** *Times* 12 Feb. 17/1 When demand for keg beer rose, they would seek to expand. **1967** C. DRUMMOND *Death at Furlong Post* xii. 151 The brewery.. had rushed out twenty-four gallons of keg beer... 'The whole bleedin' world wants keg ale.' **1968** W. GARNER *Deep, Deep Freeze* vi. 73 The Duke of York.. stocked a good line in keg bitter. **1968** 'D. RUTHERFORD' *Skin for Skin* ii. 18 Crispin ordered two pints of Keg and carried them to the dimmest corner of the Saloon. **1971** *Times* 12 June 14/5 The new drinkers who do like beer are willing to pay extra for keg. **1972** *Which?* Apr. 124/2 One way to think of 'keg' beer is as a 'bottled' beer, but in a five or 11 gallon sealed metal container. Keg is chilled, filtered and (usually) pasteurised beer which has had carbon dioxide added.

2. *attrib.*, as ***keg-buoy, -head;*** **keg-fig** (see quot.).

1868 PAXTON *Bot. Dict.*, *Keg fig* of Japan is the fruit of *Diospyros Kaki.* **1883** *Fisheries Exhib. Catal.* (ed. 4) 127 Keg Buoy, for floating drift nets. **1895** *Century Mag.* Aug. 570 He had on a keg hat, all shiny silk, and a red necktie.

Hence †**keg** *v.*, to cut up (a sturgeon) into 'kegs'.

1630 J. TAYLOR (Water P.) *Jack-a-lent* Wks. (1630) I. 117/1 The poore Anchoue is pittifully pepper'd in the fight, whilst the Sturgeon is keg'd, randed, and iold about the eares.

kegeree, variant of KEDGEREE.

keghet, keȝte, obs. ff. *caught*: see CATCH *v.*

kegler (ˈkɛglə(r), ˈkeɪglə(r)). *N. Amer.* Also **keggler.** [G. *kegler* skittle-player: cf. KAYLES *sb. pl.*] One who plays tenpin bowling, skittles, ninepins, etc.

1932 *Lincoln* (Neb.) *State Jrnl.* 9 Mar., Floyd Olds.. began calling the pin topplers, keglers, and the folk in Cleveland began looking at him askance. **1943** FALCARO & GOODMAN *Bowling for All* vii. 28 The kegler who feels that he has a 300 game.. will discover that every delivery gets tougher after that. **1956** *Wall St. Jrnl.* 22 Mar. 1/1 These sportsmen and women, known to each other as 'keglers', will spend about $250 million on their sport, 10 times as much as both major baseball leagues collected in a gate receipts last year. **1958** *Economist* 20 Dec. 1085/1 If the 'keggler' does not knock down all the pins with his two balls he is credited merely with the number of pins he does knock over. **1970** *Daily Colonist* (Victoria, B.C.) 5 Apr. 15/2 The Kokomo, Ind., kegler beat Dick Ritger, of Hartford, Wis., in the championship [bowling] match. **1974** *Plain Dealer* (Cleveland, Ohio) 27 Oct. 12-C/5 In match play, each kegler faces each other one time, with the winner of a contest receiving 30 bonus pins.

keg-meg, dial. variant of CAGMAG.

†**kegwort.** *Herb. Obs. rare*[−1]. Some plant.

1610 MARKHAM *Masterp.* II. clxxiii. 485 *Bettonicum*, which we call dogstone or kegwort.

‖**kehaya** (kɛhəˈjɑː). Forms: 6 **cahaia,** 7 **cayha, cahay, caya, kia(y(a,** 8 **kehaja, k(i)aya, kiyaya, chiaia, kaia, caia,** 8–9 **kiaja,** 9 **kiayah, kehaya.** [Turk. *kiḥayā, kekhyā*, etc., corrupt forms of Pers. (and Turk.) *katkhudā* (cf. *kad* house + *khudā* master), viceroy, vicar, deputy, etc.] A Turkish viceroy, deputy, agent, etc.; a local governor; a village chief.

1599 HAKLUYT *Voy.* II. ii. 192 A *Cahaia* of the *Andoluzes* .. and another principall Moore. **1625** PURCHAS *Pilgrims* I. III. xi. §3. 256 The seuenth day, I was sent for to the *Cayhas* garden. **1688** *Lond. Gaz.* No. 2308/2 Rageb the Caimacan, his Kiaia or Lieutenant. **1702** *Ibid.* No. 3875/2 The last having served him as his Kehaja. **1717** LADY M. W. MONTAGU *Let. to C'tess Mar* 18 Apr., The Greek lady with me earnestly solicited me to visit the *kiyaya's* lady, saying, he was the second officer in the empire. *a* **1734** NORTH *Lives* (1742) II. 450 The money demanded was.. twenty-five purses for the vizier, and five for the kaia and officers. **1819** T. HOPE *Anastasius* (1827) III. v. 122 In the capacity of the Pasha's kehaya, he enjoyed both the direction of his councils and the command of his armies. **1895** *Daily News* 21 Mar. 5/6 They had a Kehaya who led them... A Kehaya is a leader or head man.

‖**kehilla** (kəˈhɪlə). Also **kehillah, kille.** Pl. **kehi(l)lot, kehilloth.** [ad. Heb. *qěhillāh* community.] The Jewish community in a town or village.

1882 tr. *L. Kompert's Scenes from Ghetto* 67 She grew up, became beautiful, and in all the *kille* people talked of nothing but Hendel, the daughter of Rebb Paltiel Wolf. **1892** I. ZANGWILL *Childr. Ghetto* I. 126 Every town which could muster the minimum of ten men for worship boasted its Kehillah. **1950** [see JUDENRAT]. **1961** *Observer* 3 Dec. 10/6 The formal communities of Russian Jews, the *kehilot*, were abolished in 1919 and never restored. **1967** N. COHN *Warrant for Genocide* vii. 163 The official New York Jewish community organization,.. under the name Kehilla (Yiddish for 'Kahal') was chiefly concerned with protecting and educating Jewish immigrants. **1971** *Jewish Communities of World* (Inst. Jewish Affairs) (ed. 3) 29 The Buenos Aires Community (*Kehillah*) is the largest. *Ibid.* 90 There are no organized local Communities (*Kehillot*) in France. **1973** *Jewish Chron.* 2 Feb. 7/2 We have no intention.. of creating a separatist movement or a new *kehilla* or some political group.

kehoeite (kiːˈhəʊaɪt, ˈkiːhəʊaɪt). *Min.* [f. the name of Henry *Kehoe*, who discovered it + -ITE[1].] A hydrated hydroxide and phosphate of aluminium, zinc, and calcium, found as white, chalky, amorphous masses in South Dakota.

1893 W. P. HEADDEN in *Amer. Jrnl. Sci.* CXLVI. 24, I propose the name Kehoeite as the name of this mineral, after Mr. Henry Kehoe, to whom I am indebted for the material and who was the first to observe its occurrence. **1964** *Mineral. Mag.* XXXIII. 799 The hardness of kehoeite cannot be determined because of its microcrystalline nature.

kehte, obs. pa. t. of CATCH *v.*

kei-apple (ˈkaɪˌæp(ə)l). [f. *Kei*, name of a river formerly separating Cape Colony from Kaffraria.] The edible fruit of a South African shrub, *Aberia Caffra*; also, the shrub itself.
1859 HARVEY & SONDER *Flora Capensis* II. 585, *Aberia Caffra*, hab. Eastern districts and Kaffirland. A shrub or small tree,..fruit edible like a small yellowish apple. Colonial name, the Kei apple.

keiching, keie, keight, (keiȝt, keiht), keigne, keik, keil(l, obs. ff. KITCHEN, KEY, CAUGHT, CHAIN, KEEK *v.*, KEEL *sb.*², KILL *v.*

keilhauite (ˈkaɪlhaʊaɪt). *Min.* [Named 1844, after Prof. B. M. Keilhau.] A titano-silicate of calcium, yttrium, and other metals.
1846 *Amer. Jrnl. Sc.* Ser. II. II. 415 Keilhauite was found near Arendal in Norway. **1868** DANA *Min.* (ed. 5) 387 The Alve keilhauite has two cleavages inclined to one another 138°.

†**keir**, *v. Sc. Obs. rare*⁻¹. [Cf. ON. *keyra* to drive.] *trans.* To drive off.
1562 A. SCOTT *Poems* (S.T.S.) i. 150 Be thai vnpayit, thy pursevandis ar socht To pund pure communis corne, and cattell keir [*rime* ȝeir].

keir, var. KIER.

keire, var. CAIR *v. Obs.*
a **1650** *Scotish ffielde* 154 in Furniv. *Percy Folio* I. 220 He kee[peth] him in Carleile: & keire wold no further.

†ˈ**keiri.** *Obs.* Also keri, keyri, -ry. [med.L. *keiri*, *cheiri*, Arab. *khīrī*, Pers. *khīrū* (yellow) gillyflower.] The Wallflower, *Cheiranthus Cheiri*.
The generic name *Cheiranthus* was formed by Linnæus on *Cheiri* or '*Keiri* arab.', by arbitrary association with Gr. χείρ hand. *Philos. Bot.*, *Nomina* §229.
1578 LYTE *Dodoens* II. iii. 151 Of the Wallfloure... The yellow Gillofer is a kinde of violete called.. of Serapio and the Apothecaries *Keyri*. **1616** SURFL. & MARKH. *Country Farme* 237 White, yellow, and red Gillo-flowres.. especially the yellow.. commonly called of Apothecaries Keyry. **1664** EVELYN *Kal. Hort.* Mar. (1729) 196 Slip the Keris or Wallflower. **1706** PHILLIPS, *Keiri* or *Cheiri*, Wall-flower.

keiser(e, obs. ff. KAISER.

keises, *sb. pl.*: see KEYSIE.

keist, *Sc.* obs. pa. t. of CAST *v.*

keister (ˈkiːstə(r), ˈkaɪstə(r)). *U.S. slang.* Also keester, keyster. [Etym. unknown.] **1. a.** A suitcase, satchel; a handbag; a burglar's tool-case; a salesman's sample-case, etc.
[**1881** *National Police Gaz.* (U.S.) 1 Oct. 10/1 Prominent among the small army of confidence operators in this city are: 'Grand Central Pete'..'The Guinea Pig'..'Keister Bob'.] **1882** G. W. PECK *Peck's Sunshine* 227 The boy took the knight's keister and went to the elevator. **1910** G. B. MCCUTCHEON *Rose in Ring* 80 Ruby Noakes.. was directing the contortionist in his efforts to construct a table out of three 'blue seats' and a couple of property trunks, or 'keesters', as they were called. **1926** *Flynn's* 16 Jan. 637/2 All this chatter 'bout keisters with false bottoms an' mushes is mostly pipe stuff an' hopchin. **1926** *Clues* Nov. 161/2 *Keyster*, handbag or suitcase. **1933** 'P. CAIN' *Fast One* vi. 211 Hang on the front.. until you see three big pig-skin keesters go in. **1935** COLLIER & WESTRATE *Reign Soapy Smith* i. 2 An open sample case of liberal dimensions.. the typical 'keister' of the street hawker. **1935** *Jrnl. Abnormal Psychol.* XXX. III. 363 *Keyster*, a suitcase. **1950** H. E. GOLDIN *Dict. Amer. Underworld Lingo* 114/2 Ditch that keister. It draws heat (attracts police attention).
b. A strong-box in a safe; a safe (see also quot. 1924).
1913 A. STRINGER *Shadow* 36 He made a mental record of dips and yeggs and till-tappers and keister-crackers. **1921** P. & T. CASEY in *Adventure* (U.S.) 18 July 22/2 They.. breaks inter the keester o' the bank safes an' gits away with all the stored-up jack. **1924** G. C. HENDERSON *Keys to Crookdom* 409 *Keister*, bars on certain type of safe. A handbag that can be strapped and locked. **1931** *Amer. Speech* VII. 110 Can we use can-opener on this keister? **1950** H. E. GOLDIN *Dict. Amer. Underworld Lingo* 114/2 Easy on the soup (crude nitro-glycerine) with that keister or she'll jam.
2. The buttocks.
1931 *Amer. Speech* VI. 439 *Keister*, a satchel; also what one sits on. **1951** WODEHOUSE *Old Reliable* xi. 132 And then they'd leave me flat on my keister and go off and buy candy and orchids for the other girls. **1968** *McLean's Mag.* Dec. 1/1 His job at Christ the King was defined by Father Mooney as 'getting people off their keesters'. **1975** *New Yorker* 10 Mar. 90/2 Just put your keyster in the chair and shut your mouth.

‖**keitloa** (ˈkeɪtləʊə). Also ketloa. [Sechuana *kgetlwa*, *khetlwa*.] A species of South African rhinoceros (*Rhinoceros Keitloa*), having two horns of nearly equal length.
1838-47 SIR A. SMITH in *Sk. Nat. Hist.*, *Mammalia* (U.K.S., 1849) 40 The keitloa browses on shrubs and the slender branches of brushwood, using the upper lip as an organ of prehension. **1841** *Penny Cycl.* XIX. 472/2 The *Keitloa* is of a very savage disposition. **1867** J. E. GRAY in *Proc. Zool. Soc.* 1025 *Rhinaster Keitloa*, the Keitloa or Ketloa.

Kekchi (ˈkɛktʃɪ), *sb.* and *a.* Also Quecchi, Quekchi. **A.** *sb.* Name of an ancient people belonging to the Maya Empire, the modern descendants of whom now live in Guatemala. Also, a member of this people (ancient or modern); their language. **B.** *adj.* Of or pertaining to the Kekchi or their language.
1823 J. BAILY tr. *Juarros's Statistical & Commercial Hist. Guatemala* II. vi. 198 No one of the kingdoms of the New World has so many different languages as Guatemala, the following 26 being peculiar to it, *viz.* Quiché.. Quecchi. **1888** *Encycl. Brit.* XXIV. 760/1 Poconchi Group.. *Quekchi* ..Coban district, Guatemala. **1949** E. A. NIDA *Morphol.* (ed. 2) ii. 6 In Kekchi, a Mayan language of Guatemala. **1960** R. C. BELL *Board & Table Games* I. ii. 89 This is another running-fight game played by the Kekchi Indians of Central America. **1964** E. A. NIDA *Toward Sci. Transl.* iii. 46 In fact, at one time some Kekchis in Guatemala asked the missionary not to attempt to explain the 'truths of their faith', for if such matters could be explained and understood, they would then 'cease to be religion'.

keke, var. KEAK *v. Obs.*; obs. f. KEEK, KICK *v.*

kekshoes, -shose, obs. var. KICKSHAW.

Kekulé (ˈkɛkjuːleɪ). *Chem.* The name of Friedrich August *Kekulé* (1829–1896), German chemist, used *attrib.* and in the possessive with reference to a system of structural formulæ devised by him, the principal features of which are the quadrivalency of the carbon atom and the linking of carbon atoms to form chains, and esp. his conception of the benzene molecule as having a closed hexagonal ring of six carbon atoms with alternate double and single bonds between them (later extended to other conjugated cyclic carbon compounds).
1871 *Jrnl. Chem. Soc.* XXIV. 824 The author says that he acknowledges the value of Kekulé's ring formula. **1908** A. W. STEWART *Rec. Adv. Org. Chem.* i. 6 But as they actually existed in isomeric forms, the same was to be expected in benzene, if the Kekulé theory were correct. **1938** H. GILMAN *Org. Chem.* I. ii. 57 A further, rather serious objection to the Kekulé formula arose from the difficulty of understanding why, if benzene contains three ordinary double bonds, it is so inferior to the ethylenic hydrocarbons in reactivity. **1951** I. L. FINAR *Org. Chem.* I. xx. 408 The difficulty with the Kekulé formula is that it represents benzene with three double bonds, and the oscillation does not account for the difference in behaviour between these and olefinic bonds. *Ibid.* 409 The Kekulé structures contribute far more to resonance (about 80 per cent.) than do the Dewar structures (about 20 per cent.). **1961** L. F. & M. FIESER *Adv. Org. Chem.* i. 16 The Kekulé theory of structure performed valuable service for half a century before the nature of the Kekulé bond became understood. **1964** CRAM & HAMMOND *Org. Chem.* (ed. 2) xxiii. 543 Two equivalent Kekulé structures may be drawn for this $C_{18}H_{18}$ hydrocarbon [*sc.* cyclo-octadecanonaene]. **1972** E. CLAR *Aromatic Sextet* vi. 29 The VB theory assumes nine Kekulé structures for triphenylene which are supposed to contribute equally to the ground state.

kel: see KELLY, KELLY *sb.*² 2.

kelassee, kelassie, variants of KHALASI.

kelch (kɛltʃ). *slang.* Also kelt, -tch, keltz. [Etym. unknown.] A white person: only in depreciatory use.
1912 F. M. HUEFFER *Panel* I. i. 14 'Do you mean to say that you haven't got a single book of James'?' 'Never heard the name,' the bookstall boy said. 'But there's plenty by Mrs. Kerr Howe.' 'That kelch!' Major Foster exclaimed. **1938** C. HIMES *Black on Black* (1973) 173 Then he met a high-yellah gal, a three-quarter keltz, from down Harlem way. **1970** C. MAJOR *Dict. Afro-Amer. Slang* 73 *Kelt*, *keltch*, white person; Negro passing for white.

†ˈ**kelchyn.** *Sc. Obs.* In ancient Scottish law: One of the mulcts or payments exacted in compensation for homicide. (Cf. CRO.)
[*a* **1200** *Regiam Maj.* IV. lvii. (*Acts Parl. Scot.* I. 300) Kelchyn unius comitis est sexaginta sex et duæ partes unius vaccæ.] **1609** SKENE tr. *Regiam Maj.* IV. xxxviii, Item, Kelchyn of ane Earle is thriescore sax kye, and halfe ane kow... Ane husband-man [*rusticus*] has na Kelchyn. Gif the wife of ane frie man is slane, her husband sall haue the Kelchyn, and her friend[s] sall haue the Cro and Galnes. Item, gif the wife of ane husband-man [*rustici*] is slane, the Lord of the land quhare she duelles sall haue the Kelchyn, and her kinsmen sall haue the Cro and the Galnes.

†**keld**, *sb.*¹ *Obs. rare*⁻¹. [dial. form of COLD *sb.*; see KELD *v.*] Cold.
a **1310** in Wright *Lyric P.* 37 Casten y wol the from cares ant kelde.

keld (kɛld), *sb.*² *north. dial.* Also 7 kell. [a. ON. *kelda* (Sw. *källa*, Da. *kilde*).]
A well, fountain, spring. **b.** A deep, still, smooth part of a river.
Frequent in place-names in Cumbria, and Yorkshire, e.g. *Gunner-keld*, *How Keld*, *Sal(t)keld*, *Springkeld*, *Threlkeld*. In *Cartul. Prior. de Gyseburne* (Surtees) I. 48, 49, 66, *Hildekelde* is given as *Fons Sanctæ Hildæ*.
1697 A. DE LA PRYME *Diary* (Surtees) 142 This day I was at a place called Kell Well, near Aukburrow. **18..** T. D. WHITAKER *Surv. Burton Chace* (ed. 3) 35 (Craven Gloss.) From cald keld super Camb to the Top of Penigent. **1825** BROCKETT, *Kelds*, the still parts of a river which have an oily smoothness while the rest of the water is ruffled. **1828** *Craven Dial.*, *Keld*, a well. *Halikeld*, a holy fountain. A *keal keld*, a cold well. **1855** ROBINSON *Whitby Gloss.* s.v., 'The keld head', the spring head. **1891** ATKINSON *Last of Giant Killers* 203 A very remarkable spring, or fountain, or keld it was.

†**keld(e**, *v. Obs. rare.* Also chelde. [app. repr. OE. **cealdian* (see COLD *v.*). For the vowel, cf. *kelf* = calf.] *intr.* To become cold.
a **1300** *Maximian* 64 (Digby MS.) in *Anglia* III. 279 For þi min herte keldeþ And mi bodi ounbeldeþ. ? *c* **1325** *Old Age* i. in *E.E.P.* (1862) 149 Eld wold keld an cling so the clai. *Ibid.* vii, þroȝ kund i comble an kelde.

kelde, obs. pa. t. of KEEL *v.*⁴

Keldé, obs. Sc. form of CULDEE.

†ˈ**kelder.** *Obs. rare.* [a. Du. *kelder* a cellar: cf. the phrase HANS-*in-kelder*.] The womb.
1646 CLEVELAND *Kings Disguise* Poems (1647) 33 The Sun wears Midnight; Day is beetle-brow'd, And Lightning is in Kelder of a Cloud. **1658** BROME *New Acad.* II. i. Wks. 1873 II. 29 The unbegotten *Hans* that I mean to clap into thy *Kelder*.

kele, obs. f. KEEL; obs. Sc. var. KILL *v.*

‖**kelebe** (ˈkɛləbiː). *Gr. Antiq.* [Gr.] (See quot. 1890.)
1858 S. BIRCH *Hist. Anc. Pott. & Porc.* I. II. iv. 262 The Archaic *pyxis* or Apulian *stamnos*, the *kelebe*, or *crater*, with columnar handles, is seen for the first time. **1890** *Cent. Dict.*, *Kelebe*, in Greek Archæol., a large ovoid, wide-mouthed vase, with a broad flat rim and two handles connecting the rim and the body, and not extending above the rim. **1960** R. M. COOK *Greek Painted Pott.* 367 *Kelebe*, obsolete, a conventional name for a column krater.

K-electron: see K 3 e.

‖**kelek** (ˈkɛlɪk). Also 7 kilet, 9 kelleck, -ick. [Turk. *kalak*, *kelek*.] A raft or float used on rivers in Turkey in Asia, etc., formed of inflated sheep-skins, bundles of reeds, and the like.
1684 J. PHILLIPS tr. *Tavernier's Trav.* I. II. v. 72 The Merchant must be careful to spread good store of thick Felts over the *Kilet*. **1840** J. B. FRASER *Trav. Koordistan* II. iv. 74 The canal was not fordable, and the only means of crossing it was by a kellick pulled across by a rope. **1872** YEATS *Growth Comm.* 26 Such vessels are sculptured on Assyrian monuments and under the name of *keleks* continue to be used.

kelep (kəˈlɛp). [Kekchi] A Central American stinging ant, *Ectatomma tuberculatum*.
1904 W. M. WHEELER in *Science* 30 Sep. 439/1 There is little probability that the kelep can be successfully established in Texas. **1910** —— *Ants* i. 9 It [*sc.* United States Department of Agriculture] recently introduced a Guatemalan ant, the 'kelep' (*Ectatomma tuberculatum*) into Texas for the purpose of destroying the very injurious cotton-boll weevil. **1951** C. F. W. MUESEBECK et al. *Hymenoptera of Amer. North of Mexico* 783 *Ectatomma* ..*tuberculatum*... This species, known as the kelep, was introduced into Texas in the early part of this century to combat the cotton boll weevil. It has apparently become extinct.

keleusmatically (kɛljuːsˈmætɪkəlɪ), *adv.* [Rendering Gr. κελευσματικῶς by way of command: see CELEUSMA and -ICALLY.] Imperatively.
1885 W. L. ALEXANDER *Zechariah* iii. 28 Here it is used hortatorily or keleusmatically.

kelf¹, obs. dial. form of CALF¹.

†**kelf**². *Obs. rare*⁻¹. [? dialect survival of prec.: cf. CALF 1 c.] A lubber, blockhead.
1664 COTTON *Scarron.* IV. Poet. Wks. (1734) 85 One Squire Æneas, a great Kelf, Some wandring Hangman like herself.

kelf³. *Coal-mining. local.* In the Midland coal-field (Derby and Leicestersh.): 'The vertical height of the back cutting of the holing at any time during the operation of holing a stint' (Gresley *Gloss. Coal Mining* 1883).

Kelim, var. KILIM.

‖**kelis** (ˈkiːlɪs). *Path.* [a. Gr. κηλίς stain, spot.] = KELOID, q.v.
1864 W. T. FOX *Skin Dis.* 24 Lepra, lupus, kelis, and elephantiasis.

kelk. Now *dial.* The roe of a fish.
c **1420** *Liber Cocorum* 19 Take þo kelkes of fysshe anon, And þo lyver of þo fysshe. **1483** *Cath. Angl.* 201/1 Kelkys (*A.* kellys) of fyschis, *lactes*. **1655** MOUFET & BENNET *Health's Improv.* (1746) 238 Cods have a Bladder in them full of Eggs or Spawn, which the northern Men call the Kelk. **1855** ROBINSON *Whitby Gloss.*, *Kelks*, the roe or spawn of fish.

kelk, dial. var. of KECK, KEX.
1880 in BRITTEN & HOLLAND *Plant-n.*

kell (kɛl). *Obs.* exc. *dial.* Also 4–6 kelle, 7 kel. [A northern form corresp. to ME. *calle*, CAUL *sb.*¹; the difference in vowel is not easy to account for, but cf. *mell*, Sc. form of *maul*, *mall*.]
1. A woman's hair-net, cap, or head-dress: = CAUL *sb.*¹ 1.
a **1400** *Pistill of Susan* 128 (MS. A) By a wynliche welle Susan cast of hir kelle. *Ibid.* 158 (MS. I) þan had sche kast of hire kell and hire courcheffe. **1513** DOUGLAS *Æneis* VII. xiv. 82 The hair was of this damysell Knyt wyth a buttoune in a goldin kell. **1603** *Philotus* xxii, Than may ȝe haue baith Quaiffis and Kellis.. All for ȝour weiring and not ellis. ? *a* **1700** *Childe Maurice* v. in Child *Ballads* (1886) IV. lxxxiii.

264/2 As many times As knotts beene knitt on a kell. **1817** LADY MARGARET in Whitelaw *Bk. Scot. Ball.* (1875) 55/2 To braid her hair she didna care Nor sett her golden kell.

b. *dial.* The back part of a woman's cap.

1871 W. ALEXANDER *Johnny Gibb* xlvi. (1873) 256 A mutch that my wife hed ance wi' a byous muckle squar' kell.

2. A long cloak or garment; a shroud.

c **1425** *Voc.* in Wr.-Wülcker 656/15 *Hec caracalla*, kelle. [Cf. *ibid.* 571/34 *Caracalla*, a sclavayn or a cope.] ? *a* **1800** *Gay Goss-Hawk* xxx. in Child *Ballads* (1886) IV. xcvi E. 364/2 Then up and gat her seven sisters, And sewed to her a kell, And every steek that they pat in Sewd to a siller bell.

3. Gossamer threads forming a kind of film on grass. Cf. CAUL 3.

1523 FITZHERB. *Husb.* §54 Also there wyll be many kelles vppon the grasse, and that causeth the myldewe. **1576** TURBERV. *Venerie* 76 Many tymes the cobwebbes fall from the skye and are not suche as spyders make, but a kind of kell. **1614** MARKHAM *Cheap Husb.* I. III. i. (1623) 107 Those webs, kels, and flakes..lying on the earth, and a sheepe licking them vp, do breed rottennesse. **1663** J. BEAL *Let. to Boyle* 9 Nov., Boyle's Wks. 1772 VI. 357 Those kells, which like cobwebs do sometimes cover the grounds.

b. The web or cocoon of a spinning caterpillar.

1612 DRAYTON *Poly-olb.* iii. 42 Trees..With caterpillers kells, and duskie cobwebs hong. **1616** B. JONSON *Devil an Ass* II. vi, [Love could] Bury himselfe in euery Silke-wormes Kell.

4. *Anat.* An investing membrane or film: = CAUL 4.

1540 RAYNOLD *Byrth Mankynde* I. ii. (1634) 19 The fleshy skinne..is compassed of fleshinesse, more then any other kell or skin in all the body. **1630** DRAYTON *Noah's Flood* Wks. 1538 *note*, The aspick hath a kell of skin which covereth his teeth until it be angry. **1766** *Chron.* in *Ann. Reg.* 120/1 She..has a speck or kell over one eye.

fig. **1823** GALT *R. Gilhaize* I. 271 She was soon scrapit of all the scurf and kell of her abominations.

5. *spec.* **a.** The fatty membrane investing the intestines; the omentum: = CAUL 5 a.

1578 BANISTER *Hist. Man* v. 67 We call one part of the Kell the Anteriour or superiour Membran, and the other the inferiour or posteriour. **1611** BEAUM. & FL. *Philaster* v. iv, I'le have him cut to the kell, then down the seames. **1694** MOTTEUX *Rabelais* v. xvii, The inner thin Kell wherewith the Intrails are cover'd. *a* **1825** FORBY *Voc. E. Anglia*, *Kell*, the omentum or caul. **1877** in *N.W. Linc. Gloss.*

b. The amnion inclosing the fœtus, and sometimes enveloping the head at birth: = CAUL 5 b.

1530 PALSGR. 235/2 Kell in a womans belly, *taye.* **1621** BURTON *Anat. Mel.* III. iii. II. i, A silly jealous fellow..seeing his childe new born included in a kell, thought sure a Franciscan..was the father of it, it was so like the Frier's Coule. **1828** *Craven Dial.* s.v., Brand mentions several advertisements in which these kells or cauls were announced for sale. **1883** in *N.W. Linc. Gloss.* s.v., Oor ohd mare, she foal'd e' th' neet, an' th' foal could n't braak th' kell, so it was droonded.

6. *Comb.* (sense 1), as ***kell-knitter***, ***-maker***, ***-wise***.

a **1400-50** *Alexander* 3300 þis coppis opon kell-wyse knytt in þe woȝes. **14..** *Nominale* in Wr.-Wülcker 692/35 *Hec reciaria*, a kelmaker. **1483** *Cath. Angl.* 201/2 A kelle knytter, *reticularius*, *reticularia*.

Hence **kelled** (†**keld**) *a.*, webbed.

1630 DRAYTON *Noah's Flood* Wks. 1534 The otter..feeds on fish, which..He with his keld feet and keen teeth doth kill.

kell, obs. form of KALE, KILN.

kellagh (-eg, -ick, -ock), kellaut, kelle, kellidar, kellow, kellus: see KILLICK, KHILAUT, KILL *v.*, KILLEDAR, KILLOW, KILLAS.

Kellaways ('kɛləweɪz). *Geol.* Also formerly **Kellaway, Kelloway(s).** The name of a village near Chippenham in Wiltshire, used *attrib.* to designate a group of clays and calcareous sandstones of Jurassic age lying below the Oxford clay and above the cornbrash, and found in a belt extending from Dorset to Yorkshire.

1813 J. TOWNSEND *Character of Moses* I. vi. 103 Kelloway rock. The next calcareous stratum, first attracted our notice, at Kelloway Bridge. **1888** J. PRESTWICH *Geol.* II. xiv. 217 On the Continent the Kelloways Rock forms a division of almost equal importance with the Oxford Clay. **1913** *Q. Jrnl. Geol. Soc.* LXIX. 152 (*heading*) The 'Kelloway rock' of Scarborough. [*Note*] The appellation 'Kelloway' is here used for quotations from Leckenby [1859] or in reference to Yorkshire beds, and 'Kellaways' in relation to deposits in Wiltshire and elsewhere. **1933** W. J. ARKELL *Jurassic Syst. Gt. Brit.* xii. 346 The thickest development of the Kellaways Rock exposed in the West of England was seen in a short cutting on the Midland and South-Western Junction Railway at South Cerney, near Cirencester. **1946** [see CALLOVIAN *a.*]. **1969** BENNISON & WRIGHT *Geol. Hist. Brit. Isles* xiii. 307 The sandy limestone with hard flaggy bands of the Upper Cornbrash has a fauna resembling that of the overlying Kellaways Beds.

‖**keller** ('kɛlə(r)). [Ger., = cellar.] A beer-cellar in Austria or Germany. Also *attrib.*

1927 *Sat. Rev. Lit.* 3 Dec. 382 Meetings of congenial colleagues in some Keller. **1968** *Guardian* 21 Sept. 10/2 The moonlit sleigh rides, and keller bars. **1969** A. GLYN *Dragon Variation* viii. 229 Drinking beer in a keller, singing German songs. **1969** *Guardian* 11 Oct. 10/5 Austria, with its.. boisterous bars and kellers. **1973** *Daily Tel.* 3 Feb. 12/4 Ski-ing, they wear bright, crazy clothes; après-ski-ing, they whoop it up in the *kellerbars*.

Kellgren ('kɛlgrən). The name of Henrik *Kellgren* (1837–1916), Swedish physician, used *attrib.* to denote a system of massage devised by him. Hence '**Kellgrenite** *a.* and *sb.*, (one) that is a practitioner of this system.

1907 *Boston Med. & Surg. Jrnl.* CLVII. 493/1 In the Kellgren method, the fingers of the gymnast remain in contact with the skin, and thus they are enabled to really manipulate the parts beneath. **1918** G. B. SHAW in *Eng. Rev.* Jan. 14 Osteopathy, for instance, is, like Kellgren massage, a no-drug system. *Ibid.* 10 The Kellgrenites are not recognized by the Medical Gymnasts. *Ibid.*, Some time ago a Kellgrenite masseur..qualified himself for the British register. **1925** —— in *Times* 12 Nov. 10/2, I do not hold any brief for osteopathy, or Kellgren massage, or naturopathy or homœopathy. **1944** —— *Everybody's Pol. What's What?* xxiii. 205 A manipulative technique which, like Kellgren massage.., needed about two years training to acquire.

kellin, obs. var. KHELLIN.

Ke'llovian, *a.* *Geol. rare.* [ad. F. *kellovien* (A. d'Orbigny *Paléont. française. Terrains Jurassiques* (1842–9) I. 608), f. Kelloway(s), former name of KELLAWAYS.] = CALLOVIAN *a.*

1888 J. PRESTWICH *Geol.* II. i. 9 Kellovian Limestones and Marls.

Kelloway(s), varr. KELLAWAYS.

kelly ('kɛlɪ), *sb.*[1] *U.S.* [cf. CALLOW *sb.* 3, the equivalent term in England.] The top-soil which is removed in order to get at clay for brickmaking. Hence **kelly** *v.* (see quot.).

1884 C. T. DAVIS *Manuf. Bricks* 103 This vegetable soil is called in brickyard parlance, 'kelly', and the operation of removing it termed 'taking off the kelly'. *Ibid.*, The operation of placing the soil upon the places where the bricks are moulded is termed 'kellying the floors'.

Kelly, kelly ('kɛlɪ), *sb.*[2] [Prob. f. the name *Kelly*, a common Irish surname.] **1.** (With capital initial.) A type of pool (POOL *sb.*[3] 3) using fifteen balls (see quot. 1934). In full, ***Kelly pool.*** *U.S.*

1898 *Handbk. Rules of Billiards* (Brunswick-Balke-Collender Co.) (rev. ed.) 78 The game of Kelly pool is played with fifteen numbered balls, and one white ball not numbered. **1913** *Billiards Mag.* Oct. 25 (*caption*) A 'Nine' of billiard notables gathered from different states by Artist Carlson for a pictorial game at 'Kelly'. **1918** *Ibid.* Jan. 55/1 A new idea for the old game of Kelly. **1934** WEBSTER, *Kelly pool*, a variety of fifteen-ball pool in which each player draws a number and, while playing on the object balls in numerical order, aims to pocket the ball of the number corresponding to his own, thereby winning the game. **1948** MENJOU & MUSSELMAN *It took Nine Tailors* 29 The only sports I cared to indulge in personally were Kelly pool and bowling.

2. Rhyming slang for *belly*. Also ***Derby*** (or ***Darby***) ***kelly*** or ***kel***.

1906 E. DYSON *Fact'ry 'Ands* viii. 96 Er cold, proud man tumbles on his Darby Kel in ther dirt. **1928** M. C. SHARPE *Chicago May* xxxi. 287/2 *Darby Kelly*, belly. **1942** T. RATTIGAN *Flare Path* II. ii. 138 Just that ride home. Cor, I still feel it down in the old darby kel. **1967** L. DEIGHTON *London Dossier* 40 The only places now making boiled beef available to your darby kellies, or bellies, are the Jewish salt-beef bars. **1970** A. DRAPER *Swansong for Rare Bird* vi. 41 My old kelly was rumbling and I fancied a pie and chips.

3. A man's hat; *spec.* a derby hat (cf. sense 2 above). *slang* (chiefly *U.S.*).

1915 *Recruiter's Bulletin* (U.S.) Dec. 33/2 Say, old top, when you go home tonight, Pull your old brown Kelly down real tight. **1922** *Collier's* 4 Mar. 8/2, I have got to wear a brass Kelly on my head which weighs at least ten pounds. **1927** E. HEMINGWAY in *Atlantic Monthly* July 11/1 John put his kelly down on the table. It was all wet. His coat was wet, too. **1948** LAIT & MORTIMER *New York: Confindential* xxxi. 276 Some of the larger clubs reap up to $50,000 a year for the privilege of checking your kellys.

4. *slang.* (See quots. 1942 and 1963.)

1934 H. N. ROSE *Thesaurus of Slang* viii. 57/1 Oilfield slang... Hole to set the 'Kelly' in when not in use..: *rat hole.* **1939** D. HAGER *Fund. Petroleum Industry* ix. 203 In older drilling methods where the kelly was not used, the drill pipe was badly cut by the gripping devices. **1942** BERREY & VAN DEN BARK *Amer. Thes. Slang* §516/4 *Kelly*, a square joint on top of the drill stem passing through a square hole in the rotary table. **1946** *Mod. Petroleum Technol.* (Inst. Petroleum) 87 As drilling proceeds the square section of the kelley is lowered through the rotary table until its full length is below the table. The drilling string is then raised, the kelley removed, a fresh length of drill pipe is coupled up and the kelley is replaced. **1963** *Gloss. Mining Terms* (*B.S.I.*) III. 10 *Kelly*, the rod attached to the top of the drill column in rotary drilling. It passes through the rotary table and is turned by it, but is free to slide down through it as the borehole deepens. **1974** *Scotsman* 22 Apr. p. x, Only in oil can you break off kelly and set down on rams while keeping a straight face.

5. In full, ***kelly green.*** A light green colour. orig. *U.S.*

1936 *Mademoiselle* Sept. 13 (Advt.). A slipon with sleeveless sweater...rust with Churchill green, kelly with brown. *Ibid.* Nov. 49/1 (Advt.), Sweaters..in..yellow, kelly green, gray. *Ibid.* Dec. 3/2 (Advt.), Sweaters with an English pedigree..jockey red, Kelly green or natural. **1958** 'E. MCBAIN' *Killer's Choice* (1960) vi. 69 'What sort of green was it?' 'Almost a Kelly green...' **1966** G. BAXT *Queer Kind of Death* (1967) xvi. 223 Kelly green lanterns at the end of the garden. **1972** 'R. CRAWFORD' *Whip Hand* I. ix. 54 The kelly-green jungle was tangled; it hid a gunner.

6. *attrib.* and *Comb.* **kelly board, joint** (see quot. 1942); **Kelly's eye** *colloq.* (see quot. 1925).

1925 H. C. GEORGE in *Bull. U.S. Bureau of Mines* No. 224. 115 Means of escape from..the kelly board on every drilling and redrilling derrick shall be provided. **1942** BERREY & VAN DEN BARK *Amer. Thes. Slang* §516/2 *Kelly-board*, a platform at the height of the 'kelly'. *Ibid.* §516/4 *Kelly joint*, the first joint of pipe attached to the 'kelly'. **1925** FRASER & GIBBONS *Soldier & Sailor Words* 134 *Kelly's eye*, no. 1 in the game of 'House'. **1933** L. A. G. STRONG *Sea Wall* 256 A game of 'house' was in progress, and a voice monotonously droned the numbers: '..Kelly's eye.' **1945** E. WAUGH *Brideshead Revisited* II. i. 230 The voice of the officer in charge of tombola—'Kelly's eye—number one; legs, eleven; and we'll Shake the Bag.' **1962** *Daily Tel.* 25 June 11/4 Miss L. Brahmer..began calling the numbers over the loudspeakers... 'Kelly's Eye, No. 1; and Legs Eleven' echoed throughout the ship.

Kelmscott ('kɛlmzkɒt). The name of Kelmscott House, Hammersmith (named after Kelmscott Manor, Kelmscott, Oxfordshire), the home of William Morris (1834–1896), used in the name of the Kelmscott Press, which was founded there by him in 1891 and worked until 1898; also used *absol.* or *attrib.* to designate the books produced or their design.

1891 W. MORRIS *Story of Glittering Plain* 188 Here endeth the Glittering Plain, printed by William Morris at the Kelmscott Press, Upper Mall Hammersmith, in the County of Middlesex. **1896** G. B. SHAW in *Sat. Rev.* 10 Oct. 387/2 If he [*sc.* William Morris] had started a Kelmscott Theatre instead of the Kelmscott Press, I am quite confident that.. he would have produced work that would within ten years have affected every theatre in Europe. **1920** A. SMELLIE in C. Jerdan *Scottish Clerical Stories* xii. 242, I had rather be the owner of its twenty-seven volumes than have all the Elzevirs and Kelmscotts in the world. **1938** *Times Lit. Suppl.* 12 Mar. 174/1 The book has somewhat of a Kelmscott air. **1963** *Listener* 21 Mar. 522/1 There is a vigour and vitality in his decorations that make Burne-Jones's Kelmscott borders rather tame. **1966** BERRY & POOLE *Ann. Printing* 262/1 The beauty of the Kelmscott books was due to harmony of type and decoration, the spacing of words and lines, the positioning of the text on the page, the careful choice of paper and ink, and the excellent presswork... Other private presses followed which served to increase the interest in fine book printing.

keloid ('kiːlɔɪd). *Path.* [a. F. *kéloïde*: see CHELOID.] A form of skin disease, having the appearance of a hypertrophic scar; = CHELOID.

1854 [see CHELOID]. **1864** W. T. FOX *Skin Dis.* 70 Deformities of Derma. Keloid. **1876** BRISTOWE *The. & Pract. Med.* (1878) 47 Such results are seen in keloid and in some forms of arterial atheroma. **1889** BUCK *Med. Sci.* IV. 266 Keloid..is most common on the chest and neck.

attrib. **1897** W. ANDERSON *Surg. Treat. Lupus* 8 The 'keloid' thickening of the new cicatrix.

Hence **ke'loidal** *a.*, of the nature of keloid.

1888 *Medical News* LIII. 442 Slight keloidal growths sometimes follow in the wake of the largest vesicles.

kelong ('keɪlɒŋ). Also 9 **kaylong.** [Malay.] A large fish trap built with stakes, common along the coasts of the Malay Peninsula. Also *transf.*, a building erected over one.

1878 F. MCNAIR *Perak & Malays* ix. 93 The kaylongs are made of hurdles composed of strips of bamboo, some five feet long, fastened closely together with rattans. **1900** W. W. SKEAT *Malay Magic* v. 315 *Kelong* is the name given to one of the kinds of fishing-stakes (something like weirs) common on the coasts of the Peninsula. **1953** R. GRAHAM *War Damage Report* (Malaya War Damage Commission) xiv. 52 As one approaches the coast of Malaya one cannot fail to notice the large number of fish traps, or kelongs, built in some cases far out to sea. **1971** *Daily Tel.* 18 Sept. 11/3 At Ponggol Point on the north-east shore you can dine at the Sea Palace restaurant on a kelong or fish trap of stakes driven into the shallow sea bed, where fish are lured by lamps at night into a net. **1972** *Guardian* 6 Sept. 16/4 Fashionable now is a kelong visit. The kelongs are thatched huts over stakes driven into the seabed from which local fishermen cast their nets. Some of these have been 'improved' with bar, restaurant, and changing rooms for tourists to spend the day swimming and sunning and in the evening watch the fishermen bring in their haul.

kelp[1] (kɛlp). Forms: 4 culp, 7 kilpe, 7– **kelp.** [ME. *culp* or *culpe* (y), of unknown origin. Of this the normal mod. repr. would be *kilp*; *kelp* is app. a dialect variation: cf. *melt* and *milt* sb.]

1. a. A collective name for large seaweeds (chiefly *Fucaceæ* and *Laminariaceæ*) which are burnt for the sake of the substances found in the ashes.

bull-head kelp, a N.W. American species (*Nereocystis Luetkeana*) used by the Indians for fishing-lines.

1387 TREVISA *Higden* (Rolls) II. 181 As culpes of þe see waggeþ wiþ þe water. **1601** HOLLAND *Pliny* II. XXXII. vi. 437 As for the reits Kilpe, Tangle, & such like sea-weeds, Nicander saith, they are as good as treacle. **1663** BOYLE *Exp. Hist. Colours* xlix. Ann. i, In making our ordinary allom the workmen use the ashes of a sea-weed (vulgarly called kelp). **1791** NEWTE *Tour Eng. & Scot.* 112 The cutting and burning of the kelp that grows on their shores. **1840** R. H. DANA *Bef. Mast* xiv. 35 We found the tide low, and the rocks and stones covered with kelp and sea-weed.

b. *spec.* The giant or great kelp (*Macrocystis pyrifera* or *Fucus giganteus*) of the Pacific coast of America, the largest of seaweeds.

1834 DARWIN in *Voy. 'Adventure' & 'Beagle'* (1839) III. 303 There is one marine production, which from its importance is worthy of a particular history. It is the kelp or *Fucus giganteus* of Solander. **1897** F. T. BULLEN *Cruise of 'Cachalot'* 88 We were continually passing broad patches of kelp..whose great leaves and cable-laid stems made quite reef-like breaks in the heaving waste of the restless sea.

2. The calcined ashes of seaweed used in commerce for the sake of the carbonate of soda, iodine, and other substances which they

contain; large quantities were formerly used in the manufacture of soap and glass.

1678 *Phil. Trans.* XII. 1054 Kelp is made of a Sea-weed, called Tangle, such as comes to London on Oysters. **1756** C. LUCAS *Ess. Waters* I. 9 [It] is the nitre of the antients, not unlike the soda or kelp of the moderns. **1808** *Gazetteer Scotl.* (ed. 2) s.v. *Gigha*, Much sea-weed..partly employed as a manure, and partly burned into kelp. **1862** ANSTED *Channel Isl.* IV. xxii. 514 The quantity of weed required to manufacture a ton of kelp averages twenty tons.

†**3.** A name for the plants *Salsola* and *Salicornia*: cf. KALI[1] 1. *Obs. rare.*

1712 tr. *Pomet's Hist. Drugs* I. 101 A Plant..which the Botanists call Kali..and we..Kelp. **1760** J. LEE *Introd. Bot.* App. 316 Kelp, *Salicornia*.

4. *attrib.* and *Comb.*, as ***kelp-ashes***, ***-burner***, ***-burning***, ***-making***, ***-weed***, ***-wrack***; **kelp crab**, a spider crab, *Pugettia producta*, found on the Pacific coast of North America; **kelp-fish**, the name given to several fishes found on the Pacific coast of the United States; see also quot.; **kelp-goose**, **-hen** (see quots.); **kelp-pigeon**, the sheathbill, an Antarctic sea-bird; **kelp raft**, a mass of kelp floating on the sea.

1834 *Brit. Husb.* I. 420, 6 bushels of *kelp-ashes. **1895** *Outing* (U.S.) XXVI. 355/1 The long swells..only half broken by the *kelp belt a mile away. **1845** SELBY in *Proc. Berw. Nat. Club* II. No. 13. 161 These buildings have..been occupied..by the *kelp-burners. *Ibid.* 162 *Kelp-burning was carried on at Holy Island as early as the 13th century. **1884** *Bull. U.S. Nat. Museum* No. 27. 112 The *Kelp Crabs are used by the natives. **1939** RICKETTS & CALVIN *Between Pacific Tides* I. 80 A dark, olive-green, spider crab, *Pugettia producta*, occurs so frequently on strands of the seaweed *Egregia* and others that it is commonly called the kelp crab. The points on the carapace and the spines on the legs are sharp. **1954** S. F. LIGHT et al. *Intertidal Invertebr. Cent. Calif. Coast* 342 A few organisms (e.g. the kelp crab *Pugettia producta*..) graze directly on the larger attached algae. **1880** GÜNTHER *Fishes* 533 The 'Butter-fish', or '*Kelp fish' of the colonists of New Zealand (*Coridodax pullus*)... It feeds on zoophytes, scraping them from the surface of the kelp. **1883** COPPINGER *Cruise 'Alert'* 56 The *kelp-geese (*Bernicla antarctica*) were paddling about with their young ones. **1899** EVANS *Birds* 247 These Rails are semi-nocturnal..*Ocydromus fuscus* [of N.Z.] obtaining the name of *Kelp-Hen from the stretches of sea-weed that it frequents. **1884** *Harper's Mag.* VII. 706/2 They caught gulls, and tried to make them carry *kelp lines, but all was of no avail. **1810** *Edin. Rev.* XVII. 146 The introduction of *kelp-making. **1886** *Encycl. Brit.* XXI. 782/2 *note*, In the Falkland Isles it is called the '*Kelp-Pigeon'. **1897** *Outing* (U.S.) XXX. 259/1 We drew in toward the island..avoiding the great *kelp rafts. **1805** *Naval Chron.* XIV. 38 The *kelp-weed..lying upon the Shore. **1833** SIR J. E. SMITH *Eng. Flora* V. 268 It [*Fucus nodosus*] is said in the Hebrides to be preferable to all other Fuci in the manufacturing of kelp, and passes there under the name of *kelp-wrack.

Hence **'kelper**, a maker of kelp. **'kelping** *vbl. sb.*, the manufacture of kelp; *ppl. a.*, that makes kelp. **'kelpy** *a.*, abounding in kelp.

1808 FORSYTH *Beauties Scotl.* V. 100 The kelpers might employ their time between tides. **1822** P. WOODLEY *Scilly Isl.* I. v. 119 The Islanders seldom get more..than from £7 to £10, for their labours during the kelping season. **1852** RAINE *Hist. N. Durham* 146 A ridge of kelpy stone, over which it is no easy matter to pass. **1890** *Scribner's Mag.* XIX. 659/1 The mother..struck out through the kelpy waters for the shore. **1895** *Longm. Mag.* Nov. 33 The kelper's year may be reckoned from mid November. *Ibid.* 39 The old stories linger among the kelping people.

†**kelp**[2]. *Obs. rare*[−1]. [Obscure: connexion with KILP *sb.* seems unlikely.] ? Sword-belt, scabbard.

13.. *Disp. Mary & Cross* 283 in *Leg. Rood* 140 His swerd he pulte vp in his kelp.

†**kelp**[3] (kɛlp). *Obs. slang.* Also **kilp**. [Origin unknown.] A hat. Hence **kelp** *v. trans.* (see quot. 1812).

1736 J. COLE in *Ordinary of Newgate, his Account* I. 13/2, I and Thomas Campson..broke open a Hatters..and robbed it of three Dozen of Kilps. **1753** J. POULTER *Discoveries* (ed. 2) 26 We jostle him up, and one knocks his Kelp off. **1812** J. H. VAUX *Vocab. Flash Lang.* in *Mem.* (1964) 247 *Kelp*, a hat; to *kelp* a person, is to move your hat to him.

Kelper ('kɛlpə(r)), *sb.* and *a.* Also **kelper**. [f. KELP[1] + -ER[1].] **A.** *sb.* The name given locally to a native or inhabitant of the Falkland Islands, the shores of which abound in kelp. **B.** *adj.* Of or pertaining to a Kelper.

1960 M. B. R. CAWKELL et al. *Falkland Islands* viii. 93 Improved sanitation and street lighting, main drainage and a telephone exchange, were improvements the Kelper's business-like nature could readily appreciate. **1960** E. R. PETTINGILL *Penguin Summer* (1962) i. 7 Some of them were native Falklanders—'Kelpers', they called themselves. **1968** *Economist* 7 Dec. 33/2 More and more [Falkland Islands] young people are emigrating to New Zealand to escape the isolated monotony of kelper life. **1971** *Daily Tel.* 19 Jan. 10/4 Successive British Governments have laid it down firmly that the 'kelpers', all 2,000 of them, must decide their own destiny.

kelpie[1], **kelpy** ('kɛlpɪ). *Sc.* [Of uncertain etym.; Gael. *calpa*, *cailpeach*, bullock, heifer, colt, has been suggested, but positive evidence is wanting.] The Lowland Scottish name of a fabled water-spirit or demon assuming various shapes, but usually appearing in that of a horse; it is reputed to haunt lakes and rivers, and to take delight in, or even to bring about, the drowning of travellers and others. Also ***water-kelpie***.

The beliefs relating to the kelpie are essentially the same as those connected with the Danish and Norw. *nøkken*, and the Icel. *nykur* or *nennir*; but in Scotland the kelpie was sometimes held to render assistance to millers by keeping the mill going during the night.

1747 COLLINS *Pop. Superst. Highlands* 137 Drowned by the kelpie's wroth. **1792** BURNS *Let. to Cunningham* 10 Sept., Be thou a kelpie, haunting the ford or ferry. **1805** SCOTT *Last Minstr.* VI. xxiii, But the Kelpy rung, and the Mermaid sung, The dirge of lovely Rosabelle. **1813** HOGG *Queen's Wake* 192 The darksome pool..Was now no more the kelpie's home. **1881** GREGOR *Folk-lore* 66 (E.D.D.) The wife..tried to dissuade him under the fear that Kelpie would carry him off to his pool.

kelpie[2] ('kɛlpɪ). *Austral.* [f. the name of an early specimen of the breed.] A smooth-coated, prick-eared, Australian sheep-dog, which may be black, black-and-tan, blue, or red; first bred from imported Scottish collies about 1870.

1907 R. LEIGHTON *New Bk. Dog* 472/2 The Kelpie..is not perhaps an example of high, scientific breeding; but he is a useful, presentable dog. **1934** *Bulletin* (Sydney) 14 Feb. 40/2 Lassie was, like all kelpies, highly strung, with brains under her broad, thin-boned skull. **1946** [see BARB *sb.*[3] 3]. **1971** F. HAMILTON *World Encycl. Dogs* 74 Kelpies were bred back in the early days of settlement from the Collie type dogs which came to Australia with the early farmers. **1972** *Southerly* XXXII. 9 A kelpie and a blue cattle dog had raced to meet them, barking frantically.

'kelpwort. [f. KELP[1] + WORT.] = GLASSWORT b, *Salsola Kali.*

1787 WITHERING *Brit. Plants* (ed. 2), (Br. & Holl.).

kelson, keelson ('kɛlsən). *Naut.* Forms: α. 7 **kelsine, kilson,** 7– **kelson,** (9 **kelston**). β. 7 **keeleson,** 7– **keelson,** (8 **keelstone,** 9 **keelsale**). [= Du. *kolzwijn*, *kolsem*, LG. *kielswîn*, G. *kielschwein*, Da. *kølsvin*, Sw. *kölsvin*. The first element is app. KEEL *sb.*[1], but of the second the original form and meaning are obscure.

In all the equivalents cited, except Du. *kolsem*, the second element is identical with the word corresponding to E. *swine*, and it appears that in 18th c. LG. *swîn* was used by itself in the sense of 'keelson' (see Grimm). The English forms may therefore represent a ME. **kelswin*: cf. the reduction of *boatswain* to *boteson*, *boson*, *bos'n*. The reason for calling the timber by this name does not appear, but this is also the case with many similar applications of the names of animals, as *cat*, *dog*, *hog*, *horse*, etc. The original may have been an unrecorded ON. **kjǫlsvín* or **kjalsvín*, independently adopted in Eng. and LG. The corruptions *keelstone*, *kelston*, *kelsom*, *keelsale*, originate mainly in the lack of stress on the second element. Eng. *stemson* and *sternson* are app. recent formations on the analogy of *keelson*. It has been suggested that the original form may be preserved in Norw. dial. *kjølsvill* = 'keel-sill', but this may also be an alteration, by popular etymology, of the usual *kjølsvin*.

The most usual spelling from the first has been *kelson*: recently, however, there has been a tendency to spell *keelson*, though the pron. ('kɛlsən) still prevails.]

1. a. A line of timber placed inside a ship along the floor-timbers and parallel with the keel, to which it is bolted, so as to fasten the floor-timbers and the keel together; a similar bar or combination of iron plates in iron vessels.

α. *c* **1611** CHAPMAN *Iliad* I. 426 The top-mast to the kelsine then with halyards down they drew. *a* **1618** RALEIGH *Royall Navy* 4 Even from the Batts end to the very Kilson of a Ship. **1637** HEYWOOD *Royall Ship* 44 That one peece of Timber which made the Kel-son. **1711** W. SUTHERLAND *Shipbuild. Assist.* 26 Bolt the Kelson through every other Floor-timber. **1867** MACGREGOR *Voy. Alone* (1868) 6 She has an iron keel and kelson to resist a bump on rocks.

β. **1627** CAPT. SMITH *Seaman's Gram.* ii. 3 Lay your keeleson ouer your floore timbers, which is another long tree like the keele. **1706** *Wooden World Dissected* (1708) 3 Some compare her to a Common-wealth, and carry the Allegory from the Vane down to the Keelson. **1805** *Naval Chron.* XIV. 172 Placing it on the keelsale. **1840** R. H. DANA *Bef. Mast* xv. 39 Everything has been moved in the hold, from stem to stern, and from the water-ways to the keelson. **1866** *Morn. Star* 19 Mar. 2/1 The ship is built up from a keelson, formed of a huge bar of iron.

fig. **1751** SMOLLETT *Per. Pic.* IV. lxxxvii, Something shoots from your arm, through my stowage, to the very keel-stone. **1855** WALT WHITMAN *Song of Myself* 5, I know..that a kelson of the creation is love.

b. With qualifying terms: **assistant kelson** or **keelson** = *side-kelson*; **bilge-k.**, an additional strengthening beam placed fore-and-aft in the bilge of a vessel, parallel to the kelson; **boiler-k.**, a bilge- or cross-kelson supporting the boilers of a steamer (Hamersly *Naval Encycl.* 1881); **box-k.**, a kelson whose section is box-shaped; **cross-k.**, a beam placed across the kelson to support the boilers or engines of a steamer (Webster, 1864); **engine-k.**, a side- or cross-kelson supporting the engines in a steamer (Hamersly, 1881); **false k.**, an additional beam placed longitudinally above the kelson in order to strengthen it (Young *Naut. Dict.* 1846); **hog k.**, ? = false kelson; **main k.**, the kelson proper, as distinguished from the side-kelsons, etc.; **rider-k.**, a false kelson, kelson-rider (Knight *Dict. Mech.* 1875); **side-** or **sister k.**, a second kelson parallel with the main one.

1825 CLARK, etc. *Shipwrights' Scale Prices* 16 Main, Hog, or Assistant Keelsons. *Ibid.*, All Hog Keelsons under 6 inches thick to be paid plank price. **1859** J. S. MANSFIELD in *Merc. Marine Mag.* (1860) VII. 15 She was strengthened by the addition of two bilge keelsons, having been originally constructed with a kelson and two sister keelsons. **1867** SMYTH *Sailor's Word-bk.* s.v. *Keelson*, The main keelson, in order to fit with more security upon the floor-timbers, is notched opposite to each of them. *Ibid.*, *Side-keelsons*..First used in mortar-vessels to support the bomb-beds; later they have crept in to support the engines in steamers. **1869** SIR E. REED *Shipbuild.* i. 7 A large central box-keelson completed these lower strengthenings.

c. (Spelt *keelson*.) A structure in the hull of a flying-boat (or the float of a seaplane) analogous to the keelson of a ship's hull.

1920 *Flight* 2 Sept. 948/1 Such members as keelson and chines are of rock elm. **1928** CHATFIELD & TAYLOR *Airplane & its Engine* xiii. 237 Since the loads on the bottom of the float in landing are large, additional longitudinal members called keelsons are provided to stiffen it. **1930** [see KEEL *sb.*[1] 3 d]. **1942** R. H. LONGE in R. A. Beaumont *Aeronaut. Engin.* xviii. 486/1 The keelson..is the backbone of the hull [of a flying-boat], and runs the full length of the hull, from the stem or bow, to the stern-post. **1969** *Jane's 100 Significant Aircraft* 38/2 Twin-engined flying-boat... Floors notched out for two-thirds of depth to fit over solid keelson... Keelson is continuous member from stem to stern. **1974** *Flight International* 7 Nov. 646/2 The fuselage..is based on a twin-girder keelson running from nose to tail.

2. Used as = KEEL *sb.*[1] 1. *rare.*

1831 TRELAWNEY *Adv. Younger Son* II. 261, I could almost see the kelston as she rolled heavily. **1837** MARRYAT *Dogfiend* x, Lowering him down over the bows, and with ropes retaining him exactly in his position under the kelsom, while he is drawn aft by a hauling line until he makes his appearance at the rudder-chains.

3. *Comb.*, as ***kelson-bolt***, ***-plate***; **kelson-rider** = *false kelson* (Young *Naut. Dict.* 1846).

1825 CLARK, etc. *Shipwrights' Scale Prices* 4 Main Keel, exclusive of Shores, Blocks, and Keelson Bolts. **1875** KNIGHT *Dict. Mech.* 1223/2 Pigs of iron..laid over the keelson-plates.

†**kelsouns.** *Sc. Obs. rare*[−1]. [a. F. *caleçons* (in Cotgr. *calçon*, *calson*): see CALZOONS.] Drawers, linen trousers.

1568 in Hay Fleming *Mary Q. Scots* (1897) 512 Item ane curchsche [= curch]. Item ane pair of kelsounis.

kelt[1] (kɛlt). [Etym. unknown.] A salmon, sea-trout, or herling, in bad condition after spawning, before returning to the sea.

c **1340** *Durham Acc. Rolls* (Surtees) 36 In playces et keltis emp., 6s. **1793** *Statist. Acc. Scotl.*, *Forfar*. VIII. 204 No salmon; except at the end of the fishing season, when a few of what are called foul fish, or kelt, are caught. **1834** JARDINE in *Proc. Berw. Nat. Club* I. No. 3. 51 The return of the old fish or kelts to the sea. **1884** SPEEDY *Sport* vii. 80 Good runs with sea-trout kelts of considerable size. **1937** *Evening News* 15 Feb. 8/5 A kelt—that is a fish which has paid its visit to the gravel beds—is a sad wreck and is in no form to put up a fight. An otter can deal with such salmon. **1963** *Times* 26 Jan. 11/4 If the fish has shed only a few eggs..it is still technically and in law a kelt.

attrib. **1883** *Fisheries Exhib. Catal.* (ed. 4) 96 Large Kelt Salmon..with arrow-headed parasites in the gills.

Hence **'kelty** *a.*, like a kelt.

1884 *Chamb. Jrnl.* 29 Mar. 204/2 Nothing but huge, lanky, kelty-looking fish.

kelt[2]. *Sc.* and *north. dial.* [Of obscure origin. Ir. and Gael. *cealt* cloth, clothing, may be from Eng. or Sc. Cf. KELTER[1].] A kind of homespun cloth or frieze, usually of black and white wool mixed, formerly used for outer garments by country people in Scotland and N. England. Also *attrib.*

1583 *Leg. Bp. St. Androis* 573 in *Satir. Poems Reform.* xlv, Ane hamelie hat; a cott of kelt Weill beltit in ane lethrone belt. **1611** *Rates* (Jam. s.v. *Kendilling*), Kelt or kendall freese. **1791** *Statist. Acc. Scotl.* I. 356 They [farmers *c* 1750] were clothed in a homespun suit of freezed cloth, called Kelt. *a* **1833** ANDERSON *Cumbld. Ball.* (1840) 123 *note*, An oaken staff, a pair of clogs, and a kelt surtout.

b. *fig.* Applied to a sheep's fleece.

1722–8 RAMSAY *Ram & Buck* 38 Ye've a very ragged kelt on.

Kelt, -ic, -icism, etc.: see CELT[1], CELTIC.

kelt, keltch, varr. KELCH.

kelt, erroneous form of CELT[2].

1862 LATHAM *Channel Isl.* III. xviii. (ed. 2) 414 Kelts, arrow-heads..and hammers, all of stone.

kelt, obs. form of KILT *sb.*[1]

†**'kelter**[1]. *north. Obs.* [Of obscure origin; cf. KELT[2]. Ir. and Gaelic *cealtar* prob. from Eng.]

1. A coarse cloth used for outer garments. Chiefly *attrib.*

1502 *Ld. Treas. Acc. Scot.* (1900) II. 198 For making of ane cote of kelter. **1505** *Ibid.* III. 38 For ane blak keltir cote to the King. **1543** *Richmond Wills* (Surtees) 39, I gyue and beqwethe to Henry Warryner a kelter jacket. ? **16..** *Lord of Lorn* in *Roxb. Ball.* (1873) II. 350 He put him on an old Kelter coat, And Hose of the same above the knee.

2. A garment made of this cloth.

1562 *Richmond Wills* (Surtees) 152, v kelters and a blakene xliiij[s]. **1580** *Inv. T. Wilson, Kendal* (Somerset Ho.), A Romeland keltar.

Hence **keltering** *vbl. sb.*, ? lining with kelter.
1507 *Ld. Treas. Acc. Scot.* (1901) III. 254 Item for vj elne Rislis blak to be an cote to the King..vj*li*. Item, for keltering of it..iijs.

kelter^{2}, kilter ('kɛltə(r), 'kɪltə(r)). [Etym. obscure. Widely diffused in Eng. dial. from Northumb. and Cumb. to Cornwall, and occasional in literature. More frequent in U.S. (in form *kilter*).] Good condition, order; state of health or spirits. Used in the phrases ***out of kelter, in (good, high) kelter, to get into kelter.***
α. **1643** R. WILLIAMS *Key Lang. Amer.* 177 Their Gunnes they..often sell many a score to the English, when they are a little out of frame or Kelter. **1674** RAY *S. & E. Country Words* 69 *Kelter* or *Kilter*, Frame, order. *a* **1677** BARROW *Serm.* vi. Wks. 1716 I. 50 If the organs of Prayer are out of Kelter, or out of tune, how can we pray? **1722** in *Connect. Col. Rec.* (1872) VI. 335 Mending, cleansing and keeping in good kelter the firelocks left with his Honour. **1828** SCOTT *Jrnl.* 20 May, The rest are in high kelter. **1875** *Contemp. Rev.* XXV. 262 Some part of her internal economy is chronically out of kelter.
β. **1628** W. BRADFORD in *Mass. Hist. Soc. Coll.* (1856) 4th Ser. III. 235 Ye very sight of one [*sc.* a gun] (though out of kilter) was a terrour unto them. **1681** in *New Eng. Mag.* (1898) June 450/1 The seats some burned and others out of kilter. **1862** LOWELL *Lett.* I. 359, I must rest awhile. My brain is out of kilter. **1883** J. HAWTHORNE *Dust* I. 16 There's something awkward here... A joint out of kilter perhaps. **1893** STEVENSON *Let. C. Baxter* 19 July in *Lett. Fam.* etc. II. 300, I..am miserably out of heart and out of kilter. **1938** 'E. QUEEN' *Four of Hearts* (1939) xii. 173 Jack's death sort of knocked you out of kilter. **1960** M. PHILLIPS in *Analog Science Fact/Fiction* Nov. 16/1 We've had some reports that some of the government machines are out of kilter, and I'd like you to go over them for me. **1968** J. C. HOLMES *Nothing More to Declare* 77 A deeply traditional nature thrown out of kilter, and thus enormously sensitive to anything uprooted. **1973** *Times* 15 Oct. 17/3 There [*sc.* in N. Ireland], an allotment of 12 seats at Westminster is based upon electoral quotas wildly out of kilter with the quotas for England, Scotland, and Wales.

'kelter^{3}. *north. dial.* [Origin obscure. *Sheffield Gloss.* gives *kelt* in same sense.] Money, cash.
1807 in Anderson *Cumbld. Ball.* 138 His billet a bad yen, his kelter aw duin. **1825** BROCKETT, *Kelter*..also means money, cash. **1828** *Craven Dial.*, *Kelter*, a cant term for money. *W. Yorksh. dial.* He's a rich man, he is worth plenty of kelter.

'kelter^{4}. *dial.* [In dialect use from Durham to S. Lincolnsh.] Rubbish; nonsense.
1847–78 in HALLIWELL. **1870** E. PEACOCK *Ralf Skirl.* II. 48 Lookin' at their tongues, feelin' of their pulses, or ony such like kelter. *Ibid.* III. 78 What can a man like you want wi' that kelter?

Kelto-, variant of CELTO-.

†**'kelty.** *Sc. Obs.* [According to the *Stat. Acc. Scotl.* XVIII. 474 (quoted in full by Jamieson), Keltie was a Scottish laird famous for his drinking powers.]

1. A term denoting the complete draining of a glass of liquor (indicated by turning it upside down).
1664 COTTON *Scarron.* 108 With that she set it to her Nose, And off at once the Rumkin goes... Then turning Topsy [*Margin:* alias *Kelty*] on her Thumb, Says, look, here's Supernaculum. **1818** SCOTT *Rob Roy* xxviii, Are ye a' cleared kelty aff? Fill anither.

2. A glass or bumper imposed as a fine on one who does not drink fair. Also ***Keltie's mends.***
1692 *Sc. Presbyt. Eloq.* (1738) 143 Lord give thy Enemies the Papists and Prelates a full Cup of thy Fury to drink; and if they refuse to drink it off, then good Lord give them Kelty. **1796** *Statist. Acc. Scotl.*, *Perths.* XVIII. 474 Nothing is more common, at this very day, when one refuses to take his glass, than to be threatened with Keltie's Mends. *a* **1835** HOGG *Tales* (1866) 405 (E.D.D.) Gin he winna tak that, gie him kelty. **1879** P. R. DRUMMOND *Perth Bygone Days* xii. 66 To drink 'Kelty' or another glass.

keltz, var. KELCH.

Kelvin, kelvin ('kɛlvɪn). [The title of Sir William Thomson, Lord *Kelvin* (1824–1907), British physicist and inventor.] †**1.** (With lower-case initial.) A name proposed (but little used) for the kilowatt-hour, the ordinary commercial unit of electric energy. *Obs.*
1892 *Electrician* 6 May 1/1 The President of the Board of Trade having cordially approved and Lord Kelvin having acquiesced; after the word 'unit' in the Provisional Orders of this year, the words 'hereinafter called a kelvin' will be introduced. **1911** *Encycl. Brit.* XXVII. 740/1 The corresponding energy unit being the kilowatt-second, and 3600 kilowatt-seconds or 1 kilowatt-hour called a 'Board of Trade unit' or a 'kelvin'.

2. (With capital initial.) Used *attrib.* and in the possessive to designate instruments and concepts devised by Lord Kelvin, as **Kelvin balance**, an electrical measuring instrument having a set of horizontal coils arranged in the form of a balance with a sliding weight, which is used to balance the electromagnetic forces produced by a current passed through the coils and so to measure its strength; **Kelvin (double) bridge**, a modification of the Wheatstone bridge used for measuring low resistances and having two pairs of variable ratio resistors, an adjustable standard resistor, and the unknown one; **Kelvin's law**, the law that the most economical cross-sectional area of a conductor used as a transmission line is that for which the cost of the energy dissipated in any period is equal to the charges during the same period on the capital cost of the line.
1896 *Proc. Physical Soc.* XIV. 166 A convenient method for determining low resistances, such as..a Kelvin bridge. **1903** F. A. C. PERRINE *Conductors for Electr. Distribution* viii. 160 (*heading*) Kelvin's law of economy in conductors. **1904** SWENSON & FRANKENFIELD *Testing Electro-Magn. Machinery* I. 122 The Kelvin Balance is recognized as a standard instrument. **1906** *Rep. Brit. Assoc. Adv. Sci.* 119 The current leads of standard resistances intended for measurement on the Kelvin double bridge should have a resistance not greater than the standard itself. **1933** E. W. GOLDING *Electr. Measurements* ii. 14 Kelvin balances are manufactured with ten different ranges up to 2,500 amp. **1957** W. J. JOHN *Mod. Electr. Engin.* III. x. 301/2 Kelvin's law is usually expressed in terms of annual costs, though it is equally true of capitalized costs. **1967** H. COTTON *Adv. Electr. Technol.* iii. 92 Calculate the current flowing in the galvanometer of the Kelvin double-bridge circuit.

3. (With capital initial.) Used *attrib.* to designate an absolute scale of temperature (defined thermodynamically in terms of the operation of an ideal heat engine) in which the zero is identified with absolute zero and values are assigned to one or more fixed points so as to make the degrees correspond in size to those of the centigrade (Celsius) scale. So ***Kelvin temperature***, a temperature expressed in terms of this scale.
As the scale was orig. defined, the temperature interval between two fixed points (the freezing point and the boiling point of water) was made to be exactly 100 degrees, so that the value of each point was a matter of experiment (which produced values of about 273° and 373° respectively); in 1954 the scale was redefined in terms of a single fixed point, the triple point of water, to which was assigned the value 273·16° exactly (giving a figure of approximately 273·15° for the ice point).
[**1871** J. C. MAXWELL *Theory of Heat* viii. 155 (*heading*) Thomson's absolute scale of temperature. **1899** W. WATSON *Text-bk. Physics* vi. 334 The temperatures..are 283°, 293°,..on Lord Kelvin's absolute scale.] **1908** *Amer. Jrnl. Sci.* CLXXVI. 421 The derivation of the Kelvin thermodynamic scale from the expansion of nitrogen. **1922** GLAZEBROOK *Dict. Appl. Physics* I. 270/2 If the same size of degree be adopted for the Kelvin scale, then..the readings, on either scale, will be identical. **1937** M. W. ZEMANSKY *Heat & Thermodynamics* ix. 140 Two temperatures on the Kelvin scale are to each other as the heats absorbed and rejected respectively by a Carnot engine operating between reservoirs at these temperatures. *Ibid.* 144 The Kelvin temperature is therefore numerically equal to the absolute temperature and may be measured with a gas thermometer. **1958** CONDON & ODISHAW *Handbk. Physics* v. iii. 30/2 This new absolute thermodynamic scale, called the Kelvin scale, does not differ from the thermodynamic 'centigrade' scale by an amount which can be determined experimentally at the present time. **1962** *Units & Standards of Measurement: Temperature* (Nat. Physical Lab.) 3 The thermodynamic Kelvin scale..is recognized as the fundamental scale to which all temperature measurements should ultimately be referred.

b. ***degree Kelvin*** (or ***Kelvin degree***): a degree of the Kelvin scale (in size equal to the degree centigrade), symbol °K (see K 4 f); now formally called a *kelvin* (symbol K) and incorporated into the International System of Units as a basic unit.
1911 *Physical Rev.* XXXIII. 220 The writer has assumed that the degree Kelvin and the degree centigrade were equal. **1930** *Engineering* 9 May 595/3 A perfect gas of one free electron per atom would necessarily contribute three calories per gram-atom per degree Kelvin to the specific heat of the metal. **1941** *Temperature* (Amer. Inst. Physics) 11 When using the Thermodynamic Centigrade Scale one is simply expressing the number of Kelvin degrees that a particular thermal state is above or below the ice point. **1945** G. R. NOAKES *Text-bk. Heat* i. 26 The name 'degrees Kelvin' (°K.) is used for the true absolute scale temperature, and 'degrees absolute' (°A., or °abs.) for temperatures measured by other means on any other scale numbered up from absolute zero. **1962** CORSON & LORRAIN *Introd. Electromagn. Fields* iii. 108, *T* is the absolute temperature in degrees Kelvin. **1968** *Nature* 16 Nov. 651/2 Resolution No. 3 [of the thirteenth General Conference of Weights and Measures] changes the name of the 'degree Kelvin' (symbol °K) simply to 'kelvin', with symbol K... The terms of the revised definition of the unit of thermodynamic temperature are (resolution No. 4): 'the kelvin..is the fraction 1/273·16 of the thermodynamic temperature of the triple point of water'. **1971** *Physics Bull.* Mar. 144/1 The inversion transitions..indicate that the ammonia molecules are at a temperature of several tens of kelvin. **1973** *Sci. Amer.* Aug. 84/3 Only liquid hydrogen will serve, and it must be stored at an extremely low temperature (22 degrees Kelvin, or 22 degrees Celsius above absolute zero).

Kelvinside ('kɛlvɪnsaɪd). The name of a residential district of Glasgow, used *attrib.* or *absol.* to designate the supposedly affected and refined accent with which some of its residents speak.
1903 J. H. MILLAR *Lit. Hist. Scotl.* 317 A mincing and quasi-genteel lingo of their own (the sort of English known in some quarters as 'Princes Street' or 'Kelvinside'). **1928** I. C. WARD *Phonetics of English* x. 76 Some types of Scottish town speech—sometimes called 'Kelvinside' or 'High English'. **1932** N. M. GUNN *Lost Glen* II. ii. 117 A thin.. woman.., fair and full of merriment and a Kelvinside-English accent. **1935** *Trans. Philol. Soc.* 8 The artificial variety of speech which has been called Kelvinside English. **1969** G. PAYTON *Proper Names* 243 *Kelvinside*, the north-western area of Glasgow around the University and Kelvingrove Park, where the..residents were supposed to speak with a mincing ('Kelvinside')..accent.

kelyn, -yng, obs. ff. KEEL *v.*^{1}, KEELING.

kelyphite. *Min.* [f. Gr. κέλυφος a pod, shell + -ITE.] (See quot.)
1882 DANA *Min.* (1883) App. III, *Kelyphite*..Grey serpentinous coating of pyrope crystals from Kremze, near Budweis, Bohemia.

kelyt, obs. pa. pple. of KILL *v.*

kem, kemb, keme, variants of *kam(b)e*, COMB *sb.*^{1}, assimilated to KEMB *v.*
1583 *Wills & Inv. N.C.* (Surtees 1860) 83 A wyndocloth, ij kemys poiks, 16s. ?**16..** *Alison Gross* in Child *Ballads* (1857) I. 288 My sister Maisry came to me, Wi' silver bason, and silver kemb.

Kemalism ('kɛmalɪz(ə)m). [f. the name of *Kemal* Atatürk (*c* 1880–1938), Turkish soldier and statesman + -ISM.] The political, social, and economic policies advocated by Kemal Atatürk, which aimed to create a modern republican secular Turkish state out of a part of the Ottoman empire. So **'Kemalist**, one who advocates or believes in the theory of Kemalism; an adherent or supporter of Kemalism; also as *adj.*
1920 *N.Y. Times* 3 Dec., Greek troops have dispersed the Kemalists in the district of Nicee. **1921** *Manch. Guardian Weekly* 29 July 65 The Kemalists are evacuating Angora. **1925** *Ibid.* 11 Dec. 476 The anti-Kemalist revolt..has as its centre the town of Erzerum, where, curiously enough, Kemalism was born. **1927** *Observer* 18 Sept. 7 In Turkey an utter victory for the Kemalists over the Greeks supplied the opportunity for a comprehensive scrapping of Turkey's Ottoman habits... Quite the most striking of these post-war metamorphoses has been accomplished by Kemalist Turkey, the leader among Oriental nations in the race for 'Westernisation'. **1947** A. KOESTLER in *Partisan Rev.* XIV. 344 Under a de Gaulle regime of the Kemalist type you could after all go on publishing your stuff within limits. **1959** *Encounter* Sept. 36/1 The theoretical justification of Kemalism. **1963** *Times* 23 Apr. 11/3 The pamphlets were said to have been signed 'the Army of Young Kemalists'. **1966** *Tablet* 12 Mar. 299/2 The Kemalist revolution was often brutal.

kemb, *v.* *Obs.* exc. *dial.* Forms: α. 1 **cemban**, (**cæmban**), 3 **kemben**, 3–7 **kembe**, (6 **kimbe**), 6– **kemb.** *Pa. t.* and *pa. pple.* 3–8 **kembed**, 3– **kempt.** β. 4 **cemme**, 6– 7 **kemm**, 9 **kem.** γ. 4–6 **keme**, (6 **keame, keyme**), 7 **keem.** [Com. Teut.: OE. *cęmban* = OS. *kembian*, *kemmian* (MDu. *kemmen*), OHG. *chempan* (MHG. *kemben*, *kemmen*, G. *kämmen*), ON. *kemba* (Da. *kæmme*):—O.Teut. **kambjan*, f. *kamb-* COMB *sb.*^{1}. Now displaced by COMB *v.*^{1} (f. the sb.; cf. Du. *kammen*, Sw. *kamma*), but partly surviving in the pa. pple. *kempt*, and the commoner *unkempt*.
In ME. the vowel usually remained short, and the commonest spelling is *kemb* or *kemm*: forms indicating a long vowel are much less frequent. In later Sc. it is difficult to separate *kemb* or *keme* from *kame* = comb.]

1. *trans.* To disentangle and smooth (hair) by drawing a comb through it; to dress or trim (the hair, head, a person, etc.) with a comb; to curry (a horse): = COMB *v.*^{1} 1. Now *dial.*
α. *c* **1000** ÆLFRIC *Gram.* xxviii. (Z.) 168 *Pecto* ic cembe [*v.r.* cæmbe]. *a* **1225** *Ancr. R.* 422 *marg.*, Ha mot oftere weschen & kemben hire holuet. *a* **1300** *Floriz & Bl.* 562 Þat on his heued for to kembe þat oþer bringe towaille and bacin. *c* **1386** CHAUCER *Knt.'s T.* 1285 His longe heer was kembd [*v.r.* kemb, kempte] bihynde his bak. *a* **1450** *Knt. de la Tour* (1868) 99 As she kembed her hede atte a wyndow, the kinge perceiued her. **1562** BULLEYN *Def. agst. Sickness, Bk. vse Sicke men* 67 Then begin with a fine Combe, to kembe the heere up and doun. *a* **1661** FULLER *Worthies* III. (1662) 228 Not able to kembe his own head. **1725** BAILEY *Erasm. Colloq.* 35 How often do you rub 'em down, or kemb them in a year? **1832** MOTHERWELL *Poems* (1847) 131 While kembing locks like sunbeams glancing. **1874** HOLLAND *Mistr. Manse* xvi. 64 Clean and kempt, the little oaf..went forth.
β. **13..** *Gaw. & Gr. Knt.* 188 Þe mane of þat mayn hors ..Wel cresped & cemmed. *c* **1400** MAUNDEV. (Roxb.) iv. 13 He sawe a damysell kemmand hir hare. **1508** DUNBAR *Tua Mariit Wemen* 275 Weil couth I..kemm his cowit noddill. **1561** HOLLYBUSH *Hom. Apoth.* 2 Strake or kemme the heyres. **1812** W. TENNANT *Anster F.* IV. lxxvi, The mermaids..kem..Their long sleek oozy locks.
γ. **1398** TREVISA *Barth. De P.R.* VI. vi. (Tollem. MS.), Whan þe modir wascheþ and kemeþ hem. *a* **1450** *Knt. de la Tour* (1868) 45 This day we trow shalle not this lady be kemed, and arraied. **1557** SEAGER *Sch. Vertue* 74 in *Babees Bk.* 338 Thy handes se thou washe, and thy hed keame [*rime* seame]. **1618** SIR T. WILSON *Jrnl.* 21 Sept. (R. Suppl.), He [Raleigh] told me he was wont to keem his head a whole hour every day. **1639** HORN & ROB. *Gate Lang. Unl.* liii. §586 The bush of haire..is keem'd with a combe. *a* **1835** HOGG *Poems* (1865) 33 (E.D.D.) They kemed her hair.

b. *fig.* To trim, make smooth or elegant.
c **1386** CHAUCER *Sqr.'s T.* 552 So peynted he and kembde at point deuys As wel hise wordes as his contenaunce. *c* **1391** —— *Boeth.* I. met. v. 14 (Camb. MS.) The fraude couered and kembd with a fals coloure.

c. *humorously.* To beat, thrash; = COMB *v.*^{1} 3.

c **1566** *Merie T.* in *Skelton's Wks.* (1843) I. p. lix, Hys wife woulde diuers tymes in the weeke kimbe his head with a iii. footed stoole. **1769** WALLIS *Antiq. Nhb.* in *N. & Q.* (1877) 5th S. VII. 208 *Kemb*, ..often used by borderers when they threaten in a passionate tone to beat an assailant.

†**2.** To prepare (wool, flax, etc.) for spinning by parting and straightening the fibres with wool-combs or cards; = COMB *v.*[1] 2. Also *absol. Obs.*

a **1300** *Sat. People Kildare* xix. in *E.E.P.* (1862) 155 Fi a debles kaites that kemith the wolle. **1377** LANGL. *P. Pl.* B. x. 18 Carded with coueytise, as clotheres kemben here wolle. **1393** *Ibid.* C. x. 80 Boþe to karde and to kembe, to clouten and to wasche. **1543** TRAHERON *Vigo's Chirurg.* II. iv. ii. 66 Unwashed woalle..or towe wel kembed. **1627-77** FELTHAM *Resolves* II. lx. 285 We are like Flax that's dress'd, and dry'd, and kemb'd. **1715** tr. *Pancirollus' Rerum Mem.* II. xxiv. 403 They were famous for kembing silken Fleeces.

†**b.** To tear or lacerate with a comb-like instrument. *Obs.*

c **1375** *Sc. Leg. Saints* xx. (*Blasius*) 187 [He] gert þame keme his tendir flesch with Irne camys. **1483** CAXTON *Gold. Leg.* 121 b/1 Thenne the bochyers toke combes of yron and began to kembe hym on the sides within the flesshe.

†**3.** *to kemb from* or *off*: to remove or obtain by means of combing, or by a similar process. Also with *out*. Cf. COMB *v.*[1] 4. *Obs.*

1601 HOLLAND *Pliny* VI. xvii, They kembe from the leaves of their trees the hoarie downe thereof. **1605** CAMDEN *Rem.* (1637) 194 Sericum which was a doune kembed off the trees among the Seres. **1622** FLETCHER *Beggar's Bush* II. i, No impositions, taxes, grievances..Lie lurking in this beard, but all kem'd out. **1626** BACON *Sylva* §617 There are some Tears of Trees, which are kembed from the Beards of Goats.

†**kember.** *Obs.* [f. KEMB *v.* + -ER[1]; cf. MDu. *kemmer*, G. *kämmer*, Da. *kæmmer*.] One who combs (wool): = COMBER[1] 1.

1511-2 *Act 3 Hen. VIII*, c. 6 §1 The breker or kember to delyver..the same Woll so broken and kempt. **1697** *View Penal Laws* 66 Kember, Spinster or Weaver of Wooll.

kembestere, variant of KEMPSTER.

†ˈ**kembing**, *vbl. sb. Obs.* [f. KEMB *v.* + -ING[1].] **1.** The action of the verb KEMB; combing.

c **1440** *Promp. Parv.* 270/2 Kemynge of here, or wulle, *pectinacio*. **1508** DUNBAR *Tua Mariit Wemen* 182 He is.. Alse curtly of his clething, and kemmyng of his hair. **1547** BOORDE *Brev. Health* cxxxiii. 49 After keymyng of the head. **1634** PEACHAM *Gentl. Exerc.* I. xxiii. 74 Haire worthy the kembing.

2. *Comb.*, as **kembing-claith**, *Sc.*, combing-cloth; **kembing-stock**, the stock or frame on which the combs were fixed for dressing wool, rippling lint, and breaking flax.

1418 *Bury Wills* (Camden) 3, j par de wollecombes j kembyngstok. **1533** in Weaver *Wells Wills* (1890) 155 A payre of woll combes with a kemynge stoke. *a* **1568** *Wyf of Auchterm.* 84 in Laing *Anc. Poet. Scot.* 340 He fell backward into the fyre, And brack his head on the keming stock. **1578** *Inv.* in Hunter *Biggar & House of Fleming* xxvi. (1862) 332 Ane kame caiss & ane auld kimi[n]g clayth about ye same. *a* **1776** *Country Wedding* in Herd *Coll. Sc. Songs* II. 89 A keam but and a keaming-stock.

kembo, kemelin(e, -ing, etc., **kemelyng, kemes, kemester:** see KIMBO, KIMNEL, COMELING, CHEMISE, KEMPSTER.

kemp, *sb.*[1] *Obs.* exc. *dial.* Forms: 1 cempa, (cæmpa), 2 cempe, 3-5 kempe, (3 kimppe), 4-6, 9, kemp. [OE. *cęmpa* wk. masc. = OFris. *kempa*, *kampa*, OS. **kempio* (MDu. *kemp(e*, *kimp(e*, MLG. *kempe*), OHG. *chemph(i)o* (MHG. *kempfe*; G. *kämpe*, from LG., for earlier *kämpfe*):—WGer. **kampjōn-*. It is doubtful whether this is an independent formation from *kamp-* (CAMP *sb.*[1]) battle, or ad. late L. *campiōnem* (see CAMPION).]

1. A big, strong, and brave warrior or athlete; a professional fighter, wrestler, etc.; a champion.

a **700** *Epinal Gloss.* 481 *Gladiatores*, caempan [*Erfurt* cempan]. **995** *Death of Byrhtnoth* 119 Him æt fotum feoll fæʒe cempa. *a* **1175** *Cott. Hom.* 243 Gif we ofercumed heom we scule bien imersed alle gode cempen. *a* **1225** *Ancr. R.* 196 Iðe vihte aʒeines ham, heo biʒiteð þe blisfule kempene crune. *c* **1300** *Havelok* 1036 He was for a kempe told. *c* **1350** *Will. Palerne* 3352 Oþer kud kempes. **1470-85** MALORY *Arthur* VII. viii, They rasshed to gyders lyke two myghty kempys. **1527** *Ld. Treas. Acc. Scotl.* in Pitcairn *Crim. Trials* I. *271 Item, to John Drummond, callit the kingis kemp..xv li. **1562** WINȜET *Tractates* Wks. 1888 I. 33 Albeit thir twa ȝoure kempis dar not for schame ansuer in this mater. **1818** SCOTT *Burt's Lett. N. Scotl.* I. Introd. 62 Hammer Donald..(like Viga Glum and other celebrated Kemps and homicides of the North). **1832** MOTHERWELL *Poems* (1847) 7 In starkest fight where kemp to kemp, Reel headlong to the grave. **1893** *Northumbld. Gloss., Kemp*, an impetuous youth.

2. = KEMPER a.

1573 *Satir. Poems Reform.* xlii. 276 All the corne of the Countrie Be kempis hes not bene schorne, we see.

3. *Sc.* A seed-stalk of the ribwort (*Plantago lanceolata*), used in a children's game: see quot. 1825. [So Norw. *kjæmpe*, Sw. *kämpa*.] Cf. COCKS.

1825 JAMIESON s.v., Two children, or young people, pull each a dozen of stalks of rib-grass; and try who with his *kemp*, can decapitate the greatest number of those belonging to his opponent. **1853** G. JOHNSTON *Nat. Hist. E. Bord.* I. 170 It is customary with children to challenge each other to try the 'kemps'. **1893** in *Northumbld. Gloss.*

kemp (kɛmp), *sb.*[2] [app. the same as CAMP *sb.*[4], a. ON. *kamp-r* beard, moustache, whisker of a cat, lion, etc.] A coarse or stout hair, as those of the eyebrows (*obs.*); now, hair of this kind occurring among wool. Also in *comb.* **kemp-hair; kemp-haired** *a.*

c **1386** CHAUCER *Knt.'s T.* 1276 Lik a grifphon looked he aboute, With kempe [*v.r.* keempe] heeris on hise browes stoute. **1570** LEVINS *Manip.* 59/45 Kemp, haire, *grandebala*. **1641** BEST *Farm. Bks.* (Surtees) 9 To cutt of all the shaggie hairy woll..this the sheppeardes call forcinge of them, and cuttinge of kempe-haires. *Ibid.* 11 Sheepe which ..are thinne skinn'd..or kempe-hair'd. **1805** LUCCOCK *Nat. Wool* 170 Its staple was perfectly free from kemps and wild hair, so common upon the backs of northern sheep. **1849** ROWLANDSON in *Jrnl. R. Agric. Soc. Eng.* X. II. 436 The fineness of the Ryeland fleece and freedom from kemps.

†**kemp**, *sb.*[3] *Obs. rare.* ? A barrel or cask.

1391 *Earl Derby's Exp.* (Camden) 77/22 Pro ij kempes de rubiis allecibus. *c* **1440** *Promp. Parv.* 270/2 Kempe of herynge, or spyrlynge.

†**kemp**, *sb.*[4] *Obs. rare.* A kind of eel.

c **1440** *Promp. Parv.* 270/2 Kempe eel [no Latin]. **1515** BARCLAY *Egloges* iv. (1570) C iv b/2 Fed..with crudd, Or slimy kempes ill smelling of the mud. **1552** HULOET, Kempe or small eale, *anguilula*. **1884** DAY *Brit. Fishes* II. 243.

kemp, *sb.*[5] *Sc.* [f. KEMP *v.*] A contest, *esp.* of reapers when kemping.

1786 *Har'st Rig* in Chambers *Pop. Hum. Scot. Poems* (1862) 50 The master..cries with haste, 'Come, lads, forbear, This kemp let be'. **1844** RICHARDSON *Borderer's Table Bk.* VII. 372 The stormy *Kemp*, or emulous struggle for the honour of the ridge-end. **1870** HUNTER *Stud.* Pref. (E.D.D.), What ever lesson we began to, we gaed at it just like a kemp on the hairst rig.

kemp (kɛmp), *v. Sc.* and *north. dial.* [ME. *kempen* = MDu. *kempen*, *kimpen*, LG. *kämpen*, OHG. *chemfan* (MHG. *kempfen*, G. *kämpfen*), ON. *keppa* (:—**kempa*; Sw. *kämpa*, Da. *kæmpe*):—OTeut. **kampjan*, f. *kamp-*: see CAMP *sb.*[1] and KEMP *sb.*[1]] *intr.* **a.** To fight or contend in battle *with* another. **b.** To contend or strive in doing a piece of work; said esp. of a set of reapers striving to finish their 'rig' first.

a. ? *a* **1400** *Morte Arth.* 2634 There is no kynge undire Criste may kempe with hym one! **1893** *Northumbld. Gloss.* s.v. *Kemps*, They are called by children *kemps*..and are used to *kemp* or fight with.

b. **1513** DOUGLAS *Æneis* III. x. 20 We..kempand with airis in all our mane, Wp welteris watter of the salt se flude. **1685** *Lintoun Green* (1817) 95 (E.D.D.) [She] could..kemp wi' Kate or Wull, On harvest day. **1786** *Har'st Rig* in Chambers *Pop. Hum. Scot. Poems* (1862) 48 This sets the lave a-working fast—They kemp at length. *a* **1881** CARLYLE in *Mrs. C.'s Lett.* (1883) II. 192 His reapers had taken to 'kemp' and spoiled him much stuff.

kempas (ˈkɛmpəs). Also 9 **kompas, koompass.** [Malay.] A hardwood timber tree, *Koompassia malaccensis*, native to Malaya, Sumatra, and Borneo; also, the wood of this tree.

1839 T. J. NEWBOLD *Pol. & Statistical Acct. Straits of Malacca* II. viii. 100 The ore and charcoal, (of the Kompas, Kamoui, or other hard woods,) are gradually heaped up. *a* **1869** A. C. MAINGAY in *Kew Bull.* (1890) 122 Koompass. ..Wood yellowish white... Used for shipbuilding. **1935** I. H. BURKILL *Dict. Econ. Products Malay Peninsula* II. 1286 Kempas sheds all its leaves every year. **1940** E. J. H. CORNER *Wayside Trees Malaya* I. 397 The *Kempas* occurs throughout the lowland forest in swampy ground or on hillsides. **1956** *Handbk. Hardwoods* (Forest Prod. Res. Lab.) 127 Kempas normally seasons fairly well. **1959** 'M. DERBY' *Tigress* ii. 98 He waited in the fork of the kempas tree. **1965** C. SHUTTLEWORTH *Malayan Safari* i. 16 There are.. medium hardwoods such as kapur, kempas and keruing. **1972** T. C. WHITMORE *Tree Flora of Malaya* I. 266/2 Kempas is a smaller tree than tualang, it is more often cut for timber.

‖**Kempeitai** (ˈkɛmpeɪtaɪ). Also **Kempetai.** [Jap.] The Japanese military secret service in the period 1931-1945.

1947 J. BERTRAM *Shadow of War* 197 A single communication..to the *kempeitai* revealing my identity would be more than enough. **1953** J. TRENCH *Docken Dead* xiv. 217 Docken had betrayed Richard to the Kempetei. **1961** R. SETH *Anat. Spying* viii. 148 The Kempeitai, like the Nazi Gestapo, was the most powerful and most hated of all Japanese institutions. It derived its power for the most part from the semi-independent position which it held within the army. *Ibid.* 149 Wherever the Kempeitai was, its most important function was counter-espionage. **1965** B. SWEET-ESCOTT *Baker St. Irregular* v. 127 If the Gestapo or the Kempetai had kept track of his movements, they would have had a good idea of what was likely to happen. **1965** *This is Japan 1966* 107 A tough *kempeitai gendarme*, with the customary red armband, two holstered revolvers, gold-and-black teeth, and foul *daikon* breath. **1969** J. M. GULLICK *Malaysia* ii. 97 The teachers..played a leading part in maintaining the underground resistance in the towns despite torture and other reprisals by the Japanese Security Police (the Kempeitai).

ˈ**kemper.** *Sc.* or *arch.* [f. KEMP *v.* + -ER[1]; cf. MDu. *kemper*, MHG. *kempfer*, G. *kämpfer*, Da. *kæmper*.] **a.** *Sc.* One who kemps or strives for victory, esp. in reaping. **b.** *arch.* = KEMP *sb.*[1]

a. **1641** FERGUSON *Prov.* No. 70 A' the corn in the country is not shorn by kempers. **1776** C. KEITH *Farmer's Ha'* in Chambers *Pop. Hum. Scot. Poems* (1862) 28 The lasses.. Are sittin at their spinnin-wheels, And weel ilk blythsome kemper dreels. **1821** *Blackw. Mag.* Jan. 401/1 Helping to give a hot brow to this bevy of notable kempers.

b. **1891** R. W. DIXON *Hist. Ch. Eng.* IV. 469 The spirit of the northern kempers.

†ˈ**kempery.** *Obs. rare.* [f. prec.: see -ERY.] The practice of kemping or fighting. Only in **kempery-man** = KEMP *sb.*[1] 1.

a **1765** *King Estmere* liv. in Child *Ballads* III. lx. (1885) 54/1 Downe then came the kemperye man. *Ibid.* lxvi, Up then rose the kemperye men. [**1865** KINGSLEY *Herew.* (1867) I. 77, I knew you would turn Viking and kemperyman.]

ˈ**kemping**, *vbl. sb.* [f. KEMP *v.* + -ING[1].] The action of the verb KEMP.

1793 *Statist. Acc. Scotl., Dumfr.* VII. 303 A boon of shearers..turned into large grey stones, on account of their kemping, i.e. striving. **1816** SCOTT *Antiq.* xxviii, A soldier, my lord; and mony a sair day's kemping I've seen. **1851** H. STEPHENS *Bk. Farm.* (ed. 2) II. 335/2 A desire frequently arises for striving, or what is..called *Kemping*..to finish the reaping of their ridges before those who had entered theirs prior to them. **1893** *Northumbld. Gloss., Kempin*, a contest between reapers in the harvest field.

kempite (ˈkɛmpaɪt). *Min.* [f. the name of J. F. Kemp (1859-1926), American geologist + -ITE[1].] An emerald-green basic chloride of manganese, $Mn_2(OH)_3Cl$, found in California.

1924 A. F. ROGERS in *Amer. Jrnl. Sci.* VIII. 150 The name kempite is given in honor of Professor James Furman Kemp. **1949** *Bull. Geol. Soc. Amer.* LX. 1944 It seems likely that the formula of kempite is $MnCl_2.3MnO.3H_2O$. **1968** I. KOSTOV *Mineral.* 195 Kempite is orthorhombic-dipyramidal, occurring as a weathering product of a manganese deposit.

†ˈ**kempkin.** *Sc. Obs. rare*[−1]. [ad. MDu. *kimmekijn*, var. of *kindekijn* KILDERKIN; cf. KINKIN.] A small barrel, a keg.

1580 *Shipping Lists Dundee* (S.H.S.) 199 Ihone Smyth ij kempkynnis of seap [= soap].

ˈ**kemple.** *Sc.* ? *Obs.* Also 7 **kimple.** [Etym. obscure.] A Scotch measure of hay or straw, varying in amount (see quots.).

1629 *MS. Charter* (Byrehills, Fife), Et quatuor oneribus equorum straminum vulgariter nuncupatis ffour kimples of stray. **1676** *Charter* (of same lands), Ffoure kemples of strae. **1706** *Acc. Bk. Sir J. Foulis* (1894) 428 For 7 kemples of strae. **1805** *Edin. Even. Courant* 18 July (Jam.), The Kemple of straw must consist of forty windlens..so that the kemple must weigh fifteen stones trone. **1849** H. STEPHENS *Bk. of Farm* II. 347 The straw will weigh 9 kemples of 440 lbs. each [In Morton's *Cycl. Agric.* (1863) given as = 358 lbs. trone.]

kemp-shot(t, variant of CAMP-SHOT.

1795 *Act 35 Geo. III*, c. 106 §23 Any Kempshot or other such Work, for the Purpose of haling Barges. **1848** M. ARNOLD *Lett.* (1895) 12 Bathed with Hughes in the Thames, having a header off the 'Kempshott'.

†ˈ**kempster.** *Obs.* Forms: 4 **keme-**, 5 **kempstare, kembestere, cem-, kem-**, 5-6 **kemp-**, (7 **kemester**). [f. KEMB *v.* + -STER. Cf. MDu. *kemster(e*.] A comber (of wool); properly, a female comber.

a **1400** *Burgh Laws* c. 103 (*Sc. Stat.* I.) Gif ony kemestaris levis þe burgh to dwell wyth uplandys men. *c* **1400** *Promp. Parv.* 270/2 Kempstare, *pectrix*. **14..** *Voc.* in Wr.-Wülcker 601/10 *Pectrix*, a kembestere. *c* **1483** CAXTON *Dialogues* 32/12 Katherin the kempster..swore..That she kembyth never Wulle so well. **1530** PALSGR. 481/1 This felowe chattereth lyke a kempster,..*comme vne piegneresse de layne*. **1641** FERGUSON *Sc. Prov.* No. 566 Kemsters are ay creishie.

b. *Comb.*

1356 in Riley *Mem. London* (1868) 283 [8 pairs of] kemster-combes, [and one] boweshawe, 11*d*.

kempt (kɛm(p)t), *ppl. a.* Forms: 1 **cemd-**, 5 **kempte, kembyd**, 6 **kemmyt, kemt**, 5-7 **kembed**, 4- **kempt.** [f. KEMB *v.*] Of hair or wool: Combed. Also with advs., as ***well-kempt***, etc. Cf. UNKEMPT. Also *transf.*

c **1050** *Ags. Gloss.* in Wr.-Wülcker 387/23 *De stuppe stamineo*, be cemdan wearpe. *c* **1380** WYCLIF *Wks.* (1880) 426 ȝif a man haue a kempt hed þanne he is a leccherous man. **1513** DOUGLAS *Æneis* X. xiv. 19 Hys weyll kemmyt berd. **1601** HOLLAND *Pliny* I. 228 A distaffe, drest and trimmed with kembed wool. **1863** MRS. WHITNEY *Faith Gartney* iv. (1869) 30 Carefully kempt tresses. **1867** J. B. ROSE tr. *Virg. Æneid* 307 His kempt beard adown his bosom spread. **1905** *Daily Chron.* 15 June 4/4 The little girls wear clean pinafores; their hair is neatly kempt. **1929** R. ALDINGTON *Death of Hero* III. xii. 398 The street paving was badly worn, but looked marvellously smooth and kempt to Winterbourne. **1946** S. SPENDER *European Witness* I. i. 9 Gardens as well kempt as a short hair-cut. **1951** W. SANSOM *Face of Innocence* i. 1 The kempt yellow gravel of drives. *a* **1954** F. B. YOUNG *Wistanslow* (1956) 113 A spacious expanse of greensward, smooth and kempt as the ancient turf of an Oxford college. **1975** *Times* 21 July 10/7 Artificially beautified people looking kempt and highly coloured for the hairdressers' and beauticians' trade fair.

ˈ**kempy**, *sb. Sc.* and *north. dial.* [f. KEMP *sb.*[1]] A kemp or champion; one given to fighting; a rough or uncouth fellow.

1525 in Pitcairn *Crim. Trials* I. 126* John Steill, alias Kempy Steill, convicted. **1801** MACNEILL *Poet. Wks.* (1856) 172 I've heard some hair-brained kempy Growl when your chappin bottle's empty. **1822** SCOTT *Pirate* xxviii, When kempies were wont, long since, to seek the habitations of the galdragons and spae-women. **1874** WAUGH *Chimn. Corner* (1879) 158 (E.D.D.) 'Never..quiet but when he're feightin'.' 'Ay, he're a regilar kempie'.

kempy ('kɛmpɪ), *a.* [f. KEMP *sb.*² + -Y¹.] Of wool: Abounding in kemps or coarse hairs.

1805 LUCCOCK *Nat. Wool* 242 Its wool was kempy, rough and thin. **1849** ROWLANDSON in *Jrnl. R. Agric. Soc. Eng.* X. II. 427 The great quantity of kempy locks which compose the fleece of this breed. **1868** *Daily News* 8 Dec., Like a black-faced sheep, but rather kempy in the wool.

kemse, kemster: see CHEMISE, KEMPSTER.

kemstock, obs. var. of CAPSTOCK, CAPSTAN.

1653 URQUHART *Rabelais* II. xxv, Panurge took two great cables of the ship and tied them to the kemstock or capstane.

ken (kɛn), *sb.*¹ Also 7 kenn(e. [f. KEN *v.*¹]

†**1.** = KENNING *vbl. sb.*¹ 4 b. *Obs.*

1545 *St. Papers Hen. VIII*, I. 815 The place, wher we be at this present, ys thwartt of Shorham, too kennys allmoste frome the shore. **1574** BOURNE *Regim. for Sea* xviii. (1577) 48 b, Neyther is it possible to see any lande further.. wherefore 6. leagues or 9. leagues is called a ken. **1580** LYLY *Euphues* (Arb.) 250 Lette this suffice, that they are safely come within a ken of Douer. **1611** SHAKS. *Cymb.* III. vi. 6 Milford, When from the Mountaine top, Pisanio shew'd thee, Thou was't within a kenne. **1625** CARPENTER *Geog. Del.* II. vii. (1635) 121 The Fisher-man iudging by sight, could not see about a kenne at sea.

2. Range of sight or vision; in phrases ***in*** or ***within ken, beyond, out of,*** or ***past ken.*** Now *rare.*

1590 GREENE *Orl. Fur.* I. Wks. (Rtldg.) 90 The bordering islands, seated here in ken. **1594** NASHE *Unfort. Trav.* 85 Out of ken we were ere the Countesse came from the feast. **1624** MASSINGER *Bondman* IV. i, The conquering army Is within ken. **1691** RAY *Creation* I. (1692) 4 Beyond all Ken by the best Telescopes. **1725** POPE *Odyss.* v. 456 Scarce in ken appears that distant isle. **1882** F. MYERS *Renewal of Youth* 77 Thro' space, if space it be, past count or ken.

b. With possessive or equivalent.

1630 DRAYTON *Noah's Flood* (R.), On which they might discern within their ken The carcasses of birds, of beasts, and men. *a* **1677** HALE *Prim. Orig. Man.* IV. viii. 365 The Intellect.. taketh a flight out of the ken or reach of Sense. **1791** COWPER *Illiad* III. 15 The eye Is bounded in its ken to a stone's cast. **1864** H. AINSWORTH *John Law* v. x. (1881) 283 Many remarkable personages came under Evelyn's ken.

†**3.** Sight or view *of* a thing, place, etc.; possibility or capacity of seeing; chiefly in phrases ***in, within, out of ken of.*** *Obs.*

1593 SHAKS. *Lucr.* clx, 'Tis double death to drown in ken of shore. **1634** MASSINGER *Very Woman* v. v, Hardly We had lost the ken of Sicily, but we were Becalm'd. **1691** RAY *Creation* I. (1692) 86 Scarce daring to venture out of the Ken of Land. **1745** *De Foe's Eng. Tradesman* (1841) I. viii. 64, I sent out my servant to watch.. these.. strollers, and keep.. within ken of them.

4. Power or exercise of vision; look, gaze.

1666 DRYDEN *Ann. Mirab.* cxi, Each ambitiously would claim the ken That with first eyes did distant safety meet. **1736** W. THOMPSON *Nativity* xi, Faith led the van,.. Steady her ken, and gaining on the skies. **1814** CARY *Dante's Inf.* IV. 4, I.. search'd, With fixed ken, to know what place it was Wherein I stood.

b. Mental perception or recognition.

c **1560** A. SCOTT *Poems* (S.T.S.) xxxv. 28 Every gait off wicket stait Sall perreiss owt of ken. **1701** ROWE *Amb. Step-Moth.* III. iii. 1340 Whose Orb, with streaming Glories fraught, Dazles the Ken of human thought. **1836–7** SIR W. HAMILTON *Metaph.* xviii. (1870) 361 Acts of mind so rapid and minute as to elude the ken of consciousness. **1871** W. ALEXANDER *Johnny Gibb* xlii. (1892) 235 My vera memorandum book blottit oot' o' ken.

ken (kɛn), *sb.*² Also 6 kene. [Vagabonds' slang.] A house; *esp.* a house where thieves, beggars, or disreputable characters meet or lodge. Freq. with qualifying words, as ***bousing-, dancing-, smuggling-, stalling-, touting-ken*** (q.v.). Phr. ***to burn the ken*** (see quot. 1725).

1567 HARMAN *Caveat* (1869) 83 *A ken*, a house. *Ibid.* 85 Tower ye [= look you], yander is the kene. **1622** FLETCHER *Beggars' Bush* v. i, Surprising a boore's ken for grunting cheates. **1641** BROME *Joviall Crew* II. Wks. 1873 III. 388 Bowse a health to the Gentry Cofe of the Ken. **1725** *New Cant. Dict.*, *Burnt the Ken*, when Strollers leave the Alehouse, without paying their Quarters. **1800** *Sporting Mag.* XVI. 26 Called at a ken in the way home. **1851** MAYHEW *Lond. Labour* I. 351 Up she goes to any likely ken,.. and commences begging. **1860** DIXON *Pers. Hist. Ld. Bacon* v. §15 These.. skulk about the kens of Newgate Street.

‖**ken** (kɛn), *sb.*³ Also 8–9 kin. Pl. ken, occas. kens. [Jap.] A Japanese unit of length equal to six *shaku*; equivalent to approximately 71·5 inches (1·82 metres).

1727 J. G. SCHEUCHZER tr. *Kæmpfer's Hist. Japan* II. 405 The *Tsjo* contains sixty *Kin*, or Mats, according to their way of measuring, or about as many European fathoms. *Ibid.* 407 This bridge is supported, in the middle, by a small island, and consequently consists of two parts, the first whereof hath 36 *kins*, or fathoms, in length, and the second 96. **1845** *Encycl. Metrop.* XX. 486/2, 1 kin = 1 fathom. **1884** SATOW & HAWES *Handbk. for Travellers Cent. & N. Japan* (ed. 2) 17 The *chō* is further subdivided into 60 *ken* and the *ken* again into 6 *shaku*, the *shaku* being about 11·9 English inches. **1956** K. TOMIKI *Judo* i. 22 The floor space for a contest shall be 5 *ken* (30 feet) square of 50 *tatami*.

‖**ken** (kɛn), *sb.*⁴ [Jap.] A prefecture; one of the territorial divisions of Japan.

1882 *Encycl. Brit.* XIV. 490/2 His [*sc.* Sho-tai's] territory was declared first a *han* or feudal dependency and afterwards a *ken* or province of the Japanese monarchy. **1890** B. H. CHAMBERLAIN *Things Japanese* 134 There are two current divisions of the soil of the Empire—an older and more popular one into provinces (*kuni*).. and a recent, purely administrative one into prefectures (*ken*) of which at the present moment.. there are forty-three. **1899** KIPLING *From Sea to Sea* I. xviii. 378 Away in the western *kens*—districts, as you call them. **1947** E. O. REISCHAUER *Japan Past & Present* ix. 119 Two years later, in 1871, the fiefs were entirely abolished, and the land was divided into a number of new political divisions called *ken* or 'prefectures'. **1965** J. W. HALL et al. *Twelve Doors to Japan* i. 16 Today.. they [*sc.* the *kuni*] have been merged into the larger prefectures (to, dō, fu, and ken, of which there are forty-six) and have lost much of their contemporary meaning.

‖**ken** (kɛn), *sb.*⁵ [Jap.] A Japanese game of forfeits played with the hands and with gestures.

1890 B. H. CHAMBERLAIN *Things Japanese* 125 The Japanese play various games of forfeits, which they call *Ken*, sitting in a little circle and flinging out their fingers, after the manner of the Italian *mora.* **1898** A. DIÓSY *New Far East* v. 236 Dignified and sedate as if *ken*, and other rollicking games of forfeits, were frivolities far beneath her notice. **1958** *Japan* (Jap. Nat. Commission for Unesco) xxix. 1030 *Ken* is a game introduced from ancient China with many variations... The game was held at banquets and feasts in the Edo Period when *ken* meets were also held.

ken (kɛn), *v.*¹ Forms: 1 cennan, (cænnan), 3–4 kennen, (5 -yn), (3–5 kene, 3 cene, 5 keen), 3–7 kenne, 3– ken, (3, 8 kenn, 5 kyn). *Pa. t.* 3–5 kende, 3– kenned(e, kenn'd, kend; 9 *Sc.* kent. [Com. Teut.: OE. *cennan* (*cende, cenned*) = Fris. *kanna, kenna*, OS. (*ant*)*kennian* (MDu. and Du. *kennen*), OHG. (*ir-, in-, pi-*) *chennan* (MHG. and G. *kennen*), ON. *kenna* (Sw. *känna*, Da. *kjende, kende*), Goth. *kannjan*, factitive of the preterite-pres. **kann-*, I know: see CAN *v.*¹

The form is properly causative 'to cause to know', 'to make known', and was restricted to this use in Goth. and OE. At an early period, however, in all the Teutonic tongues, the verb also acquired the sense 'to know'. In Eng. this may have been taken from Norse, in which both senses were in early use. In mod. Eng. *ken* is only archaic (in sense 6) and has its pa. t. and pa. pple. *kenned* (cf. *pen, penned*); in Sc. (where it has entirely displaced *knaw* 'to know') the pa. t. and pple. are now *kent*; south Sc. *kend.*]

I. In causative senses. (All *Obs.*)

†**1.** *trans.* To make known, declare, confess, acknowledge. *Obs.*

Beowulf 1219 (Z.) Cen þec mid cræfte & þyssum cnyhtum wes lara liðe. *c* **975** *Laws K. Edgar* IV. §10 Gif he þonne cenð [§11 cænne] þæt he hit mid ȝewitnysse bohte. *c* **1000** *Ags. Ps.* (Th.) cvii[i]. 8 Ic me to cyninge cenne Iudas.. ic Idumea ealle cenne. *c* **1205** LAY. 6639 Ne der ich noht kennen.. þat ich her king weore.

†**2.** To make known, to impart the knowledge of (a thing). Usually with dat. of person (or *to*): To make a thing known to one; to teach one something. *Obs.*

a **1225** *Leg. Kath.* 1347, & tat we kennið þe wel.. þat we leaueð þi lahe. *c* **1250** *Gen. & Ex.* 216 A fruit, ðe kenned wel and wo. *a* **1300** *Cursor M.* 3644, I sal þe ken ful gode a gin. *a* **1352** MINOT *Poems* vii. 34 Calais men, now may ze care.. Sir Edward shall ken zow zowre crede. **1362** LANGL. *P. Pl.* A. I. 90 Clerkes þat knowen hit scholde techen [*v.r.* kenne] hit aboute. *c* **1425** WYNTOUN *Cron.* VI. ii. 114 Thir Papys war gud haly men, And oysyd the trowth to folk to ken. *c* **1430** *Christ's Compl.* 508 in *Pol. Rel. & L. Poems* 199 Y loued not hem þat me good kende.

†**b.** With clause expressing what is made known or taught, the dat. of the person being later taken as direct obj., and so as subject of passive. *Obs.*

a **1225** *St. Marher.* 16 Cuð me ant ken me hwi þe worldes weldent wunieð in þe. **1377** LANGL. *P. Pl.* B. I. 136 ȝet mote ye kenne me better, By what craft in my corps it comseth. *Ibid.* xv. 156 Clerkis kenne me þat cryst is in alle places. ? *a* **1500** *Chester Pl.* vii. 356 Why.. the ayre is so cleare, now shall we be kent.

†**c.** ***to ken thank***: to make known or express thanks: = CAN *v.*¹ 10, CON *v.*¹ 4. *Obs.*

c **1440** HYLTON *Scala Perf.* (W. de W. 1494) III. viii, Sothly he wyll kenne the more thanke for thy meke wesshynge of his fete. **1561** T. HOBY tr. *Castiglione's Courtyer* (1577) R viij a, Least.. he ken them the lesse thanke for doing al things contrarily. **1567** EDWARDS *Damon & Pythias* in Hazl. *Dodsley* IV. 61 All right courtiers will ken me thank.

†**3.** To direct, teach, or instruct (a person). *Obs.*

a **1300** *Cursor M.* 2694 (Cott.) Abram.. did als drightin can him ken [*Trin.* as god him hadde tauȝt]. *c* **1375** *Sc. Leg. Saints* xl. (*Ninian*) 482 Al þat ware honeste men ȝarnit he suld þare barnis ken. *c* **1400** *Destr. Troy* 5663 þen folowet all the flete.. Euyn kepyn hor course, as þai kend were. *c* **1440** HYLTON *Scala Perf.* (1494) I. lxxii, I am enformed & kenned in all thynges. **1523** SKELTON *Garl. Laurel* 824 Arrectyng my prayer to Mynerve.. me to inform and ken.

†**b.** with inf. compl.: To teach one, show one how *to do* something. *Obs.*

a **1300** *Cursor M.* 7363, I sal þe ken To knau him a-mang oþer men. **1362** LANGL. *P. Pl.* A. II. 4 Kenne me bi somme crafte to knowe þe fals. **1375** BARBOUR *Bruce* x. 544, I vndirtak.. For to ken ȝow to clym the wall. *a* **1529** SKELTON *P. Sparowe* 970 Now Phebus me ken To sharpe my pen.

†**c.** *absol.* To give instruction or directions.

c **1330** R. BRUNNE *Chron. Wace* (Rolls) 663 Parys dide as Venus kende. **1393** LANGL. *P. Pl.* C. v. 40 Thanne reson rod forth.. And dude as conscience kenned.

†**4.** To direct, guide, show the way *to* (*unto, till*) a place or person. *Obs.*

c **1200** *Trin. Coll. Hom.* 45 He is cleped king, for þat he kenneð eure to rihte. *c* **1325** *Metr. Hom.* 50, I openly Ken you till him of quaim I spek. **1362** LANGL. *P. Pl.* A. XI. 104, I schal kenne þe to my Cosyn þat Clergye is I-hoten. *c* **1440** *York Myst.* xxxiv. 350 If anye aske aftir vs Kenne thame to Caluarie. *c* **1470** HENRY *Wallace* v. 414 A trew Scot.. kend thaim to that place. *c* **1560** A. SCOTT *Poems* (S.T.S.) xxxvi. 55, I sall thame ken to consolatioun.

†**b.** *intr.* and *refl.* To direct one's course, betake oneself, proceed, go. *Obs.*

c **1205** LAY. 26467 ȝif æuer aie is swa kene.. þat us after kenne, ich hine wulle aquelle. **1297** R. GLOUC. (Rolls) App. xx. 482 þe kyng to yrlonde wende In þe monþe of octobre, and seþþe in may hom kende. *c* **1305** *St. Christopher* 212 in *E.E.P.* (1862) 65 Ouer Cristofre an arewe heng: þat toward þe king kende. *c* **1320** *Sir Beues* 334 (MS. A.) Toward his court he him kende [*v.r.* went anoon].

†**5.** *trans.* To consign, commend, deliver, bestow. *Obs.*

a **1300** *Cursor M.* 1584 (Gött.) Al mankind forsoth he wend, To his will all suld be kend. *c* **1340** *Ibid.* 8840 (Fairf.) Ne ware þai neuer þeiþen dispende Til þai ware til Iudas kende. **13..** *Gaw. & Gr. Knt.* 2067 þis kastel to kryst I kenne, He gef hit ay god chaunce! *a* **1400–50** *Alexander* 5383 With þat scho kende him a croun clustrid with gemmes. *c* **1440** *Bone Flor.* 1566 To Florence they can hur kenne, To lerne hur to behave hur among men.

II. In non-causative senses.

6. To descry, see; to catch sight of, discover by sight; to look at, scan. Now only *arch.*

c **1205** LAY. 1659 þa Goffar þe king þane castel kennede.. swiðe wa him was. *a* **1300** *Body & Soul* 109 Thine eiȝene are blinde and connen nouȝt kenne. **1340** HAMPOLE *Pr. Consc.* 4703 Takens sal be in þe son and in þe mone, And in þe sternes þat in heven men may ken. *c* **1450** HOLLAND *Howlat* 587 In a feld of siluer.. Of a kynde colour thre coddis I kend. **1593** SHAKS. *2 Hen. VI*, III. ii. 101 As farre as I could ken thy Chalky Cliffes.. I stood vpon the Hatches in the storme. **1652–62** HEYLIN *Cosmogr.* Introd. (1682) 19 So great a space of the earth, as a quick sight can ken in an open field. **1671** MILTON *P.R.* II. 286 To ken the prospect round, If cottage were in view. **1768** BEATTIE *Minstr.* I. xx, And now he faintly kens the bounding fawn, And villager abroad at early toil. **1805** WORDSW. *Waggoner* III. 67 Indistinctly may be kenned The vanguard, following close behind. **1828** SCOTT *F.M. Perth* xxxiii, Unable to ken the course of the bird of Jove. **1880** W. WATSON *Prince's Quest* (1892) 75 And far below him.. a city exceeding fair to ken.

b. *absol.* To see, look. *Obs.* or *arch.*

1577 HANMER *Anc. Eccl. Hist.* (1650) 166 Some watched diligently, kenning from towers, casements and high places. **1598** GRENEWEY *Tacitus, Ann.* III. i. (1622) 63 Places, from whence a man might farthest kenne. **1652** NEEDHAM tr. *Selden's Mare Cl.* 374 Spaces distant from them as far as a man may ken. **1755** YOUNG *Centaur* iii. Wks. 1757 IV. 186 Not the keenest discernment can ken through the second of a minute.

7. To recognize (at sight, or by some marks or tokens); to identify. Now *north.* or *Sc.*

c **1205** LAY. 21443 Nu þu scalt to hælle, þer þu miht kenne muche of þine cunne. *a* **1300** *Cursor M.* 1152 Bituix quat lede sum þat þou lend, Euer sal þou and þine bi kend. *c* **1450** *Merlin* 45 'Sirs', seide the kynge, 'yef ye myght se Merlin, cowde ye hym knowen?' 'Sire', seide thei, 'it myght not be but that we sholde hym kenne wele, yef we myght him se'. **1596** SPENSER *F.Q.* IV. x. 14 Me whenas he had privily espide Bearing the shield.. He kend it streight. **1596** DALRYMPLE tr. *Leslie's Hist. Scot.* I. 63 To ken the lione be his taes. **1606** SHAKS. *Tr. & Cr.* IV. v. 14 'Tis he, I ken the manner of his gate, He rises on the toe. *a* **1661** FULLER *Worthies* (1840) II. 506 King James, who did ken a man of merit as well as any prince in Christendom. **1800** COLERIDGE *Christabel* II. 446 He kenn'd In the beautiful lady the child of his friend! **1809** MALKIN *Gil Blas* II. iii. ¶1 He kenned me in a twinkling, though I had changed my dress. *Mod. Sc.* Ye're grown that big, I hardly kent ye.

b. To (be able to) distinguish (one person or thing *from* another). Now *Sc.*

c **1340** *Cursor M.* 23116 (Trin.), Fro comynynge of cristen men þo careful shul be eþ to ken. *c* **1400** *Destr. Troy* 3911 The ton fro þe tother was tore for to ken In sight at þat sodan. **1579** SPENSER *Sheph. Cal.* Sept. 42 The shepheards swayne you cannot wel ken, But it be by his pryde, from other men. *Mod. Sc.* They're that like, I never ken the tane frae the tither.

†**8.** To recognize, acknowledge, admit to be (genuine, valid, or what is claimed). *Obs.*

1375 BARBOUR *Bruce* III. 750 And thai as lord suld.. him ken. *c* **1400** *Apol. Loll.* 77 Now new lawis kennyn prescripcoun, þat if ani be in posessioun of oþer mennis þingis by a cercle of ȝeris, he schal ioi it as his oune. *c* **1400** in Neilson *Trial by Combat* (1890) 229 Schir, kenys thow this is thi sele and thine appele? *c* **1450** *St. Cuthbert* (Surtees) 5196 His mysse þat he moght ken.

b. *Sc. Law.* To recognize (a person) as legal heir or successor *to* an estate; usually, to serve a widow to a life-rent of the third part of her deceased husband's lands.

1468 *Burgh Rec. Aberdeen* 20 Mar. (Spalding Cl.) I. 28 Askande him to be kende to the saide lande as air til his fadir. *c* **1575** *Balfour's Practicks* (1754) 106 Ane lady havand the tierce of ony landis.. the schiref of the schire sould ken hir to hir thrid part thairof. **1754** ERSKINE *Princ. Sc. Law* II. Tit. ix. §29 She.. cannot remove tenants, till the Sheriff kens her to her terce. **1808** JAMIESON, *To ken a widow to her terce*,.. a phrase still used in our courts of law.

†**9.** To get to know, ascertain, find out. *Obs.*

c **1330** R. BRUNNE *Chron.* (1810) 270 Clerkis and lewed men suld.. trie þe soth and ken, in whom þe wrong lay. *c* **1400** *Destr. Troy* 1452 What myschefe befell, þere no cause was to ken but vnkynd wordes. **1450–70** *Golagros & Gaw.* 1325 Sa that the caus may be kend and knawin throw skill. **1586** WARNER *Alb. Eng.* I. vi. 23 Calde.. To ken of whence and where they would.

10. To know (a person); to have acquaintance with; to be acquainted with. Now *Sc.*

1375 BARBOUR *Bruce* I. 327 That he wald trawaile our the se.. And dre myscheiff quhar nane hym kend. *c* **1420** *Sir Amadace* ii, Sithun duelle here, quere I was borne.. And I am so wele kennit. *c* **1450** *Merlin* 72 He mette with a man that he nothinge kenned. *a* **1568** *Peebles to the Play* iii, Than

spak hir fallowis, that hir kend, Be still, my joy, and greit not. **1597** MONTGOMERIE *Sonn.* xxvi, In Cupids court ȝe knau I haif bene kend. **1606** HOLLAND *Sueton.* Annot. 14 Al while that I you kenned not, I cald you L[ord] & King. **1820** SCOTT *Monast.* ix, I have kend every wench in the Halidome of St. Mary's. *Mod. Sc.* 'Everybodie kens Watty the Post.' Is there oniebodie ye ken here?

11. To know (a thing); to have knowledge of or about (a thing, place, person, etc.), to be acquainted with; †to understand. Now chiefly *Sc.*

a **1300** *Cursor M.* 12148 (Gött.), I kene wele þat ilk siquar Quen þat ȝu ȝur moderis bare. *c* **1330** R. BRUNNE *Chron. Wace* (Rolls) 78 Symple men þat strange Inglis can nocht ken. *c* **1418** *Pol. Poems* (Rolls) II. 243, I have wel lever No more kyn than my a, b, c. *c* **1430** *Christ's Compl.* 489 in *Pol., Rel., & L. Poems* 198 þouȝ y cowþe al kunnynge ken. **1579** SPENSER *Sheph. Cal.* Feb. 85, I wote thou kenst little good, So vainely t'aduaunce thy headlesse hood. **1584** PEELE *Arraignm. Paris* I. iv, That kens the painted paths of pleasant Ida. *a* **1661** FULLER *Worthies* (1840) III. 281 He did ken the ambassador-craft as well as any in his age. **1702** C. MATHER *Magn. Chr.* II. App. (1852) 218 Any governour that kens Hobbianism. **1827** COLERIDGE *Sibyl. Leaves* Poems II. 300 Yet well I ken the banks where amaranths blow. **1879** J. ARMSTRONG *Kielder Hunt* (in *Northumbld. Gloss.*), He kens the hauds on Tosson hills, he kens the holes at Rae.

b. To know, understand, or perceive (a fact, etc.); to be aware of, to be aware *that* (*what*, etc.). Now chiefly *Sc.*

a **1300** *Cursor M.* 6418 Quils moyses heild vp his hend It was wel in þat bateil kend. *c* **1375** *Sc. Leg. Saints* ii. (*Paul*) 375 Ȝe suld wele ken, þat here slane has bene mony men. *c* **1400** *Sowdone Bab.* 799 Litill kennyth he what I may doo. **1567** *Satir. Poems Reform.* iii. 137, I ken rycht weill ȝe knaw ȝour dewtie. *a* **1634** RANDOLPH *Poems, Eglogue Assemblies Cotswold* (1638) 115 Dost thou ken, Collen, what the cause might be Of such a dull and generall Lethargie? **1714** GAY *Sheph. Week* III. 89 Now plain I ken whence Love his Rise begun. **1844** DICKENS *Christmas Carol* iii. (Househ. ed.) 23/1 Little kenned the lamp-lighter that he had any company but Christmas. **1865** G. MACDONALD *A. Forbes* 43, I dinna ken what ye mean, Alec.

c. With compl. (Chiefly in *pass.*) Now *Sc.*

a **1300** *Cursor M.* 6715 (Cott.) If his lauerd kenne him kene of horn. *c* **1300** *Ibid.* 25151 (Cott. Galba) For goddes sun may he noght be kend. *c* **1400** *Melayne* 1437 Ȝitt are we ten thowsande here..þat wele for kene are kende. **1721** RAMSAY *Addr. Town Counc. Edin.* iii, To you, ne'er kend to guide ill..My case I plainly tell. **1829** HOGG *Sheph. Cal.* I. 232 Ye're kenn'd for an auld-farrant man. **1869** C. GIBBON *R. Gray* iii, Ivan Carrack was ay kenned to be ready tae flee in the face o' Providence.

12. a. *intr.* or *absol.* To have knowledge (*of* or *about* something). †Also with inf.: To know how to, to be able to (*obs.*).

13.. *E.E. Allit. P.* C. 357 Þenne he cryed so cler, þat kenne myȝt alle. *c* **1400** *Destr. Troy* 1583 Of all þe craftes to ken as þere course askit. **1508** DUNBAR *Tua Mariit Wemen* 454 No creatur kernis of our doingis. **1659** T. PECKE *Parnassi Puerp.* 3 If he be happy that can Causes scan, You ken to plead our Causes. **1721** RAMSAY *Prospect of Plenty* i, A lairdship wide, That yields mair plenty than he kens to guide. **1816** SCOTT *Old Mort.* xxxix, It was his father then ye kent o'.

†**b.** *refl.* To have skill; to be accomplished *in.* (= F. *se connaître en.*) *Obs. rare.*

1362 LANGL. *P. Pl.* A. II. 202 He kennede him in heore craft and kneuȝ mony gummes. *c* **1450** HOLLAND *Howlat* 703 The Boytour callit was cuke, that him weile kend In craftis of the ketchyne.

†**ken**, *v.*[2] *Obs.* Forms: 1 cennan, 2–4 kennen. *Pa. t.* 1 cende, kende, 2 kennede, 4 kynned. *Pa. pple.* 1 (ȝe)cenned, 3–4 kenned, 4 (y)kennyd, (y)kend, kynned, 5 kynde. [OE. *cęnnan* = OS. *kennian* (pa. pple. *kennit*), OHG. (*ki*)*chęnnan*:—OTeut. **kannjan*, f. **kan-*, second ablaut grade of the series *kin-*, *kan-*, *kun-* (see KIN). See also KENE.]

1. *trans.* To generate, engender, beget; to conceive; to give birth to.

.. *Leiden Riddle* 2 Mec se ueta uong..ob his innaðae aerest caendae [*Exeter Bk.* cende]. *c* **1000** *Ags. Gosp.* Matt. i. 25 Heo cende hyre frum-cennedan sunu. *c* **1200** *Trin. Coll. Hom.* 31 Ure lafdi seinte marie kennede of holie lichame ure louerd ihesu crist. **1340** *Ayenb.* 12 Þe zone..wes y-kend of þe holi gost. *c* **1460** *Towneley Myst.* xvi. 210 He shalbe so kynde That a madyn, sothely, whiche neuer synde, Shall hym bere.

fig. *c* **825** *Vesp. Psalter* vii. 15 Sehðe cenneð unrehtwisnisse. **13..** *E.E. Allit. P.* B. 915 Hov schulde I huyde me fro hem þat hatz his hate kynned.

b. *absol.* To conceive or bear a child.

c **1000** ÆLFRIC *Gen.* xviii. 13 Sceal ic nu eald wif cennan? *c* **1205** LAY. 15789 Wimmon þurh heore cræfte kenneð anan.

2. *intr.* To be conceived or born. Of eggs: To hatch out.

13.. *E.E. Allit. P.* B. 1072 Bot much clener watz hir corse, God kynned þerinne. **13..** *St. Erkenwolde* 209 in Horstm. *Altengl. Leg.* (1881) 271 Before þat kynned ȝour Criste by cristene acounte A þousande ȝere. **1399** LANGL. *Rich. Redeles* III. 51 [She] houeth the eyren..And with hir corps keuereth hem till þat þey kenne.

ken, obs. f. KEEN *a.*

kenaf (kəˈnæf). Also **kanaff**. [Persian.] = AMBARI.

1891 *Kew Bull.* 204 Recently an announcement has been made of the discovery of a new textile plant on the shores of the Caspian. The plant known as Kanaff by the natives is said to yield a soft elastic and silky fibre... It is supposed that Kanaff fibre..will successfully compete with any other textile for sacking, ropes, and packthread. **1945** *Bot. Gaz.* CVI. 349/1 The identity of the plant [introduced into Cuba] has been established as kenaf (*Hibiscus cannabinus*, L.) which..is capable of producing more than a ton of dry fiber per acre. **1952** A. E. HAARER *Jute Substitute Fibres* i. 2 Kenaf is the name used principally in Russia, America and Cuba.. and the word is derived from the local names Kanaff, Kanap or Kanaph, given to the plant where it grows on the Persian shore of the Caspian sea. *Ibid.* i. 8 No one seems to know why this fibre plant was given the name Kenaf in the Western Hemisphere. **1967** *New Scientist* 14 Dec. 660/1 The kenaf plant which is already a leading substitute for jute fibres..is now being seriously considered..as a substitute for the hardwoods used in papermaking. **1974** *Times* 12 Jan. (Ghana Suppl.) p. iv, Achievements [in the production of raw materials] were sparse except in some agricultural sectors like cotton and kenaf.

kenbow(e: see A-KIMBO.

kench (kɛnʃ), *sb.*[1] [Special sense of *kench*, *canch*, current in various dialects with the senses of 'slice, cut, section, etc.' See *Eng. Dial. Dict.* s.v. *Canch.*] A strip or slice of an arable field containing a number of furrows.

1799 J. ROBERTSON *Agric. Perth* 62 The first deviation from run-rig was by dividing the farms into kavels or kenches, by which every field..was split down into as many lots as there were tenants.

kench (kɛnʃ), *sb.*[2] *U.S.* [perh. the same as prec.] A rectangular bin or box used for salting seal-skins: a box used in salting and packing fish.

1874 SCAMMON *Marine Mammals* 161 The [seal] skins are all taken to the salt-houses, and are salted in kenches, or square bins. **1887** *Fisheries U.S.* Sect, v. II. 370 Sliding planks, which are taken down and put up in the form of deep bins, or boxes—kenches, the sealers call them. **1897** R. KIPLING *Captains Courageous* 122 The silvery-gray kenches of well-pressed fish mounted higher and higher in the hold.

†**kench**, *v.* *Obs. rare.* [repr. OE. **cęncean*:—**kankjan*, from the root *kank-*, found in OE. *ȝecanc* mock, gibe, *cancęttan* to laugh noisily, cackle, CANK, Icel. *kank* gibing, *kankast* to jeer; the ablaut-grade **kink-* is the base of CHINK *v.*[1] and KINK *v.*[1]] *intr.* To laugh loudly.

c **1225** *Leg. Kath.* 2042 Þer me mahte iheren..þe cristene kenchen and herien þen healent. *c* **1230** *Hali Meid.* 17 Hu.. te deoueles hoppen & kenchinde beaten hondes to-gederes.

kench, variant of KINCH, noose.

kend, variant of KENT *ppl. a.*

kend(e, **kendle**, etc., **kendly**, obs. ff. KIND, KINDLE, KINDLY.

Kendal (ˈkɛndəl). [f. *Kendal* in Cumbria (formerly in Westmorland), the place of manufacture.

Rymer's Fœdera II. 825 has a letter of protection, of the year 1331, to John Kempe of Flanders, who established cloth-weaving at Kendal. See *Westmorland Note-bk.* I. 241–250.]

†**1.** A species of green woollen cloth. *Obs.*

1389 *Act. 13 Rich. II*, c. 10 §1 Certeines draps en diverses Countees Dengleterre appelez Cogware & Kendalecloth. **1410** *Rolls of Parlt.* III. 643 Draps appelles Kendales, Kerseis, Bakkes, [etc.]. **1464** *Mann. & Househ. Exp.* (Roxb.) 277 Payd for iiij. ȝerdys and iij. quarterys kendalle for a gowne and a sadyll clothe, the yerde ix. *d.* **1483** *Act 1 Rich. III*, c. 8 §18 Any Cloths called Kendals. **1497** *Ld. Treas. Acc., Scot.* I. 340 For vij elne of grene Kentdalee. **1505** *Ibid.* III. 37 For x elne Kentdale to be ane cote to the King. *c* **1570** *Pride & Lowl.* (1841) 33 Of Kendall very course his coate was made. *a* **1687** COTTON *Poet. Wks.* (1765) 82 His Breeches..Were Kendal, and his Doublet Fustian.

†**b.** *attrib.* *Obs.*

c **1425** LYDG. *Assembly of Gods* 356 On hys hede he had a thredebare kendall hood. *c* **1550** *Disc. Common Weal Eng.* (1893) 82 A servinge man was content to goe in a Kendall cote in somer. **1611** *Coryat's Crudities* Panegyr. Verses, The Mayor of Hartlepoole..Put on's considering cap and Kendall gowne.

2. Kendal green. **a.** = sense 1. Now only *arch.* or *Hist.*

1514 BARCLAY *Cyt. & Uplondyshm.* (Percy Soc.) p. vii, His costly clothing was threadebare kendall grene. **1532** MORE *Confut. Tindale* Wks. 618/2 Tyl he do of his gray garmentes and clothe him selfe cumly in gaye kendall greene. **1596** SHAKS. *1 Hen. IV*, II. iv. 246 Three misbegotten Knaues, in Kendall Greene. **1812** SCOTT *Rokeby* v. xv, A seemly gown of Kendal green.

b. The green colour of Kendal cloth; also, the plant Dyer's Greenweed, with which it was dyed.

1866 *Treas. Bot.* 526/1 The process by which was obtained the once celebrated Kendal green. **1822** J. SMITH *Dict. Econ. Pl.*, *Kendal Green*,..a low bushy shrub of the bean family... It yields a yellow dye, but by a mordant becomes a permanent green.

Hence †**kendaling** *Sc. Obs.*, Kendal cloth.

?**15..** *Aberdeen Reg.* XVI. (Jam.) Ane coitt of grene kendilling. *Ibid.*, Ane grene kendelyng cloik.

‖**kendo** (ˈkɛndəʊ). [Jap.] The Japanese sport of fencing with bamboo swords.

1921 S. K. UYENISHI *Text-bk. Ju-Jutsu* i. 14 Kendo or Ken-jutsu, 'the hard way' and 'the hard art'..is the elaboration of the old two-sword play of the *samurai* or 'two-sworded men'. **1933** *Official Guide to Japan* (Jap. Imperial Govt. Railways) p. clxxxvi, *Kenjutsu* or *Kendō* (also called *Gekken*), the art of handling a sword, corresponds to European fencing and is as old as Japanese history. **1939** R. KAJI *Japan* facing p. 56 (*caption*) *Kendô*, Japanese fencing, in which the participants use bamboo swords. **1958** *Economist* 1 Nov. 422/1 The government has reintroduced the forbidden *kendo* or military fencing in schools. **1964** R. A. LIDSTONE *Introd. Kendō* 15 Quite understandably Kendō, with its militant background, lost favour after the last war. **1966** J. BALL *Cool Cottontail* (1967) iv. 37 He had become interested in the basic Oriental martial arts: judo, kendo, aikido, and karate. **1974** *Publishers Weekly* 28 Jan. 100/1 (Advt.), Kendo, or Japanese sword fighting, is an ancient method of training body and mind that now is becoming popular throughout the world.

†**kene**, *v.* *Obs.* [ME. *kenien*, app. repr. a late OE. (W.Sax.) **cęnian* for *cęnnan* KEN *v.*[2]] *trans.* To beget, conceive, bear. *intr.* To be born.

c **1275** *O.E. Misc.* 100 Þer schal a child in þe kenyen, and springe. *c* **1290** *S. Eng. Leg.* I. 319/708 Formest þare keniez þar-of smale bollene þreo... Þis beoth þe þreo hexte limes þat formest i-kenede beoz. **1297** R. GLOUC. (Rolls) 1545 He þoȝte he wolde wite & ise hou vair þe chamber were War inne he was ikenede [*MS. B.* kenede] ar is moder him bere. *c* **1380** *Sir Ferumb.* 5724 Gode sone, þat in marye y-kened was.

kene, obs. f. KINE *sb.*[1], KEEN *a.*, KEN *v.*, KIN *sb.*

kenedom, **kenet**, **keng**, **kenine**, **-ing**, obs. ff. KINDOM, KENNET, KING, KENNING *sb.*

keneme (kɛˈniːm). *Linguistics.* Also **ceneme.** [f. Gr. κενός empty: see -EME.] (See quot. 1966.) Cf. *empty word* (EMPTY *a.* and *sb.* C). Hence **keneˈmatics**, **keˈnetics**, the aspect of language concerned with kenemes; **keneˈmatic**, **keˈnemic**, **keˈnetic** *adjs.*

The forms with initial *c-* predominate over the etymological forms with *k-*.

1939 L. HJELMSLEV in *Proc. Third Internat. Congr. Phonetic Sci.* 271 A language is a category of two members. .. One of these planes, the plerematic plane, gives form to the content..; the other, the cenematic plane, forms the expression. *Ibid.* 272 The constitutents—in plerematics: the pleremes, in cenematics: the cenemes—are usually of two types: central and marginal constituents. **1950** S. POTTER *Our Lang.* vii. 86 Beginning with the phoneme, philologists pass on to speak about *morphemes*, *taxemes* or *tagmemes*, *sememes* (including *pleremes* and *kenemes*).., as if *-eme* were a brand-new suffix meaning 'linguistic agent'. **1958** C. F. HOCKETT *Course in Mod. Ling.* lxiv. 575 Phonemes are linguistic *cenemes*; morphemes are linguistic *pleremes*. *Ibid.*, It will be better to introduce two new terms for general applicability: *cenematic* and *plerematic*. The cenematic structure of language is phonology; the plerematic structure of language is grammar. **1966** M. PEI *Gloss. Ling. Terminol.* 35 *Ceneme*, 1. Linguistically, a phoneme, or anything pertaining to phonology (Hockett). 2. The smallest unit of expression without corresponding content, differing from a phoneme in that it does not necessarily consist of sound, but may include letters and other semantic indicators (Hjelmslev). **1967** [see FUNCTOR 2]. **1967** *Word* XXIII. 469 My observations apparently support the structuralist separation of cenetics and plerematics. *Ibid.* 471 In addition to their two cenetic and two plerematic systems, bilingual children naturally have to master two sets of form-to-meaning relationships. **1969** *English Studies* L. 432 The tradition from Saussure and Hjelmslev brought about a phonemic—or cenemic—analysis based on pure relations.

Kenite (ˈkiːnaɪt), *sb.* and *a.* [f. Heb. *ḳênî* a gentilic adjective associated with Heb. *ḳayin* a weapon made of metal, Arab. *ḳayn* an ironsmith, maker of iron weapons and tools, Aram. *ḳênay*, *ḳaynāyā* smith, metal-worker, Nabatæan *ḳynw*, Old South Arabian *'ḳnw*: see -ITE[1].] **A.** *sb.* A member of an ancient nomadic people from S. Palestine, freq. mentioned in the Old Testament. **B.** *adj.* Of or pertaining to the Kenites.

From the etymology it has been conjectured that the Kenites were chiefly metal-smiths.

[*c* **1000** ÆLFRIC *Heptateuch* Gen. xv. 19 Cynei & Cenezei; Cetmonei. **1382** WYCLIF *Num.* xxxii. 12 Caleph, the sone of Jephone, Ceneze, and Josue, the sone of Nun.] **1535** COVERDALE *Gen.* xv. 19 The Kenytes, the Kenizites, the Kydmonites. —— *Judg.* iv. 11 Heber the Kenyte. *a* **1679** M. POOLE *Annotations Holy Bible* (1688) I. *Judg.* iv. 11 Which removal is here mentioned, lest any should wonder to find the Kenites in this place. **1710** M. HENRY *Exposition Five Bks. Moses Num.* xxiv, The Kenites were now the securest of the Nations. **1876** *Encycl. Brit.* IV. 763/1 The aboriginal Rephaim and three Arab tribes, the Kenites, Kenizzites, and Kadmonites. **1911** *Ibid.* XV. 729/2 Moses himself married into a Kenite family (Judges i. 16). **1962** G. A. BUTTRICK *Interpreter's Dict. Bible* III. 7/1 The last mention of the Kenites in connection with the history of Israel is during the time of David before he became king over all Israel (ca. 1000). **1968** *Encycl. Brit.* XIII. 281/1 *Kenites*, a clan closely related to the Midianites and Amalekites, frequently mentioned in the biblical narratives about the early history of Israel. The name was derived from Cain, whose descendants they were believed to be (Gen. iv).

kenk, obs. form of KINK *sb.*[1] and *v.*[2]

ˈken-mark. *Sc.* [f. KEN *v.*[1] + MARK *sb.*] A mark by which a thing may be recognized.

1885 J. BULLOCH *Geo. Jamesone* ix. 112 It needs no such kenmark. **1896** in *Academy* 12 Dec. 533/1 Good writing and clear thinking are the ken-marks of *The Children of the Hour.*

kenna *Sc.* = ken not, know not.

kennah, obs. var. HENNA; cf. ALCANNA.

1731 J. PITTS *Acc. Mahometans* 163 The Women here commonly paint their Hands and Feet with a certain Plant call'd *Kennah*, dried and beaten to Powder.

kenne, obs. form of CAIN[1].

1612 *Sc. Acts Jas. VI*, c. 10 Fewmales, kennes, annuel rents.

kenned, kend (kɛnd), *ppl. a. Sc.* [f. KEN *v.*[1] + -ED[1].] Known.

c **1450** HOLLAND *Howlat* 683 Kyngis and patriarkis kend, with cardinalis hale. **1725** RAMSAY *Gent. Sheph.* I. ii, What if..your Patie think his half-worn Meg And her ken'd kisses, hardly worth a feg? **1822** SCOTT *Pirate* ix, An auld kenn'd freend. **1895** CROCKETT *Men of Moss Hags* ix, Among his own kenned faces, his holders and cottiers.

† **kennedy** (ˈkɛnədɪ). *Obs. slang.* [Said to be f. the name of a man who was killed by being struck on the head with a poker.] **a.** A poker. **b.** A blow inflicted by a poker, freq. in the phr. *to give* (someone) *kennedy*. Also **kennedy** *v. trans.*, to strike with a poker.

1823 *Morning Herald* in *Spirit of Public Jrnls. for M.DCCC.XXIII* (1825) 77 Mr. Davis bore these irregularities as long as he could, but at last..he ventured to tell *Mykle* that he could bear it no longer! When, what does *Mykle* do but seize the *poker*, and threaten to '*Kennedy* him' (beat him with a poker). **1859** HOTTEN *Dict. Slang* 55 *Kennedy*, to strike or kill with a poker. A St Giles' term, so given from a man of that name being killed by a poker. Frequently shortened to *Neddy*. **1864** *Athenæum* 29 Oct. 559 St Giles's perpetuates the memory of a..man..who was killed by a poker by calling that instrument a kennedy.

Kennedya (kɛˈniːdɪə). [mod. bot. L. (Ventenat, 1804), from *Kennedy*, name of a gardener of Hammersmith.] A genus of perennial herbaceous climbing plants (N.O. *Leguminosæ*), natives of Australia and Tasmania, some of which are cultivated for the sake of their flowers; also (with lower-case initial) a plant of this genus. *K. prostrata* is the coral-creeper.

1845 *Florist's Jrnl.* 75 An early vinery is exactly the place in which to grow Kennedyas. **1881** MRS. C. PRAED *Policy & P.* I. 110 Vines of the crimson Kennedia trailed into the streamlet. **1885** —— *Head Station* 191 Crimson kennedia and hoya tapestried the rocks.

kennel (ˈkɛnəl), *sb.*[1] Forms: 4–6 **kenel**, 5 **-elle**, 5–6 **-ell**, (6 **cannel**), 6–7 **kennell**, 6– **kennel**. [app. a. ONF. **kenil* = F. *chenil* (16th c. in Hatz.-Darm.):—popular L. *canīle* (in Wr.-Wülcker 198/29), f. *canis* dog, with suffix as in *ovīle* sheepfold. Sense 2 may be partly due to OF. *kienaille, chienaille* (= mod.F. *canaille*) pack of dogs (Godef.).]

1. a. A house or cot for the shelter of a house-dog; a house or range of buildings in which a pack of hounds or sporting dogs are kept. Also (usu. *pl.*), an establishment where dogs are bred, or where they are cared for in the absence of their owners.

13.. [see *kennel-door* in 3]. *c* **1440** *Promp. Parv.* 271/2 Kenel for howndys,..*canicularium*. **1576** TURBERV. *Venerie* 27 In the highest place of the Courte it shall be good to buylde the kennell or lodging for the Houndes. **1594** SHAKS. *Rich. III*, IV. iv. 47 From forth the kennell of thy wombe hath crept A Hell-hound that doth hunt vs all to death. **1642** CARPENTER *Experience* II. xi. 215 The Curre taken out of the Kennell, and provoked to barke. **1735** SOMERVILLE *Chase* I. 124 First let the Kennel be the Huntsman's Care. **1882** MISS BRADDON *Mt. Royal* III. i. 16 All the other dogs are in their kennels. **1887** G. STABLES *Practical Kennel Guide* (ed. 3) xv. 145, I know some kennels..which are a disgrace to civilised society—dirty and beastly in the extreme. **1896** *Notable Dogs of Yr.* (Advt.), Borzoi kennels and sanatorium for dogs and cats. Patients treated at the kennels. **1925** J. LUCAS *Pedigree Dog Breeding* 61 Those intending to board their dogs for more than a week or two should try and visit one or two kennels before making their selection... Many kennels ..make a speciality of whelping cases. **1931** N. W. LEWIS *Your Dog* iii. 173 Good bitches can be bought..from big kennels that have become overstocked. **1969** [see *boarding kennel* s.v. BOARDING *vbl. sb.* 7]. **1974** R. RENDELL *Face of Trespass* ii. 27 I've never left her since she was a puppy... I couldn't put her in kennels. She'd fret.

b. The hole or lair of the fox.

1735 SOMERVILLE *Chase* III. 54 While from his Kennel sneaks The conscious Villain. **1774** GOLDSM. *Nat. Hist.* II. 190 The instant he perceives himself pursued, he makes to his kennel.

c. Contemptuously applied to a small and mean dwelling or hut.

1837 DICKENS *Pickw.* xlv, He got us a room—we were in a kennel before. **1887** RIDER HAGGARD *Jess* xxxi, Jess..never entered the Hottentot's kennel.

d. A woman's head-dress, of a shape suggesting a kennel.

See Fairholt's *Hist. Costume* (1885) I. 226, and cf. quot. for *kennel-shaped* in 3.

1896 *Gloucestersh. N. & Q.* No. 72. 138 On their heads they wear the kennel or angular head dress so generally worn during the latter part of the reign of Henry VII.

e. *fig.* Place to occupy.

1853 KANE *Grinnell Exp.* xxxix. (1856) 355 The last-named came on board last, and found, though he is not a very large man, a sufficiently narrow kennel between the companion-ladder and the dinner-table.

2. a. A pack of hounds, or of dogs of any kind.

c **1470** in *Hors Shepe & G.*, etc. (Caxton 1479, Roxb. repr.) 31 A brace of houndes, a kenel of recches. **1526** *Pilgr. Perf.* (1531) 49 A kenel of houndes folowynge theyr game. **1591** SHAKS. *1 Hen. VI*, IV. ii. 47. **1781** W. BLANE *Ess. Hunting* (1788) 62 It is hard to procure an even kennel of fast Hounds. **1826** SCOTT *Woodst.* iv, Hurt a dog, and the whole kennel will fall on him and worry him.

b. A pack or troop of other animals.

1641 J. JACKSON *True Evang. T.* I. 48 What a Kennell of these Wolves, Leopards, &c. was there in France. **1765** T. HUTCHINSON *Hist. Mass.* I. i. 114 The howling of a kennel of wolves. **1844** KINGLAKE *Eöthen* (1847) 217 A kennel of very fine lions..I say a kennel of lions, for the beasts were.. simply chained up like dogs.

†**c.** *fig.* A pack, crew, gang, of persons. *Obs.*

1581 SIDNEY *Apol. Poetrie* (Arb.) 39 Dionisius, and I know not how many more of the same kennell. **1649** FULLER *Just Man's Fun.* 12 Hear the whole kennel of Atheists come in with a full crie. **1720** T. GORDON *Cordial for Low Spirits* 77 We are enchanted by a stupid Kennel of Stock-Jobbers.

†**d.** Used for CANAILLE. *Obs.*

1726 *Penn's Tracts* Wks. I. 730 It has not only prevail'd with the Populace, the Kennel [*ed.* 1679 Cannale], the Vulgar. **1771** E. LONG *Trial of Dog 'Porter'* in Hone *Everyday Bk.* II. 199 A liquor the London kennel much delight in.

3. *attrib.* and *Comb.*, as *kennel-door, -groom, -huntsman, -maid, -man, -work*; *kennel-shaped* adj.; **kennel-book**, a book recording events of a kennel where dogs are bred; cf. *herd-book, stud-book*; **Kennel Club**, an organization, founded in 1873, which establishes dog breeds, records pedigrees, issues the rules for dog shows and trials, etc.; also, a branch of this organization; **kennel lameness**, a rheumatic disease in dogs, freq. affecting the forelegs.

1890 MARG. DELAND *Sidney* iii. 42 One of these researches among *kennel-books resulted in a present to Ted of the mastiff puppies. **1874** F. C. S. PEARCE *Kennel Club Stud Bk.* p. v, The Club shall be called the *Kennel Club, it shall endeavour in every way to promote the general improvement of dogs, dog shows, and dog trials. **1935** *Discovery* Oct. 310/2 The breed has been taken up by kennel clubs and the dogs are now officially called Illyrian Sheepdogs. **1959** *Listener* 12 Mar. 447/1 These details were vouched and signed for by the chief of the local kennel club. **1971** F. HAMILTON *World Encycl. Dogs* 620 Registration of a pedigree dog at the Kennel Club is a simple matter; it is usually completed by the breeder, the fee of 5s.... registers the dog for life. **13..** *Gaw. & Gr. Knt.* 1140 Þenne þise cacheres þat couþe, cowpled hor houndes, Vnclosed þe *kenel dore, & calde hem þer-oute. **1875** W. S. HAYWARD *Love agst. World* 4 The kennel-door was thrown open. **1829** *Sporting Mag.* XXIII. 208 My *kennel-groom has orders frequently to lead the dogs to little distance from the kennel. **1841** R. T. VYNER *Notitia Venatica* 45 *Kennel-lameness, or shoulder-lameness, as it is sometimes called. **1885** BEAUFORT & MORRIS *Hunting* 112 That mortal scourge which among men is known as rheumatism, and among hounds as kennel lameness. **1930** C. FREDERICK et al. *Fox-Hunting* viii. 108 Through this cause they appear to stiffen up, which is mistaken for kennel lameness. **1948** H. KIRK *Index of Treatm. in Small-Animal Pract.* II. 445 *Kennel lameness.* This layman's term is meant to indicate a condition brought about by a diet deficient in calcium which affects mainly full-grown animals kept for some weeks or months in kennels and fed chiefly on dog biscuit. **1907** *Westm. Gaz.* 5 July 9/1 In the lady's service was the prisoner, who occupied the position of *kennel-maid. **1929** *Daily Express* 16 Jan. 5/2 The showing of dogs is skilled work for a kennelmaid. **1970** *Daily Tel.* 14 Apr. 17/2 He had bought substantial quantities of veterinary preparations for the mange and had left the treatment to a young kennelmaid. **1828** *Sporting Mag.* XXIII. 23 Your *kennel-man should be constantly on the watch. **1954** C. L. B. HUBBARD *Compl. Dog Breeders' Manual* x. 103 With reliable staffing the kennel runs smoothly enough, therefore it is essential that he selects his kennelmen and kennelmaids with care. **1972** *Shooting Times & Country Mag.* 27 May 18/3 To manage such a large kennel Sheppard has two kennel-men in addition to four girls. **1898** *Yorksh. Archæol. Jrnl.* No. 57. 7 His wife Margaret..wears the *kennel-shaped head-dress. **1929** *Daily Express* 16 Jan. 5/2 *Kennelwork as a career for educated girls. **1971** DANGERFIELD & HOWELL *Internat. Encycl. Dogs* 268 Kennel work cannot be classed as an effeminate career for a male or an overly masculine job for a woman.

kennel (ˈkɛnəl), *sb.*[2] Also 6 **kenell**, 6–7 **kennell**. [Later form of CANNEL *sb.*[1] (q.v.); for the vowel, cf. *ketch, keg, kedge*, etc., from *catch, cag, cadge*, etc.] The surface drain of a street; the gutter: = CANNEL *sb.*[1] 2.

1582 STANYHURST *Æneis* II. (Arb.) 55 Thee streets and kennels are with slayne carcases heaped. **1607** ROWLANDS *Diog. Lanth.* 9 Nay ile go low enough to the kennel, thou shalt not iustle me for the wall. **1608–33** BP. HALL *Medit. & Vows* §103 A Scavenger working in the Kennel. **1764** HARMER *Observ.* XII. i. 35 Having no kennels in the streets to carry off the water, it was ancle-deep. **1879** G. MACDONALD *Sir Gibbie* I. i. 2 Raking with both hands in the grey dirt of the kennel.

fig. **1637** R. HUMPHREY tr. *St. Ambrose* Pref., I will rake no deeper into this kennell. **1678** *Yng. Mans Call.* 317 Sometime thou wert the beautiful image of God, but now the stinking and filthy kennel of Satan. **1847** LEWES *Hist. Philos.* (1867) II. 97 Descending into the kennel of obscenity and buffoonery.

b. *attrib.* and *Comb.*, as *kennel sink, water*; *kennel-muddy* adj.; **kennel-brow**, the top of the sloping side of a gutter; **kennel-dash**, a splash from the gutter; **kennel-nymph**, a girl of the streets; † **kennel wits**, muddy brains. Also KENNEL-RAKER.

1761 *Lond. Mag.* XXX. 17 The step..with a pebble or two standing up in the *kennel-brow before, would secure the posts from being moved. **1731** *Gentl. Mag.* I. 332 To walk through Rag Fair in Dirty Weather..a jostle in one place, a slip in another, a slop in a third, a *Kennel-dash in a fourth. **1607** WALKINGTON *Opt. Glass* 16 *Kennel-muddy thoughts. **1771** SMOLLETT *Humph. Cl.* 10 June, Let. i, He.. indulged himself..with one of the *kennel-nymphs. **1599** MARSTON *Sco. Villanie* I. ii. 176 The *kennell sincke of slaues. **1707** *Curios. in Husb. & Gard.* 268 Horse-dung, and *Kennel-Water, contribute beyond all belief to the forwarding of Plants. **1598** E. GILPIN *Skial.* (1878) 5 That men should haue such *kennel wits To thinke so well of a scald railing vaine.

Hence (*nonce-wds.*) † ˈ**kennelage** [cf. *drainage*] a system of kennels, gutters collectively; ˈ**kennelled** *a.*, lying in the gutter; ˈ**kennelly** *a.*, such as is found in a kennel or gutter.

1612 STURTEVANT *Metallica* 92 Kennellage is one of the chiefe kinds of Pipeage which passeth and voydeth away the stincking and filthy waters of citties and townes. **1794** COLERIDGE *To the Nightingale*, '*Sister of love-lorn Poets*', They..Mark the faint Lamp-beam on the Kennell'd mud. **1803** SIR R. T. WILSON *Brit. Exp. Egypt* 63 The miraculous qualities of the river [Nile]..the luxuries which the very kennelly waters would afford.

† **kennel**, *sb.*[3] *Obs.* In 6 **kenel**. Var. CANNEL *sb.*[1] 5: cf. CANNEL-BONE, neck-bone.

c **1532** DU WES *Introd. Fr.* in Palsgr. 902 The knot of the necke, *le neu du col*; the hole of the necke, *la fosse du col*; the kenel of the necke, *la canol du col*.

kennel, *sb.*[4], obs. form of CANNEL *sb.*[2]

17.. BLACK in Brand *Hist. Newcastle* (1789) II. 242 *note*, Parrot, or kennel coal is distinguished by producing a more copious bright flame. **1794** MRS. PIOZZI *Synon.* I. 408 One large kennel coal keeps his chamber from excess of cold.

kennel (ˈkɛnəl), *v.* [f. KENNEL *sb.*[1]]

1. a. *intr.* To lie or dwell in a kennel; to retire into a kennel. Of a fox or other wild beast: To retreat into a lair. Of a person (*contemptuous*): To lodge or lurk. Also *fig.*

1552 HULOET, *Acherusius*, a..caue in hell wherin..the dogge of hell cannelleth. *a* **1577** GASCOIGNE *Wks.*, *To such as find fault*, We see the dog that kenels in his den. **1599** J. FERNE *Let.* 4 May (Cecil MSS. Hatf. Ho. LXIX. No. 103), The book..was made by Campion while he kenelled at this house. **1603** DRAYTON *Heroic. Ep.* xiii. 156 Glad here to kennell in a Pad of Straw. **1610** GUILLIM *Heraldry* III. xiv. (1660) 166 You shall say that a Fox Kenneleth. **1726** G. ROBERTS *4 Years Voy.* 102 The rest kennelling like Hounds on Deck, or where they could. **1847** BUSHNELL *Chr. Nurt.* II. iii. (1861) 279 All foul passions that kennel in a sensual soul. **1884** E. P. ROE in *Harper's Mag.* Feb. 445/1 The dull, sodden faces of the man and woman who kennelled there.

b. With *up*. To return to one's kennel (also *fig.*); to keep quiet, to shut up. *colloq.*

1913 GALSWORTHY *Fugitive* III. i, 63 You've run her to earth; your job's done. Kennel up, hounds! **1919** W. H. DOWNING *Digger Dial.* 30 *Kennel-up*, stop talking. **1929** GALSWORTHY *Roof* ii. 37 Kennel up, Reggie! You've had too much and you know it. **1972** *Shooting Times & Country Mag.* 4 Mar. 37/3 After clean straw had been put on their benches, the order 'kennel up!' was given, though not immediately obeyed.

2. a. *trans.* To put into, or keep in, a kennel.

1592 SHAKS. *Ven. & Ad.* clii, Here kennelled in a brake she finds a hound. **1641** J. JACKSON *True Evang. T.* III. 205 Kennelling the Wolfe and the Lamb together. **1709** STEELE *Tatler* No. 62 ¶3 That Quarter of the Town where they are kennel'd is generally inhabited by stangers. **1887** *Daily News* 31 Dec. 3/8 Mr. C. kennelled the harriers at the house of a friend.

b. *transf.* and *fig.* To lodge, shut *up*; to put in a place of retreat or confinement.

1582 STANYHURST *Æneis* I. (Arb.) 28 His ships hee kenneld neere forrest vnder an angle Of rock. **1607** ROWLANDS *Diog. Lanth.* 12 Away with him,..chayne and kennell him vp in Iayle. **1677** MRS. BEHN *Adelazer* II. ii, Let's to the Queen's Apartment, and seize this Moor; I am sure there the Mongrel's kennel'd. **1840** DICKENS *Barn. Rudge* xviii, Hold the torch up till I've got to the end of the court, and then kennel yourself.

Hence ˈ**kennelled** *ppl. a.*; ˈ**kennelling** *vbl. sb.*, also *concr.* provision of kennels; also *attrib.*

1716 B. CHURCH *Hist. Philip's War* (1865) I. 65 His next kennelling Place was at the falls of Connecticut River. **1730–46** THOMSON *Autumn* 548 The kennelled hounds Mix in the music of the day again. **1870** BLAINE *Encycl. Rur. Sports* (ed. 3) §1945 The kennelling of greyhounds should equal that of foxhounds in amplitude. **1876** GEO. ELIOT *Dan. Der.* xxxv, Gwendolen had lingered behind to look at the kennelled blood-hounds.

kennelage, -nelled, -nelly: see KENNEL *sb.*[2]

Kennelly (ˈkɛnəlɪ). [Name of Arthur Edwin *Kennelly* (1861–1939), U.S. electrical engineer, who in 1902 suggested (as did Heaviside independently) that such a layer existed.)] ***Kennelly(-Heaviside) layer*** or ***region***: = *E-layer* (E II. 9), *Heaviside layer*.

1925 *Science* 22 May 540/1 (*heading*) The Kennelly-Heaviside layer. **1925** *Nature* 24 Oct. 609/2 The hypothesis of an electrically conducting stratum in the upper air was clearly enunciated in an article by Prof. A. E. Kennelly.. published in the *Electrical World and Engineer* of New York on March 15, 1902. The official date of Heaviside's disclosure of his hypothesis is December 19, 1902... If names are to be attached to the hypothetical layer it should be called, in equity, the 'Kennelly-Heaviside' layer, a name which is beginning to be used in America. **1932** *Discovery* Oct. 308/1 The Kennelly-Heaviside layer..is responsible for the reflection of long and medium wireless wavelengths. **1933** *Ibid.* Oct. 306/1 Professor Appleton..observed that there was yet another layer beyond the Kennelly layer. **1963** G. M. B. DOBSON *Exploring Atmosphere* viii. 142 These different ionized regions are usually known by the letters which have been placed alongside them in the diagram, but the *E* region is also known as the 'Kennelly-Heaviside' region, and the *F* region as the 'Appleton' region, after their discoverers. **1972** *Science* 5 May 463/2 It was not until 1926

that the existence of this 'Kennelly-Heaviside layer' was established beyond all doubt.

† **'kennel-,raker.** *Obs.* A raker of the gutter; a scavenger; also used as a term of abuse.

c **1589** *Theses Martinianæ* 27 You contemne such kenell rakers and scullions. **1618** WITHER *Motto* Wks. (1633) 552 Those gaudy Upstarts no more prize I doe Than poorest Kennell-rakers. **1731** ARBUTHNOT *Treat. Scolding* 20 You did not love Cruelty, you Kennel-raker, you Gibbet-carrier.

kennen, obs. form of KENNING *sb.*

'kenner. *rare.* [f. KEN *v.*[1]] One who kens.

1686 F. SPENCE tr. *Varillas' Medicis* 63 The accurate Kenners of military discipline judged that the Town would have been taken forthwith. [**1891** ATKINSON *Last of Giant-Killers* 224 Go, consult the Crystal, the all-kenner.]

† **kennet**[1]. *Obs.* Also 4–5 kenet, 5 -it. [a. ONF. *kennet* = OF. *chienet*, etc. (Godef.), dim. of *chien* dog.] A small dog, used in hunting.

13.. *Gaw. & Gr. Knt.* 1701 A kenet kryes þerof, þe hunt on hym calles. ? *a* **1400** *Morte Arth.* 122 The Romaynes.. Cowchide as kenetez before þe kynge selvyne. *c* **1425** *Seven Sag.* (P.) 1740 The lord a lytyl kenet hadde. **1486** *Bk. St. Albans* F iv b, Theis be the namys of houndes.. Rachys, Kenettys, Terroures. **1602** *2nd Pt. Return fr. Parnass.* II. v. 870 My father.. keepes an open table for all kinde of dogges. .. He hath your.. Leurier, your Spaniell, your Kennets. **1614** *Bk. Hauking* in Strutt *Sports & Past.* I. i. (1801) 17 Lemors, kenets, terrours.

† **kennet**[2]. *Obs. rare.* Also 5 kannette, 6 kenet(te. [prob. a. ONF. **canette*, **kenette* = OF. *chenette* (one example in Godef.), f. L. *cānus* hoary: cf. ONF. *canu*, *kenu*, F. *chenu*:—**cānūtus*.] A kind of grey cloth.

1480 CAXTON *Ovid's Met.* XIV. xii. 63 b/1 Wel semed he for age to tremble & had made his hed lyke as hit had been of kannette. **1541** *Act 33 Hen. VIII*, c. 3 A certayne kinde.. of walshe clothes called whytes, russettes, and kenettes. [In Poulton *kennets*: hence in Blount, Phillips, etc.]

b. *Comb.* † **kennet-colour** *a.*, grey-coloured.

1530 PALSGR. 235/2 Kenet coloure, *cendré*.

[**kennet.** *Naut.* Error for KEVEL (q.v.), in Kersey's Phillips 1706, whence in Bailey, Chambers, Smyth *Sailor's Word-bk.*, *Century Dict.*, etc.]

kennetic (kɛ'nɛtɪk), *a.* [f. KEN *v.*[1] 11 after KINETIC *a.*] (See quot. 1955.) Usu. in phr. *kennetic inquiry*.

1950 A. F. BENTLEY in *Science* CXII. 775/1 Kennetic inquiry is a name proposed for organized investigation into the problem of human knowings and knowns, where this is so conducted that the full range of subject matters—all the knowings and all the knowns—form a common field. *Ibid.* 775/2 To form the name 'kennetic', the Scottish 'ken' or 'kenning' has been preferred to any word in the groups centering around 'cognition'. **1955** M. REIFER *Dict. New Words* 116/1 *Kennetic adj.*, pertaining to the study of the acquisition of knowledge viewed as a transaction between the learner and the entire matter to be learned. **1960** H. C. SHANDS *Thinking & Psychotherapy* ii. 40 It is important for an understanding of the processes of kennetic inquiry to remember always the shifting nature of means and ends. **1970** —— *Semiotic Approaches to Psychiatry* 8 Natural philosophy must be primarily oriented toward the understanding of communicative process, and.. toward 'kennetic inquiry'.

‖ **kennetjie** ('kɛnəci). *S. Afr.* Also **kennetje**. [Afrikaans.] = TIP-CAT.

1947 *Cape Times Weekend Mag.* 21 June 22 Whether they were climbing in hedges.. or playing kennetjie or marbles, the youthful Miss H —— and her companions were like all healthy children. **1953** *Cape Argus* 28 Feb. 3/6 On these grassy squares we played 'rounders' and on the paths marbles, tops, hop-scotch, and kennetje. **1959** *Cape Times* 2 May 9/1 A South African in England tells me that what they call *kennetjie* in the Boland is sweeping Lancashire, where it is known as tip-cat. **1971** *Standard Encycl. S. Afr.* III. 190/2 In his delightful memoirs P. B. Borcherds mentions the games of 'kennetjie' (tip-cat) in which he took part.. at the close of the 18th century... The kennetjie itself was a piece of wood about 5 inches.. long and 1½ inch.. in diameter, tapered off at both ends.

'kenning, *sb. north. dial.* [Derivation obscure.] A dry measure: = two pecks, or half a bushel; a vessel containing this quantity.

[**1299** *Acc. Rolls Durham* (Surtees) 496 In xlvij qr. ij ken. præbendæ.] **1344–5** *Inv. Norham Castle* (in *Northumbld. Gloss.*) Kenine. [**1392** *Acc. Rolls Durham* (Surtees) 345 Will's Byng kennen bon.] *c* **1574** *Inv. Warkworth Cas.* in *Hist. Northumbld.* (1899) V. 66 A bushell mett, a keninge, ij peckes. **1576** *Wills & Inv. N.C.* (Surtees 1835) 410, I gyve .. one kennyng of wheat to the poore. **1673** *Depos. Cast. York* (Surtees) 196 A kening of wheate flower for pyes. **1825** BROCKETT, *Kennen, Kenning*, a measure of two pecks. **1893** in HESLOP *Northumbld. Gloss.*

kenning ('kɛnɪŋ), *vbl. sb.*[1] Now only *Sc.* and *north. dial.* (exc. sense 6). [f. KEN *v.*[1] + -ING[1].]

† **1.** Teaching, instruction. *Obs.*

c **1320** *Sir Beues* (MS. A) 644 Þe stedes hom to stable ran Wiþ oute kenning [*v.r.* techyng] of eni man. *c* **1330** R. BRUNNE *Chron. Wace* (Rolls) 2472 When y blamed my doughter ȝyng, & gaf no kepe til hure kennyng. **1377** LANGL. *P. Pl.* B. x. 194 Þis is catounes kennyng to clerkes þat he lereth.

† **2. a.** Sign, token. **b.** Appearance. *Obs.*

a **1300** *Cursor M.* 18332 (Cott.) Þou.. has þe kenening [*Gött.* taken of] þe rode Raised in erth of ur ranscum. *Ibid.* 24086 (Cott.) Vnethes i his kenning kneu.

† **3.** Visual cognition; sight or view: = KEN *sb.*[1] 3. Phrases ***in, within, beyond, out of kenning***. *Obs.*

c **1400** *Destr. Troy* 2837 Nawther company.. hade Kennyng of other, But past to þere purpos. **1577** HOLINSHED *Chron.* I. 490 There arriued in their sight a nauie of Shippes, which at the first kenning, they tooke to be french Shippes. **1586** R. LANE in Capt. Smith *Virginia* I. 5 The passage from thence was thought a broad sound within the maine, being without kenning of land. **1598** TOFTE *Alba* (1880) 34 He is in kenning of his wished Home. **1599** HAKLUYT *Voy.* II. I. 102 We had also kenning of another Iland called Lissa. **1630** LENNARD tr. *Charron's Wisd.* III. xxiv. (1670) 491 Again, at a kenning we cannot see of the Earth above ten or twelve leagues. *a* **1697** STRATHSPEY in *Aubrey's Misc.* (1721) 203 The Lady Gareloch was going somewhere from her House within kenning to the Road which Clunie was coming.

† **4.** Range of sight: = KEN *sb.*[1] 2. *Obs.*

1530 PALSGR. 431, I am within syght, as a shyppe is that cometh within the kennyng. **1599** T. M[OUFET] *Silkwormes* 15 Not dreaming that her loue in kenning were. **1601** HOLLAND *Pliny* I. 61 Without your kenning lyeth Sardinia fast vpon the Africke sea.

† **b.** The distance that bounds the range of ordinary vision, *esp.* at sea; hence, a marine measure of about 20 or 21 miles. Cf. KEN *sb.*[1] 1.

a **1490** BOTONER *Itin.* (Nasmith 1778) 110 Per distanciam de le narrow see.. v kennyngys, et quilibet kennyng continet .. 21 miliaria. *c* **1500** *Melusine* 104 He sawe the ship three kennynges ferre on the sea, that is, one & twenty legues ferre. **1538** LELAND *Itin.* III. 19 Scylley is a Kenning, that is to say about a xx Miles from the very Westeste Point of Cornewaulle. **1694** MOTTEUX *Rabelais* IV. xxii. (1737) 94, I see Land.. 'tis within a Kenning.

5. Mental cognition; knowledge, cognizance; recognition. Now *Sc.* and *north. dial.* † ***fleshly kenning***, carnal knowledge.

c **1400** tr. *Secreta Secret., Gov. Lordsh.* 64 Þy seluyn hadde takyn deed, þurgh þe hete of fleschly kennynge with here. *c* **1440** *Promp. Parv.* 271/2 Kennynge, or knowynge, ..*cognicio, agnicio.* **17..** in *Burns' Wks.* (Rtldg.) Life 45, I crept quietly owre the bed, out o' his kennin, and kneeled down beside him. **1828** *Craven Dial.*, *Kennin*, knowing. 'Ye're seea feafully waxen, at ye're past kennen.'

b. A recognizable portion; just enough to be perceived; a little. *Sc.* and *north. dial.*

1786 BURNS *Unco Guid* vii, Tho' they may gang a kennin wrang, To step aside is human. **1805** J. NICOL *Poems* I. 187 (Jam.) Gif o' this warl, a kennin mair, Some get than me, I've got content. **1876** *Whitby Gloss.* s.v., That string's just a kenning thicker than the other. **1893** STEVENSON *Catriona* 103 His father was.. a kenning on the wrong side of the law.

6. One of the periphrastic expressions used instead of the simple name of a thing, characteristic of Old Teutonic, and esp. Old Norse, poetry.

Examples are *oar-steed* = ship, *storm of swords* = battle. The term is adopted from the mediæval Icelandic treatises on poetics, and is derived from the idiomatic use of *kenna við* or *til*, 'to name after'.

1883 VIGFUSSON & POWELL *Corpus Poet. Bor.* II. 448 The extreme development of the 'kenning' in Northern Poetry. **1889** COOK *Judith* Introd. 59 A characteristic ornament of Old English, as well as of early Teutonic poetry in general, are the kennings. **1896** *Scott. Rev.* Oct. 342 *note*, The kennings for 'man' in Gröndal's *Clavis Poetica* extend to 33 closely printed columns.

7. *Comb.*, as † **kenning-glass**, a spy-glass, small telescope; † **kenning-place**, a place prominently in sight.

1603 *Reg. Stationers' Co.* 15 June (Arb.) III. 238 A Booke Called *A Kennyng glass for a Christian Kinge.* **1610** HOLLAND *Camden's Brit.* I. 606 It standeth forth as a Kenning place to the view of eyes.

† **'kenning**, *vbl. sb.*[2] *Obs. rare.* Also 7 kinning. [app. f. KEN *v.*[2] + -ING[1]; cf. OE. *cęnning* birth.] The cicatricula or tread of an egg.

1585 HIGGINS tr. *Junius' Nomenclator, Ovi umbilicus*, the streine or kenning of the egge. **1601** HOLLAND *Pliny* I. 298 There is found in the top or sharper end of an egge within the shell, a certaine round knot resembling a drop or a nauil, rising aboue the rest, which they call a Kinning.

kennit, obs. f. KENNED, KENT *ppl. a.*

keno ('kiːnəʊ), *sb.* (and *int.*) *U.S.* Also 9 **keeno, kino, quino**. [ad. F. *quine* set of five winning numbers in a lottery, f. L. *quīnī* distributive of *quinque* five.]

a. A game of chance based on the drawing of numbers and covering of corresponding numbers on cards, in a manner similar to lotto.

1814 B. F. PALMER *Diary* 30 May (1914) 70, I employ'd in washing & mending my messmate playing keeno. **1843** J. F. COOPER *Ned Myers* 93, I commenced operations by purchasing shares in a dice-board, a *vingt-et-un* table, and a quino table. **1870** A. S. EVANS *Our Sister Republic* xx. 462 A great shed capable of seating one thousand or fifteen hundred people, which is devoted exclusively to *quino*, played for money. The cards or tickets are pasted down upon the tables and must number at least one thousand all told. Each player is provided with a handful of corn with which to keep the game as the numbers drawn out by the dealer are called... One game.. takes about three minutes. **1871** *Figaro* 15 Apr., The police pulled every Keno establishment in the city. **1873** J. H. BEADLE *Undevel. West* iv. 95 This game, like keno, has less of the 'cutthroat' about it than the others. **1875** E. KING *Southern States N. Amer.* xx. 206 A man.. tried to shoot the keno-dealer in the back. **1879** *Scribner's Mag.* XIX. 386/1 To play cards and keno for small stakes. **1884** *Pall Mall G.* 26 June 11/2 Some of the members were lying about asleep in the gaming room, having.. been hit hard by the latest American importation, kino. **1889** K. MUNROE *Golden Days of '49* iv. 40 We'll have a drawin' over in Slim Jim's keno ranch. **1904** W. N. HARBEN *Georgians* xxiii. 218 The town's got what they call the 'White Elephant'—a gamblin', keno shebang on a giant scale. **1907** C. E. MULFORD *Bar-20* (1914) ix. 108 I'd shore look nice loping around a keno lay-out without my guns, in th' same town with some cuss huntin' me, wouldn't I? **1951** E. KEFAUVER *Crime in Amer.* (1952) xii. 144 Another huge gambling casino.. ran dice, keno and card games. **1968** R. F. ADAMS *Western Words* (ed. 2) 169 Keno.. is played with a large globe, called the keno goose.

b. *int.* An exclamation (expressing encouragement or approval).

1868 *Terr. Enterprise* (Virginia, Nevada) 30 Sept. 3/2 When they thus got three beans in a row they were to call out 'Keno!' and rake in the pot. **1884** *Pall Mall G.* 26 June 11/2 He opened a door and ushered me in, and the first exclamation I heard was 'Kino' and a grunt of satisfaction. **1907** C. E. MULFORD *Bar-20* (1914) xix. 193 He wants to know where th' cards are stacked an' why he can't holler 'Keno'. **1920** in J. M. Hunter *Trail Drivers of Texas* I. 205 Shake yer spurs an' make 'em rattle! Keno! Promenade to seats.

† **'kenodoxy.** *Obs. rare*[−0]. [ad. Gr. κενοδοξία, f. κενόδοξ-ος vain-glorious, f. κενό-ς empty + δόξα glory.] 'The love, study, or desire of vain-glory' (Blount *Glossogr.* 1656; hence in Phillips 1658, and Bailey 1730).

kenogenesis (kiːnəʊ'dʒɛnɪsɪs). *Biol.* [irreg. for *cæno-* or *kainogenesis*, f. Gr. καινός new + γένεσις genesis.] Haeckel's term for the form of ontogenesis in which the true hereditary development of a germ is modified by features derived from its environment (opposed to *palingenesis*). Hence **kenoge'netic** *a.*

1879 tr. *Haeckel's Evol. Man* I. i. 10 The term Kenogenetic process (or vitiation of the history of the germ) is applied to all such processes of the germ-history as are not to be explained by heredity from primaeval parent-forms. *Ibid.* 11 This distinction between Palingenesis or inherited evolution, and Kenogenesis or vitiated evolution, has not.. yet been sufficiently appreciated by naturalists.

‖ **kenosis** (kɪ'nəʊsɪs). *Theol.* [a. Gr. κένωσις an emptying, f. κενόειν to empty, with ref. to *Phil.* ii. 7 ἑαυτὸν ἐκένωσε 'emptied himself'.] The self-renunciation of the divine nature, at least in part, by Christ in the incarnation.

[**1844** W. H. MILL *Serm. Tempt. Christ* v. 113 Here especially we behold that κένωσις, that voluntary emptying Himself of Divinity of which St. Paul speaks.] **1873** WATSON & EVANS tr. *Oostersee's Christ. Dogmatics* (1881) 549 The idea of the Kenosis in its legitimate application. **1882** CAVE & BANKS tr. *Dorner's Syst. Chr. Doctr.* III. 393 We cannot accept a self-emptying of the Logos in the sense of the modern Kenosis. **1884** L. A. TOLLEMACHE *Stones of Stumbling* 115 My article.. is designed to show that the *kenosis* involved in the Incarnation may be a complete one. **1891** *Ch. Q. Rev.* Oct. 9 By the doctrine of Kenosis it is not held that the Divine Being in Christ is really limited.

kenotic (kɪ'nɒtɪk), *a.* *Theol.* [ad. Gr. κενωτικ-ός, f. κενόειν to empty: see prec. and -IC.] Of or pertaining to kenosis; involving or accepting the doctrine of kenosis.

1882–3 SCHAFF *Encycl. Relig. Knowl.* I. 461 The Kenotic view of Giessen is more in accordance with the facts of Christ's life. *Ibid.*, The Kenotic controversy was renewed recently. **1895** *Ch. Q. Rev.* 487 [A] leaning towards the Kenotic theories of the Incarnation.

Hence **ke'noticism**, the doctrine of, or belief in, the kenosis of Christ; **ke'noticist**, one who believes in, or maintains, the kenosis.

1882–3 SCHAFF *Encycl. Relig. Knowl.* I. 458 Baur, Dorner, Rothe, and the modern Kenoticists. **1891** *Ch. Q. Rev.* Oct. 9 The Kenoticist does not deny them, but practically he gets rid of them.. by his theory of kenosis. **1899** W. BRIGHT *Law of Faith* 337 Kenoticism may indeed be described as a solvent of faith.

kenotism ('kɛnəʊtɪz(ə)m). *Theol.* = KENOTICISM. So **'kenotist** = KENOTICIST.

1896 E. H. GIFFORD in *Expositor* Sept. 166 Speculation concerning the fulness of the Godhead in the Incarnate Christ, and the opposite doctrine of Kenotism. **1899** *Ch. Times* 3 Feb. 117 The Modern Theories of the Kenotists with reference to Our Lord's Knowledge.

kenotron ('kɛnətrɒn). *Electr.* [f. Gr. κενό-ς empty + -TRON.] A kind of highly evacuated thermionic diode designed for rectification at high voltages.

Kenotron was formerly a proprietary name in the U.S.

1915 S. DUSHMAN in *Gen. Electric Rev.* Mar. 159/2 In the case of a rectifier containing a hot filament as cathode and exhausted to as high a degree of vacuum as possible, there is no conduction except by electrons. In order to distinguish the latter type of hot cathode rectifier from other forms.. the designation, kenotron, has been specially coined. **1915** *Electrician* 21 May 242/1 A kenotron has been built capable of rectifying 250 milliamperes at 180,000 volts. **1918** *Official Gaz.* (U.S. Patent Office) 1 Jan. 291/1 General Electric Company... Kenotron... Rectifying apparatus. Claims use since about May, 1916. **1946** W. T. SPROULL *X-Rays in Pract.* vii. 120 Kenotrons are widely used in the electric circuits that are provided to supply the high voltage for x-ray tubes. *Ibid.* 121 In an x-ray tube, the space current is said to be 'emission limited', while in a kenotron the current is 'space charge limited', as in most radio vacuum tubes.

kenozooid (,kɛnəʊ'zəʊɔɪd). [f. Gr. κενό-ς empty + ZOOID *sb.*] In a colonial bryozoan of the

phylum Ectoprocta, an individual consisting of the body wall or ZOŒCIUM alone, without tentacles or an alimentary canal. Also called †**kenozo'œcium** [f. Gr. κενό-ς empty + ZOŒCIUM].

1909 G. M. R. LEVINSEN *Cheilostomatous Bryozoa* 46 We can distinguish between four main forms of individuals (Bryozooids)... *Kenozoœcia* (*Kenozooids*), which not only have no polypide, but as a rule no aperture and always no operculum. *Ibid.*, The Kenozoœcia must be regarded as supporting, fastening and connecting individuals. **1959** L. H. HYMAN *Invertebrates* V. xx. 331 Kenozooid is the name applied to heterozooids that lack zooidal differentiation and consist simply of body wall enclosing strands of tissue.

kenrik, kenschipe: see KINGRICK, KEENSHIP.

Kensal Green (kɛnsəl 'gri:n). The site of a large cemetery in London, used allusively as the type of a cemetery or as a symbol of death and burial. Also *fig.*

1842 DICKENS *Let.* 26 Apr. (1974) III. 211 What would I give if the dear girl whose ashes lie in Kensal-Green, had lived. *c* **1885** A. W. PINERO in M. R. Booth *Eng. Plays of 19th Cent.* (1973) IV. 332 In less than that, unless I am lucky enough to fall in some foreign set-to, I shall be in Kensal Green. **1903** KIPLING *Five Nations* 122 That Kensall-Green of greatness called the files. **1914** G. K. CHESTERTON *Flying Inn* xxi. 252 Before we go to Paradise by way of Kensal Green. **1967** O. LANCASTER *Eye to Future* I. 24 My mother was wholly free from the lachrymose necrophilia of the Victorians; not for her the pious outings to Kensal Green. **1975** P. SOMERVILLE-LARGE *Couch of Earth* iv. 73 The necropolis was huge... We wandered about this devasted Kensal Green, Ismael.. kicking at the piles of bones.

Kensington ('kɛnzɪŋtən). The name of a borough of London (now part of the Royal Borough of Kensington and Chelsea), used *attrib.* or quasi-*adj.* to designate speech supposedly characteristic of people living in Kensington (cf. next).

1968 J. LOCK *Lady Policeman* viii. 62 'Haymarket!' the manner is brusque and the voice exaggerated Kensington. **1971** *Guardian* 22 Oct. 10/3 One spectator exclaimed, 'all the peasants speak Baliganj Bengali!' (read: 'Kensington English').

b. ***Kensington (outline) stitch***, a needlework stitch which is formed by putting the needle into the material from the front and returning it some way back whilst splitting the thread.

1881 C. C. HARRISON *Woman's Handiwork* I. 33 Feather stitch.. is often incorrectly termed 'Kensington' or 'crewel' stitch. **1883** *Century Mag.* Sept. 787/1 They know little of Kensington stitch or of Eastern-woven portières. **1909** *Cent. Dict.* Suppl. s.v. *stitch*, *Kensington stitch*, in *embroidery*, a long and a short outline-stitch, appearing alternately. **1934** M. THOMAS *Dict. Embroidery Stitches* 186 Split stitch... Also known as Kensington Outline Stitch.

Kensingtonian (kɛnzɪŋ'təʊnɪən), *sb.* and *a.* [f. *Kensington* (see prec.) + -IAN.] **A.** *sb.* An inhabitant of Kensington.

1889 G. B. SHAW in *Star* 6 Dec. 2/5 The Kensingtonians are asses to neglect these concerts. **1951** R. CAMPBELL *Light on Dark Horse* 45 Zulus are far more important.. than dogs to Kensingtonians. **1965** G. MCINNES *Road to Gundagai* xv. 267 The whole of this great grey sun-baked continent [*sc.* Australia] she regarded much as if it were Hornsey or Tooting Bec, and she a Kensingtonian of high degree. **1968** *Listener* 6 June 733/1 Hot or cool jazz would have been just too much and might have driven out the dreary West Kensingtonians with their dim uniformed escorts. **1974** *Times* 23 May 16/7 A Kensingtonian in her eighties.. missed the style and elegance of the old shop.

b. A supposedly refined or affected manner of speech typical of people living in Kensington. *rare.*

1911 A. BENNETT *Hilda Lessways* I. x. 91 Hilda.. had been deprived of her Five Towns accent at Chetwynd's School, where the purest Kensingtonian was inculcated.

B. *adj.* Of, pertaining to, or characteristic of Kensington; *spec.* denoting refined or affected speech.

1902 A. BENNETT *Anna of Five Towns* xi. 290 His broad Five Towns speech contrasting with the Kensingtonian accents of the coroner. **1936** *Times Lit. Suppl.* 27 June 541/1 Superior Margery Seymour, with her Kensingtonian 'mothah and brothah'. **1958** *Listener* 2 Oct. 537/1 A truly Kensingtonian drawing-room. **1960** *Times* 24 Feb. 15/3 Miss Maggie Smith and Miss Moyra Fraser at times vocally suggested mere Kensingtonian refinement. **1961** WODEHOUSE *Service with Smile* (1962) v. 73 Somehow it seemed worse and more wounding coming from those Kensingtonian lips. **1971** *Listener* 28 Oct. 596/3 Kensingtonian shrieks, with fiddle, indicated Gypsies relaxing.

Kensitite ('kɛnzɪtaɪt). [f. the surname *Kensit* (see below): see -ITE[1].] A follower of John Kensit (1853–1902), a Low Church extremist who objected to alleged Romanizing aspects of the Anglican Church.

1898 *Tablet* 6 Aug. 207/1 It was disloyalty, with which Mr. Drummond and his brethren were charged by an irate and portly Kensitite with a Hyde Park voice. **1904** *Daily Chron.* 5 Mar. 6/6 The cheering of the 'Kensitites' brought a crowd quickly to the scene. **1907** *Ibid.* 14 May 5/4 Some of the audience endeavoured to expel the Kensitites. **1927** W. E. COLLINSON *Contemp. Eng.* 50 The Ritualists, strongly opposed by the Kensitites or followers of John Kensit. **1928** *Daily Express* 1 Dec. 11 (*heading*) Kensitite protests at the new Archbishop's election. **1936** A. HUXLEY *Eyeless in Gaza* iv. 29 The Ritualists and the Kensitites were at it again.

kenspeck ('kɛnspɛk), *a. dial.* Also 8 -spack, 9 -spec, -spac. [Origin obscure: the form agrees with Norw. *kjennespak*, Sw. *känspak*, quick at recognizing persons or things (cf. ON. *kennispeki* faculty of recognition); but the change from the active to a passive sense makes difficulties. Some have suggested confusion with *conspicuous*, but evidence is wanting. *Kenspecked* is given by Skinner (1671) and Ray (1674), and in Craven and other Northern glossaries.] = next.

1590 SIR T. COCKAINE *Hunting* D j, The most Buckes haue some kenspeck marke to knowe them by vpon their heads. **1715** THORESBY *Leeds* in *Craven Dial.*, A convention at some noted oak, or to use a local word, kenspack ake. **1841** DE QUINCEY *Homer* Wks. 1857 VI. 375 The Homeric metre .. is certainly kenspeck, to use a good old English word—that is, recognisable. **1855** ROBINSON *Whitby Gloss.* s.v., 'As kenspac as a cock on a church broach'.

kenspeckle ('kɛnspɛk(ə)l), *a. Sc.* and *north. dial.* Also -speckled; cf. prec. [See prec.; the ending may be -LE I, as in *brittle*, etc.] Easily recognizable; conspicuous.

1714 MRS. CENTLIVRE *Wonder* III, *Eng. Man.*.. What kind of a Woman is it you enquire after? *Gib.* Geud troth, she's ne Kenspekle, she's aw in a Clowd. **1795** BURNS *Let. to G. Thomson* May, My phiz is sae kenspeckle that the very joiner's apprentice.. knew it at once. **1820** SCOTT *Monast.* xxxiv, It is a kenspeckle hoof-mark, for the shoe was made by old Eckie of Canonbie. **1862** DARWIN *Let.* 25 Jan. in *Life* (1887) II. 385 Your notion of the Aristocrat being kenspeckle.. is new to me. **1916** J. BUCHAN *Greenmantle* xx. 259 The immediate front of a battle is a bit too public for any one to lie hidden in by day, especially when two or three feet of snow make everything kenspeckle. **1930** H. S. WALPOLE *Rogue Herries* II. 392 He.. wondered what it must be for such a boy to be in charge of so wild and tumultuous and kenspeckle an army. **1971** *Lancet* 6 Nov. 1028/2 He [*sc.* a cockerel] was.. a kenspeckle figure in the neighbourhood [*sc.* in Scotland]. **1973** *Perthshire Advertiser* 8 Aug. 13/2 There have been others.. who, if not as kenspeckle and dynamic in the public eye, have given of their time, talents and means.

†'**kensy.** *Sc. Obs. rare.* [Of unknown etym. The erron. form *kenyie* (see Jam.) is due to a misinterpretation of Ramsay's spelling *kenzie*, in his edition of *Christ's Kirk*.] A rough or rude fellow.

1500–20 DUNBAR *Poems* lx. 16 Fowll jow jourdane hedit-jevellis, Cowkin kenseis and culroun kewellis. **15..** *Christis Kirke Gr.* vii. (Bann. MS.), The kensy cleikit to the cavell, Bot, Lord, than how they luggit. **15..** *Colkelbie Sow* I. 351 (ibid.) Curris, kenseis, and knavis, Inthrang and dansit in thravis.

kent (kɛnt), *sb.*[1] *Sc.* and *north.* [Origin uncertain; in sense identical with the Kentish *quant*; for the difference in vowel cf. *kell* and *call* (CAUL *sb.*[1]).]

1. 'A long staff, properly such a one as shepherds use for leaping over ditches or brooks' (Jam.); a long pole used in leaping ditches, climbing mountains, etc.; a leaping pole.

1606 in Pitcairn *Crim. Trials* II. 519 The said W. R., haifing ane grit grene Kent and squarit batoun in his hand. *a* **1700** N. BURN in Ramsay *Tea-t. Misc.* (1733) II. 196 Shepherds.. With cur and kent upon the bent. **1721** RAMSAY *Richy & Sandy* 19 A better lad ne'er lean'd out o'er a kent. **1890** *Blackw. Mag.* Sept. 328/2 He placed his long pole or kent in front of him.

2. A punting-pole.

1844 RICHARDSON *Borderer's Table Bk.* VII. 175 *note*, When the stream is of equal depth, a *kent* or pole is used. [So on the Tweed and Teviot in 1850.]

kent, *sb.*[2] *Whaling.* = CANT *sb.*[1] II. Also *attrib.*

1820 W. SCORESBY *Acct. Arctic Regions* II. 296 The fat of the neck, or what corresponds in other animals with the neck, is called the Kent. **1837** R. HAMILTON *Nat. Hist. Whales* 106 A band of blubber two or three feet in width, encircling the fish's body at what is the neck in other animals, is called the *kent*, because by means of it the fish is turned over or *kented*. To this band is fixed the lower extremity of a combination of powerful blocks, called the *kent-purchase*, by means of which, the whole circumference of the animal is, section by section, brought to the surface. **1875** *Ure's Dict. Arts* III. 451 A band of fat, however, is left around the neck [of the whale], called the *kent*, to which hooks and ropes are attached for the purpose of shifting round the carcass.

Kent (kɛnt), *sb.*[3] [Name of a county in England.] In full, ***Kent sheep***. (See quot. 1957.)

1809 D. PRICE *Syst. Sheep-Grazing Romney Marsh* iv. 186 The New Leicester breed.. were ripe for the slaughter-house in April, whereas the South Down and the Kents would not be so till the latter end of the summer. *Ibid.* 201 The Kent sheep being 65 lb. lighter than the Leicesters.. makes the gainings of the Kent sheep in the whole 152 lb. of mutton. **1891** R. WALLACE *Rural Econ. Austral. & N.Z.* Plate LXIX (*caption*) Romney Marsh or Kent Sheep. **1894** *Country Gentlemen's Catal.* 52/1 Sheep—Kent or Romney Marsh. Bred by owner. **1957** *Encycl. Brit.* XX. 476/1 The *Romney* is a long-coarse-wool, white-face, hardy, polled sheep that originated in Kent, Eng. It is sometimes called the Kent or the Romney Marsh. **1960** *Farmer & Stockbreeder* 8 Mar. 15/1 Grassland types [of sheep] include .. Greyface and Kent. **1972** *Country Life* 16 Mar. 607/1 The sheep.. can break down organo-phosphates by blood enzymes. Among Dorset Downs 3 per cent could do this efficiently.. and among Kent 37 per cent.

kent, *ppl. a. Sc.* Also 6 kennit. [KEN *v.*[1]] Northern and western Sc. form of KENNED, known.

1513 DOUGLAS *Æneis* I. x. 52 My childe, cleith the with ȝone kennit [*v.r.* kend] childis visage. *c* **1787** BURNS *To a Painter*, You'll easy draw a weel-kent face. **1801** MACNEILL *Poet. Wks.* (1856) 146 (E.D.D.) Far frae ilk kent spot she wandered. **1888** STEVENSON in *Scribner's Mag.* May 635 A gentleman.. should mean a man of family, 'one of a kent house'.

kent, *v.*[1] *Sc.* and *north. dial.* [f. KENT *sb.*[1]; cf. CONT *v.*] *intr.* and *trans.* To punt.

1820 SCOTT *Abbot* xxxv, They will row very slow,.. or kent where depth permits, to avoid noise. **1846** RICHARDSON *Borderer's Table Bk.* VII. 175 A man had just been *kented* over the Tweed.

kent, *v.*[2] *Whaling.* = CANT *v.*[2]: cf. KENT *sb.*[2]

1820 W. SCORESBY *Acct. Arctic Regions* II. 296 By means of it, the fish is turned over or kented. **1856** STEGGALL *Real Hist. Suffolk Man* (1859) 230, I might speak of '*kenting*' the animal, that is turning him round, so that other layers of blubber might be cut off.

kental, obs. variant of QUINTAL.

kentallenite (kɛn'tælɪnaɪt). *Petrogr.* [f. *Kentallen*, name of a village in Strathclyde (formerly in Argyllshire) + -ITE[1].] An olivine-bearing monzonite.

1900 HILL & KYNASTON in *Q. Jrnl. Geol. Soc.* LVI. 532 Taking.. the Kentallen rock as our type, we propose that the term kentallenite should be substituted for olivine-monzonite. Kentallenite may be briefly defined as a coarse or medium-grained holocrystalline rock, consisting of olivine and augite, with orthoclase, plagioclase, and biotite in varying proportions. **1960** E. B. BAILEY et al. *Geol. Ben Nevis & Glen Coe* (ed. 2) xv. 192 The handsome black kentallenite, once worked as an ornamental stone, is pierced by a few white felspathic segregations. **1969** *Scottish Jrnl. Geol.* V. 11 Kentallenite is a pyroxenic member of the dominantly hornblendic Appinite Suite.. of the British Caledonian calc-alkaline igneous province.

kente ('kɛntə). Also **Kente.** [Twi, = cloth.] In full, ***kente cloth***. In Ghana, a banded material; also, a long garment made from this material, loosely draped on or worn around the shoulders and waist.

[**1881** J. G. CHRISTALLER *Dict. Asante & Fante Lang.* 228 *Kente*, country cloth, a home-made negro-dress, consisting of a number of narrow stripes of cotton-cloth sewed together.] **1957** M. BANTON *W. Afr. City* xii. 218 They may forsake western dress for Kente cloth. **1959** A. ABBS *Ashanti Boy* i. 38 The Chief was dressed in a gorgeous silk Kente... He was accompanied by some elders and friends, all wearing colourful Kentes.. with quick, characteristic swings of the right arm, each man re-arranged his cloth. *Ibid.* 255 *Kente*, cloth woven on native loom, usually in narrow strips that are sewn together. The designs are geometrical and each one has a distinctive name. **1962** *Times* 23 Nov. 4/2 The Ghanaian girls came past in their Kente dresses of gold, dark blue or deep pink and mauve. **1963** *Economist* 1 June 894/1 The confident swirling of Ghanaian *kente* robes. **1964** *Ibid.* 8 Feb. 488/2 Dr Nkrumah.. intends to clutch his people by the lapels (or kente cloths). **1969** *Times* 22 Oct. (Ghana Suppl.) p. viii/4 Not even the.. King of the Ashanti, knows much more than six weeks in advance when he is going to hold his durbah.. when the Golden Stool of the Ashanti is paraded before a crowd robed in its gaudiest *kente* cloth.

kentia ('kɛntɪə). [mod.L. (C. L. Blume 1836, in *Rumphia* II. xvii. 94), f. the name of William *Kent* (d. *c* 1828), botanical collector + -IA[1].] A palm with pinnate leaves of the genus so called, native to Australia and some Pacific islands, or one formerly included in this genus.

1870 B. S. WILLIAMS *Choice Stove & Greenhouse Ornamental-leaved Plants* 223 The *Kentias* are handsome robust plants, with pinnate leaves. **1909** *Westm. Gaz.* 8 Jan. 9/2 Over 1,000 Kentia palms from the South Sea Islands. **1937** M. JAMES *Family Garden* i. 46 *Kentias* are sometimes called curly palms. **1951** *Dict. Gardening* (R. Hort. Soc.) II. 1015/2 The Howeas (usually called Kentias in the market) are the most popular of Palms for general decorative work. **1966** E. J. H. CORNER *Nat. Hist. Palms* vii. 172 They [*sc.* pigeons] have been thought responsible.. for the wide distribution of *Areca* and *Kentia* in the South Pacific.

Kenticism ('kɛntɪsɪz(ə)m). [f. *Kent* after *Anglicism*, etc.] **a.** A word, idiom, or expression peculiar to the Kentish dialect. *rare.*

1735 PEGGE *Kenticisms* (E.D.S.) 10 Having gathered together an handfull of those Kenticisms.. I have ventured to send it to you.

b. A word, idiom, or expression peculiar to the OE. or ME. Kentish dialect; language characteristic of such dialect.

1933 *Amer. Jrnl. Philol.* LIV. 307 They show traces of the Kentish dialect, which is not surprising as there is Kenticism in the inked glosses in the manuscript. **1965** H. KÖKERITZ in Bessinger & Creed *Medieval & Ling. Stud.* 294 We can discern in his [*sc.* Wyatt's].. poems the survival of certain Kenticisms.

†'**kenting.** *Obs.* Also 7–8 kentin. [app. f. *Kent*, the English county (cf. *Kentish cloth* under KENTISH *a.* 3) + -ING[1].] A kind of fine linen cloth.

1657 R. LIGON *Barbadoes* (1673) 109 Linnen Cloth, as Canvas and Kentings. **1696** J. F. *Merchant's Ware-ho.* 31 Neck-cloaths... There is one sort more which comes from Hamborough, these are made of Kenting thread. **1712** MRS. CENTLIVRE *Perplexed Lovers* IV, Buy any British cloth or

Holland Kentins, Cambricks or Muslin? **1793** *Statist. Acc. Scot.* VII. 175 Lawns, gauzes and linens called Kentings are exported to Ireland.

b. A piece of this used as a strainer.

1725 Bradley *Fam. Dict.* s.v. *Plum*, Let the Syrup..be strain'd through a Kentin upon your Plums.

Kentish ('kɛntɪʃ), *a.* Also 1 **Centisc**, 3 **Kentisc**, **-iss**, 4 **Kentissh(e**. [OE. *Cęntisc*, f. *Cęnt*, ad. L. *Cantia* Kent + *isc*, -ish¹.]

1. Of or belonging to Kent. Chiefly of the inhabitants or speech. ***Kentish man*** (see quot. 1887).

a **1100** *O.E. Chron.* (Laud MS.) an. 999 Com þa seo Centisce fyrde þær onȝean. *c* **1205** Lay. 7441 Kentisce [*later text* Kentisse] leoden. **1387** Trevisa *Higden* (Rolls) V. 355 Þis Ethelbertus regnede among Kentisshe men fyfe and fifty ȝere. **1590** Swinburne *Testaments* 71 At last also the kentish-men yeelded. **1849** Macaulay *Hist. Eng.* iii. I. 346 The wives and daughters of the Kentish farmers. **1887** *Kent. Gloss.*, *Man of Kent*, a title claimed by the inhabitants of the Weald as their peculiar designation: all others they regard as Kentish men.

2. *absol.* as *sb.* **a.** *pl.* The natives or inhabitants of Kent. *rare.* **b.** The dialect of Kent.

905 *O.E. Chron.* (Parker MS.) an. 905 þa ætsæton ða Centiscan þær beæftan. **1670** Ray *Collect. Prov.* 233 *Kentish long-tails*..A note of disgrace on all English men, though it chanceth to stick onely on the Kentish at this day. **1735** Pegge *Kenticisms* 15 Thus the Kentish would have many particularities in their speech. **1866** Morris *Ayenb.* Introd. 6 In the Old Kentish of the Ayenbite an *e* takes the place of the Southern *u*. **1887** *Kent. Gloss.* Introd. 8 The specimens of Kentish in the Early and Middle English Periods.

3. a. Common in, or peculiar to, Kent, as ***Kentish ague, cherry, codlin, pippin, tracery, tree***; made or manufactured in Kent, as ***Kentish brick, cloth***, etc. **b. Kentish balsam**, Dog's Mercury, *Mercurialis perennis* (Britt. & Holl.); †**Kentish cap**, a species of paper (see quot.); **Kentish cousins**, distant relatives; **Kentish crow**, one of the many names of the hooded crow, *Corvus cornix*; **Kentish fire**, a prolonged and ordered salvo or volley of applause, or demonstration of impatience or dissent (said to have originated in reference to meetings held in Kent in 1828–9, in opposition to the Catholic Relief Bill: see N. & Q. series 2, I. 182, 423; VIII. 278); **Kentish glory**, a large beautiful moth, *Endromis versicolor*; †**Kentish Knocker** [f. *Kentish Knock* the sand-bank before the mouth of the Thames], a Kentish smuggler; **Kentish long-tails**, a phrase embodying the old belief that the natives of Kent had tails; also, the Bearded Wild Oat-grass, *Avena fatua* (E.D.D.); **Kentish nightingale**, the blackcap; **Kentish plover**, a ring-plover, *Ægialitis cantianus*, in Britain chiefly confined to Kent; **Kentish rag**, a hard compact limestone found in Kent, used for paving and building; **Kentish tern**, the Sandwich tern, *Sterna cantiaca*.

1703 Moxon *Mech. Exerc.* 239 Plain Work is done with the Grey *Kentish Bricks. **1766** C. Leadbetter *Royal Gauger* ii. xiv. (ed. 6) 372 Names of Paper: *Kentish Cap. Dimensions of each Sheet—Length 21½ Bread. 18. **1566** *Act 8 Eliz.* c. 6 §2 Anye Clothe commonly called *Kentyshe Clothe or Suffolke Clothe. **1803** J. Abercrombie *Ev. Man his own Gard.* 671/1 Apples,..Holland Pippin, Kentish pippin, *Kentish codlin. *a* **1796** Pegge *Kenticisms, Proverbs* (E.D.S.), *Kentish Cousins. The sense of this is much the same with that [of]..cousins germans quite remov'd. **1893** P. H. Emerson *Lagoons* (1896) 156 (E.D.D.) We saw a hawk chasing a *Kentish crow. **1834** Ld. Winchelsea *Sp.* at Dublin, 15 Aug. (Reddall *Fact, Fancy & Fable*, 1889, 301) Let it be given with *Kentish Fire. **1883** Chamberlain *Sp. at B'ham* 30 Mar., The cheers..are your prompt reply to the Kentish-fire with which Birmingham Tories are wont to solace themselves. **1775** M. Harris *Eng. Lepidoptera* 27 (*heading*) *Glory, Kentish. **1869** E. Newman *Illustr. Nat. Hist. Brit. Moths* 47 The Kentish Glory.—Fore wings of the male brown; hind wings orange-colour: all the wings of the female alike, pale smoky-brown. **1899** D. Sharp *Cambr. Nat. Hist.* VI. vi. 406 The 'Kentish glory', *Endromis versicolor*,..is a large and strong moth, and flies wildly in the daytime in birch-woods. **1971** *Times* 28 Jan. 12/6 The birch which provides the last English home of the Kentish glory moth. **1891** W. C. Sydney *Eng. in 18th C.* I. 358 Gangs of forty or fifty '*Kentish Knockers', as these smugglers were called. **1844** *Zoologist* II. 620 Blackcap... It is frequently called the '*Kentish nightingale', which epithet it deserves. **1837** Gould *Birds Europe* IV. pl. 40 The habits of the *Kentish Plover are similar to those of the Ring Dottrel. **1893** Newton *Dict. Birds* 341 The Kentish Plover..has its breeding place in Britain limited to the pebbly beach between Sandwich and Hastings. **1769** *De Foe's Tour Gt. Brit.* I. 158 From the Weald of Kent..they bring..A Kind of Paving Stone, called *Kentish-rags. **1879** Rutley *Study Rocks* iii. 20 Some..as the Kentish rag, afford good building stones. **1720** Gay *Poems* (1745) II. 100 Thy trembling lip..Red as the cherry from the *Kentish tree.

Hence '**Kentishly** *adv.*, in the Kentish manner.

1588 W. Kempe *Educ. Childr.* C iv, Yea, in one house, we heare one speake Northernly, another Westernly, another Kentishly.

kentle, obs. form of quintal.

kentledge ('kɛntlɪdʒ). *Naut.* Forms: 7 **kintledge**, **kinttlidge**, 7–8 **kintlage**, 8 **kent(i)lage**, 9 **kentledge**. [Of obsure origin. ?f. *kentle, kental, kintal*, quintal + -age; cf. *dunnage*.]

Pig-iron used as permanent ballast, usually laid upon the kelson-plates. Also *attrib.*

1607 Keeling in Purchas *Pilgrims* (1625) iii. vi. §2. 191 Our too great quantitie of kintledge goods, maketh our ship to labour marvellously. **1626** Capt. Smith *Accid. Yng. Seamen* 13 Ballast, kintlage, canting coynes. **1722** *Lond. Gaz.* No. 6116/2 The Iron Kentilage from aboard the Carnarvon. **1860** H. Gouger *Imprisonm. Burmah* x. 111 Logs of pure silver, shaped like pieces of ship's kentledge, but..wanting the handle with which kentledge is furnished for the convenience of lifting. **1892** *Pall Mall G.* 3 Oct. 3/2 In order to give..greater stability..nearly one hundred tons of iron pigs or 'kentledge' was fitted into the open spaces along the keelson between her frames.

kentrogon ('kɛntrəgɒn). *Zool.* [ad. Fr. *kentrogone* (Y. Delage 1884, in *Arch. Zool. Expér. & Gén.* 2 Sér. II. 606), f. Gr. κέντρον sharp point + γόν-ος offspring.] A larval form of parasitic barnacles of the order Rhizocephala, in which state the barnacle first attaches itself to the host.

1909 A. Sedgwick *Student's Text-bk. Zool.* III. v. 430 At this stage the young Cirripede is known as the Kentrogon larva. **1909** W. T. Calman in E. R. Lankester *Treat. Zool.* VII. v. 134 (*caption*) *Kentrogon*-stage, after the *Cypris* shell has been cast off and the 'dart' has been formed. **1940** *Chambers's Techn. Dict.* 473/1 Kentrogon (*Zool.*). A stage in the life-history of certain parasitic *Cirripedia* (e.g. *Sacculina*) which succeeds the Cypris stage and precedes the entry of the parasite into the body of the host.

kentrolite ('kɛntrəlaɪt). *Min.* [f. (1880) Gr. κέντρο-ν sharp point + -lite.] A silicate of lead and manganese, in small sharp-pointed crystals.

1882 Dana *Min.* App. iii. 65 Websky calls attention to the fact that the angles of kentrolite agree very closely with those of descloizite.

Kentuck ('kɛntʌk), *a.* and *sb. U.S.* Also **Kaintuck**. [Abbrev. of Kentucky.] = next.

1826 T. Flint *Recoll.* 15 A 'Kentuck' is the best man at a pole. **1831** *Constellation* (N.Y.) 143/2 Placing a huge lump of his favorite 'Kentuck' [tobacco] in his mouth. **1834** W. A. Caruthers *Kentuckian in N.Y.* I. 24, I gets a quid of the real Kentuck twist into my mouth. *Ibid.* 25 When we Kentuck boys get at it, it won't all end like a log rollin'. **1842** *Amer. Phioneer* I. 157, I then entered a Kentuck boat and descended the river. **1852** B. Casseday *Hist. Louisville* ii. 69 'And you waded in like a raal Kaintuck,' rejoined Nine-Eyes. **1872** W. J. Flagg *Good Investment* 544/1 You must expect me to defend myself *Kaintuck* fashion. **1941** L. D. Baldwin *Keelboat Age* 61 The Americans..considered a 'Kentuck' best at the setting poles. **1942** in H. Wentworth *Amer. Dial. Dict.* (1944) 338/2 The Kaintucks were spared a feud with the N.Y.C. police.

Kentuckian (kɛn'tʌkɪən), *a.* and *sb. U.S.* Also 8–9 **Kentuckyan**. [f. next: see -ian.] **A.** *adj.* Of or pertaining to Kentucky. **B.** *sb.* A native or inhabitant of Kentucky.

1779 G. R. Clark *Campaign in Illinois* (1869) 85 If not deceived by the Kentuckyans, I should still be able to compleat my design. **1784** [see Indianian]. **1804** C. B. Brown tr. *Volney's View Soil & Climate U.S.A.* 71, I have observed the Kentuckian bank of the river to be formed of similar ridges. **1831** [see bead *sb.* 5 d]. **1886** F. C. Baylor *On Both Sides* 145 A handsome carriage..drawn by a beautiful pair of Kentuckian thoroughbreds. **1949** B. A. Botkin *Treas. S. Folklore* p. xix, The pioneer saga of planting colonies..and creating names, legends, and ballads in that wild and wonderful country that the first Englishmen found in Virginia, the first Virginians in Kentucky, and the first Kentuckians and Virginians in Texas. **1969** I. Kemp *Brit. G.I. in Vietnam* iii. 43 Staff Sergeant Howell was..a paunchy, cheerful, easy-going Kentuckian.

Kentucky (kɛn'tʌkɪ). Chiefly *U.S.* Also **Kentucke**. [From the name of the river; the original meaning of this is uncertain.] One of the south-eastern United States, lying south of the Ohio River and east of the Mississippi; used *attrib.* to designate things originating in, or connected with, this state.

Only a selection of collocations is given here: see D.A.E. and D.A. for fuller lists.

1785 E. Denny *Mil. Jrnl.* (1859) 57 Our fleet now consists of..batteaux, besides two large flats called Kentucky boats. **1785** [see coffee-tree 2]. **1811** A. Wilson *Amer. Ornith.* III. 85 [The] Kentucky Warbler, *Sylvia Formosa*,..inhabits the country whose name it bears. **1832** in A. Nicoll *Hist. Eng. Drama 1660–1900* (1959) VI. 487 (*title of play*) The Kentucky Rifle; or, the horse and the murderer. **1835** J. H. Ingraham *South-West* II. 175 The young Mississipian ..dresses plainly,..often in pantaloons of Kentucky jean. **1849** E. Emmons *Agric. N.Y.* II. 68 An earlier kind of grass than timothy, is the Spear grass, Meadow grass, or Kentucky blue grass. **1872** Schele de Vere *Americanisms* 416 The Coffee-tree (*Gymnocladus canadensis*), often called Kentucky Coffee-tree, or Kentucky Locust, derives its name from the fact that in the days of early settlements the seeds were frequently used as a substitute for coffee. **1875** *Courier-Jrnl.* (Louisville, Ky.) 18 May 4/3 The Kentucky Derby, a dash of 1½ miles for three-year olds. **1901** *Jrnl. Chem. Soc.* LXXIX. i. 984 Several kilograms of Western Kentucky leaf, used mainly as 'fillers'. **1943** J. S. Huxley *TVA* vi. 49 The famous Kentucky blue grass (which won't grow without plenty of phosphorus). **1962** R. B. Fuller *Epic Poem on Industrialization* 40 Lawyer vice-presidents were fast being substituted For the Kentucky colonels As executive heads of industry. **1966** [see burgoo 2]. **1968** *Canad. Antiques Collector* Aug. 11/1 Their gunsmiths developed and perfected the 'Kentucky' rifle, the accuracy and superiority of which was proven. **1972** E. Thorpe *Night I caught Santa Fé Chief* xiv. 183, I went into the drug store and ordered Kentucky fried chicken.

kentum, var. centum.

Kenya ('kɛnjə, 'kiːnjə). The name of an E. African state used *attrib.*, as **Kenya Asian** = *Kenyan Asian*; **Kenya coffee**, a mild coffee grown in Kenya.

1968 *Times* 22 Feb. 1/7 The unrestricted right of entry to Britain of some Kenya Asians must be respected, insisted Mr. Heath. *Ibid.* 1/7 Some Kenya Asians were allowed to opt for British passports. **1971** *Guardian* 27 Feb. 5/1 A Kenya-Asian teacher..said that the Walsall Education Authority refused her a job because of her accent. **1926–7** *Army & Navy Stores Catal.* 3/2 Coffee. Kenya. Roasted, whole—lb. 2/5. **1937** *Discovery* Oct. p. xciii/1 Finest Kenya Coffee. **1970** *E. Afr. Standard* 2 Jan. 5/3 In 1965 some 20,000 bags of Kenya coffee were sold locally, consumption per head being around 130 grams per year.

Kenyah ('kɛnjə). Also **Kenniah**, **Kenya**. [Native name.] A member of one of the aboriginal peoples inhabiting parts of Borneo and Sarawak.

1866 C. Brooke *Ten Yrs. Sarawak* I. ii. 73 The branches [of the Malanans] inhabiting the inland and up-rivers..are Kanowit..Kenniah, Bakatan..and numerous others. **1901** Hose & McDougall in *Jrnl. Antropol. Inst.* XXXI. 174 The Kenyahs inhabit a district far inland among the head-waters of the Baram river. *Ibid.* 175 Of the many animals that the Kenyahs dare not eat or kill..the common white-headed carrion-hawk..is by far the most important. **1911** J. G. Frazer *Golden Bough*: *Magic Art* (ed. 3) II. xxi. 385 In the interior of Borneo the Kenyahs generally place before the main entrance of their houses the wooden image of Balli Atap, that is, the Spirit or God (*Balli*) of the Roof. **1957** *Encycl. Brit.* XIII. 346/1 Kenyah economy is based on the cultivation of dry rice in jungle clearings. **1960** *Guardian* 9 Nov. 10/3 The population [of Sarawak] includes..Kelebits, Kenyas, Muruts, and others.

Kenyan ('kɛnjən, 'kiːnjən), *sb.* and *a.* [f. Keny(a + -an.] **A.** *sb.* A native or inhabitant of Kenya.

1938 T. W. Wallbank in *Jrnl. R. Afr. Soc.* Suppl. Apr. 20 Perhaps a more immediate and vital problem concerns the character of the young, native-born Kenyan. **1960** *Daily Tel.* 21 Jan. 10/3 Moderate Kenyans can regard the claims of the African group only with distrust. **1969** *Listener* 8 May 634/3 This week a number of Asian Kenyans, holders of British passports, are due to arrive in Britain without work permits. **1971** *Sunday Nation* (Nairobi) 11 Apr. 8/5 We must, as Wa Kataka says, try to encourage self-analysis as part of our national political ethic, and the best people, nay the people best qualified to do this, are Kenyans themselves. **1972** *Daily Tel.* 29 Dec. 2/8 The bank clerk, Rajendrakumar Thakrar, a Kenyan, who lived in Clovelly Road, Southampton, was said to be a 'happy man' until a month ago.

B. *adj.* Of, pertaining to, or characteristic of Kenya or its people. ***Kenyan Asian***, an Asian, esp. one from India or Pakistan, resident, or formerly resident, in Kenya.

1946 R. Capell *Simiomata* i. 14 Kenyan gossip in the Aegean. **1960** *Guardian* 22 Apr. 6/5 Ex-Mau-Mau members ..padded through the Kenyan forests. **1962** *Times* 23 Aug. 11/1 Tony, the epitome of all the New Kenyan morality must destroy. **1968** *Times* 13 Feb. 9/1 That so many Kenyan Asians are now claiming their legal right of entry to Britain is embarrassing. **1968** *Guardian* 5 Sept. 18/8 The settler farmers who opted for Kenyan citizenship. **1970** *Ibid.* 24 Mar. 11/3 Europe's airport lounges are still littered with passportless Kenyan Asians. **1972** *Ibid.* 26 June 6/5 What have Ulster Catholics, Russian Jews and Kenyan Asians in common? They are all members of underprivileged minorities.

,Kenyani'zation. [f. Kenyan *a.* + -ization.] In Kenya, the replacement of settlers and Asians by Kenyan Africans in government posts, the civil service, and other occupations. So '**Kenyanize** *v. trans.*, to make Kenyan in character, organization, etc.

1963 *Times* 17 May 13/7 Nowhere will Europeans be required more than in administration, since the pace of Africanization—or Kenyanization, to use the locally preferred term—has been until recently far too slow to produce adequate numbers of trained and experienced African civil servants. **1970** *Guardian* 25 Nov. 11/6 The Kenyanisation and Ugandanisation law. **1971** *Inside Kenya Today* Mar. 7/1 The target of Kenyanizing the top management personnel will be reached sooner than later. **1973** *Daily Tel.* 11 Jan. 1/1 Kenya is to order 418 non-citizen Asian traders to shut their businesses and quit the country by June 1 under its Kenyanisation policy.

Kenyapithecus (,kɛnjə'pɪθɪkəs). [mod.L., f. Kenya + Gr. πίθηκος ape.] A fossil hominid of the genus so called, first discovered in Kenya in 1961 by L. S. B. Leakey; sometimes included in the genus *Ramapithecus*.

[**1961** L. S. B. Leakey in *Ann. & Mag. Nat. Hist.* IV. 690 The following is a diagnosis and preliminary description of this new Kenya Lower Pliocene primate. Super-Family Hominoidea. Family Incertae sedis. Genus *Kenyapithecus* gen. nov.– The type of the genus is the new species *Kenyapithecus wickeri* described below. Species *Kenyapithecus wickeri* sp. nov.] **1963** *Times* 1 June 6/1 The pelvis of *Oreopithecus*..is probably farther removed from human ancestry than its East African contemporary, *Kenyapithecus*. **1967** *Observer* 15 Jan. 9/6 Dr. Leakey.. endeavours to show..that his *Kenyapithecus* hominids are quite distinct from the ancestors of apes living at the same time. **1971** J. Z. Young *Introd. Study Man* xxxi. 440 The fossils of *Ramapithecus* are less ape-like and more human. They were first named from specimens from the late Miocene of India, but the form known as *Kenyapithecus* from East Africa..is similar.

†**kenyon**, variant of CANION, *Obs.*
1588 *Lanc. & Chesh. Wills* III. 139 One new paire of round hose..lyned wth satten and the kenyons of tuftafita.

kenyte (ˈkɛnaɪt, ˈkiːnaɪt). *Petrogr.* [f. the name of Mount *Kenya*, Kenya: see -ITE[1].] A light red to pale brown rock consisting of olivine-bearing phonolitic trachyte.
1900 J. W. GREGORY in *Q. Jrnl. Geol. Soc.* LVI. 209 It is unadvisable to include the Mount Kenya lavas among the pantellerites, and the name of kenytes is accordingly proposed for them. **1921** H. G. PONTING *Gt. White South* xi. 103 One of the most grotesque of these shapes was a monolith of kenyte... The geologists were much interested in this curiosity, and, as kenyte lava is very brittle, exhorted all not to injure it. **1954** W. C. SMITH in *Brit. Antarctic 'Terra Nova' Expedition 1910, Nat. Hist. Rep.: Geol.* II. iii. 41 It is now known that there is an important difference between the rocks of Mount Kenya named kenyte by J. W. Gregory and the lavas of Mount Erebus to which Prior extended the name. The kenytes of Mount Kenya actually contain large insets of nepheline. **1968** *Mineral. Abstr.* XIX. 323/1 A K/Ar date determined from anorthoclase indicates an age of 0·68(±0·14) m.y. for the Antarctic kenyte of the Cape Royds area.

†**keo**, variant of KAE, CO, jackdaw, *Obs.*
c **1440** *Promp. Parv.* 272/1 Keo, or chowghe, *supra in* cadaw, *et infra in* koo, bryd, *monedula.*

‖**keora** (kiːˈɔərə). *E. Ind.* [Hindī *keorā* the plant.] In *keora oil*, an essential oil obtained from the male flowers of *Pandanus odoratissimus*; also called *ketgee oil.*
1858 SIMMONDS *Dict. Trade.*

keorfen, keorven, obs. inf. of CARVE *v.*

kep (kɛp), *v. Sc.* and *north. dial.* Also 6 kepp, 8 keap, kaip, 9 cape. [Differentiated form of KEEP *v.* (cf. s.v. senses 6, 7, 8), the short vowel of the pa. t. *kept* having been carried into the present and infinitive. In some Sc. dialects, now *cape* (keːp), with abnormal lengthening.]
1. *trans.* To meet, intercept, throw oneself in the way of (a person or thing); to stop the course of; to receive the force of (a blow); †to catch hold of.
c **1400** *Destr. Troy* 6875 Eneas to Aiax angarely rode, And he keppit hym cantly with a kene spere. *c* **1420** *Anturs of Arth.* (Douce MS.) 618 Gawayne bi þe coler keppes [*Thornton MS.* clekis] þe kniȝte. **1513** DOUGLAS *Æneis* x. xiii. 97 The bytand brand vphevyt keppit he. **1596** DALRYMPLE tr. *Leslie's Hist. Scot.* II. 165 Thay prepare.. and quiklie cumis furth to kepp the Scottis in thair cuming. *c* **1620** A. HUME *Brit. Tongue* iv. (1865) 12 Thre be, as it were, hammeres stryking, and the rest stiddies, kepping the strakes of the hammeres. *Ibid.* v. 14 Behind the voual, if a consonant kep it, we sound it alwayes as a k. **1793** T. SCOTT *Poems* 364 (E.D.D.) Whare Benlomond keps, an' cleaves the cluds. **1862** G. MACDONALD *D. Elginbrod* I. 68 (E.D.D.) I'm no gaein to kep her at ilka turn.
2. To catch, in the hands or otherwise, so as to prevent from falling; to catch (falling liquid) as in a vessel.
1500–20 DUNBAR *Poems* xiii. 30 Sum standis besyd and skaild law keppis. **1573** *Satir. Poems Reform.* xxxix. 88 Thay ..keppit standfulis [of water] at the sklatis thair in. **1637** RUTHERFORD *Lett.* (1862) I. 385, I shall be glad..to kep and receive the off-fallings..that fall from His sweet fingers. **1691** RAY *N.C. Words* 40 To kep a Ball, is to catch it; to keep it from falling. ? **17..** *Song, Lords Marie* (Jam.), The Lords Marie has kepp'd her locks Up wi' a gowden kame. **1790** BURNS *Elegy Capt. Henderson* xii, Ilk cowslip cup shall kep a tear. **1795** MACNEILL *Will & Jean* I. vii, Will..just when fa'ing, Kepp'd her on his manly breast. *a* **1802** *Lanckin* x. in Child *Ballads* IV. 332/2 A bason..To cape this ladie's blood. *a* **1856** J. BALLANTYNE *Song, 'Confide ye ay in Providence'*, Ilka blade o' grass keps its ain drap o' dew.
†**b.** *to kep skaith*, to 'catch' or receive harm.
1572 *Satir. Poems Reform.* xxxi. 14 That nane of ȝow kep ony skayth For laik of Premonitioun. **1721** RAMSAY *Fygar rub her* iv, Laying a' the wyte On you, if she kepp ony skaith.
Hence **kep** *sb.*, a catch; a haul; also in *Mining* = KEEP *sb.* 4 d; **kep-ball**: see quot. 1877.
1790 A. WILSON *Poems & Lit. Prose* (1876) II. 90 She got an honest kepp Might ser't a decent miller Sax years an' mair. **1877** *N. Linc. Gloss., Kep-ball* (1) the game of catch-ball. (2) The ball with which it is played. **1893** *Northumbld. Gloss., Keps*, the catches or rests at the top of a pit-shaft on which the cage is caught... This word is often written *keeps*, but its spoken form is *keps. Mod. Sc.* Gie's a kep! [i.e. a catch of a ball]. A clever kep.

kep, obs. f. KEEP *sb.* and *v.*

kepe, var. KIPE, basket.

kephalic, -al, var. CEPHALIC, -AL.

kephalin (ˈkɛfəlɪn). *Chem.* [f. Gr. κεφαλή head + -IN[1].] Thudichum's term for a substance obtained from brain matter. Now usu. spelt *cephalin* (see CEPHALIN[2]). So **kepha'loidin.**
1878 KINGZETT *Anim. Chem.* 290 Kephaline may be purified to some extent by its repeated solution in ether. *Ibid.* 294 To that furnished by 'buttery matter' Thudichum gives the name kephaloidine.

kephalo- (ˈkɛfələʊ), var. form of CEPHALO-, combining f. Gr. κεφαλή head, preferred by some, as in *kephalograph, kephalometer, kephalotomy*, etc.
1802 *Gentl. Mag.* July 602 The ingenious contrivance of the Kephalometer, or head-measurer. **1876** *S. Kens. Mus. Catal.* No. 3731 Kephalograph. **1890** *Sat. Rev.* 15 Feb. 186/2 The violent kephalotomic method for the abatement of party spirit proposed by Swift.

kephir, variant of KEFIR.

‖**kepi** (ˈkepi). Also **képi.** [Fr. *képi* (1809 in Hatz.-Darm.), a. Ger. Swiss *käppi*, dim. of *kappe* a cap.] A French military cap, slightly tapering, with a flat top which slopes towards the front, and a horizonal peak.
1861 W. H. RUSSELL in *Times* 14 May, The head-dress is generally..a smart cap like the French kepi. **1883** DE MILLE *Castle in Spain* lvi, She wore..an officer's 'kepi'.

Kepler (ˈkɛplə(r)). The name of Johann *Kepler* (1571–1630), German astronomer, used, chiefly in the possessive, to designate things and concepts discovered or investigated by him, as **Kepler's equation**, the equation $\theta = \phi - e \sin \phi$ relating the mean anomaly θ of a planet to the eccentric anomaly ϕ and the eccentricity e of the orbit; **Kepler's laws** (see LAW *sb.*[1] 17 c (*a*)); **Kepler's nova** or **star**, a supernova which appeared in 1604 in the constellation Ophiuchus and disappeared in 1606; **Kepler('s) problem**, the problem of solving Kepler's equation for the eccentric anomaly of a planet in a known orbit given the mean anomaly, which is effectively that of finding the position of the planet at any given time.
[**1714** *Phil. Trans. R. Soc.* XXVIII. 1 (*heading*) Problematis Kepleriani, de inveniendo vero motu planetarum, areas tempori proportionales in orbibus ellipticis circa focorum alterum describentium, solutio Newtoniana.] **1721** J. KEILL *Introd. Astron.* xxiii. 287 (*heading*) Kepler's problem. **1883** *Encycl. Brit.* XV. 709/1 By far the most important problem is to find the values of θ and r as functions of t, so that the direction and length of a planet's radius-vector may be determined for any given time. This generally goes by the name of Kepler's Problem. **1890** A. M. CLERKE *Syst. Stars* vii. 97, 1604, Kepler's star. **1902** F. R. MOULTON *Introd. Celestial Mech.* v. 148 (*heading*) Geometrical derivation of Kepler's equation. **1954** C. PAYNE-GAPOSCHKIN *Introd. Astron.* (1956) xiv. 392 Attempts to identify the remains of Tycho's and Kepler's novae with stars have failed. **1958** CONDON & ODISHAW *Handbk. Physics* II. iv. 32/2 Kepler's equation defines ϕ as a function of nt.., which functional relation is the subject of a large mathematical literature. **1964** *Yearbook Astron. 1965* 49 The most brilliant 'new star' of which we have an accurate record was Tycho's Star of 1572, which was, of course, a supernova, and which became equal to Venus... Its only subsequent rival has been Kepler's Star of 1604, which also seems to have been a supernova. **1970** G. K. WOODGATE *Elem. Atomic Struct.* ii. 28 This is called an accidental degeneracy. It occurs likewise in the equivalent classical problem—the Kepler problem of planetary motion under an inverse square law of force.

Keplerian (kɛˈplɪərɪən), *a.* [f. prec. + -IAN.] Of or pertaining to Kepler or his discoveries and investigations; applied *spec.* to (*a*) motion, orbits, and trajectories such as occur when one body moves freely in the gravitational field of another (much more massive) body, viz. an ellipse (in accordance with Kepler's laws) or some other conic section; (*b*) a refracting telescope that has a positive objective and a positive eyepiece and gives an inverted image.
1851 MILL *Logic* (ed. 3) I. III. ii. 313 If the Keplerian operation, as a logical process, be really identical with what takes place in acknowledged induction, the definition of induction ought to be so widened as to take it in. **1909** WEBSTER, Keplerian telescope. **1922** A. D. UDDEN tr. *Bohr's Theory of Spectra* ii. 37 The orbit of the electron deviates a little from a simple ellipse and is no longer exactly periodic. This deviation from a Keplerian motion is, however, very small compared with the perturbations due to the presence of external forces. **1935** E. A. MILNE *Relativity, Gravitation & World-Struct.* xiv. 267 Newton..determined the nature of the possible motions of the particle and showed that it consisted of Keplerian orbits, or parabolas or hyperbolas with Keplerian properties. *Ibid.*, Newton's solution of the Keplerian problem. **1958** *Listener* 20 Nov. 839/1 The Keplerian universe, which did away with the epicycles, was systematically ignored by Galileo. **1959** K. A. EHRICKE in H. S. Seifert *Space Technol.* viii. 92 Figure 8–50 presents a survey of possible Keplerian (in distinction to powered) mission profiles for the inner and outer solar system. **1966** *McGraw-Hill Encycl. Sci. & Technol.* VII. 452/2 If the second lens has a positive power, the telescope is called a.. Keplerian telescope and the separation of the two parts is equal to the sum of the focal lengths. **1966** *Daily Tel.* 31 Oct. 9/8 True weightlessness..can best be simulated in an aircraft flying in a so-called Keplerian trajectory. **1968** R. A. LYTTLETON *Mysteries Solar Syst.* iv. 124 It is to be remembered that in computing an orbit, the aim is to obtain a Keplerian path about the sun—an ellipse, parabola, or hyperbola—that fits the observation.

keppe, obs. form of CAP *sb.*[1]

†**kepper.** *Obs. rare*⁻¹. [? f. KEP *v.* + -ER[1].] A device for catching fish.
1558 *Act 1 Eliz.* c. 17 §1 No person..withe any..Butt Tayning Kepper Lyme Crele..shall take..Spawne or Frye of Eeles Salmon Pyke or Pyckerell.

kepper, obs. form of KIPPER *sb.*[1] and *a.*

kepstone, obs. Sc. form of COPESTONE.

kept (kɛpt), *ppl. a.* [f. KEEP *v.*] In various senses derived from KEEP *v.*; *spec.*
1. a. Maintained or supported by a paramour. Also of a man or boy maintained or supported in a homosexual relationship.
1678 DRYDEN *Limberham* I. i, A kept mistress too! my bowels yearn to her already. **1741** tr. *D'Argens' Chinese Lett.* xxii. 152 Some..have Houses of their own, as do most of the Kept-Misses at Paris. **1747** WESLEY *Jrnl.* 22 Nov., About six years ago, she was without God in the world, being a kept mistress. **1897** *Allbutt's Syst. Med.* IV. 363 A kept woman ..having been deserted by her protector, took to furious drinking. **1963** *Economist* 27 Apr. 304/1 The complete failure to translate his off-beat characteristics into homosexual or kept-man terms. **1966** 'R. STANDISH' *Widow Hack* xi. 121 The appalling indignities endured by kept men pass belief. **1969** *Jeremy* I. III. 25/1 At the upper-end of the scene is the kept-boy who has little or nothing in common with the humbler 'rent-boy'.
b. Financially supported by, and in consequence under the private control of, interested persons.
1888 *Pall Mall G.* 29 Sept. 7/2 Mr. Chamberlain, speaking at Nottingham, is reported to have said, '..The Irish party is a kept party'. **1900** *Daily News* 23 Feb. 6/4 The confederacy of international financiers working through a kept Press.
2. Maintained in ordinary or good condition.
1856 OLMSTED *Slave States* 6 The kept grounds are very limited, and in simple but quiet taste. **1897** MARY KINGSLEY *W. Africa* 67 Every village having a kept piece of ground outside it which is the dancing place for the village.

†**ker, kerre**, obs. ff. CARR[2], wet marsh, fen.

ker, kerr, variant of CAR *a.*, left.

ker-. *U.S. vulgar.* Also occasionally **ke-, ca-, ka-, che-, co-.** The first element in numerous onomatopœic or echoic formations intended to imitate the sound or the effect of the fall of some heavy body, as ***kerchunk, -flop, -plunk, -slam, -slap, -slash, -souse, -swash, -swosh, -thump, -whop***, etc.
1836 *Public Ledger* (Philadelphia) 27 July (Th.), Down I came chewallop..and overset the chair. **1843** *Major Jones's Courtship* i. (Farmer), Kerslash! I went rite over Miss Stallinses spinnin' wheel onto the floor. *Ibid.* (Bartlett), Kerslosh he went into a tub of water. **1844** 'J. SLICK' *High Life N.Y.* II. 88 We drew up co-wallop right afore Jase's house. *Ibid.* 154 Ca-smash went the chair. **1850** *Americans at Home* I. (Bartlett), The dugout hadn't leaped more'n six lengths from the bank, afore..ke-souse I went. **1854** M. J. HOLMES *Tempest & Sunshine* 2 Then, again, you'll go in co-slush. **1855** *Spirit of Times* 29 Sept. 387/1 And the fust thing you knows he falls and down he comes kerflumix. **1858** S. P. AVERY *Harp of Thousand Strings* 44 He fell 'kerslap' upon the hot goose of the pressman! **1875** *My Opin. & Betsey Bobbet's* 99, I fell kerslap over a rail that lay in the grass. **1884** 'MARK TWAIN' *Huck. Finn* xxiii. 234 Jes' den, 'long come de wind en slam it to, behine de chile, ker-*blam!* **1885** J. RUNCIMAN *Skippers & Shellbacks* 85 They hoists him over and lets him go ker-whop. **1897** *Outing* (U.S.) XXX. 127/2 Across the lower end of the swamp..back we go kerslosh-kersplash for another quarter of a mile. **1899** F. T. BULLEN *Way Navy* 52 Down came the bunch of sacks kerslam on the deck below. **1903** *Outing* XLIII. 83/1 The sound made by the water when the frog dives, we used to express when we were boys, by the word 'kerplunk'. **1908** *Magnet* I. 1, 'Ker-woosh!' ejaculated the junior, as he sprawled on the floor over Harry Wharton's legs. 'What's that in the way?' **1923** *Public Opinion* 15 June 565/1 With both feet set down kerplunk he closed the interview. **1926** F. M. FORD *Man could stand Up* II. iv. 164 Kerumph—the wagons of coal would fly over until we recalled our planes. **1935** H. G. WELLS *Things to Come* xi. 96 Can I go when I grow up? And see the other side of the moon! And plump back *ker-splosh*! into the sea! **1937** *New Masses* 26 Oct. 18/1 Their [*sc.* Hollywood journalists'] vernacular divides the failures into three subdivisions: flop, flopperoo, and ker-plunk. **1939** T. S. ELIOT *Old Possum's Pract. Cats* 17 Growltiger to his vast surprise was forced to walk the plank. He who a hundred victims had driven to that drop, At the end of all his crimes was forced to go ker-flip, ker-flop. **1939** J. CARY *Mr. Johnson* 41, I go trow him..In de river Thames, kersplash. **1942** Z. N. HURSTON in A. Dundes *Mother Wit* (1973) 26/2 Ker-blam-er-lam-er-lam! And dat was de last of Brer Engine-driving Monk. **1959** M. GILBERT *Blood & Judgment* vi. 59 The boat hit the surface with a solid ker-splash. **1963** *Punch* 30 Jan. 178/2 The boot..kerplonked to the carpet as straight and true as Newton's apple. **1963** *New Yorker* 29 June 26 That's why I nearly went kerplunk when you walked out of here with him. **1970** *Observer* (Colour Suppl.) 15 Feb. 36/4 They wear..extraordinary bathing costumes with Mighty Mouse zigzags across their chests, so that one half-expects them to rush about the beach shouting 'Pow!' and 'Zap!' and 'Kerrump!'

kera, var. KRA.

kera- (ˈkɛrə), from Gr. κέρας horn, occas. used in combination in place of KERATO-, as **keracele** (ˈkɛrəsiːl), [Gr. κήλη tumour], a horny tumour of the external surface of the hoof of the horse (*Syd. Soc. Lex.* 1887). **'keralite** [-LITE], hornstone. **kera'phyllite** [Gr. φύλλον leaf], a variety of hornblende (Watts *Dict. Chem.* 1865–72). **kera'phyllous** *a. Med.*, consisting of horny laminae (*Syd. Soc. Lex.*) **'keratome** = *keratotome*: see KERATO-; hence **ke'ratomy**, keratotomy.

1811 PINKERTON *Petral.* II. 51 Keralite, with Chlorite... This combination often forms the green keralite. **1874** LAWSON *Dis. Eye* 160 Having made the section.. either with a large keratome or with Graefe's cataract knife.

keramat, var. KRAMAT.

keramic, -ist, variants of CERAMIC, -IST.

kerargyrite, variant of CERARGYRITE.

1865-72 WATTS *Dict. Chem.* V. 295 The protochloride [of silver].. occurs native as *horn-silver* or *kerargyrite*.

kerasin (ˈkɛrəsɪn). *Biochem.* Also cer-, -ine. [irreg. f. Gr. κέρας horn + -IN¹.] A cerebroside, $C_{48}H_{93}NO_8$, which gives lignoceric acid, D-galactose, and sphingosine on hydrolysis and is a white amorphous powder.

1878 Kerasine [see PHRENOSIN]. **1884** J. L. W. THUDICHUM *Treat. Chem. Constitution Brain* iv. 178 Kerasin.. is a cerebroside, namely a body which contains the sugar cerebrose, combined with at least two other radicles. **1933** CAMERON & GILMOUR *Biochem. of Med.* v. 78 In kerasin or cerasin it [*sc.* the fatty acid] is lignoceric acid, $C_{24}H_{48}O_2$. **1951** *Arch. Path.* LI. 338 A lipoprotein fraction containing 62 per cent kerasin has been isolated from two spleens removed surgically from patients with Gaucher's disease.

ˈkerasine, *a.* [Improperly f. Gr. κέρας horn + -INE; cf. Gr. κεράτινος.] 'Resembling horn, horny, corneous' (Webster, 1864).

kerasite, variant of CERASITE.

† **ˈkerate.** *Min. Obs.* [Improperly f. Gr. κέρ-ας horn + -ATE¹.] A synonym of CERARGYRITE.

1846 in WORCESTER. **1852** PHILLIPS *Min.* 613.

keratectomy: see KERATO-.

keratin (ˈkɛrətɪn). [f. Gr. κέρας, κερατ- horn + -IN¹.] An organic substance found in horn.

1847-9 TODD *Cycl. Anat.* IV. 169/1 The form in which protein exists in hair, horn, nails, and the epidermis, and called by Simon *keratine*, has been but imperfectly examined. **1873** RALFE *Phys. Chem.* 43 *Keratin*.. obtained by treating pounded horny matter.. with boiling alcohol and ether.

keratinization (ˈkɛrətɪnaɪˈzeɪʃən). [f. as next + -ATION.]

1. The change to a more horny texture of the cells of the epidermis, as they are pressed out by the growth of younger cells beneath.

1887 in *Syd. Soc. Lex.* **1891** W. A. JAMIESON *Dis. Skin* i. (ed. 3) 4 Unna regards it as connected with keratinization.

2. *Pharmacy.* The coating of pills with a horny substance, so that they may pass through the stomach without being dissolved, and act directly on the intestines (*Syd. Soc. Lex.* 1887).

keratinize (ˈkɛrətɪnaɪz), *v.* [f. Gr. κεράτιν-ος horny + -IZE.] **1.** *intr.* To grow horny.

1896 *Allbutt's Syst. Med.* I. 211 In squamous-celled carcinomata the keratinising cells themselves have been erroneously viewed as parasites. **1973** *Nature* 9 Feb. 398/1 Ambivalent cells of the vaginal squamous epithelium keratinize under oestrogenic action.

2. *trans.* To make horny, to subject to keratinization.

1909 in WEBSTER. **1924** *Q. Jrnl. Microsc. Sci.* LXIX. 33 The centre [of the tumour] is completely keratinized. **1971** J. Z. YOUNG *Introd. Study Man* xi. 146 The products of the epidermal line are ultimately keratinized.

Hence **ˈkeratinized, ˈkeratinizing** *ppl. adjs.*

1896 Keratinising [see sense 1 above]. **1904** *Trans. Ophthalm. Soc.* XXIV. 13 Meibomian secretion organisms, etc., will become adherent to the keratinised plaques. **1912** A. S. GRÜNBAUM *Essent. Morbid Histol.* ii. 11 In epithelial cancer, the result is the formation of somewhat typical cell nests, which are composed of concentric groups of keratinised cells. **1924** *Q. Jrnl. Microsc. Sci.* LXVIII. 105 Keratinized epidermis, e.g. a finger-nail, can be resolved after treatment with sulphuric acid. **1924** *Ibid.* LXIX. 49 In the keratinizing cells the volume of the cytoplasm becomes only slightly greater. **1952** *Brit. Jrnl. Dermatol.* LXIV. 424 The diagnosis of well-differentiated keratinizing squamous carcinoma. **1964** G. H. HAGGIS et al. *Introd. Molecular Biol.* i. 6 When sufficient vitamin A is present, the cells [in the tissue culture] fail to form a keratinized squamous epithelium as they usually do. **1966** *Lancet* 31 Dec. 1457/2 There is thus gradually built up a picture of increasing epidermal hyperplasia which at length becomes heaped up into a papilloma composed of the keratinising remnants of former follicles.

keratino- (ˈkɛrətɪnəʊ), used as combining form of KERATIN, as **keraˈtinocyte**, an epidermal cell which produces keratin; **keratiˈnolysis**, lysis or destruction of keratin; so **ˌkeratinoˈlytic** *a.*, bringing about keratinolysis; **ˌkeratinoˈphilic** *a. Bot.*, growing on keratinous material such as hair, feathers, etc.

1956 D. M. PILLSBURY et al. *Dermatol.* ii. 7 The epidermis .. contains two distinct cell types... The most numerous and important of these are the keratin synthesizing cells (Malpighian cells or keratinocytes) which make up 95 per cent of the epidermis. **1964** *Progress Biol. Sci. Rel. Dermatol.* II. 415 The keratinocytes are derived from the surface ectoderm. **1972** *Amer. Zoologist* XII., 35/1 Melanin pigmentation of mammalian epidermis results from the interaction of melanocytes and keratinocytes in the synthesis, transfer, transport, and ultimate disposition of melanosomes. **1956** *Experientia* XII. 309/1 Enamel minerals stimulate keratinolysis, and keratinolysis contributes to dissolution of enamel apatite. **1905** *Jrnl. Investigative Dermatol.* XLIV. 308/2 True keratinolysis is within the capability of the dermatophytes. **1952** *Mycologia* XLIV. 177 The keratinolytic power of the fungus is reduced. **1970** *Biol. Abstr.* LI. 9627/1 (*heading*) Keratinolytic and keratinophilic fungi in the immediate surroundings of cattle. **1946** J. S. KARLING in *Amer. Jrnl. Bot.* XXXIII. 751/1 Inasmuch as these species appear to be limited in occurrence and growth to tissues which contain keratin they will be described as keratinophilic chytrids. **1971** *Indian Jrnl. Med. Res.* LIX. 1699 Three hundred and thirty-one domestic animals.. were examined for the presence of dermatophytes and other keratinophilic fungi.

keˈratinous, variant of CERATINOUS, horny.

1898 MARTINDALE & WESTCOTT *Extra Pharmacopœia* (ed. 9) 296 Originating from keratinous tissue, wool fat has affinity for, and is readily absorbed by, the skin.

keratitis (kɛrəˈtaɪtɪs). *Path.* [f. Gr. κερατ- horn + -ITIS.] Inflammation of the cornea.

1858 HUTCHINSON in *Ophthalmic Hosp. Rep.* I. 229 Chronic Interstitial Keratitis. **1859** DIXON *Dis. Eye* (ed. 2) 92 True Keratitis commonly occurs in children and young persons. **1884** E. O'DONOVAN *Story of Merv* xvi. 174 Keratitis, the ophthalmic malady commonly known by the name of 'pearl'.

kerato- (ˈkɛrətəʊ), before a vowel **kerat-**, var. of CERATO-, combining form of Gr. κέρας, κερατ- horn, used in various scientific terms relating to horny substances, or to the cornea of the eye: as **keratecˈtasia** *Ophthalm.* [ECTASIA], protrusion of the cornea; **keraˈtectomy** *Surg.* [Gr. ἐκτομή cutting out], excision of part of the cornea; **keˈratic** *a. Ophthalm.*, occurring on the cornea; **ˌkeratoacanˈthoma** (pl. **-omas, -omata**) *Path.* [ACANTH(O- + -OMA], a tumour-like overgrowth of the skin, resembling a squamous carcinoma with a keratinized centre, but usually healing spontaneously; molluscum sebaceum; **ˌkeratoconjuncˈtival** *a.*, of or pertaining to the cornea and the conjunctiva, or keratoconjunctivitis; **ˌkeratoconjunctiˈvitis** *Path.*, inflammation of the cornea and conjunctiva; any disorder so characterized; **keratoˈconus** *Path.* [Gr. κῶνος cone] = conical cornea (see CORNEA); **keratoˈcricoid** *Anat.* [CRICOID] *a.*, relating to the cornua of the cricoid cartilage; also as *sb.*, a short slender muscle arising from the cricoid cartilage (Stormonth *Man. Scient. Terms* 1879); **keratoˈderma, -ia** *Med.*, a local or general thickening of the horny layer of the epidermis; **keratoˈgenic, keraˈtogenous** *adjs.*, producing, or promoting the production of, keratinous material; **keratoˈglobus** *Path.* [L. *globus*], a spherical bulging of the cornea; hydrophthalmia (*Syd. Soc. Lex.* 1887); **keratoˈhyalin(e** *Biochem.* [ad. G. *keratohyalin* (W. Waldeyer in *Beiträge zur Anat. und Embryol. als Festgabe Jacob Henle* (1882) 149], the substance which makes up the granules in the granular layer of the epidermis; **ˌkerato-iˈritis** *Path.* [IRITIS], combined inflammation of the iris and cornea; interstitial keratitis; **keraˈtoma** *Path.* [-OMA], a hard patch of thickened epidermis, due either to hypertrophy of the horny layer or to friction or pressure; a callus; **keratomaˈlacia** *Path.* [MALACIA], a disorder in which the cornea becomes soft and opaque, associated with vitamin A deficiency; **keraˈtometer** *Ophthalm.*, an instrument for measuring the radii of curvature of the front surface of the cornea by observing images reflected in it; an ophthalmometer; so **keratoˈmetric** *a.*, obtained by using a keratometer; **keraˈtometry**, measurement of the radii of curvature of the cornea; **ˌkeratomyˈcosis** *Path.*, fungal infection of the cornea; **keratoˈnyxis** *Surg.* [Gr. νύξις pricking], a method of operating for cataract; **keraˈtopathy** *Ophthalm.* [-PATHY], any of various disorders of the cornea; † **ˈkeratophyte** *Zool.* [Gr. φυτόν plant], a coral polyp with a horny axis; **keratoˈplastic** *a.*, promoting keratinization, and hence restoration, of the epidermis; **keratoˈplasty** *Surg.* [ad. G. *keratoplastik* (F. Reisinger 1824, in *Baiersche Ann. f. Abhandl.*, etc., *aus d. Gebiete d. Chir.*, etc. I. 215), f. Gr. πλάσσειν to form], artificial restoration of the cornea (*Syd. Soc. Lex.*); **ˈkeratoscope** [ad. Sp. *keratoscopio* (Placido 1880, in *Periódico de Oftalm. Prát.* Sept.-Nov. 44)], an instrument for inspecting the cornea; so **keraˈtoscopy** [ad. F. *kératoscopie* (Cuignet 1873, in *Rec. d'Ophthalm.* I. 14)], inspection of the cornea; **keraˈtosis** (pl. **-oses**) *Path.* [-OSIS], (*a*) any of various disorders characterized by circumscribed hyperkeratosis; (*b*) a keratotic lesion; hence **keraˈtotic** *a.*, of or pertaining to keratosis; **ˈkeratotome** *Surg.* [Gr. -τόμος cutting], a knife with triangular blade used for making incisions in the cornea (Mayne *Expos. Lex.* 1855); **keraˈtotomy** *Surg.*, incision of the cornea.

1887 *Syd. Soc. Lex.*, *Keratectasia. **1904** L. W. FOX *Dis. Eye* vi. 172 *Keratectasia.* The term applied to the undue protrusion of an opaque cornea as the result of some inflammatory condition. **1918** J. H. PARSONS *Dis. Eye* (ed. 3) xi. 198 As the cicatrix becomes consolidated the bulging may disappear, or it may remain permanently as an ectatic cicatrix (keratectasia from ulcer). **1972** *Biol. Abstr.* LIV. 6213/2 Differential diagnosis is discussed for keratoconus, keratectasia,.. and corneal transplant marginal degeneration. **1871** W. S. WATSON in *Lancet* 8 July, On a new operation '*Keratectomy'. **1907** J. H. PARSONS *Dis. Eye* xiii. 301 The *keratic precipitates.. consist of leucocytes which are deposited from the aqueous upon the back of the cornea and stick there. **1955** P. D. TREVOR-ROPER *Ophthalm.* xxiii. 415 The endothelial cells become distended and tacky, so that any corpuscles that have been exuded into the aqueous from the iris and ciliary vessels are liable to adhere, forming keratic precipitates. **1950** A. ROOK in *Proc. R. Soc. Med.* XLIII. 839 MacCormac and Scarff (1936, *Brit. J. Derm.*, 48, 624), in the first published account of the condition, proposed to name it molluscum sebaceum, but as this term has been employed as synonymous with molluscum contagiosum, we prefer the name *kerato-acanthoma which was suggested some years ago by Dr. Freudenthal. **1950** *Q. Cumulative Index Medicus* XLVIII. 1201/2 Kerato-acanthoma (molluscum sebaceum). **1952** *Brit. Jrnl. Dermatol.* LXIV. 425, I wonder if Dr. Ferguson Smith's cases of multiple self-healing epitheliomata.. are really very different from these kerato-acanthomata. **1954** *Jrnl. Amer. Med. Assoc.* 5 June 562/2 Keratoacanthoma enlarges rapidly to maximum size (1 to 2 cm.) in four to eight weeks. **1972** *Cancer* XXIX. 1387 Histopathologic study of 108 keratoacanthomas and 14 squamous cell carcinomas failed to reveal any consistent single feature allowing for their distinction. **1941** *Amer. Jrnl. Ophthalm.* XXIV. 900 (*heading*) *Kerato-conjunctival lesions observed at high altitudes in Bolivia. **1965** *Biol. Abstr.* XLVI. 4694/1 Diagnostic value of the keratoconjunctival test in dysentery. **1887** *Syd. Soc. Lex.*, *Keratoconjunctivitis. **1892** *Arch. Ophthalm.* XXI. 445 On kerato-conjunctivitis of rhino-pharyngeal origin. **1954** S. DUKE-ELDER *Parsons' Dis. Eye* (ed. 12) xxxiii. 554 Kerato-conjunctivitis sicca (Sjögren's syndrome), a general systemic disturbance of unknown origin usually occurring in women after the menopause.., is characterized by deficiency of the lacrimal secretion leading to dryness of the eyes. **1960** *Jrnl. Infectious Dis.* CVI. 162/1 Keratoconjunctivitis in sheep of an infectious character is prevalent in many sheep-breeding districts in Norway. **1972** *Biol. Abstr.* LIV. 325/2 An outbreak suspected to be infectious bovine keratoconjunctivitis in Zebu cattle was reported in Khartoum, Sudan. **1859** DIXON *Dis. Eye* (ed. 2) 85 Conical Cornea.. has also received various other names, as *Hyperkeratosis*,.. **Keratoconus*, &c. **1879** *St. George's Hosp. Rep.* IX. 511 Imperfect optical iridectomy by Mr. Carter's method.. for Keratoconus. **1933** *Arch. Dermatol. & Syphilol.* XXVII. 87 In man a diffuse *keratoderma is the result of a different mutation than that causing papular keratoderma. **1967** H. MONTGOMERY *Dermatopath.* I. v. 68/2 Recently a 34-year-old woman was seen who had had diffuse keratoderma of the palms and soles all of her life. **1972** C. B. S. SCHOFIELD *Sexually Transmitted Dis.* xvi. 183 Skin lesions.. are found in about 10 per cent of patients with Reiter's disease... These fully developed lesions are known as keratoderma blenorrhagica, and histologically are indistinguishable from pustular psoriasis. **1902** H. W. STELWAGON *Treat. Dis. Skin* iv. 502 Besnier divides the cases into four classes:.. (2) the symmetric *keratodermia developing in childhood, of an erythematous and irritable character..; (3) symmetric keratodermia, especially of the feet, developing primarily in isolate foci..; (4) accidental keratodermias. **1970** *Dermatologica* CXLI. 321 Localized congenital erythrokeratodermias are a separate entity of keratodermias among erythrodermias and hyperkeratoses. **1923** *Keratogenic [see ENCEPHALITOGENIC *a.*]. **1959** *Science* 26 June 1744/2 The presence of CO_2 at concentrations higher than atmospheric concentrations restricts the ability of the chorion to undergo keratogenic changes. **1971** *Dermatologica* CXLII. 14 The follicular-keratogenic properties of several fatty acids were investigated. **1887** *Syd. Soc. Lex.*, *Keratogenous. **1907** *Practitioner* Dec. 849 The keratogenous and analgesic properties of picric acid, as exhibited in the treatment of burns. **1951** *Ann. N.Y. Acad. Sci.* LIII. 474 In the hair, the fibrils.. are most pronounced in the keratogenous zone. **1962** *Jrnl. Investigative Dermatol.* XXXVIII. 237/1 Keratohyalin granules occur in abundance in epidermal cells located next to the keratogenous zone. **1887** *Syd. Soc. Lex.*, *Keratohyaline. **1889** *Brit. Jrnl. Dermatol.* I. 235 Waldeyer held that they [*sc.* granules] were composed of a solid hyalin-like substance, which he called Keratohyalin. **1937** E. WOLFF *Dis. Eye* i. 13 In the cells of the deeper layers are found numerous granules of keratohyaline. **1972** *Biochim. & Biophys. Acta* CCLXI. 416 The three most common amino acid residues in the keratohyalin material.. are glutamic acid, glycine and alanine. **1842** DUNGLISON *Med. Lex.* (ed. 3) **Kerato-iritis*, Aquo-Membranitis. **1879** P. SMITH *Glaucoma* 23, I believe the disease first becomes a 'kerato-iritis'. **1887** *Syd. Soc. Lex.*, *Keratoma. **1902** H. W. STELWAGON *Treat. Dis. Skin* iv. 498 Callositas. Synonyms—Tyloma; Tylosis; Keratoma; Callus. **1931** L. MCCARTHY *Histopath. Skin Dis.* ix. 438 Keratoma senilis is one of the factors that make up the clinical condition known as old-age atrophy of the skin. **1972** *Biol. Abstr.* LIV. 374/1 (*heading*) A case of senile keratoma on the eyelid. **1876** DUNGLISON *Dict. Med. Sci.* (rev. ed.) 565/1 *Keratomalacia. **1886** C. M. CULVER tr. *Landolt's Refraction & Accommodation of Eye* v. 413 Certain affections of the cornea, as keratomalacia, or central corneal ulcers, may bring about a notable flattening of this membrane. **1920** *Biochem. Jrnl.* XIV. 519 The histological and bacteriological evidence shows that keratomalacia among rats consists in a breakdown of the corneal tissue, caused by bacterial invasion. **1969** *New Scientist* 30 Jan. 227/1 Keratomalacia, scurvy and beriberi are also frequent aftermaths of infection in people living on diets deficient in vitamin A, ascorbic acid, and thiamine respectively. **1886** C. M. CULVER tr. *Landolt's Refraction & Accommodation of Eye*

iv. 330 Javal and Schiötz have adapted a similar disc to their *keratometer. **1927** *Amer. Jrnl. Ophthalm.* X. 683/2 In the measurement of irregular astigmatism in the center of the cornea, the keratometer is usually extremely valuable. **1972** STONE & PHILLIPS *Contact Lenses* iv. 105 Since the optic radii of a contact lens are similar to those of the cornea, a keratometer may be used to check them. **1885** *Arch. Ophthalm.* XIV. 175 The hyperbolic lenses..can be manufactured to order to suit each particular case from data furnished by the *keratometric measurements. **1927** *Amer. Jrnl. Ophthalm.* X. 678/1 The accuracy of a keratometric record..depends primarily on having a good modern instrument. **1973** W. G. SAMPSON in *Symposium Contact Lenses* (New Orleans Acad. Ophthalm.) ii. 22 Javal's rule was used in the past to estimate the predicted spectacle cylinder from keratometric measurements. **1891** *Ophthalmic Rev.* X. 250 (*heading*) Contributions to *keratometry. **1972** STONE & PHILLIPS *Contact Lenses* iv. 105 The central radius is determined by 'classical' keratometry. **1883** *Ophthalmic Rev.* II. 369 (*heading*) *Keratomycosis. **1951** H. L. BIRGE in A. Sorsby *Syst. Ophthalm.* ix. 305 Keratomycosis (moniliasis) is rarely seen in the cold climates, and usually follows some sort of trauma to the eye with an earthy substance. **1971** *Amer. Jrnl. Ophthalm.* LXXI. 1191/2 A fifth case of keratomycosis due to Allescheria boydii is reported. **1822-34** *Good's Study Med.* (ed. 4) III. 172 The anterior operation, invented by Buchorn, or rather by Conradé, has been named *Keratonyxis. **1874** LAWSON *Dis. Eye* 127 Operation by Solution—Keratonyxis—consists in breaking-up with a fine needle the central portion of the capsule of the lens. **1948** D. G. COGAN et al. in *Arch. Ophthalm.* XL. 625 The corneal changes are those generally called band keratitis, but, for obvious reasons, are more properly designated as band *keratopathy. **1958** *Circulation* XVIII. 524/2 Lipid keratopathy..consists clinically of a fatty plaque in an area of the cornea that has been previously vascularized. **1972** H. M. LEIBOWITZ in Gasset & Kaufman *Soft Contact Lenses* xxv. 202 Hydrophilic contact lenses have been found to be extremely useful in the therapy of bullous keratopathy. **1774** GOLDSM. *Nat. Hist.* VIII. 197 Corallines,..sponges, astroites, and *keratophytes. **1887** *Syd. Soc. Lex.*, *Keratoplastic. **1907** W. A. PUSEY *Princ. & Pract. Dermatol.* i. 126 The keratoplastic action that is noted from the application of various powders upon raw epithelial surfaces may be due partly to their drying action. **1951** A. GROLLMAN *Pharmacol. & Therapeutics* xxv. 522 Chrysarobin is used in skin diseases, especially in psoriasis. .. In a strength of 10 to 20 per cent it has a keratolytic action while in more dilute form (5 per cent) it exercises a keratoplastic action. **1857** DUNGLISON *Dict. Med. Sci.* (rev. ed.) 518/1 *Keratoplasty. **1888** *Arch. Ophthalm.* XVII. 524 In making his experiments on keratoplasty Wagenmann.. first took flaps from the cornea of rabbits which were left in partial communication with it. **1939** E. B. SPAETH *Princ. & Pract. Ophthalmic Surg.* xvi. 489 Circumscribed or partial penetrating keratoplasty has offered up to the present day the best permanent results. **1948** *Sci. News* VIII. 31 This problem has been resolved by keratoplasty, or corneal transplantation. **1972** *Arch. Ophthalm.* LXXXVII. 538/1 Corneas more than 50 hours old and from elderly donors are dependable for use in penetrating keratoplasties. **1886** C. M. CULVER tr. *Landolt's Refraction & Accommodation of Eye* iv. 329 This author [*sc.* Placido] uses, as a '*keratoscope', a disc of card-board, wood or zinc, 23 centimetres in diameter. On one side is drawn a series of concentric circles, alternately black and white. **1910** H. C. PARKER *Handbk. Dis. Eye* 81 The cone is observed by inspection..with an instrument known as the keratoscope. **1972** *Jrnl. Optical Soc. Amer.* LXII. 169/1 In a conventional keratoscope, light from a flat or curved target subtending about 150° at the eye is specularly reflected by the anterior surface of the cornea. **1882** C. MACNAMARA *Man. Dis. Eye* (ed. 4) ii. 40 *Keratoscopy may assist us in forming a diagnosis. **1902** E. H. LENDON *Method of Cuignet* 5 The word 'Keratoscopy' has now come..to be equivalent to 'Shadow Test'. **1972** FELDMAN & CARNEY in Gasset & Kaufman *Soft Contact Lenses* xxxiii. 269 By using photoelectric keratoscopy and lenses designed by computer to fit the measured eye, we were able to resolve these problems. **1885** *Buck's Handbk. Med. Sci.* I. 419/2 (*heading*) Laminated epithelial plugs (*Keratosis obturans*, Wreden, Burnett). **1888** *Trans. Path. Soc. London* XXXIX. 357 That the keratoses were in their turn due to arsenic no one will, I think, doubt. **1939** *Arch. Dermatol. & Syphilol.* XXXIX. 235 A unique case of tumor-like keratoses developing on the dorsum of the hands after severe sunburn is reported. **1966** WRIGHT & SYMMERS *Systemic Path.* II. xxiv. 1487/2 The type of keratosis that is caused by arsenic has a microscopical picture much less complex than that of senile and solar keratosis. **1972** *Daily Colonist* (Victoria, B.C.) 26 Jan. 2/1 These brown spots.. can be generally called senile keratoses, although they are not all of the same type. **1934** *Brit. Jrnl. Dermatol.* XLVI. 162 *Keratotic lesions..were observed with this distribution in nine of the ten cases. **1972** *Arch. Dermatol.* CV. 249/3 An 18-year-old daughter of the patient..began developing firm keratotic papules on her thighs at the age of 13. **1972** C. B. S. SCHOFIELD *Sexually Transmitted Dis.* xvi. 183 The lesions tend.., if dry, to develop keratotic crusts. **1897** *Allbutt's Syst. Med.* II. 79 Boeckmann and Kaurin have found *Keratotomy sometimes of use in saving a cornea from a growth [of leprosy] encroaching from the sclerotic.

keratode (ˈkɛrətəʊd). [ad. Gr. κερατώδης horn-like, f. κέρας, κερατ- horn.] = KERATOSE *sb.*

1872 NICHOLSON *Palæont.* 67 The ordinary sponges of commerce, in which the skeleton is composed of a horny substance called 'keratode'.

keratoid (ˈkɛrətɔɪd), *a.* [ad. Gr. κερατοειδής horn-like: see prec. and -OID.]

1. *Math.* Resembling a horn in shape. ***keratoid cusp***: a cusp at which the two branches of the curve lie on opposite sides of the common tangent; a cusp of the first species.

1873 SALMON *Higher Plane Curves* 46 These two kinds of cusps have been called keratoid and ramphoid from a fancied resemblance to the forms of a horn and a beak. **1875** TODHUNTER *Diff. Calc.* (ed. 7) xxii. §301 Cusps of the first species have been called ' keratoid cusps'.

2. Resembling horn in substance.

1885-8 FAGGE & PYE-SMITH *Princ. Med.* (ed. 2) I. 117 The analogy of keratoid carcinoma..suggests that they may be in great part made up of pre-existing tissue elements.

keratolysis (kɛrəˈtɒlɪsɪs). *Med.* [f. KERATO- + -LYSIS.] **1.** 'Auspitz's term for a diminished growth of the horny part of the epidermis' (*Syd. Soc. Lex.* 1887).

1887 in *Syd. Soc. Lex.* **1898** J. HUTCHINSON *Arch. Surg.* IX. 372 A liability to urticarious irritation in association with Keratolysis.

2. A condition in which parts of the epidermis (esp. on the palms and soles) peel off periodically.

1895 *Brit. Jrnl. Dermatol.* VII. 37 (*heading*) A case of congenital exfoliation of the skin—(keratolysis exfoliativa?). **1902** J. W. BALLANTYNE *Man. Antenatal Path. & Hygiene: Foetus* xviii. 320, I place fœtal keratolysis here among the idiopathic maladies.. simply to emphasise the fact that sometimes no such pathogenesis is possible. **1939** LEWIS & HOPPER *Introd. Med. Mycol.* ix. 102 In keratolysis exfoliativa the lesions consist of superficial scaly macules, which may coalesce and are localised to the palms and/or soles.

b. Loosening or removal of the horny layer of the epidermis through the action of chemical or mechanical agents.

1936 C. W. DODGE *Med. Mycol.* xx. 736 The infection.. extends to the thick palmar or plantar surface as a gyrate area of keratolysis. **1956** D. M. PILLSBURY et al. *Dermatol.* iv. 22 The chemical disorganization of keratin is called keratolysis. It may be brought about chiefly by two classes of chemical agents: (1) strong alkalies and (2) reducing agents. **1969** *Arch. Dermatol.* C. 10/2 Pitted keratolysis is quite common in our military patients who have spent at least several days in wet conditions.

keratolytic (kɛrətəʊˈlɪtɪk), *a.* and *sb. Med.* [f. KERATO- + -LYTIC.] **A.** *adj.* Able to destroy keratinous material, esp. the horny layer of the epidermis.

1893 P. H. PYE-SMITH *Introd. Study Dis. Skin* xi. 244 The hardened skin may be covered with salicylic acid... The best method of applying this valuable keratolytic agent is probably..as a plaister. **1917** M. B. HARTZELL *Dis. Skin* vi. 47 (*heading*) Keratolytic agents (those which soften the horny cells of the epidermis and cause its exfoliation). **1956** D. M. PILLSBURY et al. *Dermatol.* iv. 22 Common examples of this type of keratolytic agent are the thioglycate salts (reducing agents) which are the principal ingredients of home sets for the permanent (cold) waving of hair. **1961** *Sabouraudia* I. 87 Keratolytic enzymes have not yet been isolated from dermatophytes.

B. *sb.* A keratolytic agent.

1932 A. C. ROXBURGH *Common Skin Dis.* iii. 25 Keratolytics. For removal of horny thickening. **1940** BECKER & OBERMAYER *Mod. Dermatol. & Syphilol.* iv. 36/1 Resorcin. This drug is somewhat similar in action to salicylic acid, and the two are the only drugs we use as keratolytics. **1971** *Brit. Jrnl. Dermatol.* LXXXIV. 311 Keratolytics and other topical agents have proved unhelpful.

keratophyre (ˈkɛrətəfaɪə(r)). *Petrogr.* [ad. G. *keratophyr* (C. W. Gümble *Die paläolith. Eruptivgesteine des Fichtelgebirges* (1874) 44), f. KERATO-: see -PHYRE.] (See quot. 1972.)

1889 *Geol. Mag.* Feb. 71 Microscopical examination and chemical analysis show that these rocks consist, in part at least, of soda-felsites or keratophyres. The keratophyres (so named from their resemblance to hornstone) were first described by Gümbel. **1937** A. JOHANNSEN *Descr. Petrogr. Igneous Rocks* III. 49 The keratophyres are similar in appearance [to normal trachytes] but usually are much weathered and show brown or green tones. **1956** E. W. HEINRICH *Microscopic Petrogr.* iii. 51 Trachytes occur as volcanic rocks and minor hypabyssal intrusives... Albitized types (keratophyres) occur with spillites. **1972** *Gloss. Geol.* (Amer. Geol. Inst.) 385/2 *Keratophyre*, a name originally applied by Gümbel..to trachytic rocks containing highly sodic feldspars, but now more generally applied to all salic extrusive and hypabyssal rocks characterized by the presence of albite or albite-oligoclase and chlorite, epidote, and calcite, generally of secondary origin. Originally the term was restricted to lavas of pre-Tertiary age but this distinction is not recognized in current usage.

keratose (ˈkɛratəʊs), *a.* and *sb.* [f. Gr. κερατ- horn + -OSE.]

A. *adj.* Of a horny substance; applied to the texture of certain sponges.

1851-9 OWEN in *Man. Sci. Enq.* 365 They are divided.. into horny or 'keratose', flinty or 'siliceous' and limey or 'calcareous' sponges.

B. *sb.* A substance resembling horn forming part of the skeleton of certain sponges.

1865 R. PATTERSON in *Pop. Sci. Rev.* Apr. 306 In the sponges in domestic use it [the skeleton] is principally composed of a substance termed Keratose. **1877** HUXLEY *Anat. Inv. Anim.* iii. 117 A skeleton, which consists..of bands and filaments of keratose, and secondly, of silicious spicula.

Hence ˈ**keratosed** *a.*, rendered horny.

1894 *Lancet* 3 Nov. 1025 The distinguishing mark between a coccidium and an invaginated or keratosed cell.

keratosulphate (kɛrətəʊˈsʌlfeɪt). *Biochem.* Also (*U.S.*) **-sulfate.** [f. KERATO- + SULPHATE *sb.*] A mucopolysaccharide composed of galactose and sulphated acetylglucosamine units which is found in the cornea and in costal cartilage.

1953 K. MEYER et al. in *Jrnl. Biol. Chem.* CCV. 611 A polymer composed of *N*-acetylglucosamine, galactose, and sulfate in equimolar portions.., a novel type of sulfated mucopolysaccharide, we propose to name keratosulfate. **1960** G. K. SMELSER in Duke-Elder & Perkins *Transparency of Cornea* 33 Loss of metachromatic staining, following digestion of the sections with testicular hyaluronidase, suggests that keratosulphate appears late in development. **1972** *Jrnl. Pediatrics* LXXXI. 108/2 Keratosulfate was clearly visible on the chromatograms [of the urine] of three patients with Morquio's disease, whereas none of the normal subjects or patients with other mucopolysaccharidoses tested had any visible keratosulfate.

keraulophon (kɛˈrɔːləfɒn). [f. Gr. κεραύλης hornblower + φωνή voice.] A manual stop on the organ (see quot.), first used in 1843.

1876 HILES *Catech. Organ* ix. (1878) 67 *Keraulophon*, an 8 feet manual stop of metal, and of a pleasant, reedy quality of tone.

kerb (kɜːb), *sb.* Also kirb. [Variant of CURB *sb.*, used in special senses.]

1. In various uses in which *curb* is the more frequent spelling (see CURB III).

1664 [see CURB 8 b]. **1733, 1793** [see CURB 9]. **1797** *Monthly Mag.* III. 221 The skirting, or kirb, which keeps in the ground, may be cast, or framed, with the boxes. **1873** F. HALL *Mod. Eng.* p. xi, Mistaking the kerb of our own little philologic well for the far-off horizon of science.

2. a. *spec.* An edging of stone or the like, bordering a raised path, side-walk, or pavement: = CURB 12. ***on the kerb***: said of stock-exchange business done on the street-pavement, esp. after the exchange is closed for the day.

1805 *Chron.* in *Ann. Reg.* 359/2 A young man..fell down off the kirb, in Thames-street. **1851** *Illustr. Catal. Gt. Exhib.* 243 A section of a street, with improved kerb, for keeping the pavement clean. **1863** M. HOPKINS *Hawaii* 71 An ancient lava road..defined on each side with a kerb or bordering of stones. **1894** *Times* 19 Apr. 4/4 Later in the day the trading was slow, and on the Kerb cash was done at £40. 2*s.* 6*d.*

b. *Comb.*, as ***kerb-merchant***, ***-vendor***, one who sells his wares on or beside the street-kerb; ***kerb-edge***, ***-side***; ***kerb market***, ***stocks*** (see *on the kerb* in 2 a and CURB *sb.* 15); **kerb crawling** *vbl. sb.* = *gutter crawling* vbl. sb. (GUTTER *sb.*[1] 8); also as *ppl. a.*; also **kerb-crawl** *v. intr.* [as a back-formation]; **kerb-crawler**; **kerb drill**, the exercise of standing on the kerb and looking right, then left, then right again before crossing the road; **kerb service**, see *curb service* (CURB *sb.* 15); **kerb weight** (see quot. 1967).

1971 *Daily Tel.* 13 Jan. 11/1 A man who *kerb-crawls is not committing an offence. **1972** *Ibid.* 16 Oct. 3 A campaign against motorists who 'kerb crawl' in search of prostitutes. **1955** 'C. H. ROLPH' *Women of Streets* ii. 43 The solicitation of respectable women in the streets by '*kerb-crawlers'... is causing much disquiet. **1969** *Sunday Tel.* (Brisbane) 20 Apr. 3/6 Women who complain of kerb-crawlers who pester them are often hypocritical to sex. **1949** in PARTRIDGE *Dict. Slang* 1091/2 *Kerb-crawling vbl. sb. and ppl. a. **1971** *Times* 10 Aug. 2/1 The Rev. Peter Hawkins..complaining of kerb-crawling by men looking for girls. *Ibid.* 2/2 Respectable women had complained of being importuned by kerb-crawling motorists. **1948** R. BAILEY *Safety Way* iii. 17 In some schools the children practise *Kerb Drill with their teachers and learn to judge speeds. **1969** *Highway Code* 5 *Kerb drill.* Before you cross, stop at the kerb, look right, look left, look right again. **1970** R. RENDELL *Guilty Thing Surprised* ix. 105 They poured through the gates.., paying no attention to the kerb drill. **1930** D. H. LAWRENCE *Nettles* 11 Idle we stand at the *kerb-edge, Auntie, Dangling our useless hands. **1955** W. FAULKNER *Fable* 306 On through the gate into an alley, a blank wall opposite and at the kerb-edge [curb-edge, 1954 U.S. ed.] a big..car. **1905** *Daily Chron.* 28 Apr. 4/4 The *kerb market in New York reflects in a general way the tone of the stock market. **1897** *Daily News* 30 Mar. 6/4 Some *kerb merchants..were also driving a good trade in loyal buttons. **1956** P. HIGHSMITH *Blunderer* viii. 69 Walter..bought her chocolate sodas at the *kerb-service drugstore. **1905** *Daily Chron.* 11 Nov. 4/7 Fruit from the *kerbside barrow is marvellously cheap nowadays. **1923** *Daily Mail* 21 July 3 The growing tendency of motorists to avail themselves of kerb-side pumps. **1959** *Times* 8 Dec. 5/6 The all-day parker has become so accustomed to free kerbside accommodation that the very idea of having to pay a parking charge seems to him an outrage. **1969** *Daily Tel.* 19 Aug. 15/1 A kerbside cafe. **1971** SLAUGHTER & GOODMAN *Every Man should have One* ii. 18 If they succeed in looking like a model girl..it is meant as a compliment to you, not an expectation of ritzy treatment with champagne flowing and nothing less than an Aston Martin at the kerbside. **1923** *Daily Express* 30 July 2/6 *Kerb Stocks. **1894** FENN *Tiger Lily* I. 139 A silk umbrella—one of those..declared by the *kerb vendor as being better than new. **1958** *Economist* 25 Oct. (Suppl.) 10/1 With a *kerb weight of 26 cwt and 240 BHP of power from the 3.7-litre engine, the maximum speed will equal that of any four-seater car in the world, close to 150 mph. **1967** E. RUDINGER *Consumer's Car Gloss.* (ed. 2) 64 *Kerb weight*, weight of a car without occupants or luggage but with oil and water and some petrol.

kerb (kɜːb), *v.* [f. KERB *sb.* Cf. CURB *v.*[2]] *trans.* To furnish with a kerb.

1861 [see CURB *v.*[2] 3]. **1887** *Athenæum* 8 Jan. 58 The muddy streets were gravelled and kerbed.

kerbing (ˈkɜːbɪŋ), *vbl. sb.* [f. KERB *v.* + -ING[1].] **a.** The act of furnishing with a kerb. **b.** The stones collectively forming a kerb.

1869 [see CURBING *vbl. sb.*[2]]. **1884** E. O'DONOVAN *Story of Merv* xi. 124 A canal, with kerbing of brick flush with the roadway. **1885** *Law Times Rep.* LII 618/2 The requirements of the respondents as to the kerbing.

ker-blam: see KER-.

'kerb-stone. Also kirb-. [KERB *sb.*]

1. a. An edging of stone about the top of a well. **b.** One of the stones forming the kerb of a path; also, the kerb itself.

a. **1706** PHILLIPS, *Kerb-Stone*, a Stone laid round the Brim of a Well.

b. [**1795** *Statist. Acc. Scot.* XVI. 614 From 600 to 800 tons of *kerb* and carriage-way stones. *Ibid.* 628 Kirb and carriage-way stones.] **1815** W. TAYLOR in *Monthly Rev.* LXXVII. 134 He calls the edge of the foot-pavement the kerb-stone instead of curb-stone. **1830** J. W. CROKER in *C. Papers* 18 Sept. (1884), If one's foot had slipped at the edge of the kerbstone. **1882** BESANT *All Sorts* xxxv, On the kerbstone the little girls are dancing.

2. *attrib.*, as **kerb-stone broker** (*U.S.*), a broker, not a member of the stock exchange, who transacts business in the streets; **kerb-stone merchant**, a street dealer.

1860, 1886 Kerbstone-broker [see CURBSTONE]. **1896** *Daily News* 5 Aug. 3/5 Among the kerbstone brokers to-day Diamond Match were sold at 150. **1899** *Westm. Gaz.* 18 Feb. 6/1 It seems an anomaly that gentlemen of the Stock Exchange should have to sink to the level of kerbstone merchants.

†**kerch**[1], **kerche.** *Obs.* [Another form of CURCH: for vowel cf. KERCHIEF.

With ME. *keuerche, kerche* (disyllabic) cf. OF. *cuevrechié*, occas. form of *cuevrechief*, in pl. *cuevrechies*; the regular mod. repr. of this would be *kerchy*: cf. KERCHIEF 1 δ.]

= KERCHIEF 1.

c **1430** in *Pol., Rel. & L. Poems* 47 She weryd a keuerche. *c* **1430** LYDG. *Min. Poems* (Percy Soc.) 47 Upon hir hed a kerche [*v.r.* kerchef] of Valence. *c* **1440** *Generydes* 3827 With hir kerche she bekenyd hym aside. *Ibid.* 4398 Before hir eyne a kerche hanging side. **1463** *Bury Wills* (Camden) 33 A lityl grene coffre for kerchys. **1698** MARTIN *Voy. Kilda* (1749) 50 The Kerch, or Head-dress worn by herself. *a* **1800** *Sweet Willie* in Child *Ballads* (1861) II. 135 The scarlet sae red, and the kerches sae white, And your bonny locks hangin down.

Kerch[2] (kɜːtʃ). Also Kertch. The name of a town in the Crimea used *attrib.* to designate a type of ancient red-figured Greek pottery found there.

1936 G. M. A. RICHTER *Red-Figured Athenian Vases* I. vii. 213 (*heading*) Kerch style... With the Kerch period we reach the last phase of Athenian red-figured pottery. *Ibid.* 214 Kerch vases have been found at Alexandria. **1960** R. G. HAGGAR *Conc. Encycl. Cont. Pott. & Porc.* 412/2 In the Greek decadence, popular vases of so-called 'Kerch' ware, from the name of the town where they have been found, were exported to South Russia. **1965** J. V. NOBLE *Techniques Painted Attic Pott.* (1966) iii. 64 Attic chous in the Kerch style, mid fourth century B.C., in the Metropolitan Museum of Art.

'kercher. *Obs.* exc. *dial.* Forms: α. 4 kevercher, 4– kercher, (5 -ere, -yer, 6 -oer, karcher, kircher); β. 6 courcher. [ME. *curcher, kercher*, by syncope from earlier **cover-, kevercher* a. OF. *couvre-, cuevrechier* (Godef. *Compl.*), erroneous forms of *couvrechief*, etc.] = KERCHIEF.

c **1380** WYCLIF *Wks.* (1880) 65 ȝif þei ȝeuen benefis to clerkis..for palfreis or keuercheris..it is foul symonye. *c* **1450** *Cov. Myst.* v. (Shaks. Soc.) 54 With this Kerchere I kure thi face. **1483** CAXTON *Gold. Leg.* 433 b/1 Shertes, shetys and kerchyers. **1525** LD. BERNERS *Froiss.* II. xxix. 84 Oure faces wrapped in kerchers, so that we coude nat be knowen. **1571** *Wills & Inv. N.C.* (Surtees 1835) 353 A worcett kirtle, a courcher, a raile. **1573** G. HARVEY *Letter-bk.* (Camden) 12, I having..usid mi self to a hat and a karcher, culd not abide ani while to be barehed. **1649** BULWER *Pathomyot.* II. i. 88 This Muscle..Laurentius compares to a Maids Coife or Kercher. **1718** BP. HUTCHINSON *Witchcraft* 132 She..pulled off her Kercher. **1780** J. T. DILLON *Trav. Spain* 178 The women tie a kercher round their heads.

Hence **'kerchered** *a.*, covered with a kercher.

1610 G. FLETCHER *Christ's Vict.* I. xii, Pale Sicknes, with his kercher'd head up wound.

kerchief ('kɜːtʃɪf), *sb.* Forms: α. 3–4 curchef, (5 -cheff, -chyfe), 5–6 courchef(e, (6 -chief, corecheffe), 6 curtchif. β. 4–7 kerchef, (5 -cheff(e, *pl.* -cheves, 6 -chefe, -cheife), 4–6 kerchif, (5 -chife, 6–7 -chiffe, 8 -tchiff), 5– kerchief, (6 *pl.* -chievis); also 5 keercheef, kyrchef(fe, 6 kar-, car-, c(h)arschaffe. γ. 5 kerchew(e, 6 -cheu, -chow, -cho, -chu, kirchowe, -tshaw. δ. kerchy. See also KERCH, KERCHER. [ME. *curchef* and *kerchef*, syncopated forms of *coverchef* and *keverchef*, respectively a. OF. *couvrechief* and *cuevrechief*, in AF. also *courchief*: see COVERCHIEF, and, for the vowel difference, COVER *v.*[1] In northern ME. *coverchef, curchef* and CURCH were typical, while *keverchef, kerchef*, KERCHER and KERCH were (like *kever*) midland or southern. From *kerchef* came also the obs. local variants *kirchef, karchef*, while the pl. *kerchevis* app. gave rise to the forms ending in *-ew, -o(w, -u*, etc. The form *kerchy* is still used in some dialects.]

1. A cloth used to cover the head, formerly a woman's head-dress.

α. *a* **1300** *Cursor M.* 28018 (Cott.) Yee leuedis..wit curchefs crisp and bendes bright. *a* **1400–50** *Alexander* 5249 A croune & a corecheffe clustert with gemmes. *a* **1440** *Sir Degrev.* 653 Hir courchefs were curious, Hir face gay and gracyous. **1535** *Will* in *Ripon Ch. Acts* (Surtees) 359 j curtchif. **1552** CAIUS *Sweatyng Sicknes* 361 Chaucer's *couercephe*..written and pronounced comonly, *Kerchief* in yᵉ south, & *courchief* in the north.

β. **13..** *Cursor M.* 28018 (Cott. Galba) With kerchifes crisp and biletes bright. *c* **1440** *York Myst.* x. 288 Lay doune þis kyrcheffe on myn eghne. **1482** *Act 22 Edw. IV*, c. 1 They shall not suffer their wives to weare any reile called a kercheffe, whose price exceedeth twentie pence. **1584** COGAN *Haven Health* ccxli. (1636) 274 It is good also to weare a kerchiffe.. in the night on our heads. **1632** DELONEY *Thomas of Reading* in Thoms *E.E. Prose Rom.* (1858) I. 151 His Oastesse was very diligent to warme a kerchiffe and put it about his head. **1720** GAY *Poems* (1745) I. 109 Her goodly countenance..Set off with kerchief starchd and pinners clean. **1877** BRYANT *Lit. People of Snow* 99 A broad kerchief, which her Mother's hand Had closely drawn about her ruddy cheek.

γ. *c* **1440** *Generydes* 4424 Vppe he lift here kerchewe furth with all. **1482** *Croscombe Church-w. Acc.* (Som. Rec. Soc.) 10 A ryng of sylver and a kerchew. **1505** *Rep. Ambass. touching the Queen of Naples*, Clothed in black cloth, and, also in black kerchoes. **1535** COVERDALE *Ezek.* xvi. 11, I clothed the with kerchues. *c* **1540** in *Laneham's Let.* (1871) p. cxxix. *note*, Reyment off kercheus one your hed.

δ. *c* **1450** *Cov. Myst.* xxxii. (Shaks. Soc.) 318 Sche [Veronyca] whypyth his face with her kerchy... I xal them kepe from alle mysese, That lokyn on thi kerchy.

†**b.** = AMICE[1] 2. *Obs. rare.*

1552–3 *Inv. Ch. Goods Staffs.* in *Ann. Lichfield* IV. 80 One albe & karcheffe to the same..one vestement of whyte sateyn with albe & karcheffe to the same.

†**c.** A woman who wears a kerchief. *nonce-use.*

1700 DRYDEN *Fables, Wife's T.* 245 The proudest kerchief of the court shall rest Well satisfied of what they love the best [cf. CHAUCER *Wife's T.* 162].

2. A covering for the breast, neck, or shoulders; a breast-kerchief or neckerchief.

13.. *Gaw. & Gr. Knt.* 954 Kerchofes..wyth mony cler perlez Hir brest & hir bryȝt þrote bare displayed. *c* **1460** RUSSELL *Bk. Nurture* 900 On his shuldur about his nek a kercheff þere must lye. **1552** HULOET, Kerchiefe for the brest, *pectoralis fascia.* **1807–8** W. IRVING *Salmag.* (1824) 9 [If] Mrs. Oldmixon pins her kerchief a hair's-breadth awry. **1871** B. TAYLOR *Faust* (1875) I. vii. 115 Get me a kerchief from her breast.

3. A handkerchief.

1815 SOUTHEY *Roderick* XXII. 136, I ween That a thin kerchief will dry all the tears. **1821** BYRON *Two Foscari* I. i. 103 Waving kerchiefs, and applauding hands. **1847** WHEWELL tr. *Hermann und Dorothea* in *Eng. Hexam. Transl.* 66 Each one wipes his brow with his kerchief.

b. A cloth resembling a kerchief or handkerchief.

1877 J. D. CHAMBERS *Divine Worship* 273 Besides these [chalice-veils] there ought to be two other white linen kerchiefs.

4. *attrib.* and *Comb.*, as ***kerchief cloth***, † ***launder***, † ***people***, ***-taking***, ***-turban***.

1483 *Churchw. Acc. St. Mary Hill Lond.* (Nichols 1797) 97 For buryinge the Kerchiefe Launder's doghter. **1566** *Eng. Ch. Furniture* (Peacock 1866) 68 A kerchef clothe and a crosse clothe solde..by the said church wardens. **1636** DAVENANT *Platonic Lovers* v. Dram. Wks. 1872 II. 88 Many of these tiffany Young kerchief people. **1833** L. RITCHIE *Wand. by Loire* 182 Some of the women wore a kerchief-turban of the gaudiest colours. **1843** MARRYAT *M. Violet* xxvii, Kerchief-taking is a most common joke in Texas.

'kerchief, *v.* [f. prec.] *trans.* To attire or cover with a kerchief; in *pa. pple.* and *ppl. a.* **kerchiefed** ('kɜːtʃɪft).

1600 *Look About You* xxiv. in Hazl. *Dodsley* VII. 454 I'll ne'er go more untruss'd, never be kerchief'd. **1632** MILTON *Penseroso* 125 Morn..kercheft in a comely cloud. **1813** SCOTT *Trierm.* II. Interl. i, Some phantom..With limb of lath and kerchief'd chin. **1855** SINGLETON *Virgil* I. 329 Be kerchieft o'er thy tresses, muffled up In crimson hood.

†**kere**, obs. variant of *quere*, CHOIR.

c **1400** *Trevisa's Higden* (Rolls) VI. 465 Clerkes fliȝ þe travayle of þe queere [*v.r.* kere] and spended þe catel of holy cherche.

†**kere**, syncopated f. *kever*, COVER *v.*[2], to recover.

c **1475** *Anturs of Arth.* 201 (Douce MS.) If..couentes in cloistre miȝte kere..þe of care. **1515** *Scot. Field* 505 Christopher Savadge was downecaste that kere might he never!

†**kere**, variant of CAIR *v.*, *Obs.*, to go.

1515 *Scot. Field* 192 Then the mightie Lord Maxewell.. kered to his King with careful tydings.

ke'rectomy. *Surg.* [f. KER(A)- + Gr. ἐκτομή cutting out + -Y. Cf. *keratectomy.*] Excision of the outer layers of the cornea (Mayne 1855).

kerel ('kɛrəl). *S. Afr.* Also kêrel. [Afrikaans, f. Du. = CARL *sb.*[1]] A fellow, chap, young man.

1873 *Cape Monthly Mag.* Oct. 215, I have always known you to be a *slimme kerel.* **1896** H. A. BRYDEN *Tales S. Afr.* 214 *Kerel* (my boy) you have never by chance heard the story of the vrouw there and her Frenchman? **1902** J. H. M. ABBOTT *Tommy Cornstalk* 81 It is that 'kerel' French who is coming. **1939** S. CLOETE *Watch for Dawn* 41, I want no more than justice, kerels. **1974** *Cape Times* 11 Nov. 9/2 Willem Prinsloo..served his lekker peach brandy on the stoep as the kêrels gathered to bid good afternoon to the setting sun.

kereru ('kɛrəruː, ‖'kereruː). [Maori.] The New Zealand pigeon, *Hemiphaga novæseelandiæ.*

1873 W. L. BULLER *Hist. Birds N.Z.* 157 *Carpophaga Novæ Zealandiæ* (New-Zealand Pigeon)..*Native names.* Kuku, Kukupa, and Kereru. **1905, 1949** [see KUKU 1]. **1955** W. R. B. OLIVER *N.Z. Birds* (ed. 2) 440/1 New Zealand Pigeon. Kereru..was noticed and recorded by all the early explorers.

Keres ('keɪreɪs). Also Queres. [American Indian.] **a.** A Pueblo Indian people inhabiting parts of New Mexico. **b.** The language of the Keres, forming the Keresan group. Also *attrib.* or as *adj.*

1893 T. DONALDSON *Moqui Pueblo Indians* 91 The Queres group (Keresan stock) are the Pueblos of Santa Ana, San Felipe, Cochiti, San Domingo, Acoma, Zia, and Laguna. **1925** *Amer. Indian Life* 397 The Pueblo Indians..number about 10,000. They are usually classified according to language into four or five stocks, the Hopi of Arizona, the Ashiwi or people of Zuñi, the Keres of Acoma and Laguna to the west and, to the east, of five towns on the Rio Grande, and, also in the east, the Tanoans including the Tewa and the people of Jemez. **1957** *Encycl. Brit.* XVIII. 753/2 At the discovery in 1540 the Hopi, Zuñi and Keres may have been twice..as numerous as to-day. **1965** *Canad. Jrnl. Linguistics* Spring 99 Hokan-Siouan in Sapir's arrangement includes six major units... The six units are:..Keres (Powell's Keresan)..and an 'Eastern Group'.

Keresan ('kɛrəsən). [f. prec. + -AN.] A linguistic group consisting of Keres only. Also *attrib.* or as *adj.*

1893 [see KERES]. **1939** L. H. GRAY *Found. Lang.* xii. 408 In North America, twenty-five linguistic families are listed ..*Algonkin*... *Iroquois*... *Keresan* with two dialects. **1950** F. EGGAN *Social Organiz. Western Pueblos* 2 The more western Keresan-speaking villages. *Ibid.* 223 The Keresan villages of the Rio Grande. **1968** A. M. JOSEPHY *Indian Heritage Amer.* xvi. 149 Keresan-speaking people of Acoma and Laguna in western New Mexico [are] considered western Pueblos. **1969** H. E. DRIVER *Indians N. Amer.* (ed. 2) xxvii. 517 As one proceeds eastward, to Zuñi, Acoma, Laguna, and other Keresan pueblos, the system [of matriarchy] becomes more bilocal and bilateral.

kerf (kɜːf). Forms: α. 1 cyrf, 4 kyrf, 5 kirf, 6 kyrfe. β. 4–7 kerfe, (4–5 -ff(e), 4– kerf, (9 *dial.* curf, kurf). γ. See CARF. [OE. *cyrf*, app.:—**kurbi-*, f. **kurb-* (cf. ON. *kurf-r* chip, *kyrfa* to cut), ablaut-form of **kerb*, stem of OE. *ceorfan* to CARVE. Hence ME. *kirf*, giving later *kerf* and *karf*; cf. *kernel* and *carnel* from ME. *kirnel*, OE. *cyrnel*. Cf. (with different stem vowel) Du. *kerf*, Ger. *kerb, kerbe*; also ON. *kjarf*, Icel. *kerfi*, bundle (of twigs, etc.), Sw. *kärfve* sheaf.]

1. The act of cutting or carving; a cut, stroke; †power of cutting. Now *rare.*

c **1000** ÆLFRIC *Hom.* II. 406 'Ælc treow ðe ne wyrcð godne wæstm bið forcorfen...' Be ðisum cyrfe spræc se Hælend on oðre stowe. **13..** *Gaw. & Gr. Knt.* 372 'Kepe þe cosyn', quoth þe kyng, 'þat þou on kyrf sette'. **1390** GOWER *Conf.* II. 152 With sondri kerf and pourtreture Thei made of goddes the figure. **1398** TREVISA *Barth. De P.R.* XVII. clxxvii. (MS. Bodl.) lf. 234 b/1 þe kuttinge [of vines] schal be aslonte..so þat in þe oþer side afore þe knotte þe kerfe schal passe. **1892** VIZETELLY tr. *Zola's Débâcle* 289 Then, with a single kerf of the saw, he lopped them off.

†**b.** Humorous term for a company of pantry-men. *Obs.*

1486 *Bk. St. Albans* F vij, A Kerff of Panteris; a Credens of Seweris; an vnbrewyng of Kerueris. [**1678** PHILLIPS (ed. 4) App., A *Kerf* of Panthers (among some Venatory writers), is taken for a company of Panthers.]

2. The result of cutting; the incision, notch, slit, etc., made by cutting, esp. by a saw.

1523 FITZHERB. *Husb.* §136 Bycause it [a saw] is thyn, it wyll cut the narowe kyrfe. **1664** EVELYN *Sylva* (1776) 132 Cut your kerfe near to the ground, but have a care the Tree suffer not in the fall. **1792** BELKNAP *Hist. New Hampsh.* III. 156 The felling of such a tree must require much labour, since those of but one inch have eight or ten strokes, distinctly marked, and a very good kerf is allowed. **1812–16** J. SMITH *Panorama Sc. & Art* I 99 The saw, when cutting, takes away the wood at the two sides of the kerf. **1890** W. J. GORDON *Foundry* 121 A matter-of-fact place is a sawmill... Its great problem is how to minimize the 'kerf', the kerf being the track of the saw.

†**b.** *fig.* The furrow made by a ship's keel. *rare.*

c **1422** HOCCLEVE *Learn to Die* 203 As a ship þat is sayllynge..Whos kerfe nat fownden is whan past is shee.

3. The place at which a tree or branch is or has been cut across; the cut end or surface either on a felled or pruned tree.

c **1420** *Pallad. on Husb.* I. 190 Turne euery kirf aweyward from the grape; Lest droppyng do hit harm. **1664** EVELYN *Sylva* 85 A Tree..thirteen foot diameter at the Kerf, or cutting place neer the Root. *Ibid.* 92 One foot of Timber neer the Root (which is the proper kerfe, or cutting place) is worth three farther off. **1677** PLOT *Oxfordsh.* 161 The Oaks had none of them any roots, but plainly cut off at the kerf, as is used in felling Timber. **1868** BLACKLEY *Word Gossip* (1869) 161 (E.D.D.) A woodman will say that a felled tree 'measures so and so, not counting the kurf'.

4. A piece or quantity cut off; a cutting (of anything).

1678 PHILLIPS (ed. 4) App. s.v., Among Woodmen Kerf signifieth a parcel of Loppings of wood. **1730** in Swayne *Churchw. Acc. Sarum* (1896) 352 Carrying away a Kerfe of half a foot of earth. **1890** *Cent. Dict.*, *Kerf*, in a cloth-shearing machine, the wool taken off in one passage through the cutter.

5. *Comb.* as †***kerf-shears***.

1356 in Riley *Mem. London* (1868) 283 [4 small] anfeldes [for goldsmiths, and 2] kerfsheres.

Hence 'kerfed *a.*, having kerfs or slits. '**kerfing-machine**, a machine for sawing kerfs in a board (Knight *Dict. Mech.* 1875).

kerf, obs. pa. t. of CARVE *v.*

ker-flip, -flop, -flumix: see KER-.

kerfuffle (kə'fʌf(ə)l). Also **kafuffle, kufuffle,** GEFUFFLE. [Variant of the Scots CURFUFFLE *sb.* (perh. influenced by KER-?), now the general form in colloquial use.]

= CURFUFFLE *sb.*

1946 F. SARGESON *That Summer* 94, I bet it [*sc.* the domestic row] ended up in a good old kafuffle. **1959** J. FLEMING *Miss Bones* xiv. 150 The kerfuffle over the stolen jewels last week. **1960** E. W. HILDICK *Jim Starling & Colonel* viii. 62 Butcher said he didn't know what all the kerfuffle was about. **1960** A. WYKES *Snake Man* iii. 38 After this kufuffle was over and we were on our way again. **1965** *New Statesman* 30 Apr. 693/3 After..some abortive backstage kerfuffles at the National Theatre, Wedekind's *Spring Awakening* has scraped past the Lord Chamberlain. **1968** 'B. MATHER' *Springers* xii. 130 In the kerfuffle of the last half hour I had forgotten the poor soul's personal needs. **1973** K. AMIS *Riverside Villas Murder* ii. 40 A lot of our readers are going to think all this kerfuffle over an old skeleton being snatched is..a bit of a joke.

Kerguelen (kə'geɪlən, 'kɜːgələn). The name of a group of islands in the southern Indian Ocean, used *attrib.* in **Kerguelen cabbage**, a cabbage-like plant, *Pringlea antiscorbutica*, of the family Cruciferæ, which is confined to several islands in this region.

1847 J. D. HOOKER *Bot. Antarctic Voy.: Flora Antarctica* II. 240 The illustrious Cook first discovered and drew attention to the 'Kerguelen's Land cabbage' during his first voyage, when accompanied by Mr. Anderson as surgeon and naturalist. The latter gentleman drew up an account of some of the more remarkable plants which he collected there and in other islands, which are preserved in the Banksian library. *Ibid.* 241 The Kerguelen's Land cabbage, cabbage though it be, [is] a cherished object in the recollection of the mariner. **1879** H. N. MOSELEY *Notes by Naturalist on 'Challenger'* viii. 191 The feature which distinguishes the general appearance of the vegetation of Christmas Harbour ..is the presence of the Kerguelen Cabbage in large quantities. The plant grows on the slopes and bases of the cliffs in thick beds. The cabbage is in appearance like a small garden cabbage, but often with a long trailing stalk. **1952** J. A. KING in F. A. Simpson *Antarctic Today* xv. 305 The Kerguelen cabbage (*Pringlea antiscorbutica*) is not as abundant [in the Prince Edward Islands] as at Kerguelen. **1960** *Times* 20 Apr. 14/7 There are no trees or shrubs and only some 17 species of other vascular plants, the largest being the so-called Kerguelen cabbage.

‖**Keri** (kə'riː) *Heb. O.T.* Also **k'ri, qere, Qᵉre, q'ri.** [Heb., imp. of *qārā* to read.] In the Hebrew text of the O.T., the word, given in the margin, to be substituted in reading for that standing in the text (KETHIB), the latter having been retained by the Masoretes as evidenced by MSS. or tradition, though considered erroneous or unintelligible.

1644 MILTON *Areop.* (Arb.) 46 Ask a Talmudest what ails the modesty of his marginall Keri, that Moses and all the Prophets cannot persuade him to pronounce the textuall Chetiv. **1659** BP. WALTON *Consid. Considered* 112 Certain marginal notes in the Hebrew Bibles, where the Keri is the word that must be read, placed in the margin, with a ״ק: the Ketib, or word written in the text, marked with a little circle or cipher. **1881** W. R. SMITH *Old Test. in Jew. Ch.* iii. 16 These notes are called Keris, the word Keri being the imperative 'read!' The expression actually written in the text, but not uttered is called Kethîb (written). **1941** R. H. PFEIFFER *Introd. Old Testament* I. v. 93 The *kethib* (written) is the consonantal text; the *qere* (read) is an accepted reading differing from the consonantal text. *Ibid.* 95 Long after the introduction of the *qere* 'Lord' for *YHWH*..vulgar expressions in the text..were removed by substituting a euphemism in the reading (*qere*). **1958** F. KENYON *Our Bible & Anc. MSS.* (ed. 5) iv. 78 Such variations were known by the name of Qᵉre ('read') and kᵉthib ('written'), the latter being the reading of the text, and the former that of the margin, which was to be substituted for the other when the passage was read. **1968** J. BARR *Compar. Philol. & Text of Old Testament* x. 246 Here, however, there is a rather peculiar *Qere. Ibid.* 247 The translation at 1 Sam. 25. 14 makes it extremely probable that the LXX is a translation not of the present *Kethibh* at 14. 32 but of the present *Qere.* **1969** R. K. HARRISON *Introd. Old Testament* (1970) IV. ii. 213 The preferred reading was known as *Qᵉre*, meaning 'that which is to be read', as contrasted with the sacred consonantal text, the *Kᵉthîbh* or 'written' Scripture. The *Qᵉre* on occasions may have constituted a genuine variant reading.

keri(e, variants of KEIRI, KIERIE.

†**kerimery.** *Obs. rare.* Also **kermery, kyrymyry.** [a. AF. *kyrymyry, kermery.*]

? Filigree work.

1424 in Sir F. Palgrave *Antient Kal. & Invent.* (1836) II. 117 Item i hanap d ore covre del ovrage d un kyrymyry. **1437** *Ibid.* 166 Item i peire basyns d arg dorrez chacez & pounsonez..faitz de kermery. **1449** *Ibid.* 202 Item i cuppe of gold coverd of kerimery werk.

‖**kerion** ('kɪərɪən). *Path.* [a. Gr. κηρίον, lit. 'honey-comb'.] A pustular folliculitis of the scalp (Quain *Dict. Med.* 1882).

kerite ('kɪəraɪt). [f. Gr. κηρ-ός wax + -ITE¹; named by the inventor A. G. Day (1866).] A kind of artificial caoutchouc for coating telegraph wires, made with tar or asphaltum, oils and sulphur.

1875 KNIGHT *Mech. Dict.* s.v., The principal use of kerite has been as an insulating material in telegraphy.

†**kerl(e**, obs. forms of CARL *sb.*¹

c **1489** CAXTON *Blanchardyn* 173 Men sayen that 'of a kerle may nought come but poyson and fylth'. **1654** GAYTON *Pleas. Notes* III. i. 65 As the Scotch Kerle saith.

kerlew(e, obs. forms of CURLEW.

kerling, variant of *carling*, CARLINE¹.

kerloc(k, variants of CHARLOCK: cf. KEDLOCK.

a **1387** *Sinon. Barthol.* (Anecd. Oxon.) 36 *Rapistrum*, i. kerloc. **1879** BRITTEN & HOLLAND *Plant-n.*, *Kerlock* [in Gloucester, etc.].

Kerman, var. KIRMAN.

Kermanji (kə'mɑːndʒɪ). [Kurdish.] A language of the Iranian group spoken by the Kurds of Kurdistan.

1882 *Encycl. Brit.* XIV. 157/2 The present Kurdish language which is called Kermánjí..is an old Persian patois, intermixed to the north with Chaldæan words and to the south with a certain Turanian element which may not improbably have come down from Babylonian times. **1914** T. E. LAWRENCE *Home Lett.* (1954) 295 A grammar of Kermanji (Kurdish). **1959** *Chambers's Encycl.* VIII. 274/1 They [*sc.* the Kurds] speak Kermanji, derived from an old Persian dialect.

Kermanshah, var. KIRMANSHAH.

kermes ('kɜːmɪz). Forms: 6–7 **chermez**, (8 **chermes**), 7 **kermez**, (**cremes**), 7– **kermes**. See also ALKERMES. [= F. *kermès*, It. *chermes*, Sp. *carmes*, Pg. *kermes*, ad. Ar. and Pers. *qirmiz* (whence also *carmine, cramoisy, crimson*).]

1. The pregnant female of the insect *Coccus ilicis*, formerly supposed to be a berry; gathered in large quantities from a species of evergreen oak in S. Europe and N. Africa, for use in dyeing, and formerly in medicine; the red dye-stuff consisting of the dried bodies of these insects; = ALKERMES 1.

1610 W. FOLKINGHAM *Art of Survey* IV. ii. 81 Drugs, as Mechoacan, Kermez, Methium, [etc.]. **1626** BACON *Sylva* §738 The Scarlet Powder, which they call Kermez. **1741** *Compl. Fam.-Piece* I. iv. 245 To which add Juice of Chermes 1 Pound. **1774** GOLDSM. *Nat. Hist.* (1862) II. IV. vi. 551 An insect of great use in medicine, is that..known by the name of the Kermes. **1816** J. SMITH *Panorama Sc. & Art* II. 537 Kermes has not been much used since the art of brightening cochineal with tin was discovered. **1865** *Morn. Star* 5 Apr., Plants infested by the aphis grub, weevil, kermes, cochineal, or tipula.

2. The small evergreen species of oak (*Quercus coccifera*) on which this insect lives. More fully ***kermes oak.***

1598 SYLVESTER *Du Bartas* II. i. I. *Eden* 600 There grows ..the Chermez, which on each side arms, With pointed prickles, all his precious arms. **1718** OZELL tr. *Tournefort's Voy.* I. 177 The island..is fertile in fine plants, and covered with Lentisks, Kermes, and Cistus's. **1858** HOGG *Veg. Kingd.* 698 *Quercus coccifera*..is called the *Kermes Oak.*

3. Amorphous trisulphide of antimony, of a brilliant red colour. More fully ***kermes mineral.***

1753 CHAMBERS *Cycl. Supp.* s.v., The kermes mineral was a preparation of Glauber..made public in 1720. *Ibid.*, The more the kermes contains of a regulus easily revivified, the more it proves emetic. **1796** KIRWAN *Elem. Min.* (ed. 2) II. 251 Mr. Sage thinks it [Red Antimonial ore] a natural Kermes. **1831** J. DAVIES *Manual Mat. Med.* 328 When administered in the dose of a few grains, kermes acts as an emetic. **1857** SEMPLE *Diphtheria* 10 Kermes mineral.

4. *attrib.* and *Comb.*, as ***kermes-berry, grain, insect*** (= sense 1); **kermes lake** (see quot. 1850).

1671 RAY *Corr.* (1848) 46, I did not then suspect it to be anything akin to the Kermes kind. **1673** —— *Journ. Low C.* 457 As for the grains themselves they are so like the *Kermes* grains. **1676** GREW *Exper. Luctat. Menstr.* i. §15 Kermes-berries, commonly, but ignorantly, so called. **1841** *Penny Cycl.* XIX. 213/2 The Kermes insect, which yields so brilliant and permanent a blood-red dye. **1850** WEALE *Dict. Terms*, *Kermes lake*, an ancient pigment.

kermesite ('kɜːmɪzaɪt). *Min.* [Named 1832, f. KERMES + -ITE¹.] Native red antimony, a compound of the oxide and sulphide, occurring in six-sided prismatic crystals of a cherry-red colour.

1843 E. J. CHAPMAN *Min.* 61 Kermesite. Sulphuret of Oxide of Antimony. **1887** MALLET *Min. India* 62 Kermesite and cervantite are found in connection with..stibuite.

kermesse (kə'mɛs). *Cycling.* [Fr.: see KERMIS.] A circuit race.

1963 *Times* 13 June 3/5 They stopped..to put on a.. 26-mile, 10-lap kermesse (circuit race). **1965** *Times* 31 May 4/5 *Kermesse* is a Continental term which British cycling uses to describe a circuit race. It originates from Belgium and is the Flemish for the carnival which usually includes such a race. **1971** D. ARMSTRONG in N. G. Henderson *Cycling Year Bk.* xii. 101 Any rider who has ever won some little local kermesse would label it a classic event if he thought anyone would listen to him.

‖**kermis** ('kɜːmɪs). Forms: 6 **kirkemesse**, 7 **carmas, kermas, kirmish,** 7– **kermis**, 8 **kearmas**, 9 **kermess(e, kirmess(e.** [a. Du. *kermis* (earlier *ker-, kirmisse*:—orig. *kerk-, kirkmisse*), f. *kirk* KIRK + *mis* MASS: cf. MHG. *kirmesse*, G. *kirmes, kirms* (also *kirchmesse*), OFris. *tserkmisse*, ON. *kirkjumessa* (Norw. †*kjörmes, -messe*); F. *kermesse*; orig. the mass or service on the anniversary of the dedication of a church, on which also was held a yearly fair or festival. (Cf. St. Giles's Fair in Oxford.)] In the Low Countries, parts of Germany, etc.: A periodical (properly, annual) fair or carnival, characterized by much noisy merry-making. Also *U.S.* an imitation of this, usually got up for charitable purposes.

1577 HARRISON *England* II. xviii. (1877) I. 303 Albeit some of them [fairs] are not much better than the common kirkemesses beyond the sea, yet there are diuerse not inferiour to the greatest marts in Europe. **1611** L. WHITAKER in Coryat *Crambe* b ij a, Dutch *Pappigeay* and *Carmas gay* [*Margin.* A kind of drunken Dutch faire held on Sundaies and holidaies in afternoones in Sommer time]. **1641** EVELYN *Diary* 28 July, It was now Kermas, or a fair, in this town. **1695** DRYDEN *Parall. Poetry & Paint.* Wks. 1821 XVII. 305 The painting of clowns, the representation of a Dutch kermis. **1756** MRS. CALDERWOOD *Lett. & Jrnls.* (1884) 108 As we came through Harlem, it was Kearmas, which is a great fair, which all the towns in Holland hold once every year. **1818** *Blackw. Mag.* III. 406 It would.. have done the readers good, To see the pair to kerk or kermis going. **1883** G. H. BOUGHTON in *Harper's Mag.* Apr. 690/1 He arrived during the wildest powwow of the 'kermesse' [Holland]. **1888** *Boston* (Mass.) *Jrnl.* 12 Dec. 1/8 Salem Mechanic Light Infantry Kirmess..is destined to prove a brilliant success.

kern, kerne (kɜːn), *sb.*¹ Forms: 4– **kerne**, 6 **karn(e**, 6–8 **kearne**, 6– **kern.** [ad. Ir. *ceithern*, (*ceatharn*), pronounced ('kehərn) or ('keərn), OIr. *ceitern*, OCelt. *keterna*, a band of foot-soldiers; adopted in Eng. not only in its collective sense, but also to denote an individual soldier, = the Irish *ceithearnach, ceatharnach*, whence KERNAUGH. Cf. CATERAN, representing an adoption of *ceithern* or the synonymous Sc. Gael. *ceatharn*, at a time when the dental was still pronounced.

Stanyhurst (*Descr. Irel.* viii.) gives a fanciful derivation of *ceithern* from *ceath* or *cith* shower, and *ifrinn* hell. 'Kerne signifieth (as noble men of deepe iudgement informed me) a shower of hell, because they are taken for no better than for rakehels.' In later Irish *cearn* (for *ceatharn*) is used in the sense of 'banditti'.]

1. *Hist.* A light-armed Irish foot-soldier (cf. quot. 1600); one of the poorer class among the 'wild Irish', from whom such soldiers were drawn. (Sometimes applied to Scottish Highlanders.)

Stanyhurst divides the followers of an Irish chief into five classes—daltins or boys, grooms, kerns, gallowglasses, and horsemen.

1351 *Ordin. Dubl. & Kilk.* ii. in *10th Rep. Hist. MSS. Comm.* App. v. 257 Si nul..ne tiegne kernes, hobelours ne udives gentz en terre. *Ibid.*, Que kerne ou nul altre prenge nul manere des vitailles ou altre biens. **1358** *Ord Hibern.*, 31 *Edw. III*, m. 11, 12 (Blount *Law Dict.*) Nec non de illis qui dicuntur homines ociosi, et malefactoribus, qui etiam Kernys dicuntur. **1423** *Rolls Parlt.* IV. 199/1 What tyme the same Kernes hadde hym in governance, they bette hym. **1556** W. TOWRSON in Hakluyt *Voy.* (1589) 112 The South part of Irelande..The country people which were wilde Kernes. **1593** SHAKS. *Rich. II*, II. i. 156 Now for our Irish warres, We must supplant those rough rug-headed Kernes, Which liue like venom. **1600** DYMMOK *Ireland* (1843) 7 The kerne is a kinde of footeman, sleightly armed with a sworde, a targett of woode, or a bow and sheafe of arrows with barbed heades, or els 3 dartes. **1700** DRYDEN *Fables* Ded. 58 Hibernia, prostrate at your feet... The sturdy kerns in due subjection stand. **1810** SCOTT *Lady of L.* v. xiv, Soars thy presumption then so high Because a wretched kern ye slew? **1873** DIXON *Two Queens* I. IV. viii. 227 He was..bribing Irish kernes to rise against the English rule.

b. In collective sense; †*orig.* a troop or band of Irish foot-soldiers (*obs.*).

1422 tr. *Secreta Secret., Priv. Priv.* 133 He slowe the same Waltere wyth a grete kerne dyscomfitid. **1550** *Acts Privy Counc. Eng.* (1891) III. 79 To paie the waiges of the Kerne being at Chester and at London. **1612** DAVIES *Why Ireland*, etc. (1787) 182 Horsemen and kern should not be imposed upon the common people, to be fed and maintained by them. **1633** T. STAFFORD *Pac. Hib.* I. iv. (1810) 58 Iohn Fitz Thomas accompanied with one hundred Kerne. **1813** SCOTT *Rokeby* v. x, I've seen a ring of rugged kerne, With aspects shaggy, wild, and stern. **1872** *Deeside Tales* 125 (E.D.D.) The kern were makan' aff wi' a stirkie frae Rhineton as well.

2. *transf.* A rustic, peasant, boor; †*contemptuously* vagabond, rascal (*obs.*). Now *rare.*

1553 GRIMALDE *Cicero's Offices* II. (1558) 82 He commaunded a kerne and hym also..be prynted with Thracean markes, to goo beefore with a drawne swoorde. **1582** STANYHURST *Æneis* II. (Arb.) 43 What curst Myrmidones, what karne of canckred Vlisses? **1600** HOLLAND *Livy* III. lxix. 135 The countrie kernes that fled (to Rome,)..reported more foule and cruell outrages. **1656** BLOUNT *Glossogr.* s.v., We take a *Kern* most commonly for a Farmer or Country Bumpkin. **1856** W. E. AYTOUN *Bothwell* (1857) 2 The villain kernes Who keep me fettered here.

kern, *sb.*^{2} [A word of late appearance: related to KERN *v.*^{1} and KERNEL. Cf. MDu. *kern(e*, (Du. *kern*), OHG. *cherno* (MHG. *kerne*, G. *kern*), ON. *kjarni* (Da. *kærne*, Sw. *kärna*) kernel, pip, etc.; but it may repr. an OE. **cyrne*; cf. Norw. *kyrne* grain, and see CURN *sb.*]

†**1.** Kernel (of a nut). *Obs. rare.*

1570 LEVINS *Manip.* 81/39 Kerne of a nut, *nucleus.*

2. A grain (of wheat, sand, etc.). *rare.* Hence **kern-stone**, ? coarse-grained sandstone; or perh. oolite.

1753 CHAMBERS *Cycl. Supp.* s.v. *Kern-stone*, The little grains of sand are still visible in all parts of this stone, and are what induced the people to call it *kern stone*, as they call these *kerns*, or *kernels*. **1867** ROCK *Jim an' Nell* cxiii, With that Jones hullèd out a kern. **1880** BLACKMORE *Mary Anerley* I. 57 Grained with kerns of maxim'd thought.

3. *Meteorol.* [abstracted from G. *kernzähler* kern (nucleus) counter (A. Wigand 1913, in *Meteorol. Zeitschr.* XXX. 13).] A particle which acts as a condensation nucleus in a **kern counter**, a device in which a sample of air is supersaturated and condensation nuclei made visible and collected for counting: orig. intended to measure the concentration of condensation nuclei in the air, but now known to respond to particles too small to act as such under atmospheric conditions.

1941 *Jrnl. R. Aeronaut. Soc.* XLV. 72 The Aitken nucleus or 'kern' counter determines the number of nuclei in an air sample by subjecting it to a rapid expansion. This causes a considerable degree of supersaturation, and the drops which form around each nucleus fall on to a ruled slide where they may be counted. **1951** H. G. HOUGHTON in T. F. Malone *Compendium Meteorol.* 165/2 The sweeping action of the dust particles on the kerns. **1954** J. C. JOHNSON *Physical Meteorol.* vii. 206 These dusts, or kerns, as they are called, which make up most of the suspensoids in the atmosphere and are important for their light scattering effects on visibility, contribute little or nothing to the condensation process. *Ibid.* 207 Dust counts made by instruments such as the Aitken kern counter have little correlation with the number of active condensation nuclei in the atmosphere. **1967** R. W. FAIRBRIDGE *Encycl. Atmospheric Sci.* 84/2 Such nuclei counters (or kern counters..) have some distinct advantages.

kern (kɜːn), *sb.*^{3} *Printing.* [For **carn*, a. F. *carne* 'projecting angle, nib of a quill pen', a northern form (for **charne*):—L. *cardinem* hinge.] A part of a metal type projecting beyond the body or shank, as the curled head of f and tail of j, as formerly made, and parts of some italic letters. (Cf. KERNED *ppl. a.*^{2})

1683 MOXON *Mech. Exerc., Printing* xix. ⁋ 7 Every next Letter is turned with its Nick downwards, that the Kern of each Letter may lie over the Beard of its next. **1824** J. JOHNSON *Typogr.* II. 655 *Kern of a Letter*, that part which hangs over the body or shank.

kern (kɜːn), *v.*^{1} Now chiefly *dial.* Forms: 3-4 curne, 4 **kurne**, 4-7 **kerne**, 7 **kearn**, (quern), 7- kern. [ME. *kerne, curne* (cf. G. *körnen, kürnen*, Norw. *kyrna*), app. repr. OE. **cyrnan*:—OTeut. **kurnjan*, f. *kurno-*: see CORN *sb.*^{1}.

An OE. *cyrnian* is app. implied in the obscure gloss *ȝecyrnode* (*cambas*) in Napier's *O.E. Glosses* 26/15.]

1. *intr.* Of corn: To form the hard grains in the ear, to seed; = CORN *v.* 6. Also of fruit: To set.

1297 R. GLOUC. (Rolls) 10044 Þe þridde time þo grene corn in somer ssolde curne. **1422** tr. *Secreta Secret., Priv. Priv.* 141 Reyne..makyth herbis..cornys, treis and rootes sprynge, blowe, and kerne. **1591** PERCIVALL *Sp. Dict., Granar*, to kerne as corne doth, *in grana durescere.* **1699** *Poor Man's Plea* 5 The continued good Weather..gave the Corn so much time to knit and kearn, as they call it. **1744-50** W. ELLIS *Mod. Husbandm.* III. I. 150 Unless wheat blooms well, it cannot kern well. **1880** *W. Cornwall Gloss.* s.v. *Kerned*, 'The apple blowths have kerned'. **1897** BLACKMORE *Dariel* 63 While the corn began to kern.

†**b.** *trans.* To make into hard grains. *Obs.*

a **1571** JEWEL *Serm. Matt.* ix. 37-8 The corn..was ripened, and kerned by the Spirit of God. *a* **1722** LISLE *Husb.* (1752) 159, I told in those chests five compleat grains full kerned.

†**2.** *trans.* To cause to granulate; to make (salt) into grains; = CORN *v.* 1. *Obs.*

1600 HAKLUYT *Voy.* (1810) III. 147 Salt kerned on the rocks very white. **1628** *The World Enc. by Sir F. Drake* 9 Salt..is increased upon the sands by the flowing of the sea, and the heate of the Sunne kerning the same. **1726** G. ROBERTS *4 Years' Voy.* 262 If too deep, those Hollows.. could not, in so short time, kern any Salt.

b. To cover with crystalline grains of salt; to salt (meat); = CORN *v.* 3. *Obs.* exc. *dial.*

1613 PURCHAS *Pilgrimage* (1614) 333 *note*, If..a bird toucheth it with her wings they are kerned with salt. **1687** RYCAUT *Hist. Turkes* II. 101 Masts, Yards, and Decks were querned with a white Salt. **1721** BAILEY, *To Kern*, to corn, to salt or powder, as Beef, Pork, etc. **1886** ELWORTHY *W. Somerset Word-bk.* s.v. *Kerned*, That'll be a beautiful bit when he's well a kerned—not to zalt.

c. *intr.* Of salt, sugar, etc.: To crystallize in grains; to granulate; = CORN *v.* 2. *Obs.* exc. *dial.*

1657 R. LIGON *Barbadoes* (1673) 90 A liquor..which they call Temper, without which, the Sugar would continue a Clammy substance and never kerne. **1697** DAMPIER *Voy.* I. iii. 56 The Salt begins to kern, or grain, in April. **1753** in CHAMBERS *Cycl. Supp.* s.v. [of salt]. **1880** *W. Cornwall Gloss.* s.v. *Kerned*, Metal fixed or concreted around quartz is also said 'to have kerned'.

¶ Halliwell's *kerne* 'to sow with corn', copied by later Dicts., is an error: in Purvey's *Isa.* xxviii. 24, misquoted by him, the correct reading is *kerue*, carve. The old ed. of *Roland & V.* has also *kerne* for *kerue* in line 312. So in various other cases.

kern (kɜːn), *v.*^{2} *Printing.* [f. KERN *sb.*^{3}] *trans.* To furnish (a type) with a kern; to make a kern on. Hence '**kerner**, a workman who makes or adjusts kerned type.

1683 MOXON *Mech. Exerc., Printing* xix. ⁋ 5 Amongst the Italick-Letters many are to be Kern'd, some only on one side, and some both sides. The Kern'd-Letters are such as have part of their Face hanging over one side or both sides of their Shanck. *Ibid.* xiii. ⁋ 4 They..left the Letter-Kerner, after the Letter was Cast, to Kern away the Sholdering. **1824** J. JOHNSON *Typogr.* II. 23 Some founders have been more liberal than others in kerning letters. **1865** *Standard, Police News* (May) [A witness described himself as a kerner in Messrs..'s letter foundry].

kern, variant of KIRN *sb.*^{1}, ^{2}, and *v.*

†'**kernaugh.** *Obs. rare.* [a. Ir. *ceitheirneach, ceatharnach*: see KERN *sb.*^{1}] An Irish (or Highland) kern.

1535 *St. Papers Hen. VIII*, II. 242 He was inforced to leue horses, and goo to woodes, as a kernaugh. **1556** *Act 3-4 Phil. & Mary* in Bolton *Stat. Irel.* (1621) 255 No cottier nor labouring man in husbandry nor horseboy, nor kernaugh shall not buy any horse. **1822** D. STEWART *Highlander's Scot.* (1825) I. ii. 40 There was a peculiar class called Kearnachs... Some of these Kearnachs died in my remembrance.

kerned (kɜːnd), *ppl. a.*^{1} [f. KERN *v.*^{1}]

a. Of cereal grains or fruit: (Ill or well) formed, set, or hardened. Said also of a crop. †**b.** Of salt: (Small, large, hard, etc.) -grained. *Obs.* **c.** *dial.* = CORNED *a.*^{1} 2. **d.** Of ore: see quot. 1850.

1602 CAREW *Cornwall* 20b, An ill kerned, or saued Harvest, soone emptieth their old store. *c* **1682** J. COLLINS *Salt & Fishery* 53 It is a pure hard kerned Salt. **1847-78** HALLIWELL, *Kerned beef*, salted beef. *Hants.* **1850** WEALE *Dict. Terms, Kerned*, a term applied to a heap of mundic or copper ore hardened by lying exposed to the sun. **1865** *Pall Mall G.* 11 July 5/2 The straw was about six feet long, and the grain exceedingly well kerned.

kerned (kɜːnd), *ppl. a.*^{2} *Printing.* [f. KERN *v.*^{2}] Said of a type which has its top or bottom projecting beyond the square metal or shank.

1683 [see KERN *v.*^{2}]. **1688** R. HOLME *Armoury* III. 122/2 Kern, or Kerned Letter; such as have part of their face hanging over..their Shanks. **1824** J. JOHNSON *Typogr.* II. 22 In Roman, f and j are the only kerned letters; but, in Italic, *d,g,j,l,y* are kerned on one side, and *f* on boths sides of its face. *Ibid.*, Most Italic capitals are kerned on one side of their face.

[**kerned**, error for *kerued*, CARVED, castrated.

1655 MOUFET & BENNET *Health's Improv.* (1746) 126 Beasts, kerned Fowls, and barren Fish..as an Ox amongst Beasts, a Capon amongst Birds, and a Pike wounded in the Belly. **1661** LOVELL *Hist. Anim. & Min.* Isagoge, The males are more strong..but the kerned are of a better nature.]

kernel ('kɜːnəl), *sb.*^{1} Forms: α. 1 **cyrnel**, 2-6 **curnel**, (3-6 **kurnel**, 5 **curnyll**, 6- -**ell**), 5-8 **cornel**, (6 -**ell**), 6 **coornel**(l. β. 3-7 **kirnel**, (4 -**elle**, 6-7 -**ell**), 5-6 **kyrnel**, (-**ele**, etc.) γ. 5-7 **kernell**, -**e**, 4- **kernel**. δ. 4-6 **karnel**, 4-7 **carnell**, (6 -**ill**), 5-7 **carnel**. [OE. *cyrnel*, dim. of *corn* seed, grain, CORN:—OTeut. **kurnilo-*. Cf. (without umlaut) MHG. *kornel* a grain, MDu. *cornel* coarse meal; also MDu. *kernel* (f. *kern*; see KERN *sb.*^{2}). OE. *cyrnel* gave ME. *curnel* in south. and *kirnel* in midl. and north. dial.; from *curnel* came *cornel, coornel*, while *kirnel* became *kernel*, whence again *carnel*.]

†**1.** A seed; esp. the seed contained within any fruit; the pip of an apple or similar fruit; a grape-stone. *Obs.* exc. *dial.*

α. *c* **1000** ÆLFRIC *Hom.* I. 236 Men ȝeseoð oft þæt of anum lytlum cyrnele cymð micel treow. *c* **1290** *S. Eng. Leg.* I. 7/218 Ane Appel þare-of he nam And bi-tok Seth þreo curneles þar-of. **13..** *Creation* (Vernon MS.) in Horstm. *Altengl. Leg.* (1878) 226 þreo curnels of an appel þe angel tok. *c* **1420** *Pallad. on Husb.* x. 163 By cornels or sleuynge The bisynesse of settynge [apples] ful wel spende is. **1572** MASCALL *Plant. & Graff.* (1592) 61 Apples,..in a leape yeere (as some do say) the Curnelles or Pepines, are turned contrarie. **1653** J. HALL *Paradoxes* 96 They may dye by the cornel of the grape. **1738** [G. SMITH] *Curious Relat.* II. v. 150 Take some of the Cornels of Pine-Apples.

β. *a* **1300** *Cursor M.* 1385 Mani kirnels of a tre mast. *a* **1400-50** *Alexander* 2070 The kyng..on þe kirnels [= onion-seed] bote. *c* **1440** *Promp. Parv.* 276/1 Kyrnel of frute, *granum, granellum.* **1573** TUSSER *Husb.* (1878) 85 Sowe kirnels and hawe, where ridge ye did drawe. **1632** SANDERSON *Serm.* 554 A kirnel sprowt and grow into a tree.

γ. **1495** *Trevisa's Barth. De P.R.* XVII. cxxii. (W. de W.) 684 Whan the pyne appyll kernell shall be vsed: it nedyth to hete easely all the pyne appyll vpon coles. **1599** H. BUTTES *Dyets drie Dinner* C vij, *Granatum*, or Pome-granate, of his multitude of grains or kernels. **1601** SHAKS. *All's Well* II. iii. 276 **1650** FULLER *Pisgah* II. x. 219 Grapes of goodly greatness; yea the Hebrews report them to have been without any kernels. **1764** HARMER *Observ.* III. v. 209 The pounded kernels of dates. **1863** BARNES *Dorset Gloss.*, *Kernel*,..commonly applied to the pips of pomaceous fruit.

δ. *c* **1375** *Cursor M.* 1385 (Laud) Thise carnellis lest & most Come from the holy gost. **1375** *Creation* 800 in Horstm. *Altengl. Leg.* (1878) 134 þat angel ȝaf him þre Karnelis of þat appel-tre. **1534** MORE *Treat. on Passion* Wks. 1282/2 All the sowre crabes..do take theyr sowrenes of the carnell whereof the tree grew. **1609** BIBLE (Douay) *Ps.* viii. Comm., The huskes and carnels [of grapes] cast to hogges.

2. The softer (usually edible) part contained within the hard shell of a nut or stone-fruit.

c **1000** *Sax. Leechd.* III. 134 And oþera hnutena cyrnlu. *c* **1175** *Lamb. Hom.* 79 Me brekeð þe nute for to habbene þe curnel. *c* **1330** R. BRUNNE *Chron. Wace* (Rolls) 14682 Luytel notes þey toke, & holede þem, þe kerneles out schoke. **1377** LANGL. *P. Pl.* B. XI. 253 After þat bitter barke Is a kirnelle [*v.r.* curnel] of conforte. *c* **1440** *Gesta Rom.* lvi. 373 (Addit. MS.) The ape wil gladly Ete the kyrnell of the note, for it is swete. **1526** *Pilgr. Perf.* (W. de W. 1531) 5 b, As the shale of the nut to be broken that he may fede of the cornell. **1583** STUBBES *Anat. Abus.* II. (1882) 72 Bicause he cannot come by the carnell at the first, will therefore cast awaie both the nut and the carnell. **1640** QUARLES *Enchirid.* II. xxxvi, He.. casts away the Kirnell, because hee hath lost the Shell. **1780** COWPER *Progr. Err.* 419 We slight the precious kernel of the stone, And toil to polish its rough coat alone. **1865** KINGSLEY *Herew.* xii, A man..so strong that he could shake a nut till the kernel went to powder.

3. The body of a seed within its husk or integuments: **a.** A grain of wheat or other cereal or graminaceous plant.

a **1225** *Ancr. R.* 260 Heo breken þe eares bi þe weie & gniden þe cornes [*MS. T.* curnles] ut. **1483** CAXTON *Cato* 2 b, At theyre ful rypyng there is no carnel ne good corn but chaff for the mooste parte. **1599** H. BUTTES *Dyets drie Dinner* E viij b, Rize. Bright and cleare kernels, like Pearles Margarite. **1610** A. WILLET *Daniel* 195 The henne.. contemneth a pearle, and preferreth a barley curnell. **1744-50** W. ELLIS *Mod. Husbandm.* III. II. 8 Long heads [of wheat] full of plump milky kernels. **1891** S. C. SCRIVENER *Our Fields & Cities* 146 The grain could not multiply to its natural extent when thirty kernels are thrown down upon a square foot of soil.

b. Of other seeds.

1796 WITHERING *Brit. Plants* (ed. 3) II. 307 Seeds thread-shaped, containing a kernel at the base. **1838** T. THOMSON *Chem. Org. Bodies* 898 Bonastre employed the same method to analyze the husk and the kernel of the seeds [of Jamaica pepper]. **1846** J. BAXTER *Libr. Pract. Agric.* (ed. 4) II. 251 Good seed [sainfoin] may be known by the husks being of a bright colour, the kernel full and plump. **1880** GRAY *Struct. Bot.* (ed. 6) 417/2 *Kernel*, the nucleus of an ovule, or of a seed, i.e., the whole body within the coats.

4. A morbid formation of rounded form in any part of the body; *esp.* an enlarged gland in the neck or groin; an inflamed tonsil. Usually in *pl.* Now chiefly *dial.*

wax or ***waxing kernels***, a popular term for enlarged lymphatic glands in children, esp. in the neck.

c **1000** *Sax. Leechd.* II. 240 Missenlica adla..cyrnelu uneaðlacnu & þam ȝelic. *c* **1400** *Lanfranc's Cirurg.* 4 Of scrofules & glandeles þat buþ curnellys þat comyth in þe fflessch. **1483** CAXTON *Gold. Leg.* 326/1 Of kyrnellys and botches of his face. **1528** PAYNEL *Salerne's Regim.* R, By kyrnels are vnderstande impostumes, whiche commonly chance vnder ye arme pittis and in the groynes. **1607** TOPSELL *Four-f. Beasts* (1658) 197 The flesh of goats decocted in water take[s] away all bunches and kernels in the body. **1711** *Lond. Gaz.* No. 4921/4 A Kernel on the near side of his Neck. **1886** *W. Som. Word-bk.*, *Kernels* are very frequent with some individuals, and are often painful.

5. a. A gland or glandular body; a tonsil; a lymphatic gland or ganglion; a rounded fatty mass (see quot. 1790). Now *rare* or *dial.*

1398 TREVISA *Barth. De P.R.* v. lxii. (MS. Bodl.) lf. 31/2 þe curnels vnder þe tunge þat bredeþ þe spotell to saue þe mouþe tunge..[from] greete drynes. *c* **1400** *Lanfranc's Cirurg.* 84 Glandeles, þat ben kirnelis [*MS. B.* kurnellys] þat ben in þe ground [= groin]. **1533** ELYOT *Cast. Helthe* (1539) 31 b, The kernelles and gristell..if they be well digested they make good nourishment. **1607** TOPSELL *Four-f. Beasts* (1658) 530 The beginning of this disease is in the Almonds, or kernels of the throat. **1674** BOYLE *Excell. Theol.* II. iii. 148 That little kernel in the brain, called by many writers the Conarion. **1790** W. MARSHALL *Midl. Counties* (1796) II. (E.D.S.), *Kernel*, a bundle of fat before the shoulder of cattle: the *shift.* **1893** *Brit. Med. Jrnl.* 15 Apr. 812 The thyroid [in the calf] is situated at the upper part of the neck ..though the lobes are closer together than in man, they are spoken of as two, each being named a 'kernel' or 'gland'.

b. *dial.* The dug of a heifer. *Craven Dial.* (1828).

6. †**a.** A granule, as of sand or salt. *Obs.*

c **1440** *Jacob's Well* 230 þe kyrnelys of þe grauel or of sande arn wyth-oute noumbre. **1564** BECON *Nosegay* in *Early Wks.* (Parker Soc.) 206 Who having but a kernel of christian salt in his breast, will not hang wholly on this God? *a* **1825** FORBY *Voc. E. Anglia* s.v., A kernel of salt.

†**b.** *Mining.* (See quot.) *Obs. rare*$^{-1}$.

1757 tr. *Henckel's Pyritol.* 333 Kernel is the best and richest small ore.

7. a. The nucleus of any structure or formation; a core; a centre of formation.

1641 BEST *Farm. Bks.* (Surtees) 24 The lambes stones.. are accounted a very dainty dish, being fryed with parsley; ..after they are fryed browne, yow are to take of the uppermost filmes, and to eate nothinge but the very innermost kernells. **1665-6** *Phil. Trans.* I. 301 The Head.. having in its middle onely one round, but very bright and big Kernel or speck. **1692** RAY *Dissol. World* iii. (1732) 21 The middle Part or as he calls it the Kernel of the Mountain. **1793** HOLCROFT tr. *Lavater's Physiog.* xii. 63 This point may be called the kernel of the future bone. **1799** KIRWAN *Geol. Ess.* 49 The solid kernel of the globe. **1850** LEITCH tr. *C.O. Müller's Anc. Art* (ed. 2) §85 Those images of the gods..in which a kernel of wood was overlaid with ivory and gold. **1867** FREEMAN *Norm. Conq.* I. iv. 186 This settlement, the kernel of the great Norman Duchy.

b. A crystal or almond-shaped nodule of some mineral embedded in a trappean rock or the like.

1839 MURCHISON *Silur. Syst.* I. xxxvi. 500 The trap is, for the most part, an amygdaloidal greenstone, containing kernels of white calcareous spar.

c. A stone consisting of a nodule.

1892 *Skating & Curling* 344 (Badm. Libr.), If it can be secured as a boulder or kernel, it is perhaps of all stones the best.

d. *Chem.* = CORE *sb.*¹ 7 f.

1916 G. N. LEWIS in *Jrnl. Amer. Chem. Soc.* XXXVIII. 768 In every atom is an essential kernel which remains unaltered in all ordinary chemical changes. *Ibid.* 769 It must not be assumed..that the distinction between kernel and shell is absolutely hard and fast. **1927** E. N. DA C. ANDRADE *Struct. Atom* (ed. 3) xv. 552 The interaction of the outer electrons with one another is large compared to the interaction of the single electrons with the core. We may refer to it as the kernel scheme. **1927** [see CORE *sb.*¹ 7 f]. **1957** SIENKO & PLANE *Chem.* iii. 64 The letters represent the entire core, or kernel, of the atom.

8. a. *fig.* The core or central part of anything non-material; the gist of a narrative, the basis of a system, etc.

1556 J. HEYWOOD *Spider & F.* lxxviii. 73 Of my tale: the verie carnell or core, Must stand on two points. **1806** A. KNOX in *Mem.* I. 13 That which is the kernel of Christianity—to be spiritually minded. **1843** CARLYLE *Past & Pr.* IV. ii, Wherein lies for him the true kernel of the matter.

b. *Linguistics.* (i) The stem or common basis of a set of inflectional forms, such as *lach-* in the German verb *lachen*; (ii) in full ***kernel sentence*** (in an early version of transformational grammar), a relatively simple sentence that results from the application of only a few (obligatory) transformations, and to which other sentences may be related by further transformations; a set of such sentences.

1894 O. JESPERSEN *Progress in Language* vi. 143, I shall have to separate word and case-ending, as far as this is feasible... We want a special term for this distinction; and I propose to call the substantial part of the word, felt as such by the instinct of each generation as something apart from the ending (*eag* in the example chosen [*sc.* O.E. *eagel*]), the *kernel* of the word, while *eagan* is the historic 'stem'. **1918** *Amer. Jrnl. Philol.* XXXIX. 91, I think it unfortunate that the author feels it necessary to use the term *kernel* in place of the now generally used name *root*. **1933** L. BLOOMFIELD *Lang.* xiii. 225 This *lach-*, strictly speaking, is a bound form; it is called the kernel or stem of the paradigm. **1957** N. CHOMSKY *Syntactic Structures* v. 45 We define the kernel of the language (in terms of the grammar G) as the set of sentences that are produced when we apply obligatory transformations to the terminal strings. **1961** R. B. LONG *Sentence & its Parts* 494 'Kernels'. This term is applied to stripped-down nucleuses. **1963** J. LYONS *Structural Semantics* ii. 14 It appears that the kernel for English consists of simple, active, declarative sentences. **1969** *Canad. Jrnl. Linguistics* XV. 25 Sentences of the form *she is eager to please* demand that the subject, but no other nominal, of their embedded kernels be deleted. **1969** *Neuphilol. Mitt.* LXX. 204 The oft-repeated claim that all 'well-formed' sentences of a language are derivable from a single syntactic kernel is clearly unfounded.

c. *Math.* [tr. G. *kern* (D. Hilbert 1904, in *Nachrichten von d. Königl. Ges. d. Wissensch. zu Göttingen* (Math.-physik. Kl.) 49).] A function of two or more variables which, multiplied by one or more functions each of just one of the variables, constitutes the integrand of an integral with respect to these latter variables. (Orig. defined for integral equations in which the kernel is known and the other function(s) unknown, but now used in other situations also.)

1909 M. BÔCHER *Introd. Study Integral Equations* 13 Comparing Abel's equation..with Liouville's equation.. we see that they come respectively under the following types: $f(x) = \int_a^x K(x, \xi)u(\xi)d\xi$ [and] $u(x) = f(x) + \int_a^x K(x, \xi)u(\xi)d\xi$ in which $f(x)$ and $K(x, \xi)$ are to be regarded as known functions and $u(x)$ is the function to be determined. .. K is called the kernel of these equations. **1924** W. V. LOVITT *Linear Integral Equations* i. 6 An integral equation is also said to be singular if the kernel becomes infinite for one or more points of the interval under discussion. **1962** *Newnes Conc. Encycl. Nucl. Energy* 762/2 The function $P(\mathbf{r}, \mathbf{r}_0, E, E_0)$ is called the slowing-down kernel of the moderator. It cannot, in general, be calculated exactly, but various approximations have been developed. **1971** J. W. MILES *Integral Transforms in Appl. Math.* i. 1 We define $F(p) = \int_a^b K(p, x)f(x)dx$ to be an integral transform of the function $f(x)$; $K(p, x)$, a prescribed function of p and x, is the kernel of the transform.

d. *Math.* The set of all the elements that are mapped by a given homomorphism into the identity element (for the group operation in the case of groups, for addition in the case of rings).

1946 E. LEHMER tr. *Pontrjagin's Topological Groups* i. 11 The set of all the elements of the group G which go into the identity of the group G^* under the homomorphism g is called the kernel of this homomorphism. **1959** G. & R. C. JAMES *Math. Dict.* 224/2 If a homomorphism maps a ring R onto a ring R^*, then the kernel of the homomorphism is the set I of elements which map onto the zero element of R^*. **1971** G. GLAUBERMAN in Powell & Higman *Finite Simple Groups* i. 9 Since ϕ maps G into an abelian group, (G' is contained in the kernel of ϕ.

9. *attrib.* and *Comb.*, as ***kernel bed, flavour, oil, refuse***; (sense 8 b (ii)) ***kernel string, word***; ***kernel-bearing, -breaking, -like*** adjs.; †**kernel-fruit**, fruit having seeds or pips (distinguished from *stone-fruit*); so ***kernel fruit-tree***; †**kernel-relished** *a.*, flavoured with seeds or kernels; **kernel sentence**: see quot. 1968 and 8 b (ii) above; **kernel-substance**, the substance forming the nucleus of an ovum or other cell; nuclein; †**kernel-water**: see quot.; †**kernel-wort**, the figwort, *Scrophularia nodosa*.

1667 *Phil. Trans.* II. 511 Those that are *Kernel-bearing Animals, or chewing the Cud. **1693** EVELYN *De la Quint. Compl. Gard.* Dict. s.v. *Beds*, *Kernel Beds are Nursery Beds, wherein the Seed or Kernels of Kernel Fruit are sown in order to raise Stocks to Graff upon. **1887** MOLONEY *Forestry W. Afr.* 65 *Kernel-breaking machines have been introduced. **1791** E. DARWIN *Bot. Gard.* II. 92 *note*, Apricot-kernels, peach-leaves..and whatever possesses the *kernel-flavour. **1612** DRAYTON *Poly-olb.* XVIII. 298 Pippin, which we hold of *kernell-fruits the king. **1693** EVELYN *De la Quint. Compl. Gard.* I. Dict. s.v. *Fruit*, Kernel-Fruit, is Fruit that comes of Kernels or Seeds, as Apples, Pears, Quinces. **1719** LONDON & WISE *Compl. Gard.* 41 The time that Kernel Fruit-Trees require before they attain to a fit Age for Bearing. **1898** P. MANSON *Trop. Diseases* xxxi. 472 Hard *kernel-like pieces can be felt in their interior. **1877** A. B. HORTON in Moloney *Forestry W. Afr.* (1887) 41 Second Palm *Kernel Oil. **1708** J. PHILIPS *Cyder* II. 63 Blissful Cups Of *Kernell-relish'd Fluids. **1957** N. CHOMSKY *Syntactic Structures* viii. 89 Both 'the hunters shoot' and 'they shoot the hunters' are *kernel sentences. **1968** J. LYONS *Introd. Theoret. Ling.* vi. 256 A kernel sentence..is any sentence which is generated from a single kernel string without the application of any *optional* transformations. **1972** *Science* 23 June 1304/1 The basic units of information in language are the 'kernel sentences'—primitive nondecomposable sentences that can be modified and combined in various ways..to produce a very large number of different messages. **1957** N. CHOMSKY *Syntactic Structures* viii. 88 Alternative transformational developments from the same *kernel strings. **1706** PHILLIPS, **Kernel-water*,..Liquor made of the Kernels of Cherries and Apricocks, pounded and steep'd in Brandy. **1965** *Language* XLI. 392 Variants occurring under unique operators or *kernel-words. **1597** GERARDE *Herbal* II. ccxlv. (1633) 717 Figwort or *Kernel Wort is called in Latin *Scrophularia major*.

†**'kernel**, *sb.*² *Obs.* Forms: α. 3–7 **kernel**, (*pl.* 3 **kerneaus**), 4 **cernel**, 5 **kernell**. β. (*chiefly north.*) 3–6 **kirnel**, (5 **-elle**), 4–6 **kyrnell**, (5 **-elle,**) 5–6 **kyrnale**, (5 **-aill, -eill**). [a. ONF. *kernel* in same sense, variant (by metathesis) of OF. *crenel* (now *créneau*); see CRENEL. A third OF. form, *carnel*, *quarnel* (mod.F. *carneau*) gave ME. CARNEL and CORNEL¹.] An indentation or embrasure in the battlement of a wall; = CRENEL *sb.* 1. Also *pl.* (rarely *sing.*) = battlements.

a **1225** *Ancr. R.* 62 And nis heo..to folherdi, þet halt hire heaued baldeliche uorð vt iþen open kernel..þe kerneaus of þe castel beoð hire huses þurles. *a* **1300** *Cursor M.* 10016 Þe bailles thre o þat castel, þat ar sa wel wroght wit kirnel [*Gött.* cernel]. *c* **1330** R. BRUNNE *Chron.* (1810) 326 Wallis & kirnels stoute þe stones doun bette. *c* **1400** *Rom. Rose* 4195 In the kernels heere and there, Of arblasters grete plente were. *c* **1425** WYNTOUN *Cron.* II. i. 37 Ane archare in a kyrnale stude. *c* **1430** *Pilgr. Lyf Manhode* I. iii. (1869) 2 At þe kernelles ouer þe yate..j seyh þe penselles hanginge. **1560** ROLLAND *Crt. Venus* II. 586 With subtill wark it was sa roborat. Properlie alswa with kirnalis weill quadrat. **1652** URQUHART *Jewel* Wks. (1834) 196 Outjetting of kernels, erecting of prickets, barbicans, and such like.

†**kernel**, *sb.*³, obs. form of CORNEL³.

1655 MOUFET & BENNET *Health's Improv.* (1746) 301 Kernels or Corneols are of a very astringent and binding Taste.

kernel ('kɜːnəl), *v.*¹ Also 5 **kyr-**, 8 **kir-**. [f. KERNEL *sb.*¹

An OE. *cyrnlian* is implied in *ȝecyrnlude appla* (rendering L. *mala granata* (Napier *O.E. Glosses* 102/3841).]

†**1.** *intr.* To form kernels or seed. Of land: To produce grain or corn. *Obs.*

1483 *Cath. Angl.* 204/1 To kyrnelle, *granare, granere, granescere, inchoatiuum.* **1611** FLORIO, *Inglandulire*,..to glandulate, to kernell. **1707** MORTIMER *Husb.* I. v. vii. (1708) 108 In Staffordshire they sow Garden-Rouncivals in the Fields, and find them to kernel well. *a* **1722** LISLE *Husb.* 110 This ground kirnelled very fine.

2. *trans.* To enclose as a kernel in its shell.

1652 BENLOWES *Theoph.* XII. xliv, Though in rough shels our bodies kerneld are Our roof is neat. **1869** BLACKMORE *Lorna D.* xvii, The lilacs and the woodbines, just crowding forth in little tufts, close kernelling their blossom.

'kernel, *v.*² *Obs.* exc. *Hist.* Also 5 *Sc.* **kyr-**. [a. ONF. *kerneler*, variant of *carneler*, *creneler* (mod.F. *créneler*), f. *kernel*, *crenel* KERNEL *sb.*²] *trans.* To furnish with embrasures or battlements; to crenellate. (Cf. next.)

1377 LANGL. *P. Pl.* B. v. 597 Alle þe wallis ben of witte.. And kerneled with crystendome. *c* **1425** WYNTOUN *Cron.* II. i. 109 And kyrnalit it perfytly. **1610** HOLLAND *Camden's Brit.* I. 753 Licence to fortifie and kernel his mansion house, that is to embatle it. **1747** CARTE *Hist. Eng.* I. 688 It is evident..that no body could erect a castle or kernel a house ..without a license from the king. **1796** PEGGE *Anonym.* IX. xxxv. (1809) 410 The manor-houses..are called..*castles* in case they had the privilege of being *kernelled*.

Hence **'kernelled** *ppl. a.*

1706 PHILLIPS, *Kernelled Walls*, Walls built with Cranies or Notches, for the better Conveniency of shooting. **1789** BRAND *Hist. Newcastle* I. 172 The Keep, or Great Tower.. had, no doubt a kernelled battlement.

'kernellate, *v. arch. rare.* [f. ppl. stem of med.L. *kernellāre*: cf. prec. and CARNILATE *v.*] *trans.* = prec. Hence **'kernellated** *ppl. a.*

1851 TURNER *Dom. Archit.* I. vi. 260 In..1315, he obtained the license to kernellate, or fortify, his house at Bampton. **1861** C. INNES *Sk. Early Sc. Hist.* 443 A stern square keep rudely kernellated.

kernelled, -eled ('kɜːnəld), *a.*¹ [f. KERNEL *sb.*¹ + -ED².] †**a.** Of flesh: Full of kernels or glands. *Obs.* **b.** Of fruit: Having a kernel.

1398 TREVISA *Barth. De P.R.* v. lxii. (MS. Bodl.) lf. 31/2 Kerneld and knottye [flesh] filleþ and occupieþ lere and voide place and socowreþ þe veines and þe senewes. **1719** LONDON & WISE *Compl. Gard.* 89 The Anjou sweet kernell'd Apricot. **1841** MRS. LOUDON *1st Bk. Bot.* (1845) 24 Most of the kerneled fruits are indehiscent.

kernelled, *a.*², var. CORNELED², *Obs.*, cornered.

kernelless ('kɜːnəllɪs), *a.* [f. KERNEL *sb.*¹ + -LESS.] Without a kernel.

1879 tr. *Haeckel's Evol. Man* II. xvi. 51 We..assumed that the egg-cell..falls back into the kernel-less cytod stage. **1881** *Graphic* 15 Oct. 402/1 To pick up and crack the promising well-husked nut, but only to find it kernelless.

†**'kernelling**, *vbl. sb. Obs. rare.* [f. KERNEL *v.*¹ + -ING¹.] The forming of kernels or grains.

1532–3 *Act 24 Hen. VIII*, c. 10 As well in the sowing of the same corne and grayne, as at the riping and kernelling of the same.

†**'kernellish**, *a. Obs. rare*⁻¹. [f. KERNEL *sb.*¹ + -ISH¹ 2.] = KERNELLY 1; glandular.

1543 TRAHERON *Vigo's Chirurg.* I. x. 10 The other parte of the Mesenterium is kernellysh.

kernelly, -ely ('kɜːnəlɪ), *a.* Forms: see KERNEL *sb.*¹ [f. KERNEL *sb.*¹ + -Y.]

†**1.** Of flesh: Consisting of, or full of, glands; glandular. *Obs.*

1398 TREVISA *Barth De P.R.* v. lxii. (MS. Bodl.) lf. 31/2 Þere is þre manere of flessche..þe þrid is curnely. **1541** R. COPLAND *Guydon's Quest. Chirurg.* C iij, The other is.. cruddy and kyrnele. **1545** RAYNOLD *Byrth Mankynde* (1564) 46 Karnels and fatnesse spread abroade euery where on the karnelly body. **1548–77** VICARY *Anat.* ii. (1888) 22 Glandulus, knotty, or kurnelly fleshe. **1683** A. SNAPE *Anat. Horse* I. xxiii. (1686) 48 These are glandulous, or kernelly.

†**b.** Containing granular concretions. *rare*⁻¹.

c **1400** *Lanfranc's Cirurg.* 93 Þese ben þe tokenes of þe cankre..þe lippis ben grete, wan, or blak, hard, and wiþinne kirnely [*v.r.* kernelly].

2. Of the nature of, or like, a kernel.

1655 MOUFET & BENNET *Health's Improv.* (1746) 148 A Sow..her Throat [is never void] of Kernelly Apostems. **1667** *Phil. Trans.* II. 511 Kernelly and fleshy substances. **1840** *Jrnl. R. Agric. Soc.* I. IV. 384 A sweet kernelly taste.

Hence **'kernelliness**, 'fulness of kernels' (Bailey).

kerner: see KERN *v.*²

kernicterus (kɜː'nɪktərəs). *Path.* Formerly also **kern-**, **Kernikterus.** [ad. G. *kernikterus* (G. Schmorl 1903, in *Verhandl. d. Deut. Path. Ges.* VI. 112), f. *kern* nucleus + *ikterus* ICTERUS, jaundice.] The staining of nuclei of the brain cells with bilirubin, which sometimes occurs, usu. associated with rhesus incompatibility, in neonatal jaundice, and which causes permanent brain damage; the disease or condition characterized by or associated with such staining.

1912 *Brain* XXXIV. 488 An important analogy may be drawn from the occurrence of 'Kernikterus' in certain cases of familial icterus gravis neonatorum. **1933** *Amer. Jrnl. Dis. Children* XLV. 757 Opinion is almost unanimous on the subject of the pathogenesis of kernikterus, namely, that following some injury, the nerve cells are subsequently stained with the bile pigments carried to them by the blood stream. **1950** *Jrnl. Laryngol. & Otol.* LXIV. 505 Sixteen cases of perceptive deafness associated with kernicterus are reported. In fourteen of these cases the jaundice was due to Rh iso-immunization. **1953** *Lancet* 28 Mar. 613/1 Kernicterus is never found apart from jaundice. **1965** *Amer. Jrnl. Path.* XLVI. 336 Yellow ganglion and glial cells, characteristic features of human kernicterus, were demonstrated in 23 rabbits.

Hence **ker'nicteric** *a.*, afflicted or associated with kernicterus.

1956 *Jrnl. Speech & Hearing Disorders* XXI. 407 (*heading*) Clinical pathologic aspects of kernicteric nuclear 'deafness'. **1967** *Jrnl. Neurochem.* XIV. 192 The kernicteric animals are known to have pathologic lesions in the CNS comparable to those found in brain tissue of infants dying with kernicterus.

Kernig's sign ('kɜːnɪgz saɪn). *Med.* [f. the name of V. M. *Kernig* (1840–1917), Russian physician.] The inability of a patient to straighten his leg at the knee when lying on his back with the hips fully flexed, an indication of meningitis.

1901 *Brit. Med. Jrnl.* 16 Feb. 396/2 'Kernig's sign' was well marked. **1924** *Ibid.* 20 Dec. 1159/1 The angle at which Kernig's sign begins to be positive is clearly very different for a baby who can suck his own toe and a stocky middle-aged man. **1950** T. R. HARRISON *Princ. Internal Med.* viii. 94/2 If the head cannot be so flexed and Kernig's sign is positive, it is likely that the patient has either meningitis or subarachnoid hemorrhage. **1969** I. J. T. DAVIES *Postgrad. Med.* vi. 201 The cardinal signs of inflammation of the meninges are neck stiffness..and Kernig's sign which is spasm of the hamstring muscles when the knee is extended with the hips fully flexed.

kerning ('kɜːnɪŋ), *vbl. sb.*¹ [f. KERN *v.*¹ + -ING¹.] The process of forming into grains; seeding;

granulation. Also *attrib.*, as **kerning-period, -season, -time**; **kerning-ground** (see quot. 1732).

1669 Worlidge *Syst. Agric.* (1681) 135 The greater Trees, in their blossoming and kerning-time. **1699** Dampier *Voy.* II. ii. 43 The Indians whose business..is to gather the Salt thus into Heaps, wait here by turns all the Kerning Season. **1732** W. Ellis *Pract. Farmer* Gloss., *Kerning ground* is that which, drest well, will produce a great quantity of corn, as gravel does. **1744–50** —— *Mod. Husbandm.* I. i. 47 A better kerning of the blossoms. **1894** *Agric. Gaz.* 16 July, The kerning period has been so favourable that there is every reason to expect a good yield in proportion to straw.

kerning (ˈkɜːnɪŋ), *vbl. sb.*² [f. Kern *v.*² + -ing¹.] The operation of making kerns on type; the making of kerned letters. Also *attrib.* as **kerning-knife, -stick**, tools used in kerning letters.

1683 Moxon *Mech. Exerc., Printing* xix. ¶5 This Kerning-stick is somewhat more than an Handful long... He also provides a Kerning-knife. **1788** *Chambers's Cycl.* s.v. *Foundery*, These..are scraped on the broad-sides with a knife or file... This operation is called kerning. **1824** J. Johnson *Typogr.* II. 22 The kerning of letters, it must be owned, may serve many good purposes.

† **ˈkernish**, *a. Obs. rare.* [f. Kern *sb.*¹ + -ish¹.] Of, or of the nature of, a kern.

1581 Derricke *Image Irel.* ii. Eivb, To wounde the harmlesse sorte, it is the Karnishe guise. **1641** Milton *Ch. Govt.* i. vii, Ireland that was once the conquest of one single Earle with his privat forces, and the small assistance of a petty Kernish Prince.

kernite (ˈkɜːnaɪt). *Min.* [f. *Kern*, name of the county in California where it was discovered + -ite¹.] A hydrated form of sodium borate, $Na_2B_4O_7.4H_2O$, that occurs as large transparent crystals and is used as a source of borax.

1927 W. T. Schaller in *Amer. Mineralogist* XII. 24 The new mineral kernite, $Na_2B_4O_7.4H_2O$, was received through Hoyt S. Gale..and is reported to occur in quantity in the southeast corner of Kern County, California... The name kernite is proposed. **1930** *Prof. Papers U.S. Geol. Survey* No. 158. i. 146/1 The extreme abundance of kernite, its large crystals, its perfect cleavage, and its clearness and transparency render the occurrence one of almost unique character as well as of striking beauty. **1951** C. Palache et al. *Dana's Syst. Min.* (ed. 7) II. xv. 337 The material had earlier been called rasorite..but the name kernite has published priority. **1972** M. H. Battey *Mineral. for Students* 235 Borax and the related mineral kernite, $Na_2B_4O_6(OH)_2.3H_2O$, are the principal sources of borax and of boron.

kernos (ˈkɜːnɒs). *Archæol.* Pl. **kernoi.** [Gr.] An ancient Mediterranean and Near Eastern earthen vessel with small cups around the rim or fixed in a circle to a central stem.

1903 J. E. Harrison *Proleg. Study of Gk. Relig.* iv. 158 *Kernos*, a vessel made of earthenware, having in it many little cups fastened to it, in which are white poppies, wheat, barley..; and he who carries it..tastes of these things. **1955** L. Woolley *Alalakh* xii. 344 Three black impressed sherds, one from a beaker and one from a *kernos*. **1960** T. Burton-Brown *Early Mediterranean Migrations* ii. 35 The kernos shape..is known in Azarbaijan, for there is an unpublished example from there exhibited in the Tehran Museum. **1967** A. D. Lacy *Greek Pott. Bronze Age* v. 260 The kernos or cluster vase..is a composite vessel in which one or more rings of small cups are mounted upon a central stem. Kernoi have been found at Phylakopi in Milo, and in Crete. **1971** *Ashmolean Mus. Rep. Visitors 1970* 16 Purchased:..a Proto-White Painted kernos, Late Cypriot IIIB. **1972** Y. Yadin *Hazor* ii. vii. 101 The cultic aspect of the whole area is further attested by the enormous nests of vessels, which included incense-stands, 'cups and saucers', kernoi, and 'rattles'.

kern-stone: see Kern *sb.*² 2.

kero (ˈkɛrəʊ). Austral. and N.Z. colloq. abbrev. of Kerosene *sb.*

1930 *Bulletin* (Sydney) 10 Sept. 22/3 Never feed in troughs. With little stalls and cut-down kero.-tins..calves can be fed quickly enough for anybody. **1938** X. Herbert *Capricornia* ix. 129 Take it and buy some tucker and kero. **1957** 'N. Culotta' *They're a Weird Mob* (1958) vi. 78 Pat threw in..a 'kero tin' of water. **1961** P. White *Riders in Chariot* xi. 411 The rusted kero stove. **1968** *N.Z. Listener* 15 Mar. 6/2 Just picture us flicking on lights (no candles and kero to mess with). **1970** M. Kelly *Spinifex* xv. 214 The fire's all right. I put out a quart of kero and there's stacks of green stuff.

kerogen (ˈkɛrədʒən). *Petrogr.* [f. Gr. κηρό-ς wax + -gen.] Orig., the carbonaceous material in oil shale that gives rise to crude oil on distillation; in later use extended to denote any organic material in sedimentary rock which, like the oil-yielding kind, is insoluble in the usual organic solvents.

1906 D. R. Steuart in H. M. Cadell et al. *Oil-Shales of Lothians* iii. 142 We are indebted to Professor Crum Brown, F.R.S., for suggesting the term Kerogen to express the carbonaceous matter in shale that gives rise to crude oil in distillation. **1923** P. E. Spielmann *Genesis of Petroleum* ii. 17 In some cases it may have been that kerogen consisting of unicellular algae and of spores like those of the lycopods, had actually been distilled. **1941** *Jrnl. Inst. Petroleum* XXVII. 426 The term 'kerogen'..is merely a convenient name for the organic matter from which oil is obtained when rocks containing it are heated; hence the kerogens of different deposits may be chemically different. *Ibid.* 427 The insolubility of kerogen in organic solvents is a characteristic property which serves to distinguish true kerogen rocks from such materials as oil- or tar-sands, bituminous limestones, etc. **1958** *Habitat of Oil* (Amer. Assoc. Petroleum Geol.) 758 Kerogens isolated from the marine rocks were obtained as very fine, amorphous, soft powders that varied from dark brown to jet black... When the samples were heated in an open test tube only small amounts of an oily distillate were formed. **1961** *Fuel* XL. 387 Colorado oil-shale kerogen is predominantly a cyclic material, highly saturated with hydrogen, and contains oxygen, nitrogen and sulphur atoms associated with ring structures. **1963** J. P. Forsman in I. A. Breger *Org. Geochem.* v. 148 The term 'kerogen'..may be defined as the insoluble organic matter occurring in sedimentary rocks. *Ibid.*, Since the dividing line between oil shales and other rocks is rather arbitrary, there appears to be no logical reason for restricting the name 'kerogen' to a certain rock type. **1968** *Times* 16 Nov. 9/6 The most ancient kerogen yet known comes from the Fig Tree System of rocks in Swaziland, thought to be 3,100 million years old.

kerography, -lite, var. Cerography, -lite.

kerosene (ˈkɛrəsiːn), *sb.* Also **kerosine** (see note below). [irreg. f. Gr. κηρός wax + -ene.]

a. A mixture of liquid hydrocarbons, a commercial product of the distillation of petroleum; obtained also from coal and bituminous shale, and extensively used as a lamp-oil. Now important as a fuel for some kinds of internal-combustion engines, esp. jet engines.

First manufactured by Abraham Gesner, shortly after 1846 (1865 Gesner *Coal, Petrol.* etc. 9), and frequently called ***kerosene oil***. Also commonly known as *petroleum*, which properly denotes the crude mineral oil from which kerosene is obtained. *Kerosene, -ine* is now the usual name for paraffin in much of the U.S. (see quot. 1961¹) and in Australia and New Zealand; in Britain its currency is largely restricted to technical contexts. The spelling *kerosine* was adopted in 1925 by the Amer. Soc. for Testing Materials and (in Britain) by the Institute of Petroleum; the *-ene* form remains the usual one in general usage and still occurs in technical contexts.

1854 A. Gesner in *U.S. Patent Rep.* 462 The new product or composition of hydrocarbon for illuminating and other purposes called..Kerocene. **1858** Simmonds *Dict. Trade*, *Kerosene*, a liquid hydro-carbon obtained from a species of bituminous shale in New Brunswick. **1864** Eliz. Murray *Ella Norman* II. 206 He had brought in..a large tin of kerosine, to fill up and light the lamps in the bar. **1881** Watts *Dict. Chem.* VIII. 1509 Illuminating Oil, Petroleum, Kerosene, Paraffin Oil, Refined Paraffin, has a large and increasing consumption for lamps, etc. **1894** *Dublin Rev.* Oct. 434 The American oil gives about 80 per cent. of kerosene. **1925** *Proc. Amer. Soc. Testing Materials* XXV. 287 The sub-committee [on nomenclature] wishes to call particular attention to the spelling of the word 'kerosine'. This matter was brought to our attention by the Executive Committee of the Standardization Committee of the Institution of Petroleum Technologists, it being pointed out that the ending 'ene' is very generally applied to pure hydrocarbons. The suffix 'ine' already applied to gasoline is therefore also applied to kerosine. **1933** *Industr. Chemist* IX. 227/2 High sulphur, low quality, off-colour kerosene distillates..may be hydrogenated. **1949** *Thorpe's Dict. Appl. Chem.* (ed. 4) IX. 389/2 The word 'kerosene'..is an alternative name with paraffin oil (British) and coal oil (American). **1950** *Inst. Petroleum Rev.* IV. 9/1 The American Society for Testing Materials and the Institute of Petroleum..desire to reiterate their strong recommendation for international recognition of the spelling *kerosine*. **1951** C. R. Noller *Textbk. Org. Chem.* iv. 53 Previous to 1910, kerosene was the most important product derived from petroleum. *Ibid.*, The demand for the kerosene fraction is increasing again, since it is being used as the fuel for gas turbines and jet engines. **1954** *Chem. & Engin. News* 5 Apr. 1386/3 'Kerosene' is commoner than 'kerosine'. The ASTM [*sc.* American Society for Testing Materials] and ASA [*sc.* American Standards Association] have preferred 'kerosine', probably in order to make it consistent with 'gasoline', and *CA* [*sc. Chemical Abstracts*] has adopted 'kerosine' as the choice of an authoritative group in the petroleum field. **1957** Frazer & Eshelman *Tractors & Crawlers* i. 14 Kerosene and distillate..will burn satisfactorily in engines which are designed for low-grade fuels. **1960** *B.S.I. News* Dec. 25 (*heading*) Kerosine (paraffin) unflued space heaters. **1961** *Amer. Speech* XXXVI. 27 Fuel for lamps: Kurath found *kerosene* in general use through the North. The Atlas field interviewer, on the other hand, encountered *coal oil* in all three Cleveland interviews. Both terms are in widespread use today. 1. The commercial *kerosene*..increases in frequency with the youth and the cultivation of the informant. 2. *Coal oil*..appears to find its chief strength among the old and the uncultivated. **1961** D. Petrie *Petroleum* xi. 62 The heavier products condense on the lower trays, and the lighter ones like kerosine and petrol near the top. **1966** C. Orr *Particulate Technol.* ix. 439 Organic liquids like benzene, toluene, kerosine. **1966** G. W. Turner *Eng. Lang. Austral. & N.Z.* i. 22 Trade has given currency to such words as *kerosene*: an English lady surprised a New Zealand chemist by asking for four gallons of 'paraffin' and he surprised her by supplying four gallons of 'liquid paraffin'. **1967** W. A. Gruse *Motor Fuels* i. 6 The next higher-boiling fraction, kerosene, will cover the range about 180 to 290°C. **1970** *Sci. Jrnl.* Mar. 44/1 Aviation kerosine has a strong and unpleasant odour.

b. *attrib.* and *Comb.*, as ***kerosene box, bucket, case, engine, flare, lamp, -manufacturer, oil, shale, spectrum, stove, tax, tin, works***, etc.; ***kerosene-lit, -soaked*** adjs.

1948 V. Palmer *Golconda* x. 76 There was a bookcase made of *kerosene-boxes nailed together. **1929** K. S. Prichard *Coonardoo* xxiv. 235 Coonardoo had *kerosene buckets of water boiling. **1905** W. B. *Where White Man Treads* 304 He invited me to his whare, and seated me in the seat of honour—the slab bunk—while he made shift with the ubiquitous *kerosene case store-all. **1909** *Westm. Gaz.* 3 Feb. 2/2 A gasolene- or *kerosene-engine. **1920** D. H. Lawrence *Women in Love* ix. 125 The market-place was hot with *kerosene flares. **1869** *Bradshaw's Railway Manual* XXI. p. xii (Advt.), Dietz & Co., petroleum and *kerozene lamp manufacturers. **1879** *Gd. Words.* Mar. 164 Pots, pans, vessels of wood, kerosene lamps. **1945** *Coast to Coast 1944* 75 It was a dingy hole all right, with a feeble kerosene-lamp trying to soak up some of the shadows. **1974** 'I. Drummond' *Power of Bug* viii. 113 The smell of gasoline could not have come from..kerosene lamps. **1932** W. Faulkner *Light in August* v. 107 He saw himself enclosed by cabinshapes, vague, *kerosenelit. **1863** Dicey *Federal St.* I. 21 A store of *Kerozene oil had caught fire. **1896** Mrs. Croker *Village Tales* 221 Treasure, which was buried in a kerosene-oil tin. **1908** *Westm. Gaz.* 3 June 12/1 No sooner had the speeches concluded than..a light was set to the stack of *kerosene-soaked pipes. **1889** *Anthony's Photogr. Bull.* II. 395 The color sensitiveness of a photograpic plate..judged by a *kerosene spectrum. **1876** *Daily News* 22 Aug. 6 He lost his *kerosene stove, and his square sail by the upset. **1946** *Coast to Coast 1945* 175 In the shed that had been fitted up with taps and shelves, a sink and an old smoky kerosene stove, Bennie was always happy. **1928** *Manch. Guardian Weekly* 10 Aug. 113/4 Mr. Churchill was deeply chagrined by being compelled to withdraw his proposed *kerosene tax. **1891** C. Roberts *Adrift Amer.* xii. 211 There was no difficulty in cooking it as an old *kerosine tin furnished a pot, and..I soon had it boiling away. **1908** E. J. Banfield *Confessions of Beachcomber* i. i. 48 All convenient vessels available, even to the never-to-be despised kerosene tins, were utilised to store the nectar. **1937** *Discovery* June 169/2 Dozens of boys and girls..came along with calabashes, bags and kerosene tins full of locusts. **1969** *Coast to Coast 1967–68* 18 Kate had been boiling clothes in kerosene tins on the kitchen stove and carrying them outside to be rinsed in big tubs on the back veranda.

ˈkerosene, *v.* [f. prec. sb.] *trans.* To saturate with kerosene, esp. in order to render inflammable.

1883 *Pall Mall Gaz.* 20 Mar. 7/1 The cities that are, forsooth, to be kerosened and dynamited. **1894** *Blackw. Mag.* Sept. 394 The cook who strains his master's soup through a much kerosened lamp-cloth.

kerosolene (ˈkɛrəsəʊliːn). [Arbitrary f. kerosene, with insertion of -ol q.v.] An oil with anæsthetic properties, distilled from petroleum; petroleum ether.

1861 *Shrewsbury Weekly Observer* 21 Sept., Under the name of 'kerosolene' a new anæsthetic has lately been undergoing investigation in America. **1888** in *Syd. Soc. Lex.*

kerp, obs. or dial. form of Carp *v.*¹

c **1500** *Yng. Childr. Bk.* 120 in *Babees Bk.* 23 Be not besy forto kerpe. **1886** Elworthy *W. Som. Word-bk.* s.v., What's the good o' keeping on kerpin about it?

ker-plonk, -plunk: see Ker-.

Kerr (kɛə(r), kɑː(r), kɜː(r)). The name of John *Kerr* (1824–1907), Scottish physicist, used *attrib.* to designate certain devices, phenomena, and concepts discovered by him or arising out of his work, as **Kerr cell**, a transparent cell containing two plate electrodes in a substance exhibiting a strong Kerr (electro-optical) effect, by means of which an applied voltage may be made to vary the plane of polarization of plane-polarized light and hence (when the cell is placed between crossed nicols) the intensity of a beam; **Kerr constant**, a number expressing the degree to which a substance exhibits the electro-optical Kerr effect, equal to the difference between the extraordinary and ordinary indices of refraction of the substance divided by the wavelength of the monochromatic light used and by the square of the electric field strength; **Kerr effect**, (*a*) the rotation of the plane of polarization of light when it is reflected from a magnetized surface; (*b*) the production of birefringence in a substance by the application of an electric field.

[**1893** J. J. Thomson *Notes Rec. Res. Electr. & Magn.* v. 501 There is..no reason to expect that the order of the metals with respect to Kerr's effect should be the same as that with respect to Hall's.] **1909** *Chem. Abstr.* III. 2084 The theory of the Kerr effect shows that..the effect of the mirror of ferromagnetic metal placed in the magnetic field is the same as would be the face of a naturally active crystal without the magnetic field. **1910** *Hawkins' Electr. Dict.* 232/2 *Kerr effect*, the effect produced in dielectrics when subjected to electro-static stresses, so that they become double refracting. **1927** *Proc. Nat. Acad. Sci.* XIII. 506 These experiments involved measuring the differences in the lag of the Kerr effect behind the electric field for the liquids in two Kerr cells. **1927** *Phil. Mag.* III. 715 All the substances which possess a large Kerr constant have molecules which are electrically polar. **1937** G. S. Monk *Light* xvi. 318 Gases exhibit a Kerr electric effect which is about 1/1000 that for ordinary liquids. **1953** J. R. Partington *Adv. Treat. Physical Chem.* IV. x. 279 Kerr cells containing this liquid [*sc.* nitrobenzene]..are used in television and cinema apparatus as instantaneous switches or relays. **1953** J. Morgan *Introd. Geom. & Physical Optics* xvi. 361 The Kerr effect depends on the difference in the dipole moments produced by the electric field along different axes of the molecule, and such measurements give information about the molecular structure of the liquid. **1969** McGuire & Flanders in Berkowitz & Kneller *Magnetism & Metall.* I. iv. 145 The Kerr magnetooptical effect refers to polarized light reflected from a magnetized surface. The reflected light is elliptically polarized with the major axis of the ellipse rotated with respect to the original axis of the light. **1972** J. R. Meyer-Arendt *Introd. Classical*

& *Mod. Optics* III. i. 297 Kerr cells are used most often as ultra-fast shutters.

kerr, kerre: see CAR, CARR, KER.

kerria (ˈkɛrɪə). [mod.L. (A. P. de Candolle 1817, in *Trans. Linn. Soc.* XII. 154), f. the name of William *Ker* or *Kerr* (d. 1814), English botanical collector.] A deciduous shrub of the monotypic genus so called, native to China and Japan, belonging to the family Rosaceæ, and bearing single or double yellow flowers; = CORCHORUS 2; ***white kerria***, a closely related shrub, *Rhodotypos kerrioides*, which bears white flowers.

1823 J. LINDLEY *Donn's Hortus Cantabrigiensis* (ed. 10) 200 *Kerria japonica*, Kerria. Japan... 1804. **1829** J. C. LOUDON *Encycl. Plants* 455 *Kerria*. So named after Mr. William Ker, a botanical collector, who was sent some years since to China, whence he sent many curious plants. The plant named after him is the common Corchorus japonica of the gardens. **1836** *Edward's Bot. Reg.* XXII. 1873 (*heading*) Japan Kerria. **1896** J. H. VEITCH *Traveller's Notes* VII. 112 Some lovely flowering bushes of double Kerria are..to be seen. **1900** M. THORN in W. D. Drury *Bk. Gardening* xi. 407 *Rhodotypos kerrioides* (White Kerria) is a charming and easily-grown shrub. *Ibid.* 465 The double-flowered Kerria (*K. japonica flore pleno*) is a favourite wall-shrub. **1939** W. J. BEAN *Wall Shrubs & Hardy Climbers* II. 100 The typical, single-flowered kerria is a spreading, twiggy shrub. **1951** *Dict. Gardening* (R. Hort. Soc.) 1103/1 Kerria, White. See *Rhodotypos kerrioides*. **1970** C. LLOYD *Well-Tempered Garden* iv. 356 Japanese quinces, weigelas, kerrias, mahonias..are all stripped by birds at various times.

kerrite (ˈkɛraɪt). *Min.* [Named in 1873 after Prof. W. C. Kerr.] A kind of vermiculite found in North Carolina, of a pale greenish yellow colour with a tint of brown.

1873 *Amer. Philos. Soc.* XIII. 396 Kerrite..consists of innumerable fine scales, which under the microscope do not present a definite shape.

Kerry[1] (ˈkɛrɪ). [See def. 1.]

1. *attrib.* as *adj.* Belonging or native to Kerry, a county in the S.W. of Ireland. ***Kerry security, witness*** (see quots.).

1785 GROSE *Dict. Vulg. T.*, *Kerry Security*, bond, pledge, oath and keep the money. **1828** C. CROKER *Fairy Leg.* II. 18 A Kerry witness..signifies a witness who will swear to anything. **1885** LADY BRASSEY *The Trades* 99 Queer little Hindoo cattle, something like Brittany or Kerry cows.

2. *absol.* as *sb.* A cow of a breed belonging to Kerry, noted for the quality of the milk. Also, ***Kerry cow***.

1829 G. GRIFFIN *Collegians* (ed. 2) I. xi. 233 Her little cow was a kind Kerry, and had the best of grazing. **1880** *Daily News* 21 Dec. 5/5 The little Kerries are greatly prized as 'milkers'. **1888** *Blackw. Mag.* Dec. 812 The skin of a little Kerry sufficed to make two pairs. **1907** *Macm. Mag.* May 514 We saw a cattle-boat bringing Kerries to Scariff. **1929** E. BOWEN *Last September* III. xxiii. 294 Look at those little teeny black cows. Those are Kerry cows. **1975** *Irish Times* 9 May 4/6 Kerries, Ayrshires, Herefords, Charolais, and the Jerseys, the nicest of all.

3. *Comb.* **Kerry blue terrier**, a breed of Irish terrier, of medium size, with a long, silky, blue coat, found in Kerry and neighbouring counties and introduced elsewhere during the nineteen-twenties; also ***Kerry, Kerry blue***.

1922 D. MATHESON *Terriers* 145 The Kerry (Blue) Terrier. Since the close of the Great War we have had this variety of Irish Terrier introduced to us under its present title. **1930** E. C. ASH *Pract. Dog Bk.* 150 The history of the Kerry Blue is not easy to obtain. **1955** N. FITZGERALD *House is Falling* x. 169 She had firmly attached herself to the big Kerry Blue. **1971** F. HAMILTON *World Encycl. Dogs* 455 Kerry pups are born black. The blue color comes later, showing at any time after six or seven months. **1973** *Country Life* 15 Feb. 384/3 The terriers replaced the gundogs..the eventual winner the Kerry Blue terrier.

Kerry[2] (ˈkɛrɪ). The name of a town and neighbouring range of hills in the county of Powys, on the Welsh borders, used *attrib.* in **Kerry Hill sheep** to designate a breed of sheep developed there, distinguished by a thick fleece and black markings near the muzzle and feet. Also *absol.*

1908 *Daily Chron.* 1 May 4/6 Many people are under the impression that the famous Kerry Hill sheep come from Ireland. As a matter of fact, they come from Kerry in Montgomeryshire. **1937** F. B. YOUNG *Portrait of Village* v. 102 By the time he had finished stocking it with Wessex Saddleback pigs, Kerry Hill sheep, short-horn cows, runner ducks and Rhode Island Red poultry,..he had made another big hole in his dwindling capital. **1945** J. F. H. THOMAS et al. *Sheep* ii. 33 The Kerry Hill (Wales)..is a polled breed of medium size which carries a dense fleece. **1960** [see DEVON]. **1971** *Farmers Weekly* 19 Mar. 83/1 For many years we kept Kerrys at Downton, now we have commercial Cluns—with some Welsh blood.

†**kerry-merry-buff.** *Obs. rare.* Also 6–7 kiri(e-)mirie-. [app. of fanciful coinage: the last element is prob. BUFF *sb.*[1]] Some kind of blow or buffet; perhaps a loud but not severe blow, such as one given in sport with the hollowed hand.

(Halliwell's statement that the term denoted 'a kind of material of which jerkins were formerly sometimes made' appears to be quite unsupported by evidence.)

1598 FLORIO, *Tartóffola*, the..black and blue of a blow or hurt. Also a blow giuen with ones knuckles vpon ones head. Also a kirimiriebuff. **1602** MIDDLETON *Blurt, Master Const.* I. i. 223 Trickes; trickes; kerry merry buffe; how now lad, in a traunce? **1659** TORRIANO, *Buffettàre*, to buffet or clap one on the mouth, to give one a kirie-mirie-buff.

kers, -se, -ss, obs. or dial. ff. CRESS.

kersantite (ˈkɜːsəntaɪt). *Min.* Also **-yte**. [f. *Kersanton*, a hamlet near Brest in Brittany.]

A fine-grained porphyritic compound of oligoclase and mica, containing also hornblende and quartz.

1868 DANA *Min.* (ed. 5) 348 Oligoclase..occurs..in a micaceous dioryte (called *kersantyte*) at Visembach in the Vosges. **1879** [see next].

kersanton (ˈkɜːsəntən). *Min.* [See prec.: named by Rivière.] A dark-coloured rock allied to kersantite.

1862 G. P. SCROPE *Volcanos* (ed. 2) 112 The augitic rocks of this class have likewise numerous varieties, respectively called..Diabase, Kersanton, [etc.]. **1879** RUTLEY *Stud. Rocks* xii. 239 Kersantite differs mainly from kersanton in containing more or less hornblende.

kersen, dial. form of CHRISTEN *v.*

kersey (ˈkɜːzɪ). Now *rare.* Also 5 **kerseye**, 5–6 **carsey, -say**, 6 **carsy(e, -soye, -ssey, -esye, cassaye, kersay, karsey**, 6–7 **karsie, carsie, -zie**, 6–8 **kersie, -sy**, 7 **kerzie**. [Possibly named from the village of Kersey in Suffolk, (cf. *Kendal*, *Worsted*, etc., as names of fabrics); though evidence actually connecting the original manufacture of the cloth with that place has not been found. See note below.]

1. A kind of coarse narrow cloth, woven from long wool and usually ribbed.

1390 *Earl Derby's Exp.* (Camden) 89 Pro iij[bus] vlnis et di. de kersey. **1481** *Howard Househ. Bks.* (Roxb.) 17 Item, half yerd kersey for my lady. **1502** *Ld. Treas. Acc. Scot.* II. 198 For iij elne quhit carsay to be ane cote to the King xiijs. vjd. **1543–4** *Old City Acc. Bk.* in *Archæol. Jrnl.* XLIII, For iij quarters of yallow carssey for hose xv[s]. **1580** LYLY *Euphues* (Arb.) 443 The Sunne..shineth aswel vpon course carsie, as cloth of tissue. **1607** ROWLANDS *Dr. Merrie-man* (1609) 6 The Stockings that his clownish Legges did fit, Were Kersie to the calfe, and t'other knit. **1724** RAMSAY *Tea-t. Misc.* (1733) II. 170 Her stockings were of Kersy green As tight as ony silk. **1772–84** COOK *Voy.* (1790) I. 164 English broad-cloth, and red Kersey they highly esteemed. **1834** HT. MARTINEAU *Moral* I. 17 A substantial petticoat of serge or cloak of kersey.

2. With *a* and *pl.* †**a.** A piece of kersey of a definite size. *Obs.* **b.** A make or variety of kersey (chiefly in *pl.*).

In the 16–17th c. *kerseys* are commonly contrasted with *cloths* or *broad-cloth*; the size of the latter was fixed by the statute of 1465 as 24 yds. long by 2 wide, while a kersey was only 18 yds. long and a yard and a nail in width. The act of 1552 enumerates various kinds of kerseys, as ordinary, sorting, Devonshire (called dozens), and check kerseys, and fixes their length as between 17 and 18 yards; in 1557 this was reduced to between 16 and 17. About 1618 we find three kersies reckoned as equal to one cloth (see CLOTH 8).

1465 *Act 4 Edw. IV*, c. 1 Ordeignez est..que chescun drap appelle Kersie..conteigne en longeure xviij aulnes..& en laeure une aulne & la naile [etc.]. **1517** *Act Com. Counc. 8 Hen. VIII*, Broad-Cloths, Carsies, Cottons, Bridge-water Frizes, Dosseins, or any other manner of Cloth made of wool. **1545** BRINKLOW *Compl.* ii. (1874) 12 Demand the clothyer, if he lyued not better whan he sold..his carseys for xxij or xxiij pownd the pack. **1599** HAKLUYT *Voy.* II. I. 127 Also we had three kintals of cotten wooll for a carsie. **1603** BRETON *Poste with Packet* D iij, I have sent you over fourscore broadclothes and thirty carzies. **1769** *De Foe's Tour Gt. Brit.* III. 148 The great Demand of Kerseys for cloathing the Armies abroad. **1810** J. T. in *Risdon's Surv. Devon* p. xxiv, The Devonshire kersies were..in great request, and were generally known by the name of Tiverton kersies.

†**c.** *pl.* = sense 1. *Obs.*

1567 in Hay Fleming *Mary Q. of Scots* (1897) 506 Item to be cotte and hoyss of blew carsis. **1634** SIR T. HERBERT *Trav.* 146 Short wide stockings of English cloth or Kersies.

3. *pl.* Trousers made of kersey.

1831 CARLYLE *Sart. Res.* I. ix, Girt with thick double-milled kerseys; half buried under shawls and broadbrims. **1864** PAYN *Lost Sir Massingberd* 84 He was dressed in a blue lapelled coat, light waistcoat, and kerseys.

4. *attrib.* or as *adj.* Made of kersey.

1577 HARRISON *England* II. vii. (1877) I. 172 An English-man..contented himselfe with his fine carsie hosen. **1594** PLAT *Jewell-ho.* II. 41 Let the same runne through a course white karsey gellie bagge. **1602** WARNER *Alb. Eng.* IX. xlvii. (1612) 218 Blacke karsie stockings. **1714** GAY *Sheph. Week* II. 37 Thy neckcloth..o'er thy Kersey Doublet spreading wide. **1822** SCOTT *Nigel* xvii, The old gentlemen in the kersey hood.

†**b.** *fig.* Plain, homely. *Obs.*

1588 SHAKS. *L.L.L.* v. ii. 413 Henceforth my woinge minde shall be exprest In russet yeas and honest kersie noes.

5. *Comb.*, as ***kersey-clothier***, ***maker***.

1587 FLEMING *Contin. Holinshed* III. 1010/2 Now it is cheeflie inhabited with merchants, kersie-clothiers, and all sorts of artificers. **1598** STOW *Surv. London* (1754) II. v. ix. 267/1 Cloth and Kersy making decayed.

Hence †ˈ**kersey** *v.*, to clothe in kersey. *rare*[−1].

1627–47 FELTHAM *Resolves* I. xxviii. 94 When the sun-bak'd Peasant goes to feast it with a Gentleman, he washes, and brushes, and kersies himself in his holy day cloathes.

[*Note.* Historically the evidence is in favour of the name being of English origin; *Caersige* was the OE. form of Kersey in Suffolk (Earle *Land Charters* 484). *Panni cersegi* were manufactured in England in 1262; *Kerseyes* were important English exports in 1390; *drap de Kersy* is mentioned along with other fabrics named from places in 1399; *carisies d'Angleterre* are mentioned in French in 1630 (Godef. *Compl.*), and *kentischer kirsey* in German in 1716 (Grimm).

At an early date the word appears in OF. as *carizé*, *carisé* (1453 in Godef. *Compl.*), later *carisie* and *carisel*. It is also common in MDu. as *kerseye*, *kaersay*, *carcey*, etc. (mod.Du. *karsaai*), and is found in G. as *kirsei*, *kirschei* (earlier *carisey*); also Da. *kersei*, *kirsei*, and Sw. *kersing*. It. and Sp. *carisea* are app. from the older F. forms.

1262 in Gross *Gild Merch.* II. 4 (Gild Merchant of Andover) Memorandum de illis qui ponunt lanam de Ispania in pannis cersegis [*mispr.* tersegis]. **1390** *Rolls of Parlt.* III. 281/2 Les liges du Roialme qe amesnent une manere de Marchandise appellez Kerseyes as parties de dela. *Ibid.* 282/1 Touchant l'envoye des ditz Kerseyes franchement. **1399** *Ibid.* III. 437 Nul Drap de Kersy, Kendale-cloth, Frise de Coventree, Coggeware, ne nulle autre estreit ne remenant d'Engleterre, ne Drap de Gales, ne soloient..paier nul Coket ne autre Custume.]

kerseymere (ˈkɜːzɪmɪə(r)). Also **karsimir**. [A corruption of CASSIMERE (q.v.), due to erroneous association with KERSEY.]

1. a. A twilled fine woollen cloth of a peculiar texture, one-third of the warp being always above, and two-thirds below each shoot of the weft.

1798 W. TAYLOR in *Monthly Rev.* XXV. 577 The purple kerseymere, which is essentialy requisite to this senatorial toga. **1802** *Med. Jrnl.* VIII. 254 That kind of cloth called Karsimir is best calculated for retaining the moisture. **1813** SIR R. WILSON *Priv. Diary* II. 187 Waggon loads of cotton goods and kerseymeres. **1876** GEO. ELIOT *Dan. Der.* xxxix, A figure..tall and physically impressive, even in his kid and kerseymere.

b. *pl.* (rarely *sing.*). Trousers made of kerseymere.

1840 HOOD *Kilmansegg, Her first Step* ii, If he had not lost some inches clear By looking down at his kerseymere. **1848** THACKERAY *Bk. Snobs* xxiv, Stripes..proceeded to gut my portmanteau, and to lay out my black kerseymeres.

2. *attrib.* or as *adj.* Made of kerseymere.

1808 JANE AUSTEN *Let.* 30 June (1952) 204 My kerseymere Spencer is quite the comfort of our Even[g] walks. **1836** MARRYAT *Jephet* xi, Silk stockings, shoes, and white kerseymere kneed breeches. **1843** BORROW *Bible in Spain* lvii. 324/1 A man about sixty, dressed in a grey kerseymere coat.

kerseynette, corrupt form of CASSINETTE.

1846 in WORCESTER. Hence in later Dicts.

ker-slap, splash, -splosh: see KER-.

†**kersp**, variant of *kirsp*, CRISP *sb. Obs.*

1508 DUNBAR *Tua mariit Wemen* 138 A curche of kersp allther fynest.

kerss, obs. form of CARSE, CRESS.

kerstenite (ˈkɜːstənaɪt). *Min.* [f. the name of K. M. *Kersten* (1803–1850), German chemist, who first reported it + -ITE[1].] A yellow selenite or selenate of lead, of uncertain composition, with a greasy to vitreous lustre.

1868 J. D. DANA *Syst. Min.* (ed. 5) 669 Kerstenite *Dana.* **1930** J. W. MELLOR *Comprehensive Treat. Inorg. & Theoret. Chem.* X. lviii. 833 C. M. Kersten reported normal lead selenite... J. D. Dana called the mineral kerstenite—*cf.* cobalt arsenide. The data do not distinguish whether the mineral is a selenite or selenate. **1951** C. PALACHE et al. *Dana's Syst. Min.* (ed. 7) II. 640 Kerstenite was found as botryoidal masses with a fibrous fracture as an alteration of zorgite at the Friedrichsglück mine near Hildburghausen, Thuringia, Germany. **1962** W. A. DEER et al. *Rock-Forming Min.* V. 188 Several other minerals and compounds have the 'barytes structure'; among them are: $BaSeO_4$, $PbSeO_4$ (kerstenite)..and $(K, Cs)BF_4$.

kert, obs. Sc. form of CARTE[1] 2, chart, map.

†**kert**, var. of (or error for) *gert*, pa. t. of GAR *v.*

c **1375** *Sc. Leg. Saints* vii. (*Jacobus Minor*) 401 He þat kert blynd men clerly se..He helpe þe gyf it be his wil.

kertch, var. CURCH.

Kertch, var. KERCH.

kertill, -tyl, obs. forms of KIRTLE.

†**kerua**, obs. form of CARAWAY.

c **1500** LLOYD *Treas. Health* (1585) Dj, Suffumigacion of ye oyle of kerua.

keruing (ˈkɛrʊɪŋ). Also **kruin**. [Malay *kĕruing*.] The light or dark brown hardwood timber of several trees of the genus *Dipterocarpus*, found in Malaysia, Sabah, and Indonesia.

1921 F. W. FOXWORTHY in *Malayan Sci. Bull.* I. 36 Meranti and Keruing, because of their contained resinous substances, are better firewoods than some of the heavier woods. **1934** A. L. HOWARD *Man. Timbers of World* (rev. ed.) 152 In the Malay Peninsula there are many species of Dipterocarpaceæ which produce timber known as keruing. **1948** *Ibid.* (ed. 3) 282 Keruing. See Kruin. *Ibid.* 291 Kruin. —This is produced by 15 to 20 species of the genus Dipterocarpus. **1950** C. W. BOND *Colonial Timbers* 54 Keruing is not unpleasant to handle at the bench. **1966** P. F. BURGESS *Timbers of Sabah* 102 Keruing is remarkable among tropical timbers for its generally straight grain. **1970** *Timber Trades Jrnl.* 21 Mar. 54/1 There have been few 'spot' offers of keruing circulating, and this timber has been hard to buy in the popular specifications.

kerumph, ker-woosh: see KER-.

kerve, obs. and dial. form of CARVE *v*.

kervel, -ell, -ale, -yle, obs. ff. CARVEL.

‖**kerygma** (kiː'rɪgmə). Pl. **kerygmata**. [Gr. κήρυγμα proclamation, preaching, f. κηρύσσειν to proclaim.] Preaching; proclamation of religious truth.

1889 *Dublin Rev.* Apr. 315 My account of the Kerygma and the Rule of Faith. **1894** tr. *Harnack's Hist. Dogma* iv. 255 *note*, The traditional complex of the Christian Kerygma. **1899** STALKER *Christology of Jesus* i. 24 [The words of Jesus] are kerygma, not dogma; nature, not science. **1936**, etc. [see DIDACHE 2]. **1949** *Scottish Jrnl. Theol.* II. 316 And the miracle of the *kerygma* is just this that through it the once and for all event in Jesus Christ becomes event all over again in the faith of the hearer. **1953** *Ibid.* VI. 314 The essential difference from Christianity, however, lies in the place occupied by such speculations about the kosmos, its beginnings and end, its hierarchies and denizens, in the respective *kerygmata*. **1955** *Ibid.* VIII. 158 Usage in direct speech may also be due to the editor, but the ruling presumption is against that, especially in the *kerygmata*. **1958** *Times Lit. Suppl.* 23 May p. vii/1 And what he writes, without a word of justification, about the unity of the mind of the apostles with that of Christ, and of the apostolic *kerygma* with the activity of Christ, could be used by the Pope himself and welcomed by him as coming from a Protestant source. **1962** *Ibid.* 17 Aug. 628/2 It is also true that historical facts become objects of religious faith only when they belong to salvation-history and are part of the *kerygma*, the proclamation of the gospel, which presents them as sources and types of the redemption offered to mankind. **1970** WEST & FRANCIS *Scandal in Assembly* xxviii. 151 Without the *Kerygma*, the *didache* reduces itself to a system of ethics as unstable as the customs of men.

Hence **keryg'matic** *a*., belonging to or of the nature of preaching; **keryg'matically** *adv*.

1929 *Church Times* 18 Jan. 82/1 Our ministry..before all else..is 'kerygmatic', the proclamation of a Kingdom and a King. **1949** *Scottish Jrnl. Theol.* II. 88 They hold that the Scriptures of the New Testament witness to Jesus Christ Himself *kerygmatically*, that is in such a way that He Himself, by the power of His Spirit, speaks to men through them. **1955** *Ibid.* VIII. 346 The present Hexateuch represents the elaboration and the heaping up of traditions around the simple kerygmatic theme, the chief premonarchial elements of which can be discerned in old confessions. **1969** E. SIMONS in *Sacramentum Mundi: Encycl. Theol.* III. 246/1 This dialectic of mediation.. which may be termed dialogal, is a kerygmatic event. **1970** J. DONCEEL tr. *Rahner's Trinity* II. 57 Some new word..may be more precisely and easily understood, hence kerygmatically more useful than the word 'person'.

kerystic (kiː'rɪstɪk), *a*. and *sb*. [ad. Gr. type *κηρυστικός, f. κηρύσσειν to preach.] **A.** *adj*. Relating to, of the nature of, preaching. **B.** *sb*. in *pl*. The study of preaching.

1882–3 SCHAFF *Encycl. Relig. Knowl.* II. 1011 Some.. have discarded the term 'homiletics' altogether, and substituted in its stead, as more comprehensive, 'kerystics'.

kes, kesar, obs. forms of KISS, KAISER.

‖**kesa-gatame** (ˌkesaga'taːme). *Judo*. [Jap.] The 'scarf' hold, a way of holding the opponent by the edge (the so-called 'scarf') of his jacket in an attempt to immobilize him.

1932 E. J. HARRISON *Art of Ju-Jitsu* v. 68 (*heading*) 'Locking in the form of a scarf' (kesagatame; otherwise hongesa, or 'regular scarf'). **1957** TAKAGAKI & SHARP *Techniques Judo* III. viii. 112 *Kesa gatame* is one of the simplest holds to secure. **1968** P. & K. BUTLER *Judo & Self-Defence for Women & Girls* 141 (*heading*) Kesa-gatame—scarf hold. T applies kesa-gatame, U struggles then submits.

kesh, kesk, dial. forms of KEX.

Keshan, var. KASHAN.

kesh-work: see KISH *sb*.[1]

keskeedie, keskidee, varr. KISKADEE.

keskoo, keskossou, var. COUSCOUS, -COUSSOU.

1878 HOOKER & BALL *Morocco* 268 A dish of keskossou. **1891** HALL CAINE *Scapegoat* xxv, Fifty camels' load of keskoo.

keslep, -lip, -lop, northern ff. CHEESELIP, -LEP[1].

1534–5 *Durham Acc. Rolls.* (Surtees) 112 Et sol. pro le kesselopes..4*s*. **1570** LEVINS *Manip.* 70/25 Keslep, renet bag *coagulum*. **1624** *Naworth Househ. Bks.* (Surtees) 216, ij keslops, viij[d].

kesse, obs. f. KISS *v*.

kest (kɛst), *v*. Dial. var. of CAST *v*. esp. in senses 'cast aside, throw away' and (*fig*.) 'do down, outdo'.

1590 SPENSER *Faerie Queene* I. xi. 163 That infernall Monster, hauing kest His wearie foe into that liuing well. **1862** C. C. ROBINSON *Dial. Leeds* 334 A man who has been abroad in bad weather, ill-clad, says,—'Ah sal nivver kest what I've gotten to neet I knawah.' **1892** J. WRIGHT *Gram. Dial. of Windhill, W. Riding* iii. 29 In the following words we have *e* which in many of the examples is no doubt the *i*-umlaut of *a*:..*kest* (ME. *kesten*) to cast. **1893–4** R. O. HESLOP *Northumb. Words* II. I. 421 He kest his claes ower syun an' gat caad. **1913** D. H. LAWRENCE *Sons & Lovers* II. vii. 164 At seven o'clock the family heard him buy threepennyworth of hot-cross buns... He turned away several boys who came with more buns, telling them they had been 'kested' by a little lass. *Ibid.* viii. 200 Just then Wesson entered... 'I see you've kested me,' he said, smiling rather vapidly. 'Yes,' replied Barker.

kest, -e, obs. ff. CAST *sb*. and *v*.; obs. pa.t. of KISS *v*.

kësterite ('kɛstəraɪt). *Min*. Also **kesterite**. [ad. Russ. *kësterit* (Z. V. Orlova, 1956), f. *Këster*, name of its locality in Yakutia, Siberia: see -ITE[1].] A black sulphide of copper, tin, zinc, and iron, $Cu_2(Zn,Fe)SnS_4$.

1958 *Mineral. Mag.* XXXI. 963 *Kësterite*... (Cu,Sn,Zn) S, containing Cu 30·56, Sn 25·25, Zn 11·16, S 23·40%. **1968** I. KOSTOV *Mineral.* ii. 147 Sakuraiite..is considered an indium analogue of kesterite.

kesteyn, var. of CHESTEINE *Obs*.

kestrel ('kɛstrɪl). Forms: α. 6–7 castrell, 6–8 -el, 6–9 -ill, 7–8 -il, -eril; **kastrell, -il(l, -al, -el**. β. 6–7 **kist-**, 7 **kest-, kaist-, keistrell**, 6– **kestrel, -il**. γ. 7–9 **coistrell, -il, coystrel, -il**. [ME. *castrel*, app. corresp. (through **cas'rel*, **casserel*) to OF. *cresserelle, crécerelle, quercerelle*, mod. Poitevin *casserelle*. The ulterior etymology is obscure, and it is difficult to reconcile the different OF. forms with each other or the It. equivalents. See Godef., Cotgr., and Rolland *Faune popul. de la France* II. 31. The rare *coistrel* is prob. due to confusion with COISTREL, groom, varlet.]

1. A species of small hawk (*Falco tinnunculus*, or *Tinnunculus alaudarius*), also called *stannel* or *windhover*, remarkable for its habit of sustaining itself in the same place in the air with its head to the wind. The name is extended to about 15 foreign species of the restricted genus *Tinnunculus*.

α. **14..** *Turn. Totenham, Feest* ix, Ther was castrell in cambys, And capulls in cullys. **1577** B. GOOGE *Heresbach's Husb.* III. (1586) 170 There is a kinde of Hauke, that naturally is terrible to other Haukes, and preserveth the Pigion: the common people call it Castrell. **1621** BURTON *Anat. Mel.* II. ii. IV. (1651) 268 Some reclaime Ravens, Castrils, Pies, etc., and man them for their pleasures. **1726** LEONI tr. *Alberti's Archit.* I. 97/1 If in one corner..you enclose a Kastrel, it will secure your Dove-house from birds of prey. **1829** J. HOGG in *Four C. Eng. Lett.* (Camden) 421 The hills of Westmoreland that can nourish nothing better than a castrill or stone-chat!

β. **1602** *2nd Pt. Return fr. Parnass.* I. ii. 175 Those eggs which have ben filcht from the nest[s] of Crowes and Kestrells. **1608** TOPSELL *Serpents* (1658) 655 Those kind of Hawks which are called Kaistrels or Fleingals. **1766** PENNANT *Zool.* (1768) I. 149 The kestril breeds in the hollows of trees. **1816** KIRBY & SP. *Entomol.* (1828) I. ix. 288 Among the Accipitres the kestril devours abundance of insects. **1870** MORRIS *Earthly Par.* II. III. 348 As on unheard wings The kestrel hangs above the mouse. **1893** NEWTON *Dict. Birds* 479 Some of the islands of the Ethiopian Region have peculiar species of Kestrel, as the *T. newtoni* of Madagascar..and *T. gracilis* of the Seychelles;..the Kestrel of the Cape Verd Islands has been separated as *T. neglectus*.

γ. *a* **1613** OVERBURY *A Wife*, etc. (1638) 183 Like a Coistrell he strives to fill himselfe with wind, and flies against it. **1687** DRYDEN *Hind & P.* III. 1119. **1831** H. NEELE *Romance Hist.* I. 21, I would stake my noblest falcon against the vilest coystril in England.

b. *fig*., or in fig. context, applied to persons, usually with contemptuous force.

1589 GREENE *Menaphon* (Arb.) 64 Nay I thought no lesse ..that you would proue such a kinde of kistrell. **1621** FLETCHER *Pilgrim* I. i, But there is another in the wind—some castrell That hovers over her. **1820** SCOTT *Monast.* xix, Thou art thyself a kite, and kestrel to boot.

2. *attrib*., as ***kestrel bird, breed, kind***.

1590 SPENSER *F.Q.* II. iii. 4 In his kestrell kynd A pleasing vaine of glory he did fynd. **1596** NASHE *Saffron Walden* K ij, One of these kistrell birds, called a wind-sucker. **1831** H. NEELE *Romance Hist.* I. 194 A bird of such a coystril breed.

Keswick ('kɛzɪk). The name of a town in Cumbria, used to designate a variety of cooking apple, in full **Keswick codlin(g)**, which has a greenish skin tinged with red and was first introduced by John Sander, who lived in the town.

1814 *Mem. Caledonian Hort. Soc.* I. 374 (*title*) Information regarding the Carlisle and Keswick Codlin Apples. *Ibid.* 376 The Keswick Codlin tree has never failed to bear a crop since it was planted..twenty years ago. **1831** H. RONALDS *Pyrus Malus Brentfordiensis* 5 Keswick Codlin. A favourite sauce apple from the North of England. **1912** MULFORD & CLAY *Buck Peters* xxii. 198 It's Buck as sure as little apples Kesicks. **1936** H. V. TAYLOR *Apples Eng.* vii. 74 Those [apples] that became soft and frothy, even on coddling (i.e. parboiling), were known as coddlings—the Keswick Codling, English Codling. **1973** *Countryman* LXXVIII. IV. 42, I could watch the sheets billowing, and the clothes flapping and being confettied by blossom from the crabs, keswicks and white heart cherries.

ket[1]. *Obs*. exc. *dial*. Also 6 **kytte**. [a. ON. *kjǫt* (:—**ketwo*[m]), flesh, in mod.Icel. also *ket* (Sw. *kött*, Da. *kød, kjød*).] Raw flesh; carrion; also *fig*. trash, rubbish.

c **1220** *Bestiary* 438 He billeð one ðe foxes fel, Wo so telleð idel spel, And he tireð on his ket Wo so him wið sinne fet [= feeds]. **1586** *Scotter Manor Records* in *N.W. Linc. Gloss.*, That no man throwe no kytte or caryon vnto the heighe waye. **1616** SURFL. & MARKH. *Country Farme* 677 Your raw flesh meate (which amongst huntsmen is called ket). **1788** W. MARSHALL *Yorksh.* Gloss. (E.D.S.), *Ket*, carrion. **1808–80** JAMIESON, *Ket, kett*, carrion, the flesh of animals, especially sheep, that have died of disease or from accident. **1893** *Northumbld. Gloss.*, *Ket*.

Comb. **1828** *Craven Dial.*, *Ket-craw*, a carrion crow.

ket[2]. *Sc*. *rare*[−1]. [cf. COT *sb*.[2]] 'A matted, hairy fleece of wool' (Jam.).

1782 BURNS *Poor Mailie's Elegy* vi, She was nae get o' moorland tips, Wi' tawted ket, an' hairy hips.

ket[3] (kɛt). *Quantum Mech*. [f. BRAC)KET: cf. BRA[2].] A vector in Hilbert space symbolized by |>; *esp*. one representing the state of a quantized system. Freq. as ***ket vector***.

1947 P. A. M. DIRAC *Princ. Quantum Mech.* (ed. 3) i. 16 It is desirable to have a special name for describing the vectors which are connected with the states of a system in quantum mechanics, whether they are in a space of a finite or an infinite number of dimensions. We shall call them ket vectors, or simply kets, and denote a general one of them by a special symbol |>. **1957** F. MANDL *Quantum Mech.* (ed. 2) v. 102 Labels, in particular eigenvalues, distinguishing different ket vectors are written as arguments of the ket vectors. For example, we might write a set of vectors as |1>, |2>,..|*n*>, or the wave function (14.4) as |*l, m*>. **1972** J. M. JAUCH in Salam & Wigner *Aspects Quantum Theory* ix. 142 Dirac never defines what a ket vector is mathematically, he describes its physical interpretation as 'vectors which are connected with the states of a system in quantum mechanics'. From the context one concludes that they are vectors in a Hilbert space. **1973** [see BRA[2]]. **1974** P. W. ATKINS *Quanta* 30 The state of a system whose wavefunction is $\Psi_n(r)$ is represented by the ket |*n*>, and the conjugate $\Psi_n^*(r)$ by the bra <*n*|.

ket-: see KETO-.

keta ('kiːtə). Also †**keth**. [Russ.] = CHUM *sb*.[4]

1824 S. BLACK *Jrnl. Voy. from Rocky Mountain Portage* (1955) 52 In Bears River near the Lake they speared a kind of salmon he names Keth in the Rapids. **1901** A. M. B. MEAKIN *Ribbon of Iron* xviii. 263 At Nikolaevsk upwards of a hundred and ninety-three thousand pnds of a salmon called 'keta'—*salmo lagocephalus*—are salted annually. **1905** D. S. JORDAN *Guide to Study of Fishes* II. iv. 73 In Japan *keta* is by far the most abundant species of salmon. **1933** A. W. SHIELS *Seward's Ice Box* 83 Chums or keta are plentiful in all districts. **1962** *Co-op Grocery News Bull.* (Saskatoon) 1 Aug. 1 Formerly known as dog salmon, the chum, with the scientific name Oncorhynchus Keta, has also been called the qualla, keta and calico salmon. It is caught all along the coast of British Columbia.

ketal, ketamine, etc.: see KETO- a.

ketate ('kiːteɪt). *Chem*. [f. KET-ONE + -ATE[4].] An ether of ketone.

1892 MORLEY & MUIR *Watts' Dict. Chem.* III. 101/2.

ketch (kɛtʃ), *sb*.[1] *Naut*. [Later form of *cache*, CATCH *sb*.[2], with *e* for *a* as in *keg, kennel, kestrel*, etc.] A strongly-built two-masted vessel, usually from 100 to 250 tons burden, formerly much used as a bomb-vessel (see BOMB-KETCH); now a similarly rigged small coasting vessel.

[**1481** —: see CATCH *sb*.[2]] **1655** CROMWELL *Let.* 13 June in Carlyle, Those [dispatches] which were sent by a ketch immediately from hence. **1665** *Lond. Gaz.* No. 3/4 Thursday last the Drake Friggot, and a Ketch with Goods, ..were put back by the storms. **1720** DE FOE *Capt. Singleton* xviii. (1840) 315 She sailed..with square sail and mizen-mast, like a ketch. **1876** T. HARDY *Ethelberta* II. 44 Outside these lay the tanned sails of a ketch or smack.

b. *attrib*. and *Comb*., as ***ketch fashion, rig***; ***ketch-rigged*** adj.

1819 REES *Cycl.* s.v., At present only a few coasting vessels are rigged ketch fashion. **1845** NICOLAS *Disp. Nelson* II. 177 La Vierge de Consolation, one hundred and twenty tons, ketch-rigged. **1891** *Daily News* 13 Feb. 3/5 Some twelve thousand square feet of sail spread in what is known as the 'Salcombe ketch rig'.

ketch, *sb*.[2] [See JACK KETCH.] The hangman. Hence **ketch** *v*.[1] *trans*., to hang; **ketchcraft**, the hangman's craft.

1681 T. FLATMAN *Heraclitus Ridens* No. 14 'Squire Ketch rejoices as much to hear of a new *Vox*, as an old Sexton does to hear of a new Delight. *Ibid.* No. 18 Well! If he has a mind to be Ketch'd, speed him say I. **1706** *Wooden World Dissected* (1708) 80 For a running Noose, this new Ketch is but a Fool to him. **1840** *Fraser's Mag.* XXI. 210 Ignorant of many of the secrets of ketchcraft. **1859** MATSELL *Vocab.* s.v. (Farmer), I'll ketch you; I'll hang you.

ketch (kɛtʃ), *v*.[2] Dial. var. (pa. t. **ketched**) of CATCH *v*.

1815 D. HUMPHREYS *Yankey in England* I. 21, I guess, he is trying to ketch me—but it won't du. I'm tu old a bird to be ketch'd with chaff. **1865** DICKENS *Mut. Fr.* II. IV. xv. 287 Wot is it, lambs, as they ketches in seas, rivers, lakes, and ponds? *a* **1883** [see KNUCK 2]. **1911** E. WHARTON *Ethan Frome* ii. 60 You'll ketch your death. The fire's out long ago. **1916** W. O. BRADLEY *Stories & Speeches* 18 You'll never ketch me hollerin' at no Republican gatherin'. **1929** H. W. ODUM in A. Dundes *Mother Wit* (1973) 184 If so you gonna ketch hell. **1967** *Atlantic Monthly* Apr. 103/1 You heard about that joke a dollar down and a dollar when you ketch me? **1968** S. STUCKEY in A. Chapman *New Black Voices* (1972) 445 Run, nigger, run, de patrollers will ketch you.

ketch, var. CATCH *sb*.[1]; obs. f. KEACH *v*.

ketchak, var. KETJAK.

†**ketchepillar**. *Sc*. *Obs*. *rare*[−1]. [f. **ketche-*, *cachepill*, CACHESPELL + -ER[1].] A tennis-player.

1500–20 DUNBAR *Poems* xiv. 66 Sa mony rakkettis, sa mony ketche-pillaris, Sic ballis, sic nackettis, and sic tutivillaris..Within this land was nevir hard nor sene.

ketchup ('kɛtʃəp, -ʌp). Also 8 kitchup: see also CATCHUP. [app. ad. Chinese (Amoy dial.) *kôechiap* or *kê-tsiap* brine of pickled fish or shell-fish (Douglas *Chinese Dict.* 46/1, 242/1). Malay *kĕchap* (in Du. spelling *ketjap*), which has been claimed as the original source (Scott *Malayan Wds. in English* 64–67), may be from Chinese.

The Japanese *kitjap*, alleged in some recent dicts., is an impossible form for that language. (? error for *Javanese*.)]

A sauce made from the juice of mushrooms, walnuts, tomatoes, etc., and used as a condiment with meat, fish, or the like. Often with qualification, as ***mushroom ketchup***, etc.

1711 LOCKYER *Acc. Trade India* 128 Soy comes in Tubbs from Jappan, and the best Ketchup from Tonquin; yet good of both sorts are made and sold very cheap in China. **1748** MRS. HARRISON *House-kpr.'s Pocket-bk.* i. (ed. 4) 2, I therefore advise you to lay in a Store of Spices,.. neither ought you to be without.. Kitchup, or Mushroom Juice. **1817** BYRON *Beppo* viii, Buy in gross.. Ketchup, Soy, Chili-vinegar, and Harvey. **1840** DICKENS *Barn. Rudge* (1849) 91/1 Some lamb chops (breaded, with plenty of ketchup). **1874** COOKE *Fungi* 89 One important use to which several.. fungi can be applied, is the manufacture of ketchup.

ketch-word, obs. f. CATCHWORD (sense 3).

1715 M. DAVIES *Athen. Brit.* I. Pref. 4 Pamphlets become more and more.. Ketch-words to Informers,.. Heart-ease to Censurers.

†**kete**, *a.* and *adv.* *Obs.* [Early ME. *kete* (*kēte*), not known in OE.: etymology uncertain.

Perh. related to ON. *kæti* sb., cheer, gladness, f. *kátr* cheerful, merry. Kluge (*Paul's Grundr.* (ed. 2) I. 939) suggests an unrecorded ON. *kætr*, beside *kátr*, but of this there is no evidence. Cf. also Björkeman *Scandinavian Loanwds. in ME.* (1900) 174.]

A. *adj.* **1.** Of persons (or animals): Bold, forward; brave; distinguished.

c **1275** *Sayings of Bede* 47 in Horstm. *Altengl. Leg.* (1881) 506 Pikede beþ þe shete, And wormes þer beþ kete [*rimes* hete, ounimete] To don þe soule tene. *Ibid.* 131 Satanas þe kete [*rimes* strete, ounimete, biȝete] Here soule wille derien. [Cf. other versions in *Sinners Beware* 53, 143 in *O.E. Misc.* 73, 76.] *c* **1350** *Will. Palerne* 330 Whanne þou komest to kourt among þe kete lordes. *c* **1400** *St. Alexius* 201 (Laud MS.) He to a borugh com þat mychel was & kete [*rime* grete *inf.*]. *c* **1449** PECOCK *Repr.* I. i. 5 In this.. holding thei ben so kete and so smert and so wantoun.

2. Of things: Great, strong, powerful, violent.

a **1290** *Magdalena* 369 in *S. Eng. Leg.* I. 472 þe stormes beoth so kete [*rime* lete *inf.*] To quellen us huy þenchez. *a* **1300** *Fragm. Pop. Sc.* (Wright) 262 For the grete hete Of the sonne that is above, the leomes beoth so kete. *a* **1330** *Syr Degarre* 337 Thanne he herde a noise kete In o valai, an dintes grete.

B. *adv.* Boldly, bravely; quickly.

c **1380** *Sir Ferumb.* 3667 þe Sarasyn þat opon him set After Richard prikede ket. *Ibid.* 4596 A litel by-fore þe ȝeate... Charlys gan fiȝte.. And sloȝe þe Sarsyns kete.

Hence †**ketly** *adv.*, quickly, hastily. *Obs.*

c **1350** *Will. Palerne* 1986 Þhe.. kom ketly to þemperour & kurteisly him gret. *Ibid.* 3023 þan þat comli quen ketli vp rises.

†**kete** *v.*, obs. var. GET *v.* (pa. t. **kat**, pa. pple. (**y**)**kete**).

c **1420** *Chron. Vilod.* 673 For he shuld knowell þ^t he had kete of God mercy and grace, And kete w^t hurr' repentaunce hevene blys. *Ibid.* 840 Kyng Edgarus douȝter yche wene he was, Y-kete bot upon a wenche. *Ibid.* 1094 And w^e his travell his lyf lode kat.

kete, obs. f. KITE.

kete, kête, varr. KIT *sb.*[1]

ketel, ketelok, obs. ff. KETTLE, KEDLOCK.

ketene ('ki:ti:n). *Chem.* Also -en. [ad. G. *keten* (H. Staudinger 1905, in *Ber. d. Deut. Chem. Ges.* XXXVIII. 1735): see KETONE and -ENE.] **a.** Any compound containing an ethylenic double bond adjacent to a carbonyl group, i.e. the structure $>C=C=O$.

[**1905** *Jrnl. Chem. Soc.* LXXXVIII. 444 Diphenylketen $CPh_2:CO$, the first representative of a new type of compound, is prepared by the action of zinc on an ethereal solution of diphenylchloroacetyl chloride.] **1907** *Ibid.* XCI. 1941 There can.. be no doubt that the new substance is a keten, having the formula $CH_2:CO$. **1942** FUSON & SNYDER *Org. Chem.* xxi. 296 Carbonyl compounds which contain the grouping $>C=C=O$ are known as ketenes... Ketenes fall into two classes, aldoketenes and ketoketenes. **1971** *Jrnl. Chem. Soc.* (C) 3645 The addition of ketenes to conjugated dienes generally yields 1,2-adducts.

b. The simplest of the ketenes, $CH_2:C:O$, a pungent colourless gas which dimerizes on liquefaction and has wide applications in synthesis owing to its high reactivity.

1907 *Jrnl. Chem. Soc.* XCI. 1941 Keten has a peculiar penetrating smell. **1946** [see ACETYLATION]. **1964** N. G. CLARK *Mod. Org. Chem.* xi. 211 On heating acetic acid vapour at 700° to 800° under reduced pressure, it loses the elements of water to form keten. **1972** *Guardian* 16 Oct. 15/2 Although keten and its organic relations have been known and used for generations, no one had realised that they could produce salts.

keth, kethe(n, var. KITHE *v.*

ketharan, -therin, obs. ff. CATERAN *sb.*[1]

kether, dial. corr. of QUOTHA.

1698 *Unnat. Mother* (N.) Hei, hei! handsom, kether! sure somebody has been rouling him in the rice.

‖**kethib, -ibh** (kə'θi:v). *Heb. O.T.* Also ketiv, chetiv, cetib. [Heb. *k'thībh* written.] The name given to the traditional reading in the text of the Hebrew Old Testament: see KERI.

1644, etc. [see KERI].

kethubah, var. KETUBAH.

‖**Kethubim** (kɛθu:'vi:m, kɛt-), *sb. pl.* Also 7 Chetoubim, 20 Ketubim, K'tubhim, -vim. [Heb. *k'thūbīm* writings.] = HAGIOGRAPHA *sb. pl.*

1690 tr. *J. Le Clerc's Five Lett.* ii. 102 Others.. they call Chetoubim, or simply Writings; that is to say, the Psalms [etc.]. **1892** H. E. RYLE *Canon of Old Testament* vi. 127 The *Psalter* is the most important book of the 'Kethubim'. *Ibid.* 132 The Book of Job.. had no fitting place in the Canon save in the mixed group of 'the Kethubim'. **1904** *Jewish Encycl.* VI. 151/1 It can not now be ascertained when the name 'Ketubim' and the Greek designation 'Hagiographa' were first given to the collection. **1961** *Jrnl. Biblical Lit.* LXXX. 106 Tanak.. stems from the abbreviations of the three divisions, *Torah*, *Nebhi'im*, and *K'tubhim*, of the Hebrew Scriptures. **1967** D. T. KAUFFMAN *Dict. Relig. Terms* 274 *Ketuvim* or *Kethubim*, third section of the Jewish Scriptures: the Sacred Writings beginning with the Psalms and ending with the Chronicles.

ketine ('ki:taɪn). *Chem.* [f. KET(ONE + -INE[5].] An oily liquid, $C_6H_8N_2$, or one of a series of homologous bases $C_nH_{2n-4}N_2$ formed by the reduction of nitrosoacetone and its homologues by sodium (or tin) and hydrochloric acid.

1892 MORLEY & MUIR *Watts' Dict. Chem.* III. 101.

‖**ketjak** ('kɛtʃæk). Also **ketchak, 'tjak.** [Balinese, f. '*tjak-a-tjak*', the sound of the chanted refrain accompanying the dance.] A Balinese dance, with a male chorus. Also *attrib.*

1937 M. COVARRUBIAS *Island of Bali* (1972) viii. 219 *Ketjak*, large groups of men singing in chorus, moving and dancing to the rhythm of the music. **1938** DE ZOETE & SPIES *Dance & Drama in Bali* ii. 85 The *ketjak* dance is primarily a dance of exorcism. **1942** C. BARRETT *On Wallaby* ix. 176 The Monkey Dance or Ketchak Ceremonies impressed me more than all other dances and dramas... A Ketchak was held solely for our entertainment. **1954** J. COAST *Dancing out of Bali* viii. 161, I had suggested the gamelan club forming a 'Tjak, or Monkey Dance chorus. **1972** C. SIMPSON *Bali & Beyond* 26 *Ketjak* is the name of the male chorus in the *sanghyang* and this dance extends the role of that chorus to a *Ramayana*-story presentation in which the number of men is increased to about 150. **1972** *Times* 11 Nov. 13/4 The dancers you see performing the *Barong* or the *Ketchak*.. are not professionals.

ketling, -yng, obs. forms of KITLING.

ketlock, var. KEDLOCK.

ketly: see KETE *a.*

keto- ('ki:təʊ), comb. form of KETONE. **a.** (Before a vowel also **ket-**.) As an inseparable formative element of terms in *Chem.* and *Med.*: **ketal** ('ki:tæl) [after ACETAL], any compound of the type $R^1R^2C(OR^3)OR^4$, where neither R^1 nor R^2 is a hydrogen atom (see quot. 1926); **'ketamine**, a crystalline anæsthetic and analgesic substance, $C_{13}H_{16}NOCl$; 2-*o*-chlorophenyl-2-methyl-aminocyclohexanone; **'ketazine** [ad. G. *ketazin* (Curtius & Thun 1891, in *Jrnl. f. prakt. Chem.* XLIV. 162)], any compound of the type $RR'C:N{\cdot}N:CR''R'''$, made by reacting one molecule of hydrazine with two molecules of (identical or different) ketones; **'ketimine**, any compound containing the grouping $>C=NH$, formed e.g. by the action of ammonia on a ketone; **ˌketoaci'dosis**, acidosis due to enhanced production of ketone bodies; hence **ˌketoaci'dotic** *a.*, of or pertaining to ketoacidosis; **ˌketo'bemidone** [perh. f. car*be*thoxy- + M(ETHYL + -ID[4] + -ONE], an analgesic, $(C_6H_4OH)(COC_2H_5)C_5H_8N{\cdot}CH_3$, with action similar to that of morphine; **keto'genesis**, production of ketone bodies; **keto'genic**, †**-ge'netic** *adjs.*, producing ketone bodies; applied *spec.* to a diet that is rich in fats and low in carbohydrates and has been used therapeutically to produce ketosis; (*17-*)*ketogenic steroid*, any steroid which yields a (17-)ketosteroid on oxidation with a bismuthate; **α-ketoglu'taric acid**, a dibasic keto-acid, $HOOC{\cdot}CO{\cdot}CH_2{\cdot}CH_2{\cdot}COOH$, which is formed by oxidation and decarboxylation of isocitric acid in the Krebs cycle; hence **α-keto'glutarate**, a salt or ester, or the anion, of α-ketoglutaric acid; **keto'hexose**, any ketose with six carbon atoms; **α-ˌketoˌisova'leric acid**, a crystalline carboxylic acid, $(CH_3)_2CH{\cdot}CO{\cdot}COOH$, from which valine is synthesized by transamination in fungi; hence **α-ˌketoˌiso'valerate**, a salt or ester, or the anion, of α-ketoisovaleric acid; **keto'keten(e)** [a. G. *ketoketen* (Staudinger & Klever 1908, in *Ber. d. Deut. Chem. Ges.* XLI. 909)], any ketene of the type $RR'C:C:O$; **ke'tolysis**, decomposition of ketone bodies; hence **keto'lytic** *a.*, causing or pertaining to ketolysis; **keto'lytically** *adv.*; **keto'steroid**, any steroid whose molecules contain a ketone group; ***17-ketosteroid*** (see quot. 1964); **ke'toxime**, an oxime of a ketone (i.e. any compound containing the group $>C:NOH$), formed by the action of hydroxylamine on a ketone; **'ketyl** [-YL], any salt containing a free-radical anion of the type $RR'C{\cdot}O^-$, formed by dissolving a metal in a ketone.

1924 *Chem. Abstr.* XVIII. 3518 (*heading*) Velocity of hydrolysis of acetals and *ketals. **1926** *Ibid.* XX. 2937 The saponification of ketals (acetals of ketones) was studied in the presence of mineral acid catalyzers. They are liquids of disagreeable odor, insol. in water, sol. in alc., ether, etc., stable towards dil. alkali, rapidly hydrolyzed by dil. acid. **1933** *Jrnl. Amer. Chem. Soc.* LV. 3744 The method described in this paper.. furnishes a simple approach to cyclic ketals which are difficult or impossible to make by the usual method. **1965** *Nomencl. Org. Chem.* (I.U.P.A.C.) C. 104 Compounds containing the group $>C<^{OR^1}_{OR^2}$ are termed acetals. [*Note*] The name 'ketal' is abandoned. **1967** I. L. FINAR *Org. Chem.* (ed. 5) I. viii. 189 Ketones do not readily form ketals when treated with alcohols in the presence of hydrogen chloride... Ketals may, however, be prepared by treating the ketone with ethyl orthoformate. **1966** *Approved Names* (Brit. Pharmacopœia Comm.) 23 *Ketamine. **1967** *Martindale's Extra Pharmacopoeia* (ed. 25) 1530/2 Ketamine hydrochloride is a potent analgesic and anaesthetic with actions similar to those of phencyclidine hydrochloride.., to which it is chemically related. **1968** *Anesthesia & Analgesia Current Res.* XLVII. 775/2 Ketamine has both a stimulatory and a depressive effect on the cardiovascular system. The stimulation predominates with small doses. **1972** *Anesthesiology* XXXVI. 311 With the increased medical and veterinary use of ketamine, it will probably become a popular hallucinogenic street drug. **1894** *Jrnl. Chem. Soc.* LXVI. 348 (*heading*) Transformation of *ketazines into pyrazolines. **1911** *Ibid.* C. I. 571 The ketazines from the following ketones have been prepared and examined: benzophenone, fluorenone, and tetramethyldiaminobenzophenone. All the compounds are stable.. and when hydrolysed by hot mineral acids yield hydrazine and ketone. **1943** H. GILMAN *Org. Chem.* (ed. 2) I. ix. 812 Hydrazones and ketazines have also been hydrogenated by means of platinum.. catalysts. **1909** J. F. THORPE in *Proc. Chem. Soc.* XXV. 309 It is suggested that as the compounds containing the group C:NH are in many respects analogous to the ketones, the general name *ketimine should be applied to them, leaving the name imine to be applied to the secondary amines. **1938** ALLEN & BLATT in H. Gilman *Org. Chem.* I. vi. 568 Monomolecular ketimines.. have been prepared; they too are readily hydrolyzed and reduced. **1971** N. L. ALLINGER et al. *Org. Chem.* xxi. 586 Grignard reagents add to the cyano group of most nitriles to give salts of ketimines. **1958** *Diabetes* VII. 230 (*heading*) The nature and correction of diabetic *ketoacidosis. **1961** *Endocrinology* LXVIII. 815 Rather marked insulin insufficiency is necessary for the development of uncontrolled diabetic ketoacidosis. **1969** *Nature* 20 Dec. 1155/1 All the children suffered from vomiting, lethargy and ketoacidosis, and did not grow. **1966** DUNLOP & ALSTEAD *Textbk. Med. Treatm.* (ed. 10) 353 The patient in *ketoacidotic coma must be sent without delay to hospital. **1972** *Jrnl. Clin. Invest.* LI. 493/2 Intensive therapy for 72–96 hr with parenteral glucose and alkali were necessary before he recovered from his ketoacidotic episodes. **1949** *Jrnl. Pharmacol. & Exper. Therap.* XCVII. 188 *Keto-bemidone appears to be one of the most addictive drugs yet discovered. **1958** *A.M.A. Arch. Internal Med.* CI. 745 Comparison of ketobemidone with other common analgesics shows that it is one of the safest drugs to use for analgesia because of the great difference between its analgesic and euphoria-producing doses. **1972** J. BALL *Five Pieces Jade* vi. 73 Have you heard of keto-bedmidone [*sic*]? Or Claradon, that's another name for it... It is extremely addictive. Considerably more than heroin. **1915** *Arch. Internal Med.* XV. 65 Feeding of pancreas may augment *ketogenesis by determining increased absorption of fat. **1933** CAMERON & GILMOUR *Biochem. of Med.* v. 77, 1 gram by weight of glucose can be oxidized in the body along with 4·8 grams of fat, without ketogenesis. **1972** *Diabetes* XXI. 50/2 Ketogenesis from fatty acid is thus tied into the liver cell's energy metabolism. **1915** *Arch. Internal Med.* XV. 63 It seems probable that it falls in the same category as that increased sensitiveness of the diabetic organism to *ketogenetic factors after repeated pancreatic opotherapy. **1911** STEDMAN *Med. Dict.* 452/1 *Ketogenic. **1921** *Jrnl. Biol. Chem.* XLIX. 162 A method is described by which the ratio of ketogenic to antiketogenic molecules in the metabolic mixture of a subject may be calculated from the respiratory quotient. **1930** *Sci. Amer.* Nov. 391 This is called a ketogenic diet, because it tends to produce an excessive amount of ketones and their derivatives in the blood. **1952** J. K. NORYMBERSKI in *Nature* 20 Dec. 1075/1 The difference between 17-ketosteroids found before and after oxidation of urine affords a measure of '17-ketogenic steroids' which represent an important group of corticosteroids. **1968** R. F. STEINER *Life Chem.* ix. 168 Four amino acids—leucine, isoleucine, phenylanine [*sic*] and tyrosine—can give rise to ketone bodies... The.. group of amino acids are termed ketogenic. **1972** *Jrnl. Clin. Endocrinol. & Metabolism* XXXIV. 580/1 Routine urine steroid analysis showed normal excretion of 17-ketosteroids and 17-ketogenic steroids. **1973** *Nature* 2 Mar. 74/1 He was interested in the mechanism of action of ketogenic diets which were then used for the treatment of urinary tract infections. **1911** *Jrnl. Chem. Soc.* C. I. 520 Ethyl α-*ketoglutarate, b.p. 114°/13 mm., obtained by esterification of the acid in a closed tube at 120°, is a colourless liquid. **1940** *Jrnl. Biol. Chem.* CXXXVI. 302 Carbon dioxide combines directly with pyruvic acid to yield

oxaloacetic acid, the latter then combining with an additional molecule of pyruvate to form α-ketoglutarate. **1971** *Scand. Jrnl. Clin. & Lab. Invest.* XXVIII. 365/1 The known ammonia-detoxifying processes..involve amination of α-ketoglutarate to glutamate and amidation of glutamate to glutamine. **1908** *Jrnl. Chem. Soc.* XCIV. I. 713 When ethyl oxalosuccinate is treated with hydrogen chloride in the cold and the solution boiled, hydrolysis takes place and α-*ketoglutaric acid..is formed. **1937** *Biochem. Jrnl.* XXXI. 300, α-Ketoglutaric acid thus appears to arise in the course of pyruvic acid oxidation. **1938** *Ibid.* XXXII. 112 Ten human urines contained between 10 and 40 mg. α-ketoglutaric acid per 24 hr. specimen. **1968** R. F. STEINER *Life Chem.* xii. 219 α-Ketoglutaric acid represents an important junction between the metabolic pathways of carbohydrates and amino acids. **1899** *Jrnl. Chem. Soc.* LXXV. 423 With *ketohexoses (lævulose, sorbose), the purple colour appears after a few minutes. **1938** M. L. WOLFRAM in H. Gilman *Org. Chem.* I. xvi. 1442 The French scientist, Pelouze, described the isolation of a new ketohexose from the juice of the berries of the mountain ash. **1971** N. L. ALLINGER et al. *Org. Chem.* xxvii. 698 Fructose, another common hexose, has a ketone group at C-2 and is called a ketohexose. **1953** *Jrnl. Biol. Chem.* CCV. 480 Conversely, α-*ketoisovalerate accumulation is depressed whenever the supply of valine is sufficient to permit maximal growth rate. **1966** *Biochemistry* V. 409/1 A soil microorganism, *Pseudomonas* P-2, growing on pantothenate as sole carbon source, converts this in part to β-alanine, α-ketoisovalerate, and valine. **1953** *Jrnl. Biol. Chem.* CCV. 457 (*heading*) Isoleucine and valine metabolism in Escherichia coli. V. α-*Ketoisovaleric acid accumulation. **1971** *Jrnl. Nutrition* CI. 1165/1 The effect of substituting α-ketoisovaleric acid for L-valine upon the nitrogen balance of a young female was evaluated. **1908** *Jrnl. Chem. Soc.* XCIV. I. 318 The first groups are termed aldo-ketens and the second, *keto-ketens. **1937** F. C. WHITMORE *Org. Chem.* 281 The ketoketenes are colored, are easily auto-oxidized to give peroxides, and form addition cpds. with cyclic tertiary amines. **1951** I. L. FINAR *Org. Chem.* I. xii. 230 If the compound is of the type R·CH:C:O, it is known as an aldoketen; and if R_2C:C:O, then a ketoketen. **1937** *Amer. Jrnl. Physiol.* CXIX. 734 Any reduction in the ketosis consequent to carbohydrate administration must be due to either a decrease in the rate of the former ('antiketogenesis') or to an increase in the rate of the latter ('*ketolysis'). **1938** *Jrnl. Biol. Chem.* CXXVI. 106 Liver slices from a well fed monkey have a very low rate of ketolysis as compared with liver slices from well fed rats, rabbits, and guinea pigs. **1921** *Ibid.* XLVII. 435 Glucose thus exhibits, in alkaline solution *in vitro*, a '*ketolytic' action in hastening the oxidation of acetoacetic acid which would appear to be analogous to its 'antiketogenic' action in the body. **1936** *Jrnl. Nutrition* XII. 646 That aspect of the quantitative relationship of ketolytic to ketogenic factors which has interested us especially.., is the relation of carbohydrate combustion to the reduction of ketogenesis. **1938** *Jrnl. Biol. Chem.* CXXVI. 106 The large amount of work..showing the extrahepatic tissues..to be much more active *ketolytically than the liver is very convincing. **1939** *Biochem. Jrnl.* XXXIII. 931 (*heading*) The isolation of 17-*ketosteroids from the urine of normal women. **1959** *Austral. Jrnl. Exper. Biol. & Med. Sci.* XXXVII. 147 It was decided to employ enzymatic hydrolysis and separation of the individual ketosteroids in an attempt to identify and estimate them individually. **1964** A. WHITE et al. *Princ. Biochem.* (ed. 3) xlviii. 856 Since each of the various urinary metabolites of testosterone has a ketone group at C-17, these substances are referred to as 17-ketosteroids, and their concentration in the urine is a useful index of endogenous production of androgenic hormones. **1888** *Jrnl. Chem. Soc.* LIV. 443 (*heading*) Conversion of *ketoximes into pseudonitroles. **1938** C. D. HURD in H. Gilman *Org. Chem.* vii. 636 The reaction of bromine with ketoximes yields bromonitrosoparaffins. **1971** N. L. ALLINGER et al. *Org. Chem.* xxii. 605 The oximes of ketones (ketoximes) undergo an overall rearrangement to amides when heated with certain inorganic reagents, followed by treatment with water. **1914** *Chem. Abstr.* VIII. 113 (*heading*) Metal *ketyls, a large class of compounds with trivalent carbon. **1934** *Trans. Faraday Soc.* XXX. 23 By using dioxan as solvent high concentrations of the ketyls were obtained and their paramagnetism placed beyond doubt. **1971** N. L. ALLINGER et al. *Org. Chem.* xix. 493 If benzophenone is converted to the ketyl with sodium, for example, the ketyl concentration is sufficient to give the solution a beautiful blue color.

b. In Combs. in which *keto* may be used *attrib.* (without a hyphen) as an independent word or joined by a hyphen to the second element, as ***keto-acid***, ***-compound***, ***-ester***, ***-form***, etc. (in which *keto-* denotes the presence of a ketone group); also **keto-'enol** *attrib. phrase*, **-e'nolic** *a.*, applied to the tautomerism between the ketonic and enolic forms of certain compounds.

1911 *Chem. Abstr.* V. 3686 (*heading*) Preparation of amino acids from *keto acid phenylhydrazones and aluminium amalgam. **1968** R. O. C. NORMAN *Princ. Org. Synthesis* vii. 237 A dibasic acid which, as a β-ketoacid, is readily decarboxylated by heat. **1891** *Proc. Chem. Soc.* VII. 91 The resinous matters often formed in large amount on nitrating many phenols are, doubtless, products of the interaction of several molecules of the addition compounds, or of the *keto-compounds formed from them in the first instance. **1927** *Jrnl. Amer. Chem. Soc.* XLIX. 849 Acetylacetone may undergo *keto-enol tautomerism in the following way. $CH_3COCH_2COCH_3 \rightleftharpoons CH_3COCH{:}C(OH)CH_3$. **1971** N. L. ALLINGER et al. *Org. Chem.* viii. 172 Keto-enol interconversion is subject to catalysis by acid or base. **1909** *Proc. Chem. Soc.* XXV. 309 It is advisable to apply some general term to this form of isomerism, similar to the phrase *keto-enolic isomerism in use with the oxygen derivatives. **1936** *Biochem. Jrnl.* XXX. 745 The present paper contains some observations..on certain substances..which under similar conditions yield colours with this reagent [*sc.* diazotized sulphanilic acid]. The group has the common character that all its members are capable of keto-enolic tautomerism. **1937** F. C. WHITMORE *Org. Chem.* 444 Diacetosuccinic ester, as a beta *keto ester gives reactions like those of acetoacetic ester itself. **1958** *Oxf. Univ. Gaz.* 23 Apr. 882 Grignard reactions of keto-esters. **1927** *Jrnl. Amer. Chem. Soc.* XLIX. 856 Acetylacetone in 95% alcohol solution is an equilibrium mixture of the *keto and enol forms. **1968** R. O. C. NORMAN *Princ. Org. Synthesis* i. 18 For ethyl acetoacetate..two factors increase the bonding.. of the enol form relative to the keto form.

ketolic (kiːˈtɒlɪk), *a.* *Chem.* [f. KETOL + -IC.] Having the functional groups of a ketol.

1960 *Biochem. Jrnl.* LXXVII. 400/1 A method for the quantitative fractionation of..ring D α-ketolic oestrogens. **1971** *Folia Histochem. & Cytochem.* IX. 391 (*heading*) Oxidative enzymes and α-ketolic steroids in the interrenal cells of the South African clawed toad.

ketonæmia (kiːtəˈniːmɪə). *Med.* Also (chiefly *U.S.*) -nemia. [f. KETON(E + Gr. αἷμα blood: see -IA[1].] An abnormally high concentration of ketone bodies in the blood.

1917 *Amer. Jrnl. Med. Sci.* CLIII. 343 Marriott demonstrated ketonemia in such animals. **1941** *Jrnl. Biol. Chem.* CXXXVIII. 128 Ketonemia develops within 39 hours in man, as compared to 2 to 3 days in the dog. **1962** *Lancet* 29 Dec. 1350/2 The diabetic syndrome in this patient was unusual in that he had severe hyperglycæmia, insulin resistance, and no ketonæmia. **1965** LEE & KNOWLES *Animal Hormones* vii. 112 The effect of removal or destruction of the islet tissue varies in different animals... Ketonaemia does not occur in rabbits and it is slight in calves; in pigs ketonaemia may be severe, yet coma does not occur.

ketone (ˈkiːtəʊn). *Chem.* [a. Ger. *keton* (pl. *ketone*), a modification of ACETONE, introduced by Gmelin, *Handbuch d. Chem.* (ed. 4, 1848) IV. 40, 187.] **1.** The name of a class of chemical compounds formed by oxidation of the secondary alcohols or carbinols, to which they stand in some respects in the relation of aldehydes. The lowest of the series, ***dimethyl ketone***, is common ACETONE.

'The ketones, in their simplest form, contain a carbonyl group CO attached to two monad hydrocarbon radicles. If the two radicles are identical as in acetone, the compound is a *simple* ketone; if different, as in methyl-ethyl-ketone CH_3·CO·CH_2·CH_3, it is a *mixed* ketone. Compounds containing two carbonyl groups are termed *diketones*; those containing three *triketones*' (Morley & Muir *Watts' Dict. Chem.* III. 102/2).

1851 BRAZIER & GOSSLETH in *Q. Jrnl. Chem. Soc.* III. 215 A new class of bodies known under the name of acetones or ketones. *Ibid.* In preparing the ketone of caproic acid. **1852** WATTS tr. *Gmelin's Handbk. Chem.* VII. 214 (*heading*) Acetones in general or Ketones. All ketones are highly combustible. **1872** —— *Dict. Chem.* VI. 764 A peculiar penetrating smell, which deserves to be called the ketone-smell. **1873** —— *Fownes' Chem.* (ed. 11) 595 The formation of a ketone by oxidation is the essential characteristic of a secondary alcohol. **1897** *Allbutt's Syst. Med.* III. 200 Glucose ($C_6H_{12}O_6$) now regarded as a ketone of a hexatomic alcohol.

2. Special combs.: **ketone body**, any of the three related compounds acetone, acetoacetic acid, and β-hydroxybutyric acid, which are produced in the body in fatty- and amino-acid metabolism; an 'acetone body'.

1915 *Arch. Internal Med.* XV. 40 There are in the literature only casual references to the influence of organotherapy on the formation and excretion of ketone bodies. **1936** *Jrnl. Nutrition* XII. 647 The term 'rate of ketogenesis'...takes into account both the ketonemia, or level of ketone bodies in the blood, and the ketonuria, or the rate of ketone body excretion in the urine. **1959** A. WHITE et al. *Princ. Biochem.* (ed. 2) xix. 479 The total ketone body concentration in blood, expressed as β-hydroxybutyrate, is normally below 1 mg. per 100 ml., and the average total daily excretion in the urine is approximately 20 mg. **1974** *Nature* 18 Jan. 161/2 Urine samples were tested for 'ketone bodies' with a commercial preparation that contains sodium nitroprusside.

Hence **ke'tonic** *a.*, of or pertaining to ketones, as in **ketonic acid**, a compound containing the radical carbonyl, CO, and having the characteristic properties of both a ketone and an acid. So **'ketol**, a ketonic alcohol; **'ketose**, a sugar which is a ketonic alcohol, e.g. lævulose, or fruit sugar.

1876 *Jrnl. Chem. Soc.* XXIX. 926 The ketonic acids are converted by nascent hydrogen into oxy-acids. **1891** *Ibid.* LX. 1176 Ketoses. **1892** MORLEY & MUIR *Watts Dict. Chem.* III. 103/1 Certain ketonic acids part with carbon dioxide, forming ketones. **1892** E. F. SMITH tr. *V. von Richter's Chem. Carbon Compounds* (ed. 2) 498 Bromine water..oxidises the aldoses to their corresponding monocarboxylic acids..whereas the ketoses (fructose and sorbinose) are not attacked. **1894** G. MCGOWAN tr. *Bernthsen's Text-bk. Org. Chem.* (ed. 2) 237 (*heading*) Ketone-alcohols (ketols). **1899** M'GOWAN tr. *Beruthsen's Organ. Chem.* 245 These alkylated aceto-acetic ethers.. undergo either the 'ketonic decomposition' or the 'acid decomposition'. **1938** M. L. WOLFRAM in H. Gilman *Org. Chem.* I. xvi. 1442 The Lobry de Bruyn dilute alkali interconversion reaction was used..in obtaining the crystalline ketose of lactose (lactulose). **1968** R. O. C. NORMAN *Princ. Org. Synthesis* xvi. 501 Treatment [of an epoxide] with dimethyl sulphoxide gives an α-ketol. **1972** *New Phytologist* LXXI. 475 The phenomenon of ketose formation in polyol media is much better documented for bacteria where, for example, fructose may be formed from mannitol in yields of up to..95%.

ketonize (ˈkiːtənaɪz), *v.* *Chem.* [f. KETON(E + -IZE.] *intr.* Of a compound which undergoes keto-enol tautomerism: to change into the keto-form.

1937 F. C. WHITMORE *Org. Chem.* 345 The free enediol is unstable and ketonizes to the acyloin at once. **1938** L. F. FIESER in H. Gilman *Org. Chem.* I. ii. 55 The hydroxyl derivatives of benzene show much less tendency to ketonize than do the aliphatic enols. **1962** E. L. ELIEL *Stereochem. Carbon Compounds* viii. 242 The enolate..ketonizes in such a way that the proton approaches equatorially.

Hence **ketoni'zation**, the process of changing into a keto-form.

1931 *Canad. Jrnl. Res.* V. 26 The suggested formation of the lignosulphonic acids by ketonization of a phenolic nucleus is most unlikely. **1937** F. C. WHITMORE *Org. Chem.* 280 Ketonization gives acetic acid, esters, acid amides, acid chloride, etc. **1968** R. O. C. NORMAN *Princ. Org. Synthesis* i. 19 Compared with the ketonization of phenol.., the ketonization of β-naphthol is more favourable by about 11 kcal per mole. **1972** *Jrnl. Chem. Soc. Perkin Trans.* I 987/1 Kinetic control of enolisation and ketonisation is replaced by thermodynamic control at higher temperatures.

ketonuria (kiːtəˈnjʊərɪə). *Med.* [f. KETON(E + -URIA.] The excretion of abnormally large amounts of ketone bodies in the urine.

1913 *Jrnl. Amer. Med. Assoc.* 13 Dec. 2161/1 No one is justified at present in concluding that the liver is the sole organ concerned in the phenomena of ketonuria. **1923** *Glasgow Herald* 25 July 7 Daily injections of insulin.. removed entirely the ketonuria for a period of some days. **1939** *Nature* 29 Apr. 728/1 During rest after work there is a reduction in the glucose tolerance,..associated with a low respiratory quotient and ketonuria. **1972** *Drugs of Choice 1972–73* xxxi. 468/2 One of the more pernicious consequences of hypoglycemia is the hyperglycemia and ketonuria that may follow.

ketosis (kɪˈtəʊsɪs). *Med.* [f. KET(O- + -OSIS.] A condition characterized by an increased production of ketone bodies, which is associated with a predominance of fat metabolism and with diabetes.

1917 F. M. ALLEN in *Amer. Jrnl. Med. Sci.* CLIII. 335 No other name but acidosis exists for the metabolic process which it denotes. Ketonuria and ketonemia have their accurate place but do not cover the ground. Possibly the word ketosis might be suggested and used for special purposes, but the change of established usage would be difficult and seems unnecessary. **1925** *Biochem. Jrnl.* XIX. 948 In man after a relatively short period of starvation..a considerable ketosis appears. **1951** A. GROLLMAN *Pharmacol. & Therapeutics* vii. 151 The paroxysmal cerebral dysrhythmia characteristic of epilepsy may be altered by inducing ketosis by a low carbohydrate, high fat diet. **1960** *Farmer & Stockbreeder* 22 Mar. 136/1 There does appear to be a connection between the heavy feeding of kale, and the incidence of ketosis (acetonæmia), but in rather a roundabout way. **1961** [see ACETONE]. **1970** R. W. MCGILVERY *Biochem.* xxii. 530 However, the meat-fat diet does cause the appearance of an asymptomatic ketosis.

Hence **ke'totic** *a.*, suffering from or associated with ketosis.

1943 *Jrnl. Amer. Med. Assoc.* 2 Jan. 52/2 During episodes of ketotic acidosis it was necessary to give 2,360, 2,500 and 2,795 units of insulin in twenty-four hours before adequate control was accomplished. **1959** *Jrnl. Appl. Physiol.* XIV. 1028/1 The turnover time was increased also by about ⅓ in the ketotic cows. **1961** L. MARTIN *Clin. Endocrinol.* (ed. 3) ii. 52 Uncontrolled diabetics with high blood sugar levels do not as a rule suffer from anorexia unless they are also ketotic. **1972** *Jrnl. Clin. Invest.* LI. 1440/1 The cause of ketotic hypoglycemia, the commonest form of hypoglycemia in childhood, is not known.

kettal, kettule, obs. forms of KITTUL.

†**'ketterel.** *Sc. Obs.* Also kytral. [Origin obscure.] A vile or filthy wretch.

a **1572** KNOX *Hist. Ref.* Wks. 1846 I. 74 Thay kettereles, though they had but lyse, The twa part to us they will bring. *a* **1585** MONTGOMERIE *Flyting w. Polwart* 447 They kow'd all the kytral the face of it before.. They call it peild Polwart.

ketterick, -ing, corrupt ff. CATERAN.

kettie waike, obs. form of KITTIWAKE.

kettisol: see KITTISOL.

kettle (ˈkɛt(ə)l). Forms: 1 cetel, -il, (cit-, cytel), 4 ketil, 4–6 -el, 5 -ill, -yl(l, 5–7 kettell, (6 -yl, -yll), 6 ketell, ke(a)tle, catell, kyttle, (7 kittle), 6– kettle. Also 3–5 chetel, -ill: see CHETEL. [Com. Teut.: OE. *cętel* (W. Sax. *cietel*) = OS. *ketel* (in comb. *ketel-kôp*; MDu. and Du. *ketel*) OHG. *kezzil* (MHG. *kezzel*, G. *kessel*), ON. *ketill*, Goth. *katils*, prob. a. L. *catillus*, dim. of *catīnus* a food-vessel (or ad. L. *catīnus* itself).

W.Germ. *katil* regularly gave (through **cætil*, **ceætil*, **ceatil*) W.Sax. *cietel* (with palatal *c*), whence ME. *chetel*, found from Kent and E. Anglia to Devonsh. The Mercian and Northumb. form was *cętel* (palatalization either absent or lost): cf. Mercian **cæf*, *cæster*, **cælc* = southern *ceaf*, *ceaster*, *cealc*. Hence northern and general Eng. *ketel*, *kettle*. (The *k* is by some referred to Scandinavian influence.)]

1. a. A vessel, commonly of metal, for boiling water or other liquids over a fire; a pot or caldron (cf. *camp-*, *fish-*, *gipsy-kettle*); now *esp.* a covered metal vessel with a spout, used to boil water for domestic purposes, a TEA-KETTLE.

a **700** *Epinal Gloss.* 168 Caccabum, cetil. *c* **1000** *Sax. Leechd.* II. 44 Wermod ȝesodenne on wætere on niwum cytele. *Ibid.* 87 ȝenim þonne tyn-amberne cetel. *a* **1100** *Gerefa* in *Anglia* IX. 264 Lead, cytel, hlædel. *a* **1300** *E.E. Psalter* cvii. 10 [cviii. 8] Moab ketel of mi hope is. *a* **1350** *St. Anastasia* 84 in Horstm. *Altengl. Leg.* (1881) 26 Pottes and pannes & oþer slyke Als ketils, crassetes, to kechin like. *c* **1440** *Promp. Parv.* 273/2 Ketyl, or chetyle, or caudrone, *cacabus*, *lebes*. **1527** ANDREW *Brunswyke's Distyll. Waters* A ij, Take for the erthen cappell a copper cappell or kettyll

with a copper pype as before is fygured. **1697** DRYDEN *Virg. Georg.* I. 393 She..boils in Kettles Must of Wine. **1740** PINEDA *Sp. Dict.*, *Sartèn*..We say, The Kettle called the Pot Black-Arse. **1755** JOHNSON s.v., In the kitchen the name of *pot* is given to the boiler that grows narrower towards the top, and of *kettle* to that which grows wider. **1866** R. M. BALLANTYNE *Shift. Winds* i. (1881) 1 The family kettle..was singing on the fire.

b. A bowl- or saucer-shaped vessel in which operations are carried out on low-melting metals, glass, plastics, etc., in the liquid state.

a **1817** [see *potash kettle* (POTASH *sb.* 4)]. **1892** P. BENJAMIN *Mod. Mechanism* 803 A rendering and refining kettle for making..fancy toilet soap. **1895** E. L. RHEAD *Metall.* xv. 214 The ore is ground to a pulp in the mill, or arastra, and transferred to kettles with bottoms made of copper. **1929** *Industr. Chemist* V. 487/1 A Pfaudler, all cast-iron, glass-lined, 300-gallon, reaction kettle or chemical still. **1940** H. L. HIND *Brewing* II. xxiv. 576 The vessel[s] in which the mash is boiled..are usually known as kettles in America. **1952** M. R. MILLS *Introd. Drying Oil Technol.* iii. 48 Oleo-resinous varnishes are commonly produced in portable kettles of 450–3,000 lb...capacity. **1953** *Archit. Rev.* CXIV. 187/1 The raw materials used in the former process [*sc.* the manufacture of synthetic resins] are highly inflammable, and it was desirable that the 'kettles' in which this process is carried out should be in a separate building. **1955** KIRK & OTHMER *Encycl. Chem. Technol.* XIV. 653 Stationary open kettles are used to polymerize large batches of oil. **1967** J. D. GILCHRIST *Extraction Metall.* x. 259 Softening—at 750°C, in a wide, open hearth furnace or in the open saucer-shaped lead 'kettle' which presents a very large surface for oxidation, Sb, Sn and As are slowly oxidized out with air or litharge.

2. Phrase. ***a kettle of fish.***

a. On the Tweed, etc. A kettle of fish cooked *al fresco*, at a boating excursion or picnic; hence, applied to the picnic itself. Also simply *kettle*.

1791 NEWTE *Tour Eng. & Scot.* 394 It is customary for the gentlemen who live near the Tweed to entertain their neighbours and friends with a Fete Champetre, which they call giving 'a kettle of fish'. Tents or marquees are pitched near the flowery banks of the river..a fire is kindled, and live salmon thrown into boiling kettles. **1824** SCOTT *St. Ronan's* xii, The whole company go to the water-side today to eat a kettle of fish. **1881** A. CARTER in *Picturesque Scot.* 111 A 'kettle' in Berwick parlance is a picnic party with this specialty about it that fish is the chief thing consumed, and this fish is salmon taken out of the river..and cooked upon the spot.

b. Usually with adj. ironically, as ***pretty***, ***fine***, ***nice***, ***rare*** (†also simply ***a fine kettle***): A mess, muddle, disagreeable or awkward state of things. Also, ***a different*** or ***another kettle of fish***: a different state of affairs, a different matter altogether.

1742 RICHARDSON *Pamela* III. 308 He has made a fine Kettle on't—han't he! **1742** FIELDING *J. Andrews* I. xii, 'Here's a pretty kettle of fish', cries Mrs. Tow-wouse. **1749** —— *Tom Jones* XVIII. viii, Fine doings at my house! A rare kettle of fish I have discovered at last. **1800** WELLINGTON *Let. to Close* 2 Oct. in Gurw. *Desp.* (1837) I. 245 If so, we shall have a fine kettle of fish at Seringapatam. **1820** LADY GRANVILLE *Lett.* 7 Oct. (1894) I. 184 Ministers are in a nice kettle of fish, to be sure. **1854** DICKENS *Hard T.* I. iv, Your training schools, and your whole kettle-of-fish of schools. **1937** *Discovery* Nov. 353/1 H. S. Thompson's 'Garnet in Flight' is another kettle of fish. **1938** R. WARNER *Professor* vi. 141 Professor..you're very good at thinking out schemes —brainwork, I mean..if you understand what I mean; but that's only half the battle you know, in fact a different kettle of fish altogether. **1942** E. WAUGH *Put out More Flags* iii. 172 Until now the word 'Colonel' for Basil had connoted an elderly rock-gardener on Barbara's G.P.O. list. This formidable man of his own age was another kettle of fish. **1959** J. L. AUSTIN *Sense & Sensibilia* (1962) ii. 14 Looking ..at a distant village on a very clear day across a valley, is a very different kettle of fish from seeing a ghost.

3. ***a kettle of hats***: a quantity of hats dyed at the same time in a dye-kettle.

1789 *Trans. Soc. Arts* I. 184 Upon dying a Kettle of hats of twenty-four dozen. **1900** [Still in use in the trade].

4. *transf.* **a.** 'The brass or metal box of a compass' (Smyth *Sailor's Word-bk.* 1867).

b. *Sc. Mining.* A kind of shallow tub or kibble in which miners descend and ascend the shaft, or in which material is brought to the surface.

1894 *Daily News* 9 May 7/7 Four pit-sinkers were being drawn up a shaft..when the 'kettle' on which they were standing..swung from one side of the shaft to the other and three men fell off. **1894** *Labour Commission Gloss.*, *Kettle*, a Scotch mining term for the basket or kibble which takes the place of a cage in shafts not provided with 'guides'..It is like a half-barrel attached to the winding-rope.

c. A deep circular hollow scoured out in a rocky river bed, or under a glacier, etc.; a pot-hole. Cf. *giant's kettle* (GIANT 6), also HELL-KETTLE. Also (now the usual meaning in *Geomorphol.*), a *kettle hole* (see sense 6 b).

1866 *Smithsonian Contrib. Knowl.* No. 197. 3 To form an idea of the appearance of the 'potash kettle' country, we may imagine a region of drift moraines inverted, and..occupied by cavities of irregular size and depth. *Ibid.* 4 On the north of the Peshattego river..the 'kettles' are very numerous. **1874** J. GEIKIE *Gt. Ice Age* (1894) 431 Everyone who has visited the Glacier Garden at Lucerne will remember the fine display of 'kettles' seen there. **1877** T. C. CHAMBERLIN *Geol. Wisconsin: Survey of 1873–79* II. II. v. 206 The peculiar feature of this range..consists of numerous depressions in the drift variously known as 'Potash Kettles', 'Kettles', 'Potholes', 'Pots and Kettles', 'Sinks', etc. Those which have most arrested popular attention are circular in outline, and symmetrical in form... Large numbers of these depressions are not perfectly circular, but rudely oval, oblong or elliptical, or are extended into trough-like, or even winding hollows. *Ibid.* 214 If masses of the ice became incorporated within the drift,..their subsequent melting would give rise to a depression constituting one form of the kettles. **1893** *Northumbld. Gloss.*, *Kettle*, a pot-hole or circular hole, scoured out in a rocky river bed by the swirling action of pebbles. **1896** T. G. BONNEY *Ice-Work* I. i. 34 These 'kettles', when first discovered, were filled with débris, and still contained the large rounded boulders by which they had been mainly excavated. **1926** *Jrnl. Geol.* XXXIV. 315 The ice blocks that formed the kettles in pitted out-wash varied in size from a few yards to several miles in diameter. **1942** C. A. COTTON *Climatic Accidents* xxiv. 328 Both bowl-like round pits and elongated trench-like kettles are common. **1970** R. J. SMALL *Study of Landforms* xi. 384 A bare tract of boulders, gravels and sand separates the two glacier snouts, and is pitted by numerous circular water-filled hollows ('kettles') marking small masses of ice that calved from the glaciers, became trapped in the debris, and subsequently melted.

d. A watch. *slang* (chiefly *Criminals'*).

1889 BARRÈRE & LELAND *Dict. Slang* I. 516/2 *Kettle* (thieves), a watch; *red kettle*, gold watch. **1931** [see GROIN *sb.*[2] 4]. **1935** G. INGRAM *Cockney Cavalcade* xiv. 234, I pinched his 'kettle' what those two blunderers left behind. **1936** J. CURTIS *Gilt Kid* xxv. 244 Next buckshee kettle that comes my way I'll just stick to it. **1960** 'A. BURGESS' *Doctor is Sick* xvi. 122 Edwin, student of philology, knew what kettles were, cheap smuggled watches guaranteed to go for a day or two. **1970** *Brewer's Dict. Phrase & Fable* (rev. ed.) 603/2 A tin kettle is a silver watch and a red kettle a gold one.

†**5.** Short for KETTLEDRUM. *Obs.*

1602 SHAKS. *Ham.* V. ii. 286 Let the Kettle to the Trumpets speake, The Trumpet to the Cannoneer without.

6. *Comb.* **a.** Gen. combs., as (sense 1) ***kettle-boiling***, ***-hanger***, ***-hook***, ***-iron***, ***-lid***, ***-maker***, ***-prop***, ***-scrubber***, ***-stand***; (sense 4 c) ***kettle-formation***, ***-valley***. **b.** Special combs.: **kettle-bail** *U.S.*, a dredge used in taking scallops; **kettle-boiler**, an old type of steam-boiler, having a rounded top (Knight *Dict. Mech.* 1875); **kettle-bread**, home-made bread, baked under a 'kettle' or pot; **kettle-broth** (see quot.); **kettlecase**, a popular name of *Orchis mascula*; **kettledock**, a popular name of the Ragwort, *Senecio Jacobæa*; also applied to the Broad-leaved Dock, *Rumex obtusifolius* (Britt. & H., Miller *Plant-n.*); **kettle-faced** *a.*, having a face as black as a kettle; †**kettle-fats** = BATTERY 14; †**kettle-fish**, small fish; **kettle-furnace**, (*a*) a basket-furnace in which lead or solder is melted for plumbing; (*b*) a furnace for heating a kettle; **kettle-holder**, a piece of cloth or the like used in lifting a kettle, to protect the hand from the heated handle; *transf.* a kind of small bonnet; **kettle hole**, a depression in the ground thought to have been formed by the melting of an ice block trapped in glacial deposits, esp. one that is circular and deep; freq. *attrib.* in ***kettle-hole lake*** = ***kettle lake***; **kettle lake**, a lake in a kettle hole; **kettleman**, †(*a*) ? = KETTLER; (*b*) (also ***kettle man***) one who attends to a kettle in various industries; **kettle-maw**, the angler (fish); †**kettle-mill**, a device for raising water; **kettle moraine** *Geomorphol.* [orig. applied as a proper name to such a moraine in Wisconsin], moraine characterized by the presence of numerous kettle holes; **kettle-net**, a form of net used in fishing for mackerel.

1881 E. INGERSOLL *Oyster-Industry* 245 **Kettle bail*, a dredge used in catching scallops, which has the blade adjusted to swing in the eyes of the arms, in order to prevent its sinking into the mud of the soft bottom on which it is used. **1887** G. B. GOODE *Fisheries U.S.: Hist. & Methods* II. 571 The dredge for a soft bottom differs from the other in having the 'blade' adjusted to swing in the 'eyes' of the arms in order to prevent its sinking into the mud. This is called the 'kettle-bail' style of dredge. **1897** *Daily News* 9 Dec. 10/3 A question of cigar-lighting or *kettle-boiling. **1882** EDNA LYALL *Donovan* xx. 239 Donovan sat down with the farmer and his wife to broth and '*kettle bread'. **1880** ELEANOR G. O'REILLY *Sussex Stor.* II. 187 (E.D.D.) '*Kettle-broth'.. consists of pieces of stale bread liberally moistened with boiling water, and besprinkled with salt and pepper. **1680** OTWAY *Caius Marius* II. i, I'm an honest, black, tauny, *Kettle-fac'd Fellow. **1812** J. SMYTH *Pract. of Customs* (1821) 120 Metal prepared; and Battery, which are commonly called *Kettle Fats. This last is known by the dint of the mill-hammers upon the kettles. **1630** in *Descr. Thames* (1758) 69 That no Peter-man..take any Flounders, or any other short Fish which they have usually called *Kettle-Fish. **1861** GEO. ELIOT *Silas M.* 32 A small bit of pork suspended from the *kettle-hanger. **1813** M. EDGEWORTH *Let.* 1 May (1971) 32 After having admired..a picture of Cromwell and Fanny's *kettle-holder we sallied forth. **1853** MISS YONGE *Heir Redclyffe* I. 101 Charlotte worked a kettle-holder. **1867** *Morn. Star* 17 Sept. 5 The small bonnets, which are known as 'kettle-holders'. **1887** STEVENSON in *Scribner's Mag.* I. 612/2 A kettle-holder in Berlin wool. **1882** *Proc. Amer. Assoc. Adv. Sci.* XXXI. 395 The kames of Cherry Valley..are composed of stratified water-worn gravel,..and, as a series of conical hills and reticulated ridges, enclosing '*kettle holes', form conspicuous objects in the centre of the valley. **1889** G. F. WRIGHT *Ice Age N. Amer.* 11 A true terminal moraine is made up of knolls and bowl-shaped depressions called kettle-holes. **1895** J. D. DANA *Man. Geol.* (ed. 4) 970 Kettle-holes are bowl-shaped depressions, usually 30 to 50 feet deep and 100 to 500 feet in larger diameter. Each depression ..was the resting-place, and often the burial-place, of a huge mass of ice that became detached during the melting. **1902** GILBERT & BRIGHAM *Introd. Physical Geogr.* vi. 143 Many lakes with steep rims in the midst of much glacial waste are known as Kettle-hole Lakes. **1930** *Q. Jrnl. Geol. Soc.* LXXXVI. 112 Numerous lakes and pools lying in kettle-holes dot the surface of the moraine. **1957** G. E. HUTCHINSON *Treat. Limnol.* I. i. 90 The exact nature of such basins depends largely on the details of the process of deglaciation..producing an extraordinary number of kettle-hole lakes in North America. **1970** DORR & ESCHMAN *Geol. Michigan* vii. 151/2 Most of the smaller inland lakes of Michigan occupy kettle-holes. **1485** *Naval Acc. Hen. VII* (1896) 51 Potte hokes..j, *kettle hokes..ij. **1914** *Prof. Papers U.S. Geol. Survey* No. 82. 163 Till or similar impervious material appears to be present in considerable amounts, as indicated by the numerous springs, *kettle lakes, and similar features. **1968** R. W. FAIRBRIDGE *Encycl. Geomorphol.* 587/2 The hollow is frequently water filled, so that it forms a kettle lake, kettle pond or swamp. **1920** 'K. MANSFIELD' *Bliss* 44 They spent half their time..dosing him with various awful mixtures concocted by Pip, and kept secretly by him in a broken jug covered with an old *kettle lid. *c* **1483** CAXTON *Dialogues* 46/37 Ysaac the *ketelmaker Gyveth four ketellis. **1629** in *New Romney Par. Reg.*, Thomas Well, *Kittleman [buried]. **1833** B. SILLIMAN *Man. Sugar Cane* 15 The manner in which the hands are distributed during the cutting season is the following..forty hands with knives..six kettle men. **1960** *Classification of Occupations* (General Register Office) 51/2 Kettleman—gelatin, glue, size mfr... metal mfr... oil seed crushing. **1963** *Lebende Sprachen* VIII. 130/2 Kettleman. *a* **1798** PENNANT *Journ. fr. Lond. to Isle of Wight* (1801) II. 74 The common angler..from the vast width of its mouth, it is called here the *Kettle-maw. **1570** DEE *Math. Pref.* 37 The sundry wayes to force water to ascend, eyther by Tympane, *Kettell mills [etc.]. **1577** B. GOOGE *Heresbach's Husb.* (1586) 49 b, Some pump to be made, or Kettle-Mill, or such like, as may serve the turne of a naturall streame. [**1883** T. C. CHAMBERLIN *Geol. Wisconsin: Survey of 1873–79* I. I. xv. 275 That portion of the moraine which..was formed by the joint action of the Green Bay and Lake Michigan glaciers, constitutes a succession of irregular hills and ridges, locally known as the Kettle Range, from the peculiar depressions which characterize it... As this moraine will need a specific name to distinguish it from other similar accumulations, the term *Kettle Moraine may fittingly be applied to it.] **1889** G. F. WRIGHT *Ice Age N. Amer.* vii. 120 Attention was first directed..by President T. C. Chamberlin to the character and connection of the kettle-moraine in Wisconsin. **1897** W. B. SCOTT *Introd. Geol.* viii. 155 When such masses melt they form depressions in the mound and give rise to the 'kettle moraines'. **1937** WOOLDRIDGE & MORGAN *Physical Basis Geogr.* xxii. 387 Mounds and ridges of gravelly drift are referred to in British glacial literature as eskers and kames, or, generally, as kettle-drift or kettle-moraine. **1970** B. B. LUCKMAN in C. A. Lewis *Glaciations Wales* viii. 176 (*heading*) The Kington-Orleton kettle moraine. **1881** HAMERSLY *Naval Encycl. U.S.*, **Kettle-net*, a net formerly used in catching mackerel. **1843** THACKERAY *Irish Sk.-Bk.* II. 278 Thus it was I drew her Scouring of a kettle... That sweet *kettle-scrubber! **1881** C. SCHREIBER *Jrnl.* 1 Nov. (1911) II. 367 Found a fine old *kettle stand..and a few minutes after had the good luck to find the kettle to fit. **1960** H. HAYWARD *Antique Coll.* 157/1 *Kettle-stand*, a special stand which was introduced with tea-drinking in the later 17th-cent., of two main kinds. (a) A small table..with a gallery or raised edge round the top... (b) A box-like arrangement set on four legs. **1970** D. ASH *Dict. Eng. Antique Furniture* 92/2 Kettle-stands were lower than contemporary tripod tables so that the kettle, mounted on its lamp-stand, would be at a convenient height. **1881** LESLIE tr. *Nordenskiöld's Voy. 'Vega'* II. xv. 291 A high plain.. interrupted at many places by deep *kettle valleys.

Hence **'kettled** *a. Geol.*, worn into kettle-shaped hollows.

1898 *Amer. Geologist* Nov. 298 Crevasses and moulins would be formed..producing such a profusely kettled surface as in the Glacier Garden.

kettle-bottom.

1. *lit.* The bottom of a kettle. *fig.* A name given to a hill with broad flat top and sloping sides.

1746 *MS. Log of the ship 'Wake'* 13 Sept., The High Land of Pullicat from ye Kittle Bottom. **1809** HORSBURGH *Direct. Sailing* I. 322 Far inland..there is a round conical hill called the Kettle Bottom.

2. 'A ship with a flat floor' (Smyth *Sailor's Word-bk.* 1867). So **kettle-bottomed** *a.*

1840 R. H. DANA *Bef. Mast* xxix. 101 She was a good, substantial ship..wall-sided and kettle-bottomed.

kettle-de-benders: see KITTLY-*benders*.

kettledrum ('kɛt(ə)lˌdrʌm), *sb.*

1. A musical instrument of percussion consisting of a hollow hemisphere of brass or copper, over the edge of which parchment is stretched and tuned to a definite note: cf. DRUM *sb.*[1] 1.

[**1554** MACHYN *Diary* (Camden) 76 Thrumpets..and drumes mad of ketylles.] **1602** SHAKS. *Ham.* I. iv. 11 The kettle Drum and Trumpet thus bray out The triumph of his Pledge. **1730** FIELDING *Tom Thumb* II. iv, A noise, Great as the kettledrums of twenty armies. **1844** *Regul. & Ord. Army* 30 No Trumpet to sound, or Kettle-Drum to beat.

attrib. **1874** T. HARDY *Far fr. Madding Crowd* I. 68 His head being dandled up and down on the bed of the waggon like a kettledrum-stick. **1898** *Westm. Gaz.* 6 Sept. 4/3 The kettledrum boy plays his incessant pom-pom-pom.

†**2.** = KETTLEDRUMMER. *Obs.*

1542 SIR T. SEYMOUR *Let. to Hen. VIII*, in *St. Papers* IX. 501 The captaynes that your Heynes wolde retayne, the dromes and fyffes, the ketyl dromes. *a* **1548** HALL *Chron.*, *Hen. VIII* 239 b, Trompettes..twelve in nombre besyde two kettle Drommes on horsebacke. **1669** *Lond. Gaz.* No. 4012/3, 6. Trumpets and 2. Kettle-Drums in rich Liveries. **1705** VANBRUGH *Confed.* I. ii, The rogue had a kettledrum to his father. **1755** *Mem. Capt. P. Drake* I. xv. 143 One Morgrigg, a Kettle Drum to the Queen's Life-guard.

3. *colloq.* An afternoon tea-party on a large scale.

A punning term, implying that the gathering was a smaller affair than the usual 'drum' (see DRUM *sb.*[1] 10) and associating it with the tea-kettle.

1861 *Times* 1 July 12 Then the 5 o'clock tea, the sort of little assembly so happily called 'kettledrum'. **1888** *Lady* 25 Oct. 374/1 We ask them to afternoon tea, or have kettle-drums at Le Repos.

'kettledrum, *v.* [f. prec. sb.] *intr.* To beat the kettledrum; to make a noise like a kettledrum. Hence **'kettle,drumming** *vbl. sb.*

1848 B. WEBB *Continental Ecclesiol.* 277 There was a great deal too much trumpeting and kettle-drumming in the orchestra. **1893** CROCKETT *Stickit Minister* 175 He heard.. his own heart kettle-drumming in his ears.

kettledrummer ('kɛt(ə)l,drʌmə(r)). [f. as prec. + -ER[1].] One who plays the kettledrum.

1683 CLAVERHOUSE in *15th Rep. Hist. MSS. Comm.* App. VIII. 284 Licence to import.. gray cloath for the trompeters and ketledrumers. **1807** W. IRVING *Salmag.* (1824) 72 The kettle-drummers.. are confounded and lost in the military crowd.

kettleful ('kɛt(ə)lfʊl). [f. KETTLE + -FUL.] As much as a kettle will hold.

1862 H. MARRYAT *Year in Sweden* I. 273 A kettleful of powder.

†**kettle-hat.** *Obs.* A kind of helmet in use in the fourteenth and fifteenth centuries.

1380 *Exch. Rolls Scotl.* III. 654 *note*, Capelli de calibe dicti Ketilhattis. **1399** *Will* in *Hampole's Wks.* (1896) II. 449 My ketylle-hat. ?*a* **1400** *Morte Arth.* 2994 Ketelle hattes they cleve evene to þe scholdirs! *c* **1440** *Promp. Parv.* 273/2 Ketylle hat, *pelliris,.. galerus.*

kettle-pins, kettles, variants of KITTLE-PINS, KITTLES.

kettler, ketler. [f. KETTLE + -ER[1].] †**1.** One who mends or repairs kettles, a tinker. *Obs.*

1604 T. M. *Black Bk.* in *Middleton's Wks.* (1840) V. 543, I would have the sometimes go disguised (in honest apparel), and so drawing in amongst bunglers and ketlers, under the plain frieze of simplicity [etc.].

2. A colour-mixer's assistant who attends to the boiling of dyestuffs.

1921 in *Dict. Occup. Terms* (1927) §381. **1960** *Classification of Occupations* (General Register Office) 51/2 Kettler.. 106 [dyers of textiles].

'kettle-stitch. [ad. G. *kettelstich* chainstich, f. *kettel* a small chain + *stich* stitch.] In bookbinding: A knot made at the head and tail of a book in sewing it, by which the thread holding one sheet is fastened to the thread in the next.

1818 H. PARRY *Art of Bookbinding* 2 *Kettle-stitch*, the stitch at head and foot of the book, independent of the bands, to tack or fasten the sheets together. **1846**, etc.[see *catch-stitch* (CATCH- 3 a)]. **1880** ZAEHNSDORF *Bookbind.* 17 The head and tail must now be sewn in to imbed the chain of the kettle stitch. *Ibid.* 21 The needle brought out of the kettle-stitch hole on the left or tail of the sheet. **1973** *Islander* (Victoria, B.C.) 30 Sept. 11/1 Dick shewed me some of the stitches used in book binding. Among them, the kettle stitch, used in hand sewing during the early days of book binding.

†**kettlin,** obs. f. CATLING, lute-string, etc.

1578 *Richmond. Wills* (Surtees) 280 Thread lace, garters, A gros of kettlins, iij[s]. iij dos of mynykens iij[s]. vj[d].

kettling, var. CHITLING.

1869 *Overland Monthly* III. 130 Then there are the delusive 'kettlings', among the 'low-down' people... I will simply say that it is fried sausages, minus all the unhealthy and absurd meat which most people insist on stuffing into the intestinal integuments.

'ketton-stone. An oolitic limestone obtained from quarries at Ketton, in Rutland.

1796 KIRWAN *Elem. Min.* (ed. 2) I. 83 Ketton stone, whose colour is reddish brown, and consists of small rounded particles compacted together like the roe of fish. **1817** J. BRADBURY *Trav. Amer.* 287 That species of limestone called ketton-stone, or compact limestone of Kirwan. **1839** E. D. CLARKE *Trav. Russia* 116/1 The chemical analysis of this mineral is nearly that of the Ketton-stone.

kettrin, variant of CATERAN.

kettule, variant of KITTUL, jaggery palm.

ketty ('kɛtɪ), *a.* Now *dial.* [f. KET[1] + -Y[1].] Having bad flesh; carrion-like; rotten, foul, nasty; worthless. Of soil: Soft, peaty.

1607 MARKHAM *Caval.* III. (1617) 25 If your horse be grose, fat, and a foule feeder, which is calld a kettie horse. **1674–91** RAY *N.C. Words* 40 A *Ketty Cur*, a nasty stinking Fellow. **1828** *Craven Dial.*, *Ketty*, worthless. **1855** ROBINSON *Whitby Gloss.*, *Ketty*, putrid. **1872** in *N.W. Linc. Gloss.* s.v., By the river some more [land] Rotten and ketty and bad.

kettysol(l, variants of KITTISOL.

‖**ketubah** (kɛtuː'vɑː). Also **kethubah, ketuba.** [Heb. *kethūbhāh* written statement.] A formal Jewish marriage contract which includes financial provisions for the wife in the event of the husband's death or of divorce.

1841 BORROW *Zincali* I. II. vii. 344 The walking of the bride.. to the house of her betrothed.. the reading of the Ketubah. **1891** M. FRIEDLÄNDER *Jewish Relig.* II. vii. 487 The fulfilment of the conditions agreed upon in the *kethubah* .. tended to render divorce a rare event. **1960** *Commentary* June 500/1 The Rabbinical Assembly has modified the *Ketubah* (marriage contract). **1960** [see GET *sb.*[3]]. **1962** B. ABRAHAMS tr. *Life Glückel of Hameln* iv. 79 When we stood all together under the *chuppah* with the bride and bridegroom, we found that.. the Ketuba had not been drawn up! **1974** H. KEMELMAN *Tuesday Rabbi saw Red* 7, I read the *Ketubah*, that is the marriage contract, which the groom has signed previously.

†**keup.** *Obs. rare*[−1]. [a. Du. *kuip*: see COOP *sb.*[1]] A barrel, cask, tub.

c **1483** CAXTON *Dialogues* 44/16 Poule the couper Maketh and formaketh the keupis, Barellis, vessellis.

‖**keuper** ('kɔɪpə(r)). *Geol.* [A German miners' term.] The name given in Germany, and thence by English geologists, to the upper member of the Triassic system, consisting in Germany of marls, shales, sandstones, gypsum, and clays, in England chiefly of marls and sandstones.

1844 ANSTED *Geol.* I. xix. 295 The Keuper, the uppermost division of the Triassic system, is called by the French *marnes irisées.* **1858** WHEWELL *Novum Org. Renov.* IV. ix. (ed. 3) 288 The term *Pœcilite* [was] proposed by Mr. Conybeare to designate the group of strata which lies below the oolites and lias, including the new red or variegated sandstone, with the keuper above, and the magnesian limestone below it. **1863** LYELL *Antiq. Man* xvi. (ed. 3) 332 It is mottled with red and green, like the New Red Sandstone or keuper.

keurboom ('kʊəbʊm). Also **keur.** [Afrikaans, f. *keur* choice + *boom* tree.] A small South African tree of the genus *Virgilia* (*V. oroboides* or *V. divaricata*) of the family Leguminosæ, having pinnate leaves and racemes of white, pink, mauve, or red, scented flowers.

1731 G. MEDLEY tr. *Kolb's Present State of Cape of Good-Hope* II. 258 The Amaquas Tree. This Tree the Cape-Europeans call *Keur-boom.* It grows so quick, that in Two Years Time it becomes, from a Small Plant, a Tree of Eight or Nine Foot in Height. **1854** L. PAPPE *Silva Capensis* 13 *Virgilia Capensis.* Lamk. (*Keurboom*)... Wood rather light and soft. Looks well when polished. **1907** T. R. SIM *Forests & Forest Flora Cape Good Hope* 204 Keur is often cultivated for its ornamental evergreen foliage and sweetly scented flowers. **1925** R. MARLOTH *Flora S. Afr.* II. I. 72 *Virgilia capensis.* Keurboom... In favourable localities it reaches a height of 40 feet with trunks three feet in diameter. Such trees form a beautiful sight when covered with their pale rose or lilac coloured, sweet-scented flowers. **1955** J. PACKER *Valley of Vines* iv. 58 The *keurbome* toss fragrant pale-pink plumes in the wind. **1973** PALMER & PITMAN *Trees S. Afr.* II. 903 Botanists, foresters, and gardeners have not yet decided to their mutual satisfaction whether the genus *Virgilia* is composed of one, two, or three different species of keurboom.

keuvrepane, variant of COVERPANE, *Obs.*

†**keve,** *v.* *Obs. rare.* [Of obscure origin and meaning.

ON. *kefja* to dive, sink, has been suggested, but is scarcely satisfactory for the second passage.]

13.. *E.E. Allit. P.* A. 320 Þy corse in clot mot calder keue. *Ibid.* 980, I.. blusched on the burghe.. By3onde þe brok fro me-warde keued.

keve, obs. form of KEEVE.

kevel ('kɛv(ə)l), *sb.*[1] Now *Sc.* and *north. dial.* Forms: 3–4, 9 **kevel,** (3 **-il,** 5 **-yl**), 5 **-le,** 6 **kewle,** 9 **keevel,** *Sc.* **kewl.** [a. ON. *kefli* a round stick, small roller, gag (Norw. and Da. *kjevle*; cf. Sw. *käfling*), related to *kafli* a piece, bit of anything.]

1. †**a.** A gag. *Obs.* **b.** A bit or twitch for a horse's mouth.

a **1300** *E.E. Psalter* xxxi[i]. 9 In keuil and bridel þair chekes straite. *c* **1300** *Havelok* 547 A keuel of clutes.. Þat he [ne] mouhte [MS. -the] speke, ne fnaste. *c* **1440** *Promp. Parv.* 274/1 Kevle, or kevyl, for hors, *mordale, camus.* **1570** LEVINS *Manip.* 95/39 Kewle, *postonis* [read *postomis*]. **1825–80** JAMISON s.v., One who rides a horse,.. when he brings the halter under the horse's jaws and makes it pass through his mouth, is said *to put a kewl* on.

2. A rounded piece of wood; a staff, cudgel.

1807 C. WAUGH *Fisherman's Defence* 41 The pocket is knit upon a keevel from six to seven inches in circumference. **1836** J. M. WILSON *Tales Borders* III. 304 Brandishing of flails and kevels showed they were determined to act.

kevel ('kɛv(ə)l), *sb.*[2] Forms: 4 **kevile, kyvile,** 7– **kevel,** 9 **cavel, -il.** [a. ONF. *keville* (Godef. *Compl*) = Central F. *cheville* pin, peg, CHEVILLE.

The Fr. form *chevil* is given in sense 1 by Harris *Lex. Techn.* (1704), whence in Phillips (1706), Bailey, etc., but there is no independent evidence for it.]

†**1.** A pin or hasp for fastening anything; a tilepin. (Perh. not English.) *Obs.*

1251 *Liberate Roll 35 Hen. III*, 2 July (P.R.O.), Per paviari capellam nostram et in eadem kiuellos ferri ad cathenas ad claudendum fenestras vitreas fieri. [Cf. TURNER *Dom. Archit.* 1:3th *C.* (1851) v. 230 Iron kevils with chains to shut the glass windows.] **1303–40** in Rogers *Agric. & Prices* (1866) I. 490 [Tiles were fastened, as now, by pins.. These pins are also called] 'keuills' [*printed* 'kenills'], [a name found in Southampton, Westshene, Isleworth, and London].

2. *Naut.* A peg or cleat, usually fixed in pairs, to which certain ropes are belayed (see quot. 1769).

c **1330** R. BRUNNE *Chron. Wace* (Rolls) 12062 Bowlyne on bousprete to sette & hale Cordes, kyuiles [*v.r.* keuiles], atached þe [*v.r.* to] wale. *a* **1642** SIR W. MONSON *Naval Tracts* III. (1704) 345/2 The Kevels are to belay the Sheets. **1704** J. HARRIS *Lex Techn.*, *Chevils* or *Kevils*, are small Pieces of Timber nailed to the inside of a Ship to belay or fasten the Sheets and Tacks. **1769** FALCONER *Dict. Marine* (1789), *Kevels*,.. a frame composed of two pieces of timber, whose lower ends rest in a sort of step or foot, nailed to the ship's side, from whence the upper ends branch outward into arms or horns, serving to belay the.. ropes by which the bottoms of the main-sail and fore-sail are extended. **1840** MARRYAT *Poor Jack* xxvii, The bight.. he belayed.. to the main-sheet kevel. *c* **1860** H. STUART *Seaman's Catech.* 73 What are 'cavils'? Timber heads, or small bollards for belaying important ropes to, such as the main tack.

b. *Comb.*, as ***kevel-head, kevel-headed*** adj.

1815 BURNEY *Falconer's Marine Dict.*, *Kevel-Heads*, the ends of the top timbers, which, rising above the gun-wale, serve to belay the ropes, or take a round turn to hold on. *c* **1850** *Rudim. Navig.* (Weale) 98 Blocks for the.. lifts.. are kevel-headed blocks.

kevel ('kɛv(ə)l), *sb.*[3] *Sc.* and *north. dial.* [Etym. obscure. GAVEL *sb.*[4] is probably a variant of this.] A kind of hammer for rough-hewing or breaking stone (see quot. 1793); also ***kevel-hammer, -mell.*** Hence **'kevel** *v.*, to break (stones).

1360 *Fabric Rolls York Minster* (Surtees) 2 Pro factura ix. wegges et novo kevell et j melle ferri. **1368** *Durham Acc. Rolls* (Surtees) 571 Pro.. pikkis, hakkis, et kevellis faciend. **1404** *Ibid.* 397 In custodia Sementarii.. j kevyll. **1793** SMEATON *Edystone L.* §108 A tool called a Kevel, which is at one end a hammer, and at the other an axe, whose edge is so short or narrow that it approaches towards the shape of a pick. **1825–80** JAMIESON, *Kavel-mell*, a sledge-hammer, a hammer of a large size used for breaking stones. **1893** *Northumbld. Gloss.*, *Kevel, kyevel*, a stone-hammer, the common gavel. *Kyevel-hammer*, a heavy hammer used by stone-breakers to break up the large blocks of road metal.

kevel ('kɛv(ə)l), *sb.*[4] *Mining. local.* Also **keval, -il.** [Origin obscure.] The name given by Derbyshire lead-miners to a calcareous stone found mingled with the ore (see quots.).

1747 HOOSON *Miner's Dict.* Ej, Burr [is] a hard Knot or Lump in the Vein, or Sticking, of Caulk, Chirts, Kevells, &c. mixed with the Ore. **1802** MAWE *Mineral. Derbysh.* Gloss., *Kevel*, a sparry substance found in the vein, composed of calcareous spar, fluor, and barytes.

†**kevel,** *sb.*[5] *Obs.* [Given by Adanson as the native name in Senegal.] A species of antelope, now identified with the common gazelle.

1759 tr. *Adanson's Senegal.* **1774** GOLDSM. *Nat. Hist.* (1862) I. II. iii. 307–8 The.. second he calls the Kevel, which is rather less than the gazella. **1834** *Penny Cycl.* II. 83/2 The kevel [is] found only on the opposite side of the great African desert to that inhabited by the dorcas.

kevel, kevil: see CAVEL *sb.*[1] and [2].

'kevel, *v.*[1] *Obs.* exc. *dial.* In 5 **kevylle,** 6 **kewle,** 9 *dial.* **kibble.** [a. ON. *kefla* to bridle, gag, f. *kefli* KEVEL *sb.*[1]] *trans.* To bit or bridle.

a **1400** *Syr Perc.* 424 (Thornton MS. lf. 164) Brydille hase he righte nane;.. Bot a wythe hase he tane, And keuylles his stede. **1570** LEVINS *Manip.* 95/41 Kewle an horse, *os obstruere.* **1877** *N.W. Linc. Gloss.*, *Kibble*, to put the cord of a halter into a horse's mouth by way of bit.

kevel, *v.*[2]: see under KEVEL *sb.*[3]

†**'Kevenhuller.** *Obs.* Also **Khevenhullar.** [f. the name of the Austrian general, Andr. von Khevenhüller (1683–1744).]

a. *attrib.* Applied to a high cock given to a broad-brimmed hat worn in the middle of the 18th c. (see Fairholt *Costume in Eng.* (1860) 299); hence also with *hat.* **b.** *absol.* A cock of this form; a hat cocked in this fashion.

1746 *Brit. Mag.* 309 A laced Hat pinched into what our Beaux have learnt to call the Kevenhuller Cock. **1750** COVENTRY *Pompey Litt.* II. iv. (1785) 58/1 Jockey-boots, Khevenhullar-hats, and Coach-whips. **1753** *Proc. Commission of Common Sense* (Fairholt I. 377) Is not the Dettingen cock forgotten? the noble Kevenhuller discouraged? **1762** *Lond. Chron.* XI. *Chapter of Hats* (Planché), Hats are now worn, upon an average, six inches and three-fifths broad in the brim and cocked between Quaker and Kevenhuller.

kever, common ME. form of COVER *v.*[1] and *v.*[2] in midl. and south. dial.; rare obs. f. COVER *sb.*[1]

1570 LEVINS *Manip.* 74/38 Keuer, *operculum.*

keverche, -cher, var. KERCH, KERCHER, *Obs.*

†**keverfue,** obs. form of CURFEW.

14.. *Voc.* in Wr.-Wülcker 588/40 *Ignitegium*, keuerfve.

kevir, var. KAVIR.

kew. Short for THANK YOU.

1939 G. B. SHAW *Geneva* II. 30 Sit down. *Begonia* [complying]: Kew. **1961** *Times* 14 Aug. 9/4 Of 20 recipients of sitting space, five said 'Thank you' or 'Thanks'; three said 'Kew'.

kew, kewe, obs. forms of CUE *sb.*[1], [2].

Keweenawan (kiːwiː'nɔːən), *a.* Also †**Keweenawian.** [f. the name of *Keweenaw*

Peninsula, Michigan + -AN, -IAN.] Of, pertaining to, or designating the most recent division of the Proterozoic in North America, as represented by rocks in the region of the Great Lakes. Also *absol.*, the Keweenawan period or rocks.

1876 T. B. BROOKS in *Amer. Jrnl. Sci.* CXI. 210 We are therefore justified, I think, in regarding the Copper-bearing rocks of Lake Superior as a distinct and independent series, marking a definite geological period which separates the Silurian from the Huronian ages... Since Keweenaw Peninsula forms one of the most striking geographical features in Lake Superior.., I suggest the name Keweenawian for this period. **1883** R. D. IRVING *Copper-Bearing Rocks Lake Superior* ii. 25 The Keweenawan rocks form the larger part of Keweenaw Point. **1893** *Jrnl. Geol.* I. 126 The source of the lavas of the Keweenawan. **1930** *Econ. Geol.* XXV. 252 Erosion had peneplained the original folds of the Keewatin and Timiskaming rocks before Keweenawan time. *Ibid.* 262 They are distinctly younger than the Algoman and older than the Keweenawan. **1935** *Bull. Geol. Soc. Amer.* XLVI. 504 The Keweenawan lavas of the Lake Superior district form the inner border of the Lake Superior syncline. They crop out over an area of several thousand square miles, and in one section on Keweenaw Point, Michigan, form a series with a minimum thickness of 15,000 feet. **1970** DORR & ESCHMAN *Geol. Michigan* iv. 56/1 Keweenawan lavas were derived from molten magmas of the 'basic' or ferro-magnesian type.

kewery, variant of CURY[1] *Obs.*, cookery.

†**kew-kaw, kew-waw**, *adv. Obs.* [Origin obscure.] Upside down. (Used as *sb.* in quot. 1399.)

1399 LANGL. *Rich. Redeles* III. 299 In well and in woo þe werld euere turneth, ȝit þer is kew-kaw þouȝ he come late, A new þing þat noyeth nedy men and oþer. **1630** J. TAYLOR (Water P.) *Wks.* II. 233 The Picture topsie-turuie stands kewwaw: The World turn'd vpside downe, as all men know.

kewpie ('kjuːpɪ). orig. *U.S.* Also cupie. [A dim. form of CUPID.] In full, ***kewpie doll.*** A chubby doll with a curl or topknot on its head, from a design by R. C. O'Neill (1874–1944). Also *transf.*, of a person.

1909 R. O'NEILL in *Ladies Home Jrnl.* Dec. 28/1 The Kewpie wights stay up at nights, All gayly singing rum-te-tum. *Ibid.*, The reason why these funny, roly-poly creatures are called Kewpies..is because they look like little Cupids. **1912** *Ibid.* Oct. 109 The kewpies were invented by Rose O'Neill. They are always doing good, helping Dotty Darling and her Baby Brother to have a good time... So Rose O'Neill has made the Kewpie Kutouts. **1913** *Official Gaz.* (U.S. Patent Office) 13 May 536/1 Rose O'Neill Wilson... Kewpie. Particular description of goods.—Dolls. **1922** A. HADDON *Green Room Gossip* 176 The floor is strewn with at least fifty toys—teddy bears, golliwogs, bunnies, and woolly mascots galore. Kewpies, too, on the dressing-table. **1926** G. S. CHAPPELL *Younger Married Set* iv. 48, I have here..a magnificent kewpie doll. **1929** T. WOLFE *Look Homeward Angel* (1930) xxii. 324 Over the screened hearth, on a low mantel, there was a Kewpie doll, sashed with pink ribbon. **1937** *Official Gaz.* (U.S. Patent Office) 15 June 543/2 Rose O'Neill Wilson. The Kewpies. For Cartoons in Periodical Publications. Claims use since Dec. 21, 1912. **1937** J. STEINBECK *Of Mice & Men* iii. 93 They got a rag rug on the floor and a kewpie doll lamp on the phonograph. **1943** K. TENNANT *Ride on Stranger* vii. 60 Outside the turnstiles, vendors vie for custom, waving gilded cupie dolls on canes. **1946** I. L. IDRIESS *In Crocodile Land* xxvi. 180 With the little black kewpie of a piccanin aboard her tiny canoe, Wagis paddled downstream towards the river mouth. **1947** *Archit. Rev.* CI. 206/3 There are dolls for sale on the pier, too, Kewpie or cuddly or fashionable. **1952** M. MCCARTHY *Groves of Academe* (1953) ii. 18 Decorated with the same rag-dolls and teddy-bears, pink kewpies won at shooting-ranges. **1954** *Encounter* Feb. 52/1 Art Young, a white-haired little kewpie, sitting in a corner, was pointed out to me. **1957** M. MILLAR *Soft Talkers* 62 A kewpie doll. One of those tiny celluloid kewpie dolls you can buy in the dime store. **1960** *Birmingham Mail* 13 June 3/4 Each year Roo..has brought his woman..a cupie-doll. **1960** *Official Gaz.* (U.S. Patent Office) 30 Aug. TM 174/1 Cameo Doll Products Co., Inc., Port Allegany, Pa... Kewpie. For Dolls. **1961** A. CHRISTIE *Pale Horse* v. 67 A most terrible Kewpie doll from the hoop-la. **1969** N. COHN *AWopBopaLooBop* (1970) viii. 81 She'd be like some kewpie doll, all sheen and varnish and eyes that really roll. **1972** M. J. BOSSE *Incident at Naha* iii. 126 Kewpie dolls..staring at you stupidly and insanely from their glass eyes.

b. A sweet made in the form of a kewpie doll.

1916 *Daily Colonist* (Victoria, B.C.) 28 July 12/6 (Advt.), Kewpie Dolls, made of pure barley sugar, a box 10¢. **1918** *T. Eaton & Co. Catal.* Fall & Winter 385/3 Kewpie Kandy Dolls are made from the pure cane sugar... Twelve little kewpie dolls in each package.

†**kewt**, *v. Obs. rare.* [Imitative.] *intr.* To mew as a cat. Hence †**kewting** *vbl. sb.*

c **1440** *Promp. Parv.* 274/1 Kewtyn, as cattys, *catillo, glatio. Ibid.*, Kewtynge of cattys, *catillatus, glaticus.*

kex (kɛks). *Obs.* exc. *dial.* Forms: α. 4- **kex**, 6–7 **kexe**, 6 **keckes**, 8 **kecks**, (9 *dial.* **kesk, kesh**). β. 4–6 **kyx**, 6–8 **kix(e**, (6 **kickes, kykkes**, 9 *dial.* **gix, gicks, kish**). See also KECK, KECKSY, CASSHE. [Origin unknown; W. *cecys* pl., sometimes cited as the source, is no doubt from Eng.]

1. The dry, usually hollow, stem of various herbaceous plants, *esp.* of large umbelliferous plants, such as Cow Parsnip, Wild Chervil, and Marsh Angelica.

1377 LANGL. *P. Pl.* B. XVII. 219 Glowande gledes gladieth nouȝte þis werkmen..As doth a kex [C. xx. 185 kyx] or a candel þat cauȝte hath fyre & blaseth. *c* **1440** *Promp. Parv.* 277/2 Kyx, or bunne, or drye weed, *calamus.* **1530** PALSGR. 235/2 Keckes of humblockes, *tviau. Ibid.* 236/1 Kickes the drie stalke of humlockes or burres, *tvyau.* **1577** B. GOOGE *Heresbach's Husb.* (1586) 177 b, Take a peece of a reede or a kex. **1589** *Pappe w. Hatchet* C iv, Elders they may bee, which being fullest of spungie pith, proue euer the driest kixes. **1672** JOSSELYN *New Eng. Rarities* 74 The Stalkes are as hollow as a Kix, and so are the Roots. **1723** J. NOTT *Confectioner's Dict.* Pref., Upon the Battlements of the Castle [of pastry] were planted Guns made of Kexes. **1768–74** TUCKER *Lt. Nat.* (1834) II. 596 Taking for our support a withered kecks instead of the staff of life. **1842** AKERMAN *Wiltsh. Gloss.*, *Gix*, the dry stalks of hemlock. **1891** T. HARDY *Tess* (1892) 139, I should be as dry as a kex wi' travelling so far.

†**b.** Without *a*: collectively, or as a material.

In some cases perh. taken as pl. of KECK, a form which was prob. evolved from this collective sense.

1562 J. HEYWOOD *Prov. & Epigr.* (1867) 106 Of kyks for cage woorke, to builde thy house hie. **1597** GERARDE *Herbal* II. xvii. § 1. 199 The stalke is rounde, smooth and hollow, like to Kexe or Casshes. **1607** WILKINS *Miseries enforced Marriage* IV. in Hazl. *Dodsley* IX. 534 *Ilf.* Dost not know me, butler? *But.* For kex, dried kex. **1725** BAILEY *Erasm. Colloq.* 7 You're so thin, a Body may see through you, and as dry as Kecks.

2. An umbelliferous plant with a hollow stalk.

1578 LYTE *Dodoens* III. xxiii. 306 Sagapenum is the sap or gumme of a kinde of Ferula or kix. **1658** ROWLAND *Moufet's Theat. Ins.* 1003 They are commonly found in Kexes, or Asse Parsly in the summer time. **1755** *Gentl. Mag.* XXV. 29 *Cicuta.* Common Hemlock, or Kex. **1784** TWAMLEY *Dairying* 118 Kex, or water-parsnip,..grows in rivers and fens, is very noxious to cattle; also the lesser Kex called upright water-parsnip, in rivers and ditches. **1847** TENNYSON *Princ.* IV. 59 Tho' the rough kex break The starr'd mosaic. **1880** JEFFERIES *Gt. Estate* vii. 136 Cutting a dry 'gicks' so that it should be open at either end, like a tube.

†**3.** The husk, sheath, or hard case of a chrysalis.

c **1600** HOLLAND, When the kex, or husk, is broken, he proveth a fair flying butterfly. **1688** R. HOLME *Armoury* II. 371/1 Kex, or husk of Worms.

†**4.** *fig.* A dried-up sapless person. *Obs.*

1611 BEAUM. & FL. *King & No King* V. ii, I'le make these withered kexes bear my body two hours together above ground. **1659** *Lady Alimony* II. v. in Hazl. *Dodsley* XIV. 309 *Flo.* The issue madam? *Med.* None; nor ever shall With that sear, suckless kex. **1709** *Brit. Apollo* II. No. 54. 3/2 If a weighty Boss She, And a slender Kecks He. *a* **1711** KEN *Edmund* Poet. Wks. 1721 II. 360 I'll follow glorious Edmund to his Urn, The Embers of his Fire this Kix will burn.

†'**kexen**, *a. Obs. rare*[−1]. In 6 kicson. [f. prec. + -EN[4].] Made of kexes.

1579 PUTTENHAM *Parthenides* xi, One daye agayne will, in his rage, Crushe it all as a kicson cage, And spill it quite.

'**kexy**, *a. Obs.* exc. *dial.* Also 7 **kecksie**, 9 *dial.* **kecksy, kiskie.** [f. KEX + -Y. Cf. KECKY.] Like a kex; dry and brittle; withered, sapless.

1608 SYLVESTER *Du Bartas* II. iv. IV. *Schisme* 396 Thou.. Shalt play no longer thy proud Kingling's Part On such a Kixey stage. **1653** A. WILSON *Jas. I* 159 His Kecksie carkass was made to ride..with his face to the horse tail. **1660** H. MORE *Myst. Godl.* VI. x. 240 The Earth..will become more kexy, and loose of its Solidity. *a* **1825** FORBY *Voc. E. Anglia*, *Kisky*, dry, juiceless, husky. **1884** *Cheshire Gloss.* s.v., Celery, when it is inclined to run up to stalks, would be called 'very kecksy'.

key (kiː), *sb.*[1] Forms: 1 **cæȝ, cæȝe, (kæȝe, kaiȝe)**, 2 **kæie**, 3 **keiȝe**, *pl.* **keyȝen, keien**, 4 **keyȝe**; 3–4 **kai**, 3–8 **kay**, (4 **cay, kaie**, *pl.* **caiss**), 4–6 **kaye**, (5–6 *pl.* **kaies**); 3–6 **keye**, (*pl.* **keis**), 3–7 **keie**, 5–7 **kee**, 7 **kie**; 4- **key**, (*pl.* 4–6 **-es**, 4- **-s**). [OE. *cǽȝ* str. f. (pl. *cǽȝa*) and *cǽȝe* wk. f. (pl. *cǽȝan*) = OFris. *kei, kay*; not found in the other Teut. languages; ulterior etym. unknown.

The mod. pronunciation (kiː) is abnormal. The other OE. words ending in *-ǽȝ* have uniformly mod. (eɪ), as *clǽȝ* clay, *grǽȝ* grey, gray, *hwǽȝ* whey; and that *key* had the same vowel as these in ME. is proved not only by the frequent spelling *kay*, but by its constantly riming with *day, way, say, play*, etc. This was evidently the standard pron. down to the close of the 17th c.; Dryden has the rime with *way* more than once in one of his latest works (1700). On the other hand, we find even in 15th c. a (northern) spelling *kee*; and in Scottish MSS. of the same cent. the form *key* (pl. *keis*) shows that the vowel in that dialect was not the same as in *day* or *clay*; in somewhat later Scottish (16th–17th c.) the identity of the vowel with that which gives mod. (iː) is established by rimes. In mod. Southern Sc. also, *key* has the same diphthong (keɪ) as *be, me, we, dee, see, tree*, etc., proving that it must from an early period have had the same sound as *ē, ee* had at the time. The vb. *weigh* has the same history in Sc. (wiː), but in Eng. remains (weɪ). The mod. pronunciation (kiː) thus appears to be of northern origin, and it is difficult to know how it came into general Eng. use. Cf. the surname *Kaye* or *Key* (*Caius*) in *Caius* (i.e. *Key's*) College, Cambridge.]

I. 1. a. An instrument, usually of iron, for moving the bolt or bolts of a lock forwards or backwards, and so locking or unlocking what is fastened by it; usually fitted on the bit or web with more or less elaborate incisions, etc., adapted to the wards of the lock.

a **1000** *Riddles* xliii. 12 (Gr.) Hwylc þæs hordgates cæȝan cræfte þa clamme onleac. **1018** *Laws of Cnut* II. c. 76 § 1 þæra cæȝean heo sceal weardian. *c* **1290** *S. Eng. Leg.* I. 200/14 þe prior haueth þe keiȝe in warde. *a* **1300** *Cursor M.* 17357 þai sperd fast wit lok and kai [*v.rr.* kay, key] þe seles alssua þai bar away. *c* **1320** *Sir Beues* (MS. A) 3207 A..schette þe dore wiþ þe keie [*rime* veie (= fey)]. *c* **1375** *Sc. Leg. Saints* xlvii. (*Effame*) 73 þo he had þe keys brocht Vith hyme, duris opyn he [ne] mocht. **1463** *Bury Wills* (Camden) 22 A keye of the grete gardeyn gate. **1491–2** in Swayne *Sarum Church-w. Acc.* (1896) 40, j key to the Organ dore & iij keyis to the quer dorys vijd. **1535** COVERDALE *Judg.* iii. 25 (For no man opened the perler dore) they toke the keye, and opened it. **1552** HULOET, Kaye, *clauis.* **1596** SPENSER *F.Q.* IV. x. 18 Either through gifts, or guile, or such like waies, Crept in by stouping low, or stealing of the kaies. **1632** LITHGOW *Trav.* IV. 137 The doore, that he had newly locked, and taken the key with him to the ship. **1700** DRYDEN *Sigism. & Guisc.* 133 The dame, who long in vain had kept the key, Bold by desire, explored the secret way. *Ibid.* 156, 294. **1772** *Junius Lett.* lxviii. 354 A key was found in his room. **1820** KEATS *St. Agnes* xli, The key turns, and the door upon its hinges groans. **1877** J. M. PORTEOUS *Turkey* 20 A key was an emblem carried before the troops of the prophet.

b. Phrases and proverbs: †***under key***, under lock and key (see LOCK). ***as cold as a key*** (cf. KEY-COLD *a.*). ***to lay*** (or ***put***) ***the key under the door***, to shut up house and go away. ***to get*** (***have***) ***the key of the street*** (ironical), to be shut out for the night, or have no house to go to. ***key and book*** (or ***bible***), used in a method of divination. ***the King's keys*** (see quot. 1824).

13.. *Evang. Nicod.* 831 in Herrig *Archiv* LIII. 406 Yhe keped him vnder kay [*rimes* day, way, may]. **1390** GOWER *Conf.* II. 188 The Priest Thoas, which..the Palladion of Troie Kepte under keie. **1501** DOUGLAS *Pal. Hon.* 674 With quaikand voce and hart cald as a key [*rimes* fey, pley, etc.]. *a* **1541** WYATT *Poet. Wks.* (1861) 121 What 'vaileth under kay To keep treasure alway, That never shall see day. *a* **1600** MONTGOMERIE *Sonn.* xli, My lyfe..from my body fled, And left my corps als cold as ony kie [*rimes* thee, ee, thrie]. **1677** YARRANTON *Eng. Improv.* 126 The Tenant lays the Key under the Door. **1824** SCOTT *Redgauntlet* ch. xix, Constables ..considered as worthy to use what are called the king's keys. [Cf. *Antiq.* xxi. *note*, The king's keys are, in law phrase, the crow-bars and hammers used to force doors and locks, in execution of the king's warrant.] **1837** DICKENS *Pickw.* xlvii, It's too late now: you can't get in to-night; you've got the key of the street, my friend. **1894** G. PARKER *Transl. Savage* 161 A crossing sweeper early to his task, or holding the key of the street.

c. The representation of a key, in painting, sculpture, etc. ***St Peter's keys***, the cross keys borne in the Papal arms (see 4). ***Greek key***, each of the key-like bends of which the Greek fret consists.

c **1450** HOLLAND *Howlat* 345 Twa keyis our croce, of siluer so cleir, In a feild of asure flammit on fold. **15..** *Sym & his bruder* 25 in Laing *Anc. Poet. Scot.* 315 Thay..clampit vp sanct Peteris keis [*rimes* leis, weis, sleuis] Bot of ane auld reid gartane. **1688** R. HOLME *Armoury* III. 301/2 He beareth Azure, a key double Bited in Fesse. **1897** *Westm. Gaz.* 2 Sept. 3/2 Its trimmings..running in vertical lines that end in Greek keys.

2. In pregnant sense, with reference to the power of custody, control, admission of others, etc., implied by the possession of the keys of any place; hence as a symbol of office, and *fig.* the office itself. ***gold key***, the office of groom of the stole.

a **900** [see 4]. **1297** R. GLOUC. (Rolls) 3848 þe conseil of france..ȝolde him vp al þat lond & þe keyen [*v.rr.* keyȝen, keyes] of parys. *c* **1385** CHAUCER *L.G.W.* 2298 (*Philomela*) Myn yonge doughter..That beryth the keye of al myn hertis lyf. *a* **1400–50** *Alexander* 2147 þai vnȝarked him þe ȝatis & ȝald him þe keys [*MS. D.* kees]. **1546** J. HEYWOOD *Prov.* (1867) 30 The kays hang not all by one mans gyrdell. *a* **1548** HALL *Chron.*, *Hen. VI* 162 All the townes in Acquitayne (except Bayon) delivered their keys, and became vassals. **1642** G. MOUNTAGU in *Buccleuch MSS.* (Hist. MSS. Comm.) I. 299 These Lords, Holland and Essex,.. accordingly delivered their key and staff respectively to the Lord Falkland. **1676** C. HATTON in *H. Corr.* (Camden) 138 His office of Chamberlaine is here incompatible wth his other character. It is generally beleeved he will lose his Key. **1761** DK. NEWCASTLE *Lett. Dk. Devonsh.* 13 Mar. in W. E. Manners *Mrq. Granby* (1899) 196 Lord Bute told me the King wished to give the Gold Key to the Duke of Rutland and the Staff to my Lord Talbot. **1795** SOUTHEY *Joan of Arc* VI. 168 Of every captured town the keys Restore to Charles.

II. *fig.* (often in figurative context).

3. a. Something compared to a key, with its power of locking or unlocking; that which opens up, or closes, the way to something; that which gives opportunity for or precludes an action, state of things, etc.

a **1000** *Cædmon's Exod.* 524 ȝif onlucan wile lifes wealhstod..gastes cæȝon, run bið ȝerecenod. *c* **1200** *Vices & Virtues* 7 Hie is kæie of alle oðre sennes non senne ne mai bien idon bute ðurh unhersumnesse. *c* **1450** in *3rd Rep. Hist. MSS. Comm.* (1872) 280/1 And as for Maunce and Mayne, alle lordes and comons in Englond knew well that it was the keye of well faire of alle the kynge's obeisaunce in Fraunce. **1596** DRAYTON *Leg.* i. 740 His victorious Hand became the Kay, To let yee in, to my rich Treasure. **1642** FULLER *Holy & Prof. St.* IV. xxi. 352 Love, the key of hearts, will open the closest coffers. *a* **1703** BURKITT *On N.T.*, *Matt.* vii. 11 Prayer is the key that opens both His heart and His hand. **1845** FORD *Handbk. Spain* I. 58 A supply of cigars, those keys to Spanish hearts.

b. ***golden*** or ***silver key***: Money, employed as a bribe to obtain the opening of a door or to gain a purpose.

[**14..** *Purif. Marie* in *Tundale's Vis.* (1843) 130 Thowgh that sche bare of gold no key To bye a lombe.] **1679** *Hist. Jetzer* 2 The Silver Key will open the strongest Gates of the strictest Monastery. **1705** HICKERINGILL *Priest-cr.* I. (1721) 63 Will Council open their Mouths without a Golden Key? **1798** W. HUTTON *Autobiog.* 41, I was given to understand that the door, contrary to other doors, would not open with a silver key. **1842** TENNYSON *Locksley H.* 100 Every door is barr'd with gold, and opens but to golden keys.

†**c.** A name for the principal claws of a hawk's foot (see quot.) *Obs.*

1486 *Bk. St. Albans* A viij, Understond ye also that the longe Senclees be calde the key of the fote, or the Closer. For what thyng som euer it be yt yowre hawke strenyth, open that Sengle, and all the fote is oppen, for the strength ther of fortyfieth all the fote.

4. *Theol.* (With allusion to *Matt.* xvi. 19). Usually *pl.*: The ecclesiastical authority, held by Roman Catholics to be conferred by Christ on St. Peter, and transmitted to the Popes as his successors. In a wider sense: The disciplinary or spiritual power of priests, as successors of the Apostles.

a **900** *O.E. Martyrol.* 210 þæt he [se papa] heofna rices cæᵹan & helle ᵹeweald ahte. [*c* **1000** *Ags. Gosp.* Matt. xvi. 19 þe ic sylle heofona rices cæᵹia [*Lindisf.* cæᵹas, *Rushw.* kæᵹen; *Hatton* kaiᵹen.] *a* **1300** *Cursor M.* 26150 He mai þe noþer lese ne bind, forqui þat kay es giuen to nan bot preist. **1340** Hampole *Pr. Consc.* 3838 Þa cays er noght elles to se Bot playn power of his [the Pope's] dignite. **1426** Audelay *Poems* 20 Cal the clarge to ȝour counsel, that beryn Cristis kay. **1552** Lyndesay *Monarche* 4820 Those spiritual keis quhilkis Christ to Peter gaif. **1560** Daus tr. *Sleidane's Comm.* 437 Whether Priestes onlye have authoritye of the Keyes. **1653** Baxter *Chr. Concord* 43 They that distinguish between the Key of Order and the Key of Jurisdiction, do without question allow the former to the Presbyters. **1681** *Procl. Privy Counc.* in *Lond. Gaz.* No. 1670/1 The Intrinsick Spiritual Power of the Church, or Power of the Keys, as it was exerced by the Apostles. *a* **1711** Ken *Hymnotheo* Poet. Wks. 1721 III. 131 Jesus to you the ghostly Keys commits, And those you here absolve, in Heav'n acquits. **1849** Macaulay *Hist Eng.* I. iv. 466 Lewis..was in turn accused by the Pope of encroaching on the spiritual power of the keys.

5. A place which from the strategic advantages of its position gives its possessor control over the passage into or from a certain district, territory, inland sea, etc.

c **1440** Capgrave *Life St. Kath.* I. 71 Therfor þis kyng ryght as for a keye Of all hys kyngdame set hys town þer. *a* **1548** Hall *Chron., Hen. VI* 153 Which towne was the kay and passage over the ryver of Soame, from Fraunce to Normandy. *a* **1600** Montgomerie *Misc. Poems* xlviii. 115 For these tua Castells ar the only kees Of all Turkie, and do divide the sees. **1684** *Lond. Gaz.* No. 1954/3 A very Important place, which is the Key of Sclavonia. **1735** Berkeley *Querist* §266 Whether the sea-ports of Galway, Limerick, Cork, and Waterford are not to be looked on as keys of this kingdom? **1838** Thirlwall *Greece* II. xv. 291 He had now the key of Northern Greece in his hands. **1838** *Penny Cycl.* XI. 214/2 (*Gilbraltar*) Henry IV, king of Castile ..gave it the arms it still bears, viz. a castle with a key hanging to the gate, alluding to its being the key to the Mediterranean.

transf. **1869** Huxley in *Sci. Opin.* 5 May 506/1 And yet this is the key of the whole position.

6. a. That which serves to open up, disclose, or explain what is unknown, mysterious, or obscure; a solution or explanation.

c **897** K. Ælfred *Gregory's Past.* xv. 90 Ðæt word ðære ðreaunge is cæᵹ, forðæm hit oft onlycð & ᵹeopenað ða scylde þe se him self ær nyste se hie ðurhteah. *c* **1000** Ælfric *Gram.* Pref. (Z.) 2 Stæfcræft is seo cæᵹ ðe ðæra boca andᵹit unlicð. **1382** Wyclif *Luke* xi. 52 Woo to ȝou, wyse men of lawe, for ȝe han take awey the keye of kunnynge. *c* **1422** Hoccleve *Learn to Die* 12 Thow of al science berst the keye. **1597** Montgomerie *Cherrie & Slae* 411 Euer Curage keipis the keyis Of knawledge at his belt. **1642** Fuller *Holy & Prof. St.* III. iv. 158 Get the Language (in part) without which Key thou shalt unlock little of moment. **1712** Addison *Spect.* No. 435 ¶6, I have one general Key to the Behaviour of the Fair Sex. **1788** Mad. D'Arblay *Diary* 21 July, I felt his meaning, though I had no key to it. **1883** S. C. Hall *Retrospect* II. 305 It was the key to his success; he knew the value of time.

b. *spec.* The alphabet or explanatory scheme for the interpretation of a cipher, an allegorical statement, or other composition of hidden or veiled meaning; any scheme explaining the features of a picture, identifying the persons represented, etc.; an outline or simplified map or chart, intended to make a full map, etc., more intelligible; a work containing solutions of mathematical or other problems; a translation of a book or exercise in a foreign language, to facilitate the work of learners.

1605 Implied in *key-cipher* [see 17]. **1675** *Essex Papers* (Camden) I. 290 'Tis most of it in cypher, wch ye Key will unfolde. **1711** Addison *Spect.* No. 37 ¶2 The New *Atalantis*, with a Key to it. **1753** *Scots Mag.* Apr. 208/2 A burlesque upon some late..transactions; but seems to want a key. **1800** Dk. Wellington *Let. to Lieut. Col. Close* in Gurw. *Desp.* (1837) I. 151, I beg also that you will send me a key of the cipher. **1826** Syd. Smith *Wks.* (1867) II. 102 Some of the best Greek and Roman classics should be immediately published, with keys. **1827** Hare *Guesses* Ser. II. (1873) 296 Poetry is the key to the hieroglyphics of nature. **1870** A. R. Hope *My Schoolboy Fr.* (1875) 52 Where the master used a Key to Henry's Exercises.

c. *Chess.* (*a*) In full ***key move***. The first move in the solution of a set problem, upon which depends the style of the whole solution. Also *attrib.* or as *adj.* (*b*) The whole solution of a set problem.

1827 W. Lewis *Chess Probl.* Pref., I defer for the present publishing the Solutions, that the reader may solve the Problems without being tempted to refer to the Key. **1846** *Chess Player's Chron.* VI. 65 Amateurs wanting either time or perseverance to undertake the solution themselves,..may obtain the key by addressing a note to the Editor. **1878** S. Loyd *Chess Strategy* 60 Key-moves which threaten an easy mate. *Ibid.* 201 There is always a great deal of chance in solving a problem, such as hitting upon the key by accident. **1923** B. G. Laws *Artistry of Chess Probl.* 5 Key, continuations and principal mates are all of the first order... The key abandoning an important protective Pawn..is little short of being superb. **1938** C. S. Kipping *Chess Probl. Sci.* I. 51 This was followed by six dis. checks..with a check key, and J. L. Millins showed that it could be done with a quiet key... Ua Tane, using White King diagonal battery and Pawn promotion key showed that six were possible. *Ibid.* 56 Petrovic's astounding triple task has not a key which will appeal to everyone. **1945** *Chess in Schools* (Chess Educ. Soc.) 27 *Problems*, composed positions in which a key move is to be found, after which mate is forced in a specified number of moves. **1958** Mansfield & Harley *Mod. Two-Move Chess Probl.* 19 The solver's attention is drawn to it, and Key possibilities are limited. *Ibid.*, Such a Key is thematic and good.

d. The device used to 'key' an advertisement (see key *v.* 5). orig. *U.S.*

1905 Calkins & Holden *Art of Mod. Advertising* xi. 266 A variation of the 'key' in advertising is the coupon. **1915** H. W. Hess *Productive Advertising* xiii. 199 Accounts may be opened charging up to each key not only (1) number of inquiries, but (2) amount spent on that particular key, [etc.]. **1957** Clark & Gottfried *University Dict. Business & Finance* (1967) 201/1 The key may be a special street or box number, or a department to which the reply is to be addressed, or it may be a number or letter code included in the reply coupon if one is used.

7. *Mus.* †**a.** [after Guido Aretino's use of *clāvis*.] The lowest note or tone of a scale or sequence of notes; the key-note. *Obs.* Hence, **b.** A scheme or system of notes or tones definitely related to each other, according to (or *in*) which a piece of music is written; such scheme being based upon and named after some particular note (the *key-note*), as ***the key of C***. Hence, **c.** The sum of melodic and harmonic relations existing between the tones of such a system; tonality.

major, minor, natural (etc.) *key*: see these words.

[There is app. some relationship between this sense and 11, but its precise nature is not clear; its origin prob. lies outside Eng., in the use, in mediæval music, of L. *clāvis* (whence, also, through Fr., clef, q.v.).

1880 A. J. Hipkins in Grove *Dict. Mus.* I. 369 The word *clavis*, key, in the solmisation system of Guido d'Arezzo, was used for note or tone.]

1590 Shaks. *Mids. N.* III. ii. 206 Both warbling of one song; both in one key. **1597** Morley *Introd. Mus.* 4 Now I praie you shew me all the seuerall Keyes wherein you may begin your sixe Notes [i.e. hexachords]. **1609** Douland *Ornith. Microl.* 7 A Key is the opening of a Song, because like as a Key opens a dore, so doth it the Song. **1674** Playford *Skill Mus.* I. xi. 57 To shew in what Key the Song was set, and how each Musical Key had relation one to another. **1694** W. Holder *Harmony* (1731) 119 Draw a second Scale..but let the Key, or First Note be D *Sol re.* **1731** Keller *Rules for Thorow-Bass* in Holder *Harmony* 192 The extream Sharp in a sharp [i.e. major] Key, is the half Note [i.e. semitone] below the Key. **1787** Wolcott (P. Pindar) *Ode upon Ode* Wks. 1812 I. 421 To hear her pompously demand the Key Of every piece Musicians play. **1826** B'ness Bunsen in Hare *Life* I. vii. 268, I have often practised writing out parts in the different keys. **1898** Stainer *Dict. Mus. Terms* 253/2 The key of C requires no flats or sharps for this purpose, hence it is called the *normal* key.

8. *transf.* and *fig.* **a.** *transf.* (High or low) tone (of the voice); pitch.

1599 B. Jonson *Cynthia's Rev.* IV. i. Wks. (Rtldg.) 84/1 There's one speaks in a key, like the opening of some Justice's gate, or a postboy's horn. **1623** Massinger *Dk. Milan* II. i. Plays (1868) 74/1 I'll speak to her, And in a high key too. **1709** Berkeley *Th. Vision* §46 Men speak in a high or a low key. **1748** J. Mason *Elocut.* 10 Carefully to preserve the Key (that is, the Command) of your Voice. **1877** Black *Green Past.* xxxv. (1878) 282 Loudly discoursing—in a high shrill and plaintive key—of his troubles.

b. *fig.* Intensity or force, 'pitch' (of feeling or action); tone or style (of thought or expression); sometimes, prevailing tone or idea, 'key-note'. Phr. ***in key (with)***: in harmony (with); in a style that matches; ***out of key (with)***: out of harmony (with); not matching; unsuitable.

1594 Nashe *Unfort. Trav.* 36 As for my cariage, he knew hee was to tuene it at a key, either high or low, as he list. **1599** Daniel *Musoph.* Wks. (1601) B v, His passions set to such a pleasing kay. **1621** Quarles *Div. Poems, Esther* (1717) 131 Let peace and love exalt your Key of mirth. **1646** Evance *Noble Ord.* 16 Which is the right Key of obedience. **1770** Langhorne *Plutarch* (1879) II. 904 2 The key of politics, which he first touched, he kept to without variation. **1816** Keatinge *Trav.* (1817) I. 234 He returned in a high key of spirits in consequence of the reception he was favoured with. **1875** Stubbs *Const. Hist.* I. xiv. 129 The writs to the barons..are shorter but in the same key. **1919** B. Ruck *Disturbing Charm* II. xiv. 287 Everything in that drawing-room was in key with that mantelpiece. **1920** E. Pound *Hugh Selwyn Mauberley* I. 9 For three years, out of key with his time, He strove to resuscitate the dead art Of poetry. **1931** E. Wilson *Axel's Castle* ii. 34 We shall be thrown fatally out of key with reality. **1934** H. G. Wells *Exper. Autobiogr.* II. vii. 489 That was entirely out of key with James's assumptions.

c. Tone or relative intensity (of colour).

1851 H. Wilson *Compos. Light & Shade* 65 Pictures, painted in a 'light key', possess many advantages. **1876** Ruskin *Arrows of Chace* (1880) I. 174 Their harmonies of amber-colour and purple are full of exquisite beauty in their chosen key.

III. Applied to various mechanical devices, in function or form suggesting the key of a lock.

9. A piece of wood or metal which is inserted between other pieces; usually, a pin, bolt or wedge fitting into a hole or space contrived for it so as to lock various parts together; a cotter.

Also, in special senses: (*a*) A piece of timber framed between floor-joists by mortice and tenon. (*b*) A piece of wood let into the back of a board or set of boards, across the grain, to prevent warping. (*c*) In stone-work: the piece or wedge of iron used to secure a dovetail in a hole, or driven between two 'feathers' to split a stone (see quots. 1793). (*d*) In bookbinding: a metal U-shaped instrument by which each band is secured in the sewing-press.

[**1408–19** *Acc. Roll* in Raine *Brief Acc. Durh. Cath.* (1833) 88, 4*d.* each for 280 'keys', or bosses for the crossings of the beams.] *c* **1440** *Promp. Parv.* 269/2 Key, or knyttynge of ij. wallys, or trees yn an vnstabylle grownde,..*loramentum.* **1497** *Naval Acc. Hen. VII* (1896) 84 Boltes forlokkes kayes lynces and a taile pynne for the said Curtowe. **1523** Fitzherb. *Husb.* §5 The bodye of the wayne..the crosse somer, the keys and pikstaues. **1603–4** in Swayne *Sarum Church-w. Acc.* (1896) 152 Boltes and kayes for the belles. **1660** Boyle *New Exp. Phys. Mech.* ii. 37 The brass Key (formerly described as a stopple in the brass Cover). **1730** A. Gordon *Maffei's Amphith.* 213 The Stones..are pieced together..with Keys of Iron or Stones left projecting out in what was already built, the better to join them. *Ibid.* 215 Keys or Cramps of Metal. **1787** Winter *Syst. Husb.* 312 Take out the pins or keys which fasten the iron work of the brass collars. **1793** Smeaton *Edystone L.* §51 The iron stanchions..were not fixed into the rock in the method of Key and Dovetail..but were fixed in with club ends. *Ibid.* §147 A method sometimes used..for the division of hard stones, called the Key and Feather..The Key is a long tapering wedge..The Feathers are pieces of iron, also of a wedge like shape. **1838** Simms *Pub. Wks. Gt. Brit.* 15 Two wrought iron keys for fixing the rail in the chair. **1857–62** Nicholson *Dict. Archit.* II. 86 When a key is passed through..two or more thicknesses of metal or other material .. it is customary to clasp them together by gibbs, previous to inserting the key. **1892** D. A. Low *Machine Draw.* 22 Keys are wedges, generally rectangular in section, but sometimes circular; they are made of wrought iron or steel, and are used for securing wheels, pulleys, cranks, &c., to shafts.

¶In the following passages L. *clāvus* tiller, rudder, is confused with *clāvis* key.

c **1374** Chaucer *Boeth.* III. pr. xii. 81 (Camb. MS.) He is as a keye [L. *clauus*] and a stiere by which þat the edifice of this world is I-kept stable. **1423** Jas. I *Kingis Q.* c, O anker and keye of oure gude auenture.

10. a. That which completes or holds together the parts of any fabric; *esp.* the key-stone of an arch, which by its position and wedged form locks the other stones and holds together the structure.

Also (*a*) the last board laid in a floor (Nicholson *Dict. Archit.* (1857–62); (*b*) the bent bar of iron which in well-boring supports the train of rods (Knight *Dict. Mech.* 1875).

1523 Fitzherb. *Husb.* §3 The sharebeame, the whiche is the keye and the chiefe bande of all the plough. **1624** Wotton *Archit.* in *Reliq.* (1651) 290 If the great Doore be Arched with some brave Head, cut in fine Stone or Marble for the Key of the Arch. **1703** Moxon *Mech. Exerc.* 273 The under side of the Arch at the Key to rise in height 18 Inches from the level of the place, whence you begin to spring the Arch. **1723** Chambers tr. *Le Clerc's Treat. Archit.* I. 52 Keys..ought to be..a real support, and not stand for mere Ornaments as they frequently do. **1892** *Daily News* 22 Nov. 3/1 The hole will be lined all the way round with an iron plate two inches thick. This will be laid all round in 14 segments, and a 'key' at the top.

†**b.** *fig.* The leading person or mainstay of a society, etc.; one of the best dogs in a pack; a cardinal point or principle. *Obs.*

1559 *Mirr. Mag., Dk. Clarence* xviii, Where decayed the kayes of chiualrie. **1578** T. N. tr. *Conq. W. India* 319 The key of all these wars consisted in this victory. *c* **1620** A. Hume *Brit. Tongue* vii. 18 That general, quhilk I called the keie of orthographie..that is the congruence of the symbol and sound symbolized. **1652** Culpeppper *Eng. Physic.* (1809) 336 The one must keep his credit, and the other get money, and that is the key of the work. **1693** Evelyn *De la Quint. Compl. Gard.* I. 103 Which..are among our Fruits that which those called the Keys in a Pack of Hounds are in Hunting.

c. That portion of a first coat of wall-plaster which passes between the laths and secures the rest; the hold which plaster has on a wall by means of roughnesses in the surface; the roughness of a wall-surface which enables plaster to adhere to it; the roughing on the under-side of a veneer, giving the glue a better hold.

1825 J. Nicholson *Operat. Mechanic* 612 The plaster is crossed all over with the end of a lath, to give it a tie or key to the coat which is afterwards to be laid upon it. **1842–76** Gwilt *Archit.* (ed. 7) §1899 A better key is obtained upon the bricks and mortar. **1888** C. F. Mitchell *Build. Constr.* I. vii. (1889) 104 Tredgold recommends the arrises of wide timbers to be taken off, so as not to interrupt the key for plaster.

11. a. In the organ, pianoforte, and other ('keyboard') instruments: Each of the levers, or more usually only the exposed front end of each of these, which are pressed down by the fingers in playing, and actuate the internal mechanism so as to produce the various notes.

[This sense appears to be confined to Eng. It is app. related in origin to 7: see the note there.]

c **1500** *Prov.* in *Antiq. Rep.* (1809) IV. 407 He must handill the keyes all lyke. **1513** in Kerry *Hist. St. Lawr., Reading* (1883) 60 Payd for ye lokks to the same organs, one for the stopps and the oþer for the keyes. **1626** Bacon *Sylva* §158 In Clericalls, the Keyes are lined. **1632** Quarles *Div. Fancies* I The unseen Bellows, nor the hand that plays Upon

th' apparant note-dividing Kayes. **1664** Pepys *Diary* 5 Oct., The new instrument..the Arched Viall..played on with kees like an organ. **1785** Mad. D'Arblay *Diary* 16 Dec., 'Are you sure you never play?—never touch the keys at all?' **1876** F. E. Trollope *Charming Fellow* II. i. 4 [She] began to run her fingers over the keys of the piano. **1896** Hipkins *Pianoforte* 28 The lower keys are called the naturals and, where seen, are covered with ivory; the visible ends of the shorter upper keys, called sharps, are raised to the height required by blocks of ebony glued upon them.

b. In some wind instruments, as the flute, oboe, clarinet, concertina, etc.: Each of the small metal levers, actuated by the fingers, which cover or uncover the holes so as to modify the length of the vibrating column of air and thus produce the various notes.

1765 Croker, etc. *Dict. Arts*, etc. s.v. *Flute*, Stopped and opened by the little finger's pressing on a brass, or sometimes, a silver key, like those in hautboys, bassoons, &c. **1829** *Specif. Patent* 5803 Finger keys have also been added to such instruments [as the concertina]. **1851** *Illustr. Catal. Gt. Exhib.* 1105 D flute of ebony, with keys..Clarionets in B and D, in German silver, with all the keys.

†**c.** Each of the vibrating steel tongues of a musical box. *Obs.*

1823 J. Badcock *Dom. Amusem.* 67 Long bits of steel called the keys of the instrument.

12. Hence **a.** In telegraphy, A mechanical device for breaking and closing an electric circuit. **b.** In a typewriter or similar instrument, each of a set of levers pressed by the fingers in the same manner as the keys of a pianoforte or organ.

1837 *Specif. Patent* No. 7390. 4 Giving signals..by..pressure of his..fingers upon suitable buttons or finger keys. **1846** *Penny Cycl.* 1st Suppl. II. 616/1 In M. Alexander's instrument, a set of keys resembling those of a pianoforte, and corresponding to the number of needles, were arranged on a frame or table. **1867** Sabine *Electric Telegraph* 41 The transmitting key used by Morse in his later apparatus..consisted of a lever. **1876** Preece & Sivewright *Telegraphy* 58 To send dots and dashes by this key it is only necessary to tap or move it as one would the key of a piano.

13. a. An instrument for grasping a square or polygonal-headed screw, peg, or nut, and turning it by lever action; esp. (*a*) for winding a clock, watch, or clock-work machine; (*b*) for turning the wrest-pins of stringed instruments; a tuning-hammer; (*c*) for turning a valve or stop-cock; (*d*) for turning a nut; a screw-wrench or spanner.

The reference in quot. 1610 is somewhat uncertain. In quot. 1659 applied to the plug of a cock or tap.

1610 Shaks. *Temp.* I. ii. 83 Thy false vncle..hauing both the key, Of Officer, and office, set all hearts i'th state To what tune pleas'd his eare. **1659** Leak *Waterwks.* 14 The Cock D; whose barrel is pierced..to the end that the key C turning either one way or the other,..the Water..may run when the hole of the key C shall agree with one or the other of them. **1729** Swift *Direct. Servants* Wks. (1879) 559/2 Hide the key of the jack. **1755** Johnson *Dict.*, *Key*..3. An instrument by which something is screwed or turned. **1783** *Phil. Trans.* LXXIII. 443 Those stop-cocks must be turned by means of a key adapted to their square tops. **1828** Webster s.v., The key of a watch or other chronometer. **1851** *Illustr. Catal. Gt. Exhib.* 1147 Ordinary tuning-keys are generally formed in one piece of hard iron. **1884** J. F. Britten *Watch & Clockm.* 131 Capable of being wound without a key.

b. An instrument for extracting teeth, consisting of a firm handle, with a claw, beak, or hook at right angles to it, and moving upon a pivot.

1854–67 C. A. Harris *Dict. Med. Terminol.* 377/2 Since the time of Garengeot, the key has undergone a number of improvements..almost every dentist has felt the necessity of modifying the instrument. **1856** Druitt *Surgeon's Vade M.* 450 The key is..often employed for the extraction of the biscuspides and molars.

IV. 14. A dry fruit with a thin membranous wing, usually growing in bunches, as in the ash and sycamore.

1523 Fitzherb. *Surv.* xxix. (1539) 51 Ye may gette the Keys of asshes, nuttes, and suche other. **1562** Turner *Herbal* II. 6 They are called in Englishe ashe Keyes, because they hangh in bunches after the maner of Keyes. **1664** Evelyn *Sylva* (1679) 4 Oaklings, young beeches, ash, and some others, spring from the self-sown mast and keys. **1789** G. White *Selborne* (1853) 387 Many ash-trees bear loads of keys every year. **1880** Gray *Struct. Bot.* (ed. 6) 294 The Samara, sometimes called in English a Key, is an indehiscent one-seeded fruit provided with a wing.

15. ***key of the sea***, the pelican's foot shell.

1854 *Zoologist* XII. 4425 *Aporrhais pes-pelecani*..This common shell is popularly known as the 'key of the sea'.

16. [Respelling of *ki* in *kilo*.] A kilogramme of a drug. *U.S. slang.*

1968–70 *Current Slang* (Univ. S. Dakota) III–IV. 76 *Key*, kilo of any narcotic; a measurement for marijuana, 215 lbs, $300.00 +. **1970** *Time* 13 Apr. 36 A $10 or $20 'key' of Lebanese hash can fetch $1,500 or more in the U.S. **1972** J. Wambaugh *Blue Knight* (1973) iv. 45 On her coffee table she had at least half a key and that's a pound of pot and that's trouble.

V. *attrib.* and *Comb.*

17. a. General combs., as (sense 1), ***key-basket***, ***-maker***, ***-rack***; ***key-headed*** adj.; (sense 6) ***key-book***, ***-cipher***, ***-list***, ***-map***, ***-sentence***; (sense 7) ***key-centre***, ***-change***, ***-relationship***, ***-signature***, ***-system***; (senses 9 and 10) ***key-beam***, ***-course***, ***-log***, ***-piece***, ***-pile***.

1888–9 *Century Mag.* XXXVII. 841 A mob-cap covering her grey hair, and *key-basket in hand. **1865** R. Hunt *Pop. Rom. West Eng.* (1896) 112 (E.D.D.) They were playing all sorts of pranks on the *key-beams and rafters. **1826** E. Irving *Babylon* I. I. 54 These two *key-books [Daniel and Revelations] and the treasure-books, which they unlock. **1940** *Scrutiny* Sept. 122 Without establishing a *key-centre the fluctuating basses eventually soar..into another homophonic passage. **1931** G. Jacob *Orchestral Technique* iii. 24 The choice..should..rest entirely on simplicity of key—the piece as a whole with all its modulations and sectional *key-changes being taken into consideration. **1959** 'F. Newton' *Jazz Scene* 115 The free and continual key changes. **1973** J. Wainwright *Pride of Pigs* 175 He rippled through a key-change bridge passage, then moved into the beat. **1605** Bacon *Adv. Learn.* II. xvi. §6 The kinds of Ciphers..are many, according to the nature or rule of the infolding; Wheel-ciphers, *Key-ciphers, Doubles, &c. **1703** Moxon *Mech. Exerc.* 282 The middle of the *Key-course will be the middle of the Arch. **1859** C. Forster *Primev. Lang.*, *Mon. Assyria* 13 Clavi-formed or nail-headed, cleidi-formed or *key-headed, cuneiform or wedge-shaped. **1868** *Harper's Mag.* XXXVI. 423 The most vulnerable point, the *key-log of the jam is sought. **1483** *Cath. Angl.* 200/1 A *kay maker, *clauicularius*, *clauicularia*. **1851** in *Illustr. Lond. News* (1854) 5 Aug. 119 Key-maker. **1872** Proctor *Ess. Astron.* xxviii. 346 This chart..with photo-lithographed *keymaps. **1895** *Bookman* Oct. 26/2 Single page plans of small districts on a fair scale with a key-map for reference. **1891** *Pall Mall G.* 7 Nov. 2/1 Fourteen segments and a *keypiece will make up a ring 2½ ft. wide. **1882** Stevenson *New Arab. Nts.* (1884) 297 The landlord..rose from a business table under the *key-rack. **1881** Broadhouse *Mus. Acoustics* 371 So many stumbling-blocks, in the way of understanding *key-relationship. **1859** C. Forster *Primev. Lang.*, *Mon. Assyria* 207 The inscriptions terminated with their *key-sentence. **1875** Stainer & Barrett *Dict. Mus. Terms* (1898) 404/2 The *key signatures, including the clefs, are usually written on every stave. **1934** C. Lambert *Music Ho!* I. 28 His [*sc.* Debussy's] destruction of the *key-system. **1959** D. Cooke *Lang. Mus.* ii. 44 All the modes eventually became major and minor scales..; and so arose our key-system. **1879** Stainer *Music of Bible* 164 The different versions begin and end in the same *key-tonality.

b. Passing into *adj.* in the sense of 'dominant', 'controlling', 'chief', 'essential'; esp. designating some person or thing that is of crucial importance to others. See also *key man* (sense 18 below).

1913 E. C. Bentley *Trent's Last Case* xi. 207 When chance or effort puts one in possession of the key-fact in any system of baffling circumstances, one's ideas seem to rush to group themselves anew in relation to that fact. **1916** *Economic Jrnl.* XXVI. 24 We are asked to learn one essential lesson from the war, and that is, not to be caught short of any 'Key' industry. **1926** D. L. Colvin *Prohibition in U.S.* 509 Occupants of key offices such as the Presidency or the Attorney-Generalship. **1927** W. E. Collinson *Contemp. Eng.* 94 Greek was said to occupy a key-position. **1928** J. Boon *Victorians, Edwardians & Georgians* I. 203 There had been considerable difficulty in getting hold of a key witness. **1931** C. A. Lejeune *Cinema* 4 A study of these key-names, unobscured by any commercial considerations of box-office value. **1934** C. Lambert *Music Ho!* II. 110 It is Stravinsky who is the key-figure of our times. **1941** *Hutchinson's Pict. Hist. War* 19 Mar.–13 May 103 German airmen..were ensconced in key positions. **1945** K. R. Popper *Open Soc.* I. viii. 135 The key-passage of the philosopher king. **1946** *Sun* (Baltimore) 6 Mar. 1/6 The news was spread all over front pages with photographs of the key figures. **1955** *Ann. Reg.* *1954* 256 Investments in the key industries were to be gradually reduced. **1959** *Times Rev. Industry* June (London & Cambridge Econ. Bull.) p. i/1 The key factor in an assessment of the economic position and prospects of the country is Mr. Amory's Budget. **1963** *Times* 12 Feb. 7/4 A small number of key-workers among the affected men stayed away from work. **1964** *English Studies* XLV. 243 One wonders..how many of their key-questions will in fact gain in coherence. **1966** *Illustr. London News* 30 July 27/2 Australia and North America are key areas. **1969** *Times* 16 July 5/8 Key abbreviations used by mission control and the astronauts. **1970** J. Ardagh *New France* xi. 529 It was in 1943 that Sartre brought out his key philosophical work. **1970** *Physics Bull.* Nov. 493/1 Two ideas were key in the discovery of the kinoform. **1971** *Black Scholar* Dec. 55/2, I viewed myself as assisting everything that was done, and you must recognise that this is what's key in the liberation of women.

18. Special combs.: **key-action**, the mechanism by which sounds are produced in musical instruments that have a keyboard; †**key-band** *Mech*, a pin or wedge used in tightening machinery; **key-bed** *Mech.*, the part of a shaft on or in which a key rests (see quot.); **key-bit** = bit *sb.*[1] 7; **key-block**, (*a*) a block, usu. of wood, also of metal or, in lithography, stone, used in the printing of chiaroscuro and colour pictures to give the outline, and to provide a guide for the accurate registration of the tint or colour blocks; (*b*) in limestone and marble quarrying, the first block or blocks to be removed from a new layer of stone; **key-bolt** *Mech.*, a bolt which is secured in its place by a key or cotter (Hamersly *Naval Encycl.* 1881); **key-bone**, (*a*) the collar-bone, clavicle (*nonce-use*); (*b*) a bone forming the key of a structure; **key-chain**, a chain to which a key or keys may be attached; **key-check** (see quot.); **key-chord** *Mus.*, the common chord of the key-note; †**key-clock**, ? a pine cone (cf. clock *sb.*[1] 9); **key-colour**, the leading colour in a picture; **key-desk** *Mus.*, the case enclosing the keys and stops of an organ; **key-dovetailing**, a method of joining two pieces of wood, etc., by means of a key dovetailed into each; **key-drawing**, (*a*) in lithography and colour printing, an outline drawing which is transferred on to the key-plate and used as a guide to printing the colours; (*b*) *Cinematogr.* (see quot. 1940); **key-drop**, an external keyhole-guard, which falls by its own weight; **key-fastener**, any device to prevent a key from being turned in a lock (Knight *Dict. Mech.* 1875); a wedge securing the breech-block of a gun (*Cent. Dict.*); **key-file**, a flat file, of the same thickness throughout, used in filing the wards of keys; **key-frame** = keyboard *sb.* 2; **key-fruit** = key 14; **key-groove** *Mech.* = *key-seat*: hence ***key-grooving machine***; †**key-gun**, = *key-pistol*; **key-hammer**, a hammer for driving in keys or wedges; †**key-herd** *Obs.* = key-keeper; **key-holder**, (*a*) 'an electric-lamp holder or socket containing a switch' (Webster 1909); (*b*) a person who keeps the key or keys of a workshop, factory, etc.; **key-loader**, a workman who balances the wooden keys of a musical instrument by the insertion of lead pellets; †**key-locks**, lock and key; **key-log** *Logging*, a log which is so caught or wedged that a jam is formed and held by it; **key man**, **key-man**, (*a*) *Logging*, a man who finds and dislodges the key-logs in a jam (*U.S. obs.*); (*b*) an operator of telegraph keys (*U.S. obs.*); (*c*) one who plays a leading or important role in a group, an industry, etc.; **key-money**, a payment required from the tenant of a house before he is allowed to have the key; **key move** (see sense 6 c above); **key-movement**, the mechanism of the keys of an organ; **key-pattern**, a fret or meander; **key-pin**, the pin on which a pianoforte or organ key is centred; **key-pipe**, in a lock, the tubular opening in which the shank of the key turns; †**key-pistol**, a small pistol disguised in the form of a key; **key-plate**, (*a*) a key-hole escutcheon; (*b*) in colour-printing from a metal surface, the outline plate answering to a keystone in lithography; **key-point** = sense 5 (also *fig.*); **key-ring** (*a*) a finger-ring having a small key combined with it; (*b*) a ring on which a number of keys are hung; **key-screw** = sense 13; **key-seat** *Mech.*, a key-bed or key-way (see quot. for *key-bed*); hence **key-seated** *a.*; †**key-shot**, shot consisting of a bunch of pieces of metal; **key-stop**, a key fitted to a violin to assist in stopping the strings (*Cent. Dict.*); **key-stringed** *a.*, having strings which are sounded by means of keys; **key-tail**, the part of a piano or organ key which lies behind the key-pin; **key-trumpet**, a trumpet fitted with keys; **key-way** *Mech.*, a groove cut in a shaft, or in the boss of a wheel, to receive a key (see quot. for *key-bed*); **key-winding** *a.*, of a watch, that is wound up with a key; **key-word**, (*a*) a word serving as a key to a cipher or the like; (*b*) a word or thing that is of great importance or significance; *spec.* in information-retrieval systems, any informative word in the title or text of a document, etc., chosen as indicating the main content of the document; so **key-word-in-context**, used *attrib.* of an index or concordance in which key-words are listed alphabetically, preceded and followed by a fixed amount of the immediate context.

1881 Edwards *Organs* vi. (Heading) 67 *Key Action. **1734** *Phil. Trans.* XXXVIII. No. 434 *Engraving*, The Screw or *Key-band to confine all close and tight. **1892** D. A. Low *Machine Draw.* 22 The part of the shaft upon which a key rests is called the *key bed or key way, and the recess in the boss of the wheel or pulley into which the key fits is called the key way; both are also called key seats. **1875** *Ure's Dict. Arts* III. 142 By turning the handle, the *key-bit..is brought into contact with the works of the lock, so as to shoot and withdraw the bolt. *c* **1870** A. Ashley in *Jrnl. Printing Hist. Soc.* (1969) V. 73 *Key blocks. **1910** R. M. Burch *Colour Printing* v. 126 Baxter's process was simply the colouring of an impression from an outline or key block, which could be either a copper, zinc or steel plate, or a litho stone..by successive impressions from colour blocks of wood or metal, one for each tint used. **1934** O. Bowles *Stone Industries* II. ix. 212 In opening up a new floor the first blocks to be removed are known as 'key blocks'. **1937** *Discovery* Mar. 77/1 In order to get the colours fitting accurately, prints are taken from the first or key-block and pasted on to each successive block. **1966** Berry & Poole *Ann. Printing* 241/1 They vary in quality, many being spoiled by the heavy impression from the wood key block. **1967** *Amer. Speech* XLII. 290 Once this first troublesome block, called the *key block*, is out, further quarrying becomes much easier. **1791** Cowper *Iliad* v. 171 One with his huge falchion smote Fast by the *key-bone. **1854** Owen *Skel. & Teeth* in *Circ. Sc.*, *Organ. Nat.* I. 206 It..completes the neural arch, as its crown or key-bone. **1895** *Montgomery Ward Catal.* 86/2 Polished steel *key chains, 18 inches long. **1950** F. P. Walkup *Dressing the Part* (rev. ed.) 368 A ridiculous fad..

was the 'zoot suit'.. adorned with a keychain that swept the ground. **1973** K. GILES *File on Death* ii. 42 He locked the door... He had a housekeeper-like key chain attached to the top button of his fly. **1875** STAINER & BARRETT *Dict. Mus. Terms* (1898) 341 The pieces of wood on each side of the manual, to which the pin-rails are firmly fixed, are called **key-checks*. *Ibid.* 2/4 C, E, G is the *key-chord of C. **1577** B. GOOGE *Heresbach's Husb.* (1586) 95 The Pine.. is planted not muche unlike to the Almond, the Kernels of the *Keie clockes being set as the Almond is. **1899** *Westm. Gaz.* 21 Jan. 4/2 The console or *key-desk is movable. **1847** SMEATON *Builder's Man.* 90 The first method.. is called, amongst workmen, keying together; the second.. *key-dovetailing. **1937** *Discovery* Oct. 300/1 The use of several colours, flat or stippled, combined with a black or dark-coloured *key drawing. **1940** *Chambers's Techn. Dict.* 475/2 *Key drawing* (*Cinema*). In animated cartoon production, *key drawings* indicate situations at special instants, such as at beats in the bar of music, after which the in-between drawings are made to fit with the timing. **1951** D. BLAND *Illustration of Bks.* ix. 133 The artist first makes his key drawing in black, regardless of whether it is intended finally to print in black. From this non-actinic prints are prepared, one for each colour, showing the key drawing in a pale blue colour that will not photograph. **1851** *Cassell's Illustr. Exhibitor* 52 [Foucault's] Printing *key frame by which the blind may write. **1835** URE *Philos. Manuf.* 21 The dexterous hands of the filer and driller are now superseded by the planing, the *key-groove cutting, and the drilling machines. **1663** DAVENANT *Siege Rhodes* Wks. (1673) 65, I hope he wears no charms About him, *Key Guns or Pistols charg'd with White Powder. **1884** *Mil. Engineering* I. II. 59 The tools required are.. 1 rammer, 1 *key-hammer, 2 beaters. *c*725 *Corpus Gloss.* 490 *Clavicularius*, *cæȝhiorde. *c* **1200** *Trin. Coll. Hom.* 193 Ðe heuenliche keiherde sainte peter. **1928** *Daily Tel.* 11 May 5/6 Workmen were waiting outside ready to begin work for the day... The *key-holder had not arrived. **1970** P. LAURIE *Scotland Yard* iii. 66 The Inspector calls the nick to check the keyholder's register and see who can let us in. *Ibid.*, The keyholder is the caretaker of the flats. **1886** *Standard* 10 May 2/6 He had worked.. as a *key-loader. **1018** *Laws of Cnut* II. c. 76 §1 Buton hit under þæs wifes *cæȝ-locan ȝebroht wære, sy heo clæne. *a* **1687** COTTON *Poet. Wks.* (1765) 7 And here, in House, with her own Key-locks, She us'd to keep her Coach and Peacocks. **1851** J. S. SPRINGER *Forest Life & Forest Trees* 166 It may be thought best to cut off the *key-log, or that which appears to be the principal barrier. **1902** S. E. WHITE *Blazed Trail* xxxii. 211 By pulling out or chopping through certain 'key' logs which locked the whole mass. *a* **1951** B. CRONIN in *Austral. Short Stories* (1951) 173 Half-way up the kiln a key-log had swung loose. **1851** in C. M. Wilson *Aroostook* (1937) 104 The *key man then commences prying while they are pulling. **1907** *Washington Star* 30 Sept. 9 Some of the leading keymen are sounding as their shibboleth the cry of 'government ownership of the telegraph systems'. **1921** *Daily Colonist* (Victoria, B.C.) 15 Oct. 1/1 Following the conference of 'Key' men of the G.W.V.A. last July, arrangements were advanced to have in attendance at the convention the foremost leaders of the navies and armies of the allied nations in the Great War. **1949** I. DEUTSCHER *Stalin* 143 The 'handful' of Bolsheviks consisted of well-organized and disciplined 'key-men'. **1963** *Times* 18 Feb. 8/3 One of the key men in this new method of assessing needs and opportunities is the local prefect. **1898** *Daily News* 19 Dec. 6/7 The rent was higher than was stated on the rent book and the *key money exorbitant. **1906** *Westm. Gaz.* 28 Mar. 5/2 Some house-agents would still extort 'key-money' from tenants. **1963** *Times* 21 Feb. 5/2 A former property manager was alleged at Southend-on-Sea Magistrates' Court today to have exploited the housing shortage to extort key money. **1969** R. RENDELL *Best Man to Die* iii. 26 They'd had to find the key money for the flat themselves. **1881** EDWARDS *Organs* vi. (Heading) 67 The Claviers and *Key Movement. **1876** HUMPHREYS *Coin-Collector's Man.* iv, The figure known in Greek ornament as the '*key pattern'. **1887** J. R. ALLEN *Early Chr. Symbol.* 111 The cross.. is enclosed in a rectangular frame of key-pattern. **1655** MRQ. WORCESTER *Cent. Inv.* Index p. iv, A *Key-pistol [art. 44.. a Key of a Chamber door, which.. shall become a perfect pistol]. **1903** T. A. STRANGE *Hist. Guide French Interiors* 326 The *key plate is formed as a vase-shaped burning lamp. **1909** R. E. LE BLOND *Let.* in H. G. Clarke *Baxter Colour Prints* (1919) 103 These prints were first engraved on a steel plate, a key-plate, or, as I should call, a master-plate. **1969** J. GLOAG *Short Dict. Furnit.* (rev. ed.) 317 (*caption*) The simplest type of escutcheon, pivoted to cover the key-platė. **1970** *Jrnl. Printing Hist. Soc.* VI. 73 A key plate of the design was printed in black or brown, usually from an.. engraved steel or copper plate. **1870** LOWELL *Study Wind.* 256 They have not learned the art of concentrating their force on the *key-point of their hearers' interest. **1889** *Cent. Dict.* III. 3280/2 **Key-ring*. 1. A finger-ring from which projects a tongue or blade which is either fixed or movable on a hinge, and serves as the key to a lock. Such key-rings were formerly common, and were often of rich design. 2. A ring used for keeping a number of keys together by being passed through their bows. **1906** E. NESBIT *Story of Amulet* xi. 261 Jane added a key-ring. **1967** *Economist* 11 Feb. 512 An advertising firm.. has now been hired to show that gaullism washes whiter. It has begun to do so in American fashion with badges, key-rings, drum-majorettes and all. **1874** RAYMOND *Statist. Mines & Mining* 509 Upon the upper end of the sleeve.. a *key-seat of from four to six feet in length is cut..; over this sleeve a pinion.. also key-seated, is slipped. **1652** *Sea-Fight betw. Eng. & Dutch* (30 Nov.) 4 So close and thick did they ply the enemy with *Key-shot, long Chains, and Bolts of Iron. **1875** STAINER & BARRETT *Dict. Mus. Terms* (1898) 253 The striking apparatus of a *key-stringed instrument. **1870** *Eng. Mech.* 18 Mar. 652/3 The driving shaft is cut with a feather groove or *key way. **1893** *Pall Mall G.* 2 Jan. 5/2 He drilled three keyways out of solid steel in the collars and fitted steel bolts into them. **1884** F. J. BRITTEN *Watch & Clockm.* 240 The square in *key-winding watches by means of which the hands are set to time. **1859** C. FORSTER *Primev. Lang.*, *Mon. Assyria* 40 The *key-word of these inscriptions. **1885** MERRIAM *Sam. Bowles* II. xxxiv. 66 The key-word of life is 'Thy will be done'. **1922** J. C. H. MACBETH tr. *Langie's Cryptogr.* iv. 166 Suppose the key-word to be 'bankruptcy'. **1926** *Encycl. Brit.* II. 822/1 As to shop detail, the keyword to mass production is simplicity. **1948** BLUNDEN *Shakespeare to Hardy* (1964) 211 The key-word is the 116th of the Sonnets. **1956** E. W. F. TOMLIN in A. Pryce-Jones *New Outl. Mod. Knowl.* 91 Let us take the keyword 'science'. **1967** COX & GROSE *Organiz. Bibliogr. Rec. by Computer* IV. 82 The system can process documents represented by a set of keywords. **1971** *New Scientist* 1 Apr. 32/2 'Keywords'.. are supposed to describe the content of the document as concisely and exactly as possible. **1959** *Key-word-in-context [see *KWIC* (*K 4f)]. **1969** *Computers & Humanities* IV. 23 Current book catalogs of John Wiley and Sons.. among many others, already contain all the elements of data proposed for the data bank except a key-word-in-context index. **1971** *Ibid.* VI. 32 Indices and concordances.. can be unlemmatized, like the key-word in context concordance to Livy. **1975** *Studies in Eng. Lit.: Eng. Number* (Tokyo) 121 The concordance employs the KWIC (key-word-in-context) principle: Each index word appears, separated by appropriate spacing, in the middle of a line, with its context extending to the left and right.

key (kiː), *sb.*[2] Now written QUAY. Forms: 4-5 **keye**, 4-9 **key**; also 5-8 **kay**, (5-6 **kaie**, 6 **kaye**, **keay**, 8 **kea**). [a. OF. *kay*, *kai*, *cay* (1311 in Godef. *Compl.*), whence also Du. *kaai* (earlier *kad*, *kae*, *kaeye*), Ger. and Da. *kai*, Sw. *kaj*. Cognate with the OF. word is Sp. *cayo* shoal, reef (see next): for the ultimate etymology see CAY. In Eng., 14-18th c., usually written *key* (less freq. *kay*), which latterly underwent the same change of pron. as KEY *sb.*[1] In early 18th c., the spelling *quay* was introduced, after later F. *quai*, but did not finally supersede *kay*, *key* till nearly a century later; in spite of this change of spelling the pronunciation remains that of *key* (kiː).]

A wharf, a quay.

[**1306** *Rolls Parlt.* I. 200/2 Per exaltationem Caye & diversionem aquæ.] *a* **1400** *Sir Beues* (MS.S) 141/3056 Sir Saber.. went him forth also bliue Tille þe keye þere þe schip scholde ryue. **1467** *Ord. Worcester* in *Eng. Gilds* 374 That the slippe and the keye, and the pavyment ther, be ouerseyn and repared. **1495** *Naval Acc. Hen. VII* (1896) 265 Ankers Receyved at the Kay in Hampton. *a* **1548** HALL *Chron.*, *Hen. VIII*, 209 The water rose three foote above the wharfe, where the Key stode in Andwarpe. **1593** NORDEN *Spec. Brit.*, *M'sex* I. 34 Billingsgate is a harbor or kaye for shipping. **1621** QUARLES *Div. Poems*, *Esther* (1717) 8 The Keel begins t' obey Her gentle Rudder, leaves her quiet Key. **1628** WITHER *Brit. Rememb.* I. 75 At her Ports and Keyes, Take in the wealth of Kingdomes and of Seas. **1718** *Freethinker* No. 16 ¶4 A young Fellow.. fell from a Key into the River, and was drowned. **1721** PERRY *Daggenh. Breach.* 24 To lade and unlade their Goods.. at the Keas of the City. **1759** MARTIN *Nat. Hist. Eng.* II. *Suffolk* 48 It is clean, and has a good Kay on the River Ald. **1773** BRYDONE *Sicily* ii. (1809) 25 The key [at Messina] exceeds anything I have yet seen, even in Holland. **1779-81** JOHNSON *Lives*, *Drake* Wks. 1787 IV. 413 The people.. ran in crowds to the key with shouts and congratulations. **1809** R. LANGFORD *Introd. Trade* 132 *Key*, *kay*, or *quay*, a wharf for loading or unloading vessels.

fig. **1666** DRYDEN *Ann. Mirab.* ccxxxi, A Key of fire ran all along the shore, And lightened all the river with a blaze.

†**b.** *transf.* A harbour, haven. *nonce-use.*

1621 QUARLES *Argalus & P.* (1678) 41 That thou maist safely slide Into the bosome of thy quiet Key, And quit thee fairly of th'injurious Sea.

c. *attrib.* and *Comb.*, as ***key-duty***, ***-gate***, ***-master***, ***-side***, ***-wall***; **key-wood**, wood landed at a quay (see quot. 1467).

1425 *MS. Found. Chart. Thornton's Hosp.*, *Newcastle*, A via regia voc. le keyside. **1467** *E.E. Gilds* 383 That better guernaunce and rule be hadd, and better ouersight, vppon keywood, crates, and colez. **1477** *Waterf. Arch.* in *10th Rep. Hist. MSS. Comm.* App. v. 313 To stoppe the saide key yate with lyme and stone. **1638** *Plan walls Newcastle* in *Archæol. Æliana* XII. Pl. xiii. 230 The Newe Key Wall. **1764** *Newcastle Chron.* No. 1. 2/2 Capt. Giles, Key-master here. **1778** *Eng. Gazetteer* (ed. 2) s.v. *Watchet*, The late Sir William Wyndham built the pier of the harbour, and had the key-duties.

key (kiː), *sb.*[3] Also 8-9 **kay**. [var. of CAY, ad. Sp. *cayo* shoal, reef. The spelling and pron. are due to the influence of prec.] A low island, sand-bank, or reef, such as those common in the West Indies or off the coast of Florida. Cf. the place-name *Key West.*

1697 DAMPIER *Voy.* I. 22 These Islands or Keys, as we call them, were first made the Rendezvous of Privateers in the year 1679. *Ibid.* 249 A mile and half from the shore there is a small Key, and within it is a very good Harbour. **1726** G. ROBERTS 4 *Yrs. Voy.* 345 The Rock is.. flat on the Top like a Key, which the Inhabitants call Kaay. **1761** *Descr. S. Carolina* 63 There a pretty many Indians among the Kays, about the Cape of Florida. **1828** W. IRVING *Columbus* (1831) 167 He soon got entangled in a complete labyrinth of small islands and keys. **1885** C. F. HOLDER *Marvels Anim. Life* 22 The group, comprising seven or eight Keys, made up of coral, is surrounded by a long reef.

b. Special Comb. **key deer**, a subspecies of the North American white-tailed deer, *Odocoileus virginianus clavium*, found in the Florida keys.

1955 *Sci. News Let.* 29 Oct. 277/2 The Key deer is the smallest of all North American deer, only about 26 to 29 inches tall, 38 inches from nose to tail, and averaging only about 30 pounds. **1964** L. S. CRANDALL *Managem. Wild Mammals in Captivity* 590 Size seems to decrease from north to south, ranging.. down to tiny creatures such as the Florida key deer.

†**key**, *sb.*[4] Obs. pl. of COW, q.v. Hence †**keywhit** (= -quit), money paid in lieu of the tithe of milk.

1507 *Pilton Church-w. Acc.* (Som. Rec. Soc.) 54 Item Receved of Willyam Townysende and Iohn Dore for Key Whyt.. ixs vd.

key (kiː), *v.* [ME. *keiȝe(n*, *keie(n*, etc. f. *keiȝe*, KEY *sb.*[1] An OE. *cǽȝian* is alleged by Somner.]

1. *trans.* To lock with a key; to lock up; to fasten securely. Also *fig. rare.*

1362 LANGL. *P. Pl.* A VI. 103 Þe dore I-closet, I-keiȝet and I-kliketed, to kepe þe þer-oute. *c* **1425** *Disp. Mary & Cross* 241 in *Leg. Rood* (1871) 205 Heuene gate was keiyed [*printed* keiþed] clos. **1433** LYDG. *St. Edmund* I. 1072 Cloos in his herte ech uertu was I-keied [*v.r.* ykeyed]. **1555** ABP. PARKER *Ps.* cxix. 352 Keyd fast thy word: was so to me: in hope that I have done. **1780** *Newgate Cal.* V. 201 Mrs. Penleaze swore that the windows were constantly barred and keyed every night. **1791** COWPER *Odyss.* XXI. 286 Be the palace-door Thy charge,.. key it fast.

2. a. To fasten by means of a pin, wedge, bolt, or wooden cross-piece.

1577 HARRISON *England* II. xi. (1877) I. 227 An ax, keied or fastened with iron into the wood. **1654** WHITELOCKE *Jrnl. Swed. Emb.* (1772) I. 196 The bodyes of great trees squared, and.. keyed togither by other great pieces of timber. **1793** SMEATON *Edystone L.* §302 To key home the plates of the cupola to the ribs. **1839** R. S. ROBINSON *Naut. Steam Eng.* 57 It is keyed or wedged in, and rusted in so as to be immoveable. **1881** YOUNG *Every Man his own Mechanic* §550 Immovably keyed upon the cranked shaft is a heavy wooden cone pulley.

b. To cause (plaster) to adhere (to laths).

1881 YOUNG *Every Man his own Mechanic* §1383 When the mortar is put over the laths, part of it penetrates between them, and when hard keys, as it were, the plaster to the laths and renders it difficult of removal.

c. To cause (glued surfaces, pigments, etc.) to adhere.

1922 *Encycl. Brit.* XXX. 34/2 Roughing of the surfaces to be glued was adopted to secure keying. **1963** R. R. A. HIGHAM *Handbk. Papermaking* ix. 226 Adhesives are used in coating to 'key' the pigment to the surface of the paper.

3. a. To regulate the pitch of the strings of a musical instrument. Hence *fig.*: To give a certain tone or intensity (to feelings, thoughts); ***to key up***, to stimulate, to raise to a high pitch; also, to render (someone) nervous or tense, freq. as ***keyed-up*** ppl. adj.; so ***to key down***: to lower in pitch or intensity.

1636 HEYWOOD *Challenge Beautie* Prol., And Poets strive to key their strings more loud. **1655** H. VAUGHAN *Silex Scint.* I. *Affliction* 36 Thus doth God key disorder'd man.. Tuning his brest to rise or fall. **1866** ALGER *Solit. Nat. & Man* IV. 257 The fervid quickness and strength of Rousseau's feelings keyed him on so high a pitch that [etc.]. **1888** HURLBERT *Irel. under Coerc.* I. I. 46 If Mr. Balfour keys up the landlords to stand out. **1889** *Cent. Dict.* s.v., *Keyed up*, high-strung; excited. **1904** ADE *True Bills* 35 He was all keyed up for Matrimony, and the next thing to do was to choose the Lucky Bride. **1922** R. S. WOODWORTH *Psychol.* vii. 126 It is the state of *excitement*, or of being 'all keyed up'. **1923** D. H. LAWRENCE *Phoenix II* (1968) 251 Everything that everybody feels is keyed down, and muted, so as not to impinge on anybody else's feelings. **1926** H. CRANE *Let.* 5 Jan. (1965) 231 One really has to keep one's self in such a keyed-up mood for the thing. **1927** *Daily Tel.* 16 Aug. 12/5 He has keyed down his playing to such a pitch that we get no impression at all of his character as a man. **1961** C. MCCULLERS *Clock without Hands* ix. 187 Although he was emotionally keyed up, Sherman yawned.

b. To fix the strings of a musical instrument upon the pegs or keys.

1872 W. SKEEN *Early Typogr.* 90 They were as useless to him as unstrung harp-strings are unmusical until they are keyed and stretched and tuned.

4. To insert the keystone in (an arch). Also with *in.*

1735 J. PRICE *Stone-Bridge Thames* 8 After the Arches are thus turn'd and key'd. **1751** LABELYE *Westm. Br.* 75 The last Arch was key'd in. **1770** *Chron.* in *Ann. Reg.* 97/2 The new bridge.. fell down after it was key'd in.

5. To distinguish (an advertisement) by some device which will identify responses to it. orig. *U.S.*

1905 CALKINS & HOLDEN *Art of Mod. Advertising* xi. 264 The advertiser likes to know which particular mediums pull best. To accomplish this the advertising is 'keyed'. Some form of address is used which can be varied in each magazine. **1927** *Daily News* 7 June 5/5 Advertisers who key their advertisements report their best results from the 'Daily News'. **1943** C. S. FORESTER *Ship* 56 How often had he devised ingenious methods by which to 'key' advertisements to discover which had the greatest pulling power. **1952** *Economist* 20 Sept. 718/1 This 'coupon sales' technique in a limited area.. has the virtue in terms of publicity of being elaborately 'keyed'; the sales technicians can follow the success of their advertising and promotion schemes round by round. **1967** *Times Rev. Industry* Oct. 82/2 One keys advertisements and measures returns.

6. *Electronics.* **a.** To switch on or off, or from one state to another, by means of a key or relay, as in telegraphic transmission. **b.** To provide (electronic equipment) with means by which it may be switched abruptly from one state to another. Cf. KEYING *vbl. sb.* 1.

1929 K. HENNEY *Princ. Radio* xvii. 443 (*heading*) Keying a transmitter. **1930** *Proc. IRE* XVIII. 1691 The transmitters are started or stopped and keyed locally or from Burnham. **1933** K. HENNEY *Radio Engin. Handbk.* XVIII. 460 Keying the output is accomplished by means of a magnetic modulator. **1943** F. E. TERMAN *Radio Engineers'*

Handbk. IX. 629 Unless the oscillator is keyed, the low-power portions of the transmitter operate continuously. **1954** E. MOLLOY *Radio & Television Engineers' Ref. Bk.* IX. 16 Means must be found..to minimize any 'thumps' in the receiver when the transmitter is keyed. **1961** GRAY & GRAHAM *Radio Transmitters* vi. 137 Where 'break-in' is needed it may be necessary to key the transmitter oscillator to avoid generating an interfering signal..in the receiver. **1966** M. SCHWARTZ et al. *Communication Syst. & Techniques* vii. 280 The carrier is 'keyed' on and off to describe the two telegraph states.

7. To cause (something) to fit *in* with something else or *into* a group, pattern, etc. Also *intr.*

1947 *Sun* (Baltimore) 13 Nov. 18/2 (*heading*) Mr. Reuther's victory keys into a world-wide pattern. *Ibid.*, The Socialist Premier..went so far as to speak of an invisible 'orchestra leader' keying these strikes into a symphonic program whose purpose seemed clear. **1949** *Ibid.* 14 Feb. 8/4 (*heading*) Keying labor law into the facts of life. **1958** *Times Lit. Suppl.* 14 Mar. 133/3 It [*sc.* the Book of Mormon] is much longer than the New Testament. Moreover, it is elaborately 'keyed-in' to the Bible. **1960** E. BOWEN *Time in Rome* i. 14 Lean young skyscrapers..key in with Rome's general virtuosity. **1969** *Guardian* 21 July 1/4 A carefully planned schedule which keys into the two-hourly orbit of their mother craft.

8. *trans.* To operate on (esp. to transfer (data) or to set (copy)), or to produce, by manipulating the keys of a keyboard. Also with various advbs.

1963 GREGORY & VAN HORN *Automatic Data-Processing Syst.* (ed. 2) v. 145 The user makes an inquiry by keying in an address in high-speed or bulk storage. **1964** C. DENT *Quantity Surveying by Computer* vii. 100 Checking can be done using a comparator machine or by reading over the print-out against the dimensions; this last method has the advantage of requiring the data to be keyed only once, instead of twice. **1967** COX & GROSE *Organiz. Bibliogr. Rec. by Computer* IV. 101 Messages requesting search information are printed out directly on the console typewriter. The search criteria are then keyed back through the console and the keyword file is searched. **1972** *Physics Bull.* Sept. 531/3 Instead of manually selecting individual type slugs from a case..the compositor keys in the copy at a specially laid out keyboard.

key, var. KAY *a.*, left (hand or foot).

keyage ('kiːɪdʒ). Now written QUAYAGE. Also 6 kei-, 7 kay-, caiage. [a. OF. *kaiage*, *caiage*, etc. (1295 in Godef.; med.L. *caiagium* is found in 1167); see KEY *sb.*² and -AGE.] Quay-dues; quayage.

[**1324** in Gross *Gild M.* I. 195 note 4 De hujusmodi theolonio..anchoragio, terragio, kayagio.] *c* **1440** *Promp. Parv.* 269/2 Keyage, or botys stondynge, *ripatum.* **1511** *Waterf. Arch.* in *10th Rep. Hist. MSS. Comm.* App. v. 325 Noo man..shall reise keiage of noo kaye nor othre place..except it be buylded as a keay. **1610** FOLKINGHAM *Art of Survey* IV. i. 80 Profits of Faires, Markets,..Pontage, Caiage, Cranage. **1681** W. ROBERTSON *Phraseol. Gen.* (1693) 784 Keyage or kayage, *portorium.* **1778** *Eng. Gazetteer* (ed. 2) s.v. *Fowey*, The toll of the market and fairs, and keyage of the harbour.

‖**keyaki** (ke'aki). Also **kiaki.** [Jap.] An important Japanese timber tree, *Zelkova serrata*, or its pale, elm-like wood.

1904 [see HINOKI]. **1907** *Yesterday's Shopping* (1969) 203/1 Japanese Trays..Kiaki..Inlaid Wood..Polished. **1948** A. L. HOWARD *Man. Timbers of World* (ed. 3) 653 While there is some resemblance to the keyaki of Japan (*Z[elkova] serrata*), there is an entire absence of that beautiful sheen or lustre which the Japanese wood possesses in a high degree. **1965** J. OHWI *Flora Japan* 381/1 *Zelkova serrata*... Keyaki. Tall trees with gray-brown smooth bark.

'key-ˌbearer. [f. KEY *sb.*¹ + BEARER: OE. had *cǽᵹbora* in same sense.]

1. One who bears a key or keys. (Cf. KEY *sb.*¹ 2.)

14.. *Nominale* in Wr.-Wülcker 684/9 *Hic claviger*, a kayberere. **1486** *Lichfield Gild Ord.* (E.E.T.S.) 22 The foure kayberers or ther deputies. **1552** HULOET, Kaye bearer or keper. **1778** BP. LOWTH *Transl. Isaiah* Notes (ed. 12) 254 The priestess of Juno is said to be the key-bearer of the Goddess. **1846** ELLIS *Elgin Marb.* I. 120 The figure of a key-bearer.

2. *fig.* One who is entrusted with authority symbolized by keys. Cf. KEY *sb.*¹ 4 and KEY-KEEPER 2.

a **1540** BARNES *Wks.* (1573) 262/2 S. Petter..commaundeth you that you shoulde bee alonely but ministers, & key-bearers of these keyes. **1669** BAXTER *Power Mag. & Ch. Past.* II. xi. (1671) 29 Christ made these Officers the Key-bearers of his Churches. **1895** *Tablet* 2 Nov. 700 The Prince of the Apostles, the key-bearer of eternal life.

So **'key-bearing** *sb.* and *a.*

1669 BAXTER *Power Mag. & Ch. Past.* II. xii. (1671) 29 This Key-bearing power (never denyed them from Christs time). **1863** W. CORY *Lett. & Jrnls.* (1897) 93, I should have lost the respect of the key-bearing woman [= guide].

keyboard ('kiːbɔəd), *sb.* [KEY *sb.*¹ 11.]

1. a. The set or row of keys in such musical instruments as the organ and piano.

1819 *Pantologia* s.v. *Organ*, Worked by..a treadle, which comes out in the front of the instrument, under the key board. **1856** MRS. C. CLARKE tr. *Berlioz' Instrument.* 126 A large organ generally possesses five key-boards one above the other. **1896** HIPKINS *Pianoforte* 5 The keyboard with its ivory and ebony notes [is seen] when the front of the instrument is opened.

fig. **1884** tr. *Lotze's Metaph.* 491 In this case the soul would stand..before the open key-board of the central nerve-terminations. **1892** STEVENSON *Across the Plains* 79 Uproar that runs..up and down the long key-board of the beach.

attrib. **1896** HIPKINS *Pianoforte* 46 The various keyboard instruments. *Ibid.* 65 A keyboard psaltery of a harp-shaped disposition.

b. *pl.* Musical instruments that have keyboards. *colloq.*

1971 *Ink* 12 June 19/2 Toni Brown wrote most of the songs..and plays keyboards. **1971** *Melody Maker* 13 Nov. 40/6 Rod's been playing keyboards since he was six. **1974** *Ibid.* 30 Nov. 46 The other four are the originals: Darryl Way on violin, Francis Monkman on keyboards and guitar, [etc.].

2. The set of keys in a type-writing machine. Also, a similar set in other kinds of machine.

1846 H. HIGHTON *Brit. Pat. 11,070* 3 Feb., Each terminus of telegraphic communication..is provided with..one of the key boards in use in single magnetic needle electric telegraphs. **1851** *Illustr. Catal. Gt. Exhib.* 1187 A printing keyboard, by which the blind are enabled to write. **1859** *Abridgments of Specifications relating to Printing* (Patent Office) 594 By depressing any one of the several keys on a key-board a lever is acted on,..thus giving motion to certain guide pulleys and cords which work the pistons by which the type is thrust out on to the guide plate. **1881** *Spon's Dict. Indust. Arts* 1608 The 'Remington' machine has in front a key-board holding the letters and numerals. **1892** A. POWELL *Southward's Pract. Printing* (ed. 4) xxxii. 310 *Hattersley's Composing Machine.* The type..is contained in the upper part of an iron framework about 3 feet square and 5 feet high. In the lower part of this framework is the key board. **1893** *Times* 25 Sept. 2/6 A machine..possessing remarkable capabilities for printing and adding up figures has recently reached this country from the United States... The keyboard has a number of buttons or keys, each representing a figure, and these are actuated for pounds, shillings, and pence just in the same way as a typewriter. **1911** *Encycl. Brit.* XXVII. 545/1 Composing machines in which the compositor put together types in the required order..by operating a keyboard which liberated them from magazines and assembled them in the order in which the keys had been struck. **1958** GOTLIEB & HUME *High-Speed Data Processing* iii. 57 A keyboard transcriber for preparing magnetic tapes offers the advantage of eliminating records intermediate to the source document and the tape. **1970** O. DOPPING *Computers & Data Processing* xix. 321 The programmer sits at an electric typewriter connected to the computer, and keys in his program with the keyboard.

keyboard ('kiːbɔəd), *v.* [f. the sb.] *trans.* = KEY *v.* 8. Also *absol.* or *intr.*

1961 H. W. LARKEN *Compositor's Work in Printing* xii. 166 Concentration on the task of keyboarding the copy to the exclusion of any concern over the performance of the operations of matrix assembly, casting and distribution, gives a remarkably clean proof with a high setting speed. **1965** *Rep. Proc. Computer Typesetting Conf. London Univ. 1964* v. 153 She is now keyboarding at a rate of 120 to 150 words a minute. **1967** COX & GROSE *Organiz. Bibliogr. Rec. by Computer* II. 43 Let me now digress..to illustrate some keyboards and photocomposing machines, for the more conventional way of generating character codes is to keyboard them. **1967** KARCH & BUBER *Offset Processes* ii. 40 The RCA-301 computer accepts punched paper tape and produces a new tape, adding justification (otherwise keyboarded by the Teletypesetter operator). **1969** *Sci. Amer.* May 68 After the encyclopedia..has been keyboarded into the computer. **1973** *Ann. N.Y. Acad. Sci.* CCXI. 284 It is now possible..to keyboard matter on an ordinary IBM Selectric typewriter..and feed it into an OCR machine where the characters are read automatically ..and then transcribed onto magnetic tape.

Hence **'keyboarded** *ppl. a.*; **'keyboarding** *vbl. sb.*, the action or process of keyboarding something; manipulation of the keys of a keyboard.

1926 *Sans Tache* in E. Mayer *Clin. Applications of Sunlight* 470 There are two processes, the 'keyboarding' of the MS and the casting of the type. **1965** *Rep. Proc. Computer Typesetting Conf. London Univ. 1964* iv. 143 Due to the rather inferior setting in the first hand keyboarded material counted, we probably opened up the computer parameters a little too widely. **1965** *Practical Printing & Binding* (ed. 3) iii. 41/1 An attachment to speed up the keyboarding of lines which require to be letter-spaced. **1967** V. STRAUSS *Printing Industry* ii. 96/2 The product of keyboarding is a punched tape which is used to assemble lines of justified type images on composing machines equipped for tape operation. **1970** *Brit. Printer* Mar. 67/3 No operator with less than five years' keyboarding experience scored higher than 87 per cent in the test.

'key-ˌbugle. A bugle fitted with keys to increase the number of its sounds.

(Invented by James Halliday about 1815, and by him named the Kent Bugle.)

1836-9 DICKENS *Sk. Boz* (1850) 249/1 The loud notes of a key-bugle broke the monotonous stillness of the street. **1884** J. COLBORNE *Hicks Pasha* viii. 86 Each battalion marched out to the inharmonious braying of their key-bugles.

'key-clog. A piece of wood tied to a key, to prevent it from being easily lost.

1552 HULOET, Kaieclogge. [No Latin.] **1555** R. SMITH in Foxe *A. & M.* (1684) III. 343, I have sent you a key-clog for a token. **1632** I. L. *Wom. Rights* 19 She is able..to have the key clog at her girdle. **1805** G. ELLIS *E.E. Metr. Rom.* II. 381 The active princess..seized the *key-clog* which hung from his shoulder.

'key-cold, *a.* Now *rare.* [Cf. KEY *sb.*¹ 1 b.] As cold as a key; devoid of heat; *esp.* cold in death.

1529 MORE *Dyaloge* II. Wks. 185/2 That body bereth them yet about sicke and noughty and cay colde as thei be. **1593** *Tell-Troth's N.Y. Gift* 4 Joyning burning sommer with kea-cold winter. **1594** SHAKS. *Rich. III*, I. ii. 5 Poore key-cold Figure of a holy King. **1667** DRYDEN *Sir Martin Mar-all* III. ii, *Mill.* Feel whether she breathes, with your hand before her mouth. *Rose.* No, madam, 'tis key-cold. **1894** HALL CAINE *Manxman* VI. xiii. 405 The word was scarce out of his mouth when he was key-cold.

b. *fig.* Entirely devoid of warmth of feeling; having no zeal or fervour; apathetic.

1534 MORE *Comf. agst. Trib.* III. xxvii. (1847) 313 The consideration of his incomparable kindness could not..fail to inflame our key-cold hearts. **1565** STAPLETON *Fortr. Faith* 123 *Kaye colde christians. *a* **1659** BP. BROWNRIG *Serm.* (1674) I. xxxi. 393 Men are many times..luke-warm, yea, key-cold in the execution of justice. *a* **1734** WODROW *Sel. Biog.* (1845-7) I. 397 (E.D.D.) The nobility..are either key-cold, or ready to welcome Popery.

†**B.** As *sb.* (jocularly): A severe cold. *Obs.*

1602 DEKKER *Satirom.* Wks. 1873 I. 206 Sir Adam is best you hide your head for feare Your wise braines take key-colde.

Hence †**key-coldness**, utter coldness.

1641 R. BAILLIE *Unlawf. Lim. Episc.* 5 The greatest part of your professed vertue, we find to consist in a key-coldnes.

keyed (kiːd), *a.* [f. KEY *sb.*¹ or *v.* + -ED.]

1. Of a musical instrument: Furnished with keys. ***keyed bugle*** = KEY-BUGLE.

1796 BURNEY *Mem. Metastasio* II. 320 *note*, Pieces for keyed-instruments. **1806** CALLCOTT *Mus. Gram.* II. i. 99 Both which are, upon Keyed Instruments, performed with the same Keys. **1849** LONGF. *Kavanagh* xxix, Silas, who breathed his soul out upon the air of summer evenings through a keyed bugle.

2. In carpentry, engineering, etc.: Secured, fastened, or strengthened by means of a key.

1823 P. NICHOLSON *Pract. Build.* 587 *Keyed-dado*, dado secured from warping by bars grooved into the back. **1874** THEARLE *Naval Archit.* 79 A keyed and riveted scarph, joining two arms.

3. Of an arch: Constructed with a keystone.

1841 W. SPALDING *Italy & It. Isl.* I. iv. 155 In the time of Pericles..we discover in at least one of the great temples of Greece the keyed arch. *Ibid.* v. 183 The keyed arch was introduced for strength.

4. ***keyed-up***: see KEY *v.* 3 a.

5. *Electronics.* **a.** Of electronic equipment or devices: provided with a means by which it may be rapidly switched on or off, or 'keyed' (see KEY *v.* 6). **b.** Of a signal: intermittent, abruptly stopped and started, as in telegraphic transmissions.

1942 *Proc. IRE* XXX. 15/1 Among the novel features of the design [of the television camera] are..keyed diodes for black-level setting. **1943** *Gloss. Terms Telecomm.* (*B.S.I.*) 65 *Type A1 waves* (*keyed continuous waves*), continuous waves which are keyed according to a telegraphic code. **1943** F. E. TERMAN *Radio Engineers' Handbk.* IX. 630 Keying causes the load placed on a power-supply system by the keyed stages to change abruptly. **1961** GRAY & GRAHAM *Radio Transmitters* vi. 138 Frequency variation of a keyed oscillator..can be reduced by making the oscillator frequency independent of supply voltages.

keyer ('kiːə(r)). *Electronics.* [f. KEY *v.* + -ER¹.] A device for switching the signal supply to electronic equipment on and off.

1933 K. HENNEY *Radio Engin. Handbk.* XVIII. 466 (*heading*) Tube keyer for transmitter. **1965** L. E. FOSTER *Telemetry Syst.* iv. 195 The signals are passed through a keyer which converts them from varying-amplitude to constant-amplitude signals of varying pulse width, or pulse duration. **1967** *Electronics* 6 Mar. 346/2 (Advt.), Electronic musical instrument engineer. Should have knowledge of transistor and diode keyer, wave shapers, [etc.].

keyhole ('kiːhəʊl), *sb.*

1. a. The hole by which the key is inserted into a lock.

In an ordinary house- or room-door the keyhole usually goes right through, and thus affords opportunities of peeping, listening, etc. which are often alluded to: see the quots.

c **1592** MARLOWE *Jew of Malta* II. Wks. (Rtldg.) 138/2 Yet through the key-hole will he talk to her. **1592** NASHE *P. Penilesse* (1843) 57 If I would raunge abroad, and looke in at Sluggards' key-holes. **1635** ? HERRICK *Fairy Queen* ii. in *Hesper.* (1869) App. 478 When mortals are at rest.. Through key-holes we do glide. *a* **1715** BURNET *Own Time* (1766) II. 212 He looked through the key-hole and there saw him lying dead. **1833** N. ARNOTT *Physics* (ed. 5) II. 222 A candle carried past a key-hole, throws its light on the opposite wall. **1887** RUSKIN *Præterita* II. ii. 52 An ominously Æolian keyhole in a vile inn.

b. (See quots.) *slang.*

1896 FARMER & HENLEY *Slang* IV. 95/1 *Keyhole*, the female *pudendum*. **1927** *Jrnl. Abnormal & Social Psychol.* XXII. 14 Another term for the female organs is *cabbage*... Other symbols are *keyhole* and *bread*. The former is found infrequently.

c. *Astronautics.* A comparatively narrow area through which a spacecraft must pass to reach its objective. *colloq.*

1962 *Times* 21 Feb. 10/1 He swept towards the so-called 'keyhole in the sky', through which he had to pass if orbit was to be achieved. **1968** *Daily Tel.* 27 Dec. 1/2 It must hit a corridor only 35 miles wide. If it dips below this tiny 'keyhole in space', Apollo 8 and its crew will be burned up.

2. A hole made to receive a peg or key used in carpentry or engineering.

1703 T. N. *City & C. Purchaser* 33 Round-bolts..with a Head at one end, and a Key-hole at the other. *c* **1860** H. STUART *Seaman's Catech.* 61 The lower keyholes should be clear, to allow the water to run out freely.

3. In New Brunswick: A round harbour or cove with narrow entrance.

1896 W. F. GANONY in *Trans. R. Soc. Canada* Ser. II. II. ii. 210.

4. *attrib.*, as ***key-hole prospect, slit, view***; **key-hole escutcheon**, an escutcheon-shaped plate of metal surrounding a keyhole; **keyhole guard, -protector**, a metal plate which falls over (or into) and closes a keyhole; **keyhole limpet**, a gastropod of the family *Fissurellidæ*, having a shell with an aperture at the apex; **keyhole saw**, a narrow saw for cutting keyholes, etc.; **key-hole urchin**, a flattened North American sea-urchin, with openings in the test, belonging to the genus *Mellita* or closely related genera; **keyhole whistler** *slang* (see quot.).

1889 *Sci. Amer.* LXI. 195 Bennett's improved *key-hole guard.. preventing any view through the keyhole. **1869** J. G. WOOD *Common Shells* 96 In the Tusk-shells there is an aperture at the peak, and the same is the case with the *Key-hole Limpet *Fissurella reticulata*. **1885** *Stand. Nat. Hist.* I. 320 The *Fissurellidæ*, or key-hole limpets, are structurally closely allied to the.. *Haliotidæ*. **1851** H. MELVILLE *Whale* xvii. 92 The *key-hole prospect was but a crooked and sinister one. **1816** J. SMITH *Panorama Sc. & Art* I. 107 A small kind of compass-saw, called a *Key-hole-saw, is used for quick curves such as key-holes. **1881** *Gentl. Mag.* Jan. 65 A man standing on his head to keep him quiet, and another cutting a '*keyhole' slit in his ear. **1897** in WEBSTER, *Key-hole urchin. **1904** H. L. CLARK in *Bull. U.S. Fish. Comm. 1902* XXXII. 565 *Mellita pentapora* (Gmelin). Key-hole Urchin. **1962** D. NICHOLS *Echinoderms* v. 76 Among the gnathostomes the clypeasteroid sand-dollars achieve probably the greatest specialization, some, such as the Key-hole Urchin, *Rotula*, becoming remarkably flat and possessing holes through the test. **1851** MAYHEW *Lond. Labour* I. 311 '*Keyhole whistlers*', the skipper birds are sometimes called... They start early to good houses for victuals, when gentlefolk are not up.

Hence **'keyhole** *v. intr.*, (of a bullet in target-practice) to strike the target in such a way as to make a hole of the form of a key-hole.

1890 *Cent. Dict.* cites REYNOLDS. **1905** *Kynoch Jrnl.* Oct.–Dec. 172 Some of these weapons.. shot wildly, the bullet invariably keyholing. **1910** KIPLING *Land & Sea Tales* (1923) 190 The bullet must have ricochetted short of the butt, and it has key-holed, as we say. **1957** *Amer. Speech* XXXII. 194 *Keyhole*, of a bullet: to enter the target with the side foremost so that a rectangular or oblong hole is cut; of a handgun: to shoot bullets that keyhole.

keying ('kiːɪŋ), *vbl. sb.* [f. KEY *sb.*[1] and *v.*]

1. The action of the verb KEY in various senses.

1596-7 in Swayne *Sarum Church-w. Acc.* 302 One Chiboll for his laboʳ for the keyinge of a bell, 6*d.* **1862** G. P. SCROPE *Volcanos* 290 The 'keying' of their flexures by the intrusion of molten matter from beneath, and its consolidation there. **1878** MARG. STOKES *Early Chr. Archit. Irel.* 10 Finished at the top by selecting a thicker or thinner stone, as the case might require, for keying. **1918** W. H. ECCLES *Wireless Telegr.* (ed. 2) 247 When the high voltage in the repeat side does not exceed 100 or 200 volts it is easy to interrupt that circuit by aid of a morse key. Other suggestions for keying will be found in the section on Wireless Telegraphy. **1931** L. B. TURNER *Wireless* v. 131 To start a Poulsen arc it must be struck... In keying, therefore, the oscillation cannot be started and stopped as in a spark transmitter. Instead, the Morse key—or.. the set of relay contacts controlled by the key—is made to alter the wavelength slightly. **1966** S. STEIN in M. Schwartz et al. *Communication Syst. & Techniques* vii. 280 With rectangular modulation, the states are described by which of a pair of possible frequencies is transmitted. The system is commonly known as frequency-shift keying (FSK). Phase-shift keying (PSK) is the analog of phase modulation.

†**2.** Stone-work serving as the key of an arch. *Obs. rare*⁻¹.

1483 *Churchw. Acc. St. Mary hill, London* (Nichols 1797) 97 Keyenge of a gate of ston 8 fote of heyghte withynne boght of William Gemet mason.

'key-ˌkeeper.

1. One who has the custody or control of the key of a house, room, chest, etc. Cf. *key-herd*, KEY *sb.*[1] 18.

1534 in W. H. Turner *Select. Rec. Oxford* 219 To the Key Kepers to thuse of the body of the Town. **1576** *Ibid.* 388 The Key Kepers of thys Cytie shall delyver them xˡⁱ in money. **1669** WOODHEAD *St. Teresa* II. App. 10 He must enquire, whether any money comes to the hands of the Superioress, without the Key-keeper's knowledge. *a* **1711** KEN *Psyche* Poet. Wks. 1721 IV. 205 That Angel.. Of the Abyss Key-keeper made, Rules the infernal Shade. **1892** *Antiquary* Oct. 141 His application.. was refused by the key-keeper.

2. = KEY-BEARER 2.

1563-87 FOXE *A. & M.* (1596) 87/1 Left with Peter the holie keie keeper.

†**3.** A regulator. *Obs.*

1674 N. FAIRFAX *Bulk & Selv.* 122 The best key-keeper of motion is an elater or bear.

keyl, obs. form of KEEL *sb.*[2], *sb.*[3], *v.*[1]

keyless ('kiːlɪs), *a.* [f. KEY *sb.*[1] + -LESS.] Without a key or keys. **a.** Of a door or lock.

1823 BYRON *Island* IV. vi, A spacious cave, Whose only portal was the keyless wave. **1860** READE *Cloister & H.* xciv, Faith and simplicity had guarded that keyless door.

b. Of a watch or clock which is wound up otherwise than by means of a key. Hence of a mechanism, method of winding, etc.

1828 *Mech. Mag.* IX. 66 Berrollas' keyless watch or clock. **1884** F. J. BRITTEN *Watch & Clockm.* 133 The simple keyless mechanism used for going barrels is not suitable for the fusee. *Ibid.* 247 The ordinary method of keyless winding.

c. Of a musical instrument.

1875 tr. *Blaserna's Th. Sound* v. §8 The primitive keyless trumpet.

d. Without explanatory key.

1861 J. PYCROFT *Ways & Words* 83 Such compositions have.. a voice only for the initiated, but are keyless mysteries to all others. **1892** *Pall Mall G.* 22 Sept. 2/1 We find your work so abstruse, your parables so keyless.

keylet ('kiːlɪt). [f. KEY *sb.*[1] + -LET.] A little or tiny key.

1860 *Artist & Craftsman* 367 To open the rose-wood case with the precious keylet she had left him.

keyll, obs. form of KEEL *sb.*[3], KYLE.

keyme, keynard, var. KEMB, CAYNARD.

Keynesian ('keɪnzɪən), *a.* and *sb.* [f. the name of J. M. *Keynes* + -IAN.] **A.** *adj.* Of or pertaining to the English economist John Maynard Keynes (1883–1946) or his economic theories, esp. regarding State control of the economy through money and taxes. **B.** *sb.* An adherent of these theories. Hence **'Keynesianism**.

1937 *Economic Jrnl.* XLVII. 153 The latest Keynesian analysis does indeed justify.. such policies as redistribution of income. **1942** *Fortune* May 61 Mr. Keynes is now a Director of the Bank of England, and he is not the only Keynesian on the Board. **1946** *Ann. Amer. Acad. Pol. & Soc. Sci.* Nov. 284 The distinctive feature of this textbook.. is Keynesianism. **1947** A. P. LERNER in S. E. Harris *New Economics* (1948) IX. xlv. 654 The very simplified form of the Keynesian system.. speaks as if there were only one kind of asset. *Ibid.* 655, I say, as a Keynesian, that the rate of interest is determined by the supply and demand for cash. **1951** R. F. HARROD *Life J. M. Keynes* x. 414 Not prepared to accept Keynesian doctrine. **1960** *Commentary* June 463/2 The war left a legacy of wild Keynesianism that continues in a new war economy to sustain prosperity. **1965** *New Statesman* 9 Apr. 560/1 Devious and vulgarised Keynesian calculations of the 'inflationary gap'. **1974** *Times Lit. Suppl.* 20 Sept. 1022/4 The notion of Keynesianism as a system might have been attractive to his vanity but it would have been repellent to his intelligence.

key-note ('kiːnəʊt), *sb.* Also **keynote**.

1. a. *Mus.* The first, i.e. lowest, note of the scale of any key, which forms the basis of, and gives its name to, the key; the tonic. (Formerly called simply *key*: see KEY *sb.*[1] 7 a.) In quot. 1776 applied to the lowest tone of an ancient Greek scale or 'mode.'

1776 BURNEY *Hist. Mus.* I. v. 460 The key-note of the Dorian mode. **1782** *Ibid.* II. ii. 97 Transposed keys.. represented by other sounds in the same relation to the key-note. **1859** JEPHSON *Brittany* iv. 41 They never leave off on the key-note; the ear is left unsatisfied. **1875** OUSELEY *Mus. Form* ii. 11 A melodic perfect cadence must end with the key-note.

b. *transf.* = KEY *sb.*[1] 8 a. *rare.*

1762 KAMES *Elem. Crit.* XVIII. iv. (1774) II. 104 In reading, whether verse or prose, a certain tone is assumed, which may be called the key-note; and in that tone the bulk of the words are sounded.

2. *fig.* **a.** The leading idea of a discourse, composition, or course of action; the prevailing tone of thought or feeling.

1783 BLAIR *Rhet.* II. xxxi. 166 Much of the Orator's art and ability is shown, in thus striking properly at the commencement, the key note, if we may so express it, of the rest of his Oration. **1825** SCOTT *Diary* 22 Dec. in *Lockhart*, I wrote a few verses.. taking the key-note from the story of Clavers leaving the Scottish Convention of estates in 1688–9. **1862** J. SKELTON *Nugæ Crit.* ix. 404 This moderation was the key-note of Canning's character. **1875** STUBBS *Const. Hist.* III. xviii. 14 The keynote of the Lancastrian policy. **1888** BURGON *Lives 12 Gd. Men* I. II. 140 Such was the frequent keynote of his discourses in public.

b. *attrib.*, as **keynote address** or **speech** orig. *U.S.*, a speech, usu. an opening address, designed to state the main concerns or to set the prevailing tone for a conference or the like; often used at political rallies merely to arouse enthusiasm or promote unity; so **key-note speaker**, one who gives a keynote speech.

1905 *Milwaukee Jrnl.* 28 July 8/1 His address tonight will undoubtedly be a keynote speech. *c* **1908** *Great Issues & National Leaders of 1908* 54 He.. began his 'keynote' address. *Ibid.* 133 The 'Keynote' Speech of Democracy. **1948** *Times* 21 June 5 The first two days [of the Republican Convention] will be taken up with.. the 'keynote' speech. To heighten suspense and increase the mystery, the 'keynoter' is Governor Green. **1957** *Observer* 13 Oct. 2/5 Mr. Eugene Black, president of the International Bank for Reconstruction and Development, will deliver the 'keynote address' to-morrow. **1967** *Economist* 23 Sept. 1072/2 Mr Thorpe decided to set the tone for the week with a short keynote speech. **1968** *Globe & Mail* (Toronto) 3 Feb. 3/6 A first-rate keynote speaker from the party. **1973** *Observer* 14 Jan. 44/3 Roy Jenkins, MP, will give the keynote speech. **1973** *Black World* Mar. 49 A number of speakers are scheduled for each panel following keynote addresses.

keynote ('kiːnəʊt), *v. colloq.* (orig. *U.S.*). [f. the sb.] *trans.* To express the prevailing tone or idea of (something); to address (a meeting) as a keynote speaker. Hence **'keynoting** *vbl. sb.*

1934 in WEBSTER. **1945** *News Review* 10 May 14 Keynoting the surface atmosphere, a Daily Express cartoon showed strap-hanging travellers reading splash-headlined newspapers. **1955** E. LOWRY in Sperber & Trittschuh *Amer. Pol. Terms* (1962) 226/1 Keynoting implies the ability to make melodic noises and give the impression of passionately and torrentially moving onward and upward while warily standing still. **1963** *Amer. Mineralogist* XLVIII. 959 Dr. Ira Cram.. will keynote the meeting [of the Society of Exploration Geophysicists]. **1965** *Daily Tel.* 9 June 21/6 Keynoting the meeting, Dr. —— high-lighted the need for [etc.]. **1974** *State* (Columbia, S. Carolina) 5 Mar. 9-B/2 Judge George N. Leighton, Howard University and Harvard Law School graduate, will keynote the symposium.

keynoter ('kiːnəʊtə(r)). *colloq.* (orig. *U.S.*). [f. KEY-NOTE *sb.* + -ER[1].] A keynote speaker.

1926 *S.P.E. Tract* XXIV. 123 *Keynoter*, one who outlines the policy of a campaign, sounds the key note. **1948** [see KEY-NOTE *sb.* 2 b]. **1962** *Economist* 3 Nov. 462/1 The same evangelistic style he displayed as keynoter of the 1960 Republican convention.

keypad ('kiːpæd). Also **key pad.** [f. KEY *sb.*[1] + PAD *sb.*[3], after KEYBOARD.] A small, sometimes hand-held, panel carrying an array of push-buttons identified by numbers, letters, or symbols and used to select a television channel remotely, make a telephonic connection, etc.

1975 [see PAGE *sb.*[2] 1 d]. **1978** *Sci. Amer.* Mar. 60/2 (*caption*) Push-button telephone now in use is much the same.. except that a key pad has replaced the dial. **1978** *Pract. Computing* July–Aug. 43/3 The hexadecimal keypad is constructed from high-quality key mechanisms. **1984** *Times* 4 July 5/3 With the assistance of a small keypad the cable television subscriber will be able to order from a 'menu' displayed on the television screen. **1984** *Sunday Times* (Colour Suppl.) 28 Oct. 118/3 Pressing the mute button on the keypad temporarily cuts off your caller. **1985** *Which Computer?* Apr. 64/1 There are.. seven separate clusters of keys, including a large keypad on the left hand side dedicated to word processing. **1986** *Computer Bull.* June 3/2 This new terminal has.. a numeric keypad, a function keypad and a tamper-resistant pinpad.

keypunch ('kiːpʌntʃ), *sb.* Also **key-punch, key punch.** [f. KEY *sb.*[1] + PUNCH *sb.*[1]] A device for punching holes or notches in cards or paper tape in which one of a set of keys is pressed to produce the hole or holes corresponding to a particular character.

1933 L. J. COMRIE *Hollerith & Powers Tabulating Machines* 7 The Powers automatic key punch.. has automatic feeding and ejection. **1948** *Math. Tables & Other Aids to Computation* III. 127 Data, transferred by keypunch operators onto teletype tapes. **1970** O. DOPPING *Computers & Data Processing* iii. 57 Tape can be punched in keypunches. **1970** *Honey* June 18/2 (Advt.), A keypunch operator.. prepares the cards that tell computers what to do.

keypunch ('kiːpʌntʃ), *v.* Also **key-punch.** [f. prec. sb.] **1.** *trans.* **a.** To produce holes or notches in (a card or paper tape) by means of a keypunch.

1947 *Jrnl. Chem. Education* XXIV. 62/1 A master table of cards, bearing *x* and *f*(*x*), is key-punched from printed tables. **1959** *Science* 16 Oct. 958/1 A number of other items were then added from cards which had been especially key-punched for the purpose.

b. To put into the form of punched cards or paper tape by means of a keypunch.

1959 *Jrnl. Assoc. Computing Machinery* VI. 13 The completed output definition form is.. keypunched directly into cards. **1960** E. DELAVENAY *Introd. Machine Transl.* 119 The text of the foreword was given in French typescript to Mr Brown... He proceeded to the I.B.M. headquarters where he keypunched it. **1971** *Computers & Humanities* V. 304 The computer phase of the project consists of key-punching an Old Church Slavonic-English composite glossary. **1973** *Ann. N.Y. Acad. Sci.* CCXI. 319 There have been thousands of lines of poetry.. keypunched in order to produce concordances.

2. *intr.* To operate or use a keypunch.

1970 O. DOPPING *Computers & Data Processing* iii. 59 In keypunching for automatic data processing, checking methods other than verification punching are normally used.

So **'keypunching** *vbl. sb.* Also **'keypunchable** *a.*, capable of being represented on punched cards or paper tape.

1954 *Jrnl. Assoc. Computing Machinery* I. 155/1 The punched-card input makes it possible to use key-punching and verifying techniques. **1965** L. E. FOSTER *Telemetry Syst.* iv. 221 Card-handling equipment provides keypunching, verifying, sorting.. and listing services. **1969** P. B. JORDAIN *Condensed Computer Encycl.* 395 Programming.. may end with coding (writing in keypunchable form). **1970** *Computers & Humanities* IV. 210 Gould adapted the *Plaine & Easie* keypunchable notation of 48 characters to a code specifically for the uniquely-written chant.

keypuncher ('kiːpʌntʃə(r)). Also **key puncher.** [Partly f. KEY *sb.*[1] + PUNCHER, partly f. KEYPUNCH *v.* + -ER[1].] **a.** = KEYPUNCH *sb.*

1965 L. E. FOSTER *Telemetry Syst.* iv. 224 The semi-automatic area consists of.. two oscillograph readers with six associated card punchers, 13 key punchers, four verifiers, three *X-Y* plotters, [etc.].

b. One who operates or uses a keypunch.

1967 COX & GROSE *Organiz. Bibliogr. Rec. by Computer* 144 The keypuncher should transcribe this.

keyre, obs. form of KIER.

keyry, variant of KEIRI *Obs.* wall-flower.

Keys (kiːz). [Pl. of KEY *sb.*[1] in specialized use.] A body of twenty-four members which forms the elective branch of the Legislature of the Isle of Man. More fully ***House of Keys***. (The reason

of the title is not quite clear. It appears in Latin form *clāves* in 1418, and in Eng. form in 1422. But it is not the recognized name in the Manx Statutes till 1585; from that date to 1734 the title is 'The Twenty-four Keys'; after this simply 'The Keys'. The Manx popular name is *Yn Kiare as Feed*, 'The Four-and-twenty.' The suggestion that *Keys* was some kind of corruption of *Kiare as* 'Four-and' has no historical basis.)

[**1417–18** in Gill *Statutes I. of Man* (1883) I. 2 Hæc Indentura facta inter Thurstanum de Tyldesley [etc.] ex unâ parte, et..xxiiij Claves Mann. ex altera, Testatur qd. predicti xxiiij Claves legis cum judice Mann. dicunt, etc.] **1422** *Ibid.* I. 11 Alsoe we give for Law, that there was never xxiiij Keys in Certainty, since they were first that were called Taxiaxi, those were xxiiij free Houlders..Without the Lord's Will, none of the 24 Keys to be. **1585** *Order of Henry Earl of Derby* ibid. 59 To..impart your Proceedings to the 24 Keyes of that my Isle. **1594** *Art. of Doubt by R. Stanley* ibid. 67 The two Deemsters and 24 Keys of this Isle. **1706** PHILLIPS s.v., In the Isle of Man, the twenty four chief Commoners, being as it were the Keepers of the Liberties of the People, are call'd The Keys of the Island. **1715** Gov. HORNE *Let.* in A. W. Moore *Hist. I. of Man* 835 To the Gentlemen of the Twenty-four Keys. **1718** in Keble *Life Bp. Wilson* xii. (1863) 397 A complaint of this nature is not cognizable before the 24 Keys. **1739** in Gill *Statutes I. of Man* I. 239 By and with the Advice and Consent of the Governor, Councel, Deemster, and Keyes, in this present Tynwald Court assembled. **1883** *Encycl. Brit.* XV. 452/2 The Keys were at one time self-elected, but in 1866 they consented to popular election. **1900** A. W. MOORE *Hist. I. of Man* 824 *note*, The right to try questions of the rights of members to their seats was specially reserved by the House of Keys Election Act of 1866.

keysar, -ser, -zar, obs. variants of KAISER.

keyse, keysie, keyshie, local ff. CASSIE[1].

keysender ('kiːsɛndə(r)). *Teleph.* [f. KEY *sb.*[1] + SENDER.] A device for applying electric impulses representing a telephone number to a circuit by means of a set of keys (numbered 0 to 9), in place of a dial.

1929 *Telegraph & Telephone Jrnl.* XVI. 34/1 The light, airy switchroom, the tap-tap of the keysenders and the humming of the dials, this is my introduction into the subscriber's Paradise— an Automatic Exchange. **1934** *Post Office Electr. Engineers' Jrnl.* XXVII. 32/1 It has recently been decided..to provide mechanical keysenders both for P.B.X. operators and, if desired, for individual telephones. **1948** J. ATKINSON *Herbert & Procter's Telephony* (new ed.) I. xi. 216/2 The keysender..is a device introduced as an alternative to the dial on large type private branch exchange switchboards to reduce the time expended by a P.B.X. operator when dialling numbers from the switchboard. By its use, the P.B.X. operator is free to attend to other calls whilst the keysender is still transmitting the digits which have been keyed up. **1970** *New Scientist* 5 Nov. 275/1 Tests at the St Albans exchange showed that the keysender was markedly quieter than the rotary dial and saved an average of 2–3 seconds on each call.

So **key-sending**, the use or operation of a keysender.

1928 C. W. BROWN *Automatic Telephony Simplified* viii. 143 Key sending, and not dial sending, would, of course, be provided at manual exchanges when necessary. **1930** *Gloss. Terms Telegraphs & Telephones (B.S.I.)* 26 *Key-sending B-position*, a B-position equipped with digit keys for the purpose of making calls direct to an automatic exchange. **1938** HERBERT & PROCTER *Telephony* II. ix. 393 Each manual exchange adopting direct 7-digit keysending utilizes a suitable automatic exchange as a routing centre for the whole of its indirectly routed traffic. **1950** J. ATKINSON *Herbert & Procter's Telephony* (new ed.) II. xvii. 558/2 There are three alternative arrangements of the keysending equipment.

keyster, var. KEISTER.

keystone ('kiːstəʊn), *sb.*

1. a. The stone at the summit of an arch, which, being the last put in, is looked upon as locking the whole together.

a **1637** B. JONSON *Underwoods, Misc. Poems* xxx. *To Sir E. Sackville*, 'Tis the last key-stone That makes the arch. **1703** MOXON *Mech. Exerc.* 279 If you will add a Keystone..to the Arch..let the breadth of the upper part of the Keystone be the height of the Arch. **1790** BURNS *Tam o' Shanter* 206 Now, do thy speedy utmost, Meg, And win the key-stane of the brig. **1851** RUSKIN *Stones Ven.* I. x. §4 One voussoir is as much a keystone as another; only people usually call the stone which is last put in the keystone; and that one happens generally to be at the top or middle of the arch. **1858** MRS. OLIPHANT *Laird Norlaw* III. 272 The narrow door, with some forgotten noble's sculptured shield upon its keystone.

b. *fig.* Something occupying a position compared to that of a keystone in an arch.

1641 J. JACKSON *True Evang. T.* III. 182 Christian Society is..like stones in an arch,..Christ himselfe being the key-stone. **1790** BURNS *Tam o'* 69 That hour, o' night's black arch the key-stane. **1839** BAILEY *Festus* i. (1852) 10 The sun, centre and sire of light, The keystone of the world-built arch of Heaven. **1866** HOWELLS *Venet. Life* (1883) I. xiii. 245 At the other end of the saloon sat one of the fathers, the plump key-stone of an arch of comfortable young students.

c. *esp.* The central principle of a system, course of action, etc., upon which all the rest depends.

1817 COLERIDGE *Biog. Lit.* 96 Religion, as both the corner stone, and the key-stone of morality. **1832** LEWIS *Use & Ab. Pol. Terms* xvii. 163 The keystone on which all government must ultimately rest. **1849** MACAULAY *Hist. Eng.* vii. II. 166 The tenet of predestination was the keystone of his religion. **1876** ROGERS *Pol. Econ.* ix. (ed. 3) 108 The principle of unlimited liability is the keystone of the system.

d. *ellipt.* = *Keystone State* (see sense 5). Also *attrib.* *U.S.*

[**1803** in H. M. Jenkins *Pennsylvania* (1903) II. xii. 316 Pennsylvania is the Keystone of the democratic arch.] **1844** *Congress. Globe* 4 June 662/3 The old Key-stone has never furnished the Union with either President or Vice President. **1948** *Time* 21 June 22/3 The control of keystone Pennsylvania was one of the big question marks of the convention.

2. A bond-stone.

1823 P. NICHOLSON *Pract. Build.* 339 *Key-Stones*, a term frequently used for bond-stones.

3. In chromolithography: see quots.

1875 *Ure's Dict. Arts* III. 135 A drawing of the subject, in outline,..is made..when transferred to a stone, this drawing is called the keystone, and it serves as a guide to all the others, for it must be transferred to as many different stones as there are colours in the subject. **1889** *Pall Mall G.* 23 Jan. 3/1 'Offsets'..are tracings of those portions of matter in the keystone which are to go in each colour, an offset for the red, one for the blue, and so on.

4. A block of cast-iron used to fill up certain spaces in a Scotch lead smelting furnace.

1857 TOMLINSON in *Encycl. Brit.* (ed. 8) XIII. 300/1 (*Lead*) The space at each end of the fore-stone is closed by a cube of cast-iron called a key-stone: two similar stones fill up the space between the fore-stone and the back part of the furnace.

5. a. *attrib.* and *Comb.*, as ***keystone-mask***; **keystone effect**, in *Cinemat.*, the formation of a trapezial projected image as a result of the line of projection not being normal to the screen; a similar distortion of a television picture in which a rectangular object gives a trapezial image; **keystone-mill**, a kind of mill used for grinding tanning materials; **Keystone State** *U.S.*, popular appellation of Pennsylvania, as being the seventh or central one of the original thirteen states.

1914 J. B. RATHBUN *Motion Picture Making* vi. 135 With the projector installed at one side of the screen, the keystone effect will be horizontal instead of vertical. **1940** D. G. FINK *Princ. Television Engin.* iv. 142 When such a scanned image is reproduced in the receiver, all the picture elements in the lower lines are spread out too far relative to those in the top line. This is the so-called keystone effect. **1967** *Electronics* 6 Mar. 79/1 (Advt.), The electron gun is set at an angle to the phosphor and the deflection system compensates for keystone effects. **1890** *Daily News* 26 Nov. 7/3 The quite famous sculptured *keystone-masks on the east and west sides of the central arch of Henley Bridge. **1881** *Spon's Dict. Indust. Arts* 1227 The well known American '*keystone' mill. **1836** *Southern Lit. Messenger* II. 277 The little German farmer..in the Key Stone State. **1948** *Daily Ardmoreite* (Ardmore, Okla.) 27 Apr. 6/2 Republican aspirants matched strength in the politically important keystone state.

b. Used *attrib.* (with capital initial) in allusion to the slapstick comedy films produced by the Keystone film company, formed by 'Mack Sennett' in 1912; esp. of films featuring the 'Keystone Cops', a group of bumbling policemen. Hence ***Keystones***, slang for 'police'.

1913 *Writer's Mag.* Nov. 188/2 If you have never written burlesque or vaudeville material..you will do well to watch a dozen of the Keystone comedies. **1918** R. H. KNYVETT *Over There* 54 We received at this time the nickname 'Keystone soldiers', some genial ass conceiving that we looked as funny as the Keystone police. **1935** A. J. POLLOCK *Underworld Speaks* 66/2 *Keystone*, a special, uniformed police officer. **1964** W. MARKFIELD *To Early Grave* x. 168 He was straddling the running board like a Keystone cop. **1967** [see JAMES BOND]. **1969** J. WAINWRIGHT *Big Tickle* 162 Get the keystones in the act. They watch. We perform. **1971** A. HUNTER *Gently at Gallop* i. 6 The local Keystones move in demanding alibis. **1974** N. FREELING *Dressing of Diamond* 107 The extreme infantilism of mentalities unable to distinguish between the Keystone Kops and a shattered child.

Hence **'keystoned** *a.*, having a keystone.

1887 T. HARDY *Woodlanders* I. iv. 52 Under that keystoned doorway.

keystone ('kiːstəʊn), *v.* *Television.* [f. the sb.] *trans.* To subject to a keystone effect (see KEYSTONE 5). Hence **'keystoning** *vbl. sb.*

1940 ZWORYKIN & MORTON *Television* xv. 473 If the complete sawtooth..is a modulation, the shape will be keystoned. **1940** D. G. FINK *Princ. Television Engin.* iv. 142 (*caption*) Trapezoidal distortion ('keystoning') of scanning pattern in the iconoscope. **1951** S. DEUTSCH *Theory & Design Television Receivers* xv. 495 This characteristic is counteracted by keystoning the CRT picture in the opposite sense by means of two permanent magnets. **1972** R. G. MIDDLETON *Transistor Television Servicing Guide* (rev. ed.) vii. 86 A thermistor in the vertical-deflection coil circuit will occasionally..develop an abnormal resistance characteristic that will produce keystoning.

keystroke ('kiːstrəʊk), *sb.* Also **key-stroke, key stroke**. [f. KEY *sb.*[1] + STROKE *sb.*[1]] A depression of a key on a keyboard, esp. as a measure of work.

c **1910** *Comptometer* (Felt & Tarrant Manufacturing Co.) 4 Because a simple key-stroke does it all, the Comptometer saves 60% of time on addition. **1914** E. M. HORSBURGH *Mod. Instruments & Methods of Calculation* 101 A beginner ..might by a slurred or partial key-stroke make it add a wrong amount. **1921** J. A. V. TURCK *Origin. Mod. Calculating Machines* 160 Felt was interested in the solution of the problem for detection and correction of the errors in key-strokes. **1966** E. J. & J. A. MCCARTHY *Integrated Data Processing Syst.* v. 122 Most work is figured on the basis of 100 key strokes a minute. **1972** *Sci. Amer.* May 14/1 (Advt.), Although it's only 3 by 6 inches and weighs 9 ounces..it computes transcendental functions with a single keystroke in less than a second.

Hence **'keystroke** *v. trans.* = KEY *v.* 8; **'keystroking** *vbl. sb.* Also **'keystroker**, one who operates the keys of a keyboard, esp. of a keypunch.

1966 *Ann. Rev. Information Sci.* I. 192 One of the impediments to greater use of automation in library and information center operations is the formidable prospect of keystroking an existing corpus of text. **1967** *Library Jrnl.* 1 Mar. 975 *All* publications..have to be key-stroked at some stage in their life-cycle. **1971** J. B. CARROLL et al. *Word Frequency Bk.* p. xix. The samples [of text] were keystroked freeform onto IBM cards using IBM 029 keypunch equipment. **1971** *Computers & Humanities* VI. 40 If key-stroking plays a part in data entry, the keystroker's own deviations will be added to those already in the text.

keyth, var. KITHE *v.* *Obs.*, to make known, etc.

† **'key-turner.** *Obs.* A turnkey.

1607 DEKKER *Knt.'s Conjur.* (1842) 45 Hee's as surly as those Key-turners are. **1618** MYNSHUL *Ess. Prison* (1638) 29 The master of a prison is the primum mobile..and those key-turners and street-walkers are the petty and necessary slavish wheeles. **1786** J. ROBERTS *Life* 83 A piece of service I did him..officiating as key-turner, and preventing two notorious robbers from breaking out.

keytyf, -teyves, obs. forms of CAITIFF, -S.

key-whyt: see KEY *sb.*[4]

‖ **kgotla** (k'gɒtlə). Also 9 **cotla, kotla**. [Tswana.] An assembly of tribal elders among some Bantu peoples; also, the place of such assembly (see also quot. 1857). Cf. KUTA.

1840 B. SHAW *Memorials of S. Afr.* xx. 303 Morokos Kotla had no attractions yesterday; we went and sat down in it, but we could not bear to remain. **1846** H. H. METHUEN *Life in Wilderness* viii. 253 We threaded our way between the wattle hedges..and reached the cotla, or place of assembly, set apart in all native tribes for the purpose of holding public meetings. **1857** D. LIVINGSTONE *Missionary Trav. & Res. S. Afr.* i. 15 Near the centre of each circle of huts there is a spot called a 'kotla', with a fireplace; here they work, eat, or sit and gossip over the news of the day. **1896** H. A. BRYDEN *Tales S. Afr.* 192 They reached the large *kotla*, or enclosure, in the centre of the town, where Tapinyani's own residence stood. **1949** *Cape Times* 10 Nov. 2/8 Chief Bathoen, of the Bangwaketse tribe, gave evidence about the June *kgotla*, saying that the Assistant Government Secretary had told the tribesmen that they were gathered to discuss the right of succession of chieftainship. **1966** *New Statesman* 15 Apr. 531/2 The *kgotla*..until recently the arena of decision in Bechuanaland. **1972** *Times* 11 Sept. (Botswana, Lesotho & Swaziland Suppl.) p. iii/4 Until now, the traditional place for dealing with such matters has been the *kgotla*.

khab(b)ar, variant of KHUBBER.

khad, var. KHUD.

‖ **khadar** ('kɑːdə(r)). *India.* Also **kadir, khádar, khaddar, khâder, khadir**, and with capital K. [Hindī.] **a.** A flood-plain; land susceptible to flooding.

1832 G. C. MUNDY *Pen & Pencil Sk.* I. v. 269 The road continued partly along the khâder of the river. **1879** MEDLICOTT & BLANFORD *Man. Geol. India* I. xvii. 404 The alluvial plain itself..is composed of *bhángar*, or high land.. and *khádar*, or low land, the low plain through which each river flows. **1882** W. THEOBALD *Mason's Burma* I. 4 The delta..of the Ganges, the richest land of Lower Bengal, being composed of *Khadir* land. **1887** J. M. BROWN *Shikar Sk.* 247 Pig-sticking in the Kadir, or old bed of the Ganges. **1887** *Encycl. Brit.* XXII. 98/2 Eastward of the khádar lies the sandy central tableland. **1904** A. KNOX *Gloss. Geogr. & Topogr. Terms* 193 *Khadar* (Hind.), low lands fit for rice-growing. **1929** *Blackw. Mag.* Oct. 526/2 There is more game and greater variety of game in a kadir country than in any other kind. **1955** BROWN & DEY *India's Mineral Wealth* (ed. 3) xix. 691 In the Brahmaputra valley, and the whole of the Assam plain is one great *khadar* or strath.

b. Recently deposited alluvium.

1919 D. N. WADIA *Geol. India* xxii. 251 The Khadar deposits are, as a rule, confined to the vicinity of the present channels. **1945** H. L. CHHIBBER *India* I. xiv. 187 The Newer Alluvium is confined to the river channels and their flood plains and is locally termed as *Khaddar*. **1949** M. S. KRISHNAN *Geol. India & Burma* xx. 519 The Newer Alluvium (called *Khadar* in the Punjab) is light coloured and poor in calcareous matter.

khaddar ('kædə(r)). Also **khadder, khadi**. [Hindī.] Indian home-spun cotton cloth.

1921 *Glasgow Herald* 27 Dec. 7 This tent will be made of hand-spun 'khadder'. **1922** *Ibid.* 22 Dec. 9 Delegates are already pouring into Neaya for the session of Congress that opens on December 26, and a huge marquee of khaddar (homespun) material has been erected. **1923** *Daily Mail* 23 Feb. 8 No person wearing clothes other than those made from 'Khadder'—Mr. Gandhi's own favourite brand of hand-woven cloth—is tolerated in the 'presence'. **1924** C. D. GROTH tr. *Rolland's Mahatma Gandhi* 72 Tagore, too, praised this *khaddar*, or *khadi*. **1925** E. S. JONES *Christ of Indian Road* v. 116 The whole city was dressed in white home-spun khaddar, the sign of the Nationalist. **1936** J. NEHRU *Autobiogr.* xv. 106 Khadi clothes and third-class railway travelling demand little money. **1960** KOESTLER *Lotus & Robot* 278 The produce of the cotton mills is cheaper than homespun khaddar. **1971** *Illustr. Weekly India* 18 Apr. 6 He alighted, this huge khadder-clad mountain of a man, his eyes alert and smiling. **1974** *New Yorker* 3 June 28/2 Gandhi called on all Indians..to raise cotton and to

spin and weave it, so that there would be no shortage of *khadi*, or homespun cloth. **1975** *Bangladesh Times* 22 July 5/2 There may be easily manageable industries such as handloom, Khadi, village industries, handicrafts, [etc.].

||**khair** (kaɪə(r)). Also **kheir, kiar.** [Hindī *khair*, *khayar*, = Skr. *khadirá*.] The *Acacia Catechu* of India, from which cutch is obtained.

1831 TRELAWNEY *Adv. Younger Son* II. 198 The kiar backstays, strong and elastic as they are, snapped like cast iron. **1835** BURNES *Trav. Bokhara* (ed. 2) I. 112 Clumps of tamarisk, *khair*, *lan*,..and such other shrubs as are to be found in the Thurr. **1862** *Catal. Internat. Exhib.* III. *India* 105 Kheir-gum. **1866** *Treas. Bot.* 646/1 Khair-tree.

||**khakan** (kɑːˈkɑːn). Also **khacan.** [Turkī (hence Pers. and Arab.) *khāqān* king, emperor, Great Khan: see CHAGAN and KHAN[1].] A Tartar ruler: a khan.

1777 J. RICHARDSON *Dissert. East Nat.* 26 The Khakan used often to preside at their exercises of genius. **1859** C. FORSTER *Primeval Lang., Mon. Assyria* 314 *note*, When the present khacan shall have departed, this man will succeed to the throne.

Hence **khaˈkanship**, the office of khakan.

1859 C. FORSTER *Primeval Lang., Mon. Assyria* 314 *note*, They give the khacanship only to Jews.

||**khaki** (ˈkɑːkiː), *a.* and *sb.* Also **khakee, ka(h)ki, kharki(e, karkee,** etc. [Urdū (Pers.) *khākī* dusty, f. *khāk* dust.]

A. *adj.* **a.** Dust-coloured; dull brownish yellow, drab. **b.** (*attrib.* use of B.) Made of khaki cloth.

1863 *Cornh. Mag.* Jan. 45 As to dress.. he [Capt. Cureton] confined himself to causing their clothes to be dyed khakee, or mud-colour. **1869** E. A. PARKES *Pract. Hygiene* (ed. 3) 395 The comfortable gray or dust-coloured native Khakee cloth. **1884** J. COLBORNE *Hicks Pasha* 2 We had to provide ourselves with..Karkee jackets. **1884** *Health Exhib. Catal.* 35/2 The new Khaki cloth, the material adopted by the War Office for the troops on active service. **1890** WATT *Dict. Econ. Prod. India* IV. 566 It is needless to attempt an enumeration of all the Khaki dyes of India. **1898** B. BURLEIGH *Sirdar & Khalifa* ix. 128 The Kharkie trousers of the Lincolns and Warwicks. **1900** *Daily News* 24 Mar. 6/5 Stockings, gloves, sunshades, all are to be khaki.

B. *sb.* A fabric of this colour now largely employed in the British army for field-uniforms. Originally of stout twilled cotton (*khaki drill*), but more recently made also of wool (*khaki bedford, k. serge*). Also (usu. *pl.*), a uniform or garment made from this fabric.

In India, khaki was used for uniforms by the Guide Corps under Lumsden and Hodson in 1848, by the troops in the Mutiny of 1857, in the Afghan campaigns of 1878–80, etc. It was worn in the Sudan Wars of 1883–98, and esp. by the British troops in South Africa in 1899–. (Quots. 1857–59 may mean simply the colour: cf. 'dressed in white'.)

1857 H. B. EDWARDES *Let.* 21 July in Lumsden & Elsmie *Lumsden of Guides* (1899) 200 The whole of the troops here are dressed in khâkee. **1859** SIR J. MURRAY *Disp.* 27 Apr. in *Delhi Gaz.* 23 June, The Infantry were dressed in khakee. **1879** E. S. BRIDGES *Round the World in 6 Months* 203 The troops here are dressed in khaki..It is a kind of strong brown holland, and appears to me to be made of flax. **1883** *Times* 11 July 7 Marksmen..in the case of some of the Indian team, in the light serviceable dust-coloured khakee. **1886** YULE s.v., The original khakee was a stout cotton cloth, but the colour was also used in broad-cloth. **1892** *Pall Mall G.* 25 Apr. 7/1 Khaki is not showy enough except when it is new and well made up, and if constantly worn it tends to promote slovenliness. **1899** S. CRANE in *Cornh. Mag.* Dec. 749 In came Casper, thin, yellow, and in soiled khaki. **1936** *Amer. Speech* XI. 50 Unless he learns..to restrict the use of *khaki* to cotton uniforms of that shade..he is still a *John* [*viz.* a recruit]. **1956** *Ibid.* XXXI. 192 A marine's uniform wardrobe consists of *greens*, *blues*, *khakis*. **1956** H. GOLD *Man who was not with It* (1965) xviii. 157 Once I sat wearing nothing but a pair of shiny starched new khakis. **1961** *Harper's Mag.* Oct. 43/2 The only clothing I owned was four pairs of khakis, three sweat shirts, a tweed jacket. **1970** 'T. COE' *Wax Apple* (1973) i. 8 He was short and wiry, dressed in khakis and T-shirt.

b. Used for a soldier clothed in khaki.

1899 LUMSDEN & ELSMIE *Lumsden of Guides* 85 There used to be a good deal of rivalry between the Guides and the 1st Punjab Rifles..the former were styled 'Khâkis' from their dust-coloured clothing. *Mod. Newspr.*, Before daylight the Khakis were at them again.

C. As *adj.*, *adv.*, or *sb.* in such constr. as ***to vote khaki, a khaki election, a khaki policy, the khaki loan*** (***khakis***), etc., used in reference to the South African War of 1899–1902, and the war spirit in England at the time. Also as ***khaki election, vote***, also used of the general elections of 1918 and 1931.

1900 G. FABER *Sp.* in *Yorksh. Herald* 5 Jan. 6/2 Are you ..going to..vote solid for our Government? Or may I put it in another way,..will you vote khaki? **1900** *Westm. Gaz.* 7 Feb. 2/2 The electors at York have voted khaki, as Mr. Faber invited them to do. *Ibid.* 8 Mar. 9/1 The market does not know whether the new war loan, Khakis, will be offered at 97, 98, 99, or 100. *Ibid.* 10 Mar. 2/2 The financial aspects of the 'Khaki' Loan of £30,000,000. *Ibid.* 23 Mar. 1/3 Complications of all kinds are likely to arise as the khaki feeling dies down. *Ibid.* 26 May 2/2 The result in South Manchester is a great deal more khaki than that in the Isle of Wight. **1900** *Dundee Advertiser* 21 Aug. 4 What right has the Government to attempt to ride back to power on 'khaki'? **1900** *St. James's Gaz.* 21 Sept. 6/1 Khaki and Imperialistic allusions are worked in [to a play] to the entire satisfaction of the audience. **1913** *Everyday Phrases Explained* 164 *The Khaki Election.* This was the General Election of 1900, when the Government appealed successfully to the country for its approval of the South African War. **1917** G. B. SHAW *What I really wrote about War* (1930) x. 273 You may look forward with exultation to a century of triumphant khaki elections. **1918** *Times* 23 Aug. 8/4 Parliament clearly contemplated a khaki election in the best sense, with every soldier, sailor,..and Red Cross worker voting on the sole but splendid qualification of national service. *Ibid.*, Above all, in 1900 there was no khaki vote. That is the great dividing line which the Reform Act has drawn between 1900 and 1918. **1958** *Times* 15 Feb. 8/4 In November, 1918, she was adopted..as a candidate for Parliament. At the 'khaki election' she stood as a Coalition candidate. **1963** *Times* 6 Feb. 15/1 The 'khaki election' of 1900, when the Conservatives swept the country. **1968** A. MARWICK *Brit. in Cent. of Total War* iii. 94 The election of 14 December 1918 ..was a 'Khaki' election in which the dominant element was patriotic hysteria. **1971** D. AYERST *Guardian* xxx. 472 Sir Warren Fisher..remained at the Treasury..and Ramsay Macdonald at 10 Downing St. He decided to hold a khaki election.

D. *Comb.*, as ***khaki-bound, -clad, -clothed, coloured, -hued*** adjs.; **khaki bos, bush** *S. Afr.*, (*a*) one of several herbs of the family Compositæ, *Tagetes minuta, Inula graveolens*, or *Schkuhria pinata*; (*b*) = *khaki weed*; **khaki weed,** *Alternanthera repens*, a member of the family Amaranthaceæ which has spread from South America to South Africa and Australia.

1900 *Academy* 14 Apr. 313/1 A little *khaki-bound collection of ditties about fighting and fighting-men. **1947** H. C. BOSMAN *Mafeking Road* xix. 108 He seemed to have picked out all the useless bits for his pictures—a krantz and a few stones and some clumps of *khaki-bos. **1907** R. W. THORNTON in *Agric. Jrnl. Cape of Good Hope* 7 Jan. 76 The *Khaki Bush is a species of *Aplopappus*... The plant is an annual shrub, rising on a straight main stem to a height of about from two to three feet, with fine pointed leaves and light yellow flowers, which yield an enormous quantity of fine seed. **1913** C. PETTMAN *Africanderisms* 258 Khakibush. A species of *Aplopappus*. The name has reference to the dull fawn colour the withered leaves assume... The name is also applied to *Alternanthera Achyrantha*, R. Br., a troublesome weed now spread widely throughout South Africa, the seeds having been introduced from the Argentine Republic with imported fodder. The name was given to this plant because it made its appearance in military camps during the late war in places where it was previously unknown. **1932** R. MARLOTH *Flora S. Afr.* III. II. 239 Species [of *Schkuhria*] 12, one as a weed in S.A., *S. bonariensis*, Tr., *khaki bush.* **1932** WATT & BREYER-BRANDWIJK *Medicinal & Poisonous Plants S. Afr.* 192 *Inula graveolens* Desf., Khaki bush, Khaki weed, Stinkweed (Australia) is an introduced species. *Ibid.* 195 *Tagetes minuta* L., an introduced weed, known as Khaki bush, Mexican marigold, and Kakiebos, is frequently referred to in the daily Press as an excellent parasiticide for cattle. **1956** A. G. MCRAE *Hill called Grazing* ii. 15, I had never in all my life seen such a profusion of cockle burr, Scotch thistle and 'khaki bush'. **1896** C. DOYLE in *Westm. Gaz.* 9 Apr. 2/1 We had speech with three *khaki-clad men. **1899** *Keene's Bath Jrnl.* 2 Dec. 6/1 It was impossible to distinguish the *khaki-clothed firing line. **1879** F. POLLOK *Sport Brit. Burmah* II. 177 *Khakie-coloured cloth is the best for shooting purposes. **1900** *Westm. Gaz.* 16 Feb. 3/2 The eleven will wear *khaki-hued jerseys. **1900** *Westm. Gaz.* 30 Oct. 8/1 What boys they looked, some of the sunburnt *khaki-men. **1907** H. G. MUNDY in *Transvaal Agricultural Jrnl.* V. 939 *Khaki-weed or Amaranthus weed (*Alternanthera echinata*). **1932** R. MARLOTH *Flora S. Afr.* III. II. 239 Species [of *Tagetes*] about 40, Amer., one as a weed in S.A., *T. minuta* (*khaki weed*). **1953** P. LANHAM *Blanket Boy's Moon* II. vi. 131 *Matekoane* is a weed resembling the khaki weed. **1958** N. GORDIMER *World of Strangers* xiv. 212 Khaki-weed, the growth of neglect and desolation, standing dead and high. **1965** *Austral. Encycl.* I. 167/2 The South American annual needle burr (*Amaranthus spinosus*) and khaki weed (*Alternanthera repens*) have become serious pests in Queensland.

Hence (often with capital initial) **ˈkhakied** (ˈkɑːkɪd) *pa. pple.*, dressed in khaki; *fig.* possessed by a militant spirit or policy; **ˈkhakiism,** militant spirit or policy; **ˈkhakiite,** an enthusiast for a war policy; **ˈkhakiness** = *khakiism*. (All *temporary*.)

1900 *Westm. Gaz.* 4 May 2/2 The Portsmouth electors.. did not allow themselves to be persuaded..into khakiness. **1900** *Daily Express* 26 June 5 (Cassell's Suppl.), The departure of khakied troops for the front. **1900** *National Rev.* June 535 There is no reason to suppose that Lord Salisbury has, so far, surrendered to Khakiism. *Ibid.*, The Khakiites are strenuous and determined. **1904** *Westm. Gaz.* 19 Nov. 2/1 The last election, when certainly the confidence-trick was indeed played on a Khakied nation. **1945** *Brit. Jrnl. Psychol.* Jan. 34 These millions of Khakied citizens run the whole gamut of traditional military gradation.

||**khal** (kɑːl). *India.* [Bengali.] (See quot. 1958[2].)

1903 *Jrnl. Trop. Med.* VI. 200/2 This [*sc.* the anahar plant] is steeped in the big khal at Ishapur, and during the fermenting stage mosquitoes are generated very plentifully. **1904** A. KNOX *Gloss. Geogr. & Topogr. Terms* 193 *Khal* (Bengali), a creek. **1958** N. AHMAD *Econ. Geogr. E. Pakistan* I. i. 15 The upper part of the plain between the Garai-Madhumati and the Padma,..is full of rivers, streams, and *khals* of various sizes. *Ibid.* 338 *Khāl*, narrow natural channel of water.

khalasi (kəˈlæsɪ). Also **calassie, kalashi, -y** (-ʃ-), **kalas(s)i, khalishee, khelasse,** etc. [Hind.] A native servant or labourer, esp. one employed as a seaman. Also *attrib.* in **khalasi watch** (see quot. 1911).

1800 F. GLADWIN tr. *Ayeen Akbery* I. II. 232 The tundeil is the chief of the khelasses, or sailors. **1848** *Alfred in India* 44 Alfred saw the *calassies*, or tent-pitchers, beginning to take down the tent to pack it on the cart. **1848** J. H. STOCQUELER *Oriental Interpreter* 115/1 *Kalashy*, an Indian menial. His business is, properly speaking, confined either to what relates to camp equipage, or to the management of the sails and rigging on board a budjrow or river boat. *a* **1865** SMYTH *Sailor's Word-bk.* (1867) 421 *Khalishees*, native Indian sailors. **1907** M. ROBERTS *Flying Cloud* 22 He had sailed with Khalasi crews for ten years. **1911** *Coast Seamen's Jrnl.* 9 Aug. 1/2 There is growing up a system, mostly in steamers, sometimes called Kalashi watches. This means that certain men are kept on the regular watch-and-watch while the other members of the crew are what is called 'day men'. The 'day men' work all day and are supposed to sleep all night. **1917** *Yachting Monthly* XXII. 197/1 Nothing loth the Kalassis [*sc.* bunder boat crews at Karachi] obeyed. **1931** W. H. PARKER *Leaves from Unwritten Log-Bk.* xi. 95 All hands were kept on deck (or keeping Kalasi watches) for two days and nights. **1957** D. G. O. BAILLIE *Sea Affair* 237 The Lascars, known as *khalassies*, belong to the Deck Department. They are Moslems. **1963** P. J. ABRAHAM *Last Hours* 9, I noticed some of the seamen, or Khalassis, in their blue dungaree uniforms. **1973** *Times of India* 16 Oct. 4/5 Those on strike include..winch operators, khallasis, tindals and other workmen.

Khaldian (ˈkældɪən). [f. *Khaldis* or *Khaldi* the name of the supreme god in Urartu + -AN, -IAN.] **a.** Also **Khaldæi, Khaldean.** Orig. the divine offspring of Khaldi; more usually, a native or inhabitant of the ancient Armenian kingdom of Urartu. **b.** Also **Khaldic.** The language spoken by this people. Also as *adj.*

1882 A. H. SAYCE in *Jrnl. R. Asiatic Soc.* XIV. 412 Khaldis..was also the father of other gods who were called 'the Khaldians' after him. **1898** —— in J. Hastings *Dict. Bible* I. 140/1 The supreme god of Armenia was Khaldis.. from whom the inhabitants of the country took the name of 'people of Khaldis'. From this was derived the name of Khaldæi or Khaldeans. **1901** *Westm. Gaz.* 29 July 5/2 The Khaldians..are to be identified with the Chaldaioi of the Greek writers, who figure prominently in Xenophon. **1908** A. H. SAYCE in *Encycl. Relig. & Ethics* I. 793/1 The present article deals with Proto-Armenian religion as revealed in the Vannic or 'Khaldian' cuneiform inscriptions. **1925** —— in *Cambr. Anc. Hist.* III. viii. 170 If another title is wanted in place of Vannic, Alarodian would be preferable to Khaldian. **1939** L. H. GRAY *Foundations of Lang.* xii. 381 *Khaldic* (also called *Urartaean* or *Vannic*), the language of a kingdom which flourished between 900 and 600 B.C...is known from nearly two hundred inscriptions in Akkadian cuneiform. **1952** O. R. GURNEY *Hittites* vi. 124 A direct descendant of Hurrian is the language of the kingdom of Urartu, sometimes called Vannic or Khaldian. **1959** *Chambers's Encycl.* XIV. 243/1 The people were called Khaldis, they worshipped a sun-god and an air-god. **1966** *Ibid.* XIV. 179/1 Urartu was an ancient kingdom in the highlands of Armenia... The people called themselves 'children of Khaldi' (their national god) and so have sometimes been called Khaldians by modern historians.

||**khalifa** (kəˈliːfə). [Variant of CALIPH, representing more closely the Arab. *khalīfah.*]

1. = CALIPH. So **khalifat(e, khaleefate,** variants of CALIPHATE.

1728 MORGAN *Algiers* I. iv. 153 From Alexandria..came all the Mighty Armadas set on Foot by the Saracen Khalifas. **1844** LD. HOUGHTON *Palm Leaves* 10 The just successor of the Khaleefate. **1898** *Manch. Guard.* 14 Oct., The Khalifate had belonged to the Khalifa, and not to the Khedive.

2. *S. Afr.* Also **califa, chalifah, kalifa.** A Malay sword-dance which originally had religious significance. Also *attrib.*

1856 *Cape Monitor* 16 Jan. 2/3 (*heading*) Checking the Malay 'Califa'. *Ibid.*, Several Malay priests have been examined..and it would seem from their evidence that the Califa is by no means part of the Mahomedan religion, and ..ought only to be played on a certain night in each year. **1861** *Cape Monthly Mag.* Dec. 356 The most characteristic of their customs is the 'Khalifa', a religious ceremonial of the highest solemnity. **1867** M. KOLLISCH *Mussulman Population Cape Good Hope* 59 The feats which the 'Khalifa' involved were highly amusing. **1900** *Diamond Fields Advertiser* (Kimberley) 31 May 2/3 Town Hall, Kimberley. Khalifa Representation in aid of the fund for the relief of the sick and wounded in the Transvaal war. **1950** M. MASSON *Birds of Passage* xv. 142 But the *pièce de résistance* of the whole affair was a kalifa dance by two hundred Malays. **1953** DU PLESSIS & LÜCKHOFF *Malay Quarter* iii. 62 During the previous century..there were many bands of Chalifah-players. *Ibid.*, The chief priest..is designated by the term *Chalifah*, which has now, through common usage, come to be applied to the performance itself. **1972** *Standard Encycl. S. Afr.* VII. 147/1 The most spectacular custom of the Cape Malays is the performance of the Chalifah.

Khalkha, Khalka (ˈkɑːlkə), *sb.* and *a.* [Native name.] **A.** *sb.* **a.** One of a Mongol people in Outer Mongolia; the people themselves. **b.** The language spoken by them. **B.** *adj.* Of or pertaining to this people, their language, or the territory they inhabit.

1873 *Jrnl. R. Geogr. Soc.* XLIII. 122 The *K* of *Kuren* being pronounced *H* by the Kalkas,..would leave a word having..a much greater affinity than many Chinese names have to those in use amongst the natives of the soil. **1876** H. H. HOWORTH *Hist. Mongols* I. viii. 468 Lamaism had spread very greatly among the Mongols, and it was a subject of pride among the Khalkha chiefs to have a..regenerate Buddha among them. **1926** A. N. J. WHYMANT *Mongolian Gram.* i. 1 The Khalka (or as it is generally spelt according to Russian orthography, Khalkha) Mongolian possesses seven vowels and twenty consonants. *Ibid.* 4 The Kalmuck presents consonantal difficulties over the Khalkha. *Ibid.* 5 A common word in all dialects of Mongolian is one mostly heard as *chichik* (a flower) among the Khalkhas. **1948** D. DIRINGER *Alphabet* 318 The three principal [Mongolian] dialects, Khalkha, Kalmuck and Buriat. **1967** D. S. PARLETT *Short Dict. Lang.* 87 Modern literature based mainly on Khalkha dialect in an alphabet based on Cyrillic. **1970** H.

ELVIN *Incredible Mile* xlviii. 132 If Bernard Shaw..had known as much about Mongolian costume as about English dialects..he could have told me..that blue and brown meant a Khalka,..that if a woman's sleeves had horizontal pleats they would be of a Khalka.

‖**khalsa(h** (ˈkɑːlsə). *East Ind.* [Urdū (Pers.) *khāliçah, khālça(h*, fem. of Arab. *khāliç* pure, real, proper, properly belonging.]

1. The revenue department of the government in Indian states; the state exchequer. Also *attrib.*, as ***khalsa-grain, -land.***

1776 *Trial Joseph Fowke* B 14/1, I will procure for you the Kallaut of the Aumeen [= Aumil] of the Khalsa. **1801** R. PATTON *Asiat. Mon.* 129 The injunctions on this head from the *khalsa*, or revenue department, are imperious and strong. *Ibid.* 157 The nankar lands of the zemindar, which have..been converted into khalsah lands. **1862** BEVERIDGE *Hist. India* II. v. vi. 418 The officers of the khalsa (revenue office). **1897** LD. ROBERTS *41 Yrs. India* liii. 427 The herdmen..refused to deliver the khalsa grain.

2. The Sikh community or sect.

1790 G. FORSTER *Journ. Bengal to Eng.* (1798) I 267 *note*, The government at large, and their armies, are [by the Sicques] denominated *Khalsa*, and *Khalsajee*. **1882** WOOD tr. *Barth's Relig. India* 246 Govind Singh..completed the transformation of the sect, or, as it was henceforth called..the Khâlsâ, 'the property, the portion (of God)'.

khalukah, var. CHALUKAH.

Khamba (ˈkæmbə). Also **Kamba, K(h)ampa.** [f. Tibetan *Kham* East Tibet + suffixal element *-ba* or *-pa*.] **a.** A Tibetan people from Kham; one of this people. **b.** The language spoken by this people. Also *attrib.* or as *adj.*

1928 C. BELL *People of Tibet* i. 4 Eastern Tibet... This area is known as Kam, the people as Kam-pa. *Ibid.* vi. 59 The Lhasa men, they used to say, were fonder of talking than of working; the Kam-pas (eastern Tibetans), irritable and quarrelsome. **1955** G. T. BULL *When Iron Gates Yield* iv. 58 The soldiers..were looking forward to a good scrap, for such is the Tibetan Khamba's temperament. *Ibid.* v. 67 A Kamba Tibetan..would rather his blood be spilt in the snow..than to be found alive and defamed. **1957** R. FORD *Captured in Tibet* i. 22, I had picked up enough words of the Khamba dialect to be able to talk to the local inhabitants. *Ibid.* iii. 47 When Radio Peking switched its Tibetan broadcasts to a more suitable hour, it still had no audience, for the news-reader spoke with a Khamba accent. **1960** 'S. HARVESTER' *Chinese Hammer* ii. 31 The only fighting in the country is in the east and restricted to Khambas. **1962** H. E. RICHARDSON *Tibet & its Hist.* i. 11 The Khampas..live between the upper Yangtse and the Chinese border. *Ibid.* xii. 201 The Chinese..exploited the traditional mistrust of Lhasa officialdom existing among the Khampa and Amdowa tribes to the east of the upper Yangtse. **1973** *Times* 20 Oct. 3/2 The fourteenth Dalai Lama is..now 38 and has lived in exile in the Indian Himalayas since 1959, when Khamba rebels persuaded him to flee from Lhasa with them after their abortive uprising against the Chinese occupation.

Khamitic, var. HAMITIC *a.*

‖**khamsin** (ˈkæmsɪn). Forms: 7 **camsim**, 8–9 **campsin**, (9 **kampseen**), 9 **kamsin, khamsin, -seen.** [Arab. *khamsīn*, mod. colloquial form (= oblique case) of *khamsūn* fifty (see def.).] An oppressive hot wind from the south or south-east, which in Egypt blows at intervals for about 50 days in March, April, and May, and fills the air with sand from the desert.

1685 BOYLE *Salub. Air* 74 A kind of Dew, which..purifies the Air from all the Infection of Camsims. **1757** HUXHAM in *Phil. Trans.* L. 428 The wind we had, like the Campsin, actually blew hot. **1804** C. B. BROWN tr. *Volney's View Soil U.S.* 142 The kamsin, or south wind, in Egypt and the south-west at Bagdat and Bussora, have the same properties. **1883** E. F. KNIGHT *Cruise 'Falcon'* (1887) 65 The atmosphere is hot, dry, and oppressive as that of North Africa when the khamsin blows. **1923** F. S. MARVIN *Sci. & Civiliz.* 29 Physical contrasts of seasonal and regional fertility are abrupt; solar heat contends with Nile water, sea breeze with scorching 'hamseen'.

attrib. **1896** *Blackw. Mag.* Sept. 332 The hot khamseen winds parch the fields.

‖**khan**[1] (kæn, kɑːn). Forms: 4 **caan**, 4–6 **cane**, 4–7 **can**, 6 **canne**, 7 **caunn**; 4–5 **chaan**, 4–6 **chane**, 7 **chahan, chawn**, 4, 7–9 **chan**; 7–8 **han**; 9 **khaun, khan (kan, kaan).** See also CHAM. [a. Turkī (hence Pers. and Arab.) *khān* lord, prince, generally regarded as a modified form of *khāqān*: see KHAKAN and CHAGAN.

The title became known in Europe partly through the Mongol invasions in the first half of the thirteenth century (appearing in med.L. as *chanis, canis*, Gr. *κάνης, κάνις*, OF. *chan, cham*, etc.), but more esp. through the European missions to the Mongol court in the same century (1245–55) and by the narrative of Marco Polo (1298). In the original French text of the latter the spelling *Kan, Can* or *Chan* varies with *Kaan* or *Caan*, apparently intended to represent Tartar *qā'ān*, the special title adopted by Oktai, the son of Chingīz Khan, and his successors. *Caanus* is also found in med.L. (Du Cange, s.v. *Cagan*), but the usual forms in the European languages are based on *Khān*.]

a. *Hist.* The specific title (usually with *great*, †*grand*, or the additions *of Tartary, of Cathay*) given to the successors of Chingīz Khan, who were supreme rulers over the Turkish, Tartar, and Mongol tribes, as well as emperors of China, during the middle ages. **b.** In later use: A title (now of slight import) commonly given to rulers, officials, or men of rank in Central Asia, Afghanistan, etc.

c **1400** MAUNDEV. (Roxb.) xiv. 64 Þis Tartary es halden of þe Grete Caan of Cathay. **1494** FABYAN *Chron.* VII. 331 The Great Chaan of Tartharys..sent an hooste into the lande of Hungry. **1534** MORE *Comf. agst. Trib.* III. Wks. 1241/1 Both Prester Iohns land, and the graunde Canes too. **1555** EDEN *Decades* 253 They haue much knowleage of the great cane of Cathay. **1623** *St. Papers, Col.* 1622–4. 211 Sold the small ship to the 'Caunn, being very desirous of her'. **1634** SIR T. HERBERT *Trav.* 52 A Citie..under the Jurisdiction Royall of Emang Ally, the Chawn or great Duke of Shyras. **1667** MILTON *P.L.* XI. 388 Cambalu, seat of Cathaian Can. **1682** *Lond. Gaz.* No. 1724/1 The last Week arrived here an Envoy from the Kam of Tartary. **1705** *Ibid.* No. 4102/2 The old Han of Tartary is lately dead. **1788** GIBBON *Decl. & F.* xlii. (1869) II. 562 The pride of the great khan survived his resentment. **1798** MALTHUS *Popul.* (1878) 67 The power of the Chan being absolute. **1815** ELPHINSTONE *Acc. Caubul* (1842) I. 213 The chief of an Oolooss is called Khaun... In some Ooloosses, the Khaun is elected by the people. **1857** MAX MÜLLER *Selected Ess.* II. 269 One of the Tatar Khans..sent for the Buddhist pilgrim. **1897** LD. ROBERTS *41 Yrs. India* xiv. (1898) 101 He was a grand specimen of a frontier Khan.

‖**khan**[2] (kæn, kɑːn). Forms: α. (4 **alchan**), 7 **c(h)ane, kan(ne**, 8 **k(h)ane**, 8– **khan.** β. 7– **han(e**, 7–8 **hawn**, 8 **hann.** [Arab. *khān* inn.] In the East: A building (unfurnished) for the accommodation of travellers; a caravanserai.

α. *c* **1400** *Three Kings Cologne* 22 He dischargeþ hym his hors..of his berthen and so sendeth hym into swich a hows þat is cleped þere also alchan. [**1612** *Trav. Four Englishm.* 77 In Cities they haue very stately Canes, but not for trauellers, but for themselues to dwell in; for every rich man calleth his house a Cane.] **1615** G. SANDYS *Trav.* 57 Legacies for..building of Canes for the reliefe of passengers. **1682** WHELER *Journ. Greece* I. 37 There is a Kanne there, which serveth for a Warehouse. **1759** RUSSELL in *Phil. Trans.* LI. 533 At Seidon, great part of the Frank kane was overthrown. **1775** R. CHANDLER *Trav. Asia M.* (1825) I. 193 We stopped at the khan, while our men purchased provisions. **1880** A. H. HUTH *Buckle* II 161 The badly-cooked, indigestible stuff which most Eastern travellers eat at the Khans. **1947** *Archit. Rev.* CII. 99 (*caption*) The nearest building, with a row of small domes, is the khan or shopping centre. **1951** A. CHRISTIE *They came to Baghdad* i. 8 Captain Crosbie..turned down a small alleyway into a large Khan or Court. **1958** R. LIDDELL *Morea* II. vii. 165 The buses going to Arcadia pull up at a khan near the village of Alepochori.

β. **1642** HOWELL *For. Trav.* (Arb.) 84 They are great Founders of Hospitalls, of Hanes to entertain Travellers. **1653** GREAVES *Seraglio* 182 Divers Hawns (commonly called Canes) in which wayfaring men do lodge. **1704** J. PITTS *Acc. Mahometans* 173 A Hawn or Inn adjoyning to the Harbour. **1717** LADY M. W. MONTAGU *Let. to Mrs. Thistlethwayte* 1 Apr., Their mosques are all of freestone, and the public hanns, or inns, extremely magnificent. **1903** *Westm. Gaz.* 10 Feb. 3/1 The *hans* are large, rambling inns, with a courtyard in the middle. **1920** *Q. Rev.* Apr. 395 Four hundred emaciated forms, the remnant of such convoys, are lying in one of the hans.

‖**khana** (ˈkɑːnə). *India.* [Hind. *khánā* food, dinner.] Food, a meal.

1859 G. F. ATKINSON *Curry & Rice* Plate 23 (*caption*) There, now, an invitation to dinner!—to a 'Burra Khanah', literally a grand feed. **1888** KIPLING *Phantom 'Rickshaw* 33 The *khansamah* went to get me food. He did not go through the pretence of calling it '*khana*'—man's victuals. **1933** *Discovery* Nov. 349/1 Vital ingredients for the preparation of the *khana* for the Sahib. **1953** E. M. FORSTER *Hill of Devi* 73 The cooking of our Indian khana. **1953** L. IREMONGER in *Caribbean Anthol. Short Stories* 19 At noon they would be eating their *khana*, sitting over the open fire.

khanate (ˈkæn-, ˈkɑːneɪt). Also **khanat.** [f. KHAN[1] + -ATE[1].] A district governed by a khan; the position of a khan.

1799 W. TOOKE *View Russian Emp.* II. 37 This state split..into several petty khanates. **1841** *Penny Cycl.* XX. 375/1 Samarcand is a town in Asia, in the khanat of Bokhara. **1849** E. B. EASTWICK *Dry Leaves* 74, I was forthwith employed to draw up a full report of his son's claim to the Khanate. **1893** MCCARTHY *Dictator* I. 80 In the Khanate of some Central Asian despot.

‖**khanda**, var. KHANJAR.

khandgea, variant of CANGIA, a Nile-boat.

1819 T. HOPE *Anastasius* ii. (1827) 31, I resolved, after three or four days march along the banks of the Nile, to contend with its adverse current, myself in a light khandgea.

khang, variant of CANG.

‖**khanga** (ˈkaŋgə). Also **kanga.** [Swahili.] In East Africa, a fabric printed in various colours and designs with borders, used esp. for women's clothing.

1967 *Sunday Times* 15 Jan. 31/5 *Kangas*..are the most riotous with words and even jokes printed on them. **1969** *Flamingo* (E. Afr.) x. 18/2 They often wear the two-piece dress, kanga, and this allows the smoke to pass everywhere. **1970** [see KITENGE]. **1971** *Daily Nation* (Nairobi) 10 Apr. 5/1 (Advt.), Kitenge Khanga Kikoy..at African Drapering. **1975** *Daily Tel.* 7 July 9 Khangas..come from Kenya, and are fine soft cotton rectangles about 60 in by 44 in, printed in literally hundreds of the most fabulous colours and designs... Wear them as a stunning beach dress or sarong type skirt knotted dead front.

‖**khanjar** (ˈkændʒə(r)). Also 7 **canjare**, 8 **-jer**, 8–9 **-jar**, 9 **-jiar, -giar, cunjur, khanda, kandjar, khunjur.** See also HANDJAR. [Pers. (Arab., Turk., Urdū) *khanjar, ḥanjar* dagger.] An Eastern dagger.

1684 J. PHILLIPS tr. *Tavernier's Trav.* I. II. III. 200 The Canjare which he had in his hand, was a kind of Dagger, the blade whereof toward the Handle was three fingers broad. **1797** *Encycl. Brit.* (ed. 3) XII. 346/2 A sabre and canjer (or dagger) worn in a bandelier. **1825** SCOTT *Talism.* xxvii, A sapphire, which terminated the hilt of his canjiar. **1828** *Kuzzilbash* I vii. 89 All wore the khunjur, or common dagger. **1845** LADY H. STANHOPE *Mem.* I. iii. 108, I always slept with a khanjàr..by my side. **1888** KIPLING *From Sea to Sea* (1899) I. vii. 53 'And what do you make in Udaipur?' 'Swords,' said the man..throwing down an armful of..*kuttars*, and *khandas*. **1957** *Encycl. Brit.* XX. 647/2 In that rite, with a two-edged dagger (*khanda*) sugar is stirred up in water. **1971** *Daily Tel.* 11 June 3 (*caption*) An alternative to the kirpan is the khanda, a small dagger.

‖**khanjee** (ˈkɑːndʒiː). Also **hanjee, khandjee, khanjhi.** [Turk. *khānjī*, f. *khān* KHAN[2] + *-jī*, agent-suffix.] The keeper of a khan or inn.

1839 MISS PARDOE *Beauties Bosphorus* 141 There is a certain foppery about the khanjhi of a first-rate Caravanserai. **1884** BOND in *Mission. Herald* (Boston) Dec. 515, I spent the last night at a village *khan*,..in the night the *khandjee* received a note from brigands, demanding £200. **1920** *Cornhill Mag.* Oct. 438 The hanjee was taking down his shutters.

‖**khansamah, -saman** (ˈkɑːnsamaː(n, kanˈsaːma(n). *East Ind.* Forms: 7 **consaorman**, 8 **chan-, caun-sumaun, consumma, -sumah**, (9 **-somah**), 8–9 **khaunsaman**, 9 **khaunsaumaun, khansama(h, kansamah.** [Urdū (Pers.) *khānsāmān*, f. *khān* master, ruler, KHAN[1] + *sāmān* household goods.] In India: A house-steward; a native male servant (usually a Muslim), the head of the kitchen and pantry department.

c **1645** HOWELL *Lett.* I. xxviii. (1705) 39, I met with Camillo your Consaorman here lately. **1759** in R. O. Cambridge *War in India* (1761) 231 Order, under the Chan Sumaun, or Steward's seal. *Ibid.* 232 Caun Samaun, or Steward to his Majesty. **1776** *Trial Joseph Fowke* 6/1, I put the arzee under the care of the Consumma. **1788** GLADWIN tr. *Mem. Kh. Abdulkurreem* 56 [He] asked the Khansaman, what quantity was remaining of the clothes. **1813–14** MRS. SHERWOOD *Lit. Henry & Bearer* 7 His mamma's khaunsaumaun had told him so. **1845** STOCQUELER *Handbk. Brit. India* (1854) 116 The khansama, or butler, acts the part which, in a moderate English establishment, is acted by the mistress and the cook together.

‖**khansu** (kanˈzu). Also **khanzu.** [Swahili *kanzu* shirt, f. Arab. *kasā* to clothe.] A loose outer garment worn in East Africa.

1969 M. HASTINGS *Killing in Black & White* i. 5 Steel watched the Africans in the street below. Only the older men..wore loose-fitting khanzus; the young favoured European dress. **1971** D. CREED *Trial of Lobo Icheka* I. ii. 23 Salim..went away, his white khansu swishing agitatedly about his legs. **1973** *Daily Tel.* (Colour Suppl.) 30 Nov. 63/1 A servant at a club was going to be wearing a *khanzu*, somewhat resembling a nightshirt.

‖**khanum** (ˈkɑːnəm). Also **caño, canum, hanim, hanum.** [Pers. *khānum*, Turk. *hanim*: see KHAN[1].] In the near East, a lady of rank, the wife of a khan. Also = Mrs., madam, as a title or term of address.

1824 J. MORIER *Adventures Hajji Baba* I. xxiv. 256 My situation is that of hand-maid to the *khanum*, so my mistress is called. **1826** LEYDEN & ERSKINE tr. *Mem. Zehir-Ed-Din* 12 The second daughter [of Shir Haji Beg], Kullûk Nigâr Khanum, was my mother. **1834** [see KHATUN]. **1848** J. H. STOCQUELER *Oriental Interpreter* 125/2 *Khanum*, the feminine of Khan, 'Lord', and signifies Lady, the wife of a Khan. **1859** C. R. MARKHAM tr. *Gonzalez de Clavijo's Narr. Embassy to Court of Timour* vi. 145 The first wall and tents were for the use of the chief wife of the lord, who was called *Caño*. **1900** *Daily News* 9 Jan. 7/2 The Queen of Greece..won the hearts of the Moslem feminine world by returning in person all the visits of the harem ladies..and was smothered with gifts from these enthusiastic hanums. **1929** *Spectator* 21 Aug. 276/1 Closely-veiled figures of Turkish *Khanums*. **1950** I. ORGA *Portrait of Turkish Family* xi. 123 Hasan..peered at my mother..and said uncertainly: 'I went to your house first... I did not know it was like that, hanim efendi...'

khapra (ˈkɑːprə). [ad. Hindi *khaprā* destroyer, f. *khapna* to destroy.] In full, ***khapra beetle.*** A small, brownish-black beetle, *Trogoderma granarium*, of the family Dermestidæ, native to India but widely found elsewhere as a pest of stored grain.

1896 E. C. COTES in *Indian Museum Notes* III. 119 It [*sc.* a dermestid beetle] is known as *Kapra* in the Delhi bazaar, where it is said sometimes to destroy as much as six or seven per cent. of wheat stored in godowns. **1928** *Bull. Entomol. Res.* XVIII. 251 (*title*) Investigations on the control of the Khapra beetle. **1955** *Hilgardia* XXIV. 1 The khapra beetle, *Trogoderma granarium* Everts, was first identified in the United States in stored wheat and barley..in October, 1953. **1959** *Jrnl. Econ. Entomol.* LII. 313/1 Each food sample was placed in a plastic cell with a single khapra-beetle egg. **1971** *New Scientist* 27 May 503/2 Khapra beetles may be baited by merely suspending large pieces of jute fabric on the top of the infested grain.

‖**kharaj** (kæˈrɑːdʒ), **khaˈratch.** [Arab. *kharāj*, in Egypt *kharāg*, in Turkish *kharātch* tribute.] Tribute; rent; poll-tax: see CARATCH.

1860 *Times* 25 June 10/6 The allegation that the word 'tribute' is incorrectly used..'kharatch' or 'poll-tax' being

the expression in the original. **1881** *Edin. Rev.* Apr. 342 Unable to pay their kharag or rent.

kharif (kæˈriːf). [(Hind. a.) Arab. *ḵarīf* gathered, autumn, harvest, autumnal rain.]

1. In India, the autumn crop, sown at the beginning of the summer rains.

1845 *Encycl. Metrop.* XXIII. 785/1 [Hindustan's] harvests..are equally profitable both in Spring (rabí) and Autumn (kharíf). **1882** W. W. Hunter *Indian Empire* 385 The *kharif* or autumn harvest. **1886** A. H. Church *Food-Grains India* 99 Where indigo is grown in the kharif, barley is its usual accompaniment in the rabi. **1911** *Encycl. Brit.* XXVII. 610/2 The *kharif*, or autumn crops, sown in June and reaped in October or November. **1969** *Pioneer* (Lucknow) 13 Aug. 2/3 There has been no kharif sowing in about 2,000 villages in Western Rajasthan due to failure of monsoon this year, according to official sources here. **1975** *Bangladesh Observer* 22 July 5/4 In spite of improved irrigation facilities most areas of India are dependent on rainfall for cultivation. Timely and adequate rainfall is essential for good kharif crops.

2. Also **khareef**. The rainy season in the Sudan.

1920 *Blackw. Mag.* Nov. 668/1 The gazelle here do not drink from khareef to khareef, a period of very nearly ten months. **1951** R. A. Hodgkin *Sudan Geogr.* ii. 10 If we plant a grass seed and a tree seed at the beginning of the *kharif* in a semi-desert they will both start to grow during the months of rain. *Ibid.* vi. 61 If there is..enough rain during..the *kharif*, there will be a good crop. **1961** L. D. Stamp *Gloss. Geogr. Terms* 280/1 *Kharif*, applied to the rainy season in the northern Sudan.

Kharoshti (kəˈrɒʃtɪ). Also **Kharoshthi, Kharosthi, Kharosti.** [Skr. *kharoṣṭī*.] The name of one of the two oldest alphabets in India, derived from Aramaic and used for about seven centuries from *c* 300 B.C. in north-western India. Cf. Brahmi.

1891 A. Cunningham *Coins Anc. India* 36 A script named *Kharosti*, which was read from right to left, is said to have been one of the forms taught to the youthful Buddha. *Ibid.* 37 As the name was derived from the inventor of the writing, I think it probable that the name of Zoroaster, or *Zardusht* himself, may have been preserved in the term *Kharosti*, as the inventor or introducer of that particular form of writing. The *Kharosti* alphabet, under this view of its origin, would naturally have penetrated into every country under Akhæmenian rule. **1902** [see Brahmi]. **1934** A. Toynbee *Study of Hist.* III. 130 In India, the Kharoshti script is certainly derived from the Aramaic alphabet. **1948** D. Diringer *Alphabet* II. v. 301 Many Indian scripts..exist to-day used for tongues belonging to various linguistic groups... All these scripts seem to have descended from two prototypes, the *Kharoshthi* and the *Brahmi*. **1958** L. Woolley *Hist. Unearthed* 123 The documents..were in strangely different scripts and languages... Many were in Kharoshthi, a script known from..inscriptions of north-west India. *Ibid.* 129 Most of the Kharoshthi documents were written on wooden tablets. **1972** W. B. Lockwood *Panorama Indo-Europ. Lang.* 193 Two alphabetic scripts were in use in ancient India. One of these, the Kharosthi,.. is found only from the middle of the third century B.C. to the third century A.D... It seems certain that the Brahmi script, like Kharosthi, also goes back to a Semitic model.

Khasi (ˈkɑːsɪ). Also †**Cossyah, Khas, Khasia(n), Khasiya.** [f. the name *Khasi* (see below).]

a. Name of a Mongoloid people found in the Khasi and Jaintia Hills in north-eastern India; also, an Indo-Aryan people inhabiting the hills of Kumaon and Garhwal; a member of one of these peoples. **b.** A language of the Mon-Khmer group spoken by them. Also *attrib.* or as *adj.*

1789 in Seton-Karr & Sandeman *Selections from Calcutta Gaz.* (1865) II. 218 We understand the Cossyahs, who inhabit the hills to the north-westward of Sylhet, have committed some very daring acts of violence. **1824** R. Heber *Narr. Journey Upper Provinces India* (1828) I. xvii. 479 The Khasiyah nation pretend to be all Rajpoots of the highest caste. **1855** W. Pryse *Introd. Khasia Lang.* p. iii, The Khasia or Cossyah is the dialect of a small tribe, reckoning.. somewhat under 200,000 souls. *Ibid.* p. vi, It is hoped that the majority of the Khasia words..will be found in the Vocabulary. **1882** *Encycl. Brit.* XIV. 295/1 The true Khas can be distinguished from the Laos only by the lobe of the ear. **1907** P. R. T. Gurdon *Khasis* 11 We can..suppose that the Khasis are an offshoot of the Mon people of Further India. **1911** *Encycl. Brit.* VIII. 830/2 In language 27,272,895 of the inhabitants [of Eastern Bengal and Assam] speak Bengali, 1,349,784 speak Assamese, and the remainder Hindi and various hill dialects, Manipuri, Bodo, Khasi and Garo. **1918** *Trans. Scottish Ecclesiol. Soc.* V. 230 A barbaric tribe of the Khasias burn their dead and raise to their honour menhirs... If a Khasian is in distress of any kind, he prays to some deceased ancestor. **1926** *Other Lands* July 151/2 There are six Khasis, five Nepalis, and two Lepchas from the Darjeeling Hills. **1936** *Discovery* July 205/2 The Khasis and Syntengs are an isolated group of the great Mon-Khmer family. **1937** H. W. Tilman *Ascent Nanda Devi* i. 7 The..Khasiyas, a race of a caste lower than the Brahmans or Rajputs..yet generally allowed to be also immigrants from an Aryan source, adore..the mountain god Siva. **1967** D. S. Parlett *Short Dict. Lang.* 73 *Khasi*,.. a dialect apparently transitional between Mon-Khmer and Munda language types.

khas-k(h)as: see khus-khus.

Khaskura (kɑːˈskuːrə). Also **Khaskra.** [Native name.] An Indic dialect spoken in Nepal.

1911 [see Gurkhali]. **1928** R. L. Turner in Northey & Morris *Gurkhas* iv. 70 The Indo-Aryan dialect,..variously called Khaskurā, Parbatiyā, Gurkhālī, or officially and preferably, Nepālī. **1943** E. Shipton *Upon that Mountain* vi. 112 We had two main occupations on the voyage out. One was to learn Khaskra, a language spoken by the Sherpas. **1950** T. Longstaff *This my Voyage* v. 93 Besides speaking Khaskura, the common tongue of Nepal. **1971** J. Pemble *Invasion of Nepal* i. 10 Nepali is but one dialect among a number of related tongues known generically as *Khas kura* (Khas speech) or *Parbatiya* (relating to the hills). Modern Nepali is often referred to by either of these names.

khassadar (ˈkæsədɑː(r)). Also **kassidar.** [Native name.] In the border region of north-western India and Afghanistan, a local militiaman (see quots. 1930 and 1950).

1901 T. H. Holdich *Indian Borderland* xii. 273 An Afghan force of about 1,000 men, half of whom were Kassidars (irregulars)... The Kassidars were but half-trained troops. **1909** *Daily Chron.* 13 Apr. 3/5 The Khyber Pass will be closed to caravans..due to the aggressive attitude of the Khassadars, or Militia, on the Afghan border. **1923** *Glasgow Herald* 16 July 6 The object of the murder is to discredit the Khassadar movement. **1930** *Aberdeen Press & Jrnl.* 22 Apr. 5/2 The khassadar is an extremely irregular soldier, performing a sort of police duty on caravan routes on the North-West Frontier. **1950** W. K. Fraser-Tytler *Afghanistan* xiii. 260 Khassadars were tribal police responsible for the general safety of the roads running through the areas of their respective tribes. **1965** K. P. S. Menon *Many Worlds* 94 These outposts are manned by Khassadars, a kind of irregular tribal police, formed for the purpose of enforcing the security of the road.

khat, var. kat.

‖**khatak** (kæˈtɑːk). Also **khata, khatag.** [Tibetan *k'a-btågs* a scarf of salutation.] In Tibet, a scarf presented to visitors.

[**1863** E. Schlagintweit *Buddhism in Tibet* xiii. 190 The silken scarfs inscribed with sentences which Tibetan politeness requires should be offered by visitors or enclosed in letters..are called in Tibetan Khatak, or Tashi Khatak, 'scarf of benediction'.] **1902** *Daily Chron.* 23 Oct. 3/1 Having presented his *khatag*, and placed in the lap of the Dalai Lama a piece of gold..he took his seat..about ten feet distant from the Grand Lama. **1960** 'S. Harvester' *Chinese Hammer* vii. 70 The traditional ceremony of exchanging white silk *khatas*, scarf tokens of goodwill usually decorated with swastikas.

khatib (kæˈtiːb). Also **khateb.** [ad. Arab. *ḵaṭīb*.] A Muslim preacher; one who recites the khutbah.

1625 Purchas *Pilgrimes* II. ix. xix. 1661 These Atollons are subdiuided into many Ilands, in each of which..is a Doctor called Catibe, superior in the Religion of that Ile, who hath vnder him the particular Priests of the Moschees. **1821** J. Leyden tr. *Malay Annals* v. 50 The letter was read by the khateb. **1839** T. J. Newbold *Pol. & Statistical Acct. Straits of Malacca* I. v. 249 The Khatib..recites the khatbeh, an oration or sermon, in praise of God..on Friday, in the mosque. **1875** T. P. Hughes *Notes Muhammadanism* 131 The Khatib or preacher then seats himself on the *Mimbar* (pulpit). **1971** R. Lewis *Everyday Life in Ottoman Turkey* 43 The khatib, who delivered the Friday sermon and led the invocation of God's protection on the Sultan and his family.

‖**Khatri** (ˈkætriː, ˈkʌtriː). Also 7 **cuttery, quetery,** 8 **katri, khettrie, kittree,** 9 **ketra, khatrí.** [Hindī *khatrī*:—Skr. *kshatriya*.] A member of the second or military caste among the Hindus (cf. Kshatriya).

1630 Lord *Banians & Persees* i. 5 And because Cuttery was of a Martiall temper, God gaue him power to sway kingdomes with the Scepter. **1665** Sir T. Herbert *Trav.* (1677) 52 The *Cutteries*..being men of War they scruple not to shed blood, eat flesh, and..are for the most part called Rajaes or great men. **1698** Fryer *Acc. E. India & P.* 193 Opium is frequently eaten in great quantities by the Rashpoots, Queteries, and Patans. **1723** R. Millar *Hist. Propag. Chr.* II. vii. 208 The Katris are degenerate into Merchants. **1776** *Trial of Nundocomar* 36/1 Another letter came to me with a peon and kittree, from Roopnarrain Chowdree. **1814** W. Brown *Hist. Propag. Chr.* II. 170 The Hindoos were originally divided into 4 casts or tribes; the Brahmin, the Ketra, the Bice, and the Sooder. **1885** *Panjab Notes & Q.* II. 75/1 These ceremonies are observed by Bráhmans, Khatrís, and Baises.

Khatti, var. Kheta.

‖**khatun** (ˈkɑːtuːn). Also **kadun.** [Pers.] A lady. Also used as a title of courtesy.

1834 J. Morier *Ayesha* I. iv. 80 She once made the sign of the cross..but now she is a kadûn—a khanûm, a head of a harem. **1927** *Blackw. Mag.* Nov. 687/2 My wife and other senior *khatuns*. **1959** P. N. Bazaz *Daughters of Vitasta* vi. 144 The next queen to be noticed by contemporary historians is Gul Khatun. *Ibid.* vii. 153 The last of the Muslim queens to whose harem was Habba Khatun.

khaya (ˈkaɪjə, ˈkeɪjə). [mod.L. (A. de Jussieu 1830, in *Mém. Mus. Hist. Nat.* XIX. 249), ad. Wolof *khaye*.] A tropical African tree of the genus so called, belonging to the family Meliaceæ; the timber of a tree of this kind, better known as African mahogany.

1910 H. Thompson *Gold Coast: Rep. Forests* 38 in *Parl. Papers* (Cd. 4993) LXV. 201 *Khayas* and *Pseudocedrelas* were frequently met with in this direction [*sc.* to the east of N'kwansia]. **1916** C. E. Lane-Poole *List of Trees Sierra Leone* 53 The Khayas yield the African Mahogany so esteemed in Europe. **1936** J. D. Kennedy *Forest Flora S. Nigeria* 157 A characteristic of *Khaya* seedlings is the very long drip-tip on the primary leaves. **1956** *Handbk. Hardwoods* (Forest Prod. Res. Lab.) 138 Mahogany, African... Other names..khaya (United States). **1962** Watt & Breyer-Brandwijk *Medicinal & Poisonous Plants S. & E. Afr.* (ed. 2) 1406/3 *Khaya grandifoliola*... African mahogany, Bigleaf mahogany (Uganda), Khaya mahogany. *Ibid.*, *Khaya nyasica*... Khaya mahogany. **1964** R. W. J. Keay et al. *Nigerian Trees* II. 259 Although known to the trade as 'Benin Mahogany', this species [sc. *Khaya grandifolia*] is not the typical Khaya of the southern Benin forests.

Khazar (kəˈzɑː(r)). Also **Chazar, Chozar, Khozar.** [Heb.] A member of a people of Turkish origin who from the 8th to the 10th or 11th century occupied a large part of southern Russia. Also *attrib.*

1854 J. H. Newman *Lect. Hist. Turks* II. i. 63 The horde of Chozars, as this Turkish tribe was called,..transported their tents..into Georgia. **1854** R. G. Latham *Native Races Russ. Empire* x. 143 The Khazars poured themselves over eastern Europe in the 7th, 8th, 9th, 10th, and 11th centuries. **1863** [see Turkic *a.*]. **1878** R. G. Latham *Russian & Turk* viii. 210 The Khazars seem to play the same part in the history of Eastern Russia that the Avars played in that of Southern Bavaria... We meet the term *Chazaria* as the land of the *Khazars*. **1882** *Encycl. Brit.* XIV. 60/1 Merchants from every nation found protection..in the Khazar cities. **1903** *Jewish Encycl.* IV. 1/1 The Chazars..established themselves in the territory bounded by the Sea of Azov, the Don and the lower Volga. **1930** C. A. Macartney *Magyars in 9th Cent.* 62 From a short time after the arrival of the Khazars, the Cuban Bulgars disappear from history. **1934** A. G. Chater tr. *Undset's Stages on Road* i. 29 The Khozars of the Crimea..were Tartars who had been converted to Judaism and were ruled by a Jewish king. **1952** E. Hyams *Soil & Civilization* 171 The Jewish religion was adopted by the Chazar princes. **1965** [see Bulgar *sb.*].

‖**kheda, keddah** (ˈkeɪdə, ˈkɛdə). Also **khedda(h), (kiddah).** [Hindī *khedā*.] An enclosure used in Bengal, Assam, etc., for the capture of wild elephants; corresp. to the corral of Sri Lanka.

1799 Corse in *Phil. Trans.* LXXXIX. 38 She was driven by Mr. Leeke's elephant hunters into a keddah. **1827** D. Johnson *Ind. Field Sports* 55 Elephants are numerous,.. The principal Keddah for catching them is in the district of Tipperah. **1879** F. Pollok *Sport Brit. Burmah* I. 80, I remember, when kheddahs were started in Burmah, nearly a hundred elephants had been driven into an inclosure. **1889** *Daily News* 27 Nov. 5/4 A kheda..has been formed in the jungle near an elephant cover.

‖**Khedive** (kɪˈdiːv). (Also 7 quiteue.) *Hist.* [a. F. *khédive*, a. Turk. (from Pers.) *khedīv*, *khidēv* prince, sovereign.] The title of the viceroy or ruler of Egypt, accorded to Ismail Pasha in 1867 by the Turkish government.

[**1625** Purchas *Pilgrims* II. iv. 1537 (Stanf.) He is called Quiteue a title royall and no proper name.] **1867** *Times* 24 May 11/1 At a council of the Turkish Cabinet, held on the 14th inst., the title to be granted to the Pasha of Egypt was at length definitely settled. His Highness is to be called 'Khedive', which is regarded as the Arabic equivalent of 'King'. **1878** *N. Amer. Rev.* CXXVI. 187 A description..of the political system of the khedive. **1892** Milner *Eng. in Egypt* 44 The power of the Khedive is an emanation from the power of the Sultan.

Hence **Khediva** (-ˈdiːvə), **Khediviah** (-ˈdiːvɪə) [Arab. *khedīvyah*], wife of the Khedive; **Kheˈdival, Kheˈdivial** *a.*, of or pertaining to the Khedive; **Kheˈdivate, Kheˈdiviate**, the office, authority, or government of the Khedive.

1890 *Daily News* 7 Feb. 5/4 Miss E. M. Merrick..last year had the honour of painting a portrait of her Highness the Khediviah. **1899** *Ibid.* 4 Dec. 6/3 The Khedivah, the Khedivah mère, and their enormous entourage. **1882** *Sat. Rev.* 17 June 749/1 The Khedival and Turkish portion of the Government got away..to Alexandria. **1882** *Standard* 24 July 5 The fine Khedivial Library..grew..into a collection of fame. **1880** *Daily News* 12 July 5/6 It seems almost as though Midhat Pacha wishes to establish a Khediviate in Syria, with himself as Khedive. **1892** *Times* 15 Apr. 3/1 Turkish intrigues for reducing Egypt from the status of a Khedivat..to a vilayet.

khellin (ˈkɛlɪn). Also †**kellin.** [Orig. coined as F. *kelline* (I. Mustapha 1879, in *Compt. Rend.* LXXXIX. 442), f. *kell*, given as the Arabic name of *Ammi visnaga*; the *h* originated with Samaan (1931), who gave the Arabic name as *khella*: see -in[1].] A tricyclic crystalline compound, $C_{14}H_{12}O_5$, obtained from the fruit of the North African umbelliferous plant *Ammi visnaga* and formerly used in the treatment of angina pectoris.

The name was orig. given to the glucoside of this compound.

1879 *Jrnl. Chem. Soc.* XXXVI. 1041 The author proposes for this glucoside the name *kellin*, from the Arabic name of the Ammi Visnaga. **1931** K. Samaan in *Q. Jrnl. Pharmacy* IV. 14 Ibrahim Mostapha described a crystalline principle which he named Khellin. **1938** *Chem. Abstr.* XXXII. 2120 Fantl and Salem..obtained from the fruits of *Ammi visnaga* a compd., kellin, $C_{14}H_{12}O_5$. **1947** *Lancet* 26 Apr. 557/2 Khellin causes a conspicuous and long relaxation of all the visceral smooth muscle—the intestines, uterus, bile-ducts, bronchi, and especially ureters. *Ibid.*, In 1945 a fresh interest in khellin arose as the result of the discovery that it acts as an extremely potent coronary vasodilator which, in doses used, has no effect on the general blood-pressure and does not increase the oxygen requirements of the heart. **1957** M. Plotz *Coronary Heart Dis.* xvii. 301/2 Favorable results with khellin therapy in man have been reported by many investigators. *Ibid.*, The most important factor limiting the use of khellin orally has been the high incidence of toxic reactions. **1964** *To-Day's Drugs* (B.M.A.) 132 Khellin had a brief period of popularity about ten years ago, but when the drug was evaluated by controlled clinical trials and by objective methods it was found that it was no better than a placebo.

khemkaub, khettrie, Khevenhuller, var. KINCOB, KHATRI, KEVENHULLER.

‖**khet** (keɪt). [Hind., Hindi.] In India, a tract of cultivated land.

1878 P. ROBINSON *In my Indian Garden* 176 In the still air could be heard..from the scattered *khets*, the bark of the prowling fox. **1886** —— *Valley of Teetotum Trees* 63 In all the swampy jheels and crop-grown khets. **1922** *19th Cent.* Oct. 589 The land is divided by one broad distinction into the khet and the jungle—that is to say, into the cultivated and the wild.

Kheta (ˈkɛtə, ˈxɛtə). Also **Khatti, Khita.** [Egyptian name.] Name of an ancient people and kingdom in the Near East: now usually equated with the Hittites. See HITTITE *sb.* and *a.*

1884 W. WRIGHT *Empire of Hittites* ii. 19 The war between Egypt and Kheta was brought to a close by a treaty of peace concluded between Rameses I. and Saplel the Hittite king. **1890** T. ELY *Man. Archæol.* v. 76 On the monuments [of the Hittites] the name *Khita, Kheta*, or *Khatti*..frequently occurs. **1948** D. DIRINGER *Alphabet* 89 Egyptian inscriptions mention the powerful Kheta-empire. **1952** O. R. GURNEY *Hittites* 2 Who could doubt that the Kheta-folk of the Egyptian texts and the Hittites of the Old Testament were one and the same? **1957** *Encycl. Brit.* XI. 599/1 Egyptian evidence shows that in the time of the 18th to the 20th dynasties, between the years 1500–1190 B.C., a powerful northern kingdom *Kheta* sought perpetually to obtain political influence over Syria and therefore often fought with Egypt. Already the Pharaoh Thutmosis III. (1501–1447), who had conquered Syria as far as the Upper Euphrates, received presents from the prince of Kheta. **1970** BRAY & TRUMP *Dict. Archaeol.* 104 *Hittites, Hatti* or (to the Egyptians) *Kheta*, a people who infiltrated Anatolia and in smaller numbers the Levant from the north *c* 2000 BC, but the details of their origin are more than somewhat obscure.

‖**khidmutgar** (ˈkɪdmʌtgɑː(r)). Also 8–9 **kid-, kis(t)-,** 9 **k(h)itmutgar;** 8 **khidmidgar,** 9 **khid-, khitmatgar, khid-, khed-, khitmutghar, khitmutkar,** etc. [Urdū (from Pers.) *khidmatgār*, = *khidmat* service + *-gār*, agent-suffix.] In India: A male servant who waits at table.

1765 HOLWELL *Hist. Events* (1766) I. 60 They were taken into the service of Soujah Dowla..: Hodjee, in capacity of his first Kistmutgar (or valet). **1776** *Trial of Nundocomar* 56/1 *Q.* Who came with Bollakey Doss? *A.* He came alone, only his kidmutgar. **1824** [SHERER] *Sketches in India* 247 His father had been a Khidmutgar to a British Colonel. **1873** MISS THACKERAY *Wks.* (1891) I. 269–70 A Kitmutghar who had drained off a bottle of her eau-de-Cologne.

Khilafat (kɪˈlɑːfət). [ad. Arab. *ḵilāfat* caliphate, office or rule of a caliph.] The spiritual headship of Islam, residing in the person of the Turkish Sultan; used *attrib.* to designate the Muslim anti-British movement in India after the treaty of Sèvres in 1920. Hence **Khila·fatist,** a supporter of this agitation.

1921 [see EXTREMIST]. **1923** *Edin. Rev.* Jan. 182 The *Khilâfat*..is the Vice-gerency of the Prophet. **1925** *Contemp. Rev.* Apr. 430 An influential section of the Moslem community, dissociating itself from the Khilafatist section. **1926** *Encycl. Brit.* Suppl. II. 429/2 The 'Khilāfat' agitation. **1950** R. C. MAJUMDAR et al. *Adv. Hist. India* (ed. 2) 985 The two brothers Muhammad Ali and Shaukat Ali, and Maulana Abul Kalam Azad organized a mass movement of the Muslims known as the Khilafat movement. **1957** M. D. KENNEDY *Short Hist. Communism in Asia* vi. 58 The movement thus launched for creating disaffection among Moslems in India was known as the Khilafat movement. **1964** A. SWINSON *Six Minutes to Sunset* ix. 163 Nair and many others considered that it had been Gandhi's espousal of the Khilafat cause which had triggered off the rebellion. **1972** P. HARDY *Muslims of Brit. India* 190 The philosophy of the *Khilafat* movement was not that of territorial nationalism, but of community federalism, and of a federalism wherein one party, the Muslim, looked outside the common habitat, India, for the *raison d'être* of the federal relationship.

‖**khilat, khelat** (ˈkɪlʌt). *East Ind.* Forms: 7 **calaat, collat,** 8 **kall-, kellaut,** 8–9 **khilat, khelaut,** 9 **khelat, khellât, khillaut, calatte, (khelut, khillut, killut, -laut).** [Urdū (Pers.) *khilʿat, khalʿat*, a. Arab. *khilʿah (-at).*] A dress of honour presented by a king or other dignitary as a mark of distinction to the person receiving it; hence, any handsome present made by an acknowledged superior.

1684 J. PHILLIPS tr. *Tavernier's Trav.* I. III. v. 108 The Garment of Honour, or the Calaat, the Bonnet, and Girdle. **1698** FRYER *Acc. E. India & P.* 87 He had a Collat or Seerpaw, a Robe of Honour from Head to Foot, offered him from the Great Mogul. **1774** BOGLE in Markham *Narr. Mission Tibet* (1876) 25 A flowered satin gown was brought me. I was dressed in it as a *khilat*. **1803** EDMONSTONE in Owen *Mrq. Wellesley's Desp.* (1877) 325 He is admitted to the privilege of investing the Peishwa with a khelaut. **1845** STOCQUELER *Handbk. Brit. India* (1854) 239 The king.. maintains the royal privilege of conferring *khillauts.* **1876** JAS. GRANT *Hist. India* I. xxxvii. 191/1 No peishwa could be appointed without first receiving the *khelat.* **1886** YULE, *Killut, Killaut.*

Khilim, var. KILIM.

Khirbet Kerak (ˈkɜːbət ˈkɛrək). *Archæol.* Name of a town on the south-west edge of Lake Tiberias in Syria, used *attrib.* to designate a type of early Bronze Age pottery first found there in the 1940s, which is red and black in colour with highly burnished finish and fluted decorations.

1949 W. F. ALBRIGHT *Archaeol. of Palestine* iv. 76 The most interesting new pottery of this age is the lustrous red and black burnished 'Khirbet Kerak' ware, which first became known at the site which bore this name, ancient Beth-Yerah, at the south-west corner of the Sea of Galilee. **1952** V. G. CHILDE *New Light Most Anc. East* xi. 219 The pottery includes wheel-made red-slipped and lattice-burnished vases and—but only in the last phase of a long occupation—hand-made particoloured black and red vases of 'Khirbet Kerak ware'. **1960** K. M. KENYON *Archaeol. in Holy Land* v. 124 Side by side with the native wares are vessels of Khirbet Kerak ware... This type of pottery is also found in northern Syria. **1968** *Encycl. Brit.* II. 610/2 This Khirbet Kerak ware is characteristically Anatolian, but is distinguished by its ornament of ribs and flutings and of raised geometrical patterns, especially spirals.

Khirgese, var. KIRGHIZ *sb.* and *a.*

Khita, var. KHETA.

khiva, var. KIVA.

Khlist (xlɪst). Also **Chlist, Khlyst.** Pl. **Chlists, Khlisti, Khlysts, Khlysty.** [Russ., lit. a whip.] A member of a sect of ascetic Russian Christians, formed in the 17th century, who believed that Christ could be reincarnated in human beings through their suffering.

1856 R. FARIE tr. *A. von Haxthausen's Russ. Empire* I. viii. 254 On Easter night the Skoptzi and Khlisti all assemble for a great solemnity, the worship of the Mother of God. **1874** J. H. BLUNT *Dict. Sects* 250/1 *Khlisti*, a name signifying 'Flagellants' given to a Russian sect..formed about 1645 by a deserter from the army named Daniel Philipitch. **1920** A. PAGET tr. *Nekludoff's Diplomatic Reminisc.* vii. 71 Rasputin was in fact a *Khlyst, i.e.* half 'Shaker', half Flagellant—a strange sect which from time to time rises in Russia from the common depths to the upper classes of society. **1929** A. HUXLEY *Do what you Will* 152 None but heretics have preached it [*sc.* humility]. The Russian Khlyst, for example. *Ibid.* 153 Rasputin practised what he preached, and sinned —most conspicuously, as was the custom of the Khlysty, in relation to the seventh commandment. **1967** D. T. KAUFFMAN *Dict. Relig. Terms.* 274 *Khlysts, Chlists*, or *Klysty flagellants*, Russian ascetics originating in the seventeenth century.

Khmer (k(ə)mɛə(r)), *sb.* and *a.* [Native name.] **A.** *sb.* **a.** A native or inhabitant of the ancient kingdom of Khmer in south-east Asia, which reached the peak of its power in the 11th century and was destroyed by Siamese conquests in the 12th and 14th centuries; also (from 1863) such a person in Cambodia; subsequently, a native or inhabitant of the Khmer Republic (established 1970). **b.** The monosyllabic language of this people, belonging to the Mon-Khmer group of the Austro-Asiatic family. **B.** *adj.* Of or pertaining to the Khmers or their language.

1876 *Encycl. Brit.* IV. 723/2 The name given by the people of Camboja to their own race is *Khmér.* **1881** C. J. F. S. FORBES *Compar. Gram. Lang. Further India* I. iv. 48 The Cambodians acknowledge..the Kouys, as the most ancient stock, and style them the 'Khmerdom', or ancient Khmers. **1921** *Edin. Rev.* July 172 If the Khmêrs were the ancient people of Cambodia, here we have an important land mark in common between them and the Khasis. **1921** E. SAPIR *Lang.* iv. 71 The use of prefixed elements to the complete exclusion of suffixes, is far less common. A good example is Khmer (or Cambodgian). **1932** W. L. GRAFF *Lang.* 417 Mon-Khmer comprises the three civilized languages Mon, Khmer, and Cham. **1943** *Burlington Mag.* Aug. 198/1 Of imitations of Khmer bronzes, on the other hand, a number have passed through my hands. **1959** *Chambers's Encycl.* VII. 499/2 What the Khmer and Indians called this state is not known. **1966** *Listener* 22 Sept. 409/1 The Khmers, as the people of Cambodia are known, have a maturity about their nationalism. **1967** *Economist* 23 Sept. 1088/1 Prince Sihanouk has been at odds with the Chinese since April, when he accused the *Khmers rouges*, his local communists, and their foreign friends of launching a guerrilla campaign in north-western Cambodia. **1970** *Guardian* 5 May 9/5 The men were being lectured, in both French and Khmer, on tactical formations. **1970** M. PEREIRA *Pigeon's Blood* iv. 48 The closest resemblance..was the medieval Khmer craftsmanship of Cambodia. **1971** *Nat. Geographic* Mar. 316/1 When the Khmer people were docile, the Vietnamese would withdraw all but a token force. **1972** M. SHEPPARD *Taman Indera* 6 Funan was eventually conquered by a Khmer prince of Kambuja,..in the middle of the sixth century. **1973** *Times* 10 Apr. 6/7 Khmer Rouge and Vietcong guerrillas have launched several rocket attacks.

Khoikhoi (ˈkɔɪkɔɪ). *S. Afr.* Also **Khoi Khoi, Khoi Khoin, †Quaiquae,** etc. [Hottentot, lit. 'men of men'.] The Hottentots' name for themselves; also used by others in the sense 'Hottentots'; the language which they speak. Also *attrib.* or as *adj.*

1791 tr. *Le Vaillant's Travels into Interior Parts of Africa* II. 154 A Hottentot man..Khoé-Khoep. **1801** J. BARROW *Acct. Trav. S. Afr.* I. iii. 151 [The name] by which the whole nation was distinguished, and which at this moment they bear among themselves in every part of the country, is *Quaiquae.* **1880** *Encycl. Brit.* XII. 309/2 The common denomination adopted by themselves was Khoi-Khoin (men of men). **1881** T. HAHN *Tsuni‖Goam* i. 1 These Khoikhoi generally go by the name of *Hottentots. Ibid.* 5 The Khoikhoi language is entirely void of prefixes. **1897** A. J. BUTLER tr. *Ratzel's Hist. Mankind* II. 247 The Khoi-Khoi (Bushmen and Hottentot) group of languages. **1910** G. M. THEAL *Yellow & Dark-Skinned People of Afr.* iv. 79 Those destitute Hottentots..had more Bushman than pure Khoikhoi blood in their veins. **1930** I. SCHAPERA *Khoisan Peoples of S. Afr.* i. 5 The term [*sc.* Khoisan] is compounded of the names *Khoi-Khoin*, by which the Hottentots call themselves, and *San*, applied by the Hottentots to the Bushmen. **1969** *Oxf. Hist. S. Afr.* I. i. 10 Blood group studies suggest, however, that certain Khoikhoi speakers are closely allied in their blood-group patterns to African negroids. *Ibid.* ii. 43 There were also groups of herders, most of whom spoke Khoikhoi. *Ibid.* 56 The Khoikhoi may have been shepherds before they were cattle-men.

‖**Khoja** (ˈkəʊdʒə). Forms: 7 **hoiah, hodgee, -gia, hugie, hoggie,** 7–8 **hogi,** 8 **hoage, hogia, cojah,** 9 **hoja(h, hodja, khodgea, khodja, -djo, khoja.** [Turk. and Pers. *khōjah*, prop. *khwājah.*]

1. A professor or teacher in a Muslim school or college; a schoolmaster; a scribe, clerk.

1625 PURCHAS *Pilgrims* IX. xv. §8. II. 1598 From fiue yeers of age vntill ten..they haue their Hoiah (that is, their Schoole-master) appointed them by the King to teach them. **1630** *R. Johnson's Kingd. & Commw.* 525 The third, are Hogi, Writers of Bookes; for they have no Printing. **1704** J. PITTS *Acc. Mahometans* 21 Rides in the Van of the Army, with two Hoages, or Clerks. **1786** *Art. Charge W. Hastings* in Burke *Writ.* (1852) VII. 27, I sent for Retafit Ali Khân, the Cojah. **1834** *Ayesha* I. xi. 265 They collected all that the city possessed of wisdom and learning,—Khodjas, Mollahs, Hakims, Imams. **1887** *L'pool Daily Post* 14 Feb. 5/4 This last savant brings a Khoja, who has just arrived from Bombay.

2. A member of a Muslim sect of converts from Hinduism, found mainly in western India and retaining some Hindu customs. Also *attrib.*

1882 *Encycl. Brit.* XIV. 64/1 Only the military class, the priesthood, and the khodjas are exempt from the payment of taxes. The khodjas consider themselves descendants of the prophet. **1921** C. ELIOT *Hinduism & Buddhism* III. lviii. 455 The sects known as Khojas and Bohras owe their conversion to the zeal of Arab and Persian missionaries who preached in the eleventh century. **1931** G. MACMUNN *Relig. & Hidden Cults India* 97 A portion of the Assassins escaped to India where they have developed into a wealthy trading fraternity known generally as the Khojas or 'worthy men'. **1937** L. BROMFIELD *Rains Came* I. vi. 41 The prospect of putting over a sharp deal in Bombay on the Khojas and Parsees. **1970** D. G. MANDELBAUM *Soc. in India* II. VII. xxix. 555 There are several Isma'ili jatis, the Bohras and Khojas of Gujarat being the major groups among them... Khoja doctrine held..that the Aga Khan was an incarnation of the 'glorious Tenth Avatar'.

khoker, var. KOKER.

Khond (kɒnd). Also **Kandh, Kond, Kondh.** [Native name.] **a.** A Dravidian people inhabiting Orissa in eastern India; one of this people. **b.** The language spoken by the Khonds. Also *attrib.* or as *adj.*

1852 S. C. MACPHERSON in *Jrnl. R. Asiatic Soc.* XIII. 217 The ancient state of Orissa was formed chiefly from the territories of..the Khonds, the Koles, and the Sourahs. *Ibid.* 221 The Khond religion exists in oral traditions alone. **1867** [see GOND *sb.* and *a.*]. **1881** *Encycl. Brit.* XII. 778/2 Bishop Caldwell recognizes twelve distinct Dravidian languages:—(1) Tamil,..(10) Khond. **1909** E. THURSTON *Castes & Tribes S. India* III. 398 A Kondh funeral dance in the Ganjam Māliahs. **1937** H. G. RAWLINSON *India* viii. 128 Among the Khonds, one of the primitive tribes, a human victim known as the *meriah* was until recently sacrificed in order to secure fertility for the fields. **1946** R. C. MAJUMDAR et al. *Adv. Hist. India* 826 To the first Lord Hardinge's Government belongs the credit of taking steps to stop the human sacrifices practised by the Khonds in Orissa. **1959** *Chambers's Encycl.* VII. 480/2 The most eastern member of the Central group [of Dravidian languages] is the language of the Khonds or Kandhs. *Ibid.* X. 244/2 The most interesting of the aboriginal races are the Konds. **1970** D. G. MANDELBAUM *Soc. in India* II. xxii. 422 His trade is carried on with men of the Kond tribe who are rated as a clean jati by the neighbouring Oriyas.

khookheri, obs. form of KUKRI.

‖**khor** (kɔː(r)). [Arab. *khurr, khorr.*] A watercourse, ravine, nullah, dry bed of a stream.

1884 *Times* 28 Mar. 5 Our route lay..along the bottom of the valley leading to the khor. *Ibid.*, The khor winds considerably, and splits into two or three smaller ravines. **1896** *Westm. Gaz.* 12 June 2/1 A swarm of Arabs came down upon them through a neighbouring khor.

Khorassan (kɒrəˈsɑːn). Also **-asan, Khurasan.** Name of a province in north-east Iran, used *attrib.* and *ellipt.* to designate a carpet or rug made there, usu. with vivid colouring and fine silky texture.

1900 J. K. MUMFORD *Oriental Rugs* xi. 218 The realism which marks certain carpets of the Feraghan group is fairly outdone in many of the proper Khorassans. **1904** M. B. LANGTON *How to know Oriental Rugs* ii. 68 The Khorasan is a most satisfactory rug, beautiful in colour, durable, and pliable. **1931** A. U. DILLEY *Oriental Rugs & Carpets* Pl. 25 (*caption*) Khorassan Prayer Rug. Characteristic minute floral pattern, Herati, with border of narrow bands. **1931** C. TATTERSALL *Carpets of Persia* 39 Mashhad. Much like Khorasans, but with shorter and closer pile. **1962** C. W. JACOBSEN *Oriental Rugs* 238 No rugs have been imported as Khurasans in the past 20 years. **1971** K. WATSON tr. *Hubel's Bk. Carpets* 213 Another peculiarity of the ground-weave of the Khorassan carpet is the weft: the thick straight weft is covered by the thin sinuous weft threads accompanying it.

Khotan (kəʊˈtɑːn). Also **Khoten.** Name of a city and district on the south of the Takla Makan desert in Chinese Turkestan, used *attrib.* and *ellipt.* to designate a carpet or rug made there,

usu. with Chinese geometrical patterns or stylized natural designs.

1871 R. B. SHAW *Visits to High Tartary* xii. 259 There is a large covered reception-place with a verandah in front of all. Here an immense Khoten carpet is spread with rugs along the back. **1899** KIPLING *From Sea to Sea* I. xvi. 362 The English can only be artistic in spots and by way of the art of other nations—Sicilian tapestries, Persian saddle-bags, Khoten carpets. **1904** M. B. LANGTON *How to know Oriental Rugs* viii. 228 Bayard Taylor, in his Travels, speaks of the beautiful Khotan carpets which were spread on divans in the 'royal rest' rooms near Yarkand. **1920** E. & P. SYKES *Through Deserts & Oases Cent. Asia* iv. 82 The old Khotan carpets, their colours made from vegetable dyes, were attractive, and the silk carpets are highly prized and very difficult to obtain. **1931** A. U. DILLEY *Oriental Rugs & Carpets* x. 224 Khotan rugs of the ancient vintage, with geometric blocked design, numerous borders, half-Chinese and half-Persian,..are the outstanding jewels of the Chinese Turkestan family. **1960** G. & C. W. DIGBY tr. *Haack's Oriental Rugs* vii. 56 Kashgar and Khotan are the names by which these carpets are more properly known; they show a strong Chinese influence in their design. **1967** *Times* 21 Feb. 21/4 (Advt.), An extremely rare and beautiful 18th century Khotan carpet, 12 ft. 7 in. × 7 ft. 4 in.

Khotanese (kəʊtə'ni:z), *sb.* and *a.* [f. *Khotan* (see prec.) + -ESE.] **A.** *sb.* The people of Khotan; one of this people; the Middle Iranian language of Khotan. **B.** *adj.* Of or pertaining to Khotan.

1882 *Encycl. Brit.* XIV. 67/2 The Khotanese keep camels, horses..and fowls. **1907** A. STEIN *Anc. Khotan* I. 141 It is a point of special interest that dancing..is a pastime freely indulged in by Khotanese of both sexes and of all classes. *Ibid.* 144 In the case of the Khotanese there has been, besides a slight admixture of Turkī blood, an admixture also of Tibetan. **1939** C. H. GRAY *Foundations of Lang.* 320 Besides Middle Persian proper, we have a fair amount of material in some other Middle Iranian dialects, notably Middle Parthian..and Khotanese or Middle Sakian..in the southern part of East Turkistān. **1948** D. DIRINGER *Alphabet* II. vi. 350 The material contained in Khotanese manuscripts is of great variety; there are official and business documents, translations of Indian tales, [etc.]. *Ibid.*, There are some indications to show that Khotanese began to be used in writing in the second century A.D. **1957** *Archivum Linguisticum* IX. II. 128 The most likely source would seem to be Khotanese. **1961** H. W. BAILEY *Khotanese Texts* IV. 14 The Buddhist literature of which complete or partial translations existed in Khotanese is of large extent. *Ibid.* 17 A celebrated Khotanese painter of Buddhist subjects.

khotbah, -beh, variants of KHUTBAH.

Khowar ('kəʊwɑ:(r)). A Dardic language spoken in Chitral in north-west Pakistan. Also *attrib.* or as *adj.*

1882 *Encycl. Brit.* XIV. 9/2 Their [*sc.* inhabitants of Chitral's] language, *Khowâr*, is closely allied to the dialects of the Kafir tribes. **1950** T. LONGSTAFF *This my Voyage* x. 199 The singing must be in Khowar, the tongue of Chitral, which sounds like Romany. **1964** *Language* XL. 304 A native Khowar speaker. **1967** D. S. PARLETT *Short Dict. Lang.* 73 *Khowar*.., 7 th[ousand] speakers of a dialect in N.W. India related to Kalash and probably (less closely) to Kafir. **1974** 'S. HARVESTER' *Forgotten Road* i. 11 He had a working acquaintance with dialects of most Kafir valley tribes, even Khowar and the almost extinct Domali language.

Khozar, var. KHAZAR.

Khrushchevism ('krʊstʃəfɪz(ə)m). [f. the name of Nikita Sergeevich *Khrushchev* (1894–1971), Soviet statesman + -ISM.] The practice or principles of Khrushchev, notable for his denunciation of Stalin and his advocacy of peaceful coexistence with the Western powers. So **Khrush'chevian** *a.*, of, pertaining to, or characteristic of Khrushchev or his policies.

1957 *Amer. Speech* XXXII. 294 The party has switched from Stalinism to Khrushchevism. **1961** *Listener* 28 Dec. 1107/2 The world of romance and fairy tale is never far away from the Khrushchevian Utopia. **1962** *Ibid.* 18 Jan. 112/1 There are several kinds of communism in the world—Titoism, Khrushchevism, Maoism in China. **1963** *Economist* 3 Aug. 418/2 Khrushchevism is..to be preferred by the West to Maoism. **1964** *New Statesman* 17 Apr. 592/2 What strikes one in the record of Krushchevism is the great number of vital issues which Krushchev and his men have posed but not tackled. **1973** *Daily Tel.* 22 Nov. 10/6 We know now that 'Ivan Denisovich' was not the harbinger of better things, but the high point of Khruschevian 'liberalism' from which there has since been a steady retreat.

khubab: see KEBAB.

‖**khubber** ('kʌbə(r)). *East Ind.* Also khuber, khab(b)ar. [Urdū (Pers., Arab.) *khabar.*] Information, news, report, rumour.

1878 *Life in the Mofussil* I. 159 (Y.) Khabar of innumerable black partridges has been received. **1879** *Vanity Fair* 29 Nov. 299 (Y.) He will not tell me what khabbar has been received. **1891** R. KIPLING *City Dreadf. Nt.* 75 Just fancy, among these five thousand people, what sort of effect the *khuber* of an accident would produce!

‖**khud** (kʌd). *East Ind.* Also khad. [Hindī *khaḍ.*] **a.** A deep ravine or chasm; a precipitous cleft or descent in a hill-side.

1837 BACON *First Impr. Hindustan* II. 146 (Y.) To look over the edge of the narrow footpath into the Khud. **1870** *Gd. Words* 133/2 The depth of the khuds is very great, and the slope so rapid that you can scarcely find footing when once off the beaten road. **1886** R. KIPLING *Departm. Ditties*, etc. (1899) 87 Death..drops the reckless rider down The rotten rain-soaked khud. **1925** *Dollar Mag.* Mar. 35 Our bungalow is situated on a little knoll with steep khads on three sides down to the river about 150 feet below. **1961** L. D. STAMP *Gloss. Geogr. Terms* 279/2 *Khad*, a torrent in the hills.

b. *attrib.*, as *khud-climbing, -side, -stick.*

1896 SARAH J. DUNCAN *His Honor & a Lady* xix. 244 The tin roofs of the cottages down the khud-side. **1906** *Westm. Gaz.* 13 Aug. 7/1 Killed..in India while khud-climbing. **1925** A. G. ARBUTHNOT in G. Burrard *Big Game Hunting* 118 Take your telescope, rest it on a rock or on your 'khud stick'. **1928** *Blackw. Mag.* Jan. 25/2 He jabbed his khudstick into the ground.

khukri, khunjur: see KUKRI, KHANJAR.

khurta, var. KURTA.

‖**khus-khus** ('kʌskʌs). *East Ind.* Also **khaskas, kuskos, kus-kus, kuss-kuss**; see also CUSCUS[2]. [Urdū (Pers.) *khas-khas.*] The sweet-scented root of an Indian grass, largely used in the manufacture of mats or screens ('tatties'), which are wetted to cool the air passing through them. Also *attrib.*

1810 [see CUSCUS[2]]. **1851** *Art Jrnl. Illustr. Catal.* in Forbes *Veg. World* II. p. iv†. Deliciously fragrant screens are made by the Hindoos from khus-khus, the *Andropogon muricatum*. **1886** *Offic. Catal. Ind. Exhib.* 33 (Stanf.) Fans made of the fragrant root of the khaskas grass. **1890** SIR S. BAKER *Wild Beasts* I. 233 With good tents, kuskos tatties, and cool drinks, the heat was bearable.

‖**khutbah** ('kʊtbə). Also **kootbah, khootba, khotbah, -beh.** [Arab. *khutbah, khotbeh*, f. *khataba* to preach.] A form of sermon or oration used at the Friday service in Muslim mosques.

1800 *Asiat. Ann. Reg., Misc. Tr.* 49/1 He repeatedly read the kootbah, or prayer, containing the name and titles of the prince of the age. **1815** ELPHINSTONE *Acc. Caubul* (1842) I. 112 *note*, Inserting a prince's name in the Khootba, and inscribing it on the current coin, are reckoned in the East the most certain acknowledgments of sovereignty. **1841** *Penny Cycl.* XX. 325 His lieutenant deposed the Fatimite dynasty by a simple ordinance that the *khotbah* or public prayer should be read in the name of the Abbasside caliph Mostadhi. **1860** GARDNER *Faiths World* II. 467/2 In the mosque on the Friday, which may be termed the Mohammedan Sabbath, the Khotbeh..is regularly recited.

khyal (ki:'ɑ:l). Also **kheal.** [Skr.] A traditional type of song in northern India, with instrumental accompaniment, usually containing two main themes.

1882 N. A. WILLARD in R. S. M. Tagore *Hindu Mus.* (ed. 2) I. 102 In the *Kheal* the subject generally is a love tale, and the person supposed to utter it, a female. **1914** A. H. F. STRANGWAYS *Mus. Hindostan* vi. 165 Both are *Khyāls*, and by Rabindranath Tagore. **1921** H. A. POPLEY *Mus. India* vi. 89 The *Khyāl* was introduced later than the Dhrupad, in order to find a place for the graces which are not allowed in the former. *Ibid.*, Khyal singers and Dhrupad singers are usually different. **1971** *Shankar's Weekly* (Delhi) 4 Apr. 24/4 Lines of a khyal are ordinarily made to sprawl over several matras each of a long duration.

Khyber Pass ('kaɪbə pɑ:s, -æ-). [The chief pass in the Hindu Kush mountains between Afghanistan and north-west Pakistan.] *Rhyming slang* = ARSE *sb.* 1. Also *ellipt.* **Khyber.**

1943 M. HARRISON *Reported Safe Arrival* 32 Not knowin' wevver they wz on their 'eads or their Kybers [*sic*]. **1960** J. FRANKLYN *Dict. Rhyming Slang* 88 *Khyber Pass*, arse, not the buttocks but the anus. Usually 'He can (you can) (they can) stick it up his (your) (their) Khyber!' It is an expression of disapproval. **1966** *New Statesman* 16 Sept. 408/3 Can it really be..that 'Khyber' is genuine rhyming slang for the posterior? **1968** *Crescendo* Jan. 6/3 If we sit on our Khybers, we will miss out on all the things that make our lives the richer.

‖**ki** (ki:). [Hawaiian, = general Polynesian *ti.*] A liliaceous plant, *Cordyline terminalis*, found in China and the islands of the Pacific, of which the root is baked and eaten in the Sandwich Islands; the fermented juice yields an intoxicating drink.

1860 *Merc. Marine Mag.* VII. 295 A kind of liquor..a deadly stuff, expressed from the *ki* root. **1889** *Tablet* 18 May 762/2 Drinking fermented ki-root beer, home made alcohol.

kia, var. KYA.

kiaat (kɪ'jɑ:t). *S. Afr.* Also **coyatte hout** (*hout* = wood), **kajat, kajatenhout, kiatt, kijaat.** [Afrikaans, f. Du., f. Malay *ki djati, kajoe djati* good wood.] The tree *Pterocarpus angolensis*, belonging to the family Leguminosæ, and found in southern Africa; the timber of this tree.

1801 J. BARROW *Acct. Trav. S. Afr.* I. v. 339 Catalogue of Useful Woods... Coyatte hout... Tough. [Uses:] Staves for butter firkins. **1862** L. PAPPE *Silva Capensis* (ed. 2) 29 *Atherstonea Decussata* (Cape Teak, or Kajatenhout)... This tree grows 20–25 feet high. **1921** D. E. HUTCHINS in T. R. Sim *Native Timbers S. Afr.* 108 The stem of Kajatenhout is not wanting in thickness. **1947** *Cape Times* 8 Nov. 12/3 Desks: Large selection in imbuia, kijaat, African mahogany and teak. **1956** *Handbk. Hardwoods* (Forest Prod. Res. Lab.) 159 Muninga—*Pterocarpus angolensis*. Other names..kajat, kajatenhout, kiatt (Union of South Africa). **1957** *Cape Times* 3 Sept. 3/3 There was not a scrap of wool in sight in the theatre-like, kiaat-panelled hall. **1973** PALMER & PITMAN *Trees S. Afr.* II. 937 The kiaat is a medium-sized deciduous tree.

kiabooca, -bouca, variants of KYABUKA.

‖**kiack** (kɪ'æk). [Burmese.] A Burmese Buddhist temple.

1599 HAKLUYT *Voy.* II. I. 261 The people send rice and other things to that *kiack* or church of which they be.

kiaja, variant of KEHAYA.

kiaki, var. KEYAKI.

kian, early form of CAYENNE.

1794 A. THOMAS *Newfoundland Jrnl.* 13 May (1968) 39 The Cook was holding, at an unseasonable moment, the Saucepan of Mock Turtle to season it higher with Kian. **1845** B. UPTON *Let.* 10 Sept. in *Amer. Hist.* (1966) XVII. IV. 87/2 Cayenne pepper (kian) grows wild here on the prairies.

‖**kiang** (kjæŋ *monosyll.*). Also **kyang.** [Tibetan *kyang, rkyang.*] A species or sub-species of equine quadruped (*Equus kiang*), a wild horse or ass, inhabiting the high table-lands of Tibet.

Blanford, *Fauna Brit. Ind., Mammals* 476, treats it as a variety of the *koulan*.

1869 A. A. A. KINLOCH *Large Game Shooting* I. iv. 13 Kyang are found all over the elevated plateaux and valleys of Thibet. **1882** OGILVIE (Annandale), *Kiang*. **1885** *Stand. Nat. Hist.* V. 251 Three forms [of the wild horse], which are known as the kulan, the djiggetai, and the kiang. *Ibid.*, The Kiang is only found in the mountainous regions of Thibet. **1894** C. P. WOLLEY *Big Game Shooting* (Badm. Libr.) II. 361 The kyang..is an ugly donkeyfied fiddle-headed brute, with straight shoulders. **1906** [see *desert-frequenting* adj.]. **1934** *Times Educ. Suppl.* 22 Sept. p. iv/3 The father is a very old Kiang, a true wild donkey from Tibet. **1960** 'S. HARVESTER' *Chinese Hammer* xii. 118 The risk of being reincarnated as a female *kyang*, the wild asses who roamed the *tangs* and high plateaux. **1970** *Guardian* 26 Mar. 3/1 Tibet's wild donkeys..known as kiangs. **1973** *Times* 20 Feb. (India Suppl.) p. xi/3 The plateau of Ladakh in the high Himalayas harbours forms related to those in Tibet such as the wild yak, the kiang, and the chiru.

‖**kia ora** ('kia ɔra). *N.Z.* [Maori.] An exclamation of good will: good health! be well!

1896 in E. E. Morris *Austral Eng.* (1898) 247 You will hear any day at a Melbourne bar the first man say *Keora ta-u*, while the other says *Keora tatu*... These expressions are corruptions of the Maori, *Kia ora taua*, 'Health to us too!' and *Kia ora tatou*, 'Health to all of us!' **1905** W. B. *Where White Man Treads* 273 Kia ora, oh coloured brother! **1914** A. A. GRACE *Tale of Timber Town* v. 32 The digger put his pint to his hairy lips, [and] said, '*Kia ora*. Here's fun.' **1933** 'E. MILTON' *Waimana* II. iii. 82 Good-byeee, and kia-ora! **1938** R. FINLAYSON *Brown Man's Burden* 66 They smiled sweetly and said 'Kia ora', as they bought bunches of the bitter cherries. **1966** G. W. TURNER *Eng. Lang. Austral. & N.Z.* viii. 169 Some of these [*sc.* Maori terms] seem to have been commoner in the past than they are now, e.g. *Kia ora* 'good health', more often seen in England (as a brand name for soft drinks) than in New Zealand now. **1970** *N.Z. Listener* 12 Oct. 12/5, I heard her soft, sad voice: 'This is the kia ora, Dave.'

‖**kiap** ('ki:əp). [Native name.] In New Guinea, a European patrol officer or policeman.

1923 W. R. HUMPHRIES *Patrolling in Papua* xv. 162 They had been told by their 'Kiap' to make a road. **1943** S. W. REED *Making of Mod. New Guinea* v. 174 Fear and respect for the *kiap* seem to be mingled in the native mind: fear of punishment..at the *kiap's* command, and respect..for the authority of the officer. **1969** *New Guinea & Austral.* IV. III. 9/1 Those who are subservient to Kiap doctrine. *Ibid.*, We cannot be expected to remain within the fence of racial integration whose fencing materials—the persuasiveness of the Kiap, the teaching of the church, and the legislation of a colonial administration—show distinct signs of weathering. *Ibid.* 10/1 His motion was defeated in a council whose views were predictably Kiap-dominated. **1970** *Times* 31 Mar. (Austral. Suppl.) p. ii/4 Australia was content to provide an underpaid administration whose *kiaps* (patrol officers) were largely concerned with exploration of one of the world's wildest countries.

kiapootee, anglicized phonetic spelling of *cajuputi*, Malay *kayu-putih*, CAJUPUT.

1831 TRELAWNEY *Adv. Younger Son* xxiii. III. 280 Among the rest was a large proportion of Kiapootee and colalava oil.

kiar ('kaɪə(r)), variant of KHAIR.

kiaugh (kjɑx), **kauch** (kɑx). *Sc.* In other Sc. dialects **caigh, keach, keagh** (kex). [Origin obscure.] Trouble, worry.

1786 BURNS *Cotter's Sat. Nt.* iii, His clean hearth-stane, his thrifty wifie's smile, The lisping infant, prattling on his knee, Does a' his weary kiaugh and care [*ed.* 1787 carking cares] beguile. **1794** *Poems, Eng. Scotch & Latin* 97 (Jam.) Your caigh and care ahint you fling. **1824** MACTAGGART *Gallovid. Encycl.* s.v., *To be in a kauch*, to be in an extreme flutter, not knowing which way to turn; over head and ears in business. **1825–80** JAMIESON, *Keach, Keagh*, uneasiness of mind,..bustle, anxious exertion. Dumfr[ies]. **1881** MRS. WALFORD in *Gd. Words* 402/1 Me in a kauch of work, an' Meg kirnin', an' a' the hooss wrang side up maist.

kiawe (ki:'æveɪ). [Hawaiian.] = ALGARROBA.

1915 W. A. BRYAN *Nat. Hist. Hawaii* xvii. 241 (*caption*) A fine Algaroba tree (Kiawe) (*Prosopis juliflora*). **1917** *Nature* 20 Sept. 57/2 One of the introduced trees of great economic importance is the algaroba tree (*Prosopis juliflora*) or kiawe, as the Hawaiians call it. It is found in a belt on the lowlands along the shores of all the islands, and occupies the soil almost to the exclusion of other plants. The pods are very nutritious, and are eagerly eaten by all kinds of stock. Its flowers furnish an excellent quality of honey. **1937** D. & H. TEILHET *Feather Cloak Murders* v. 102 The feathery boughs of a Kiawe tree. **1965** M. C. NEAL *Gardens of Hawaii* 413 The kiawe, a fairly large tree, seldom reaching a height of 60

feet...is the commonest and most valuable tree introduced to Hawaii.

kibab, kibaub, variants of KEBAB.

kibble ('kɪb(ə)l), *sb.*[1] *dial.* Also 5 **kyble**, 7 **keble**. [Origin obscure: cf. KEBBIE and KIBBO.] A stout staff or cudgel; a hooked stick.

1411 *Nottingham Rec.* II. 86, j. kyble, ob.; j. hacstok, jd.; j. horsmall'. **1570** LEVINS *Manip.* 113/22 Kibble, *baculus.* **1674-91** RAY *N.C. Words* (E.D.S.), *Keble*, a timber-log. **1800** S. PEGGE *Anecd. Eng. Lang.* Suppl. (1814) 383 *Kibble*, a strong thick stick.

kibble ('kɪb(ə)l), *sb.*[2] [Origin unascertained: ?from the surname *Kibble*.] More fully ***kibble-hound***: A kind of hound, a cross between the beagle and the old English hound.

1590 COKAINE *Treat. Hunting* Bj, You must breed fourteene or fifteene couple of small Kibble hounds, lowe and swift. **1831** JOHNSON *Sportsm. Cycl.* s.v., The first remove from the southern-hound is the kibble.

kibble ('kɪb(ə)l), *sb.*[3] *Mining.* Also 7 **keeble**, 8 **kible**. [prob. ad. Ger. *kübel* 'tub,' in Mining used in the same sense as the Eng. word.] **a.** A large wooden or (later) iron bucket, for conveying ore or rubbish to the surface.

1671 *Phil. Trans.* VI. 2104 A Winder with two Keebles (great buckets made like a barrel with iron hoops..) which as one comes up, the other goes down. **1684** *Phil. Trans.* XVII. 744 The Rate..for getting of Copper-Ore was.. from 8*s.* a Kibble to 2*s.* 6*d.*, every Kibble being near a Horse-Load in weight. **1747** HOOSON *Miner's Dict.* Y ij, Some-what below the Rope is placed a Hook, whereon to hang the Corfe or Kible. **1874** J. H. COLLINS *Metal Mining* 74 The kibble is simply an iron bucket made of boiler plates, riveted together... They..vary in capacity from 1 to 25 cwt. **1901** G. L. KERR *Pract. Coal Mining* iii. 35 The centre of the cradle contains an opening which provides space for two buckets or 'kibbles' passing each other. **1924** *Hist. Rev. Coal Mining* (Mining Assoc. Gt. Brit.) iii. 38 The advantages of running two kibbles simultaneously are generally more than overbalanced by the increased complications of guides and shaft fittings required. **1967** *Gloss. Mining Terms* (*B.S.I.*) IX. 10 *Kibble*, a large steel bucket used to remove debris and to transport men and materials in a shaft sinking.

b. *attrib.* and *Comb.* **kibble-chain**, the chain by which the kibble is drawn up and let down in the shaft.

1834 *Chambers's Jrnl.* 9 Aug. 223/2 He had been a kibble-boy in the mine. **1843** *Ainsworth's Mag.* IV. 507 Huge quantities of iron, boiler and kibble plates. **1851** KINGSLEY *Yeast* viii, At the shaft's mouth, reaching after the kibble-chain. **1881** *Instructions to Census Clerks* (1885) 84 Copper Miner... Kibble Filler.

kibble, *sb.*[4] [? Altered form of *cobble*, or related to KIBBLE *v.*[1]] = COBBLE *sb.*[1]

1891 *Times* 12 Oct. 4/5 The demand for coal, kibbles, and slack..is very active. **1893** *Daily News* 8 May 2/7 House coal is quiet,..kibbles 8*s.* 3*d.* to 8*s.* 6*d.*, with superior sorts approximately dearer.

kibble ('kɪb(ə)l), *v.*[1] [Etym. obscure: the form is dim. or freq., but the root does not appear; cf. KIBBLE *sb.*[4]] *trans.* To bruise or grind coarsely; to crush into small pieces. Also *absol.* Hence **'kibbled** *ppl. a.*; **kibbling-mill**, a hand-mill for kibbling grain, beans, etc.

1790 in W. MARSHALL *Midl. Counties* (E.D.S.). **1826** *Sporting Mag.* XVII. 352 A question in your last Magazine, respecting kibbled corn for hunters. *Ibid.* XVIII. 75 There is no kibbling mill equal to the horse's grinders. *c* **1880** *Sale Catal.*, Those [corn crushing machines]..will kibble beans, peas, Indian corn.

kibble ('kɪb(ə)l), *v.*[2] [f. KIBBLE *sb.*[3]] To convey ore or rubbish in a kibble.

1891 *Labour Commission Gloss.*, *Kibbling.*

kibbler ('kɪblə(r)). [f. KIBBL(E *v.*[1] + -ER[1].] A machine which kibbles or grinds coarsely; also, one who operates or tends such a machine. So **'kibblerman**.

1882 OGILVIE *Imp. Dict.*, *Kibbler*, one who or that which kibbles or cuts, especially a machine for cutting beans and peas for cattle. **1921** *Dict. Occup. Terms* (1927) §159 *Kibbler, kibblerman*;..attends and feeds machine in which he breaks up oil cake into nodular pieces before grinding into meal. **1922** *Glasgow Herald* 21 Feb. 3 Chaff and root cutters, grinding mills, or kibblers. **1945** J. F. LOCKWOOD *Flour Milling* i. 42 Wheat should always be ground into a coarse meal before testing... A small hand kibbler, such as a coffee grinder, is suitable for this purpose. **1968** *Encycl. Brit.* VI. 804/2 *Crushers or kibblers* are used mainly for oats, corn and linseed, which are bruised, broken or flattened without being ground into a meal.

kibbo ('kɪbəʊ). *dial.* ? *Obs.* [Obscure: cf. KEBBIE and KIBBLE *sb.*[1]] A stick, cudgel.

1688 SHADWELL *Sqr. Alsatia* II. i, And I tak kibbo, I'st raddle the Bones o' thee. *c* **1746** J. COLLIER (Tim Bobbin) *View Lanc. Dial.* (1862) 52 With o Wythen Kibbo he had in his Hont.

‖**kibbutz** (kɪ'bʊts). Pl. **kibbu'tzim** (-iːm) (occas. **kibbutzes**). [ad. mod.Heb. *ḳibbūṣ* gathering.] A collective settlement in Israel, owned communally by its members, and organized on co-operative principles. Also *attrib.*

1931 tr. *Ann. Rep. Central Tenuvah Federation* (Palestine) *1930* i. 3 'Tenuvah' is a co-operative marketing association. .. Its members are the kvutzoth (collective farms), moshavim (smallholders' settlements), and kibbutzim (large farm training groups). **1944** H. F. INFIELD *Co-operative Living in Palestine* 22 The term Kvutza is used alternately with Kibbutz, which has practically the same meaning... The present study uses Kvutza only for the rural settlements and Kibbutz for the superior co-ordinating organization. *Ibid.* viii. 119 (*heading*) Kibbutzim—the roof-organizations. **1957** *Observer* 29 Sept. 13/2 Miss Helga Pilarczyk..danced the Dance of the Seven Veils..with sturdy acrobatics that suggested rather more of the kibbutz than the necrophile. *Ibid.* 1 Dec. 5/2 We saw..people in *kibbutzim*, the voluntary collective farms—some of the serenest people I have ever met. **1958** *Times Lit. Suppl.* 20 June 341/4 It describes how a London-bred girl, with a carping and snobbish mama, ups and joins a *kibbutz* in Israel. **1960** *Times* 15 Oct. 7/6 The kibbutz movement, whose jubilee occurs tomorrow, has been slumping. **1962** L. R. BANKS *End to Running* I. iv. 57 Kibbutzes, I remembered from somewhere, were some kind of communistic settlements in Israel, where children were raised away from their parents and nobody owned anything. **1964** M. ARGYLE *Psychol. & Social Probl.* xvi. 204 Some communities have arranged for children to be brought up in groups... The best-known example of this is the *kibbutz* system in Israel. **1968** C. A. DOXIADIS *Between Dystopia & Utopia* ii. 46 Alfonso Reyas, who states that even 'America is a Utopia'.. and the Kibbutzim in Israel are the results of utopian theories. **1972** *Sci. Amer.* Dec. 43/2 Children in the kibbutz are cared for from infancy in small, one-age peer groups by trained personnel. They live apart from their parents for most of the day and in most kibbutzes during the night as well. **1973** *Jewish Chron.* 6 July 3/1 (*heading*) Kibbutzim back land appeal by sheikh.

‖**kibbutznik** (kɪ'bʊtsnɪk). [Yiddish, f. prec. + -NIK, Pol. and Russ. noun suffix denoting person connected with (something).] A member of a *kibbutz*.

1949 KOESTLER *Promise & Fulfilment* II. ii. 221 We..had the treat of an hour's moonlight journey across the Sea of Galilee, with *kibbutzniks* from Ein Geb sprawling all over the deck and singing Hebrew songs. **1950** G. MIKES *Milk and Honey* III. 129 The main characteristics of *Kibbutz*-life are:—(*a*) *Kibbutzniks* have no money at all;..(*c*) *Kibbutzniks* eat their soup at the end of their meals. **1959** F. M. WILSON *They came as Strangers* III. iii. 203 The kibbutzniks believed that by redeeming the soil of the Holy Land..they were.. redeeming..the Jewish people. **1965** *New Statesman* 3 Sept. 314/2 Kibbutzniks played chess in the shade. **1967** *Listener* 13 July 62/1, I wandered along the tranquil shores of Galilee, stepping over trenches and talking to armed *kibbutzniks.* **1973** *Jewish Chron.* 6 July 10/2 (*caption*) Ehud Adiv, kibbutznik and paratrooper.

kibe (kaɪb), *sb.* Also 5-7 **kybe**. [Of uncertain origin; not from OE.; cf. Welsh *cibi* (also *cibwst*) of the same meaning, which, if native, may be the source of the English word.]

1. A chapped or ulcerated chilblain, *esp.* one on the heel.

1387 TREVISA *Higden* (Rolls) VIII. 227 Also wiþ his penne he made þris croys on a kybe [L. *anthracem*] þat he hadde, and hit vansched awey. *c* **1400** *Lanfranc's Cirurg.* 5 Of wryncles, & chynes of handes, and kybis on þe ffete. **1544** PHAER *Bk. Childr.* (1553) R vij b, Sedes of nettels..sodden in oile..is verye good to heale the kybes of heeles. **1770** FOOTE *Lame Lover* I. Wks. 1799 II. 61, I..have no fear of corns, kibes, or that another man should kick my shins. **1822-34** *Good's Study Med.* (ed. 4) II. 82 When the inflammation becomes ulcerated or forms a kibe.

b. *fig.* in phrases, as: ***to gall*** or ***tread on*** (***one's***) ***kibes***, to press upon closely so as to irritate or annoy, to hurt one's feelings; ***to tread*** or ***follow on the kibes of***, to come closely at the heels of; etc.

1602 SHAKS. *Ham.* V. i. 153 The toe of the Pesant comes so neere the heeles of our Courtier, hee galls his Kibe. **1771** SMOLLETT *Humph. Cl.* 29 May, The hod-carrier, the low mechanic..the citizen, and courtier, 'all tread upon the kibes of one another'. **1820** BYRON *Blues* I. 157 We shall have the whole crew on our kibes. **1883** *Contemp. Rev.* June 907 How closely this spectre [suicide] follows on the kibes of pleasure and extravagance.

2. *transf.* **a.** A sore on a horse's foot (see CREPANCE and cf. KIBY quot. 1886). ? *Obs.*

1639 T. DE GREY *Compl. Horsem.* 38 Swellings in the hinder legs, foundrings, selenders, scratches, kybes [etc.]. **1725** BRADLEY *Fam. Dict.*, *Scratches*, a distemper incident to Horses.. being distinguished indeed by several names, viz. Crepances, Rats tails, Mules, Kibes, Pains, etc.

b. A breaking out at the top of the hoof in sheep. (So Welsh *cibi.*)

1846 J. BAXTER *Libr. Pract. Agric.* (ed. 4) II. 282 The foot-rot and kibe. *Ibid.* 283, I consider the kibe to be.. contagious, and all sheep attacked with the disorder should ..be removed from the flock.

†**c.** A hump or swelling. *Obs. rare.*

1567 MAPLET *Gr. Forest* 75 There are two kindes of Cammels, one which is onely in Arabie, which hath two kibes in his back: the other in many other countries, al plain in his back.

3. *Comb.*, as ***kibe-heel***; ***kibe-heeled*** adj.

1630 DAVENANT *Cruel Bro.* II. Dram. Wks. 1872 I. 136 How they..trip On their wanton toes, like kibe-heel'd fairies. **1658** ROWLAND *Moufet's Theat. Ins.* 1104 Their ashes..laid on with oyl of Roses cures Kibe-heels. **1741** *Compl. Fam. Piece* I. i. 17 Nothing so effectually cures Kibe Heels.

kibe (kaɪb), *v. rare.* [f. prec.] *trans.* To affect with kibes or chilblains; *incorrectly*, to kick or gall (with allusion to quot. 1602 in prec. 1 b).

1757 MRS. GRIFFITH *Lett. Henry & Frances* (1767) IV. 206, I had walked..to London-House, with..the Boots that had kibedme at Windsor on my Legs. **1887** A. BIRRELL *Obiter Dicta* Ser. II. 267 The toe of the peasant is indeed kibing the heel of the courtier.

kibed (kaɪbd), *a.* Also 6-8 **ky-**. [f. KIBE *sb.* + -ED[2].] Affected with chilblains on the heels.

c **1500** *How Plowman lerned Pater-Noster* 108 in Hazl. *E.P.P.* I. 213 No wonder yf he halted, for kybed were his helys. **1546-62** J. HEYWOOD *Prov. & Epigr.* (1867) 134 How euer kybde heeles doo, kybd hartis do not weele. **1720** W. STUKELEY in *Mem.* (1882) I. 13, I used to be troubled in my youth..with kyb'd heels. **1822** LAMB *Elia* Ser. I. *Praise Chimneysweepers*, A pair of kibed heels.

‖**kibitka** (kɪ'bɪtkə). Also 8-9 **-ki**, 9 **-ke**. [Russ. *kibitka*, tent, tilt-wagon, f. Tartar *kibits*, with Russ. suffix *-ka*: cf. Arab. *qubbat* 'tent covered with skins'.]

1. A circular tent made of lattice work and covered with thick felt, used by the Tartars; *transf.* a Tartar household or family.

1799 W. TOOKE *View Russian Emp.* II. 86 The nether horde..consisting of 30,000 kibitkas. **1814** tr. *Klaproth's Trav.* 162 The Russians determine the number of families by that of the felt jurtes or kibitkes. **1884** E. O'DONOVAN *Story of the Merv* v. 55, I was conducted to the kibitka of the village smith. **1899** *Daily News* 14 Jan. 2/1 His typical studio should be a kibitka of the Steppes.

2. A Russian wagon or sledge with a rounded cover or hood; a sledge with a tilt or covering.

1806 HEBER *Let.* 4 Jan. in *Sat. Mag.* No. 444. 215/1 We performed the journey in Kibitkas, the carriages usually employed by the Russians in their winter journies. **1823** BYRON *Juan* IX. xxx, There in a kibitka he roll'd on, (A cursed sort of carriage without springs). **1855** *Englishwoman in Russia* 79 They were hurried off to Siberia, in the prisoners' kabitkas that stood ready to receive them.

kibitz ('kɪbɪts), *v. slang* (orig. *U.S.*). Also **kibbitz**. [Yiddish, f. G. *kiebitzen* to look on at cards, f. *kiebitz* lapwing, pewit; interfering onlooker at cards.] *intr.* To look on at cards, or some other activity, esp. in an interfering manner (e.g. by standing close to the shoulders of the players); to offer gratuitous advice to a player; to act as a kibitzer. Also *trans.*, to watch (a game, person, etc.), esp. in an officious or meddling way. Hence **'kibitzing** *vbl. sb.* and *ppl. a.*

1927 in *Amer. Speech* (1928) IV. 159 The trade journal.. devotes an editorial..to the 'kibbitzer'. It defines 'kibbitzing' as a slang expression used to indicate the act of offering gratuitous advice by an outsider. **1951** M. MCLUHAN *Mech. Bride* 67/1 The children..have retired to a philosophic knoll to do a little uneasy kibitzing. **1955** I. FLEMING *Moonraker* iv. 43 Drax..[sorted] his cards..only into reds and blacks, ungraded, making his hand very difficult to kibitz. **1957** R. STOUT *If Death ever Slept* (1958) viii. 106 Corey Brigham stood behind them, kibitzing. **1961** A. SMITH *East-Enders* vi. 96 Do you remember the café proprietor with whom I kibbitzed on the soarers? **1966** P. J. NICHOLSON *Rat Race* I. iii. 66 Harry moved about, kibitzing on conversations here and there. **1967** *Sci. Amer.* Sept. 64/2 (Advt.), Reilly—with one shipmate posing and two others kibitzing—is finishing off a watercolor. **1972** *New Yorker* 26 Aug. 51/1 Even when the equipment is operating smoothly, the temptation is all but irresistible to gather around the polygraph and kibitz.

kibitzer ('kɪbɪtsə(r), kɪ'bɪtsə(r)). *slang* (orig. *U.S.*). Also **kibbitzer**. [Yiddish *kibitser*; cf. prec.] An onlooker at cards, etc., esp. one who offers unwanted advice; a busybody, an officious meddler.

1927 Kibbitzer [see KIBITZ *v.*]. **1935** A. J. POLLOCK *Underworld Speaks* 66/2 *Kibitzer*, an onlooker of a card game who seldom plays but frequently criticizes the play of the contestants, and offers advice freely. **1936** WODEHOUSE *Laughing Gas* xii. 135 The fiend leaped on to the porch and immediately dispelled any notion that might have been lurking in the minds of the checker players that here was a mere kibitzer who had come to breathe down the backs of their necks and offer advice. **1948** *Chess Rev.* Sept. 1, I tried to outline several plans of attack, but, in the excitement, with many kibitzers moving the pieces, I was unable to concentrate. **1950** J. DEMPSEY *Championship Fighting* x. 52 Keep your eyes closed to the kibitzers or wise guys. **1966** H. YOXALL *Fashion of Life* ix. 85 A member of the club was sitting watching... I went one down and the kibitzer added, 'If I'd known how you played I'd have bet..you wouldn't make it.' **1970** *Globe & Mail* (Toronto) 25 Sept. 30/6 The spectators held their breaths like kibitzers watching a pinball player try to coax the ball into a pocket. **1970** L. M. FEINSILVER *Taste of Yiddish* iii. 294 It was not until the growth of radio and films that Yiddishisms like *Kibitzer*, [etc.],..began to achieve wider circulation.

‖**kiblah** ('kɪblə). Also **kebl, kebla, keblah, kebleh, kibla, kiblé, qibla(h.** [Arab. *qiblah*, that which is placed opposite, f. *qabala* to be opposite.] **a.** The point (the temple at Mecca) to which Muslims turn at prayer. Also *transf.*

For a short period in the early history of Islam the kiblah was at Jerusalem.

1704 J. PITTS *Acc. Mahometans* 40 They all stand with their Faces one way, i.e. toward the Kiblah, or the Temple at Mecha. **1740** W. STUKELEY *Stonehenge* v. 24 A *kebla*, or a place towards which we are to address the Deity. **1825** SCOTT *Talisman* in *Tales Crusaders* III. iii. 91 The Moslem turned towards his *kebla*, the point to which the prayer of each follower of the prophet was to be addressed. **1855** MILMAN *Lat. Chr.* VII. vi. (1864) IV. 172 The prophet had wavered between Mecca and Jerusalem as the Kebla of prayer for his disciples. **1876** R. D. OSBORN *Islam under Arabs* I. iii. 82 There have been few incidents more disastrous in their consequences to the human race than this decree of Muhammed changing the *kibla* from Jerusalem to Mekka. **1883** *Encycl. Brit.* XVI. 553/2 Mohammed..

altered the direction of prayer (kibla)..towards Mecca. **1883** E. O'DONOVAN *Merv* xi. 106 Other pilgrims were standing on their little carpets with their faces towards the *keblah*..commencing their evening devotions. **1895** A. MENZIES *Hist. Relig.* 231 This setting of a new 'kiblah', as it is called, declared that Islam..had an Arab not a Jewish centre. **1902** M. ROBERTS *Immortal Youth* i. 1 Ah, yes, to be in London, at the centre of things,..at the kebleh of the universe. **1911** *Encycl. Brit.* XVII. 420/2 In prayer the worshipper faces the *qibla*. **1973** *Times Lit. Suppl.* 28 Dec. 1590/1 A concatenation of aisles on one side of the building indicated the qiblah. *Ibid.* 1590/5 Attested early associations with 'David's Sanctuary' and the first Qiblah.

b. A niche in a Muslim building on the side towards Mecca.

1775 R. CHANDLER *Trav. Asia M.* (1825) I. 143 The inside is mean, except the kiblé, or portion towards Mecca. **1825** [SHERER] *Impr. Egypt & Italy* 78 We alighted at a cool, clean serai..having its kiblah in the wall.

kiboko (kɪ'bəʊkəʊ). *Africa.* [Swahili, = hippopotamus.] A strong, heavy whip made of hippopotamus hide. Cf. SJAMBOK *sb.*

1921 *Chambers's Jrnl.* 118/1 One of those who had long ruled them with the *kiboko* (sjambok) in times gone by. **1922** C. T. CAMPION tr. *Schweitzer's On Edge Primeval Forest* iv. 67 A kiboko (or sjambok) of hippopotamus hide. **1947** J. STEVENSON-HAMILTON *Wild Life S. Afr.* vii. 62 The whips made of the skin of the hippopotamus, variously known in Africa as sjamboks, kibokos, kourbashes, and so on, have considerable value. **1969** *Tanzania Notes & Records* July 11 There were also many references to the 25 or 30 strokes of the *kiboko* used as a punishment in German days.

kibosh ('kaɪbɒʃ, kɪ'bɒʃ), *sb. slang.* Also **kybosh, kye-bosh.** [Origin obscure.

(It has been stated to be Yiddish or Anglo-Hebraic: see *N. & Q.* 9th ser. VII. 10.)]

1. In phr. ***to put the kibosh on***: to dispose of finally, finish off, do for.

1836 DICKENS *Sk. Boz, Seven Dials,* 'Hoo-roar', ejaculates a pot-boy in a parenthesis, 'put the kye-bosk [*sic*] on her, Mary'. **1846** *Swell's Night Guide* 124 *Kybosh on, to put the,* to turn the tables on any person, to put out of countenance. **1856** *Punch* XXXI. 139 (To put the cibosh upon). **1891** C. ROBERTS *Adrift in America* 9 It was attending one of these affairs which finally put the 'kibosh' on me. **1896** H. G. WELLS *Wheels of Chance* xli, 'I put the kybosh on *his* little game,' he remarks. **1924** *Chambers's Jrnl.* May 296/2 Standofer's fairly put the kybosh on us this time. **1952** J. CLEARY *Sundowners* iii. 122 Well, that puts the kybosh on it. **1956** H. G. DE LISSER *Cup & Lip* xxii. 246 Good for you... You have put the kybosh on them. **1971** *Times Lit. Suppl.* 7 May 531/2 Not only did the First World War liquidate the Edwardian douceur de vivre. It also put the kybosh on the rationalist's faith in progressive social evolution. **1975** *Sunday Post* (Glasgow) 10 Aug. 7/3 She'd been looking forward to some salmon fishing, but the heatwave's put the kybosh on that.

2. Nonsense, 'rot', stuff, humbug.

1873 *Slang Dict.* s.v., 'It's all kibosh', i.e. palaver or nonsense. **1885** *Punch* 3 Jan. 4/1 Still I wish you a 'Appy New Year, if you care for the kibosh, old Chappie.

3. The proper style or fashion; 'the thing'.

1889 in *Cent. Dict.* **1896** in FARMER *Slang.*

4. (See quots.)

1845 G. W. M. REYNOLDS *Mysteries of London* I. xxiii. 60/1 The Thieves' Alphabet... *K* was a kye-bosh [*f.n.* 1s. 6d.], that paid for his treat. **1968** *Gloss. Brit. Argot, Kybosh,* one and a half shillings.

Hence **'kibosh** *v. trans.*, to finish off, 'do for'.

1884 'CRUCK-A-LEAGHAN' & 'SLIEVE GALLION' *Lays & Legends N. of Ireland* 87 The Rector pull'd out an' oul' fourpinny-bit..An' handed the pill that wid kibosh the fun. **1890** *Punch* 16 Aug. 74/3 Wy, they'd queer the best pitches in life, if they kiboshed the Power of the Quid! **1892** MILLIKEN *'Arry Ballads* 50 (Farmer) A dig in the ribs and a 'owl, Seemed to kibosh the Frenchmen completely. **1933** J. CARY *Amer. Visitor* iv. 41 The question is, can I kybosh the whole scheme at the same time? **1969** *Listener* 27 Feb. 264/2 What a pity that the stipend has not kept pace..with the fall in the value of money (and it even comes to you less PAYE, thus kiboshing manoeuvrability in the field of expenses!).

‖**kibrit.** *Alch.* [Arab. *kibrīt* sulphur.]

1706 PHILLIPS, *Kibrit,* a Word sometimes us'd by Chymists for Sulphur. **1730** in BAILEY (folio).

kibsey, obs. var. KIPSEY, small basket.

kiby ('kaɪbɪ), *a.* Now *dial.* In 6 **kyby,** 7 **kibie,** 9 *dial.* **kibby.** [f. KIBE *sb.* + -Y.] Affected with kibes.

1523 SKELTON *Garl. of Laurel* 502 He halteth often that hath a kyby hele. **1611** COTGR., *Mulard,* one that hath kibie heels. **1886** ELWORTHY *W. Som. Word-bk., Kibby heels,* chapped heels—of horses.

kiche, obs. form of KEACH *v.*

†**'kichel.** *Obs. rare.* [OE. *cicel,* of obscure etymology. The retention of unpalatalized *c* (k) can be explained only by taking *cicel* as = **cycel*:—**kukilo-*; in which case this word would not be related to *cœcil,* KECHEL; but the identity of sense makes this difficult to accept.] A small cake.

In the quot. from Chaucer, all the MSS. of the six-text edition have *kechel.* The Harleian reading, however, is also that of Thynne's ed., and from these sources the word has passed into mod. dicts.]

c **1000** *Sax. Leechd.* III. 30 þonne se cicel colize, þonne wyrc þu ma. *Ibid.* 134 Nim ʒetemsud melu and bac hym anne cicel of. *c* **1386** CHAUCER *Sompn. T.* 39 (Harl. MS.) Yif us a busshel whet, or malt, or reye, A Goddes kichil, or a trip of chese. [**1598** SPEGHT *Chaucer's Wks.* Bbbb, A cake.. called a God's kichell, because godfathers and godmothers vsed commonly to giue one of them to their godchildren, when they asked a blessing. **1616** BULLOKAR *Eng. Expos., Kitchell,* a kinde of cake. Also in Blount, Phillips, and later dicts.] [*a* **1825** FORBY *Voc. E. Anglia, Kickel,* a sort of flat cake with sugar and currants strewn on the top. **1875** *Sussex Gloss., Kickel.*]

kichine, obs. form of KITCHEN.

Kichua, var. QUECHUA.

kick (kɪk), *sb.*[1] [f. KICK *v.*[1]]

I. 1. a. An act of kicking; a blow or knock with the foot. In *Football,* the act of striking the ball with the foot. ***free kick***: see quots. 1961. ***drop-, penalty-, place-kick***: see these words.

1530 PALSGR. 236/1 Kicke of an horse, *ruade.* **1599** MARSTON *Sco. Villanie* III. xi. 225 Robrus sprauling kicks, Fabius caper, Harries tossing tricks. **1709** STEELE *Tatler* No. 11 ¶3 A Tall Man with a Hat and Feather, who gives his first Minister, who stands just before him, an huge Kick. **1759** JOHNSON *Idler* No. 55 ¶10, I lost my patience, and gave him a kick. **1856** KANE *Arct. Expl.* II. v. 65 This imp..has always had a relishing fancy for the kicks and cuffs. **1882** in Charles-Edwards & Richardson *They saw it Happen* (1958) 299 A free kick awarded for a handling of the ball enabled Suter to place it well to the right wing forwards. **1892** *Outdoor Games & Recr.* 538 *Laws of Assoc. Football,* A Free Kick is a kick at the ball in any way the kicker pleases, when it is lying on the ground, none of the kicker's opponents being allowed within six yards of the ball. **1893** *Rugby Union Football Handbk.* 33 All free-kicks may be place-kicks, drop-kicks, or punts... If taken by drop or punt the catcher must take the kick. **1961** F. C. AVIS *Sportsman's Gloss.* 26/1 *Free kick,* an uninterrupted kick allowed to a team for an infringement against it, the opposing players having to stand ten yards away. *Ibid.* 268/2 *Free kick,* in Rugby Union football, an optional drop-kick, place-kick, or punt, taken as the result of a fair catch, the player free-kicking from the mark. **1972** *Guardian* 16 Mar. 23/3 From a free kick on the right, Foggo chipped on and the net bulged with relief.

b. *fig.* Esp. in phr. ***a kick in the pants***: a grave or humbling set-back; an expression of severe criticism or disapproval; similarly, ***a kick in the teeth.***

1627–77 FELTHAM *Resolves* I. xi. 16 For we can never throughly try him, but in the kick of malignant Chance. **1833** LYTTON in *Hansard* XV. 1234 His [Irish] policy was wittily described..as a 'quick alternation of kicks and kindness'. [**1836** D. CROCKETT *Exploits & Adv. Texas* i. 14 If a man is only determined to go ahead, the more kicks he receives in his breech the faster he will get on his journey.] **1925** D. H. LAWRENCE *Refl. Death Porcupine* 105 The novel itself gives Vronsky a kick in the behind. **1933** E. O'NEILL *Ah, Wilderness!* (1934) IV. ii. 134 Aw, you deserved a kick in the pants..making such a darned slob of yourself. **1937** PARTRIDGE *Dict. Slang* 881/1 It's better than a kick in the pants. **1940** R. A. J. WALLING *Why did Trethewy Die?* i. 25 Giving the Methusalahs a kick in the pants. **1963** *Listener* 24 Jan. 152/2 General de Gaulle's statement on the Common Market was described by the East German Deutschlandsender as 'a kick in the pants' for Britain. **1970** *Globe & Mail* (Toronto) 25 Sept. 41/4 As some philosopher once noted, the only difference between a pat on the back and a kick in the pants is about eight inches. **1972** *Guardian* 28 Oct. 12/1 The Liberals' proud victory at Rochdale..has given the two major parties the kick in the teeth that each of them deserves.

c. In phr. ***more kicks than halfpence***: more harshness than kindness: cf. MONKEY *sb.*

1824 SCOTT *St. Ronan's* xxxiv, 'Which is like monkey's allowance, I suppose', said the traveller, 'more kicks than halfpence'. **1853** DARWIN in *Life* II. 39 Though I shall get more kicks than halfpennies, I will, life serving, attempt my work. **1887** T. A. TROLLOPE *What I remember* I. i. 22 A life, in which the kicks might be more superabundant than the half-pence.

d. Ability or disposition to kick.

1885 W. J. FITZPATRICK *Life T. N. Burke* I. 14 If..the horse had any kick in him, a sensation scene took place. **1898** F. T. BULLEN *Cruise 'Cachalot'* xxv. (1900) 323 He had not a kick in him.

e. *fig.* Opposition, objection, repugnance.

1839 *Chemung* (N.Y.) *Democrat* 25 Dec. (Th.), Take the hint without a kick, and shut the open door. **1887** F. FRANCIS *Saddle & Mocassin* xviii. 308, I haven't got any kick against Don Juan. **1893** *Westm. Gaz.* 3 Mar. 9/1 There is a strong kick among the few sportsmen here at this wholesale murder. **1904** F. LYNDE *Grafters* xii. 155 To-day he came around and gave me back my opinion, clause for clause as his own. But I have no kick coming. **1910** C. E. MULFORD *Hopalong Cassidy* viii. 57 'We ain't got no kick, have we?' retorted Cavalry. **1948** *Gainesville* (Texas) *Daily Reg.* 3 July 6/2 The admission price will be upped to six-bits, which shouldn't draw any kicks from fans.

f. ***the kick*** (in phr. ***to get*** or ***give the kick***): Discharge, dismissal, 'the bag', 'the sack'. *slang.*

1844 JAMIE *Muse* 100 (E.D.D.) She was soon to get the kick. **1885** FRASER *Poems* 50 (E.D.D.) Should a brither be sick, They'll no gie him the kick.

2. *transf.* **a.** The recoil of a gun when discharged.

1826 J. F. COOPER *Mohicans* (1829) I. vii. 95 The kick of the rifle disconcerts your aim. **1846** GREENER *Gun* 294 It is ..only when the 'Kick', as it is called, becomes painful, that it is essential to avoid or lessen it.

b. A jerk, jolt; jerking motion. Hence, a pulse or surge of electricity capable of producing a jerk in a detecting or measuring instrument. ***B kick Telegr.*** (see quot. 1928[1]).

1835 URE *Philos. Manuf.* 187 The back of the trough being curved, permits the cloth to turn upwards before each successive kick. **1897** MARY KINGSLEY *W. Africa* 337 Our noble craft..had a cataclysmic kick in her. **1898** R. KIPLING *Fleet in Being,* The twin-screws gave us more kick than was pleasant. **1910** *Hawkins's Electr. Dict.* 233/1 *Kick.* 1. In general, a recoil. 2. Any impulsive movement imparted in telegraphy to delicate instrument parts by a discharge from the line. *Ibid., Kick of coil,* a discharge taking place from an electromagnet coil. **1928** A. E. STONE *Text Bk. Telegr.* xiii. 191 With the non-polarised relays a different method has had to be adopted, in order to eliminate the effects of what is known as the B kick. This term is applied to the break in the continuity of signals received on the non-polarised relays, due to the momentary demagnetisation of their cores when the current in the line is reversed. *Ibid.* 194 The 'kick' observed on the galvanometer. **1930** *Proc. R. Soc.* A. CXXIX. 214 An ambiguity arises in determining the residual range of an α-particle from the magnitude of the 'kick' recorded by the counter. *Ibid.* 216 The third record.. shows the kicks smaller and more uniform in size. **1957** [see KICKSORTER]. **1959** J. W. FREEBODY *Telegr.* vii. 200/2 Another difficulty found in the operation of diplex and quadruplex circuits was known as the B-kick which occurred when the B-side relay was operated by a marking current and the current was then reversed by the operation of the A-side key.

c. A strong or sharp stimulant effect, esp. that of liquor or drugs; *spec.* something that makes a drink potent; a thrill, excitement, pleasure; a feeling of marked enjoyment or the cause of such enjoyment; esp. in phr. ***to get a kick out of*** (something), to be excited or pleased by, to enjoy; ***for kicks,*** purely for pleasure or excitement, freq. recklessly or irresponsibly.

1844 *Bentley's Misc.* XVI. 597, I then demanded a common cocktail. 'With the kick in it?' said he. 'Oh, by all means,' I replied... It was..somewhat strong; but then that was my fault, for having ordered it 'with the kick in it'. **1899** R. WHITEING *No. 5 John St.* xxi. 216 'My Gawd! won't them chaps from the Collynies 'ave the kick!' he observes, in allusion to their entertainment at the public expense. **1903** *Daily Chron.* 16 Jan. 5/1 With cayenne and mustard (to give their food the missing 'kick' [of alcohol]). **1924** P. MARKS *Plastic Age* xi. 101 'Who wrote "La Belle Dame sans Merci"?'..'I think Jawn Keats wrote it. It's one of those bedtime stories with a kick.' **1927** W. E. COLLINSON *Contemp. Eng.* 81 Home-brew with a kick in it. **1928** *Daily Express* 4 Dec. 10/3, I was told I should get a kick out of that journey—and I certainly did. **1929** *Evening News* 18 Nov. 15/6 A cocktail basis with a real kick (42 deg. proof spirit). **1933** D. L. SAYERS *Murder must Advertise* ix. 159 There's a kick in being afraid. **1935** S. SPENDER *Destructive Element* 82 Strether accepts even the fact that he is living with Madame de Vionnet; in fact, he gets a kick out of it. **1941** *Jazz Information* Nov. 22/2 A man who..worked hard and got his kicks and saved a little money. **1942** *R.A.F. Jrnl.* 2 May 35 We get a great kick out of wearing it. **1946** MEZZROW & WOLFE *Really Blues* (1957) 373 *For kicks,* for pleasure's sake. **1951** *Manch. Guardian Weekly* 28 June 2 To seek a heftier 'kick' from real narcotics. **1956** [see CRAMP *v.* 5 c]. **1961** WODEHOUSE *Service with Smile* (1962) x. 155 He added that the beverage had a kick, and Lord Ickenham agreed that its kick was considerable. **1963** *Listener* 17 Jan. 133/1 Antisocial, sexually ruthless, stealing cars for kicks. **1967** M. M. GLATT et al. *Drug Scene* iii. 39 He no longer got a 'kick' or 'flash' from taking drugs. **1974** *Advocate News* (Barbados) 5 Mar. 3/2 The pusher can more easily persuade him to try something with a bit more kick to it.

d. An interest or enthusiasm, esp. one that is temporary; a fashion, fad (cf. sense 4); a subject, line of thought, or manner of behaving; = BAG *sb.* 1 d; esp. in phr. ***on the —— kick*** = doing, or enthusiastic about, the thing specified by the prefixed word or words. orig. *U.S. slang.*

[**1942** BERREY & VAN DEN BARK *Amer. Thes. Slang* §233/2 The fashion; rage,..*the kick.*] **1946** *Jazz Record* July 8 The whole jazz world was on a Hawkins kick. **1955** M. MCCARTHY *Charmed Life* ii. 34 He had been..a magazine editor. He was on that kick, as he called it, when he met Martha. **1955** B. BAILEY in Shapiro & Hentoff *Hear Me Talkin' to Ya* xviii. 298 When I was starting up, they used to say the two races couldn't get along playing. They used to say stuff like they were afraid we'd go after their women. All that's been proved false, and everything else on that prejudice kick has been proved false. **1957** M. MILLAR *Soft Talkers* ii. 20 'He's rather sensitive about being caught by the cops in bed with another man's wife.' 'For Pete's sake, Esther, get off that kick, will you?' **1959** C. MACINNES *Absolute Beginners* 88 Mannie wasn't in on the Angries kick. *Ibid.* 93 They didn't like it when little Emmanuel got on the writing kick? **1963** B. S. JOHNSON *Travelling People* iv. 66 The star of the production is Maurice Bunde,..fifty-ish but on a tremendous Back-to-Youth kick. **1970** *Globe Mag.* (Toronto) 26 Sept. 8/3 We must get off this kick that every job is a career—it isn't. **1971** *Times Lit. Suppl.* 12 Nov. 1409/1 Somewhere behind the cumulative high, the peace-kick, the good vibes, efficient entrepreneurs..were smiling their mean smiles all the way to the bank.

e. *Athletics.* A sharp burst of speed, esp. towards the end of a middle-distance race.

1955 F. STAMPFL *On Running* vii. 108 By making his final burst of 300 yards from home Bannister could hope to draw the sting of Nielsen's powerful kick and late finish. **1966** R. CLARKE *Unforgiving Minute* xvi. 143, I was obviously holding his finishing 'kick' with no effort whatever and I certainly ran faster when I did sprint. **1972** *N.Y. Times* 4 June 4/5 Instead, Wottle overtook Bob Wheeler of Duke starting the stretch run and turned back a belated kick by Jerome Howe of Kansas State, who finished second in 3:39.8.

3. One who kicks. Usually with adj.: A (good or bad) kicker, *esp.* in football.

1857 HUGHES *Tom Brown* I. v, He's cock of the school.. and the best kick and charger in Rugby. **1893** *Assoc. Football Handbk.* 57 Very safe with his hands and a fine kick.

II. Slang senses of which the relationship is obscure.

4. *the kick*: the fashion, the newest style.

a **1700** B. E. *Dict. Cant. Crew* s.v., *A high Kick,* the top of the Fashion. **1731** *Gentl. Mag.* I. 56 About the latter end of Queen Anne's reign, a rev. gentleman wrote a Treatise call'd

A farewell to French Kicks.. The author of it dissuades his countrymen from the use of French fashions. **1787** G. COLMAN *Inkle & Yarico* III. i, I march'd the lobby, twirled my stick..The girls all cry'd 'He's quite the kick'. **1804** *Europ. Mag.* June 413 This [head-dress] obtained the name of Nancy Dawson's new kick. **1894** MRS. LYNN LINTON *One too Many* I. viii. 190 Mrs. West naturally wanted 'the last new kick'.

5. A sixpence.

c **1700** *Street Robberies Consider'd, Kick*, Sixpence. **1725** in *New Cant. Dict.* **1812** J. H. VAUX *Flash Dict., Kick*, a sixpence, when speaking of compound sums only, as three and a kick, is three and sixpence. **1834** H. AINSWORTH *Rookwood* III. xiii. (1878) 260 Half a bull, three hogs, and a kick. **1871** *Echo* 15 May (Farmer), 'What do you mean by telling me that you will take it away for a kick?'.. 'I'll do the job for sixpence'.

6. a. *pl.* Breeches, trousers. ? *Obs.* Cf. KICKSEYS.

a **1700** in B. E. *Dict. Cant. Crew.* **1725** *New Cant. Dict.* s.v., Tip us your Kicks, we'll have them as well as your Lour. **1819** MOORE *Tom Crib* 13 Old Georgy's bang-up togs and kicks.

b. *pl.* Shoes. orig. *U.S.*

1904 'No. 1500' *Life in Sing Sing* 250/1 *Kicks*, shoes. **1936** K. MACKENZIE *Living Rough* xi. 160 My new kicks, every time I took a step, made a sound like the back of a bird store. **1937** PARTRIDGE *Dict. Slang* 601/1 *Pair o(f) kicks*, boots, shoes: tramps' c[ant]. **1964** L. HAIRSTON in J. H. Clarke *Harlem* 285 After I brushed my kicks, I looked my wig over in the mirror. **1973** *Black World* Apr. 63 My terrible blue-and-white kicks.

7. A pocket.

1851 MAYHEW *Lond. Labour* I. 52, I having some ready in my kick, grabbed the chance, and stepped home with my swag. **1869** GREENWOOD *Night in Workhouse* (Farmer) I rifled his kick of his shiners so fine. **1938** WODEHOUSE *Summer Moonshine* i. 18 'She slung your brother Joe out.' 'And with only ten dollars in his kick, mind you.' **1962** R. COOK *Crust on its Uppers* (1964) iii. 27 I'm about to stuff my pony in my kick. **1968** *Sunday Truth* (Brisbane) 22 Sept. 22/8 One of Luke's jobs was to see that the money was banked every week. Luke put it in his own kick.

8. *Comb.*, as **kick-boxer**, one who participates in kick-boxing; **kick-boxing**, a form of boxing incorporating elements of karate, in which kicking with bare feet is permitted as well as punching with gloved fists; **kick-pleat** (or **plait**), a pleat in a narrow skirt to allow freedom of movement; **kick-stand**, 'a device for holding up a bicycle or motorcycle when not in use consisting of a metal bar or rod that is attached by a swivel device to the frame and may be kicked to a vertical position as a prop' (Webster, 1961); **kick-start, -starter**, a device for starting an internal combustion engine, esp. on a motorcycle, by a downward thrust on a pedal; hence **kick-start** *v. trans.* and *intr.*, to start (an engine) thus; **kick-turn** *Skiing*, a form of standing turn; **kick-wheel**, a potter's wheel worked by a foot pedal.

1978 *Times* 4 Mar. 17 In the featherweight contest.. Griffin..came out somewhat perplexed against Oxford's former Thai *kickboxer. **1984** *Toronto Star* 28 Mar. A7/3 Spadafora,..a one-time professional kick-boxer. **1971** *Sports Illustr.* 26 Apr. 38/1 He's the heavyweight *kickboxing champion of the United States. **1972** *Observer* (Eastchester, N.Y.) 20 July 4 From karate, Mr. Rothman and his friends have graduated to the more dangerous kickboxing, an Americanized karate. **1979** CHOI HONG HI *Taekwon-Do* (ed. 4) 11 There are numerous styles of 'hand and foot fighting'. In China it is given the names Koon-Tao, Kung Fu, or Daeji-Chen;..in Thailand, Kick boxing. **1984** *Toronto Star* 28 Mar. A7/4 Spadafora said he fought a couple of professional kick-boxing matches in the early 70s. **1934** WEBSTER s.v. *plait*, A *kick plait is a variation of the latter [*sc.* box plait] used to give breadth to a narrow skirt. **1960** *Sunday Express* 20 Nov. 14/2 Pencil skirt with back '*kick' pleat. **1947** *Cycling Handbk.* (League of Amer. Wheelmen, Inc.) 23 Heavyweights are generally equipped with coaster brakes,..*kickstands, and other accoutrements dear to the hearts of juvenile Americans. **1963** D. BROUN *Subject of Harry Egypt* i. 8 There was a metered space..and he eased the cycle into it and over onto the kickstand. **1914** *Motor Cycle* 2 Apr. 138/1, 1912 P. and M., free engine, 2-speed, *kick start. **1928** *Manch. Guardian Weekly* 15 June 474/2 The biggest boy is demonstrating..how to kick-start an engine. **1959** I. JEFFERIES *Thirteen Days* i. 17, I..turned my bike down the slope to save kick-starting. *Ibid.* xi. 188, I kick-started and zoomed up the rock-slope. **1962** 'D. WILSON' *Search for Geoffrey Goring* viii. 170 He kickstarted the motor and rode on. **1916** *Motor Cyclists' A.B.C.* 107 A *kick starter is fitted to a machine for the purpose of allowing the engine to be started whilst the rider is in the saddle by a downward kick of a pedal. **1919** C. P. THOMPSON *Cocktails* 235 She mounted on the kickstarter and stamped on it with resolute vigour. **1961** *Engineering* 13 Oct. 486 The clutch, gearbox, kickstarter, transmission and rear stub axle are combined with the engine into a single unit. **1910** W. R. RICKMERS *Ski-ing* 27 People with stiff or short legs should take short ski, as otherwise certain necessary movements (*i.e.*, the *kick-turn) become difficult or impossible. **1960** *Sunday Express* 18 Dec. 15/4 Kick-turns, in which you stand on one ski on a slope, lift the other and turn it right round, and then bring the second ski round too so that you are facing in the opposite direction. **1893** E. A. BARBER *Pott. & Porc. U.S.* xii. 250 Such wares..were produced in large quantities by negro men and boys, who employed the old-fashioned '*kick-wheel' in their manufacture. **1949** K. S. WOODS *Rural Crafts Eng.* v. xvi. 233 A kick-wheel is driven by a horizontal movement of one foot on a treadle. **1968** J. ARNOLD *Shell Bk. Country Crafts* 15 With the employment of an improved kick-wheel for 'throwing', they were able to make tremendous advances. **1972** *Islander* (Victoria, B.C.) 30 July 5/1 The pottery produced is hand built. However, the group does work with a kick-wheel, as well as an electric-wheel.

kick (kɪk), *sb.*[2] [Origin obscure: sense 1 may be humorously from KICK *sb.*[1]]

1. An indentation in the bottom of a glass bottle, diminishing the internal capacity. Cf. KICK-UP 5.

1861 MAYHEW *Lond. Labour* II. 451 You must know, sir, that some bottles has great 'kicks' at their bottoms. **1876** BLACKMORE *Cripps* x. (1877) 59 He kept them in bottles without any 'kicks'. **1899** *Blackw. Mag.* Feb. 396/1 These were the 'kicks' of bottles whose long snouts were thrust into wooden racks.

2. The projection on the tang of a pocket knife blade, which prevents the edge of the blade from striking the spring.

1864 in WEBSTER.

3. In brickmaking: The piece of wood fastened to the upper side of a 'stock-board' to make a depression in the lower face of a brick as moulded. (Knight *Dict. Mech.* 1875.)

†**kick**, *sb.*[3] *Obs. rare.* In 6 kik, 7 kicke. [ad. Gr. κίκι.] The castor-oil plant.

1597 GERARDE *Herbal* II. cxxxi. §1. 400 *Ricinus*, Palma Christi, or Kik, hath a great round hollow stalke. **1611** COTGR., *Paulme de Christ*, Kicke, Ricinus, Palma Christi.

kick (kɪk), *v.*[1] Forms: 4 kike, 4–6 kyke, 6 keke, kicke, 5– kick. [ME. *kike, kyke*, of unknown origin. The W. *cicio*, often cited as the source, is from English (Prof. Rhŷs).]

I. 1. a. *intr.* To strike out with the foot.

c **1386** CHAUCER *Wife's T.* 85 Ther is noon of vs alle If any wight wol clawe vs on the galle That we nel kike [*v.r.* kyke]. **1387** TREVISA *Higden* (Rolls) V. 355 þere þou myȝte assaye how strongliche þese mares konneþ kyke [*v.r.* kike]. **1398** —— *Barth. De P.R.* VI. v. (MS. Bodl.) lf. 36 b/1 Whanne the modre wasscheþ and kemeþ ham [children] þei kikeþ and praunseþ. *a* **1529** SKELTON *Elynour Rummyng* 450 Of the tewsday in the weke Whan the mare doth keke. **1548** LATIMER *Ploughers* (Arb.) 23 If they be prycked, they wyll kycke. **1599** B. JONSON *Ev. Man out of Hum.* Induct., They.., like galled camels, kick at every touch. **1733** POPE *Hor. Sat.* II. i. 87 'Tis a Bear's talent not to kick, but hug. **1862** CARLYLE *Fredk. Gt.* IX. vi. (1872) III. 125 A dead horse, or a dying, in the next stall,..he at least will not kick upon us, think the neighbouring Kings.

b. *slang.* To die. Also *to kick it.* Cf. *kick up* (13 b), *one's heels* (5), *the bucket* (4), *k. out* (12 c).

1725 *New Cant. Dict., Kick'd*, gone, fled, departed. **1858** TROLLOPE *Dr. Thorne* III. vii. 123 There are fellows have done ten times worse than I; and they are not going to kick ..you are trying to frighten me. **1892** HUME NISBET *Bail Up* 105 (Farmer) Four on them sickened all at once..and after they had kicked it, my two mates went with me. **1899** E. PHILLPOTTS *Human Boy* 10 Then they get microbes on the chest, and kick.

c. Phrases. ***to kick against the pricks*** (***spur, goad***): to strike the foot against such sharp-pointed or piercing weapons; also *fig.* to be recalcitrant to one's own hurt. ***to kick over the traces***: (of a horse) to get a leg over the traces so as to kick more freely and vigorously; *fig.* to throw off the usual restraints.

c **1380** WYCLIF *Sel. Wks.* III. 436 It is hard to kyke aȝen þe spore. **1382** —— *Acts* ix. 5 It is hard to thee, for to kyke aȝens the pricke. **1755** SMOLLETT *Quix.* (1803) IV. 214 Advising that honest man is kicking against the pricks. **1861** H. KINGSLEY *Ravenshoe* xlii, I'll go about with the rogue. He is inclined to kick over the traces, but I'll whip him in a little. **1871** E. F. BURR *Ad Fidem* i. 4 Kicking against the pricks of the constitution, and course of nature. **1876** L. STEPHEN *Hours in Library* II. 354 The effervescence of genius which drives men to kick over the traces of respectability. **1882** BESANT *Revolt Man* i. 32 Always..some kicking over the limits of convention.

2. *intr. fig.* To show temper, annoyance, defiance, dislike, etc.; to rebel, be recalcitrant. ***to kick against*** or ***at***, to object strongly to, rebel against, reject with anger or scorn; to spurn.

1388 WYCLIF *Deut.* xxxii. 15 The louede puple was maad fat, and kikide aȝen. **1549** LATIMER *4th Serm. bef. Edw. VI* (Arb.) 126 He is none of these wynkers, he kyckes not when he heares hys fault. **1596** BELL *Serv. Popery* I. I. x. 33 The wicked do euer kicke against the preachers. **1611** BIBLE *1 Sam.* ii. 29 Wherefore kicke ye at my sacrifice, and at mine offering? **1631** SANDERSON *Serm.* (1681) II. 8 Our proposals are suspected; our counsels..scorned and kickt at. **1847** TENNYSON *Princ.* IV. 393 A rampant heresy, such as.. Would make all women kick against their Lords. **1871** FREEMAN *Hist. Ess.* Ser. II. iii. 116 Human nature craves for something like religion, and it does not always kick at a little superstition. **1887** BESANT *The World went* i, He was compelled to taste the medicines, and his stomach kicked thereat.

3. *transf.* **a.** Of firearms: To recoil when fired.

1832 BABBAGE *Econ. Manuf.* ii. (ed. 3) 23 If a gun is loaded with ball it will not kick so much as when loaded with small shot. **1837** DICKENS *Pickw.* xix, I had no idea these small fire-arms kicked so. **1858** GREENER *Gunnery* 322 Dirty guns ..kick violently, simply from the greater friction.

b. *Cricket.* Of the ground: To cause a ball to rebound in a more nearly vertical direction than usual. (Cf. 13 c.) Said also of the ball, and of the bowler. Also with *up*.

1866 'CAPTAIN CRAWLEY' *Cricket* 25 You will most likely get a run whether the ball shoots or kicks. **1877** C. BOX *Eng. Game Cricket* 453 The ground is said to kick when the ball, after being pitched, rises almost perpendicularly. **1882** *Standard* 29 Aug. 3/2 The rain had made the wicket 'kick' a good deal. **1888** STEEL & LYTTELTON *Cricket* 152 Spofforth was bowling rather more than medium pace, bringing the ball back a foot or more very quickly from the pitch, sometimes kicking to the height of the batsman's head and at others shooting. **1899** *Westm. Gaz.* 21 July 5 The turf.. played..without the slightest trace of a desire to 'kick'. **1904** P. F. WARNER *How we recovered Ashes* xiii. 246 The ball was always turning, and one or two deliveries kicked up rather awkwardly. **1963** A. ROSS *Australia 63* i. 33 McKenzie got one to kick in the next over.

c. *Telegr.* Of a relay: to break contact momentarily.

1928 A. E. STONE *Text Bk. Telegr.* xiii. 192 If during this period the tongue of the relay 'kicks', the local circuit is momentarily broken. **1959** J. W. FREEBODY *Telegr.* vii. 195/2 In a duplex circuit this surge flows through the line coil of the relay and would cause the relay to 'kick' if a similar balancing surge were not also allowed to pass through the relay balance coil.

4. a. *trans.* To strike (anything) with the foot. ***to kick the wind*** or ***clouds***, to be hanged (*slang*). ***to kick the bucket***, to die (*slang*): see BUCKET *sb.*[2] ***to kick one's heels***: see HEEL *sb.*[1] 18.

1590 SHAKS. *Com. Err.* III. i. 17, I should kicke being kickt, and being at that passe, You would keepe from my heeles. **1598** FLORIO 96/1 *Dar de' calci a Rouaio*, to be hang'd, to kicke the winde. **1711** STEELE *Spect.* No. 2 ¶1 Sir Roger.. had..kick'd Bully Dawson in a Coffee-house. **1711** ADDISON *Spect.* No. 112 ¶4 An idle Fellow, and at that Time was kicking his Heels for his Diversion. **1787** 'G. GAMBADO' *Acad. Horsemen* 39 By mounting thus, you avoid all danger of being kicked, or bit. **1811** *Lex. Bal.* s.v., To kick the clouds before the hotel door, *i.e.* to be hanged. **1842** MACAULAY *Ess., Fredk. Gt.* (1858) I. 528 He reviled his Chancellor. He kicked the shins of his Judges. **1890** G. ALLEN *Tents of Shem* x, Sir Arthur..will do the right thing in the end before he kicks the bucket.

b. To work (a printing-press) with the foot (*Cent. Dict.*).

c. *U.S. slang.* To dismiss, discharge (cf. KICK *sb.*[1] 1 f); to reject (a suitor).

1860 BARTLETT *Dict. Amer.* s.v., 'Miss A has kicked the Hon. Mr. B, and sent him off with a flea in his ear.' (Confined to the South.) **1895** *Outing* (U.S.) XXVII. 74/2 Some years ago, when a Suffolk gal kicked me.

d. *transf.* Of things: To strike (anything) with a violent impact. Of a gun: To strike in the recoil. ***to kick the beam***: see BEAM *sb.*[1] 6 b.

1667 MILTON *P. L.* IV. 1004 The latter [weight] quick up flew, and kickt the beam. **1748** SMOLLETT *Rod. Rand.* ix, A straw thrown into either scale would make the Balance kick the Beam. **1875** JOWETT *Plato* (ed. 2) III. 101 Riches are thrown into the scale, and virtue kicks the beam. *Mod.* The gun kicked my shoulder, and has made it all black.

e. *refl.* To reproach or be angry with (oneself); to be annoyed at something one has done or omitted to do.

1891 *Voice* (N.Y.) 29 Jan., In the absence of any of the committee to kick I went home kicking myself. **1892** W. S. WALSH *Handy-bk. Lit. Curiosities* 584 To kick one's self, often used with an infinite variety of adjuncts,—*i.e.*, to kick one's self 'all over the house', 'all over the place', etc.,— means to feel or express violent dissatisfaction with one's self. **1903** *Independent* (N.Y.) 15 Jan. 148/2 He goes away kicking himself. **1907** A. BENNETT *Let.* 5 May (1966) I. 90 Those who persuade themselves to act on this assumption from the start will have least cause to kick themselves in the distant future. **1955** L. P. HARTLEY *Perfect Woman* xxi. 188 All the way to Tilecotes he could have kicked himself for not having made the engagement for next week. **1966** B. KIMENYE *Kalasanda Revisited* 48 Mrs. Mulindwa could have kicked herself for making the suggestion in the first place. **1973** *Times* 27 Dec. 13/4 Rangers were rightly kicking themselves afterwards.

f. *trans.* To give up or overcome (a habit, esp. drug-taking). Also *intr. colloq.* (orig. *U.S. slang*).

1936 *Amer. Speech* XI. 123/2 *To kick the habit*, to stop using drugs. **1951** *Nat. Educ. Assoc. U.S. Jrnl.* May 342/2 Later on they find themselves hooked and can't kick the habit unless they receive medical and psychiatric help. **1956** B. HOLIDAY *Lady sings Blues* (1973) xiv. 121 Along about the end of the war I went to Joe Glaser's office and told him I wanted to kick and I'd need help. **1958** *Oxford Mail* 29 July 6/5 Harmony would again be restored if Johnny could 'kick' his craving. **1964** S. BELLOW *Herzog* (1965) 334 Between his false teeth (to help him kick the smoking habit, as he had once explained to Herzog) he kept a plastic toothpick. **1971** *Black World* Mar. 56/1 I'll help you, man, cuz I know you want to kick. *Ibid.* Apr. 22/1 Let's kick that habit, let's use soul music. **1972** *Times* 3 Jan. 8/3 In a moment of weakness, I watched an episode of this [television serial] after having kicked the habit for more than 12 months.

5. a. With adv. or prep. (see also II.): To impel, drive, or move, by or as by kicking. ***to kick down the ladder***: see LADDER. ***to kick up one's heels***: see HEEL *sb.*[1] 24.

1598 FLORIO, *Fare il pane*, to dye, to kick vp ones heeles. **1604** [See HEEL *sb.*[1] 24]. *a* **1626** FLETCHER *Nice Valour* I. Wks. (Rtldg.) 456/1 If he were not kick'd to th' church o' th' wedding day, I'll never come at court. **1711** ADDISON *Spect.* No. 57 ¶3 [She] threatens to kick him out of the House. **1749** FIELDING *Tom Jones* I. xiii, When once you are got up, to kick the stool from under you. **1775** J. TRUMBULL *McFingal* I. 96 Some muskets..though well aim'd..Bear wide and kick their owners over. **1841** LANE *Arab. Nts.* I. 98 The 'Efreet then kicked the bottle into the sea. **1871** L. STEPHEN *Playgr. Europe* iii. (1894) 86 Every little bit of snow that we kicked aside started a young avalanche on its own account. **1886** STEVENSON *Treasure Isl.* IV. xviii, Ball after ball flew over or fell short, or kicked up the sand in the enclosure.

b. To drive forcibly and contemptuously; to drive or force (*out of, into*, etc.). ***to kick downstairs***, to turn out, eject unceremoniously or ignominiously; hence, jocularly, ***to be kicked***

upstairs, to be removed from the scene of action by promotion to an ostensibly higher post; also, *to kick* (someone) ***upstairs***.

1678 MARVELL *Growth Popery* Wks. 1776 I. 643 In this manner they [the Parliament] were kickt from adjournment to adjournment. **1685** WOOD *Life* 27 Feb. (O.H.S.) III. 133 *Musae repudiatae*, 'Muses kickt downe staires'. *c* **1697** [see UPSTAIRS *adv.* 1 b]. *c* **1728** EARL OF AILESBURY *Mem.* (1890) 640 Forgetting, like good Christians.. their kicking us out of the pepper trade in the Indies. **1750** C'TESS OF SHAFTESBURY *Let.* 28 Nov. in Earl of Malmesbury *Lett.* (1870) I. 78 The Bedfordian set will be honourably kicked up or down stairs. **1809** J. QUINCY *Life* 19 Jan. 175 To use a strong but common expression, it [the majority in Congress] could not be kicked into such a declaration [of war] by either nation. **1821** CROKER *Diary* 31 May in *C. Papers* (1884) I. vii. 186 Lord Melville informs me that he is about to be kicked upstairs (his expression) to be Secretary of State for the Home Department. **1834** J. HALLEY in *Life* (1842) 21 The Faculty.. kicked us out of college. **1952** 'W. COOPER' *Struggles of Albert Woods* III. v. 197 The plot was devastatingly simple—Dibdin was to be kicked upstairs and Albert was to take his place. **1962** R. B. FULLER *Epic Poem on Industrialization* 27 Kicking the bosses upstairs—high out of the way. **1967** G. F. FIENNES *I Tried to run a Railway* vii. 78, I got eventually kicked upstairs to Paddington. **1970** *Guardian* 11 Nov. 20/6 Which party has kicked more people upstairs?

6. To accomplish, make, or do, by kicking. **a.** *Football.* To win (a goal) by a kick. **b.** To force or make (one's way) by kicking. Also *fig.*

1857 HUGHES *Tom Brown* I. v, It is all Lombard-street to a China orange that the School-house kick a goal. **1891** *Times* 15 Oct. 5/3 From this try Shorland easily kicked a goal. **1893** R. KIPLING *Many Invent.* 156 The Rathmines kicked her way northward through the warm water.

II. With adverbs, in special senses (see also 5).

7. kick about or **around. a.** *intr.* To walk or wander about; to go from place to place, esp. aimlessly. *colloq.* (orig. *U.S.*).

1839 C. M. KIRKLAND *New Home* xxv. 195 We heard that he was better, and would be able to 'kick around' pretty soon. **1846** B. UPTON *Let.* 12 Dec. in *Amer. Heritage* (1966) June 93/2, I have been kicking about with scarcely leisure enough to take my meals. **1946** F. SARGESON *That Summer* 56 We're going to have a good time just kicking around.

b. ***to be kicking about*** or ***around***: to lie scattered around, esp. in a casual or untidy fashion; to be available, unused, or unwanted.

1867 'T. LACKLAND' *Homespun* I. 80 The.. doctor, whose instruments.. lie kicking about like ordinary household trumpery. **1877** E. PEACOCK *Gloss. Words Manley & Corringham, Lincolnshire* 148/2 When I went ower to Rotterdam, bacca was that cheap, it was kickin' aboot i' th' streets. **1906** J. F. KELLY *Man with Grip* 99 Now kindly remove that old radium, It's been kicking around for a week. **1955** W. GADDIS *Recognitions* II. viii. 658 Too much gold, that was their difficulty, gold kicking around all over the place. **1967** 'V. SILLER' *Biltmore Call* 128 'Is there a sandwich kicking around?' 'Oh, sure, and I just made a fresh pot of coffee.'

c. *trans.* To kick in all directions; also *fig.*, to treat (someone) harshly, unfairly, or contemptuously. Chiefly *U.S.*

1938 C. PORTER *Most Gentlemen don't like Love*, Most gentlemen don't like love,—They just like to kick it around. **1939** J. STEINBECK *Grapes of Wrath* ii. 8 A good guy and also he was not one whom any rich bastard could kick around. *a* **1940** F. SCOTT FITZGERALD *Last Tycoon* (1949) i. 25 You seem to take things so personally... You just ask to be kicked around.

d. To discuss or examine (a subject, idea, etc.); to try out. *colloq.* (orig. *U.S.*).

1939 *Esquire* May 75 Speaking again of Swing: few tunes deserve its name till they've been 'kicked around' by good performers. **1947** F. WAKEMAN *Saxon Charm* vi. 118 He agreed to write the scene experimentally. 'Maybe I'll get excited about it when I start kicking it around.' **1966** 'D. SHANNON' *With a Vengeance* (1968) iii. 42 They.. drifted over by the other side of the big room to kick it around a little. **1971** 'G. DOUGLAS' *Time to Die* xv. 159 They kicked the details around for a few more minutes and then left them to stew.

8. kick back. a. *intr.* (See quot. 1909.)

1909 WEBSTER, *To kick back, Mech.*, to start backwards;—said of an internal-combustion engine in starting with the crank when the spark is advanced and a too early ignition is effected. **1935** T. E. LAWRENCE *Let.* 13 Feb. (1938) 855 We launched the Dinghy: the quietest and sweetest tick-over of any Dinghy yet! It kicked back, when cold. So we put the ignition back a trifle.

b. *trans.* and *intr.* To return (money, stolen goods, etc.) to the person from whom they were obtained; to pay (money), esp. as a kick-back (see KICK-BACK). *colloq.* (orig. *U.S.*).

1926 MAINES & GRANT *Wise-Crack Dict.* 10/2 *Kick-back*, have to return a sucker's money. **1930** *Amer. Mercury* Dec. 456/2 Kick back with that hooch or we give you the works. **1934** *Atlantic Monthly* Aug. 139 The kick-back operates in the following manner. A wage scale is set either by law, as in government contracts, or by agreement between capital and labor. The worker assumes that he is to get so much per day or per hour for his work. At the end of the week, he is required to return or kick-back part of his wages to a designated person, often a foreman or a bookkeeper. **1970** 'B. MATHER' *Break in Line* v. 59 The luggage coolies.. kicked back half of their take to the Pathan hall porter.

9. kick down. *trans.* and *intr.* To operate a kick-down device (see KICK-DOWN).

1909 *Cent. Dict.* Suppl. s.v., *To kick down*, to bore (a well) by a drill worked as follows: A wooden casing is sunk in the ground or rock for a few feet and the boring-tool works inside of and is guided by this casing... The tool is moved or kicked down by the pressure of the operators' feet. **1959** *Observer* 1 Mar. 21/5 Second can be obtained by kicking down the accelerator. **1963** *Which?* Oct. (Car Suppl.) 116/2 More effort was needed to 'kick-down' on the Zephyr 6.

10. kick in. a. *trans.* To break down (a door, etc.) by kicking against the outer side; *spec.* (*U.S. slang*), to break into (a building).

1881 R. L. STEVENSON *Treas. Isl.* (1883) v. 39 Then there followed a great to-do.., furniture thrown over, doors kicked in. **1926** J. BLACK *You can't Win* vii. 78 I'll kick in the first private house that looks good. We'll surely find a coat and maybe a few dollars. **1931** *Detective Fiction Weekly* 17 Jan. 23/1 Harold G. Slater's big jewelry store safe had been 'kicked in' and robbed of twelve thousand dollars.

b. *trans.* and *intr.* To contribute (money, etc.); to pay (one's share). *slang* (orig. *U.S.*).

1908 K. MCGAFFEY *Sorrows of Show-Girl* 45 The lawyer guy kicked in with the balance of the ten thousand. **1908** H. GREEN *Maison de Shine* 282 If somebody else will get 'em to kick in I'll play the show. **1928** [see CHIN *sb.*[1] 1 d]. **1936** WODEHOUSE *Laughing Gas* xxiv. 254 To encourage the Christmas spirit in whoever was supposed to kick in with my ransom. **1948** *Lawton* (Okla.) *Constitution* 2 July 8/1 The spectators 'kicked in' with a little cash. **1972** *Fortune* Jan. 112/2 Hillard Elkins, producer of *Oh! Calcutta!*, asked him to help back his productions of two Ibsen plays; Lufkin kicked in $10,000.

11. kick off.

a. *trans.* To throw off (shoes) by kicking or jerking the foot. (So *kick on.*)

1840 DICKENS *Old C. Shop* xlix, He.. kicked off his shoes, and groped his way up-stairs. **1890** G. GISSING *The Emancipated* III. II. xvii. 289 He kicked off his boots, kicked on his slippers.

b. *Football. intr.* To give the first kick. Also *fig.*, to start, begin. Freq. const. *with.*

1857 HUGHES *Tom Brown* I. v, The School are going to kick off. **1880** *Daily Tel.* 20 Dec., The Southern captain kicked off with the wind against him. **1911** R. BROOKE *Let.* 25 Apr. (1968) 300 'Are you ready to kick off?' he said... I *gathered* it merely meant was she ready to go out to San Lorenzo. **1942** F. SARGESON in *N.Z. New Writing* I. 5 To kick off with we'd fool about in the water. **1954** L. DURRELL *Let.* 14 Mar. in *Spirit of Place* (1969) 124, I will kick off with Freya Stark and Sir Harry Luke. **1968** *Blues Unlimited* Nov. 17 It kicked off with Bob Hite.. ranged through Dave Kelly's bottleneck playing. **1969** G. E. EVANS *Farm & Village* xii. 131 The old bo's would come in, and my father and I used to go down to the bar to *kick off with.*

c. To die. *slang* (orig. *U.S.*).

1921 J. DOS PASSOS *Three Soldiers* II. i. 61 Another kid's kicked off with that—what d'they call it?—menegitis. **1948** E. WAUGH *Loved One* 22 'It belonged to some old Britisher who's just kicked off.' 'I am that Britisher and I have not kicked off.' **1969** C. BURKE *God is Beautiful, Man* (1970) 29 If he don't come back his old man will get sick and kick off too. **1970** R. LOWELL *Notebk.* 122 The old bitches Live into their hundreds, while I'll kick off tomorrow.

12. kick out.

a. *trans.* To expel or turn out with a kick, or in an ignominious fashion.

1697 DRYDEN *Virg. Past.* IX. 8 Kick'd out, we set the best face on't we cou'd. **1794** LD. SHEFFIELD in *Ld. Auckland's Corr.* (1862) III. 168 You would be all kicked out before the end of the session. **1807–8** W. IRVING *Salmag.* (1824) 254 A few noisy patriots,.. who have crept into office, and a few noisy patriots,.. who have been kicked out.

b. *Rugby Football. intr.* To re-start the game by kicking the ball towards the opposite goal from the 25-yard line, after the defending side has touched down or the attacking side has failed to make a goal from a try.

In the old Rugby school-game (to which quot. 1857 refers) the term was differently used. If one side touched down the ball behind the goal-line of the other, a player of the attacking side had the right to 'kick out' from the goal-line, giving to his own side (under certain conditions) the chance of a kick at goal.

1857 HUGHES *Tom Brown* I. v, He will not kick out till they are all in goal.

c. *intr.* To die. *slang.*

1898 *United Service Mag.* Mar. 649 'Here comes the parson', I once heard a man say; 'he thinks I'm going to kick out, but I'm not'.

d. *Surfing.* (See quots.)

1962 T. MASTERS *Surfing Made Easy* 64 *Kicking out*, turning up and over the wave to end a ride. **1965** J. POLLARD *Surfrider* ii. 20 First let's 'kick out'—shift the weight to the rear of the board and pull it over the top of the wave.

13. kick up.

a. *trans.* To raise (dust, etc.) by or as by kicking; hence, to make (any disturbance or nuisance).

1756 FOOTE *Eng. fr. Paris* II. i, You must know he intended to kick up a riot tonight, at the play-house. **1786** BURNS *Ordination* iii, This day the Kirk kicks up a stoure. *c* **1800** RHODES *Bomb. Fur.* i. (1830) 11 Begone, brave army, and don't kick up a row. **1801** in Anderson *Cumbld. Ball.* 20 Robbie he kick'd up a dust in a crack. **1844** W. H. MAXWELL *Sports & Adv. Scot.* ix. (1855) 88 The wind.. had.. kicked up more sea than was.. agreeable. **1857** HUGHES *Tom Brown* II. iii, He had been kicking up horrid stinks for some time in his study. **1886** J. K. JEROME *Idle Thoughts* (1889) 1 They kick up such a shindy.

†**b.** *intr.* To die (cf. 1 b). *Obs.*

a **1658** CLEVELAND *Poems, Obsequies* 82 The rest that kick'd up were the smaller Fry. **1813** PICKEN *Poems* I. 46 (E.D.D.) Soud ye kick up an' slip awa, They'll scrimply find anither As guid.

c. *Cricket. intr.* Of a ball: To rebound more or less vertically. (Cf. 3 b.)

1895 *Daily News* 29 May 8/5 A knock on the hand from a ball.. which kicked up a little.

III. 14. Phrases used as sbs. or adjs.; *spec.* **kick-about**, an irregular form of football; **kick-and-rush**, used *attrib.* to describe football played with more vigour than art; **kick-ball** orig. *Sc.*, a football, or the game of football; **kick-out**, (*a*) (see 12 b); (*b*) *Surfing* (see quots. and cf. sense 8 d above); **kick-the-can** (or **-tin**, etc.), a children's game in which a tin can is kicked (fully described in I. & P. Opie *Children's Games* (1969) 164–6). See also KICK-OFF, KICK-UP.

1877 *Day of my Life at Eton* 97 There's kick-about going on in the passage. **1899** E. PHILLPOTTS *Human Boy* 9 The halfhour 'kick-about' in the playground. **1906** *Daily Chron.* 26 Nov. 9/2 It was a kick-and-rush game, played badly. **1930** *Daily Express* 9 Sept. 12/5 The football they played was of the kick-and-rush order. **1828** MOIR *Mansie Wauch* v, Fleeing down the street, with the kickba' at their noses. **1854** E. H. CHAPIN *Humanity in the City* vii. 200 They are running about at kick-ball and cricket. **1893** STEVENSON *Catriona* viii. 94, I will be a kick-ball between you and the Duke no longer. **1971** E. SHORRIS *Great Spirit* i. 17 You played kickball in the streets. **1972** J. E. FRANKLIN in W. King *Black Short Story Anthol.* 354 During recess the children played kick-ball, tag, and other games. **1862** THACKERAY *Philip* I. x. 172 Phil, for his part, adopted towards his cousin a kick-me-down-stairs manner. **1801** WOLCOTT (P. Pindar) *Odes to Ins & Outs* vi. Wks. 1812 IV. 359 The tumult on that kick-out day Was mob-like at a house on fire. **1889** *Standard* 23 Dec., Following the kick-out, Christopherson got possession and narrowly missed dropping a goal. **1967** J. SEVERSON *Great Surfing* Gloss. *s.v.*, A kick-out is a last-ditch effort to keep from losing your board. **1970** *Studies in English* (Univ. Cape Town) I. 32 The *kick-out*.. involves stepping on the rear of the surfboard with considerable force and, at the same time, raising the lead foot, lifting the nose of the surfboard out of the water, and making it possible to pivot the board on its tail. **1971** *Ibid.* II. 27 The *kick-out* is an act of desperation. The surfer turns his board violently from the tail and as he leaves the board kicks it—so he hopes—over the top of the wave. **1909** *N. & Q.* 5 June 445/2 Children's games in Orkney... Kick the tinnie. **1959** I. & P. OPIE *Lore & Lang. Schoolch.* xviii. 377 Orthodox games like 'Kick the Can' and 'Jacky Shine a Light'. **1959** B. SUTTON-SMITH *Games N.Z. Children* II. 58 More popular were those games in which the players helped one another to fight the He, and of these the most widespread was the game known as *Kick the Tin.* **1966** 'L. LANE' *ABZ of Scouse* 59 *Kick-ther-can*, a form of street football, using old tin cans. **1971** *Stornoway Gaz.* 10 July 1/8 Children are inventive folk, They make their own best ploys. Smooring, leevo, kick the can, Sufficed when we were boys. **1973** B. BROADFOOT *Ten Lost Years* viii. 86 My father called me in from outside, kick the can or one of those games we used to play.

kick (kɪk), *v.*[2] *slang.* [Possibly a transferred use of prec.] **a.** *intr.* To make a demand or request for money, work, etc. **b.** *trans.* To appeal to, dun (a person) *for* something; to obtain (something) by asking.

1792 GALLOWAY *Poems* 31 (E.D.D.), I kik'd a saxpence frae my master. **1829** *Sporting Mag.* XXIII. 293 They do not like two coachmen kicking in fifty miles. **1858** A. MAYHEW *Paved with Gold* 254 (Farmer) Ned Purchase suggested that they might as well try and kick him for some coppers. *Mod. Sc.* (tailors' slang) He cam into the shop yesterday to kick the cork [= master] for a job.

kickable ('kɪkəb(ə)l), *a.* [f. KICK *v.*[1] + -ABLE.] That may be kicked.

1647 WARD *Simp. Cobler* (1843) 26 Fitter to be kickt, if shee were of a kickable substance. **1876** GEO. ELIOT *Dan. Der.* II. xii, He was not unconscious of being held kickable.

Kickapoo ('kɪkəpuː). *U.S.* [Amer. Indian.]

a. (A member of) a North American Indian people of the Algonquian family, now resident in reservations in Kansas, Oklahoma, and Mexico. **b.** The language of this people. Also *attrib.* or as *adj.*

1722 D. COXE *Descr. Carolana* 50 Nations to the West of this Lake, besides the beforemention'd, are Part of the Outogamis, Mascoutens, and Kikpouz. **1835** C. F. HOFFMAN *Winter in West* I. 276 The Indians that frequent the neighbourhood of Chicago.. are chiefly Pottawattamies and Ottawas, with a few Chippewas.., and a straggling Kickapoo. **1933** L. BLOOMFIELD *Lang.* 72 The languages of ..the Great Lakes region (Ojibwa,.. Kickapoo,.. and so on). **1960** B. KEATON *Wonderful World of Slapstick* (1967) 19 He had a Kickapoo squaw on one side of him, a Kickapoo brave on the other.

kick-back, kickback ('kɪkbæk). orig. *U.S. colloq.* [f. phr. *to kick back* (KICK *v.*[1] II).]

a. A refund, a rebate; the return of money, goods, etc.; a payment (usu. illegal) made to a person who has made possible or facilitated a transaction, appointment, etc. Also *attrib.*

1932 *Editor* 6 Feb. 112/2 *Kick-back*, a return of money. **1934** [see *kick back* b s.v. KICK *v.*[1] II]. **1934** *Sun* (Baltimore) 24 Jan. 1/3 The 'kick-back' system of cutting PWA workers' pay. *Ibid.* 1 Feb. 1/5 These 'kickbacks' were described as levies amounting to from $15 to $25 a week on the musician's salary. **1935** N. ERSINE *Underworld & Prison Slang* 49 *Kickback*, loot that must be returned to avoid arrest. 'They took a grand off the hoosiers, but they had to make a kickback when the marks beefed.' **1939** *Ibid.* 13 Feb. 16/5, 150,000 persons and companies throughout nation get 'kickback'... Several hundred Maryland Corporations and individuals received tax refunds during the last fiscal year. **1940** F. RIESENBERG *Golden Gate* 308 Longshoremen were finding it tougher than ever to get jobs, even through kick-backs of pay, bottles of liquor, and cigars. **1958** M. DICKENS *Man Overboard* xiv. 218 With Mr Pearse and his little kick-backs out of the picture, the food budget was reduced. **1959** *Listener* 3 Dec. 960/1 A number of employers were prepared to offer bribes, pay 'kickbacks'. **1971** *Courier Mail* (Brisbane) 8 Mar. 4/7 The [U.S. official tax] guide says:

'Bribes and kickbacks (a form of bribe) to non-government officials are deductible.' **1972** *Daily Tel.* 19 June 10/5 The promoter claims that another member of the committee approached him demanding a kick-back on the profits and, after he had refused this proposal, the permit was somehow no longer forthcoming.

b. A strong reaction or repercussion; an undesirable result.

1935 M. M. ATWATER *Murder in Midsummer* xxii. 210 His bluster was the kick-back of his strained nerves. **1940** *Amer. Speech* XV. 64 This kickback of the idea into the word, wherein..the word is..vested with unusual suggestive power. **1953** WODEHOUSE *Performing Flea* 177 The feeling that he showed a lack of public spirit in getting away and leaving us to receive the kick-back. **1954** R. KNOX *Retreat for Lay People* xiv. 140 Even as a matter of psychology, isn't it probable that all this negative business has a kick-back which is bad for us? **1965** *Listener* 6 May 658/1 We can over-mechanize it [*sc.* education]. One of the kick-backs of this is the University of California situation, over-planning, the over-administering of education.

c. *Railways.* A device whereby the direction of wagons, etc., can be reversed.

1947 *Richmond* (Virginia) *Times Dispatch* 1 Apr. 6/1 The empty [coal] car is then kicked off the dumper by the next loaded car, rolls by gravity to a high 'kickback' at the outshore end of the pier and thence by gravity to the yard for empty cars. **1962** *Times* 26 Oct. (Spencer Steelworks Suppl.) p. xviii/2 The gravity operated kick-back which reverses the wagon's direction.

d. In timber preservation (see quots.).

1947 *N.Z. Timber Jrnl.* Sept. 61/2 *Kick back* (wood preservative), surplus antiseptic released from the wood when pressure is withdrawn after impregnation. **1968** *Gloss. Terms Timber Preservation (B.S.I.)* 21 *Kickback*, the amount of preservative forced out of the timber when pressure is released.

kick-down ('kɪkdaʊn). [f. KICK *v.*[1] + DOWN *adv.*] A device that is operated by the foot; *spec.*, on a motor vehicle, a device whereby one can change to a lower gear, esp. by pressing right down on the accelerator pedal in a vehicle with automatic transmission; also, the act of thus changing to a lower gear. Freq. *attrib.*

1909 *Cent. Dict.* Suppl., *Kick-down*, the apparatus used in kicking down. See *to kick down.* **1954** *New Automotive Encycl.* 35e/1 A valve operated by a solenoid magnet, which is connected to a governor and kickdown switch. **1958** *Times* 15 July 7/6 The unduly light pressure required for the kick-down. *Ibid.*, The ease with which the kick-down change occurred. **1959** *Times* 17 Mar. 14/7 The accelerator kick-down is an over-riding control that can be brought into play for maximum acceleration at any speed up to about 65 m.p.h. **1971** *Daily Tel.* 24 Mar. 11/4 The kick-down switch on the accelerator was unusually light and pleasant to use.

kickee (kɪ'kiː). [-EE[1].] One who is kicked.

1832 *Examiner* 148/1 One man kicked another, and afterwards disclaimed personality... The kickee..was content with the explanation. **1864** *Daily Tel.* 21 Dec. 4/6 It was..the kicker not the kickee who was entitled to the sympathy of the public.

kicker ('kɪkə(r)), *sb.* [f. KICK *v.*[1] + -ER[1].]

1. a. One that kicks; *spec.* a horse or other animal given to kicking.

1573-80 BARET *Alv.* K 45 A kicker or winser, *calcitro.* **1611** BEAUM. & FL. *King & No King* IV. iii, The boy..being thorowly kick'd, laughs at the kicker. **1660** SANDERSON *Serm.* II. 411 The Persecutors..kick against the pricks..which pierce into the heels of the kicker. **1884** *St. James's Gaz.* 10 Sept. 4/2 The camel..is a powerful kicker.

b. *fig.* One who protests, objects, or rebels; one who breaks away from his party. Chiefly *U.S.*

1888 BRYCE *Amer. Commw.* II. III. lxiii. 459 He who takes his own course is a Kicker or Bolter. **1893** *Harper's Mag.* Apr. 709/2 The pioneer is radical, impatient of dogmas, and a 'kicker' by instinct.

2. A cricket-ball that rises more than usual in rebounding from the pitch.

1894 N. GALE *Cricket Songs, Ode to W. G.*, Nothing comes amiss, Kicker, shooter, yorker.

3. *Mining.* 'A liberating catch made in the form of a bell crank lever rocking on a horizontal axis' (Gresley *Gloss. Coal Mining* 1883).

4. *Mining.* See quots. [perh. a distinct word.]

1747 HOOSON *Miner's Dict.* Lj, *Kicker* [is] a Branch or small Piece of Wholes, left for the support of some Rider or large Stone, or else some Lid. **1881** RAYMOND *Mining Gloss.*, *Kicker*, ground left in first cutting a vein, for support of its sides.

5. *Poker.* A high third card retained in the hand with a pair at the draw.

1892 W. J. FLORENCE *Handbk. Poker* 91 To keep two small cards and an ace is called holding up 'a kicker'. This draw is made by the player, hopeful of getting two pairs, with the additional ace or king. **1895** 'TEMPLAR' *Poker Manual* 57 Sometimes a player raises on a single pair and a kicker, *i.e.* a high card. **1946** MOREHEAD & MOTT-SMITH *Penguin Hoyle* 127 To keep an ace or other high card as a 'kicker' seriously decreases the chances of improving.

6. An outboard motor, or a boat driven by one. Also *attrib. N. Amer. colloq.*

1928 L. R. FREEMAN *Nearing North* II. i. 132 The kicker is hung in a hole cut at a proper height in the long overhang of the stern. **1937** *Times* 13 Oct. 15/6 At Fort Simpson..four of us went upstream to a creek in a 'kicker' (which is a canoe powered by an out-board motor) and swam luxuriously. **1942** L. RICH *We took to Woods* (1944) ii. 33, I want to cut the stern off square, when I get the price of an outboard motor, and make a kicker-boat out of it. **1953** BERREY & VAN DEN BARK *Amer. Thes. Slang* (1954) §82a/1 *Kicker*, an auxiliary motor on a boat. **1963** R. D. SYMONS *Many Trails* xvi. 165 Travelling downstream with a good 'kicker' (outboard motor) pushing the canoe at a good speed is easy. **1967** E. B. NICKERSON *Kayaks to Arctic* iv. 30 Soon we learned to..differentiate outboard motors, or 'kickers' as they are universally called here.

7. *Printing.* (See quots.)

1930 K. E. OLSON *Typogr. & Mechanics of Newspaper* xiii. 421 Every fiftieth or one-hundredth paper is turned slightly askew by an automatic 'kicker' in order to facilitate the making up of bundles of given content. **1967** V. STRAUSS *Printing Industry* vi. 384/1 Counting of newspapers is made easier by the 'kicker', a metal arm which pushes, say, every 25th or every 50th paper out of line, thereby dividing the flow of papers into smaller batches.

†**kickie-wickie.** *Obs. rare*[−1]. [app. a humorous formation: cf. KICKSEY-WINSEY. Mod. editors usually adopt *kicksy-wicksy*, after the later folios.] A jocular or ludicrous term for a wife.

1601 SHAKS. *All's Well* II. iii. 297 He weares his honor in a boxe vnseene That hugges his kickie wickie [*2–4th folios* kicksie-wicksie] heare at home.

kick-in ('kɪkɪn), *sb. Football.* [f. KICK *v.*[1] + IN *adv.*] Practice goal-shooting before the start of a match.

1961 *Times* 10 Feb. 19/7 Previously the British method had demanded a general kick-in before the toss-up. **1972** G. GREEN *Great Moments in Sport: Soccer* ii. 33 The moment the Hungarians..began their 'kick-in' before the start one got the distinct feeling that something unusual was in store. **1973** *Shoot!* 1 Dec. 15/1 The home team's goalkeeper is injured during the pre-match kick-in.

kicking ('kɪkɪŋ), *vbl. sb.* [f. KICK *v.*[1] + -ING[1].]

a. The action of the vb. KICK, in various senses.

1552 HULOET, Kyckynge, *calcitratio.* **1612** SIR H. NEVILL in *Buccleuch MSS.* (Hist. MSS. Comm.) I. 112 Much kicking there is both against you and me severally, but more against the coupling of us together. **1842** S. LOVER *Handy Andy* iii, Her sobs, and..stampings and kickings, amazed young gallipot. **1869** LD. CLERMONT *Fortescue-Family Hist.* II. ix. 138 Having missed every shot..from the excessive 'kicking' of the gun.

b. *attrib.*, as ***kicking-distance, room***, etc.; **kicking-muscle**, the muscle which raises the femur in kicking; **kicking plate**, a metal plate fixed to the lower part of a door, etc., to prevent damage or wear; **kicking-strap**, (*a*) a strap adjusted to prevent a horse from kicking; also *fig.*; (*b*) *Naut.* a rope lanyard fixed to the boom to prevent it from rising.

1897 *Century Mag.* 562/2 Not to allow one's horse to approach within *kicking-distance of another. **1866** W. B. HAWKINS *Artistic Anat. Horse* (ed. 3) 72 Prominent on the front and outer part of the haunch is the *glutæus medius*... It has been called the '*kicking muscle'. **1940** *Chambers's Techn. Dict.* 476/1 **Kicking plate* (Join.), a plate fixed on the face of the bottom rail of a door, to prevent the damage caused by persons kicking the door to open it. **1959** *Engineering* 16 Jan. 94/3 At the base of each frame is a kicking plate of porcelain-enamelled sheet steel. **1838** J. L. STEPHENS *Trav. Greece*, etc. 40/1, I..measured off space enough to fit my body, allowing turning and *kicking room. **1861** HUGHES *Tom Brown at Oxf.* vi. (1889) 56 They had..his belly-band buckled across his back, and no *kicking strap. **1951** G. PENNANT *Young Sailor* v. 70 It is to prevent the boom from lifting that a kicking strap is fitted. **1961** R. M. TETLEY *Sailing* ii. 47 It is in a gybe that a kicking-strap proves its worth, since it holds down the after end of the boom thereby allowing complete control to be maintained over the sail at all stages of the manœuvre.

'**kicking**, *ppl. a.* [-ING[2].] **a.** That kicks, in senses of the verb; also in colloq. phr. ***alive and kicking***: indubitably alive; very lively and active.

1552 HULOET, Kyckynge horse. *c* **1610** *Women Saints* 25 The wanton or kicking flesh of yong maydes, she would represse with often or double fastings. **1797** BURKE *Regic. Peace* iii. Wks. VIII. 272 The Turk..gave him two or three lusty kicks... Our traveller..begged the kicking Mussulman 'to accept his perfect assurances of high consideration'. *c* **1831** J. R. PLANCHÉ *Olympic Devils* in *Extravaganzas* (1879) I. 71 *Plu.* Alive? *Char.* And kicking. **1840** *New Monthly Mag.* LVIII. 497 He is (as the Irishman says), 'alive and kicking'. **1860** *Grandmother's Money* I. 124 So I started off to Stamford Street, just to shew that I was alive and kicking. **1890** *Boston* (Mass.) *Jrnl.* 20 Feb. 2/2 A kicking Democratic Senator in Ohio threatens to upset the ..apportionment scheme. **1930** R. LEHMANN *Note in Music* 130 He seemed to imply with amusement how particularly alive they were. 'Father, mother, two young brothers, and sister Clare, all alive and kicking.' **1966** L. SOUTHWORTH *Felon in Disguise* xi. 158 I'd feel happier if I knew Donaldson was alive and kicking.

b. *Cricket.* Of the ground, a bowler, or his bowling: causing the ball to 'kick' (see KICK *v.*[1] 3 b). Also of a lawn-tennis service.

1885 J. LILLYWHITE *Cricketers' Compan.* 53 The Gloucestershire batsmen found Palmer unplayable on a 'kicking' wicket. **1888** *Daily News* 5 July 5/2 He says that good batsmen to-day cannot play on a rough kicking wicket. **1891** W. G. GRACE *Cricket* iii. 67 My brother was the faster [bowler], and on a rough kicking wicket met with great success. **1924** F. G. LOWE *Lawn Tennis* 12 The only way to take a fast kicking service.

kickininee, var. KOKANEE.

'**kickish**, *a. Obs.* exc. *dial.* [f. KICK *v.*[1] + -ISH.] Given to kicking; irritable.

1589 *Pappe w. Hatchet* 9 If he ride me, let the foole sit fast, for my wit is verie kickish. **1622** DEKKER & MASSINGER *Virg. Mart.* II. i But that is a kickish jade, fellow Spungius. **1647** WARD *Simp. Cobler* (1843) 59 Is *Majestas Imperii* growne so kickish, that it cannot stand quiet with *Salus Populi*? **1828** *Craven Dial.*, *Kickish*, irritable.

kick-off (kɪk'ɒf, -ɔː-). [See KICK *v.*[1] 7 b.] **a.** The first kick to the ball in a football match.

1857 HUGHES *Tom Brown* I. v, Hasn't old Brook won the toss..and got choice of goals and kick-off? **1895** WELLDON *G. Eversley's Friendsh.* 161 The match was hotly contested from the kick-off to the finish.

b. *fig.* The start, beginning; an inaugural or opening event.

1875 *Punch* 27 Feb. 88/2 Sir H. James asked the Attorney-General three questions, by way of kick-off. **1919** WODEHOUSE *My Man Jeeves* 200 The kick-off was scheduled for one o'clock in the morning, when the household might be expected to be..asleep. **1969** *New Yorker* 11 Oct. 43/2 The kickoff starts tonight, with a dinner for the living benefactors of the Museum. **1973** M. TRUMAN *Harry S. Truman* i. 20 The first major crisis came on Labor Day, when we went to Detroit to make the traditional kickoff speech in Cadillac Square.

kicksey, variant of KECKSY.

kickseys, kicksies ('kɪksɪz), *sb. pl. slang.* Also -es. [Cf. KICK *sb.*[2] 2.] Breeches; trousers.

1812 J. H. VAUX *Flash Dict.*, *Kickseys*, breeches;..a purse ..got from the kickseys... To *turn out* a man's *kickseys* means to pick the pockets of them. **1834** H. AINSWORTH *Rookwood* III. v. (1878) 189 Jist twig his swell kickseys and pipes. **1851** MAYHEW *Lond. Labour* I. 52 A pair of Kerseymere Kicksies, any colour, built very slap up.

†**kicksey-winsey**, *sb.*, *a.*, and *adv. Obs.* Also **kicksie winsie, kicksy wincy, kicksee winsee**, *pl.* **kickshiwinshes.** [app. a whimsical formation, suggested by *kick* and *wince*; but the recorded senses seem to connect it with *kickshaws.*]

A. *sb.* A fantastic device; a whim or erratic fancy. (In quot. 1635 app. used interjectionally.)

1599 NASHE *Lent. Stuffe* 74 The lousy riddle..with eight score more galliard cross-points, and kickshiwinshes, of giddy ear-wig brains. **1619** J. TAYLOR (Water P.) *title*, The Scourge of Basenesse; a Kicksey Winsie or a Lerry come Twang. **1635** BROME *Sparagus Gard.* III. xi, *Wife.* [I long to be] here, and there, and here againe; and all at once. *Brit.* Hey kicksie winsie.

B. *adj.* Fantastic, whimsical, erratic.

c **1650** ? CLEVELAND *Obseq. J. Prideaux* in R. Fletcher *Epigr.*, etc. (1656) 168 Perhaps an *Ignis fatuus* now and then Starts up in holes, stincks and goes out agen. Such Kicksee winsee flames shew but how dear Thy great Light's resurrection would be here. *a* **1652** BROME *Covent Gard.* I. i. Wks. 1873 II. 17 This kicksy wincy Giddibrain will spoil all. I'le no more Italian tricks.

C. *adv.* ? Topsy-turvy.

1622 J. TAYLOR (Water P.) *Farew. Tower bottles* Wks. (1630) III. 126/2 And (but for me) apparantly 'tis knowne You had beene kicksie winsie ouerthrowne.

kickshaw, -shaws ('kɪkʃɔː, -ʃɔːz). Forms: α. *sing.* 6-8 (in 7 *pl.*) **quelque chose**; *pl.* 7 **quelque(s)-, quelk-, kick-choses, quelque choices; kicke-shoses, -chawses.** β. *pl.* 6-7 **kick-shawes**, 7 **kick-shose, -shoes, -showes, -shores, -shews, -chawes, (quick-chaws); kek-, kecshose, ke(c)k-, queck-shoes;** 7- **kickshaws.** γ. *sing.* 7- **kickshaw.** [ad. F. *quelque chose* something.

The original Fr. spelling was frequent in the 17th c., but the commonest forms follow the pronunciation *que'que chose* formerly regarded as elegant, and still current in colloquial French. The word was sometimes correctly taken as sing., with plural *-choses*, etc.; more commonly it was treated as a pl., and a sing. *kickshaw* afterwards formed from it.]

1. A fancy dish in cookery. (Chiefly with contemptuous force: A 'something' French, not one of the known 'substantial English' dishes.)

α. **1598** FLORIO, *Carabozzada*, a kinde of daintie dish or quelque chose vsed in Italie. **1611** COTGR., *Fricandeaux*, short, skinlesse, and daintie puddings, or Quelkchoses. **1612** DEKKER *If it be not good* Wks. 1873 II. 285 Ile teach..to make caudels, Iellies..cowslip sallads, and kickchoses. **1642** FEATLY *Dippers Dipt* (1645) 199, I made bold to set on the board kicke-shoses, and variety of strange fruits. **1655** MOUFET & BENNET *Health's Improv.* (1746) 366 Over curious Cookery, making..*quelque-choses* of unsavoury.. Meat. **1655** E. TERRY *Voy. E. Ind.* (1665) 408 With these *quelque chose*, was that entertainment made up. *a* **1656** BP. HALL *Rem. Wks.* (1660) 4 Longing after fine quelque choices of new and artificial composition.

β. **1597** SHAKS. *2 Hen. IV*, vi. i. 29 (Qo. 1) A ioynt of Mutton, and any pretty little tinie Kick-shawes. **1621** BURTON *Anat. Mel.* II. ii. II. (1651) 319 That scarce at first had course bread..must now feed on kickshoes and made dishes. **1709** ADDISON *Tatler* No. 148 ¶ 10 That substantial English Dish banished in so ignominious a Manner, to make Way for French Kickshaws. **1824** MISS MITFORD *Village* Ser. I. (1863) 195 The kickshaws were half raw, the solids were mere rags. **1874** HELPS *Soc. Press.* xiii. 187 You have a nice cut of wholesome leg of mutton..none of your made dishes and kickshaws.

γ. **1674** tr. *Scheffer's Lapland* xviii. 92 Another kick-shaw that pleaseth them very much they make of Angelica. **1714** MACKY *Journ. Eng.* (1724) II. xvi. 227 They go to a Cooks Shop, and ask for a Kickshaw. **1840** THACKERAY *G. Cruikshank* (1869) 303 The Chef is instructing a kitchen-maid how to compound some rascally French kickshaw.

fig. **1653** GAUDEN *Hierasp.* 63 Dished up to the mode of Familistick hashes, and Socinians..Keckshoes. **1659** —— *Tears Ch.* II. xix. 204 Enough..of these late Hashshes, Olives, and Queckshoes of Religion.

2. Something dainty or elegant, but unsubstantial or comparatively valueless; a toy, trifle, gew-gaw. In 1654 applied to a person.

1601 SHAKS. *Twel. N.* I. iii. 122 *A.* I delight in Maskes and Reuels sometimes altogether. *T.* Art thou good at these kicke-chawses Knight? *a* **1626** FLETCHER *Nice Valour* IV. i, At my wives' instigation..(As women loue these Heralds' kickshawes naturally) I bought 'em. **1654** in *Ludlow's Mem.* (1894) I. 382 You..may think he had power, but they made a very kickshaw of him in London. **1722–3** SWIFT in *Pope's Wks.* (1871) VII. 36 Has he [Pope] some *quelque chose* of his own upon the anvil? **1823** SCOTT in *Four C. Eng. Lett.* 403 He may be desirous of offering some test of his gratitude in the shape of a reprint, or such like kickshaw. **1886** E. L. BYNNER *A. Surriage* xxxi. 378 Go buy some kickshaws to send home to your mother.

3. A fantastical, frivolous person. *Obs.* exc. *dial.*

1644 MILTON *Educ.* ad fin., The Monsieurs of Paris to take our hopeful Youth..and send them over back again transformed into Mimicks, Apes, and Kickshoes. *a* **1656** USSHER *Ann.* (1658) 708 Xuthus a musitian, Metrodorus a dancer, and all the Asian comicks and kickshaws crept into the Court. **1828** *Craven Dial.*, *Kickshaw*, a proud, vain person.

4. *attrib.* as *adj.* Frivolous, trifling.

1658 SIR T. MAYERNE *Archimag. Anglo-Gall.* Pref. 4 The Kick-shaw Language, which these Chamæleon-Times love to feede on. **1663** GERBIER *Counsel* e iv a, Waving all quick-chaws-like-devices. **1778** MISS BURNEY *Evelina* xix. (1784) 127 It's all kickshaw work. **1870** DICKENS *E. Drood* xii, He sang..no kickshaw ditties.

Hence **kickshawed** ('kɪkʃɔːd) *a.*, consisting of or treated with kickshaws.

1622 H. SYDENHAM *Serm. Sol. Occ.* (1637) 111 Beware then of this..kick-shawed luxury. **1862** A. VANCE tr. *Hist. Jehan de Saintré* Introd. 29 Good..reading..risen at of our greasy palates as is plum porridge of a kickshawed stomach.

kicksies: see KICKSEYS.

kicksie-wicksie: see KICKIE-WICKIE.

kicksorter ('kɪksɔːtə(r)). *colloq.* Also **kick sorter.** [f. KICK *sb.*¹ + SORTER.] An instrument that classifies electrical pulses according to their amplitude and registers the number received in each amplitude range; a pulse-height analyser.

1947 *Rev. Sci. Instruments* XVIII. 90/2 Five instruments, which have been named Pulse Analysers, Pulse Amplitude Analysers, or 'Kicksorters', have been developed in England and Canada. **1957** *Economist* 7 Sept. 767/2 (Advt.), But why 'kick sorter'? Because it sorts out electrical 'kicks' or impulses according to their amplitude—more than 16,000 of them in each of 100 channels and at speeds up to 1,250 pulses per second. **1968** *Brit. Med. Bull.* XXIV. 259/1 The same equipment can also be used to generate a histogram of spike amplitude, comparable to the pulse-height analyser or 'kick sorter' used by the nuclear physicist.

kickster ('kɪkstə(r)). [f. KICK *sb.*¹ 2 c + -STER.] One whose behaviour is governed principally or solely by the desire for 'kicks'.

1963 *Guardian* 4 Oct. 20/6 Christine is a kickster... She will go with 15 or 18 men at a time. **1967** J. G. MORGAN *Involved* 57 'He looked a real kink, you know, a regular kickster.' 'Educate me,' Frankie said, 'I want to be with you.' 'A nut,' Janet explained, 'a kink who likes going to a scene but won't participate, he gets his kicks out of watching everyone else knocking themselves out.' **1972** *New Society* 9 Nov. 346/3 Apart from the bovver-boy type, there are some girl gangs..and middle class kickster groups... There's a theory it's best to have something to steal, rather than nothing, but this is no help with kicksters.

† **'kickumbob.** *Obs.* *rare*⁻¹. [A humorous formation: cf. *jiggumbob*, *thingumbob*.] (See quot.)

1630 J. TAYLOR (Water P.) *Taylor's Trav.* Wks. (1630) III. 86/1 If any one or more do rob Gardens or Orchards..he or they are put into this same Whirligig, or Kickumbob, and the gybbet being turned, the offender hangs in this Cage [etc.].

kick-up (kɪ'kʌp, 'kɪkʌp). [f. the phr. *kick up*: see KICK *v.*¹ 13.]

1. The act of lifting the legs in, or as in, kicking.

1861 DICKENS *Gt. Expect.* iii, With a kick-up of his hind-legs and a flourish of his tail. **1882** BESANT *All Sorts* xxx. (1884) 210 You used to sing..at the Canterbury, with a character dance and a topical song and a kick-up at the finish.

2. a. A violent disturbance or row; a great to-do.

a **1793** J. HUNTER in Jeaffreson *Bk. ab. Doctors* xxiii. (1862) 257, I knew nothing of this kick-up, and I ought to have been informed of it beforehand. **1812** *Sporting Mag.* XXXIX. 246 No chance of a kick-up, or row being plann'd. **1877** BESANT & RICE *With Harp and Crown* iv. 33 Who stood between you and my lady when you had the kick-up?

b. A dance or party. *colloq.* (orig. *U.S.*).

1778 W. BEATTY *Jrnl.* 1 Dec. in *Maryland Hist. Mag.* (1908) III. 116 We Collected the Girls in the neighbourhood and had a kick up in the Evening. **1796** GROSE *Dict. Vulgar T.* (ed. 3) s.v. *kicks*, A kick up; a disturbance, also a hop or dance. **1899** R. WHITEING *No. 5 John St.* x. 100 There's a little bit of a kick-up to-night with a few of us—sort of sing-song. **1910** 'G. B. LANCASTER' *Jim of Ranges* vi. 126 'What d'yer do at a kick-up, Jim?' 'Oh, hide-an'-seek..an' kiss-in-the-ring,' explained Jim.

3. A name given in Jamaica to two species of thrush, *Siurus noveboracensis* (***Bessy kick-up***), and *Siurus aurocapillus* (***land kick-up***).

1847 GOSSE *Birds of Jamaica* 151 When walking or standing, the tail is continually flirted up in the manner of the Wagtails, whence the local name of Kick-up. *Ibid.* 152 Land Kick-up..His manners are much like those of his cousin Bessy.

4. (See quots.)

1883 W. S. GRESLEY *Gloss. Terms Coal Mining* 147 *Kick-up*, see *tipper*. **1893–4** R. O. HESLOP *Northumberland Words* II. 423 *Kick-up*, an apparatus at a pit bank, made like an iron cradle, by which a tram is turned upside down and emptied on to the screen. **1909** H. LOUIS *Dressing of Minerals* 451 In larger mines it is more usual to use cars with fixed sides and to use some form of 'Tippler' or 'Tumbler' for turning the car over and thus emptying out its contents. Tipplers are of two kinds: end tipplers or 'Kick-ups' and side tipplers.

5. = KICK *sb.*² 1.

1901 in *N.E.D.* s.v. *Kick sb.*² 1. **1923** H. J. POWELL *Glass-Making in Eng.* ii. 22 Feet of goblets, showing hem and kick-up. *Ibid.* v. 74 Stability had been given by pushing upwards and inwards the base of the bulb to form the familiar 'kick-up' of modern wine-bottles.

kicky ('kɪkɪ), *a.* [f. KICK *v.*¹ + -Y¹.] **1.** (See quot. 1808.) Also, clever, lively; provoking, teasing, annoying. *Sc.*

1790 A. SHIRREFS *Poems* 213 Auld Meg hersel' began the play, Clad in a bran-new hudden gray, And in't, I wat, she look'd fu' gay, And spruce and kicky. **1806** G. S. in J. Cock *Simple Strains* 93 Fu' mony a witty touch, and kicky line, Wad won the praise o' langer heads than mine. **1808** JAMIESON, *Kicky*. 1. Showy, gaudy... 2. High-minded, aiming at what is above one's station. **1910** in *Sc. Nat. Dict.* (1960) V. 395/1 Isna' that kicky 'at I canna min' fat comes neest.

2. *Cricket.* Causing the ball to 'kick' (see KICK *v.*¹ 3 b).

1888 STEEL & LYTTELTON *Cricket* iii. 150 It is a slow easy wicket he has to bat on, and not a 'caked', kicky one. **1903** *Windsor Mag.* Sept. 393/2 A very kicky wicket generally averages matters somewhat by supplying one dead shooter.

3. Providing 'kicks', exciting, lively. *N. Amer. colloq.*

1968 *N.Y. Times* 15 Aug. 42 It brought out some kicky styles to preview its new fur boutique. **1969** *New Yorker* 20 Dec. 79 (Advt.), One of our kids said it would be 'kicky' to have one of those 'blow-up' chairs. **1970** J. G. VERMANDEL *Dine with Devil* i. 5 Yes, all right, let's do the kicky stuff first and then try some high fashion. **1972** M. J. BOSSE *Incident at Naha* i. 60 At first impressed, she seemed doubtful after I had unloaded our theories. 'It's kicky and all..but where's it lead to?' **1973** *Time* (Canada ed.) 25 June 8/1 The designs are variously casual, racy, sporty—or kicky, trendy and funky.

kid (kɪd), *sb.*¹ Forms: 3–5 **kide**, 4–5 **kyde**, **kede**; 4–6 **kyd(de**, (5 **kydd**), 4–7 **kidde**, 4– **kid**. [ME. *kide*, *kede*, *kid*, commonly regarded as ad. ON. *kið* (Sw., Da. *kid*):—OTeut. **kiðjo*ᵐ, related to G. *kitz*, *kitze* from OHG. *chizzî*, *kizzîn*:—OTeut. **kittîn* from orig. **kiðnîn*.

The final *-e* of ME. *kîde* is not explicable from ON. *kið*, but the initial *k* makes it still more difficult to refer the word to any OE. type.]

1. a. The young of a goat (cf. quot. 1562).

c **1200** ORMIN 7804 þe firrste callf, þe firrste lamb, þe firrste kide, and swillke. *c* **1250** *Gen. & Ex.* 1535 Two kides he fette and brogt es hire. *a* **1300** *Cursor M.* 3672 (Gött.) Iacob went in to þe fold, And broght þe kiddes. **1382** WYCLIF *Exod.* xxiii. 19 A kydde. *c* **1386** CHAUCER *Miller's T.* 74 She koude skippe and make game As any kyde [*v. rr.* kede, kid(e] or calf folwynge his dame. **1450–80** tr. *Secreta Secret.* 32 Kedis, lambis, and geldid shepe. **1562** BULLEYN *Bk. Simples* (1579) 75 They remaine Kiddes for six monethes, and afterward..be called Goates. **1590** SPENSER *F.Q.* I. vi. 14 Leaping like wanton kids in pleasant Spring. **1667** MILTON *P.L.* IV. 344 Sporting the Lion rampd, and in his paw Dandl'd the Kid. **1720** GAY *Poems* (1745) I. 78 Neither lamb nor kid nor calf..Dance like Buxoma. **1887** BOWEN *Virg. Eclogue* I. 23 Puppies resembled the hound, and the kids their mother the goat.

† **b.** A young roe-deer during its first year. *Obs.*

So G. *kitz* in various districts (Bavaria, Tyrol, etc.); cf. OHG. *rêchkizzi*, MHG. *rêchkitze*.

1486 *Bk. St. Albans* E iv, Iff ye of the Roobucke will knaw ..The first yere he is a kyde soukyng on his dame. [Hence in Turberville (1576), Manwood (1598), and later writers.] **1597** *2nd Pt. Return fr. Parnass.* II. v. 891 The Roa-bucke is the first yeare a Kid, the second yeare a Girle, the third yeare a Hemuse. **1891** C. WISE *Rockingham Castle* 152.

c. A young antelope.

1884 *Harper's Mag.* Aug. 365/2 There are five of them [antelopes]—two bucks, a doe, and two kids.

2. The flesh of a young goat.

c **1430** *Two Cookery-bks.* 13 Take Vele, Kyde, or Henne, an boyle hem in fayre Water. **1547** BOORDE *Introd. Knowl.* xvi. (1870) 274 Yonge Kyddes flesshe is praysed aboue all other flesshe..Olde kydde is not praysed. **1888** *Harper's Mag.* June 82/2 Our attendants now produced some kid and dried dates, which..formed our meal.

3. a. The skin of a kid. **b.** Leather made from kid-skins, or from lamb-skins, or other substitutes; chiefly used in the manufacture of gloves and shoes; *pl.* gloves (or boots) made of this leather.

1677 GREW *Anat. Fruits* vi. §9 Having as it were, only a Coat of Kid, but this of good thick Buff. **1686** *Lond. Gaz.* No. 2124/4 Stolen..., about 350 of the best Kids, some ready pared, and some in the Crust. **1837** THACKERAY *Ravenswing* iv, His..hands are encased in lemon-coloured kids. **1876** GEO. ELIOT *Dan. Der.* xxxix, A figure..tall and physically impressive even in his kid and kerseymere. **1891** N. GOULD *Doub. Event* 151 A pair of yellow kids on his delicate hands.

4. *sing.* or *pl.* (Rendering L. *hædus* or *hædi.*) A pair of small stars in the constellation *Auriga*, represented as kids held in the hand of the charioteer. Cf. *kid-star* below.

1609 HOLLAND *Amm. Marcell.* XIX. ix. 134 Considering it grew toward the end of Autumne, and the starre named the Kids were risen. **1615** G. SANDYS *Trav.* 206 The setting Kid, sad Hyads, he safe sees.

5. *slang.* **a.** A child, esp. a young child. (Originally low slang, but by the 19th c. frequent in familiar speech.)

[**1599** MASSINGER, etc. *Old Law* III. ii, I am old, you say, Yes, parlous old, kids, an you mark me well!] **1690** D'URFEY *Collin's Walk* IV. 183 At her Back a Kid that cry'd, Still as she pinch'd it, fast was ty'd. **1719** —— *Pills* (1872) II. 193 Send your kid home to me, I will take care on 't. **1841** LD. SHAFTESBURY *Jrnl.* 16 Aug. in *Life* (1886) I. ix. 347 Passed a few days happily with my wife and kids. **1861** MORRIS in Mackail *Life* (1899) i. 161 Janey and kid are both very well. **1894** MRS. LYNN LINTON *One too Many* I. vi. 132 The mother cannot live, and the poor little kid must have gone to the workhouse.

b. In low sporting or criminal circles: A term of admiration for an expert young thief, pugilist, etc.

1812 J. H. VAUX *Flash Dict.*, *Kid*,..particularly applied to a boy who commences thief at an early age; and when by his dexterity he has become famous, he is called by his acquaintances *the kid* so and so. **1820** *Sporting Mag.* VI. 79 The heavy torrents of rain informed the kids upon opening their peepers, that the game would again be put to the test. **1823** BEE *Dict. Turf.* s.v., People who imagine that all kids are thieves—carry the joke too far. **1834** H. AINSWORTH *Rookwood* (Farmer), Two milling coves..Vere backed to fight for heavy stake; But..Both kids agreed to play a cross.

† **c.** In American Colonies (see quots.) *Obs.* (Cf. KIDNAP.)

1724 H. JONES *Virginia* 53 The Ships..often call at Ireland to victual, and bring over frequently white Servants, which are of three Kinds... 2. Such as come bound by Indenture, commonly call'd Kids, who are usually to serve four or five Years. **1895** J. C. BALEAGH *White Servit. Virginia* 34 The class of so-called 'Kids' was supplemented by a smaller class of persons who went on agreements for fixed wages for a definite time.

d. A young man or woman. *colloq.* (orig. *U.S.*).

1884 *Cheyenne* (Wyoming) *Sun* 3 Nov. 3/1 There were some strange pranks played by the Cheyenne 'Kids' on the occasion of the 'Halloween'. **1896** *Emporia* (Kansas) *Gaz.* 15 Aug. 15 We have discovered a kid without a law practice and have decided to run him for attorney general. **1926** J. BLACK *You can't Win* iv. 26 I'll tell you what I'll do with you, kid. **1949** *N.Y. Times* 9 Oct. 50/3 A kid [*sc.* a college freshman] from anywhere immediately feels that he belongs to a great family. **1955** J. D. MACDONALD *Brass Cupcake* v. 46 Kathy came into my office... I spoke out of the corner of my mouth. 'We can't talk here, kid.' **1974** N. FREELING *Dressing of Diamond* 127 You got to learn. That's a kid's job. Make yourself useful.

6. *attrib.* and *Comb.*, as (sense 1) ***kid-fell***, ***-flesh***, ***-leather*** (also *attrib.*), ***-milk***; ***kid-like*** adj.; **kid brother** orig. *U.S.*, one's younger brother; **kid-brush**, a soft brush used in the process of finishing goatskins; † **kid-crow** [CREW *sb.*²], a pen for kids; † **kid-fox**, ? a young fox (in quot. *fig.*); **kid sister** orig. *U.S.*, one's younger sister; **kid-star** = sense 4; **kid** (also **kid's, kids'**) **stuff** *colloq.* (orig. *U.S.*), something suitable for children; a very simple or trivial task, etc. Also KID-GLOVE, -SKIN.

1895 J. L. WILLIAMS *Princeton Stories* 143 The evenings would pass pleasantly enough in fighting with Helen, his married sister, across the table, and in guying his *kid brother. **1941** *Penguin New Writing* IX. 106 She..lived with her parents and kid brother in Kennington. **1971** B. COBB *I fell among Thieves* iii. 39 He was the kid-brother whom I helped as far as I could, seeing that we had no mother. **1885** C. T. DAVIS *Manuf. Leather* xxxii. 532 The skins..are then wet over with gum-water and brushed with a very soft brush, called a '*kid-brush'. **1669** WORLIDGE *Syst. Agric.*, *Dict. Rust.* (1681) 328 A **Kid-crow*, a place for a sucking Calf to lye in. **1346** in Riley *Mem. London* (1868) 234 [For the hundred skins of] hyndes-calves, 8s.; *kiddefelles 8s. **1436** *Pol. Poems* (Rolls) II. 160 Wolle, wadmole, gotefel, kydefel also. *c* **1400** *Lanfranc's Cirurg.* 95 Good fleisch, as motoun of a weþer, *kide fleisch sowkynge. **1599** SHAKS. *Much Ado* II. iii. 44 The musicke ended, Wee'll fit the *kid-foxe with a penny worth. **1687** CONGREVE *Old Bach.* IV. viii, The daughters only tore two pair of *kid-leather gloves with trying them on. **1851** *Illustr. Catal. Gt. Exhib.* 581 Ladies' and gentlemen's coloured kid gloves,.. Kid leather gloves..manufactured from French dressed kid skins. **1881** TROLLOPE *Ayala's Angel* I. vii. 85 Then Ayala did go away, escaping by some *kid-like manoeuvre among the ruins. **1920** F. SCOTT FITZGERALD *This Side of Paradise* (1921) I. i. 36, I let people impose on me..entertain their *kid sisters. **1939** 'N. BLAKE' *Smiler with Knife* xi. 159 His manner towards them was affectionate, teasing, whimsical. .. They might have been his kid sisters just out of the schoolroom. **1962** 'M. INNES' *Connoisseur's Case* xiv. 172, I don't sound a very nice kid sister. But I'm quite fond of him. **1866** CONINGTON *Æneid* IX. 314 The *Kid-star lowering overhead. **1929** F. D. BROOKS *Psychol. Adolescence* xviii. 605 The little fellow looked at the book a minute,..and in a very caustic, critical manner sneered, '*Kid stuff.' **1959** J. BRAINE *Vodi* ii. 39 He only had to say, 'Bloody nonsense' or 'Kid's stuff, Coverack' and close his ears to Tom. **1962** L. DEIGHTON *Ipcress File* xxi. 141 Communists..won't be using kids' stuff like this bomb. **1967** *Spectator* 7 July 9/3 One addiction specialist described it [*sc.* marijuana] to me contemptuously as 'kid-stuff'. **1974** M. BABSON *Stalking Lamb* viii. 50 I've taught you the only system that makes real money... Anything else is just kids' stuff.

kid (kɪd), *sb.*² Now *dial.* Forms: 4–5 **kidde**, 5 **kyd**, 5–6 **kydde**, **kyde**, 7 **kidd**, 5– **kid**. [Of unknown origin: W. *cedys* pl., faggots (sing. *cedysen*) is prob. from English.] A faggot or bundle of twigs, brushwood, gorse, etc., used either for burning, or for embedding in a bank, beach, or

muddy bottom to give firmness to loose soil, to stop shingle or sand from shifting, etc.

a **1350** *St. Matthew* 354 in Horstm. *Altengl. Leg.* (1881) 136 Sone he gert ordayn a fire Of kiddes and brandes birnand schire. *c* **1440** *Promp. Parv.* 274/1 Kyd, fagot, *fassis.* **1485** *Nottingham Rec.* III. 230 For fellyng of wodde..þat þe kyddes were made of. **1523** FITZHERB. *Husb.* §135 Than the vnder bowes wolde be cut away, and made kyddes thereof. **1611** MARKHAM *Countr. Content.* I. xvi. (1668) 77 Shake down into the bottom of your Ponds good long Kids or Faggots of brush-wood. **1795** *Trans. Soc. Arts* XIII. 151 The plants are supplied with much nourishment from the decay of the Kids in which they were planted. **1821** CLARE *Vill. Minstr.* II. 31 The woodman..bent away home with his kid on his back. **1851** *Jrnl. R. Agric. Soc.* XII. II. 352 Many are allowed to grow up bushy for the purpose of making long faggots or kids.

b. *attrib.* and *Comb.*, as ***kid-bearer***, ***-faggot***, ***-pile***, ***-stack***, ***-wood***; †**kid-helm**, a faggot-shed.

1477 in *York Myst.* (1885) Introd. 21 *note*, Kidberers, Garthyners, erthe wallers,..ground wallers with erthe. **1501** *Searchers Verdict* in *Surtees Misc.* (1888) 22 Ather of theym shall have theyr esyng drop upon other..yat is to wit ye said Ric' Thornton for his kid helme upon ye tenement or ground of ye said William Whyte. **1523** FITZHERB. *Husb.* §134 To sell..the great woode by it self, and the kydde woode by it selfe. **1653** *Manchester Crt. Leet Rec.* (1887) IV. 105 No gorse Stacks or Kid-stackes should bee sett within or neare the houses in Towne. **1886** *S.W. Linc. Gloss.* s.v., 'The rats find harbour undernean the kid-stack'.

kid (kɪd), *sb.*³ *south. dial.* [Related to COD *sb.*¹, perh. representing an OE. **cydde* (:—**kuddjo-*).] A seed-pod of a leguminous plant; sometimes used of other seed-vessels.

a **1722** LISLE *Husb.* (1757) 95 *Kid*, a pod. **1744-50** W. ELLIS *Mod. Husbandm.* VII. II. 98 [The seed of hornbeam] grows in kids or keys like the ash. **1776** [see KID *v.*³]. **1805** R. W. DICKSON *Pract. Agric.* (1807) II. 81 The ripening of the beans is shewn by the pods or kids turning of a black colour. **1881** *Isle of Wight Gloss.*, *Kids*, pods of peas, beans, and vetches.

kid (kɪd), *sb.*⁴ [? variant of KIT *sb.*¹]

1. A small wooden tub for domestic use; esp. a sailor's mess-tub.

1769 FALCONER *Dict. Marine* (1789), *Corbeillon*, a small kid, or tub, to contain the biscuit..distributed to the several messes. **1833** MARRYAT *P. Simple* xii, One of the ship's boys going forward with a kid of dirty water to empty in the head. **1873** *Act 36 & 37 Vict.* c. 88 Sched. i, A greater quantity of mess tubs or kids than are requisite for the use of the crew.

2. A pannier or basket for rubbish. *dial.*

1847-78 HALLIWELL *Dict.*

3. A box or wooden pen constructed on the deck of a fishing-vessel to receive fish as they are caught (*U.S.*).

1890 in *Century Dict.*

Hence **'kidful**, as much as a kid will hold.

1811 W. MARSHALL *Review* III. 111 (E.D.D.) A kidful of the thick water.

kid (kɪd), *sb.*⁵ *slang.* [f. KID *v.*⁴] Humbug, 'gammon'. In colloq. phr. ***no kid***, no kidding, I am not kidding.

1873 *Slang Dict.* 207 'No kid, now?' is a question often asked by a man who thinks he is being hoaxed. **1876** HINDLEY *Cheap Jack* 64 (Farmer) One of these brother boys was well-known for his kid, that is gammon and devilry. **1880** *Punch* Dec., 'Arry. My gloves was the cheese no kid. **1894** G. MOORE *Esther Waters* 18, I should think the trial was at three-quarters of the mile. The mile was so much kid. **1899** R. WHITEING *No. 5 John St.* xxiii. 234 He do seem to enjoy hisself, no kid! **1916** J. B. COOPER *Coo-oo-ee* i. 14, I tell you, Nelly, she's a woman as will blaze a track right enough, no kid. **1922** JOYCE *Ulysses* 418 Got a prime pair of mincepies, no kid. **1964** *Amer. Folk Music Occasional* I. 91 True story, no kid.

†**kid, kyd,** *ppl. a. Obs.* Also 3-4 **kud(de,** 4 **ked.** [pa. pple. of KITHE *v.*] Made known, mentioned, declared, renowned; well-known; famous; notorious: see also KITHE *v.* 5. (Freq. in alliterative poetry.)

a **1225** *Ancr. R.* 342 Habbeð..to ower bihoue, þesne lutle laste ende, of alle kudde and kuðe sunnen. **1340-70** *Alisaunder* 556 Whan his menskfull menne might nought fynde Hur ked King in Egipt, carefull þei were. *c* **1350** *Will. Palerne* 111 þe kud king of spayne was kindely his fader. *c* **1375** *Sc. Leg. Saints* xliii. (*Cecile*) 393 Iubitere..þe name of a murtherere & of a kyd houlloure. ? *a* **1400** *Morte Arth.* 65 Aftyre at Carlelele a Cristynmese he haldes, This ilke kyde conquerour. *a* **1400-50** *Alexander* 1229 Caulus, an other knyght on a ked stede. *c* **1400** *Destr. Troy* 2124 Knightes in our cuntre kyddist in Armys. *c* **1425** WYNTOUN *Cron.* II. v. 388 Threpyt thai ware spyis Or to the kyng kyd innymys. **15..** *Proph. Merling* in *Whole Proph. Scot.* (1603), He shall be kid conquerour, for he is kende Lord, Of all Bretaine that bounds to the broad Sea. [**1875** J. A. H. MURRAY *Thomas of Erceldoune* Introd. 28 The belief in the 'kyd conqueror' yet to come must have cheered the Cumbrian Britons during the long struggle.]

kid (kɪd), *v.*¹ [f. KID *sb.*¹ Cf. Norw. *kia* (= **kida*).] **a.** *trans.* To give birth to (a kid). **b.** *intr.* To bring forth a kid or kids. Hence **'kidding** *vbl. sb.* Also *attrib.*

c **1400** *Master of Game* iv. (MS. Digby 182) þan þe femell [the doe]..goþe to kydde hir kiddes fer þens. *Ibid.*, Men shulde leue hem þe femels..into þe tyme þat þei haue kiddede. **1528** PAYNEL *Salerne's Regim.* G ij, Mylke of a gootte, nat to nere kyddynge tyme..shulde be chosen. **1611** COTGR., *Chevreter*, to kid, or bring forth yong kids. *Ibid.*, *Chevreté*, kidded, fallen as a young kid. **1614** MARKHAM *Cheap Husb.* IV. v. (1668) 98 Goats above all other cattle are troubled with hardness in kidding. **1756** *Phil. Trans.* XLIX. 802 They found the goat was kidding by its cries. **1842** MARRYAT *Masterman Ready* II. 72 He had brought with him the other goat, which had kidded during the storm.

kid (kɪd), *v.*² Now *dial.* Also 6 **kydde.** [f. KID *sb.*²] *trans.* **a.** To bind up (brushwood, etc.) in kids or faggots; also *absol.* to make faggots. **b.** To secure (loose soil, etc.) by means of kids.

1504 in *Nottingham Rec.* III. 315 Item payd vnto Stubley ..for feling..and kyddyng for a dey..viijd. **1523** FITZHERB. *Husb.* §132 Kydde the smal bowes & set them on ende. **1664** EVELYN *Sylva* (1776) 514 Set apart the largest for the Wheelwright, the smallest for the Cooper..and the brush to be kidded. **1814** W. MARSHALL *Review* IV. 161 (E.D.D.) The refuse is kidded up for the bakers. **1877** *N.W. Linc. Gloss.*, *Kid*,..(2) to use faggots for staithing, or for securing sod walls against the attacks of rabbits. **1886** *S.W. Linc. Gloss.*, s.v., He is kidding all the winter. **1897** R. E. G. COLE *Hist. Doddington* 149 Labourers..paring the sods and 'kidding' many hundreds of gorse 'kids'.

Hence **'kidding** *vbl. sb.* Also *concr.* kids used to secure loose soil, etc.; work in which kids are used.

1504 [see above]. **1566** in Harwood *Lichfield* (1806) 526 Payd, for choppynge the asshes, and kydding of the same, —ijs. xd. **1799** A. YOUNG *Agric. Linc.* 383, 2½ miles kidding at a kidd a yard. **1864** *Faversham Merc.* 13 Feb., A small length of kidding..necessary at the west side of the creek.

kid (kɪd), *v.*³ *south. dial.* [f. KID *sb.*³ (If it were an old word, it might go back to an OE. **cyddan*:—**kuddjan*, f. **kuddo-z*, whence OE. *cod(d*, COD *sb.*¹).] *intr.* Of plants: To form pods (chiefly with *advs.*). Hence **'kidding** *vbl. sb.*

1677 PLOT *Oxfordsh.* 242 [It] seldom fails of a good burthen, though sometimes it doth not kid very well. **1776** T. BOWDEN *Farm. Direct.* 53 If the vetches are not cut green ..many farmers allow them to stand till they kid and the kids begin to fill. **1883** *Hampsh. Gloss.* s.v., 'They beans have kidded uncommon well'.

kid (kɪd), *v.*⁴ *slang.* [perh. f. KID *sb.*¹ in sense 'make a kid of'; cf. KIDDY *v.*; also COD *v.*³] *trans.* To hoax, humbug, try to make (one) believe what is not true. Also, to joke with, tease. Also *intr.* or *absol.*, and const. *along* or *on*; freq. in phr. ***no kidding***, I am not kidding; that is the truth. Hence **'kidding** *vbl. sb.*; **'kidder**, one who hoaxes or humbugs; also, one who jokes or teases.

1811 *Lex. Bal.*, *Kid*, to coax or wheedle... To amuse a man or divert his attention while another robs him. **1812** J. H. VAUX *Flash Dict.* s.v. *Kid-rig*, To kid a person out of any-thing, is to obtain it from him by means of a false pretence. **1839** H. BRANDON in W. A. Miles *Poverty, Mendicity & Crime* 163/2 *Kidding on*, to entice one on. **1851** MAYHEW *Lond. Labour* I. 473 (Farmer) He kids them on by promising three times more than the things are worth. **1879** *Macm. Mag.* XL. 505, I thought they was only kidding (deceiving) at first. **1888** *Sporting Life* 15 Dec. 3/2 The champion kidder. **1891** J. NEWMAN *Scamping Tricks* xi. 88 [He] was a beautiful kidder and could patter sweet and pretty. **1895** *Daily News* 27 Nov. 2/5 The prisoner had told him that since he had been in Holloway he had 'kidded' the doctor into the belief that he was insane, and that he intended to 'kid' the judge. **1899** ADE *Fables in Slang* 84 They wanted a..Name .., so the Side-Show-Announcer, who was something of a Kidder..gave them Zoroaster. **1901** [see DOWN AND OUT *adj. phr.*]. **1903** G. B. SHAW *Man & Superman* II. 70 Garn! youre kiddin. **1906** S. FORD *Shorty McCabe* xiii. 273 I'll stand for all the private kidding you can hand out. **1914** E. E. CUMMINGS Let. 27 July (1969) 9 There's a dead monkey-fish hard by the boat club... No kidding! **1916** C. J. DENNIS *Moods of Ginger Mick* 89, I can see ole Ginger..Grinnin' a bit to kid 'is wound don't pain. **1920** S. LEWIS in *Sat. Even. Post* 11 Dec. 11/2 The boss ain't such a bad pill if you know how to kid him along. **1922** WODEHOUSE *Clicking of Cuthbert* ix. 223 'Mr Winklethorpe told me I was very good with the wooden clubs,' she said defiantly. 'He's a great kidder,' said Ramsden. **1928** D. L. SAYERS *Lord Peter views Body* 287 Really? No kidding? **1932** J. T. FARRELL *Young Lonigan* iv. 154 'You wouldn't fool us, Gov'nor, would you?' kidded Johnny. Studs thought it wasn't every guy who could kid with his old man, like Johnny could. **1936** J. L. HODSON *Our Two Englands* vi. 103 'No, we don't even get kidded (chaffed) for doin' the housework any more,' a man of thirty told me. **1947** W. STEVENS *Let.* 20 Aug. (1967) 565 Next to the passion flower I love fuchsias, and no kidding. **1952** 'J. TEY' *Singing Sands* xii. 205 'I'm a policeman.' 'No kidding!' **1959** *Times* 27 June 7/7 If the Australian had not..'kidded himself along',..then his heart might have broken. **1963** J. N. HARRIS *Weird World Wes Beattie* (1964) xvii. 196 Mr. Herbert Jackson was known as a real salesman, a man with personality, a great kidder, a hot sport and a number of other things. **1969** *Listener* 9 Jan. 34/3 Mrs O'Hare has, of course, come in for a lot of kidding and wry jokes. **1969** *New Yorker* 30 Jan. 18/3 We asked some reclining youths where the Festival was, and they pointed across a vast valley to some tiny lights... 'You're kidding!'.. We sank to the grass. **1974** *Titbits* 30 May 22/4, I have always known I was impotent but kidded myself that if I could find the right wife everything would miraculously become O.K.

kid, obs. f. KITH; pa. t. and pple. of KITHE.

‖**kidang** (kɪ'dæŋ). Now usually **kijang.** Also **kejang.** [Javanese.] The Malay name for the Indian muntjac or barking deer, *Muntiacus muntjak.*

1783 W. MARSDEN *Hist. Sumatra* 94 Deer: *rooso*: *keejang*. These are variety [*sic*] of the deer species. **1824** HORSFIELD *Zool. Res. Java*, *Cervus Muntjak*, The chace of the Kidang, by means of dogs, affords occasionally a favourite amusement to the natives of rank in Java. *Ibid.* In the Javanese language..the name is Kīdang, which with a slight modification—Kījang—is also employed in the Malayan language. **1839** T. J. NEWBOLD *Pol. & Statistical Acct. Straits of Malacca* I. vii. 436 Of the genus Cervus, are the Kijang or Cervus Muntjac, the Rúsa etc. **1880** *Encycl. Brit.* XIII. 602/2 The kidang or mintjac (*Cervulus muntjac*) and the rusa (*Rusa hippelaphus*) are the chief representatives of the deer kind [in Java]. **1900** W. W. SKEAT *Malay Magic* v. 251 The Gold spirit being supposed to take the shape of a *kijang* or roe-deer. **1958** J. SLIMMING *Temiar Jungle* ii. 28 They'll eat *Rusa*, *Pelandok*, and *Kijang*. **1965** C. SHUTTLEWORTH *Malayan Safari* iii. 38 The first visitor to the salt-lick was a *kijang* or barking deer.

†**'kidcot(e.** *Obs.* Also 6 **kydcote, -cott(e, kidcot,** 7-8 **-coat.** [app. f. KID *sb.*¹ + COT, COTE.

The origin of the appellation is not certain; perhaps facetious; possibly transferred from one prison so named to others, as in the case of *Bridewell*. Cf. KITTY⁴.]

The name formerly given in various towns (as York, Lancaster, etc.) to the lock-up or prison.

c **1515** *Test. Ebor.* (Surtees) V. 70 To the kydcotte and the masyndew, viijd. *c* **1540** *Surv. Bridlington Priory* in *Archæol.* XIX. 271 In the north syde of the same gatehouse ys there a prison for offenders within the towne called the kydcott. **1605** T. BELL *Motives Rom. Faith* 106 Did not old Sir John in the kidcote at Yorke so agree with Comberforth the priest? **1772** in Stark *Hist. Gainsborough* 285 That they procure a pair of moveable stocks to be kept in the kidcoat. **1886** E. PEACOCK *Let. to Editor*, My father could remember the old kidcote at Gainsborough. It was not used as a prison in his time, but there was a tradition that it had been.

kidd, kidde, pa. t. and pple. of KITHE *v.*

kiddah, variant of KHEDA.

†**kiddaw** ('kɪdɔː). *Ornith. Obs.* [Cf. CADDOW, *cadaw*.] A Cornish name for the guillemot.

1674 RAY *Collect. Words* 61 In Cornwal they call the guilliam a kiddaw. **1678** — *Willughby's Ornith.* 324 The Bird called by the Welsh and Manks-men, a Guillem;..by the Cornish, a Kiddaw.

kidded ('kɪdɪd), *a.* [f. KID *sb.*¹ 3 + -ED².] Covered or furnished with kid-gloves.

1879 CABLE *Old Creole Days*, *'Tite Poulette* (1883) 52 The manager waited too, rubbing his hat and brushing his clothes with the tips of his kidded fingers.

†**'kidden,** *a. Obs. rare*⁻¹. [f. KID *sb.*¹ + -EN⁴.] Made of kid-skin.

1714 *Smock-race at Finglas* in Steele *Poet. Misc.* 201 Kidden Gloves shall by the third be worn.

†**'kidden,** *v. Obs. rare*⁻¹. [f. KID *sb.*¹ + -EN⁵.] *trans.* = KID *v.*¹ b.

1607 TOPSELL *Four-f. Beasts* (1658) 181 There is no beast that is more prone and given to lust then is a Goat..Seven dayes after it is yeaned and kiddened, it beginneth and yeeldeth seed.

kidder¹, ²: see KID *v.*⁴, and KIDDIER.

Kidder³ ('kɪdə(r)). Short for next.

1893 PEEL *Spen Valley* 343 The manufacture of Kidder carpets. **1899** MISS BROUGHTON *Game & Candle* 158 Her eyes perusing the threadbare Kidder which is good enough for Willy's den.

Kidderminster ('kɪdəmɪnstə(r)). [The name of a town in Worcestershire.]

1. *attrib.* Of or pertaining to Kidderminster; *spec.* the distinctive name of a kind of carpet, originally manufactured there, in which the pattern is formed by the intersection of two cloths of different colours: also called *two-ply* and *ingrain* carpet.

1670-1 *Act 22 & 23 Chas. II*, c. 8 *Preamble*, Abuses..in the makeing of Stuffes called Kidderminster Stuffes. **1685** *Reflect. Baxter* 25 When the Writings of these excel those of R. B. as much as the richest Arras, the meanest Kedderminster-Stuff. **1832** *Encycl. Brit.* (ed. 7) VI. 173/1 Double or Kidderminster carpeting is composed of two plies of cloth. *Ibid.* 174/1 Two-ply Kidderminster Carpet Loom. **1836** *Penny Cycl.* VI. 314/1 Kidderminster or Scotch carpets, or, as the Americans more descriptively term them, ingrain carpets, are wholly of worsted or woollen.

2. *absol.* = Kidderminster carpet or carpeting. Also *attrib.*

1836 *Penny Cycl.* VI. 314/2 In Kidderminsters the shoot forms by far the greatest portion of what is visible. **1839** URE *Dict. Arts* 263 Figured Venetian carpets are woven in the two-ply Kidderminster looms. **1892** L. T. MEADE *Medicine Lady* I. viii. 123 A carpet made of faded Kidderminster covered the floor.

Hence **'Kidderminstered** *a.*, carpeted with a Kidderminster.

1852 SAVAGE *R. Medlicott* III. i. (D.), The tradesman's contracted and Kidderminstered parlour.

kiddie, var. KIDDY *sb.*

'kiddier. *Obs.* exc. *dial.* Also **kidder.** [Origin obscure.] One who buys provisions from the producers and takes them to market to sell; = BADGER *sb.*¹ (q.v.).

By the statute of 1552 the kiddier required a licence, and was forbidden to keep the provisions he bought for more than a month. Such carriers were commonly charged with *regrating* or *forestalling*, hence the def. quoted by Johnson from Ainsworth, 'an ingrosser of corn to enhance its price'; cf. under BADGER.

1551-2 *Act 5 & 6 Edw. VI*, c. 14 §5 The buying of anye Corne Fyshe Butter or Chese, by any suche Badger Lader Kyddier or Carrier. **1562-3** *Act 5 Eliz.* c. 4 §5 Every person ..not..being in Service wᵗʰ any Kyddyer or Carryoʳ of any

Corne Grayne or Meale. **1674–91** RAY *S. & E. Country Words*, A *Kidder*, Badger, Huckster, or Carrier of Goods on Horse-back. **1755** BURN *Just. Peace* s.v. *Butter & Cheese*, Licence to be a badger, lader, kidder, carrier, buyer or transporter coastwise, of butter and cheese. *a* **1825** FORBY *Voc. E. Anglia*, *Kiddier*, *kidger*, one who buys up fowls, eggs, pork, &c. at farm-houses..and carries them to market. [**1895** *E. Anglian Gloss.*, *Kidder*,..a pork-butcher, sausage-maker, a low dealer in poultry and provisions.]

fig. **1603** HARSNET *Pop. Impost.* 26 Meeting with the Common badger or Kiddier for Devils, Mr. Peckham at the L.-Staffords house in London.

kidding, *vbl. sb.*: see KID *v.*[1–4]

kiddish (ˈkɪdɪʃ), *a. rare.* [f. KID *sb.*[1] + -ISH[1].]

1. Of or pertaining to a kid; kid-like.

1552 HULOET, Kyddyshe, or of a kydde, *hædinus.* **1651** OGILBY *Æsop* (1665) 183 He oft drank kiddish gore.

2. *slang.* Childish.

1897 *Daily News* 13 Dec. 8/5 The Sunday school he deserts, partly because it is uninteresting, partly because it is 'kiddish'.

kiddle (ˈkɪd(ə)l). Forms: 5–6 kiddell, 5, 7 kydle, 6 kydell, kedel(l, 6–7 kiddel, 7 kidle, (7–9 kettle, 8 kedle, 9 keddle), 6– kidel, kiddle. [a. AF. *kidel*, *kydel* (whence med.(Anglo-)L. *kidellus*), OF. *quidel* (1289 in Godef. *Compl.*), later *quideau* 'a Wicker Engine whereby fish is caught' (Cotgr.), also *guidel* (1322 in Godef.), mod.F. *guideau*, a stake-net, also, a line of sloping planks placed to direct a current; Breton *kidel* stake-net (Le Gonidec).]

a. A dam, weir, or barrier in a river, having an opening in it fitted with nets or other appliances for catching fish. **b.** An arrangement of stake-nets on the sea-beach for the same purpose (see quot. 1891).

The word is chiefly found in some early statutes (Latin and Anglo-French) and in later references to these: there is no clear evidence that it was actually current in sense a later than *c* 1550.

[**1215** *Magna Carta* xxxiii. in Stubbs *Sel. Charters* (1895) 300 Omnes kydelli de cetero deponantur penitus de Thamisia, et de Medewaye, et per totam Angliam, nisi per costeram maris. **1275** in *Bundello Escaet.* de an. 3 Edw. I. (Du Cange) Et fuit seisitus de uno Kidello vocato a were, ac de libera piscaria in Potlok. **1350** *Act 25 Edw. III*, stat. 4. c. 4 Gortz molins estanks Estackes & kideux. **1393** *Act 1 Rich. II*, c. 9 §1 Touz les Kydels en les ewes de Tamise.] **1477** NORTON *Ord. Alch.* v. in Ashm. (1652) 71 Fishes love Soote smell, also it is trewe, Thei love not old Kydles as thei doe the new. **1529** in Picton *L'pool Munic. Rec.* (1883) I. 25 Weirs and kedells erect made or inhaunced within any of the said streams. **1556** *Chron. Grey Friars* (Camden) 10 Alle the kydelles and trungkes thorowghout the Temse. **1651** N. BACON *Disc. Govt. Eng.* II. v. (1739) 26 The Lord Admiral gained the same within the low-water mark..and in all places where Kiddels were set. **1670** BLOUNT *Law Dict.*, *Kiddle*, *kidel*, or *kedel*,..Some Fishermen corruptly call them *Kettles*. **1724** *Col. Rec. Pennsylv.* III. 233 An act for demolishing and removing Fishing Dams, Wears and Kedles set across the river Schuykill, was read. **1891** LD. HERSCHELL in *Law Times Rep.* LXV. 566/1 A kiddle consists of a series of stakes forced into the ground occupying some 700 feet in length, with a similar row approaching them at an angle. The stakes are connected by network, and at the angle, where the two rows approach, a large net or bag is placed for the purpose of catching the fish.

c. *attrib.* and *Comb.*, as ***kiddle-ground***, ***-net***.

1629 in Boys *Sandwich* (1792) 749 Certain kidel grounds ..where nets do use to hang upon poles..set in the sands above the low water mark to catch fish. **1741** T. ROBINSON *Gavelkind* II. ix. 274 For the Use of their Kidel-Nets. **1880** BUCKLAND *Fishes* 132 (E.D.D.) The mackerel here [at Rye] are caught in large fixed nets called kettle-nets. **1889** *Fishing Gaz.* 31 Aug. 126 (ibid.) The stake nets..locally [in Kent] called 'keddle' nets.

kiddleywink (ˈkɪdlɪwɪŋk). *dial.* Also kiddle-a-wink, kiddle-e-wink, kiddleliwink, kiddlewink, kiddley wenk, kiddlywink, kidley-wink. [Origin unknown; cf. TIDDLYWINK 1.] An ale-house, esp. in the West Country; a low or unlicensed public house (see also quot. 1859).

1830 *Royal Cornwall Gaz.* 25 Dec. 4/6 One hundred and forty public-houses..opened..are called 'Kidley Winks'. *Ibid.*, A gentleman..suggested to the late Chancellor of the Exchequer the idea of retail-breweries. His name is Kidley Wink—hence the term 'Kidley Wink', as applied to the new beer shops. **1859** HOTTEN *Dict. Slang* 56 *Kiddleliwink*, a small shop where they retail the commodities of a village store. **1864** 'F. DERRICK' *Kiddle-a-Wink* ii. 92 The dreary little chamber allotted to him..bad as it was,..was better than many a Kiddle-a-wink could boast of. **1865** R. HUNT *Pop. Romances W. of Eng.* 2nd Ser. 109 A drunken frolic.. at a low beer shop or 'Kiddle-e-Wink'. **1890** *N. & Q.* 18 Jan. 48/2 Can any of your correspondents inform me what is the derivation of the word 'kiddlewink', or 'tiddledy winks'? A friend tells me in the Midland Counties it denotes a house where beer is sold without a licence. **1964** C. DAVEY *Cornish Holiday* ii. 20 The potency of the drink sold in the innumerable public houses in Downlong, and in the 'kiddleywinks' or ale-houses near the mines. *Ibid.* x. 140 A tin-miner, laced with courage from the 'kiddley-wink', saw lights amongst the rocks.

kiddo (ˈkɪdəʊ). *colloq.* [f. KID *sb.*[1] + -O.] = KID *sb.*[1] 5 a, b, and d; freq. as a familiar form of address.

1896 A. MORRISON *Child of Jago* xiii. 135 Josh was up almost before Kiddo Cook reached him. **1905** *Dialect Notes* III. 85 Say, kiddo, what are you going to do this evening? **1916** [see GUESS *v.* 6]. **1938** M. ALLINGHAM *Fashion in Shrouds* xix. 340 'Have I ever let you down, kiddo?' The pseudo-American accent was slick. **1959** [see BAT *v.*[1] 4]. **1961** *John o' London's* 9 Nov. 517/3 When it comes to choosing between the balance of power and unborn babies, I'm for the kiddos, every time. **1974** N. FREELING *Dressing of Diamond* 128 'How long do I have to stay?'..'Just as long as we thinks right, kiddo.'

kiddush (ˈkɪdʊʃ). Also K-. [Heb. *qiddūš*, sanctification.] A ceremony of prayer and blessing over bread and wine, performed by the head of a Jewish household at the meal ushering in the Sabbath or a holy day. Also *attrib.*

1753 *Jewish Ritual* 34 All together with him in Concert, say the *Keedush*, i.e. the Sanctification. **1891** M. FRIEDLÄNDER *Jewish Relig.* 254 On Friday evening, before the meal, we praise God for sanctifying the Sabbath by a prayer called *Kiddush*, 'sanctification'. **1932** A. Z. IDELSOHN *Jewish Liturgy* II. x. 133 The text of the *Kiddush* consists of Gen. 1:31 and 2:1–3. Then there follows the blessing over wine and the closing paragraph... In the home, the benediction over bread follows. **1945** G. DIX *Shape of Liturgy* iv. 88 On festivals there was another common cup blessed and partaken of, besides the cup of blessing, both at a *chabûrah* meeting and at the ordinary family meal of a pious Jewish household. This was the *kiddûsh*-cup. **1960** *Commentary* June 500/1 Perhaps only one out of every two families begin the meal with the *kiddush*. **1973** *Jewish Chron.* 18 May 50/2 A service was conducted..at the Friern Hospital Synagogue and a kiddush was provided for the patients.

kiddushin (kɪˈduːʃiːn). Also K-. [Aramaic *qiddūšīn*, pl. of KIDDUSH.] The section of the Jewish Mishnah treating of betrothal and marriage; also the ceremony of betrothal, and the money or article given by the groom to effect the betrothal.

1883 *Encycl. Brit.* XVI. 505/2 Kiddushin (betrothal and marriage), in four chapters. **1904** *Jewish Encycl.* VII. 485/2 'Kiddushin' is the rabbinical term for betrothal, because the wife becomes thereby the sacrosanct possession of the husband... In the Mishnah, Kiddushin is divided into four chapters and comprises..forty-seven paragraphs. **1936** H. FREEDMAN in I. Epstein *Babylonian Talmud* VIII. p. xi, The Hebrew name Ḳiddushin ('Consecration') for betrothal, is worthy of note. The Talmud defines it as an act whereby the bride is rendered sacrosanct. *Ibid.* 51 There it was given her as a deposit... But here he gave it to her as *kiddushin*: if she did not want it [as such], she should have thrown it away. *Ibid.* 218 Her father [alone can accept *ḳiddushin* on her behalf] but not she herself. **1971** *Encycl. Judaica* X. 986 *Kiddushin*.., the last tractate in the order *Nashim*... It deals with matrimonial matters... There is no corresponding word for *kiddushin* in English. It is more than an 'engagement'.., as it can be dissolved only by divorce, and moreover the law of adultery..applies from the moment of *kiddushin*.

kiddy (ˈkɪdɪ), *sb.* Also kiddie, *Sc.* keddie. [f. KID *sb.*[1] + -Y[4].]

1. A little kid (young goat).

1579 SPENSER *Sheph. Cal.* May 249 Well heard Kiddie all this sore constraint. **1597** *Witchcraft* in *Spald. Club Misc.* I. 129 At thy incumming, the keddie lap vpon the. **1810** *Sporting Mag.* XXXV. 30 Our poor kiddy..which died yesterday of the shab.

attrib. **1855** KINGSLEY *Westw. Ho!* iv. (1881) 79 The goats furnished milk and 'kiddy-pies'.

2. *slang.* and *colloq.* A little child. [f. KID *sb.*[1] 5.]

1889 BOLDREWOOD *Robbery under Arms* xx, They'd heard all kinds of rough talk ever since they was little kiddies. **1892** R. KIPLING *Barrack-r. Ballads, Route Marchin'* iii, While the women and the kiddies sit an' shiver in the carts.

3. *Thieves' slang.* **a.** A professional thief who assumes a 'flashness' of dress and manner; one who dresses in a similar style. [cf. KID *sb.*[1] 5 b.]

1780 TOMLINSON *Slang Past.* i, My time, O ye Kiddies, was happily spent. **1812** J. H. VAUX *Flash Dict.*, *Kiddy*, a thief of the lower order, who..dresses in the extreme of vulgar gentility. **1823** BYRON *Juan* XI xvii, Poor Tom was once a kiddy upon town. **1863** COWDEN CLARKE *Shaks. Char.* xiv. 362 That such a kiddy should have made his public exit from the Tyburn stage in an embroidered dress ..was befitting his 'exquisite' nature.

b. A hat of a form fashionable among 'kiddies'.

1865 *Lond. Rev.* 2 Sept. 241/2 The last fashion being a hat, apparently bred between an archdeaconal and a 'kiddy', with a broad ribbon passing in front through a large black buckle.

4. *attrib.* as *adj.*: **a.** Pertaining to, appropriate to, 'kiddies'; fashionable among persons of that class.

1805 *Sporting Mag.* XXVI. 56 The horse-dealer..in the kiddy phrase, had both his eyes closed up. **1823** in *Newcastle Daily Jrnl.* (1891) 31 Mar. 3/3 Replete with prime chaunts, rum glees, and kiddy catches. **1836–9** DICKENS *Sk. Boz, Making a night of it* (1850) 164/2 It was his ambition to do something in the celebrated 'kiddy' or stage-coach way.

b. *Comb.*, as **kiddy brother** = *kid brother*; **kiddy car** orig. *U.S.*, (*a*) a small toy car for a child; (*b*) a perambulator; **kiddy sister** = *kid sister.*

1963 C. MACKENZIE *My Life & Times* II. 82 That was my *kiddy brother. He's a new boy. **1918** *Sears, Roebuck Catal.* Index, *Kiddy car. **1951** I. SHAW *Troubled Air* xx. 331 There wasn't enough left of the cab to make a kiddie car. **1953** WODEHOUSE *Performing Flea* 58 You'll hear them call for Mr. Warner's bicycle, Mr. Lasky's kiddie car and Mr. Louis B. Mayer's roller-skates. **1959** *Times* 24 Feb. 13/4 A toy making factory..for the manufacture of fibreglass toys, kiddy cars, and rocking horses. **1973** *Sci. Amer.* Jan. 10/2 The invention by her [*sc.* Fräulein Gretel Steiff] of the 'Teddy Bear Doll' will go down in history with the kiddie car and other things that make life happy for children. **1913** C. MACKENZIE *Sinister St.* I. I. vii. 103 He also learnt to speak..of..'my people' and 'my *kiddy sister'. **1915** A. BENNETT *Those Twain* (1916) I. ix. 159 'He's taken a terrific fancy to Maud, my kiddie sister,' said Daisy. **1963** C. MACKENZIE *My Life & Times* II. 60 Still laughing uncontrollably..in a fresh recollection of the face of our kiddy sister and the tone of her voice.

kiddy (ˈkɪdɪ), *v. slang.* [Cf. prec. and KID *v.*[4]] *trans.* To hoax, humbug, take in (a person).

1851 MAYHEW *Lond. Labour* I. 462 (Hoppe) There they met with beggars who kiddied them on to the lurk. *a* **1864** DICKENS (Webster), Some of the swell mob..so far kiddied us as to hire a horse and shay, start away from London by Whitechapel, and..come into Epsom from the opposite direction,..while we were waiting for them at the rail.

kiddy-wink, kiddywink (ˈkɪdɪwɪŋk). *colloq.* Also **kiddiewinkie, kiddywinkle, kiddywinky.** [Familiar extension of KIDDY *sb.*] = KIDDY *sb.* 2 (usu. jocular or affected). Also *attrib.*

1957 P. WILDEBLOOD *Main Chance* 201 Delicious milky-boo for the kiddy-winks. **1959** P. BULL *I know Face* x. 183 My performance..was pretty macabre, and must have frightened the bejesus out of the kiddy-winks. **1962** *Spectator* 22 June 827/2 Morality plays for the kiddie-winkies. **1968** L. BERG *Risinghill* 250 The approach was fine. None of this kiddywinky stuff. They became grownup emotionally and mentally well in advance of their years. **1970** M. TRIPP *Man without Friends* xiii. 142 He's at Bognor with his kiddiewinkie. **1974** *Times* 13 Aug. 8/8 Dad Robinson..puts off the average incompetent father. Still, the kiddywinkles aren't to know.

kide, obs. f. KITH; pa. pple. of KITHE.

kideneire, -nere: see KIDNEY.

kidful: see KID *sb.*[4]

kidge, var KEDGE *a.*

†**kidgell**, obs. north. form of CUDGEL.

c **1570** *Durham Depos.* (Surtees) 264 He cutt 4 kidgells or houghells to hange salmon netts upon. **1575–6** *Ibid.* 295 [He] lyfted up his staff or kidgell.

kid glove, ˈkid-ˌglove.

1. A glove made of kid-skin, lamb-skin, or other similar leather. ***with kid gloves***, in a gentle, delicate, or gingerly manner.

1832 MARRYAT *N. Forster* xxxii, A new pair of grey kid gloves. **1834** W. HULL *Hist. Glove Trade* 69 Men and women's fine gloves, or those that pass in the shops under the denomination of kid-gloves, but which are really made from lamb-skins..dressed at Yeovil. **1888** BRYCE *Amer. Commw.* II. III. lviii. 410 The Americans who think that European politics are worked, to use the common phrase, 'with kid gloves'.

2. *attrib.* as *adj.* Characterized by wearing kid-gloves; dainty or delicate in action or operation; avoiding real exertion or every-day work; free from roughness or harshness.

1856 H. H. DIXON *Post & Paddock* vii. 115 He was, in fact, a mere kid-glove sportsman. **1888** T. W. HIGGINSON *Women and Men* 296 Anti-kid-glove literature is really no better than the kid-glove literature at which it affects to protest. **1892** ZANGWILL *Bow Mystery* 81, I don't like your kid glove philanthropists meddling in matters they don't understand.

Hence **ˈkid-ˌglove** *v. trans.*, to cover (the hands) with kid-gloves. **ˈkid-ˌgloved** *a.*, wearing kid-gloves; also *fig.*, refined, dainty, delicate, etc.

1848 CLOUGH *Bothie* v. 117 Dancing and pressing the fingers kid-gloved of a Lady Maria. **1859** SALA *Gas-light & D.* xxiv. 276 You can descry a kid-gloved hand, with rings outside the glove. **1860** O. W. HOLMES *Elsie V.* (1887) 11 The richer part of the community that..kid-glove their hands. **1899** STEAD in *Daily News* 19 July 5/5 He was always somewhat of a kid-gloved gentleman.

kidknapper, obs. form of KIDNAPPER.

kidlet (ˈkɪdlɪt). [f. KID *sb.*[1] + -LET.] A young child. Also *fig.*

1899 'J. FLYNT' *Tramping with Tramps* ii. 31 The other 'kidlets', as they were nicknamed, were as deformed morally as was the adopted girl physically. **1903** J. DEWEY *Let.* Mar. in R. B. Perry *Tht. & Char. W. James* (1935) II. lxxxi. 521 We won't attempt to father you with all the weak kidlets which are crying in the volume to be born. **1959** C. MACINNES *Absolute Beginners* 165 A lot of kidlets helping him to do so.

kidley-wink, var. KIDDLEYWINK.

kidling (ˈkɪdlɪŋ). [f. KID *sb.*[1] + -LING. Cf. ON. *kiðlingr*, Norw. and Sw. *kidling.*]

1. A little kid.

1586 WEBBE *Eng. Poetrie* (Arb.) 78 O were thou content.. trym kydling flocke with me to driue to the greene fieldes. **1613–16** W. BROWNE *Brit. Past.* II. i, Mountaines where the wanton Kidling dallies. *a* **1732** GAY *Acis & Galatea*, O Nymph..Like kidlings blithe and merry! **1814** SOUTHEY *Roderick* xi, At yonder door Behold the favourite kidling bleats unheard.

2. *slang.* A little child; a baby.

1899 *Daily News* 11 Feb. 3/7 The poor little kidlings' feet would suffer, I should think.

kidmutgar, variant of KHIDMUTGAR.

kidnap (ˈkɪdˌnæp), *v.* [f. KID *sb.*[1] 5 c + NAP *v.*, to snatch, seize (cf. NAB); possibly as a back-formation from KIDNAPPER. The words no doubt originated among the class which followed the practice of kidnapping. Bailey,

Johnson, Ash, etc. stress *kid'nap*, which is still usual in the north.] Originally, to steal or carry off (children or others) in order to provide servants or labourers for the American plantations; hence, in general use, to steal (a child), to carry off (a person) by illegal force.

1682 LUTTRELL *Brief Rel.* (1857) I. 183 Mr. John Wilmore haveing kidnapped a boy of 13 years of age to Jamaica, a writt *de homine replegiando* was delivered to the sheriffs of London against him. **1688** *Lond. Gaz.* No. 2360/3 John Dykes..Convicted of Kidnapping, or Enticing away, His Majesty's Subjects, to go Servants into the Foreign Plantations. **1693** I. MATHER *Cases Consc.* (1862) 241 A Servant, who was Spirited or Kidnapt (as they call it) into America. **1723** DE FOE *Col. Jack* (1840) 266, I will kidnap her and send her to Virginia. **1809** J. ADAMS *Wks.* (1854) IX. 316 The practice in Holland of kidnapping men for settlers or servants in Batavia. **1849** JAMES *Gipsy* xviii, You go kidnapping people's children, you thieves of human flesh. **1884** PAE *Eustace* 103, I am not a common seaman, to be kidnapped in this fashion.

fig. **1732** SWIFT *Corr.* Wks. 1841 II. 669 We [the Irish] have but one dunce of irrefragable fame,..and the Scots have kidnapped him from us. **1850** KINGSLEY *Alton Locke* x, The people who see their children thus kidnapped into hell.

Hence **'kid,napped** *ppl. a.*, **'kid'napping** *vbl. sb.* and *ppl. a.*, **kidnappingly** *adv.*

1798 *Anti-Jacobin* 22 Jan. (1852) 47 Courteny's *kidnapp'd rhymes. **1861** *Times* 10 July, Full freights of kidnapped Chinamen. **1878** GLADSTONE *Prim. Homer* 110 The kid-napped victims whom Phœnician vessels brought from abroad. **1682** LUTTRELL *Brief Rel.* (1857) I. 187 The witnesses..were..to prove that there was..such a trade as *kidnapping or spiriting away children. **1769** BLACKSTONE *Comm.* IV. xv. 219 The other remaining offence, that of kidnapping, being the forcible abduction or stealing away of man, woman, or child from their own country, and selling them into another. **1830** SCOTT *Demonol.* iv. 127 This kidnapping of the human race, so peculiar to the whole Elfin people. **1867** FREEMAN *Norm. Conq.* I. v. 365 The kidnapping of persons of free condition was not unknown. **1887** *Athenæum* 19 Mar. 375/3 The *kidnapping grandmother..is not so repellent as might be supposed. **1838** *Tait's Mag.* V. 206, I hold it to have been wickedly,..crimpingly, *kidnappingly done.

kidnap ('kɪdnæp), *sb.* [f. the vb.] The act of kidnapping. Also *attrib.*

1961 WEBSTER *s.v.*, A kidnap plot. The kidnap car. **1973** 'I. DRUMMOND' *Jaws of Watchdog* xv. 204 There was no money in killing you, but maybe a lot in a kidnap. **1973** *Observer* 12 Aug. 1/2 (*heading*) Jet kidnap was attempt to capture top guerrilla. **1974** N. FREELING *Dressing of Diamond* 201 A kidnap case—yes..we had it on our telex last night.

kidnapper ('kɪd,næpə(r)). Also 7 **-knapper, -nabber,** (*U.S.*) **kidnaper.** [f. as KIDNAP *v.* + -ER[1]. Originally *kid'napper* (quot. 1679); also in Johnson, Ash, etc.; so still in northern use.] One who kidnaps children or others; a stealer of human beings. Also *fig.*

1678 PHILLIPS (ed. 4), *Kidknappers* [**1696–1706** *Kidnappers*], those that make a trade of decoying and spiriting away young children to Ship them for foreign Plantations. *c* **1679** *Roxb. Ball.* (1890) VII. 13 How like kidnappers all the day In every corner they survey. **1684** BUNYAN *Pilgr.* II. 109 Thou practises the craft of a Kidnapper, thou gatherest up Women, and Children, and carriest them into a strange Countrey. **1778** A. HAMILTON *Wks.* (1886) VII. 541 For punishing kidnappers or persons who aid the enemy in carrying off the peaceable inhabitants. **1834** LYTTON *Pompeii* II. i, The Thessalian kidnapper had stolen the blind girl from gentle parents. **1865** LIVINGSTONE *Zambesi* xxi. 434 It is dangerous to remain in their villages at this time of year when kidnappers are abroad. **1909** O. JESPERSEN *Mod. Eng. Gram.* I. 149 Americans write *kidnaper*, which to an Englishman would suggest [kidneipə] or [-nəpə]. **1969** *Eugene* (Oregon) *Register-Guard* 3 Dec. 3A/2 The two men..freed themselves moments after the kidnaper abducted Miss Birdsong and called police. **1973** *Philadelphia Inquirer* 7 Oct. 19 The kidnapers agreed to call the Millers back several hours later.

Hence **kid'nappery**.

1890 *Murray's Mag.* Apr. 463 The regions of kidnappery, slave-trading, and freebooting!

kidney ('kɪdnɪ). Forms: 4 **kidenei,** 4–6 **kydney** (5 ? **kidneye,** 6 **kydne**), 6– **kidney.** ? *Sing.* or *Pl.* 4 **kydnere.** *Pl.* α. 4 **kideneiren, kydeneyren;** β. 4 **kide-, kydeneris, kidneris, -nares, kydneers, -ners;** γ. 6 **kidneies, -neis, kydneys, -nes,** 6–7 **kidneyes,** 6–9 **kidnies,** 6– **kidneys.** [Of obscure formation.

On the supposition that the sing. was *kid(e)nere*, this has been inferred to be a compound, having as its second element ME. *nere* kidney; and it has been conjectured that *kid(e)-* might represent OE. *cwið, cwiða*, or ON. *kvið* belly, womb. But this is on many grounds improbable; above all, because the ordinary sing. in ME. was in *-ei, -ey*, the solitary instance of *kydnere*, c 1420 (1 b below), being probably a pl. for *kydneren*. It is thus possible that *kidenei*, pl. *kideneiren*, had as its second element *ey*, pl. *eyren, eiren, eyre, eyer*, EGG. (Cf. Ger. *eier* testicles.) The pl. *kid(e)neris* might possibly owe its form to association with *neres, neeres*, pl. of *nere*; the later *kidneies, -neys*, was a new pl. from the unanalysed singular. But the first element remains uncertain.]

1. One of a pair of glandular organs situated in the abdominal cavity of mammals, birds, and reptiles, which excrete urine and so remove effete nitrogenous matter from the blood. Also a gland with similar functions found in some animals of lower organization. The kidneys of cattle, sheep, and pigs are an article of food.

a. *sing.*

c **1325** *Gloss. W. de Bibbesw.* in Wright *Voc.* 149 L'etplen (*the milte*), boueles (*neres*), et reinoun (*kidenei*). **13..** *Metr. Voc.* in Wr.-Wülcker 627/8 *Ren*, kedney. *c* **1400** *Pol. Rel. & L. Poems* (1866) 37 The Ire in the gawle. Auaryce in the kydney. **1520** WHITINTON *Vulg.* (1527) 39 They may be wel compared to the kydne that lyeth rolled in fatte, and yet is lene hym self. **1601** HOLLAND *Pliny* XI. xxxvii. 343 The right kidney in all creatures is the bigger. **1646** SIR T. BROWNE *Pseud. Ep.* 82 The stones or calculous concretions in kidney or bladder. **1871** M. COLLINS *Mrq. & Merch.* I. ix. 293 Waiter, bring me a kidney and some stout.

b. *Of doubtful number.*

c **1420** *Liber Cocorum* 10 Take þo hert and þo mydruv and þe kydnere, And hew hom smalle, as I þe lere.

c. *pl.*

α. **1388** WYCLIF *Exod.* xxix. 13 And thou schalt take..the calle of the mawe, and twey kidneris [3 *MSS.* kideneiren, **1382** the two kydneers]. *Ibid.* 22 Twey kideneris [3 *MSS.* kideneiren, **1382** the two reynes]. —— *Lev.* iii. 4 [see β]. *a* **1400** *Prymer* (1891) 104 For thou haddest my kydeneyren.

β. *a* **1325** *Prose Psalter* lxxii[i]. 21 Myn kidnares [*v.r.* kydners] ben chaunged. **1382** WYCLIF *Exod.* xxix. 13 [see α]. **1388** —— *Lev.* iii. 4 Thei schulen offre twey kydeneris [*v.r.* kideneiren, **1382** the two reyns].

γ. *c* **1510** MORE *Picus* Wks. 20/1 My reynes or kidneis, hath chiden me vnto the night. *c* **1532** DU WES *Introd. Fr.* in Palsgr. 904 The kydneys, *les rognons.* **1535** COVERDALE *Lev.* iii. 10 The two kydneys with the fat..and the nett on the leuer vpon the kydneys also. **1581** MULCASTER *Positions* xxii. (1887) 93 It driueth also the stone from the kidneies into the bladder. **1732** ARBUTHNOT *Rules of Diet* 256 It is suspected to be hurtful to the Kidneys. **1803** *Med. Jrnl.* X. 82 Affections of the bladder and kidnies. **1857** G. BIRD *Urin. Deposits* (ed. 5) 424 Few remedies are so capricious in their action as those which..influence the functions of the kidneys. **1891** S. MOSTYN *Curatica* 27 Don't you think the kidneys will be spoiled if they are not eaten at once?

fig. **1591** SYLVESTER *Du Bartas* I. ii. 585 If heav'ns bright torches, from earth's kidneys, sup Sum somwhat dry and heatfull Vapours up. **1710** STEELE *Tatler* No. 268 ¶2 A Youth, who officiates as the Kidney of the Coffee-house.

2. *fig.* **a.** Temperament, nature, constitution, disposition; hence, kind, sort, class, stamp.

a **1555** LATIMER *Serm. & Rem.* (Parker Soc.) 312 To pronounce all to be thieves to a man, except myself, of course, and those men..that are of my own kidney. **1598** SHAKS. *Merry W.* III. v. 116 Thinke of that, a man of my Kidney;..that am as subiect to heate as butter. **1652** J. HALL *Height Eloq.* p. lxxxii, Is it not better for us that are men of this Kidney to have a Ruler set over us then to be left to our freedome. **1733** FIELDING *Don Quixote in Eng.* III. iv, This fellow is not quite of a right kidney, the dog is not sound at the bottom. **1880** DISRAELI *Endym.* xvii, It was a large and rather miscellaneous party, but all of the right kidney.

†**b.** Proper condition or state, order. *colloq. Obs.*

1763 COLMAN *Terræ Filius* No. 1 Attempt to put their Hair out of Kidney.

3. Something resembling a kidney in shape, etc.

†**a.** An ovary. *Obs. rare*$^{-1}$.

1576 TURBERV. *Venerie* lxvi. 186 The kydneys whiche gelders take awaye from a bytche when they spaye hir.

b. More fully ***kidney potato***; an oval variety of potato.

1796 C. MARSHALL *Garden.* xv. (1813) 249 The red nosed kidney..is a great favorite. **1839** *Penny Cycl.* XIII. 291/2 The earliest potato is called the Superfine White Kidney. **1840** HOOD *Up the Rhine* 111 The next dish..was of very small, very waxy kidney potatoes. **1892** ZANGWILL *Child. Ghetto* II. 6 Kidneys or regents, my child?

†**4.** ***kidneys of wheat***, an imperfect reproduction of the Scriptural expression 'fat of kidneys of wheat' Deut. xxxii, 14: cf. Ps. cxlvii. 14 'the fat of wheat', the finest of the wheat, in allusion to the fat, and esp. the kidney-fat, as the choicest part of an animal, which was therefore offered in sacrifice.

1611 BIBLE *Deut.* xxxii. 14. **1663** JER. TAYLOR *Serm. Death Ld. Primate Irel.* 10 If the Corn dyes and lives again..in the verdure of a leaf, in the fulness of the Ear, in the Kidneys of the wheat. *a* **1673** G. SWINNOCK in Spurgeon *Treas. Dav.* Ps. xxxvi. 8 [Bread] made of the kidneys of the wheat, of the finest flour.

5. *attrib.* and *Comb.* **a.** attributive: Of or belonging to the kidneys, as ***kidney disease, fat, form, substance, suet, -tube, -vein***, etc.; made of or containing kidneys, as ***kidney pie, soup***. **b.** similative, as ***kidney-form, kidney-shaped*** adjs.

1889 *Sci. Amer.* LXI. 48 Liver and *Kidney Diseases. **1806** A. HUNTER *Culina* (ed. 3) 213 The *kidney fat of a loin of veal. **1885** HAYTER *Carboona* 3 Great virtues are attributed by the Australian aborigines to the kidney-fat of their enemies. **1796** KIRWAN *Elem. Min.* (ed. 2) I. 30 *Kidney-form, or reniform, round elevations. **1811** PINKERTON *Petral.* II. 123 They are quite different from rolled pebbles, and are often of a flattened, sometimes a *kidney form. **1836–9** DICKENS *Sk. Boz, The Streets* (1850) 33/2 The *kidney-pie man has just walked away with his warehouse on his arm. **1757** PULTNEY in *Phil. Trans.* L. 67 The receptacle is convex on both sides, and *kidney-shaped. **1887** W. PHILLIPS *Brit. Discomycetes* 17 Lobes deflexed, kidney-shaped. **1887** *Spons' Househ. Man.* Index, *Kidney soup. **1873** T. H. GREEN *Introd. Pathol.* (ed. 2) 283 The capsule..cannot be removed without tearing the *kidney substance. **1822** in Cobbett *Rur. Rides* (1885) I. 93 Their skins, colour of veal *kidney-suet. **1847–9** TODD *Cycl. Anat.* IV. 254 The epithelium of the *kidney-tubes. **1597** A. M. tr. *Guillemeau's Fr. Chirurg.* 30/1 The fourth is the mediane, or *kidney-vayne, situated belowe the foote. **1888** ROLLESTON & JACKSON *Anim. Life* 110 The pulmonary vein..is joined..before it enters the auricle by the efferent kidney veins.

c. Special combs.: **kidney-cotton**, a variety of *Gossypium barbadense*, a cotton plant of which the seeds are in kidney-shaped masses; **kidney dressing-table**, a dressing-table with a kidney-shaped top; **kidney fern** *N.Z.*, a fern, *Cardiomanes reniforme*, with kidney-shaped leaves; †**kidney-fetch** = *kidney-vetch*; **kidney graft**, the operation of transplanting a kidney from one person to another (see GRAFT *sb.*[1] 3); **kidney-link**, a coupling below the collar of the harness of a horse; †**kidney-lipped** *a.*, hare-lipped; **kidney machine**, a machine for effecting hæmodialysis; = *artificial kidney* (ARTIFICIAL *a.* 5), HAEMODIALYSER; **kidney ore**, hæmatite occurring in kidney-shaped masses; **kidney-paved** *a.*, paved with cobble stones; **kidney-pie**, (*a*) a pie containing kidneys; (*b*) *Austral.* and *N.Z. slang*, flattery, humbug, deceit; **kidney-piece**, a cam with a kidney-shaped outline; **kidney-potato**: see 3 b; **kidney punch** (see quot. 1954); **kidney-rotter** *Austral.* and *N.Z. slang* (see quot. 1958); **kidney-stone**, a stone of a kidney shape, a cobble; *spec.* see quot. 1861; **kidney table**, a table having a kidney-shaped top; **kidney-vetch**, a leguminous herb (*Anthyllis vulneraria*), Lady's-fingers; **kidney worm**, either of two parasitic nematodes, *Stephanurus dentatus*, which attacks pigs, or *Dioctophyma* (or *Dioctophyme*) *renale*, which attacks man, dogs, and other mammals.

1789 *Trans. Soc. Arts* I. 256, I prepared a parcel of the silk, and also a parcel of the *kidney, or Brazilian cotton. **1932** *Times Lit. Suppl.* 9 June 429/3 A walnut suite with a *kidney dressing-table. **1965** D. TORR *Diplomatic Cover* iii. 46 She leant over her frilly kidney dressing-table. **1867** E. SAUTER tr. *F. von Hochstetter's New Zealand* vi. 133 The singular form of the *Kidney-fern (*Trichomanes reniforme*). **1926** J. DEVANNY *Lenore Divine* xx. 185 The kidney-fern was everywhere, sprawling over ground and trees. **1951** J. FRAME *Lagoon* 7 My..grandmother..could find kidney fern. **1966** *Encycl. N.Z.* I. 645/2 The kidney fern, *Cardiomanes reniforme*, with undivided leaves fringed with prominent sori, is common throughout the country. **1671** SKINNER *Etymol. Ling. Angl., Bot.*, *Kidney-fetch. **1794** MARTYN *Rousseau's Bot.* xxv. 353 Ladies-Finger or Kidney Fetch is not uncommon in chalky pastures. **1962** *Daily Tel.* 26 Nov. 1/3 (*headline*) *Kidney graft doctor worse. **1970** Kidney graft [see GRAFT *sb.*[1] 3]. **1883** J. P. GROVES *From Cadet to Captain* xxii. 223 Harnessing..Nellie's ponies..he managed to get the hames upside down, with the *kidney-links on the top of the collars. **1648** HERRICK *Hesper., Upon Jollie's Wife*, Squint-ey'd, hook-nos'd; and lastly *kidney-lipt. **1966** *Daily Tel.* 28 Sept. 19/4 Kidney patients would be able to use an artificial *kidney machine in their own homes. **1972** *Guardian* 9 Feb. 20/2 Patients who rely on electrical machinery (such as kidney machines) in their homes. **1750** R. POCOCKE *Trav.* (1888) 15 Three sorts of ore, the finest is the *kidney ore. **1852** TH. ROSS *Humboldt's Trav.* I. xiii. 441 The metals appear only in kidney-ores, and present the most delusive appearances. **1889** *Daily Tel.* 19 Apr. 6/4 The principal street..emerged from the *kidney-paved condition and got itself macadamised. **1836–9** *Kidney-pie [see KIDNEY 5]. **1937** PARTRIDGE *Dict. Slang* 455/1 *Kidney-pie*, insincere praise. **1884** F. J. BRITTEN *Watch & Clockm.* 43 On the arbor of the annual wheel is fixed a brass cam or '*kidney piece'. **1896** ADE *Artie* i. 3 Artie..gave him a friendly blow, known to ringside patrons as a '*kidney-punch'. **1954** F. C. AVIS *Boxing Reference Dict.* 61 *Kidney punch*, a blow falling at the kidneys—a foul punch liable to result in disqualification. **1964** Kidney punch [see CAPER *sb.*[2] 1 c]. **1958** *Tararua* XII. 27 The frameless pack..being more familiarly known by that elegant term, **kidney-rotter*. **1971** *N.Z. Listener* 22 Feb. 51/2 Twenty-odd years ago..we slogged along in hobnailed boots, carried 'kidney-rotter' packs, [etc.]. **1861** BRISTOW *Gloss. Min.*, **Kidney-stones*, a local name for small hard nodules..washed out of the cliffs on the north shore of Weymouth. **1890** *19th Cent.* Nov. 842 Regimental highlows will not stand the rough kidney stones of the barrack stables for more than six months. **1845** DISRAELI *Sybil* (1863) 193 He was seated in an easy chair, before a *kidney table at which he was writing. **1706** PHILLIPS, **Kidney-vetch* and *Kidney-wort*, several sorts of Herbs. **1893** W. B. E. MILLER et al. *Dis. Live Stock* vi. 410 Various symptoms are popularly attributed to '*kidney worms', especially a weakness or partial palsy of the hinder limbs, inclination to lie down, and awkwardness in the gait. **1905** MOUSSU & DOLLAR *Dis. Cattle* iii. 539 This so-called kidney worm of hogs (*Sclerostoma pinguicola*) should not be confounded with the kidney worm (*Dioctophyme viscerale*) of dogs and man. **1934** H. O. MÖNNIG *Vet. Helminthol. & Entomol.* III. 170 The 'kidney-worm' of swine occurs in the perirenal fat. **1963** JUBB & KENNEDY *Path. Domestic Animals* II. vi. 272/1 *Dioctophyma renale* is the giant kidney worm, the largest of parasitic nematodes... It is usually found in dogs, mink, and other fish-eating mammals, but is recorded in ox and horse.

kidney bean, kidney-bean.

1. The ordinary name given to two species of *Phaseolus* (N.O. *Leguminosæ*), known as the dwarf French bean (*P. vulgaris*), and the Scarlet Runner (*P. multiflorus*), of which the unripened pods and the ripe seeds are used as food: see BEAN *sb.* 3.

1548 TURNER *Names of Herbes* 75 *Smilax hortensis*..may be called in english Kydney beane, because the seede is lyke a Kydney. **1548–62** [see BEAN *sb.* 3]. **1601** HOLLAND *Pliny* I. 570 The Pulse called Phaseoli, *i.* Kidney Beans vse to be eaten cod and al together. **1732** ARBUTHNOT *Rules of Diet* i. in *Aliments*, etc. 251 Beans and Kidney-Beans have the same Qualities. **1882** *Garden* 1 Apr. 222/2 Few plants are more tender early in the season than Kidney Beans.

2. kidney-bean tree. A climbing shrub of the leguminous genus *Wistaria* as the American

species, *W. frutescens*, and the Chinese, *W. chinensis*, both grown as wall-climbers in Great Britain.

1741 *Compl. Fam.-Piece* II. iii. 380 There are several other Trees and Shrubs which are now in Flower, as.. Catesby's Climber, or Carolina Kidney-Bean-tree. **1760** J. LEE *Introd. Bot.* App. 316 Kidney Bean-tree of Carolina, *Glycine*. **1897** BRITTON & BROWN *Flora North. States Canada* II. 294 *Krauntia frutescens*—American Wisteria.. Called also Kidney-bean Tree.

'kidneywort. *Herb.* [See WORT.] The plant *Cotyledon Umbilicus*, also called Navelwort; see also quot. 1866.

1640 PARKINSON *Theat. Bot.* 741 Wall Pennywort, Hipwort, Kidneywort. **1854** GISSING in *Pharmac. Jrnl.* XIII. 459 One of the common names.. is kidney-wort. **1866** *Treas. Bot.* 646/2 Kidney-wort, *Umbilicus pendulinus*, also *Saxifraga stellaris*.

kidology (kɪ'dɒlədʒɪ). *colloq.* [f. KID *v.*^{4} + -OLOGY.] The art of 'kidding' or deceiving; knowing or studied deception, mockery, humbug; teasing.

1964 *Times* 21 Feb. 9/4 Abolition would lead to the whole box of tricks based on 'kidology', with gimmicks of every kind and stamps of every colour. **1965** [see MADAM *sb.* 3 c (e)]. **1969** J. WAINWRIGHT *Take-over Men* ix. 161 It is even doubtful whether they [*sc.* the police] can indulge in large-scale kidology with the Press. **1973** *Times* 15 Feb. 18/4 But all this is kidology and both the Government and the CBI know it! **1984** *Listener* 9 Aug. 36/2 The BBC commentary team showed great resourcefulness in improvising a form of kidology known as the 'perhaps' factor. This involves using the fact that the British hopeful is out of camera shot to intimate that they are 'perhaps in second place' when actually they are fourth or fifth.

'kid-skin. The skin of a kid, esp. such skin tanned and used for gloves; also applied to skins of lambs and other animals used for this purpose. Also *attrib.*, as ***kid-skin glove***.

c **1645** HOWELL *Lett.* xiv. (1765) 19 A dozen pair of the best white Kid-skin Gloves the Royal-Exchange can afford. **1657** THORNLEY tr. *Longus' Daphnis & Chloe* 29 Daphnis saw Chloe in her Kidskin, and her Pine coronet. **1719** W. WOOD *Surv. Trade* 94 Kid-skins, Paper, Pruans, Linens and wrought Silks. **1826** SCOTT *Woodst.* i, What is a glover but a tailor working on kid-skin? **1826** LAMB *Elia* Ser. II. *Pop. Fallacies* xv, Another had dipped his scooped palm in a kid-skin of wild honey.

kid-stakes, kidstakes ('kɪdsteɪks). *Austral.* and *N.Z. slang.* Also **kidsteaks**. [Cf. KID *sb.*^{5}] Humbug, pretence.

1916 C. J. DENNIS *Songs Sentimental Bloke* 124 *Kid stakes*, pretence. **1919** W. H. DOWNING *Digger Dial.* 30 *Kid-stakes*, insincere flattery; inveiglement; a wheedling or deceitful speech or action. **1922** A. WRIGHT *Colt from Country* 201 'It was no kid stakes,' declared Bucks. 'The old man had the roll ready.' **1945** G. CASEY *Downhill is Easier* 138 All his kidstakes during the afternoon had probably been caused by his jealousy of Peter South. **1949** F. SARGESON *I saw in Dream* II. xiv. 154 But it looked as if it was all kidsteaks. **1960** A. KIMMINS *Lugs O'Leary* ii. 17 This isn't kid-stakes... This is deadly serious.

kidyer, variant of KIDDIER.

kie, variant of *kye*, pl. of COW.

kief, kiefekil, variants of KEF, KEFFEKILL.

Kieffer ('ki:fə(r)). The name of Peter *Kieffer* (d. 1890), American gardener, used *attrib.* in **Kieffer pear** to designate a variety of yellow-skinned pear (*Pyrus pyrifolia* var. *culta* × *P. communis*) developed by him. Also *absol.*

[**1879** *Amer. Agriculturist* Jan. 21/1 (*heading*) A New Pear —Kieffer's Hybrid. *Ibid.*, Mr. Parry secured the original tree, and has called the new variety 'Kieffer's Hybrid'.] **1880** *Gardener's Monthly* Feb. 49/1 The Kieffer Pear.—A contemporary asks what evidence there is that this is a hybrid between the Chinese Sand Pear, and the ordinary garden variety? **1901** L. H. BAILEY *Cycl. Amer. Hort.* III. 1242/2 The Kieffer Pear originated with Peter Kieffer, of Roxborough, Philadelphia, an Alsatian gardener. *Ibid.*, The Kieffer Pear is now very popular in many parts of the country because of its great vigor, healthfulness, productiveness, and the keeping qualities of the fruit. *Ibid.*, 1243/1 Such varieties as Kieffer and Bartlett are usually classed as self-sterile kinds. **1916** —— *Pruning-Manual* v. 116 Young pear trees, particularly of the Kieffer type, make very long and erect growths. **1948** W. STEVENS *Let.* 19 Aug. (1967) 610, I.. asked him to try to find Kieffer pears for me this autumn. **1961** M. W. BLACK in Hyams & Jackson *Orchard & Fruit Garden* xxix. 160/1 Each of the other export varieties [of pear] (Beurré Hardy,.. Winter Nelis, Kieffer, Josephine de Malines, Doyenné du Comice, etc.) are tested individually.

‖**kie-kie** ('ki:ki:). Also **kee-kee**. [Maori.] A New Zealand climbing plant, *Freycinetia Banksii* (N.O. *Pandanaceæ*), the leaves of which are woven into baskets, etc. Also *attrib.*

1847 *N.Z. Jrnl.* No. 191. 106/1 Passed.. through a wet wood of supplejack and kiekie. **1854** GOLDER *Pigeon's Parlt.* Notes 77 The trees were.. covered with a kind of parasite plant, called a keekee, having a thick cabbage-like stock. **1873** BULLER *Birds New Zeal.* (1888) II. 317, I drew out the nest materials, consisting of shreds of kiekie-leaves and other dry litter. **1882** T. H. POTTS *Out in the Open* 20 (Morris) The unused food.. together with the empty kie-kie baskets. **1905** W. B. *Where White Man Treads* 16 Aye, and kie kie also, with its two kinds of sweet-meats, both on the same vine. **1966** *Encycl. N.Z.* II. 785/1 The only non-berry fruit of significance was that of kiekie (*Freycinetia banksii*), the flavour of which has been likened to that of a pear.

‖**kielbasa** (ki:l'bæsə, kɪ-). Also **kolbasa, -i**. [Pol. *kiełbasa* sausage, Russ. *kolbasa* sausage.] (See quot. 1965.)

1953 S. BELLOW *Adventures of Augie March* xx. 435 All these poor punks.. with immigrant blood and washday smells and kielbasa and home-brew beer. **1958** 'RYSIA' *Old Warsaw Cook Bk.* 2 (*heading*) Kielbasa, Polish sausage cut in small pieces and served on tooth-picks with a drink of vodka. *Ibid.* 49 Until the sixteenth century.. the preferred meat was.. Polish sausage—'kielbasa', or 'bigos'. **1959** *Times* 23 Jan. 12/6 Attaché cases—which must surely contain the innermost secrets of the Kremlin, but which usually turned out to harbour a lump of black bread and a petrified portion of kolbasa. **1965** *House & Garden* Jan. 60 *Kielbasa* or *kolbasi* (Polish sausage), a highly seasoned garlicky sausage. It comes fresh, smoked, uncooked and cooked, but usually must be poached before it is eaten. **1969** R. & D. DESOLA *Dict. Cooking* 133/2 *Kielbasa*, red-cased Polish sausage.. often served with sauerkraut.

kiele, obs. f. KEEL *v.*^{1}, KILN *sb.*

kiell, obs. f. KEEL, *sb.*^{2}

kien, obs. f. *kine*, pl. of COW.

kier (kɪə(r)). Forms: 6 **keare, keyre**, 7 **keere**, 9 **keir, kier**. [Known only from second half of 16th c.: cf. ON. *ker* vessel, tub (Norw. *kjer*, Sw., Da. *kar*) = OHG. *char*, Goth. *kas*.] †**a.** A brewing-vat (also ***boiling-, brewing-, gyle-, gyling-kier***). *Obs.* **b.** A large vat in which cloth is boiled for bleaching or other purposes (***bleaching-kier***).

1573 *Lanc. & Chesh. Wills* (Chetham, 1884) 64 One brewinge keare, and a troghe for yᵉ same ijs. A yailinge keare xijd. **1579** *Ibid.* (Chetham, 1861) 101 Six great vessels of tymber called keares wᵗʰ other ffurnyture for the brewehouse and backehouse. **1582** *Lanc. Wills* (1857) I. 132 Dyverse stone trowes keyres and arkes. **1635** BRERETON *Trav.* (Chetham) 104, I took notice of that common brew-house.. and observed there.. boiling keeres. [*c* **1746**, **1775**: see GYLEKER.] **1839** URE *Dict. Arts* 138 The wooden kieve, or kier, containing the cloth. **1879** *Spons' Encycl. Indust. Arts* I. 515 For yarn and thread, it is very usual to have the false bottom of the bleaching kier, or pot, movable. **1883** *Manch. Exam.* 30 Oct. 7/2 This kier.. was used for boiling.. cotton flock and other substances used in paper-making.

Hence **'kierful**.

1879 *Spons' Encycl. Indust. Arts* I. 515 A whole kierful of yarn or thread is chemicked at once. **1884** *Times* 15 Apr. 8 A large kierful of cloth of about 30 cwt.

‖**kierie** ('kɪərɪ). Also 8–9 **kirri**, 9 **kierie, kiri, keeri(e, keri(e**. [Hottentot or Bushman. Kolbe 1745 has '*Kirri* a stick or staff', Arbousset *Bushman Vocab.* 'Club, *Keri*'.] A short club or knobbed stick used as a weapon by natives of South Africa. See also KNOBKERRIE.

1731 MEDLEY *Kolben's Cape G. Hope* I. 188 The *Kirri* is about three foot long; and about an inch thick. **1785** G. FORSTER tr. *Sparrman's Voy. Cape G. Hope* (1786) II. 9 They were all of them armed with.. javelins, which they call hassagais, as well as with short sticks, to which they gave the name of *kirris*. **1815** BARROW *Trav. S. Africa* 367 The Keerie, or war-club. **1824** BURCHELL *Trav. S. Afr.* I. 354 A *keeri* or *kirri* (a short knob-stick) in his hand. **1885** HAGGARD *K. Solomon's Mines* x. (1887) 160 Savage-looking men.. with spears in one hand and heavy kerries in the other. **1939** A. W. WELLS *S. Afr.: Planned Tour* 410/1 Some Afrikaans words are used in English conversation, e.g.:.. *kierie*, walking-stick. **1953** *Cape Times* 5 Jan. 1/7 There were about 1,000 fighting with kieries. **1970** *Cape Herald* 15 May 3/3 He found.. a kierie, a two-piece pink costume, a night gown... The costume and gown had blood spots on them.

attrib. **1731** MEDLEY *Kolben's Cape G. Hope* I. 330 The women rarely trouble themselves to interpose when the men fight only with *Kirri* sticks. **1959** *Cape Times* 10 Nov. 1/1 Two other Europeans had been discharged after being treated for kierie wounds.

kiering ('kɪərɪŋ), *vbl. sb.* [f. KIER + -ING^{1}.] Boiling in a kier or vat.

1922 *Encycl. Brit.* XXX. 590/2 A uniform process of 'kiering' (boiling under pressure with a lye of caustic soda) was introduced. **1954** *Textile Terms & Definitions* (Textile Inst.) 22 *Kier boil* (*Kiering*), the process of prolonged boiling of cotton or flax materials with alkaline liquors in a.. Kier. **1963** A. J. HALL *Textile Sci.* iv. 162 Kiering and bleaching. In the first [bleaching stage] the textile material is boiled.. within a.. kier.

Kierkegaardian (kɪəkə'gɑ:dɪən, -'gɔəd-), *a.* and *sb.* [f. the name of Sören *Kierkegaard* (1813–55), a Danish philosopher + -IAN.] **A.** *adj.* Of or pertaining to Kierkegaard or his philosophy. **B.** *sb.* An adherent or admirer of Kierkegaard's philosophy.

1943 *Horizon* Oct. 260 The great psychological crisis has now been given its actual material content, and one of the most important keys.. to the inner Kierkegaardian room, has been found. **1947** *Partisan Rev.* Mar.–Apr. 187 The terminology of the neo-Kierkegaardian, Karl Barth. **1950** *Mind* LIX. 415 What possible appeal.. could a Kierkegaardian Christianity have for children? **1963** AUDEN *Dyer's Hand* 444 In some of Brand's speeches, however, there is an emphasis on the human will which is Nietzschean rather than Kierkegaardian. **1964** *English Studies* XLV. Suppl. 243 A kierkegaardian must be struck by the radical and extreme position taken by Pater. **1971** G. STEINER *In Bluebeard's Castle* III. 57 The Kierkegaardian concept of 'total possibility', of a fabric of reality open at all points to the rift of absurdity and disaster, has become a commonplace.

‖**kieselguhr** ('ki:z(ə)lgu:r). [Ger. (named by Ehrenberg), f. *kiesel* gravel, CHESIL^{1} + GUHR.] An earth composed of the siliceous remains of diatoms, used as an absorbent of nitroglycerine in the manufacture of dynamite; diatomite.

1875 *Ure's Dict. Arts* II. 176 A porous, infusorial, silicious earth known in Germany as 'Kieselguhr'. *Ibid.*, None of these [absorbents] appeared thoroughly equal to Kieselguhr in their power of retaining a very large proportion of the oil. **1885** MARTINDALE & WESTCOTT *Extra Pharmacop.* (ed. 4) 226 Kieselguhr, a diatomaceous earth, known as white peat.

kieserite ('ki:zəraɪt). [Named (1861) after D. G. Kieser, of Jena.] Hydrous magnesium sulphate, usually occurring in fine, granular, white masses, in the salt-mines at Stassfurt in Prussia and elsewhere. Used in making Epsom Salts, and in the manufacture of potash salts.

1862 *Amer. Jrnl. Sc.* Ser. II. XXXIV. 214. **1875** *Ure's Dict. Arts* III. 17 Kieserite appears likely to prove a valuable accession to our.. useful minerals. **1876** PAGE *Adv. Text-bk. Geol.* xvi. The kieserite is in beds from 9 to 12 inches thick.

kiest, kiestein, kiever: see KEEST, KYESTEIN, KIVER.

Kievan (ki:'ɛfən, ki:'ɛvən), *a.* Also **Kievian**. [f. *Kiev*, a city in Russia + -AN.] Of or pertaining to the city of Kiev, esp. with reference to the historical period (*c* 900–*c* 1150) when it dominated European Russia.

1927 D. S. MIRSKY *Hist. Russia* ii. 8 The golden age of the Kievian political power occurred in the reigns of Vladimir and of his son Yaroslav (1019–1054). **1957** K. A. WITTFOGEL *Oriental Despotism* x. 418 In Medieval Sweden and Kievan Russia the decisive social relations.. never seem to have matured... We may view them as.. 'marginal' feudal society. **1959** *Listener* 26 Mar. 564/1 The rise of the Kievan State in the tenth and eleventh centuries. **1965** *Language* XLI. 140 A recent study.. includes some [foreign] loanwords as borrowed in the.. Kievan period.

kieve, var. KEEVE, KIVE 1.

kiewiet ('ki:vɪt). *S. Afr.* Also **kievietjie, kiewietjie, kiewit, kiewitje, kivit**. [Echoic.] The crowned lapwing, *Vanellus* (or *Stephanibyx*) *coronatus*.

1785 G. FORSTER tr. *Sparrman's Voy. Cape Good Hope* I. iv. 153 Flocks of *keuvitts*.. towards the dusk of the evening, screamed out a disagreeable sound resembling that of the name they bear. **1818** C. I. LATROBE *Jrnl. Visit S. Afr.* vi. 131 Some kivits, or plovers, were the only birds.. we saw, during several hours' ride. **1867** E. L. LAYARD *Birds S. Afr.* 294 The 'Kiewit' makes known its presence by its loud plaintive call. **1896** H. A. BRYDEN *Tales S. Afr.* 121 The cry of one or two night birds may be heard—the dikkop and kiewitje plovers. **1936** E. L. GILL *First Guide S. Afr. Birds* 139 Crowned Lapwing, Kiewiet; *Stephanibyx coronatus*. The commonest and most generally distributed of the dry-land plovers in South Africa. **1939** [see DIKKOP 1]. **1957** MCLACHLAN & LIVERSIDGE *Roberts's Birds S. Afr.* 131 Crowned plover. Kiewietjie... Widespread but local all over South Africa to north-eastern Africa. **1964** P. A. CLANCEY *Birds Natal & Zululand* 156 *Vanellus coronatus*... Not normally shy, but extremely vociferous, uttering a harsh cry which has given rise to its local name of 'kiewit'. **1974** *Eastern Province Herald* (S. Afr.) 7 Nov. 5 The wide-eyed appearance of this 'kiewietjie' yesterday, nesting on a lawn.., is understandable after it had to sit through the surrounding Guy Fawkes celebrations this week.

kif, var. KEF 2.

kiff: see KITH *sb.*

kight, kijt, obs. forms of KITE.

ki-hi: see KI-YI.

kiht, obs. f. *caught*, pa. t. of CATCH *v.*

kijaat, var. KIAAT.

kijang: see KIDANG.

‖**kikar** ('kɪkə(r)). [Hindī *kīkar*.] The name in India of species of Acacia, esp. *A. arabica*, yielding much of the best gum arabic.

1883 *Cassell's Fam. Mag.* Oct. 685/1 The *Coccus lacca*.. is also found on.. the Kikar (*Acacia arabica*). **1899** *Westm. Gaz.* 17 Aug. 2/1 One evening.. he called me to where he stood by the kikar tree.

kike (kaɪk). *slang* (orig. *U.S.*). [Said to be an alteration of *-ki* (or *-ky*), a common ending of the personal names of Eastern European Jews who emigrated to the U.S. at the turn of the 20th c.] A vulgarly offensive name for a Jew. Also *attrib.* or as *adj.*

1904 R. L. MCCARDELL *Show Girl & her Friends* 49 And what do you think? He had the impudence to tell me that Louie Zinsheimer was a kike! **1912** *McClure's Mag.* XXXIX. 230/2 'It's a mascot, be-dad! Jam it, ye kike!' screeched Tracy. **1919** F. HURST *Humoresque* 211 A little red-haired kike like her! **1919** MENCKEN *Amer. Lang.* 115 An Englishman.. knows nothing of our common terms of disparagement, such as *kike*.. and *rube*. **1924** P. MARKS *Plastic Age* xviii. 201 You go chasing around with kikes and micks. **1932** J. DOS PASSOS *1919* 164 The little kike behind the desk had never been to sea. **1940** R. STOUT *Over my Dead Body* vi. 84, I don't care if the background is wop or mick or kike.. so long as it's American. **1956** D. KARP *All Honorable Men* 74 If you repeat that lie, I'll wring that skinny kike neck of yours with my own hands! **1963** V.

NABOKOV *Gift* iii. 179 My better half.. was for twenty years the wife of a kike and got mixed up with a whole rabble of Jew in-laws. **1963** *Spectator* 21 June 815 He knocks down Stern's wife, calls her a kike. **1972** *National Observer* (U.S.) 27 May 17/3 When kikes are shrewd and dagos or wops are sly and murderous, it is only one step from the epithet to contempt.

kike, obs. form of KEEK *v.*, KICK *v.*

†**kikelot**. *Obs. rare*⁻¹. [Form and origin uncertain: cf. *gigelot*, GIGLET.] A tattling woman, a magpie.

a **1225** *Ancr. R.* 88 Me seið upon ancren, þet euerich mest haueð.. ane rikelot [*MS. C.* kikelot (piot)] þet cakeleð hire al þet heo isihð oðer ihereð.

‖**kikoi** (kɪ'kɔɪ). [Swahili.] In East Africa, a striped cloth of distinctive design with an end fringe, worn round the waist. Also *attrib.*

1942 *E. Afr. Ann.* *1941–2* 27/1 His loin-cloth, 'kikoi', was edged with stripes of red, black and yellow, and showed below his shirt. **1970** *Vogue* Jan. 96/4 Mwembe Tayari is a lively, open free-for-all, with *kikois* (Arab-style sarongs), beaded jackets.. and handicrafts. **1971** *Daily Nation* (Nairobi) 10 Apr. 5/1 (Advt.), Kikoy Shirts and Dresses.

Kikuchi (kɪ'ku:tʃɪ). *Physics.* [Name of Seishi *Kikuchi* (b. 1902), Japanese physicist, who first observed the lines.] ***Kikuchi line***: each of a series of lines in electron diffraction patterns which are attributed to the elastic scattering of previously inelastically scattered electrons and may be used to determine the orientation of crystalline specimens; so ***Kikuchi pattern***.

1934 *Physical Rev.* XLV. 43/1 The [electron scattering] patterns from stibnite consist of spots, Kikuchi lines, bands, circles and parabolas. **1948** *Proc. Physical Soc.* LX. 343 The elementary diffraction theory for single scattering also leads to a Kikuchi-line breadth proportional to the corresponding plane spacing *d/n*. **1966** D. G. BRANDON *Mod. Techniques Metallogr.* ii. 113 Kikuchi line patterns can be used to give a more accurate estimate of the specimen orientation than can be determined from the normal spot pattern. **1968** *Mineral. Abstr.* XIX. 83/2 A simplified stereographic projection from a Kikuchi pattern is used to determine the orientation of a crystal. **1970** *New Scientist* 23 July 176/2 Kikuchi patterns, well known to users of the transmission electron microscope.

Kikuyu (kɪ'ku:ju:). [Native name.] **a.** The name of an agricultural Negroid people, the largest Bantu-speaking group in Kenya; a member of this people; the language they speak. Also *attrib.* or as *adj.*

1894 N. BELL tr. *L. von Höhnel's Discovery Lakes Rudolf & Stefanie* II. vi. 298 Our attention was called to another party of about forty natives approaching us... Whether they were Masai or Kikuyu neither we nor our guide could tell, so the Count went off with one of our Kikuyu friends to ascertain. **1904** H. HINDE *Vocab. Kamba & Kikuyu Lang.* p. v, Both the Kamba and Kikuyu languages belong to the Bantu group and their construction is precisely similar to that of Swahili. *Ibid.* p. xviii, It is not unfrequent, in general conversation, both in Kamba and Kikuyu, to ignore the conjugated forms of the verb. **1911** J. G. FRAZER *Golden Bough: Magic Art* (ed. 3) I. iii. 76 This curious pretence of being born again regularly formed part of the initiatory rites through which every Kikuyu lad and every Kikuyu girl had to pass before he or she was recognised as a full-grown member of the tribe. **1920** *New Statesman* 10 July 391/1 The Kikuyu, bending over their cultivated plots. **1935** E. HEMINGWAY *Green Hills Afr.* (1936) III. i. 173 Kamau, the driver, was a Kikuyu. **1936** *Discovery* June 195/1 Brought up to speak Kikuyu from childhood. **1950** D. JONES *Phoneme* 20 In one form of the Kikuyu language of Kenya the sounds ɸ, β and b appear to be.. constituting a single phoneme. **1955** *Times* 7 June 6/5 The weakening of the Mau Mau is most noticeable to the east of Mount Kenya, where its Meru and Embu supporters are less determined than the Kikuyus. **1958** *Times* 8 Jan. 6/7 After warnings in Kikuyu had been given over a loudhailer and ignored, the staff opened fire on the rioters' barricade. **1967** M. J. COE *Ecol. Alpine Zone Mt. Kenya* 1 Kikuyu folk-lore tells how, when the earth was formed, a man named Mogai made a great mountain. **1973** *Nature* 11 May 107/1 At Cambridge he studied Modern French, Medieval French and Kikuyu for Part 1 of the Tripos.

b. Kikuyu grass, a creeping perennial grass, *Pennisetum clandestinum*, native to the highlands of Kenya, and cultivated elsewhere as a lawn and fodder grass.

1913 *Rep. Dept. Agric. Union S. Afr.* *1910–11* 241 Kikuyu grass... We received in good condition a rooted plant of the Kikuyu-grass of British East Africa. This has been planted out and has made vigorous growth; it has not yet flowered, and I am therefore unable to name it. **1921** *Kew Bull.* 85 (*heading*) Kikuyu grass. *Ibid.* 93 Kikuyu grass in the presence of water will put on top-growth. **1934** *Bulletin* (Sydney) 31 Oct. 22/2 Now is the time in N.S.W. to plant Kikuyu grass, which is suitable to any class of soil that is not binding. **1951** EDWARDS & BOGDAN *Important Grassland Plants of Kenya* II. 62 In the Highland Forest regions Kikuyu grass occupies the land for a period following clearance of the forest climax. **1970** W. SMITH *Gold Mine* xxviii. 67 Rod escorted the Steyners down across the vivid green lawns of Kikuyu grass.

c. A controversy in the Anglican Church, which first arose at the Kikuyu Conference of 1913, regarding the admissibility to Holy Communion of the members of other Christian churches. Also *attrib.*

1914 H. HENSON (*title*) The issue of Kikuyu. **1915** C. KELWAY *Story of Kikuyu* 8 The mission field is, in fact, full of potential 'Kikuyus'.. the vital questions which emerge from the Kikuyu Conference. **1915** L. PULLAN *Missionary Princ. & Primate on Kikuyu* 31 This pronouncement on the Kikuyu question is considered official. **1965** S. NEILL *Anglicanism* (ed. 3) xiii. 366 The years after the First World War introduced a new period of more dramatic possibilities and intenser strains. The trouble started with the Kikuyu controversy.

‖**kikyo** ('ki:kjo). Also **kikiyo, kikuyo.** [Jap.] A local name for *Platycodon grandiflorum*, a herbaceous perennial of the family Campanulaceæ, native to China and Japan; the Chinese bell-flower.

1884 tr. *J. J. Rein's Japan* I. vii. 145 The splendid blue-flowered Kikiyo (Platycodon grandiflorum DC.).. appear in numbers only at a height of about 1,000 metres. **1899** L. HEARN *In Ghostly Japan* ii. 15 The crest upon the robe was the *kikyō*-flower. **1911** *Encycl. Brit.* XV. 162/1 If some familiar European flowers are absent, they are replaced by others strange to Western eyes.. the *kikyo* (*Platycodon grandiflorum*). **1965** J. OHWI *Flora Japan* 853/1 *Platycodon grandiflorum*... Kikyō... Frequently planted as an ornamental and for medicine.

kil, obs. form of KILL *v.*, KILN *sb.*

kilampere ('kɪlæmpɛə(r)). *Electr.* [f. *kil-* (see KILO-) + AMPERE.] A thousand amperes.

1892 BARN, SMITH & HUDSON *Arithm. for Schools* 147 A thousand milliamperes make an Ampere, a thousand amperes make a Kilampere.

kilbrickenite (kɪl'brɪkənaɪt). *Min.* [Named from Kilbricken, co. Clare, Ireland, where found: see -ITE¹.] Sulph-antimonide of lead, of a lead-grey colour and metallic lustre; GEOCRONITE.

1840 *Proc. R. Irish Acad.* I. 472 *Kilbrickenite*, as Dr. Apjohn proposed to call this mineral, is obviously what Berzelius denominates a sulphur salt.

kilbuck: see KILLBUCK.

kilch (kɪlʃ). [Swiss German *kilch.*] The Swiss name for a small whitefish, *Coregonus pidschian*, found in northern Europe, Asia, and Canada.

1881 K. SEMPER *Nat. Conditions of Existence* 320 The little fish of the Lake of Constance known as the Kilch. **1931** J. R. NORMAN *Hist. Fishes* ix. 175 One of the White-fishes (*Coregonus*), an important food-fish of Lake Constance, known locally as the Kilch. **1962** D. W. TUCKER tr. *Sterba's Freshwater Fishes of World* 56 The following may be kept successfully... the Blaufelchen or Grosse Schweberenke (*Coregonus wartmanni* Bloch) from the lakes of the Voralpen, and even the very rare Kleine Schweberenke or Kilch (*Coregonus acronius* Rapp).

kilchoanite (kɪl'xəʊənaɪt). *Min.* [f. *Kilchoan*, name of the village in the Highlands near which it was first found + -ITE¹.] A colourless, orthorhombic polymorph of a calcium silicate, $Ca_3Si_2O_7$, of which rankinite is another polymorph.

1961 AGRELL & GAY in *Nature* 4 Mar. 743/1 A mineral corresponding to phase *Z* has been found in limestones thermally metamorphosed by gabbro at Ardnamurchan, Scotland, and Carlingford, Eire. It has been named kilchoanite after the village in Ardnamurchan near where it was first found. *Ibid.*, Kilchoanite has always been found as a replacement of rankinite and no crystal form has been observed. **1969** *Mineral. Mag.* XXXVII. 517 Two polymorphs of tricalcium disilicate, rankinite and kilchoanite, have been discovered near Tokatoka, New Zealand. **1969** *Trans. Brit. Ceramic Soc.* LXVIII. 225/1 The morphology of synthetic kilchoanite made at ~ 200°C, as revealed by transmission electron microscopy, is platy with a characteristic lozenge shape.

kilcow, kildee, -deer: see KILL-COW, KILLDEE, -DEER.

kilderkin ('kɪldəkɪn). Forms: α. 4 **kyner-**, 5 **kynder-**, 6 **kynterkyn, kinderkind**, 6–7 **kinderkin**. β. 4–6 **kilderkyn**, 5–6 **kylder-**, (6 **kilde-**), **-kyn, -kin**, (6 **-ken**), 6– **kilderkin**. [Of Du. or LG. origin: cf. MDu. *kinderkin*, more commonly *kindeken*, *kinneken* (or *-kijn*), also *kyntken*, *-kijn*, *kimmekijn* (see KEMPKIN, KINKIN), the fourth part of a tun, etc. (cf. Du. *kinnetje*, a firkin): a dim. form, referred to *kintal*, *quintal*, med.L. *quintāle*, Ger. dial. *kindel*, *kindle* (13th c. *chindel*): see -KIN. (Cf. Grimm s.v. *Kindlein*², Verwijs & Verdam s.v. *Kindekijn*².) The change of *kin-* to *kil-* is app. peculiar to Eng., and is found already in 14th c.]

1. A cask for liquids, fish, etc. of a definite capacity (half a barrel).

By the statute of 1531–2 the kilderkin for beer had to contain 18 gallons, that for ale 16 gallons.

α. **1530** *Yatton Church-w. Acc.* (Som. Rec. Soc.) 146 Payd for ij kynterkynnys to yᵉ cherche howse.. viijᵈ. **1598** BARRET *Theor. Warres* v. iii. 135, 50 kinderkins and barrels to cary the small cordage. **1673** S. PARKER *Reproof Reh. Transp.* 11 Some kinderkins, some hogsheads, some tuns.

β. **1390** *Letter Bk. H., Guildhall London*, lf. 247 Omnes anguille in undecim barellis et uno kilderkyn. *Ibid.*, Dicti barelli et kilderkyn cum anguillis in eisdem. **1530** PALSGR. 236/1 Kylderken, a vessell, *cacque*. **1531–2** *Act 23 Hen. VIII*, c. 4 The Ale bruers.. have used.. to make.. theyr barrels kilderkyns and firkyns of moche lasse quantitie contente rate and assisse than they ought to be. **1639** in T. Lechford *Note-bk.* (1885) 118 Divers goods.. wᶜʰ were put up in foure chests, three butts,.. three kilderkins. **1869** W. MOLYNEUX *Burton on Trent* 249 These casks consist of kilderkins, barrels, hogsheads, and butts.

attrib. **1565** *Act 8 Eliz.* c. 9 § 1 Cowpers might have bowght .. a thowsand of Kilderkin Boordes for nyne shillings.

2. A cask of this size filled with some commodity; the quantity contained in such a cask; hence, a measure of capacity for various kinds of goods.

It varied, according to commodity, from 16 to 18 old wine gallons; a kilderkin of butter weighed 112 lbs.

α. **1391** *Earl Derby's Exp.* (Camden) 96 Pro iij kynerkynes de salmone salso. *Ibid.* 97 Pro j kynerkyn anguillarum. **1423** *Rolls Parlt.* IV. 256/2 Nether kynderkyns, Tercianes, and firdekyns of Heryng. **1587** in Wadley *Bristol Wills* (1886) 252 A kynterkin of heringes nowe Laden abourd the Peter of Milford.

β. **1392** *Earl Derby's Exp.* (Camden) 158 Clerico coquine per manus Johannis Baunche de Linne pro j kilderkyn di. de storgon. **1410** *E.E. Wills* (E.E.T.S.) 17 Y be-queþe XL. penyworth bred, & I. kylderkyn of ale, to be spended at my dirige. **1594** *Compt Bk. Dav. Wedderburne* (S.H.S.) 44 Sauld.. 3 kildekins feggis. **1670** EACHARD *Cont. Clergy* 85 The last kilderkin of drink is near departed. **1737** BERKELEY *App. to Querist* III. § 158 Twopence advance in a kilderkin of corn. **1871** M. COLLINS *Mrq. & Merch.* I. ix. 290 A huge.. kettle,.. holding about a kilderkin.

3. *transf.* and *fig.*

1593 PEELE *Edw. I* Wks. (Rtldg.) 383/1 Then.. pluck out thy spigot, and draw us a fresh pot from the kinder-kind of thy knowledge. **1600** NASHE *Summer's Last Will* in Hazl. *Dodsley* VIII. 57 To broach this little kilderkin of my corpse. **1682** DRYDEN *Mac Fl.* 196 A tun of man in thy large bulk is writ, But sure thow'rt but a kilderkin of wit.

kile, variant of KYLE¹.

kilerg ('kɪlɜg). *Physics.* [f. *kil-* (see KILO-) + ERG.] A measure of work in the centimetre-gramme-second system, equal to a thousand ergs.

1873 *Rep. Brit. Assoc.* 224 The gramme-centimetre is rather less than the kilerg, being about 980 ergs.

kiles, Sc. variant of KAYLES.

kiley. *Austral.* [var. KYLIE.] = BAT *sb.*² 3 e.

1945 [see BAT *sb.*² 3 e].

Kilhamite ('kɪləmaɪt). [f. the surname *Kilham*: see -ITE¹.] An appellation sometimes given to members of the 'New Connexion' of Methodists, after Alex. Kilham the founder of the body in 1797.

1815 WILLIAMS *Dict. Relig.*, *Kilhamites*; thus the Methodists of the New connection are sometimes called, from Mr. Alex. Kilham, who was a considerable preacher among them. **1860** J. GARDNER *Faiths World* II. 440/2 This decided refusal on the part of the Conference to allow the introduction of the lay element into their body, gave rise to the formation of a new society of Methodists, commonly known by the name of Kilhamites, or as they styled themselves the Methodist.. New Connexion.

kilhig ('kɪlhɪg). *U.S. Logging.* Also **killig.** [Origin unknown.] A short stout pole used as a lever or brace to direct the fall of a tree.

1905 *Terms Forestry & Logging* (U.S. Dept. Agric. Bureau Forestry) *Kilhig*, a short stout pole used as a lever or brace to direct the fall of a tree (N.W.). **1913** R. C. BRYANT *Logging* 83 Kilhig or sampson... It consists of a pole.. either sharpened or armed on one end with a spike. **1971** F. C. FORD-ROBERTSON *Terminol. Forest Sci.* 148/2 *Killig* (USA), *Pushpole* (Cw), a stout pole, sometimes notched into the tree stem at one end and braced against the base of a peavey handle at the other, used to push a small tree manually in the desired direction of fall.

kilian ('kɪlɪən). *Ice-dancing.* Also **killian.** [Origin unknown.] A fast ice-dance executed by a pair of skaters side by side.

1935 *Skating* Dec. 34 The Killian is one of the new English dances and has been described by Mrs. Willie Frick. It is a fast tenstep, done side by side. **1936** *Skating Rev.* III. 13 The lady's mohawk is an ordinary.. mohawk, right foot crossed behind, and not as done in the Kilian, crossed in front. **1938** T. D. RICHARDSON *Ice Rink Skating* vii. 50 The Kilian is a delightful dance, but is strictly more of a pair skating step. **1941** *U.S. Figure Skating Assoc. Rulebk.* *1940–41* 76 The Killian is of Austrian origin. It analyzes as a snappy side by side Man's Fourteenstep—using a choctaw in place of a spread eagle turn. **1962** *Times* 3 Mar. 3/5 A fine tango by the British champions.. enabled them to make up ground which they had lost on the kilian. **1968** *Daily Tel.* 29 Feb. 13/8 Skating both the kilian and blues with advanced techniques and deportment too impeccable to criticise, Ford and Miss Towler look well set for a third successive victory in tomorrow's free style.

kilie-vert, kilie-vine: see KEELIVINE.

Kilim (kɪ'li:m). Also **Kelim, Khilim.** [Turk., f. Pers. *kilīm.*] In full ***Kilim carpet, rug***, etc. A pileless woven carpet, rug, etc., made in Turkey, Kurdistan, and neighbouring areas.

1881 C. C. HARRISON *Woman's Handiwork* III. 139 A Kelim rug.. may be bought at a reasonable price.. to lay before the fire. **1884** J. R. G. GRIFFITT *Turkey Carpets & their Manufacture* 12 Carpets without a pile, known as Kilims. *Ibid.*, The Oushak Kilims.. differ from the many varieties of Kilims made by the Nomad tribes throughout Asia-Minor. **1895** *Brit. Warehouseman* Feb. 25/2 Arabian 'Kelims' or hand-woven woollen tent hangings. **1900** J. K. MUMFORD *Oriental Rugs* (1901) Pl. XXIII (*caption*), The real color value of Khilims must become very clear to everyone who sees this plate. **1923** *Daily Mail* 27 June 14 The heavier Kurdish Kelim rugs make the best floor covering. **1926** T. E. LAWRENCE *Seven Pillars* (1935) II. xix. 124 Feisal would

buckle on his ceremonial dagger and walk across to the reception tent, which was floored with two horrible kilims. **1931** A. U. DILLEY *Oriental Rugs & Carpets* i. 4 Theoretically, the product of this weaving was flat-surfaced, and would be classified by us as khilim or tapestry. **1960** S. FOOT *Emergency Exit* xiv. 113 The front hall, with its gay Kelims. **1967** [see *goat hair*]. **1972** *Vogue* Jan. 10/2 Kurdish Kelim rugs from £22. **1972** *Country Life* 3 Feb. 258/3 A fine collection of woven goods and felts: carpets, Kilims, tent bands.

kilin, variant of KYLIN.

Kilkenny (kɪl'kɛnɪ). Name of a county and city in Leinster in the Republic of Ireland, used *attrib.*, as in **Kilkenny cat**, one of a pair of cats fabled to have fought until only their tails remained; *transf.*, of combatants who fight until they annihilate each other; so ***Kilkenny fight***. Also **Kilkenny coal**, an Irish name for anthracite; **Kilkenny marble** (see quot. 1959).

1822 *Hive* I. II. 32/2 (*heading*) Kilkenny cats. *Ibid.*, One gentleman stated his opinion, that a *Kilkenny* cat was, of all other animals, the most ferocious;..'..I once,' said he, 'saw two of these animals fighting..and..drove them into a deep saw-pit, and..left them to their amusement. Next morning, ..what d'ye think I saw?..there was nothing left in the pit *but the two tails and a bit of flue.*' **1849** *Pict. Guide Birmingham* 162 Whatever may be the ultimate fate of the combatants—and it once seemed likely to be that of the Kilkenny cats. **1861** MRS. BEETON *Bk. Househ. Managem.* 33 Of *coal* there are various species: as, pit, culm, slate, cannel, Kilkenny, sulphurous, bovey, jet, &c. **1900** J. LONDON *Let.* 2 May (1966) 105 If Russia and England played the Kilkenny cat act, there would be peace in the world. **1901** *Graphic* LXIV. 288/1 The fate of the Kilkenny cats will meanwhile have overtaken the villains. **1910** *Encycl. Brit.* II. 105/2 Other terms [for anthracite]..are..'blind coal' in Scotland, and 'Kilkenny coal' in Ireland. **1930** F. J. NORTH *Limestones* 145 Black Kilkenny Marble is widely used. **1931** *Sun* (Baltimore) 7 Mar. 8/2 He has been in the center of a good old-fashioned Democratic kilkenny fight. **1931** *Times Lit. Suppl.* 23 July 578/2 All these excitable disputants have disappeared like the Kilkenny cats through the excess of their own zeal. **1959** *Chambers's Encycl.* VIII. 217/1 The Kilkenny marbles are greyish crystalline limestones which become deep blue or black on polishing. **1970** I. ORIGO *Images & Shadows* ii. 40 The home of my mother's Anglo-Irish parents..was an Italianate house built towards the end of the eighteenth century of the grey local limestone known as 'Kilkenny marble'. **1972** *Guardian* 10 Mar. 1/3 Mr Heath and Mr Wilson..guard the rival despatch boxes with the mutual respect and tolerance of a pair of Kilkenny cats.

kill (kɪl), *sb.*[1] Also 3 cul (*ü*). [f. KILL *v.*]

†**1.** A stroke, blow. *Obs. rare*⁻¹.

a **1225** *Ancr. R.* 128 Ase swin ipund ine sti uorte uetten, & forte greaten aȝein þe cul of þer eax.

2. a. The act of killing an animal hunted as game.

1852 R. S. SURTEES *Sponge's Sp. Tour* ix. 48 A run with a kill. **1883** E. PENNELL-ELMHIRST *Cream Leicestersh.* 404 The second run..led to a charming scamper, with a clean kill at the end. **1890** SIR R. PAYNE GALLWEY *Lett. to young Shooters* 145 *note*, In all-round shooting, fifteen kills to twenty shots is rarely done.

b. Phr. *in at the kill*: present at the killing of an animal; also *transf.* and *fig.*

1814 PRINCE WILLIAM *Let.* 18 Feb. in P. Ziegler *King William IV* (1971) ix. 115 The game is up with Bonaparte and I shall be in at the kill. **1969** *Amer. Heritage Dict.* s.v., *In at the kill*, present at the moment of triumph.

c. *Lawn Tennis* and *Rackets*. The striking of a ball in such a way that it cannot be returned. Cf. KILL *v.* 7 a.

1903 *Westm. Gaz.* 31 Aug. 8/1 Grant put in some mighty 'kills' from the service line. **1908** *Baily's Mag.* June 483/1 They both of them fairly bombarded the wall, often.. bringing off beautifully low ' kills'. **1920** W. T. TILDEN *Lawn Tennis* 87 The server covers and strives for a kill at once. **1969** *New Yorker* 14 June 68/2 Graebner delivers a Wagnerian kill. The ball digs a hole in the turf near Ashe's left foot.

d. The destruction or putting out of action of an enemy aircraft, submarine, etc.; the aircraft, etc., so destroyed. *colloq.*

1944 *Times* 7 Mar. 2/3 The men of this station..can show plenty of evidence of 'kills'. **1951** N. MONSARRAT *Cruel Sea* v. vi. 360 But this was to be no swift kill: perhaps, indeed, it was to be no kill at all. **1962** *Daily Tel.* 20 July 1 (*headline*) Atlas rocket 'kill' by anti-missile. **1969** G. MACBETH *War Quartet* 60 We had sailed five weeks Without a kill. **1971** *Daily Tel.* 22 Nov. 7 (*caption*) Mr H. M. Stephen.. examining..parts of a Messerschmitt 109 fighter which, as a pilot officer, he shot down on Nov. 30, 1940, while operating from Biggin Hill. It was the wartime base's 600th 'kill'.

e. *Boxing.* (See quots.) *colloq.*

1950 J. DEMPSEY *Championship Fighting* xxv. 200 His opponent will be after him quickly for 'the kill'—for the knockout. **1954** F. C. AVIS *Boxing Reference Dict.* 61 *Kill*, a knock out.

3. A killed animal, esp. one killed by sportsmen or by beasts of prey.

1878 J. INGLIS *Sport & Work* xxi. 287 In beating for tiger, ..the appearance of the kill..often affords valuable indications to the sportsman. **1893** SELOUS *Trav. S.E. Africa* 424, I cherished a hope that the lions..would return and drive the hyænas off their kill.

4. kill ratio *U.S.*, the proportion of casualties on each side in a military action.

1968 *N.Y. Times* 11 Aug. I. 3 Those Nigerians who had escaped the cross-fire had fled northward into the forest, leaving behind 41 dead, the Biafrans said. They put their own losses at three killed and a dozen wounded. The lieutenant was pleased with the kill ratio. **1973** *New Yorker* 17 Feb. 89/1 Our military..can produce sickeningly effective 'kill ratios'.

kill (kɪl), *sb.*[2] *U.S. local.* [a. Du. *kil*, MDu. *kille* river-bed, channel.] A stream, 'creek', or tributary river: so called in parts of N. America originally settled by the Dutch (esp. in place-names, as *Schuylkill*).

1669 *Pennsylv. Archives* I. 29 A Certain Island..lying and being in a Kill which runnes into the Scholekill. **1796** MORSE *Amer. Geog.* I. 494 A little pleasant stream, called Eusopus kill or creek. **1879** J. BURROUGHS *Locusts & W. Honey* 169 Kills and dividing ridges.

kill (kɪl), *sb.*[3] Also kil. [a. Ir. and Gael. *cill*, OIr. *cell* (a. L. *cella* CELL), cell, church, burial place (esp. as first element of place-names).] The cell of an old Celtic monk or hermit; an ancient Irish or Scottish church.

1827 G. HIGGINS *Celtic Druids* 190 Ripon..where was a kil or cel of the Culdees in the time of Bede. **1851** H. NEWLAND *The Erne* 191 It once contained a cell, or kill, and is the real Enniskillen.

kill, *sb.*[4] Also kiln. [Origin unascertained.] On the Thames: An eel-trap or weel.

1630 in *Descr. Thames* (1758) 66 No Fisherman..shall lay any Weels called Kills in any Place of the River. **1879** in *N. & Q.* 5th Ser. XI. 245 *Kiln*, an eel-trap, called also a 'weel' or 'weal'. In use on the Thames.

kill (kɪl), *v.* Pa. t. and pa. pple. killed (kɪld). Forms: *α.* 3–4 culle(n, kulle(n(*ü*). *β.* 4 kille(n, 4–5 kylle, 6 kyll, 6–7 kil, 6– kill. *γ.* 5–6 kelle. *δ. Sc.* 5–6 kele, keill. *Pa. t.* 3–4 culde, 4–6 kild(e, 5 kyld(e, (5–6 kelit, etc.); 4– killed. *Pa. pple.* 4 (y-)culled, (i-)kilde), y-keld, 4– killed (5–6 kyld, kelyt, keild, etc., 6 kylt, 6– kilt). [Of obscure origin; not found in the cognate langs.

If in OE., its type would be **cyllan*, conjecturally referred to an OTeut. **kuljan*, ablaut-variant of **kwaljan*, whence OE. *cwellan* to QUELL; but the original sense is against this. Known first in Layamon, and in southern texts, in form *cüllen, küllen*. In midl. dial. normally *kille(n, kill*, the common form in ME.; *kelle* is rare. The usual Sc. form in 15–16th c. was *kele, keill*, the vowel of which is difficult to account for. In ME. the pa. t. and pa. pple. varied between *killed* and *kild*; exceptionally the pple. appears as *kilt* (cf. *spilt*), now regarded as an Irishism, and sometimes used jocularly, esp. in sense 6 b.]

†**1. a.** *trans.* To stirke, hit; to beat, knock. Also with *off*, and *absol.* or *intr.* Also *fig. Obs.*

c **1205** LAY. 20319 Ofte me hine smæt mid smærte ȝerden; ofte me hine culde; swa me deð crosce. *a* **1225** *Ancr. R.* 126 þauh a word culle þe [= thee] ful herde up o þine heorte. **13** .. *E.E. Allit. P.* B. 876 We kylle of þyn heued. *a* **1375** *Joseph Arim.* 545 He starte vp and streiȝte to his hache, culles on mennes hedes þat þei doun lyen.

†**b.** To cast or throw *out*; to clear *out*.

(For a similar connexion between the notions of striking and throwing, cf. the senses of G. *schlagen* (Da. *slaa*) SLAY, and *schmeissen* (Da. *smide*) SMITE.)

a **1225** *Ancr. R.* 346 Auh to hire owune schrift-feder, oðer to summe oðre lif-holie monne: ȝif heo mei hine habben, kulle al ut þet is iðe krocke [*v.r.* culle al þe pot ut].

2. a. To put to death; to deprive of life; to slay, slaughter. In early use implying personal agency and the use of a weapon; later, extended to any means or cause which puts an end to life, as an accident, over-work, grief, drink, a disease, etc.

α. *c* **1330** *King of Tars* 179 The Sarazins withouten fayle The Cristene culde in that batayle. **13**.. *Song Yesterday* 146 in *E.E.P.* (1862) 137 ȝif þi neiȝebor þe manas, Oþur to culle, oþur to bete. **1377** LANGL. *P. Pl.* B. Prol. 185 Thouȝ we culled [*C-text* 199 hadde ycullid] þe catte, ȝut sholde þer come another. *Ibid.* XVI. 137 Thei casten & contreueden To kulle hym whan þei miȝte.

β. *c* **1374** CHAUCER *Anel. & Arc.* 53 Yche other for to kylle With blody speris. **1382** WYCLIF *Luke* xx. 15 This is the eyr, sle we him... And thei killiden him. **1387** TREVISA *Higden* (Rolls) VIII. 5 At Wycombmalban þey were i-kilde [*v.r.* y-keld]. *c* **1400** *Destr. Troy* 1343 þaire kyng was kylt. **1538** STARKEY *England* I. iii. 98 Commynly they be other kyld where they are brede or sold. **1590** SPENSER *F.Q.* I. v. 26 What art thou, that telst of Nephews kilt? **1632** LITHGOW *Trav.* x. 479 Men are rather killed with the impatience they have in adversity, then adversity it selfe. **1697** DRYDEN *Virg. Georg.* IV. 758 Orpheus..Whom ev'n the savage Beasts had spar'd, they kill'd, And strew'd his mangled Limbs about the Field. **1774** GOLDSM. *Nat. Hist.* (1776) I. 358 This terrible blast..instantly kills all those that it involves in its passage. **1848** THACKERAY *Van. Fair* xlv, He was killing himself by late hours and intense application. **1895** *Law Times* C. 133/2 A man who had been killed at a level crossing by a railway train.

fig. **1614** SAUL *Game Chesse* A iv b, But as they [pawns] march who so they finde doe in their colour stand, Such may they kill.

γ. **1387** [see *β*]. *a* **1400** *Octouian* 1063 Thy fader hath keld Well many a bole and doun yfeld. *c* **1440** *Partonope* 1054 Kelle these peuple of fals lawe. **15**.. in *Bann. MS.* lf. 145 a, Telyeouris ar tyrranis in kelling of lyiss.

δ. *c* **1470** HENRY *Wallace* VI. 651 His brothir Hew was kelyt thar full cald. **1508** KENNEDIE *Flyting w. Dunbar* 271 The feild, Quhair twelve thowsand trew Scottismen wer keild. **1572** *Satir. Poems Reform.* xxxiii. 46 Sair boistit thay my husband common-weill, And maid thair vowis and aithis him for to keill. *a* **1605** MONTGOMERIE *Misc. Poems* lii. 29 Vncourtesly thus kill thay mo Than I.

b. With adverbial extensions, as ***kill out*** (*away*, †*down*, †*up*), ***kill off***, to cut off completely, to remove, extinguish, or get rid of (a number, a whole tribe, etc.) by killing.

a **1400–50** *Alexander* 2377 þe kyng of þaire kythe was killid doun & heded. *c* **1450** HOLLAND *Howlat* 566 He..Kelit dovne thar capitanis. **1530** PALSGR. 598/2, I kyll up, as one that kylleth the resydewe where many have ben kylled afore. **1607** TOPSELL *Four-f. Beasts* (1658) 520 Although the fœcundity of Swine be great, yet it is better to kill off two or three,..then to permit them to suck their dam. **1641** HINDE *J. Bruen* xiv. 47 Hee presently killed up the game, and disparked the Parke. **1849** *Tait's Mag.* XVI. 90/1 The wars of the Roses killed them out. **1876** TENNYSON *Queen Mary* III. v, Sometimes I have wish'd That I were caught, and kill'd away at once Out of the flutter. **1894** H. DRUMMOND *Ascent Man* 264 [Nature] produces fitness by killing off the unfit. **1966** R. M. LOCKLEY *Grey Seal, Common Seal* x. 147 In New Zealand I saw how the red deer are killing out the young native forest trees in the South Island Alps. **1970** *New Scientist* 31 Dec. 576/1 Broilers are 'killed out' at eight weeks. **1972** *Country Life* 30 Nov. 1504/2 These small birds [*sc.* turkeys]..are killed out at 10–12 weeks of age.

c. With complement expressing the result: ***to kill to*** (†***into, unto***) ***death, to kill dead***. (Cf. Ger. *todtschlagen*, Du. *doodslaan*.)

1362 LANGL. *P. Pl.* A. XI. 282 Poule þe apostil þat no pite ne hadde, Cristene kynde to kille to deþe. *c* **1400** *Destr. Troy* 1734 The Grekes..kyld all our kynnesmen into colde dethe. **1614** BP. HALL *No Peace with Rome* 21 (L.) In the popish churches..their very walls kill us dead. **1670** COTTON *Espernon* I. I. 35 Some of the company..found the Horse.. kill'd stone dead. **1700** FARQUHAR *Constant Couple* IV. ii, Are you sure you killed him dead? **1882** J. C. MORISON *Macaulay* iii. 92 Bentley did kill his adversary dead.

d. *absol.* To perform the act of killing; to commit murder or slaughter.

1535 COVERDALE *Exod.* xx. 13 Thou shalt not kyll. **1593** SHAKS. *2 Hen. VI*, IV. iii. 8 Thou shalt haue a License to kill for a hundred lacking one. **1653** HOLCROFT *Procopius, Pers. Wars* I. 2 Which gives such force to the Arrow, that where it lights it kils. **1810** *Sporting Mag.* XXXV. 300 They killed in one of the new plantations near Blankney. **1883** W. BLACK in *Harper's Mag.* Dec. 64/2 They had not been 'killing' at any of the farms.

e. *intr.* in passive sense: To be killed; to suffer killing. Of an animal: To yield (so much meat) when killed. Also, *to kill out*.

1857 *Jrnl. R. Agric. Soc.* XVIII. I. 162 On inquiry of butchers..I find that one characteristic of a beast which kills well, is to have a little stomach. **1888** *Whitby Gaz.* 25 Feb. 4/7, I saw the cow in the slaughter-house... She killed 34 stones. **1950** *N.Z. Jrnl. Agric.* Apr. 364/1 The Southdown has the advantage over the Leicester in that its progeny are quicker maturing and kill out at prime weight and at an earlier age (3 to 4 months). **1971** *Country Life* 30 Dec. 1857/3 Limousin-sired fat cattle killed out at 68 per cent; far above our national average for our native breeds.

f. *trans.* To procure (meat) by killing animals.

1560 BIBLE (Genev.) *1 Sam.* xxv. 11 My bread, & my water, & my flesh that I haue killed for my sherers. **1689** LUTTRELL *Brief Rel.* (1857) I. 511 The lords of the admiralty have sent orders..to kill beefe and pork for 65 men of war. **1838** JAMES *Robber* vi, The beef was not killed at the end of the table.

g. To represent as killed or as dead. *to kill off*: to remove the names of dead officers from the navy-list (Smyth *Sailor's Word-bk.* 1867).

1867 FREEMAN *Norm. Conq.* I. iii. 199 *note*, Richer seems to kill him [Rolf] at Eu in 925. *Mod.* A novelist who always kills the hero in the last chapter.

3. *transf.* **a.** To destroy the vitality of (any organism or organic substance), the activity of (a disease, etc.). Also, in later use, To destroy, break up, or ruin anything.

1530 PALSGR. 598/2, I kyll, as any freatynge medecyne kylleth deede flesshe. **1558** WARDE tr. *Alexis' Secr.* (1568) 40 a, An oyntment to kill the plague. **1608** TOPSELL *Serpents* (1658) 725 With this they kill hair, for upon the place where the hair was puld off, they pour this bloud, and then it never groweth more. **1658** A. FOX *Wurtz' Surg.* II. ix. 83 A Surgeon made experiment on him with the white of Eggs and Bole, whereby the Eye was killed. **1697** DRYDEN *Virg. Georg.* I. 225 Tough Thistles choak'd the Fields, and kill'd the Corn. **1799** YOUNG *Agric. Lincs.* 145 (E.D.D.) Potatoes have quite killed the land. **1872** HUXLEY *Phys.* i. 18 A burn may kill more or less of the skin. *Mod.* With us the fuchsia is killed down every winter, and so never grows to a shrub in the open air.

b. To destroy the active quality of (a substance); e.g. the fluidity of mercury, the ductility of wire.

1613 PURCHAS *Pilgrimage* (1614) 724 *note*, Some thinke that Quicke-silver cannot quite be killed. **1694** SALMON *Bate's Dispens.* (1713) 661/2 The Quick-silver, before it can be mixed with the other Ingredients, is to be killed with the Turpentine. **1865** *Morn. Star* 1 June, If the phosphorus had not been properly 'killed' by being mixed with gum, it would probably explode when chloride of potass was added. **1875** *Ure's Dict. Arts* III. 846 The lye will have lost its causticity, or, in technical language,..it is killed. **1876** PREECE & SIVEWRIGHT *Telegraphy* 177 The wire..to be then stretched ('killed') to the extent of two per cent. by passing round drums, either varying in diameter or differentially geared as to speed. **1881** YOUNG *Every man his own Mechanic* § 1406 Dampness in the air technically speaking kills the size, that is to say deprives it of its binding power.

c. To neutralize the effect of.

1858 O. W. HOLMES *Aut. Breakf.-t.* (1865) 122 Indefinite quantities of black tea to kill any extra glass of red claret he may have swallowed.

d. To consume; to eat or drink; *spec.* to empty (a bottle of liquor). *colloq.* (orig. *U.S.*).

1833 *Sk. & Eccentr. D. Crockett* xi. 145, I can kill more lickur..and cool out more men than any man you can find in all Kentucky. **1887** *Lantern* (New Orleans) 20 Aug. 2/2 The lady had killed a dozen [oysters]. **1934** J. T. FARRELL *Young Manhood* xviii. 291 'We'll drink to that,' said Fat. They killed the bottle. **1967** N. FITZGERALD *Affairs of Death*

vii. 125 We drank with maudlin solemnity to Stella's memory, killing the bottle in the process.

e. In printing or journalism, to cancel or delete (matter) before publication; to discard (type); to suppress or deny (a story, etc.). *colloq.* (orig. *U.S.*).

1865 *Wilkes' Spirit of Times* 16 Dec. 256/1 Two galleys of equal length, one being marked 'Must', the other 'Kill this'. **1887** *Courier-Journal* (Louisville, Ky.) 29 Jan. 5/4 Please kill the deer story sent by Associated Press this morning. **1903** E. L. SHUMAN *Pract. Journalism* 62 The editor can make room by killing the last paragraphs of the other stories. **1929** [see *copy-desk* s.v. COPY *sb.* C]. **1938** E. WAUGH *Scoop* II. i. 133 We're killing this story... Go round to the Press Bureau and have Benito issue an official *dementi*. **1967** KARCH & BUBER *Offset Processes* ii. 40 'Dead' ads are killed. **1972** *Human World* May 75 This is a dull and confused book. (We killed our review of it as not worth the space.)

f. To turn off or stop (an engine, esp. the motor of a car). *colloq.* (orig. *U.S.*).

1886 *Philadelphia Even. Tel.* 20 Mar., The hose was cut.. and engines killed so that it will take days to bring them to life again. **1907** E. S. FIELD *Six-Cylinder Courtship* 9, I lost no time in starting. What a blessing that I hadn't killed my engine! **1935** M. M. ATWATER *Murder in Midsummer* iv. 41 Jim killed the engine and switched off the lights. **1971** D. MACKENZIE *Sleep is for Rich* vi. 196, I moved the hired car into the cobbled courtyard... I killed the motor.

g. *Metallurgy.* To treat (steel when molten) so as to prevent the evolution of oxygen on solidification (now done by adding a reducing agent: cf. KILLED *ppl. a.* 2 b); to remove (iron oxides) from the molten metal by this means.

1906 W. MACFARLANE *Princ. & Pract. Iron & Steel Manufacture* iv. 46 Higher class steel requires 'killing'—that is, it requires to be kept in the furnace for about half an hour .. after it has become fluid and it must be poured at a proper temperature. **1918** A. W. & H. BREARLEY *Ingots & Ingot Moulds* x. 172 When cast steel was made by the crucible process.. it was necessary to continue the heating, and.. increase the temperature as far as possible, in order to 'kill' the steel. **1926** *Jrnl. Iron & Steel Inst.* CXIV. 407 On account of the titanium alloy being of only 17 per cent. strength, it is not practicable to kill a heat of steel with titanium only. **1940** SIMONS & GREGORY *Steel Manuf.* vi. 31 There are several ways of killing steel. One.. is the addition in the ingot mould before teeming of about 0·02 per cent of metallic aluminium (Al) to the melt. **1969** R. STEPHEN *Iron & Steel for Operatives* xii. 56/1 All the iron oxide has been removed, or killed by de-oxidation, and has entered the slag in the ladle.

h. To extinguish or obscure (a light); also, to extinguish (a cigarette). *colloq.*

1934 *Tit-Bits* 31 Mar. 12/1 'Niggers' are not men of colour, but blackboards used to 'kill' unwanted reflections from the powerful lights. **1939** *Evening News* 7 Nov. 4/5 'Kill that baby and put a nigger in its place.' ('Put out that small spotlight and substitute a black screen'). **1940** *Chambers's Techn. Dict.* 476/2 *Kill* (Cinema), colloquialism for extinguish lights. **1942** R. CHANDLER *High Window* (1943) xix. 135 She killed her cigarette in Morny's copper goldfish bowl, speared the crushed stub absently with the letter opener and dropped it into the waste-basket. **1959** M. PUGH *Chancer* 153 Could you kill that cigarette..? It's smouldering somewhere. **1967** J. WAINWRIGHT *Worms must Wait* lxxvii. 200 The window shattered and the lights were killed almost simultaneously.

4. *fig.* **a.** To destroy, do away with, put an end to, suppress (a feeling, desire, project, or other non-material thing).

1435 MISYN *Fire of Love* 81 Well vsyd in prayinge.. all wykkydnes kylland & vnclennes. **1573** CARTWRIGHT *Repl. Answ. Admonit.* 26 Sufficient to quench her thirst and kill her hunger. **1579–80** NORTH *Plutarch* (1595) 236 Too sodaine honour in youth killeth further desire of fame. **1617** R. WILKINSON *Barwick-bridge* 22 Yea, warre and contention kill up even conscience it selfe. **1710** *Tatler* No. 191 ¶1 The monstrous Affectation of being thought artful, immediately kills all Thoughts of Humanity and Goodness. **1851** D. JERROLD *St. Giles* iv. 31 [He] detected his wife painfully endeavouring to kill a laugh. **1872** LIDDON *Elem. Relig.* vi. 214 In the Jew of the age of Tiberius, the national feeling.. had almost killed out the human. **1873** BLACK *Pr. Thule* xix, You have killed her faith as well as ruined her life.

b. To neutralize, destroy, or spoil (an appearance or quality) by contrast or incongruity.

1859 GULLICK & TIMBS *Paint.* 117 The necessity of using body-colour, in order, by its opacity, to 'kill'—using the painter's phrase—.. the unpleasant hue of the photograph. **1877** J. C. COX *Ch. Derbysh.* II. 378 The high blank walls.. kill the grace of the lancet windows on the.. sides of the chancel.

c. *Theatr. colloq.* (See quot. 1952.)

1933 [see COMEDY[1] 2 c]. **1952** GRANVILLE *Dict. Theatr. Terms* 106 *Kill a laugh*, to start a fresh line before the laugh evoked by the preceding one has died down.

d. *Athletics.* To put (a rival runner) out of contention in a race by setting a fast pace, or suddenly accelerating. Also with *off*.

1962 B. HEWSON *Flying Feet* xi. 132 Derek.. slowed the pace to a crawl, obviously hoping to use his finishing kick to kill off Mike and myself. **1968** G. GRETTON *Out in Front* v. 74 He set a fast pace which 'killed' Heino, who collapsed and retired.

5. To consume or spend (time, or any portion of time), so as to bring it to an end. Said of a person, or an occupation or amusement.

1728 VANBR. & CIB. *Prov. Husb.* I. i, What think you, if we three sat soberly down to kill an hour at ombre? **1768–74** TUCKER *Lt. Nat.* (1834) II. 578 It is ridiculous to see how many shifts are made to kill time, as it is called. **1826** DISRAELI *Viv. Grey* I. v, A sawney who was killing the half-holiday by looking out of the window. **1874** L. STEPHEN *Hours in Library* (1892) I. ii. 64 Tapestry, in which ladies employed their needles by way of killing time.

6. In hyperbolic use: To come near to killing. **a.** To overwhelm (a person) by a strong impression on the mind, as of admiration, astonishment, alarm, grief, etc.: to impress with irresistible force. Also, to convulse (someone) with laughter; to excite, thrill, delight.

1634 [see KILLING *ppl. a.* 2 c]. **1711** STEELE *Spect.* No. 144 ¶1 If they [Handsom People] do not kill at first Sight, as the Phrase is, a second Interview disarms them of all their Power. **1712–14** POPE *Rape Lock* v. 68 Chloe stepp'd in and kill'd him with a frown. **1783** MAD. D'ARBLAY *Diary* Jan., He behaves to me with a kind of deference that kills me. [**1856** C. M. YONGE *Daisy Chain* II. viii. 414 Ethel saw Meta in fits of laughing... 'Ethel! you will kill me!' said Meta, sinking back on the sofa.] **1938** C. CALLOWAY *Hi De Ho* 16 *Kill me*, show me a good time, send me. **1942** BERREY & VAN DEN BARK *Amer. Thes. Slang* §591/5 Delight the audience, .. *kill 'em*. **1951** J. D. SALINGER *Catcher in Rye* x. 82, I took her to see this French movie... It killed her. *Ibid.* 83 She killed Allie, too. I mean he liked her, too. **1960** C. DALE *Spring of Love* ix. 176 He kills me sometimes, the things he says. **1971** *Melody Maker* 13 Nov. 31/6 During the Elton John tour in the States, which was a gas, man, we killed them night after night.

b. To injure seriously; to affect with severe pain or suffering.

1800 MAR. EDGEWORTH *Castle Rackrent* 158 My lady Rackrent was all kilt and smashed, and they lifted her into a cabin hard by.. and they say my lady can't live any way. **1816** JANE AUSTEN *Emma* III. vi. 106 Nothing killed him like heat—he could bear any degree of cold. **1824** C. K. SHARPE *Corr.* (1888) II. 303, I am so kilt all over with rheumatism, as Irishmen speak, that I can scarcely hold a pen. **1899** G. W. PECK *Uncle Ike* (1903) xix. 172 'Now wouldn't that kill you,' said the boy... 'That breaks up my scheme to fight the French.' *a* **1953** E. O'NEILL *Long Day's Journey* (1956) II. i. 53 No wonder my feet kill me each night. **1962** J. CANNAN *All is Discovered* i. 19 My feet are killing me anyway and this dam' strapless bra is rubbing me raw. *Ibid.* vi. 140 The 'middy'-heeled shoes which after the long walk along the hot roads had been 'killing' her. **1965** J. PORTER *Dover Two* v. 61 The long cold walk.. did nothing to lighten Dover's mood. His feet were killing him.

c. Used in the infinitive form after another verb with adverbial force = 'to a great or impressive degree'; esp. in phr. ***dressed*** (***got up***, etc.) ***to kill***, dressed showily or impressively. *colloq.*

1818 KEATS *Let.* 23 Jan. (1958) I. 216 One chap was dressed to kill for the King in Bombastes. **1845** *N.Y. Even. Express* 5 Mar. 2/4 Mrs. Polk.. dresses 'to kill'. **1848** BARTLETT *Dict. Amer.* 194 To do anything *to kill*, is a common vulgarism, and means to do it to the uttermost; to carry it to the fullest extent; as, 'He drives to kill'; 'she dances to kill'. **1862** J. R. LOWELL *Biglow Papers* 2nd Ser. 36 'T was Concord Bridge a-talkin' off to kill With the Stone Spike thet's druv thru Bunker Hill. **1922** JOYCE *Ulysses* 280 Got up to kill: on eighteen bob a week. **1957** N. MITFORD *Voltaire in Love* xviii. 218 Mme du Châtelet.. always took the part of the leading lady, dressed up to kill and covered with diamonds. **1970** G. W. BARRAX in S. Henderson *Understanding New Black Poetry* (1973) III. 358 Dress to kill Shoot to kill Love to kill If you will But write to bring back the dead.

7. In various phrases. **a.** ***to kill a ball***: (*a*) in tennis, to strike a ball so as to prevent it from being returned (see quot. 1883); (*b*) in football, to stop a ball dead.

1883 *Daily News* 26 June 6/6 Posting themselves close to the net, to intercept the ball as it came over, and by a severe downward stroke to hit it in such a manner that it could not possibly be returned—or, in other words, to 'kill' it. **1900** *Ibid.* 23 Apr. 8/1 The ball had come in from the right, and McLuckie killed it, and shot a goal.

b. ***to kill a bill*** (in parliament): to defeat it totally; to prevent it from passing; to veto it.

1832 J. W. CROKER in *C. Papers* 14 Apr. (1884), I have just had Haddington with me. He is confident of killing the bill. **1888** BRYCE *Amer. Commw.* I. I. vi. 75 By 'killing' more bills than all his predecessors put together had done, Mr. Cleveland raised himself in public opinion.

†**c.** ***to kill one's heart***: to depress or discourage one completely. *Obs.*

1470–85 MALORY *Arthur* x. lviii, Fy vpon treason said sir Trystram, for hit kylleth my herte to here this tale. **1579–80** NORTH *Plutarch* (1676) 343 For their hearts were killed, because.. they were ever overthrown. **1654** SIR E. NICHOLAS in *N. Papers* (Camden) II. 124 To see us totally ruined rather then deale with people according to their deserts, it kills our harts.

d. ***to kill with kindness***: to destroy or fatally harm by mistaken and excessive kindness.

c **1558** *Enterlude of Welth, & Helth* sig. D1v, With kindnes my her ye do kyll. **1582** G. WHETSTONE *Heptameron of Civil Discourses* sig. T4v, You will kill her with kindnesse. **1596** SHAKS. *Tam. Shr.* IV. i. 211 This is a way to kil a Wife with kindnesse. **1607** T. HEYWOOD (*title*) A woman kilde with kindnesse. **1698** FRYER *Acc. E. India & P.* 100 Tom Coriat .. was killed with Kindness by the English Merchants. **1698** FARQUHAR *Love & Bottle* III. i, I bear her an amorous grudge still.. I could kill her with kindness. **1761** G. COLMAN *Jealous Wife* IV. i. 67 You absolutely kill Him with Kindness. **1842** F. A. KEMBLE *Let.* 31 Mar. in *Rec. Later Life* (1882) II. 189 Lord Morpeth.. has a.. mother and sisters, and really should not, on their account, be killed with kindness. **1898** F. P. DUNNE *Mr. Dooley in Peace & War* 38 'They'll kill him with kindness if he don't look out,' said Mr. Hennessy. **1925** A. HUXLEY *Along Road* 61 The country.. has not been killed by the deadly kindness of those who, like myself, are nature's townsmen. **1935** I. BROWN *Heart of England* viii. 84 Now we purge by persuasion that new Beelzebub, the complex, or kill it by kindness.

e. ***kill or cure***, with reference to medical treatment or remedies, which either cure or prove fatal; also *attrib.*, and *absol.* as *sb.*

1764 FOOTE *Mayor of G.* I. Wks. 1799 I. 162 Your Worship knows, that, kill or cure, I have contracted to physic the parish-poor by the great. **1778** in James *Dissert. Fevers* (ed. 8) 114 Dr. James's Powder, which I was determined to take, kill or cure. **1875** JOWETT *Plato* (ed. 2) III. 39 Asclepius.. adopted the rough 'kill or cure' method. **1898** *Folk-lore* IX. 14 The Lebanon mother knows no other remedy than the kill-or-cure of a dip in the sea for her babe.

f. ***to kill two birds with one stone***: see STONE *sb.* 16 b.

g. Ironical phr. ***it won't*** (etc.) ***kill you*** (or ***him***, ***us***, etc.): that would not be too much to endure.

1858 TROLLOPE *Three Clerks* I. vii. 130 'We are both used to that, I fancy,' said Tudor, 'so it won't kill us.' **1913** J. VAIZEY *College Girl* vi. 83 Suppose I ask them? Twopence three farthings each would not kill them! **1945** A. KOBER *Parm Me* 123 Even if your father's gonna lay out a few dollars, O.K., so it's not gonna kill him! **1967** 'G. NORTH' *Sgt. Cluff & Day of Reckoning* ii. 16 'You could have stopped in bed...' 'Lie there awake?' 'It wouldn't have killed you.' 'Getting my own breakfast didn't either.'

h. ***to kill the goods***: in soap-making, to emulsify the melted fat by a partial saponification.

1885 W. L. CARPENTER *Treat. Manuf. Soap* 167 The boiling, and the addition of fat and lye, must be continued until a small sample.. has a tolerably firm consistence... Practice alone will enable the operator to judge of the completion of this first operation, called 'pasting'. In English phraseology, it is called 'killing the goods' or raw material. **1888** J. CAMERON *Soaps & Candles* 82 Saponification, pasting, or killing the goods. **1894** C. R. A. WRIGHT *Animal & Veg. Fixed Oils* 468 The effect of the action of the hot ley on the melted fatty matter is to 'kill the goods'—*i.e.*, to emulsify the whole, so that no distinct layer of melted fat swims up on taking a sample.

kill, obs. form of KILN.

kill-, vb. stem, prefixed to sbs., forming *sbs.* (chiefly 17th c. *nonce-wds.*) with sense 'one who or that which kills...', and *adjs.* = 'that kills ..., -killing.' **A.** *sbs.*, as **kill-bishop**; **kill-Christ**, one who took part in putting Christ to death; **kill-courtesy**, a boorish person; **kill-crow**, (*a*) ? a good shot, one who can hit the mark well; (*b*) *dial.* = KILL-COW 3; **kill-herb**, a parasitic plant, Broomrape; **kill-lamb**, an American species of Andromeda (*A. mariana*) poisonous to sheep; **kill-man**, a man-slayer; also *adj.* man-slaying; **kill-pot**, a hard drinker. **B.** *adjs.* as **kill-calf**; **kill-duck**, suited for killing ducks; **kill-me-quite**, irresistibly bewitching or fascinating. Also **kill-curing**, that cures by killing. See also KILL-BUCK, -COW, -DEVIL, etc.

1672 WOOD *Life* 19 Nov. (O.H.S.) II. 253 Chester is a *kill-bishop. **1628** CLAVELL *Recant. ill-led Life* 35 Then take heed of those Base Padding Rascalls, for their *kill-calfe law I am not priuy to. **1630** J. TAYLOR (Walter P.) *Wks.* (N.), There they make private shambles with kil-calfe cruelty, and sheepe-slaughtering murther. **1647** TRAPP *Comm. Acts* v. 28 They should be counted *kill-Christs. **1590** SHAKS. *Mids. N.* II. ii. 77 This lacke-loue, this *kill-curtesie. **1593** *Pass. Morrice* (1876) 83, I will tell you my reason, and if it iumpes with your conceite, say you mette with a *kill Crowe. **1616** J. LANE *Contn. Sqr.'s T.* VIII. 56 That suche feirce surgeons tooles should exercise On mans soft fleshe, *kill-curinge buttcheries. **1675** COTTON *Scoffer Scoft* 31 Yonder is the Bird of prey, I see him in a *Kill-duck place. **1671** SKINNER *Etymol. Ling. Angl., Bot.*, *Kill-herb. **1874** DUNGLISON *Med. Dict.*, *Kill Lamb. *c* **1611** CHAPMAN *Iliad* II. 573 Warlike Idomen.. co-partner in the fleet, With *kill-man Merion. **1638** BRATHWAIT *Ps.* cli, Gath flesht in battles, broiles, and blood, A kill-man from his youth. **1842** S. LOVER *Handy Andy* v. 50 He sang too with a *kill-me-quite air, as if no lady could resist his strains. **1616** B. JONSON *Masque Christmas*, This Carol plays, and has been in his days A chirping boy, and a *kill-pot.

killable ('kɪləb(ə)l), *a.* [f. KILL *v.* + -ABLE.]

1. Fit to be killed for food or other use.

1817–18 COBBETT *Resid. U.S.* (1822) 91 What animal produces flesh meat like the hog?.. The animal killable at all ages. **1823** COL. HAWKER *Diary* (1893) I. 267, I.. honestly bagged 46 killable trout.

2. Capable of being killed; easy to kill.

1823 *Mirror* I. 296/1 That killable species of ghost that could be shot with a sixpence. **1877** T. A. TROLLOPE *Life of Pius IX*, III. viii. II. 84 The experience.. would have gone far to kill any man killable by disappointment and sorrow.

‖**killadar** ('kɪlədɑː(r)). *East Ind.* Also 8 **killahdaur**, 8–9 **kelli-**, **kille-**, **keeledar**. [Urdū (Pers.) *qilʻadār*, f. Arab. *qalʻah* (pl. *qilāʻ*) fort + Pers. *-dār* holder.] The commandant or governor of a fort or castle.

1778 ORME *Hist. Indostan* II. 217 The fugitive garrison.. returned, with 500 more, sent by the Kellidar of Vandiwash. **1783** *Hist. Eur.* in *Ann. Reg.* 97/1 The killedar or governor, with his rabble.. fled into the fort. **1803** WELLINGTON *Let. to Col. Murray* 16 July in Gurw. *Desp.* (1837) II. 95 It is imagined that the Killadar of Perinda is not unfaithful to the Nizam's government. **1862** BEVERIDGE *Hist. India* I. III. xi. 622 The native governor or killedar.

Hence 'killadary, the governorship of a fort.

1803 WELLINGTON in *Desp.* (1844) I. 355 The letters respecting the killadary of Darwar.

Killarney (kɪ'lɑːnɪ). The name of a town in Co. Kerry, Ireland, used *attrib.* in **Killarney fern**,

the bristle fern, *Trichomanes radicans*, which was formerly abundant in the neighbourhood of Killarney.

[1844 E. NEWMAN *Hist. Brit. Ferns* 313 It has lately been supposed by many excellent botanists, that there are two Irish species of *Trichomanes*,—the Killarney and the Glouin Caragh plants.] 1863 *Fern Manual* 160 It is not only a native of Ireland, as the popular name (Killarney Fern) would lead us to believe, but is found also in many other parts of the world. 1888 C. T. DRUERY *Choice Brit. Ferns* vi. 59 We have been very successful in the culture of the Killarney Fern. 1891 L. T. MEADE *Sweet Girl Graduate* x. 89 I'll take you into our fern-house... We have got such exquisite maidenhairs, and such a splendid Killarney fern. 1910 C. T. DRUERY *Brit. Ferns* 257 In Ireland it has been found so frequently as to have acquired the popular name of the Killarney Fern. 1960 P. TAYLOR *Brit. Ferns & Mosses* 88 The Killarney Fern has a most unusual distribution, being found chiefly in the tropics of the Old and New Worlds, with an extension northwards in Europe to the Pyrenees and Ireland. 1973 *Times* 17 Dec. 2/7 Picking wild plants prohibited in peer's Bill... The 20 flowers are..in danger of extinction... The plants are:..Killarney fern,..Snowdon lily, spiked speedwell, spring gentian, Teesdale sandwort.

killas ('kɪləs). Also 7-9 **kellus**, 8 **killos**. [Cornish.] The Cornish Miners' term for clay-slate; geologically, the clay-slate of Cornwall, of Devonian age, which rests on the granite.

1674-91 RAY *Coll. Words* Prepar. Metals (E.D.S.) 11 Above the spar lies another kind of substance like a white soft stone, which they call *kellus*. 1758 BORLASE *Nat. Hist. Cornwall* 92 Round the town of Marazion..there rises a very tender killas, of the cinereous, and also of the yellow colour. 1833 LYELL *Princ. Geol.* III. 370 At the junction of the granite and killas in St. Michael's Mount. 1875 GEIKIE *Life Murchison* I. 301 The Devonshire killas answered in point of geological time to the old Red Sandstone.

attrib. 1807 VANCOUVER *Agric. Devon* (1813) 11 *note*, The shillot or killas rock..will always be found accompanied with a similar soil or covering.

†**killat.** *Obs. rare.* [a. Sp. or Pg. *quilate* carat.] = CARAT.

1580 FRAMPTON *Dial. Yron & Steele* 170 At the tyme they melt yᵉ gold,..that it may fine and ryse of more killats,..they cast it [etc.]. 1589 R. PARKE tr. *Mendoza's Hist. China* (1854) II. 303 Pearles..which..do in many killats exceede them that are brought from Baren.

†'**killbuck.** *Obs. rare.* Also 7 **kilbuck**. [f. KILL *v.* + BUCK *sb.*[1] Cf. next.]

1. A fierce-looking fellow.

1612 CHAPMAN *Widowes T.* I. iv, *Thar.* Well, have you done now, Ladie? *Ars.* O my sweet kilbuck. *Thar.* You now in your shallow pate thinke this a disgrace to mee. 1660 HEXHAM, Kilbuck, or fierce-look, *Suyr gesicht*.

2. Applied to the keeper of a deer-park. *nonce-use.*

1826 SCOTT *Woodst.* iii, A poor kill-buck that never frightened anything before save a dun deer.

'**kill-cow**, *sb.* and *a.* *Obs.* exc. *dial.* Also 6-7 **kilcow(e**. [f. KILL *v.* + COW *sb.*[1]]

A. *sb.* **1.** A swashbuckler, bully, braggadocio; a terrible or great person; a man of importance.

1589 R. HARVEY *Pl. Perc.* (1590) A iij, What neede all this stir? this banding of kilcowes to fight with a shadow? 1639 EARL STRAFFORD *Lett. & Disp.* (1739) II. 307 A captain he is, but no such great Kill-Cow as they would have him. 1650 BAYLY *Herba Parietis* 127 One Hamon (a notable kill-cow and noted dueller). *a*1734 NORTH *Lives* (1826) I. 91 Well known to be one of the greatest kill-cows at drinking in the nation. 1896 *Dial. Notes* I. 22 (E.D.D.) 'He's no great killcow', i.e. he doesn't amount to much (of a person who thinks himself somebody).

2. *dial.* A serious affair; a matter involving great trouble or loss. (Usually in negative phr.)

1825-80 JAMIESON s.v., Ye needna mind, I'm sure it's nae sic great kill-cow. 1886 ELWORTHY *W. Som. Word-bk.* s.v., Twadn no such kill-cow job arter all.

3. A nickname for a butcher. *rare.*

.. *Old Ballad* (N.), I would not be a butcher..For..He shall be call'd Kill-cow, and so shall be named.

4. A kind of spike-rush: see quot.

1898 BRITTON & BROWN *Flora North. Canada*, Index, *Eleocharis tenuis.* Slender Spike-rush, Kill-cow.

B. *adj.* Bragging, bullying; terrifying. ***kill-cow fray***, something made up to terrify.

1589 NASHE *Ded. to Greene's Menaphon* (Arb.) 6 The ingrafted overflow of some kilcow conceipt. 1592 —— *P. Penilesse* (ed. 2) 11 b, In this vaine of kilcow vanitie. 1613 PURCHAS *Pilgrimage* I. II. xii. 145 Like Semiramis Elephants which were but stuffed oxe-hides, kill-cow-frayes. 1633 SHIRLEY *Young Admiral* IV. iii, You are afraid Of him, belike: 'tis such a kill-cow gentleman!

Hence †'**killcow** *v. trans.*, to terrify with threatening looks; to cow.

1592 G. HARVEY *Pierce's Super.* in *Archaica* II. 142 A new art to kill-cow men with peremptory termes, and buggeswordes.

kill-crazy ('kɪl 'kreɪzɪ), *a. colloq.* (orig. *U.S.*). [f. KILL *v.* + CRAZY *a.* 4.] Insanely desirous of killing; murderous.

1942 BERREY & VAN DEN BARK *Amer. Thes. Slang* § 184/14 *Kill Crazy Dillinger*.., John Dillinger, Midwest outlaw. 1949 *Sun* (Baltimore) 1 Dec. 3/4 All the prior plans to kill me have been made by the same man—a kill-crazy man. 1959 G. JENKINS *Twist of Sand* xiii. 280 Scientists don't go kill crazy..just for the sake of one lost species. *Ibid.* xiv. 306, I had no plan. I was as kill-crazy as he. 1972 'J. RIPLEY' *My Word you should have seen Us* 179, I was pure animal, and kill-crazy.

'**killcrop.** *rare.* [ad. LG. *kîlkrop*, G. *kielkropf*, of uncertain etym. (see Grimm).] An insatiate brat, popularly supposed to be a fairy changeling substituted for the genuine child.

1652 H. BELL *Luther's Colloq.* 387 Near unto Halberstad, was a man that also had a Killcrop, who sucked the mother and 5 other women drie; and besides devoured very much. 1681 T. FLATMAN *Heraclitus Ridens* No. 28 They may talk of ..Canibals, Man-eaters, Killcraps, and the Devil and all. 1836 W. IRVING in *Life & Lett.* (1866) III. 90 Those little fairy changelings called Killcrops, which eat and eat, and are never the fatter. *a*1843 SOUTHEY *The Killcrop* xvi, If killcrops look like children, by what power Know you they are not?

kill-cu ('kɪlku:). *U.S. local.* [Imitative.] A name of two American species of yellowshanks (*Totanus melanoleucus* and *T. flavipes*), related to the snipes.

1888 TRUMBULL *Names & Portr. Birds* 168.

killdee, killdeer ('kɪldi:, -dɪə(r)). Also **kil-**. [Imitative of its note.] The largest species of ring-plover (*Ægialitis vocifera*) of North America.

1731 MORTIMER in *Phil. Trans.* XXXVII. 176 The Chattering Plover. In Virginia they are called Kildeers, from some Resemblance of their Noise to the Sound of that Word. 1796 MORSE *Amer. Geog.* I. 214 Kildee or Chattering Plover. *a*1862 THOREAU *Cape Cod* vii. (1865) 123 The kildeer plover..fills the air above with its din. 1888 J. C. HARRIS *Free Joe*, etc. 26 As happy..as a killdee by a mill-race.

'**kill-devil**, *sb.* (*a.*) [f. KILL *v.* + DEVIL.]

A. *sb.* †**1.** A recklessly daring fellow. *Obs.*

*c*1590 MARLOWE *Faust.* iv, 'Did ye see yonder tall fellow..? he has killed the devil.' So I should be called Kill-devil all the parish over.

2. A colloq. name for rum (see also quot. 1846). *Obs.* exc. *Hist.*

Hence prob. F. *guildive* (1722: 'origine inconnue', Littré and Hatz.-Darm.). N. Darnell Davis in *Trans. Philol. Soc.* 1885-7, 714.

1639 J. JOSSELYN *Jrnl.* 24 Sept. in *Acct. Two Voy.* (1674) 26 Captain Thomas Wannerton..drank to me a pint of kill-devil *alias* Rhum at a draught. *c*1651 in N. D. Davis *Cavaliers & Roundheads Barbados* (1887) 112 The chiefe fudling they make in the Island is Rumbullion, alias Kill-Devill, and this is made of suggar canes distilled, a hott, hellish and terrible liquor. 1654 *Connect. Col. Rec.* (1850) I. 255 Berbados Liquors, commonly called Rum, Kill Deuill, or the like. 1740 *Hist. Jamaica* II. 31 Rum-punch is not improperly called Kill-devil; for Thousands lose their Lives by its means. 1796 STEDMAN *Surinam* I. 96 The furnace which distils the kill-devil. 1846 *Swell's Night Guide* 123/2 *Kill-devil*, new rum, from its pernicious quality. 1885 *Century Mag.* Apr. 884/2 Rum, or 'kill-devil', as it was everywhere called, was rendered plentiful by the trade with the West Indies and by the New England stills. 1970 M. SLATER *Caribbean Cooking* 7 From sugar came rum, 'kill-devil', the spirit of cane.

3. An artificial bait used in angling, made to spin in the water like a wounded fish.

1833 *Bowlker's Art Angling* 33 There are..three modes of Trolling... The third is called the kill-devil, and..it answers I think the best of all. 1839 COL. HAWKER *Diary* (1893) II. 161 Lord Saltoun's brass 'Kill-devil,' the only artificial bait the I ever found to take in our river. 1860 C. SIMEON *Stray Notes Fishing* 22, I have fished with artificial spinning-baits (killdevils) of nearly every kind.

B. *adj.* That would kill devils; deadly.

1831 TRELAWNEY *Adv. of a Younger Son* III. xxxvi. 252 We distributed this kill-devil hell-paste in several parts of the vessel,..destroying 'at one fell swoop', all the reptiles which infested and annoyed us.

killed (kɪld), *ppl. a.* [f. KILL *v.* + -ED[1].]

1. a. Deprived of life; put to death. Usually of meat, with qualifying word, as ***fresh-***, ***country-killed***, etc.

*c*1440 *Promp. Parv.* 274/2 Kyllyd, *interfectus.* 1812 *Examiner* 5 Oct. 628/1 We have found here 2000 killed or amputated Russians. 1886 *Daily News* 16 Sept. 2/5 The small supply of fresh killed meat. 1887 *Ibid.* 11 May 2/6 The heaviest decline being on country-killed beef.

b. with *adv.* (In quot. as *sb.*)

1825 BENTHAM *Offic. Apt. Maximized, Indications* (1830) 84 The deaths of Jefferies's killed-offs were speedy.

c. *Med.* Applied to bacteria and viruses that have been killed or rendered non-infectious, and hence to preparations containing them.

1919 *Med. Ann.* XXXVII. 493 A special series of vaccines have been prepared... They are standardized emulsions in normal saline of killed bacteria. 1925 J. W. BIGGER *Handbk. Bacteriol.* xiii. 152 Workers have found it possible to immunize monkeys against experimental pneumonia by the intratracheal inoculation of killed cultures. 1930 *Syst. Bacteriol.* (Med. Res. Council) VII. vii. 117 There remains a considerable doubt whether immunity..can be produced by the use of killed virus. 1964 M. HYNES *Med. Bacteriol.* (ed. 8) xxv. 385 The killed vaccine [of poliomyelitis] does not necessarily prevent subsequent intestinal infection, but it evokes sufficient neutralizing antibodies to prevent the viræmia which precedes central nervous system involvement. 1964 H. JOLLY *Dis. Children* xvi. 343 Salk vaccine is a killed preparation containing all three types of virus. 1971 BEESON & MCDERMOT *Cecil-Loeb Text-bk. Med.* (ed. 13) 416/2 Killed poliomyelitis vaccine is now used very infrequently.

2. a. Of a substance: Deprived of active property.

1894 BOTTONE *Electr. Instr. Making* (ed. 6) 5 Chloride of zinc (killed spirits of salt). *Ibid.* 7 Soldering with chloride of zinc ('killed spirits', 'soldering fluid').

b. *Metallurgy.* Of steel: treated when molten so as to prevent the evolution of oxygen on solidification and the consequent formation of blow-holes (now done by adding a reducing agent).

1884 W. H. GREENWOOD *Steel & Iron* xviii. 425 When the metal throws out sparks or teems fiery, it is said not to be 'killed', and it is indicative of the metal not having been sufficiently long in the fire after fusion, and such steel will yield unsound or honey-combed ingots. 1926 *Jrnl. Iron & Steel Inst.* CXIV. 406 In the application of titanium to killed steel the conditions are entirely different, and a complete absence of gas evolution as well as the maximum degree of deoxidation are generally desired. 1935 *Jrnl. R. Aeronaut. Soc.* XXXIX. 1121 Scientific metallurgists would like to see all steels fully killed,..but economic considerations at present compel the manufacture of rimming and partly-killed steel. 1970 A. CIBULA in O. Kubaschewski et al. *Gases & Metals* ii. 31 Small amounts of hydrogen and nitrogen are detected, and in killed ingots these gases predominate over carbon dioxide.

killedar, variant of KILLADAR.

killer ('kɪlə(r)). [f. KILL *v.* + -ER[1].]

1. a. One who or that which kills; a slayer, butcher.

1535 COVERDALE *Tobit* iii. 9 Thou kyller of thy huszbandes. 1552 HULOET, Kyller of mise and rattes, *myoph[o]nos.* 1696 *Statutes* (Scottish) c. 33 *title*, Act against killers of black fish, and destroyers of the fry and smolts of salmon. 1741 MIDDLETON *Cicero* I. vi. 538 One Licinius, a killer of the victims for sacrifice. 1829 CARLYLE *Misc., Voltaire* (1872) II. 131 He has his coat of darkness,..like that other Killer of Giants. 1872 O. W. HOLMES *Poet Breakf.-t.* ix. (1885) 225 She is a killer and a cannibal among other insects.

b. *fig.* in various senses.

1555 L. SANDERS *Let.* in Foxe *A. & M.* (1631) III. XI. 141/2 Christ the killer of death. 1819 *Hermit in Lond.* II. 170 She is the most desperate killer of time I ever met with. 1838 MARY HOWITT *Birds & Fl., Ivy-bush* iv, What a killer of care, old tree, wert thou!

c. In many combinations, as ***dragon-***, ***giant-***, ***lady-***, ***lion-***, ***pain-killer***, etc.: see these words.

2. A name of the grampus, *Orcinus orca*, and other ferocious cetaceans of kindred genera. In full, ***killer whale***. Also *fig.*

1725 DUDLEY in *Phil. Trans.* XXXIII. 265 These Killers are from twenty to thirty Feet long, and have Teeth in both Jaws... They..set upon a young Whale, and will bait him like so many Bull-dogs. 1884 G. B. GOODE *Fisheries U.S.: Nat. Hist. Aquatic Animals* 17 The Killer Whales are known the world over by their destructive and savage habits. 1897 F. T. BULLEN *Cruise 'Cachalot'* 196 A large bowhead rose near the ship... Three 'Killers' were attacking him at once, like wolves worrying a bull... The 'Killer' or *Orca gladiator*, is a true whale, but, like the cachalot, has teeth. 1931 W. G. CARR *By Guess & by God* 89 The British had been developing the mechanical killer-whales since 1904, when, unescorted, a flotilla of A-boats engaged in fleet manœuvres. 1937 NORMAN & FRASER *Giant Fishes, Whales, & Dolphins* xiii. 290 The colour of the Killer is well marked and is distinctive for the species. The back is black and the belly white. *Ibid.* 291 A feature unusual in cetaceans is the great discrepancy in size between the male and female Killer Whale. 1973 R. BURTON *Life & Death Whales* i. 23 Killer whales live in small groups and feed mainly on fish but they also kill seals and other whales.

3. An effective angler's bait.

1681 CHETHAM *Angler's Vade-m.* xxxv. § 4 (1689) 207 An admirable Fly, and in great repute for a killer. 1787 BEST *Angling* (ed. 2) 109 There are likewise two Moths..great killers about twilight in a serene evening. 1867 F. FRANCIS *Angling* v. (1880) 155 If he cannot find a killer among them his hopes of sport are very small.

4. a. A club of hard wood for killing fish with.

1890 in *Cent. Dict.*

b. A contrivance for killing a large ferocious animal (e.g. a wolf, a shark); also, an explosive implement for the painless killing of cattle, horses, etc. Cf. HUMANE *a.* 1 d.

1892 *9th Ann. Rep. U.S. Bureau Amer. Ethnol. 1887-88* 259 (*heading*) Whalebone wolf-killers. 1901 *Amer. Anthropologist* Apr.-June 391 Eskimo and Samoan 'Killers'. 1901 *Morning Leader* 18 Dec. 3/7 The deadly instrument known as 'Greener's Killer',..for the painless destruction of old and incapacitated horses, is the invention of the well-known gun manufacturer, Mr. W. W. Greener... The 'killer' consists of a noiseless explosive apparatus resembling a short rifled barrel, which contains a small cartridge with steel-pointed bullet. 1919 T. HARDY *Let.* 7 Nov. in *One Rare Fair Woman* (1972) 187, I am a strange member of the Wessex Pig Society. I accepted the nomination entirely in the hope of helping to popularize the 'killer'. 1968 A. WILSON *Pract. Meat Inspection* i. 1 Cattle are usually stunned by a captive-bolt pistol (Humane Killer). The types usually employed are..3. Schermer mechanical killer.

5. An agent used to neutralize the active property of anything, e.g. to neutralize a colour, to remove spots or stains, prevent pitch-stains on pine-boards, or the like.

1893 in *Funk's Standard Dict.*

6. A cow, sheep, etc., that is killed or destined to be killed for food. Usu. *pl. colloq.* (chiefly *Austral.* and *N.Z.*).

1897 I. SCOTT *How I stole over 10,000 Sheep in Austral. & N.Z.* 9 'You know the killers, don't you?'..i.e. the sheep the boss used for his own mutton at the house. 1907 W. H. KOEBEL *Return of Joe* 294 We were to be treated to a portion of a valuable stud ram for supper in place of the ordinary 'killer'. 1931 V. PALMER *Separate Lives* 124 He had put it [*sc.* the bullock] among the herd of killers in the home paddock in the hope that the new overseer might use it for beef in mistake. 1937 *Amer. Speech* XII. 104 As killing cattle or

killers (cattle ready for killing) they are inferior to corn-fed stock. **1952** *Coast to Coast 1951–52* 210 One afternoon they had brought in some killers to the yards, and Murray went over to the kitchen for the bucket and the knives. **1972** P. Newton *Sheep Thief* iii. 27 The yarding of the killers.. was regarded as a tryout for new dogs—with the stench of blood sheep are loth to approach the yard.

7. a. An impressive, formidable, or excellent person or thing; one who 'kills' people (see KILL *v.* 6a). Cf. *lady-killer* (LADY *sb.* 16). *slang* (orig. *U.S.*).

[**1900** *Dialect Notes* II. 44 *Killer.* 1. One who does things easily. 2. One who recites perfectly.] **1937** *Metronome* Apr. 55 That Zutie drummer-man is really a killer! **1940** *Swing* Jan. 26 *Farewell Blues* is another of those very fast killers. *Ibid.* May 10/3 I'm a killer with my new shepherd plaid suit. **1968** *Blues Unlimited* Sept. 6 'They were going to put out some records, and Luther went to see about it' said Percy, 'his "Dust my broom" was sure a killer.' **1970** *Melody Maker* 19 Sept. 28/6 George Khan has a solo on the up-tempo passage of the same track which is an absolute killer.

b. *attrib.* or as *adj.* Very effective; excellent, 'sensational' (freq. applied to popular music). Cf. KILLER-DILLER. *slang.*

1979 *Melody Maker* 12 May 26/2 That the band were going to deliver a killer set was evident. **1983** *Washington Post* 11 Nov. 37 It can be most easily compared with what Quincy Jones does when he isn't producing another killer album for someone else. **1986** *City Limits* 9 Oct. 17 Sometimes James Brown's albums stank, but there was always one killer track.

8. *attrib.* and *Comb.*, as ***killer instinct***; **killer submarine** (see quot. 1955); **killer whale** (see 2 above).

1931 Visct. Knebworth *Boxing* 78 He [*sc.* Dempsey] had more fighting spirit and more of the sheer *killer instinct in him than was in all four of them rolled together. **1960** J. Fingleton *Four Chukkas to Austral.* vi. 64 Unless Peter May can instil into his men the killer-instinct they so plainly lack, the next two Tests.. will be lost. **1973** *Times* 20 Feb. 12/2 Already he has given Oxford a lift with his drive, enthusiasm, attack and killer instinct. **1955** M. Reifer *Dict. New Words* 116/2 **Killer submarine*, a small submarine designed for hunting down and sinking enemy submarines. **1960** *Economist* 31 Dec. 1378/2 The other kind of vessel that the Navy wants to build in larger numbers is the 'killer' submarine driven by atomic power and equipped with vastly improved sonar devices to seek out and destroy enemy submarines under water.

killer, mod. dial. variant of KEELER[2].

killer-diller (ˌkɪlə'dɪlə(r)). *slang* (orig. *U.S.*). [Rhyming reduplication of KILLER 7.] = KILLER 7. Also *attrib.* or as *adj.*

1938 *Life* 8 Aug. 56 The hot musician.. shudders when he hears Benny Goodman announce his next radio number as a 'killer-diller'. **1939** R. P. Dodge in Ramsey & Smith *Jazzmen* xv. 341 The fast 'killer-diller' arrangement. **1957** W. C. Handy *Father of Blues* x. 147 My old friend Wilbur Sweatman—a killer-diller and jazz pioneer. **1970** *Melody Maker* 3 Oct. 15/6 The inevitable concessions to the gallery made by the band in some of the more 'killer-diller' specialities.

'killesse, -ese, var. CULLIS *sb.*[2], a groove or gutter; *spec.* in a cross-bow, or in a roof. Hence **'killes(s)ed** *a.*, having a killesse.

1649 in Nichols *Progr.* II. 418 One barn of four bayes of building well tyled and killesed on two sides and one end thereof. **1867** Smyth *Sailor's Word-bk.*, *Killese*, the groove in a cross-bow.

killian, var. KILIAN.

killick, killock ('kɪlɪk, -ək). *Naut.* Also 7 kelleck(e, -ock, 8–9 -ick, 9 -agh, eg, keeleg. [Of obscure origin; the spelling is unfixed, but most favour *killick* or *killock*.] **a.** A heavy stone used on small vessels as a substitute for an anchor; also a small anchor. †***to come to a killick***: to come to anchor (*obs.*). ***up killick***: to weigh anchor.

1630 Winthrop *New Eng.* (1825) I. 40 The wind overblew so much at N.W. as they were forced to come to a killock at twenty fathom. **1632** T. Morton *New Eng. Canaan* (1883) 262 The inconstant windes shiftinge at night did force the kellecke home, and billedge the boat. **1643** R. Williams *Key Lang. Amer.* 111 *Kunnosnep*, a Killick, or Anchor. **1670** Narborough *Jrnl.* in *Acc. Sev. Late Voy.* I. (1711) 107 Instead of Anchors, they have modern Crab-claws, or Kellocks. **1758** *Ann. Reg.* 292/1 They sent out another float, with killicks and ropes. **1768** J. Byron *Narr. Paragonia* (ed. 2) 82 We hove up our.. Kellick, which we had made to serve in the room of our grapnel. **1837–40** Haliburton *Clockm.* viii. (1862) 29, I shall up killoch and off to-morrow to the Tree mont. **1840** R. H. Dana *Bef. Mast* xiv. 32 We usually keep anchored by a small kedge, or keeleg. **1883** *Times* 18 May 7 With some bits of wood and a large stone.. [is] fashioned a very good kedge or killick. **1897** R. Kipling *Captains Courageous* 63 Dad says next one [anchor] he loses.. he'll give him the kelleg.

b. A leading seaman's badge, bearing the symbol of an anchor; hence, a leading seaman. Also *attrib.* or as *adj.*, leading, chief. *colloq.*

1915 'Bartimeus' *Tall Ship* iii. 62 He paid for the misplaced generosity of his well-wisher with his 'Killick'. (*footnote*) Anchor. The distinctive badge of a leading rating. **1920** —— *Unreality* II. iii. 115 Picked up my killick. *Ibid.* iv. 126 The sight-setter raised his brows at the red worsted anchor adorning Bill's sleeve. 'Killick, eh!' he ejaculated. **1925** Fraser & Gibbons *Soldier & Sailor Words* 135 *Killick* .., the lower deck term for the Petty Officers' Anchor arm badge. **1930** G. Wells *Naval Customs* 91 *Killick*,.. a slang term for a 'leading seaman'. **1945** 'Tackline' *Holiday Sailor* xiv. 143 Been in barracks for a matter of six months. Killick then, o' course. **1949** Partridge *Dict. Slang* Add. 1092/2 *Killick-scribe*, a Leading Writer.

killickinnick, variant of KINNIKINNIC.

killifish ('kɪlɪfɪʃ). Also killy-. [Commonly supposed to be f. KILL *sb.*[2] + FISH; but cf. KILLING *ppl. a.* 1 b.] The name given to several genera of small fish of the family *Cyprinodontidæ*, found in sheltered places on the east coast of North America, and used as bait; esp. *Fundulus heteroclitus*, the ***green killifish***.

1836 J. Richardson *Fishes N. Amer.* 56 This Stickleback is said, by Dr. Mitchell, to inhabit the salt waters of New York, and to consort with the Killifish. **1885** *Stand. Nat. Hist.* III. 170 The large family of Cyprinodontidæ or killifishes, is distinguished.. by the structure of its mouth.

'killigrew. *local.* Also kille-. An old name for the Cornish chough.

1668 Charleton *Onomasticon* 68 The Cornish Chough (..*in Cornubia*..*vulgo nuncupatur* the Killegrew). **1893** Newton *Dict. Birds*, *Killigrew*.

killin(e, killing, obs. forms of KEELING[1].

killing ('kɪlɪŋ), *vbl. sb.* [f. KILL *v.* + -ING[1].]

1. a. The action of the vb. KILL, in various senses.

c **1440** *Destr. Troy* 6635 þere was kyllyng of knyghtis, crusshyng of helmys. **1590** Shaks. *Mids. N.* III. i. 15, I beleeue we must leaue the killing out, when all is done. **1607** Hieron *Wks.* I. 208 All delaies are euen a very killing to the soule. **1737** Bracken *Farriery Impr.* (1757) II. 247 It is a very odd.. Notion, which the Vulgar entertain, with relation to (what they call) killing of Quick-silver. **1748** *Anson's Voy.* III. iii. 325 The killing and preparing of provisions. **1890** Boldrewood *Col. Reformer* (1891) 306 Killing is not the fashion much in this country.

b. *attrib.* and *Comb.*, as ***killing-clothes***, ***-floor***, ***-ground***, ***-house***, ***-tackle***, ***-yard***; also **killing bottle**, a bottle containing a poison for killing captured insects, etc.; **killing-circle**, the area within which, at a certain range, the charge of shot from a gun is sufficiently compact to kill the game; cf. PATTERN *sb.* 11; **killing-sheep**, a sheep intended or fit to be killed for food; **killing-time**, (*a*) the time at which an animal is (fit to be) killed; (*b*) in *Sc. Hist.*, part of the year 1685, during which many covenanters were put to death (by later writers extended to 1683–85, or even the whole period 1679–88); **killing-value**, the value of stock when killed for food.

1877 *Encycl. Brit.* VI. 134/2 Beetles when caught may.. be dropped.. into what is known as the '*killing bottle', the bottom of which contains cyanide of potassium covered over with a layer of gypsum. **1960** B. K. Wilson *Lovely Summer* ii. 21 He could not understand how his mild-mannered father could trap the butterflies in his killing-bottle with such enthusiasm. **1974** *Guardian* 20 Sept. 17/8 Insects hitting a panel dangling below the tent will fly up into the dome, where they will be anaesthetised by fumes being given off by a killing bottle. **1886** Walsingham & Payne-Gallwey *Shooting: Field & Covert* vi. 94 The charge of a 20-bore is smaller, lighter, and has a less *killing circle than has a 12-bore. **1892** W. W. Greener *Breech-Loader* 148 For ordinary sporting purposes a gun which shall give its largest killing circle at 30 yards with the first barrel, and at 40 with the second, will be found the most convenient of good shots. **1828** Moir *Mansie Wauch* v. 40 Out flew the flesher in his *killing-claiths. **1855** Whitman *Leaves Grass*, *Songs of Myself* 12 The butcher-boy puts off his killing-clothes. **1897** R. Kipling *Seven Seas*, *Rhyme Three Sealers* 70 He'll lie down on the *killing-grounds. **1578** *Nottingham Rec.* (1889) IV. 180 No butcher shall put into yᵉ medowes aboue fiue score *killinge shepe. **1687** A. Shields *Hind let loose* 200 In the beginning of this *killing-time, as the Country calls it, the first author and authorizer of all these mischiefs, Charles II, was removed by death. **1732** P. Walker *Life Cargill* 90 He was taken in November 1684, the two slaughter years of Killing-Time being begun in the 15th day of August before. **1818** Scott *Hrt. Midl.* xviii, It was in killing time, when the plowers were drawing alang their furrows on the back of the Kirk of Scotland. **1842** J. Aiton *Domest. Econ.* (1857) 236 The pig.. will be about a year old at killing time.

2. A large profit; a quick and profitable success in business, etc. *slang* (orig. *U.S.*).

1888 *Texas Siftings* 24 Mar. 13/2 Fred Jarvis.. getting $15,000 in The Louisiana State Lottery drawing... Many .. would like to know something relative to the man who was fortunate enough to 'make a killing'. **1912** T. Dreiser *Financier* xxx. 340 Railroad securities.. were considered weak under the present circumstances, and a great killing was expected. **1938** 'N. Shute' *Ruined City* i. 11 I'm a banker, of course. I don't take tips, and I don't make any great killings, but in my quiet way I get along all right. **1959** F. Hobson *Death on Back-Bench* x. 136 Instead of making a financial killing which would have made him far wealthier and more powerful than ever before, he was going to be worse off than he had ever been. **1967** M. McCarthy in *Observer* 30 Apr. 12 Their personal.. aim.. was to make a killing.. in Vietnamese real estate. **1972** Wodehouse *Pearls, Girls & Monty Bodkin* iv. 52 If Soapy Molloy made a killing nobody could be more eager to celebrate than Dolly. **1972** *Times Lit. Suppl.* 12 May 544/2 Authors hold on in the hope of making a killing on film rights.

killing ('kɪlɪŋ), *ppl. a.* [f. KILL *v.* + -ING[2].]

1. a. That kills or deprives of life. *lit.* and *fig.*

1435 Misyn *Fire of Love* 89 Bittyr hony & kyllande fruyte. **1609** Bible (Douay) *Jer.* xxii. 7, I wil sanctifie upon thee a killing man and his weapons. **1613** Shaks. *Hen. VIII*, III. ii. 355 The third day, comes a Frost; a killing Frost. **1646** P. Bulkeley *Gospel Covt.* I. 95 These are the killing and destroying sinnes, that leave no remedy. **1703** Kelsey *Serm.* 130 The killing Interpretations of Pharisaical Pride. **1821** Shelley *Hellas* 234 Apollo, Pan, and Love.. Grew weak, for killing Truth had glared on them.

b. Of bait, etc.: Deadly; sure to kill.

1681 Chetham *Angler's Vade-m.* iv. §25 (1689) 56 As killing a Bait as any whatever. **1867** F. Francis *Angling* i. (1880) 46 Fishing with the young frog is a very killing method of fishing for chub.

2. In hyperbolic use: Able to kill. **a.** Crushing, oppressive; fatal.

1615 G. Sandys *Trav.* 194 Where they say that the blessed Virgine.. fell into a trance at the sight of that killing spectacle. *a* **1711** Ken *Serm.* Wks. (1838) 184 It was a killing consideration, to lie buried in such a sorrow. **1790** Burke *Fr. Rev.* Wks. V. 193 The killing languor.. of those who have nothing to do. **1841** Catlin *N. Amer. Ind.* (1844) II. xxxvii. 37 Unshackled by the killing restraints of society. **1848** Thackeray *Van. Fair* xxix, The General went on with killing haughtiness.

†**b.** Of a proof or argument: That 'settles' an opponent; overpowering, fatal. *Obs.*

1654 Bramhall *Just Vind.* (1661) 249 To this supposed killing argument I give three clear solutions. **1673** *Ess. Educ. Gentlewom.* 32 This is the killing Objection. **1676** Marvell *Mr. Smirke* 30 Away he goes with it.. and knocks all on the head with a killing Instance.

c. Overpoweringly beautiful or attractive.

1634 Sir T. Herbert *Trav.* Ded. A ij b, Those who are suddenly taken with a killing beautie. **1676** Wycherley *Pl. Dealer* II. Wks. (Rtldg.) 115/2 With you ladies too, martial men must needs be very killing. **1768–74** Tucker *Lt. Nat.* (1834) I. 40 The maid.. tiffing out her mistress in a killing attire. **1840** Dickens *Barn. Rudge* xx, Curling her hair on her fingers,.. and giving it some killing twists.

d. Physically overpowering; exhausting.

1850 T. A. Trollope *Impress. Wand.* xxv. 383 The last three hours of our journey were the most killing part of the day's work. **1855** W. H. Russell *The War* xxvii. 17 The pace at which they went was really 'killing'.

e. 'Excruciatingly' funny; that makes one 'die' with laughing. *colloq.*

1844 'J. Slick' *High Life N.Y.* I. xvi. 255 Then the tall man in whiskers would begin to look as if he raly had been a killing critter with the women folk. **1874** L. Troubridge *Life amongst Troubridges* (1966) 83 She was in her dressing-gown and looked too killing, exactly like those fat chinamen flying kites on Amy's Japanese screen. **1889** 'Mark Twain' *Connecticut Yankee* 111 A lecturer.. flooded an audience with the killingest jokes for an hour. **1923** [see DINE *v.* 1 b]. **1960** M. Spark *Bachelors* iii. 47 'That's exactly what I expected you to say,' Marlene said. 'I think you're killing.'

3. As *adv.* = KILLINGLY.

1670 Dryden *Conq. Granada* II. i, Having seen you once so killing Fair, A second Sight were but to move Despair. **1883** Stevenson *Silverado Sq.* (1886) 3 The ocean breeze blew killing chill.

Hence **'killingly** *adv.*, in a killing manner; **'killingness**.

[**1593** Nashe *Christ's T.* (1613) 134 Sight-killingly.] **1641** Milton *Animadv.* Pref., Nothing could be more killingly spoken. **1642** J. Eaton *Honey-c. Free Justif.* 124 We must all preach it [the Law].. as killingly as we can. **1730** Lillo *George Barnwell* I. ii, *Mill.* How do I look to-day, Lucy? *Lucy.* Oh, killingly, madam! A little more red, and you'll be irresistible. **1839** Bailey *Festus* xx. (1852) 313 There are three things I love half killingly. **1840** R. Bremner *Excurs. Denmark*, etc. I. 314 A large bunch of flowers in the hand, or on the breast, which most of the young fellows displayed with conscious killingness.

killinite ('kɪlɪnaɪt). *Min.* [Named, 1818, after Killiney Bay near Dublin: see -ITE[1].] A mineral of a pale-green colour, an alteration product of spodumene.

1818 *Trans. R. Irish Acad.* XIII. 4 Killinite occurs imbedded, in elongated prisms. **1878** Lawrence tr. *Cotta's Rocks Class.* 19 Killinite is a product of the weathering or decomposition of spodumene.

'kill-joy, *sb.* and *a.* **A.** *sb.* One who or that which destroys joy or pleasure; one who throws a gloom over social enjoyment.

1776 Burney *Hist. Mus.* (1789) I. 455 The Gods were not then, says M. Rousseau, regarded as kill-joys and shut out of convival meetings. **1863** Geo. Eliot *Romola* xxv, Licentious young men, who detested him as the kill-joy of Florence. **1896** J. P. Mahaffy in *Chautauquan* Oct. 49/2 Reserve, if apparent, is the real kill-joy of conversation.

B. *adj.* That kills or puts an end to joy.

1822 Scott *Pirate* i, His kill-joy visage will never again stop the bottle in its round.

killock, variant of KILLICK.

killogie, -logy (kɪ'ləʊgɪ). *Sc.* Now *rare* or *Obs.* Also 7, 9 kiln-logie. [f. *kill*, KILN + LOGIE, sometimes used in the same sense as *killogie*.] The covered space in front of the fireplace of a kiln, serving to give draught to the fire and to shelter the person attending to it; formerly often used as a place for sheltering or hiding in.

15.. *King Berdok* (Bann. MS.) 31 Berdok fled in till a killogy. **1563** *Edin. Town Council Rec.* 18 June, Ihonne Knox was apprehendit and tane forth of ane killogye. *a* **1670** Spalding *Troub. Chas. I* (1829) 27 This night he was laid in the kiln-logie. **1815** Scott *Guy M.* vi, The muckle chumlay in the Auld Place reeked like a killogie in his time. **1881** W. Gregor *Folk-lore* 84 (E.D.D.) This clue was cast into the kiln-logie.

killos, variant of KILLAS.

†**killow.** *Obs.* Also 7 kellow, 8 cullow. [Of unknown origin.

Mod. dicts., into which the word has passed from Johnson, Todd, etc., repeat the suggestion of Woodward (cited by J.) that *killow* may be connected with COLLOW, soot, grime; but the form is against this.]

A name formerly given (orig. in Cumberland) to black-lead, plumbago, or graphite.

1666 MERRETT *Pinax Brit.* 218 Lapis cæruleus Killow dictus ducendis lineis idoneus. **1698** PLOT in *Phil. Trans.* XX. 183 The Mineral substance, called, Black Lead.. found only at Keswick in Cumberland, and there called, Wadt, or Kellow. **1706** PHILLIPS, *Killow*, a sort of Mineral Stone. **1763** W. LEWIS *Comm. Phil. Techn.* 324 The black earthy substance called Killow... The killow has somewhat of a bluish or purplish cast mixed with its blackness.

ˈkill-time, *sb.* (*a.*) [See KILL *v.* 5.] An occupation or amusement intended to 'kill time'.

1748 RICHARDSON *Clarissa* (1811) VIII. 397 The more active and lively amusements and kill-times. **1811** COLERIDGE *Lect. Shaks.* (1856) 3 Where the reading of novels prevails as a habit.. it is not so much to be called pass-time as kill-time. **1865** *Ch. Times* 11 Mar. 76/1 One of the pretty kill-times which consume modern society.

B. *adj.* Adapted to kill time.

1897 *Westm. Gaz.* 25 Jan. 5/1 Play at this very scientific kill-time game [chess].

killut, killyfish: see KHILAT, KILLIFISH.

Kilmarnock (kɪlˈmɑːnək). **1.** The name of a town in Ayrshire (now Strathclyde), used (freq. *attrib.*) to designate various articles made there, or practices characteristic of its inhabitants; *spec.* **Kilmarnock bonnet, cowl,** a cap resembling a tam-o'-shanter.

1643 *Edinburgh Testaments* (MS.) LX. 292b (D.O.S.T.), Sextene pair of Kilmarnock stokinges estimat ale to fyftie pundis. **1681** S. COLVIL *Mock Poem, or, Whiggs Supplication* 15 He used to take lives With Whingers, and Kilmarnock Knives. **1713** R. WODROW *Analecta* (1842) II. 262 Ther ar some of your Kilmarnock whittles, that, though they look not soe fair on it as your English knives, yet have a better edge. **1789** D. DAVIDSON *Thoughts on Seasons* 84 An honest wabster.. Whase haffet a Kilmarnock hood Kept warm an' snug. **1790** A. WILSON *Poems* 72 His fearsome blue Kilmarnock cowl. **1806** J. PATTERSON in J. Greenshields *Ann. Lesmahagow* (1864) App. 46 And some.. with subtle wrist, Give to their stane, the true 'Kilmarnock twist'. **1822** H. AINSLIE *Pilgrimage to Land of Burns* 6 The manner in which the whole man was so properly roofed in with the ancient Kilmarnock bonnet. *Ibid.* 31 Flourishing.. their 'Kilmarnocks' manfully round their heads. **1828** *Blackw. Mag.* Jan. 40 Kilmarnock bonnets, pixie caps, and mittens. **1833** CARLYLE *Sart. Res.* in *Fraser's Mag.* Dec. 670/1 Even the Kilmarnock nightcap is not forgotten. **1877** J. M. NEILSON *Poems* 49 He.. cover'd the bald pow o' Willie Shakspeare Wi's big blue Kilmarnock. **1902** *Daily Chron.* 20 Dec. 5/2 The Scottish team of curlers who have departed for Canada wanted to be rigged out with old-style Kilmarnocks. **1946** *Glasgow Herald* 24 Aug., Having recently taken up bowling, I have heard players saying, 'That's a Kilmarnock one' when a shot has shown evidence that the player was determined to run no risks in disturbing the head. **1949** J. DRUMMOND *Behind Dark Shutters* i. 21 They agreed to pipe a water line from Townhead and put in a 'Kilmarnock well' in the Row. **1951** J. MASTERS *Nightrunners Bengal* ix. 94 The two infantry regiments tried to get the new white Kilmarnock caps to replace their heavy shakos. **1953** J. E. SHAW *Ayrshire* 32 The Kilmarnock bonnet manufacturers strike a specially sentimental note in the hearts of all Scotsmen... It was at one time a national headwear. **1960** H. HAYWARD *Antique Coll.* 157/2 *Kilmarnock carpets*, double-cloth carpeting was made in Kilmarnock from 1778 and three-ply was perfected in 1824.

2. Kilmarnock willow, a pendulous form of the goat willow, *Salix caprea* forma *pendula*, first discovered by James Smith (*c* 1760–1840), a Scottish botanist, and subsequently distributed by Thomas Lang, a Kilmarnock nurseryman.

1854 *Gardeners' Chronicle* 17 June 392/1 The name Kilmarnock Willow was bestowed upon it to distinguish it from the common Weeping Willow. **1869** *Rep. Comm. Agric. 1868* (U.S. Dept. Agric.) 202 Kilmarnock willow (*Salix caprea* var. *pendula*).. becomes one of the most distinct of the hardy weeping plants which we possess. **1892** A. C. APGAR *Trees Northern U.S.* 166 The Goat-willow is the one generally used for the stock of the artificial umbrella-formed 'Kilmarnock Willow'. **1913** ELWES & HENRY *Trees Gt. Brit. & Ireland* VII. 1746 [*Salix caprea*] Var. *pendula*... Pendulous in habit, usually grafted on a stock about 4 ft. high, and forming a weeping shrub, which is known as the Kilmarnock Willow. This was discovered in 1840 on the banks of the river Ayr, and was propagated by Lang, nurseryman at Kilmarnock. **1972** S. C. WARREN-WREN *Willows* iii. 61 It [*sc.* a pendulous variety] is *S*[*alix*] *caprea* forma *pendula* Th. Lang, and is commonly referred to as the Kilmarnock willow. Its branches are stiffly pendulous.

kiln (kɪl, kɪln), *sb.* Forms: α. 1 cyline, -ene, cyln(e, 4 kulne, 4–5 kylne (kyllne), 6–8 kilne, 6– kiln. β. 5–6 kylle, 6–7 kyll, 7 kil, 5–8 kill. γ. 6–8 (9 *dial.*) kell. δ. 6–7 keele, 7 kiele. [OE. *cylene*, etc.:—*ˈ*culina*, a. L. *culīna* kitchen, cooking-stove, burning-place; with usual shifting of Latin stress (cf. *kitchen*).

Outside of English known only in Scand., ON. *kylna* (Norw. *kjølne*, Sw. *kölna*, Da. *kølle*), prob. adopted from Eng. (as Welsh *cilin*, *cil* certainly are). In ME. the final *-n* became silent (in most districts), hence the frequent spelling *kill* in place of the etymological *kiln*; cf. *miln*, MILL.]

1. A furnace or oven for burning, baking, or drying, of which various kinds are used in different industrial processes: e.g. (*a*) a furnace for burning a substance, as in calcining lime (LIME-KILN) or making charcoal; (*b*) an oven or furnace for baking bricks (BRICK-KILN), tiles, or clay vessels, or for melting the vitreous glaze on such vessels; (*c*) a building containing a furnace for drying grain, hops, etc. or for making malt.

α. *c* **725** *Corpus Gloss.* 906 *Fornacula*, cyline, heorðe. *c* **1050** *Suppl. Ælfric's Voc.* in Wr.-Wülcker 185/30 *Siccatorium*, cyln, *uel* ast. *c* **1325** *Gloss. W. de Bibbesw.* in Wright *Voc.* 158 *Toral* (kulne). *c* **1420** *Avow. Arth.* xv, As kylne other kechine, Thus rudely he rekes. *c* **1440** *Promp. Parv.* 274/2 Kylne for malt dryynge (*P.* kill), *ustrina.* **1625** *Markham's Farew. Husb.* 108 Having your Kilne well ordered and bedded, you shall lay as many sheaues thereon, as it can containe. **1683** *Lond. Gaz.* No. 1789/4 A Kilne for making of Mault. **1703** MOXON *Mech. Exerc.* 242 Lime.. newly drawn out of the Kiln. **1719** DE FOE *Crusoe* I. ix, A Kiln, such as the Potters burn in. **1851** LONGF. *Gold. Leg* i, A smouldering, dull, perpetual flame, As in a kiln, burns in my veins.

β. **1471** *Yatton Church-w. Acc.* (Som. Rec. Soc.) 107 For makyng a kylle and yᵉ lyme-berner xˢ. **1509** BARCLAY *Shyp of Folys* (1570) 107 As one potter maketh of one clay Vessels diuers, but when he must them lay Upon the kill [etc.]. **1577** HARRISON *England* II. vi. (1877) I. 156 They carrie it [barley] to a kill couered with haire cloth. **1611** BIBLE *Jer.* xliii. 9 Hide them in the clay in the bricke kill. **1663** GERBIER *Counsel* 52 A Kill.. for the making of twenty thousand of Bricks. **1728** RAMSAY *Monk & Miller's Wife* 48 Step ye west the kill A bow-shot, and ye'll find my hame. **1777** H. GATES in C. Gist *Jrnls.* (1893) 280 The extensive Buildings and Kills.. are also laid in Ashes. **1828** *Craven Dial.* s.v., A lime kill, a maut kill.

γ. **1577** HARRISON *England* III. viii. (1878) II. 53 The Chiues.. are dried vpon little kelles couered with streined canuasses. **1625** LISLE *Du Bartas, Noe* 46 The Tyler bakes within his smoakie kell this clay to stone. **1706** PHILLIPS, *Kell* or *Kiln*. **1875** *Sussex Gloss.*, *Kell*, a kiln.

δ. **1573–80** BARET *Alv.* B 1232 To make bricke in a keele. **1577** B. GOOGE *Heresbach's Husb.* (1586) 28b, When it [barley] is watred I drie it upon a floore or a keele. **1626** BACON *Sylva* §648 The drying [of malt] upon the Keele.

b. In phrases and proverbs: esp. ***to set the kiln on fire*** (Sc. ***a-low***), ***to fire the kiln***, to cause a serious commotion or turmoil; so ***the kiln's on fire***.

1590 LODGE *Euphues Gold. Leg.* in Halliwell *Shakespeare* VI. 42 Tush, quoth Ganimede, all is not malte that is cast on the kill. **1603** FLORIO *Montaigne* (1634) 503 It is that which some say prouerbially, 'Ill may the Kill call the Ouen "burnt taile"'. **1705** HICKERINGILL *Priest-cr.* I. (1721) 47 As for my Peck of Malt, set the Kiln on fire. **1722** WODROW *Hist. Suff. Ch. Scot.* II. 206 They.. told him, that his opposing the Clause, excepting the King's Sons and Brothers, had fired the Kiln. **1818** SCOTT *Hrt. Midl.* xlv, The Captain's a queer hand, and to speak to him about that.. wad be to set the kiln a low. **1819** —— *Leg. Montrose* xx, He has contrived to set the kiln on fire as fast as I put it out.

c. = KILNFUL.

1744–50 W. ELLIS *Mod. Husbandm.* VI. I. 21 They fetch five quarters of lime from the kiln, which they call a kiln of lime, because it is all they burn at once.

2. *attrib.* and *Comb.*, as ***kiln-board***, ***-burning***, ***-dust***, ***-fire***, ***-man***, ***-mouth***, ***-wife***; ***kiln-burnt*** adj.; **kiln-barn**, a barn containing a kiln; †**kiln-cloth**, a cloth on which the grain was laid in a kiln; **kiln-eye**, (*a*) an opening for removing the lime from a lime-kiln; (*b*) = *kiln-hole*; †**kiln-haire** = *kiln-cloth*; †**kiln-hamer** (?); **kiln-hole**, the fire-hole of a kiln (see also quot. 1828); **kiln-house**, a kiln, or building containing one; **kiln-logie** (see KILLOGIE); **kiln-pot**, ? the floor of a malting or drying kiln; **kiln-rib**, **-stick**, **-tree**, one of the sticks on which the grain is laid in a kiln. Also KILN-DRY *v.*

a **1670** SPALDING *Troub. Chas. I* (Spald. Cl.) I. 61 Thay.. schot hir self with hir barnes to duell in the *kilbarne. **1882** *Standard* 16 Sept. 8/2 Brickmakers plant and stock, comprising.. hack planks, *kiln boards. **1854** J. SCOFFERN in *Orr's Circ. Sc.*, *Chem.* 418 The mere process of *kiln-burning. **1850** GOSSE *Rivers Bible* (1878) 174 *Kiln-burnt bricks. **1877** RAYMOND *Statist. Mines & Mining* 98 Kiln-burned coal would, it is estimated, weigh 20 pounds per bushel. **1573–80** BARET *Alv.* K 60 The *kill cloth of haire, *cilicium.* **1660** HEXHAM, A Kill-cloath of hair. **1763** *Museum Rust.* I. 114 To distinguish the genuine malt-dust from that which is called *kiln-dust, which falls through the gratings from the malt whilst it is drying. **1603** OWEN *Pembrokeshire* (1891) 70 A kill.. havinge two lope holes in the bottome which they call the *kill eyes. **1875** KNIGHT *Dict. Mech.* II. 1228 The *kiln-fire is supplied with warm air. **1567** *Richmond Wills* (Surtees) 211 In the kilne, one seastron and one *kilne hare. **1551** *Wills & Inv. N.C.* (Surtees, 1835) 134 In the kyell.. a *kyllhameʳ and a wyndooclothe xˢ. **1598** SHAKS. *Merry W.* IV. ii. 59 Creepe into the *Kill hole. **1828** *Craven Dial.*, *Kill-hole*, the hole of, or a hovel adjoining, the kill. **1417** *Surtees Misc.* (1888) 12 The *kylne howse of the same Sir John. **1544** in W. H. Turner *Select. Rec. Oxford* 174 The kyll howses beneyth the [Oseney] mylls. **1598** SYLVESTER *Du Bartas* II. ii. *Babylon* 164 There, busie *Kil-men ply their occupations For brick and tyle. **1874** T. HARDY *Far fr. Madding Crowd* I. 86 The room inside was lighted only by the ruddy glow from the *kiln mouth. **1785** BURNS *Halloween* xi. *note*, An answer will be returned from the *kiln-pot, by naming the Christian and surname of your future spouse. **1790** FISHER *Poems* 149 (E.D.D.) She straught gaed to a deep kiln pot Her fortune for to try. **1737** BRACKEN *Farriery Impr.* (1757) II. 150 His Body as dry as a *Kiln-stick. *c* **1475** *Pict. Voc.* in Wr.-Wülcker 792/39 *Hec ustrinatrix*, a *kylme wife.

Hence **ˈkilnful**, as much as a kiln can hold. *rare.*

1724 RAMSAY *Tea-t. Misc.* (1733) I. 9 A kilnfu' of corn I'll gi'e to thee.

kiln (kɪl, kɪln), *v.* [f. prec.] *trans.* To burn, bake, or dry in a kiln; to kiln-dry.

1715 LEONI *Palladio's Archit.* (1742) I. 4 It must be employ'd as soon as kiln'd, otherwise it wastes.. away. *Ibid.* II. 54 Lime, the manner of killing it. **1725** BRADLEY *Fam. Dict.* s.v. *Malt*, There is also another Error in drying and kilning of Malt. **1881** BLACKMORE *Christowell* xxv, The clay was so inferior, and they were kilned in such a doltish manner.

kiln, variant of KILL *sb.*⁴

ˈkiln-dry, *v. trans.* To dry in a kiln.

c **1540** *Plumpton Corr.* 237 As for barly, is now much redy & in chambers.. Yowr men also kiln dry. **1573** TUSSER *Husb.* (1878) 127 The hop kell dride, will best abide. **1649** BLITHE *Eng. Improv. Impr.* (1653) 260 Drying it up, and housing it, and kilne-drying it. **1727** BRADLEY *Fam. Dict.* s.v. *Bean*, The best way is to kiln-dry them [beans], or to dry 'em well in the Sun. **1846** MCCULLOCH *Acc. Brit. Empire* (1854) I. 363 Much.. of the corn of Ireland could not be preserved, unless it were kiln-dried.

Hence **ˈkiln-dried** *ppl. a.*, **ˈkiln-ˈdrying** *vbl. sb.*

1823 J. BADCOCK *Dom. Amusem.* 28 Heat, i.e. kiln-drying, .. will not answer the end proposed. **1854** RONALDS & RICHARDSON *Chem. Technol.* (ed. 2) I. 189 Kiln-dried earthy lignite (20 per cent moisture and no ash).

Kilner jar (ˈkɪlnə ˈdʒɑː(r)). The proprietary name of a type of preserving jar. Also ***Kilner preserving jar***.

1930 *Trade Marks Jrnl.* 19 Nov. 1777 The 'Kilner' jar... Glass fruit preserving jars. Kilner Brothers, Limited,.. London,.. manufacturers. **1972** 'S. WOODS' *They love not Poison* vi. 82 Jenny came through from the kitchen with a Kilner jar about one third full of cream which she proposed to shake until it separated. **1973** *Listener* 25 Jan. 117/2 The old-fashioned Kilner preserving jar lent itself to both wet and dry methods of bottling. **1974** *Times* 16 Nov. 11/1 Old-fashioned vinegar crocks can be things of beauty... You can otherwise simply use a Kilner jar.

kilo¹ (ˈkɪləʊ). Abbrev. of KILOGRAM.

1870 *Daily News* 2 Dec., They provide the bread at 35 cent. a kilo, the same price as.. in Belgium. **1887** MOLONEY *Forestry W. Afr.* 77 The price for each hundred kilos of oil produced.. varies according to the pressures.

kilo² (ˈkɪləʊ). Abbrev. of KILOMETRE, -METER.

1888 E. DOWSON *Let.* 13 Nov. (1967) 17, I hope.. that you are now.. laying in a stock of hygiene many kilos from this foggy, pestilent metrop. **1948** G. H. JOHNSTON *Death takes Small Bites* viii. 195 They drove five kilos in silence. **1973** *Evening Standard* 11 Oct. 1/2 After bogging down in the sand by a wrecked tank, we dug ourselves out and hastily retreated a few kilos until we reached a tank laager.

kilo-. **a.** An arbitrary derivative of Gr. χίλιοι a thousand, introduced in French in 1795, at the institution of the Metric system, as a formative of weights and measures containing 1000 times the simple unit, as *kilogram*, *kilometre*, etc.

b. ***kilo-ampere***, ***-bar*** [BAR *sb.*⁶ 1, 2], ***-bit*** [BIT *sb.*⁴], ***-byte***, ***-curie***, ***-electron volt***, ***-gauss***, ***-hertz***, ***-joule***, ***-parsec***. Also ***kilobuck*** (joc.) [BUCK *sb.*⁸], a thousand dollars.

1901 J. A. FLEMING *Handbk. for Electr. Laboratory* I. i. 68 The standard *kilo-ampere balance. **1972** *Physics Bull.* Mar. 152/3 A few calculations, taking into account material and engineering limitations show that the voltage produced is low, say up to 10 V, but currents of kiloamperes are readily achieved. **1928** N. SHAW *Man. Meteorol.* II. p. xxxii, **Kilobar*, a name which it is proposed to substitute for the word 'millibar' to express a pressure of 1000 dynes per square centimetre, on the ground that the word 'bar' had been used in Physical Chemistry to denote the C.G.S. unit of pressure (1 dyne per square centimetre) before it was employed in meteorology to express a million dynes per square centimetre. **1971** I. G. GASS et al. *Understanding Earth* iii. 60/2 Olivine Mg_2SiO_4 can recrystallize at pressures of over 150 kilobars to a new polymorphic form called a spinel structure. **1961** GRAY & GRAHAM *Radio Transmitters* i. 3 In the case of the transmission of business-machine or telemetered data, it is more usual to express the speed in bits or *kilobits (1,000 bits) per second. **1972** *Sci. Amer.* Sept. 126/3 High-speed leased lines provide a data speed of 48 to 240 kilobits per second. **1951** *N.Y. Times Mag.* 22 Apr. 35 '*Kilobuck'.. is a scientist's idea of a short way to say 'a thousand dollars'. **1955** *Sci. Amer.* June 126/2 This instrument became the prototype of a commercial spectroscope which sells for about a kilobuck. **1970** *Times* 30 June 22/7 Its storage capacity could be 2,048 *kilobytes compared with a maximum of 512 kilobytes for the 360/50. **1973** *Physics Bull.* Oct. 626/1 It has a 64 kilobyte store with 4·8 megabytes of exchangeable disc storage. **1946** *Science* 2 Aug. 92/1 We came to the Project thinking in terms of millicuries and found that we had to face problems of curies and sometimes.. even *kilocuries. **1968** *Listener* 27 June 828/1 This power package contained as its energy source 17 kilocuries of Plutonium 238. **1950** GLASSTONE *Sourcebk. Atomic Energy* iii. 82/1 One [*sc.* energy unit], equal to a thousand electron volts, called the *kilo-electron volt, is represented by Kev. **1971** D. W. SCIAMA *Mod. Cosmol.* ii. 31 The distinction between X- and γ-rays is a somewhat arbitrary one, but.. we may take the dividing line to be an energy of 100 keV (kilo-electron volts). **1895** F. C. BAILY in *Rep. Brit. Assoc. Adv. Sci.* 206 Gaussage would be about 50 in small transformers, up to 40,000 in large dynamos. The latter could be conveniently reckoned in *kilogausses. **1973** *Sci. Amer.* Oct. 21/1 If the magnetic field at the surface of a continuous-sheet guideway is 20 kilogauss (about the field strength at the pole face of a good magnet), the lift force is 60 pounds per square inch. **1929** *Daily Express* 11 Jan. 3/6 A national common frequency of 1,040 *kilohertz (288·5 metres). **1935** TURNER & BANNER *Electr. Measurements* i. 4 Cycle per second. [*Note*] For radio purposes this is sometimes termed the 'Hertz' and a practical unit called the 'Kilohertz' or 1000 cycles per second used. **1967** *Electronics* 6 Mar. 183/1 Since the power is limited, the bandwidth has

to be restricted to 500 kilohertz. **1893** T. O' C. SLOANE *Stand. Electr. Dict.* 317 *Kilojoule. **1938** *Jrnl. R. Aeronaut. Soc.* XLII. 885 Formation of frost on the wing is accompanied by a rise in temperature which raises the deposit to 0°C. A curve is given showing the energy in kilojoules necessary to remove ice. **1974** *Times* 20 Feb. 12 Each of the colourfully illustrated cards shows a different food, together with its value in carbohydrate, calories and kilo-joules (the measurement that will be used instead of calories when Britain goes metric). **1922** *Encycl. Brit.* XXX. 301/2 The most remote cluster known is distant 67 *kiloparsecs or 200,000 light years. **1970** *Sci. Jrnl.* Mar. 71/3 The solar system is located on the mid-plane of the disc 10 kiloparsecs from the galactic centre.

kilocalorie (ˈkɪləˌkælərɪ). Also **-calory** (*rare*). [f. KILO- + CALORIE.] = CALORIE a.

1894 J. H. RAYMOND *Human Physiol.* ii. 166 It is estimated that an average man produces daily 2500 kilo-calories, which is about 100 kilo-calories per hour. **1909** *Cent. Dict.* Suppl., *Kilocalory*. **1923** H. MOORE *Textbk. Intermediate Physics* xxii. 202 The Continental Engineers' Unit is..the kilogram-calorie or kilocalorie. **1969** *Listener* 16 Jan. 67/3 The food intake was very low, 1,600 kilo-calories per head per day, but the population was healthy and apparently active. **1971** *Nature* 12 Nov. 112/3 Moreover, SI units are nowhere mentioned, the traditional Torr and kilocalories being preferred. **1974** *Sci. Amer.* Sept. 162/3 The 'calorie' of nutritional parlance is actually a kilocalorie.

kilocycle (ˈkɪləsaɪk(ə)l). [f. KILO- + CYCLE *sb.*] **a.** One thousand cycles (of an oscillation or other periodic phenomenon). **b.** *ellipt.* One thousand cycles per second: = *kilohertz*.

1921 *Wireless Board List Radio Telegr. Waves* 3 Frequency is expressed in 'Kilo-cycles' (K.C.). **1926** E. B. MOULLIN *Theory & Pract. Radio Frequency Measurements* iii. 73 (*heading*) Interpolated frequency in kilocycles per sec. **1927** *Daily Tel.* 14 June 5/3 The decision of the B.B.C. to adopt forthwith the kilocycle method of stating frequencies instead of the wave-length method. **1950** *Engineering* 7 Apr. 379/2 The high-velocity sound-level recorder... is designed for inputs with frequencies between 50 cycles and 15 kilocycles per second. **1959** R. L. SHRADER *Electronic Communication* iv. 86 A frequency of 3,500,000 cycles can be expressed as 3,500 kilocycles (3,500 kc), or 3·5 megacycles (3·5 Mc).

kilodyne (ˈkɪləʊdaɪn). [f. KILO- + DYNE.] A measure of force equal to a thousand dynes.

1873 *1st Rep. Brit. Assoc.* 224 The weight of a gramme.. is about 980 dynes, or rather less than a kilodyne.

kilogram, -gramme (ˈkɪləgræm). Also 9 chiliogramme. [a. F. *kilogramme* (1795): see KILO- and GRAM², GRAMME.] **1. a.** A unit of mass (formerly also taken as a unit of weight) that was introduced as a fundamental unit of the metric system and is now one of the base units of the International System of Units, being equivalent to approximately 2·205 lb.; it was intended to be the mass (or weight) of a cubic decimetre of distilled water, but in practice has been defined almost from its inception as the mass of a unique physical standard (orig. the 'Kilogramme des Archives', and since 1889 the International Prototype of the Kilogramme).

1797 *Jrnl. Nat. Philos.* I. 197 The kilogramme [is] equal to 2 pounds 5 gros 49 grains. **1810** *Naval Chron.* XXIV. 299 The French weight called Kilogramme. *Ibid.* 301 Killogram (weight of cubic decimeter of water). **1825** J. NICHOLSON *Operat. Mechanic* 53 A man going up stairs for a day raises 205 chiliogrammes to the height of a chiliometre. **1871** [see next]. **1898** H. O. ARNOLD-FORSTER (*title*) The Coming of the Kilogram, or the Battle of the Standards. **1946** *Proc. R. Soc.* A. CLXXXVI. 171 The kilogram was originally defined by reference to a 'natural' standard, i.e. the mass of the cubic decimetre of water. The material representation of this standard was the Kilogramme des Archives, a simple cylindrical piece of platinum which was constructed in the latter part of the eighteenth century. **1964** H. S. HVISTENDAHL *Engin. Units* iii. 20 Study of the archives of the BIPM [*sc.* the Bureau International des Poids et Mesures] has shown that whilst due to the lack of precision in scientific terminology at that time, the word 'poids' (weight) was improperly used as a synonym of 'mass', the kilogramme étalon was definitely intended to represent the unit of what we now always call mass, and not the force by which that mass unit was attracted to the earth. **1969** *Changing to Metric Syst.* (Nat. Physical Lab.) (ed. 3) 5 The spellings of the units of length (metre) and mass (kilogramme) given above are those used by the General Conference of Weights and Measures. In North America the spellings are meter and kilogram. **1969** *Symbols, Signs, & Abbreviations* (R. Soc.) 22 Kilogramme. **1971** *Quantities, Units, & Symbols* (R. Soc.) 22 Kilogram. **1971** *Nature* 8 Jan. 80/1 A thousand kilogrammes of ice. **1972** *N.Z. News* 26 Jan. 1/5 The prices for all classes of fleece wool showed an improvement of from 10c to 16c per kilogram. **1973** *SI Units* (Internat. Stand. ISO 1000) 20 The kilogram is the unit of mass; it is equal to the mass of the international prototype of the kilogram.

b. An object having a mass of one kilogram and made as a standard of mass or weight.

1831 *Jrnl. R. Inst. Gt. Brit.* II. 65 The rather unsightly appearance of the standard kilogramme of Monsieur Fortin's making. **1856** *Phil. Trans. R. Soc.* CXLVI. 875 Permission was obtained from the French Government to compare the pound with the standard kilogramme of platinum deposited in the Archives on the 22nd of June, 1799, known as the 'kilogramme des Archives'. *Ibid.* 878 The kilogramme, after having been washed with alcohol, was suspended from the right-hand pan of the balance. **1922** *Nature* 19 Oct. 622 During the nineteenth century..serious doubt arose as to whether the accepted standard kilogramme [*sc.* the 'Kilogramme des Archives' made by Lefèvre-Gineau and Fabbroni in 1799] actually did comply with the original definition of the kilogramme... A proposal to construct a new standard kilogramme brought the whole subject under review in 1872, and the Commission Internationale du Mètre..decided that the international kilogramme should be a copy of the 'Kilogramme des Archives'. **1936** *Rep. Board of Trade Standards Dept. Comparisons Imperial Standards* 3 The opportunity was.. taken to undertake..the comparison of the national copy of the kilogram with the principal standard kilograms of the Board of Trade. **1946** *Proc. R. Soc.* A. CLXXXVI. 172 Some forty or more copies of the international kilogram were constructed. The principal copies..are preserved at the International Bureau of Weights and Measures, Sèvres, Paris... One such copy, No. 18, designated the British Copy of the Kilogram, is kept in this country. **1962** *Brit. Jrnl. Appl. Physics* XIII. 456/1 The international kilogramme, which is a platinum-iridium weight at the head of an extensive hierarchy of similar kilogrammes, was known to be extremely stable.

2. *attrib.* and *Comb.*, as **kilogram calorie** = CALORIE a; **kilogram-force** (pl. *kilograms-force*), a unit of force equal to the weight of a mass of 1 kilogram, esp. under standard gravity.

1900 E. BUCKINGHAM *Outl. Theoret. Thermodynamics* ii. 12 The small or gram calorie, in distinction from the large or *kilogram calorie, which is one thousand times as large. **1930** *Engineering* 21 Nov. 640/1 Curve I shows the maximum liberation of heat in kilogram-calories per cubic metre per hour. **1951** B. L. GOODLET *Basic Electrotechnics* i. 4 Heat energy is measured in kilogram-calories, one of which equals 4186 joules. **1960** *McGraw-Hill Encycl. Sci. & Technol.* VII. 347/1 The kilogram is also sometimes defined as a unit of force, that is, the weight of a 1-kilogram mass, hence the expression *kilogram-force. **1972** *Physics Bull.* May 285/1 The addition of small weight pieces by hand to the scalepan system permits forces in newtons and kilograms-force to be obtained readily.

kilogrammetre, -meter (ˌkɪləgræmˈmiːtə(r)). [a. F. *kilogrammètre*: see prec. and METRE.] The quantity of energy required to raise a weight of one kilogram to the height of one metre.

1886 ODLING *Anim. Chem.* 104 It is convenient to apply the expression kilogram-metre to the product of the kilogrammes lifted into the metres of height. **1871** B. STEWART *Heat* (ed. 2) §314 The unit of work being always the amount represented by raising one kilogramme one mètre against terrestrial gravity, or the Kilogrammetre. **1878** TOLHAUSEN *Technol. Dict.*, Kilogrammeter.

kilolitre, -liter (ˈkɪləliːtə(r)). [a. F. *kilolitre* (1798): see KILO- and LITRE.] In the Metric system, a measure of capacity containing 1000 litres.

1810 *Naval Chron.* XXIV. 301 Killolittre, Metercube. **1828** WEBSTER, *Kiloliter*. **1871** C. DAVIES *Metr. Syst.* 14 The kilolitre, or stere, is the cube constructed on the metre as an edge. Hence, the litre is one-thousandth part of the kilolitre.

kilometre, -meter (ˈkɪləmiːtə(r)). Also with pronunc. (kɪˈlɒmɪtə(r)), prob. under the influence of such words as *speedometer*, *thermometer*. [a. F. *kilomètre* (1795): see KILO- and METRE. (The stress is marked by Webster (1828), Craig, and Cassell as *ki'lometre*.)] In the Metric system, a measure of length containing 1000 metres, or 3280.89 feet, or nearly five-eighths of a mile. Also *Comb.*, as ***kilometre-stone*** (cf. *mile-stone*).

1810 *Naval Chron.* XXIV. 301 Killometer, 1000 M. **1868** *Morn. Star* 25 Feb., The tunnel will cost 160,000*l.* per kilometre. **1881** HALSTED *Mensuration* 2 The kilometer is used as the unit of distance. **1888** PENNELL *Sent. Journey* 166 The kilometre-stones no longer marked the distance.

kilometric (kɪləʊˈmɛtrɪk), *a.* [f. prec. + -IC: = F. *kilométrique* (1878 in *Dict. Acad.*).] Of or pertaining to a kilometre; marking a kilometre on a road; ***kilometric guarantee***, a guarantee of gross receipts per kilometre of line conceded by the Turkish government in the late 19th and early 20th centuries to (foreign) companies constructing railways within the then Empire. So **kiloˈmetrical** *a.*, in same sense.

1867 *Even. Standard* 6 Aug. 5 The Public Conveyance Company of Paris invited, in 1861, designs for a kilometrical measuring machine. **1881** HALSTED *Mensuration* 2 Along roads and railways are placed kilometric poles or stones. **1902** *Daily Chron.* 24 Jan. 3/3 The revenues to be assigned for the service of the kilometric guarantee have not yet been specified. **1909** *Westm. Gaz.* 16 Dec. 2/1 The Bagdad Railway (with the iniquitous kilometric guarantee). **1909** D. FRASER *Short Cut to India* iii. 39 A heavy kilometric guarantee was provided. *Ibid.* 45 When the kilometric receipts exceed..4500 francs, the whole of the surplus goes to the government. **1943** *Gloss. Terms Telecomm.* (*B.S.I.*) 64 Radio-waves are classified as follows: A. According to wavelength, in metres... Kilometric 10 000 to 1 000. **1973** *Nature* 21 Sept. 144/2 Urey assumes that the..heart-and-soul of a comet is a solid nucleus of kilometric size.

kilo-stone (ˈkɪlə-, ˈkiːləʊstəʊn). Also **kilostone**. [f. KILO² + STONE *sb.*] = *kilometre-stone*.

1925 *Brit. Weekly* 1 Jan. 342/2 Down the road..a woman was crying with maternal, anxious voice, 'Louise! Louise!' The cry was wafted up to the kilostone. **1936** *Discovery* Feb. 63/2 We dispute the author's recollection of the kilo-stones on the Seres Road [in Macedonia].

kiloton (ˈkɪlətʌn). [f. KILO- + TON¹.] **a.** One thousand tons. Somewhat *rare*. **b.** A unit of explosive power, equal to that of one thousand tons of T.N.T. Freq. *attrib.*

1950 J. O. HIRSCHFELDER et al. *Effects of Atomic Weapons* i. 14 It is necessary for about 3 × 10^{24} atoms to suffer fission to release the energy equivalent to 20 kilotons of TNT. **1952** *Birmingham* (Alabama) *News* 24 Apr. 14/5 According to informed forecasts, the new bomb will have an explosive power of between 200 and 300 kilotons. **1956** A. H. COMPTON *Atomic Quest* v. 303 A 20 kiloton explosion (i.e., energy released equivalent to 20,000 tons of conventional explosives). **1959** *Times Lit. Suppl.* 22 May 306/4 The atomic strategy..relies on technology rather than on men and reckons fire-power in terms of kilotons of explosive. **1971** I. G. GASS et al. *Understanding Earth* xxiv. 333/1 The difficulties of discriminating between minor 'background' Earth tremors and the effects of [nuclear] tests of a few kilotons were seen to be formidable. **1973** *Sci. Amer.* Oct. 47/3 One of the aerial bombs, a comparatively low-yield weapon, had an explosive force equal to 'a few hundred kilotons' of TNT.

kilovolt (ˈkɪləvəʊlt). [f. KILO- + VOLT *sb.*] **a.** One thousand volts.

In quot. 1861 the sense is 'a milliohm'.

1861 *Electrician* 9 Nov. 3/2, 1 Farad per second = 1 Volt, or unit of resistance. 1/1000 Volt = 1 Kilovolt. **1905** *Nature* 7 Dec. 142/1 The disruptive voltage is V kilovolts. **1927** *Glasgow Herald* 8 Dec. 13 Kilovolt transformers. **1938** R. W. LAWSON tr. *Hevesy & Paneth's Man. Radioactivity* (ed. 2) v. 65 The hardest characteristic radiation known, viz. the *K*-radiation of uranium, has a wavelength of 101 X.U. and requires an excitation potential of 115 kilovolts. **1948** *Sci. News* VII. 103 The thickness of metal which can be penetrated is directly related to the kilovoltage of the X-ray set, and a modern portable industrial unit employing 400 kilovolts will penetrate up to 5 inches of steel. **1973** *Sci. Amer.* Nov. 133/1 Bigger sizes are foreseen, but 10 kilovolts at low current is not attractive.

b. *attrib.* and *Comb.*, as **kilovolt-ampere**, a unit of apparent electric power, used when an alternating current is not in phase with the voltage, equal to the product of an r.m.s. voltage of 1000 volts and an r.m.s. current of 1 amp; **kilovoltmeter**, a voltmeter for measuring thousands of volts.

1909 *Cent. Dict.* Suppl., Kilovolt-ampere. **1933** EDGCUMBE & OCKENDEN *Industr. Electr. Measuring Instruments* xxii. 443 These quantities..are directly proportional to the kilo-watts and the reactive kilo-volt-amperes, respectively. **1950** *Engineering* 6 Oct. 281/3 Automatic control is provided to enable either the power factor or the reactive kilovolt-amperes to be maintained constant. **1923** R. KNOX *Radiogr. & Radio-Therapeutics* (ed. 4) I. i. 45 The kilovoltmeter for measuring the high-tension current. **1971** STERN & LEWIS *X-Rays* xiii. 232 The kilovoltmeter is connected across the primary of the high-voltage transformer.

Hence **ˈkilovoltage**, voltage expressed in, or of the order of, thousands of volts.

1933 *Proc. R. Soc.* B. CXII. 366 A kilovoltage of 78 was used..to ensure the production of the characteristic K radiation of tungsten. **1948** [see KILOVOLT a above]. **1971** STERN & LEWIS *X-Rays* xiii. 233 The quality and quantity of x-ray output for a tube are..not described uniquely in terms of the kilovoltage and milliampere meter readings.

kilowatt (ˈkɪləwɒt). *Electr.* [f. KILO- + WATT.] **a.** A thousand watts. Also *attrib.*

1884 *Engineering* 17 Oct. 358/1 Professor Koyle thought the term kilowatt sufficiently explicit. **1892** BARN. SMITH & HUDSON *Arithm. for Schools* 147 A Kilowatt is about 1⅓ Horse-power. **1895-6** *Calendar Univ. Nebraska* 196 Dynamos and motors from 25 Kilo-watts capacity down.

b. *Comb.* **kilowatt-hour**, a unit of energy equal to that produced in one hour by a power of one kilowatt, viz. 3·6 million joules.

1892 BARN. SMITH & HUDSON *Arithm. for Schools* 147 This is a Kilowatt-hour and is equivalent to 3.6 Megajoules. **1905** *Daily Chron.* 20 July 6/4 If he uses this 300 kilowatts for every minute he is working throughout the quarter, say ..720 hours, he will use 300 × 720 kilowatt hours or 'units'. **1951** B. L. GOODLET *Basic Electrotechnics* i. 11 Electrical energy is sold commercially by the kilowatt-hour—1000 watts acting for 1 hour. **1965** OWENS & SANBORN *Fund. Electr.* vii. 366 If a lighting circuit uses 2000 watts for a period of one hour, the amount of electric energy consumed is 2 kilowatt-hours.

Hence **ˈkilowattage**, power expressed in kilowatts; also *fig.*

1935 *Daily Express* 5 Apr. 8 A human dynamo of enormous kilowattage. **1971** *Sci. Amer.* Sept. 212/1 (Advt.), There was a time when 'the more, the better' was a national attitude—when a surging yearly increase in kilowattage scored prestige points.

kilp. *north. dial.* Forms: 5-6 **kylpe**, 5 **kelpe**, 6 **kilpe**, 7-9 **kilp**, 9 **kelp**. [cf. ON. *kilpr* handle, loop; also CLIP *sb.*¹ sense 2.] The movable or detachable handle (pair of clips) of a pot or cauldron; also, a pot-hook or crook from which a pot is suspended; the bail or hoop-handle of a pot or kettle; rarely, a hook in general.

1425 *Mem. Ripon* (Surtees) III. 156 Item pro scitulis emptis Ebor., 10*d*. Item pro uno kylpe de ferro ad eosdem, 1*d*. **1483** *Cath. Angl.* 203/1 A kylpe (*A*. kelpe) of a caldron, *perpendiculum*. **1590** *Inv. John Nevil of Faldingworth*, One brasse pot with kilpes. **1674-91** RAY *N.C. Words* 40 *Kilps*, pothooks. **1855** ROBINSON *Whitby Gloss.*, *Kelps*, the iron pothooks suspended in the chimney; also the bow or circular handle of the pot itself. **1881** J. SARGISSON *Joe Scoap* 287 (Cumberl. dial.) T' kilps an' creuks fer t' back band.

kilp, var. KELP³.

Kilroy ('kɪlrɔɪ). The name of a mythical person, popularized by American servicemen in the war of 1939–45, who left such inscriptions as 'Kilroy was here' on walls, etc., all over the world.

The explanation in quot. 1946 is one of numerous unverifiable accounts of the origin of the name.

1945 *Sat. Even. Post* 20 Oct. 6/2 On the crib hung a hand-lettered sign which asserted: 'Kilroy slept Here'... Wherever he was, Kilroy had been there and left his mark behind: 'Kilroy Was Here', or 'Kilroy Passed Through' or 'You're in the Footsteps of Kilroy'. **1946** *N.Y. Times* 24 Dec. 18/4 As far as the American Transit Association is concerned, the identity of the elusive Kilroy of 'Kilroy Was Here' fame has been established, and in token of this recognition a street car was shipped today to James J. Kilroy of Halifax, Mass. *Ibid.* 18/5 In brief, Mr. Kilroy's claim is based on the following: During the war he was employed at the Bethlehem Steel Company's Quincy shipyard, inspecting tanks, double bottoms and other parts of warships under construction. To satisfy superiors that he was performing his duties, Mr. Kilroy scribbled in yellow crayon 'Kilroy was here' on inspected work. Soon the phrase began to appear in various unrelated places, and Mr. Kilroy believes the 14,000 shipyard workers who entered the armed services were responsible for its subsequent world-wide use. **1951** *Here & Now* (N.Z.) May 10/1 United Nations forces wonder what the jolly rodger they're doing [*sic*] to do when they reach the northernmost point. Mark 'Kilroy' in the snow and come back again perhaps. **1952** P. ATKEY *Juniper Rock* xvii. 149 Such English as was possessed by the C.Q.M.S. was of a somewhat dated military character... 'Kilroy was 'eah,' said the C.Q.M.S. helpfully. **1962** *Guardian* 27 Nov. 7/5 For a long time Kilroy was the exclusive possession of the American forces. **1966** *Sunday Times* (Colour Suppl.) 4 Dec. 73/2 GI Jargon '*Kilroy was here*', standard graffito. **1968** M. ALLINGHAM *Cargo of Eagles* iii. 48 'A lot of people would like to know where he is just now. I wonder why he left that little pointer behind?' 'A "Kilroy was here" sign..?' **1969** L. DURRELL *Spirit of Place* 162 When I am rich I shall have a memorial plaque placed ..on Inverness station..reading 'Kilroy was here—but oh so briefly'!

kilt (kɪlt), *v.* Also 5 **kylte**. [app. of Scand. origin: cf. Da. *kilte* (also *kilte op*) to tuck up, Sw. (dial.) *kilta* to swathe, swaddle; ON. had *kilting*, *kjalta* skirt, lap.]

1. *trans.* To gird up; to tuck up (the skirts) round the body. Also with *up*.

a **1340** HAMPOLE *Psalter* lxiv. 7 [lxv. 6] Graythand hilles in þi vertu kiltid in powere [*accinctus potentia*]. **1483** *Cath. Angl.* 203/1 To kylte,..*suffercinare, succingere.* **1513** DOUGLAS *Æneis* I. vi. 27 Venus..With..Hir skirt kiltit till hir bair kne. **1535** LYNDESAY *Satyre* 1380 Then help me for to kilt my clais. *a* **1724** in Ramsay *Tea-t. Misc.* (1733) II. 144 Come kilt up ye'r coats And let us to Edinburgh go. **1792** BURNS *Braw Lads Galla Water* iii, I'll kilt my coats aboon my knee, And follow my love thro' the water. **1853** READE *Chr. Johnstone* ii. 25 Of their petticoats, the outer one was kilted or gathered up towards the front.

2. To fasten or tie up; to pull or hoist up; to 'string up', to hang.

1697 CLELAND *Poems* 30 (Jam.) Their bare preaching now Makes the thrush-bush keep the cow, Better than Scots or English kings Could do by kilting them [the thieves] with strings. **1810** COCK *Simple Strains* 69 (Jam.) Many ane she's kiltet up Syne set them fairly on their doup. **1828** SCOTT *Jrnl.* 20 Feb., Our ancestors brought the country to order by kilting thieves and banditti with strings.

3. *intr.* To go lightly and expeditiously (i.e. as with the loins girded).

1816 SCOTT *Bl. Dwarf* xvii, He..maun kilt awa' wi' ae bonny lass in the morning, and another at night,..but if he disna kilt himself out o' the country, I'se kilt him wi' a tow. **1894** IAN MACLAREN *Bonnie Brier Bush* IV. iii. 150 Kiltin' up the braes.

4. *trans.* To gather in vertical pleats, fastened at the top and free at the bottom, as in a kilt.

1887 J. ASHBY STERRY *Lazy Minstrel* (1892) 171 The skirt is of flannel most cunningly kilted.

kilt (kɪlt), *sb.* Also 8 **quelt**, **kelt**. [f. KILT *v.*] A part of the modern Highland dress, consisting of a skirt or petticoat reaching from the waist to the knee: it is usually made of tartan cloth, and is deeply plaited round the back and sides; hence, any similar article of dress worn in other countries.

c **1730** BURT *Lett. N. Scot.* xxii. (1754) II. 185 Those among them who travel on Foot..vary it [the Trowze] into the Quelt..a small Part of the Plaid is set in Folds and girt round the Waste to make of it a short Petticoat that reaches half Way down the Thigh. **1746** *Act 19–21 Geo. II*, c. 39 §17 The..philebeg or little kilt. **1771** SMOLLETT *Humph. Cl.* 3 Sept., His piper..has a right to wear the kilt, or ancient Highland dress, with the purse, pistol, and durk. **1771** PENNANT *Tour Scot.* (1790) I. 211 The feil beag, i.e. little plaid, also called kelt..is a modern substitute for the lower part of the plaid. **1814** SCOTT *Wav.* xvi, The short kilt, or petticoat, showed his sinewy and clean-made limbs. **1850** R. G. CUMMING *Hunter's Life S. Afr.* (ed. 2) I. 231 The dress of the [Bechuana] women consists of a kaross depending from the shoulders, and a short kilt. **1874** BOUTELL *Arms & Arm.* viii. 147 Thus was formed a species of kilt of armour, or iron petticoat.

kilt, obs. or dial. pa. pple. of KILL *v.*

‖**kilta** ('kɪltə). Also **kilter**. [Origin unknown.] In India, a kind of wicker basket. Also *attrib.* = made of wicker.

1876 C. F. G. CUMMING *From Hebrides to Himalayas* II. v. 134 Our provisions were packed..in long native baskets, called *kilters*. **1896** S. J. STONE *In & beyond Himalayas* 39 The provisions and cooking apparatus were carried in kiltas (wicker baskets covered with leather). **1901** KIPLING *Kim* xiii. 338 He skipped nimbly from one *kilta* to the next, making pretence to adjust each conical basket. **1927** *Blackw. Mag.* Mar. 312/1 A *kilta* carrying-chair, carried on the back of one man.

kilted ('kɪltɪd), *a.* [f. KILT *sb.* + -ED².] Wearing a kilt.

1809 BYRON *Eng. Bards & Sc. Review.* 526 The kilted goddess kissed Her son, and vanish'd in a Scottish mist. **1848** CLOUGH *Bothie* IX. 149 This is the letter of Hobbes, the kilted and corpulent hero. **1900** *Scott. Antiq.* XV. 31 The earliest kilted force..in the king's pay was the Black Watch.

kilted ('kɪltɪd), *ppl. a.* [f. KILT *v.* + -ED¹.]

1. Tucked up; having the skirts tucked up.

1724 RAMSAY *The Toast* ii, If ye bare-headed saw her, Kilted to the knee. **1865** HAMILTON *Poems* 88 (E.D.D.) Wi' kilted coats, knee-deep among the heather.

2. Gathered in a series of vertical pleats.

1896 *Daily News* 19 Mar. 6/5 Kilted silk, net, and lace will be largely used for capes. **1900** *Westm. Gaz.* 20 Sept. 3/2 The bodice is made with this same very closely-kilted chiffon drawn into a wide berth of cream lace.

kilter ('kɪltə(r)). *Poker.* [prob. var. of dial. KELTER⁴.] A hand consisting only of cards of little or no value.

1895 'TEMPLAR' *Poker Manual* 55 Suppose you have an utterly valueless hand dealt you, for example, deuce, four of hearts, six of clubs, seven of spades and nine of diamonds; this sort of hand is termed a 'kilter'. **1904** R. F. FOSTER *Pract. Poker* 126 The Southern custom of raising the ante on a kilter, and then standing pat. **1948** O. JACOBY *On Poker* xii. 144 There are any number of additional combinations of cards which are given rank in various localities. Some of these are the Dog, the Tiger, the Skeet, the Kilter, [etc.].

kilter, var. KILTA, KELTER².

kilting ('kɪltɪŋ), *vbl. sb.* [f. KILT *v.* + -ING¹.] The action of the vb. KILT; the act of girding or tucking up, or of plaiting like a kilt; the result of this. Also *attrib.*, as ***kilting-belt***, **-*machine***.

1521 *Churchw. Acc. St. Michaels, York* (Nichols 1797) 309 P^d for Kilting Belts 1^d. **1721** KELLY *Sc. Prov.* 300 *note*, Women, when they go to Work, truss up their Petti-coats with a Belt, and this they call their Kilting. **1880** *Cassell's Mag.* June 441 Kiltings are yielding to box-plaits. **1884** *West. Morn. News* 9 Aug. 1/3 Kilting machine, work-room tables.

kilty ('kɪltɪ). *colloq.* Also **-ie**. [f. KILT *sb.* + -Y⁶.] One who wears a kilt; esp. a nickname for a Highland soldier. Also, *attrib.* and as *adj.*

1842 D. VEDDER *Poems* 112 In double quick time did the kilties career. **1900** S. R. CROCKETT *Little Anna Mark* xii. 103 Yon's nae lassie! Yon's a kiltie lad. **1902** J. MILNE *Epistles of Atkins* xi. 208 A second Gordon communicates the views of a second Boer also upon the Gordon men. 'The "kilties" are devils to fight.' **1906** *Daily Chron.* 6 Aug. 3/6 A picturesque touch..is given to the town by the presence of the 'kilties' and other regiments of soldiers. **1921** *Daily Colonist* (Victoria, B.C.) 18 Oct. 3/7 (Advt.), St. Margaret Kiltie Dresses for girls 2 to 10 years, in navy, brown, saxe and green, [etc.]. **1927** *Scots Observer* 14 May 16/4 The Kilty piping for money. **1927** H. A. VACHELL *Dew of Sea* 261 She..assured him..that he was the 'kiltiest' boy she had ever met.

kimbe, obs. form of KEMB *v.*

kimberlite ('kɪmbəlaɪt). *Min.* [Named, 1886, from *Kimberley* in Cape Colony + -ITE¹ 2 b.] The eruptive rock, or 'blue ground', which is the matrix of the diamond at Kimberley and elsewhere in South Africa; it occurs in cylindrical 'pipes', often having a diameter of several hundred feet, and of unknown depth.

1887 H. CARVILL LEWIS in *Papers on the Diamond* (1897) 50 There appears to be no named rock-type having at once the composition and structure of the Kimberley rock... It is now proposed to name the rock *Kimberlite*... Kimberlite is a rock *sui generis*, dissimilar to any other known species. **1899** *Edin. Rev.* Apr. 319 This 'blue' rock—named 'Kimberlite' by Professor Carvill Lewis—is really of a dull green tint, due to its impregnation with iron oxides.

kimbling, var. *kimlin(g*: see KIMNEL.

'kimbo, in phr. *on kimbo*: see A-KIMBO.

†**'kimbo**, *a.* *Obs.* *rare*⁻¹. [f. A-KIMBO.] Resembling an arm a-kimbo.

1697 DRYDEN *Virg. Past.* III. 67 Two [Bowls]... The Kimbo Handles seem with Bears-foot carv'd.

†**'kimbo**, *v.* *Obs. rare.* Also 8 **kembo**. [f. A-KIMBO.] *trans.* To set a-kimbo. Hence †**'kimboed** *ppl. a.*

1748 RICHARDSON *Clarissa* (1811) IV. xxxvi. 240 For a wife to come up with kemboed arm. **1754** —— *Grandison* IV. xxxvii, He kemboed his arms and strutted up to me. **1808** SEDLEY *Asmodeus* I. 41 Who thrusts herself into every company with kimboed arms.

kimchi ('kɪmtʃɪ). Also **kimchee**, **kimch'i**. [Korean.] A raw strongly-flavoured vegetable pickle, the Korean national dish.

1898 I. L. BISHOP *Korea & her Neighbours* I. vii. 98 Wine, soup, eggs, and *kimchi*..were produced, and had to be partaken of. **1898** J. S. GALE *Korean Sk.* iii. 100 We found a Korean hut and, to our delight, dined on rice and *kimch'i* (pickle) once more. **1905** J. LONDON *Jacket* (1915) xvi. 210, I know *kimchi*. It is a sort of sauerkraut. **1925** *Blackw. Mag.* Mar. 320/1 Then five different sorts of *Kimchee*, a horrible dish made out of vegetables which have become rotten. **1951** C. OSGOOD *Koreans & their Culture* v. 85 The women prepare cucumber kimch'i by washing the vegetables, then cutting small pieces off their ends, and slitting the sides in three or four places. **1966** S. MCCUNE *Korea* iv. 33 A unique part of the diet and important for its vitamin content is *kimchi*, an unbelievably 'hot' pickle. **1972** P. M. BARTZ *S. Korea* 40/2 Korea emphasizes pickled cabbage (*kimchi*), hot peppers, and other seasonings. **1972** *Korea Times* 19 Nov. 6/3 With the onset of the kimchi-making season, housewives are concerned about preparing jars in which the pickled vegetables are stocked.

†**kime.** *Obs.* *rare*⁻¹. Also **kyme**. [Etym. obscure; app. the roof of AKIMED; cf. also western dial. *kimet* silly, stupid, dizzy.] A simpleton, fool.

c **1395** *Plowman's Tale* II. 695 The emperour yaf the pope somtyme So hyghe lordship him about, That, at [the] laste, the sely kyme [*later edd.* kime], The proude pope putte him out.

kimenell, obs. form of KIMNEL.

Kimeridge, var. KIMMERIDGE.

kim-kam, *a.* and *adv.* *Obs.* exc. *dial.* Also 8 **chim-cham**. [app. f. *kam*, CAM *a.*, crooked, awry, reduplicated as in *flim-flam*, *jim-jam*, etc.]

A. *adj.* Crooked, awkward, perverse, contrary.

1582 STANYHURST *Æneis* II. (Arb.) 44 Thee wauering Commons in kym kam sectes ar haled. *a* **1734** NORTH *Exam.* I. iii. §47 (1740) 151 Now the Reason of all this Chim-Cham Stuff, is the ridiculous Undertaking, of the Author, to prove Oates' Plot..out of Coleman's Papers. **1879** MISS JACKSON *Shropsh. Word-bk.* s.v., Let's a none o' yore kim-kam ways.

B. *adv.* Crookedly, awry; in a wayward, perverse, or contrary way.

1603 HOLLAND *Plutarch's Mor.* 452 Every thing then was turned upside downe, and..all went kim kam. **1658** J. HARRINGTON *Prerog. Pop. Govt.* I. xii. (1700) 310 He presumes [etc.]..Kim Kam to the Experience of all Common-wealths. **1691–2** AUBREY *Brief Lives* (1898) I. 47, [1666] This yeare all my businesses and affaires ran kim-kam. **18..** WHITTAKER in *Lancash. Gloss.*, *Kim-kam*, (to walk) with a throw of the legs athwart one another.

kimlin(g, **kimmel**: see KIMNEL.

kimmen, **-in**, **ond**, var. CUMMING *Sc.* (Cf. KIMNEL.)

kimmer, variant of CUMMER.

Kimmerian, var. CIMMERIAN *a.* and *sb.*

Kimmeridge ('kɪmərɪdʒ). Also **Kimeridge**. A village on the Dorsetshire coast, where extensive beds of the Upper Oolite formation are developed. Hence, ***Kimmeridge clay***, a bed of clay in the Upper Oolite containing bituminous shales. ***Kimmeridge coal***, shale of the Kimmeridge clay containing so much bitumen that it may be burnt as coal; ***Kimmeridge coal money***, disks of shale found near Kimmeridge, popularly supposed to have been used as coins by the ancient inhabitants.

Although the village name is now spelt *Kimmeridge*, the form *Kimeridge* is current in geological usage, reflecting the former spelling of the name; cf.:—**1933** W. J. ARKELL *Jurassic Syst. Gt. Brit.* xiv. 441 The spelling *Kimeridge* was used by H. B. Woodward.., by Damon.., and by most earlier authorities. The new form *Kimmeridge* was not heard of before Webster and Buckland introduced it in the [early] nineteenth century and seems to have no justification. **1947** —— *Geol. Country around Weymouth* (Mem. Geol. Survey Gt. Brit.) v. 68 Inland towards Kimmeridge village. [*Note*] The name of this village was Cameric in Domesday Book and Kymerich by 1293; by the time of Hutchins' great work on Dorset it had become Kimeridge... The Ordnance map of 1811 (Sheet 16, Old Series) retained one 'm', and so did Damon in his *Geology of Weymouth* (1860 and 1884–8) and H. B. Woodward in '*The Jurassic Rocks of Britain*', (vol. v, 1895), *Mem. Geol. Survey*. In the resurvey of 1892 (Sheet 342, New Series), two 'm's' were adopted and the Geological Survey followed suit in 1898.

1760 *Phil. Trans. R. Soc.* LI. 549 The Kimeridge [*printed* Kimendge] coal..appears in most of the cliffs of the isle of Purbeck. **1774** J. HUTCHINS *Hist. & Antiquities Dorset* I. 194/1 He says the Kimeridge coal, of which I sent him some pieces, is very much like, but not so large as, the Bovey coal. **1814** T. WEBSTER in *Trans. Geol. Soc.* II. 167 Clay with limestone and bituminous shale, containing the Kimeridge coal. **1816** —— in H. C. Englefield *Descr. Isle of Wight* 187 The whole of the Kimmeridge strata, consisting of a series of argillaceous and calcareous layers, are situated below the Portland oolite. **1818** W. PHILLIPS *Selection of Facts Geol. Eng. & Wales* 61 The shale is so bituminous as to form a coaly matter of considerable extent near Kimmeridge, whence it is termed the Kimmeridge coal. **1830** *Phil. Mag.* VII. 198 The manner in which the fossils are disposed in the Kimmeridge clay at Havre. **1832** DE LA BECHE *Geol. Man* (ed. 2) 319 The Kimmeridge clay..has a considerable range, particularly over England and France. **1851** D. WILSON *Preh. Ann.* (1863) I. II. vi. 438 Objects on which the name of Kimmeridge coal-money was conferred. **1855** *Q. Jrnl. Geol. Soc.* XI. 125 The present example from the Kimmeridge shales appears to be a distinct species. **1860** R. DAMON *Handbk. Geol. Weymouth* 54 From the coast of Dorsetshire the Kimeridge clay extends inland, with little interruption, to the coast of Norfolk. **1872** *Imperial Gazetteer Eng. & Wales* I. 1104/2 Bracelets made of the Kimmeridge coal were found in an ancient burial place at Dorchester in 1839. **1923** L. D. STAMP *Introd. Stratigr.* xiv. 230 In the upper part is a band of oil-shale ('Kimmeridge

Coal'). **1931** GREGORY & BARRETT *Gen. Stratigr.* x. 155 The Kimeridge Clay varies in thickness from 100 ft. in the Midlands to 1250 ft. in the Wealden bore near Hastings. **1946** L. D. STAMP *Britain's Struct.* xii. 135 Almost everywhere the Kimeridge clay coincides with low ground. **1967** D. H. RAYNER *Stratigr. Brit. Isles* ix. 303 The thickest sequences of Kimeridge Clay come from Wessex and the Weald;..near the type locality of Kimeridge Bay in east Dorset 1,650 feet are known. **1970** *Oxford Times* 12 June 14 This field was mostly Kimmeridge clay, with some sand at the bottom, and not so intractable as the Oxford clay.

Kimmeridgian, *a.* (*sb.*) *Geol.* Also **Kimeridgian**. [ad. F. *kimméridgien* (A. d'Orbigny *Paléont. francaise. Terrains Jurassiques* (1842–9) I. 610), replacing earlier *kimméridien* (J. Thurmann *Essai sur les Soulèvemens jur. du Porrentruy* (1832) I. 11).] The specific epithet of that subdivision of the Upper Oolite which is prominent at Kimmeridge. Hence, of or pertaining to this subdivision (which is a stage of the Upper Jurassic next below the Portlandian). Also *absol.*

1851 *Q. Jrnl. Geol. Soc.* VII. II. 75 The characteristic condition of most of the Jurassic formations (Sequanian, Kimmeridgian, and Portlandian). **1863** DANA *Man. Geol.* 449 The British subdivisions are for the most part recognized in France..in the Oolite—1, Bajocian..6, Kimmeridgian. **1931** GREGORY & BARRETT *Gen. Stratigr.* x. 155 In places the Kimeridgian becomes sandy towards the top before passing into the Portlandian. **1967** D. H. RAYNER *Stratigr. Brit. Isles* ix. 303 The onset of marine muds at the beginning of Kimeridgian times brought in a period of exceptionally uniform sedimentation in the Jurassic shelf seas of Great Britain. **1969** *Proc. Geol. Soc. London* Aug. 153 It is recommended that the beginning/base of the Age-Standard Stage Kimmeridgian be taken at the base of the Baylei Chronozone at the bottom of bed 26 of Arkell (1947) in Ringstead Bay, Dorset, England.

ˈ**kimnel.** *Obs.* exc. *dial.* Forms: α. 3 (**kembelina**), 4 **kym-**, **kemelyn**, 5 **kymlyn(e**, 5–6 **kemelin(e**, 5–7 **-ing**, 6 **kymlen**, **-ling**, **gim-**, 7 **kimline**, **-linge**, **-blinge**, **kemelling**, 9 (*dial.*) **kimlin(g**, **gimlin**. β. 5–6 **kymnell(e**, 6 **kimen-**, **kimn-**, **kimmell**, 7 **kym-**, **kimnel(l**, **kemell**, 9 (*dial.*) **kimnel**. [ME. *kem(b)elin*, *kim(e)lin*, and *kim(e)nel*, of somewhat obscure formation, but app. related to OE. *cumb*, ME. *combe*, COOMB[1]: see sense 2 there.

The earlier form is that in *-lin*; for that in *-nel*, cf. *cracknel* from F. *craquelin* (also surviving as *cracklin(g)*. More obscure is the Sc. *kimmon(d* CUMMING, which also has a parallel in *cracon(d* = cracknel. Mätzner compares med.L. *cimiline*, *ciminile*, but this denotes a basin for washing the hands in, and is regarded by Du Cange as an aphetized form of *aqui-* or *aquamanile* used in the same sense.]

A tub used for brewing, kneading, salting meat, and other household purposes.

α. [*c* **1275** *Roll* 2–5 *Edw. I* in *Promp. Parv.* 274 *note*, Stephano le Ioignur, pro j. Kembelina subtus cisternam Regis, vii *d.*] **1335** in Riley *Lond. Mem.* (1868) 194, 5 kemelynes..10*d.* *c* **1386** CHAUCER *Miller's T.* 362 Anon go gete vs..A knedyng trogh or ellis a kymelyn [*v.r.* kemelyn(e, kemelyng]. **1485** *Inv.* in *Ripon Ch. Acts* (Surtees) 371 j kymlyn pro carnibus salsandis. **1545** *Richmond Wills* (Surtees) 59 Towe kymlings for salting of beefe, the one of woode, the other of leade. **1599** *Acct. Bk. W. Wray* in *Antiquary* XXXII. 243 Item, one gimlinge. **1641** H. BEST *Farm. Bks.* (Surtees) 105 Our kimblinge is a just bushell. **1824** *Craven Gloss.*, *Gimlin*, a large, shallow tub, in which bacon is salted. **1855** ROBINSON *Whitby Gloss.*, *Kimlin*, a large dough tub.

β. *c* **1425** *Voc.* in Wr.-Wülcker 662/32 *Hec cima*, kymnelle. **1509** in *Market Harb. Rec.* (1890) 233, iiij payllys and iij kymnells. **1551–60** *Inv. Sir H. Parker* in H. Hall *Elizab. Soc.* (1887) 152 In the Brewehouse..sixe Kimenelles iij[s]. *a* **1613** BEAUM. & FL. *Coxcomb* IV. vii[i], Shee's somewhat simple indeed, she knew not what a Kimnell was. **1879** MISS JACKSON *Shropsh. Word-bk.*, *Kimnel*, the shallow tub in which butter is washed and salted when fresh from the churn.

‖**ki-mon** (ˈkiːmɒn). [Jap., f. *ki* demon, devil + *mon* gate.] In Japanese tradition, the name given to the north-east, supposed to be the source of evil.

1871 A. B. MITFORD *Tales Old Japan* II. 57 The Temple Tô-yei-zan..faces the Ki-mon, or Devil's Gate, of the castle. **1901** F. BRINKLEY *Oriental Series: Japan* III. iii. 111 Prominent among the ancient superstitions of Japan was a belief that all evil influences had their abode in the northeast, the Demons' Gate (Kimon). **1904** L. HEARN *Japan: Attempt at Interpretation* vii. 144 In almost every garden, on the north side, there is a little Shintō shrine, facing what is called the *Ki-Mon*, or 'Demon-Gate',—that is to say, the direction from which, according to Chinese teaching, all evils come... The belief in the Ki-Mon is obviously a Chinese importation. **1972** *Nat. Geographic* May 689/2 The avoidance of *kimon*, the devil's gate..not a single doorway faced in a north-easterly direction.

‖**kimono** (kɪˈməʊnəʊ). Also occas. **kimona**. [Jap.] A long Japanese robe with sleeves. Now freq. applied to a similar loose, wide-sleeved garment, fastened with a sash, and worn as a dressing gown, coat, etc., in Western countries. Also *attrib.*, as ***kimono blouse, coat, gown, shirt, sleeve***.

1886 W. CONN *Japanese Life, Love, & Legend* xii. 134 There were no unwieldy articles difficult to carry, no useless luxury; the *tatami*, the *kimono*, a few musical instruments, a collection of cooking and household utensils constituted the bulk. **1887** *Pall Mall G.* 17 Nov. 5/2 A troupe of geisha dancing girls..dressed in pink, flower-variegated kimonos. **1891** A. M. BACON *Jap. Girls & Women* vii. 188 The old-fashioned embroidered *kimonos* which are now entirely out of style in Japan. **1894** *Yng. Gentlew.* 168 At a fancy ball one frequently sees real Japanese kimonos, of exquisite material. **1902** *Daily Chron.* 11 Jan. 8/3 Over a soft skirt a silken kimono makes a new looking tea-gown. **1903** *Ibid.* 11 July 8/4 Lightweight canvas cloths..are used for kimono coats. **1908** *Westm. Gaz.* 9 May 13/2 Tailors are trying to get their clientèle away from the kimono line of bodice or of coat. They are weary of it; and no wonder, when one comes to think of the hundreds they must have turned out—kimono blouses, kimono bodices, kimono coats. **1919–20** *T. Eaton & Co. Catal.* Fall & Winter 153 Slip-over nightgown.., short kimona sleeves. *a* **1922** T. S. ELIOT *Waste Land Drafts* (1971) 33 line 137 A bright Kimono wraps her as she sprawls In nerveless torpor on the window seat. **1922** JOYCE *Ulysses* 554 Under the umbrella appears Mrs. Cunningham in Merry Widow hat and kimono gown. **1949** WODEHOUSE *Uncle Dynamite* viii. 127 When a housemaid in curling pins and a kimono finds herself in a drawing-room..with her employer.., she should as soon as possible make a decorous exit. **1960** B. LEACH *Potter in Japan* ii. 51 She wiped the bowls..and folded and replaced the napkin in the breast of her kimono. **1968** *Guardian* 13 June 10/2 Kenneth Tynan, in a kimono shirt. **1968** J. IRONSIDE *Fashion Alphabet* 57 *Kimono [sleeve]*, a sleeve cut in one with the body of the garment and hanging loose. **1970** *Times* 9 Mar. 7/7 The Japanese bride has always worn the traditional wedding kimono. **1971** *Guardian* 28 Dec. 9/3 Japanese influenced dresses with kimona sleeves. **1972** V. C. CLINTON-BADDELEY *To study Long Silence* i. 15 The green kimono wrapped across her bosom.

Hence **kiˈmonoed** *a.*, dressed in a kimono.

1894 *Yng. Gentlew.* 168 One accustomed to the kimonoed beauties of Japan.

kimple, variant of KEMPLE *Sc.*

Kim's game (kɪmz geɪm). Also **Kim game**. [Developed from the 'Jewel Game' in ch. ix of Kipling's *Kim* (1901); as *Kim's Game* introduced by R. S. S. Baden-Powell in the Scouting movement.] A memory-testing game (see quots.).

1908 BADEN-POWELL *Scouting for Boys* I. i. 54 *Kim's Game.* Place about twenty or thirty small articles on a tray ..and cover them over... Then uncover the articles for one minute... The boy who remembers the greatest numbers wins the game. **1948** 'J. TEY' *Franchise Affair* vii. 73 She has a photographic memory... When we played the Kim game —you know? the objects on the tray—we had to put Betty out of the game because she invariably won... She would remember what she saw. **1972** 'M. INNES' *Open House* II. viii. 74 Kim's Game consists in enumerating as many as possible of a miscellaneous assemblage of objects briefly glimpsed shortly before. **1973** *Times* 1 Oct. 13/1 We can, for example, play Kim's game, looking at a collection of objects on a table for 30 seconds before covering them up.

kimzeyite (ˈkɪmzɪaɪt). *Min.* [f. the name of the *Kimzey* family (see quot. 1958) + -ITE[1].] A dark brown zirconian garnet.

1958 MILTON & BLADE in *Science* 6 June 1343/3 This mineral..is here named 'kimzeyite'. The Kimzey family has been actively associated with mineralogical developments in Magnet Cove for almost a century... Notably William J. Kimzey, his son Joe Kimzey, former state geologist of Arkansas, and Lawton D. and John Kimzey. **1960** *Bull. Geol. Soc. Amer.* LXXI. 1930 Kimzeyite, $Ca_3(Zr, Ti, Mg, Fe'', Nb)_2 (Al, Fe''', Si)_3 O_{12}$, is a new type of garnet occurring as dodecahedrons modified by trapezohedron [*sic*] at Magnet Cove, Arkansas. **1967** *Amer. Mineralogist* LII. 773 The garnet compositions synthesized include the end-compositions.. $Ca_3Zr_2Fe_2SiO_{12}$ (kimzeyite).

kin (kɪn), *sb.*[1] Forms: 1 **cyn(n**, **cinn**, 1–6 **kyn(n**; 2–3 **cun**, 3–4 **kun**; 2 **cen-**, 2–4 **ken(ne**; 4–6 **kynne**, *Sc.* **kine**, **kyne**, 5–7 **kinne**, 3– **kin**. [Com. Teut.: OE. *cyn(n*, neuter, = OFris. *kin*, *ken*, *kon*, OS. *kunni* (MDu. *kunne*, *konne*, Du. *kunne*), OHG. *chunni* (MHG. *künne*, *kunne*), ON. *kyn* (Da., Sw. *kön*), Goth. *kuni*:—OTeut. **kunjo*[m], from the weak grade of the ablaut-series *kin-*, *kan-*, *kun-* = Aryan *gen-*, *gon-*, *gn-*, 'to produce, engender, beget', whence also Gr. γένος, γόνος, γίγνομαι, L. *genus*, *gignĕre*, etc. Cf. KEN *v.*[2]

In the Teutonic word, as in Latin *genus* and Greek γένος, three main senses appear, (1) race or stock, (2) class or kind, (3) gender or sex; the last, found in OE. and early ME., but not later, is the only sense in mod.Du., Da., and Sw.]

I. Family, race, blood-relations.

1. a. A group of persons descended from a common ancestor, and so connected by blood-relationship; a family, stock, clan; †in OE. also, people, nation, tribe (freq. with defining genitive, as *Israela*, *Caldea cyn*); = KIND *sb.* 11, KINDRED 2. Now *rare*.

c **825** *Vesp. Psalter* lxxvii[i]. 8 Ne sien swe swe fedras heara, cyn ðuerh and bitur. *c* **897** K. ÆLFRED *Gregory's Past.* xiv. 84 ȝe sint acoren kynn Gode. *a* **1000** *Cædmon's Exod.* 265 (Gr.) Mid yrmðum Israhela cyn. *c* **1000** *O.E. Chron.* (Laud MS.) an. 449 Of Iotum comon Cantwara..& þæt cyn on West Sexum þe man nu ȝit hæt Iutna cynn. *a* **1175** *Cott. Hom.* 227 Þa wes hweðere an meȝie cynn [ÆLFRIC I. 24 mæȝð] þe nefer ne abeah to nane deofel ȝyld..and þes cenne [ÆLFRIC mæȝðe] god sælde and ȝesette ae. **1297** R. GLOUC. (Rolls) 9137 So þat of þulke kunne þer nas þo no fere. *c* **1369** CHAUCER *Dethe Blaunche* 438 By tho figuris mowe al ken.. rekene and novmbre. **1604** ROWLANDS *Looke to it* 11 You that deny the stocke from whence you came, Thrusting your selfe into some Gentle kin. **1879** HEARN *Aryan Househ.* xii. 280 By the natural expansion of the Household kins are formed; and these kins in turn form within themselves smaller bodies of nearer kinsmen, intermediate..between the Household and the entire kin.

†**b.** The family or descendants *of* a specified ancestor; offspring, progeny, posterity; = KIND *sb.* 11 b, KINDRED 2 b. *Obs.*

c **950** *Lindisf. Gosp.* Matt. iii. 7 Cynn ætterna [L. *progenies viperarum*]. **971** *Blickl. Hom.* 23 Hie wæron of Dauides cynnes strynde. *c* **1000** ÆLFRIC *Hom.* II. 190 Ðin cynn [L. *semen tuum*] sceal ælðeodiȝ wunian on oðrum earde. *c* **1200** ORMIN 9837 We sinndenn Abrahamess kinn & Abrahamess chilldre. *c* **1320** *Cast. Love* 179 Alle the kynne that of hym come Shulde have the same dome. **1567** *Gude & Godlie B.* (S.T.S.) 8 Than pray..That ȝe may be of Isackis kin.

†**c.** The group of persons formed by each stage of descent in a family or clan; a generation; = KIND *sb.* 11 c, KINDRED 2 c. *Obs.*

c **825** *Vesp. Psalter* lxxxiv. 6 Ne aðene ðu eorre ðin from cynne in cynn. *c* **1000** *Ags. Ps.* (Th.) lxxvii. 7 þæt hi heora bearnum budun..and cinn oðrum cyððen. *a* **1300** *Cursor M.* 11401 (Cott.) Þis writte was gett fra kin to kin. *Ibid.* 1464 (Gött.), Iaraeth þat was þe fift kin fra seth.

†**d.** Genealogy, descent; = KIND *sb.* 11 d, KINDRED 2 d. *Obs.*

c **892** *O.E. Chron.* (Parker MS.) an. 716 Eawa [wæs] Pybing, þæs cyn is beforan awriten. *c* **1200** ORMIN 2059 Ne talde þeȝȝ nohht teȝȝre kinn..Bi wimmenn,..& all forrþi wass Cristess kinn..Bi Josæp reccnedd. *a* **1225** *Leg. Kath.* 464 ȝef þu wult cnawen my cun, ich am kinges dohter. *c* **1330** R. BRUNNE *Chron. Wace* (Rolls) 14975 Of Ethelbright haue I told þe kyn.

2. a. Ancestral stock or race; family. Usually without article and with descriptive adj. or sb., *esp.* in phr. (*come*) *of good* (*noble*, etc.) *kin*; = KIND *sb.* 12, KINDRED 3. *Obs.* exc. *dial.*

c **1100** *O.E. Chron.* (MS. D) an. 1067 Of ȝeleaffullan & æðelan cynne heo wæs asprungon. *c* **1200** *Vices & Virtues* 7 ȝif hie bieð of heiȝe kenne. *c* **1320** *Sir Tristr.* 1233 þe leuedi of heiȝe kenne. *c* **1380** *Sir Ferumb.* 442 What ys þy riȝte name; & of wat kyn þou ert y come; tel me al þat soþe. *c* **1440** *Gesta Rom.* II. xci. 416 (Add. MS.) Some are prowde, that they come of noble kynne, and sayne they are Gentil-men. **1591** SPENSER *Teares Muses* 345 Some one perhaps of gentle kin. **1856** BALLANTINE *Poems* 206 (E.D.D.) He comes o' gude kin.

b. *by* or *of kin*, by birth or descent. *rare.*

c **1400** *Chaucer's Melib.* ¶601 (Harl.) A free man by kyn [6 *texts* kynde] or burthe. *c* **1450** *Bk. Curtasye* 13 in *Babees Bk.* 299 Yf he be gentylmon of kyn, The porter wille lede the to hym. *c* **1470** *Golagros & Gaw.* 191, I am your cousing of kyn. **1898** CROCKETT *Standard Bearer* 76 (E.D.D.) She was gentle of kin and breeding.

3. The group of persons who are related to one; one's kindred, kinsfolk, or relatives, collectively. (Now the chief sense.) **a.** with possess. pron. (rarely *the*).

c **875** *Sax. Gen.* in *O.E. Texts* 179 Ða wæs agan..ccc ond xcvi wintra ðæs ðe his cynn ærest westseaxna lond on walum ȝeeodon. **971** *Blickl. Hom.* 175 For hwon wæron ȝyt swa treowlease, oþþe incer cynn. *c* **1175** *Lamb. Hom.* 35 Ga to þine feder burinesse oðer þer eni of þine cunne lið in. **1297** R. GLOUC. (Rolls) 253 Al þe kun þat him iseiȝ adde of him ioye. **1362** LANGL. *P. Pl.* A. I. 166 Vn-kuynde to heare kun and to alle cristene. **1413** *Pilgr. Sowle* (Caxton 1483) IV. xxiii. 69, I mett in the weye moche dyuerse peple..my frendes and my kyn and also many other. **1550** CROWLEY *Last Trump* 296 Thy chyld, nor any other of thy kynne. **1601** SHAKS. *Twel. N.* I. v. 123 One of thy kin has a most weake *Pia-mater.* *a* **1700** DRYDEN (J.), The father, mother, and the kin beside, Were overborn by fury of the tide. **1742** YOUNG *Nt. Th.* IV. 543 Nor are our brothers thoughtless of their kin, Yet absent. **1807** CRABBE *Par. Reg.* III. 737 His kin supposed him dead. **1891** BLAKISTON in *Colleges Oxford* (1891) 329 Sir Thomas Pope..did not saddle [Trinity College] with any of the preferences for founder's-kin which proved fertile in litigation elsewhere.

b. Without article or pronoun. Now *rare*, exc. in *kith and* (*or*) *kin*: see KITH.

c **1250** *Hymn to God* 30 in *Trin. Coll. Hom.* App. 259 Fader forȝif vs..Al swo we doð..to freómede & kunne. *c* **1325** *Chron. Eng.* 92 (Ritson) Bruyt hade muche folk with him, Bothe fremede and eke kun. *c* **1450** *St. Cuthbert* (Surtees) 4326 Þai spared nouthir kynn na kyth. *a* **1592** GREENE *Jas. IV*, v. ii, What was I born to be the scorn of kin? **1607** SHAKS. *Timon* I. i. 121 One onely Daughter haue I, no Kin else. **1836** W. IRVING *Astoria* II. 63 One of those anomalous beings..who seem to have neither kin nor country.

c. Used of a single person: Kinsman, relative; = KINDRED 4 b. *arch.*

c **1200** *MS. Digby* 59 in *Opera Symeon Dunelm.* (Surtees) I. 190 Sic dicitur vulgariter *Nother kyn nor wyn*, id est neque cognatum neque amicum. *c* **1205** LAY. 13730 He wes heore cun & heore freond. *Ibid.* 21462 Hercne me Cador; þu ært min aȝe cun. **1382** WYCLIF *Ruth* ii. 20 And eft she seith, Oure nyȝ kyn is the man. *c* **1475** *Partenay* 6278 Ny kyn he is to king off norway, For of Melusine discended all thay. **1601** SHAKS. *Twel. N.* v. i. 237 Of charity, what kinne are you to me? **1790** SHIRREFS *Poems* 78 (E.D.D.) Were he a Laird, he'd be nae kin to me. **1864** SWINBURNE *Atalanta* 398 O sweetest kin to me in all the world.

d. In predicative use passing into *adj.* = Related, AKIN (*to*). Also *fig.*

1597 SHAKS. *2 Hen. IV*, II. ii. 120 Like those that are kinne to the King. **1601** —— *All's Well* II. i. 41 My sword and yours are kinne. **1606** —— *Tr. & Cr.* III. iii. 175 One touch of nature makes the whole world kin: That all with one consent praise new borne gaudes. **1695** tr. *Colbatch's New Light Chirurg. Put out* 37, I do not find it any the least Kin to a Miracle. **1726** G. ROBERTS *4 Years Voy.* 9 It is next kin to an Impossibility..to have their Water brought out of the Country. **1788** REID *Aristotle's Log.* ii. §2. 26 They are indeed Kin to each other. **1870** DISRAELI *Lothair* I. ix. 59 But we are kin; we have the same blood in our veins.

4. The quality, condition, or fact of being related by birth or descent; kinship, relationship, consanguinity. Now *rare*.

a **1548** HALL *Chron., Edw. IV* 190 He.. rode in poste to his kynsman,.. verefiyng the old proverbe: kynne will crepe, where it maie not go. **1628** WITHER *Brit. Rememb.* I. 1161 The brother to the brother growes a stranger. There is no kin, but Cousnage. **1678** BUTLER *Hud.* III. i. 1294 'Cause Grace and Virtue are within Prohibited Degrees of Kin. **1700** DRYDEN *Pal. & Arc.* II. 108 Palamon, Whom Theseus holds in bonds.. Without a crime, except his kin to me. **1858** MRS. OLIPHANT *Laird Norlaw* III. 156 The Mistress herself, after that first strange impulse of kin and kindness.. relapsed into her usual ways.

II. Class, group, division.

†**5.** A large natural group or division of animals or plants, having presumably a common ancestry; the race (of men, fishes, etc.); a race (of plants); = KIND *sb.* 10. *Obs.*

In OE. freq. as the second element in compounds, as *déorcynn, fisccynn, fuʒolcynn, manncynn, wifcynn*, etc.

971 *Blickl. Hom.* 5 Seo æreste modor þyses menniscan cynnes. *Ibid.* 83 Him biþ beforan andweard eal engla cynn & manna cynn. *a* **1000** *Boeth. Metr.* xi. 67 Merestream ne dear ofer eorðan sceat eard ʒebrædan fisca cynne. *c* **1175** *Lamb. Hom.* 97 He walde monna cun on þisse deie isundian. *c* **1340** *Cursor M.* 22084 (Fairf.) Alle mannis kin he [antechrist] salle for-do.

†**6. a.** A class (of persons, animals, or things) having common attributes; a species, sort, kind; = KIND *sb.* 13. *Obs.*

c **950** *Lindisf. Gosp.* Matt. xvii. 21 Ðis soðlice cynn ne bið fordrifen buta ðerh ʒebedd and fæstern. *c* **960** *Rule St. Benet* (Schröer) i. 9 Feower synt muneca cyn. Ðæt forme is mynstermonna.. Oþer cyn is ancrena. *c* **1175** *Lamb. Hom.* 135 Feole cunne beoð of weldede. *a* **1250** *Owl & Night.* 1396 Hi beoþ tweire cunne. *c* **1450** *St. Cuthbert* (Surtees) 488 Many Fysches of kynes sere. **1500** *Nottingham Rec.* III. 450 Any kinnes of corne bought for merchandise.

†**b.** In this sense, chiefly in a genitive phrase, dependent upon following sb. Cf. KIND *sb.* 14.

In OE. the genitive might be either sing. or pl., according to sense; e.g. *ælces* or *ʒehwylces cynnes déor*, animals of each or every kind, *moniʒra cynna scipu*, ships of many kinds, *þreora cynna treowu*, trees of three kinds. In ME., *cynnes* became *kunnes, kynnes, kyns, kins*; *cynna* became *kunne, kynne, kyn, kin*. For the latter the genitive sing. was often substituted; and conversely, *kynne, kin*, appeared in the sing., esp. in the north, where it was prob. viewed as an uninflected genitive, as in *man son, fader broder*, etc. The preceding adjectival word agreeing with *kynnes, kins*, dropped its gentival *s* somewhat early; sometimes it was transferred to *kinnes*, thus *alle skynnes* (= *alles kynnes, alle kynnes*), *no skynnes*, etc. Usually however the two words were at length combined, as in the later forms *alkin(s, anykin(s, fele-kin(s, manykin(s, nokin(s* or *nakin(s, otherkin(s, sere-kin(s, swilkin(s, same-kin(s, thiskin(s, whilk-kin (hwilkyn), whatkin(s*. Few of these came down to 1500, though in the north *whatkin* is found in the 16th c., and survives in Sc. and north Eng. as *what'n*, beside *siccan* from *swilk kin*.

The reduction of *kin* to its simple uninflected form may have been assisted by the equivalent use of *manere* (MANNER) from OFr., which is thus found, as *threo maner men* = men of three kinds or sorts. In this, at an early period, we find *of* inserted: *an manere of fisce, al maner o suet spices*, the syntactical relation between the words being thus reversed, and although this appears to have rarely extended to *kin* itself, it affected its later representative *kind*, also *sort, species*, etc., so that we now say 'all kinds of things' = things of all kinds. This may have been facilitated by the fact that in the order of the words (as distinct from their syntactical relation) 'al kins thinges' is more closely represented by 'all kinds of things' than by 'things of all kind'. See KIND, MANNER, SORT, etc., and, for the special combinations of *kin* with preceding adj., ALKIN, ANY-KYN, etc.

a **900** *O.E. Martyrol.* 18 Apr. 58 Moniʒra cyna wil deor. **971** *Blickl. Hom.* 63 þreora cynna syndon morþras. *c* **1175** *Lamb. Hom.* 51 þer wunieð fower cunnes wurmes inne. *Ibid.* 79 Alles cunnes wilde deor. *c* **1200** ORMIN 2260 On alle kinne wise. *Ibid.* 9759 An kinness neddre.. Iss Vipera ȝehatenn. *a* **1250** *Owl and Night.* 886 Mi muth haveth tweire kunne salve. *a* **1300** *Cursor M.* 27901 (Cott.) It es funden bodili foure kin maner [*v.r.* fowrkins maners] of glotony. *c* **1340** *Ibid.* 12346 (Fairf.) Alle þai.. honoured him on þaire kin wise. **1362** LANGL. *P. Pl.* A. x. 2 A Castel.. I-mad of foure kunne [*v.rr.* foure skenis, skynnes, kynnes] þinges. *c* **1384** CHAUCER *H. Fame* III. 440 Alle skynnes condicious. *c* **1440** *Gesta Rom.* lxi. 254 (Harl.) He shall telle yow what kynne tidynges that he hathe browte. *Ibid.* lxix. 316 (Harl.) What kynnys treson is þis? **15..** SIR A. BARTON in *Surtees Misc.* (1888) 68 Ye wott not what kine a man he is. **1572** *Lament. Lady Sc.* 325 in *Satir. Poems Reform.* xxxiii, Counterfuting hir in all kin things.

III. †**7.** Gender; sex; = KIND *sb.* 7. *Obs.*

c **1000** ÆLFRIC *Gram.* vi. (Z.) 18 Æfter ʒecynde syndon twa cyn on namum.. werlic and wiflic. *c* **1000** *Sax. Leechd.* III. 144 þæt þu meht witan on bearn-eacenum wife hwæþeres cynnes bearn heo cennan sceal. *c* **1200** ORMIN 3056 Till ezzþerr kinn onn eorþe, Till weppmann & till wifmannkinn.

IV. Phrases. (from 3, 4.)

8. a. of kin = AKIN: Related by blood-ties. Also, Related in character or qualities.

1486 *Surtees Misc.* (1888) 47 For my sake and othre unto whome he is of kin. **1607–12** BACON *Ess., Atheisme* (Arb.) 338 Man is of Kin to the beastes by his body, and if he be not of kin to God by his spiritt, he is a base and ignoble Creature. **1642** FULLER *Holy & Prof. St.* IV. xix. 339 Kings, how nearly soever allied, are most of Kinne to their own interest. **1741** MONRO *Anat. Bones* (ed. 3) 306 The Bones of the toes are much of kin [*ed.* 1782 a-kin] to those of the Thumb and Fingers. **1877** C. GEIKIE *Christ* lvi. (1879) 685 You are of kin in heart to the prophet-murderers!

b. ***near of kin***, closely related. ? *Obs.*

1491 *Act 7 Hen. VII*, c. 22 *Preamble*, They be ner of kyn. **1611** BIBLE *Ruth* ii. 20 The man is neere of kin vnto vs. **1651** HOBBES *Leviath.* II. xix. 101 The neerer of kin, is the neerer in affection. **1767** BLACKSTONE *Comm.* II. xiv. 219 The uncle is certainly nearer of kin to the common stock, by one degree, than the nephew. **1768** TUCKER *Lt. Nat.* (1834) I. II. xxvi. 564 This probability, being so near of kin to certainty.

c. ***next*** (†***nearest***) ***of kin***, most closely related; chiefly *absol.* the person (or persons) standing in the nearest degree of blood-relationship to another, and entitled to share in his personal estate in case of intestacy.

[**1426** *E.E. Wills* (E.E.T.S.) 76 My brethren and my sustren and next of my kyn. **1540** *Sc. Acts Jas. V*, c. 40 (1814) II. 377/2 þe nearest of þe kin to succeid to þaim sall haue þair gudis.] *a* **1548** HALL *Chron., Hen. VI* 104 b, The next of kynne to the lord Cawny chalenged the enheritaunce. *c* **1600** *K. Leir* in *Percy's Reliques*, Being dead, their crowns they left Unto the next of kin. **1695** *Sc. Acts Will. III*, c. 72 In the Case of a moveable Estate left by a defunct, and falling to his nearest of kin. **1827** JARMAN *J. Powell's Devises* II. 65 For the next of kin it was argued, that the estate was to be sold out and out. **1881** *Encycl. Brit.* XIII. 198/1 The next of kin must be ascertained according to the rules of consanguinity.

fig. *a* **1770** JORTIN *Serm.* (1771) IV. ii. 13 As for lying which is next of kin to perjury.

V. 9. *attrib.* and *Comb.*, as ***kin-bond, -marriage, -sphere***; **kinfolk** chiefly *U.S.*, = KINSFOLK, -FOLKS; **kin group**, a group of people related by blood or marriage; †**kin-rest**, a general cessation from labour (with reference to the Jewish sabbatical year).

1890 GROSS *Gild Merch.* I. 169 When the old *kin-bond (the 'maegth') dissolved, various new institutions arose. **1873** 'MARK TWAIN' & WARNER *Gilded Age* ii. 33 No father, no mother, no *kin folks of no kind. **1947** S. J. PERELMAN *Westward Ha!* (1949) xii. 153 We managed to unsnarl our respective kinfolk. **1959** *Listener* 24 Dec. 1128/1 They [*sc.* the Bwamba] were organized into self-contained patrilineal villages, consisting of a group of male kinfolk with their wives and children. **1964** MRS. L. B. JOHNSON *White House Diary* 8 Apr. (1970) 103, I had asked Mrs. MacArthur and her son, and the Ambassador and all the kinfolks, to stop by the White House to warm up and have a cup of tea. **1970** *Daily Progress* (Charlottesville, Virginia) 21 Mar. c 2/1 Two willing young women have started 'The Bride's Workshoppe' to cope with everything from choosing a gown to picking up kinfolk at the airport. **1973** *Publishers Weekly* 20 Aug. 75/3 He was always surrounded by affectionate and eccentric kinfolk. **1942** A. R. JOHNSON *One & Many in Israelite Conception God* 25 The conception of the individual may not be dissociated from that of his kin-group (conceived in ever-widening circles of relationship). **1951** R. FIRTH *Elem. Social Organiz.* ii. 55 Differential family growth.. affects the control of wealth by kin groups. **1957** E. BOTT *Family & Social Network* v. 117 Bilateral descent cannot give rise to enduring corporate kin groups. **1970** G. A. & A. G. THEODORSON *Mod. Dict. Sociol.* 220 *Kin group*, a group united by ties of blood or marriage. **1881** E. B. TYLOR in *Academy* 9 Apr. 265 Exogamy is connected both with wife-capture and with barring *kin-marriage. **1387–8** T. USK *Test. Love* I. v. (Skeat) l. 103, I pray that.. this eighteth [yere] mowe to me bothe be *kinrest and masse-day after the seven werkedays of travayle. **1839** BAILEY *Festus* xxii. (1852) 394 Fear The fate of your *kin-sphere.

kin (kɪn), *sb.*² *north. dial.* Forms: 4 kyn(n)e, 8 kinn, 8–9 **kin**, 9 **keen**. [var. of *chin, chene*, CHINE *sb.*¹, repr. OE. *cine, cinu*. For the *k-*, cf. *kedlock, keslop, kirk, kirn*, etc.] A crack, chink, or slit; *esp.* (*a*) a chasm or fissure in the earth; (*b*) a chap or crack in the skin.

c **1330** R. BRUNNE *Chron. Wace* (Rolls) 1720 þey leye in dykes & in kynes [*rime* Peyteuyns]. *Ibid.* 13976 In chynes [*v.r.* kynnes], in creuesses, & in semes. **1737** BRACKEN *Farriery Impr.* (1757) II. 244 Subject to what's called a Kin, or Crack in the lower Lip. **1781** J. HUTTON *Tour to Caves* Gloss. (E.D.S.), *Kinns*, chinks and crevices in rocks, or breaks in the skin of the human body. **1878** *Cumbld. Gloss.*, *Kins, Keens*, cracks in the hands caused by frost.

Hence **kin** *v.*, to chap or crack; **kinned** *a.* or *pa. pple.*, cracked, chapped; chilblained.

1825 BROCKETT s.v. *Keen*, The hands are said to be keened with the frost, when the skin is broken or cracked, and a sore induced. **1855** ROBINSON *Whitby Gloss.*, 'Kinn'd hands', chopped hands. 'Kinn'd feet', chilblained feet.

kin (kɪn), var. CAN *v.*¹ A. I. Common in written Black English.

Also in many representations of regional English.

1875 *Independent* (N.Y.) 2 Sept. 25/4 I'll bet you I kin ride um. **1880** J. C. HARRIS *Uncle Remus* i. 20, I speck de ole 'oman en de chilluns kin.. git up sump'n fer ter stay yo' stummuck. **1880** [see LALLYGAG *v.*]. **1894** F. D. BANKS in *Jrnl. Amer. Folklore* VII. 148 Ef she can look him squar in de face when she talks to him, den she kin be trusted. **1936** M. MITCHELL *Gone with Wind* v. 77 You kin allus tell a lady by dat she eat lak a bird. **1952** V. WILKINS *King Reluctant* I. iii. 46, I kin 'spicion wat Miz Fell gwine ter say. **1964** J. H. CLARKE *Harlem* 263 Don' sent fer m'gal 'n Alabama, So she kin marry me. **1967** in A. Dundes *Mother Wit* (1973) 272/1 She kin throw 'em out the window. **1973** *Black World* Oct. 58/2 How much kin you like Boston when you used to the Bayou?

kin var. KEN *sb.*³

-kin (kɪn), *suffix*, forming diminutives, corresp. to MDu. *-kijn, -ken*, MLG. *-kîn* = OHG. *-chîn*, MHG. *-chîn, -chein, -chin, -chen* (G. *-chen*), as in MDu. *kindekijn, -ken*, MLG. *kindekîn*, MHG. *kindichîn*, G. *kindchen* little child; MDu. *husekijn, huusken*, MHG. *häusichin*, G. *häuschen* a little house. No trace of the suffix is found in OE.

The suffix has only a limited use in English. It appears to occur first in some familiar forms of personal (chiefly male) names, which were either adoptions or imitations of diminutive forms current in Flanders and Holland, where such forms appear already in the 10th c. The earliest ME. examples noted are *Janekin, Malekin, Watekin*, and *Wilekin*, found as early as 1250 (*O.E. Misc.* 188–191), and evidently then in familiar use. These and others of the kind were no doubt common in 13–14th c. (for *Jankin* and its variants see Nicholson *Pedigree of 'Jack'*), but are not prominent in literature till the second half of the 14th. The A-text of 'Piers Plowman' has *Malkin* and *Perkin*, the B-text adds *Haukyn*, and the C-text *Watkyn*; Chaucer uses *Jankin, Malkin, Perkin, Simkin*, and *Wilkin*; and in the 'Tournament of Tottenham' there occur *Dawkyn, Hawkyn, Jeynkyn, Perkyn*, and *Tymkyn*. The 'Earliest English Wills' have *Idkyne* (1397), *Jankyn* (1417–22) and *Watkyn* (1433). As Christian names these seem to have mostly gone out of fashion shortly after 1400, though instances occur later (e.g. *Wilkin* in Lyndesay's 'Satyre', 2180); most of them have, however, survived as surnames, usually with the addition of *-s* or *-son*, as *Jenkins, Watkins, Wilkinson, Dickens, Dickinson*, etc.

Instances of the suffix being added to common nouns in the 14th c. are rare; but Langland has *baudekin, fauntekin*, and *feudekin*, perhaps on the analogy of the personal names. Other words in *-kin* from the same or immediately succeeding period are either adopted from Du. or are of obscure origin; and it is doubtful whether the ending was in every case felt as a diminutive: such are *barmkin, bodkin, dodkin, firkin, kilderkin, napkin*. Considerable obscurity attaches to many later words (16–17th c.) of the same type, as *jerkin, bumpkin, pipkin, gaskin, griskin, bumkin, gherkin, ciderkin*, etc.: in some of these the ending may be of different origin, or due to assimilation, as in *pumpkin, tamkin* for earlier *pumpion, tampion*. Apparently from Du. are the 16–17th c. words *minikin, cannikin, catkin*, and *mannikin*. Outside of these, and some forms used in oaths, as *lakin* (? for *ladykin*), *bodykin, pittikin*, the suffix is comparatively rare; the only example which has obtained real currency is *lambkin* (1579), though a few others are occasionally employed, as *boykin* (1547), *devilkin, godkin, ladykin*, and nonce-words such as *glenikin, headikin, handikin* (after *mannikin*). *Bootikin* (18th c.) is not clearly a diminutive in origin, and in Sc. *cutikin, thumbikin* (cf. also *greenkin*) the force of the suffix is different.

kina = CHINA³, cinchona bark: cf. QUINA.

1706 PHILLIPS, *Kina*, the Jesuits Bark.

kinæsthesis (kaɪnɪsˈθiːsɪs). Also **kinæsthesia, kinesthesis.** [f. Gr. κῑν-εῖν to move + αἴσθησις sensation ÆSTHESIS.] The sense of muscular effort that accompanies a voluntary motion of the body. Also, the sense or faculty by which such sensations are perceived. So **kinæsthetic** (-ˈθɛtɪk) *a.*, belonging to kinæsthesis; also, involving or utilizing kinæsthesis; **kinæsˈthetically** *adv.*

1880 BASTIAN *Brain as an Organ of Mind* xxv. 543 We may .. speak of a Sense of Movement, as a separate endowment. [*Note*] Or in one word, Kinæsthesis... To speak of a 'Kinæsthetic Centre' will certainly be found more convenient than to speak of a 'Sense of Movement Centre'. **1891** V. HORSLEY in *19th Cent.* June 859 Bastian coined the term 'kinæsthesis',.. further, he.. postulated the view that such kinæsthesis, or sense of movement, strain, effort, &c., must naturally find its seat or localisation in the so-called motor or Rolandic region of the brain. *Ibid.* 868 Given that the cortex of the Rolandic region is kinæsthetic, from which element of it does the efferent impulse start? **1939** [see HAPTIC *a.* (and *sb.*)]. **1942** E. G. BORING *Sensation & Perception* xiv. 532 The fact that such small angular displacements can be sensed at such relatively slow speeds did much to direct attention upon the importance of kinesthesis. **1952** *Dance Observer* Jan. 9 A happy gang of young people being kinesthetically hypnotized by a clarinetist. **1953** H. HABER *Man in Space* 149 Whenever we move a limb or perform more complex physical tasks we rely on the delicate co-ordination of these three senses, and the so-called 'kinesthetic' sensations we derive from them serve as a very effective means of control. **1953** *Jrnl. Psychol.* XXXVI. 51 (*heading*) Kinesthetically guided movements of head and arm. **1955** *Sci. News Let.* 26 Mar. 200/2 Although these children initially learn best kinesthetically, their visual perception eventually develops so that they then learn readily by visual methods. **1958** S. H. BARTLEY *Princ. Perception* xiv. 321 This being the case, kinesthesis is responsible for more than appreciation of muscle position, movement and tension. It is the mediator of general well-being or general discomfort and malaise. **1960** *Aeroplane* XCIX. 804/2 Control is kinesthetic (body leaning) and top speed approximately 20 m.p.h. **1968** F. LEUKEL *Introd. Physiol. Psychol.* vii. 128/2 The general senses are somesthesis (pressure, pain, warmth, and cold), and kinesthesis. The special senses are olfaction, vision, gustation, audition, and vestibular sensitivity. **1970** *Nature* 20 June 1173/2 A species endowed with vision as the chief distance-sense and kinaesthesia (the muscle-and-joint sense commonly confused with touch) as the sense that chiefly guides his movements. **1970** *Motoring Which?* July 111/1 The steering was 'kinesthetic' (.. it means that you have to lean over and move your weight to make the craft go round corners).

‖**kinaki** (kiˈnaki). *N.Z.* [Maori.] A relish; a tasty or savoury addition to a meal.

1820 *Gram. & Vocab. Lang. N.Z.* (Church Missionary Soc.) 164 *Kinaki*, victuals, added for variety's sake. **1873** T. CHAPMAN in W. L. Buller *Hist. Birds N.Z.* 93 Norway rats .. by diving for these freshwater pipis, provide a *kinaki* (relish) for their vegetable suppers. **1878** *Trans. N.Z. Inst.* XI. 76 Fifty years back it would have been a poor *hapu* that could not afford a slave or two as a *kinaki*, or relish, on such an occasion. **1905** W. B. *Where White Man Treads* 17 If his kinaki (relish) were fish, his predatory instincts invented the means to catch them. **1921** H. GUTHRIE-SMITH *Tutira* x. 70 This man's body.. was eaten as a relish—*kinaki*—with the fern-root. **1949** P. BUCK *Coming of Maori* (1950) II. i. 110 Less difficulty was experienced in providing the meat complement, or *kinaki*, to go with the vegetable foods.

kinase (ˈkaɪneɪz, -s). *Biochem.* [f. Gr. κιν-εῖν to move + -ASE.] **a.** Any substance which converts

an inactive precursor (a zymogen) into an active enzyme.

1902 W. H. THOMPSON tr. *Pawlow's Work of Digestive Glands* ix. 160 When a tube was introduced into the fistula, and the succus entericus afterwards collected in separate portions, the amount of kinase in the secretion became steadily less and less. **1903** *Jrnl. Chem. Soc.* LXXXIV. II. 497 When kinase is mixed with inactive pancreatic juice, it forms a powerful proteolytic mixture. **1923** [see *enterokinase* (ENTERO-)]. **1956** I. L. FINAR *Org. Chem.* II. xiii. 502 Many enzymes are inactive unless an activator is present. The inactive enzyme is known as a zymogen, and the activator as a kinase (if this is inorganic), *e.g.*, trypsinogen (the zymogen) together with enterokinase (the kinase) forms the enzyme trypsin.

b. Any enzyme capable of catalysing the transfer of a phosphate group from adenosine triphosphate (or other nucleoside triphosphate) to another molecule; also used with preceding sb. or prefix indicating the accepting molecule, as in HEXOKINASE (from which this use derives).

1953 *Jrnl. Biol. Chem.* CC. 187 The enzyme myokinase, or adenylate kinase, which catalyses the establishment of an equilibrium between the three nucleotides, adenosinetriphosphate (ATP), adenosinediphosphate (ADP), and adenylic acid (AMP). **1962** P. D. BOYER et al. *Enzymes* (ed. 2) VI. i. 7 Enzymes transferring phosphoryl groups from ATP to acceptors have been termed kinases, phosphokinases, [etc.]... The term kinase stems from Meyerhof's designation of the enzyme that activates glucose as hexokinase. **1964** FLORKIN & STOTZ *Comprehensive Biochem.* (ed. 2) XIII. 34 A number of special words are used to indicate reaction types, e.g. 'kinase' to indicate a phosphate transfer from ATP to the named substrate (not 'phosphokinase'). **1970** *New Scientist* 29 Jan. 196/1 Elegant methods of joining large oligonucleotide sequences of DNA to one another using the enzymes polynucleotide kinase and ligase have, in fact, been worked out.

kinate, obs. form of QUINATE.

†**kinboot.** *Sc. Obs.* Forms: 5 **kynbwt, -bute,** 6 **kinbute,** 7 **-but,** (9 **-bot**). [f. KIN *sb.*¹ + BOOT *sb.*¹ 9.] A wergeld or man-boot paid by a homicide to the kin of the person slain. (Not the same as the OE. *cynebót* or royal compensation.)

c **1425** WYNTOUN *Cron.* VI. xix. 2282 For a yhwman twelf markis ay þe slaare suld for kynbwt pay. **1478** *Acta Dom. Concil.* (1839) 9/1 Þᵗ walter blare sall..pay to Robert of Cargill..xxv mercis..for a kynbute. **1606** LD. ROXBURGH in *14th Rep. Hist. MSS. Comm.* App. III. 32 [He then..offers a sum of money..for] kinbut and satisfaction. [**1876** A. LAING *Lindores Abbey* xxv. 328 He shall be free on payment of twenty-four merks of Kinbot.]

kincajou, variant of KINKAJOU.

kinch (kɪnʃ), *sb. Sc.* Also 6– **kinsch, kinsh,** 9 **kench.** [In sense 1, a parallel form to KINK *sb.*¹: cf. *benk, bench,* etc. Sense 3 may be unconnected.]

1. A loop or twist on a rope or cord, esp. the loop of a slip-knot; a noose.

? *a* **1800** *Surv. Moray* Gloss. (Jam.), *Kinsch,* a cross rope capped about one stretched along and tightening it. **1808–80** JAMIESON, *Kinsch,* the twist or doubling given to a cord or rope, by means of a short stick passed through it, in order to draw it tighter. **1828** MOIR *Mansie Wauch* xix. 280 Having fastened a kinch of ropes beneath her oxters. **1844** CROSS *Disruption* xxviii. (E.D.D.), I hae maist got my neck intil a kinch for my pains. **1861** M'LEVY *Curios. Crime Edinburgh, Handcuffs* 29, I put his right hand into the kench.

2. *fig.* A catch, hold, advantage. ? *Obs.*

1635 D. DICKSON *Pract. Wks.* (1845) I. 78 Everyone seeking a kinsh of his neighbour. ? *a* **1800** *Surv. Moray* Gloss. (Jam.), *Kinsch,* an advantage unexpectedly obtained.

†**3.** ? (One's) lot. *Obs.*

a **1600** MONTGOMERIE *Cherrie & Slae* 1100 The man may ablens tyne a stot That cannot count his kinsch. —— *Sonn.* xxxvii, I can not chuse; my kinsh is not to cast. **1606** BIRNIE *Kirk-Buriall* (1833) 11 Our Heroik burials are oft led like a martiall triumphe..But alas, if in death we could count our just kinsh, we might rather dismay and feare.

Hence **kinch** *v.,* (*a*) (see quot. 1808–18); (*b*) to put a string noose on the tongue of (a horse), in order to exercise control over it.

1808–18 JAMIESON, To *Kinsch,* to twist and fasten a rope. **1864** LATTO *Tammas Bodkin* xxvi. (E.D.D.), The tooth cud be easily pu'd oot by means o a rosety string, kinched roon the root o't. **1891** *Scot. Leader* 17 Apr. 5 The cruelty attached to 'Kinching' a pit pony..to hold that kinching in no cases should be resorted to.

kinchin ('kɪntʃɪn). *Cant.* Also 6 (**kitchin**), **kynchen, -ching,** 7 **-chin,** 9 **kinchen.** [The form of the word and the history of some other early words of the same class suggest that it was a corrupt form of G. *kindchen* or MLG. *kindekin,* MDu. *kindeken,* LG. *kindken,* little child.]

1. †**a.** *attrib.* in *kinchin-co(ve), -mort,* the terms used by 16th c. tramps to denote respectively a boy and girl belonging to their community. *Obs.* **b.** *absol.* A child, a 'kid'. (Now convicts' slang.)

1561 AWDELAY *Frat. Vocab.* 5 A Kitchin Co is called an ydle runagate Boy. **1567** HARMAN *Caveat* xxii. 76 A Kynching Morte is a lytle Gyrle: the Mortes their mothers carries them at their backes in their slates, which is their shetes. *a* **1700** B. E. *Dict. Cant. Crew, Kinchin,* a little Child. *Kinchin-cove,* a little Man. **1815** SCOTT *Guy M.* xxviii, I'll pray for nane o' him, said Meg..The times are sair altered since I was a kinchen-mort. **1838** DICKENS *O. Twist* xlii, The kinchins..is the young children that's sent on errands by their mothers. **1897** P. WARUNG *Tales Old Regime* 231 There yer are now, making the woman snivel, and you have frightened her kinchins too.

2. *attrib.* in **kinchin-lay**, the practice of stealing money from children sent on errands. Also *fig.*

1838 DICKENS *O. Twist* xlii, 'Ain't there any other line open?' 'Stop', said the Jew..'The kinchin lay'. **1888** *Academy* 29 Sept. 203/1 'The detective business', which is, at the best, the kinchin lay of fiction.

kincob ('kɪŋkɒb). *East Ind.* Also **king-, khem-, keem-, quin-, -kaub, -quaub, -qwab, -quab, -caub.** [ad. Urdū (Pers.) *kimkhāb.*] A rich Indian stuff, embroidered with gold or silver; also (with *a* and *pl.*), A piece or variety of this.

1712 [see b]. **1786** *Art. agst. Hastings* in *Burke's Wks.* (1852) VII. 23 (Y.) She would ransack the zenanah..for Kincobs, muslins, cloths. **1813** J. FORBES *Oriental Mem.* I. 224 Drawers of crimson and gold Keemcab. **1829** J. SHIPP *Mem.* vi. (1890) 86 We had glorious plunder, shawls, silks, satins, khemkaubs, money, &c. **184.** MRS. SHERWOOD *Lady of Manor* III. xxi. 241 Many cushions of the richest kinquaub. **1845** STOCQUELER *Handbk. Brit. India* (1854) 210 Gold and silver brocades, called Kincaubs. **1882** *Cornh. Mag.* Jan. 103 Shawls, scarves, and pieces of silk and kincob.

b. *attrib.*

1712 *Spect.* (*Advt.*), One Isabella colour Kincob Gown, flowered with Green and Gold. **1781** *India Gaz.* 24 Feb. (Y.), A rich Kingcob Waistcoat. **1885** MRS. LYNN LINTON *Chr. Kirkland* I. 21 That green shawl with the kincob pattern.

kincough, variant of KINKCOUGH.

kind (kaɪnd), *sb.* Forms: [1 **ȝecynde, ȝecynd,** 2–3 **i-cunde, i-kunde,** (2 **i-chinde**);] 1 **cynd,** 2–4 **cunde,** 2 **cuinde,** 3 **kuinde, kund,** 3–4 **kuynde, kunde,** 3–5 **kende,** (5 **keende**), 3–6 **kynd,** 3–7 **kinde,** 4–7 **kynde,** (5 **kyynde**), 3– **kind.** [OE. *ȝecynde* n., *ȝecynd* fem. and n., f. *ȝe-* (see I-, Y-) + **cynd*(*e:—***kundi-z,* f. the root *kun-* (see KIN¹) + *-di-,* Aryan *-ti-.* OE. instances of *cynd* are doubtful, but the prefix disappeared early in ME., 1150–1250.

The only cognate sb. out of Eng. is a doubtful OS. *gicund* (suggested in *Hel.* 2476). But the adj. ending, Goth. *-kunds,* OS. *-cund,* OHG. *-chund, -kund* = OE. *-cund* 'of the nature of', is found in the other langs.]

I. Abstract senses.

†**1. a.** Birth, origin, descent. *Obs.*

a **1000** *Hymns* ix. 52 (Gr.) Þurh clæne ȝecynd þu eart cyning on riht. *c* **1200** ORMIN 7133 An child..þatt shall ben þiss Iudisskenn king All þurrh rihht aþell kinde. *c* **1386** CHAUCER *Melib.* ¶ 601 A free man by kynde or by [*v.r.* of] burthe. *c* **1415** *12 Art. Faith* (MS. Soc. Antiq.), Iesu Christ his owne son through kind. *c* **1425** WYNTOUN *Cron.* IX. xxvi. 41. 2751 His aire, that of kynd wes kyng. *c* **1463** G. ASHBY *Dicta Philos.* 122 That they be free, nat bonde in kynde. **1649** MILTON *Eikon.* xxviii. 238 His Grand-mother Mary, Queen of Scots,..from whom he seems to have learnt, as it were by heart, or els by kind,..his words and speeches heer.

†**b.** Hence, through the phrases *through, by, of kind*: Right of birth, right or position derived from birth, inherited right. *Obs.*

c **1205** LAY. 25043 Heo..nu axeð mid icunde [*c* **1275** þorh cunde] gauel of þissen londe. **1297** R. GLOUC. (Rolls) 2231 Þer nis no mon þat kunde abbe þer to. *Ibid.* 6664 He adde somdel to engelond More kunde þan þe oþer. *Ibid.* 7276 Wo so were next king bi kunde, me clupede him aþeling.

†**2. a.** The station, place, or property belonging to one by birth; one's native place or position; that to which one has a natural right; birthright, heritage. *Obs.*

c **888** K. ÆLFRED *Boeth.* xxv, Seo sunne..secð hire ȝecynde, & stiȝð..ufor & ufor oððe hio cymð swa up swa hire yfemest ȝecynde bið [cf. quot. *Boeth. Metr.* s.v. KIND *a.* 1 c]. *a* **1100** *O.E. Chron.* (Laud MS.) an. 1086 Normandiȝe þet land wæs his ȝecynde. *c* **1205** LAY. 16279 Þat ich mote..biȝite mine ikunde [*c* **1275** cunde]. *Ibid.* 21492 Cador cuðe þene wæi þe toward his cunde læi. **1340** *Ayenb.* 37 Þe children..þet hi heþ be spousbreche, berþ away þe kende.

†**b.** That which naturally belongs to or befits one. *Obs.*

c **1470** HENRY *Wallace* I. 217 Ane Ersche mantill it war thi kynd to wer. *a* **1670** SPALDING *Troub. Chas. I* (Spald. Cl.) I. 199 Thay took ane of the tounes cullouris of Abirdein, and gave it to the toune of Abirbrothokis soldiours..quhilk wes not thair kynd to cary.

3. a. The character or quality derived from birth or native constitution; natural disposition, nature. (Common down to *c* 1600; in later use rare, and blending with sense 4.)

c **888** K. ÆLFRED *Boeth.* xxxiv. § 11 Þa stanas..sint stillre ȝecynde & heardre. *Ibid.* xxxv. § 4 ȝif hio hire cynd [*Bodl. MS.* ȝecynd] healdan wille. *c* **1175** *Lamb. Hom.* 51 Þis fis is of swulc cunde, þet [etc.]. *c* **1200** ORMIN 2675 Marȝess child wass mann & Godd, An had i twinne kinde. *a* **1225** *Ancr. R.* 120 He uorleoseð monnes kunde, &..uorschuppeð him into bestes kunde. *c* **1250** *Gen. & Ex.* 189 And euerilc on in kinde good, Ðor quiles adam fro sinne stod. *a* **1300** *Cursor M.* 8452 Þe kind o thinges lerd he, Bath o tres, and gress fele. **1387** TREVISA *Higden* (Rolls) VI. 131 In Crist beeþ tweie willes and tweie kyndes of þe Godhede and manhede. *c* **1491** *Chast. Goddes Chyld.* 12 In some men the bodely kynde is feblid by a soden heuynes. *a* **1547** SURREY *On Lady refusing to dance* in *Tottell's Misc.* (Arb.) 219 My kinde is to desire the honoure of the field. **1590** SPENSER *F.Q.* II. ii. 36 But young Perissa was of other mynd..And quite contrary to her sisters kynd. **1697** DRYDEN *Virg. Georg.* II. 326 Sweet Grapes degen'rate there, and Fruits..renounce their Kind. **1784** COWPER *Tiroc.* 6 Th' associate of a mind Vast in its pow'rs, ethereal in its kind. **1857** BUCKLE *Civiliz.* I. viii. 524 For as to the men themselves, they merely acted after their kind.

†**b.** *of his* (*own*) *kind*: by its (own) nature, of itself, naturally. *Obs. rare.*

1399 LANGL. *Rich. Redeles* III. 19 Þis beste, of his kinde, Secheth and sercheth þo schrewed wormes. **1530** RASTELL *Bk. Purgat.* II. x, The soule shall..perceyve of hys owne kynde. **1578** LYTE *Dodoens* II. lx. 227 Hyssope groweth not of his owne kinde in this countrey. **1610** SHAKS. *Temp.* II. i. 163 Nature should bring forth, Of it owne kinde, all foyzon.

†**c.** *to do* (or *work*) *one's kind*: To act according to one's nature; to do what is natural to one; *spec.* to perform the sexual function. *Obs.*

c **1230** *Hali Meid.* 25 Leasse þen beastes ȝet, for þeos doð hare cunde..in a time of þe ȝer. **1297** R. GLOUC. (Rolls) 6576 Þat water dude uorþ is kunde & was euere uaste. *Ibid.* 8353 Mid wimmen of painime hii dude hor foule kunde. *c* **1430** *Hymns Virg.* 83 Þe kinde of childhode y dide also, Wiþ my felawis to fiȝte and þrete. **1554–9** *Songs & Ball.* (1860) 1 Fortune worketh but her kynde, To make the joyfull dolorus. *a* **1612** HARINGTON *Salerne's Regim.* (1634) 36 The stones of young beasts that be not able to doe their kinde. **1647** CRASHAW *Poems* 184 Let froward dust then do its kind.

†**d.** *to grow* (also *go, swerve,* etc.) *out of kind*: To lose the character appropriate to one's birth and family; to degenerate. *Obs.*

a **1547** SURREY *Æneid* II. 714 Neoptolem is swarved out of kind. **1549** COVERDALE, etc. *Erasm. Par. Heb.* 20 Neither dyd Ioseph growe out of kynde, & become vnlike his auncestours in faith. **1573** TUSSER *Husb.* (1878) 100 So garden with orchard and hopyard..That want the like benefit, growe out of kinde. **1587** GOLDING *De Mornay* xvi. 254 God created man to be to him as a child, and man is growne out of kinde.

†**4. a.** Nature in general, or in the abstract, regarded as the established order or regular course of things (*rerum natura*). Rarely with *the.* Freq. in phr. *law* or *course of kind. Obs.* (exc. as conscious archaism.)

c **888** K. ÆLFRED *Boeth.* xiv. § 1 On swiðe lytlon hiera hæfð seo ȝecynd ȝenoȝ. *Ibid.* xvi. § 3 Seo ȝecynd hit onscunað þæt [etc.]. *c* **1230** *Hali Meid.* 45 Ichulle halde me hal þurh þe grace of godd, as cunde me makede. *a* **1300** *Cursor M.* 28491 Ic..haf i broken..þe lagh o kynd thoru licheri. **1387** TREVISA *Higden* (Rolls) I. 335 Kynde bryngeþ hem [barnacle-geese] forþ wonderliche out of trees, as it were kynde worchynge aȝenst kynde. *c* **1400** MAUNDEV. (Roxb.) xxxii. 144 Many..diez for pure elde withouten sekeness, when þe kynde failez. ? *a* **1412** LYDG. *Two Merch.* 75 So strong of nature is the myhty corde. Kynde is in werkyng a ful myhty lorde. **1583** T. WATSON *Centurie of Loue* lxxviii, Venus..will have it so That Louers wanting sight shall followe kinde. **1596** SHAKS. *Merch. V.* I. iii. 86. **1674** N. FAIRFAX *Bulk & Selv.* Contents, God holds us by laws of kind as we do others by those of right. *Ibid.* 124 Those bounds that Dame Kind before had pitcht upon. **1868** MORRIS *Earthly Par.* I. 90 O ye who sought to find Unending life against the law of Kind.

†**b.** Phrases. *by* (*by way of*), *of, through,* (rarely *in*) *kind,* by nature, naturally; *against* or *out of kind,* contrary to, or in violation of, nature.

In these phrases the distinction between 3 and 4 tends to fade away.

a **1000** *Boeth. Metr.* xiii. 17 Þara micles to feola..winð wið ȝecynde. *a* **1000** *Hymns* vii. 24 (Gr.) Þin weorc..þurh ȝecynd clypiað and crist heriað. *a* **1121** *O.E. Chron.* (Laud MS.) an. 1107 Maneȝe sædon þet hi on þam monan..tacna ȝesawon, & onȝean cynde his leoman wexende & waniende. *c* **1200** ORMIN 2320 All swa maȝȝ Godd don þe full wel To childenn gæness kinde. *a* **1225** *Leg. Kath.* 297 Engles & sawlen, þurh þet ha bigunnen, Ahten..endin þurh cunde. *a* **1300** *Cursor M.* 2889 Oute of kind þe sin was don. *c* **1384** CHAUCER *H. Fame* II. 241 Every Ryver to the see Enclyned ys to goo by kynde. *c* **1386** —— *Frankl. T.* 40 Wommen of kynde desiren libertee. **1493** *Festivall* (1515) 66 b, At mydnyghte our lorde was borne, for by kynde all thynge was in peas and rest. **1575** *Gamm. Gurton* in Hazl. *Dodsley* III. 210 She is given to it of kind. **1658** J. JONES *Ovid's Ibis* 55 When bloud toucheth bloud in this kind, it is abominable out of kind. **1714** GAY *Sheph. Week* Thursday 37 Last Valentine, the day when birds of kind Their paramours with mutual chirpings find. **1792** BURNS *She's Fair & Fause* ii, Nae ferlie tis tho' fickle she prove, A woman has't by kind.

†**5. a.** Natural state, form, or condition. *Obs.*

a **1000** *Boeth. Metr.* xxviii. 62 Sona ȝecerreð ismere..on his aȝen ȝecynd, weorðeð to wætere. *a* **1340** HAMPOLE *Psalter* cxviii. 70 Mylk in þe kynd is fayre & clere, bot in lopirynge it waxis soure. *a* **1380** *St. Ambrose* 538 in Horstm. *Altengl. Leg.* (1878) 16 His face..lyk to snouh hit wox al whit, But aftur to his oune kynde [L. *ad suam speciem*] turned hit. *c* **1400** MAUNDEV. (Roxb.) iv. 12 Þan sall scho turne agayne to hir awen kynde [F. *estat*] and be a woman [*cf.* 14 in to hir riȝt schappe, F. *fourme*].

†**b.** *in kind,* in proper or good condition; *out of kind,* out of order, in bad condition. *Obs.*

1393 LANGL. *P. Pl.* C. III. 247 Thi kyngdom þorw here couetyse wol out of kynde wende. *c* **1400** *Lanfranc's Cirurg.* 2 Of a wounde bollid and out of kynde. **1602** CAREW *Cornwall* 31 The countrie people long retained a conceit, that in summer time they weare out of kind. **1623** COCKERAM III. s.v. *Isæan Riuer,* Salmon, which is euer in kind all times of the yeare.

†**6.** A natural quality, property, or characteristic.

c **888** K. ÆLFRED *Boeth.* xxxiii. § 5 Vðwitan secȝað þæt hio [sio sawul] hæbbe þrio ȝecynd... Twa þara ȝecynda habbað netenu swa same swa men. *c* **1220** *Bestiary* 15 An oðer kinde he haueð, wan he is ikindled Stille lið ðe leun. *a* **1225** *Ancr. R.* 126 Þe pellican..haueð anoðer cunde: þet is, þet hit is euer leane. *c* **1340** HAMPOLE *Prose Tr.* 8 The bee has thre kyndis. Ane es that scho es neuer ydill. *c* **1400** MAUNDEV. (1839) xxx. 302 And thei han this kynde [F. *nature*] that thei lete nothing ben empty among hem.

†**7. a.** Gender; sex; = KIN¹ 7. (L. *genus.*) *Obs.*

a 1000 *Phœnix* 356 God ana wat..hu his ȝecynde byð, wifhades þe weres. **a 1380** *Virgin Antioch* 387 in Horstm. *Altengl. Leg.* (1878) 32 In to wyn Crist torned þe watur, And nou he leueþ not beohynde For to chaunge monnes kynde [L. *sexum*]. **1393** LANGL. *P. Pl.* C. IV. 339 As adiectif and substantyf vnite asken, Acordaunce in kynde, in cas and in numbre. **1551** ROBINSON tr. *More's Utopia* II. ix. (1895) 293 All they which be of the male kind..sitte before the goodman of ye house, and they of the female kynde before the goodwyfe. **1584** COGAN *Haven Health* (1636) 136b, The opinion which some hold, that every hare should bee of both kindes, that is, male and female. **1590** SPENSER *F.Q.* III. ii. 4 To aske ..what inquest Made her dissemble her disguised kind.

†**b.** The sexual organs. (L. *natura*.) *Obs. rare.*

c **1000** ÆLFRIC *Gen.* ix. 23 Sem and Iafeth..beheledon heora fæderes ȝecynd [cf. 22 ȝesceapu]. **a 1325** *Life Adam* 110 in Horstm. *Altengl. Leg.* (1878) 140 Aiþer of oþer aschamed was And hiled her kinde wiþ more and gras.

†**c.** The semen. *Obs. rare.*

a 1450 MYRC 1046 Take also wel in mynde, ȝef þou haue sched þyn owne kynde Slepynge or wakynge. **1552** HULOET, Kynde naturall of euerye thynge, *semen.*

8. a. The manner or way natural or proper to any one; hence, mode of action; manner, way, fashion. Freq. in phr. ***in any, no, some, that, this kind***; ***in a kind***, in a way. Common in 17th c.; now *arch.*

a 900 *O.E. Martyrol.* 25 Dec. 2 Þy ȝeare maniȝ seah.. lamb spæcan on mennisc ȝecynde. **a 1000** *Salomon & Sat.* 499 Swa ðonne feohteð se feond on feower ȝecynd. **a 1330** *Roland & V.* 310 Braunches of vines Charls sett, In marche moneþ..As was þe riȝt kende. *c* **1374** CHAUCER *Troylus* II. 904 (855) Þis þyng stant al in a noþer kynde. **1483** CAXTON *G. de la Tour* xxi. L iij, An ordenaunce of a moche sauage and wyld guyse and ageynst the kynde of the tyme. *c* **1560** A. SCOTT *Poems* (S.T.S.) iii. 4 Cast ȝow to conqueiss luve ane vþir kind. **1593** DRAYTON *Eclogues* x. 71 The Birds and Beasts yet in their simple Kinde Lament for me. **1631** GOUGE *God's Arrows* III. §75. 325 Such was Deborahs and Baraks kind of praising God. **1646** EVANCE *Noble Ord.* 29 The worke..tended in a kinde to Gods honour. **1691** T. H[ALE] *Acc. New Invent.* 31 Being in no kind desirous that his Majesty should be under any Obligation. **1709** STEELE *Tatler* No. 47 ⁋3, I have done Wonders in this Kind. **1766** FORDYCE *Serm. Yng. Wom.* Pref., Nothing in the kind.. having been endeavoured before. **1803-6** WORDSW. *Intimations* vi, Yearnings she hath in her own natural kind. **1859** TENNYSON *Elaine* 321 Mirthful he, but in a stately kind.

b. ***the worst kind*** used advb. = severely, extremely, very badly. *U.S. colloq.* ? *Obs.*

1839 F. MARRYAT *Diary Amer.* II. 227 he loves Sal, the worst kind. **1877** BARTLETT *Dict. Amer.* (ed. 4) *Worst Kind.* Used in such phrases as..'I licked him the worst kind', *i.e.*, in the worst manner possible, most severely. **1892** *Harper's Mag.* Feb. 437/2, I want something to read the worst kind. **1901** M. E. RYAN *That Girl Montana* xvii. 221 Now that you have got here, I'd hate the worst kind to lose you. **1904** *N. Y. Tribune* 26 June, 'So you want to go to Cuba, do you?'.. 'I do, worst kind.'

9. Character as determining the class to which a thing belongs (cf. sense 13); generic or specific nature or quality; esp. in phr. ***in kind*** (rendering L. *in genere* or *in specie*), used with reference to agreement or difference between things, and freq. contrasted with *in degree*.

1628 FORD *Lover's Mel.* III. iii, Pray, my lord, [*Gives the paper-plot*] Hold and observe the plot; 'tis there express'd In kind, what shall be now express'd in action. **1663** BUTLER *Hud.* I. iii. 1279 Though they do agree in kind, Specifick difference we find. **1665** BOYLE *Occas. Refl.* II. iii. (1848) 104 'Tis all one..whether our Afflictions be the same with those of others, in Kind, or not Superiour to them in Degree. **1827** POLLOCK *Course T.* VIII, All faith was one: in object, not in kind, The difference lay. **1868** NETTLESHIP *Browning* iii. 105 There are such wide differences in degree as to constitute almost differences in kind.

II. A class, group, or division of things.

In this branch the senses of *kind* originally ran closely parallel with those of KIN; but later usage has so differentiated the words that there is now very little overlapping.

10. a. A race, or a natural group of animals or plants having a common origin; = KIN[1] 5. Cf. MANKIND, etc.

c **888** K. ÆLFRED *Boeth.* xxxv. §4 Nis nan ȝecynd þe wið hire scippendes willan winne buton dysiȝ mon. **971** *Blickl. Hom.* 37 Ne forseoh þu næfre þine ȝecynd. **a 1000** *Elene* 735 Ne mæȝ þær manna ȝecynd of eorðweȝum up ȝeferan. **a 1300** *Cursor M.* 14909 (Gött.) Þat he for manes [*Cott.* mans] kind wil dei. **13..** *Leg. Rood* 145 Til God þat dyed for vch a kuynde For Monnes kuynde deyde. *c* **1400** *Destr. Troy* 4300 Goddes son of heuyn..come to our kynde throgh a cleane Maydon. **a 1577** SIR T. SMITH *Commw. Eng.* (1633) 25 Without this society of man and woman the kind of man could not long endure. **1592** SHAKS. *Ven. & Ad.* 1018 Till mutual overthrow of mortal kind. **1610** —— *Temp.* v. i. 23 My selfe, one of their kinde. **1667** MILTON *P.L.* VI. 73 As when the total kind Of Birds..Came summond over Eden. **1697** DRYDEN *Virg. Geog.* I. 95 Whence Men, a hard laborious Kind were born. **1726** G. ROBERTS *4 Yrs. Voy.* 153 They would sooner starve than eat any Thing that lived upon human Kind. **1774** GOLDSM. *Nat. Hist.* (1862) I. 239 The Rabbit kind. **1784** COWPER *Task* v. 69 The sparrows.. often scared As oft return, a pert voracious kind. **1816** BYRON *Ch. Har.* III. xxxi, Each..a ghastly gap did make In his own kind and kindred. **1876** MORRIS *Sigurd* III. 212 The cunning of the Dwarf-kind.

b. Used in poetry, with defining word, in the general sense of 'race'.

1362 LANGL. *P. Pl.* A. XI. 282 Poule þe apostil þat no pite ne hadde, Cristene kynde to kille to deþe. **1599** SHAKS. *Hen. V*, II. i. 80 Fetch forth the Lazar Kite of Cressids kinde. **1735** SOMERVILLE *Chase* III. 309 Thus Man innum'rous Engines forms, t' assail The savage Kind. **1739** COLLINS *Ep. Hanmer* 138 Poets ever were a careless kind. **1847** EMERSON *Poems* (1857) 207 The men are ripe of Saxon kind To build an equal state.

†**c.** A class (of human beings or animals) of the same sex; a sex (in collective sense). *Obs.*

1552 HULOET s.v., *Sexus fœmineus*, womankinde, or the female kynde. **1564** tr. *Jewel's Apol.* Ded., J.'s Wks. (Parker Soc.) 51 Besides the honour ye have done to the kind of women..ye have done pleasure to the author of the Latin work. **1697** DRYDEN *Virg. Georg.* III. 332 Far from the Charms of that alluring Kind. **1735** POPE *Ep. Lady* 207 In Men, we various Ruling Passions find; In Women, two almost divide the kind.

†**11. a.** A subdivision of a race of the same descent; a family, clan, tribe, etc. Also (with possessive pron.), One's family, clan, kin, or kinsfolk. = KIN[1] 1, KINDRED 2. *Obs.*

c **1205** LAY. 23176 King heo wolden habben of seoluen heore cunden. **1297** R. GLOUC. (Rolls) 3434 King he was of westsex, & is ofspring al so, & atte laste þulke kunde alle þe oþere wan þer to. **13..** *Minor Poems fr. Vernon MS.* 249 At þe grete day of dome..þei schul sitte on twelf seges wel And Iugge þe twelf kuyndes of Israel. **1513** DOUGLAS *Æneis* XII. xiii. 111 The kynd of men discend from thir Troianis, Mydlyt with kyn of the Italianis. **1596** DALRYMPLE tr. *Leslie's Hist. Scot.* I. 76 The affectione that ilk had to his awne kinde. **1697** DRYDEN *Virg. Georg.* III. 433 The Parent Wind, Without the Stallion, propagates the Kind.

†**b.** Offspring, brood, progeny; descendants; = KIN[1] 1 b, KINDRED 2 b. *Obs.*

c **1000** *Narrat. Angl. Conscript.* (Cockayne) 35 Hyra ȝecynda on weorold bringaþ. *c* **1250** *Gen. & Ex.* 650 And or he was on werlde led, His kinde was wel wide spred. **a 1300** *Cursor M.* 14864 Vr crist suld be born o bethleem, o dauid kind. **1393** LANGL. *P. Pl.* C. XIX. 224 A book of þe olde lawe, þat a-corsed alle couples þat no kynde forth brouhte. *c* **1460** *Towneley Myst.* vi. 21, I shall thi seede multyply,..The kynd of the shall sprede wide. **1582** N. T. (Rhem.) *Acts* xvii. 28 Of his kinde also we are.

†**c.** A generation; = KIN[1] 1 c, KINDRED 2 c. *Obs. rare.*

a 1325 *Prose Psalter* lxxxviii[i]. 2 Y shal tellen þy soþe-nesses in my mouþe fro kynde to kynde. **1526** TINDALE *Luke* xvi. 8 The chyldren of this worlde are in their kynde, wyser then the chyldren of light [so *Geneva* 1557].

†**d.** Descent, genealogy; = KIN[1] 1 d, KINDRED 2 d. *Obs. rare.*

c **1330** R. BRUNNE *Chron. Wace* (Rolls) 363 Þys þe kynde, fro gre til gre, Bytwyxten Eneas & Noe.

12. The family, ancestral race, or stock from which one springs; = KIN[1] 2, KINDRED 3. *arch.*

a 1300 *Cursor M.* 10161 Sir Ioachim o kinges kind Was commin. *c* **1330** *Amis & Amil.* 8 Here faders were barouns hende, Lordynges y-come of grete kende. *c* **1386** CHAUCER *Sec. Nun's T.* 121 Cecilie..Was comen of Romayns and of noble kynde. **1608** SHAKS. *Per.* v. i. 68 [If she] came of a gentle kind and noble stock. **1724** RAMSAY *Tea-t. Misc.* (1733) I. 114 My Cromie is a useful cow And she is come of a good kyne. **1816** SCOTT *Antiq.* xl, The oyster loves the dredging sang, For they come of a gentle kind. **1854-6** PATMORE *Angel in Ho.* II. II. (1866) 244 Good families are so, Less through their coming of good kind, Than [etc.].

13. a. A class of individuals or objects distinguished by attributes possessed in common; a genus or species; also, in vaguer sense: A sort, variety, or description. (= L. *genus*.) Now the chief sense.

something of the kind, something like the thing in question; ***nothing of the kind***, nothing at all like it. ***of a kind***, of some sort, not a typical or perfect specimen of the class.

a 1000 *Guthlac* 15 (Gr.) Of wlite wendað wæstma ȝecyndu. **a 1300** *Cursor M.* 8040 Bi frut and leef bath moght man see O quatkin kind was ilk[a] tre. **13..** *E.E. Allit. P.* B. 507 He..heuened vp an auter..& sette a sakerfyse þer-on of vch a ser kynde. *c* **1400** *Apol. Loll.* 90 Þe heþun men had sex kyndis of similacris. *c* **1400** *Destr. Troy* 8746 The tabernacle ..was atiryt..with triet stones, Of all kyndes. **1529** *Supplic. to King* (E.E.T.S.) 22 The Apostle Paul..descrybeth two kyndes of doctrynes. **1652** CULPEPPER *Eng. Physic.* 8 The most usual Kindes of Apples. **1694** *Acc. Sev. Late Voy.* II. (1711) 79, I saw but this one of the Kind. **1732** BERKELEY *Alciphr.* II. §7 Suppose you saw a fruit of a new untried kind. **1774** GOLDSM. *Nat. Hist.* (1776) IV. 321 Of the bear, there are three different kinds. **1845** M. PATTISON *Ess.* (1889) I. 13 Barbarisms and solecisms of all kinds abound. **1862** TROLLOPE *Orley F.* xiv. 111 There was never anything of the kind before. **1871** FREEMAN *Norm. Conq.* (1876) IV. xvii. 55 Something of the kind had been done. **1875** JOWETT *Plato* (ed. 2) IV. 6 Before we can reply with exactness, we must know the kinds of pleasure and the kinds of knowledge. **1895** *Scot. Antiq.* X. 79 They had haversacks of a kind with them, but very little in them.

b. *Eccl.* In phrase ***in*** (***under***, †***with***) ***one kind***, ***both kinds*** (= med.L. *species*), referring to each of the elements (bread and wine) used in the sacrament of the Eucharist.

1539 *Act 31 Hen. VIII*, c. 14 Whether it be necessary.. that al men should be communicate with bothe kindes or no. **1635** PAGITT *Christianogr.* I. iii. (1636) 104 They must communicate in both kindes, both of the bread and the wine. **a 1770** JORTIN *Serm.* (1771) V. xiii. 293 The Church of Rome gives the Communion in one kind. **1869** FREEMAN *Norm. Conq.* III. xi. 16 *note*, Communion in both kinds was certainly usual at this time. **1880** LITTLEDALE *Plain Reas.* xxviii. 76 Christ is received entire under each kind.

c. A literary genre.

1667 DRYDEN *Annus Mirabilis 1666* Pref., Those who write correctly in this kind [*sc.* quatrains] must needs acknowledge, that the last line of the Stanza is to be consider'd in the composition of the first. **1908** H. JAMES *Awkward Age* Pref. p. xvii, 'Kinds' are the very life of literature, and truth and strength come from the complete recognition of them. **1943** J. T. SHIPLEY *Dict. World Lit.* (1945) 346 *Kind*, term used esp. in 17th and 18th c. Eng. for genre or class of work, *e.g.* epic, tragedy. **1966** G. HOUGH *Ess. on Crit.* xiii. 83 The impetus to the theory of kinds was initially given by Aristotle, who discussed tragedy, comedy and epic as separate genres.

14. a. Kind of. Later usage transposes the syntactical relation in such constructions as ***all kinds of trees*** = 'trees of all kinds', ***this kind of thing*** = 'a thing of this kind'. For the history of this, see KIN[1] 6 b.

As the original genitive phrase was in attrib. relation to the following sb., the natural tendency is still to treat *all kind of*, *no kind of*, *what kind of*, etc. (like ME. *alkin*, *nakin*, *whatkin*), and, hence also, the simple *kind of* (colloq. *kind o'*, *kind a*, *kinder*), as an attrib. or adj. phrase qualifying the sb. Hence the uses in b, c, d.

c **1470** *K. Estmere* 193 in *Percy's Rel.*, He lett for no kind of thyng. **15..** *Sir Andrew Barton* xxxviii. in *Surtees Misc.* (1888) 74 They came fore noe kind of thinge, But Sir Andrewe Barton they would see. **a 1548** HALL *Chron.*, *Hen. VII* 3b, A newe kynde of sicknes came sodenly..into this Isle. **a 1568** ASCHAM *Scholem.* II. (Arb.) 157 A grekysh kind of writing. **1583** T. WATSON *Centurie of Loue* xcviii, Learne of me, what kinde a thing is Loue. **1596** DALRYMPLE tr. *Leslie's Hist. Scot.* IV. 244 Vtterlie abiecteng al kynd of hope of ony helth. *c* **1645** HOWELL *Lett.* II. liv, 'Twixt the rind and the Tree there is a Cotton or hempy kind of Moss. **1705** ADDISON *Italy* Pref., Vast Collections of all Kinds of Antiquities. **1798** FERRIAR *Illustr. Sterne* vi. 166 They must be a different kind of people. **1840** DICKENS *Old C. Shop* ii, In a secret, stealthy..kind of way. **1857** MAURICE *Ep. St. John* ii. 25 See whether this is not the kind of thing that he is telling us in all of them. *Mod.* Few people have any notion what kind of life many of the poor live.

b. The feeling that *kind of* was equivalent to an adj. qualifying the following sb., led to the use of *all*, *many*, *other*, *these*, *those*, and the like, with a plural verb and pronoun, when the sb. was plural, as in ***these kind of men have their use***. This is still common colloquially, though considered grammatically incorrect.

(Cf. the ME. use of *alkin*, *manykin*, *serekin*, etc.: see KIN. In quot. 1648, *other kind* is for the earlier *other kin*.)

1382 WYCLIF *Matt.* xiii. 47 A nette sent in to the see, and of alle kynd of fishis gedrynge. **1564** *Brief Exam.* B iv b, It is not lawfull to vse these kinde of vestures. **1586** LD. BURGHLEY in *Leycester Corr.* (Camden) 360 Fittest to impeche thos kind of havens. **1605** SHAKS. *Lear* II. ii. 107 These kind of Knaues I know. **a 1648** LD. HERBERT *Hen. VIII* (1683) 543 Because of his Nephew's minority, and other kind reasons. **1672** WILKINS *Nat. Relig.* 378 Of vertues containing in their very essence these kind of inward felicities. **1681** T. FLATMAN *Heraclitus Ridens* No. 43 (1713) II. 27 Such kind of Pamphlets work Wonders with the credulous Multitude. **1797** HOLCROFT *Stolberg's Trav.* (ed. 2) III. lxxxii. 323 These kind of barracks..are..more expensive. *Mod.* What kind of trees are those?

c. ***a kind of***..: A sort of..; a (person or thing) of a kind; an individual that is, or may be, included in the class in question, though not possessing its full characteristics.

A kind of gentleman and *a gentleman of a kind* differ in that the former expresses approach to the type, admitting failure to reach it, while the latter emphasizes the non-typical position of the individual. Hence, *a kind of* may be used as a saving qualification, as in 'a kind of knave'.

1591 SHAKS. *Two Gent.* III. i. 262, I haue the wit to thinke my Master is a kinde of a knaue. **1598** —— *Merry W.* I. i. 215 There is as 'twere a tender, a kinde of tender, made a farre-off by Sir Hugh here. **1670** NARBOROUGH *Jrnl.* in *Acc. Sev. Late Voy.* I. (1711) 81 Very little Grass, the Woods are so thick; much kind of long sedgy Grass. **1719** DE FOE *Crusoe* II. xvi, I..thought myself a kind of a monarch. **1734** tr. *Rollin's Anc. Hist.* (1827) II. II. 110 Only a kind of huts were built there. **1761** WESLEY *Jrnl.* 10 June, One, a kind of gentleman, seemed displeased. **1824** MISS MITFORD *Village* Ser. I. (1868) 94 Dash is a sort of a kind of a spaniel. **1832** L. HUNT *Poems, Pomfret's 'Choice'*, A pretty kind of sort of kind of thing. **1860** TYNDALL *Glac.* I. ix. 62 The rock..bent by the pressure so as to form a kind of arch.

d. *colloq.* ***kind of*** (vulgarly ***kind o'***, ***kind a'***, ***kinder***, etc.) is used adverbially: In a way, as it were, to some extent. Also ***kind of sort of***, ***kinder sorter*** (see SORT *sb.*[2] 8 c).

The adverbial use arises out of the adjectival: cf. 'She was a mother *of a kind* to me', 'She was a *kind of* mother to me', 'she *kind o'* mothered me'.

1804 T. G. FESSENDEN *Orig. Poems* 100, I kind of love you, Sal—I vow. **1830** *Massachusetts Spy* 6 Jan. 1/5, I was kind of provoked at the way you came up. **1834** C. A. DAVIS *Lett. Jack Downing* 90 This kinder corner'd me, and made me a little wrathy. **1849** DICKENS *Dav. Copp.* lxiii, 'Theer's been kiender a blessing fell upon us', said Mr. Peggotty. **1855** T. C. HALIBURTON *Nat. & Hum. Nat.* I. vi. 190, I rather kinder sorter guess so, than kinder sorter not so. **1857** HOLLAND *Bay Path* x. 120, I kind a' backed him down, I thought. **1861** LEVER *One of them* xvi. 125 This is a kinder droll way to welcome a friend. **1871** ALEXANDER *Johnny Gibb* ix. (1892) 56 He's jist a kin' o' daumer't i' the heid like. **1885** HOWELLS *Silas Lapham* (1891) I. 105 Didn't you like the way his sack-coat set?..kind of peeling away at the lapels? **1889** BOLDREWOOD *Robbery under Arms* xxxi, I kinder expected it. *Mod.Sc.* It had a kind o' sour taste. **1901** F. NORRIS *Octopus* I. iii. 102 Makes it go down kind of sort of slick. **1963** J. N. HARRIS *Weird World Wes Beattie* iii. 28 He was one of these handsome guys with a kind of ugly expression. **1967** *Boston Sunday Herald Mag.* 30 Apr. 34/3, I kind of want to choose my war since it's my life. **1973** *Washington Post* 5 Apr. B.2 Introducing him as 'my old man' and adding, 'We're kind of a middle-aged Sonny and Cher.'

15. ***in kind*** (rendering L. *in specie*: see SPECIE).

a. In the very kind of article or commodity in question; usually payment: In goods or natural produce, as opposed to money.

1622 BACON *Hen. VII*, Mor. & Hist. Wks. (Bohn, 1860) 426 He did..give the goods of all the prisoners unto those that had taken them; either to take them in kind, or compound for them. **1670** WALTON *Lives* II. 125 His very Food and Raiment were provided for him in kind. **1727**

SWIFT *To Earl of Oxford*, The farmers.. Force him to take his tythes in kind. *a* **1862** BUCKLE *Civiliz.* (1869) III. v. 329 Their revenues were mostly paid, not in money, but in kind, such as corn, wine and cattle.

b. Of repayment: In something of the same kind as that received. Chiefly *fig.*

1726 G. ROBERTS *4 Yrs. Voy.* Ded. A ij, Obligations you have laid me under,.. I despair of ever having the Opportunity to return them in Kind. **1819** SCOTT *Ivanhoe* xli, The best of them are most willing to repay my follies in kind. **1867** FREEMAN *Norm. Conq.* I. iv. 199 These incursions were more than repaid in kind.

III. 16. *attrib.* and *Comb.*, as †**'kind-blind** *a.*, blind by nature; †**'kindlike** *a.*, of like nature or character; natural; **kind payment**, payment in kind, or in natural produce instead of coin.

1608 SYLVESTER *Du Bartas* II. iv. IV. *Decay* 923 Imitating right The *Kinde-blinde Beast [the mole], in russet Velvet dight. **1579** J. STUBBES *Gaping Gulf* B viij b, Shall a French hart be *kindlike enough to rule our Queene? **1823** SCOTT *Quentin D.* vii, It was but natural and kindlike to help your young kinsman. **1828** P. CUNNINGHAM *N.S. Wales* (ed. 3) II. 81 The Bank establishment.. will, in all probability, ultimately extirpate even *kind payments in part. **1883** G. CULLEY in *Trans. Highland Soc. Agric.* Ser. IV. XV. 7 That part of my district in which the kind payment is most developed.

kind (kaɪnd), *a.* Forms: 1 ȝecynde (? cynde), 3 i-cunde, kunde, 3–4 cunde, kuynde; 4–5 kende, 5 keend; 3–6 kynde, 3–7 kinde, 4–6 kynd, 3– kind. [OE. *ȝecynde* (:—OTeut. **gakundjo-z*), f. **gakundi-*, *ȝecynd* nature, KIND *sb.*]

I. Natural, native.

†**1.** Of things, qualities, etc.: Natural, in various senses. *Obs.* **a.** That is, or exists, in accordance with nature or the usual course of things; = KINDLY *a.* 1 a.

c **888** K. ÆLFRED *Boeth.* xxxix. § 10 þone deað þe eallum monnum is ȝecynde to þolianne. *c* **1250** *Gen. & Ex.* 78 His firme kinde dei.. Of foure and twenti time riȝt; Ðes frenkis men.. It nemnen 'un iur natural'. *c* **1290** *St. Michael* 563 in *S. Eng. Leg.* I. 315 Bi-tweone somer and wynter.. þanne is þe þondre kuynde Inov. *c* **1320** *Sir Beues* (MS. A) 3662 Kende hit is, wimman te be Schamfaste and ful of corteisie. *c* **1330** R. BRUNNE *Chron. Wace* (Rolls) 10610 Of hym more men fynde In farre bokes, als ys kynde, þan we haue in þys lond. **1579** GOSSON *Ephem. Phialo*, It is but kinde for a Cockes heade to breede a Combe.

†**b.** Implanted by nature; innate; inherent; = KINDLY *a.* 1 b. Const. *to*, *for*, or dat. *Obs.*

Beowulf 2696 Ellen cyðan, cræft and cenðu, swa him ȝecynde wæs. *c* **1000** *Cædmon's Gen.* 2771 (Gr.) Swa him cynde wæron. *c* **1200** ORMIN 8336 Herode king,.. wass ifell mann inoh, & well it wass himm kinde. **1362** LANGL. *P. Pl.* A. I. 127 'Yit haue I no kuynde knowing' quod I, 'þou most teche me betere'. *c* **1430** *Pol. Rel. & L. Poems* 198 And how kinde and propir it is to þee,.. On hem to haue mercy and pitee. **1522** *World & Child* in Hazl. *Dodsley* I. 245 All recklessness is kind for thee.

†**c.** Naturally pertaining to, or associated with, a person or thing; proper, appropriate, fitting; = KINDLY *a.* 1 c. In later use const. *for*. *Obs.*

a **1000** *Boeth. Metr.* xiii. 63 Oð his eft cymeð þær hire yfemesð bið eard ȝecynde. **1297** R. GLOUC. (Rolls) 5900 þat child.. dude is kunde fulþhede. *a* **1300** *Cursor M.* 9380 Til alkin thing he gafe, þair kinde scrud al for to haue. *c* **1374** CHAUCER *Troylus* IV. 768 (740) How sholde a plaunte or lyues creature, Lyue with-oute his kynde noriture? *c* **1400** *Destr. Troy* Prol. 70 A Romayn.. That Cornelius was cald to his kynde name. **1540** HYRDE tr. *Vives' Instr. Chr. Wom.* (1592) X ij, No honest women.. but such as be sham-lesse, and worthy of kind rebuke. **1663** J. BEAL *Let.* in *Boyle's Wks.* (1772) VI. 357 What hay is kindest for sheep. **1694** WESTMACOTT *Script. Herb.* 9 Cyder is a kind vehicle and proper menstruum for medical matters.

†**2. a.** Belonging to one by right of birth, descent, or inheritance; lawful, rightful; = KINDLY *a.* 2. *Obs.*

a **1000** *Daniel* 3 ȝefræȝn ic Hebreos.. cyningdom habban, swa him ȝecynde wæs. *c* **1205** LAY. 18158 Nim þu þene kinhelm; he is þe icunde. *c* **1320** *Sir Beues* (MS. A) 2940 Ȝif ich miȝte wiþ eni ginne Me kende eritage to winne. *c* **1470** HENRY *Wallace* x. 1055 And tak the croun; till ws it war kyndar, To bruk for ay, or fals Eduuard it war. **1570** *Satir. Poems Reform.* xiii. 130 Ȝe.. Baneist his Gud-schir from his kynde heritage.

†**b.** Native (country or language). *Obs.*

c **1250** *Gen. & Ex.* 1279 [It] was noȝt is kinde lond. **13..** R. GLOUC. (Rolls) 7544 (MS. β) In þe world ne is.. countrey none þat he ne holdeþ his kynde speche, bote engelond now one. *c* **1440** *Eng. Conq. Irel.* 7 Man thynkyth no Place so Myrry lyghtly as in his Kynd Place. **1513** DOUGLAS *Æneis* v. xiii. 82 As thi kind ground and cuntre naturale.

†**3.** Of persons. *Obs.* **a.** Lawful, rightful (lord, heir, tenant, etc.). Cf. KINDLY *a.* 3.

a **1000** *Boeth. Metr.* i. 6 Gotan.. hæfdan him ȝecynde cyningas tweȝen. *a* **1100** *O.E. Chron.* (Laud MS.) an. 1014, Him nan leofre hlaford nære þonne heora ȝecynde hlaford. **1297** R. GLOUC. (Rolls) 6429 þe kunde eirs to bitraye. *c* **1320** *Sir Beues* (MS. A) 1398 Ariseþ vp.. And wolcomeþ ȝour kende lord. *c* **1440** *Bone Flor.* 1259 And crowne Mylys my brodur.. For kyndyst heyre ys hee.

†**b.** Native; = KINDLY *a.* 3 b. Also with *to*. *rare*. *Obs.*

1297 R. GLOUC. (Rolls) 851 Many kundemen of þis lond Mid king Leir hulde also. *Ibid.* 937 þe kunde volc of þe lond adde to hom onde. **1375** BARBOUR *Bruce* IX. 448 Thai war kynde to the cuntre.

†**c.** Having a specified character by nature, or a specified status by birth; by birth, natural, born.

c **1350** *Will. Palerne* 241 A kowherde, sire, of þis kontrey is my kynde fader. *Ibid.* 513 þouȝh he were komen of no ken, but of kende cherls. **1484** CAXTON *Fables of Æsop* v. v, Suche supposeth to be moche wyse whiche is a kynd and a very foole. **1589** GREENE *Menaphon* (Arb.) 63, I thought no lesse .. that you would proue such a kinde kistrell.

†**d.** Related by kinship; of kin (*to*); one's own (people). *Obs.*

1297 R. GLOUC. (Rolls) 8240 þe sarazins.. wende toward antioche, to helpe hor kunde blod. **1387–8** T. USK *Test. Love* I. vi. (Skeat) I. 49 How turned the Romaine Zeodories fro the Romaines, to be with Haniball ayenst his kind nacion. **1509** BARCLAY *Shyp of Folys* (1874) I. 285 Than shall he rewarde them in heven right gloriously So mayst thou be callyd unto thy maker kynde.

II. Of good birth, kind, nature or disposition.

(Sense 4 forms the link between I and II. Cf. L. *generōsus*.)

4. †**a.** Well-born, well-bred, of generous or gentle birth, gentle (*obs.*). **b.** Of a good kind; hence, good of its kind, having the natural (good) qualities well developed. Now only *dial.* Cf. KINDLY *a.* 4.

c **1250** *Gen. & Ex.* 1451 Ysaac he let al his god, For he was bigeten of kinde blod. *c* **1300** *St. Margarete* 2 Ibore heo was in Antioche, icome of cunde blod. **1393** LANGL. *P. Pl.* C. III. 29 Ne on croked kene þorne kynde fygys wexe. *a* **1400–50** *Alexander* 2459 þai crosse ouir toward þe kyng, as kyndmen [*Dubl. MS.* kene men] suld. **1579** GOSSON *Sch. Abuse* (Arb.) 58 The kindest Mastife, when he is clapped on the back, fighteth best. *a* **1656** HALES *Gold. Rem.* (1688) 218 As Men graff Apples and kind fruits upon Thorns. **1756** P. BROWNE *Jamaica* 136 It is a hardy and kind pasturage. **1890** *Gloucester Gloss.*, *Kind*, healthy, likely, in perfection, thriving. A kind barley is one that malts well. **1891** S. C. SCRIVENER *Our Fields & Cities* 143 The cultivation so far having been perfect, the barley crop will be 'kind'.

5. Of persons: Naturally well-disposed; having a gentle, sympathetic, or benevolent nature; ready to assist, or show consideration for, others; †generous, liberal, courteous (*obs.*). Also of disposition. (This (with c and d) is now the main sense.)

a **1300** *Cursor M.* 20033 Sua kind.. ar þou þat þou nu will mi wil a-lou. *c* **1386** CHAUCER *Clerk's T.* 796 How gentil and how kynde Ye semed, by youre speche, and youre visage. *c* **1430** *Syr Tryam.* 240 An olde knyght.. That curtes was and kynde. **1567** *Gude & Godlie B.* (S.T.S.) 19 We thank our God baith kynde and liberall. **1610** SHAKS. *Temp.* III. iii. 20 Giue vs kind keepers, heauens. **1681** DRYDEN *Sp. Friar* Prol. 1 Now, luck for us, and a kind hearty pit. **1732** POPE *Ep. Cobham* I. 110 Who does a kindness, is not there-fore kind. **1781** COWPER *Truth* 251 Some mansion.. By some kind, hospitable heart possessed. **1849** MACAULAY *Hist. Eng.* iii. I. 424 We have.. become, not only a wiser, but also a kinder people.

fig. **1576** GASCOIGNE *Philomene* (Arb.) 98 Could no kinde coale, nor pitties sparke Within thy brest be plaste. **1634** MILTON *Comus* 187 Such cooling fruit As the kind hospitable Woods provide. **1676** DRYDEN *Aurengz.* III. i. 1502 Your kinder Stars a Nobler Choice have giv'n. **1704** POPE *Windsor For.* 53 In vain kind seasons swell'd the teeming grain. **1840** DICKENS *Old C. Shop* i, Night is kinder in this respect than day.

†**b.** Well or favourably disposed *to*; bearing good will *to*. *Obs.*

1664 CHAS. II in Cartwright *Madame* (1894) 175 The Comte de Gramont will give you this, and he will tell you how kind I am to you. **1666** SIR J. TALBOT *Let.* in *Slingsby's Diary* (1836) 369, I hope you are not soe little kind to mee as to censure this freedome I use. **1680–90** TEMPLE *Ess., Ireland* Wks. 1731 I. 125 It is.. little to be hoped, that a Breach with Spain should make us any kinder to the War than we were.

c. Exhibiting a friendly or benevolent disposition by one's conduct *to* a person or animal. Also *fig.*

c **1315** SHOREHAM 90 Ha wole be the so kende, He wole be fo to thyne fon, And frend to thyne frende. **1362** LANGL. *P. Pl.* A. XI. 243 þat is, iche cristene man be kynde to oþer, And siþen hem to helpe. ? **1507** *Communyc.* (W. de W.) B iij, Euer the kynder to me thou arte The more unkynder I am agayne. **1590** SHAKS. *Mids. N.* III. i. 167 Be kinde and curteous to this Gentleman. **1606** —— *Ant. & Cl.* III. ii. 40 The Elements be kind to thee. **1707** LADY M. W. MONTAGU *Let. to Anne Wortley* 2 May, I hope you intend to be kinder to me this summer than you were the last. **1807** CRABBE *Par. Reg.* III. 842 Kind to the poor, and ah! most kind to me. **1840** DICKENS *Barn. Rudge* (1849) 96/1 'You had as good be kinder to me'.. said Hugh. *Mod.* They were exceedingly kind; they insisted upon our staying till our clothes were dry.

d. Of action, language, etc.: Arising from or displaying a kind disposition.

c **1400** *Destr. Troy* 2155 Myche comforth he caght of þaire kynd speche. **1551** CROWLEY *Pleas. & Pain* 27 You.. gaue me wordis curteyse and kynde. **1670** EARL ANGLESEY in *12th Rep. Hist. MSS. Comm.* App. v. 15 My sonne is at Newmarket.. or else would acknowledge your Ladyship's kind mention of him. **1779–81** JOHNSON *L.P.*, *Milton* Wks. II. 134 *Paradise Lost* broke into open view with sufficient security of kind reception. **1846** TENNYSON in *Mem.* (1897) 239 Your kind letter gave me very sincere pleasure.

6. Of persons, their actions, etc.: Affectionate, loving, fond; on intimate terms. Also *euphemistically*. Now *rare* exc. *dial.*

1297 R. GLOUC. (Rolls) 724 þine sostren ssolleþ abbe al, vor hor herte is so kunde, & þou ssalt vor þin vnkundhede be out of al min munde. *c* **1350** *Will. Palerne* 3474 Wiþ clipping & kessing & alle kinde dedus. **1526** *Pilgr. Perf.* (W. de W. 1531) 4 b, If they had ben kynde & louynge to god. **1594** CONSTABLE *Diana* VIII. i, Women are kind by kind, but coy by fashion. **1698** FRYER *Acc. E. India & P.* 110 The next Moon their Women flock to the Sacred Wells; where, they say, it is not difficult to persuade them to be kind. **1704** POPE *Autumn* 52 Do lovers dream, or is my Delia kind? **1735** —— *Ep. Lady* 94 A Spark too fickle, or a Spouse too kind. **1825** BROCKETT, *Kind*, intimate—*not kind*, at enmity. **1870** TENNYSON *Window* 184 Stiles where we stay'd to be kind, Meadows in which we met.

†**7.** Acceptable, agreeable, pleasant, winsome; = KINDLY *a.* 6. *Obs.*

In early use transl. L. *grātus*, which in med.L. had the sense of 'gentle, kind' as well as its correct sense of 'pleasing'. In later use passing into fig. use of 5, 5 d.

c **1340** *Cursor M.* 6509 (Trin.) þis moyses was dere & kynde To god. **1398** TREVISA *Barth. De P.R.* XVII. xcvii. (Tollem. MS.), This flexe is nouȝt moste stronge, but ..þerof is kynde [L. *gratissimæ*] vestimentes made for prestes. **1703** ROWE *Ulyss.* I. i. 98, I have the kindest Sounds to bless your Ear with. **1774** GOLDSM. *Nat. Hist.* (1862) I. 15 Though at a kinder distance.

8. Grateful, thankful. *Obs.* exc. *dial.*

c **1450** tr. *De Imitatione* II. x. 54 Be kynde þerfore for a litel þinge, & þou shalt be worþi to take gretter. **1530** PALSGR. 316/2 Kynde that remembreth a good torne, *grat.* **1563** *Homilies* II. *Time of Prayer* I. (1859) 339 He should declare himself thankful and kind, for all those benefits. **1610** B. JONSON *Alch.* v. iv, *Sob.* Why doe you not thanke her Grace? *Dap.* I cannot speake, for ioy. *Sob.* See, the kind wretch! **1877** *N.W. Linc. Gloss.* s.v., I'm very kind to Mrs...'cause she sent me them coals i' th' winter.

9. *dial.* or *techn.* Soft, tender; easy to work.

1747 W. HOOSON *Miner's Dict.* U ij b, We drive at the Vein Head in the first Place, because there it is likely that the Vein may be the most Kind or Leppey. **1828** *Craven Dial.*, *Kind*, soft. 'As kind as a glove.' *Kind-harled*, soft-haired. **1831** J. HOLLAND *Manuf. Metal* I. 243 To distinguish between hard and kind steel, that is, between steel that has been more or less carbonated. **1848** KEARY in *Jrnl. R. Agric. Soc.* IX. II. 429 Breeders.. are now fully alive to the importance of kind hair and good flesh in a feeding beast. **1883** GRESLEY *Gloss. Coal Mining* 147 *Kind* generally signifies tender, soft, or easy to work.

III. 10. As *adv.* = KINDLY. (Here perh. belongs the phr. *to take it kind*.) Now *colloq.* or *vulgar*.

1607 SHAKS. *Timon* I. ii. 225, I take all, and your seuerall visitations So kinde to heart. **1725** RAMSAY *Gent. Sheph.* I. i, Ye.. wha have sae kind Redd up my ravel'd doubts. **1750** H. WALPOLE *Lett.* (1845) II. 354 He took it mighty kind. **1781** JOHNSON 3 June in *Boswell*, Tell him, if he'll call on me ..I shall take it kind. **1800** MRS. HERVEY *Mourtray Fam.* III. 102 All this would be mighty well.. if Lady C. behaved kind and tenderly to you. **1849** DICKENS *Dav. Copp.* xlii, 'How kind he puts it!' said Uriah.

IV. 11. *Comb.*, as ***kind-minded***, ***-tempered***, ***-thoughted***, ***-witted***; ***kind-contending***; ***kind-cruel***.

1377 LANGL. *P. Pl.* B. XII. 109 Namore kan a kynde witted man.. Come for al his kynde witte to crystendome and be saued. **1591** SYLVESTER *Du Bartas* I. vi. 48 Pierc't with glance of a kinde-cruell eye. **1727–46** THOMSON *Summer* 39 The kind-temper'd change of night and day. **1728–46** —— *Spring* 596 The thrush And woodlark o'er the kind-contending throng Superior heard. **1858** FABER *Spir. Confer.* (1870) 25 The kind-thoughted man has no.. self-importance to push.

†**kind**, *v.* *Obs. rare.*

1. [app. f. prec. adj.] *trans.* ? To treat kindly.

a **1450** *Knt. de la Tour* (1868) 112 The hynde.. whanne the moder of other bestis be slaine, yet wolle she gladly of her gentille nature norishe the yonge.. and kindithe hem tille they may susteine hem selff.

2. [f. KIND *sb.*] In *pa. pple.* Sprung, begotten. ? *pseudo-arch.*

1596 SPENSER *F.Q.* V. v. 40 Not borne of Beares and Tygres, nor so salvage mynded As that.. She yet forgets that she of men was kynded.

kinda ('kaɪndə), colloq. shortening of *kind of* (see KIND *sb.* 14).

1912 *Collier's* 12 Oct. 18/2 He.. started whistling to himself kinda soft. **1925** T. DREISER *Amer. Trag.* (1926) I. xii. 83 He's kinda soft on me, you know. **1935** 'R. WEST' *Harsh Voice* ii. 132, I kinda like being way out beyond everywhere. **1945** A. KOBER *Parm Me* 17, I feel kinda stuffed up. **1953** A. BARON *Human Kind* 185 Movies, shows, do you get a lot of that kinda thing? **1966** L. COHEN *Beautiful Losers* (1970) I. 72 Thank you, my friend, I guess you kinda saved my life. **1972** *Punch* 1 Mar. 278/2 This some new kinda gimmick? **1973** *Black World* July 56/1 Bop ain't goan bless me no kinda way.

kindcough, erron. variant of KINKCOUGH.

†**'kinded**, *a.* *rare.* [f. KIND *sb.* + -ED².] In *comb.* Of (such a) kind, as ***lean-kinded***.

1601 J. HARRINGTON *Let.* in *Monthly Rev.* XLII. 55 Many lean kinded beastes and some not unhorned.

kinder = *kind of*: see KIND *sb.* 14 d.

kindergarten ('kɪndəˌgɑːt(ə)n). [a. Ger. *Kindergarten*, lit. 'children's garden'.] **1.** A school for the instruction of young children according to a method devised by Friedrich Froebel (1782–1852), for developing the intelligence of children by interesting object-lessons, exercises with toys, games, singing, etc. Also *attrib.* and *fig.*

The word was coined by Froebel in German in 1840: 'Entwurf.. eines Kinder-Gartens' 1 May 1840 in *Kindergarten-Briefe* (1887) 132.

('*Johannes Ronge*.. took refuge in England in 1850, and, with the assistance of his wife, established at his house a kinder-garten.' Allibone *Dict. Authors*.)

1852 MOTLEY *Corr.* (1889) I. v. 145 Mary has not yet found a school. We have sent her to a kindergarten. **1854** *Rep. to Governor of Connecticut* in *Encycl. Brit.* XIV. 80 The first kindergarten was opened at Blankenburg, near Rudolstadt, in 1840. **1855** RONGE (*title*) Practical Guide to

the English Kinder Garten. **1869** *Macm. Mag.* July 221/1 Singing a few Kinder Garten songs with movements in unison. **1874** H. Hoffmann *Kindergarten Toys* 31 Having become well acquainted with the first Six Gifts of the Kindergarten, children will be fitted to proceed to the more advanced Kindergarten Amusements. **1878** *N. Amer. Rev.* CXXVI. 370 Such as would be of use in a Kindergarten. **1890** W. James *Princ. Psychol.* I. xi. 443 In kindergarten instruction one of the exercises is to make the children see how many features they can point out in such an object as a flower or a stuffed bird. **1926** T. E. Lawrence *Seven Pillars* xxxiv. 195 We kindergarten soldiers were beginning our art of war in the atmosphere of the twentieth century. *Ibid.* lxxxiii. 442 They refused to learn from me.. and I could not be bothered to set up a kindergarten of the imagination for their benefit. **1942** *Tee Emm* (Air Ministry) II. 148 We can still do with a few more chaps.. but be fit, because this ain't no kindergarten. **1945** E. Waugh *Brideshead Revisited* II. i. 207 The painted panels of the walls were like kindergarten work in flat, drab colours. **1961** *Facts about Korea* (Pyongyang, N. Korea) 156 For the working women and their children, a great number of creches and kindergartens are established in factories. **1968** *Harrods Christmas Catal.* 22/1 A kindergarten toy which is lots of fun.

2. *transf.* The nickname given to a group of young men with imperialist ideals who were recruited by Alfred, Lord Milner (1854–1925), High Commissioner of South Africa, to aid with reconstruction work after the South African war of 1899–1902. Freq. ***Milner's kindergarten.***

1902 *Cape Times* 12 Sept. 6/10 Lord Milner described the nature of the government that was to be set up, which was a Council. He (Mr. Merriman) wondered what sort of rag-tag and bob-tail they would have got to sit on that Council. .. What did he expect to set up? A sort of kindergarten of young Balliol men—laughter—to govern this great country. **1913** W. B. Worsfold *Reconstruction New Colonies* I. x. 259 Mr Curtis was one of the most flagrant examples of Lord Milner's 'kindergarten'. **1958** *Spectator* 22 Aug. 244/3 The ideas of Milner and his dedicated 'kindergarten' about the treatment of the African. **1958** *Listener* 6 Nov. 739/3 Those were the days when the group of Englishmen who helped to bring order out of chaos and to prepare the way for the future came to be nicknamed Lord Milner's 'kindergarten'. **1971** *Oxf. Hist. S. Afr.* II. vii. 331 Locally he appointed young Oxford graduates—'Milner's kindergarten'—to the administrative positions. *Ibid.* 346 To Selborne and the members of the Kindergarten.. unification was desirable.

Hence **'kinder'garten, -'gartenize** *vbs.*, to employ the kindergarten method; **'kinder,gartener (-gärtner)**, a kindergarten teacher; also, a pupil at a kindergarten; **'kinder,gartenism**, the kindergarten system.

1872 *Daily News* 1 Aug., You have been reading that article on Kinder Gartenism. [**1881** Fitch *Lect. Teaching* 198 Your thorough going *Kindergärtner*.] **1889** *Jrnl. Educ.* 1 Aug. 410/2 A band of kindergarteners who teach them the rudiments of education. **1893** J. Strong *New Era* xv. 340 There is.. no sectarian way of kindergartening. **1919** G. A. Miller *Prowling about Panama* ix. 129 *(caption)* Happy kindergartners, Panama. **1937** D. Aldis *Time at her Heels* v. 103 The procession would end with the kindergarteners, looking very bustling and important as they hurried towards the little red chairs reserved for them. **1967** *Boston Sunday Herald* 26 Mar. I. 35/7 There will be no school sessions for currently enrolled kindergarteners on that day. **1973** *Jrnl. Genetic Psychol.* CXXII. 255 Eighty children, 40 kindergarteners and 40 third-graders.

kinderkin(d, obs. variants of kilderkin.

‖**kinder, kirche, küche** ('kɪndə(r), 'kɪrçə, 'kʏçə). Also in different order. [G.] 'Children, church, kitchen'; a phrase, freq. used ironically, to denote the interests and preoccupations of a housewife.

1899 [See K 1.] **1935** D. L. Sayers *Gaudy Night* xxii. 453 The Nazi doctrine that woman's place in the State should be confined to the 'womanly' occupations of *Kinder, Kirche, Kuche*. **1953** E. Simon *Past Masters* III. iii. 155 Good heavens! *Kinder, Kirche, Küche*, however you pronounce it. Still.. at least you haven't given up smoking. **1963** *Economist* 10 Aug. 519/2 Her countrywomen are unhappy housewives trapped in the home by an ideal of *Kinder, Küche, Kirche* which is vigorously pressed by American educators,.. and husbands. **1965** R. Rendell *To fear Painted Devil* x. 124 He was an awfully *kinder, küche, kirche* sort of person, house-proud, passionately neat and tidy. **1968** R. Harris *Nice Girl's Story* xv. 112 As a wife, I should expect you to make it [*sc.* the bed]—*kinder, kirche, küche*, you know. **1970** W. Garner *Puppet-Masters* v. 40 He subscribed wholeheartedly to Hitler's womanly ideal of *Kinder, Küche, Kirche*. **1970** G. Greer *Female Eunuch* 303 The women students.. had not yet formed any clear idea of the disabilities which increasingly encumber women as they move.. towards *kinder* and *küche*.

kinderspiel ('kɪndəʃpi:l). [G.] A dramatic piece performed by children.

1902 *Daily Chron.* 19 Dec. 5/2 An opera.. and a kinderspiel are being rehearsed. **1930** *Aberdeen Press & Jrnl.* 28 Feb. 3/2 'Blossom Time', a pretty kinderspiel, was part of a delightful entertainment given.. by the Sunday School children.

† **'kindhead.** *Obs. rare.* Forms: see kind *a.* [f. kind *a.* + -head.] **a.** Kinship. **b.** Kindness.

1297 R. Glouc. (Rolls) 756 Þe king of scotlonde vor reuþe & for kundhede [*v.rr.* kundede, kyndehede, kuyndhede] Hym nom to hym in to his hows. *Ibid.* 10589 Heyemen of engelond.. Vor kundede hor herte to king henry bere. *Ibid.* 11834 Vor kundede of blode.

kind-hearted, *a.* [kind *a.* 11.] Having naturally a kind disposition.

1535 Coverdale *Song 3 Childr.* 67 O geue thankes therfore vnto yͤ Lorde: for he is kynde harted. *c* **1600** Shaks. *Sonn.* x, Be.. gracious and kind, Or to thy selfe at least kind harted proue. **1681** Dryden *Prol. Univ. Oxford* 6 Of our sisters, all the kinder-hearted [are] To Edenburgh gone. **1787** Sir J. Hawkins *Johnson* 336 He was by nature a friendly and kind-hearted man. **1860** G. H. K. in *Vac. Tour.* 116 Donald, kindest-hearted and keenest of stalkers.

Hence **kind'heartedness.**

1583 Golding *Calvin on Deut.* li. 303 That God had no pitie nor kindeheartednesse. *a* **1735** Arbuthnot *Gulliver Decypherd* Misc. Wks. 1751 I. 84 Noted for her kindheartedness to her Husband's Patients. **1896** Anne Elliott *Ld. Harborough* II. 264 All this gratified her importance.. and also her kindheartedness.

kind'heartedly, *adv.* [-ly².] In a kindhearted manner.

1900 H. C. Beeching in *Monthly Rev.* Nov. 91 The brass lectern, which the good sister.. kindheartedly uncovered for him. **1957** B. Spock *Common Sense Bk. Baby & Child Care* (new ed.) 148 Whenever her child has a crying spell in the daytime or wakes at night, she kind-heartedly makes another bottle for him. **1972** A. W. Read in *Current Trends in Linguistics* X. 588 Wentworth (1931) complained that *kindheartedly* was missing from all dictionaries, though he knew it from all sources; it was thereupon inserted into the Merriam-Webster of 1934.

† **'kindlaik.** *Obs. rare.* [f. kind *a.* + -laik.] Kindness.

a **1400–50** *Alexander* 2718 Quat bounte þou shewis, Quat curtassy & kyndlaike I ken alto-gedire.

kindle ('kɪnd(ə)l), *sb.* Forms: 3 kundel, *pl.* -les, 4 *pl.* kyndles, -(e)lis, 5 -yll, kindil, 7, 9 kindle. [Appears in early ME. (along with the cognate kindle *v.*²): app. a deriv. of *cynd-*, stem of *ȝecynd*, kind *sb.* Cf. G. *kind* child.]

† **1. a.** The young (of any animal), a young one. **b.** *collect.* A brood or litter (of kittens). *Obs.*

c **1220** *Bestiary* (Elephant) 620 Ðanne ȝe sal hire kindles beren, In water ȝe sal stonden. *a* **1225** *Ancr. R.* 82 Heo is neddre kundel. *Ibid.* 200 Þe Neddre of attri Onde haue[ð] seoue kundles. *c* **1380** Wyclif *Wks.* (1880) 2 Joon baptist and crist clepede hem ypocritis and serpentis and addir kyndles. **1486** *Bk. St. Albans* F vj, A Litter of welpis, a kyndyll of yong Cattis. **1688** R. Holme *Armoury* II. 132/1 [A company of] Cats [is] a Kindle. [An error of Holme.]

2. *in kindle* (of a hare): With young.

1877 *Daily News* 23 July 2 A fine hare, and.. a doe in kindle. *Mod. Advt.* 3 pure Belgian hare does, in kindle.

kindle ('kɪnd(ə)l), *v.*¹ Forms: *α.* 3 kundlen, kindlen, (*Orm.* kinndlenn), 3–5 kindel(l, kyndel(l, -il(l, -yl(l, (4 kinl-, kynl-), 5–6 kyndle, 5– kindle (*mod.Sc.* kynnle, kinnle). *β.* 4–6 kendyl, (6 *Sc.* -yll), 5–6 *Sc.* -ill. [app. f. ON. *kynd-a* to kindle (*trans.* and *intr.*) + -le: cf. ON. *kyndill* a candle, torch.]

In most of the senses *up* may be added as an intensive.

1. *trans.* To set fire to, set on fire, ignite, light (a flame, fire, or combustible substance).

c **1200** Ormin 16135 Hat lufess fir.. Iss kinndledd i þatt herrte. *a* **1300** *E.E. Psalter* xvii. 9 Koles.. Kindled ere of him glouand. *c* **1300** *Havelok* 915 Stickes kan ich breken and kraken, And kindlen ful wel a fyr. **1388** Wyclif *Judg.* xv. 4 He.. boond brondis in the myddis, whiche he kyndlid with fier. *c* **1475** *Rauf Coilȝear* 107 Dame.. kendill on ane fyre. **1484** Caxton *Fables of Æsop* I. xiii, [He] put to gyder grete habondance of straws.. and kyndeled it with fyre. **1582** Stanyhurst *Æneis* I. (Arb.) 24 Soom doe set on caldrons, oothers doe kendel a bauen. **1607** Shaks. *Cor.* III. i. 197 Fie, fie, fie, this is the way to kindle, not to quench. **1646** Boyle *Let. to Marcombes* 22 Oct., Wks. 1772 I. p. xxxi, These two flints are striking such sparks, as are likely to kindle a fine bonfire for the English. **1707** Watts *Hymn 'Come Holy Spirit, Heavenly Dove'* i, Kindle a Flame of sacred Love In these cold Hearts of ours. **1732** Berkeley *Alciphr.* I. §11 A man must be a long time kindling wet straw into a vile smothering flame. **1800** tr. *Lagrange's Chem.* I. 40 Kindle the phosphorus with a piece of bent iron brought to a state of ignition in the fire. **1863** Fr. A. Kemble *Resid. in Georgia* 31 Bidding the elder boys and girls kindle up the fire. **1871** R. H. Hutton *Ess.* II. 122 Wordsworth seems to kindle his own poetic flame like a blind man kindling his own fire.

2. *intr.* Of a fire, flame, or combustible matter: To begin to burn, catch fire, burst into flame.

a **1225** *Ancr. R.* 296 Þe sparke.. keccheð more fur.. And þe deouel bloweð to from þet hit erest kundleð. *a* **1300** *E.E. Psalter* lxxvii[i]. 25 [21] Fire kindeled ful brinnand þare In Iacob. **1495** *Trevisa's Barth. De P.R.* XVII. iv. (W. de W.) 606 Gleymy fatnesse.. of this tree Abies kyndlyth full soone and brennyth wyth lyght leyle. *a* **1533** Ld. Berners *Gold. Bk. M. Aurel.* (1546) P iij b, In great thycke and dry busshes, the fyres kendle moste easyly. **1679** Bedloe *Popish Plot* 15 They know not how it [a fire] came to kindle there. **1719** Young *Busiris* II. i, Think not, Mandane, this a sudden start; A flash of love, that kindles and expires. **1820** W. Irving *Sketch Bk.* I. 45 A spark of heavenly fire.. which kindles up and blazes in the hour of adversity. **1848** C. Bronte *J. Eyre* xii, My eye.. caught a light kindling in a window.

3. *fig. trans.* **a.** To inflame, excite, rouse, inspire (a passion or feeling).

a **1300** *Cursor M.* 6791 And sal mi wrath be kindeld sua. *c* **1380** Wyclif *Sel. Wks.* II. 240 Þis wolde kyndele oonhede and love. *a* **1450** *Knt. de la Tour* (1868) 64 It is the synne of pride, and engenderithe and kendelithe lechery. **1547–8** *Ordre of Commvnion* 9 We kyndle Gods wrathe ouer vs. **1638** *Penit. Conf.* viii. (1657) 235 Kindling in his heart faith, whereby he is justified. **1759** Robertson *Hist. Scot.* II. Wks. 1813 I. 145 The protestant army, whenever it came, kindled or spread the ardour of reformation. **1874** Green *Short Hist.* iii. §5. 141 The wholesale pillage kindled a wide spirit of resistance.

b. To inflame, fire, excite, stir up (a person, the mind, etc.); to make ardent or eager. Const. †*in* (†*of*), *to*, or with *inf.*

a **1300** *Cursor M.* 19436 (Cott.) Eth es to kindel þat es kene. *c* **1340** *Ibid.* 15390 (Trin.) Of al venym and of envye ful kyndeled he was. *c* **1440** *Pol. Rel. & L. Poems* (ed. 2) 227/620 Kindele þou me in charitee. *a* **1547** Surrey *Æneid* II. 131 This kindled us more egre to enquire. **1600** Shaks. *A.Y.L.* I. i. 179 Nothing remaines, but that I kindle the boy thither. **1657** Trapp *Comm. Nehem.* i. 4 These good men.. by mutual confidence kindle one another. **1775** Johnson *Tax. no Tyr.* 21 Some discontented Lord.. would.. have quickly kindled with equal heat a troop of followers. **1824** Byron *Juan* XVI. xli, The thrilling wires Died from the touch that kindled them to sound. **1871** R. Ellis *Catullus* xvi. 9 It shall kindle an icy thought to courage.

c. To arouse or give rise to (†care, trouble, etc. (*obs.*), war, strife).

a **1300** *Cursor M.* 24149 Ye Iuus þat kindeld all þis care. *c* **1325** *Metr. Hom.* 37 Thai kindel baret wit bacbiting. *c* **1470** *Golagros & Gaw.* 1121 It semyt be thair contenance that kendillit wes care. **1513** Douglas *Æneis* IX. viii. 99 As scho thus kyndillis sorow and wo. **1567** *Satir. Poems Reform.* xi. 48 Throw the is kendlit ciuil weir. **1761** Hume *Hist. Eng.* II. xxix. 151 He took measures for kindling a war with England. **1764** Goldsm. *Hist. Eng. in Lett.* (1772) I. 95 The wars that were now kindled up between England and France. **1847** Mrs. A. Kerr *Hist. Servia* 312 Time was gained for kindling the revolution in the neighbouring districts.

4. *intr.* **a.** Of passion or feeling (†care or trouble): To rise, to be aroused, to be excited.

c **1340** *Cursor M.* 6791 (Trin.) Þenne shal my wreche kyndel [*other MSS.* be Kindeld]. *a* **1352** Minot in *Pol. Poems* (Rolls) I. 62 Rough-fute riveling, now kindels thi care. *a* **1400–50** *Alexander* 2724 Myn angire on þine arrogance sall at þe last kindill. **1508** Dunbar *Tua Mariit Wemen* 94 Quhen kissis me that carybald, than kyndillis all my sorow. **1788** Gibbon *Decl. & F.* xlii. (1869) II. 553 Their mutual resentment again kindled. **1845** M. Pattison *Ess.* (1889) I. 18 As their fury kindled, they pushed into the nave of the building.

b. To become inflamed, ardent, or warm; to glow with passion or excitement; to become eager or animated.

c **1400** *Destr. Troy* 6575 Then Alcanus, the kyng, kyndlit in yre. **1513** More in Grafton *Chron.* (1568) II. 775 The Queene.. began to kindle and chafe, and speake sore byting wordes. **1666** Bunyan *Grace Ab.* §91 The words began thus to kindle in my spirit. **1794** Godwin *Cal. Williams* 27 We are both apt to kindle, warm of resentment. **1820** W. Irving *Sketch Bk.* II. 97 He kindled into warmth with the ardour of his contest. **1888** Burgon *Lives 12 Gd. Men* II. xii. 383 Very pleasant it was.. to see the dear fellow kindle at the mention of Hebron and Jerusalem.

†**c.** To spread like fire. *Obs. rare.*

a **1350** *St. Matthew* 28 in Horstm. *Altengl. Leg.* (1881) 132 Þe meruailes of þir mawmettes two Thwrgh all þe cuntre kindeld so.

5. *trans.* To light up as with fire; to make bright or glowing. Also with *up*.

1715–20 Pope *Iliad* II. 537 The fires expanding.. Shoot their long beams, and kindle half the skies. **1852** Mrs. Stowe *Uncle Tom's C.* xxii, One of those intensely golden sunsets which kindles the whole horizon into one blaze of glory. **1860** Hawthorne *Marb. Faun* 364 Brilliant costumes largely kindled up with scarlet. **1881** Freeman *Sk. Venice* 95 The mighty campanile of Spalato rises, kindled with the last rays of sunlight.

b. *intr.* To become glowing or bright like fire.

1797 Campbell *Wounded Hussar* iii, Dim was that eye,.. That melted in love, and that kindled in war! **1810** Southey *Kehama* VII. v, The Orient,.. Kindles as it receives the rising ray. **1823** F. Clissold *Ascent Mt. Blanc* 23 The western arc of the misty circle kindled, from a rosy to a deep reddening glow. **1865** Kingsley *Herew.* xvii. Hereward's face reddened and his eyes kindled.

Hence **kindled** ('kɪnd(ə)ld) *ppl. a.*

c **1440** *Promp. Parv.* 275/1 Kynlyd, as fyyr.., *accensus, succensus.* **1561** Norton & Sackv. *Gorboduc* II. ii. (1847) 120 The fiery stedes did drawe the flame With wilder randon through the kindled skies. *c* **1632** *Poem* in *Athenæum* No. 2883. 121/3 When the furious Doggstarr raves throughout the Spanish soyle, which smoakes like kindled flax. **1767** Sir W. Jones *Seven Fountains* in *Poems* (1777) 48 The magick water pierc'd his kindled brain. **1898** *Daily News* 2 Apr. 5/5 The kindled sentiments of the Spaniards.

kindle ('kɪnd(ə)l), *v.*² Now *dial.* Forms: 3 kundlen, 5 kyndlyn, kyndel, -il, (6 -yll), 5–6 kyndle, 7 kindel(l, 6–8 kindle; 4–6 kendle; 4 kynel-, kinel-, 5 kynle(n, kinlyn, 8 kinnel, 9 *dial.* kinnle, kennel. [Cf. kindle *sb.*] *trans.* Of a female animal: To bring forth, give birth to (young). Also *fig.*

c **1220** *Bestiary* 16 Wanne he is ikindled Stille lið ðe leun. *a* **1225** *Ancr. R.* 328 Euerich on [sin] kundleð more and wurse kundles þen þe sulue moder. *a* **1300** *E.E. Psalter* vii. 15 Bihald, he kyneld [*v.r.* kineled] un-rightwisnesse, Onfang sorwe and bare wickednesse. **1579–80** North *Plutarch* (1895) III. 275 A rat was taken full of young, and kendled five young rats in the trappe. **1600** Shaks. *A.Y.L.* III. ii. 358 As the Conie that you see dwell where shee is kindled. **1725** Bradley *Fam. Dict.* s.v. *Rabbit*, When a Doe has kinnell'd one Nest, and then kinnell'd another, the first must be taken from her.

b. *absol.* (Of hares or rabbits.)

c **1310** *Prophecy* (MS. Harl. 2253) in *Thomas Erceld.* (1875) Introd. 18 When hares kendles oþe herston. **1486** *Bk. St. Albans* E iij, Now of the hare.. Other while he is male.. And other while female and kyndelis by kynde. **1530** Palsgr. 598/2 A konny kyndylleth every moneth in the yere. **1614** Markham *Cheap Husb.* (1623) 131 The Females [of Rabbits or Conies] after they have kindled, hide their young ones. **1781** W. Blane *Ess. Hunt.* (1788) 102 The Doe makes choice of some thick dry brake.. to kindle in. **1810** *Treat. Live Stock* 170 (E.D.D.) The males or bucks should be

parted from the does, or females, till the latter kindle. **1828** *Craven Dial.*, *Kinnle*, to bring forth young.

†**c.** *intr.* To be born. *Obs. rare.*

a **1400–50** *Alexander* 696 Þat euer he kyndild [*Dubl. MS.* come] of his kynde kend he bot litill.

†**'kindle-coal.** *Obs.* [f. KINDLE *v.*¹ + COAL.] A kindler of strife; a mischief-maker. Cf. next.

1632 SHERWOOD, Kindle-cole (or stirre-suit). **1635** R. N. *Camden's Hist. Eliz.* IV. an. 42. 534 Essex..hearkened to Cuffe and other kindle-coles of sedition. **1650** HUBBERT *Pill Formality* 5 Art thou a kindle-coal and an incendiary? **1655** GURNALL *Chr. in Arm.* I. 175 In these civil wars among Saints, Satan is the great kindle-coal.

†**'kindle-fire.** *Obs.* [f. as prec. + FIRE. Cf. F. *boute-feu.*] = KINDLE-COAL.

1601 DANIEL *Civ. Wars* VI. xiii, Warwick..The fatall kindle-fire of those hot daies. **1613–18** —— *Coll. Hist. Eng.* (1626) 42 The Bishop..became the onely kindle-fire to set them all into more furious combustion. **1655** GURNALL *Chr. in Arm.* xxv. §4 Such a kindlefire sin is that the flames it kindles fly..from one nation to another.

kindler ('kɪndlə(r)). [f. KINDLE *v.*¹ + -ER¹.]

1. One who kindles; one who sets anything on fire.

a **1450** *Knt. de la Tour* (1868) 54 Delycious metes and drinkes..kindelers of the brondes of lecherye. **1483** *Cath. Angl.* 203/2 A kyndyller, *incensor*, *incendiarius.* **1600** FAIRFAX *Tasso* XVIII. lxxxv, A sudden..blast The flames against the kindlers backward cast. **1726** CAVALLIER *Mem.* I. 99 They discover'd great Fires every where, but cou'd not find out the Kindlers of them. **1821** BYRON *Diary* in *Juan* I. cxiv. *note* (Wks. 1846), The kindler of this dark lantern.

2. One who or that which inflames, incites, or stirs up.

1577–87 HOLINSHED *Chron.* III. 184/2 The sedition (where-of he himselfe had beene no small kindler). **1639** J. CORBET *Ungird. Scot. Arm.* 27 Be not the kindlers of this unlawfull war. **1714** GAY *Trivia* III. 321 Kindlers of riot, enemies of sleep. **1878** *N. Amer. Rev.* CXXVII. 497 The kindler of endless wars.

3. Something that will kindle readily, used for lighting a fire.

1851 S. JUDD *Margaret* ii, Put some kindlers under the pot. **1854** KNIGHT *Once upon a Time* II. 276 In those days there was a bundle of green sticks called a kindler, which no power but that of the bellows could make burn.

b. An arrangement to assist in kindling the fire in a stove (Knight *Dict. Mech.* 1875).

kindless ('kaɪndlɪs), *a.* [f. KIND *sb.* + -LESS.]

†**1.** Without natural power, affection, feeling, etc.; unnatural. *Obs. rare.*

c **1200** ORMIN 2310 Elysabæþ..þatt ta wass swiþe winntredd wif, And kindelæs to tæmenn. **1599** PEELE *David & Bethsabe* Wks. (Rtldg.) 466/2 Amnon's lusty arms Sinew'd with vigour of his kindless love. **1602** SHAKS. *Ham.* II. ii. 609 Remorselesse, Treacherous, Letcherous, kindles villaine!

2. [As if f. KIND *a.*] Devoid of kindness. *rare.*

1847 *Graham's Mag.* Mar., Calculated to draw out their true nature, whether it were kind or kindless. **1881** G. MACDONALD *Mary Marston* xxxvii, It was a sad, gloomy, kindless November night. **1887** SWINBURNE *Locrine* III. ii. 75 One that had No thought less kindly—toward even thee that art Kindless—than best beseems a kinsman's part.

Hence **'kindlessly** *adv.*, without affection.

1883 R. W. DIXON *Mano* I. xi, 32, I was..by my parents kindlessly designed To marry one whom fate my equal made.

kindlily ('kaɪndlɪlɪ), *adv.* [f. KINDLY *a.* + -LY².] In a kindly manner; with good nature and sympathy.

1826 SOUTHEY *Lett.* (1856) III. 544, I have taken very kindlily to every thing in Holland. **1842** LONGF. in *Life* (1891) I. 441 He thanks you most kindlily for your poems. **1868** *Contemp. Rev.* VIII. 610 The golden chain linking it closely but kindlily with all that has gone before.

'kindliness. [f. as prec. + -NESS.]

1. The quality or habit of being kindly. **b.** with *pl.* An instance of this, a kindly deed.

c **1440** *Promp. Parv.* 271/2 Kendlynesse of a gentyl herte ..,*gratitudo.* **1561** NORTON & SACKV. *Gorboduc* I. i, In kinde a father, not in kindlinesse. **1645** MILTON *Tetrach.* Wks. (1847) 185/2 (Gen. ii. 24) The fleshly act indeed may continue, but..more ignoble than that mute kindliness among the herds and flocks. **1791** BOSWELL *Johnson* 17 Apr. an. 1778, A kindliness of disposition very rare at an advanced age. **1883** BLACK *Shandon Bells* xxxi, Their life.. was..full of cheering activities and kindlinesses.

2. Mildness or amenity (of climate and season) favourable to vegetation.

1654 WHITLOCK *Zootomia* 427 Fruits, and Corn are much advanced by temper of the Aire, and Kindlinesse of Seasons. **1794** G. ADAMS *Nat. & Exp. Philos.* III. xxxv. 456 We ascribe..kindliness to dews.

kindling ('kɪndlɪŋ), *vbl. sb.*¹ [f. KINDLE *v.*¹]

1. The action of KINDLE *v.*¹ in various senses.

a **1300** *Cursor M.* 14389 (Gött.) His gode werkes ai to þaim ware Bot soru and kindling of care. *c* **1440** *Promp. Parv.* 275/1 Kynlynge, as fyyr, and oþer lyke.., *accensio, succensio.* **1550** BALE *Eng. Votaries* II. (R.), That the publicacion..of that vyce, gaue kyndelinges to the same in the hartes of ydel persons. **1694** KETTLEWELL *Comp. Persecuted* 66 To warm ourselves at imaginary Fires..of our own kindling. **1871** MACDUFF *Mem. Patmos* v. 60 So that there are no kindlings of soul as once there were.

2. Material for lighting a fire. In *U.S.* usually *pl.*

1513 DOUGLAS *Æneis* IX. ii. 89 Eftyr the fyre and kyndillyng did he cry. *a* **1568** *Wyf of Auchterm.* (Bann. MS.) 89 Than he beur kendling to the kill. **1824** MACTAGGART *Gallovid. Encycl.* 308 If I had got a spunk o' kennelling on t it wad hae become my ain. **1878** MRS. STOWE *Poganuc P.* ix. 71 Backlog and forestick were soon piled and kindlings laid. **1889** JESSOPP *Coming of Friars* ii. 90 Brakes and waste afforded turf..and kindling which all had a right to carry away.

3. *attrib.* and *Comb.*, as ***kindling brand, irons, matter***; **kindling-coal**, a piece of burning coal left banked in overnight in order to start the fire in the morning; so **kindling-peat**; **kindling-wood**, dry split wood suitable for lighting fires; wood only fit for lighting fires; hence ***kindling-wood machine***, an apparatus for splitting such wood.

1559 *Richmond Wills* (Surtees) 134 One pare of tongs,..ij kenling irons, one standing, one lying. **1577** HELLOWES *Gueuara's Chron.* 334 Stubble, stalkes, and strawe, and other kindling matter to burne. **1592** BRETON *Pilgr. Paradise* D ij, Thou kindling cole of an infernall fire, Die in the ashes, of thy dead desire. **1850** SCORESBY *Cheever's Whalem. Adv.* vi. (1859) 82 The first whale..knocked them [boats] into kindling wood. **1851** STOCKHARDT *Chem.* (1852) 105 The reason of its being so commonly used for all kindling purposes. **1883** *Harper's Mag.* Oct. 673/1 The farmer sits by the hour splitting kindling-wood.

'kindling, *vbl. sb.*² [f. KINDLE *v.*²]

1. The bringing forth of young.

c **1440** *Promp. Parv.* 275/2 Kenlynge, or forthe bryngyng of yonge beestys (*K.* kindeling, *P.* kyndlinge), *fetura.* **1725** BRADLEY *Fam. Dict.* s.v. *Rabbit*, The Tame [Coneys] at one Kindling, bringing forth more than the Wild do.

2. a. *collect.* A brood or litter; progeny, issue. **b.** *sing.* One of a brood or litter; a young animal.

13.. *K. Alis.* 5680 Swich is this addres kyndlyng. **1324** *Charter in Verse* in *Rel. Ant.* I. 168 Iche Edward Kynge Have yeoven of my forest the keping..To Randolph Peperking ant to his kyndlyng. *c* **1380** WYCLIF *Wks.* (1880) 315 Crist & baptist..clepeden hem kyndlyngis of eddris. *c* **1440** *Promp. Parv.* 275/2 Kynlynge, yonge beeste (*S.* kyndelynge), *fetus.* **1563** WINȜET *Four Scoir Thre Quest.* Wks. 1888 I. 118 *note*, The auld Serpent, and his poysonit Kenling Juliane the Apostate. **1781** W. BLANE *Ess. Hunt.* (1788) 103 The three Leverets were the most in number I ever saw, that in appearance were the same Kindling.

kindling ('kɪndlɪŋ), *ppl. a.* [f. KINDLE *v.*¹] That kindles, in senses of the vb. (chiefly *intr.*).

1483 *Cath. Angl.* 203/2 Kyndyllynge, *incendens.* **1728–46** THOMSON *Spring* 184 Swift fancy..Beholds the kindling country colour round. **1791** COWPER *Iliad* II. 113 A kindling rumour..Impelled them. **1810** SCOTT *Lady of L.* III. viii, Before the kindling pile. **1833** HT. MARTINEAU *Vanderput & S.* i. 18 'Yes', added the pastor, gravely meeting the kindling eyes of Christian.

Hence **'kindlingly** *adv.*

1885 G. MEREDITH *Diana* III. viii. 137 Man's nuptial half is kindlingly concerned in the launch of a new couple.

kindly ('kaɪndlɪ), *a.* Forms: see KIND. [OE. *ȝecyndelic*, f. *ȝecynde*, KIND + *-lic*, -LY¹.]

I. Pertaining to nature or birth.

†**1.** Natural, in various senses. *Obs.* **a.** That is, exists or takes place according to natural laws; consonant or congruent with nature; natural, as opposed to artificial; = KIND *a.* 1 a.

c **888** K. ÆLFRED *Boeth.* xxxix. §1 Hwy ne maȝon ȝe ȝebidon ȝecyndelices deaðes. *c* **1000** *Sax. Leechd.* I. 90 Swa þæt þæt blod ne mæȝ hys ȝecyndelican ryne habban. *a* **1225** *Leg. Kath.* 964 Hit is aȝein riht, and aȝein leaue of euch cundelich lahe. **1340** HAMPOLE *Pr. Consc.* 1686 Bodily ded, þat is kyndely, Es twynyng betwene þe saule and þe body. *c* **1400** MAUNDEV. (Roxb.) iii. 10 Þai say also þat fornicacion es na dedly bot a kyndely thing. *Ibid.* xviii. 82 Simulacres er ymages made to þe liknes of sum thing þat es kyndely. **1496** *Dives & Paup.* (W. de W.) I. xlvii. 88/2 It is a kyndly thynge in somer tyme to thondre. *a* **1547** SURREY *Æneid* IV. 929 Neither by lot of destiny Nor yet by kindly death she perished. **1607** TOPSELL *Four-f. Beasts* (1658) 130 The whole estate of kindly hunting consisteth principally in these two points, in chasing the beast that is in hunting, or in taking the bird that is in fowling.

†**b.** Implanted by nature; innate; inherent in the nature of a person or thing; = KIND *a.* 1 b.

971 *Blickl. Hom.* 7 Seo ȝecyndelice hætu..ȝestilleþ on þe. **1340** HAMPOLE *Pr. Consc.* 2003 Þe dede fra a man his mynd reves And na kyndely witte with hym leves. **1480** CAXTON *Descr. Brit.* 14 It accordeth better to kendly reson. **1587** GOLDING *De Mornay* i. 9 To loue company, and to clad himself.., (which things wee esteeme to be verie kindlie). **1590** SPENSER *F.Q.* I. iii. 28 The earth shall sooner leave her kindly skil To bring forth fruit..Then I leave you. **1607** SHAKS. *Timon* II. ii. 226 'Tis lacke of kindely warmth, they are not kinde.

†**c.** Naturally belonging to or connected with a person or thing; own, proper, suitable; = KIND *a.* 1 c. Const. *for, to. Obs.*

c **888** K. ÆLFRED *Boeth.* xiv §2 Þincð him ȝenoȝ on..Þam fodre þe him ȝecyndelic bið. *a* **1300** *Cursor M.* 1912 Þe beist thoght selcut li god þat þai hade raght þair kindle fode. **1387–8** T. USK *Test. Love* Prol. (Skeat) I. 36 Lette frenchemen in their frenche also enditen their queinte termes, for it is kyndely to their mouthes. *c* **1400** *Destr. Troy* 2412 Thou shalbe wisest of wit..And know all the conyng, þat kyndly is for men. **1470–85** MALORY *Arthur* XIX. x, Here we muste begynne at kynge Arthur, as is kyndely to begynne at hym that was the moost man of worshyp..at that tyme. *a* **1586** SIDNEY *Arcadia* III. (1627) 350 Doe you not know that daintinesse is kindly vnto vs? **1647** WARD *Simp. Cobler* 69 Ropes and hatchets are not the kindliest instruments to set it. **1674** N. FAIRFAX *Bulk & Selv.* 79 The kindliest attribute of time, which is successiveness in abiding. **1727** BRADLEY *Fam. Dict.* s.v. *Cheese*, The Season of the Year denies a kindly Drying or Hardening thereof.

†**2.** That belongs to one by birth; native; hereditary; = KIND *a.* 2. *Obs.*

a **1300** *Cursor M.* 3914 (Gött.) To wend into þair kindly land. **1413** *Pilgr. Sowle* (Caxton) IV. xxxviii. (1859) 64 He hadde thus oppressyd his owne kyndely peple of his owne countre. **1536** BELLENDEN *Cron. Scot.* (1821) II. 314 It pertenit to him be kindly heritage. **1572** *Satir. Poems Reform.* xxx. 201 King Roboam..tynt his kyndlie Trybes ten. *a* **1670** SPALDING *Troub. Chas. I* (1850) I. 3 James erll of Moray..had cassin them out of thair kindlie possessions quhilk (past memorie of man) their predicessoris and they had keipit.

†**b.** Existing between kinsfolk. *Obs. rare*⁻¹.

1567 *Satir. Poems Reform.* iv. 6 Traisting with ane..Quha was the ruite quhair of I did spring, In honour to liue be kyndelie allyance.

3. Having a right to one's position in virtue of birth or descent; rightful, lawful (= KIND *a.* 3 a). Of children: Lawfully born, legitimate. Of a tenant (*Sc.*): Holding a lease of land which his ancestors have similarly held before him: such a tenant usually held his land on favourable terms, and the name was also extended to others admitted as tenants on similar conditions.

c **900** tr. *Bæda's Hist.* III. viii. (1890) 172 Þæs ylcan cyninges ȝecyndelice dohtor. *c* **1275** *O.E. Misc.* 90 Crist, kundeliche kyng, cuþ þu þi mayht Rihtwise louerd. *c* **1425** *Eng. Conq. Irel.* 12 Trywly with hym for to hold frome þat tym forward, as har kyndly lord. **1513** MORE *Rich. III*, Wks. 67/2 As though the killing of his kinsmen could..make him a kindly king. **1548** UDALL, etc. *Erasm. Par. Matt.* v. 44 To be the kyndely children of the heauenly father. **1563** *Sc. Acts Mary* c. 13 Na kyndlie lauchfull possessour tennent or occupyar of ony of the saidis Kirk landis be remouit fra thair kyndelie rowme. **1600** *Rental* in *Orig. Paroch. Scot.* (1851) I. 517 [The teinds of the parish of Lintoun] quhairof my Lord of Mortoun is kyndlie takisman. **1773** ERSKINE *Inst. Law Scotl.* II. vi. §37 A rental is a particular species of tack, now seldom used, granted by the landlord, for a low or favourable tack-duty, to those who are either presumed to be lineal successors to the ancient possessors of the land, or whom the proprietor designs to gratify as such: and the lessees are usually styled *rentallers*, or *kindly tenants.* **1816** SCOTT *Old Mort.* vii, Your service is not gratuitous—I trow ye hae land for it. Ye're kindly tenants. **1879** HEARN *Aryan Househ.* 73 He must be a genuine or kindly son..one born in lawful marriage.

transf. **1786** MACKENZIE *Lounger* No. 87 ¶4 It was tenanted by kindly daws and swallows.

b. Native-born; = KIND *a.* 3 b. *arch.*

1820 SCOTT *Monast.* iii, God keep the kindly Scot from the cloth-yard shaft, and he will keep himself from the handy stroke. ? *a* **1833** *Otterburn* in Child *Ballads* III. 300 Let never living mortal ken That ere a kindly Scot lies here.

II. Characterized by good nature.

4. Of good nature or natural qualities; excellent of its kind; of a good sort; in good condition, thriving; goodly. Cf. KIND *a.* 4. *arch.* or *dial.*

Quot. 1548–9 is doubtful; some take it in sense 1.

c **1400** MAUNDEV. (Roxb.) vii. 26 Balme þat es kyndely and gude es riȝt clere and ȝalow. **1541** R. COPLAND *Galyen's Terapeut.* 2 A iij b, It behoueth than that the sayd flesshe be kyndely. **1548–9** (Mar.) *Bk. Com. Prayer, Litany*, To geue and preserue to our use the kyndly fruytes of the earth. **1574** R. SCOT *Hop Gard.* (1578) 9 The good and the kindely Hoppe beareth a great and a greene stalke. **1697** DAMPIER *Voy.* (1729) I. 419 The fattest and kindliest Beef, that I did ever taste. **1772** *Ann. Reg.* 106/2 What the graziers call a *kindly* sheep; one that has always an inclination to feed. **1772–84** COOK *Voy.* (1790) IV. 1222 There is a large plain.. producing a thick, kindly grass. **1887** *S. Chesh. Gloss.*, *Kindly*,..healthy. 'My plants binna very kindly.'

5. Of persons: Having a friendly benevolent disposition; kind-hearted, good-natured. Hence also of character, feelings, actions, etc. Cf. KIND *a.* 5.

1570 LEVINS *Manip.* 100/14 Kyndly, *benignus.* **1606** SHAKS. *Ant. & Cl.* II. v. 78 Melt Egypt into Nyle; and kindly creatures Turne all to serpents. **1697** DRYDEN *Virg. Georg.* III. 411 Nor cou'd his Kindred, nor the kindly Force Of weeping Parents, change his fatal Course. **1797–1803** J. FOSTER in *Life & Corr.* (1846) I. 242 How much kindly, friendly softness of heart. **1842** BARHAM *Ingol. Leg.*, *Wedding-day*, Your father was a kindly man. **1871** R. ELLIS *Catullus* lxv. 9 Ah! no more to address thee, or hear thy kindly requital! **1889** JESSOPP *Coming of Friars* ii. 89 Those legacies..were left by kindly people a century or two ago.

b. *transf.* and *fig.* Of things, esp. of the weather, climate, or soil: Genial, benign; favourable to growth or *for* a particular crop.

1655 FULLER *Ch. Hist.* III. vi. §44 In a kindly spring, bite it bare over night, next morning the grass will be grown to hide a wande therein. **1697** DRYDEN *Virg. Georg.* I. 29 You, who swell those Seeds with kindly Rain. **1699** DAMPIER *Voy.* II. I. 25 This [Rice] serves them for Bread-corn; and as the Country is very kindly for it, so their Inhabitants live chiefly of it. **1732** POPE *Ess. Man* II. 275 Behold the child, by Nature's kindly law, Pleas'd with a rattle. **1789** G. WHITE *Selborne* i. (1853) 14 A kind of white land..neither fit for pasture nor for the plough, but kindly for hops.

6. Acceptable, agreeable, pleasant, genial. In later use, of conditions, influences, etc., blending with 5 b.

1382 WYCLIF *Lev.* iv. 7 Of moost kyndli encense to the Lord. **1600** SHAKS. *A.Y.L.* II. iii. 53 Therefore my age is as a lustie winter, Frostie, but kindely. **1696** WHISTON *The. Earth* IV. (1722) 359 The Heat in the one, and the Cold in the other, were more kindly. **1828** CARLYLE *Misc.*, *Burns* (1872) II. 5 The kindliest era of his whole life. **1850** TENNYSON *In Mem.* c, But each has pleased a kindred eye, And each reflects a kindlier day. **1854** MRS. OLIPHANT *Magd. Hepburn* III. 41 Standing before the kindly hearth.

III. 7. *Comb.*, as **kindly-dispositioned, -hearted, natured** adjs.; †**kindly-born** *a.*, native; **kindly-like** *adv.* in a manner suggesting kind feeling.

1413 *Pilgr. Sowle* (Caxton) IV. xxxviii. (1859) 64 Nought only straungeours, but also the kyndely borne men of this same land. **1716** *Wodrow Corr.* (1843) II. 136 [They] never carried more friendly and kindly-like than they did. **1859** TENNYSON *Enid* 514 So spake the kindly-hearted Earl. **1871** SMILES *Charac.* viii. (1876) 227 It is the kindly-dispositioned men who are the active men of the world.

kindly ('kaɪndlɪ), *adv.* Forms: see KIND *a.* [OE. *ȝecyndelíce*, f. as prec. + *-líce*, -LY².]

I. †1. a. In accordance with nature; naturally; by natural disposition; characteristically. *Obs.*

*c*888 K. ÆLFRED *Boeth.* xxxv. §3 Ealla ȝesceafta ȝecyndelice.. fundiað to cumanne to Gode. *a* **1225** *Ancr. R.* 124 Þer ase muchel fur is, kundeliche hit waxeð mid winde. *a* **1300** *Cursor M.* 9431 Þe first lagh was kald 'o kind', þat es to sai kindli to do, Al þat him was biden to. *c* **1350** *Will. Palerne* 111 Þe kud king of Spayne was kindely his fader. *c* **1400** tr. *Secreta Secret., Gov. Lordsh.* 114 Kepe þe fro a man þat kyndly is ȝalow and blew. **1575** *Mirr. Mag., Fall blacke Smith* vi, Nature hath so planted in ech degree, That Crabs like Crabs will kindly crall and crepe. *a* **1586** SIDNEY *Arcadia* (1622) 248 Because that out of the circumstance of her present behauiour, there might kindly arise a fit beginning of her intended discourse.

b. In the way suitable or appropriate to the nature of the thing; properly, fittingly. In later use, esp. said of processes which successfully follow their natural course. Now *rare.*

13.. *E.E. Allit. P.* B. 1 Clannesse who-so kyndly cowþe comende. **1486** *Bk. St. Albans* Cj, Who so will that an hawke endure and mew kyndli. **1548-77** VICARY *Anat.* v. (1888) 42 The Lippes.. keepe the mouth close tyl the meate were kindly chewed. **1582** STANYHURST *Æneis* II. (Arb.) 46, I vowd to be kindlye reuenged. **1641** H. BEST *Farm. Bks.* (Surtees) 50 It is a very rare thinge to see oates ripe kindely, for usually the ridges will bee ripe and ready to shake when the furres are greene. **1758** J. S. *Le Dran's Observ. Surg.* (1771) 250 The Suppuration proceeding kindly, the Wound became a simple Wound. **1842** J. AITON *Domest. Econ.* (1857) 197 The butter and the cheese.. are kindliest dealt with at home.

c. In an easy, natural way; readily; congenially; spontaneously. Now *dial.* or *colloq.*

14.. *Sir Beues* (MS.M) 95/1917 He gaue hym a dynt than, His sworde so kyndly yode, That at the breste the dynt stode. *c* **1400** *Destr. Troy* 8601 Thay knew hym full kyndly be caupe of his sworde. **1563** HYLL *Art Garden.* (1593) 5 Every ground doth not kindlie bring up Garden hearbes. **1658** MANTON *Exp. Jude* verse 2 As we say of children that take the dug kindly, they will thrive and do well enough. **1793** SMEATON *Edystone L.* §259 The ground chain now came in kindly. **1886** *Sat. Rev.* 6 Mar. 327/2 One often hears it said, 'Such and such an animal knows So-and-so the moment he gets up, and always goes kindly with him'.

†**d.** Properly; thoroughly, exactly. *Obs.*

1340 HAMPOLE *Pr. Consc.* 221 If he hym-self knew kyndely, He suld haf knawyng of God almyghty. **13..** *E.E. Allit. P.* B. 319 A wyndow wyd In þe compas of a cubit kyndely sware. **1362** LANGL. *P. Pl.* A. VI. 29, I knowe him as kuynde-liche as Clerk doþ his bokes. **1401** *Pol. Poems* (Rolls) II. 65 Sich as ben gaderid in couentis togidere.. this clepe we monasticall, that kendly is knowun. **1592** SHAKS. *Rom. & Jul.* II. iv. 59 *Rom.* Meaning to cursie. *Mer.* Thou hast most kindly hit it.

II. 2. With natural affection, affectionately, lovingly; with sympathy, benevolence, or good nature.

c **1250** *Gen. & Ex.* 2500 He it for-gaf hem mildelike, And luuede hem alle kinde-like. *c* **1350** *Will. Palerne* 1613 Eiþer oþer keste kindeliche þat time. *c* **1400** *Destr. Troy* 657 The Knight was curtas, & kendly he saide:—'Most louesom lady, your lykyng be done!' **1535** COVERDALE *Bible* Prol., How kyndly and fatherly he [God] helpeth the. **1600** SHAKS. *A.Y.L.* I. i. 144, I thanke thee for thy loue to me, which.. I will most kindly requite. **1611** BIBLE *Gen.* I. 21 Hee comforted them, and spake kindly vnto them. **1697** DAMPIER *Voy.* I. 52, I was aboard twice or thrice, and very kindly welcomed both by the Captain and his Lieutenant. **1722** DE FOE *Col. Jack* (1840) 151 They would be.. used kindlier. **1766** GOLDSM. *Vic. W.* xiv, Mr. Thornhill having kindly promised to inspect their conduct himself. **1875** JOWETT *Plato* (ed. 2) III. 206, I must earnestly request that you will kindly answer. *a* **1882** ABP. TAIT in *Daily News* (1891) 26 June 7/2 Tell him he is an ass,—but say so kindly.

b. *fig.* Benignly, genially.

1792 BURNS *Bessy & her Spinnin Wheel* ii, The sun blinks kindly in the biel'.

3. In a way that is pleasant or agreeable to the recipient or object; agreeably, pleasantly.

1596 SHAKS. *Tam. Shr.* Ind. i. 15 Let him come, and kindly. **1609** F. N. *Fruiterer's Secr.* 19 There be pippins.. that haue the warmth of the sunne.. they last long and eate kindly. **1863** KINGLAKE *Crimea* I. xiv. 210 How it was possible.. that the coarse Bonaparte yoke of 1804 could be made to sit kindly upon the neck of France. **1875** H. C. WOOD *Therap.* (1879) 688 Thus, purgatives act much more kindly when a number of them are united together.

4. Phrases.

a. ***to take kindly***, to accept pleasantly, or as a kindness. **b.** ***to take kindly to***, to be naturally attracted to or pleased with. **c.** ***to thank kindly***, to thank heartily, with appreciation of the kindness shown.

a. *a* **1622** MABBE tr. *Aleman's Guzman d' Alf.* (K.O.), Take it kindely at your hands. **1677** LITTLETON *Lat. Dict.*, To take a thing kindly,.. *æquo, bono animo accipere.* **1709** STEELE *Tatler* No. 14 ¶1, I took his Admonition kindly.

b. **1809** MALKIN *Gil Blas* x. x. ¶26, I took very kindly to my condition. **1866** MRS. GASKELL *Wives & Dau.* I. 330 They don't take kindly to me.. and so I suppose I'm not generous enough to take kindly to them.

c. **1662** in Chr. Wordsworth *Scholæ Acad.* (1877) 293 *note*, Mother I kindly thank yᵒ for yʳ Orange pills yᵒ sent me. **1785** BURNS *Ep. to Lapraik* II. v, Yet ye'll neglect to shaw your parts, An' thank him kindly! **1838** JAS. GRANT *Sk. Lond.* 207, I thaunk'd her kindly for her condescension, and hoped she was weel hersel'.

5. *Comb.* with pples. and adjs., as ***kindly-meant, -sheltering, -soft.***

1599 H. BUTTES *Dyets drie Dinner* A a iv, Then Whiffe, and smoke Tobaccos antidot From out thy kindly traunced Chimny-head. **1868** J. H. NEWMAN *Verses Various Occas.* 36 In the Church's Kindly-sheltering fold. **1885** RUSKIN *Let.* in *Pall Mall G.* 24 Apr., Your kindly-meant paragraphs on my resignation.

kindness ('kaɪndnɪs). Forms: see KIND *a.*; also 5 **kyndynes, kyndinesse.** [f. KIND *a.* + -NESS. (OE. had *ȝecyndnys* in sense 'generation, nation'; but the existing word is of later formation.)]

†1. Kinship; near relationship; natural affection arising from this. *Obs.*

c **1425** WYNTOUN *Cron.* VII. viii. 228 Bathe kyn and kyndnes he foryhet. **1511-12** *Act 3 Hen. VIII*, c. 22 *Preamble*, The Kyng of Scottis.. not regarding the kyndenesse and nigh aliaunce of your Grace. **1677** GILPIN *Demonol.* (1867) 39 The engagements of kindness, blood, affinity, and relation.

†2. *Sc.* Natural right or title derived from birth or descent; the status of a kindly tenant. *Obs.*

1536 BELLENDEN *Cron. Scot.* (1821) I. 221 The nobillis of Britane gaif to Fincormak.. all the landis of Westmureland and Cumber. with clame and kindnes thairof perpetually. **1574** in *Exch. Rolls Scotl.* xx. (1899) 365 Forasmekill as I haif the present possessioun and kyndnes of the landis of Maristoun. **1578** *Sc. Acts Jas. VI* (1814) III. 112 To sie that the saidis kyndlie tennentes be satisfeit for thair kyndnes.

†3. Natural inclination, tendency, disposition, or aptitude. *Obs. rare.*

a **1400-50** *Alexander* 1982 To ken þe to knaw my kyndnes here-eftir Bath my grace & my glori & my grete strenthe. *Ibid.* 4700 All ȝoure lefing & ȝoure lare, at ȝe so loude prayse, It comis bot of a kyndnes, & of na clene thewys. **1674** N. FAIRFAX *Bulk & Selv.* 17 Either we want a kindness for the business.. or else that we want respect enough for the Author.

b. Good natural quality or aptitude.

1834-43 SOUTHEY *Doctor* cxliii. (1848) 367/1 Kindness of disposition in a beast, importing in their language, that it fattens soon. **1875** *Encycl. Brit.* I. 171/1 A good loaf should have kindness of structure, being neither chaffy, nor flaky, nor crummy, nor sodden.

4. The quality or habit of being kind; kind nature or disposition, or the exhibition of this in action or conduct.

c **1350** *Will. Palerne* 321 [They] han al kindenes me kyd, & y ne kan hem ȝelde. **1413** *Pilgr. Sowle* (Caxton 1483) IV. xx. 66 Is there in the no drope of kyndenesse? **1513** MORE in Grafton *Chron.* (1568) II. 757 The common people, which oftentymes more esteme, and take for great kindnesse a little courtesye then a great benefite. **1567** *Gude & Godlie B.* (S.T.S.) 52 Na tung sic kyndnes can expres. **1605** SHAKS. *Macb.* I. v. 18 Yet doe I feare thy Nature, It is too full o' th' Milke of humane kindnesse, To catch the neerest way. **1750** JOHNSON *Rambler* No. 75 ¶10 They.. inflict pain where kindness is intended. **1871** SMILES *Charac.* viii. (1876) 228 Kindness does not consist in gifts, but in gentleness and generosity of spirit.

b. With *a* and *pl.*: An instance of this; a kind act; †a benefaction (*obs.*).

c **1290** *S. Eng. Leg.* I. 204/157 We ne beoth nouȝt so onkuynde, þat we it nellez ȝelde þe bliue For þe kundenesse þat þov to us come. **1377** LANGL. *P. Pl.* B. v. 441 The kyndenesse þat myne euene-cristene kidde me fernȝere. *c* **1380** WYCLIF *Sel. Wks.* III. 435 For þise sixe kyndenessis. *c* **1440** *York Myst.* xl. 149, I thanke youe of þis kyndinesse ȝe kydde me. **1588** SHAKS. *Tit. A.* v. iii. 171 Do him that kindnesse, and take leaue of him. **1608** —— *Timon* III. ii. 22, I haue receyued some small kindnesses from him, as Money, Plate, Iewels. **1697** DAMPIER *Voy.* I. 460 This Tide, which did us a kindness in setting us through. **1862** TROLLOPE *Orley F.* i. (1873) 8 All those numberless kindnesses which a lady with comfortable means and no children is always able to bestow.

†**c.** A benefit, an advantage. *Obs. rare.*

1727 BRADLEY *Fam. Dict.*, *Belching* is a Kindness to the Person whose Belly is fill'd with Wind, and when he can do it, he always finds some Relief by it.

5. Kind feeling; a feeling of tenderness or fondness; affection, love. Also, Good will, favour, friendship. Const. *for* (†*to*). Now *rare.*

c **1385** CHAUCER *L.G.W.* 665 (*Cleopatra*), But herkenyth ȝe that spekyn of kyndenesse.. Here may ȝe sen of wemen which a trouthe. **1508** DUNBAR *Tua Mariit Wemen* 483 Sum kissis me; sum clappis me; sum kyndnes me proferis. **1662** J. DAVIES tr. *Olearius' Voy. Ambass.* 126 Hence.. the Muscovites love the Greeks, and have a kindnesse for them. **1667** PEPYS *Diary* 2 Sept., Sir C. Carteret.. tells me he is sure he hath no kindness from the king. **1683** *Pennsylv. Archives* I. 59 Unwilling to withdraw my kindness to the General Good. **1709** LADY M. W. MONTAGU *Let. to Miss Wortley* 21 Aug., It is not in my power.. to hide a kindness where I have one. **1779-81** JOHNSON *L.P.*, *Milton* Wks. II. 87 He left the university with no kindness for its institution. **1807-8** W. IRVING *Salmag.* v. (1860) 112 A lady for whom he had once entertained a sneaking kindness.

†6. (See quot.) *Obs.*

a **1603** MOYSES *Mem.* (1755) 43 Upon the 25th of June [1580].. the inhabitants of Edinburgh contracted a strange sickness, which was called *Kindness.*

7. *Comb.*, as ***kindness-proof*** adj.

1692 SOUTH *12 Serm.* (1697) I. 514, I may truly say of the Mind of an Ungrateful person, that it is Kindness-proof.

†**'kindom.** *Obs.* Forms: 1 cyni-, cyne-, cine-, 2-4 kine-, 3-4 kyne-, (4 kene-), 3-5 kyndom, 4 kin-, kyndam, kyndome, -dum, kindome, (5 coindom). [OE. f. *cyne-*, KINE-¹ + -DOM: of parallel formation to *king-dom*, and of much more frequent use in OE.] = KINGDOM, in various senses.

a **700** *Epinal Gloss.* 859 *Respuplica*, cynidom. *c* **855** *O.E. Chron.* an. 47 (Parker MS.) Claudius.. Orcadus þa ealond Romana cynedome [*Bæda* rice] under þeodde. *c* **1121** *O.E. Chron.* (Laud MS.) an. 1107 Ymbe vii ȝear þæs þe se cyng Henri cynedomes onfeng. *c* **1200** ORMIN 12104 To seon off all þiss middellærd þe kinedomess alle. *a* **1225** *Ancr. R.* 198 Þe kinedom þet he haueð bihoten his icorene. *c* **1305** *Kenelm* 79 in *E.E.P.* (1862) 50 In þe four & tuenti ȝer of his kynedom Kenulf wende out of þis wordle. *c* **1330** R. BRUNNE *Chron. Wace* (Rolls) 13411 Bretaygne.. ys Hed of þritty kynedames. **1426** AUDELAY *Poems* 9 God wyl.. in his kyndom the restore the lyf that lastyth ay. *Ibid.* 22 Thai wyl ȝow leede Into his court and his coindom.

kindred ('kɪndrɪd), *sb.* and *a.* Forms: *α.* 2 cunredden, 2-3 kun-, cunn-, 3-5 kyn-, kin-, -reden(e, -redin, -yn, -raden, -radin, 5 -redynge, -radone, -oun; 3 kindreden. *β.* 3 cun-, kun-, 3-6 kyn-, 3-7 kin-, 4-5 ken-, 4-6 kynne-, kinne-, 5-7 kine-, 3-5 -rede, 3-7 -red, (4 -rade, 6 -raid, -reid); 4, 6- kindred, (6 kyndrede, 6 -reade, 7 kindered). *γ.* 5-6 (*Sc.*) kyn-, kinrent. [Early ME. f. KIN¹ + *-rǣden*, -RED, OE. *rǣden*, condition, reckoning. The occasional early ME. variant *kindred(en* may have been a parallel formation on *kynde*, KIND *sb.*; but the modern *kindred*, which first became common in the 17th c., appears to have arisen through phonetic development of *d* between *n* and *r*, as in *thunder, Hendry*, etc.]

A. *sb.* 1. a. The being of kin; relationship by blood or descent (occasionally, but incorrectly, by marriage); kinship.

c **1200** *Trin. Coll. Hom.* 83 Hie giuen here elmesse noht for godes luue, ac for neheboreden oðer for kinraden. **1297** R. GLOUC. (Rolls) 9552 Þe kunrede iproued was, so þat king lowis þere & elianore is quene vor kunrede departed were. **1387** TREVISA *Higden* (Rolls) V. 29 Þese tweyne were y-ioyned to gidres boþe by kynrede and affinite. **1393** LANGL. *P. Pl.* C. XI. 258 Of kyn ne of kynredene a-counteþ men bote lytel. **1483** *Cath. Angl.* 203/2 A kynredynge *cognacio, consanguenitas, geneologia* [etc.]. **1587** GOLDING *De Mornay* xvi. 253 The kinred that is betweene all men, deriued from the father of their Soules, moueth vs very little, but the vile kinred of the flesh moueth vs very much. **1632** HEYWOOD *1st Pt. Iron Age* v. i. Wks. 1874 III. 339 Wee plead not kinred Or neare propinquity. **1678** BUTLER *Hud.* III. iii. 451 Tho' we're all as near of Kindred As th' outward man is to the Inward. **1776** PAINE *Com. Sense* (1791) 49 Every day wears out the little remains of kindred between us and them. **1874** GREEN *Short Hist.* iii. §7. 148 A secret match with.. the King's sister.. raised him to kindred with the throne.

b. *fig.* Affinity in respect of qualities; resemblance, agreement.

1577 B. GOOGE *Heresbach's Husb.* (1586) 60 b, The smoke, for the Kinred it hath with the Onyon. **1638** ROUSE *Heav. Univ.* iv. (1702) 29 Yet have we other fruits that by some kindred may seem to counterfeit som Lineaments of that taste. **1850** TENNYSON *In Mem.* lxxiv, I.. know Thy likeness to the wise below, Thy kindred with the great of old.

2. a. A group or body of persons related to each other by blood; a family, clan, tribe, etc.; = KIN¹ 1, KIND *sb.* 11. Now *rare.* †***the human kindred***, the human race (*obs.*).

c **1175** *Lamb. Hom.* 141 Þa twelf kunreden sculden þermide heore þurst kelen. *c* **1250** *Gen. & Ex.* 4127 Ðo twelue kinderedes.. He gaf bliscing. **13..** *K. Alis.* 6423 Unlossom is that kynrede. **1382** WYCLIF *Matt.* xxiv. 30 Alle kynredis [*gloss* or lynagis], of erthe schulen weyle. **1480** CAXTON *Chron. Eng.* cxcvii. 175 One kynred had no more pite of that other than an hungary wolfe hath of a shepe. *c* **1532** DU WES *Introd. Fr.* in Palsgr. 1065 To dye for the humaine kyndred. **1674** N. FAIRFAX *Bulk & Selv.* To Rdr., A patcht up Tongue from Lands and Kinreds round about. **1874** STUBBS *Const. Hist.* I. iii. 57 The little territory of Dithmarschen was colonised by two kindreds from Friesland and two from Saxony.

†**b.** The family, offspring, or descendants *of* a specified ancestor; = KIN¹ 1 b, KIND *sb.* 11 b. *Obs.*

a **1300** *Cursor M.* 6624 Als was þe kinred o sir leui. *c* **1340** *Ibid.* 10730 (Gött.) Þe kin of dauid kindred all. *c* **1330** R. BRUNNE *Chron.* (1810) 9 Kynewolf, of the kynred of Adelardes blode. *c* **1400** MAUNDEV. (Roxb.) vi. 22 He was successour of Macomete and of his kynredyn. **1513** DOUGLAS *Æneis* I. v. 39 Bot we thi bluide, thy kinrent and afspryng.. Hes lossit our schippis. **1581** MARBECK *Bk. of Notes* 323 Vnder the title of Circumcision and the kinred of Abraham. **1662** J. DAVIES tr. *Olearius' Voy. Ambass.* 208 To signifie that they were of the posterity and kinred of their Prophet Aaly.

†**c.** A generation; = KIN¹ 1 c, KIND *sb.* 11 c. *Obs.*

a **1340** HAMPOLE *Psalter* ix. 28, I sall noght be stirid fra getynge in getynge [*v.r.* kynreden into kynreden]. *c* **1380** WYCLIF *Sel. Wks.* II. 405 Þis kynrede shal not passen til alle þingis be doon. **1450** *Paston Lett.* I. 122 That youre blood may.. from kynrede to kynrede multeplye. **1450-1530** *Myrr. Ladye* 160 Hys mercy ys from kynred in to kynredes.

†**d.** Descent, pedigree; = KIN¹ 1 d, KIND *sb.* 11 d. ***kindred's tree***, a genealogical tree. *Obs.*

1387 TREVISA *Higden* (Rolls) IV. 289 Þe genelegies of þe Hebrewes and rekenynge of kynrede [*v.r.* kynrad] of oþer nacIouns were i-write in bookes. **1598** SYLVESTER *Du Bartas* II. ii. III. 543 So far the branches of his fruitfull Bed Past all the names of Kinreds-Tree did spread.

†3. Race, family, or stock, from which one springs; = KIN¹ 2, KIND *sb.* 12. *Obs.*

c **1250** *Meid Maregrete* x, Yef ho is boren of cunnraden free. *c* **1300** *St. Margarete* 62 Tel me of wham þu ert icome, and of what cunrede. *c* **1374** CHAUCER *Troylus* v. 979 þat ȝe ben of noble and heigh kynrede. *c* **1450** *Bk. Curtasye* 279 in *Babees Bk.* 307 And he be comen of gret kynraden, Go no be-fore þawgh þou be beden. **1513** DOUGLAS *Æneis* v. v. 75 Of Creit, as to hir kynrent, born was sche.

4. a. The family, clan, etc. of which one is a member. Usually with possessive pron.: One's kinsfolk or relatives, collectively; = KIN¹ 3. ***of one's kindred***: related to one.

a **1225** *Juliana* 61 þu leddest þurh moyses.. þurh þe reade sea al his cunredden. *a* **1250** *Owl & Night.* 1675 Alle heo beoth of mine kunrede. **1387** TREVISA *Higden* (Rolls) VII. 161 For hatreden of hir kynrede. *c* **1450** *Merlin* 79 The kynge sente to alle the Dukes kenrede.. that thei sholde come to hym. *c* **1470** HENRY *Wallace* II. 196 On our kynrent, deyr God, quhen will thou rew? **1538** WRIOTHESLEY *Chron.* (1875) I. 77 An Irishman of my Lord Garrattes kynnered. **1653** HOLCROFT *Procopius, Goth. Wars* III. 94 Sending others, and one of his own Kinred with them. **1725** POPE *Odyss.* xv. 20 Her kindred's wishes, and her sire's commands. **1870** F. R. WILSON *Ch. Lindisf.* 61 In the grassy spot where Grace Darling sleeps with her kindred.

†**b.** Applied to one person: A kinsman or kinswoman; = KIN¹ 3 c. *Obs.*

c **1430** *Syr Gener.* (Roxb.) 2211 He had wedded hir nigh kynrede, He was the more trew to hir in dede. **1599** MASSINGER, etc. *Old Law* III. ii, *Cleanthes.* Be I ne'er so well, I must be sick of thee. *Eu.* What ails our kindred? **1631** T. POWELL *Tom All Trades* 24 Some such helpe, as To be a Favourite, A Kindred. **1728** YOUNG *Love Fame* VI. 392 Wives.. ask, what kindred is a spouse to them?

B. *attrib.* passing into *adj.*

1. a. Of the same kin; related by birth or descent; cognate.

1530 PALSGR. 624, I make kynred, or make one a kynne to an other, *jemparente.* **1697** DRYDEN *Virg. Georg.* IV. 546 The bright Quire their kindred Gods invoke. **1781** GIBBON *Decl. & F.* xxx. III. 161 The countries towards the Euxine were already occupied by their kindred tribes. **1809** CAMPBELL *Gertr. Wyom.* III. viii, Nay meet not thou.. thy kindred foe! **1887** BOWEN *Virg. Æn.* III. 15 Ancient ally of the Trojans, with kindred gods to our own.

fig. **1687** DRYDEN *Hind. & P.* II. 396 The dame.. looking upward to her kindred sky. **1814** SCOTT *Ld. of Isles* III. ix, I long'd for Carrick's kindred shore. **1871** R. ELLIS *Catullus* lxiv. 160 Yet to your household thou, your kindred palaces olden, Might'st have led me.

b. Belonging to, existing between, or done by, relatives.

1593 SHAKS. *Rich. II*, II. i. 182 (Qo. 1) His hands were guilty of no kinred [1623 kindreds] bloud. **1718** ROWE tr. *Lucan* 10 The tender Ties of Kindred-love were torn. **1739** SMOLLETT *Regicide* IV. vi, What kindred crime, alas! am I decreed To expiate. **1850** TENNYSON *In Mem.* lxxix, Ere childhood's flaxen ringlet turn'd To black and brown on kindred brows.

2. Allied in nature, character, or properties; possessing similar qualities or features; cognate. Esp. in phr. ***kindred spirit*** (see quot. 1950).

1340 *Ayenb.* 228 'O', zayþ he, 'huet is uayr chasteté kenrede mid briȝtnesse'. **1595** SHAKS. *John* III. iv. 14 Who hath read, or heard Of any kindred-action like to this? **1697** DRYDEN *Alexander's Feast* 95 'Twas but a kindred sound to move, For pity melts the mind to love. **1781** GIBBON *Decl. & F.* xviii. II. 79 The kindred names of Constantine, Constantius, and Constans. **1849** GEO. ELIOT *Let.* 13 Sept. (1954) I. 307 She says, 'You won't find any kindred spirits at Plongeon, my dear.' **1878** HUXLEY *Physiogr.* 38 To study the formation of rain and kindred phenomena. **1898** E. HOWARD *To-Morrow* viii. 83 They can see their way to join with a sufficient number of kindred spirits. **1950** PARTRIDGE *Dict. Clichés* (ed. 4) 124 *Kindred spirit, a*, a person like another in character and temperament.

Hence **'kindredless** *a.*, having no kindred or relatives. **'kindredly** *adv.*, in a kindred way, cognately. **'kindredness, 'kindredship**, the quality or state of being of kin or akin; kinship.

1835 LYTTON *Rienzi* v. iv, Shouldst thou be friendless, *kindredless, alone.. I may claim thee as my own. **1864** A. B. GROSART *Lambs all Safe* (1865) 85 Many *kindredly inscrutable and tremendous things. **1838** CHALMERS *Wks.* XIII. 96 A *kindredness in their heart with its flavour and phraseology is a kindredness with heaven. **1882** C. E. TURNER *Stud. Russ. Lit.* i. 10 The resemblance consists only in the form and in the kindredness of subject. **1769** ROBERTSON *Chas. V* (1796) I. 256 He was deemed to have renounced all the rights and privileges of *kindredship. **1885** E. F. BYRRNE *Entangled* I. I. v. 69 A certain kindredship of soul and likeness of quality.

†**'kindsfolk.** *Obs. rare*⁻¹. [Cf. KIND *sb.* 11.]

= KINSFOLK.

1587 RALEIGH in *Collect.* (O.H.S.) I. 203 My Lady's frends and kindsfolkes.

†**'kindship.** *Obs.* [f. KIND *a.* + -SHIP.]

= KINDNESS.

1390 GOWER *Conf.* I. 170 He.. seide hem for the kindeschipe, That thei have don him felaschipe, He wole hem do som grace ayein. **1591** *2nd Pt. Troub. Raigne K. John* (1611) 85 What kindship, lenitie, or Christian raigne, Rules in the man to bear this foul impeach? *a* **1641** BP. MOUNTAGU *Acts & Mon.* (1642) 252 Herod, out of high stomach,.. or distrust of his honesty, refused his kindship.

kindtcough, obs. form of KINKCOUGH.

kindy ('kɪndɪ). Austral. and N.Z. colloq. abbrev. of KINDERGARTEN.

1966 G. W. TURNER *Eng. Lang. Austral. & N.Z.* viii. 173 If a child eats his vegies as he should, he is soon ready for kindy. **1968** *Wanganui* (N.Z.) *Photo News* 8 June 78 (*caption*) Kindy Ball. Guests of honour at the recent Wanganui Free Kindergarten Ball. **1973** *Courier-Mail* (Brisbane) 4 June 15/6 (*heading*) Off to kindy.. at home. A new scheme under consideration by the State Education Department will provide children in isolated areas with a pre-school education... A scheme for 'kindy by correspondence' would be available by the start of 1974. **1975** *Telegraph* (Brisbane) 28 Feb. 12 Self-help is basis for special kindy.

kine, *sb.*¹ Archaic pl. of COW *sb.*¹ (see 1 b β); occas. *attrib.* or in *Comb.*, as ***kine-killing, -pox.***

1800 B. WATERHOUSE (*title*) A Prospect of exterminating the Small-Pox; being the History of the.. Kine-Pox, commonly called the Cow-Pox. **1894** *Daily News* 23 Apr. 3/5 The kine-killing practice of the Mohammedans at their festivals.

kine (kaɪn), *sb.*² *Linguistics.* [Back-formation from KINE(SICS.] An isolable element of body movement or gesture made in non-vocal communication. Also *attrib.*

1952 R. L. BIRDWHISTELL *Introd. Kinesics* (U.S. Dept. State, Foreign Service Inst.) 15 Most users of kinesic material will not be able to record and analyze every kine played by the actor in any given situation. **1955** *Etc.: Rev. Gen. Semantics* XIII. I. 13 The least isolated particle with discriminational meaning we call a *kine.* **1965** OSGOOD & SEBEOK *Psycholinguistics* iv. 84 A particular motion or posture of a given part of the organism (facial or bodily) is called a *kine* (equivalent to *phone*). *Ibid.* 85 Various 'minimal pairs' of kine patterns (for example, variations in eyebrow position with the rest of the facial pattern constant).

†**kine-**¹ (also rarely **kyne-, kini-, cune-**), the representative in early ME. of OE. *cyne-, cyni-*, used in numerous combs. with the sense of 'kingly, royal', as *cyne-bearn, -cynn, -dóm*, etc., also in personal names as *Cynebald, -gils, -mund, -wulf*, etc., corresponding to OHG. *chuni-* in *chunirîche, Chunipald, -per(h)t, -gund, -mund*, etc. (But in OHG., combs. are usually formed with *chuninc-*, king, as *chunincduom, -helm, -rîche, -stuol*, whereas those formed with *cyning-* are comparatively rare in OE.: e.g. *cyning-cynn, -dóm, -feorm, -stán.*) Most words of Greek etymology beginning with *kine-* are now commonly pronounced with (ɪ).

[Neither OE. *cyne* nor OHG. *chuni* is found as a separate word, and two views are possible as to the exact etymology of the element; either that it is the simple stem of OTeut. **kunjo-*, Goth. *kuni*, OE. *cynn*, KIN, race, in combination, or that it represents a masculine derivative of this, of form **kuni-z*, equivalent to ON. *konr* 'man of race, man of gentle or noble birth', taken also by some as the immediate source of OHG. *chuning*, OE. *cyning*, KING. For the former view, cf. the combining use of *dryht*, 'people, folk, army', in sense 'lordly', in *dryht-bearn* lordly or princely child, lit. child of the folk, etc.]

The following combinations of *kine-* are found in early ME.; few of them survived the middle of the 13th c. **kine-ærd** [ERD], kingdom. **kine-be(a)rn** [BAIRN], child of royal birth. **kine-bench**, throne. **kine-born** *a.*, of royal birth. **kine-burh** [BURGH], royal city. **kine-erþe** [EARTH], kingdom. **kine-helm, -halm**, crown. **kine-laverd, -loverd** [LORD], royal master, king. **kinelich** *a.*, royal. **kine-lond** [LAND], kingdom, realm. **kine-mede** [MEED], royal reward. **kine-merk** [MARK], a mark indicating royal birth. **kine-mote** [MOOT], royal council or court. **kine-ring**, royal ring. **kine-sæte** [SEAT], throne. **kine-scrud** [SHROUD], royal robes. **kine-setle** [SETTLE], **kine-stol** [STOOL], throne. **kine-þeod** [THEDE], kingdom. **kine-worþ, -wurþ** [WORTH] *a.*, royal; hence **kine-wurþliche** *adv.*, royally. **kine-ȝerde** [YARD], sceptre, royal power. See also KINDOM, KINRICK.

c **1205** LAY. 19433 He.. letten beoden uerde ȝeond al his *kine-ærde [*c* **1275** kine-erþe]. *c* **1000** *Andreas* 566 (Gr.) Synniȝe ne mihton oncnawan þæt *cynebearn. *c* **1200** *Trin. Coll. Hom.* 47 Seinte Marie.. bar hire holie cunebern. *a* **1240** *Wohunge* in *Cott. Hom.* 273 Kine bearn.. of dauiðes kin. *c* **1205** LAY. 9693 þus seide þe king,.. þer he sæt.. an his *kine-benche. *c* **1000** ÆLFRIC *Lives Saints* ii. 326 þa wæs on rome byriȝ sum *cyne-boren mæden. *c* **1205** LAY. 22142 þer come þreo ibroðeren, þe weore kiniborne. *a* **1225** *Leg. Kath.* 1882 Under þis, come þe þurs Maxence.. aȝein to his *kineburh. *c* **1275** *Kine-erþe [see *kine-ærd*]. **971** *Blickl. Hom.* 23 þa wundan beaȝ of þornum & hine setton on heafod for *cynehelme. *c* **1205** LAY. 6766 He his kinehelm on-feng. *Ibid.* 18158 Nim þu þene kinehalm. *c* **1000** in Kemble *Cod. Dipl.* IV. 266 þurh hæse his *cynehlafordes Æðelredes cynges. *c* **1205** LAY. 2501 For Locrines lufe, þe wes hire kine louerd. *Ibid.* 9831 þu ært me swa leof swa mi kine-lauerd. *c* **900** tr. *Bæda's Hist.* IV. xxvi[i]. (1890) 358 Seo *cynelice fæmne Ælflæd. *c* **1205** LAY. 14130 Bi-tache me ænne castel oðer ane kineliche burh. *Ibid.* 183 He wes king & heo quen, & *kine-lond heo welden. *Ibid.* 2523 Heo ȝef Madan an hond Al his fader kine-lond. *a* **1225** *Leg. Kath.* 399 And tu schalt.. to curt cumen seoðen, and *kinemede ikepen. *c* **1300** *Havelok* 604 On his rith shuldre a *kyne merk. *a* **1225** *Leg. Kath.* 1979 And te king heold ta. hise *kinemotes. *Ibid.* 409 He.. sende iseelede writes wið his ahne *kinering. *c* **1200** ORMIN 2224 þatt illke *kinesæte þatt Daviþþ kinng hiss faderr held. *a* **1240** *Ureisun* in *Cott. Hom.* 193 þu ham ȝiuest *kinescrud, beies, and gold ringes. *c* **893** K. ÆLFRED *Oros.* III. vii. §6 þæt hehste *cynesetl and heafod ealles eastrices. *a* **1225** *Leg. Kath.* 45 He set o kine setle. *a* **900** CYNEWULF *Crist* 1217 (Gr.) þonne Crist siteð on his *cynestole. *c* **1205** LAY. 4517 Stille he wes iswoȝen On his kine-stole. *Ibid.* 22300 Arður letten beoden ȝeond al his *kine-þeoden. *c* **1275** *Ibid.* 11026 þat he.. his *kineworþe lond Sette Custance an hond. *c* **1320** *Cast. Love* 14 Worschupe him.. þat kineworþe kyng [is] vs aboue. *a* **1225** *Juliana* 62 þus þu.. of þe þreo kinges were *kinewurðliche iwurȝet. *c* **1000** ÆLFRIC *Hom.* II. 502 Hi to þæs caseres *cyne-ȝyrde ȝebuȝon. *c* **1200** ORMIN 8182 And himm wass sett inn hiss rihht hannd An dere kineȝerrde. **1306** *Sir Simon Fraser* in *Pol. Songs* (Camden) 215 Hii.. token him a kyne-ȝerde, so me kyng sholde, to deme.

kine-² ('kɪniː), var. CINE (reverting to the Gr. initial κ).

1899 *Daily Chron.* 31 Aug. 3/2 The British Museum authorities have made arrangements for the safe custody of kinenegatives dealing with events of national importance. **1923** *Chambers's Jrnl.* 603/2 The kinegraph registers the short intake of the breath marking his embarrassment. **1927** *Bulletin* 12 Aug. 14/2 An enthusiast for the kine camera. **1928** *Daily Express* 28 Mar. 13 He has turned the music-hall into a home of kine-variety. **1959** *Listener* 3 Sept. 356/2 Kine-recordings are used in large numbers to help distribution.

kinema ('kɪnɪmə, kaɪ'niːmə). Variant of CINEMA with initial *k* from the Greek original. Now *rare.*

1914 *Evening News* 29 Sept. 4/5 It was my first step in the path of the kinema actor. **1921** *19th Cent.* Apr. 672 Properly handled, the Kinema could be made to endear the two races to one another. **1928** *Western Morning News* 28 Dec., The new kinema on the site of the old Post Office at Totnes. **1942** *Electronic Engin.* XIV. 708/1 The commercialisation of the sound film in the kinema over twelve years ago. **1954** A. CORNWELL-CLYNE *3-D Kinematogr.* 8 Commercial kinemas had only exhibited coloured short films which had to be viewed through spectacles. **1974** *Listener* 22 Aug. 252/1 A period's grandest buildings.. indicate a community's current concern: medieval castles.. 1920s Kinemas.

b. *attrib.* and *Comb.*, as ***kinema-camera, drama, film, producer, projection, theatre***; **'Kinemacolo(u)r**, proprietary name of a method of producing motion pictures in the natural colours by means of revolving colour screens.

1927 *Manch. Guardian Weekly* (Suppl.) 2 Dec. p. xvi/2 The kinema-camera. **1909** *Trade Marks Jrnl.* 19 May 830 Kinema Color.. Kinematographic apparatus and photographic films bearing finished pictures in natural colours for use therewith. Charles Urban,.. Wardour Street, London; manufacturer. **1909** *Daily Chron.* 3 June 7/2 'Kinema-color', or animated scenes in nature's actual tints. **1914** *Times* 29 Jan. 4/3 These lectures might perhaps be illustrated by kinemacolour photographs. **1918** H. CROY *How Motion Pictures are Made* 288 By the Kinemacolor process colored motion pictures were made of the Coronation. **1949** R. LOW *Hist. Brit. Film 1906–14* iii. 101 As the sheer novelty of colours wore thin the company perforce became more ambitious and in September 1910 it was announced that the first drama in Kinemacolor was being filmed. **1916** A. BAKSHY *Path Mod. Russ. Stage* 221 The kinema-drama raises some of the most fundamental problems of art. **1915** *Truth* 6 Oct. 567/1 A levy of 1d. per foot on all imported kinema film. **1929** *Melody Maker* Apr. 418/2 A mixed programme of kinema films and variety acts. **1921** *19th Cent.* Apr. 672 The Kinema-producers in California. **1916** *Chambers's Jrnl.* 26 Feb. 207/1 [The lamp's] suitability for kinema projection. **1929** *Melody Maker* Apr. 418/2 In nearly all kinema theatres which have been converted from Music Halls. **1932** B. B. HAMPTON *Hist. Movies* xii. 257 Tally.. sold his Kinema Theater and First National franchise to Gore Brothers and Lesser.

kinematic (kaɪnɪ'mætɪk), *a.* and *sb.* [f. Gr. κίνημα, κῑνηματ- a motion (f. κῑνεῖν to move) + -IC.]

A. *adj.* **1. a.** Relating to pure motion, i.e. to motion considered abstractly, without reference to force or mass.

1864 *Athenæum* No. 1924. 340/3 Kinematic effects of revolution and rotation. **1879** THOMSON & TAIT *Nat. Phil.* I. I. 483 The design of a kinematic machine.. essentially involves dynamical considerations. **1880** *Nature* XXI. 244/1 M. Mannheim has recently introduced the expression kinematic geometry.. dealing with motion independently of forces and times.

b. *spec.* in *Mech.* Applied to a set of mechanical elements so disposed in relation to each other that the relative position and motion of each is uniquely determined by the relative position and motion of the other(s).

1876 A. B. W. KENNEDY tr. *Reuleaux's Kinematics of Machinery* i. 43 A machine consists solely of bodies which thus correspond, pair-wise, reciprocally. These form the kinematic or mechanismal elements of the machine. *Ibid.*, If a kinematic pair of elements be given, a definite motion can be obtained by means of them if one of the two be held fast or fixed in position. *Ibid.* 46 The whole now forms a linkage returning upon itself... A combination of pairs of elements in this way we shall call a chain, or more fully a kinematic chain. **1915** R. F. MCKAY *Theory of Machines* viii. 92 When one of the links of the kinematic chain is fixed, the chain is called a mechanism. When the mechanism transmits force.. it is called a machine. **1957** R. M. PHELAN *Fund. Mech. Design* i. 1 A chain.. in which with one link fixed every point in every other link must move in a definite path is called a constrained or kinematic chain.

2. ***kinematic viscosity***: see VISCOSITY.

B. *sb.* = KINEMATICS.

1873 W. K. CLIFFORD *Pure Sciences* in *Contemp. Rev.* (1874) Oct. 717 These rules are called the laws of kinematic, or of the pure science of motion.

kinematical (kaɪnɪ'mætɪkəl), *a.* [f. as prec. + -AL¹.] Of or pertaining to kinematics; kinematic.

1864 in WEBSTER. **1879** THOMSON & TAIT *Nat. Phil.* I. I. §91 These and kindred curves, which give good instances of kinematical theorems. **1884** *Health Exhib. Catal.* 143/2 Kinematical Apparatus.

kinematically (kɪnɪˈmætɪkəlɪ), *adv.* [f. KINEMATIC, -ICAL *adjs.*: see -ICALLY.] From the point of view of kinematics.

1876 A. B. W. KENNEDY tr. *Reuleaux's Kinematics of Machinery* vi. 234 Thus..the force-closed beam-chains became the imperfect but still kinematically far more complete 'parallel motion'. **1915** R. F. MCKAY *Theory of Machines* viii. 93 A direct-acting steam engine and a quick-return motion are kinematically identical, though their general appearance would not suggest such a connection. **1955** J. S. BEGGS *Mechanism* vi. 194 The kinematically equivalent chain thus obtained has all lower pairs, and Eq. (6-5) may be applied. **1971** D. W. SCIAMA *Mod. Cosmol.* xvi. 198 The rotation of the Galaxy can be detected not only dynamically from its flattened shape but also kinematically by observing the motions of stars..far out from the centre.

kineˈmatics. [In form a pl. of KINEMATIC: see -IC 2, and quot. 1840.] **a.** The science of pure motion, considered without reference to the matter or objects moved, or to the force producing or changing the motion. (Cf. KINETICS 1.)

1840 WHEWELL *Philos. Induct. Sc.* I. 146 M. Ampère, in his Essai sur la Philosophie des Sciences (1834)..proposes to term it Kinematics (*Cinématique*). **1859** J. R. LUNN *Motion* v, The phænomena of Motion..what has hitherto been called (though not universally) Kinematics. **1879** THOMSON & TAIT *Nat. Phil.* (ed. 2) Pref. 6 We adopt the suggestion of Ampere and use the term Kinematics for the purely geometrical science of motion in the abstract. **1882** MINCHIN *(title)* Uniplanar Kinematics of Solids and Fluids.

b. The kinematic features or properties of something. Const. as *sing.* or *pl.*

1955 J. S. BEGGS *Mechanism* ix. 273 The kinematics of the area wheel is shown in Fig. 9-11. **1973** *Sci. Amer.* Aug. 33/1 The kinematics of the decay required that the mass of the particle be very small, perhaps even zero.

kinematograph (kaɪˈniːmətəʊgrɑːf, -æ-, kɪnɪˈmætəʊgrɑːf, -æ-). [ad. Fr. *cinématographe*, f. Gr. κίνημα, κινηματο- motion + -GRAPH.] A contrivance (invented by Messrs. Lumière of Paris) by which a series of instantaneous photographs taken in rapid succession can be projected on a screen with similar rapidity, so as to give a life-like reproduction of the original moving scene.

The spelling with a *k* has been virtually superseded, for this word and all the derivatives listed below, by the French form with a *c*.

1896 *19th Cent.* July 135 The Kinematograph is already at more than one of them [*sc.* the music-halls], showing a stormy sea, the Thames at Waterloo Bridge, the race for the Derby. **1897** *Westm. Gaz.* 5 May 8/1 It was the lamp of the kinematograph which set the place on fire. **1899** *Harper's Mag.* Feb. 385 What is called 'the American Biograph'—an improved form of the kinematograph. **1969** T. H. GUBACK *Internat. Film Industry* v. 102 The Kinematograph Renters Society..brought action against the two Maltese films.
fig. **1899** *Month* Apr. 378 Reducing to order and viewing synoptically the kinematograph of life.

Hence ˌ**kineˈmatograph** *v. trans.*, ˌ**kinemaˈtographer**, **kiˌnematoˈgraphic** *a.*, ˌ**kinematoˈgraphical** *a.*, ˌ**kinematoˈgraphically** *adv.*, ˌ**kinemaˈtography**.

1900 *N. & Q.* 9th Ser. VI. 206/2 A novel by..Galdós..with a wonderful kinematographic style. **1900** *Nature* 15 Feb. 384/2 Prof. R. W. Wood will exhibit..the Kinematographical Demonstration of the Evolutions of Reflected Wave-fronts. **1907** *Westm. Gaz.* 24 Aug. 6/3 Acting, Sir, is mere kinematography. What we require is something more static, reposeful, and intellectual. **1908** *Daily Chron.* 26 Sept. 7/2 Mr. Charles Urban during the past five months has enjoyed facilities to kinematograph the efforts made during this period to salve the Gladiator. **1911** *Chambers's Jrnl.* 412/1 Here, however, the scientific kinematographer has gone farther. **1925** *Daily Mail* 13 Apr. 6/5 One..important thing..is to get into the hiding-place unobserved by the birds which he happens to be kinematographically on the track of. **1954** A. CORNWELL-CLYNE *3-D Kinematogr.* 7 Colour kinematography and synchronized sound. **1971** *(title)* British kinematography sound and television.

kinematoscope. = CINEMATOSCOPE. (*Disused.*)

1898 *Windsor Mag.* VIII. 113/1, I knew that conjurors were to be obtained there,..and the kinematoscope. **1926** *Encycl. Brit.* Suppl. II. 960/2 This machine was patented in the United States as the Kinematoscope Feb. 5 1861.

kineme (ˈkaɪniːm). *Linguistics.* [f. Gr. κίνη(σις movement + -EME.] A meaningful unit of body movement or gesture made in non-vocal communication.

1952 R. L. BIRDWHISTELL *Introd. Kinesics* (U.S. Dept. State, Foreign Service Inst.) 22 Phone: Allophone Phoneme. Kine: Allokine (? Kineme?). **1955** *Etc.: Rev. Gen. Semantics* XIII. I. 13 Each of these *classes* of allokines or variants within a range, we define as *kinemes*. **1965** OSGOOD & SEBEOK *Psycholinguistics* iv. 85 The second step in analysing any gestural 'language'—again, in parallel with linguistics—would be to determine what movements are significant in the code, i.e., what classes of kines constitute *kinemes* (equivalent to *phonemes*) by virtue of having the same significance. **1972** B. G. COOKE in T. Kochman *Rappin' & Stylin' Out* 34 In this paper the gestures of giving and getting skin shall be considered as *kinemes* according to Birdwhistell's classification.

kinemics (kaɪˈniːmɪks). [f. KINEM(E + -ICS.] (See quot. 1954.)

1953 J. B. CARROLL *Study of Lang.* 279 Kinemics. **1954** PEI & GAYNOR *Dict. Ling.* 115 *Kinemics*, the study of units of gestural expression.

kineograph (ˈkaɪnɪəʊgrɑːf, -æ-). Also cineograph. [irreg. f. Gr. κινέ-ειν to move + -GRAPH.] A picture representing objects in motion, produced by bringing separate pictures before the eye in such quick succession as to blend the images into one continuous impression.

1891 *Anthony's Photogr. Bull.* IV. 100 A simpler optical illusion still is that known as the 'kineograph'. **1899** *Daily News* 14 July 6/4 Cineograph, or better, Kineograph, means a picture of movement—of moving objects.

kine-pox: see KINE *sb.*[1]

kinescope (ˈkɪnɪskəʊp). *Television.* [f. Gr. κίνη(σις movement + -SCOPE.] **1.** A cathoderay tube specially constructed for use in a television set. Chiefly *U.S.*

The registration as a proprietary name was cancelled in 1950.

1930 *Sci. Amer.* Feb. 147/3 Dr. Zworykin developed an entirely new type of cathode-ray tube for his receiving apparatus which he calls a 'kinescope'. **1932** *Official Gaz.* (U.S. Patent Office) 17 May 568/1 RCA Victor Company, Inc., Camden, N.J. Filed Feb. 6, 1931. *Kinescope* for Cathode Ray Tubes and Thermionic Tubes. **1933** V. K. ZWORYKIN in *Proc. IRE* XXI. 1656 The name 'kinescope' has been applied to the cathode ray tube used in the television receiver to distinguish it from ordinary cathode ray oscilloscopes because it has several important points of difference. **1949** B. GROB *Basic Television* ix. 144 The picture tube, or kinescope, has the funnel-shaped form and internal structure of a conventional cathode-ray tube. **1971** H. E. ENNES *Television Broadcasting* viii. 357 The kinescope upon which the image to be recorded is displayed is a special type of tube employing a flat face, with phosphor and brightness characteristics that allow use of inexpensive film.

2. A film recording made from a television broadcast.

1949 *Richmond* (Va.) *News Leader* 25 Oct. 30/1 Kinescope or television recording, the process of filming a television show off the receiving tube. **1953** *Manch. Guardian Weekly* 2 July 15/1 On June 2 a United States television network transmitted a kinescope version of the B.B.C.'s television of the Abbey Coronation service. **1957** *Economist* 19 Oct. 226/1 It buys a programme or series of programmes from, say, station KETC in St Louis, and then makes it available to all the other ETV outlets on kinescope. **1957** P. FRANK *Seven Days to Never* ii. 20 He took a course in American television and radio. Every Tuesday afternoon he listened to recordings, and watched kinescopes, of the most popular programs. **1964** L. A. WORTMAN *Closed-Circuit Television Handbk.* v. 93 The major advantage in kinescope recording is that the final film can be shown wherever there is a 16-mm projector.

Hence ˈ**kinescope** *v. trans.*, to make a kinescope of; ˈ**kinescoped** *ppl. a.*, reproduced from a kinescope recording; ˈ**kinescoping** *vbl. sb.*

1949 *Life* 17 Oct. 75 Each show is kinescoped (filmed and sound-tracked) and re-telecast from stations in the rest of the country. **1961** P. LEWIS *Educ. Television Guidebk.* iv. 70 *(heading)* Kinescoping possibilities. **1964** L. A. WORTMAN *Closed-Circuit Television Handbk.* v. 93 One can usually recognize a kinescoped telecast by virtue of its visual quality. **1967** *Telegraph* (Brisbane) 3 Mar. 12/1 The only way then to record a show was by a film technique called 'kinescoping'. .. At that time the quality was diabolical.

kinesi- (kaɪniːsɪ), before a vowel also **kines-**, combining form of Gr. κίνησις motion, used in certain scientific and medical terms: as **kinesiˈatric** *a.* [see IATRIC], relating to kinesiatrics (Ogilvie 1882). **kinesiˈatrics** [see -IC 2], the treatment of diseases by means of gymnastics or muscular action. **kinesiˈometer**, 'an instrument for determining quantitatively the motion of a part' (Gould *Med. Dict.* 1890). **kiˈnesipath** [cf. ALLOPATH], one who treats diseases by kinesipathy. **kinesiˈpathic** *a.*, pertaining to kinesipathy. **kineˈsipathist** = *kinesipath* (Webster 1864). **kineˈsipathy** = *kinesiatrics*. **kiˈnesiscope**, an electrical instrument (invented by Capt. McEvoy) placed at the sea bottom to detect the presence of steam vessels in the neighbourhood. **kinesiˈtherapy** [Gr. θεραπεία medical treatment; cf. F. *kinésithérapie*] = *kinesiatrics*. **kineˈsodic** *a.* [Gr. ὁδ-ός a path; cf. F. *kinésodique*], transmitting motor impulses from the brain, efferent. **kineˈsopathy**, erroneous form of *kinesipathy*.

1856 M. ROTH *Movem. Cure* (L.), The treatment by movements (which is also called kinesitherapy, *kinesiatrics). **1860** *All Year Round* No. 45. 450 One of these *Kinesipaths invented the amusing theory that 'synovia' was the cause of all bodily ailments. **1855** MAYNE *Expos. Lex.*, **Kinesipathy*,..a system of athletic exercises and feats of muscular strength, invented by..a fencing master and teacher of gymnastics in Stockholm. **1860** RUSSELL REYNOLDS *Yes & No* II. 139 He has gone the round of the 'pathies',..he has tried homœopathy, hydropathy, kinesipathy,..and I know not what besides. **1893** *Daily News* 8 June 5/8 The hydrophone, in connection with a new instrument named a *kinesiscope. **1874** DUNGLISON *Med. Dict.*, **Kinesodic*. **1878** FOSTER *Phys.* III. v. §3. 488 They speak of it accordingly as kinesodic and æsthesodic, as simply affording paths for motor and sensory impulses. **1864** MISS MULOCK *Ld. Erlistoun* 231 He..tried allopathy, homœopathy, *kinesopathy, and heaven knows how many pathies besides.

kinesic (kaɪˈniːsɪk), *a. Linguistics.* [f. Gr. κίνησ(ις movement + -IC.] Of or pertaining to communication effected non-vocally through movements or gestures. Hence **kiˈnesically** *adv.*

1952 R. L. BIRDWHISTELL *Introd. Kinesics* (U.S. Dept. State, Foreign Service Inst.) 15 It is suggested that any student beginning kinesic recording work on but one part of the body at a time. **1952** *Rep. 3rd Ann. Round Table Meeting Ling. & Lang. Teaching* (Georgetown Univ. Inst. Lang.) 66 A rather thorough preliminary study of *kinesics* has indicated that the kinesic system can be analyzed and described. **1955** *Etc.: Rev. Gen. Semantics* XIII. I. 18 He was kinesically more 'mature' than the other boys. **1959** *College English* XX. IV. 172 Kinesic and paralinguistic phenomena constitute separate patterned systems, which differ in their structure from culture to culture. **1964** CRYSTAL & QUIRK *Prosodic & Paralinguistic Features Eng.* ii. 18 Those kinesic phenomena which are unintended by the individual. **1965** L. PEDERSON in *Lang. Programs for Disadvantaged* (U.S. Nat. Council Teachers of English) 247 Most speech occurs in the form of dialogue with two or more participants actively cooperating at the structural, paralinguistic, kinesic, proxemic, and haptic level. **1967** L. THAYER *Communication* 61 Inspection of the working transcript of the linguistically and kinesically recorded data revealed repetitive and apparently systematic body behaviors. **1968** *Amer. Speech* XLIII. 202 There are many conventionalized kinesic systems, each with its own hierarchy. **1972** J. L. DILLARD *Black English* v. 203 It is quite believable..that gestural and kinesic cues might 'give away' a member of the Negro subculture to people who knew that culture.

kinesics (kaɪˈniːsɪks). *Linguistics.* [f. Gr. κίνησ-ις movement + -ICS.] The study of those body movements and gestures by which, as well as by speech, communication is made; body movements and gestures which convey meaning non-vocally.

1952 R. L. BIRDWHISTELL *(title)* Introduction to kinesics: an annotation system for analysis of body motion and gesture. **1955** *Etc.: Rev. Gen. Semantics* XIII. I. 12 Kinesics may be defined as the systematic study of the visually sensible aspects of non-verbal interpersonal communication. **1957** *Psychiatry* XX. 74 Kinesics, or gestures and motions, are not instinctive human nature but are learned systems. **1958** A. A. HILL *Introd. Ling. Struct.* xxi. 409 The vocal qualifiers together with kinesics make up the paralinguistic system. **1970** J. FAST *Body Lang.* (1971) i. 11 To understand this unspoken body language, kinesics experts often have to take into consideration cultural differences and environmental differences. **1972** W. M. AUSTIN in A. L. Davis *Culture, Class, & Lang. Variety* viii. 152 Kinesics is the study of body posture, tonus, and movement in man and the other animals.

kinesimeter (kaɪnɪˈsɪmɪtə(r)). [f. KINESI- + -METER.] An instrument for investigating the properties of different areas of the skin, by which a movable point whose position can be measured may be applied to the surface with a known force.

1885 H. H. DONALDSON in *Mind* X. 402 This machine was devised by Prof. [G.] Stanley Hall, and will be described in a forthcoming paper, under the name of the 'Kinesimeter'. **1901** E. B. TITCHENER *Exper. Psychol.* I. II. 145 *(caption)* Arm-rest, designed for use with kinesimeter.

kinesiology (kaɪniːsɪˈɒlədʒɪ). [f. KINESI- + -OLOGY.] The field of study concerned with the mechanics of (human) bodily movement.

1894 N. POSSE *Special Kinesiology* p. v, I have deemed it desirable to change the title into *Special Kinesiology*,—it being a treatise on the mechanics, effects, and classification of special exercises. **1936** *Nature* 14 Mar. 438/2 This book [sc. *Mechanics of Normal and Pathological Locomotion in Man*] should take a prominent place in the literature of kinesiology. **1941** *Res. Q. Amer. Assoc. Health & Physical Educ.* XII. 163 While kinesiology borders on the field of several sciences, its greatest practical interest is in the field of physical education. **1963** M. G. SCOTT *(title)* Analysis of human motion: a textbook in kinesiology.

Hence **kinesioˈlogic**, **-ˈlogical** *adjs.*, **kinesiˈologist**, a person who studies kinesiology or kinesics.

1941 *Res. Q. Amer. Assoc. Health & Physical Educ.* XII. 167 He presents a concise kinesiological analysis. *Ibid.* 165 The importance of the part he [*sc.* Aristotle] played as a founder of the study of the mechanics of movement is hardly realized by many contemporary kinesiologists. **1950** K. F. WELLS *Kinesiology* xvi. 350 *(heading)* The kinesiologic analysis of a movement. **1952** R. L. BIRDWHISTELL *Introd. Kinesics* (U.S. Dept. State, Foreign Service Inst.) 3 The term *social* kinesiologist has been selected as the term for one attempting to analyze systematically the data covered by kinesic investigation. *Ibid.* 15 This is particularly difficult for the average American mover when working with the kinesiological systems of other Americans. **1965** OSGOOD & SEBEOK *Psycholinguistics* iv. 85 Kinesiologists require training in objective looking—the untrained observer will be likely to perceive only those movements which are significant in his own 'language'.

kinesis (kaɪ-, kɪˈniːsɪs). Pl. **kineses**. [mod.L., f. Gr. κίνησις motion.] † **1.** *Cytology.* Karyokinesis, mitosis. *Obs. rare.* (Cf. KINETIC *a.* 4.)

1904 *Jrnl. R. Microsc. Soc.* 529 At the first metaphase there is a second division (? longitudinal) which appears preparatory to the second kinesis. **1906** *Ibid.* 282 The two constitutive branches of the definitive chromosomes..separate from one another in each chromosome at the first kinesis.

2. *Biol.* [Adopted (in G.) by W. Rothert 1901, in *Flora* LXXXVIII. 374, after its use as a suffix in *photokinesis*.] An undirected movement of an

organism that occurs in response to a particular kind of stimulus.
1905 *Jrnl. Compar. Neurol.* XV. 139 Kinesis is a term which seems to have been first used by Engelmann for the increase or decrease of activity produced by certain agencies. The fact that certain bacteria increase or decrease movement in the light he called photokinesis. Rothert accepted the term kinesis for such changes in the amount of activity produced by chemicals, calling this chemokinesis. **1940** FRAENKEL & GUNN *Orientation of Animals* i. 10 The term *taxis* is to-day used for directed orientation reactions. .. Undirected locomotory reactions, in which the speed of movement or the frequency of turning depend on the intensity of stimulation, we call kineses. **1955** STORER & USINGER *Elem. Zool.* xxiii. 394 Taxes and kineses.. enable insects and many other animals to find and inhabit the small environmental niche or microclimate in which each kind is most successful. **1960** L. PICKEN *Organization of Cells* x. 450 The formation of cell aggregates is undoubtedly favoured by a non-directional movement of the cells, by a kinesis, with thigmotaxis taking over once contact is established.

kinesthesia, -esthetic: see KINÆSTHESIS.

kinetheodolite (kɪnɪθiːˈɒdəlaɪt). Also (with hyphen) **kine-theodolite**. [f. Gr. κίνη(σις movement + THEODOLITE.] A telescope used to follow the path of a projectile, aircraft, or the like, and mounted so that its elevation and azimuth angles are indicated.
1941 *Illustr. London News* CXCVIII. 380/2 The girls work with two kine-theodolites set far apart and connected at the firing position by a central control post which photographs the shell-bursts. **1946** *Jrnl. R. Aeronaut. Soc.* L. 925/1 Bombs of differing weights were dropped... They were followed visually by kine-theodolites, which gave the flight path. **1958** *New Scientist* 21 Aug. 655/1 The contributions.. on the tracking of the Russian satellites.. were quite outstanding. Thus the data obtained using kine-theodolites by scientists of the Ministry of Supply were the most accurate optical observations reported. **1961** *Engineering* 26 May 750/3 Woomera has a number of double kinetheodolite sites, one instrument tracking the missile, the other the target aircraft. **1965** K. J. TURNER in M. A. Perry *Flight Test Instrumentation* III. 229 The model trajectories are recorded by.. kine-theodolites.

kinetic (kaɪˈnɛtɪk), *a.* (*sb.*) [ad. Gr. κῑνητικός moving: see -IC.]
A. *adj.* **1.** Producing or causing motion. *rare*—⁰.
1855 MAYNE *Expos. Lex.*, *Kinetic*..(*Physiol.*), exciting to move, or to act.
2. a. Of, pertaining or relating to, motion; due to or resulting from motion. ***kinetic energy***: see ENERGY 6. ***kinetic heating***, heat generated by the compression and acceleration of air by a fast-moving body. ***kinetic theory of heat, of gases***: the theory that heat, or the gaseous state, is due to motion of the particles of matter.
1864 *Reader* 2 Apr. 429/3 Till and about the year 1780.. the weightiest authorities inclined towards the kinetic theory of heat. **1866** *Lond. Rev.* 2 June 615/2 Correct principles of kinetic science. **1870** P. G. TAIT in *Nature* 29 Dec. 163/2 The grand modern ideas of Potential and Kinetic Energy cannot be too soon presented to the student. **1871** SIR W. THOMSON in *Daily News* 3 May, The kinetic theory of gases, shadowed forth by Lucretius, definitely stated by Daniel Bernoulli, largely developed by Herapath, made a reality by Joule, and worked out to its present advanced state by Clausius and Maxwell. **1879** THOMSON & TAIT *Nat. Phil.* I. I. §357 If, from any one configuration, two courses differing infinitely little from one another have again a configuration in common, this second configuration will be called a kinetic focus relatively to the first: or.. these two configurations will be called conjugate kinetic foci. **1881** STEVENSON *Virg. Puerisque* (ed. 8) 111, I still remember that the spinning of a top is a case of Kinetic Stability. **1954** *Aircraft Engineering* XXVI. 138/3 Kinetic heating is caused by two related phenomena; first the adiabatic compression of the air as it is brought up to the velocity of the leading edge or nose of the body and second the frictional heating which takes place in the boundary layer as the air adjacent to the surface tends to accelerate the air, through which the plane is passing, up to the flying speed. **1959** L. BROGLIO in *Adv. Aeronaut. Sci.* I. 216 The design of an aircraft or missile is often ruled by the transient-temperatures of its external surface, due to kinetic heating and radiation. **1970** *Progr. Aerospace Sci.* XI. 64 Another effect which occurs in flight.. concerns the influence of kinetic heating.
b. *Biol.* Of or pertaining to a kinesis (sense 2).
1905 *Amer. Naturalist* XXXIX. 167 It has been found convenient to distinguish between two factors in the effect of light on Drosophila, a kinetic effect and a directive one. **1914** *Jrnl. Exper. Zool.* XVII. 273 Animals, such as the blowfly larva, which respond phototactically to horizontal light show a simple kinetic response when subjected to uniform illumination from above. **1941** S. O. MAST in Calkins & Summers *Protozoa Biol. Res.* v. 277 Kinetic responses.—If an amoeba is kept for some time in very weak light it becomes inactive; if the light is then increased, the organism gradually becomes active again.
c. *transf.* and *fig.*, esp. active, dynamic, full of energy.
1931 H. G. WELLS *Work, Wealth & Happiness of Mankind* (1932) ix. 382 In every preceding phase where there has been a concentration of wealth it has been far less easily converted into kinetic purchasing power. **1934** —— *Exper. Autobiogr.* II. ix. 658 For the purposes of the state I proposed a division into four types of character, the poietic, the kinetic, the dull and the base. A primary problem of government was to vest all the executive and administrative work in the kinetic class. **1939** —— *Holy Terror* III. i. 218 They were at least kinetic, they wanted to make things happen even if they did not quite know what or how. **1956** N. CARDUS *Close of Play* 89 His life was short and kinetic. **1957** L. DURRELL *Justine* II. 134 It was these very defects of character—these vulgarities of the psyche—which constituted for me the greatest attraction of this weird kinetic personage. **1961** *Listener* 20 Apr. 707/3 His was an aural and kinetic imagination, not a visual one.
3. *Chem.* Of, pertaining to, or governed by the kinetics of a reaction.
1882 *Nature* 21 Dec. 183/2 What may perhaps be called the kinetic theory of chemical actions, the theory, namely, that the direction and amount of any chemical change is conditioned not only by the affinities, but also by the masses of the reacting substances, by the temperature, pressure, [etc.]. **1926** C. N. HINSHELWOOD *Kinetics Chem. Change Gaseous Syst.* ii. 48 We are concerned now with the kinetic measurements only. **1964** ROBERTS & CASERIO *Basic Princ. Org. Chem.* xiii. 402 Carbon-deuterium bonds are normally broken more slowly than carbon-hydrogen bonds and this so-called kinetic isotope effect provides a very general method for determining whether or not particular carbon-hydrogen bonds are broken in slow reaction steps. **1968** G. E. COATES et al. *Princ. Organometallic Chem.* i. 11 The 'kinetic stability' of carbon compounds has a variety of causes. **1968** R. O. C. NORMAN *Princ. Org. Synthesis* xiv. 458 The *para*-derivative is formed the faster (kinetic control).
4. *Cytology.* Pertaining to or involved in mitotic division; undergoing division. (Cf. KINESIS 1.)
1894 *Jrnl. R. Microsc. Soc.* 581 Nuclear division takes place under the control of the kinetic centres. **1910** G. N. CALKINS *Protozoöl.* i. 29 Definite, active, kinetic bodies closely associated with the mechanism of nuclear division and of locomotion. **1931** J. GRAY *Test-bk. Exper. Cytol.* viii. 141 The chromatic constituents of the kinetic nucleus. **1940** G. S. CARTER *Gen. Zool. Invertebr.* iii. 43 The centrosome seems to control the kinetic activities of the cell at division. **1960** L. PICKEN *Organization of Cells* iv. 150 Navashin (1933).. suggested that the number of kinetic bodies (centromeres) is primary and conditions the number of chromosomes. **1965** C. D. DARLINGTON *Cytology* II. i. 657 *Holomastigotoides tusitala*, whose giant chromosomes.. are always attached to the kinetic body or centriole [during mitosis].
5. *Phonetics.* Of consonants, vowels, etc.: changing in quality during utterance as opposed to being held constant.
1931 *Programme for Vacation Course for Foreign Students Cambridge* 3 Static and kinetic vowels. **1939** L. H. GRAY *Foundations of Lang.* iii. 53 Consonants can be.. static (or continuant), i.e. can be held continuously without changing quality..; or are kinetic, i.e., cannot be so held (plosives, affricates, and flaps). **1956** *English Studies* XXXVII. 68 The rise can be continued until the next kinetic tone is reached. **1961** Y. OLSSON *On Syntax Eng. Verb* ii. 21 Kingdon distinguishes between two types of intonation, static, with pitch kept level, and kinetic, with pitch changed in the course of the same note.
6. Of, pertaining to, or producing an artistic construction which depends upon movement for its effect. Esp. in phr. ***kinetic art***.
1957 J. LYNCH *Metal Sculpture* v. 105 It might be easier to define constructions, stabiles, mobiles and kinetic sculpture by what they are *not*. **1964** *Times Lit. Suppl.* 3 Sept. 775/3 The 'kinetic art' which is occupying so many of the younger artists today.. is largely based on a quasi-mathematical analysis of variation and motion. **1966** *Cambr. Rev.* 28 May 449/1 Schöffer.. claims that kinetic works of art are 'man's biological and psychological extension'. **1967** *Listener* 30 Mar. 434/1 At the Indica Gallery there is a kinetic exhibition. **1968** S. BANN tr. *Popper's Orig. & Devel. Kinetic Art* vii. 156 The majority of kinetic works composed on plane surfaces bring white or coloured light into play. **1969** *Listener* 16 Jan. 93/1 Modern developments fall more or less exactly into two groups which might roughly be called kinetic and psychedelic. **1971** J. WILLETT in A. Bullock *20th Century* x. 244/2 Serialism in every art owed an obvious debt to Schönberg and Webern; the kinetic artists to Calder and Moholy-Nagy. **1973** *Times* 27 Nov. 12/6 A good deal of European kinetic art was mere flashy mechanics (the light machines of Nicolas Schöffer, for example) but one of the best kinetic artists has been the German, Gerhard von Graevenitz, who now works in Amsterdam. **1974** *Evening News* (Edinburgh) 10 Apr. 1/8 The kinetic sculpture—the first of its kind in Scotland—was erected by Edinburgh Corporation and the Scottish Arts Council at a cost of £11,000. The structure blends perfectly with the rows of scaffolding masking the north side of Picardy Place.
B. *sb.* = KINETICS 1.
1873 CLIFFORD *Syllabus Lect.* in *Math. Papers* (1882) 516 Dynamic.. is divided into two parts; Static.. and Kinetic.. Properly speaking, Static is a particular case of Kinetic which it is convenient to consider separately.

kinetical (kaɪˈnɛtɪkəl), *a.* [f. as prec. + -AL¹.] Of or pertaining to kinetics.
1882 MINCHIN *Unipl. Kinemat.* 107 D'Alembert, in enunciating the kinetical principle known by his name, speaks of force of inertia as effective force. *Ibid.* 190 To introduce here a proposition which is not kinematical but kinetical.

kinetically (kaɪˈnɛtɪkəlɪ), *adv.* [f. KINETIC *a.*: see -ICALLY.] By kinetics; from the point of view of kinetics.
1909 in *Cent. Dict.* Suppl. **1926** C. N. HINSHELWOOD *Kinetics Chem. Change Gaseous Syst.* ii. 42 The thermal decomposition of nitrous oxide is kinetically bimolecular. **1941** [see CONTOUR *sb.* 1 e]. **1964** J. W. LINNETT *Electronic Struct. Molecules* vi. 101 This would mean that 1:2 addition would be favoured kinetically relative to 1:4 addition. **1967** *Oceanogr. & Marine Biol.* V. 198 An enzyme reaction that can readily be studied kinetically and the results analysed using the theory of absolute reaction rates. **1968** R. O. C. NORMAN *Princ. Org. Synthesis* iii. 92 In most reactions which can proceed by two or more pathways each of which gives a different set of products, the products isolated are those derived from the pathway of lowest free energy of activation... These reactions are described as being kinetically controlled.

kineticism (kaɪˈnɛtɪsɪz(ə)m). [f. KINETIC *a.* + -ISM.] = *kinetic art*; also, in *Music*, a mechanical and inexpressive style.
1939 B. FLES tr. *Křenek's Music Here & Now* iii. 84 A modern trend.. which, through its misinterpretation of neoclassicism, fell in with a streamlined kineticism. **1966** *Time* 28 Jan. 44 Manhattan's avant-garde Jewish Museum is currently showing 102 works by kineticism's established practitioners, Jean Tinguely and Nicolas Schöffer. **1972** *Daily Tel.* 28 Nov. 12/7 Dada was fostered by its nihilist aspects and from there we can trace the seeds of multi-media kineticism, underground cinema, and even the liquid theatre.

kineticist (kaɪˈnɛtɪsɪst). [f. KINETIC(S + -IST 2.]
1. An expert in or student of kinetics (sense 2) or gas kinetics.
1960 S. W. BENSON *Found. Chem. Kinetics* p. ix, I should like to acknowledge my most profound indebtedness to the many kineticists whose work has served as guide and inspiration. **1972** J. C. POLANYI *Chem. Kinetics* p. ix, The earliest concern of the kineticist was the overall rate of chemical reactions. **1972** *Nature* 17 Mar. 99/2 It is also very likely that the stem cells of a tumour.. are not estimated by the averaged measurements easily available to the kineticist. **1973** *Ibid.* 16 Feb. p. xv (Advt.), Applicants should be either gas kineticists, with an interest in photochemistry and spectroscopy, or have experience in mass spectroscopy.
2. A kinetic artist. Cf. KINETIC *a.* 6.
1970 *Guardian* 10 Feb. 8/4 Like a lot of the kineticists, she went on record.. with some dauntingly pretentious statements.. [about] the need to create constellations in her 'Perspex' and liquid reflections. **1971** *Guardian* 24 June 10/3 In the late fifties.. many kineticists.. were enraged by the élitism of the gallery system. **1971** J. WILLETT in A. Bullock *20th Century* x. 245/1 The Swiss kineticist Jean Tinguely's prodigally ingenious self-destructive machines.

kiˈnetics. [In form a pl. of KINETIC: see -IC 2.]
1. The branch of dynamics which investigates the relations between the motions of bodies and the forces acting upon them; opposed to *Statics*, which treats of bodies in equilibrium.
1864 in WEBSTER. **1866** *Lond. Rev.* 2 June 615/2 Between whiles he has kinetics to get up for the next morning. **1882** MINCHIN *Unipl. Kinemat.* 59 The particular case in which the resultant acceleration of a moving point is always directed towards a fixed.. centre is deserving of special notice on account of the part which it plays in kinetics.
2. a. A field of study concerned with the mechanisms and rates of chemical reactions or other kinds of process; see also *gas kinetics*.
1884 M. M. P. MUIR *Treat. Princ. Chem.* p. ix, The second part of the book is devoted to the subjects of dissociation, chemical change and equilibrium, chemical affinity, and the relations between chemical action and the distribution of the energy of the changing system. These, and cognate questions, I have ventured to summarise in the expression Chemical Kinetics. **1898** C. L. SPEYERS *Text-bk. Physical Chem.* vi. 125 Chemical kinetics.—Sometimes called chemical dynamics. It treats of the velocity of chemical reactions. **1910** *Encycl. Brit.* VI. 28/2 The law of chemical mass-action not only defines the conditions for chemical equilibrium, but contains at the same time the principles of chemical kinetics. **1953** FROST & PEARSON *Kinetics & Mechanism* i. 1 Kinetics deals with the rate of chemical reaction, with all factors which influence the rate of reaction, and with the explanation of the rate in terms of the reaction mechanism. **1956** G. R. KEEPIN *Physics Nucl. Kinetics* i. 2 The fields of fission physics and reactor kinetics have developed in the main as quite distinct and separate disciplines. **1972** CAPELLOS & BIELSKI *Kinetic Syst.* i. 1 The raw data of chemical kinetics are the measurements of the rates of reactions.
b. Those aspects of a particular process that relate to the rate at which it occurs; the details of the way a process occurs, esp. as regards its rate. Const. as *sing.* or *pl.*
1907 *Chem. Abstr.* I. 2763 (*heading*) The kinetics of nitration. **1924** *Jrnl. Gen. Physiol.* VII. 280 Studies on the kinetics of growth. **1926** C. N. HINSHELWOOD *Kinetics Chem. Change Gaseous Syst.* vii. 193 The kinetics of a reaction taking place on such a surface would be almost the same as on a surface of uniform structure. **1931** J. GRAY *Text-bk. Exper. Cytol.* xiii. 337 (*heading*) The kinetics of osmotic equilibria. **1939** *Chem. Abstr.* XXXIII. 4851 The kinetics of evaporation of droplets, and surfaces of pure liquids and of solns. of surface-inactive and surface-active substances.. are treated mathematically. **1946** *Proc. R. Soc.* A. CLXXXVII. 129 The kinetics of these reactions are not well understood. **1961** *Federation Proc.* XX. 437/2 The kinetics of infection by the virus of foot-and-mouth disease was determined as a function of virus cell concentration. **1968** *Brit. Med. Bull.* XXIV. 245/2 The techniques of investigating cell kinetics include gross measurement of increase in size, of a tumour cell colony for instance. **1968** R. O. C. NORMAN *Princ. Org. Synthesis* iii. 75 We have assumed the mechanism of the reaction in order to show how it leads to the observed kinetics. *Ibid.* 76 Although the complete kinetics are complex, they are given approximately by $-d[CH_3CHO]/dt = k[CH_3CHO][OH^-]$.

kinetin (ˈkaɪnɪtɪn). *Biochem.* [f. KINET(O- + -IN¹.] 6-Furfurylaminopurine, $C_{10}H_9N_5O$, a compound that is a decomposition product of the deoxyadenosine present in DNA and promotes cell division in plants.
1955 C. MILLER et al. in *Jrnl. Amer. Chem. Soc.* LXXVII. 1392/1 The name *kinetin* is proposed for this substance. *Ibid.* 2662/2 It was concluded that kinetin most probably is 6-furfurylaminopurine... The correctness of this structure has now been verified by synthesis. **1957** *Times* 11 Sept. 6/2 The practical uses of such substances as gibberellic acid and kinetin could not be forecast until further experiments were completed. **1971** I. D. J. PHILLIPS *Introd. Biochem. & Physiol. Plant Growth Hormones* i. 32 Kinetin does not occur

naturally in plants. **1973** *McGraw-Hill Yearbk. Sci. & Technol.* 277/1 Enlargement of [cambial] rays, both in height and width, was also obtained in pine plants by the application of a mixture of kinetin and auxin.

kinetite ('kaɪnɪtaɪt). [f. KINET(O- + -ITE¹.] A disused kind of explosive (see quot. 1918).

1887 *Jrnl. Soc. Chem. Industry* 29 Jan. 3/1 The so-called kinetite is virtually one of what Dr. Sprengel terms his 'safety explosives'. **1918** E. DE W. S. COLVIN *High Explosives* 142 Kinetite, an explosive which was considerably used from about 1885 to 1900, consisted of potassium chlorate incorporated with nitrobenzene and gelatinised with collodion cotton and sulphur.

kineto- (kaɪniːtəʊ), repr. Gr. κῑνητο-, comb. form of κινητός movable, used in several terms of recent origin, as **ki'netochore** (-kɔə(r)) *Cytology* [Gr. χῶρ-ος place] = *centromere* (*b*) (s.v. CENTRO-); **kineto'desma** (pl. **-desmas, -desmata**) *Biol.* [ad. F. *cinétodesme* (Chatton & Lwoff 1935, in *Compt. Rend. hebd. d. Séances et Mém. de la Soc. de Biol.* CXVIII. 1069), f. Gr. δεσμ-ός band, bond], in ciliates and flagellates, a thin fibre situated to one side of a row of kinetosomes and composed of a number of fibrils each of which terminates in one of them; hence **kineto'desmal** *a.*; **kineto'genesis**, the (theoretical) origination of animal structures in animal movements; **ki'netogram**, a motion picture taken by a kinetograph; **ki'netograph**, an apparatus for photographing a scene of action in every stage of its progress; *v. trans.*, to make a cinematographic record of; hence **ki,neto'graphic** *a.*; **kine'tographer** = CINEMATOGRAPHER; **kine'tography** = CINEMATOGRAPHY; **ki,neto'nucleus** *Biol.* = KINETOPLAST a; **ki'netophone**, an apparatus combining the functions of a kinetoscope (*b*) and a phonograph; **ki,neto'phonograph**, a kinetograph with mechanism for recording sounds; **ki'netoscope**, (*a*) 'a sort of movable panorama' (Webster 1864); (*b*) an apparatus for reproducing the scenes recorded by the kinetograph; (*c*) an instrument by which arcs of different radii are combined in the production of curves (Knight *Dict. Mech.* 1875); hence **ki,neto'scopic** *a.*; **ki,neto'skotoscope** [Gr. σκότος darkness: see -SCOPE] (see quot.).

1934 L. W. SHARP *Introd. Cytol.* (ed. 3) ix. 116 The region ..has been variously called the 'fiber-attachment point', 'insertion region', 'primary constriction', 'kinetic constriction', 'attachment constriction', and 'Trennungstelle'... The convenient term *kinetochore (= movement place) has been suggested to the author by J. A. Moore. The use of the term is recommended. **1936** *Biol. Bull.* LXX. 484 The mitotic movement of chromosomes is closely associated or perhaps even dependent on the activities of the kinetochore. **1961** WILSON & MORRISON *Cytol.* iv. 90 In many chromosomes, segments near or adjacent to the kinetochore are covered by this definition [of heterochromatin] and are also frequently heteropycnotic in the purely cytological sense. **1970** AMBROSE & EASTY *Cell Biol.* ix. 296 Each chromosome carries a distinct region known as a centromere or kinetochore which plays a fundamental role in chromosome movements during mitosis. **1949** *Kinetodesma [see KINETY]. **1953** *Biol. Bull.* CIV. 419 The kinetodesmas on the right ventral side of the animal. **1967** E. J. W. BARRINGTON *Invertebr. Struct. & Function* iii. 49 One special problem..is presented by the existence in ciliate Protozoa of patterns of fibres, called kinetodesmata, which lie in the ectoplasm and which are closely associated with the basal bodies of the cilia. *Ibid.*, The kinetodesma is visible as a fibre with the light microscope,..but electron microscopy is needed to elucidate fully its complex relationships. **1950** A. LWOFF *Probl. Morphogenesis Ciliates* vii. 54 *Kinetodesmal fibers. **1953** Kinetodesmal [see KINETOSOMAL *a.*]. **1884** E. D. COPE *Orig. Fittest* (1887) 423 The 'law of use and effort'..that animal structures have been produced, directly or indirectly, by animal movements, or the doctrine of *kinetogenesis. **1893** OSBORNE in Williams *Geol. Biology* (1895) 324 The changes *en route* [in the Mammalia] lead us to believe either in predestination..or in kinetogenesis. **1897** *Knowledge* Sept. 217/2 When making the original kinetograms. **1891** *Times* 29 May 5/1 [Mr. Edison said] The *kinetograph is a machine combining electricity with photography. **1897** *Knowledge* 218/1 Slow movements may be *kinetographed. **1897** *Knowledge* 217/2 Reproduced through the labours of 'special' *kinetographers. *Ibid.* 217/1 Kinetography is based upon the principle of the well-known zoetrope. **1894** DICKSON *Life Edison* 316 The *dramatis personæ* of the *kinetographic stage. **1906** H. M. WOODCOCK in *Q. Jrnl. Microsc. Sci.* L. 182 The resulting body, which may be termed the *kinetonucleus, passes into the now rounded trophonucleus. **1920** W. E. AGAR *Cytol.* vi. 193 This view was founded partly on analogy with certain Protista; for example Trypanosomes, where a darkly staining body ('kinetonucleus') which is in close anatomical relation to the flagellum and therefore apparently concerned with the function of locomotion, is supposed by many to have been derived from the nucleus. **1938** [see KINETOPLAST]. **1960** L. PICKEN *Organization of Cells* vi. 240 The kinetonucleus of trypanosomes and of the bodonids normally multiplies by division. **1896** *19th Cent.* July 135 The *Kinetophone is not at the [music-] halls yet, perhaps; but is probably on the way to them. **1894** DICKSON *Life Edison* 303 The comprehensive term for this invention is the *kineto-phonograph. *Ibid.*, The kinetograph and the *kinetoscope..relate respectively to the taking and reproduction of movable but soundless objects. *Ibid.* 311 A popular and inexpensive adaptation of *kinetoscopic methods. **1896** *Westm. Gaz.* 18 Mar. 2/1 The *kinetoskotoscope... By means of this barbarously termed piece of apparatus it is possible, so we are told, to see the motions of the bones of the finger when bent backwards and forwards.

kinetoplast (kaɪ'niːtəʊplɑːst, -æ-). *Biol.* [ad. F. *kinétoplaste* (A. Alexeieff 1917, in *Compt. Rend. hebd. d. Séances et Mém. de la Soc. de Biol.* LXXX. 512): see KINETO- and -PLAST.] **a.** A structure lying close to a kinetosome in some protozoa, esp. trypanosomes. **b.** This structure together with the kinetosome; now *rare* or *Obs.*

1925 *Manson's Trop. Dis.* (ed. 8) 636 This composite body is known as the kinetoplast, and is composed of a minute blepharoplast, or basal body, and a parabasal body. **1938** *Trans. R. Soc. Trop. Med. & Hygiene* XXXII. 333 In referring to the prominent dark-staining structure at the base of the flagellum in trypanosomes I have at one time used the term *parabasal*, later changing to *kinetonucleus*, while the name *kinetoplast* has been employed to denote the complex kinetonucleus (or parabasal) + blepharoplast (or basal granule)... While the conception of the nuclear nature of this element (hence 'kinetonucleus') has been discarded long ago, considerable doubt has also been thrown on its interpretation as a parabasal body... In the present paper the term *kinetoplast* has accordingly been employed in its original sense, to denote the kinetonucleus alone (without the blepharoplast). **1961** MACKINNON & HAWES *Introd. Study Protozoa* ii. 101 In the Trypanosomidae and some other protomonads..there is a body lying near the blepharoplast which..is generally well preserved by acetic acid fixatives like Bouin; it is F +; it is self-perpetuating, divides when the blepharoplast divides, and one of its daughters goes to each product of fission... To it the name kinetoplast is applied... The term parabasal body (unfortunately applied at times to the structure just defined as a kinetoplast) is here reserved for an organelle best seen in the Trichomonadida... It is more complex than the kinetoplast, usually compound, F −, and rarely if ever completely preserved except by 'cytological' fixatives. It is not self-reproducing. **1971** *New Scientist* 13 May 370 Certain single-celled organisms are propelled forwards in the water by flagellae, which draw their power from a single huge mitochondrion called a kinetoplast.

kinetosome (kaɪ'niːtəʊsəʊm). *Biol.* [f. KINETO- + -SOME⁴.] A cytoplasmic structure which forms the base of a cilium or flagellum.

1912 C. E. ALLEN in *Archiv für Zellforschung* VIII. 134 It seems plain..that the plates and the groups of smaller bodies—which will be referred to as kinetosomes—are mutually equivalent. **1934** L. W. SHARP *Introd. Cytol.* (ed. 3) xiv. 203 The granules and plates in the earlier spermatogenous cells [of bryophytes] were called 'kinetosomes' and 'kinoplasmic plates' by Allen (1912). **1949** *Growth* XIII. Suppl. 61 In all animals or plants, as well as in flagellates or ciliates, at the basis of each flagellum or cilium, a spherical corpuscle is to be seen: the kinetosome. **1960** L. PICKEN *Organization of Cells* vii. 273 In molluscan, amphibian, and ciliate kinetosomes, but not in those in mammalian ciliated tissues, there is a prolongation of the kinetosome base as a single or double, striated fibre. *Ibid.*, In the ciliates, kinetosomes appear to generate not only cilia but (and alternatively, only) trichocysts and a variety of types of fibril. **1961** MACKINNON & HAWES *Introd. Study Protozoa* ii. 71 Asexual reproduction is universal [among the Mastigophora]... The basal granule (blepharoplast or kinetosome) of the flagellum divides, and it frequently acts as a centriole. **1974** BROWN & BERTKE *Textbk. Cytol.* (ed. 2) xiii. 273/2 At the base of the shaft of a cilium or flagellum but within the cell itself is the basal body... This structure is called the kinetosome by protozoologists or the blepharoplast by some phycologists.

Hence **kineto'somal** *a.*

1949 *Growth* XIII. Suppl. 77 (*heading*) Genetic continuity of kineties. Organization of kinetosomal populations. **1953** *Biol. Bull.* CIV. 418 The kinetodesmal bundles lie to one side of the kinetosomes and..the individual fibrils curve laterally from their kinetosomal origins to join the main bundle.

kinety ('kaɪnətɪ). *Biol.* [ad. F. *cinétie* (Chatton & Lwoff 1935, in *Compt. Rend. hebd. d. Séances et Mém. de la Soc. de Biol.* CXVIII. 1069), f. Gr. κινητ-ικός for putting in motion: see -Y³.] In ciliates and flagellates, a kinetodesma together with its row of associated kinetosomes.

1949 *Growth* XIII. Suppl. 62 Consider..a classical and simple ciliate of the *Leucophrys* type... The cilia are organized in 29 somatic rows. These rows, or kineties, are complex structures. You see: 1) a fiber: the kinetodesma; 2) a line of kinetosomes. **1953** *Biol. Bull.* CIV. 408 The primary fibrillar apparatus of ciliates consists of a number of parallel structural units, the kineties. **1967** J. H. WILMOTH *Biol. Invertebr.* ii. 19 The connecting kinetosomes and kinetodesma form a functional and structural unit called a kinety.., but are not connected to other kineties. *Ibid.*, It is of extreme significance that flagellates at cell division cleave parallel to the kineties, while among ciliates the cleavage plane crosses kineties.

kinfolk: see KIN *sb.*¹ 9.

king (kɪŋ), *sb.* Forms: 1 cyning, (-incg), kyning, cining, cyniȝ, 1–2 cyng, cing, (1 cyncg, ching), 1–6 kyng, 4–6 kynge, (4 kinge, kin, 5 kynnge, kink, keng), 2– king. [A Com. Teut. word: OE. *cyning* = OFris. *kin-*, *ken-*, *koning*, OS. *kuning* (MDu. *coninc*, Du. *koning*, MLG. *kon(n)ink*), OHG. *chun-*, *kuning*:—OTeut. **kuningo-z*, a derivative of **kunjo-*, Goth. *kuni*, OE. *cynn*, KIN, race, etc. The ON. equivalent was *konong-r*, *-ungr* (Sw. *konung*). Finnish *kuningas* king, and Lith. *kuningas* lord, priest, were early adoptions from Teut. In most of the Teut. languages two reduced forms appear: 1) OE. *cyniȝ* = OFris. *kinig*, etc., OS. *kunig* (MDu. *conich*), OHG. *chun-*, *kunig* (MHG. *künic*, *künec*, G. *könig*, †*künig*); 2) OE. *cyng*, *cing* = MHG. *künc* (obs. G. *küng*, *kung*), ON. *kóngr* (Sw. *kung*, Da. *konge*). Compare OE. *peniȝ* (G. *pfennig*) PENNY, for *pening*; ON. *þengar* pl. (Da. *penge*) for *peningar*.

As to the exact relation, in form and sense, of *king* to *kin*, views differ. Some take it as a direct derivative, in the sense either of 'scion of the kin, race, or tribe', or 'scion of a (or the) noble kin', comparing *dryhten* (:—**druhtino-z*) 'lord' from *dryht* (:—**druhti-z*) 'army, folk, people', *dryht-bearn* 'lordly or princely child, prince', lit. 'child of the nation', ON. *fylkir* 'king' from *folk*, Goth. *þiudans* 'king', from *þiuda* people, nation. Others refer **kuningo-z* immediately to the supposed masc. **kuni-z*, preserved in comb. in OHG. *chuni-*, OE. *cyne-* (see KINE-¹), taking it as = 'son or descendant of one of (noble) birth'. See Hildebrand in Grimm, and Kluge, s.v. *König*; Franck s.v. *Koning* etc.]

(The genitive plural in southern ME. was *kingene*, *-en*, *-yn*.)

I. 1. a. The usual title of the male sovereign ruler of an independent state, whose position is either purely hereditary, or hereditary under certain legal conditions, or, if elective, is considered to give to the elected the same attributes and rank as those of a (purely or partly) hereditary ruler.

In OE. the title appears first as the name of the chiefs of the various Anglian and Saxon 'kins', tribes, or clans, who invaded Britain, and of the petty states founded by them, as well as of the native British chiefs or princes with whom they fought, and of the Danish chiefs who at a later time invaded and occupied parts of the country. Among the Angles and Saxons the kingship was not strictly hereditary, according to later notions; but the *cyning* was chosen or accepted in each case from a recognized kingly or royal *cynn* or family (usually tracing its genealogy up to Woden). With the gradual ascendancy and conquests of Wessex in the 9th and 10th c., the king of the West Saxons became the king of the Angelcynn, Angelþéode, or English (*Angligenarum*, *gentis Angligenæ*, *Anglorum*), and the tribal kings came to an end. But there still remained a King of Scotland, and several petty kings in Ireland. In European and other more or less civilized countries, *king* came to be the title of the ruler of an independent organized state called a *kingdom*; but in mediæval times, as subsequently in the German Empire, some *kings* were really or nominally subordinate to the Emperor (as ostensibly representing the Roman *Cæsar* or *Imperator*), and a King was held to rank below an Emperor. In reference to ancient times the name is applied, like L. *rex*, Gr. βασιλεύς, Heb. *melek*, to the more or less despotic rulers not only of great dominions like Assyria, Persia, Egypt, but of petty states or towns such as Jericho, Ai, Mycenæ, Ithaca, Syracuse, and Rome. It is still applied to the native rulers of petty African states, towns, or tribes, Polynesian islands, and the like.

king designate, possessive: see the adjs. ***uncrowned king***, one who has the power, though not the rank, of a king.

*a***855** *O.E. Chron.* an. 577 Her Cuþwine and Ceawlin fuhton wiþ Brettas, and hie .iii. kyningas ofsloȝon, Coinmail, and Condidan, and Farinmail. **858** *Charter* in *O.E. Texts* 438 Se cyning sealde..wullafe fif sulung landes. **875** *O.E. Chron.*, And for Godrum and Oscytel and Anwynd, þa .iii. cyningas, of Hreopedune to Grantebrycge mid micle here, and sæton þær an ȝear. **971** *Blickl. Hom.* 69 Hi..hine weorþodon swa ciniȝe ȝeriseþ. *Ibid.* 71 He wæs to cinge onȝyten & ȝehered. *c***1001** *O.E. Chron.* (Parker MS.) an. 1001 þæs cynincges ȝerefa. *a***1131** *O.E. Chron.* an. 1123 Se kyng alihte dune of his hors. *Ibid.* an. 1124 Se king let don þone eorl..on heftnunge. *c***1175** *Lamb. Hom.* 115 Ðes kingges rihtwisnesse areteð his kine setle. *c***1205** LAY. 24609 þider weoren icumen seouen kingene sunen. *c***1250** *Gen. & Ex.* 834 Neȝ ilc burȝe hadde ise louereding, Sum was king, and sum kumeling. **1297** R. GLOUC. (Rolls) 8179 He smot þoru out wiþ a launce on of hor hexte kinge. *a***1300** *Cursor M.* 3382 Ysmael had wijfs thrin þat kinges twelue þar come of him. *Ibid.* 4243 To putifer, þe king stiward. **1387** TREVISA *Higden* (Rolls) V. 263 Wel nygh al þe kyngyn lynage of straunge naciouns come of þis Woden. *Ibid.* VI. 151 Cedwalla, a stalworþe ȝongelyng of kyngene kynde. *c***1400** *Rom. Rose* 6851 These emperours..Or kyngis, dukis, & lordis grete. *c***1430** *Syr Gener.* (Roxb.) 888 Of the Rodes he was a king son. *c***1460** FORTESCUE *Abs. & Lim. Mon.* v. (1885) 119 What dishonour is this, and abatynge of the glorie of a kynge. **1535** COVERDALE *1 Pet.* ii. 17 Feare God. Honoure the kynge [**1382** WYCLIF Make ȝe the kyng honourable; **1388** onoure ȝe the king]. **1602** SHAKS. *Ham.* IV. v. 123 There's such Diuinity doth hedge a King. **1605** —— *Lear* IV. vi. 109, I, euery inch a King, When I do stare, see how the Subiect quakes. **1613** PURCHAS *Pilgrimage* (1614) 836 Their Kings were no other then the chiefe in every Cottage, which consisted of one kindred. **1624** CAPT. SMITH *Virginia* II. 37 The forme of their [Indians'] Common-wealth is a Monarchicall government, one as Emperour ruleth ouer many Kings or Governours. **1718** PRIOR *Power* 275 What is a king?—a man condemn'd to bear The public burden of the nation's care. **1784** COWPER *Task* V. 188 War's a game, which were their subjects wise, Kings would not play at. **1794** COLERIDGE *Relig. Musings*, The great, the rich, the mighty men, The Kings and the chief captains of the world. **1847** PRESCOTT *Peru* (1850) II. 20 The title of King, by which the earlier Aztec princes are distinguished by Spanish writers, is supplanted by that of Emperor in the later reigns. **1872** E. W. ROBERTSON *Hist. Ess.* 206 Thus he [Henry I of Germany] was a king, but not an anointed sovereign.

b. In phrases and proverbs. ***king and country***: the objects of allegiance for a patriot in a monarchy.

1539 TAVERNER *Erasm. Prov.* (1552) 4 Kynges haue manye eares and manye eyes. **1546** J. HEYWOOD *Prov.* (1867) 39 Where as nothing is, the kynge must lose his right. **1591** *2nd Pt. Troublesome Raigne K. John* (1611) 106 A king is a king though fortune do her worst. **1625** BACON *Ess.* xxiii. 135 Be so true to thy Selfe, as thou be not false to Others;

Specially to thy King, and Country. **1659** HOWELL (N.), The king's cheese goes half away in paring, viz., among so many officers. **1694** MOTTEUX *Rabelais* IV. xvi. (1737) 65 Which made the Dog get on his Legs, pleas'd like a little King. *a* **1732** [see HAPPY 4]. **1765** BLACKSTONE *Comm.* I. vii. 246 The king can do no wrong... The prerogative of the crown extends not to do any injury: it is created for the benefit of the people, and therefore cannot be exerted to their prejudice. **1773** C. JENNENS *Saul* III. 204 O Jonathan! how nobly didst thou die, for thy King and Country Slain! **1788** BURNS *Let. to Mrs. Dunlop* 16 Aug., The old Scottish proverb says well, 'Kings' caff is better than ither folks' corn'. **1803** M. WILMOT *Russ. Jrnls.* (1934) 11 Tis pleasant to see how true the Britons are to their King & Country. **1814** SCOTT *Waverley* III. v. 60 Colonel Talbot was in every point the English soldier. His whole soul was devoted to the service of his king and country. **1913** BARRIE *Quality St.* I. 15 If..death or glory was the call, you would take the shilling, ma'am... For King and Country. **1933** *Times* 11 Feb. 8/4 After a debate at the Oxford Union Society on Thursday, a motion 'that this House will in no circumstances fight for its King and country' was carried by 275 votes to 153. **1941** 'G. ORWELL' in *Partisan Rev.* Mar.–Apr. 109 There does not effectively exist any policy between being patriotic in the 'King and Country' style and being pro-Hitler. **1965** A. NICOL *Truly Married Woman* 48 Kill for food, kill dangerous things, kill for King and country.

c. ***the three kings***, the Wise Men who came from the East to worship the new-born Christ.

Frequently called ***the (three) kings of Cologne***, from a prevalent belief that their bodies were preserved at that city, having been removed thither in 1164 from Milan, where they were alleged to have been discovered in 1158.

c **1200** *Trin. Coll. Hom.* 45 þe þre kinges þe comen of estriche. *c* **1350** *Winner & Waster* 503 To þe kirke of Colayne þer þe kynges ligges. **1387** TREVISA *Higden* (Rolls) IV. 283 þe þre kynges [L. *magi*] come to Ierusalem. *Ibid.* VIII. 43 Rauph bisshop of Coloyne brouȝt þe bodies of þe (þre) kynges of Coloyne out of Melan. *c* **1400** *Three Kings Cologne* 2 [þe] þree holy and worshipfull kyngis of Coleyn: Iaspar, Melchyor, and Balthaser. **1583** *Leg. Bp. St. Androis* 669 As Culen Kyngis that Christ adorned, *Per aliam viam* he returned.

d. ***the Books of Kings***: certain books of the Old Testament which contain the history of the Kings of Israel and Judah. Also ellipt. ***Kings.***

In the original Hebrew text there was only one book so called, corresponding to 1st and 2nd Kings in the present English Bible. In the Septuagint, followed by the Vulgate, and so by the older English versions, these two are reckoned as the 3rd and 4th, the two books of Samuel being called 1st and 2nd Kings.

1382 WYCLIF *1 Kings* [i.e. *1 Samuel*] Prol., In this book of Kingis the first is contened, how Anna..axide of God to haue a sone. *c* **1460** FORTESCUE *Abs. & Lim. Mon.* i. (1885) 110 The viij[th] chapiter of the first boke of kynges [1 Sam. viii.]. **1535** COVERDALE, The first boke of the kynges, otherwyse called the first boke of Samuel. **1611** BIBLE, The first Booke of Samuel, otherwise called, The first Booke of the Kings. *Ibid.*, Contents..1 Samuel, 2 Samuel, 1. Kings, 2. Kings, 1 Chronicles [etc.].

2. With additions: **a.** As a title, now placed immediately before a personal name, as *King Edward*, †in OE. (rarely in later use) immediately after it, as *Ælfred cyning*, *Harold cyng*; formerly also *the King*, before or after the name.

In *OE. Chron.* (Laud MS.) the annal of 1066 has *se cyng Eadweard, Harold eorl, Harold cyng, Willelm eorl, þe cyng Willelm.*

O.E. Chron. an. 588 Her Ælle cyning forþ ferde. *Ibid.* 604 East Seaxe..under Sæbrihte cinge and Mellite bisceope. **836** *Charter* in *O.E. Texts* 453 Ecȝhard..ðes friodom waes biȝeten aet Wiȝlafe cyninge. *c* **888** K. ÆLFRED *Boeth.* i, þa.. yfel þe se cyning Ðeodric..dyde. **971** *Blickl. Hom.* 161 On Herodes daȝum þæs cyninges. *a* **1020** in Kemble *Cod. Dipl.* IV. 9 Cnut cing gret Lyfing arcebisceop. *a* **1100** *O.E. Chron.* an. 1066 þe cyng Willelm ȝeherde þæt secgen. *a* **1150** *Ibid.* an. 1132 Ðis ȝear com Henri king to þis land. **1297** R. GLOUC. (Rolls) 7574 King Macolom spousede Margarete so; Ac king Willam..Wende aȝen to normandie. *c* **1400** *Three Kings Cologne* 12 Kyng Ezechias was syke to þe dethe. *Ibid.* 14 þerfore god sent to Ezechias þe kyng. **1535** COVERDALE *Matt.* i. 6 Dauid the kynge begat Salomon. **1591** SHAKS. *1 Hen. VI*, II. v. 66 The lawfull Heire of Edward King, the Third of that Descent. *Ibid.* 76 Third Sonne To King Edward the Third. *a* **1635** NAUNTON *Fragm. Reg.* (Arb.) 28 The people hath it to this day in proverb, King Harry loved a man. **1711** ADDISON *Spect.* No. 129 ¶10 We fancied ourselves in King Charles the Second's reign. **1784** COWPER *Task* VI. 663 Two staves, Sung to the praise and glory of King George. **1785** GROSE *Dict. Vulg. T.* s.v., He is one of king John's men, eight score to the hundred: a saying of a little undersized man. **1876** FREEMAN *Norm. Conq.* V. xxii. 16 The two great notes of time [in Domesday] are 'the time of King Eadward', and 'the time when King William came into England'. **1895** *Newspr.* King Khama's visit to England.

b. With specification of the people or country over which a king's rule extends, as *King of the Romans*, *of Italy*. Also ***king of kings***, a king who has other kings under him, an emperor: often assumed as a title by Eastern monarchs. ***king of men***, translating Gr. ἄναξ ἀνδρῶν.

a **855** *O.E. Chron.* an. 488 Her Æsc feng to rice, and was .xxiiii. wintra Cantwara cyning. *Ibid.* an. 508 Her Cerdic and Cynric ofsloȝon ænne Brettisc cyning, þam was nama Natanleod. *c* **975** *O.E. Chron.* (Parker MS.) an. 975 Eadgar Engla cyning ceas him oðer leoht. *a* **1100** *O.E. Chron.* (Laud MS.) an. 1079 Melcolm cyng of Scotlande. *c* **1154** *Ibid.* an. 1129 Se kyng of France. *c* **1205** LAY. 13320 þe king of Norewæiȝe..& þere Densemonne king. *c* **1330** R. BRUNNE *Chron. Wace* (Rolls) 11945 First com Epistrot þe kyng of Grece..Pandras þe kyng of Egipte. **1382** WYCLIF *Ezra* vii. 12 Artaxerses, king of kingus, to Esdre the prest. —— *Dan.* ii. 37 Thou art kyng of kyngus, and God of heuen ȝaue to thee kingdam. **1405** *Rolls Parlt.* III. 605/1 The Wyrshipful Prince Robert the King of Scotland. *a* **1552** LELAND *Collect.* (1774) II. 547 Edwarde de Bruse,..proclayming hym self King of Kinges yn Ireland. **1647** WARD *Simp. Cobler* 51 There is a quadrobulary saying, which passes current in the Westerne World, That the Emperour is King of Kings, the Spaniard, King of Men, the French King of Asses, the King of England, King of Devils. **1715–20** POPE *Iliad* XIX. 54 The king of men, Atrides, came the last. **1835** THIRLWALL *Greece* I. v. 129 He leads an army against Augeas, king of Elis. **1876** A. ARNOLD in *Contemp. Rev.* June 32 The King-of-Kings.. signified his willingness.

c. ***King Charles***, short for *King Charles's Spaniel* (see SPANIEL): ***King Harry***, the goldfinch.

1808 M. WILMOT *Russ. Jrnls.* (1934) III. 352 One of Princess D's great passions..is that for Dogs of the King Charles's breed. [*a* **1825** FORBY *Voc. E. Anglia* s.v., King Harry Redcap, is the gold-finch..King Harry Blackcap, is the bird which is commonly called simply the blackcap.] **1848** *Zoologist* VI. 2186 The goldfinch..is the King Harry from its beautiful crown. **1848** THACKERAY *Van. Fair* lxiv. 589 A King Charles in her lap, a white parasol swaying over her head. **1858** GEO. ELIOT *Scenes Clerical Life* I. 56 A little 'King Charles', with a crimson ribbon round his neck..is jumping on the sofa. **1883** *Cassell's Nat. Hist.* II. 132 The King Charles of the present day is an interesting example of deterioration.

3. Applied to a woman, esp. one who rules or bears herself like a king. *rare.*

1297 R. GLOUC. (Rolls) 869 Hennin & Morgan..adde despit þat womman king ssolde alonde beo. **1796** BURKE *Regic. Peace* iv. Wks. IX. 53 The Hungarian Subjects of Maria Theresa..called her..a King... She lived and died a King. **1898** *Daily News* 30 Aug. 4/5 After the King died his consort determined that her daughter should be a King, not a Queen.

4. Applied to God or Christ. Freq. in phr. ***King of heaven, of bliss, of glory, King of kings***, etc.

871–89 *Charter* in *O.E. Texts* 452 ȝehalde hine heofones cyning in þissum life. **971** *Blickl. Hom.* 203 To þæm cyninga cyninge, to Criste sylfum. *a* **1300** *Cursor M.* 8100 Pine on þat tre thole he sal, þe king o blis. *a* **1325** *Te Deum* in *Prose Psalter* 192 þou, Christ, art kynge of glorie [**1535** in *Goodly Prymer*, Thou art the kyng of glory O Christe]. *c* **1375** *Sc. Leg. Saints* ii. (*Paul*) 966 He..[at the] last Iugment sall bryng nere hand all men befor þe kyng. **1382** WYCLIF *Rev.* xvii. 14 For he is Lord of lordes and kyng of kyngis [**1611** For he is Lord of Lords, and King of kings]. **1387** TREVISA *Higden* (Rolls) VIII. 189 Kyngene Kyng schal destroye þis rewme wiþ double meschef. *c* **1400** MAUNDEV. (Roxb.) Pref. 1 He þat was King of heuen and of erthe. **1500–20** DUNBAR *Poems* x. 28 To him that is of kingis King. **1548–58** *Bk. Com. Prayer* (Prayer Queen's Majesty), O Lord our heuenly father, high and mighty king of kynges, Lorde of lordes, the onely ruler of princes. **1667** MILTON *P.L.* v. 640 Th' all-bounteous King, who showrd With copious hand. **1781** COWPER *Truth* 179 What purpose has the King of Saints in view? **1871** E. F. BURR *Ad Fidem* iv. 68 The King whose twin names are Light, and Love.

5. A title given to certain persons holding a real or pretended supreme authority or rank, or to one who plays the king.

e.g. ***King Cæsar***, a children's game (see quot. 1849); ***King of Heralds***, the King Herald or King-of-Arms; ***King of Ribalds***: see RIBALD; ***King of the Sacrifices***, one of the Roman priests (*rex sacrorum*); esp. the leading person in some game or sport, as ***King of the Bean, of the Cockneys, of May, of Misrule***: see BEAN *sb.*, etc.; ***King Arthur, King I am, King of Cantland, King of the Castle***, certain games (see quots.) so called from the chief player.

1656 BLOUNT *Glossogr.*, *King of Heralds*..is an Officer at Arms, that hath the preheminence of this Society. **1709** *Grecian Plays* 43 [The Greeks] had likewise their Basilinda, representing our Questions and Commands, or King I am. **1781** GIBBON *Decl. & F.* xxviii. III. 71 The King of the Sacrifices represented the person of Numa, and of his successors, in the religious functions, which could be performed only by royal hands. **1808–25** JAMIESON, *King of Cantland*, a game of children in which one of a company being chosen King o' Cantland, and two goals appointed [etc.]. **1847–52** HALLIWELL, *King-Arthur*, a game used at sea, when near the line, or in a hot latitude. It is performed thus [description follows]. **1849** *Boy's Own Bk.* 36 *King Cæsar*,..the ground is divided into three parts... The spaces at the end, called bases, being much smaller than the middle one. The..players..all go into one of the bases, except 'the King'..; he places himself..between the two bases, and the others run from base to base... Should the King..succeed in intercepting one of them, he claps him on the head with his hand three times, and each time repeats the words, 'I crown thee, King Cæsar'... This game is sometimes called 'Rushing Bases'. **1890** *J.G. Wood's Boy's Mod. Playmate* 147 *King of the Castle*... One player stands upon a mound, crying, 'I am king of the castle', and the others try to pull him down. **1969** I. & P. OPIE *Children's Games* iii. 140 The Victorian schoolboys' excuse for a rough-house called 'King Caesar' or 'Rushing Bases'.

6. a. One who in a certain sphere or class has supremacy or pre-eminence compared to that of a king. Since the 19th cent. often applied to great merchants, manufacturers, etc., with defining word prefixed, as *alkali-*, *fur-*, *railway-king.*

1382 WYCLIF *Job* xli. 25 [34] He [Leviathan] ys king vpon alle the sones of pride. **1508** KENNEDIE *Flyting w. Dunbar* 326 Confess thy crime, hald Kenydy the king. **1567** *Gude & Godlie B.* (S.T.S.) 12 Distroy the Deuill..Quhilk of this warld is Prince and King. **1592** DAVIES *Immort. Soul* XXXII. lx, Why made he Man, of other Creatures, King? **1623** H. HOLLAND *Lines Shaks.*, Those bayes, Which crown'd him Poet first, then Poets King. *a* **1649** DRUMM. OF HAWTH. *Poems* 46 What those kings of numbers did conceive By muses nine. **1789** BURNS *Willie brew'd* iv, Wha first beside his chair shall fa' He is the King among us three. **1792** —— *Auld Rob Morris* i, He's the King o' gude fellows and wale of auld men. **1806** *Guide to Watering Places* 14 Richard Nash, the first King of Bath, was a native of Swansea. **1821** SHELLEY *Adonais* xlviii, The kings of thought Who waged contention with their time's decay. **1846** J. G. SAXE *Progress* (1847) 28 How would she [*sc.* the Muse] strive, in fitting verse, to sing The wondrous Progress of the Printing King! **1847** E. D. BANCROFT *Lett. from England* (1904) 113 We both went to a concert at Mr. Hudson's, the great railway 'king', who has just made an immense fortune from railway stocks. **1884** S. E. DAWSON *Handbk. Dom. Canada* 154 Here the fur-kings of the North-West lived and spent their profits in generous hospitality. **1894** *Outing* (U.S.) XXIII. 380/2 Relics of the palmy days of the old sugar kings of Jamaica. **1898** *Daily News* 23 Mar. 6/3 Mr. Audubon, you are the king of ornithological painters. **1919** F. HURST *Humoresque* 194 You've never met Mr. Feist, have you, the film king? You two ought to get acquainted—one makes the films and the other makes them famous. **1927** WODEHOUSE *Small Bachelor* ii. 25 She had also been the relict of the late P. Homer Horlick, the Cheese King, and he had left her several million dollars. **1966** 'J. HACKSTON' *Father clears Out* 83 He began to tell me what the sheep kings had to put up with. *Ibid.* 123 The young sheep king.

b. Applied to things personified as ***King Caucus, King Cotton. king of day***, the sun. ***king of terrors***, death (see TERROR). ***King Willow***, the game of cricket. Cf. quot. 1876 s.v. WILLOW *sb.* 5.

1592 SHAKS. *Rom. & Jul.* II. iii. 27 Two such opposed Kings encampe them still, In man as well as Hearbes, grace and rude will. *c* **1820** CAMPBELL *Last Man* 36 Yet mourn I not thy parted ray, Thou dim discrowned king of day. **1868** BREWER *Dict. Phrase & Fable* (ed. 3), *King Cotton*... The expression was first used by James H. Hammond in the senate of the United States 1858. **1881** tr. *von Holst's Const. Hist. U.S.* I The undemocratic 'King Caucus' was already so thoroughly hated that..his days were numbered. **1933** A. G. MACDONELL *England, their England* xvii. 285 The evening papers were already beginning to talk of the Advent of King Willow. **1936** S. R. JONES *Eng. Village Homes* iii. 36 Football thrives lustily, and King Willow reigns on the old turf of the greens in summer. **1972** P. DICKINSON *Lizard in Cup* vi. 92 Loyalty to..the imagined spirit of King Willow.

7. *fig.* Something to which there is attributed supremacy or chief excellency in its class. **a.** Of animals. ***king of beasts***, the lion; ***king of birds***, the eagle. Sometimes forming part of an ordinary or popular name; e.g. ***king of six***, the male of certain polygamous South African birds.

king of the ant-eaters, a South American bird (*Grallaria rex*). ***king of the breams***, the Spanish Bream (*Pagellus erythrinus*). ***king of the herrings***, (*a*) the Northern Chimæra (*C. monstrosa*); (*b*) the opah (*Lampris guttata*); (*c*) the oarfish (*Regalecus glesne*); (*d*) the allice shad. ***king of the mullets***, (*a*) a Mediterranean fish (*mullus imberbis*); (*b*) the common bass. ***king of the salmon***, a deep-sea fish of the Pacific coast of America, *Trachypterus altivelis*. ***king of the sea-breams***, the becker or braize.

1390 GOWER *Conf.* III. 74 As leon is the king of bestes. **1398** TREVISA *Barth. De P.R.* XVIII. lxiv. (MS. Bodl.), Hatte leo kinge for he is kinge and prince of al oþer bestes. **1481** CAXTON *Reynard*, *Table*, Hoow the kynge of alle bestes the lyon helde his court. **1486** *Bk. St. Albans* E iij, Now for to speke of the hare..That beest kyng shall be calde of all venery. **1503** DUNBAR *Thistle & Rose* 103 The King of Beistis mak I the [the lion]. *Ibid.* 120 Syne crownit scho the Egle King of Fowlis. **1602** CAREW *Cornwall* (1811) 94 Lastly the salmon king of fish, Fills with good cheer the Christmas dish. **1753** CHAMBERS *Cycl. Supp.*, *King of the mullets*, see *Mullus imberbis*. **1836** King of the Herrings [see HERRING 1 c]. **1880** GÜNTHER *Fishes* 522 *Regalecus*..the largest of all Ribbon-fishes..frequently called 'Kings of the herrings', from the erroneous notion that they accompany the shoals of herrings. **1885** *Stand. Nat. Hist.* III. 207 The popular name of opah, and king of the herrings. **1913** C. PETTMAN *Africanderisms* 260 *King of six*, a King Williamstown name for the Rooibekje... The reference is to the number of females by which the male is generally accompanied during the breeding season. **1931** R. C. BOLSTER *Land & Sea Birds S.-W. Cape* 133 Of the two Bishop Birds, the Black and Yellow one is said to be polygamous, whence the name 'King of Six' in the vicinity of Cape Town.

b. Of trees, plants, or fruits.

1697 DAMPIER *Voy.* I. 311 The Plantain I take to be the King of all Fruit, not except the Coco it self. **1786** BURNS *Scotch Drink* iii, John Barleycorn, Thou King o' grain. **1791** COWPER *Yardley Oak* 50 Time made thee what thou wast, king of the woods. **1842** TWAMLEY in *Visitor* 131/1 The pine is king of Scottish woods. **1846** J. BAXTER *Libr. Agric.* I. 59 Winter Sauce Apples..King of the pippins.

c. Of things, places, etc.

1608 SHAKS. *Per.* I. i. 13 Her thoughts the king Of every virtue gives renown to men! **1728** POPE *Dunc.* II. 273 Thames, The king of dykes. **1796** ELIZA HAMILTON *Lett. Hindoo Rajah* I. 185 The King of worshipped places, the renowned Allahabad. **1833** MARRYAT *P. Simple* xiv, He taught me a fisherman's bend, which he pronounced to be the king of all knots. **1881** C. A. EDWARDS *Organs* 3 The organ..has..earned the title of the 'King of Instruments'.

8. †**a.** Applied by earlier writers, after Latin, to the queen bee. *Obs.* **b.** A fully developed male termite or white ant.

a. *c* **1386** CHAUCER *Pers. T.* ¶394 Thise flyes, that men clepeth bees, whan they maken hir kyng they chesen oon that hath no prikke, wherwith he may stynge. **1600** SURFLET *Countrie Farme* I. x. 48 He shall make cleane their hiues verie carefully and kill their kings. **1642** PRYNNE *Sov. Antid.* i. 4 Though all other Bees have stings,..yet the King among the bees hath no sting at all, for nature would not have him to be cruell. **1710** *Brit. Apollo* III. No. 87. 2/1 The Kings are bred of the Brains.

b. **1895** SHARP *Insects* I. in *Cambridge Nat. Hist.* V. 361 Termites live in communities..The king and queen may be recognised by the stumps of their cast wings.

9. In games.

a. In chess: The piece which each player must protect against the moves made by the other, so as to prevent it from being finally checkmated.

King's Gambit: see GAMBIT. *King's Bishop, Knight, Rook*, the pieces placed on the king's side of the board at the commencement of the game. *King's Pawn*, the pawn immediately before the king at the commencement of the game. *king's side*, the half of the board on which both kings stand at the commencement of the game.

1411-12 HOCCLEVE *De Reg. Princ.* 2120 Somwhat I knowe a kynges draught. **1413** *Pilgr. Sowle* I. xxii. (Caxton 1483), Whan that a pown seyith to the kyng, chekmate. **1474** CAXTON *Chesse* IV. ii. K ij, Al these yssues hath the kyng out of his propre place whan he begynneth to meue. **1562** ROWBOTHAM *Cheasts* A viij, Yf checke be geuen to the Kyng, the Paune can not marche asyde..for to couer his Kynge. **1645** Z. BOYD *Holy Songs* in *Zion's Flowers* (1855) App. 13/1 Kings, Pawnes, Knights, Aphens, heere and there stand, yet there wood is one. **1735** J. BERTIN *Chess*, The King's Pawn ..must move before the Knights. **1841** G. WALKER *New Treat. Chess* 2 The pieces on the King's side of the line are called..King's Bishop, King's Knight, and King's Rook. **1882** MEYER *Guide to Chess* 21 The King is never taken; all the other pieces can be.

b. In ordinary playing-cards: One card in each suit, bearing the representation of a king, and usually ranking next to the ace. †Hence (with humorous allusion to 1 d) ***the books*** (or ***history***) ***of the four kings***, a pack of playing cards (*obs.*).

1563 FOXE *A. & M.* 1298 Thoughe it were the Kyng of Clubbes. *c* **1592** MARLOWE *Massacre Paris* I. ii, Since thou hast all the cards within thy hands..thou deal thyself a king. **1593** SHAKS. *3 Hen. VI*, v. i. 44 Whiles he [Warwick] thought to steale the single Ten, The King was slyly finger'd from the Deck. **1653** URQUHART *Rabelais* I. xxii, After supper were brought in..the books of the foure Kings. **1760** FOOTE *Minor* I. (1781) 31 Come, shall we have a dip in the history of the Four Kings this morning? **1848** THACKERAY *Van. Fair* lxiv, Caned..for carrying four kings in his hat besides those which he used in playing. **1879** 'CAVENDISH' *Card Ess.*, etc. 231 He can hardly think that ace and king are held up against you.

c. In draughts: A 'crowned' piece (see quot.).

1820 *Hoyle's Games* 313 When any man gets onwards to the last row on the end of the board opposite to that from whence his colour started, then he becomes a king and is crowned by placing one of the captives upon him, and he thereby obtains the privilege of moving and taking either backwards or forwards in any angular direction. **1899** *N. & Q.* 11 Feb. 115/1.

†**d.** In billiards. (See quots.) *Obs.*

1688 R. HOLME *Armoury* III. 262/2 The King is the little Pin or Peg standing at one end of the Table, which is to be of Ivory. **1873** CAVENDISH & B. *Billiards* 4 The peculiarity of the game at this time consisted in the use of a small arch of ivory called the 'port' , which was placed where the pyramid spot now stands, and of an ivory peg or king, placed on a corresponding spot at the other end of the table.

10. Technical uses.

a. *pl.* A trade-name for one of the classes into which fullers' teasels are sorted (see quot. 1836). **b.** A kind of salmon-fly for angling.

1798 BILLINGSLEY *Somerset* 111 Teasels are sorted into kings, middlings, and scrubs. **1830** J. L. KNAPP *Jrnl. Nat.* 43-4 The terminating heads are ready first, and called 'kings': they are larger and coarser than the others and fitted only for the strongest kinds of cloth. **1867** F. FRANCIS *Angling* x. (1880) 396, I would prefer Purple and Green Kings.

11. *ellipt.* **a.** A toast in which the king's health is drunk. **b.** A king-post.

1763 CHURCHILL *Conference*, The King gone round. **1858** *Skyring's Builders' Prices* (ed. 48) 18 Truss framed with king post..Ditto with king and queens.

c. (Usu. with capital initial.) The British national anthem, 'God Save the King'.

1932 *Week-end Rev.* 30 Apr. 554/2 Programme to-night as follows:—British Movietone News. Sunshine Susie. Mickey Mouse. The King. **1959** I. JEFFERIES *Thirteen Days* vii. 95 The band played the King and we all stood up. **1967** R. HARRIS *All my Enemies* iii. 34 We applauded, stood for 'The King'.

II. *attrib.* and *Comb.*

12. a. appositive, 'that is a king': as ***king-bishop, -brother, -cardinal, -dauphin, -devil, -emperor, -folk, -god, -industry, -parliament, -pedagogue, -poet, -pope, -sovereign***, etc.

1890 J. HEALY *Insula Sanctorum* 608 Cormac Mac Carthy, himself a *king-bishop. **1862** H. MARRYAT *Year in Sweden* I. 446 Horrified at the domestic misery of her *king-brother. **1613** SHAKS. *Henry VIII*, II. ii. 20 This is the Cardinals doing: The *King-Cardinall. **1577-87** HOLINSHED *Chron.* III. 1184/1 The *king Dolphin and queene of Scots his wife. *c* **1440** *Jacob's Well* 9 þe *kyng deuyl seyde to hym [etc.]. **1902** *Westm. Gaz.* 27 Feb. 11 The *King-Emperor is honoured among us [*sc.* Americans] because he stands for the great people whom he rules. **1971** R. RUSSELL tr. *Ahmad's Shore & Wave* xv. 159 'Have you ever attended the King-Emperor's levée?' asked the Diwan Bahadur. **1876** MORRIS *Sigurd* III. 175 He is born of the Volsung *king-folk. **1614** SYLVESTER *Bethulia's Rescue* v. 437 My *King-God, weary of War's tedious toile, In Ninive..Made Publique Feasts. **1875-7** TENNYSON *Q. Mary* I. v, So your *King-parliament suffer him to land. **1850** H. ROGERS *Ess.* (1874) II. iv. 199 The first James..was fit for nothing except to be *king-pedagogue of a nation of pedants. **1890** J. HEALY *Insula Sanctorum* 618 This *King-poet..met with an untimely end. **1826** W. E. ANDREWS *Rev. Fox's Bk. Martyrs* II. 198 On the second day the *king-pope [Henry VIII] came down to the house. **1908** H. H. JOHNSTON *George Grenfell & Congo* I. xx. 448 The Governors-General or heads of departments representing the *King-Sovereign in Africa.

b. simple attributive, 'of the king, royal': as ***king-gear, -house***.

1840 CARLYLE *Heroes* v. (1858) 322 Strip your Louis Quatorze of his *king-gear, and there is left nothing but a forked radish with a head fantastically carved. **1483** *Cath. Angl.* 203/2 A *kynghouse, *basilica, regia*.

c. objective and obj. genitive, as ***king-bane, -deposer, -murderer, -worship; king-becoming, -deposing, -dethroning, -ennobling, -murdering, -upholding***, etc., adjs. See also KING-KILLER, -KILLING, -MAKER, -MAKING.

1643 PRYNNE *Sov. Power Parlt.* I. (ed. 2) 21 Perswaded, while that *King-bane breathed, peace could never be maintained in the Realme. **1605** SHAKS. *Macb.* IV. iii. 91 The *King-becoming Graces,..I haue no rellish of them. **1780** COWPER *Table-t.* 57 That were indeed a *king-ennobling thought. **1605** SYLVESTER *Du Bartas* II. iii. iv. *Captains* 1262 The *King-maiming Kinglings of Bezec. *a* **1711** KEN *Hymns Festiv.* Poet. Wks. 1721 I. 311 A Persecution..From the traduc'd, *King-murd'ring Sect. **1844** MACAULAY *Ess., Chatham* (1887) 821 The Tories..who had always been inclined to *King-worship. **16..** SIR R. BERKELEY in Hurd *Dial., Const. Eng. Govt.* (1759) 300 *note*, [Sir Robert Berkeley..affirmed that] the law knows no such *king-yoking policy.

d. instrumental and locative, as ***king-born, -descended, -favoured*** adjs.; †***to the kingward***, towards the king.

1670 MILTON *Hist. Eng.* IV. Wks. (1847) 528/2 Under a thorn..lieth poor Kenelm *kingborn. **1832** TENNYSON *Œnone* 125 A shepherd all thy life but yet kingborn. **18..** CHR. ROSSETTI *Royal Princess*, I, a Princess, *king-descended. **1614-15** SYLVESTER *Panaretus* 543 That *King-favour'd Place. **1461** CLEMENT PASTON in *P. Lett.* II. 53 Come to the *Kinge wards or ye meet with him. **1480** CAXTON *Chron. Eng.* cxlix, Whan the tydyng came to the pope..tho was he to the kyngward ful wrothe.

13. a. Special combs.: †**king-ale**, a feasting or ale-drinking on some royal anniversary; **king-ball**, a ball at which others are aimed in bagatelle; †**king-bee**, the queen-bee: see 8 a above; **king-card** (see quot.); **king-carp**, a variety of the common carp, *Cyprinus carpio*; **king-closer** (see quot. and CLOSER² 3); **king-cobra** = HAMADRYAD 2; **king-conch, -conk**, a collector's name for a variety of conch (see quots.); **King Country** *N.Z.*, an extensive region in the North Island of New Zealand formerly allotted to the Maoris under a king; so ***King movement, party***, etc., referring to the followers of this king; **king-fluke**, *Sc.* the turbot; †**king-game**, ? = *king-play*; †**king-geld**, scutage; **king-herald** (see HERALD 1 e); **king-hit** *Austral. slang*, (*a*) a knock-out blow; a hard punch; (*b*) a fighter or bully; a leader; hence as *v. trans.*, to punch hard or knock out; **king-hood** = *king's-hood*; †**king-key**, the main keystone or point of support; †**king-land**, a kingdom; **king-list**, a list of the names of kings; **king mackerel**, a game fish of the eastern U.S. coast, *Scomberomorus cavalla*, also called Spanish mackerel or king-fish; **king-mullet**, the goat-fish (*Upeneus maculatus*) of the West Indies; †**king-play**, a performance of the old drama of the Three Kings; **king-pot**, the largest crucible in a brass-smelting furnace; **king-rod**, an iron rod used in place of a king-post (= KING-BOLT a); **king-roller**, the middle roller in a sugar-press; **king-row**, the row of pieces next to the end of the draught-board; †**king-sacrificer**, the Roman king of the sacrifices (see 5 above); **king salmon**, the Californian Salmon (*Oncorhynchus quinnat*); *N. Amer.*, the Chinook or quinnat salmon, *Oncorhynchus tshawytscha*; **king-side** *a. Chess*, made or done on the king's side of the board; also applied to men situated on that side; **king-size** *a.*, of an extra large size; of larger size than normal; *spec.* designating an extra large cigarette; hence *ellipt.* as *sb.*, a king-size cigarette; also ***king-sized*** adj.; **king-snake**, a large North American snake (esp. *Ophibolus getulus*) which attacks other snakes; **king-truss**, a roofing-truss which has a king-post; †**king-wand**, a sceptre; †**king-wasp**, a queen wasp; **king-wood**, a Brazilian wood, prob. from a species of *Dalbergia*. See also KING-BOLT, KING-CRAB, KING-CRAFT, etc.

1470-73 in *Rec. Andover* 18 Recᵈ of William plomer and Alice ffewar for a *Kyngale xxiijˢ. **1600** *Wottone* (*Hants.*) *Acc.*, Receipts for the Kingale as followeth, for the Sunday after Midsomer Day, Junij xxix⁰. [Also for July 6.] **1679** M. RUSDEN *Further Discov. Bees* 2 The Royal Race of *King-Bees, being natural Kings. **1876** A. CAMPBELL-WALKER *Correct Card* (1880) Gloss., **King-card*, the best card left in each suit. Thus if the ace and King were out, the King-card would be the queen. **1908** *Westm. Gaz.* 7 Aug. 10/3 Yesterday a *king carp was hooked. **1930** E. PARKER et al. *Fine Angling for Coarse Fish* 162 A very heavy king-carp.. weighed 18¼ lb. This fish is rarer than the common carp. **1971** B. J. MUUS *Freshwater Fish Brit. & Europe* 136/1 Scaled carps (often known as king carps) are covered by small uniform scales. **1888** MITCHELL *Building Construction* I. ii. (1889) 18 *King Closers are bricks cut so that one end is half the width of a brick. **1894** E. H. AITKEN *Naturalist on Prowl* 39 A Hamadryad, or *King Cobra,..the most terrible of the whole serpent tribe. **1851** MAYHEW *Lond. Labour* (1861) II. 22 (E.D.D.) The shells of this man's stock-in-trade he called 'conks' and '*king-conks'. **1885** LADY BRASSEY *The Trades* 303 The queen-conch..has gone quite out of favour, and nothing but the king-conch—which, though smaller, is far richer in its colouring of dark chocolate and reddish brown—is looked upon with favour as an article of commerce. **1884** J. H. KERRY-NICHOLLS (*title*) The *King Country; or, explorations in New Zealand, a narrative of 600 miles of travel through Maoriland. **1910** J. COWAN *Maoris of N.Z.* xxvii. 294 The men..finally faced death..in the famous redoubt at Orakau, on the borders of what afterwards came to be known as the King Country. **1917** G. H. SCHOLEFIELD *New Zealand* iii. 19 A railway ran from Auckland..until it touched..the boundary of the native preserve known as the 'King Country', which stretched like a neutral zone across the island. **1944** A. MULGAN *From Track to Highway* ii. 58 In the end he took refuge in the King country, below the military frontier in the Waikato, where the defeated Kingites had been left unmolested. **1966** *Encycl. N.Z.* II. 223/2 The King Country, or Rohe Potae, was originally a large tract of the western central North Island... Europeans called the area 'the King Country' because it was here that Tawhiao sought refuge following the Maori Wars. **1895** *Sea Fishing* (Badm. Libr.) 367 They [turbot] are called on the east coast of Scotland *king-fleuk. **1504** *Churchw. Acc.* in Lysons *Env. Lond.* (1810) I. 165 At the geveng out of the *Kynggam by [the] cherchewardens, amounted clerely £4. 2*s.* 6*d.* of that same game. **1706** PHILLIPS, **Kingeld*, Escuage, or Royal Aid. **1923** G. COLLINS *Valley of Eyes Unseen* i. 29 Neither blow was a true *king hit, however, and neither Chink was anything near knocked out. **1941** BAKER *Dict. Austral. Slang* 41 *King hit*, a knock-out blow. (2) As for 'king dick' [= a leader, boss]. **1944** L. GLASSOP *We were Rats* xiii. 76 'Do this galah over,' he whispered in my ear. 'He's a king-hit merchant.' **1945** BAKER *Austral. Lang.* vi. 120 To bump, comb down,..king hit. **1962** S. GORE *Down Golden Mile* 277 'King-hit me, the bastard,' he muttered. 'With me own gun.' **1970** *Sunday Truth* (Brisbane) 16 Aug. 32/6 You king-hit him with what appears to be savage brutality. **1974** *Sunday Mail* (Brisbane) 29 Sept. 28 D/2 A piece of legislation that has been described as..a king-hit to human rights. **1654** VILVAIN *Theol. Treat.* vii. 194 This is the *King-key of al the Fabric. *c* **1250** *Gen. & Ex.* 1262 His .ix. [son] was tema, for-ðan Is ðor a *ku[n]glond teman. **1914** E. A. W. BUDGE *Short Hist. Egyptian People* iii. 27 The famous *King-List drawn up for Seti I, and cut upon a wall in a temple built by him at Abydos. **1962** J. GRAY *Archaeol. & Old Testament World* ii. 34 In the king-lists the 'Flood' demarcates between historical dynasties and the early ages. **1939** J. O. LA GORCE *Bk. Fishes* (ed. 2) 338/2 *King mackerel serves as Spanish, and bonito may be served as either Spanish or King mackerel. **1953** F. ROBB *Sea Hunters* vii. 104 Old Drum Watts says these aren't barracouta at all —says they're king-mackerel or something. **1965** A. J. MCCLANE *Standard Fishing Encycl.* 449/2 King mackerel reach a much larger size than any other American Spanish mackerel. **1970** M. SLATER *Caribbean Cooking* 11 *Kingfish*, a game fish, sometimes called King Mackerel which can weigh up to 100 lb. **1858** *King movement [see HUI]. **1860** T. BUDDLE *Maori King Movement* 3 This chief..initiated a Maori King movement in the South. **1884** J. H. KERRY-NICHOLLS *King Country* 6 In 1854,..Te Heuheu.. summoned a native council at Taupo, when the King movement began in earnest. **1959** K. SINCLAIR in J. E. Gorst *Maori King* p. xxiii, The King movement survives today, though its followers are less numerous than a century ago. **1860** T. BUDDLE *Maori King Movement* 72 It becomes..the duty of those entrusted with native interests..to enter promptly into negociations with the *King party. **1944** A. MULGAN *From Track to Highway* ii. 55 The King party wanted to keep their king and their flag. **1519** *Churchw. Acc. St. Giles, Reading* 4 Recᵈ in gatheryng wᵗ the *kyngplay at Witsontide. **1791** LYSONS *Environs Lond.* (1810) 165 *note*, It appears by the churchwardens' accounts in the parish of St. Lawrence at Reading, that the ancient drama of the three Kings of Cologne was..performed at that place, and that it was called the King-game or King-play. **1879** *Cassell's Techn. Educ.* IV. 262 Nine great pots of fire-clay, the largest, or *king-pot, being in the centre. **1847** LONGF. *Ev.* I. iii. 80 Laughed when a man was crowned, or a breach was made in the *king-row. **1601** HOLLAND *Pliny* I. 340 What time as L. Posthumius Albinus was *king sacrificer at Rome. **1881** *Amer. Naturalist* XV. 177 These species [in the North Pacific] may be called the quinnat or *king salmon. **1893** *Arena* Mar. 490 Great numbers of king salmon ascend the streams to spawn. **1959** *Vancouver Sun* 28 Aug. 5/1 Fall is also in the return of the salmon to their rivers—not in the early king salmon runs that come to a few rivers in May. **1941** F. REINFELD *Keres' Best Games of Chess* 86/1 Not only winning a Pawn, but devaluating the remaining Black *King-side Pawns. **1954** H. GOLOMBEK *Game of Chess* 12 In the case of King side castling, the King is moved two squares to the right. **1973** *Times* 13 Aug. 12/7 Hartston won quickly with a strong king-side attack against Mestel. [**1825** J. CONSTABLE *Let.* 10 Dec. in *Corr.* (1964) II. 419 Sir Thomas has done 4 pictures in Paris—the two of the King & Dolphin are very large *King size, & fine—the others, are the Dolphiness and Duchess of Berry head size.] **1942** *Time* 7 Sept. 18/1 (Advt.), Regent Cigarettes, King Size. *Ibid.*, King Size Regent's the cigarette for *moderns* like you. **1949** *Sun* (Baltimore) 1 July 2/1 He..allowed Stryker to read the king-size question summarizing the life of Whittaker Chambers. **1957** H. ROOSENBERG *Walls came tumbling Down* iv. 88 We..had a king-size meal. **1957** P. WILDEBLOOD *Main Chance* 159 'Have you got a cigarette?' 'King-size,' said Mrs. Tull. 'Oh, I can't stand them big ones.' **1966** King size [see ECONOMY 9]. **1971** *New Scientist* 17 June 707/2 It's a pity that Rudolph de Salis..never had the advantage of his king-size burgers. **1971** WODEHOUSE *Much Obliged, Jeeves* xiii. 133 The snag which had raised its ugly head was one of formidable—you might say king-size—dimensions. **1943** in *Amer. Speech* (1944) XIX. 111/2 So that's it for *king-sized beauties. **1953** *Manch. Guardian Weekly* 24 Apr. 7 A kingsized defence programme. **1883** COUES in *Cassell's Nat. Hist.* IV. 319 Both Rattlesnakes and Mocassins will endeavour to get away from the '*King Snake'. *a* **1300** *Cursor M.* 22266 His corun and his *king wand. **1724** DERHAM in *Phil. Trans.* XXXIII. 54 The Queen, or Female-Wasp (by many called the *King-Wasp). **1851** *Dict. Archit.*, **King Wood*..is beautifully streaked in violet tints ..and is principally used for turning and for small cabinet work. **1885** *Cassell's Techn. Educ.* II. 26 Violet-wood and king-wood, which come to this country..from the Brazilian forests.

b. in names of birds, as **king-auk** [tr. Norw. *alkekonge*], the little auk or rotche; **king-crow**, the leader of a flock of crows; also the name of several species of drongo, esp. *Dicrurus ater*; **king-duck**, **king-eider**, *Somateria spectabilis*, allied to the eider-duck; **king-hunter**, several species of African and Australian birds related to the king-fisher, but which do not feed on fish; **king-lory** = *king-parrakeet* (Newton *Dict. Birds* 1893); **king-ortolan** (see quot.); **king-parrakeet**, **king-parrot**, the name of several species of small parrots of the genus *Aprosmictus*, kept as cage-birds; **king-penguin**, *Aptenodytes longirostris*; **king-rail** (see quot.); **king-tyrant** = KING-BIRD 3; **king-vulture**, *Gypagus* (*Cathartes*) *papa*, of tropical America, having a gaudy-coloured head.

1885 *Stand. Nat. Hist.* IV. 69 The little sea-dove..or *king-auk, as it is styled by the Norsemen. **1866** *Intell. Observ.* No. 50. 106 The *King crows, or drongo shrikes. **1883** E. H. AITKEN *Tribes on my Frontier* 143 (Y.) The King-crow..leaves the whole bird and beast tribe far behind in originality and force of character. **1856** KANE *Arct. Expl.* I. xxi. 270 A noble specimen of the *king duck. **1876** DAVIS *Polaris Exp.* xvi. 378 The Esquimaux shot three king-ducks. **1893** DIXON *Game Birds* 447 The *King Eider..is occasionally found in fresh water. **1837** SWAINSON *Nat. Hist. Birds* II. 154 These are the habits of the European kingfisher..and travellers affirm that the *king-hunters..pursue the same method. **1885** *Stand. Nat. Hist.* IV. 401 The giant kinghunter of Australia. **1893** SELOUS *Trav. S.E. Africa* 64, I saw a pair of the great African Kingfishers, and a handsome Kinghunter. **1888** TRUMBULL *Bird Names* 122 *Gallinula galeata*..At Washington *King-Ortolan..The name King-ortolan is given by Coues and Prentiss..as an alias of *Rallus elegans*. **1883** *Cassell's Nat. Hist.* III. 315 Several..well known as cagebirds, such as the *King Parrakeet. **1879** GOULD *Birds N. Guinea* V. pl. 9 Yellow-winged *King Parrot. **1890** LYTH *Golden South* 127 The brilliant scarlet and green king parrot. **1885** *Stand. Nat. Hist.* IV. 59 The *king penguin of the Falkland Islands..and some other rocks and islands of the Antarctic Ocean. **1888** TRUMBULL *Bird Names* 125 The present species [*Rallus elegans*]..being the *King Rail of 'the books'. **1837** SWAINSON *Nat. Hist. Birds* II. 7 Bees appear to be a favourite food with..the *king tyrant of North America (*Tyrannus intrepidus*). **1883** *Cassell's Nat. Hist.* III. 263 The tree on which the *King Vulture roosts. **1885** *Stand. Nat. Hist.* IV. 268 The bird of this group whose appearance is most striking is the king-vulture.

c. in names of plants, as †**king-apple**, an old variety of apple, of red colour and large size; **king-cob** = KING-CUP; **king-cure**, name for American species of *Pyrola* and *Chimaphila*; **king-devil**, *Hieracium præaltum*, a troublesome weed, common in some parts of America, but originally introduced from Europe; **King Edward** (**VII potato**), an oval variety of potato with a white skin mottled with red, introduced in 1902 by J. Butler; **king fern**, (*a*) the royal fern (*Osmunda regalis*); (*b*) *N.Z.*, a large fern, *Marattia salicina*, with a swollen, starchy rhizome; (*c*) *Todea barbara*, a fern closely related to the royal fern, *Osmunda regalis*, found in Australia, New Zealand, and South Africa; **king-nut**, the name of a species of hickory; †**king-pear**, an old variety of pear; **king-pine**, †(*a*) the pine-apple; (*b*) a large and stately Himalayan fir, *Picea Webbiana*; **king-plant**, a Javan Orchid, *Anæctochilus setaceus*, having purple-brown leaves marked with yellow lines (Miller *Plant-n.*); **king-tree** (see quot.).

1707 MORTIMER *Husb.* I. (1708) 519 The *King Apple, tho' not common, yet is by some esteemed an excellent Apple. **1597** GERARDE *Herbal* II. ccli. 805 Crowfoote is called..in English *King kob. **1874** DUNGLISON *Med. Dict.*, *King cure, *Pyrola maculata*. **1898** BRITTON & BROWN *Flora North. U.S.* III. Index, King-cure. A name of *Chimaphila umbellata*. *Ibid.* 284 *King-devil..in north-central New York..a troublesome weed. Naturalized from Europe. **1926** R. N. SALAMAN *Potato Varieties* xxvi. 274 (*heading*) *King Edward VII. *Ibid.* 275 King Edward, whose parentage is unknown, was raised by a gardener in Northumberland... This variety is today the most popular in England. **1949** —— *Hist. & Social Influence Potato* x. 170 The 'King Edward' became a favourite in the kitchen. **1963** *Times* 22 Apr. 2/6 The three most popular potato varieties grown in England and Wales are all relatively old. Arran Pilot..was introduced just over 40 years ago. Majestic..was introduced in 1912 and King Edward VII, with about 25 per cent [of the maincrop acreage], in 1902. **1911** W. R. GUILFOYLE *Austral. Plants* 354 *Todea barbara*. '*King Fern' or 'Swamp Sponge Fern'. **1921** H. B. DOBBIE *N.Z. Ferns* (ed. 2) xxix. 374 *M*[*arattia*] *fraxinea* (like an ash leaf). 'Para', 'King Fern', 'Horseshoe Fern'. The largest herbaceous fern in New Zealand; plentiful in the early days, now becoming scarce. **1962** J. H. WILLIS *Handbk. Plants Victoria* I. 10 *T*[*odea*] *barbara*... Austral King-Fern (King Fern)..all States except W.A. (but very localized in S.A.), N.Z., S. Afr. **1963** B. PEARSON *Coal Flat* xxii. 379 The three of them huddled under a king fern. **1898** BRITTON & BROWN *Flora North. U.S.* I. 486 *Hicoria laciniosa*. Big Shag-bark, *King-nut. **1585** HIGINS tr. *Junius' Nomenclator* 99 b *Pirum regium*..A *king peare with a very little stalke. **1668** EVELYN *Diary* 19 Aug., That rare fruit call'd the *King-pine, growing in Barbados. **1863** BATES *Nat. Amazon* ii. (1864) 38 The Moira-tinga (the White or *King tree) probably the same as, or allied to, the Moira Excelsa which Sir Robert Schomburgk discovered in British Guiana.

14. Combinations with *king's*. **a.** Used in numerous titles or appellations, in the sense Of, belonging to, in the service of the king, as head of the State (in which use it interchanges, during the reign of a female sovereign, with *queen's*), royal; as ***king's coin***, ***commission***, ***court***(***s***, ***customs***, ***soldiers***, ***taxes***, ***tower***, etc.; also *King's* ADVOCATE, BEADSMAN, COUNSEL, ENGLISH, EVIDENCE, HIGHWAY, KEYS, PEACE, PRINTER, REMEMBRANCER, SCHOLAR, SCHOOL, SHIP, THANE, WIDOW, WRIT, for which see these words. **king's blue**, a shade of blue (see quots.); a substance giving that colour; **King's messenger**: see MESSENGER 3; **king's peg**, a drink consisting of brandy and champagne; **King's** (**National**) **Roll**, a roll of employers pledged to employ at least a fixed proportion of disabled ex-service men after the war of 1914–18. **b.** †**king's ale**, the strongest ale brewed; **king's** (**bad**) **bargain** (see quots.); †**king's bird**: see KINGBIRD 1; †**king's books**, the taxation lists; **king's chair** = *king's cushion*; **king's cup**, lemonade; **king's cushion**, a seat made by the crossed hands of two persons; †**king's day**, the King's birthday, coronation-day, and similar anniversaries; †**king's fish** (see quots.); †**king's freeman**, *Sc.*, one who, in return for services rendered to the king, had the right to trade as a freeman without being member of a gild; †**king's friends**, *Hist.*, a political party which supported George III in his attempts to increase the power of the crown; **king's-hood** *Sc.* [cf. Da. *kongehætte*], the second stomach of ruminants; †**king's language** = *King's* ENGLISH; **king's letter men**, a former class of officers of similar rank with midshipmen (Smyth *Sailor's Word-bk.* 1867); †**king's piece**: see KING-PIECE; †**king's silver**, (*a*) silver blessed by the king, and intended for cramp-rings; (*b*) money paid in the Court of Common Pleas for licence to levy a fine; †**king's stroke**, the touch of the royal hand for king's evil; †**king's wand**, a sceptre; **king's yellow**, orpiment or yellow arsenic used as a pigment. See also KING'S BENCH, KING'S EVIL, KING'S MAN.

1574 *Burgh Rec. Glasgow* (1876) I. 25 That thair be na derare aill sauld nor sax penneis the pynt, and that the samyn be *kingis aill and werraye guid. **1785** GROSE *Dict. Vulg. T.* s.v., One of the *king's bad bargains: a malingeror, or soldier who shirks his duty. **1867** SMYTH *Sailor's Word-bk.*, *King's bargain, Good or Bad*; said of a seaman according to his activity and merit, or sloth and demerit. **1908** C. MAYER tr. *Zerr & Rübencamp's Treat. Colour Manuf.* II. 200 The blue cobalt compounds known in commerce as smalt, *king's blue, cobalt blue, [etc.]. **1951** R. MAYER *Artist's Handbk.* ii. 52 *King's blue*, cobalt blue; formerly smalt. **1970** *Canad. Antiques Collector* Oct. 17/1 Very little, if any, Bristol-blue glass was made between about 1800 and about 1820, when it again came into vogue under the name of king's blue. This was a loyal gesture to George IV. *c* **1600** DAY *Begg. Bednall Gr.* II. ii. (1881) 39 You are more in the *Kings Books than he, and pay more Scot and lot a fair deal, so ye do. **1892** *Cooley's Pract. Receipts* 948 *Lemonade. Syn.* Lemon-sherbet, *King's cup. **1818** SCOTT *Hrt. Midl.* vii, He was now mounted on the hands of two of the rioters, clasped together, so as to form what is called in Scotland, 'The *King's Cushion'. **1622** *Direct. Conc. Preachers* in Rushw. *Hist. Coll.* (1659) I. 64 Upon the *Kings days, and set Festivals. **1705** BOSMAN *Guinea* 278 Vast Shoals are taken of the Saffer, or *Kings-fish. **1712** W. ROGERS *Voy.* 77 La Plata..and Uraguay abound so with Fish,..one of the choicest, call'd the Kings-Fish, is small without Bones, and taken only in Winter. **1770** BURKE *Pres. Discont.* Wks. 1815 II. 258 The name by which they chuse to distinguish themselves, is that of king's men or the *king's friends. **1844** LD. BROUGHAM *Brit. Const.* viii. (1862) 103 'King's friends'—men for the most part attached to his service, by holding military or household places. **1685** *Lintoun Green* (1817) 92 (E.D.D.) Pow's-sowdy, *king's-hoods, mony-plies, Sheep's trotters. **1782** A. MONRO *Compar. Anat.* (ed. 3) 39. The second stomach, which is the anterior and smallest, is called ..the *bonnet*, or *king's-hood*. *c* **1620** A. HUME *Brit. Tongue* Ded. 2 Your courteoures, quha..sum tymes spilt (as they cal it) the *king's language. **1890** *King's peg [see HEIDSIECK]. **1899** C. J. C. HYNE *Further Adv. Capt. Kettle* xi. 265 Cranze kept up a steady soak on king's peg—putting in a good three fingers of the liqueur brandy before filling up the tumbler with champagne. **1958** M. PROCTER *Man in Ambush* xiii. 148 This was the shy man who drank champagne laced with brandy, a millionaire's drink... It was called King's Peg. **1919** HAIG in *Times* 11 Nov. 10/5, I ..appeal to employers..to give a pledge of their sympathy by enrolling their names on the *King's National Roll under the national scheme for the employment of disabled men. **1920** *Times* 16 Feb. 9/4 The King's Roll. First edition, with 9,500 firms, now in the press. **1463** *Bury Wills* (Camden) 35 A rowund ryng of the *kyngis silvir. **1617** MINSHEU *Duct. Ling.*, *Kings siluer*, is properly that money, which is due to the King in the Court of common plees, in respect of a licence there granted to any man for passing a fine. **1888** W. RYE *Records and Rec.-search* 39 *note*, The King's Silver (or the Post Fine) was the fine paid to the King for liberty to compromise the imaginary suit. **1613** ZOUCH *Dove* 30 O! may some Royall Heau'n grac'd hand asswage This swelling Euils *Kings-stroke-asking rage! *a* **1300** *Cursor M.* 7864 þai sett a ceptre in his hand þat man clepes *kyngs wand. *c* **1790** IMISON *Sch. Art* II. 72 *King's Yellow is the most useful and most brilliant. **1823** P. NICHOLSON *Pract. Build.* 414 King's Yellow is a pure orpiment, or arsenic, coloured with sulphur.

c. in names of plants, as **king's bloom**, the peony; **king's crown**, (*a*) = Melilot or King's Clover; (*b*) *Viburnum Opulus*; **king's ellwand**, the foxglove (Britt. & Holl.); **king's feather**, London Pride (Miller *Dict. Plant-n.* 1884); **king's flower**, a S. African liliaceous plant, *Eucomis regia*; **king's knob** = KING-CUP (Britt. & Holl.); **king's spear**, **kingspear**, *Asphodelus luteus* and *A. ramosus*; **king's taper**, the Great Mullein. Also *king's* CLOVER, CONSOUND, etc. q.v.

1611 COTGR., *Peone*, Peonie, *Kings-bloome, Rose of the Mount. **1597** GERARDE *Herbal* App., *King's crowne is *Melilotus*. **1879** BRITTEN & HOLLAND *Plant-n.*, King's Crown,..*Viburnum Opulus*. **1597** GERARDE *Herbal* I. lxiv. §1. 88 The leaues of the *Kings speare are long, narrow, and chamfered or furrowed. **1625** B. JONSON *Pan's Anniv.*, Bright crown imperial, kingspear, hollyhocks. **1892** AGNES M. CLERKE *Fam. Stud. Homer* viii. 213 The tall white flowers of the king's spear. **1861** MRS. LANKESTER *Wild Fl.* 102 Great Mullein..The common name, 'Torchblade', or '*King's taper', may have arisen from its candle-like appearance.

15. Phraseological combinations, as **King Charles's head** [with reference to Mr. Dick in Dickens's *David Copperfield* xiv], an obsession or fixed idea; **King Charles's Spaniel** (see SPANIEL); †**King Harry cut** (see quot. 1611); **King Henry's shoestrings**, a dish in cookery; **King James('s) translation** or **version**, the Authorized Version of the Bible (1611); also ***King James***; **King William's cravat**, a cravat of the kind worn by King William III (1689–1702).

1882 W. How *Let.* in H. Barnett *Canon Barnett* (1918) I. xxii. 275 Like King Charles's head, there was no keeping you out. **1889** G. B. SHAW *London Music 1888–89* (1937) 124, I am afraid I shall have to drag in the subject of music rather often in this column. I know that it is my King Charles's head. **1929** C. MACKENZIE *Gallipoli Memories* xii. 198 And then, of course, he produced his King Charles's head, which was the landing at Bulair. **1972** F. M. LÓPEZ-MORILLAS in R. Highfield *Spain in 15th Cent.* xiv. 441 His King Charles' head was the role played on the first voyage by Martín Alonso Pinzón. **1973** *Times* 30 June 13/5 My own King Charles's head is the use of 'nerve-wracking' for 'nerve-racking'. **1611** COTGR., *Balafre*, a slash ouer the face; a king Harry cut. **1887** *Spon's Househ. Man.* 413 King Henry's Shoestrings. Make a batter with ¼ lb. flour [etc.]. **1835** *Penny Cycl.* IV. 374/2 The period of King James's translation. **1931** *Sunday School Times* (Philadelphia) 22 Aug. 458/1 A good English translation should be in good English idiom, and the old King James was that at least. **1932** *Jrnl. R. Anthrop. Inst.* LXII. 283 He made 'a serpent of brass', as the King James version says. **1973** *Sci. Amer.* Aug. 98/3 Add the number on the top of *A* to the number on the bottom of *B*, then find the chapter of Genesis (in a King James Bible) that corresponds to the sum. **1748** RICHARDSON *Clarissa* II. i. 7 A King-William's-Cravat, or some such antique chin-cushion as by the pictures of that prince one sees was then the fashion.

king (kɪŋ), *v.* [f. prec. sb.]

1. *intr.* (mostly with *it*). To act the king; to perform the part of a king; to rule, govern.

c **1420** HOCCLEVE *De Reg. Princ.* 3307 Out of pitee, growith mercy and springiþ,..What prince hem lakkith, naght aright he kyngeth. *c* **1645** HOWELL *Lett.* (1650) II. 41 The Lord Deputy Kings it notably in Ireland. **1701** ROWE *Amb. Step-Moth.* IV. i. 1677 You King rarely! You mean to be renown'd for early Justice. **1883** E. F. KNIGHT *Cruise 'Falcon'* (1887) 162 Some sacred bull of Memphis, kinging it in his manger.

2. *trans.* To make (one) a king.

1593 SHAKS. *Rich. II*, V. v. 36 Then crushing penurie, Perswades me, I was better when a King: Then am I king'd againe. **1656** S. H. *Gold. Law* 24 It un-king'd him, and King'd his un-kingers in point of Power. *a* **1716** SOUTH *Twelve Serm.* (1744) II. 51 Those traiterous Captains of Israel, who kinged themselves by slaying their masters. **1843** LYTTON *Last Bar.* VIII. viii, The recreant whom I kinged.

3. To rule over, to govern, as a king. *rare.*

1599 SHAKS. *Hen. V*, II. iv. 26 Shee [France] is so idly king'd, Her Scepter so phantastically borne. **1839** BAILEY *Festus* ii. (1852) 15 Why mad'st Thou not one spirit, like the sun, To King the world?

4. quasi-*trans.* To mention the name of 'king'. (Cf. BUT *v.*) *nonce-use.*

1605 *Tryall Chevalry* I. i. in Bullen *O. Pl.* III. 271 King me no Kings.

Hence **ˈkinging** *vbl. sb.*, the act of making, or fact of being made, a king.

1656 S. H. *Gold. Law* 64 Solomon also opprest the people so,..as it obstacled his son Rehoboams Kinging. **1708** T. WARD *Eng. Ref.* (1716) 95 Till once again he fell to Kinging, And then he got a Rope to swing in.

King-at-arms: see KING-OF-ARMS.

king-bird.

1. (Also *king's-bird*, *king bird of paradise*.) A species of bird of paradise, *Cicinnurus regius.*

1779 FORREST *Voy. N. Guinea* 141 The late Linneus, as well as Count Buffon, reckon the King's bird among the birds of paradise. **1828** WEBSTER, *Kingbird*, a fowl of the genus *Paradisea*. **1862** WOOD *Nat. Hist.* II. 418 The Manucode, or King Bird of Paradise, so called because it was thought to exercise a regal sway over the other species. **1958** G. DURRELL *Encounters with Animals* II. 47 Here [*sc.* in a Brazilian zoo]..three king birds of paradise were living... The male is about the size of a blackbird, with a velvety

orange head contrasting vividly with a snow-white breast and a brilliant scarlet back.

2. A royal bird; ? the eagle.

1840 BROWNING *Sordello* VI. 583 As the king-bird with ages on his plumes Travels to die in his ancestral glooms. **1926** D. H. LAWRENCE *David* viii. 65 *Jonathan*: .. Shall not the leader shine forth? *Saul*: Even so. And the young King-bird shall moult his feathers in the same hour.

3. One of several North American tyrant fly-catchers of the genus *Tyrannus*.

1778 J. CARVER *Trav. N. Amer.* 475 The King Bird is like a swallow, and seems to be of the same species as the black martin or swift. **1801** *Massachusetts Spy* 25 Nov. 1/2 Just as a parcel of King-birds will pick at a Crow. **18..** in *Encycl. Brit.* (ed. 7) XVI. 569/1 With spring's return the king-bird hither hastes. **1858** O. W. HOLMES *Aut. Breakf.-t.* (1865) 28 If you ever saw a crow with a king bird after him, you will get an image of a dull speaker and a lively listener. **1896** NEWTON *Dict. Birds* 1000 The glory of the Family may be said to culminate in the king of King-birds, *Muscivora regia*. **1959** VAN TYNE & BERGER *Fund. Ornith.* vii. 205 The Gray Kingbird (*Tyrannus dominicensis*) and the Black-whiskered Vireo (*Vireo altiloquus*)..leave Cuba to winter in South America.

4. A sailor's name for various species of tern (Newton *Dict. Birds* s.v.).

'king-bolt. A main or large bolt in a mechanical structure.

a. An iron rod in a roof, used instead of a king-post. **b.** A vertical bolt passing through the axle of a carriage or railway car, and forming a pivot on which the axle swings in taking curves. **c.** A bolt from which the cage of a mining shaft is suspended.

1825 J. NICHOLSON *Operat. Mechanic* 563 Constructed with one king-bolt in the middle. **1874** KNIGHT *Dict. Mech.* 839/2 The king-bolt is the center of oscillation, and the fifth-wheel forms an extended support to prevent the careening of the carriage-bed. **1882** *Rep. to Ho. Repr. Prec. Met. U.S.* 591 As soon as these arms become engaged and fixed in the guides, the whole weight of the cage is transferred to the king-bolt by which it is suspended. **1888** C. F. MITCHELL *Building Constr.* I. ix. (1889) 129 Feet of King or Queen Bolts. These may pass through cast-iron sockets which are indented into the tie-beam.

†'king-by-your-'leave. *Obs.* A variety of the game of hide-and-seek (see quot. 1572).

1572 HULOET, *Kinge by your leaue*, a playe that children haue, where one sytting blyndefolde in the midle, bydeth so tyll the rest haue hydden them selues, and then he going to seeke them, if any get his place in the meane space, that same is kynge in his roume. **1611** FLORIO, *Abomba*, is properly the place, where children playing hide themselves, as at a play called king by your leave. [**1884** BLACK *Jud. Shaks.* iii, Is it anything worse than the children..having a game of 'King by your leave'?]

kingcough, variant of KINKCOUGH.

'king-crab. [f. KING + CRAB *sb.*[1]]

1. A large arthropodous animal of the genus *Limulus*, having a convex carapace somewhat of the shape of a horseshoe; the horseshoe or Molucca crab.

Formerly classed among the *Crustacea*, but now generally placed under the *Arachnida* or Spiders; in structure it differs considerably from the typical form of both classes, and is considered to be the nearest living representative of the extinct Trilobites.

1698 J. PETIVER in *Phil. Trans.* XX. 394 A King Crab of the Molucos Island. **1782** ANDRE *ibid.* LXXII. 440 The *Monoculus Polyphemus*, or *King Crab*..frequently grows to a very large size. **1847** ANSTED *Anc. World* ix. 188 The prawns and the king-crabs of the existing seas.

2. The British thornback-crab (*Maia squinado*).

1890 in *Cent. Dict.*

'king-craft. The art of ruling as a king; the skilful exercise of royalty; *esp.* the use of clever or crafty diplomacy in dealing with subjects.

[**1650** WELDON *Crt. Jas. I*, 102 Nor must I forget to let you know how perfect the King [Jas. I] was in the art of dissimulation, or to give it his own phrase (*King-craft*).] **1643** PRYNNE *Sov. Power Parlt.* II. 34 In this dissembling age; when King-craft is improved to the utmost. **1677** GALE *Crt. Gentiles* IV. 4 Solomon was endowed with this natural sagacitie..which kind of sagacitie Politicians cal King-craft. **1827** HALLAM *Const. Hist.* (1876) III. xviii. 376 The king-craft and the priest-craft of the day taught other lessons. **1874** GREEN *Short Hist.* viii. §7. 534 With Charles they were simply counters, in his game of king-craft.

'king-cup. A name given in many parts of England to the common species of buttercup, *Ranunculus acris*, *bulbosus*, and *repens*; also to Marsh Marigold, *Caltha palustris*.

1538 TURNER *Libellus*, *Ranvnculvs*,.. Kyngecuppe. **1551** —— *Herbal* I. I v b, A yellow floure like vnto the kyngcuppe called Ranunculus. **1634** PEACHAM *Gentl. Exerc.* II. vii. 124 A garland of Bents, King-cups, and Maidens haire. **1784** COWPER *Task* VI. 303 To gather king-cups in the yellow mead. **1802** WORDSW. *Small Celandine* I Pansies, lilies, kingcups, daisies, Let them live upon their praises! **1833** TENNYSON *Poems* 38 Methinks that I could tell you all The cowslips and the kingcups there.

kingdom ('kɪŋdəm), *sb.* Forms: 1 cyning-, 3 kung-, 4–5 kyng-, 4– kingdom; also 4 king-, 4–5 kyngdam(e; 4–5 kinge-, 5 kynge-, 4–7 kyng-, 6–7 kingdome, (7 -doume), (4 kingdon, 5 kyngham). [OE. *cyningdóm* = OS. *kuningdôm* (MDu. *koninghdom*, Du. *koningdom*), G. *königtum* (only since 18th c.), ON. *konungdóm-r*: see KING and -DOM.

OE. *cyningdóm* is found only in the poem of *Daniel*, the usual word being *cynedóm*, whence ME. *kinedom*, KINDOM. The use of *kingdom* in ME. was further limited by the existence of KINGRICK and KINRICK, with the same senses.]

†1. Kingly function, authority, or power; sovereignty, supreme rule; the position or rank of a king, kingship. *Obs.* **a.** Without article.

a **1000** *Daniel* 567 Se [metod] þec aceorfeð of cyningdome. *Ibid.* 680 þa wæs endedæᵹ, þæs þe Caldeas cyningdom ahton. *c* **1325** *Know Thyself* 76 in *E.E.P.* (1862) 132 þauȝ þou haue kyngdam and empyre. **1529** RASTELL *Pastyme, Hist. Rom.* (1811) 13 Put downe from his dignyte of kyngdome. **1533** BELLENDEN *Livy* I. (1822) 12 Avarice and desire of kingdome. *a* **1679** HOBBES *Rhet.* viii. (1681) 19 Monarchy..which Government, if he limit it by Law, is called Kingdom; if by his own will, Tyranny.

b. With poss. pron. or *the* (passing into 2 or 3).

a **1300** *Cursor M.* 7613 He dred his kingdom [*v.r.* -dome] to lese, þat þai to king suld dauid chese. **1390** GOWER *Conf.* I. 142 Thus was he from his kingdom Into the wilde Forest drawe. *c* **1425** *Eng. Conq. Irel.* 28 Sume of hys eldre to-fore hym hadden somtyme the kynge-dome of all Irland. **1535** COVERDALE I *Sam.* xiv. 47 Whan Saul had conquered the kyngdome ouer Israel. **1594** SHAKS. *Rich. III*, IV. ii. 62 Else my Kingdome stands on brittle Glasse. **1631** WEEVER *Anc. Fun. Mon.* 767 Sigebert..resigned vp his kingdome.

2. An organized community having a king as its head; a monarchical state or government.

Latin Kingdom (see LATIN). *Middle Kingdom*, a translation of Chinese *chung kwoh* 'central state', originally the name given, *c* B.C. 1150, under the Chan dynasty, to the imperial state of Honan, in contrast to the dependencies surrounding it. In mod. use the term is sometimes confined to the eighteen provinces of China Proper, but is also used to denote the whole Chinese Empire. *United Kingdom*, Great Britain and Ireland, so called since the Act of Union of 1800.

a **1300** *Cursor M.* 2127 (Cott.) þe mast cite..And mani riche kingdon [*Gött.* mani a noþer riche kingdame]. **1387** TREVISA *Higden* (Rolls) I. 31 Somtyme þere were foure principal kyngdoms..þe firste kyngdom was vnder oure fore fadres from Adam to Moyses. **1657–8** *Burton's Diary* (1828) II. 403 The Commons of England will quake to hear that they are returning to Egypt, to the garlick and onions of ..a kingdom. **1672** TEMPLE *Ess., Government* Wks. 1731 I. 102 If..a Nation extended it self over vast Tracts of Land and Numbers of People, it thereby arrived in time at the ancient Name of Kingdom, or modern of Empire. **1734** POPE *Ess. Man* IV. 133 This world..Contents us not. A better shall we have? A kingdom of the Just then let it be. **1790** BURKE *Fr. Rev.* Wks. V. 48 There is ground enough for the opinion that all the kingdoms of Europe were at a remote period elective. **1801** *Proclamation* 22 Jan., George the Third,..of the United Kingdom of Great Britain and Ireland, King. **1883** S. W. WILLIAMS *Middle Kingdom* I. 4 A third [name] is *Chung Kwoh*, or Middle Kingdom. **1883** *Standard* 6 Apr. 5/2 The Middle Kingdom has forwarded the..articles. **1900** *Westm. Gaz.* 15 Oct. 4/2 His invitation having been..only the second to a foreigner, by the Kingdom of the Chrysanthemum [Japan].

3. a. The territory or country subject to a king; the area over which a king's rule extends; a realm.

c **1250** *Gen. & Ex.* 1260 A kungriche his name bar; And of duma his sexte sune, A kungdom dirima. *c* **1340** *Cursor M.* 5567 (Trin.) þenne commaundide kyng pharao..Ouer al his kyngdome euery where [etc.]. *c* **1400** *Three Kings Cologne* 8 In all þe londys and þe kyngdoms of þe eest. *a* **1450** *Cov. Myst.* (Shaks. Soc.) 210 Naverne and the kyngdom of Spayn. **1591** SHAKS. *Two Gent.* II. vii. 10 A true-deuoted Pilgrime is not weary To measure Kingdomes with his feeble steps. **1667** MILTON *P.L.* II. 361 The utmost border of his kingdom. **1794** BURKE *Corr.* (1844) IV. 255, I wish he may be able to find his kingdom in the map of the British territories. **1841** W. SPALDING *Italy & It. Isl.* III. 71 The Kingdom of Naples consisted of the same provinces on the mainland which had been governed by the Bourbons.

b. A familiar name for the Scotch county of Fife, which was one of the seven Pictish kingdoms.

1710 SIBBALD *Hist. Fife & Kinross* 3 It was from the large Extent of Fife of old, that the Vulgar are wont to call it The Kingdom of Fife. **1845–52** BILLINGS in *Ordnance Gaz. Scotl.* III. 19/1 A ramble amongst the grey old towns which skirt the ancient Kingdom of Fife. **1886** (*title*) The Kingdom; a handbook to Fife (ed. 3). **1899** *Westm. Gaz.* 21 Jan. 1/3 (*heading*) 'Kodaks from the Kingdom'.

4. *trans.* and *fig.* **a.** The spiritual sovereignty of God or Christ, or the sphere over which this extends, in heaven or on earth; the spiritual state of which God is the head.

The conception and the different phrases expressing it are of frequent occurrence in the first three gospels. In Matthew the common form is ***the kingdom of heaven***, sometimes merely ***the kingdom***; in Mark and Luke, as well as in the epistles of St. Paul, the constant phrase is ***the kingdom of God***. Cf. also Ps. cxlv, Daniel ii. 44, vii. 27, etc.

a **1300** *Cursor M.* 1615 (Gött.) Forto bring þaim..Als his aune his kingdam tille. **1340** HAMPOLE *Pr. Consc.* 1408 þe way of lyfe..þat ledes us til our contre-warde þat es þe kyngdom of heven bright. *Ibid.* 8778 þat land es cald..þe kyngdom of God alle-myghty. **1377** LANGL. *P. Pl.* B. Prol. 105 þere crist is in kyngdome..to opne it to hem and heuene blisse shewe. **1382** WYCLIF *Matt.* iii. 2 Do ye penaunce for the kyngdom of heuens shal neiȝ. —— *John* xviii. 36 Jhesu answeride, My kyngdom is not of this world. **1567** *Gude & Godlie B.* (S.T.S.) 116 The gloriousnes of thy kingdome [they] teiche. **1671** MILTON *P. R.* III. 199 What concerns it thee, when I begin My everlasting Kingdom? *a* **1822** SHELLEY *Chas. I*, III. 28 Until Heaven's kingdom shall descend on earth. **1852** MRS. STOWE *Uncle Tom's C.* xix. 197 'Augustine, sometimes I think you are not far from the kingdom', said Miss Ophelia.

b. Used in reference to the spiritual rule or realm of evil or infernal powers.

a **1300** *Cursor M.* 18245 Nu es all vr kingdom for-dune, O man-kind mon we gett ful fune. **1588** SHAKS. *Tit. A.* V. ii. 30, I am Reuenge sent from th' infernall Kingdome. **1594** —— *Rich. III*, I. iii. 144 Hight thee to Hell..Thou Cacodemon, there thy Kingdome is. **1629** MILTON *Hymn Nativ.* 171 Th' old Dragon..wrath to see his Kingdom fail. **1667** —— *P.L.* VI. 183 Reign thou in Hell thy Kingdom.

c. A realm, region, or sphere in which some condition or quality is supreme or prevails.

[**1362** LANGL. *P. Pl.* A. II. 65 Wiþ þe kingdom of Couetise I Croune hem to-gedere.] *a* **1380** *St. Ambrose* 755 in Horstm. *Altengl. Leg.* (1878) 20 To þe kyngdom of blis þat euer schal laste. **1594** SHAKS. *Rich. III*, I. iv. 47, I past (me thought) the Melancholly Flood..Vnto the Kingdome of perpetuall Night. **1637** MILTON *Lycidas* 177 In the blest kingdoms meek of joy and love. **1872** RUSKIN *Eagle's N.* §33 The elastic and vaporous kingdom of folly. **1875** E. WHITE *Life in Christ* III. xxiii. (1876) 361 The Kingdom of Darkness is man's arena of action separated from his God.

d. Any sphere in which one has dominion like that of a king. ***to come (in) to one's kingdom***: to acquire authority, power, attractiveness, or the like. Cf. Luke xxiii. 42.

c **1600** SIR E. DYER *Poems* (ed. Grosart) 21 My mynde to me a Kyngdome is. **1781** COWPER *Truth* 406 His mind his kingdom, and his will his law. **1784** —— *Tirocin.* 12 Hers [the soul's] is the state..An intellectual kingdom all her own. **1825** SCOTT *Talism.* vii, The sick-chamber of the patient is the kingdom of the physician. **1892** KIPLING & BALESTIER *Naulahka* xviii. 211 Now we are come to our Kingdom..Little it profits us. **1930** L. G. MOBERLY *Eternal Dustbin* xiv. 194 That woman has come into her kingdom. **1973** R. RENDELL *Some lie & Some Die* iii. 30 Good luck. Remember me when thou comest into thy kingdom.

e. Anything compared to a realm or country ruled by a king; a domain.

1595 SHAKS. *John* IV. ii. 246 The body of this fleshly Land, This kingdome, this Confine of blood, and breathe. **1597** —— *2 Hen. IV*, IV. iii. 118 All the rest of this little Kingdome (Man). *a* **1822** SHELLEY *Chas I*, II. 385 To dispeople your unquiet kingdom of man. **1832** TENNYSON *Pal. Art* 228 The airy hand..divided quite The kingdom of her thought.

5. A realm or province of nature; *esp.* each of the three great divisions of natural objects, the ***animal***, ***vegetable***, and ***mineral kingdoms***.

[**1642** M. R. BESLER (*title*) Gazophylacium Rerum Naturalium, e regno vegetabili, animali, et minerali depromptarum.] *a* **1691** BOYLE *Chr. Virtuoso* II. I. i. §3 The mineral kingdom, as, after the chemists, most writers now call it. **1692** BENTLEY *Boyle Lect.* iv. 131 If they confine the Earth to Pigmie Births in the Vegetable Kingdom. **1706** PHILLIPS (ed. Kersey) s.v., Chymists..call the three Orders of Natural Bodies, viz. Animal, Vegetable, and Mineral, by the name of Kingdoms. **1746–7** HERVEY *Medit.* (1818) 153 Another subject of the verdant kingdom..demands my particular notice. **1776** WITHERING *Brit. Plants* (1796) I. 5 The Animal, the Vegetable, and the Fossil or Mineral Kingdom. **1802** PLAYFAIR *Illustr. Hutton. The.* 178 The bodies of amphibious animals which now make part of the fossil kingdom. **1849** MACAULAY *Hist. Eng.* iii. I. 411 No kingdom of nature was left unexplored.

6. ***kingdom-come*** (from the clause *thy kingdom come* in the Lord's Prayer).

a. Heaven or paradise; the next world. *slang.*

1785 GROSE *Dict. Vulg. T.* s.v., He is gone to kingdom come, he is dead. **1789** WOLCOTT (P. Pindar) *Subj. Paint.* Wks. 1812 II. 180 Sending such a Rogue to Kingdom-come. **1870** MISS BRIDGMAN *R. Lynne* I. xii. 184 So old aunt Duncan has gone to kingdom come at last.

b. The millennial kingdom of Christ. Also *attrib.*

1848 CLOUGH *Amours de Voy.* III. 76 It would seem this Church is indeed of the purely Invisible, Kingdom-come kind. **1873** MISS THACKERAY *Wks.* (1891) I. p. x, A future.. bound to us by a thousand hopes and loving thoughts—a Kingdom-come for us all.

7. *attrib.* and *Comb.*, as ***kingdom-quake*** (after *earthquake*), ***-making***, etc.

a **1711** KEN *Urania* Poet. Wks. 1721 IV. 463 In Kingdom-quakes the wise Feel no disquieting surprise. **1872** A. DE VERE *Leg. St. Patrick, Disbelief of Milcho* 161 Exile, or kingdom-wearied king. **1882** *Times* 18 Mar. 4/2 The Russian intrigue which they say pushed on the kingdom-making.

Hence **'kingdomful**, as much as a kingdom can hold; **'kingdomless** *a.*, having no kingdom; **'kingdomship**, a kingdom; a kingship.

1547 BOORDE *Introd. Knowl.* Index, The thyrd chapter treateth of..the kyngdomeshyp of Irland. *Ibid.* ii. (1870) 132 Irland is a Kingdomship longing to the Kyng of England. **1882** FARRAR *Early Chr.* II. 319 Provincial governors..here characterised as kings yet kingdomless.

kingdom ('kɪŋdəm), *v.* [f. prec. sb.]

†1. *intr.* (with *it*). To pose or figure as a kingdom. *Obs. nonce-use.*

a **1618** SYLVESTER *Dialogue* 24 Every Countie Kingdomes it a-part.

2. *trans.* **a.** To take possession of, as a kingdom. **b.** To furnish with a kingdom (only in *pass.*).

1887 J. SERVICE *Life Dr. Duguid* 270, I was..Haunted for ever by a fleeting face..whose lips So often as I slept, would kingdom mine. *a* **1891** LD. LYTTON *King Poppy* xi. 480 King henceforth Thou art, and bravely kingdom'd.

kingdomed ('kɪŋdəmd), *a.* [f. prec. sb. or vb.]

1. Furnished with, or constituted as, a kingdom.

1606 SHAKS. *Tr. & Cr.* II. iii. 185 Twixt his mentall and his actiue parts, Kingdom'd Achilles in commotion rages,

and batters gainst it selfe. **1838** S. BELLAMY *The Betrayal* 22 Empire in its regal seat..And kingdom'd character.

2. Consisting of or divided into (so many) kingdoms: in parasynthetic compounds.

1854 *Tait's Mag.* XXI. 265 The much-lacerated, many-kingdomed, state-splintered 'Fatherland'. **1898** M. BAXTER in *Daily News* 11 June 7/4 A Ten-kingdomed Confederacy.

'king-fish. 1. A name given to several fishes remarkable for their size, appearance, or value as food; esp. (*a*) the opah (*Lampris guttatus* or *luna*), a brilliantly-coloured fish of the mackerel family, occasionally found in British waters; (*b*) a carangoid fish (*Seriola Lalandii*) of New Zealand and New South Wales, also called 'yellow-tail'; (*c*) a scombroid fish of Florida (*Scomberomerus regalis* or *Cybium regale*); (*d*) an American sciænoid fish (*Menticirrus nebulosus* or related species); (*e*) a sciænoid fish of S. Australia (*Sciæna antarctica*).

1750 *Phil. Trans., Abridg.* (1756) X. 879 Plate v. The Opah, or King Fish. **1775** ROMANS *Florida* App. 7 Groopers are in great plenty, king-fish, Spanish mackrel and Barrows are also often caught towing. **1798** T. HINDERWELL *Scarborough* II. ii. 229 The Opah or king-fish (very rare) was seen here a few years ago. **1827** P. CUNNINGHAM *N.S. Wales* I. 68 (Morris) King-fish, mullet, mackarel..are all found plentifully about. **1859** *All Year Round* No. 4. 82 The deep sea fish—the 'schnapper', the 'king fish', the 'grounder', and the rock cod—were beyond their reach. **1880** *Rep. R. Comm. Fisheries N.S. Wales* 22 The 'King-fish' [*Elacata nigra*] is about the most voracious and destructive of all the predacious fishes of these seas. **1897** *Outing* (U.S.) XXIX. 330/2 Second in importance is the kingfish, whom the Fish Commissioners call a *Scomberomorus regalis*..He is wholly unrelated to the kingfish of the North, but is a variety of mackerel. He abounds off the coast of Florida.

2. A leader, chief, boss; freq. used as a nickname for a particular person, notably for Huey Long (1893–1935), Governor and Senator from Louisiana. *U.S. slang.*

1933 HUEY P. LONG *Every Man a King* xxvii. 277 We from time to time termed various of our political enemies the 'Kingfish', most prominent of which was..a certain corporation lawyer. *Ibid.*, I am participating here anyway, gentlemen. For the present you can just call me the Kingfish. **1934** *Sun* (Baltimore) 21 Aug. 10/2 The Kingfish [*sc.* Huey Long] is ideally equipped for a dictator's rôle. **1939** *Ibid.* 17 July 11/1 King Levinsky, the Kingfish, who earned a fortune..during four spectacular years in the ring. **1946** *Richmond* (Va.) *Times Dispatch* 26 Dec. 1/5 Mr. Brown ..is sometimes referred to as the 'kingfish' of City Council. **1968** *Word Study* Dec. 4/1 The term *kingfish* may be applied to an undisputed leader or master. It has been used as a personal appellation, self-applied I believe, to Huey Long, and to a character in the enduring radio show of Amos 'n' Andy.

kingfisher ('kɪŋˌfɪʃə(r)). Forms: α. 5 **kyngys fischare**, 6 **kinges fisher**, 6–8 **king's fisher**. β. 7– **kingfisher**.

1. A small European bird (*Alcedo ispida*) with a long cleft beak and brilliant plumage, feeding on fish and aquatic animals which it captures by diving. Hence, extended to other birds of the family *Alcedinidæ* or *Halcyonidæ*, esp. the Belted Kingfisher of N. America (*Ceryle alcyon*), and the Laughing Jackass of Australia (*Dacelo gigas*).

Various superstitions have been associated with the Common Kingfisher, some of which it shares with the HALCYON (which has been generally identified with it), esp. the belief that a dried specimen hung up indicated by its position the direction in which the wind was blowing.

α. *c* **1440** *Promp. Parv.* 275/2 Kyngys fyschare, lytylle byrde, *isida*. **1567** MAPLET *Gr. Forest* 108 b, Beare a naturall grudge the one to the other: as doth the Eagle and the Kings Fisher. **1622** MAY *Virg. Georg.* III. (1628) 89 When..dew refreshing on the Pasture fields The Moone bestowes, Kings-fishers play on shore. **1646** SIR T. BROWNE *Pseud. Ep.* b ij, That a Kings fisher hanged by the bill sheweth where the winde is. **1688** J. CLAYTON in *Phil. Trans.* XVII. 989 The Fishing Hauk is an absolute Species of a Kings-fisher. **1797** BURKE *Regic. Peace* iii. Wks. VIII. 326 This sanguine little king's-fisher (not prescient of the storm, as by his instinct he ought to be).

β. **1658** PHILLIPS, *Halcyon*, a bird called a King-fisher. *a* **1667** COWLEY *On Poverty*, Here sad King-fishers tell their Tales. **1789** G. WHITE *Selborne* II. xlii. (1853) 271 The king-fisher darts along like an arrow. *a* **1821** KEATS *Imit. Spenser* ii, There the Kingfisher saw his plumage bright Vieing with fish of brilliant dye below. **1893** NEWTON *Dict. Birds* 488 In habits Kingfishers display considerable diversity.

2. The name of an artificial salmon-fly. ? *Obs.*

1787 BEST *Angling* (ed. 2) 109 Two salmon flies, which are the principal ones, called the Dragon and Kings-fisher..of the most gaudy feathers there are, especially the peacock's.

3. In full, ***kingfisher blue***. A brilliant blue colour.

1922 *Daily Mail* 11 Dec. 1 (Advt.), All the leading colours including Ivory, Apricot, Jade, Kingfisher, [etc.]. **1956** G. DURRELL *My Family* v. 58 The sea smooth and opalescent, kingfisher-blue. **1970** *Observer* 18 Jan. 1/8 (Advt.), Both dresses in navy, deep oatmeal or kingfisher. **1971** R. RENDELL *One Across* vi. 55 A wool dress of brilliant kingfisher blue.

†**'kinghead.** *Obs.* In 4 -hed(e. [f. KING *sb.* + -HEAD.] **a.** = KINGHOOD. **b.** = KINGDOM.

c **1340** *Cursor M.* 9549 (Trin.) Wiþouten þese kyng haþ no miȝt For to reule his kynghede. **1390** GOWER *Conf.* III. 143 A king, which hath to lede The people, for his kinghede.

kinghood ('kɪŋhʊd). [f. KING *sb.* + -HOOD.] Kingship; the rank, authority, or office of king; kingly spirit or character.

c **1350** *Will. Palerne* 4059 King, i þe coniure..bi alle þe kud customes to kinghod þat longes. *c* **1380** WYCLIF *Wks.* (1880) 471 Crist koude ensaumple kynghod. **1440** J. SHIRLEY *Dethe K. James* (1818) 12, I am undir youre kynghood and yn the service of Love. **1656** S. H. *Gold. Law* 69 What did any of their aforesaid Kings..for their King-hoods? **1837** CARLYLE *Misc. Ess., Mirabeau* (1888) V. 211 This gift was precisely the kinghood of the man, and did itself stamp him as a leader of men. **1875** TENNYSON *Q. Mary* IV. i, Your father was a man Of such colossal kinghood.

'kinginess. *nonce-wd.* [f. **kingy* (like *doggy, horsy*) + -NESS.] The quality of being 'the king'.

a **1849** H. COLERIDGE *Ess.* (1851) II. 159 There is an intense Kinginess about the elder Harry [Shakspere's Hen. IV] which takes from our sympathies with his sufferings.

†**'kingist.** *Obs. rare*$^{-1}$. [f. KING *sb.* + -IST, after *papist*.] A partisan of the king.

1563 WINȜET *Four Scoir Thre Quest.* Wks. 1888 I. 59 Thai wald mok ws on lyke manere, and call ws Kingistis and Queneistis.

Kingite ('kɪŋaɪt). *N.Z.* [f. KING *sb.* + -ITE[1] 1 b.] A follower of the Maori king (see *King Country* s.v. KING *sb.* 13 a). Also *attrib.* or as *adj.*

1860 T. BUDDLE *Maori King Movement* 60 On this point the kingites carry with them the sympathies of the majority. **1884** J. H. KERRY-NICHOLLS *King Country* 6 In 1857 Kingite meetings were held in Paetai. *Ibid.* 9 Sir George Grey..opened up communication with the chiefs of the Kingites. **1910** J. COWAN *Maoris of N.Z.* xxvii. 286 This Kingite war-song..is still on the lips of the Waikato people. *Ibid.* 289 All might have gone well had the Kingites been able to restrain their more turbulent spirits. **1959** K. SINCLAIR in J. E. Gorst *Maori King* p. xiv, He was driven out by the Kingites on 18 April, 1863. *Ibid.* 263 There were no large Kingite meetings, at which he could have been formally 'installed'.

'king-ˌkiller. One who kills a king; a regicide.

1607 SHAKS. *Timon* IV. iii. 382 O thou sweete King-killer, and deare diuorce Twixt naturall Sunne and sire. **1681** T. FLATMAN *Heraclitus Ridens* No. 24 (1713) I. 158 They'll give you leave to roast them at Temple-Bar with their Brother King-killer the Pope. **1726** DE FOE *Hist. Devil* (1822) 244 No less than a King-Killer and an assassinator.

'king-ˌkilling, *sb.* The killing of a king or kings.

1606 *Proc. agst. late Traitors* 105 That King-killing and Queen-killing was not indeed a doctrine of theirs. **1662** *Rump Songs* (1874) II. 98 Murther and Lyes, King-Killing, Hypocrisy, Cheats. **1667** J. CORBET *Disc. Relig. Eng.* 4 The Jesuits Doctrine of king-killing, hath made them odious.

attrib. **1643** PRYNNE *Sov. Power Parlt.* I. (ed. 2) 3 This King-deposing, King-killing Popish Doctrine.

'king-ˌkilling, *a.* That kills a king or kings; regicidal.

1598 SYLVESTER *Du Bartas* II. ii. II. *Babylon* 4 King-killing Treacheries Succeed a-row, with Wrack of Israel. *a* **1732** ATTERBURY *Serm.* (1737) IV. 21 They outstripped..even the bloodiest of their king-killing neighbours.

kingklip ('kɪŋklɪp). In full, **kingklipfish** (**-visch**). [Afrikaans, f. Du. *koningklipvisch*: see KLIPFISH.] One of several South African marine food fishes, esp. *Epinephelus andersoni*, of the family Serranidæ.

[**1843** J. C. CHASE *Cape of Good Hope* 169 Koning Klip Fish, King Rock Fish. Scarcer than the preceding, very considerably larger, and less delicate, but in much repute.] **1876** H. BROOKS *Natal* iv. 141 Klipvisch, kingklip fish..are held in very high estimation. **1878** K. JOHNSTON *Africa* xxiii. 393 Not fewer than forty-four varieties of edible fishes have been enumerated, including..'King Klip'. **1893** H. A. BRYDEN *Gun & Camera S. Afr.* xx. 449 Many of the fish in Cape waters furnish excellent eating; the Roman, kingklipvisch, stomneus, steenbras, and klipvisch being among the choicest. **1923** *Nature* 24 Feb. 271/1 The kingklip (in appearance like a ling). **1930** C. L. BIDEN *Sea-Angling Fishes of Cape* 2 Angling for..kabeljou, stockfish, and king klipfish. **1950** M. MASSON *Birds of Passage* xii. 121 Vendor and buyer alike haggled over the merits of.. Kingclipfish. **1971** *Rand Daily Mail* 4 Sept. 1/3 Kingklip, soles and Cape salmon were almost unobtainable.

King Kong ('kɪŋ'kɒŋ). [Name of the ape-like monster featured in the film *King Kong* (1933).]

a. Used as a nickname for anyone of outstanding size or strength. (In quot. 1966 used ironically.)

1955 E. WAUGH *Officers & Gentlemen* I. vi. 62 He looks like a gorilla. They..sent him here to teach us to climb. We call him King Kong. **1966** 'L. LANE' *ABZ of Scouse* 59 *King Kong*, derisory name for a weedy, undersized individual. **1970** M. KELLY *Spinifex* vi. 103 'What about King Kong?' ..'He's just an honest murderer.' **1970** K. PLATT *Pushbutton Butterfly* (1971) xi. 123 'He looked like a big ape.' ..'Make it a gorilla... That way we can pin it on King Kong.' **1974** *Guardian* 23 Aug. 8/4 Finn MacCool was a legendary Irish giant, a King Kong with a generous heart.

b. Cheap alcohol. *slang.*

1946 MEZZROW & WOLFE *Really Blues* 357/2 *King Kong*, cheap moonshine, corn whisky. **1950** H. E. GOLDIN *Dict. Amer. Underworld Lingo* 117/1 *King Kong*, (South) a potent drink made from the skimmings of boiling sugar cane.

kingless ('kɪŋlɪs), *a.* [f. KING *sb.* + -LESS; cf. ON. *konunglauss*, G. *königlos*.] Without a king; having no king.

1297 R. GLOUC. (Rolls) 2289 þe king lai ded þar, þo was þis lond kingles. *a* **1300** *Cursor M.* 9344 Kyngles sal yee be fra þat dai. *c* **1450** *Merlin* 24 Sir, we ben Kyngeles, for he that we haue is naught worth. **1683** WILLIAMS *Answ. Hunt's Postscr.* 17, I find no approbation of such as the Kingless Keepers of the Liberty of England. **1812** BYRON *Ch. Har.* I. lxxxvi, They fight for freedom who were never free; A Kingless people for a nerveless state. **1871** TYLOR *Prim. Cult.* I. 353 The kingless Turkoman hordes say of themselves 'We are a people without a head'.

Hence **'kinglessness**.

1850 CARLYLE *Latter-d. Pamph.* i. 7 Open 'kinglessness', what we call anarchy,..is everywhere the order of the day.

kinglet ('kɪŋlɪt). [f. KING *sb.* + -LET.]

1. A petty king; a king ruling over a small territory. Mostly *contemptuous*. Cf. KINGLING 1.

1603 FLORIO *Montaigne* I. xlii. (1632) 143 Cæsar termeth all the Lords..to be Kinglets, or pettie Kings [= *reguli*]. *Ibid.* (1634) 146 So many petty-kings, and petty-petty kinglets have we now adayes. **1807** G. CHALMERS *Caledonia* I. III. vii. 388 Sitrig, the kinglet of Northumberland. **1831** CARLYLE *Misc., Early Germ. Lit.* (1872) III. 198 Who.. ventured into the field against even the greatest of these kinglets. **1865** *Pall Mall G.* 12 Aug. 11/1 The Kinglets of Tuscany, Modena, and Parma. **1882** *Daily News* 16 Aug. 5/2 The Zulu King is to be restored under conditions..the same as those that Sir Garnet Wolseley imposed upon his thirteen Kinglets.

2. A popular name of the Golden-crested Wren, *Regulus cristatus*: also of two allied N. American species, *R. satrapa* and *R. calendula*.

1839–43 YARRELL *Hist. Birds* I. 347 The little Golden-Crested Regulus, or Kinglet..has a soft and pleasing song. **1869** J. BURROUGHS in *Galaxy Mag.* Aug., Wilson called the Kinglets Wrens. **1884** E. P. ROE in *Harper's Mag.* Mar. 614/2 The golden-crested kinglet is a little mite of a bird.

kinglihood ('kɪŋlɪhʊd). *rare*$^{-1}$. [f. KINGLY *a.* + -HOOD.] Kingly or royal state; royalty.

1869 TENNYSON *Coming of Arthur* 50 He neither wore on helm or shield The golden symbol of his kinglihood.

kinglike ('kɪŋlaɪk), *a.* and *adv.* [f. KING *sb.* + -LIKE.] **A.** *adj.* Resembling a king; characteristic of, or befitting, a king; kingly; regal.

1561 T. NORTON *Calvin's Inst.* IV. xix. (1634) 726 *marg.*, Rasure of the crowne [is] ministred in token of spiritual Kinglike dignitie. **1636** MASSINGER *Bashf. Lover* III. iii, 'Tis truly noble, having power to punish,—Nay, kinglike—to forbear it. **1661** GAUDEN in Birch *Milton's Wks.* (1738) I. 67 What was done like a King, should have a Kinglike Retribution.

B. *adv.* Like, or in a manner befitting, a king.

1884 TENNYSON *Becket* IV. ii, He..kinglike fought the proud archbishop—kinglike Defied the Pope.

kingliness ('kɪŋlɪnɪs). [f. KINGLY *a.* + -NESS.] Kingly quality or character.

1548 UDALL, etc. *Erasm. Par. Mark* iii. 28 Shewed no poynte of Kingliness. *a* **1618** RALEIGH *Apol.* 71 To that grace, and goodnesse, and Kinglynesse I referre my self. **1843** LYTTON *Last. Bar.* II. ii, Warwick, thou deemest ill of thy king's kingliness. **1876** FREEMAN *Norm. Conq.* V. xxiv. 388 The kingliness was in the whole kin; one son of Woden was as kingly as another.

kingling ('kɪŋlɪŋ). [f. KING *sb.* + -LING.]

1. A little or petty king. (Less contemptuous than *kinglet*.)

1598 SYLVESTER *Du Bartas* II. i. IV. *Handie-Crafts* 381 Prince of some Peasants..And silly Kingling of a simple Village. **1658** CLEVELAND *Rustic Rampant* Wks. (1687) 477 This Upstart Kingling would not wholly move by Example. **1764** CHURCHILL *Candidate* 82 Enough of Kinglings, and enough of Kings. **1812** SOUTHEY *Omniana* II. 193 The romantic adventures of a little Kingling of Ithaca. **1884** TENNYSON *Becket* Prol., You could not see the King for the kinglings.

†2. (See quot.) *Obs. rare.*

1658 *2nd Narr. late Parlt.* 2 A Catalogue of the Kinglings, or the names of those Seventy persons (most of them being the Protectors Kinsmen, and Sallery-men) that voted for Kingship.

kingly ('kɪŋlɪ), *a.* Also 4–6 **kyng-**. [f. KING *sb.* + -LY[1]. Not in OE., which had *cynelic* royal, kingly; but cf. OFris. *kining-*, *kenenglik*, MDu. *coninc-*, *koninglijc* (Du. *koninklijk*), OHG. *chuninclîh* (MHG. *küniclîch*, G. *königlich*), ON. *konungligr* (Da. *kongelig*, Sw. *kong(s)lig*).]

1. Of the nature of a king or kings; royal; of royal rank.

1382 WYCLIF *1 Pet.* ii. 9 ȝe ben a kynde chosun, kyngly presthod, holy folk. **1535** COVERDALE *Hos.* v. 1 Geue eare, o thou kingly house. **1611** SHAKS. *Wint. T.* III. ii. 167 He..to my Kingly Guest Vnclasp'd my practise. **1618** LITHGOW *Pilgr. Farew.* in Farr. *S.P. Jas. I*, 338 Wer'st thou a kinglie sonne, and vertue want, Thou art more brute than beastes. **1652** SIR E. PEYTON (*title*) The Divine Catastrophe of the Kingly Family of the House of Stuarts. **1877** FREEMAN *Norm. Conq.* (ed. 3) I. iii. 108 In every Kingdom there was a kingly house, out of which..alone kings were chosen.

2. Of or belonging to a king; held, exercised, or issued by a king; fit or suitable for a king; royal, regal.

1387–8 T. USK *Test. Love* I. v. (Skeat) l. 126 Dauid that from keping of shepe, was drawen vp in to the order of kingly gouernaunce. *c* **1430** *Life St. Kath.* (1884) 29 Lettres seled wyth his kyngly ryng. **1535** COVERDALE *Esther* i. 19 Yf it please the kynge, let there go a kyngly commaundement from him. **1585** T. WASHINGTON tr. *Nicholay's Voy.* I. xviii. 20 b, Governours..did chase them away with al the other kinglie officers. **1601** SHAKS. *Jul. C.* III. ii. 101, I thrice presented him a Kingly Crowne, Which he did thrice refuse. **1780** COWPER *Table-Talk* 174 Leave kingly backs to cope with kingly cares. *a* **1826** HEBER *Hymn*, The Son of God goes forth to war, A kingly crown to gain. **1855** MACAULAY

Hist. Eng. xvii. IV. 42 Whether the magistrate to whom the whole kingly power was transferred should assume the kingly title.

b. Of government: Monarchical.

1658 *2nd Narr. late Parlt.* in *Select. fr. Harl. Misc.* (1793) 421 To change the government from kingly to parliamentary. **1676** TOWERSON *Decalogue* 232 Aristotle.. was no friend of the kingly government. **1835** THIRLWALL *Greece* I. vi. 163 The kingly form of government appears to have been the only one known in the heroic age. **1899** *Daily News* 8 May 8/4 [Mommsen's] conclusions regarding capital punishment in Kingly, Republican, and Imperial Rome.

3. Having the character, quality, or attributes of a king; kinglike; dignified, majestic, noble. Of persons, their actions, etc.

1593 SHAKS. *2 Hen. VI*, v. i. 29, I am farre better borne then is the king: More like a King, more Kingly in my thoughts. **1605** *Play Stucley* 2138 in Simpson *Sch. Shaks.* (1878) I. 243 What a high spirit hath this Englishman He tunes his speeches to a kingly key. *a* **1618** RALEIGH *Prerog. Parl.* (1628) 5 There is nothing more kingly in a King, then the performance of his word. **1687** DRYDEN *Hind & P.* III. 881 A generous, laudable, and kingly pride. **1858** HAWTHORNE *Fr. & It. Jrnls.* II. 24 The possession of this kingly look implies nothing whatever as respects kingly and commanding qualities.

fig. **1853** KANE *Grinnell Exp.* xlix. (1856) 461 The kingly bergs began their impressive march. **1877** TENNYSON *Harold* III. i. 79 The kingliest Abbey in all Christian lands.

'kingly, *adv.* [f. as prec. + -LY². Cf. MDu. *coninclîke*, ON. *konungliga*.] In a kingly manner, royally; regally.

1586 MARLOWE *1st Pt. Tamburl.* III. iii, Each man a crown! Why, kingly fought, i'faith. **1658** CLEVELAND *Rustic Rampant* Wks. (1687) 442 This Way he could not but dye Kingly, at least, like a Gentleman. **1742** POPE *Dunc.* IV. 207 Low bow'd the rest: He, kingly, did but nod. **1872** TENNYSON *Gareth & Lynette* 124 When I was frequent with him in my youth, And heard him Kingly speak.

'king-ˌmaker. One who makes or sets up kings; *spec.* an epithet of Richard Neville, Earl of Warwick, in the reigns of Henry VI and Edward IV. Also *transf.* and *fig.*

1599 DANIEL *Civ. Wars* v. xvi, That great King-maker Warwick, so far growne In grace with Fortune, that he gouerns it, And Monarchs makes. **1603** *Archpr. Controv.* II. 236 The kingmakers designes will come, as is the old prouerbe, from a wyndmill post to be pudding pricke. **1856** FROUDE *Hist. Eng.* II. viii. 259 Sir Edward Poynings was sent to Dublin to put down this new king-maker. **1878** STUBBS *Const. Hist.* III. xviii. 212 Warwick.. filled.. a place which never before or after was filled by a subject, and his title of Kingmaker was not given without reason. **1887** *Dict. Nat. Biog.* IX. 67/1 William Thompson, the great Maori chief and 'king-maker'. **1899** E. WHARTON *Greater Inclination* 162 John Oberville? I'll tell you what he is—the power behind the throne, the black Pope, the King-maker. **1949** *Sun* (Baltimore) 10 Aug. 1/6 Hunt boasted of responsibility for getting so many Government officials their jobs that he was known 'socially' as 'the kingmaker'. **1959** *Manch. Guardian* 4 Aug. 4/2 Governor Ribicoff, of Connecticut.. has launched his career as a kingmaker by taking command of the Kennedy forces. **1968** 'G. BAGBY' *Another Day* iv. 76 This was a young man who was clearly destined to make his mark... The kingmakers had their eye on him. He was going to go places. **1972** *Times* 27 Dec. 5/8 This was a sad example of a politician still trying to play the kingmaker long after his influence had waned.

So **'king-ˌmaking** *sb.* and *a.*

1816 BYRON *Ch. Har.* III. xvii, And is this all the world has gain'd by thee, Thou first and last of fields! king-making Victory? **1865** KINGSLEY *Herew.* I. Prel. 11 Leofric had the first success in king making.

King-of-Arms. Also (less correctly) **King-at-Arms.** [See ARM *sb.*² 14]

The title of the three chief heralds of the College of Arms, viz. Garter, the principal King of Arms, and Clarenceux and Norroy, provincial Kings of Arms, the former of whom has jurisdiction south of the Trent, and the other north of that river. Besides these there are the Lyon King of Arms of Scotland, and the Ulster King of Arms of Ireland; also Bath King of Arms (see BATH *sb.*¹ 19). The appellation is given also to similar officers in other countries.

1449-50 *Will of W. Bruges* in Sir H. Nicolas *Testamenta Vetusta* (1826) I. 266 William Bruges, Garter Kyng of Armes, at London, Feb. 26, 1449. My body to be brought and buryed in the Church of Saynt George within Staunford, [etc.]. **1464** *Rolls Parlt.* V. 530/2 John Smert, otherwise called Garter King of Armes. **1530** PALSGR. 236/1 Kyng of armes, *roy de armes*. **1565** in Gross *Gild Merch.* (1890) II. 55, I Clarenciux, King of Armes of the Sowth est and West parts. *a* **1614** J. MELVILL *Diary* (Wodrow Soc.) 58 William Stewart, sumtyme Lioun King of Armes. **1702** *Lond. Gaz.* No. 3804/1 Then the Deputy Garter King of Arms with his Coronet. **1806** A. DUNCAN *Nelson's Fun.* 33 Garter, Principal King of Arms,.. with his Sceptre. **1874** *N. & Q.* 5th Ser. I. 146 The Crown of a Herald King of Arms.

β. *a* **1548** HALL *Chron., Edw. IV*, 244 Causing Gartier, principal kyng at armes, to make a publique Proclamacion. *Ibid.* 245 They sent Lyon Kyng at Armes to the duke of Glocester. **1713** STEELE *Englishm.* No. 35. 224 The King.. dispatches Garter King at Arms with a Letter of Defiance. **1808** SCOTT *Marm.* IV. viii. *note*, It was often an office imposed upon the Lion King-at-arms, to receive foreign ambassadors. **1861** M. PATTISON *Ess.* (1889) I. 37 We find, from a household book of Edward I, that.. Herthelm, king-at-arms of the 'King of Almaine', receives a present.

†**king-piece.** *Obs.* Also **king's-piece.** = KING-POST 1.

1664 EVELYN tr. *Freart's Archit.* 133 The Hyperthyron which the Italians call Soppra frontale, and our Carpenters the King-piece. **1679** MOXON *Mech. Exerc.* 169 King peece, see Joggle peece. **1688** R. HOLME *Armoury* III. 450/1 Kings piece.. which stands upright in the middle of the Gable end [of a wooden house].

'king-pin.

†**1.** The tallest (central) pin in the game of kayles.

1801 STRUTT *Sports & Past.* III. vii. 239 One of them.. is taller than the rest, and this, I presume, was the king-pin.

2. = KING-BOLT. Hence *fig.*, that which holds together any complex system or arrangement; also, the most important or outstanding person in a party, organization, etc.

1867 *Harper's Weekly* 14 Sept. 590/2 His best position was as a batter. He was a 'King-pin' there. **1895** *Libr. Jrnl.* (U.S.) June 202 Mr. Vinton.. believed cataloging to be the king-pin of the library system. **1898** R. KIPLING *Fleet in Being* vi. 76 The newer generation.. know that he is the king-pin of their system. **1914** *Chambers's Jrnl.* Jan. 62/1 The cars are mounted on bogie trucks, the connection being by means of a central or 'king-pin'. **1915** C. J. DENNIS *Songs of Sentimental Bloke* 102 But 'struth!' 'E is king-pin! The 'ead serang! **1926** K. S. PRICHARD *Working Bullocks* (1956) 206 'My!' Mary Ann gasped incredulously, 'and you was the king pin last week.' **1957** J. WATEN *Shares in Murder* 99 Then he must be the biggest fence of the lot. The kingpin. The daddy of all fences. **1957** *Economist* 5 Oct. 22/1 The balloting for the seven seats filled by the constituency parties revealed that, with the kingpin removed, the former Bevanite machine is showing signs of disintegration. **1958** *Engineering* 28 Feb. 265/3 Another remarkable feature of the design is a front suspension which uses telescopic dampers as the king pins and steering swivels. **1970** *Daily Tel.* 30 Oct. 2/6 The owner of three shops was the kingpin behind a wholesale shoplifting plot. **1971** M. TAK *Truck Talk* 96 *Kingpin*, the bolt on the underside of the front of a trailer that fits into the tractor's fifth wheel to couple the tractor and the trailer together.

'king-post. 1. *Carpentry.* **a.** An upright post in the centre of a roof-truss, extending from the ridge to the tie-beam.

1776 G. SEMPLE *Building in Water* 115 The King-post, h. may be the same. **1817** B. HALL *Voy. Loo Choo* (1820) 54 The roof was well constructed, the rafters being mortised into the ends of the horizontal beams, and braced to the middle by a perpendicular beam or king-post. **1891** A. WHITE *Tries at Truth* iii. 15 In building a porch, the king-post is the beam on which the whole structure rests.

b. *attrib.*, as ***king-post roof, truss.***

1845 *Ecclesiologist* I. 149 Tie-beams, which sustain a low king-post roof. **1886** E. S. MORSE *Japanese Homes* i. 10 [He] fairly loathes a structure that has no king-post.. truss.

2. On a ship (see quots.).

1927 G. BRADFORD *Gloss. Sea Terms* 95/2 *King post*, a short derrick mast to support the smaller cargo booms. **1948** R. DE KERCHOVE *Internat. Maritime Dict.* 385/1 *King post*. 1. A short heavy mast which serves to support a boom. 2. The centerline pillars in a ship's hold. **1961** F. H. BURGESS *Dict. Sailing* 127 *Kingpost*, a vertical post, sometimes resembling a mast, erected near the hatches, to support and top a derrick boom.

†**'kingrick, -rik, -rich.** *Obs.* Forms: *α.* 1 **kynyng-**, 3 **kung-, kinge-**, 4 **king-, kyng(e)- riche.** *β.* 4 **kinge-**, 4-5 **kyngrik(e**, (5 **-ryke**), 4, 6 **kingrik(e**, 7 **-rick.** [OE. *cyningrīce* (f. *cyning* KING + *rīce* kingdom, RICHE, RIKE) = MDu. *coninc̄rike* (Du. *koninkrijk*), OHG. *chunincrîchi* (MHG. *künicrîche*, G. *königreich*), ON. *konungríki* (Sw. *konungrike*, Da. *kongerige*). Cf. KINRICK.] = KINGDOM, in various senses.

α. *a* **1067** in Kemble *Cod. Dipl.* IV. 229 For ælre ðere kynga sawle ðe æfter me ðyses kynyngriches wældeð. *c* **1250** *Gen. & Ex.* 1258 A kungriche his name bar. *a* **1300** *K. Horn* 17 In none kinge-riche Nas non his iliche. **1377** LANGL. *P. Pl.* B. Prol. 125 Crist kepe þe, sire kyng, And þi kyng-riche.

β. *a* **1300** *Cursor M.* 416 Als mighti king in his kingrike. **1375** BARBOUR *Bruce* I. 57 Thai said, successioun of kyngrik Was nocht to lawer feys lik. *c* **1470** HARDING *Chron.* CLXXXVII. iii, Aboue all men within his hole kyngrike. **1579** J. STUBBES *Gaping Gulf* C vij b, Our Elizabeth.. hauing the kingrike in her owne person.

attrib. **1663** BP. GRIFFITH *Serm. 4 Admir. Beasts* 10 The Regal or Kingrick office of Christ.

King's Bench. [See BENCH *sb.* 2 b.] A former court of record and the supreme court of common law in the kingdom; now, under the Judicature Act of 1873, represented by the King's Bench division of the High Court of Justice.

1362- [see BENCH *sb.* 2 b].

b. In full, *King's Bench Prison.* A jail formerly appropriated to debtors and criminals confined by authority of the supreme courts at Westminster, etc.

1428 *E.E. Wills* (1882) 78 The prisons of Ludgate, Marchalsie, Kyngesbenche, And the Countours in London. **1436** *Ibid.* 106 The Prisoners of the Kynggis bench. **1501** *Bury Wills* (Camden) 89 To the prisoners in Newgate, Ludgate, to the Kyngs Benche, and to the Marshalsy, to eche of them vj *s.* viij *d.* **1849** DICKENS *Dav. Copp.* xlix, My feet will naturally tend towards the King's Bench Prison. **1898** BESANT *Orange Girl* II. xxvi, A Newgate bird and a bird of the King's Bench.

king's evil. [tr. med.L. *regius morbus* (in classical L. = jaundice); cf. MDu. *conincsevel*, OF. *le mal le roy*.] Scrofula, which in England and France was formerly supposed to be curable by the king's (or queen's) touch. (Cf. EVIL *sb.* 7 c.)

The practice of touching for the king's evil continued from the time of Edward the Confessor to the death of Queen Anne in 1714. The Office for the ceremony has not been printed in the Prayer-book since 1719.

1387 TREVISA *Higden* (Rolls) V. 49 [God] destroyed the secounde witnesse by the Kynges evel [**1432-50** the kynges sekenesse]. **1398** —— *Barth. De P.R.* XVII. cxxxiii. (MS. Bodl.) lf. 224/1 þe smel of leke.. helep þe kinges yuel and þe dropsie. **1533** ELYOT *Cast. Helthe* (1541) 90 a, Swellinges in the neck ful of matter, called the kinges evyll. **1580** LYLY *Euphues* (Arb.) 322 There is nothing that can cure the Kings Euill, but a Prince. **1615** CROOKE *Body of Man* 340 The seauenth Sonne is able to cure the Kings Euill. **1660** PEPYS *Diary* 23 June, Staid to see the King touch people for the King's evil. **1722** W. BECKETT (*title*) A Free and Impartial Inquiry into the Antiquity and Efficacy of Touching for the King's Evil. **1791** BOSWELL *Johnson* (1887) I. 41-2 Young Johnson had the misfortune to be much afflicted with the scrophula, or King's-evil,.. His mother.. carried him to London where he was actually touched by Queen Anne [1712]. **1839** KEIGHTLEY *Hist. Eng.* I. 66 The Confessor was the first who touched for the King's evil. **1898** BESANT *Orange Girl* I. iv, Rheumatism, gout, and the King's Evil.

fig. **1692** WASHINGTON tr. *Milton's Def. Pop.* v. M.'s Wks. (1851) 134 You had not then been bribed with Charles his Jacobusses. You had not got the King's-Evil.

Hence †**king's-'evil'd, -'evilly** *adjs.*, affected with the king's evil.

1706 BAYNARD in Sir J. Floyer *Hot & Cold Bath.* II. (1709) 257 Their children.. Rickety, King's Evil'd, or Consumptive. *Ibid.* 335 Miserable small King's-Evilly.. Infants.

King's Highway: see HIGHWAY.

kingship ('kɪŋʃɪp). [f. KING *sb.* + -SHIP; cf. MDu. *conincscap* (Du. *koningschap*), G. *königschaft*. OE. had *cynescipe* (see KINE-¹). The early occurrence of the word in one MS. of *Cursor Mundi* is remarkable.]

1. The office and dignity of a king; the fact of being king; reign.

c **1325** *Cursor M.* 8583 (Cott.) In his kingscip [*Fairf.*, *Trin.* kingdome; *Gött.* king-riche] þe fourte [*other MSS.* forme, former] daus, O-mang his folk he sett his laus. **1642** SIR E. DERING *Sp. Relig.* 96 The Kingship and Priestship of every particular man. **1765** BLACKSTONE *Comm.* I. vii. 249 Immediately upon the decease of the reigning prince.. his kingship or imperial dignity.. is vested at once in his heir. **1869** FREEMAN *Norm. Conq.* III. xiv. 374 The few days of life and kingship which still were his.

fig. **1865** RUSKIN *Sesame* 121 The kingship.. which consists in a stronger moral state.. than that of others.

2. The rule of a king; monarchical government.

1648 *Eikon Bas.* x. 78 They designed, and proposed to me the new modelling of Soveraignty and Kingship. **1692** SOUTH *12 Serm.* (1697) I. 409 While his army believed him real in his Zeal against Kingship. **1840** CARLYLE *Heroes* vi. In rebellious ages, when Kingship itself seems dead and abolished, Cromwell, Napoleon step forth again as Kings.

3. With poss. pron.: The personality of a king; (his) royal majesty. Also *fig.*

1648 HERRICK *Hesper., Past. Birth Pr. Chas.*, I a sheep-hook will bestow To have his little King-ship know, As he is prince, he's shepherd too. **1660** A. SADLER *Subj. Joy* 28 Though.. his fifty Boyes Do run before his Kingship. **1832** J. WILSON in *Blackw. Mag.* XXXI. 870 Then shall we skirt his kingship [Scafell] all the way to the head of Seathwaite Tarn. **1861** DU CHAILLU *Equat. Afr.* xii. 183 His ebony kingship.

4. The dominion or territory of a king.

1864 DASENT *Jest & Earnest* (1873) II. 158 So long as countries are split into small kingships, and each valley has its chief.

king's man, 'kingsman.

1. a. A partisan of the king; a royalist. In *Sc. Hist.*, (see quot. 1862).

a **1639** SPOTTISWOOD *Hist. Ch. Scotl.* (1655) 253 [anno 1571] One professing to be the Kings man, another the Queens. **1659-60** *Hist. 2nd Death Rump* 1/1 Two Kings-men Last week to the Country did gallop. **1770** BURKE *Pres. Discont.* Wks. 1815 II. 256 The name by which they chuse to distinguish themselves, is that of king's men, or the king's friends. **1862** HUNTER *Biggar & Ho. Fleming* xxviii. 357 In the year 1571.. the people of Scotland were divided into two inveterate factions, called respectively Queensmen and Kingsmen.

b. ***the King's men***: a name for the dramatic company otherwise known as 'the King's Majesty's Servants' under James I.

1613 R. DABORNE *Let.* 29 Oct. in P. Henslowe *Henslowe Papers* (1907) 76 They shall have the play or noe, they rale upon me I hear bycause the kingsmen hav given out they shall hav it. *Ibid.* 77 Eight pound besyds my rent which J will fully satisfy yᵘ eather by them or the kings men as yᵘ please. **1886** *Dict. Nat. Biogr.* VII. 286/1 Burbage's position justifies the conjecture.. that he had been connected with the lord chamberlain's men, subsequently called the king's men, and originally called Lord Strange's company. **1923** E. K. CHAMBERS *Eliz. Stage* II. 218 The King's men gave eight plays at Court.. during the winter of 1614-15. **1951** M. CHUTE *Shakespeare of London* xi. 233 The King's Men gave a Sunday production of *The Merry Wives of Windsor* and then followed it on St. Stephen's night with *Measure for Measure*.

c. *U.S.* One who supported the British cause at the time of the American Revolution. *Obs.* exc. *Hist.*

1809 P. FRENEAU *Poems* II. 11 Whate'er some angry king's-men say, You play a game that must be won. **1857** *Ladies' Repository* XVII. 83/1, I never feed kingsmen if I can help it. **1949** *Sat. Even. Post* 2 Apr. 98/4, I am neither king's man nor rebel.

2. A custom-house officer.

1814 SCOTT *Diary* 25 Aug. in *Lockhart*, We observed a hurry among the inhabitants, owing to our being as usual suspected for king's men. **1824** MACTAGGART *Gallovid. Encycl.* (1876) 362 He was one of the greatest smugglers on..the Solway, and outwitted the most sagacious kingsmen.

3. *slang.* (see quot.).

1851 MAYHEW *Lond. Labour* I. 51 The man who does not wear his silk neckerchief—his 'King's-man' as it is called—is known to be in desperate circumstances.

4. A member of King's College, Cambridge.

1803 C. SMART in *Gradus ad Cantabrigiam* 81 Ev'n gloomiest Kings-men, pleas'd awhile, Grin horribly a ghastly smile. **1852** C. A. BRISTED *Five Yrs. in Eng. Univ.* (ed. 2) 127 He came out the winner, with the Kingsman and one of our three close at his heels. **1968** *Tablet* 17 Aug. 820/1 He was anxious, like many Kingsmen, to be recognised as a Fabian. **1973** *Observer* 1 July 32/3 He was a fellow of King's College, Cambridge..and immediately after his death he received what must have been regarded by most Kingsmen as the ultimate accolade. **1974** *Times Lit. Suppl.* 29 Nov. 1346/3 Basileon. A Magazine of King's College, Cambridge... The founder-editors believed that facility in writing resulted from early practice, and their rather solemn purpose was to give Kingsmen a chance of trying their hand. ..To a Kingsman of between the wars they still give off that faint but delightful savour.

King's Peace: see PEACE.

kingston[1] ('kɪŋstən). Also 7 **kingstone**, 8 **king's stone**, **kinson**. A name for the angel-fish or monk-fish (*Rhina squatina*).

1666 MERRETT *Pinax* 186 *Squatina*, a Kingstone. **1747** MRS. GLASSE *Cookery* xxi. 163 Fish in Season.. Thornback, and Homlyn, Kinson, Oysters [etc.]. **1769** HEWSON in *Phil. Trans.* LIX. 205, I next went to Brighthelmstone, where I found kingston, or monk-fish, a species of skate. **1836** YARRELL *Brit. Fishes* II. 407 It is common on the coasts of Kent and Sussex, where it is called a kingston.

Kingston[2] ('kɪŋstən). *Naut.* The name of John *Kingston*, 19th-century British dockyard foreman, used *attrib.* and *absol.* (†and in the possessive) to designate a kind of conical valve he invented for use in the sides of ships below the water-line which opens outwards with a screwing action.

1846 J. BOURNE *Treat. Steam Engine* xi. 223/1 In modern steam vessels Kingston's valves are..used, which consist of a spindle or plate valve fitted to the exterior of the ship, so that if the internal pipe or cock breaks, the external valve will still be operative. **1859** *Reed's New Guide Bk. Local Marine Board Exam.* 62 (*heading*) Boiler valves and cocks... Kingston valves. **1883** A. E. SEATON *Man. Marine Engin.* xvi. 301 For all large inlets the Kingston valve is preferable, as it acts as a non-return valve in case of the spindle breaking, and can then always be worked by simply forcing it outwards. *Ibid.* 303 A valve may be fitted in lieu of a cock to even the smallest Kingston. *Ibid.*, In the Navy, Kingston valves are fitted to all inlets and blow-off pipes. **1905** E. M. & B. DONKIN tr. *Bauer's Marine Engines & Boilers* 418 Most of the valves in merchant ships consist of ordinary valves opening inwards, but on warships the old so-called 'Kingston' valves are still frequently met with. **1933** 'L. LUARD' *All Hands* 124 Drop of air in three main. Open three Kingston. Close air. Open three vent. **1966** P. E. SEGDITSAS *Elsevier's Naut. Dict.* 111 Kingston valve; sea cock.

King Street ('kɪŋ striːt). [Name of the street near Covent Garden, London, in which the headquarters of the Communist Party of Great Britain Executive Committee has been situated since 1920.] Used *transf.* to designate the Communist Party of Great Britain, its members, or its leaders. Also *attrib.*

1958 C. COCKBURN *Crossing Line* iii. 49 The place did good business in those days..because the *Daily Worker* staff and the people from King Street..used it. *Ibid.* v. 83 This was a situation which gave many people at King Street nightmares. **1961** *Guardian* 5 June 8/4 The Labour party.. shunning the support of King Street. **1964** C. DRIVER *Disarmers* iii. 72 If the King Street commissars were not so invincibly stupid, they would have insisted that the movement be left severely alone. **1970** *Times Lit. Suppl.* 18 Sept. 1016/3 Even if not a card-carrying member of the Communist Party, Strachey was at this time the grey eminence of King Street. **1972** *Observer* 8 Oct. 29/2 One version of events is that 'King Street' had decided the miners wouldn't end the strike unless they were given 25 per cent. King Street means the headquarters of the Communist Party.

kingy ('kɪŋɪ). [f. KING *sb.* + -Y[6].] A children's game resembling 'He' but played with a ball; the winner is declared King.

[**1916** N. DOUGLAS *London Street Games* 5 There are other ball-games, such as hot rice..and king and missings out.] **1959** B. SUTTON-SMITH *Games N.Z. Children* ii. 150 Kingy. In this game the players begin by standing round in a circle with their arms on one another's shoulders. The ball is dropped in the middle of the circle. When it touches someone's foot that person is He. **1969** I. & P. OPIE *Children's Games* ii. 95 'Kingy' is a ball game in which those who are not He have the ball hurled at them, without means of retaliation. **1972** *Where* Apr. 102/2 Transferred to playground or playing field, such games as 'kingy' can lose much of their colour and point, since the existence of natural and human obstacles and hazards are of their essence.

†**kinhead.** *Obs. rare.* In 4 **kunhede, kinhed.** [f. KIN[1] + -HEAD.] Kinship: cf. KINDHEAD a.

c **1350** *Will. Palerne* 4515 To litel þow me knowest or kinhed me kiþes. *c* **1400** *R. Glouc.'s Chron.* (1724) 447 (Harl MS.) Erl Roberd..held hem boþe aȝe þe kyng, to þenche on kunhede [*other MSS.* kundhede] Vor [þe] emperesse was hys soster.

† '**kinhood.** *Obs. rare*$^{-1}$. In 5 **kynhod.** [f. KIN[1] + -HOOD.] Kindred.

c **1440** CAPGRAVE *Life St. Kath.* I. 526 The kynhod of hir Had fovnded this Cite.

kinic, *Chem.*, obs. form of QUINIC.

kinin ('kaɪnɪn). [f. Gr. κιν-εῖν to set in motion + -IN[1]; in sense 1 abstracted from *bradykinin* (s.v. BRADY-).] **1.** *Biochem.* Any of a group of polypeptides of low molecular weight which are formed in tissue (from inactive precursors in the blood) in response to injury and have local effects that typically include pain and the dilatation of blood vessels.

1954 SCHACHTER & THAIN in *Brit. Jrnl. Pharmacol.* IX. 352/1 Since this substance in wasp venom cannot as yet be identified with any substance hitherto described, it is tentatively designated as wasp (or venom) kinin, or simply as kinin. **1962** *New Scientist* 4 Oct. 35/2 If the kinins get into the general circulation they are destroyed before they can produce general effects throughout the body. **1963** *Listener* 7 Nov. 741/2 An important factor in rheumatism may be an accelerated formation and release of certain compounds known as kinins, which are formed from amino-acids. The kinins may cause many of the painful symptoms, such as the swollen joints that are a prominent part of the disease. **1970** PASSMORE & ROBSON *Compan. Med. Stud.* II. xvii. 1/2 In addition to the above kinins, bradykinin homologues..are found in many parts of the animal kingdom, e.g. in wasp and scorpion venoms..and in the plasma of reptiles and birds.

2. *Plant Physiol.* = CYTOKININ.

1956 C. O. MILLER et al. in *Jrnl. Amer. Chem. Soc.* LXXVIII. 1375 A substance which markedly promotes cell division in various plant tissue cultures..has been shown.. to be 6-furfurylaminopurine. The specific name *kinetin* has been applied to this substance, and the generic term *kinin* is suggested for any substance which similarly stimulates cytokinesis. **1965** *New Scientist* 25 Mar. 788/3 The third and most recently investigated group of plant growth substances is that of the kinins. **1971** F. C. STEWARD *Plant Physiol.* VIA. iii. 356 The photoperiodic responses to red light may also involve kinin effects.

kininogen (kaɪ'nɪnədʒən). *Biochem.* [f. KININ + -OGEN.] Any biologically inactive precursor of a kinin (sense 1).

1963 *Jrnl. Physiol.* CLXIX. 45P The plasmin preparation ..did not form kinin from purified kininogen. **1970** PASSMORE & ROBSON *Compan. Med. Stud.* II. xvii. 2/1 Although plasma and tissues contain readily activated kinin-forming enzymes and kininogens, free active kinin is rarely detected in biological fluids.

kinjal (kɪn'dʒɑːl). [Native name in the Caucasus (= Russ. *kinzhál*), a. Pers. (Arab., Turk., Urdū) KHANJAR.] (Among Caucasians and Kurds) = HANDJAR, HANJAR, KHANJAR.

1862 *Harper's Mag.* XXVI. 803/1, I laid aside revolver and kindshall. **1889** J. ABERCROMBY *Trip E. Caucasus* 130 At his waist hung a *kinjal* and a long native sabre. **1897** R. D. BLACKMORE *Dariel* viii. 86 His hand was playing with his *kinjal* all the time, for so they call those deadly bits of steel, without which they never think their attire complete. **1924** *Blackw. Mag.* Feb. 149/1 The scar of a Kurdish kinjal.

kink (kɪŋk), *sb.*[1] Also 7 **keenk**, 8 **kenk**. [prob. a. Du. *kink* twist, twirl, = G. *kink, kinke*, Da., Sw. *kink*, app. from a root **kink-*, **kik-*, to bend, twist; cf. Icel. *kikna* to bend at the knees, *keikr* bent back.]

1. a. A short twist or curl in a rope, thread, hair, wire, or the like, at which it is bent upon itself; esp. when stiff so as to catch or cause obstruction. (Orig. nautical.) Also *transf.* of a 'crick' or stiffness in the neck, etc.

1678 PHILLIPS (ed. 4) App., *Keenk* (in Navigation), is when a Rope which should run smooth in the Block, hath got a little turn, and runs as it were double. **1769** FALCONER *Dict. Marine* (1789), *Kink*, a sort of twist or turn in any.. rope, occasioned by it's being very stiff or close-laid; or by being drawn too hastily out of the roll. **1778** NAIRNE in *Phil. Trans.* LXVIII. 834 Where there happened to be kenks in the wire. *a* **1825** FORBY *Voc. E. Anglia*, *Kink*, an entanglement in a skein. **1833** MARRYAT *P. Simple* xx, Your back with a bow like a kink in a cable. **1848** *Yale Lit. Mag.* XIV. 82 (Th.), Come! wake up, and shake the kinks out of your land legs. **1851** H. MELVILLE *Whale* iii, I tore myself out of it in such a hurry that I gave myself a kink in the neck. **1857** MAYNE REID *War Trail* xiii. 67 Yes, there was the same negress with..the little well-oiled kinks hanging like corkscrews over her temples! **1893** G. D. LESLIE *Lett. Marco* xxv. 167 The clematis, tomato, and some others, form kinks in their leaf-stems, which secure the plants very effectively. **1894** BOTTONE *Electr. Instr. Making* (ed. 6) 125 Care should be taken to wind this wire evenly, closely, and without kinks. **1930** [see CRONK *a.*]. **1962** *Kenyon Rev.* XXIV. 94 Don't worry about Saturday night. Play around. Work the kinks out. **1970** G. F. NEWMAN *Sir, You Bastard* 259 There existed kinks in the man's career; it was only a question of drawing on the right one.

b. A sudden bend in a line, course, or the like that is otherwise straight or smoothly curved.

1899 S. BARING-GOULD *Furze Bloom* 27 That [wall] on the left makes a kink to respect 'The Brothers' Grave'. **1928** L. S. PALMER *Wireless Princ. & Pract.* v. 132 The curve sometimes exhibits a sudden 'kink' or discontinuity. **1965** G. MCINNES *Road to Gundagai* v. 74 Below the kink the street degenerates rapidly. **1971** *Sunday Express* (Johannesburg) 28 Mar. 7/1 A new grandstand for 2,000 spectators at the kink on the main straight.

2. *fig.* **a.** A mental twist; an odd or fantastic notion; a crotchet, whim. In recent use also = a state of madness; an instance of, the practice of, or suffering resulting from sexual abnormality. **b.** An odd but clever method of doing something; a 'dodge', 'wrinkle'.

18.. CARLTON *New Purchase* (Bartlett), It is useless to persuade him to go, for he has taken a kink in his head that he will not. **18..** *Major Jones's Courtship* 20 (ibid.), I went down to Macon to the examination, whar I got a heap of new kinks. **1803** T. JEFFERSON *Let.* 24 Nov. in *Writings* (1897) VIII. 280 Should the judges take a kink in their heads. **1876** W. CORY *Lett. & Jrnls.* (1897) 414, I have done a little towards bringing up young people without kinks. **1889** *Anthony's Photogr. Bull.* II. 110 The hundred and one recent valuable wrinkles, dodges and kinks that float through the photographic press. **1915** F. M. HUEFFER *Good Soldier* IV. ii. 229 By a kink, that I could not at the time understand, Miss Hurlbird insisted that I ought to keep the money all to myself. **1924** [see ENSNARL *v.*[1]]. **1950** T. S. ELIOT *Cocktail Party* II. 120 And so you suppose you have what you call a 'kink'? **1959** *Encounter* Mar. 22 Hates kissing. Undertakes most kinks..but no buggery. **1959** M. GEE in C. K. Stead *N.Z. Short Stories* (1966) 279 He's got a kink I reckon. He'll end up in the nuthouse. **1965** *Movie* Summer 44/4 The result is the story of the sexual hallucinations of a young girl..played for flat-out kink.

3. *U.S.* A human being in various slang applications. **a.** A Black person, a Negro. *Obs.*

1865 J. H. BROWNE *Four Yrs. in Secessia* xxxix. 288 'Coming the kink' was to steal a negro from the country, and dispose of him in town. **1944** *Amer. Speech* XIX. 173 *Kink* shows an obvious allusion to the Negro's hair.

b. A criminal.

1914 JACKSON & HELLYER *Vocab. Criminal Slang* 52 *Kink*, a crook; a larcenous criminal. Also used by yeggs to designate a non-criminal tramp, or one who is not initiated into the particular craft of the speaker. **1950** H. E. GOLDIN *Dict. Amer. Underworld Lingo* 117/2 *Kink* (scattered areas of East and near South), a thief, especially an expert in stealing automobiles.

c. A sexually abnormal person; one who practises sexual perversions; loosely, an eccentric, a person wearing noticeably unusual clothes, behaving in a startling manner, etc.

1965 *Harper's Bazaar* Jan. 54/1 His phone is ex-directory because of all the kinks who used to phone at 2 a.m. **1967** [see KICKSTER]. **1968** B. TURNER *Sex Trap* xv. 149, I believe the psychiatrists have other ideas about what makes a kink kinky. **1972** 'J. RIPLEY' *My Word you should have seen Us* 35, I have known queers. I have known kinks.

kink (kɪŋk), *sb.*[2] *Sc.* and *north. dial.* [f. KINK *v.*[1]: cf. the equivalent CHINK *sb.*[1]] A fit or paroxysm, as of laughter or coughing, that for the moment catches the breath.

1788 W. MARSHALL *Yorksh.* Gloss. s.v. (E.D.S.), A kink of laughter. **1790** MORRISON *Poems* 215 (Jam.) We value their frowns not a kink. **1822** HOGG *Perils of Man* I. xii. 311 The honest man's gane away in a kink. **1880** *Antrim & Down Gloss.*, *Kink, keenk*, a paroxysm of coughing or of laughter.

kink (kɪŋk), *v.*[1] *Sc.* and *north. dial.* Forms: (1 **cincian**), 4 **kinc**, 5 **kynke**, 7 **kinck**, 7- **kink**. [Northern form of CHINK *v.*[1], OE. *cincian*, corresp. to LG. *kinken*, app. a nasalized variant of Teut. **kīk-an*, whence MHG. *kīchen*, Ger. *keichen*, Sw. *kikna*, Norw. *kikje*, to gasp, pant, fetch breath with difficulty. Occurs in most modern Teutonic langs., as the first element of the name of the *chincough*, *kinkcough*, or *kinkhost*.]

intr. To gasp convulsively for breath, lose the breath spasmodically, as in hooping-cough or a severe fit of laughing. **a.** with laughing.

c **1050** *Suppl. Ælfric's Voc.* in Wr.-Wülcker 171/39 *Cachinnatio*, ceahhetung *uel* cincung. *c* **1325** *Metr. Hom.* 83 Full ille bers us lah and kinc Quen apon this bischop we think. *c* **1460** *Towneley Myst.* xxx. 152 Peasse, I pray the, be still, I laghe that I kynke. **1607** WALKINGTON *Opt. Glass* 90 Hee laughs and kinckes like Chrysippus when he saw an asse eate figs. **1802** SIBBALD *Sc. Poetry* Gloss., *Kink*,..to laugh immoderately. **1894** HALL CAINE *Manxman* VI. iv. 368 The child..laughed and squealed till she 'kinked'.

b. as in hooping-cough.

1674–91 RAY *N.C. Words*, To *Kink*,..spoken of Children when their Breath is long stopped through eager crying or coughing. **1863** *Mod. Yorksh. Dial.*, Poor child coughs till it kinks again. **1883** C. F. SMITH *Southernisms* in *Trans. Amer. Philol. Soc.* 51 *Kink*..used in West Virginia, and perhaps elsewhere, of a child's losing its breath by coughing especially, or crying, or laughing. **1886** *S.W. Linc. Gloss.*, *Kink*, to..labour for breath, as in the whooping-cough. *Mod. Sc.* She does not kink much, she has it lightly.

Hence '**kinking** *vbl. sb.*[1] and *ppl. a.*[1]

c **1050** [see a above]. **1607** WALKINGTON *Opt. Glass* 81 With ever-kincking vaine The bellowes of his breath he tore in twaine.

kink (kɪŋk), *v.*[2] Also 8 **kenk**. [prob. a. Du. *kinken* (Hexham), f. *kink* KINK *sb.*[1]]

1. *intr.* To form a kink; to twist or curl stiffly, esp. at one point, so as to catch or get entangled: said of a rope or the like.

1697 DAMPIER *Voy.* I. II. 17 The Line in drawing after him chanc'd to kink, or grow entangled. **1787** BEST *Angling* (ed. 2) 48 Always have one, or more swivels on the line, which will prevent its kenking. **1867** F. FRANCIS *Angling* iv.

(1880) 107 The running line snarls, and kinks. **1891** H. L. WEBB in *Electr. in Daily Life, Making a Cable* 193 Occasionally a sounding was spoiled by the wire kinking.

2. *trans.* To cause to kink; to form a kink upon; to twist stiffly. Also *fig.* (Usually in passive.)

1800 JEFFERSON *Writ.* (1859) IV. 346 Arguments..such as none but a head, entangled and kinked as his is, would ever have urged. **1886** J. M. CAULFEILD *Seamanship Notes* 4 Cable is full of turns and kinked. **1897** *Allbutt's Syst. Med.* III. 651 The shortened bowel may be kinked or twisted.

Hence **kinked** (kɪŋkt) *ppl. a.* (also in extended use), **'kinking** *vbl. sb.*² and *ppl. a.*²; also **'kinkable** *a.*, liable to kink.

1794 *Rigging & Seamanship* 55 *Kinking*, the twisting or curling of a rope, by being twisted too hard. *c* **1865** J. WYLDE in *Circ. Sc.* I. 250/2 That there may be no loose or 'kinked' places. **1891** *Daily News* 24 June, Garden hose..non-kinkable hose is preferred. **1897** *Allbutt's Syst. Med.* III. 489 Pyloric kinking may occur with rapid aggravation of the state. **1966** *Punch* 5 Oct. 521/1 Others were delighted by the elegance of the language and the sinister kinked logic governing the behaviour of the characters. **1967** A. HUNTER *Gently Continental* viii. 127, I *am* scared. I can't protect Trudi. Frieda is kinked. **1969** D. C. HAGUE *Managerial Econ.* iv. 92 The kinked demand curve is derived from the.. curves we have already been using in our analysis of trade association pricing. **1970** D. UHNAK *Ledger* (1971) vii. 97 Stoner Martin massaged the back of his neck. 'This kind of work can sure leave you kinked up.'

‖**kinkajou** ('kɪŋkədʒuː). Also 8 kincajou. [a. F. *quincajou* (Denis 1672), from N. American Indian: cf. Algonquin *Kwingwaage*, Otchipwe *gwingwaage*, the wolverine. The same word orig. as CARCAJOU, which is still applied to the wolverine; but erroneously transferred by Buffon to the quadruped indicated below. (J. Platt, in *N. & Q.* 9th s. VII. 386, 18 May 1901.)] A carnivorous quadruped (*Cercoleptes caudivolvulus*) of Central and South America, allied to the racoon; it is about the size of the common cat, has a prehensile tail, and is nocturnal in its habits. Also called *potto* or *honey-bear*.

[**1672** N. DENIS *Descr. des côtes de l' Amerique* 330 Le kinkajou ressemble à un chat.] **1796** MORSE *Amer. Geog.* I. 198 Kincajou..makes havoc among the deer. **1863** BATES *Nat. Amazon* xii. (1864) 400 A curious animal, known to naturalists as the kinkajou,..has been considered by some authors as an intermediate form between the lemur family of apes, and the plantigrade carnivora or bear family. **1900** BARTLETT *Wild Beasts in the 'Zoo'* 41 The voice of the panda, kinkajou, otter and coati are wonderfully alike.

kinkcough ('kɪŋk,kɒf). *north. dial.* Also 7–9 **kincough**, 9 **king-cough**. [f. KINK *v.*¹ + COUGH *sb.*; cf. CHINCOUGH, and the earlier KINKHOST.

(By Turner and others erroneously referred to Ger. *kind* child, and misspelt accordingly; cf. Kilian's *kind-hoest*.)] The hooping-cough.

1568 TURNER *Herbal* III. 54 The cough that yonge childer have, called in right English The kindt cough: for kindt is a chyld in Duche. **1674–91** RAY *N.C. Words* s.v. *Kink*, The Kink-cough, called in other places the Chin-cough, by adding an Aspirate. **1741** A. MONRO *Anat. Nerves* (ed. 3) 54 The *Tussis convulsiva*, Kinkcough. **1773** W. BUTLER (*title*) Treatise on Kinkcough with appendix on Hemlock. **1825** BROCKETT, *Kin-cough, Kink-cough*, Ching-cough or King-cough, the hooping-cough. **1886** *S.W. Linc. Gloss.*, *Kincough*, or kink-cough, the whooping-cough.

kinker ('kɪŋkə(r)). [f. KINK *sb.*¹ + -ER¹.] An acrobat, a contortionist (see also quot. 1948).

1926 *Amer. Speech* I. 282/2 *Kinker*, a performer or acrobat. **1931** *Amer. Mercury* Nov. 353/1 *Kinkers*, circus performers. **1948** MENCKEN *Amer. Lang.* Suppl. II. 684 A contortionist is a *frog*, *bender* or *Limber Jim*, a freak or snake-charmer is a *geek*, and all performers are *kinkers*.

kinkhost ('kɪŋkhɒst). *Obs.* exc. *Sc.* [f. KINK *v.*¹ + HOAST, cough, corresp. to MLG. *kinkhôste*, LG. *kinkhôst*, Du. *kink-*, *kiek-*, *kikhoest*, G. *keichhusten*, Da. *kighoste*, Sw. *kikhosta*: all containing the Teut. stem *kik-*, Saxon *kink-*.] = KINKCOUGH.

c **1190** REGINALD *Vita Godrici* (Surtees) 373 Quod genus infirmitatis *Kinkehost* vocant Angli. *a* **1584** MONTGOMERIE *Flyting w. Polwart* 307 The kinkhost, the charbuckle, and the wormes in the cheiks. **1830** GALT *Lawrie T.* I. ii. (1849) 6 In teethings and kink host. **1858–61** RAMSAY *Remin.* v. (1870) 115 I've had..the kinkhost.

†**kinkin.** *Sc. Obs.* Also 6 kynkyn, 7 kinkine, 8 kinken. [a. MDu. *kintken*, *kinneken*, var. of *kindeken* KILDERKIN. See also KEMPKIN.] 'A small barrel, a keg, a kilderkin' (Jam.).

c **1500** in Cosmo Innes *Scot. in Mid. Ages* viii. (1860) 248 [The Abbot of Holyrood is charged for a] kynkyn [of olives]. **1594** *Compt Buik D. Wedderburne* (S.H.S.) 132 To by a kynkyn seap. *a* **1670** SPALDING *Troub. Chas. I* (1851) II. 469 He cumis down Die syd..plunderis about 20 barrellis or kinkenis of pulder. **1685** in *Scott. N. & Q.* (1900) Dec. 92/1 Half kinkin soap.

kinkina, obs. f. QUINQUINA, Peruvian bark.

[**kin-kind, ken-kind**, in Sc. phr. *a' kin-kind*, by erroneous analysis of *a'-kin kind*, ALKIN *kind*.

a **1774** FERGUSSON *Poems, Leith Races*, We drink o' a' kin-kind. **1819** W. TENNANT *Papistry Storm'd* (1827) 17 Wi' leifsam pictures a' kinkind. **1833** SANDS *Poems* 116 (E.D.D.) Cannon o' a ken kinds.]

kinkiness ('kɪŋkɪnɪs). [f. KINKY *a.* + -NESS.] The quality or habit of being kinky; a kinky state.

1924 W. DEEPING *Three Rooms* ii. 15 His black hair was wavy even to kinkiness. **1951** G. C. SHATTUCK *Dis. Tropics* lvii. 694 The hair loses its luster... The natural kinkiness disappears. **1959** C. MACINNES *Absolute Beginners* 22 'What kind of print might you be needing?' I went on, not sure yet what kinkiness I had to cater for. **1966** *Punch* 28 Sept. 483/1 Normally he [*sc.* a cat] prefers to bite men and scratch women, which seems to point to some kinkiness in his make-up. **1968** R. V. BESTE *Repeat Instructions* x. 104 What's wrong with her? Or is a certain kinkiness in spelling now evidence of a security risk? **1971** S. JEPSON *Let. to Dead Girl* iii. 23 If black vinyl thigh boots under a slit midi skirt.. wasn't kinky on purpose, he'd be glad someone else would tell him what it was... Trust Fatty to look for kinkiness. **1972** *Daily Tel.* 27 Apr. 9/2 His book..is too smuttily concerned with 'kinkiness' to justify its sub-title.

kinkle ('kɪŋk(ə)l), *sb.*¹ [f. KINK *sb.*¹ Cf. E.Fris. *kinkel* kink.]

1. A little or slight kink or twist; also *transf.*

1862 LOWELL *Biglow P.* Ser. II. ii. 7 To shake the kinkles out o' back an' legs. **1881** BLACKMORE *Christowell* xvi, He stroked the cow; but she..made no other movement than a kinkle in her tail.

2. A herring-bone or zigzag arrangement in which bricks are laid in a kiln, etc., the alternate courses being inclined at an angle of 45° in opposite directions: *attrib.*, as in *kinkle form*, *shape*, *course*.

1855 MORTON *Cycl. Agric.* II. 161/1 s.v. *Kiln*, The next is the stretcher and kinkle or skinkle course..in which the stretcher..lies over the solid arch, and the kinkle..over the hollow work. *Ibid.*, Roofing-tiles [are laid] in the kinkle shape. *Ibid.*, The large paving bricks are either laid up in the kinkle form, on their ends, or flat, like common bricks.

3. *fig.* A 'wrinkle', a hint. Cf. KINK *sb.*¹ 2 b.

a **1873** LYTTON *Parisians* II. viii, I am not without a kinkle that you will be enthused.

kinkled ('kɪŋk(ə)ld), *a.* [f. prec. sb. + -ED².] Having kinkles or kinks; of hair: Frizzed, crisped like the fibre of crape.

1890 *Cent. Dict.* s.v. *Glass*, *Kinkled glass*, the surface of which is raised in small rounded elevations produced by blowing the glass into a mold formed of a more or less fine netting of wire. **1899** *Chamb. Jrnl.* II. 692/2 They [Philippine islanders] had the kinkled hair of the race (not wool).

kinkless ('kɪŋklɪs), *a.* [f. KINK *sb.*¹ + -LESS.] Without a kink: applied in *Electronics* to a kind of tetrode designed so as to eliminate the irregularity of the current-voltage characteristic of an ordinary tetrode (which shows up as kinks in the characteristic curve).

1943 C. L. BOLTZ *Basic Radio* x. 164 The second method of suppressing the secondary emission is to align the control grid and screen very carefully so that the wires are opposite. .. Such a valve is a kinkless tetrode. **1953** F. LANGFORD-SMITH *Radio Designer's Handbk.* (ed. 4) I. i. 8 Some 'kinkless' tetrodes are also used as v-f and i-f amplifiers. **1958** W. F. LOVERING *Radio Communication* viii. 170 To avoid the kink in the E_a–I_a characteristic it is necessary to return the secondary electrons to the anode even when the screen is positive to anode... The first solution to this problem was the pentode... A later solution was the kinkless tetrode (or Beam tube).

kinky ('kɪŋkɪ), *a.* and *sb.* Also **kinkey**. [f. KINK *sb.*¹ + -Y.]

A. *adj.* **1.** Having, or full of, kinks; closely curled or twisted: said esp. of the hair of some races. Also *Comb.*, as *kinky-bearded*, *-haired*, *-headed*, *-tailed* adjs.

1844 *Congress. Globe* 6 Jan. App. 42/3 [The Negro's] skull is as thick, his hair is as kinkey, his nose as flat..as they were the day he was first introduced. **1848** W. T. THOMPSON *Major Jones's Sk. Trav.* 146, I happened to call one of the nigger waiters 'boy'. The kinky-headed cuss looked at me sideways, and rolled the whites of his eyes at me. **1861** in *Rebellion Rec.* (1862) I. III. 137 A marked distinction is laid Between the rights of the mistress, And those of the kinky-haired maid. **1865** *Publ. Opin.* 31 Dec. 726 Sambo the blubber-lipped..the kinky-haired. **1872** 'MARK TWAIN' *Innoc. Abr.* viii. 55 With heads clean-shaven, except a kinky scalp-lock back of the ear. **1885** *Century Mag.* XXIX. 644 The hair more kinky, yet altogether unlike the woolly headed negro of the Guinea coast. **1925** W. DEEPING *Sorrell & Son* xxix. 290 The hard-bitten, kinky-haired casualty-sister assisting him with critical and voiceless composure. **1937** *Time* 16 Aug. 58/2 Ill lay kinky-bearded, 64-year-old Thorvald Stauning, Premier of Denmark, after breaking a leg. **1956** C. AUERBACH *Genetics in Atomic Age* 93 When a female mouse is irradiated during the second week of pregnancy, some of her young may be born with kinky tails. Unlike true mutations to kinky tail, these deformities are not inherited. If, later on, visible mutants should turn up in the progeny of such a kinky-tailed mouse, they are not more likely to affect the tail than the eyes or the ears or the coat.

2. *fig.* (*colloq.*) 'Queer, eccentric, crotchety' (Bartlett *Dict. Amer.* 1860): cf. KINK *sb.*¹ 2.

1889 *Sportsman* 2 Jan. (Farmer), The kinky ones and the worthy ones who play hole-and-corner with society. **1907** E. M. FORSTER *Longest Journey* viii. 100 This jaundiced young philosopher, with his kinky view of life, was too much for him. **1929** W. J. LOCKE *Ancestor Jorico* xix. 263 A fellow ought to know something about the funny kinky ways of ordinary men and women. **1950** T. S. ELIOT *Cocktail Party* II. 120 But when everything's bad form, or mental kinks, You either become bad form, and cease to care, Or else, if you care, you must be kinky.

b. Lively, spry, energetic. *U.S. local.*

1903 G. S. WASSON *Cap'n Simeon's Store* vi. 107 'He ain't over and above kinky, though, I s'pose likely?' 'No,.. nothin' very antic about him...there must be some buckram left into him, too, the way he keeps a-going.' **1914** *Dialect Notes* IV. 4 *Kinky*, in high spirits. 'You seem to be feeling pretty kinky to-day.'

c. *Criminals' slang.* Of things: dishonestly come by (see also quot. 1954). Cf. CROOKED *a.* 3 b, BENT *ppl. a.* 5 a, b.

1927 *Collier's* 23 July 15/1 'Why, you can't tell me that you didn't know those five big cars were kinky.' 'Kinky?' ..'Those cars were bent.' **1931** G. IRWIN *Amer. Tramp & Underworld Slang* 117 *Kinky*, criminal; crooked; unlawful. Said of stolen goods, or of an individual known to be without the law. **1942** BERREY & VAN DEN BARK *Amer. Thes. Slang* §470/1 *Booty*,..killing, kinky goods, lift. **1954** W. R. & F. K. SIMPSON *Hockshop* 275 Canfield..was never accused..of having 'kinky' gambling paraphernalia. By that I mean dice and cards and roulette wheels that gave the house an unfair advantage.

d. In senses corresponding to KINK *sb.*¹ 3 c. Of persons: perverted, esp. sexually; *spec.* homosexual. Of things or situations: suggestive of sexual perversion, as of certain items or styles of dress (e.g. *kinky boots*); in weakened sense, bizarre.

1959 C. MACINNES *Absolute Beginners* 16 Suze..meets lots of kinky characters..and acts as agent for me getting orders from them for my pornographic photos. **1960** 'A. BURGESS' *Doctor is Sick* xviii. 145 'If you think I'm perverted you're completely mistaken. I'm quite normal.' 'Normal? You? That's a laugh. You're kinky, the same as what I am.' **1960** F. NORMAN *Fings ain't wot they used t' Be* II. i. 52 Fancy anyone being so kinkey about a brown teapot. **1963** *Daily Tel.* 11 Dec. 19/2 The phrase 'kinky advert'..meant that she acted as an advertisement for irregular sexual practices. **1964** *Ann. Reg. 1963* 1 It [*sc.* 1963] was the year..that women adopted the fashionable long 'kinky' boot. **1964** J. BURKE *Hard Day's Night* i. 11 She was dead kinky for sweetbreads. **1964** *Times Lit. Suppl.* 8 Oct. 925/1 Zoo men receive a constant stream of kinky letters. **1966** *Listener* 6 Jan. 23/1 One of the girls—a buxom specimen in kinky patent leathers. **1966** J. PORTER *Sour Cream* ix. 117 On the one hand I had to trust Zinaida, on the other I knew she was perfectly capable of fabricating the whole scheme just to get rid of Katia whom she loathed. It was like something out of Greek tragedy, only kinkier. **1967** A. DIMENT *Dolly Dolly Spy* ii. 19 He produced a pack of Black Russian cigarettes, dead kinky, and tossed me one. **1968** [see KINK *sb.*¹ 3 c]. **1971** *Daily Tel.* 16 July 11/4 In a moment of excessively kinky passion a husband strangles his mistress. **1972** F. WARNER *Lying Figures* III. 36 Kinky sex makes them feel inadequate.

B. *sb.* **a.** A person with 'kinky' hair. **b.** An object dishonestly obtained. **c.** A sexually abnormal or perverted person. **d.** *pl.* Kinky boots.

1926 J. F. DOBIE *Rainbow in Morning* 4 One considers the negro as a shining apostle of sweetness and light, another as a gentle old darkey, and still another as a 'phallic kinky'. **1926** G. THOMAS in *Ibid.* 154 The Fayette County and other South Texas 'kinkies' whose songs I have been noting. **1927** *Collier's* 23 July 14/1 *A kinky*, any stolen car. **1941** *Amer. Mercury* Mar. 349/2 The titles of every car Joe sold could be searched clear back to the factory... Yet the cars were strictly kinkies. **1942** BERREY & VAN DEN BARK *Amer. Thes. Slang* §430/2 *Curly-headed person*, curly, curly-locks, curly-pate, kinks, kinky. **1950** 'N. BELL' *I am Legion* vii. 216 O Good Lord... Quite half of them *are* kinkies. **1959** *Encounter* July 83/1 No prostitutes, no queers, no kinkies. **1965** *Punch* 19 May 755/1 Palm memory of the agreeable feel of the two-in-hand will come back, and if snakeboots replace kinkies, the thrill of the double slalom round the sprigs above the eyeletholes. **1967** A. DIMENT *Dolly Dolly Spy* vi. 82 Porny photos, various drugs and birds for kinkies at Oxford.

kinless ('kɪnlɪs), *a.* [f. KIN¹ + -LESS.] Having no relatives; without kin or kindred.

1720 T. BOSTON *Fourfold State* (1797) 219 The base things of this world, the kinless things (as the word [ἀγενῆ] imports. **1840** THORPE *Anc. Laws* I. 79 A man, kinless of paternal relatives. **1882** *Fraser's Mag.* XXVI. 500 Cromwell's kinless judges were the first pure judges in Scotland. **1882** OGILVIE *Imperial Dict.*, *Kinless loons*, a name given by the Scotch to the Judges sent by Cromwell, because they distributed justice solely according to the merits of the cases, being uninfluenced by family or party ties.

†**kinlin.** *Obs. rare.* In 5 kynlyn(e, -lym, kymlyn. [? f. *kynle*, KINDLE *v.*¹] = HEAD-BLOCK 1.

c **1440** *Promp. Parv.* 237/2 Herthe stok or kynlym (*K.*, *P.* stocke; *S.* kynlyn), *repofocilium*. *Ibid.* 275/1 Kynlyne, or herthestok (*K.* kynny, erthestock, *H.*, *P.* kymlyn).

†**kinnaut**, obs. variant of CANAUT.

1800 *Asiat. Ann. Reg.*, *Misc. Tr.* 59/1 The seat was surrounded by a kinnaut, or tent wall.

kinned, *dial.* chapped: see KIN *sb.*²

kinnen, obs. Sc. variant of *cunning*, CONY.

16.. *Johnie Armstrang* ii, Make Kinnen and Capon ready then, And Venison in great Plenty. **1783** *My Auld Man* in Whitelaw *Bk. Sc. Song* (1875) 571/1 Wheitbreid and wine, and a kinnen new slain.

‖**kinnikinnic, kinnikinnik** (,kɪnɪkɪ'nɪk). Also 8 killegenico, 9 kanickanick, kanikanik, killickinnick, kin(n)ikin(n)ick, -kineck, -kennic, kinnakinnec, and many other varr. [Algonquin; lit. 'mixture'.]

1. A mixture used by North American Indians as a substitute for tobacco, or for mixing with it; the commonest ingredients are dried sumach-leaves and the inner bark of dogwood or willow. Also *attrib.*

1799 J. Smith *Acc. Remark. Occurr.* (1870) 16 A pouch, which..contained tobacco, killegenico, or dry sumach leaves which they mix with their tobacco. **1805** J. Ordway in Lewis & Ordway *Jrnls. Western Explor.* (1916) 199 Some Indians had hung up..a Scraper a paint bag.., kinikaneck bags, flints, [etc.]. **1817** J. Bradbury *Trav. Amer.* 91 They did not make use of tobacco, but the bark of *Cornus sanguinea*, or red dog wood, mixed with the leaves of *Rhus glabra*, or smooth sumach. This mixture they call kinnikineck. **1827** T. L. McKenney *Sk. Tour to Lakes* 181 The pipe of an Indian..and a pouch made of the skin of some animal, in which he carries his *kinnikanic*, a kind of fragrant weed that has a leaf like our box wood. **1839** J. K. Townsend *Narr. Rocky Mts.* ii. 146 He smokes the article called *kanikanik*,—a mixture of tobacco and the dried leaves of the poke plant. **1839** C. A. Murray *Trav. N. Amer.* II. 22 We took out our kinnekinik-bag. **1844** —— *Prairie-bird* II. 179 Volumes of *kinnekenik* smoke. **1847** C. Lanman *Summer in Wilderness* xiv. 87 A bag of ka-nick-a-nick and tobacco was circulated and a cloud of fragrant smoke ascended to the sky. **1860** H. Y. Hind *Narr. Canad. Red River Expedition* I. 315 A sandy ridge..was covered with the bear-berry from which kinnikinnik is made. **1865** Visc. Milton & Cheadle *Northwest Passage* 275 What the Indians call kinnikinnick—the inner bark of the dogwood. **1867** 'Mark Twain' *Amer. Drolleries* (1875) 41 The most popular..smoking tobacco is..Killikinick. **1883** P. Robinson in *Harper's Mag.* Oct. 710/2 The 'kinnikinic' of travellers, a pale yellow pile of stuff resembling 'granulated' tobacco. **1889** K. Munroe *Golden Days* xxvi. 284 Put that in your pipe and smoke it, along with your killikinick. **1890** E. Custer *Following Guidon* viii. 101 Kinnikinnic..is a mixture of willow bark, sumach leaves, sage leaf, and tobacco, and is thoroughly mingled with marrow from buffalo bones. **1920** *Chambers's Jrnl.* 31 Jan. 136/1 The curling wisps of *kinickinick* smoke. **1969** *Islander* (Victoria, B.C.) 23 Nov. 13/2 Since their canoe had been swamped, the two pipe-smoking canoeists had been without tobacco. They used kinnikinik..which the Indians smoke.

2. Any of the various plants used for this, as the Silky Cornel, *Cornus sericea*, Red-osier Dogwood, *Cornus stolonifera*, and esp. Bearberry, *Arctostaphylos Uva-ursi* (also ***trailing k.***, ***k.-vine***). Also *attrib.*

1822 A. Eaton *Man. Bot.* (ed. 3) 178 *Arbutus uva-ursi*, bear berry kinnikinnick... Dry, barren sand plains. **1839** Marryat *Diary Amer.* Ser. I. I. 198 The Kinnakinnec, or weed which the Indians smoke as tobacco, grew plentifully about it. **1853** J. W. Bond *Minnesota & its Resources* 303 Some dry Kinne-kin-nick bark is generally carried along, cut very fine for the purpose of smoking. **1883** *Lit. World* (U.S.) 20 Feb. 55/2 The vine on the pretty cover design is the kinnikinnick, a Colorado creeper. **1886** *Ogoutz Mosaic* Jan. 7/2 A soft carpet of pine needles and trailing killickinnicks. **1910** *Anthropos* V. 420 Nor should we forget to mention the fruit of the *kinnikinik* or bearberry bush (*Arctostaphylos uva-ursi*), which, though insipid enough to a white man, is of such importance in the eyes of some tribes, as the Chilcotins, that it gives its name to one of their minor seasons. **1938** M. Thompson *High Trails of Glacier Nat. Park* 86 As we climb into the Hudsonian zone we find extensive carpets of kinnikinnick. **1956** V. Fisher *Pemmican* xxviii. 259 They went another day, and another, eating nothing but rose hips, leaves, kinnikinnik bark, moss, water cress. **1963** *Vancouver Sun* 23 Nov. 21/1 The rolling hills.. are park-like with their copses of fir, tamarack, poplar and willow, dotted through open stretches of bitterbrush and kinnikinnik.

kinning, variant of KENNING[2].

kino[1] ('kiːnəʊ). [app. of W. African origin: cf. Mandingo *cano* = Gambia kino, the first kind used, called by Fothergill in 1757 (*Med. Obs.* I.) *gummi rubrum astringens Gambiense*, in Edinb. Pharmacop. 1774 *Gummi Kino*, and in London Pharmacop. 1787 *Resina Kino*.]

1. A substance resembling catechu, usually of a brittle consistence and dark reddish-brown colour, consisting of the inspissated gum or juice of various trees and shrubs of tropical and sub-tropical regions; used in medicine and tanning as an astringent, and also (in India) for dyeing cotton. Sometimes called ***gum kino***.

African or **Gambia kino** (the kind first known in Europe, but now out of use) is the produce of *Pterocarpus erinaceus* (N.O. *Leguminosæ*); **Bengal k.**, of *Butea frondosa* and *B. superba* (N.O. *Leguminosæ*); **Botany Bay k.** or **Australian k.**, of *Eucalyptus resinifera* (N.O. *Myrtaceæ*) and other species; **East Indian k.**, **Malabar k.**, or **amboyna k.** (the kind most used), of *Pterocarpus Marsupium*; **West Indian k.** or **Jamaica k.**, of *Coccoloba uvifera* (N.O. *Polygonaceæ*).

[**1738** Stibbs *Voy. Gambia* 267, I shall now describe the Pau de Sangue, or Blood-wood, so called from a red gum which issues from it; it grows abundantly all up the river.. and by the Mandingoes called Cano.] **1788** *Lond. Pharmac.* (ed. 2) 21 Kino, *Kino, Gummi Gambiense*. **1811** A. T. Thomson *Lond. Disp.* (1818) 216 Botany Bay kino is inodorous; tastes bitterish and more austere than the African. **1830** Lindley *Nat. Syst. Bot.* 91 Gum Kino is the produce of *Pterocarpus erinacea*. **1852** Morfit *Tanning & Currying* (1853) 69 African Kino,..Asiatic Kino,.. American Kino, from a decoction of the fibrous wood of *Coccoloba uvifera*. The African, which is the most common kind, differs from the rest in coming in small, angular, glittering, black granules. **1879** *St. George's Hosp. Rep.* IX. 200 After five days' treatment by kino with opium and ipecacuanha.

b. *attrib.*

1881 Watts *Dict. Chem.* VIII. 1158 Kino-red yields by dry distillation a small quantity of watery and oily distillate. **1897** *Allbutt's Syst. Med.* II. 743 Compound kino powder in 10 grain doses is also very useful.

2. Any of the trees or plants which yield this substance: see above.

1876 Harley *Mat. Med.* (ed. 6) 644 Kino is a lofty tree.. native of Ceylon, and the adjacent part of India. **1887** Moloney *Forestry W. Afr.* 324 African or Gambia Kino.. Tree often 40 to 70 feet high, with a very hard, fine-grained red wood suitable for naval construction, planking, &c.

Hence **kinofluous** (kɪ'nɒfluːəs) *a.* [after *mellifluous*], 'exuding kino' (*Cent. Dict.*); **ki'noic** *a.*, of or pertaining to kino; **kinoin** ('kiːnəʊɪn), *Chem.*, a crystalline substance ($C_{14}H_{12}O_6$) obtained from East Indian kino; ***kino-tannic acid***, **kino-tannin**, the varieties of tannic acid and tannin occurring in kino.

1853 *Pharm. Jrnl.* XIII. 79 Hennig calls this substance kinoic acid. **1881** Watts *Dict. Chem.* VIII. 1158 By repeatedly crystallising..pure colourless crystals of kinoïn are obtained..Kinoïn is anhydrous; it dissolves sparingly in cold water, easily in hot water and in alcohol. **1888** *Syd. Soc. Lex.*, *Kinotannic acid*, a reddish-brown translucent substance forming some 95 per cent. of kino. **1852** Morfit *Tanning & Currying* (1853) 69 Kino-tannin forms a red mass, and yields no pyrogallic acid in dry distillation.

kino[2], variant of KENO *sb.* (and *int.*).

kino- ('kaɪnəʊ), comb. form of Gr. κινεῖν to set in motion, as in **kino'cilium** (pl. **-cilia**) *Biol.*, a cilium which is capable of moving (in contrast to an immobile cilium, called a stereocilium), *spec.* such a cilium borne singly on each hair cell of the maculæ of the inner ear amid a group of about a hundred stereocilia; **'kinoform** *Physics*, a transparent plate with a contoured surface so made as to introduce phase differences into an incident parallel beam in such a way as to form a single three-dimensional image of the particular object for which the calculation of the surface was made; **'kinoplasm** *Cytology* [ad. G. *kinoplasma* (E. Strasburger *Histol. Beiträge* (1892) IV. 60)], a supposed special kind of cytoplasm which was formerly held to be fibrillar in nature and to give rise to the active parts of a cell (such as the membrane and the mitotic apparatus); hence **kino'plasmic** *a.*

1933 M. Fernán-Núñez tr. *Ramón y Cajal's Histol.* x. 148 These cilia [of ciliated epithelium] are completely free and carry out spontaneous vibratory and whip-like movements, both of flexion and extension in the greater number of cases (kinocilia); in other cases, as in the epididymis, they appear immobile (stereocilia). **1956** *Acta Oto-Laryngol. Suppl.* No. 126. 46 The kinocilium in each cell is closely consistent in structure with the kinocilia that have been observed in the trachea, the fallopian tube, and in a number of unicellular organisms. **1971** *New Scientist* 29 July 283/1 The kinocilium, an apparently active hair among the passive hairs of each hair cell on the basilar membrane of the ear. **1968** P. M. Hirsch et al. *Digital Holograms & Kinoforms* in *IBM Technical Symposium on Laser Applic., Sept. 1968* (typescript) 244 Our efforts have been in making digital holograms and a new kind of imaging element, which we call a kinoform. **1969** L. B. Lesem et al. in *IBM Jrnl. Res. & Devel.* XIII. 150/1 The kinoform is a new, computer-generated wave-front reconstruction device which, like the hologram, provides the display of a three-dimensional image. In contrast, however, the illuminated kinoform yields a single diffraction order and, ideally, all the incident light is used to reconstruct this one image. *Ibid.* 151/2 Unlike the making of holograms, which can be physical recordings of actual wavefront interference patterns.., it does not appear possible to create a kinoform using completely optical techniques. **1970** *Physics Bull.* Nov. 493/1 Kinoforms, like digital holograms, are also made by calculating the wavefront scattered from the numerically defined object, but instead of adding in a reference beam, the amplitude of the scattered wavefront is assumed constant. A photographic plot of the phase distribution (mod 2π) is made, and translated into a phase plate. *Ibid.* 495/2 Kinoforms can be used as arbitrarily shaped phase plates in lens applications. **1894** *Jrnl. R. Microsc. Soc.* 581 Prof. E. Strasburger concludes that in the cytoplasm two constituents are contrasted in their activity. To one of these, the kinoplasm, the radiations round the centro-spheres, the spindle-fibres, and the combining filaments..owe their origin... The other constituent..is the trophoplasm. **1910** G. M. Calkins *Protozoöl.* i. 29 Some [observers]..have endeavored to show that archoplasm, or, in a larger sense, kinoplasm, is not only specific, but a kind of 'superior' protoplasm, self-perpetuating and distinct. **1934** L. W. Sharp *Introd. Cytol.* (ed. 3) ii. 45 It appears to be the kinoplasm that is responsible for protoplasmic streaming; it flows through the relatively stationary trophoplasm, carrying with it the plastids and chondriosomes. **1965** K. Esau *Plant Anat.* (ed. 2) iii. 57 The old concept of the existence of a special kind of active, fibrous cytoplasm, the kinoplasm. **1900** E. B. Wilson *Cell* (ed. 2) vi. 322 Beyond this the two forms of protoplasm show a difference of staining-reaction, the kinoplasmic fibrillæ staining deeply with gentian-violet and iron-hæmatoxylin, while the trophoplasm is but slightly stained. **1905** *Rep. Brit. Assoc. Adv. Sci.* 577 Strasburger considers them [*sc.* blepharoplasts] as kinoplasmic in nature, and thus brings them into relation with his other kinoplasmic structures, the centrosome and spindle. **1927** *Protoplasma* II. 201 The kinoplasmic spheres from which the contractile vacuoles arise in *Spirogyra*.

kinology (kaɪ'nɒlədʒɪ). [irreg. f. Gr. κινέειν to move + -(O)LOGY.] That branch of physics which treats of motion; kinematics.

1890 in *Cent. Dict.*

kinone, kinovic, kinoyl, kinquina, etc.: see QUIN-.

†**kinrick, -rik, -rich.** *Obs.* Forms: α. 1 cynerice, 2–3 kine-, 3 kyne-, kune-, kinne-, cunn-, 4 kinriche, kynryche. β. 3 kun(e)rike, 4–5 kynryk, 5–6 -rik, (5 -rike, 6 -rick), 4–6 kinrik, (4 -ric, -rike, 5–6 -ryk, -ryke, 7 -rick); 6 kenrik. [OE. *cynerice*, f. *cyne-*, KINE-[1] + *rice*, RICHE, RIKE, rule, realm: cf. KINGRICK.] = KINGDOM, in various senses.

α. *c* **892** *O.E. Chron.* (Parker MS.) an. 871 On þy cynerice be suþan Temese. *a* **1100** *Ibid.* (Laud MS.) an. 1076 Harold ..feng to þe kynerice. *c* **1175** *Lamb. Hom.* 77 Hit scal king bon on þet endelese kineriche. **1258** *Eng. Proclam. Hen. III*, Ouer al þære kuneriche on Engleneloande. **1393** Langl. *P. Pl.* C. I. 148 Crist kep þe, sire kyng and þy kynryche.

β. *a* **1300** *Cursor M.* 21822 (Edin.) þu mun me kaste of kinrik oute. *c* **1300** *Havelok* 2804 Aþelwold was king of þis kunerike. *c* **1325** *Metr. Hom.* 23 Kinric sal rohly rise Igain kinric. **1424** *Sc. Acts Jas. I* (1814) II. 7 Of his kynrik þe xix ȝer. **1535** Stewart *Cron. Scot.* II. 7 His croun agane and kinrik for to win. **1609** Skene *Reg. Maj.* 112 Disherished.. of all the lands in the Kinrick, that his father held.

-kins, *suffix.* Variant of -KIN, as in *babykins*, *boykins*, etc., and formerly in certain oathwords, as *bodikins*, *lakens* (see LAKIN[2]), *maskins*, *pit(t)ikins*.

kinsfolk, -folks ('kɪnzfəʊk, -fəʊks). Now *rare.* [f. KIN[1] + FOLK, after *kinsman.*] Persons of the same kin; relations by blood; relatives.

α. *c* **1450** *Paston Lett.* (K.O.), Kynsefolke. **1526** Tindale *Luke* ii. 44 They..sought hym amonge their kynsfolke and acquayntaunce. **1546** Heywood *Prov.* (1867) 37 Many kyns-folke and few freends, some folke saie. **1598** Grenewey *Tacitus, Germanie* i. (1622) 260 Their family and friends, and kinsfolcke. **1855** Kingsley *Heroes, Argon.* I. 76 That I may go home to my fathers and to my kinsfolk.

β. **1514** *E.E. Gilds* (1870) 144 Hys kynfalkes benefactours and alle crysten saules. *Ibid.* 145 There kynsfolkes, benefactours. **1555** Eden *Decades* 70 The prosperitie of owre contrey and kynsefolkes. **1652** C. B. Stapylton *Herodian* 161 Their Friends and kinsfolks them upbraid.

kinship ('kɪnʃɪp). [f. KIN[1] + -SHIP. A modern word: not in Johnson, Todd, Webster 1828.] The quality or state of being of kin.

1. a. Relationship by descent; consanguinity.

1833 Mrs. Browning *Prom. Bound* Poems 1850 I. 141 An awful thing Is kinship joined to friendship. **1868** Stanley *Westm. Abb.* iii. 172 In consideration of her kinship with no less than twelve sovereigns. **1880** Dixon *Windsor* III. xiii. 119 She was of kinship with the queen.

b. *Anthropology.* The recognized ties of relationship, by descent, marriage, or ritual, that form the basis of social organization. So *attrib.* and *Comb.*, as ***kinship category***, ***group***, ***structure***, ***term***; **kinship system**, the system of relationships traditionally accepted in a culture and the rights and obligations which they involve.

1866 J. F. M'Lennan in *Fortn. Rev.* 15 Apr. 580 Kinship through the mother had been in Homer's time undisputed among the Greeks. **1910** J. G. Frazer *Totemism & Exogamy* I. 20 The Psylli, a Snake clan in Africa, had a similar test of kinship. **1914** W. H. R. Rivers (*title*) Kinship and social organization. *Ibid.* 1 The aim of these lectures is to demonstrate the close connection which exists between methods of denoting relationship or kinship and forms of social organisation. **1937** R. H. Lowie *Hist. Ethnol. Theory* x. 171 In 1909 Kroeber, while fruitfully paving the way for work on the linguistic categories embodied in kinship systems, denied any social determinants. **1945** G. & M. Wilson *Analysis of Social Change* vi. 162 Any attempt to bolster up a legal system based on kinship is doomed to failure in an expanding society. **1949** E. E. Evans-Pritchard in M. Fortes *Social Struct.* 101 Nuer themselves ..see that it is undesirable to obliterate..the boundaries between kinship categories. **1949** F. Eggan in *Ibid.* 121 One of the most significant advances in the study of kinship systems in modern times has been Professor A. R. Radcliffe-Brown's method of structural or sociological analysis. **1951** R. Firth *Elem. Social Organiz.* i. 32 Other basic relations.. are due to position in a kinship system. **1955** M. Gluckman *Custom & Conflict in Afr.* iv. 99 Children are desired by a Zulu kinship-group because they strengthen it. **1957** V. W. Turner *Schism & Continuity in Afr. Soc.* iii. 77 In most primitive societies social control at the local level is associated with position in the kinship structure. **1958** A. R. Radcliffe-Brown *Method in Social Anthropol.* II. iv. 171 The kin of any given person were classified into a limited number of categories, each denoted by one kinship term. **1969** M. Fortes *Kinship & Social Order* (1970) p. vii, My thesis is that the structuralist theory and method of analysis in the study of kinship and social organization..stems directly from Morgan's work. **1970** E. Leach *Lévi-Strauss* vi. 99 Ties of filiation and..ties of siblingship..provide the basic bricks out of which kinship systems are built up. **1971** *World Archaeol.* III. 217 Ethnographic evidence therefore focuses on metalworking as a kinship or descent group-organized activity.

2. *fig.* Relationship in respect of qualities or character.

1873 M. Arnold *Lit. & Dogma* (1876) 239 We see how far it has any kinship with that doctrine of the Godhead of the Eternal Son. **1878** R. W. Dale *Lect. Preach.* iv. 90 Those mysterious instincts which vindicate our kinship to God. **1899** W. M. Ramsay in *Expositor* Jan. 42 Peter was..among the older apostles..the one with whom Paul felt most kinship in spirit.

†**kinsing**, *vbl. sb. Obs. rare*[−1]. [Origin and meaning obscure: see Nares, and quot. 1899.]

1598 Bp. Hall in *Marston's Sco. Villanie* III. x. (1599) 223, I ask't Phisitions what their counsell was For a mad dogge, or for a mankind Asse? They told me..The dogge was best cured by cutting and kinsing. [**1899** E. Gosse *Life of John Donne* I. 33 Marston..liked to be known by the nickname of Kinsayer, as one who 'kinsed' or docked the tails of wandering dogs and stray social abuses.]

kinsman ('kɪnzmən). Forms: 3-4 cunnes-, kun(n)es- (3-5 kenes-, 5 kennes-, -ys-), 3-5 kinnes(s-, 3-6 kynnes-, 4-5 kines-, 4-7 kinse-, 5-6 kyns(e-, 6- kinsman. [Early ME. f. *cunnes, kinnes*, gen. of KIN + MAN.] A man of one's own kin; a relative by blood (or, loosely, by marriage). (Now chiefly literary.)

[*c* **1052** *O.E. Chron.* (MS. C.) an. 1052 Hit wæs heom mæst eallon lað þat hiȝ sceoldon f[e]ohtan wið heora aȝenes cynnes mannum.] *c* **1200** *Vices & Virtues* 75 Ne ðine breðren..ne ðine kenesmen, ne ðine neihibures. *c* **1200** ORMIN 7613 Cristess kinness menn þær brohhtenn Crist to kirrke. *c* **1290** *S. Eng. Leg.* I. 456/3 His freond and is cunnes-men þe gretteste maystres were. *a* **1300** *Cursor M.* 6434 Ietro..was moyses kynnes-man [*Gött.* kinesman]. *c* **1400** tr. *Secreta Secret., Gov. Lordsh.* 106 My kennysmen and ancestres yn þe self lawe dwellyd. *c* **1477** CAXTON *Jason* 50 That my kinnesmen and frendes be assembled. **1555** EDEN *Decades* 2 No..kynseman for kynseman..coulde do more. **1613** PURCHAS *Pilgrimage* (1614) 273 Hali, Mahomets nearest kinsman and sonne in lawe. **1768** STERNE *Sent. Journ.* (1778) II. 31 (*Captive*) Nor had the voice of friend or kinsman breathed through his lattice. **1855** MACAULAY *Hist. Eng.* xv. III. 605 It was no pleasant task to accuse the Queen's kinsman in the Queen's presence. **1865** KINGSLEY *Herew.* i, He is your mother's kinsman.

fig. **1590** SHAKS. *Com. Err.* v. i. 80 Moodie and dull melancholly, Kinsman to grim and comfortlesse despaire. **1635** SWAN *Spec. M.* v. §2 (1643) 148 Dew..being a near kinsman to rain.

Hence '**kinsmanly** *a.*, appropriate to or characteristic of a kinsman.

1838 J. MARTIN *Rem. & Serm.* vii. 168 True kinsmanly affection to our brethren in Christ. **1885** *Spectator* 31 Jan. 154/2 The claims of New England upon the kinsmanly interest and affection of all travellers from the mother-country.

kinsmanship ('kɪnzmənʃɪp). [f. prec. + -SHIP.] The relation of kinsmen; kinship. Also *fig.*

1842 *Tait's Mag.* IX. 563 Little..did I surmise your kinsmanship with a man so disgraced. **1874** SAYCE *Compar. Philol.* v. 189 The surest 'differentia' of linguistic kinsmanship.

kinson, variant of KINGSTON.

'**kinspeople.** *U.S.* = KINSFOLK.

1866 HOWELLS *Venet. Life* xviii. 267 Kinspeople of herself or her husband. **1881** *Harper's Mag.* July 266/1 Pike was.. free-handed, especially to his kinspeople. **1891** J. WINSOR *Columbus* v. 86 Here his kinspeople ruled.

'**kinswoman.** Forms: see KINSMAN. [f. as *kinsman* + WOMAN.] A woman of one's own kin; a female relative. (Now only literary.)

c **1400** MAUNDEV. xxviii. (1839) 288 Hire othere kynnes-wommen [*Roxb.* sibbe wymmen]. *c* **1460** *Towneley Myst.* xi. 15 My dere kyns Woman. **1586** Q. ELIZ. in Ellis *Orig. Lett.* Ser. I. III. 23 Yow have not in the World a more lovinge kinswoman..then my self. **1699** BENTLEY *Phal.* 88 Autonoe, a Kinswoman of the Tyrant's. **1741-70** ELIZ. CARTER *Lett.* (1808) 353, I wish,..in the next edition Mr. Richardson would leave out the grievous old-fashioned word *kinswoman.* **1855** MACAULAY *Hist. Eng.* xviii. IV. 168 He tried to restore harmony between his kinswomen. **1868** FREEMAN *Norm. Conq.* II. vii. 54 The murdered prince had married a kinswoman of the Earl.

kintal, early form of QUINTAL, a weight of one hundred pounds.

kintecoy: see KANTIKOY.

kintlage, -ledge, -lidge, obs. ff. KENTLEDGE.

kintra, kintry, Sc. forms of COUNTRY.

† **kinyng**, var. *cuning*, obs. f. CONY, rabbit.

c **1450** *Inv.* in *Archæologia* XXI. 264 Item, j redde panne of kinyng skynnys.

kinzigite ('kɪntsɪgaɪt). *Petrogr.* [ad. G. *kinzigit* (H. Fischer 1860, in *Neues Jahrb. f. Min.* 797), f. the name of the *Kinzig* valley, W. Germany: see -ITE[1].] A metamorphic schistose rock containing garnet, biotite, and varying amounts of quartz, plagioclase, sillimanite, and cordierite. Hence **kinzi'gitic** *a.*, containing kinzigite.

1878 *Jrnl. Chem. Soc.* XXXIV. 208 Garnet-graphite-gneiss was hitherto unknown [in the Black Forest],..being formerly known by the name of Kinzigite. **1947** *Bull. Geol. Soc. Amer.* LVIII. 1024 The kinzigites of the Askainen-Lemu zone are fine- to medium-grained and contain garnet as well as cordierite. **1965** *Mineral. Abstr.* XVII. 227/2 A kinzigitic formation..occurs in the district of Miglierina (Catanzaro). This formation is composed of kinzigites, kinzigitic gneiss, and amphibolic kinzigites.

Kioko (kɪ'əʊkəʊ). Pl. Kioko, -os. [Native name.] The name of an African people inhabiting Zaïre and Angola, and their language; a member of this people. Also *attrib.* or as *adj.*

1884 *Encycl. Brit.* XVII. 319/1 *Equatorial Group*:..Wa-Lunda, Kioko, Wa-Shinsh, [etc.]. **1897** A. J. BUTLER tr. *Ratzel's Hist. Mankind* II. 376 It is otherwise with the Songos and Kiokos, who let you deal with them in the usual way. *Ibid.* 404 Here, Lunda will be spoken; there, perhaps only half a mile away, Kioko. **1908** H. H. JOHNSTON *George Grenfell & Congo* I. xi. 194 Round him [*sc.* a person of Hima descent] a community would group itself... Thus..the kingdoms..of the Luba, Lunda, Kioko, and other Bantu countries came into existence. **1948** M. GUTHRIE *Classification Bantu Lang.* Index 86/1 Kioko (A[ngola]). **1966** *Chambers's Encycl.* III. 50/1 Among the African Kioko, however, it is the availability of criminals for food that seems paramount.

kiore (kɪ'ɔːreɪ). *N.Z.* [Maori.] In full, ***kiore rat.*** A small vegetarian rat, *Rattus exulans*, native to New Zealand. Also *transf.*

1838 J. S. POLACK *New Zealand* I. ix. 314 The *kiore*, or rat, has been introduced at an early period by European vessels. **1840** —— *Manners & Customs New Zealanders* II. xiii. 125 A thin person [is termed] Kioré or rat. **1843** E. DIEFFENBACH *Trav. N.Z.* II. I. vii. 114 The fat of the native rats (Kiore) killed on such lands should be given to the principal proprietor. **1883** in A. R. Wallace *Australasia* (ed. 3) xxvi. 559 The native rat, called Kiore, has been destroyed by the imported European rat. **1949** P. BUCK *Coming of Maori* (1950) II. i. 102 The Polynesian rat (*kiore, Mus exulans*) arrived in the voyaging canoes... They were probably stowaways. **1959** TINDALE & LINDSAY *Rangatira* 203 The kiore rat, taken to New Zealand by the ancestors of the Maori..was a small vegetarian animal..now extinct.. except on a small island off the coast. **1966** *Encycl. N.Z.* III. 50/1 By the early 1920s it was believed that the kiore had become extinct. Today it is known to have survived in a few localities in widely separated areas.

‖**kiosk** ('kiːɒsk, kɪ'ɒsk). Also 7 (chouske), chiosque, 7-9 kiosque, 8 kioske, kiosc, chiosk, 9 keoschk. [= F. *kiosque* (It. *chiosco*), a. Turk. *kiūshk* pavilion, Pers. *kūshk* palace, portico.]

1. An open pavilion or summerhouse of light construction, often supported by pillars and surrounded with a balustrade; common in Turkey and Persia, and imitated in gardens and parks in Western Europe.

1625 PURCHAS *Pilgrims* II. ix. 1581 Some [Rooms] also vpon the Sea side, which are called *Kiosks*, that is Roomes of faire prospect, or (as we terme them) banquetting Houses. *Ibid.* 1626 Banquetting Houses, which they call *Chouskes.* **1682** WHELER *Journ. Greece* II. 204 A stately Chiosque, or Summer-house. **1717** LADY M. W. MONTAGU *Let. to Mrs. Thistlethwayte* 1 Apr., In the public gardens there are public *chiosks*, where people go..and drink their coffee, sherbet, etc. **1816** J. SCOTT *Vis. Paris* (ed. 5) 289 The great Cedar.. Before it lost its top..must have nearly equalled the brass kiosk in elevation. **1863** KINGLAKE *Crimea* (1876) I. i. 20 The summer kiosks, and the steep shady gardens looking down on the straits between Europe and Asia.

2. A light ornamental structure resembling this, used for the sale of newspapers (orig. in France and Belgium), for a band-stand, or for other purposes.

1865 *Daily Tel.* 5 Dec. 3/4 A 'kiosk'—*i.e.*, a place for the sale of newspapers. **1868** *Morn. Star* 26 Feb., The kiosques in which the two military bands were stationed, were illuminated by lampions and electric light. **1870** W. CHAMBERS *Winter Mentone* i. 13 At kiosks on the Quai.. several Paris daily newspapers may be purchased. **1933** P. MACDONALD *Mystery of Dead Police* xvii. 186 His quarry was at the change kiosk. **1963** V. NABOKOV *Gift* iii. 156 There was..a triangular island with a kiosk, at which tram conductors regaled themselves with milk. **1964** G. JOHNSTON *My Brother Jack* 36 Somehow we were able to get to the big kiosk-restaurant behind the point. *Ibid.* 37 The kiosk had been very late Victorian, with imitation turrets and spires. **1966** *South Australian Yearbk.* No. 1, 169 There are refreshment kiosk facilities. **1966** *Listener* 18 Aug. 227/2 Breaking into a tobacco kiosk. **1971** *E. Afr. Standard* (Nairobi) 10 Apr. 7/8 Most of the food sold in the kiosks is approved by medical officers.

3. = *telephone kiosk.*

1928 *Daily Mail* 25 July 19/4 It is expected that nearly 500,000 new lines will be laid, several thousand new kiosks erected, and several hundred telephones fixed at rural railway stations. **1972** 'H. BUCKMASTER' *Walking Trip* 197 'I'd better call Norman..he has a right to know.' 'Here's a kiosk. Have you enough change?' **1974** M. BABSON *Stalking Lamb* xxiv. 179 He broke off the connection, swung open the door and stepped out of the kiosk.

kiotome ('kaɪəʊtəʊm). *Surg.* Also ciotome. [irreg. for *kionotome, f. Gr. κίων pillar + τομός cutting. (Cf. CIONOTOME.)] An instrument invented by Desault for dividing pseudo-membranous bands in the rectum or bladder; also used for removing the tonsils.

1842 DUNGLISON *Med. Lex.* (ed. 3). **1855** MAYNE *Expos. Lex., Kiotome*, see *Ciotome.* **1888** *Syd. Soc. Lex., Kiotome.*

Kiowa ('kaɪəwə, 'kaɪəwɔː), *sb.* and *a.* Also Kiawa, Kyaway, etc. [Native name.] **A.** *sb.* **a.** An Indian people of the south-western U.S.; a member of this people. **b.** The language of this people.

1810 Z. M. PIKE *Acct. Expeditions Sources Mississippi* App. II. 16 The only nations with whom the Pawnees are now at war, are the Tetaus, Utahs, and Kyaways. **1849** G. A. F. RUXTON *Life in Far West* vii, The Kioway loves the pale-face, and gives him warning. **1856** W. W. WHIPPLE in *Rep. Explor. Route to Pacific* (U.S. War Dept.) III. v. 80 Some resemblances are likewise to be observed between the Kioway and the languages of the southern and western tribes of the Sioux or Dakota stock. **1874** [see COMANCHE *sb.* 2]. **1928** *U.S. Bureau Amer. Ethnol. Bull.* No. 84. 2 Six vowel qualities and twenty-two consonants are found in Kiowa. **1959** E. TUNIS *Indians* 106/1 The fingers of one hand, held up and moved in a shaking circle, was the Kiowa —rattlebrained. **1965** *Canad. Jrnl. Linguistics* Spring 78 Kiowa (Powell's 'Kiowan'), a language of the western Plains, seems now to have been reasonably well established as a part of the Aztecan-Tanoan phylum. **1969** *Observer* (Colour Suppl.) 18 May 25/4 When the son of a wealthy Kiowa achieved an exploit, everyone heard about it.

B. *adj.* Of or pertaining to any of the above; ***Kiowa Apache***, an Athapascan people associated with the Kiowa; a member of this people; also, their language.

1821 J. FOWLER *Jrnl.* (1898) 64 The Kiowa cheef with his nation had stoped and intended we shold stop with them. **1865** J. PIKE *Scout & Ranger* iv. 64 Houston's design was to carry the war into the Comanche and Kiowa country. **1885** W. P. CLARK *Indian Sign Lang.* 33 This gesture refers to the Apaches living with the Kiowas at the Wichita Agency, Indian Territory..frequently called Kiowa Apaches. **1928** *U.S. Bureau Amer. Ethnol. Bull.* No. 84. 2 (*heading*) Vocabulary of the Kiowa language. **1937** J. G. MCALLISTER in F. Eggan *Social Anthropol. N. Amer. Tribes* iii. 100 Communication was carried on by means of the sign language, and most of the old Kiowa-Apache knew a little Kiowa, though very few of the Kiowa had any knowledge of the Kiowa Apache tongue. **1963** *Univ. Calif. Publ. Linguistics* XXIX. 102 Western Apache..is one of the Apachean languages. Others are Chiricahua, Mescalero, Jicarilla, Kiowa Apache, Navaho, and Lipan. **1969** *Observer* (Colour Suppl.) 18 May 25/4 A Kiowa warrior was forced by custom to give away some of his wealth.

kip (kɪp), *sb.*[1] Also 6 kyppe, keippe, kepe, 7 kipp(e. [Of uncertain origin. Sense 2 corresponds to MDu. *kip, kijp*, pack or bundle, esp. of hides (see Verwijs and Verdam); but there is no direct evidence that sense 1 was developed from 2.

Hardly to be connected with Flem. *kippe* new-born or young calf, G. *kippe* ewe.]

1. The hide of a young or small beast (as a calf or lamb, or cattle of small breed), as used for leather.

1530 PALSGR. 236/1 Kyppe of lambe a furre [no Fr.]. **1617** *Nottingham Rec.* IV. 353 A kipp to make a cover for the charter. **1776** *Excise-book* in *Dorset County Chron.* (1881) 2 June, [Kinds of hides] sheep and lamb, butts and backs, calves and kips. **1852** MORFIT *Tanning & Currying* (1853) 146 Kips, consisting of the younger growth of the above animals [oxen, horses, cows, bulls, and buffaloes]. **1875** *Ure's Dict. Arts* III. 24 The tanners call the skins of young animals kips. The skins of full-grown cattle of small breed are also so called. *a* **1882** KENDALL *Poems* (1886) 192 A hero in moleskin and kip.

2. A set or bundle of such hides, containing a definite number: see quots.

c **1525** *Northumbld. Househ. Bk.* (1827) 355, ij Keippe and a half [of lamb skin] after xxx Skynnes in a Kepe. **1612** A. HOPTON *Concord. Yeares* 164 The skins of Goats are numbered by the Kippe, which is 50. **1674** JEAKE *Arith.* (1696) 67 Skins of Goats. In 1 Kippe, 50 Skins. *c* **1890** *Correspondent*, A kip of chamois skins is now 30.

3. *attrib.*, as ***kip leather*** (used chiefly for the uppers of shoes), ***kip-skin.***

1828 *Craven Dial.*, *Kip-leather*, the tanned hide of a stirk. **1833** *Act 3 & 4 Will. IV*, c. 56 Calf Skins and Kip Skins, in the Hair, not tanned. **1844** *Port Phillip Patriot* 25 July 3/6 Half ton Hobart Town kip leather. **1891** *Auckland* (*N.Z.*) *Star* 1 Oct. 1/4 A hundred gross of Kip Leather Laces.

kip, *sb.*[2] *Sc.* Also kipp. [Cf. Germ. (prop. LG.) *kippe* point, peak, tip.]

1. 'A term denoting anything that is beaked' (Jam.), e.g. the tip of the lower jaw of a male salmon at the time of spawning (cf. KIPPER *sb.*[1] and *a.* etym. note).

2. A sharp-pointed hill; also, a jutting point, on the side of a hill, etc. (Jam.)

1815 ARMSTRONG in Pennecuik *Descr. Tweeddale* 228 (Jam.) The kipps, above this, are remarkably steep and pointed hills.

attrib. **1868** J. HARDY in *Proc. Berwick. Nat. Field Club* 376 Kip rocks are numerous in Scotland, the name being applied to jutting eminences or upright points of rocks.

3. *Gymnastics.* (See quot. 1972[1].) *U.S.*

1909 in WEBSTER. **1967** [see KIP *v.*[3]]. **1972** W. VINCENT *Gymnastic Routines for Men* 123 A kip is a vigorous and rapid extension of the hip joint for the purpose of developing momentum to raise the center of gravity of the body. It may be performed on all the events in gymnastics in one form or another. *Ibid.*, Kips may be performed forward (clockwise) or backward (counter-clockwise) with either the legs or the upper body as the moving part and the other as the stabilizing part. **1972** B. TAYLOR et al. *Olympic Gymnastics for Men & Women* v. 108/2 The movement begins with the gymnast jumping to a glide swing on the low bar and continuing into a glide kip position.

kip, *sb.*[3] *slang.* [Cf. Da. *kippe* mean hut, low alehouse; *horekippe* brothel.]

1. A house of ill-fame, a brothel. Also *Comb.*

1766 GOLDSM. *Vic. W.* xx, My business was to attend him at auctions..to take the left hand in his chariot when not filled by another, and to assist at tattering a kip, as the phrase was, when we had a mind for a frolic. [S. BALDWIN *Note* Tattering a kip: we have never heard this expression in England, but are told that it is frequent among the young men in Ireland. It signifies, beating up the quarters of women of ill fame.] **1922** JOYCE *Ulysses* 541, I saw him, kipkeeper! Pox and gleet vendor! **1965** BROPHY & PARTRIDGE *Long Trail* 140 *Kip-shop*, a brothel.

2. A common lodging-house; also a lodging or bed in such a house; hence, a bed in general; a sleep, the action of sleeping. Also (*rare*) **kipp**, and *Comb.* as ***kip-house, -shop.***

1879 *Macm. Mag.* XL. 501/1 So I went home, turned into kip (bed). **1883** *Pall Mall G.* 27 Sept. 4/1 The next alternative is the common lodging-house, or 'kip', which, for the moderate sum of fourpence, supplies the applicant with a bed. **1889** BARRÈRE & LELAND *Dict. Slang* I. 521/2 *Kip house*, a tramps' or vagrants' lodging-house. **1892** M. WILLIAMS *Round London* (1893) 38 The sort of life that was led in 'kips', or 'doss-houses'. **1893** *Sessions Papers Cent. Criminal Court* 16 Nov. 39 He said, 'I only came here for a *kip*.'.. *Kip* means sleep, I believe. **1908** J. M. SULLIVAN *Criminal Slang* 14 *Kipp*, a lodging house. **1925** FRASER & GIBBONS *Soldier & Sailor Words* 136 *Kip*: A sleep. Rest. A

bed. A hammock, *e.g.*, 'To do a kip—to have a sleep.' **1932** *Fortn. Rev.* Mar. 325 The jake drinker's.. earning capacity is nil, and if he has no lair of his own there is the 'doss house' or 'kip shop'. **1936** J. Curtis *Gilt Kid* i. 12 He had spent a few nights in kip-shops. **1938** —— *They drive by Night* ix. 103, I got to have a rest. I ain't had no kip. **1943** M. Harrison *Reported Safe Arrival* 18 Like the Professor, Harry was 'partial to a kip'. **1946** *Penguin New Writing* XXVIII. 123 Conditions under which the transport drivers work, of their cafés and kip-houses. **1962** *Observer* 11 Mar. 34/3 (*caption*) Dossers at a London kip-house. **1971** B. W. Aldiss *Soldier Erect* 78, I had to stay with the captain.. while the other lucky sods settled down for a brief kip.

kip, *sb.*[4] *Coal-mining.*

1883 Gresley *Gloss. Coal Mining Terms, Kip* (N.), a level or gently sloping roadway going *outbye* at the extremity of an engine plane, upon which the full tubs stand ready for being sent up the shaft.

kip, *sb.*[5] Also kipp. A local name for a tern.

1802–3 in Col. Hawker *Diary* (1893) II. 358 Kipps.. 5. [*Note*, A kipp is a genus of tern peculiar to the vicinity of Romney.] **1885** Swainson *Prov. Names Birds*, Common Tern.. also called.. Kip.

kip (kɪp), *sb.*[6] *Austral.* and *N.Z.* [Origin unknown.] A small piece of wood from which pennies are spun in the game of two-up.

1898 *Bulletin* (Sydney) 17 Dec. Red Page/2 The *kip* is the piece of wood used in 'two-up', otherwise pitch and toss. **1933** *Ibid.* 5 July 20/1, I see the pennies in the air, The outstretched hand that holds the kip. **1945** [see bat *sb.*[2] 3 e]. **1948** V. Palmer *Golconda* xxx. 250 He [was] .. becoming more convinced every day that his whole future lay in winning the [Parliamentary] seat. At first the idea had been hardly more than a toss of the kip to him; now it was woven into his daily fantasies. **1964** A. Wykes *Gambling* iii. 62 In this game [*sc.* two-up], two pennies are placed on a flat stick (called the 'kip') and are thrown into the air by the 'spinner'.

kip (kɪp), *sb.*[7] *Engin.* orig. *U.S.* [Prob. f. ki(lo- + p(ound *sb.*[1]] A unit of force equal to the weight of 1,000 lb., used in expressing loads.

1915 H. R. Thayer *Struct. Design* II. vi. 87 Shear in kips. [*Note*] 1 Kip = 1000 lbs. *Ibid.* 250 Maximum shear 110 kips. **1949** S. Butterworth *Struct. Analysis* ii. 30 The actual sway force is 3 kips. **1959** L. C. Urquhart *Civil Engin. Handbk.* (ed. 4) v. 45 The panel load on the upper lateral system is 25 × 150 = 3,750 lb = 3·75 kips. **1962** *Engineering* 8 June 746/3 Each of these pavement designs could be expected to carry a million applications of the 18 kip axle load.. before serviceability dropped to 2·5.

kip (kɪp), *sb.*[8] [Thai.] The basic monetary unit of Laos.

1955 *Britannica Bk. Year* 265/1 The Laotian unit of currency had its name changed from *piastre* to *kip*, without any effect on its purchasing power. **1959** *Economist* 24 Jan. 305/2 The *kip* has been devalued. **1965** *Ibid.* 20 Nov. p. xxxvi/1 An indelible public impression of foreign exchange dealers.. inhabiting a rarefied world of eight-ball arbitrage and private jokes about the baht, the kip and the won.

†**kip,** *v.*[1] *Obs.* Forms: 3–4 **kippe**, 4 **kip, kyp**, 4–5 **kyppe**; *pa. t.* 3 **kypte**, 3–4 **kipte, kipt**, 4 **kyppid**. [ME. *kippen*: cf. ON. *kippa* to snatch, tug, pull; also MDu. *kippen* to catch, grip, G. dial. (Swiss) *kippen* to steal, 'prig'.] *trans.* To take hold of, take in the hand, seize, snatch, catch.

c **1250** *Gen. & Ex.* 3164 Ðo was non biging of al egipte lich-les, so maniȝe dead ðor kipte. **1297** R. Glouc. (Rolls) 2667 'Nimeþ ȝoure sexes', & is men þer wiþ Echon Kipte hor longe kniues. *c* **1300** *Havelok* 1050 He.. kipte up þat heui ston. **13..** *E.E. Allit. P.* B. 1510 Kyppe kowpes in honde kyngez to serue. *c* **1400** *Sege Jerus.* (E.E.T.S.) 27/478 Cayphas of þe kyst kyppid a rolle & radde. *c* **1440** *Promp. Parv.* 276/1 Kyppyn, *idem quod* hynton.

b. ? *absol.* or *intr.*

c **1460** *Towneley Myst.* xii. 253 Be God, he bot syppys, begylde thou art; Behold how he kyppys. *Ibid.* xiii. 557 Any lord myght hym haue This chyld to his son. When he wakyns he kyppys, that ioy is to se.

¶ In many passages, *kip, kipte*, appear to be = *kepe, kepte*, from keep *v.*

c **1300** *Beket* 1841 That was signe of his baner, for other ne kipte he non [*S. Eng. Leg.* I. 158/1805 kepte]. *c* **1305** *St. Dunstan* 64 in *E.E.P.* (1862) 36 He ne kipte of hem non hure. *c* **1311** *Pol. Songs* (Camden) 152 Thus y kippe ant cacche careful colde. *c* **1330** R. Brunne *Chron.* (1810) 182 Togidir I rede we kip. *c* **1340** *Cursor M.* 3079 (Trin.) Whenne [Ismael] hadde good elde kipte he spoused a wif.

Hence **'kipping** *vbl. sb.*; also *attrib.*, as in **kipping-line**, ? some kind of fishing line; cf. kip-.

c **1440** *Promp. Parv.* 276/1 Kyppynge, or hyntynge (*K., P.* hentynge), *raptus.* *c* **1689** *Depred. Clan Campbell* (1816) 104 Ane long fishing lyne.. and three kipping lynes.

kip (kɪp), *v.*[2] *slang.* [f. kip *sb.*[3]] *intr.* To go to bed, sleep. Also, to lie *down*. So **'kipping** *vbl. sb.*; also *attrib.*, as **kipping-house**, a lodging-house.

1889 Barrère & Leland *Dict. Slang* I. 522/1 *Kip, to* (popular and thieves), to sleep or lodge. **1899** C. Rook *Hooligan Nights* i. 10 Next door.. that's where me and my muvver kipped when I was a nipper. **1919** *Athenæum* 1 Aug. 695/2 'To kip' is to go to bed—or what serves for a bed. **1925** E. Jervis *25 Yrs. in Six Prisons* xix. 243, I used to conduct services in the 'kippin'-'aases', or common lodging-houses. **1929** J. B. Priestley *Good Companions* I. iv. 116 Yes, we'll have to kip down for an hour or two, Annie. **1938** J. Curtis *They drive by Night* iv. 46 I'm kipping here tonight and all. **1939** *Airman's Gaz.* Dec., This will be very useful if you forced-land and have to kip out in a field. **1961** *New Statesman* 26 May 830/3 Nancy.. set her persuasive charms to work to get Billy, Bob and Nick a free sky-sheltered bench to kip on. **1973** *Weekly News* (Glasgow) 11 Aug. 14/4 A driver whose van broke down near Bristol, decided to kip down in the driver's seat.

kip (kɪp), *v.*[3] *Gymnastics. U.S.* [f. kip *sb.*[2] 3.] *intr.* To perform a kip.

1909 in Webster. **1967** Loken & Willoughby *Compl. Bk. Gymnastics* (ed. 2) ii. 12 Go to the bridge from the kip position on back of the shoulders using the kipping action.

†**kip-**, the stem of kip *v.*[1] in comb., as **kip-hook, kip-net**, some kind of hook and net used in fishing; **kip-string**, some part of the harness of a draught horse; **kip-tree**, a wooden lever used in drawing water from a well.

1615 E. S. *Britain's Buss* in Arb. *Garner* III. 642 Each man fishing for Cod and Ling useth at once two *Kip-hooks. **1622** Whitbourne in Capt. Smith *Virginia* vi. 245, 10 *Kip-net Irons, 10*s.* Twine to make kipnets and gagging hooks, 6*s.* *c* **1330** *Durham Acc. Rolls* (Surtees) 518 In 40 capistris.. cum 2 *Kypstringges. **1364–5** *Ibid.* 568 In Kypstringes pro carectis. **1453–4** *Ibid.* 147 Pro.. j kipstryng et iij capistris. *c* **1440** *Promp. Parv.* 276/1 *Kyptre of a welle, *telo.*

Kipchak (kɪp'tʃɑːk). Also **Qipchak**. [Russ., ad. Jagatai.] **A.** *sb.* **a.** A member of a Mongolian people of central Asia. **b.** The language of this people, a Turkic dialect. **B.** *adj.* Of or pertaining to this people, or their language.

1865 J. & R. Michell tr. *Valikhanof's Russians Cent. Asia* iii. 62 The towns of Almalyk.. were chief stations on the high road traversed by the Genoese traders.. as well as by the Kipchak ambassadors on their.. missions to the great Khan. **1879** *Encycl. Brit.* IX. 85/2 The nomads are mainly Kipchaks and Kara Kirghiz or Buruts. **1898** A. J. Butler tr. *Ratzel's Hist. Mankind* III. 319 The Kiptchaks, whose fame for extraordinary valour is known throughout Central Asia. *Ibid.* 348 The Kiptchaks are only a clan of the Kara-Kirghis. **1953** O. Caroe *Soviet Empire* I. iii. 37 The migrations of the Oghuz may have been prompted by Kipchak pressure. *Ibid.* 38 The Kipchak language was of the Turkic family. **1959** *Chambers's Encycl.* VI. 426/2 *Golden Horde*, or West Kipchak Horde, the name given to the western division of the great Mogul empire.. after.. 1241... The neighbouring East Kipchak Horde was known as 'White'. **1970** D. M. Lang *Armenia* xi. 273 Other Armenian communities of the diaspora adopted the Mkhitar Code as their own, so that it was translated into Latin, Polish, Georgian, Russian and even Qipchak. **1972** G. Clauson *Etym. Dict. pre-13th-Cent. Turkish* p. xix, In XI the Kipçak were west of the Oğuz in southern Russia.

kipe (kaɪp), *sb.* Now *dial.* Forms: 1 **cype**, 3–4 (?) **cupe(ü)**, 4 **kype**, 6 **kepe**, 8–9 **kipe**. [OE. *cýpe* wk. f., app. = LG. *küpe* (*keupe*) basket carried in the hand or on the back. LG. has also *kîpe, kiepe* (recorded from 15th c., also spelt *kype, kypp*); whence mod.G. *kiepe*, Du. *kiepe*(*korf*). The relationship of the forms is obscure, as is that between LG. *küpe* basket and *kûpe* tub, cask, and that of OE. *cýpe* to ME. *cūpe*: see coop *sb.*[1]]

A basket; †*spec.* an osier basket used for catching fish (*obs.*); a basket used as a measure (*dial.*).

c **1000** *Ags. Gosp.* Luke ix. 17 Man nam þa ȝebrotu þe þar belifon, twelf cypan fulle. *a* **1100** in Napier *O.E. Glosses* xviii. 3 *Corbes*, cypan. *c* **1320** *Cast. Love* 1278 Twelf cupeful weoren vp i-bore. **1387** Trevisa *Higden* (Rolls) IV. 359 He was i-lete a doun in a cupe [*v.r.* kype] over þe wal. **1398** —— *Barth. De P.R.* xvii cxlii[i]. (MS. Bodl.) lf. 227 b/2 Wylowe .. þerof beþ made diuers nedefulle þinges to house-hold as stoles sotels panyers and kuypes. **1558** *Act 1 Eliz.* c. 17 §3 No.. Person.. shall fish.. with any manner of Net, Tramel, Kepe, Wore [etc.]. **1706** Phillips (ed. Kersey), *Kipe*, a Basket made of Osiers, broader at Bottom, and narrow'd by Degrees to the Top, but left open at both Ends; which is used for taking of Fish, particularly at Otmore in Oxfordshire, where this manner of Fishing is called Kiping, and going to Kipe. **1879** Miss Jackson *Shropsh. Word-bk.*, *Kipe*, a strong osier basket with a twisted handle on each side, of circular form, but wider at the top than the bottom. *Ibid.* Intr. 85 A kype is often used as a measure for potatoes, apples, etc. When filled level with the top it equals a half-strike heaped.

Hence **kipe** *v. intr.*, to catch fish with a kipe. **'kiping** *vbl. sb.*

1706 [see above].

Kiplingese (kɪplɪ'ŋiːz). [-ese.] The literary style and characteristics of the writer Rudyard Kipling (1865–1936). Also **Kipling'esque** *a.* [see -esque], resembling Kipling in style; so **Kipling'esquely** *adv.*; **'Kiplingish** *a.*, typical of Kipling or his works; **'Kiplingite** [see -ite[1] 1 b], an admirer of Kipling; as *adj.*, characteristic of Kipling; **'Kiplingize** *v.* [see -ize] *trans.*, to make Kipling-like.

1894 *'Sunlight' Year Bk. 1895* 77 A glance at the adaptation is enough to reveal its Kiplingesque roll and emphasis. **1898** *Windsor Mag.* Dec. 131/1 True Kiplingites. **1899** 'G. F. Monkshood' *Kipling* 188 Perhaps the most distinctly Kiplingite piece of prose in the whole book. **1899** *Westm. Gaz.* 28 June 3/1 Thorpe.. is, merely, the primitive Kiplingesque type of man transferred from the battle-field or the plains of India to the Stock Exchange. **1899** *Daily News* 1 Dec. 8/2 The account of the making of the first axe .. is told quite in the heroic style of Kingsley and Morris, flavoured here and there with more than a dash of 'Kiplingese'. **1903** *Times Lit. Suppl.* 2 Oct. 277/3 The whole poem.. has another claim upon the attention of the reader as an example of Kiplingized Longfellow. **1905** Chesterton *Heretics* iii. 45 The modern army is not a miracle of courage; it has not enough opportunities, owing to the cowardice of everybody else. But it is really a miracle of organization, and that is the truly Kiplingite ideal. *Ibid.* xx. 292 No man has any business to be a Kiplingite without being a politician, and an Imperialist politician. **1909** H. G. Wells *Tono-Bungay* iv. iii. 492 They served me up to the public in turgid degenerate Kiplingese. **1921** G. B. Shaw *Back To Methuselah* iv. i. 170 You have actually Kiplingized me... He is said to have invented the electric hedge. I consider that in using it on me you have taken a very great liberty. **1928** *Weekly Dispatch* 24 June 15/3 The road to home these days lies across the 49th degree of latitude between Bishops Rock and Nantucket. It is a sad, un-Kiplingish thought. **1931** *Times Lit. Suppl.* 17 Sept. 692/3 It contains also quite a number of amusing and quite Kiplingesque 'Just So' stories. **1966** *Punch* 8 June 826/1 Nor am I sure that the anonymous genius who originally picked 'East of Suez' to describe the sphere of our Asian involvement chose wisely. It's so emotively Kiplingesque, so redolent of imperial splendours and miseries. **1969** *Guardian* 27 Nov. 14/6 No one ran Kiplingesquely amuck; no shot was fired in anger. **1972** J. Wainwright *Night is Time to Die* 53 *The Green Eye of the Yellow God*... It's Kiplingish... But it was written by J. Milton Hayes. **1973** *Daily Tel.* 24 Nov. 16 Kiplingites will be interested to learn that Kipling Terrace, a Victorian development at Westward Ho!, North Devon, is to be auctioned next month.

Kiplingism ('kɪplɪŋɪz(ə)m). [-ism.]

†**1.** *Cambridge Univ. slang.* A sarcastic term for the errors and solecisms alleged to occur in the edition of the 'Codex Bezæ' (1793) by Thomas Kipling (d. 1822), afterwards Dean of Peterborough.

1803 *Gradus ad Cantabrigiam* 81 A *Kiplingism*; a blunder-*bus* levelled at poor Priscian's head by the *learned* Dr. Kipling. The opposition wits at Cambridge have composed an epigram of *Kiplingisms.* **1899** 'G. F. Monkshood' *Kipling* 15 A 'Kiplingism' was long an expression for a Latin blunder. **1950** M. Marples *University Slang* 110 An anthology of *Kiplingisms*, somewhat on the lines of modern collections of *howlers*, is said to have been current in Cambridge for some years.

2. Views or opinions or style of expression characteristic of Rudyard Kipling (see Kiplingese).

1898 *Daily News* 7 Oct. 6/3 The manner otherwise may degenerate into sheer mannerism, a Kiplingism of Kipling. **1901** *Speaker* 26 Jan. 469/1 Sportsmen may be divided into two classes—those who care more for the chase than the killing and those who merely make 'bags' and break records. But the latter are not sportsmen.. and their method is nothing but Kiplingism out of place. **1920** H. G. Wells *Outl. Hist.* 524/1 The crude Darwinism and the Kiplingism of the later Victorian years.

Kipp (kɪp). *Chem.* The name of Petrus Jacobus *Kipp* (1808–64), German chemist, used in the possessive (less commonly *absol.* or *attrib.*) to denote an apparatus for the generation of gas by the action of a liquid on a solid as and when gas is required.

The apparatus consists essentially of three glass bulbs, of which the upper and lower ones are connected and contain the liquid and the middle one is connected with the lower one and contains the solid; while a tap in the middle bulb is open, liquid rises into the bulb and gas is evolved, whilst closing the tap causes the pressure of the gas to increase until the liquid is forced out of the middle bulb into the lower and upper ones, out of contact with the solid.

1879 *Proc. Cambr. Philos. Soc.* III. 160 A gentle current of hydrogen from the Kipp's apparatus *A*.. was led into *D*. **1901** F. G. Benedict *Chem. Lect. Exper.* 3 The Kipp generator, or one of its various modifications, remains today the only portable gas generator for the lecture table... The simpler and less expensive the form of Kipp used, the better. **1912** J. W. Mellor *Mod. Inorg. Chem.* iii. 45 Kipp's apparatus is very convenient when a steady current of hydrogen is needed for some time. **1921** J. R. Partington *Text-bk. Inorg. Chem.* xi. 185 Instead of a flask, a Kipp's apparatus may be used, the metal being placed in the central globe *B* and acid poured in the top funnel until the lower bulb *A* is full and the metal covered with acid. **1965** D. Abbott *Inorg. Chem.* xi. 535 It [*sc.* hydrogen sulphide] is most conveniently prepared for laboratory use in a Kipp's apparatus by the action of dilute hydrochloric acid on ferrous sulphide.

kippage ('kɪpɪdʒ). *Sc.* [Aphetic ad. F. *équipage* equipage.]

†**1.** 'The company sailing on board a ship, whether passengers or mariners' (Jam.). Cf. equipage 13.

1578 *Sc. Acts Jas. VI* (1814) III. 104 Considder diligentlie how mekill flesche may serve euerie schip and thair kippage for that present veyage.

2. 'Disorder, confusion' (Jam.); a state of excitement or irritation.

Cf. such F. phrases as *mettre en piteux équipage* to wreck or destroy (Littré).

1814 Scott *Wav.* liii, The Colonel's in an unco kippage. **1818** —— *Br. Lamm.* xxvi, Dinna pit yoursell into a kippage. **1825–80** Jamieson s.v., One is said to be in a sad kippage, when reduced to a disagreeable dilemma, *Loth.*

kippeen, kippin (kɪ'piːn, 'kɪpɪn). *Irish.* [a. Irish *cipín*: cf. Gael. *cipean, cipein* stump, peg, wooden pin.] A stick or dibble used for planting; a short thin stick.

1830–2 Carleton *Traits* (1843) I. 133 A good root-growing kippeen. **1841** S. C. Hall *Ireland* I. 122 The tree beside it grew out of the Kippin of the spancel which she carried in her hand.

kipper ('kɪpə(r)), *sb.*[1] and *a.* Forms: (1 **cypera**), 4 **kypre**, 6–7 **kypper**, 6–8 **kepper**, 6– **kipper**. [Etymology uncertain; it is also doubtful how sense A. 2, which goes with kipper *v.*, is

connected with 1, and indeed whether it is the same word.

At the approach of the breeding season, the lower jaw of the male salmon becomes hooked upward with a sharp cartilaginous beak known as the *kip*, which is used as a weapon by the fish when two or more fight for the same female; from this 'kip', the name 'kipper' is currently explained; but this is not compatible with the identity of *kipper* and OE. *cypera*, ME. *kypre*, which, itself, though phonetically unobjectionable, is also unproved, since the exact sense in which these words were used does not appear from the context. Moreover, in the quots. of 1376 and 1533–4, in B. 1, *kipper* appears to include both sexes.]

A. *sb.* **1.** A name given to the male salmon (or sea trout) during the spawning season. (The female is then called a *shedder*.)

Some recent writers give as the meaning 'the male salmon when spent after the spawning season', thus making the term equivalent to KELT; but this is not borne out by the earlier instances, which, when clear, evidently relate to the time when the fish is full of milt, and needs protection on account of its breeding value; nor does it harmonize with some later authorities, e.g. Jamieson, who says, '*kipper*, salmon in the state of spawning'; it is directly challenged by some (cf. quot. 1879); and it seems to have arisen from misapprehension of such qualifications as 'unseasonable', 'not wholesome', really applied to fish from the approach of the spawning season. For this Pennant seems largely responsible: see quot. 1766 in B. 1.

a **1000** *Boeth. Metr.* xix. 12 Hwy ȝe nu ne settan on sume dune fiscnet eowru, þonne eow fon lysteð leax oððe cyperan. *c* **1567** *Surv. Warkworth* in *Hist. Northumbld.* (1899) V. 151 The salmon fishing mainteyned, no kipper slayne alonge the water of Cockett. **1581** LAMBARDE *Eiren.* IV. iv. (1588) 450 Any Salmons or Trouts, out of season, that is being kippers or shedders. **1597** *Sc. Acts Jas. V* §72 (ed. Skene) *heading*, Of slauchter of redde fish or Kipper. **1624** in *N. Riding Rec.* (1885) III. II. 228 For killing salmon in time of kipper. **1705** *Act 4 & 5 Anne* c. 21 The old Salmon or Kippers, which, during that Season [1 Jan. to 10 Mar.] are out of kind, and returning to the Sea. **1848** *Chambers' Inform. for People* I. 687 The adult fish [salmon] having spawned, being out of condition, and unfit for food.. are.. termed kelts; the male fish is sometimes also called a kipper, and the female a shedder or baggit. **1861** J. BROWN *Horæ Subs.* Ser. II. 243 The poaching weaver who had.. leistered a prime kipper. **1879** T. T. STODDART in *Academy* 30 Aug. 151/2 On the banks of our Scottish salmon rivers, the designation *kipper* is applied to the male fish before parting with its milt, when the beak is fully developed. After spawning, it shares along with the female fish the term *kelt*. **1898** *Westm. Gaz.* 14 Oct. 7/2 The heaviest salmon.. was a fine 'kipper', weighing close on 30 lb., which he captured on Saturday last [8th Oct.].

2. A kippered fish (salmon, herring, etc.); now *esp.* a herring so cured: see KIPPER *v.*

(It is doubtful whether the quots. from the Durham Acc. Rolls belong here; they may relate to the fish in sense 1, without reference to any particular mode of preparation.)

1326 *Durham Acc. Rolls* (Surtees) 15 In 11 Kypres emp., 3*s.* 4*d.* **1340** *Ibid.* 37 In 6 kypres emp. et 1 salmone salso, 2*s.* 2*d.* **1769** *De Foe's Tour Gt. Brit.* III. 336 Preserving Salmon by making it into what they call Kipper: This is done by dividing it in the Middle from Head to Tail, and drying it slowly before a Fire. **1815** SCOTT *Guy M.* v, Ye're no eating your meat; allow me to recommend some of the kipper. It was John Hay that catcht it. **1824** CARLYLE in Froude *Life* (1882) I. 263 His heart.. is as dry as a Greenock kipper. **1837** M. DONOVAN *Dom. Econ.* II. 231 Some people, in order to give the kipper a peculiar taste.. carefully smoke it with peat-reek or the reek of juniper bushes.

3. a. A person, esp. a young or small person, a child. *slang.*

1905 *Daily Chron.* 30 Mar. 4/7 The expression 'giddy kipper', which Mr. Charles Brookfield has introduced to Mr. Justice Darling's notice. **1907** *Punch* 10 Apr. 254/2 Half-a-dozen dreadfully common young bicyclists were commenting on her discomfiture with delighted exclamations of 'Giddy old Kipper', 'Sweet Seventeen', 'Cheero, Maudie—you'll win!' **1923** M. M. GIBB *Hetherington's Affinity* xx. 175 If you're enterprizing enough to climb one of the trees christened by usage 'The Kipper's Tree', which hardly needs to be translated into plainer terms. **1959** I. & P. OPIE *Lore & Lang. Schoolch.* ix. 170 A chap who has got duck's disease is most often labelled 'Tich'... Alternatively: ankle biter,.. kipper, microbe, midge, [etc.].

b. An Englishman, an English immigrant in Australia. *Austral. slang.*

1946 R. RIVETT *Behind Bamboo* 397/1 *Kipper*, Englishman. **1946** *Sunday Sun* (Sydney) 8 Aug. Suppl. 15 An able seaman on a kipper warship called the Eagle. **1963** *Times Lit. Suppl.* 24 May 370/2 Quite often they [*sc.* English immigrants in Australia] are referred to as Kippers. **1967** K. GILES *Death & Mr Prettyman* ii. 57 You kippers—no guts and two faces—are only strong under the armpits... What about the east of Suez caper, eh?

4. a. *Naut. slang.* A torpedo. Cf. FISH *sb.*[1] 1 h.

1953 A. MARS *Unbroken* iii. 74 As she was only crawling along I aimed my first 'kipper' just a fraction ahead of her bows. **1959** G. JENKINS *Twist of Sand* v. 86, I evaluate its firing power at eighteen torpedoes—I think kipper is a distressing piece of naval slang—in thirty minutes.

b. kipper kite *R.A.F. slang* (see quot. 1943); **kipper tie** [see quot. 1969], a gaudy and very wide neck-tie.

[**1941** L. WALMSLEY *Fishermen at War* ix. 138 Kipper, I discovered, was airman's slang for a fishing boat. The chief function of this particular station was the escorting of convoys and fishing fleets, and the section which had the latter duty to perform was known as the 'Kipper Patrol'.] **1942** *Gen* 1 Sept. 14/1 A Coastal Command plane is a 'kipper kite'. **1943** HUNT & PRINGLE *Service Slang* 42 *Kipper-kites*, aircraft engaged on convoy escort duties over the North Sea and usually giving protection to the fishing-vessels. **1966** *Daily Tel.* 20 Jan. 15/6 Neckties are slightly wider and pointed, though not yet as floppy as London's Carnaby Street kipper ties. **1969** *Guardian* 16 Sept. 9/4 Michael Fish [*sc.* a London designer of mens-wear].. can.. take credit for popularising the wide tie, named 'kipper' after him. **1973** *Times* 30 May 18/3 He had come from his Suffolk home wearing a kipper tie and black and white patterned shirt, full of energy and ideas.

B. *adj.* (attrib. use of sb.)

1. Said of a male salmon (or sea trout), at the breeding season: see A. 1. In quots. 1376 and 1533–4 'kipper' appears to include both sexes.

[**1376** *Rolls Parlt.* II. 331/2 Qe null Salmon soit pris en Tamise entre Graveshend & le Pount de Henlee sur Tamise en temps q'il soit kiper: C'est assavoir, entre les Festes de l'Invention del Crois, & le Epiphanie.] **1533–4** *Act 25 Hen. VIII*, c. 7 That no maner of persone or persones.. frome the feaste of the exaltation of the holy crosse to the feaste of Seynt martyn in wynter.. kyll or distroye any Salmons not in season called kepper Salmons. **1558** *Act 1 Eliz.* c. 17 §1 Any Salmons or Trouts, not being in Season, being Kepper-Salmons or Kepper-Trouts, Shedder-Salmons or Shedder-Trouts. **1603** OWEN *Pembrokeshire* (1891) 118 In wynter, when.. they are found kipper, leane and vnhole-some. **1653** WALTON *Angler* vi. 136 The He Salmon.. is more kipper, & less able to endure a winter in the fresh water, than the She is. **1766** PENNANT *Zool.* (1769) III. 242 After spawning they [salmon] become very poor and lean, and then are called kipper.

2. *transf.* Shaped like the lower jaw of a kipper salmon: see etymological note above.

1822 HOGG *Perils of Man* II. ii. 50 Tam and Gibbie, with their long kipper noses, peeping over his shoulder.

C. *attrib.* and *Comb.*, as †**kipper-time**, the period of close-time for salmon.

1706 PHILLIPS, *Kipper-Time*, a Space of Time between the Festival of the Invention of the H. Cross May 3d. and Twelfth-Day; during which, Salmon-fishing in the River Thames was forbidden by Rot. Parl. 50 Edw. 3. [See quot. 1376 in B. 1.] **1894** HALL CAINE *Manxman* III. xii. 171 The ould kipper-box rolling on a block for a boat at sea—do you mind it? **1899** *Daily News* 27 Oct. 2/3 At Great Yarmouth, where there are some 350 boats and some 4,000 fishermen and kipper-girls engaged in the great herring fishery.. some 800 girls are curing the enormous catches for the Continental and the other markets of the world.

'kipper, *sb.*[2] *Austral.* [Native name.] A young Aboriginal who has been initiated and is admitted to the rights of manhood.

1841 C. EIPPER *Statement German Mission to Aborigines* 8 With these weapons the natives invest their young men at the age of from fourteen to sixteen years... These young men are then called *kippers*, and for the first time enjoy the privilege of taking an active part in the fight. **1853** H. B. JONES *Adventures Austral.* 126 Around us sat 'Kippers', i.e. 'hobbledehoy blacks'. **1885** R. C. PRAED *Austral. Life* i. 24 A ceremony at which the young men.. receive the rank of warriors and are henceforth called *Kippers.* **1966** W. S. RAMSON *Austral. Eng.* vi. 129 *Bora*, 'a rite of initiation', *kipper*, used of a youth who has passed through such a rite, and *boyla* and *koradji*, 'an aboriginal medicine-man or witchdoctor', are used only in their original and specific senses.

kipper, *v.* [? f. KIPPER *sb.*[1]

If really derived from the sb., it seems most reasonable to infer that this process was originally used for the preservation of 'kipper' salmon; but no direct evidence has been found.]

trans. and *intr.* To cure (salmon, herring, or other fish) by cleaning, rubbing repeatedly with salt and pepper or other spice, and drying in the open air or in smoke. Also *transf.* and *fig.*

1773 [see KIPPERED below]. **1835** SOUTHEY in C. Southey *Life* VI. 281 Salmon which he had kippered the preceding night. **1848** *Life Normandy* (1863) II. 56 [Salmon out of season] are.. more frequently kippered; that is to say, they are cured with salt, sugar, and spice, and then dried in the smoke. **1885** *Times* (weekly ed.) 2 Oct. 15/1 Smoking and kippering them [mackerel] for winter use. **1894** KIPLING *Seven Seas* (1896) 36 The Leevin' God, That does not kipper souls for sport or break a life in jest. **1909** R. BEACH *Silver Horde* 129 He's an awful spender. I'm half kippered [= drunk] myself. **1924** *Glasgow Herald* 28 Jan. 10 Oily cotton-waste was picked up at the gates of yards and factories, and our hands were duly kippered over smoking lumps of this stuff. **1930** R. CAMPBELL *Adamastor* 20 Hang him up to kipper in the sun. **1963** *Times* 14 May p. ii/3 (Advt.), Central heating designed to prevent the average household from being kippered on one side and frozen on the other. **1969** *Daily Tel.* 30 Dec. 6/5 On the last day of addiction, smoke twice or thrice as many cigarettes as normal. The next morning you should feel sufficiently kippered as to see the sense of your new plan.

Hence **'kippered** *ppl. a.*; **'kippering** *vbl. sb.*

1773 MRS. GRANT *Lett. fr. Mount.* (1807) I. ii. 20 We had.. kippered salmon. **1795** *Statist. Acc. Scot., Stirlings.* XVI. 122 The kippering of salmon is successfully practised in several parts of the parish. **1863** in *Tyneside Songs* 91 A cask o' the best kipper'd herrins. **1885** *Pall Mall G.* 11 June 9/2 A large kippering establishment at Stornoway. **1892** E. REEVES *Homeward Bound* 31 Fisher-girls.. at Grimsby, splitting herrings for kippering, seven a minute.

'kipperer. [-ER[1].] One who kippers herrings.

1902 *Nature* 4 Sept. 435/2 The 'kipperer' and the 'gutter' have their peculiar troubles. **1920** *Glasgow Herald* 10 July 6 Joint meetings of fishermen, curers, salesmen, freshers, and kipperers were held at both places. **1930** *Aberdeen Press & Jrnl.* 21 Mar. 6/5 A shed.. standing alongside a kippering kiln.., occupied by Mr. David Mackenzie, kipperer. **1955** *Times* 3 May 6/3 Merchants and kipperers refused to pay the new minimum price of 91s. a cran.

'kipperish, *a. rare.* [f. KIPPER *a.* + -ISH[1].] Characteristic of a 'kipper' fish: see KIPPER *sb.*[1] and *a.* 1.

1658 R. FRANCK *North. Mem.* (1821) 296 [The salmon] is then prohibited the benefit of salt-water to bathe her fins.. which is the natural cause of her kipperish infirmity.

kipper-nut. [Origin unknown.

The conjecture of Hempl (*Publ. Mod. Lang. Assoc. America* XIV. 455) that *kipper* is here a variant of *pepper*, *pickle*, in sense 'pungent', does not seem justified.]

1. = EARTH-NUT 1.

1597 GERARDE *Herbal* II. ccccxv. 905 Earth Nut, Earth Chestnut, or Kipper Nut. **1611** COTGR., *Noix chastaigne*, the earth nut, Kipper nut, earth Chestnut. **1722** QUINCY *Lex. Phys. Med.* (ed. 2) 348 The Earth-nut, Kipper-nut or Pig-nut. **1846** SOWERBY *Brit. Bot.* (ed. 3).

2. The tuber of the Heath-pea: = EARTH-NUT 2.

1863 PRIOR *Pop. Names Brit. Plants.* **1879** BRITTEN & HOLLAND *Plant-n.*

kippersol ('kɪpəsɒl). *S. Afr.* Also **kiepersol.** [Corrupt f. KITTISOL.] A small evergreen African tree of the genus *Cussonia*, belonging to the family Araliaceæ.

1893 'R. IRON' *Dream Life* 26 A kippersol tree. *Ibid.* 29 She.. cut at the root of a kippersol, and got out a large piece.. and sat down to chew it. Kippersol is like raw quince. *Ibid.* 34 When one has had no food but kippersol juice for two days. **1921** T. R. SIM *Native Timbers S. Afr.* 194 Kipperkol [*sic*]. *Cussonia*, all species. **1954** K. COWIN *Bushveld, Bananas & Bounty* v. 78 According to legend the [*Cussonia*] *umbellifera*, with its broad flat leaves, was first called Kiepersol by the Cape Malays, whose word for monkey is *kie* and for umbrella is the Afrikaans word *persols* and the combination results in the picturesque name of Monkey's Umbrella. **1973** PALMER & PITMAN *Trees S. Afr.* III. 1691 Most of the species [of *Cussonia*] are known as 'kiepersol'... The name travelled to the Cape where it was first used for the *Cussonia* species common around Cape Town, *Cussonia thyrsiflora* Thunb., and is now a general name for all the cussonias with their parasol-like mops of leaves at the ends of the branches.

kippe-sole, corrupt f. KITTISOL.

kipple, Sc. and dial. f. COUPLE *sb.* and *v.*

†**kipsey, kibsey.** *Obs.* exc. *dial.* Also 7 **kybzey.** [Origin uncertain: cf. KIPE.] A small wicker-basket.

1615 MARKHAM *Eng. Housew.* III. i. (1668) 96 With a gathering hook, gather those which be full Ripe, and put them into your Cherry-pot, or Kybzey, hanging by your side or upon any bough you please. **1706** PHILLIPS, *Kibsey*, a kind of Wicker-basket. **1754** MARTIN *Eng. Dict.* (ed. 2), *Kibsy*, a sort of wicker basket. **1879** HORSLEY in *Macm. Mag.* XL. 501, I was coming home with my kipsy (basket).

kipsie, kipsy ('kɪpsɪ). *Austral.* [f. KIP *sb.*[3] + -Y[6], -IE.] A house (see also quot. 1919).

1916 C. J. DENNIS *Songs Sentimental Bloke* 124 *Kipsie*, a house, the home. **1919** W. H. DOWNING *Digger Dial.* 31 *Kippsie*—lean-to; shelter; house; dugout. **1943** *Coast to Coast 1942* 91 He turned and looked our little weather-beaten kipsie over. **1946** *Coast to Coast 1945* 236 Our little kipsy breathed a heavy stillness like that leaden hush that hangs over tree and earth before a storm breaks. **1969** *Courier-Mail* (Brisbane) 29 Nov. 13/1 Our kipsy was an aloof-looking little place.

Kipsigis ('kɪpsɪgɪs). [Native name.] The name of a people inhabiting western Kenya, and their Nilotic language; a member of this people. Also *attrib.* or as *adj.*

1931 *Africa* IV. 467 The Kipsigis and the other tribes speaking an almost identical language.. are really pastoral in custom and thought, though they have ceased to be truly nomadic, like the Masai. **1939** E. E. EVANS-PRITCHARD in J. G. Peristiany *Social Inst. Kipsigis* p. xx, The Kipsigis are Nandi-speaking. *Ibid.* p. xxxi, The Kipsigis clan (*oret*) is a totemic non-exogamous group of persons. **1939** J. G. PERISTIANY *Ibid.* i. 1 The Kipsigis, also called Kipsigi or Kipsigisiek, are better known to the European as Lumbwa, a misnomer of unknown origin, as none of the neighbouring tribes seems to be responsible for this name. *Ibid.* xii. 231 The Kipsigis text accompanies the translation for the better understanding of Kipsigis thought. **1947** *E. Afr. Ann. 1946–7* 43/1 Nilo-Hamitic tribes such as the Nandi, Suk and Kipsigis. **1964** A. N. TUCKER in D. Abercrombie et al. *Daniel Jones* 445 The Kalenjin languages are spoken by two groups of non-Bantu speakers in the Rift Valley Province.. the Nandi Group, comprising Nandi, Kipsigis, Keyo ('Elgeyo'), Tugen ('Kamasia'), Kony ('Elgon'), Sabiny ('Sabei'), and others. *Ibid.*, The languages chosen here as representative are Nandi (with occasional reference to Kipsigis) and Western Päkot. **1971** *E. Afr. Standard* (Nairobi) 10 Apr. 7/4 A fight.. broke out between Kipsigis and Kisii tribesmen.

kir (kiːr). Also **Kir.** [The name of Canon Felix *Kir* (1876–1968), mayor of Dijon, who is said to have invented the recipe.] A drink made from dry white wine and crème de cassis.

1966 *Times Lit. Suppl.* 19 May 456/5 M. Follain's work should be read with a kir, a benedictine or a calvados. **1967** *Sat. Rev.* (U.S.) 22 Apr. 50/2 In 1967 the drink.. is *Kir*, which the pros call *blanc Cassis*, or if they are *really* switched on, a *blancass.* **1967** L. DEIGHTON *Expensive Place* x. 74 'Waiter,' he called. 'Four kirs.'.. The white wine and cassis came. **1967** A. LICHINE *Encycl. Wines* 172 Around Dijon it [*sc.* Cassis] is used as a popular aperitif, a little Cassis being put in a glass that is then filled with a fairly neutral, dry white wine... Also called kir. **1968** M. TRIPP *One is One* xvii. 159 You couldn't get Kir, his customary drink, anywhere. **1974** *Guardian* 22 Aug. 11/6 The summer aperitif 'Kir'.

kiradjee, var. KORADJI.

kirat, obs. form of CARAT.

1568 TURNER *Herbal* III. 50 If one kirat of it be geven in wine, it maketh a man wonderfully dronken. **1616**

BULLOKAR *Eng. Expos.*, *Kirat*, an Arabian word signifying the weight of three graines.

kirb, kirble, kirb-roof, var. CURB, KERB, CURBLE, CURB-ROOF.

Kirby ('kɜːbɪ). The name of Charles *Kirby*, 17th-c. English fish-hook maker, used *attrib.* and *absol.* (†and in the possessive) to denote a design of fish-hook originated by him.

[**1655** WALTON *Compleat Angler* (ed. 2) xvii. 313 But if you will buy choice hooks, I wil one day walk with you to Charles Kerbyes in Harp Alley in Shooe-lane, who is the most exact and best Hook-maker that the Nation affords.] **1804** T. BEST *Conc. Treat. Art of Angling* (ed. 6) ii. 23 Ford and Kirby's hooks are excellent ones. **1823** T. F. SALTER *Angler's Guide* (ed. 5) xvi. 140 In choosing Eel hooks, prefer the single ones whose shank is similar to the Kirby hook, to those which have a loop shank. **1870** H. CHOLMONDELEY-PENNELL *Mod. Pract. Angler* i. 9 The round and Kirby bends are very deficient in penetrating power, and disproportionately short in the shank as compared to their breadth of bend, either for appearance or use, more particularly in the matter of flies. **1967** B. KNOX *Blacklight* ii. 32 The box held a collection of wickedly barbed Kirby hooks.

kirby-grip ('kɜːbɪ grɪp). Also **Kirbigrip** (proprietary name), **kirbigrip**. A type of sprung hair-grip.

1926 *Trade Marks Jrnl.* 6 Jan. 12 Kirbigrip... Hair-pins of ordinary Metal. Kirby, Beard & Co., Limited,.. Birmingham; Manufacturers. **1945** 'A. GILBERT' *Don't open Door* xi. 95 Two plain brown combs and a kirbigrip. **1949** 'J. TEY' *Brat Farrar* xxiii. 214 The aged kirby-grip that kept Jane's hair off her face. *a* **1953** DYLAN THOMAS *Adventures Skin Trade* (1955) I. 18 Mrs. Probert next door,.. butting the air with her kirby-grips. **1955** [see *hair-grip* s.v. HAIR *sb.* 9 b]. **1959** *Woman's Own* 12 Dec. 21/3 Ribbon bows fixed to kirby-grips or combs. **1960** C. STORR *Marianne & Mark* i. 20 Marianne bought a card of kirbigrips. **1973** B. BAINBRIDGE *Dressmaker* i. 20 Nellie, when put out, could appear to be suffering, her white hair plastered to her head in waves and a kirby grip to keep it neat.

kirch, var. CURCH.

kirchenwasser: see KIRSCHWASSER.

kircher, -chowe, obs. ff. KERCHER, KERCHIEF.

Kirchhoff ('kɪətʃɒf, ǁ'kɪrxhɔf). Also (erron.) Kirchoff. The name of Gustav Robert *Kirchhoff* (1824–87), Ger. physicist, used in *Kirchhoff's law*: **a.** *Electr.* Either of two laws concerning electric networks in which steady currents are flowing: (*a*) (the first law) the algebraic sum of the currents in all the conductors that meet in a point is zero; (*b*) (the second law) the algebraic sum of the products of current and resistance in each part of any closed path in a network is equal to the algebraic sum of the e.m.f.s in the path.

1869 R. MAIN *Rudimentary Astron.* (new ed.) 164 (*heading*) Kirchhoff's law. *Ibid.* p. xx (*heading*) Application of Kirchhoff's law. **1876** H. R. KEMPE *Handbk. Electr. Testing* v. 45 Kirchoff's laws.., though exceedingly simple .., are not so well known as they ought to be. **1905** W. C. D. WHETHAM *Theory Exper. Electr.* v. 117 The principles of continuous current-flow which we have now established may conveniently be applied to complex circuits and networks of conductors in the form of two statements known as Kirchhoff's laws. **1970** M. NELKON *Electr.* v. 130 Kirchhoff's first law is a mathematical statement of the fact that the charges do not accumulate at any junction of an electrical circuit. *Ibid.* 132 We need to apply Kirchhoff's second law to two complete circuits as there are two unknowns.

b. *Physics.* The law that the absorptivity of a body for radiant energy of any particular wavelength is equal to its emissivity at the same temperature for the same wavelength.

1901 G. K. BURGESS tr. *Le Chatelier & Boudouard's High-Temperature Measurements* viii. 140 (*heading*) Kirchoff's law. **1945** F. A. BERRY et al. *Handbk. Meteorol.* IV. 288 It is an immediate consequence of Kirchhoff's law that the intensity emitted by a body can never exceed the black-body intensity and can equal it only in the spectral regions where the body is opaque. **1967** R. W. FAIRBRIDGE *Encycl. Atmospheric Sci.* 793/1 We assume black-body radiation which is that of a body that is characterized by maximum possible absorption at all incident wavelengths, insuring maximum emissivity according to Kirchoff's Law.

Kirghiz (kɪə'giːz), *sb.* and *a.* Also **Khirgese, Kirghis, Kirgiz.** [ad. Russ. *Kirgiz.*] **A.** *sb.* A widespread Mongolian people of west central Asia, now chiefly inhabiting the Kirghiz Soviet Socialist Republic; a member of this people; their Turkic language. **B.** *adj.* Of or pertaining to the Kirghiz; *spec.* **Kirghiz pheasant** = *Mongolian pheasant* (MONGOLIAN *a.* 4). Also **Kir'ghizian** *a.* and *sb.*

1652 P. HEYLYN *Cosmographie* III. 190 These again subdivided into severall Tribes, which they call their Hordes, of which the most considerable are, 1. the Nagaian Tartars, 2. the Zavolhenses, 3. the Thumenenses, 4. the Kirgessi. **1837** DE QUINCEY in *Blackw. Mag.* July 109/2 The murderous attacks of their cruel enemies the Bashkirs and the Kirghises. **1888** *Encycl. Brit.* XXIII. 661/2 Tatar dialects (Kirghizian, Bashkiri, Nogai). **1898** A. J. BUTLER tr. *Ratzel's Hist. Mankind* III. 326 The Kirghiz women adorn their plaits with beads, shells, and copper buttons. **1908** T. G. TUCKER *Introd. Nat. Hist. Lang.* 134 *Kirghiz*, comprising the speeches of the Black Kirghiz (or *Buruts*) in the part of Turkestan bordering on China, and of the Cossack Kirghiz to the north of the Caspian, the sea of Aral and Lake Balkash. **1921** *19th Cent.* May 871 Kirghizes, Lesghiens, Mingrelians. **1922** C. W. BEEBE *Monogr. Pheasants* III. 96 On the south-east the enormous Tian-Shan serve as the boundary between the Kirghiz Pheasant and both *shawi* and *tarimensis.* **1922** *Contemp. Rev.* Sept. 342 The Kirgisian population has retained its nomadic habits. **1924** *Blackw. Mag.* Aug. 256/1 The Russians, who were conscripting young Khirgese men for use on the railway. **1931** A. U. DILLEY *Oriental Rugs & Carpets* x. 226 Kirghiz rugs.. are country-bred, vigorous and coarse. **1932** R. JOHN tr. *Popoff's City of Red Plague* iii. 46 One could not help being struck by the large number of Mongolian types—torn by their Muscovite masters from the remote steppes and forests of Siberia and Asiatic Russia;.. Kalmucks, Kirghiz, Yakuts, and similar obscure, semi-barbaric tribes. **1935** HUXLEY & HADDON *We Europeans* vii. 212 Ethnologists use the word [*sc.* Turki] loosely and in several different senses:—..(*b*) To designate a certain ethnic group of which the Turks, the Kirghis and the Tatars are best known. **1946** G. MILLAR *Horned Pigeon* i. 12 A dashing White Russian officer.. spoke frequently of the Kirghesian sheep that drag their fat-containing tails behind them on little sleighs. **1955** V. CRONIN *Wise Man from West* xiii. 243 In this country of chasms and precipices roamed the Kirghiz, a predatory tribe. **1961** L. F. BROSNAHAN *Sounds of Lang.* viii. 177 A palatalisation of syllables.. occurs in most of the Turco-Tartar languages of.. Kirghiz, Turkmenian, etc. **1963** [see *Mongolian pheasant* s.v. MONGOLIAN *a.* 4]. **1967** D. S. PARLETT *Short Dict. Languages* 73 *Kirgiz*.., apparently one of the oldest (or oldest attested) Turkic tribes. **1971** *Whitaker's Almanack 1972* 966 The Kirghiz S.S.R. occupies the north-eastern part of Soviet Central Asia and borders in the south-east on China.

ǁ**kiri** ('kɪərɪ). [Jap.] = PAULOWNIA.

1727 J. G. SCHEUCHZER tr. *Kæmpfer's Hist. Japan* I. I. ix. 119 *Kiri*, is a very large but scarce Tree. **1822** F. SHOBERL tr. *Titsingh's Illustr. Japan* 255 Sometimes this cane is made of the wood of the *kiri*-tree. **1877** *Trans. Asiatic Soc. Japan* V. I. 9 The second of the Imperial badges is a representation of the leaf and flower of the *kiri*, or *Paulownia Japonica.* **1893** A. M. BACON *Jap. Interior* xiv. 237 The blossoms and leaves of the kiri-tree, (paulownia imperialis), which is the sign of the imperial family. **1928** BLUNDEN *Jap. Garland* 22 The broad-leaved *kiri.* **1972** *Nat. Geographic* Sept. 374 Miss Hori still goes into the forests to select the best *kiri*, or Paulownia wood.

kirie-mirie-buff: see KERRY-MERRY-BUFF.

ǁ**kirin** ('kɪərɪn). Also **Kirin.** [Jap., f. Chinese (see KYLIN).] A fabulous beast of composite form, freq. portrayed in Japanese pottery and art (see quots.); = KYLIN.

1727 J. G. SCHEUCHZER tr. *Kæmpfer's Hist. Japan* I. I. x. 123 *Kirin*, according to the description and figure, which the Japanese give of it, is a winged Quadruped, of incredible swiftness, with two soft horns standing before the breast, and bent backwards, with the body of a Horse, and claws of a Deer, and a head which comes nearest to that of a Dragon. **1875–80** AUDSLEY & BOWES *Keramic Art Japan* I. p. xxxviii, The Japanese have described the *kirin* as a supernatural animal, requiring for its creation the concurrence of a certain constellation in the heavens. **1900** F. LITCHFIELD *Pott. & Porc.* vii. 172 Figure subjects are not common in this kind of china, but one finds representations of.. the *Kirin*.., a monster with the body and hoofs of a deer, the tail of a bull, and a horn on his forehead. **1908** H. L. JOLY *Legend in Jap. Art* 148 The Chinese *Shang Huen Fujen*, female Sennin, shown riding upon a Kirin. **1963** [see HO-HO]. **1971** L. A. BOGER *Dict. World Pott. & Porc.* 170/2 Included among other popular [porcelain] motifs were.. the five fabulous creatures:.. Kirin (Japanese unicorn), [etc.].

Kiriwinian (kɪrɪ'vɪnɪən), *sb.* and *a.* [f. *Kiriwin(a*, the name of the largest of the Trobriand Islands + -IAN.] **A.** *sb.* A native or inhabitant of Kiriwina; the Austronesian language spoken there. **B.** *adj.* Of or pertaining to Kiriwina.

1916 *Jrnl. R. Anthrop. Inst.* XLVI. 356 There is very little of the universally reported native's dread of darkness among the Kiriwinians. *Ibid.* 354 He.. acquired sufficient knowledge of the Kiriwinian language to be able to dispense with the services of an interpreter. *Ibid.* 391 Archaic expressions.. the natives only partially understand, and.. it is extremely difficult to make them translate the meaning correctly into modern Kiriwinian. **1922** B. MALINOWSKI *Argonauts W. Pacific* xx. 480 The Kiriwinians have to go inland to the industrial districts of Kuboma.. to acquire the articles needed. **1964** *Language* XL. 308 These Kiriwinian and English sentences.

kirk (kɜːk, *Sc.* kɪrk), *sb.* Forms: 3 (*Orm.*) kirrke, 3–7 kirke, 4–6 kyrke, 4–7 kyrk, (4 kirc, 6 kerke, 6–9 kurk), 4– kirk. [Northern form of CHURCH: cf. OE. *circe*, and ON. *kirkja*, Da. *kirke*, Sw. *kyrka.*]

1. The Northern English and Scotch form of the word CHURCH, in all its senses.

a. In Northern English: formerly used as far south as Norfolk; and still extending in dialect use to north-east Lincolnshire: see E.D.D. Frequent in proper names all over its original area.

c **1200** ORMIN 3533 Hallȝhedd inn hiss kirrke. *c* **1330** R. BRUNNE *Chron.* (1810) 92 Clerkes of holy kirke. *a* **1340** HAMPOLE *Psalter* Prol., þis boke.. is mast oysed in halykyrke seruys. *c* **1400** *Melayne* 29 In kirkes and abbayes that there were. *c* **1450** *Mirour Saluacioun* 1422 After the trewe kyrkes vsage. *c* **1550** CHEKE *Matt.* xvi. 18 *note*, Yis word church.. commeth of yᵉ greek κυριακόν.. as ye north doth yet moor truli sound it, yᵉ kurk, and we moor corruptli and frenchlike, yᵉ church. **1579** SPENSER *Sheph. Cal.* July 97 To Kerke the narre, from God more farre, Has bene an old-sayd sawe. *a* **1656** USSHER *Power Princes* II. (1683) 234 That place which.. all men did call a Kirk. **1674–91** RAY *N.C. Words* 41 *Kyrk*, Church, κυριακόν. **1785** HUTTON *Bran New Wark* (Westmld.) 14 Be serious and devout, net come to kirk with a moon belief. **1802** in Anderson *Cumbld. Ball.* 24 Helter skelter frae the kurk. **1828** *Craven Dial.* s.v., He's as poor as a kirk mouse. **1877** *Holderness Gloss.*, *Kirk*, a church. Not much used. That at Owthorne on the coast is called the 'Sister Kirk'.

b. Used in literary Sc. till 17th c., and still retained in vernacular use in the general sense of 'church'.

1375 BARBOUR *Bruce* II. 71 Quhen he.. In-till the kyrk Schyr Ihone haid slayn. *c* **1475** *Rauf Coilȝear* 574 The hie Mes was done, The King with mony cumly out of the Kirk is gane. **1567** *Gude & Godlie B.* (S.T.S.) 11 We trow the kirk Catholik be Ane Faithfull Christin cumpanie. **1643** *Petit. Ass. Kirk Scot.* in Clarendon *Hist. Reb.* VI. §340 The Kirk of England (which We ought to tender as our own Bowels). **1648** in *Rec. Kirk of Scot.* (1838) I. 507 All the corruptions that have been formerly in the Kirks of God in these Lands [England and Scotland]. *a* **1649** DRUMM. OF HAWTH. *Poems* Wks. (1711) 49 The Scottish kirk the English church do name; The English church the Scots a kirk do call. *a* **1653** BINNING *Serm.* (1743) 607 Unless their prayers do it, or their keeping the kirk. *a* **1704** T. BROWN *Cupid turn'd Tinker* Wks. 1730 I. 112 At play-house and kirk Where he slily did lurk. **1786** BURNS *Twa Dogs* 19 At kirk or market, mill or smiddie. **1894** 'IAN MACLAREN' *Bonnie Brier Bush, Lachlan Campbell* iii. 145 Away on the right the Parish Kirk peeped out from a clump of trees.

c. In official use, the name 'Kirk of Scotland' gave place to 'Church of Scotland' at the date of the Westminster Assembly: see quots. 1645, 1648. But (**d**) in subsequent English (as opposed to Scottish) usage, the term 'kirk' has often been opposed to 'church' to distinguish the Church of Scotland from the Church of England, or from the Episcopal Church in Scotland. So ***Free Kirk*** for the Free Church of Scotland.

c. 1560 (*title*) The Booke of the Universall Kirk of Scotland. **1637–50** ROW *Hist. Kirk* (1842) 3 Instructed.. in the exact knowledge of the Estate of this Kirk of Scotland. **1645** in *Rec. Kirk of Scot.* (1838) I. 431/1 Subscribed in name of the General Assembly of the Kirk of Scotland, by the Moderator of the Assembly. [**1648** *Ibid.* I. 506 (*title*) A Declaration and Exhortation of the General Assembly of the Church of Scotland, to their Brethren of England. **1691** (*title*) The principal Acts of the General Assembly of the Church of Scotland conveened at Edinburgh the 16th day of October, 1690.]

d. *a* **1674** CLARENDON *Hist. Reb.* XII. §121 Nor did she [the queen] prefer the glory of the church of England before the sordidness of the kirk of Scotland. **1708** SWIFT *Sacram. Test* Wks. 1755 II. I. 135 To swear.. as they do now in Scotland, to be true to the kirk. **1791** HAMPSON *Mem. Wesley* II. 19 A member of the kirk. **1831** MACAULAY *Ess., Hampden* (1887) 219 This government.. called a general assembly of the Kirk. **1850** WHIPPLE *Ess. & Rev.* (ed. 3) I. 213 Examples which tell against kirk as well as against church. **1854** KINGSLEY *Let.* 22 Feb. in *Life* xii. (1879) I. 321 Erskine and others think [the lectures] will do much good, but will infuriate the Free Kirk.

2. Sometimes affected to render Du. *kerk*, LG. *kerke*, or Ger. *kirche.*

1673 RAY *Journ. Low C.* 25 Here [Delft] are two large Churches, the one called the old, the other the new Kirk. **1851** LONGF. *Gold Leg.* II. *Village Ch.* 69, I may to yon kirk go, To read upon yon sweet book.

3. Phr. (*Sc. colloq.*) ***to make a kirk and a mill of***: to put to any use one pleases, to do what one will with. But Kelly gives what may have been the earlier meaning.

1721 KELLY *Sc. Prov.* 252 Make a Kirk and a Mill of it, that is, make your best of it: It does not answer to the English, 'Make a Hog or a Dog of it': For that means, bring it either to one use, or another. **1822** GALT *Entail* I. xviii. 147 The property is my own conquesting.. and surely I may make a kirk and a mill o't an I like. **1887** MRS. ALEXANDER *Mona's Choice* II. vii. 173, I doubt but the man I let the land to is just making a kirk and a mill of it.

4. *attrib.* and *Comb.* (see also, in many cases, corresponding combinations of CHURCH): as ***kirk act, bell, door, -goer, government, preacher, rent, steeple, stile, vassal, writer***; ***kirk-greedy, kirk-like*** adjs.; **kirk-assembly,** Assembly of the Church of Scotland; **kirk-burial,** burial within a church; **kirk-fast,** a fast ordained by the Church; †**kirk-feuar** *Sc.* = *church-feuar* (CHURCH *sb.* 18); **kirk-gate,** the high-way or street leading to a church; **kirk-keeper** *Sc.*, a constant attendant at the kirk; †**kirk-lair** *Sc.*, 'a lair or burial place within a church, the right of burial within a church' (Jam. *Suppl.*); †**kirk-loom,** church machine or utensil; **kirk-shire** (see quot.); **kirk-skail, -skailing** *Sc.*, the dispersion of the congregation after divine service; **kirk-work** *Sc.* = CHURCHWORK a.; **kirk-wynd,** the lane leading to a church. Also KIRK-ALE, -GARTH, -YARD, etc.

1606 BIRNIE *Kirk-Buriall* xix, The *Kirk acts against *Kirk-buriall. **1752** CARTE *Hist. Eng.* III. 425 Going.. to the *Kirk-assembly at Edenburgh. **1830** GALT *Lawrie T.* VI. ii. (1849) 257 To hear the far-off *kirk-bell ringing. **1814** SCOTT *Wav.* xxx, He would drive a nail for no man on the Sabbath or *kirk-fast. **1820** —— *Monast.* xvii, The son of a *kirk feuar is not the stuff that lords and knights are made of. **1643** *Declar. Commons* (*Reb. Ireland*) 56 Desires for establishing Unity of Religion, and Uniformity of *Kirk-government. **1882** J. WALKER *Jaunt to Auld Reekie*, etc. 42 He neir was godly nor *kirk-greedy. **1815** SCOTT *Guy M.* xi, A constant *kirk-keeper she is. **1606** BIRNIE *Kirk-Buriall* xix, Secluding all from the *Kirk-laire. *c* **1450** HOLLAND

Howlat 82 The plesant Pacok... Constant and *kirklyk vnder his cler cape, Myterit, as the maner is. **1819** W. TENNANT *Papistry Storm'd* (1827) 201 The mickle pulpit;.. was the Cardinal's ain *kirk-loom, He brocht it in a ship frae Rome. **1844** LINGARD *Anglo-Sax. Ch.* (1858) I. iv. 144 *note*, These districts allotted to priests were called priestshires, shrift-shires, or *kirkshires. **1843** BETHUNE *Sc. Fireside Stor.* 283 Hame again At *kirk-skail time she came. **1819** LOCKHART *Peter's Lett.* lxxiii. III. 265 When the service is over..(for which moment the Scotch have, in their language, an appropriate and picturesque term, the *kirk-skailing). **1826** J. WILSON *Noct. Ambr.* Wks. 1855 II. 312 The cock on a *kirk-steeple. **1552** LYNDESAY *Monarche* 4729 Thay hauld the Corps at the *kirk style. **1820** SCOTT *Monast.* iii, To hear ye even the Lady of Avenel to seeking quarters wi' a *kirk-vassal's widow! **1430** in *14th Rep. Hist. MSS. Comm.* App. III. 21 [A penalty of £20 Scots to be paid to the] *kirkwerk [of Glasgow]. **1467** [see CHURCH WORK]. **1680** G. HICKES *Spirit of Popery* Pref. i, Citing out of the *Kirk-Writers their Papal,.. Schismatical and Rebellious Principles. **1888** BARRIE *When a Man's single* i, A kitchen in the *kirk-wynd of Thrums.

kirk, *v.* Now *Sc.* [f. KIRK *sb.*]

1. *trans.* = CHURCH *v.* 1.

c **1425** WYNTOUN *Cron.* v. xii. 4904 In honoure off that madyn clere That wes kyrkkyd as that day. *c* **1470** [see CHURCH *v.* 1 b]. **1818** SCOTT *Hrt. Midl.* xliii, I'm to be married the morn, and kirkit on Sunday. **1825** JAMIESON, A bride is said to be *kirkit*, the first time she goes to church after she has been married; on which occasion she is usually attended by some of the marriage-company... A family is also said to be *kirkit*, the first time they go to church after there has been a funeral in it. **1891** BARRIE *Little Minister* xliv, All he had to do was to re-marry him, and kirk him.

†**2.** To lay *up* or deposit in a church. (Cf. CHURCH *v.* 2.) *Obs.*

1606 BIRNIE *Kirk-Buriall* xi, The wel deseruing by the purse,.. was in vse to be Kirked vp in burial.

3. To send or drive (the ball) to the church, as a goal.

1834 T. BROWN in *Proc. Berw. Nat. Club* I. No. 2. 46 The person who succeeded in kirking or in milling—such are the phrases—the.. golden ball.

Hence **'kirking** *vbl. sb.* (also *attrib.*).

c **1470** HENRY *Wallace* XI. 352 It was bot till a kyrkyn fest. **1818** *Edinb. Mag.* Nov. 414 On Sunday comes the kirking. The bride and bridegroom, attended by their office-bearers, .. walk to the kirk. *Mod. Sc. saying*, 'A bride is a bride fra' her crying to her kirking' (i.e. from the proclamation of banns to her first attendance at church).

†**kirk-ale.** *Obs.* In 5 kirkehale, 6 kirkall. = CHURCH-ALE. (But in quot. 1470 (if not simply an error) app. used as = CHURCHING 1: cf. quots. 1568 s.v. CHURCH *v.* 1 b, 1297 s.v. CHURCH-GANG.)

c **1470** HARDING *Chron.* CXXII. iii, To light His Candill then,.. at his kirkehale and puryficacion. *c* **1570** *Durham Depos.* (Surtees) 243 This examinate being at a kirkall at the said Anne father's house.

†**kirked,** *a. Obs.* ? a dialectal variant of CROOKED (or perh. a scribal error for *kroked*).

c **1400** *Rom. Rose* 3137 His nose frounced fulle kirked stoode.

kirkemesse, obs. variant of KERMIS.

kirker ('kɜːkə(r)). *rare.* [f. KIRK *sb.* + -ER[1].] A member or adherent of the 'kirk', i.e. the Church of Scotland. Now *Obs.* exc. *colloq.* in comb., as ***Auld Kirker*** (an adherent of the 'auld kirk'), ***Free Kirker.***

1680 G. HICKES *Spirit of Popery* 5 Which is the Kirk, and Kirkers usual sence of free grace, according to the Assemblies larger and shorter Catechisms. **1716** M. DAVIES *Athen. Brit* II. 310 Twenty Episcopals.. to one Kirker of the Calvinistical Order. **1893** *Daily News* 10 June 5/8 'What aboot.. the ministers wha are na' auld Kirkers?' his companion,.. a Free Kirker, rejoined.

kirkereve, north. var. CHURCH-REEVE *Obs.*

kirk-garth. *north. dial.* Also 3 (*Orm.*) kirrkegærd. [f. KIRK *sb.* + GARTH, an enclosure: cf. Icel. *kirkju-garðr*, Da. *kirkegaard.* Cf. also CHURCH-GARTH and KIRK-YARD.] Northern English = Churchyard: formerly prevalent from Cumberland to Lincolnshire; now much restricted.

c **1200** ORMIN 15254 To birrʒenn ʒuw i kirrkegærd. *a* **1300** *Cursor M.* 27198 In kyrcgarth, chapell or kyrk. **1417** *Surtees Misc.* (1888) 11 Anent Al Halow Kyrk garth wall on the Pament. **1483** *Cath. Angl.* 204/1 Kyrkegarthe, *cimitorium.* **1508** *Will* in *N.W. Linc. Gloss.* s.v., My body to be beried in the kirkgarth of our lady of ffrothingham. **1708** T. WARD *Eng. Ref.* III. (1710) 18 Crosses In Kirk-Garths, and in Market places. **1785** HUTTON *Bran New Wark* 14 A covetous man trapes to th' kirk-garth on a sunday morning. **1839** *Cumbld. & Westmld. Dial.* 47 What they see i th Kirk-garth. [In *Swaledale Gloss.* 1873, *Cumbld. Gloss.* 1878.]

kirkify ('kɜːkɪfaɪ), *v. rare.* [f. as prec.: see -FY: cf. CHURCHIFY.] *trans.* To imbue with the principles of the 'kirk' or Church of Scotland; to make like a Scottish church.

1661 R. L'ESTRANGE *Relaps'd Apostate* 6 Your Kirkify'd Reformers;.. that made such Conscience of a Ceremony. **1854** HAWTHORNE *Eng. Note-bks.* II. 286 St. Giles's Cathedral,.. having been kirkified into three interior divisions by the Covenanters.

kirkin-head. *Arch.* [app. f. KIRK *sb.*] The end of a building in which the upper half of the gable is hipped off; the truncated gable and the triangular piece of roof above it; = JERKIN-HEAD, of which it is app. the original form.

1703 T. N. *City & C. Purchaser* 22 All Buildings, where there is either a Gable or a Kirkin-Head. **1727** BRADLEY *Fam. Dict.* s.v. *Barge-course.* **1851** *Dict. Archit.* I. 53 Any building where there was a gable or Kirkin-head.

†**'kirkist.** *nonce-wd.* [f. KIRK *sb.* + -IST.] An adherent of the 'kirk' or Scottish church.

1652 URQUHART *Jewel* Wks. (1834) 277 What hath been done by kirkists these last dozen of yeers.

'kirkland. *Sc.* and *north.* = CHURCH-LAND.

c **1450** HOLLAND *Howlat* 784 Thai ete of the corne in the kirkland. *c* **1500** *Rowlis Cursing* 31 in Laing *Anc. Poet. Scot.* 212 Kirkland hay, or gerss to a waill. **1633** *Sc. Acts Chas. I* (1817) V. 128 With all manssis gleibs kirklands.

kirkless, *a.* Sc. form of CHURCHLESS *a.*

1801 H. MACNEILL *Poet. Wks.* (1856) 171 After a Sunday's feast—or pascal, Wi' you, ye kirkless, canty rascal. **1895** *Westm. Gaz.* 8 Jan. 8/1 The kirkless ministers of his country.. will applaud him.

kirkman ('kɜːkmən). [Sc. and north. form of CHURCHMAN.]

1. An ecclesiastic; = CHURCHMAN 1. (In later use only *Sc.*)

c **1340** [see CHURCHMAN 1]. *c* **1375** *Sc. Leg. Saints* xl. (*Ninian*) 560 In quhat wyse þe kirkmen did þar seruice. **1440** in *Corr*, etc. *Priory Coldingham* (Surtees) 113 Baith temporal lords and kirkmen. *a* **1548** HALL *Chron., Hen. VIII*, 255 b, Their Kirkmen preached, that in Englande was neither Masse, nor any service of God. **1638** *Act Assembly* in *Coll. Conf.* II. 115 (Jam.) The civil places and powers of Kirkmen declared to be unlawful. **1733** NEAL *Hist. Purit.* II. 238 That part of it [the Act] which referred to the Apparel of Kirkmen. **1853** CADENHEAD *Bon-Accord* 188 (E.D.D.) Nane but kirkmen daur'd to preach.

2. A member or adherent of the 'kirk', i.e. the Church of Scotland: see CHURCHMAN 4.

1650 *Nicholas Papers* (Camden) 205 The Kirkmen and their faction adhering still very rigidly to their mad principles. **1660** R. COKE *Power & Subj.* 262 The English Presbyterians (who had most basely accepted a canting thing called the Covenant from the Kirkmen of Scotland). **1752** CARTE *Hist. Eng.* III. 425 A number of the most zealous kirkmen, meeting at Leonard's Craig near Edenburgh. **1893** *Dict. Nat. Biog.* XXXIII. 1002 Rothes had never been a fanatical puritan; he was a politician and a patriot rather than a kirkman.

kirk-master, -maister. *north. dial.*

1. In northern English, A churchwarden.

1429 *Test. Ebor.* (Surtees) I. 417 Item to the kyrkmasters a nobill. **1512** *Churchw. Acc. Wigtoft, Linc.* (Nichols 1797) 205 Ye cayrke maysters of Wygtoft. **1674-91** RAY *N.C. Words* 41 *Kyrkmaster*, Churchwarden. **1876** *Mid. Yorksh. Gloss.* s.v. *Kirk*, Kirkmaister.. often heard from old Mid-Yorkshire people.

†**2.** *Sc.* **a.** 'A deacon in the church, one who has the charge of ecclesiastical temporalities' (Jam.). **b.** The deacon of an incorporated trade: see DEACON 3. *Obs. rare.*

1505 in Pennecuik *Blue Blanket* (1756) 44 Compeired.. the Kirk-Master and Brether of the Surgeons and Barbaris. **1522** in *Charters of St. Giles, Edin.* (Bann.) 213-16 Kirk-maisters of the confrary and altare of the haly blude. **1572** *Sc. Acts Jas. VI* (1814) III. 76* Thair was not Kirkmaisteris or Deaconis appointit in the Parochinnis to ressaue the taxatioun appointit.

†**kirkomanetic,** *a. nonce-wd.* Labouring under 'kirkomania'; adhering fanatically to the 'Kirk'.

1652 URQUHART *Jewel* Wks. (1834) 211 New Palestine, as the Kirkomanetick Philarchaists would have it [Scotland] called.

kirk-scot: another form of CHURCH-SCOT, q.v.

kirk-session (kɜːk'sɛʃən). The lowest court in the Established Church of Scotland and other Presbyterian Churches, composed of the minister and elders of the parish or congregation.

(The Free Church having revived the office of *deacon*, has as its lowest court a Deacons' Court.)

1717 DE FOE *Mem. Ch. Scot.* (1844) 6 The Subordination of Judicatories is such, and the Proceedings so nicely accounted for by the Kirk-Sessions to the Presbyteries, by the Presbyteries to the Provincial Synods, and by the Synods to the General Assemblies, that there can no Mistake pass unobserved. **1806** *Gazetteer Scot.* (ed. 2) Introd. 19 The Kirk Session, composed of the minister, elders, and deacons of every parish, forms the lowest ecclesiastical court of Scotland. **1871** SIR H. MONCRIEFF *Pract. Free Ch. Scotl.* 7 The Pastor or Pastors of each Congregation, along with a suitable number of elders who are not pastors, constitute a governing body which is called the Kirk-session.

kirkset: see KIRSET.

†**'kirkship.** *nonce-wd.* [See -SHIP.] A humorous title for a church dignitary (? after *worship*).

1710 *Pol. Ballads* (1860) II. 95 To know what his Kirkship wou'd have em to do.

[†**kirk-shot:** known only in the ballad cited; taken as = Churchyard (but prob. a corruption of some kind).

a **1827** *Ballad, Weary Coble o' Cargill* x. (Motherwell *Minstrelsy* 232) And there they got the bonnie lad's corpse, In the kirk shot o bonnie Cargill.]

kirk-shot: see CHURCH-SCOT.

kirk-town. *Sc.* Also **kirk-ton.** The town, village, or hamlet in which the parish church is: = *church-town* (CHURCH *sb.* 18). **b.** A glebe.

1706 SEMPILL *Piper Kilbarchan* in *Chambers Pop. Hum. Scot. Poems* (1862) 24 Or who can for our kirk-town cause Stand us in stead? **1864** *Glasgow Herald* 16 May, The word Kirktoun.. applied to all collections of houses, not farm touns, which surrounded parish kirks. **1872** E. W. ROBERTSON *Hist. Ess.* 136 The ordinary amount of Kirktown or glebe assigned to the church.. was a half-davoch. *a* **1894** STEVENSON *Olalla* Wks. 1895 III. 313 The mountain village, which was, as we say in Scotland, the kirk-ton of that thinly peopled district.

†**'kirkward,** *sb. Hist.* = CHURCH-WARD *sb.* 1.

1883 I. G. SMITH & P. ONSLOW *Worcester* 31 The kirkward of St. Peter's peaceably handed over the keys.

'kirkward, *adv.* (*a.*) [See -WARD.] Towards the kirk or church; churchward.

18.. *Ballad* in Scott *Hrt. Midl.* xl, When six braw gentlemen Kirkward shall carry ye. **1832** A. CUNNINGHAM in *Blackw. Mag.* XXXI. 996 Much they talked upon their kirkward way.

kirk'yard. Now *Sc.* Also 4 **kyrk-yarde,** 4-5 **kirk(e)-ʒerd(e,** 5 **kyrkʒerd, kyrkeʒerde, kyrk-yharde,** 7- *Sc.* **kirkyaird.** [f. KIRK *sb.* + YARD.] Northern form of CHURCHYARD: now confined to Scotland: cf. KIRK-GARTH.

a **1300** *Cursor M.* 29349 In kyrk-yarde aght naman him deluen. [**1377** LANGL. *P. Pl.* B. XIII. 9 No corps in her kirkeʒerde ne in her kyrke was buryed. **14..** *Nominale* in Wr.-Wülcker 722/12 *Hoc semitorium*, a kyrkʒerd. *c* **1475** *Pict. Voc.* ibid. 803/5 *Hoc atrium*, a kyrkeʒerde.] *a* **1636** B. JONSON *Sad Sheph.* II. iii, Our dame Hecate Made it her gaing-night, over the Kirk-yard. **1816** SCOTT *Old Mort.* Introd., The Cameronian monuments, in the old kirkyard of Kirkchrist. **1896** *New-York Scot. American* Oct., The auld kirkyaird on the grey hillside.

kirle, obs. form of CURL *sb.*

1612 tr. *Benvenuto's Passenger* (N.), Artes to stiffen their kirles on the temples, and to adorne their foreheads.

Kirlian ('kɪəlɪən). The name of S. D. and V. K. *Kirlian*, 20th-cent. Russian electricians, used *attrib.* with reference to the process invented by them of directly recording corona discharges from the surfaces of objects on photographic material.

1970 OSTRANDER & SCHROEDER *Psi Psychic Discoveries behind Iron Curtain* xvi. 218 In the color Kirlian pictures of plant leaves we saw the same basic colors: blue and reddish-yellow. **1973** *Popular Photogr.* LXXII. 90 Examples of Kirlian photographs—that is, images obtained on film without camera or lens by direct recording of an electric charge transmitted by the given object, to which a high-frequency charge has been applied. **1974** *Sciences* Jan.-Feb. 19/2 Kirlian photographs may also offer a measure of interpersonal relations.

Kirman (kɪr'mɑːn, kə'mɑːn). Also **Karman, Kerman.** The name of a province and town in south-east Iran, used (freq. *attrib.*) to designate a carpet or rug made there, usu. having soft delicate colouring and naturalistic designs.

1876 O. B. ST. JOHN in F. J. Goldsmid *Eastern Persia* I. vi. 101 Not only flowers and trees, but birds, beasts, landscapes, and even human figures are found on the Karmán carpets. **1900** J. K. MUMFORD *Oriental Rugs* xi. 187 It has been customary, until very lately, among the rug dealers of the West and Constantinople as well, to attribute the Kirman rugs to Kermanshah. **1931** A. U. DILLEY *Oriental Rugs & Carpets* iv. 94 Of all the villages weaving Kerman rugs, Rawar only has general rug fame. **1953** A. C. EDWARDES *Persian Carpets* xiii. 208/2 The new styles were dictated by America, which is by far the largest consumer of Kermān carpets. **1953** R. GODDEN *Kingfishers catch Fire* xv. 184 It was a Kirman rug: a Kirman is the only Persian carpet that looks feminine. **1957** R. STOUT *If Death ever Slept* (1958) iii. 30 Through the reception room, across a Kirman twice as big as my room at home. **1967** S. REED *Oriental Rugs & Carpets* v. 69 By the turn of the century some very good Tabriz and Kirman pieces were being made. **1969** C. W. JACOBSEN *Check Points How to buy Oriental Rugs* vii. 132 Take the name Kirman, which is one of the highest priced and best of new rugs being woven today... Many people bought these as Kirmanshah (also spelled Kermanshah). **1970** *Canad. Antiques Collector* Dec. 22/2 On the floor is a fine pile pink Persian Kerman rug [etc.].

Kirmanshah (kɪmɑːn'ʃɑː, kə-). Also **Kermanshah.** The name of a city in west Iran, used confusedly (freq. *attrib.*) to designate a carpet made in Kirman, usu. one with white field and flowered medallion and borders. See prec. word.

The confusion with *Kirman* seems to have arisen because of the similarity of the two names and the great importance of Kirmanshah as a wool-trading town.

1900 J. K. MUMFORD *Oriental Rugs* xi. 188 In design, the best of the Kermanshahs affect the floral treatment. **1904** M. B. LANGTON *How to know Oriental Rugs* ii. 78 There are a few antiques in this country; but the modern Kirman or Kermanshah rug, made throughout the district, rivals the old. **1931** A. U. DILLEY *Oriental Rugs & Carpets* Pl. 20 (*caption*), Kerman, Southeast Persia (mistakenly called Kermanshah). *Ibid.* iv. 94 Some fifty years ago, large flower-strewn medallion patterns with graceful pendants and floriated corners were devised and applied to large carpets by weavers working for Tabriz rug-merchants who saw in the fine Kerman workmanship opportunity for commercial enterprise. These rugs and carpets were called

Kermanshah, to permanent confusion with the rug-weavings of the city of that name located miles to the west. **1969** C. W. JACOBSEN *Check Points How to buy Oriental Rugs* vii. 133 The Kirmanshah was never a correct name for these rugs because they were woven in and around Kirman, while the town of Kirmanshah was 1,000 miles to the west.

kirmess, -mish, variants of KERMIS.

†**kirmew.** *Obs.* [a. Ger. *kirrmeve*, f. *kirren* to coo, chirp, cry with a harsh sound + *meve* gull, MEW.] The common Tern.

It is doubtful whether the word has any standing in English except as occurring in quot. 1694 (transl. from German), which is also the source cited by Pennant, from whom subsequent writers get the name. Montagu (*Ornith. Dict.* 1802–33) gives also *kirman*, prob. an error.

1694 *Acc. Sev. Late Voy.* II. (1711) 82, I have heard the Kirmew and Kutyegehf cry. *Ibid.* 92 The Kirmew hath a thin sharp-pointed bill as red as blood... It is commonly called Kirmew from its Cry. **1766** PENNANT *Zool.* (1768) II. 428.

kirn (kɜːn, *Sc.* kɪrn), *sb.*[1] *Sc.* and *north. dial.* Also 4–6 **kirne,** 5–6 **kyrn(e**; *north. Eng.* 7 **kerne,** 7–9 **kern, kurn.** [Northern form of CHURN *sb.*: cf. ON. *kirna*, in same sense.]

1. A churn.

1338–9 *Acc. Rolls Durham* (Surtees) 311 In j kirne emp. pro eadem [dayeria], 5*d.* **1483** *Cath. Angl.* 204/1 (MS. A.) A kyrne, *cimba, fiscina.* **1562** *Wills & Inv. N.C.* (Surtees 1835) 207, j kirne with staffe xiiij[d]. **1681** *Inv.* in Hunter *Biggar & Ho. Fleming* vi. (1862) 62 Ane say, ane kerne and two four gallon trees. **1728** RAMSAY *Betty & Kate* vii, Sae may your kirn with fatness flow. **1785** BURNS *Addr. Deil* x. Countra wives.. May plunge an' plunge the kirn in vain. **1820** SCOTT *Monast.* xxxv, I see it is ill done to teach the cat the way to the kirn. **1825** BROCKETT, *Kern.* **1876** *Mid Yorksh. Gl.*, Kurn.

2. *fig.* 'Applied to a mire' in which the mud is churned up; 'a disgusting mixture'. 'The ground's a mere kirn.' (Jam.)

3. *Comb.*, as *kirn-milk, -staff*: see CHURN.

1549 *Compl. Scot.* vi. 43 Thai maid grit cheir of.. reyme, flot quhaye, grene cheis, kyrn mylk. **1674–91** RAY *N.C. Words, Kern-milk*, butter-milk. **1684** G. MERITON *Praise Ale* 160 (E.D.D.) Sheel kedge our kites with good kirne-milk and whig. **1724** RAMSAY *Evergreen, Wyfe of Auchtermuchty* xii, He tuke the kirnstaff be the shank. *a* **1774** FERGUSSON *Poems* (1807) 225 My kirn-staff now stands gizzened at the door. **1818** SCOTT *Hrt. Midl.* xxvii. *note*, He dealt in the whole-some commodity called kirn-milk.

kirn (kɜːn, *Sc.* kɪrn), *sb.*[2] *Sc.* and *north. dial.* Also 9 **kern, kurn, curn.** [Of uncertain etymology: see Note below.]

1. A feast or merry-making held on the completion of the harvest; a harvest-home or harvest-supper. (Thing and name are passing out of use.)

1777 [see KIRN-BABY]. **1786** BURNS *Twa Dogs* 124 As bleak-fac'd Hallowmass returns, They get the jovial, ranting kirns, When rural life, o' ev'ry station, Unite in common recreation. **1806** DOUGLAS *Poems* 143 (E.D.D.) Hame they gang to get the kirn. **1808** SCOTT *Marm.* IV. Introd. 101 Who envies now the shepherd's lot,.. His rustic kirn's loud revelry. **1883** *Longm. Mag.* Apr. 657 The oldest rustic festival here [in Lothian] is the harvest home, or 'kirn'.

2. The cutting of the last handful of corn (the kirn-cut) on the harvest-field. Chiefly in the phrases ***to win*** (***get***) ***the kirn***: to gain the distinction of cutting down the last armful of corn; to succeed in finishing the harvest; ***to cry*** or ***shout the kirn***: to cheer or shout in token of this. (Now *rare.*)

1808–18 JAMIESON, *Kirn*, the last handful of grain cut down on the harvest-field. **1821** *Blackw. Mag.* 400 (Jam.), I shall either gain a kiss from some fair lip for winning the kirn, or some shall have hot brows for it. **1836** J. M. WILSON *Tales Bord.* II. 209 (E.D.D.) An hour would be sufficient to terminate their harvest toils and win the kirn. **1866** HENDERSON *Folk-lore N. Counties* 66 When the sickle is laid down, and the last sheaf of golden corn set on end, it is said that they have 'got the kern'. [The words I have heard used in crying the kirn in Roxburghshire, *a* 1860, were 'The corn's shorn, the kirn's won, Kirnie, kirnie, coo-oo-oo!' the last word much prolonged. J.A.H.M.]

3. *attrib.* and *Comb.*, as ***kirn-bannock, -feast, -night***; **kirn-cut** = sense 2; **kirn-supper,** the harvest-home supper (see also *churn-supper*, s.v. CHURN *sb.* 5); **kirn-winning** = sense 2.

1824 MACTAGGART *Gallovid. Encycl.* (1876) 405 A piece.. of the *kirn-bannock. **1810** CROMEK *Rem. Nithsdale Song* 259 From the same pin depended the *kirn-cut of corn, curiously braided and adorned with ribbons. **1862** J. GRANT *Capt. of Guard* xlv, Above the mantelpiece hung the.. kirn-cuts of corn gaily ornamented with ribbons—the trophies of the last year's harvest home. **1846** *Drummond's Muckomachy* 32 (E.D.D.) At fairs, *kirn-feasts, and penny weddins. **1789** BURNS *Let. Lady Glencairn*, At gala-times, such as New-year's day, a christening, or the *kirn-night,.. my punch-bowl is brought from its dusty corner. **1777** *Kern Supper [see KIRN-BABY]. **1822** BEWICK *Mem.* 26 The man.. when he met me had been on his way to a 'kirn supper'. **1864** *Chambers' Bk. of Days* II. 379/2 In Scotland, under the name of the Kirn or Kirn-supper. **1819** in Anderson *Cumbld. Ball.* 65 To murry-neets, *kurn-winnins, Hannah ne'er went.

[*Note.* The instances of the word *kirn* or *kern* are quite recent, and leave us in the dark as to its earlier history. The popular notion often associates it with KIRN *sb.*[1], CHURN; and there are positive statements that a churnful of cream was a prominent item in the harvest-supper (J. Nicol *Poems* (1805) I. 154; Hone *Year-bk.* (1832) 10 Sept. 534/2; Haliburton *Puir Auld Sc.* (1887) 148–9). See also *churn-supper*, s.v. CHURN *sb.* 5. But this may be due only to popular etymology. If the word were old, it might in form represent an OE. **ȝecyrn* = OHG. *gikurni*, shortened *kurni, churni*, MHG. *kürne, kürn*, 'corn collectively or of all kinds' (see Grimm, s.v. *Korn* 1 d). But this hardly suits the sense, unless indeed **ȝecyrn* could have meant something like 'completion (of the reaping or ingathering of all the corn)'. (Prof. E. Sievers.)]

kirn (kɜːn, *Sc.* kɪrn), *v.* Also *dial.* **kern, kurn.** [Northern form of CHURN *v.*]

1. a. *trans.* and *absol.* To churn; to make butter by churning. **b.** *intr.* Of butter: To form by churning, to 'come'.

15.. *Wyfe of Auchtermuchty* v, Scho kyrnd the kyrne, and skwmd it clene. **1725** RAMSAY *Gent. Sheph.* II. iii, Tibby kirn'd, and there nae butter came. *a* **1774** FERGUSSON *Poems* 74 (Jam.) Nae mair the thrifty gudewife sees Her lasses kirn. **1801** in Anderson *Cumbld. Ball.* 19 For tou can kurn, and darn, and spin. **1856** HENDERSON *Pop. Rhymes* 56 (E.D.D.) The gudewife's butter wadna kirn.

2. *transf.* **a.** *trans.* To mix or stir by a process like that of churning cream; to keep turning *over, up*, etc. **b.** *intr.* To perform the act of stirring something; to puddle, etc.

1822 GALT *Sir A. Wylie* xxxiv. (E.D.D.) It would hae been mair to the purpose had ye been kirning drogs with the pistle and mortar in your ain shop. **1869** R. LEIGHTON *Scotch Wds.* 20 I've just been kirnin' through the Word o' God. **1892** N. DICKSON *Auld Min.* (1896) 106 Busy kirnin' among clay an' makin' bricks.

Hence **kirned** *ppl. a.*; **'kirning** *vbl. sb.*, churning: *attrib.* as ***kirning-day***; **kirning-rung** = *kirn-staff* (KIRN *sb.*[1] 3).

1790 A. WILSON *Pack* Poems 59 Gin ye please our John an' me, Ye'se get the kirnan rung To lick, this day. **1808** ELIZ. HAMILTON *Cottagers Glenburnie* (Jam.), The very first kirning after, her butter was burstet and gude for naething. **1824** MACTAGGART *Gallovid. Encycl.* (1876) 39 'Twas fed on new kirned butter-milk. **1899** CROCKETT *Kit Kennedy* 217 The morn.. is kirning-day.

'kirn-,baby. Also kern-. [f. KIRN *sb.*[2] + BABY *sb.* 2, 'doll, puppet'.] A rude semblance of a human figure made out of the last handful of corn cut on the harvest-field, and dressed as a female, which formerly played a part in the ceremonial of the kirn or harvest-home, and was afterwards often hung up on the farmer's kitchen wall until the next harvest, when its place was taken by a new one. Also called ***kirn-doll*** or ***-dolly, maiden*** or ***kirn-maiden, harvest-queen***, and, in books, after a mistaken suggestion of Brand (quot. 1777), ***corn-baby.***

In the most usual form, the cluster of ears formed the head of the figure, while part of the stalks were plaited into two arms, and the rest expanded as a body in skirts, the whole being decorated with ribbons or gaily dressed in doll's clothes.

1777 BRAND *Pop. Antiq.* xxxi. 307 *Kern Baby*.. the northern Word is plainly a Corruption of *Corn Baby* or *Image*, as is the *Kern* or *Churn* Supper of *Corn* Supper. **1787** GROSE *Prov. Gloss., Kern-baby*, an image dressed up with corn, carried before the reapers to their mell-supper, or harvest home. **1813** ELLIS *Brand's Antiq.* I. 422 *note*, An old woman.. informed me that, not half a century ago, they used every where [in Northumberland] to dress up something, similar to the figure above described, at the end of Harvest, which was called a Harvest Doll, or *Kern Baby.* **1826** in Hone *Every-day Bk.* II. 1166. **1846** RICHARDSON *Borderer's Table-Bk.* VII. 375 The corn-baby or kirn-dolly. **1866** W. HENDERSON *Folk Lore N. Counties* 66 When the sickle is laid down and the last sheaf set on end.. an image is at once hoisted on a pole.. crowned with wheat ears and dressed up in gay finery, a white frock and coloured ribbons being its conventional attire. The whole group [of reapers] circle round this harvest queen or Kernbaby, curtseying to her, and dancing and singing. **1868** ATKINSON *Cleveland Gloss., Kern baby*, an image, or possibly only a small sheaf of the newly cut corn, gaily dressed up and decorated with clothes, ribbons, flowers, &c.

kirnel, -ell, -elle, obs. forms of KERNEL.

kirombo (kɪ'rɒmbəʊ). [Malagasy.] The cuckoo-roller, *Leptosomus discolor*, a large grey or black and brown bird found only in Madagascar and the Comoro Islands.

1891 *Ibis* Apr. 224 The natives of the north-west of Madagascar give this bird the name of *Kiròmbo*. It has the curious habit of hovering in the air and uttering a very loud note, striking its wings against the body as it calls. **1915** J. SIBREE *Naturalist in Madagascar* x. 138 The *Vorondreo*, or Kiròmbo roller. **1964** A. L. THOMSON *New Dict. Birds* 172/1 Cuckoo-roller: *Leptosomus discolor*, sole member of the Leptosomatidae (Coraciiformes, suborder Coracii). This monotypic family is restricted to Madagascar and the nearby Comoro Islands; the bird is called 'Courol' in some works, and less frequently 'Kirombo'.

‖**kirpan** (kɪə'pɑːn). [ad. Panjabi and Hindi *kirpān*, f. Skr. *kṛpaṇa* sword.] The sword or dagger worn by Sikhs as a religious symbol.

1904 J. J. H. GORDON *Sikhs* iv. 41 Every true Sikh must always have five things with him, their names all commencing with the letter *k*—namely,.. *kard* (knife), and *kirpan* (sword). **1923** *Contemp. Rev.* Sept. 293 Guru Govind Singh.. prescribed for his Singhs five symbols, of which it is sufficient to note here.. the *kirpan*, a weapon which is sometimes a miniature carried in the hair, sometimes a dagger not more than a foot in length, sometimes a sword. **1952** J. MASTERS *Deceivers* v. 45 He whipped a twelve-inch dagger, the Sikh kirpan, from his belt. **1964** A. SWINSON *Six Minutes to Sunset* vi. 120 It is possible that many people, especially the Sikhs, were armed with their *kirpans* or short swords. **1969** H. R. F. KEATING *Inspector Ghote plays Joker* vii. 99 At his side there hung a kirpan, traditional knife of the Sikhs. **1971** *Daily Tel.* 11 June 3 (*caption*) Sant Mann Singh,.. a visiting Sikh religious leader who has agreed not to carry his kirpan, a sword, in public.

kirre, obs. f. QUARRY *sb.*[1] (hunting term).

‖**kirsch** (kɪrʃ). Also **kirsh.** [F. *kirsch*, abbrev. of KIRSCHWASSER.] = KIRSCHWASSER.

1869 *Daily News* 25 Aug., Distillers of the cherry-stone liquor, called kirsh. **1874** T. G. APPLETON in *Longfellow's Life* (1891) III. 229, I tried coffee and kirsch, and they had the good old taste.

Kirschner ('kɪəʃnə(r)). [Name of Aage *Kirschner* (fl. 1905), Da. chemist.] ***Kirschner value***, a number expressing the proportion of certain fatty acids (esp. butyric acid) in a fat (see quot. 1961).

1911 *Analyst* XXXVI. 337 The Kirschner value is practically a measure of the butyric acid content of the mixture. **1928** E. R. BOLTON *Oils, Fats & Fatty Foods* iv. 83 Although in general practice the Kirschner value is a measure of the amount of butter fat present, yet there are a few vegetable oils that give large Kirschner and Reichert-Meissl, and low Polenske values. **1961** *Methods for Chem. Analysis of Butter* (*B.S.I.*) 8 The Kirschner value is the number of millilitres of 0·1N aqueous alkali solution required to neutralize the water-soluble volatile fatty acids which form water-soluble silver salts distilled from 5g of the fat under the precise conditions specified in the method. **1973** D. PEARSON *Laboratory Techniques Food Analysis* vi. 156 Genuine butter fat gives Kirschner values from 20·5 to 26·4.

kirschsteinite ('kɪəʃstaɪnaɪt). *Min.* [f. the name of Egon *Kirschstein* (see quot. 1957) + -ITE[1].] Iron-monticellite, esp. as a naturally occurring mineral.

1957 SAHAMA & HYTÖNEN in *Mineral. Mag.* XXXI. 698 For this natural $CaFeSiO_4$ the name kirschsteinite is proposed, in honour of the German geologist, the late Dr. Egon Kirschstein, who died in the events of the World War I in East Africa. *Ibid.*, The analysis corresponds to the following molecular composition: $CaFeSiO_4$ 69·4 mol. %, $CaMnSiO_4$ 4·3, $CaMgSiO_4$ 22·6, excess Fe_2SiO_4 3·7. Accordingly, the mineral is to be called magnesian kirschsteinite. **1962** W. A. DEER et al. *Rock-Forming Min.* I. 1 The iron analogue of monticellite, kirschsteinite, $CaFeSiO_4$, is known from slags, but has not been reported from a natural occurrence, and a magnesium-rich kirschsteinite containing 69 per cent. $CaFeSiO_4$ is the most iron-rich mineral of the Fe_2SiO_4—$CaFeSiO_4$ series yet reported. **1966** *Amer. Mineralogist* LI. 1192 Mineralogical studies on the debris formed during the underground Gnome nuclear explosion in a salt horizon of the Salado formation near Carlsbad, New Mexico have shown that significant quantities of olivine and kirschsteinite are present in the water insoluble fraction.

‖**kirschwasser** ('kɪrʃvasər). Also **kirschen-.** [Ger. *kirsch(en)wasser*, f. *kirsche* cherry + *wasser* water.] An alcoholic spirit distilled in Germany and Switzerland from a fermented liquor obtained by crushing wild cherries.

1819 SCOTT *Leg. Montrose* ii, We had drunk.. about two mutchkins of *kirschenwasser.* **1826** DISRAELI *Viv. Grey* VIII. iv, A bottle of Kerchen Wasser, from the Black Forest. **1855** 'E. S. DELAMER' *Kitchen Garden* (1861) 148 The famous cordials known as kirschwasser and maraschino.

kirsen, -dom, obs. or dial. ff. CHRISTEN *v.*, CHRISTENDOM.

†**kirset**[1]. *Sc. Law. Obs.* Also **kerset, kirseth, kyrset(t.** [app. a. ON. *kyrrseta* or *kyrrsæti*, sitting in peace and quiet, freedom from disturbance.] Exemption from the payment of taxes, granted for one year to a new burgess (see quot.).

In some MSS. of the *Burgh Laws* the erroneous form *kirksett* is found: see Jamieson, s.v.

14.. *Burrow Lawes* c. 27 Quha sum evir be made new burges of a waste lande and he hafe na lande wythin þe burgh herberyt in þe fyrst ȝere he sall haf kyrset [*Latin text* kirseth] And efter þe fyrst ȝere he sall haf herberyt lande and byggyd. [**1609** SKENE *Reg. Maj.* 122 He may haue respit, or continuation for payment of his burrow mailes for ane zeare, quhilk is called hyrsett (*sic*).]

†**kirset**[2], **kyrsede, -ett(e,** obs. ff. CRESSET.

1459–60 *Acc. Rolls Durham* (Surtees) 88 Le Kirsettez in domo capitulari et Refectorio. *c* **1497** *Inventory* in *MS. Ashmole* 1519, lf. 141 b, In coquina: a chawfere, a brandlet, a kirset. **1505–6** *Acc. Rolls Durham* (Surtees) 104 De 11 petr. feodi [coquinæ] pro le kyrsett ad portam abbathie. **1569** *Inv.* in *Trans. Cumbld. & Westmld. Arch. Soc.* X. 34 On Kyrsede & ij trepetts price vs.

Kir-Shehr ('kɜːʃɪə(r)). Also **Kirshehir.** The name of a town in Central Turkey, used *attrib.* and *ellipt.* to designate the brightly coloured prayer rugs made there.

1900 J. K. MUMFORD *Oriental Rugs* x. 139 Border medallions,.. are found in Kir-Shehrs of old date. *Ibid.*, Some of the small Kir-Shehr mats have several particolored tufts at each end. **1931** A. U. DILLEY *Oriental Rugs & Carpets* vi. 165 Kir-Shehr.. prayer rugs [are distinguished] by central panels covered by 'flight of stairs roofs'. **1967** *Times* 21 Feb. 21/4 (Advt.), Several fine prayer rugs: *Ladik, Mudjur, Kirshehir*, [etc.]. **1971** K. WATSON tr. *Hubel's Bk. Carpets* 86 Cherry red and grass green are noticeable in the colour scheme of Kirshehirs.

Kirsine, -some, obs. corruptions of CHRISTIAN.

kirsp, variant of CRISP *sb.*

kirtan ('kɪətɑːn). Also **keertan, kirtana.** [Skr.] (See quots.)
1898 B. A. PINGLE *Indian Mus.* (ed. 2) vii. 313 The *Kirtana* or *Hari-kirtana* is a musical performance, vocal and instrumental, of a sacred character, the theme of which is always a moral... The *Kirtana* is a beautiful combination of *rhetoric, rhyme* and *rhythm.* **1960** KOESTLER *Lotus & Robot* I. i. 65 During Kirtans her body got stiff and benumbed. **1966** J. & R. GODDEN *Two under Indian Sun* iii. 82 Indian singing too was usually about the gods, kirtans or sacred poems that told these epics of Krishna, or Rama and his love Sita. **1967** SINGHA & MASSEY *Indian Dances* xv. 129 The poet Jayadeva, author of the *Gita Govinda* who composed numerous keertans or devotional songs, and whose wife expressed them through dance. **1970** *Listener* 24 Sept. 404/3 The Kirtan.. is the traditional song that seems to be always about spiritual love and pain. **1971** *Illustr. Weekly India* 18 Apr. 10/2 *Tamashas*..consisted of long-drawn recitations from mythology and legend, interspersed with *bhajans, keertans* and folk songs.

kirtle ('kɜːt(ə)l), *sb.*[1] Forms: α. 1 cyrtel, 3 cuer-, cuyrtel, 3-6 cur-, kur-, -tel(l(e, -til, -tyll; 4-5 cortel, -yl. β. 2 cer-, kier-, 2-5 kertel, (5 -tyl), 6 kertle, 6-7 -tell. γ. 3 cirtil, 3-8 kir-, kyr-, -tel, -til, etc., 5- kirtle, (6-8 kyrtle). [OE. *cyrtel* = ON. *kyrtill* tunic (Da. *kjortel* tunic, gown, Sw. *kjortel* skirt, petticoat):—**kurtil-*, app. a dim. of **kurt-* 'short', commonly regarded as an early adoption of L. *curtus.* The sense 'short coat', as opposed to 'long gown', would suit the ordinary meaning of the ON. word, but does not apply to the use in Eng.]

1. A man's tunic or coat, originally a garment reaching to the knees or lower, sometimes forming the only body-garment, but more usually worn with a shirt beneath and a cloak or mantle above.

In early instances freq. transl. L. *tunica.* As the common name for an article of male attire, *kirtle* seems to have gone out of use about or shortly after 1500; writers of the 16th and 17th c. use it chiefly in describing robes of state. It survived to some extent in dialects, applied to a short jacket or blouse (see quots. 1706 and 1828).

c **893** K. ÆLFRED *Oros.* I. i. §17 Se byrdesta sceall ȝyldan ..berenne kyrtel oððe yterenne. *c* **1000** ÆLFRIC *Hom.* I. 64 Nimað þis gold.. Bicȝað eow pællene cyrtlas. *c* **1160** *Hatton Gosp.* Matt. vii. 15 Warnieð eow wið leasan witeȝen, þe cumeð to eow on sceapene kertlen. *c* **1200** *Trin. Coll. Hom.* 139 He ches.. Stiue here to shurte and gret sac to curtle. *c* **1200** *Vices & Virtues* 127 Se þe benimð ðe þine kiertel, ȝif him þine mantel. *c* **1290** *Becket* 1155 in *S. Eng. Leg.* I. 139 Is Cuyrtel ȝwijt blaunket. *a* **1300** *Cursor M.* 4161 His kyrtil [*Gött. MS.* cirtil] sal we riue and rend. *c* **1386** CHAUCER *Miller's T.* 135 I-clad he was.. Al in a kirtel of a lyght waget. **1387** TREVISA *Higden* (Rolls) VII. 307 Þe curtelle of wolle and a pilche. *a* **1440** *Sir Eglam.* 1255 To onarme hym the knyght goys In cortyls, sorcatys and schorte clothys. **1494** FABYAN *Chron.* VII. ccxxxvii. 276 A man.. barefote, and in a whyte kyrtell. **1552** HULOET, Kyrtyll of a kynge worne vnder the mantyll of estate, *trabea.* **1577** HARRISON *England* II. v. (1877) I. 116 Giuing them [knights of the Garter] a kirtle, gowne, cloke, chaperon [etc.]. **1706** PHILLIPS, *Kirtle,* a kind of short Jacket. **1791** COWPER *Odyss.* XIII. 485 In such a kirtle as the eyes of all Shall loath to look on. **1828** *Craven Dial, Kytle,* a kirtle, or a short coat without laps or skirts. **1870** MORRIS *Earthly Par.* II. III. 341 A white-haired elder clad in kirtle red.

2. A woman's gown. **b.** A skirt or outer petticoat. (See quot. *a* 1825.)

App. in common use down to about 1650, and now, as an archaism, much more frequent than sense 1.

α. *c* **995** in Kemble *Cod. Dipl.* VI. 133 Hio becwið Æðelf[læde] Elhhelmmes dehter.. hyre twili brocenan cyrtel. *c* **1205** LAY. 4993 Heo nom hire on anne curtel [*v.r.* cuertel].. hire hem heo up i-tæh, hire cneon he was swiðe nehi. *c* **1330** R. BRUNNE *Chron.* (1810) 122 Scho ȝede out in hir smok.. Withouten kirtelle or kemse. **13..** *E.E. Allit. P.* A. 203 Her cortel.. With precios perlez al umbe-pyghte. *c* **1440** *Generydes* 4395 The quene dede on hir kirtill fayre and well. *c* **1485** *Digby Myst.* v. 165 Here entreth v. virgynes in white kertelys. **1546** J. HEYWOOD *Prov.* (1867) 23 Though ny be my kyrtell, yet nere is my smocke. *c* **1550** *Image Hypocr.* I. 417 in *Skelton's Wks.,* Your curtles be of silke With rochetes white as mylke. **1650** HOWELL *Giraffi's Rev. Naples* ii. (1664) 9 Ladies and gentlewomen were for-bidden likewise to go abroad with wide-hoop'd gowns or kirtles. **1742** SHENSTONE *Schoolmistr.* 65 A russet kirtle fenc'd the nipping air. *a* **1825** FORBY *Voc. E. Anglia, Kirtle,* an outer petticoat to protect the other garments from dust, &c. in riding... Scarcely, if ever, heard of now that pillions are so gone out of use. **1873** OUIDA *Pascarèl* I. 117 In her ruddy serge kirtle and her great Tuscan hat.

3. *fig.* A coat or covering of any kind; a coating of paint.
1398, 1582 [see CURTEL]. *c* **1420** *Pallad. on Husb.* I. 417 Thre kyrtils do theron, of marbul greyne; But first let on be drie, and then engre[y]ne A smaller cote aboue on that. **1878** GILDER *Poet & Master* 14 The gray rock had not made Of the vine its glistening kirtle.

4. *attrib.* and *Comb.*
1530 in Weaver *Wells Wills* (1890) 118 To by a kyrtilcloth for my mother. **1725** *Cock-laird* in *Orpheus Caledonius* (1829), I maun hae a silk hood, A kirtle-sark, wyliecoat, And a silk snood. *a* **1800** *Clerk's Twa Sons* in Child *Ballads* (1857) II. 67 Ben it came the Mayor's dauchters Wi' kirtle coat alone.

†**kirtle,** *sb.*[2] *Obs.* ? An error for *kintle,* QUINTAL.
1688 R. HOLME *Armoury* III. 106/2 Kirtle Flax is twelve heads in a bunch, and is about an hundred pounds in weight. **1726** *Dict. Rust.* (ed. 3), A *Kirtle* of Flax is the quantity of about 100 pounds Weight, containing 12 Heads in a Bunch.

kirtle ('kɜːt(ə)l), *v.* [f. KIRTLE *sb.*[1]]
trans. To cover or envelop as with a kirtle.
1888 A. S. WILSON *Lyric of Hopeless Love* lxviii, Dreams Kirtle thee in robes too fair For jealous Dawn to see thee wear. **1896** J. LUMSDEN *Poems* 198 Corn fields.. Kyrtle This God's acre like a queen.

kirtled ('kɜːt(ə)ld), *a.* [f. KIRTLE *sb.*[1] + -ED[2].] Clothed in a kirtle: often in parasynthetic comb.
1634 MILTON *Comus* 254 Amid'st the flowry-kirtl'd Naiades. **1812** BYRON *Ch. Har.* II. lviii, The wild Albanian kirtled to his knee. *a* **1850** ROSSETTI *Dante & Circ.* I. (1874) 141 A lady.. sweetly kirtled and enlac'd.

kirve (kɜːv), *v.* Also **kerve, curve.** [a. ON. *kyrfa* to carve:—**kurbjan*: see KERF.]
†**1.** To carve. Hence ***kirving-knife,*** carving-knife. *Obs. rare.*
1484-5 *Acc. Rolls Durham* (Surtees) 649 Pro emundacione de le kirvyngknyffez d'ni Prioris, 12*d.*

2. *Coal-mining.* To undercut a seam; to hole. Cf. KIRVING *vbl. sb.*
1827-1865 [implied in KIRVING *vbl. sb.*]. **1883** GRESLEY *Gloss. Coal Mining, Kirve,* to hole.
Hence †**kirver** (in 6 **kyrvour**), a carver. *Obs.*
1536-7 *Acc. Rolls Durham* (Surtees) 703 Sol. Thome Whythed, kyrvo^r^, 20*s.*

kirving, *vbl. sb.* [f. KIRVE *v.*] *Coal-mining*
a. The wedge-shaped excavation made with the pick at the bottom of a seam, previous to blasting or bringing down the coal. Cf. KIRVE *v.* 2.
1827 WILSON *Pitman's Pay* II. xxvii, What he gat was varry sma', Frae out the kirvens and the nickens. **1851** GREENWELL *Coal-trade Terms Northumb. & Durh.* 33 The coals obtained from the kirving are always small; and as the size of the kirving is pretty constant.. it follows that a greater per centage of small is made in working a thin than a thick seam of coal. **1865** JEVONS *Coal Quest.* (1866) 72 The waste of coal in the 'kirving' or cut made by the hewer.
b. *pl.* Coal dust or small pieces of coal produced during mining operations.
1956 [see GUMMING *vbl. sb.*[2] b].

kirwanite ('kɜːwənaɪt). *Min.* [Named after R. Kirwan, an Irish mineralogist (1733-1812): see -ITE[1].] A fibrous, green, chlorite-like mineral, found in the basalt of the North of Ireland.
1811 PINKERTON *Petral.* I. 561 Kirwanite. **1833** *Philos. Mag.* III. 85 Kirwanite—Found by Mr. P. Doran in the Greenstone and Porphyry of Mourne, and named by Dr. Thomson.

†**kis.** *Obs. rare*$^{-1}$. [a. Gr. κίς.] A weevil.
1658 ROWLAND *Moufet's Theat. Ins.* 1086 The English call the Wheat-worm Kis, Pope, Bowde, Weevil, and Wibil.

‖**kisaeng** ('kiːsaŋ, -ɛŋ). Also **gesang, ki-saing, kisang.** [Korean.] In Korea, a trained female entertainer, the Korean equivalent of the geisha girl.
1895 L. J. MILN *Quaint Korea* vi. 155 The Korean word for the class of women of whom I am writing is ki-saing; but they are generally called gesing. **1904** C. J. D. TAYLER *Koreans at Home* ix. 50 The favourite entertainment for those who can afford it is the dancing of 'gesang'. **1905** J. LONDON *Jacket* (1915) 212 Tell us more about the *kisang* and the curries. **1908** H. N. ALLEN *Things Korean* viii. 125 The best performances.. consist of dances by the class of public dancing girls or gesang. **1951** C. OSGOOD *Koreans & their Culture* xiv. 259 The kisaeng entertainments seem to have started as a court institution. **1953** D. PORTWAY *Korea* vi. 107 The Korean married woman is much too home-bound to be expected to sit down at a public dinner, and the kisaeng girl takes her place... The kisaeng girl is definitely not a prostitute, though probably the height of her ambition is to become the concubine of some wealthy man. **1973** *Guardian* 31 Jan. 4/6 In South Korea they [*sc.* Japanese tourists] are herded to mock 'kisaeng' parties designed to camouflage courtesans as trained 'kisaeng' (traditionally skilful, geisha-like entertainers).

kisan (kɪ'sɑːn). [Hindi *kisān,* f. Skr. *kṛṣāṇa* one who ploughs.] In India, a peasant, an agricultural worker.
1935 *Ann. Reg. 1934* 152 The Communist Party of India ..had through a *kisan* (peasant) organisation in the Punjab sought to make propagandist capital out of economic discontent. **1936** J. NEHRU *Autobiogr.* ix. 62 The Indian *kisans* have little staying power, little energy to resist for long. *Ibid.* x. 63 Agrarian troubles are frequently taking place in various parts of India.. and the *kisan* agitation in certain parts of Oudh in 1920 and 1921 was but one of them. **1959** M. BRECHER *Nehru* iii. 69 Jawaharlal's discovery of the *kisans* (peasants) spurred him to action on their behalf. *Ibid.* 70 His [*sc.* Nehru's] reputation as a friend of the *kisan* spread into the interior. **1969** *Hindu* (Madras) 28 July 9/8 Eleven Communist kisans were arrested yesterday by the Kilayur Police when they obstructed the ploughing with tractor of some fields in Kazhakkarai village. **1969** *Pioneer* (Lucknow) 13 Aug. 5/2 The whole legal system should be overhauled to make dispensation of justice speedy and cheap, specially to the poor kisans.

kish[1] (kɪʃ). Also 8 **kesh.** [a. Ir. *cis* (kiʃ), *ceis* (keʃ) basket, hamper: cf. KISHEN.] A large wickerwork basket, used in Ireland chiefly for carrying turf; sometimes mounted on a car.
1780 A. YOUNG *Tour Irel.* I. 61 A kish of turf burns 2 barrels of lime. **1802** EDGEWORTH *Irish Bulls* x. (1803) 180 An Irish boy.. saw a train of his companions leading their cars loaded with kishes of turf. **1841** S. C. HALL *Ireland* II. 125 *note,* He pointed to the potatoe Kish which was placed upon the table. **1842** S. LOVER *Handy Andy* xix. 166 The cars were in great variety.. some bore kishes in which a woman and some small children might be seen.
b. Used, like gabions, in building the piers of bridges, etc. (see quot.). Hence **kish-work.**
1776 G. SEMPLE *Building in Water* 59 Kesh-work, that is, a kind of large Baskets, made of the Boughs and Branches of Trees, about the size of four or five Feet Square; these they sink in rows, by throwing stones.. into them till they ground, and then filling them up. *Ibid.* 60 They.. so begin to build their Piers, banking the Kishes all round with other Stones and hard Stuff thrown in.

kish[2] (kɪʃ). [Etym. obscure. Cf. F. *chiasse,* in Normandy *quiasse, kiasse* scum of metals.] A form of impure graphite, which separates from certain kinds of iron in the process of smelting, floating on the top in the form of scales. Also, A dross on the surface of melted lead. Hence **'kishy** *a.* (see quot. 1825).
1812 SIR H. DAVY *Chem. Philos.* 391 There is a substance formed in iron foundries called *kish,* of a brilliant appearance, usually in thin scales, analogous to plates of polished steel. It consists chiefly of carbonaceous matter united to iron. **1825** J. NICHOLSON *Operat. Mechanic* 330 The appearance of this substance, called by the workmen *kish,*.. is so common an attendant on the production of the most highly carbonized iron, that the workmen have applied the term *kishy* to that peculiar sort of iron. **1881** RAYMOND *Mining Gloss., Kish,* the blast-furnacemen's name for the graphite-segregations seen in pig-iron and in the cinder of a furnace making a very gray iron.

‖**kishen** ('kɪʃən). *I. of Man.* Also **kischen, kishon.** [Manx *kishan* = Ir. *cisean,* dimin. of *cis,* KISH[1].] A measure containing eight quarts.
1825 *Pious Manx Peasant* in *Houlston Tracts* I. No. 17. 8 She.. brought him two fat hens, and.. a kishon of oats to feed them. **1890** HALL CAINE *Bondman* I. vii, The April rain would bring potatoes down to sixpence a kishen.

kishke ('kɪʃkə). Also **kishka, kishkeh, kishker.** [Yiddish.] **a.** Beef intestine casing stuffed with a sausage-like savoury filling. **b.** In *sing.* and *pl.* The guts. *slang.*
1936 MENCKEN *Amer. Lang.* (ed. 4) 217 In New York City the high density of Eastern Jews in the population has made almost every New Yorker familiar with a long list of Yiddish words *e.g.,*.. *kishkes, kittl,* [etc.]. **1951** L. W. LEONARD *Jewish Cookery* xiv. 190 Stuffed kishke may be roasted with chicken, duck, goose or turkey. **1959** B. KOPS *Hamlet of Stepney Green* I. 12 You sweat your *kishkers* out to give them a good education. **1964** *Amer. N. & Q.* Jan. 72/1 Ishka, pishka, Hit him in the *kishka.* **1967** G. SIMS *Last Best Friend* vi. 53 They had.. dined at Bloom's in Whitechapel High Street on beetroot bortsch and stuffed kishka. **1968** *Guardian* 8 Oct. 2/6 It is not every city where you go into a café and find yourself offered 'knishes, blintzes, kishka, [etc.]'. **1968** L. ROSTEN *Joys of Yiddish* 181, I laughed until my *kishkas* were sore. **1970** L. M. FEINSILVER *Taste of Yiddish* iii. 293 Gentiles are learning to enjoy and pronounce such typical dishes as *kishke* and *tsimmes.* **1972** *Listener* 16 Mar. 341/3 Kishkeh vaguely resembles a kosher haggis.. stuffed with a mixture of flour meal, grated onion and fat.

Kisii ('kɪsiː). [Name of a district on the east side of Lake Victoria, Kenya.] A Bantu people from Kisii; a member of this people. Also *attrib.* or as *adj.*
1905 C. ELIOT *E. Afr. Protectorate* vii. 131 The Kisii people are practically unknown to Europeans. *Ibid.,* Igizzi (the language of the Kisii) would appear from these vocabularies to have some resemblance to the Kikuyu tongue. **1934** N. K. STRANGE *Kenya To-Day* vi. 82 The ornamental bead belts.., and Kisii ware, various shaped vases and bowls made from soapstone.. are amongst the attractive curios to be bought throughout Kenya. **1939** J. G. PERISTIANY *Social Inst. Kipsigis* p. xxi, The traditional enemies of the Kipsigis are the Masai to the south and the Kisii and Luo to the west. **1963** *Times* 31 May 10/2 Mr. Sagini is a Kisii. **1971** *E. Afr. Standard* (Nairobi) 10 Apr. 7/4 Kisii farmer killed in fight after stock theft.

kiskadee (kɪskə'diː). Also **keskeedie, keskidee.** [Echoic, f. the call of the bird.] A tyrant flycatcher, *Pitangus sulphuratus,* found in Central and South America; also used for related birds of the family Tyrannidæ.
1891 *Timehri* V. 61 One of the most common of birds.. is a brown and yellow Tyrant-shrike called the keskeedie (*Pitangus sulphuratus*). *Ibid.* 88 The large kiskadee (*Pitangus sulphuratus*).. whose loud, harsh and fierce cry of kis-kis-kiskadee is to be heard at all times of the day. **1922** *Blackw. Mag.* July 16/1 Glorious clumps of bamboo with kiskadees clinging like yellow blossoms to the bending plumes. **1941** *Penguin New Writing* VI. 75 Some keskidees were singing in the mango tree. **1953** E. R. BLAKE *Birds Mexico* 347 While mainly insectivorous like their relatives, Kiskadees also commonly catch small fish. **1958** J. CAREW *Wild Coast* i. 7 Hector watched the birds and remembered.. a pair of kiskadees. **1964** A. L. THOMSON *New Dict. Birds* 316/1 Some larger species with shrike-like or terrestrial habits, such as the Kiskadee Flycatcher (or Great Kiskadee) *Pitangus sulphuratus*.. take lizards, frogs, mice, and small birds.

‖**kiskitomas** (-'tɒməs). Also **kiskatom, kisky-Thomas.** [Corruption of an Amer. Indian name.] ***kiskitomas nut***, a hickory nut.

1809 A. Ritson *Poetical Pict. Amer.* 161 Their nuts, black walnuts, persimins, Kiscatoma nuts, and Chinquapins. [**1810** F. A. Michaux *Histoire des arbres forestiers* I. 20 *Shell bark hickery* [*sic*]..nom le plus en usage dans tous les Etats-Unis... *Kiskythomas*, par les Hollandois du New-Jersey.] **1832** D. J. Browne *Sylva Americana* 184 The Dutch settlers ..near the city of New York, call it Kisky Thomas Nut. **1836** W. Dunlap *Mem. Water Drinker* (1837) I. 48 While the rustic jest, or the tale of..wars..mingle with the cracking of the kisskatomasses..and walnuts. **1850** *Literary World* 2 Nov. (Bartlett), Hickory, shell-bark, kiskitomas nut, Or whatsoever thou art called. **1858** Hogg *Veg. Kingd.* 691 The fruit of *Carya alba*, or Shell-bark Hickory, are called Kisky Thomas Nuts, and are also much esteemed in America. **1894** *Jrnl. Amer. Folk-Lore* VII. 98 *Carya alba*, kiskytom, Otsego Co., N.Y.

Kislev ('kɪslɛf, -ljuː). Also 4-7 **Casleu,** 6-7 **Chisleu,** 8- **Kislew.** [Heb.] The third month of the Jewish civil year and the ninth of the ecclesiastical year, corresponding to parts of November and December.

1382 Wyclif *Zech.* vii. 1 The word of the Lorde is maad to Zacharie, in the fourthe day of the nynthe monethe, that is Casleu [*later version* Caslew; **1535** Coverdale Casleu]. **1388** —— *Neh.* i. 1 It was doon in the monethe Casleu [**1535** Coverdale Chisleu], in the twentithe ȝeer. **1611** *Bible* 1 Macc. i. 54 The fifteenth day of the moneth Casleu. **1838, 1876** [see Hesvan]. **1880** *Encycl. Brit.* XIII. 421/2 Upon the great altar of burnt offering a small altar to Jupiter Capitolinus was erected, on which the first offering was made on 25th Kislev 168. **1904** *Jewish Encycl.* VII. 515 On the twenty-fifth of Kislew the *Hanukkah* festival.. commences. **1940** *Universal Jewish Encycl.* II. 632/2 If the day is subtracted, it is taken from the month of Kislev, and the year is termed *haserah.* **1962** D. Bridger *New Jewish Encycl.* 269 *Kislev*, the third month of the Jewish calendar, corresponding to November-December, and consisting of 30, and sometimes 29 days.

‖**kismet** ('kɪsmɛt, 'kɪzmɪt). Also **kismat, kismut.** [Turk. *kismet*, Pers. *qismat*, a. Arab. *qisma(t)* portion, lot, fate, f. *qasama* to divide.] Destiny, fate.

1849 E. B. Eastwick *Dry Leaves* 46 One day a man related to me a story of Kismat or destiny. **1865** Mrs. Gaskell in *Cornh. Mag.* Feb. 219 It's a pity when these old Saxon houses vanish off the land; but it is 'kismet' with the Hamleys. **1883** F. M. Crawford *Mr. Isaacs* i. 19 The stars or the fates..or whatever you like to term your kismet.

kiss (kɪs), *sb.* Forms: α. 1-4 cos, coss, 3-5 cosse, 4-6 kosse. β. 4 cuss, 5 cus, cusse, kus, 6 kusse. γ. 4-7 kisse, 5 kys, 5-6 kysse, 4, 7- kiss. [OE. *coss* = OFris. *kos*, OS. *cos*, *kus* (MDu. *cus, cuss*, Du. *kus*), OHG. *chus* (MHG. *kus, kos*, G. *kuss*), ON. *koss*:—OTeut. **kuss-oz.* ME. *cuss* (kʊs) was app. developed from *coss*, as it appears to have had (ʊ) not (Y), and occurs in texts which do not use *cusse* (*cüsse*) for the vb. The mod.Eng. form (like Da. *kys*, Sw. *kyss*) is from the vb.]

1. A touch or pressure given with the lips (see kiss *v.* 1), in token of affection, greeting, or reverence; a salute or caress given with the lips.

α. *c* **1000** Ælfric *Hom.* II. 32 Ic hine to minum cosse aræ̃rde. *c* **1000** *Ags. Gosp.* Luke xxii. 48 Mannes sunu þu mid cosse sylst. *a* **1100** *Ags. Voc.* in Wr.-Wülcker 309/8 *Osculum*, cos. *a* **1225** *Ancr. R.* 194 Wo wurðe his cos: vor hit is Judases cos þet he ou mide cusseð. **13..** *Gaw. & Gr. Knt.* 1300 He had craued a cosse, bi his courtaysye. **1382** Wyclif *Song. Sol.* i. 1 Kisse he me with the cos of his mowth. **1482** *Monk of Evesham* (Arb.) 25 He..with cossis and terys watryd the fete of the crosse. *a* **1553** Udall *Royster D.* i. iii. 24, I will not sticke for a kosse with such a man as you.

β. **1390** Gower *Conf.* II. 348 Yit wol he stele a cuss or tuo. *c* **1430** *Hymns Virgin* 12 Ful curteis was þi comeli cus [*rime* ihesus]. *c* **1440** *Partonope* *3236 Ther with she yaf hym a swete cus. *a* **1529** Skelton *P. Sparrow* 361 Many a prety kusse Had I of his swete musse.

γ. *c* **1340** *Cursor M.* 15779 (Gött.) Wid a kiss [*other MSS.* coss, cosse] has þu mannes sune vnto þi bandun broght. *Ibid.* 17198 (Gött.) Kisse of saghtling þu me bedis. *c* **1440** *Promp. Parv.* 277/1 Kys, or kus, *osculum, basium.* *c* **1489** Caxton *Blanchardyn* ix. 39 To haue a kysse or cusse of her mouth. **1526** *Pilgr. Perf.* (W. de W. 1531) 278 b, Kysse me lorde, with the kysse of thy mouth. **1599** Shaks. *Much Ado* ii. i. 322 Speake cosin, or..stop his mouth with a kisse, and let not him speake neither. **1667** Milton *P.L.* iv. 502 He.. press'd her Matron lip With kisses pure. **1796-7** Coleridge *To Sara* 4 Ah why refuse the blameless bliss? Can danger lurk within a kiss? **1833** Tennyson *Fatima* iii, He drew With one long kiss my whole soul thro' My lips. **1852** Hook *Ch. Dict.* (1871) 424 The kiss of peace..was one of the rites of the eucharistic service in the primitive church. **1871** R. Ellis *Catullus* vii. 1 Ask me, Lesbia, what the sum delightful Of thy kisses.

2. *fig.* A light touch or impact.

1588 Shaks. *L.L.L.* iv. iii. 26 So sweete a kisse the golden Sunne giues not, To those fresh morning drops vpon the Rose. **1821** Shelley *Epipsych.* 547 Where the pebble-paven shore, Under the quick, faint kisses of the sea Trembles and sparkles. **1850** Tennyson *In Mem.* cxvii, Every kiss of toothed wheels.

b. *Billiards*, etc. (See kiss *v.* 3 c.)

1836 T. Hook *G. Gurney* III. 154 'That is a cannon however'. 'Not a bit of it!..a kiss!' **1859** Crawley *Billiards* 95 All these canons are made by a kiss from the cushion. **1874** J. D. Heath *Croquet Player* 35 A proper laying of the balls will preclude the undesirable kiss.

3. Name for a small sweetmeat or piece of confectionery; a sugar-plum.

1825 Brockett, *Kisses*, small confections or sugar plums. Perhaps the same as Shakspeare's kissing-comfits. **1887** Stevenson in *Scribner's Mag.* I. 612/2 Munching a 'barley-sugar kiss'.

4. A fanciful term for a drop of sealing-wax accidentally let fall beside the seal.

1829 *Young Lady's Bk.* 337 No drops, or, as our country cousins designate them, kisses, will fall in the passage of the wax from the taper to..the seal. **1848** Thackeray *Van. Fair* xxvii, 'It's Peggy O'Dowd's fist', said George, laughing. 'I know it by the kisses on the seal'. **1850** Dickens *Detective Police Party* Wks. (Libr. ed.) VIII. 307, I observed that on the back of the letter there was what we call a kiss—a drop of wax by the side of the seal.

5. *pl.* A local name for the heartsease (*Viola tricolor*); cf. *kiss-me*, etc., in kiss-, kiss-me-quick 3.

1840 Spurdens *Suppl. Forby*, *Kisses*, the pansy; heart's-ease.

6. *attrib.* and *Comb.*, as ***kiss-giver, -thrower; kiss-worthy*** adj.; **kiss impression** *Printing* (see quot. 1960); **kissproof** *a.*, of lipstick, that will not smudge, come off, etc., if its wearer kisses or is kissed; also *fig.*; **kiss-wise** *adv.*, in the manner of a kiss.

1735 *Fanshaw's* tr. *Guarini's Pastor Fido* ii. i, She, that is The best kiss-giver, shall receive her mead. **1946** B. Dalgin *Advertising Production* 89 If a high-light dot carries little ink, only contact ('kiss impression', we call it) would be required. **1960** G. A. Glaister *Gloss. Bk.* 208 *Kiss impression*, one in which the ink is deposited on the paper by the lightest possible surface contact and is not impressed into it. This technique is required when printing on coated papers. **1962** F. T. Day *Introd. to Paper* ix. 98 The letterpress process employs various machines all of which operate on the same principle, that of bringing inked type surfaces together in a 'kiss impression' with the paper. **1967** Karch & Buber *Offset Processes* ix. 446 Long press runs with a single plate are possible because the offset plate does not touch the paper but contacts the blanket with a very light 'kiss' impression. **1967** V. Strauss *Printing Industry* vii. 448/2 The inking cylinder should be set for a 'kiss impression', a term indicating that the least pressure compatible with proper image transfer is to be used. **1934** Dylan Thomas *18 Poems* 26 Happy Cadaver's hunger as you take The kiss-proof world. **1937** M. Sharp *Nutmeg Tree* iii. 40 She exchanged her more subdued..lipstick for a new Kiss-proof in flamingo red. **1940** 'N. Shute' *Landfall* ii. 37 'You don't use lipstick.' 'That's all you know. They told me it was kissproof in the shop.' **1959** *Punch* 19 Aug. 39/2 Eight refills of genuine English kissproof lipstick, in the new, passionate tangerine shade. **1962** *New Scientist* 27 Sept. 686/3 Kissproof lipstick was among the most profitable inventions of the present century. **1974** V. Canning *Painted Tent* ix. 194 You can give me a kiss. It's all right—don't fret—the stuff's kiss-proof. **1860** T. L. Peacock *Gryll Gr.* 298 A most beautiful kiss-thrower. **1875** Lanier *Poems, Symphony* 291 Lips kiss-wise set. *a* **1586** Sidney *Astr. & Stella* lxxiii, Thy most kisse-worthy face.

b. Phr. ***the kiss of death*** [f. the association with the kiss of betrayal given to Jesus by Judas in the Garden of Gethsemane (Matthew xxvi. 48-50)], a seemingly kind or well-intentioned action, look, association, etc., which brings disastrous consequences; ***the kiss of life***, the mouth-to-mouth method of artificial respiration; also *attrib.* and *fig.*

1948 'N. Shute' *No Highway* iv. 113, I told you that he'd put the kiss of death on it. **1952** H. Waugh *Last seen Wearing* (1953) 141 I'm starting to take a liking to that guy. .. The kiss of death. **1960** *Times* 20 July 13/3 Military assistance from Rhodesia would be the kiss of death to Mr. Tshombe. **1960** *Guardian* 10 Dec. 5/1 Let us hope that the critics' approval does not, at the box-office, prove a kiss of death. **1970** *New Scientist* 27 Aug. 405/1 In some countries state participation is essential for a scientific programme, in others it often seems the kiss of death.

1961 *Daily Mail* 22 Sept. 1/7 Mrs. Alice Lowe..used the 'kiss-of-life' to save her 19-month-old nephew Geoffrey Ahmed at Oldham yesterday. **1962** *Guardian* 25 June 4/4 Two children..were given the 'kiss of life' artificial respiration treatment. **1964** *Ibid.* 21 Apr. 18/4 Here was Mr Houghton giving the debate the kiss of life, and Mr Boyd-Carpenter responding to treatment. **1969** P. Dickinson *Pride of Heroes* i. 28, I cut the rope..and lowered him to the floor to administer the kiss of life, a technique in which I have taken instruction. **1969** *Private Eye* 5 Dec. 17/2 Finding her six years old goldfish 'Bubbles' on the carpet beside its tank, a Nottinghamshire woman gave it the kiss of life. **1972** *Daily Tel.* 6 Jan. 15/6 Firemen rescued them from their first-floor flat..and tried to revive them on the footpath with the kiss of life and oxygen.

kiss (kɪs), *v.* Pa. t. and pple. **kissed (kist).** Forms: α. 1-2 **cyssan,** 2-5 **kyssen,** 3-6 **kysse,** (4 **kyse, kise,** 4-6 **kys, kis),** 4-7 **kisse,** 4- **kiss.** β. 2-6 **cusse,** 3-4 **kusse,** 4 **cus, kus** (*ü*); 4-6 **cus, kus, kuss,** 9 *dial.* **kuss.** γ. 3-5 **kesse,** 4 **kes.** δ. 1 **cossian;** 4 **cosse,** 6 **kos.** *Pa. t.* 1 **cyste,** 2-5 **kyste, kiste, custe, keste;** 4-6 **kyst,** etc.; 4- **kist;** 3-4 **cussede, cossede, kyssede,** 4-5 **-ide, -ed, -id;** 4- **kissed.** *Pa. pple.* 1 **cyssed,** 4-6 **(y)cussed, cossed, (i)cust, kest, kost,** etc.; 4- **kist, kissed.** [OE. *cyssan* (pa. t. *cyste*, pa. pple. *cyssed*) = OFris. *kessa*, OS. *kussian* (MDu. *cussen*, Du. *kussen*), OHG. *chussen, kussen* (MHG. and G. *küssen*), ON. *kyssa* (Sw. *kyssa*, Da. *kysse*):—OTeut. **kussjan*, f. **kuss-*: see prec. Both vb. and sb. are wanting in Gothic, which has, in the same sense, *kukjan* (cf. E.Fris. *kükken*). Of the ME. forms those in *y, i*, were orig. Midland and Northern; of those in *u*, the earlier, down to *c* 1400, had *ü* as regular southern ME. repr. of OE. *y*; the later (in *u* not *ü*) are to be compared with the form *kuss* of kiss *sb.*; those in *e* have partly *e* from *ü* as in Kentish; partly *e* as a broadening of *i*. The rare OE. *cossian* (pa. t. *cossode*), was a distinct formation, from the sb.; but the later examples (14-16th c.) of *coss, koss*, appear to be merely the ordinary vb. assimilated to the sb. in its vowel.]

1. a. *trans.* To press or touch with the lips (at the same time compressing and then separating them), in token of affection or greeting, or as an act of reverence; to salute or caress with the lips; to give a kiss to.

α. *c* **900** tr. *Bæda's Hist.* iii. iv. (1890) 166 He..ȝenom hine þa biȝ þære swiðran honda and cyste. *c* **1000** Ælfric *Gram.* xix. (Z.) 122 *Et osculor a te* and ic eom fram ðe cyssed. *c* **1000** *Ags. Gosp.* Matt. xxvi. 48 Swa hwæne swa ic cysse se hyt is. *Ibid.* 49 He cyste hyne. *c* **1250** *Gen. & Ex.* 2355 Euerilc he kiste, on ilc he gret. *a* **1300** *Cursor M.* 17649 (Cott.) He kist [*Gött.* kisced, *Trin.* cust, *Laud* kyst] þaim all. *c* **1375** *Sc. Leg. Saints* i. (*Petrus*) 111 þan kissit þai ilk oþer sammyne. *c* **1400** Maundev. iv. (Roxb.) 13 He schuld kisse hir mouthe and hafe no drede of hir. **1480** Caxton *Chron. Eng.* cxciv. 170 He fell doune..and thryes kist the grounde. **1589** Puttenham *Eng. Poesie* iii. xxiv. (Arb.) 292 With vs the wemen giue their mouth to be kissed, in other places their cheek, in many places their hand. **1660** F. Brooke tr. *Le Blanc's Trav.* 187 Where perceiving a Crosse, he kissed it with tears. **1721** Amherst *Terræ Fil.* No. 3 (1754) 12 He takes the oaths of allegiance and supremacy:..some have thought themselves sufficiently absolved from them by kissing their thumbs, instead of the book. **1847** Tennyson *Princ.* vi. 208 Kiss her; take her hand, she weeps. **1871** R. Ellis *Catullus* ix. 9 Kiss his flowery face, his eyes delightful.

β. *c* **1200** *Trin. Coll. Hom.* 145 Hie his fet..mid hire muðe custe. *a* **1225** *Ancr. R.* 102 Ure Louerd mid his cosse ne cusseð none soule þet lueð ei þing bute him. **1297** R. Glouc. (Rolls) 310 Brut hire clupte and kuste [*v.rr.* cussede, kyssyd]. *c* **1340** *Cursor M.* 5003 (Trin.) þei him cussed swiþe soone And dude her sackes to be vndone. **1362** Langl. *P. Pl.* A. Prol. 70 þe lewede Men..comen vp knelynge and cusseden his Bulle. **1387** Trevisa *Higden* (Rolls) III. 127 Oon þat hadde ycused [*v.rr.* y-cussed, kysshed, kisside] his douȝter in þe hiȝe weye. **1389** in *Eng. Gilds* (1870) 6 (St. Katherine, London) Euerich brother and suster..atte resceyuynge schule kusse euerich other. *c* **1450** *Cov. Myst.* (Shaks. Soc.) 88, I crye the mercy, Lord, and thin Erthe cus. *a* **1553** Udall *Royster D.* i. iii. (Arb.) 23 Ill chieue it dotyng foole, but it must be cust [*rime* must]. **1567** Drant *Horace, De arte poet.* B vj, Thou mightst..hugge, and busse, and cull, and cusse thy darling apishe fruite. **1825** Brockett, *Kuss*, to kiss.

γ. *c* **1200** *Vices & Virtues* 117 Rih(t)wisnesse and Sibsumnesse kesten hem to-gedere. *a* **1300** *Cursor M.* 24533, I kest him þan bath frunt and chek. *c* **1330** R. Brunne *Chron. Wace* (Rolls) 6804 þe Romayns þem keste, & wente þer weye. *c* **1375** *Sc. Leg. Saints* xviii. (*Egipciane*) 1050 Zozimas ran To kes hyre fete. *c* **1449** Pecock *Repr.* 270 Thei kessiden the feete of the ymage.

δ. *c* **1000** Ælfric *Hom.* I. 566 Heo ða mid micelre blisse hit awrehte, and wepende cossode. **1382** Wyclif *Gen.* xxvii. 27 He com nerre, and cossyde hym. **1555** Phaer *Æneid* i. 11 And swetely kost his doughter dere. [So **1584** Twyne].

b. *transf.* Of birds: To touch lightly with the bill by way of a caress.

1398 Trevisa *Barth. De P.R.* xii. vii. (MS. Bodl.) lf. 117 b/2 þe culuere is a lecherous bridde and kusseþ euerich oþer tofore ye tredinge. *a* **1529** Skelton *Sp. Parrot* 269 Now kus me, Parrot, kus me.

2. a. *intr.* or *absol.*: usually of two persons, in reciprocal sense.

a **1300** *Cursor M.* 9750 (Cott.) And dom and pes do samen kys. *c* **1330** R. Brunne *Chron.* (1810) 86 He said þan his avis, 'Kisse & be not wroþe'. At þe first þei kiste, as frendes felle to be. **1390** Gower *Conf.* II. 27 Therupon thei kisten bothe. **1470-85** Malory *Arthur* ii. vi, Whan they were mette they putte of her helmes and kyssed to gyders. **1604** E. G[rimstone] *D'Acosta's Hist. Indies* v. iv. 339 To make a certaine sound with their mouthes (like people that kissed). **1660** F. Brooke tr. *Le Blanc's Trav.* 156 Then kissing in sign of peace. **1710-11** Swift *Lett.* (1767) III. 89 Kiss and be friends, sirrah. **1847** Tennyson *Princ.* vi. 271 Kiss and be friends, like children being chid! **1850** —— *In Mem.* Concl., Farewell, we kiss, and they are gone.

b. *trans.* with cognate obj.; also, to express by kissing.

? **1830** Tennyson *Sea-Fairies* 34 We will kiss sweet kisses, and speak sweet words. **1864** —— *Aylmer's Field* 472 He pluck'd her dagger forth..Kissing his vows upon it like a knight. **1883** E. P. Roe in *Harper's Mag.* Dec. 51/2 Coming to kiss good-night?

3. *fig.* **a.** *trans.* To touch or impinge upon lightly, as if in affection or greeting.

a **1420** [see 6 b]. **1592** Shaks. *Ven. & Ad.* 872 As she runnes, the bushes in the way, Some catch her by the necke, some kisse her face. **1593** —— *Rich. II*, iii. iii. 191 You debase your Princely Knee, To make the base Earth prowd with kissing it. **1596** —— *Merch. V.* v. i. 2 When the sweet winde did gently kisse the trees. **1627** Feltham *Resolves* ii. [i.] i. (1628) 1 When a Rich Crowne ha's newly kiss'd the Temples of a gladded King. **1805** Scott *Last Minstr.* ii. xi, The moon-beam kissed the holy pane. **1820** Shelley *Love's Philos.* ii, See the mountains kiss high heaven..And the moonbeams kiss the sea. **1829** Hood *Eug. Aram* xxxvi, While gentle sleep The urchin's eyelids kiss'd.

b. *intr.* (in reciprocal sense).

1592 Shaks. *Rom. & Jul.* ii. vi. 11 Like fire and powder; Which as they kisse consume. **1818** Shelley *Woodm. & Night.* 54 Where high branches kiss. **1847** Emerson *Poems, Hafiz* Wks. (Bohn) I. 478 Let us make our glasses kiss. **1870** Tennyson *Window* 24 Rose, rose and clematis, Trail and twine and clasp and kiss.

c. *spec.* in *Bowls, Billiards*, etc., said of a ball touching another ball lightly, esp. after it has struck it once, as in a 'cannon' at billiards.

Const. *trans.* of the one ball, or (in causal sense) of the player; or *intr.* (in reciprocal sense) of the two balls.

1579 GOSSON *Sch. Abuse* (Arb.) 60 At Bowles euery one craues to kisse the maister. **1611** SHAKS. *Cymb.* II. i. 2 When I kist the Iacke vpon an vp-cast, to be hit away. **1873** BENNETT & CAVENDISH *Billiards* 181 If played a true half ball, the red and white will kiss and spoil the cannon. **1874** J. D. HEATH *Croquet Player* 35 The roll of pressure of the mallett must not send the rear ball so as to catch or 'kiss' the front one. **1894** *Cornh. Mag.* Mar. 275 The balls kissed and glided off gently at the exact angle required. **1897** *Daily Chron.* 16 Feb. 5/7 Roberts made a pretty cannon off the red, kissing the white out of balk.

4. *trans.* with *adv.*, *prep.*, or *compl.* To put, get, or bring by kissing: as *to kiss away* = to remove, put away, or lose by kissing. (*lit.* and *fig.*)

1606 SHAKS. *Ant. & Cl.* III. x. 7 We haue kist away Kingdomes, and Prouinces. **1820** SHELLEY *Sensitive Plant* II. iv, The morn kissed the sleep from her eyes. **1832** TENNYSON *Miller's Dau.* xix, Dews, that would have fall'n in tears, I kiss'd away. **1842** —— *The Day-dream* L'Envoi iii, That I might kiss those eyes awake! **1856** MRS. BROWNING *Aur. Leigh* I. 52 Kissing full sense into empty words.

†**5.** *trans.* To cause to kiss, fraternize, or associate. *Obs.*

1562 A. SCOTT *New Year Gift Q. Mary* 127 Sic Christianis to kis wᵗ Chauceris kuikis God gife þe grace.

6. Phrases.

a. *to kiss the book*, i.e. the Bible, New Testament, or Gospels, in taking an oath (cf. Book *sb.* 4 a). **b.** *to kiss the cup*, to take a sip of liquor; to drink. **c.** *to kiss the dust*, to be overthrown, humiliated, ruined, or slain; to yield abject submission. **d.** *to kiss the ground*, (*a*) to prostrate oneself on the ground in token of homage; (*b*) *fig.* to be overthrown or brought low. **e.** *to kiss the hand* (*hands*) of a sovereign or superior, as a ceremonial greeting or leave-taking, or on appointment to an office of state under the sovereign; formerly, in complimentary speech or writing, merely = to pay one's respects, to salute or bid farewell. **f.** *to kiss the hare's foot*: see HARE *sb.* 2. **g.** *to kiss* (*the*) *pax*: see PAX. **h.** *to kiss the post*, to be shut out in consequence of arriving too late. **i.** *to kiss the rod*, to accept chastisement or correction submissively. †**j.** *to kiss the stocks*, to be confined in the stocks: so †*to kiss the clink, the counter* (see CLINK *sb.*², COUNTER *sb.*³ 7). **k.** *to kiss and be friends, to kiss and make up*: to become reconciled; also as a substantival phr. **l.** *to kiss* (a person's) *arse, behind, bum*: to behave obsequiously towards (a person). As *imp.*, esp. in phr. *kiss my arse*: a vulgar rejoinder, stronger than 'go to hell'. **m.** *to kiss and tell*: to recount one's sexual exploits. **n.** *to kiss better* (or *well*): to comfort (a sick or injured person, esp. a child) by kissing him, esp. by kissing the sore or injured part of the body; also *fig.* **o.** *to kiss goodbye*: to bid farewell with a kiss; freq. used *fig.* and ironically. **p.** *to kiss off slang*, (*a*) *trans.* to dismiss, get rid of, kill (see also quot. 1935²); (*b*) *intr.* to go away, die.

a. 1523 FITZHERB. *Surv.* 20 b, I shall true constable be.. so helpe me god and my holydome, and kysse the boke. **1610** SHAKS. *Temp.* II. ii. 145 Come, sweare to that: kisse the Booke. **1765** BLACKSTONE *Comm.* I. vi. (1809) 235 After this the king or queen.. shall say, 'The things which I have here before promised I will perform and keep: so help me God': and then shall kiss the book. **1899** BESANT *Orange Girl* II. xii, After kissing the Testament.. he turned an unblushing front to the Prosecutor.

b. *a* **1420** HOCCLEVE *De Reg. Princ.* 3815 More is.. honurable, a man compleyne of thrist, Than dronken be, whan he þe cuppe haþ kist. **1579** GOSSON *Sch. Abuse* (Arb.) 25 Kissing the cupp too often. **1623** COCKERAM *Delibate*, to sippe, or kisse the cup. **1808** SCOTT *Marm.* v. xii, The bride kissed the goblet; the knight took it up, He quaffed off the wine, he threw down the cup.

c. 1835 I. TAYLOR *Spir. Despot.* x. 410 To kiss the dust before monstrous superstitions. **1867** TROLLOPE *Chron. Barset* II. lvi. 129 She had yielded, and had kissed the dust.

d. 1589 *Pasquil's Ret.* B, Ouerthrow the state, and make the Emperiall crowne of her Maiestye kisse the ground. **1601** R. JOHNSON *Kingd. & Commw.* (1603) 149 In the Church he kisseth the grounde with his forehead. **1782** COWPER *Boadicea* 19 Soon her pride shall kiss the ground. **1841** LANE *Arab. Nts.* I. 86 He went again to the King, and kissed the ground before him.

e. *c* **1575** *Diurn. Occurr.* (Bannatyne Club) 332 The castell men kust thair hand with schutting of small artailyerie. **1593** SHAKS. *Rich. II*, III. iii. 104 Thy thrice-noble Cousin, Harry Bullingbrooke, doth humbly kisse thy hand. **1654** SIR E. NICHOLAS in *N. Papers* (Camden) II. 94 My sonne will kiss your hands in a letter of his owne by the next post. **1670** LADY MARY BERTIE in *12th Rep. Hist. MSS. Comm.* App. v. 21 The Dutchesse.. presented mee to kisse the Queene's hand. **1680** LADY CHAWORTH *ibid.* 55 Mr. Vice-chamberlaine.. kisses your hands and begs your commands if any into France sudainly. **1710** *Lond. Gaz.* No. 4722/2 He had this Day the Honour of kissing Her Majesty's Hand. **1768** in *Priv. Lett. Ld. Malmesbury* I. 159, I had intended to set off, as soon as I could kiss hands. **1809** G. ROSE *Diaries* (1860) II. 434 The Marquis could not kiss hands for the Seals. **1854** CDL. WISEMAN *Fabiola* II. xxx. 325 Fulvius.. kissed the emperor's hand and slowly retired. **1955** H. NICOLSON *Diary* 6 Apr. (1968) 281 Anthony [Eden] drives to the Palace and kisses hands on his appointment as Prime Minister. **1963** *Times* 31 Jan. 14/2 Mr. F. J. Blakeney was received in audience by The Queen this morning and kissed hands upon his appointment as Her Majesty's Ambassador Extraordinary and Plenipotentiary for the Commonwealth of Australia at Bonn. **1974** *Guardian* 7 Mar. 26/4 Mr Foot.. started work to settle the miners [*sic*] dispute even before kissing hands with the Queen.

h. *c* **1515** BARCLAY *Egloges* ii. (1570) B iv/2 Thou shalt lose thy meat and kisse the post. **1600** HEYWOOD *1st Pt. Edw. IV*, Wks. 1874 IV. 47 Make haste thou art best, for feare thou kiss the post. **1681** W. ROBERTSON *Phraseol. Gen.* (1693) 475 You must kiss the post, or hares foot, *Sero venère bubulci*.

i. *a* **1586** SIDNEY *Arcadia* II. (1867) 190 Yet he durst not but kiss his rod and gladly make much of his entertainment. **1628** SHIRLEY *Witty Fair One* I. iii, Come, I'll be a good child, and kiss the rod. **1774** MAD. D'ARBLAY *Early Diary* (1889) I. 271 If you will so far favour me, I will gladly kiss the rod. **1800** I. MILNER in *Life* xii. (1842) 209 When the fits of illness come, I do not, I believe, properly kiss the rod.

j. 1575 *Gamm. Gurton* v. i. in Hazl. *Dodsley* III. 235 Well worthy.. to kisse the stockes. **1588** J. UDALL *Diotrephes* (Arb.) 22, I will make thee kiss the Clinke for this geare. **1620** ROWLANDS *Night Raven* (1872) 11 You kisse the Counter sirra. **1626** *Letter* (N.), Some constables, for refusing to distrain have kissed the Counter.

k. *a* **1654** J. SELDEN *Table-Talk* (1689) 36 The People and the Prince kist and were Friends, and so things were quiet for a while. **1657** W. DENTON *Let.* 5 Feb. in M. M. Verney *Mem.* (1894) III. ix. 301 Go, kisse and be friends, which is the advice of Wᵐ. D. **1834** G. CORNISH *Let.* 8 Feb. in G. Battiscombe *John Keble* (1963) x. 191 After knocking each other down half-a-dozen times, kiss and be friends. **1942** BERREY & VAN DEN BARK *Amer. Thes. Slang* §334/3 *Become reconciled*; *make up*.., kiss and make up. **1958** *Listener* 2 Oct. 508/1 The party to which I had invited myself was a sort of Kiss-and-make-up. **1969** M. PUGH *Last Place Left* xviii. 128 Play the argument bit again.. and then play the kiss-and-make-up bit.

l. 1705 in *N. & Q.* (1971) Feb. 46/1 You can father it.. just as you did another man's philosophical essay upon the wind .. when you made bold with several pages from the learned Dr. Bohun, without saying so much to the Dr. for his assistance as kiss my a-se. **1749** FIELDING *Tom Jones* I. VI. ix. 288 The Wit.. lies in desiring another to kiss your A— for having just before threatened to kick his. **1934** H. MILLER *Tropic of Cancer* (1948) 207 If it weren't that I had learned how to kiss the boss's ass, I would have been fired. **1937** 'G. ORWELL' *Road to Wigan Pier* x. 196 You 'get on'.. by.. kissing the bums of verminous little lions. **1938** L. MACNEICE *Earth Compels* 34 Let us thank God for valour in abstraction For those who go their own way, will not kiss The arse of law and order. **1956** B. HOLIDAY *Lady sings Blues* (1973) vi. 60 You've got to kiss everybody's behind to get ten minutes to do eight sides in. *Ibid.* vii. 66, I threw the money at him and told him to kiss my ass and tell Miss Waters to do the same. **1963** *Amer. Speech* XXXVIII. 169 To curry favor with a professor... There are three occurrences of *kiss ass*. **1972** *Fairbanks* (Alaska) *Daily News-Miner* 3 Nov. 1/5 McGovern had told an airport antagonist to 'kiss my a..'. The candidate's national political director ..joked that the remark had been rather natural for a Democratic nominee. 'After all,' Mankiewicz said, 'he can't say kiss my elephant.'

m. 1695 CONGREVE *Love for Love* II. 30 Oh fie Miss, you must not kiss and tell. **1846** *Swell's Night Guide* 88 Let those who wish to know her qualifications as *une coucheuse*, try her; for we will not, on all occasions, *kiss* and *tell*. **1921** G. B. SHAW *Let.* 30 Dec. in *B. Shaw & Mrs. Campbell* (1952) 235 A gentleman does not kiss and tell.

n. 1808 A. TAYLOR *Original Poems for Infant Minds* (1814) 72 Who ran to help me when I fell, And would.. kiss the place to make it well? My Mother. **1929** E. BOWEN *Last September* xvi. 207 She kept.. feeling the bump: David must 'kiss it better' for her. **1966** *New Society* 23 June 19/1 Mothers.. welcome the opportunity of being able to 'kiss their baby better'. They find it easier to have the sick child at home. **1972** *Guardian* 6 May 9/1 I've got this old pain back. 'You must go to the doctor's,' Maggie said, when she'd failed to kiss it better.

o. 1935 C. DAY LEWIS *Time to Dance* 33 On January 8, 1920, their curveting wheels kissed England goodbye. **1944** 'N. SHUTE' *Pastoral* ix. 209 I'll tell Proctor he can kiss his truck good-bye for the rest of the day. **1959** *Listener* 8 Jan. 50/1 It would be exaggerating the trend to say that the Chinese are almost ready to kiss the Soviet experts goodbye. **1970** V. GIELGUD *Candle-Holders* v. 45 If she chooses one of the Eltham team for a partner, poor George can kiss the trophy goodbye.

p. 1935 *Amer. Speech* X. 22/1 *To throw* (*someone*) *down*... Modern *to kiss* (*someone*) *off* (usually restricted in use to a person of the opposite sex). **1935** A. J. POLLOCK *Underworld Speaks* 68/1 *Kissed off*, defrauded of share of loot or plunder. **1945** L. SHELLY *Jive Talk Dict.* 28/1 *Kiss off*, to die. **1946** 'J. EVANS' *Halo in Blood* xi. 134 I'm a private eye and I've got a customer who wants to know who kissed off Marlin.. and why. **1948** —— *Halo for Satan* (1949) vi. 83 The man who ..had kissed off all raps except.. the one.. for income tax evasion. **1967** D. SKIRROW *I was following this Girl* xxxvi. 219 'Kiss off,' he said... 'I told you, the girl's not here.' **1970** C. MAJOR *Dict. Afro-Amer. Slang* 73 *Kiss-off*,.. to die. **1973** M. & G. GORDON *Informant* xviii. 74 The same FBI agents.. getting tough. Well, kiss them off. **1973** W. MCCARTHY *Detail* iii. 216 'I thought you had stopped smoking.' 'Kiss off, I just started again.'

7. Used in various collocations to denote the comparative ease of an action, etc.; as in (*as easy as*) *kiss my* (or *your*, etc.) *hand*, *finger*, etc.

1891 [see THUMB *sb.* 5 i]. **1909** P. WEBLING *Story of Virginia Perfect* xxv. 249 It isn't so easy to make respectable friends, and so Miss Malet will find out, though she finds it as easy as kiss-your-'and to drop them! **1924** KIPLING *Debits & Credits* (1926) 167 The 'ole Somme front washed out as clean as kiss-me-'and! **1926** F. M. FORD *Man could stand Up* I. ii. 21 The prospect had seemed as near—as near as kiss your finger! **1949** J. SYMONS *Bland Beginning* 187 He wanted us to do a little job for him. It was as easy as kiss your hand. **1961** *Sunday Express* 12 Feb. 9/4 The cars have to be insured and that's as easy as kiss your hand. **1968** *Punch* 4 Sept. 330/3 The furs.. dropped down like kiss-your-arm into net provided. **1973** V. CANNING *Flight of Grey Goose* v. 92 You might be on to a bit of all right here. Yes... Sweet and easy as kiss your hand.

Hence **kissed** (kɪst, *poet.* 'kɪsɪd), *ppl. a.*

c **1440** *Promp. Parv.* 277/1 Kyssed, *osculatus, basiatus.* **1591** SPENSER *M. Hubberd* 730 He.. unto all doth yeeld due curtesie; But not with kissed hand belowe the knee. **1868** D. COOK *Dr. Muspratt's Patients*, etc., *Milly Lance* ii, It was hard to say which was the more.. confused, the kisser or the kissed.

kiss- In *Comb.*, forming *sbs.* and *adjs.* [*Kiss* is the imperative or stem of the vb.] †**kiss-cheeks** *a.*, kissing or lightly touching the cheeks; †**kiss-cloud** *a.*, so high as to 'kiss' or touch the clouds, cloud-kissing; **kiss-cow** *a.*, that kisses the cow for the sake of the milk, that stoops to indignities for a consideration; **kiss-curl**, a small flat curl worn on the forehead, in front of the ear, or at the nape of the neck; **kiss-me**, local name for the wild heartsease; also, for London Pride, Herb Robert, and Spur Valerian (*Centranthus ruber*) (H. Friend *Devonsh. Plant Names* 1882); **kiss-me-at** (or **behind**)**-the-**(**garden-**)**gate**, the cultivated heartsease, also London Pride; **kiss-me-ere-I-rise**, heartsease; **kiss-me-twice-before-I-rise**, Love-in-a-mist, *Nigella damascena*: **kiss-my-loof** (*Sc.*), a person given to compliment (cf. KISS *v.* 6 e); **kiss-sky** *a.*, so high as to 'kiss' or touch the sky. See also KISS-IN-THE-RING, KISS-ME-QUICK.

a **1586** SIDNEY *Arcadia* (1622) 85 In rowes of *Kisse-cheeks teares they raine. **1605** SYLVESTER *Du Bartas* II. iii. III *Law* 234 Driving forth to *kisse-cloud Sina's foot His fleecy Flock. **1840** *New Monthly Mag.* LVIII. 498 If we are ..to allow that the hope of living renowned in story is a sufficient motive for all sorts of despised labours.. we have no such *kiss-cow tastes. **1856** *Punch* 29 Nov. 219/1 Those pastry-cook's girl's ornaments called *kiss-curls. **1867** H. SPICER *Bound to Please* II. 15 Bob Jessamy.. was nursing a kiss curl, though it hung limperer than what it usually did do. **1930** *Daily Express* 8 Sept. 3/6 Any kind of curls from Nell Gwynn ringlets to kiss curls. **1966** *Punch* 21 Dec. 933/3 'It's the little touches,' he murmurs.., faintly disordering his kisscurl before pretending to be laid low by a heart attack. **1968** J. IRONSIDE *Fashion Alphabet* 194 Although a kiss curl is usually regarded as being on the cheek, like a 'confidante', sometimes it can hang in the middle of the forehead. **1974** *Guardian* 27 Mar. 12/6 Haley.. came on looking much the same as ever, the kiss curl immaculately in place. **1877** *N.W. Linc. Gloss.*, **Kiss-me*, the wild heart's-ease. **1787** WITHERING *Brit. Plants* (1796) II. 262 Viola tricolor.. Heart's-ease.. *Kiss me at the garden gate. *a* **1825** FORBY *Voc. E. Anglia*, *Kiss-me-at-the-garden-gate*. **1884** BLACK *Jud. Shaks.* vii, Did you never hear it called 'Kiss-me-at-the-gate'? **1597** GERARDE *Herbal* App., **Kisse me ere I rise* is Pansies. **1664** R. TURNER *Botanol.* 223 [Nigella] is also called.. of some, *Kiss me twice before I rise. **1894** CROCKETT *Raiders* 97 [The smuggler shouted] 'such a set of *kiss-my loofs, you king's men!' **1603** FAIRFAX *Eclogues* iv, Cypress with his *kiss-sky tops.

kissable ('kɪsəb(ə)l), *a.* [f. KISS *v.* + -ABLE.] Capable of or adapted for being kissed; such as to invite kissing.

1815 SOUTHEY *Lett.* (1856) III. 3 Love from all to all, and kisses as many as you please to give to the kissable part of the family. **1871** M. COLLINS *Mrq. & Merch.* II. ii. 34 Her.. quiet kissable mouth. **1891** R. KIPLING *Light that failed* viii, Maisie looked more than usually kissable.

Hence **kissa'bility**; **'kissably** *adv.*

1884 G. ALLEN *Philistia* I. ii. 51 [Her lips] suggested to a critical eye the distinct notion of kissability. **1888** J. C. JEAFFRESON *Lady Hamilton & Ld. Nelson* I. vi. 86 The lips that curled so kissably.

kissage ('kɪsɪdʒ). [f. KISS *v.* + -AGE.] Kissing.

1886 KIPLING *Departmental Ditties* (ed. 2) 1 Ere they hewed the Sphinx's visage Favouritism governed kissage Even as it does in this age. **1898** G. B. SHAW *Let.* 5 Jan. in *Ellen Terry & Shaw* (1931) 287 The best thing for the knee is kissage; for the heart, careful wrapping round by the arms of a rather tall man, with, if possible, a red beard. **1960** F. FRANKFURTER *Felix Frankfurter Reminisces* iii. 28 This system, the objectivity of the marking, and the other considerations—no kissage by favors has always been the slogan there—creates an atmosphere and habits of objectivity and disinterestedness.. and a zest for being very good at this business which is law.

kissar ('kɪsə(r)). [ad. colloq. Arab. *kīsār*.] (See quot. 1964.) Also *attrib.*

1864 C. ENGEL *Music Most Anc. Nations* ii. 41 A kissar from Abyssinia.. is so far different from the common Nubian kissar, that its body is square, without sounding-holes. *Ibid.* iv. 158 The songs with the kissar accompaniment.. are called by the Nubians ghouna. **1941** J. PULVER tr. *Panum's Stringed Instruments Middle Ages* 12 Engel.. points to the striking likeness existing between the type of lyre depicted here and the lyre which, under the name of *Kissar*, is still used by several North African peoples. **1964** S. MARCUSE *Mus. Instruments* 291/1 *Kissar* (Gk. *kithara*), bowl lyre of E. Africa, a survival of the ancient Gk. lyra, still found in Ethiopia, Sudan, and Uganda. The body is shallow, of wood, covered with a sheepskin membrane laced to the back of the body.

kissee (kɪ'siː). [f. KISS *v.* + -EE.] One who is kissed; the receiver of a kiss.

1827 LYTTON *Pelham* I, This Hebe, Mr. Gordon greeted with a loving kiss which the kissee resented. **1887** *Athenæum* 1 Jan. 39/2 The shy *espièglerie* of the kissee and the innocent grace and audacity of the kisser.

‖**kissel** ('kɪsəl, ki'sjɛl). Also **keessel**. [ad. Russ. *kiséľ*.] A sweet dish made from fruit juice mixed with sugar and water, which is boiled and thickened with potato or cornflour.

1924 A. GAGARINE *Russ. Cook Bk.* x. 191 When eaten hot, the keessel should be thick as honey; when cold, like custard. **1943** E. M. ALMEDINGEN *Frossia* vii. 266 A hut odorous of freshly baked rye loaves, singed chicken feathers, and cranberry jelly, '*kissel*', and pickled cucumbers lying in a wooden bowl. **1952** M. MCCARTHY *Groves of Academe* (1953) iii. 34 The small presents she was in the habit of bringing them—a dish of Russian kissel with a white napkin over it. **1969** *Guardian* 15 Aug. 7/4 *Blackberry kissel*... Blend the cornflour with a little cold water, and with the brandy, stir into the blackberry puree. **1971** *Times* 9 Aug. 5/8 Moscow housewives are buying up huge amounts of berries just now—mostly blackcurrants, redcurrants and cranberries—to preserve them as jam or make a thin jelly (*kissel*).

kisser ('kɪsə(r)). [f. KISS *v.* + -ER[1].] **1.** One who kisses; the giver of a kiss.

1537 LATIMER *Serm. bef. Convoc.* D j b, Some brought forth..pedaries for pilgrimes, some oscularies, for kyssers. **1552** HULOET, Kysser, *basiator, osculator.* *a* **1625** FLETCHER *Love's Cure* II. i, A kisser of men, in drunkenness, and a betrayer in sobriety. **1788** LD. AUCKLAND *Diary* in *Corr.* (1861) II. 88 Everybody kissed everybody's hands..there were 335 kissers, and eight that were kissed. **1832** L. HUNT *Poems* 169 Kissers of flow'rs, lords of the golden bowl.

2. The mouth; the face. orig. *Boxing slang.*

1860 *Chambers's Jrnl.* XIII. 348/1 His mouth is his 'potato-trap'..or 'kisser'. **1892** P. H. EMERSON *Son of Fens* iv. 43 'Oh,' he say, and dabbed the wet mittens across my kisser kind of smart. **1927** W. E. COLLINSON *Contemp. Eng.* 27 In speaking of parts of the body we might use..the boxer's term claret-jug or conk, but we did not..use 'I'll hit you on the kisser (*mouth*)'. **1938** D. RUNYON *Furthermore* v. 81 He is a tall skinny guy with a long, sad, mean-looking kisser, and a mournful voice. **1953** R. CHANDLER *Let.* 15 Mar. in *R. Chandler Speaking* (1966) 28 Chandler..consumed three double gimlets and fell flat on his kisser. **1973** J. WAINWRIGHT *High-class Kill* 156 Open that sweet little, lying little, kisser of yours, and start saying something that makes sense.

Kissi ('kɪsɪ), *sb.* and *a.* [Native name.] **A.** *sb.* An agricultural people inhabiting the regions of Guinea, Sierra Leone, and Liberia near the headwaters of the Niger; one of this people; also, their language. **B.** *adj.* Of or pertaining to the Kissi.

1884 *Encycl. Brit.* XVII. 319/1 *Felup Group*,..Kissi. **1916** [see KONO[2]]. **1949** E. A. NIDA *Morphol.* (ed. 2) v. 107 In Kissi, a language of French Guinea,..the distinction between monosyllabic and polysyllabic verbs is pertinent. **1957** M. BANTON *W. Afr. City* ii. 36 The Army had..recruited a high proportion of its soldiers among the Koranko, Kono, and Kissi tribes in the farthest corners of the Protectorate. *Ibid.* vii. 122 The Kissi, who speak a separate language similar to that of the Bulom but now much influenced by Mandinka, live far inland in the high ground where the French, British, and Liberian frontiers meet. **1970** *Western Folklore* XXIX. 241 Among some of the Liberian Kissi of the frontier regions the musical bow accompanies tribal initiation rites in the forest, being utilized in place of the wooden drum.

kissing ('kɪsɪŋ), *vbl. sb.* [f. KISS *v.* + -ING[1].]

1. a. The action of the verb KISS.

a **1300** *Floriz & Bl.* 513 Here kessinge ileste amile And þat hem þuȝte litel while. *a* **1310** in Wright *Lyric P.* xxv. 70 Thin heved doun boweth to suete cussinge. *c* **1400** *Destr. Troy* 2931 Acoyntyng hom with kissyng & clippyng in Armes. **1526** *Pilgr. Perf.* (W. de W. 1531) 284 b, Goostly embracynges, clepynges, kyssynges. **1697** VANBRUGH *Relapse* v. ii, Kissing goes by Favour; he likes you best. *a* **1714** BURNET *Hist. Ref.* (1820) III. 101 So many bowings, crossings, and kissings of the altar. **1860** PUSEY *Min. Proph.* 82 Kissing in the East was a token of Divine honour, whether to an idol or to God.

b. Phr. (*when*) *the kissing had* (or *has*) *to stop*: (when) the 'honeymoon' period finished (or finishes); (when) one is forced to recognize harsh realities.

1855 BROWNING *Toccata of Galuppi's* xiv, in *Men & Women* I. 61 What of soul was left, I wonder, when the kissing had to stop? **1960** C. FITZGIBBON (*title*) When the kissing had to stop. **1965** *Guardian* 20 Aug. 12/3 In the past 15 years more than 190,000 adult Jamaicans have come to settle in this country... Now the kissing has to stop. **1973** *Times* 28 Dec. 8/3 If left wing extremists continue to exploit ..grievances..we should not have to wait long for the emergence of extremists of the right... It is then a few short steps to the place where the kissing has to stop.

2. *attrib.* and *Comb.*, as ***kissing scene, -stuff***; **kissing-ball, -bough, -bunch, -bush,** a Christmas wreath or ball of evergreens, freq. arranged with fruit and ribbons, which is hung from the ceiling and under which a kiss may be taken; † **kissing cause** (app.) = next; † **kissing-comfit,** a perfumed comfit for sweetening the breath; **kissing dance** = CUSHION-DANCE; **kissing-gate,** a small gate swinging in a U- or V-shaped enclosure, so as to allow only one person to pass at a time; † **kissing-strings** *sb. pl.*, a woman's bonnet- or cap-strings tied under the chin with the ends hanging loose; **kissing time,** the time to kiss, freq. used as a joc. reply to children who ask the time.

1970 *Canad. Antiques Collector* Dec. 10/1 A *kissing ball, consisting of evergreen, wrapped round a cluster of apples, provides the 'mistletoe'. **1956** B. CHUTE *Green Willow* viii. 91 In some houses..*kissing-boughs hung over doorways. **1969** E. WILKINS *Rose-Garden Game* viii. 191 The old English Christmas globe, called a kissing-bough, which was made up of three interlocking hoops of greenery, hung from the ceiling and lit up with candles. **1857** T. WRIGHT *Dict. Obsolete & Provincial English* II. 614/2 *Kissing-bunch, a bush of evergreens sometimes substituted for mistletoe at Christmas. **1913** D. H. LAWRENCE *Sons & Lovers* vi. 116 It [*sc.* the kitchen] was small and curious to her, with its glittering kissing-bunch. **1859** C. W. WILSON *Mapping the Frontier* (1970) i. 77 It will be a hard matter if we cannot get something wherewith to drink success to the '*kissing bush'. **1879-81** G. F. JACKSON *Shropshire Word-Bk.* 237 *Kissing-bush*, a bunch of evergreens or mistletoe garnished with ribands and fruit, which is hung in the kitchen, or hall, at Christmas-tide. **1620** *Swetnam Arraigned* (1880) 12 Their very breath Is sophisticated with Amber-pellets, and *kissing causes. **1598** SHAKS. *Merry W.* v. v. 22 Let it..haile *kissing-Comfits, and snow Eringoes. **1660** R. MAY *Accompl. Cook* (1665) 271 To make Muskedines, called Rising Comfits or Kissing Comfits. **1899** *Daily News* 14 Sept. 7/1 There was the famous *kissing dance, 'Joan Saunderson'. **1875** PARISH *Sussex Gloss.*, *Cuckoo Gate*,..called in Hampshire a *kissing-gate. **1886** ELWORTHY *W. Som. Word-bk.*, *Kissing-gate*..It is only made to open far enough for one person to pass at a time. **1896** *Westm. Gaz.* 7 Nov. 7/1 The disappearance of the last of the kissing-gates on Parliament Hill. *a* **1735** ARBUTHNOT *John Bull* III. Misc. Wks. 1751 II. 89 The *kissing-Scene being at an end. **1705** *London Ladies Dressing-room* (N.), Behind her back the streamers fly, And *kissing-strings hang dangling by. **1818** SCOTT *Hrt. Midl.* xlv, The old-fashioned terms of manteaus, sacques, kissing-strings, and so forth, would convey but little information even to the milliners of the present day. **1690** CROWNE *Eng. Frier* III. 30 Fy Sir: you are a Priest, you have no *kissing-stuff about you. **1875** W. ALEXANDER *Sk. Life among my Ain Folk* v. ii. 245 When the leading fiddler pushes his fourth finger far up his first string..this is '*kissing time'; and, after an attempt more or less successful on the part of each male dancer to kiss his partner's cheek, at it they go! **1916** F. NORTON (*song-title*) Any time is kissing time. **1922** JOYCE *Ulysses* 354 Edy asked her the time and Miss Cissy..said it was half past kissing time, time to kiss again. **1935** T. S. ELIOT *Murder in Cath.* i. 25 If you will remember me, my Lord, at your prayers, I'll remember you at kissing-time below the stairs. **1947** W. DE LA MARE *Coll. Stories for Children* 165 Nobody ever wasted *any* time (except kissing-time). **1959** I. & P. OPIE *Lore & Lang. Schoolch.* xii. 247 It is kissing time after four o'clock. If the girls trip you up they say you have got to kiss them after four o'clock.

kissing, *ppl. a.* [f. as prec. + -ING[2].] **a.** That kisses: see the verb.

1590 SHAKS. *Mids. N.* III. ii. 140 Thy lips, those kissing cherries. **1784** COWPER *Let. to J. Newton* 29 Mar., A most loving, kissing, kind-hearted gentleman. **1864** W. CORY *Lett. & Jrnls.* (1897) 132 In the wood we met just one kissing shower.

b. *Comb.* **kissing bug** *U.S.*, a blood-sucking bug of the family Reduviidæ; **kissing cousin,** a relative or friend with whom one is on close enough terms to greet with a kiss; also *transf.*; **kissing-crust** (*colloq.*), the soft part of the crust of a loaf where it has touched another in baking; 'also the under-crust in a pudding or pie' (Farmer *Slang*); **kissing gourami,** a small Malaysian freshwater fish, *Helostoma temmineki*, often kept in aquaria; **kissing kind** *a.*, kind or friendly enough to kiss, on affectionate terms; **kissing trap** *slang*, the mouth.

1899 *Pop. Sci. Monthly* Nov. 33 Several persons suffering from swollen faces visited the Emergency Hospital in Washington and complained that they had been bitten by some insect while asleep... Thus began the 'kissing bug' scare. **1904** *N.Y. Even. Post* 4 Aug. 1 The doctors were unable to decide whether he had been bitten by a mosquito or a kissing bug. **1932** METCALF & FLINT *Fund. Insect Life* viii. 222 Family Reduviidæ. The Assassin or Kissing Bugs. —This is a very large family of mostly flattened, oval bugs. .. The assassin bugs catch small insects and suck their blood as food. Some species, when handled, inflict painful bites on man. **1973** L. E. CHADWICK tr. *Linsenmaier's Insects of World* 120/1 The bite of many reduviids is very painful, even to man; in warm countries certain species even enter homes on occasion at night and suck the blood of people. In North America this may be done by the black 'kissing bug' (*Melanolestes picipes*). About 0·6 inch long, this bug prefers to bite the face, especially in the region of the mouth. **1974** A. DILLARD *Pilgrim at Tinker Creek* xiii. 232 The cone-nose bug, or kissing bug, bites the lips of sleeping people, sucking blood and injecting an excruciating toxin. **1708** W. KING *Cookery* 191 (R.) These brought him kissing-crusts. **1822** LAMB *Elia* Ser. I. *Praise Chimneysweepers*, How he would recommend this slice of white bread, or that piece of kissing-crust. **1842** BARHAM *Ingol. Leg.*, *Nell Cook*, A mouldy piece of kissing-crust as from a Warden-pie. **1951** in Wentworth & Flexner *Dict. Amer. Slang* (1960) 306/2 You guys talk like kissing cousins. **1961** *John o' London's* 20 Apr. 436/3 Marianne Spottiswoode, who is also a kissing cousin of the publishing Spottiswoodes. **1961** *Economist* 18 Nov. 676/2 The relationship will be more on the order of 'kissing cousins'—the experience gained will be valuable for later and more serious efforts. **1970** *Guardian* 31 Aug. 7/4 We resemble the Dutch more than we resemble the people of any other country—we are truly kissing cousins. **1973** *Publishers Weekly* 25 June 33/2 (Advt.), From cream pies to their kissing cousins, soufflés. **1935** W. T. INNES *Exotic Aquarium Fishes* 360 *Helostoma temmineki*... Popular name, Kissing Gourami. **1952** H. R. AXELROD *Tropical Fish* iii. 59 The Kissing Gourami [is]..so named for the unusual shape of its mouth when eating or sucking debris from the sides of the tank. **1962** D. W. TUCKER tr. *Sterba's Freshwater Fishes of World* 794 There is an unpigmented variety of the Kissing Gourami which is a uniform dull pink. **1852** R. S. SURTEES *Sponge's Sp. Tour* (1893) 153 Our friends..seemed more inclined to fraternize. Not that they were as yet kissing kind. **1886** *Pall Mall G.* 16 Dec. 3/1 Russia and Germany are once more kissing kind. **1854** 'C. BEDE' *Further Adventures Verdant Green* iv. 31 To one gentleman he would pleasantly observe..in the still more elegant imagery of the Ring, ..'How about the kissing-trap?' **1887** G. D. ATKIN *House Scraps* 54 The 'off-side' of his 'kissing-trap' Displays an ugly mark! **1942** BERREY & VAN DEN BARK *Amer. Thes. Slang* §121/66 *Mouth*,..kissing trap, loud-speaker, maw, [etc.].

Hence **'kissingly** *adv.*

1836 E. HOWARD *R. Reefer* xxxix, The breeze came so freshly and kissingly on my cheek. **1892** *Pall Mall Mag.* 7 Sept., She pouted her lips kissingly.

kiss-in-the-ring. An open-air game played by young people of both sexes, who stand in a ring with hands joined, except one who runs round outside the ring and touches (or drops a handkerchief behind) one of the opposite sex, who thereupon leaves the ring and runs after the first, kissing him or her when caught.

1801 J. STRUTT *Sports & Pastimes* IV. iv. 285 A boy must touch a girl, and a girl a boy, and when either of them be caught they go into the middle of the ring and salute each other; hence is derived the name of *kiss in the ring.* **1825** HONE *Every-day Bk.* I. 691 There were several parties playing at 'Kiss in the ring'. **1862** *Guardian* 23 Apr. 386/2 Kiss-in-the-ring once so popular at Sydenham was decidedly at a discount. **1899** *Westm. Gaz.* 10 Aug. 8/2 A peculiar custom on Hampstead Heath for the week following Bank Holiday is the playing of kiss-in-the-ring on a large scale on a special part of the West Heath. **1925** W. DE LA MARE *Broomsticks* 26 There were quantities of things to eat and lots to see, and Kiss-in-the-Ring. **1936** 'R. CROMPTON' *Sweet William* vii. 171 The games were to be Kiss in the Ring, Postman's Knock, Turn the Trencher,.. and others of similar kind. **1957** J. MASTERS *Far, Far the Mountain Peak* i. 5 Why don't I suggest a game of ring-a-ring-a-roses or kiss-in-the-ring? **1969** I. & P. OPIE *Children's Games* vi. 201 Throughout the nineteenth century 'Kiss in the Ring' was a favourite game at Christmas time and midsummer.

kissless ('kɪslɪs), *a.* [f. KISS *sb.* + -LESS.] Without a kiss, unkissed.

1708 *Brit. Apollo* No. 48. 3/2 Poor Lovesick, kissless Spark. **1892** *Temple Bar Mag.* Oct. 158 He had been tucked in, kissless because unrepentant.

kiss-me-quick. [See KISS-.]

1. A small bonnet standing far back on the head, formerly fashionable. (Also *attrib.*)

1852 G. W. BUNGAY *Crayon Sk.* (1854) 372 She wears..a Kossuth hat instead of a 'kiss-me-quick'. **1855** HALIBURTON *Nat. & Hum. Nat.* I. 287 She has a new bonnet on... It has a horrid name, it is called a kiss-me-quick. **1886** BARING-GOULD *Court Royal* ii, This Dolly Varden with panniers..and a kiss-me-quick bonnet.

2. A ringlet in front of the ear. (Also *attrib.*)

1893 Q. [COUCH] *Delectable Duchy* 16 Her hair..had..been..twisted in front of either ear, into that particular ringlet locally called a kiss-me-quick.

3. Local name for several plants, also called *kiss-me* (see KISS-). So ***kiss-me-quick-and-go***, Southernwood (*Artemisia Abrotanum*).

1882 H. FRIEND *Devon. Plant N.*, Kiss-me, Kiss-me-love, or Kiss-me-quick, (1) *Saxifraga umbrosa*... (2) *Geranium Robertianum*... (3)..*Centranthus ruber*. *Ibid.*, Kiss-me-quick-and-go, *Artemisia Abrotanum*. Doubtless in reference to the other common names of Boy's Love, Maiden's Ruin. **1886** ELWORTHY *W. Som. Word-bk.*, *Kiss-me-quick* the pansy or heart's-ease. The wild variety.

4. ***kiss-me-quick hat***: a hat bearing the words 'kiss me quick' (or some other, usu. jocular, phrase) on the front.

1963 *Guardian* 12 July 9/6 Mature matrons..now..wear kiss-me-quick hats. **1974** J. WAINWRIGHT *Evidence I shall Give* xxiv. 120 Whitby... Genuine Olde Worlde charm, wearing a Kiss-Me-Quick hat. A fishing community, taken over by day-trippers.

kissogram ('kɪsəgræm). Also **Kissagram** (proprietary), **Kiss-a-Gram,** etc. [f. KISS *sb.* or *v.* + -*o*- + GRAM[4].] A novelty telegram or greetings message sent through a commercial agency, which is delivered (usu. by a provocatively-dressed young woman) with a kiss, esp. to amuse or embarrass the recipient.

A 'Kissogram Post Card' (Valentine Series) was available in the 1900s. The sender could leave the imprint of a kiss on the face of the card, above a sentimental verse ('..But it's you that I'd rather be "kissing".').

1982 *Standard* 9 Aug. 4/1 Kissagrams. 286 9531. **1984** *Times* 11 Aug. 3/2 A kissogram employer who parked his car illegally rather than allow his scantily-clad girls to walk too far was fined £10 on each of nine charges. **1984** *Daily Tel.* 30 Oct. 3/3 A sex-change Kiss-a-Gram girl stepped into the Marlborough Street dock yesterday clad in a see-through bra, black knickers, and fishnet stockings with suspender belt. **1985** *Sunday Express Mag.* 14 Apr. 22/2 People mostly send Kissagrams to mark birthdays, anniversaries and vasectomies.

kisstiȝ, variant of CUSTI *Obs.*, munificent.

kist (kɪst), *sb.*[1] *Sc.* and *north. dial.* Forms: (1 cest, cist, cyst), 3–5 kiste, 4– kist, (4–6 kyst(e, 4 kystte, 6 keste). [Northern form of CHEST *sb.*[1]; either directly from Scandinavian, or owing its form to Norse influence; cf. ON. *kista*, Sw. *kista*, Da. *kiste*; also Du. *kist*, Ger. *kiste*. With the various senses, cf. CHEST 1, 3, 4, 5.]

1. a. A chest, box, coffer. (In Sc. the specific term for a servant's trunk.)

c **1300** *Havelok* 2018 Al þat he milhen [= hy mihten] fynde Of hise, in arke or in kiste. **13..** *E.E. Allit. P.* C. 159 Ouerborde bale to kest,..Her kysttes & her coferes. *c* **1420** *Sir Amadace* (Camden) xliv, Kistes and cofurs bothe ther stode,..fulle of gold precius and gode. **1535** STEWART *Cron. Scot.* II. 21 All tha buikis tha kist hes brocht till. **1792** A. WILSON *Watty & Meg* in *Chambers' Pop. Hum. Scot. Poems* (1862) 82 On a kist he laid his wallet. **1825** BROCKETT, *Kist*, a chest. **1888** *Pall Mall G.* 9 June 3/2 It bears the strongest family resemblance to carvings on the old Cumberland kists. **1958** *Personality* 4 Dec. 27/3 Ancient brass-bound *kists* of teak help to furnish the back stoep. **1959** *Star* (Johannesburg) 22 Jan. 7/4 (Advt.), Heavy bowfronted *kists* price cut to £15:19:6. **1971** *Cape Times* 13 Feb. 21/3 (Advt.), Furniture and effects..walnut bedroom suite, easy chairs..several large teak glass fronted cupboards, 2 carved Zanzibar camphor-wood kists. **1971** *Leader* (Durban) 7 May 15 (Advt.), Imbuia Kist..R29.00.

†**b.** Applied to the 'ark' of bulrushes in which Moses was placed; and to Noah's ark. *Obs.*

a **1300** *Cursor M.* 5614–17 (Cott.) A rescen [*MS.* An esscen] kyst [*Gött.* a kist of rises] sco did be wroght,.. In þis kist þe barn sco did. **13..** *E.E. Allit. P.* B. 449 'Now Noe', quoth oure lorde, '..Hatz þou closed þy kyst with clay alle aboute?'

c. ***kist o' whistles, whustles***, an organ (ORGAN *sb.*¹ 2). Now *rare.*

1772 A. RAMSAY *New Misc. Scots Sangs* [*Tea-Table Misc.*] 141 The Kist fou of Whistles, That make sic a Cleiro. **1828** J. RUDDIMAN *Tales & Sk.* 60 To cram down our craigs, will we, nill we, their kists o'whistles. **1866** ENGEL *Nat. Mus.* viii. 272 The instances where an organ—or a 'a kist o' whistles', as this noble instrument has been termed—has gained favour in a Scotch congregation, are exceptional. **1889** G. B. SHAW *London Music in 1888–89* (1937) 116 M. Gigout, who was performing on the 'Kist o' whustles'. **1891** R. FORD *Thistledown* vi. 106 There was no such thing as an organ, or 'kist o' whustles', in any Presbyterian kirk in the land. **1936** *Discovery* July 223/2 The normal 'kist of whistles' would spoil the architectural effect. **1947** 'H. MACDIARMID' (*title*) A kist of whistles. **1969** C. GEESON *Northumberland & Durham Word Bk.* 118 *Kist o' whistles*, an organ in Scotland and Northumberland.

2. A basket. (Cf. CHEST *sb.*¹ 4.)

1724 in Ramsay *Tea-t. Misc.* (1733) I. 29 Ane auld kist made with wands, And that sall be your coffer. **1861** CLINGTON *F. O'Donnell* 35 Servant maids..were collected around a kist or basket of potatoes..peeling them for the colcannon.

3. A chest or place in which money is kept; a treasury; also *transf.* the store of money itself.

1619 FLETCHER *Loy. Subj.* III. iii, When the kist increased not. **1816** SCOTT *Antiq.* xxiv, Yon kist is only silver, and I aye heard that Misticot's pose had muckle yellow gowd in 't.

4. a. A coffin; a stone coffin or sarcophagus.

a **1300** *Cursor M.* 21018 Siþen was his bodi..laid in kist o marbil stan. *c* **1450** *St. Cuthbert* (Surtees) 3439 Þar ligges a kist on þe north syde. *a* **1555** LYNDESAY *Tragedie* 266 Thay Saltit me, syne cloist me in ane kyste. **1596** DALRYMPLE tr. *Leslie's Hist. Scot.* VII. 35 In a kist of leid he is laid. **1721** KELLY *Sc. Prov.* 6 A' that you'll get will be a kist and a sheet after all. **1855** ROBINSON *Whitby Gloss.* s.v., 'A kirk garth kist', a churchyard chest, a coffin.

b. *Archæol.* = CIST¹, KISTVAEN.

1853 PHILLIPS *Rivers Yorksh.* viii. 208 In a conspicuous barrow..The kist contained a female skeleton. **1866** LAING *Preh. Rem. Caithn.* 45 This kist contained an extended male skeleton with a rude flint spear-head. **1868** G. STEPHENS *Runic Mon.* I. 255 In this kist lay four glazed pots or urns.. full of ashes and bones and charcoal.

Hence **'kistful**, as much as fills a kist.

?*c* **1644** *Lesly's March* in Scott *Minstr. Scott. Bord.*, The kist-fou of whistles, That mak sick a cleiro. **1816** SCOTT *Antiq.* xxiv, Sic another kistfu' o' silver.

‖**kist**, *sb.*² *East Indies.* [Urdū (Pers., Arab.) *qisṭ* portion, instalment.] An instalment (of the yearly land revenue or other payment). Hence **kist-bundy**: see quot. 1764.

1764 *Ann. Reg.* 192/2 Kistbundee, a contract for the acquittance of a debt by stated payments. **1799** MRQ. WELLESLEY in Owen *Desp.* (1877) 188 Purneah had discharged the first monthly kist of the subsidy stipulated by the late treaty. **1805** SIR J. MALCOLM in Sir J. Kaye *Life* (1856) I. xiii. 346 We expect three or four lakhs of the kist due a twelvemonth hence to be paid immediately. **1818** JAS. MILL *Brit. India* VI. vii. (1830) VI. 63 Those districts, which are pledged for the security of his kists.

kist, *v.* *Sc.* and *north. dial.* [f. KIST *sb.*¹ Cf. Du. and Ger. *kisten.*] *trans.* To put into a 'kist' or coffin.

a **1670** SPALDING *Troub. Chas. I* (1851) II. 390 Johne Logei's heid wes first keppit and kistet, and both togidder wes convoyit to the Gray Freir kirkyaird and bureit. **1808–18** JAMIESON, *Kistin'*, *Kisting*, the act of putting a corpse into a coffin, with the entertainment given on this melancholy occasion. **1876** *Whitby Gloss.* s.v. *Kisted*, 'I wad fain see thee kisted'..I should like to see you dead. **1882** J. WALKER *Jaunt to Auld Reekie* 179 Kisted mummies from the tombs of Thebes.

kist, occas. pa. t. and pa. pple. of KISS *v.*

kist(e, obs. pa. t. of CAST *v.*

kistvaen, cistvaen ('kɪstvaɪn). *Archæol.* [Anglicized spelling of Welsh *cist faen*, i.e. *cist* chest, cist + *faen* (pron. *vaen*) aspirated form of *maen* stone.] = CIST I.

1715 PENNECUIK *Wks.* (1815) 121 (E.D.D.), In trenching the ground for a garden was discovered another tomb, kistivaen..of five flags, without an urn, or any remains of bones. **1807** G. CHALMERS *Caledonia* I. I. ii. 84 Among the varieties, in the manner of burial,..the *Cistvaen* is remarkable. **1827** G. HIGGINS *Celtic Druids* 217 In the Welsh language called Kist-vaens, or stone-chests. **1842** BRANDE *Dict. Sci., Lit.* etc. s.v., Cistvaens are commonly three stones placed on edge, like the three sides of a box, with a stone cover. **1881** *Athenæum* No. 2826. 857 The great megalithic forms of interment, consisting of kistvaens, or sepulchral underground chambers, formed of four huge slabs, covered with an immense capstone.

Kiswa ('kɪswa). Also **Kiswah**. [Arab.] The black cloth which covers the Kaaba.

1599 HAKLUYT *Voyages* II. I. 203 Moreouer he deliuereth vnto him ye *Chisua Talnabi*, which signifieth in the Arabian tongue, The garment of the Prophet. *a* **1817** J. L. BURCKHARDT *Trav. Arabia* (1829) I. 254 The four sides of the Kaaba are covered with a black silk stuff, hanging down, and leaving the roof bare. This curtain..is called *kesoua.* **1855** R. F. BURTON *Pilgrimage* II. xvi. 82 The Kiswa is a black, purple, or green brocade, embroidered with white or with silver letters. **1912** A. J. B. WAVELL *Mod. Pilgrim in Mecca* viii. 152 The 'Ihram'..remains till the day of the festival, when the 'Kiswah', that is the covering itself, is changed. **1928** E. RUTTER *Holy Cities Arabia* I. xiii. 178 The beautiful silk and wool kiswa with its gold-embroidered band..not having been sent this year, Ibn Sa'ûd had supplied a covering of black Bedouin hair cloth. **1959** *Chambers's Encycl.* IX. 192/2 Each old Kiswa is cut up and sold to pilgrims. **1963** *Ann. Reg. 1962* 375 Saudi refusal to accept the *kiswa*, the traditional holy cloth for the Kaaba shrine in Mecca sent annually from Cairo.

Kiswahili (kiːswa'hiːlɪ). [Native word, f. *ki-* prefix designating an abstract or inanimate object + SWAHILI.] A major language of the Bantu family, spoken widely in Kenya, Tanzania, and elsewhere in East Africa, where it serves as a lingua franca.

1864 J. A. GRANT *Walk across Afr.* p. xvi, *Kisuahili*, the dialect of the Wasuahili on the east coast of Africa. **1936** *Discovery* June 196/1 A record of certain Bena customs, written in Kiswahili. **1966** C. SWEENEY *Scurrying Bush* ii. 23 He could read Swahili... He knew little English, but this was an advantage as it forced me to learn Kiswahili. **1967** C. W. RECHENBACH *Swahili-Eng. Dict.* p. v, The Swahili language (*Kiswahili*) is a Bantu language spoken by perhaps as many as forty million people throughout a large part of East and Central Africa. **1969** *Nationalist* (Dar Es Salaam) 25 Jan. 6/2 (Advt.), Candidates must be Tanzanian Citizens fluent in both Kiswahili and English. **1971** *Inside Kenya Today* Mar. 39/1 The School..manages to arrange the course for Kiswahili speakers from time to time. **1972** G. WIGG *George Wigg* v. 110 Facilities for learning Kiswahili were made available in Chinyanja speaking units.

kit (kɪt), *sb.*¹ Forms: 4–5 **kyt**, 4–7 **kitt**, 5–6 **kytt(e**, 6– **kit**. [app. a. MDu. *kitte* a wooden vessel made of hooped staves (Du. *kit* tankard): ulterior etymology uncertain.]

1. a. A circular wooden vessel, made of hooped staves; in different localities applied to vessels of various sizes, with or without a lid, and usually having a handle or handles; as, a small open tub with one or two of the staves fashioned into handles, used for holding water or 'washing up'; a deeper vessel with a lid used as a milking-pail; a tub- or pail-shaped vessel, often with a lid, used for holding or carrying milk, butter, fish, or other commodities; whence, by extension, sometimes, a square box used for the same purpose.

1375 BARBOUR *Bruce* XVIII. 168 Thai strak his hed of, and syne it Thai haf gert salt in-till a kyt [*v.r.* kitt] And send it in-till Ingland. **14..** *Nominale* in Wr.-Wülcker 696/14 *Hoc multrum*, a kytt. **1485** *Inv.* in *Ripon Ch. Acts* (Surtees) 371, j kitt cum cooperculo. **1565** *Inv.* in *Trans. Cumbld. & Westmld. Arch. Soc.* X. 31 In the brew howse A Leade, a mashe fat... Two Kytts. **1570** LEVINS *Manip.* 148/43 Kit, a litle vessel, *cantharus, fidelia.* **1633** in Cramond *Ann. Banff* (1891) I. 71 Paid for three Kittis of Salmound. **1649** BLITHE *Eng. Improv. Impr.* ix. (1653) 56 As a man doth with a hand-scoop, pail, or kit, cast water out of a ditch. **1674** RAY *N.C. Words* 27 A *Kit* or milking Pail..with two Ears and a Cover. **1701** C. WOLLEY *Jrnl. New York* (1860) 55, I..ordered him to fetch a kit full of water and discharge it at them. **1771** SMOLLETT *Humph. Cl.* 3 Sept., The following articles formed our morning's repast; one kit of boiled eggs; a second, full of butter; a third full of cream. **1795** J. RICHARDSON in J. Robertson *Agric. Perth* (1799) 378 Salmon was..preserved in vinegar, and packed up in small wooden vessels called kits. **1802** MAWE *Min. Derbysh.* Gloss. (E.D.S.), *Kit*, a wood vessel of any size. **1825** BROCKETT, *Kit*, properly a covered milking-pail with two handles, but often applied to a small pail of any sort. **1832–53** *Whistle-Binkie* Ser. III. 114 We've kits fu' o' butter—we've cogs fu' o' brose. **1878** *Cumbld. Gloss.*, *Butter kits*, square boxes used for conveying butter to market in a wallet on horseback. **1883** *Fisheries Exhib. Catal.* 72 Samples of Red Herrings in kits. **1888** *Sheffield Gloss.*, *Kit* or *Kitty*,..a wooden tub with one handle, in which..grinders cool their knives, saws, etc.

b. A kind of basket, *esp.* one made of straw or rushes for holding fish. Also in extended use, and, by metonymy, the contents of a kit, used as a measure of weight.

1847–78 in HALLIWELL. **1859** SALA *Tw. round Clock* (1861) 20 Crabs are sold by the 'kit' (a long shallow basket) and by the score. **1906** *Daily Chron.* 12 Apr. 6/3 One vessel alone brought in a thousand kits of fish. **1934** 'TAFFRAIL' *Seventy North* ix. 185, 20,000 to 25,000 'kits' of fish, each weighing ten stone might be landed from the trawlers—say 125 to 150 tons. **1935** 'L. LUARD' *Conquering Seas* ii. 20 Within two hours of berthing, with a full two thousand kit aboard..over a hundred tons of fish. **1961** *Guardian* 18 Jan. 9/2 He was pushing a barrow on the fish dock, wheeling aluminium 'kits' which, when full, each contain 10 stone of fish.

2. a. A collection of articles (called ***articles of kit***) forming part of the equipment of a soldier, and carried in a valise or knapsack; also, the valise containing these, or this with its contents; sometimes = outfit, 'turn-out', uniform.

1785 GROSE *Dict. Vulg. T.* s.v., The kit is likewise the whole of a soldier's necessaries, the contents of his knapsack. **1813** SIR R. WILSON *Priv. Diary* II. 18 Considering that we were conspicuous *à cheval*, and in glittering kits, it is wonderful that no marksman fired with unerring aim. **1820** J. W. CROKER in *C. Papers* 16 June (1884), Several [soldiers]..removed their kits from the barracks. **1855** THACKERAY *Newcomes* xxvi, His kit is as simple as a subaltern's. **1868** *Regul. & Ord. Army* ¶602 c, The Articles of Kit to be worn and carried in the different orders. **1870** *Illustr. Lond. News* 29 Oct. 446 They came without muskets or kits, but the officers had their swords.

b. A collection of personal effects or necessaries, esp. as packed up for travelling.

1833 MARRYAT *P. Simple* xiv, I hardly need say that my lord's kit was valuable; and what was better, they exactly fitted me. **1849** THACKERAY *Pendennis* I. xvi. 160 The widow and Laura..set about the preparation for Pen's kit, and filled trunks with his books and linen. **1862** F. HALL *Hindu Philos. Syst.* 107 He thereupon dressed, tied up his kit, and set off. **1866–7** LIVINGSTONE *Last Jrnls.* (1873) I. v. 111, I sent a man to carry his kit for him.

c. The outfit of tools required by a workman, esp. a shoemaker.

[**1825** BROCKETT, *Kit*,..the stool on which a cobbler works.] **1851** S. JUDD *Margaret* I. iii. 17 The workshop.. contained a loom, a kit where the father of Margaret sometimes made shoes. **1858** M. PORTEOUS *Souter Johnny* 10 The Souter..Liv'd wi' his kit, And made gude shoon. **1881** *Pharmaceut. Jrnl.* 165 The kit of tools for a nipple maker consists of a small slanting case [etc.] **1885** *Harper's Mag.* Jan. 282/2 The laster is about the only shoemaker left who can still talk..of his 'kit'.

d. A set or outfit of tools, equipment, etc.; *spec.*, a collection of parts sold for the buyer to assemble. Also *fig.* and *attrib.*

1859 G. W. MATSELL *Vocabulum* 48 *Kit*..the implements of a burglar. **1907** *Yesterday's Shopping* (1969) 277/2 The Army & Navy Boot Kit contains 3 shoe brushes,..1 tin of boot polish, complete in leather case. **1935** A. J. POLLOCK *Underworld Speaks* 68/1 *Kit*, a safe-cracker's tools. **1955** *Amer. Speech* XXX. 226 Kit, all the necessary parts to assemble one section of the plane. **1955** A. HUXLEY *Genius & Goddess* 51 A make-up kit and a bottle of cheap perfume. **1961** PARTRIDGE *Dict. Slang* Suppl. 1160/1 *Kit*, paint-kettle and -brushes: house-painters' coll. **1967** *Listener* 3 Aug. 148/2 Beckett forces upon you a do-it-yourself Tantalus-kit. He requires you to seek and not to find. **1970** *House & Garden* Mar. 77/2 'Cena' chair... Comes in kit form (see components below)..from £14 19s. plus tool kit. **1970** *Times* 26 Sept. 18/1 Make your own sausages... Kit includes hand-filler, recipes and full instructions, also herbs, spices, skins. **1970** D. MARLOWE *Echoes of Celandine* i. 12, I have also a penchant for vintage-car kits... I have constructed the 1929 Mercedes Benz SSK three times.

e. An outfit of drums, cymbals, and other percussion devices and accessories used by a drummer in a dance-band, jazz-group, or the like.

1929 *Melody Maker* Mar. 259/3 Lyman plays the drums in the band—at least he sits behind a nice kit. **1934, 1965** [see *drum kit* s.v. DRUM *sb.*¹ 12 a]. **1971** *Melody Maker* 27 Nov. 47/3 It's more important to think about the music than the colour of your kit. A good drummer is going to sound good even if he plays on the table top.

f. A quantity of printed matter on a specified topic for students, etc.

1968 *Globe & Mail* (Toronto) 17 Feb. 36 (Advt.), Savannah's full of colonial names... Why not add your name to an illustrious list? Write for our free travel kit. **1971** J. B. CARROLL et al. *Word Frequency Bk.* p. vi, The materials themselves include text-books, periodicals, encyclopedias, novels, student workbooks, kits, and so on, all of which contain vocabulary to which students are exposed. **1971** *Guardian* 7 June 6/7 The SACK—School and Community Kit—is made up of information and ideas on community projects for schools, together with reference material. **1974** *Catholic Herald* 4 Oct. 4/2 The study kits come in colourful folders and contain pictures, taped songs, fact sheets and quotations from Church leaders.

3. *colloq.* A number of things or persons viewed as a whole; a set, lot, collection; esp. in phr. ***the whole kit.*** Also, ***the whole kit and boiling*** (***boodle, caboodle, cargo***). (Cf. CABOODLE.) *U.S.*

1785 GROSE *Dict. Vulg. T.*, *Kit*,..is also used to express the whole of different commodities; as, Here, take the whole kit; i.e. take all. **1788** R. GALLOWAY *Poems* 170 (Jam.) 'Twas whiskey made them a' sae crouse;..But now I wad na gi'e ae louse For a' the kit. **1821** SHELLEY *Œdipus Tyr.* I. 92 I'll sell you in a lump The whole kit of them. *a* **1852** F. M. WHITCHER *Widow Bedott Papers* (1856) xxiii. 257 The hull kit and cargo on 'em had conspired together. **1859** BARTLETT *Dict. Amer.* (ed. 2) 32 *Biling*, a vulgar pronunciation of *boiling*. The phrase *the whole* (or more commonly *hull*) *kit and bilin*, means the whole lot, applied to persons and things. **1861** DICKENS *Gt. Expect.* xl, A better gentleman than the whole kit on you put together. *a* **1861** T. WINTHROP *John Brent* (1883) xxviii. 237, I motioned we shove the hul kit an boodle of the gamblers ashore on logs. 'Twas kerried. **1888** *Boston Globe* 5 Feb. 1/3 If any 'railroad lobbyist' cast reflections on his character he would wipe out the whole kit and caboodle of them. **1908** *Dialect Notes* III. 327 (East Alabama) *Kit an(d) bilin*, the crowd. Usually in the expression 'the whole kit and bilin'. Cf. *kit and cargo* of the middle west. **1920** S. LEWIS *Main St.* 50 The whole kit and bilin' of 'em are nothing in God's world but socialism in disguise. **1946** *Newsweek* 16 Sept. 32/2 It gave the farm and the whole kit and boodle to Stanley. **1969** *Listener* 22 May 707/3 The whole kit and caboodle of us were then investigated by the FBI to see how many subversives there were among us.

4. *attrib.* and *Comb.* **a.** (sense 1) **kit-dressing** (see quot.); **kit-haddock**, an inferior sort of haddock, sent away in kits for curing; **kit-trade**, the trade of putting up fish in kits for the market. **b.** (sense 2) ***kit-inspection***; **kit-bag**, a stout bag in which to carry a soldier's or traveller's kit; **kit-car**, a motor car sold in parts for assembly by the owner; a build-it-yourself car; **kit-drill** (see quot.); **kitset** *N.Z.*, the components and aids for assembling an article (radio, furniture, etc.) or model (aeroplane, etc.).

a. 1831 *Glover's Hist. Derby* I. 261 The rural festival of *kit dressing took place on the 4th of August 1829... Twigs of willow were bent over the tops of the kits... The maidens carried the kits on their heads. **1894** *Daily Free Press*

(Aberdeen) 18 May 7/6 *Kit haddocks, 10s. to 13s. per box. **1866** MITCHELL *Hist. Montrose* xvi. 136 The Berwick-on-Tweed companies..commenced the boiling and *kit-trade. **b. 1898** *Westm. Gaz.* 7 Apr. 4/1, I looked at the marching boots..and wished they were in my *kit-bag along with the wonderful assortment of articles..technically described as 'small kit'. **1899** *Ibid.* 25 Sept. 3/1 An exceedingly handy form of knapsack or kit-bag that I bought..in Germany for the modest sum of 1s. 9d. **1953** G. DURRELL *Overloaded Ark* xiii. 216, I..set off early one morning in the back of the Schiblers' *kit-car. **1964** *Sunday Times* (Colour Suppl.) 29 Nov. 53/3 The modern kit car... All you need is practical application, a few hand tools. **1970** *Sunday Truth* (Brisbane) 18 Jan. 60/3 Here we loaded the kit-car..and travelled south to Biafra. **1890** *19th Cent.* Nov. 849 The man condemned to *kit drill marches up and down the barrack square for two hours a day carrying his entire kit in his valise, including boots, his sword, carbine, and cloak. **1892** *Pall Mall G.* 3 Dec. 6/3 Two corporals and eleven privates..absented themselves from a *kit inspection. **1963** *Weekly News* (Auckland) 8 May 56/5 *Transistor radio *kitsets.* New low prices. Easy-to-build range from crystal set, £1, to 7T portables, £9/19/6. **1966** *Ibid.* 26 Jan. 6/6 Many other clubs throughout the Auckland province assist the young yachtsman with kitsets and drawings for home building [of yachts].

kit (kɪt), *sb.*[2] Now *rare.* [Origin obscure.

Perh. repr. the initial part of Gr. κιθάρα CITHARA, or some derivative form of that word.]

A small fiddle, formerly much used by dancing masters.

1519 *Interl. Four Elem.* in Hazl. *Dodsley* I. 48 This dance would do mich better yet, If we had a kit or taberet. **1562** PHAER *Æneid* IX. Cc iv b, His pastime chief was harpe and kit. **1637** B. JONSON *Sad Sheph.* I. ii, Each did dance, some to the kit or crowd, Some to the bag-pipe. **1709** STEELE *Tatler* No. 34 ¶4 Pray let me see you dance: I play upon the Kit. **1852** DICKENS *Bleak Ho.* xiv, Prince Turveydrop then tinkled the strings of his kit with his fingers, and the young ladies stood up to dance.

attrib. **1634** W. CARTWRIGHT *Ordinary* I. ii. in Hazl. *Dodsley* XII. 220 Do you not hear her guts already squeak Like kit-strings?

kit (kɪt), *sb.*[3] Also 6 **kytte, kitt.** A shortened form of KITTEN.

1562 J. HEYWOOD *Prov. & Epigr.* (1867) 203 Thy cat great with kytte. **1599** *Life Sir T. More* in Wordsw. *Eccl. Biog.* (1853) II. 112 She would now and then show herself to be her mother's daughter, kitt after kinde. **1729** MRS. DELANY *Lett., to Mrs. A. Granville* 225, I forgot to say my cat had four kits. **1844** E. FITZGERALD *Lett.* (1889) I. 127 Thank Miss Barton much for the kit;..my old woman is a great lover of cats, and hers has just kitted. **1957** Kitt [see KITTEN *sb.* 1 b]. **1970** *Times* 8 Sept. 11/3 The kits [*sc.* young mink] are fully grown at six months. **1974** A. DILLARD *Pilgrim at Tinker Creek* ii. 15 You crouch motionless on a bank..and are rewarded by the sight of a muskrat kit paddling from its den.

Kit (kɪt), *sb.*[4]

1. Abbreviated pet form of the name Catherine or Kate (cf. KITTY[1]), used *esp.* in the obs. phr. ***Kit has lost her key.***

1533 MORE *Apol.* xxiv. Wks. 888/2 Certaine letters whiche some of the brethrene let fall of late, and lost theim of likelyhedde as some good kitte leseth her kayes. **1548** W. PATTEN *Exp. Scotl.* Pref. in *Eng. Garner* III. 71 Oblations and offerings..for deliverance of bad husbands, for a sick cow, to keep down the belly, and when 'Kit had lost her key'.

†**2.** A light woman. *Obs.* (Cf. KITTOCK.)

a **1577** GASCOIGNE *Dan Bartholomew* Wks. (1587) 67 Kits of Cressides kinde. **1600** BARTON *Pasquil's Fooles-cappe* (1879) 21 Such foolish Kittes of such a skittish kinde, In Bridewell booke are euery where to finde.

Kit, *sb.*[5] [abbr. of *Christopher.*] In phr. ***Kit with the canstick*** or ***candlestick*** = JACK-O'-LANTERN.

1584 R. SCOT *Discov. Witchcr.* VII. xv. (1886) 122 They have so fraied us with bull beggars, spirits, witches, urchens, elves, hags,..kit with the cansticke. [*a* **1626** MIDDLETON *Witch* I. ii.]

kit (kɪt), *sb.*[6] *Naut.* [a. G. *kitt* cement, mastic, putty, etc., whence also Da. *kit*, Sw. *kitt.* There is little evidence of the use of the term in Eng.] A composition of resin, pitch, and tallow applied to the canvas used for covering carcasses (see CARCASS 7).

1815 in *Falconer's Marine Dict.* **1885** in *Cassell's Encycl. Dict.*

kit (kɪt), *sb.*[7] A local name for the fish also called mary-sole, smear-dab, and sand-fluke.

1836 YARRELL *Brit. Fishes* II. 241 The Kit of Jago is the smooth or small-headed dab. **1880–84** DAY *Fishes Gt. Brit.* II. 29 *Pleuronectes microcephalus*,..[in] Cornwall..it has likewise been known as *kit*;..at Hove, as 'the kit'.

kit (kɪt), *sb.*[8] *Photogr.* A thin frame inserted in a plate-holder to hold plates smaller than those for which the holder was originally constructed.

1885 in *Cassell's Encycl. Dict.* **1889** *Anthony's Photogr. Bull.* II. 74 A 5 × 8 is the best size for general use, and with a few 3 × 4[4] kits is all that is needed.

kit, *sb.*[9]: see KIT-FOX.

kit, *sb.*[10] [app. ad. Ger. dial. *kitte, kütte*, covey, flight of doves, etc.: see Grimm 2895/1.] A school of pigeons.

1880 *Times* 24 Nov. 10/3 Mr. Cotton's handsome birds from Sunningdale, and the Macclesfield tipplers, which fly in schools or 'kits' for hours against another school.

kit (kɪt), *sb.*[11] *N.Z.* Also **kete, kête.** [ad. Maori *kete.*] A basket plaited from flax. Hence **'kitful.**

1834 E. MARKHAM *N.Z. or Recollections of It* (MS.) 44 They make Baskets or Kits as we call them for potatoes. **1841** W. COLENSO *Jrnl.* (typescript) I. 120 Opening his *kete* and taking out his Blanket. **1856** E. B. FITTON *New Zealand* 68 Neatly made baskets, plaited from flax, and known by the name of 'Maori kits'. **1877** W. T. PRATT *Colonial Experiences* 31 Potatoes were procurable from the Maories [*sic*] in flax kits, at from one to five shillings the kit. **1882** W. D. HAY *Brighter Britain!* I. ii. 38 [The well-to-do Maori] stops and ..examines the kitful of fruit. **1884** LADY MARTIN *Our Maoris* 44 My heart is like an old kête (*i.e.*, a coarsely-woven basket). **1902** W. SATCHELL *Land of Lost* xviii. 161, I will give you a kitful when you go away. **1936** 'R. HYDE' *Check to your King* xiii. 156 Great flax-kits of *Kumaras*..were left outside the door. **1938** R. FINLAYSON *Brown Man's Burden* 75 So the three men got enough kitfuls [of shellfish] long before Hira came back. **1941** BAKER *N.Z. Slang* vi. 55 We have also put into wide use the term *kit* for a shopping basket. **1958** S. ASHTON-WARNER *Spinster* 41 When I comes to this word 'basket' in my book I never says 'basket'... I always says 'kit'. **1969** F. SARGESON *Joy of Worm* iii. 105 Between the two of them they carried a flax kit of food.

kit (kɪt), *v.*[1] [f. KIT *sb.*[1]] **1.** *trans.* To put or pack in a kit or kits; esp. fish for the market. Hence **'kitted** *ppl. a.*, placed or packed in a kit.

1725 RAMSAY *Gent. Sheph.* IV. ii, To leave his ram-horn spoons, and kitted whey. **1776** PENNANT *Zool.* IV. 290 The fish [salmon] is..boiled, pickled, and kitted, and sent to the London markets. **1845** *New Statist. Acc. Scot., Caithness* XV. 45 The salmon are kitted in the usual way and sent to London.

2. To equip (someone or something) with a uniform, an outfit, personal effects, equipment, etc. Freq. with *out, up.* So **kitted (out, up),** provided with clothing, accessories, etc.; **kitting (up)** *vbl. sb.*

1919 W. LANG *Sea-Lawyer's Log* ii. 13 It is pleasant to march down to the kitting-up store and have garments thrown at you..without price. *Ibid.* 16 Now we have been 'kitted up', as the nautical expression has it. **1925** T. E. LAWRENCE *Let.* 25 Aug. (1938) 481 Sergeant take this man to the Q.M. Stores, kit him at once, and put him into the first train for Cranwell. **1945** *Times* 25 May 2/2 In a day or so these men would be kitted up in smart new uniform and go on leave. **1948** 'N. SHUTE' *No Highway* ii. 50 I'll get a letter through to Ottawa asking them to kit you up for the trip. **1958** *Technology* May 68/3 Some firms may wish to give students a 'kitting up allowance'. **1960** K. AMIS *New Maps of Hell* (1961) iv. 95 There are cases on record of writers having to kit out contemporary narratives with aliens and space-ships in order to make a sale. **1962** *Guardian* 7 Aug. 5/1 A child can have ten days skiing for under £25 and be kitted out by Moss Brothers into the bargain. **1963** *Times* 18 Jan. 3/6 The cars—numbered, polished and kitted with every conceivable gadget to compete against time and the elements—will set course for the Côte d'Azur. *Ibid.* 20 Apr. 3/4 Probably the business locality this weekend will be Bristol, where the England players for the short Antipodean tour will foregather to be kitted and generally vetted. **1970** *New Society* 5 Mar. 384/1 Voluntary labour repaired and kitted out about 20 houses in three months. **1973** *Daily Tel.* 21 Nov. 14/3 The 1500 TC offers good value at £1,295 for a well kitted-out four-door 1½-litre.

kit, *v.*[2] *rare.* [f. KIT *sb.*[3]] *trans.* and *absol.* To kitten, kittle.

1758 *Brit. Chron.* 1 May 410 a few days ago a cat at Brinkley..kitted two squirrels, which are now both alive. **1844** [see KIT *sb.*[3]].

kit, obs. inf., pa. t. and pa. pple., of CUT *v.*

Kitab (kɪ'tɑːb). [Arab. *kitāb*, lit. writing, book.] The Koran; also, a sacred book of certain other revealed religions, e.g. the Bible.

[**1652** J. NOTSTOCK tr. *Andrés's Confusion Muhamed's Sect* ii. 53 O Moore,..what thinkest thou of the Scripture which you so much reverence, that..ye..keep it like a God, and call it *Alkitib Alhazim*, (i.e.) a glorious book and *Alcoran alhadin*, (i.e.) the Mighty *Alcoran*.] **1885** T. P. HUGHES *Dict. Islam* 280/2 *Al-Kitāb*.., 'the Book', a term used for the Qur'ān, and extended to all inspired books of the Jews and Christians, who are called *Ahlu'l-Kitāb*, or believers in the book. *Ibid.* 484/1 The Muhammadan Scriptures..are usually appealed to and quoted from as..*al-Kitāb*, 'the Book'. **1912** *Moslem World* II. 168 Mohammed..knew of the existence of the Holy Scriptures of both Testaments, and..fully intended to refer to them... In the first place, *Al Kitâb*, 'the Book', is a clear reference to 'the Bible'. **1927** *Encycl. Islam* II. 1044/2 The 'Book' par excellence is..the Kur'ān itself; it is the revelation of God... As the Kitāb is the word of God it has also the meaning in the Kur'ān of 'a decree of God' or it becomes the 'impression' which God stamps upon the hearts of man. **1959** S. & N. RONART *Conc. Encycl. Arabic Civilization* 297 *Al-Kitāb* as a specifically Moslem term denotes the Holy Book, i.e. the Koran, but is also extended to the Scriptures of..Christianity and Judaism, whose adherents are called *Ahl al-Kitab* (People of the Book). *Ibid.* 298 (*heading*) Koran,..the Holy Book of Islam, frequently spoken of by Moslems simply as The Book (*al-kitāb*).

‖**ki'tar.** *rare.* Also **kittar.** [Arab. *qītār*, a. Gr. κιθάρα CITHARA.] A guitar or lyre.

c **1640** SHIRLEY *Capt. Underwit* I. in Bullen *O. Pl.* (1883) II. 330, I can play well o' the kittar. **1817** MOORE *Lalla R., Parad. & Peri* Introd., Striking a few careless but melancholy chords on his kitar.

kit-cat[1] ('kɪtkæt). Now *dial.* [Reduplicated from CAT *sb.*, or with KIT *sb.*[3]] The game of tip-cat.

1664 COTTON *Scarron.* IV. Poet. Wks. (1734) 88 Then in his Hand he takes a thick Bat, With which he us'd to play at Kit-Cat. *a* **1825** FORBY *Voc. E. Anglia, Kit-cat*, a game played by three or more players. The cat is shaped like a double cone.

b. *Comb.* *kit-cat-roll* (see quot.), probably so called from the shape of the 'cat' in the game.

a **1825** FORBY *Voc. E. Anglia, Kit-cat-roll*, a bellied roller for land;..going in the furrow, and the roller acting on the sloping surface of the ridge on each side.

Kit-cat[2] ('kɪtkæt). Also 8–9 **kit-kat.** [f. *Kit* (= Christopher) *Cat* or *Catling*, the keeper of the pie-house in Shire Lane, by Temple Bar, where the club originally met.]

1. *attrib.* with *Club*: A club of Whig politicians and men of letters founded in the reign of James II.

1705 HEARNE *Collect.* 6 Dec. (O.H.S.) I. 116 The Kit Cat Club came to have it's Name from one Christopher Catling. [*Note*, a Pudding Pye man.] **1710** *Acc. Tom Whig* 31 Your Kit-Cat Clubs, Calf's-Head Clubs, Junto's, and other infernal Cabals. **1821** (*title*) Portrait and Memoirs of the Celebrated Persons composing the Kit-Cat Club. **1829** LYTTON *Devereux* II. vi, That evening we were engaged at the Kit-Cat Club.

b. *absol.* in same sense.

1704 *Faction Displ.* 15, I am the founder of your lov'd Kit-Kat, A Club that gave Direction to the State. **1719** D'URFEY *Pills* VI. 349 The Kit Cat, and the Toasters, Did never care a Fig. **1749** FIELDING *Tom Jones* IV. ii, Thou mayest remember each bright Churchill of the gallaxy, and all the toasts of the Kit-cat.

attrib. *c* **1706** BLACKMORE *Poem Kit-cat Club*, Hence did th' Assembly's Title first arise, And Kit-Cat Wits spring first from Kit-Cat's Pyes.

c. A member of this club.

1704 *Faction Displ.* 14 Tosters, Kit-Kats, Divines, Buffoons and Wits. **1722** MARY ASTELL *Enq. after Wit* Ded., To the most Illustrious Society of the Kit-Cats. **1883** *Harper's Mag.* July 181/2 The Kit-Kats were the greatest gentlemen of the day.

2. *attrib.* with *size, portrait*, etc.: A particular size of portrait, less than half-length, but including the hands.

Said to have been so called because the dining-room of the club at Barn Elms was hung with portraits of the members and was too low for half-size portraits.

1754 A. DRUMMOND *Trav.* i. 31 There is..a kit-cat size of St. Ignatius holding a crucifix. **1778** PENNANT *Tours in Wales* (1883) I. 15 Here is another picture..a kit-cat length of Sir Roger Mostyn. **1875** MISS BRADDON *Strange World* II. i. 4 It was a kit-kat picture of a lad in undress uniform.

b. *absol.* in same sense.

1800 MALONE *Dryden* 534 *note*, The canvas for a Kit-kat is thirty-six inches long, and twenty-eight wide. **1840** *Polytechnic Jrnl.* II. 322 The portraits..will be of the proportion of what is termed a Kit-Kat. **1883** D. C. MURRAY *Hearts* I. 92 All the portraits in the Shire Hall are Kit-cats.

c. *fig.*

1803 *Edin. Rev.* II. 427 As Virgil did with his verses, leaving some half lengths, others kit-cat. **1822** COLERIDGE *Lett., Convers.*, etc. II. 144, I destroyed the Kit-cat or bust at least of the letter I had meant to have sent you.

kitchen ('kɪtʃɪn), *sb.* Forms: *α.* 1 **cycene, kycen(e, cicen(e;** 3 **kycchen,** (4–5 **-yne**), 3–4 **kichene,** (3–7 **-ine,** 7 **-en**), 4–5 **kychene,** 5 **-en, -ing, -o(u)n,** 5–6 **-yn(e,** 6 **kytchyn(e, -in(e, -en, kitchyn(e, -ine, (kitschine, chit-, citchen),** 6– **kitchen,** (6–8 **-in, -ing,** 7 **-ein**). *β.* 3 **ku-,** 3–4 **cuchene(ü);** 5 **cochyn(e,** 5–6 **kochyn.** *γ.* 4–5 **kechene, -ine, -yne,** 4–7 **-ing,** 5 **-ynne,** 5–6 **-yn, -en,** 6 **-in,** (4–5 **keitch-, keiching; ketchyne, chechyn).** [OE. *cycene* wk. fem. = OLG. **kukina* (MDu. *coken(e, koekene, kuekene*, Du. *keuken*; MLG. *kokene*, LG. *köke(n, kök*; hence Da. *kökken*, also dial. *köken*, Sw. *kök*), OHG. *chuhhîna* (MHG. *küche(n, kuche(n*, G. *küche*, and obs. or dial. *küch, kuch(e)*:—vulg. L. *cucina, cocina*, var. of *coquīna*, f. *coquĕre* to COOK. Of the ME. forms, those in *y, i* were orig. midland and north.; those in *u* southern and esp. s.w., with *ü* = OE. *y*; those in *e* partly Kentish with *e* for OE. *y*, partly north. and midl. with *e* widened from *i*.]

I. 1. a. That room or part of a house in which food is cooked; a place fitted with the apparatus for cooking. ***Clerk of the Kitchen***: see CLERK *sb.* 6.

α. *c* **1000** *Ags. Voc.* in Wr.-Wülcker 283/12 *Coquina*, cycene. *c* **1000** ÆLFRIC *Hom.* II. 166 þa wurpon hi ðа anlicnysse inn to heora kycenan. *c* **1050** *Suppl. Ælfric's Voc.* in Wr.-Wülcker 184/11 *Coquina, uel culina*, cicen. *c* **1275** LAY. 3316 We habbeþ cocus to cwecche to kichene. *c* **1300** *Havelok* 936 He bar it in, A[l] him one to the kichin. *c* **1380** WYCLIF *Serm.* Sel. Wks. I. 215 Sum men ben proude in her herte..of hiȝe kycchynes. **1450** *Rolls Parlt.* V. 192/1 John Hardewyk Clerk of oure Kechon, William Pecke Clerk of our Spicerye. **1481** CAXTON *Reynard* xxxii. (Arb.) 90 Therwyth the wulf was had to kychen and his lyuer taken out. **1552** HULOET s.v., All kindes of meat dressed in the kitchen. **1616** SURFL. & MARKH. *Country Farme* 3 The first foundation of a good House must be the Kitchin. **1656** FINETT *For. Ambass.* 168 Giving him a lodging to lye in and no Kitching to dress his meate in. **1728** NEWTON *Chronol. Amended* v. 337 Kitchins to bake and boil the Sacrifices for the People. **1832** G. DOWNES *Lett. Cont. Countries* I. 189 The dishes were conveyed from the kitchen by a kind of windlass, erected in the dining-hall.

β. *c* **1205** LAY. 24602 þas beorn þa sunde from kuchene. *a* **1225** *Ancr. R.* 214 He stikeð euer iðe celere, oðer iðe kuchene. *c* **1380** *Metr. Hom.* (Vernon MS.) in *Herrig's Archiv* LVII. 260 Vre Cuchene schaltou make clene. *c* **1450** *Bk. Curtasye* 44 in *Babees Bk.*, Spare brede or wyne..To

thy messe of kochyn be sett in sale. *Ibid.* 553 The clerke of the cochyn shalle alle þyng breue.

γ. **13..** *Coer de L.* 3429 Fro kechene come the fyrst course. *c* **1375** *Sc. Leg. Saints* xxx. (*Theodera*) 430 Nedful thing to þe keching. *c* **1489** CAXTON *Sonnes of Aymon* x. 255 Mawgys.. went to the kechyn for to haste the mete. **1562** WINȜET Wks. 1888 I. 11 Mair cure had of the keching nor of the queir.

b. *fig.* (chiefly with ref. to the stomach.) † ***the worms' kitchen***, the grave (*obs.*). ***hell's kitchen***, an area or place that is regarded as very disreputable or unpleasant; *spec.* a district of New York City once regarded as the haunt of criminals; ***thieves' kitchen***, a place inhabited by thieves or other criminals; also *transf.*

c **1470** HENRYSON *Mor. Fab.* VIII. (*Preach. Swallow*) xlv, The bodie to the wormes keitching go, The saule to fire. **1594** T. B. *La Primaud. Fr. Acad.* II. To Rdr., The stomacke ..being as it were the kitchin of the body. **1651** BURTON *Anat. Mel.* I. i. II. iv. 17 The Ventricle or Stomack..the Kitchin (as it were) of the first concoction. **1806** A. HUNTER *Culina* (ed. 3) 11 The Stomach is the kitchen that prepares our discordant food. **1838** N. HAWTHORNE *Amer. Notebks.* (1932) 15 He..swore fervently in favor of driving the British 'into Hell's kitchen' by main force. **1868** A. J. MUNBY *Diary* 29 Jan. in D. Hudson *Munby* (1972) 248 We went to see the Thieves' Kitchen,..a large long antique cellar,..men and lads, perhaps 15 in all, lounging on benches. All thieves. **1894** *Harper's Mag.* July 223/2 Her father had moved into.. a ramshackle old barrack just at the edge of Hell's Kitchen. **1894** W. J. LOCKE *At Gate of Samaria* (1895) xxvii. 319 They went together to East End music halls, bank holiday gatherings, thieves' kitchens, night clubs in the West End. **1900** 'FLYNT' & WALTON *Powers that Prey* 98 'Think Hell's Kitchen 'ud learn him?' Hell's Kitchen, in the speech of people who do not know what it means to work there, is the foundry. **1909** J. R. WARE *Passing Eng.* 243/2 *Thieves' kitchen* (London Street, 1882), the name satirically given to the then new Law Courts. **1941** C. O. SKINNER *Soap behind Ears* 168 She asked me a few routine questions..in the manner of someone questioning a welfare worker concerning life in Hell's Kitchen. **1949** *Sat. Even. Post* 15 Jan. 39/1 It stands between a greasy garage and a tawdry row of brownstone tenements on the edge of Hell's Kitchen, west of Eighth Avenue on 49th Street. **1960** *Observer* 24 Jan. 5/5 Where did I think the biggest thieves' kitchen was today? **1973** P. GEDDES *Ottawa Allegation* iii. 32 A Whitehall trusty, too, once away from the thieves' kitchen of intelligence and admitted to the counsels of the mandarins. **1974** D. RAMSAY *No Cause to Kill* II. 141 A bar on the East Side, almost the width of Manhattan Island away from Hell's Kitchen. **1974** 'M. INNES' *Mysterious Commission* xviii. 162 The place was certainly no thieves' kitchen. Honeybath..became aware of its respectable opulence.

c. Allusively, with reference to the furnishing of supplies for the kitchen.

1551 ABP. HAMILTON *Catech.* (1882) 99 That the giffar of that benefice may get in the laif to thame self and thair keching. **1562** WINȜET *Cert. Tractates* Wks. 1888 I. 8 Approprying the Kirk landis..to zour awin kechingis. **1677** W. HUGHES *Man of Sin* III. iv. 132 Purgatory makes the Popes Kitching hot, and his inferior Clergies too.

†**d.** Culinary art; cooking. *Obs. rare.*

13.. *K. Alis.* 4933 [4917] (MS. Laud) Flesshe hij eten Raw & hoot Wiþouten kycchen.

e. The culinary department; = CUISINE.

1679 *Gentlem. Calling* x. 80 Cookery is become a very mysterious Trade, the Kitchin has almost as many Intricacies as the Schools. **1752** CHESTERF. *Lett.* (1792) III. 274 The German kitchen is..execrable, and the French delicious; how-ever never commend the French kitchen at a German table.

f. Phr. *to go into* (or *to take tea in*) *the kitchen*: see quots. ? *Obs.*

1889 BARRÈRE & LELAND *Dict. Slang* I. 415/2 *To go into the kitchen* (popular), to drink one's tea out of the saucer; an allusion to the vulgar method of drinking very common among servants. **1894** G. F. NORTHALL *Folk-Phrases* 30 To take tea in the kitchen = To pour tea from the cup into the saucer, and drink it from this.

g. A part of a casino at Monte Carlo where gamblers place smaller bets than in the *salles privées*.

1931 W. HOLTBY *Poor Caroline* i. 25 In the kitchen the whirring of wheels, the jangle of voices..had grown intolerable. **1932** WODEHOUSE *Louder & Funnier* 255 It may be that your neighbours at the Le Touquet tables have a winsomeness lacking in those who congest the 'kitchen' at Monte Carlo. **1964** A. WYKES *Gambling* xii. 288 The old Winter Casino has 11 rooms. The smallest (i.e., the ones where the stakes are smallest) are known collectively as 'the Kitchen'. This is where the majority of Monte Carlo's 'amateur' gamblers play.

h. The percussion section of an orchestra or band. *slang.*

1931 G. JACOB *Orchestral Technique* vii. 68 We now come to a consideration of the percussion group (commonly known as 'the kitchen'), chief among which stand the *Timpani* (or kettledrums). **1934** S. R. NELSON *All about Jazz* ii. 49 Next in the rhythm section we will have a look at the 'gentlemen of the kitchen'.

†**2.** A utensil in which food is prepared.

a. Name in New England for a Dutch oven. **b.** *Sc.* A tea-urn. *Obs.*

1782 SIR J. SINCLAIR *Obs. Scot. Dial.* 171 *A kitchen*, a tea-urn, or vase. **1828** WEBSTER, *Kitchen*, a utensil for roasting meat; as, a tin kitchen. **1858** RAMSAY *Remin.* v. (1870) 118 The kitchen [tea-urn] is just coming in.

3. (Formerly also ***kitchen meat***.) Food from the kitchen; hence, any kind of food (as meat, fish, etc.), eaten with bread or the like, as a relish; by extension, anything eaten with bread, potatoes, porridge, or other staple fare to render it more palatable or more easily eaten. Thus butter or cheese is 'kitchen' to bare bread, milk is 'kitchen' to porridge. Chiefly *Sc.* or *north. Ir.* (= Welsh *enllyn.*)

14.. *Sir Beues* (MS. C.) 96/1917 And seruyd hym..of the kechyne metys fyne. **1596** DALRYMPLE tr. *Leslie's Hist. Scot.* I. 91 A verie smal portione of kitschine meit, buttir, milke, or cheis. **1721** KELLY *Scot. Prov.* 127 Hunger is good kitchen meat.

1535 STEWART *Cron. Scot.* I. 81 Herbis grene and frutt.. And quhilis milk..Without kitching or ony kynd of kaill. **1562** TURNER *Herbal* II. L vj b, The most part vse Basil and eate it with oyle and gare sauce for a sowle or kitchen. **1567** *Earl Mar's Househ. Bk.* in Chalmers *Mary* (1818) I. 178 Kiching to the violaris; Item, ij quarteris of muttoun; ij powterie; with potagis, and fische [etc.] **1795** *Statist. Acc. Scotl.* XIV. 401 The cottagers..have not always what is called kitchen, that is, milk or beer, to their meals. *Ibid.* XVI. 39 Salt herrings too made great part of their kitchen (*opsonium*), a word that here signifies whatever gives a relish to bread or porridge. **1862** *Hislop's Prov. Scot.* 41 Butter to butter's nae kitchen. **1886** STEVENSON *Kidnapped* xxiii. 227 We were glad to get the meat and never fashed for kitchen. *Mod. Sc. Prov.* Hunger is the best kitchen.

4. In a smelting-furnace: see quot.

1881 RAYMOND *Mining Gloss.*, *Laboratory*, the space between the fire and flue-bridges of a reverberatory furnace in which the work is performed; also called the kitchen.

II. *attrib.* and *Comb.*

5. Simple *attrib.* Of, pertaining to, or connected with, a kitchen.

a. With names of persons, denoting esp. those employed in a kitchen, as ***kitchen-artist, -boy, -clerk, -drudge, -folk, -girl, -lass, Malkin, -man, -mechanic, -page, -slave, -slut, -trull, -vestal, -woman.***

a **1661** HOLYDAY *Juvenal* 235 The great Roman *kitchin-artist Apicius. **1470–85** MALORY *Arthur* VII. ix, Why folowest thou me thou *kechyn boye? **1588** J. UDALL *Diotrephes* (Arb.) 11 He tooke me up as if I had bin but a kitchin boye. **1712** ARBUTHNOT *John Bull* III. vi, Frog, that was my father's kitchin-boy, he pretend to meddle with my estate! *c* **1380** WYCLIF *Sel. Wks.* III. 277 Stiwardis, or *kechene clerkis. **1615** J. STEPHENS *Satyr. Ess.* A vij b, Make him judge, Betwixt rare beauties and a *kitchin-drudge. **1901** M. FRANKLIN *My Brilliant Career* iii. 13 The dashing snake yarns told by our *kitchen-folk at Bruggabrong. **1912** W. OWEN *Let.* 1 Feb. (1967) 114, I.. must unpack a Crate of *China*... Fit occupation for me, who have far more knowledge of these matters than the kitchen-folk. **1700** W. KING *Transactioneer* 8 Every *Kitchen Girl about the Town knows Jamaica Pepper. **1835** J. H. INGRAHAM *South-West* II. 253 There are some Yankee 'kitchen girls',..who can do more house work..than three or four negro servants. **1957** M. SPARK *Comforters* ii. 33 The kitchen girls grumble about the work. **1826** GALT *Lairds* i. (E.D.D.), Jenny Clatterpans, the *kitchen-lass, answers the summons. **1607** SHAKS. *Cor.* II. i. 224 The *Kitchin Malkin pinnes Her richest Lockram 'bout her reechie necke. **1849** I. TAYLOR *Loyola & Jes.* (1857) 187 He would be *kitchenman. **1910** *Granta* 11 June 10 His door was sported, but on a covered dish left outside by a *kitchen-man I observed three slices of cold beef. **1930** Kitchen man [see BED *sb.* 1 g]. **1887** *Lantern* (New Orleans) 23 July 2/2 A..dirty looking *kitchen mechanic called Maggie Howard. **1931** 'D. STIFF' *Milk & Honey Route* 215 A hobo camp cook, a kitchen mechanic. **1942** Z. N. HURSTON in A. Dundes *Mother Wit* (1973) 224/2 Best you can do is to confidence some kitchen-mechanic out of a dime or two. **1969** L. G. SORDEN *Lumberjack Lingo* 67 *Kitchen mechanic*, a dishwasher in a logging camp. Cookee. **1470–85** MALORY *Arthur* VII. v, Torne ageyn bawdy *kechyn page. **1530** TINDALE *Answ. More* I. iv. Wks. III. 88 The kitchen-page, turning the spit. **1538** BALE *Thre Lawes* 381 Where are these vyllen knaues, The deuyls owne *kychyn slaues? **1859** G. MEREDITH *R. Feverel* 393 He got among them *kitchen sluts. **1611** SHAKS. *Cymb.* v. v. 177 Our bragges Were crak'd of *Kitchen-Trulles. **1590** —— *Com. Err.* IV. iv. 78 The *kitchin vestall scorn'd you. **1861** MRS. CARLYLE *Lett.* III. 77 The Welsh housemaid, whom I have decided to make *kitchen-woman.

b. With terms denoting the building containing the kitchen, its parts or surroundings, etc., as ***kitchen-building, -chimney, -court, -door, -gutter, -hatch, -hearth, -lum*** (Sc.), ***-stair, -yard.***

1886 WILLIS & CLARK *Cambridge* III. 553 The *kitchen-building of S. John's College. **1711** SHAFTESB. *Charac.* (1737) III. 219 Who took the *kitchin-chimney and dripping-pan for their delight. **1634** RAINBOW *Labour* (1635) 24 Let all the..heards..lay downe their life at his *kitching doore. **1848** THACKERAY *Van. Fair* xxxii, A knock might have been heard at the kitchen door. *c* **1440** *Promp. Parv.* 274/1 *Kychyne gotere, *alucium.* **1750** CARTE *Hist. Eng.* II. 64 A poor Irish scholar..begging some relief at the *Kitchen-hatch. **1790** *Laws Harvard Coll.* 40 The Waiters shall take the victuals at the kitchen-hatch, and carry the same to the several tables. *a* **1800** COWPER tr. *Bourne's Cricket* 2 Little inmate full of mirth, Chirping on my *kitchen hearth. **1819** SCOTT *Bride of Lamm.* xi, The thunner's come right down the *kitchen-lumm. **1844** C. M. YONGE *Abbeychurch* ix. 188 Katherine, seeing Elizabeth go towards the *kitchen stairs. **1902** *Granta* 3 May 287 It was the Fancy Dress Ball of the season, and the Duchess of Billingsgate was waiting at the head of the kitchen-stair to receive her guests.

c. With names of utensils, articles of furniture, etc., belonging to the kitchen, as ***kitchen-board, -boiler, -chair, -clock, cupboard, -dresser, -fire, -furniture, -goods, -grate, -implement, -jack, -knife, -poker, -range, scissors, stool, -stove, -table, unit, -utensil, -vessel, -ware.***

1552 HULOET, *Kytchen bourdes, or instrumentes perteyninge to the kytchen, *magida.* **1853** HICKIE tr. *Aristoph.* (1887) I. 188 A hole in the *kitchen-boiler. **1847** C. BRONTË *J. Eyre* xviii, In its place stood a deal table and a *kitchen chair. **1856** EMERSON *Eng. Traits, Race* Wks. (Bohn) II. 24 The *kitchen-clock is more convenient than sidereal time. **1865** *Trans. Illinois Agric. Soc. 1862* V. 161 The warm *kitchen cupboard. **1916** *Daily Colonist* (Victoria, B.C.) 4 July 12/2 (Advt.), Kitchen cupboard with closed cupboard and drawers in base, separate open shelving on top. *a* **1643** SUCKLING *Poems* (1646) 12 No *Kitching fire, nor eating flame. **1785** *Daily Universal Reg.* 1 Jan. 2/2 Two waggons, loaded with his Majesty's *kitchen furniture. **1726** SWIFT *Gulliver* II. iv, The *kitchen grate, the prodigious pots and kettles [etc.]. **1969** M. PUGH *Last Place Left* xi. 68 She turned with a *kitchen knife in her hand. **1785** *Daily Universal Reg.* 1 Jan. 3/2 Perpetual ovens, in *Kitchen Ranges..upon an entirely new construction, heated without the assistance of any flue. **1807** SOUTHEY *Espriella's Lett.* (1808) I. 158 Took me into his kitchen..to show me what he called the kitchen-range. **1907** *Yesterday's Shopping* (1969) 214/2 Scissors, *kitchen—6½ in., 0/11½. **1966** *Olney Amsden & Sons Ltd. Price List* 33 Kitchen Scissors..10/6. **1926–7** *Army & Navy Stores Catal.* 140/2 **Kitchen stools*..Made of Deal..height 14 in.—3/9. **1968** A. LASKI *Keeper* ii. 15 ' Now, tell me all about it,' she commanded, perched..on the kitchen stool. **1738** F. MOORE *Trav.* I. 17 (Jod.) Like a turtle on its back upon the *kitchen table of an alderman. **1937** *N.Y. Times* 21 Mar. III. 9/2 The demand for electrical *kitchen units is greatest in the Midwest. **1958** *House & Garden* Mar. 120 (Advt.), You can start with an EZEE Sink Unit and gradually build your dream kitchen around it... EZEE are the only kitchen units you can buy in a complete range. **1596** DALRYMPLE tr. *Leslie's Hist. Scot.* I. 94 Pottis, panis, and vthir *kitchine veshels. **1722** DE FOE *Plague* (1884) 188 Some *Kitchin-ware for ordering their Food. **1930** H. CRANE *Bridge*, I ran a donkey engine..In Panama..Then Yucatan selling kitchen-ware. **1967** *Times* 11 Nov. 13/8 It was common ground that 'kitchen-ware' meant 'ware' of such a class as to be appropriate to use in a kitchen, but that consumer goods and mere packaging were excluded. **1974** J. DRUMMOND *Boon Companions* xxv. 78 The display windows were still lit. He looked past kitchen-ware and crockery.

d. With products or requisites of the kitchen, as ***kitchen-brewis, -fare, foil, -grease, -herb, -lee, match, paper.***

1872 TENNYSON *Gareth & Lynette* 760 All The *kitchen brewis that was ever supt. *a* **1715** WYCHERLEY *Bill of Fare* Posth. Wks. 1728 I. 175 But with him on his *Kitchen-Fare to fall. **1958** *Observer* 21 Sept. 8/5 Stud the joint with a few cloves..before wrapping it up generously in *kitchen foil. **1961** *Guardian* 24 Mar. 12/6 Wrapping the fish in well-buttered kitchen foil. **1823** J. BADCOCK *Dom. Amusem.* 149 Tallow, vegetable oils, or *kitchen grease. **1638** FORD *Fancies* v. ii, To thrust my head into a brazen tub of *kitchen-lee. **1955** J. D. MACDONALD *Brass Cupcake* iii. 29 Chief Powy stood nibbling on a *kitchen match. **1973** R. THOMAS *If you can't be Good* (1974) xix. 165 He would stick a cigarette between his lips and light it with a kitchen match. **1846** *Jewish Manual, or Pract. Information Jewish & Mod. Cookery* 186 Tie with pack-thread white *kitchen paper, so as to prevent the paste coming off. **1962** F. T. DAY *Introd. to Paper* viii. 87 Household rolls, plain or with printed designs, tile and kitchen papers..are a few of the varieties which are rewound on the winding machine from the larger diameter rolls. **1974** D. FLETCHER *Lovable Man* i. 37 A wad of absorbent kitchen paper.

e. With abstract sbs., as ***kitchen-aphorism, -commentary, -invention, -science, -similitude, -skill, -term, -vassalage.***

1646 SIR T. BROWNE *Pseud. Ep.* I. x. (1686) 30 Culinary prescriptions and *Kitchin Aphorisms. **1586** T. B. *La Primaud. Fr. Acad.* I. 197 We..studie *kitchin commentaries, as much as any good science. **1711** SHAFTESB. *Charac.* (1737) II. 423 You wou'd be apt..to have less appetite, the more you..descended into the *kitchin-science. **1605** CAMDEN *Rem.* (1636) 17 We first taught the French all their *Kitchen-skill. **1872** TENNYSON *Gareth & Lynette* 156 Thro' villain *kitchen-vassalage.

f. *Comb.*, as ***kitchen-bed-sittingroom, -diner, -dining-room, -living-room.*** A room serving both as a kitchen and as a room of the type designated in the second (or further) element.

1951 KOESTLER *Age of Longing* ix. 152 The 'study' had at first been a corner of their kitchen-bed-sittingroom, partitioned off by a sheet. **1961** *Times* 11 Dec. 13/7 The kitchen-diner is much favoured and consequently catered for. **1974** *Country Life* 28 Feb. (Suppl.) 30/2 Bathroom, lounge, kitchen/diner, cloakroom. **1963** N. MARSH *Dead Water* (1964) vi. 161 Nobody had visited the kitchen-dining-room while she drank her coffee. **1974** *Times* 3 May 11/3 The kitchen-dining room..is 19 ft. by 8 ft. **1904** *Westm. Gaz.* 13 Dec. 8/1 Three bedrooms, kitchen-living room, scullery, and out-houses. **1955** D. CHAPMAN *Home & Social Status* ii. 32 Houses built in pairs or small rows, with a kitchen or kitchen-living-room..bedrooms and bathroom. **1963** N. MARSH *Dead Water* (1964) v. 121 The old kitchen..had been converted into a kitchen-living-room.

6. Objective and locative, as ***kitchen-haunter, plunderer; kitchen-bred*** adj.

1647–8 WOOD *Life* 15 Feb. (O.H.S.) I. 140 Those greedie dogs and kitchin-haunters, who noint their chops every night with greese. **1676** MARVELL *Mr. Smirke* Wks. 1875 IV. 83 He is a meer Kitchin-plunderer, and attacks but the baggage. **1775** SHERIDAN *Rivals* II. i, You little, impertinent, insolent, kitchen-bred [etc.].

7. Special Combs.: †**kitchen-bob** (BOB[1] 9), a wood-louse or myriapod; †**kitchen-cordial** = KITCHEN-PHYSIC; **kitchen Dutch** [tr. Du. *kombuis-Hollands*], now *rare*, the dialect of Afrikaans spoken by Cape Coloured people in the Western Province of S. Africa; later, used by English speakers as a contemptuous term for Afrikaans; **kitchen evening** *Austral.* and *N.Z.*, a party to which guests bring gifts of kitchenware for a bride-to-be; †**kitchen-gain** = KITCHEN-FEE; †**kitchen-garth, -ground**, a kitchen-garden; **kitchen Kaffir**, now *rare*, a *lingua franca* of southern Africa; = FANAGALO; **kitchen-Latin**, inferior Latin, dog-Latin; **kitchen meat**:

see sense 3; †**kitchen-medicine** = KITCHEN-PHYSIC; **kitchen-parlour**, a room serving both as kitchen and parlour; **kitchen-plot** = *kitchen-ground*; **kitchen-pokerness** *nonce-wd.*, a stiffness like that of a kitchen-poker; **kitchen police**, in the U.S. army, enlisted men detailed to help the cook, wash dishes, etc.; the work of these men; **kitchen shower** *U.S.*, = *kitchen evening*; **kitchen tea** *Austral.* and *N.Z.*, = *kitchen evening*; †**kitchen-tillage**, vegetables for the kitchen; †**kitchen-trade**, a set of kitchen-utensils. Also KITCHEN-FEE, -GARDEN, etc.

1610 GUILLIM *Heraldry* III. xvii. (1660) 210 *Kitchin bobs, which being touched gather themselves round like a Ball. **1597-8** BP. HALL *Sat.* II. iv. 31 If nor a dram of treacle sovereign,.. Nor *kitchen cordials can it remedy, Certes his time is come. **1894** F. A. BARKLY *Boers & Basutos* (ed. 2) vii. 109 By this time they [*sc.* our two children] could both speak Sesuto and 'Low' or '*Kitchen Dutch' (as it is called in those parts) well. **1899** W. S. LOGEMAN *How to speak Dutch* (ed. 2) Pref., My friend J. F. van Oordt, who has tried to strike the happy medium between 'High Dutch', not often understood by the people, and the 'Kombuis-Hollands' (Kitchen-Dutch) of the uneducated coloured servants. **1959** *Chambers's Encycl.* XII 763/2 By 1875, when the spoken language was firmly established, S. J. du Toit founded a 'Society of True Afrikaners' to propagate the written language; this met at first with violent opposition from the peasant and the politician—both English and Dutch—and Afrikaans was called kitchen Dutch, as the Greek of the Bible was once supposed to be 'bad' Greek. **1964** V. POHL *Dawn & After* 102 What delighted us most was the originality of Gashep's speech. To us he spoke a kind of kitchen Dutch into which he introduced English and Sesuto words. **1931** *Auckland Star* 22 Mar. 7/2 A *kitchen evening was given by Mr. and Mrs. A. R. Gillett at their residence ..in honour of Miss Sabina Gardner, whose marriage..to Mr. P. Richardson takes place shortly. **1589** GREENE *Menaphon* (Arb.) 86 Thy sweat vpon thy face dooth oft appeare, Like to my mothers fat and *Kitchin gaine. **1520** in *Laing Charters* (1899) 82 A gardyne, called..the *kitchengarthe. **1712** J. JAMES tr. *Le Blond's Gardening* 3 These make the Perfection of the Art of Gardening..to consist in a *Kitchen-Ground. **1862** G. H. MASON *Zululand* iv. 38 In adopting [the official dialect]..no doubt, the Bishop has been guided by one of the chief clerks in the native department; who was born and reared amongst the Cape Colony Caffres, and, consequently, prefers it to learning Zulu proper; which, of course, is held in contempt by all officials, and sneeringly called '*Kitchen Kaffir'. **1924** *Cape Argus Mag.* 2 Feb. 5 A wonderful language is kitchen Kafir, a weird medley of dialects, interspersed with English words. **1936** [see BAROTSE]. **1962** 'D. WILSON' *Search for Geoffrey Goring* vii. 144 He speaks a bit of English and some Kitchen Kaffir as well as Swahili. **1971** T. SHARPE *Riotous Assembly* (1973) ii. 15 She had spoken to him in Kitchen Kaffir, a pidgin Zulu reserved only for the most menial and mentally retarded black servants. **18..** CARLYLE *Misc., Boswell's Johnson* (1872) IV. 129 Some Benedictine priests, to talk *kitchen-latin with. **1737** GRIFFITH JONES *Lett. to Mrs. Bevan* 526, I..Incline to try *Kitchen Medicines with stricter Rules of liveing. **1848** THACKERAY *Van. Fair* xxvi, Her mother..dived down to the lower regions of the house to a sort of *kitchen-parlour. **1843** HT. MARTINEAU *Hill & Valley* 50 Another portion of his garden was half *kitchen-plot. **1836-9** DICKENS *Sk. Boz, Watkins Tottle* (1839) 460 He..had a clean-cravatish formality of manner, and *kitchen-pokerness of carriage. **1917** *Kitchen police [see *K.P.* s.v. K 4 f]. **1918** *Wells Fargo Messenger* Jan. 87/3 My present position does not require me to perform any of the so-called dreaded duties, such as guard duty, kitchen police, stable orderly. **1918** FARROW *Dict. Mil. Terms* 330 *Kitchen police*, those charged with the scullery work of the kitchen. **1929** F. A. POTTLE *Stretchers* (1930) 33 Before first call, six or more unfortunates crept out of bed and went on kitchen police... 'K.P.' is for good reason the most hated detail in the army. **1936** *Amer. Speech* XI. 51 When you have reached the stage where you know that an M.P. is not a Member of Parliament and that kitchen police do not carry clubs, no one can send you to the warehouse to bring back a skirmish line. **1924** H. CROY *R.F.D. No. 3* 89 It was a '*kitchen shower'. The glittering array was piled high, like a special sale in a racket store—dishpans, saucepans, pie pans,..and so on. **1974** *News & Reporter* (Chester, S. Carolina) 22 Apr. 2-A/5 Mrs. J. J. Key and Miss Mary Smyre were joint hostesses last Wednesday evening when they honored Miss Marilyn Hicks, bride-elect of the season, with a kitchen shower at the Key home on Columbia Street. **1948** N. SCANLAN *Rusty Road* xvii. 195 A 'linen tea' for the bride-elect, and a '*kitchen tea' and a 'China tea' followed. **1965** *Sunday Mail* (Brisbane) 28 Nov. 26 Michelle Bowes and Patricia Donovan..gave the bride a kitchen tea on Friday. **1970** G. GREER *Female Eunuch* 116 The more class the families can pretend to the more they can exact in the way of presents at showers, kitchen teas and the like. **1669** WORLIDGE *Syst. Agric.* (1681) 45 They are sowen..in the Spring with other the like *Kitchen-Tillage. **1693** DRYDEN *Juvenal* x. (1697) 250 Pans, Cans, and..a whole *Kitchin Trade.

Hence '**kitchendom**, '**kitchenful**; '**kitchenward** *adv.*

1859 W. COLLINS *Q. of Hearts* (1875) 50 A whole kitchenful of people. **1872** TENNYSON *Gareth & Lynette* 1044 Our good King Who lent me thee, the flower of kitchendom. **1876** LANIER *Clover* 28 in *Poems*, And, kitchenward, the rattling bucket plumps Souse down the well.

kitchen ('kɪtʃɪn), *v.* [f. prec. sb.]

1. †**a.** *trans.* To entertain in the kitchen, to furnish with kitchen-fare. *Obs. rare*$^{-1}$.

1590 SHAKS. *Com. Err.* v. i. 415 There is a fat friend at your masters house, That kitchin'd me for you to day at dinner.

b. *intr.* To do the work of the kitchen, to cook.

1893 *Month* Apr. 522 The indefatigable Brother..was kitchening under difficulties.

2. *Sc. trans.* To serve as 'kitchen' or relish for (see prec. 3); to give a relish to, to render palatable, to season.

1721 RAMSAY *Poet's Wish* iii, I can be well content To eat my bannock on the bent, And kitchen 't wi' fresh air. **1786** BURNS *Scotch Drink* vii, His wee drap parritch or his bread, Thou kitchens fine. **1835-40** J. M. WILSON *Tales Borders* (1851) XX. 205, I kitchened my loaf..with a penny-worth of butter. **1865** LIVINGSTONE *Zambesi* 271 There is an unpleasant sensation of wanting what the Scotch know by the word kitchen, ὄψον. We made the fat kitchen the lean.

b. *Sc.* To use sparingly as 'kitchen' with food; to make (a thing) go far; to husband carefully.

1787 in GROSE *Prov. Gloss.* **1825-80** in JAMIESON.

Hence '**kitchening** *vbl. sb.*, cooking, cookery.

1883 *Athenæum* 11 Aug. 172 Crying out for old books, and good kitchening, and good manners.

kitchenable ('kɪtʃɪnəb(ə)l), *a.* [f. KITCHEN *sb.* or *v.* + -ABLE.] Suitable for cooking and serving at table.

1905 *Chambers's Jrnl.* Feb. 193/2 There is probably no bird upon our game-list which is more eagerly sought after than the wood-cock..for his kitchenable qualities. **1913** G. BOLAM *Wild Life Wales* vi. 50 In judging of the probable kitchenable qualities of a bird.

†'**kitchenary**, *a. Obs. rare*$^{-1}$. In 7 -inary. [f. KITCHEN *sb.* + -ARY.] Of, or resembling that of, a kitchen; culinary.

1662 J. CHANDLER *Van Helmont's Oriat.* 180 The Schooles do understand that there is in the heart a kindled, Kitchinary and smoakie fire.

kitchen cabinet. orig. *U.S.* [f. KITCHEN *sb.* + CABINET.] **1.** *Politics.* A group of unofficial advisers (orig. of the President of the U.S.A.), popularly believed to have greater influence than the actual Cabinet (or the elected representatives, etc.). Hence, a private or unofficial group of advisers to the holder of an elected office.

1832 W. S. ARCHER *Let.* 8 July in A. C. Cole *Whig Party in South* (1913) 13 If there be no other mode of preventing its being given to the most despicable of all the Protegees of the Kitchen Cabinet. **1842** *Ainsworth's Mag.* Dec. 554 We will hurl the kitchen cabinet tyrants from their stools. **1860** J. PARTON *Life A. Jackson* III. xvi. 183 These were the gentlemen—Lewis, Green, Hill and Kendall—who, at the beginning of the new administration, were supposed to have most of the President's ear and confidence, and were stigmatized by the opposition as the Kitchen Cabinet. **1893** 'MARK TWAIN' in *Century Mag.* Dec. 237 Her master left a couple of dollars lying unprotected on his desk... She covered the tempter with a book, and another member of the kitchen cabinet got it. **1904** *N.Y. Herald* 14 Sept. 5 The kitchen cabinet is a development of the ascendency of Governor Odell in republican affairs. It consists of the body guard of his closest friends and advisers. **1952** *Manch. Guardian Weekly* 27 Nov. 3 Mr. Brownell is part of the Dewey 'kitchen cabinet'. **1969** *Guardian* 21 Mar. 1/1 Key policy decisions were being taken by the Prime Minister and a kind of 'Kitchen Cabinet' of intimates. **1975** *Times Lit. Suppl.* 23 May 576/4 Every ruler operates on two levels, the personal and the official, that is, he has a kitchen cabinet and a body of ministers.

2. A cabinet for domestic and culinary utensils, etc., in a kitchen.

1895 *Montgomery Ward Catal.* 607/1 Kitchen Cabinets. Very useful about a house where a 'shortage' of closets or cupboards is felt. *Ibid.* 612/1 Kitchen Cabinet Table... Has a molding board, spice and cutlery drawer, sugar and groceries drawer, flour drawer..and a cupboard for cooking utensils. **1911** *Daily Colonist* (Victoria, B.C.) 29 Apr. 4/4 (Advt.), These Kitchen Cabinets have revolutionized labor-saving in the kitchen of today. **1922** S. LEWIS *Babbitt* vi. 68 Babbitt picked up his partner..at his kitchen-cabinet works. **1933** *Discovery* July 219/2 Most houses and flats are fitted as a matter of course with kitchen cabinets and refrigerators, hanging cupboards in bedrooms and so on. **1972** M. J. BOSSE *Incident at Naha* 14 The sugar bowl would have gone back into a kitchen cabinet.

kitchener[1] ('kɪtʃɪnə(r)). [f. KITCHEN *sb.* + -ER[1].]

1. One employed in a kitchen; *esp.* in a monastery, he who had charge of the kitchen.

c **1440** *Relig. Pieces fr. Thornton MS.* 53 Penance sall be kychynnere. **1614** *Nottingham Rec.* IV. 319 To the black gard the kitchinners *vs.* **1820** SCOTT *Monast.* xv, Two most important officers of the convent, the kitchener and refectioner. **1884** *19th Cent.* Jan. 110 Capons, eggs, salmon, eels, herring, &c..passed to the account of the kitchener.

2. A cooking-range fitted with various appliances such as ovens, plate-warmers, water-heaters, etc.

1851 *Catal. Exhib.* Class 22, No. 38 This kitchener or cooking grate is remarkable for economy in fuel. **1867** *Civil Serv. Gaz.* 29 June 402/1 Improved London-made Kitcheners. **1884** *Health Exhib. Catal.* 68/1 Patent Kitchener with two low ovens, boiler, gas hob, &c.

Kitchener[2] ('kɪtʃɪnə(r)). The name of Herbert Horatio *Kitchener*, first Earl Kitchener of Khartoum and of Broome (1850-1916), British soldier, used *absol.*, *attrib.*, or in the possessive to denote a man of his imposing and taciturn personality, soldiers recruited while he was Secretary of State for War (1914-16), or aspects of appearance or of dress characteristic of him or of these troops. Also allusively. So '**Kitchenerism**, a quality characteristic of Kitchener.

1903 *Westm. Gaz.* 31 Aug. 1/2 The outer man of this 'Kitchener of Russian finance'..is in keeping with his personality. **1916** J. N. HALL *Kitchener's Mob* i. 1 'Kitchener's Mob' they were called in the early days of August, 1914, when London hoardings were clamorous with the first calls for volunteers. *Ibid.* iii. 23 'Kitchener's Rag-Time Army I calls it!' growls the veteran of South African fame. *Ibid.* viii. 125 It was not until the arrival on active service of Kitchener's armies that the construction of the double line of reserve or support trenches was undertaken. **1916** H. G. WELLS *Mr. Britling* I. iii. 74 He was presented as a monster of energy and self-discipline; as the determined foe of every form of looseness, slackness, and easy-goingness... 'It's Kitchenerism.'.. 'It's the army side of the efficiency stunt.' **1925** FRASER & GIBBONS *Soldier & Sailor Words* 136 *Kitchener's blue*, a name given to the blue serge uniform served out to recruits in the autumn of 1914 in consequence of the shortage of khaki. **1928** BLUNDEN *Undertones of War* 43 The first Kitchener battalion, they said, to hold the sector. **1929** *Papers Mich. Acad. Sci. Arts & Lett.* X. 304/1 *Kitcheners*, a name given by the Regulars to soldiers enlisting for the emergency. **1930** C. D. BAKER-CARR *From Chauffeur to Brigadier* ix. 127 The new Kitchener Divisions were now beginning to arrive. **1937** PARTRIDGE *Dict. Slang* 458/1 *Kitchener wants you!* A military c.p. to a man selected for filthy, arduous or perilous work. **1965** BROPHY & PARTRIDGE *Long Trail* 139 *K1* (*K One*), the first 100,000 of the New (Kitchener's) Army of 1914 volunteers. **1969** 'A. CADE' *Turn up Stone* i. 20 A large European wearing a pink shirt, baggy grey trousers and a drooping Kitchener moustache. **1971** D. MEIRING *Wall of Glass* viii. 62 He wore summer khaki drill, with Kitchener helmet and Sam Browne.

kitchenette (kɪtʃɪ'nɛt). orig. *U.S.* [See -ETTE.] A small room or alcove in a house, flat, etc., combining kitchen and pantry. Also *attrib.*

1910 *Variety* 7 May 10/4 Mr. and Mrs. Nellie are going to have a swell apart. and they call the 'cook house' in a swell apart. a kitchenette. **1919** *Ladies' Home Jrnl.* Oct. 117 Ovenette and kitchenette cookery. **1921** *Daily Colonist* (Victoria, B.C.) 2 Oct. 26/7 Kitchenettes and bathrooms are also installed. **1922** *Hotel World* 25 Mar. 10/2 Kitchenette suites of 2 rooms. **1922** *Glasgow Herald* 28 Apr. 5 The New York business woman..wants her kitchenette and her home cooking, be it ever so simple. **1929** F. KILBOURNE *Dot & Will* 188 They had a little kitchenette apartment on the North Side. **1930** J. CANNAN *No Walls of Jasper* iii. 56 She had never thought it..too much trouble to..bustle away into the kitchenette to make up something nice and tasty for her George. **1934** [see *drying-rack*]. **1955** [see DINETTE]. **1960** *Times* 25 Feb. 1/3 Bed-sitter, with kitchenette, in private house Kensington. **1974** *Country Life* 30 May (Suppl.) 20 Granny annexe comprising: living room, kitchenette, bedroom and shower room.

kitchen-fee. [See FEE *sb.*[2] 8. So called as being a perquisite of the cook.] The fat which drips from meat in roasting; skimmings of fat; dripping.

1485 *Inv.* in *Ripon Ch. Acts* (Surtees) 371, ij petræ et iiij lb. de kychyn fee, vijd. **1560** *Richmond Wills* (Surtees) 147 In tallowe, kytchynfye and butterr, x^{s}. **1614** MARKHAM *Cheap Husb.* II. xxiii. (1668) 79 Anoint the place with Tarr, Turpentine, and Kitchin-fee, mixt together. **1824** SCOTT *St. Ronan's* ii, The diet-loaf, raised wi' my ain fresh butter.. and no wi greasy kitchen-fee.

kitchen-garden.

1. A garden in which fruit and vegetables for the table are grown. Also *attrib.*

1580 HOLLYBAND *Treas. Fr. Tong*, *Iardin à herbes & arbres*, a kitchin garden. **1629** PARKINSON *Paradisus Terrestr.* title-p., With a Kitchen garden of all manner of herbes, rootes, & fruites for meate or sause. **1793** *Trans. Soc. Arts* (ed. 2) V. 45 Dutch Turneps, sowed on beds in my Kitchen garden. **1884** J. HATTON in *Harper's Mag.* July 234/2 There is a kitchen-garden with..asparagus beds and potato-patches.

attrib. **1664** EVELYN *Kal. Hort.* (1729) 193 Kitchen-Garden Herbs may now be planted as Parsley, Spinage, Onions, Leeks. **1712** J. JAMES tr. *Le Blond's Gardening* 3 A Garden..fill'd with Kitchen-Garden Stuff.

2. A kindergarten in which house-work, esp. kitchen-work, is taught. *U.S. local.*

1893 in *Barrows' Parlt. Relig.* II. 1483 Kindergartens, kitchengartens, and nightschools..are among the methods employed.

Hence **kitchen-'gardener, -'gardening.**

1766 ENTICK *London* IV. 191 The upper part is occupied as a warehouse by fruiterers and kitchen-gardeners. **1822-34** *Good's Study Med.* (ed. 4) II. 643 It was not..till the beginning of the sixteenth century that any great progress was made in the art of kitchen-gardening in our country. **1893** *Daily News* 26 Jan. 5/5 'Kitchen-gardening' is the curious name bestowed upon their labours by the ladies of an American city, who teach a class of poor children to sew, cook, dust, sweep, make beds, and wash clothes.

†'**kitchenist.** *nonce-wd.* [See -IST.] One employed in a kitchen; a cook.

a **1618** SYLVESTER *Tobacco Battered* 427 Limeburners, Alchymists, Brickmakers, Brewers, Colliers, Kitchenists.

kitchen-knave. *arch.* A scullion.

c **1440** *Promp. Parv.* 274/1 Kechyne knave, *lixa.* **1470-85** MALORY *Arthur* VII. vii, This is but a kechyn knaue that was fedde in kynge Arthurs kechyn for almesse. **1872** TENNYSON *Gareth & Lynette* 395 Grant me to serve For meat and drink among thy kitchen-knaves.

'**kitchen-maid.** A female servant employed in a kitchen, usually under the cook.

1550 BALE *Votaries* II. N iv, The king toke al their wiues, otherwise called their kichine maides..and put them all in the tower of London. **1675** WOOD *Life* 31 Mar. II. 311

Disinherited..because debauched and married his kitchin maid. **1892** MRS. OLIPHANT *Cuckoo in Nest* II. xxv. 133 The dinner, which an eager kitchen-maid..had the charge of.

kitchen-midden ('kɪtʃɪn,mɪd(ə)n). [A transl. of Da. *kjökken-* or *kökkenmödding*: see KITCHEN and MIDDEN, dung-hill, refuse-heap.] A refuse-heap of prehistoric date, consisting chiefly of the shells of edible molluscs and bones of animals, among which are often found stone implements and other relics of early man. Also *fig.* and *attrib.*

Such mounds are especially characteristic of the Danish coast, and were first brought into scientific notice by Danish archæologists, but they are also found in many other parts of the world.

[**1862** LATHAM *Channel Isl.* III. xviii. (ed. 2) 415 Just as in the Danish *kjokkemiddings* whole heaps of shells of the edible mollusca have been preserved.] **1863** LYELL *Antiq. Man* xix. 372 The old refuse-heaps, or 'kitchen-middens'. **1877** DAWSON *Orig. World* xiv. 311 The accumulation of kitchen-midden stuff in the course of the occupancy of caverns. **1883** *Contemp. Rev.* June 788 The mental kitchen middens of generations of savages.

'kitchen-'physic. *humorous.* Nourishment for an invalid, suitable for 'feeding up'.

1592 GREENE *Upst. Courtier* in *Harl. Misc.* (ed. Park) V. 406 If I be ill at ease, I take kitchyn physicke, I make my wife my doctor, and my garden my apoticaries shop. **1658** *Sir. T. Mayerne's Archim. Anglo-Gall.* Pref. 2 The Excellency of Kitchin-physick, beyond all Gally pots. **1738** SWIFT *Pol. Conversat.* ii. 154 Well, after all, Kitchen-Physic is the best Physic. **1863** J. R. W. *By-gone Days* 5 The Manse..being the resort of the sick and aged..when in want of what the minister's wife termed 'kitchen physic'.

So **'kitchen phy'sician**.

1797 MRS. A. M. BENNETT *Beggar Girl* IV. i. 21 The fever took its departure, and left Rosa in the hands of an excellent kitchen physician.

Kitchen rudder. [Named after J. G. A. *Kitchen*, Englishman, who patented the device in 1914.] A steering device for small craft consisting of a pair of curved deflectors either side of the propeller whose position is altered to change the course or speed of the vessel or to cause it to go backwards.

1920 *Engineer* 6 Feb. 149/1 The essential parts of the Kitchen rudders consist of two curved deflectors generally formed as parts of a circular cylinder, partly enclosing the propeller. **1920** *Shipbuilding & Shipping Rec.* 12 Feb. 200/2 (*caption*) Admiralty pinnace with Kitchen rudder. **1923** *Man. Seamanship* (Admiralty) II. 200 Boats are fitted with a clutch and reverse gear, clutch and reversing propellers, or clutch and Kitchen rudder. **1961** F. H. BURGESS *Dict. Sailing* 127 *Kitchen rudder*, one comprising two curved blades that may completely enclose the propeller; they are rotated by a wheel on the tiller to open or close for going either ahead or astern; the direction and speed are thus controlled from the tiller, while the engine runs unattended at one speed.

kitchenry ('kɪtʃɪnrɪ). *rare.* Also 7 **kitchinree.** [f. KITCHEN *sb.* + -RY.]

†**1.** The body of servants employed in a kitchen.

1609 HOLLAND *Amm.-Marcell.* XIV. vi. 12 Next unto whom goeth the blacke guard and kitchinree [L. *atratum coquinæ ministerium*]. **1658** W. SANDERSON *Graphice* 26 The Hall with Paintings of Neat-heards,..Milke-maides Minding Cattle, in proper degrees, some other also, of Kitchenry.

†**2.** The art of cooking, cookery. *Obs.*

1610 HOLLAND *Camden's Brit.* I. 450 Those..who beeing deinty toothed are iudicious clerkes in Kitchenrie.

3. Kitchen-utensils.

1890 in *Cent. Dict.*

kitchen sink. [f. KITCHEN *sb.* + SINK *sb.*¹ 1 c.]

a. A sink in which dirty dishes, vegetables, etc., are washed. Freq. used as a symbol of women's enslavement to the kitchen.

1873 *Young Englishwoman* May 259/3 Unwholesome smells—which I found all proceeded from (what Miss Nightingale calls) that abomination, the kitchen sink. **1930** *Archit. Rec.* Jan. 13/1 Until a few years ago, the kitchen sink would have been made of sheet zinc fitted over a box made by the carpenter. **1969** *Guardian* 6 Nov. 9/5 A situation in which married women find it impossible to return to work and have to return once more to the kitchen sink. **1973** J. CLEARY *Ransom* iii. 67 It was the housewives' hour... Perry Como..sang of the past; housewives dreamed with him over their kitchen sinks and unmade beds. **1973** *Guardian* 14 Feb. 11/2 Women stayed right where they were: for the most part at the kitchen sink, or in low-paid clerical or light manual work.

b. *fig.*

1888 KIPLING *Under Deodars* (1889) 5 All his ideas and powers of conversation..are taken from him by this—this kitchen-sink of a Government.

c. ***everything but the kitchen sink*** and similar phr.: everything imaginable.

1948 PARTRIDGE *Dict. Forces' Slang* 106 *Kitchen sink*, used only in the phrase indicating intense bombardment—'They chucked everything they'd got at us except, or including, the kitchen sink.' 'The kitchen stove' was also used. **1958** *Wall St. Jrnl.* 23 Oct. 4/4 Gen. Trudeau said the military services often slow down development of new weapons 'because we are such perfectionists that we want everything but the kitchen sink in a weapon'. **1965** 'E. MCBAIN' *Doll* x. 128 Brown began searching. 'Everything in here but the kitchen sink,' he said. **1966** —— *Eighty Million Eyes* xi. 189 We'll throw everything but the god-damn kitchen sink at you. **1967** L. WHITE *Crimshaw Memo.* (1968) iii. 61 He goes out and buys himself an XKE Jaguar..it had everything but the kitchen sink on it.

d. Used (with hyphen) *attrib.* or *absol.* to designate a group of English realistic painters of the 1950s and later, or their type of art, or a group of English realistic authors (chiefly playwrights) of the same period or their plays or publications.

1954 D. SYLVESTER in *Encounter* Dec. 61 (*title*) The kitchen sink. *Ibid.* 62/1 The post-war generation takes us back from the studio to the kitchen... The kitchen sink too. *Ibid.* 62/2 It is evident that neither objectivity nor abstraction is the aim of the young painters of the kitchen-sink school. **1956** L. MCINTOSH *Oxford Folly* 69 On the walls were several drawings and paintings of the 'Kitchen Sink' school of modern English painters, whose sordid subject matter contrasted with their luxurious setting. The one above the mantelpiece depicted a lavatory. **1959** *Listener* 19 Feb. 340/3 'Kitchen sink' painting is not an exclusive English phenomenon: it originated in France, with Rebeyrolle and Minaux. **1960** *Times* 15 Mar. 13/6 Mr. Ronald Duncan is reported as saying that the English Stage Company..presents only left wing 'kitchen sink' drama. **1960** *Guardian* 28 Oct. 9/5 The day of the social-realist, kitchen sink advertisement has dawned. **1963** *Times* 16 Feb. 9/3 If the British new wave were interested only in easy money they would stick to the slag-heap and the kitchen sink. **1965** *Punch* 26 May 762/1 The 'Kitchen-Sink' tag.. began as descriptive heading for a post-war school of painters (nudity, violence, squalor, blasphemy, subversiveness and distortion are somehow morally OK qualities in the visual arts) and only later became a pejorative title for a school of playwrights. **1973** *Black World* Apr. 41, I wasn't going to write any more Black 'kitchen sink' dramas.

So **,kitchen-'sinkery**.

1964 *Listener* 16 Apr. 624/1 We've been attacked for too much pessimism, sordidness, and kitchen-sinkery. **1969** B. TURNER *Circle of Squares* i. 7 The longest-ever season of kitchen-sinkery on our stages.

kitchen stove. [f. KITCHEN *sb.* + STOVE *sb.*¹ 5 a.]

a. A stove in a kitchen.

1845 *Knickerbocker* XXV. 106 He wished her in the south of France or the kitchen stove, rather than there. **1925** F. AYSCOUGH *Chinese Mirror* 386 Ts'ao Chün, Lord of the Kitchen-Stove. **1959** P. H. JOHNSON *Humbler Creation* xvi. 108 'Mrs. Fisher is a most awful stick,' Lucy said. 'One might as well say one's lines to the kitchen stove.' **1974** *Times* 21 Sept. 7/2 The kitchen stove, a low stout Rayburn of chipped yellow enamel.

b. ***everything but the kitchen stove*** and similar phr. = KITCHEN SINK c.

1927 E. WALLACE *Feathered Serpent* i. 9 'Got everything on except the kitchen stove,' said Mr. Crewe pleasantly... 'You're a fool to go out with all that stuff on you.' **1928** [see BOB *v.*³ 2 b]. **1948** [see KITCHEN SINK c]. **1959** *Listener* 8 Jan. 63/2 The assumption that, since Christmas is the only time children go to the theatre, they must therefore be given everything, including the kitchen-stove. **1960** M. CECIL *Something in Common* xxi. 235 'I suppose you haven't an ulcer?' Colin said that—apart from the kitchen stove—it was the one item he'd forgotten to bring. **1964** C. DALE *Other People* x. 178 There's Mum, hair tinted, face done up, everything on bar the kitchen stove.

'kitchen-stuff.

1. Material used in cooking; requisites for the kitchen, *esp.* vegetables.

1606 *Sir G. Goosecappe* III ii. in Bullen *O. Pl.* (1884) III. 52 To sooth their pallats with choyce kitchin-stuff. *c* **1710** CELIA FIENNES *Diary* (1888) 299 Another Garden for Kitchen Stuff. **1744** (*title*) Adam's Luxury and Eve's Cookery..Containing..Receipts for Dressing all sorts of Kitchen-Stuff.

2. The refuse or waste products of the kitchen; *spec.* dripping, kitchen-fee.

1577 B. GOOGE *Heresbach's Husb.* (1586) 904 All those that smell of grease or kitchingstuffe. **1583** STUBBES *Anat. Abus.* II. (1882) 49 They make them [candles] of all kind of kitchen stuffe, and other stinking baggage. **1697** DAMPIER *Voy.* (1729) I. 537 When they want Oil, they make use of Kitchin-stuff. **1719** D'URFEY *Pills* (1872) VI. 125 Come Maids bring out your Kitchen-stuff, Old Rags, or Women's Hair. **1836–9** DICKENS *Sk. Boz* v. (1849) 43/2 Shops for the purchase of rags, bones, old iron, and kitchen-stuff.

b. *fig.* Of persons or things. *contemptuous.*

1637 HEYWOOD *Royall King* III. Wks. 1874 VI. 46 Where be those kitchinstuffes here, shall we have no attendants? **1654** VILVAIN *Theol. Treat.* Suppl. 216 [They] scorn the book of Homilies as most cours contemptible Kitchin-stuf. **1754** WARBURTON *Ld. Bolingbroke's Philos.* (R.), Would you easily believe his lordship could pride himself in cooking up this old kitchin-stuff?

3. *attrib.* and *Comb.*

1603 DEKKER *Wonderfull Yeare* F ij, All the way he went, was more greazie than a kitchin-stuffe-wifes basket. **1608** MIDDLETON *Trick to Catch Old One* III. iv, Thou Kitchen-stuff-drab of beggary, roguery, &c. **1681** W. ROBERTSON *Phraseol. Gen.* (1693) 789 A kitchin-stuff-wench.

'kitchen-wench. *arch.* A girl employed in the kitchen, a kitchen-maid. *contemptuous.*

1590 SHAKS. *Com. Err.* III. ii. 96 She's the kitchin wench, & al grease. **1678** OTWAY *Friendship in F.* II. i, Chloris dwindles into a Kitchen-Wench. **1840** BARHAM *Ingol. Leg.*, *The Ghost*, His wife would..strike with all her might, As fast as kitchen-wenches strike a light.

kitcheny ('kɪtʃɪnɪ), *a.* [f. KITCHEN *sb.* + -Y.] Of or pertaining to the kitchen.

1874 MRS. WHITNEY *We Girls* v. 100 A specialty..hers was a very womanly..not to say kitcheny one. **1926** KIPLING *Debits & Credits* 328 We eat kitcheny food. **1971** P. DICKINSON *Sleep & his Brother* vi. 137 Doll had left the room..and was making kitcheny noises beyond. **1973** *Times* 16 Nov. 15 (*caption*) Most of the things are decidedly kitcheny.

kitchin, obs. var. of KINCHIN.

kite (kaɪt), *sb.* Forms: 1 **cyta**, 4 **kete**, **kijt**, **kuytte**, 4–5 **kuyte**, 4–7 **kyte**, (6 **kight**, **-e**, **kyght**, *Sc.* **kyt**), 5– **kite**. [OE. *cýta* (:—**kūtjon-*); no related word appears in the cognate languages.]

1. A bird of prey of the family *Falconidæ* and subfamily *Milvinæ*, having long wings, tail usually forked, and no tooth in the bill. **a.** *orig.* and *esp.* the common European species *Milvus ictinus* (*M. regalis*, *M. vulgaris*), also distinctively called *fork-tailed kite*, *royal kite*, or (from its reddish-brown general colour) *red kite*, and *glede*, formerly common in England, but now very rare.

c **725** *Corpus Gloss.* 333 *Butio*, cyta. **13..** *K. Alis.* 3048 Nultow never late ne skete A goshauk maken of a kete. *c* **1386** CHAUCER *Knt.'s T.* 321 Ther cam a kyte, whil they weren so wrothe, And baar awey the boon bitwixe hem bothe. *c* **1450** *Bk. Hawkyng* in *Rel. Ant.* I. 298 Draw hym oute of the mewe and put him in a grove, in a crowys neste, other in a kuytes. **1539** TONSTALL *Serm. Palm Sund.* (1823) 74 Their carkases there to lye to be deuoured by kytes & crowes. **1593** SHAKS. *2 Hen. VI*, III. i. 249 Wer't not all one, an emptie Eagle were set, To guard the Chicken from a hungry Kyte. **1663** COWLEY *Verses & Ess.*, *Ode Liberty* vi, To kites and meaner Birds he leaves the mangled Prey. **1766** PENNANT *Zool.* (1768) I. 141 The kite generally breeds in large forests, or wooded mountainous countries. **1828** SCOTT *F.M. Perth* xix, Her ear for bad news was as sharp as a kite's scent for carrion. **1870** MORRIS *Earthly Par.* II. III. 301 With wide wing The fork-tailed restless kite sailed over her, Hushing the twitter of the linnets near.

b. Applied with qualifying words to other species of the genus, or of the subfamily *Milvinæ*.

Arabian k., *Milvus ægyptiacus*; **Australian** or **square-tailed k.**, *M. isurus* (*Lophoictinia isura*); **black k.**, *M. ater* of southern Europe and northern Africa; **black-winged k.**, *Elanus cæruleus* of northern Africa; **brahminy k.**, *Haliastur indus* of Hindustan; **Indian** or **pariah k.**, *Milvus govinda*; **Mississippi k.**, *Ictinia mississippiensis*; **pearl** or **white-tailed k.**, *Elanus leucurus* of N. America; **swallow-tailed k.**, *Elanoides forficatus* of N. America.

Also locally applied (or misapplied), with or without qualification, to birds belonging to other divisions of *Falconidæ*, as the Buzzard (**bald k.**), Hen-harrier, and Kestrel.

1611 COTGR., *Buzart*, a Buzzard, or Bald-kite. *c* **1813** [see BRAHMINEE *a.*]. **1843** YARRELL *Brit. Birds* I. 72 The Swallow-tailed Kite..is only an occasional visitor to this country. **1847** LEICHHARDT *Jrnl.* x. 321 We had to guard it by turns..from a host of square-tailed kites (*Milvus isurus*). **1893** NEWTON *Dict. Birds* 491 There is a second European species..the *Milvus migrans* or *M. ater* of most authors, smaller in size... In some districts this is much commoner than the red Kite.

2. *fig.* A person who preys upon others, a rapacious person; a sharper; also more indefinitely as a term of reproach or detestation.

a **1553** UDALL *Royster D.* v. v. (Arb.) 83 Roister Doister that doughtie kite. **1599** SHAKS. *Hen. V*, II. i. 80 Fetch forth the Lazar Kite of Cressids kinde, Doll Teare-sheete. **1605** —— *Lear* I. iv. 284 Detested Kite, thou lyest. **1606** —— *Ant. & Cl.* III. xiii. 89 Ah you Kite. *c* **1614** FLETCHER *Wit without Money* I. i, Maintaining hospitals for kites and curs. **1841** CARLYLE *Misc.*, *Baillie* (1872) VI. 235 Food for learned sergeants and the region kites!

3. a. [From its hovering in the air like the bird.] A toy consisting of a light frame, usually of wood, with paper or other light thin material stretched upon it; mostly in the form of an isosceles triangle with a circular arc as base, or a quadrilateral symmetrical about the longer diagonal; constructed (usually with a tail of some kind for the purpose of balancing it) to be *flown* in a strong wind by means of a long string attached. Also, a modification of the toy kite designed to support a man in the air or to form part of an unpowered flying machine (cf. AEROPLANE 1).

Kites are also used of special shapes, or with special appliances, for various scientific and other purposes, e.g. the bird-kite, used to frighten partridges (see KITE *v.* 2); cf. also ELECTRIC *a.* 2 b, quot. 1898 here, and combs. in 9 b.

1664 BUTLER *Hud.* II. III. 414 As a Boy one night Did flie his Tarsel of a Kite, The strangest long-wing'd Hawk that flies. **1672** MARVELL *Reh. Transp.* I. 58 He may make a great Paper-kite of his own Letter of 850 pages. **1789** MRS. PIOZZI *Journ. France*, etc. I. 129 Boys flying kites, cut square like a diamond. **1826** VINEY & POCOCK *Brit. Pat. 5420*, This Patent is obtained for an Invention by which kites are made to act as..sails, for the purpose of navigating or drawing vessels.., for the purpose of raising weights or persons in the air,..or for the hoisting of flags. The peculiarities of these kites are:—..they have four lines by which their power is controlled or their course directed. **1827** D. JOHNSON *Ind. Field Sports* 22 A frame-work of split bamboos, resembling the frame of a paper kite. **1875** A. M. CLARK *Brit. Pat. 169*, This Invention relates to a kind of kite or ærial apparatus to be used for military and other purposes, its chief object being to raise to the desired height in the air, and to support in a sufficiently tranquil position for reconnoitring a scout, look out man, or sentry. **1880** *Daily News* 1 Sept. 5/2 The kite has been fiercely attacked as..a mean advantage to take of the birds [partridges]. **1889** H. S. MAXIM *Brit. Pat. 16,883*, My invention is chiefly designed..to provide for the construction of an aëronautic machine which can, while moving forward in the air, be caused to rise or descend at any desired velocity or to travel at any predetermined height

above the ground... I provide an adjustable covered framework or kite of very large dimensions... For convenience of description I will hereinafter term this covered framework or kite an 'aëroplane'. **1893** *23rd Rep. Aeronaut. Soc.* 17 What we have to do is to make the wings, whether fixed or flapping, in the requisite form, and add aëroplanes or kites, and find the necessary power to drive them along at their proper angles. **1894** *Proc. Internat. Conf. Aerial Navigation, Chicago, 1893* 253 Among the different free-flying models which I exhibited.. in the large hall of the Engineering Society in Vienna there was a model of my gliding aeroplane or kite, which illustrated the support to be obtained from the air. **1898** *Westm. Gaz.* 8 Mar. 10/1 Our own War Office have intimated that they are not prepared.. to make further trials with kites for military purposes.

fig. **1781** *Bell's Poets* I. *Life King* p. xxiii, Some of the political kites which flew about at that time.

b. ***to fly*** (or ***send up***) ***a kite*** (*fig.*): to try 'how the wind blows', i.e. in what direction affairs are tending. (See also 4.) A proposal or suggestion offered or 'thrown out' tentatively in order to 'see how the wind blows'. (Cf. BALLON D'ESSAI.) See also FLY *v.*[1] 5 a.

1831 PALMERSTON in Sir H. Lytton Bulwer *Life* (1871) II. 65 Charles John [King of Sweden] flew a kite at us for the Garter the other day, but without success. **1902** *Nature* 14 Aug. 380/2 A few suggestions have been thrown out by various students which must be regarded more as trial hypotheses than as definite conclusions, indeed they should be looked upon rather as 'Kites'. **1904** *Westm. Gaz.* 5 Aug. 2/2 The new Army scheme.. is to be debated on Monday, but whether as a Government proposal or the private kite of the Minister for War remains wholly obscure. **1973** A. MACVICAR *Painted Doll Affair* ii. 29 'I'm sorry ye're lumbered wi' me,' he said, sounding anything but sorry. I ignored this blatant kite.

c. An aeroplane. *slang*, esp. *Services'*.

The popular use of *kite* in this sense prob. originated with the 'box-kite' aeroplane (see BOX *sb.*[2] 24); but the uses in quots. 1838, 1909 are direct applications of *kite* in sense 3.

[**1838** J. H. PENNINGTON *Aerostation, (caption)* Steam-kite, or inclined plane, for navigating the air.] **1909** S. F. CODY in *Aeronaut. Jrnl.* XIII. 15/2, I had to turn my hobby into manufacturing a kite in order to raise money to build a flying machine, or to put 'power' into my kite, consequently the term 'Power Kite'. *Ibid.* 19/1 This is the finished power kite ready to start. The screws are not really propellers. You may call them tractors or propellers, which you like. **1917** in A. J. L. Scott *Hist. Sixty Squadron R.A.F.* (1920) 100 He told me that he had managed to fly his kite back with great difficulty. **1934** T. E. LAWRENCE *Let.* 19 Mar. (1938) 793 The German kites will be new and formidable. **1942** T. RATTIGAN *Flare Path* I. 33 A kite from the Polish squadron. **1952** M. TRIPP *Faith is Windsock* xii. 183 The Squadron hasn't lost a single kite in the last three raids. **1969** [see HARRY *sb.*[2] 8 b].

d. Phr. ***high as a kite***: see HIGH *a.* 16 b.

4. a. *Commercial slang.* (With jocular allusion to a paper kite, sense 3.) A bill of exchange, or negotiable instrument, not representing any actual transaction, but used for raising money on credit; an accommodation bill. A person thus raising money is said to ***fly a kite***: see FLY *v.*[1] 5 a.

1805 *Sporting Mag.* XXV. 290 Flying a kite in Ireland is a metaphorical phrase for raising money on accommodation bills. ?**1817** MAR. EDGEWORTH *Love & Law* I. i, Here's bills plinty.. but even the kites, which I can fly as well as any man, won't raise the wind for me now. **1859** *Riddles & Jokes* 98 Plunkett.. used to say there was this difference between boys' kites and men's kites—that with boys the wind raised the kites, but with men the kites raised the wind. **1894** J. C. JEAFFRESON *Bk. Recoll.* I. v. 84 The wretched piece of paper, with my autograph upon it. But no harm came to me from the little kite.

b. *Criminals' slang.* A communication (esp. one that is illicit or surreptitious); *spec.* a letter or verbal message smuggled into, out of, or within a prison.

1859 G. W. MATSELL *Vocabulum* 49 *Kite*, a letter; fancy stocks. **1923** J. F. FISHMAN *Crucibles of Crime* ix. 203 Sometimes.. prisoners manage to plant notes in various parts of the prison which are to be picked up by the intended recipient. This practice of 'shooting' contraband notes is known among the prisoners as 'flying a kite'. **1925** *Flynn's* 3 Jan. 665/2 *Kite*, a message per lip. *Kite*, a letter or note. **1927** [see sense 4 c]. **1953** H. BRYAN *Inside* (1954) xvii. 279 Having settled on the girl, one would send her a 'kite', or love letter. **1960** WENTWORTH & FLEXNER *Dict. Amer. Slang* 194/2 *Fly a kite.* 1. To write a letter; esp. to smuggle a letter into or out of prison. *Underworld use.* 2. To send an airmail letter, often requesting money or assistance. *Modern use, mainly underworld but gaining some popularity.* **1971** *N.Y. Times* 21 Oct. 52/2 *Kite*, a complaint to the police about an illegal operation, often originating with a disgruntled gambler.

c. *slang.* A cheque (sense 3), *esp.* a blank cheque or a cheque drawn on insufficient funds or forged from a stolen cheque-book.

1927 *Dialect Notes* V. 446 *Fly a kite*, v. (1) To pass a bad cheque. (2) To sell worthless stocks and bonds. (3) To write mournful letters, as of prisoners, to sympathetic old women and charitable institutions. **1928** E. WALLACE *Gunner* xxx. 243 He had spent the afternoon searching London for the right 'kites'. There is quite a brisk trade in blank cheque forms. **1936** J. CURTIS *Gilt Kid* iv. 45 Used to say that he'd been done for kites, but everyone reckoned it was for poncing. **1962** R. COOK *Crust on its Uppers* i. 21 The real morries.. flying dodgy kites with each other at bent spielers till the punter.. outs his kiting-book too and scribbles a straight one. **1969** T. PARKER *Twisting Lane* 41 He's in for what they call 'kites', dud cheques, you know.

5. *Naut.* **a.** (*pl.*) A name for the highest sails of a ship, which are set only in a light wind. Also ***flying-kites***.

1856 EMERSON *Eng. Traits* ii. 33 Our good master keeps his kites up to the last moment, studding-sails alow and aloft. **1867** SMYTH *Sailor's Word-bk.*, *Flying-kites*, the very lofty sails, which are only set in fine weather, such as sky-sails, royal studding-sails, and all above them. **1875** BEDFORD *Sailor's Pocket Bk.* iv. (ed. 2) 90 When the glass falls low, Prepare for a blow; When it rises high, Let all your kites fly.

b. On a minesweeper, a device attached to a sweep-wire submerging it to the requisite depth when it is towed over a minefield.

1915 *Chambers's Jrnl.* June 386/1 Between the vessels of each pair is the sweep-wire, sunk to the necessary depth in the water by means of towed 'kites', wooden arrangements acting on the same principle as the ordinary air-kites. **1923** *Man. Seamanship* (Admiralty) II. 172 The present form of kite consists of a specially shaped metal plate which has a tendency to dive when towed. This is towed over the stern by a kite wire.

6. Local name of a fish, the Brill.

1836 YARRELL *Brit. Fishes* II. 241 The Kite of the Devonshire and Cornish coasts is the same as the Brill. **1884** DAY *Brit. Fishes* II. 16.

7. Name for a variety of the Almond Tumbler pigeon, having black plumage with the inner webs of the quill-feathers passing into red or yellow.

1867 TEGETMEIER *Pigeons* xi. 118 Kites, though seldom regarded as exhibition birds are exceedingly valuable as breeding stock... An Almond and a Kite will often produce an Almond and a Kite in each nest.

8. *Geom.* A quadrilateral figure symmetrical about one diagonal (from its resemblance to the form of a toy kite, sense 3); also called DELTOID.

1893 in FUNK.

9. *attrib.* and *Comb.* **a.** in sense 1, as ***kite-and-crow***, ***-colour***; ***kite-coloured***, ***-like*** adj.; **kite bar**, a bar or stripe of an undesirable colour in the plumage of a fancy pigeon; **kite-eagle**, name for *Neopus* (*Ictinætus*) *malayensis*, an East Indian hawk; **kite-falcon**, a hawk of the genus *Baza*, having a crested head and two teeth in the beak; **kite-fish**, a species of gurnard; † **kite-key** (*erron.* **kit-key**), a name for the 'key' or fruit of the ash-tree; **kite-tailed** *a.*, having a long tail like that of a kite, as the ***kite-tailed widgeon***, a species of duck (*Dafila acuta*) found in Florida; † **kite-wolf**, rendering of Gr. ἰκτῖνος (properly 'a kite', also a kind of wolf). **b.** in sense 3, as ***kite expert***, ***-line***, ***-maker***, ***-string***; ***kite-faced***, ***-like***, ***-shaped*** adjs.; **kite-balloon**, a balloon with a long string or wire attached, used for scientific or other purposes; **Kite mark**, **Kitemark**, a quality mark, similar in shape to a kite, granted for use on goods approved by the British Standards Institution; also *transf.*; hence **kite-mark** *v. trans.*, to use the Kite mark on; **kite-marked** *ppl. a.*, bearing the Kite mark; **kite-photograph**, a photograph taken by means of a camera attached to a kite or kite-balloon; **kite-tail (plug)**, name for an obstetric dressing made with pledgets of lint or gauze affixed at intervals to a string or tape, like the pieces of paper in the tail of a kite; **kite-track** (see quot.). **c.** in sense 4, **kite-man**, a person who obtains money against bills of exchange or cheques that will not be honoured; *spec.* (see quot. 1967).

1887 *Academy* 7 May 319/1 *Kite-and-crow struggles of Swabian and Würtemberger. **1876** R. FULTON *Illustr. Bk. Pigeons* 108 A softer shade of blue, with brown, or what are called by Pouter fanciers '*kite' bars. **1898** *Westm. Gaz.* 8 Mar. 10/1 The German military authorities are experimenting with *kite-balloons. **1682** *Lond. Gaz.* No. 1736/4 Stolen or Strayed.., two Mares, one of a *Kite-colour. **1702** *Ibid.* No. 3814/4 A large Sandy or Kite-colour Grey Gelding. **1676** *Ibid.* No. 1092/4 A *Kite-coloured Roan Nag. **1883** *Cassell's Nat. Hist.* III. 283 The *Kite Eagle is about thirty inches in length. **1898** *Westm. Gaz.* 8 Mar. 10/1 *Kite experts, who.. are building up an art.. destined to be of the greatest utility to science and warfare. **1922** JOYCE *Ulysses* 537 Alone on deck,.. yellow *kitefaced, his hand in his waistcoat opening, declaims. **1684** LITTLETON *Lat. Dict.*, The *Kite-fish, *Milvus piscis.* **1578** LYTE *Dodoens* VI. lxx 748 The huskes or fruite thereof [the Ash] are called in shoppes *Lingua anis*, and *Lingua passerina*: in English, *Kytekayes. **1620** VENNER *Via Recta* (1650) 136 Ash-keys, commonly called Kite-keys of the Ash. **1656** BULLOKAR *Eng. Expos.*, *Kitkaies*, the fruit of the ashen tree. **1901** KIPLING *Kim* xiv. 365 From the edge of the sheep-pasture floated a shrill, *kite-like trill. **1909** *Daily Graphic* 26 July 10/1 When floating on an up-draught they [*sc.* the planes] will be expanded as a fan expands, and will present a larger kite-like surface. **1828** *Kaleidoscope* 12 Aug. 48/2 There is no obstacle to interfere with the *kite-lines. **1876** 'MARK TWAIN' *Tom Sawyer* xxx. 304 He took a kite-line from his pocket. **1926** M. LEINSTER *Dew on Leaf* v. 211 The *kite-makers were busy making fantastic objects in bamboo and paper. **1928** E. WALLACE *Double* v. 64 This was a favourite rendezvous of the swell mob, the '*kite' men, the confidence artists. **1967** J. PHELAN *Nine Murderers & Me* 162 *Kite-man*, one who passes forged cheques. **1952** *B.S.I. Monthly Information Sheet* Oct. 16 (*heading*) The '*Kite' mark on consumer goods. *Ibid.*, In March, 1952, when the Utility schemes for textiles and clothing were brought to an end, most of the industries concerned undertook to co-operate with the B.S.I. in preparing voluntary standards.. to ensure that at least the same levels of quality could be maintained. It was also agreed that wherever possible the B.S.I. 'Kite' mark would replace the former Utility mark as a guarantee to consumers that the goods bearing the mark were, in fact, 'up to standard'. **1956** *Observer* 12 Feb. 6/4 It is hoped that eventually the B.S. Kite-Mark will certify the quality of many.. consumer goods. **1957** *Times* 23 Sept. 11/4 The first fireguards bearing the kite mark of the British Standards Institution will be in the shops this autumn. **1957** *Economist* 12 Oct. 157/1 'Shoppers' Guide' discusses articles against the measure of the BSI Kite-mark, which is a guarantee only of minimum satisfactory performance. **1958** *B.S.I. News* Nov. 3 Buyers, particularly large-scale purchasers, can do much to safeguard their workpeople from injury by insisting, wherever possible, that the safety equipment which they buy should be Kite-marked. *Ibid.* 17/1 We hear from Kirk and Company (Tubes) Ltd., that they have recently been granted a licence to Kite-mark their malleable cast iron and cast copper alloy pipe fittings under B.S. 1256. **1960** *Ibid.* Apr. 5/2 (*heading*) Kitemarking should be extended. **1966** *New Scientist* 12 May 338/3 The findings will be used by the British Standards Institution when it publishes the 'rules' for 'kite-marked' toothpastes later this year. **1971** *Brit. Standards Yearbk.* p. xvi, The British Standards Mark (known as the Kitemark) is a registered certification trade mark owned by BSI. Manufacturers may apply to BSI to use the mark on their products when their quality control arrangements are considered satisfactory and they have agreed to comply with a Scheme of Supervision and Control involving.. inspection, sampling and testing. **1971** *Daily Tel.* 24 Nov. 11/5 The annual Civic Trust Awards,.. emphasising architectural and design excellence in a total lived-in environment, have become sought-after kitemarks for planners.. and architects. **1972** *Ibid.* 12 June 2/6 It will be illegal for shops to sell crash helmets which do not have the BSI's 'kitemark' seal of approval. **1972** *Which?* June 192 So far, no cabinets with mirrors have been given the Kitemark... If we hear of any Kitemarked cabinets, we will mention them. **1897** *Daily News* 4 Nov. 6/4 A view of the City Hall, New York, with a portion of Lower Broadway and adjacent streets.. what is called 'a *kite photograph'. **1828** TYTLER *Hist. Scot.* (1864) I. 321 The *kite-shaped shield of the Normans. **1841** THOREAU *Jrnl.* 6 Aug. in *Writings* (1906) VII. 266 Like pasteboards on a *kite string. **1971** *N.Z. Listener* 22 Mar. 13/1 Get seen around with a good woman on your kite-string and no-one bothers you regardless. **1869** L. M. ALCOTT *Little Women* II. x. 150 The others are torn up to.. bandage cut fingers, or make *kite-tails. **1896** *Allbutt's Syst. Med.* I. 439 For supporting the uterus and packing round the cervix several of these rolls are attached to the one string, forming the 'kite-tail' plug. **1893** *Outing* (U.S.) XXII 97/2 A *kite track [for racing] consists of two stretches of one-third of a mile each, with a connecting curve of one-third of a mile. **1607** TOPSELL *Four-f. Beasts* (1658) 570 One of them hath a back of a silver colour,.. this is *Ictinus canus*, a gray *Kite-wolf.

kite, *v.* [f. prec. sb.]

1. a. *intr.* To fly, soar, or move through the air, with a gliding motion like that of a kite; also, *fig.* of a person. To move quickly, to rush; to rise quickly. Const. *around*, *off*, *up*, etc. *colloq.*

1854 'O. OPTIC' *In Doors & Out* (1876) 92 You did not use to be fond of 'kiting' round in this manner. **1863** LE FANU *Ho. by Churchyard* II. 66 He has been 'kiting' all over the town. **1864** L. N. BOUDRYE *Jrnl.* 21 Aug. in *Hist. Rec. Fifth N.Y. Cavalry* (1865) 165 A well directed shell.. sent them 'kiting' to the woods again. **1870** W. W. FOWLER *Ten Yrs. Wall St.* 504 Would seem to be enough to start a panic, or send the market 'kiting' up among the tall figures. **1894** J. J. ASTOR *Journ. other Worlds* II. iii. 145 Whenever a large mass seemed dangerously near the glass, they.. sent it kiting among its fellows. **1908** KIPLING *Lett. to Family* viii. 72 We have seen a financial panic.. send whole army corps of aliens kiting back to the lands whose allegiance they forswore. **1931** WODEHOUSE *Big Money* viii. 181 The stock kited sixty points the first day. **1935** C. S. FORESTER *Afr. Queen* vi. 116 Bet they were surprised to see the old *African Queen* come kiting past. **1965** J. POTTS *Only Good Secretary* i. 13 Yes, and her too, kiting off to Long Island when she ought to be here.

b. *trans.* To cause to fly high like a paper kite.

1865 E. BURRITT *Walk Land's End* 379 We pulled in our kited fancies soaring so high. **1868** BUSHNELL *Serm. Liv. Subj.* 62 We are going.. to be kited or aerially floated no more.

2. To terrify grouse or partridges by flying a paper kite, shaped like a hawk, over their haunts, so as to make them lie close till the guns come near.

1880 *Daily News* 1 Sept. 5/2 The practices known as driving and kiting.

3. *Commercial slang.* **a.** *intr.* To 'fly a kite': see KITE *sb.* 4. **b.** *trans.* To convert into a 'kite' or accommodation bill. Now usually, to write or cash a dud or temporarily unbacked cheque. Hence **'kiting** *vbl. sb.*, the raising of money on credit; the passing of forged or unbacked cheques. Cf. KITE-FLYING *vbl. sb.* 2.

1839 C. F. BRIGGS *Adventures H. Franco* II. iv. 35 He stuffed half a dozen blank checks into his hat, and said he must go out and kite it to save his credit. **1864** WEBSTER, *Kite, v.i.* (Literally, to fly a *kite.*) To raise money, or sustain one's credit, by the use of mercantile paper which is fictitious. **1866** *Congress. Globe* 29 June 3482/1 Every kiting charter like this one—I speak of the National Telegraph Company. **1872** *Ibid.* 3 Apr. 2128/2 (Th.), They may hold the bonds, as has often been done in kiting corporations, and then take the property they have thus swindled the public out of. **1901** *Dundee Advertiser* 10 Jan. 6/2 It seemed.. as if every one in London who had a six-pence to purchase a stamp had 'kited' paper with my signature forged to it. **1934** H. N. ROSE *Thesaurus of Slang* iii. a. 21/1 Issue a check which hasn't sufficient backing: *to kite.* **1942** BERREY & VAN DEN BARK *Amer. Thes. Slang* §556/1 Kiting, kite flying, extending credit or sustaining a balance in the bank by means of 'kites'. **1950** H. E. GOLDIN *Dict. Amer. Underworld Lingo* 118/1 *Kite*, v. 1. To issue or pass, as a forged check or bond; (more accurately) to issue or pass a check against insufficient funds... *Kite checks* (New England States). 1. To issue forged checks. 2. To write checks, usually post-dated, against insufficient funds. 3. To raise illegally the face value of otherwise good checks. **1959** N. MAILER *Advts. for Myself* (1961) 438 Her ideas about.. those investors with some credit rating whom an exurban

bank, proud of its personal touch, might allow to kite a cheque for twenty-four hours..intrigued the banker. **1960** F. Gibney *Operators* vi. 158 Check kiting..is a different and more complex process than forging... Few up-and-coming businessmen..can claim to have resisted the temptation to write a pressing check just a day or two before some money is due, in the prayerful expectation that their deposit will get into the bank's ledgers before the check they have cashed comes home to roost. **1962** R. Cook *Crust on its Uppers* x. 90 We'll kite 'em at the airport! **1963** J. N. Harris *Weird World Wes Beattie* (1964) xv. 184 He was up to his ears in debt—always kiting checks before payday. **1969** 'E. Lathen' *Murder to Go* (1970) xvii. 173 If it had been a question of..kiting a cheque—well, that wouldn't surprise you at all. Clyde cut corners all his life. **1970** R. Lewis *Wolf by Ears* iii. 137 The technical terms..are 'kiting' and 'lapping'. Money is transferred between two accounts, recording the receipt prior to the balancing date and the payment after the balancing date. That's 'kiting'.

c. To send a communication; *spec.* to smuggle a letter into, out of, or within a prison. (Cf. kite *sb.* 4 b.)

1925 *Flynn's* 3 Jan. 665/2 *Kite*, to send a signal; to send a message. **1936** *Detective Fiction Weekly* 4 Jan. 116 A letter which I had 'kited' out of the prison. **1945** L. Shelly *Jive Talk Dict.* 13/2 *Kite*, to air mail or exchange.

kite, obs. f. cut *v.*: var. kyte, belly.

kite-flying, *vbl. sb.* [kite *sb.* 9 b.] **1.** *lit.* The flying of a kite on a string. Also *attrib.*

1804 T. A. Ward *Diary* 5–6 Oct. in *Peeps into Past* (1909) viii. 51/1 He went away..to renew the sport of kite-flying. **1827** D. Johnson *Ind. Field Sports* 168 This..man spent..his time in..pigeon flying, or paper kite flying. **1849** Dickens *Dav. Copp.* (1850) xvii. 179 He never took an active part in any game but kite-flying. **1926** M. Leinster *Dew on Leaf* v. 199 Towards the end of the kite-flying season, numerous Chinese had made their way to various pieces of rising ground with these toys. **1962** W. O. Mitchell *Kite* ii. 14 Kite-flying would be a lot like taking a drive on Sunday or going on a picnic.

2. *slang.* The raising of money (*a*) by persons collusively exchanging accommodation bills or cheques on different banks, in none of which they possess sufficient funds; (*b*) by one person transferring accounts between banks and creating an illusory balance against which he cashes cheques; (*c*) by a person passing forged, stolen, or unbacked cheques.

1834 *Blackw. Mag.* XXXVI 500/2 Some accommodating associate in the noble art and mystery of 'kite-flying'. **1848** Bartlett *Dict. Amer.* 195 *Kite flying*,..a combination between two persons, neither of whom has any funds in bank, to exchange each other's checks, which may be deposited in lieu of money, taking good care to make their bank accounts good before their checks are presented for payment. *Kite flying* is also practised by mercantile houses... A house in Boston draws on a house in New York at 60 days or more, and gets its bill discounted. The New York house, in return, meets its acceptance by re-drawing on the Boston house. **1850** Thackeray *Pendennis* II. xxiv. 244 That kite-flying, you know, Mr. M., always takes two or three on 'em to set the paper going. Altamont put the pot on at the Derby, and won a good bit of money. **1951** 'H. Cecil' *Painswick Line* vi. 55 'Kite flying' is a method of borrowing money from a bank, which is not prepared to lend it to you. **1964** Z. Progl *Woman of Underworld* xix. 178 Passing dud cheques (kite-flying) calls for unwavering nerve and audacity. **1970** M. Kenyon *100,000 Welcomes* iv. 23 Forgery? Fraudulent conversion? Kite-flying?

3. Sending up a 'kite' or *ballon d'essai*. Also *attrib.*

1898 'A. Hope' in *Daily News* 4 Apr. 7/1 Principally it [*sc.* the press interview] was said to be used as a means of what might be called kite-flying. **1899** *Ibid.* 29 June 5/4 The object of Boer diplomacy is to prolong the kite-flying stage indefinitely until commercial interests..urge England to accept anything. **1927** *Daily Tel.* 30 Aug. 8/6 These suggestions are dismissed in British circles as mere 'kite-flying'. **1958** *Economist* 20 Dec. 1058/2 The Belgrade newspaper, *Borba*, which is often the government's mouthpiece, has emphasised..that if other countries would accept immigrants from Jugoslavia these would be allowed to leave... If this was kite-flying, the kite has been allowed to drop to the ground with a thud. **1969** *Courier-Mail* (Brisbane) 2 May 3/8 State D.L.P. secretary (Mr. J. Judge), said: 'This is nothing but kite-flying. The D.L.P. will be making no decision on preferences until the Central Council meets next Tuesday.'

So (as a back-formation) **'kite-fly** *v. trans.* and *intr.*; **'kite-flyer.**

1844 *Knickerbocker* XXIV. 258 The most persevering kite-flyers that I know of, are the Reformers. **1860** Bartlett *Dict. Amer.* (ed. 3) 231 *Kite-flier*, a financier who practises the operation of '*kite-flying*'. **1876** *Monthly Packet* June 577 Heavy bets are laid on the best kite-flyers. **1896** *Daily News* 1 Dec. 8/5 Franklin's experiences as a scientific kite-flyer. **1935** 'D. Hume' *Gaol Gates are Open* 8 Higher in the hierarchy of crime come the 'kite flyers', who cash worthless cheques. **1965** *Listener* 22 July 111/2 The irrelevance of his office to foreign affairs..stressed that he was merely kite-flying. **1968** 'L. Egan' *Serious Investigation* (1969) iii. 34 Right now we've got a con man operating on the pensioners, and a kite flyer passing all the rubber checks. **1972** *Daily Colonist* (Victoria, B.C.) 16 Jan. 2/7 Sarasota, Fla... Some 89 contestants jammed Lido Beach for the Association's 4th Annual International Flyoff, held in honor of America's foremost kiteflyer Ben Franklin.

†**kitekin.** *Obs.* [f. kit *sb.*[3] or *kitty* = *kitten* + -kin.] = catkin.

1578 Lyte *Dodoens* vi. lxvii. 743 A Chatton, Kitekin, or Catteken.

‖**kitenge** (kɪˈtɛŋgiː). Pl. kitenges, vitenge(s. [Swahili.] In East Africa, a fabric, usu. of cotton and printed in various colours and designs with distinctive borders, used esp. for women's clothing.

1969 *Daily Nation* (Nairobi) 31 Oct. 5/1 Betty was taking a good look at the lovely things on sale, but had almost made up her mind to wear traditional kitenge on the 'Big Day'. **1970** *Sunday News Mag.* (Tanzania) 30 Aug. 8 Take the case of a polygamous peasant whose wives have been turned into working machines to bring wealth to him while all they get in return are pieces of kitenge or khanga. **1971** *Inside Kenya Today* Mar. 42/1 Local fabrics such as Kitenges and Kangas are also used to make clothes at the Institute. **1971** *Standard* (Tanzania) 7 Apr. 1/8 UWT members have been urged to reflect the African culture in their dress and other items that convey our intrinsic values. May Day vitenges will be on sale at 19/20.

kite's-foot, kitefoot.

†**1.** Name of some herb. *Obs.*

1580 Hollyband *Treas. Fr. Tong*, *Pied de milan*,..an herbe called kitesfoote. **1611** in Cotgr. s.v. *Milan*. **1706** in Phillips.

2. Name of a variety of tobacco, from its colour.

[**1688** J. Clayton in *Phil. Trans.* XVII. 943 Aranoko Tobacco, whose Scent is not much minded, their..aim being..to procure it a bright Kite's-foot colour.] **1788** *Mass. Centinel* 4 June 94/2 Crowley & Clark Have just received a quantity of Kitefoot Tobacco, of a *superior quality* for smoking. **1796** Morse *Amer. Geog.* I. 544 The kitefoot tobacco. **1835** H. C. Todd *Notes Canada & U.S.A.* 50 Maryland produces..the Bright Kite's Foot Tobacco.

kitesoll: see kittisol.

kit-fox. [perh. from kit *sb.*[3], in reference to its small size.] A small fox (*Vulpes velox*), peculiar to North-western America, scarcely half the size of the common fox, of a prevailing yellowish grey colour, with a black-tipped tail; the American corsak or swift-fox. Also, by ellipsis, *kitt.*

1812 J. Cutler *Topogr. Descr. Ohio* 139 The Christenoes..traffic in beaver, otter, lynx,..small fox or kitts, dressed elk, and moose deer skins. **1815** Lewis & Clarke *Trav.* xxiv. III. 29 The kit-fox or small red fox of the plains. **1829** Richardson *Fauna Bor. Amer.* I. 98 It has long been known to the Hudson Bay fur-traders, its skins forming a portion of their annual exports, under the name of *kit foxes.*

kitful: see kit *sb.*[11]

kith (kɪθ), *sb.* Forms: 1 **cyþþo, cyþ(þ,** 2 **ceþ, cheþ,** 3–4 **cuþþe,** (4 **cuþþhe, kuþþe,** cuth), 4 **keþþe, kiþþe, kiþ, kyþ,** (**kyþthe, kitth, -e, kiyth, kuith, kuythe, kygth, kid, kidh**), 4–5 **kithe, kythe,** (**kyght, -e,** 5 **kyghth, kide**), 4–6 **kyth,** 4– **kith.** *β.* 6–7 **kiffe,** 6–8 **kiff.** [OE. *cýðð*, *cýð*, earlier *cýððu* = OHG. *chundida*:—OTeut. **kunþiþā*, abstr. sb. from **kunþ-* known, OE. *cúð*, couth. In ME. the *u*(*ü*) forms were s.w., the *e* forms Kentish.]

†**1.** Knowledge, acquaintance with something; knowledge communicated, information. *Obs.*

c **900** tr. *Bæda's Hist.* v. xxii[i.], Of minre sylfre cyþþe. *c* **1000** Ælfric *Hom.* I. 396 Þe nane cyððe to Gode næfdon. *a* **1400** *Sir Perc.* 1281 So kyndly takes he that kyth, That up he rose and went hym wyth. *c* **1450** *Rel. Ant.* I. 308 Spare noȝth an hauke yf he lye in thy kyth.

†**2.** Knowledge how to behave; rules of etiquette. *Obs.*

c **1350** *Will. Palerne* 331 Whanne þou komest to kourt among þe kete lordes, & knowest alle þe kuþþes þat to kourt langes. *c* **1470** *Gol. & Gaw.* 320 The king cumly in kith, couerit with croune. **1804** Tarras *Poems* 32 (Jam.) But nature, thy feature, An' mien o' various kythe.

†**3.** The country or place that is known or familiar; one's native land, home; hence *gen.* country, region, quarter. *Obs.*

c **888** K. Ælfred *Boeth.* xxvii. §4 Þæt hi on heora aȝenre cyþþe ealne weȝ mæȝen. *Ibid.* xxxiii. §4 Þæs wæteres aȝnu cyþ is on eorþan. *a* **1175** *Cott. Hom.* 231 Þa sende se king his ærndraches of fif ceðen to alle his underþeoden. *Ibid.* 235 Isent of fif cheðen. *c* **1205** Lay. 2435 Guendoleine he sende into hire fader londe,..into hire cuððe. *a* **1300** *Cursor M.* 5452 (Cott.) Drightin þan was our eldres wit, He mon yow bring in to your kyth [*Gött.* kid]. *Ibid.* 9074 (Cott.) Far wil i fle In vncuth kygth [*Fairf.* kiþ] fra þis cuntre. **1362** Langl. *P. Pl.* A. iii. 197 He hedde beo lord of þat lond..And eke kyng of þat cuþþe. ?*a* **1400** *Morte Arth.* 3997 Þe kyng..kayres furthe with þe cors in kyghte þare he lenges. *c* **1440** *York Myst.* xviii. 91 Us most flee Owte of oure kyth where we are knowyn. **1513** Douglas *Æneis* vii. iii. 59 Sers and inquyr..of this kith quhair standis the cheif citee.

†**4.** The persons who are known or familiar, taken collectively; one's friends, fellow-countrymen, or neighbours; acquaintance; in later use sometimes confused with *kin*: see 5. *Obs.* or *arch.* exc. as in 5.

c **1000** *Ags. Gosp.* Luke ii. 44 Hiȝ..hine sohton betux his maȝas & his cuðan [*Lindisf.* cuðo, *Rushw.* cyððo]. *c* **1325** *Metr. Hom.* 108 Thai him soht Imang thair kith. *c* **1330** R. Brunne *Chron. Wace* (Rolls) 8443 Þe men of kuythe þat he wel knewe, þat he wyste were gode and trewe. *c* **1615** W. Browne *Yng. Willie & Old Wernock* (R.), My near kith. **1825** Brockett, *Kith*, acquaintance... Not obsolete as stated in Todd's John. **1848** Lytton *Harold* iii. iii, High persons of his own kith.

5. Phr. *kith and kin*: *orig.* Country and kinsfolk (see 3); in later use, Acquaintance and kinsfolk, one's friends and relatives; in mod. use often taken merely as a pleonastic phrase for Kinsfolk, relatives, family connexions. (Formerly sometimes corrupted to ***kiff and kin.***)

a. **1377** Langl. *P. Pl.* B. xv. 497 How riȝtwis men..Fer fro kitth and fro kynne yuel yclothed ȝeden. *a* **1400** *Octouian* 1822 I-dryue Ywas,..From ken and kyghth. *c* **1450** *St. Cuthbert* (Surtees) 23 Of saynt cuthbert kyth and kynne. **1570** Levins *Manip.* 150/36 Kith or kin, *cognatio.* **1794** Burns '*My Lady's gown*' ii, My lady's white, my lady's red, And kith and kin o' Cassillis' blude. **1824** Byron *Juan* xv. xxxi, Daughters, brothers, sisters, kith or kin. **1872** Black *Adv. Phaeton* viii, If any extra bit of comfort or kindness is wanted for their own kith and kin.

β. **1573** Tusser *Husb.* (1878) 22 For kiffe nor for kin. **1584** *3 Ladies Lond.* i. in Hazl. *Dodsley* VI. 250 They forsake..prince, country, religion, kiff and kin. **1620** Middleton *Chaste Maid* iv. i. 86 A mayd that's neither kiffe nor kin to me. **1719** D'Urfey *Pills* IV. 151 To visit Kiff and Kin.

fig. **1851** Mrs. Browning *Casa Guidi Wind.* i. 888 Mark the natural kiths and kins Of circumstance and office. **1861** Max Müller *Sci. Lang.* iv. 156 That Greek and Latin were of the same kith and kin as the language of the black inhabitants of India.

†**kith**, *v.* *Obs.* Forms: 3 **cuððen,** (*Orm.*) **kiþþenn,** 4 **kuþþe(n, keþþe.** [Early ME. *cuððen* (*ü*), repr. an OE. **cýððan*, f. *cýð*(*ð*, kith *sb.*] *trans.* To make friendly or familiar; *refl.* to become acquainted, or associate oneself (*with*); to greet each other as friends or familiar acquaintances.

c **1200** *Trin. Coll. Hom.* 45 Wille we..mid swiche weldede cuððen us wið alre kingene king. *c* **1200** Ormin 16979 Þatt he wiþþ Crist i sunnderrrun Himm awihht haffde kiþþedd. *c* **1350** *Will. Palerne* 1011 Þan eiþer hent oþer hastely in armes, And wiþ kene kosses kuþþed hem to-gidere. *Ibid.* 4964 Whan þei samen mette, With clipping and kissing to keþþe hem to-gadere.

kithe, kythe (kaɪð), *v.* Now *Sc.* and *north. dial.* Forms: see below. [Com. Teut.: OE. *cýðan* (ME. *cüþen, kyþen, kiþen, keþen*) = OFris. *ketha, keda*, OS. *kûðian*; MLG. *kunden*, MDu. *conden*, (Du. (*ver*)*konden*), f. **kundian* = OHG. *chundian, chunden* (MHG. *kunden, künden*, G. *künden*), ON. *kynna*, Goth. **kunþjan* (cf. *gasvikunþjan*):—OTeut. **kunþjan*, f. *kunþ-*, known, couth.]

A. Illustration of Forms.

1. *Pres. t.* *α.* 1 **cýðu, cýðe,** 1–2 **kýðe, kýþe,** 3–5 **kyþe, kiþe,** 4–9 **kythe, kithe,** (4 **kiþ, kyeth,** 4–6 **kith,** 4–8 **kyth,** 5–6 **kyith,** 6 **keyth, kaithe**); 3rd pers. sing. 1 **cyþ,** 2–3 **kyþ,** 3 **ciþ, kiþ.** *β.* 2–4 **cuþe, kuþe, cuiþe,** 4–5 **cuyþe, kuyþe, kuiþe,** (4 **couth**); 3rd pers. sing. 3 **cuþ.** *γ.* 4 **keþe, kethe, keth.**

a. *c* **825** *Vesp. Psalter* xlix. [l.] 7 Ic cyðu ðe ðætte god god ðin ic eam. *c* **1000** *Ags. Gosp.* Matt. xxviii. 10 Farað and cyðað minum ȝebroþrum. *c* **1160** *Hatton Gosp.* (ibid.), Fareð and kyðeð mine ȝebroðre. *c* **1200** *Trin. Coll. Hom.* 59 Þat he cið on alle wise. *Ibid.* 139 To kiðen cristes to cume. *a* **1300** *Cursor M.* 12164 Nathing wald yee to me kyth [*v. rr.* kiþe, kiþ]. *Ibid.* 22737 His come to kyeth. *c* **1385** Chaucer *L.G.W.* 912 *Thisbe*, I schal a-non it kythe. *c* **1475** *Rauf Coilȝear* 107 Kyith I am cummin hame. **1486** *Bk. St. Albans* E vij b, That he wolde hym kith. **1530** Lyndesay *Test. Papyngo* 128 To keyth hir craftynes. **1573** *Satir. Poems Reform.* xli. 34 Thair ioukers durst not kyith thair cure. **1594** *Battell Balrinness* in *Scot. Poems 16th C.* II. 349 Giue he into this countrie kaithe [*rime* blaithe].

β. *c* **1175** *Lamb. Hom.* 109 His leoman him cuþað þet he ne bið quic longe. *c* **1200** *Trin. Coll. Hom.* 181 Ðat child..cuð mid his wope. *a* **1240** *Lofsong* in *Cott. Hom.* 215 Cuið in me hwat is milce. **1297** R. Glouc. (Rolls) 2963 Cuþeþ nouþe þat ȝe beþ men [*v. rr.* Kithe, Cuyþe]. *c* **1320** *Cast. Love* 590 Þat so muche loue hi kuiþe wolde. **1377** Langl. *P. Pl.* B. v. 181, I couth [*v.r.* kiþe] it in owre cloistre þat al owre couent wote it.

γ. *c* **1315** Shoreham 7 God þorwe miracles keþeþ hit. *Ibid.* 20 To keþen ous hiis ryche. *c* **1330** *Arth. & Merl.* 2131 Merlin..bad him orpedliche he schuld kethe [*rime* dethe]. *c* **1375** *Sc. Leg. Saints* vii. (*Jacobus minor*) 387 For-þi þi crafte þu keth one me, And waryse myn Infyrmyte.

2. *Pa. t.* *α.* 1 **cýðde,** 1–2 **cydde,** 2, 4–5 **kydde,** 3–6 **kidde,** (3–4 **kidd**), 4–5 **kydd(e, kyd,** 4–6 **kid,** (5–6 **kyde**); 4 **kiþed, -id, kyþed,** (4–6 **-it, -yt, -yd**), 4– **kythed, kithed.** *β.* 2–4 **cudde,** 3–4 **kudde,** 4 **kud.** *γ.* 3–5 **kedde,** 4 *Sc.* **kethit.**

a. *a* **900** Cynewulf *Crist* 65 [Hi] Cyðdon cristes ȝebyrd. *c* **1000** *Ags. Gosp.* Matt. viii. 33 Ða hyrdas..cyddon [*c* **1160** *Hatton Gosp.* kydden] ealle þas þing. *a* **1175** *Cott. Hom.* 227 Se ængel..cydde hyre þat godes sune sceolde beon acenned of hire. *c* **1250** *Gen. & Ex.* 1394 Rebecca..kidd it to hire broðer. *c* **1330** R. Brunne *Chron.* (1810) 281 Þe werre bigan, and kid it so couth. *c* **1350** *Will. Palerne* 5287 Þe messangers..kiþed here arnd. **1387** Trevisa *Higden* (Rolls) IV. 411 He turned to and kydde [*v.r.* kudde] al the myght of his wicche craft. **1535** Stewart *Cron. Scot.* II. 100 The grit wonder and miraclis that tha kid. **1560** Rolland *Crt. Venus* ii. 790 Sen ȝe on me befoir kyde sic kindnes. **1637–50** Row *Hist. Kirk* (Wodrow Soc.) 438 He kythed such great gifts.

β. *c* **1200** *Trin. Coll. Hom.* 35 Þe engel cudde þe herdes..þat þe helende was..iboren. **1297** R. Glouc. (Rolls) 2379 Þere he kudde wat he was. **1387** Kudde [see *a*].

γ. *c* **1200** *Moral Ode* 193 (Trin. MS.) Muchel luue he us kedde. *c* **1330** *Arth. & Merl.* 3910 Thai kedden her noble might. *c* **1375** *Sc. Leg. Saints* xii. (*Mathias*) 232 Þat kethit wele þat he was meke. *c* **1460** *Launfal* 580 Gyfre kedde he was good at nede.

3. *Pa. pple.* *α.* 1 **ȝe)cýþed,** 4 **i-kid,** (**kide, keid**), 4–5 **y-kyd, y-kidde, kyd, kydd(e, kidd(e, kid,** 5 **y-kydde, y-kid, kyde,** (**kyth,** 6 **kyith**); 4–9 **kythed, kithed,** 5–6 **-it,** 6 **-yd, kyithit.** *β.* 3 **ikudd,** 3–5 **kud,** 4–5 **icud, ikud, ykud.** *γ.* 4 **ked,** 5 **kedd(e.**

α. *c* **900** tr. *Bæda's Hist.* v. xvii. [xix.] (1890) 460 Eallra heora dome wæs cyþed, þæt [etc.]. *c* **1000** ÆLFRIC *Saints' Lives* IV. 348 þæt heo næfre on hire life ȝecyðed wære. *a* **1300** *Cursor M.* 6609 It sal be kydd [*v.r.* kidd]. *c* **1300** *Havelok* 1060 It was loude kid. **1387** TREVISA *Higden* (Rolls) VII. 393 He hadde y-kyd [*v. rr.* kidde, ykud, kydde] his woodnesse. *c* **1460** *Pol., Rel. & L. Poems* 254 Cowþe ykid in euery cost. *c* **1470** HARDING *Chron.* XXXIX. xii, Vnto no manne was it kyde [*rime* hid]. **1528** LYNDESAY *The Dreme* 1050 Dame Fortune..hes lairgli kyith on the hir cure. *a* **1529** SKELTON *Poems agst. Garnesche* 8 What, have ye kythyd yow a knyght? **1567** *Gude & Godlie B.* (S.T.S.) 46 Christ hes vs kyithit greit conforting. **1640** R. BAILLIE *Canterb. Self-convict.* 33 Whereto the faction hath not kythed too passionate a love.

β. *a* **1225** *Juliana* 24 Hit were sone iseid þe keiser ant ikudd to þe kinge. **1297** R. GLOUC. (Rolls) 1328 He miȝte abbe.. ikud me loue. **1387** Ykud [see α].

γ. *c* **1430** *Syr Tryam.* 1386 But they be kedd.

B. Signification.

1. *trans.* To make known. †**a.** To make known in words; to announce, proclaim, declare, tell. (With *simple obj.* or *obj. clause.*) *Obs.*

c **725** *Corpus Gloss.* 1150 *Intimandum*, to cyðenne. *c* **1000** *Ags. Gosp.* John xvii. 26 Ic him cyðde ðinne naman & ȝyt wylle cyþan. *c* **1175** *Lamb. Hom.* 117 þat þu..mine speche heom cuðe. *c* **1200** ORMIN 632 He comm dun wiþþ Godess word, To kiþenn itt onn eorþe. *c* **1330** *King of Tars* 341 Heore sorwe couthe no mon kithe. *c* **1450** HOLLAND *Howlat* 235 Confess cleir can I nocht, nor kyth all the cass. **1530** PALSGR. 599/1, I kythe, I shewe or declare a thyng, as he kytheth from whence I am (Lydgate), *je demonstre.* This terme is nat vsed in comen spetche.

b. To make known by action, appearance, etc.; to manifest, show, prove, demonstrate, indicate. (With *simple obj.*, *obj. clause*, or *obj.* and *compl.*) Also *refl.*

c **1175** *Lamb. Hom.* 99 Elches monnes weorc cuðað [*printed* cuðan] hwilc gast hine wissað. *a* **1300** *Cursor M.* 13983 Iesus ..mani a-pert meracle did, Quar-wit to mankind he him kid. *c* **1385** CHAUCER *L.G.W.* Prol. 492 Sche kytheth what she is. *c* **1460** *Towneley Myst.* i. 45 Trees to florish & frute furth bryng, Thare kynde that it be kyd. **1515** *Scot. Field* in *Chetham Misc.* (1856) II. Introd. p. xii, He kidde himselfe no coward. **1640-1** *Kirkcudbr. War-Comm. Min. Bk.* (1855) 156 They bothe..did kythe thameselffes enemeis to the gude caus. *a* **1734** WODROW *Scl. Biogr.* (1845) I. 100 (E.D.D.) He began to kyth his sickness the first of March. **1785** BURNS *Halloween* iii, Their faces blythe, fu' sweetly kythe Hearts leal, an' warm, an' kin. [**1822** SCOTT *Nigel* v, It would have kythed Cellini mad, had he never done ony thing else out of the gate.]

c. To make manifest to the sight, to show, exhibit, discover; *refl.* to show oneself, appear.

1297 R. GLOUC. (Rolls) 5098 Wanne þe relikes of halwen yfounde were and ykud. *a* **1300** *Cursor M.* 13095 Hu lang siþe Sal he him hide and not kiþe. *c* **1330** *Arth. & Merl.* 3869 The other no might ben y-kidde Behinden hem thai werren y-hidde. **1508** DUNBAR *Tua Mariit Wemen* 433 As the new mone..Kythis quhilis her cleir face, through cluddis of sable. **1594** JAS. VI *Let. Q. Eliz.* 13 Apr. in Tytler *Hist. Scot.* (1864) IV. 216 Ever plainliest kything himself where greatest confluence of people was. **1846** DRUMMOND *Muckomachy* 68 (E.D.D.) When the moon begoud to keek From Thetis rim and kythe her disk.

2. *intr.* for *refl.* To show oneself or itself, come forth to sight; to manifest or display itself; to become known; to appear.

a **1300** *Cursor M.* 4276 (Cott.) Luken luue at þe end wil kith. *Ibid.* 11416 (Gött.) þe last þis stern it kid. **1535** STEWART *Cron. Scot.* I. 18 The langer ay the better it did kyth. **1585** *Papers Jas. Carmichael* in *Wodrow Soc. Misc.* 430 Our true humility shall appear, and the fruit of our forming to that work kythe. *c* **1635** W. SCOT *Apol. Narrat.* (Wodrow Soc.) 80 They were insisting with his Majesty to kythe in action against the forfaulted Earles. **1821** GALT *Ann. Parish* xii. (1895) 83 A kindly spirit, which would sometimes kythe in actions of charity. **1822** *Blackw. Mag.* XII. 309 In what colours other ladies intended to kithe before Majesty. **1829** HOGG *ibid.* XXV. 750 The evening star kithed like a gem. **1862** in *Hislop's Prov. Scot.* 108 If you loe me, let it kythe.

b. with *compl.* To show oneself or itself in some specified aspect; to appear, seem, or prove to be.

c **1330** R. BRUNNE *Chron.* (1810) 240 With Leulyn gan he kith to be þe kynges traytour. **1513** DOUGLAS *Æneis* I. vi. 167 Hir habeit fell down couering to hir feit, And..ane verray god did hir kith. **1565** *Sc. Metr. Ps.* xviii. 26 Pure to the pure, froward thou kythst Unto the froward wight. **1637-50** ROW *Hist. Kirk* (1842) 169 Such as hes kythed favourers of the forefeited rebells. *a* **1639** SPOTTISWOOD *Hist. Ch. Scot.* II. (1677) 89 Nor did any kithe so foolish as the Priests. [**1818** SCOTT *Hrt. Midl.* xii, It kythes bright to the ee, because all is dark around it.]

†**3.** *trans.* To exhibit, display, or manifest practically (a feeling, quality, capacity, etc.); hence, to exercise, practise, perform, do. *Obs.*

Beowulf 2695 Andlongne eorl ellen cyðan. *c* **1175** *Lamb. Hom.* 153 Mildheortnesse God kudde monne. **1297** R. GLOUC. (Rolls) 1297 þer hii kudde hor prowesse. *c* **1330** R. BRUNNE *Chron.* (1810) 132 Warre on him gan he kithe. **1387** TREVISA *Higden* (Rolls) II. 341 He kydde his tyrauntyse on his gestes. *c* **1440** *York Myst.* xl. 149, I thanke youe of þis kyndinesse ȝe kydde me. **1500-20** DUNBAR *Poems* xxviii. 37 In erd ȝe kyth sic mirakillis heir. **1613** W. BROWNE *Sheph. Pipe* i. (1869) 187 Your bountee on me kythe. **1641** R. BAILLIE *Parall. of Liturgy with Mass-bk.* 77 None of all the reformed Churches have kythed more zeale against Images. **1724** in Ramsay *Tea-t. Misc.* (1733) II. 164 Well can my Jocky kyth His love and courtesy.

†**4.** To acknowledge, confess, own; to recognize. (With *simple obj.* or *obj.* and *compl.*) *Obs.*

c **1000** *Ags. Gosp.* Matt. x. 32 Ælcne..þe me cyð beforan mannun, ic cyðe hyne beforan minum fæder [*c* **1160** *Hatton Gosp.* kyð, ic kyðe]. **13..** *E.E. Allit. P.* B. 1368 Vche duk.. Schulde com to his court to kyþe hym for lege. *c* **1374** CHAUCER *Anel. & Arc.* 231 He..his trouthe me had iplyght, For everemore hys lady me to kythe. *c* **1425** WYNTOUN *Cron.* VI. vi. 16 Nane persayvyd hyr woman Bot all kythyd hyr as man. **1570** LEVINS *Manip.* 152/3 Kythe, acknowledge, *agnoscere.* **1613** JACKSON *Creed* I. viii. §1 That the sons of Isaac and Ishmael..should kithe each other with as little scruple as if they were full cousin germans.

5. *Pa. pple.* **kid, kyd, i-kyd,** etc. Made known, declared; hence, Known, well known, famed, renowned; with *compl.* Well-known as.., acknowledged to be... (See also KID *ppl. a.*)

a **1225** *Ancr. R.* 64 Heo..wolde..sone beon mit te wise icud [*v. rr.* cuððet, icuððet] and icnowen. **1297** R. GLOUC. (Rolls) 1929 Seint eleine ys moder þat wis was wide ikud [*v. rr.* ykud, kydde, kud]. *c* **1350** *Will. Palerne* 110 Komen was he of kun þat kud was ful nobul. *c* **1380** *Sir Ferumb.* 274 In many a lond my name ys kud aboute. *c* **1386** CHAUCER *Merch. T.* 699 That ye nat discouere me; For I am deed, if that this thyng be kyd. *c* **1450** HOLLAND *Howlat* 504 Throwout Cristindome kid War the deidis that he did. **1486** *Bk. St. Albans* E iv b, The Robucke as hit is weele kyde At holyrode day he gooth to Ryde.

kithing, kything ('kaɪðɪŋ), *vbl. sb.* [f. prec. + -ING[1].]

1. The action of the verb KITHE, KYTHE; a making known, telling, showing, manifestation, etc.

a **1300** *Cursor M.* 11656 Forth þair wai þai went..Witvten kithing of ani man. **1591** R. BRUCE *Serm.* (1843) 215 The manner or form of the Kything of the Sign. **1823** GALT *Gilhaize* i. (E.D.D.), His abundant hair..was also clouded and streaked with the kithings of the cranreuch of age.

†**2.** Acquaintance, recognition; also *concr.* Acquaintance, kith. *Obs.*

a **1300** *Cursor M.* 4817 Cuth [*v.r.* cowde] þai wit him na kything tak, And vncuthli to þam he spak. *Ibid.* 11080 All mad þai mirth at his bering, Fader and moder and þair kything.

kithless ('kɪθlɪs), *a.* [f. KITH *sb.* + -LESS.] Without kith or acquaintances; having no one whom one knows. (Cf. KINLESS.)

c **1750** in Ld. Campbell *Chancellors* (1857) VI. cxxxiv. 250 No thanks to them [Cromwell's Judges] kithless loons! **1861** *Times* 27 Mar. 8/4 The kithless outcasts of every country. **1887** FARJEON *Tragedy Featherstone* I. I. i. 6 He was alone in the world, kinless and kithless.

†**kithly,** *adv. Obs.* Forms: 3 *Orm.* **kiþþeliȝ,** 3-4 **kithli.** [f. KITH *sb.* + -LY[2]. Perh. distinct formations. (OE. *ȝecyðelíc* 'manifest', in Bosw.-Toller is an error for *ȝecyndelíc* natural.)]

1. Familiarly.

c **1200** ORMIN 16532 Ne lætenn kiþþeliȝ wiþþ hemm.

2. In a way that is known or manifest; manifestly.

a **1300** *Cursor M.* 22742 His oþer cuming sal he scau kithli til þis werld.

kiting: see KITE *v.* 3 b.

kitish ('kaɪtɪʃ), *a.* [f. KITE *sb.* + -ISH[1].] Resembling or of the nature of a kite; greedy.

1566 W. ADLINGTON *Golden Asse* (1893) 131, I could not escape the kitish eyes of the old woman. **1567** TURBERVILE *Aunsw. Wom. to hir Louer* Epitaphs, etc. 32 All your maners more agree vnto the Kytish kinde. **1608** T. MORTON *Preamb. Encounter* Pref. 3 Is not your Defence..a Kitish Doue?

kitist ('kaɪtɪst). *nonce-wd.* [f. KITE *sb.* + -IST.] One skilled in flying kites.

1844 *P. Parley's Ann.* V. 313 The great kitist turned to the boys who held her..alleging..that they held her too tight.

†**kit-key:** see *kite-key* s.v. KITE *sb.* 9.

'kitless, *a.* [f. KIT *sb.*[1] + -LESS.] Having no kit (KIT *sb.*[1] 2 b); without (adequate, suitable) clothing.

The definitions in the work cited in quot. 1846 are often unsatisfactory; it nevertheless seems to provide a genuine example of the sense defined above.

1846 *Swell's Night Guide* 123/2 *Kitless*, a bare, naked fellow. **1936** J. BUCHAN *Island of Sheep* ix. 160 [He] went off with the women..to look after her wardrobe, for she also was kit-less.

kitling ('kɪtlɪŋ). Now *dial.* Forms: 3 **kiteling,** 4 **keetlyng,** 5 **kytylyng, cytlyng,** 5-6 **kytling, -lyng(e,** 6 **kytlyn, kitlyng, -linge,** *Sc.* **-lyne,** 6-7 **ketlyng, -ling,** 6-9 **kitlin, -ling, kittling,** 7-9 **-lin,** 8 *Sc.* **-len.** [Commonly identified with ON. *kettling-r, ketling-r* (Norw. *kjetling*) kitten, dim. of *kǫttr* (stem *kattu*); though the form of the earliest Eng. instance, and the fact that the sense is not confined to 'young cat' make difficulties. But if from OE., the form would be **cyteling*, of which no explanation appears.]

†**1.** The young of any animal; a cub, a whelp.

a **1300** *E.E. Psalter* lvi. 5 þe kitelinges of liouns. **1382** WYCLIF *Deut.* xxxiii. 22 Dan, keetlyng of a lyon. *c* **1440** *Gesta Rom.* I. lix. 243 (Harl. MS.) Thenne saide the sarpent, 'I am a beste, and I have her in myn hole kytlingis, that I have browt forthe'. *c* **1450** [see KITTEN 1 b, quot. 1495]. **1603** HOLLAND *Plutarch's Mor.* 218 They [sea-weasels or sea-dogs] breed their young whelpes or kitlings alive within their bellies, and when they list, let them foorth.

2. A young cat, a kitten. Now *dial.*

a **1530** *Johan & Tyb* (Brandl) 591, I haue sene the day that pus my cat Hath had in a yere kytlyns eyghtene. **1530** [see KITTLE *v.*[2] 1]. **1605** B. JONSON *Volpone* v. xi, Whether goe you, now?..to drowne kitlings? **1783** JOHNSON *Let. to Miss S. Thrale* 18 Nov., Bickerstaff..gives..an account of his cat. I could tell you as good things of Lily the white Kitling. *a* **1825** FORBY *Voc. E. Anglia, Kitling*, a young cat. **1894** CROCKETT *Lilac Sunbonnet* 187 I'm ower auld a Pussy Bawdrons to learn new tricks o' sayin' 'miauw' to the kittlins.

†**3.** Applied to a person; either = child, offspring (cf. *cub, whelp*); or as resembling or acting like a kitten in some way. *Obs.*

1541 *Aberd. Reg.* XVII. (Jam.) Calling of him theiff.. howris geyt, preistis kitlyne. **1621** FLETCHER *Wild-Goose Chase* IV. iii, Out, kittlings! What catterwauling's here! **1702** DE FOE *Good Advice to Ladies* 84 Come, says the patient Kitling, Husband come. *a* **1745** SWIFT *Wks.* (1841) II. 59 Bid your mistress go hang herself..you whore's kitling.

B. *attrib.* or *adj.* Resembling a kitten or that of a kitten; inexperienced; diminutive.

1604 MIDDLETON *Father Hubbards T.* Wks. 1840 V, Like an old cunning bowler to fetch in a young ketling gamester. **1648** HERRICK *Hesper., Oberon's Feast*, His kitling eyes. **1689** PHILOPOLITES *Grumblet. Crew* 3 A new Oath of Allegiance..which every Kitling Critic..takes upon him to censure.

kitmutgar, var. KHIDMUTGAR.

kitool: see KITTUL.

kitoun, obs. f. KITTEN.

‖**kitsch** (kɪtʃ). Also **Kitsch.** [G.] Art or *objets d'art* characterized by worthless pretentiousness; the qualities associated with such art or artifacts. Also *attrib.*, *Comb.*, and *transf.*

1926 B. HOWARD *Let.* in M. J. Lancaster *Brian Howard* (1968) ix. 166 A healthy week..riding, chasing dogs and listening to 'Kitsch' on his wireless. **1939** *Partisan Rev.* VI. 40 Kitsch is mechanical and operates by formulas. Kitsch is vicarious experience and faked sensations. Kitsch changes according to style, but remains always the same. Kitsch is the epitome of all that is spurious in the life of our times. **1941** AUDEN *New Year Let.* III. 59 Reason's depravity that takes The useful concepts that she makes As universals, as the kitsch. **1949** KOESTLER *Insight & Outlook* 410 The more romantic a work of art, or a landscape, the quicker its repetitions are perceived as *kitsch* or 'slush'. **1955** *20th Cent.* June 541 In a time of crassness and stridency perhaps unique in history, a time when an alternative civilization of *kitsch* is not only available to all but clamantly thrust upon them, it is imperative to strive for agreement, order, and coherence in the ranks of the cultivated. **1958** *Observer* 23 Feb. 14/1 What is so extraordinary about some of these *kitsch* masterpieces is the way they can be enjoyed on two planes, both as themselves and as their own parodies. **1958** *Times* 4 July 13/4 Few attempts are made in England to mount productions of plays of the *commedia dell' arte* tradition; and such attempts are in danger of being dismissed as 'art theatre *kitsch*'. **1961** *Times* 11 May 10/4 There are the same highbrows as in England, who consider that the quality of the pure entertainment as such is generally *kitsch* or trash. **1962** *Times* 6 Apr. 17/3 Their attitude to this *kitsch*-culture is highly equivocal. **1965** *Spectator* 22 Jan. 108/1 If leaders of the state choose their job..they must choose to be the victims of the kitsch and whitewash and balderdash. **1967** *Ibid.* 29 Dec. 812/2, I have never seen such kitsch, not even in French provincial towns or Irish church bazaars. **1972** *Listener* 24 Aug. 236/1 A galloping fancy for Victoriana, a sophisticated and uncritical taste for Kitsch and the cute. **1972** *New Yorker* 30 Sept. 24/3 This is one of the liveliest and most popular of their *kitschfests.*

So **kitsch** *v. trans.* (*rare*), to render worthless, to affect with sentimentality and vulgarity; **'kitschy** *a.*, possessing the characteristics of kitsch.

1951 W. SANSOM *Face of Innocence* ii. 16 Situations that have for many become unendurably hackneyed, spoiled by bad artists or kitsched by politics. **1967** *Time* 17 Feb. 104 The kitschy existential slogan: 'Things just happen. No reason, no reason, just a happening.' **1969** R. PETRIE *Despatch of Dove* i. 19 Her family owned a furniture factory. 'We make..mostly kitschy bits fit to furnish Grimm's fairy tales.' **1973** *Times* 27 Aug. 5/6 Costumed in a distressingly 'kitschy' manner.

kitsol(l, kittasole: see KITTISOL.

kittel ('kɪt(ə)l). [Yiddish (G., overall, smock), ad. MHG. *kitel, kietel* cotton or hempen outer garment, prob. ad. Arab. *quṭn* cotton.] A white cotton or linen robe worn by orthodox Jews on certain holy days; also used as a shroud.

1891 M. FRIEDLÄNDER *Jewish Relig.* 492 The *kittel* or *sargenes* is part of the raiment in which the dead are clothed. .. In some countries..the bride presents the bridegroom with this article on the wedding-day: and it is worn by the husband on New-Year's Day and on the Day of Atonement and on the *Seder*-evening during the service. **1972** C. RAPHAEL *Feast of Hist.* i. 11/2 A Yementie Seder... The celebrants are wearing their traditional festive clothes, the men in white '*kittels*'. **1973** *Synagogue Light* Sept. 46/2 Garbed in the white Kittel, head wrapped in a Tallith, he who blows stands near the Rabbi.

kitten ('kɪt(ə)n), *sb.* Forms: 4 **kitoun, ketoun,** 4-5 **kyton,** 5 **kytton,** 7- **kitten.** [ME. app. a. AFr. **kitoun*, **ketun* = OF. *chitoun, cheton*, obs. var. of F. *chaton* kitten.

The F. form *chitoun* occurs in Gower *Mirour de l'omme* 8221: Teut ensement comme du chitoun, Qi naist sanz vieue et sanz resoun.]

1. a. The young of the cat; a young cat (not full-grown).

1377 LANGL. *P. Pl.* B. Prol. 190 þere þe catte is a kitoun þe courte is ful elyng. *c* 1400 *Master of Game* ix. (MS. Digby 182) þei beer hir kitouns.. as oþer cattes, saue þei haue not but two ketouns at ones. *c* 1450 *Merlin* 665 He caste his net into the water, and drough oute a littil kyton as blakke as eny cool. 1596 SHAKS. *1 Hen. IV*, III. i. 129, I had rather be a Kitten, and cry mew, Then one of these same Meeter Ballad-mongers. 1776 WHITEHEAD *Variety* 9 The Kitten too was comical, She play'd so oddly with her tail. 1852 MISS MULOCK *Agatha's Husb.* i, Carrying not only the real black kitten, but the.. allegorical 'little black dog' on her shoulder.

b. *transf.* Applied to the young of some other animals.

1495 *Trevisa's Barth. De P.R.* XVIII. lxxiv. (W. de W.) 829 The wesell.. nouryssheth her kyttons [*MS. Bodl.* (*c* 1450) ketelinges] in howses and bereth them fro place to place. 1899 *Blackw. Mag.* Jan. 41/1 Each beaver-plew of full-grown animal or 'kitten' fetched six to eight dollars overhead. 1957 J. H. F. STEVENSON *Mink in Britain* (ed. 2) v. 18 Once the kittens, or kits as they are called, are able to fend for themselves, they do so. 1964 R. M. LOCKLEY *Private Life Rabbit* iv. 54 It was possible to handle and weigh week-old kittens without causing their desertion by the doe. 1972 R. ADAMS *Watership Down* xlii. 356 Clover's had her litter. All good, healthy kittens. Three bucks and three does.

c. *fig.* Applied to a young girl, with implication of playfulness or skittishness. In extended use: a girl-friend; a young woman; often as a form of address.

1870 D. J. KIRWAN *Palace & Hovel* xliii. 612 The 'Kitten' is a blonde, with black eyes, a pretty, babyish face,.. a profusion of golden hair. 1894 H. NISBET *Bush Girl's Rom.* 74 After fishing all she could, artful, artless little kitten that she is. 1908 W. DE MORGAN *Somehow Good* xii. 119 'Kitten,' said Sally's mother to her suddenly, 'I think I shall go away to bed.' 1938 W. G. HARDY *Turn back River* iii. 28 'You'll have to go, kitten,' Clodia whispered hurriedly... For an instant she held her sister close. 1961 'E. LATHEN' *Banking on Death* (1962) vii. 59 He.. accepted a sherry from June with a somewhat absent, 'Thanks, Kitten.' 1970 G. GREER *Female Eunuch* 266 There are the cute animal terms like ..*kitten* and *lamb* [to signify a woman].

2. Short for *kitten-moth*: see 3.

1874 NEWMAN *Brit. Moths* 210 The Alder Kitten.

3. *attrib.* and *Comb.*, as ***kitten days***, ***face***; ***kitten-like*** adj.; **kitten-hearted** *a.*, faint-hearted, timorous; **kitten-moth**, a collector's name for the bombycid moth *Cerura furcula*; also for species of *Dicranura*, as *D. bifida* (**poplar-kitten**), *D. bicuspis* (**alder-kitten**).

1821 CLARE *Vill. Minstr.* I. 166 The gamesome plays That mark'd her happy *Kitten-days. 1813 *Sketches Character* (ed. 2) I. 157, I see her *kitten face looking about, trying to understand what's going forwards. 1831 T. ATTWOOD 19 Sept. in *Life* xi. (1885) 171 The tame *kitten-hearted slaves. 1838 DICKENS *Nich. Nick.* xxxiv, Pouncing with *kitten-like playfulness upon a stray sovereign. 1819 SAMOUELLE *Entom. Useful Comp.* 248 *Cerura Vinula* (puss moth), *Cerura Furcula* (*kitten moth).

4. Slang phr. (orig. *U.S.*), ***to have kittens***: to lose one's composure; to get into a 'flap'.

1900 *Dialect Notes* II. 44 *Kitten.* In phrases 'get kittens', 'have kittens'. 1. To get angry. 2. To be in great anxiety, or to be afraid. 1937 *Times* 15 Feb. 13/4 Mr. Partridge allows 'jitters'.. but not 'having kittens'. 1940 K. M. KNIGHT *Rendezvous with Past* xx. 141 If he knew what I know about you he'd have kittens. 1943 HUNT & PRINGLE *Service Slang* 38 *Having kittens*, perturbed. 'The Colonel is having kittens'—the Colonel is upset and he is very, very angry. 1950 M. KENNEDY *Feast* II. ix. 42 She's been having kittens all day because Mrs. Siddal says she's got to empty slops. 1952 W. PLOMER *Museum Pieces* xxv. 210 My doctor nearly had kittens when I suggested my being dropped to the *maquis* by parachute. 1959 'A. GILBERT' *Third Crime Lucky* ii. 28 Gertrude was going to have kittens when she discovered that extravagance. 1967 N. FREELING *Strike Out* 76 When one of the horses has something wrong with it—then everybody has kittens.

Hence **'kittendom**, **'kittenhood**, the state or condition of being a kitten.

1886 BESANT *Childr. Gibeon* II. xxii, A man whom they [the cats] had known and respected since kittendom. *a* 1843 SOUTHEY *Nondescripts* i. 50 Thou art beautiful as ever cat That wanton'd in the joy of kittenhood.

'kitten, *v.* [f. prec. sb.] Of a cat: To bring forth kittens; also of some other animals: To bring forth young, to litter. (*intr.* and *trans.*) Hence **'kittening** *vbl. sb.*

1495 *Trevisa's Barth. De P.R.* XVIII. lxxiv. (W. de W.) eevj/1 Theyr opynyon is false.. that wesels conceyue atte mouth and kytneth [*MS. Bodl.* whelhiþ] att the eere. 1597 SHAKS. *1 Hen. IV*, III. i. 19 If your Mothers Cat had but kitten'd. 1824 MISS MITFORD *Village* Ser. I. (1863) 191 Two as fine litters of rabbits as ever were kittened. 1859 MRS. GASKELL *Round the Sofa* 335 My cat has kittened, too.

kittenish ('kɪt(ə)nɪʃ), *a.* [f. KITTEN *sb.* + -ISH[1].] Like a kitten, or that of a kitten; having the qualities or characteristics of a kitten; playful.

1754 RICHARDSON *Grandison* (1812) IV. 115 Such a kittenish disposition in her. 1844 DICKENS *Mart. Chuz.* ii, She was all girlishness, and playfulness, and wildness, and kittenish buoyancy. 1895 M. E. FRANCIS *Frieze & Fustian* 45 The kittenish grace of her small slight figure.

Hence **'kittenishly** *adv.*

1896 LOCKE *Demagogue & Lady Phayre* iii. 22 The little blue ribbon.. with the bow tied kittenishly under her ear.

'kittenishness. [f. prec. + -NESS.] Kittenish characteristics or behaviour.

1905 *Smart Set* Sept. 15/1 Monsieur de Latour felt, as well as saw, that Madame de Beauregard, for all her kittenishness, was really a very great lady. 1926 *Chambers's Jrnl.* Aug. 610/1 Ages back the American girl abjured all that was in the nature of kittenishness. 1974 F. NOLAN *Oshawa Project* xv. 99 'What do you mean..?' she said, every trace of the kittenishness falling away.

kittereen (kɪtə'riːn). Also **kittar-**, **kitur-**. [Origin unascertained.

The statement in Gardener's *Hist. Jamaica* (1873) 163, that it was named from being made at *Kettering*, proves to be unfounded; that in quot. 1880 is prob. not more reliable.]

A kind of covered vehicle. †**a.** In West of Eng., A kind of omnibus (*obs.*). **b.** In West Indies, A kind of one-horse chaise or buggy.

1792 *Descr. Kentucky* 42 In 1787 were exported Chaises 40, Kittareens 10, Sulkeys 7. 1831 JANE PORTER *Sir E. Seaward's Narr.* II. 336, I desired Drake to.. hire a kittereen—a sort of one-horse chaise. 1865 R. HUNT *Pop. Romances W. Eng.* Introd. 14 Within my own memory [born 1807] the ordinary means of travelling from Penzance to Plymouth was a van called a 'kitterine', and three days were occupied in the journey. 1880 J. W. in *W. Cornw. Gloss.* s.v., The Kit-Tereen was an open car that ran between Penzance and Truro, set up by Christopher Treen. [Jago adds Kit Treen.] 1885 LADY BRASSEY *The Trades* 224 We.. packed ourselves into buggies.. the body being in some cases sheltered by a movable hood, when they are called 'Kittereens'.

kith, -e, obs. forms of KITH.

†**kittisol** ('kɪtɪsɒl). *Obs.* Forms: 6–7 **quitasole**, 7 **quita-**, **quitta-**, **quittusol**; **kittasole**, **kittisal**, **kitesoll**, (**kippe-sole**, **kettysol**), **kitsol(l**, 8 **kitysol**, 8–9 **kittisol**, (9 **ketty-**, **kettisol**). [a. Pg. and Sp. *quitasol*, f. *quitar* to take away, ward off + *sol* sun.] A sunshade, parasol, umbrella: almost always in reference to the East Indies or China; *spec.* a Chinese umbrella made of bamboo and oiled paper.

'This word survived till lately in the Indian Tariff, but it is otherwise long obsolete' (Yule).

1588 PARKE tr. *Mendoza's Hist. China* (Hakluyt Soc.) II. 105 Two quitasoles of silke, and a horse. 1611 HAWKINS in Purchas *Pilgrims* (1625) I. 217 Of *Kittasoles* of state, for to shaddow him, there bee twentie [in the treasury of Akbar]. 1615 R. COCKS *Diary* (Hakluyt Soc.) I. 28 The China Capt. ..brought me a present from his brother, viz., 1 faire *kitesoll*. 1625 PURCHAS *Pilgrims* I. iv. 559 Many Canopies, Quittusols and other strange ensignes of Maiesty. 1662 BP. NICHOLSON *David's Harp*, The Lord is thy shade—*umbraculum*—a quittasol upon thy right hand. 1687 *Let. Crt. Directors* in Wheeler *Madras in Olden Time* (1861) I. 200 (Y.) They [Aldermen of Madras] may be allowed to have Kettysols over them. 1698 FRYER *Acc. E. India & P.* 110 A great Attendance with Pageants, Mirxhals, and Kitsols. 1706 *Wooden World Dissected* (1708) 19 [He] believes a Kittisol a nobler Piece of Magnificence, than a good Table. 1813 MILBURN *Orient. Comm.* II. 464 (Y.) Kittisols, large, 2,000 to 3,000. 1875 *Indian Tariff* (Y.), Umbrellas, Chinese, of paper, Kettysolls. *Ibid.*, Chinese paper Kettisols.. duty 5 per cent.

Kittitian (kɪ'tɪʃən), *sb.* and *a.* Also **Kittician**. [f. *St. Kitt(s* + *-itian* as in *Haitian*.] **A.** *sb.* A native or inhabitant of the island of St. Kitts, in the West Indies; also, the form of regional English spoken in St. Kitts. **B.** *adj.* Of or pertaining to St. Kitts or its inhabitants.

1966 *Listener* 26 May 754/2 The factors which drew Kitticians to this particular area. 1970 J. BROWN *Unmelting Pot* vii. 104 They also came as islanders: Jamaicans, Barbadians, Kittitians, or Grenadans. 1973 *Observer* (Colour Suppl.) 16 Dec. 25/1 Carol Browne's brother will not speak Kittitian.. but he will speak the Jamaican dialect. 1973 *Country Life* 31 May 1544/1 Rodney Lad.. carried off a considerable amount of Kittitian property, leaving the local whites in an unpatriotic mood. 1974 *Advocate-News* (Barbados) 19 Feb. 9 By rescuing sugar the Government was in fact rescuing Kittitians.

kittiwake ('kɪtɪweɪk). Forms: 7 **cattiwake**, **kittie wark**, 8 **kettie waike**, **kittiwaik**, (? *pl.*, **kittawaax**, 7– **kittiwake**, 9 **kittywake**. [Named in imitation of its cry. Early spellings show that the last syllable was meant to be (wɑːk).] Any sea-gull of the genus *Rissa*; esp. (and primarily) *R. tridactyla*, the common species of the North Atlantic and Arctic Oceans, a small gull having generally white plumage with black markings on the primaries, very long wings, and the hind toe very short or rudimentary. Also ***kittiwake gull***.

1661 RAY *Three Itin.* II. in Lankester *Mem. John Ray* (1846) 155 The other birds which nestle in the Basse are these; the scout,.. the cattiwake. 1684 SIBBALD *Scotia Illustr., Nat. Hist.* II. III. vi. 20 Avis *Kittiwake*, ex Larorum genere, egregii saporis. 1698 in Warrender *Marchmont* (1894) 184 Kittie warks, 12.. Rost rabets 6. 1744 PRESTON in *Phil. Trans.* XLIII. 61 Many Sorts of Wild fowl;.. the Dunter Goose,.. Solan-Goose,.. Kittiwaiks.. etc. 1769 *De Foe's Tour Gt. Brit.* IV. 341 In the mouth of the river Forth lie several islands.. which abound with Fowl, particularly those called.. Kittawaax.. about the size of a Dove. 1877 W. THOMSON *Voy. Challenger* I. iii. 199 A few kittiwakes followed the ship for the first days after we left Teneriffe. 1881 R. BUCHANAN *God & the Man* II. 263 Innumerable terns and kittiwake gulls were hovering over the vessel.

†**kittle,** *sb. Obs. rare.* [app. shortened from KITLING.] A kitten.

1566 DRANT *Horace, Sat.* v. (1567) M, I knowe who plaies the catte, and howe her ioly kittles mouses.

kittle ('kɪt(ə)l), *a.* orig. *Sc.* and *north. dial.* Also 6 **kittil(l**. [f. KITTLE *v.*[1]; the use of the simple verbal stem as an adjective is unusual.] Ticklish; difficult to deal with, requiring great caution or skill; unsafe to meddle with; as to which one may easily go wrong or come to grief; risky, precarious, 'nice', delicate.

1560 [implied in *kittleness*: see below]. 1568 *Satir. Poems Reform.* xlvi. 60 Scho will be kittill of hir dok. 1571 *Ibid.* xxvii. 22 Thow may hir tyne in turning of a tyde; Cast weill thy courss, thow hes ane kittle cwir. 1596 JAS. VI *Let. to Earl Huntley* in Spottiswood *Hist. Ch. Scot.* (1655) 438 If your conscience be so kittle, as it cannot permit you. 1600 in Pitcairn *Crim. Trials* II. 284 My brother is 'kittle to shoe behind', and dare not enterprise for fear. 1641 BEST *Farm. Bks.* (Surtees) 80 If an ewe bee kittle on her yower, or unkinde to her lambe. 1721 RAMSAY *To Dalhousie* 22 Till frae his kittle post he fa'. 1728 —— *Rob. Richy & Sandy* 78 Kittle points of law. 1765 A. DICKSON *Treat. Agric.* (ed. 2) 232 *note*, Every common plowman will tell you, that, when the plough- irons are short, his plough goes kittle. By this he means, that it is easily turned aside, and is difficult to manage. 1815 SCOTT *Guy M.* xxii, I maun ride, to get to the Liddel or it be dark, for your Waste has but a kittle character. 1818 —— *Hrt. Midl.* xii, These are kittle times.. when the people take the power of life and death out of the hands of the rightful magistrate into their ain rough grip. 1830 *Blackw. Mag.* XXVII. 829 The kittler a question is, the mair successfully do you grapple wi't. 1869 C. GIBBON *R. Gray* xiv, Metaphors are kittle things to handle. 1890 *Truth* 11 Sept. 526/2 Cleopatra is a kittle character for a London theatre, unless played by some French actress who has no character to lose.

Hence **'kittleness.**

1560 ROLLAND *Seven Sages* 185 Ye may persaue.. Of wemen the gret brukilnes And of thair kynde the kittilnes.

kittle ('kɪt(ə)l), *v.*[1] Now *dial.* and chiefly *Sc.* Forms: (1 *vbl. sb.* **kitelung**, 4 *vbl. sb.* **kitlynge**), 5 **kytill**, **-ylle**, (? **kitell**, **ketil**), 6 **kyttyl(l**, **-il**, **kittil(l**, **kitill**, (3*rd sing.* **kytlis**, *vbl. sb.* **kitling**), 7– **kittle**. [ME. *kytylle*, *kityll*; cf. late OE. sb. *kitelung*, ME. *kitlynge*; cognate with OS. *kitilôn* (MDu. *kitelen*, *kittelen*, *ketelen*, Du. *kittelen*, *kietelen*), OHG. *chizzilôn*, *chuzzilôn* (MHG. *kitzeln*, *kütz-*, mod.G. *kitzeln*), ON. *kitla* (Sw. *kittla*); not known outside Teutonic, and generally supposed to be of onomatopœic origin, with a double form in *kit-* and *kut-*.

The history of the word in English is not clear. The verb itself is not found before the date of the *Catholicon*, 1483; and it is now used dialectally from Scotland to East Anglia. Hence it might, as well as the sb. *kitlynge* in Hampole, *c* 1340, be of Norse origin. But the sb. *kitelung* occurring once in a late OE. gloss (*c* 1000), naturally suggests an OE. sb. **kitelian*, which could only stand for **cytelian*, parallel to the OHG. form in *chu-*. An original OE. **citelian* = OS. *citilôn*, would not have been written with *k*, and would have given ME. **chittle*. It thus remains uncertain whether *kittle*, the date and locality of which are consistent with Norse derivation, is of Scandinavian or OE. origin.]

1. *trans.* To tickle (in physical sense).

c 1000 [see KITTLING]. 1483 *Cath. Angl.* 204/2 To kytylle, *titillare*. 1483 CAXTON *Gold. Leg.* 265/2 She.. felt hym and ketild hym. 1564 SIR J. MELVIL *Mem.* (Bann. Club 1827) 120 Sche culd not refrain from putting hir hand in his nek to kittle him. *c* 1575 *Balfour's Practicks* (1754) 509 Gif.. the band quhairwith thay ar bund tuich or kittle his sair bak. 1683 KENNETT tr. *Erasm. on Folly* 22 How a man must hug, and dandle, and kittle.. his bed-fellow. 1822 GALT *Steam-boat* x. 250 Kittling him in the ribs with his fore-finger. *a* 1825 FORBY *Voc. E. Anglia*, *Kittle*, to tickle. 1855 ROBINSON *Whitby Gloss.*, *To kittle*, to tickle.

b. *transf.* Used of actions humorously or ironically likened to tickling, as the friction of the strings of a fiddle with a bow, a stab with a weapon, etc.

1785 BURNS *To W. Simpson* v, I kittle up my rustic reed. 1814 SCOTT *Wav.* xxix, 'Her ain sell', replied Callum, 'could ..kittle his quarters wi' her skene-occle'. 1820 *Blackw. Mag.* July 386/1, I wad kittle the purse-proud carles under the fifth rib wi' the bit cauld steel. 1824 SCOTT *Redgauntlet* Let. x, The best fiddler that ever kittled thairm with horse-hair. 1828 *Craven Dial.* s.v., 'To kittle the fire', to stir it.

2. *fig.* To stir with feeling or emotion, usually pleasurable: to excite, rouse; to 'tickle'.

a 1340 [see KITTLING]. 1513 DOUGLAS *Æneis* v. xiv. 2 Glaidnes and confort.. Begouth to kittill Eneas thochtfull hart. *Ibid.* XII. Prol. 229 Quhen new curage kytlis all gentill hartis. 1534 HACKET *Let. to Hen. VIII* in *St. Papers* VII. 556 Able to cawse the Kyng of Denmark to kyttyll Inglonde with out any infrangyng of peace betwix the Emperour and Your Hyghnys. 1725 RAMSAY *Gent. Sheph.* II. i, I've gather'd news will kittle your heart wi' joy. 1819 SCOTT *Br. Lamm.* xiii, He kittles the lugs o' a silly auld wife wi' useless clavers. 1873 MURDOCH *Doric Lyre* 97 (E.D.D.) The corn-riggs kittle the farmer's e'e.

3. To puzzle with a question, a riddle, etc.

1824 SCOTT *St. Ronan's* xv, To kittle the clergymen with doubtful points of controversy. *a* 1832 —— in *Lockhart's Scott* (1839) VII. 195 [To a remark.. that he seemed to know something of the words of every song.. he replied] I daresay it wad be gay ill to kittle me in a Scots one at any rate.

'kittle, *v.*[2] Now *Sc.* and *north. dial.* Also 6 **kyt(t)ell**. [perh. a back formation from KITLING: but cf. Norw. *kjetla*, in the same sense.]

1. = KITTEN *v.*

1530 PALSGR. 599/1 Whan your catte kytelleth, I praye you, let me have a kytlynge. 1611 COTGR., *Chatonner*, to kittle. ? 17.. in Scott *Minstr. Scot. Bord.* II. 285 (Jam.) The hare sall kittle on my hearth stane. 1825 BROCKETT, *Kittle*, to bring forth kittens.

2. *fig.* (*intr.* and *pass.*) To be engendered or produced; to come into being.

1823 GALT *Entail* II. xxx. 282, I would be nane surprised if something had kittled between Jamie and a Highland lassie. **1824** SCOTT *St. Ronan's* ii, Before ony of them were born, or ony sic vapouring fancies kittled in their cracked brains. **1827** J. WILSON *Noct. Ambr.* Wks. 1855 I. 277 The cursedest kintra that ever was kittled.

kittle, obs. form of KETTLE *sb.*

kittle cattle ('kɪt(ə)l kæt(ə)l). orig. *Sc.* [f. KITTLE *a.* + CATTLE *sb.*] Used to denote people or animals that are capricious, rash, or erratic in behaviour; also *transf.*, objects, concepts, etc., that are difficult to use, sort out, or comprehend.

Initially in phr. (*kings are*) *kittle cattle to shoe behind*, an elaboration of *kittle to shoe behind* (see quot 1600 s.v. KITTLE *a.*).

1818 SCOTT *Heart Midl.* in *Tales my Landlord* 2nd Ser. IV. i. 5 Kings are kittle cattle to shoe behind, as we say in the north. **1876** GEO. ELIOT *Dan. Der.* xxv, She is kittle cattle to shoe, I think. **1881** H. SHANKS *Peasant Poets Scotl., & Musings* 342 Now, women are (compared wi' men), More contumacious; and when Their 'birse' is up,—my certy! then They're kittle cattle. **1888** *Trans. Highland Soc.* 197 Even as machines are easily deranged so sheep are 'kittle cattle'; no more delicate animal breathes. **1900** E. T. FOWLER *Farringdons* i. 15 She knew a great portion of the Methodist hymn-book by heart, and pondered long over the interesting preface to that work, wondering much what 'doggerel' and 'botches' could be—she inclined to the supposition that the former were animals and the latter were diseases; but even her vivid imagination failed to form a satisfactory representation of such queer kittle-cattle as 'feeble expletives'. **1926** FOWLER *Mod. Eng. Usage* 717/1 It is well known that *and which* & *but which* are kittle cattle, so well known that the more timid writers avoid the dangers associated with them. **1935** *Times Educ. Suppl.* 28 Dec. p. iv/1 It helps to discount the general impression that, as a race, they [*sc.* lilies] are kittle-kattle. **1942** F. SMYTHE *Alpine Ways* 14 The 'he man' mountaineer who scorns tourists as mere kittle kattle, the tourists who jeer at the mountaineer as mad, have yet to gain that fuller understanding which abhors intolerance. **1966** *Sunday Express* 13 Mar. 16/7 Princesses in love.. are at times Kittle Cattle.

'kittle-pins, 'kettle-pins, *sb. pl.* Now only *dial.* [The relation of this to SKITTLE has not been determined.] Skittles, nine-pins.

1649 G. DANIEL *Trinarch., Hen. V*, clxiii, Quoyts, and Kettle-pins. **1649** SADLER *Rights Kingd.* 43 When shall our kittle-pins return again into the Grecian skyttals. **1679** *Trial Langhorn* 32, I saw him in the Garden with a Lay-Brother at Kittle-pins in the view of all the Colledge. **1801** STRUTT *Sports & Past.* III. vii. (1810) 239 Loggatts..is the same which is now called kittle-pins, in which the boys often make use of bones instead of wooden pins. **1886** ELWORTHY *W. Somerset Word-bk.*, *Kittle-pins*, skittles—applied to the pins and not to the game.

So **'kittles** *sb. pl.*, skittles.

1697 *View Penal Laws* 329 If any person..shall by any Fraud..at..Kittles..Win Money. **1719** D'URFEY *Pills* III. 162 We merrily Play At Trap, and Kettles.

'kittling, *vbl. sb. Sc.* and *north. dial.* [OE. *kitelung*: see KITTLE *v.*[1]] The action of KITTLE *v.*[1]; tickling (*lit.* and *fig.*).

c **1000** *Ags. Voc.* in Wr.-Wülcker 278/6 *Titillatio*, kitelung. *a* **1340** HAMPOLE *Psalter* ii. 4 Dissayued thurght quayntis of þe deuel and kitlynge of þaire flesch [*MS. Coll. Eton.* 10, lf. 4, kitellynge of thaire flesshe]. **1483** *Cath. Angl.* 204/2 A kytyllynge, *titillacio*. **1822** HOGG *Perils Man* II. vi. 234 A kind o' kittling, a sort o' prinkling in my blood like. **1830** GALT *Lawrie T.* VII. vi. (1849) 330 Ye'll never laugh or smile At the kittling o' your knee.

kittling, kittlin, obs. forms of KITLING.

kittly ('kɪtlɪ), *a. Sc.* and *U.S.* [f. KITTLE *v.*[1] + -Y; cf. Norw. *kitlug*, Sw. *kitlig*, LG. *kitlich*, G. *kitzlich*. For the sense 'risky' in the compound *kittly-benders*, cf. KITTLE *a.*] Easily tickled; susceptible or sensitive to tickling; ticklish; tickly.

1822 GALT *Steam-boat* viii. 155, I was no so kittly as she thought, and could thole her progs and jokes. **1830** —— *Lawrie T.* v. ii. (1849) 199 It made the very soles of my feet kittly to hear it.

b. kittly-benders (also corruptly ***kettle-de-benders***), thin ice which bends under one's weight; the sport of running over this. (*U.S. colloq.*)

1854 THOREAU *Walden* 353 Let us not play at kittly-benders. **1872** E. E. HALE *How to Do it* iii. 46 You will, with unfaltering step, move quickly over the kettle-de-benders of this broken essay.

'kittock. *Sc.* ? *Obs.* [f. as KIT *sb.*[4] + -OCK *dim.*] A familiar or disrespectful term for a girl or young woman; esp. a woman of loose character, a wanton; a mistress.

c **1470** HENRYSON *Mor. Fab.* III. (*Cock & Fox*) xx, He was sa lous and sa lecherous: He had..kittokis ma than sevine. *c* **1538** LYNDESAY *Against Syde Taillis* 108 He did lift ane Kittokis claithis. **1603** *Philotus* iv, Ha, ha, quha brocht thir kittocks hither The mekill feind resaue the fithir. **1706** R. SEMPILL *Piper of Kilbarchan* in *Chambers' Pop. Hum. Scot. Poems* (1862) 26 He was convoyer of the bride, With kittock hinging at his side.

kittree, obs. variant of KHATRI.

‖**kittul, kitool** (kɪ'tuːl). Also 7 kettule, 9 kettal, (?-ul), kittool. [Cingalese *kitūl*.] The jaggery palm, *Caryota urens*; hence, a strong black fibre obtained from the leaf-stalks of this, used for making ropes, brushes, etc.

1681 R. KNOX *Hist. Ceylon* 15 The next Tree is the Kettule. It groweth streight, but not so tall or big as a Coker-Nut-Tree. **1857** R. TOMES *Amer. in Japan* ii. 47 Ceylon abounds in..trees of great utility; among which,.. there is the kettul-tree, from the sap of which is produced a coarse sugar. **1866** *Treas. Bot.* 647 *Kittool, Kittul*, a Cinghalese name for *Caryota urens*; also for the strong fibre obtained from its leaf-stalks. **1884** *Pub. Opinion* 11 July 47/1 Ropes made of kitool are used to tether and secure wild elephants... Kitool fibre is [used]..in the manufacture of brooms and brushes.

kitty[1] ('kɪtɪ). Also 6 *Sc.* **kittie**. [One of the pet forms of the female name Catherine; cf. KATE, KATY, KIT *sb.*[4] (Cf. also CUTTY *sb.*, senses 2 and 3.)]

†**1.** A girl or young woman; a wench; sometimes (= *kittie unsell*) a woman of loose character. (Cf. KITTOCK.) *Sc. Obs.*

1500–20 DUNBAR *Poems* xiv. 76 Sa mony ane Kittie, drest vp with goldin chenȝe. *a* **1550** *Christis Kirke Gr.* i, Thair come our kitteis weschin clene, In thair new kirtillis. *c* **1560** A. SCOTT *Poems* (S.T.S.) xxvi. 19, I can thame call bot kittie vnsellis, That takkis sic maneris at thair motheris. **1572** *Lament Lady Scotl.* 112 in *Satir. Poems Reform.* xxxiii, Bot at the last, throw filthy speiche and Counsell, That scho did heir of sum curst Kittie vnsell.

2. Local name for the wren; also ***kitty-wren***.

1825 BROCKETT, *Kitty-wren*, or *Jenny-wren*, the wren. **1860** *All Year Round* No. 63. 295 The male wrens of North America..build 'cock-nests'..like the males of our distinct kitty-wrens. **1885** SWAINSON *Prov. Names Brit. Birds* 35 Wren... Familiar names. Kitty, Jenny. **1893** NEWTON *Dict. Birds*, *Kitty*, a local nickname of the Wren.

b. Also prefixed to, or forming part of the local names of other birds, as **kitty-coot**, the moorhen (*Gallinula chloropus*); **kitty-needy**, the sandpiper; **kitty-witch** = KITTIWAKE; also name of a small swimming crab, *Porcellana platycheles*.

1850 *Zoologist* VIII. 2644 *note*, 'Kittie-needie' [Aberdeenshire]..the common sandpiper. **1876** SMILES *Sc. Natur.* vii. (ed. 4) 125 The piping of the kittyneedy..the boom of the snipe, were often heard at night. **1885** SWAINSON *Prov. Names Brit. Birds* 178 Moor Hen... Kitty coot (Dorset).

kitty[2]. [f. as KIT *sb.*[3] + -Y.] A kitten; used esp. as a pet name.

1719 D'URFEY *Pills* II. 82 A pretty young Kitty, She had that could Purr.

kitty[3]. Short for KITTIWAKE.

1806 R. FORSYTH *Beauties Scotl.* IV. 460 Some people are fond of eating the young kitties.

kitty[4]. *north. dial.* and *slang.* [Origin uncertain: cf. KIDCOTE.]

1. A prison, jail, or lock-up; a house of correction.

1825 BROCKETT, *Kitty*, the house of correction. Newcastle. **1832** W. STEPHENSON *Gateshead Local Poems* 28 We had a nice tollbooth,..And in its stead we've got..A vile pernicious kitty. **1864** *Daily Tel.* 22 Sept., The Provost [of Jedburgh] ordered another man to be taken into custody; said the crowd, 'If ane gangs t' the kitty, we'll a' gang'. **1888** *Monthly Chron. N.C.* June 285/1 Wey, man, that's a fine kitty.

2. 'A pool into which each player in a card-game puts a certain amount of his winnings, to be used in meeting expenses, as for room-rent, refreshments, etc.' (*Cent. Dict.*) Also, the money (freq. placed in the centre of the table) taken by the winner of a game or round (the usual sense). So *transf.*, earnings, liquid capital, a reserve fund; a sum of money made up of contributions by people involved in a common activity.

1887 J. W. KELLER *Game of Draw Poker* 12 *Widow*, or *Kitty*—A percentage taken out of the pool to defray the expenses of the game or the cost of refreshments. **1891** E. DOWSON *Let.* 1 July (1967) 206, I shall..refuse to associate myself with penny nap & an unlimited Kittie. **1892** *Daily Chron.* 5 Mar. 9/2 (Farmer *Slang*) Five or six men playing 'Nap', with a kitty for drinks, kitty being the pool and the payment to it of a half-penny. **1903** 'J. FLYNT' *Rise of Ruderick Clowd* iii. 106 'Forty [cents] out of every dollar you cop out—understand?'—'Who gets the rest?'—'The mob an' the kitty. The kitty is the fall-money reserve. A mob like ours ought to carry a $3000 kitty all the time. It's drawn on when one of us gets arrested an' has to hire lawyers an' get bail. If you get a tumble, for instance, the rest of us'll have to stand by you—see?' **1905** *Daily Chron.* 12 Sept. 4/7 'Kitty wins everything,' is the bookmakers' plaint. **1909** 'O. HENRY' *Roads of Destiny* xiii. 213 Your thousand dollars is gone into the kitty of this corrupt country on that last bluff you made. **1924** T. ROHAN *Confessions of Dealer* iv. 51 The King of the Knock-Out..counts out banknotes to the tune of £1,000, and places these notes in the bowl or kitty which occupies the centre of the table. The first man to help himself from the kitty is the dealer who bid £100 at the sale. **1929** [see FULL HOUSE 2]. **1935** A. J. POLLOCK *Underworld Speaks* 68/1 *Kitty*, money taken from virtually every gambling pot for purpose of profits or expenses, or whangdoodles at the end of a friendly home game. **1969** *Listener* 17 July 77/1 In 1949, the authorities at the hall had enough money in the kitty to install a new aluminium roof. **1971** *Ink* 12 June 14/1 Bernie's salesmen kept bringing in the lolly..until by 1970 they had $2.4 billion in their management kitty.

3. *Bowls.* The jack.

1898 D. WILLOX *Poems & Sk.* 174 Now, in throwing up the 'Kitty', Oor first player's quite a card, But in playing tae't he seldom Ever gangs within a yard. **1909** *Westm. Gaz.* 6 Sept. 4/1 When the bowl goes near the kitty. **1926** H. HENDRY *Poems* 98 Kitty, that licht and lively quean, Wha links athort the bowling-green. **1959** *Chambers's Encycl.* II. 476/1 The small white earthenware ball, known as the jack or 'kitty', at which the bowls are aimed, must not be more than 8 in. in circumference or 10 oz in weight.

kittydid, var. KATYDID.

kitysol: see KITTISOL.

kiva ('kiːvə). Also **khiva, kiver.** [Hopi.] A chamber, built wholly or partly underground, used by the male Pueblo Indians for religious rites, etc.; ESTUFA. Also *attrib.* and *transf.*

1871 in *Utah Hist. Q.* (1939) VII. 54 Found pieces of pottery and arrowheads... Also saw a 'kiver' or underground 'clan room'. **1875** *Scribner's Monthly* Dec. 205/2 This kiva, as it is called in their own tongue, is called '*Estufa*' by the Spaniards, and is spoken of by writers in English as the 'Sweat House'. **1898** *17th Ann. Rep. U.S. Bureau Amer. Ethnol. 1895–6* 611 A pueblo of the size of Awatobi..would no doubt have ceremonial chambers or kivas. **1927** W. CATHER *Death comes for Archbishop* IV. ii. 132 It was a smothered fire in a clay oven, and had been burning in one of the kivas ever since the pueblo was founded. **1931** *Discovery* Sept. 279/2 The 'khiva' as they are called by the present Hopi Indians... It seems clear that their purpose was to provide a meeting place for councils and ceremonies for the men of the clan. **1950** F. EGGAN *Social Organiz. Western Pueblos* ii. 28 Between the members of the kiva groups there are no special kinship ties. **1958** J. CLEUGH tr. *Jungk's Brighter than Thousand Suns* xviii. 295 The mechanism used took the form of a 'critical assembly' under remote control. Processes going on inside the 'Kivas'—the buildings had been called after the sacred ceremonial chambers of the Pueblo Indians, which could only be approached, with the greatest awe, by their priests—were to be observed solely on television screens. **1964** E. A. NIDA *Toward Sci. Transl.* viii. 169 For the Zuñis, uttering *melika* in a kiva ceremony would be as out of place as bringing a radio into such a meeting.

kive, variant of KEEVE, tub, vat.

kiver ('kɪvə(r)). *Obs.* exc. *dial.* Also 5 **kevere**, 7 **keuer, keaver, kiever**, 8 **keever**. [app. connected with KEEVE, *kive*: but the force of the suffix is unexplained.] A shallow wooden vessel or tub.

α. **1407** in Kennett *Par. Ant.* (1818) II. 212 Et pro novo Cowele empto, ix[d]. Et pro novo Kevere empto, viii[d]. **1609** C. BUTLER *Fem. Mon.* x. 1, Wiping the Bees,..into a keuer or other vessel. **1610** *Althorp MS.* in Simpkinson *The Washingtons* (1860) p. vii, Itm little keavers..iiij. **1676** WORLIDGE *Cyder* (1691) 109 Either a tub or kiever or else a square chest. **1706** PHILLIPS, *Keeve* or *Keever*, a kind of Tub.

β. **1623** C. BUTLER *Fem. Mon.* (ed. 2) x. 11, A Ridder, resting vpon Tongs ouer a cleane Pan or Kiuer that will not leake. **1744–50** W. ELLIS *Mod. Husbandm.* III. I. 129 Divide [the milk] into several pans, or leads, or kivers. **1750** —— *Country Housew.* 19 Kneading-kiver, or trough, or tub. **1876** *S. Warwicksh. Gloss.*, *Kiver*, the tub that the butter is made up in. **1881** *Oxfordsh. Gloss.* Suppl., *Kiver*, a trough to make dough, butter, &c. in. **1884** *W. Sussex Gaz.* 25 Sept., Brew vat and stand, oval Kiver, two 50-gallon casks.

kiver, obs. and dial. form of COVER *sb.* and *v.*

‖**kiwach**, another form of COWAGE.

1876 HARLEY *Mat. Med.* (ed. 6) 635 The Kiwach or Cowhage Plant..is a lofty climber.

Kiwanis (kɪ'wɑːnɪs). [Origin obscure.] In full, ***Kiwanis Club***. A society of business and professional men formed in Detroit in 1915 for the maintenance of commercial ethics, and as a social and charitable organization; any similar society formed later elsewhere in the U.S.A. or in Canada. Also **Ki'wanian**, a member of a Kiwanis Club.

1921 *Daily Colonist* (Victoria, B.C.) 16 Mar. 5/4 An initiation ceremony for the purpose of welcoming into the organization three new members took place at the weekly luncheon of the Kiwanis Club yesterday. *Ibid.* 30 Mar. 7/5 As Kiwanians and citizens, Mr Smith claimed, it was a duty to look after the children. **1922** *Collier's* 29 Apr. 5/2 It had a civic association, and Rotary, Kiwanis, and Lion Clubs. **1926** *Glasgow Herald* 18 Sept. 4 Take Galveston, for example... A newspaper describes how the local Kiwanians and their lady friends..rounded off an evening's delight by indulging in a hand-shaking competition. **1948** *Daily Ardmoreite* (Ardmore, Okla.) 30 Mar. 3/1 A class of older girls recently entertained the local Kiwanis club. **1949** *Amer. Speech* XXIV. 29 Virginians..show little of the exuberant affability of a Midwestern Rotarian or Kiwanian. **1964** MRS. L. B. JOHNSON *White House Diary* (1970) 5 Jan. 30 We drove to the little house in Johnson City.., which we are having restored as a Community Center, where, hopefully, 4-H youngsters or the PTA, or Kiwanis, or Lions, or ladies' groups, or whatever can hold their meetings. **1972** *Fairbanks* (Alaska) *Daily News-Miner* 3 Nov. 1/2 Alaska Attorney General John Havelock analyzed and approved the moral basis of Alaska's Oil Legislation in an address before a joint Kiwanis banquet here last night.

‖**kiwi** ('kiːwɪ). Also **kiwi-kiwi, kivi.** [Maori.]

1. The native New Zealand name of the APTERYX, now commonly used in English.

1835 W. YATE *Acc. New Zeal.* 58 (Morris) Kiwi—the most remarkable and curious bird in New Zealand. **1852** *Zoologist* X. 3409 On the Habits of the Kiwi-kiwi. **1873** BULLER *Birds New Zeal.* (1888) I. 237 Last Sunday I dined on stewed Kiwi, at the hut of a lonely gold-digger.

2. (With capital initial.) A New Zealander, esp. a New Zealand soldier; also, a New Zealand sportsman. Also *attrib.*

1918 *N.Z.E.F. Chrons.* 24 May 179/1 In the evening the 'Kiwis' gave a performance to a crowded hall. *Ibid.* 21 June 225/1 The New Zealand boys.. will find the 'Kiwi' A.D.S. as reasonably safe as is possible. **1945** BAKER *Austral. Lang.* ix. 178 New Zealand football representatives acquired the names *All Blacks, Fernleaves,* and *Kiwis.* **1947** B. MASON in D. M. Davin *N.Z. Short Stories* (1953) 333 We were Kiwis, and a long way from home. **1958** R. FRANCE *Race* 12 Laurie was not a real Kiwi, or hard-bitten New Zealander. **1960** B. CRUMP *Good Keen Man* 58, I suspect she was a real Kiwi mum, with a soft spot for her little Harry. **1961** in J. Reid *Kiwi Laughs* 10 Told in a homely Kiwi idiom. **1963** N. HILLIARD *Piece of Land* 35 They fill the place with immigrants... A Kiwi'd never look at the prices some of them want. **1974** *Times* 17 June 12/7 It is hurtful to many Australians to see the Kiwis take all the credit for Antipodean anti-Pom feelings.

3. Also **Kiwi.** A non-flying member of an air force (see also quot. 1938). *slang.*

1918 B. HALL *Diary* 22 Jan. in Hall & Niles *One Man's War* (1929) xxxii. 289 Visited the Avenue Montaigne Headquarters. It is full of non-flying aviators. The American pilots call them Kiwis. **1925** FRASER & GIBBONS *Soldier & Sailor Words* 137 *Kiwi,* Air Force slang for a man on ground duty and not qualified for flying service. **1931** *Vanity Fair* (N.Y.) Nov. 78/3 There are terms with which to plaster the green pilot and the non-flyer. *Quirks* or *kiwis* are beginners—sometimes the terms are broadened to include the layman. The origin of *quirk* is somewhat obscure.. but *kiwi* is a derogatory reference to the Australian [*sic*] kiwi-bird, which, having only stub wings, is unable to fly. **1938** *Amer. Speech* XIII. 156/2 *Kiwi,*.. a person with no practical flying experience; often used as a term of disparagement toward one who speaks with authority concerning flying but whose knowledge is entirely theoretical. **1943** HUNT & PRINGLE *Service Slang* 43 *Kiwi,* a word brought over by the New Zealand airmen with a new meaning: men who do not belong to air crews. **1960** WENTWORTH & FLEXNER *Dict. Amer. Slang* 307/1 *Kiwi,* an air force man, esp. an officer who cannot, does not, or does not like to fly.

4. = *kiwi berry, fruit.*

1972 *Daily Colonist* (Victoria, B.C.) 2 Aug. 19/1 Have you noticed a small brown fruit called kiwi in local markets lately?.. Sometimes called a Chinese gooseberry. **1973** *Sat. Rev. Soc.* (U.S.) Mar. 53/1 Twenty-six different crops, most of them fruit—almonds, apples.. kiwis, nectarines, olives.

5. *attrib.* and *Comb.*, as ***kiwi feather, -hunter, -preserve***; **kiwi berry, fruit** = *Chinese gooseberry* (CHINESE *a.* 2).

1968 *N.Z. News* 23 Oct. 2/4 New Zealand exports of chinese gooseberries will enter the United States—where they are called 'giant Kiwi-berries'—almost duty-free from next season. **1905** *Daily Chron.* 7 July 6/5 The presents included.. a rug of kiwi feathers from New Zealand, and three rare engravings. **1938** R. D. FINLAYSON *Brown Man's Burden* 47 They had covered his shrunken body with fine kiwi-feather cloaks. **1966** *N.Y. Times* 13 Aug. 12 Chinese gooseberries, also known as kiwi fruit, are in metropolitan markets for the third season in increased quantities. **1970** *N.Z. News* 7 Jan. 4/4 A storage technique first developed for bananas has been tested on Chinese gooseberries, now renamed 'Kiwi fruit'. *Ibid.* 4/5 A 20 lb. pack of Kiwi fruit. **1973** *Massey Ferguson Rev.* (N.Z.) Mar./Apr. 3/4 Chinese gooseberries or 'kiwi fruit', bear extravagantly. **1873** BULLER *Birds New Zeal.* (1888) II. 313 Old experienced Kiwi-hunters. *Ibid.* 315 The heights of Rangitoto, where.. there exists another Kiwi-preserve.

kix, kixen, obs. or dial. ff. KEX, -EN.

kiyaya, variant of KEHAYA.

ki-yi ('kaɪ'jaɪ), *v.* *U.S. colloq.* Also **ki-hi.** [Echoic. According to Farmer, of Negro origin.] *intr.* To howl or yelp as a dog, or utter a sound compared to this.

1869 MRS. STOWE *Oldtown* 332 (Cent.) Hang him [a dog] we did, and he ki-hied with a vigor that strikingly increased the moral effect.

Hence **ki-yi** *sb.*, (*a*) the howl or yelp of a dog; a whoop; a shout of exultation; (*b*) a dog.

1884 *Breadwinners* 210 You ought to have heard the ki-yi's that followed. **1886** *Detroit Free Press* 4 Aug. (Farmer), Now and then you will hear a joyous ki-yi come from the direction of a woolly-headed worker. **1895** *Harper's Mag.* Nov. 962/1 I'm not really a ki-yi, and while I don't like bicyclists,.. I won't bite you. **1904** *Buffalo* (N.Y.) *Express* 20 June 4 A butcher in Brussels made sausage of the carcass of a zoo elephant which had been killed. Doubtless the Brussels kiyis yelped for joy. **1913** J. LONDON *Valley of Moon* I. x, But them sickenin', sap-headed stiffs, with the grit of rabbits and the silk of mangy ki-yi's, a-cheerin' me—*me*!

kiyn, obs. pl. of COW.

kiyth, obs. f. KITHE *v.*

Kizil (kɪ'zɪl), *a.* and *sb.* Also **Kyzyl.** [ad. Turk. *kizil* red.] **A.** *adj.* Of or pertaining to a Turkic Tartar people of southern Siberia. **B.** *sb.* A member of this people.

1898 A. J. BUTLER tr. *Ratzel's Hist. Mankind* III. v. xiii. 336 The Kizil Tartars on the Upper Chulym. *Ibid.* 342 The Kizil tribe of the Tomsk Kirghises. **1909** WEBSTER, Kizil *n.* **1964** tr. *Levin & Potapov's Peoples of Siberia* 358 The Kyzyls belonged to a large Turkic-speaking group living in the Chulym Basin. *Ibid.* 360 The language of the present-day Kyzyls is identical with Kachin.

Kizilbash ('kɪzɪlbɑːʃ). (Also used as *pl.*) Also 8 -bac, 9- Kizzil-, -bashi. [ad. Turk. *kizilbaş*, f. *kizil* red + *baş* head.] **a.** A Persianized Turk of Afghanistan. **b.** A member of any of several cultural or religious minorities in Asian Turkey.

1727 J. G. SCHEUCHZER tr. *Kæmpfer's Hist. Japan* I. I. vi. 88 The *Kizilbacs*, or Noblemen, and great Families, in Persia value themselves mightily upon their being of Turcoman extraction. **1815** [see TURK[1] 1]. **1875** *Encycl. Brit.* I. 235/1 The *Kizilbâshes* may be regarded as modern Persians, but more strictly they are Persianised Turks. **1898** A. J. BUTLER tr. *Ratzel's Hist. Mankind* III. v. xv. 365 In Persia and Afghanistan the Turks, Kizilbashes, Usbeks, Turcomans, are even more sharply distinguished from the Persians. **1902** *Encycl. Brit.* XXV. 120/1 The Kizzilbashes of Kabul. **1920** *Blackw. Mag.* Jan. 121/2 Hosts of Tartar, and Afghan, Persian and Kizilbash. **1960** *Guardian* 28 June 8/5 Mingled with the Pathans of the south [of Afghanistan] ..are.. Turkomans, Kizilbashes, Kirghis. **1960** *Spectator* 2 Dec. 889/3 Religious sects living apart like the Kizil Bashis, Shiah, Tartars and Kára Papachs [in Turkey, *c* 1912].

Kjeldahl ('kɛldɑːl). *Biochem.* The name of Johann *Kjeldahl* (1849–1900), Danish brewing chemist, used *attrib.* and in the possessive to denote a method of estimation of nitrogen invented by him, in which the organic substance to be analysed is treated with concentrated sulphuric acid and the ammonium sulphate so formed is converted by excess alkali to ammonia, which is then titrated; **Kjeldahl flask,** a glass flask having a round bottom and a long wide neck, used in the Kjeldahl method.

1885 *Jrnl. Chem. Soc.* XLVIII. 688 (*heading*) Nitrogen determinations by Kjeldahl's method. **1909** P. B. HAWK *Pract. Physiol. Chem.* (ed. 2) xxii. 382 Place 5 c.c. of urine in a 500 c.c. long-necked Jena glass Kjeldahl flask. **1964** [see COLORIMETRICALLY *adv.*]. **1970** R. W. MCGILVERY *Biochem.* xxviii. 704 The Kjeldahl method has the advantage of being applicable to insoluble materials, such as most foodstuffs, and the disadvantage of not distinguishing proteins from other sources of nitrogen, such as nucleic acids, urea, and the like.

kjerulfin(e ('kjɛːrʊlfɪn). *Min.* [Named in 1873, after Prof. Kjerulf, a Norwegian mineralogist.] A variety of Wagnerite, occurring in large crystals and cleavable masses; found at Bamle in Norway.

1875 WATTS *Dict. Chem.* VII. 715 Kjerulfin differs from wagnerite, which it resembles in many respects, by containing less fluorine and sodium, and more calcium.

kl-, occasional ME. spelling for *cl-*, as in *klath, klawe, kleane, klee,* for *clath* (*cloth*), *claw, clean, clee,* etc.; now only in words of foreign origin.

Klá, var. KULLAH.

Klaas (klɑːs). The name of a servant who travelled with the French explorer, François Le Vaillant (1753–1824), used in the possessive in **Klaas's cuckoo,** a bronze and green cuckoo, *Chrysococcyx klaas,* found in the southern part of Africa.

1867 E. L. LAYARD *Birds S. Afr.* 250 Klaas's cuckoo is not uncommon in most wooded parts of the colony. **1903** A. C. STARK *Birds S. Afr.* III. 188 This cuckoo was first obtained by Levaillant and named by him after his faithful Hottentot servant Klaas... Klaas' Cuckoo frequents both bush and thorn lands. **1936** E. L. GILL *First Guide S. Afr. Birds* 108 Among the birds parasitized by Klaas's Cuckoo are various sunbirds, warblers and kingfishers. **1951** R. CAMPBELL *Light on Dark Horse* x. 143 The bird known to this day as Klaas's Cuckoo.. is the ruby cuckoo. **1964** P. A. CLANCEY *Birds Natal & Zululand* 222 The young Klaas' cuckoo ejects the nestlings of the foster parent a few days after hatching.

klaberjass, var. KLOBBIYOS.

Klamath ('klæməθ). Also †**Clamet.** [ad. Chinook *ƚámaƚ* Klamath.] **A.** *sb.* A Penutian Indian people of the Oregon-California border; a member of this people; also, their language. **B.** *adj.* Of or pertaining to this people.

1826 J. MCLOUGHLIN *Lett.* (1941) I. 33 Mr. Ogden [goes] .. thence towards Lac Sale makes a Circuit West and comes Out above the Clamet tribe. **1853** H. R. SCHOOLCRAFT *Hist. & Stat. Information Indian Tribes* III. 133 The goods destined for the Klamath Indians had been sent to Trinidad. **1881** *Encycl. Brit.* XII. 826/2 The *Klamath* family,.. comprises the Lutuami or Klamaths proper. *Ibid.*, *Californian Races.*—This is mainly a geographical grouping, but with three large ethnical and linguistic families—the Klamath, Pomo, and Runsien. **1890** A. S. GATSCHET *Klamath Indians* I. 209 Triphthongs are not infrequent, since Klamath has a greater tendency to accumulate consonants than vowels. **1923** [see DAKOTA *sb.* 2]. **1965** *Canad. Jrnl. Linguistics* Spring 123 The last family represented in Oregon is Klamath-Modoc. Klamath speakers are found in fairly large numbers... Modoc is represented by only about seven or eight speakers.

C. Klamath weed, the local name of a species of St. John's wort, *Hypericum perforatum.*

1922 F. J. SMILEY *Weeds Calif.* 54 (Hypericum perforatum L.) English names:.. Common St. John's-wort .. Klamath weed. **1949** *Sunday World-Herald Mag.* (Omaha) 1 May 10/1 Klamath weed probably can be controlled or destroyed chemically. **1971** DEBACH & HUFFAKER in C. B. Huffaker *Biol. Control* v. 118 Figure 1.. shows the degree of biological control achieved in California of the formerly serious Klamath weed, *Hypericum perforatum* L., by colonization of an imported exotic beetle which feeds upon it.

Klan. Short for KU-KLUX-KLAN. Also ***Klansman,*** occas. ***Clansman.***

1867 [see KU-KLUX 1]. **1868** *Century Mag.* XXVIII. 409/1 The Klan now, as in the past, is prohibited from doing such things. **1884** [see INVISIBLE *a.* 1 c]. **1905** T. DIXON (*title*) The Clansman. **1924** J. M. MECKLIN *Ku Klux Klan* i. 3 The modern Klan was organized by William J. Simmons in 1915. *Ibid.* 5 Masked men leaped from their cars clad in Klan regalia. *Ibid.* 6 Public sentiment.. seems to have supported the Klansmen. **1953** *Manch. Guardian Weekly* 31 Dec. 11 A klansman from Georgia. **1973** *Freedomways* XIII. 31 The.. killings and the Attica prison slaughter are remindful of the post-Civil War Klan days. **1973** *Guardian* 23 Mar. 15/2 A former member of the Klan, Senator Byrd has a dismal voting record on social and civil rights issues. **1973** *Black Panther* 1 Sept. 8/3 The Assistant District Attorney tossed out the charges saying that although the law prohibits Klansmen from appearing in public, the faces of the 24 were visible.

‖**klang** (klaŋ, klæŋ). [G., = sound.] A musical tone composed of fundamental and overtones; = CLANG *sb.* 3. Hence '**klangfarbe** (-'farbə) [G. *farbe,* colour], musical quality of a note, timbre, 'clang-tint' (see CLANG *sb.* 4); **klangfarbenmelodie,** melody of timbres.

1867 [see CLANG *sb.* 3]. **1890** J. KLAUSER *Septonate* i. 37 (Funk), In music a tone or a *klang* is thought, heard, and treated as a unit. **1959** *Listener* 12 Nov. 834/2 It is possible that some of the mannerisms—disjointed rhythms, 'Klangfarbenmelodie' (the playing of notes that have no connection with each other one by one), etc., may fall by the wayside. **1966** *Ibid.* 19 May 736/3 No. 3.. is systematically subjected to *klangfarbenmelodie,* emphasis of instrumental timbre.

klapper ('klæpə(r)). *S. Afr.* [perh. ad. Malay *kĕlapa* coconut or Afrikaans *klapper* rattle.] = *Kaffir orange* (KAFFIR 4); also used for other shrubs or trees with similar fruit.

1863 W. C. BALDWIN *Afr. Hunting* vi. 199 We had a capital lunch from some wild fruit about three times the size of an orange, called a clapper. It has a hard shell outside, which one must batter against a tree to crack or break. **1921** T. R. SIM *Native Timbers S. Afr.* 120 *Strychnos pungens*... Klopper [*sic*], Wild Orange. **1932** WATT & BREYER-BRANDWIJK *Medicinal & Poisonous Plants S. Afr.* 140 The pulp of the fruit of *Strychnos pungens* Solered., Wild orange, Kaffir orange, Klapper.. *Strychnos spinosa* Lam. (*Brehmia spinosa* Harv.), Kaffir orange, Klapper.. and *Strychnos gerrardi* N.E. Br... is acidulous from the presence of citric acid, and is very refreshing. **1939** tr. *E. N. Marais's My Friends the Baboons* iii. 29 Wild peaches, sour klappers (unknown in the south), medlers, moepels, and various other kinds of fruit made our wilderness a veritable orchard. **1966** E. PALMER *Plains of Camdeboo* x. 177 The spekboom, the wild plum and the klapper, now bright with colour. **1973** PALMER & PITMAN *Trees S. Afr.* III. 1857 The monkey orange, or klapper as it is often known,.. is an evergreen tree.

†'**klaprothine.** *Min. Obs.* [Named in 1811, after Prof. M. H. Klaproth of Berlin.] = LAZULITE.

1837 PHILLIPS *Min.* 159 *Klaprothine,* a synonym of Azurite. **1852** *Ibid.* 524 Klaprothine... Is found in crystals, but more frequently massive.

'**klaprothite.** *Min.* [f. as prec. + -ITE[1].] **a.** = KLAPROTHINE. **b.** = KLAPROTHOLITE.

1872 [see next].

klaprotholite (klæ'prəʊtəlaɪt). *Min.* [f. as prec. + -LITE. Changed in 1872 from *klaprothite,* the name given by Petersen in 1868.] A sulphide of bismuth and copper related to Wittichenite, occurring in steel-grey orthorhombic crystals.

1872 G. J. BRUSH in *Dana's Min.* App. I. 8 Klaprotholite is generally associated with a cobalt-tetrahedrite... The name klaprothite was given to lazulite by Beudant in 1824, we therefore change Petersen's name to klaprotholite.

‖**klatsch** (klatʃ). Also **klatch.** [G., tittle-tattle, gossip.] A visit; a coffee-party. Cf. *coffee-klatsch,* KAFFEEKLAT(S)CH.

1953 A. MILLER *Crucible* (1956) I. 34 There are accounts of similar *klatches* in Europe, where the daughters of the towns would assemble at night and.. give themselves to love. **1967** E. B. NICKERSON *Kayaks to Arctic* xvi. 155 So later, when the men returned and set up their camp we had them over for a klatch.

klaxon ('klæksən), *sb.* orig. *U.S.* Also **Klaxon.** [Name of the manufacturing company.] An (electric) horn or warning hooter, orig. one on a motor vehicle. Also ***klaxon-horn.***

1910 *Sat. Even. Post* 17 Sept. 48 The Klaxon has never taken a life; it has saved thousands. **1911** *N.Y. Times* 16 Oct. 12/7 Speedometer, slip covers, pigskin upholstery and klaxon. **1917** 'CONTACT' *Airman's Outings* 66 A signal rocket streaked from the first Boche biplane, and the trio dived almost vertically, honking the while on Klaxon horns. **1918** R. H. KNYVETT *Over There with Australians* IV. xx. 199 These noises were made chiefly with klaxon horns. **1920** *Motor Manual* (ed. 23) xv. 150 The electrically-operated Klaxon horn. **1924** B. GILBERT *Bly Market* 343 Emery Stamp sounded his klaxon. **1949** *Reader's Digest* Apr. 140/2 It was a gray Pierce Arrow, equipped with two bulb horns and an electric Klaxon. **1965** 'J. LE CARRÉ' *Looking-Glass War* 8 He heard the klaxons,.. moaning out over the godforsaken airfield like the howl of starving animals. **1973** P. EVANS *Bodyguard Man* i. 14 The evening traffic was thick, shrill with sudden braking and klaxon noise.

Hence '**klaxon** *v. intr.*, to sound a klaxon; also *trans.*; '**klaxoning** *vbl. sb.*

1922 E. V. LUCAS *Genevra's Money* vi. 38 The almost constant clatter and Klaxoning of motor-cars and lorries on the high-roads. **1924** G. FRANKAU *Gerald Cranston's Lady* iv. 48 Lees, Klaxoning furiously, slackened pace round the dangerous stone-wall turning. **1971** *Daily Tel.* 15 Sept. 12 There are two sides to every situation, once the Press, television and radio have 'klaxoned' the story to the general public. **1973** G. BEARE *Snake on Grave* vii. 35 A little white Fiat klaxoning shrilly.

Kleagle ('kli:g(ə)l). [f. KL(AN + EAGLE *sb.*] A title given to an officer of the KU-KLUX-KLAN.

1924 J. M. MECKLIN *Ku Klux Klan* i. 8 The head of the promotion department as a whole was Imperial Kleagle E. Y. Clarke.. The head of the 'realm', or state, was called a King Kleagle, and the house-to-house solicitors, or legwork men, were called Kleagles. **1924** E. T. BYNUM *Personal Recoll.* 8 The Kleagle showed considerable irritation in the conversation which followed. **1929** *Sun* (Baltimore) 31 Jan. 1/2 There was a time when Johnston could have called the roll of the kleagles and merely waited for donations to roll in. **1949** *Time* 13 June 24/1 Samuel Green, the Grand Dragon of the Ku Klux Klan, was frantically exhorting his Kleagles and Cyclops to mass for a big night of cross-burning and hate-spieling.

klebsiella (klɛbzɪ'ɛlə). [mod.L. (V. Trevisan 1885, in *Atti Accad. Fisio-Medico-Statistica Milano* 4th Ser. III. 105), f. the name of *Klebs* (see next) + L. *-ella* (see -EL²).] A coliform bacterium of the ill-defined genus so called, which includes Friedländer's bacillus, *Klebsiella pneumoniæ*, and others associated with respiratory, urinary, and wound infections and occas. with hospital epidemics.

1928 W. GILTNER *Elem. Text Bk. Gen. Microbology* [sic] xxv. 337 (*heading*) Klebsiella infections. **1948** H. F. DOWLING *Acute Bacterial Dis.* xx. 364 Cholecystitis and cholangitis are frequently the site of klebsiella infections. **1957** R. Y. STANIER et al. *Microbial World* xvi. 341 The members of the *Klebsiella* group are encapsulated. **1962** *Lancet* 12 May 989/1 In 1 patient with a urinary-tract infection a klebsiella strain was isolated. **1973** A. L. SMITH *Princ. Microbiol.* (ed. 7) xxiii. 351 *Klebsiella* are non-motile, gram-negative, aerobic organisms.

Klebs-Löffler (klɛbz'lœflə(r)). The names of T. A. E. *Klebs* (1834-1913) and F. A. J. *Löffler* (1852-1915), German bacteriologists, used *attrib.* to designate the bacterium (*Corynebacterium diphtheriæ*) which is the cause of diphtheria in man and similar diseases in other animals.

1895 *Lancet* 21 Dec. 1577/1 The difference between it and the Klebs-Löffler bacillus [were] pointed out. **1897** *Ibid.* 5 June 1533/1 We might now fitly speak of conjunctival inflammations as due to gonococci, to trachomacocci, to Weeks bacilli, to streptococci, to Klebs-Löffler bacilli, or to pneumococci. **1897** MUIR & RITCHIE *Man. Bacteriol.* xv. 329 The organism is.. known as the Klebs-Löffler bacillus, or simply as Löffler's bacillus. **1935** *Discovery* XVI. 244/1 An enormous number of cases, mostly drain throats, are rushed off to hospital because the Klebs-Loeffler (diphtheria) bacillus has been found. **1972** PELCZAR & REID *Microbiol.* (ed. 3) xxix. 567 Diphtheria is an acute febrile infection caused by *Coryne-bacterium diphtheriae*, also known as the Klebs-Löffler bacillus.

||**kleenebok** ('kle:nəbɒk, 'kli:nbɒk). [S. Afr. Du., = little buck (antelope).] A small S. African antelope (*Cephalophus monticola*, Thunb.), also called Blue Duiker.

1834 *Penny Cycl.* II. 82 The Kleenebok (*A. perpusilla*, H. Smith) very improperly called *guevi* by M. Desmarest, is about a foot high at the shoulder. **1867** *Nat. Encycl.* I. 809 The Kleeneboc.. in the thick brushes of South Africa.

Kleenex ('kli:nɛks). orig. *U.S.* The proprietary name of an absorbent disposable cleansing paper tissue. Also *attrib.*

1925 *Picture-Play Mag.* Apr. 107/2 (Advt.), This secret of famous stage beauties... is simply the use of Kleenex in removing cold cream and cosmetics... This soft velvety absorbent is made of Cellucotton... Use it once, throw it away. **1925** *Trade Marks Jrnl.* 15 July 1545 Kleenex... Absorbent pads or sheets (not medicated) for surgical or curative purposes or in relation to the health. Cellucotton Products Company.., City of Neenah,.. Winnebago, State of Wisconsin, United States of America; Manufacturers. **1936** N. COWARD *Play Parade* (1954) IV. 90 They stuff wads of Kleenex paper in between their collars and their necks to prevent the make-up soiling their ties. **1942** M. MCCARTHY *Company She Keeps* (1943) 197 The tears streamed from her eyes... He took a box of Kleenex from the drawer and handed it to her. **1956** E. AMBLER *Night-Comers* iv. 84 She had a box of Kleenex... She began to wipe off the grease. **1957** 'GYPSY ROSE LEE' *Gypsy* xxiv. 315 She dabbed at her eyes with a tattered Kleenex, then shoved it back in her purse. **1967** *Listener* 16 Mar. 368/3 The Master himself fulminates in California against some of his more conservative juniors, in an essay not yet reprinted in England (it dismisses Britten's War Requiem as *Kleenex Music*). **1969** G. GREENE *Trav. with my Aunt* xvii. 179 She wiped her fingers on the Kleenex and opened the yellow envelope. **1971** *Trade Marks Jrnl.* 12 May 910/1 Kleenex... Babies' disposable napkins, diapers and lining sheets for all such goods... Kimberly-Clark Corporation.., Neenah, State of Wisconsin, United States of America; Manufacturers. **1974** *Listener* 11 July 61/3 The almost unpopulated wilderness of Maine, where TV dinners and Kleenex are in short supply.

kleet, variant of CLEAT.

1883 *Fisheries Exhib. Catal.* 45 Model of Collapsible Kleet, for instantly liberating entangled ropes.

kleig, Kleig, varr. KLIEG.

Klein bottle (klaɪn-). [Named after Felix *Klein* (1849-1925), Ger. mathematician.] A closed non-orientable surface that can be represented in three dimensions by passing the neck of a bottle through its side and joining its end to a hole in the base.

1941 COURANT & ROBBINS *What is Math.?* v. 262 Another interesting one-sided surface is the 'Klein bottle'. **1950** *Astounding Sci. Fiction* Dec. 75/2 'The Möbius band', Turpelo said, 'has unusual properties because it has a singularity. The Klein bottle, with two singularities, manages to be inside of itself.' **1965** H. EVES *Survey of Geom.* II. xv. 357 The surface is homeomorphic to a sphere with two crosscaps, and is called a Klein bottle, after Felix Klein who first called attention to it in 1882. *Ibid.*, Show that a Klein bottle can, by one cut, be converted into a disc and a Möbius strip.

||**kleindeutsch** ('klaɪndɔɪtʃ), *a.* [G.] Referring to or favouring a United Germany, excluding Austria. Also as *sb.*, a supporter of such a policy. Cf. GROSSDEUTSCH *a.*

1916 A. W. WARD *Germany 1815-90* I. vi. 484 The Austrian members.. formed a faction.. coalescing.. on the question of the exclusion of Austria.. under the attractive name *Grossdeutsche*, and designating their opponents (who ..included E. M. Arndt) as *Kleindeutsche*. **1945** F. DARMSTAEDTER *Germany & Europe* iv. 53 In the Frankfurt Assembly the adherents of the 'kleindeutsche' solution (exclusion of Austria) gained the upper hand over those of the 'grossdeutsche' (inclusion of Austria). **1946** [see GROSSDEUTSCH *a.*]. **1968** F. EYCK *Frankfurt Parl. 1848-9* vii. 255 The exclusion of Austria from Germany (which was to become the programme of the *Kleindeutsche* who proposed the King of Prussia as hereditary German Emperor). *Ibid.* viii. 363 The antithesis of *Kleindeutsch* (Lesser German) and *Grossdeutsch* (Greater German) is not sufficiently subtle to describe the real difference between the parties.

Kleinian ('klaɪnɪən), *a.* and *sb.* *Psychol.*

A. *adj.* Of or pertaining to Melanie *Klein* (1882-1960) or her theories which, though basically Freudian, differed particularly in the field of child psychoanalysis. **B.** *sb.* A follower of the theories of Melanie Klein.

1955 R. L. MUNROE *Schools of Psychoanal. Thought* 663/1 Introjection,.. in Kleinian theory. **1959** *Encounter* Apr. 41/1 A.. comprehensive interpretation of various aspects of art in terms of Kleinian theory. **1960** R. WAELDER *Basic Theory Psychoanal.* xi. 233 Analysts of the Kleinian school of thought have made different claims. **1961** J. A. C. BROWN *Freud & Post-Freudians* iv. 79 The biological emphasis further stressed by the Kleinians, who are now regarded by many as the main movement in orthodox psychoanalysis. **1963** *Times Lit. Suppl.* 15 Feb. 111/2 It has become almost impossible to write even a lyric poem without being diagnosed as a Freudian, a Kleinian, [etc.]. **1972** *Guardian* 6 July 15/3 The Kleinian examination of infantile development.

kleinite ('klaɪnaɪt). *Min.* [ad. G. *kleinit* (A. Sachs 1905, in *Sitzungsber. d. preuss. Akad. d. Wissensch.* 1094), f. the name of J. F. C. *Klein* (1842-1907), German geologist: see -ITE¹.] A hydrous chloride and sulphate of mercury and ammonia, occurring as transparent or translucent crystals of a yellow to orange colour.

1907 *Chem. Abstr.* I. 2454 Kleinite may be a mixture of a mercury-ammonium chloride.. in great preponderance, with an oxychloride and sulphate or oxysulphate of mercury. **1932** *Amer. Mineralogist* XVII. 547 Specimens of kleinite, terlinguaite, montroydite, and mosesite from the Texas locality were then prepared for *x*-ray examination. **1954** *Mineral. Abstr.* XII. 433 Comparison of the data for kleinite.. with those of mosesite.. suggests that the former has a three-dimensional structure of $[Hg_2N]^{1+}$.. with a formula $[Hg_2N](Cl,SO_4)xH_2O$, where *x* is about ½.

Kleistian ('klaɪstɪən), *a.* [After Ger. *kleistisch* (*kleistische, kleistsche flasche* a Leyden jar), f. name of Domherr von Kleist, one of the discoverers of the properties of the jar: see -AN.] *Kleistian jar*, a Leyden jar.

1881 ROSENTHAL *Muscles & Nerves* 31 A simple electric shock, such as is afforded by the discharge of a Kleistian jar.

kleistogamous, variant of CLEISTOGAMOUS.

kleket: see CLICKET.

klementite (klə'mɛntaɪt). *Min.* [ad. G. *klementit* (G. Tschermak 1891, in *Sitzungsber. d. kaiserl. Akad. d. Wissensch.* (*Math.-nat. Cl.*) Abt. I. C. 40), f. the name of Constantin *Klement* (b. 1856), curator of the Natural History Museum, Brussels: see -ITE¹.] A variety of thuringite containing more magnesium than iron.

1892 E. S. DANA *Dana's Syst. Min.* (ed. 6) 656 *Klementite.* In thin scales in quartz veins at Vielsalm in Belgium. Probably monoclinic.. Color dark olive-green. **1954** *Mineral. Mag.* XXX. 279 It may be found convenient to retain the name klementite as a variety of thuringite with Mg>(Fe'' + Fe'''); the original klementite analysis falls in this field. **1968** *Ibid.* XXXVI. 753 This chlorite has been identified as klementite, a variety of thuringite... In thin flakes the mineral is light green but deeper coloured in aggregates... The composition approximates to $Mg_{3.3}Fe_{1.8}Al_{2.8}Si_{2.3}(O,OH)_{18}$.

klendusity (klɛn'dju:sɪtɪ). *Bot.* [f. Gr. κλ-είς bar, bolt + ἔνδυσις entry: see -ITY.] The resistance of a plant to disease, through the presence of some characteristic that inhibits infection. So **klen'dusic** *a.*, showing resistance of this kind.

1940 J. I. WOOD et al. in *Phytopathology* XXX. 362 The.. continued misuse of such words as *immunity*, *resistance*, *tolerance* and *klendusity* (with *resistance* as a catch-all) tends definitely to confuse readers. *Ibid.* 364 Klendusity: Ability of a susceptible variety to escape infection because of possession of some quality preventing or hindering successful inoculation under conditions conducive to infection in other varieties. **1943** *Phytopathology* XXXIII. 19 A few seedlings in subsequent generations that were derived indirectly from the almost sterile hybrid were about as capable of escaping infection as *L[ycopersicon] chilense* itself, thus showing heritability of klendusity. *Ibid.* 692 This klendusic seedling did not fruit for some time. **1950** *Trans. Brit. Mycol. Soc.* XXXIII. 156 On this side of the Atlantic 'klendusity' and 'suscept' were each thrown out without a hearing, because they are the very opposite of comfortable words. **1958** *Virology* VI. 303 The nature and inheritance of the tendency to escape infection (klendusity) was investigated. **1967** R. K. S. WOOD *Physiol. Plant Path.* xii. 400 Before these different forms of resistance are dealt with in detail, it is as well to refer to what some pathologists regard as a form of resistance, and which is usually referred to as 'disease escape'. Less frequently the term 'klendusity' is used for the same thing. **1973** *Guide Use Terms Plant Path.* (Federation Brit. Plant Pathologists) 22 Klendusity: the failure of a susceptible host to become infected, in the presence of the pathogen, because of qualities preventing or hindering the operation of a vector or other inoculating agent... Klendusity may be considered a form of disease escape.

klene, klenge: see CLEAN, CLENGE.

klep (klɛp), *sb.* Slang abbrev. of KLEPTOMANIAC. Hence as *v. intr.*, to steal.

1889 BARRÈRE & LELAND *Dict. Slang* 523/1 *Klep*, a thief; to *klep*, to steal. **1896** FARMER & HENLEY *Slang* IV. 117/2 *Klep* (popular), a thief. Short for kleptomaniac. **1949** 'N. R. NASH' *Young & Fair* 20 The kleps have started!

klepht (klɛft). Also **kleft.** [ad. mod. Gr. κλέφτης, ancient Gr. κλέπτης thief.] One of the body of Greeks who refused to submit to the Turks after the conquest of Greece in the fifteenth century, and maintained their independence in the mountains. After the war of independence (1821-28) those who continued this existence became mere brigands. Hence, A brigand, bandit.

1820 T. S. HUGHES *Trav. Sicily*, etc. I. vi. 178 Here we pitched our tent and dined, but the tatar would not permit us to sleep under it for fear of the kleftes or banditti. **1847** CHURCH in *Life & Lett.* 20 Apr. (1894) 106 The difficulty of the road,.. and the fear of klephts. **1888** BLACKIE in *Times* 7 Apr. 7/2 The assertors of Greek independence.. were, in fact, a sort of patriotic brigands, known as klephts.

Hence **'klephtic** *a.*, belonging to or characteristic of klephts; **'klephtism**, brigandage.

1834 LD. HOUGHTON *Mem. Many Scenes, Suliot to Frank* (1844) 28 The Suliot character and method of life.. the rash impartiality with which they conducted their klephtic enterprises. **1858** FREEMAN in W. R. W. Stephens *Life* (1895) I. 239 Plenty of evils, peculation, klephtism, what not —but good stuff at the bottom.

klepsydra, variant of CLEPSYDRA.

kleptic ('klɛptɪk), *a.* *rare*⁻¹. [ad. Gr. κλεπτικ-ός thievish: see next.] Thievish.

1865 *Pall Mall G.* 7 Apr., A laugh at the thief's clever impudence and a joke about his kleptic propensities.

klep'tistic, *a.* *rare*⁻¹. [f. Gr. κλέπτ-ης a thief + -ISTIC.] Related to or consisting in stealing.

1742-3 FIELDING *Phil. Trans.* Wks. 1775 IX. 231 Indeed there is a method [of subdividing the guinea] called the *Kleptistic*.. but this is too dangerous.

klepto ('klɛptəʊ). Slang abbrev. of KLEPTOMANIAC.

1958 *New Yorker* 25 Jan. 29 Some befuddled guest (or klepto, more likely) abstracted a hat. **1962** *Punch* 4 July 24/1 Playwrights of the imminent Klepto school. **1964** 'E. V. CUNNINGHAM' *Lydia* (1965) xii. 178 You got it.. right out of Helen Sarbine's purse... What are you—some kind of nut or klepto?

kleptobiosis (ˌklɛptəʊbaɪ'əʊsɪs). *Zool.* In quots. clepto-. [f. Gr. κλέπτης thief, κλέπτειν to steal + βίωσις way of life.] Among ants and certain other social insects, an association in which a small species feeds on the refuse of a neighbouring nest inhabited by a larger species, or robs returning workers of the host species of the food they are carrying. Hence ˌ**kleptobi'otic** *a.*

1901 W. M. WHEELER in *Amer. Naturalist* XXXV. 516, I have therefore adopted the following headings... Cleptobiosis. Wasmann's 'Diebsameisen'; first regular form of compound nest. *Ibid.* 529 All the known cleptobiotic ants are of minute size and of subterranean habits. **1927** H. ST. J. K. DONISTHORPE *Guests of Brit. Ants* iii. 78 Ants exhibit a variety of associations, symbiotic, mutualistic, and parasitic... Such associations consist of—Cleptobiosis (originally used to denote thievery, now applied to brigandage by Wheeler); Lestobiosis [etc.]. **1971** E. O. WILSON *Insect Societies* xix. 377/2 As a rule, cleptobiotic aculeates prey on only one or a very few species of other aculeates. *Ibid.* 381/2 Members of the melipomine genus *Lestrimelitta* do engage in nest robbing, or 'cleptobiosis'.

kleptocracy (klɛp'tɒkrəsɪ). [f. as KLEPTOMANIA + -CRACY.] A ruling body or order of thieves. Also, government by thieves; a nation ruled by this kind of government.

1819 L. HUNT *Indicator* No. 12 (1822) I. 95 Titular ornaments, common to the Spanish *kleptocracy*. **1968** S. L. ANDRESKI *African Predicament* vii. 109 The essence of kleptocracy is that the functioning of the organs of authority is determined by the mechanisms of supply and demand rather than the laws and regulations. **1971** *Guardian Weekly* 10 July 18 The Federal Republic of Cameroon, which he [*sc.* Leonard Barnes] seems to regard as one of the less wicked kleptocracies. **1975** *Times Lit. Suppl.* 4 July 740/4 The role of corruption within the [Franco] regime..and the growth of a virtual kleptocracy within the administration.

kleptolagnia (klɛptəʊ'lægnɪə). [mod.L., f. Gr. κλεπτο-, combining form of κλέπτης thief + λαγνεία lust; formed by analogy with ALGOLAGNIA.] A morbid desire, associated with fetishism, to achieve sexual gratification through theft.

1917 J. C. KIERNAN in *Urologic & Cutaneous Rev.* **1928** H. ELLIS *Stud. Psychol. Sex* VII. viii. 491 Kleptolagnia..is an effort to attain the direct gratification of the sexual impulse by the aid of emotional energy generated by the excitement of the theft. **1960** HINSIE & CAMPBELL *Psychiatric Dict.* (ed. 3) 414/1 *Kleptolagnia*, a morbid desire to steal. **1969** E. M. BRECHER *Sex Researchers* (1970) ii. 55 *Psychopathia Sexualis* presents cases of satyriasis and nymphomania,.. kleptolagnia (sexual arousal through stealing), [etc.]. **1972** *Cumulated Index Medicus* XIII. 7662/2 A case of kleptolagnia.

kleptomania (klɛptəʊ'meɪnɪə). Also clepto-. [f. Gr. κλεπτο-, combining form of κλέπτης thief + MANIA.] An irresistible tendency to theft, actuating persons who are not tempted to it by necessitous circumstances, supposed by some to be a form of insanity.

1830 *New Monthly Mag.* XXVIII. 15 Instances of this *cleptomania* are well known to have happened in this country, even among the rich and noble. **1861** *Critic* 19 Oct. 410 Persons..subject to what has been characterised as 'Kleptomania'. **1872** GEO. ELIOT *Middlem.* xxiii, When a youthful nobleman steals jewellery we call the act kleptomania.

Hence **klepto'maniac**, one affected with kleptomania (also *attrib.* or as *adj.*); **klep'tomanist**.

1861 R. F. BURTON *City of Saints* 74 The Dakota of these regions are expert and daring kleptomaniacs. **1874** MAUDSLEY *Respons. in Ment. Dis.* iii. 82 Many kleptomaniacs have..been moral imbeciles. **1884** *Graphic* Christm. No. 21/1 A kleptomaniac ape. **1862** M. B. EDWARDS *John & I* xliv. (1876) 321 No more..than a kleptomanist can keep his fingers off the goods on a shop-counter.

kleþe, kleþinge, obs. ff. CLEAD, CLEADING.

‖**kletterschuh** ('klɛtəʃuː). Pl. -schuhe. [G.] A cloth- or felt-soled light boot worn esp. for rock-climbing; usu. in *pl.* Sometimes colloquially abbrev. to *klets*. Also *attrib.*

1920 J. P. FARRAR in G. W. Young *Mountain Craft* ii. 96 Kletterschuhe are much used in the Dolomites, and..they can be used..not only on dry rocks but also in great climbs. .. A good kind is the so-called Sexten pattern, the soles of which are built up of layers of cloth. **1950** tr. *Mountaineering Handbk.* (Assoc. Brit. Members Swiss Alpine Club) ii. 23 Kletterschuhe (cloth soled boots) are an advantage for difficult rock climbs because they hold and do not slip. **1951** C. D. MILNER *Dolomites* 88 The usual wear in the Dolomites for many years has been felt-soled *kletterschuhe*... Today *kletterschuhe* and rubber tennis shoes are both used... An interesting compromise..is to have Vibram soles, over a thin leather undersole, on *kletterschuhe* soft uppers. **1963** *Climber* Aug. 11/1 Beginners come to climbing without being aware that there is any kind of mountain footwear other than 'vibs'—barring..the P.A.'s or kletterschuhe to which they eventually hope to aspire. *Ibid.* 12/2 If you're a rock climber rather than an all-round mountaineer..then Vibrams, P.A.'s or 'klets' are the wear for you.

kley, obs. f. CLAY.

kleywang ('kleɪwæŋ). Also †**calewang**; **kelewang**. [ad. Malay *kĕlewang*.] A single-edged Indonesian sword.

1783 W. MARSDEN *Hist. Sumatra* 277 There are.. weapons of a make between that of a scimitar, and a knife.. as..the calewang. **1839** T. J. NEWBOLD *Pol. & Statistical Acct. Straits of Malacca* I. i. 39 The crew are armed with.. swords (the parang and kleywang). **1900** W. W. SKEAT *Malay Magic* 24 The articles of Malay regalia usually consist of a *silasila*..and a few weapons, generally a *kris*, *kleywang*, or spear. **1936** G. B. GARDNER *Keris & Other Malay Weapons* 73 *Golok jambu* or the Kĕlantan *kĕlewang*. This is short and curved. *Ibid.* 75 The *sula kĕlewang*. A single edge sword that gets wider and heavier towards the point.

klick, -er, -et, obs. ff. CLICK, etc.

klieg (kliːg). *Cinemat.* Also kleig and with capital initial. [f. the name of two brothers, A. T. and J. H. *Kliegl*, who invented it in the U.S.] In full, *klieg light*. **a.** Orig., a kind of arc lamp invented for use as a studio light; hence, any powerful electric light used in film-making, or in television.

1925 *Movie Mag.* Nov. 57/1 The scene in a motion picture studio is eternally the same. It doesn't matter what difference there is in the set which raises its skeleton wings towards the Kleigs. **1927** U. SINCLAIR *Oil!* xiv. 355 The kleigs glare upon them, and a dozen moving picture cameras grind. **1931** A. NADELL *Projecting Sound Pict.* xiv. 250 Klieg (arc) lights are passé; they made too much noise; 1,000-watt incandescents are used. **1932** S. GIBBONS *Cold Comfort Farm* xvii. 237 The sunshine, vivid as a Kleig light, revealed every wrinkle in his melancholy..face. **1947** AUDEN *Age of Anxiety* II. 39 The polychrome Oval With its kleig lights and crowd engineers. **1951** 'J. WYNDHAM' *Day of Triffids* viii. 141 At the first blink it was as dazzling as a klieg light. **1957** *New Yorker* 13 July 21/1 My brother and I [*sc.* Mr. John H. Kliegl] invented the klieg light around 1911—the first practical light for taking motion pictures indoors. It projected a beam, by means of carbons, that emitted a light of high actinic power. **1967** *Economist* 7 Jan. 40/2 Inaugurated in a blaze of familiar kleig lights. **1969** *Rolling Stone* 28 June 13 The kleig lights shine for a mercifully brief moment upon an aging cosmetic face.

b. klieg eyes, an eye condition caused by exposure to very bright light, characterized by watering and conjunctivitis. Hence ***klieg-eyed*** adj.

1923 *Sci. Amer.* Oct. 243/1 The burning of the eyeball by the ultra-violet rays... This malady appears so freely among motion-picture actors..that a name, 'Kleig eyes', has been coined for it. **1941** *Amer. Cinematographer* Dec. 589 The ultra-violet glare from those unshielded arcs..literally sunburned the actors' eyeballs and created the dread malady, 'kleig eye'. **1973** *Rolling Stone* 30 Aug. 38 Most folks got back to San Clemente sated, klieg-eyed and tired.

Kline (klaɪn). *Med.* The name of Benjamin S. *Kline* (b. 1886), U.S. pathologist, used *attrib.* to designate a diagnostic test for syphilis devised by him in which serum, blood, or spinal fluid is mixed on a slide with a lipid antigen and examined under a microscope for precipitation.

1929 *Amer. Jrnl. Syphilis* XIII. 583 (*heading*) The Kline slide precipitation test for syphilis..with a clinical evaluation in syphilitic and non-syphilitic cases. **1944** J. H. STOKES et al. *Mod. Clin. Syphilol.* (ed. 3) x. 471 The Kline finger-puncture blood test procedure avoids the objection of donors to a double venipuncture. **1963** *Amer. Jrnl. Clin. Path.* XL. 551/2 The Kline test with cardiolipin-synthetic lecithin antigen yielded more accurate results in terms of TPI-reactivity than did the tests with cardiolipin-natural lecithin antigens.

Klinefelter ('klaɪnfɛltə(r)). *Med.* The name of Harry Fitch *Klinefelter* (b. 1912), U.S. physician, used in the possessive (less commonly *attrib.*) to designate a syndrome he described (with others) in 1942 which affects males and becomes evident at puberty or after, being characterized by small testes, eunuchoidism, gynæcomastia, and infertility, usu. now restricted to those cases in which the cells have an extra X sex chromosome (most commonly in an XXY constitution, in contrast to the XY of normal males and the XX of normal females).

[**1946** *Med. Jrnl. Austral.* 28 Sept. 446/1 (*heading*) The Klinefelter-Reifenstein-Albright syndrome.] **1950** *Jrnl. Clin. Endocrinol. & Metabolism* X. 630 (*heading*) Dystrophia myotonica, with special reference to endocrine function (Klinefelter's syndrome). *Ibid.* 635 In the 2 male patients the diagnostic criteria for the so-called Klinefelter syndrome were satisfied. **1958** H. J. ROBERTS *Difficult Diagn.* I. i. 37 The evolution of the belief that micro-orchidism with gynecomastia (the Klinefelter syndrome) probably represents a genetic defect in the sex chromosomes. **1964** L. MARTIN *Clin. Endocrinol.* (ed. 4) vi. 209 Apart from these two main XXY and XY types, Klinefelter's syndrome has also been described in variants possessing the chromosomal constitutions of XXXY, XXXXY, and XXYY. **1969** *Nature* 16 Aug. 680/2 Züblin and Pasqualini noted a childishness, shyness, lack of drive and a degree of intellectual impairment in patients with Klinefelter's syndrome. **1970** PASSMORE & ROBSON *Compan. Med. Stud.* II. xxxi. 15/2 The most important findings were that abnormal females with Turner's syndrome were sex chromatin negative like normal males, and that abnormal males with Klinefelter's syndrome were sex chromatin positive like normal females. **1971** *Daily Tel.* (Colour Suppl.) 10 Dec. 20/1 One of the most common physical intersex conditions affecting a minimum of 2·65 males out of every 1,000 is the Klinefelter syndrome.

b. *ellipt.*

1961 DAVIDSON & ROBERTSON SMITH *Proc. Conf. Human Chromosomal Abnormalities* ii. 23 In 5 of the Klinefelter cases our observations were consistent with the belief that the chromosome number was regularly 47. **1967** BARTALOS & BARAMKI *Med. Cytogenetics* x. 155 In Hornstein's experience, only a few of the Klinefelter patients were free from some form of psychopathological traits. **1971** *Daily Tel.* (Colour Suppl.) 10 Dec. 20/1 In Klinefelter there is an extra X chromosome added to the male XY.

Kling (klɪŋ). [Malay *Keling* Tamil, ad. *Kalinga* an old name for a strip of coast along the Bay of Bengal.] A disparaging term applied to Indian settlers in Malaysia.

1606 E. SCOTT *Exact Discourse E. Indians* sig. F 4 If it were not for the Sabyndar, the Admirall, and one or twoe more, which are Clyn men borne, there were noe liuing for a Christian amongst them. **1625** PURCHAS *Pilgrimes* I. IV. ii. 385 The fifteenth of Iune, heere arriued Nockhoda Tingall a Cling-man from Banda, in a Iaua Iuncke. **1839** T. J. NEWBOLD *Pol. & Statistical Acct. Straits of Malacca* I. i. 8 The Chinese, and the natives from India (Chuliahs and Klings,) are by far the most useful class. **1868** C. COLLINGWOOD *Rambles of Naturalist on Shores & Waters China Sea* xv. 245 The Klings are, indeed, the only people who can contest the field with the Chinese. **1869** A. R. WALLACE *Malay Archipelago* I. ii. 31 The Klings of Western India are a numerous body of Mahometans, and, with many Arabs, are petty merchants and shopkeepers. **1890** KIPLING *Barrack-Room Ballads* (1892) 135 The frigate-bird shall carry my word to the Kling and the Orang-Laut. **1968** *Encycl. Brit.* XIII. 400/1 In Malay usage 'Kling' carried associations of disparagement from the start. It..was replaced by 'Tamil' early in the 20th century.

kling: see CLING.

kling-kling ('klɪŋklɪŋ). Also **cling-cling, clinkling, klinkling**. [Echoic.] A Jamaican name for a grackle, *Quiscalus niger*.

1847 GOSSE & HILL *Birds Jamaica* 219 It is to the first of these notes that the bird before us owes his local names of Tinkling, Tintin, Clinkling. **1949** *Caribbean Q.* I. IV. 42 What to Miss Bottome is a tropical bird, is to Vic Reid a pechary or a klinkling. **1955** R. G. TAYLOR *Introd. Birds Jamaica* 11 Kling-kling, a bird of medium size with shining black plumage, pointed beak, a pale yellow eye and long boat-shaped tail. **1960** J. BOND *Birds W. Indies* 217 Greater Antillean Grackle *Quiscalus niger*. Local names: Tinkling; Cling-cling; Ting-ting (Jamaica). **1965** I. FLEMING *Man with Golden Gun* v. 75 Two large black birds..whirled in... She said, 'We call them kling-klings but learned folk call them Jamaican grackles.'

†'**klingstone**. *Min. Obs.* [ad. G. *klingstein*.] = CLINKSTONE.

1800 HENRY *Epit. Chem.* (1808) 364 Soda [has been found] in basalt; in pitch-stone; and in kling-stone. **1811** PINKERTON *Petral.* I. 175 The klingstone employed in the preceding experiments was from the Donnersberg.

klino- (klaɪnəʊ), var. of CLINO-, as in *klinoclase*, *-crocite*, *-humite*, *-meter*, *-phæite*, *-pinacoid*, *-rhombic*, etc.; also **klinocephalic** (-sɪ'fælɪk), **-cephalous** (-'sɛfələs), *adjs.*, having a saddle-shaped depression at the vertex of the skull; hence **klino'cephalism, -'cephaly; klinoki'nesis** [KINESIS 2], a kinesis in which the movement is one of turning; hence **klinoki'netic** *a.*, **klinoki'netically** *adv.*; similarly **klinostat** ('klaɪnəʊstæt), a stand on which germinating seeds or growing plants are placed, and which is made to revolve so as to counteract the influence of gravity on their growth; **klino'taxis** [TAXIS 6], a taxis in which the movement is one of turning.

1878 BARTLEY tr. *Topinard's Anthrop.* v. 177 *Klinocephalic, skull with vault in form of a saddle. **1937** D. L. GUNN et al. in *Nature* 18 Dec. 1064/2 We propose to divide kineses into (*a*) ortho-kineses..and (*b*) *klino-kineses ..—variations in angular velocity. **1954** *New Biol.* XVII. 49 A klino-kinesis (a higher rate of turning in dry than in moist air) is also present [in woodlice]. **1970** R. A. & B. M. MAIER *Compar. Animal Behavior* v. 81 A second category of kinetic response—klinokinesis—involves changes in the rate of turning associated with shifts in the intensity of stimulation. **1940** FRAENKEL & GUNN *Orientation of Animals* v. 45 In some animals there is a *klino-kinetic response in which the rate of random turning, or angular velocity, depends on the intensity of stimulation. **1964** *Oceanogr. & Marine Biol.* II. 478 Unoriented klinokinetic movements occur [in two species of Erycinidæ] under uniform overhead light. **1946** *Nature* 13 July 58/2 When behaving photopositively *Hydra* orientates itself *klinokinetically. **1866** BRANDE & COX *Dict. Sci.*, etc., *Klinometer. **1875** BENNETT & DYER tr. *Sachs' Bot.* 50 It is uncertain whether they belong to the hexagonal or the *klinorhombic system. **1855** MAYNE *Expos. Lex.*, *Klinorhomboid, -rhomboidal. **1880** C. & F. DARWIN *Movem. Pl.* 93 Seven seeds were allowed to germinate..in a *klinostat, by which means geotropism was eliminated. **1940** FRAENKEL & GUNN *Orientation of Animals* vi. 59 The kind of reaction in which these regular deviations are a necessary part of the orientation mechanism is here named *klino-taxis. *Ibid.* 75 Klino-taxis is an uncommon type of reaction to light. **1958** *New Biol.* XXVII. 72 A fly larva with a single median eye moves away from a single source of light. .. The movement involves swinging from side to side; as the eye is illuminated from one side so the swing is away from that side... This swinging motion is a klinotaxis. **1970** R. A. & B. M. MAIER *Compar. Animal Behavior* v. 81 The first type [of taxis]—klinotaxis—involves a series of successive comparisons of the intensity of stimulation.

klip (klɪp), *sb.* *S. Afr.* Also dim. **klippie**. [Afrikaans, a. Du. *klip* cliff, rock, stone.]

1. A diamond; †micaceous iron ore (quot. 1835). Also, ***blink klip*** [Afrikaans *blink* shining].

1835 A. SMITH *Diary* 22 Jan. (1939) I. 225 [The Bechuana] mix fat with the blink klip and rub it over the body in moderate quantities, but in great quantities upon the head. **1887** J. W. MATTHEWS *Incwadi Yami, or Twenty Yrs. S. Afr.* xiii. 186 The natives had not yet acquired a knowledge of the value of diamonds or *klips* as they were then termed. **1892** J. R. COUPER *Mixed Humanity* vi. 48 Flogged to death for stealing a 'klip' (as the Dutch and many of the Kaffirs call a diamond). **1893** T. REUNERT *Diamonds & Gold S. Afr.* I. 6 By this time the attention of every one in that neighbourhood was turned to seeking *blink klippe*.. and during the following year several diamonds were picked up. **1897** *Pearson's Mag.* July 67/1 Fifteen years on that blathted breakwater, just for being found with a few little klips on you. **1911** L. COHEN *Remin. Kimberley* 35 'I'll show you the klip. Here it is.' With that he pulled out his snuffbox ..; inside was a fairly sized beautiful octahedron diamond. **1967** L. G. GREEN *Like Diamond Blazing* xiii. 144, I met old Hottentots who remembered Luderitz; they said he had two little boxes of *blink klippies*..and that he carried these diamonds with him.

2. A stone, pebble.

1852 C. BARTER *Dorp & Veld* vi. 50 Stooping to set large *klips* (stones) behind the wheel, to prevent the wagon from slipping back. **1899** A. WERNER *Captain of Locusts* 63 She left me when we were on the trek over into Basutoland.. and the boys and I could only cut a cross on the thorn-tree.. and put a heap of klippies to mark the spot.

Hence **klip** *v. trans.*, to place a stone behind (a wheel) in order to prevent a vehicle from rolling backwards.

1878 H. A. ROCHE *On Trek in Transvaal* iv. 91 We crawling into the wagon, the wheels of which were 'klipped', to keep us from running down the hill, trying to nap at intervals.

klipbok ('klɪpbɒk). Also **klipbokkie, klipbuck.** [Afrikaans, f. Du. *klip* rock + *bok* buck.] = KLIPSPRINGER.

1886 G. A. FARINI *Through Kalahari Desert* i. 4 Not even the beasts of the desert, the klip-bok (rock buck), or steinbok (stone buck).. are to be seen. **1895** J. G. MILLAIS *Breath from Veldt* 92 The most curious thing about the klipbuck is the shape of its feet and the manner in which it uses them in springing up and down its native rocks. **1939** tr. *E. N. Marais's My Friends the Baboons* v. 59 The troop must often have had the chance of catching little klipbuck, dassies, and red hares. **1947** *Cape Argus* (Magazine Section) 23 Oct. 1/9 The dog.. brought down a klipbok. **1953** J. R. ELLERMAN et al. *S. Afr. Mammals* 188 *Oreotragus oreotragus* Zimmerman, 1783. Klipspringer. Klipbokkie.

klipdas ('klɪpdæs). [Afrikaans, f. Du. *klip* rock + *das* badger.] = DASSIE 1.

1853 *Edin. New Philos. Jrnl.* LV. 214 Basking themselves on the sunny side of the krantzes.. may generally be seen several of the Klipdas, Cony, Rock Rabbit, or Cape Hyrax (*H. capensis*). **1886** P. GILLMORE *Hunter's Arcadia* xxvi. 248 From this descendant of Holland.. I bought.. the skins of some rock rabbits, the *klip das* of the Dutch. **1953** J. R. ELLERMAN et al. *S. Afr. Mammals* 157 *Procavia capensis* Pallas, 1766. Dassie; Hyrax. Klipdas. Distribution: one of the commonest mammals in the Union.

klipfish ('klɪpfɪʃ). Also **clipfish, klepvis, klippfish, -fisch, klipvissie.** [ad. Du. *klipvisch* (f. *klip* rock) and Da. *klipfisk* (f. *klippe* rock).]

1. *S. Afr.* A viviparous, brightly-coloured, marine fish of the family Clinidæ, living in shallow water or rock pools.

[**1731** G. MEDLEY tr. *Kolb's Present State Cape Good-Hope* I. xx. 256 The Hottentots frequently take Abundance of a Sort of Fish, call'd Rock-fish. These are Fish without Scales.] **1790** E. HELME tr. *Le Vaillant's Trav. Afr.* I. ii. 22 The *klepvis*.. is without scales, and taken among the rocks on the sea shore. **1806** J. BARROW *Trav. S. Afr.* (ed. 2) II. i. 38 The *Klip* or rock-fish, the *Blennius viviparus*, makes no bad fry. **1838** J. E. ALEXANDER *Expedition Interior Afr.* I. iv. 88 Abundance of excellent fish are to be procured here; such as the delicious Roman fish, Hottentot, 'Jacob Fever', mullet, stump nose, and clip fish. **1876, 1893** [see KINGKLIP]. **1902** *Trans. S. Afr. Philos. Soc.* XI. 224 Several names, or parts of names, are derived from the localities in which the fish are found. Thus we have.. Klip Visch, Steen Klip Visch (a peculiar redundancy). **1953** U. KRIGE *Dream & Desert* i. 14 They had.. gazed into rockpools full of starfish, slowly waving sea plants and green-and-gold *klipvissies* drifting lazily from crevice to crevice. **1969** *Nature* 8 Nov. 540/1 The shores of South Africa are enlivened by a group of typically littoral viviparous fishes known locally as klipfishes (but as clinids to the academic). **1973** *Farmer's Weekly* (S. Afr.) 18 Apr. 102 The klipfish is fried in butter and carefully filleted on the plate with knife and fork.

2. A codfish split open, boned, salted, and dried.

1835 *Penny Cycl.* IV. 273/2 The klip-fish is cut along the back, and the back-bone taken out, after which it is salted down in the bottom of the vessel. **1881** S. WALPOLE in *20th Ann. Rep. Salmon Fisheries 1880* 23 in *Parl. Papers* (C 2901) XXIII. 299 Cod are either cured as stock fisch or as klipp fisch... The klipp fish are split and boned before they are salted. **1925** J. T. JENKINS *Fishes Brit. Isles* 136 The bulk of the cod caught in the northern fisheries is split open, washed, and salted in pickle and then dried on rocks (Klippen). This is the so-called Klipp-fish. **1961** H. ANGERMAN et al. in Borgstrom & Heighway *Atlantic Ocean Fisheries* 80/2 The klipfish is subjected to more complicated treatment than the stockfish.

klipkous ('klɪpkəʊs). *S. Afr.* Also **klipkoes, klipkos.** [Afrikaans, f. Du. *klip* rock + *kous* stocking.] = SEA-EAR 1; ABALONE.

1731 G. MEDLEY tr. *Kolb's Present State Cape Good-Hope* II. 209 The *Klip-Kousen* are sometimes call'd, by the Virtuosi, *Nabel*-Snails. **1785** G. FORSTER tr. *Sparrman's Voy. Cape Good Hope* I. ii. 26 A sort of snail or cockle, *klipkous* (*Haliotis*, Linn.) from half a foot to a foot and a half diameter, is usually stewed, but makes in my opinion a very unsavoury dish. **1843** J. C. CHASE *Cape of Good Hope* vii. 168 Klip Kous... A shell fish, most delicious, but requiring much trouble in the preparation. **1910** D. FAIRBRIDGE *That which hath Been* xxv. 303 The first muscadel grapes and the finest klip-kous from the rocks had invariably found their way across the sands to Meerlust. **1930** C. L. BIDEN *Sea-Angling Fishes of Cape* xviii. 260 The crushed remains of klipkoes or venus ear—a shellfish, *Haliotis*. **1947** L. G. GREEN *Tavern of Seas* viii. 66 The perlemoen or klipkous, largest and most beautiful of Cape shellfish. **1950** M. MASSON *Birds of Passage* iii. 41 Souvenirs, among which was a Venus ear or klipkos whose brown crust had been scraped away to reveal the iridescent shell. **1966** H. J. DUCKITT *Bk. Recipes* 73 The Perlemoen, or Klipkous (stone-stocking) a species of shellfish found on many parts of the South African coast, adhering to the rocks.

klippe ('klɪpə). *Geol.* Also Klippe. Pl. **klippes,** ‖-en. [a. G. *klippe* partly or totally submerged rock.] A part of a nappe which has become detached from its parent mass by sliding or by erosion of intervening parts.

1902 *Encycl. Brit.* XXV. 333/2 These [structures], called Klippen, are abrupt pyramidal masses, the beds in the upper part being not only older than those in the lower, but also 'contorted, fractured, crushed, and mixed up', while the newer are comparatively undisturbed. **1912** *Smithsonian Misc. Coll.* LVI. No. 31. 12 It is well known that some of these isolated masses, those of the Klippes, are 'exotic'; that is to say, no strata of the same facies have ever been found in place. **1942** O. D. VON ENGELN *Geomorphol.* xv. 332 Klippen are peculiar in that, unlike the outliers which persist beyond the main front of a weathering escarpment, and which have younger beds capping older strata, they have older beds over younger beds. **1954** W. D. THORNBURY *Princ. Geomorphol.* x. 273 Chief Mountain, Montana, is a well-known example of a klippe, in which an isolated mass of Pre-Cambrian rock rests upon Cretaceous beds. **1969** M. G. RUTTEN *Geol. W. Europe* xi. 239 Further southwest, these isolated klippen.. merge into a continuous nappe.

klippie: see KLIP *sb.*

‖**klipspringer** ('klɪpˌsprɪŋə(r)). [S. African Du., f. *klip* rock + *springer* SPRINGER.] A small African antelope, *Oreotragus oreotragus.*

1785 G. FORSTER tr. *Sparrman's Voy. Cape G. Hope* II. 224 The klip-springer has obtained the name it bears from its running with the greatest velocity, and making large bounds even on the steepest precipices. **1834** PRINGLE *Afr. Sk.* vi. 204 Several species of beautiful wild animals—such as the quagga, zebra,.. klipspringer. **1885** *Macm. Mag.* Feb. 280/1 The klip-springer, the little chamois that is so clever at eluding dogs and men. **1907** P. FITZPATRICK *Jock of Bushveld* 245 The dainty little klipspringers led them many a crazy dance along the crags and ledges of the mountain face, jumping from rock to rock. **1936** R. CAMPBELL *Mithraic Emblems* 68, I always thought to be A klipspringer or chamois. **1947** J. STEVENSON-HAMILTON *Wild Life S. Afr.* xvi. 115 The klipspringer (*Oreotragus oreotragus*). *Ibid.*, The ubiquitous klipspringer, truly the chamois of Ethiopia. **1960** *Times* 29 Sept. (Nigeria Suppl.) p. xxi/5 But two other local races special to Nigeria, of that curious little pithy-haired antelope, the Klipspringer,.. seem doomed. **1972** L. VAN DER POST *Story Like Wind* vi. 180 This man in front of him wore nothing except a loin-cloth of soft yellow klipspringer leather.

klipsteinite ('klɪpstaɪnaɪt). *Min.* [Named 1866 after Prof. A. von Klipstein of Giessen.] A hydrous silicate of manganese and iron, amorphous and of a dark brown colour.

1868 DANA *Min.* (ed. 5) 511.

Klischograph ('klɪʃəʊgrɑːf, -æ-). *Printing.* [f. G. *klischee* stereotype or electrotype plate: see -GRAPH.] The proprietary name of a type of electronic engraving plate (see quots. 1955 and 1963).

1955 *Trade Marks Jrnl.* 16 Mar. 288/1 Klischograph... Machines for making printers' blocks, printers' cliches and printers' formes; and plain and engraved printers' plates. Dr. Ing. Rudolf Hell.., Kiel-Dietrichsdorf, Germany; Manufacturer. **1963** *Times* 17 July 6/7 In the field of electronic engraving a German firm, Dr. Ing. Rudolf Hell, are demonstrating their latest type of klischograph. This consists of an electronic scanning instrument, capable of dealing with both black and white and multi-colour reproductions, which operates an engraving stylus to produce a gravure cylinder. Preparation of gravure cylinders can be a lengthy business, and this process, it is claimed, can reduce the time taken from several days to a matter of hours. **1967** KARCH & BUBER *Offset Processes* ii. 20 These machines [*sc.* electronic platemakers] include the models of.. Klischograph, Photo-lathe and Elgramma.

klister ('klɪstə(r)). *Skiing.* [Norw. *klister* paste.] A soft wax for applying to the running surface of skis to facilitate movement, used esp. in warm weather.

1936 B. LUNN tr. *Hallberg & Mückenbrünn's Compl. Bk. Ski-ing* iv. 39 We specially recommend the following waxes: Ostbye (Medium.. Klister); Bratlie (Nysnö.. Klister). **1948** —— *Ski-ing Primer* xix. 95 Klister.. is generally sold in tubes. There are many brands. **1951** EUGEN & ATWATER *Ski with Sverre* xi. 94 For wet snow, well above freezing, use a soft klister type wax.

klob: see next.

klobbiyos ('klɒbɪjɒs). *Cards.* Also **klaberjass, klobbyosh, klobiosk,** etc. [ad. G. *klaberjass*, f. Du. *klaverjas* a type of piquet.] A type of piquet, esp. popular with eastern European Jews. Also in shortened form **klob.**

1892 I. ZANGWILL *Childr. Ghetto* I. 124 They played loo, 'klobbiyos', napoleon, vingt-et-un. **1928** *Daily Tel.* 6 Nov. 9/2 Dice, nap, and klobiosk were played... The Magistrate: What is klobiosk? Inspector Dyer: It is similar to the English game known as 'Five hundred'. **1937** D. RUNYON *More than Somewhat* 10, I find Little Isadore playing klob with a guy. **1946** MOREHEAD & MOTT-SMITH *Penguin Hoyle* 94 Klaberjass, a game for two players, is better-known under corrupted names—Clobber, Clob, and the like and particularly under the name Kalabrias, which is a popular Hungarian game. **1946** MEZZROW & WOLFE *Really Blues* ii. 20 Easygoing guys who spent half their lives playing klabiasch, pinochle, and tarok. **1961** A. SMITH *East-Enders* ix. 159 They will create a few private gambling hells... There will be klobby-osh and strip poker.

klockmannite ('klɒkmænaɪt). *Min.* [ad. G. *klockmannit* (P. Ramdohr 1928, in *Centralbl. f. Mineral.* A. 226), f. the name of F. F. H. *Klockmann* (1858-1937), Ger. mineralogist: see -ITE[1].] A slate-grey selenide of copper, CuSe, found impure as granular aggregates and synthesized as crystal plates.

1939 *Mineral. Mag.* XXV. 295 Another copper selenide from the same locality [*sc.* Sierra de Umango, Argentina] has since been named klockmannite. **1969** *Acta Crystallogr.* XV B.2420 (*heading*) Twinning in the superlattice structure of CuSe, synthetic klockmannite.

‖**klomp** (klɒmp). *S. Afr.* Also **clompie, clumpjie, klompie, klompje, klumpjie.** [Afrikaans, f. Du. *klomp*: see CLUMP *sb.*] A group, esp. of animals.

1853 W. R. KING *Campaigning in Kaffirland* 215 Even at three quarters of a mile, we were able to disperse small 'clumpjies' of Kaffirs and cattle. **1861** T. BAINES *Jrnl.* 25 Nov. in *Explor. S.-W. Afr.* (1864) ix. 241 Snyman also saw nothing except one 'klumpjie' of kameels. **1896** H. A. BRYDEN *Tales S. Afr.* 70 Rather suddenly we came upon a *klompje* of giraffe. **1920** F. C. CORNELL *Glamour of Prospecting* xi. 170 Next day we were off well before sun-up, anxious to shoot something for the pot, but it was not till late in the afternoon that Poulley spotted a *klomp* of springbok. **1937** S. CLOETE *Turning Wheels* xxviii. 434 We saw some of them [*sc.* cattle].. a big clompie of a thousand head or more. **1963** —— *Rags of Glory* v. 44 Great *klompies* of them [*sc.* stallions] could live together with hardly a serious quarrel till a female came along.

klompie ('klɒmpɪ). *S. Afr.* Also **klompje.** [Afrikaans, f. Du. *klomp* a small blue brick + Afrikaans *-ie* a dim. ending.] A type of brick.

1926 S. G. MILLIN *South Africans* IV. ii. 111 Open hearths outlined in stone or in the small bricks called *klompjes*. **1949** L. G. GREEN *In Land of Afternoon* xv. 199 When you step on to the klompie brick stoep and into the low cool rooms.. you are in a more leisurely world. **1950** *Cape Times* 4 Mar. 11/8 (Advt.), Golden Brown Klompies 9 in. × 4 in. × 1¾ in. and 2,500 face bricks.

Klondike ('klɒndaɪk), *sb.* Also **Klondyke.** [f. the Kutchin name *tron-duik* hammer river, a tributary of the Yukon River.] **1.** The name of a region (and river) in the Yukon, NW. Canada, the scene of a gold-rush in the years following 1896. Hence many *attrib.* uses, as ***Klondyke fever, (gold) rush,*** etc., applied to this period and to the life lived during it. **b.** *ellipt.* as *sb.*, a mine or quarry of valuable material.

1897 *Slocan* (B.C.) *Pioneer* 31 July 4/2 The Klondike fever has struck Slocan City in a mild form. **1897** *Athenæum* 9 Oct. 483/3 The rich Klondyke of Malory and Geoffrey of Monmouth had not escaped the eyes of previous prospectors. **1898** *Century Mag.* Mar. 697/2 These men made their way home, as best they could, out of the wreckage of the first Klondike rush. **1898** *T. Eaton & Co. Catal.* Spring & Summer 124 Men's Klondike mining coats... Men's Klondike sleeping bag... Men's Klondike shirts. **1912** H. FOOTNER *New Rivers of North* 192 We guessed that we were upon the spot where our last white predecessors had made camp in the year of the Klondike rush. **1948** *Life* 2 Feb. 49/3, 78-year-old Emil J. N. Ott,.. a veteran of the Klondike Rush, who smelts rough gold into ingots. **1958** *Encycl. Canadiana* VI. 15 (*caption*) Hundreds watch as the *Australia*.. leaves Seattle for the North at the height of the Klondike fever. **1961** *Tamarack Rev.* XIX. 4 For a long time, before the Klondike days, there was a feud and a battle between them two logging camps. **1964** *Edmonton* (Alberta) *Jrnl.* 11 July 3/6 The past 60 years have obscured or distorted the extraordinary strength and endurance, and the Klondike wealth of the erstwhile sourdough who became a legendary character during his own lifetime. **1965** *Star Weekly* (Toronto) 2 Jan. 37/2 Mrs. MacCleave was a young girl at the height of the Klondike gold rush. **1973** *Times* 1 Feb. 12/8 He combed the reports of Congressional committees rarely read or reported by others. It was a new Klondike.

2. A card-game played with a single pack of fifty-two, the object being to see how many cards can be built up in sequence and suit on a row of aces. *N. Amer.*

1902 L. MCKEE *Land of Nome* 163 All the games were going—roulette, vingt-et-un,.. Klondike, and craps. **1908** U. SINCLAIR *Metropolis* vi. 91 The smoking-room, where the stout little Major had gotten a group of young bloods about him to play 'Klondike'. **1910** R. SERVICE *Trail of '98* 183 There were crap-tables,.. the Klondike game, Keno, stud poker, roulette and faro outfits. **1946** MOREHEAD & MOTT-SMITH *Penguin Hoyle* 174 Klondike is probably the most widely known solitaire game. **1953** J. WALKER *Pardon my Parka* (1958) 127 We sat around.. and we played a vicious gambling patience called Klondike.. which cost me a vast amount of money. **1968** *Encycl. Brit.* XX. 875/2 Many solitaires can be played by two, but Klondike is by far the favourite for this purpose.

3. The name given to a herring fishery off the W. coast of Scotland. (Cf. KLONDIKE *v.*)

1929 W. KEIR *Herring Trade on Continent 1928* 16 In the early part of the season the trawlers fished mostly on the 'Klondyke' grounds off the West Coast of Scotland.

'Klondike, *v.* Also **Klondyke,** and with small initial. [See prec., sense 3.] *trans.* To export (fresh herring) (as opp. to pickled herring).

1923 *Glasgow Herald* 25 Oct. 6 A regular fleet of steamers 'Klondyking' or running the fresh fish direct from the various landing ports to Germany. **1930** *Aberdeen Press & Jrnl.* 30 Jan. 8 If a boycott was attempted, they would klondyke their supplies into the Dutch and other markets. **1930** *Morning Post* 2 Aug., Reference is made to the quantities of herrings 'klondyked'—which means despatched fresh to the Continent. **1945** [see BISMARCK 3].

Klondiker ('klɒndaɪkə(r)). Also **Klondyker**. [f. KLONDIKE *sb.* + -ER[1].] **1.** A prospector in the Klondike. Also *transf.*

1897 *Brit. Columbia Mining Jrnl.* (Ashcroft, B.C.) 9 Oct. 1/6 The venturesome Klondiker who may select this valley as his road to the diggings may rest assured that his daily bill of fare will not only be ample but of good variety. **1901** *Daily Colonist* (Victoria, B.C.) 5 Nov. 3/2 Steamer Amur arrived from Skagway and way ports early this morning, with gold, salmon, and many Klondikers, among her 78 passengers. **1904** BURGESS & IRWIN *Picaroons* 102 The Story of the Returned Klondyker. **1917** *Dialect Notes* IV. 420 Terms from New Orleans. *Klondiker*, an heiress-hunter. **1954** A. M. BEZANSON *Sodbusters invade Peace* 4 There's an old trail that some Klondikers tried to take their outfits over.

2. An exporter of or dealer in fresh herring from the Scottish fisheries; a ship used for this.

1926 *Glasgow Herald* 19 Dec. 8 The 'Klondykers' are.. the German boats which buy the herring and transport them for sale in Germany. **1938** L. MACNEICE *I crossed Minch* II. xii. 166 The herring fishing was nothing here now. He remembered when the German Klondikers used to come into Loch Seaforth and buy [herrings] from the natives on the spot. **1953** *Press & Jrnl.* (Aberdeen) 17 June, The klondykers, however, sent only about one-third of the 1951 quantity of fresh herring to Western Germany. **1971** *Stornoway Gaz.* 7 Aug. 3/3 The first Klondyker of the season, from Norway, arrived at Stornoway during the week-end for a cargo of herring.

Klondiking ('klɒndaɪkɪŋ), *vbl. sb.* Also **Klondyking**, and with small initial. [f. KLONDIKE *v.* + -ING[1].] **1.** Prospecting in the Klondike during the gold-rush period.

1900 J. LONDON *Let.* 31 Jan. (1966) 87, I spoke at length in previous letter concerning my tramping and Klondiking.

2. Dealing in or exporting fresh herring from the Scottish fisheries.

1927 J. T. JENKINS *Herring* 146 While trawled herring are unsuitable for pickling, they are well adapted for 'Klondyking'—a method of preparing herring for export practically fresh by sprinkling them with salt and ice. **1930** P. F. ANSON *Fishing Boats & Fisher Folk E. Coast Scotl.* 20 On an average about 12 per cent [of the herring catch] is exported fresh to Germany. This freshing export trade is known as 'klondyking'. **1973** *Stornoway Gaz.* 27 Jan. 1/1 The herring was disposed of as follows: Freshing and kippering—27 crans; klondyking—3,565 crans. **1973** *Courier & Advertiser* (Dundee) 21 Feb. 9/1 Ullapool.—Herring 3420 crans—1430 crans for home market, £5·50 to £6·70; 220 for freezing, £4·60 to £5; 120 for canning, £4·50 to £5; 1650 for klondyking.

klong (klɒŋ). Also **khlong**. [Thai.] In Thailand, a canal. Also *attrib.*

1898 E. YOUNG *Kingdom Yellow Robe* ii. 26 When agricultural enterprise led to the formation of inland settlements, no roads were made.. but canals or 'khlongs' were cut instead. **1928** *Daily Express* 13 Mar. 12/4 A broad flat field.. beribboned with klongs (canals). *Ibid.*, Millions of happy frogs sing in high shrill voices, perched on the banks of the klongs. **1967** *Nat. Geographic* July 81 Where were the *klongs* of yesteryear, all those colorful canals, criss-crossing the city, that had made travel agents abroad burble about Bangkok as the Venice of the East? **1970** M. PEREIRA *Pigeon's Blood* i. 10 A wooden jetty on the banks of one of the numerous klongs, or canals, which intersected the city. **1972** *Nation* (Bangkok) 22 Nov. 4/4 He had made a survey of the plant and found that the water released from the ponds into the nearby klongs and later to the Chao Phya river needed to be medically treated.

‖**klonkie** ('klɒŋkɪ). *S. Afr.* [Afrikaans, a blending of *klein* small and *jong* small boy + dim. suff. *-kie*.] A coloured boy; occas., an African boy; a coloured man.

[**1913** PETTMAN *Africanderisms* 268 *Klong*.. is in common use in various parts of South Africa, and is applied to coloured males without reference to age, much as the word 'boy' is among the English colonists.] **1953** A. PATON *Too Late the Phalarope* viii. 58 The small *klonkies* from the black people's location.. liked to hang around the store. **1955** D. JACOBSON *Trap* i. 32 Strained and shy, the boy's voice came: 'Good night, baas. Thank you, baas.' 'Good night, *klonkie*,' Van Schoor replied. **1960** D. LYTTON *Goddam White Man* iv. 102 But don't tell me the coloured klonkie living in those huts on the farm feels shame at his failure to provide better for his kids.

klooch (klu:tʃ). *NW. Amer.* Also **klootch**. [Chinook Jargon (from Nootka) *klootchman* woman.] An Indian woman. Also (variously spelt) '**kloochman**.

Quot. 1861 illustrates the erroneous form *kloochwoman*.

1837 H. BEAVER *Let.* 10 Mar. (1959) 38 'Klout-che-man' is the term used to express the whole female sex, in whatever degree of relationship, whether rational or irrational. **1860** *Brit. Colonist* (Victoria, B.C.) 24 Mar. 2/3 About 75 Cape Flattery Indians arrived in canoes yesterday.. on a visit to the Songish tribe, for the purpose of buying a *clootchman* for their chief. **1861** in C. Maiden *Lighted Journey: Story of B.C. Electric* (1948) 1, I perceived two clootch-vimmen a' standin' outside of a 'ouse, and they was a-laughing at me. **1865** G. STUART *Montana as it Is* 83 Oregon is the place to hear the 'Chinnook' in all its glory; it has 'played' the English language 'square out' in that land of.. 'cloockmans' and camus. **1897** M. H. E. HAYNE *Pioneers of Klondyke* 25 The klūtch (short for klūtchman, the local name for squaws) dress exactly like the men. **1901** *Daily Colonist* (Victoria, B.C.) 8 Oct. 3/1 Old klootchmen were to be seen with their arms filled with all kinds of goods. **1907** R. DUNN *Shameless Diary of Explorer* iv. 28 Starved dogs, half-naked children, shawled klootches, bucks in prospectors' old clothes, all gathered, stared, shook hands, clucked questions. **1945** R. W. SERVICE *Ploughman of Moon* 176 In the old days he had taken up with a klootchman, and had written home, saying he was married to an Indian Princess. *Ibid.*, On one side of me I had a klootch with a papoose tied to her back. **1956** *Beaver* Summer 44 The Indians had respected the promises of the Great White Queen—or as she was known—'King George's Klootchman'—and they relied upon the word of the Hudson's Bay Company. **1966** H. MARRIOTT *Cariboo Cowboy* vi. 58 An Indian 'klootch' with three kids playing around the tent. **1969** *Islander* (Victoria, B.C.) 31 Aug. 10/2 Jenny, a Klootchman as Indian women were called, washed, ironed, sewed on buttons and mended.

kloof (klu:f). [a. Du. *kloof* (klo:f) cleft: see CLOVE *sb.*[5]] In South Africa: A deep narrow valley; a ravine or gorge between mountains.

1731 MEDLEY *Kolben's Cape G. Hope* II. 18 The Lion is separated from the Table-Hill by a small Kloof, as the Dutch call it, i.e. a Cleft or Descent. **1775** MASSON in *Phil. Trans.* LXVI. 273 We ascended the mountains by an exceedingly steep rugged path, which the peasants call Hottentot Holland Kloof. **1834** PRINGLE *Afr. Sk.* v. 209 Lofty hills.. broken by kloofs, or subsidiary dales. **1849** E. E. NAPIER *Excurs. S. Afr.* II. 20 On a nearer approach, dark glens and gloomy 'kloofs' are found to furrow the mountain sides.

attrib. **1899** RIDER HAGGARD *Swallow* iv, Her face was rich in hue as a kloof lily.

klop (klɒp), *sb.* Also **clop**. [Echoic: cf. CLIP-CLOP, and Du. *klop*, G. *klopf*. In quot. 1893 prob. suggested by the Du. word.] The sound of the impact of something solid on a hard surface: see quots. Also reduplicated *klop-klop*.

1841 J. H. SEALY *Porcelain Tower, Marr. in Mask* 206 A rustle of pig-tails and a klop-klop of [Chinese] ladies' feet. **1854** W. COLLINS *Hide & Seek* i, He heard the heavy clop-clop of thickly-booted feet. **1891** *Pall Mall G.* 10 Jan. 2/3 A hard road beats musically to the klop-klop of galloping horse or march of men. **1893** *Blackw. Mag.* Sept. 444 The crack was heard, again followed by the fatal 'klop' [of a beast falling].

So **klop** *v.*, *intr.* to produce a somewhat hollow sound by striking a hard surface.

1841 J. H. SEALY *Porcelain Tower, Hyson & Bohea* 99 The sad Bohea, who stay'd awake to weep, Rose from her couch, and lest her shoes should klop, 'Padded the hoof', and sought her father's shop.

klopemania (kləʊpɪ'meɪnɪə). [f. Gr. κλοπή theft + MANIA.] = KLEPTOMANIA.

1855 in MAYNE *Expos. Lex.*: whence in mod. Dicts.

klops (klɒps). [Ger.] A type of meat-ball or meat-loaf.

1936 I. S. ROMBAUER *Joy of Cooking* (ed. 2) 89/2 German meat balls. (Koenigsberger Klops). **1966** L. DAVIDSON *Long Way to Shiloh* ix. 132 The proprietor was eating a plate of klops at the next table. **1972** N. FROUD *Some of our Best Recipes are Jewish* 75 Klops is an East European improved version of a meat loaf.

‖**kloster** ('kləʊstə(r)). [Ger.: cf. CLOSTER.] A convent, a monastery (in Germany, Flanders, etc.).

1844 LONGF. *Norman Baron* iv, Bells, that from the neighboring kloster Rang for the Nativity. **1878** WHITTIER *Vision Echard* 12 On minster tower and kloster cross, The westering sunshine fell.

klote, klotte, klowet (kloyt), etc., obs. ff. or var. of CLOTE, CLOT, CLOUT.

Klucker, var. KLUXER.

kludge (klu:dʒ). *slang* (orig. *U.S.*). Also **kluge**. [J. W. Granholm's jocular invention: see first quot.; cf. also BODGE *v.*, FUDGE *v.*] 'An ill-assorted collection of poorly-matching parts, forming a distressing whole' (Granholm); esp. in *Computing*, a machine, system, or program that has been improvised or 'bodged' together; a hastily improvised and poorly thought-out solution to a fault or 'bug'.

1962 J. W. GRANHOLM in *Datamation* Feb. 30/1 The word 'kludge' is.. derived from the same root as the German *Kluge*.., originally meaning 'smart' or 'witty'... 'Kludge' eventually came to mean 'not so smart' or 'pretty ridiculous'. *Ibid.* 30/2 The building of a Kludge.. is not work for amateurs. There is a certain, indefinable, masochistic finesse that must go into true Kludge building. **1966** *New Scientist* 22 Dec. 699/1 Kludges are conceived of man's natural fallibility, nourished by his loyalty to erroneous opinion, and perfected by the human capacity to apply maximum effort only when proceeding in the wrong direction. **1976** *Electronic Design* 5 Jan. 120 The technique uses some kluge wiring, which must be carefully done to avoid shorts and noise problems. **1979** *Personal Computer World* Nov. 71/3 *Kludge*, a local modification or patch in a computer program to overcome some error or design fault. **1983** *Austral. Personal Computer* Sept. 43/2 A well constructed and neat PCB with no obvious 'kludges' or last minute changes of mind. **1984** *Which Micro?* Dec. 21/4 The QL is at last available.. and without 'kludges' tacked on to make it work. **1987** *Electronics* 25 June 67 They have to get this performance with simple air-cooled designs, not with liquid-cooled kluges.

Hence as *v. trans.*, to improvise with a kludge or kludges; also **kludged** *ppl. a.*; '**kludgemanship**, skill in designing or applying kludges.

1962 *Datamation* Feb. 30/2 It is in the lashing together of whole modules of equipment that the opportunity for applied kludgemanship presents itself to the hilt. **1966** L. HARRISBERGER *Engineersmanship* vii. 108 The noble art of Kludgemanship capitalizes upon the design engineer's affinity for asininity and deals with the techniques for how to miss the perfect opportunity and succeed in achieving optimum imperfectability. **1983** *Verbatim* Winter 17/1 *To kludge* means to put together some hardware (or write a program) by combining parts of existing computers or their programs. **1984** *QL User* Dec. 19 Its history was most unfortunate to start with: production delays, 'kludged' machines, extra ROMs hanging off the back.

kluke: see CLUTCH.

†**klumene** ('klu:mi:n). *Chem. Obs.* [f. mod.L. *kalium* potassium (see quot. 1900) + -ENE.] = ACETYLENE.

1853 H. WATTS tr. *Gmelin's Hand-bk. Chem.* VIII. 150 A carbide of potassium.. gives off, when immersed in water, a peculiar combustible gas, which is klumene gas. **1900** V. B. LEWES *Acetylene* iii. 63 Edmund Davy, in 1836, named the newly-discovered gas bicarburet of hydrogen..; whilst later the name 'klumene' was bestowed upon it, because it had been derived from a kalium compound—potassium carbide. **1901** *Oxf. Univ. Gaz.* 3 Dec. 204 Olefine and Klumene Compounds. **1902** *Encycl. Brit.* XXV. 35/1 *Acetylene*, klumene or ethine, is one of the gaseous compounds of hydrogen and carbon.

klumst: see CLUMSED.

klunk (klʌŋk). *U.S. slang.* Also **clunk**. [Of unknown origin.] A derogatory designation for a person.

1942 BERREY & VAN DEN BARK *Amer. Thes. Slang* §396 Klunk [in list of terms of disparagement for a person]. **1959** N. MAILER *Advts. for Myself* (1961) 399 What was unique about Jones was that he had come out of nowhere, self-taught, a clunk in his lacks. **1964** S. BELLOW *Herzog* (1965) 78 He sat there, in her own words, like a clunk, bored, resentful. **1964** *N.Y. Herald-Tribune* 2 Jan. 8/1 Mr. Wagner has been a remarkably good mayor, and the klunks who don't realize this, they add, understand neither the Mayor himself nor the nature of his responsibilities.

klutz (klʌts). *U.S. slang.* Also **klotz, kluhtz**. [Yiddish, f. G. *klotz*, lit. = wooden block. Cf. CLOT *sb.*] A clumsy, awkward person, esp. one considered socially inept; a fool. Also as *vb.* So '**klutzy** *a.*, awkward, foolish.

1965 *Sat. Rev.* (U.S.) 28 Aug. 51/2 The dancers look good and the artists look a little *klutzy*. **1968** F. MULLALLY *Munich Involvement* i. 10 Look, I feel a bit of a klutz in this crumpled day suit. **1968** L. ROSTEN *Joys of Yiddish* 185 Two *klutzes* were discussing their wives. **1970** L. M. FEINSILVER *Taste of Yiddish* 276 Recent bilingual jokes about Christmas, like 'Santa *Kluhtz*'. *Ibid.* 303 Choreographer Kenneth MacMillan has attempted a compromise between dancing and acting that too often leaves Nureyev.. with nothing to do but klutz around the stage. **1970** *New Yorker* 17 Jan. 72 The sad, klutzy ballerinas of the Music Hall pollute children's first live experience of dance. **1970** *Time* 2 Nov. 83 Basically I'm the klutz who makes a terrific entrance to the party and then trips and falls and walks around with food in her hair. **1973** E.-J. BAHR *Nice Neighbourhood* ix. 99 Janet is an utter klotz.

Kluxer ('klʌksə(r)). *U.S.* Also **Klucker**. [f. (KU-)KLUX(-KLAN) + -ER[1].] A member of the Ku-Klux Klan. Also *attrib.*

1879 A. W. TOURGÉE *Fool's Errand* xxvii. 141 Ef dere's any mo' Kluckers raidin' roun' Burke's Corners, dar'll be some funerals tu. **1923** *Nation* (N.Y.) 21 Nov. 570 We are not much impressed with the desireability of organizations specially formed to fight the 'Kluxers'. **1929** *Sun* (Baltimore) 31 Jan. 1/2 Johnston is disowned by the kluxers or whatever is left of them in Oklahoma. **1944** J. S. PENNELL *Hist. Rome Hanks* 176 Are you a Klucker, Mr. Ocamb? **1948** *Daily Ardmoreite* (Ardmore, Okla.) 25 July 20/4 Some 20 more noted Kluxers.. and similar ragtag and bobtail were on hand. **1963** D. B. HUGHES *Expendable Man* (1964) v. 146 There's not going to be any color business in this case. I'm not going to have it messed up with Kluxers or with bleeding hearts. **1965** C. COLTER in A. Chapman *New Black Voices* (1972) 72 Jus' ask her t' pull up that Kluxer sheet and show you her arm.

Hence '**Kluxery**, conduct or behaviour characteristic of members of the Ku-Klux Klan; '**Kluxism**, the principles and practice of the Ku-Klux Klan or of similar organizations.

1929 *Sun* (Baltimore) 31 Jan. 2/2 When Henry Johnston announced for Governor, carrying the flambeau of kluxism, Mrs. Hammonds became his Joan of Arc. **1949** *Richmond* (Virginia) *Times-Dispatch* 23 Jan. IV. 2-D/2 There have been too many episodes in the Old Dominion of late which reflect the spirit of kluxery.

klyack: see CLIACK.

klydonograph (klaɪ'dəʊnəʊgrɑ:f, -æ-). *Electr. Engin.* [f. Gr. κλύδων wave, billow + -O + -GRAPH.] An instrument for making a photographic record from which the voltage and polarity of a surge can be inferred, consisting of a point electrode resting (in darkness) on a stationary or moving film behind which is a plate electrode.

1924 J. F. PETERS in *Electr. World* 19 Apr. 769 (*heading*) The Klydonograph. An instrument for accurately measuring and recording voltage surges. *Ibid.* 769/1 The word 'klydonograph' was coined by Dr. Roscoe M. Ihrig of the Carnegie Institute of Technology. **1940** *Nature* 22 June 982/1 Three klydonographs were coupled to the line by means of concentric-cylinder type capacitance 'potential-dividers'. **1963** D. J. MALAN *Physics of Lightning* xi. 92 Since the Klydonograph indicates voltage, it is necessary to know the surge impedance of the system of conductors in order to calculate the peak current.

klyfft, klyppe: see CLIFT, CLIP.

klystron ('klaɪstrɒn). *Electronics.* Also **Klystron** (now *rare*). [f. Gr. κλύζειν (stem κλυσ-) to wash or break over + -TRON.] An electron tube for amplifying or generating microwave signals in which a beam of electrons from a thermionic cathode is passed through a gap in a cavity resonator across which is applied a high-frequency voltage, so that the electrons collect into bunches and on reaching a second gap induce a (larger) high-frequency voltage across it. Freq. *attrib.*, as ***klystron oscillator, tube.***

1939 R. H. & S. F. VARIAN in *Jrnl. Appl. Physics* X. 324/1 Such an apparatus we call a 'klystron', from the Greek verb 'klyzo', expressing the breaking of waves on a beach. **1945** H. D. SMYTH *Gen. Acct. Devel. Atomic Energy Mil. Purposes* xi. 118 The varying electric field..introduces small, periodic variations in ion velocity, and has the effect of causing the ions to 'bunch' at a certain distance down the tube. (This same principle is used in the klystron high-frequency oscillator...) **1959** G. TROUP *Masers* i. 1 In conventional microwave amplifiers and oscillators such as the Klystron, an alternating electromagnetic field interacts with elementary particles, electrons, by virtue of their charge. **1959** *New Scientist* 19 Nov. 982/3 The Jodrell radar pulses originated in a big ultra-high-frequency valve of the type known as a klystron. **1964** *Listener* 16 Apr. 626 (Advt.), EEV 25 kW klystrons are being supplied to the British Broadcasting Corporation for use in the new UHF television transmitters. **1973** *Sci. Amer.* Sept. 74/3 The microwaves are produced by a pair of 30-kilowatt klystron tubes powered by a diesel generator.

K(-)meson. *Nuclear Physics.* Also (*rare*) **k meson.** [f. *K* (in K(-)PARTICLE) + MESON[3].] = KAON.

1954 *Phil. Mag.* XLV. 1219 The mass of the K-meson, measured by ionization-range is 970 ± 100 m_e. **1954** *Physical Rev.* XCIV. 1794/2 All the *K* mesons observed lived at least 2 × 10^{-9} sec before coming to rest in the emulsion. **1964** *Listener* 30 Apr. 711/1 Usually the beams consist of particles called pi-mesons which have 270 times the mass of the electron, or the more exotic K-mesons with about 1,000 electron masses. K-meson beams have been particularly valuable recently in the production of further new particles. **1968** M. S. LIVINGSTON *Particle Physics* iv. 81 The new particles were of two basic types: *k* mesons with mass values less than nucleon mass, now called kaons; and hyperons, with masses greater than the nucleon mass. **1973** L. J. TASSIE *Physics Elem. Particles* ix. 84 There are two kinds of neutral *K*-mesons, the K^0 and the $\bar{K}^0$.

Hence **K-'mesic** *a.* = KAONIC *a.*

1958 *Phil. Mag.* III. 33 Negative K-mesons captured by the heavy nuclei in nuclear emulsion form K-mesic atoms. **1967** *Comments Nucl. & Particle Physics* I. 112 *K*-mesic x-rays from Li, Be, B, and C.

kn-, an initial combination common to all the Teutonic langs. and still retained by most. In English, the *k* is now silent, alike in educated speech and in most of the dialects; but it was pronounced app. till about middle of the 17th c. In the later 17th and early 18th c., writers on pronunciation give the value of the combination as = *hn, tn, dn* or simple *n*. The last was prob. quite established in Standard English by 1750. The *k* is still pronounced in some Scottish dialects; in others the guttural is assimilated to the dental, making *tn-*, esp. after vowels, as *a tnife, my tnee.*

knab (næb), *v. Obs.* exc. *dial.* [Imitative: cf. KNABBLE and KNAP *v.*[2]]

1. *trans.* To bite lightly, to nibble.

1668 R. L'ESTRANGE *Vis. Quev.* (1708) 134 After this Manner these Asses Knab and Curry one another. **1694** —— *Fables* 11, I had much rather lie knabbing of crusts..in my own little hole. **1879** MISS JACKSON *Shropsh. Word-bk.*, *Knab*, to bite gently and playfully. Horses knab each other when in good temper. **1887** *S. Chesh. Gloss.*, *Knab*, to bite, of a horse... 'I räther think hey knabs a bit'.

2. *intr.* To bite, nibble. Const. *on, upon.*

1630 J. TAYLOR (Water P.) *Dogge of War* Wks. II. 227/2 He seru'd his Master..In Holland, Zealand, Brabant..And if his fare were but a Crust, Hee patiently would knab on't. **1692** R. L'ESTRANGE *Fables* cccxvii. 277 An Ass was Wishing..for..a Mouthful of Fresh Grass to Knab upon.

knab: see NAB *sb.* and *v.*

†**'knabble**, *v. Obs.* Also 6 **knable**, 7 **gnab(b)le, nabble.** [dim. or freq. of KNAB *v.*: cf. Du. *knabbelen*, LG. *knabbeln* (G. *knabbern*), also NIBBLE *v.*] To bite, gnaw, nibble. Usually *intr.* or *absol.* with *at, upon.* Hence †**'knabbling** *ppl. a.*

1567 DRANT *Horace, Ep.* xvi. E viij, The puttocke from the bayted hooke her knabling neb will spare. **1580** HOLLYBAND *Treas. Fr. Tong, Ronger*, to knaw, to knabble. **1612** T. TAYLOR *Comm. Titus* iii. 3 No companie freeth it selfe but a man may obserue some mens names nibled at, and gnabled vpon. **1622** WARD *Woe to Drunkards* Serm. (1862) 159 Take us these little foxes..for they gnabble our grapes. **1666** HARVEY *Morb. Angl.* ix. 76 Left as a bone for every Readers discretion to knabble at. **1684** OTWAY *Atheist* I. i, Asses..are always ready to nabble, because it is the certain way to be nabbled again.

knack (næk), *sb.*[1] Forms: 4–6 **knak**, 6–7 **knacke**, 7– **knack.** [ME. *knak*: in senses 1 and 2 = Du. *knak*, G. (orig. LG.) *knack, knacke* (also *gnacke*), *knacks*, Norw. *knak*; also Gael. *cnac* (? from Sc.). Of echoic origin: cf. the associated KNACK *v.*]

†**1.** A sharp sounding blow, stroke, or rap. Cf. KNAP *sb.*[2] 1. *Obs. rare.*

c **1380** *Sir Ferumb.* 4599 Charlis lokedem be-hynde ys bak, and saw dele þar many a knak, & myche noyse make.

2. A sharp sound or noise such as is made in striking a stone with a hammer; a crack or snap.

1565–73 COOPER *Thesaurus, Concrepare digitis*, ..to make a fillip or knack with the fingers. **1607** TOPSELL *Four-f. Beasts* (1658) 331 [Which] made the bone to return into his right place, with such a loud knack or crack, as it might be heard a great way off. **1609** B. JONSON *Sil. Wom.* I. ii, The fellow trims him silently, and has not the knacke with his sheeres, or his fingers. **1831** J. HOLLAND *Manuf. Metal* I. 214 The knack of the fly [used by nail-cutters]..nearly equals in the rapidity of its repetition the ticking of a watch.

†**3.** A taunt, gibe, sharp repartee. *Sc. Obs.*

1513 DOUGLAS *Æneis* Dyrectioun 21 Perpetualy bechydit with ilk knak. **1560** ROLLAND *Crt. Venus* IV. 386 Pointand thair hand with mony scorne & knak [*S.T.S. ed. prints* knax]. *a* **1568** in *Bannatyne MS.* 321/18 Than will thay mak at him a knak.

knack (næk), *sb.*[2] Forms: 4–6 **knak, knakke** (*pl.* **knakkes**, 5 **knax**), 5–7 **knacke**, 6– **knack**, (4 **gnack(e**, 6 **neck**, 9 **nack**). [Origin obscure: in age and forms agreeing with KNACK *sb.*[1], and possibly the same word; but the connexion of sense is not clear.]

1. A trick; a device, artifice; formerly often, a deceitful or crafty device, a mean or underhand trick; later *esp.* an adroit or ingenious method of doing something, a clever expedient, a 'dodge'.

c **1369** CHAUCER *Dethe Blaunche* 1033 She ne used no suche knakkes smale. *c* **1380** WYCLIF *Wks.* (1880) 184 Coueitous laweieris wiþ here gnackis & iapis. *a* **1420** HOCCLEVE *De Reg. Princ.* 1395 Al þis..Is but a iape, who seith, or a knak. *c* **1470** HENRYSON *Mor. Fab.* v. (*Parl. Beasts*) xxx, 'Let be, lowrence', quod scho, 'your courtlie knax'. *c* **1540** EARL SURREY *Poems* (1854) 68, I have found a neck To keep my men in guard. **1548** UDALL *Erasm. Par. Luke* Pref. 13 Swete pleasaunte knackes and conceiptes. **1568** *Jacob & Esau* II. ii. in Hazl. *Dodsley* II. 214 That ever son of thine should play such a lewd knack! **1584** R. SCOT *Discov. Witchcr.* XII. xviii. (1886) 225 A knacke to knowe whether you be bewitched or no. **1660** *Dial. Tom & Dick* 1 If George does not do the knack, Ne're trust good-fellow more. *a* **1677** BARROW *Serm.* Wks. 1716 I. 174 Slander seemeth..a fine knack, or curious feat of policy. **1735** POPE *Ep. Lady* 155 How should equal Colours do the knack? **1829** CARLYLE *Misc., Germ. Playwrights* (1872) II. 91 He has some knack, or trick of the trade.

2. The 'trick' of dexterous performance; an acquired faculty of doing something cleverly, adroitly, and successfully. (Now the leading sense.)

1581 MULCASTER *Positions* v. (1887) 34 They that haue any naturall towardnesse to write well, haue a knacke of drawing to. *a* **1661** FULLER *Worthies* (1840) III. 287 Our Holland had the true knack of translating. **1710** SHAFTESB. *Charac.* (1737) II. I. i. 189 A violent Desire..to know the Knack or Secret by which Nature does all. **1713** STEELE *Guard.* No. 10 ¶6 He who hath no knack at writing sonnets. **1824** W. IRVING *T. Trav.* I. 54 He always had a knack of making himself understood among the women. **1834** BECKFORD *Italy* II. xv. 83 Sister Theresa has an admirable knack for teaching arithmetic. **1845** FORD *Handbk. Spain* I. 68 Most Spaniards have a peculiar knack in making omelettes. **1851** D. JERROLD *St. Giles* v. 48 You think the knack to do this does you good. **1870** EMERSON *Soc. & Solit., Work & Days* Wks. (Bohn) III. 68 Look up the inventors. Each has his own knack.

b. A 'trick' of action, speech, etc.; a personal habit of acting or speaking in a particular way.

1674 N. FAIRFAX *Bulk & Selv.* To Rdr., If the knack of borrowing, or robbing and pilfering rather, gets but a little further ground amongst us,..it will..be harder for an English-man to speak his own tongue without mingling others with it, than to speak a medly of sundry others without bringing in his own. **1709** STEELE *Tatler* No. 31 ¶9 The Lady..has only, with a very brisk Air, a Knack of saying the commonest Things. **1741** RICHARDSON *Pamela* (1824) I. 160, I have got such a knack of writing, that when I am by myself, I cannot sit without a pen in my hand. **1861** MISS BRADDON *Trail Serpent* I. v, The Sloshy has quite a knack of swelling and bursting.

3. *concr.* An ingenious contrivance; a toy, trinket, trifle, KNICK-KNACK. ? *Obs.*

1540 HEYWOOD *Four P.P.* in Hazl. *Dodsley* I. 349 Needles, thread, thimble, shears, and all such knacks. **1596** SHAKS. *Tam. Shr.* IV. iii. 67 Why 'tis a cockle or a walnut-shell, A knacke, a toy, a tricke, a babies cap: Away with it. *a* **1677** BARROW *Serm.* (1683) II. vii. 104 Springs, and wheels, and such mechanick knacks. **1715** tr. *C'tess D'Aunoy's Wks.* 557 A Thousand pretty Knacks..which she made with Fish-Bones and Shells, with Reeds and Rushes. **1825** LAMB *Elia* Ser. II. *Superannuated Man*, All the glittering and endless succession of knacks and gew-gaws. **1863** COWDEN CLARKE *Shaks. Char.* xiv. 360 The pedlar's knacks and gaudy trash [*Wint. T.* IV. iv.] absorb Mopsa's whole gloating vision.

†**b.** A choice dish; a delicacy, a dainty. *Obs.*

1548 UDALL, etc. *Erasm. Par. Mark* viii. 56 The knackes and junckettes of the Rhetoricians, the royall dishes of the Philosophers. **1592** GREENE *Disc. Coosnage* III. 10 Hee wanted no ordinarie good fare, wine and other knackes. **1616** SURFL. & MARKH. *Country Farme* 574 The flower of meale,..whereof the pasterers..doe make wafers, and such like daintie knackes. **1642** MILTON *Apol. Smect.* i. Wks. (1851) 283 (tr. Horace *Sat.* I. i. 24) As some teachers give to Boyes Junkets and Knacks, that they may learne apace.

†**c.** An ingeniously contrived literary composition; a quaint device or conceit in writing. *Obs.*

1605 CAMDEN *Rem., Rythmes* 26 Our Poets hath their knacks..as Ecchos, Achrostiches, Serpentine verses [etc.]. **1641** DENHAM *Petit. to Five Members* 41 All those pretty knacks you compose—Alas! what are they but poems in prose? **1644** BULWER *Chiron.* 98 Ovid that grand Master of love knacks. **1660** H. MORE *Myst. Godl.* X. xiii. 532 You.. reproach them..that they have not taken up your Allegorical knacks.

4. *local.* = KIRN-BABY. See also NECK[2].

1813 ELLIS *Brand's Pop. Antiq.* I. 433 *note*, At Werington, in Devonshire,..when a farmer finishes his reaping, a small quantity of the ears of the last corn are twisted or tied together into a curious kind of figure,..which is called 'a knack'.

5. *attrib.* and *Comb.*, as ***knack-maker, -shop***; †**knack-hardy** *a.*, bold in the use of trickery.

1549 COVERDALE, etc. *Erasm. Par.* 2 *Pet.* 18 They.. contemne those that be set in public authoritie, being knacke hardie and shameless. **1607** TOPSELL *Serpents* (1658) 783 Not one dare be so knack-hardy as to break into their friends and fellowes fence and enclosure. **1649** *Mercurius Aulicus* (*Thomason Tracts* (B.M.) Vol. 438 No. 2. 14) Resolved by the supreme knack-makers that a knack be brought in for settling the college of Westminster. *a* **1700** B. E. *Dict. Cant. Crew, Knacks*, or Toies, *a Knack-shop*, or Toy-shop.

knack (næk), *v.* Also 4–7 **knacke**, 5–6 **knak.** [In senses 2 and 3 = Du. *knakken* (first in Kilian), MHG. *knacken* (also *gnacken*), MLG. *knaken* (hence prob. Sw. *knaka*, Da. *knage*); cf. also Sw. *knäcka*, Da. *knække*, Norw. *knekkja*, to break, snap. Of echoic origin: cf. CLACK, CRACK.]

†**1.** *intr.* To deal (sharp sounding) blows. *Obs.* Cf. KNACK *sb.*[1] 1.

1575 R. B. *Appius & Virg.* in Hazl. *Dodsley* IV. 121 Nay then, by the mass, it's time to be knacking.

2. *trans.* To strike (things or their parts) together so as to produce a sharp abrupt noise; to gnash (the teeth); to snap (the fingers). Now *dial.*

c **1489** CAXTON *Sonnes of Aymon* xix. 406 He knacked his teeth for angre. **1577** H. RHODES *Bk. Nurture* in *Babees Bk.* 79 Cast not thy bones vnder the Table, nor none see thou doe knack. **1611** COTGR., *Matassiner des mains*, to moue, knacke, or waggle the fingers, like a Iugler. **1735** E. CHICKEN *Collier's Wedd.* (Northumbld. Gloss.), The pipes scream out her fav'rite jig, She knack'd her thumbs and stood her trig.

†**b.** To break or crack with a sharp sound. [Cf. Swed. *knacke-brod*, a sort of biscuit or cracknel.]

1562 J. HEYWOOD *Prov.* (1867) 66 Knak me that nut. **1573–80** BARET *Alv.* K 85 To knacke, or breake a nut.

3. *intr.* To make a sharp abrupt noise, as when stones are struck together. Now *dial.*

1603 HOLLAND *Plutarch's Mor.* 1276 Knacking (as it were) with his fingers over his head. **1617** BP. HALL *Quo Vadis?* §20 If they can heare their beads knacke vpon each other. **1646** FULLER *Wounded Consc.* (1841) 282 Sheep..fly without cause, scared (as some say) with the sound of their own feet: their feet knack because they fly, and they fly because their feet knack. **18..** *Colliers' Pay Week* in Brockett *N.C. Gloss.*, He jumps, and his heels knack and rattle.

†**4.** *trans.* To 'break' (notes: see BREAK *v.* 2 h, NOTE *sb.*); to sing with trills or runs; to sing in a lively or ornate manner, to trill forth. *Obs.*

c **1380** WYCLIF *Wks.* (1880) 192 þre or foure proude & lecherous lorellis schullen knacke þe most deuout seruyce þat noman schal here þe sentence..& þanne strumpatis & þeuys preisen sire iacke or hobbe,..how smale þei knacken here notis. *c* **1388** in *Wyclif's Sel. Wks.* III. 482 God seis not þat he is blessid þat syngus or knackus swete notis. *c* **1460** *Towneley Myst.* xiii. 659 For to sing vs emong right as he knakt it, I can.

†**b.** *intr.* To sing or speak in a lively manner; to 'descant'. *Obs.*

a **1529** SKELTON *Agst. Comely Coystrowne* Wks. 1843 I. 15 Curyowsly he can both counter and knak of Martyn Swart and all hys mery men.

c. *intr.* To talk finely or mincingly. *dial.*

1674–91 RAY *N.C. Words, Knack*, to speak finely. And it is used of such as do speak in the Southern dialect. **1825** BROCKETT, *Knack*, to speak affectedly, to ape a style beyond the speaker's education. **1855** ROBINSON *Whitby Gloss.* s.v., She knacks and knappers like a London miss.

†**5.** *trans.* To mock, taunt. *Obs.* (chiefly *Sc.*).

c **1425** WYNTOUN *Cron.* VIII. x. 1728 This Kyng Edward all wyth gawdys Knakkyd Robert the Brws wyth frawdis. *a* **1500** *Ratis Raving* II. 371 Thai wyll men..scorn & knak. **1513** DOUGLAS *Æneis* II. iii. [ii.] 13 A multitude ȝong Troianis Byssy to knak and pull the presoneir.

†**'knackatory.** *Obs. rare.* A shop for knick-knacks. Cf. KNICK-KNACKATORY.

1709 *Brit. Apollo* II. No. 56. 3/2 You keep a Knackatory.

knacker ('nækə(r)), *sb.*[1] Also (sense 3) **nacker.** [f. KNACK *v.* + -ER[1].]

†**1.** One who sings in a lively manner. *Obs.*

c **1380** WYCLIF *Wks.* (1880) 191 ȝif þes knackeris excusen hem bi song in þe olde lawe.

2. Something that makes a sharp cracking noise; *spec.* a castanet. Now *dial.*

16.. MIDDLETON & ROWLEY *Span. Gipsy* III. ii, Our knackers are the fifes and drums. Our knackers are the shot that fly. **1647** R. STAPYLTON *Juvenal* 220 Castinetta's; knackers of the form of chesnuts, used to this day by the Spaniards in their dances. **1649** W. CAVENDISH *Varietie* III. 43 A Bachanalian dancing the Spanish Morisco, with knackers at his fingers. **1877** *N.W. Linc. Gloss., Knackers*, flat pieces of wood with which children beat time.

3. *pl.* The testicles. *slang.*

1866 T. EDMONDSTON *Etym. Gloss. Shetland & Orkney Dial.* 76 *Nackers*, testes, S. **1877** in E. PEACOCK *Gloss. Words Manley & Corringham, Lincolnshire* 150/2. **1889** BARRÈRE & LELAND *Dict. Slang* I. 523/2 *Knackers*.. (Butchers, &c.), the testicles, also 'knuckers'. **1922** JOYCE *Ulysses* 576 Eh, Harry, give him a kick in the knackers. **1940** J. CARY *Charley is my Darling* xlv. 261 I'll murder the bastards... I'll take the knackers offen them. **1951** *Landfall* Sept. 177 Sling your hook out of this dump before it gets you by the knackers. **1958** M. PUGH *Wilderness of Monkeys* 79 Oh, smart boy, eh? .. Festival Hall fiddle! Nackers! **1969** G. GREENE *Travels with my Aunt* I. v. 42, I may regret him for a while tonight. His knackers were superb.

†**knacker**, *sb.*² *Obs.* [Cf. KNACK *sb.*² 1.] A trickster, deceiver.

c **1380** WYCLIF *Wks.* (1880) 156 He þat.. can helpe to anoie a pore man by knackis or chapitris.. siche knackeris ben as proude of here veyn kunnynge as lucifer.

knacker ('nækə(r)), *sb.*³ [Origin obscure. In sense 1, the knacker may orig. have made only the *knacks* or smaller articles belonging to harness, and hence have taken his name; but this is doubtful, as is also the connexion of sense 2.]

1. A harness-maker; a saddler. *dial.*

1573 TUSSER *Husb.* (1878) 137 Plowwrite, cartwrite, knacker and smith. **1622** F. MARKHAM *Bk. War* III. iv. §6. 96 Men of these trades, as Codders, or Knackers, Cartwrights, Smiths, and the like. **1691** RAY *S. & E. Country Words* 104 A *Knacker*, One that makes Collars and other Furniture for Cart-horses. *Mod. Northampton Dial.*, You must take this collar to the knacker's to be altered, it wrings the horse's shoulders so much.

[Ainsworth *Lat. Dict.* (1736) has 'A Knacker, *Restio*'. (*Restio* is a ropemaker.) Johnson (1755) has *Knacker* '1. A maker of small work' (quoting 1573 above). '2. A rope-maker' (quoting Ainsworth). Craig 1847 has 'A maker of knacks, toys, or small work; a rope-maker; a collar-maker'. All these dictionary-explanations or misunderstandings seem to arise out of the sense 'harness-maker'.]

2. a. One whose trade it is to buy worn out, diseased, or useless horses, and slaughter them for their hides and hoofs, and for making dog's-meat, etc.; a horse-slaughterer. ***knacker's yard***: Also *transf.* and *fig.*

1812 *Sporting Mag.* XXXIX. 209 He was a knacker [*note*, A purchaser of worn-up horses]. **1824** *Monthly Mag.* LVII. 109 The nackers' and catgut-makers' yards. **1875** HELPS *Soc. Press.* ii. 9 Four or five hundred horses are carried to the knacker's yard each week in London. **1961** F. H. BURGESS *Dict. Sailing* 128 *Knacker's yard*, the shipbreaker's yard. **1966** 'L. LANE' *ABZ of Scouse* 59 *Knacker's yard*: said of a place that looks a complete mess. **1967** T. GUNN *Touch* 42 The graveyard is the sea... They have all come who sought distinction hard To this universal knacker's yard.

b. One who buys old houses, ships, etc., for the sake of their materials, or what can be made of them.

1890 *Times* 23 Aug. 4/6 Worm-eaten hulks.. sent by ship knackers to find freight or a grave in the North Atlantic. **1899** *Daily News* 2 Feb. 3/1 The old house knacker was bad enough,.. but he was innocence itself, compared with the new house knacker that has risen up. *Ibid.* 12 June 8/4 Lovers of old London have been grieved by the news that No. 47, Leicester-square.. where the painter [Reynolds] lived and worked.. was to be made over to the house-knackers.

3. *transf.* An old worn-out horse. *dial.*

1864 MAYHEW *German Life* I. 127 Such spavined knackers. **1867** OUIDA *Under Two Flags* (1890) 122 The famous English horse was dead beat as any used-up knacker.

knacker ('nækə(r)), *v. slang.* [f. KNACKER *sb.*³ 2 or KNACKER *sb.*¹ 3.] *trans.* To kill; to castrate; usu. in weakened sense, to exhaust, to wear out. So as an imprecation. Freq. as *pa. pple.* or *ppl. a.*

1886 H. BAUMANN *Londinismen* 90/2 *Knacker*, umbringen; he's knackered, er ist abgemurkst worden. **1936** B. PENTON *Inheritors* ix. 72 Coons is cheap. They'd knacker us white bushmen if they got the chance and let them Chows and Jimmy Tannas breed like rabbits. **1946** *Penguin New Writing* XXVII. 79 His eyes narrowed but he knew I had him knackered. **1959** M. PUGH *Chancer* vi. 86 'Wasn't it Major Fleming with the Bren-gun?' 'Major Fleming be knackered. It was Ramsay.' **1963** *New Society* 22 Aug. 5/1 Other adoptions are 'get knotted' and 'knackered' which have come to mean innocently enough, 'go to hell', and '*kaput*'. **1971** B. W. ALDISS *Soldier Erect* 258 Gor-Blimey came up, panting like a dog. 'I'm knackered,' he said. Blood was streaming down his face from a cut on his temple. **1971** *Times* 21 May 8/7, I kept thinking I should whip up the pace and then I'd think 'I'm knackered, I'll leave it for another lap.' **1973** C. BONINGTON *Next Horizon* xxi. 283 We've been above Base Camp for twenty-eight days. If we had to go back to carrying now we'd have to go all the way back down for a rest. We're just too knackered to carry. **1975** *Sunday Times* (Colour Suppl.) 23 Feb. 25/2 Oot a' mornin' daein' thae miracles. I'm *knackered*! Gie's a glass o' that wine. Nae kiddin' son, I'm knackered.

knackery ('nækərɪ). [f. prec., sense 2: see -ERY.] A knacker's yard.

1869 E. A. PARKES *Pract. Hygiene* (ed. 3) 114 Evidence to show that the workmen in knackeries are in no way injured. **1888** W. WILLIAMS *Veterin. Med.* (ed. 5) 765 Dogs that frequent knackeries and slaughter-houses.

†'**knacking**, *vbl. sb. Obs.* [f. KNACK *v.* + -ING¹.] The action of the verb KNACK in various senses.

c **1380** WYCLIF *Wks.* (1880) 9 Veyn songis and knackynge and harpynge. *c* **1388** in *Wyclif's Sel. Wks.* III. 484 Þai wole no ferþer þen holy writte and olde seintus teche, for no newe knackynge of sotile cavellaciones. **1548** W. PATTEN *Exp. Scotl.* in Arb. *Garner* III. 71 Knakkynge of beadstones in every pew. **1607** TOPSELL *Serpents* (1658) 633 A certain significant noise, made by knacking of the fingers. **1644** BULWER *Chirol.* 176 To compresse the middle-finger with the Thumbe by their complosion... This knacking with the Fingers.

†'**knacking**, *ppl. a. Obs.* [f. as prec. + -ING².] That knacks: in senses of the verb. ***knacking earnest***, downright earnest.

1496 *Dives & Paup.* (W. de W.) I. lix. 102/1 This curyouse knackynge songe of the vycyouse mynystres in the chirche. **1526** SKELTON *Magnyf.* 33 *Fel.* Here you not howe this gentylman mockys. *Lyb.* Ye, to knackynge ernyst what an it preue? *a* **1553** UDALL *Royster D.* III. ii. (Arb.) 41 Sure, the partie is in good knacking earnest. **1644** BULWER *Chiron.* 82 This knacking adjunct of expression. *Mod. Yorksh. Dial.*, He is a knacking sort of talker.

†'**knackish**, *a. Obs. rare.* [f. KNACK *sb.*² + -ISH¹.] Characterized by knacks or tricks; artful, tricky; artificial.

1660 H. MORE *Myst. Godl.* IX. viii, Beating the Air with knackish forms of gracious speeches and vain grandiloquence. **1694** S. S. *Loyal & Impart. Satirist* 20 With knackish Prayer he does the Poor undoe: So Cain could Sacrifice and Murder too.

Hence †'**knackishness**, artificiality.

1660 H. MORE *Myst. Godl.* x. xiv, A set Form will prevent all Pride and knackishness, and preserve the publick worship in its due reverence and honour.

knackwurst ('nakvuːrst). Also **knockwurst**. [Ger.] A type of German sausage.

1939 M. BRINIG *Anne Minton's Life* (1940) 241 This very second, with us full of beer and knackwurst and sauerkraut .., there's nothing to worry about. **1965** *House & Garden* Jan. 60 *Knockwurst, knackwurst*, a sausage similar to but larger than the frankfurter, and more highly seasoned. **1968** *Washington Post* 5 July A 19/3 (Advt.), Foremost knockwurst, kosher style. **1968** A. WHITNEY *Every Man has his Price* xvii. 147 The waiter came, and they ordered—Knackwurst for Deb, and a dish improbably called Kalbshaxe for Robin. **1970** 'E. LATHEN' *Pick up Sticks* (1971) x. 86 Beer and knockwurst. **1971** *Sunday Times* (Colour Suppl.) 27 June 50/2 *Knackwurst*: not unlike a thicker Frankfurter lightly flavoured with garlic, and also best served hot.

knacky ('nækɪ), *a.* Also 8 **nacky**. [f. KNACK *sb.*² + -Y.] Characterized by or having a knack; artful, clever, adroit, ingenious.

1710 RUDDIMAN *Gloss. Douglas's Virgil* s.v. *Knak*, A knacky man; *i.e.* witty and facetious. **1719** HAMILTON *2nd Ep. Ramsay* xi, Mony a bonny nacky tale. **1828** *Craven Dial.*, *Knacky*, ingenious, fond of knick-knacks. **1880** *Jubilee of Rev. W. Orr Fenwick* 72 His sermons—often exceedingly knacky in their division—were always logical in their structure. **1900** *Daily News* 11 Jan. 7/3 He stoops, with his back to the derailed trucks, and with a knacky sort of jerk gets them on the line again.

knag (næg), *sb.*¹ Forms: 5 **knage**, 5–7 **knagge**, 5, 9 **knagg**, 6– **knag**. [ME. *knag* or *knagge* = G. (orig. LG.) *knagge* knot, peg, etc., whence prob. Da. *knag*, Sw. *knagg*. Gael. *cnag* may be from Sc. KNAG *v.* and KNAGGED, regarded as derivatives of this word, are evidenced before it.]

1. A short spur or stiff projection from the trunk or branch of a tree, as the stunted dead branch of a pine or fir; hence, a peg or hook for hanging anything on.

c **1440** *Syr Gowghter* 194 in Utterson *Early Poetry* I. 169 He made prestes and clerkes to lepe on cragges, Monkes and freres to hong on knagges. *c* **1440** *Bone Flor.* 1795 Take here the golde in a bagg, I schall hyt hynge on a knagg, At the schypp borde ende. **1483** *Cath. Angl.* 204/2 A knage. **1535** LYNDESAY *Satyre* 3090 (Bannatyne MS.) It will hurt bettir, .. Richt now, quhen ye hing on a knag. **1662** in Pitcairn *Crim. Trials* III. 605 It wes hung wp wpon an knag. **18..** HOGG *Tales & Sk.* (1838) III. 250 Where is my cloak?.. It is hanging on one of the wooden knags in the garret.

†**2.** One of the knobs or points of a stag's horn; a tine. *Obs.*

1578 BANNISTER *Hist. Man* I. 3 Sharpe but not so slender, as the knagge of a hartes horne. **1601** HOLLAND *Pliny* II. 324 The ashes of Harts horn serueth.. the very tip and points of the knags are thought more effectuall. **1603** —— *Plutarch's Mor.* 1276 Wonderfull hornes for bignesse, and most dangerous by reason of their sharpe and branching knagges. **1657** W. COLES *Adam in Eden* ccxxxviii, [Leaves] gashed in on both sides into three or four gashes, and pointed at the ends, resembling the Knaggs of a Bucks-horne.

3. A knot in wood, the base of a branch.

1555 W. WATREMAN *Fardle Facions* I. iii. 37 Trees.. of a wondrefull heigth, smothe, and without knagge or knotte. **1639** T. DE GREY *Compl. Horsem.* 41 If the staffe have knags or knots upon it. **1706** PHILLIPS, *Knag*, a Knot in Wood. **1852** SEIDEL *Organ* 44 The knots and knags in the wood are glued over with leather.

4. A pointed rock or crag.

1552 HULOET, Knagge, *scopulus.* **1825** BROCKETT, *Knaggs*, pointed rocks, or rugged tops of hills.

knag, *sb.*² *Sc.* [Origin uncertain: cf. NOGGIN.] A small cask or barrel; a keg.

a **1585** POLWART *Flyting w. Montgomerie* 790 Buttrie bag, fill knag! thou will rag with thy fellows. **1596** *Compt Buik Dav. Wedderburne* (S.H.S.) 46 Ane Knag of Vinacre. **1703** *Rules Edin. Fire Co.* in Maitland *Hist. Edinb.* v. (1753) 329 Threttie sex Stings with Knags.. whereof sex standing full of Water. **1804** W. TARRAS *Poems* 8 (Jam.) To slock our drouth's a knag o' berry brown.

Hence '**knaggie** (*dim.*), a small wooden vessel (of the capacity of a pint or so) with an upright handle. *Sc.*

†**knag**, *sb.*³ *Sc. Obs.* The Woodpecker.

1639 SIR R. GORDON *Gen. Hist. Earls Sutherland* 3 In these fforests.. steares or stirlings, lair-igigh or knag (which is a foull like unto a paroket or parret, which makes place for her nest with her beck in the oak tree). **1769** *De Foe's Tour Gt. Brit.* IV. 261.

†**knag**, *v. Obs.* Also 5 **gnag**. [f. KNAG *sb.*¹] *trans.* To hang, fasten up.

13.. *Gaw. & Gr. Knt.* 577 Greuez With polaynez piched þer-to,.. Aboute his knez knaged wyth knotez of golde. *c* **1450** *Cov. Myst.* xli. (Shaks. Soc.) 384 Sweche schul ben.. gnaggyd up by the gomys tyl the devyl doth hem grone.

knag, etc., early var. NAG *v.*, etc.

†'**knagged**, *a. Obs.* Also 5 **gnaggid**. [f. KNAG *sb.*¹ + -ED².] Furnished with protuberances, knobs, or knots; knobbed, toothed, jagged.

c **1400** *Destr. Troy* 4973 A tre, þat was tried, all of tru gold, .. And frut on yt fourmyt fairest of shap, Of mony kynd þat was knyt [*ed.* 1874 kuyt], knagged aboue. *c* **1430** *Virg. 2nd Compl.* 97 in *Pol., Rel. & L. Poems* 211 Thou scourge maad of ful touȝ skyn, Knottid & gnaggid. **1601** HOLLAND *Pliny* XI. xxxvii, In some she hath made them [horns] knagged and branched, as in Deere. **1631** R. H. *Arraignm. Whole Creature* v. 32 A knagg'd staffe. **1711** J. PETIVER in *Phil. Trans.* XXVII. 394 Narrow, knagged Alatern.

knaggy ('nægɪ), *a.* [f. KNAG *sb.*¹ + -Y.] Abounding in pointed protuberances, knobs, or knots: knotty, rough, rugged.

1552 HULOET, Knaggye, or full of knagges, *scopulosus.* **1569** STOCKER tr. *Diod. Sic.* III. xv. 131 The place was.. so knaggy and hanging that the wayes were inaccessible. **1647** FULLER *Good Th. in Worse T.* (1841) 153 The head of a flail, or flagel, knaggy and knotty. **1729** HOOLE *Comenius' Vis. World* (1777) 38 The elke.. hath knaggy horns. **1853** G. JOHNSTON *Nat. Hist. E. Bord.* I. 96 Old bushes.. all knaggy and wormed.

Hence '**knagginess**.

1727 BAILEY vol. II, *Knagginess*, fulness of Knots, as Wood.

knaidel ('kneɪdəl). Also **knaydl**. Usu. in pl. **knaidlach** ('kneɪdlaç), **kneidlach**. [f. Yiddish *kneydel*, ad. MHG. (and mod.G.) *knödel* KNÖDEL.] A type of dumpling eaten esp. in Jewish households during Passover. Also *transf.*

1951 L. W. LEONARD *Jewish Cookery* i. 6 The *Seder* is a home festival, and every part of it, from *Haggada* to *Knaidlach*, has been enriched with traditions that are passed along to the children from generation to generation. **1955** —— *Jewish Holiday Cook Bk.* 87 Drop.. into rapidly boiling clear soup.. and cook.. till Knaidlach rise to the top. **1960** S. H. RIVKIN *Mama's Meichulim: Trad. Jewish Cooking* 150 Looking down at our faces after the long prayers, Papa would say perceptively, 'Children! They are not so hungry for religion as they are for knaidlach.' **1968** L. ROSTEN *Joys of Yiddish* 185 *Knaydl* is used affectionately for a child.. or to describe a round, fat, chubby woman. **1973** *Times* 3 Feb. 13/4 You can try the kneidlach soup (with matzo-meal dumplings).

knaif, etc., obs. Sc. form of KNAVE, etc.

†**knaifatic**, *a. Sc. Obs. nonce-wd.* [f. *knaif*, KNAVE, after *dogmatic*, etc.] Of the condition or character of a knave; low-born; knavish.

c **1550** LYNDESAY *Peder Coffeis* 33 Knaifatic coff misknawis him sell, Quhen he gettis in a furrit goun.

†**knal**. *Obs. rare*⁻¹. [Echoic: cf. G. *knall* loud report, blow (hence Da. *knald*, Sw. *knall*), Du. *knal*; cf. KNELL *sb.* Mod. dial. (Lincolnsh. etc.) has *knowl*, *knoll* in same sense.] A stroke, knock, esp. on the head.

c **1380** *Sir Ferumb.* 463* On þyn heued y ȝeue þe a knal.

knall-gas ('knælgæs). *Chem.* Also **knallgas** and with capital initial. [a. G. *knallgas*, f. *knall* bang, detonation + *gas* gas.] Any explosive mixture of gases, esp. one of two volumes of hydrogen with one of oxygen.

1899 R. E. BAYNES tr. *Meyer's Kinetic Theory of Gases* iii. 86 (*table*) Knallgas. [*Note*] This is the mixture of hydrogen and oxygen produced by electrically decomposing water. **1923** *Jrnl. Chem. Soc.* CXXIII. 1026 Berthelot measured the *initial* rates of the flame in hydrogen and in carbon monoxide Knall-gas..; he also made a similar series with hydrogen and with ethylene Knall-gas. **1924** *Nature* 8 Mar. 373/2 The explosion of an undiluted 2 CO + O_2 'knall-gas'. **1927** BONE & TOWNEND *Flame & Combustion in Gases* xxxiv. 432 In cases where excess of either hydrogen or oxygen was present in the system, the observed rate was still.. proportional to the partial pressure of the '*knall-gas*' present. **1969** OTTAWAY & IRVINE tr. *Netter's Theoret. Biochem.* iii. 72 The reverse reaction (the Knall-gas reaction) $2H_2 + O_2 = 2H_2O$ releases the same energy [as is absorbed in the forward reaction].

knap (næp), *sb.*¹ Forms: α. 1 **cnæpp**, **cnepp**, 1–2 **cnæp**, 6 **knappe**, (**knape**), 7 **knapp**, 6– **knap**, (7, 9 **nap**). β. **knop**. [OE. *cnæp(p*, top, summit (of a hill); perh. cognate with ON. *knapp-r* knob, head of a stick, button, etc. (see KNOP *sb.*¹). Irish, Gael., and Welsh *cnap*, knob, knop, boss,

button, lump, knap, hillock, knoll, may be from Norse or Eng.]

1. The head, crest, or summit of a hill; a small hill, hillock, or knoll; a rising ground; a short steep ascent. Chiefly *dial.* (Cf. KNOB *sb.*[2], NAB.)

α. *c* **1000** ÆLFRIC *Exod.* xix. 20 Drihten eode uppan þæs muntes cnæp. *c* **1000** *Ags. Gosp.* Luke iv. 29 Hiȝ..læddon hine ofer ðæs muntes cnæpp. **1538** LELAND *Itin.* I. 109 The Castelle..standith..on the very Knape of an highe Hille, stepe up eche way. **1600** F. WALKER *Sp. Mandeville* 102 b, Three men setting vp a poast, vpon a little knap close by the high-way. **1685** *1st Cent. Hist. Springfield* (1899) II. 176 To the first Pine Tree upon the knap or Hill by Stony Brooke side. **1778** *Eng. Gazetteer* (ed. 2) s.v. *Knebworth*, Its situation is on a hill or knap, from whence it has its name. **1876** T. HARDY *Ethelberta* II. xlvi. 235 'Now where's the inn?' said Mountclere... 'Just on the knap', Sol answered. **1887** *Cycl. Tour. Club Gaz.* 215/2 With the exception of a steepish knap on leaving the Doubs Valley,..the road was good and nearly level. **1893** Q. [COUCH] *Delect. Duchy* 19 A ..pathway..winding..around the knap of a green hill.

β. *a* **1548** HALL *Chron., Hen. VI*, 136 The toune of Auraunches, standyng upon the knop of an hill. **1623** BINGHAM *Xenophon* 62 There remained yet a little knop aboue them..where the enemies guards did sit.

2. *fig.* ***knap of the case*** (*obs. Rogues' Cant*), the head or goodman of the house. [Doubtfully placed here.]

c **1550** *Dice-Play* (Percy Soc.) 29 The knapp of the case, the goodman of the house calleth secretly unto him the third person. *Ibid.* 34 A reward unto her by knap of the case, & the cut-throats his accomplices.

knap, *sb.*[2] *Obs.* exc. *dial.* Also 9 nap. [Echoic: goes with KNAP *v.*[1]: cf. KNACK *sb.* and *v.*, and Sw. *knäpp*, Da. *knep*, a rap, fillip. Gael. *cnap*, a sharp blow, may be from Sc.]

1. An abrupt stroke or blow; a smart knock.

c **1400** *Destr. Troy* 6437 Mony strokes,..þo stithe men hym gefe, Till þe knight, vndur knappis, vppon knes fell. **14..** *Sir Beues* (MS. N) 1895 + 4, I wol fonde to ȝeue þe a knap. **1535** STEWART *Cron. Scot.* I. 143 At that counter wes mony crwell knap. **1575** TURBERV. *Faulconrie* 100 You myght chaunce to catch a knappe of hir beake. **1603** OWEN *Pembrokeshire* (1892) 280, I have by it gotten store of Knappes on my head and shoulders. **1737** RAMSAY *Scot. Prov.* (1750) 109 When the lady lets a pap, the messan gets a knap. **1828** *Craven Dial.*, *Knap*, a blow.

b. The sound of a sharp blow.

1870 LUBBOCK *Orig. Civiliz.* ix. (1875) 408 Sounds..The collision of hard bodies..as clap, rap, tap, knap, snap.

2. The clapper of a mill.

1622 J. TAYLOR (Water P.) *A Thiefe* Wks. (1630) II. 119/2 A fellow..hearing neither noyse of knap or tiller, Laid downe his corne, and went to seeke the miller.

†**3.** A cheating trick with dice: see quots. s.v. KNAPPING *vbl. sb. Obs.*

a **1658** CLEVELAND *Wks.* (1687) 200 Doublets? or Knap? The Cog? low Dice? or high? *a* **1680** BUTLER *Rem.* (1759) I. 83 Engages blind and senseless Hap 'Gainst High, and Low, and Slur, and Knap.

knap, variant form of KNOP *sb.*[1] and [2].

knap (næp), *v.*[1] Now *dial.* Forms: α. 5– knap, 5–6 knapp, 9 nap. β. 5–7 knop. [Echoic, going with KNAP *sb.*[2]; cf. Du. and G. (orig. LG.) *knappen* to crack, crackle, etc.; to break (a thing) with a sharp crack. Gael. *cnap* to strike, knock, is prob. from Sc. As in the case of other words that express an action by an imitation of its sound, the sense diverges in various directions, according as the sound or the action is prominent. In *knack* we think more of the sound, in *knap* of the stroke and its result.]

1. *trans.* To strike with a hard short sound; to knack, knock, rap.

α. *c* **1470** HENRYSON *Mor. Fab.* IX. (*Wolf & Fox*) iii, Thow can knap doun caponis on the nicht. **1550** COVERDALE *Spir. Perle* vi. (1588) 63 The heuenly scholemaster knappeth vs on the fingers, til we apprehend and learne his will. **1626** BACON *Sylva* §133 Knap a pair of Tongs some depth within the Water, and you shall hear the Sound of the Tongs well. **1895** CROCKETT *Men of Moss Hags* iii. 27 It was ever his wont.. to knap his toes on the edge of the step.

β. *c* **1460** *Towneley Myst.* xxi. 408, I can my hand vphefe and knop out the skalys.

b. *absol.* or *intr.*

1535 STEWART *Cron. Scot.* II. 467 This Gregour gaif him feild,..knappit on quhill mony ane wes keild. **1676** WISEMAN *Surg.* VII. v. (R.), The people standing by heard it knap in, and the patient declared it by the ease she felt. **1886** *Gd. Words* 86 The noise my crutches made knap, knapping up and down the deck.

2. *trans.* To break into parts or pieces with a sharp cracking sound; to snap or break by a smart blow. Now used *spec.* of the breaking of flints or of stones for the roads: cf. KNAPPER[3].

1535 COVERDALE *Ps.* xlv[i]. 9 He hath knapped the speare in sonder. *a* **1572** KNOX *Hist. Ref.* Wks. 1846 I. 147 Rockettis war rent, typettis war torne, crounis war knapped. **1647** FANSHAWE *Pastor Fido* (1676) 120 Pil'd in one heap dogs slain, spears knapt, men wounded. **1648** HERRICK *Hesper., Bracelet to Julia*, 'Tis but silke that bindeth thee, Knap the thread and thou art free. **1820** J. CLELAND *Glasgow* 107, 330 persons knapping stones for the road. **1862** *Instructor* I. 122 Picking up flints and knapping them, as the method of breaking them is called.

β. **1675** *Depos. Cast. York* (Surtees) 218, 8 halfe crownes, ..the said Auty clipt that night, for she heard the knoping of them, being in the next room.

b. *intr.* To break off short; to snap.

1545 ASCHAM *Toxoph.* II. (Arb.) 111 The string..beynge sore twined must nedes knap in sunder. **1623** GOUGE *Serm. Extent God's Provid.* §15 The Summier..being overburdened..knapt suddenly asunder in the midst.

3. *trans.* To break *off* by a smart blow, stroke, or tap; to strike or knock *off*.

1600 HOLLAND *Livy* I. liv. 38 With his rod..he knapt of the uppermost heads and tops of the poppies. **1710** T. FULLER *Pharm. Extemp.* 170 A Scorbutic Foment.. knappeth off the sharp points of the Salt. **1830** GALT *Lawrie T.* IV. i. (1849) 143 He took the cigar from his lips, and knapped off the ashes.

4. To utter smartly; to talk, chatter (a language): = CRACK *v.* 5. Also *intr. Sc.* and *north. dial.*

In quot. 1886 said of the stonechat, 'so called from the similarity between its alarm note and the striking together of two pebbles' (Swainson *Prov. Names Brit. Birds* 1885).

1581 J. HAMILTON *Facile Treat., Quest. Ministers* xiii, King James the fyft,..hering ane of his subjectis knap suddrone, declarit him ane traiteur. **1681** COLVIL *Whigs Supplic.* I. (1695) 56 Like Highland Lady's knoping speeches. *c* **1690** *Lintoun Addr. to Prince of Orange* in Watson *Coll. Sc. Poems* (1706) I. 20 English Andrew, who has Skill, To knap at every word so well. **1812** SCOTT *Let. to Morritt* 29 Nov. in *Lockhart*, He answered..that he could knap English with any one. **1816** —— *Old Mort.* vii, Ilka auld wife in the chimley-neuk will be for knapping doctrine wi' doctors o' divinity. **1886** MARY LINSKILL *Haven under Hill* II. xi. 147 There was a stone-chat knapping out its song.

knap (næp), *v.*[2] Now *dial.* [Cf. GNAP *v.* and KNAB *v.*; also Du. and G. (orig.LG.) *knappen* to crack, snap, bite, which unites the senses of this and the prec. In Eng. also, the sense 'snap' seems to unite this with sense 2 of KNAP *v.*[1] See also KNEP *v.*]

intr. and *trans.* To bite in a short or abrupt way; to snap; to nibble.

1575 TURBERV. *Faulconrie* 141 If she chaunce to knappe or byte at the sticke let hir bite hardly. **1596** SHAKS. *Merch. V.* III. i. 10 As lying a gossip..as euer knapt ginger. **1611** COTGR., *Brouter*, to brouze; to knap, or nible off the sprigs, buds, barke &c., of plants. **1617** *Janua Linguarum* 22 Mules knap one another. **1721** STRYPE *Eccl. Mem.* I. I. xxxi. 222 These Eliot compared to a galled horse..always knapping and kicking at such examples and sentences as they felt sharp. **1819** W. TENNANT *Papistry Storm'd* (1827) 52 Some knapp'd awa' at kebbuck-stumps. **1821** CLARE *Vill. Minstr.* II. 106 Horses..turn'd to knap each other at their ease.

knap, obs. form of NAP *sb.* and *v.*

†**'knap-bottle.** *Herb. Obs.* The Bladder-campion, *Silene inflata*, so called from its inflated calyx which snaps when suddenly compressed.

1640 PARKINSON *Theat. Bot.* 263 Some with us call it Knap bottle, and others Spatling or Frothy Poppy.

knape. *Obs.* exc. *dial.* Forms: 1 cnapa, 2–3 cnape, 3–6 (8 *dial.*) knape, 6 *Sc.* knaip, 7 (9 *dial.*) knap. [OE. *cnapa* = OFris. *knapa*, ODu. *knapo* (MDu. *knape*, Du. *knaap*), MLG. (hence MHG.) *knape*, ON. *knapi* (ODa. and OSw. *knape*):—OTeut. **knapon-*. The ulterior etym. and relation to OE. *cnafa*, knave, are uncertain: see note to KNAVE.]

†**1.** A male child, a boy (= KNAVE *sb.* 1); a lad, young man, youth, fellow. *Obs.*

c **1000** ÆLFRIC *Gen.* xxi. 19 Heo of þam sealde þam cnapan drincan. *c* **1200** ORMIN 4106 To clippenn swa þe cnapess shapp. *c* **1250** *Gen. & Ex.* 2573 Ðe knapes to deade giuen, And leten ðe mayden childre liuen. *c* **1300** *Arth. & Merl.* 7821 Ac right now a litel knape To Bedingham com with iape. **13..** *Gaw. & Gr. Knt.* 2136 þaȝe he be a sturn knape.

†**2.** A man-servant, male attendant, 'man': = KNAVE *sb.* 2. *Obs.*

c **1000** ÆLFRIC *Gen.* xxii. 19 Abraham þa ȝecyrde sona to hys cnapum. *c* **1000** *Ags. Gosp.* Matt. viii. 6 Min cnapa lið on minum huse lama. *c* **1250** *Gen. & Ex.* 477 His knape wende it were a der. **1390** GOWER *Conf.* III. 321 This cherles knape Hath lad this maiden ther he wolde. **1508** DUNBAR *Tua Mariit Wemen* 125, I dar nought keik to the knaip that the cop fillis. **1513** DOUGLAS *Æneis* XII. ii. 87 The byssy knaipis and verlettis of his stabill.

b. *dial.* A thatcher's requisite. (See quots.)

1764 BURN *Poor Laws* 127 The thatchers to this day have an instrument that holds their straw, which they call a knape. **1895** *East Anglia Gloss.*, *Knape* or *Knave*, the frame which contains the straw which is carried up the ladder to the thatcher.

3. As term of contempt or reprobation (also jocularly): A rascal, rogue, knave: = KNAVE *sb.* 3. *Obs.* exc. *dial.*

a **1450** LYDG. *Merita Missæ* 190 Prowde knapys, That make in holy chyrche Iapis. **1513** DOUGLAS *Æneis* IX. ix. 77 Turnus..Thus dyd hym chyde: O cative rakles knaip. *a* **1553** UDALL *Royster D.* v. vi. (Arb.) 88 Good night Roger olde knaue, knaue, knap. **1855** ROBINSON *Whitby Gloss.*, *A Knap*, a person not strictly honest. .. 'A regular knap'.

4. *attrib.*, as †**knape child** (= KNAVE-CHILD).

c **1200** ORMIN 7903 Forr cnapechild is afledd wel Affterr weppmanne kind. *c* **1250** *Gen. & Ex.* 2585 Euerilc knape child of ðat kin, ben a-non don ðe flod wið-in.

knapholt, knappald, var. KNAPPLE *sb. Obs.*

†**'knappan.** *Obs.* [Welsh *cnapan*, deriv. of *cnap* knob, lump, round piece.] An old Welsh game in which a wooden ball was hurled through the air by successive players, each side endeavouring to drive it as far as possible in one direction; also the ball with which this game was played.

1573 PHAER *Æneid* VII. *marg.*, This play is yet used in Wales, and the ball is called Knappan. **1603** OWEN *Pembrokeshire* (1892) 271 Of these Knappan daies in Penbrokshere there were wont to be fyve in nomber. *Ibid.* 273 There is a rounde bowle prepared..of some massye wood,..and should be boyled in tallow, for to make it slipperye, and harde to be holden, this bowle is called Knappan, and..he that catcheth it hurleth it towardes the countrey he playeth for, for gole, or appointed place.

Hence †**'knappaner**, a player at this game.

1603 OWEN *Pembrokeshire* (1892) 280 Saw none but himselfe and this old rude Knappaner in place.

knapped (næpt), *ppl. a.* [f. KNAP *v.*[1] + -ED[1].] Broken by a sharp blow, broken off short.

1861 *Times* 28 Sept., Advt., Freehold Villa Residence,.. in the style of the domestic architecture of the 14th century, most substantially built of knapped flints, interlaced with brickwork and with dressings of Bath stone. **1899** *Daily News* 16 Sept. 7/6 The fragment of a bridge;..a fine piece of work, with alternations of stone and knapped flints.

knappell, var. KNEPPEL *Obs.*, clapper of a bell.

†**knapper**[1]. *Sc. Obs. rare.* In 6 -ar. [Jamieson suggests derivation from KNAPE.] 'A boor, a menial' (Jam.).

1513 DOUGLAS *Æneis* VIII. Prol. 121 Grathit lyke sum knappar [*Camb. MS.* gnappar].

†**knapper**[2]. *Obs.* [f. KNAP *v.*[2] + -ER[1].] One who bites abruptly, or snaps.

1500–20 DUNBAR *Poems* xxvii. 10 Off seme byttaris and beist knapparis. **1611** COTGR., *Rongeur*, a gnawer, knapper, nibler.

knapper[3] ('næpə(r)). *dial.* and *local.* [f. KNAP *v.*[1] + -ER[1].] One who or that which 'knaps'; one who knaps or breaks stones, flints, or the like; *esp.* one whose occupation is the shaping of flints by strokes of a hammer.

1870 *Spectator* 13 Aug. 976 They [flints] then pass into the hands of the 'knapper'. His implements are a small anvil, called a 'stake', set obliquely..and a 'knapping-hammer' of fine steel, of which the face is set obliquely also... One smart blow strikes off the rough end, another detaches a piece of the proper size for a gun-flint. **1894** *Athenæum* 27 Jan. 111/1 'Knapping' flints, as practised on Brandon Heath, in Suffolk, is exceedingly hard work, though there the 'knapper' labours for 'his own hand'.

b. A hammer used for shaping flints; also, *Sc.* a stone-breaker's hammer; a knapping-hammer.

1787 SHIRREF *Jamie & Bess* IV. i, A finer lad..ne'er cocked his knapper to the lift. **1882** *Athenæum* 16 Dec. 818/1 Palæolithic implements,..together with the flint tools, or knappers, by which they were shaped. *Ibid.* 818/2 Neolithic knappers were shown,..with knapping hammers of the seventeenth or eighteenth century.

'knapper[4]. *slang.* or *dial.* Also **knepper, napper.** The knee.

1764 T. BRYDGES *Homer Travest.* (1797) I. 237 The bully on his bare Kneppers knelt down. *Ibid.* II. 243 On his knappers down he dropp'd. **1877** *N.W. Linc. Gloss.*, *Nappers*, the knees.

'knapping, *vbl. sb.* [f. KNAP *v.*[1] + -ING[1].] The action of KNAP *v.*[1]; the action of striking or knocking; **a.** *spec.* a form of cheating in throwing dice (see quots., and cf. KNAP *sb.*[2] 3); **b.** in mod. local use, the action of breaking stones or flints.

a. 1680 KIRKMAN *Eng. Rogue* IV. 226 Knapping, is when you strike one Die dead. **1822** SCOTT *Nigel* xxiii, Men talk of high and low dice,..topping, knapping, slurring.

b. 1835 CARLYLE *Let.* in Froude *Life in Lond.* (1884) I. i. 24 Walk out of this if even into the knapping of stones. **1887** *Magazine of Art* X. 406 The third process, or 'knapping'... Holding the flake or strip of flint with its face uppermost upon a 'stake' of iron [etc.]. **1892** *Daily News* 2 Dec. 6/1 There has never been a cessation of the Brandon flint 'knapping'.

c. *attrib.*, as ***knapping-hammer, -machine, -tool.***

1785 BURNS *1st Ep. to Lapraik* xi, Ye'd better taen up spades and shools Or knappin-hammers. **1883** *Archæol. Cant.* XV. 103, I have..discovered numerous flint hammers, and knapping tools.

†**'knappish**, *a. Obs.* exc. *dial.* [f. KNAP *v.*[2] + -ISH[1]. Cf. *snappish.*] Rudely abrupt or froward, testy.

1513 MORE in Grafton *Chron.* (1568) II. 809 He rejected the Dukes request with many spitefull and knappishe wordes. **1542** UDALL *Erasm. Apoph.* (1877) 165 A certaine saucie or knappishe young springall. **1577–87** STANYHURST in Holinshed *Chron.* I. 35/1 Answering your snappish 'Quid' with a knappish 'Quo'. **1629** Z. BOYD *Last Battell* 169 Your spirit is so knappish and way-ward.

Hence †**'knappishly** *adv.*, †**'knappishness.**

1549 CHALONER *Erasm on Folly* T iij b, If ought shall seeme to you to have been saied..more knappishely. **1573–80** BARET *Alv.* F 1154 Frowardly..malapertly, knappishly, *proteruè.* **1617** MINSHEU *Ductor*, Knappish, knappishnesse.

†**knapple, knappel**, *sb. Sc. Obs.* Also **knappald, knapholt.** [Scotch variant of *clappalde, -olde,*

CLAPHOLT; app. with substitution of *knap* for *clap*.] = CLAPBOARD.

1496 *Ld. Treas. Acc. Scot.* I. 285 Item, for leding of ixᵉ knapholtis furth of Leith to the Castel of Edinburgh..iijs. iiijd. *Ibid.* 278 Item..for ixᵉ knappaldis..iiij *li.* xs. *c* **1575** *Balfour's Practicks, Custumis* (1754) 88 The great hundreth knapple, contenand xxiiij small hundrethis. **1661** *Sc. Acts Chas. II*, c. 33 (Jam.) That the whole coupers..make the said salmond barrels of good and sufficient new knappel. **1707** G. MIEGE *St. Gt. Brit.* II. 30 Pitch, Steel-Kits, Knapple, Oak, Wainscoat. **1753** MAITLAND *Hist. Edinb.* III. 248 For every hundred of Dantzic Knappel..4 pennies. [**1898** *Compt Buik Dav. Wedderburne* (S.H.S.) Introd. 44 The Norwegian timber consisted of..roofspars, knapholt and burnwood.]

† **'knapple,** *v.*¹ *Obs.* In 7 knaple. [Frequentative of KNAP *v.*²: see -LE and cf. KNABBLE.] To bite shortly and repeatedly; to nibble.

1611 COTGR., *Grignoter*,..to gnaw, knaple, or nible away. **1847-78** HALLIWELL, *Knapple*, to bite, or nibble. *North.*

† **'knapple,** *v.*² *Obs. rare*⁻⁰. [Frequentative of KNAP *v.*¹; see -LE.] = KNAP *v.*¹ 2, 3.

1755 JOHNSON, *Knapple*, to break off with a sharp quick noise. *Ainsworth.*

'knappy, *a.* Now *dial.* [f. KNAP *sb.* and *v.* + -Y.] (See quots.)

1552 HULOET, Knappye, or full of knappes, *verrucosus.* **1855** ROBINSON *Whitby Gloss.*, *Nappy*, ill-natured, testy. 'As nappy and as nasty as you please.' [E.D.D. *Knappy*, snappish.] **1887** JAMIESON *Suppl.*, *Knappy*, in small roundish lumps, abounding in small lumps; Orkn.

knappy, obs. form of NAPPY.

knapsack ('næpsæk). [a. LG. *knapsack* (Du. *knapzak*, G. *knappsack*), first recorded in 16th c. The first element is somewhat obscure, but is generally taken as LG. and Du. *knappen* = KNAP *v.*², G. *knapp* eating, food; cf. also SNAPSACK. Also adopted in F. (about 1600) as *canapsa* (now obs.).]

a. A bag or case of stout canvas or leather, worn by soldiers, strapped to the back and used for carrying necessaries; any similar receptacle used by travellers for carrying light articles.

1603 DRAYTON *Bar. Wars* I. (R.), Each one fills his knapsack or his scrip With some rare thing that on the field is found. **1608** CAPT. SMITH *True Relat.* Wks. (Arb.) 20 One that vsually carried my Gowne and Knapsacke after me. **1645** *Mass. Col. Rec.* (1854) III. 40 Every souldier..with muskett, sword, bandaleers, and knapsacke. **1793** BURNS *Sodger's Return* i, My humble knapsack a' my wealth, A poor but honest sodger. **1858** LYTTON *What will He do* I. xix, He packed up his knapsack, and started for the train. **1868** *Regul. & Orders Army* §604 d, The havresack is to be worn on all occasions when the knapsack is worn.

fig. *a* **1658** CLEVELAND *Char. Country-Comm.-man* Wks. (1687) 76 A short-handed Clerk, tack'd to the Rear of him to carry the Knapsack of his Understanding. **1841-4** EMERSON *Ess., Nature* Wks. (Bohn) I. 224 The knapsack of custom falls off his back.

b. *attrib.* **knapsack pump** = *knapsack sprayer*; **knapsack sprayer** (or **spray**), a sprayer consisting of a hand-held nozzle supplied from a pressurized reservoir that is carried on the back like a knapsack.

1633 SHIRLEY *Yng. Admiral* I. ii, *Vittori.* He is valiant truly That dares forget to be rewarded. *Soldier.* This Is but cold comfort for a knapsack-man. **1823** CRABB *Technol. Dict.* s.v. *Drill*, 'Knapsack-Drill', a sort of punishment for minor offences, which consists in marching soldiers round the barrack-yard, &c. for a certain time, with 6 or 12 lb. shot tied to their knapsacks. **1894** *Country Gentlemen's Catal.* 302/2 Vermorel's knapsack pumps. **1897** *Sears Roebuck Catal.* 162/3 The Celebrated Myers Knapsack Spray Pump. **1899** *Westm. Gaz.* 16 Nov. 12/2 An Oxford Bible..printed on Oxford India paper..and bound in khaki..will be known as the Knapsack Bible, and is specially designed for use by soldiers and sailors. **1909** *Cent. Dict.* Suppl. s.v. *sprayer, Knapsack sprayer.* **1944** *Living off Land* vii. 153 Firefighting weapons are many and varied... The knapsack pump—a 4-gallon container with shoulder straps, brass hand pump and nozzle—is most effective. **1950** *N.Z. Jrnl. Agric.* Feb. 177/2 Obtaining complete coverage of tall [orchard] trees with a knapsack sprayer is most difficult. **1971** *Community* (E. Afr. Community) Apr. 8/1 The new method could well replace the present widespread use of knapsack sprayers which was considered inefficient in insecticide application.

Hence **'knapsacking** *vbl. sb.* (cf. *coaching, training*), travelling with a knapsack; **'knapsackwise** *adv.*, in the manner of a knapsack.

1877 H. DRUMMOND in G. A. Smith *Life* v. (1898) 115, I was glad to..go knapsacking with Professor Geikie. **1886** *Ibid.* xi. 269, I have often marked this spot in my knapsacking days. **1899** *Blackw. Mag.* Aug. 162/1 A large basket carried knapsackwise.

knapsacked ('næpsækt), *a.* [f. KNAPSACK + -ED².] Equipped with a knapsack.

1905 *Westm. Gaz.* 26 Aug. 3/1 The knapsacked mountaineers come and go. **1908** HARDY *Dynasts* III. II. ii. 76 The sunset slants an ochreous shine Upon the English knapsacked line. **1926** R. MACAULAY *Crewe Train* I. i. 5 Knapsacked British walkers.

† **knapscall.** *Sc. Obs.* Forms: 5 knapescall, 6 knapscall, -scull, -shal, -ska, -skaw, -scha, knopska, 6-7 knapiskay, 7 knapskall, -schaw, 9 *arch.* knapskull. [The first element has been supposed to be KNAPE *sb.*, lad, attendant, man, or its possessive *knap's*; the second is doubtful.]

Some kind of helmet or headpiece; generally worn by persons of inferior rank; perhaps originally by the servants of the men-at-arms.

1498 in *Durham Eccl. Proc.* (Surtees) 42 Galea, Anglicè a Salet or knapescall. *a* **1572** KNOX *Hist. Ref.* Wks. 1846 I. 150 To address thame selves in thare most warlyk array, with jack, knapscall, splent, speir, and axe. **1572** *Satir. Poems Reform.* xxxiii. 264 To ride furth to the weir, With Jak and Sword, gude hors, Knapscull, and speir. **1586** J. CARMICHAEL *Let.* in *Wodrow Soc. Misc.* (1844) I. 442 He did use you to go before uthers..with the reade Knapska. **1609** SKENE *Reg. Maj.* 6 b (*Acts Will.* c. 23) Ane habergeon, ane knapiskay of iron, ane sword, ane dagger. [**1820** SCOTT *Abbot* xxvi, Get on your jacks, plate-sleeves, and knapsculls.]

† **'knapscap.** *Sc. Obs.* App. an altered form of prec.; conformed to *cap*.

a **1802** *Jamie Telfer* xxxv. in Child *Ballads* VII. cxc. (1890) 7/2 Willie was stricken ower the head, And through the knapscap the sword has gane. **1830** R. CHAMBERS *Jas. I*, I. iii. 94 We find..knapscaps burnished up.

knapweed ('næpwi:d). [Orig. *knopweed*, f. KNOP *sb.*¹ + WEED *sb.*; from the hard rounded involucre.] The common name of species of *Centaurea* (N.O. *Compositæ*), esp. *C. nigra*, a common weed with a hard tough stem, and light purple flowers set on a hard rough dark-coloured globular 'head' or involucre.

α. **14..** *MS. Laud* 553 lf. 13 *Iasia nigra*..is an herbe yᵗ me clepitth maidfeloun or bolwes or yrnehard or knopwed. **1530** PALSGR. 236/2 Knoppe wede an herbe. **1691** RAY *Coll. Words* Postscr. 171 For Knapweed, Knopweed, because of the knops at the top. **1787** WITHERING *Brit. Plants* (ed. 2), Knopweed. **1863** PRIOR *Plant-n.*, Knap-weed, Knop-, or Knob-weed.

β. **1597** GERARDE *Herbal* II. ccxxxviii. 588 Matfellon or blacke Knapweede is doubtlesse a kinde of Scabious..the flowers do grow at the top of the stalks, being first small scaly knops, like to the knops of Corne flower. **1656** W. COLES *Art of Simpling* 38 Some grow in knaps like bottles as knapweed. **1785** MARTYN *Rousseau's Bot.* xxvi. (1794) 401 Common or Black Knapweed..which the country people in some places call Hard-heads. **1896** R. F. HORTON in *Sunday Mag.* Nov. 722 Within the enclosure were ragwort, knapweed, and scabious.

knar (nɑ:(r)). Forms: 3-4 knarre, 7, 9 knare, 9 knar, knaur; 5, 7 gnarre 9 gnar(r, 9- gnaur. [ME. *knarre* = LG. *knarre(n*, Du. *knar* stump (of an old tree), knot, knob. Cf. KNUR.

The history in Eng. is obscure. From 14th to 19th c. there are app. no genuine examples of its use, Dryden's *knare* (copied by later writers) being based on *knarie*, KNARRY in Chaucer. The spelling with *gn-*, usual in recent glossaries, may be partly due to *gnarled*.]

1. A rugged rock or stone. Now *dial.*

a **1250** *Owl & Night.* 999 That lond nis god,..Ac wildernisse hit is and weste, Knarres and cludes. **13..** *Gaw. & Gr. Knt.* 2166 Hyȝe bonkkez & brent..& ruȝe knokled knarrez, with knorned stonez. **1837** THORNBER *Hist. Blackpool* 184 (E.D.D.) Gnarrs are large beds of stones, covered with incrustations formed by insects for their habitations.

2. A knot in wood; *spec.* a mass orginating in an abortive branch, forming a protuberance covered with bark, on the trunk or root of a tree.

1382 WYCLIF *Wisd.* xiii. 13 A crokid tree, and ful of knarres [**1388** knottis]. **1623** COCKERAM, *Gnarre*, a hard knot in wood. **1700** DRYDEN *Palamon & Arc.* 1146 Prickly stubs, instead of trees,..Or woods with knots and knares deformed and old. **1805** MISS SEWARD in Polwhele *Trad. & Recoll.* (1826) II. 572 The..knots and knares with which it was covered. **1814** CARY *Dante's Inf.* XIII. 4 Not light The boughs and tapering, but with knares deform'd. **1854** MISS BAKER *Northampt. Gloss.* s.v. (E.D.D.), The stick with which the game is played, having a gnar or knot at the end of it. **1869** MASTERS *Veg. Terat.* 419 Knaurs may occasionally be used for purposes of propagation. **1869** M. T. MASTERS *Veget. Teratol.* 158 The huge gnaurs and burrs met with occasionally on some trees often produce great quantities..of roots. **1900** B. D. JACKSON *Gloss. Bot. Terms*, *Gnaurs*, burrs or knotty excrescences on tree-trunks or roots, probably from clusters of adventitious buds. **1903** F. W. BURBIDGE *Let. to W. T. Thiselton-Dyer* 20 June (MS.), I beg to hand you a 'gnaur' or swollen, arrested branch of a Tulip tree.

† **3.** A knotted, thick-set fellow. *Obs.*

c **1386** CHAUCER *Prol.* 549 He was short scholdred, brood, a thikke knarre [*so most MSS.*; *Lansd.* gnarre].

Hence **knarred** (nɑ:d) *a.*, knotted, gnarled.

1849 LONGF. *Building of the Ship* 59 The knarred and crooked cedar knees. **1856** AIRD *Poet. Wks.* 19 Gnared with knots and knobs.

knark (nɑ:k). *slang.* [Cf. Da. *knark* an old crabbed person; but see also NARK *sb.* 2.] A hard-hearted, unfeeling person.

1851 MAYHEW *Lond. Labour* I. 343 (Hoppe) He was a good man; he couldn't refuse a dog,..but he had a butler, a regular 'knark'.

knarl (nɑ:l). *rare.* [Related to KNAR; cf. *knur* and *knurl*.]

† **1.** A tangle, knot. *Obs.*

1598 GRENEWEY *Tacitus, Ann.* III. ii. (1622) 65 The poison was found hidden in a knarle of her haire.

2. *dial.* 'A hunch-backed or dwarfish man' (Brockett *N.C. Gloss.* 1825).

knarle, knarled, obs. ff. GNARL, -ED.

knarr, var. KNORR.

knarry ('nɑ:rɪ), *a.* *rare.* Also 7, 9 **gnarry**. [f. KNAR + -Y.] Having knars or knots; knotty.

c **1386** CHAUCER *Knt.'s T.* 1119 A forest..With knotty knarry [*Thynne's ed.* knarie] bareyne trees olde, Of stubbes sharpe. **1567** TURBERV. tr. *Ovid's Epist.* 22 This rygor to the woods and knarrie trees expell. *Ibid.* 23 My brothers bones with baleful blowes of knarrie clubbe he brake. **1613** R. CAWDREY *Table Alph.*, *Knarry*, knotty, stubbie. **1623** COCKERAM II, Knotty, *Gnarry.* **1882** SWINBURNE *Athens* 7 in *Tristr. Lyonesse* 179 Boughs all gaunt and gnarry.

knash, obs. or erron. variant of GNASH *v.*

c **1600** BUREL *Pilgr.* in Watson *Coll. Sc. Poems* (1706) II. 25 Sick hashing and knashing, Cums not of cleinlie cukis. **1826** J. DOYLE *Ess. Cath. Claims* 248 Some tub for a whale of prejudice to knash its teeth against.

knast, variant of GNAST *sb.*

c **1440** CAPGRAVE *Life St. Kath.* I. 159 Ovre wyt on-to his wyt is but a knast.

‖ **'knaster,** German spelling of CANASTER 2, a kind of tobacco.

1798 FERRIAR *Illustr. Sterne* 306-7 Who Knaster loves not, be he doom'd to feed With Caffres foul, or suck Virginia's weed... But Knaster always, Knaster is my song, In studious gloom, or 'mid th' assembly's throng. **1853** *Blackw. Mag.* LXXIV. 132 The dried leaves, coarsely broken, are sold as canaster or knaster. **1858** CARLYLE *Fredk. Gt.* v. vii. (1872) II. 118 Long Dutch pipe in the mouth of each man; supplies of knaster easily accessible.

knat, obs. form of GNAT¹ and ².

knatch, variant of KNETCH *v.* *Obs.*

knau(e, knaulag(e, obs. ff. KNOW *v.*, KNOWLEDGE.

knauling: see KNAVE-LINE.

† **knavate.** *Obs. nonce-wd.* A knave.

a **1529** SKELTON *Epitaphe* Poet. Wks. 1843 I. 170 *Fratres, orate*, For this knauate, By the holy rode, Dyd neuer man good.

knave (neɪv), *sb.* Forms: 1 cnafa, 3 cnafe, 3-4 cnaue, 3-7 knaue, (4-5 knawe, knaf(e, 5 knaffe, 5-6 *Sc.* knaif(f), 4- knave. [OE. *cnafa* = OHG. *knabo*, *chnabe* (MHG. and G. *knabe*):—OTeut. **knabon-*. The relation between this and the synonymous *cnapa*, KNAPE (q.v.) is not clear.

OHG. had also *knappo* (MHG. and G. *knappe*): on the supposed relationship between this and *knabo*, see Streitberg *Urgerm. Gram.* p. 151.]

† **1.** A male child, a boy. *Obs.*

a **1050** *Liber Scintill.* lv. (1889) 172/19 Na ȝedafenað þam se to fulfremednysse hoȝað, gamenian mid cnafan [L. *cum paruulo*]. *c* **1205** LAY. 292 þa þe time com: þat þe cnaue wes iboren. *c* **1250** *Gen. & Ex.* 1151 So ðat he haueð..on eiðer here a knaue bi-geten. *a* **1300** *Cursor M.* 10267 þe lagh.. Biclepis þat man for maledight þat has na barn, ne mai ne knaue. *c* **1375** *Sc. Leg. Saints* xvi. (*Magdalena*) 362 Grant ws grace a barne to hafe, othire a madyne or a knaf. *c* **1460** *Towneley Myst.* xiii. 554 Is youre chyld a knave?

2. A boy or lad employed as a servant; hence, a male servant or menial in general; one of low condition. (Freq. opposed to *knight*.) Now *arch.*

c **1000** *Ags. Ps.* (Spelman) lxxxv. 16 (Bosw.) Syle mihte cnafan þinum [L. *puero tuo*]. *a* **1225** *Ancr. R.* 380 þe kokes knaue, þet wassheð þe disshes iðe kuchene. *a* **1300** *Cursor M.* 3153 He bad cum wit him knaues tua. **1393** LANGL. *P. Pl.* C. VI. 54 Men sholde constreyne no clerke to knauene werkes. *a* **1420** HOCCLEVE *De Reg. Princ.* 506 There may no lord take up a newe gise, But that a knave shalle the same uptake. **1509** HAWES *Past. Pleas.* xxix. (1845) 135 Icham a gentylman of much noble kynne, Thoughe Iche be clad in a knaves skynne. **1600** DYMMOK *Ireland* (1843) 7 Every Horseman hath two or thre horses, and to every horse a knave. **1697** DRYDEN *Virg. Past.* III. 22 What Nonsense wou'd the Fool thy Master prate, When thou, his Knave, canst talk at such a rate! **1820** SCOTT *Monast.* xii, A man seeks but his awn, and yet folk shall hold him for both miller and miller's man, that is miller and knave. **1825** —— *Talism.* xx, Thou art an apt, and wilt doubtless be a useful, knave.

3. An unprincipled man, given to dishonourable and deceitful practices; a base and crafty rogue. (Now the main sense. Often contrasted with *fool*.)

In early use the sense may have been 'one of low or ignoble character', 'a mean person'.

c **1205** LAY. 16303 For vnwis is þe king,..& a cnaue is his broðer. **13..** *E.E. Allit. P.* B. 855 What! he wonded no woþe of wekked knauez. **1481** in *Eng. Gilds* (1870) 315 Yf any Brother..dysspysse anoder, callenge hym knaffe, or horson, or deffe, or any yoder mysname. **1500-20** DUNBAR *Poems* xxviii. 39 In Hevin ȝe salbe sanctis full cleir, Thocht ȝe be knavis in this cuntre. **1555** EDEN *Decades* 33 His accusers were nowghtye felowes, abhominable knaues & vylaynes. **1668** PEPYS *Diary* 29 Jan., The veriest knave and bufflehead that ever he saw in his life. **1726** SWIFT *Gulliver* I. vi, The honest dealer is always undone, and the knave gets the advantage. **1800** WELLINGTON *Let. to Lieut. Col. Close* in Gurw. *Desp.* (1837) I. 258 The common practice is to accuse a man of being either a fool or a knave. **1847** TENNYSON *Princ.* IV. 110 Knaves are men, That lute and flute fantastic tenderness, And dress the victim to the offering up.

b. In various proverbial expressions.

1546 J. HEYWOOD *Prov.* (1867) 29 Two false knaues neede no broker, men say. *Ibid.*, Some saie also, it is mery when knaues meete. *Ibid.* 47 An olde knaue is no childe. **1617**

MORYSON *Itin.* III. 5 Thus the English Prouerb saith, No knaue to the learned knaue.

c. Jocularly, or without seriously implying bad qualities (cf. *rogue*, *rascal*). Now *rare*.

a **1553** UDALL *Royster D.* III. iii. (Arb.) 46 Good night Roger olde knaue! **1605** SHAKS. *Lear* I. iv. 107 How now, my pretty knaue, how dost thou? **1670** EACHARD *Cont. Clergy* 4 Lads, that are arch knaves at the nominative case. **1848** THACKERAY *Van. Fair* v, A roar would follow from all the circle of young knaves, usher and all.

4. In playing-cards: The lowest court card of each suit, bearing the representation of a soldier or servant; the jack.

1568 FULWELL *Like Will to Like* in Hazl. *Dodsley* III. 309 (*Stage direction*) Here entereth Nichol Newfangle..and hath a knave of clubs in his hand. *a* **1612** HARINGTON *Epigr.*, A sawcy Knave, to trump both King and Queene. **1712–14** POPE *Rape Lock* III. 87 The Knave of Diamonds tries his wily arts, And wins..the Queen of Hearts. **1796** ELIZA HAMILTON *Lett. Hindoo Rajah* I. 150 If any one of the figures has any claim to European origin, it is that of Knaves. **1868** PARDON *Card Player* 11 The old German cards had neither queen nor knave.

†**5.** A contrivance in which a spool or spindle revolves. *Obs. rare.*

1564 *Inv.* in Noake *Worcestersh. Relics* (1877) 13 In the weaving shoppe ij pare of shuttels, a swiste and a knave to the quiltourne. **1688** R. HOLME *Armoury* III. 287/2 The Reeling Pin (which some call a Knave..) is for the Spool to run or turn upon whilst it is Reeling upon the Reel.

6. *attrib.* and *Comb.*, as ***knave-fool***; ***knave-born*** adj.; †**knave-seller**, a slave-dealer; †**knave's grease**, a flogging; †**knave's mustard**, some cruciferous plant. Also KNAVE-BAIRN, -CHILD.

1860 GEN. P. THOMPSON *Audi Alt.* III. cxxxviii. 112 Get up *knave-born falsehoods against the people and governors of foreign countries. **1627** DRAYTON *Moon-calf* Poems (1810) 129/1 Whilst that *knave-fool..Smiles at the coxcomb, which admires him so. **1552** HULOET, *Knaue seller, or he that selleth knaues or slaues. **1608** *Withal's Dict. Childr.* 73 *Mastigophorus*,..that is worthie to bee beaten, or scourged, they cal it *knaues grease. **1597** GERARDE *Herbal* II. xix. 206 The thirde kinde of treacle Mustarde, named *knaues Mustard (for that it is too bad for honest men).

knave (neɪv), *v.* [f. KNAVE *sb.*] *trans.* In various nonce-uses: **a.** To call (any one) knave. **b.** To make a knave of. **c.** To steal like a knave. **d.** To force knavishly. Hence **'knaving** *vbl. sb.*

1545 *1st Exam. Anne Askewe* in *Bale's Sel. Wks.* (Parker Soc.) 173 Dog's rhetoric and cur's courtesy, knavings, brawlings, and quarrellings. **1598** J. M. *Seruingmans Comf.* (1868) 162 What cares a Gentleman now adayes to knaue and rascall his Man at euery worde? **1605** KYD *1st Pt. Jeronimo* in Hazl. *Dodsley* IV. 361 He's a great man, therefore we must not knave him. **1658** SIR T. BROWNE *Hydriot.* ii, To be knav'd out of our graves. **1732** *Gentle-man Instructed* (ed. 10) 477 (D.) How many nets do they lay to ensnare the squire and knave themselves. **1821** CLARE *Vill. Minstr.* I. 18 Sad deeds bewailing of the prowling fox; How in the roost the thief had knav'd his way.

†**knave-bairn.** *Sc.* and *north. Obs.* = next.

a **1300** *Cursor M.* 2668 Do your knauebarns to circumces. *c* **1375** *Sc. Leg. Saints* xii. (*Mathias*) 31 Gyf I consawyt haf þis nycht a knafe barne. *c* **1425** WYNTOUN *Cron.* VII. xiii. 115 Þe Erlys awyn wyf wes lychtare Of a Knaive Barne. *a* **1800** *Tam-a-Line* in Child *Ballads* (1857) I. 366 If it be a knave bairn, He's heir o' a' my land. **1815** SCOTT *Guy M.* xi, He tell'd the Laird that the Evil One wad have power over the knave-bairn.

†**'knave-child.** *Obs.* A male child.

c **1175** *Lamb. Hom.* 77 Þu scald..bare Knaue child. *c* **1275** LAY. 15526 ȝef man funde..eny cnaue child, þat neuere fader nadde. *c* **1320** *Sir Beues* (MS. A) 3714 Fond he þer noþer ȝong ne elder, Boute twei heþene knaue childer. *c* **1440** *Gesta Rom.* I. lxxii. 390 (Add. MS.) With in few dayes after she was delyuered of a fayre knave childe.

†**'knave-line.** *Naut. Obs.* In 7 **knauling, knaueline.** One of the small lines in the tackling of a vessel (see quot. 1627).

1626 CAPT. SMITH *Accid. Yng. Seamen* 15 Small cordage, as head lines, the knaulings, gassits or furling lines. **1627** —— *Seaman's Gram.* v. 24 The Knaue-line is a rope [that] hath one end fastened to the crosse trees, and so comes downe by the ties to the Rams head..to keepe the ties and Halyards from turning about one another when they are new. **1678** PHILLIPS (ed. 4), *Knave Line.* **1867** in SMYTH *Sailor's Word-bk.* s.v. *Line.*

†**'knavely,** *adv. Obs. rare*$^{-1}$. [f. KNAVE *sb.* + -LY².] In the manner of a knave.

c **1592** MARLOWE *Jew of Malta* IV. v, Knavely spoke, and like a man at arms.

knavery ('neɪvərɪ, 'neɪvrɪ). Also 6 *Sc.* **knaifrie.** [f. KNAVE *sb.* + -ERY.]

1. Performance characteristic of a knave; dishonest and crafty dealing; trickery, roguery. With *a* and *pl.*, A knavish deed or practice.

1528 TINDALE *Obed. Chr. Man* Wks. (1573) 147/2 Because of a litle knauery which a Deacon at Constantinople plaide thorough confession with one of the chiefe wiues of the citie. **1546** BALE *Eng. Votaries* I. (1560) 64 All suche knaueryes must haue a pretensed colour. **1612** DEKKER *If it be not good* Wks. 1873 III. 312 The Sun sees much Knauery in a yere, and the Moone more in a quarter. **1673** TEMPLE *Ess., Ireland* Wks. 1731 I. 115 The Unskilfulness, or Carelesness, or Knavery of the Traders. **1724** RAMSAY *Vision* xiii, Knaivry, and slaivrie, Ar equally dispysd. **1747** WESLEY *Prim. Physic* (1762) p. xiv, Either through the Ignorance or Knavery of Physicians. **1870** SPURGEON *Treas. Dav.* Ps. xxxiii. 10 He frustrates their knaveries, and makes their promising plots to end in nothing.

b. As a mock title: = KNAVESHIP 1.

1871 R. ELLIS *Catullus* xxxiii. 5 Please your knaveries hoist a sail for exile, Pains and privacy?

†**2.** In weakened sense: Roguishness, waggishness, playing of tricks. *Obs.*

1590 SHAKS. *Mids. N.* III. ii. 346 This is thy negligence, still thou mistak'st, Or else committ'st thy knaueries wilfully. **1599** —— *Hen. V*, IV. vii. 52 He was full of iests, and gypes, and knaueries, and mockes. **1646** EVELYN *Diary* 7 Oct., Yet are they chereful and full of knavery.

†**b.** *concr.* Tricks of dress or adornment. *Obs.*

1596 SHAKS. *Tam. Shr.* IV. iii. 58 With Scarfes, and Fannes, and double change of brau'ry, With Amber Bracelets, Beades, and all this knau'ry.

†**3.** A popular name for the plant *Narthecium ossifragum*, Bog Asphodel. (Cf. *honesty*, *pride*, *thrift*.) *Obs.*

[**1547** BOORDE *Brev. Health* § 151 Put no Lubberworte into theyr potage, and beware of knauerynge aboute theyr hert.] **1640** PARKINSON *Theat. Bot.* 1219 My good friend Doctor Anthony Salter of Exeter,..could understand of the countrey people no other name thereof, or propertie appropriate unto it but knavery.

knaveship ('neɪvʃɪp). Also (*Sc.*) 6 **knaship, knaifschip,** 7 **knawship.** [f. KNAVE *sb.* + -SHIP.]

1. The condition of being a knave: used with a possessive, as a mock title.

1589 *Pappe w. Hatchet* B, Your Knaueship brake you[r] fast on the Bishops. **1680** *Revenge* I. i. 6 What, Mr. Trickwell, does your Knaveship dare walk the street? **1767** THORNTON tr. *Plautus* II. 322 Let him try the cause..whether too your knaveship Should not be clapt in prison. **1887** SWINBURNE *Locrine* II. ii. 28 The liar will say no more—his heart misgives His knaveship.

†**2.** *Sc.* The quantity of corn or meal payable to a miller's servant (cf. KNAVE *sb.* 2, quot. 1820) as one of the sequels or small dues levied on each lot of corn ground at a thirlage mill. *Obs.*

15.. *Aberdeen Reg.* (Jam.), Prewing of the auld statutis & vse that thai hed wownt to hef of the multur of ilk boll, and quhat knaship. **1575** *Burgh Rec. Glasgow* (Mait. Cl. 1832) 37 Taking furth þairof of v multours and thre knaifschips of malt. **1596** *Reg. Mag. Sig.* (1890) 176/1 Cum astrictis multuris acrarum de F. vocat. le knaifschip. **1609** SKENE *Reg. Maj.* 3 (*Act Will.* c. 9) Ane free man or ane free halder, sall gif for multure at the milne..of tuentie bolles, ane firlot (as knawship). **1754** ERSKINE *Princ. Sc. Law* II. ix. § 19 The sequels are the small parcels of corn or meal given as a fee to the servants, over and above what is paid to the multurer; and they pass by the name of knaveship. **1818** SCOTT *Hrt. Midl.* viii, Regular payment of..multure, lock, gowpen, and knaveship, and all the various exactions now commuted for money.

'knavess. *nonce-wd.* [See -ESS.] A she-knave.

1833 CARLYLE *Ct. Cagliostro* in *Misc. Ess.* (1872) V. 89 Cullies, the easy cushions on which knaves and knavesses repose and fatten.

†**knavi'gation.** *Obs.* [Jocular, after *navigation.*] A knavish invention or relation.

1613 PURCHAS *Pilgrimage* VII. viii. 693 For my part..I could wish such complaints to be but calumnies, and to be the knavigations of false discouerers.

†**knavinge,** obs. form of GNAWING.

c **1440** *Promp. Parv.* 279/1 Knavynge, or gnavynge (*K., H., P.* knawynge), *corrosio.*

knavish ('neɪvɪʃ), *a.* [f. KNAVE *sb.* + -ISH¹.] Characteristic of or appropriate to a knave, having the character of a knave.

†**1.** Low, vulgar; obscene. *Obs.*

c **1386** CHAUCER *Manciple's T.* 101 His wyf anoon hath for hir lemman sent. Hir lemman? certes, þis is a knauyssh speche. Forȝeueth it me. *a* **1529** SKELTON *Col. Cloute* 653 Howe ye were wonte to drynke Of a lether bottell With a knauysshe stoppell.

†**2.** Roguish, rascally, mischievous, impertinent.

1552 HULOET, Knauishe, *proteruus.* **1573** BARET *Alv.* K 87 A Knappish, or knauish tongue, *lingua proterua.* **1590** SHAKS. *Mids. N.* II. i. 32 That shrew'd and knauish spirit Cal'd Robin Good-fellow. *Ibid.* III. ii. 440 Cupid is a knauish lad, Thus to make poor females mad. **1603** DEKKER *Grissil* (Shaks. Soc.) 15 You may be ashamed to lay such knavish burden upon old age's shoulders.

3. Basely unprincipled, fraudulent, rascally.

1570 LEVINS *Manip.* 145/33 Knauish, *peruersus.* **1602** SHAKS. *Ham.* III. ii. 250 'Tis a knauish peece of worke. *a* **1704** T. BROWN *Two Oxf. Schol.* Wks. 1730 I. 8 Some..are poor and cannot pay, and others knavish and will not pay. *a* **1800** COWPER *Ep. Protest. Lady* 6 Praise is the medium of a knavish trade. **1856** FROUDE *Hist. Eng.* (1858) I. v. 405 It was a knavish piece of business. *a* **1859** MACAULAY *Hist. Eng.* xxiii. V. 38 He had employed a knavish Jew to forge endorsement of names.

knavishly ('neɪvɪʃlɪ), *adv.* [f. prec. + -LY².] In a knavish manner; villainously, dishonourably, dishonestly, fraudulently; roguishly, trickily.

1481 CAXTON *Reynard* (Arb.) 94 Alas there rauysshyd he and forcyd my wyf so knauisshly that I am ashamed to telle it. **1552** HULOET, Knauishly, *proterue, proteruiter.* **1603** HOLLAND *Plutarch's Mor.* 423 One of those slaves..had behaved himselfe somewhat too insolently and knavishly against him. *c* **1720** PRIOR *Viceroy* 95 That he did likewise traitorously..Enrich himself most knavishly. **1825** MCCULLOCH *Pol. Econ.* II. ii. 84 As it has been sometimes ignorantly or knavishly represented.

knavishness ('neɪvɪʃnɪs). [f. as prec. + -NESS.] The quality of being knavish; knavery; petty villainy, dishonesty, trickery.

1515 BARCLAY *Egloges* III. (1570) C ij b/2 If thou haue one with knauishenes infect, Then all the other shall folowe the same secte. **1783** *Ainsworth's Lat. Dict.*, Knavishness, *nequitia, scelus.*

knavyn, knaw(e, obs. forms of GNAW.

knaw, knawe(n, knawledge, obs. var. KNOW, KNOWN, KNOWLEDGE.

knawel ('nɔːɪl). [a. Ger. *knauel, kneuel* knot-grass; cf. Ger. *knauel, knäuel* clew, ball of yarn: see Grimm.] A book-name of the knot-grass, *Scleranthus*, a weed frequent in sandy soil.

1578 LYTE *Dodoens* I. lxvii. 97 Amongst the kindes of Knot grasse, we may well recken that herbe, whiche doth so wrap and enterlace it self, and is so ful of ioynts, that the base Almaignes cal it Knawel, that is to say, Knot weede. **1640** PARKINSON *Theat. Bot.* 446 The Germanes Knawell sendeth forth from a small slender threddy roote, divers small branches. **1760** J. LEE *Introd. Bot.* App. 316 Knawel, *Scleranthus.* **1816–43** KIRBY & SP. *Entomol.* I. 270 The scarlet grain of Poland..is found on the roots of the perennial knawel.

knawin, knawyn, obs. ff. GNAW, KNOW.

knax, obs. pl. of KNACK.

knaydl, var. KNAIDEL.

kne, obs. f. KNEE.

knead (niːd), *v.* Pa. t. and pa. pple. **kneaded.** Forms: see below. [Orig. a strong vb.: OE. *cnedan*, pa. t. *cnæd*, pl. *cnǣdon*, pa. pple. *cneden*, = OS. *knedan* (found in pa. pple. *giknedan*: MDu. and Du. *kneden*), OHG. *chnetan, cnetan* (MHG. *kneten*, Ger. *kneten*):—OTeut. type **kned-, knad-, knǣdum, knedano-*. A different formation of the present stem, with weak grade of root-vowel, appears in ON. *knoða* (Norw. *knoda*, Sw. *knåda*); cf. *troða* = Goth. *trudan*, to TREAD.

The modern form *knead* corresponds in spelling to *tread*:—OE. *tredan*, but has the original short unstopped vowel lengthened to (iː) as in *mead, cat, meat*. In some dialects, e.g. in Sc., the *e* remains short (nɛd) as in *tread*. The pa. t. **knad* does not appear to be known in ME., where also the pa. pple. *kneden* was partly displaced by *knoden* (cf. *trodden*; also, ONorthumbr. *ȝecnoeden*); and eventually both pa. t. and pple. assumed the weak form *kneaded*. The shortened pa. pple. *kned* (*knead*) might arise out of either *kneden*, or *kneded* (*kneaded*).]

A. Illustration of Forms.

1. *Present stem.* 1 **cnedan,** 2–4 **-en,** 4–5 **kneden, -yn,** 5 **cnede,** 5–6 **knede,** 6–7 **kneade,** 6–8 **kneed,** (6–8 **kned**), 6– **knead.**

c **1000** *Sax. Leechd.* III. 134 Nim cumin and merces sæd and cnede to þan hlafe. *c* **1200** [see B. 1]. *c* **1440** *Promp. Parv.* 279/1 Knedyn paste, *pinso* [v.r. *pistrio*]. **14..** *Voc.* in Wr.-Wülcker 594/23 *Malaxo*, to cnede. **1535** COVERDALE *Jer.* vii. 17 The fathers kyndle the fyre, the mothers kneade the dowe, to bake cakes. **15..** *Wyfe of Auchtermuchty* v, First ye sall sift, and syne sall kned. **1573–80** BARET *Alv.* K 91 To knead dowe: waxe: or other things, *depso.* **1606** Knede [see B. 3]. **1653** WALTON *Angler* viii. 171 You may kneade with your Paste..white or yellowish wool.

2. *Pa. t.* *α.* 1 ***cnæd,** *pl.* **cnǣdon,** 2–4 ***knad,** 4 ***knod.** *β.* 6 **kneed, kneded,** 7– **kneaded.**

1537 BIBLE (Matthew) *1 Sam.* xxviii. 24 The woman..toke flower & kneed it. **1539** BIBLE (Great) *ibid.*, The woman..toke flowr and kneded it. **1660** JER. TAYLOR *Worthy Commun.* ii. § 2. 134 The fine meal that Sarah kneaded for the Angels entertainment.

3. *Pa. pple.* *α.* 1 **ȝecnoeden, cneden,** 2–4 (i-) **cneden,** 5 **kneden,** 7 **knedden.** *β.* 4–6 **knoden,** (-yn, -on), 5–7 (*dial.* -9) **knodden,** 6 **knodde.** *γ.* 5 **knedid,** 6 **knedded,** (**knoded**), 7 **kneeded,** 7– **kneaded.** *δ.* 4–5 **ikned(de,** 5 **knedde,** 5–7 **kned,** 7 **knead.**

α. *c* **950** *Lindisf. Gosp.* Luke xiii. 21 Dærste þ..wif gehydeð in meolo..oððæt sie ȝedærsted *vel* ȝecnoeden [*c* **975** *Rushw. Gosp.* cneden] all. **13..** *Propr. Sanct.* (Vernon MS.) in Herrig's *Archiv* LXXXI. 83/31 Þenne is hit..grounden to mele, ffeire I-kneden. **1495** *Trevisa's Barth. De P.R.* XVII. lxvii. 643 Mele..kneden and moulde to shape of louys and bake. **1616** SURFL. & MARKH. *Country Farme* 472 Verie choice earth..verie cleane and verie well kneaden.

β. *c* **1380** WYCLIF *Sel. Wks.* I. 223 Þat þis be not knodyn..in þe whete flour. *c* **1440** *Promp. Parv.* 280/1 Knodon, *pistus.* **14..** *Noble Bk. Cookry* (1882) 47 A paist of pured flour knoddene with mylk of almondes. **1550** LEVER *Serm., at Shrouds* (Arb.) 46 Wheate..knoden into dough. **1550** VERON *Godly Sayings* (1846) 40 When ye were baptized, ye were as a man should say, knode together. **1562, 1688** Knodden [see B. 1]. **1855** ROBINSON *Whitby Gloss.* s.v., Clay or any soft substance is said to be knodden when indented with the fingers.

γ. *c* **1490** *Promp. Parv.* 280/1 (MS. K) Knedid, *pistus.* **1550** R. HUTCHINSON *Image of God* vii. (1842) 37 The liquor of water knoded into dough. **1577–87** HOLINSHED *Chron.*, *Irel.* 88 Hauing well nighe knedded the dough. *c* **1645** HOWELL *Lett.* (1705) 289 No Creature that's kneeded of Clay. **1819** Kneaded [see B. 2].

δ. **1398** TREVISA *Barth. De P.R.* xvii. 67 (MS. Bodl.) lf. 206/2 Mele..is iknedde and ymolded to þe schap of loues and ibake. *c* **1400** Kned [see B. 2]. **1625** TUKE *Conc. Holy Euchar.* in Farr *S.P. Jas. I* (1848) 313 Wheat-flower, ground

with man's hand, and knead. **1657** TRAPP *Comm. Esther* vii. 6 Dirt kned with blood.

B. Signification.

1. *trans.* To mix and work up into a homogeneous plastic mass, by successively drawing out, folding over, and pressing or squeezing together; *esp.* to work up (moistened flour or clay) into dough or a paste; to make (bread, pottery, etc.) by this process.

c **950** [see A. 3 *a*]. *c* **1000** [see A. 1]. *c* **1200** ORMIN 1486 Siþþenn winndwesst tu þin corn,..and grindesst itt, and cnedesst itt. *c* **1386** CHAUCER *Reeve's T.* 174 He half a busshel of hir flour hath take, And bad his wyf go knede it in a cake. **1398** TREVISA *Barth. De P.R.* XVII. cxlvii[i]. (MS. Bodl.) lf. 228 b/1, Storase..moche and grete in quantite.. may be tempered and made rowe wiþ handelinge and knedinge in hande. **1562** TURNER *Herbal* II. 160 Hellebore.. knodden wyth mele and honye. **1573** TUSSER *Husb.* (1878) 166 Maides, three a clock, knede, lay your bucks, or go brew. **1688** R. HOLME *Armoury* III. vi. §56 A Simnell is a thick copped cake, or loaf made of white bread, knodden up with saffron and currans. **1698** FRYER *Acc. E. India & P.* 331 Courser Wool of their Sheep stand[s] them in some stead, they kneading it into Felts. **1796** MRS. GLASSE *Cookery* xiv. 263 Take some flour and knead it with oil. **1878** SMILES *Robt. Dick* iii. 18 The flour is mixed with yeast and salt and water laboriously kneaded together.

2. *fig.* **a.** To blend, incorporate, weld together, or reduce to a common mass, as if by kneading. **b.** To manipulate, mould, shape, form, as by kneading.

c **1400** *Rom. Rose* 4811 It [love] is a sykenesse of the thought, Annexed and kned betwixe tweyne. **1582** STANYHURST *Æneis* II. (Arb.) 45 Had gods or fortun no such course destenye knedded. **1647** H. MORE *Song of Soul* I. Introd. 12/2 No earth or other Orb as yet kned together. **1819** SHELLEY *Prometh. Unb.* I. 614 Mighty realms..Whose sons are kneaded down in common blood. **1848** H. ROGERS in *Edin. Rev.* Apr. 329 Inconsistencies..incapable..of being kneaded into any harmonious system. **1871** B. TAYLOR *Faust* (1875) I. vii. 1 15 Knead and shape her to your thought.

3. *transf.* **a.** To operate on or manipulate by an action similar to that in working dough, etc. Said esp. in reference to massage.

1606 SHAKS. *Tr. & Cr.* II. iii. 231, I will knede him, Ile make him supple. **1841** LANE *Arab. Nts.* I. 121 And kneads his flesh. **1861** GEO. ELIOT *Silas M.* v. 76 He turned his bed over, and shook it, and kneaded it. **1898** *Allbutt's Syst. Med.* V. 997 The muscles of the extremities and of the thorax should be gently kneaded.

b. *trans.* and *intr.* To manipulate or paw repetitively with or as with the action of (the claws of) a cat.

1954 G. DURRELL *Bafut Beagles* iii. 69 The cloud seemed to move,..padding and kneading the mountain crests like a cat on the arm of a gigantic chair. **1967** 'T. WELLS' *Dead by Light of Moon* (1968) ii. 27 He..began to purr and knead at the blanket. **1968** V. CANNING *Melting Man* vi. 144 The cat woke me by kneading determinedly on my chest. **1968** R. SAWKINS *Snow along Border* xii. 102 It began kneading dough, claws exposed.

Hence **'kneaded**, **'kneading** *ppl. adjs.*; also **'kneadingly** *adv.*, in the manner of one who kneads.

1603 SHAKS. *Meas. for M.* III. i. 121, I, but to die!.. This sensible warme motion, to become A kneaded clod. **1738** G. LILLO *Marina* II. i. 23 To bury kneaded earth for dead Marina. **1818** L. HUNT *Foliage, Nymphs*, She..pressed kneadingly, As though it had been wine in grapy coats. **1860** J. F. CAMPBELL *Tales W. Highland* (1890) I. 163 He reached the kneading wife.

knead, *sb. rare*⁻¹. [f. prec. vb.] An act of kneading; an application of pressure in massage.

1854 KANE *Grinnell Exp.* xxxvi. 326 James Stewart..had to wag his leg half an hour..each wag being accompanied by a shampooing knead.

kneadable ('niːdəb(ə)l), *a.* [f. KNEAD *v.* + -ABLE.] Capable of being kneaded.

1804 R. JAMESON *Mineralogy* I. 309 It does not form so kneadable a mass as the preceding. **1840** *Fraser's Mag.* XXI. 612 A stiff but kneadable paste. **1892** *Field* 19 Mar. 412/1 The whole [was] stirred..until it became kneadable on a board.

Hence **kneada'bility**.

1791 NICHOLSON *Chem.* 101 A remarkable..ductility or kneadability serve to distinguish moistened clays.

'knead-cake. *dial.* [f. *knead*, pa. pple. of KNEAD *v.*] Kneaded cake; griddle-cake.

1810 J. HODGSON in Raine *Mem.* (1857) I. 66 We had.. excellent oat-cake and knead-cake of fine white bread.

kneader ('niːdə(r)). [f. KNEAD *v.* + -ER¹.] One who, or that which, kneads; *spec.* a kneading-machine.

c **1440** *Promp. Parv.* 279/1 Knedare of paste. **1552** HULOET, Kneder, *pinsor, pistor.* **1851** *Illustr. Catal. Gt. Exhib.* 1199 A mechanical kneader for the use of bakers. **1885** *Truth* 21 Aug., Two huge revolving blades within the kneader then perform their important task of thoroughly mixing the ingredients. **1894** *Daily News* 18 Dec. 5/4 The Panama grand lottery prize..has..been won by a 'kneader' ..who works in a bakery belonging to his uncle.

kneading ('niːdɪŋ), *vbl. sb.* [f. as prec. + -ING¹.] The action of the vb. KNEAD.

1398 [see KNEAD *v.* B. 1]. *c* **1440** *Promp. Parv.* 279/1 Knedynge, *pistura.* **1711** ADDISON *Spect.* No. 211 ¶ 1 That when Prometheus made his Man of Clay, in the kneading up of his Heart, he season'd it with some furious Particles of the Lion. **1893** A. S. ECCLES *Sciatica* 48 Vigorous kneading of the calf and hamstring muscles should be practised.

†**b.** *concr.* Yeast. *Obs.*

1638 PENKETHMAN *Artach.* G iv b, For Yeast or kneading.

c. *attrib.* and *Comb.*, as ***kneading-friction***, ***-machine***; † **kneading-tub**, **-vat** = next.

c **1386** CHAUCER *Miller's T.* 408 Tomorwe at nyght.. In to our knedyng tubbes wol we crepe. **1472-3** *Rolls Parlt.* VI. 38/1 Item, 11 knedyng Fates. **1563** *Richmond Wills* (Surtees) 169 A kneadinge tube..a kneadinge bassyn. **1822-34** *Good's Study Med.* (ed. 4) III. 336 The kneading-friction or shampooing of the Egyptians and Turks. **1858** SIMMONDS *Dict. Trade, Kneading-machine*, an apparatus for working dough by means of a revolving spiral. **1896** *Allbutt's Syst. Med.* I. 376 Kneading movements, chiefly with the heel and palm.

'kneading-trough. A wooden trough or tub in which to knead dough.

c **1386** CHAUCER *Miller's T.* 362 Go gete vs faste in to this In A knedyng trogh. **1411** *Nottingham Rec.* II. 86, j. knedyngtrow. **1611** BIBLE *Exod.* xii. 34 The people tooke their dough before it was leauened, their kneading troughes being bound up in their clothes vpon their shoulders. **1894** *Daily News* 18 Dec. 5/4 He had just been released..from military service and had returned to the kneading trough.

kneaf, dial. form of NIEVE, fist.

knealing, erron. f. NEALING, annealing.

1723 *Lond. Gaz.* No. 6203/3 That temperate Heat, that prevents the Knealing of the Combs or Burning of the Wooll.

knebelite ('knɛbəlaɪt). *Min.* [ad. Ger. *Knebelit*, named in 1817 after Major von Knebel: see -ITE¹.] Hydrous silicate of iron and manganese, usually of a red-brown, greyish, or black colour.

1818 *Ann. Philos.* XII. 391 Knebelite. This is a name given by Dobereiner. **1892** DANA *Min.* (ed. 6) 467.

† **kneck**, *Naut. Obs.* or *erron.* var. of KINK.

1706 PHILLIPS, *Knecks*, the twisting of a Cable or Rope, as it is veering or putting out. **1867** in SMYTH *Sailor's Word-bk.*

kned, knede, obs. forms of KNEAD.

knede, obs. erron. form of NEED *v.*

knee (niː), *sb.* Forms: *α.* 1-3 **cneow, cnew**, (1 **cneu, kneu**), 3 **cno(u)w**, (*Orm.*) **cnewwe**, 4 **know(e, knew**; *pl.* 1 **cneow, -u, -a**; 3 **-en**; 2-4 **-es**. *β.* 1-3 **cneo**, 3 **cne**, 3-5 **kneo**, 3-6 **kne**, 5- **knee**; *pl.* 1 **cneo**; 1-5 **-en, -n**; 3- **-s**. [Com. Teut.: OE. *cnéow, cnéo* neut., = OFris. *kniu, kni, knē*, OS. *knio, kneo* (Du. *knie* fem.), OHG. *chniu, kneo* (MHG. *kniu, knie*, Ger. *knie*), ON. *knē* (Sw. *knä*, Dan. *knæ*), Goth. *kniu*, gen. *kniwis*:—OTeut. **knewoᵐ* = pre-Teut. **gneuo-*: cf. L. *genu*, Gr. γόνυ, Skr. *jānu* knee; also Goth. *knu-ssjan* to kneel, Gr. γνύξ with bent knee, Skr. *abhi-jnu* to the knee. These forms point to an orig. ablaut stem *geneu-, goneu-, gneu-*, liable to shortening of the second syllable.]

I. The part of the limb, etc.

1. a. The joint, or region about the joint, between the thigh and the lower leg; by extension, the part of the thigh of a sitting person over the knee.

α. *c* **825** *Vesp. Psalter* cviii. 24 Cneow min ȝeuntrumad sind fore festenne. **971** *Blickl. Hom.* 43 Hine besencton..æt his cneowa. *c* **1000** *Ags. Ps.* (Th.) cviii. 24 Me synt cneowu swylce cwicu unhale. *c* **1000** *Sax. Leechd.* I. 186 Beþe þonne þa fet & þa cnewu. *c* **1200** *Vices & Virtues* 51 He ðat alle cnewes to cnelið. *c* **1290** *St. Michael* 725 in *S. Eng. Leg.* I. 320 þe kneuwene in eiþur eiȝe. **1377** LANGL. *P. Pl.* B. v. 359 Clement the cobelere..leyde hym on his knowes.

β. *a* **1000** *Phoenix* 514 þonne anwald eal..ban ȝeȝædrað.. fore cristes cneo. *c* **1200** ORMIN 4775 Cnes, & fet, & shannkess. *c* **1275** *XI Pains Hell* 96 in *O.E. Misc.* 149 þat stondeþ vp to heore kneow. *a* **1300** *Cursor M.* 12685 Hes knes war bolnd sua þat he ne moght vnnethes ga. *c* **1400** *Trevisa's Higden* (Rolls) V. 461 He wolde..lenye on his kneon [*v.r.* knees]. *c* **1470** HENRY *Wallace* I. 323 On kneis he faucht. ? *a* **1500** *Chester Pl.* (E.E.T.S.) 403 Hym honour we and all men, devoutly kneling on our knen. **1597** SHAKS. *2 Hen. IV*, II. iv. 247 Sit on my Knee, Dol. **1711-12** SWIFT *Lett.* (1767) III. 291 The queen has the gout in her knee. **1800** WORDSW. *Pet Lamb* 7 With one knee on the grass did the little maiden kneel. *a* **1835** MRS. HEMANS *Graves of a Househ.* vii, Whose voices mingled as they prayed, Around one parent knee. **1841** H. SMITH *Addr. Mummy* xi, Have children climbed those knees and kissed that face? **1858** GEN. P. THOMPSON *Audi Alt.* (1859) II. lxxix. 36 One of the earliest stories learned at a mother's knee.

b. A damaged condition of the knee. Cf. *housemaid's knee* (HOUSEMAID c), *tennis-knee* (TENNIS *sb.* 3 b).

1921 J. C. JENKINS in E. H. D. Sewell *Rugby Football* ix. 195 Unfortunately developed a 'knee' and had to retire in his prime. **1922** JOYCE *Ulysses* 127 'Are you hurt? I'm in a hurry.' 'Knee,' Lenehan said. He made a comic face and whined, rubbing his knee. **1971** I. PEEBLES *Denis Compton* x. 97 Denis, handicapped by his knee, was no longer able to get down the pitch to the slower bowlers.

2. In various phrases: **a.** ***knee by knee***, side by side and close together; ***knee to knee***, = prec.; also, facing each other with the knees touching. **b.** *to offer* or *give a knee*, to act as second in a pugilistic encounter, it being customary for a second to give a principal the support of his knee between the rounds. **c.** ***on the knees of the gods*** (Gr. θεῶν ἐν γούνασι, Hom.), dependent on superhuman disposal, beyond human control. **d.** ***across one's knee***, (of someone, esp. a child) placed face-down on the knee(s) to be spanked.

a. *a* **1759** COOPER in *Phil. Trans.* LI. 39 Another old woman sitting knee to knee with her companion. **1798** COLERIDGE *Anc. Mar.* v. xii, The body of my brother's son Stood by me, knee to knee. **1842** TENNYSON *Vision of Sin* 84 Sit thee down,..Cheek by jowl, and knee by knee. **1899** *Daily News* 27 June 5/7 Men were wedged tightly knee-to-knee as they rode at a gallop.

b. **1848** THACKERAY *Van. Fair* v, Every body was anxious to have the honour of offering the conqueror a knee. **1857** HUGHES *Tom Brown* II. v, Tom..with Martin to give him a knee, steps out on the turf.

c. **1879** BUTCHER & LANG *Odyssey* I. 9 Howbeit these things surely lie on the knees of the gods, whether he shall return or not. **1900** *Daily News* 17 Aug. 6/5 Such things are yet upon the knees of the gods.

d. **1866** [see WHIPPING *vbl. sb.* 1 a]. **1916** 'TAFFRAIL' *Pincher Martin* ix. 154 If yer don't stop it I'll put yer across my knee an' give yer wot for. **1936** 'N. BLAKE' *Thou Shell of Death* xiii. 230 Manny's the time I've had him across me knee—and Miss Judith, too—and belted them with a slipper. **1959** I. FLEMING *Goldfinger* ix. 126 This one has got to go dead or I'll put you across my knee.

3. *esp.* In phrases having reference to kneeling or bowing in worship, supplication, or submission.

a. With governing prep.: ***on*** or ***upon the*** (***one's***) ***knee***(***s***; ***to fall, go, kneel***, †***lie***, †***set oneself***, †***sit down on one's knees*** (†***on knee***(***s***), ***to bring one to his knees***; see also AKNEE, FALL *v.* 20. **b.** With governing vb.: ***to bend, bow, drop***, †***fold, put the*** (***one's***) ***knee***; see also BOW *v.*¹ 9 c, BENDED. **c.** As the part of the limb used in kneeling or bowing; ***to owe a knee***, to owe reverence or adoration; † ***with cap and knee***: see CAP *sb.*¹ 4 h.

a. *c* **893** K. ÆLFRED *Oros.* III. ix. §14 þeh þe hie hiene meðiȝne on cneowum sittende metten. *a* **1000** *Elene* 1136 (Gr.) Cwene willa heo on cneow sette. *c* **1200** ORMIN 6627 Buȝhenn himm o cnewwe. *Ibid.* 6467 þeȝȝ..fellenn dun o cnewwess. *c* **1205** LAY. 12685 ȝe bidden for me on eower bare cneowen. *Ibid.* 12941 He..feol on his cneowen. *c* **1386** CHAUCER *Knt.'s T.* 1017 Doun on knees wente every maner wight. **1390** GOWER *Conf.* I. 286 Sche began merci to crie, Upon hire bare knes. *a* **1548** HALL *Chron., Hen. V*, 50 On theyr knes desired to have theyr lives saved. **1717** LADY M. W. MONTAGUE *Let. to C'tess Bristol* 1 Apr., A minister of state is not spoken to, but upon the knee. **1800** I. MILNER in *Life* xii. (1842) 204 In a very short time you may be on your knees to this very B[uonaparte]. **1855** MACAULAY *Hist. Eng.* xx. IV. 402 The Marshal reasoned: he implored: he went on his knees. **1887** *Times* (weekly ed.) 4 Nov. 10/3 A very efficacious method of bringing a..troublesome class of offenders to their knees.

b. *c* **950** *Lindisf. Gosp.* Matt. xxvii. 29 Cnew [*c* **975** *Rushw. Gosp.* kneu] ȝebeȝed bifora him. *c* **1000** *Ags. Gosp.* ibid., Biȝdon heora cneow beforan him. *a* **1240** *Ureisun* in *Cott. Hom.* 191 To þe ich buwe and mine kneon ich beie. **1382** WYCLIF *Acts* xx. 36 His knees putt, he preiede with alle hem. **1567** *Gude & Godlie B.* (S.T.S.) 51 The kneis of my hart sall I bow. **1580** SIDNEY *Ps.* v. iii, I..in Thy feare, knees of my heart will fold. **1593** SHAKS. *Rich. II*, IV. i. 165, I hardly yet haue learn'd To insinuate, flatter, bowe, and bend my Knee. **1611** BIBLE *Prayer Manasses*, I bow the knee of mine heart, beseeching thee of grace. **1667** MILTON *P.L.* v. 788 Will ye submit your necks, and chuse to bend The supple knee? **1715** R. NELSON tr. *A Kempis' Chr. Exerc.* III. vi. 116 When with knees bended, thou entreatest for the Pardon of thy Sins. **1857** KEBLE *Euchar. Ador.* 3 If we kneel and bow the knees of our hearts to receive a blessing.

c. **1513** MORE in Grafton *Chron.* (1568) II. 761, I would never have wonne the curtesie of so many mens knees with the losse of so many mens hands. **1596** SHAKS. *1 Hen. IV*, IV. iii. 68 The more and lesse came in with Cap and Knee. **1607** —— *Cor.* v. iii. 57 What's this? your knees to me? To your corrected son? **1640** BP. REYNOLDS *Passions* xiii, I cannot but think that..the reed and knees of those mocking and blasphemous Jews were so many drops of full cup. *a* **1699** KIRKTON *Hist. Ch. Scot.* (1817) 210 (E.D.D.) When they came to town they were so attended with salutations, caps, and knees.

4. A joint in an animal likened to, or regarded as corresponding in position or shape to, the human knee. **a.** The carpal articulation of the foreleg of the horse, cow, cat, or other quadruped. **b.** The tarsal articulation or heel of a bird. **c.** The joint of an insect's leg between the femur and the tibia.

c **1450** *Two Cookery-bks.* 116 Lete a fesaunt blode in the mouth..& kutt a-wey..the legges by the kne. **1486** *Bk. St. Albans* B j, The federis that bene at the Ioynte: at the hawkes kne thay stonde hangyng. **1626** BACON *Sylva* §45 A pottage of strong nourishment..made with the knees and sinews of beef, but long boiled. **1753** CHAMBERS *Cycl. Supp.*, *Knee* in the *Manege*, is the joint of the fore quarters, that joins the fore thigh to the shank. **1831** YOUATT *Horse* (1848) 339 In examining a horse for purchase the knees should be very strictly scrutinised. **1858** FRED. SMITH *Catal. Brit. Foss. Hymenopt.* 111 *Didineis lunicornis*..Female..the legs simple, with the knees of the anterior femora..of a testaceous yellow. **1893** NEWTON *Dict. Birds* 498 *Knee*, a term commonly misapplied by many ornithological writers to the intertarsal (often called tibio-tarsal) joint.

5. The part of a garment covering the knee.

1662 PEPYS *Diary* 12 June, I tried on my riding-cloth suit with close knees..I think they will be very convenient, if not too hot to wear any other open knees after them. **1844** J. T. HEWLETT *Parsons & W.* x, His coat and waistcoat off, and his knees unbottoned. **1887** MISS BRADDON *Like & Unlike* I. iv. 107 There is always a new man coming to the front, with advanced theories upon the cutting of the knee. **1896** MRS. CAFFYN *Quaker Grandmother* 30 The very knees of your flannels won't flop and bag.

II. Something resembling the knee in position or shape.

6. a. Part of a hill, tree, etc., regarded as corresponding to the knee.

c **1586** C'TESS PEMBROKE *Ps.* LXXII. vii, The woods, where enterlaced trees..Joyne at the head, though distant at the knees. *c* **1640** J. SMYTH *Hundred of Berkeley* (1885) 4 The sydes, knees, and feete of those hills. **1842** TENNYSON *Talking Oak* 29 Hail, hidden to the knees in fern, Broad Oak of Sumner-chace!

b. A natural prominence, as a rock or crag. *rare.*

1590 SPENSER *F.Q.* I. ix. 34 All about old stockes and stubs of trees..Did hang upon the ragged rocky knees.

7. A piece of timber having a natural angular bend, or artificially so bent; also a piece of metal of the same shape. **a.** *Shipbuilding* and *Naut.* A piece of timber naturally bent, used to secure parts of a ship together, esp. one with an angular bend used to connect the beams and the timbers; by extension, a bent piece of iron serving the same purpose; †formerly applied to any naturally grown bent timber used in shipbuilding. ***knee of the head***, a cutwater: cf. HEAD[1] 21.

Hence CARLINE-, CHEEK-, DAGGER-, HEAD-, HEEL-, STANDARD-, STERNPOST-KNEE: q.v.

1352 *Excheq. Acc. Q.R.* (Bundle 20. No. 27. P.R.O.) Pro iij. lignis maer[emii] curvis vocatis 'knowes' sic emptis et positis in nave predicta. **1497** *Naval Acc. Hen. VII* (1896) 293 Boltes of yron for Knees in the seid Ship. **1600** HAKLUYT *Voy.* III. 864 Carpenters to set knees into her, and any other tymbers appertaining to the strengthening of a shippe. **1626** CAPT. SMITH *Accid. Yng. Seamen* 9 All the beames to be bound with two knees at each ende. **1706** PHILLIPS s.v., The Cut-water of a Ship is also called the Knee of the Head. **1769** FALCONER *Dict. Marine* (1789), *Knees* are either said to be lodging or hanging. The former are fixed horizontally... The latter are fixed vertically. **1878** A. H. MARKHAM *Gt. Frozen Sea* i. 3 Extra iron knees were introduced in order more effectually to resist the enormous pressure of the ice.

b. *Carpentry* and *Mech.* A piece of timber or metal naturally or artificially shaped, so as to fit into an angle; also, the bend in such a piece, or one made by the junction of any two pieces.

1677–83 MOXON *Mech. Exerc.* (1703) 142 Knees of the principal Rafters, to be made all of one piece with the principal Rafters. *Ibid.* 162, *Knee*, a piece of Timber growing angularly, or crooked. **1703** T. N. *City & C. Purchaser* 146 When Rafters are cut with a Knee, these Furrings are pieces that go straight along with the Rafter from the top of the Knee to the Cornish. **1825** J. NICHOLSON *Operat. Mechanic* 103 Two knees of cast-iron, to support the posts that the gates are fixed to.

c. *spec.* (*a*) An elbow-piece connecting parts in which the side plates are let into the pieces of timber and bolted thereto. (*b*) 'A piece framed into and connecting the bench and runner of sled or sleigh'. (*c*) 'An elbow or toggle-joint' (Knight *Dict. Mech.* 1875).

8. *Arch.* (See quots.)

1823 P. NICHOLSON *Pract. Build.* 201 A Knee, in a dog-legged and open-newelled stair-case, is the lower end of a hand-rail. **1842–76** GWILT *Archit.* (ed. 7) Gloss., *Knee*, a part of the back of a handrailing, of a convex form, being the reverse of a ramp, which..is concave. **1850** PARKER *Gloss. Archit.*, *Knee*,..the *projectura* or projection of the architrave mouldings, at the ends of the lintel in the dressings of a door or window of classical architecture.

9. *Bot.* †**a.** An articulation or joint; esp. a bent joint in some grasses (cf. KNEED 1 b, *knee-sick*). *Obs.* **b.** A spur-like process on the roots of the bald cypress (*Taxodium distichum*) and tupelo (*Nyssa*), rising above the water in which the tree grows: cf. *cypress-knee* (CYPRESS 4).

[**1597** GERARDE *Herbal* I. xii. 14 Kneed grasse..is so called, bicause it hath ioints like as it were knees.] **1678** PHILLIPS (ed. 4), *Knees*, in the Art Botanick, are those Partitions, which in some Kinds of Plants are like Knees or Joynts. **1878** *Folk-Lore Rec.* I. 221 (E.D.D.) Find a straw with nine knees. **1889** *Science* (U.S.) XIII. 176/2 Inquiries concerning the knees of the swamp cypress..led me to the supposition that these peculiar processes from the roots served in some manner to aerate the sap. *Ibid.* 177/1 At this stage..if the crown be permanently wet, the knees [of *Nyssa uniflora*] become an extremely conspicuous feature.

10. *Anat.* (See quots.)

1840 G. V. ELLIS *Anat.* 33 [In the brain] The part of the corpus callosum that bends is called the *knee*, and the prolonged portion the *beak*. **1881** *Syd. Soc. Lex.*, *Beak of corpus callosum*, the recurved anterior termination of the corpus callosum of the brain beyond what is called the knee.

†**11.** *fig.* A degree of descent in a genealogy.

c **1000** *Laws of Ethelred* VI. c. 12 in Schmid *Gesetze*, Ne ȝeweorðe, þæt cristen man ȝewifiȝe in vi. manna sib-fæce, on his aȝenum cynne, þæt is binnan feorðan cneowe. *c* **1250** *Gen. & Ex.* 444 Lamech is at ðe sexte kne, ðe seuende man after adam. **1297** R. GLOUC. (Rolls) 4691 Yde,..com of woden þe olde louerd, as in þe teþe kne. *c* **1340** *Cursor M.* 9260 (Trin.) Who so wol se fro adam þe olde How mony knees to crist are tolde.

12. An abrupt obtuse or approximately right-angled bend in a graph between parts where the slope varies smoothly.

1880 *Proc. R. Soc.* XXX. 513 An interval of constant stress of even five seconds produces a perceptible 'knee' in the curve. *Ibid.* 514 We get a stepped curve, having a number of 'knees' upon it. **1904** *Physical Rev.* XIX. 114 On the rising curve there is seen to be a more or less well defined 'knee' where the relation of stress to strain undergoes a marked change. This 'knee' might be said to mark the elastic limit. **1926** R. W. HUTCHINSON *First Course Wireless* viii. 144 Consider now the parts of the curve where the bending is greatest, i.e. the 'knees'. **1957** G. E. HUTCHINSON *Treat. Limnol.* I. vii. 429 From the upper plane of maximum curvature, termed by Munk and Anderson the knee of the thermocline, to the lower plane of maximum (inverse) curvature. **1967** L. G. LAWRENCE *Electronics in Oceanogr.* iii. 56 The arrangement makes special use of the knowledge that the saturation 'knee' of a *B-H* loop of a given material can be modified by allowing the magnetism of the earth to contribute to the effective operating point of this knee.

III. *attrib.* and *Comb.*

13. General Comb., as ***knee-apron***, ***-band***, ***-bath***, ***-bolt***, ***-buckle***, ***-cords***, ***-end***, ***-giver***, ***-grip***, ***-height***, ***-labour***, ***-line***, ***-muscle***, ***-pad***, ***-pants***, ***-room***, ***-shorts***, ***-smalls***, ***-sock***, ***-splint***, ***-sprain***, †***-stead***, ***-tribute***, ***-trick***, ***-trousers*** (U.S.), ***-ward***, ***-way***, ***-worship***; ***knee-crooking***, ***propt***, ***-shaped***, ***-worn*** adjs.; ***kneewards*** adv.

1885 *Daily News* 22 Jan. 3/3 A *knee-apron and cape belonging to..the driver of the cab. **1822–34** *Good's Study Med.* (ed. 4) I. 330 A narrow tub for a *knee-bath, just wide enough to hold the feet and reach the knees. **1874** THEARLE *Naval Archit.* 36 The whole of the fastenings of the shelf, including the *knee bolts. **1754** *South Carolina Gaz.* 1–8 Jan. 4/3 To be sold...shoe and *knee buckles, snuffers, gun hammers. **1772** HENLEY in *Phil. Trans.* LXII. 135 His stock, shoe, and knee-buckles,..were all uninjured. **1837** DICKENS *Pickw.* xiv, It had long been his ambition to stand in a bar of his own, in a green coat, *knee-cords, and tops. **1604** SHAKS. *Oth.* I. i. 45 A dutious and *knee-crooking knaue. **1869** SIR E. REED *Shipbuild.* xv. 286 The *knee-ends of the girder are connected with the bulkheads by double vertical angle-irons. **1903** *Westm. Gaz.* 12 Feb. 2/4 The bridle-rein light in the hand, The *knee-grip steady and sure. **1925** E. T. BROWN *Compl. Moter-Cyclist* 126 The non-essential accessories include a luggage grid, speedometer, leg-shields.., knee-grips, handle-bar gloves. **1834** H. MILLER *Scenes & Leg.* xxiii. (1857) 334 The white table..raised *knee-height over the floor. **1640** BROME *Antipodes* v. vi. Wks. 1873 III. 330 She kneeles. Tis but so much *knee-labour lost. **1858** J. A. WARDER *Hedges & Evergreens* 71 As it is easier to work on your knees, you will provide thick *knee-pads for them. **1955** E. POUND *Classic Anthol.* I. 71 Saw I white knee-pads decent misery I'd know one man still feels and thinks as I. **1972** P. DRISCOLL *Wilby Conspiracy* (1973) xi. 145 September, on all fours with a pair of rubber knee-pads on, was vigorously polishing the slate floor. **1869** *Atlantic Monthly* July 74/2, I made my initial bow before the foot-lights, in my small Canton flannel *knee-pants. **1916** *Daily Colonist* (Victoria, B.C.) 1 July 12/4 (Advt.), Boys' Straight Knee Pants, of good quality English tweeds. **1942** *Short Guide Gr. Brit.* (U.S. War Dept.) 20 There are..youngsters in knee pants..who have lived through more high explosives..than many soldiers saw..in the last war. **1969** WIDDOWSON & HALPERT in Halpert & Story *Christmas Mumming in Newfoundland* 162 More modern costumes reported alongside the older disguises include service uniforms, ice-hockey clothing (presumably with padded shoulders and knee pants), [etc.]. **1798** SOTHEBY tr. *Wieland's Oberon* (1826) II. 124 Rests on her *knee-propt arm her drooping head. **1958** *Times* 19 Aug. 11/6 The headroom is only just sufficient, and the same reservation applies to the *kneeroom in the back when the driver's seat is pushed back for a fairly tall driver. **1970** *Times* 16 Apr. 18 More front headroom and rear kneeroom could be devised by reducing the bulk of their cushions and back-rests. **1847–9** TODD *Cycl. Anat.* IV. 545/2 The same *knee-shaped bend. **1844** DICKENS *Mart. Chuz.* xxvi, A flannel jacket, and corduroy *knee-shorts. **1838** —— *Nich. Nick.* xxiii, Played some part in blue silk *knee-smalls. **1964** *Punch* 19 Aug. 284/3 Green plaid *knee-socks end in sling-back shoes. **1966** T. PYNCHON *Crying of Lot 49* ii. 41 A long-leg girdle and a couple pairs of knee socks. **1591** GREENE *Farew. Folly* Wks. 1881–3 IX. 294 Sugar candie she is,..fro the wast to the *kneestead. **1667** MILTON *P.L.* v. 782 Coming to receive from us *Knee-tribute yet unpaid, prostration vile. **1899** T. HALL *Tales* 162 Since she was a little girl in short dresses and he a boy in *knee trousers. **1575** TURBERV. *Faulconrie* 349 Knit it on the side towards the leg to the *kneeward. **1926** *Brit. Weekly* 24 June 250/5 On the patterned skirt the design grew larger as it reached *kneewards. **1968** G. JONES *Hist. Vikings* III. iv. 255 Ibn Rustah notes the full baggy trousers gathered kneewards vouched for by Scandinavian picture stones. **1900** *Westm. Gaz.* 18 Sept. 10/1 There are umbrella-stands at the ends of the seats, and plenty of *knee-way is given. **1832** R. CATTERMOLE *Beckett* 8 My prayers rose from no *knee-worn cell. **1630** SANDERSON *Serm.* II. 262 The *knee-worship, and the cap-worship, and the lip-worship they may have that are in worshipful places and callings.

14. Special Combs.: **knee-action**, (*a*) in a horse, the action or coordination of movement of the knee joint; (*b*) exaggerated raising of the knee by an athlete; (*c*) in motor vehicles, a form of independent front-wheel suspension; **knee apparatus**, surgical apparatus for fracture, etc., of the knee; **knee-ball**: see quot.; **knee-bend**, the action of bending the (human) knee, esp. used of a physical exercise in which the body is raised and lowered without use of the hands; so **knee-bend** *v. intr.*; **knee-bent**, **-bowed** *adjs.*, of grasses and straws, bent or bowed at the knees or joints (see 9 a); **knee-board**, (*a*) the part of the leg at the back of the knee, the back of the thigh or hough; (*b*) in a cotton-yarn winding-machine (see quot.); **knee-bone**, the patella, knee-cap; **knee-boot**, (*a*) a boot reaching to the knee; (*b*) a leathern apron to draw over the knees in a carriage; **knee-boss**, a piece of armour used in the Middle Ages to protect the knee, consisting of a cap of leather or other material; **knee-brace** *Engin.*, a strut fixed diagonally between the lower chord of a truss and one of its supporting columns; hence **knee-braced** *ppl. a.*, **-bracing** *vbl. sb.*; **knee-breech**, sing. of *knee-breeches*; **knee-breeches** (*Sc.* **-breeks**), breeches reaching down to, or just below, the knee (hence **knee-breeched** *a.*, wearing knee-breeches); **knee-brush**, (*a*) a tuft of long hair, immediately below the carpal joint, on the legs of some antelopes; (*b*) a hairy mass covering the legs of bees, on which they carry pollen (cf. BRUSH *sb.*[2] 4); **knee-chest position**, a position adopted by some women in sexual intercourse (see quot. 1936); **knee-drill**, kneeling to order for prayers: a term of the Salvation Army; **knee-elbow position**, 'the prone position of the body when supported on a bed or couch by the knees and the elbows, so that the face is lower than the pelvis, and the abdominal muscles become relaxed' (*Syd. Soc. Lex.* 1888); †**knee-evil** = *knee-ill*; **knee-fringe**, a fringe on the bottom of knee-breeches; †**knee-grass**: see KNEED 1 b; **knee-guard**, a genouillère; **knee-hobbling** *vbl. sb.*, fastening an animal's knees with a hobble; **knee-hul(l**, †**-hulver** = KNEE-HOLLY; **knee-ill**, **-iron**: see quots.; **knee-jerk**, see quots.; also *attrib.*, and *fig.*, predictable, automatic, stereotyped; **knee-jump**, **-kick** = *knee-jerk*; **knee-knaps**, 'leathers worn over the knees by thatchers' (Barnes *Gloss. Dorset* 1864); **knee-length** *attrib.*, reaching down (or up) to the knee; also *ellipt.*, (a garment of) such a length; **knee-piece**, (*a*) a bent piece of timber used in shipbuilding: = sense 7 a; (*b*) = *knee-rafter*; (*c*) a genouillère; **knee-pine**, a dwarf variety of the European mountain pine; **knee-plate**, (*a*) a broad steel plate worn from the 15th to the 17th c. as a protection for the thigh; (*b*) *Shipbuilding*, an angled metal plate used as a knee (sense 7 a); **knee-process** = 9 b; **knee-punch**: see quot.; **knee-rafter**, a rafter the lower end of which is bent downwards; **knee-reflex** = *knee-jerk*; **knee-roof** = CURB-ROOF; †**kneeshive** [Ger. *kniescheibe*, Du. *knieschijf*], the knee-cap; **knee-sick** *a.*: see quot.; **knee-slapper** *U.S.*, an uproariously funny joke; **knee-sprung** *a. Farriery* (see quot. 1905); **knee-stake** *v. trans.*, in *Leather manuf.*, to soften (a skin) by aid of the knee; **knee-stop** = *knee-swell*; **knee-strap**, (*a*) the strap used by a shoemaker to keep a boot in position on his knee; (*b*) *U.S.* 'in a railroad-car, a wrought-iron facing to a knee-timber, connecting the end-sill and the stirrup or drawbar carry-iron' (*Cent. Dict.* 1890); **knee-strings**, strings worn round the knee at the bottom of knee-breeches; **knee-swell**, in the harmonium and American organ, a lever operated by the performer's knee for producing crescendo and diminuendo effects; **knee-table**, a knee-hole table; †**knee-ties** = *knee-strings*; **knee-trembler** *slang*, an act of sexual intercourse between persons in a standing position (so **knee-tremble**). Also KNEE-CAP, -DEEP, -HALTER, etc., q.v.

1868 H. W. WOODRUFF *Trotting Horse* iv. 62 [The colt] continually hit himself in the elbows, by reason of excessive *knee-action as it appeared. **1903** A. ADAMS *Log of Cowboy* xv. 100 They will discuss how to shoe that filly so as to give her certain knee action which she seems to need. **1908** *Westm. Gaz.* 22 July 2/1 My action is low and sweeping, mainly from the hips, but many men..have a lot of what may be called 'knee-action'. **1935** A. C. BAUGH *Hist. Eng. Lang.* x. 370 Of late we have heard a good bit about *free-wheeling*, *safety-glass*, *knee-action*, while *service stations* and *tourist camps* are everywhere along the road. **1963** R. F. WEBB *Motorists' Dict.* 144 *Knee-action suspension*... The front wheels are supported on upper and lower radius arms, the upper of which has an action like the human knee joint where it joins the king pin link support. **1826** KIRBY & SP. *Entomol.* III. 385 *Molula* (the *Knee-ball), the convex and sometimes bent head of the Tibia, armed with a horny process on each side, by which it is attached to the thigh. **1941** *Penguin New Writing* IX. 62, I practise the *knee-bend, the stare, and the slow roll. **1961** A. MILLER *Misfits* xi. 119 Guido half knee-bends with his rope over his thighs and pulls. **1963** I. FLEMING *On H.M. Secret Service* xi. 117 He proceeded to a quarter of an hour of knee-bends and press-ups. **1972** *Village Voice* (N.Y.) 1 June 26/2 La Lanne moves from knee bends and neck stretches to pitching his mattresses and reducing aids without the slightest break in his pace or enthusiasm. **1776–96** WITHERING *Brit. Plants* (ed. 3) II. 119 *Straw* not only ascending, but *knee-bent. **1895** R. MARSDEN *Cotton Weaving* 257 The board..generally called the *knee-board, an incorrect name if regard be had to its function. This board is usually covered with flannel, and forms a check upon the too easy delivery of the yarn to the draught of the spindle, thereby securing uniformity of tension in the winding. **1886** ELWORTHY *W. Somerset Word-bk.*, **Knee-bowed*, said of corn after much rain. *c* **1425** *Voc.* in Wr.-Wülcker 637/13 *Hec fragus*, *kneborde. *c* **1410** *Chron. Eng.* 758 Hys legges hy corven of anon, Faste by the *kneo-bon. **1898** *Westm. Gaz.* 21 July 7/1 [He] stated that successful cases of the binding of the knee-bone had been known after a fortnight's delay. **1794** W. FELTON *Carriages* (1801) I. 205 At the top of some *knee-boots, an iron-jointed rod is sewed in the leather, which fixes in spring sockets on the elbow-rail. **1892** *Gentlewomen's Bk. Sports* I. 97, I wear a waterproof skirt, and india-rubber knee-boots. **1912** A. MORLEY *Theory of Struct.* xv. 423 The

*kneebraces meeting the stanchions 4·75 feet below the caps. **1959** L. C. Urquhart *Civil Engin. Handbk.* (ed. 4) v. 3 Frequently..trusses are stiffened in their own vertical planes by inserting knee braces at both ends between the bottom chord and supporting columns. **1915** H. R. Thayer *Struct. Design* II. xii. 448 (*heading*) The *knee-braced steel frame. **1940** *Archit. Rev.* Mar. 102/2 The roof unit and ceiling members..in the 27 ft. wide blocks [form] a knee-braced truss. **1950** *Engineering* 31 Mar. 366/1 By using a knee-braced portal structure, broad-flange beams may be employed for spans up to about 70 ft. **1912** H. R. Thayer *Struct. Design* I. iii. 53 It is sometimes necessary to use *knee bracing..but it is not as strong as the X bracing..and it introduces large bending stresses. **1904** *Daily Chron.* 11 Oct. 3/5 Men do not dress now, they merely clothe themselves, and they will not alter this fact by adopting the *knee-breech. **1927** *Observer* 22 May 12 (*heading*) A blow to the knee-breech crusade. **1826** J. Wilson *Noct. Ambr.* Wks. 1855 II. 275 There he is,—wi' his..licht casimer knee-breeks wi' lang ties. **1833** Ht. Martineau *Loom & Lugger* I. i. 4 It is so odd to see such a little fellow with knee-breeches. **1860** Fairholt *Costume Eng.* Gloss. (ed. 2) 400 The plain tight knee-breeches, still worn as court-dress. **1884** *Harper's Mag.* Jan. 303/1 Some two hundred and fifty apostles of the *knee-breeched cultus. **1833** *Penny Cycl.* II. 75/2 Another [species of antelope] differs from the general type in the possession of *knee-brushes. **1936** H. M. & A. Stone *Marriage Manual* vii. 249 The woman in the so-called '*knee-chest' position, that is kneeling face downward. **1968** R. Kyle *Love Lab.* ix. 127 The arm can be set for only two positions, the supine and knee-chest. **1882** Besant *All Sorts* xii, The brave [Salvation Army] warriors were now in full blast, and the fighting, '*knee-drill', singing ..were at their highest. **1898** *Allbutt's Syst. Med.* V. 768 If the patient..assume the *knee-elbow position for a short time, the dulness disappears. **1827** *Sporting Mag.* XX. 73 F. Bacon..called it the *knee evil, and seemed to consider it as a new complaint among race-horses. **1674** Dryden *Prol. open. New House* 27 The dangling *knee-fringe and the bib-cravat. **1706** Phillips, **Knee-grass*, a sort of Herb. **1869** Boutell *Arms & Arm.* vii. (1874) 113 These secondary defences were entitled *coudières* and *genouillières*, elbow-guards, that is, and *knee-guards. **1894** H. Speight *Nidderdale* 208 Upon the knee-guards are depicted small raised shields. **1908** *Animal Managem.* 150 Grazing should be afforded at every opportunity, and for this purpose *knee-hobbling is the best plan to adopt. **1808–18** Jamieson, **Knee-ill*, a disease of cattle, affecting their joints. **1884** Knight *Dict. Mech.* Suppl., **Knee-iron*, an angle-iron at the junction of timbers in a frame. **1876** Foster *Phys.* (1888) 913 Striking the tendon below the patella gives rise to a sudden extension of the leg, known as the *knee-jerk. **1897** *Allbutt's Syst. Med.* II. 367 The physiological deep reflex called the 'knee-jerk' or 'patellar reflex'. **1951** J. Holloway *Lang. & Intelligence* v. 79 The knee-jerk reflex may be more or less rapid. **1963** *N.Y. Times* 7 Oct. 30 The place has always been full of liberals... In Washington, we call them crack-pots, knee-jerks, do-gooders. **1969** *Time* 30 May 22/3 'What you have here,' he said, 'is the opposite of the knee-jerk liberal—the knee-jerk conservative.' **1970** *Daily Tel.* 2 June 19 In spite of knee-jerk reactions speculating on a Swiss franc revaluation, the Swiss franc never reached its 'ceiling' against the dollar. **1973** *Washington Post* 5 Apr. B. 2 There is also some tired business about 'educating abroad' and a knee-jerk Mafia joke because Candoli is Italian. **1898** J. Hutchinson *Archives Surg.* IX. 135 His *Knee-jump was poor. **1895** *Montgomery Ward Catal.* 483/3 Horsehide leggings, either '*knee' or 'thigh' lengths. **1897** *Sears, Roebuck Catal.* 240/1 Ladies'..Union suit..shaped form fitting waist, knee length. **1909** *Daily Chron.* 6 Jan. 7/1 Both sexes wear deerskin breeches and knee-length coats. **1922** Joyce *Ulysses* 517 To lace up crisscrossed to knee-length the dressy kid footwear. **1958** B. Nichols *Sweet & Twenties* xvi. 206 The taste of the twenties was not entirely represented by knee-length frocks and bobbed fringes. **1966** *Guardian* 25 July 6/2 A hovering knee-length is generally expected to be the winter norm. **1967** *Punch* 4 Jan. 1/1 The lengths of female laid bare by minis are apt to be covered anew by costly knee- and thigh-length boots, thick tights and miscellaneous 'warms'. **1889** T. Hardy *Mayor Casterbr.* xliii, Fresh leggings, *knee-naps, and corduroys. **1666** *Lond. Gaz.* No. 68/1 One [Fly-boat] of 300 Tuns, with ..Deal, *Knee-pieces, and other Oak timber for ships. **1677–83** [see *knee-rafter*]. **1869** Boutell *Arms & Arm.* x. (1874) 190 The *pouleyns, genouillières*, or knee-pieces became general before the close of the 13th century. **1884** Miller *Plant-n.* 231 *Pinus Mugho var. nana*, *Knee Pine. **1858** J. Grantham *Iron Ship-Building* 217 Bulkheads to be five in number;..to have brackets, or *knee plates, riveted horizontally against the ship's side. **1969** *Jrnl. Abstr. Brit. Ship. Res. Assoc.* XXIV. 218 (*heading*) Determination of the effectiveness of a knee plate by plastic theory. **1889** *Science* (U.S.) XIII. 176/2 The trees [swamp cypresses] which grew upon high ground failed to develop any *knee processes. **1884** F. J. Britten *Watch & Clockm.* 135 **Knee Punch*, a cranked punch for removing plugs from cylinders. **1677–83** Moxon *Mech. Exerc.* (1703) 162 A piece of Timber growing angularly, or crooked..being made out of one piece of stuff: It is called a Knee-piece, or *Knee-rafter. **1845** Parker *Gloss. Archit.*, *Knee-rafter*, a rafter in the principal truss of a roof. **1888** *Syd. Soc. Lex.*, **Knee reflex.* Same as *knee-jerk.* **1898** J. Hutchinson *Archives Surg.* IX. 336 His knee-reflexes were good. **1599** A. M. tr. *Gabelhouer's Bk. Physicke* 224/1 Heerwith must the Woman annoyncte herselfe in and rownde about her Navle, and *kneeshive. **1794** T. Davis *Agric. Wilts.* in *Archæol. Rev.* (1888) Mar., *Knee-sick*, wheat is *knee-sick [when] weak in the stalk and dropping on the first joint. **1966** *New Yorker* 5 Nov. 128 'How's the World Treating You', an English comedy at the Music Box, is full of *knee-slappers like that one. **1970** W. Burroughs, Jr. *Speed* 84, I needed a phone book which the guard thought a real knee slapper. **1875** *Scribner's Monthly* June 208/1 Particularly when that animal's foundered and *knee-sprung. **1905** J. W. Axe *Horse* I. 74 When the knee is displaced forward in advance of the vertical line it is said to be 'bowed', or the horse 'stands over', 'knee sprung'. **1903** L. A. Flemming *Pract. Tanning* 51 When in just the right condition, the skins are *knee-staked for the purpose of softening them to get rid of the stretch. **1876** Stainer & Barrett *Dict. Mus. Terms*, **Knee Stop*, a mechanical contrivance on harmoniums, by which certain shutters are made to open gradually when the knees are pressed against levers. **1897** *Mus. Times* 1 Jan. 57/1 American organ..11 stops including two knee-stops. **1812** *Sporting Mag.* XL. 14 A significant dangle of my *knee-strap. *a* **1892** Walt Whitman *To Working Men* 6 The awl and knee-strap. **1712** Addison *Spect.* No. 317 ¶4 Tied my *Knee-strings, and washed my Hands. **1768–74** Tucker *Lt. Nat.* (1834) I. 67 When we set ourselves to think intensely, few of us leave our limbs entirely at rest;..some play with their buttons, some twist their knee-strings. **1852** R. S. Surtees *Sponge's Sp. Tour* (1893) 286 The knee-strings were generally also loose. **1882** Ogilvie, **Knee-swell.* **1890** *Eng. Illustr. Mag.* Christm. No. 157 He..took a seat at the *knee table. **1825** H. T. B. in Hone *Every-day Bk.* I. 563 *Knee-ties depending half-way down to the ancles. **1896** Farmer & Henley *Slang* IV. 119/1 **Knee-trembler*, a standing embrace; a fast-fuck; a perpendicular. **1965** G. Melly *Owning-Up* vi. 67 A member of the band..gave her a knee tremble at the back of the building. **1966** F. Shaw et al. *Lern Yerself Scouse* 62 *We wen up der jigger fera kneetrembler*, we went courting in lovers' lane. **1971** B. W. Aldiss *Soldier Erect* 18 They would be going to the pub for a pint and afterwards Nelson would get her against our back wall for a knee-trembler... He claimed that knee-tremblers were the most exhausting way of having sex.

knee (niː), *v.* Forms: 1 cneowian, 2 knewien, 3 kno(u)wien; 6– knee. [In sense 1, OE. *cnéowian*, f. *cnéow*, knee *sb.* Cf. OHG. *chniuwen, knewen*, MHG. *kniuwen, kniewen, knien*, Ger. *knien.* But the orig. verb does not appear after 13th c.; the existing vb. being a new formation of 16th c. from knee *sb.*]

1. a. *intr.* To go down on, or bend, the knee or knees; to kneel or bow, esp. in token of reverence or submission. Const. *to* (a person), whence indirect passive *to be kneed to.*

c **1000** Ælfric *Hom.* II. 154 Benedictus..mid wope on his ȝebedum cneowode. *c* **1175** *Lamb. Hom.* 121 þet folc.. knewede to-foren him on bismer. *c* **1250** *Passion our Lord* 387 in *O.E. Misc.* 48 Seþþe hi knowede and seyde, hayl gywene king.

1577 tr. *Bullinger's Decades* (1592) 122 To bowe downe is to cap and to knee, to ducke with the heade. **1612** W. Parkes *Curtaine-Dr.* (1876) 42 The Lawyer whilst he liues may..be capt and kneed to like a Prince.

b. *trans.* with complement or cognate obj.

1607 Shaks. *Cor.* v. i. 5 Go..fall downe, and knee The way into his mercy. **1864** Earl Derby *Iliad* xxii. 409 Knee me no knees, vile hound! nor prate to me Of parents! **1869** *Pall Mall G.* 22 July 4 It was a rare sight to see the throng ..kneeing their way up stair by stair.

2. *trans.* To supplicate, or do obeisance to, by kneeling or bending the knee. *arch.*

1592 Nashe *P. Penilesse* (1842) 45 Thou has capd and kneed him..for a chipping. **1605** Shaks. *Lear* ii. iv. 217, I could as well be brought To knee his Throne, and Squire-like pension beg. **1784** Cowper *Task* vi. 937 Sycophants, who knee Thy name, adoring. **1888** R. Buchanan *City of Dream* viii. 162 They knee strange gods.

3. a. To strike or touch with the knee; *spec.*, to strike a person (esp. in the groin) deliberately with the knee. Also *fig.*, implying foul play.

1892 *Pall Mall G.* 23 Mar. 2/1 B...whilst defending the College goal..was 'kneed a violent blow in the groin'. *Ibid.*, P.B. received injuries in an Association game..it is fair to infer that the injury was received from kneeing the ball. **1899** M. Hewlett in *Blackw. Mag.* Feb. 333 Evenly forward she came..without so much as kneeing her skirt. **1953** *Time* 20 July 13/1 Like most successful rough and tumble fighters, Senator Joe McCarthy always presses in, and is adept at forensic kneeing, gouging and butting. **1955** [see butt-end *v.* 2]. **1967** K. Giles *Death in Diamonds* ix. 176 He belted the P.C., kneed another in the stomach and tried to bolt. **1968** 'R. Raine' *Night of Hawk* xxvi. 174, I.. knee'd him in the groin. **1972** J. Mosedale *Football* ix. 122 Guyon..spun round and kneed Halas, breaking three of his ribs. **1973** *N.Y. Times* 6 Oct. 4/5 One plainclothesman repeatedly kneeing Mr Ogden in the back.

b. To urge (a horse) on by pressing the knees against its flanks. *U.S.*

1924 C. E. Mulford *Rustlers' Valley* iii. 33 Then he.. turned his own animal southward and kneed it forward. **1926** —— *Cassidy's Protégé* x. 133 The herder,..kneeing his horse, rode swiftly back and forth several times for a hundred feet each way.

4. *Carpentry.* To fasten with a knee or knees.

1711 W. Sutherland *Shipbuild. Assist.* 71 To be Dove-tail'd into the Clamps and double Knee'd. *c* **1850** *Rudim. Navig.* (Weale) 129 The clamps..are..supplied, the beams knee'd.

5. *Sc.* **a.** *trans.* To give a knee-like or angular bend to. **b.** *intr.* To bend in an angle.

1808–18 Jamieson s.v., The wind is said to knee corn, when it breaks it down so that it strikes root by the stalk. **1825–80** *Ibid.*, *To knee irne*, to bend iron into an angular form. *Ibid.*, *To knee*, to bend in the middle, as a nail in being driven into the wall. **1851** *Jrnl. R. Agric. Soc.* XII. i. 117 When bulky the culms knee over above the first joint from the ground.

6. *trans.* To make a cut in the knee of (a beast), in order to disable it.

1890 L. C. D'Oyle *Notches* 37 (U.S.)'Dandy' took out his knife, and, had I not been close by, would have 'kneed' the steer before letting him up.

7. To renew the knees of (a garment). *U.S.* and *dial.*

1847 H. Howe *Hist. Coll. Ohio* 348 After wearing out their woollen pantaloons, [they] were obliged to have them seated and kneed with buckskin. **1891** R. Kerr *Maggie o' Moss* 36 Corduroys! and them sae clouted, Backside, foreside, knee'd an a'.

Hence 'kneeing *vbl. sb.*

a **1240** *Ureisun* in *Cott. Hom.* 199 þu miht forȝelden..Al mi swinc and mi sor and mine kneouwunge.

knee-cap ('niːkæp). [f. knee *sb.* + cap.]

1. A cap or protective covering for the knee; *spec.*, a genouillère.

1660 *Survey Arm. Tower Lond.* in *Archæologia* XI. 98 Cushes, Knee capps. **1827** Scott *Jrnl.* 23 Jan., I have got a piece of armour, a knee-cap of chamois leather. **1858** Simmonds *Dict. Trade*, *Knee-cap*, a cover or protection for the knee of a stumbling horse. **1860** Fairholt *Costume Eng.* (ed. 2) 128 Small plates of metal also begin to appear at the elbows and knees... The knee-caps were styled *genouillères.* **1884** *Mil. Engineering* (ed. 3) I. ii. 72, 4 pairs of knee-caps. **1886** T. Hardy *Mayor Casterbr.* iv, Thatcher's knee-caps, ploughman's leggings.

b. (*Surgical.*) A water- or ice-bag for topical appliances to the knee.

1884 in Knight *Dict. Mech.* Suppl.

2. The convex bone in front of the knee-joint; the patella, knee-pan.

1869 Huxley *Elem. Phys.* (ed. 3) 186 The ligament of the knee-cap, or patella. **1884** Bosanquet tr. *Lotze's Metaph.* 506 If we touch any part of the skin that is stretched above a bone, whether it be the forehead, the knee-cap, or the heel, feelings are..aroused which have a common tone.

Hence **kneecap** *v. trans.*, to shoot a person in the knee (or leg) as a form of punishment; so **kneecapping** *vbl. sb.*

1975 *Daily Tel.* 12 Aug. 2/7 Man 'kneecapped' in Carrickfergus. **1975** *Observer* 8 June 4/3 Ulster's gunmen have found they can get hold of Government cash by giving victims a 'knee-capping'—their grim colloquialism for a bullet in the legs... Kneecapping..has replaced tarring and feathering as the province's most common form of terrorist punishment... 'This so-called kneecapping is really a misnomer, because the kneecap itself is rarely touched.'

kneed (niːd), *a.* [f. knee *sb.* and *v.* + -ed.]

1. a. Furnished with knees: chiefly in parasynthetic compounds, as ***broken-***, ***feeble-***, ***weak-***, knock-kneed.

1652 Gaule *Magastrom.* 186 That loose kneed, signifies lascivious, and baker kneed effeminate. **1719** De Foe *Crusoe* i. iv, My breeches..were..open knee'd. **1904** E. M. Forster in *Independent Rev.* Mar. 280 They are so weak-chested and anæmic and feeble-kneed.

b. *Bot.* Having joints like knees; bent like a knee; knee-jointed; geniculate. ***kneed grass***, a name of *Setaria verticillata.*

1597 Gerarde *Herbal* i. iii. 4 Slender bentie stalks, kneed or jointed like those of corne. *Ibid.* i. xii. 13 Kneed grasse hath straight and vpright strawie stalks. **1853** G. Johnston *Nat. Hist. E. Bord.* I. 214 The branchlets..of the Oak [are] irregular, kneed, and spreading. **1861** Miss Pratt *Flower. Pl.* VI. 57 Stem kneed at the joints.

c. Having an angle like a knee; also *techn.*, Having a knee or knees (in senses 7, 8 of the sb.).

1775 Lind in *Phil. Trans.* LXV. 353 This cover and the kneed tube are connected together by a slip of brass. **1823** P. Nicholson *Pract. Build.* 201 The same part of a rail may therefore be both ramped and knee'd. **1848** B. Webb *Continental Ecclesiol.* 151 The gables are universally kneed; i.e. the lines of the gable..spread outwards in a larger angle towards the bottom.

†**2.** Having the knees bent, as in kneeling. (In quot. *fig.*) *Obs.*

1637 N. W[hiting] *Albino & Bellama* Ep. Ded. (1639) A ij b, These lines, In which..shines Your worth, en-fired by my kneed quill.

3. Of trousers: Bulged at the knees.

1887 *Trade testimonial*, If the trousers are kneed it has the effect of taking it out.

kneed, obs. form of knead.

knee-deep, *a.*

1. So deep as to reach to the knee. Said of water, snow, mud, grass, etc.; also of the ground submerged or covered by these.

1535 Stewart *Cron. Scot.* II. 619 In wynter in ane kne deip snaw. **1555** Eden *Decades* 116 They make a hole in the earth knee deape. **1647** H. More *Insomn. Philos.* xii, Great fields of Corn and Knee-deep grasse were seen. **1748** *Anson's Voy.* ii. iv. 160 Her decks were almost constantly knee-deep in water. **1862** Beveridge *Hist. India* III. vii. v. 148 Rice fields and plains knee-deep in water.

2. Sunk to the knee (*in* water, mud, etc.). Also *fig.*

c **1400** *Sege Jerus.* (E.E.T.S.) 32/573 Kne-depe in þe dale, dascheden stedes. **1611** Shaks. *Wint. T.* i. ii. 186 Ynch-thick, knee-deepe; ore head and eares a fork'd one. **1646** Evance *Noble Ord.* 42 Wee have bin but ankle-deepe in the one, but wee have bin knee-deepe in the other. **1721** Amherst *Terræ Fil.* No. 48 (1754) 256 To keep his court knee-deep in a bog. **1862** Mrs. H. Wood *Mrs. Hallib.* ii. ix. 194 Half the women round us are knee-deep in Bankes's books. **1895** Suffling *Land of Broads* 51 Hundreds of oxen ..standing knee-deep in the cool water.

'knee-,halter, *v. local*, esp. in S. Afr. To fasten a cord or halter from the head of a beast to its knee, so as to restrain its movements. Hence **'knee-,haltered** *ppl. a.*, **'knee-haltering** *vbl. sb.* Also **'knee-,halter** *sb.*, the cord or halter used in doing this.

1835 A. Steedman *Wanderings S. Afr.* I. vii. 215 While the servants knee-haltered and watched the horses, we returned on foot to where the corpse lay. **1849** E. E. Napier *Excurs. S. Afr.* II. 16 Whilst the 'knee-haltered' horses, and out-spanned oxen, were busily engaged. **1850** R. G. Cumming *Hunter's Life S. Afr.* (ed. 2) I. 129 Having off-saddled our horses, we knee haltered them. **1868** Atkinson *Cleveland Gloss.*, *Knee-halter*, to apply restraint to an animal's motions by means of tying. **1892** *Cradock* (S. Afr.) *Reg.* 4 Mar. 2 Brown mare..marks of kneehalter on left

front leg below knee. **1898** *Daily News* 13 June 5/5 Should one man be shot, the others would kneehalter their horses and go on working the gun. **1908** *Animal Managem.* 126 The practice of grazing may be taken advantage of to accustom horses to knee haltering. **1926** T. E. LAWRENCE *Seven Pillars* (1935) xi. 85, I was rolled up in my cloak and asleep in a most comfortable little sand-grave before Tafas had done knee-haltering my camel. **1939** S. CLOETE *Watch for Dawn* ii. 23 Dismounting, he off-saddled, knee-haltered his horse.

knee-high, *a.* [f. KNEE + HIGH *a.*.] Reaching as high as the knees. Freq. in jocular phrase (orig. *U.S.*) ***knee-high to a grasshopper*** (and varr.), i.e. very short.

1743 W. ELLIS *Mod. Husbandman* Aug. xvi. 64 By Michaelmas following they were Knee high. **1799** C. B. BROWN *Arthur Mervyn* I. xv. 141, I never cried in my life, since I was knee-high. **1814** *Portsmouth* (New Hampsh.) *Oracle* 2 Apr. 3/2 One..who, as farmer Joe would say, is 'about knee high to a toad'. **1824** *Microscope* (Albany, N.Y.) 12 June 55/1 (Th.), He has lived with me ever since he was 'knee high to a musquitoe'. **1833** *Louisville Herald* 20 Mar., It is really the best version of an old story we have heard 'ever since we were knee-high to a frog'. **1833** J. NEAL *Down-Easters* I. 78 A bit of a rogue he was too, when he wa'n't more'n knee high to a bumbly-bee. **1841** W. G. SIMMS *Kinsmen* II. 63 (Th.), Ever since I was knee high to a splinter. **1843** *Jrnl. R. Agric. Soc.* IV. II. 309 Heath growing knee-high. **1851** *Democratic Rev.* XXVIII. 301 You pretend to be my daddies; some of you who are not knee-high to a grasshopper! **1887** *Harper's Mag.* Oct. 754/2 Their myriads of gray trunks stood knee-high in water. **1892** *Dialect Notes* I. 230 Knee high to a duck. **1925** R. GRAVES *Welchman's Hose* 25 He gibed at modern poets, 'Show me one Knee-high in stature to a Tennyson.' **1937** *Discovery* June 170/2 The grass grows in thick tufts and is knee high. **1942** *R.A.F. Jrnl.* 18 Apr. 2 Air gunners..envisage him [*sc.* a gremlin] as something fairly big—say, knee-high to an air-gunner. **1957** I. CROSS *God Boy* (1958) xxii. 187 Sister Theresa, who is not much more than knee-high to a grasshopper. **1973** H. CARVIC *Miss Seeton Sings* (1974) 35 A little Italian cock sparrow about knee-high to a grasshopper.

ˈknee-hole. A hole or space between the pedestal drawers of a writing-table, to receive the knees and enable one to sit close up to it. Also *attrib.* **b.** *ellipt.* A knee-hole table.

1862 LYTTON *Str. Story* I. 214 The arm-chair by the fireplace; the knee-hole writing-table beside it. **1893** *Westm. Gaz.* 22 Apr. 6/3 His desk of mahogany..with knee-hole and drawers, stood in the recess. **1895** *British Weekly* 10 Oct. 395/2 [His] writing table is a plain, substantial kneehole.

ˈknee-ˌholly. In OE. cnéow-holen. [f. KNEE *sb.* (perh. in reference to its height) + *holen*, HOLLY (as a prickly evergreen).] A name of Butcher's Broom (*Ruscus aculeatus*).

c **1000** *Sax. Leechd.* I. 162 Wið þone dropan,..ȝenim tweȝen scenceas fulle woses ðysse wyrt þe man.. cneowholen nemneð. *c* **1265** *Voc. Names Pl.* in Wr.-Wülcker 557/33 *Frisgonem*, i. fresgun, i. cnehole. **1661** LOVELL *Hist. Anim. & Min.* 448 Asparagus, grasse, knee holly, marsh-mallows. **1785** MARTYN *Rousseau's Bot.* xxix. (1794) 461 Butcher's Broom, or Knee Holly, bears its flowers in the middle of the leaves. **1866** *Treas. Bot.* 999.

ˈknee-holm. [f. as prec. + HOLM².] = prec.

1562 TURNER *Herbal* II. 121 b, Ruscus is named..in English Kneholme, or Knehull, and of other Bucher broume. **1610** MARKHAM *Masterp.* II. clxxiii. 485 *Brusco*, which we cal butchers broome, or knee holm. **1712** tr. *Pomet's Hist. Drugs* I. 66 Berries of the Bigness of Holly-Oak, or Knee-Holm. **1864** PRIOR *Plant-n.*, *Knee-holm*, *-hulver*, or *-holly*, referred to the holms or hollies on account of its evergreen leaves.

†**knee-hull, -hul, -hulver.** *Obs.* [See HULL *sb.*³, HULVER.] = prec.

1562 [see prec.]. **1578** LYTE *Dodoens* VI. xiii. 674 In English, Kneeholme, Kneehul..and Petigree. **1864** [see prec.].

†**ˈkneeify**, *v. Obs. nonce-wd.* To make a knee of: in quot., to attach (the toe of a shoe) to the knee by a chain, as was the fashion in the 14th c.

c **1630** *Trag. Rich. II* (1870) 50 This chayne doth (as it were) soe tooefy the knee, and so kneefye the tooe, that betweene boeth it makes a most methodicall coherence.

ˈknee-joint.

1. The joint of the knee.

1648 WILKINS *Math. Magick* I. v. 36 The weight of the body doth bear most upon the knee-joints. **1831** YOUATT *Horse* (1848) 337 Many horses are sadly blemished..by wounds in the knee-joint. **1876** *Clin. Soc. Trans.* IX. 176, I ordered..an evaporating lotion to be kept applied to the knee-joint. **1891** FLOWER *Horse* 148.

2. *Mech.* A joint formed of two pieces hinged together endwise so as to resemble a knee, a toggle-joint. †Formerly applied to a ball-and-socket joint. Also *attrib.*, as ***knee-joint press***.

1712 J. JAMES tr. *Le Blond's Gardening* 81 The Semi-circle is mounted upon a Knee-Joint, or Ball, for the Conveniency of turning it every way. **1851** *Illustr. Catal. Gt. Exhib.* 287 The introduction of the knee-joint gives to the dies a variable motion, and causes the greatest force..at the closing of the joint. **1875** KNIGHT *Dict. Mech.*, *Knee-joint Press*, one in which power is applied by means of a double knee-joint articulated at the top to the upright framework, and at the bottom to a cross-head, from which proceeds the shaft which applies the force.

So **ˈknee-jointed** *a.*, geniculate: cf. KNEED 1 b.

1776–96 WITHERING *Brit. Plants* (ed. 3) II. 120 *Alopecurus geniculatus*, spiked straw knee-jointed. *Ibid.* 454 *Geum*.. Seeds many, with a knee-jointed awn. **1855** *Loudon's Encycl. Plants* Gloss. 1101 *Kneed* or *knee-jointed*, bent like the knee-joint.

kneel (niːl), *v. Pa. t.* and *pple.* kneeled (niːld), knelt (nɛlt). Forms: *α.* 1 **cnéowlian**, 2–4 **cnewlen**, 3 **cneoulen**, **kneuli(ȝen**, 3–4 **kneulen**, 4 **knewlen**. *β.* 2 **cnylen**, 2–3 **cneolen**, **cnelen**, 3 **cneoli**, **-ly**, **kneolien**, **-ly**, **-len**, 3–4 **knelen**, (**kn-**, **cnely**), 3–6 **knele**, (5–6 **knyl**, *Sc.* **kneil(l)**, 6–7 **kneele**, 7– **kneel**. [Early ME. *cneolen*:—OE. *cnéowlian* = Du. *knielen*, MLG., LG. *knelen*; deriv. of *cnéow*, *knie*, KNEE *sb.* The pa. t. and pple. *knelt* appear to be late (19th c.) and of southern origin. Cf. *feel*, *felt*.]

intr. To fall on the knees or a knee; to assume, or remain in, a posture in which the body is supported on the bended knees or on one of them, as in supplication or homage. Const. *to*; also, with indirect passive, ***to be knelt to***. Sometimes of the knee: To bend to the ground in supplication or reverence.

α. ? *a* **1000** *Canons of K. Edgar* (MS. Cott. Tiberius A. iii. lf. 96), Silf he on diȝlum cneowlie [*v.r.* (Thorpe *Anct. Laws* II. 282) ȝecneowiȝe] ȝelome and hine on eorðan swiðe aþenie. *c* **1200** *Trin. Coll. Hom.* 25 After þe forme word of þe salme [þu] abuȝest gode and cnewlest toȝenes him. *c* **1300** *Beket* 540 The Bischop of Northwich..Kneulede tofore him wepinge. *c* **1320** *Sir Beues* (MS. A) 259 Þerl knewlede to þemperur.

β. *c* **1200** *Vices & Virtues* 51 He ðat alle cnewes to cnelið. *Ibid.* 145 Cnyle ðar niðer to-foren hise fet. *c* **1205** LAY. 19976 Þer to gon cneoli [*c* **1275** cneoly] þe king. *a* **1225** *Ancr. R.* 20 Et tis word..buweð oðer kneoleð. **1297** R. GLOUC. (Rolls) 7607 Þis heyemen, in chirche me may yse Knely [*v.rr.* Kneleþ, Kneuliȝeþ] to god. *c* **1386** CHAUCER *Knt.'s T.* 39 Ther Kneled in the weye A compaignye of ladyes. *c* **1394** *P. Pl. Crede* 124 Þou chuldest cnely bifore Crist. *c* **1470** HENRY *Wallace* VII. 578 The hardy Scottis..Be fors off hand gert mony cruell kneill. **1548–9** (Mar.) *Bk. Com. Prayer*, *Communion*, Make your humble confession to almightie God..mekely knelyng upon your knees. **1610** SHAKS. *Temp.* II. i. 128 You were kneel'd too, & importun'd otherwise By all of vs. **1637** POCKLINGTON *Altare Chr.* 154 His knees may not buckle to Baal, nor kneele at the Communion. **1756–7** tr. *Keysler's Trav.* (1760) II. 231 On these stones St. Peter kneeled. **1818** CRUISE *Digest* (ed. 2) III. 14 The clerk kneels before the ordinary, whilst he reads the words of the institution. **1840** DICKENS *Old C. Shop* xvii, The homely altar where they knelt in after-life. **1884** F. M. CRAWFORD *Rom. Singer* I. ii. 25 Most of the people around him kneeled.

fig. **1633** HERBERT *Temple*, *Businesse* 38 Who in heart not ever kneels. **1821** SHELLEY *Prometh. Unb.* I. i. 378 Let the will kneel within thy haughty heart. **1855** BROWNING *Childe Roland* xx, Low scrubby alders kneeled down over it [the river].

b. With *down* (*adown*): To go down on the knees. So ***to kneel up***, to rise on the knees.

a **1225** *St. Marher.* 20 Heo bigon on hire cneon to cneolin adun. *a* **1300** *Cursor M.* 4816 Dun þai kneld [*v.rr.* knelid, kneled] at his fette. *c* **1450** *St. Cuthbert* (Surtees) 1145 Þai knelyd doune at þe water syde. **1587** FLEMING *Contn. Holinshed* III. 1321/1 Who..falling downe prostrate on his face, and then kneeling up, concluded this noble exercise with these words to her Majestie. **1606** SHAKS. *Ant. & Cl.* III. ii. 19 But as for Cæsar, Kneele downe, kneele downe, and wonder. **1750** N. LARDNER *Wks.* (1838) III. 292 They kneeled down to the elect to ask their blessing. **1817** SHELLEY *Rev. Islam* X. xxxix, He knelt down upon the dust. **1849** DICKENS *Dav. Copp.* ii, When I kneel up, early in the morning, in my little bed..to look out.

c. With refl. pron. (see HIM 4 b). *arch.*

c **1430** *Life St. Kath.* (1884) 9 A lord aroos..and kneled hym doun before þe queen. **1595** DANIEL *Civ. Wars* II. lxiii, He kneeles him downe euen at his entering. **1805** SCOTT *L. Minstr.* VI. xxix, There they kneeled them down.

d. With impers. object: ***to kneel it***.

1656 S. H. *Gold. Law* 91 We beg and entreat, and bend also; yea and kneel it.

kneeler (ˈniːlə(r)). [f. prec. + -ER¹.]

1. One who kneels, esp. in reverence; *spec.* in 16–17th c., one who received the Lord's Supper kneeling.

c **1380** WYCLIF *Serm.* Sel. Wks. II. 3 Whos knelere, I, am unworþi to unbinde þe lace of his shoon. **1551** RECORDE *Cast. Knowl.* (1556) 264 Hercules, whom the greekes do call Engonasin, as it were the kneeler, bicause of his gesture. **1665** LIVINGSTONE *Charac.* in *Sel. Biog.* (1845) I. 344 They would not communicat with Kneelers. **1748** RICHARDSON *Clarissa* II. 332 Down the ready kneeler dropped between me and the door. **1864** J. WALKER in *Faithful Ministry* iv. 84 He then retired..waving his hand and blessing the kneelers.

2. *Ch. Hist.* **a.** One belonging to the third class of penitents in the early Eastern church, so called because they knelt between the ambo and the church-door during the whole of divine service. **b.** In the Apostolic Constitutions, one of the second class of catechumens, who received the bishop's blessing on bended knee.

1719 T. LEWIS *Consecr. Churches* 95 In this Part of the Church..stood the Class of the Penitents, who were call'd Kneelers. *a* **1773** A. BUTLER *Moveable Feasts* (1852) I. 279 The third rank of penitents was that of the kneelers or prostrators. **1882–3** SCHAFF *Encycl. Relig. Knowl.* I. 202 The Catechumens proper, both the *Audientes*..and *Genuflectentes* (kneelers).

†**3.** *Arch.* **a.** The return of the dripstone at the spring of an arch: cf. KNEE *sb.* 10. **b.** Each of the terms or steps of the 'fractable' of a gable; a crow-step or corbie-step. *Obs.*

1617 in Willis & Clark *Cambridge* (1886) I. 204 Doorsteedes with..heddes and cornishes and kneelers over yᵉ same. *Ibid.* 205 Cornises and kneelers over everie windowe. **1688** R. HOLME *Armoury* III. 472 A *kneeler*,.. stones that stand upright, that makes a Square outward aboue, and inward below.

4. A board, stool, or hassock on which to kneel. Also *attrib.* in ***kneeler chair***.

1848 J. H. NEWMAN *Loss & Gain* III. x. 381 At the lower end of the church were about three ranges of movable benches, with backs and kneelers. **1894** *Daily News* 22 May 7/1 There are also fauld-stools and kneelers. **1909** M. B. SAUNDERS *Litany Lane* I. xi, She would follow the Stations of the Cross with a slow dreaminess, and lean longer over her kneeler chair when the services had finished. **1969** E. H. PINTO *Treen* 94 The traditional U-shaped elm kneeling mat or 'kneeler'..had many uses on the farm. It was also used until early in this century in the house. **1972** S. BURNFORD *One Woman's Arctic* (1973) iii. 70 Some beautiful inset work sewn in to the sealskin kneelers.

5. *Mining.* (See quot.)

1883 GRESLEY *Gloss. Coal Mining Terms*, *Kneeler*, a quadrant by which the direction of pump rods is reversed.

ˈkneeless, *a. rare.* [f. KNEE *sb.* + -LESS.] Without a knee or knees: in quot. (*nonce-use*) That refuses to kneel.

1631 G. WIDDOWES (*title*) The lawlesse kneelesse schismaticall Puritan.

ˈkneelet. *rare.* [f. KNEE *sb.* + -LET: cf. *armlet*, *earlet*.] A piece of armour or clothing protecting or covering the knee; *spec.*, a genouillère.

a **1843** SOUTHEY *Doctor* clxxxviii. (1848) 497 A necessary part of a suit of armour was distinguished by this name (*genouillères*) in the days of chivalry; and the article of dress which corresponds to it may be called *kneelets*, if for a new article we strike a new word. **1896** *Westm. Gaz.* 31 Mar. 3/2 This is, properly speaking, not a garter at all: it is a kneelet, if I may coin the term.

kneeling (ˈniːlɪŋ), *vbl. sb.* [f. KNEEL *v.* + -ING¹.]

1. The action of the vb. KNEEL; a falling down, or remaining, on the knees in worship, submission, etc.; in quot. 1631, advancing on the knees; formerly often with *pl.*, a genuflexion.

c **1200** *Vices & Virtues* 127 Oððer mid cnewlinge, oððer mid swinke. *c* **1400** MAUNDEV. (Roxb.) xxvi. 122 Þai do grete wirschepe also to þe sonne, and mase many knelinges þerto. **1509** FISHER *Fun. Serm. C'tess Richmond* Wks. (1876) 294 The blessyd Martha is commended, in orderynge of her soule to god, by often knelynges. **1631** WEEVER *Anc. Fun. Mon.* 202 There was..such creeping and kneeling to his Tombe. **1769** *Junius Lett.* xv. (1835) 72 A Court, in which prayers are morality and kneeling is religion. **1881** MISS YONGE *Lads Langley* ii. 69 The next time there was a kneeling; that is to say, when the children and Miss Dora went down on their knees, as Frank had never seen any one ..except perhaps the clergyman, kneel before.

2. *transf.* A place or space for kneeling in a place of worship.

1587 in Picton *L'pool Munic. Rec.* (1883) I. 105 Highest place in that form where they have been and are accustomed to be and have their kneeling. **1645** HABINGTON *Surv. Worc.* in *Worc. Hist. Soc. Proc.* III. 507 In the..highest windowe, under which Habington's auncesters haue formerly had theyre kneelinge. **1852** *Ecclesiologist* XIII. 309 The Chapel of the Holy Trinity, which..is also furnished with similar kneelings. **1861** BERESF. HOPE *Eng. Cathedr. 19th C.* 116 Space beyond that which is required for the sittings or kneelings of the average place of worship.

3. *Comb.*, as ***kneeling-cushion***, ***-desk***, ***-mat***, ***-place***, ***-stool***, ***-support***; † **kneeling-rail**, a rail of triangular section, to the vertical face of which the pales or boards of a fence are nailed; **kneeling-sap**, a mode of sapping in military engineering (see quot.).

1876 T. HARDY *Ethelberta* (1890) 368 Chickerel turned towards the chancel, his eye being attracted by a red *kneeling-cushion. **1647** in *Archives of Maryland* (1887) IV. 321 A *kneeling desk, & a picture of Paules. **1853** DALE tr. *Baldeschi's Ceremonial* 200 *note*, An uncovered kneeling-desk before the Altar. **1907** *Yesterday's Shopping* (1969) 231/4, 2 Housemaid's *Kneeling Mats—0 2 [s] 6 [d]. **1969** Kneeling mat [see KNEELER 4]. *a* **1847** ELIZA COOK *Thanksgiving* ii, My temple dome is Thy broad sky, my *kneeling-place Thy sod. **1703** T. N. *City & C. Purchaser* 217 Making and setting up of Palisado-pales (if the Heads are handsomely cut,..and the Rails, *Kneeling-rails) is worth 14*s.* per Rod. **1884** *Mil. Engineering* I. II. 72 The mode of executing the sap..is done in two ways, called, *kneeling sap, and standing sap, from the attitude in which the leading sappers work... In the kneeling sap it is imperative to use shields for the protection of the sappers. **1844** C. M. YONGE *Abbeychurch* v. 64 Do you not remember how much trouble Rupert took to find a pattern for the *kneeling-stools? **1881** YOUNG *Every Man his own Mechanic* (ed. 8) 798 Carpeting of a sober pattern..for kneeling stools in a church. **1954** W. HANNAH *Christian by Degrees* xii. 167 To the west of the Sepulchre is a kneeling-stool.

ˈkneeling, *ppl. a.* [f. as prec. + -ING².] That kneels (*lit.* and *fig.*).

1587 FLEMING *Contn. Holinshed* III. 1317/2 The bowed knees of kneeling hearts. **1593** SHAKS. *Rich. II*, v. iii. 132 O happy vantage of a kneeling knee. **1855** MACAULAY *Hist. Eng.* xx. IV. 387 On the day when he told the kneeling fellows of Magdalene to get out of his sight.

Hence **ˈkneelingly** *adv.*, in a kneeling posture, on one's knees.

1388 WYCLIF *Jer.* xxxviii. 26 Knelyngli y puttide forth my preiris bifore the kyng.

knee-pan (ˈniːpæn). [f. KNEE *sb.* + PAN.]

1. The bone in front of the knee-joint; the patella, knee-cap.

14.. *Voc.* in Wr.-Wülcker 590/18 *Internodium*, the knepanne, or wherlebon. **1565** GOLDING *Ovid's Met.* VIII. (1593) 206 Hir leannesse made her joints bolne big and kneepannes for to swell. **1688** *Lond. Gaz.* No. 2406/4 The Bone in one of his Legs sticks out below his Knee-Pan. **1881** MIVART *Cat* 109 The articular surfaces of the condyles.. form an elongated, transversely concave, ascending articular surface for the knee-pan.

2. *Entom.* 'A concavity at the apex of the thigh, underneath, to receive the base of the Tibia' (Kirby & Sp. *Entomol.* (1826) III. 384).

kneesberry, variant of NASEBERRY.

knees up, Mother Brown. A light-hearted popular song beginning thus; a popular dance in which the knees are vigorously raised to the accompaniment of the song. So *ellipt.*, as **knees-up** *sb.*, *spec.* a lively party or gathering. Also occas. in extended uses.

1939 WESTON & LEE *Knees up Mother Brown!* 3 Ooh! Knees up Mother Brown! Well! Knees up Mother Brown! ..knees up, knees up! Don't get the breeze up Knees up Mother Brown. **1945** *Daily Mirror* 8 May 1/2 We are dancing the Conga and the jig and 'Knees up, Mother Brown'. **1958** *Times* 15 Aug. 9/4 'Knees up, Mother Brown' is an injunction to apprehend nothing but jollity. **1961** A. WILSON *Old Men at Zoo* iv. 213 Matthew..was involved with a circle of old women out on the spree who were doing 'Knees up Mother Brown'. **1963** P. WILLMOTT *Evolution of Community* vii. 75 We went to another house on the banjo for a 'knees-up'. **1966** K. MARTIN *Father Figures* iv. 88, I happened to get leave on Armistice Day and crossed to London in time to witness the glorification in Trafalgar Square. We danced round and round all night long, singing 'Knees up, Mother Brown' and other fragments from English folklore. **1966** A. PRIOR *Operators* xvi. 259 He.. turned to see Emmie doing a knees-up, her skirt held high. **1967** L. DEIGHTON *London Dossier* 54 As indigenous to London as a Saturday-night knees-up in the boozer. **1969** *Guardian* 31 Jan. 22/3 An irrepressible bunch of girls chanted 'Knees up Barbara Castle'. **1971** *Ibid.* 18 Sept. 8/5 He and Mr [Harold] Wilson finished up doing Knees Up Mother Brown together. **1974** *New Scientist* 3 Oct. 39/1 Two new video discs were demonstrated last month during the annual video industry knees-up at Cannes. **1975** *Oxford Times* 3 Jan. 16/5 (Advt.), Saturday January 4th. 8 pm. (New Year's Knees-Up).

kneesy, -ie ('niːzɪ). *colloq.* [Jocular dim. of *knees*: see -Y[6].] Amorous play with the knees; the relationship implied by such activity. Also redupl.

1951 'M. SPILLANE' *Big Kill* v. 102 We got back to the table and played kneesies while we talked. **1954** A. MELVILLE *Simon & Laura* in *Plays of Year* XI. 83 Ramming Le Touquet down *my* throat, as though you'd never heard of kneesy-kneesy under a table at the Café de Paris. **1970** *New Yorker* 26 Sept. 36/3 Ha! No kneesies, no invitations to a midtown matinée?

'knee-,timber. Timber having a natural angular bend, suitable for making knees in shipbuilding or carpentry; = KNEE *sb.* 7. Also *fig.*

1607-12 BACON *Ess., Goodness & Goodness of Nat.* (Arb.) 206 Like to knee-tymber that is good for Shipps..but not for building houses. **1673** E. BROWN *Trav. Germ.*, etc. (1677) 55 It is built with large Knee Timber, like the ribs of a Ship. **1791** COWPER *Yardley Oak* 99 Thy tortuous arms.. Warped into tough knee-timber. **1898** *Archæol. Æliana* XIX. III. 265 A plantation of oaks growing to provide 'knee-timber' for his ships.

b. with *pl.* A bent piece of timber used in carpentry or shipbuilding.

1739 LABELYE *Short Acc. Piers Westm. Br.* 24 Every Angle ..had three Oaken Knee-Timbers, properly bolted and secured. **1795-1814** WORDSW. *Excurs.* VII. 606 Many a ship ..to him hath owed Her strong knee-timbers.

kneidlach: see KNAIDEL.

‖**Kneipe** ('knaɪpə). Also *erron.* **Kneip, Knipe.** Pl. **-en, -es.** [Ger.] A convivial meeting of German university students (and the like) at a tavern or restaurant. So **kneip** *v. intr.* [after G. *kneipen*] to indulge in this conviviality.

1854 I. ALDRIDGE *Diary* 9 June in Marshall & Stock *Ira Aldridge* (1958) 189 Visited a Knipe or a Society of German Students. **1864** H. MAYHEW *German Life & Manners* II. 243 Youths whose lives are apparently given up to the mere conviviality of '*Kneiping*' or beer-drinking. **1874** J. M. HART *German Univ.* ix. 139 In whatever other respects the German student may be irregular, he always *kneips* according to rule. **1880** 'MARK TWAIN' *Tramp Abroad* iv. 43 Kneips are held, now and then [at the University of Heidelberg], to celebrate great occasions,—like the election of a beer king. **1911** R. BROOKE *Let.* 31 Jan. (1968) 275 Last night he took me to a '*Kneipe*'. The students who are working at some special subject band together to form a club... Every Monday evening this Verein has a 'Kneipe', a meeting. **1924** A. GEIKIE *Long Life's Work* vii. 217 After the meetings during the day, every night a 'Kneipe' at which Zirkel, Lossen, Reusch..and a host of younger men took part.

Kneipp (naɪp). The name of Sebastian *Kneipp* (1821–97), Bavarian priest, used *attrib.* to designate (a system of) hydropathic treatments advocated by him, a special feature of which was walking barefoot through dewy grass. Hence **'Kneippism.**

[**1891** A. DE F. tr. *Kneipp's My Water-Cure* p. xviii, It is evident that in Germany, at least, Pfarrer Kneipp's cure is going to influence the present state of medicine to a considerable extent.] **1895** *N.Y. Med. Jrnl.* LXII. 523/2 Is the Kneipp cure injurious? **1900** DORLAND *Med. Dict.* 341/1 Kneippism. **1901** J. H. KELLOGG *Rational Hydrotherapy* I. 28 The leading features of the so-called 'Kneippism' are simply a revival of these rude practices of ignorant peasants a century and a half ago. **1911** STEDMAN *Med. Dict.* 454/2 *Kneipp method*, the treatment of disease by hydrotherapy in various forms—douches, wet packs, full and local baths, compresses, vapor baths, walking barefoot in the dew of early morning, etc. **1933** H. F. WOLF et al. *Textbk. Physical Therapy* xxiii. 268 Such headaches are promptly relieved.. by walking barefooted in wet grass (Kneipp cure). **1966** *Punch* 2 Feb. 161/2 Bavaria also offers a range of Kneipp cures. The good Father Kneipp..knew that walking barefoot on wet stone floors would cure constipation.

knele, knely, obs. forms of KNEEL.

knell (nɛl), *sb.* Forms: α. 1–3 **cnyll,** (1 **cnyl**), 3 **cnul,** 5–6 **knyll,** (6 **knyle**), 7 **knill;** β. 4 **knel,** 6– **knell.** [OE. *cnyll* masc.:—**cnulli-*, from stem of *cnyllan*, KNELL *v.* (perh. a late formation, after orig. *i-* sbs. from strong vbs.): thence app. Welsh *cnul, cnull*, 'death-bell, passing-bell, knell'. The later form *knell* goes with the same form in the vb. Cf. Ger. and Du. *knoll* 'clap, loud report' from *knellen.*] The sound made by a bell when struck or rung, *esp.* the sound of a bell rung slowly and solemnly, as immediately after a death or at a funeral.

α. *c* **961** ÆTHELWOLD *Rule St. Benet* xlviii. 74 Siðþan hy þone forman cnyl to none ȝehyren, gangen hy ealle from hyra weorce. *c* **1000** *Ælfric's Colloq.* in Wr.-Wülcker 103 Hwilon ic ȝehyre cnyll, and ic arise. *c* **1300** *Vox & Wolf* 251 in *Rel. Ant.* II. 277 Thi soul-cnul ich wile do ringe. *a* **1512** FABYAN *Will* in *Chron.* Pref. 5, I will that my knyll be rongyn at my monethes mynde after the guyse of London.

β. *c* **1325** *Gloss. W. de Bibbesw.* in Wright *Voc.* 149 Laste knel, *le dreyne apel.* **1530** *Aberd. Counc. Reg.* (1844) Pref. 37 The watch that beis in Sanct Nicholass stepill..quhen he seis ony man cummand to the toun ridand..[sal] gif bot a knell with the bell, and gif thair beis tua, tua knellis. *a* **1541** WYATT *Louer showing continual paines* (R.), The dolefull bell that still doth ring The woful knell of all my ioyes. **1591** SPENSER *Daphnaida* 334 Let..the ayre be fil'd with noyse of dolefull knells. **1605** SHAKS. *Macb.* II. i. 63 The Bell inuites me. Heare it not, Duncan, for it is a Knell, That summons thee to Heauen, or to Hell. **1750** GRAY *Elegy* I The curfew tolls the knell of parting day. **1814** SCOTT *Ld. of Isles* IV. xx, The Convent bell Long time had ceased its matin knell. **1881** BESANT & RICE *Chapl. of Fleet* I. 3 All the morning the funeral knell has been tolling.

b. *fig.* A sound announcing the death of a person or the passing away of something; an omen of death or extinction. Also, allusively, in phrases expressing or having reference to death or extinction.

β. **1613** SHAKS. *Hen. VIII*, II. i. 32 Brought agen to th' Bar, to heare His Knell rung out, his Iudgement. **1784** COWPER *Task* IV. 148 No stationary steeds Cough their own knell. **1878** EMERSON *Misc., Fort. Repub.* Wks. (Bohn) III. 393 Men whose names are a knell to all hope of progress.

c. *transf.* A sound resembling a knell; a doleful cry, dirge, etc.

α. **1647** H. MORE *Song of Soul* I. III. xxi, Ever and anon a dolefull knill Comes from the fatall Owl.

β. **1820** SHELLEY *Witch of Atlas* xxv, A knell Of sobbing voices came upon her ears.

d. *Comb.*, as †*knell-man, -voice.*

1611 G. VADIANUS *Panegyr. Verses* in *Coryat's Crudities*, Bell-man and knell-man gentrie of the steeple. **1900** *Speaker* 9 June 276/1, I still must only hearken To these knell-voices in the blood.

knell (nɛl), *v.* Now chiefly *arch.* Forms: α. 1 **cnyllan,** 4 **knulle** (*ü*), 4–5 **knylle;** β. 4–5 **knelle,** 6 **knel,** 7– **knell.** [OE. *cnyllan*:—**knulljan*; app. in ablaut relation to MHG. *er-knellen* (OTeut. **knell-, knall-, knoll-*: see Grimm s.v. *knellen*): thence app. Welsh *cnulio* to toll (a bell). The later *knell* was prob. an onomatopœic modification.]

†**1.** *trans.* To strike with a resounding blow, to knock; also *absol. Obs.*

α. *c* **950** *Lindisf. Gosp.* Matt. vii. 7 Cnysað *vel* cnyllas ȝe [*pulsate*] & un-tyned bið iuh. *c* **975** *Rushw. Gosp.* Luke xi. 10 Ðæm cnyllende ontyned bið. *Ibid.* xii. 36 Miððy cymeð & cnyllað [*Lindisf.* cnyllsað] sona ontyned bið him. *c* **1311** *Pol. Songs* (Rolls) 193 Ther hy were knulled y the put-falle, This eorles ant barouns ant huere knyhtes alle.

β. **13..** *Propr. Sanct.* (Vernon MS.) in Herrig's *Archiv* LXXXI. 84/70 Whos heued þei knelled wiþ moni a knoc.

†**2.** *trans.* To ring (a bell); in later use *esp.* to ring slowly and solemnly, as for a death or at a funeral, to toll; also *absol. Obs.*

α. *c* **961** ÆTHELWOLD *Rule St. Benet* xlviii. 74 Hy ealle.. don hy ȝearuwe, þæt hy maȝon to cirican gan, þonne mon eft cnylle. *a* **1400** *Sir Perc.* 1349 Now knyllyne thay the comone belle. *c* **1400** MAUNDEV. (Roxb.) xxii. 102 He knyllez a lytill bell of siluer.

β. **1494** in *Eng. Gilds* (1870) 189 When the more Bell at Powles church is knelled. **1530** *Aberd. Counc. Reg.* (1844) Pref. 37 And quhowsone the watch..heirs him knelland continuall and fast, than he sall jow the comond bell. **1563-7** BUCHANAN *Reform St. Andros* Wks. (1892) 11 At ten he sal knel; at half hour to xi knel; at xi ryng to the dennar. *a* **1651** CALDERWOOD *Hist. Kirk* (1843) II. 362 A little before midnight..the trumpets were blowin, the commoun bell knelled.

3. *intr.* **a.** Of a bell: To ring; now esp. for a death or at a funeral; to toll.

α. *c* **1430** *Freemasonry* 689 When thou herest to masse knylle, Pray to God with herte stylle.

β. *a* **1375** *Lay Folks Mass Bk.* App. IV. 571 Ʒit schul ȝe preye..Til þat þe belle knelle. **1567** *Gude & Godlie B.* (S.T.S.) 231 O hirdis of Israel, heir ȝe the Lordis bell, Knelland fast in ȝour eir. **1622** FLETCHER *Span. Curate* V. ii, Not worth a blessing, nor a bell to knell for thee. **1820** BYRON *Mar. Fal.* IV. ii. 182 The sullen huge oracular bell, Which never knells but for a princely death.

b. *gen.* To give forth a reverberating or a mournful sound. Usually *transf.* or *fig.* from a.

α. *a* **1400-50** *Alexander* 775 So knellyd [*Ashm. MS.* kinlid *for* knilid] þe clarions þat all þe clyff rongen.

β. *a* **1450** HOLLAND *Howlat* 764 Claryonis lowde knellis, Portatiuis, and bellis. **1808** SCOTT *Hunting Song* i, Hawks are whistling, horns are knelling. **1887** DOWDEN *Shelley* II. xii. 499 The waves began to cry and knell against the rocks.

c. *fig.* To sound ominously or with ominous effect. Also said allusively in reference to death or extinction. (Cf. KNELL *sb.* b.)

1816 SCOTT *Bl. Dwarf* vii, The words of the warlock are knelling in my ears. **1880** G. MEREDITH *Tragic Com.* (1881) 161 Her natural blankness of imagination read his absence as an entire relinquishment: it knelled in a vacant chamber.

4. *trans.* To summon or call by or as by a knell; to ring (*into*, etc.).

1800 COLERIDGE *Christabel* II. 2 Each matin bell, the Baron saith, Knells us back to a world of death. **1831** LYTTON *Godolphin* 65 Ladies who become countesses are knelled into marriage.

b. To proclaim by or as by a knell.

1840 LADY C. BURY *Hist. of Flirt* iii, Mr. Flynn's requiem was knelled in the hearts of the elders. **1847** EMERSON *Poems* (1857) 137 Let..the bell of beetle and of bee Knell their melodious memory. **1859** G. MEREDITH *R. Feverel* x, Benson's tongue was knelling dinner.

Hence **'knelling** *vbl. sb.* and *ppl. a.*

c **1440** *Promp. Parv.* 279/2 Knyllynge of a belle, *tintillacio.* **1662** T. W. *Thorny Abb.* 14 Are these sounds the knelling obsequies You use to keep at a King's Funerall? **1863** THORNBURY *True as Steel* III. 142 The knelling shots of the harquebusses. **1865** *Pall Mall G.* 12 June 4 The mournful knelling of the bells from the steeples of Cronstadt and St. Petersburg.

kneo, kneol(i)en, obs. ff. KNEE, KNEEL.

kneot, obs. form of KNIT *v.*

knep, *v.* Also 7 **kneppe.** Dial. var. KNAP *v.*[2]

1641 BEST *Farm. Bks.* (Surtees) 118 Horses,..are on mendinge hand when they kneppe one with another. *c* **1746** COLLIER (Tim Bobbin) *View Lanc. Dial.* Wks. (1862) 67 Os greadly o Lad as needs t' knep oth 'Hem of a keke. **1828** *Craven Dial.*, *Knep, knipe*, to crop with the teeth, to bite easily. **1855** ROBINSON *Whitby Gloss.* s.v., 'They [sick cattle] are nobbut just yabble to knep a bit', only able to eat a little at a time.

†**'kneppel.** *Obs.* In 5–6 **knepill, knappell.** [a. LG. *knäpel, knepel*, Du. *knepel, kneppel*, var. of *kleppel* (see Grimm).] The clapper of a bell.

c **1500** *Churchw. Acc. Heybridge* (Nichols 1797) 152 For the makynge of the cage of the great bell Knepill. *c* **1560** *Ibid.* 154 For newe mendynge of the third bell Knappell agense Hallowmasse.

Knesset ('knɛsɪt). [Heb., lit. gathering.] The parliament of the State of Israel. Also *attrib.*

1949 *Jewish Chron.* 11 Feb. 1/2 On Monday next Israel's newly elected Constituent Assembly, to be known as the Knesset Gedola, will hold its first meeting in Jerusalem. **1956** *Ann. Reg.* 1955 283 The General Election for the Knesset. **1959** *New Statesman* 14 Nov. 648/1 At the other political pole, the Communists slumped heavily, losing three of their six Knesset seats. **1972** *Guardian* 27 Mar. 4/4 Arab propagandists are wrong in claiming that a map hangs in the Knesset building showing the land from the Nile to the Euphrates.

knet, knete, obs. forms of KNIT *v.*

†**knetch,** *v. Obs.* Also 6 **knatch.** [app. a phonetic variant or deriv. of KNACK *v.*] *trans.* To knock (on the head), destroy, crush, suppress.

a **1564** BECON *Common-pl. Holy Script.* in *Prayers*, etc. (1844) 339 He that killeth a sheep for me knetcheth a dog. **1579** GOSSON *Sch. Abuse* 29b, With a great clubbe [Commodus] knatched them all on the hed, as they had been Giauntes. **1609** BP. W. BARLOW *Answ. Nameless Cath.* 17 Now for vs to feret and knetch these Vermin. **1633** T. ADAMS *Exp. 2 Peter* iii. 3 That treason was knetched before it was fully hatched.

knettle: see KNITTLE.

knevel, erroneous form of KEVEL *sb.*[2]

1627 CAPT. SMITH *Seaman's Gram.* ii. 7 Kneuels are small pieces of wood nailed to the inside of the ship, to belay the sheats and tackes vnto. **1678** PHILLIPS (ed. 4), *Knivels* [**1706** (ed. Kersey), *Knevels* or *Kevels*].

knevel, var. NEVEL *v.*

knew, knewleche, knewlen, obs. ff. KNEE, KNOWLEDGE, KNEEL.

‖**knez** (knɛz). Also 6–9 **knes,** 9 **knias.** [A Slavonic word: Servian, Slov. *knez*, Boh. *kněz*, Sorbian *knjez*, Russ. *knjazь*:—Old Slav. *kŭnenzĭ*, prehistoric a. OTeut. **kuning-* KING. From Slov., also Romanian *knêz*, Alban. *knez*, Magyar *kenez.*] A former title among Slavonic nations = 'prince'; sometimes implying

sovereignty, as in Montenegro and formerly in the various Danubian Principalities; sometimes merely rank, as in Russia: often rendered in western langs. by 'duke': cf. the title *velikiĕ knjazъ* 'great prince', usually englished 'grand duke'.

1586 T. B. *La Primaud. Fr. Acad.* I. (1594) 596 The great Knes, or duke of Moscovia. **1642** HOWELL *For. Trav.* xi. (Arb.) 57 Mosco, the court of the great Knez. **1650** —— *Lett.* II. To Rdr., The Knez of them may know, what Prester John Doth with his Camells in the torrid Zone. **1698** A. BRAND *Emb. Muscovy to China* 41 These three Women.. were the Wives of so many Knezes or Dukes of the Ostiacky. **1710** WHITWORTH *Acc. Russia* (1758) 31 They are divided into three ranks, the Nobility, called *Kneas*; the Gentry.. and the Peasants. **1847** MRS. A. KERR *Hist. Servia* 45 After consultation with the Kneses, the tax was imposed proportionably on the respective districts. *Ibid.* 409 It was of advantage to the enemies of the Knias, that neither Russia nor the Porte was satisfied with his political administration.

knib, obs. form of NIB *sb.* and *v.*

†**knick**, *sb.*[1] *Obs. rare.* [= MDu. *cnic*, Du. *knik*, MLG. (whence mod.G.) *knick*. Orig. echoic. *Knick* bears the same relation to *knack*, that *click*, *snip*, bear to *clack*, *snap*.] A light-sounding snap or crack as with the fingers.

1580 HOLLYBAND *Treas. Fr. Tong*, *Niquet*,..a knicke made with the thombes, nailes, and teeth. **1611** COTGR., *Niquet*, a knicke, klicke, snap with the teeth, or fingers.

knick (nɪk), *sb.*[2] *Geomorphol.* Also **nick**. [a. G. *knick* bend, kink, break.] **a.** = KNICKPOINT.

1932 *Bull. Geol. Soc. Amer.* XLIII. 416 If one convex nick can not be produced in the profile of a stream that is eroding its valley in an enlarging dome of continuously accelerated upheaval, all the less can a series of nicks be produced. **1941** C. A. COTTON *Landscape* xx. 233 Even where nicks occur at resistant outcrops, this is quite commonly a result merely of retardation at such points of headward erosion due to rejuvenation. The most widely accepted explanation of nicks in valley profiles is that they are the effects of successive lowerings of base-level. **1970** I. CORNWALL *Ice Ages* i. 35 At the point where renewed erosion begins there will be a sharp increase in rate of fall, showing a 'knick', or downward break in gradient.

b. The angle formed by a pediment and the adjacent mountain slope.

1936 *Zeitschr. für Geomorphol.* IX. 132 Massive rocks, on weathering, produce steep mountain slopes because of their widely spaced joints. They are also characterized by a relatively sharp 'Knick', whereas in the same area more closely jointed rocks have lower slopes and there is a more gradual transition into the pediment at the base. **1952** *Ann. Assoc. Amer. Geogr.* XLII. 305 Johnson..pointed to the sharp angle (knick) between pediment and inselberg as an indication that lateral corrosion and not weathering-retreat is the cause of destruction of the feature. **1963** D. W. & E. E. HUMPHRIES tr. *Termier's Erosion & Sedimentation* ii. 36 Pediments are surfaces cut into hard rocks at the foot of mountains which they continue to erode. At their highest point, they join the mountain side at a break of slope called a 'knick'.

knick (nɪk), *v.* [Goes with KNICK *sb.*[1] = MDu. *cnicken* (Du. *knikken*), MLG. (whence mod.G.) *knicken*.] *trans.* and *intr.* To snap, or crack lightly (the fingers, etc.); to 'knack' lightly.

1731 *Gentl. Mag.* I. 350 O Gout! thou puzzling knotty point Who knick'st man's frame in every joint. **17..** *Laird o Logie* in Child *Ballads* VI. clxxxii E. (1889) 455 May Margaret sits in the queen's bouir, Knicking her fingers ane be ane. **1887** JAMIESON and Suppl. s.v., He can gar his fingers knick.

knick, variant of NICK *v.*, to deny.

knick-a-knock. [Cf. prec. and KNOCK; also KNICKETY-KNOCK.] An echoic word expressing a succession of knocks of alternating character.

1600 *Look About You* xxiv. in Hazl. *Dodsley* VII. 457 Our gates are like an anvil; from four to ten, nothing but knick-a-knock upon't.

knicker ('nɪkə(r)). [In sense 1, understood to be a. Du. *knikker*, local Ger. *knicker*, marble (used in school-boy play), app. agent-n. from *knikken*, *knicken* to crack, snap, KNICK; adopted in U.S. But NICKER (q.v.) in this or a similar sense is much earlier in Eng. The connexion of the other senses, and their spelling with *kn-* or *n-* is also uncertain.]

1. A boys' 'marble' of baked clay; esp. one placed between the forefinger and thumb, and propelled by a jerk of the latter, so as to strike at another marble.

1860 BARTLETT *Dict. Americanisms*, *Knicker* or *Nicker*, a boy's clay marble; a common term in New York.

2. (Also ***nicker***). A large flat button or disk of metal, used as a pitcher, in the boys' game 'on the line', played with buttons.

1899 *N. & Q.* 9th Ser. III. 185/2 The buttons of the coach-man type, with the shank battered down, made a good 'nicker', or 'knicker'.

3. A game played in Suffolk with stones (of the same nature as *duck* or *duck-stone*). Also the stone thrown by each player.

1900 F. HALL in *Eng. Dial. Dict.*

knicker, variant of NICKER *v.*

knickerbocker ('nɪkəbɒkə(r)). Also 9 **nicker-**. [The name of the pretended author of Washington Irving's *History of New York*.]

I. (*with capital initial*). **1.** A descendant of the original Dutch settlers of the New Netherlands in America, hence, a New Yorker.

[**1809** W. IRVING (*title*) History of New York...By Diedrich Knickerbocker.] **1848** *Ibid.* Author's Apol., When I find New Yorkers of Dutch descent priding themselves upon being 'genuine Knickerbockers' [etc.]. **1876** S. OSGOOD in D. J. Hill *Bryant* (1879) 158 We can all join,.. whether native or foreign-born, Knickerbockers, or New-Englanders.

2. *attrib.* or as *adj.* Of or pertaining to the Knickerbockers of New York.

1856 LONGF. in *Life* (1891) II. 303 The dreadful Knickerbocker custom of calling on everybody. **1887** *Pall Mall G.* 29 Jan. 10/1 A descendant of one of the Knickerbocker families.

II. 3. a. (*with lower-case initial*). *pl.* Loose-fitting breeches, gathered in at the knee, and worn by boys, sportsmen, and others who require a freer use of their limbs. The term has been loosely extended to the whole costume worn with these, = *knickerbocker suit*. (Rarely in *sing.*) Cf. KNICKERS *sb. pl.* 1

The name is said to have been given to them because of their resemblance to the knee-breeches of the Dutchmen in Cruikshank's illustrations to W. Irving's *History of New York*.

1859 LD. ELCHO in *Times* 23 May 12/3 The suggestion.. is that volunteers should not wear trowsers, but I would recommend as a substitute what are commonly known as *nickerbockers*, i.e. long loose breeches generally worn without braces, and buckled or buttoned round the waist and knee. **1859** KINGSLEY in *Life* (1878) II. 90 The puffed trunk-hose..in the country, where they were ill made, became slops, i.e. knickerbockers. **1860** THACKERAY *Round. Pap.*, *De Juventute* 71 Children in short frocks and knickerbockers. **1862** MRS. FRESHFIELD *Tour Grisons* i. 3 Mountain solitudes..undisturbed by visions of crinoline and knickerbockers. **1883** E. PENNELL-ELMHIRST *Cream Leicestersh.* 202 In cases not few the knickerbocker has of late been more familiar than the buckskin. **1962** *Times* 14 Apr. 9/4 Plus-fours, or knickerbockers, as the Americans prefer to call them. **1967** *Daily Tel.* 26 Aug. 7/2 Boots were all around Paris and so were tweed..knickerbockers as the logical successor to the now-almost-boring trouser suits. **1969** J. LAVER *Concise Hist. Costume* ix. 251 The new baggy knickerbockers were known as 'plus-fours'.

attrib. **1861** *Times* 12 July, One knickerbocker company, wearing the same uniform as the London Scottish. **1864** MISS YONGE *Trial* II. 236 A little knickerbocker boy, with floating rich dark ringlets. **1894** *Pall Mall G.* 15 June 4/2 The assumption that the knickerbocker ladies [cyclists] were doing something confessedly unseemly. **1897** *Westm. Gaz.* 14 Jan. 2/1 A talent..quite ignored in knickerbocker days.

b. = KNICKERS *sb. pl.* 2.

1872 *Young Englishwoman* Oct. 554/2 *Lady's longcloth knickerbockers.* These drawers fasten behind. **1887** *Lady's World* Oct. 403 It [*sc.* a peasant's blouse] is girdled at the waist by a leather belt, and falls over the short woollen skirt, which just reaches the knees, where it meets the linen knickerbockers. **1895** *Home Chat* 20 Apr. 176 We spoke of satin knickerbockers in connection with this trousseau. **1913** B. L. BLACKMORE *ABC of Cutting Garments* 140 In girls' knickerbockers, the back band is sometimes buttoned to the front band, instead of the whole garment being attached to the under-bodice or to stays. **1969** R. T. WILCOX *Dict. Costume* (1970) 234 (*caption*) Muslin knickerbockers—girl's 6 to 8—buttoned at sides—pleated cambric frill.

c. *Comb.* **knickerbocker suit** (see sense 3 a); **knickerbocker yarn**, a yarn flecked with different colours.

1868 C. L. EASTLAKE *Hints Household Taste* xi. 264 The knickerbocker suit..has been adopted for wear in many country gentlemen's houses. **1879** C. M. YONGE *Burnt Out* iii. 52 A knickerbocker suit, just Charlie's size, had been turned over to his cousin Ada. **1911** *Encycl. Brit.* XXVIII. 906/2 *Flaked Yarn* has cloudy appearance imparted to it.. as in *Knickerbocker Yarn*, by dropping small quantities of dyed fibres into two..rovings at the spinning machine. **1932** E. MIDGLEY *Technical Terms Textile Trade* II. 81 True 'knickerbocker' yarn is obtained by flecking the spotting material during carding. **1950** '*Mercury*' Dict. Textile Terms 303 *Knickerbocker tweeds*, rough-faced wool and cotton mixture dress goods made with nub yarns, in mixed colours. The yarn is known as knickerbocker yarn.

d. Knickerbocker Glory, a quantity of ice cream served with other ingredients in a tall glass.

1936 G. GREENE *Gun for Sale* i. 11 Have a *parfait*... They do a very good Maiden's Dream. Not to speak of Alpine Glow. Or the Knickerbocker Glory. **1941** M. TREADGOLD *We couldn't leave Dinah* xvi. 256 'Lyons' Corner House,' capped Caroline, envisaging the increasing possibilities of Knickerbocker Glories. **1963** *Times* 25 Feb. 11/4 Knickerbocker Glory oddly has become the name of a specially luscious mixture of ice-creams and the 'plus fours' deserved a similar grandeur of title. **1973** *Times* 20 Oct. 12/7 At five in the morning it must have had all the charm of a pre-breakfast Knickerbocker Glory.

Hence **'knickerbockered** (-əd), *a.*, wearing knickerbockers.

1869 *Echo* 28 Sept., The tall, knickerbockered Q.C. from Dublin. **1897** *Outing* (U.S.) XXX. 462/2 A knicker-bockered, travel-stained, dusty-shoed guest.

knickered ('nɪkəd), *a.* [f. KNICKERS *sb. pl.* + -ED[2].] Clothed in knickerbockers.

1897 *Punch* 28 Aug. 85/1 Three human legs..hygienically knickered.

knickers, *sb. pl.* ('nɪkəz). [Short for KNICKERBOCKERS.] **1. a.** Colloq. contraction of KNICKERBOCKERS. Now *U.S.*

1881 JEFFERIES *Wood Magic* I. i. 15 It was not in that pocket,..nor in his knickers. **1900** *Times* 29 Jan. 10/3 The Imperial Yeomanry..In their well-made, loosely-fitting khaki tunics and riding knickers.

b. *attrib.* and *Comb.* (in form *knicker*) as ***knicker fabric, hose, skirt, suit; knicker-pink*** adj.; **knicker yarn**, = *knickerbocker yarn* (KNICKERBOCKER 3 c).

1974 *News of World* 22 Sept. 14/4 Faiman's in Southampton sold us a skirt in nasty 'knicker' fabric. **1899** *Northern Times* (Golspie, Sutherland) 22 June 1/2 (Advt.), In the Gents. Department..Hand-Knitted knicker hose a speciality. **1973** *Sunday Times* 7 Oct. 36/5 Alive and well in a spanking new knicker-pink emporium at 100 Mount Street. **1912** *Woman's Weekly* 27 Jan. p. iii/2 (Advt.), Knicker Skirts, Nightdresses, Pyjamas, &c. **1899** *Daily News* 13 July 6/6 A well-known North Country flockmaster, ..in a light check knicker suit. **1929** *Encycl. Brit.* XXIII. 879/2 'Knicker yarns' are produced by throwing little bits of highly coloured material into the last cylinders of the card so that instead of being broken up by carding they are carried forward as 'knickers' into the spun thread. **1951** *Good Housek. Home Encycl.* 327/2 'Knicker' yarns may be produced by including bits of coloured material in the final cording.

2. a. A short-legged (orig. knee-length), freq. loose-fitting, pair of pants worn by women and children as an undergarment. In extended use, the shorts worn by boxers, footballers, etc. Also occas. in *sing.* Cf. DIRECTOIRE *a.* 1, KNICKS *sb. pl.*

1882 *Queen* 7 Oct. 328/3, I recommend..flannel knickers in preference to flannel petticoat. **1895** *Home Chat* 2 Nov. 301/2 Serge knickers..for girls from twelve to sixteen. **1926** *Ibid.* 22 May 507 French Knicker made in Grafton's Voile and Grafton's Chiffonelle. Trimmed with lace. Elastic waistband. **1926** *Vogue* Late Nov. p. xxiii, An Original Directoire Knicker of milanese. **1928** G. B. SHAW *Intelligent Woman's Guide Socialism* i. 2 Laws..are amended and amended and amended like a child's knickers until there is hardly a shred of the first stuff left. **1938** DYLAN THOMAS *Let.* 16 June (1966) 201, I find a tripper's knicker in the gully. **1951** *Good Housek. Home Encycl.* 156/1 Iron knickers lengthwise, one leg at a time. **1954** F. C. AVIS *Boxing Reference Dict.* 62 *Knickers*, boxing shorts. **1966** F. SHAW et al. *Lern Yerself Scouse* 49 *Ee's got both legs in one knicker*, he is not playing [football] well. **1968** 'C. SAINT-LAURENT' *Hist. Ladies Underwear* x. 145 (*caption*) Little girls wore short knickers before women did. **1974** *Guardian* 19 Feb. 1/5 Women workers in a lingerie factory..waved yellow knickers at Mr Thorpe as a gesture of support.

b. *pl.* as *int.* An expression of exasperation, surprise, contempt, etc.

1971 *TV Times* 23 Sept. 6/1 When things go wrong then I'll say: 'Knickers. I'll have another go.' **1974** *Pacifist* June 20/2 This is where the revolution's happening, man, and knickers to the metropolis! **1974** *Daily Tel.* 5 Oct. 5/3 Asked whether she would tell them more about the man.., she said: 'Knickers. I have told you all I know.'

knickety-knock ('nɪkɪtɪ'nɒk). [Echoic: cf. KNICK-A-KNOCK.] An echoic word imitating an alternation of knocking sounds; hence adverbially: striking from side to side with alternation of sound.

1812 H. & J. SMITH *Rej. Addr.*, *Rebuilding*, His head as he tumbled went knickety-knock Like a pebble in Carisbrook well. **1825** CHR. WORDSWORTH in *Life* (1888) 28 You know that the pebbles cry nickety-nock when they arrive at the bottom.

knick-knack, nick-nack ('nɪknæk). Also 7-9 **knick-nack, knicknack**; 7-9 **nicknack**, 9 **nic-nac, nicnac**. [Redupl. of KNACK *sb.*, with first element lightened as in *crick-crack*, etc.]

†**1.** A petty trick, sleight, artifice, subterfuge.

1618 FLETCHER *Loyal Subj.* II. i, If you use these knick-knacks, This fast and loose. *a* **1625** FLETCHER *Hum. Lieutenant* I. i, These foolish mistresses do so hang about ye, So whimper and so hug... Soft vows and sighs, and fiddle-faddles, Spoils all our trade [of war]! You must forget these knick-knacks. **1673** MARVELL *Reh. Transp.* II. 312 You by the advantage of some knick-knacks have got the ascendant over them.

2. A light, dainty article of furniture, dress, or food; any curious or pleasing trifle more for ornament than use; a trinket, gimcrack, kickshaw.

α. **1682** N. O. *Boileau's Lutrin* I. *Argt.*, Miss won't come in to Buy, before She spies the Knick-knacks at the Dore. **1686** GOAD *Celest. Bodies* II. ii. 179 Two Knick-nacks of the fair. **1725** BAILEY *Erasm. Colloq.* (1877) 377 (D.) He found me supporting my outward tabernacle..with some knick-knacks..at the confectioner's. **1748** CHESTERF. *Lett.* (1792) II. clvii. 61 Knick-knacks, butterflies, shells, insects, &c. are the objects of their most serious researches. **1822** W. IRVING *Braceb. Hall* iii. 25 The many little valuables and knick-knacks treasured up in the housekeeper's room. **1866** MRS. STOWE *Lit. Foxes* 27 Knick-nacks.

β. *a* **1692** POLLEXFEN *Disc. Trade* (1697) 93 Toys and Nick-nacks, to a very great value. **1714** MANDEVILLE *Fab. Bees* (1725) I. 349 Watchmakers and others that sell toys, superfluous nicknacks, and other curiosities. **1820** W. IRVING *Sketch Bk.* (1849) 386 He is a plain John Bull, and has no relish for frippery and nick-nacks. **1823** W. COBBETT *Rural Rides* (1885) I. 347 Two or three nick-nacks to eat instead of a piece of bacon and a pudding. **1836-9** DICKENS *Sk. Boz.* ii. (1850) 6/1 The little front parlour,..the little nicnacs are always arranged in precisely the same manner. **1861** HUGHES *Tom Brown at Oxf.* xliii, There was an elegance in the arrangement of all the nick-nacks and ornaments. **1889** J. K. JEROME *Idle Thoughts* 131 All your little nick-nacks spread around you.

attrib. **1860** SALA *Lady Chesterf.* v. 74 Not mere millinery and gloves and nicknack shopping.

b. A feast or social meal to which each guest contributes in kind.

1772 FOOTE *Nabob* I. Wks. 1799 II. 298 Robins has a rout and supper on Sunday next... A nick-nack,..we all contribute, as usual.

3. An alternation of knacking sounds; an instrument that produces such, as the bones.

1650 H. MORE *Observ. Anima Magica* (1655) 144 Some idle boy playing on a pair of Knick-knacks. **1708** *Brit. Apollo* No. 56. 3/1 Death-Watches perplex, With repeated knick-knacks.

Hence **'knick-knacked** (-nækt) *a.*

1891 *Faith of Our Fathers* Sept. 201 Furnituted, and knick-knacked, as though its hospitable inmates had been in since Quarter-day.

knick-knackatory, nick-nackatory. (nɪk'nækətərɪ). Also 8 **nick-kn-**. [f. KNICK-KNACK after *conservatory*, *laboratory*, etc.] A repository of knick-knacks. Also *loosely*, a knick-knack.

a **1704** T. BROWN *Wks.* (1760) II. 15, I keep a nicknackatory, or toy-shop. **1721** AMHERST *Terræ Fil.* No. 34. (1754) 178, I went..to the [Ashmolean] musæum, vulgarly called the nicknackatory. *a* **1734** NORTH *Lives* (1826) II. 180 He was single, and his house a sort of knick-knackatory. **1812** SCOTT *Let. to Miss Baillie* 4 Apr. in *Lockhart*, You see my nick-nackatory is well supplied. **1819** W. TAYLOR in *Monthly Rev.* XC. 13 Collecting the.. nicknackatories of every virtuoso within reach.

Hence **knick-knacka'torian, -'tarian** *sb.* and *a.*: (*a*) *sb.*, one (also **nicknackitorian, -arian -aterian**) who keeps a 'knick-knackatory'; a dealer in knick-knacks; (*b*) *adj.*, devoted to knick-knacks.

1802 in Hone *Every-day Bk.* I. 1284 The plaintiff was a *nicknackitarian*, that is, a dealer in curiosities. **1802** *Chron.* in *Ann. Reg.* 445/1 A profession technically called a Nicknackitorian, that is a dealer in all manner of curiosities, such as Egyptian mummies, Indian implements,..antique shields, helmets, &c. **1842** *United Service Mag.* II. 7 Those of a knicknackaterian tendency.

† **'knick-,knacker.** *Obs. rare*⁻¹. [f. KNICK-KNACK + -ER.] A trifler.

1622 BRETON *Strange Newes* (1879) 6/2 Other kind of knick-knackers..which betwixt knaue and foole can make an ilfauourd passage through the world.

,knick-'knackery, nick-nackery. [f. KNICK-KNACK + -ERY.] **a.** Knick-knacks collectively. **b.** A slight or trifling ornament. **c.** A fanciful dish or confection, = KNICK-KNACK 2.

α. **1812** G. COLMAN *Poet. Vagaries, Lady of Wreck* Advt., A short epic poem, stuffed with romantic knick-knackeries. **1813** MOORE *Horace, Odes* I. xxxviii, Boy, tell the Cook that I hate all nick-nackeries. **1848** *Fraser's Mag.* XXXVIII. 130 They eagerly collected all sorts of knick-knackery. **1876** MRS. WHITNEY *Sights & Ins.* II. xxxi. 588 She took the duster..and went round whisking among knicknackery and books.

β. **1800** *Ann. Reg.* 2362 Too much drapery, ornament, and various nick-nackery. **1870** MISS BRIDGMAN *R. Lynne* II. iii. 58 Nicknackeries from China and Japan.

knick-'knacket. *Sc.* [f. KNICK-KNACK + -ET¹ dim. suffix.] A little knick-knack.

1789 BURNS *Capt. Grose's Peregrin.* vi, He has a fouth o' auld nick-nackets: Rusty airn-caps and jinglin jackets. **1892** KEENE in *Life* ix. 212 An omnivorous collector of knick-knackets.

knick-'knackically, *adv. nonce-wd.* In a knick-knackish way, frivolously.

1749 CHESTERF. *Lett.* (1792) II. cxcv. 234 Do not run through it, as too many of your young countrymen do, musically, and (to use a ridiculous word) knick-knackically.

knick-knackish ('nɪk,nækɪʃ), *a.* [f. KNICK-KNACK + -ISH.] Of the character of a knick-knack; light, trifling, flimsy.

1824 *New Monthly Mag.* X. 165 A fondness for all that is neat, effeminate, finical, and nick-knackish. **1844** *Fraser's Mag.* XXX. 55/1 The plan of this dinner..was..a trifle too knick-knackish [*mispr.* -ashish].

'knick-,knacky. *a.* Also **nick-nacky.** [f. as prec. + -Y¹.] Of, pertaining to, knick-knacks; addicted to knick-knacks; affected, trifling.

1797 MRS. A. M. BENNETT *Beggar Girl* (1813) I. 30 The parsonage, which the knick-knackey taste of the late incumbent had rendered like [etc.]. **1821** *Blackw. Mag.* X. 201 That any nick-knacky gentleman, like Hope, could.. inhale from Byron's works the spirit of his bold, satirical, and libertine genius. **1824** MISS FERRIER *Inher.* viii, His dressing-room is..so neat and nicknacky. **1828** MISS MITFORD *Village* Ser. III. (1863) 519 John Hallett..was rather knick-knacky in his tastes; a great patron of small inventions.

knickpoint ('nɪkpɔɪnt). *Geomorphol.* Also **nickpoint** and as two words. [Partial tr. G. *knickpunkt*, f. *knick* (see KNICK *sb.*²) + *punkt* point.] A break of slope in a river profile, esp. one where a new curve of erosion arising from rejuvenation intersects an earlier curve.

1924 *Bull. Geol. Soc. Amer.* XXXV. 638 Since erosion progresses headward when a region is uplifted by a uniform tilting movement.., the longitudinal profiles of those streams will record a knickpoint at the headward limit of quickened erosion. **1937** WOOLDRIDGE & MORGAN *Physical Basis Geogr.* xv. 220 The rate of upstream recession of knickpoints will evidently vary with the character of rocks eroded. **1954** W. D. THORNBURY *Princ. Geomorphol.* v. 110 Along some streams..nickpoints are found which do not seem to be related to more resistant rock. **1967** J. CHALLINOR *Dict. Geol.* (ed. 3) 142/2 To the present writer it seems that nearly all knick points are due to some commoner and more compelling cause [than rejuvenation], such as the outcropping of a hard bed or glacial erosion. **1968** C. R. TWIDALE *Geomorphol.* vi. 190 Not all falls and rapids indicate nick points, for hard-rock strata crossing the river's path may well produce a break of slope. **1973** *Nature* 9 Nov. 75/1 Recession of valley nickpoints inland from the coastal margin was followed by valley widening, scarp retreat and pedimentation.

knicks (nɪks), *sb. pl.* Colloq. shortening of *knickers* or *knickerbockers*.

1895 *Punch* 15 June 285/2 One young piece in grey knicks and cream cloth..took my fancy perdigious, dear boy. **1923** J. MANCHON *Le Slang* 173 Knicks..s. pl., un pantalon de femme. **1937**, **1952** [see CAMI-]. **1972** J. WILSON *Hide & Seek* vi. 105 Mary, if you'd just stand up I could take your wet knicks off.

'knicky-,knackers. [f. KNACKER, with varied reduplication.] (See quot.) Cf. KNICK-KNACK *sb.* 3.

1875 STAINER & BARRETT *Dict. Mus. Terms*, *Knicky-knackers*, the common instrument of percussion known as bones.

knie, obs. form of KNEE.

knife (naɪf), *sb.* Pl. **knives** (naɪvz). Forms: 1–3 **cnif**, 3–7 **knif**, (3 **cnife, cniue, kniue**), 3–4 **knijf**, 3–5 **knyue**, 4–5 **knyf, knyff(e**, 4–6 **knyfe**, 4– **knife**. *Pl.* 3 **cniues, -fes, -fen**, 3–6 **kniues**, (5 **knyfes, -ys**, 6–7 **knifs**), 7– **knives**. [Late OE. *cníf* (11th c.) = Fris. *knif*, MDu. *cnijf* (Du. *knijf*), MLG. *knîf* (LG. *knîf*, *knief*, *knif*), Ger. *kneif* (prob. from LG.), ON. *knif-r* (Sw. *knif*, Da. *kniv*):—OTeut. **knîƀo-z*, of uncertain etym. Forms with *p* are also found in Du. *knijp*, LG. *knîp*, *kniep*, G. *kneip* (also *kneupe*, *gneip*, *gnippe*): as to the relation between these and the forms with *f*, cf. *knape* and *knave*. F. *canif* (1441 in Godef. *Compl.*) is from Teut.]

1. a. A cutting instrument, consisting of a blade with a sharpened longitudinal edge fixed in a handle, either rigidly as in a ***table-***, ***carving***, or ***sheath-knife***, or with a joint as in a ***pocket-*** or ***clasp-knife***. The blade is generally of steel, but sometimes of other material, as in the silver fish- and fruit-knives, the (blunt-edged) PAPERKNIFE of ivory, wood, etc., and the flint knives of early man.

a **1100** *Ags. Voc.* in Wr.-Wülcker 329/17 *Artauus*, cnif. *c* **1200** ORMIN 4128 þatt cnif wass..Off stan, and nohht of irenn. *c* **1305** *Pilate* 234 in *E.E.P.* (1862) 117 Len me a knyf þis appel to parie. *c* **1386** CHAUCER *Prol.* 369 Hir knyues [*v.r.* knyfes] were chaped noght with bras But al with siluer wroght ful clene and wel. *c* **1460** *Stans Puer* 58 in *Babees Bk.* 30 Brynge no knyves vnskoured to the table. **1552** HULOET, Knife to cut vynes, or graffynge knyfe. **1573–80** BARET *Alv.* K 100 A Shoemakers paring knife. **1663** PEPYS *Diary* 23 Oct., Bought a large kitchen knife, and half a dozen oyster knives. **1708** W. KING *Cookery* iii, Silver and gold knives brought in with the dessert for carving of jellies. **1796** C. MARSHALL *Garden.* xii. (1813) 142 A slip of the knife may wound a neighbouring branch. **1846** BRITTAN tr. *Malgaigne's Man. Oper. Surg.* 214 Lisfranc uses a double-edged knife, and passes it round the limb so as to carry it with its point downwards on the anterior surface of the tibia. **1874** KNIGHT *Dict. Mech.*, *Double-knife*, a knife having a pair of blades which may be set at any regulated distance from each other, so as to obtain thin sections of soft bodies. One form of this is known as Valentin's knife, from the inventor.

b. A knife used as a weapon of offence or defence; a knife-like weapon; applied to a short sword, cutlass, or hanger. ***war to the knife***: war to the last extremity, fierce or relentless war (*lit.* and *fig.*).

c **1175** *Lamb. Hom.* 69 We ne maȝen be fond from us driue Ne mid sworde ne mid kniue. **1297** R. GLOUC. (Rolls) 2286 He drou is knif, & slou þe king. **1377** LANGL. *P. Pl.* B. v. 165 Hadde þei had knyues, bi cryst, her eyther had killed other. *c* **1475** *Rauf Coilȝear* 864 Ilk ane a schort knyfe braidit out sone. *c* **1507** DUNBAR *7 Deadly Sins* 32 Than Yre come in with sturt and stryfe; His hand wes ay vpoun his knyfe. **1590** SPENSER *F.Q.* I. iii. 36 The worthie meed Of him that slew Sansfoy with bloody knife. **1606** SHAKS. *Tr. & Cr.* I. i. 63 Thou lai'st in euery gash that loue hath giuen me, The Knife that made it. **1704** F. FULLER *Med. Gymn.* (1711) 255 If I had been Stab'd, or had had my Flesh cut with Knives. **1812** BYRON *Ch. Har.* I. lxxxvi, War, war is still the cry, 'War even to the knife!' **1876** GLADSTONE *Relig. Thought* i. in *Contemp. Rev.* June 7 'Catholicism' has..declared war to the knife against modern culture. **1894** MRS. H. WARD *Marcella* II. 5 If Westall bullies him any more he will put a knife into him.

†**c.** ***pair of knives***, a set of two knives, esp. as carried in one sheath. *Obs.*

Davies and others following him have explained the term as = 'a pair of scissors', but this is apparently erroneous.

[**1302–3** *Durham Acc. Rolls* (Surtees) 504 In uno pare de Cultell. empt. pro Priore, 5*s*.] **1575** LANEHAM *Let.* (1871) 38 A payr of capped Sheffield kniuez hanging a to side. **1594** BARNFIELD *Aff. Sheph.* II. xvii, A paire of Kniues,..New Gloues to put vpon thy milk-white hand Ile giue thee. **1610** F. COCKS *Diary* 1 Oct. (1901) Paide for a paire of knyves for my va[lentine]: 2*s*., a string for them 10*d*. *c* **1645** HOWELL *Lett* I. I. xiv, Half a dozen pair of Knifs. *a* **1658** FORD, etc. *Witch of Edmonton* II. ii, But see, the bridegroom and bride come, the new pair of Sheffield knives, fitted both to one sheath. **1893** *N. & Q.* 8th Ser. IV. 17/2 At a meeting of the British Archæological Association, in 1860, was exhibited a pair of wedding knives in their embossed sheath of courbouilli.

d. A sharpened cutting-blade forming part of a machine, as of a straw-cutter, turnip-cutter, rag-engine, etc.

1833 J. HOLLAND *Manuf. Metal* II. 261 These knives are placed obliquely to the axle..so as to operate with a sort of draw cut upon the matter presented at the end of the box. **1853** *Catal. R. Agric. Soc. Show Gloucester* 31 The knives are as easily sharpened and set as in an ordinary chaff cutter. **1873** J. RICHARDS *Wood-working Factories* 105 It would be impossible to change the cylinders when a machine has a variety of work to do, but by having some extra knives ground at different bevels it becomes an easy matter to change them.

e. Phr. ***before (one) can say knife***: very quickly or suddenly. Also ***while (one) would say knife***. *colloq.*

1874 M. CLARKE *His Natural Life* II. III. viii. 170 He was over the wall before you could say 'knife'. **1880** MRS. PARR *Adam & Eve* xxxii. 443 'Fore I could say knife he was out and clane off. **1893** R. KIPLING *Many Invent.* 334 We'll pull you off before you can say knife. **1922** JOYCE *Ulysses* 158 Toss off a glass of brandy neat while you'd say knife. **1954** A. MACRAE *Both Ends Meet* in *Plays of Year* X. 509 With a couple like that you'll be in a lawsuit before you can say 'knife'. **1973** M. MUGGERIDGE *Infernal Grove* i. 71 Like alcoholics after taking the cure—never another drop; well, just a taste perhaps, and then, before you could say knife, back on the meths.

f. ***the knife***: used as typical of surgical operations. Also *attrib.*

1880 TENNYSON *Ballads* 88 But they said too of him He was happier using the knife than in trying to save the limb. *Ibid.* 95 My sleep was broken besides with dreams of the dreadful knife. **1932** KIPLING *Limits & Renewals* 350 And leave you knife-*wallahs* to kill our patients? **1961** [see KNIFE-MAN].

g. ***to get*** or ***have one's knife into*** (a person): to exhibit a malicious or vindictive spirit towards; to persecute unrelentingly.

1890 D. C. MURRAY *John Vale's Guardian* III. xxxvi. 173, I reckon you've got your knife into Mr. Jousserau. **1911** H. S. WALPOLE *Mr. Perrin & Mr. Traill* vi. 116 This was to be the beginning of persecution. The Reverend Moy-Thompson had got his knife into him. **1930** J. B. PRIESTLEY *Angel Pavement* ix. 440 You got your knife into him the first time he came here, and after that of course he had to be blamed for everything. **1963** N. MARSH *Dead Water* (1964) i. 26, I don't know what's got into you. Why've you got your knife into this reporter chap?

h. ***night of the long knives***: see LONG KNIFE 2.

i. ***you*** (or ***one***) ***could cut*** (something) ***with a knife***: colloq. phr. used to describe an atmosphere (*lit.* or *fig.*) so thick that it seems capable of being cut with a knife.

1892 A. W. PINERO *Magistrate* I. 18 There's a fog on the line—you could cut it with a knife. **1954** M. SHARP *Gipsy in Parlour* (1955) xiii. 111 The smell was chiefly cabbage..and one could have cut it with a knife. **1973** G. MOFFAT *Deviant Death* v. 68 You could have cut the atmosphere with a knife.

2. *Comb.* **a.** *attrib.*, as ***knife-age*** (see AGE *sb.* 11), ***-back*** (also *attrib.*), ***-basket***, ***-blade***, ***-box***, ***-case***, ***-cut***, ***-feat***, ***-girdle***, ***-haft***, ***-shaft***, ***-stab***, ***-stroke***, ***-thrust*** (also *fig.*), ***-tray***, ***-trick***, etc.; objective, obj. gen., and instrumental, as ***knife-cleaning***, ***-eater***, ***-fancier***, ***-hafter***, ***-juggling***, ***-maker***, ***-sticking***, ***-swallower***, ***-throwing***; similative, etc., as ***knife-backed***, ***-featured***, ***-happy***, ***-jawed***, ***-like***, ***-sharp***, ***-shaped***, ***-skewed***, ***-stripped*** adjs.

1889 R. B. ANDERSON tr. *Rydberg's Teut. Mythol.* 94 The third patriarch begins the '*knife-age and the axe-age with cloven shields'. **1844** J. T. HEWLETT *Parsons & W.* vi, A cook..and *knife-and-shoe-boy. **1737** BRACKEN *Farriery Impr.* (1757) II. 124 Shoulders..no thicker than a *knife back. **1886** *Harper's Mag.* June 119/2 Between these knife-back ledges are plots of sea-green grass. **1966** *Listener* 2 June 789/1 Miniature trains of rubber-tyred, electrically-driven cars (with knife-back seats or flat decks for standing passengers) would run on set routes. **1683** MOXON *Mech. Exerc.*, *Printing* Dict., **Knife backt Sculptor*, is a Sculptor with a thin edge on its back. **1858** SIMMONDS *Dict. Trade*, **Knife-basket*, a tray for holding table-knives. **1848** THACKERAY *Van. Fair* vii, An old-fashioned crabbed *knife-box on a dumb waiter. **1790** *Pennsylvania Packet* 6 Jan. 1/4 Steel and gilt hat buckles, and A few inlaid mahogany *knife cases. *c* **1807** JANE AUSTEN *Watsons* (1954) 344 Nanny..was beginning to bustle into the parlour with the Tray & the Knife-case. **1971** *Canad. Antiques Collector* May 3 (Advt.), Rare and elegant pair of circular inlaid mahogany Knife Cases of the highest quality. English. Circa 1800. **1869** *Daily News* 11 Dec., *Knife-cleaning machine maker. **1883** STEVENSON *Treas. Isl.* IV. xvi, With a *knife-cut on the side of the cheek. **1822–34** *Good's Study Med.* (ed. 4) I. 117 The medical journals..are numerous in their descriptions of London *knife-eaters. **1895** *Century Mag.* Aug. 638/2 A tall, lanky, sharp-boned, *knife-featured fellow. **1865** J. H. INGRAHAM *Pillar of Fire* (1872) 190 *Knife-girdle of lion's hide. **1720** STRYPE *Stow's Surv.* (1754) II. v. xii. 298/1 The skill of making fine Knives and *Knive-hafts. **1864** *Leeds Merc.* 24 Oct., Richard Rhodes, *knife hafter. **1961** *Amer. Speech* XXXVI. 147 **Knife happy*, overeager to resort to operation, said of a surgeon. **1964** *New Statesman* 21 Feb. 306/3 Sacha Pitoeff scowls away as a canapé-ferrying, knife-happy villain. **1896** LYDEKKER *Roy. Nat. Hist.* V. 349 The *Knife-Jawed Fishes... A small genus..(*Hoplognathus*).. characterised by the jawbones having a sharp cutting edge. **1874** LISLE CARR *Jud. Gwynne* I. vii. 202 Some terrible feats of *knife-juggling. **1856** KANE *Arct. Expl.* I. xxiv. 315 Her great fault was her *knife-like bow. **1860** *Illustr. Lond. News* 14 Apr. 362/3 [The simoom's] passage leaves a narrow 'knifelike' track. **1632** SHERWOOD, A *knife maker. **1704**

Lond. Gaz. No. 4082/4 William Dickenson,..Scizer or Knife-maker. *a* **1763** SHENSTONE *On Taste* Wks. 1764 II. 320 A *knife-shaft made from the royal oak. **1835–6** TODD *Cycl. Anat.* I. 312 Compressed *knife-shaped bill. **1955** E. POUND *Classic Anthol.* I. 73 Down from the spring the *knife-sharp waters run. **1973** J. WAINWRIGHT *Devil you Don't* 145 The wind came in, knife-sharp, from the North Sea. **1974** H. R. F. KEATING *Bats fly Up* ix. 95 Ghote felt a knife-sharp happiness. *a* **1918** W. OWEN *Coll. Poems* (1963) 41 Your slender attitude Trembles not exquisite like limbs *knife-skewed. **1851** MAYNE REID *Scalp Hunt.* xxvii. 204 Dogs..growling over the *knife-stripped bones. **1822–34** *Good's Study Med.* (ed. 4) I. 117 Cummings, the *knife-swallower. **1923** G. COLLINS *Valley of Eyes Unseen* i. 28 If there's shooting or *knife-throwing. **1894** *Daily Tel.* 27 June 6/7 That successful *knife-thrust. **1959** *Times* 24 June 13/1 The *knife-thrusts of Ibsen's dialogue. **1967** *Coast to Coast 1965–6* 228 The first knife-thrusts of hunger had developed into a permanent ache of emptiness. **1851** C. CIST *Cincinnati* xiii. 215 Among the principal articles are..*knife trays. **1939–40** *Army & Navy Stores Catal.* 168/1 Knife-trays. Japanned and filleted.

b. Special Combs.: **knife-bar**, a bar bearing the knives in a cutting machine; **knife-bayonet**, a combined knife and bayonet, carried when not in use in a sheath, a small sword-bayonet; **knife-blade**, (*a*) the blade of a knife; (*b*) something sharp or pointed; (*c*) in *Mountaineering*, a kind of piton (see quot. 1968); also *attrib.* and *Comb.*; **knife-boy**, a boy employed to clean table-knives; **knife-cleaner**, a machine for cleaning and polishing knives; **knife-dagger**, an ancient form of one-edged dagger, having a long and heavy blade; **knife-file**, a thin and tapering file, with a very sharp edge; **knife-fish**, a species of carp (*Cyprinus cultratus*); **knife-grass**, a stout American sedge (*Scleria latifolia*) with sharp-edged leaves; **knife-guard**, a small metal piece or arm hinged to the back of a carving-fork to protect the hand against the slipping of the knife; **knife-head**, 'that piece in the cutting apparatus of a harvester to which the knife is fastened, and to which the pitman-head is connected' (Knight *Dict. Mech* Suppl. 1884); †**knife-hook**, a sickle; **knife-lanyard**, a lanyard to which a sailor's knife is fastened; **knife-money**, an ancient Chinese currency consisting of bronze shaped like a knife; **knife-pleat**, a narrow sharply creased pleat (in a garment, esp. a skirt); so **knife-pleated** *a.* (see also PLEATED *ppl. a.*), **knife-pleating** *vbl. sb.*; **knife-polisher** = *knife-cleaner*; **knife-rest**, (*a*) a small pillow of metal or glass on which to rest a carving-knife or -fork at table; also, a support to keep a knife in position while it is being ground; (*b*) *Mil. slang*, a barrier or obstruction composed of barbed wire and timber; **knife-scales**, the sides of the haft of a knife; **knife-sharpener**, an instrument, usually of steel, for sharpening knives; **knife-smith**, a maker of knives, a cutler; †**knife-stone**, a hone; **knife switch** *Electr. Engin.*, a switch consisting of a conducting blade or set of blades hinged at one end so that it may be swung out of or into a fixed contact or set of contacts at the other end; **knife-thrower**, one who throws knives (*spec.* as a form of entertainment); also *U.S. slang* (see quot. 1905); **knife-tool**, (*a*) a knife-shaped graver, (*b*) a minute disk used to cut fine lines in seal-engraving; †**knife-warper**, a knife-thrower, a juggler; **knife-work**, the use of knives as weapons or instruments; also *fig.*; **knife-worm**, a caterpillar that cuts leaves. See also KNIFE-BOARD, -EDGE, -GRINDER, -HANDLE, etc.

1867 *Trans. Illinois Agric. Soc.* VII. 312 By the arrangement of its parts the *knife-bar is placed further forward than in most machines. **1881** *Spon's Encycl. Indust. Arts* 1603 Knife-bar, with diagonal slots, to give the lateral movement as it descends. **1799** G. SMITH *Laboratory* I. 231 To etch 100 or more *knife-blades at once. **1902** *Daily Chron.* 12 Sept. 3/2 The snowy knife-blade *arête*. **1911** J. A. THOMSON *Biol. Seasons* I. 44 The knife-blade-like larvæ of the eel. **1950** J. DEMPSEY *Championship Fighting* x. 49 All fingers, including the thumb, pressing tightly against each other to form a 'knife blade'. **1955** E. POUND *Classic Anthol.* II. 106 A shallow basin gives the fish no shade, Dive as they will, there's flash of fin's knife-blade. **1968** P. CREW *Encycl. Dict. Mountaineering* 75/2 *Knife-blade*, a long thin piton. The name is mainly applied to chrome-molly pitons of this type. **1971** D. HASTON in C. Bonnington *Annapurna South Face* xvii. 206 It was a long and tortuous pitch done in one run-out on one of our big ropes. Firstly knee-deep mushy snow, then hard ice to exit, with one miserable knife-blade for protection. **1848** THACKERAY *Van. Fair* vi, The *knife-boy was caught stealing a cold shoulder of mutton. **1869** L. M. ALCOTT *Little Women* II. i. 12 A *knife-cleaner that spoilt all the knives. **1891** *Month* LXXII. 19 The apple-parer and knife-cleaner are American. **1683** MOXON *Mech. Exerc., Printing* Dict., **Knife-file*, a file with a thin edge. **1799** W. TOOKE *View Russian Emp.* III. 176 The *knife-fish. *a* **1599** SPENSER *F.Q.* VII. vii. 38 In his one hand, as fit for harvests toyle, He held a *knife-hook. **1901** *Chambers's Jrnl.* Apr. 255/2 Between 1122 and 224 B.C. a very curious *knife-money was used in the state of Tsi. This coin was of copper, shaped like a bill-hook, and about seven inches long, with the handle terminating in a ring, doubtless for the purpose of stringing the coins together. **1891** *Cassell's Family Mag.* Nov. 753/2 '*Knife-pleats'—as the Americans call them, to distinguish the single from the box-pleat—are turned towards the centre of the back [of the mantle]. **1928** *Daily Mail* 31 July 1/2 Well made with smart knife pleats at sides. **1964** *McCall's Sewing* ii. 30/1 *Knife pleats*, series of pleats that turn in the same direction, are usually equal in width and are pressed straight to the hem. **1905** *Knife-pleated [see PLEATED *ppl. a.*]. **1937** *Times* 27 Sept. 19/2 A knife-pleated vermilion dinner gown. **1965** *Punch* 12 May p. xvii, Knife-pleated travel skirts. **1895** *Montgomery Ward Catal.* 37/1 Fast Black Sateen Waists... 2 rows *knife pleating from shoulder to belt. **1937** *Times* 27 Sept. 19/2 Knife pleating was used in several graceful gowns. **1858** SIMMONDS *Dict. Trade*, **Knife-rest*. **1919** *Athenæum* 15 Aug. 759/1 Knife-rests, *chevaux de frise*. **1921** F. W. BEWSHER *Hist. 51st Div.* vii. 114 Stooks of cut strands of wire and over-turned knife-rests lay everywhere. **1958** P. KEMP *No Colours or Crest* iv. 54 The entrance to the courtyard was blocked by a heavy 'knife-rest' barbed wire entanglement. **1964** A. H. FARRAR-HOCKLEY *Somme* ii. 83 Gaps had been filled with wired knife-rests and concertina rolls pegged down with iron pickets. **1884** *Yorksh. Post* 9 Jan., '*Knife-scales' are those parts of a knife that form the sides of the handle..of horn, bone, ivory, or tortoiseshell. **1858** SIMMONDS *Dict. Trade*, **Knife-sharpener*. **1738** WESLEY *Wks.* (1872) I. 131 Augustine Neusser, a *knife-smith. **1886** J. PENDLETON *Hist. Derbysh.* 195 The knifesmith's homely forge. **1571** *Wills & Inv. N.C.* (Surtees 1835) 352, ij dosen *knyff stones and iiij dosen rebstones. **1907** H. H. NORRIS *Introd. Study Electr. Engin.* ix. 225 Open *knife switches as described are not commonly used for circuit-breaking purposes above 500 volts and a few hundred amperes. **1962** *Newnes Conc. Encycl. Electr. Engin.* 726/2 Air-break isolators are made in a large variety of forms and range from the simple knife switch to those suitable for the highest transmission voltages. **1905** *Smart Set* Oct. 3/1 'They got a new *knife-thrower up to the hotel,' he announced... (A 'knife-thrower', be it known, is parlance for waitress.) **1953** WODEHOUSE *Performing Flea* 190 He would shoot all round you till you felt like a knife-thrower's assistant, but you were really quite safe. **1973** *Listener* 19 July 80/1 Electrons are fired at an object, and they trace its outline like a knife-thrower at a fair. *a* **1225** *Ancr. R.* 212 He is his *knif-worpare, & pleieð mid sweordes. **1845** W. G. SIMMS *Wigwam & Cabin* 2nd Ser. 143 But none of your *knife-work, le'me tell you. **1931** D. L. SAYERS *Five Red Herrings* xxii. 255 Copying a canvas isn't the same thing as painting direct... It's the technique that's a nuisance... I don't feel handy with so much knife-work. **1954** J. R. R. TOLKIEN *Two Towers* 141 It has been knife-work up there. **1955** J. MORRISON in *Austral. Short Stories* (1963) 2nd Ser. 147 Collins the overseer did all the knife-work—castrating, ear-marking, and tailing. **1965** J. LAWLOR in J. Gibb *Light on C. S. Lewis* 76 Then proceed to the knife-work of murdering to dissect, in order to sweep the vile body aside to make room for the certified masterpieces. **1860** EMERSON *Cond. Life, Fate* Wks. (Bohn) II. 327 Such an one has curculios, borers, *knife-worms.

knife (naɪf), *v.* [f. KNIFE *sb.* (See also KNIVE.)]

1. a. *trans.* To use a knife to; to cut, strike, or stab with a knife.

18.. *Greatheart* III. 174, I should get you pistoled or 'knifed' as sure as eggs are eggs for this insolence. **1865** *Daily Tel.* 18 Apr. 3 Pirate..who was only 'knifed' just prior to winning at Doncaster, secured the judge's fiat easily at the finish. **1883** 'ANNIE THOMAS' *Mod. Housewife* 72, I knew better than to knife my oyster. **1890** DOYLE *Sign of Four* xi. (ed. 3) 209, I would have thought no more of knifing him than of smoking this cigar.

b. To lift (food) to the mouth with a knife.

1897 *Outing* (U.S.) XXX. 460/1 These knowledge-seekers ..knife their food, feeding both brain and stomach simultaneously. What they lost in manners, they gained in time.

c. *U.S. slang.* To strike at secretly; to endeavour to defeat in an underhand way.

1888 *Nation* (N.Y.) 5 July 3/1 He speaks favourably of them in a leading article, and 'knifes' them slyly in paragraphs. **1892** *Boston* (Mass.) *Jrnl.* 5 Nov. 12/7 The idea is to knife Moise for Congress. **1895** *Times* 19 Dec. 8 The liberal knifing of Senators Lodge and Chandler will confirm wavering Irish voters to support the 'Grand Old Party'.

2. *Techn.* **a.** To spread or lay *on* (paint) with a knife. **b.** *Boot-making.* To trim (soles and heels) with a knife.

1887 *Ch. Times* 24 June 516/3 The pigments..are knifed on to the canvas. **1888** *Times* (weekly ed.) 18 May 17/3 For boots..1*s.* a dozen [was paid to the finisher] for knifing.

3. *intr.* To move as with the action of a knife cutting or passing through.

1920 W. CAMP *Football without a Coach* 107 If any of these three center men lunges through—'knifes' through, as it is called—he opens the door on either side of him. **1950** J. DEMPSEY *Championship Fighting* xx. 120 Deflection of the blow by..knifing with the forearm. **1958** *Times* 25 Sept. 3/2 The principal advantage of the American yacht seemed to be her ability to sail closer to the wind and knife more smoothly through the water than Sceptre. **1965** *Harper's Bazaar* June 68/2 If you come across a Salon 1959..knife on to it. **1971** *Flying* (N.Y.) Apr. 30/3 Skirting the coast for awhile before knifing northwest to Bordeaux.

knife and fork.

1. a. *lit.* as used in eating at table. Hence in various phrases referring to eating, as *to play a good knife and fork*, to eat heartily.

1727–38 GAY *Fables* I. *Farmer's Wife & Raven*, Then, to contribute to my loss, My knife and fork were laid across. **1809** MALKIN *Gil Blas* I. vi. ¶2 Domingo, after playing a good knife and fork..took himself off. **1852** DICKENS *Bleak Ho.* xlv, My digestion is much impaired, and I am but a poor knife and fork at any time. **1888** ANNIE S. SWAN *Doris Cheyne* i. 21 I'll be glad to see you over to a knife and fork. **1889** BOLDREWOOD *Robbery under Arms* xlv, Moran..played a good knife and fork.

b. *attrib.* (with hyphens).

1812 *Sporting Mag.* XL. 25 These dextrous knife-and-fork men. **1838** *Manch. Guardian* 26 Sept. 3/2 This question of universal suffrage is a knife-and-fork question, a bread-and-cheese question, after all. **1841** GRESLEY *C. Lever* 183 With one class, it is what has been termed a knife-and-fork question; with the other, a moral or political affair. **1895** PÉRONNE *Veil of Liberty* ix. 182 A good knife-and-fork breakfast. **1909** J. R. WARE *Passing Eng.* 163/2 *Knife and fork tea* (middle class, 1874). Vulgarisation of high tea. **1929** J. B. PRIESTLEY *Good Companions* III. vi. 624 A sound specimen of their knife-and-fork tea. **1963** BIRD & HUTTON-STOTT *Veteran Motor Car* 150 The first model of Lutzmann was a knife-and-fork copy of the Benz.

2. A popular name of Herb Robert (*Geranium Robertianum*) and the common club-moss (*Lycopodium clavatum*).

1879 in BRITTEN & HOLLAND.

Hence **knife-and-forker**, one who plays a good knife and fork, a hearty eater.

a **1845** HOOD *Literary & Literal* vi, Not a mere pic-nic.. But tempting to the solid knife-and-forker.

knife-board.

1. A board on which knives are cleaned.

1829 in A. Mathews *Mem. Charles Mathews* (1839) IV. ii. 26 *Joe Merriman*,—formerly imp of the ring, slave of the knife-board, and footman of Mr. Jenkins. **1848** THACKERAY *Vanity Fair* xxxvii, Raggles rose from the knife-board [= position of knife-boy] to the foot-board of the carriage. **1858** SIMMONDS *Dict. Trade*, *Knife-board*, a piece of wood, plain, or cased with leather for cleaning and polishing table-knives.

2. A popular name for the original roof-seat on buses consisting of a double bench placed lengthways on the top. Also *attrib.* and *transf.*

1852 LEECH in *Punch* 15 May (Cartoon), You don't catch me coming out on the knife board again to make room for a party of swells. **1869** TROLLOPE *He knew*, etc. xxxiii, He sat smoking on the knife-board of the omnibus. **1894** SALA *London up to Date* 135 There was added to the top of the 'bus two long rows of seats..which soon acquired the popular designation of the 'knife-board'. **1931** *Times Lit. Suppl.* 24 Dec. 1043/2 The photograph..is delightful..of a very primitive 'knifeboard' omnibus with its top-hatted travellers. **1963** *Times* 6 Feb. 11/4 Those devoted to seeing Shakespeare on his home-ground and taking the full treatment will no doubt be thankful that the Stratford Theatre is not of the old and austere style with hard benches in the pit and knife-board seats in the gallery.

ˈknife-ˌedge.

1. The edge of a knife; also *transf.*, anything keenly cutting. Also *attrib.* = *knife-edged*.

1876 GEO. ELIOT *Dan. Der.* xxiii, Her pride had felt a terrible knife-edge. **1877** E. R. CONDER *Bas. Faith* ii. 80 To insert the knife-edge of a sharp discrimination. **1884** TENNYSON *Becket* II. i. 140, I would creep, crawl over knife-edge flint Barefoot. *a* **1930** D. H. LAWRENCE *Last Poems* (1932) 39 The sudden dripping down of the knife-edge cleavage of the lightning. *a* **1935** T. E. LAWRENCE *Mint* (1955) II. xii. 132 He creases everybody's trousers with the knife-edge that Stiffy demands. **1969** *Sci. Jrnl.* Nov. 35/2 Steel wheels or even solid rubber tyres..give a knife-edge response which would render driving at speeds over 80 km/h impossibly dangerous.

2. a. A wedge of hard steel, on which a pendulum, scale-beam, or the like, is made to oscillate.

1818 CAPT. KATER in *Phil. Trans.* 35 For the construction of the pendulum, it became of..importance to select a mode of suspension..free from objection. Diamond points, spheres, and the knife edge, were each considered. **1851** *Illustr. Catal. Gt. Exhib.* 1266 The pendulum is suspended on a knife-edge of very hard bronze. **1854** J. SCOFFERN in *Orr's Circ. Sc., Chem.* 4 Delicate balances have their points of oscillation composed of a steel knife-edge working on agate planes.

b. *transf.* and *fig. Esp.* a sharp crest of rock, ice, sand, or the like. Also *attrib.*, as ***knife-edge ridge***.

1871 L. STEPHEN *Playgr. Europe* v. (1894) 120 Balancing ourselves on a knife-edge of ice between two crevasses. **1897** *Pall Mall Mag.* Aug. 524 She had come to the party..on the knife-edge of anticipation and alarm. **1907** *Westm. Gaz.* 26 Nov. 3/2 The road thereto lies along a 'knife-edge'. **1925** W. J. MILLER *Introd. Physical Geol.* viii. 252 A knife-edge ridge may also develop where glaciers in two parallel valleys erode and steepen the valley sides until only a very sharp divide separates the valleys. **1925** E. F. NORTON *Fight for Everest, 1924* I. ii. 31 A ridge which begins in a knife-edge of rock worthy of the Chamounix Aiguilles. **1945** BAKER *Austral. Lang.* iii. 58 Knife edges, as certain razor-back sandhills are known. **1963** *Times* 24 Jan. 10/3 Mr. John Brass, chairman of the West Midlands Division of the N.C.B., said yesterday that west Midland coal supplies were poised 'on a knife edge' at the present. **1964** C. WILLOCK *Enormous Zoo* v. 74 The immediate foreground beneath the sandstone cliff.. was eroded into a series of gullies and knife-edges like row upon row of yellowed shark's teeth. **1969** C. R. LONGWELL et al. *Physical Geol.* xii. 266/2 An arête is a jagged, knife-edge ridge created where two groups of cirque glaciers have eaten into the ridge from both sides. **1971** *Country Life* 25 Feb. 408/3 The ridge goes easily at first on firm snow..and finally ends in a snow knife-edge. **1972** *Guardian* 18 Feb. 24/5 The Government's knife-edge victory for the European Communities Bill in the Commons last night. **1974** *Times* 12 Oct. 1/1 A government with a knife-edge majority. *Ibid.* 1/2 Mr Wilson intends to govern on a parliamentary knife-edge for at least two or three years.

3. *Diamond-cutting.* (See quot.)

1909 J. WODISKA *Bk. Precious Stones* 349 *Knife-edge.* The girdle of a brilliant cut to a sharp edge and polished.

Hence **knife-edged** *a.*, having a thin sharp edge like a knife.

1863–76 CURLING *Dis. Rectum* (ed. 4) 46 A pair of knife-edged scissors. **1865** GEIKIE *Scen. & Geol. Scot.* vi. 118 A

mere knife-edged crest, shelving steeply into the glens on either side. **1883** *Harper's Mag.* Aug. 445/2 A knife-edged craft with wide keel.

knifeful ('naɪffʊl). [-FUL.] As much as a knife will hold or carry.

1850 B. TAYLOR *Eldorado* ix. (1862) 86 Every knifeful brought out a quantity of grains and scales. **1894** R. MANSFIELD *Chips* 187 He proceeded to shovel knifefuls of fat into his throat.

knife-grinder.

1. One whose trade it is to grind knives and cutting-tools, esp. in the process of making these; also, an itinerant grinder or sharpener of knives and scissors.

1611 FLORIO, *Arruotatore*, a sheare or knife grinder. **1797** CANNING *Knife-Grinder* iii, Tell me, Knife-grinder, how you came to grind knives? **1813** *Examiner* 17 May 317/2 Tricks that are called nervous,—such as..playing the knife-grinder with your leg. **1878** *N. Amer. Rev.* CXXVII. 265 The case of the Sheffield knife-grinders.

2. A grind-stone, emery-wheel, or other appliance for grinding steel cutting tools.

1875 in KNIGHT *Dict. Mech.*

3. a. A name for a species of cicada. **b.** The Night-jar or Goatsucker (*Cent. Dict.*); see GRINDER 7.

1859 TENNENT *Ceylon* (1860) I. 267 The cicada..makes the forest re-echo with a long sustained noise so curiously resembling that of a cutler's wheel that..it has acquired the highly appropriate name of the knife-grinder.

'knife-ˌhandle.

1. The handle or haft of a knife.

1798 WILCOCKE tr. *Stavorinus' Voy. E. Ind.* I. vi. 377 *note*, The iron point..together with the blade of a knife..set in a knife-handle, common to them both.

2. Popular name of species of Razor-shell, *Solen siliqua* or *S. ensis*. Chiefly *U.S.*

1755 *Gentl. Mag.* XXV. 33 Knife-Handles, *Solen s.* Their figure..resembles the handle of a knife.

'knifeless, *a. rare.* In 6 kniueles. Without a knife.

1573 TUSSER *Husb.* (1878) 188 Some knjueles their daggers for brauerie weare. **1916** H. G. WELLS *Mr. Britling* III. ii. 412 Knifeless and forkless meals.

†**'knifely,** *a. Obs. rare*$^{-1}$. [-LY[1].] Of the nature of a knife.

1548-67 THOMAS *Ital. Dict.*, *Coltellate*, strypes with a sword, or other knifely weapon.

'knife-man. One who uses a knife as an instrument, a tool, or a weapon; *spec.* †(*a*) in the parlance of N. American Indians, an Englishman (*obs.*); (*b*) *slang*, a surgeon.

1643 R. WILLIAMS *Key Lang. Amer.* (1866) 126 They call English-men Chauquaquock, that is, Knive-men, stone formerly being to them in stead of Knives. **1852** W. WILLISON in *Midland Florist* VI. 9 Serving as knife-man in the Gateshead nursery. **1901–2** *Ann. Brit. Sch. Athens* VIII. 294 The few picked 'knife-men' who lay or crouched in the trenches cutting through the compost of bones and pottery inch by inch. **1923** *Dialect Notes* V. 235 *Knifeman*, a man who fights with a knife... Not common. **1956** J. MASTERS *Bugles & Tiger* i. 19 There was always the sense-sharpening chance of a sudden storm of bullets, a rush of knifemen. **1961** *Woman* 18 Mar. 10/4 Had she seen the new nurse on women's surgical? The knife men always had the luck. **1964** *Amer. Speech* XXXIX. 271 *Cutter man, knife man*, a worker who operates the cutter. **1973** 'R. MACLEOD' *Burial in Portugal* v. 110 A third man..was coming in at a rush with a knife... Gaunt..felt the jar as his heel took the knife-man low in the stomach.

'knife-ˌplaying. †**a.** Tossing and catching knives, as practised by jugglers. *Obs.* **b.** Wielding a knife as a weapon.

13.. *K. Alis.* 1044 (Bodl. MS.) Knijf pleyeyng and syngyng. **1855** MOTLEY *Dutch Rep.* VI. i. (1866) 784 'We came nearly to knife-playing', said the most distinguished priest in the assembly.

knifer ('naɪfə(r)). [f. KNIFE *v.* + -ER[1].] **1.** *Boot-making.* One who knifes or trims the soles and heels of boots.

1888 *Pall Mall G.* 18 Apr. 7/2 Charles Solomon, a Jew, described himself as a knifer or 'master', taking boots to make at 4*s.* per dozen pairs, out of which he got 2*s.* per dozen for knifing. **1890** EARL DUNRAVEN *Draft Rep. Sweating Syst.* 3 An inferior master in the boot trade, or what is called a 'knifer'.

2. One who carries or uses a knife as a weapon.

1870 DICKENS *E. Drood* xxiii. 188 Jacks. And Chayner men. And hother Knifers. **1905** *Times* 11 Dec. 5/2 This is a new move of the hooligans and knifers, who lately committed attacks on enlightened working men.

knifey, knifie ('naɪfɪ), *sb.* Chiefly *Sc.* [f. KNIFE *sb.* + -Y[6], -IE.] Either of two games played by boys with knives: (*a*) = MUMBLE-THE-PEG; (*b*) (see quot. 1969).

1896 E. TURNER *Little Larrikin* iv. 40 An angel in little blue knickerbockers playing knifey on a heap of builders' sand. **1901** *Scottish Antiquary* XVI. 49 'Bonnety' and 'Knify'..are the 'Hatty' and 'Knifey' which..the Edinburgh Academy once knew so well. **1934** G. M. MARTIN *Dundee Worthies* 179 'Knifie'..[was] played with a knife with open blade on any grass plot. **1939** F. L. COMBS *Harrowed Toad* 90 Another fieldsman who may have seen the ball but had been indulging spasmodically in 'knifey'. **1951** *Banffshire Advertiser* 16 Aug., I eest tae be the best knifey player in the toonie squeel. **1969** I. & P. OPIE *Children's Games* vii. 221 The first boy throws a knife..so that it sticks in the ground not more than twelve inches to the left or right of one of his opponent's feet. The other boy ..plucks the knife out of the ground, and moves his nearest foot to the place where the knife went in... Throughout Scotland..it is 'Knifie'. **1973** 'J. PATRICK' *Glasgow Gang Observed* xii. 113 A game of 'knifey' began with Rose's front door as target. Bayonets and commando knives..sank into the woodwork.

knifey ('naɪfɪ), *a.* [f. KNIFE *sb.* + -Y[1].] Resembling the edge of a knife in narrowness or sharpness; also *fig.* (see quot. 1937).

1906 G. A. B. DEWAR *Faery Year* 258 Hovering, he presents to the wind but a knifey edge of wing. **1937** PARTRIDGE *Dict. Slang* 459/2 *Knifey*, (of a person, esp. a customer) that cuts things painfully fine when dealing in the money-market: stockbrokers'. **1955** H. SMITH *Horseman through Six Reigns* xix. 192 Withers that are neither rounded nor knifey.

†**kniff-knaff.** *Obs. slang.* A kind of jest.

1683 E. HOOKER *Pref. Pordage's Mystic Div.* 15 What shal wee sai..of..Railleries and Drolleries, Quirks and Quillets, Trics and Trangams, Kniff-knaffs, Bimboms, &c.?

knight (naɪt), *sb.* Forms: α. 1–3 cniht, (1 cnæht, cneoht, 3 *Orm.* cnihht), 4 cniȝt, (3 cnih, 5 cnect); 1–5 knyht, (2 knicht, 3 kniȝt, knict), 3–4 kniht, 3–5 kniȝt, knyȝt, (5 knyȝht), 4–6 knyght, (5–6 knygt, *Sc.* knicht, knycht), 4– **knight.** (β. 3 cniþt, knicth, 4 knitht, knytht, knigth, kniȝth, 5 knygth; 3–4 knith, 4– 5 (6 *Sc.*) knyth. γ. 3 knit, 4 knite, 4–5 knyte, 6 knytt.) [A common WGer. word: OE. *cniht, cneoht* = OFris. *knecht, kniucht*, OS. *(in)knecht* (MDu. and Du. *knecht*), OHG., MHG. *kneht* (G. *knecht*). In the continental tongues the prevailing senses are 'lad, servant, soldier'. The genitive pl. in ME. was occas. *knighten(e)*]

I. †**1.** A boy, youth, lad. (Only in OE.) *Obs.*

c **893** K. ÆLFRED *Oros.* III. vii. §2 Philippus, þa he cniht wæs, wæs Thebanum to ȝisle ȝeseald. *c* **925** *Laws of Ine* c. 7 §2 Tyn-wintre cniht mæȝ bion þiefðe ȝewita. *c* **950** *Lindisf. Gosp.* John vi. 9 Is cnæht an her. **971** *Blickl. Hom.* 175 He wearþ færinga ȝeong cniht & sona eft eald man.

†**2.** A boy or lad employed as an attendant or servant; hence, by extension, a male servant or attendant of any age. *Obs.*

c **950** *Lindisf. Gosp.* Luke xii. 45 Onginneð..slaa ða cnæhtas & ðiuwas. *a* **1000** *Boeth. Metr.* xxvi. 180 Cnihtas wurdon, ealde ȝe ȝiunge, ealle forhwerfde to sumum diore. *c* **1000** *Ags. Gosp.* Matt. ix. 15 Þæs brydguman cnihtas. *c* **1205** LAY. 3346 Heo sende..to þare cnihtene inne, heo hehte hem faren hire wei. *Ibid.* 29636 Þus spac ure drihten wið Austin his cnihten. *c* **1250** *Hymn Virgin* 16 in *Trin. Coll. Hom.* App. 255 Swete leuedi, of me þu reowe & haue merci of þin knicht [*cf.* 22 ic am þi mon].

3. With genitive, or poss. pron.: A military servant or follower (of a king or some other specified superior); later, one devoted to the service of a lady as her attendant, or her champion in war or the tournament; hence also *fig.*, and even applied to a woman (quot. 1599).

This is logically the direct predecessor of sense 4, the 'king's knight' having become the 'knight' *par excellence*, and a lady's knight being usually one of knightly rank.

a **1100** *O.E. Chron.* (Laud MS.) an. 1087 Þa wæron innan þam castele Oda bisceopes cnihtas. *Ibid.* an. 1094 Rogger Peiteuin..& seofen hundred þes cynges cnihta mid him. *c* **1369** CHAUCER *Dethe Blaunche* 1179 That she wolde holde me for hir knyght, My lady that is so faire. *a* **1450** *Le Morte Arth.* 328, I my self wille wyth you abyde, And be youre servante and youre knight. **1535** STEWART *Cron. Scot.* (1858) I. 14 Syne thus he said, in presence of his men, 'My knichtis kene [etc.]'. **1592** SHAKS. *Rom. & Jul.* III. ii. 142 O find him, giue this Ring to my true Knight. **1599** —— *Much Ado* V. iii. 13 Pardon goddesse of the night, Those that slew thy virgin knight. **1712–14** POPE *Rape Lock* III. 129 So Ladies in Romance assist their Knight, Present the spear, and arm him for the fight. **1859** TENNYSON *Elaine* 958 In all your quarrels will I be your knight.

4. Name of an order or rank. **a.** In the Middle Ages: Originally (as in 3), A military servant of the king or other person of rank; a feudal tenant holding land from a superior on condition of serving in the field as a mounted and well-armed man. In the fully-developed feudal system: One raised to honourable military rank by the king or other qualified person, the distinction being usually conferred only upon one of noble birth who had served a regular apprenticeship (as page and squire) to the profession of arms, and thus being a regular step in this even for those of the highest rank. **b.** In modern times (from the 16th c.): One upon whom a certain rank, regarded as corresponding to that of the mediæval knight, is conferred by the sovereign in recognition of personal merit, or as a reward for services rendered to the crown or country.

The distinctive title of a knight (mediæval or modern) is *Sir* prefixed to the name, as 'Sir John Falstaff': *Knight* (also abbrev. *Knt.* or *Kt.*) may be added, but this is now somewhat unusual. A knight who is not a member of any special order of knighthood (see 12 b below) is properly a *Knight Bachelor* (see BACHELOR 1 b). Various ceremonies have at different times been used in conferring the honour of knighthood, esp. that of the recipient kneeling while the sovereign touches his shoulder with the flat of a sword; knights of the higher orders are now frequently created by letters-patent. In point of rank the mediæval knight was inferior to earl and baron; modern knights rank below baronets, and the dignity is not hereditary.

In early use the *knight*, as the type of the military profession, was freq. contrasted with *clerk, merchant*, etc., and, in point of rank, with *king*. The characteristic qualities expected in a knight, as bravery, courtesy, and chivalrous conduct, are frequently alluded to, and the name (esp. with adjs., as *a good knight*) often implied these qualities as well as the mere rank.

a **1100** *O.E. Chron.* (Laud MS.) an. 1086 Þænne wæron mid him ealle þa rice men..abbodas & eorlas, þeȝnas & cnihtas. *a* **1124** *Ibid.*, Þes kinges stiward of France..& fela oðre godre cnihte. *a* **1250** *Owl & Night.* 1573 Moni chapmon, and moni cniht, Luveth and halt his wif ariht. **1297** R. GLOUC. (Rolls) 11608 Þo turnde grimbaud pauncefot to sir edward anon & was imad kniȝt. *c* **1315** A. DAVY *Dreams* 4 A kniȝth of mychel miȝth, His name is ihote sir Edward þe kyng. **1340** *Ayenb.* 36 Hi..makeþ beggeres þe knyȝtes and hemen þet uolȝeþ þe tornemens. *c* **1386** CHAUCER *Prol.* 72 He was a verray parfit gentil knyght. **1411** *Rolls of Parlt.* III. 650/2 All the Knythes and Esquiers and Yomen that had ledynge of men on his partie. *c* **1425** *Eng. Conq. Irel.* 92 Now we wyllen turne ayeyne to our knyghten gestes yn Irlande. **1470–85** MALORY *Arthur* I. xv, He was a passyng good knyght of a kynge, and but a yong man. **1556** *Chron. Gr. Friars* (Camden) 22 There was slayne kynge Henrys sone and many other lordes and knyttes. **1577** HARRISON *England* II. v. (1877) I. 114 Knights be not borne, neither is anie Man a Knight by succession. **1596** DALRYMPLE tr. *Leslie's Hist. Scot.* VIII. 57 Alex[r] Leuingstoun knicht..is elected gouernour of the Realme. **1648** *Art. Peace* c. 7 The estates..of the lords, knights, gentlemen, and free-holders..of Connaught. **1771** SMOLLETT *Humph. Cl.* 3 Oct., We found the knight sitting on a couch, with his crutches by his side. **1800** COLERIDGE *Love* iv, She leaned against..The statue of the armed knight. **1818** *Letters Patent* in Nicholas *Hist. Ord. Knighthood* (1842) IV. 7 The said Distinguished Order of Saint Michael and Saint George, shall..consist of Three Classes of Knights of the said Order.

c. More fully ***Knight of the Shire***: A gentleman representing a shire or county in parliament; originally one of two of the rank of knight; with the abolition of almost all distinctive features of the county representation, the term has lost its distinctive meaning and is only used technically and *Hist.*: cf. BURGESS 1 b. Formerly sometimes ***Knight of the Commonty*** or ***of Parliament***.

1399 LANGL. *Rich. Redeles* IV. 41 Thei must..mete togedir, þe knyȝtis of þe comunete and carpe of the maters, With Citiseyns of shiris. **1444** *Rolls of Parlt.* V. 110/2 All other that will be atte the assessyng of the wages of the Knyghtes of the Shire. **1538** FITZHERB. *Just. Peas* (1554) 132 b, Sherifes must returne such persons knights of the parliament which be chosen by þe greater nombre of the freholders. [**1544** *Act 35 Hen. VIII*, c. 11 The Knights of all and euery Shire..chosen for their assembly in the Kings high Court of Parliament.] **1617** MINSHEU *Ductor*, Knights of the Shire,..otherwise bee called Knights of the Parliament, and be two Knights, or other Gentlemen of worth, that are chosen in *Pleno Comitatu*, by the Freeholders of euery County. **1648** PRYNNE *Plea for Lords* B iij b, The King..might call two Knights, Citizens and Burgesses to Parliament. *Ibid.* C j b, There could be no Knights of Shires..to serve in Parliament. **1679** EVELYN *Mem.* 4 Feb., My Brother, Evelyn, was now chosen Knight for the County of Surrey. **1711** STEELE *Spect.* No. 109 ¶7 He served his Country as Knight of this Shire to his dying Day. **1765** BLACKSTONE *Comm.* I. ii. 128 With regard to the elections of knights, citizens, and burgesses. **1844** LD. BROUGHAM *Brit. Const.* iii. (1862) 47 The knights are to represent the 'community of the counties', the citizens and burgesses the 'community of the towns'.

d. Name of an order or rank in the political association called the 'Primrose League'.

1885 *Primrose League* 10 Obtain thirteen Signatures to the form of Declaration as Knights, or Dames. *Ibid.* 12 After having been a Member of the League for twelve months,.. a Knight, as a special reward for meritorious service, may be elevated to the rank of Knight Companion. **1885** *Primrose Rec.* 17 Sept. 109 It is needless to say that they will induce as many as possible to enrol themselves as Knights, Dames, or Associates of the League.

e. Fig. phr. ***knight in shining armour***: in informal or ironic use, a person regarded as a medieval knight in respect of his chivalrous spirit, especially towards women.

1965 V. CANNING *Whip Hand* xv. 188 A man..didn't have to be a knight in shining armour. **1967** M. SUMMERTON *Memory of Darkness* x. 124 Most people regard him as a crank. I'm afraid, so far as Dilys is concerned, he makes a very ineffectual knight in shining armour. **1968** A. DIMENT *Gt. Spy Race* i. 8, I was one of the new knights in shining PVC armour. Come to rescue the lower-middle class maiden from the dragon of boredom. **1973** *Ottawa Jrnl.* 16 Aug. 1/6 'Throughout his whole brief, Mr. Cassidy has attempted to portray himself as a knight in shining armor but on close examination it portrays our whole judicial system as something less than perfect,' said Chief Seguin.

†**5. a.** Applied to personages of ancient history or mythology, viewed as holding a position or rank similar to that of the mediæval knight. *Obs.*

c **1205** LAY. 406 Assaracus wes god cniht; Wið Grickes he heold moni fiht. *c* **1250** *Gen. & Ex.* 283 Ðo wurð he drake ðat ear was kniȝt. *c* **1330** R. BRUNNE *Chron. Wace* (Rolls) 4185 Hardy Iulius, knyght war & wys. *c* **1400** *Destr. Troy* 2740 Parys the pert knight, and his pure brother Comyn vnto courtte with company grete, Of thre thowsaund þro knightes. **1513** DOUGLAS *Æneis* IX. xi. 48 Equicolie A lusty knycht in armis rycht semly. **1535** COVERDALE *2 Kings* ix. 25 And Iehu sayde vnto Bidekar the knyghte. **1606** SHAKS. *Tr. & Cr.* IV. v. 86 This Aiax..This blended Knight, halfe Troian, and halfe Greeke.

b. freq. transl. L. *mīles*, a common soldier.
Miles was the regular med.L. equivalent of 'knight'.
c **1200** ORMIN 8185 Hise cnihhtess alle imæn Forþȝedenn ..Wiþþ heore wæpenn alle bun. *c* **1300** *Cursor M.* 19824 Cornelius..calde til him tua men and a knite. **1382** WYCLIF *Matt.* xxvii. 27 Thanne kniȝtis of the president takynge Jhesu in the mote halle, gedriden to hym all the cumpanye of kniȝtis. **1483** CAXTON *Gold. Leg.* 14 b/2 He is delyverd to knyghtis for to be beten. **1563** WINȜET *Four Scoir Thre Quest.* Wks. 1888 I. 77 That knycht quha peirsit our Lordis syde with the speir.
fig. *c* **1375** *Sc. Leg. Saints* ii. (*Paul*) 218, I am cristis lauchtful knycht. **1382** WYCLIF *2 Tim.* ii. 3 Trauele þou as a good knyȝt [Vulg. *miles*, TINDALE, etc. soudier, souldier] of crist ihesu. **1526** *Pilgr. Perf.* (W. de W. 1531) 293 In parte they be weyke, and not of the strongest knyghtes of god.

6. a. *Roman Antiq.* (tr. L. *eques* horseman). One of the class of *equites*, who originally formed the cavalry of the Roman army, and at a later period were a wealthy class of great political importance.
1375 BARBOUR *Bruce* III. 210 Off Ryngis..That war off knychtis fyngerys tane He send thre bollis to Cartage. **1601** HOLLAND *Pliny* II. 459 There were none at Rome vnder the degree of a knight or gentleman that carried rings on their fingers. **1850** MERIVALE *Rom. Emp.* (1852) I. 79 The leader of the senate, the patron of the knights,..Pompeius.

b. *Greek Antiq.* (tr. Gr. ἱππεύς horseman). A citizen of the second class at Athens in the constitution of Solon, being one whose income amounted to 300 medimni.
1820 T. MITCHELL *Aristophanes*, The Knights, or, The Demagogues. **1836** THIRLWALL *Greece* II. xi. 37 The members of the second class were called knights, being accounted able to keep a war-horse. **1885** STEWART & LONG *Plutarch's Lives* III. 498 The knights rode..in solemn procession to the temple of Zeus.

7. In games: **a.** One of the pieces in the game of chess, now usually distinguished by the figure of a horse's head; fig. ***knight's move***, an indirect or devious move.
c **1440** *Gesta Rom.* xxi. 71 (Harl. MS.) The chekir or þe chesse hath viij poyntes in eche partie..þe knyȝt hath iij poyntes. **1474** CAXTON *Chesse* II. iv. C iij b, The knight ought to be maad al armed upon an hors in such wise that he have an helme on his heed [etc.]. **1562** ROWBOTHAM *Play of Cheastes*, The knight hath his top cut asloope, as thoughe beynge dubbed knight. **1689** *Young Statesmen* vi. in *Coll. Poems Popery* 8/2 So have I seen a King on Chess, (His Rooks and Knights withdrawn). **1870** HARDY & WARE *Mod. Hoyle, Chess* 39 The knight has a power of moving which is quite peculiar. **1958** P. SHORE in N. Mackenzie *Conviction* 37 The favoured entrant moves, to quote the current jargon, by a series of 'knight's moves' over the management board. **1959** *Listener* Jan. 219/2 Mankind does move forward, even if it is often by the Knight's move. **1963** V. NABOKOV *Gift* iv. 228 Any genuinely new trend is a knight's move, a change of shadows, a shift that displaces the mirror. **1967** G. SIMS *Last Best Friend* xviii. 168 We took a kind of Knight's move, one step forward and a jump to the side. **1972** W. MCGIVERN *Caprifoil* (1973) ii. 37 You've made a knight's move in thought.

†**b.** The knave in cards. *Obs.*
1585 HIGINS tr. *Junius' Nomenclator* 294 b, Playeng cards ..*Eques*, the knight, knaue, or varlet.

†**8.** *Naut.* Each of two strong posts or bitts on the deck of a vessel, containing sheaves through which were passed the jeers or halyards used in raising and lowering sails. (See quot. 1627.) *Obs.*
1495 *Naval Acc. Hen. VII* (1896) 200 Shyvers of brasse.. in the Knyght of the fore castell. **1611** COTGR., *Teste de More*,..the Knights, a crooked peece of timber in the fore-castle of a ship. **1627** CAPT. SMITH *Seaman's Gram.* ii. 7 The Ramshead,..to this belong the fore Knight, and the maine Knight, vpon the second Decke... They are two short thicke peeces of wood, commonly carued with the head of a man upon them, in those are foure shiuers apeece, three for the halyards and one for the top rope to run in. *a* **1642** SIR W. MONSON *Naval Tracts* III. (1704) 345/2 The Knights belong to the Halyards.

9. in *pl.* A boys' game.
'Two big boys take two smaller ones on their shoulders; the big boys act as horses, while the younger ones seated on their shoulders try to pull each other over' (Alice Gomme *Dict. Brit. Folk-lore* 1894).

II. Sense 4, with descriptive additions.

10. Followed by an appositive sb. †***knight adventurer*** = KNIGHT-ERRANT. †***knight baronet*** = BARONET. †***knight brother***, a brother in a society or order of knights. †***knight wager***, a mercenary soldier. See also BACHELOR 1 b, BANNERET 1 c, COMMANDER 4, COMPANION 5, HARBINGER 2, HOSPITALLER 3, TEMPLAR.
1636 MASSINGER *Bashf. Lover* II. ii, *Knight adventurers are allowed Their pages. *a* **1652** BROME *Queenes Exch.* v. Wks. 1873 III. 547 With Knights adventurers I went in quest. **1621** BURTON *Anat. Mel.* III. ii. VI. v. (1651) 579 A Gentlemans daughter and heir must be married to a *Knight Barronets eldest son at least. **1706** PHILLIPS, *Knight Baronet*, a Combination of Title, in regard the Baronetship is generally accompany'd with that of the Knighthood; but the latter was made a distinct Order by K. James I... These Baronets were to have Precedency.. before all ordinary Knights Banneret, Knights of the Bath, and Knights Batchelors. **1687** *Lond. Gaz.* No. 2251/3 That Order [of the Thistle], consisting of the Soveraign and Twelve *Knights Brethren. **1513** DOUGLAS *Æneis* II. i. [I. xii.] 12 Quhat Marmidon.. Or *knycht wageor to cruell Vlixes.

11. With adj. (before or after the sb.). †***knight adventurous*** = KNIGHT-ERRANT. †***knight caligate of arms***: see CALIGATE. ***military*** (†***naval, poor***) ***knight of Windsor*** (see 12 b).
1429 *Rolls of Parlt.* IV. 346/2 The said Chapelle [of St. George] was founded by the right noble and worthy Kyng Edward the Thridde syn the Conquest..upon a Wardein, Chanons, poure Knyghtes, and other Ministres. *c* **1440** *Promp. Parv.* 279/2 Knyghte awnterows (*S.* knyht a-ventowrs), *tiro*. **1470–85** MALORY *Arthur* IV. xviii, Here am I redy, an auentures knyghte that wille fulfylle ony aduenture that ye wylle desyre. **1577** HARRISON *England* II. v. (1877) I. 124 The thirteene chanons and six and twentie poore knights haue mantels of the order [of the garter]. **1724** *Lond. Gaz.* No. 6290/3 First went the Poor Knights.

12. Followed by a genitive phrase.

a. Denoting a special set or class of knights (real or by courtesy). †***knight of adventurers*** = KNIGHT-ERRANT. †***knight of arms*** (see 11). ***Knight of Grace***, a knight of Malta, of a lower rank in the order. ***Knight of Justice***, a knight of Malta possessing full privileges. ***knight of the carpet*** (see CARPET *sb.* 2 c). †***knight of the chamber*** = prec. †***knight of the community*** or ***parliament*** = Knight of the Shire (see 4 c). ***Knight of the Round Table***, one of King Arthur's knights (see TABLE). †***Knight of the Shire*** (see 4 c). †***Knight of the Spur***, a knight bachelor. †***knight of the square flag***, a banneret. Also, ***Knight of the Rueful Countenance***: see quot.
1530 PALSGR. 236/2 *Knyght of adventures, *cheualier errant*. **1762–71** H. WALPOLE *Vertue's Anecd. Paint.* (1786) I. 206 Another person of some note..was Sir John Godsalve, created *knight of the carpet at the king's coronation. **1672** COWELL *Interpr.*, **Knights of the Chamber*, ..seem to be such Knights Batchelors as are made in time of Peace, because knighted commonly in the Kings Chamber. **1788** *Picturesque Tour thro' Europe* 18 The *Knights of Justice are alone eligible to the posts of Bailiffs, Grand Priors, and Grand Masters; the *Knights of Grace are competent to all excepting these. *c* **1400** *Ywaine & Gaw.* 5 Ywayne and Gawayne..war *knightes of the tabyl rownde. **1774** WARTON *Hist. Eng. Poetry* iii. (1840) I. 113 The achievements of king Arthur with his knights of the round table. **1614** SELDEN *Titles Hon.* 305 *Knights of the Spurre, or those which generally are known by the name of Knights. **1718** MOTTEUX *Quix.* I. xvi, The champion that routed them is..the famous Don Quixote de la Mancha, otherwise called the *Knight of the Rueful Countenance.

b. Denoting a member of some order of knighthood, as ***Knight of the*** BATH, GARTER, THISTLE, etc., q.v. ***Knight of St. John, of Malta, of Rhodes*** = HOSPITALLER 3. ***Knight of the Temple*** = TEMPLAR. ***Knight of Windsor***, one of a small number of military officers (***Military Knights of W.***) who have pensions and apartments in Windsor Castle. (From 1797 to 1892 there were also ***Naval Knights of W.***; cf. 11.) †Also, jocularly, ***knight of the forked order***: see FORKED 4 b; ***knight of the order of the fork***, one who digs with a fork (cf. 12 c).
a **1500** [see GARTER *sb.* 2]. **1530** PALSGR. 236/2 Knight of the order of saynt Michaell. **1608** MIDDLETON *Mad World, my Masters* II. v, Many of these nights will make me a knight of Windsor. **1630** J. TAYLOR (Water P.) *Great Eater of Kent* 4 Some get their living by their..feet, as dancers, lackeyes, footmen, and weavers, and knights of the publicke or common order of the forke. **1631** T. POWELL *Tom All Trades* (1876) 171 A poore Knights place of Windsor. **1632** MASSINGER *Maid of Hon.* I. i, You are, sir, A Knight of Malta, and, as I have heard, Have served against the Turk. **1704** *Collect. Voy.* (Churchill) III. 690/1, 8 Persian Horses led by eight Knights of the Golden Sun. **1711** *Lond. Gaz.* No. 4799/1 The Marquis de Suza..was lately Install'd Knight of the Order of St. Maurice. **1783** *Royal Warrant* in Nicholas *Hist. Ord. Knighthood* (1842) IV. 6 Letters Patent ..for creating a Society or Brotherhood, to be called Knights of the Most Illustrious Order of Saint Patrick. **1803** *Naval Chron.* IX. 158 Seven Lieutenants of the Navy are to be installed Naval Knights of Windsor. **1856** EMERSON *Eng. Traits, Manners* Wks. (Bohn) II. 49 The Knights of the Bath take oath to defend injured ladies.

c. Forming various jocular (formerly often slang) phrases denoting one who is a member of a certain trade or profession, has a certain occupation or character, etc.
In the majority of these the distinctive word is the name of some tool or article commonly used by or associated with the person designated, and the number of such phrases may be indefinitely increased. Examples are:
†***knight of the blade***, 'a Hector or Bully' (B. E. *Dict. Cant. Crew*, *a* 1700). ***knight of the brush***, a painter, an artist. ***knight of the cleaver***, a butcher. †***knight of the collar***, one who has been hanged. ***knight of the cue***, a billiard-player. †***knight of the elbow***, a cheating gambler. †***knight of the field***, a tramp. †***knight of the grammar***, a schoolmaster. †***knight of (the) industry***, a sharper or swindler (F. *chevalier d'industrie*). †***knight of the knife***, a cutpurse. ***knight of the needle, shears, thimble***, a tailor. ***knight of the pen***, a clerk or author. ***knight of the pencil***, a bookmaker. ***knight of the pestle***, an apothecary. ***knight of the quill***, a writer, author. ***knight of the road***, (*a*) a highwayman; (*b*) a commercial traveller; (*c*) a tramp; (*d*) the driver of a lorry, taxicab, etc. ***knight of the spigot***, a tapster or publican. †***knight of the vapour***, a smoker. ***knight of the whip***, a coachman. ***knight of the wheel***, a cyclist. ***knight of the whipping-post***, a sharper or other disreputable person. See also KNIGHT OF THE POST.
1885 *Longm. Mag.* Nov. 78 A distinguished *knight of the brush. *c* **1554** *Interl. Youth* in Hazl. *Dodsley* II. 15 Thou didst enough there For to be made *knight of the collar. **1887** *Graphic* 15 Jan. 55/2 The '*knights of the cue' keep the balls a-rolling. **1693** *Humours Town* 92 Sharpers are divided into Bullies and *Knights of the Elbow. **1508** KENNEDIE *Flyting w. Dunbar* 430 Because that Scotland of thy begging irkis, Thow scapis in France to be a *knycht of the felde. **1692** WASHINGTON tr. *Milton's Def. Pop.* viii. M.'s Wks. (1851) 185 A Stipend large enough for a *Knight of the Grammar, or an Illustrious Critick on Horseback. **1658** CLEVELAND *Rustic Rampant* Wks. (1687) 475 Our Hacksters Errant, of the Round Table, *Knights of Industry. **1668** ETHEREDGE *She wou'd if She cou'd* III. iii, Let me commend this ingenious Gentleman to Your Acquaintance; he is a Knight of the Industry. **1751** SMOLLETT *Per. Pic.* (1779) III. lxxxiv. 310 Our hero was a professed enemy to all knights of industry. **1614** B. JONSON *Barth. Fair* II. iii, Is this..a *knight of the knife?.. I meane..a cutpurse. **1778** FOOTE *Trip Calais* I. 24 The *knights of the needle are another sort of people at our end of the town. **1885** *Punch* 7 Mar. 109 The *Knights of the Pencil, Sir, hold that backers, like pike, are more ravenous in keen weather, and consequently easier to land. **1927** *Daily Express* 11 June 7/3 We have mentioned the knights of the pencil. Bookmakers are not permitted to take up positions at will on racecourses under Greyhound Racing Association jurisdiction. *a* **1735** ARBUTHNOT *Ess. Apoth.* Wks. 1751 II. 111 There being no part of Mankind, that affords a greater variety of uncommon Appearances than the *Knights of the Pestle. **1691–2** *Gentl. Jrnl.* Mar. 2, I know some of your sturdy, tuff *Knights of the Quill, your old Soakers at the Cabbaline Font. **1665** R. HEAD *Eng. Rogue* xxvi. 86 An Oath, which every young Thief must observe..at his investation into the honour of one of the *Knights of the Road. **1889** J. BURNLEY *Romance Mod. Industry* 317 Customers used to come out miles upon summer evenings to meet the 'knights of the road',..and the old travellers on their part would spend two or three days with some of their clients. **1928** *Sunday Express* 12 Feb. 11/4 Secrets of the Commercial Traveller's Bag. By John S. Banks, for twenty years a 'Knight of the Road'. **1928** *Daily Express* 8 Aug. 3/5 If something of this spirit could be instilled into the regular 'knights of the road', if they could be inspired with some notion of the dignity of work and the shame of alms-taking. **1971** R. REISNER *Graffiti* vi. 82 Truck drivers are notorious for their..loudly expressed admiration for women. They are true knights of the road. **1974** L. DEIGHTON *Spy Story* ii. 20 Finally some knight of the road deigned to do a Gloucester Road to Fulham. **1821** SCOTT *Kenilw.* viii, When an old song comes across us merry old *knights of the spigot, it runs away with our discretion. **1812** *Sporting Mag.* XXXIX. 139 A gallant *knight of the thimble. **1630** J. TAYLOR (Water P.) *Great Eater of Kent* 5 Some [live] by smoake; as tobacconists, *knights of the vapour, gentlemen of the whiffe, esquires of the pipe. **1813** *Examiner* 8 Feb. 84/2 We cannot too often caution the *Knights of the Whip against so dangerous..a practice. **1819** SCOTT *Let. to Son Walter* 4 Sept. in *Lockhart*, Blacklegs and sharpers, and all that numerous class whom..we [call] *knights of the whipping-post.

d. ***Knights of Columbus***, a society of Roman Catholic men founded at New Haven, Connecticut, in 1882; ***Knights of Labour***, an extensive association in the United States, embracing many of the Trade Unions; ***Knights of Pythias***, a secret order, founded at Washington in 1864 (Funk *Stand. Dict.*).
1886 *Harper's Weekly* 3 Apr. 213/3 The order of the Knights of Labour was founded in 1869 by five workmen of Philadelphia. **1888** BRYCE *Amer. Commw.* II. III. lvi. 370 The enormous organization or league of trades unions known as the Knights of Labour. **1901** *N.Y. Tribune* 22 July 3/4 Wednesday the Knights of Columbus and Utah people will unite their forces; on Thursday another double-header. **1929** F. A. POTTLE *Stretchers* (1930) iv. 66 Besides the enormous structures of the Y.M.C.A. and..Knights of Columbus,..the general public had provided at Merritt many other agencies of relaxation and amusement quite peculiar to the camp. **1948** *Green Bay* (Wisconsin) *Press-Gaz.* 12 July 16/7 Members of the Green Bay lodge Knights of Columbus were reminded today that the annual Fish Fry will be held at the Shorewood Country club next Tuesday. **1974** *Listener* 21 Nov. 683 The Knights of Columbus are associated with lodge meetings and bingo.

III. 13. *attrib.* and *Comb.*

a. With *knight-*, as ***knight-martyr***; †**knight-bairn**, a male child; †**knight-cross** = *knight's cross*; †**knight-money** = *knighthood-money*; †**knight-weed**, the dress of a knight; †**knight-wered**, a band of warriors; †**knight-wife**, a female knight or warrior.
c **1205** LAY. 15526 Ȝif mon funde..æuer æi *cniht bærn, þe næuere fæder no ibæd. **1725** BRADLEY *Fam. Dict.*, *Jerusalem-Cross*, called by some the *Knight, or Scarlet Cross. **1826** W. E. ANDREWS *Exam. Fox's Cal. Prot. Saints* 49 The condemnation of this..gentlewoman and *knight-martyr. **1643** PRYNNE *Sov. Power Parlt.* II. 31 *Knight-mony, Ship-mony, with sundry other unlawfull Taxes. **1340–70** *Alisaunder* 544 Hee cast of his *Knightweede, & cloþes hym neew. *c* **1205** LAY. 26766 Al þa *cniht-weorede fluen an heore steden. **1483** *Cath. Angl.* 205/2 A *knyghte wyffe, *militissa*.

b. With *knight's*, chiefly in names of plants: **knight's cross**, Scarlet Lychnis, *L. chalcedonica*; †**knight's milfoil**, a yellow species of *Achillea*; †**knight's pondwort**, Water-soldier, *Stratiotes aloides*; **knight's star, -star lily**, the amaryllidaceous genus *Hippeastrum*; †**knight's water-sengreen, wort, woundwort** = *knight's pondwort*. See also KNIGHT'S FEE, KNIGHT-SERVICE.
1760 J. LEE *Introd. Bot.* App. 316 *Knight's Cross, *Lychnis*. **1578** LYTE *Dodoens* I. ci. 143 The second is called ..in English *Knights Milfoyle: souldiers Yerrow, and yellow knighten Yerrow. *Ibid.*, The first is called..in English Knights worte, Knights wounde worte, or Knightes water woundworte, *Knights Pondeworte, and of some Knights water Sengreene. **1855** *Loudon's Encycl. Plants* 1176 *Knight's Star. **1866** *Treas. Bot.* 590/2 The Knight's Star Lily, a genus..consisting of South American and West Indian bulbs, remarkable for their showy flowers.

c. With *knighten* (ME. gen. pl.): **knighten court** (also **knights-court**): see quot. 1701; **knighten-gild**, a gild of knights; **knighten-milfoil** = *knight's milfoil*; **knightenspence**, some local rate; **knightenway**, a military road; **knighten-yarrow** = *knight's milfoil*.

c **1050** *Charter Edw. Confessor* in *Calendar Letterbks., Guildhall London* (1891) III. 218 Mine men on Anȝioce cnihte ȝilde [*read* mine men on Englisce cnihte gilde.] **1398** TREVISA *Barth. De P.R.* XIX. cxxix. (Add. MS.) lf. 332 Agger is an huple of stones or a tokene in þe hihe way and histories clepiþ such a wey knyȝweye [*viam militarem*]. **1467** in *Eng. Gilds* (1870) 390 That then he pay taske tallage, knyghtenspence, wacches, and other charges. **1578** LYTE *Dodoens* I. ci. 143 Yellow knighten Yerrow. *Ibid.*, The other with the thousand leaues, called Knighten Mylfoile. **1631** WEEVER *Anc. Fun. Mon.* 426 King Edgar established here without Aldgate a Knightengield or Confrery, for thirteene knights or souldiers. **1701** *Cowell's Interpr.*, *Knighten-Court*, Is a Court-Baron or Honor-Court, held twice a Year under the Bishop of Hereford at his Palace there; wherein those who are Lords of Manours, and their Tenants..are Suiters.

knight (naɪt), *v.* Also 3 **kniȝti**, 3-4 **kniȝte**, 4 **knyhte, knyȝte**. [ME., f. prec.] *trans.* To dub or create (one) a knight.

a **1300** *K. Horn* 492 Hit nere noȝt forlorn For to kniȝte child Horn. *Ibid.* 644 Nu is þi wile iȝolde, King, þat þu me kniȝti woldest. **1362** LANGL. *P. Pl.* A. I. 103 And crist king of kinges kniȝtide [*v.r.* knyhtide] tene, Cherubin and Seraphin [etc.]. **1577-87** HOLINSHED *Chron.* III. 1236/1 This man..was knighted by the king. **1627** DRAYTON *Agincourt*, etc. 192 This Drone yet neuer braue attempt that dar'd, Yet dares be knighted. **1712** ADDISON *Spect.* No. 299 ¶2, I was knighted in the thirty fifth Year of my Age. **1876** J. SAUNDERS *Lion in Path* xii, Sir Richard Constable had been knighted by King James.

Hence **'knighted** *ppl. a.*

1656 S. HOLLAND *Don Zara* II. iv. 101 That his Isabel and Mortimer was now compleated by a Knighted Poet. **1896** J. H. WYLIE *Hist. Eng. Hen. IV*, III. 321 The flood of knighted names in the lists of fighting men.

knightage ('naɪtɪdʒ). [f. KNIGHT *sb.* + -AGE.] **a.** A body of knights; the whole body of knights. **b.** A list and account of persons who are knights.

1840 DOD (*title*) The Peerage, Baronetage, and Knightage, of Great Britain and Ireland. **1858** CARLYLE *Fredk. Gt.* I. III. v. 238 He rode thither with his Anspach Knightage about him, 'four-hundred cavaliers'. **1900** *Whitaker's Peerage* 44 Wherever in the Knightage the husband is styled 'Sir', the wife, in conventional usage, has the title 'Lady' or 'Dame'.

'knight-'errant. *Pl.* **knights-errant.** In 7 erron. **-errand.** [See ERRANT *a.* I.]

1. A knight of mediæval romance who wandered in search of adventures and opportunities for deeds of bravery and chivalry.

13.. *Gaw. & Gr. Knt.* 810 He calde, & sone þer com A porter..& haylsed þe knyȝt erraunt. *a* **1440** *Sir Degrev.* 1311 Ȝondur ys a knyȝthe erraunt. **1612** SHELTON *Quix.* i. (1652) 2 The Knight-Errant that is lovelesse, resembles..a body without a soul. **1641** BROME *Joviall Crew* III. Wks. 1873 III. 394 Never did Knight Errants..merit more of their Ladies. **1712** STEELE *Spect.* No. 540 ¶4 In Fairy-land, where knights-errant have a full scope to range. **1713** BERKELEY *Guard.* No. 83 ¶5 From what giants and monsters would these knight-errants undertake to free the world? **1847** PRESCOTT *Peru* (1850) II. 224 A cavalier, in whose bosom burned the adventurous spirit of a knight-errant of romance.

attrib. **1768-74** TUCKER *Lt. Nat.* (1834) I. 668 This knight-errant humour of seeking adventures and perilous encounters. **1868** W. CORY *Lett. & Jrnls.* (1897) 223 The armies which resisted Bonaparte, and made us the knight-errant nation.

2. *transf.* One compared to a knight-errant in respect of a chivalrous or adventurous spirit. Sometimes used in ridicule, with allusion to the character or action of Don Quixote.

[**1597** SHAKS. *2 Hen. IV*, v. iv. 24 Come, come, you shee-knight-arrant, come.] **1751** EARL ORRERY *Remarks Swift* (1752) 115 Descartes was a knight errant in philosophy, perpetually mistaking windmills for giants. *a* **1857** R. A. VAUGHAN *Essays & Rem.* (1858) I. 38 Reason was the knight-errant of speculation.

Hence **knight-'erranting** *gerund* or *pr. pple.*, playing the part of a knight-errant.

1860 GEN. P. THOMPSON *Audi Alt.* III. cvii. 21 You are not to go out knight-erranting in all corners of the town.

knight-'errantry. [f. prec. + -RY.]

1. The practice of a knight-errant; the action of knights who wandered in search of adventures.

1654 GAYTON *Pleas. Notes* 9 This order of Knight-errantry is very ancient; when there were but three persons in the World, one was of this order, even Cain. **1764** REID *Inquiry* I. Ded. 95 If all belief could be laid aside, piety, friendship, &c., would appear as ridiculous as knighterrantry. **1814** SCOTT *Chivalry* (1874) 9 They achieved deeds of valour..only recorded in the annals of knight-errantry. **1860** ADLER *Fauriel's Prov. Poetry* xv. 342 In the poetical monuments of Southern France I find the most ancient indications of knight-errantry.

attrib. **1645** EVELYN *Diary* 11 Apr., The prizes being distributed by the ladies after the knight-errantry way.

2. Conduct resembling that of a knight-errant; readiness to engage in romantic adventure. Often depreciative: Quixotic behavior.

1659 *Gentl. Calling* (1696) 104 But to anticipate the Proposal, to go in quest of such Opportunities, looks with them like a piece of Knight-errantry. **1711** STEELE *Spect.* No. 168 ¶5 It is a noble Piece of Knight-Errantry to enter the Lists against so many armed Pedagogues. **1831** BREWSTER *Newton* (1855) II. xv. 73 The charge of knight errantry which Newton has made against Leibnitz..for challenging the English to the solution of mathematical problems. **1853** WHITTIER *Prose Wks.* (1889) II. 427 That spiritual knight-errantry which undertakes the championship of every novel project of reform.

3. The body of knight-errants. *rare.*

1860 C. SANGSTER *Hesperus*, etc. 35 He, Prince of Love's knight-errantry. **1872** TENNYSON *Gareth* 613 That old knight-errantry Who ride abroad and do but what they will.

knight-'errantship. *rare.* [See -SHIP.] The condition or personality of a knight-errant.

1640 BROME *Sparagus Garden* I. iii. Wks. 1873 III. 125 My house shall bee no enchanted Castle to detaine your Knight-errandship from your adventures. **1736** LEDIARD *Life Marlborough* I. 59 There was a more daring set of People, with whom His Knight-Errantship had to encounter.

knightess ('naɪtɪs). *rare.* [f. KNIGHT *sb.* + -ESS[1].] **a.** A woman who fights like a knight. **b.** A female member of a knightly order. **c.** The wife of a knight.

a **1553** UDALL *Royster D.* IV. viii. (Arb.) 78 Too it agaїne, my knightesses, downe with them all. **1693** tr. *Emilianne's Hist. Monast. Ord.* II. ii. 238 The Order of the Nuns Knightesses, Sword-bearers of St. James in Spain. **1843** *Mirror* II. 161/2 There is reason to believe that as well as Knights there were knight-*esses*, or ladies, of that order. **1845** DISRAELI *Sybil* II. ii, The 'honourable baronetess'..or the 'honourable knightess'.

'knightfully, *adv. nonce-wd.* [cf. *manfully*.] Like a knight, bravely.

1845 NEALE *Mirr. Faith* 82 Gallantly and knightfully They toil'd the live-long day.

knight-head ('naɪtˌhɛd). *Naut.* **a.** One of two large timbers in a vessel that rise obliquely from the keel behind the stem, one on each side, and support the bowsprit, which is fixed between them; called also bollard timbers. †**b.** A windlass-bitt (*obs.*). †**c.** = KNIGHT 8 (*obs.*).

1711 W. SUTHERLAND *Shipbuild. Assist.* 115 They are reev'd through Knight-heads, and so hal'd home. **1769** FALCONER *Dict. Marine* (1789), *Knight-Heads*, two strong pieces of timber, fixed on the opposite sides of the main-deck, a little behind the fore-mast... They are sometimes called the *bits*, and in this sense their upper parts only are denominated knight-heads,..being formerly embellished with a figure designed to resemble a human head... *Knight-heads*, was also a name formerly given to the lower jear-blocks, which were then no other than bits. **1883** *Cent. Mag.* Oct. 946/2 Her..bows would be buried in a smother of foam clear to the knight-heads.

†**'knighthed, -hede.** *Obs.* Also **kniht-, kniȝt-,** etc. (see KNIGHT *sb.*); 4 **-ed(e,** 5-6 *Sc.* **-heid.** [f. KNIGHT *sb.* + -HEAD. Cf. next.]

1. The rank of a knight: = KNIGHTHOOD 2.

c **1325** *Metr. Hom.* 139 A kniht That thoru kind was bond and thralle Bot knihthed gat he wit catelle. *c* **1475** *Rauf Coilȝear* 960 Schir Rauf gat rewaird to keip his Knichtheid. **1500-20** DUNBAR *Turnament* 56 To comfort him, or he raid forder, The Devill off knychtheid gaif him order.

2. The vocation of a knight: = KNIGHTHOOD 3.

c **1375** *Sc. Leg. Saints* xvi. (*Magdalene*) 70 To k[n]ychthed hyre bruþir lazare Halely hyme gafe, & lytil rocht Of landis. **1490** CAXTON *Eneydos* lvi. 153 He hadde lefte his offyce and hadde taken hym self to the fayttes of knygthed. *c* **1500** *Lancelot* 822 He goith ymong them in his hie curage, As he that had of knyghthed the wsage.

3. Knightly character or accomplishments: = KNIGHTHOOD 4.

a **1300** *Cursor M.* 8422 To be lered him-self to lede, Wit clerge bath and wit knighthede. *c* **1400** *Destr. Troy* 5549 Of knighthede to count þere was the clene floure. **1450-70** *Golagros & Gaw.* 376 Thai war courtes and couth thair knyghthed to kyth. **1513** DOUGLAS *Æneis* VI. vi. 39 Eneas, ful of piete and knychtheid. **1535** STEWART *Cron. Scot.* I. 575 Suppois he was of all knychteid the floure.

4. A body of knights, or (= L. *mīlitia*) of fighting men: = KNIGHTHOOD 5.

c **1375** *Sc. Leg. Saints* xxix. (*Placidas*) 68 A knycht callit placydas Prynce of his knychted was. **1382** WYCLIF *Jer.* viii. 1 The sunne, and the moone and al the knyȝthed [**1388** knyȝthod, L *militia*] of heuene.

knighthood ('naɪthʊd). Forms: 1 **cnihthád;** 3- **kniht-,** etc. (see KNIGHT), 3-6 **-hod, -hode,** 5-6 **-hoode,** 6- **hood.** [OE. *cnihthád*, f. *cniht* boy, lad + *-hád* -HOOD. In ME. following the current sense of KNIGHT.]

I. (OE. *cnihthád*.) †**1.** Boyhood, youth. *Obs.*

c **893** K. ÆLFRED *Boeth.* xxxviii. §5 Þa hwile þe hit on cnihthade bið, & swa forð eallne ȝioȝoðhad. *c* **1000** ÆLFRIC *Gram.* ix. (Z.) 56 *Pubis*, cniht oð ðe cnihthad.

II. (ME. and mod.Eng.)

2. The rank or dignity of a knight.

a **1300** *K. Horn* 440 Þat he me ȝive dubbing Þanne is mi þralhod Iwent in to kniȝthod **1362** LANGL. *P. Pl.* A. XI. 222 Kinghod and kniȝthod..Helpiþ nouȝt to heuene. **1503-4** *Act 19 Hen. VII*, c. 31 *Preamble*, Divers of the Kinges Subgiettes..ar commaunded..to take uppon them the honour & degree of Knyghthode. **1597** SHAKS. *2 Hen. IV*, v. iii. 132, I would not take a Knighthood for my Fortune. **1617** MORYSON *Itin.* II. 277 A gentleman..who had long been earnestly ambitious of the honour of Knighthood. **1733** POPE *Hor. Sat.* II. i. 22 You'll gain at least a Knighthood, or the Bays. **1885** *Pall Mall G.* 24 Feb. 9/1 It is expected that several knighthoods will be conferred.

b. *transf.* Applied to one having this rank; a knight.

1598 SHAKS. *Merry W.* v. v. 76 [The Garter] Buckled below faire Knight-hoods bending knee.

c. With poss. pron. as a mode of address.

1828 SCOTT *F.M. Perth* xxxii, I only desired to know if your knighthood proposed the chivalrous task.

d. The ceremony of knighting a person.

1711 MADOX *Exch.* i. 2 There Coronations, Marriages and Knighthoods of the King's Children..were celebrated.

3. The profession or vocation of a knight.

c **1325** *Song Mercy* 155 in *E.E.P.* (1862) 123 Corteis knihthod and clergye... Are now so roted in rybaudye. **1481** CAXTON *Myrr.* I. vi. 31 Yf the studye [of science] wente out of ffraunce, knyghthode wold goo after. **1593** SHAKS. *Rich. II*, I. i. 75 By that, and all the rites of Knight-hood else, Will I make good against thee..What I haue spoken. **1700** DRYDEN *Pal. & Arc.* III. 10 The champions..Who knighthood loved, and deeds of chivalry. **1856** R. A. VAUGHAN *Mystics* (1860) I. 145 The old virtues of knighthood—its truth and honour, its chastity and courage.

†**b.** (tr. L. *mīlitia*.) Military service; soldiery; warfare. *Obs.*

1382 WYCLIF *2 Cor.* x. 4 The armers of oure knyȝthod ben not fleischly. —— *2 Tim.* ii. 4 No man holdinge knyȝthod to God [Vulg. *militans Deo*], inwlappith him silf with worldli nedis. *c* **1450** tr. *De Imitatione* III. l. 122 Þis frayl lif, þat is all temptacion and kniȝthode. **1535** COVERDALE *Judith* vi. 4 Then shal the swerde of my knyghthode [*militiæ meæ*] go thorow thy sydes. **1552** HULOET, Knighthode, *militia*.

4. The character and qualities appropriate to a knight; chivalrousness.

1377 LANGL. *P. Pl.* B. XVIII. 96 Cursed caytyue! kniȝthod was it neuere To mysdo a ded body. *c* **1386** CHAUCER *Monk's T.* 652 He was of knyghthod and of fredom flour. *c* **1450** *Merlin* 56 Ther Pendragon dide merveloise knyghthode a-monge his enmyes. **1523** LD. BERNERS *Froiss.* I. ccxcviii. 441 The noble knighthode that was in them reconforted them. **1865** KINGSLEY *Herew.* iii, Would it grow and bear the noble fruit of 'gentle, very perfect knighthood'? **1873** HAMERTON *Intell. Life* VIII. ii. (1876) 290 The perfect knighthood of Sydney.

5. The collective body of knights; a company of knights. ***knighthood-errant*** (cf. KNIGHT-ERRANT).

1377 LANGL. *P. Pl.* B. Prol. 116 The kyng and knyȝthode and clergye bothe Casten þat þe comune shulde hem-self fynde. **1477** EARL RIVERS (Caxton) *Dictes* 11 b, By whiche..the people be susteyned the knyghtehode multiplied and the houses full of richesse. **1605** CHAPMAN, etc. *Eastw. Hoe* v, The knighthood now-a-days are nothing like the knighthood of old time. **1859** TENNYSON *Guinevere* 457, I was first..who drew The knighthood-errant of this realm..together under me. **1874** GREEN *Short Hist.* ii. §4. 76 It was against the centre of this formidable position that William arrayed his Norman knighthood.

†**b.** (tr. L. *mīlitia*.) Military force, host. *Obs.*

1382 WYCLIF *Isa.* xiii. 4 The Lord of ostes comaundide to the knyȝthod of the bataile. —— *Luke* ii. 13 A multitude of heuenly knyȝthod, heriynge God, and seyinge, Glorie be in the hiȝeste thingis to God. —— *Acts* vii. 42 To serue to the knyȝthod of heuene.

6. *attrib.* †**knighthood-money**, a fine exacted from persons who refused to be knighted. (Abolished by Act 16 Chas. I, c. 20.)

c **1670** WOOD *Life* Jan. an. 1643 (O.H.S.) I. 79 He was fined in October 1630 for refusing the honour of knighthood, a matter then lately brought up to obtaine money for his majestie's use. This money which was paid by all persons of 40*li.* per an. that refused to come in and be dub'd knights, was called knighthood-money.

'knightify, *v. nonce-wd. trans.* = KNIGHT *v.*

1682 MRS. BEHN *Round-heads* v. i, I wonder with what impudence Noll and Dick could Knightifie your husbands.

'knighting, *vbl. sb.* [f. KNIGHT *v.* + -ING[1].] The action of making one a knight; the fact of being knighted.

1550 CROWLEY *Epigr.* 491 Woulde God all our knightes dyd minde colinge no more, than this Colier dyd knyghtyng. **1614** SELDEN *Titles Hon.* 308 The Honor of taking armes (which in our present idiom may be calld Knighting). **1705** HEARNE *Collect.* 28 Sept. (O.H.S.) I. 50 Upon the Knighting of Dr. Hann's and..Dr. W[m] Read. **1876** FREEMAN *Norm. Conq.* V. xxiii. 324 Randolf of Chester was at Henry's knighting, and did homage to David.

b. *attrib.*, as ***knighting sword***; †**knighting-money** = *knighthood money*.

1625 in *Crt. & Times Chas. I* (1848) I. 15 On Monday, Maurice Abbot..had the maidenhead of the king's knighting sword. **1641** *Jrnls. Ho. Comm.* XI. 145 For the Judges, unto which the Consideration of Knighting-money is referred.

†**'knightless,** *a. Obs. rare.* [f. KNIGHT *sb.* + -LESS.] Unbecoming a knight; unknightly.

1590 SPENSER *F.Q.* I. vi. 41 Thou cursed miscreaunt, That hast with knightlesse guile..Faire knighthood fowly shamed, ?**17..** *Ld. Ingram* xxiii. in Child *Ballads* III. lxvi E. 134/2, I laugh at the knightless sport That I saw wi my ee.

knightlihood, -ness, etc.: see KNIGHTLY *a.*

knightlike ('naɪtlaɪk), *a.* and *adv.* [See -LIKE.]

A. *adj.* Like or befitting a knight; knightly.

c **1425** WYNTOUN *Cron.* VII. viii. 20 In Tornementis, and Justyngis, And mony oþir Knychtlyk Thyngis. **1574** HELLOWES *Gueuara's Fam. Ep.* (1577) 204 Agreeable to the last rule, which was the better and more Knightlike. **1612** DRAYTON *Poly-olb.* XII. 202 That great and puissant Knight (in whose victorious dayes Those knight-like deeds were

done). **1847** TENNYSON *Princ.* IV. 577 He knightlike in his cap instead of casque..assumed the Prince.

B. *adv.* = KNIGHTLY *adv.*

1375 BARBOUR *Bruce* XV. 53 Thai mantemyt that gret melle So knychtlik apon athir syde. *c* **1470** HENRY *Wallace* IX. 1047 Rycht knychtlik he thaim kend, In that jornay othir to wyn or end. *a* **1649** DRUMM. OF HAWTH. *Poems* Wks. (1711) 22 If he die, he knight-like dies in blood. **1808** SCOTT *Marm.* III. xviii, If, knight-like, he despises fear.

knightling (ˈnaɪtlɪŋ). *rare.* [See -LING.] A petty knight.

1640 BROME *Sparagus Garden* III. iv. Wks. 1873 III. 159 Tis such a Knightling, Ile but give yee his Character, and he comes, I warrant thee. **1845** *Lives Eng. Saints, Aelred* iv. 57 It was found that every knightling possessed not only a castle, but a seal, like the king of England himself.

knightly (ˈnaɪtlɪ), *a.* [f. KNIGHT *sb.* + -LY[1].]

I. (OE. *cnihtlíc.*) †**1.** Boyish. *Obs.*

a **1000** *Prose Life Guthlac* ii. (Goodwin) 12 Ne he cnihtlice galnysse næs begangende.

II. (ME. and mod.Eng.)

2. Having the rank or qualities of a knight; noble, chivalrous. Now *rare.*

1382 WYCLIF *2 Macc.* viii. 9 A kniȝtly man, and in thingus of bateil most expert. **1390** GOWER *Conf.* I. 184 Elda the kinges Chamberlein, A knyhtly man after his lawe. *c* **1430** *Pilgr. Lyf Manhode* III. lxiii. (1869) 173 He is michel the more corageows after, and the more knightlich. **1813** BYRON *Ch. Har.* Add. Pref., He was..knightly in his attributes.

3. Of things, actions, etc.: Of, belonging to, suitable, or appropriate to a knight. †*knightly fee* = KNIGHT'S FEE.

c **1375** *Sc. Leg. Saints* xxxiii. (*George*) 386 His knychtly clething..he gef away for godis sak. *c* **1480** HENRYSON *Test. Cres.* 519 For knichtly pietie and memoriall Of fair Cresseid. **1590** SPENSER *F.Q.* I. i. 1 As one for knightly giusts and fierce encounters fitt. *c* **1630** RISDON *Surv. Devon* §334 (1810) 346 William Fitz-Morice held Haginton by one knightly fee. **1700** DRYDEN *Theod. & Honoria* 389 Preferr'd above the rest, By him with knightly deeds. **1834** L. RITCHIE *Wand. by Seine* 55 The use of the knightly sword or lance.

4. Consisting or composed of knights. *rare.*

1845 S. AUSTIN *Ranke's Hist. Ref.* I. 127 The knightly order had taken no part in the diet. **1877** MISS YONGE *Cameos* IV. xii. 131 The romances of chivalry which were the delectation of the knightly world in those days.

Hence **ˈknightlihood** (†**-hede**), **ˈknightliness**, knightly condition or qualities.

1390 GOWER *Conf.* III. 212 Wherof his knyhtlihiede Is yit comended overal. **1596** SPENSER *F.Q.* IV. vii. 45 Some gentle swaine..Traind vp in feates of armes and knightlinesse. **1890** 'ÆLIAN PRINCE' *Of Joyous Gard* ii. 47 Sir Tristram yearned to largely breathe again Sharp air inspiriting of knightlihood. **1900** *Longm. Mag.* July 227 Scott has created for us a true type of Saracen knightliness in the Talisman.

knightly (ˈnaɪtlɪ), *adv.* [f. KNIGHT *sb.* + -LY[2].] After the fashion of, or in a manner befitting, a knight; gallantly, chivalrously.

c **1385** CHAUCER *L.G.W.* 2085 *Ariadne*, God..synde ȝow grace..ȝow to defende & knyghtly slen ȝoure fo. *c* **1477** CAXTON *Jason* 79 b, They dyde so knyghtly and cheuaulerously. **1593** SHAKS. *Rich. II*, I. iii. 12 Say..why thou com'st thus knightly clad in Armes? **1822** BYRON *Werner* IV. i, Whose plume nods knightlier? **1859** TENNYSON *Guinevere* 40 He..Made such excuses as he might, and these Full knightly without scorn.

Knight Marshal (a title of certain marshals who were knights): see MARSHAL.

knight of the post. [i.e. (?) of the whipping-post or pillory: see quots.] A notorious perjurer; one who got his living by giving false evidence; a false bail.

1580 E. KNIGHT *Trial Truth* 39 b, Men,..who will not let to sweare vpon a booke,..beyng hyred therevnto for money ..called..Knightes of the poste, more fitter for the Gallowes, then to liue in a common wealth where Christ is professed. **1592** CHETTLE *Kinde-harts Dr.* (1841) 11 A knight of the post, whome in times past I haue seen as highly promoted as the pillory. **1592** NASHE *P. Penilesse*, A Knight of the Post,..a fellow that will sweare you any thing for twelve pence. **1597** E. S. *Discov. Knights Post* B, Knightes of the Poste, Lords of lobs pound, and heires apparant to the pillory: who are ready to baile men out of prison. **1641** BROME *Joviall Crew* Wks. 1873 III. 366 He was taken up a Knight o' the Post; and so he continued, till he was degraded at the whipping-post. *a* **1716** BLACKALL *Wks.* (1723) I. 330 When once Men have by frequent use lost the reverence that is due to an Oath, they easily become Knights of the Post and may be hir'd to swear any-thing. **1772** WESLEY *Wks.* (1872) XI. 45 Does not the publisher..deserve to lose his ears more than a common knight of the post? **1819** R. CHAPMAN *Jas. V*, 132 They hired knights of the post, who were evidences against him.

ˈknight-ˌservice. Also **knight's service.**

1. Under the Feudal System: The military service which a knight was bound to render as a condition of holding his lands; hence, the tenure of land under the condition of performing military service.

α. **1439** *Rolls of Parlt.* V. 31/2 Eny of youre said Comunes, holdyng of you by Knyghtes service. *c* **1500** *Corte Barune* in *Book of Brome* 155 If they holde be skwage, that is knytes serwyce. **1513** MORE in Grafton *Chron.* (1568) II. 774 He hath nothing by dissent holden by knightes service, but by socage. **1628** COKE *On Litt.* i. 74 Tenure by homage, fealty & Escuage, is to hold by Knights Seruice.

β. *c* **1500** *Corte Barune* in *Book of Brome* 155 The chylde ..þat holdith be þat tenuer of knyte serwisse. **1523** FITZHERB. *Surv.* 11 b, What fees they holde..and wheder it be by socage or by knight seruyce. **1767** BLACKSTONE *Comm.* II. v. 63 This tenure of knight-service had all the marks of a strict and regular feud. **1874** STUBBS *Const. Hist.* I. x. 305 As a special boon to tenants by knight-service, their demesne lands are freed from all demands except service in the field. **1876** DIGBY *Real Prop.* i. 39 Tenure *per militiam*, in chivalry or by knight-service.

2. *fig.* Such service as is rendered by a knight; hence, good service.

α. *a* **1716** SOUTH *Serm.* VI. vi. (R.), He [the devil] never knights any one, but he expects more than knights-service from him in return.

β. **1675** tr. *Machiavelli's Prince* (1883) 263, I have done you knight-service. **1874** T. HARDY *Far fr. Mad. Crowd* I. xxv. 283 Doing the mistress of the farm real knight-service by this voluntary contribution of his labour.

knight's fee. Under the Feudal System: The amount of land for which the services of an armed knight were due to the sovereign.

Historical writers now agree that the different knight's fees were not equal in extent (see quots. 1876, 1893); whether they were approximately equal in value is still doubtful.

1387 TREVISA *Higden* (Rolls) VII. 309 How meny knyȝtene fees, how meny teme lond [etc.]. **1427** *Rolls of Parlt.* IV. 318/2 Ye subsidees of ye saide Knyghtes Fees with ye rate yrof. **1494** FABYAN *Chron.* VII. ccxxii. 246 *marg.*, viij. hydes make a knyghtes fee, by the whiche reason, a knyghts fee shuld welde. c. lx. acres. **1602** CAREW *Cornwall* 36 Commonly thirtie Acres make a farthing land, nine farthings a Cornish Acre, and foure Cornish Acres a Knight's fee. **1761** HUME *Hist. Eng.* I. App. ii. 251 *note*, The relief of a barony was twelve times greater than that of a knight's-fee. **1876** DIGBY *Real Prop.* i. 36 Where land is held by military service every portion amounting to twenty pounds in annual value constitutes a 'knight's fee', for which the service of a knight fully armed and equipped must be rendered. **1895** POLLOCK & MAITLAND *Hist. Eng. Law* I. 235 The term 'knight's fee' does not imply any particular acreage of land. The knight's fee is no unvarying areal unit; some fees are much larger than others.

knightship (ˈnaɪt-ʃɪp). [See -SHIP.]

1. †**a.** The performance of a knight or soldier; military service. *Obs.* †**b.** Knightly character; valour. *Obs.* **c.** The rank or position of a knight; knighthood. **d.** The territory of a knight.

a **1175** *Cott. Hom.* 243 Cnihtscipe [L. *militia*] is manes lif upen eorðe. *c* **1205** LAY. 26747 Cuðeð eouwer cniht-scipe. *c* **1325** *Poem Times Edw. II* 265 in *Pol. Songs* (Camden) 335 Knihtshipe is acloied and deolfulliche i-diht; Kunne a boy nu breke a spere, he shal be mad a kniht. *c* **1330** R. BRUNNE *Chron. Wace* (Rolls) 14405 Of knyght-schipe nobely he proued. **1620** in *Crt. & Times Jas. I* (1849) II. 214 Sir James Whitelocke is gone to be judge of Wales and Chester, which place came not to him gratis, though perhaps his knightship was cast into the bargain. **1845** S. AUSTIN *Ranke's Hist. Ref.* II. 123 A..government..formed out of the several knightships which were now become absolute and independent sovereignties.

2. With poss. pron. as a title or form of address.

1694 MOTTEUX *Rabelais* v. v. (1737) 17 We have not the Honour to be acquainted with their Knightships. **1831** *Keepsake* 307 Gout and sixty well-spent years Had made his knightship tame.

†**knightte.** *Obs. rare.* In 4 **knyȝtte.** [f. KNIGHT *sb.* + ? *-te*, -TY: but perh. some error.] A knight's estate or property.

c **1380** WYCLIF *Wks.* (1880) 384 In þe same wise as þe baron or the knyȝte occupieþ & gouerneþ his baronrye or his knyȝtte, so after þe amortesynge occupieþ þe clerke..þe same lordeschip.

knill, obs. form of KNELL.

†**knip,** *v.* *Sc. Obs. rare.* [Parallel to GNIP, NIP; cf. LG. and Du. *knippen* to clip, snip; also north. dial. KNEP, *knipe* to nibble.] *trans.* Of cattle: To bite or crop (grass). Also *absol.*

1500-20 DUNBAR *Poems* lxi. 13 With gentill horss quhen I wald knyp, Than is thair laid on me ane quhip. **1513** DOUGLAS *Æneis* XII. Prol. 94 As far as catal..Had in thar pastur eyt and knyp away.

Knipe, var. KNEIPE.

kniphofia (nɪpˈhəʊfɪə). [mod.L. (C. Moench *Methodus Plantas Horti Botanici et Agri Marburgensis* (1794) 631), f. the name of Johann Hieronymus *Kniphof* (1704-63), German physician and botanist + -IA[1].] A perennial herb of the genus so called, native to southern or eastern Africa, belonging to the family Liliaceæ, and bearing spikes of red, yellow, or orange flowers; also called red-hot poker, torch lily, and formerly TRITOMA, a synonymous generic name.

1854 *Curtis's Bot. Mag.* LXXX. 4816 Serrulated-leaved Kniphofia... Of late years visitors to the Royal Gardens of Kew have been much struck with the beauty of the flower-spikes of a *Kniphofia* (*Tritoma* of most authors), planted in several of the beds. **1900** W. D. DRURY *Bk. Gardening* x. 336 Kniphofias may be accommodated in shrubberies and wide borders. **1935** A. G. L. HELLYER *Pract. Gardening* x. 81 Delphiniums, kniphofias, and ordinary lupins may be planted from 2 feet to 2 feet 6 inches apart. **1971** *Country Life* 2 Sept. 567/2 You will probably put your emphasis..on delphiniums, kniphofias, [etc.].

†**knip-knap.** *Obs. rare*[−1]. [Redupl., app. based on KNAP *sb.*; cf. *snip-snap.*] (?)

1599 HARSNET *Agst. Darell* 179, I told him..that if he would not leave I would set such a paire of knip-knaps upon him as should make him rue it. [**1600** DARRELL *Detect. Harsnet* 128 Wee are to observe heere that Shepheard threatened Somers with a Payre of Knip-Knaps if he were in a Fit again.]

knipper, variant of NIPPER.

knipperdolling (ˈnɪpərdɒlɪŋ). *Ch. Hist.* Also 6 **cnipper-, kniper-,** 6-7 **-dolin(g, -dollin.** An adherent of Bernhard Knipperdolling, a leader of the Münster Anabaptists in 1533-35; an Anabaptist; hence, a religious fanatic.

1594 NASHE *Unfort. Trav.* 56 All the Crue of Cnipperdolings and Muncers. *a* **1600** HOOKER *Eccl. Pol.* VIII. vi. §14 Some Kniperdoling, with his retinue, must take this work of the Lord in hand. **1653** J. LILBURN *Tryed & Cast* 107 Tyrants, Traytors, Murderers, Knipperdolings. **1690** D'URFEY *Collin's Walk* I. 38 Hold, quoth Collin, I am not such a Knipperdollin; Not to allow.. That you are stronger of your hands. [**1823** SCOTT *Peveril* xliv, Four Germans..right Knipperdolings and Anabaptists.]

knipperkin, variant of NIPPERKIN.

†**knipse,** *v.* *Sc. Obs. rare*[−1]. In 6 **knypse.** [prob. a. G. *knipsen* in same sense.] *trans.* To strike sharply, to rap.

a **1572** KNOX *Hist. Ref.* I. Wks. 1846 I. 147 Rockettis war rent, typpetis war torne, crounis war knapped [*MS. G.* knypsed].

knish (knɪʃ). [Yiddish, f. Russ. *knish, knysh* a kind of cake.] A dumpling of flaky dough filled with chopped liver, potato, or cheese, and baked or fried.

1930 A. GROSS *Kibitzer's Dict.* 47 Knishes—Dyspepsia. **1932** L. GOLDING *Magnolia St.* III. vii. 560 There would be *knishehs* to eat. **1960** *New Yorker* 29 Oct. 36/3 Have a canapé. The knishes are especially delicious. **1965** 'E. QUEEN' *Fourth Side of Triangle* iv. 164 We take one of these thin little pancakes, or knishes—almost like tortillas, aren't they? **1973** *Times* 12 Apr. 18/7 Arthur Goldberg, the Democratic candidate, was running a gauntlet of knishes, pizza and egg-roll wherever he went. **1973** *Daily Colonist* (Victoria, B.C.) 27 May 2/4 He consumed three meat knishes, two blueberry knishes, four potato knishes and two cream-filled knishes.

knit (nɪt), *v.* Forms: 1 **cnyttan,** 3-4 **knutte(n** (*ü*), 4 **kneotte(n,** 4-5 **knette(n,** 4-6 **knytte, knyt(e, knitte,** 6- **knit** (*dial.* **knet**). *Pa. t.* 1 **cnytte,** 3-4 **knutte** (*ü*), 4 **knette,** 4-5 **knyt(te,** 4- **knit** (*dial.* **knet**), 5-6 **knytted,** 5- **knitted.** *Pa. pple.* 1 **(ȝe)cnyted,** 3 **i-knut,** 4 **i-, y-knyt, (y-knitte),** 4-6 **(-9** *dial.*) **knet,** (5 **-tte, -te**), **cnyt, knyt, (-ytte, -yȝt, -ut(t),** 4-5 **knytted,** 4- **knitted, knit,** (4-7 **knitt(e,** 6 **nit,** 7 **knite).** *β. Pa. t.* 6- (*north. dial.*) **knat.** *Pa. pple.* 3 **i-cnutten, i-cnute,** 5-6 (9 *dial.* and *arch.*) **knitten.** [OE. *cnyttan*, weak vb. = MDu. and MLG. *knutten*, G. *knütten*:—OTeut. **knuttjan*, f. stem *knutt-*, of OE. *cnotta*, KNOT *sb.* The pa. pple. is regularly *knitted*, contr. *knit*; but *knitten*, after the analogy of strong vbs., has also been used, and (in the north) a strong pa. t. *knat*; cf. *sit, sat, sitten.*]

†**1. a.** *trans.* To tie in or with a knot; to tie, fasten, bind, attach, join, by or as by knotting. With cogn. obj. *to knit a knot. arch.* and *dial.*

c **1000** ÆLFRIC *Gram.* xxxvi. (Z.) 214 Ic cnytte, *necto.* *c* **1000** *Sax. Leechd.* I. 218 Cnyte mid anum ðræde on anum clænan linenan claþe. *a* **1225** *Ancr. R.* 396 Mon knut his kurtel uorte habben þouht of one þinge. *c* **1230** *Hali Meid.* 33 Beo þe cnot icnute anes of wedlac. **1377** LANGL. *P. Pl.* B. Prol. 169 To bugge a belle of brasse..And knitten on a colere..And hangen it vp-on þe cattes hals. *c* **1386** CHAUCER *Man of Law's T.* 209 Thou knyttest [*v.r.* knettest] thee ther thou art nat receyued. **14..** in *Pol. Rel. & L. Poems* (1866) 249 Cryst for vs on croys was knet. *c* **1450** *St. Cuthbert* (Surtees) 1356 For him behoued knyt þe knott [of monkhood]. **1523** FITZHERB. *Husb.* §122 Thre or four splentes that the bees may knitte theyr combes vnto. **1526** TINDALE *Acts* x. 11 A greate shete knytt at the iiij. corners. **1595** SHAKS. *John* IV. i. 42, I knit my hand-kercher about your browes. **1607** HIERON *Wks.* I. 404 Look to the first marriage that euer was; the Lorde Himselfe knit the knot. **1697** DRYDEN *Virg. Past.* VIII. 107 Knit with three Knots the Fillets, knit 'em straight. **17..** *Ploughman* i. in *Burns' Wks.*, His garters knit below his knee. **1805** *Log H.M.S. 'Prince'* 21 Oct. in Nicolas *Disp. Nelson* (1846) VII. 189 *note*, Knitting fore and mizen rigging, and securing the masts.

b. To fasten up, shut up. Cf. 10 a and b. *Obs.*

1398 TREVISA *Barth. De P.R.* XVII. clxxxv. (1495) 726 His tonge is bounden and knytted. *c* **1400** *Rom. Rose* 2092 Alle my jowelle loke and knette, I bynde undir this litel keye. *c* **1425** *Seven Sag.* (P.) 677 Ye have hys tonge cnyt. *c* **1460** *Towneley Myst.* iii. 451 Now ar the weders cest and cateractes knyt. **1509** *Parl. Devylles* xxiii, Thy conclusyon knytteth me so feruently.

c. To geld (a ram) by tying the scrotum. *Obs.*

1607 TOPSELL *Four-f. Beasts* (1658) 482 Then do they use to knit them [rams], and so, in time, their stones, deprived of nourishment..by reason of knitting, do dry and consume away. **1744-50** W. ELLIS *Mod. Husbandm.* IV. I. 129 When he is five years old, he is to be knit and fatted off.

d. *intr.* To attach, itself, adhere. *Obs.*

1571 GOLDING *Calvin on Ps.* xxxvi. 11 Heereunto knitteth rightuousnesse, as the effect of the cause.

2. *trans.* †a. To knot string in open meshes so as to form (a net); to net. *Obs.*

c 1290 *S. Eng. Leg.* I. 436/168 Ase man knut a net: i-knut swiþe harde and stronge. a 1687 WALLER *Mrs. Baughton* Wks. (1730) 41 Those curious nets..thy slender fingers knit.

b. To form (a close texture) by the interlooping of successive series of loops of yarn or thread.

Now the chief specific sense. App. so called from a general resemblance to the formation of network.

1530 PALSGR. 599/2, I knyt bonettes or hosen. 1591 SHAKS. *Two Gent.* III. i. 312 She can knit him a stocke. 1660 *Seas. Exhort.* 11 In Knitting, and Sewing of garments. 1776 ADAM SMITH *W.N.* I. xi. III. (1869) I. 259 In the time of Edward IV. the art of knitting stockings was probably not known in..Europe. 1834–7 SOUTHEY *T' terrible Knitters*, We knat quorse wosset stockings. 1865 MRS. CARLYLE *Lett.* III. 288, I have knitted myself a pair of garters. 1889 *N.W. Linc. Gloss.* s.v., Oor Sarah's knitten yards an' yards on it.

c. *absol.* or *intr.* To do knitting (as in b); *spec.* to do knitting in plain stitch as opposed to purl.

1530 PALSGR. 599/2, I knyt, as a matte maker knytteth. 1591 SHAKS. *Two Gent.* III. i. 310 Item she can knit. 1859 DICKENS *T. Two Cities* III. xv, A number of women, busily knitting. c 1890 tr. *T. de Dillmont's Encycl. Needlewk.* 196 Piqué pattern..1st and 2nd row—purl 7, knit 1, purl 1, knit 1, [etc.]. 1902 [see PURL *v.*[1] 4]. 1944 A. THIRKELL *Headmistress* iii. 61 She was well settled into knit two, purl two. 1972 'B. GRAEME' *Tomorrow's Yesterday* xiv. 142 She would have to undo three rows of knitting. Knit two, purl two, the pattern called for, but she had knitted one and purled three.

3. *trans.* To interlock, interlace, intertwine; to twine, weave, or plait together. *arch.* or *Obs.*

1470–85 MALORY *Arthur* VIII. xxii, Kynge Mark and sire Tristram toke eyther other by the handes hard knyte to gyders. 1526 *Pilgr. Perf.* (W. de W. 1531) 139 The aungell sate downe & knyt roddes, & wrought on yᵉ basket. 1634 MILTON *Comus* 143 Com, knit hands. *Ibid.* 862 In twisted braids of lilies knitting The loose train of thy amber-dropping hair.

4. a. To draw closely together; to contract in folds or wrinkles; †to clench (the fist).

c 1386 CHAUCER *Knt.'s T.* 270 This Palamon gan knytte his browes tweye. c 1489 CAXTON *Sonnes of Aymon* i. 48 He frompeled his forhede and knytted his browes. 1593 SHAKS. *2 Hen. VI*, III. i. 15 He knits his Brow, and shewes an angry Eye. 1602 MARSTON *Antonio's Rev.* v. i. Wks. 1856 I. 132 They all..knit their fists at him. 1611 COTGR., *s'Acroupir*, a Horse to knit, or draw vp, or gather togither, his hinder parts. 1710 *Tatler* No. 253 ¶8 May a Man knit his Forehead into a Frown? 1817–18 COBBETT *Resid. U.S.* (1822) 41, April 18. Cold and raw... The lambs don't play, but stand knit up. 1874 BURNAND *My Time* iv. 34 Knitting his eyebrows.

b. *intr.* said of the brows.

1815 [see KNITTING *ppl. a.*]. 1862 J. GRANT *Capt. of Guard* xx, His brows knit and his eyes loured.

5. a. *trans.* To make compact or firm by close contraction or consolidation of parts; to make close, dense, or hard; to compact; to concentrate.

1423 JAS. I *Kingis Q.* cxciv, Go litill tretise..And pray the reder..Of his gudnese thy brukilnese to knytt. c 1560 A. SCOTT *Poems* (S.T.S.) ii. 31 William wichttar wes of corss Nor Sym, and bettir knittin. 1590 SPENSER *F.Q.* I. i. 19 Knitting all his force, [he] got one hand free. 1607 MARKHAM *Caval.* I. (1617) 4 The..sharpenesse..[of] winter..will..harden and knitte him [a foal]. a 1848 R. W. HAMILTON *Rew. & Punishm.* v. 231 With striving we knit our strength. 1872 J. L. SANFORD *Estim. Eng. Kings, Chas. I* 335 His mind was much more firmly knit..than that of his father.

b. *intr.* (for *refl.*) To become compact, firm, or strong by close consolidation of parts; to become consolidated.

1605 BACON *Adv. Learn.* I. v. §4 Young men, when they knit and shape perfectly, do seldom grow to a further stature. 1614 MARKHAM *Cheap Husb.* (1623) 45 After your mares have beene covered,..you shall let them rest three weeks, or a moneth, that the substance may knit. 1662 R. MATHEW *Unl. Alch.* §111. 182 Warm water,..sprinkle this powder thereon, and keep it stirring with a stick, otherwise it wil knit to a stone in the bottom. 1727–46 THOMSON *Summer* 1264 Hence the limbs Knit into force. 1821 CLARE *Vill. Minstr.* I. 67 Weakness knits stubborn while it's bearing thee.

c. *intr. spec.* Of fruit: To form, 'set'. Also of the tree, or of the blossom: To form fruit. (Said also of corn and potatoes.)

c 1400 *Destr. Troy* 2737 In the moneth of May..frutes were knyt [*ed.* 1874 *mispr.* kuyt]. *Ibid.* 4973. 1577–87 HOLINSHED *Chron.* (1807–8) II. 317 The fruit was knit before the growth..could be hindered. 1601 HOLLAND *Pliny* I. 473 Some trees..doe not knit nor shew their fruit immediatly vpon their blooming. 1699 *Poor Man's Plea* 5 Continued good Weather..gave the Corn..time to knit and kearn, as they call it. 1719 LONDON & WISE *Compl. Gard.* 33 The new Shoots..blossom extremely, but little of the Fruit knits. 1884 *Cheshire Gloss.* s.v., Potatoes also are said to knit when the tubers begin to form. 1894 *Cath. News* 1 Dec. 8/1 A friend..remarked..that the gooseberries he had planted in his garden were 'knitting' well.

†d. Of a female animal: To conceive, form fruit: cf. quot. 1614 in b, and KNIT *ppl. a.* 3. *Obs.*

1732 W. ELLIS *Pract. Farmer* 139 At five weeks end let her take buck, that the former brood may go off before she knits, about a week.

6. a. *trans.* To conjoin or unite closely and firmly (contiguous members, broken parts). Cf. KNITTED, quot. 1855.

1578 BANISTER *Hist. Man* I. 3 The vpper head of the thighe, where it is knit with the Bone of the hippe. 1676 WISEMAN *Surg.* (J.), Nature cannot knit the bones while the parts are under a discharge. 1715–20 POPE *Iliad* VIII. 393 There, where the juncture knits the channel bone. 1811 PINKERTON *Petral.* II. 624 A piece..which had at some former time been separated from it..was again knitted to the stock in such a perfect manner that the joint was scarcely perceptible. 1849 MURCHISON *Siluria* iii. 41 The whole of the beds are so knit together. 1862 STANLEY *Jewish Ch.* (1877) I. xviii. 346 The good physicians who knit together the dislocated bones of a disjointed time. 1887 BOWEN *Virg. Æneid* II. 786 Huge timbers of oak knitted to timbers, a fabric that reaches to heaven.

b. *intr.* To become closely united; to grow together.

1612 WOODALL *Surg. Mate* Wks. (1653) 91 Leaving of the grief undressed for two daies, that the veins may knit. 1621 DONNE *Serm.* xv. 150 And invites the severall Ioynts to knit again. *Mod.* In young people fractured bones soon knit.

c. *intr.* Of bees: To cluster together in a mass. Now *dial.*

[1523 FITZHERB. *Husb.* §122 Whan the swarme is knytte, take a hyue and splent it within.] 1577 B. GOOGE *Heresbach's Husb.* (1586) 181 Bowes and branches,..whereupon they may knit and settle themselves. 1648 MARKHAM *Housew. Gard.* III. x. (1668) 77 If your swarm knit in the top of a tree. 1831 W. HOWITT *Seasons* 144 The queen-bee alights..and the rest of the bees clustering, or as it is termed knitting, about her, form a living, brown, dependent cone. 1879 MISS JACKSON *Shropsh. Word-bk.* s.v., I never like to see the bees knit on the ground—it's a sure sign of a berrin' [= burial].

d. *trans.* To form out of parts compacted. *rare.*

1896 A. E. HOUSMAN *Shropsh. Lad* xxxii, From far, from eve and morning And yon twelve-winded sky, The stuff of life to knit me Blew hither: here am I.

7. *fig.* a. To conjoin as by knotting or binding together; to bind, join, or connect firmly; to unite or combine intimately.

1340 HAMPOLE *Pr. Consc.* 1855 God,..First body and saul togyder knyt. c 1386 CHAUCER *Frankl. T.* 258 Ne shal I neuere been vntrewe wyf..I wol been his to whom þat I am knyt. 1450–1530 *Myrr. our Ladye* 295 Manhode was knytte unto godhed in his persone. 1547 J. HARRISON *Exhort. Scottes* A ij, So nere neighbors..knitte in Christes faithe. 1662 STILLINGFL. *Orig. Sacr.* III. i. §6 The mind may..knit some things together in fictitious Ideas. 1711 ADDISON *Spect.* No. 69 ¶6 They [merchants] knit Mankind together in a mutual Intercourse of good Offices. 1871 R. ELLIS *Catullus* lxiv. 335 Never [hath] love so well his children in harmony knitten. 1879 DIXON *Windsor* II. vii. 69 These lords were closely knit by marriage.

b. *intr.* (for *refl.*) To join; to grow together, unite closely.

a 1548 HALL *Chron., Edw. IV* 206 b, To..allure the hartes of other men, to ioyne and knit with hym, against all hostilitie. 1627 E. F. *Hist. Edw. II* (1680) 69 And then retreat to knit with their Confederates. 1770 LANGHORNE *Plutarch* (1879) I. 252/1 The city..is broken into two parts which will never knit again. 1832–4 DE QUINCEY *Cæsars* Wks. 1859 X. 10 Everywhere the members of this empire had begun to knit; the cohesion was far closer.

8. *trans.* To make or constitue by joining (a covenant, agreement, or the like); to make fast or firm, to establish (a relation of union); to 'tie', 'cement'.

13.. *E.E. Allit. P.* B. 564 He knyt a couenaunde..with monkynd þere. c 1400 *Destr. Troy* 11863 Soche acord was here knyt with knynges. a 1541 WYATT *Defence* in *Wks.* (1861) p. xxxiii, Them that knit company with Chappins. 1600 HOLLAND *Livy* XXV. xxix. 570 When peace was knit again. 1818 CRUISE *Digest* (ed. 2) V. 296 It was the very issue, knit by the express words of the plea.

9. *intr.* To effervesce, form froth, as wine or beer. In *pa. pple.*, effervescing, brisk; not still or dead.

[Perh. related to intrans. senses under 5. But it may be a different word, and properly written *nit*: cf. a 1700 B. E. *Dict. Cant. Crew*, *Nit*, wine that is brisk, and pour'd quick into a Glass. 1725 in *New Cant. Dict.*]

1743 *Lond. & Country Brew.* III. (ed. 2) 220 In Winter they commonly heat their Parcels to invigorate the new Drink..and then..the Malt-Liquor will knit and sparkle in a Glass, though drawn out of a Barrel. 1766 GOLDSM. *Vic. W.* xvi, If the gooseberry wine was well knit, the gooseberies were of her gathering.

10. **knit up.** a. *trans.* To tie up; to fasten up; to string up, to hang; to compose or repair by knitting. *lit.* and *fig.*

c 1400 *Destr. Troy* 2014 þai..knitten vp þe saile, Atyrit the tacle. *Ibid.* 11460 All..knit vp þere couenaunte. 1509 BARCLAY *Shyp of Folys* (1570) 241 All my vesture is of golde pure,..In siluer net my heare up knet. 1530 PALSGR. 599/2, I knytte up a man, I holde hym shorte or kepe hym from his lybertye. 1605 SHAKS. *Macb.* II. ii. 37 Sleepe that knits vp the rauel'd Sleeue of Care. 1610 —— *Temp.* III. iii. 89 These (mine enemies) are all knit vp In their distractions. 1725 RAMSAY *Gent. Sheph.* I. ii, They're fools that slav'ry like, and may be free; The chiels may a' knit up themselves for me. 1846 TRENCH *Mirac.* xxvii. (1862) 371 We see how entirely his own life is knit up with his child's.

†b. To 'shut up', take up; to snub. *Obs.* Cf. 1 b.

1530 PALSGR. 599/2, I knyt one up, I take hym up, I reprove hym. 1571 EDWARDS *Damon & Pithias* in Hazl. *Dodsley* IV. 46 So sternly he frowned on me, and knit me up so short.

c. To close up; to conclude, finish, or end.

1530 PALSGR. 599/2, I knytte up a mater, I make an ende or conclusyon of a matter. 1566 ADDISON *Apuleius* VIII. xxxii. (1893) 163 To end and knit up all sorrow. 1587 THYNNE in *Holinshed's Scot. Chron.* (1805) II. 377 Before I knit up this exordium. 1622 F. MARKHAM *Bk. War* v. ix. 196, I will heere knit vp this Epistle. 1879 FROUDE *Cæsar* xxv. 434 The tragedy was being knitted up in the deaths of the last actors in it.

†d. To sum up; to express concisely. *Obs.*

1553 *Short Catech.* in *Lit. & Doctr. Edw. VI* (Parker Soc.) 499 Will you that I knit up in a brief abridgment all that belongeth both to God and men? 1560 DAUS tr. *Sleidane's Comm.* 84 b, To knit up the matter in fewe wordes. 1610 HOLLAND *Camden's Brit.* (1637) 280 Briefly to knit up their succession.

11. *Comb.* **knit-back**, **knit-wort**, the herb Comfrey; **knit-beggar** = COUPLE-BEGGAR.

1597 GERARDE *Herbal* II. cclxxiv, It is called..in English, Comfrey..of some Knitbacke. 1611 COTGR. s.v. *Asne*, *Oreille d'asne*, th' hearbe Comfrey, knit-backe, knit-wort, blacke-wort. 1700 *Wilmslow Parish Register* Aug. 25, in Earwaker *E. Cheshire* (1877) I. 99 Were married by [a] knit-begger, Daniel Hulme and Esther Hunt.

knit (nɪt), *sb.* [f. KNIT *v.*]

1. a. The style or stitch in which anything is knitted; knitted work; texture. Also, a knitted fabric. **knit stitch**, the plainest stitch in knitting.

1596 SHAKS. *Tam. Shr.* IV. i. 95 Let..their garters [be] of an indifferent knit. 1603 *Q. Eliz. Wardr.* in *Leisure H.* (1884) 739/2 A paire of sleeves of gold and silver knytt. 1897 *Sears, Roebuck Catal.* 217/3 Turtle Neck Sweater. Extra heavy knit. All wool. 1932 D. C. MINTER *Mod. Needlecraft* 68/2 (*caption*) Rows of plain knitting... Smooth knit stitch; ..rough purl stitch. 1960 *Guardian* 19 Feb. 8/6 Dress and jacket of corded cotton knit. 1960 *News Chron.* 22 Mar. 11/3 Textured nylon is making news with new chunky knits, and fur fabrics. 1963 *New Yorker* 29 June 44 It looks like sharkskin, but it's really a knit. 1964 *Guardian* 22 Jan. 8/4 Knits are used for dresses, coats, suits.., so that it is possible to dress in knitwear from dawn to dark. 1964 *McCall's Sewing* iv. 53/1 When buying a knit, remember that it is a resilient fabric.

b. The action or process of knitting.

1926 E. K. MIDDLETON *New Knitting* Pref., Left hand knit and left hand purl are simpler and quicker than the old right hand knit.

c. A knitted garment. Freq. in *pl.*

1938 D. BAKER *Young Man with Horn* I. iv. 38 His brother Henry..was selling jersey knits. 1965 *Harper's Bazaar* June 66 Sportive, can't-wait-for-winter knits. 1972 *Daily Tel.* 30 Oct. 13/1 Glitter knits are one of the top fashions for winter.

2. Knitting, uniting of parts. *rare.*

1892 *Pall Mall G.* 4 Oct. 7/1 A palmist on Mr. G. G... He has the knits of order but no science.

3. Contraction or wrinkle (of the brow).

1895 *Daily News* 29 Jan. 5/4 He..has..a permanent knit of the brow.

4. *Mining*: see quot. (Perh. properly *nit.*)

1881 RAYMOND *Mining Gloss.*, *Knits* or *Knots*, small particles of ore.

knit (nɪt), *ppl. a.* [Pa. pple. of KNIT *v.*]

1. a. Knotted, tied, fastened together; contracted together: see the verb.

c 1440 *Promp. Parv.* 279/2 Knytte, *nodatus, nexus, connexus.* 1605 VERSTEGAN *Dec. Intell.* iii. (1628) 79 The knit vnitie and conioyned concord of the Saxons. 1715–20 POPE *Iliad* XX. 554 Where the knit nerve the pliant elbow strung. 1851 D. JERROLD *St. Giles* xiv. 139 He turned with knit eyebrows to his wife.

b. With qualifying adv., as ***well-knit***.

1725 POPE *Odyss.* XVIII. 259 Thy well-knit frame..Speaks thee an hero, from an hero sprung. 1871 TYLOR *Prim. Cult.* II. xiv. 122 Well-knit harangues full of the poetic figure and metaphor of the professional orator.

2. Formed as a texture by knitting: see KNIT *v.* 2 b. [Or a use of KNIT *sb.* 1.]

Formerly sometimes hyphened, as ***knit-stockings***.

[1488 *Will* in *Ripon Ch. Acts* (Surtees) 286, j knyt gyrdyll.] 1587 HARRISON *England* II. xxii. (1877) I. 342 In colouring their knit hosen. 1612 STURTEVANT *Metallica* 71 Knit stockings with loome, which is a late Inuention of one Maister Lee. 1720 DE FOE *Capt. Singleton* xviii. (1840) 302 He..obtained it for a knit cap. 1818 LADY MORGAN *Autobiog.* (1859) 86 A knit silk scarf. 1895 *Montgomery Ward Catal.* 283/1 Children's Knit Undershirts. Ladies' Jersey Knit Ribbed Vests. 1897 *Sears, Roebuck Catal.* 203/1 Lumberman's Knit Socks. a 1901 *Mod. Trade Rep.*, The knit goods market is in a flourishing condition. 1922 E. E. CUMMINGS *Enormous Room* vii. 155 A knit sweater of a strangely ugly red hue. 1962 F. I. ORDWAY et al. *Basic Astronautics* xiii. 517 The inner liner of the suit is of neoprene-coated fabric with knit stretch sections. 1970 *Catal. L. L. Bean* (Freeport, Maine) Fall 32 Deluxe insulated coverall... Knit cuffs at wrists. 1970 *Women's Wear Daily* 23 Nov. 31/2 So many knit pants in the market are dumb, missy looks.

†3. Having conceived, pregnant. *Obs.*

1603 HOLLAND *Plutarch's Mor.* 218 No sooner doth she perceive herselfe to be knit with egge, but she falleth presently to build her nest. 1781 W. BLANE *Ess. Hunting* (1788) 118 The Doe..seldom holds an end, unless knit; or at the end of the season has kindled.

knit, variant of NIT *sb.*[1] and *v.*[1]

knitch (nɪtʃ). Now *dial.* Forms: α. 4 **knucche, knohche, knycche**, 4–6 **knytche**, 5 **knyche**, 6 **knoche**, 6– **knitch**. β. 6 **nytche**, 8– **nitch**. [ME. *knücche, knycche*:—OE. *ȝecnycc(e* (occurring in the sense 'bond'); from same root as LG. *knuck(e*, Ger. *knocke*, a bundle of heckled flax. Ultimate etym. obscure: cf. *tocnuicte* and *ȝecnyht* from a vb. *cnycc(e)an* in Lindisf. Gl.] A bundle (of wood, hay, corn, etc.) tied together; a sheaf or faggot.

α. [c 950 *Durham Ritual* (Surtees) 59 From synna usra ȝicnyccum [L. *a peccatorum nostrorum nexibus*]. *Ibid.* 66 Deaðes ȝicnyccum [L. *mortis nexibus*].] 13.. *XI Pains of Hell* 77 in *Minor Poems fr. Vernon MS.* 253 Ligate per fasciculos..Byndeþ hem in knucchen [*MS.* knucchenus]. ? 13.. *Coer de L.* 2985 The ffootmen kast in knohches of hay, ..And ffylde the dyke fful upryghte. 1382 WYCLIF *Matt.* xiii. 30 Gedre ȝe to-gedre dernels,..and byndeth hem to gidre in knytchis [*gloss* or smale bundelis]. 1398 TREVISA

Barth. De P.R. xvii. xcvii. (Tollem. MS.), [Flax] bounde in knytches [**1535** nytches] and bondeles. **1481** *Nottingham Rec.* II. 320, xvj. knitche de strey lates. **1519** *Churchw. Acc. Stratton* in *Archæologia* XLVI. 207 Paid for strow v knochys jd. **1552** Huloet, Knytche or bownche of woode, *fascis*. **1603** Holland *Plutarch's Mor.* 203 Himselfe tooke out of the sheafe or knitch the darts.. one by one. **1850** Kingsley *Alt. Locke* xxviii, If I dared break a hedge for a knitch o' wood, they'd put me in prison.

β. **1535** [see **1398** in *a*]. **1725** *Lond. Gaz.* No. 6447/4 Taking Straws out of a Nitch of Straw. **1823** *Examiner* 574/1 He was seen to go towards the thicket, for the purpose.. of getting a nitch of fern. **1882** *West. Morn. News* 25 Nov. 4/2 Wanted, 200 Nitches of well-made good reed, for thatching. **1888** *Edin. Rev.* July 129 Nitch is a faggot of wood which a hedger has.. a right to carry away at night.

'knitchel. [f. prec. + -EL.] A small bundle.

1500-20 Dunbar *Poems* xxii. 72 Twa curis or thre hes vpolandis Michell, With dispensationis bund in knitchell. **1901** *Eng. Dial. Dict.*, *Knitchell*, a bundle,.. a cluster.

†**knitchet.** *Obs. rare*⁻¹. [f. KNITCH + -ET¹.] A small knitch; a handful (of reeds, etc.).

But in quot. perh. misprint for *knitches*, usual in Holland. **1601** Holland *Pliny* II. xx. xvii. 100 The said stems are slit and clouen.. when they be dried, they ought to be made up into knitchets or handfuls.

'knit-knot. *rare.* [f. KNIT *ppl. a.* + KNOT, with effect of alternative reduplication, as in *knick-knack*.] A knitted or knotted piece of work.

1703 *Country Farmers Catech.* (N.), Not to spend their time in knit-knots, patchwork,.. and such like fooleries.

†**'knitster.** *Obs. rare*⁻¹. [f. KNIT *v.* + -STER.] = KNITTER 2. (In form, feminine.)

1648 Mayne *Amorous War* v. viii, My two Troilus's transform'd to Knitsters.

knitted ('nɪtɪd), *ppl. a.* (and *sb.*) [f. KNIT *v.* + -ED¹.] = KNIT *ppl. a.* Also as *sb.*, a knitted garment; freq. in *pl.*

1855 Mayne *Expos. Lex.*, *Knitted*, applied to that stage in the union of fractured bones in which ossification has so far advanced as to give a certain degree of firmness to a broken limb. **1858** Simmonds *Dict. Trade*, *Knitting-machine*, a machine for weaving and making knitted work. **1866** J. B. Rose tr. *Ovid's Met.* 263 She sate, Cross-legged and knitted-fingered in the gate. **1870** Morris *Earthly Par.* II. iii. 20 She Set her slim hand upon her knitted brow. **1958** *Woman* 9 Aug. 31/4 Briony is going to Ardoaghy to buy more knitteds. **1960** *Woman's Own* 19 Mar. 34/2 Two elegant knitteds from one set of instructions. **1963** *Harper's Bazaar* Feb. 41 The knitteds we can't do without.

knitter ('nɪtə(r)). [f. KNIT *v.* + -ER¹.]

1. One who or that which ties, knots, unites, or closely joins together. *lit.* and *fig.*

c **1440** Capgrave *Life St. Kath.* iv. 2311 On oo god I beleue.. I beleue on Ihesu.. I leue in the goost, knettere of hem too. **1587** Golding *De Mornay* xiv. 225 Wee see in mans body.. a greate nomber of sinewes, Fleshstrings, and knitters. **1604** Dekker *Honest Wh.* Wks. 1873 II. 74 He means this day to be married.. Frier Anselmo is the Knitter.

2. One who knits or works up yarn or thread into a looped texture, for hosiery, etc.

c **1515** *Cocke Lorell's B.* 10 Spynsters, carders, and cappe knytters. **1601** Shaks. *Twel. N.* ii. iv. 45 The Spinsters and the Knitters in the Sun. **1723** *Lond. Gaz.* No. 6224/9 Thomas Pratchitt, late of Nottingham, Frame Work Knitter. **1778** Johnson in *Boswell* 7 Apr., A knitter of stockings. **1834-7** Southey *Doctor*, (*title*) T' terrible Knitters e' Dent. **1844** G. Dodd *Textile Manuf.* vii. 209 A frame-work knitter (the technical name for a stocking maker).

b. A knitting-machine.

1890 *Chicago Advance* 12 June, Some sort of an invention .. a knitter.

†**3.** (app.) Some knitted article of dress. *Obs.*

1530 in Weaver *Wells Wills* (1890) 145 My wyfes best cap, her best gowne, her best kyntter. **1532** *Ibid.* 105 His eldest dowter a cape and a knytter—to the ijnd dowter a aprone and a knytter. **1534** *Ibid.* 107 A cap with a knytter.

knitting ('nɪtɪŋ), *vbl. sb.* [f. as prec. + -ING¹.]

1. a. The action of the verb KNIT. Fastening in or with a knot, tying, binding, conjunction, compacting, etc. *lit.* and *fig.*

a **1420** Hoccleve *De Reg. Princ.* 4542 Opne hem [bags]; hir knyttynge al to sore annoyeth. *c* **1430** *Life St. Kath.* (1884) 42 þe lawfull knyttyng of matrymony. **1550** Bale *Image Both Ch.* (1560) A iij, The very complete summe and whole knyttyng up. **1617** Bp. Hall *Quo Vadis?* §4 Wks. (1628) 691 Blossomes.. nipped.. with an Aprill frost when they should come to the knitting. **1874** Green *Short Hist.* iii. §4. 131 The knitting of Christian nations together into a vast commonwealth.

†**b.** *concr.* A tie, fastening, knot (*lit.* and *fig.*). *Obs.*

13.. *Sir Beues* (MSS. S. and N.) 149/3220 On hur gurdul ȝhe made a knyttyng riding [*other MSS.* knotte riding], Aboute his necke ȝhe hit þrew Him to honge hard and fast. **1495** *Trevisa's Barth. De P.R.* xvii. clxxiv. (W. de W.) V iv b/1 Bendes and knyttynges [*Bodley MS.* knyttels] made to bynde vp vynes. *a* **1548** Hall *Chron.*, *Hen. VIII*, 96 Betweene the knittynges Flowers of Golde. **1610** Barrough *Meth. Physick* i. xxv. (1639) 43 Apply it to the Hanches, and to the.. Knittings of the joynts.

c. A girl or girls. *slang.*

1943 C. H. Ward-Jackson *Piece of Cake* 39 *Knitting*, girl or girls. **1946** J. Irving *Royal Navalese* 104 *Knitting*, girls in the plural. The singular of this is '*A Piece of Knitting*'. **1962** Granville *Dict. Sailors' Slang* 68/2 *Knitting*, girl friend or girls collectively.

2. a. *spec.* The formation of a fabric by looping (see quot. 1883). **b.** *concr.* Work so done or made, knitted work.

1711 Addison *Spect.* No. 108 ¶3 A Pair of Garters of his own knitting. **1880** Miss Braddon *Just as I am* vii, Aunt Dora was occupied with her knitting. **1882** Caulfeild & Saward *Dict. Needlework* s.v., The art of Knitting was unknown in England until the sixteenth century. **1883** *Chambers' Encycl.* V. 810 *Knitting* consists in using a single thread, and with it forming a continual series of loops across the whole fabric; the next row [of loops] passes through these; and they in their turn receive another set, until the whole is completed. **1892** Mrs. Alexander *For his Sake* I. 220 Please bring me my knitting.

3. *attrib.* and *Comb.*, as ***knitting bag, bee, book, -cotton*** (cotton thread for knitting), ***frolic, machine, -mill, pattern, -silk, wire, wool, -work***; **knitting-case**, (*a*) = *knitting-sheath*; (*b*) a case for keeping knitting-needles in; †**knitting-cup**, a cup of wine handed round at a marriage feast; **knitting-pin**, †**knitting-prick**, **knitting-wire** = KNITTING-NEEDLE; **knitting sheath**, a cylindrical sheath for holding a knitting-needle steady in the act of knitting; **knitting-stick**, an elongated form of the knitting-sheath. Also KNITTING-NEEDLE.

1789 W. Cowper *Let.* 31 Jan. in *Corr.* (1904) III. 347 A basket.. [which] contained.. a *knitting bag, and a piece of plumcake. **1939** J. Cary *Mister Johnson* 209 The accomplished.. traveller.. sets up her household, complete with family and knitting bag, even in trains and tram shelters. **1971** A. Christie *Nemesis* ii. 20 Taking her knitting out of its embroidered knitting bag. **1851** *Illustr. Catal. Gt. Exhib.* 786 Complete fancy *knitting-basket. **1855** *Chicago Times* 19 Mar. 2/6 This girl had been at a *knitting bee, at the house of a friend. **1880** *Harper's Mag.* Sept. 508/1 In winter they sometimes had knitting bees. **1843** A. Lambert (*title*) My *knitting-book. **1873** *Young Englishwoman* June 311/3 We must refer you to Madame Goubaud's Knitting and Netting Book. **1973** Horne & Bowden *Bk. Knitting & Crochet* i. 10 The contents of the knitting books of the 1840s differed greatly from those of today. **1851** *Illustr. Catal. Gt. Exhib.* 785 *Knitting cases. **1888** E. Eggleston *Graysons* xxx. 332 She paused to take the end of one needle out of the quill of her knitting-case. **1851** *Illustr. Catal. Gt. Exhib.* 1106 *Knitting and sewing cotton yarn. **1632** B. Jonson *Magn. Lady* iv. ii, Doe, doe, and mind The Parsons pint.. A *knitting Cup there must be. **1818** H. B. Fearon *Sk. Amer.* 223 They are invited to the preacher's house, to partake of a supper... This is termed a *knitting frolic. **1858** *Knitting-machine [see KNITTED]. **1875** Knight *Dict. Mech.* I. 1236/2 The Bickford knitting-machine.. is a specimen of the circular system. **1927** M. Ostenso *Mad Carews* (1929) iv. 44 Her mother had sent to the city for a knitting machine in the hope that she might be able to supply her neighbours with woollen socks. **1974** *Times* 12 Feb. 11/5 He started.. with a couple of hand frame knitting machines. **1898** *Folk-lore* Sept. 219 The old *knitting-parties which once formed centres of social life in winter evenings. **1885** C. M. Yonge *Nuttie's Father* ii. i. 7, I couldn't get a *knitting pattern Miss Headworth was to send Lady Ronnisglen. **1961** M. Stewart *Ivy Tree* iii. 46 The colourless voice.. might have been discussing a knitting pattern. **1973** 'J. Ashford' *Double Run* xi. 85 Nina, at a critical point in the intricate knitting pattern,.. dropped a stitch. **1857** C. M. Yonge *Dynevor Terrace* I. iv. 49 He had in the other pocket.. wools.. the long *knitting-pins under his arm like a riding-whip. **1870** Miss Bridgman *R. Lynne* I. xi. 178 The.. click of the knitting-pins ceased. **1597** *Wills & Inv. N.C.* (Surtees 1860) 283, ij lbs. and a half of *knitting prickes 2s. 1d. **1755** Smollett *Quix.* (1803) IV. 82 In making *knitting-sheaths and plain-work. **1867** 'T. Lackland' *Homespun* i. 23 A great tear trembles on her cheek as she adjusts her needle in the knitting sheath she wears. **1897** *Sears, Roebuck Catal.* 321/2 *Knitting and Crochet Silk.. is used for knitting mittens, stockings and other articles which require washing. **1850** *Rep. Comm. Patents 1849* (U.S.) 491 The needle itself, and thimble will be exhibited in museums with distaffs, spinning-wheels, *knitting-wires, [etc.]. **1860** Geo. Eliot *Mill on Floss* III. vi. vi. 87 Maggie's ball of *knitting-wool rolled along the ground. **1965** A. Christie *At Bertram's Hotel* xii. 114 She had a splendid time rounding up knitting patterns, new varieties of knitting wool, and suchlike delights. **1852** Mrs. Stowe *Uncle Tom's C.* xix. 187 Miss Ophelia.. pulled out her *knitting-work, and sat there, grim with indignation.

knitting ('nɪtɪŋ), *ppl. a.* [f. as prec. + -ING².] That knits, in various senses: see the verb.

1387-8 T. Usk *Test. Love* Prol. (Skeat) I. 3 The deliciousnesse of iestes and of ryme, by queynt knittinge coloures. **1587** Golding *De Mornay* x. (1617) 152 The knitting parts, that is to wit, the bones, the skin, the sinewes and such like. **1599** A. M. tr. *Gabelhouer's Bk. Physicke* 342/2 Knitting and congealinge Playsters. **1815** Byron *Parisina* x, With downcast eyes and knitting brow. **1837** Ht. Martineau *Soc. Amer.* III. 88 Four knitting young ladies and their knitting mother.

knitting-needle. A long straight blunt 'needle' or slender rod used, two or more at a time, in knitting; either of steel for fine work, or of wood, ivory, etc., with a knob at one end, for larger work.

These are sometimes distinguished as *kn.-needles* and *kn.-pins*. In Scotland steel *kn.-needles* are called *wires*.

1598 Florio, *Agucchiare*, to knit with knitting needles. **1712** Arbuthnot *John Bull* iii. ii. She would prick him with her knitting needle. **1889** 'J. S. Winter' *Mrs. Bob* (1891) 48 She plied her knitting-needles.

knittle ('nɪt(ə)l). Also 7 knettel, 7-8 -le, (8 nittle, 9 nettle). [A derivative of KNIT *v.*: see -LE, -EL¹. OE. *cnyttels* is found once as a gloss to L. *nervus.*]

†**1.** A string or cord for tying or fastening. *Obs.* in gen. sense.

1398 Trevisa *Barth. De P.R.* xvii. xcvii. (Tollem. MS.), þred to sewynge, ropes to bindynge, and strenges to schetynge, knittels to knittynge [*Ligamina ad connectendum*]. *Ibid.* xvii. clxxv. (Bodl. MS.), Of persche beþ nedefulle bondes and knyttels [*ed.* 1495 knyttynges] made to binde up vines.

2. *spec.* **a.** *Naut.* A small line made of yarn, used on board ship. Also *attrib.*

1627 Capt. Smith *Seaman's Gram.* v. 25 Knettels are two rope yarnes twisted together, and a knot at each end, whereunto to sease a blocke, a rope, or the like. **1762** Falconer *Shipwr.* ii. 194 The reef enwrapp'd, th' inserted nittles [*ed.* 1769 inserting knittles] ty'd. *c* **1860** H. Stuart *Seaman's Catech.* 30 Cut a nettle about two feet long. **1867** Smyth *Sailor's Word-bk.*, *Knittle*, see *Nettle*. *Ibid.*, *Nettles*, small line used for seizings, and for hammock-clues. **1885** J. Runciman *Skippers & Shellbacks* 185 If any hammock looked baggy or if the 'knittles' were not hauled taut.

b. (See quots.)

1847-78 Halliwell, *Knittle*, a string fastened to the mouth of a sack to tie it with. *Sussex.* **1875** in Parish *Sussex Gloss.* **1875** Knight *Dict. Mech.* 1239/1 *Knittle*.. 2. a draw-string of a bag. **1881** in *Isle of Wight Gloss.*

knitty, variant of NITTY.

knitwear ('nɪtwɛə(r)). [f. KNIT *ppl. a.* + WEAR *sb.*] Knitted articles of clothing.

1925-6 *Army & Navy Co-op. Soc. Price List* 698 'Braemar' Knitwear for Gentlemen. **1928** *Daily Express* 7 May 4 Two-piece suits, knitwear, leather coats and raincoats. **1957** L. F. R. Williams *State of Israel* 111 There is already some considerable export of cotton goods, as well as of knitwear. **1966** *Illustr. London News* 26 Feb. 5 The knitwear is made of Shetland wool and is fully fashioned with raglan sleeves. **1973** J. Thomson *Death Cap* vi. 91 He was in Bradford, seeing some knitwear manufacturers on business.

knitwork ('nɪtwɜːk). [f. KNIT *ppl. a.*] Knitted work; knitting.

1628 *World encomp. by Sir F. Drake* 74 His attire vpon his head was a cawle of Knitworke. **1661** Morgan *Sph. Gentry* i. viii. 105 Garments of Knit-work. **1862** Lytton *Str. Story* I. 202 Resuming her knitwork while I read.

knive (naɪv), *v.* [f. KNIFE *sb.*, on analogy of *wife, wive; strife, strive*, etc.] = KNIFE *v.*

1850 F. Walpole *The Ansayrii* II. 8 A brute who in cold blood knived and tortured them with his own hand. **1883** E. F. Knight *Cruise 'Falcon'* (1887) 53 These race-meetings, .. he said, end as a rule in considerable kniving.

knived (naɪvd), *a.* [f. KNIFE *sb.* + -ED².] Armed with a knife or knives.

1893 *Westm. Gaz.* 7 Oct. 2/1 The whole gang of us, belted and knived, bronzed to the elbows.

kno, obs. form of KNOW *v.*

knob (nɒb), *sb.* Forms: *α.* 4-6 **knobbe**, (7 **knobb**, **knobe**), 6- **knob**. *β.* 5-7 **nobbe**, 7-9 **nob**. [ME., = MLG. and mod.G. *knobbe* knot, knob, bud, etc., Flem. *knobbe(n* lump (of bread, etc.): cf. KNOP, NOB, KNUB, NUB.]

1. a. A small rounded lump or mass, esp. at the extremity or on the surface of something, as on a stick, a branch or trunk of a tree, a plate of glass (see BULL'S-EYE 1), the antenna of an insect, the pistil of a flower, etc.; a rounded protuberance, boss, stud; the handle of a door or drawer, the hinder end of a gun (see CASCABEL).

1398 Trevisa *Barth. De P.R.* xvii. clxi. (MS. Bodl.) lf. 230 b/2 Hurden,.. is clensing of offal of hempe oþer of flaxe ..þerof is þrede sponne þᵗ is fulle grete: vneuen and ful of nobbes. *c* **1440** *Promp. Parv.* 280/1 Knobbe, or knotte yn a tre, *vertex*. **1557-8** Phaer *Æneid* vii. U j b, Another caught a clubbe, with heauy knobbes. **1611** Coryat *Crudities* 15 He had a long staffe in his hand with a nobbe in the middle, according to the fashion of those Pilgrims staffes. **1774** Foote *Cozeners* iii. Wks. 1799 II. 190 That.. is a watch; if you touch the nob that juts out, it strikes.. like a clock. **1776-96** Withering *Brit. Plants* (ed. 3) I. 184 Pist[il] ... Style thread-shaped... Summit a knob. **1833** J. Holland *Manuf. Metal* II. 278 The bolt is moved by.. a fixed knob or handle, as in the common door catch. **1840** *Civil Eng. & Arch. Jrnl.* III. 400/1 A certain article which forms.. a handsome nob for parlour and other doors. **1842-76** Gwilt *Archit.* (ed. 7) §1872 *a*, The great advantage of sheet glass is that of.. avoiding the waste arising from.. the knob or bull's eye in the centre. **1844** H. Stephens *Bk. Farm* III. 928 A wooden cover..., with nobs for the convenience of lifting it out. *Ibid.* 936 It has a nob-handle standing upward. **1875** Knight *Dict. Mech.* 1530/2 *Nob* (Artillery), the plate under the swing-bed for the head of an elevating screw. **1894** R. Bridges *Feast Bacchus* v. 1574 A little knob of a nose.

b. A rounded protuberance or swelling on the skin or on a bodily organ; a bump, hump, wart, pimple, pustule, etc. *Obs.* or merged in 1.

c **1386** Chaucer *Prol.* 633 The knobbes sittynge on his chekes. *c* **1490** *Promp. Parv.* 280/1 (MS. K) Knobbe of a mannys hande, or in another part of him [*a* **1485** *MS. S.* knoble; **1499** *ed. Pynson* knolle], *callus*. **1530** Palsgr. 326/2 Kyrnell or knobbe in the necke or otherwhere, *glandre*. **1599** Shaks. *Hen. V*, iii. vi. 108 His face is all bubukles and whelkes, and knobs, and flames a fire. **1747** Wesley *Prim. Physic* (1762) 39 It also dissolves any Knob or swelling in any part. **1792** Hunter *Obs. Anim. Œcon.* (ed. 2) 80 The hen had nobs on her toes. **1822-34** *Good's Study Med.* (ed. 4) II. 517 The dark-coloured or hepatised knobs.

c. The bud or rudiment of a horn; in quot. *fig.*

1664 BUTLER *Hud.* II. i. 658 Those knobs that grow Much harder on the marry'd brow.

d. *Arch.* A rounded prominence or boss of carved work, esp. at the end of a raised moulding or at the intersection of ribs.

1730 W. WARREN *Collectanea* in Willis & Clark *Cambridge* (1886) I. 230 The Cieling being Timber-work, Pannels and Knobs. **1850** WEALE *Dict. Terms, Knot* or *Knob*, a boss; a round bunch of leaves or flowers, or other ornament of a similar kind.

e. ***with knobs on***: jocular slang phr. = 'that and more' (indicating ironic or emphatic agreement, or in retort to an insult, etc.).

1930 M. KENNEDY *Fool of Family* xiii. 129 'I'm waiting for the Marchese Ferdinando Emanuele Maria Bonaventura Donzati.' 'With knobs on,' agreed Gemma airily. 'Who's he?' **1931** J. J. FARJEON *House Opposite* ii, 'You are nothing,' said the Indian. 'And so are you, with knobs on!' barked Ben, and slammed the door. **1938** WODEHOUSE *Code of Woosters* viii. 196 '"Ha jolly ha!" to you, young Stiffy, with knobs on,' I retorted with quiet dignity. **1941** M. TREADGOLD *We couldn't leave Dinah* xv. 232 '*Schweinhund*,' screamed Nannerl. '*Schweinhund* yourself with knobs on,' returned Petit-Jean tartly. **1959** I. & P. OPIE *Lore & Lang. Schoolch.* iii. 45 Same to you with knobs on. **1969** *Guardian* 22 Feb. 9/6 They shouted something... 'The same to you with knobs on,' Jim shouted back. **1970** A. PRICE *Labyrinth Makers* xiv. 179 If the A.S. 12 was the answer to Egypt's Russian missile boats, the A.S. 15 was the answer with knobs on.

2. A prominent isolated rounded mound or hill; a knoll; a hill in general; esp. in *U.S.*

1650 T. B. *Worcester's Apoph.* 30 The ground..is said to rise up, in a round Knob; whereupon St. David pitched his Crosse. **1791** W. BARTRAM *Carolina* 338 The surface of the land..is..uneven, occasioned by natural mounds or rocky knobs. **1812** BRACKENRIDGE *Views Louisiana* (1814) 108 Those dividing ridges of streams, which in Kentucky, are called knobs. **1863** E. HITCHCOCK *Remin. Amherst Coll.* 241 Hilliard's Knob, the highest point of the Holyoke range. **1872** JENKINSON *Guide Eng. Lakes* (1879) 81 The rocky knob called Whitemoss Howe. **1895** *Century Mag.* Aug. 621/2 One of the many knobs from which Daniel Boone is said to have looked first over the Blue Grass land.

3. A small lump (of sugar, coal, etc.). Also KNUB, NUB.

1676 WORLIDGE *Cyder* (1691) 150 Bottling it with a knob of sugar. **1768–74** TUCKER *Lt. Nat.* (1834) I. 70 Is your tea bitter? You may sweeten it by putting in a knob of sugar. **1801** WOLCOTT (P. Pindar) *Ep. to Ct. Rumford* Wks. 1812 V. 144 Rummage the dark Coal-hole of his brain But not one Knob is in it. **1865** *Gd. Words* Feb. 125/1 These children.. when they are 'very good', and work hard,..sometimes get a 'knob o' suck'..on Saturday.

4. *slang.* **a.** The head. Usually NOB, q.v.

1725 *New Cant. Dict., Knob*, the Head or Skull. **1888** M. ROBERTSON *Lombard St. Myst.* xvi, It were s'posed the guilty deed were one too much for 'is knob. **1899** R. WHITEING *No. 5 John Street* xxvii, They invariably..'ketch it in the knob' in the form of bilious headache.

b. *Austral.* and *N.Z.* A double-headed penny. Also *nob*.

1928 J. DEVANNY *Dawn Beloved* xv. 163 Sometimes two pennies are filed down to half their thickness and then joined together. A double-tailer is called a 'grey'; a double-header a 'nob'. Of course, anyone caught cheating is liable to get bashed about a bit. **1941** BAKER *Dict. Austral. Slang* 41 *Knob*, a double-headed penny.

5. A small collection of widgeons, dunbirds, teals, or the like.

1875 'STONEHENGE' *Brit. Sports* I. I. ix. §1 A 'knob' is a still smaller number [than 30] of the above birds [wildfowl].

6. = KNOBSTICK 2.

1838 *Ann. Reg.* 204/1 *note*, The chastisement of 'knobs', the assassination of oppressive and tyrannical masters.

†7. Phr. ***to make no knobs***: to make no difficulty, not to hesitate. (Cf. 'to make no bones'.)

1677 CARY *Chronol.* II. ii. III. xvi. 259 Instead of 6 Centuries defalked by the Jews, they make no Knobs in cutting off 9 of them together.

8. *attrib.* and *Comb.*, as ***knob-end, tail, -twiddling, -twister, -twisting***; ***knob-billed, -like, -nosed*** adjs.; **knob-cone pine**, *Pinus attenuata*, a species native to California; **knob-fly**, a kind of fly used in angling; **knob-hole**, a hole for the insertion of a knob; **knob-lock**, a lock which is opened with a knob; **knob-nose** *S. Afr.*, name applied to (a member of) a people having this distinguishing feature; also *attrib.* (or as *adj.*); **knob-nosed** *a.*, having a knob-shaped nose; *spec.* = *knob-nose*. Also KNOBSTICK, -WEED, etc.

1878 GOULD *Birds N. Guinea* V. pl. 50 *Knob-billed Fruit-Pigeon. [**1882** A. KELLOGG *Forest Trees of California* in *Rep. State Mineralogist California* Appendix II. 51 Knobby-cone Pine... The Knobby Pine is a lofty tree of much beauty.] **1884** C. S. SARGENT *Rep. Forests N. Amer.* 196 *Pinus tuberculata*... *Knobcone pine. **1905** —— *Man. Trees N. Amer.* 22 *Pinus attenuata*, Lemm. Knob-cone pine. .. Fruit..becoming light chestnut-brown, with thin flat scales rounded at the apex, those on the outer side being enlarged into prominent transversely flattened knobs. **1932** W. DALLIMORE in *Conifers in Cultivation* (R. Hort. Soc.) 28 *Pinus... attenuata* Lemm. (*P. tuberculata* Gord.)—Knob-cone Pine—Oregon to California. **1967** N. T. MIROV *Genus Pinus* iii. 170 *Pinus attenuata* is known as 'knobcone pine'. Its area is chiefly in California, although..it extends northward to the mountains of southwestern Oregon. **1894** 'J. S. WINTER' *Red Coats* 65 He came to a door on which he rapped with the *knob-end of his stick. **1829** *Glover's Hist. Derby* I. 177 The following..are well known to the expert angler; viz. barm fly, black fly,..*knob fly. **1851** *Illustr. Catal. Gt. Exhib.* 1458 The *knob holes of the curtains form, in stitching, the grape leaf. **1861** BENTLEY *Man. Bot.* 51 In touching a nettle lightly, the *knob-like head is broken off, and the sharp point of the sting enters the skin. **1813** *Examiner* 10 May 294/2 J. Charlesworth,..*knob-lock-maker. **1900** A. H. KEANE *Boer States* vii. 99 Hence the extraordinary differences that are observed between..the degraded Magwamba ('demons' or 'devils'), called '*Knobnoses' by the Transvaal Boers, and the Basutos. **1943** D. REITZ *No Outspan* iv. 59 We went up along the Sami river to Sibasa's country and then to the chief of the knob-nose kaffirs. **1839** W. C. HARRIS *Wild Sports S. Afr.* xxxix. 350 A friendly tribe of natives, whom, from a peculiarity in the nasal prominence, they dignified with the appellation of '*knob-nosed Kafirs'. **1864** J. A. GRANT *Walk across Afr.* 93 A knob-nosed duck. **1887** RUSKIN *Præterita* II. ix. 331 A.. snub- or rather knob-nosed..simpleton. **1905** *Westm. Gaz.* 2 Oct. 8/2 The knob-nosed lizard (*Lyriocephalus scutatus*) from Ceylon. **1836** T. HOOK *G. Gurney* I. 212 An old buck-rabbit with a *nob tail. **1968** *Times* 29 Nov. 1/1 Some are hi-fi maniacs, *knob-twiddling perfectionists. **1973** *Times* 7 June 18/6 He thinks commercial competition could benefit the BBC..by encouraging them to do more knob-twiddling, instead of staying tuned to one programme all day. **1940** *Chambers's Techn. Dict.* 478/2 **Knob-twister*. A casual reference to monitor man or recordist in motion-picture production. **1950** *People* (Austral.) 7 June 50/2 He believes that 90 per cent of the 'knob-twisters', as they are called, favor the abolition of the [betting] boards. **1929** *Radio Times* 8 Nov. 450/2 'Earth's End' stations can be received..if you..find your fun in *knob twisting. **1958** *Listener* 13 Nov. 799/2 Audiences for a number of these [programmes] have dropped considerably since they were transferred from their old places in the Light Programme. This might be blamed on mass inertia, as applied to knob-twisting.

knob (nɒb), *v.* [f. prec. sb.]

1. *trans.* To furnish with a knob or knobs; to form knobs upon.

1879 *Spon's Encycl. Indust. Arts* I. 701 A thin sheet of copper, whose surface has been 'knobbed', or raised into rows of oval knobs, by the application of a blind punch.

2. *intr.* To form a knob or knobs, to bunch; to bulge *out*.

1566 [see KNOBBING below]. **1631** MARKHAM *Way to Wealth*, To make Hasty Pudding..when it boils put in a spoonful of Flower, but not let it knob. **1876** BLACKMORE *Cripps* xxiv, Tapering straight as a fishing-rod, and knobbing out on either side with scarcely controllable bulges.

3. *trans.* To free from knobs, to rough-dress (stone in the quarry).

1890 in *Cent. Dict.*

4. *trans.* To hit. *slang.*

1818 *Sporting Mag.* II. 211 He knobbed his adversary well.

Hence **'knobbing** *ppl. a.*

1566 DRANT *Horace* I. ix. (1567) N ij b, Stitche, or coughe, or knobbing gowt.

knobbed (nɒbd, -ɪd), *a.* Also 9 **nobbed**. [f. KNOB *sb.* or *v.* + -ED.] Furnished with or having a knob or knobs; formed into or ending in a knob.

c **1440** *Promp. Parv.* 280/1 Knobbyd, as hondys or other lymmys, *callosus*. Knobbyd, or knottyd as trees, *vertiginosus, verticosus*. **1563** SACKVILLE in *Mirr. Mag., Induct.* xxxix, His knuckles knobd. **1673** GREW *Anat. Roots* i. §6 Round [roots] are Tuberous, or Simply Knobbed, as Rape-Crowfoot. **1776–96** WITHERING *Brit. Plants* (ed. 3) I. 230 Pist[il]... Summit knobbed. **1794** G. ADAMS *Nat. & Exp. Philos.* IV. xlix. 333 Experiments on the preferable utility of pointed or knobbed conductors, for preserving buildings from lightning. **1839** URE *Dict. Arts* 583 The workman [glass-blower] having..taken possession of the globe by its bottom or knobbed [*ed.* 1875 II. 657 knobbled] pole attached to his punty rod. **1850** H. MILLER *Footpr. Creat.* x. (1874) 188 The knobbed surface of the thong.

knobber ('nɒbə(r)). *Venery.* ? *Obs.* [f. KNOB *sb.* 1 c + -ER[1].] A male deer in its second year: cf. KNOBBLER 1; a brocket.

a **1700** B. E. *Dict. Cant. Crew, A Knobber*, the second [year]. **1891** C. WISE *Rockingham Cast. & Watsons* 152 The Hart of the second year was a 'Knobber'.

knobbiness ('nɒbɪnɪs). [f. KNOBBY *a.* + -NESS.] The quality of being knobby.

1611 COTGR., *Nodosité*, knottinesse, knobbinesse. **1755** in JOHNSON. **1885** *Harper's Mag.* Mar. 614/1 The knobbiness of her spine. **1893** W. H. HUDSON *Patagonia* v. 61 The surface carved to almost symmetrical knobbiness.

knobble ('nɒb(ə)l), *sb.* [dim. of KNOB *sb.* = Du. and LG. *knobbel* knob, knot: cf. G. *knobel* (*knöbel, knübel*) knuckle, knot.] A small knob.

a **1485** [see KNOB *sb.* 1 b quot. 1490]. **1577** *Lanc. Wills* (1857) II. 92 One standeinge cup..w[th]..roses upon the knobble off the cover. **1849** ALB. SMITH *Pottleton Leg.* (repr.) 46, I always endeavour to act right by gentlemen's coals, and wouldn't rob them of a knobble.

Hence **'knobbled** *a.*, knobbed.

1875 [see KNOBBED, quot. 1839].

'knobble, *v. dial.* and *techn.* [f. KNOB *sb.*]

a. To knock, etc.: *spec.* = KNAP *v.*[1] 2, KNOB *v.* 3. **b.** *Metallurgy.* To shingle; also NOBBLE, q.v.

1842–76 GWILT *Archit.* (ed. 7) Gloss., *Knobbling*, knocking off the rough protuberances of hard rock stone at the quarry. **1863–9** *Dict. Archit.*, *Knobbling*, the term used near London and in the west of England for..reducing a mass of stone in the quarry to a somewhat square block... In flint work it is called 'knapping'. **1876** *Whitby Gloss.*, *Knobble*, v. to strike with a club. **1879** MISS JACKSON *Shropsh. Word-bk.*, *Knobble*, to hammer; to knock, but not forcibly. **1881** RAYMOND *Mining Gloss.*, *Knobbling-fire*, a bloomary for refining cast-iron.

knobbler ('nɒblə(r)). [f. KNOBBLE *sb.* + -ER[1].]

1. = KNOBBER.

1686 BLOME *Gent. Recreat.* II. 75 The Hart is called the first year a Calf,..the second year a Knobler. *a* **1832** SCOTT (Webster 1864), He has hallooed the hounds upon a velvet-headed knobbler. **1971** *Country Life* 19 Aug. 431/2 They were all dead, six of them: five hinds and calves and a small knobbler.

2. *Metallurgy.* A shingler; also NOBBLER, q.v.

knobbly ('nɒblɪ), *a.* Also **nobbly**. [f. KNOBBLE *sb.* + -Y[1].] Full of or covered with knobbles; of the nature of a knobble; knobby. Esp. of knees; ***knobbly-knees competition***, a competition in which a prize is awarded to the competitor with the 'knobbliest' knees.

1859 SALA *Gaslight & D.* xxv. 284 To clink his boot-heels upon the nobbly stones. **1862** TYNDALL *Mountaineer.* xii. 98 The snow was steep but knobbly. **1894** IOTA *Yellow Aster* I. xv. 184 He..returned shortly with a big knobbly parcel in one hand. **1958** *Times* 15 Aug. 9/4 These knees are.. knobbly and..unsightly. **1968** *Listener* 12 Sep. 349/3 When I witness a theatrical 'happening' and 'audience participation' is urged upon me, I generally feel that I would sooner enter for a knobbly-knees competition at Butlin's.

knobby ('nɒbɪ), *a.* Also 6–7 **knobbie**, 9 **nobby**. [f. KNOB *sb.* + -Y[1].]

1. Full of, abounding in, bearing, or covered with knobs or protuberances; knotty.

1543 TRAHERON *Vigo's Chirurg.* 166 Ovide sayth..no medicine can heale the knobbie gout. **1607** HIERON *Wks.* I. 235 A crooked and knobby tree must first be hewed and squared. **1647** H. MORE *Song of Soul* III. App. xxxiii, Humours did arrive His knobby head, and a fair pair of horns contrive. *a* **1722** LISLE *Husb.* (1752) 140 The smooth loose land should be first rolled, and the rough knobby land be deferred. **1844** DICKENS *Mart. Chuz.* xxxiii, His face was almost as hard and knobby as his stick.

fig. **1640** HOWELL *Dodona's Gr.* (1645) 124 The Informers continued in a knobby kind of obstinacy.

2. Of the nature of a knob, knob-shaped.

1764 GRAINGER *Sugar Cane* IV. 274 When no more Round knobby spots deform, but the disease Seems at a pause. **1848** DICKENS *Dombey* x. (C.D. ed.) 82 The captain..brought out his wide suit of blue..and his knobby nose in full relief.

3. Full of rounded knolls or hills; hilly. *U.S.*

1869 'MARK TWAIN' *Innoc. Abr.* liii. 558 It is as knobby with countless little domes as a prison door is with bolt-heads.

knobby ('nɒbɪ), *sb. Austral.* [f. the adj.] An opal.

1921 K. S. PRICHARD *Black Opal* I. i. 8 'Look at this..and this!' he cried eagerly, going over the two or three small knobbies in his hand... 'I'm going in now,' he said, thrusting the opals into the bag. *Ibid.* iii. 23 Paul was holding up a good-looking knobby so that red, green, and gold lights glittered through its shining potch as he moved it. **1971** J. S. GUNN *Opal Terminol.* 24 *Knobby*, opal which is found as a solid lump..rather than in a seam formation.

knobkerrie ('nɒbˌkɛrɪ). Also **knobkeerie, -kerri, -kerry, -kier(r)ie, -kirrie, -kurrie, knopkierie.** [f. KNOB *sb.* + *kerrie*, var. of KIERIE, after Cape Du. *knopkirie, -kieri.*] A short thick stick with a knobbed head, used as a weapon or missile by South African peoples. Also extended to similar weapons used by other peoples, e.g. in Polynesia and Australia.

1844 *United Service Mag.* July 337 With the precious book..in one hand, and his knob-kurrie in the other, away he trudged. **1849** E. E. NAPIER *Excurs. S. Afr.* II. 82 The 'knob keerie'..hurled with unerring aim, brings the smaller animals to the ground. **1850** R. G. CUMMING *Hunter's Life S. Afr.* (ed. 2) I. 231 Their [the Bechuana's] arms..consist of a shield, a bundle of assagais, a battle-axe, and a knobkerry. **1879** *Athenæum* 6 Dec. 731 Two aboriginal Australian skulls with occipital thickening, supposed to be induced by the blows of the native knobkerries. **1899** HOWARTH *Shield & Assegai* 93 The Kaffirs were armed with assegais and knobkerries. **1926** T. E. LAWRENCE *Seven Pillars* (1935) VI. lxix. 384 Spattering the brains of a cornered mob of Germans one by one with his African knob-kerri. **1940** BAUMANN & BRIGHT *Lost Republic* 220 When a Basuto beats his wife, he does it with a knopkierie. **1949** *Cape Argus* 10 Nov. 1/6 Motibeli was struck on the head with a knobkierie. **1961** *Reader's Digest* Feb. 142/1 On the river-bed lay the weapon—an African knopkierie. **1973** *Times* 8 Feb. 1/5 The chanting Africans, waving knobkerries, were cordoned off by police. **1974** *Eastern Province Herald* 2 Sept. 1 Miners attacked each other with knobkerries.

knobstick ('nɒbstɪk).

1. A stick, cane, or club, having a rounded knob for its head; a knobbed stick.

1824 [see b]. **1867** *Crim. Chronol. York Castle* 190 Beating him over the head with knobsticks. **1887** JESSOPP *Arcady* vii. 192 With the knob sticks of the mob.

b. Such a stick used as a weapon; a knobkerrie.

1824 BURCHELL *Trav. S. Afr.* I. 354 A keeri..(a short knobstick) in his hand. **1859** BURTON *Centr. Afr.* in *Jrnl. Geog. Soc.* XXIX. 266 Terrifying the enemy with maniacal gestures, while stones and knobsticks fly through the air. **1894** B. MITFORD *Curse Clement Waynflete* vii. 241 The warrior's heavy knobstick, hurled with deadly precision.

2. A name given, by workmen, to one who during a strike or lock-out continues to work on the master's terms; a black-leg. (See also quot. 1892.) Also *attrib.*

1826 *Examiner* 663/2 Skirmishes..between the turn-outs and those whom they call 'knobsticks'. 1826 *Ann. Reg.* 151/2 One man, a weaver, was accused of being 'a knobstick spinner'. 1848 MRS. GASKELL *Mary Barton* xvi, Taken up last week for throwing vitriol in a knob-stick's face. 1892 *Labour Commission Gloss.*, A *knobstick* is one who takes the work of an operative on strike, or refuses to go out on strike along with his fellow-workmen... Workmen..who are not members of a trade union are frequently called knobsticks by the unionist workmen. The term is also applied to men who work at a trade to which they served no apprenticeship.

b. A master who employs men on terms not recognized by a trade-union.

1851–61 MAYHEW *Lond. Labour* III. 220 (Hoppe), I next went to work at a under-priced hatter's termed a 'knob-stick's'.

knobweed ('nɒbwi:d). [f. KNOB *sb.* + WEED *sb.*] **a.** = KNAPWEED; also applied to other British species of *Centaurea*. **b.** Name for *Collinsonia canadensis*, a N. American labiate plant.

1785 MARTYN *Rousseau's Bot.* xxvi. (1794) 401 Common or Black Knapweed, perhaps more properly Knobweed. 1879 BRITTEN & HOLLAND *Plant-n.*, Knobweed (in allusion to the hard, round flower-heads), *Centaurea nigra*, *C. Cyanus*, and *C. Scabiosa*. 1888 *Syd. Soc. Lex.*, *Knobweed*, the *Collinsonia canadensis*.

knobwood ('nɒbwʊd). A local name of the Wild Cardamom of S. Africa, *Xanthoxylon capense*, the hard close-grained wood of which is used for implements.

1887 in *Kew Bulletin* Sept. 11. 1894 SIM *Flora of Kaffraria* 27.

knoccle, obs. form of KNUCKLE.

knock (nɒk), *v.* Forms: 1 **cnucian, cnocian**, 2 **cnokien**, 4 **cnoke, knoke, knokke**, 4–6 **knok**, 4–7 **knocke**, 4, 6– **knock**. [Late OE. *cnocian*, beside usual WS. *cnucian*; cf. ON. *knoka*; prob. of echoic origin. The relations between the *u* and *o* forms are obscure.]

I. 1. a. *intr.* To strike with a sounding blow, as with the fist or something hard; *esp.* to rap upon a door or gate in order to call attention or gain admittance (const. *at*, †*on*, †*upon*).

c 1000 ÆLFRIC *Hom.* II. 382 He..cnucode æt ðære dura. *c* 1000 *Ags. Gosp.* Matt. vii. 7 Cnuciað and eow biþ ontyned. —— Luke xii. 36 þonne he cymð and cnucað. 10.. in Assmann *Angels. Homil.* (Kassel) 1889 Heo..fæstlice on þære cytan duru cnocode. *c* 1160 *Hatton Gosp.* Matt. vii. 7 Cnokieð and eow beoð untyned. —— Luke xii. 36 þanne he cymð and cnokeð. *c* 1320 *Orfeo* 363 Orpheo knocked at the gate. 13.. *E.E. Allit. P.* B. 726 Quen such þer cnoken on þe bylde, Tyt schal hem men þe ȝate vnpynne. 1382 WYCLIF *Matt.* vii. 7 Knocke ȝe, and it shal be opnyd to ȝou. *c* 1386 CHAUCER *Miller's T.* 246 Clepe at his dore, or knokke with a stoon. *c* 1425 WYNTOUN *Cron.* VIII. xxxv. 72 þare knokide he Wyth-owte þe Dure. 1596 SHAKS. *Tam. Shr.* v. i. 16 What's he that knockes as he would beat downe the gate? 1608 ARMIN *Nest Ninn.* (1842) 13 They knockt to the dresser, and the dinner went up. 1703 MOXON *Mech. Exerc.* 195 To knock upon the back of the Cleaving Knife. 1828 SCOTT *F.M. Perth* xix, She stood before her lover's door and knocked for admittance. 1891 E. PEACOCK *N. Brendon* I. 115 He knocked at the door.

fig. *c* 1374 CHAUCER *Compl. Mars* 84 With torch in honde of whiche the stremes briȝt On venus Chaumbre knokkide ful lyȝt. 1563 WINȜET *Four Scoir Thre Quest.* To Rdr., Wks. 1888 I. 61 Sa grete is the guidnes of God to knok at the breist of man. 1610 SHAKS. *Temp.* I. ii. 8 The cry did knocke Against my very heart. 1858 HAWTHORNE *Fr. & It. Jrnls.* II. 2 A sense of his agony..came knocking at my heart.

b. Without reference to the sound produced: To give a hard blow, to beat; to give blows; †*ellipt.* To strike upon the breast (*obs.*).

a 1300 *Cursor M.* 29092 Knock on brest wit hand. 13.. *Gaw. & Gr. Knt.* 414 Ta now þy grymme tole to þe, & let see how þou cnokez. 1562 in Strype *Ann. Ref.* (1824) I. I. xxix. 503 Divers communicants..superstitiously both kneel and knock. 1583 BABINGTON *Commandm.* ii. (1590) 87 To fall downe before a stocke and a stone, and to doo it reuerence, capping, kneeling, knocking,..and such like.

c. *trans.* with indefinite obj. *it*, To give knocks; also, with cognate obj.

1613 SHAKS. *Hen. VIII*, I. iv. 108 Let the Musicke knocke it. 1682 N. O. *Boileau's Lutrin* II. 183 He resolv'd at a Dead pinch to knock it. 1840 DICKENS *Old C. Shop* xxxv, We have knocked double-knocks at the street-door. 1865 J. H. NEWMAN *Gerontius* §1 A visitant Is knocking his dire summons at my door.

2. a. *trans.* To give a hard blow or blows to; to hit, strike, beat, hammer; †to beat into small pieces, pound (*obs.*). Also with extension expressing result, as *to knock to* (or *in*) *pieces*, etc., *to knock a hole*, *gap*, etc.; *to knock daylight into* (cf. DAYLIGHT 1 c).

c 1000 *Sax. Leechd.* I. 142 ȝenim þonne þa leaf, cnuca on anum mortere. *Ibid.* 168 ȝenim þa wyrte ȝecnucude [*MS. B.* ȝecnocode]. *Ibid.* 382 Cnuciȝe ealle ða wyrta. *c* 1075 *Indicia Monasterialia* in *Techmer's Zeitschrift* II. 125 þonne weȝe þu þine fyst, swilce þu wyrta cnocian wille. 1377 LANGL. *P. Pl.* B. v. 397 He bygan *benedicite* with a bolke, and his brest knocked. 1398 TREVISA *Barth. De P.R.* XVII. xcvii. (Tollem. MS.), It [flax] is..knokked and bete, breyed and carfled. *c* 1400 *Destr. Troy* 2601 Kylle of hor knightes, knocke hom to dethe. *a* 1400–50 *Alexander* 639 Him wald he kenely on þe croune knok with his tablis. *a* 1548 HALL *Chron.*, *Hen. VIII* 172 b, Some knocked other on the elbow, and said softly he lieth. 1599 SHAKS *Hen. V*, II. i. 58, I haue an humor to knocke you indifferently well. 1602 —— *Ham.* II. i. 81 His knees knocking each other. 1698 FRYER *Acc. E. India & P.* 37 The Bar knocking in pieces all that are inflexible. 1822–34 *Good's Study Med.* (ed. 4) I. 424 [He] runs to open the door when it is knocked. 1881 *Punch* 17 Sept. 124/1 Ready at the call of duty to frame a new programme or knock daylight into an old one. 1890 A. CONAN DOYLE *Sign of Four* iv. 68 He knocked a hole..in the lath and plaster ceiling. 1906 SOMERVILLE & 'ROSS' *Some Irish Yesterdays* 85 You may see him skilfully 'knocking a gap' (*i.e.* unbuilding a wall).

†**b.** *fig.* To strike with astonishment, alarm, or confusion; to confound; to 'floor'. *Obs. colloq.*

1715 S. SEWALL *Diary* 1 Feb. (1882) III. 37 Mr. Winthrop was so knockt that he said it could not be done.

c. To 'strike' forcibly, make a strong impression on; to move to admiration, 'fetch'. *slang.*

1883 *Referee* 6 May 3/3 (Farmer) 'It's Never too Late to Mend', with J. H. Clynds as Tom Robinson, is knocking 'em at the Pavilion. 1885 J. K. JEROME *On the Stage* 97 There is nothing knocks a country audience like a hornpipe. 1892 CHEVALIER *Song*, Knocked 'em in the Old Kent Road. 1898 A. BENNETT *Man from North* xi. 95 Two guineas the suit, my boy! Won't I knock 'em in the Wal-worth Road! 1910 WODEHOUSE *Psmith in City* xix. 167 He told him that he had knocked them at the Bedford the week before. 1947 K. TENNANT *Lost Haven* vii. 97 The skirt was flared with cunning little tucks at the waist, so that it fitted her like a glove... 'That ought to knock them,' Mark's granddaughter said aloud. 1954 'N. BLAKE' *Whisper in Gloom* I. vi. 83 Wasn't she in pantomine?.. Bet she knocked them.

d. To copulate with; also, to make pregnant. So in phr. *to knock a child* (or *an apple*) *out* (*of*).

1598 FLORIO *Worlde of Wordes* 94/1 *Cunnuta*, a woman nocked. 1604 MARSTON *Malcontent* III. iii. sig. E2ᵛ Haue beate my Shoomaker, knockt my Sempstres, cuckold my Pottecary, and vndone my Taylor. 1785 GROSE *Dict. Vulgar T.*, *Knock*, to knock a woman, to have carnal knowledge of her. 1818 KEATS *Let.* 5 Jan. (1931) I. 80 They call good Wine a pretty tipple, and call getting a Child knocking out an apple. 1922 JOYCE *Ulysses* 401, I cannot but extol the virile potency of the old bucko that could still knock another child out of her. 1936 J. STEINBECK *In Dubious Battle* iv. 45 Sooner or later some girl'd get knocked higher than a kite. 1963 T. PARKER *Unknown Citizen* v. 120 You give your missus so much money a week, you knock a few kids out of her, and that's about it, really. 1967 D. PINNER *Ritual* ix. 96 I've knocked some girls in my time but I've never had such a rabbiter as you. The cruder it is, the more you like it.

e. To rob (esp. a safe or till). *Underworld slang.*

1767 *Sessions Papers* IV. 151/2, I heard him say he got twelve shillings once by *knocking the lobb*... What is that?.. That is breaking open a place. 1924 G. C. HENDERSON *Keys to Crookdom* App. B. 397 Blowing a peter. Blowing a safe open with explosives. Also called knocking a peter, blowing a pete, getting a box. 1963 *Times* 25 May 12/2 The appellant had been asked if he had told someone in the 'Norfolk' that he got the money by safe breaking. The appellant had replied: 'Aye but you will never prove that I got it by knocking a safe.'

f. To speak ill or slightingly of, disparage, find fault with, criticize captiously. Also *intr.* and *absol. colloq.* (orig. *U.S.*).

1892 'J. MILLER' *Workingman's Paradise* 85 Admit it's a business concern and that everybody growls at it, it's the only paper that dares knock things. 1896 ADE *Artie* xii. 106 There's a lot o' people in the ward that's got their hammers out, and they're knockin' him all they can. *Ibid.* 110 He's got to make good with 'em to keep 'em from knockin. 1901 'H. MCHUGH' *John Henry* 54 I'm not knocking, remember; I'm only saying what I think. I hate a knocker. 1904 *Sun* (N.Y.) 4 Aug. 5 'Of course there'll be plenty of cranks to knock this scheme,' said he. 1906 *Daily Colonist* (Victoria, B.C.) 16 Jan. 4/3, I refer to the practice of allowing any kicker in the city to avail himself of newspaper space to knock some public man or some public institution. 1919 'IAN HAY' *Last Million* iii. 36 A certain licence is permitted to professional grouchers; but 'knocking' the Cause is the one thing that the New Crusaders will not permit. 1926 *Spectator* 3 Apr. 635/2 A reputation for 'knocking' is enough to ensure being blackballed from some of the best clubs. 1930 WODEHOUSE *Very Good, Jeeves!* ii. 44 Where does a valet get off, censoring vases? Does it fall within his province to knock the young master's chinaware? 1958 K. AMIS *I like it Here* xvi. 205, I shouldn't like you to get the idea I'm trying to knock Portugal and the Portuguese. 1958 *Spectator* 12 Dec. 865/1 On the last page he protests about 'the growing tendency in some newspapers today to write only "knocking" stories about stars as big as Tommy'. But..almost any publicity is good publicity: you can knock around the clock and the moon-faced masses will only hear applause. 1970 *New Scientist* 5 Mar. 478/2 They're knocking Concorde again, the cads. 1974 *Observer* 22 Sept. 14/5 It's fashionable nowadays to 'knock' England for its shortcomings.

3. *to knock on* (†*in*) *the head* (also rarely *at head*): **a.** *lit.*; *esp.* to stun or kill by a blow on the head; often *loosely*, to kill in any summary way, dispatch, put to death.

c 1537 *Thersites* in Hazl. *Dodsley* I. 427, I care not if the old witch were dead: It were an almsdeed to knock her in the head. 1641 J. JACKSON *True Evang. T.* II. 117 S. James..was knockt in the head like an Oxe, or Calfe, after he had been thrown down from a Pinacle of the Temple. 1711 ADDISON *Spect.* No. 99 ¶5 The Knight goes off,..seeks all Opportunities of being knock'd on the Head. 1737 BRACKEN *Farriery Impr.* (1756) I. 316, I had better knock the Horse o' th' Head, and dispatch him at once. 1840 BARHAM *Ingol. Leg.*, *Grey Dolphin*, To lie snoring there when your brethren are being knocked at head.

b. *fig.* To put an end to, bring to nothing.

1579 W. FULKE *Heskins' Parl.* 327 To knocke his..mallice in the head. 1584 R. SCOT *Discov. Witchcr.* VIII. iii. (1886) 129 Witchcraft,..is knocked on the head. 1677 YARRANTON *Eng. Improv.* 63 Endeavour to knock all on the head, urging that it will be of great prejudice to the King. 1724 DE FOE *Mem. Cavalier* (1840) 186 One unlucky action knocked it all on the head. 1852 MRS. CARLYLE *Lett.* II. 158 We were to have gone to Germany, but that is all knocked on the head.

4. a. *trans.* To drive or bring (a thing) violently against something else; to strike against or upon something else; to bring into collision.

a 1340 HAMPOLE *Psalter* cxxxvi. 12 Blisful he þat shal holde, and knok his smale [*paruulos suos*] til þe stone. 1599 SHAKS. *Hen. V*, IV. i. 54 Ile knock his Leeke about his Pate. 1698 FRYER *Acc. E. India & P.* 111 Buffola's..knock Foreheads with a Force adequate to such great Engines.

b. † *to knock heads with*: to congregate thickly or associate closely with (*obs.*). *to knock one's head against*: to strike with one's head; *fig.* to hurt oneself by coming into collision with resisting facts or conditions; *to knock head* = to KOTOW.

1530 PALSGR. 599/2, I knocked my heed agaynst the poste. 1615 CHAPMAN *Odyss.* Ep. Ded., Our patrician loves, That knock heads with the herd. 1662 STILLINGFL. *Orig. Sacr.* III. i. §17 In danger of knocking their heads against the Stars. 1824 BYRON *Juan* XV. xci, I always knock my head against some angle About the present, past, or future state. 1837 DICKENS *Pickw.* xxxiii, I hear him a-knockin' his head again the lath and plaster now. 1876 GRANT *Hist. India* I. xcii. 497/1 The ambassador who refused to 'knock-head'. *Mod.* An angular man—always knocking his head against stone walls.

5. a. *intr.* To come into violent collision with something; to strike, collide, bump, clash.

1530 PALSGR. 599/2, I knocke, or hyt agaynst a thing. 1633 T. JAMES *Voy.* 18 Our Ship beating and knocking.. fearefully. 1724 BENTLEY *Serm.* (T.), The atoms..must needs knock and interfere. 1881 *Standard* 19 Dec. 6/3 Olive Branch has been assisted into Harwich very leaky, having knocked over the Knock Sand.

b. Of mechanism: To rattle on account of parts being loose and striking each other. Also, (i) of an internal-combustion engine, to suffer from knock caused by faulty combustion (see KNOCK *sb.*[1] 1 c). (ii) Of fuel for an internal-combustion engine: to give rise to knock when burnt in an engine.

1869 *Eng. Mech.* 19 Mar. 579/3 There was less 'knocking' where a little play..had..begun. 1896 R. KIPLING *Seven Seas* 32 They [engines] knock a wee—the crosshead-gibs are loose. 1905 *Daily Chron.* 5 May 3/5 You advance your spark ..to the point at which your engine does not knock. 1909 *Motor Cycling* 22 Nov. 32/1 If the engine begins to 'knock', a few vigorous thrusts at the pedals should be given immediately. 1916 EIGHINGER & HUTTON *Steam Traction Engineering* v. 156 The main shaft boxes..will often knock. 1925 R. J. B. SELLAR *Sporting Yarns* 186, I shall have to pull up, old chap. Cylinder's knocking! 1927 *Industr. & Engin. Chem.* Jan. 145/1 There is at present no satisfactory method of expressing the tendency of a fuel to 'knock', or detonate. 1937 WODEHOUSE *Lord Emsworth & Others* ix. 299, I became aware that the engine was not humming so smoothly. It had begun to knock. 1960 V. B. GUTHRIE *Petroleum Products Handbk.* IV. 21 Engine designers..have done a great deal to minimize the tendency of engines to knock. 1966 *McGraw-Hill Encycl. Sci. & Technol.* III. 309/2 Hydrocarbon fuels with compact molecular structures are less likely to knock.

†**c.** *to knock under board*, *under* (*the*) *table*: to succumb in a drinking-bout; to give in, submit, yield; = *knock under* (17). *Obs.*

1691–2 *Gentl. Jrnl.* Mar. 10 He that flinches his Glass, and to Drink is not able, Let him quarrel no more, but knock under the Table. 1662 SOUTH *Serm.* (1724) VI. 17 For the Government to knock under-board to the Faction. 1700 ASGILL *Argument* 105, I..knock under table That Satan hath beguiled me to play the Fool with my self. 1703 *Levellers* in *Harl. Misc.* (ed. Park) V. 447 We will not knock under-board to the men.

d. with *adv.* or *advb. phr.*: To stir or move energetically, clumsily, and noisily, or in random fashion, about a place. (See also *knock about*, *around*, 7 b, 8). *colloq.*

a 1825 FORBY *Voc. E. Anglia*, *Knock*, to stir or to work briskly. Ex. 'He came knocking along the road in a great hurry'. 1839 W. E. FORSTER 20 Dec. in T. W. Reid *Life* v. (1888) 134 A true hearty old Navy Captain,..who has knocked about Africa half his life. 1886 G. ALLEN *Maimie's Sake* ii, Knocking up and down all over..the country.

6. a. *trans.* With extension: To drive by striking; to force or send by means of a blow (*away*, *into*, *out of*, *off*, etc. something, or *into* or *out of* some state or condition). See also 7–18. Also *fig.*

1610 SHAKS. *Temp.* III. ii. 69 Ile yeeld him thee asleepe, Where thou maist knocke a naile into his head. 1669 STURMY *Mariner's Mag.* v. 85 Knock the Fuse up to the head within one quarter of an Inch. 1719 DE FOE *Crusoe* I. iv, I knocked pieces into the wall of the rock, to hang my guns..up. 1880 TROLLOPE *Duke's Childr.* xlvii. 272 He was completely 'bowled over',—'knocked off his pins!'

b. Phr. *to knock the bottom out of*: (*fig.*) to render invalid, make of no effect, bring to nought. (Cf. 'It won't hold water'.) *colloq.* Also (*slang*) *to knock the end in* or *off*: to spoil the whole affair (? *obs.*).

1875 W. MCILWRAITH *Guide to Wigtownshire* 93 This explanation knocks the bottom out of a great many theories. 1887 LD. R. CHURCHILL in *Times* (weekly ed.) 24 June 9/3 We shall have knocked the bottom out of Home Rule. 1919 *Athenæum* 8 Aug. 727/2 To 'knock the end in' is to spoil the whole show. 1925 FRASER & GIBBONS *Soldier & Sailor Words* 138 *Knock the end off*, *to*, to spoil anything.

†**c.** To 'knock down' at an auction: see 8 c.

1623 FLETCHER & ROWLEY *Maid in Mill* v. i. Thy maiden-head Shall not be worth a chequin, if it were Knock'd at an out-cry.

d. To rouse or summon (a person, esp. from sleep) by knocking at his door. (Usually with extension: see also *knock up*, 18 f.) *colloq.*

1706 BAYNARD in Sir J. Floyer *Hot & Cold Bath.* II. 344, I have been..sometimes knock'd out of Bed, to Children just dying. *Mod.* He asked to be knocked at seven o'clock.

e. In various slang or colloq. phrases, as *to knock into a* COCKED HAT, *to knock* SPOTS *out of*, *to knock into the middle of next* WEEK, etc. Also *to knock all of a* HEAP, *down with a* FEATHER, *for a* LOOP, *for* SIX; *to knock* SILLY, COLD, ENDWAYS, ROTTEN, SIDEWAYS; ***to knock the nonsense***, etc., ***out of***.

1856 C. M. YONGE *Daisy Chain* I. v. 48 The girlishness and timidity will be knocked out of him by the boys. **1892** 'MARK TWAIN' *Amer. Claimant* v. 63 'When I came to breakfast Miss Gwendolen—well, she knocked everything out of me, you know—.' 'Wonderful girl, wonderful.' **1931** *Times Lit. Suppl.* 15 Oct. 787/1 The boy returned to Turin, where his royal relatives did their best to get his revolutionary notions knocked out of him. **1935** L. & A. MAUDE tr. *Tolstoy's Iván Ilých & Hadji Murád* 273 They'd have knocked the nonsense out of you in the army, and he was worth five of such as you at home!

II. In combination with adverbs.

7. knock about. a. *trans.* To strike hither and thither by a succession of blows; hence, to treat roughly and without respect.

a **1817** JANE AUSTEN *Persuasion* (1818) III. iii. 44 They [*sc.* sailors] are all knocked about, and exposed to every climate, and every weather, till they are not fit to be seen. **1876** FERGUSSON *Ind. & East. Archit.* 198 The building..has been so knocked about and altered. **1889** CONSTANCE F. WOOLSON *Jupiter Lights* i. 4 Great waves began to toss her and knock her about. **1926** T. E. LAWRENCE *Seven Pillars* (1935) lxxvi. 424 Young Mustafa refused to cook rice; Farraj and Daud knocked him about until he cried. **1969** *Listener* 24 July 103/2 After being knocked about to an appalling extent in the first week of the war, the Poles were rallying until the Russians came in on the other side.

b. *intr.* To move about, wander, or roam, in an irregular way; also to lead an irregular life. *colloq.*

1833 *Sk. & Eccentr. D. Crockett* i. 31 David, collecting his clothes,..began to knock about. **1834** W. G. SIMMS *Guy Rivers* II. viii. 98 I've been a matter of some fifteen or twenty years knocking about..in one way or another. **1851** MAYHEW *Lond. Labour* II. 87 (Farmer) I've been knocking about on the streets. **1855** SMEDLEY *H. Coverdale* i. 3 I've.. no dog-cart to knock about in. **1900** J. HUTCHINSON *Archives Surg.* XI. 267 The man admits that in youth he 'knocked about a little'. **1929** C. MACKENZIE *Gallipoli Memories* iii. 21 He had knocked about all over the Pacific and would have been a splendid companion. **1937** M. SHARP *Nutmeg Tree* xx. 265 You're older, and you've knocked about a bit.

c. ***to knock the balls about***: to strike a (billiard, croquet, etc.) ball idly; to play (such a ball game) in a casual fashion.

1864 C. M. YONGE *Trial* II. vi. 123 Tom..had seen the Andersons knocking about the balls in the new gardens.. and proposed to..try to get up a match. **1872** TROLLOPE *Golden Lion* xviii. 305 He knocked the balls about with his cue. **1907** F. E. E. BELL *At Works* vi. 130, I have seen a club with two free tables, where men..have been happily knocking the balls about from 9 a.m. onwards. **1916** A. BENNETT *These Twain* II. xiv. 271 'Shall we knock the balls about a bit?' They began a mild game of croquet.

d. To lie around, to be available or in the vicinity; to impend.

1866 F. HUNT *25 Yrs. Experience N.Z.* ix. 45 My carpet bag I left knocking about amongst them with utmost carelessness. **1870** R. P. WHITWORTH *Martin's Bay Settlement* 23/1, I have commenced to make a dingy..out of old boards that are knocking about. **1889** G. B. SHAW *London Music 1888–89* (1937) 116 There is plenty of musical talent knocking about misused or misdirected. **1897** P. A. PHILIPS *Memories of Past* 21 When we did have them they were pretty severe [fires], such as..W. S. Grahame's in Fort Street (any amount of drink knocking about), the fire in High Street. **1902** CONRAD *Typhoon* ii. 22 Observing the steady fall of the barometer, Captain MacWhirr thought, 'There's some dirty weather knocking about.' **1908** W. H. KOEBEL *Anchorage* ii. 45 Do you know of a billet knockin' about anywhere that 'ud suit him, boss? **1916** A. BENNETT *These Twain* I. v. 60 'There are one or two ordinaries knocking about the place,' said Edwin, 'but we haven't got a proper bicycle-house.' **1939** [see EYE *sb.*[1] 3 b]. **1948** R. FINLAYSON *Tidal Creek* i. 17 I'll just see about a box that ought to be knocking about.

e. ***to knock about with***: to be a habitual companion of.

1915 T. BURKE *Nights in Town* 323 We talked of Love, Wines, Dinners, Music-halls, of the men we had knocked about with, the girls we had loved. **1924** M. KENNEDY *Constant Nymph* viii. 122 Look at the sort of people the poor child has knocked about with.

8. knock around, round = *knock about* (sense 7 b). Also *fig.*

1848 W. T. THOMPSON *Major Jones's Sk. Travel* 8 I'm gwine..to New York,..and Boston and all about thar, and spend the summer until pickin time, nockin round in them big cities, mong them peeple what's so monstrous smart. **1856** C. E. DELONG in *Calif. Hist. Soc. Q.* (1930) IX. 65 Got up late knocked around. **1874** V. PYKE *Adventures G. W. Pratt* (1890) I. vi. 27 Seems that there's a joke knocking around somewhere. **1884** *Marcus Clarke Memor. Vol.* 88, I thought it advisable to 'knock round' in search of him. **1924** C. MACKENZIE *Heavenly Ladder* iii. 55 Not that I'm against your style of services myself. But most of the people round here haven't knocked around like I have. **1938** G. GREENE *19 Stories* (1947) 76 He's knocking around somewhere. **1959** P. MCCUTCHAN *Storm South* xiii. 198 Mrs. van Neyland's been a married woman, and she's knocked around.

9. knock back. a. *trans.* To refuse, to rebuff. *Austral.* and *N.Z. colloq.*

1930 V. PALMER in *Bulletin* (Sydney) 19 Feb. 51/1 Not the sort of man we want... I knocked him back. **1939** K. TENNANT *Foveaux* IV. ii. 368 Why, she knocks back the boss where she works, if he gets gay. **1944** L. GLASSOP *We were Rats* xviii. 104 Still goin' to keep knockin' back the sheilas? **1948** V. PALMER *Golconda* xi. 85 Most of them knocked his appeals back lightly and watched the proceedings with tolerant amusement. **1952** J. CLEARY *Sundowners* ii. 108 He wouldn't knock it [*sc.* money] back if you offered it to him. **1957** 'N. CULOTTA' *They're a Weird Mob* (1958) vi. 86 Never knock back O.P.'s [*sc.* other people's smokes]. **1969** *Private Eye* 12 Sept. 14 *(caption)* Knocking back a free night at the *flea-pit* too. **1973** *Nation Rev.* (Melbourne) 24–30 Aug. 1398/6 Never knock back a dollar, I guess.

b. *trans.* To drink (esp. intoxicants) or eat heartily or heavily; to swallow a drink at a gulp. Also in phr. ***to knock it back***. *colloq.*

1931 BROPHY & PARTRIDGE *Songs & Slang 1914–18* (ed. 3) 326 *Knock it back.*—To eat; sometimes, to drink. **1939** *Eastbourne Herald* 6 May 13/2 Thirsty Eastbourne really does 'knock back' thousands of gallons in the course of a year. **1947** 'A. P. GASKELL' *Big Game* 8 'Boy oh boy oh boy,' he chanted, 'won't I knock back those handles tonight.' **1951** J. B. PRIESTLEY *Festival at Farbridge* III. ii. 476 That's why he knocked a few back—and he doesn't as a rule. **1951** 'J. WYNDHAM' *Day of Triffids* i. 26, I knocked back the last of my brandy, and went out. **1953** X. FIELDING *Stronghold* III. iv. 221, I hear you knock it back a bit. Well, so do I. **1957** C. MACINNES *City of Spades* I. ix. 69 My two friends knocked back their gins. **1957** 'N. CULOTTA' *They're a Weird Mob* (1958) iii. 42 'What is this pin one on, Joe?' 'Knock one back. Gunna 'ave a drink?' **1961** M. KELLY *Spoilt Kill* ii. 71 When you were fourteen you knocked back a whole jar..at one sitting. **1968** M. RICHLER in R. Weaver *Canad. Short Stories* 2nd Ser. 194 Hod was knocking back large snifters of brandy.

c. *trans.* To retard, to check. *Austral.* and *N.Z.*

1945 J. PASCOE in *N.Z. Geographer* I. 27 An early winter will knock his flock back. **1946** F. SARGESON *That Summer* 85 The two sprees had knocked me back considerably [financially].

10. knock down. a. *trans.* To strike or fell to the ground with a blow or blows; *fig.* to overcome, vanquish, cause to succumb. Also, to bring down by a shot, or by artillery, etc., fire.

c **1450** tr. *De Imitatione* III. xxxix. 110 Brynge to nouȝt folkes, þat wol haue bateiles. Knocke hem doun in þy miȝt. **1593** SHAKS. *2 Hen. VI*, IV. vi. 9 Knocke him downe there. **1659** D. PELL *Impr. Sea* 479 Cut down Hammoks, knock down wooden stanchions. **1733** W. BYRD *Journey Land of Eden* in *Writings* (1901) 311 We pursued our Journey thro' uneven and perplexed Woods, and in the thickest of them had the Fortune to knock down a young Buffalo, 2 Years old. **1787** WOLCOTT (P. Pindar) *Ode upon Ode* Wks. 1812 I. 443, I would rather be knocked down By weight of argument, than weight of Fist. **1809** M. L. WEEMS *Life F. Marion* xi. 98 Many a family goes without dinner unless the father can knock down a squirrel in the woods. **1893** FORBES-MITCHELL *Remin. Gt. Mutiny* 261 Mackie, who had been knocked down by the sun the day before and had died that afternoon. **1940** *War Illustr.* 12 Apr. 366/3 But before the Germans had managed to recover from their surprise that only three British 'planes dared to attack them, the young flight leader had knocked down two of them.

b. To drive (a stake, etc.) into the ground by blows; to fasten (a rivet) by knocking the end flat.

1657 AUSTEN *Fruit Trees* I. 64 If the plants are in danger to be shaken by the winds, then knock down a stake close to every one. **1869** SIR E. REED *Shipbuild.* xvii. 329 The various modes of forming the rivet-point, or, in technical language, of 'knocking-down' the rivet.

c. To dispose of (an article) to a bidder at an auction sale by a knock with a hammer or mallet.

1760 C. JOHNSTON *Chrysal* (1822) III. 205 It was.. knocked down to the last bidder. **1777** SHERIDAN *Sch. Scand.* IV. i, This shall be your hammer, and now you may knock down my ancestors. **1884** *Illustr. Lond. News* 20 Dec. 603/1 The first Aldine Horace, of 1501..was knocked down for fifteen guineas.

d. To call upon, nominate (*for* some function, etc.); from the chairman at a dinner, etc., doing this with the knock of a hammer or mallet. *colloq.*

1759 GOLDSM. *Ess., Clubs* Wks. (Globe) 284/2 The Grand ..had knocked down Mr. Spriggins for a song. **1789** G. PARKER *Variegated Char.* (Farmer), He was knocked down for the crap [gallows] the last sessions. **1842** S. LOVER *Handy Andy* v, The call is with you, Ned,..knock some one down for a song.

e. To summon (a person) downstairs by knocking at his door. (Cf. *knock up*, 18 f.) *rare.*

1881 *Athenæum* 3 Sept 303/2 At an early hour..the farmer's wife said to her son, 'Thomas, go and knock your father down'.

f. To disconnect the parts of (a structure that is 'knocked together': see 16 c) by blows; to take to pieces. Cf. KNOCK-DOWN *a.* 3, *knocked-down* s.v. KNOCKED *ppl. a.* 2. (The opposite of *knock up*, 18 d.)

1776 [see KNOCKED *ppl. a.* 1]. **1875** KNIGHT *Dict. Mech.* 1239/2 A chair complete and box to hold a dozen knocked down. **1945** B. MACDONALD *Egg & I* (1946) xix. 194 The six-hundred-gallon water tank arrived, knocked down and looking disappointingly like a bundle of faggots. **1958** *Times Rev. Industry* Dec. 65/3 Motor-car body shells..knocked down for export. **1973** *Amer. Speech 1969* XLIV. 206 *Knock down*, disassemble freight or merchandise.

g. To lower effectively in amount or degree. *colloq.*

1867 *Jrnl. R. Agric. Soc.* Ser. II. III. II. 533 A very plentiful season has knocked down prices. **1895** *Times* 27 Apr. 12/2 When the picture leaves the exhibition, whether it would not be well to 'knock down', as they say, those somewhat too brilliant tones.

h. *Austral.* and *N.Z. slang.* To spend in drink or riot. Hence ***knocking down*** *vbl. sb.*

1852 in *Occasional Papers Univ. Sydney Austral. Lang. Res. Centre* (1966) No. 9. 15 They then go 'upon the burst' as they call it, and drink until all their earnings are 'knocked down'. **1861** H. W. HARPER *Lett. from N.Z.* (1914) 65 [Station hands] proceed to 'knock down their cheque', giving it to the landlord and bidding him treat all comers as long as it lasts. **1866** *Bk. Canterbury Rhymes* 19, I knock my earnings down [at the Royal Hotel]. **1869** MARCUS CLARKE *Peripat. Philos.* (reprint) 80 (Morris) Knocked down thirteen notes, and went to bed as tight as a fly. **1874** A. BATHGATE *Colonial Experiences* xi. 142 He would get amongst a bad lot and knock down every penny of our hard-earned cash. **1879** J. GREY *His Island Home* iii. 32/1 They were 'knocking down' their cheques and living at the rate of ten thousand a year. *Ibid.*, They appear to derive intense satisfaction from the knocking down process until their resources were exhausted. **1884** BOLDREWOOD *Melb. Memories* xiii. 99 They could earn money, and..proceeded to 'knock down' the same by means of..alcoholic indulgence. **1884** *Marcus Clarke Memor. Vol.* 135 At shearing time, when the 'hands' knocked down their cheques. **1904** M. CRADOCK *Sport in N.Z.* I. i. 10 Their rabbit cheques generally find their way to the nearest public house, to be 'knocked down' as soon as received. **1965** J. S. GUNN *Terminol. Shearing Industry* I *Knock down*, to spend a cheque, usually in one quick celebration.

i. *U.S. slang.* To appropriate or embezzle (esp. passengers' fares).

a **1854** J. F. KELLEY *Humors of Falconbridge* (1856) 86 No knocking down, sir! **1864** T. L. NICHOLS *40 Yrs. Amer. Life* I. 89 The omnibus-drivers were expected to 'knock down' a certain proportion of the receipts. **1872** J. D. MCCABE *Lights & Shadows N.Y. Life* xi. 214 In order to make up the deficiency between their actual wages and their necessities, the conductors and drivers have fallen into the habit of appropriating a part of the money received from passengers to their own use... This practice of 'knocking down', or appropriating money, begins with the conductor, as he alone receives the money paid for fares. **1882** MCCABE *New York* 158 The driver of a stage was furnished with a cash-box,.. he had frequent opportunities of 'knocking down', or appropriating a modest sum to his own use. **1888** *Boston Jrnl.* 31 Oct. 2/4 The street car conductors..have been 'knocking down' from $100 to $200 a day, and several have been arrested. **1892** BALESTIER *Average Woman*, He's knocking down fares every day. **1949** 'J. EVANS' *Halo in Brass* xx. 172 Some..clerk who was knocking down on the till.

j. *intr.* To deal a knock or blow downwards (e.g. on the floor, to arouse a person below).

1724 R. WODROW *Life Prof. Wodrow* (1828) 166 He had given a groan, and the person in waiting knocked down. When I came up, I observed his lips quivering.

k. *pass.* Of a ship (see quots. 1891 and 1948). *U.S.*

1873 G. H. PROCTER *Fisherman's Memorial* 128 A severe gale, which knocked the vessel down and nearly swamped her. **1891** H. PATTERSON *Illustr. Naut. Dict.* 104 *Knocked down*, said of a vessel when, by the force of the wind acting upon her sails and spars, she is careened to such an extent that she does not recover herself. **1948** R. DE KERCHOVE *Internat. Maritime Dict.* 387/1 *Knocked-down*, the situation of a vessel listed over by wind to such an extent that it does not recover.

l. To earn, get paid. *U.S.*

1929 M. LIEF *Hangover* vi. 100 She and Humphrey rented a cottage in Westport..where authors who knocked down $3,000 for knocking out a short story of 5,000 words, built such magnificent houses. **1949** *New Yorker* 5 Nov. 76/2 You wanna know hommuch that animal knocks down a week?

11. knock in. a. *trans.* To drive or force in by blows or as by blows.

1669 STURMY *Mariner's Mag.* v. 87 Put down a piece of Paste-board, and knock it in hard. **1891** T. HARDY in *Harper's Mag.* Apr. 704 They knocked in the victuals and drink till they could hold no more.

b. *intr.* (*Univ. slang.*) To knock so as to gain admission to college after the gate is closed.

1825 C. M. WESTMACOTT *Eng. Spy* I. 155 Close the oak, Jem, and take care no one knocks in before [etc.]. **1829** J. R. BEST *Pers. & Lit. Mem.* 103 Mr. Langton, you knock in very often: why do you visit so much out of college? **1861** HUGHES *Tom Brown at Oxf.* xli, There's twelve striking, I must knock in.

12. knock off. a. *trans.* To strike off by or as by a blow; also *fig.* ***to knock off a person's head***, to 'beat' or surpass him.

1611 SHAKS. *Cymb.* v. iv. 199 Knocke off his Manacles. **1666** BOYLE *Orig. Formes & Qualities*, If a parcel of Matter be knockt off from another. **1719** YOUNG *Busiris* II. i. (1757) 35 'Till death shall knock them [chains] off. **1862** *Cornh. Mag.* June 655, I could knock his head off in Greek Iambics.

b. To cause to desist or leave off from work; to discharge or dismiss from employment, to 'lay off'.

1651 GATAKER in *Fuller's Abel Rediv., Ridley* (1867) I. 230 He returned..to his study, where he sat, unless suitors or some other affairs knocked him off. **1881** A. BATHGATE *Waitaruna* xii. 172 [The boss] would growl at the offending shearer and make use of some vague threat of 'knocking him off'. **1889** *Times* (weekly ed.) 13 Dec. 3/2 The men were knocked off earlier. **1896** 'M. RUTHERFORD' *Clara Hopgood* xxvi. 256 As reg'lar as winter comes Longwood is knocked off—no work. **1955** *Times* 9 June 8/3 The Cunard company put the main restaurant at his service and the staff captain 'knocked off all the men from their duties'.

c. *intr.* To desist, leave off; to cease from one's work or occupation; *slang* to die.

1649 G. Daniel *Trinarch., Hen. V*, ccxliii, The Sun (who quafft French blood, to Harrie's health) knock's of And can noe more. **1688** Bunyan *Heavenly Footman* (1886) 159 If thou do not.. knock off from following any farther. *a* **1704** *Let.* in *T. Brown's Wks.* (1760) IV. 183 Perverse people.. that would not knock off in any reasonable time, but liv'd long, on purpose to spite their relations. **1842** *Spirit of Times* 4 June 158/2 My tackle being very light I had to humor him, and 'twas full half an hour before I killed him. Knocked off, and set Joe to work to boil rock [i.e. fish]. **1851** H. Melville *Moby Dick* II. xii. 95 Do you want to sink the ship, by knocking off at a time like this? **1890** Clark Russell *Ocean Trag.* III. xxix. 110 We were forced to knock off through sheer fatigue. **1916** 'Boyd Cable' *Doing their Bit* iii. 49 The factory was knocking off for dinner as we came away. **1969** M. Crouch *Essex* ii. 28 One who has just knocked off for his tea-break.

d. *trans.* To stop, discontinue, give up (work).

1767 'A. Barton' *Disappointment* i. i. 10 As for McSnip, he intends to knock off business, home to England and purchase a title. **1840** R. H. Dana *Bef. Mast* xxiii. 71 After we had knocked off work and cleared up decks for the night. **1884** Clark Russell *Jack's Courtship* xvii, I heard that you had knocked off the sea some years ago. **1885** R. Buchanan *Matt.* viii, He at once knocked off painting for the day.

e. To dispatch, dispose of, put out of hand, accomplish; to complete or do hastily; *spec.* to write, paint, etc., in a hurried and perfunctory fashion. *colloq.*

1817 Peacock *Melincourt* III. 68 He had.. to dispose of.. a christening, a marriage, and a funeral; but he would knock them off as fast as he could. **1820** J. W. Croker *Let.* in Smiles *Mem. J. Murray* (1891) II. xxiii. 87, I am anxious to knock off this task whilst.. it is fresh in my recollection. **1879** F. W. Robinson *Coward Conscience* i. xiii, If you have any business.. with me, the sooner we knock it off the better. **1886** in *Amer. Speech* (1950) XXV. 35/1 When he knocked off a few stanzas of poetry. **1925** R. Fry *Let.* 11 Nov. (1972) II. 584 Derain.. lets 'em [*sc.* dealers] have any old thing, or rather, what's much worse, any new thing which he's knocked off. **1970** W. Garner *Puppet-Masters* xv. 124 Look, you could knock off a few hundred words on Baxx without so much as scratching the surface of your *magnum opus*.

f. To strike off, deduct from an amount or sum.

1811 Jane Austen *Let.* 6 June (1952) 288 As *you* knock off a week from the end of her visit, & *Martha* rather more from the beginning, the thing is out of the question. *a* **1817** —— *Persuasion* (1818) III. ii. 26 Every comfort of life knocked off! Journeys, London, servants, horses, table. **1858** *Jrnl. R. Agric. Soc.* XIX. ii. 305 The saltpetre diminished the yield 5 bushels.. and the salt.. also knocked off 3 bushels. **1869** *Bradshaw's Railway Manual* XXI. 384 A great deal is knocked off from our claim against the Grand Trunk. **1889** Jessopp *Coming of Friars* v. 244 The steward graciously knocked off seventy-five per cent. **1892** Sir W. Grantham in *Law Times* XCIV. 63/2 Most of the plaintiff's bill was passed by the Taxing Master, and only £63 knocked off. **1926** J. Buchan *Dancing Floor* i. i. 11 First string of the 'Varsity mile. Believed.. to be going to knock five seconds off his last year's time. **1966** *Melody Maker* 15 Oct. 19 (Advt.), Quality instruments at knocked-off prices. **1972** *Daily Tel.* 30 Mar. 19/2 The gloomy assessment.. knocked 12p off ICI's share price in London.

g. *Cricket.* Of batsmen, to score the runs requisite for victory, or to oblige (a bowler) to be taken off by scoring heavily from his bowling.

1851 J. Pycroft *Cricket Field* ii. 30 If in the field.. and trying hard to prevent these few runs being knocked off by the last wickets, I know of no excitement so intense. **1860** *Baily's Monthly Mag.* Mar. 34 These two gentlemen scored 123 runs between them, knocking off Caffyn, Jackson, Parr, [etc.]. **1963** A. Ross *Australia 63* 18 Pullar and Cowdrey knocked off the 49 required to win without actually being separated.

h. [*imp.* use of 12 c.] ***knock it off!***: leave off! stop it!

1902 *N.Z. Illustr. Mag.* V. 488 Knock it off, boys. **1945** D. Dempsey *It ain't Brooklyn* in *Best One-Act Plays 1944* 28 Will you knock it off, please? **1961** J. Heller *Catch-22* (1962) xxvii. 294 'Hey, knock it off down there,' a voice rang out from the far end of the ward. 'Can't you see we're trying to nap?'

i. *slang.* To steal, to rob. Also *transf.*

1919 *Athenæum* 8 Aug. 729/1 A curious term used by a Tommy, in 'explaining' his deficiencies of kit, is 'Someone knocked it off' for 'Someone pinched (or made away with) it'. **1925** E. Wallace *Mind of Mr. J. G. Reeder* vi. 224 A big-shouldered man whose speciality was the 'knocking-off' of unattended motor-cars. **1938** F. D. Sharpe *Sharpe of Flying Squad* i. 14 They learn to 'knock things off'. **1956** C. Willock *Death at Flight* iv. 42 Mr. Goss had shown himself willing to knock off a pheasant himself. **1959** *New Statesman* 26 Sept. 404/2 After quietly knocking off a couple of retail shoe chains at the end of 1958, he entered the public takeover lists and won control of a Connoisseur's gobbet —Temperance Billiard Halls. **1960** *Observer* 24 Jan. 5/2 The boys either knocked off a hut where they knew gelly was kept or straightened a quarry man. **1963** J. Prescot *Case for Hearing* i. 16 Always dropping in on me.. with search-warrants.. and turning over that place of mine as if they expected to find some knocked-off gear there. **1969** *Sunday Truth* (Brisbane) 20 July 30/5 Only a few weeks after he finished up at St. Laurence's Christian Brothers College, Luzzcek knocked the place off. **1973** A. Hunter *Gently French* iii. 24 Just met a bloke.. in the nick... Him what was in there for knocking-off cars.

j. *slang* (orig. *U.S.*). To kill; to murder.

1919 E. Streeter *Same Old Bill* 28 Im goin to rite just as much as I can. Thats partly sos you wont worry an partly so that if I get knocked off you will have something to amuse you in case you go into a convent. **1929** *Papers Mich. Acad. Sci., Arts & Lett.* X. 304 *Knocked off*, killed. **1942** E. Paul *Narrow St.* xxiv. 217 Hitler.. ordered the blood purge which knocked off Roehm, Von Schleicher, and others among his former pals. **1943** P. Cheyney *You can always Duck* iv. 75 A United States Army officer was knocked off in a joint of his off Mount Street. **1948** Partridge *Dict. Forces' Slang* 107 *Knock off*, to kill. **1959** H. Hobson *Mission House Murder* xxii. 145 One of my boys.. got knocked off— an' nobody does a damn' thing about who knocked him off. **1973** C. Mullard *Black Britain* i. ii. 24 In one village a white launched a murder campaign because 'he liked knocking off blacks'.

k. *Underworld slang.* To arrest (a person); to raid (an establishment).

1926 F. D. Wilkinson in *Flynn's* 6 Feb. 58/1 'Willie of Detroit is here and is knocking everybody off.' (Meaning, arresting them.) **1930** *Amer. Mercury* Dec. 456/2 *Knock off*, to raid; to arrest. 'The feds knock off the scatter.' **1930** G. Smithson *Raffles in Real Life* xix. 256 About ten days or so after being 'knocked off'.. the Chief Warder came to my cell. **1939** 'D. Hume' *Heads you Live* ii. 24 You.. acted as a so-called hostess at the Angel Club in Dean Street for a year before it was knocked off. **1960** J. Stroud *Shorn Lamb* iii. 33 There was two other boys wiv Egg when you knocked him off, why ain't they 'ere? **1969** R. V. Beste *Next Time I'll Pay* xi. 157 You're the sort who'd knock off his mother because she hadn't got a lamp on her bike five minutes after lighting up time.

l. *slang.* To copulate with, to seduce (a woman).

1952 S. Kauffmann *Philanderer* (1953) viii. 134 Hell, she isn't much,.. but she's all there is around here. And if you don't want her, I don't mind knocking her off. **1965** A. Prior *Interrogators* v. 69 Do you think that young twit Wilkinson is knocking her off? **1970** G. Greer *Female Eunuch* 265 The vocabulary of impersonal sex is peculiarly desolating. Who wants to.. 'knock off a bit? of belly? of crumpet?' **1974** *Times Lit. Suppl.* 11 Oct. 1109/4 Knocking off his best friend's busty wife during boozy sprees on leave in Soho.

13. knock on. *trans.* To drive on or forward by a blow (also *fig.*); *spec.* in *Rugby Football*: To propel (the ball) with hand or arm in the direction of the adversary's goal (thereby committing an infringement of the rules); also *absol.*

1642 Fuller *Holy & Prof. St.* iv. xxi. 353 Loving Subjects.. being more kindly united to their Sovereigne then those which are onely knock'd on with fear and forcing. **1660** Milton *Free Commw.* Wks. (1851) 442 Shackles lock'd on by pretended Law of Subjection, more intolerable.. than those which are knock'd on by illegal Injury and Violence. **1894** *Daily News* 7 Sept. 5/1 If a full back 'knocked on' when a try was otherwise inevitable. **1900** *Westm. Gaz.* 12 Dec. 7/3 Hind spoiled a chance of scoring by knocking-on a pass from Jones.

14. knock out. a. *trans.* To strike or dash out by a blow; to stun or kill by a blow.

1591 Shaks. *1 Hen. VI*, iii. i. 83 Many haue their giddy braynes knockt out. **1727** Gay *Beggar's Op.* i. x. (1729) 14, I shall knock your brains out if you have any. **1887** I. R. *Lady's Ranche Life Montana* 102 Knocking the ashes out of his pipe. **1903** *Sun* (N.Y.) 2 Dec. 1 Scott's reputation is excellent, and the managers fear that he has been knocked out and robbed. *a* **1918** W. Owen *Coll. Poems* (1963) 7 Ye get knocked out; else wounded—bad or cushy; Scuppered; or nowt except yer feelin' mushy.

†**b.** To stop or drown the voice of (a speaker) by making a knocking noise. *Obs.*

1574 in Peacock *Obs. Stat. Camb.* App. p. vi, If the Father shall upon his Chyldrens Aunswer replie and make an Argument, then the Bedel shall knocke hym out.

c. (See quots., and knock-out *a.* and *sb.*)

1876 W. Green *Life Cheap Jack* 203 The concern would.. be 'knocked out' at once, that is resold by auction among themselves and the profit divided. **1896** Farmer *Slang, Knock-out*, a man frequenting auction rooms and joining with others to buy at a nominal price. One of the gang is told off to buy for the rest... At the end of the sale the goods are taken to a near hand public-house, where they are resold or knocked-out among the confederates.

d. *fig.* To drive out of the contest; to vanquish, exhaust. ***to knock out of time*** (Pugilistic), to disable an opponent so that he is unable to respond to the call of 'Time'; also in extended use.

1874 Trollope *Phineas Redux* II. xxviii. 228 You'll come all right after a few weeks. You've been knocked out of time; —that's the truth of it. **1883** *Pall Mall G.* 16 Apr. 4/1 (Farmer) Foxhall.. was second favourite for some time, but he has now been knocked out to comparatively long odds. **1884** *Sat. Rev.* 16 Jan. 108/1 A man of weak physique.. knocked out of time by a more robust.. adversary. **1888** *Pall Mall G.* 20 Apr. 11/2 The light-weight champion 'knocked out' his two first opponents. **1890** W. A. Wallace *Only a Sister?* 95 They call it.. 'knocked out of time', when a fellow doesn't come to at once. **1891** *Young Man* Apr. 140/2 A [bicycle] ride of ten miles within the hour may mean comfort and the capability of doing another twenty easily; a ride of eleven miles in the hour may just mean knocking a man out of time. **1894** *Daily News* 26 Feb. 5/1 Two years ago Aston Villa [football club] knocked out Sunderland. **1900** *Ibid.* 21 Apr. 7/3 You have to have your horses fit, otherwise you knock them out. **1970** *Brewer's Dict. Phr. & Fable* (ed. 12) 613/2 *To knock out of time*, to settle one's hash, to double him up.

e. To make roughly or hastily. (Cf. 12 e.) *colloq.*

1856 Dickens *Lett.* (1880) I. 422 We may knock out a series of descriptions.. without much trouble. **1881** T. Hardy *Laodicean* iii. v. (1882) 185, I wish.. you could knock out something for her before you leave town.

f. *intr.* (*Univ. slang.*) To gain exit from a college by knocking at the gate after it has been shut.

1861 Hughes *Tom Brown at Oxf.* xlv. (1864) 503 'Hullo!' he said, getting up; 'time for me to knock out'. **1862** H. Kingsley *Ravenshoe* vii. I. 82 Five out-college men had knocked out at a quarter to three.

g. 'To lose the scent: said of hounds in fox-hunting' (*Cent. Dict.*).

h. *trans.* To earn. *Austral.*, *N.Z.*, and *U.S. slang.*

[**1871** C. L. Money *Knocking about in N.Z.* ii. 18 They knocked out in this day as much gold as sufficed to make them afterwards two rings.] **1873** V. Pyke *Story Wild Will Enderby* (ed. 4) i. xiv. 62 Two industrious young men who worked very hard for a bare living—'just knocking out tucker', as the phrase went. **1874** —— *Adventures G. W. Pratt* 12/2, I can knock out tucker enough for the pair of us. **1920** *Sat. Even. Post* 27 Mar. 3/2 At that I was knocking out about eighteen hundred dollars per annum selling cigars out of South Bend. **1959** Baker *Drum* (1960) ii. 123 *Knock out*, to earn (a sum of money).

i. *trans.* To eliminate, remove forcibly, get rid of, destroy. orig. *U.S.*

1883 'Mark Twain' *Life on Mississippi* 465 The religious feature has been pretty well knocked out of it [i.e., Mardi-Gras at New Orleans]. **1889** *Kansas City* (Missouri) *Times & Star* 17 May, By a vote of 11 to 9 the Missouri senate knocked out the legislative reduction of tolls here by the Bell Telephone Company. **1904** *Sun* (N.Y.) 5 Aug. 4 In power, the Democrats wouldn't knock out protection if they could. **1927** J. N. McIlwraith *Kinsmen at War* xvii. 170, I will have to knock that idea out of Lucy's head too, straightway. **1933** F. Baldwin *Innocent Bystander* (1935) ii. 30, I got a good deal of it knocked out of me. **1944** *Return to Attack* (Army Board, N.Z.) 15/1 In the Bir el Gubi area the 22nd Armoured Brigade.. knocked out forty-five enemy tanks. **1955** *Times* 28 June 4/4 It is now believed that even if all the major ports of the United Kingdom were knocked out by atomic attack sufficient food for the population could still be passed through minor ports. **1971** *Daily Tel.* 17 Dec. 1 India claimed to have knocked out forty tanks in a major battle on the Kashmir front.

j. *trans.* (*Founding.*) To separate (a flask) from a casting contained inside it, or (a casting) from a flask containing it.

1906 *Jrnl. Iron & Steel Inst.* LXX. 174 The castings were all made in green sand, and were allowed to cool before being 'knocked out', *i.e.* taken from the sand. **1942** *Engineering* 6 Mar. 195/2 One difficulty was to get cool sand after the castings had been knocked out. **1955** H. E. Crivan in W. C. Newell *Casting of Steel* vi. 227 Heavier, dry sand work can be knocked out over a grid using hammers to loosen the sand.

k. ***to knock oneself out***: to make a considerable effort, to apply oneself energetically (to the point of exhaustion).

1936 *Mademoiselle* Mar. 43/2 All the fancier lassies.. are practically knocking themselves out in an effort to get to Hollywood. **1951** Green & Laurie *Show Biz* p. xxi, They like 'knocking themselves out' for *Variety*.

l. To give (a person) enjoyment, to excite. Often *refl.* and in *pass.* *slang* (orig. *U.S.*).

1942 *Amer. Mercury* July 95 *Knock yourself out*: have a good time. **1944** *New Yorker* 8 July 27/1 There are times when Duke laughs naturally and exuberantly; for example, when the boys.. are competing to see who can whistle the lowest note. 'I knock myself out,' he says. **1947** *Band Leaders & Record Rev.* Feb. 20 'When I heard it,' Ella Mae says, 'it knocked me out.' **1953** D. Wallop *Night Light* xix. 236 It's pretty hard to be knocked out with a baby when you know its old man is bored with the whole idea. **1956** B. Holiday *Lady sings Blues* (1973) ii. 26, I used to make them crazy dishes... This used to knock him out. When my time was running out, he made me an offer to stay on and cook for him. **1957** J. Kerouac *On Road* (1958) iii. iv. 202 A man who knocked himself out every evening and let the others put the quietus to him in the night. **1966** *Melody Maker* 7 May, I only heard half an hour of Ornette but I wasn't knocked out at all.

15. knock over. a. *trans.* To overthrow by, or as if by, a blow; to prostrate. Also *fig.*

1814 S. Pegge *Anecd. Eng. Lang., Suppl. Grose's Prov. Gloss.* 384 *To Knock a man over*, to knock him down. *North.* **1852** Dickens *Bleak Ho.* (1853) xxix. 285 Such a resemblance.. that it completely knocked me over. **1855** Russell *War in Crimea* xxiv. 167 The 'Sampson' pitched shell after shell right in among the tents, knocking them over right and left. **1857** Lady Canning in Hare *2 Noble Lives* (1893) II. 343 Sunstroke.. knocks them over quite suddenly. **1882** W. D. Hay *Brighter Britain!* I. vii. 184 If a single bushman could not have knocked that tree over before dinner time, he would not have been worth wages. **1893** Selous *S.E. Africa* 69 That evening two of my Kafirs.. were knocked over with fever.

b. *intr.* To succumb; to die. *colloq.* or *slang.*

1892 Stevenson in *Illustr. Lond. News* 9 July 42/1 Captain Randall knocked over with some kind of a fit or stroke.

c. *trans.* In warp knitting: to cause (a stitch) to pass *over* the head of the needle on which it was held.

a **1877** Knight *Dict. Mech.* II. 1238/1 *Knocking-over bar*, the bar against which the loops and fabric are drawn as the needles retreat, so that the loops shall be thrown or knocked over the heads of the needles. **1885** W. T. Rowlett tr. *Willkomm's Technol. Framework Knitting* II. iii. 145 These sinkers.. must move up and down, and backwards and forwards, so as to sink the thread into loops, bring them forward under the needle beards, land and knock over the old stitches, and.. lock in the new stitches, and take them to the back of the needles. **1952** D. F. Paling *Warp Knitting Technol.* i. 6 The presser is now withdrawn and the needle bar continues its downward motion, thus causing the fabric loops to pass further up the needle beards until finally they are knocked-over the needle heads as the latter pass below the level of the sinkers. **1964** H. Wignall *Knitting* ii. 28 The old loop is now cast-off or knocked over.

d. *trans.* (*Underworld slang.*) To rob (a person), to burgle (a building); to steal (from).

1928 *Detective Fiction Weekly* 7 June 52/2, I just got knocked over for that wad we jest lifted... My pocket was picked... I was tapped, touched, if that's any plainer. **1932** *Ibid.* 6 Feb. 129/2, I ain't knocked nothin' over for some

little time now. **1937** C. R. COOPER *Here's to Crime* iv. 89 There's the real fun of bank-robbing—running the roads. Old Harve used to love it. I've seen him run roads when he had no intention of ever knocking over a can. **1940** *Illustr. London News* 26 Oct. 548/2 The job looks easy enough—a big hotel at Tropico Springs that any fool could 'knock over'. **1941** K. TENNANT *Battlers* i. 9 Life 'on the track' was not so bad, with good places to camp and 'cockies' sheep to knock over.

16. knock together. a. *trans.* To drive or bring into collision or contact.

1398 [see KNOCKING *vbl. sb.* 1 b]. **1598** SHAKS. *Merry W.* III. i. 122 Let us knog our praines together to be reuenge on ..the Host of the Garter. **1609** BIBLE (Douay) *Jer.* li. 20 Thou doest knocke together the vessels of warre.

b. *intr.* To come into collision.

1641 J. JACKSON *True Evang. T.* III. 209 Two pots floting upon a pond,..with this word, If we knock together, we sink together. *a* **1609** LADY A. HALKETT *Autobiog.* (1875) 44 Our heads knockt together.

c. *trans.* To put together, or construct, hastily, rudely, as for a temporary purpose.

1874 FARRAR *Christ* (1894) 612 It [the Cross] would..be ..knocked together in the rudest fashion. **1893** KATH. L. BATES *Eng. Relig. Drama* 226 A temporary stage has been roughly knocked together.

17. knock under. *intr.* Short for *knock under board*, 5 c. To acknowledge oneself beaten; to give in, yield, submit, 'knuckle under'.

1670 *Merry Drollery* II. *Capt. Hick* 288 He..Made the wits at the board to knock under. **1684–94** tr. *Plutarch's Mor.* III. 219 (L.) He knocked under presently, and a single glass dozed him. **1728** MAD. D'ARBLAY *Diary* 10 Nov., Is not this a triumph for me..? Pray let my daddy Crisp hear it, and knock under. **1852** THACKERAY *Esmond* III. i, When he heard this news..Colonel Esmond knocked under to his fate, and resolved to surrender his sword. **1887** RIDER HAGGARD *Jess* xxvii, Our government is not going to knock under because it has suffered a few reverses.

18. knock up. a. *trans.* To drive upwards, or fasten up, by knocking; *spec.* in *Bookbinding*, etc. to make even the edges of (a pile of loose sheets) by striking them on a table; in *Bootmaking*, to cut or flatten the edges of the upper after its attachment to the insole.

1660 PEPYS *Diary* 30 Jan., Knocking up nails for my hat and cloakes. **1683** MOXON *Mech. Exerc., Printing* xxv. ¶3 Having thus Gathered one Book, he Knocks it up. *Ibid.* p. 382 *Knock up a Letter*..a Letter may be worn so low that it will not Print well..The Workman then..beats lightly upon the Foot of the Shank, till he have battered Mettle enough out of the Shank, to raise it higher against Paper. **1888** JACOBI *Printers' Vocab.* 71 *Knock up*, to make the edges of a heap of paper straight and square by knocking up to one edge. **1905** *Westm. Gaz.* 30 Oct. 7/3 A mechanical device for trimming off the surplus material from the lasted boot before it is 'knocked up', and a machine for the 'knocking-up' process itself, the latter guaranteed to 'knock-up' between 400 and 500 pairs of boots per week.

b. *intr.* To be driven up so as to strike something. ***to knock up against***, to come into collision with; *fig.* to meet with, come across, encounter.

1887 A. BIRRELL *Obiter Dicta* Ser. II. 264 When Montaigne was in Rome..he complained bitterly that he was always knocking up against his own countrymen. **1895** *Times* (weekly ed.) 27 Dec. 1034/3 One can't remember all the people one knocks up against in one's holiday-making. **1898** *Daily News* 24 Nov. 7/2 The smack eventually knocked up high on the shore under the cliffs.

c. *trans.* To make up (hastily or off-hand), to arrange summarily.

c **1580** JEFFERIE *Bugbears* I. iii. 30 We wile knocke vp this maryage. **1812** *Sporting Mag.* XXXIX. 138 A match was knocked up betwixt Dogherty..and a man named Burn. **1852** H. ROGERS *Ecl. Faith* (1853) 167 This gentleman, with whom Harrington..has knocked up an acquaintance. **1872** F. W. ROBINSON *Coward Conscience* I. viii, Why didn't they knock up a match between you and Ursula?

d. To put together hastily; = 16 c. Also, to prepare (food) quickly (*U.S.*).

1683 MOXON *Mech. Exerc., Printing* xxiv. ¶10 The Balls are well Knockt up, when the Wooll is equally dispersed about all the Sides. **1812** L. HUNT in *Examiner* 12 Oct. 642/2 The carpenters that knock up our hustings. **1850** *Jrnl. R. Agric. Soc.* XI. I. 271 A range of farm buildings can be roughly knocked up. **1869** L. M. ALCOTT *Little Women* II. v. 61 Don't cry, dear, but just exert yourself a bit, and knock us up something to eat. **1890** *Harper's Mag.* May 894/2, I jest killed a chicken, and knocked up a few biscuit. **1931** H. NICOLSON *Diary* 14 Aug. (1966) 87 He has got out several tenders for printing... He and Joseph have..knocked up a dummy lay-out. **1967** *Official Jrnl. Patents, Trade Marks & Designs* (Austral.) XXXVII. 1538/2 Plumbing means can be purchased ready made by factories whereas they once might have to be 'knocked up'..from basic materials. **1972** *Shooting Times & Country Mag.* 4 Mar. 21/2 They will knock you up a meal to hold you through the coldest day's fishing or wildfowling.

e. To get or accumulate by labour or exertion; *spec.* in *Cricket*, to run up (a score), make (so many runs) by striking the ball. *colloq.*

1837 WHITTOCK *Bk. Trades* (1842) 360 [He] obtains almost full employment,..and 'knocks' up £3 or £4 or more weekly. **1860** *Baily's Monthly Mag.* Oct. 41 Tinley in a trice knocked up 8. **1888** *Sporting Life* 10 Dec. (Farmer), With only 29 to win, White at his next attempt knocked up the necessary item. **1891** *Times* 12 Oct. 11/5 The Englishmen.. knocked up 305 runs before their innings closed. **1955** *Publ. Amer. Dial. Soc.* xxiv. 37 This adds up to over $1500 per week which must be *knocked up*—just to meet operating expenses.

f. To arouse by knocking at the door. (This sense is not current in the U.S.)

1663 PEPYS *Diary* 11 Sept., This morning, about two or three o'clock, knocked up in our back yard;..I found it was the constable and his watch. **1737** POPE *Hor. Epist.* II. i. 161 Time was, a sober Englishman would knock His servants up, and rise by five o'clock. **1851** THACKERAY *Eng. Hum., Steele* (1858) 121 They knock up the surgeon. **1973** *National Observer* (U.S.) 3 Feb., Fielding's guide-book considerately explains that a male host may quite casually tell a female American house guest that he will 'knock you up at 7:30 tomorrow morning'. The term, of course, conveys nothing more than a rapping at the door until one is awakened.

g. To overcome or make ill with fatigue; to exhaust, tire out. (Esp. in *pass.*)

1737 BRACKEN *Farriery Impr.* (1757) II. 167 Where the Horse is young,..it would splint him, or knock him up (as we say) if the Rider were to make his Flourishes upon his Back like a Rope-dancer. **1770** MAD. D' ARBLAY *Early Diary* 7 Feb., Here is a lady who is not at all tired,..and here am I knocked up. **1856** T. A. TROLLOPE *Girlhood Cath. de Medici* xvi. 253 He is completely knocked up from over-work. **1883** LD. R. GOWER *My Remin.* II. 244 Walter was too knocked up to join those who rode to the grove.

h. *intr.* To become exhausted or tired out; to become unserviceable; to break down.

1771 SMOLLETT *Humph. Cl.* 12 Sept., In passing the sands without a guide, his horse had knocked up. **1849** ALB. SMITH *Pottleton Leg.* (repr.) 255 Every literary man, however great his success, knocks up at last. **1897** A. BEARDSLEY *Let.* 25 Feb. (1971) 259, I am aghast at the amount of travelling she [*sc.* his sister Mabel] has to get through before the tour comes to an end. I do hope she won't 'knock up' while she is over there. **1941** I. L. IDRIESS *Great Boomerang* x. 78 They travelled fast then, taking the chance. But their horses knocked up.

i. *trans.* To break up, destroy, put an end to.

1764 FOOTE *Mayor of G.* I. Wks. 1799 I. 173 This plaguy peace..has knock'd up all the trade of the Alley. **1776** in *New York during Amer. Rev.* (1861) 99 The arrival of the fleet, since which almost all business in town is knocked up. **1857** DE QUINCEY *Whiggism in Relat. to Literature* Wks. VI. 67 The establishment was knocked up, and clearly from gross defects of management.

j. To make (a woman) pregnant; (*less commonly*) to have sexual intercourse with (a woman). *slang* (orig. *U.S.*).

1813 C. EARLE *Diary* 12 Apr. in J. McPhee *Pine Barrens* (1971) ii. 33 William Mick's widow arrived here in pursuit of J. Mick, who she says has knocked her up. **1836** D. CROCKETT *Exploits & Adv. Texas* vii. 97 Nigger women are knocked down by the auctioneer, and knocked up by the purchaser. **1860** HOTTEN *Dict. Slang* (ed. 2) 166 *Knocked up.* In the United States, amongst females, the phrase is equivalent to being *enceinte*, so that Englishmen often unconsciously commit themselves when amongst our Yankee cousins. **1925** E. HEMINGWAY *In Our Time* (1926) 165 Hell, no girls get married around here till they're knocked up. **1934** H. MILLER *Tropic of Cancer* 241 Nearly all the co-eds had been knocked up some time or other. **1952** B. MALAMUD *Natural* 133 You haven't knocked up a dame maybe? **1971** H. C. RAE *Marksman* I. vi. 51 He screwed her, knocked her up first go and..married her..before she could even contemplate abortion. **1973** E. BULLINS *Theme is Blackness* 170 The girls all got knocked-up and set up homes, got married, went on the block or on welfare or turned into booze hounds.

knock, *sb.*[1] Forms: 4–5 knokk(e, 4–6 knok, 6 knoke, 6–7 knocke, 7– **knock**. [f. KNOCK *v.*]

1. a. An act of knocking; a sounding blow; a hard stroke or thump; *spec.* a rap at a door to call attention or gain admittance.

1377 LANGL. *P. Pl.* B. x. 327 Þanne shal þe abbot of Abyndoun and alle his issu..Haue a knokke of a kynge. **1460** CAPGRAVE *Chron.* (Rolls) 284 He schal for his spoilyng have as good knokkis as evyr had Englischman. **1526** *Pilgr. Perf.* (W. de W. 1531) 223 b, As a nayle, the moo knockes it hath, the more sure it is fixed. ? *a* **1550** *Freiris of Berwik* 154 in *Dunbar's Poems* (1893) 290 His knok scho kend, and did so him in lett. **1663** BUTLER *Hud.* I. i. 200 And prove their Doctrine Orthodox By Apostolick Blows and Knocks. **1742** POPE *Dunc.* IV. 443 A drowsy Watchman, that just gives a knock, And breaks our rest, to tell us what's a-clock. **1819** KEATS *Let.* 13 Mar. (1958) II. 46 The variations of single and double knocks. *a* **1844** L. HUNT *Our Cottage* 10 No news comes here,..not a postman's knock. **1866** MRS. CARLYLE *Lett.* III. 317 The telegraph boy gave his double-knock. **1883** C. J. MATHEWS *Patter versus Clatter* ii. 10 (*Double knock*, L.H.) There, someone come to call. Polly, go and see who it is; stop, child, take off your apron, it's a double knock.

b. A misfortune, a rebuff, a blow; adverse criticism. Freq. in phr. ***to take the knock***: to sustain a severe financial or emotional blow, to suffer a setback.

1649 T. FORD *Ludus Fort.* 92 Our bodies are but fraile, earthen vessels, subject to every knock of sicknesse. **1890** *Globe* 21 Apr. 6/1 A broken backer of horses who has taken, what is known in the language of the turf, as the knock. **1898** DOYLE *Trag. Korosko* ii. 37 We get hard knocks and no thanks, and why should we do it? **1900** E. WELLS *Chestnuts* xxiii. 226 When a prominent backer takes the knock racing, he sometimes has the greatest difficulty to avoid his creditors. **1905** 'H. MCHUGH' *You can search Me* iii. 50 There are only four people in New York city who can write criticisms—the rest of the bunch are slush-dealers, and a knock from any one of them is a boost. **1906** GALSWORTHY *Man of Property* III. iv. 322 Here's a poor devil whose mistress has just been telling him a pretty little story of her husband... He's taken the knock, you see. **1929** D. RUNYON in *Hearst's International* Nov. 73/1 It will be a knock to his reputation. **1930** V. PALMER in *Bulletin* (Sydney) 30 Apr. 38/3 [McCurdie] lay there... 'He's taken the knock,' said a cattle-buyer... In a moment a change came into the atmosphere around the sleeping man. **1930** D. RUNYON in *Collier's* 13 Sept. 7/1 They are always doing something which is considered a knock to the community, such as robbing people. **1936** A. HUXLEY *Eyeless in Gaza* vi. 54 'One's had a pretty bad knock,' he added self-consciously, in that queer jargon which he imagined to be colloquial English... That 'bad knock' was a metaphor drawn from the boxing contests he had never witnessed. **1948** V. PALMER *Golconda* xiv. 111 He saw himself..ready to stand up and take the knock if they got into trouble with the john. **1955** *Times* 19 Aug. 2/5 In a dress suit much too large for him, he is on top of the world by submitting with such cheerful readiness to its knocks. **1959** *Encounter* Aug. 7/1 Like other institutions of the Establishment, it has taken a knock or two in recent years. **1962** *B.S.I. News* June 9/1 Advertising has had some hard knocks from its critics recently. **1973** A. BEHREND *Samarai Affair* ii. 24 The pilot ..in the event of an accident will..[be] summoned to appear before the Pilotage Committee to explain his actions and take the knock if held to blame.

c. A knocking noise, or knocking noises, in an engine; *spec.* in a reciprocating internal-combustion engine, noise caused by a very abrupt rise in pressure in the cylinder as a result of too rapid combustion (in spark-ignition engines, the sudden spontaneous ignition of all the unburnt portion of the mixture before the flame from the sparking plug reaches it); faulty combustion of this character. Cf. KNOCK *v.* 5 b.

1899 J. PERRY *Steam Engine* v. 115 In double-acting engines we can often utilise the inertia forces to alter the point in the crank pin path at which the knock occurs, so that it shall not produce such serious effects. **1903** M. P. BALE *Gas & Oil Engine Managem.* iv. 61 Knocking in the Cylinder.—This often arises from premature firing of the charge before the end of the compression stroke is reached, thus throwing a greater pressure than usual on the piston before it commences the power stroke, and causing a jar or knock as the crank turns the dead centre. **1903** *Cassell's Cycl. Mech.* 3rd Ser. 264/1 Locating 'Knock' in Steam Engine. **1908** *Motor Cycle* 15 Jan. 46/1, I have had a number of letters lately referring to the existence of 'knock' in engines that have run a year or two in private hands. **1920** *Cornh. Mag.* Sept. 314 The carbon knock, the ignition knock, and the bearing knock are fairly simple propositions. **1927** W. DEEPING *Doomsday* xxv. 265 Half-way up the long hill..'Cherry's' engine developed a sudden and rather fearsome 'knock'. **1933** [see *compression-ignition*]. **1939** CROFT & TANGERMAN *Steam-Engine Princ.* (ed. 2) xiii. 410 By far the commonest causes of knocks are water in the cylinder and loose bearings. **1956** MOLLOY & LANCHESTER *Automobile Engineer's Ref. Bk.* v. 5 The well-known effect of ignition timing on knock is due to the fact that the relative timing of the piston and the spark-ignited flame controls the pressure in the end-gas. **1963** C. CAMPBELL *Sports Car Engine* ix. 181 During knock more heat is transferred to the cylinder walls. **1973** A. PARRISH *Mech. Engineer's Ref. Bk.* II. 17 Correct choice of mixture strength, ignition timing, fuel (octane number) and good combustion chamber design will allow smooth combustion without knock which occurs if the end gas reaches the condition where self-ignition causes an explosion of all the mixture remaining in the chamber.

2. A clock. *Sc.*

1502 *Ld. Treas. Acc. Scot.* II. 159 To Schir James Petegrew, to his expens cumand to Strivelin to divis ane knok iijli. xs. **1559** KENNEDY *Lett. to Willock* in *Wodrow Misc.* (1844) 270 Att ten houris of the knoke. **1826** J. WILSON *Noct. Ambr.* Wks. 1855 I. 272 Do you put back.. the lang hand o' the knock.

Comb. **1540** *Ld. Treas. Acc. Scot.* in Pitcairn *Crim. Trials* I. 305* William Purves, Knok-maker and smyth. **1663** *Inv. Ld. J. Gordon's Furnit.*, A going knock and knockcaice. **1885** EDGAR *Old Ch. Life Scot.* I. 29 The Knock house stood in a little gallery called the Knock loft.

3. *Cricket.* An innings; a spell at batting (in a match or at practice).

1889 J. LILLYWHITE *Cricketers' Ann.* 72 Surrey were fortunate to get first 'knock', and..were able to just reach the second hundred. **1898** G. GIFFEN *With Bat & Ball* i. 2 At last..I would..bowl for a little while; and then they began to give me an occasional knock. **1900** *Captain* III. 200/1 'You play cricket yourself, then?' 'Oh, I have an occasional knock.' *Ibid.* 210/1 'W. G.' advises every batsman to have a knock..before going in. An over or two at the nets loosens your muscles. **1909** *Pearson's Mag.* Aug. 180/1 Crofton's had won the toss and taken first 'knock'. **1927** *Observer* 27 Nov. 28 His knock..included eight boundaries. **1958** 'N. BLAKE' *Penknife in my Heart* iii. 50 I'm taking first knock. I've got to be sure you'll go in when it's your turn. **1970** *Times* 26 Aug. 11/8 A fine knock by Mushtaq, who batted for two hours and hit ten fours.

4. ***knock for knock***: applied to an agreement between insurers that each will pay his own policy-holders without regard to the question of liability.

1906 *Daily Chron.* 26 July 6/6 Mr. Fairbank said that the 'knock for knock' agreement had never paid with the horse vehicles. **1927** B. C. HOSKINS *Insurance Lexicon* 127 *Knock for knock agreement.*—An arrangement made between Companies..for dealing automatically with collisions between vehicles owned by their respective insureds; each Company undertakes to pay for the damage to its own insured's vehicle irrespective of the question of liability as between the parties in collision. **1958** *Manch. Guardian* 11 June 9/6 The knock-for-knock agreement is an arrangement whereby when two insured vehicles have been in collision each insurance company pays for the damage to the car it has insured,..without regard to the degree of blame, if any, of the driver. **1972** *Mod. Law Rev.* XXXV. I. 18 Some types of cases which are handled by small claims courts in other jurisdictions are dealt with in England in ways which obviate the necessity for a claim. Perhaps the most significant example is knock-for-knock agreements among motor-vehicle insurers.

5. a. (An act of) copulation; so ***on the knock***, engaged in prostitution. **b.** *Austral.* Phr. ***to do a knock with***: (see quot. 1941).

1933 N. LINDSAY *Saturdee* 138 Supposin' I was to do a knock with girls, what 'ud I say to them? **1937** PARTRIDGE *Dict. Slang* 460/2 *Knock*, a copulation. **1941** BAKER *Dict. Austral. Slang* 23 *Do a knock (line) with*: to take an amorous

interest in a member of the opposite sex. **1969** D. BAGLEY *Spoilers* i. 11 Maybe she was on the knock.

6. Special Comb.: **knockmeter**, an instrument for measuring the intensity of knock in the cylinder of an internal-combustion engine; **knock rating**, (the determination of) the insusceptibility of a fuel to knock.

1934 *Jrnl. R. Aeronaut. Soc.* XXXVIII. 353 Knock intensity is measured by a bouncing pin, in conjunction with either a knockmeter or a gas-evolution burette. **1960** V. B. GUTHRIE *Petroleum Products Handbk.* IV. 17 The test engine is equipped with a pressure-sensitive pickup mounted in the cylinder head in direct contact with the combustion chamber. A knockmeter is used in conjunction with this pressure-sensitive element to indicate on a scale the intensity of the engine knock... A fuel that is to be tested is brought up to a standard knock intensity, as indicated on the knockmeter, by adjustment of the engine compression ratio. **1932** *Engineering* 8 July 45/3 The marked effect of cylinder temperature upon the relative knock ratings of fuels was observed by Heron in 1928. **1933** *Aircraft Engineering* Aug. 177/1 To have an agreed scale of knock-rating for aviation fuels is no less important. **1959** *B.S.I. News* Aug. 14 Two draft ISO recommendations covering the motor and research methods of determining knock rating.

knock (nɒk), *sb.*^{2} *Sc.* [In sense 1, a. Gael. (also Ir.) *cnoc* knoll, rounded hill. With 2 cf. Danish dial. *knok* little hillock (Molbech).]

1. A hill; a hillock, a knoll.

?**17..** *Jacobite Relics* II. 148 (Jam.) Round the rock, Down by the knock. **1820** *Glenfergus* I. 108 The knock, an insulated hill behind the church.

2. A name given on the coast of Lincolnshire, etc., to sand-banks. Cf. ***Kentish Knock***, a sand-bank near the mouth of the Thames; also ***Knock Sand***.

1587 FLEMING *Contn. Holinshed* III. 1538/2 To make [at Dover] certeine groins or knocks, which at the havens mouth should cause such a depth, as thereby the whole harborough should lie drie at a low water. **1881** Knock Sand [see KNOCK *v.* 5]. **1898** *Westm. Gaz.* 1 Dec. 7/2 The surf boat ..when near Kentish Knock was taken in tow by a tug..no vessel can be found on the Knock.

†**knock, knok**, *sb.*^{3} *Obs. rare*$^{-1}$. [app. a. LG. *knocke* in same sense: see KNITCH *sb.*] A bundle of heckled flax.

1573 *Lanc. Wills* III. 62, xx knokes of hatchelled lyne.

knock, variant of NOCK.

knock-, the vb.-stem or noun of action in Comb. **knock-bark** (*Mining*), ore that has been crushed; **knock-knock** *sb.*, *v.*, and *int.* in various senses (see quots.); **knock-stone**, a stone (or cast-iron plate) on which ore is broken; **knock-toe**, a galley-punt. Also with adverbs, as **knock-under**, an act of 'knocking under' (see KNOCK *v.* 17); **knock-'upable** *a.* (*nonce-wd.*), likely to be 'knocked up' or weak; **knock'upedness** (*nonce-wd.*), the state of being 'knocked up' or weak. See also KNOCK-ABOUT, KNOCK-DOWN, KNOCK-KNEE, etc.

1653 MANLOVE *Lead Mines* 266 Fell, Bous, and *Knock-barke. **1747** [see *knock-stone*]. **1828** *Craven Dial.*, *Knock-bark*, ore after it is reduced by the hand or machine. **1904** *Daily Chron.* 2 July 8/1 The *knock-knocking at the door sending a thrill through the pulse. **1936** *Variety* 19 Aug. 25/5 Manager Russell Bovim, of Loew's Broad, Columbus, cashed in handsomely on the 'Knock Knock' craze now sweeping the country. **1941** C. GRAVES *Life Line* 179 Certain trawlers have the job of sweeping for magnetic mines (known as 'Maggies') and the latest acoustic mines (known as 'knock-knocks'). **1957** O. NASH *You can't get there from Here* 151 Who, rapped Mr. Webster, escapes an escapee? That, knock-knocked Mr. Merriam, is what puzzles me. **1959** I. & P. OPIE *Lore & Lang. Schoolch.* v. 82 A craze for Wellerisms is apt to develop in a school in the same way that there are still sometimes crazes for limericks, Little Audrey jokes, Knock-knocks, and Shaggy-dog stories. **1961** PARTRIDGE *Dict. Slang* Suppl. 1161/1 *Knock! knock!* A c.p., dating from the middle of Nov. 1936... Orig. ex U.S. It is used, esp. among busmen, by a person about to tell a dirty story or, esp., to make a pun, gen. in doubtful taste. **1974** *Radio Times* 19–25 Oct. 59 'Knock, knock.' 'Who's there?' 'Richard Milhous.' 'Richard Milhous who?' 'Ah...how quickly people forget.' **1747** HOOSON *Miner's Dict.* Lj, Knockbark [is] all that is carried to the *Knock-Stone and there knocked down with the Bucker. **1839** URE *Dict. Arts* 749 A very hard stone slab, or cast-iron plate,..called a knock-stone. **1903** W. C. RUSSELL *Overdue* vi. 104 It is the Deal galley-punt too, called in the parts she belongs to '*knocktoe'. **1929** F. C. BOWEN *Sea Slang* 80 Knock-toe, an old name for the Deal lugger-rigged galley punt, in which there was little room for the feet. **1894** BLACKMORE *Perlycross* 51 They seem to have brought him down to a flat *knock-under. **1857** GEO. ELIOT *Let.* 5 Apr. (1954) II. 314 For some time I have been unusually weak and *knock-upable. **1855** D. G. ROSSETTI *Let.* 19 Sept. (1965) I. 271, I am very sorry indeed to hear of your *knockupedness but I warned you about that window.

'knock-about, knockabout, *a.* and *sb.* [The phrase *knock about* (see KNOCK *v.* 7), used attrib., and hence by ellipsis as sb.]

A. *adj.* **1. a.** Characterized by knocking about, or dealing blows; rough, violent, boisterous.

1885 *Pall Mall G.* 4 Apr. 4/1 The rage for this knockabout sport [football]. **1891** *Ibid.* 4 Aug. 7/1 Prize fights, and street-fights, and knockabout performances.

b. *Theatr. slang.* Of noisy and violent character. Also *transf.*

1892 *Daily News* 10 May 3/4 The 'knockabout' character of sketches. **1893** *Times* 25 Dec. 6/2 Two very droll and daring knock-about comedians. **1897** G. FLOYD in *Compl. Cyclist* vi. 156 The intelligent foreigner..imagines that the type of English humour is a knockabout entertainment. **1914** A. HUXLEY *Let.* Feb. (1969) 57 The whole city is permeated with the Mission to Undergraduates—the Bp of Oxford being heard twice nightly in a knock-about sermon at St. Mary's. **1924** J. BUCHAN *Three Hostages* xiii. 183 He liked plays with shooting in them, and knockabout farce. **1969** *New Yorker* 31 May 110/2 His strong colloquial flavour and knock-about verbiage cannot be conveyed in French. **1974** *Daily Tel.* 5 Oct. 16/1 One would have expected the argument in the Election campaign to have been conducted with a high level of rigour and seriousness, which would not be incompatible with some of the traditional knockabout fun.

2. a. Characterized by being driven to and fro, or wandering irregularly about.

1886 MORRIS in Mackail *Life* (1809) II. 158 Such a knock-about day as I had on Monday! **1890** BLACKMORE *Kit* III. xvi, A knockabout fellow swore to find out all about you.

b. Of a garment, etc.: Suitable for travelling or 'knocking about'.

1880 *Echo* 23 Nov. 4/4 Knockabout Corduroy Cloth. **1895** M. E. FRANCIS *Daughter of Soil* 130 Any make,..from knock-about suits to dress-clothes. **1900** *Daily Tel.* 25 Aug. 3/2 Concocting with their own nimble fingers tasteful blouses, useful knockabout skirts, and dainty trifles of lace and muslin.

c. *Australia.* Applied to a labourer on a station who is ready to turn his hand to any kind of work. Cf. ROUSEABOUT *sb.*

1876 W. HARCUS *S. Australia* 275 (Morris) Knockabout hands, 17s. to 20s. per week. **1890** BOLDREWOOD *Col. Reformer* xix, We're getting rather too many knockabout men for a small station like this.

3. a. *N. Amer.* Designating a class of sloop-rigged sailing-yacht (see quots. 1894, 1897); also, designating a sailing-yacht without a bowsprit. Also as *sb.*

1894 in *Forest & Stream* (1895) 12 Jan. 35/2 A knock-about boat is a seaworthy keel boat (not to include fin-keels) decked or half-decked, of fair accommodations, rigged simply, without bowsprit, and with only mainsail and one head sail. **1897** *Outing* (U.S.) Dec. 235/1 The knockabout class, which originated in Boston a few seasons ago, has much to recommend it... It is free from all freakiness. It has no fin-keel... With a moderate sail area it is under control at all times... This class is limited to five hundred square feet of sail. All are keel-boats, and all must be under twenty-one feet on the load water-line. **1919** *Canad. Fisherman* 695/1 The fine new knockabout schooner, General Haig, the first of her kind ever built here. **1970** *Amer. Neptune* XXX. 196 The term knockabout soon was restricted to the type lacking a bowsprit and was further used attributively to designate any rig in which a long fore overhang took the place of a bowsprit. *Ibid.* 197 The single knock-about yawl was *Arapahoe*, built in 1893.

b. More generally, descriptive of small yachts or dinghies. Also as *sb.*

1904 [implied at sense 3 of the sb.]. **1921** *Yachting Monthly* XXXII. 105/2 The usual lug and mizen clinker built 'knockabout' boats, common to seaside watering places. **1970** *Motor Boat & Yachting* 16 Oct. 39/2 It [*sc.* the balanced lug] is a powerful sail and very well suited to knockabout dinghies.

B. *sb.* **1.** *Theatr. slang.* A 'knockabout' performer or performance: see A. 1 b. Also *transf.*

1887 *Pall Mall G.* 17 Sept. 3/2 Bounding brothers, knock-abouts, step-dancers. **1892** *Daily News* 7 June 6/3 Singers, dancers, knockabouts, and quick-change artistes. **1899** ADE *Fables in Slang* (1900) 83 These two Troupers began their Professional Career with a Road Circus..doing a Refined Knockabout in the Grand Concert or Afterpiece. **1930** *Observer* 2 Mar. 15/3 The actors attack both the recitative and knockabout delightfully. **1955** *Times* 9 Aug. 2/5 One called The Cold War, in which Mr. Wisdom, suffering from a fever, tries out different miraculous cures evincing immediately their different after-effects, is the most intricate piece of knockabout seen on the London stage for some time. **1959** *Ann. Reg. 1958* 50 The proceedings were wound up by a forcible speech from the leader of the party, Mr Grimond, in a style of party-political knockabout in which he demonstrated that it was easier to abuse the other parties than to explain the purposes of one's own. **1970** *New Society* 5 Mar. 406/3 For while there is some knockabout.. most of the pieces here are technically of a high order.

2. *Australia.* A 'knock-about' man: see A. 2 c.

1889 BOLDREWOOD *Robbery under Arms* xvi, The knock-abouts and those other three chaps won't come it on us.

3. *N. Amer.* A 'knock-about' boat: see A. 3 a, b.

1904 *N.Y. Even. Post* 21 May 6 There are numerous knockabouts and other small yachts in the Pawcatuck River. **1927** G. BRADFORD *Gloss. Sea Terms* 96/1 *Knock-about*, a sloop or schooner without a bowsprit and whose jib sets from a stay at the stern.

4. A small motor vehicle for casual use.

1956 W. H. WHYTE *Organization Man* (1957) vi. 71 A little knock-about for the wife to run down to the station in.

knock-back, knockback. *dial.*, and *Austral.* and *N.Z. colloq.* [Phr. *to knock back* (see KNOCK *v.* 9 a) used as sb.] A refusal, a rebuff.

1898 *Evesham Jrnl.* 21 May 7/1 He..objected to the powers of the guardians being relegated to the officers. It was a knock-back. **1902** *Eng. Dial. Dict.* III. 478/2 It was a nasty reply—a complete knock-back. **1919** W. H. DOWNING *Digger Dial.* 31 *Knock-back*, a refusal. **1933** *Bulletin* (Sydney) 18 Jan. 17, I sought casual work... Result, six flat knockbacks. **1941** K. TENNANT *Battlers* xvii. 182 She could take a 'knock-back' as though it didn't matter. **1943** F. SARGESON in *Penguin New Writing* XVII. 56 And I said to myself, well, a knock-back from one of yous isn't going to make me lose any sleep. **1960** N. HILLIARD *Maori Girl* II. xiv. 161 She had mentioned the knock-back from the Tallahassee Milk Bar. **1962** [see DADDY 2]. **1972** *Sunday Mail* (Brisbane) 9 Jan. 5/2 When he lead[s] the conversation ..on to Jesus and Christianity we don't get any knockbacks.

knock-down, *a.* and *sb.* [The phr. *knock down* (see KNOCK *v.* 10) used attrib. and as sb.]

A. *adj.* **1. a.** Such as to knock down or fell to the ground; *fig.* irresistible, overwhelming.

1690 DRYDEN *Amphitryon* I. i, This same Arbitrary Power is a knock-down Argument. **1794** *Sporting Mag.* IV. 78/2 After the first knock-down blow, Johnson attempted to shift. **1802** WOLCOTT (P. Pindar) *Ld. Belgrave & his Motions* Wks. 1812 IV. 514 You've learnt to face a knock-down laugh. **1840–1** DE QUINCEY *Style* Wks. 1859 XI. 220 These ..are knock-down blows to the Socratic..philosophy. **1885** COURTHOPE *Liberal Movement Eng. Lit.* iv. 114 The view that Johnson propounded in his direct 'knock-down' style. **1971** *Nature* 15 Oct. 441/1 They are used against houseflies, mosquitoes and cockroaches..; their great advantage is that pyrethrin I has a high kill rate and pyrethrin II a high knock down rate.

b. Adapted to be fastened by being knocked flat at the end: see KNOCK *v.* 10 b.

1869 SIR E. REED *Shipbuild.* xvii. 383 It is advantageous to have plain knockdown or conical points to steel rivets.

2. ***knock-down price***, the price below which an article will not be 'knocked down' at an auction; the reserve price. Also, ***knock-down book, fee*** (*U.S.*).

1888 *Harper's Mag.* Nov. 934/2 Bills for knock-down fees are presented for payment to auctioneers every month. *Ibid.* 937/2 The knock-down book records the price, buyer, and all particulars of every sale in the Auction-room. **1895** *Daily News* 6 May 6/5 Fairy, favourite spaniel of Lady Bulwer's, ..40 gs.;..the knockdown price last year was 54 gs.

3. Constructed so as to be easily 'knocked down' or taken in pieces for removal (see KNOCK *v.* 10 f); sold as, or in the form of, a number of separate parts that require to be assembled.

1795 W. WINTERBOTHAM *Hist. View Amer. U.S.* III. 305 Articles of exportation [were]..231,776 Barrels of dried and pickled fish..48,860 Shook or knock-down casks. **1875** KNIGHT *Dict. Mech.* 1239/2 The shook may be said to be a knock-down barrel. **1888** *Sci. Amer.* LIX. 187 To make a knockdown wigwam, the framing should be lashed together with ropes or twine, and the bark tied to the rafters with twine. **1952** *Archit. Rev.* CXI. 241/1 Swedish 'knock-down' furniture. *Ibid.*, The production of 'packaged' furniture (an adjective which is preferable to either knock-down or demountable, since it not only sounds better, but is more definitive). **1969** *Sunday Mail* (Brisbane) 2 Feb. 26/6 Cars imported in the complete knockdown form. **1971** *Rand Daily Mail* 4 Sept. 10/3 The boat is imported in a knock-down form and is assembled here. **1972** 'E. LATHEN' *Murder without Icing* (1973) vii. 65 Millions of Americans..had stayed up late Christmas Eve to struggle with knockdown toys.

B. *sb.* **1.** Something that knocks one down; something overpowering; *e.g.* strong liquor. *slang.*

1698 W. KING tr. *Sorbière's Jrnl. Lond.* 35 He answer'd me that he had a thousand such sort of liquors,..Old Pharaoh, Knockdown, Hugmatee [etc.]. *a* **1700** B. E. *Dict. Cant. Crew*, *Knock-down*, very strong Ale or Beer.

2. An act of knocking down; a blow that knocks down or fells to the ground; *fig.* an overwhelming blow; a stand-up or free fight. Also (*U.S. colloq.*) ***knock-down (and) drag-out***: a free-for-all, a rough-and-tumble fight; also *transf.* and *attrib.*

1809 *Sporting Mag.* XXXIII. 6 This round produced the first blood, and first knock-down. **1818** LADY MORGAN *Autobiog.* (1859) 85 It is a knockdown to all Morgan's arguments and mine. **1827** J. F. COOPER *Prairie* I. iv. 93 Making it a real knock-down and drag-out! **1834** *Amer. Railroad Jrnl.* III. 304/1 He was one of our careless unconcerned knock down and drag out looking sort of fellows. **1837** DICKENS *Pickw.* xxxvii, 'I'll try and bear up agin such a reg'lar knock-down o' talent' replied Sam. **1845** E. MIALL *Nonconf.* V. 437 Let us turn to and have a real Irish knockdown. **1932** *Tulsa* (Okla.) *World* 13 Mar. v. 2/3 A knock-down-and-drag-out battle betwen Roosevelt and Smith forces. **1941** AUDEN *New Year Let.* II. 34 The hard self-conscious particles Collide, divide like numerals In knock-down drag-out laissez-faire. **1949** B. A. BOTKIN *Treas. S. Folklore* II. iii. 251 When it comes to knock-down-and-drag-out..political bickering..well, as Donald Davidson's typical Middle Georgia country gentleman, 'Cousin Roderick', puts it, 'Politics is for lawyers.' **1952** B. ULANOV *Hist. Jazz in Amer.* (1958) viii. 89 Whole choruses ..and ensemble sections..are delightful..in knockdown and dragout choruses. **1968** *Punch* 1 May 624/1 An elderly bum who's just sold him the Lincoln Centre at the knock-down drag-out price of fourteen bucks.

3. A 'knock-down' piece of furniture: see A. 3.

1875 KNIGHT *Dict. Mech.* 1239/2 *Knock-down*, a piece of furniture or other structure adapted to be disconnected at the joints so as to pack compactly.

4. The heeling of a ship by the force of the wind.

1888 *Scribner's Mag.* May 526/1 Every bit of that water came in through the hatch at the time of the knock-down. **1926** H. HOWARD *Yacht 'Alice'* 13 Raised deck amidships which gives excellent room below, increases the structural strength and adds greatly to her stability and righting moment in case of a knockdown. **1951** H. I. CHAPELLE *Amer. Small Sailing Craft* 242 Such a maneuver takes room and also might lead to a knockdown when the boa pays off, as she has no way on. **1973** J. R. L. ANDERSON *Death on Rocks* xi. 201 Anthea had seen our knockdown... They stood by us until it was clear that we were not going to sink.

5. An introduction. *U.S.*, *Austral.*, and *N.Z. slang.*

1865 'D. Rattlehead' *Adventures of Fudge Fumble* v. 61, I asked the young man if he would go down some night and give me a 'knock down' to the family, and Miss Kate, more especially. **1885** 'Phudge Phumble' *Adventures Greenhorn in Gotham* 39 He loved Lucy at first sight and couldn't help it. So he managed to get a knock down to her. **1896** Ade *Artie* iii. 24 Take me over and gi' me a knock down to the queen in the corner. **1916** C. J. Dennis *Songs Sentimental Bloke* 125 *Knock-down*, a formal introduction. **1930** *National Education* (N.Z.) May 197/2, I heard one young fellow ask another to 'give him a knockdown to that tart in the green skirt'. I gathered that he was asking for an introduction to a young lady!! **1937** J. Weidman *I can get it for you Wholesale* xvi. 156 'Meet the stable,' he said, waving his hand to take in the girls.. 'You want a knockdown to something?' **1945** *Chicago Daily News* 7 Sept. 31/3, I know her well! I'll sell you a knockdown to her for two-bits. **1946** F. Sargeson *That Summer* 66 He called me over and gave me a knock-down, and she was certainly the goods. **1974** *Telegraph* (Brisbane) 28 May 24/1, I think you should meet Fred. And maybe Bert, too. So here's for the knock-down.

knocked (nɒkt), *ppl. a.* [f. Knock *v.* + -ed[1].]

1. Struck, hit, beaten, etc.: see Knock *v.*

† ***knocked bear***, barley beaten in a stone mortar in order to remove the hulls (*Sc. Obs.*). ***knocked knees***, knees turning inwards: cf. Knock-kneed. Also with adverbs as ***knocked-down, -up***, etc.: see Knock *v.* II.

c **1537** *Thersites* in Hazl. *Dodsley* I. 405 Thou shalt have knocked bread and ill-fare. **1583** *Leg. Bp. St. Androis* 467 Knocked beir, Herbis to the pot, and all sic geir. **1784** J. Barry in *Lect. Paint.* ii. (1848) 94 Knocked or baker knees. **1890** Boldrewood *Col. Reformer* (1891) 257 His.. knocked-up horses showed.. the effects of a long journey.

2. knocked-down. In the form of a number of separate parts that require to be assembled.

1776 *Rhode Isl. Col. Rec.* (1862) VII. 571 Shaken or knocked down casks. **1908** *Sears, Roebuck Catal.* 371/1 The patent knocked down construction.. give [*sic*] this splendid rocker additional strength and rigidity and permit its shipment in a package 33 inches long. **1950** *Engineering* 3 Feb. 139/2 For carriage in merchant vessels all vehicles.. should possess a 'knocked-down' height of less than 7 ft. 9 in. **1960** *Times Rev. Industry* July 74/1 Cars.. imported.. in completely knocked down packs. **1971** *Timber Trades Jrnl.* 14 Aug. 58/1 Filters in a new 'knocked down' kit form.

knockel, obs. form of Knuckle.

'knock-'em-'down, 'knockem,down. [A phrase used as a name.] A stick with a coconut or the like stuck on it to be aimed at.

1828 J. Bee *Pict. Lond.* 263 The charms of nine pins—whether they be skittles, knock-em-down, bowl-and-tip, dutch-pins, or the more sturdy four-corners. **1847** R. Brown in *Mem.* vii. (1866) 126 The fair and whirligigs and knockemdowns. **1870** *Daily News* 4 June, At the deserted knock-'em-down grounds the sticks stood in melancholy rows, protesting against the public contempt for cocoa nuts.

knocker ('nɒkə(r)). [f. Knock *v.* + -er[1].]

1. a. One who or that which knocks; *esp.* one who knocks at a door in order to gain admittance; also = *knocker down* (see 5).

1388 Wyclif *Pref. Ep. Jerome* viii, To the askere me ȝyueth, and to the knockere me openeth. *c* **1425** *Found. St. Bartholomew's* 5 The asker.. schall resceyue, the seker shall fynde, and the rynger or knokker shall entre. **1552** Huloet, Knocker, *percussor, pulsator*. **1652** Sparke *Scintilla Altaris* (1663) 103 Lest with those untimely knockers at the bride-chamber door, we.. be repulsed. **1821** Byron *Juan* iii. xxxiv, Rocks bewitch'd that open to the knockers. **1888** *Pall Mall G.* 20 Apr. 11/2 Cardiff sent up two boxers. .. The more terrible.. eventually succumbed to a talented Irishman, who knocked out the would be knocker.

b. A spirit or goblin imagined to dwell in mines, and to indicate the presence of ore by knocking.

1747 Hooson *Miner's Dict.* L ij b, Miners say that the Knocker is some Being that Inhabits in the.. Hollows of the Earth. **1885** *Chamb. Jrnl.* II. 371/2 In the Cardigan mines, the knockers are still heard, indicating where a rich lode may be expected. **1898** Watts-Dunton *Aylwin* iii. (1899) 24 She had not only heard but seen these knockers. They were thick-set dwarfs.

c. *slang.* A person of 'striking' appearance, or who moves others to admiration. (Cf. Knock *v.* 2 c, and Stunner.)

1612 Field *Woman a Weather-cocke* i. C ij, You should be a Knocker then by the Mothers side. **1620** Middleton *Chaste Maid* ii. ii, They're pretty children both, but here's a wench Will be a knocker. **1664** Cotton *Scarron.* 88 That old Knocker good Anchises.

d. A knock-down blow. *rare.*

1674 N. Fairfax *Bulk & Selv.* 96 The backstroke will be sure to give him a knocker. **1842** *Newcastle Song Bk.* 148 (E.D.D.) He lifted up his great long airm, Me soul he gave him sec a knocker.

e. A fault-finder, one who is addicted to captious criticism. (Cf. Knock *v.* 2 f.) *colloq.* (orig. *U.S.*).

1898 in Wentworth & Flexner *Dict. Amer. Slang* (1960) 308/2 That pack of knockers and snapping curs. **1901** [see Knock *v.* 2 f]. **1911** *Daily Colonist* (Victoria, B.C.) 22 Apr. 4/2 The Cranbrook Herald says that the 'pestilential knocker' has been doing his best to injure the Southeast Kootenay by misrepresenting the condition of a party of English settlers. **1923** J. Moses *Beyond City Gates* 154 The 'knocker' of his home town is, on this line of deduction, a 'knocker' of his Empire, a destroyer of thought, labour, and enterprise. **1928** *Sunday Express* 18 Mar. 5/2 All the knockers were there,.. yearning to find fault. **1956** W. H. Whyte *Organization Man* (1957) ix. 124 This system virtually ensures that the over-zealous or the 'knocker' type of man will not get ahead. **1958** *Times Lit. Suppl.* 24 Jan. 37/3 Today it would be difficult to get together such a team of 'knockers' as Harold Stearns did for his *Civilization in the United States*. Cheerfulness has been creeping in among the intelligentsia. **1962** M. Harris in P. Coleman *Austral. Civilization* 57 It is said that Australians are 'knockers'; that is, they gain pleasure from seeing superiority in talent, intellect or energy reduced to the scale of average mediocrity. **1969** *Telegraph* (Brisbane) 5 Dec. 3/2 Knockers are people who identify the ordinary Australian bloke as an easy-going, irresponsible oaf who spends more time drinking and arguing with his mates than working. **1972** *Shooting Times & Country Mag.* 1 July 26/3 Today the 'knockers' seem to delight in slamming anything British.

2. a. An appendage, usually of iron or brass, fastned to a door, and hinged so that it may be made to strike against a metal plate, to attract the attention of those within. (The most usual sense; cf. Knock *v.* 1.)

1598 Florio, *Picchiatoio*, a hammer to knocke at a doore with, a striker, a knocker. **1709** Steele *Tatler* No. 77 ⁋2 One could hardly find a Knocker at a Door in a whole Street after a Midnight Expedition of these *Beaux Esprits*. **1791** Mrs. Radclife *Rom. Forest* ii, La Motte,.. advanced to the gate and lifted a massy knocker. **1863** Geo. Eliot *Romola* xviii, Tito found the heavy iron knocker on the door thickly bound round with wool. **1898** J. T. Fowler *Durham Cath.* 63 The famous bronze knocker on the great north door.

Comb. **1844** J. T. Hewlett *Parsons & W.* vi, Knocker-wrenching and sign-removing were in vogue in my day.

† b. *colloq.* or *slang.* A kind of bob or pendant to a wig. *Obs.*

1818 *La Belle Assemblée* XVII. No. 106. 27 The physicians with their great wigs had disappeared, and had given place to those who wore a wig with a knocker. **1837** *New Monthly Mag.* XLIX. 550 Pig-tails and 'knockers' superseded the ponderous 'clubs'.

c. Phr. ***up to the knocker***: in good condition; in the height of fashion; 'up to the mark'. *slang.*

1844 Selby *London by Night* i. ii, *Jack.* How do you feel? *Ned.* Not quite up to the knocker. **1896** *Westm. Gaz.* 24 Dec. 1/3 We was dressed up to the knocker.

d. *Austral.* and *N.Z.* (See quots.)

1933 L. G. D. Acland in *Press* (Christchurch, N.Z.) 4 Nov. 15/7 *Knocker*, a small leather pad fixed near the heel of shears to keep the blades from closing too far. **1938** R. M. Burdon *High Country* viii. 84 A piece of rawhide known as a knocker is now used to prevent the shears clashing when closed, but before this was introduced the clack and snap of steel meeting steel was a noise inseparable from any busy shearing shed. **1941** Baker *Dict. Austral. Slang* 42 *Knocker*, a leather pad fixed near the heel of a pair of hand shears to prevent the blades closing too deeply. **1959** H. P. Tritton *Time means Tucker* 31/1 Shears do not click. The gullets of the blades are filled with soft wood, or sometimes with cork. These are called 'knockers', and they stop the heels of the blade from meeting. **1965** J. S. Gunn *Terminol. Shearing Industry* i. 34 *Knockers*, small pads, usually of leather or softwood, inset near the heel of hand shears. These stopped jarring and prevented the blades from closing too far and cutting the shearer's hand... It is likely that the name developed because they knocked together, but it could be a misspelling of 'nock'.

e. One who buys from, or sells to, persons at their residences; a door-to-door salesman; also, the action of selling (etc.) from door to door. Phr. ***on the knocker*** (and varr.), (engaged in buying from, selling to, or canvassing) from door to door; also, (obtained) on credit.

1934 P. Allingham *Cheapjack* xiii. 166 A 'knocker-worker' is one who sells things at people's front doors. *Ibid.* xv. 186 'The knocker's the only game in the winter' said London Joe. **1936** *Evening News* 11 Dec. 11/1 A valued and regular lady customer drives up.. and.. orders petrol.. finds she has left her handbag at home... The hand.. yells out: 'Oi, there's a lidy 'ere wants some juice on the knocker!' **1959** *Listener* 7 May 802/2 That record of progress in Blackpool shows what can be done if we work, in the first place, as our canvassers say, on the knocker. **1959** G. Savage *Antique Collector's Handbk.* 156 'Knockers' are jewellery and antique dealers who operate by calling from door to door in search of something to buy, and their purchases are sold to larger dealers. **1960** A. Prior in *Pick of Today's Short Stories* XI. 185 If I kept getting as much jewellery for him on the knocker then perhaps he wouldn't have to sell. **1963** J. F. Straker *Final Witness* viii. 81 Once she got a whole pile of stuff on the knocker, and then the firm came and took it back. **1967** *Sun* 17 July 7/2 The 'knocker boys'.. trick old ladies into parting with family heirlooms for a fraction of their value. **1968** M. Allingham *Cargo of Eagles* ix. 116 I've worked the knocker if you know what that means—the door-to-door selling racket. **1970** *Sunday Times* 18 Jan. 37 A knocker was a specially trained salesman working, not under the authority and generally not in the pay of a district sales agent, but for the company itself, out of the Dayton executive offices.

f. *pl.* The female breasts. *vulgar.*

1941 J. Smiley *Hash House Lingo* 25 Fix the knockers—look at the nice breasts on that woman. **1948** N. Mailer *Naked & Dead* (1949) iii. ii. 484 Look at the knockers on her, Murray says. **1967** J. Kennaway *Some Gorgeous Accident* i. 15 She was slight.. but with great little knockers—breasts being for mothers. **1970** *Private Eye* 11 Sept. 16 Hello, luv! Phew, look at them knockers!! **1972** M. J. Bosse *Incident at Naha* 24 I'm jealous. She has those big knockers, and I'm afraid you like them.

† 3. A castanet: cf. Knacker *sb.*[1] 2. *Obs.*

1648 Gage *West Ind.* xi. (1655) 37 Capering and dancing with their castannettas, or knockers on their fingers.

4. 'An attachment in a flour-bolt to jar the frame and shake the flour from the meshes of the bolting-cloth' (Knight *Dict. Mech.* 1875).

5. With adverbs, as ***knocker-down***, also = Knock-down B. 1; ***knocker-off***, (*a*) = Knock-off A 1.; (*b*) *Underworld slang*, a thief; ***knocker-up***, a person who goes round the streets in the early morning to awaken people.

1611 Cotgr., *Assommeur*, a knocker, feller, or beater, downe. **1638** Ford *Lady's Trial* i. i, A taker-up, Rather indeed a knocker-down. **1688** R. Holme *Armoury* iii. 315/1 The Axe, which is the right form of the Butchers Knocker Down. **1697** *Praise Yorksh. Ale* (Craven Gloss.), We've ale also that is called knocker-down. **1861** E. Waugh *Lake Country* 223 (E.D.D.) That curious Lancashire character the 'knocker-up'. **1875** Knight *Dict. Mech.*, *Knocker-off.* (*Knitting.*) A wheel with projections to raise the loop over the top of the needle and discharge it therefrom. **1884** *Pall Mall G.* 14 Oct. 3/2 The stock in trade of the 'knocker-up' consists of a long pole.. with pieces of wire at the end. This pole is raised to the bedroom, and the wires are rattled against the window pane. Knockers-up charge 2*d.* a week for this service. **1926** E. Wallace *Door with Seven Locks* iii. 28 Tommy Cawler had been a notorious 'knocker-off' of motor-cars. **1952** 'J. Henry' *Who lie in Gaol* iv. 61 They are mostly house-breakers and petty thieves, or 'knockers-off' in prison parlance.

knockered ('nɒkəd), *a.* [See -ed[2].] Of a house door: fitted with a knocker.

1921 *United Free Ch. Miss. Rec.* May 137/1 We entered by those massive brass-studded and knockered doors. **1928** *Daily Tel.* 24 Apr. 12/7 Knockered front doors and curtained windows.

knocking ('nɒkɪŋ), *vbl. sb.* [-ing[1].]

1. a. The action of the verb Knock, q.v.

a **1340** Hampole *Psalter* lxi. 8 In knokynge of brest. *c* **1500** *Adam Bel* 226 Who is there nowe, sayde the porter, That maketh all this knocking? **1546** *Supplic. Poore Commons* (E.E.T.S.) 63 Lightyng of candels to images, knockyng and knelyng to them. **1605** Shaks. *Macb.* ii. ii. 74 Wake Duncan with thy knocking: I would thou could'st. **1662** Stillingfl. *Orig. Sacr.* iii. ii. §17 There is no such knocking of particles. **1762** Foote *Orator* ii. Wks. 1799 I. 210 Certain thumpings, knockings, scratchings. **1845** M. Pattison *Ess.* (1889) I. 22 Roused by a loud and continued knocking at the door of the house. **1899** J. Perry *Steam Engine* ii. 30 Knocking or Back-lash.—It will be noticed that however good may be the fit of a brass to a pin, when the forces between them are suddenly reversed, there is a blow. **1903** M. P. Bale *Gas & Oil Engine Managem.* iv. 61 Knocking may also arise from the key of the flywheel becoming loose. **1928** [see Decoke *v.*]. **1946** *Mod. Petroleum Technol.* (Inst. Petroleum) 245 All reciprocating petrol engines, if run on unsuitable fuel, will produce a characteristic noise known as knocking, the quality of the sound varying from a sharp pink to a low thud according to the design of the engine and the composition of the fuel. **1971** *Guardian* 13 Dec. 1/4 Steam injection could eliminate 'knocking' on unleaded fuel even in high compression engines.

b. With adverbs: see Knock *v.* II. (Also *attrib.*)

1398 Trevisa *Barth. De P.R.* vii. v. (MS. Bodl.) lf. 49/2 Grysbating and knokking togedres of teeþ. **1768–74** Tucker *Lt. Nat.* (1834) II. 472 It seems.. probable.. that bowing the knee answers to the very vulgar expression of knocking under. **1840** *N.Z. Jrnl.* 1 Aug. 183/1 Any one coming out must expect to have a good knocking about. **1868** in Hughes *Tom Brown* (ed. 6) Pref., The old delusion.. that knocking about will turn a timid body into a bold one. **1897** *Organ Voicing & Tuning* 9 A knocking-up cup, similar in form to the cone... It is of great substance, and, therefore, heavy, that it may the more readily effect its mission, namely, that of 'knocking up' or reducing the wind-hole of the pipe. **1905** *Westm. Gaz.* 19 Aug. 15/2 It is always the brim that matters in one's knocking-about hat. **1922** A. E. Crawley *Lawn Tennis Do's & Don'ts* 42 As in many other games, it is not normal to get into your stroke at once; hence the need of a few minutes' knocking-up before a game. **1924** F. G. Lowe *Lawn Tennis* 10 When a new stroke has been learnt.. it is an excellent idea to practise it against a wall until it becomes perfect. This 'knocking up' will also materially improve footwork and quicken up the player. **1970** *Country Life* 20 Aug. 469/3 (*caption*) 'Knocking-up' slate in front of a miner's house.. Co. Durham. **1973** *Oxf. Mag.* 4 May 9/2 *Knocking-up* is notoriously not done in America, even by tennis players trying to warm up their partners before a match.

c. knocking-off: (i) = Knock-off *sb.* 2; also (in full ***knocking-off time***), the time laid down for the end of a spell of work.

1886 in *Amer. Speech* (1950) XXV. 35/1 The entire mill is kept on operation long after knocking off.. to make up for time lost during the day. **1887** in *Ibid.*, Saturday evening last, just about knocking off time. **1894** in *Leeds Mercury Weekly Suppl.* 11 Aug. (E.D.D.). **1922** C. E. Montague *Disenchantment* ix. 123 He.. knocked off work for the day. There was no knocking off for the army. **1944** *R.A.F. Jrnl.* Aug. 292 At knocking-off time.. the hooter sounds and everyone climbs thankfully out of their overalls. **1958** *Times* 14 Apr. 6/1 It is not all *that* difficult to control tea-breaks, knocking-off times or shift changes without upsetting your employees. **1974** N. Freeling *Dressing of Diamond* 45 Another cubic metre to shift before knocking-off time.

(ii) *Spinning.* Automatic stopping of the bobbin and flyer frames when a sufficient length of yarn has been wound on to the bobbin.

1883 H. E. Walmsley *Cotton Spinning* 15 See that the saddles and weights are accurate, and that both front and back knocking-off motions are in perfect working order. **1901** —— *Cotton Spinning* II. iii. 67 It is still more difficult to invent a motion that will prevent tenters from doffing bobbins before knocking-off does take place. **1908** H. Priestman *Princ. Woollen Spinning* x. 282 If a mule were empty, and were run with the knocking-off gear out of action,.. the rollers would revolve at all kinds of varying speeds. **1927** T. Thornley *Cotton Spinning* (ed. 4) iii. 61 This completes the knocking-off motion and the lap may now be doffed.

(iii) *Weaving.* Automatic stopping of the loom when the shuttle fails to reach the box.

1912 T. Roberts *Tappet & Dobby Looms* ix. 198 In order to reduce the vibration and strain on the various parts of the loom when knocking-off takes place, strong springs.. are employed which serve as cushions for the frogs. **1935** J. W. Hutchinson *Mod. Looms* xxix. 265 The sudden knocking-

off of the loom may crack the cast iron brushes on the sword pin.

d. knocking over. *Machine-knitting.* = KNOCK-OVER.

*a*1877 KNIGHT *Dict. Mech.* II. 1237/1 The stripping or knocking-over wheel.. then throws the old loops entirely over the tops of the needles. **1964** H. WIGNALL *Knitting* ii. 28 The needle now moves to its lowest position drawing the new loop through the fabric loop which is now cast off. On the original Lee knitting frame this called for physical effort and this action was called knocking over.

e. Phr. ***the last knockings***, the last earnings; so ***to be on the last knockings***, to approach the end of one's employment or earnings.

1939 H. HODGE *Cab, Sir?* iii. 31, I.. have left it late, and come in 'at the last knockings'. **1958** F. NORMAN *Bang to Rights* III. 137 When I was on the last knockings I tried to get my bird out earning again.

2. *pl.* **a.** (See quot. 1678.) **b.** *Mining.* Ore that has been broken with a hammer before being crushed. **c.** Small pieces broken off from stone by hammering or chiseling.

1678 *Phil. Trans.* XII. 1063 A third sort of Salt we have which we call Knockings, which doth candy on the Stailes of the Barrow. **1747** HOOSON *Miner's Dict.* P ij, To break the Knockings, and crush them to Knockbark, to make the Ore merchantable. **1875** KNIGHT *Dict. Mech.* 1240/1 The sorting of lead ore by the sieve develops three qualities, *knockings, riddlings*, and *fell*. The former are large scraps, which are picked out.

3. *Comb.*, as ***knocking-bucker*** (see BUCKER^2), ***-mell, -mill, -room, -stone, -trough***: see quots.

1686 PLOT *Staffordsh.* 166 Three sorts, viz. round Ore, small Ore, and Smithum; the two last whereof are first beaten to pieces with an instrument called a *Knocking-bucker. **1847–78** HALLIWELL, **Knocking-mell*, a large wooden hammer used for bruising barley. **1858** *N. & Q.* 2nd Ser. VI. 8 A strong knockin-mell or wooden pestle. **1727–41** CHAMBERS *Cycl.*, *Stamping-mill*, or **knocking-mill*, an engine used in the tin-works, to bruise the ore small. **1887** N. D. DAVIS *Cavaliers & Roundheads Barbados* 9 The pots were removed to the *Knocking Room. Here they were knocked with force against the ground, causing the sugar to come out in a loaf. **1805** RAMSAY *Scot. in 18th C.* (1888) II. ii. 70 Its place was supplied by knocked bear. Every family had therefore its *knocking-stone. **1825** BROCKETT, **Knocking-trough*, a conical trough in which the rind is beat off barley with a mallet.

ˈknocking, *ppl. a.* [f. as prec. + -ING^2.]

a. That knocks (see the verb); †*fig.* violent, forcible, 'thumping'; 'knock-down', clinching, decisive.

1597 A. M. tr. *Guillemeau's Fr. Chirurg.* 17 b/1 Prickinge, knockinge, or beatinge payne. **1624** GEE *Foot out of Snare* v. 33 Heere is a knocking and long-lasting lie, worthy to be nailed vpon a post or pillory. **1711** SWIFT *Jrnl. to Stella* Lett. 1767 III. 269 The lords.. they say, are preparing some knocking addresses. **1732** POPE *Ep. Cobham* 236 Still to his wench he crawls on knocking knees.

b. ***knocking copy***, advertising which claims that the product of another manufacturer is inferior to one's own. (Cf. KNOCK *v.* 2 f.)

1958 *Times* 1 July 11/5 Certain types of announcement covering such things as.. politically and religiously controversial statements, 'knocking' copy, and so on. **1960** *Guardian* 19 Dec. 3/2 In advertising, the pamphlet advocates the ending of the 'no knocking copy rule', which restricts competition by preventing one advertiser from 'fairly disparaging' another's product. **1966** G. N. LEECH *Eng. in Advertising* iv. 37 'Knocking copy', designed to discredit competing products, offends against the principle of 'positiveness' mentioned earlier, and is besides considered bad form. **1969** *Listener* 23 Jan. 127/3 Knocking copy means advertisements which point out clearly that one brand is better than another brand.

ˈknocking-shop. *slang.* [Cf. KNOCK *v.* 2 d and *Eng. Dial. Dict.* s.v. *knocking-house*.] A brothel.

1860 HOTTEN *Dict. Slang* (ed. 2) 166 *Knocking-shop*, a brothel, or disreputable house frequented by prostitutes. **1938** 'J. SPENSER' *Crime against Soc.* xiii. 126 She might wonder if you hadn't been gettin' scragged in a knockin' shop for not payin' yer dues. **1945** E. WAUGH *Brideshead Revisited* 300 This eye-sore.. always reminds me of one of the costlier knocking-shops. **1959** 'O. MILLS' *Stairway to Murder* xiv. 149 I'm a clean-living man... I wouldn't go to any back-street knocking shop. **1969** L. KENNEDY *Very Lovely People* ii. 111 Yes, it seems that some of the girls are running a knocking-shop on the side. **1971** B. W. ALDISS *Soldier Erect* 115 Somewhere there must be a woman whose longings corresponded to mine. Perhaps she could be found, that unknown She, even within the confines of a knocking shop.

knock-knee (ˈnɒkniː). [f. KNOCK *v.* + KNEE *sb.*] *pl.* Knees that knock together in walking from inward curvature of the legs. Also *sing.* the condition of being knock-kneed.

1827 HONE *Every-day Bk.* II. 857 With knock-knees, and a.. large head. **1879** *St. George's Hosp. Rep.* IX. 614 Knock-knee.. treated by the long-continued application of splints.

ˈknock-kneed, *a.* [f. prec. + -ED^2.] **a.** Having the legs bent inwards so that the knees knock together in walking. (The opposite of *bandy-legged*.)

1774 in *Maryland Hist. Mag.* (1911) VI. 41 Charles Blundell, an Englishman,.. a very slender made fellow much knock-kneed, with light brown hair very short. **1806** W. TAYLOR in *Ann. Rev.* IV. 720 Parents, whose children from bad nursing are become knock-kneed. **1838** DICKENS *O. Twist* xlii, Those long-limbed, knock-kneed, shambling, bony people. **1862** SALA *Seven Sons* I. vii. 142 The knock-kneed horse.

b. *fig.* Halting; feeble.

1865 DICKENS *Mut. Fr.* III. iv, It was constitutionally a knock-knee'd mind. **1887** SAINTSBURY *Hist. Elizab. Lit.* i. 5 So stumbling and knock-kneed is his [Wyatt's] verse. **1898** *Westm. Gaz.* 7 Dec. 4/1 There are no shambling, knock-kneed verses.

knock-knock: see KNOCK-.

knockle, obs. variant of KNUCKLE.

ˈknockless, *a.* [See -LESS.] **a.** *nonce-wd.* That enters without knocking on a door. **b.** Of an engine: free from knock (KNOCK *sb.*^{1} 1 c).

1907 W. DE MORGAN *Alice-for-Short* xlvii. 500 Alice was interrupted by the advent of the doctor, knockless but with musical boots. **1928** *Daily Chron.* 9 Aug. 11 (Advt.), A 'knockless', livelier engine; reduced vibration and less wear and tear of engine parts.

ˈknock-me-ˈdown, *a.* and *sb.* *colloq.*

A. *adj.* Such as to knock one down (*lit.* or *fig.*); violent, riotous; overbearing, defiant; prostrating, overpowering.

1760 FOOTE *Minor* I. Wks. 1830 I. 35 No knock-me-down doings in my house. **1848** J. H. NEWMAN *Loss & Gain* II. xviii. (1858) 250 He's so positive, so knock-me-down. **1863** OUIDA *Held in Bondage* (1870) 104 The overbearing, knock-me-down Marchioness.. who gave the law to everybody. **1896** *Allbutt's Syst. Med.* I. 691 The term 'knock-me-down fever' (applied sometimes to dengue). **1922** JOYCE *Ulysses* 300 And Bloom, of course, with his knockmedown cigar putting on swank with his lardy face. **1944** DYLAN THOMAS *Let.* 31 Dec. (1966) 270, I haven't read more than a scattered few of the poems.. stopping with delight.. at many knock-me-down lines. **1958** *Times Lit. Suppl.* 26 Dec. 757/1 Its current number deals with the very subject.. and it does so in a brisk, knock-me-down way which is extremely refreshing. **1967** *Listener* 16 Feb. 235/1 It was not yet fashionable for poets to present themselves as knock-me-down sales representatives of verse.

B. *sb.* = KNOCK-DOWN B. 1.

1756 W. TOLDERVY *Hist. Two Orphans* II. 112. **1828** *Craven Dial.*, *Knock-me-down*, strong ale. **1892** *Daily News* 3 Aug. 6/1 A savant who muddled my poor brains with geological knock-me-downs which he declares will be heard in Section C.

ˈknock-ˈoff, *sb.* and *a.*

A. *sb.* **1.** A contrivance for knocking something off, or point at which something is knocked off.

1875 KNIGHT *Dict. Mech.* 1240/1 *Knock off* (*Knitting-machine*), the piece which, at the proper moment, removes the loops from the tier of needles. **1883** GRESLEY *Gloss. Coal Mining Terms*, *Knock off*. (1) The point upon an engine plane at which the set is disconnected from the rope, or where a jockey comes into play. (2) A joint for disconnecting the bucket sword from the pump rods.

2. The act of leaving off one's work or occupation; the signal for doing this. See sense 1 of the adj.

1902 *Daily Chron.* 13 June 6/3 Just at that moment the officer in charge gave what is technically known as the 'knock-off', or the signal to discontinue the play of water on the building. **1948** D. BALLANTYNE *Cunninghams* (1963) i. 13 From early morning to morning smoko, to lunch, to afternoon smoko, then to knockoff.

3. *slang.* A robbery; *concr.* (see quot. 1963); phr. ***on the knock-off***, engaged in stealing.

1936 J. CURTIS *Gilt Kid* x. 100 They [*sc.* gloves].. gave away the fact that he was still on the knock-off. **1963** *Austral. T.V. Times* 18 Apr. 10/2 *Knock-off*, loot or illegally found goods. **1969** J. GARDNER *Complete State of Death* vi. 94 The really profitable knock-offs, like the Train Robbery.

4. A copy or reproduction of a design, e.g. of a textile, china, etc. *U.S.*

1966 *N.Y. Times* 25 Jan. 44 Copying designs to sell for less has a name in the industry. It is called the 'knockoff'. **1970** *Washington Post* 30 Sept. B. 14/1 People who appreciate genuine pate de foie gras.. might like to serve it on a decently designed plate, and not on a knock off.. of 18th Century English china. **1971** *Time* 25 Jan. 38 [Coco] Chanel had long since refused to join the cabal of Paris designers who tried to prevent style piracy... Private customers paid $700 for the original; buyers, intent on knockoffs, paid close to $1,500.

B. *adj.* **1.** ***knock-off time***, time to 'knock off' or leave off work. Also ***knock-off signal, whistle***, etc. See sense 2 of the sb.

1899 F. T. BULLEN *Log of Sea-waif* 108 It was 'knock-off' time. **1902** *Daily Chron.* 13 June 6/3 After the 'knock-off' signal had been given. **1947** K. TENNANT *Lost Haven* xvi. 249 The knock-off whistle blew at the mill.

2. a. *Machine-knitting.* ***knock-off lap*** (see quot. 1957).

1884 W. T. ROWLETT tr. *Willkomm's Technol. Framework Knitting* I. ii. 102 In the second lap.. the loops are simply taken back into the throats of the sinkers with the old stitches. This second lap is called a 'knock off lap', because it does not form stitches. *Ibid.*, The purpose of such knock off laps is manifestly to bring as much thread as possible into the fabric, which thus becomes thick and soft, and suitable for underclothing or linings for shoes, &c. **1926** J. CHAMBERLAIN *Hosiery, Yarns & Fabrics* vii. 173 As a lap is formed without pressing and clearing the knock-off lap it is in every sense a parallel to the tuck-stitch of ordinary knitting. **1952** D. F. PALING *Warp Knitting Technol.* viii. 106 Knock-off laps can be used in conjunction with striped warps to produce purely vertical stripes on the face of the fabric without any overlap between adjacent colours. **1957** *Textile Terms & Definitions* (Textile Inst.) (ed. 3) 55 *Knock-off lap* (*warp knitting*), a length (or lengths) of yarn received by a needle and not pulled through the loop of the previous course.

b. Designating a mechanical part (e.g. of a vehicle) that may be removed or disengaged by knocking.

1896 W. E. HIPKINS *Wire Rope* 47 They are connected and disconnected.. by means of suitable couplings. When the rope is under considerable tension 'knock-off' hooks have to be used. **1905** C. HURST *Valves & Valve-Gearing* (ed. 4) vii. 130 In high-class Corliss engines it is often necessary to fit an automatic knock-off gear in connection with the governer, so that should the speed of the engine exceed or fall below certain limits the trips will be thrown into such a position that will prevent engagement of the catches,.. the engine thus [being] brought to rest. **1958** *Sunday Times* 26 Jan. 27/1, I would recommend that knock-off hubs are fitted in future; they can be changed in thirty seconds. **1963** A. F. W. COULSON et al. *Man. Cotton Spinning* II. II. v. 122 The doffing cycle commences when the desired length of lap has been made; the measuring plate ..on the measuring motion releases the spring-loaded knock-off lever, which.. disengages the brake on the rack-shaft. **1967** *Guardian* 12 Sept. 3/4 Knock-off wheels with proper splined hub and graduated spokes.

c. *Spinning.* Associated with or bringing about knocking off (KNOCKING *vbl. sb.* 1 c(ii)).

1927 T. THORNLEY *Cotton Spinning* (ed. 4) iii. 56 It is customary to apply a full lap automatic stop motion.. to automatically stop the feed and delivery parts every time a lap is sufficiently full... The favourite.. knock-off motion is worked from one of the calenders on the Hunter cog principle.

knock-on, *sb.* and *a.* [f. the vbl. phr. *to knock on*: see KNOCK *v.*, esp. sense 13.] **A.** *sb.* (ˈ*knock-*ˈ*on.*) *Rugby Football.* The act of knocking the ball forward or 'on': see KNOCK *v.* 13.

1845, 1881 [see PUNT *sb.*^{3} 1]. **1888** *Daily News* 5 Oct. 5/2 A knock-on gives a free kick. **1905** *Daily Chron.* 29 Dec. 9/5 The alleged incident of the referee in the New Zealanders–Newport match sounding the whistle when a knock-on by an All Black proved to the advantage of the Welsh team was.. contrary to law. **1960** *Times* 11 Jan. 17/1 A body of dedicated Scots thought that France's last [try] followed a knock-on. **1974** *Sunday Tel.* 23 June 35/7 The referee did not see the knock-on.

B. *adj.* (ˈ*knock-on.*) **1.** *Physics.* Ejected, produced, or caused as a result of the collision of an atomic or sub-atomic particle with an atom.

1940 *Nature* 13 July 65/2 A few particles of energy greater than 10^8 ev... were therefore considered to be mesons responsible for the production of 'knock on' showers. **1953** *Jrnl. Brit. Interplanetary Soc.* XII. 203 These [*sc.* nuclear fragments] may be accompanied by knock-on particles (or shower particles) which also move with velocities comparable to the original particle. **1967** A. H. COTTRELL *Introd. Metall.* ii. 14 There are three main types of radiation damage... (3) Knock-on damage in which atoms inside the material are knocked from their sites by the impacts of nuclear particles. **1971** *Nature* 6 Aug. 422/2 Knock-on protons produced by 3MeV neutrons would not.. produce visible flashes.

2. Designating a mechanical part (e.g. of a vehicle) that may be attached or fastened by knocking. Also *absol.*

1952 *Motor Manual* (ed. 34) vii. 150 There are two principal types of wheel fastening. The less common, known as the knock-on, has at its centre a large nut with two lugs or projections. *Ibid.* p. x, Knock on wheel fastening. **1959** *Times* 12 Sept. 3/3 Moss's car has knock-on wheels. **1965** *Punch* 20 Oct. 567/2 The imitation knock-on hubs had been knocked off by genuine thieves. **1967** I. HAMILTON *Man with Brown Paper Face* ii. 24 The strengthened knock-on wire wheels were original M.G.

ˈknock-ˈout, *a.* and *sb.*

A. *adj.* Characterized by 'knocking out' (see KNOCK *v.* 14); *spec.* **a.** of, or in connexion with, an auction sale (see quots.); **b.** of a blow, etc.: Such as to disable or knock out of the contest; also *fig.*

a. 1818 *Chron.* in *Ann. Reg.* 373/1 Combinations, by a set of men who attend real sales, and drive, by various means, respectable purchasers away, purchase at their own price, and afterwards privately sell the same, under a form of public auction, termed 'Knock-out Sales'. **1895** W. ROBERTS *Bk.-Hunter in London* iii. 121 This auction [1726] is interesting.. as being the genesis of the knock-out system. **1896** FARMER *Slang* s.v., The lot is knocked down to the knock-out bidders.

b. 1898 *Times* 24 Dec. 8/5 The effect of the 'knock-out' blow,.. delivered, not straight from the shoulder, but sideways and on the tip of the chin, was to produce unconsciousness. **1938** *Ann. Reg. 1937* 90 The task of the Government.. was to make impossible the greatest danger to civilisation—the knock-out blow. **1955** *Times* 9 May 19/1 A new fashion has, however, arisen—the cry for knock-out competition in private enterprise.

c. Designating (a system used in) a competition or tournament in which the defeated competitors in each round are eliminated.

1896 W. BROADFOOT et al. *Billiards* i. 40 Scarcely a dozen really important handicaps on the old 'knock-out' principle have been played in the last twenty years. **1897** K. S. RANJITSINHJI *Jubilee Bk. Cricket* 281 The first elevens meet in a series of matches, played on the 'knock-out' system. **1920** *Motor Cycle* 22 July 114/1 Competitors in the motor cycle events were run off in pairs on the knock-out principle. **1921** E. B. TURNER in E. H. D. Sewell *Rugby Football* xiv. 244 The competition was run on 'knock-out' lines as it is at the present time, the teams which entered being drawn in ties, and those left in after each round being again paired by lot until only two were left in the final. **1928** *Daily Mail* 25 July 16/4 The singles championship held by the Ayton Tennis Club.. was played on the knock-out principle. **1953** E. SMITH *Guide Eng. Traditions* 94 Besides the League there

is also a 'knock-out' competition for the English Cup. **1955** *Times* 18 Aug. 4/3 Leeds, Huddersfield, Halifax, and Hull will be expected to go a long way in the various knock-out competitions again. **1966** *Listener* 30 June 936/1 The British Isles are to be invaded by football fans from all over the world bent on seeing the knock-out international competition known as the World Cup. **1974** *Country Life* 2 May 1070/2 By mid-summer we are left with 32 [cricket] clubs who fight it out on a knockout basis.

d. ***knock-out drops*** (also occas. *sing.*), a liquid drug of which drops are put into liquor to render a person unconscious or stupefied (e.g. in order to rob him). Also *fig. colloq.* (orig. *U.S.*).

1895 J. S. Wood *Yale Yarns* 152 Our dandy team played a logy, tired sort of game, as if each man had been given knock-out drops, and we all felt blue! **1904** Ex-Inspector Elliott *Tracking Glasgow Criminals* 23 The use of drugs.. or what is more familiarly known in criminal circles as 'knock-out' drops is common enough in most cities. What is known as 'knock-out' drops is chloral hydrate, and from fifteen to thirty grains of it produces a sleep that lasts three hours. **1926** J. Black *You can't Win* xii. 152 Here I learned to beware the crafty shanghaier with his knockout drops. **1955** 'N. Shute' *Requiem for Wren* viii. 242 About midnight ..I took one of Aunt Ellen's things. It was a knock-out drop all right because I didn't wake up till half past nine. **1958** *Sunday Times* 10 Aug. 8/3 The first [film] was a typical knock-out drop—a study of 'inter-specific inter-dependence'.

e. *Mech.* Designating or pertaining to a knock-out (see B. 5 a, b).

1907 *Installation News* Nov. 6/2 The 'knock-out' principle as applied to junction boxes. **1925** Hodkin & Cousen *Textbk. Glass Technol.* xxxii. 439 The knock-out arm moves outwards, so that the bottle falls off the mould base into the trough. **1946** Du Bois & Pribble *Plastics Mold Engin.* iii. 104 As the press continues to open, the pin attached to the knockout bar rises and pushes the wedge, with molded piece attached, up out of the cavity. **1955** *Die Design Handbk.* (Amer. Soc. Tool Engineers) v. 23 Knockout slugs should be readily removable from the outside of the box; so care should be exercised to see that the material is pierced from the proper side. *Ibid.*, Knockout dies. **1963** H. R. Clauser *Encycl. Engin. Materials* 104/1 If necessary knockout pins are cast into the mold.

f. *Founding.* Used in or pertaining to the knocking out of castings and flasks (see knock *v.* 14 j).

1942 *Engineering* 6 Mar. 195/2 With continuous casting with a mould conveyor, there was great difficulty in adjusting the whole conveyor for uniform speed, so that, when the castings came to the knock-out grid, they would be cool enough for knocking out. **1958** *Ann. Rep. Chief Inspector of Factories on Industr. Health 1957* 15 in *Parl. Papers 1958–9* (Cmnd. 558) XIII. 183 Various types of exhaust systems used to control dust and fumes at central knock-out positions..have been examined. **1973** *Steel Castings Abstr.* XXII. 24 (*heading*) Improving the knock-out properties of silicate bonded sands.

g. *colloq.* Of a person or thing: of overwhelming or surpassing quality. Cf. B. 4.

1966 *Crescendo* Aug. 41 (Advt.), Chasing a real knockout sound? You'll find the most rewarding instrument..is the Hammond organ. **1968** *Listener* 5 Sept. 307/2 The wit and repartee of the DJ... 'Hi there— it's great to be with you and welcome to another knock-out show.'

B. *sb.* **1.** The practice of 'knocking out' at auction sales or in similar transactions; a knock-out sale; also, one of the confederates who 'knock out': see A. a, knock *v.* 14 c.

1854 *Illustr. Lond. News* 7 Oct. 342/2 A knock-out is a combination of bidders at a sale, who, deputing one to bid, save the increase of price which further competition causes, and subsequently have a private sale among themselves. **1864** *East London Observer* 25 June, Witness said a knock-out was where a sum of money was divided among the contractors, and the officials generally,..out of the contract price over and above what ought to be paid for the work... Those who did not get the work had money for putting in tenders so that the favored one got it, and the officials also. **1883** A. Lang in *Longm. Mag.* II. 522 The auctioneer put up lot after lot, and Blinton plainly saw that the whole affair was a knock-out.

2. A knock-out blow: see A. b. Also *transf.*

1887 in *Amer. Speech* (1950) XXV. 35/1 A knock-out was no more possible with these youngsters. **1891** *Sporting Life* 25 Mar. 7/3 The Barrier man was nearly helpless, and Choynski tried frantically to pull himself together for one good knock out. **1894** Morrison *Tales Mean Streets, Three Rounds* 138 It was a hard fight, and both the lads were swinging the right again and again for a knock-out. **1895** G. B. Shaw *Let.* 17 Sept. (1965) 560 Got up [after cycling smash] within the prescribed ten seconds, but had subsequently to admit knock-out. *a* **1918** W. Owen *Coll. Poems* (1963) 71 One of us got the knock-out, blown to chops. **1944** *Return to Attack* (Army Board, N.Z.) 23/2 The tanks, which had suffered three knockouts from 88-millimetre guns.

3. *Polo.* (See quot.) *U.S.*

1894 *Rules of Amer. Polo Assoc.* in M. H. Hayes *Mod. Polo* (1896) 314 When the ball goes out ends, the side defending that goal is entitled to a knock out from the point at which it crossed the line. When the player having the knock out causes unnecessary delay, the Referee may throw a ball on the field and call play.

4. *colloq.* A person or thing of overwhelming or surpassing quality. Cf. A. g.

1892 *Idler* June 549 'E's a knockout! **1898** J. D. Brayshaw *Slum Silhouettes* 28 Got a rippin' good voice, ain't he? It's a knock-out. **1908** *London Mag.* June 473/2 The tent is a knock-out. **1918** A. Quiller-Couch *Foe-Farrell* xi. 163 The view from the top is a knock-out. **1920** Wodehouse *Jill the Reckless* (1922) xiv. 213 He had a respect for Wally's opinion, for Wally had written 'Follow the Girl' and look what a knock-out that had been. **1935** A. Huxley *Let.* *c* May (1969) 394 The greatest knockout is the 'Assumption' at S. Vincente, where there are also some small pictures of absolutely staggering beauty. **1953** R. Lehmann *Echoing Grove* 190 A *whizzing* beauty! Really but really a knock-out. **1958** *Daily Mail* 1 Sept. 10/8 The clever, wicked face of Emlyn Williams expressing the words of Dylan Thomas was once again a knock-out. **1970** A. Cameron et al. *Computers & O.E. Concordances* 24 I've got a version of *Paradise Lost* that is a knock-out. **1971** *Daily Colonist* (Victoria, B.C.) 11 June 2/1 I'm sick to death of women's liberation. I don't see any real knockouts running around with those placards, just a bunch of unhappy uggas. Nobody would want to spend an evening—much less a lifetime—with them.

5. a. *Mech.* A device for 'knocking out' or ejecting something, esp. from a mould or die.

1893 *Funk's Stand. Dict.*, *Knock-out*, a device for throwing out finished work from a punching- or stamping-machine. **1896** O. Smith *Press-Working of Metals* xii. 243 There is a distinct class of ejecting press- or die-attachments known by the general name of 'knockouts', or sometimes and if limited to the lower die, as 'knockups'. **1915** F. D. Jones *Diemaking & Die Design* vii. 282 The mechanically operated knockout..applied to a punch press..operates more satisfactorily than a rubber bumper. **1919** F. A. Stanley *Punches & Dies* vii. 152 The die is made..with a knock-out which ejects the work after the trimming operation. **1946** Du Bois & Pribble *Plastics Mold Engin.* ix. 371 The knockout pins may be made as sleeve knockouts working over a core pin. **1960** Eary & Reed *Techniques Pressworking Sheet Metal* xviii. 377 Basically, there are two main types of knockouts: the spring knockout and the solid knockout.

b. A part of a box or other article designed to be forced out to form a hole.

[**1907**: implied in A. e above.] **1939** H. P. Richter *Pract. Electr. Wiring* x. 124 Around the sides [of the outlet box] and in the bottom are found 'knockouts'—sections of metal that can be easily knocked out to form openings for wire to enter. The metal is completely severed around these sections except at one small point. **1955** *Die Design Handbk.* (Amer. Soc. Tool Engineers) v. 23 Typical single and double dies for producing knockouts in conduit boxes, enclosing boxes, and similar products. **1962** *Gloss. Terms Glass Industry* (*B.S.I.*) 36 *Button* (cap, knockout), a portion of a piece of pressed ware so designed that it can be knocked out or off to make a hole.

c. *Founding.* The process of separating a casting from the flask and sand in which it was made (cf. knock *v.* 14 j); the place where, or equipment with which, this is carried out.

1942 *Engineering* 6 Mar. 195/3 The method of dealing with mould-making, closing and knock-out must depend upon the nature of the product. *Ibid.*, The cooling of the sand on its way from the knock-out to the reconditioning mill presented some difficulty. **1955** H. E. Crivan in W. C. Newell *Casting of Steel* vi. 227 Mechanical jolt knock-outs are in operation. **1972** P. R. Beeley *Foundry Technol.* viii. 417 The interval before knockout is important from the points of view of moulding box utilisation and of the temperature of the sand in the system. **1973** *Steel Castings Abstr.* XXII. 11 The redesign of castings..and alterations to the plant layout, including the knock-out, have reduced the labour required.

6. A 'knock-out' competition: see A. c.

1928 *Observer* 4 Mar. 22 Pembroke..have won the finals ..of both the football 'knock-outs'. **1959** A. Wesker *Roots* iii. 66 The fireman's whist drive. Won seven'n six in the knockout.

'knock-over. *Machine-knitting.* [f. vbl. phr. *to knock over* (knock *v.* 15 c).] The act or process of causing a stitch to pass over the head of the needle on which it was held. Also *attrib.*

1952 D. F. Paling *Warp Knitting Technol.* i. 6 A forward movement of the sinker bar combined with a further downward movement of the needle bar ensures a gradual knock-over. **1964** H. Wignall *Knitting* ii. 29 The frame needle goes down to its first knock-over. *Ibid.* 39 When the needle and point are locked together below the top of the knock-over bit they rise and the needle passes through the transferred loop.

'knock-up, *sb.* and *a.* **A.** *sb.* A practice or casual game at lawn tennis, squash rackets, etc.

1884 E. W. Hamilton *Diary* 4 May (1972) II. 609 In the afternoon had a little 'knock up' at lawn tennis. **1922** F. Hamilton *P.J.: Secret Service Boy* iii. 89 Shall we have a little knock-up against the wall of the stables? It doesn't make half a bad squash court. **1930** W. S. Maugham *Breadwinner* ii. 73 Why don't you and Dinah go and have a knock-up? **1946** *Penguin New Writing* XXVIII. 29 Expecting to find the three of them having a knock-up while they waited for him. **1973** G. Mitchell *Murder of Busy Lizzie* xiv. 159 'I think I *will* go to bed.'.. 'All right, unless you'd like a knock-up at table tennis first.'

B. *adj.* Designating a knock-up: see above.

1928 *Weekly Dispatch* 24 June 21/7 Many of the world-famous players engaged in final 'knock-up' games at Wimbledon yesterday.

knockwurst, var. knackwurst.

knocle, knokel, etc., obs. ff. knuckle.

knod, knodden, obs. or dial. pa. pple. of knead *v.*

knödel ('knœdəl). Also **knoedel**. Pl. **-s**, ‖**-n.** [Ger.] In Germany, a type of dumpling. Cf. knaidel.

1827 M. Wilmot *Jrnl.* 23 July in *More Lett.* (1935) 276 [H]oltzknecht Knödel—Woodcutter's dumpling, a sort of rice moistened with butter..fried..in little round balls. **1873** *German Nat. Cookery for Eng. Kitchens* x. 176 'Klösse' or 'Knödeln'... The bread used for them must be light, and without crust, either grated, crumbled, or soaked in cold milk or water. **1948** R. Sysonby *Cook Bk.* (ed. 2) 144 Mariller Knoedel... Wrap some peeled fresh apricots each in a square of the paste... Drop the dumplings into.. boiling water. **1968** L. Deighton *Continental Dossier* §45 Baden-Württemberg... 'Knödel' ('dumplings') are famous. **1971** A. R. Daniel *Baker's Dict.* (ed. 2) 108/2 *Knödel*, Bavarian name for a special kind of small dumpling.

Knoevenagel ('knœvənɑːgəl). *Chem.* The name of Emil *Knoevenagel* (1865–1921), German chemist, used *attrib.* and occas. in the possessive to designate various reactions in organic chemistry, *esp.* the reaction between an aldehyde or ketone and malonic acid or a related compound containing active hydrogen, catalysed by ammonia or an amine, to yield an acid with the group –CH·CH·COOH.

1907 J. B. Cohen *Org. Chem. Adv. Students* I. vii. 285 (*heading*) Knoevenagel's reaction. **1931** *Jrnl. Chem. Soc.* 745 Catalytic action..effected by the salts of bases with mineral acids in the malonic acid condensation and the Knoevenagel reaction generally. **1938** G. H. Richter *Textbk. Org. Chem.* xvi. 289 The Knoevenagel reaction is the condensation of the carbonyl group of aldehydes and ketones with *active methylene* hydrogens; the reaction takes place in the presence of primary and secondary amines, especially diethylamine or piperidine. Knoevenagel was the first to point out the great catalytic power of ammonia and amines for this type of condensation. **1967** *Organic Reactions* XV. 204 (*heading*) The Knoevenagel condensation. **1969** R. C. Denney *Named Org. Reactions* 52 An interesting development has been the use of the Knoevenagel condensation to increase the chain length of sugars.

knok(e, knokk(e, obs. ff. knock.

knoledge, -lege, obs. forms of knowledge.

Knole sofa (nəʊl 'səʊfə). [f. the name of the prototype at *Knole* Park, Kent, *c* 1605–20.] A sofa designed in the style of an early 17th-century model, having adjustable sides that may be lowered to make it into a day-bed. So ***Knole couch, settee.***

[**1868** C. L. Eastlake *Hints Household Taste* vi. 142 The sofa at Knole..is an example of thoroughly good design... The sides can be raised or lowered..thus enabling the sofa to be used as a couch or a settee, at pleasure.] **1942** R. King *Design in Evil* xxi. 207 A Knole sofa sheened with lemon-colored damask. **1943** D. Welch *Maiden Voy.* xv. 122 Two fringed and tasselled Knole settees. **1945** *Burlington Mag.* LXXXVI. 114/1 The famous Knole couch..is the first comfortable type of couch that was made in England. **1951** A. Christie *They came to Baghdad* ii. 17 That Knole settee ..in electric blue satin.

knoll (nəʊl), *sb.*[1] Forms: 1–2 **cnol(l**, 3–5 **knol**, 5 (9 *dial.*) **knolle**, 7 (9 *dial.*) **knowle**, (**nowle**), 7–9 **knole, knowl**, 6– **knoll**. [OE. *cnoll* hill-top, cop, summit, hillock, from same root as Du. *knol*, formerly *knolle* clod, ball, turnip, Ger. *knollen*, MHG. *knolle* clod, lump, knot, tuber; Norw. *knoll*, Sw. *knöl*, Da. dial. *knöl, knöld* hillock.

OE. *cnoll* might represent an OTeut. **knoð-lo*, with usual assimilation of *ðl* to *ll*, and thus be radically connected with knot. Cf. for the form Ger. *knödel* dumpling.]

1. The summit or rounded top of a mountain or hill (*obs.* exc. *dial.*).

c **888** K. Ælfred *Boeth.* xii, Se þe wille fæst hus timbrian, ne sceall he hit no settan upon þone hehstan cnol. *c* **1000** Ælfric *Gen.* viii. 5 On þam teoþan monþe æteowodon þæra munta cnollas. *c* **1250** *Gen. & Ex.* 4129 At munt nemboc on ðat knol fasga,.. Saȝ ðe lond of promission. **1706** Phillips, *Knoll*, the top of a Hill, a Word much us'd in the West; especially in Hereford-shire. **1825** Brockett, *Knoll, Knowl, Knowe*, the top of a hill, a bare rounded hillock.

b. *Naut.* 'The head of a bank, or the most elevated part of a submarine shoal' (Smyth *Sailor's Word-bk.* 1867).

2. A small hill or eminence of more or less rounded form; a hillock, a mound.

c **1000** *Ags. Ps.* (Th.) xli. 7 On þam lytlan cnolle, þe Ermon hatte. *c* **1200** *Trin. Coll. Hom.* 111 He cumeð stridende from dune to dune, and ouer strit þe cnolles [L. *colles*]. *a* **1300** *E.E. Psalter* lxiv. 13 [lxv. 12] Gird sal be knolles with faines. **1513** Douglas *Æneis* v. ii. 5 Eneas..Syne spak thir wordis on a knollis hycht. **1523** Fitzherb. *Husb.* §128 To cary grauell & fyll it vp as hygh as yͤ other knolles be. **1604** Edmonds *Observ. Cæsar's Comm.* 84 A knowle exceedingly fortified. **1628** Le Grys tr. *Barclay's Argenis* 82 A Knole fitly placed..for a Cittadell. **1686** Evelyn *Diary* 23 Oct., It stands on a knowle..insensibly rising. **1780** A. Young *Tour Irel.* I. 92 A knole of lawn rises among them. **1816** W. Smith *Strata Ident.* 21 Rounded low hills, which are called knolls or knowls. **1865** Geikie *Scen. & Geol. Scot.* vii. 153 Hills and crags of every size, down to mere hummocks and knolls. **1884** Q. Victoria *More Leaves* 64 At half-past two we five ladies lunched on a heathery knoll.

†**b.** (See quot. and cf. hummock 1 b.) *Obs.*

1772 J. G. W. De Brahm *Hist. Georgia* (1849) 45 The second Species of Pine..is only met with on the Knowls (small Islands in Swamps).

†**3.** A swelling upon the skin; = knob *sb.* 1 b.

1499 *Promp. Parv.* 280/1 (Pynson) Knolle (*K.*, *H.* Knobbe) of a mannys hande or in another part of him.., *callus*.

†**4.** A turnip. *Obs. dial.*

1669 Worlidge *Syst. Agric.* (1681) 328 *Knolls*, Turnips. **1674** Ray *S. & E.C. Words* 70 *Knolles*; Turneps, *Kent*.

5. A lump, a large piece. *Sc.*

1829 Hogg *Sheph. Cal.* II. 19 The auld wife..brought a knoll o' butter like ane's nieve.

knoll (nəʊl), *sb.*² Also 5 knolle, 7 knole. [Formed with next, from same root as KNELL, perh. with later onomatopœic modification.]

1. An act, or the action, of 'knolling' or tolling a bell; the sound of a large bell. *arch.* and *dial.*

1379 *Mem. Ripon* (Surtees) III. 100 Pro factura campanæ del knoll. **1497** BP. ALCOCK *Mons Perfect.* E j, At the fyrst knolle of yᵉ bell they departe fro theyr celles. **1615** G. SANDYS *Trav.* IV. 233 The watch of one Fort giues two or three Knoles with a bell. **1795–1814** WORDSW. *Excurs.* VI. 801 The bells..before The last hath ceased its solitary knoll.

†**2.** A large bell; a church-bell. *Obs.*

1379 *Mem. Ripon* (Surtees) III. 99 In viij stanges meremii sarrandis..pro le knoll [*margin*, Custus del klank knoll]. **1412–13** *Durham Acc. Rolls* 403 Pro reparacione del knoll.

knoll (nəʊl), *v.* Forms: 5 knollen, (-yn), 5–6 knolle, 6–7 knol, 6–8, 9 *dial.* knowl, (8 knowll), 7– knoll. [Goes with KNOLL *sb.*²]

1. *trans.* To ring, toll (a bell); = KNELL *v.* 2. Also *fig.* Now *arch.* and *dial.*

1467 *Eng. Gilds* 401 As often as they shallen here the grete belle of the parisshe of Seint Androwe to be knolled..and after that rongen out. *a* **1485** *Promp. Parv.* 280/2 (MS. S.) Knollyn, *pulso.* **1605** SHAKS. *Macb.* V. viii. 50, I would not wish them to a fairer death; And so his Knell is knoll'd. **1871** BROWNING *Pr. Hohenst.* 1942 So do the old enthroned decrepitudes Acknowledge, in the rotten hearts of them, Their knell is knolled. **1877** *N.W. Linc. Gloss.*, *Knowl*, to knoll; to toll a bell.

2. *intr.* Of a bell or clock: To sound, ring a knell, toll; = KNELL *v.* 3. Now chiefly *dial.*

1582 MUNDAY *Eng. Rom. Life* in *Harl. Misc.* (Malh.) II. 179 Soon after, the bell knowleth againe, when as the students..walk to the Romayne colledge. **1600** SHAKS. *A.Y.L.* II. vii. 114 Where bels haue knoll'd to Church. **1612** *Two Noble K.* I. i, Remember that your fame Knolls in the ear o' the world. **1815** BYRON *Parisina* xv, For a departing being's soul The death-hymn peals and the hollow bells knoll. **1876** *Whitby Gloss.*, *Knoll*, to toll as a bell. **1886** *S.W. Linc. Gloss.* s.v., I heard the bell knoll a piece sin [= a bit since].

b. *trans.* To ring a knell for. **c.** To ring or toll out.

1597 SHAKS. *2 Hen. IV*, I. i. 103 His Tongue Sounds euer after as a sullen Bell Remembered, knolling a departing Friend. **1842** TENNYSON *Gardener's D.* 180 All that night I heard The heavy clocks knolling the drowsy hours.

3. *trans.* To summon by the sound of a bell.

1600 SHAKS. *A.Y.L.* II. vii. 121 We haue seene better dayes, And haue with holy bell bin knowld to Church. **1820** BYRON *Juan* V. l, They heard No Christian knoll to table. **1844** LYTTON tr. *Schiller's Fridolin* 90 From the church-tower clangs the bell Knolling souls that would repent To the Holy Sacrament. **1894** *Times* 17 July 9/3 Every woman who ever has been knolled to church.

Hence **'knolling** *vbl. sb.*; also **'knoller**, one who knolls.

1480 *Waterf. Arch.* in *10th Rep. Hist. MSS. Comm.* App. v. 315 The knollyng of the bell in the chappell. **1538** *Injunctions* in Strype *Eccl. Mem.* (1721) I. xlii. 322 The Knoling of Aves after service..henceforth to be left. **1611** COTGR., *Carillonneur*, a chymer, or knowler, of bels. **1837–9** HALLAM *Hist. Lit.* (1847) III. 122 The knolling of Church bells. **1877** LEE *Gloss. Liturg.*, *Knoller*, 2. a sexton or sacristan.

knolled (nəʊld), *a.* Also 7 nol'd. [f. KNOLL *sb.*¹ + -ED².] Having a knoll or knolls: in parasynthetic combs., as ***high-knolled***.

1602 MARSTON *Antonio's Rev.* IV. iii, I have a mount of mischiefe clogs my soule, As waightie as the high-nol'd Appenine.

knolly ('nəʊlɪ), *a.* [f. KNOLL *sb.*¹ + -Y.] Full of or abounding in knolls or hillocks.

1821 CLARE *Vill. Minstr.* II. 68 While Dobbin..patient goes to gate or knowly brake. **1870** MISS BROUGHTON *Red as Rose* I. 151 A grassy, knolly park.

Knoop (nu:p, knu:p). The name of Frederick *Knoop* (1878–1943), U.S. instrument-maker, used *attrib.* with reference to an indentation test devised by him, in which hardness is measured by the size of the indentation produced in a substance by a pyramidal diamond indenter of specified shape under a known load.

The pronunc. (knu:p) is used by members of the Knoop family.

1940 *Metals & Alloys* Sept. 292/1 The article is a description of the Knoop Indenter, a new instrument for determining the micro-hardness of thin layers of metals. **1945** *Amer. Mineralogist* XXX. 595 The Knoop hardness of gypsum is approximately 32 to 45 or more, depending on orientation. **1961** E. CAMERON *Ore Microsc.* iv. 75 The Knoop hardness (*KV*) is given by the formula *KV* (in kg/mm²) = 14230 × P/l^2 where *P* is the test load in grams, and *l* is the long diagonal of the indentation in 0·001 mm. **1971** *Nature* 14 Nov. 661/1 A study..on anisotropy in the hardness of crystals using the Knoop indenter. **1971** *Brit. Jrnl. Nutrition* XXVI. 234 The Knoop test of hardness..was applied to human nails.

knoop, dial. var. of KNOP *sb.*¹

knop (nɒp), *sb.*¹ Forms: α. 4–6 **knoppe**, 5–6 **knopp, knope**, (6 **noppe**), 5– **knop**; 9 (*dial.*) **knoop**. β. 4–6 **knappe**, (5 **cnap**), 6 **knapp**, (**knepp**), 5– **knap**, (7–8 **nap**). [ME. *knop* = OFris. *knop*, MDu. *cnoppe*, *cnop* (Du. *knop*), MLG. *knoppe* (hence Da. *knop*, Sw. *knopp*), OHG. *chnoph*, *chnopf* (G. *knopf* knob, head, knot, button, etc.) The form *knap* may repr. ON. *knapp-r* knob, stud, button (Sw. *knapp*, Da. *knap*), perh. cognate with OE. *cnæp*, KNAP *sb.*¹ The ulterior etymology is obscure.]

1. a. A small rounded protuberance, a knob (esp. one of an ornamental character, *e.g.* upon the stem of a chalice, a candlestick, etc.); a boss, stud, button, tassel, or the like; in *Arch.* = KNOB *sb.* 1 d. *Obs.* or *arch.* exc. in specific applications.

(Sometimes prob. a carved representation of a flower-bud; cf. 2 below.)

α. ? *a* **1366** CHAUCER *Rom. Rose* 1080 With a bend of gold tasseled, And knoppis fyne of gold enameled. **1455** in Rymer *Foedera* (1710) XI. 369 With Knopps and Tassells. **1483** *Cath. Angl.* 205/2 A knoppe of a scho, *bulla*. **1527** *Test. Ebor.* (Surtees) V. 225 Sex silver spones with knopis of oure Ladie. **1535** COVERDALE *Jer.* lii. 22 Vpon the rope were brasen knoppes. **1676** WORLIDGE *Cyder* (1691) 182 A knop at the end of a slender handle or stick. **1861** *Times* 12 July, The crown and the knops which adorn the turret were gilt by him. **1865** S. EVANS *Bro. Fabian* 105 Ornan..Unlooped the ruby knops Loosing her kirtle.

β. [*a* **1000** in Wr.-Wülcker 238/33 *Fibula*, cnæp, sigl, spennels.] **1362** LANGL. *P. Pl.* A. VII. 257 His cloke of Calabre, with..knappes of Gold. **1420** *E.E. Wills* (1882) 45 A becure of seluer y-keueryd, ..þe cnap of þe couercle ys an-amylyd with blewe. **1563–87** FOXE *A. & M.* (1596) 80/2 Scourge him then with whips..with knaps of lead at the ends. **1577** *Lanc. Wills* (1857) II. 92 Twelve silver spones with kneppes gilt wrought with a lyon. **1623** HART *Arraignm. Ur.* v. 27 To snatch and pull the naps of the coverlid. **17..** in Child *Ballads* VIII. 295/2 The naps of gold were bobbing bonnie.

b. A loop or tuft (often of different colour) formed in a strand of yarn for ornament. Also *attrib.* in ***knop yarn*** (see quots.).

1904 GOODCHILD & TWENEY *Technol. & Sci. Dict.*, Knop yarn. **1914** BARKER & MIDGLEY *Analysis Woven Fabrics* 272 *Knop yarn.*—A yarn upon which knops or lumps of yarn of one or more colours appear at intervals. **1929** *Encycl. Brit.* XXIII. 879/2 The knop yarn—in which knops are formed at any required intervals on an otherwise level thread by holding one thread tightly and allowing the second thread to run in slackly to form knops of the required size. **1964** *Which?* Sept. 284/2 *Knop or nub*, a compound yarn with lumps or balls of yarn at regular or irregular intervals. **1968** E. GALE *From Fibres to Fabrics* iv. 44 *Knop yarn.* Two threads are twisted together, with one at regular intervals being given in very rapidly so that it is wound round and round the first thread in the form of a hard knop or lump.

2. a. The bud of a flower; a compact or rounded flower-head or seed-vessel. (Cf. KNAPWEED.) *arch.*

α. **1388** WYCLIF *Num.* xvii. 8 Whanne knoppis weren greet, the blossoms hadden broke out. *c* **1440** *Promp. Parv.* 280/2 Knoppe, or bud of a tre. **1495** *Trevisa's Barth. De P.R.* XVII. cxxxvi. (W. de W.) 692 The fruyte of the rose is smalle rounde knoppes [*Bodl. MS.* knappes] and harde. **1508** DUNBAR *Gold. Targe* 22 The rosis yong, new spreding of thair knoppis. **1597** GERARDE *Herbal* II. xxv. §2. 217 At the top of the stalke growe small knops, from which come flowers. **1697** *Phil. Trans.* XIX. 793, I have..wondered..to see those little Snails..on the Knops and Branches of the Vine. **1871** G. M. HOPKINS *Jrnls. & Papers* (1959) 209 Then the knot or 'knoop' of buds some shut, some just gaping. **1894** R. BRIDGES *Shorter Poems* 97 The chestnut holds her gluey knops upthrust.

β. **1398** TREVISA *Barth. De P.R.* XVII. xxiv. (MS. Bodl.) lf. 196 b/1 þe cipresse..haþ leere knappes in stede of frute. **1578** LYTE *Dodoens* I. xxxii. 45 The floures..do likewise turne into little knappes, or heads. **1656** W. COLES *Art of Simpling* xii. 38 Some [seeds] grow in Knaps like Bottles, as Knap-weed. **1879** BRITTEN & HOLLAND *Plant-n.*, *Knap*, flowers of *Trifolium pratense*.

b. Hence, A popular name of Red Clover. *U.S.*

1897 BRITTEN & BROWN *Flora North States* II. 276 *Trifolium pratense*..Honeysuckle Clover, Knap, Suckles.

†**3. a.** The rounded protuberance formed by the front of the knee or the elbow-joint. *Obs.*

α. **14..** *Nominale* in Wr.-Wülcker 678/29 *Hoc internodium*, the knope of the kne. **1590** W. BURCH *MS. Scrap Bk.* in *Chapter Libr. Canterb. Cathedr.*, The Arme in lenghthe must com shorte of yᵉ knop of the kne.

β. **1652** *Burgh Rec. Glasgow* (Burgh Rec. Soc.) II. 242 The knap of hir elbow. **1734** *Act Crt. Session* in *N. & Q.* 3rd Ser. IV. 125/2 Heads, knaps, tongues, and marrow bones cut out by themselves. *c* **1817** HOGG *Tales & Sk.* IV. 146 His breeches came exactly to the knap of the knee.

b. A swelling upon the skin; a wart, pimple, etc.: = KNOB *sb.* 1 b. *Obs.*

1556–8 PHAER *Æneid* IV. L j, From a tender colt they take the knapp. **1562** TURNER *Baths* 4 It is good..for suche as have any knoppes or hard swellinges upon any membre. **1598** FLORIO, *Verruche*,..also wartes or knops of flesh rising in the bodie.

4. *attrib.* and *Comb.*, as **knop-fly** (*Angling*) = *knob-fly*; **knop-sedge**, the bur-reed, *Sparganium*.

1562 TURNER *Herbal* II. 143 b, It maye be called bede sedge or knop sedge. **1582** STANYHURST *Æneis* IV. (Arb.) 113 For to snip, in the foaling, from front of fillye the knap-knob. **1799** G. SMITH *Laboratory* II. 310 Knop-fly. Dubbing, of the down of an otter-cub.

knop (nɒp), **knap** (næp), *sb.*² *north. dial.* [Origin obscure.] A large wooden tub.

α. **1563** *Richmond Wills* (Surtees) 169 A kneadinge bassyn, a knoppe, a gielfatte. **1588** *Lanc. Wills* (1857) II. 75 The great brewinge knopp. **1614** *Inv.* in *Trans. Cumbld. & Westmld. Arch. Soc.* III. 114 One knopp one handle 2 salt pres dishes. **1802** in Anderson *Cumbld. Ball.* 51, I dung owre the knop.

β. **1614** *Inv.* in *Trans. Cumbld. & Westmld. Arch. Soc.* III. 114 In the butterye 3 barrells 2 staues one Knapp. **1821** *Blackw. Mag.* VIII. 432 But stoups are needed, tubs, and pails, and knaps.

†**knop**, *v. Obs.* [f. KNOP *sb.*¹]

1. *trans.* To furnish or adorn with knops; to stud.

c **1400** *Rom. Rose* 7260 High shoes knopped with dagges. **1483** *Cath. Angl.* 205/2 To Knoppe, *bullare*. **1505** *Ld. Treas. Acc. Scot.* (1901) III. 40 For ij pypanes blak silk to knop the said hat. **1539** in *Inv. R. Wardrobe* (1815) 52 Ane capparisone..bordourit with silvir and knoppit with silvir & yallow silk.

2. *intr.* To put forth 'knops', to bud. *Sc.*

a **1584** MONTGOMERIE *Cherrie & Slae* 40 Sum knopping, sum dropping Of balmie liquor sweit. *c* **1600** BUREL *Pilgr.* in Watson *Coll. Sc. Poems* (1706) II. 23 Ranie Orion, That dropit and knopit, Baith upon tre and stone.

knop, obs. form of KNAP *sb.*¹, *v.*¹

knopite ('nɒpaɪt, 'knɒpaɪt). *Min.* [ad. Sw. *knopit* (P. J. Holmquist 1894, in *Geol. För. Förh.* XVI. 73), f. the name of Adolf *Knop* (1828–93), Ger. mineralogist: see -ITE¹.] A variety of perofskite occurring in lead-grey crystals, in which calcium is partly replaced by cerium.

1896 *Mineral. Mag.* XI. 158 Minerals at first thought to be perofskite and dysanalyte are here described under the new name knopite. **1927** *Mineral. Abstr.* III. 412 Knopite, a mineral new to Canada, occurs sparingly in small bunches in a basic pegmatite. **1947** *Ibid.* X. 138 Knopite is here a rock-forming mineral of primary magmatic origin, in contrast to its other occurrences as a contact mineral or in pegmatite. **1962** W. A. DEER et al. *Rock-forming Min.* V. 50 A variety [of perovskite] rich in rare earths, chiefly cerium, has been called knopite... In addition to rare earths of the cerium group, the lanthanum group is usually present.

knopkierie: see KNOBKERRIE.

knopped (nɒpt, *poet.* 'nɒpɪd), *a.* [f. KNOP *sb.*¹ or *v.* + -ED.] **a.** Having knops; knobbed; bearing buds, or compact rounded flower-heads. ? *Obs.*

c **1394** *P. Pl. Crede* 424 Wiþ his knopped schon clouted full þykke. **1434** *E.E. Wills* (1882) 101 A litell basyn knopped. **1501** DOUGLAS *Pal. Hon.* Prol. 76 The knoppit syonis with leuis aggreabill. **1601** HOLLAND *Pliny* II. 447 With knopped Majoram or Sauorie. **1655** MOUFET & BENNET *Health's Improv.* (1746) 320 The unset Leek, or Maiden-leek, is not so hot as the knopped ones.

b. Formed into a knop or knob; knob-shaped; *spec.* of the stem of a glass.

1578 LYTE *Dodoens* II. xii. 161 Lyke to..Cyanus floures..in his Scaly knopped buttons. **1869** G. M. HOPKINS *Jrnls. & Papers* (1959) 193 A fine sunset..; along the earth-line a train of dark clouds of knopped or clustery make. **1960** H. HAYWARD *Antique Coll.* 158/2 Knopped stem, a type of stem found on 18th cent. drinking glasses composed of a varying number of knops. **1963** *Times* 30 Apr. 14/4 C. Davis bought ..a cylinder-knopped wine glass for £155. **1973** *Times Lit. Suppl.* 6 Apr. 374/5 There are knopped and wrythen wine glasses.

c. ***knopped yarn***, yarn ornamented with knops or tufts. See KNOP *sb.*¹ 1 b.

1911 *Encycl. Brit.* XXVIII. 906/2 *Knopped Yarn* is formed by twisting together several strands, one of which is at intervals delivered in greater lengths than the others, in order to allow a loop to be made.

knopper ('nɒpə(r)). Pl. **knoppern, knoppers.** [Ger., = gall-nut.] A kind of oak-gall caused by an insect of the genus *Cynips*, formerly used in tanning and dyeing.

1879 *Encycl. Brit.* X. 44/1 The 'knoppern' galls of *Cynips polycera*, Gir., are cones having the broad, slightly convex, upper surface surrounded with a toothed ridge. **1903** H. R. PROCTER *Princ. Leather Manuf.* xviii. 262 *Knoppern* are galls produced on the immature acorns of various species of oaks, principally *Q[uercus] Cerris* in Hungary... They..have been largely replaced by valonia. **1908** E. T. CONNOLD *Brit. Oak Galls* 143 *Cynips calicis*... 'The Knopper Gall'... It occurs principally on *Quercus pedunculata*, but also on *Q. sessiliflora*. **1953** F. N. HOWES *Vegetable Tanning Materials* xxxvii. 260 The best known European galls are those obtained from eastern Europe (the Balkans and adjoining regions), which are commonly known as 'knoppers' or 'knoppern' or 'acorn galls'... There are various kinds of knoppern recognized, such as those formerly obtained from Hungary, Bohemia, Dalmatia and Serbia.

knopple ('nɒp(ə)l), *v. rare*⁻¹. [? f. KNOBBLE *sb.* or KNOP *sb.*¹] *trans.* = KNOB *v.* 1.

1870 G. M. HOPKINS *Jrnls. & Papers* (1959) 201 Herds of towering pillow clouds, one great stack..was knoppled all over in fine snowy tufts and pencilled with bloom-shadow.

'knoppy, *a.* ? *Obs.* [f. KNOP *sb.*¹ + -Y. Cf. G. *knöpfig*.] Full of knops; knop-like; knobby.

1562 TURNER *Herbal* II. R, Polygonum..hath many knoppy ioyntes. **1578** LYTE *Dodoens* II. xvii. 167 Whan this seede is ripe, his knoppie head openeth. **1597** GERARDE *Herbal* II. clxv. 458 This kinde hath certaine knoppie tufts.

knopweed, obs. or dial. form of KNAPWEED.

knor, -re, knorry, obs. ff. KNUR, KNURRY.

knorcock, Anglicized form of next.

‖**'knorhan.** *Obs.* [Du. *knorhaan*, f. *knorren* to growl, snarl + *haan* cock.] A name of a S. African species of bustard: = KORAN².

1731 MEDLEY *Kolben's Cape G. Hope* II. 139 *The Knorhan.* Among the wild fowls at the Cape there is a sort of

birds, a male of which the Europeans there call *Knor-cock*; a female they call *Knor-hen*. **1777** G. Forster *Voy. round World* I. 85 The Knorhan, which is..the African bustard.

knorr (nɔːr). Also **knarr, knörr**. [ad. ON. *knörr* ship, merchant ship.] A mediæval type of ship of Northern Europe, having a single sail (see quots.).

1889 P. B. du Chaillu *Viking Age* II. xiii. 212 We find them [*sc.* trading ships] mentioned under their different names—viz., Knörr, Kugg, Byrding (ship of burden), Vistabyrding, [etc.]. **1932** C. M. Smith *Northmen of Adventure* xiv. 320 The round ships went under a variety of names. The largest class was the *knorr*. **1967** H. Harrison *Technicolor Time Machine* xi. 114 Where the dragon-prowed Viking ship was long and narrow, this *knorr* was wide and stood high out of the water—and was at least a hundred feet long. **1968** G. Jones *Hist. Vikings* III. ii. 188 Captain Folgar ..in 1932 took a replica of a 60-foot knörr across the Atlantic. **1971** S. E. Morison *European Discovery Amer., Northern Voys.* iii. 35 The Norse discoverers of Greenland and Vinland did not use a long Viking ship... There is ample evidence that they used the *knarr*, a beamy type propelled principally by one big square sail made of a coarse woolen cloth called 'wadmal', rigged with an additional sprit to set well close-hauled. **1973** *Country Life* 17 May 1373/2 A Knarr, the cargo ship in which the great [Viking] voyages to Greenland and North America were made.

knosp (nɒsp). *rare.* [ad. Ger. *knospe* a bud, boss, knob.] An architectural (or other) ornament in the form of a bud, or forming a bunch-like or rounded protuberance; a knop, knob, boss, stud.

1808 Scott *Marm.* v. Introd. iv, Ere from thy mural crown there fell The slightest knosp or pinnacle. **1820** —— *Abbot* xxxii, The black letter Bible..adorned with massive silver clasps and knosps. **1855** Milman *Lat. Chr.* xiv. viii. (1864) IX. 297 Prodigality of ornament, knosps, shrine work, corbels, gurgoyles.

Hence **knosped** (nɒspt, *poet.* ˈnɒspɪd) *a.*, furnished with knosps.

1818 Milman *Samor* 290 The iron or the knosped brass.

Knossian (ˈknɒsɪən, ˈknəʊ-), *a.* Also **Cnossian**. [f. Gr. Κνωσσός Knossos or Cnossos + -ian.] Of or pertaining to Knossos, a city in ancient Crete, where, according to classical tradition, King Minos ruled and kept the Minotaur in a labyrinth; historically, the centre of the Minoan civilization as revealed by the ruins of a vast labyrinthine palace (18th–14th centuries b.c.). Also as *sb.*

1894 A. J. Evans in *Jrnl. Hellenic Stud.* XIV. 283 The incised marks on the slabs of the Knôsian building do not.. stand alone. **1895** H. S. Jones tr. *Sel. Passages Anc. Writers* I. i. 4 The Knossians also possess the dance of Ariadne, a relief in white marble. **1900** A. J. Evans in *Ann. Brit. Sch. Athens* VI. 16 An artistic advance which..was not reached till the fifth century before our era, some eight or nine centuries later than the date of this Knossian fresco. *Ibid.* 59 Out of about 25 distinct signs..near parallels to about 6 occur in the Knossian linear series. **1909** —— *Scripta Minoa* I. i. iii. 21 A perfect clay bar of the same general class as some of those from the Knossian deposit..had been acquired... The first stage represented by the existing West Wing of the Knossian palace goes far back into the Second Middle Minoan Age. **1939** J. D. S. Pendlebury *Archaeol. Crete* iv. 180 L.M. II vases of Knossian fabric in L.M. I deposits at Pseira. **1950** G. E. Daniel *100 Yrs. Archaeol.* vi. 192 To the great Bronze Age civilisation which he discovered in Crete, Sir Arthur Evans gave the name Minoan... Other names were suggested, such as Knossian, Cretan, or Aegean. **1962** *Times* 21 Apr. 9/6 Deposits are 'telescoped', material of several Knossian periods being represented in a single layer of rubbish... It cannot be assigned..to any particular subdivision of the Knossian system. **1963** *Listener* 21 Mar. 495/1 The Cnossian ruler's contemporaries in Egypt.

knot (nɒt), *sb.*[1] Forms: 1 cnotta, 3 cnot, 3–5 cnotte, 3–7 knotte, 5–8 knott, 3– knot. [OE. *cnotta* = Du. *knot*, LG. *knütte*, MG. *knotte*, MHG. *knotze* knob, knot, etc.:—OTeut. **knutton-*, (whence knit *v.*); cf. OHG. *chnodo*, *chnoto* (MHG. *knode*, *knote*, G. *knoten*) :—OTeut. **knôpon-*, *knoðón-*, with variation of consonant due to difference of stress.

ON. had *knútr* knot, knob, *knúta* knucklebone (Sw. *knut* Da. *knude* knot), which may be connected with the above forms, but the difference in vowel makes difficulties. The relationship (if any) of ON. *knǫttr* (:—**knattu-z*) ball, and L. *nōdus* (perh. for *gnōdus*) knot, is also obscure.]

I. 1. a. An intertwining or complication of the parts of one or more ropes, cords, or strips of anything flexible enough, made for the purpose of fastening them together or to another object, or to prevent slipping, and secured by being drawn tight; a tie in a rope, necktie, etc.; also, a tangle accidentally drawn tight. ***to make, †knit,*** or ***tie a knot (in)***, to knot a piece of string or a handkerchief, esp. as a reminder. Also in allusions to the knot in a halter for hanging.

c **1000** Ælfric *Hom.* II. 28 He afunde..þa snode mid eallum cnottum swa fæste ȝewriðen swa heo ær wæs. *c* **1290** *Beket* 1445 in *S. Eng. Leg.* I. 148 Þe knottes gnowen al is flechs: a-boute bi eche side. **14..** *Chaucer's Sqr.'s T.* 663 (Lansd.) Bot I wil here nowe maake a knotte To þe time it come next to my lotte. *c* **1449** Pecock *Repr.* II. v. 166 Make a knot on his girdil. **1542–3** *Act 34 & 35 Hen. VIII*, c. 3 The bonde of euerywhiche faggotte to conteine three quarters of a yarde at the leaste, besyde the knotte. **1601** Shaks. *All's Well* IV. iii. 163 This is Mounsieur Parrolles the gallant militarist,..that had the whole theoricke of warre in the knot of his scarfe. **1631** R. Bolton *Comf. Affl. Consc.* (1635) 333 One knot in a thread will stay the Needle's Passage as well as five hundred. **1647** Cowley *Mistr.*, *The Tree* v, Go tye the dismal Knot (why shouldst thou live?). **1838** Thirlwall *Greece* II. xiv. 200 He tied sixty knots in a leathern thong, and bade them unfasten one every day, till the prescribed interval had expired. **1873** *Act 36 & 37 Vict.* c. 71 §39 Such mesh [in a net] shall not be less than one and a half inch from knot to knot.

b. Often with qualifying word, naming different forms of knots, as ***barber's k., bowline k., diamond k., draw-k., fisher's k., French k., granny's k., loop-k., reef-k., †riding k., running k., slip-k., surgeon's k., wall-k., water-k., weaver's k.***, etc.; for the more important of these, see the first element.

c **1320** *Sir Beues* (MS. A) 3220 On a towaile ȝhe made knotte riding, Aboute his nekke ȝhe hit prew. **1552** Huloet, Knotte whiche runneth to, called a rydynge knot, *capulum*. **1726** G. Roberts *4 Years Voy.* 112 And making a running bowling Knot on the End of another Rope, I cast it over. **1769** Falconer *Dict. Marine* (1789), *Knot*, a..knob formed on the extremity of a rope, by untwisting the ends..and interweaving them..amongst each other. There are several sorts, which differ in..form and size: the principal of these are the diamond-knot, the rose-knot, the wall-knot, or walnut. **1795** Hutton *Math. Dict.* s.v., Fig. 11, a *Barber's knot*, or a knot for cawls of wigs. **1813** J. Thomson *Lect. Inflam.* 267 We passed,..a crooked needle under the artery, threaded with a double waxed thread, part whereof we passed above the aperture in the vessel, and the other below, which were afterwards tied with a double knot called the surgeon's knot. **1860** *All Year Round* No. 66. 382 'Which knot?' asked Toby. 'Single or double wall, single or double diamond, Matthew Walker, spritsail-sheet, stopper, or shroud?' **1881** Hamersly *Naval Encycl.* 421 They [knots].. are named either from the manner in which they are made, or the use to which they are applied, as *stopper* knot, *diamond* knot, *double-diamond* knot, *single* and *double wall* knots, etc. *c* **1885** *Weldon's Pract. Needlework* III. 3/1 Flowers are mostly worked in satin stitch highly raised, embellished with French knots. **1899** W. G. P. Townsend *Embroidery* vi. 90 French Knots.—A very ancient stitch, much used by the Chinese for all kinds of elaborate embroidery.

†c. *Astron.* The star α Piscium, situated in the 'tie' of the lines or ribbons imagined to connect the two fishes in the constellation Pisces. *Obs.*

1551 Recorde *Cast. Knowl.* (1556) 267 The Fysshes, tyed by the tayles with a common Lyne:..and where those two lines are knitte togyther, there is one starre more, whiche is called the Knotte. **1727–41** Chambers *Cycl.* s.v. *Pisces*, That [star] next the knot in the north. line... 1st before the knot in the south. line.

2. a. Such a tie used or worn as an ornament or adjunct to a dress; a bow of ribbon; a cockade or epaulette; esp. in obs. phrase ***a suit of knots***.

Often with distinctive word prefixed: as *breast*, *shoulder*, *sword*, *top*, *true-love knot*, q.v.

a **1400–50** *Alexander* 4917 With cumly knottis & with koyntis & knopis of perle. **1552** Huloet, Knotte of a capbande, or hatbande, or lace. **1668** Etheredge *She would if she could* III. i, We will only fancy a suit of Knots or two at this shop. **1708** *Brit. Apollo* No. 75. 4/2 The Officers to wear ..a mourning Knot on their left Arm. **1713** Gay *Guard.* No. 149 ¶ 18 A lady of genius will give a genteel air to her whole dress by a well-fancied suit of knots. **1891** Mrs. Newman *Begun in Jest* I. 209 Her grey morning gown, with its soft frillings of lace and knots of pale, coral-coloured ribbon.

b. *Her.* (See quot. 1892.)

1828–40 Berry *Encycl. Her.* **1865** Kingsley *Herew.* Prel., The badge in the 'Wake Knot', in which..two monks' girdles are worked into the form of the letter W. **1892** Woodward & Burne *Heraldry* II. 585 Knots of particular form were not infrequently used as badges; *e.g.* the Stafford knot, the Bourchier knot, the Wake and Ormond knot; in all these the silk is twined having some resemblance to the initial letter of the family name. In the Bowen knot the allusion is double, it is formed of four *bows*, or loops, and each bears a resemblance to one form of the Greek letter B. Knots were also used to unite the badges of two families which had merged into one; or the badge of an office to a personal one.

3. a. *Naut.* A piece of knotted string fastened to the log-line, one of a series fixed at such intervals that the number of them that run out while the sand-glass is running indicates the ship's speed in nautical miles per hour; hence, each of the divisions so marked on the log-line, as a measure of the rate of motion of the ship (or of a current, etc.). Also *attrib.* with prefixed numeral = 'running (so many) knots'.

1633 T. James *Voy.* 24 It did runne two knots. **1669** Sturmy *Mariner's Mag.* IV. 146 The distance between every one of the Knots must be 50 Foot; as many of these as run out in half a Minute, so many Miles or Minutes the Ship saileth in an Hour. **1760–72** tr. *Juan & Ulloa's Voy.* (ed. 3) I. 9 The distance between the knots on the log-line should contain $\frac{1}{120}$ of a mile, supposing the glass to run exactly half a minute. **1840** R. H. Dana *Bef. Mast* xxvi. 87 A light wind ..carrying us at the rate of four or five knots. **1860** *Merc. Marine Mag.* VII. 169 A ten-knot breeze was blowing. **1900** *Daily News* 10 Jan. 5/1 A torpedo-boat destroyer..had made a record speed of $35\frac{1}{2}$ knots, which was almost exactly equal to 41 miles an hour.

b. Hence loosely used as if equivalent to 'nautical mile', in such phrases as *20 knots an hour*.

1748 *Anson's Voy.* I. iii. 24 The ship went ten knots an hour. **1772–84** Cook *Voy.* (1799) V. 1828 The strong tide, though even here it ran five knots an hour. **1833** Marryat *P. Simple* xxxviii, We were going twelve knots an hour, and running away from them as fast as we could.

c. ***at the rate of knots***, very fast, quickly. *colloq.*

1892 R. Wardon *Macpherson's Gully* vi. 40 When she's [*sc.* the Teremakau river has] got her back up, travellin' in a hurry, like—tearin' along at the rate o' knots like she is to-day—..she's got to be treated with all doo respeck. **1921** 'T. Collins' *Rigby's Romance* xxxii. 222, I went for it at the rate of knots, with the fire lathering along behind me roaring like fury. **1932** Kipling *Limits & Renewals* 80 A natty little grey and black self-driven coupé came from Brighton way at the rate of knots. **1941** Baker *N.Z. Slang* vi. 53 To travel at the rate of knots.

4. A definite quantity of thread, yarn, etc., varying with the commodity, being a certain number of coils tied by a knot.

c **1540** *Churchw. Acc. St. Dunstan's, Canterbury* (MS.) For a knott of sylke ijd. **1641** Best *Farm. Bks.* (Surtees) 16 A loose kinde of two plettes, which is usually sold for 3 half-pence and sometimes for 2^{d}. a knotte; there should bee in everie knotte 18 fathames. **1688** R. Holme *Armoury* III. vi. 288/2 A knot is a Hundred Threds round the Reel, at which place Housewives make a Katch, as some call it, or a Knot, or an Hank. **1875** Temple & Sheldon *Hist. Northfield, Mass.* 161 A run of yarn consisted of twenty knots, a knot was composed of forty threads, and a thread was seventy-four inches in length, or once round the reel.

5. More fully ***porter's knot***: 'A kind of double shoulder-pad, with a loop passing round the forehead, the whole roughly resembling a horse-collar, used by London market-porters for carrying their burdens' (*Cassell's Encycl. Dict.*).

(Perh. originally a rope tied or knotted into a loop.)

1719 D'Urfey *Pills* (1872) V. 75 Tom the Porter, Companion of the Pot, Who stands in the Street with his Rope and Knot. *c* **1737** in Boswell *Johnson* an. 1737 Mr Wilcox..eyed his robust frame attentively, and with a significant look, said, 'You had better buy a porter's knot'. **1840** Dickens *Barn. Rudge* xlix, Preceded by a man who carried the immense petition on a porter's knot through the lobby to the door of the House of Commons. **1866** *Daily Tel.* 12 Jan. 5/5 Fathers of families who should have carried porters' knots, so heavy was their fardel of toys.

6. A design or figure formed of crossing lines; an intricate flourish of the pen. ***†endless knot***, the five-pointed figure consisting of a continuous self-crossing line, otherwise called *pentacle*, *pentagram*, or *pentangle*.

13.. *Gaw. & Gr. Knt.* 630 Fyue poyntez, & vche lyne vmbe-lappez & loukez in oþer, & ay quere hit is endelez, & englych hit callen Ouer-al, as I here, þe endeles knot. **1638** Sir T. Herbert *Trav.* (ed. 2) 197 In blew, red, and yellow tinctures, commixt with Arabiq knots and letters. *a* **1680** Butler *Rem.* (1759) I. 210 As Scriveners take more Pains to learn the Slight Of making Knots, than all the Hands they write.

7. A flower-bed laid out in a fanciful or intricate design; also, more generally, Any laid-out garden plot; a ***flower-knot***. Now chiefly *dial.*

1494 Fabyan *Chron.* VII. ccxxxviii. 277 An howse wrought lyke vnto a knot in a garden, called a mase. **1502** *Acc.* in A. Amherst *Gardening* (1895) 84 For diligence in making knottes in the Duke's garden. Clypping of knottes, and sweeping the said garden. **1577** B. Googe *Heresbach's Husb.* (1586) 66 Basyell..is an hearbe that is used to be set in the middest of knottes,..for the excellent savour that it hath. **1622** Peacham *Compl. Gentl.* xix. (1634) 235 Here are the goodliest walkes in Europe, for the trees themselves are placed in curious knots as we use to set our herbes in gardens. **1667** H. More *Div. Dial.* II. v. (1713) 97 They do not water the Walks of the Garden, but only the Beds or Knots wherein the Flowers grow. **1737** G. Smith *Cur. Relat.* I. i. 49 The Borders of the Beds were lin'd with Box, and beautifully garnish'd with choice Flowers, as were the Knots, in each of which stood a handsome Pot of a choice foreign Plant. **1758** L. Temple *Sketches* 14 More pleasing and beautiful than that insipid, childish, uncomfortable Bauble called a Flower-knot. **1824** Miss Ferrier *Inher.* lxviii, I must see if my flower knots are arranged according to rule.

8. A central thickened meeting-point of lines, nerves, etc.; *esp.* in *Phys. Geog.*, an elevated point or region in which several mountain-chains meet.

1861 Herschel *Phys. Geog.* §144 The knot of Pasco, a great ganglion, as it were, of the system [of the Andes]. **1865** *Chambers' Encycl.* VII. 436/1 The Knot [of Cuzco in Peru] comprises six minor mountain-chains, and has an area thrice larger than that of Switzerland.

fig. **18..** Stevenson *Manse* Wks. 1894 Misc. I. 160 He [grandfather] moves in my blood..and sits efficient in the very knot and centre of my being.

9. *Geom.* A unicursal curve in three-dimensional space, which, on being distorted in any way so as to bring it into a plane without passing one part through another, will always have nodes.

1877 Tait in *Trans. R. Soc. Edin.* XXVIII. 145, I was led to the consideration of the forms of knots by Sir W. Thomson's Theory of Vortex Atoms. *Ibid.* 164 Thus this 4-fold knot, in each of its forms, can be deformed into its own perversion. In what follows all knots possessing this property will be called Amphicheiral. **1884** Kirkman *ibid.* XXXII. 281 Nothing general seems to have been written on knots of more than seven crossings.

II. Figurative applications of 1.

10. *fig.* **a.** Something intricate, involved, or difficult to trace out or explain; a tangle or difficulty; a knotty point or problem. ***Gordian knot***: see Gordian 1 c. ***to tie*** (a person) ***(up) in(to) knots*** (or ***a knot***): to confuse or nonplus (someone).

c **1000** Ælfric *Hom.* II. 386 ȝet her is oðer cnotta ealswa earfoðe, þæt is, 'Nan man ne astihð to heofenum, buton se ðe of heofenum astah'. *a* **1225** *Leg. Kath.* 1157 Ich habbe uncnut summe of þeos cnotti cnotten. *c* **1400** *Rom. Rose* 4698

Unto hym that love wole flee, The knotte may unclosed bee. **1638–48** G. Daniel *Eclog.* iii. 185 All the Subtle Knotts, which crabbed Heads Have twist. **1676** Temple *Lett., to Sir J. Williamson* Wks. 1731 II. 397 This Knot is of those that must be cut through, and cannot be untied. **1784** Cowper *Task* II. 520 Knots worthy of solution, which alone A Deity could solve. **1860** *Baily's Mag.* Aug. 368 Never before.. were bowlers or fielders so 'tied up in a knot'. **1876** Freeman *Norm. Conq.* V. xxvii. 719 The death of John cut the knot. **1876** T. Hardy *Ethelberta* (1890) 129 'Tis one of the greatest knots in service—the smoke question. **1888** A. G. Steel in Steel & Lyttelton *Cricket* iii. 167 The team was beginning to get tied up into a knot. **1957** D. Robins *Noble One* (1960) xx. 191 He is tied up in knots. He's fighting himself as well as me. **1974** I. Murdoch *Sacred & Profane Love Machine* 154, I could tie you into such knots, but I won't bother... You won't tell me the truth even now.

b. The central or main point of something intricate, involved, or difficult; the main point in a problem; the complication in the plot of a tale or drama; that in which the difficulty of anything centres.

c **1386** Chaucer *Sqr.'s T.* 393 The knotte why þat euery tale is toold If it be taried til that lust be coold.. The sauour passeth euer lenger the moore. *c* **1418** *Pol. Poems* (Rolls) II. 243 He that can be Cristes clerc, And knowe the knottes of his crede. **1573–80** Baret *Alv.* K 122 The knot and principall point of the matter. **1653** Urquhart *Rabelais* I. xiii, By and by shall you.. know the whole mysterie and knot of the matter. **1881** Gladstone *Sp.* 7 Apr., The small holdings.. the very knot of the difficulty not yet overcome.

11. a. Something that forms or maintains a union of any kind; a tie, bond, link.

1393 Langl. *P. Pl.* C. xviii. 127 [Holy Church is] Charite, .. Lyf, and loue, and leaute, in o by-leyue and lawe, And loue a knotte of leaute, and of leel by-leyue. *c* **1460** G. Ashby *Dicta Philos.* 1142 Thre thinges be in a right simpul knot, First goode counseil in hym that is not herde [etc.]. **1526** *Pilgr. Perf.* (W. de W. 1531) 285 b, And therfore it is called of Saynt Paule the knot of perfeccyon. **1538** Starkey *England* II. ii. 178, I remembyr the knot betwyx the body and the soule. **1587** Fleming *Contn. Holinshed* III. 1576/2 Ingratitude.. and treason.. linked togither with manie knots of other shameful sinnes. **1692** Dryden *St. Euremont's Ess.* 362 Policy had not as yet united Men by the Knots of a reasonable Society. **1701** Rowe *Amb. Step-moth.* I. i, To draw The Knot, which holds our common Interest, closer.

b. *spec.* The tie or bond of wedlock; the marriage or wedding knot.

a **1225** *Leg. Kath.* 1525 Swa wit beoð ifestnet & iteiet in an, & swa þe cnotte is icnut bituhhen unc tweien. *c* **1230** *Hali Meid.* 33 Beo þe cnot icnute anes of wedlac. **1592** Shaks. *Rom. & Jul.* IV. ii. 24 Send for the Countie,.. Ile haue this knot knit vp to morrow morning. **1698** Fryer *Acc. E. India & P.* 94 But the Cazy.. can loose the Knot when they plead a Divorce. **1828** *Craven Dial.* s.v., 'To tie a knot wi the tongue, at yan cannot louze wi yan's teeth', i.e. to get married.

†**12.** A bond or obligation; a binding condition; a spell that binds. *Obs.*

c **1460** *Towneley Myst.* vii. 107 Shall I now syng you a fytt, With my mynstrelsy; loke ye do it well in wrytt, And theron a knot knytt, ffor it is prophecy. **1534** More *Treat. on Passion* Wks. 1286/1 All these supernaturall giftes he gaue him with the knot of thys condicion, that yf hee brake hys commaundement, then shuld he leese them al. *a* **1627** Middleton *Witch* I. ii, Knit with these charms and retentive knots, Neither the man begets nor woman breeds. **1651** Hobbes *Leviath.* IV. xlvii. 384 This was the first Knot upon their Liberty. **1813** Scott *Trierm.* Introd. viii, Of the dread knot a wizard tied, In punishment of maiden's pride.

III. *transf.* A hard or firm mass such as is formed by a knot tied in a string, etc.

13. A hard lump in an animal body, either in a softer tissue, or on a smooth surface; a swelling or protuberance in a muscle, nerve, gland, etc.; a knob or enlargement in a bone; a tumour, ganglion, wart, pimple, or the like; the lump that seems to gather in the throat in strong emotion.

a **1225** *Ancr. R.* 2 þe on riwleð þe heorte, þe makeð hire efne & smeðe, wiðute knotte & dolke of woh inwit. **13..** *Gaw. & Gr. Knt.* 1334 þen brek þay þe bale, þe balez out token Lystily forlancyng & bere of þe knot. *c* **1400** *Beryn* 2513 Strecching forth his fyngirs, in siȝt,.. Without[en] knot or knor, or eny signe of goute. *c* **1440** *Promp. Parv.* 280/2 Knotte yn the fleshe, vndyr the skynne, *glandula.* *a* **1533** Ld. Berners *Gold. Bk. M. Aurel.* (1546) L vj, Thei found his handes hard and ful of hard knottes. **1606** Shaks. *Tr. & Cr.* v. iii. 33 Let grow thy Sinews till their knots be strong. **1688** *Lond. Gaz.* No. 2351/4 A Sorrel Horse,.. a dry knot on the near Leg behind. **1718** Rowe tr. *Lucan* Notes 32 The Knots of Love. These are little Excrescences of Flesh upon the Forehead of Foals. **1774** Goldsm. *Nat. Hist.* (1776) III. 62 They [the horns of the ibex] are bent backward, full of knots; and it is generally asserted that there is a knot added every year. **1859** Tennyson *Elaine* 736 The Queen, who sat With lips severely placid, felt the knot Climb in her throat.

14. a. A thickened part or protuberance in the tissue of a plant; an excrescence on a stem, branch, or root; a node on a stem, esp. when of swollen form, as the joints in grasses; the hard mass formed in a trunk at the insertion of a branch or round the place of insertion of an abortive or dead branch, causing a rounded cross-grained piece in a board, which is apt to fall out, and leave a *knot-hole*. Also, a bud; *in (the) knot*, in bud, budding. *pl.*, a disease which attacks plum and cherry trees (see quot. 1845).

1398 Trevisa *Barth. De P.R.* xvii. i. (MS. Bodl.) lf. 105 b/1 Euerich tree herbe and gras haþ a rote: and in euerich rote manye maner knottes and stringes. *Ibid.* lxxiii. lf. 207/2. *c* **1400** *Lanfranc's Cirurg.* 118 He may not breke a knotte of a straw wiþ hise teeþ. **1523** Fitzherb. *Husb.* §25 Quyche.. hath many knottes towarde the roote. *Ibid.* §130 Apple trees that haue knottes in the bowes. **1601** Holland *Pliny* (1634) II. 165 If any person.. gather one of these tender knots or buds [of the pomegranate] with 2 fingers only. **1606** Shaks. *Tr. & Cr.* I. iii. 316 Blunt wedges riue hard knots. *a* **1670** Hacket *Abp. Williams* II. 88 The Citron Tree.. It bore some ripe ones [fruits], and some sour ones, some in the Knot, and some in the Blossom altogether. **1703** Moxon *Mech. Exerc.* 111 In Deal-boards, those Boughs or Branches are Knots. **1787** Winter *Syst. Husb.* 51 Couch and some other weeds vegetate at every joint or knot. **1796** C. Marshall *Garden.* ii. (1813) 21 The flowers of many proceed from a bud or knot. **1845** Downing *Fruits Amer.* 270 The knots is a disease attacking bark and wood.. [with] the appearance of large, irregular black lumps, with a hard, cracked, uneven surface, quite dry within. *Mod. dial.* The may is in knot.

†**b.** Phr. ***to seek (search for, look for, find) a knot*** or ***knots in a rush*** or ***bulrush*** (Lat. *nodum in scirpo quærere*), to seek or make difficulties where there are none; also, ***to seek a knot in a ring***. *Obs.*

1340 *Ayenb.* 253 þet zekþ þet uel ine þe aye oþer þane knotte ine þe resse. **1563–87** Foxe *A. & M.* (1684) II. 387 To strain at gnats, to stumble at straws, to seek knots in rushes. *a* **1592** Greene *Jas. IV*, III. ii, They seek a knot in a ring that would wrong my master or his servants in this court. **1625** Hart *Anat. Ur.* I. iii. 36 To enquire after [this], were to search for a knot in a rush. **1712** Oldisworth *Odes Horace* II. 7/2 The Grammarians therefore do in this place look for a Knot in a Bull-rush. *a* **1734** North *Exam.* III. vii. §43 (1740) 533 Those, that sought Knots in Bulrushes to obstruct the King's Affairs in Parliament.

15. A knob or embossed ornamentation in carved or hammered work; a stud employed as an ornament or for fastening; a boss; also, the carved foliage on the capital of a column (Parker *Gloss. Archit.* 1875). ***friar's knots***: see friar 9.

13.. *Gaw. & Gr. Knt.* 577 Greuez, With polaynez piched þer-to, policed ful clene, Aboute his knez knaged wyth knotez of golde. *c* **1394** *P. Pl. Crede* 161 þe pileres weren.. queynteli i-coruen wiþ curiouse knottes. **1412–20** Lydg. *Chron. Troy* II. xi, Eche caruer and curious ioyner To make knottes w^t many a queynt floure. **1534** in Peacock *Eng. Ch. Furniture* (1866) 191 Item a shaft of siluer for the same crosse with a roll gilte & iij knottes gilte of the whiche knottes euery one hath vj roses enamelid with asure. **1664** in Bradshaw & Wordsworth *Lincoln Stat.* (1897) 645 Vehemently suspected to haue secretly purloyned.. much of the lead and soulder.. and many of the ould window knotts; and to haue sould them to diuerse pewterers. **1683** Moxon *Mech. Exerc., Printing* xx. ¶3 These Knots are small square pieces of Box-wood. **1812–16** J. Smith *Panorama Sc. & Art* I. 163 A boss or knot at the centre intersections. **1849–50** Weale *Dict. Terms, Knot* or *Knob*, a boss; a round bunch of leaves or flowers, or other ornament of a similar kind.

16. A hill or eminence of moderate height; esp. a rocky hill or summit. Frequent in proper names of hills in the north-west of England. Cf. knob 2.

13.. *Gaw. & Gr. Knt.* 1431 In a knot, bi a clyffe, at þe kerre syde, þer as þe rogh rocher vn-rydely watz fallen. **1594** Norden *Spec. Brit., Essex* 11 Sundrie valleis ther are, which of necessitie require hills; but they are but small knottes,.. makinge a difference betwene the valley and the higher grounde. **1785** Hutton *Bran New Wark* Prol. 10 Whilst I grovel amongst these knots and barrows. **1828** *Craven Dial., Knot*, a rocky summit, as Bolland knot, Nursaw knot. **1887** *Pall Mall G.* 25 June 6/1 The loyal bonfires were descried by the watchers on Arnside Knott... Some mischievous boys had set light to the gorse and undergrowth at the foot of the knott.

17. A mass formed by the aggregation and cohesion of particles; esp. one that has formed as a hard kernel in the surrounding softer material; a lump, clot, concretion.

Glass-making: in crown glass, = knob *sb.* 1, bull's eye 1 (*Dict. Archit.* 1863–9); in flint glass, a defect caused by the presence of foreign matter. *Geol.*: a concretion of foreign matter in some schistose rocks. (Quot. 1625 is doubtful.)

1625 B. Jonson *Staple of N.* II. iii, I haue lost two stone Of suet.. posting hither, You might haue followed me like a watering pot, And seene the knots I made along the street. **1703** Moxon *Mech. Exerc.* 250 It must be extreamly beaten, which will break all the knots of Lime. *a* **1728** Woodward *Nat. Hist. Fossils* (1729) I. 186 A Knot of Black-Lead, that, happening to be form'd within the Verge of another, has a Sinus. **1821** Clare *Vill. Minstr.* I. 135 Insects of mysterious birth.. Doubtless brought by moisture forth, Hid in knots of spittle white. **1838** *Encycl. Brit.* (ed. 7) XVII. 7 The straining of the stuff [pulp], and thereby keeping out of the paper all the knots and hard substances.

18. A small group, cluster, band or company of persons or things (gathered together in one place, or associated in any way). ***of a knot***, in union or combination, associated together.

a. Of persons.

13.. *E.E. Allit. P.* B. 787 Sant Iohan hem syȝ al in a knot, On þe hyl of Syon. *a* **1548** Hall *Chron., Edw. IV*, 216 All they came together in one knot to the citie. **1601** Shaks. *Jul. C.* III. i. 117 So often shall the knot of vs be call'd, The Men that gaue their Country liberty. **1639** W. Mountagu in *Buccleuch MSS.* (Hist. MSS. Comm.) I. 278 My Lord Sey and my Lord Brooke, and some of that knott. **1662** Pepys *Diary* 16 Dec., All do conclude M^r. Coventry, and Pett, and me, to be of a knot. **1704** Swift *Mech. Operat. Spir.* Misc. (1711) 287 A Knot of Irish Men and Women. **1849** Macaulay *Hist. Eng.* vii. II. 225 There was scarcely a market town in England without at least a knot of separatists. **1874** Green *Short Hist.* viii. §9. 557 Within the House.. a vigorous knot of politicians was resolved to prolong its existence.

b. Of things.

1607–12 Bacon *Ess., Fortune* (Arb.) 376 The Milken Way in the Sky.. is a meeting or knot of a number of smalle Starres. **1698** Fryer *Acc. E. India & P.* 6 We were close under St. Iago, another Island of the same Knot. **1825** Scott *Talism.* ii, They had now arrived at the knot of palm-trees. *a* **1853** Robertson *Lect.* ii. (1858) 84 You will have.. not an institution, but a knot of clubs. **1875** Whitney *Life Lang.* xii. 263 A host of lesser knots of idioms.

IV. 19. *attrib.* and *Comb.*, as ***knot-bed***, ***-garden*** (see sense 7); ***knot-maker***, ***-tier***, ***-tightener***; ***knot-free***, ***-green***, ***-haired***, ***-like*** adjs.; **knot-catcher** (see quot.); **knot-gall**, a species of oak-gall produced by the cynipid *Andricus noduli*; **knot-head** *N. Amer.*, a stupid person (see also quot. 1940); also, a stupid horse; **knot-hole**, (*a*) a hole in a board, etc., caused by the falling out of a knot; (*b*) the hollow formed in the trunk of a tree, by the decay of a branch; (*c*) a hole formed by the excavation of clay; **knot-horn** = *knot-horn moth*; **knot-horn moth**, a moth of the genus *Phycita*; **knot-ribbon**, ribbon used in making bows or knots; **knot-stitch**, a stitch by which ornamental knots are made; **knot-wood**, wood that is full of knots; *esp.* pine; **knot-writing**, a mnemonic aid consisting of strings in which a number of knots are made.

1665–76 Rea *Flora* (ed. 2) 232 Directions for the.. making of a *Knot-bed. **1927** T. Woodhouse *Artificial Silk* 100 The threads or yarn from the cone cheeses are first led up through coils in wires termed *knot catchers. **1648** Herrick *Hesper.*, *Charm for Stables*, The Manes shall be, Of your horses, all *knot-free. **1894** C. R. Straton tr. *Adler's Alternating Generations* 34 The *knot gall is found in June on *Q[uercus] pedunculata*, *Q. sessiliflora*, and *Q. pubescens.* **1908** E. T. Connold *Brit. Oak Galls* 65 The Knot Gall. **1519** Horman *Vulg.* 172 The *knot-garden serueth for pleasure: the potte garden for profitte. *a* **1722** Lisle *Husb.* (1757) 208 (E.D.S.) Red-straw wheat must be gathered *knot-green, that is, whilst the knots in the straw are green. **1659** T. Pecke *Parnassi Puerp.* 125 *Knot-hair'd Sicambrians And Natures frisled Æthiopians. **1940** *Amer. Speech* XV. 447/2 **Knot head*, low intelligence. **1961** Webster, *Knothead*, a dull-witted blunderer. **1961** R. P. Hobson *Rancher takes Wife* i. 21 Harold called in a loud voice to the horse. 'Step up there, you old knothead.' **1962** A. Fry *Ranch on Cariboo* xv. 160 I'd the repertoire of a mule skinner, developed behind a wide variety of knothead horses. **1972** J. Aiken *Butterfly Picnic* ix. 163 Why hadn't he *said* he was going to, the silly knothead? **1726** G. Roberts *4 Years Voy.* 284, I found one great Leak, which was a *Knot Hole. **1889** Baring-Gould *Arminell* (1890) I. i. 12 Fanny.. detected an eye inspecting her through a knot-hole, laughed, and then turned crimson. **1903** *Westm. Gaz.* 31 Dec. 3/2 The little coons.. climbed up to the knot-hole, and scrambled down inside. **1964** E. Huxley *Back Street New Worlds* x. 98 There are craters.. called knot-holes, and from them clay has been scooped and loaded into tub-like steel wagons to proceed.. to the kilns. **1967** M. Chandler *Ceramics in Mod. World* i. 29 The underlying Lower Oxford clay.. is taken from the claypit or 'knot-hole' by a mechanical excavator. **1899** D. Sharp in *Camb. Nat. Hist.* VI. 424 The males frequently have the basal-joint of the antennæ swollen; hence the term '*Knot-horns' applied by collectors to these moths. **1894** *Spectator* 18 Aug. 216/1 The various species of *knot-horn moths (*Phycidæ*). **1776–96** Withering *Brit. Plants* (ed. 3) II. 347 Leaves with *knot-like joints. **1888** *Pall Mall G.* 26 Jan. 10/1 The trade of '*knot-maker', or 'tier of cravats', is not one of the least lucrative callings in Paris just now. **1851** *Illustr. Catal. Gt. Exhib.* 1145 Ribbon for military decorations. *Knot ribbon. **1881** C. C. Harrison *Woman's Handiwork* I. 84 Beginning with the hemstitch of our grandmothers, we may add.. lace stitches, herring-bone, buttonhole.. darning and *knot stitch. **1964** *McCall's Sewing* ii. 30/1 *Knot-stitch*, stitch used to secure thread at beginning and end of stitching. **1645** Milton *Tetrach.* Wks. (1851) 163 (Gen. ii. 24) This vers.. is the great *knot tier, which hath undon by tying, and by tangling, millions of guiltles consciences. **1896** A. J. Butler tr. *Ratzel's Hist. Mankind* I. 344 In West Australia,.. a network of reed serves for a messenger's credentials,—a reminiscence of the once more widely-developed *knot-writing.

knot (nɒt), *sb.*² Also knott. [Found from 15th c.; varying from 17th c. with *knat*, gnat²; origin unknown.

The conjecture of Camden, adopted by Drayton, and commemorated by Linnæus in the specific name *Canutus*, that the bird was named after King Cnút or Canute, 'because believed to be a visitant from Denmark', is without historical or even traditional basis.]

A bird of the Snipe family (*Tringa Canutus*), also called Red-breasted Sandpiper; it breeds within the Arctic Circle, but is common on the British coasts during the late summer and autumn.

[**1422** in Rogers *Agric. & Prices* III. 136/2.] **1452** *Bill of fare* in A. Wood *Hist. Univ. Oxf.* 26, 3rd Table. Plover, Knottys, Styntis, Quayles. **1572** J. Jones *Bathes Buckstone* 10 Rayle, Curlyew, Cnotwyppe [= Cnot, Wyppe], Wodcocke, Snype, or any other clouen footed fowles. **1586** Camden *Brit.* (1607) 408 *Knotts*, i. *Canuti aves* vt opinor, e Dania enim aduolare creduntur. **1622** Drayton *Poly-olb.* xxv. (1748) 368 The Knot, that called was Canutus Bird of old, Of that great King of Danes, his name that still doth hold. **1774** Goldsm. *Nat. Hist.* VI. 28 The long legged plover, the knot and the turnstone, are rather the guests than the natives of this island. **1863** C. A. Johns *Home Walks* 21 Mixed with them in the same flock we repeatedly saw Sanderlings, purple Sandpipers and Knots. **1881** *Spectator* 27 Aug. 1108 In the Nares Arctic Expedition Capt. Fielden discovered the breeding ground of the sanderling and the knot.

knot (nɒt), *v.* [f. KNOT *sb.*[1]]

1. *trans.* To tie in a knot; to form a knot or knots in; to do up, fasten, or secure with a knot.

a **1547** SURREY *Æneid* IV. (1557) Ej, Her quyuer hung behinde her back, her tresse Knotted in gold. **1649** G. DANIEL *Trinarch., Hen. IV*, clxiv, Perhaps those Elves Abuse them rather,.. And Knot their Hearts in their owne Handkercheife. **1702** ADDISON *Dial. Medals* ii. Wks. 1721 I. 515 No costly fillets knot her hair behind. **1832** MARRYAT *N. Forster* xlvii, The seamen were employed in knotting the rigging. **1833** RENNIE *Alph. Angling* 65 Begin with three hairs, put them level at top and knot them. **1842** TENNYSON *St. Sim. Styl.* 64, I wore The rope..Twisted as tight as I could knot the noose. **1894** HALL CAINE *Manxman* v. v. 295 A cardboard box, tied about with a string, which was knotted in a peculiar way.

b. *intr.* To form a knot or knots; to be or become tied or twisted into a knot.

1611 HEYWOOD *Gold. Age* I. i. 15 Henceforth my vnkem'd lockes shall knot in curles.

2. *intr.* To make or knit knots for fringes; to do the fancy work called KNOTTING.

a **1701** SEDLEY *Song, Hears not my Phillis* i, Phillis..Sat and knotted all the while. **1713** STEELE *Guard.* No. 41 ⁋4 Lady Char—te is taken knotting in Saint James's chapel during divine service. **1824** MISS FERRIER *Inher.* xv, Miss P. gabbled and knotted. **1869** ROGERS *Hist. Gleanings* I. 58 Caroline sat during these recitals, sometimes yawning, sometimes smiling, but always knotting.

b. *trans.* To make or form by this art.

1750 MRS. DELANY *Life & Corr.* (1861) II. 606 Till I have finished a plain fringe I am knotting. **1781** MRS. BOSCAWEN *ibid.* Ser. II. III. 64 You would contrive to knot them some quipos of remembrance!

3. *trans.* To form protuberances, bosses, or knobs on or in; to make knotty; to emboss; to knit (the brows).

1509 HAWES *Past. Pleas.* XXXVII. (Percy Soc.) 195 The gate, Whiche all of sylver was knotted proprely. **1697** R. PEIRCE *Bath Mem.* II. viii. 372 The Gout had knotted all his Joynts, both of Toes and Fingers. **1844** MRS. BROWNING *Drama Exile* Poems 1864 I. 28 This Eve..Knots her fair eyebrows in so hard a knot. **1865** DICKENS *Mut. Fr.* II. xiv, Bradley Headstone knotted his brows.

fig. *a* **1541** WYATT *Poems* (1557) 46 Make plaine thine hart, that it be not knotted With hope or dreade.

†**b.** *intr.* Of plants: To form knots or nodes; to bud; to form a close head, as clover; to begin to develop fruit; to 'set' (= KNIT *v.* 5 c). *Obs.*

1611 COTGR., *Nouer*,..also, to knot (as a tree thats in growing). **1651-3** JER. TAYLOR *Serm. for Year* I. vi. 78 You must..let it blossom and knot, and grow and ripen. **1658** EVELYN *Fr. Gard.* (1675) 153 The false flowers which will never knot into fruit, are to be nipped off. **1660** SHARROCK *Vegetables* 20 The time of cutting [clover] will be knowne, by observing when it begins to knot.

4. *trans.* To combine or unite firmly or intricately; to associate intimately; to entangle, complicate.

1611 SPEED *Hist. Gt. Brit.* IX. xvi. 657 There were three score thousand of them rebelliously knotted together. **1624** BACON *War with Spain* Wks. 1879 I. 536/1 The party of the papists in England are become more knotted, both in dependence towards Spain, and amongst themselves. **1670** MARVELL *Corr.* Wks. 1872-5 II. 339 The House also thought fit to adjourn itselfe... Thus we are not yet knotted. **1859** HAWTHORNE *Marb. Faun* xix, The deed knots us together for time and eternity, like the coil of a serpent. **1898** G. MEREDITH *Odes Fr. Hist.* 29 Thy [armies] clash, they are knotted; and now 'tis the deed of the axe on the log.

†**b.** *intr.* To unite or gather together in a knot; to assemble, congregate; to form a compact mass, to concrete. *Obs.*

1604 SHAKS. *Oth.* IV. ii. 62 A Cesterne, for foule Toades To knot and gender in. **1639** SALTMARSH *Policy* 289 A little Physicke will disperse a gathering Disease, which if it knot, hath more danger and difficulty. **1662** PEPYS *Diary* 24 Aug., A great many young people knotting together, and crying out 'Porridge!'

5. *techn.* **a.** To cover the knots in (wood) before painting (see KNOTTING *vbl. sb.* 4). **b.** To cover (metal, etc.) with knotting (sense 4 b). **c.** To remove knots from (cloth, etc.): cf. KNOTTER 2, KNOTTING *vbl. sb.* 5.

knot, obs. form of NOT *a.*, shorn, round-headed.

knotberry. Also **knoutberry.** [? f. KNOT *sb.*[1] + BERRY.] A local name of the Cloudberry, *Rubus Chamæmorus*.

1633 JOHNSON *Gerarde's Herbal* App. 1630 Knot, or Knout-berrie, or Cloud-berrie. **1671** SKINNER *Etymol. Ling. Angl.*, Knot-berry-bush, *Chamæmorus*. **1778** LIGHTFOOT *Flora Scot.* (1789) I. 266 Cloud-berries, Knot-berries, or Knout-berries. **1828** *Craven Dial., Knout-berry*. **1859** W. S. COLEMAN *Woodlands* (1862) 103 The Cloudberry... Called also the Mountain Bramble and Knotberry.

knotch, variant of NOTCH.

knote (nəʊt). *Mech.* [a. G. *knoten*, MHG. *knote* knot, node.] 'The point where ropes, cords, etc., meet from angular directions in funicular machines.'

1885 in *Cassell's Encycl. Dict.*

'knotfulness. *Geom.* [f. **knotful* (KNOT *sb.*[1] + -FUL) + -NESS.] The number of knots of less knottiness of which a more complex knot is made up: see KNOT *sb.*[1] 9.

1877 TAIT *Knots* in *Trans. R. Soc. Edin.* (1879) XXVIII. I. 177 The term *Beknottedness* will be used to signify the peculiar property in which knots, even when of the same order of knottiness, may thus differ... Another property, which may be called *Knotfulness*—to indicate the number of knots of lower orders (whether interlinked or not) of which a given knot is in many cases built up. **1885** *Ibid.* (1887) XXXII. III. 504 This is a difficulty of a very formidable order. It depends upon the property which I have called knotfulness.

knot-grass. [f. KNOT *sb.*[1] + GRASS: from the knotted stem.]

1. The plant *Polygonum aviculare*, a common weed in waste ground, with numerous intricately-branched creeping stems, and small pale pink flowers; an infusion of it was formerly supposed to stunt the growth. Called by early herbalists †*male knot-grass*. Also extended to other species of *Polygonum*, as ***seaside knot-grass***, *P. maritimum*; ***Virginian knot-grass***, *P. virginianum*, etc.

[*a* **1500** *Gl. Sloane* 5 (*Sax. Leechd.* III. 319/1) Knotting grass.]

1538 TURNER *Libellus, Poligonon*,..knotgyrs. **1544** PHAER *Regim. Lyfe* (1553) C vij, It is good for the paciente to.. drinke the iuice of knotgrasse. **1590** SHAKS. *Mids. N.* III. ii. 329 You dwarfe You minimus, of hindring knot-grasse made. **1597** GERARDE *Herbal* II. clxi. §1. 451 The common male knot grasse creepeth along vpon the ground, with long slender weake branches, full of knots or ioints, whereof it tooke his name. *a* **1706** EVELYN *Kal. Hort.* Jan. (1729) 189 Knot-grass, the very worst of Garden-weeds. **1860** O. W. HOLMES *Prof. Breakf.-t.* x. (Paterson) 212 The wiry, jointed stems of that iron creeping-plant which we call 'knot-grass'.

2. Applied to various other plants with knotty stems, etc.

a. Various grasses, as the Fiorin Grass or Marsh Bent (*Agrostis stolonifera* or *alba*) with creeping rooting stems, and the varieties with knotty rootstock of the False Oat (*Arrhenatherum avenaceum*) and a species of Oat-grass (*Avena elatior*). **b.** Any species of the genera *Illecebrum* or *Paronychia*. † **c.** ***female knot-grass***, Lyte's name for Mare's-tail (*Hippuris vulgaris*). **d.** ***German knot-grass***, name for Knawel (*Scleranthus annuus*).

1578 LYTE *Dodoens* I. lxvii. 97 Of Knotgrasse... There be two kindes..The second kinde whiche they call female Knot grasse, hath..stemmes..much like to the stalkes and ioyntes of *Hippuris*, or Horse tayle, but not so rough... Amongst the kindes of Knot grasse, we may well recken that herbe, whiche doth so wrap and enterlace itself, and is so ful of ioynts, that the base Almaignes cal it knawel, that is to say, knot weede. **1634** MILTON *Comus* 542 The chewing flocks Had ta'n their supper on the savoury Herb Of Knot-grass dew-besprent. **1744-50** W. ELLIS *Mod. Husbandm.* IV. I. 53 (E.D.S.) *Avena elatior*, knot or couch grass. **1760** J. LEE *Introd. Bot.* App. 316 Knot Grass, Mountain, *Illecebrum*. **1787** tr. *Linnæus' Fam. Plants* I. 304 *Scleranthus*..German Knot-grass. **1806** GALPINE *Brit. Bot.* §109 *Illecebrum*. Knot-grass. I. *Verticillatum*, whorled. **1808** BATCHELOR *Agric. Bedfordsh.* 324 The creeping bent-grass (*Agrostis stolonifera*)..the same, I believe, as that called knot-grass in this county.

3. *attrib.* **knot-grass moth**, *Acronycta rumicis*.

a **1658** CLEVELAND *Cl. Vindic.* (1677) 104 He is much of the size of those Knot-grass Professors. **1819** G. SAMOUELLE *Entomol. Compend.* 250 Knot-grass moth. **1859** NEWMAN *Brit. Moths* 255 The Knot-Grass.—The antennæ are simple in both sexes... It feeds on the common knot-grass.

knotless ('nɒtlɪs), *a.* [f. KNOT *sb.*[1] + -LESS.] Without a knot, free from knots (in various senses of the sb.); unknotted. In first quot. quasi-adv. = like a thread without knots, smoothly, without check or hindrance.

c **1374** CHAUCER *Troylus* v. 769 Bothe Troylus and Troye toun Shal knotles thorugh out here herte slyde. **1589** FLEMING *Virg. Georg.* II. 21 Or else the knotles trunks are cut againe. **1717** CONGREVE tr. *Ovid's Met., Orph. & Euryd.*, Here silver firs with knotless trunks ascend. **1792** BURNS *My Tocher's the Jewel*, Ye'll slip frae me like a knotless thread. **1822** *Blackw. Mag.* XII. 711 The manufacture of threadless, knotless, endless, useless mysteries. **1849** MRS. CARLYLE *Lett.* II. 70, I slipt away from them like a knotless thread.

knotted ('nɒtɪd), *a.* [f. KNOT *sb.*[1] and *v.* + -ED.]

1. a. Having a knot or knots tied on it; tied in a knot; fastened with a knot.

c **1154** *O.E. Chron.* an. 1137 Me did cnotted strenges abuton here hæued. *a* **1225** *Leg. Kath.* 1551 Het..beaten hire bare flesch & hire freoliche bodi mit cnottede schurgen. *c* **1400** MAUNDEV. (1839) xviii. 197 He hath abouten his Nekke 300 perles oryent gode & grete, & knotted, as Pater Nostres here of Amber. **1509** HAWES *Past. Pleas.* XXXII. (Percy Soc.) 156 In her hand she had a knotted whyp. **1597** A. M. tr. *Guillemeau's Fr. Chirurg.* 15/1 The first is called the knotted suture or sowinge, because every stitche is cutt of, and both the endes of the thread knitte together. **1607** ROWLANDS *Guy Warw.* 41 The Dragon winds his crooked knotted tail About the Lyon's legs. **1788** COWPER *Negro's Compl.* 29 Ask him, if your knotted scourges,..Are the means that duty urges Agents of his will to use? **1831** J. HOLLAND *Manuf. Metal* I. 183 These knotted chains, as they are called, are now made by all the chain-makers.

b. *fig.* Knit together as with knots; formed like network; entangled, intricate.

1648 MILTON *Observ. Art. Peace* Wks. (1851) 576 No breach of any just privilege, but a breach of their knotted faction. **1664** BUTLER *Hud.* II. iii. 18 They're catch'd in knotted law like nets. **1892** MARIE CORELLI *Wormwood* III. viii. 160 Little by little, I unravelled my knotted thoughts.

c. Colloq. phr. ***to get knotted***, to 'go to hell'. Usu. in *imp.*, stop annoying me!

1963 *New Society* 22 Aug. 5/1 Other adoptions are 'get knotted' and 'knackered' which have come to mean innocently enough, 'go to hell', and '*kaput*'. **1964** B. W. ALDISS *Dark Light Years* iii. 39 Get knotted, Duffield, you ruddy trouble-maker. **1965** M. FORSTER *Bogeyman* viii. 144 'You are to behave properly.' 'Get knotted,' said Natalie, deliberately. **1968** 'H. CALVIN' *Miranda must Die* ii. 19, I don't know why the hell you didn't tell him to get knotted and be done with it. **1969** O. BLAKESTON *For crying out Shroud* v. 46 'That boy in Rome said we looked like a hero.' ..'Get knotted. We might as well be dead.' **1972** G. LYALL *Blame the Dead* xii. 80 'I'll lend you a good book about security.' 'Get knotted, Major.'

2. a. Formed or decorated with knots or bosses. **b.** Of a garden, laid out in knots (see KNOT *sb.*[1] 7).

1588 SHAKS. *L.L.L.* I. i. 249 The West corner of thy curious knotted garden. **1830** N. S. WHEATON *Jrnl.* 411 A double colonnade of clustered pillars..spanned above by a richly ribbed and knotted arch. **1863-9** *Dict. Archit.*, *Knotted shaft*, a peculiarity in the carving of the shafts of columns in the early part of the mediæval period in Italy, representing a knot; sometimes two shafts are knotted together. **1896** *Edin. Rev.* July 169 The term 'knots' or 'knotted garden' came to be used for any grouping of flower beds of other than simple shape.

3. a. Characterized by knobs, protuberances, excrescences or concretions; gnarled, as a trunk or branch; having swollen joints, as a stem; gathered into wrinkles, knitted (as the brows): cf. KNOT *sb.*[1] 13, 14; KNOT *v.* 3.

c **1440** *Promp. Parv.* 280/1 Knobbyd, or knottyd as trees, *vertiginosus*. **1606** SHAKS. *Tr. & Cr.* I. iii. 50 The splitting winde Makes flexible the knees of knotted Oakes. **1632** MASSINGER & FIELD *Fatal Dowry* III. i. M.'s Wks. (Rtldg.) 278/1 He has a knotted brow, would bruise A court-like hand to touch it. **1664** POWER *Exp. Philos.* I. 7 The Gray, or Horse-Fly. Her legs all joynted and knotted like the plant called *Equisetum* or Horse-tayl. **1701** SIR H. C. FLOYER *Hot & Cold Bathing* I. iv. 102 He was afflicted with the Gout.. his Joints were so knotted, that he could scarcely go. **1776-96** WITHERING *Brit. Plants* (ed. 3) IV. 49 Branches.. Sometimes smooth and regular, sometimes knotted. **1843** LYTTON *Last Bar.* I. vii, A formidable knotted club in his hand.

b. †Compacted, formed into a knot or compact close mass, as a bud (*obs.*); forming a close head of blossom (*dial.*).

1626 BACON *Sylva* §414 Pulling off the Buds of the Rose, when they are newly knotted, for then the side Branches will bear. **1744-50** W. ELLIS *Mod. Husbandm.* III. I. 83 (E.D.S.) [Clover, when fit for mowing, is] known by its being full knotted. **1821** CLARE *Vill. Minstr.* I. 209 Knotted flowers of thyme.

knottedness ('nɒtɪdnɪs). [f. KNOTTED *a.* + -NESS.] The character or manner of being formed into a knot.

1909 in WEBSTER. **1962** C. S. OGILVY *Tomorrow's Math* vi. 109 Does the system of lines of magnetic force in space surrounding the knot reflect topologically the knottedness of the curve?

knotter ('nɒtə(r)). [f. KNOT *v.* + -ER[1].]

1. One who knots or ties knots; a machine or contrivance for doing this.

1712 ADDISON *Spect.* No. 536 ⁋2 The satisfaction these male-knotters will find, when they see their work mixed up in a fringe [etc.]. **1881** *Mark Lane Express* 8 Aug. 1076 The string approaches the knotter as the knot is tightened. **1884** *Thorley's Illustr. Farmers' Almanack* 39 The 'binder',..after passing the binding string around the bundle, leaves its end in the grasp of the 'knotter'. Finally, this clever device first ties and then cuts the twine band. **1889** in Mackail *W. Morris* I. 316 A carpet-knotter was got from Glasgow, to teach the girls the method of working.

2. A person or contrivance employed to remove knots: see quots.

1875 *Ure's Dict. Arts* III. 490 (Manufacture of Paper) The pulp is strained by means of a sieve or 'knotter', as it is called,..having fine slits cut in it to allow the comminuted pulp to pass through, while it retains all lumps and knots. **1893** *Labour Commission Gloss., Knotters*, young females employed to cut the knots of yarn off the pieces before they undergo the processes of 'milling' and 'finishing'.

3. With prefixed numeral: a boat or ship that makes (so many) knots.

1908 *Pall Mall Gaz.* 20 Apr. 6/1 Not many of the so-called '30-knotters' could steam at this speed. **1929** 'SEAMARK' *Down River* i, Essex noted the stolid little ten knotter ahead.

knottily ('nɒtɪlɪ), *adv. rare.* [f. KNOTTY + -LY[2].] In a knotty manner.

1699 BENTLEY *Phal.* 216 Four marks of Parentheses, () () like Knots upon a String, to make it look the more Knottily.

knottiness ('nɒtɪnɪs). [f. KNOTTY + -NESS.]

1. The quality or condition of being knotty (*lit.* and *fig.*).

1607 HIERON *Wks.* I. 409 Such children, the knottines of whose nature is refined and reformed and made smooth by grace. **1616** DONNE *Serm.* (ed. Alford) V. cxxxvii. 463 The wryness, the knottiness, the entangling of the serpent. **1662** HERNE in *Collect.* (O.H.S.) I. 246 The bark of such pollards cannot be gotten off because of its knottyness. **1868** BROWNING *Ring & Bk.* II. 1167 Never was such a tangled knottiness, But thus authority cuts the Gordian thro'.

2. *Geom.* The minimum number of nodes in the projection of a knot (sense 9) on a plane or similar surface.

1877 TAIT in *Trans. R. Soc. Edin.* XXVIII. 148 There are, therefore, projections of every knot which give a *minimum*

number of intersections, . . this minimum number . . we will call *Knottiness*.

knotting ('nɒtɪŋ), *vbl. sb.* [f. KNOT *v.* + -ING[1].]

1. The action of tying a knot, or of tying or entangling in a knot.

1758 J. BLAKE *Plan Mar. Syst.* 7 Exercising those who are received into the service, in knotting and splicing, in handing and reefing of sails. **1884** SIR S. ST. JOHN *Hayti* v. 196 The peculiar knotting of their curly wool. **1898** P. MANSON *Trop. Diseases* xxxvii. 587 The affected hairs are bent and twisted and tend to produce matting and knotting.

2. The knitting of knots for fancy-work, similar to TATTING *sb.*; *concr.*, fancy work done by knitting threads into knots.

1697 [see 6 below]. **1712** ADDISON *Spect.* No. 536 ⁋2 Knotting is again in fashion. **1750** MRS. DELANY *Life & Corr.* (1861) II. 616, I have sent you by Mr. Dubourg, . . all the knotting and knotting thread I have. **1784** JOHNSON in *Boswell* 3 June, Next to mere idleness, I think knotting is to be reckoned in the scale of insignificance; though I once attempted to learn knotting. **1801** *Monthly Rev.* XXXV. 342 The young females of the Cape . . are expert at . . all kinds of lace, knotting, and tambour work. **1826** MISS MITFORD *Village* Ser. II. (1863) 317 The whole fringe of the bed and window curtains being composed of her knotting. **1879** MRS. MACQUOID *Berksh. Lady* 123 Taking her knotting out of a black velvet reticule.

3. The formation of knots or protuberances; the production of buds, etc., budding.

1611 COTGR., *Nouëment de jeunes arbres*, the knotting of young trees; their springing, or shooting out from knot to knot. **1620** Brinsley *Virg. Ecl.* 119/2 In the new flower (viz. at the first knotting). **1848** B. WEBB *Continent. Ecclesiol.* 116 It is like a finger deformed by the knotting of the knuckles.

4. The process of covering the knots in wood with a special preparation, previously to painting; *concr.*, the preparation used for this.

1823 P. NICHOLSON *Pract. Build.* 587 *Knotting*; in painting, the process for preventing knots from appearing in the finish. **1852** *Nicholson's Dict. Archit.* s.v., Knotting is a composition of strong size, mixed with red lead. **1881** YOUNG *Every Man his own Mechanic* §1578 All the knots in the wood must be killed with knotting. . . Knotting is a preparation of red lead, litharge, boiled oil, and a little turpentine.

b. A preparation used as a cement or covering for metals.

5. The process of removing knots from cloth, pulp, etc.: see quots.

1875 KNIGHT *Dict. Mech.* 1240/2 *Knotting* . . . 2. (*Cloth-making.*) Removing weft knots and others from cloth by means of tweezers. **1880** SIR E. REED *Japan* II. 44 The processes of straining, knotting (the separation of knots, impurities, or of matted fibre which has formed into strings, or is insufficiently ground,) making [pulp into paper].

6. *attrib.* and *Comb.* (chiefly in sense 2).

1697 in Doran *Ann. Eng. Stage* (1864) I. xii. 250 A black taffety cap, together with . . a knotting needle, and a ball of sky-colour and white knotting. **1763** MRS. HARRIS in *Priv. Lett. Ld. Malmesbury* I. 94 Lady Weymouth . . and the Duchess of Ancaster sat knotting, with a knotting-bag hanging on their left arm. *a* **1847** MRS. SHERWOOD *Lady of Manor* II. x. 26, I then . . seated myself at the table, with my knotting-shuttle in my hand.

†**'knottish,** *a. Obs. rare*$^{-0}$. [f. KNOT *sb.*[1] + -ISH[1].] Knotty.

1530 PALSGR. 317/1 Knottysshe, knorisshe, or full of knottes, *neueux*.

†**'knottle.** *Obs.* [dim. of KNOT *sb.*[1]: see -LE.] A small knot; a knob; a tangle (of rope).

?*a* **1500** *Life Alexander* (in *MS. Lincoln* A. i. 17 lf. 1) (Halliwell), He hade a heued lyke a bulle, and knottilles in his frount, as thay had bene the bygynnyng of hornes. **1568** FULLWELL *Like will to Like* in Hazl. *Dodsley* III. 333 A bag and a bottle, or else a rope knottle.

knotty ('nɒtɪ), *a.* [f. KNOT *sb.*[1] + -Y.]

1. Of a cord, etc.: Having or full of knots; tied or entangled in knots.

a **1240** *Wohunge* in *Cott. Hom.* 281 þu wes . . wið cnotti swepes swungen. *c* **1440** *Promp. Parv.* 280/2 Knotty, *nodosus*. **1576** GASCOIGNE *Philomene* 112 She bare a skourge, with many a knottie string. **1602** SHAKS. *Ham.* I. v. 18 Make . . Thy knotty [*Qo.* knotted] and combined locks to part, And each particular haire to stand an end. **1634** SIR T. HERBERT *Trav.* 14 Their haire curld, . . blacke and knotty. **1852** R. S. SURTEES *Sponge's Sp. Tour* (1893) 310 Regardless of . . the crack of his little knotty whip.

2. *fig.* Full of intellectual difficulties or complications of thought; hard to 'unravel', explain, or solve; involved, intricate, perplexing, puzzling. (Sometimes with mixture of sense 4.)

a **1225** *Leg. Kath.* 1157 Ich habbe uncnut summe of þeos cnotti cnotten. **1573–80** BARET *Alv.* K 122 Knottie, full of knots, or difficulties. **1625** BACON *Ess., Regim. Health* (Arb.) 59 Auoid . . Anger fretting inwards; Subtill and knottie Inquisitions. **1638** *Penit. Conf.* vii. (1657) 192 Reckoned amongst the knotty pieces of Christian Religion. **1701** *Stanley's Hist. Philos.* Biog. 14 Æschylus, the most knotty and intricate of all the Greek Poets. **1702** POPE *Jan. & May* 140 The knotty point was urg'd on either side. **1874** CARPENTER *Ment. Phys.* I. ii. §79 (1879) 83 The man who is . . in a complete reverie, unravelling some knotty subject.

3. Abounding in or covered with knots, knobs, or rough protuberances; rugged, gnarled; containing knots, as a board.

c **1386** CHAUCER *Knt.'s T.* 1119 A forest, . . With knotty knarry bareyne trees olde. *c* **1420** *Pallad. on Husb.* III. 377 Ffertile, & fressh, ek knotty, sprongen newe Thy graffes be. *c* **1440** *Promp. Parv.* 280/2 Knotty, wythe-in the flesche, *glandulosus*. **1594** BLUNDEVIL *Exerc.* III. I. viii. (1636) 287 Like knots in a knotty board. **1692** BENTLEY *8 Serm.* (1724) 331 The scragged and knotty Backbone. **1762** R. GUY *Pract. Obs. Cancers* 75 A Cancer in her Breast, rough on the Surface, with knotty Vessels. **1821** CLARE *Vill. Minstr.* I. 122 The wild shelter of a knotty oak. **1881** MISS YONGE *Lads & Lasses Langley* ii. 97 She knelt upon the grass, with her bare hard-working knotty hands clasped.

4. Hard and rough in character; rugged.

a **1568** ASCHAM *Scholem.* I. (Arb.) 34 A witte . . that is not ouer dulle, heauie, knottie and lumpishe. **1643** MILTON *Divorce* Pref., Wks. (1851) 19 To doe this . . with a smooth and pleasing lesson, which receiv'd hath the vertue to soften and dispell rooted and knotty sorrowes. **1663** J. SPENCER *Prodigies* (1665) 341 A kind of blunter wedges provided by divine Wisdom to work upon those knotty tempers, upon which those instruments of a finer edg . . can do no good. **1821** LAMB *Elia* Ser. I. *Imperf. Symp.*, They beat up a little game peradventure—and leave it to knottier heads . . to run it down.

5. *Comb.*, as ***knotty-pated*** adj. [perh. associated with *not-headed, not-pated* (1 Hen. IV, II. iv. 78)], blockheaded.

1596 SHAKS. *1 Hen. IV*, II. iv. 251 Thou Clay-brayn'd Guts, thou Knotty-pated Foole.

knotweed ('nɒtwi:d). [f. KNOT *sb.*[1] + WEED *sb.*]

†**a.** Lyte's name for Knawel (*Scleranthus annuus*). *Obs.* **b.** Name for various species of *Centaurea* (Knapweed, etc.), from the knobby 'heads'. **c.** Name for various species of *Polygonum*.

1578 LYTE *Dodoens* I. lxvii. 97 The base Almaignes cal it knawel, that is to say, knot weede. **1827** CLARE *Sheph. Cal.* 49 They pull the little blossom threads From out the knot-weed's button heads. **1884** MILLER *Plant-n.*, Knotweed, . . Alpine, *Polygonum alpinum*. . . Amphibious, *Polygonum amphibium*.

knotwork ('nɒtwɜ:k).

1. Ornamental work consisting of, or (as in *Arch.*) representing, cords or the like intertwined and knotted together.

1851 D. WILSON *Preh. Ann.* (1863) II. IV. ii. 237 The interlaced knotwork so favourite a device of Celtic Art. *Ibid.* II. IV. iv. 292 The ornamentation vulgarly called Runic knot-work. **1863–9** *Dict. Archit.*, *Knot work*, the term lately given to a species of ornament of great variety and beauty, met with in manuscripts, on articles of attire, on monuments, and in the architecture, of the middle ages. **1868** G. STEPHENS *Runic Mon.* I. 389 The borders themselves, with their varied sculpture of knotwork and rope work, seem decidedly British.

2. A kind of fancy needlework.

1882 CAULFEILD & SAWARD *Dict. Needlework*, *Knot Work*, this is an old work recently introduced from the continent into England . . the modern Knot Work is made with fine silk on thread knotted over crochet cotton or cord, with its edging made with crochet.

knotwort ('nɒtwɜ:t). [See WORT.] **a.** The common knot-grass (*Polygonum aviculare*). **b.** *pl.* Lindley's name for the N.O. *Illecebraceæ*.

1845 LINDLEY *Veg. Kingd.* (1853) 499 Order . . *Illecebraceæ* . . Knotworts. **1864** PRIOR *Plant-n.*, *Knot-grass*, or *Knot-wort*, the centinode, from its trailing jointed stems and grass-like leaves.

knou(e, knouleche, obs. ff. KNOW, KNOWLEDGE.

knout (naʊt, nu:t), *sb.* Also 8 **knoute, knowt,** 8–9 **knoot.** [a. French spelling of Russ. *knut.*] A kind of whip or scourge, very severe and often fatal in its effects, formerly used in Russia as an instrument of punishment.

1716 J. PERRY *State Russia* 218 *note*, The Knout is a thick hard Thong of Leather of about three Foot and a half long, fasten'd to the end of a handsome Stick about two Foot and a half long, with a Ring or kind of Swivle like a Flail at the end of it, to which the Thong is fasten'd. **1753** *Scots Mag.* Jan. 6/1 The Russian government has been rendered more mild, by an abolition of the severe punishment of the knout. **1780** *Gentl. Mag.* Dec. 578/1 Death is often the consequence of a punishment apparently more mild, viz. the knoot. **1808** SIR R. R. PORTER *Trav. Sk. Russ. & Swed.* (1813) II. xxviii. 20, I have been to witness the execution of the Knout, to a height of torture which very seldom is now inflicted. **1855** TENNYSON *Maud* I. IV. viii, Shall I weep if . . an infant civilisation be ruled with rod or with knout?

knout, *v.* [f. prec.] *trans.* To flog or punish with the knout.

1772–84 COOK *Voy.* (1790) VI. 2162 At 16 years of age he was knowted, had his nose slit, and was banished to Siberia. **1863** SALA *Murderous Ischoostchik* 91 One was knouted to death only the other day, at the top of the Nevski, for the murder of a German commercial traveller.

Hence **'knouted** *ppl. a.*, **'knouting** *vbl. sb.*

1851 MRS. BROWNING *Casa Guidi Wind.* II. 644 Hast thou found . . No repose, Russia, for knouted Poles? **1887** *Daily News* 8 Oct. 6/1 Happily M. Verestschagin, who paints a Russian hanging, did not paint a Russian knouting.

knoutberry, variant of KNOTBERRY.

know (nəʊ), *v.* Pa. t. **knew** (nju:). Pa. pple. **known** (nəʊn). Forms: *Inf.* 1 **cnáwan,** 3–4 **cnawe(n;** 2–4 **cnowe(n,** 3 **cnoue(n,** 4–5 **cnow;** 3–5 **knawe(n,** 3–4 **knaun,** 5 *Sc.* **knaue,** (5–7 **knau);** 3–5 (3– *Sc.* and *dial.*) **knaw;** 3–4 **knowen,** (3 **kneowen,** 3–5 **knoue(n,** 5–6 **knou,** 6 **knowne),** 3–7 **knowe,** (6–7 **kno),** 5– **know.** *Pa. t.* 1–3 **cnéow,** 3 **cneou, cnew, cneu,** 3–4 **kneow,** 3–6 **kneu,** (4 **kneuȝ, kneuh, kneȝ, knev, knuȝ,** 5 **kneew, knogh),** 4–6 **knewe,** 3– **knew.** Also 3 **cnawed,** 5 **knowede,** 9– *dial.* **knowed.** *Pa. pple.* 1 **cnáwen,** 3–5 **knawen,** 3–4 **knauen,** (3 **knaun(e),** 4 **knawe,** 6 **knaw,** 7 *Sc.* **knawne,** 9 *Sc.* and *north.* **knawn;** 3–5 **cnowe(n,** 4–7 **knowen,** (4 **-un,** 4–5 **-yn),** 4–5 **know(e,** (5 **kno,** 6 **knouin, knoen,** 7 **knouen),** 6–7 **knowne,** 6– **known.** Also 2–3 **i-cnawe(n,** 3 **-cnowe(n,** 2–4 **i-, ykna(u)we(n, -knowe(n.** Also 3 **knawed, knaued, knaud,** 4 (9 *dial.*) **knowed.** [A Com. Teut. and Com. Aryan vb., now retained in Eng. alone of the Teut. languages: OE. (*ȝe*)*cnáwan*, pa. t. (*ȝe*)*cnéow*, pa. pple. (*ȝe*)*cnáwen* = OHG. *-cnâan, -chnâan, -chnâhan*, ON. pres. ind. *kná*, pl. *knegum*, Gothic type **knáian*, **kaiknô*, **knáians*, a redupl. vb. not found in existing remains. Outside Teut., = OSlav. *zna-tĭ*, Russ. *zna-t* to know; L. **gnō-*, whence the inceptive (*g*)*nōscĕre*, perf. (*g*)*nōvi*, pa. pple. (*g*)*nōt-us*; Gr. **γνω-*, whence redupl. and inceptive *γι-γνώ-σκειν*, 2 aor. *ἔ-γνω-ν*; Skr. *jnā-* know. Generally held to be from the same root (*gen-, gon-, gn-*) as CAN *v.*, and KEN. Already in early times the simple vb. had sustained various losses; in L. and Gr. the pres. stem survived only in derived forms; in Gothic the word is not recorded; in ON. the pres. inf. was obs.; in ON. and OHG. the orig. strong pa. t. and pa. pple. were lost; in OHG. and OE. the vb. was app. known only in composition, as in OE. *ȝecnáwan, oncnáwan, tócnáwan*. The first of these may be considered as the historical ancestor of ME. and mod. *know*, for although it came down in southern ME. as *i-knowen, y-knowe*, the prefix was regularly dropped in midl. and north., giving the simple stem form *cnawen, knawe(n, knowe(n*, which was well-established in all the main senses by 1200 (a single instance being known *a* 1100). The verb has since had a vigorous life, having also occupied with its meaning the original territory of the vb. WIT, Ger. *wissen*, and that of CAN, so far as this meant to 'know'. Hence Eng. *know* covers the ground of Ger. *wissen, kennen, erkennen*, and (in part) *können*, of Fr. *connaître* and *savoir*, of L. *nōvisse, co-gnōscĕre*, and *scīre*, of Gr. *γιγνώσκειν* and *εἰδέναι* (*οἶδα*). But in Sc. the verb KEN has supplanted *knaw*, and come to be the sense-equivalent of 'know' in all its extent of signification. As *ȝecnáwan* came down as late as 1400 in form *iknowen* YKNOW, the pa. pple in *i-, y-*, in southern ME., may belong to either form.]

Signification. From the fact that *know* now covers the ground formerly occupied by several verbs, and still answers to two verbs in other Teutonic and Romanic languages, there is much difficulty in arranging its senses and uses satisfactorily. However, as the word is etymologically related to Gr. *γιγνώσκειν*, L. (*g*)*nōscere* and (*g*)*nōvisse*, F. *connaître* (:—L. *cognōscĕre*) to 'know by the senses', Ger. *können* and *kennen*, Eng. *can, ken*, it appears proper to start with the uses which answer to these words, rather than with those which belonged to the archaic vb. to WIT, Ger. *wissen*, and are expressed by L. *scīre* and F. *savoir*, to 'know by the mind'. This etymological treatment of the word, and the uses to which it has been put, differs essentially from a logical or philosophical analysis of the notion of 'knowing', and the verbal forms and phrases by which this is expressed, in which the word 'know' is taken as an existing fact, without reference to the history of its uses.

Know, in its most general sense, has been defined by some as 'To hold for true or real with assurance and on (what is held to be) an adequate objective foundation'. Mr. James Ward, in *Encycl. Brit.* XX. 49 s.v. *Psychology*, assigns to the word two main meanings: 'To *know* may mean either to perceive or apprehend, or it may mean to understand or comprehend. . . Thus a blind man, who cannot *know* about light in the first sense, may *know* about light in the second, if he studies a treatise on optics.' Others hold that the primary and only proper object of knowing is a fact or facts (as in our sense 10), and that all so-called knowing of things or persons resolves itself, upon analysis, into the knowing of certain facts about these, as their existence, identity, nature, attributes, etc., the particular fact being understood from the context, or by a consideration of the kind of fact which is usually wanted to be known about the thing or person in question. Thus, 'Do you know Mr. G.?', 'Do you know Balliol College?' have different meanings according to the kind of facts about Mr. G. or Balliol College, which are the objects of inquiry.

I. 1. a. *trans.* To perceive (a thing or person) as identical with one perceived before, or of which one has a previous notion; to recognize; to identify. Sometimes with *again*; also, later, with *for*.

[*Beowulf* 2047 Meaht ðu, min wine, mece ȝecnawan þone þin fæder to ȝefeohte bær. *c* **1000** Ælfric *Gen.* xxvii. 12 ȝif min fæder me handlaþ and me ȝecnæwþ. *Ibid.* xxxviii. 26 Ða he ða lac ȝecneow.] *a* **1100** in Napier *O.E. Glosses* 76 *Noscuntur*, .i. *intelleguntur*, þa beoð cnawene. *c* **1200** Ormin 1314 Lamb.. cann cnawenn swiþe wel Hiss moderr þær ȝho blæteþþ. *c* **1250** *Gen. & Ex.* 2162 Ðe .x. comen.. To Iosep, and he ne knewen him nogt. *a* **1300** *Cursor M.* 4209 Quen his fader his kirtell kneu Moght na gamen him com to gleu. *c* **1460** *Towneley Myst.* xxvii. 348 All sone he hym with-drogh, ffro he saw that we hym knogh. **1560** Daus tr. *Sleidane's Comm.* 232 This question,.. whether that in the life everlasting, we shal know one an other. **1634** Sir T. Herbert *Trav.* 11 After two leagues pursuit, they knew her for a Portugall Carrack. **1706** Pope *Let. to Wycherley* 10 Apr., They would not be chang'd so much, but any one would know them for the same at first sight. **1724** De Foe *Mem. Cavalier* (1840) 26 For four days more I knew nobody. **1865** Kingsley *Herew.* v. (1877) 111, I knew you, in spite of your hair, by your eyes. **1867** Howells *Ital. Journ.* 63, I wonder how he should have known us for Americans?

b. To recognize or distinguish, or be able to distinguish (one thing) *from* (another) = OE. *tócnáwan*.

c **1375** *Cursor M.* 6402 (Fairf.) Mony atte.. knawes noȝt þe gode fra þe ille. **1406** Hoccleve *La male regle* 23 Now can I knowe feeste fro penaunce. **1598** Shaks. *Merry W.* iii. iii. 44 We'll teach him to know Turtles from Iayes. **1704** Pope *Windsor For.* 175 Scarce could the Goddess from her nymph be known. **1843** Macaulay *Mme. D'Arblay* Ess. 1865 III. 295 Burney loved his own art passionately; and Johnson just knew the bell of Saint Clement's church from the organ.

(*b*) Phrases: ***not to know one's arse from one's elbow*** (and similar phrases): a coarse expression suggestive of complete ignorance or innocence; (***not***) ***to know from nothing*** (*U.S.*): to be totally ignorant (about something).

1930 R. Blaker *Medal without Bar* xiii. 69 'But nor 'an 'un' (this phrase was his masterpiece of thoughtful emphasis), 'nor 'an 'un of us knows 'is ears from 'is elbow when it comes to learning—learning like you orficers have got up your sleeves.' **1936** *Mademoiselle* Mar. 43/1, I find I belong to the wrong gender to take part in such confabulations, and know from nothing. **1942** Berrey & Van den Bark *Amer. Thes. Slang* §150/3 *Be ignorant*, know from nothing. **1944** 'N. Shute' *Pastoral* iv. 75, I wish I'd had a crowd like that for my first crew. We none of us knew arse from elbow when they pushed me off. **1945** 'F. Feikema' *Boy Almighty* (1950) xvii. 162 Them San dietitians, they don't know from nuthin'. **1945** T. Shor in Mencken *Amer. Lang.* (1948) Suppl. II. 695 A *square* don't know from nothin' and a *creep* is worse'n a jerk. **1966** 'L. Lane' *ABZ of Scouse* 29 Don't know Thairsday from brekfuss-time. *Ibid.*, Don't know 'is arse from 'is elbow. **1968** *Encounter* Sept. 22/1 He knows from nothin'.

c. *intr.* To distinguish *between*. *rare.*

1864 Lowell *Fireside Trav.* 3 Let him know between the good and evil fruits.

†**2.** *trans.* To recognize in some capacity; to acknowledge; to admit the claims or authority of: = beknow 3. *Obs.*

a **1225** *Leg. Kath.* 2066 To him we kennið & cnaweð to lauerd. **1297** R. Glouc. (Rolls) 3995 Þat þou nelt him iknowe [*v.r.* knowe] ne do þin seruage. **13..** *E.E. Allit. P.* C. 519 Wyȝez wyl torne, & cum & cnawe me for kyng. **1382** Wyclif *1 Thess.* v. 12 We preien ȝou, that ȝe schulen knowe hem that trauelen among ȝou, and.. that ȝe haue hem more haboundantli in charite [1611 and *R.V.* to know them]. *c* **1450** *Cov. Myst.* (Shaks. Soc.) 169, I.. know the for my lorde. **1560** Daus tr. *Sleidane's Comm.* 38 Thinke you that they wyll knowe or obey any civill Magistrate?

†**3. a.** *trans.* To acknowledge, confess, own, admit: = acknow 2, beknow 2. *Obs.*

c **1200** Ormin 9818 Ne wollden þeȝȝ nohht cnawenn Ne ȝatenn þatt teȝȝ wærenn ohht Sinnfulle. *a* **1300** *Cursor M.* 5107 Þat we haue misdon we will knau. *c* **1375** *Lay Folks Mass Bk.* (MS. B.) 51 Lered & lewed þat wil.. knowe to god þat þai are ille. *c* **1440** *Jacob's Well* 67 Knowe þi synne to vs, ȝif þou be gylty. **1467** *Burgh Rec. Aberdeen* 2 Dec. (Spald. Cl) I. 27 The said Thomas sal.. opynly knaw that he has offendit til him.

b. *refl.* To make confession, confess; also with *compl.*, to confess oneself (to be) something.

a **1225** *Leg. Kath.* 132 Al ha cneowen [*v.r.* icneowen] ham crauant & ouercumen. *a* **1300** *Cursor M.* 18488 Loues nu vr lauerd dright, And knau yow til him o yur plight. *c* **1375** *Ibid.* (Fairf. MS.) 26959 Qua buxumli him-self knawes [*Cott.* be-knaus] sal haue mercy. **14..** *Masse* in *Tundale's Vis.* (1843) 148 Sey ye with hym *Confiteor* Or ellis in Ynglysch thus therfor I know me to God. **1478** *Croscombe Church-w. Acc.* (Som. Rec. Soc.) 7 Comes.. and cnowth hym dettar to the Cherch for his servant xx[d].

c. *intr.* (for *refl.*) *Obs.*

c **1200** *Trin. Coll. Hom.* 71 Kneoweð ure louerd [*confitemini domino*]. *a* **1350** *Cursor M.* 18488 (Gött.) Louis nu vr lauerd dright, An knau til him of ȝur plight. **1362** Langl. *P. Pl* B. xi. 273 For he kneuȝ on þe crois & to crist shref hym.

d. *pass.* = b. Const. *of*, *that*. = acknow 4, beknow 4. *Obs.*

c **1200** *Vices & Virtues* 21 Ðat ic scolde bien icnawe of mine sennes. *c* **1200** *Trin. Coll. Hom.* 123 Þe man.. þe beð is gultes cnowe. *c* **1205** Lay. 26433 ȝif þu wulle icnawen beo þat Arður is king ouer þe. *c* **1310** *Marina* 53 in Böddeker *Alt. Eng. Dicht.* 258 He nolde be knowe for no þyng þat hit wes a mayde ȝyng. *c* **1330** *Assump. Virg.* 534 (Br. Mus. Add. MS.), ȝif.. he wille on his last þrowe Schryue him & ben y-knowe.

†**4.** *trans.* To perceive (with the senses). *Obs.*

c **1330** R. Brunne *Chron. Wace* (Rolls) 1684 Coryneus.. busched þem on a rowe þat þe Frensche moughte þem nought knowe. **1398** Trevisa *Barth. De P.R.* iii. xxi. (1495) 69 The sighte knoweth hewe and colour and the taast knoweth sauour. *a* **1400-50** *Alexander* 63 He saȝe þam in þe hiȝe see.. Carrygis comand he knew keruand þe ithis.

II. 5. a. To be acquainted with (a thing, a place, or a person); to be familiar with by experience, or through information or report (= F. *connaître*, Ger. *kennen*). Sometimes, To have such familiarity with (something) as gives understanding or insight. ***to know like a book*** (see like *adv.* 1 c).

c **1175** *Lamb. Hom.* 137 For hereword to habbene and beon iwurðeȝede fir and neor ðer þe heo icnawene beoð. *c* **1205** Lay. 4623 Ne þas strond we ne cnoweð þe we isoht habbeð. **1362** Langl. *P. Pl.* A. ii. 202 He kennede him in heore craft and kneuȝ mony gummes. *c* **1386** Chaucer *Prol.* 240 He knew the Tauernes wel in al the toun. **1485** Caxton *Pref. Malory's Arthur*, Alysaunder the grete, &.. Iulyus Cezar.. of whome thystoryes ben wel kno and had. **1598** Shaks. *Merry W.* ii. ii. 188 You haue been a man long knowne to me, though I had neuer so good means as desire, to make my selfe acquainted with you. **1634** Milton *Comus* 311, I know each lane, and every alley green,.. of this wilde Wood. **1710** Addison *Tatler* No. 192 ¶5 A Story that is very well known in the North of England. **1800** *Med. Jrnl.* IV. 400 The external use of cold water has been known and practised from the earliest periods. **1849** Macaulay *Hist. Eng.* iii. I. 365 Whoever could make himself agreeable to the prince,.. might hope to rise in the world.. without being even known by sight to any minister of state.

b. *refl.* To know oneself; esp. in *imper.* *arch.* phr. ***know thyself***.

c **1200** *Trin. Coll. Hom.* 123 Þe man cnoweð him seluen þe þencheð of wu medeme þinge he is shapen. *c* **1305** *Knowe þi self* 3, in E.E.P. (1862) 130 Vche cristen creature knowen hym self ouht. **1484** Caxton *Æsop* ii. Fable 17 Who that knoweth hym self lytel he preyseth hym self. *c* **1527** tr. *Erasmus's Dicta Sapientium* sig. A3v *Nosce te ipsum*, know thy selfe. **1531** Elyot *Gov.* iii. iii, *Nosce te ipsum*, whiche is in englysshe, know thy selfe. **1707** Norris *Treat. Humility* ii. 58 We say of proud men that they do not understand themselves, or that they ought to be made to know themselves better. **1849** Lytton *Caxtons* III. xvi. x. 183 'Know thyself,' said the old philosophy. 'Improve thyself,' saith the new. **1860** Pusey *Min. Proph.* 455 In order to repent, a man must know himself thoroughly. **1905** A. Maclaren *Gospel St. Matthew* i. 43 The proud old saying of the Greeks, 'Know thyself'.. would result in this profound abnegation of all claims, in this poverty of spirit. **1929** A. Huxley *Let.* 7 Jan. (1969) 306 'Know thyself' was probably one of the stupidest pieces of advice ever given. *a* **1930** D. H. Lawrence *Last Poems* (1932) 266 When at last we escape the barbed wire enclosure of *Know Thyself*, knowing we can never know. **1941** *N. & Q.* Feb. 138 The folly of that impossible precept 'Know thyself'.

c. To have personal experience of (something) as affecting oneself; to have experienced, met with, felt, or undergone. Also *fig.* of inanimate things. Chiefly in negative forms of expression.

1390 Gower *Conf.* I. 7 Justice of lawe tho was holde.. The citees knewen no debat. **1591** Shaks. *Two Gent.* i. iii. 16 In hauing knowne no trauaile in his youth. **1697** Dryden *Virg. Georg.* iii. 530 Whole Months they wander, grazing as they go; Nor Folds, nor hospitable Harbour know. **1877** E. R. Conder *Bas. Faith* iv. 151 'He has never known trouble'; 'He knows no fear', meaning that the person spoken of is not familiar with these feelings. **1879** R. K. Douglas *Confucianism* iii. 71 Running water which knows no stagnation. **1896** A. E. Housman *Shropshire Lad* l, And lads knew trouble at Knighton When I was a Knighton lad.

d. ***to know as***, to be familiarly acquainted with under the name of; *pass.*, to be commonly called.

1887 *Co-operative News* XVIII. 242 The timbers.. are not what is technically known as 'blue'.

6. a. To be personally acquainted with (a person); to be familiar or intimate with; †to become acquainted with (*obs.*).

1377 Langl. *P. Pl.* B. vi. 222 If þow fynde any freke þat fortune hath appeyred,.. fonde þow suche to cnowe; Conforte hem with þi catel. *c* **1386** Chaucer *Knt.'s T.* 345 Duc Perotheus loued wel Arcite And hadde hym knowe at Thebes yeer by yere. *a* **1400** *Pistill of Susan* 170 Hir kinrede, hir cosyns and al þat hire knewe. *a* **1548** Hall *Chron., Hen. VIII* 244 [He] curssed the tyme that ever he knewe Doctor Barnes. **1575** Laneham *Let.* 1, I am.. acquainted with the most, and well knoen too the best, and euery officer glad of my company. **1726** G. Roberts *Four Yrs. Voy.* 313 [He asked] If I was acquainted with any of the Signores of the City? I told him, I knew some of them. **1872** W. Coleman in *Rep. 42nd U.S. Congress 2 Sess. Joint Select. Comm. Condition of Affairs Late Insurrectionary States* XI. 484 Of course I knowed him. **1892** Mrs. H. Ward *David Grieve* III. 131 As to knowing people, you won't take any trouble at all! *Mod.* They are neighbours of ours, but we do not know them.

†**b.** *pass.* ***to be known***, to be personally acquainted or on familiar terms *with*. *Obs.*

a **1225** *Juliana* 14 Ne ich neuer þat ich wite nes wið him icnawen. **1380** *Lay Folks Catech.* (Lamb. MS.) 178 He was homly and knowyn with þis lady. *c* **1475** *Rauf Coilȝear* 532, 'I am knawin with the Quene', said Schir Rolland. **1560** Daus tr. *Sleidane's Comm.* 117b, He was so well knowen with the Emperour Soliman.

†**c.** *intr.* Of two persons: To be (mutually) acquainted. (= F. *se connaître.*) *Obs.*

1606 Shaks. *Ant. & Cl.* ii. vi. 86 You, and I haue knowne sir. **1611** —— *Cymb.* i. iv. 36 Sir, we haue knowne togither in Orleance.

7. *trans.* To have carnal acquaintance or sexual intercourse with. *arch.*

Chiefly a Hebraism which has passed into the mod. langs., but found also in Gr. and L. So Ger. *erkennen*, F. *connaître*.

c **1200** Ormin 2406 Ȝho.. seȝȝde; Hu maȝȝ þiss forþedd ben þurrh me þatt nan weppmann ne cnawe? *c* **1325** *Metr. Hom.* 38 It was igain the lawe His brother wif fleyslic to knawe. *c* **1330** R. Brunne *Chron.* (1810) 155 He stode, & proued it.. þ at his fader Henry þat ilk Aleyse had knowen. **1382** Wyclif *Gen.* iv. 1 Adam forsothe knewe Eue his wijf. **1535** Joye *Apol. Tindale* (Arb.) 48 Before she knew (that is) slept with hir howsbonde. **1572** *Depos. Canterb. Cath. Libr.* bk. 18 lf. 166 (MS.) To haue to doo with her, meaning carnallye to knowe this deponentes boddye. **1601** Shaks. *All's Well* v. iii. 288 By Ioue, if euer I knew man, 'twas you. **1603** —— *Meas. for M.* v. i. 203 That is Angelo, Who thinkes he knowes, that he nere knew my body. *c* **1613** Middleton *No Wit like a Woman's* ii. iii, Will you swear here you never yet knew woman?

III. 8. To have cognizance of (something), through observation, inquiry, or information; to be aware or apprised of (= F. *savoir*, Ger. *wissen*); †to become cognizant of, learn through information or inquiry, ascertain, find out (*obs.*).

a **1225** *Leg. Kath.* 463 Ȝef þu wult cnawen mi cun, ich am kinges dohter. *c* **1350** *Will. Palerne* 577 Ȝit couþe non by no craft knowen hire sore. **1362** Langl. *P. Pl.* A. ix. 63 'What art þou', quod I 'that my nome knowest?' *c* **1375** *Quon. Attach.* c. 48 §5 in Skene *Reg. Maj.* 85 b, All hurdes and treasures hid vnder the earth.. quhereof the awner is not knawin. *c* **1425** Lydg. *Assembly of Gods* 175 He hit desyryd to knowe hys offence. **1531** Elyot *Gov.* iii. xxvi, Galene.. exhorteth them to knowe exactly the accustomed diete of their patientes. **1669** Sturmy *Mariner's Mag.* i. 38 How to divide a Triangle (whose Area or Content is known) into two Parts. **1706** Pope *Let. to Wycherley* 10 Apr., Pray let me know your mind in this. **1776** *Trial of Nundocomar* 23/1, I do not know his age exactly. **1871** Morley *Voltaire* (1886) 10 The free-thinker [would fain pass] for a person with his own orthodoxies if you only knew them.

9. a. To be conversant with (a body of facts, principles, a method of action, etc.) through instruction, study, or practice; *esp.* to have practical understanding of (a science, language, profession, etc.); to have learnt by study or practical experience; to be versed or skilled in; †to acquire skill in, to learn (*obs.*).

a **1400** *Pistill of Susan* 24 Þus thei lerne hire þe lawe, Cleer Clergye to knawe. *c* **1400** *Lanfranc's Cirurg.* 20 Galienus seiþ, þat it is necessarie a surgian to knowe anatomie. **1598** Florio *Ital. Dict.* Ep. Ded., Well to know Italian is a grace of all graces. **1639** Massinger *Unnat. Combat* i. i. Wks. (Rtldg.) 27/1 Nay, if a velvet petticoat move in the front, Buff jerkins must to the rear, I know my manners. **1749** Johnson *London* 115 All sciences a fasting Monsieur knows. **1762** Goldsmith *Cit. W.* lxi, To know one profession only, is enough for one man to know. **1808** Scott *Marm.* i. viii, Each, chosen for an archer good, Knew hunting-craft by lake or wood. *c* **1813** Mrs. Sherwood *Stories on Catechism* x. (1873) 83 Know you not the commandments of God? **1872** L. Carroll *Through Looking Glass* ix. 192 Of course you know your ABC.

b. Phr. ***to know better*** (†***better things***), to have learnt better from experience; hence, to be more prudent or discreet (*than to do* something).

a **1704** L'Estrange (J.), One would have thought you had known better things than to expect a kindness from a common enemy. **1782** Mad. D'Arblay *Let. to S. Crisp* Aug., You and I know better than to hum or be hummed in that manner. **1872** *Punch* 24 Feb. 78/2 Some persons who should know better than to talk nonsense. **1886** Ruskin *Præterita* I. 431 Nothing to blame themselves in, except not having known better.

c. To have learnt by committing to memory; more fully, ***to know by heart***: see heart *sb.* 32.

1855 Pusey *Doctr. Real Presence* Note S. 602 Sozomen mentions a celebrated Ascetic.. who.. knew the Holy Scriptures by heart. *Mod.* To know one's lesson; to know one's part, as in a play.

†**d.** *refl.* (in later use *pass.*) To be versed or skilled *in*. (= F. *se connaître en.*) *Obs.*

c **1330** R. Brunne *Chron. Wace* (Rolls) 11064 Þer were chanons of clergye, & knewe þem wel in astronomye. *Ibid.* 11198, Y ne knowe me nought in swylk chaffare. *c* **1470** Henry *Wallace* xi. 412 Wallace beheld, quhilk weill in weir him knew. **1630** Lord *Banians & Persees* 33 To bee knowne onely in his owne busynes, and not to enquire after the things of the world. **1655** [see known 2].

e. ***to know one's*** ——: to be well acquainted with something, to be well up in something. E.g. ***to know one's business***, ***onions*** (see onion *sb.*), ***stuff*** (see stuff *sb.*[1]).

10. a. To apprehend or comprehend as fact or truth; to have a clear or distinct perception or apprehension of; to understand or comprehend with clearness and feeling of certainty. Formerly, sometimes, †to get to understand, to find out by reasoning.

When the feeling of certainty is emphasized, *know* is often contrasted with *believe*.

c **1200** Ormin 15624 He cnew hemm alle wel & alle þeȝȝre þohhtess. **1387** Trevisa *Higden* (Rolls) III. 217 Meny þinges beeþ þat mowe be knowe by manis kynde wytt. **1413** *Pilgr. Sowle* (Caxton 1483) iv. xxviii. 75 Why is it thenne that he vseth nought discours of reason to knowe oute the trouthe? **1601** Gill *Treat. Trinitie* in *Sacr. Philos.* (1625) 215, I conclude, that there is nothing which is beleeved, but it may also be knowen. **1667** Milton *P.L.* ix. 804 Mature In knowledge, as the Gods who all things know. **1744** Berkeley *Siris* §253 We know a thing when we understand it. **1845** Trench *Huls. Lect.* i. (1854) 16 We must pass into, and unite ourselves with, that which we would know, before we can know it more than in name. **1855** Macaulay *Hist. Eng.* xvii. IV. 56 It seems probable that.. he did not know his own mind. **1874** Blackie *Self-Cult.* 14 Count yourself not to know a fact when you know that it took place, but then only when you see it as it did take place.

b. *absol.* or *intr.* To have understanding or knowledge.

c **1200** Ormin 13811 Þu cnawesst rihht & trowwesst. **1377** Langl. *P. Pl.* B. x. 464 Suche lewed iottes.. þat imparfitly here knewe, And eke lyued. **1561** T. Norton *Calvin's Inst.* iii. 277 When menne do with minde and vnderstanding conceyue the knowlege of things, they are thereby sayd (*Scire*) to know. **1669** Sturmy *Mariner's Mag.* i. 22 By

Speculation we know that we may the better know. **1832** TENNYSON *Pal. Art* xli, Large-brow'd Verulam, The first of those who know. **1850** —— *In Mem.* Prol. vi, We have but faith: we cannot know; For knowledge is of things we see. **1892** MRS. H. WARD *David Grieve* II. 164 A word, a look from a real artist—from one of the great men who *know*.

11. To be cognizant, conscious, or aware of (a fact); to be informed of, to have learned; to apprehend (with the mind), to understand.

* With various constructions:

a. with dependent statement, usually introduced by *that*.

†Formerly sometimes passive, ***to be known that***, in same sense.

[*a* **1000** *Juliana* 356 þæt þu..sylf ȝecnawe þæt þis is soð.] *c* **1200** *Trin. Coll. Hom.* 127 þo nam he ȝeme of mannes liflode and cnew þat here dedes weren iuele. *a* **1425** *Cursor M.* 1905 (Trin.) þenne was noe wel I knawe þat þe flood hit was wiþdrawe. *c* **1470** HENRY *Wallace* III. 273, I knaw he will do mekill for his kyne. **1479** *Surtees Misc.* (1888) 37 Be it knawen to all maner of men to whom this present writyng commys, that Robert Elwalde..is a trewe Ynglish man. **1560** DAUS tr. *Sleidane's Comm.* 375 You knowe, howe they were both letted by the war..and..also by sicknes. **1602** SHAKS. *Ham.* IV. iii. 69 Till I know 'tis done, How ere my happes, my ioyes were ne're begun. **1669** STURMY *Mariner's Mag.* I. 15 The Hollander..knows it right well, that there are none like English for Courage at Sea. **1702** ADDISON *Medals* i. Wks. 1721 I. 437 You do not know but it may have its usefulness. **1712** —— *Spect.* No. 415 ¶3, I know there are Persons who look upon some of these Wonders of Art as Fabulous. **1748** RICHARDSON *Clarissa* Wks. 1883 VI. 336, I know you will expedite an answer. **1849** MACAULAY *Hist. Eng.* vi. II. 158 Tyrconnel threatened to let the king know that the lord president had..described his majesty as a fool. **1878** J. COOK *Lect. Orthod.* vi, You know that you know that nothing can be known! How do you know that you know? **1879** HARLAN *Eyesight* iii. 41 It is now known that the increased refraction..is the result of an increase in the convexity of the lens. **1889** J. K. JEROME *Three Men in a Boat* 275, I know for a fact that they are there.

dial. **1848** J. R. LOWELL *Poet. Wks.* (1873) 252/1 My! when he made Ole Hunderd ring, She *knowed* the Lord was nigher. **1929** *Amer. Mercury* Sept. 50/1 Got in trouble one time... Knowed officers couldn't 'rest me. **1942** *Ibid.* July 87, I knowed you'd back up. **1949** in B. A. Botkin *Treas. S. Folklore* III. i. 434, I knowed dad-blamed well they wa'n't no fox in that sourwood.

b. with dependent question, introduced by *who*, *what*, *when*, *where*, *how*, and the like; as *I know who did it, I know where he lives.* Often *ellipt.*, giving rise to subst., adj., and advb. phrases, as *I know not who, I know not how, dear knows where*, etc. ***not to know what hit one***: see HIT *v.* 8e. Also, ***you know***: a phrase used with aposiopesis (the implication to be imagined) or const. *what*, *whom*, etc. (as a means of avoiding naming the person, etc., referred to).

The fact known is the answer to the question directly or indirectly expressed.

c **1200** *Trin. Coll. Hom.* 81 Warbi we mihten cnowen gif hit soð were þat þu seist. *c* **1275** LAY. 4621 Ne cnowe non of þis gomes..in woche londe he beoþ icome. **1387** TREVISA *Higden* (Rolls) I. 47 ȝif helle is in myddel of þe erþe doun riȝt, me myȝte knowe how meny myle is to helle. *c* **1391** CHAUCER *Astrol.* II. §1 Rekene and knowe which is the day of thi monthe. **1406** HOCCLEVE *La male regle* 41 Myn vnwar yowthe kneew nat what it wroghte. **1531** ELYOT *Gov.* I. xviii, I coulde neuer knowe who founde firste that disporte. **1567** MAPLET *Gr. Forest* 28 Othersome..arise up of their owne accord not known how. **1649** MILTON *Eikon.* xvii. Wks. (1847) 317/1 Timothy and Titus, and I know not whom thir Successors. **1736** BUTLER *Anal.* II. v. Wks. 1874 I. 211 We do not know what the whole natural or appointed consequences of vice are. **1867** TROLLOPE *Phineas Finn* (1869) I. x. 84 She told me once..it would lead to my being everlastingly—you know what. She isn't so squeamish as I am, and said it out. **1875** GEO. ELIOT *Let.* 13 Jan. (1956) VI. 116, I had a letter from 'you know whom' last night. **1875** JOWETT *Plato* (ed. 2) V. 44 He who does not know what is true will not know what is good. **1892** MRS. ALEXANDER *Mammon* II. 95 Chief manager, a millionaire, and I don't know what. **1911** D. H. LAWRENCE *White Peacock* II. i. 219 It's the way she swings her body—an' the curves as she stands. It's when you look at her—you feel—you know. **1925** *New Yorker* 7 Mar. 19/1 Of course there's no use me asking you if you took in all the revues where the girls come out—you know. **1937** C. DAY LEWIS *Starting Point* iii. 44 Never mind, kick him in the you know where—he's used to it. **1948** D. BALLANTYNE *Cunninghams* ii. 12 She is you know [*sc.* in the family way] to a Maori. **1949** D. M. DAVIN *Roads from Home* 99 Too much you know what last night, eh? **1970** *Harrap's French-Eng. Dict. Slang* 201 *Qui-vous-savez*, (said of person one does not wish to name) you know who.

c. with accusative and infinitive, as *I know him to be a friend*; also in the corresponding passive, as *he is known to be friendly.*

The infin. *to be* is sometimes omitted; its place may be taken by *as* or *for*.

a **1300** *Cursor M.* 6715 If his lauerd kneu him kene o horn ..If he sla man or womman, þis ox þan sal be taght to slan. **1377** LANGL. *P. Pl.* B. IV. 164 Who-so wilneth hir to wyf.. But he be knowe for a koke-wolde kut of my nose. *c* **1400** *Apol. Loll.* 29 So knaw bischopis hem to be..þe more þer soureyns. *c* **1420** *Anturs of Arth.* 139, I haue kinges in my kyne, knowene for kene. **1560** DAUS tr. *Sleidane's Comm.* 353 b, He would urge..those thinges chiefly, wherewith he knawe theyr myndes to be moste offended. **1603** SHAKS. *Meas. for M.* v. i. 505 You sirha, that knew me for a foole, a Coward. **1611** —— *Cymb.* I. i. 76, I will be knowne your Aduocate. **1769** GOLDSM. *Hist. Rome* (1786) I. 263 An enemy whom he knew more powerful than himself. **1809** *Med. Jrnl.* XXI. 479 It would be an insult to common reason to suppose..that you would encourage prejudices which you knew to exist. **1817** LD. ELLENBOROUGH in *Maule & Selwyn's Rep.* VI. 316 When he knew himself insolvent. **1891** SIR R. BALL in *Contemp. Rev.* Sept. 440 The stars were known to be bodies more or less congenerous with our sun.

d. The perfect tenses with acc. and inf. have the sense, To have had perception or experience of something as a contemporary fact.

Here the infin. *to* is usually omitted after the active voice (*I have known them fall*), but is retained after the passive (*they have been known to fall*). Cf. HEAR *v.* 3.

1703 EARL ORRERY *As you Find it* I. i, I have known some of 'em dog-cheap. **1711** ADDISON *Spect.* No. 29 ¶11, I have sometimes known the Performer..do no more in a Celebrated Song, than the Clerk of a Parish Church. **1849** THACKERAY *Pendennis* xv, I never knew a man die of love,.. but I have known a twelve-stone man go down to nine stone five under a disappointed passion. **1850** MCCOSH *Div. Govt.* III. ii. (1874) 397 Criminals have been known..to jest even upon the scaffold. **1884** MRS. H. WARD *Miss Bretherton* vii. 86, I never knew anyone do so much in so short a time.

e. *absol.* Often parenthetically, esp. in colloquial use, in ***you know*** (cf. 'you see'; now freq. as a mere conversational filler.), ***we know***, ***do you know***. Also, ***don't you know?***, a variant of *you know* (cf. DONCHER).

Grammatically the parenthetic clause is often the chief sentence, and the fact stated its object; but it can often be taken as = *as you know to be the fact*.

c **1350** *Will. Palerne* 1174 He is my lege man lelly þou knowes. *c* **1386** CHAUCER *Man of Law's Prol.* 50 Chaucer.. Hath seyd hem in swich englissh as he kan Of olde tyme as knoweth many a man. **1599** H. BUTTES *Dyets drie Dinner* A a iv b, Yet Time (you know) is *Edax rerum.* **1712** ADDISON *Spect.* No. 475 ¶5 How can he help that, you know? **1798** JANE AUSTEN *Northang. Abb.* vi. (1833) 24 Do you know, I saw the prettiest hat you can imagine. **1880** 'MARK TWAIN' *Tramp Abroad* App. D. 611 Nothing gives such an air of grace and elegance and unconstraint to a German or an English conversation as to scatter it full of 'Also's' or 'You-knows'. **1885** ANSTEY *Tinted Venus* i. 7 Ought I to have cried both my eyes out? You haven't cried out either of yours, you know. **1885** A. EDWARDES *Girton Girl* II. iii. 40 Attack me? Why that was only a foolish joke, don't you know? **1896** F. C. PHILIPS *Undeserving Woman* 104 'When?' said George. 'I'd like to put the thing right at once, don't you know.' **1924** D. H. LAWRENCE *Phoenix II* (1968) 304 Little smart man of the shabby world, very much on the spot, don't you know. **1926** G. HUNTING *Vicarion* iv. 63 This represents some years of study, you know, this little exhibition I have given you. **1930** 'SAPPER' *Finger of Fate* 225 My wife is such a nervous woman, don't you know. **1947** [see BOUDIN]. **1965** *Listener* 2 Dec. 914/1 A. They're supposed to be, you know, sexy. B. That's all right, but all men are the same, after one thing, but sometimes, you know, it can be wonderful. **1968** *Ibid.* 16 May 626/2 Too often one hears people on the wireless beginning an elaborate sentence—they flounder about for a bit and then break off with: 'you know'. **1969** WIDDOWSON & HALPERT in Halpert & Story *Christmas Mumming in Newfoundland* 151 You could buy them in St. John's, you know, the false faces. **1974** *Sunday Times* (Colour Suppl.) 3 Feb. 66/4 People get the wrong idea, thinking we might be, you know, glamorous or brilliant or something.

f. with a word or phrase standing in place of a fact referred to.

e.g. to know *it, that, what has been said, the fact, all about it, the existence of the book, the goodness of his heart* (= that his heart is good). (This last passes into 8). ***not if I know it***, a colloquial phrase intimating that one will take care not to do the thing referred to.

[*c* **1000** *Juliana* 443 Ic ðat sylf ȝecneow to late micles.] **1386** *Rolls of Parlt.* III. 225/1 Nichol Brembre..with stronge honde, as it is ful knowen..was chosen Mair. *c* **1386** CHAUCER *Man of Law's T.* 857 The Romayn Emperour.. hath by lettres knowe The slaughtre of cristen folk. *c* **1400** *Destr. Troy* 11721, I haue comynt in this case, knowith hit your-selfe. *a* **1425** *Cursor M.* 14949 (Trin.) þese iewes ben, ȝe hit knowen [*Cott.* Yon Iues ar, wel wat ȝee it]. *c* **1489** CAXTON *Sonnes of Aymon* xxvi. 549 Whan the kyng charlemagn knewe the comyng of reynawd. **1560** DAUS tr. *Sleidane's Comm.* 177 b, But that time knew I none of all this gere. **1610** HEALEY *St. Aug. Citie of God, Vives Comm.* (1620) 103 This I think is knowne to all. **1697** DRYDEN *Virg. Georg.* II. 639 O happy, if he knew his happy State! **1715** DE FOE *Fam. Instruct.* I. i. (1841) I. 6 How do we know that he dwells there?..we know it in two ways. **1865** TROLLOPE *Miss Mackenzie* I. ii. 33 'Tom,' said I, when he asked me to go down to Drunder Street, 'not if I know it.' **1874** T. HARDY *Far fr. Madding Crowd* (1889) 32 After that do you think I could marry you? Not if I know it. **1891** MRS. NEWMAN *Begun in Jest* I. 47 As soon as Dorothy wished it to be known. **1892** W. S. GILBERT *Mountebanks* I. 24 *Ni.* I say —don't lose that. *Pie.* Not if I know it. **1897** HINDE *Congo Arabs* 147 Oh, we know all about Mohara.

** In various phrases, arranged in the chronological order of their first recorded use in English as far as this is determinable:

g. ***to know little*** (or ***nothing***) ***and care less***: to be unconcerned *about*; to be studiously ignorant of.

1814 JANE AUSTEN *Mansf. Park* II. xi. 251 'I know nothing of the Miss Owens,' said Fanny calmly. 'You know nothing and you care less, as people, say. Never did tone express indifference plainer.' **1853** LYTTON *My Novel* II. VIII. iv. 322 'Ah!' said Egerton, who, as it has been before said, knew little, and cared less, about the Hazeldean pedigree, 'I..had forgotten it.' **1893** R. L. STEVENSON *Catriona* xxii. 267, I tell ye I ken naething and care less either for him or his breed. **1924** R. H. MOTTRAM *Spanish Farm* I. 71 Madeleine knew little and cared less as to what this might mean, except as it affected the work of the farm. **1925** F. HARRIS *My Life & Loves* III. xii. 183 The great London doctors knew nothing about leprosy and cared less. **1925** O. W. HOLMES in *Holmes-Laski Lett.* (1953) I. 741, I think he generally was kind in his judgment of me, except when Roosevelt was so angry at my dissent in the *Northern Securities* case (about which you probably know little and care less). **1931** F. L. ALLEN *Only Yesterday* v. 88 The shock troops of the rebellion were not alien agitators, but the sons and daughters of well-to-do American families, who knew little about Bolshevism and cared distinctly less. **1937** N. COWARD *Present Indicative* VIII. v. 321 Even at the time we realised in our hearts that the bulk of the public knew nothing about *Sirocco* and cared less.

h. ***to know the reason why***: to demand (and get) an explanation. Cf. REASON *sb.*[1] 5.

1825 R. S. HAWKER *Cornish Ballads* (1869) 1 And shall Trelawney die? Here's twenty thousand Cornish men Will know the reason why! **1894** SOMERVILLE & 'ROSS' *Real Charlotte* III. xxxix. 87 She had laid out a good deal of money on the house and farm, but she was going to get a good return for it, or know the reason why. **1934** G. B. SHAW *On Rocks* II. 68 My Union Jack men would keep order, or theyd know the reason why. **1941** *Punch* 20 Aug. 155/2 Two months ago Herr Hitler said his armies would sweep through Russia or he would know the reason why. **1942** *Ibid.* 11 Feb. 113/2, I caught him in the wash-house for an explanation or I'd know the reason why, and it appeared I'd ruined his life.

i. ***and knows*** (or ***knew***, etc.) ***it***: is clearly aware of (what has been stated).

1848 MRS. GASKELL *Mary Barton* I. vi. 103 The son was strikingly handsome and knew it. **1898** G. B. SHAW *Mrs. Warren's Profession* III. 208 I'm not a young man, and I know it. **1930** J. B. PRIESTLEY *Angel Pavement* v. 248 Well, she's pretty enough, and knows it, the little monkey. **1932** E. V. LUCAS *Reading, Writing & Remembering* xi. 182 Meredith was very handsome, and he knew it.

j. ***to know what one likes***: a phrase used to imply that the speaker knows which works of art, poems, etc., he like without necessarily having an informed opinion to support his view.

1873 H. JAMES *Compl. Tales* (1962) III. 72, I went with Harold a great deal to the Louvre, where he was a very profitable companion. He had the history of the schools at his fingers' ends, and, as the phrase is, he knew what he liked. **1881** —— *Portrait of Lady* II. v. 67, I don't care anything about reasons, but I know what I like. **1959** *Listener* 9 July 75/3 In reality, she was just a wealthy collector. She knew what she liked. **1974** R. HILL *Very Good Hater* xi. 93 'Are you interested in art?' asked Mrs Housman politely. 'I know what I like,' he answered.

k. ***don't I know it***: I am well aware of it, you need not tell me.

1874 M. CLARKE *His Natural Life* (1875) II. iii. 192 The old trick. Ha! ha! don't I know it? **1899** KIPLING *Stalky & Co.* 151 'We didn't always knock him about, though!' 'You did when you could catch him... Don't I know it!' **1936** 'R. WEST' *Thinking Reed* xii. 419 'I hate it,' she said. 'I hate it.' ..'Don't I know it,' said Alan. **1964** J. CREASEY *Look Three Ways* x. 96 'He's in a mess..that poor devil is.' 'And don't I know it?' **1970** B. COBB *Catch Me* i. 13 'They've only been married a few months. She's still starry-eyed.' 'Don't I know it!'

l. ***before you know where you are*** (and similar phrases): very soon, very quickly.

1916 A. HUXLEY *Let.* 30 June (1969) 104 Steps must quickly be taken, or we shall find the place full of effigies and all the money spent before we know where we are. **1930** W. S. MAUGHAM *Bread-Winner* ii. 102 Almost before you know where you are, they're young men and women with characters of their own. **1936** WODEHOUSE *Laughing Gas* i. 9 And little by little and bit by bit, before you know where you are—why, there you are, don't you know. **1956** A. WILSON *Anglo-Saxon Att.* II. ii. 341 Gerald said at the end of her story, 'Yes, that's certainly jolly sad,' and, before he knew where he was, he had given her a cheque for the dispensing of charity. **1970** C. WHITMAN *Death out of Focus* xii. 183 You're a clever devil... You'll be an Inspector before you know where you are.

m. ***not to know whether one is coming or going*** (see COME *v.* 27e).

n. ***to know too much***: used in a context of murder, or of a threat to kill, because the victim knows too much to be allowed to live.

1922 CHESTERTON (*title*) The man who knew too much. **1953** A. CHRISTIE *After Funeral* xxi. 163 'And why should anyone want to kill you, beautiful Rosamund?'.. 'Because I know too much, of course.' **1966** 'S. WOODS' *Enter Certain Murderers* xii. 191 At the risk of being melodramatic..you know too much.

o. ***to know where one stands*** (or ***is***) ***with*** (someone): to know how one is regarded by (someone); to know a person's views (on a issue).

1950 J. CANNAN *Murder Included* ii. 33 'Those blunt, downright people are never irritating—you know where you are with them.' 'They're irritating to some people.' **1951** E. PAUL *Springtime in Paris* iv. 90 An honest whore knew where she stood. **1954** L. P. HARTLEY *White Wand* 37 One never quite knew where one was with her. **1966** *Oxf. Univ. Gaz.* 23 Dec. 433/2 If the majority now rise and say they support Council's paragraph (*a*), we shall know where we stand—we shall all be standing! **1972** F. WARNER *Lying Figures* II. 9, I wasn't a pushover. All I wanted was to know where I stood.

p. ***(do) you know something?***: shall I tell you this surprising fact?, I am going to tell you something.

1965 I. FLEMING *Man with Golden Gun* viii. 113 Mr. Paradise..said softly 'You know something?' **1971** J. BRUNNER *Honky in Woodpile* v. 37 'You know something?' We looked expectant. **1972** P. DICKINSON *Lizard in Cup* x. 159 You know something? She was reared in a home. **1972** J. WILSON *Hide & Seek* ii. 29 Do you know something, Mary? Mr Harris is the nicest man I know, except for my father.

*** Misc. phrases in which *know* is used *intr.* or *absol.* (usually with something implied and sometimes with specific idiomatic force):

q. ***I want to know***: well, well! *U.S. colloq.*

1833 J. NEAL *Down-Easters* I. 45, I *want* to know! exclaimed the other down-easter. Well, you *do* know, replied the southerner. **1840** *Knickerbocker* XVI. 20 'I want to know!' said the lady; 'precious soul!' **1888** *Harper's Mag.* Sept. 530/1 'Why, Jered Hopkins!' she said, looking up at him; 'I want to know!' **1904** J. C. LINCOLN *Cap'n Eri* iii. 39

'I want to know!' exclaimed Captain Perez. 'You don't tell me!' said Captain Jerry. **1911** —— *Cap'n Warren's Wards* x. 154 'She said she would be delighted!' 'I want to know!' **1923** R. D. PAINE *Comrades of Rolling Ocean* 169 And you come from North Dakoty! I want to know.

r. ***that's all you know***: you do not know the facts, you do not understand (used censoriously of the person to whom the phrase is addressed). Also, ***that's all you know about it***.

1876 TROLLOPE *Prime Minister* III. xi. 183 'They may do foolish things, dear; and yet.. not interfere with politics.' 'That's all you know about it, Plantagenet.' **1879** C. M. YONGE *Magnum Bonum* III. xxxiv. 723 'She thought you a catch in the old days.' 'That's all you know about it!' **1930** E. H. YOUNG *Miss Mole* ii. 20 'And breakfast in bed is not what you want, Hannah.' 'That's all you know about it,' Hannah said. **1961** I. FLEMING *Thunderball* ii. 19 'I wouldn't have thought these people would be interested.'.. The young man snorted, 'That's all you know.' **1973** 'S. WOODS' *Enter the Corpse* 165 '*He* hasn't been near them,' said Boney Nelson confidently... 'That's all you know,' Meg retorted.

s. ***what do you know?***: used as an expression of mild surprise = 'Isn't that amazing?' 'Well I never!' 'Just fancy!' Also, ***what do you know about that?***

1914 [see GET *v.* 21 d]. **1916** 'B. M. BOWER' *Phantom Herd* ii. 33 Now what do you know about that, Mig? **1933** E. E. CUMMINGS *eimi* 245 What do you know—out of every 50 chances to make a mistake, those greedy tovariches took advantage of 4 (versus 1 mistake out of 10,000 chances in America). **1943** K. TENNANT *Ride on Stranger* vii. 72 Why, the louse!.. He's glad to get rid of us. What do you know about that? **1947** 'N. SHUTE' *Chequer Board* iii. 63 Say, what do you know? They ain't got no sewer here. **1952** 'C. BRAND' *London Particular* xvi. 216 Well, what do you know, boys?—let's call it a day. **1957** J. KEROUAC *On Road* (1958) xii. 80 And that thousand dollars was.. right there on top of the safe, what do you know about that? **1959** 'M. NEVILLE' *Sweet Night for Murder* xxi. 200 'Yeah... That's right... I'll say! What do you know!' Which crescendo of surprise was a clear.. statement of agreement. **1968** 'A. GILBERT' *Night Encounter* v. 80 'Well,' marvelled Frankie, 'what do you know?' **1971** R. DENTRY *Encounter at Kharmel* (1973) v. 89 Well! What do you know? So the Company has been getting off its well-padded bum at last.

t. ***wouldn't you*** (or ***he***, etc.) ***like to know?***: I have no intention of telling you.

1923 G. ATHERTON *Black Oxen* xx. 105 'Look here!' he said. 'How far do you go?' 'Wouldn't you like to know?' 'I should. Not for personal reasons, for girls.. bore me.' **1941** I. BAIRD *He rides Sky* 123 The old crumpet fires off a lot of bilge like.. 'What do you do in your spare time?' (wouldn't *he* like to know?)... And so on and on. **1942** BERREY & VAN DEN BARK *Amer. Thes. Slang* §205/6 *I won't tell you*, don't you wish you knew?.. wouldn't you like to know?, you'd like to know? **1963** M. BORRELLI *Street Lamp & Stars* xiv. 127 'And what did *you* do, Naso Stuorto?' 'Wouldn't you like to know.' 'I can guess.'

u. ***you never know*** or ***one never knows***: something unexpected or surprising may occur.

1924 G. B. SHAW *St. Joan* vi. 94 A flaw in the procedure may be useful later on: one never knows. **1926** F. W. CROFTS *Inspector French & Cheyne Mystery* viii. 103 'I don't see that we should gain much by looking at the outside of the house.' 'You never know... If we see nothing no harm is done.' **1948** 'J. TEY' *Franchise Affair* xiv. 147 It would be too great luck that he should be staying at the Midland, but one never knows. **1972** E. BERCKMAN *Fourth Man on Rope* iii. 38 Among the most unpromising debris there might lurk.. some jewel as yet undiscovered. *You never know*, faithfully she invoked the formula that spurred the weariest.. *you never know*. **1974** J. MANN *Sticking Place* viii. 129 'I'll come with you,' Edward said... He added in a low, ominous voice.. 'You never know.'

v. ***for all I know*** (or ***he knows***, etc.): as far as I am aware, since I know nothing to the contrary.

1930 E. WAUGH *Vile Bodies* viii. 143 But these young people have got hold of another end of the stick, and for all we know it may be the right one. **1934** F. W. CROFTS *12.30 from Croydon* xxi. 292 They stood to gain by Mr. Andrew Crowther's death, and though they didn't stand to gain so much as the other two, for all we know to the contrary any one of them may have been in greater need. **1937** D. RUNYON *More Than Somewhat* v. 104 Leaving the wop yelling very loud, and maybe cussing us in wop for all I know. **1954** W. S. MAUGHAM *Ten Novels* i. 3 Everybody skips, but to skip without loss is not easy. It may be, for all I know, a gift of nature, or it may be something that has to be acquired by experience. **1954** E. CALDWELL *Love & Money* (1955) xiii. 171 How do I know you're telling the truth? For all I know, this might be some more scheming between you and Tess. **1955** D. GARNETT *Aspects of Love* iv. 119 Well, if you believe in mermaids I might be one, for all you know.

w. ***I wouldn't know***: I cannot be expected to know, that is outside the range of my knowledge. Also, ***I wouldn't know about that***.

1939 W. M. RAINE *River Bend Feud* x. 72 Faint wrinkles creased the forehead of the engineer. 'Has he fixed up an alliance with the outside ranchmen?' he asked. 'I wouldn't know about that,' Raleigh answered. 'But if he hasn't, he will.' **1950** J. CANNAN *Murder Included* iii. 44 'The bedroom.. was only locked by the deceased during her ablutions.' 'As you say nowadays—I wouldn't know,' said Sir Charles. **1952** M. R. RINEHART *Swimming Pool* xii. 110, I wouldn't know. I've never had one. **1960** L. P. HARTLEY *Facial Justice* xvi. 133 'Every man has his type, of course—.' 'I wouldn't know about that.' **1961** J. B. PRIESTLEY *Saturn Over Water* v. 64, I wouldn't know... I'm just a painter. **1968** B. FOSTER *Changing Eng. Lang.* i. 42 As an avowal of ignorance, British English has long used 'I couldn't say', but this is often replaced now by the *I wouldn't know*... In Britain it started making headway in the 'thirties, and in a British serial film (*Pimpernel Smith*) of 1940 the late Leslie Howard remarked 'In the deplorable argot of the modern generation, "I wouldn't know".' **1969** M. PUGH *Last Place Left* vii. 45 'That's why married people get so complicated in bed, isn't it?' 'Do they? I wouldn't know.'

x. ***wouldn't you (just) know?***: 'just fancy!' 'imagine that!'; as one might have foreseen. orig. *U.S.*

1946 H. P. M. BROWN *Sound of Hunting* I. 52 Wouldn't you know? Of all the days to get stuck out there, he has to pick this one. **1966** *Listener* 3 Mar. 325/2 George Scott is an English professor (wouldn't you know?) who's engaged in the *bellum sexuale* with his wife. **1973** *Washington Post* 13 Jan. B. 8/7 Wouldn't you just know. Lorne Greene, also known as Ben Cartwright, has gone right out and gotten himself another steady job; this time with the ABC network.

y. ***I don't*** (or ***he***, etc., ***doesn't***) ***want to know***: I am not interested. Occas. const. with person as object.

1948 'N. SHUTE' *No Highway* iii. 79, I was trying to tell her what to do if things look bad. But if she doesn't want to know, I can't do more. **1967** *Listener* 14 Sept. 326/1 After doing a hard week's work I had nothing in my pocket.. nothing at all and that went on for four years... After that I said: 'Well, that's it. I don't want to know. I can get a living a lot easier than going to work.' **1969** *Focus* Feb. 16/2 But if you are paying it all in on a Friday, and taking it all out again on Saturday, do not be surprised if the building society does not want to know you. **1973** *Observer* 14 Jan. 7/3 It remains to add that all this, and much more, was well enough known at the time. But the fellow-travellers didn't want to know. **1973** *Times* 19 Sept. 13/4 (Advt.), Graduates you have a problem. If you wanted the summer following graduation free, you missed out on the 'milk round'. Many employers don't want to know by the autumn.

IV. 12. a. ***to know how*** (formerly also simply ***to know***): to understand the way, or be able (*to do* something): cf. CAN *v.*[1] 3.

a **1548** HALL *Chron., Hen. VIII* 174 We have so many clothes in our handes, that we knowe not how to utter them. **1566** W. ADLINGTON tr. *Apuleius' Golden Ass* IX. xl. (1893) 188 By and by the old woman which knew well to babble, began to tell as followeth. **1594** MARLOWE & NASHE *Dido* I. ii, Abandon fruitless fears, Since Carthage knows to entertain distress. **1610** SHAKS. *Temp.* I. ii. 364, I know how to curse. **1634** SIR T. HERBERT *Trav.* 147 Not one.. of a thousand among them, knowing how to write. *a* **1763** SHENSTONE *Elegies* iii. 13 He little knew to ward the secret wound. **1808** J. BARLOW *Columb.* III. 107 Tell them we know to tread the crimson plain. **1885** *Manch. Exam.* 11 Nov. 3/2 Told by a lady who knows exactly how to write for children. **1893** *Bookman* June 82/2 Nobody writes moral-allegorical tales now, because nobody knows how.

b. *ellipt.* in colloq. phr. ***all one knows***, all one can; also *advb.*, to the utmost of one's ability.

1872 *Punch* 27 Jan. 40/2 Both men will do all they know, and a clinking good contest is expected. **1883** D. C. MURRAY *Hearts* II. 206 He was not accustomed to be badgered in this way, and it cost him all he knew to restrain his anger. **1889** BOLDREWOOD *Robbery under Arms* II. ii. 21 A good many men tried all they knew to be prepared and have a show for it. **1889** R. S. S. BADEN-POWELL *Pigsticking* 173 If they find themselves being pursued.. they will shoot round on the instant, and make the running 'all they know' back again.

†13. To make known: **a.** To disclose, reveal, manifest; *refl.* to make oneself known; **b.** to make (a person) acquainted or (a thing) familiar.

a **1300** *Cursor M.* 1161 Caym sagh his sin was knaud, And wist þat þe erth had scaud. *a* **1350** *Ibid.* 3838 (Gött.) Iacob.. kneu him þar wid mayr rachel. *a* **1400** *Hymn Virgin* iii. in Warton *Hist. Eng. Poetry* x. (1840) II. 109 Heil reson of al rihtwysnesse, To vche a caityf comfort to knowe. *c* **1400** *Rom. Rose* 6090 For certeyn, they wolde hate me, If ever I knewe hir cruelte. *a* **1400–50** *Alexander* 2872 (Ashm.) He knew his kniȝtis þat cas. **1422** tr. *Secreta Secret., Priv. Priv.* 143 Of falsnes and vntrowth he shal be Proclamyd and knowe. *a* **1450** *Knt. de la Tour* (1868) 110 Whanne this was opened, know, and tolde thorughe the kingges court.

14. In biblical language, used to render Heb. *yd'* in various inferential senses: To take notice of, regard, care for; to look after, guard, protect; to regard with approval, approve.

1382 WYCLIF *Ps.* i. 6 For the Lord hath knowe the weie of the riȝtwise. **1535** COVERDALE *Ps.* xxxi. 7 Thou hast considred my trouble, thou hast knowne my soule in aduersite. **1611** BIBLE *Gen.* xxxix. 6 And he left all that he had, in Ioseph's hand: and he knew not ought he had, saue the bread which he did eate. **1662** SOUTH *Serm.* (1823) I. 77 To know, in scripture language, is to approve; and so, not to know, is to reject and condemn.

15. Used (chiefly in sense 8) in various colloq. and slang phrases expressing sagacity, cunning, or 'knowledge of the world', as ***to know what's what***, ***to know a thing or two***, ***to know the time of day***, etc. ***to know it all***: not to be aware of one's deficiencies, ***to think one*** (or ***he***, ***she***, etc.) ***knows it all***; cf. *know-all*, *know-it-all* s.v. KNOW-. Also ***to know the ropes*** (see ROPE *sb.*[1] 4 c); ***to know all the answers*** (see ANSWER *sb.* 6 b); ***not to know beans*** (see BEAN *sb.* 6 e).

c **1520** *Vox Populi* 373 in Hazl. *E.P.P.* III. 281, I knowe not whates a clocke. **1546** J. HEYWOOD *Prov.*, He knew which way the winde blew. *a* **1553** UDALL *Royster D.* I. ii. (Arb.) 17 Mary, nowe I see you know what is what. **1562** J. HEYWOOD *Prov. & Epigr.* (1867) 71, I know on which syde my bread is buttred. **1631** POWELL *Tom All Trades* 171 He knowes how many dayes goe to the weeke. **1663** BUTLER *Hud.* I. i. 149 He knew what's what, and that's as high As metaphysick wit can fly. **1792** HOLCROFT *Road to Ruin* (Farmer), You know a thing or two, Mr. Selby. **1817** SCOTT *Search after Happiness* xviii, She loved a book, and knew a thing or two. **1867** *All Year Round* 13 July 56 The tramp who knows his way about knows what to do. **1870** E. G. WHITE *Testimonies for Church* No 19. 73 You have so long thought, with the peculiar class I have mentioned, that you knew it all, that you will not see your deficiencies when they are presented before you. **1929** J. B. PRIESTLEY *Good Companions* I. iii. 24 Ted.. admitted that he knocked about a bit and knew a thing or two. **1944** E. CALDWELL *Tragic Ground* (1947) iii. 31 Jim Howard Vance is a pretty smart fellow. He was talking in there just a while ago like he knows a thing or two. **1972** G. DURRELL *Catch me a Colobus* vi. 111 As I had warned Long John, there comes a time on every collecting trip when you begin to think that you know it all. This is a moment of great danger, for you *never* know it all, however hard you try. *Ibid.*, I made a mistake once by thinking I knew it all, and got bitten by a snake. **1973** WODEHOUSE *Bachelor Anonymous* iv. 33 The serfs and vassals now know a thing or two and prefer to make their living elsewhere. **1973** *Black World* Sept. 97/1 To my once respected student who has taken over the pompous entitlement as chief white critic of inferior Black literature, let me say..: 'Stop knowing it all.'

V. With prepositions.

(For other constructions in which the vb. and prep. had their ordinary independent meanings, see the simple senses.)

16. know about ——. To have information about. Often used to express a knowledge of externals, as opposed to real understanding or actual acquaintance.

1854 KINGSLEY *Alexandria* ii. 50 It is better to know one thing than to know about ten thousand things. **1876** J. P. NORRIS *Rudim. Theol.* I. iv. 70 Knowing God is an infinitely better thing than knowing about God.

†17. know for ——. To be aware of. *Obs. rare*$^{-1}$.

1597 SHAKS. *2 Hen. IV*, I. ii. 6 He might haue more diseases than he knew for.

18. know of ——. **†a.** In various obsolete senses: To be or become assured of, to have or obtain information about or experience of, etc. *Obs.*

c **1400** *Destr. Troy* 354 Þe pepull.. Haden.. wilfulde desyre To knowe of þere comyng and the cause wete. *Ibid.* 10862 Pantasilia.. purpost.. The grekes to greue.. And of maidyns might make hom to know. *c* **1420** *Anturs of Arth.* xix, Certis or thay hethun fare, Thay knaue of mekil care.

b. To be cognizant of (something as existing, an event as having occurred); †to become cognizant of (*obs.*).

1390 GOWER *Conf.* I. 192 Therto we be swore, That non bot only thou and we Schal knowen of this privete. **1573** BARET *Alv.* To Rdr., Knowing then of no other Dictionarie to helpe vs, but Sir Thomas Eliots Librarie. **1597** SHAKS. *2 Hen. IV*, II. iv. 19 Sir Iohn must not know of it. *a* **1691** BOYLE (J.), There is but one mineral body that we know of, heavier than common quicksilver. **1818** CRUISE *Digest* (ed. 2) IV. 40 He knew of no case where an agreement, though all written with the party's own hand, had been held sufficient, unless it had been likewise signed by him. **1857** TROLLOPE *Three Clerks* i, All the English world knows, or knows of, that branch of Civil Service which is popularly called the Weights and Measures. *Mod.* I know *of* him, of course; but I do not know him.

c. Colloq. phrases. ***not that I know of***, not so far as I know, not to my knowledge. **†*not that you know of***, an expression of defiance addressed to a person in reference to something he is about to do (*obs.*).

1742 RICHARDSON *Pamela* III. 310 As Mr. B. offer'd to take his Hand, he put 'em both behind him—Not that you know of, Sir! **1753** FOOTE *Englishm. in Paris* II. Wks. 1799 I. 49 May I flatter myself that your Ladyship will do me the honour of venturing upon the fatigue of another minuet this morning with me? *Buck.* Not that you know of, Monsieur.

†19. know upon ——. To take (judicial) cognizance of. *Sc. Obs.* Cf. F. *connaître de*.

1457 *Sc. Acts Jas. II* (1814) II. 47/2 The caussis þ[t] þe lordis of þe Sessione sall knaw apone. **1609** SKENE *Reg. Maj.* 118 (*Form Baron Couris* c. 81) The Judge may of law, gar knaw vpon the dead be ane assise.

†know, *sb.*[1] *Obs.* In 3 cnaw. [Early ME. *cnaw*, prob. repr. an OE. **ȝecnáw*, f. *ȝe)cnáwan* to KNOW: cf. *ȝefeoht*, *ȝeheald*, *ȝesc(e)ád*, *ȝeweald*, *ȝewinn*, etc.; also OE. *ȝecnǽwe* adj. 'conscious of, acknowledging'.]

Acknowledgement, confession; in early ME. phr. (*soð*) ***cnawes beon***, to acknowledge truthfully, to confess. *Obs.*

a **1225** *Leg. Kath.* 1078 Beo nu soð cnawes, ȝef ich riht segge. *Ibid.* 2041 Beo nu ken & cnawes, of þat þat tu isehen hauest. *a* **1225** *Juliana* 54 Sei me ant beo soð cnawes hwer weren þe itaht þine wichecreftes. *c* **1230** *Hali Meid.* 25 Beo nu soð cnawes for to kele þi lust wið fulðe of þi licome.. for gode hit is wlateful þing.

know (nəʊ), *sb.*[2] [f. KNOW *v.* A new formation.] The fact of knowing; knowledge. Now chiefly in colloq. phr. ***in the know***, in possession of information which is not generally known.

1592 WYRLEY *Armorie* 119 What booteth it of Gentries brag to boast,.. When we ourselues no warlike practise trow, But rest ourselues with this old idle know? **1602** SHAKS. *Ham.* v. ii. 44 That on the view and know of these Contents.. He should the bearers put to sodaine death. *a* **1825** FORBY *Voc. E. Anglia* s.v., 'Poor fellow! he has but little know'. **1827** *Sporting Mag.* XXI. 42 The mare.. was jockied by a raw young lad.. who had not that kind of know about him to enable her to win. **1883** *Daily News* 21 Sept. 2/2 People in the 'know' are playing with loaded dice. **1885** *Times* 19 Mar. 3 To those in the know the spectacle was painful in the extreme.

know, var. KNOWE, knoll; obs. f. KNEE.

know-, the vb.-stem in comb. forming adjs. and sbs. mostly nonce-words. **know-all**, one who knows or professes to know everything; also

attrib. or as *adj.*, full of knowledge; esp., deaf to advice or instruction; so **know-it-all**; **know-all-about-it** *a.*, having the air of knowing all about something; **know-every-thingism**, pretension to universal knowledge; **know-little**, a simpleton; **know-not-what**, an indescribable something; †**know-thy-master**, a name given to the sweating sickness; †**know-worth** *a.*, worth knowing. Also KNOW-NOTHING.

1881 TENNYSON *Tiresias* (1885) 49 *We* have knelt in your *know-all chapel. **1895** *Westm. Gaz.* 29 Nov. 3/1 Nothing must be hidden from this Imperial Know-All. **1906** *Daily Chron.* 30 Aug. 3/4 He..maintains in his know-all manner that the two counties of Wigtown and Kirkcudbright..were integral parts always of the kingdom of Scotland. **1923** D. H. LAWRENCE *Birds, Beasts & Flowers* 185 Fool, in spite of your pretty ways, and quaint, know-all, wrinkled old aunty's face. **1895** *Outing* (U.S.) XXVII. 65/1, I have no desire to send a young *know-it-all to the shop. **1935** WODEHOUSE *Blandings Castle* ix. 225 These know-it-all directors make me tired. **1956** H. GOLD *Man who was not with It* (1965) ii. 16 He looked over the apprehensive afternoon crowd with its know-it-all faces. **1959** *Encounter* XIII. II. 57 All big smart know-it-all Marxists. **1974** *Times* 23 Jan. 1/8 We didn't realize, until it was too late, how our know-it-all attitude was undermining the self-assurance of parents. **1887** RUSKIN in Spielmann *Life* (1900) 193 Their girls have an energetic and business-like '*know-all-about-it' kind of prettiness. **1868** G. STEPHENS *Runic Mon.* I. p. xvii, The ignorance and insolence of modern *know-every-thingism, that is of modern sciolism. **1651** WITTIE tr. *Primrose's Pop. Err.* IV. xliii. 386 The same might be said of some *know-littles that practice Physick. **1877** FURNIVALL *Introd. Leopold Shaks.* p. cxix, Wooden-heads and pert know-littles, we've had in plenty. *a* **1641** SUCKLING *Fragm. Aurea, Sonn.* ii, I ask no red and white..Black eyes, or little *know-not-whats, in faces. *a* **1681** ALLESTREE *Serm.* 297 (L.) Exact features, perfect harmony of colours,..a graceful presence, cheerful air, and all those other know not whats. **1551** in *Archæologia* XXXVIII. 107 The Swatt called new acquyntance, alles Stoupe knave and *know thy Master, began the xxiiij[th] of this monethe [June] 1551. **1598** E. GILPIN *Skial.* Ep. xliv, Phrix hath a nose: who doubts what ech man knowes? But what hath Phrix *know-worth besides his nose?

knowable (ˈnəʊəb(ə)l), *a.* (*sb.*) [f. KNOW *v.* + -ABLE.] That may be known; capable of being apprehended, understood, or ascertained.

c **1449** PECOCK *Repr.* I. viii. 41 Fyndeable and knoweable bi mannis resoun. **1652** GAULE *Magastrom.* 24 Pretending and presuming..to foreknow all things knowable. **1692** LOCKE *Toleration* III. ix. Wks. 1727 II. 417 Who is it will say ..that it is knowable, that any National Religion..is that only true Religion? **1748** HARTLEY *Observ. Man* I. iii. 349 Reasoning concerning the knowable Relations of unknown things. **1817** BENTHAM *Parl. Ref. Catech.* (1818) 26 The direction taken by the vote is in each instance known or knowable. **1856** R. A. VAUGHAN *Mystics* (1860) I. 69 A spiritual art whereby the possible is forsaken for the impossible—the knowable for the unknowable. **1874** L. STEPHEN *Hours in Library* (1892) I. viii. 270 An insatiable curiosity as to all things knowable and unknowable.

b. Capable of being recognized.

1654-66 EARL ORRERY *Parthen.* (1676) 582 We were hardly knowable to each other. **1687** BOYLE *Martyrd. Theodora* i. (1703) 10 Not being knowable by his fair Mistress. **1737** BRACKEN *Farriery Impr.* (1757) II. 296 Counterfeits..are knowable in a very little time. **1806** W. TAYLOR in *Monthly Mag.* XXII. 29 The body..was too much hacked and disfigured to be knowable.

B. *absol.* or *sb.* A knowable thing; usually in *pl.* knowable things.

1661 GLANVILL *Van. Dogm.* Pref. Bj, I doubt not but the opinionative resolver, thinks all these easie Knowables. **1725** WATTS *Logic* I. vi. §1 To distinguish well between knowables and unknowables.

Hence **knowa'bility**, **'knowableness**, the quality of being knowable.

1660 N. INGELO *Bentivolio & Urania* I. (1682) 162 God is the most Knowable and most Lovely Thing in the world; excess of Knowableness following the Greatness of his Essence. **1679** J. GOODMAN *Penitent Pardoned* I. iii. (1713) 58 Respect is had to the knowledge or knowableness of that rule. **1865** MILL *Exam. Hamilton* 48 The argument is only tenable as against the knowability and the possible existence of..'The Infinite' and 'The Absolute'. **1872** *Contemp. Rev.* XX. 828 Not the unknowability, but the knowability of his 'ultimate scientific ideas'. **1883** A. BARRATT *Phys. Metempiric* 172 Without ideas there is no perception, no knowableness.

knowe, know (naʊ, *Sc. dial.* nou, nʌu), Sc. and North. Eng. form of KNOLL, hillock, rising ground.

1513 DOUGLAS *Æneis* VIII. iii. 37 From a hyll or a know To tham he callis. *a* **1585** MONTGOMERIE *Flyting* 73 Many ȝeald ȝow hast thou cald ouer a know. **1719** D'URFEY *Pills* (1872) II. 167 Riding over a Knough, I met with a Farmer's Daughter. **1804** J. GRAHAME *Sabbath* 295 He roam'd O'er hill and dale, o'er broomy knowe. **1879** E. WAUGH *Chimney Corner* 252 (*Lancash. dial.*) Till I geet at th' top of a bit of a knowe. **1893** STEVENSON *Catriona* xxx. 352 The path rose and came at last to the head of a knowe. [In E.D.D. from the six northern counties of England.]

b. *Comb.*, as *knowe-head*, *-top*.

15.. *Wife of Auchtermuchty* xiii, Then up he gat on a know heid, On hir to cry, on hir to schout. **1818** SCOTT *Hrt. Midl.* xlv, I will just show mysell on the knowe-head.

knowe, -en, pa. pple. of KNOW *v.*

knowed, widespread dial. pa. t. of KNOW *v.*

knower (ˈnəʊə(r)). [f. KNOW *v.* + -ER[1].] One who knows (in senses of the vb.).

1382 WYCLIF *Job* xvi. 20 Forsothe in heuene is my witness; am I knowere of myself in heiȝtis? *a* **1533** LD. BERNERS *Huon* 449 Y[e] beste lapidary and knower of stones that was in all the world. **1575-85** ABP. SANDYS *Serm.* (Parker Soc.) 122, I will not be a knower, but a doer of thy law. **1681** TEMPLE *Mem.* III. Wks. 1731 I. 334 The pretending Knowers among them,..pretended now to know nothing of it. *c* **1728** EARL OF AILESBURY *Mem.* (1890) 277 An honest man, but no knower of men. **1881** P. BROOKS *Serm.* 88 Like the knowledge of the rocks or the stars, something quite independent of moral conditions in the knower.

†**b.** One who has or takes cognizance, a judge (L. *cognitor*). *Obs.*

c **1374** CHAUCER *Boeth.* IV. pr. iv. 100 (Camb. MS.) Yif thow weere..yset a Iuge or a knowere of thinges, trowestow þat men sholden tormenten hym þat hath don the wrong or elles hym þat hath suffred the wrong? **1581** STYWARD *Mart. Discipl.* I. 65 God is the knower and deteminer.

'knowful, *a. dial.* [See -FUL.] Endowed with knowledge, well-informed.

1855 ROBINSON *Whitby Gloss.* s.v., 'He was skilful and knowful.' 'A knowful kind of a body.' **1891** ATKINSON *Last of Giant-Killers* 140 His canny and knowful counsellor.

Hence **'knowfulness**.

1891 ATKINSON *Last of Giant-Killers* 196 If one had knowfulness and experience enough.

know-how (ˈnəʊhaʊ). orig. *U.S.* [f. vbl. phr. *to know how* (KNOW *v.* 12).] Knowledge of how to do some particular thing; technical expertness, practical knowledge.

1838 *New Yorker* 14 July 260/2, I promise, 1st. To do the duties of the office to the best of my know-how, and have a stouter man than myself to help me. **1857** *Spirit of Times* 26 Dec. 270/3 'No, no, Massa,' replied the gentleman from Africa, 'charge fifty cents for killing, and fifty for the know how.' **1899** KIPLING *From Sea to Sea* II. 95 He has the money. We have the know-how. He comes in winter to play poker... When he's lost his money we make him drunk and let him go. **1936** J. DOS PASSOS *Big Money* 282 Charley Anderson, the boy with the knowhow. **1944** H. A. WALLACE *Century of Common Man* 52 We have the 'know how' to help many of the poverty-stricken peoples to set their feet on the path of education, manual dexterity, and economic literacy. **1946** *Times* 10 Dec. 2/6 With regard to American investments in this country the Government welcomed such applications if they brought to this country real industrial knowledge, the 'know how', which otherwise we should be without. **1947** AUDEN *Age of Anxiety* (1948) i. 26 A modern product Of nerve and know-how with a new thrill. **1949** *Listener* 15 Sept. 451/3 A manager may have knowledge of a process in his charge, but not the know-how possessed by the foreman who controls it. **1952** R. M. HARE *Lang. Morals* x. 159 Everything that we are taught how to do must..be reducible to principles, though these may be 'know-hows' hard to formulate in language and more easily taught by example. **1953** *Encounter* Oct. 68/2 There were some who were persuaded that technical knowledge—that intangible but wonderful thing called American 'know-how'—could somehow be made a substitute for capital in the poor countries. **1967** L. B. ARCHER in Wills & Yearsley *Handbk. Managem. Technol.* 129 It takes special talent and know-how on the part of a properly trained designer to create a successful house style. **1972** P. M. HUBBARD *Whisper in Glen* ix. 91 She hasn't got the mere social know-how to carry it off.

knowing (ˈnəʊɪŋ), *vbl. sb.* [f. KNOW *v.* + -ING[1].] The action or fact denoted by the verb KNOW.

†**1.** Acknowledgement; recognition. *Obs.*

a **1225** *Ancr. R.* 280 Edmod cnowunge of þin owune wocnesse & of þine owune unstrencðe. **1362** LANGL. *P. Pl.* A. II. 206 Freres..fetten him þennes; For knowynge of Comers kepten [*B.* coped] him as a Frere.

†**2.** Personal acquaintance. *Obs.*

fleshly knowing, carnal knowledge.

a **1300** *Cursor M.* 11749 þar þai fand nan o þair knaing, At þat þai cuth ask at þair gesting [*Fairf.* þer þai fande na knawinge of quam þai muȝt aske gesteninge]. *c* **1385** CHAUCER *L.G.W.* 2155 *Ariadne*, Ther as he had a frend of his knowinge. *c* **1430** *Hymns Virg.* 105 Lete fleischeli knowynge from þee be lent Saue oonli bi-twene man & wijf: þis is þe sixte comaundement.

3. The action of getting to understand, or fact of understanding; mental comprehension of truths or principles; knowledge; †understanding *of* or skill *in* something (*obs.*).

c **1330** R. BRUNNE *Chron. Wace* (Rolls) 166 Geffrey.. made it alle in Latin þat clerkes haf now knawyng in. **13..** *E.E. Allit. P.* A. 858 Al-thagh oure corses in clottez clynge, ..We thurgh-outly haven cnawyng. **1450-1530** *Myrr. our Ladye* 147 The spyryte of knowynge and of pytye. **1480** CAXTON *Chron. Eng.* I. (1520) 6/1 Athlas..is lykened to bere up heven on his sholders bycause of his knowynge in sterres. **1658** A. FOX *Wurtz' Surg.* I. ix. 35 The Knowing of the Medicine and of the Disease must go hand in hand. **1874** BLACKIE *Self-Cult.* 15 He did not mean to assert that mere indiscriminate knowing is always good. **1875** JOWETT *Plato* (ed. 2) I. 451 Knowing is the acquiring and retaining knowledge and not forgetting.

4. The fact of being aware or informed of any thing; acquaintance with a thing or fact; cognizance, knowledge; †notice, intimation (*obs.*). Now chiefly in the phrase, ***there is no knowing***, one cannot know, no one can tell.

a **1300** *Cursor M.* 5495 (Gött.) A neu king, þat of ioseph had na knouyng. *c* **1386** CHAUCER *Sqr.'s T.* 293 Deyntees mo than been in my knowyng. *c* **1400** *Destr. Troy* 13199 When hit come to the knowyng of hir kid brother, Poliphemus prudly preset hir after. *c* **1485** *Digby Myst.* III. 1273, I send hym knowyng of crystes deth. **1611** SPEED *Hist. Gt. Brit.* IX. xix. (1623) 929 Without the knowing and assent of the Lords. **1794** MRS. RADCLIFFE *Myst. Udolpho* xii, There is no knowing how young women will act. **1800** *Asiat. Ann. Reg., Proc. E. Ind. Ho.* 60/2 There was no knowing what it might lead to. **1860** GEO. ELIOT *Mill on Fl.* II. ii, There's never any knowing where that'll end.

†**b.** A means whereby to know something; a sign, an indication. *Obs.*

c **1400** *Lanfranc's Cirurg.* 271 Whanne þe bowels fallip þoruȝ dindimum, he makiþ þe ballok leþir neuere þe lengere, & þis is a good knowinge.

†**c.** Something known, an experience. *Obs.*

1605 SHAKS. *Macb.* II. iv. 4 This sore Night Hath trifled former knowings.

knowing (ˈnəʊɪŋ), *ppl. a.* [f. KNOW *v.* + -ING[2].] That knows.

1. That knows or has knowledge; conscious; mentally perceptive; cognitive.

1649 JER. TAYLOR *Gt. Exemp.* II. Sect. x, We believe a story which we love..in which cases our guides are not our knowing faculties, but our affections. **1655** H. VAUGHAN *Silex Scint.* II. *Quickness* iii, Life is a fix'd discerning light, A knowing joy. **1662** H. MORE *Philos. Writ.* Pref. Gen. (1712) 16 This Spirit..being the natural Transcript of that which is knowing or perceptive. **1690** LOCKE *Hum. Und.* IV. x. (1695) 355 There has been also a knowing Being from Eternity. **1865-75** M. ARNOLD *Ess. Crit.*, A matter which does not fall within the scope of our ordinary knowing faculties.

2. a. That has knowledge of truths or facts; understanding, intelligent, instructed, enlightened, well-informed.

c **1375** *Cursor M.* 27153 (Fairf.) Prest agh be skilful soft & meke Knawande, riȝtwise, loueli in speke. **1483** *Cath. Angl.* 204/2 Knawynge, *scius, sciolus*. **1606** SHAKS. *Ant. & Cl.* III. iii. 26 He's very knowing, I do perceiu't. **1648** BOYLE *Seraph. Love* xii. (1700) 61 Like rare Musick, which..the knowingst Artists still do highliest value. **1652** BP. HALL *Invis. World* I. §5 So perfectly knowing are the angels that the very heathen philosophers have styled them by the name of Intelligences. **1737** J. CHAMBERLAYNE *St. Gt. Brit.* II. II. iii. 359 Adults..are not catechised, when they are found to be sufficiently knowing. **1875** JOWETT *Plato* (ed. 2) I. 34 He is the most knowing of all living men. *Ibid.* III. 200 A man who is knowing about horses.

b. Skilled or versed *in* something.

1651 CLEVELAND *Poems* 35 To return knowing in the Spanish shrug. **1700** DRYDEN *Pref. Fables* Wks. (Globe) 497 Both of them were knowing in astronomy. **1866** FELTON *Anc. & Mod. Gr.* I. I. vii. 113 In such drugs was Helen knowing.

†**c.** Of an act, etc.: Showing knowledge or skill. *Obs.*

1793 GOUV. MORRIS in Sparks *Life & Writ.* Wks. 1832 II. 307 Dumouriez writes that the retreat was a knowing or skilful one. **1827** SCOTT *Jrnl.* 5 Feb., There is a very knowing catalogue [of pictures] by Frank Grant himself.

3. Of persons, their actions, look, etc.: Having or showing discernment or cunning; shrewd, cunning, acute, 'wide-awake'. (Often implying the air of possessing information which one does not or will not impart.) Also *Comb.*, as ***knowing-looking*** *ppl. a.*

knowing one, much used *c* 1750–1820 for a person professing to be well up in the secrets of the turf or other sporting matters.

1503 *Act 19 Hen. VII*, c. 6 Knowing Thieves and other Pickers that steal..Pewter and Brass. **1712** STEELE *Spect.* No. 314 ¶2 He is the most knowing infant I have yet met with. **1749** *Whitehall Evening Post* No. 537 The Odds being very high for Booby, the Knowing Ones were taken in. *a* **1817** JANE AUSTEN *Northanger Abbey* (1818) I. vii. 81 A gig, driven along on bad pavement by a most knowing-looking coachman. **1818** *Sporting Mag.* II. 22 The knowing ones were perfectly satisfied. **1832** LYTTON *Eugene A.* IV. ii, When I saw my master, who was thought the knowingest gentleman about court, taken in every day. **1833** HT. MARTINEAU *Berkeley the Banker* I. i. 13 'But he takes out a part by the way', interrupted Enoch, with a knowing look. **1852** R. S. SURTEES *Sponge's Sp. Tour* lxvi. 371 'I believe you', replied George, with a knowing jerk of his head. **1927** H. V. MORTON *In Search of England* i. 9 [Newbury, in Berkshire] is, like all towns which have any traffic with race-horses, a knowing-looking, bandy-legged town.

4. Showing knowledge of 'what is what' in fashion, dress, and the like; stylish, smart. *colloq. Obs.* or merged in 3.

1796 JANE AUSTEN *Sense & Sens.* xix, Many young men.. drove about town in very knowing gigs. **1800** MRS. HERVEY *Mourtray Fam.* II. 135 Not a knowing man in the room! —and, as to the women,—look at their horrid figures! **1826** DISRAELI *Viv. Grey* III. viii, Colonel Delmington is at Cheltenham, with the most knowing beard you can possibly conceive. **1837** MRS. SHERWOOD *Henry Milner* III. iii. 43 A little foot-boy, dressed in a very knowing costume.

5. Cognizant, informed, aware. Const. *of*, *in* (both ?*obs.*) *to* (now *U.S.*).

1659 *Burton's Diary* (1828) IV. 480 Every man that lives under a law is supposed to be knowing of it. **1664** SIR C. LYTTELTON in *Hatton Corr.* (Camden) 37 To them who are commonly knowing enough in the affaires of that kind. **1752** J. STEWART in *Scots Mag.* (1753) 294/2 It was a premeditated thing, to which I must have been knowing. **1790** in Dallas *Amer. Law Rep.* I. 24 He was not knowing to any corrupt agreement. **1841** CATLIN *N. Amer. Ind.* (1844) II. liv. 187, I must be supposed to be knowing to and familiar with the whole circumstances. **1905** *Springfield* (Mass.) *Weekly Republ.* 29 Dec. 16 Some of the neighbors were knowing to the event. **1906** *Dialect Notes* III. 144 I'm knowing to that; you're wrong. **1913** *Ibid.* IV. 2 You are knowing to that. **1913** H. KEPHART *Our Southern Highlanders* xiii. 297 Reckon Pete was knowin' to the sarcumstance?

knowingly (ˈnəʊɪŋlɪ), *adv.* [f. prec. + -LY[2].] In a knowing manner; with knowledge; intelligently, consciously, intentionally, etc.: see prec.

1382 WYCLIF *Wisd.* xiii. 5 Of the mykilnesse of fairnesse, and of creature, knowendeli shal moun the creatour of these

ben seen. **1435** MISYN *Fire of Love* 103 He truly þat knawyngly & wilfully fallis in-to þe lest [sin], vnauisyd to gretter oft-tymes sal fall. **1526** *Pilgr. Perf.* (W. de W. 1531) 94 b, Wylfully & knowyngly..to chose..yᵉ thynge that is of lesse goodnes. **1611** SHAKS. *Cymb.* III. iii. 46 Did you but know the Citties Vsuries, And felt them knowingly. **1682** BURNET *Rights Princes* Pref. 8, I have not knowingly left anything unobserved. *a* **1708** BEVERIDGE *Thes. Theol.* (1710) II. 362 Then perform these duties,..knowingly. **1827** SCOTT *Two Drovers* ii, A good-looking, smart little man upon a pony, most knowingly hogged and cropped, as was then the fashion. **1861** GEO. ELIOT *Silas M.* vi, His eyes twinkled knowingly. **1875** FREEMAN *Hist. Ess.* Ser. I. viii. 213 It is not likely that any such feeling was knowingly present to the mind of any man.

knowingness (ˈnəʊɪŋnɪs). [f. as prec. + -NESS.] The quality or state of being knowing.

1. The quality or state of being intelligent or well-informed; cleverness, cunning, shrewdness, appearance or air of shrewdness; also affectation of knowing, sciolism.

1727 BAILEY vol. II, *Knowingness*, knowledge. **1812** J. H. VAUX *Flash Dict.*, A thief..who..affects a knowingness in his air and conversation. **1877** T. A. TROLLOPE *Peep beh. Sc. at Rome* iv. 41 The glossy cylindrical hat..stuck with somewhat cynical knowingness over his left ear.

2. The state of being conscious, consciousness. *rare.*

1839 CARLYLE *Chartism.* v. 138 It grows to be the universal belief, sole accredited knowingness. **1841** L. HUNT *Seer* II. (1864) 28 We are not conscious of the reason: that is to say, we do not feel it with *knowingness.*

knowl. *Sc.* Also mod.Sc. **knool, knule.** [Cf. LG. *knull, knulle* knot, hump, swelling, etc.] A knob, knot, swelling, excrescence. *attrib.* in **knowl taes**, toes with swollen joints.

1500–20 DUNBAR *Poems* xxviii. 19 That hes vpoun his feit a wyrok, Knowll tais, nor mowlis in no degrie.

knowledge (ˈnɒlɪdʒ), *sb.* Forms: (*north.*) 3–7 **knau-**, 4–7 **knaw-**, (5–6 **knawe-**); (*midl. and south.*) 4–5 **knou-**, 4– **know-**, (4–6 **knowe-**, 5–7 **kno-**); 3–6 **-lage**, (4–6 **-lag**, 5–6 **-leage**, 6 **-lauge**), 4–5 **-lache**, (4 **-lach**), **-leche** (**-lech**, 5 **-lich(e**, **-lych**), 5–7 (8) **-lege**, (5 **-legge**); 5 **-ledge**, (6–8 **-ledg**). [ME. (north. dial.) *knaulage*, in Wyclif *knowleche*. The first element is identical with KNOW *sb.*[1], and the stem of KNOW *v.*; for the formation of the word and its relation to KNOWLEDGE *v.*, see *Note* below. The second element was presumably, as in the vb., originally *-leche*; but the earliest cited instances (northern, *c* 1300) have already *-lage*; *lache*, *-leche*, appear in southern Eng. late in the 14th c. The shortening of *o* in the first syllable is phonetically normal; cf. the 15–17th c. spelling *knoledge*; (ˈnəʊlɪdʒ) used by some, is merely a recent analytical pronunciation after *know*.]

Signification. The earliest sense goes with the original sense of KNOWLEDGE *v.* But the word was app. soon laid hold of to supply a noun of action to KNOW *v.*, for which *cnowunge*, KNOWING, was in earlier use, and continued to be used in part.

I. Senses related to KNOWLEDGE *v.* and early uses of KNOW *v.*

†**1. a.** Acknowledgement, confession. **b.** Acknowledgement or recognition of the position or claims (of any one). *Obs.*

a **1300** *Cursor M.* 11193 (Cott.) To mak knaulage [*Gött.* knowlage, *Trin.* knowleche] with sum-thing Til sir august, þair ouer-king. *Ibid.* 12162 (Cott.) Mang barns als barn i wit yow spac, To me knaulage [*Gött.* knauleche, *Fairf.* knawlage, *Trin.* knowleche] nan wald ye tac. *Ibid.* 27355 (Cott.) For nakin scam þat he ne mak Opine knaulage of all his sak. *c* **1375** *Ibid.* (Fairf.), Bid him opin knawlage make & lette for na shame to shew his sake. **1491** *Act 7 Hen. VII*, c. 18 If the..seid knowledge had never be made. **1531–2** *Act. 23 Hen. VIII*, c. 6 §1 The maires of the Stapull..might laufully take reconisance or knowledge for dettes. *a* **1533** LD. BERNERS *Huon* xlii. 142 To pay me for a knowlege euery yere .iiii. drams of gold. *a* **1548** HALL *Chron., Hen. VIII* 253 b, In knowledge of our superioritie over them.

†**2.** The fact of recognizing as something known, or known about, before; recognition. *to take knowledge of*, to recognize. *Obs.*

a **1350** *Cursor M.* 4817 (Gött.) To Ioseph siþen þai soght, ..Coud þai of him na knaulag [*Cott.* kything] take. *a* **1400** *Sir Perc.* 1052 Now hase Percyvelle..Spokene with his emes twoo, Bot never one of thoo Took his knawlage. *c* **1480** HENRYSON *Test. Cres.* 393 Sum had na knawlege Of hir, becaus sho was sa deformait. **1579–80** NORTH *Plutarch* (1676) 337 Demetrius..stole away secretly, disguised in a threadbare cloak..to keep him from knowledge. **1600** HOLLAND *Livy* XXXIV. xx. 865 The Lacetanes, when they took knowledge of their armor and colours,..sallied out upon them. **1611** BIBLE *Acts* iv. 13 They tooke knowledge of them, that they had been with Iesus.

†**3.** Legal cognizance; judicial investigation or inquiry. Chiefly *Sc. Obs.*

1398 *Sc. Acts Robt. III* (1814) I. 211/2 Þe Justice sal tak knaulage of þe officeris how þai gowerne þaim in þair offcis. **1424** *Sc. Acts Jas. I* (1814) II. 4/2 Lele men and discret;.. the quhilkis sall byde knawlege befor þe king gif þai haif done thair deuoir. **1472–3** *Rolls Parlt.* VI. 5/1 After suche serches, enquerres, and knoweleche taken and had. **1526** TINDALE *Acts* xxv. 21 When Paul had appealed to be kept vnto the knowledge [so COVERD., *Great, Rheims*; WYCLIF knowynge, *Genev.* examination, **1611** hearing, *R.V.* decision] off Cesar. **1600** HOLLAND *Livy* IV. xxvi. 156 The taking knowledge of such, as pretended to bee freed,..was put off untill the war was ended. **1732** LOUTHIAN *Form of Process Scotl.* 272 And remit them and the Libel, as found relevant, to the Knowledge of an Assize.

†**4.** *gen.* Cognizance, notice: only in phr. ***to take knowledge of***, to take cognizance or notice of, to notice, observe; in quot. 1609, to become aware of (cf. 8). *Obs.*

1602 SHAKS. *Ham.* II. i. 13 Take you as 'twere some distant knowledge of him. **1609** HOLLAND *Amm. Marcell.* XXVII. ii. 305 When knowledge was taken with exceeding great sorrow, of this overthrow. **1611** BIBLE *Ruth.* ii. 10 Why haue I found grace in thine eyes, that thou shouldest take knowledge of me, seeing I am a stranger? —— *Isa.* lviii. 3 Wherefore haue wee afflicted our soule, and thou takest no knowledge? **1611** B. JONSON *Catiline* IV. vi, A state's anger Should not take knowledge either of fools or women. **1623** J. ROBINSON *Let.* 19 Dec. in W. Bradford *Plymouth Plantation* (1856) 163 So are we glad to take knowledg of it in that fullnes we doe.

II. Senses derived from the verb KNOW, in its later uses.

* *The fact or condition of knowing.*

5. a. The fact of knowing a thing, state, etc., or (in general sense) a person; acquaintance; familiarity gained by experience.

a **1300** *Cursor M.* 15931 Coth petre, 'knaulage [*Gött.* cnaulage, *Fairf.* knawlage] of him had i neuer nan'. *a* **1350** *Ibid.* 5061 (Gött.) Mi fadir faris wele, sir, I wat. Knaulage [*Cott.* knauing] of ȝoures haue I nan. **1375** BARBOUR *Bruce* I. 337 Knawlage off mony statis, May quhile awailȝe full mony gatis. **1484** CAXTON *Fables of Alfonce* i, I herd of two marchaunts whiche neuer had sene eche other..but they had knowleche eche of the other by theyr lettres. **1535** COVERDALE *2 Chron.* viii. 18 Hiram sent him shippes by his seruauntes which had knowlege of the See. **1662** J. DAVIES tr. *Olearius' Voy. Ambass.* 169 The Antient Geographers.. had no knowledge of these Tartars. **1771** *Junius Lett.* liv. 281 His knowledge of human nature must be limited indeed. **1860** TYNDALL *Glac.* I. x. 67 Thus expanding my knowledge of the glaciers.

†**b.** *absol.* in phr. ***to grow out of*** (***one's***) ***knowledge***: to cease to be known, to become unknown or unfamiliar. *Obs.*

1578 LYTE *Dodoens* v. xliii. 167 Albeit it be nowe growen out of knowledge, yet we haue thought it good to describe the same. **1623** LISLE *Ælfric on O. & N. Test.* Pref. 6 The Hebrew it selfe..grew so out of knowledge among the people that they understood not our Saviours Eli, Eli, lammasabactani. **1722** DE FOE *Col. Jack* (1840) 199, I was grown out of everybody's knowledge. **1754** FOOTE *Knights* I. (1778) 3/1 Master Timothy is almost grown out of knowledge, Sir Gregory. **1864** D. G. MITCHELL *Sev. Stor.* 33 Now, he must have grown out of my knowledge.

†**6. a.** Personal acquaintance, friendship, intimacy. **b.** Those with whom one is acquainted, one's acquaintances; = ACQUAINTANCE 3. *Obs.*

1388 WYCLIF *Luke* ii. 44 Thei..souȝten hym among hise cosyns and his knouleche [1382 knowen]. **1389** in *Eng. Gilds* (1870) 4 Þe brethren and sustren of þe bretherhede..shul euery ȝer..hold to-geder, for to norishe more knowelech and loue, a fest. *c* **1483** CAXTON *Dialogues* 4/13 And ye mete ony That ye know Or that they be of your knoweleche [*de vostre cognoissance*]. **1509** BP. FISHER *Fun. Serm. C'tess Richmond* Wks. (1876) 290 She was bounteous and lyberall to euery persone of her knowlege or aquayntaunce. **1600** SHAKS. *A.Y.L.* I. ii. 297, I shall desire more loue and knowledge of you.

7. Sexual intimacy. Const. *of* (†*with*). Now only in ***carnal knowledge***. (*archaic* and *legal.*)

a **1425** *Cursor M.* 11056 (Trin.) Þe ton was ȝonge mayden þon, þe toþer had knowleche wiþ mon. *c* **1450** *Merlin* 17 Neuer erthely man hadde I of knowleche, wherethrough I sholde haue childe. **1540** *Act 32 Hen. VIII*, c. 38 §2 Such mariages beyng..consummate with bodily knowlage. **1686** *Col. Rec. Pennsylv.* I. 176 He was accused of having Carnall Knowledge of his Brother in Law's women Servants. **1883** *Wharton's Law Lex.* (ed. 7) 691/1 *Rape*, the carnal knowledge of a woman by force against her will.

8. a. Acquaintance with a fact; perception, or certain information of, a fact or matter; state of being aware or informed; consciousness (of anything). The object is usually a proposition expressed or implied: e.g. the knowledge that a person is poor, knowledge of his poverty.

c **1375** *Sc. Leg. Saints* xxvi. (*Nycholas*) 114 He t[h]ocht to wak..for til get knawlag & to se quha It wes helpyt hyme sa. **1422** tr. *Secreta Secret., Priv. Priv.* 208 By the eeris we haue knowlech of Sovne. *a* **1548** HALL *Chron., Edw. IV* 200 So that this civill warre should seme to all men, to have been begon without his assent or knowledge. **1604** E. G[RIMSTONE] *D'Acosta's Hist. Ind.* IV. viii. 230 They labour in these mines in continuall darkenes and obscuritie, without knowledge of day or night. **1725** POPE *Odyss.* II. 185 Till big with knowledge of approaching woes The prince of augurs, Halitherses, rose. **1796** JANE AUSTEN *Pride & Prej.* ii, Till the evening after the visit was paid she had no knowledge of it. **1832** HT. MARTINEAU *Demerara* ii. 16 The knowledge that he might at any hour be called upon.. stimulated his studies of his duties.

b. *absol.* Acquaintance with facts, range of information, ken. Esp. in phrases as ***to one's knowledge***, so far as one is aware; also, as one is aware, as one can testify (in latter sense, also, ***of one's k.***); ***to come to one's knowledge***, to become known to one.

1542 N. UDALL in *Lett. Lit. Men* (Camden) 3 To my knowlege I have not eftsons offended. **1576** FLEMING *Panopl. Epist.* 103 According to the measure of your knowledge, and proportion of your policie. *c* **1592** MARLOWE *Massacre Paris* I. ii, Of my knowledge, in one cloister keep Five hundred fat Franciscan friars. **1662** J. DAVIES tr. *Olearius' Voy. Ambass.* 168 Who,..if ever it should come to their knowledge, that they had sold any fish. **1820** *Examiner* No. 652. 641/2 A better paid witness..had never come to his knowledge. **1872** E. PEACOCK *Mabel Heron* II. i. 17 What came to my knowledge.

c. *Philos.* ***knowledge about***, ***knowledge by description***: knowledge of a person, thing, or perception gained through information or facts about it rather than by direct experience (opp. *knowledge by* (or *of*) *acquaintance*, see ACQUAINTANCE 1 b).

1885, etc. [see ACQUAINTANCE 1 b]. **1945** E. MAYO *Social Probl. Industr. Civilization* (1949) I. i. 15 The student is required to relate his logical *knowledge-about* to his own direct acquaintance with the facts. **1952** B. MAYO *Logic of Personality* iii. 30 Knowledge *about* something is called knowledge by *description*. **1954** [see ACQUAINTANCE 1 b]. **1967** *Encycl. Philos.* IV. 350/1 Parallel to this on the side of knowledge of things is the distinction between knowledge by acquaintance and knowledge by description. **1968** A J. AYER *Origins Pragmatism* II. iii. 293 The mind has 'knowledge about' an object not immediately there.

9. a. Intellectual acquaintance with, or perception of, fact or truth; clear and certain mental apprehension; the fact, state, or condition of understanding. †Formerly, also, the faculty of understanding, intelligence, intellect.

1387 TREVISA *Higden* (Rolls) III. 217 God wole þat meny þinges passe þe knoweleche of man. **1422** tr. *Secreta Secret., Priv. Priv.* 212 A stronge argument to Shewe..the Sotilte of thy knowleche. **1508** DUNBAR *Tua Mariit Wemen* 300 Ay the fule did forȝet, for febilnes of knawlege. **1593** Q. ELIZ. tr. *Boeth.* pr. v. 115 That is not opinion, but an included purenes of the hyest knoledge that is shut in no lymites. **1690** LOCKE *Hum. Und.* IV. i. §2 Knowledge..seems to me to be nothing but the perception of the connexion and agreement, or disagreement and repugnancy of any of our ideas. **1748** HARTLEY *Observ. Man* II. Introd. 1 The Infinite Power, Knowledge, and Goodness of God. **1828** WHATELY *Logic* (1857) 164 *note*, Knowledge..implies..firm belief,.. of what is true,..on sufficient grounds. **1836–7** SIR W. HAMILTON *Metaph.* (1859) I. iii. 58 Philosophical knowledge,..is thus the knowledge of effects as dependent on their causes. **1857** BUCKLE *Civiliz.* I. v. 246 The knowledge on which all civilization is based, solely consists in an acquaintance with the relations which things and ideas bear to each other and to themselves. **1877** E. R. CONDER *Bas. Faith* iv. 193 Knowledge is composed of judgments: the criteria of the judgments composing it being truth and certainty.

b. Const. *of* (something). Also in *pl.* (now *rare*).

1398 TREVISA *Barth. De P.R.* II. ii. (1495) 27 Mannes vnderstondynge & inwytte gadreth knowlege of some thynge of the knowlege of other thynges. **1477** EARL RIVERS (Caxton) *Dictes* 73 Disputing & arguing for to haue knowlech of yᵉ trouth of a thing. **1670** A. ROBERTS *Advent. T.S.* 146 They do it by the Knowledges that they have of Nature. **1878** JEVONS *Prim. Pol. Econ.* iii. 31 Knowledge of nature consists, to a great extent, in understanding the causes of things.

c. with *pl.* A mental apprehension; a perception, intuition, or other cognition. *rare.*

1563 *Homilies* II. *Rogation Week* I. (1859) 470 To have a knowledge of the power and divinity of God. **1626** T. H. *Caussin's Holy Crt.* 123 To proceed..by such knowledges, as are common, with brute beastes, and forsake those of men. **1825** COLERIDGE *Aids Refl.* (1848) I. 128 It is the office ..of reason, to bring a unity into all our conceptions and several knowledges. **1836–7** SIR W. HAMILTON *Metaph.* (1859) I. iii. 57 These two cognitions or knowledges have, accordingly, received different names. **1872** LOWELL *Wks.* (1890) IV. 184 With Dante wisdom is the generalization from many several knowledges of small account by themselves.

†**d.** *Med.* Diagnosis: cf. KNOWLEDGE *v.* 5. *Obs.*

1541 R. COPLAND *Guydon's Quest. Chirurg.* etc. N ij, Is the Cyrurgyen bounde to haue the knowledge of the blode that is drawen?.. No, but the beholdynge of the saide blode belongeth to Physycyens. **1655** CULPEPPER, etc. *Riverius* X. v. 292 The Knowledg in general is manifest... That Parts sending have a more difficult Diagnosis or way of Knowledg.

†**e.** ***to come to*** (***one's own***) ***knowledge***, to recover one's understanding; to come to one's senses. *Obs.*

13.. *E.E. Allit. P.* B. 1702 Þenne he wayned hym his wyt ..þat he com to knawlach & kenned hym seluen. *c* **1489** CAXTON *Blanchardyn* xiv. 49 Euyn at these wordes cam the prouost tyl his owne knowlege ageyne.

10. Acquaintance with a branch of learning, a language, or the like; theoretical or practical understanding *of* an art, science, industry, etc.; †skill *in* or *to do* something (*obs.*). (Rarely in plural.)

c **1375** *Sc. Leg. Saints* xl. (*Ninian*) 130 Þane trawalit he besyli, til he in knavlage of clergy..wes wise Inuch. *c* **1475** *Rauf Coilȝear* 325 The King had greit knawledge the countrie to ken. **1508** DUNBAR *Tua Mariit Wemen* 455 Folk a cury may miscuke, that knawledge wantis. **1560** DAUS tr. *Sleidane's Comm.* 201 He had no greate knowledge in the latyn tongue. **1669** STURMY *Mariner's Mag.* I. 15 Mariners brought up in Practical Knowledge of Navigaton at Sea. *a* **1774** GOLDSM. *Surv. Exp. Philos.* (1776) I. 210 Nor were the ancients without a great knowledge in this art. **1782** WOLCOTT (P. Pindar) *Ode to R.A.'s* iii. Wks. 1812 I. 20 With scarce more knowledges than these He earns a guinea every day with ease. **1841** LANE *Arab. Nts.* I. 85 A knowledge of all the medical and other sciences. **1851** *Illustr. Catal. Gt. Exhib.* 1278 This article is..made by young women who have no knowledge of drawing.

11. In general sense: The fact or condition of being instructed, or of having information acquired by study or research; acquaintance with ascertained truths, facts, or principles; information acquired by study; learning; erudition.

1477 EARL RIVERS (Caxton) *Dictes* 27 Knowlege is better than ignoraunce. **1559** W. CUNNINGHAM *Cosmogr. Glasse* 46 Knowledge hath no enemie but ignoraunce. **1596** DALRYMPLE tr. *Leslie's Hist. Scot.* VIII. 71 In gret honour for his eruditioun and knawledge. **1611** BIBLE *Eccles.* i. 18 Hee that increaseth knowledge increaseth sorrow. **1784** COWPER *Task* VI. 96 Knowledge is proud that he has learned so much; Wisdom is humble that he knows no more. **1856** RUSKIN *Mod. Paint.* III. IV. iii. §17 The highest knowledge always involves a more advanced perception of the fields of the unknown. **1870** M. D. CONWAY *Earthw. Pilgr.* xviii. 220 One might say that no kind or amount of human knowledge were too much for a woman.

** *The object of knowing; that which is known or made known.*

†**12.** Information; intelligence; notice, intimation. *Obs.*

1417 HEN. V in Ellis *Orig. Lett.* Ser. III. I. 62 We remitte hem to have ful declaracion and verrai knaweleche of you in that matere. *c* **1440** *Generydes* 1160 Whan she hadde tideng And trew knowlage of Auferius. **1473** WARKW. *Chron.* 11 He yaff knoleage to his peple that he wulde holde withe the Erle of Warwyke. **1568** GRAFTON *Chron.* II. 317 He imediatly sent knowledge into the whole countrie. **1600** HOLLAND *Livy* XXVI. XXVI. 603 There hee published and gave knowledge, That hee would shape his course from thence for Anticyra. **1722** DE FOE *Plague* (1756) 49 Shall give knowledge thereof to the Examiner of Health.

13. The sum of what is known.

1534 STARKEY *Let.* in *England* (1878) p. x, I..passyd ouer in to Italy, whereas I so delytyd in the contemplacyon of natural Knolege. **1559** W. CUNNINGHAM *Cosmogr. Glasse* 142 The proper nature of suche in whose mynde knoweledge have once builded her Boure. *a* **1628** PRESTON *New Covt.* (1634) 446 You..may have abundance of emptie and unprofitable knowledge, without Grace. **1667** MILTON *P.L.* VII. 126 Knowledge is as food, and needs no less Her Temperance over Appetite, to know In measure what the mind may well contain. **1753** JOHNSON *Adventurer* No. 85 ¶7 He is by no means to be accounted useless or idle who has stored his mind with acquired knowledge. **1823** DE QUINCEY *Lett. to Young Man* Wks. 1860 XIV. 58 All knowledge may be commodiously distributed into science and erudition. **1833** (*title*) The Penny Cyclopædia of the Society for the Diffusion of Useful Knowledge. **1877** E. R. CONDER *Bas. Faith* iv. 139 We speak of knowledge as stored up in books. But in reality what books contain is not knowledge, but only symbols of knowledge. *Mod.* Every branch of knowledge.

14. (with *pl.*) A branch of learning; a science; an art. (Rarely in *sing.*)

1581 SIDNEY *Apol. Poetrie* (Arb.) 20 Poetry,..the..first nurse, whose milk by little and little enabled them to feed afterwards of tougher knowledges. **1605** BACON *Adv. Learn.* II. xvii. §9 The mathematics, which are the most abstracted of knowledges. **1662** J. CHANDLER *Van. Helmont's Oriat.* To Rdr., Many clear fundamental Knowledges and Arts. **1825** COLERIDGE *Aids Refl.* (1848) I. Pref. 19 A land abounding with men, able in arts, learning, and knowledges manifold. **1860** MARSH *Eng. Lang.* 28 The superior attractions and supposed claims of other knowledges.

†**15.** A sign or mark by which anything is known, recognized, or distinguished; a token.

1483 *Cath. Angl.* 204/2 A knawlege, *nota,..specimen, experimentum.* **1523** LD. BERNERS *Froiss.* I. cclxxviii. 416 At theyr departyng they thought to make a knowledge that they had ben there; for they set the subbarbes afyre. **1555** W. WATREMAN *Fardle Facions* II. iv. 141 Thei deuised.. circumcision, because thei would haue a notable knowledge betwene them and other nacions.

III. 16. *attrib.* and *Comb.*, as ***knowledge element, power, -tree; knowledge-full, -kindled, -proof*** adjs.; **knowledge base** *Computing*, the underlying set of facts, assumptions, and inference rules on which a computer system operates; a store of information (as in a database) available to draw on; **knowledge-based** *ppl. a.*, of an academic discipline: founded on an accumulation of facts, non-empirical; of a computer system: incorporating a set of facts, assumptions, or inference rules derived from human knowledge; **knowledge-box, -casket**, humorous names for the head; **knowledge factory**, term applied pejoratively to a university or college, etc., which places undue emphasis on vocational training; **knowledge industry**, term applied fancifully or pejoratively to the development and use of knowledge, *spec.* in universities, polytechnics, etc.

1971 *Symp. über Computer Graphics* (Berlin) 1 Steps toward this goal are being made within a particular context —architecture—that furnishes a '*knowledge base' or 'assumption base' from which programs can procure..those heuristics necessary to handle two dimensional and three dimensional ambiguities. **1986** *Times Higher Educ. Suppl.* 13 June (Journals Suppl.) p. vii/2 He sees the explosion in knowledge gathering, based on computer storage and retrieval, as providing a knowledge base for teachers. **1986** *Financial Times* 16 Oct. (Information Technol. Surv.) p. x/2 Once a way is found to represent the knowledge, it is no problem to add extra rules to the knowledge base. **1970** C. A. MYERS *Computers in Knowledge-Based Fields* i. 8 Education is clearly the leading *knowledge-based industry. **1975** *IEEE Trans. Software Engin.* I. 26/1 The planner project is constructing a programming apprentice to assist in knowledge based programming. **1980** *Jrnl. R. Soc. Arts* Feb. 151/2 Management education..has inevitably become much more knowledge-based. **1983** *Austral. Microcomputer Mag.* Dec. 69/7 Computers based on the 16-bit Motorola 6800 microprocessor were adequate for knowledge-based systems. **1796** *Mod. Gulliver's Trav.* 194 His head being differently formed to that of others, by producing what had been his *knowledge-box, my word could not be doubted. **1874** BURNAND *My time* v. 42 With all these odds and ends, my knowledge-box was fairly stored. **1879** BAIN *Education as a Science* xii. 402 The work of teaching *knowledge elements. **1928** *World's Work* May 55 Next day we visited the *knowledge factory, and..the head teacher asked if I had ever been sent to school. **1968** *Listener* 4 July 6/2 Some students who rioted on British campuses (like some in France and Italy) have been protesting at having found themselves in a knowledge factory when they thought they were headed for something else. They find themselves being trained for the managerial and technocratic élites, whereas what they demand is the right to question the structure of society which makes such élites necessary. **1969** C. DAVIDSON in Cockburn & Blackburn *Student Power* 341 The production of an increase in socially useful and necessary labour power is the new historic function of our educational institutions that enables us to name them, quite accurately, knowledge factories. **1879** *St. George's Hosp. Rep.* IX. 793 In his concise but *knowledge-full work on the pathology of the ear. **1962** F. MACHLUP *Production & Distribution of Knowledge in U.S.* iii. 45 If the phrase '*knowledge industry' were to be given an unambiguous meaning, would it be a collection of industries producing knowledge or rather a collection of occupations producing knowledge in whatever industries they are employed. **1963** C. KERR *Uses of University* iii. 87 Basic to this transformation is the growth of the 'knowledge industry', which is coming to permeate government and business. **1968** *Economist* 28 Feb. 51/3 This is a book for the serious investor who..wants to learn something about the operations of the New York Stock Exchange and the 'knowledge industry', with its analysts, theorists..and numerous other 'ists'. **1970** *Globe & Mail* (Toronto) 25 Sept. B2/2 The report notes the emergence of the knowledge industry, growing emphasis on people values. **1886** LOWELL *Wks.* (1890) VI. 150 There are some pupils who are *knowledge-proof. **1598** ROWLANDS *Poems on Passion, Christ to Wom. Jerus.*, Life's arbour next, which grace did fill; And *knowledge-tree of good and ill.

[*Note.* The origin of *knowledge* sb. and vb. and the question of the original relations between the sb. and vb. themselves, are a difficult problem. According to the extant evidence, the vb. is exemplified nearly a century before the sb., and is found only in southern Eng., with a form in *-lechien, -leche*, while the sb., when it appears *c* 1300, is found only in northern dialect, and has its earliest form in *-lage*. Thus the northern MSS. of *Cursor Mundi* have numerous examples of the sb.—the earliest known,—but do not use the vb. Late in the 14th c., the sb. is found in midl. and south. (first in Wyclif, a northern man), with the forms *-lache, -leche*; in the 15th c. the vb. appears sparingly in the north, with the form *-lage, -lege*. If the sb. were at first only northern, the want of earlier examples may be explained by there being no northern literature of the 12th and the early 13th c.; but this does not account for the app. absence of the sb. from southern literature before Wyclif, and leaves the early relations between the vb. and sb. very perplexing. It can hardly be doubted, in view of the earliest sense of both, that they have a common origin; but what this was it is not easy to determine. The sb. has no parallel in Eng., nor app. in any Teutonic lang. Some have thought it related to ONorse derivative sbs. in *-leik-r* 'play, exercise, action', e.g *kunnleik-r* knowledge. The OE. cognate ending was *-lác*, as in *wedlác* wedlock; but neither the ON. nor OE. form could have given an early ME. *-leche*; this would have required an OE. *-lǽce*, of which there is no trace. If, on the other hand, we start from the vb. *i)cnawlechien*, there are difficulties in explaining the formation of this also. It has been proposed to associate it with OE. verbs in *-lǽc(e)an*, pa. t. *-lǽhte*, a few of which came down into early ME. in *-lêchen, -lêhte*. In OE. these usually go with derivative adjs. in *-líc* (from an adj. or sb.), to which they are supposed to stand somehow in ablaut relation; e.g. *cúðlic* friendly, *cúðlǽcan* be friendly with, to treat like a friend, *efenlíc* equal, *efenlǽcan* to make equal, imitate, *néahlíc* near, *néahlǽcan* to draw nigh, approach, *rihtlic* right, correct, *ȝe)rihtlǽcan* to make right, correct, *sumorlic* summerlike, *sumorlǽcan* to draw near to summer, *winterlíc* winterly, *winterlǽcan* to draw near to winter, etc. Here the radical part is an adj. or sb. If now early ME. *cnaw*, KNOW *sb.*[1], 'acknowledgement, confession', went back to an OE. *ȝecnáw*, it is possible that, either immediately by analogy, or through an adj. **ȝecnáwlíc* = *ȝecnǽwe* 'conscious of, acknowledging', there was formed a derivative vb. **ȝecnáwlǽcan* 'to become conscious of, make acknowledgement or confession of', which would give an early ME. **i-cnawlechen, -lehte*. True, these are not the ME. forms actually found; but some variation in the formation of these verbs appears in the instances cited by Sievers (*Ags. Gram.*, ed. 3, §407, Ann. 17, 18), including a pa. pple. *ȝerihtlǽced*, in the West Saxon *Past. Care*, beside *ȝerihtlǽht*, while the Rushw. copy of the Lindisfarne Gloss shows, for *néahlǽcan*, a form *neoliciȝa*, pa. t. *néolicade, néalocode*, pa. pple. *ȝinéolicad*; so that, perhaps, the early ME. *i)cnawlechien, i-cnoulechien, -lechede*, may be taken as having this origin. If this was so, the verb *to knowledge* was first formed, and the sb. was derived from it, which would also agree with the extant historical data for the two words, and account for the original sense of the sb.]

†'**knowledge**, *v. Obs.* Forms: 3 **cnaw-, cnou-**, (5 **cnow-**), 3–5 (6) **knou-**, (4 **kneu-**, 5 **knew(e-)**, 3–7 **know-**, (4–5 (6) **knowe-**, 5–6 **kno-**; *north.* 5–7 **knaw-**, (5 **kna-**); 3 **-lechi(en**, 3–5 **-leche(n**, (4–5 **-lech, -lich(e, -lych(e, -lach(e)**, 5–6 **-lege**, (5 **-legh**, 6 **-lage**), 6–7 **-ledge**, (6 **-ledg**). [Early ME. *cnawlechien*, in 14th c. *knowleche(n*, prob. f. *cnaw*, KNOW *sb.*[1], and ultimately from *cnáw-an, know-en*, to KNOW, with a second element of obscure origin: see note to prec. A single example of *i-cnoulechien* in same sense, from *ȝecnáw-, i-know-*, is known in the 13th c. Northern instances of the vb. are unknown before the 15th c., and are rare at all times. The unstressed ending *-leche*, became by 1400 *-lege*, whence the later *-ledge*. (Cf. *Grinnidge* = *Greenwich, Swanage* from *Swanewíc, Swanwich*.) See also the sb.]

1. *trans.* To own the knowledge of; to confess; to recognize or admit as true: = ACKNOWLEDGE *v.* 1.

c **1230** *Hali Meid.* 9 ʒif ha..cnawlecheð soð; Ich habbe ham to witnesse ha lickeð huni of þornes. *a* **1240** *Lofsong* in *Cott. Hom.* 205 Al þis ich i-cnoulechie þe. *a* **1380** *St. Ambrose* 672 in Horstm. *Altengl. Leg.* (1878) 18 þus þis gode mon..Knouleched þat al þat was his Was pore mennes at heore nede. **1428** *Surtees Misc.* (1888) 5 He knawleged and graunted his trespas. **1438** *Waterf. Arch.* in *10th Rep. Hist. MSS. Comm.* App. v. 330 John Franches..didd knolech hym to ow to William Lyncoll..x. *li.* of money currant. **1439** *Sc. Acts Jas. II*, c. 3 (1814) 54 (Jam.) The said princess ..knawlegis that quhat thing the said personis did,..thai dide it of gude zele and motife. *c* **1440** *Partonope* 3522, I knowlech a traytoure am I. *a* **1450** *Knt. de la Tour* (1868) 37 Thanne she knowleged her misdede. **1483** *Cath. Angl.* 205/1 To knawlege, *fateri, confiteri* [etc.]. **1537** *Act 28 Hen. VIII* in Bolton *Stat. Irel.* (1621) 129 Them that..doe professe and knowledge Christs religion. **1551** ROBINSON tr. *More's Utop.* Transl. Ep. (1895) 18 Knowing, and knowledging the barbarous rudenes of my translation. **1582** STANYHURST *Æneis* II. (Arb.) 48 My flight from prison I knowledge. [**1660** STILLINGFL. *Iren.* II. viii. §2 The Cleregie..did knowledge and confesse according to the truth, that the Convocations of the same Cleregie hath ben and ought to be assembled by the Kings writt.]

b. *absol.* or *intr.* To make confession or acknowledgement; to confess. Const. *to* (a fault, etc.).

1382 WYCLIF *John* i. 20 And he knowelechide, and denyede not, and he knowlechide, For I am not Crist. **1393** LANGL. *P. Pl.* C. VIII. 148 For dedes þat we han don ille, dampned sholde we be neuere Yff we knewelechid and cryde crist þer of mercy. *a* **1450** MYRC 916 When thow herest what thow hast do, Knowlache wel a-non ther to. **1526** TINDALE *Rom.* x. 10 To knowledge with the mougth maketh a man safe.

†**c.** *intr.* with *to* (in biblical versions): To give thanks to, to praise. *Obs.*

A literal rendering of L. *confitērī* of Vulg., repr. Heb. *yōdāh*, Gr. ἐξομολογεῖσθαι.

1382 WYCLIF *Gen.* xxix. 35 She conseuyde, and bare a sone, and seith, Now I shal knowlech [Cov. geue thankes] to the Lord. —— *Ps.* xli[i]. 12 Hope I in god, for ʒit shal knoulechen to hym. —— *Matt.* xi. 25, I knowleche to thee, fadir..for thou hast hid these thingis fro wijse [men] and ware and hast shewid hem to litil men. **1535** COVERDALE *Rom.* xiv. 11 All tunges shal knowlege vnto God [WYCLIF Ech tunge schal knowleche to God].

2. *trans.* To recognize or confess (a person or thing to be something); **a.** with *complement.* **b.** *simply*: To recognize (one) to be what he claims; to own the claims or authority of: = ACKNOWLEDGE 2.

a **1225** *Leg. Kath.* 1352 Her we cnawlecheð him soð godd, and godes sune. *a* **1300** *Body & Soul* in *Map's Poems* (Camden) 335 That thouȝ woldest God knouleche. **1377** LANGL. *P. Pl.* B. XII. 193 He..knewleched hym gulty. **1382** WYCLIF *Luke* xii. 8 Ech man which euer schal knowleche me byfore men,..mannis sone schal knowleche him bifore þe aungelis of God. *c* **1450** *Cov. Myst.* (Shaks. Soc.) 138 Knowlyche thiself ffor a cockewold. **1535** *Goodly Primer* (1834) 82 They knowledge thee to be the Father of an infinite majesty. **1582** STANYHURST *Æneis* III. (Arb.) 89 A Greeke my self I doe knowledge. **1631** WEEVER *Anc. Fun. Mon.* 113 Knowledging, and affirming..the same Bishop to be supreme. **1643** PRYNNE *Sov. Power Parlt.* App. 28 Charles dying, his sonne Charles the eight, was..reputed and knowledged King.

3. To own as genuine, or of legal force or validity; to own, avow, or assent in legal form to (an act, document, etc.), so as to give it validity: = ACKNOWLEDGE *v.* 3.

1531–2 *Act 23 Hen. VIII*, c. 6 §1 The cognisor ne the cognisee, that did knowledge and take the same reconisances. **1581** LAMBARDE *Eiren.* II. iii. (1588) 136 Assaults..do draw after them the forfaiture of a Recognusance, knowledged for the keeping of the Peace. **1594** WEST *2nd Pt. Symbol.*, The said L. M. his heires and assignes shall..do, make, knowledge, and suffer, or cause to be made, knowledged and suffered al and everie act and acts [etc.]. **1797** *Burn's Eccl. Law* (ed. 6) III. 204 If any ecclesiastical person knowledge a statute merchant or statute staple, or a recognizance in the nature of a statute staple.

4. *refl.* To make oneself known to, or bring oneself into acquaintance *with* a person. **b.** *intr.* To have carnal knowledge *with*.

c **1375** *Cursor M.* 11056 (Fairf.) The tone was yong maidyn þan The tothir had knowlechid with man [*Trin.* had knowleche wiþ mon]. *a* **1425** *Ibid.* 3838 (Trin.) Iacob.. knowleched him [*Cott.* kythed him, *Gött.* knew him] þere wiþ rachel.

5. *trans.* To recognize; in *Med.* to recognize and identify (a disease), to diagnose.

1541 R. COPLAND *Galyen's Terap.* 2 C iij, It is leful yᵉ moste often to knowlege the dysease at the begynnynge, and it is necessary that the indication be taken of the sayd dysease. *a* **1618** SYLVESTER *Mayden's Blush* 442 Vouchsafe mee,..As in a glasse to see and knowledge Him.

6. To take legal cognizance of (a cause, etc.).

1609 SKENE *Reg. Maj.* 105 (Form Baron Courts c. 15) Gif it [the judgement] be againe said in the Schiref Court, it sould be knawledged in the justice Court.

Hence †'**knowledged** *ppl. a.*, known, acknowledged.

c **1450** *Bp. Grossetest's Househ. Stat.* in *Babees Bk.* 330 That they admitte youre knowlechyd men, familiers frendys, and strangers.

knowledgeable (ˈnɒlɪdʒəb(ə)l), *a.* Also knowledgable. [f. KNOWLEDGE *sb.* and *v.* + -ABLE.]

†**1.** [From the verb.] Capable of being perceived or recognized; recognizable; noticeable. *Obs.*

1607 TOPSELL *Four-f. Beasts* (1658) 575 Let him but set up a stick or staffe, or some such other knowledgable mark, in the middle space betwixt him and the Wolf, and it will scare him away. **1619** T. MILLES tr. *Mexia's, etc. Treas. Anc. & Mod. T.* 49 They took a branch cut off from a fruite tree, which they would cut into diuers peeces, with certaine very knowledgable markes made vpon them.

2. [From the sb.] Possessing or showing knowledge or mental capacity; well-informed; intelligent. Also, cognisant *of*.

1829 G. GRIFFIN *Collegians* (ed. 2) I. xi. 233 She went.. to Shaun Lauther, the knowledgeable man, and put a half-a-crown into his hand, and asked his advice. **1831** S. LOVER *Leg. Irel.* 45 'A gintleman like you, that ought to be knowledgable'. **1854** MRS. GASKELL *North & S.* xxviii, 'If yo, sir, or any other knowledgeable patient man..says he'll larn me what the words mean..why, in time I may get to see the truth of it'. **1859** W. H. GREGORY *Egypt* II. 17 A very intelligent, knowledgeable man, thoroughly understanding the business and the machinery. **1897** *Spectator* 18 Sept. 367 Inquiries..conducted in a careful, a reasonable, and a knowledgeable spirit. **1901** *Academy* 21 Sept. 240/2 The review..is not only able and knowledgable; it is also..fair. **1903** *Daily Chron.* 4 Aug. 3/2 His manner is so knowledgable and convincing that they will question nothing of his theories. **1905** *Westm. Gaz.* 2 Feb. 2/1 If any official English politician has a knowledgable opinion of how these Powers are likely to combine or to clash..he should be sought. **1908** *Daily Chron.* 13 Feb. 5/7 All 'knowledgable opinion'..is against the Bill. **1945** MENCKEN *Amer. Lang.* Suppl. I. 423 The English have many counter-words that fail to make the Atlantic journey, *e.g.*, *knowledgeable*. **1955** *Sci. Amer.* June 102/2 It will be a great day for mankind when we become equally knowledgeable about the lives of microbes. **1973** *Times* 31 July 6/7 Mr Dean drew the erroneous conclusion that the President was fully knowledgeable of the cover-up at the time of the March 13 meeting.

Hence **knowledgeaˈbility**; **ˈknowledgeableness**; **ˈknowledgeably** *adv.*

1865 *Pall Mall G.* 21 Aug. 3/1 Many's the lady they've beguiled—there is fifty-six sorts of Patience as can be played with 'em [cards] on a tea-tray placed knowledgeably on the bed. **1886** *Illustr. Lond. News* 6 Mar. 232/3 Feelings of sympathy and good-fellowship, which almost took the place of 'knowledgeableness' in art matters. **1946** *Time* 19 Aug. 98 His portrait shows Caesar to be a man as far beyond mere knowledgeability as a Hitler or a Stalin. **1957** N. FRYE *Anat. Criticism* 263 This has a truth that the myopia of knowledgeability is more apt to overlook. **1965** F. SARGESON *Mem. Peon.* iv. 62, I had impressed my host by my.. knowledgeability.

knowledged (ˈnɒlɪdʒd), *a. rare.* [f. KNOWLEDGE *sb.* + -ED².] Furnished with knowledge.

1548 GESTE *Pr. Masse* in H. G. Dugdale *Life* (1840) App. i. 71, I am slenderly knowledged in Scripture matters. **1595** tr. *Saviolo's Practise* N j a, Is it possible that he which neuer saw the warres can be better knowledged than he which hath spent his life wholye therein? **1864** *Times* 10 Oct. 7/4 He is turned out..a schoolboy knowledged up to the highest mark the material and the system of mental-facture would admit.

ˈknowledgefully, *adv. rare.* [f. KNOWLEDGE *sb.* + -FUL + -LY².] Cf. *knowledge-full* adj. s.v. KNOWLEDGE *sb.* 16.] In the manner of one who is fully informed.

1906 *Harper's Mag.* Feb. 474/2 He has written of this very knowledgefully, of course, and very justly.

ˈknowledgeless, *a.* [f. KNOWLEDGE *sb.* + -LESS.] Devoid of knowledge, ignorant.

1856 R. A. VAUGHAN *Mystics* (1860) I. VI. v. 196 He will ..bid you be knowledgeless, desireless, motionless. **1900** F. W. BULLEN *With Christ at Sea* iv. 101 So helpless, so utterly knowledgeless..is the new born Christian.

ˈknowledgement. [f. KNOWLEDGE *v.* + -MENT.]

†**1.** Formal acknowledgement; legal cognizance.

a **1625** SIR H. FINCH *Law* (1636) 260 No writ shall be abated by knowledgement of villenage. **1628** COKE *On Litt.* 158 b, *Cognitio* is knowledge, or knowledgement, or opinion, and recognition is a serious acknowledgement or opinion vpon such matters of fact as they shall haue in charge, and there-upon the Iurors are called *Recognitores assisæ.* **1641** *Cases of Treason* in *Harl. Misc.* (Malham) V. 27 [These justices] do take knowledgement of all fines.

2. Knowledge, cognizance. *arch.*

1650 HUBBERT *Pill Formality* 153 They can look no further then after the things of this world; their knowledgement is bounded here. **1889** R. S. FERGUSON *Carlisle* ix. 158 No record has come to our knowledgment of the reception this letter met with.

†**ˈknowledger.** *Obs.* In 4 -lechour, -lechere. [f. KNOWLEDGE *v.* + -ER¹ (earlier -OUR: see -ER¹ 2.)] One who acknowledges or confesses.

13.. *Propr. Sanct.* (Vernon MS.) in Herrig's *Archiv* LXXXI. 106/126 Þat is þat God, vr saueour, þat ȝaf so to his knowelechour. **1382** WYCLIF *Ecclus.* xx. 1 Hou good..to not forbeden the knoulechere in orisoun.

†**ˈknowledging**, *vbl. sb. Obs.* [f. KNOWLEDGE *v.* + -ING¹.]

1. The action of the vb. KNOWLEDGE; acknowledgement, confession; formal acknowledgement; also (rendering L. *confessio* of Vulg.), Thanksgiving, praise.

a **1225** *Leg. Kath.* 1388 Iþe cnawlechinge of his kinewurðe nome. *c* **1330** R. BRUNNE *Chron. Wace* (Rolls) 10778 Knowlechyng til hym þey bed. *c* **1380** WYCLIF *Wks.* (1880) 327 Confession generaly is knowlechynge made wiþ wille. **1382** —— *Ps.* cxlviii. 14 The knoulechinge of hym vpon heuene and erthe. **1523** LD. BERNERS *Froiss.* I. ccxii. 259 The kynges of Englande..shall..holde all the forenamed countreys..without any knowledgynge of any soueraayntie, obeysaunce..or subieetion..to the crowne of Fraunce. **1539** TONSTALL *Serm. Palm Sund.* (1823) 48 Peter,..the fyrst that with his mouthe vttered that confessyon and knowlegynge by which all Christen men must be saued. **1594** WEST *2nd Pt. Symbol.* §59 At the knowledging of every fine, if the Justice..do not know the cognisors, it is requisite that some other credible person..be present.

2. The action, condition, or faculty of knowing; = KNOWLEDGE *sb.*; understanding, cognition, cognizance, notice, recognition, acquaintance, etc.

a **1225** *Ancr. R.* 92 God wule..ȝiuen ou liht..him uorto iseonne & icnowen; & þuruh þe cnoulechunge, ouer alle þing him luuien. *c* **1330** *Spec. Gy Warw.* 725 What mannes soule ..þurw dedli sinne ifiled is, His knowelaching is al gon. *a* **1425** *Cursor M.* 15931 (Trin.) Petur seide knowlechyng of him had I neuer none. *c* **1430** *Syr Gener.* (Roxb.) 6896 On his finger she knew the ring, Of him had shee noo knowleching. *c* **1450** LONELICH *Grail* xliii. 155 Was neuere Child In wommannes body with-Owten mannes knowlechinge. **1470–85** MALORY *Arthur* xix. i, They bare.. no maner of knoulechynge of their owne armes but playne whyte sheldes. *Ibid.* xx. xiv, Ye shall..lete hym haue knowlechynge that..I my self shall brynge my lady Quene Gueneuer vnto hym. **1500–20** DUNBAR *Poems* lxv. 18 Ȝe clarkis..Fullest of science and of knawlegeing. **1509** HAWES *Conv. Swearers* 3 How sholde we nowe haue ony knowledgynge Of thynges past but by theyr endytynge. **1560** ROLLAND *Crt. Venus* IV. 154 Traistant richt weill be perfite knawleging, ȝe will not thoill.

3. Meaning, signification. *rare*⁻¹.

1387–8 T. USK *Test. Love* Prol. (Skeat) l. 29 Many termes ther ben in Englyshe [of] whiche vnneth we Englishe men connen declare the knowleginge.

knowman, perverted form of GNOMON.

known (nəʊn), *ppl. a.* (*sb.*) [pa. pple. of KNOW *v.*]

A. *ppl. a.* **1. a.** Become an object of knowledge; apprehended mentally, learned; familiar; often, in pregnant sense, familiar to all, generally known or recognized.

a **1300** *Cursor M.* 15895 A knaun freind he had þare-in, in he did him late. **1495** *Trevisa's Barth. De P.R.* XIII. i. (W. de W.) 440 There is noo ryuer but the spryngeth of some welle knowen or vnknowen. **1513** MORE in Grafton *Chron.* (1568) II. 789 Those that by their favors more resembled other knowen men then him. **1622** S. WARD *Life of Faith in Death* Serm. (1862) 53 Death is the knownest and unknownest thing in the world. **1647–8** COTTERELL *Davila's Hist. Fr.* (1678) 22 Men of known courage. **1673** PENN *The Chr. a Quaker* iii. Wks. (1726) 525 Paul..is very express in that known Passage to the Romans. *a* **1704** T. BROWN *Sat. French King* Wks. 1730 I. 59 Thou mak'st me swear, that am a known Non-juror. **1860** TYNDALL *Glac.* II. iii. 241 All known bodies possess more or less of this molecular motion. **1881** JOWETT *Thucyd.* I. 116 Some man of known ability and high reputation.

b. ***the known***, that which is known; that which is objective in knowledge; the totality of known things.

1863 E. V. NEALE *Anal. Th. & Nat.* 142 The condition of clear thought upon metaphysical subjects, is the separation of the two elements of knowledge, the knowing and the known. **1884** F. HARRISON in *19th Cent.* Mar. 502 Knowledge is of course wholly within the sphere of the Known.

c. ***known to the police***: applied to a person with a criminal record. Also ellipt. *known* (itself occas. used as *sb.*).

1909 GALSWORTHY *Silver Box* III. 75 Is she known here? .. No, your Worship, they're neither of them known, we've nothing against them at all. **1924** A. CHRISTIE *Poirot Investigates* ix. 255 Billy Kellett?.. He's known to the police! **1938** F. D. SHARPE *Sharpe of Flying Squad* ix. 112 A long communication telling us that Mrs. Cousins was not 'known to the police'. **1971** E. MCGIRR *No Better Fiend* 69 The late Mantel had been 'known' since 1928. It was a dismal dirty story. **1973** K. GILES *File on Death* vi. 149 A lot of Irish boys in Granchester... I spotted a couple of 'knowns'.

†**2.** Possessed of knowledge; acquainted with something; learned or skilled *in*; informed or aware *of*. ***known men***, a name assumed by the Lollards. *Obs.*

c **1449** PECOCK *Repr.* 53 Thei besien hem silf forto leerne & knowe the Bible,..thei..clepen hem silf knowun men as thouȝ alle othere than hem ben unknowun. **1563** FOXE *A. & M.* (1583) 820 After the great abiuration aforesayd, which was vnder William Smith Bishop of Lincolne: they were noted and termed among themselues by the name of knowne men, or iust fast men. **1655** FULLER *Ch. Hist.* v. ii. §42 The two Lord chief Justices were in the same Treason (whose Education made them more known in the Laws of the Land).

B. *absol.* or as *sb.*

†**1.** With *poss. adj.* One's acquaintance. *Obs.*

a **1325** *Prose Ps.* lxxxvii[i]. 8 Thou madest my knowen fer fram me. **1382** WYCLIF *Luke* ii. 44 Thei..souȝten him a mong his cosyns and knowen [1388 his knouleche].

2. A well-known person. *colloq.*

1835 *Court Mag.* VI. 47/1 It is chiefly from among this latter band of Small Knowns that we shall take the liberty of drawing the Sketches.

Hence †**ˈknownly** *adv.*, in a known manner.

a **1643** LD. FALKLAND *Infallibility* (1646) 194 Lawes,..to be obeyed, unless they should be publiquely and knownely found contrary to a greater authority.

†**ˈknowness.** *Obs. rare*⁻¹. In 3 cnownesse. [? f. KNOW *sb.*¹, or stem of KNOW *v.*, + -NESS.] Acknowledgement.

c **1200** *Trin. Coll. Hom.* 25 Þu seist þat on gode bileuest, and dost cnownesse þat he is þi louerd.

know-nothing (ˈnəʊnʌθɪŋ), *sb.* and *a.* [f. KNOW *v.* + NOTHING; cf. DO-NOTHING.]

A. *sb.* **1. a.** One who knows nothing, a very ignorant person, an ignoramus. **b.** One who holds that nothing can be known; an agnostic.

1827 J. F. COOPER *Red Rover* I. ii. 42 The fellow is a know-nothing! **1839** J. ROGERS *Antipopopr.* 140 Knownothing appears a desirable word to signify one very ignorant. **1871** R. H. HUTTON *Ess.* (1877) I. 24 The know-nothings really feel towards God as if they knew something of Him. **1875** JOWETT *Plato* (ed. 2) II. 443 Socrates is represented in the character of a know-nothing.

2. A member of a political party in the United States, called also the American party, prominent during the years 1853–56; so named because, having been originally organized as a secret society, its members, to preserve this character, professed to outsiders complete ignorance regarding it.

The chief principle of the party was that none but native citizens should be permitted to share in the government. It disappeared about 1859.

1854 *Harper's Mag.* Aug. 400/1 A secret combination designated as 'Know-Nothings'..have operated with much success in local elections in many of the larger places. **1856** OLMSTEAD *Slave States* 15 Washington is, at this time, governed by the Know Nothings. **1878** *N. Amer. Rev.* CXXVI. 22 In the campaign of 1855..the Know-nothings carried the state again by a large majority. **1884** T. W. BARNES *Mem. Thurlow Weed* 224 (Cent.) If a member of the order was asked about its practices or purposes, he answered that he knew nothing about them, and 'Americans', for that reason, soon came to be called Know Nothings.

B. *attrib.* or *adj.*

1. a. That knows nothing; grossly ignorant. **b.** That holds that nothing can be known; agnostic.

a **1825** FORBY *Voc. E. Anglia* s.v., A poor know-nothing creature! **1837** MARRYAT *Dog-Fiend* xx, I'm..a know-nothing ninny. **1858** GEN. P. THOMPSON *Audi Alt.* I. xxx. 116 The know-nothing or deceptive government at home. **1860** EMERSON *Cond. Life* vi. (1861) 121 Here are know-nothing religions, or churches that proscribe intellect. **1897** *Dublin Rev.* Apr. 334 A rationalistic and know-nothing philosophy. **1959** *Encounter* XII. II. 32 He..sounds most like a know-nothing native writer. **1972** *Computers & Humanities* VII. 13 Robert Wachal has offered a humorous account of the problems encountered by the know-nothing humanist who wishes to learn about computing.

2. Of or pertaining to the American Know-nothings: see A. 2.

1854 *Southern Lit. Messenger* XX. 540/1 This Know Nothing movement will prove to be..a giant evil. **1856** OLMSTED *Slave States* 172 The *Richmond Whig*—the leading Know-nothing newspaper in the Southern States. **1875** *N. Amer. Rev.* CXX. 394 The great Know-Nothing movement. **1885** LALOR & MASON tr. *Von Holst's Const. Hist. U.S.* 116 One-half of the Know Nothing programme was unacceptable to the South.

ˈknow-ˌnothingism. [f. prec. + -ISM.]

1. The profession of knowing nothing, the practice of wilful ignorance; the doctrine of agnostics, agnosticism.

1866 *Reader* 15 Dec. 1007 He must have long felt that the ignorance which is sedulously kept up of practical physiology adequately reflects the 'knownothingism' of middle-class Englishmen. **1871** R. H. HUTTON *Ess.* I. 27 A sort of know-nothingism, or Agnosticism, or belief in an unknown and unknowable God. **1881** *Standard* 7 Feb., The age is..face to face..with Agnosticism or Know-nothingism.

2. The political doctrine of the American Know-nothings: see KNOW-NOTHING A. 2.

1854 W. G. SIMMS *Southward Ho!* 252 Know-Nothingism had not then become a fixed fact in the political atmosphere. *a* **1860** *New York Times* (Bartlett *Amer.*), The Know-Nothings have had their day... The earth hath bubbles, and Know-Nothingism was one of them. **1885** LALOR & MASON tr. *Von Holst's Const. Hist. U.S.* 112 Know-Nothingism had very ardent partisans in the southern states.

ˈknow-ˌnothingness. [f. as prec. + -NESS.] The state or quality of knowing nothing; complete ignorance.

1884 *N. & Q.* 21 June 493/1 Jo..scandalized by his distressing know-nothingness the coroner and jury at the inquest..in *Bleak House.* **1899** *Chamb. Jrnl.* II.92/1 One meets with more of this curious, half-reticent know-nothingness, real or assumed.

knowperts. *Sc.* A local name of the Crowberry, *Empetrum nigrum*.

1863 *Phytologist* New Ser. VI. 474 *Empetrum nigrum* (Crowberry), 'Knowperts'. **1886** G. MACDONALD *What's Mine's Mine*, Heather, ling, blueberries, knowperts, and cranberries.

Knoxian (ˈnɒksɪən), *sb.* and *a.* [f. the proper name *Knox* (see below) + -IAN.] **A.** *sb.* An adherent or follower of John *Knox* (*c* 1505–72), the Scottish Reformer who was mainly

responsible for establishing the Presbyterian Church. **B.** *adj.* Of or pertaining to John Knox.

1714 J. COLLIER *Eccl. Hist. Gt. Brit.* II. v. 394/2 In this Abstract, the Knoxians make a scandalous Representation of some Part of the Litany. **1905** *Westm. Gaz.* 4 Mar. 12/3 His Knoxian project was dropped in favour of his works on Cromwell. **1906** *Daily Chron.* 22 May 3/3 Buchanan, in fact, never was a Reformer in the Knoxian sense. **1933** *Times Lit. Suppl.* 30 Nov. 848/2 In Scotland—after the Knoxian supremacy was established—'not one single adherent of the Roman Communion was martyred because of his faith'. **1937** E. PERCY *John Knox* IV. xv. 253 A strong anti-clerical party.. who would have nothing to do either with Knoxians or with sectaries. **1961** C. H. & K. GEORGE *Protestant Mind of Eng. Reformation* II. v. 177 Knoxian precepts from Geneva had altered the entire course of Scottish history.

knoxvillite (ˈnɒksvɪlaɪt). *Min.* [Named from Knoxville in California, where found: see -ITE[1].] Hydrous sulphate of chromium, iron, and aluminum, of a greenish-yellow colour.

1889 G. F. BECKER in *Geol. Surv. U.S.* Monogr. XIII. 343.

knub (nʌb), *sb.* Now *dial.* or *techn.* Also 6 knubbe, 7 knubb. See also NUB. [Early mod.E. = LG. *knubbe*, MLG. *knubbe*, *knobbe*, knot, knob, protuberance, lump, etc., Da. *knub* block, log, stump: see KNOB.]

1. A small lump, a protuberance; *esp.* a small swelling on the body, a boil; = KNOB *sb.* 1, 1 b.

1570 LEVINS *Manip.* 181/31 Knubbe, *bruscum, callum.* **1575** TURBERV. *Faulconrie* 344 If a hawkes feete be but swolne and have not any Knubs in the ball of the foote. **1601** HOLLAND *Pliny* II. 434 Frogs.. with two knubs bearing out in their front like horns. *Ibid.* 196 The same juice.. healeth the clifts and swelling knubs in the fundament. **1662** R. MATHEW *Unl. Alch.* 137 A Woman far gone in a Scurvie,.. ful of spots and knubs as big as French Nuts about her body. *a* **1825** FORBY *Voc. E. Anglia*, *Knub*, a knob. **1897** F. T. BULLEN *Cruise 'Cachalot'* 178, I came butt up against something solid, the feel of which gathered all my scattered wits into a compact knub of dread.

†**2.** A stag of the second year, a knobber. *Obs.*

1617 ASSHETON *Jrnl.* (Chetham Soc.) 61 A knubb was killed and a calf.

3. The innermost wrapping of the chrysalis in a silk cocoon: usually NUB.

1812 J. SMYTH *Pract. of Customs* (1821) 214 Husks and Knubs are the refuse, which is thrown aside by the windster, during the process of winding the Silk from the cocoons. **1858** SIMMONDS *Dict. Trade* s.v., A large quantity is imported under the names of 'knubs' and 'husks' which is carded and spun up into various common silk stuffs.

†**knub**, *v. dial. Obs.* [Kindred in origin to KNAB *v.*[1]]

1. *trans.* To bite gently, nibble.

a **1652** BROME *City Wit* IV. i. Wks. 1873 I. 344 As you have beheld two Horses knubbing one another; Ka me, Ka thee.

2. To beat; to strike with the knuckle. Also NUB.

1721, **1828** [see KNUBBLE *v.*].

ˈ**knubbed**, *a. rare*[−1]. [f. KNUB *sb.* + -ED[2].] Having 'knubs', or of the nature of a 'knub'; knobbed.

1565 GOLDING *Ovid's Met.* VII. (1593) 173 If of cornell tree, It would be full of knubbed knots.

†**knubble**, *sb. dial. Obs.* [dim. of KNUB *sb.* = LG. *knubbel*, dim. of *knubbe*: see also NUBBLE.] = KNOBBLE *sb.*: in quot., a knuckle.

1671 SKINNER *Etym. Ling. Angl.*, Knubble, knub, *Nodus seu Condylus digiti.*

knubble (ˈnʌb(ə)l), *v. dial.* [dim. and freq. of KNUB *v.*: see also NUBBLE.] = KNOBBLE *v.* a: see quots.

1721 BAILEY, *To Knub, Knuble*, to beat with the Fist or Knuckles. **1783** MORELL *Ainsworth's Lat. Dict.* 1, To knubble, *Pugnis contundĕre.* *a* **1825** FORBY *Voc. E. Anglia*, *Knubble*, to handle clumsily; using thumbs and knuckles, as in kneading dough. **1828** WEBSTER, *Knub, knubble*, to beat; to strike with the knuckle. [*Not used.*]

knubbly (ˈnʌblɪ), *a. dial.* [f. KNUBBLE *sb.* + -Y.] Full of or covered with 'knubbles' or small knobs: more usually NUBBLY.

1858 MAYHEW *Upp. Rhine* i. §2 (1860) 35 A queer-looking knubbly little angel. **1860** *All Year Round* No. 42. 363 Up and down the knubbly street. **1883** *Gd. Words* Nov. 711/2 The grand old gnarled knubbly beech. **1910** W. DE LA MARE *Three Mulla-Mulgars* iv. 55 Three big knubbly cudgels. **1917** W. J. LOCKE *Red Planet* xxi. 277 He held out his hand, a dirty, knubbly, ragged-nailed hand. **1939** 'A. BRIDGE' *Four-Part Setting* vii. 79 Two loose knubbly little cushions.

knubby (ˈnʌbɪ), *a.* [f. KNUB *sb.* + -Y.] Full of 'knubs', or of the form of a 'knub'.

1882 *Standard* 14 Dec. 5/3 [Jamaica], On the other side of the.. bamboo fence rise.. 'knubby cabbages', with their bullet heads.

knublet (ˈnʌblɪt). [dim. of KNUB *sb.*: see -LET.] A small knub or lump.

1884 *Pall Mall G.* 27 Aug. 1/2 Putting knublets of ice into my coffee.

knucche, ME. form of KNITCH, bundle.

knuck (nʌk). Also occas. nuck. [Shortening of KNUCKLE *sb.*, KNUCKLER.] **1.** *slang.* A thief, a pickpocket. Cf. KNUCKLE *sb.* 2 c, KNUCKLER 1. ? *Obs.*

1812 J. H. VAUX *Vocab. Flash Lang.* in *Mem.* (1819) II. 184 *Knuck, knuckler*, or *knuckling-cove*, a pickpocket, or person professed in the knuckling art. **1848** 'N. BUNTLINE' *Mysteries & Miseries N.Y.* I. 33 There is a house in Cherry street.. [that] has been known to the 'crossmen' and 'knucks' of the town as 'Jack Circle's Watering place' and 'fence'. **1903** A. H. LEWIS *Boss* 168 But knucks, dips, sneaks, .. an' strong-arm men have got to quit. **1904** 'NO. 1500' *Life in Sing Sing* 251/1 *Nuck*, a thief. **1935** A. J. POLLOCK *Underworld Speaks* 68/2 *Knuck*, a thief.

2. *pl.* 'A game of marbles in which the winner shoots at his adversary's knuckles' (Clapin). *U.S.*

1840 *Southern Lit. Messenger* VI. 385 To the game of marbles he devotes much of his leisure time, and is counted a proficient particularly in knucks and five in the ring. *a* **1883** G. W. BAGBY *Sel. Misc. Writings* (1885) II. 20 He tries to keep somebody's country store, but will close the doors whenever the weather is fine to 'ketch chub' or play knucks. **1886** *Harper's Mag.* Dec. 41/2 They were playing 'knucks' together. **1935** *Amer. Speech* X. 159/1 More on Marble Names and Games... Knucks Down. A variant of *knuckle down.*

3. Shortening of KNUCKLE-DUSTER.

1897 *Sears, Roebuck Catal.* 593/1 Knucks, heavy nickel plated and polished. $0.30 per pair. **1918** C. SANDBURG *Cornhuskers* 88, I slipped my fingers into a set of knucks. **1966** WODEHOUSE *Plum Pie* i. 48 To reason successfully with that king of the twisters one would need brass knucks and a stocking full of sand. **1973** D. WESTHEIMER *Going Public* ix. 130 He produced a two foot length of stout nylon cord with brass knucks at either end. 'You can hit or strangle with it ..' he explained.

knuckle (ˈnʌk(ə)l), *sb.* Forms: 4 knokel, 5 -il, -yl(le, 6 -ulle, knoc(c)le, knockel, nuckul, 6–7 (9 *dial.*) knockle, 7 knucle, 8 nuckle; 6– knuckle. [ME. *knokel* = OFris. *knok(e)le*, MDu. *knökel* (Du. *kneukel*), MLG. *knokel* (LG. *knukkel*), MHG. *knuchel*, *knüchel* (G. *knöchel*); app. dim. of a word for 'bone' which appears as MLG. *knoke* (Du. *knook*, *knok*), MHG. *knoche* (G. *knochen*).]

†**1.** The end of a bone at a joint, which forms a more or less rounded protuberance when the joint is bent, as in the knee, elbow, and vertebral joints. *Obs.*

c **1375** *Rel. Ant.* I. 190 Bynethe the knokelys of the fete Wyth two weynis thow myȝt mete. *c* **1425** *Voc.* in Wr.-Wülcker 636/10 *Hic nodus*, knokylle. **1565** GOLDING *Ovid's Met.* I. (1593) 24 With wearie knockles on thy brim she kneeled sadly downe. **1594** T. B. *La Primaud. Fr. Acad.* II. 42 The backebone.. consisteth of manie bones,.. which are called the knuckles or turning ioyntes of the backebone. **1607** TOPSELL *Four-f. Beasts* (1658) 359 His [a lion's] neck very stiffe, because it consisteth but of one bone without joynts,.. There are no knuckles or turning joynts in it called *Spondyli*, and therefore he cannot look backward. **1658** A. FOX *Wurtz' Surg.* II. xxv. 152 Sometimes the Elbows-Knockle is broken.

2. *spec.* The bone at a finger-joint, which forms a rounded protuberance when the hand is shut; esp. applied to those at the roots of the fingers. (Sometimes in *sing.* for collective plural.)

c **1440** *Promp. Parv.* 280/1 Knokyl of an honde.., *condilus.* **1519** HORMAN *Vulg.* 25 b, In euery fynger be .iii. ioyntes, and as many knokulles: saue in the thome, that hath but ij. **1580** HOLLYBAND *Treas. Fr. Tong*, *Condyle*, the roundenesse or knots in the knee, ankle, elbow, and knuckles. **1658** A. FOX *Wurtz' Surg.* II. xxv. 153 A Fracture near the Knockles is worse than that in the middle. **1753** HOGARTH *Anal. Beauty* x. 65 The dimples of the nuckles. **1792** COWPER *Lett.* 11 June, Adieu! My knuckles ache with letter writing. **1867** A. DAWSON *Rambl. Recoll.* (1868) 4 He switched their shoulders and knuckles with his cane. **1884** PAE *Eustace* 96 The leader and spokesman of the party gave a low but distinct tap with his hard knuckle.

b. Hence several colloquial phrases. ***near the knuckle***: near the permitted limit (esp. in regard to decency); ***to go the knuckle*** (*Austral. slang*), to punch, to fight.

1579 J. STUBBES *Gaping Gulf* C iij b, Assuring ourselues that if they went up to the knocles in french blood, they wyll vp to the elboes in English blood. **1759** DILWORTH *Pope* 78 Some who did not absolutely deserve that appellation, he has rapped over the knuckles. **1790** WOLCOTT (P. Pindar) *Adv. Fut. Laureat* I. 79 He sighs—upon his knuckles he is down. **1809** MALKIN *Gil Blas* v. ii. ¶3 The boiling courage of knighthood, pledged up to the knuckles or the chin on the behalf of female innocence. **1812** *Sporting Mag.* XL. 161 The father-in-law had everything arranged to his own knuckle. **1866** GEO. ELIOT *F. Holt* ii, When he's had plenty of English exercise, and brought out his knuckle a bit, he'll be a Lingon again as he used to be. **1895** W. P. RIDGE *Minor Dialogues* vii. 72, I can stand a joke as well as anyone, but whispering's a bit *too* near the knuckle. If you've got anything to say, say it. **1897** MARY KINGSLEY *W. Africa* 390 A severe rap on my moral knuckles from my conscience. **1909** *Westm. Gaz.* 4 May 2/2 A series of articles entitled 'Crimes of Passion', full of abominable details 'as near the knuckle' as the police would allow. *Ibid.* 6 Sept. 1/3 If a play shows that its author has.. a sincere respect for his art, it must be stopped if it goes at all 'near the knuckle'. **1930** W. S. MAUGHAM *Cakes & Ale* 147 What I like about 'er is that she gives you a good laugh. She goes pretty near the knuckle sometimes, but she never jumps over the fence. **1944** J. DEVANNY *By Tropic Sea & Jungle* xviii. 160, I always got on well with the blacks, because I never went the knuckle on them, and never interfered with their women. **1945** L. A. G. STRONG *Othello's Occupation* iv. 89 Did you notice how she stiffened, when I slipped in that bit about remembering what she was looking at—what was on the table? I got a bit near the knuckle there. **1962** S. GORE *Down Golden Mile* i. 26 Then he said: 'Want to watch out for them quiet snoozers. Sometimes they can go the knuckle a bit themselves!' **1973** D. JORDAN *Nile Green* xiii. 58 He ho-ho'd jovially to show he was joking. It was a little close to the knuckle for my taste.

†**c.** = PICKPOCKET *sb.* 1. Cf. KNUCK 1. *Obs.*

1781 G. PARKER *View of Soc.* II. i. 73 *Knuckle*, in the flash language, signifies those who hang about the Lobbies of both Houses of Parliament, the Opera-House and both Play-Houses, and in general wherever a great crowd assemble. They steal watches, snuff-boxes, &c. **1785** GROSE *Dict. Vulgar T.*, *Knuckles*, pickpockets who attend the avenues to public places, to steal pocket books, watches, &c., a superior kind of pickpockets. **1846** *Swell's Night Guide* 124/1 *Knuckles*, pickpockets.

3. The projection of the carpal or tarsal joint of a quadruped; hence, a 'joint' of meat, *esp.* veal or ham, consisting of the knuckle joint with the parts immediately above and below it. In a leg of mutton, the rounded muscular part adjacent to the knuckle joint of the animal.

1625 MASSINGER *New Way* II. ii, 'Tis the quintessence Of five cocks of the game,.. Knuckles of veal, potato-roots, and marrow. **1626** BACON *Sylva* §45 Jelly.. which they use for a restorative, is chiefly made of knuckles of veal. **1726** GAY in *Swift's Lett.* (1766) II. 65 Take a knuckle of veal.. In a few pieces cut it: In a stewing-pan put it. **1771** SMOLLETT *Humph. Cl.* 5 June, One wit, like a knuckle of ham in soup, gives a zest and flavour to the dish. **1840** DICKENS *Old C. Shop* xxvi, The tea-things, including.. a cold knuckle of ham.

4. Something shaped or protruding like a knuckle of a bone. *spec.* †**a.** A thickened joint of a plant, a node. **b.** *Anat.* A projecting bend of the intestine. **c.** *Mech.* The projecting tubular part of a hinge through which the pintle runs. **d.** *Ship-building.* An acute angle in certain timbers.

1601 HOLLAND *Pliny* II. 255 The swellings or blind piles appearing like bigs or knuckles within the fundement, are cured with five-leafe grasse. **1611** COTGR., *Les nerfs*, the knuckles that sticke out on the backe of a booke. **1626** BACON *Sylva* §589 Divers Herbs.. have Joynts or Knuckles.. As have.. Pinks,.. Corn,.. and Canes. **1825** J. NICHOLSON *Operat. Mechanic* 591 The knuckle of the hinge is a portion contained under a cylindrical surface, and is common both to the moving part and the part which is at rest. **1835–6** TODD *Cycl. Anat.* I. 503 *note*, A knuckle of the intestine. *c* **1850** *Rudim. Navig.* (Weale) 128 *Knuckle*, a sudden angle made on some timbers by a quick reverse of shape, such as the knuckle of the counter timbers, &c. **1894** CROCKETT *Raiders* 230, I.. sat on a solid knuckle of rock that shot up from the ribs of the mountain. **1897** *Clin. Soc. Trans.* IX. 108 A knuckle of bowel having been exposed by incision.

5. = KNUCKLE-DUSTER (see quot. 1861 s.v.).

6. *attrib.* and *Comb.*, as ***knuckle-hinge***, ***-length***, ***-rap***, ***-summons***, ***-work***; ***knuckle-rapper***, ***-rapping*** vbl. sb. and ppl. adj.; **knuckle ball**, **knuckleball** *Baseball* (see quots.); **knuckle-bow**, **-guard**, a guard on a sword-hilt to cover the knuckles; **knuckle-end**, the lower or small end of a leg of mutton or pork; **knuckle-head**, a slow-witted or stupid person; **knuckle-kneed** *a.*, having prominent or bulging knees; **knuckle sandwich** *slang*, a punch in the mouth; **knuckle-thread**, a rounded thread in a screw; **knuckle timber**, a timber having or forming a knuckle (see 4 c.).

1927 *Secrets of Baseball* iii. 37 If you're worrying about when to use a '*knuckle ball'. **1929** *Encycl. Brit.* III. 163/1 There is what is known as the knuckle ball, in which the knuckles of the pitcher's hand play a prominent part in giving the ball erratic motion. **1970** *New Yorker* 24 Oct. 39/2 The knuckleball is thrown not with the knuckles but with the fingertips. **1972** *N.Y. Times* 4 June v. 2/5 Phil Niekro baffled the Mets with his celebrated knuckleball, allowing them only three hits. **1975** *Cleveland* (Ohio) *Plain Dealer* 6 Apr. 13-C/3 Oakland, aiming for a fourth straight world championship, opens at home with Vida Blue pitching against Chicago's veteran knuckleball specialist, Wilbur Wood. **1895** *Proc. Soc. Antiq.* 7 Feb. 297 There is a *knucklebow with an extra guard attached by a ring. *a* **1845** SYD. SMITH in *Mem.*, Scotland, that garret of the earth—that *knuckle-end of England. **1883** 'ANNIE THOMAS' *Mod. Housewife* 48 A good leg of Welsh mutton.. its knuckle-end makes a pretty little extra dish braised and stewed brown with celery and haricot beans. **1944** in WENTWORTH & FLEXNER *Dict. Amer. Slang* (1960) 310/2 You *knuckle-heads. **1948** *Amer. Speech* XXIII. 249/1 Knucklehead, a slow or stupid person. **1971** R. PARKES *Line of Fire* xvii. 158 What I'm trying to get across to you knuckleheads is that it was *not* murder! **1973** J. CLEARY *Ransom* i. 25 He's a knuckle-head, he knows nothing and doesn't want to know. **1866** G. MACDONALD *Ann. Q. Neighb.* v. (1878) 54 They [the horses] were so fat and *knuckle-kneed. **1906** *Daily Chron.* 29 Mar. 6/4 A man.. proceeded to measure it with the *knuckle-length of his closed fist. **1938** *Times* 9 Mar. 19/4 The knuckle-length coat is in stripes of various sizes. **1837** WHEELWRIGHT tr. *Aristophanes* II. 176 With *knuckle-raps, we will put out the lamps. **1910** H. G. WELLS *Hist. Mr. Polly* iv. 56 The aunt.. was.. a *knuckle-rapper and sharp silencer: no friend for a slovenly little boy. **1944** R. LEHMANN *Ballad & Source* 243 'No,' he said shortly, but not in the *knuckle-rapping way I had half feared. **1968** *Globe & Mail Mag.* (Toronto) 13 Jan. 3/1 Anti-Dow demonstrations at U of T drew just polite knuckle-rapping. **1968** *Listener* 18 July 75/1 Did you ever suggest to him.. how a field commander might feel when he got one of these knuckle-rappings? **1974** *Farm & Country* 26 Mar. 4/2 Your knuckle-rapping will teach him to think before he is carried away on a flow of words. **1973** A. BUZO *Norm & Ahmed* 12 He tried to hang one on me at Leichhardt Oval once, so I administered a *knuckle sandwich to him. **1973** *Ottawa*

Jrnl. 17 July 23/3 Give the guy a knuckle sandwich and let the teeth fall where they may. **1864** BROWNING *Sludge the Medium* 720 Suppose I blunder in my guess at the true sense O' the *knuckle-summons, nine times out of ten. **1887** D. A. Low *Machine Draw.* (1892) 15 The angles of the square thread are frequently rounded... If this rounding is carried to excess we get the *Knuckle thread shown at (*d*). **1711** W. SUTHERLAND *Shipbuild. Assist.* 54 The Planks under the *Nuckle Timbers forward. *c* **1850** *Rudim. Navig.* (Weale) 128 *Knuckle-timbers*, those top-timbers in the fore body whose heads stand perpendicular, and form an angle with the hollow of the topside. **1885** T. MOZLEY *Remin. Towns*, etc. I. 298 All the communications between the postal officials and the public were done through an aperture fifteen inches by twelve,..to be opened after some *knuckle-work.

knuckle (ˈnʌk(ə)l), *v.* [f. prec. sb.]

1. *intr.* To place one's knuckles upon the ground in shooting or casting the taw in playing at marbles; see sense 4. Usually ***knuckle down***.

1740 DYCHE & PARDON, *Knuckle* or *Knuckle down* (v.)..is a particular phrase used by lads at a play called taw, wherein they frequently say, *Knuckle down to your taw*, or fit your hand exactly in the place where your marble lies. **1784** COWPER *Tiroc.* 307 As happy as we once, to kneel and draw The chalky ring, and knuckle down at taw. **1842** TENNYSON *Will Waterpr. Monol.* xvii, A something-pottle-bodied boy, That knuckled at the taw.

2. a. *intr.* (*fig.*) To acknowledge oneself beaten; to give way, give in, submit. Usually ***knuckle down*** or ***knuckle under***.

1740 DYCHE & PARDON, *Knuckle* or *Knuckle down*, to stoop, bend, yield, comply with, or submit to. **1791** WOLCOTT (P. Pindar) *Remonstrance* 73, I knuckle not—I owe not to the great A thimble-full of obligation. **1871** CARLYLE in *Mrs. C's Lett.* II. 237 He had to knuckle and comply in all points. **1882** MISS BRADDON *Mt. Royal* II. iv. 63 They must all knuckle under to him. **1888** *Times* (weekly ed.) 2 Nov. 12/3 He would not knuckle down under the attacks of the Land League. **1955** *Times* 19 May 15/4 He replied that there was no power on earth to make a local party accept a candidate. He was rather sorry they knuckled under to Transport House in this division. **1964** *Ann. Reg. 1963* 10 Britain, he said, had 'knuckled under' to threats of African violence, but there was little he could constitutionally do about it. **1973** *Nation Rev.* (Melbourne) III. 31 Aug. 1444/1 Now the last group of any size..has knuckled under following a series of splits and coups.

b. ***to knuckle down to***, to apply oneself earnestly or vigorously (Webster 1864).

3. a. *trans.* To tap, strike, press, or rub with the knuckles.

a **1793** J. PEARSON *Polit. Dict.* 49 Little Shiells, who is a mercenary dog, knuckles them [reporters] just as he pleases. *c* **1825** BEDDOES *Poems, Life a Glass Window*, Uncourteous Death Knuckles the pane. **1842** H. SMITH *Addr. Mummy* vi, I need not ask thee if that hand, when arm'd, Has any Roman soldier maul'd and knuckled. **1890** CLARK RUSSELL *Ocean Trag.* I. xii. 251 The seaman knuckled his forehead and wheeled round.

b. To dig (one's hand) into a specified position, knuckles first.

1890 HALL CAINE *Bondman* I. i. 10 Thrusting his head beneath his chin, he knuckled his left hand under the islander's rib.

4. *trans.* To propel or shoot (a marble, etc.) from between the knuckle of the thumb and the bent forefinger.

1803 W. TAYLOR in *Ann. Rev.* I. 354 Flying kites, knuckling marbles, chuck-halfpenny, etc. **1897** CROCKETT *Lads' Love* x. 90 'Go on', she said, knuckling little stones at a puddock.

5. *intr.* To protrude or project like a knuckle.

c **1862** in *Circ. Sc.* I. 272/2 There is no danger of the conductor knuckling through the gutta-percha.

6. *Farriery.* With *over*, of the knee or fetlock: ? to project through weakness of the ligaments. Also with *forwards*. (Cf. *knuckle-kneed* adj. s.v. KNUCKLE *sb.* 6.)

1877 A. SEWELL *Black Beauty* (*c* 1878, ed. 5) xl. 198 The knees knuckled over, and the forelegs were very unsteady. **1877** M. H. HAYES *Vet. Notes for Horse Owners* i. 30 'Knuckling over', as a result of hard work, appears to be due to relaxation of the capsular and lateral ligaments [of the fetlock joint]. **1906** J. W. AXE *Horse* IV. 53 The animal knuckles over at the joints. **1907** *Ibid.* V. 298 The movements of the hind-limbs are for a time weak, and the fetlocks knuckle over now and again during progression. **1907** *Ibid.* VI. 347 In young horses it is common to meet with a knuckling forwards of the hind fetlocks.

7. *Golf.* To bend (the knee) inward. Also *absol.*

1909 *Times* 23 Apr. 16/2 An elaborate knuckling of the right knee in putting. *Ibid.*, The 'knuckling' habit in putting has long been exposed as fallacious. **1909** *Westm. Gaz.* 11 May 12/3 You may 'knuckle' if knuckling conduces to comfort, provided that..you get the process over before beginning the actual stroke.

Hence **knuckle-down** as *sb.*: (*a*) a game at marbles (see prec. 1 and 4); (*b*) submission; as *adv.* = submissively.

1859 RUSKIN *Two Paths* iv. (1891) 178 How that vagabond child at the street corner is managing his game of knuckle-down. **1878** E. JENKINS *Haverholme* 215 Our people are bent on nothing but a complete knuckle-down. **1880** BLACKMORE *Mary Anerley* III. 184 Long sighs only lead to turn-up noses. He plays too knuckle-down at it.

ˈknuckle-ˌbone.

1. Any bone forming a knuckle; the rounded end, at the joint, of any of the bones of the fingers; also, †the projecting bone of the knee or elbow (*obs.*). ***down on the knuckle-bone***, hard-up (*slang*).

1577 DEE *Diary* (Camden) 3 My fall uppon my right nuckul bone. **1690** DRYDEN *Amphitryon* II. i, Bless me, what an arm and a fist he has..; and knuckle-bones of a very butcher. **1883** *Daily Tel.* 4 Aug. 2/1 Some one who was 'down on the knuckle-bone' in consequence of having been 'put away' since the previous October.

2. In an animal: **a.** A limb-bone with a ball-like knob at the joint-end, or the rounded end of such a bone; also, a joint of meat consisting of this part of an animal's leg; = KNUCKLE *sb.* 3.

c **1440** *Promp. Parv.* 280/2 Knokylle bone of a legge, *coxa.* **1530** PALSGR. 236/2 Knoccle bone, *joincte de la hanche.* **1677** *Lond. Gaz.* No. 1226/4 A black brown Gelding..[having] a white spot upon one of his knuckle bones. **1857** HUGHES *Tom Brown* II. iii, He..hauled out an old knuckle-bone of ham, and two or three bottles of beer.

b. One of the metacarpal or metatarsal bones of a sheep or the like; hence, (usually *pl.*) a game played with these, by tossing them up and catching them in various ways; also called *huckle-bones* or *dibs*.

1759 tr. *Adanson's Voy. Senegal* 52 The girls had for ornament round their waist a girdle of glass toys, or,..of a *requien's* knuckle-bones, or of cockle-shells. **1880** C. R. MARKHAM *Peruv. Bark* xii. 106 Courtyards very neatly paved with round pebbles and llama's knuckle-bones in patterns. **1884** J. SHARMAN *Hist. Swearing* iv. 63 School-boys still play at the game of knuckle-bones. **1885** *New Bk. Sports* 316 Knucklebones..is pre-eminently a game for man-by-himself-man.

knuckled (ˈnʌk(ə)ld), *a.* [f. KNUCKLE *sb.* + -ED[2].]

†**1.** Having projections or protuberances, knobbed, rugged; thick-jointed, as the stem of a plant. *Obs.* in gen. sense.

13.. *Gaw. & Gr. Knt.* 2166 Hyȝe bonkkez & brent,..& ruȝe knokled knarrez, with knorned stonez. **1626** BACON *Sylva* §656 The Reed or Cane is a Watry Plant,..Knuckled, both Stalke, and Root.

2. Having (prominent) knuckles; protuberant like a knuckle. Also with defining word, Having knuckles of a specified kind.

1842 *Tait's Mag.* IX. 289 His forehead high, broad, bony, knuckled, and shiny. **1852** R. S. SURTEES *Sponge's Sp. Tour* lxvi. 365 His red knuckled hands thrust a long way through his tight coat. **1854** *Fraser's Mag.* XLVIII. 158 His knees slighty knuckled over through the wear and tear of time and excessive exercise. **1897** *Outing* (U.S.) XXX. 125/1 The feet should be round,..toes well-knuckled, close and compact.

ˈknuckle-ˌdeep, *adv.* Up to the knuckles; with the whole hand in; hence *fig.*, deeply, 'up to the hilt'.

1589 *Pappe w. Hatchet* (1844) 41 Haue with thee knuckle deepe, it shall neuer bee said that I dare not venter mine eares where Martin hazards his necke. **1629** MASSINGER *Picture* III. i, Methinks I am already Knuckle-deep in the flesh-pots. **1765** COWPER *Lett.* Wks. 1837 XV. 4, I dare say you were knuckle-deep in contrabands. **1829** SCOTT *Anne of G.* xiii, Shall we..be knuckle-deep in the English budgets.

ˈknuckle-dust, *v.* [Back-formation from KNUCKLE-DUSTER.] *trans.* To strike with a knuckle-duster. So **ˈknuckle-dusting** *vbl. sb.*

1909 *Daily Chron.* 29 Dec. 1/7 One boy..got the robber's head under his arm and gave it a knuckle-dusting. **1962** V. NABOKOV *Pale Fire* 151 The brief affray during which two of the attackers were knuckledusted and knocked out by the brave Lorrainer.

ˈknuckle-ˈduster. [f. KNUCKLE *sb.* + DUSTER. (orig. criminals' slang, U.S.)]

A metal instrument made to cover the knuckles, so as to protect them from injury in striking, and at the same time to add force to a blow given with the fist thus covered.

1858 *Times* 15 Feb. (Farmer), Knuckle-duster..a formidable American instrument, made of brass, which slips easily on to the four fingers of the hand, and having a projecting surface, across the knuckles, is calculated..to inflict serious injury on the person against whom it is directed. **1861** *All Year Round* 13 July 372 But what the crew most feared, was the free use of the 'brass knuckles' or 'knuckle-dusters'... These are brass finger-guards, not unlike what the Roman gladiators called the cestus; they constitute a regular portion of the equipment of an officer of the American mercantile marine. **1862** *Illustr. Lond. News* 11 Jan. 51/2 The American 'shoulder-hitters', 'knuckle-dusters', and 'gum-ticklers'. **1862** *Ann. Reg.* 193 One of them struck him a fearful blow with a 'knuckle-duster'. **1873** *Slang Dict.* s.v., Sometimes a knuckle-duster has knobs or points projecting, so as to mutilate and disfigure the person struck.

attrib. **1870** *Standard* 15 Dec., I have been in many mobs, and have been charged both by cavalry and the knuckleduster brigade in Paris.

ˈknuckle-ˌjoint.

1. *lit.* Each joint of the knuckles (of the hands), or the joint of the leg of an animal called a knuckle.

2. *Mech.* A joint or coupling forming a connexion between two parts of a mechanism, in which a projection in one is inserted into a corresponding recess in the other (like the knuckles of the two hands when clasped or placed together); also extended to other joints, such as universal joints.

1863-9 *Dict. Archit.*, *Knuckle Joint*, an old name for a Rule Joint. **1873** *Spon's Dict. Engineering* 2663 The knuckle-joint, at the back of the vibrating form-frame. **1881** YOUNG *Every Man his own Mechanic* §819 Some of these racks are fitted in the centre with a grooved joint technically called a 'knuckle joint'. **1887** D. A. LOW *Machine Draw.* (1892) 100 Form of ordinary knuckle joint.

Hence **knuckle-ˈjoint** *v.*

1900 *Westm. Gaz.* 27 Dec. 5/3 The plates will be placed on in dovetail fashion,..the Herreshoffs having decided that the plan of *knuckle-jointing them was not feasible.

ˈknuckler. [agent-n. f. KNUCKLE *v.*]

1. *Thieves' slang.* A pick-pocket.

1834 H. AINSWORTH *Rookwood* III. v, No knuckler so deftly could fake a cly.

2. A schoolboy's marble used in knuckling.

1896 CROCKETT *Cleg Kelly* ii. 7 One noble knuckler of alabaster.

3. *Baseball.* A knuckle ball (see KNUCKLE *sb.* 6).

1928 G. H. RUTH *Babe Ruth's Own Bk. Baseball* vi. 79 Eddie used to toss 'knucklers' until he had the hitters blue in the face. **1972** *N.Y. Times* 4 June v. 2/5 The Mets, meanwhile, were subdued by Niekro's knuckler.

knucklesome (ˈnʌk(ə)lsəm), *a. rare.* [See -SOME[1].] Having prominent knuckles. Also *transf.*

1919 W. DE MORGAN *Old Madhouse* xx. 306 That young woman was bony and knucklesome. **1922** C. E. MONTAGUE *Disenchantment* xii. 170 The twisty valley and knucklesome banks of the Somme.

ˈknuckle-walker. [f. KNUCKLE *sb.* + WALKER *sb.*[1]] Any primate, such as the gorilla or chimpanzee, which has a quadrupedal gait involving the backs of the knuckles (rather than the tips of the fingers or flat of the palm) making contact with the ground. So **ˈknuckle-walk** *v.*, **ˈknuckle-walking** *vbl. sb.*

1859 R. OWEN *On Classification & Geographical Distribution of Mammalia* 75 Of the broad-breasted quadrumana, are the knuckle-walkers or the brachiators, i.e. the long-armed gibbons, most nearly and essentially related to the human subject? **1874** WOOD *Nat. Hist.* I. 25 When these creatures [the gorilla, chimpansee, and orang-outan] aid their steps by placing the hands on the ground, they have the curious habit of resting the knuckles on the ground.. From this peculiarity, the three apes have received the appropriate title of knuckle-walkers. **1967** R. H. TUTTLE in *Amer. Jrnl. Physical Anthropol.* XXVI. 171 (*title*) Knuckle-walking and the evolution of Hominoid hands. *Ibid.*, Most orang-utans assume one of a variety of flexed hand postures, but they cannot knuckle-walk. *Ibid.* 171/2 The knuckle-walking posture of chimpanzees and gorillas is unique among primates. **1967** S. L. WASHBURN in *Proc. R. Anthrop. Inst.* 23/1 Both chimpanzees and gorillas are knuckle walkers. *Ibid.*, It appears that our ancestors were arboreal apes for many millions of years, that they then shared a common knuckle-walking stage with the ancestors of the chimpanzee and gorilla, and that only later they became bipeds. **1969** A. H. SCHULTZ *Life of Primates* v. 56 In the orang-utan the mode of using the hands in walking..is more in the form of a clenched fist, rather awkwardly twisted sideways, and rarely like real knuckle-walking. **1972** O. J. LEWIS in R. H. Tuttle *Functional & Evolutionary Biol. Primates* ix. 212 Thick palmar radiocarpal ligaments are not the exclusive property of knuckle-walkers... It thus seems that knuckle-walking requires no especially striking modifications of the wrist joint. **1973** *Nature* 10 Aug. 373/2 The first component separates quadrupedal cercopithecoids from both knuckle-walkers (*Pan* and *Gorilla*) and the quadrupedal arm-swinger..*Ateles.*

ˈknuckly, *a.* [f. KNUCKLE *sb.* + -Y.] Having large or prominent knuckles.

1870 *Daily News* 3 June 5 Such hands!.. The sturdy, the knuckly, the wrinkled, and the scarred—all handing in their written bits of paper. **1886** STEVENSON *Dr. Jekyll* x. 121 The hand which I now saw,..was lean, corded, knuckly.

†**knuckyl'bonyard.** *Obs.* [app. f. KNUCKLEBONE (or f. **knuckle-bony*) + -ARD.] A clumsy fellow.

1526 SKELTON *Magnyf.* 485 A knokylbonyarde wyll counterfet a clarke, He wolde trotte gentylly, but he is to stark. **1546** J. HEYWOOD *Prov.* (1867) 33 He is a knuckylbonyard veraie meete, To match a minion nother fayre nor sweete.

Knudsen (ˈknʊdsən). The name of Martin H. C. *Knudsen* (1871–1949), Danish physicist, used *attrib.* (or occas. in the possessive) to designate apparatus, phenomena, and concepts connected with his work.

a. *Physics.* **Knudsen cell**, a vessel in which a substance is heated in equilibrium with its vapour, which is allowed to diffuse out of a small orifice; **Knudsen effect, flow**, the effusion from an orifice (also called ***Knudsen effusion***) or the flow through a tube of a gas with a high Knudsen number, so that the resistance to flow arises principally from collisions of the molecules with the walls rather than with one another; **Knudsen gas**, any gas in a state characterized by a Knudsen number much greater than one; **Knudsen gauge** or **manometer**, an instrument for measuring the absolute pressure of a rarefied gas by means of the transfer of momentum by the gas molecules between two fixed plates at different temperatures and a suspended vane, which undergoes a rotation dependent on the pressure; **Knudsen number**, the ratio of the mean free path of the molecules of a gas to a length derived

from the dimensions of the apparatus in which or past which it is flowing.

1954 *Jrnl. Chem. Physics* XXII. 1414/2 The vapor pressure was determined by collecting a known fraction of the vapor effusing from a Knudsen cell. **1960** *Ibid.* XXXIII. 530/1 The equilibrium vapor from a Knudsen cell was collimated into a molecular beam and allowed to pass through the ionizing region of a mass spectrometer. **1953** *Physical Rev.* LXXXIX. 796/1 The Knudsen effect occurs when two portions of a gas are separated by a very fine capillary or a porous plate with openings so small that collisions between the gas molecules in the capillary or the pores are infrequent compared with the collisions of the gas molecules with the walls. **1954** *Jrnl. Chem. Physics* XXII. 1414/1 The vapor pressure has been redetermined over a temperature range from 1630 to 1970°K. As in the previous measurements the Knudsen effusion method was used. **1937** *Bull. Chem. Soc. Japan* XII. 199 If the mean free path is large in comparison with the diameter the flowing quantity is independent of the viscosity but inversely proportional to the square root of the molecular weight of the gas, and such flow is called Knudsen's or the molecular flow. **1958** R. D. PRESENT *Kinetic Theory of Gases* iv. 61 Effusion through a circular orifice can be considered as a special case of Knudsen flow in which the length of tube is small compared to its diameter. **1958** *Encycl. Physics* XII. 212 Another example which is more intuitive is afforded by a Knudsen gas. This is a gas which is sufficiently rarefied so that intermolecular forces can be completely ignored. **1972** *Chem. Abstr.* LXXVI. 87851 A collision-free Knudsen gas was considered between 2 parallel plates with a time-dependent temp. gradient. **1918** *Physical Rev.* XII. 452 Delicate equilibria at low pressures in this way make it possible to measure exceedingly small quantities of emission products even with the use of a less sensitive form of Knudsen gauge. **1925** F. H. NEWMAN *Production & Measurement Low Pressure* viii. 155 These investigators have also constructed Knudsen gauges capable of measuring pressures as high as 10^{-2} mm. **1959** *Chambers's Encycl.* XI. 188/1 Knudsen gauges can be constructed to cover ranges from 10^{-3} to 10^{-7} mm Hg. **1961** J. THEWLIS et al. *Encycl. Dict. Physics* IV. 185/2 The functions of the Knudsen manometer essentially depend on the variation of the thermal conductivity of a gas with pressure, provided the pressure is low enough, i.e. the mean free path is sufficiently great. **1956** G. N. PATTERSON *Molecular Flow of Gases* v. 159 In both high-vacuum systems and high-altitude flight, the Knudsen number becomes large. **1957** LIEPMANN & ROSHKO *Elem. Gas Dynamics* xiv. 353 For flow similar to Couette flow, i.e., flow that is confined between walls, one can easily define these two limiting cases by the ratio of mean free path Λ to channel diameter d. Λ/d is often called the Knudsen number; if $\Lambda/d \ll 1$, intermolecular collisions dominate; if $\Lambda/d \gg 1$, collisions with the boundaries dominate.

b. *Oceanogr.* **Knudsen burette**, **pipette**, special types of burette and pipette for use in Knudsen titrations; **Knudsen method**, **titration**, a method for determining the chlorinity and hence salinity of sea-water by titration against silver nitrate solution and reference to a set of tables, ***Knudsen's tables***, first published by Knudsen in 1901.

1959 H. BARNES *Apparatus & Methods Oceanogr.* I. iv. 86 *The Knudsen burette.* The silver nitrate solution contained in a reservoir is delivered from a special burette, with an automatic zero. **1966** B. B. BAKER et al. *Gloss. Oceanogr. Terms* (ed. 2) 32/1 By using normal water as a comparison standard, Knudsen burettes and pipettes for the analysis, and Knudsen's Tables to compute the results, determinations as accurate as those of a time-consuming gravimetric analysis can be made with a rapid titration of the sea water against silver nitrate solution, employing potassium chromate or other suitable indicator for the end-point. **1954** *Jrnl. Marine Res.* XIII. 246 The keystone of the Knudsen method is the adjustment of the silver nitrate concentration so that at the end of the titration the number representing the burette reading is approximately equal to the chlorinity in per mille. [**1923** GLAZEBROOK *Dict. Appl. Physics* III. 677/2 The pipette..generally used is of the Knudsen pattern, with a three-way tap instead of a mark.] **1951** *Jrnl. du Conseil Internat. Explor. de la Mer* XVII. 223 By means of a Knudsen pipette 15 ml. were taken out of a number of sea-water samples. **1966** Knudsen pipette [see *Knudsen burette* above]. **1923** GLAZEBROOK *Dict. Appl. Physics* III. 677/2 The salinity and density can, of course, be determined from the 'chlorine' content by Knudsen's Tables. **1966** Knudsen's Tables [see *Knudsen burette* above]. **1962** *Nature* 10 Feb. 520/1 The precision of measuring conductivity on a good salinometer is at least five times better than that of the standard Knudsen titration.

knuffe, variant of GNOFF *Obs.*, churl.

knulling, variant of NULLING: cf. KNURLING.

1842-76 GWILT *Archit.* (ed. 7) Gloss., *Knulling*, a moulding nearly flat, and similar in character to a bead and reel ornament. It is chiefly used in cabinet work.

knur, knurr (nɜː(r)). Also 5- knor, 5-6 knorre, 6 knour, 6-7 knurre, 7-9 (*dial.*) knorr, 9 nurr. [ME. *knorre*, *knurre*, corresp. to MDu., MLG., MHG. *knorre* (Du. *knor*, G. *knorre(n)*, Sw. dial. *knurr*, *knurra* hard swelling, knot, knob; ulterior etym. uncertain. The ME. word may be older than the quotations show: cf. the related KNURNED.]

†**1.** A hard excrescence, swelling, or concretion in the flesh. *Obs.* Cf. KNOB *sb.* 1 b.

c **1400** *Beryn* 2513 Strecching forth his fyngirs,..Withouten knot or knor or eny signe of goute. **1547** BOORDE *Brev. Health* (1575) cix, Knottes, knobbes, knorres, or burres, the which is in man's flesh or fatnesse. **1621** MOLLE *Camerar. Liv. Libr.* I. v. 11 Hard knurs or knobs in his hands with working in the fields.

2. A knot or hardened excrescence on the trunk of a tree, a KNAR; a hard concretion or kernel in stone; any swollen formation, a bur.

1545 ELYOT *Dict.*, *Bruscum*, a bunche or knur in a tree. **1548** COOPER, *Centrum*,..an hard knotte or knurre in tymbre [1565-73 *adds* or stone]. **1563-87** FOXE *A. & M.* (1596) 1429/2 The euil tree of our harte,..with al the crooks, knots and knoures. **1601** HOLLAND *Pliny* I. 467 The bunch or knurre in the Maple, called Bruscum, is passing faire. **1664** EVELYN *Sylva* (1679) 28 Oaks bear also a knur, full of cottony matter. **1725** BRADLEY *Fam. Dict.* s.v. *Seminary*, If you raise your Trees of such sorts as bear a Knur or Burry Swelling, set that part into the Ground. **1853** G. JOHNSTON *Nat. Hist. E. Bord.* I. 143 The knots or knurs on the stem are in repute for making snuff boxes. **1861** C. A. JOHNS *Forest Trees Gt. Brit.* 150 We may often see, on the bole of a beech, scattered excrescences called knurs, varying in size from a pea to a large marble.

3. A wooden ball or a hard knot of wood used in the north country game of ***knur and spell*** or ***spell and knur***, resembling 'bat and trap', or trap-ball. Also, A similar ball used in other games, as hockey.

1852 *Househ. Words* 23 Oct. 139 The mysterious game of Nurr and spell. **1855** ROBINSON *Whitby Gloss.*, *Knor* or *Gnar*, a small ball of *lignum vitæ* for playing at cricket with, or a similar game which is called 'Spell and Knor'. **1868** *Morning Star* 10 Feb., A well-known Yorkshire game known as 'knurr and spell', in which an ordinary stick some two feet in length has a solid piece of wood 3 in. long and 2 in. in depth screwed on for the purpose of striking a marble. **1872** PRIOR *Croquet* 15 Bandy is the same game as hockey, and is played..with a wooden ball that..is cut from a blackthorn bush and called a 'knurr'. **1877** *N.W. Linc. Gloss.*, *Knur*, a hard wooden ball with which children play. *Ibid.*, *Nur*, a small ball, such as that used in the game of hockey. **1967** *Antique Finder* Aug. 11/3 Knur and Spell. This Georgian tavern game must really be a forerunner of darts. **1972** *Daily Tel.* (Colour Suppl.) 14 Jan. 22/3 In fact Knur and Spell is simply a formalisation of something that every male person in the world must have done at some time throwing a ball or stone in the air and giving it a tremendous clout with a stick. How maddening when you miss! What a marvellous eye you feel you have when you do it fair and square! The Spell is the device that throws the ball (the Knur) into the air. It is an iron contraption that lies on the ground looking a bit like a rat trap; the framework holds a flat horizontal spring, held down by a catch. On the releasable end of the spring is a little cup containing the knur, a tiny white ball (porcelain, of all things), one inch across and weighing half an ounce. You stand about four feet away from the spell, armed with a 'stick', rather like a billiard cue with a hammer head (called the 'pommel'). You tap the catch on the spell, the knur jumps up about four feet; the object is to hit it farther, over a fixed number of goes, than anyone else.

4. *north. dial.* = KNURL 2. (See quots.)

1691 RAY *N.C. Words* 135 *A Knor* or *Knurre*, a short stubbed dwarfish Man. **1869** *Lonsdale Gloss.*, *Knorr*, a dwarfish fellow, a hard fellow.

knurl, nurl (nɜːl), *sb.* Also 7-9 knurle. [app. a derivative (? dim.) of KNUR; but cf. also KNARL, GNARL *sb.*]

1. A small projection, protuberance, or excrescence; a knot, knob, boss, nodule, etc.; a small bead or ridge, esp. one of a series worked upon a metal surface for ornamentation or other purpose.

1608 *2nd Pt. Def. Ministers' Refus. Subscript.* 131 [It] grew up naturally from the roote,..without knot or knurle, right and streight. **1611** COTGR., *Goderonner*,..to worke, or set with knurles. *Ibid.*, *Neud*, a knot..a knurre, or knurle in trees. **1651** J. F[REAKE] *Agrippa's Occ. Philos.* 272 From the crown of the head to the knurles of the gullet is the thirteenth part of the whole altitude. **1658** R. WHITE tr. *Digby's Powd. Symp.* (1660) 117 A knurle either of waxe, gumme, or glue. **1773** *Phil. Trans.* LXIII. 374 Those small fine blue knobs, that are to be seen round the rim or upper knurl of the coat [of a sea-anemone]. **1806** J. GRAHAME *Birds Scot.* 48 The nest deep-hollowed, well-disguised as if it were a knurll in the bough.

2. A thick-set, stumpy person; a deformed dwarf. *dial.*

1674-91 RAY *S. & E.C. Words*, *Knurl*, a little dwarfish person. **1793** BURNS *Meg o' the Mill* ii, The laird was a widdiefu', bleerit knurl. **1811** WILLAN *W. Riding Gloss.*, *Knurl*, a hunch-backed dwarf.

3. A knurling-tool.

1879 *Sci. Amer.* XL. 224 Knurls of various patterns..are employed in 'beading', 'milling', or knurling the heads of screws, the handles of small tools, &c. *Ibid.*, Examples of knurling done with the different knurls.

knurl, nurl, *v.* [f. prec. sb. The vbl. sb. *knurling* is recorded long before the simple vb.] *trans.* To make knurls, beadings, or ridges (on the edge of a coin, a screw-head, etc.); to mill, to crenate.

1875 KNIGHT *Dict. Mech.* 1536/2 A sunken groove, indented so as to form the counter-part of the bead which is to be nurled on the head of the temper-screw. **1879** [see KNURL *sb.* 3].

knurled, nurled (nɜːld), *a.* [f. as prec. + -ED².] Having knurls wrought on the edge or surface; crenated, milled.

1611 COTGR., *Goderonné*,..knurled, wrought or set with knurles. **1696** *Lond. Gaz.* No. 3224/4 Lost,..a large Knurl'd Cup and Cover of French work. **1705** *Ibid.* No. 4162/4 Two small Silver Salts nurl'd. **1884** F. J. BRITTEN *Watch & Clockm.* 118 There is a knurled lock-nut to ensure the hand being held fast.

knurling, nurling ('nɜːlɪŋ), *vbl. sb.* [See KNURL *v.*] The action of the verb KNURL; also *concr.* knurled work.

1611 COTGR., *Goderon*,..a fashion of imbossement vsed by Goldsmithes, &c., and tearmed knurling. **1862** MAYHEW *Lond. Labour* IV. 377 Then you file the edges of the coin to perfect the 'knerling'. **1875** KNIGHT *Dict. Mech.* 1536/2 *Nurling*, the indentations or fluting on the edges of coins, the heads of temper and set screws, and similar objects.

attrib. **1875** KNIGHT *Dict. Mech.* 1536/2 *Nurling-tool*, a milling-tool. One for indenting the heads of temper and tangent screws, etc. **1879** *Sci. Amer.* XL. 223 Knurling tool.

'knurling, -lin, *sb. Sc.* [f. KNUR *sb.* 4, or KNURL 2: see -ING, -LING.] = KNURL *sb.* 2.

1794 BURNS *Pastoral Poetry* iii, Wee Pope, the knurlin, 'till him rives Horatian fame. **1899** J. LUMSDEN *Edinburgh Poems & Songs* 149 Ouphes, knurlins, goblins, ghouls.

'knurly, *a.* [f. KNURL *sb.* + -Y.]

a. Having knurls or knots; gnarled. **b.** Of the nature of a knurl, dwarfish.

1602 MARSTON *Antonio's Rev.* IV. iii, Till by degrees the tough and knurly trunke Be riv'd in sunder. **1610** W. FOLKINGHAM *Art of Survey* I. iii. 6 The high timbring Oake ..denotates a rich and battle soile:..the knurly, crooked and crabbed..starueling bewraies his barren and hungrie bedde. **1758** J. ADAMS *Diary* 3 Dec., Wks. 1850 II. 51 A little knurly, ill-natured horse. **1882** *Garden* 18 Mar. 182/2 This ..apple..is knurly and imperfect at first.

†**'knurned**, *a. Obs.* In 3 cnurnede, 4 knorned. [From *knurn, deriv. form of KNUR or parallel form of KNURL.] = next.

a **1225** *St. Marher.* 10 His twa honden to his cnurnede cneon heteueste ibunden. **13..** *Gaw. & Gr. Knt.* 2166 Hyȝe bonkkez & brent, vpon boþe halue, & ruȝe knokled knarrez, with knorned stonez.

'knurred, *a.* ? *Obs.* Also 5 knorred, 6 knurd. [f. KNUR + -ED².] Knotted; rugged, gnarled.

c **1430** *Pilgr. Lyf Manhode* II. cxxi. (1869) 120 It is a staf for a cowheerde,..for it is hard, and knorred, and writhen. **1577** STANYHURST *Descr. Irel.* in Holinshed *Chron.* II. 18/2 To cleaue knurd knobs with crabbed wedges. **1582** —— *Æneis* I. (Arb.) 27 Thee gates of warfare wyl then bee mannacled hardly With steele bunch chayne knob, clingd, knurd, and narrolye lincked.

†**'knurrish**, *a. Obs. rare*$^{-0}$. [f. KNUR + -ISH¹.] Knurry.

1530 PALSGR. 317/1 Knottysshe knorisshe or full of knottes, *neueux*.

†**'knurry**, *a. Obs.* [f. KNUR + -Y.]

1. Full of knurs, knotty, gnarled.

1513 DOUGLAS *Æneis* VII. ix. 71 Wyth ane knotty club and knorry heid. **1582** STANYHURST *Æneis*, etc. (Arb.) 143 Thee knurrye knob oake tree,..in strength surpasseth a smooth slip. **1601** DEACON & WALKER *Spirits & Divels* To Rdr. 7 Knottie or knurrie hard logs doe craue strong yron wedges. **1664** EVELYN *Sylva* (1776) 217 Poplars and Abeles [on] coming to be very old are apt to grow knurry and out of proportion.

2. *fig.* 'Knotty', perplexing.

1615 CROOKE *Body of Man* 304 The second Question is more obscure and the more knurrie knotte a great deale to riue. **1652** URQUHART *Jewel* Wks. (1834) 225 Set all their braines awork how to contrive the knurriest arguments.

†**knush**, *v. Obs. rare.* [Cf. OE. *cnyssan* to strike, dash, beat; OHG. *knusjan*, *knussan* to dash, Ger. *knüssen* to push, beat, Du. *kneuzen* to bruise; also Ger. dial. *knuschen* to crush, to knock or strike with the fist; Icel. *knúska* to knock, ill-treat.] *trans.* To crush.

13.. *K. Alis.* 1844 (Bodl. MS.) In justes & fiȝttes nys oþere rente Bot bones knusshed & hard dent.

knut, jocular variant, often pronounced (kə'nʌt), of NUT *sb.*¹ 9 (a fashionable or showy young man). Hence **'knutty** *a.*

1911 *Granta* 25 Nov. 136/2 He, Timothy Gray, bhoy, lad, knut. **1913** L. A. HARKER *Ffolliots of Redmarley* v. 57 He was ..a 'knut' of the nuttiest flavour. **1914** *Scotsman* 5 Oct. 8/1 It is clear that he has once been a 'knut' in spite of his oil-stained khaki service jacket and trousers. **1915** A. WIMPERIS *Gilbert the Filbert (song)*, I'm Gilbert, the Filbert, The Colonel of the Knuts. **1916** E. V. LUCAS *Vermilion Box* 52 Among the people staying here is a knut. He must be almost the last of the tribe; but here he is, just as knutty as though the Algies and Berties were still ruling the roast, and not Mars at all. **1919** C. ORR *Glorious Thing* xvii. 212 He was trying to be knutty, he said. **1929** G. STOWELL *Hist. Button Hill* 183 The Knut was an urban and suburban phenomenon of the years 1912 to 1914 inclusive. **1973** *Listener* 6 Sept. 320 The 'silly asses', the 'knuts' who were wiped out on the Somme.

knyl, obs. f. KNEEL.

knyll(e, obs. ff. KNELL.

knypse: see KNIPSE.

‖**ko**¹ (kəʊ). *N.Z.* [Maori.] A digging-stick.

1843 E. DIEFFENBACH *Trav. N.Z.* II. III. 367 *Ko*—a tool with which the natives plant their sweet potatoes. **1868** W. COLENSO in *Trans. N.Z. Inst.* I. Essay 15 A *ko*, a rude kind of narrow and pointed spade with a very long handle, to which, at about 18 inches or more from the point, they [*sc.* Maoris] fitted a small crooked bit of carved wood, as a rest for the foot. **1905** W. B. *Where White Man Treads* 2 Plantations of kumara..which the Maori with his primitive ko (native wooden spade) had brought under tillage with much labour. **1941** ALLEY & HALL *Farmer in N.Z.* i. 3 His [*sc.* the Maori's] instant casting aside of his poor crude *ko*

and *timo* (or grubbing stick) in favour of European spades and hoes. **1955** W. J. PHILLIPPS *Maori Carving Illustr.* 16 Designs carved on the upper ends of ko or digging sticks.

‖**Ko**² (kəʊ). *Ceramics.* [Chinese, = elder brother. See quot. 1954.] In full, *Ko iú* or *yao* [Chinese, = ware], *Ko ware*. A crackled Sung ware closely related to Southern Kuan; also, a name for other crackled porcelains.

1882 *China Rev.* X. v. 310/1 Speaking of porcelain ware .., it is absolutely necessary to distinguish the kinds called Ch'ái porcelain.., Ü porcelain.., Government porcelain.., Ko porcelain. **1882** *Ibid.* XI. III. 176/2 Ko-iú (Ko porcelain) has, on its ground, hidden lines like spawn. **1904** E. DILLON *Porcelain* v. 63 The word Ko yao is used as a general name for many kinds of [Sung] crackle ware... In a more restricted sense it includes only the early pieces with a greyish white glaze and well-marked crackles. **1954** G. SAVAGE *Porcelain* I. i. 67 *Ko yao* was, by tradition, made by the elder of two brothers Chang... The type has a very dark stoneware body. **1972** *Collector's Guide* June 95/3 Traditionally there is Northern Kuan, Southern Kuan, Altar Kuan and the related Ko ware.

ko, = *quo'*, abridged f. QUOTH: cf. KA.

‖**koa** ('kəʊə). [Native Hawaiian name.] A valuable forest-tree of the Sandwich Islands, a species of Acacia, yielding a beautiful dark wood which is used in building and cabinet-work; the bark is employed in tanning. Also *attrib.*

1850 SCORESBY *Cheever's Whalem. Adv.* ii. (1859) 19 Over-grown with huge roots of the kamani and koa trees. **1860** *Merc. Marine Mag.* VII. 270 Koa, a kind of Hawaiian mahogany. **1887** *Science* X. 115 The remarkable boards of koa-wood,.. standing on which they rode through the surf. **1954** J. SHERIDAN in J. Macdonald *Lethal Sex* (1962) 181 Four men carried the pigs on huge *koa* platters carved with supporting feet. **1965** *N.Z. Listener* 17 Dec. 4/2 The commoners [in Hawaii] were permitted only the heavier and less buoyant Koa boards.

koaftah var. KOFTA.

koala (kəʊ'ɑːlə). Also 9 coola(h, kool-la, koolah. [Native name: given as *kūlla* in Dippil, *kūlā* on George's River (Ridley *Kámilarói*, pp. 64, 104); *koala* was perhaps orig. a misreading of *koola*. Hence the name of the town *Coolah* in New South Wales.] In full, ***koala bear***. An arboreal marsupial mammal of Australia (*Phascolarctos cinereus*), of an ashen-grey colour, small, clumsy, and somewhat resembling a sloth in form, and feeding on the leaves of eucalyptus. Also called the *Australian* or *Native Bear*.

1808 HOME in *Phil. Trans.* XCVIII. 305 The koala is another species of the wombat. The natives call it the koala wombat; it..was first brought to Port Jackson in August, 1803. **1813** *Hist. N.S. Wales* (1818) 432 (Morris) The koolah or sloth is likewise an animal of the opossum species, with a false belly. **1827** CUNNINGHAM *N.S. Wales* I. 317 (Morris s.v. *Bear*) Our coola (sloth or native bear) is about the size of an ordinary poodle dog, with shaggy, dirty-coloured fur, no tail, and claws and feet like a bear. **1859** DARWIN *Orig. Spec.* xiv. (1878) 382 The climbing, leaf-eating koala. **1902** *Daily Chron.* 3 July 3/4 The koala of Australia, has also a very big cæcum. **1937** C. KEARTON *I visit Antipodes* x. 132 The Koala Bear was first seen by a young explorer who journeyed to the Blue Mountains in 1798. **1944** A. RUSSELL *Bush Ways* xix. 95 There was.. scarce a gum tree but that sheltered an opossum or a koala. **1966** G. DURRELL *Two in Bush* v. 173 Fortunately, before it became too late, the Government stepped in and passed laws strictly protecting the Koalas, and slowly over the years their numbers have built up again.

‖**koan** ('kəʊɑːn). [Jap., f. *kō* public + *an* matter, material for thought.] In Zen Buddhism, a paradox put to a student to stimulate his mind.

1946 R. BENEDICT *Chrysanthemum & Sword* (1947) xi. 246 The significance of the koan does not lie in the truths these seekers after truth discover. **1957** *Time* 4 Feb. 66/2 A less physical shock technique is the *koan*, a problem designed to shock the mind beyond mere thinking. **1958** A. HUXLEY *Let.* 11 Jan. (1969) 844 They might act as Zen koans and cause sudden openings into hitherto unglimpsed regions. **1960** KOESTLER *Lotus & Robot* II. x. 236 The koan—the logically insoluble riddle which the pupil must try to solve. *Ibid.* 237 There are said to exist some one thousand seven hundred koans, divided into various categories... The oldest-known koans are the 'Three Barriers of Hung-Lun', an eleventh-century Zen master. **1972** *Times Lit. Suppl.* 28 Jan. 85/1 What he comes up with—his runes and enigmas and impromptu koans—builds gradually into a supplementry creation.

koatuku, obs. var. KOTUKU.

‖**kob**¹ (kɒb). Also cob. [Given by Adanson as the native name (among the Joloffs) in Senegal.] In full, ***kob antelope***. An African water antelope of the genus *Kobus*, represented by several distinct species; esp. the species *Kobus kob*.

1774 GOLDSM. *Nat. Hist.* (1862) I. 308 The Gazelles, of which there are several kinds... The first he calls the *koba*, and the sixth the *kob*. **1834** *Penny Cycl.* II. 79/2 The Kob (*A[ntilope] koba*, Erxleben) called *Petite Vache brune*, or little brown cow, by the French settlers on the western coast of Africa, is described as being about the size of the fallow-deer. **1850** *Proc. Zool Soc.* 133 It is called Dacoi, or White Mouth, by the Mandingoes, Kob and Koba by the Joliffs. **1897** SCLATER & THOMAS *Bk. Antelopes* II. VII. 139 The first specimen of the Kob Antelope that reached Europe alive, so far as we know, was that presented to the Zoological Society of London by Mr. John Foster in 1836. *Ibid.* 140 From Senegal and the Gambia and Kob extends through the interior of West Africa to Togoland. **1920** *Blackw. Mag.* May 656/2 The tawny Uganda cob, a very handsome antelope. **1961** *Listener* 7 Sept. 348/2 The host of antelopes, such as..impala, cob, kudu, and a score more. **1964** C. WILLOCK *Enormous Zoo* iv. 40 The kob... To look at, this lovely creature with the back-raked horns is a little like a larger version of the impala... In fact its nearest relative is the large, shaggy, big-horned waterbuck. **1964** G. B. SCHALLER *Year of Gorilla* (1965) iii. 75 Rwindi, near the southern end of Lake Edward,..is the central location from which to see the herds of buffalo, elephant, hippopotamus, waterbuck, kob antelope. **1967** *Listener* 6 Apr. 459/2 Among the Ugandan kob males may defend small territories... By tradition a certain number of kob are associated with each breeding ground. **1974** *Nature* 29 Nov. 345/3 In the Uganda kob antelope there exists a system of social behaviour designed to prevent clandestine matings.

kob² (kɒb). *S. Afr.* = KABELJOU.

1906 *East London (Cape Province) Dispatch* 26 June 3/7 Our well-known and very common kabeljaauw, called for briefness 'cob' or 'kob'. **1913** W. W. THOMPSON *Sea Fisheries Cape Colony* 155 Kabeljaauw..; Cob or Kob (East London). **1930** C. L. BIDEN *Sea-Angling Fishes of Cape* v. 108 Kabeljou; Kob (abbreviated name). **1950** *Cape Times* 17 Nov. 13/8 Kob are well worth a try from the usual spots around the sandy sweep of the bay. **1959** *Ibid.* 16 Nov. 2/5 Visitor Lands Big Kob. **1974** *South-Western Herald* (S. Afr.) 2 July 5 'I am now after kob,' said Mr. Thomson.

2. kob water, disturbed, discoloured water in which the kob is often found.

1930 C. L. BIDEN *Sea-Angling Fishes of Cape* v. 113 On the south-east coast particularly they keep a watchful eye on what is known as 'kob-water'—a discoloration of the sea, either milky, dirty yellow, or what one would liken to pea soup. **1957** S. SCHOEMAN *Strike!* iii. 71 Kob-water usually results from a disturbance of the seabed. **1974** *Argus* (Cape Town) 31 Dec. 4/2 The familiar, ginger-beer coloured water known to anglers as 'kob water' is moving in along parts of the Strandfontein coast-line.

kob, obs. form of COB *v.*

‖**koba** ('kəʊbə). [Given by Barth and Reichardt, as the native name in Fulah.] = KOB¹. But by earlier naturalists often taken as the name of a distinct species.

1774 [see KOB¹]. **1834** *Penny Cycl.* II. 79/1 The Koba (*A[ntilope] koba*) called *Grande vache brune*, or large brown cow, by the French of Senegal, is in size equal to the European stag.

‖**kobang** ('kəʊbæŋ). Also 7 coban, 8 cupang. [Jap. *ko-ban*, f. *ko* little + *ban* (a. Chinese *fan*) division: cf. OBANG.] An oblong gold coin, rounded at the corners, formerly current in Japan. The original weight was 222 grains troy, but it was afterwards reduced to about a quarter of this owing to the unfavourable rate of exchange. Also *attrib.* in †*coban gold*.

1616 COCKS *Diary* 17 Sept. (1883) I. 176, I receved two bars Coban gould with ten ichibos, of 4 to a coban. **1727** A. HAMILTON *New Acc. E. Ind.* II. 86 My Friend.. complimented the Doctor with five Japon Cupangs, or fifty Dutch Dollars. **1860** *Merc. Marine Mag.* VII. 57 The exportation of the gold coin called kobangs is permitted. **1897** *Blackw. Mag.* Dec. 842/1 Bus were essential for another purpose, the purchase of kobangs.

kobeite ('kəʊbiːaɪt). *Min.* [Partial tr. Jap. *kobeishi* (J. Takubo et al. 1950, in *Jrnl. Geol. Soc. Japan* LVI. 512), f. *Kobe*, name of a locality in Kyoto prefecture, Japan + *ishi* mineral (formative suffix of names of minerals): see -ITE¹.] A black, prismatic, hydrated multiple oxide of formula close to $AB_2(O,OH)_6$ (where A represents mainly yttrium, iron, and uranium and B represents mainly titanium, zirconium, hafnium, niobium, and tantalum), but with much less $(Nb,Ta)_2O_5$ than minerals of the euxenite-polycrase series and more TiO_2.

1950 J. TAKUBO et al. in *Jrnl. Geol. Soc. Japan* LVI. 513 [Eng. abstr. of article in Jap.] The content of TiO_2 is.. exceedingly high compared with that of polycrase or blomstrandite. So the writers propose here to call this mineral 'Kobeite' after the name of the locality. **1957** *Amer. Mineralogist* XLII. 342 The kobeite-bearing cobble..was collected while panning sands and gravels in the Paringa River, South Westland, New Zealand. **1961** *Mineral. Jrnl.* III. 146 The writers are inclined to recognize kobeite as a distinct mineral species belonging to multiple oxides rich in titanium, zirconium and yttrium group rare earths.

kobellite ('kəʊbəlaɪt). *Min.* [Named 1839, after Professor F. von Kobell, a German mineralogist: see -ITE.] Sulph-antimonide of bismuth and lead, occurring in lead-grey radiated masses.

1844 DANA *Min.* (ed. 2) 496 Kobellite comes from the cobalt mine of Hvena in Sweden. **1886** *Amer. Jrnl. Sc.* Ser. III. XXXI. 73 Kobellite from Colorado.

kobil, obs. form of COBLE, fishing-boat.

kobo ('kəʊbəʊ). Pl. kobo. [See quot. 1972¹.] A unit of currency in the Federal Republic of Nigeria, equal to $\frac{1}{100}$ naira.

1972 *N.Y. Times* 9 Aug. 14 Kobo..is a corruption of the word 'copper' and the popular term here [*sc.* Nigeria] for a penny, a copper coin... The kobo, symbolized by a lower-case k, will be produced in coins of one-half kobo, 1, 5, 10 and 25 kobo. **1972** *Times* 9 Oct. (Nigeria Suppl.) p. viii/4 The new currency being introduced by the Central Bank of Nigeria consists of naira and kobo... Kobo was the popular name for the old penny pieces... The new kobo is the same size as the old Nigerian shilling and carries a depiction of cocoa seeds. **1973** *Whitaker's Almanack 1974* 985 Nigeria (Federal Republic of)... Naira = 100 Kobo.

‖**kobold** ('kəʊbəld). [G. *kobold*, *kobolt* (dial. *kob(b)elt*, *kubbelt*), MHG. *kobolt* (*chowolt*) = MDu. *cobout* (*cobbout*, *coubout*, Du. *kabouter*); ulterior etymology uncertain.

Hildebrand, in Grimm, favours an original **kobwalt*, f. *kobe* house, COVE *sb.*¹ + stem of *walten* to rule, WIELD; cf. OE. *cofgodas*, *-godu* as renderings of L. *lares* and *penates*.]

In German folklore: **a.** A familar spirit, haunting houses and rendering services to the inmates, but often of a tricky disposition; a brownie. **b.** An underground spirit haunting mines or caves; a goblin or gnome.

[**1635** HEYWOOD *Hierarch.* IX. 568 The Parts Septentrionall are with these Sp'ryts Much haunted.. About the places where they dig for Oare. The Greekes and Germans call them Cobali. *Ibid.* 574 Kibaldi.] **1830** SCOTT *Demonol.* 121 The Kobolds were a species of gnomes, who haunted the dark and solitary places, and were often seen in the mines. **1849** A. J. SYMINGTON *Harebell Chimes* 11 Witch, kobold, sprite..and imp of every kind. **1870** EMERSON *Soc. & Solit., Work & Days* Wks. (Bohn) III. 65 What of the grand tools with which we engineer, like kobolds and enchanters?

fig. **1870** LOWELL *Among my Bks.* Ser. I. (1873) 217 There in the corner is the little black kobold of a doubt making mouths at him.

kobold, obs. form of COBALT.

kocatrice, obs. form of COCKATRICE.

†**kocay.** *Obs. rare.* (See quot.)

c **1440** *Promp. Parv.* 281/1 Kocay, priuy, *cloaca*.

Koch (kɒx, kɒk). The name of Robert *Koch* (1843–1910), Ger. bacteriologist, used in the possessive (less commonly *attrib.*) to designate certain things related to his work on tuberculosis, as **Koch's bacillus**, *Mycobacterium tuberculosis*, which causes tuberculosis in man, and was first isolated by Koch; **Koch's laws** = *Koch('s) postulates*; **Koch('s) phenomenon**, the altered reaction to an inoculation of (living or dead) tubercle bacilli of an animal already infected with tuberculosis from that of a healthy animal, the infected animal showing a reaction which is quicker and locally more severe but which is not followed by a general infection; (now regarded as a classic example of delayed hypersensitivity); **Koch('s) postulates**, a set of four criteria which should be satisfied before a given disease is attributed with certainty to any particular micro-organism, viz. (*a*) the organism concerned is present in each case of the disease; (*b*) it is possible to isolate it from the diseased animal in a pure culture; (*c*) the introduction of such a culture into a suitable healthy animal produces the disease in it; and (*d*) the organism is recoverable from the animal so infected; **Koch's tuberculin**, either of two kinds of tuberculin (***Koch's old*** and ***new tuberculin***) orig. devised by Koch; formerly also called ***Koch's fluid, liquid, lymph***, and now usually just *tuberculin*.

1885 *Jrnl. R. Microsc. Soc.* 557 (*heading*) Staining of Koch's bacillus. **1890** *Lancet* 22 Nov. 1119/2 He drew attention to the advantage of being able, by the injection of Koch's fluid, to diagnose whether a serious laryngeal affection was carcinomatous..or tubercular. *Ibid.* 1120/1 Experiments with Koch's lymph. *Ibid.* 1121/1 He was inoculated with Koch's liquid for distinct facial lupus, and at the same time for pulmonary tuberculosis. **1891** Dr. Koch's lymph [see TUBERCULIN]. **1897** MUIR & RITCHIE *Man. Bacteriol.* ix. 229 (*heading*) Koch's tuberculin. **1898** R. T. HEWLETT *Man. Bacteriol.* ii. 31 With regard to the pathogenic organisms..Koch has laid down the following conditions, which have been termed Koch's Postulates, which must be complied with before the relation of an organism to a disease process can be said to be completely demonstrated. **1899** Koch's lymph [see TUBERCULIN]. **1910** MUIR & RITCHIE *Man. Bacteriol.* (ed. 5) x. 284 (*heading*) Koch's old tuberculin. *Ibid.* 288 Another preparation has.. been introduced, known as 'Koch's new tuberculin'. **1911** *Encycl. Brit.* XX. 783/1 Koch's tuberculin has been of inestimable value in the early diagnosis of tuberculosis, especially in animals. **1929** TOPLEY & WILSON *Princ. Bacteriol. & Immunity* II. xlix. 729 There are two classical examples, which provide striking illustrations of this double aspect of the allergic reaction. One of these is the well-known Koch's phenomenon (Koch 1891). **1939** K. L. BURDON *Med. Microbiol.* ii. 20 These principles have become known as 'Koch's laws' or 'Koch's postulates'. **1944** L. E. H. WHITBY *Med. Bacteriol.* (ed. 4) i. 2 Very few organisms pathogenic to man fulfil Koch's postulates rigidly. **1955** *Sci. Amer.* June 103/1 Koch found the bacillus in body tissues, in sputum and in urine. He was able to grow the microbe in an artificial culture, to reproduce tuberculosis by injecting it into new animals and to recover it again from the infected tissue—a procedure which has become standard for connecting a given disease with a germ and is known by the name Koch's Laws. **1963** HUMPHREY & WHITE *Immunol. for Students of Med.* x. 322 The injection into a normal guinea-pig of as much as 2 ml of Koch's old tuberculin has little effect. But the injection of 0·1 [*printed* 0·0] ml into a guinea-pig, in the eighth or tenth week of tuberculous infection, may kill it within a few hours. **1964** WHEELER & VOLK *Basic Microbiol.* xxiii. 263/2

Mycobacterium tuberculosis (more commonly called the tubercle bacillus and sometimes Koch's bacillus) was shown by Robert Koch to be the causative agent of tuberculosis. **1970** PASSMORE & ROBSON *Compan. Med. Stud.* II. xxi. 17/1 This Koch phenomenon is a specific example of cellular immune response. **1973** *Sci. Amer.* Oct. 28/1 Thus the famous 'Koch postulates' have been satisfied, and the tumor is firmly placed among those transmitted by an infectious agent.

kochubeïte (kɒ'tʃuːbɪaɪt). *Min.* Also kotschubeite. [ad. G. *kotschubeit* (N. von Kokscharow 1863, in *Bull. de l'Acad. Imp. des Sci. de St.-Pétersbourg* V. 369), f. the name of Count P. A. *Kochubei*, 19th-century Russian mineralogist: see -ITE[1].] A mineral of the chlorite group that is a chromiferous variety of clinochlore and occurs as rose-red rhombohedral crystals.

1868 J. D. DANA *Syst. Min.* (ed. 5) 500 *Kotschubeite*..in the district of Ufaleisk, Southern Ural. **1910** *Encycl. Brit.* VI. 256 Alumina may also be partly replaced by chromic oxide, as in the rose-red varieties [of chlorite] kämmererite and kotschubeite. **1954** *Mineral. Mag.* XXX. 280 The chromiferous chlorites include three varieties: kämmererite ..; chrome-clinochlore, with less than 4% Cr_2O_3; and kochubeïte, a variety of clinochlore with more than 4% Cr_2O_3. **1958** [see KÄMMERERITE].

Koch-Weeks bacillus. *Med.* [f. the names of Robert *Koch* (see KOCH) and J. E. *Weeks* (1853–1949), American ophthalmologist: see BACILLUS.] The bacterium, *Hæmophilus ægyptius*, which is a common cause of infectious conjunctivitis.

[**1897** *Arch. Ophthalmol.* XXVI. 102 Peters and Fuchs claimed never to have been able to find the Koch-Weeks's bacillus.] **1898** R. T. HEWLETT *Man. Bacteriol.* xx. 359 Conjunctivitis is usually of three kinds—viz. the acute, caused by the Koch-Weeks bacillus; the gonorrhœal; and the chronic. **1974** PASSMORE & ROBSON *Compan. Med. Studies* III. II. xxxiii. 8/1 Conjunctivitis may occur in epidemic form in schools, offices, etc., the classical epidemic pink-eye, being caused by *H. aegyptius* (the Koch-Weeks bacillus).

kock(e, kockerell, etc., obs. forms of COCK, COCKEREL, etc.

kockowe, obs. form of CUCKOO.

kocks nownes, perversion of *God's wounds* as an oath: see COCK *sb.*[8]

a **1553** UDALL *Royster D.* I. iv. (Arb.) 26 Kocks nownes what meanest thou man.

kocok-pyntyl, obs. form of CUCKOO-PINTLE.

a **1400** *Stockh. Medical MS.* ii. 731 (*Anglia* XVIII. 325) Of dragans arn spycis iij..Kocok pyntyl is þe ton.

kod, obs. form of COD *sb.*[3], QUOTH *v.*

Kodachrome ('kəʊdəkrəʊm). [f. KODA(K *sb.* + *-chrome* (Gr. χρῶμα colour).] The registered trade name of a method of colour photography used by Kodak Ltd. Also, a colour film manufactured by this method; a photograph or slide produced from a Kodachrome film. Also *attrib.*

The spellings in quots. 1915 and 1966 are *erron.*

1915 *Chambers's Jrnl.* 25 Sept. 687/2 The kodachchrome process offers a means of enabling the former [*sc.* the amateur] to realise his ambition. **1926** *Trade Marks Jrnl.* 22 Sept. 2158 Kodachrome... All Goods included in Class 8 [*sc.* philosophical instruments, scientific instruments, apparatus for useful purposes, etc.]. Kodak, Limited,.. London, W.C.2; Manufacturers and Dealers. **1930** C. W. ACKERMAN *George Eastman* viii. 285 Ever since the advent of the Kodak system, Eastman had dreamed of photographs in natural colors and the research workers..had just succeeded in a color process for portraiture, which was called Kodachrome. **1935** *Discovery* July 190/2 Recently Kodak have introduced a very interesting three-colour subtractive film for sub-standard cinematography which is to be known as 'Kodachrome'. **1936** *Times* 10 Jan. 7/5 Among other short films shown was one which illustrated the results obtained by the new Kodachrome process. **1951** L. Z. HOBSON *Celebrity* (1953) ii. 22 Each grandchild, whether in the flesh or on Kodachrome, was Beauty and Goodness personified. **1960** A. COREN in *Introduction: Stories by New Writers* 102 Brash teased-up Kodachrome lupins and a postcard sky. **1961** G. SMITH *Business of Loving* xv. 271 The air had a tint of Kodachrome blue in it. **1966** *Guardian* 28 Dec. 4/6 Pope Pius, in Kodakchrome, smiled at stacks of institutional china. **1969** *Focal Encycl. Photogr.* 815/2 *Kodachrome*, pioneer subtractive process of colour photography worked out by L. D. Mannes and L. Godorosky and introduced by Kodak... It makes use of an integral tripack in which the emulsions contain no colour formers but are subjected to individual dye development. **1970** *Daily Tel.* (Colour Suppl.) 7 Aug. 7 A vivid Kodachrome of the coach roaring down a hillside became the background for the new cheques. **1971** R. DENTRY *Encounter at Kharmel* (1973) ix. 148 Bloody marvellous country... I've got a box of Kodachromes to prove it.

Kodak ('kəʊdæk), *sb.* [An arbitrary word invented by Mr. G. Eastman for trade-mark purposes.] The proprietary name of a range of cameras produced by Kodak Ltd.

1888 *Official Gaz.* (U.S. Patent Off.) XLIV. 1072/1 Photographic Cameras and Sensitized Plates and Film Therefor.—The Eastman Dry Plate and Film Company... 'The word "Kodak".' **1890** *Kodak Man.* 9 The principal thing to learn in using the Kodak is to hold it steady. **1890** *Rev. of Rev.* II. 489/2 The use of even a Kodak is attended with considerable difficulty. **1893** MRS. C. PRAED *Outlaw & Lawmaker* III. 124 A clever young 'new chum'..who had brought a Kodak, took photographs. **1899** MERWIN & WEBSTER *Short Line War* v. 62 Near the box was a kodak picture of Miss Porter. **1907** W. JAMES *Pragmatism* viii. 290 We want a Kodak-picture and we press a button. **1913** F. A. TALBOT *Pract. Cinematogr.* 22 Contrary to general belief, taking the 'movies' is quite as simple as snapshot photography with a Kodak. **1933** R. L. SUTTON *Arctic Safari* 43 We had to exercise considerable self-restraint in the matter of kodak portraiture... I think that we did not use up more than three packs of film. **1966** J. BETJEMAN *High & Low* 47 These are the walls adorned with portraits, Camera studies and Kodak snaps. **1974** *Times* 26 Jan. 8/3 Americans walk the length of the street market in the Portobello Road snapping it with Kodaks.

fig. **1899** F. C. GOULD in *Westm. Gaz.* 6 Sept. 1/3 Printed on the endless roll of sensitised material with which our brain kodaks are fitted.

b. *transf.* A photograph taken with a Kodak.

1895 *Westm. Gaz.* 22 Oct. 2/3 That a photographer in ambush could get..a 'Kodak' of the document, which would be legible under a microscope. **1898** *N.Y. Observer* 3 Mar. 258/1 Some of the rest took kodaks of us. **1901** E. HORNBY *Jrnl.* 22 Mar. in *Sinai & Petra* (1907) 180 M. at once took two kodaks of it. **1930** B. WILLIS *Living Afr.* vii. 98 After I had taken a couple of kodaks.

c. *attrib.*

1890 *Kodak Man.* 76 Any Kodak negative that will make a good contact print, will make a good enlargement. **1893** F. HARRISON in *Westm. Gaz.* 10 Apr. 3/2 The Kodak school of romance, the snap-shots at every day realism with a hand camera.

Kodak ('kəʊdæk), *v.* Now *rare.* Also kodak. [f. prec. sb.] *trans.* and *intr.* To photograph with a Kodak.

1891 *Anthony's Photogr. Bull.* IV. 59 A next door neighbor, who is just beginning to 'kodak'. **1892** *Ill. Sport. & Dram. News* 23 July 695/2 Chloe..insisted upon kodaking us all in every conceivable position. **1924** *New Republic* 24 Dec. 120 Our Main Street is the happy-hunting ground of the ill-willed camera. Picture ahead, Kodak as you go. **1928** *Ibid.* 12 Dec. 90 The young cook who had been one of the last to leave the ship, Kodaking as he went. **1936** *Time* 14 Dec. 21 A French actress who recognizes Mrs. Simpson and tries to Kodak her gets a blow from the British bodyguard knocking her camera from her hand. **1954** *Life* 26 Apr. 155 Kodaked by friend as he himself aimed a Kodak, Eastman was photographed on a ship in 1890 by early model which took round pictures.

b. *fig.* To 'catch' or describe quickly or vividly.

1892 *Daily News* 2 Dec. 6/1 His only aim having been to 'kodak'..with camera and pen a few phases of life in Japan. **1897** *Ibid.* 2 Mar. 8/2 The President of the Transvaal, as recently kodaked by Labouchere out of Rhodes. **1900** *Westm. Gaz.* 22 Jan. 1/2 His writing had, naturally enough, the defects of its qualities—there are obvious drawbacks in the process of kodaking. **1934** J. COLLIER *Defy Foul Fiend* 318 Willoughby's eye had kodaked the attitude of a beaten child, sulking in tears. **1948** H. M. GLOSTER *Negro Voices Amer. Fiction* 165 McKay's second novel, *Banjo* (1929), an impressionistic kodaking of life among the colored boys of the Marseilles breakwater.

Hence **'Kodaker, 'Kodakist**, one who photographs with a kodak; **'Kodakry**. (All app. *obs.*)

1890 *Kodak Man.* 51 If..the Kodaker wishes to develop and print his own negatives, he can easily learn to do so. **1898** *Westm. Gaz.* 25 Mar. 9/2 The Prince had to pass through a triple file of kodakers, each anxious to get a good shot. **1895** WORKMAN *Algerian Mem.* 13 The opportunity here offered the kodakist is a rare one. **1893** YORK POWELL in *Classical Rev.* May 229/1 In these days of Kodakry, a little photograph can usually be secured of any larger object on the spot.

kode, kodeling, obs. ff. COD *sb.*[1], CODLING[1].

1340 *Durham Acc. Rolls* (Surtees) 37 in..7 kodeling.

Kodet (kəʊ'dɛt). [Arbitrarily f. KOD-AK + -ET[1].] A smaller variety of KODAK.

1894 *Forum* (N.Y.) June *Advt.*, The Kodet is the youngest member of the Kodak family. **1895** *Westm. Gaz.* 23 May 7/1 All the latest aids to war, such as..the field telephone, the Kodet.

Kodiak ('kɒdjæk). Also **Kadiak** ('kædjæk). The name of an island off Alaska, used *attrib.* to designate the large brown bear, *Ursus arctos middendorffi*, found there, as well as in Alaska itself and on other islands off the coast. Also *absol.*

1899 R. WARD *Rec. Big Game* (ed. 3) 474 Even more gigantic is the Kadiak bear..of Kadiak Island, Alaska. **1904** C. R. E. RADCLYFFE *Big Game Shooting in Alaska* 268 The Kodiak brown bear (*Ursus middendorffi*). **1930** *Sat. Even. Post* 13 Dec. 11/2 A Kodiak bear looks as big as an elephant as he ambles..through vegetation that comes only to his stomach. **1955** *Arctic Terms* 47/1 Kodiak bear. The world's largest carnivore, *Ursus middendorfi*, occasionally weighs 1,500 pounds, yellowish to dark brown in color, ranging from the Alaska Peninsula south-east on coasts and adjacent islands to British Columbia. Also called the 'big brown bear', 'brownie', 'Alaskan brown bear', 'Kadiak bear'. **1966** R. PERRY *World of Polar Bear* ix. 111 In both size and weight polar bears approximate to the giant Alaskan and Kodiak bears. **1974** 'R. B. DOMINIC' *Epitaph for Lobbyist* xx. 173 He was going to walk..into the Zoo... Kodiaks and Himalayas, the tourist booklet said.

kodlomb, obs. f. *cade-lamb*: see CADE *sb.*[2]

kodpeasid; see COD-PIECED.

koechlinite ('kœːçlɪnaɪt). *Min.* [f. the name of Rudolf *Koechlin* (1862–1939), curator of the mineral collection, Hof-Museum, Vienna + -ITE[1].] A molybdate of bismuth, Bi_2MoO_6, found as minute, greenish-yellow plates, and in soft white to yellow masses.

1914 W. T. SCHALLER in *Jrnl. Washington Acad. Sci.* IV. 354 Koechlinite (bismuth molybdate), a new mineral from Schneeberg, Saxony. **1943** *Amer. Mineralogist* XXVIII. 537 Koechlinite also was found as soft white to yellow masses associated with bismoclite on specimens from Bygoo, New South Wales. Here, too, the mineral has formed by the alteration of a pre-existing bismuth mineral. **1966** *Jrnl. Inorg. & Nucl. Chem.* XXVIII. 1125 The lattice parameters were equal to those of natural koechlinite within the experimental error.

koedoe: see KUDU.

koek(oe)makranka, varr. KUKUMAKRANKA.

‖**koeksister** ('kuːsɪstə(r)). *S. Afr.* Also koeksuster, koesijster, koesister. [Afrikaans *koe(k)sister.*] A kind of sugared doughnut popular in South Africa.

1904 *Hilda's Where is it? of Recipes* (Pettman) 128 *Koesisters* (Batavian or old Dutch sweetmeat recipe). **1913** C. PETTMAN *Africanderisms* 272 *Koesijsters*,—a confection or sweetmeat which has been boiled in fat and dipped in powdered sugar. **1947** L. G. GREEN *Tavern of Seas* viii. 72 There was a koesister (doughnut) specialist. **1953** *Cape Times* 24 Mar. 16/1 Tea and coffee, *boerebeskuit, koeksusters, melktart*, and scores of other platteland delicacies. **1959** H. GERBER *Trad. Cookery Cape Malays* 9 Some of them [*sc.* Malay housewives] turn out lighter pastries, spongier *koesisters* than others. **1967** E. M. SLATTER *My Leaves are Green* 9 The coffee was hot and strong and the flaky koeksisters melted in my mouth. **1974** *Sunday Times* (Johannesburg) (Colour Suppl.) 3 Mar. 7 Those delicious onions with a sour sauce, melk snysels, koeksisters.

‖**koel** ('kəʊɪl). Also coel, koïl. [Hindī *kóīl*, f. Skr. *kokila.*] A cuckoo of the genus *Eudynamis*, esp. the *E. honorata* of India, and the *E. flindersi* of New Guinea and Australia.

1826 ERSKINE tr. *Baber's Mem.* 323 *note*, The koel..has a kind of song, and is the nightingale of Hindustân. **1834** A. PRINSEP *Baboo* I. ii. 18 The ever-green shrubberies formed ..a sheltered choir for the mango-bird, the meina, and the coel. **1865** GOULD *Handbk. Birds Australia* I. 632 Australian Koel. **1886** R. KIPLING *Departm. Ditties*, etc. (1899) 113 The rose has lost its fragrance, and the *köil's* note is strange. **1888** GOULD *Birds New Guinea* IV. pl. 41 The Koels or Black Cuckoos of the genus *Eudynamys*.

koelie: see COOLIE, COOLY 2 b.

koelreuteria (kœːlrɔɪ'tɪərɪə). [mod.L. (E. Laxmann 1772, in *Nov. Comm. Acad. Sci. Imp. Petrop.* XVI. 561), f. the name of Joseph G. *Koelreuter* (1733–1806), German naturalist + -IA[1].] A deciduous tree of the east Asian genus so called, belonging to the family Sapindaceæ, esp. *K. paniculata*, from northern China, which has large panicles of yellow flowers and pinnate leaves which turn bright yellow in autumn.

1789 W. AITON *Hortus Kewensis* II. 7 Panicled Kœlreuteria. Nat[ive] of China. **1818** *Bot. Reg.* IV. 330 (*heading*) Panicled Koelreuteria. **1914** W. J. BEAN *Trees & Shrubs Hardy in Brit. Isles* II. 687 Mr Wilson introduced from China, in 1900, a rather distinct Koelreuteria with very large and often quite bipinnate leaves. **1920** A. D. WEBSTER *London Trees* 71 The Koelreuteria is readily propagated by cuttings or either root or branch. **1946** L. J. F. BRIMBLE *Trees in Brit.* xxvii. 209 *Koelreuteria* is a native of northern China, but it is sometimes cultivated in Britain for ornamental purposes since its yellow flowers and autumnal foliage are so attractive.

koembang, var. KUMBANG.

koenenite (kɜː-, 'køːnənaɪt). *Min.* [ad. G. *koenenit* (F. Rinne 1902, in *Centralblatt f. Mineral.* 493), f. the name of Adolph von *Koenen* (1837–1915), German geologist who first found it: see -ITE[1].] A hydroxide and chloride of magnesium, aluminium, and sodium (formerly thought to be an impurity), which forms pale yellow scales when pure, but is normally red owing to enclosed hæmatite.

1902 *Jrnl. Chem. Soc.* LXXXII. II. 611 Koenenite. This new mineral was found..in crevices in the clay of the salt deposits at Volpriehausen, in the Sollinger Wald, Hanover. It is red in colour. **1952** *Mineral. Abstr.* XI. 459 Koenenite is widely distributed in the German salt deposits, occurring in salt-clay with blue halite, in anhydrite 'Hartsalz', and carnallite. **1968** *Zeitschr. für Kristallogr.* CXXVI. 7 Koenenite, $4NaCl.4(Mg,Ca)Cl_2.5Mg(OH)_2.4Al(OH)_3$, is built up of two trigonal substructures: $[Na_4(Ca,Mg)_2Cl_{12}]^{4-}$ and $[Mg_7Al_4(OH)_{22}]^{4+}$. **1968** I. KOSTOV *Mineral.* II. iii. 195 Koenenite is trigonal with perfect {0001} cleavage.

kœnleinite ('kœnlaɪnaɪt). *Min.* [Named (*Könleinit*) 1838, after Kœnlein, its discoverer: see -ITE.] A reddish-brown hydrocarbon, found in the brown coal of Uznach, Switzerland.

1861 in BRISTOW *Gloss. Min.*

koesijster, koesister, varr. KOEKSISTER.

kœttigite ('kœtɪgaɪt). *Min.* [Named, 1850, after O. Köttig: see -ITE.] Hydrous arsenate of zinc, containing also cobalt and nickel.
1850 DANA *Min.* (ed. 3) 487 Köttigite.. [occurs] in crusts with a crystalline surface.

kof, var. of COF(E *a.* and *adv. Obs.*, quick(ly.

‖**koff** (kɒf). *Naut. rare.* Also kuff. [Du. *kof.*] A clumsy sailing-vessel with two masts, used by the Dutch, Germans, Danes, etc.
1794 *Rigging & Seamanship* I. 238 *Koffs* are Dutch vessels of burthen, with a main and fore mast, and a large spritsail set abaft each. **1858** in SIMMONDS *Dict. Trade.* **1895** *Times* 19 Nov. 10/5 Danish kuff 'Gebrœders' Nyhuis.. is ashore at Thisted.

koffle, variant of COFFLE, a caravan.

†**koffry**. *Sc. Obs. rare*⁻¹. In 5 koffre. [? f. COFE *sb.* bargain, pedlar + -RY.] Bargaining, peddlery.
c **1470** HENRY *Wallace* VIII. 526 Thai sawft na Sotheroun for thair gret riches; Off sic koffre he callit bot wretchitnes.

‖**koft**. *E. Indian.* Also 9 kuft. [See KOFTGARI.] *attrib.* in ***koft-work*** = KOFTGARI.
1880 BIRDWOOD *Ind. Arts* 163 One of the finest examples of the *kuft* work of the Panjab. **1883** J. L. KIPLING in *Harper's Mag.* June 62/2 Modern damascening, or *koft*-work, is apt to degenerate into.. meaningless ornament. **1883** *Daily News* 3 July 2/2 This.. can be well studied in the 'Koft', or steelware inlaid with silver and gold.

‖**kofta** ('kɒftə). Also koaftah, kooftah. [Hind. *kofta* pounded meat.] A rissole, made of meat or fish, popular in the East. Also *attrib.*
1888 W. H. DAWE *Wife's Help to Indian Cookery* 71 *Koftá kabáb.* [Recipe given.] **1932** M. R. ANAND *Curries* 49 In Kofta Curry.. all the tomatoes should be put in at once to form the gravy. **1936** E. P. VEERASAWMY *Indian Cookery* 51 Kooftahs.. are usually balls of minced mutton or beef, blended with onions, garlic, ginger and certain spices, and cooked in a curry sauce. **1955** H. DAY *Curries of India* iii. 27 Koaftah curry is quite simple to make and is a universal favourite all over India and Pakistan. **1971** *Femina* (Bombay) 16 Apr. 57/2 Put *koftas* in it [*sc.* the water] and cook till soft enough.

‖**koftgari** (kɒftgə'riː). *E. Indian.* Also koftgaree. [Urdū (Pers.) *kuft-*, *koftgarī* 'beaten-work,' f. *kuftan* to beat + *garī* making, work.] A kind of Indian damascene-work, in which a pattern traced on steel is inlaid with gold.
1874 BIRDWOOD in Cole *Obj. Indian Art* 60 Even European tradesmen gave their orders for koftgaree through me. **1874** COLE *ibid.* 121 Armour of kuftgari.. was worn by the Sikh horsemen. **1887** HUNTER *Imp. Gaz. India* XII. 447 The famous *koftgári* or damascene work manufactured at Kotli.

kog, kogg(e, obs. ff. COG¹ and ².

‖**kogai** ('kəʊgaɪ). [Jap.] Environmental pollution in Japan.
1970 *New Yorker* 23 May 94 Although *kogai* is one of the most controversial and thoroughly covered topics in the Tokyo press, the daily seminars [on pollution] were closed to Japanese reporters. **1971** *Peace News* 17 Sept. 1 (*heading*) Basic theory of Kogai. *Ibid.*, 'Kogai' is the Japanese word which is used to identify the pollution problem. It cannot be literally translated, for it is also used to refer to environmental problems above and beyond simple pollution: factory noise, vibration, obstruction of sunlight, traffic congestion, water shortage, etc.

kogh, obs. f. COG *sb.*¹

koghe, koghwhe, obs. ff. COUGH.

‖**kogia** ('kəʊdʒɪə). [Mod.L.] A genus of pygmy sperm-whales.
1898 F. T. BULLEN *Cruise Cachalot* x. (1900) 127 It was but a school of kogia or 'short-headed' cachalots. **1900** *Daily News* 22 Mar. 6/3 One of the whales, known as the Kogia, is peculiar from the inferior position of its mouth. This gives to the creature,.. a curiously shark-like aspect.

kohekohe ('kɔhekɔhe, kəʊɪ'kəʊɪ). *N.Z.* [Maori.] A deciduous tree, *Dysoxylum spectabile*, of the family Meliaceæ, which has pinnate leaves and panicles of fragrant white flowers.
1835 W. YATE *Acct. N.Z.* (ed. 2) ii. 48 Kohekohe (*Laurus kohekohe*).—A fine handsome tree, with a trunk free of branches to a height of forty feet. **1855** H. R. RICHMOND *Let.* 11 Aug. in *Richmond-Atkinson Papers* (1960) I. iv. 173 There is a beautiful view of the splendid kohekohe bush on your ridge. **1910** L. COCKAYNE *N.Z. Plants* iii. 29 In some few cases the flowers of a tree are produced on the thick branches, as in the kohekohe (*Dysoxylum spectabile*), and not, as usual, from amongst the leaves. **1950** *N.Z. Jrnl. Agric.* Sept. 215/3 The main-range forest, consisting of tawa, beech, rimu.. kohekohe. **1966** *Encycl. N.Z.* II. 234/2 Kohekohe is a medium-sized tree usually 30–40 ft in height, with a trunk 1–3 ft in diameter.

‖**koh-i-noor** ('kəʊhɪnʊə(r)). [Pers. *kōh-i nūr* mountain (*kōh*) of light (*nūr*).] An Indian diamond, famous for its size and history, which became one of the British Crown jewels on the annexation of the Punjaub in 1849; hence, *allusively*, any magnificent large diamond; *fig.* something that is the most precious or most superb *of* its kind.
1849 THACKERAY *Pendennis* lxvi, Miss Laura Bell.. had such a sparkling and brilliant koh-i-noor in her bosom, as is even more precious than that famous jewel. **1863** A. B. GROSART *Small Sins* (ed. 2) 34 The tiniest flaw or fracture in a diamond vitiates the whole gem—be it a very Koh-i-noor. **1892** *19th Cent.* Feb. 213 The great kohinoor of reciprocated affection. **1897** *Westm. Gaz.* 23 June 2/3 A scene at once so varied, so magnificent... It is, verily, the Koh-i-Noor of spectacles.

‖**kohl**¹ ('koːh(ə)l, kəʊl). Also 8 kohhel, 9 kochhel, kohol, cohol. [Arab. *kuḥ'l*, *koḥ'l*; see ALCOHOL.] A powder used in the East to darken the eyelids, etc., usually consisting of finely powdered antimony.
1799 W. G. BROWNE *Trav. Africa*, etc. xxi. 318 If any thing be applied in these *flussioni*.. it is generally *kôhhel* (calx of tin mixed with sheep's fat). **1817** MOORE *Lalla R., Veiled Proph.* 11, Others mix the Kohol's jetty die, To give that long, dark languish to the eye. **1875** EMERSON *Lett. & Soc. Aims* viii. 195 The cohol, the cosmetic by which pearls and eyebrows are indelibly stained black. **1877** A. B. EDWARDS *Up Nile* viii. 215 Their eyes were blackened round with Kohl.
attrib. **1900** *19th Cent.* Feb. 319 The Louvre possesses a beautiful Kohl pot.
Hence **kohl** *v. trans.*, to darken with kohl. So **kohled** *ppl. a.*
1947 *Penguin New Writing* XXIX. 10 Altogether the face.. of an actor roughed and kohled. **1964** *Punch* 26 Feb. 298/2 She had appeared.. in her most glamorous *sari*.. eyelids kohl-ed. **1971** R. DENTRY *Encounter at Kharmel* (1973) x. 183 Ten-year-old boy sopranos with kohl-ed eyes.

kohl², abbrev. of next.
1880 *Daily News* 18 Oct. 3/1 No bright green leaf of beet or turnip, or paler tops of kohl or swede.

‖**kohlrabi, kohl-rabi** (kəʊl'rɑːbɪ). Also *erron.* khol-. [G. *kohlrabi* (also formerly *kol-*, *kal(i)-*, *kaulirabi*, and dial. *koll(e)râwî*) 16th c. ad. It. *cavoli* (or *cauli*) *rape*, pl. of *cavolo rapa* (F. *chou-rave*) 'cole-rape'; the first element being assimilated to G. *kohl* (earlier ad. L. *caulis*, COLE *sb.*¹).] A cabbage with a turnip-shaped stem, varieties of which are cultivated as food for cattle in England, and as a vegetable in India and Germany; the turnip-cabbage.
1807 VANCOUVER *Agric. Devon* (1813) 191 The khol rabi, or above ground turnip cabbage. **1808** J. C. CURWEN *Hints Econ. Feeding* 50 The ground was cropped with.. one [acre] of kohlrabi. **1851** STEPHENS *Bk. of Farm* (ed. 2) II. 88/2 Two varieties of Kohl rabi are cultivated—the green and the purple. **1887** *Times* (weekly ed.) 9 Sept. 17/1 A large breadth of kohl-rabi, which was a fair plant. **1899** RIDER HAGGARD in *Longm. Mag.* 512 The kohlrabi are coming up on the new-drained field.

Kohlrausch ('kəʊlraʊʃ). *Physical Chem.* [The name of Friedrich Wilhelm *Kohlrausch* (1840–1910), German physicist.] ***Kohlrausch's law***: that the equivalent electrical conductivity of an electrolyte at infinite dilution may be represented as the sum of two constants, viz. the ionic mobilities of the cation and the anion respectively.
1888 *Jrnl. Chem. Soc.* LIV. 331 Kohlrausch's law that the conductivity of a neutral salt may be represented as a sum of two constants, one of which depends on the nature of the acid and the other on that of the base. **1924** H. J. CREIGHTON *Princ. & Applications Electrochem.* v. 91 This additive relationship.. is called Kohlrausch's law or 'the law of the independent migration of ions'. **1964** G. I. BROWN *Introd. Physical Chem.* xxxiii. 369 The immediate usefulness of Kohlrausch's law is that it provides a method for finding the Λ_∞ [*sc.* the equivalent conductivity at infinite dilution] value for weak electrolytes from Λ_∞ measurements on strong electrolytes. **1969** R. A. HORNE *Marine Chem.* iii. 117 Kohlrausch's law.. of the additivity of conductivities.. is valid only in the limiting case. Solutions of finite concentration exhibit an appreciable departure from the law.

Kohs block (kəʊz blɒk). *Psychol.* Also Kohs' block. [f. the name of Samuel *Kohs* (b. 1890), U.S. psychologist.] One of a set of coloured cubes used in psychiatric testing with which the subject is required to reproduce patterns presented to him.
1930 *Child Development* I. 341/2 The Kohs block design test was given to 29 children in the Child Institute of Johns Hopkins University. **1941** *Jrnl. Appl. Psychol.* XXV. 420 The Kohs Block Designs test.. has found extensive application in clinical psychological work. **1954** A. ANASTASI *Psychol. Testing* x. 245 In the Kohs Block Design.., the subject is presented with a set of identical one-inch cubes, whose six sides are painted red, blue, yellow, white, yellow-and-blue, and red-and-white, respectively. Colored designs are presented on each of 17 test cards, the subject being required to reproduce each design by assembling the proper blocks. **1964** M. CRITCHLEY *Developmental Dyslexia* ix. 57 Constructional tasks.. include the assembling of jig-saw puzzles, a game which may not be easy for some of these dyslexics. This difficulty is readily assessed by the test of Kohs' blocks, where some dyslexics fare badly.

‖**kohua** ('kɔːhʊa). *N.Z.* [Maori *kōhua.*] **a.** A Maori oven. **b.** A three-legged iron pot or kettle. Cf. *go-ashore* (c) (GO *v.* VIII).
1843 E. DIEFFENBACH *Trav. N.Z.* II. iv. 43 The native oven, *hangi* or *kohua*, made in the well-known manner with heated stones. **1901** A. A. GRACE in D. M. Davin *N.Z. Short Stories* (1953) 53 Soon the *kohua* was sizzling over a bright fire. **1905** W. B. *Where White Man Treads* 72 The last day of all he [*sc.* Captain Cook] gave Toia another pot, and.. with much pointing at it, said: 'Now go ashore.' So we took that to be its name; for do we not call it at this distant day a 'kohua'? (corruption of 'go ashore'). **1949** P. BUCK *Coming of Maori* (1950) II. i. 112 The early trade goods included three-legged iron pots which from their function were also termed *kohua*.

koi (kɔɪ). [Jap.] A local name in Japan for the common carp, *Cyprinus carpio.*
1727 J. G. SCHEUCHZER tr. *Kæmpfer's Hist. Japan* I. I. 136 *Koi* is another sort of it [*sc.* Steenbrass], which also resembles a Carp. **1875** H. W. BATES *Illustr. Trav.* VI. 140/2 Some *koi*, a coarse-tasted fish of the carp species. **1884** tr. *J. J. Rein's Japan* I. viii, 197 The most conspicuous [of the Cyprinodontidæ] in size and importance are the Carp or Koi (Cyprinus carpio L.) and the Japanese Crucian or Funa. *Ibid.* II. ii. 440 In every house in which during the previous year a boy has been born, a flag waves on a long bamboo staff, consisting of a large painted koi (carp) of paper. **1896** L. HEARN *Kokoro* vi. 89 The real koi, the great Japanese carp, ascends swift rivers against the stream. **1971** S. ELIOVSON *Gardening Jap. Way* 86 The carp (*koi*) is a symbol of strength and perseverance.

‖**koi-cha** ('kɔɪtʃə). Also koi cha, koicha. [Jap.] In Japan, powdered tea mixed to a thick brew and drunk ceremonially.
1727 J. G. SCHEUCHZER tr. *Kæmpfer's Hist. Japan* II. App. I. 15 This powder is mix'd with hot water into a thin pulp, which is afterwards sip'd. This Tea is call'd *Koitsjaa*, that is, thick Tea, by way of distinction from the thinner Tea, made only by infusion, and it is that which all the rich people and great men in Japan daily drink. **1890** B. H. CHAMBERLAIN *Things Japanese* 338 The resulting beverage resembles pea-soup in colour and consistency. There is a thicker kind called *koi-cha*, and a thinner kind called *usu-cha*. **1960** B. LEACH *Potter in Japan* iii. 66 That was the first time I have had 'Koi Cha'. It is a variant of the Tea Ceremony in which the powdered tea is mixed to a thick brew and the bowl is passed from hand to hand. **1965** W. SWAAN *Jap. Lantern* xvi. 182 It is *koi-cha*, or thick tea, made from leaves which have been ground to a powder. **1970** J. KIRKUP *Japan behind Fan* 206 The host is ready to serve his guests with the *koi-cha*, or thick tea.

‖**koi hai**, var. QUI-HY.

koilonychia (kɔɪləʊ'nɪkɪə). *Path.* [a. G. *koilonychia* (J. Heller 1897, in *Dermatol. Zeitschr.* IV. 490), f. Gr. κοῖλ-ος hollow + ὄνυξ, -υχος nail + -IA¹.] A condition of the finger-nails in which the outer surfaces are concave instead of convex; spoon-nail.
1902 *Trans. Med. Assoc. Missouri* XLV. 157 The disease.. is known technically as koilonychia and ordinarily as 'spoon' nails... Koilonychia may be observed in one or more of the nails of the fingers of one or both hands. **1934** J. M. VAUGHAN *Anaemias* iii. 43 Koilonychia is not found in 'splenic anaemia', while some degree is extremely common in idiopathic hypochromic anaemia. **1970** *Jrnl. Pediatrics* LXXVII. 1057/2 There is a significant correlation between koilonychia and iron deficiency in infants 9 to 13 months of age.

koine ('kɔɪniː). [Gr. κοινή, fem. sing. of κοινός common, ordinary.] **a.** Originally the common literary dialect of the Greeks (ἡ κοινὴ διάλεκτος) from the close of classical Attic to the Byzantine era. Now extended to include any language or dialect in regular use over a wide area in which different languages or dialects are, or were, in use locally.
[**1886** *Encycl. Brit.* XXI. 653/1 As might be expected, this κοινή, like the κοινή of the Greeks, has a comparatively limited vocabulary.] **1913** D. B. DURHAM *Vocab. Menander* 8 The year 600 A.D. is a convenient date at which to divide the Koine from the Greek of the middle ages. **1926** *Germanic Rev.* I. IV. 297 Assuming that all our dialects had given way to a High German *koiné*, we should still recognize the characteristic distinctions of the former dialects. **1927** A. H. MCNEILE *Introd. New Testament* 278 Such [constructions] as were rapidly making their way into the *Koine* Greek. **1933** *Amer. Speech* VIII. Oct. 5/1 The American *koiné* in eliminating the extreme variations in English dialects nevertheless absorbed enough of their peculiarities to make it a highly varied unity. **1956** A. TOYNBEE *Historian's Approach to Relig.* xix. 270 In the first century of the Christian Era the dissemination of the books of the New Testament in the Attic *koinê*—the 'standard Greek' of the day—ensured their finding readers as far afield.. as Britain.. and India. **1958** D. WHITELOCK *Changing Currents Anglo-Saxon Stud.* 6 The general use of the West Saxon literary *koine* in the tenth and eleventh centuries. **1964** S. M. ERVIN-TRIPP in J. A. Fishman *Readings Sociol. of Lang.* (1968) 197 Superposed varieties [of speech] include many types, from occupational argots to koines used for trade and regional communication, such as Melanesian Pidgin and Swahili. **1965** *Times Lit. Suppl.* 22 Apr. 317/2 A 'disc-jockey' found himself saying 'take time *out*', in accordance with the conventional mid-Atlantic koine these people have to use. **1966** K. H. ALBROW in C. E. Bazell *In Memory of J. R. Firth* 2 F. Roberts is in the habit of speaking standard Welsh with a Northern accent as his Welsh koine except at home.
b. A set of cultural or other attributes common to various groups. Also *attrib.*
1924 A. J. B. WACE in *Cambr. Anc. Hist.* II. xvi. 466 During the last two centuries, at least, of the Mycenaean dominion in Greece and the Aegean, there was a cultural *koiné*, and it is at least likely that there was a linguistic *koiné* as well. **1939** J. D. S. PENDLEBURY *Archaeol. Crete* vi. 358 Crete had entered the Hellenistic *koine* and its individuality is nearly lost. **1962** *Economist* 28 Apr. 340/3 The

Mauretanian and Numidian kingdoms..were centres of an Afro-European 'koine'.

||**koinonia** (kɔɪ'nəʊnɪə). *Theol.* [Gr. κοινωνία communion, fellowship.] Christian fellowship or communion, either with God or, more commonly, with fellow Christians.

1907 W. P. Du Bose *Gospel according to St. Paul* xvii. 243 As the first two truths of our faith in Christ might be called those of the Father and the Son, so the third may be designated that of the Spirit. Or, to put it in the other way, as the first two may be called those of the divine love and the divine grace, so the third may be named that of the divine *koinonia*. **1920** 'W. S. Palmer' *Christianity & Christ* 177 Thinking of the Church I am reminded of the 'Koinonia', the fellowship of early Christians which came of the Pentecostal inflowing of the Spirit of God. **1938** *Theology* XXXVI. 211 The Church's tradition of social and economic justice; the primitive koinonia, the medieval just price and condemnation of usury. **1949** *Scottish Jrnl. Theol.* II. 67 We exist in the Image of the Living God who Himself confronts Himself to become one God in the *koinonia* of the Holy Spirit. **1967** J. Macquarrie *Dict. Christian Ethics* 73/1 The point of departure for Christian thinking about ethics is the concrete reality in the world of a community, a *koinonia*, called into being and action by Jesus of Nazareth.

kointise, koir, obs. ff. quaintise, coir.

||**koji** ('kəʊdʒɪ). [Jap.] An enzyme preparation derived from various moulds, esp. *Aspergillus oryzæ* and closely related species, and used to bring about the fermentation involved in the production of saké, soy sauce, etc.

1878 R. W. Atkinson in *Nature* 12 Sept. 522/2 The rice-grains are found to be covered with large quantities of fine hair-like threads, the mycelium of the fungus added. In this state it is called 'kōji'. **1926** Thom & Church *Aspergilli* vi. 64 Koji in its various forms is used in several fermentations. **1953** J. Ramsbottom *Mushrooms & Toadstools* xxiii. 275 The Koji for the enormous fermentation industries of Japan is *Aspergillus Oryzae*, or closely allied species. **1960** A. E. Bender *Dict. Nutrition* 122/1 Takadiastase. Or Koji, an enzyme preparation produced by growing the fungus, *Aspergillus oryzae*, on bran, leaching the culture mass with water and precipitating with alcohol. **1965** Raper & Fennell *Genus Aspergillus* xviii. 358 *A. flavus*..had been encountered frequently among cultures received from Japanese workers as isolates from commercial inoculum, or 'koji', for fermentation industries. *Ibid.* 391 The manufacture of saké is dependent upon the use of *A. oryzae* for the preparation of the koji used to digest rice starch and protein.

kojic ('kəʊdʒɪk), *a. Chem.* [f. koji: see -ic.] *kojic acid*: 5-hydroxy-2-hydroxymethyl-γ-pyrone, $HO{\cdot}C_5H_2O_2{\cdot}CH_2OH$, a crystalline pyrone derivative produced from dextrose by some fungi of the genus *Aspergillus* and having mild antibacterial properties.

[**1912** T. Yabuta in *Orig. Communications 8th Internat. Congr. Appl. Chem.* XXV. 455, I have given the name 'Koji acid' to this substance.] **1913** *Jrnl. Chem. Soc.* CIV. i. 180 Kojic acid..obtained from finely powdered *Aspergillus oryzae* forms colourless needles or prisms. **1947** *New Biol.* II. 88 Kojic acid is a mild disinfectant of the same order of activity as phenol. **1971** *Jrnl. Trop. Med. & Hygiene* LXXIV. 164/1 Kojic acid production which is supposed to be a constant property of *A[spergillus] flavus*.

kok, obs. form of cock, cook.

||**kokako** ('kɔːkakɔ). [Maori.] The New Zealand Wattle-crow or Wattle-bird, *Glaucopis cinerea* and *G. wilsoni*.

1873 Butler *Birds N. Zeal.* (1888) I. 3 In disposition the Kokako inherits the true characteristics of the Crow family. *Ibid.* II. 316 The rich flute-notes of the Kokako..in the low timber at the edge of the forest. **1882** T. H. Potts *Out in Open* 194 (Morris) The kokako loving a moist temperature will probably soon forsake its ancient places of resort.

kokall, obs. f. cockle.

kokam, var. of cocum[1].

kokama, var. kukama.

kokanee ('kəʊkænɪ). Also kickininee. [ad. Interior Salish *kikinee*.] A landlocked dwarf subspecies, *Oncorhynchus nerka kennerlyi*, of the sockeye salmon.

1875 in *Okanagan Hist. Soc. Rep.* (1953) 17 There we would fill our basket with the shining kik-e-ninnies. **1937** *Kootenay & City of Nelson, B.C.* 62 The Kokanee or 'Silver Trout', which is in reality a landlocked Sockeye salmon abounds in the larger lakes of the districts. **1940** *Nature* 3 Aug. 172/1 Attempts to explain the origin of kokanee (a variety of sockeye salmon) were made. **1963** *New Scientist* 31 Jan. 228/2 The kokanee, *Oncorhynchus nerka kennerlyi*, might increase overall production when cultured with trout. **1963** *Globe & Mail* (Toronto) 2 Mar. 8/6 The kokanee (or kickininee) is a sockeye salmon that does not migrate to the ocean. Its life span is similar to that of the sockeye in that it returns to the nursery stream after three or four years, at which time it weighs about a pound. **1965** A. J. McClane *Standard Fishing Encycl.* 457/2 The kokanee was originally found in Oregon, Idaho, Washington, British Columbia, and northward into Alaska... In Japan it is found in Lake Akan in northern Hokkaido... Morphologically the kokanee and sockeye are identical. **1970** D. Waterfield *Continental Waterboy* i. 2 Enabling the silver trout to kokanee..to reach the formerly inaccessible river.

kokatrice, obs. f. cockatrice.

koke = *quoke*, obs. pa. t. of quake *v.*; obs. f. cook *sb.*

†'**kokell**, *a. Obs.* [Cf. cockle *a.*, cockle *v.*[2]] ? Unsteady, wavering, shaky.

a **1400-50** *Alexander* 2588 (MS.D) Commandes hys knyghtez ouer to carye; þai hed kokell hertes, Seghen þe streme be so styff, þai stoned [*A.* stonaid] þe helder.

†**koken**. *Sc. Obs. rare*⁻¹. [? a. F. *coquin*.] ? Rogue, rascal.

1500-20 Dunbar *Poems* lxiii. 48 Thrimlaris and thriftaris [? thristaris] as thay war woid; Kokenis, and kennis na man of gude.

kokeney, obs. f. cockney.

||**koker** ('kəʊkə(r)). *Guyana.* Also khoker. [Du.] A sluice-gate, a lock-gate; the narrow stretch of water between such gates.

1851 J. A. Tinne *Rep. Outfall Drainage Brit. Guiana* 11 By means of a koker or sluice near the sea, the drains are emptied at low tide and the sluices are shut when the tide rises higher than the water in the drains. **1893** J. Rodway *Hand-bk. Brit. Guiana* 9 Through openings in the front dams, closed at high water by marine gates called kokers, the canals empty themselves into the sea. **1944** *Drainage & Irrigation Schemes* (Brit. Guiana Bureau of Publicity) 3 Investigations have to be made concerning..Capacity of sluices and kokers. *Ibid.* 5 The surplus water being discharged through..kokers when the tide is sufficiently low. **1951** E. A. Mittelholzer *Shadows move among Them* ii. ix. 240 The ditch was wide and..where it entered the stream stood what seemed to be a sluice-gate. 'That's the *koker*... It's a Dutch word... The *koker* is left open so that the tide can rise and fill the ditch... Then at high tide the *koker* is shut.' **1958** J. Carew *Black Midas* iv. 61 The procession moved out of sight down the path by the khoker and towards the river. **1965** 'Lauchmonen' *Old Thom's Harvest* iii. 34 The dereck of the first koker from the sea toppled over.

koker, obs. f. cocker.

kokerboom ('kʊəkəbʊəm). *S. Afr.* [Afrikaans, f. Du. *koker* quiver + *boom* tree.] A large aloe, *Aloe dichotoma*, the size of a small tree, whose branches were formerly used to make quivers for arrows; = *quiver-tree* (quiver *sb.*[1] 2).

1774 F. Masson *Jrnl.* 2 Nov. in *Phil. Trans R. Soc.* (1776) LXVI. 309 We found a new species of aloe here, called by the Dutch Koker Boom, of which the Hottentots make quivers to hold their arrows. **1812** W. J. Burchell *Jrnl.* 14 May in *Trav. S. Afr.* (1824) II. vii. 199 The natives more towards the western coast, frequently use the branches of the *Aloë dichotoma*, which is therefore called by the Hottentots and Colonists, *kokerboom* or quiver tree. **1920** F. C. Cornell *Glamour of Prospecting* 116 We outspanned about sunset on an open plateau covered with vegetation and studded with many of the queer looking aloes known as *koker boomen*, or 'quiver trees'. **1950** *Cape Argus* 5 Aug. 7/5 As you drive northwards through the mountains to Springbok you may see that weird tree-aloe, the kokerboom, flowering beside the road. **1959** J. D. Clark *Prehist. S. Afr.* ix. 226 The arrows were usually kept in a quiver made from leather..or bark, in particular the bark of the 'Kokerboom' tree which is a species of aloe. **1974** *Eastern Province Herald* (S. Afr.) 28 Jan. 11 Those who lived in houses built of Kokerboom trunks stood back and watched as..the flames leapt and crackled through the wooden structures.

kokerel(le, kokery, obs. ff. cockerel, cookery.

||**kokeshi** ('kɔːkeʃi). [Jap.] A kind of wooden Japanese doll.

1959 R. Kirkbride *Tamiko* xxii. 172 He bought Tamiko a kokeshi doll. **1970** J. Kirkup *Japan behind Fan* 63 Some stalls were selling celluloid masks and *kokeshi*. **1973** R. Littell *Defection of A. J. Lewinter* iv. 19 Sarah's 'things'—sea shells..Japanese *kokeshi* dolls, paperweights.

kokeswayne, obs. f. cockswain.

koket, var. cocket *sb.*[2] *Obs.*, leavened bread.

kokewold(e, obs. forms of cuckold *sb.*[1]

||**kokila** ('kəʊkɪlə). Also 8 cocila, 9 kokeela. [Skr. *kokila*.] = koel.

1791 Sir W. Jones *Lett.* (1821) II. 157 (Stanf.) The cocila sing charmingly here in the spring. **1812** Maria Graham *Jrnl. Resid. India* 22 The *mina*, the kokeela, and a few other birds of song. **1931** L. H. Myers *Prince Jali* iii. 37 A kokila-bird was sounding its single, inexpressive note.

kokkewiet (kɒkə'viːt). *S. Afr.* Also cock-o-veet, kook-a-vic. [Afrikaans, echoic.] = bokmakierie.

1896 E. Clairmonte *Africander* vii. 126 The kook-a-vic was piping his shrill note in a bush hard by. 'Kook-a-vic, kook-a-vic, kook-a-vic.' **1926** O. Schreiner *From Man to Man* 49 A cock-o-veet came flying up to her. *Ibid.*, Kokkewiet: The Bush-shrike, a very handsome bird with resonant call notes of great beauty. **1936** E. L. Gill *First Guide S. Afr. Birds* 49 Bokmakierie, Bacbakiri, Kokkewiet. .. The calls are duets by the inseparable pair. **1970** *Standard Encycl. S. Afr.* II. 401/1 Bokmakierie..is sometimes locally referred to as bakbakiri, kokkewiet, janpierewiet or bush-shrike.

kokko, var. koko[2].

koklas(s ('kəʊkləs). Also cocklass, kuklass. [Nepalese, var. of *pokras, pukras*.] The pheasant, *Pucrasia macrolopha*, several subspecies of which are found in the Himalayas and China and have been introduced elsewhere.

1864 T. C. Jerdon *Birds of India* III. 525 The Cocklass is of a rather retired and solitary disposition. *Ibid.* 524 *Koklas* or *Kokla*, in various hill dialects. **1898** *Ibis* Jan. 39 The Koklass was not uncommon in the forest above Gund. **1922** *Blackw. Mag.* Mar. 323/2 In the woods below a kuklass crowed hoarsely. **1952** Bates & Lowther *Breeding Birds Kashmir* 278 The Koklas is the commonest pheasant in Kashmir. **1965** P. Wayre *Wind in Reeds* xv. 219, I recognised them at once as Koklass Pheasants. *Ibid.*, Koklass are high mountain birds and come from the western Himalayas and North Eastern Tibet across to Eastern and Northern China. **1974** *Country Life* 25 July 244/3 From a dealer's shop in London, came a pair of Koklass pheasants ..[which] the Trust succeeded in breeding..in captivity.

||**koko**[1]. Also coco, cocco. [*Koko*, native name in Fanti lang.] The taro-plant, *Colocasia esculenta*, of West Africa; = cocoyam.

1874 C. A. Gordon *Life Gold Coast* 30 Another root that was used for the table deserves to be mentioned;..their ordinary name, indeed, was Cocos. **1897** Mary Kingsley *W. Africa* 292 Koko is better than yam, I may remark, because it is heavier. *Ibid.* 601 A plantation of giant kokos mid-leg deep in most excellent fine mould. **1938** *Jrnl. R. Anthrop. Inst.* LXVIII. 125 These [*sc.* cultivated crops] are ..koko yams (*Colocasia antiquorum*), maize, [etc.].

koko[2] ('kəʊkəʊ). Also kokoh, kokko. [Burmese name for the tree.] The brown hardwood obtained from *Albizia lebbeck*, a tropical, deciduous tree of the family Leguminosæ, or the tree itself.

1862 E. Balfour *Timber Trees of India* (ed. 2) 30/2 In the Prome district a special tax was levied on the felling of 'Kokoh' and 'Padouk' under the Burmese rule. **1881** J. S. Gamble *Man. Indian Timbers* 157 *A[lbizzia] Lebbeck*... The Siris Tree. Vern[acular]... Kokoh, Burm. **1911** J. H. Holland *Useful Plants Nigeria* II. 299 *Albizzia Lebbek*... East Indian Walnut, Kokoh or Kokka (Rangoon). Wild in Tropical Asia..; distributed to Tropical Africa. **1930** *Observer* 29 June 18/2 In respect of woods the building itself is an exhibition: every piece of joinery..has come from India... Most of the floors are of a pleasant brown wood called koko. **1937** J. M. Dalziel *Useful Plants W. Trop. Afr.* 211 *Albizzia Lebbek*... The timber is sometimes called East Indian Walnut, and is marketed as Kokko or Koko. **1947** J. C. Rich *Materials & Methods Sculpture* x. 290 *Koko* or East Indian Walnut is a hard, dense, close grained tropical wood imported from Burma. It is dark brown and is usually available in log form. **1956** *Handbk. Hardwoods* (Forest Prod. Res. Lab.) 128 Kokko varies considerably in size according to locality. *Ibid.* 129 Kokko is said to be used for sliced veneers and in the furniture industry.

||**kokoon** (kəʊ'kuːn), **kokong** (kəʊ'kɒŋ), *sb.*[1] [Sechuana *kgokoñ* or *khokong*.] A large antelope (*Antilope taurina*) of South Africa.

1806 Sir J. Barrow *Journ. Leetakoo* 409 It was called by the Booshuanas the Kokoon. **1822** Burchell *Trav.* II. x. 278 The Bichuanas call it Kokun (Kokoon), or rather, with a nasal sound of the N, Kokung (Kokoong). **1834** *Penny Cycl.* II. 91/1 The habits and manners of the kokoon closely resemble those of the gnu, but it possesses neither the speed, spirit, nor activity of that animal. **1857** Livingstone *Trav.* vii. 135 The kokong or gnu, kama or hartebeest..and the giraffe.

||**kokoon** (kəʊ'kuːn), *sb.*[2] [Sinhalese.] A large forest tree, *Kokoona zeylanica*, growing in the central provinces of Ceylon.

1866 *Treas. Bot.* 650/1.

kokopan, var. cocopan.

||**kokopu** ('kɔːkɔpʊ). *N.Z.* [Maori.] A small freshwater fish, *Galaxias fasciatus*.

1886 R. A. Sherrin *Handbk. Fishes N.Z.* 138 'Kokopu', Dr Hector says, is the general Maori name for several very common fishes in the New Zealand streams and lakes, belonging to the family of *Galaxiidæ*. **1929** W. Martin *N.Z. Nature Bk.* I. xix. 175 The Kokopu or 'Native Trout' (*Galaxias fasciatus*) is known from all parts of New Zealand south of the Bay of Islands. **1949** P. Buck *Coming of Maori* (1950) ii. viii. 236 The *kokopu* do not run until March. **1962** *Post-Primary School Bull.* (Wellington, N.Z.) XV. i. 27 Kokopu, *Galaxias fasciatus*, live in most of our streams and smaller rivers. **1966** *Encycl. N.Z.* I. 675/2 *Galaxias fasciatus*, the kokopu or banded galaxias, is found throughout the country.

||**kokowai** ('kɔːkɔːwai). *N.Z.* [Maori.] Red ochre, burnt red clay (see quot. 1949).

1836 J. A. Wilson *Jrnl.* July in *Missionary Life & Work N.Z.* (1889) iii. 43 Two large totara posts..daubed with *kokowai*. **1840** J. S. Polack *Manners & Customs New Zealanders* I. xix. 210 The *powâka* is kept neatly painted red with *kokowai*. **1845** E. J. Wakefield *Adventure N.Z.* I. 124 A carved post which was painted with *kokowai*, or red ochre. *Ibid.* II. 87 The *kokowai*-painted monuments which I have mentioned. **1878** *Trans. N.Z. Inst.* XI. 75 *Kokowai* is a kind of pigment, burnt, dried, and mixed with shark-liver oil. **1905** W. B. *Where White Man Treads* 7 The rafters painted with kokowai (iron-ore rust), for a ground colour in red, and adorned with intricate volutes in pipe-clay for white. **1949** P. Buck *Coming of Maori* (1950) ii. xiii. 319 The decorative painting of woodwork did not advance very far in Polynesia. In New Zealand, red ochre, or haematite, was termed *karamea* and after it was burnt and powdered it became *kokowai* or *horu*. The *kokowai* was mixed with shark oil to form a red paint. **1963** T. Barrow *Life & Work Maori Carver* 28 The red clay or haematite used by the Maori for paint was first burnt, then powdered, when it became *kokowai*.

kok-saghyz (kɒksa'gɪz). [ad. Russ. *kok-sagÿz*, of Turkic origin.] A kind of dandelion,

Taraxacum koksaghyz, whose roots contain a latex used for making rubber.

1932 *Bull. Rubber Growers' Assoc.* Sept. 534 The Kak-Saugyiz, gave a material with even more resilience, but it has a lower content of caoutchouc. **1945** K. E. Knorr *World Rubber* x. 182 Experiments with *kok-saghyz*, the Russian dandelion, and *Cryptostegia* were soon abandoned. **1954** H. J. Stern *Rubber* i. 18 Kok saghyz (*Taraxacum kok saghyz.* Rodin). This plant was discovered in 1931... The roots contain about 90 per cent. of the total rubber in the plant. *Ibid.*, The amount of information [about Krim Saghyz] available is less than in the case of Kok Saghyz. **1959** J. C. T. Uphof *Dict. Econ. Plants* 354/2 *Taraxacum kok-saghyz* Rodin., Kok-saghyz. (Compositae).—Herbaceous perennial. Turkestan. Roots are a source of rubber. Cultivated in some parts of Russia. **1971** Roff & Scott *Fibres, Films, Plastics & Rubbers* 681/2 (*index*) Kok-saghyz.

koktaite (ˈkɒktəaɪt). *Min.* [ad. Czech *koktait* (J. Sekanina 1948, in *Acta Acad. Sci. Nat. Moravo-Silesiacae* XX. I. 1), f. the name of Jaroslav *Kokta*, Czech mineralogist (see quot. 1948): see -ite[1].] Hydrated calcium ammonium sulphate, $(NH_4)_2Ca(SO_4)_2.H_2O$, occurring in acicular monoclinic crystals and identical with artificial ammonium syngenite.

1948 *Mineral Abstr.* X. 352 Artificial ammonium-syngenite..has the composition $(NH_4)_2Ca(SO_4)_2.H_2O$ (analysis by J. Kokta..), and agrees in the optical data with the mineral, named koktaite, from Žeravice. **1968** I. Kostov *Mineral.* II. ix. 504 Syngenite and koktaite are isotypic.

‖**koku** (ˈkoːku). [Jap.] **a.** A Japanese unit of capacity equal to ten *to*, used for liquids and solids (esp. of rice as a monetary measure); equivalent to approximately 39·7 gallons (180 litres) or 4·96 bushels. **b.** A Japanese unit of capacity equal to ten cubic *shaku*, used for vessels; equivalent to approximately 9·8 cubic feet (0·278 cubic metres).

1727 J. G. Scheuchzer tr. *Kæmpfer's Hist. Japan* I. II. v. 199 The Emperor..order'd, that three *koku's* of rice should be given, or lent to any family, that stood in need of it. **1871** A. B. Mitford *Tales Old Japan* I. 96 His revenue of eight million kokus reverted to the Government. *Ibid.*, The koku of rice, in which all revenue is calculated, is of varying value. **1892** Kipling *Lett. of Travel* (1920) 42 Five Japanese dollars (fifteen shillings) per *koku* of 330 lbs. **1896** L. Hearn *Kokoro* x. 170 The seat of a daimyō of three hundred thousand koku. **1904** *Daily Chron.* 30 Mar. 4/5 Jeyas.. reduced the civil list to 9,000 kokus, or 44,500 bushels of rice, which was the way then that revenue was paid. **1911** *Encycl. Brit.* XV. 193/1 Any vessel having a capacity of more than 500 *koku* (150 tons). **1931** G. B. Sansom *Japan* II. viii. 168 Any who could produce from the new fields one thousand *koku* of rice were promised lifelong immunity to tax. **1938** D. T. Suzuki *Zen Buddhism & its Influence on Jap. Culture* I. vii. 153 Hideyoshi gave him three thousand *koku* of rice for his service to him as tea-master.

kokum, var. cocum[1].

kokur, obs. f. cocker *sb.*[1], a quiver.

kokylle, obs. f. cockle.

Kol (kəʊl). *India.* Also Col(e), Kole. [Of disputed origin.] Mundu-speaking tribes of Chota Nagpur and Bengal in India (see also quot. 1896); a member of any of these tribes. Also *attrib.* or as *adj.*, of or relating to any of these tribes or their languages.

1795 J. T. Blunt Jrnl. 2 Feb. in *Asiatick Res.* (1803) III. 61 Not wishing to injure the *Coles* by encamping on the little spots, which, with much care and toil, they had cleared..we took up our abode..in the jungle. **1827** R. Jenkins *Rep. Territories Rajah of Nagpore* ii. 30 The Koorkoo dialect is found to resemble that spoken by the Lurka Koles, on the frontier of Singbhoom. **1847** B. H. Hodgson *On Aborigines India* p. ii, The Kól or Dhánger race. *Ibid.* iii. 149 The Kóls are indeed, as enterprising as industrious. *Ibid.* iii. 150 Kól is an old and classical name, and the best I think for the great mass of aborigines intervening between the Bhils, the Gonds, and the Ganges—at least till we know them better. **1866** *Jrnl. Asiatic Soc. Bengal* XXXV. II. 154 The present population..are of the race best known to us by the name of 'Kol'. **1871** [see Dravidian *adj.*]. **1872** E. T. Dalton *Descr. Ethnol. Bengal* v. i. 125 The Kols rejecting all change adhered to their impurity of life. **1896** W. Crooke *Tribes & Castes N.W. Provinces & Oudh* III. 294 *Kol*, a Dravidian tribe found in considerable numbers along the Vindhya Kaimūr plateau. **1903** Risley & Gait *Rep. Census India 1901* I. 282 The Kol language has..two main dialects, Mundari and Ho. **1931** E. A. H. Blunt *Caste System N. India* xiv. 287 The Kol is a tribe of aboriginal jungle folk, akin to the Bengal Mundas. **1957** C. B. Mamoria *Tribal Demogr. India* iv. 62 In the iron-ore industry..the labour force..consists of largely Santhals and Kols.

kola[1]. A frequent spelling of cola, used to refer to two trees of the genus *Cola*, *C. acuminata* or *C. nitida*, or their seeds, also called kola nuts.

1830 Lindley *Nat. Syst. Bot.* 39 The Kola spoken of by African travellers. **1868** *Curtis's Bot. Mag.* XCIV. 5699 (*heading*) Kola-nut tree. *Ibid.*, The Kola has been introduced into the Royal Gardens, Kew. **1890** *Kew Bull.* 255 Kola nuts contain some constituent analogous to caffeine. **1932** J. Cary *Aissa Saved* xv. 82 A family of kola-nut traders, father, mother, sister, and two children, hurrying to Kolu to sell at good prices. **1937** J. M. Dalziel *Useful Plants W. Trop. Afr.* 101 Elephants eat the fruits of kola and damage the tree. *Ibid.* 103 Kola is generally supposed to contain about equal quantities of caffeine and theobromine. *Ibid.* 104 Amongst some peoples a kola tree is planted to commemorate a joyful event. **1957** M. Banton *W. Afr. City* ix. 170 That afternoon he will 'pin flour'—a small ceremony for which he will invite an *alfa* and some respected local Muslims to pray for the deceased; after praying they will eat kola and balls of rice flour mixed with sugar and water. **1964** E. Huxley *Back Street New Worlds* xiv. 141 Had I been a Nigerian, he'd have offered me a kola nut, symbol of hospitality among his people.

Kola[2] (ˈkəʊlə). *India.* (See quot. 1873.)

1873 E. Balfour *Cycl. India* (ed. 2) III. 255/1 *Kola*, Beng. A class of hindoos whose principal avocations are basket and mat-making. **1916** [see Kolam]. **1937** L. Bromfield *Rains Came* III. xxvii. 412 There were Kathis and Kolas.

kolach (ˈkɒlɑːtʃ). Also **kolache, kolachi, kolachy.** Pl. **kolache** (ˈkɒlɑːtʃiː), **kolaches.** [ad. Czech *koláč*, f. *kolo* wheel, circle.] A small tart or pie popular in Czechoslovakia, topped or filled with a sweet mixture, preserve, etc.

1918 W. Cather *My Antonia* (1926) v. i. 381 'Show him the spiced plums, mother. Americans don't have those,' said one of the older boys. 'Mother uses them to make *kolaches*,' he added. **1947** M. Given *Mod. Encycl. Cooking* I. 528 (*heading*) Fillings for kolachy. **1953** A. Heath *Internat. Cookery Bk.* 187 Cover the kolach with it [*sc.* pastry]..and bake in a hot oven. **1961** H Watney tr. *Břízová's Cooking Czech Way* 143 Kolache (flat fruit buns) and filled rolls made from yeast dough are typically Czech. **1967** Mrs. L. B. Johnson *White House Diary* 7 July (1970) 545 For dessert a typical specialty of the area—'kolaches', a rich pastry that has a center of dried apricots or prunes. **1969** O. Hesky *Sequin Syndicate* xviii. 169 Mamma's sent you some of her *kolachis.* I don't know if they'll let you eat them?

Kolam (ˈkəʊlɑːm). Also **Kolamb.** [Origin unknown.] In India, a group of people (whose name for themselves is *Kōlavar*) speaking a Dravidian language similar to that of the Parji of Bastar.

a **1863** S. Hislop *Papers Aboriginal Tribes Cent. Provinces* (1866) I. 10 The Kolâms and the common Gonds do not intermarry... Their dress is similar; but the Kolâm women wear fewer ornaments. **1885** E. Balfour *Cycl. India* (ed. 3) II. 593 *Kolam* or *Kolamb*, a Gond tribe, along the Kandi Konda or Pindi Hills, on the south of the Wardha, and along the table-land stretching east and north of Manikgarh, and thence south to Dantanpilly, running parallel to the right bank of the Pranhita... The Kolam race are found also in the Amraoti, Wun, and Maiker districts as a wild race. **1916** Russell & Lal *Tribes & Castes Cent. Provinces India* III. 521 Mr. Hīra Lāl suggests that the Kolāms may be connected with the Kolas,..who regard the Kolamallai hills as their original home. He further notes that the name of the era by which the calendar is reckoned on the Malabar coast is Kolamba.

Hence ˈ**Kolami**, the language spoken by these people.

a **1863** R. Temple in S. Hislop *Papers Aboriginal Tribes Cent. Provinces* (1866) II. p. i, The English words having been..classified, the design was to ascertain and record.. the equivalents in..Gondi, Gayeti,..Kolami. **1916** Russell & Lal *Tribes & Castes Cent. Provinces India* III. 520 The Kolāms..have a language of their own, called after them Kolāmi. **1968** *Encycl. Brit.* VII. 655/1 Five of the Central Dravidian languages..form a closely related group—Kolami, Naiki, Parji, Ollari and Poya Gadaba.

Kolarian (kəʊˈlɛərɪən). [f. *Kolar* (see quot. 1869) + -ian.] A non-Aryan linguistic stock of India, the Munda group. Also as *adj.*, of or pertaining to this stock.

1866 G. Campbell in *Jrnl. Asiatic Soc. Bengal* XXXV. II. 28, I propose then to call the northern tribes Kolarian or Coolee Aborigines. **1869** —— in *Jrnl. Ethnol. Soc. London* I. 130, I designate these tribes 'Kolarian' (as distinguished from the Dravidians), from the name Kol, Kolee or Coolee, applied to many of them, and the old name 'Kolar' by which India was known in very ancient times. **1915** Risley & Crooke *People of India* (ed. 2) i. 48 The hypothesis of the north-eastern origin of the Kolarians depends on the fancied recognition of Mongolian characteristics among the people of Chutia Nāgpur. **1923** A. L. Kroeber *Anthropol.* iii. 46 Typical representatives [of Indo-Australian people] are the Vedda of Ceylon; the Irula and some of the Kolarian tribes of India. **1928** V. G. Childe *Most Anc. East* iii. 52 Early Indian races, particularly the Dravidians, the Kolarians, and even the Veddahs of Ceylon. **1957** G. S. Ghurye *Mahadev Kolis* i. 6 Kolis of Bombay..do not show the slightest trace of Kolarian tongue in their languages. **1972** W. B. Lockwood *Panorama Indo-Europ. Lang.* 226 Munda or Kolarian are names given to a group of languages spoken today in the central part of India.

kolbasa, kolbasi, varr. kielbasa.

Kolbe (ˈkɒlbə). *Chem.* The name of A. W. H. *Kolbe* (1818–84), German chemist, used *attrib.* and in the possessive to designate two syntheses devised by him: (*a*) the electrolysis of a salt of a carboxylic acid, R·COOH, to yield a (substituted) paraffin R_2; and (*b*) the reaction between sodium phenoxide and carbon dioxide to yield sodium salicylate.

1885 *Jrnl. Chem. Soc.* XLVIII. 982 The successive reactions in Kolbe's process are then (1) the formation of sodium phenyl carbonate..; (2) the conversion of this substance into sodium salicylate..; and (3) the formation of disodium salicylate and phenol. **1915** *Chem. Abstr.* IX. 294 The K and NH_4 salts, on electrolysis, give first an alk. and later an acid reaction, the electrolysis probably proceeding in accordance with Kolbe's..reaction. **1926** J. Read *Text-bk. Org. Chem.* xxvi. 570 Kolbe's reaction is also given by other phenols. **1942** Fuson & Snyder *Org. Chem.* xi. 133 Still higher members [of the dibasic acid series] may be made by the Kolbe electrolysis of the potassium salt of an acid ester. **1951** I. L. Finar *Org. Chem.* I. xxviii. 557 The original industrial method of preparing salicylic acid was Kolbe's synthesis (1859)... The method now used is a modification of the Kolbe synthesis..known as the Kolbe-Schmidt method. It is carried out by heating sodium phenoxide with carbon dioxide at 120–140° under pressure. **1969** R. C. Denney *Named Org. Reactions* xxiii. 76 Woolford has used the Kolbe reaction to prepare long-chain ω, ω′-dibromohydrocarbons which can only be obtained with considerable difficulties by other methods.

kolbeckite (ˈkɒlbɛkaɪt). *Min.* [ad. G. *kolbeckit* (F. Edelmann 1926, in *Jahrb. f. d. Berg- u. Hüttenwesen in Sachsen* C. A74), f. the name of Friedrich *Kolbeck* (1860–1943), German mineralogist: see -ite[1].] A blue hydrated silicate-phosphate of beryllium, calcium, and scandium (and possibly aluminium).

1928 *Mineral. Mag.* XXI. 568 *Kolbeckite.* Beryllium phosphate or silicophosphate as cyan-blue monoclinic crystals from Saxony. **1959** *Bull. Geol. Soc. Amer.* LXX. 1649 Sterrettite and kolbeckite are the first known scandium-bearing phosphates. **1966** Z. Lerman tr. *Vlasov's Geochem. & Mineral. Rare Elements* II. vi. 219 Kolbeckite is distinguished by its marked pleochroism. It is a very rare mineral.

kold, kole, obs. ff. cold, coal, cool.

kolea (kəʊˈlɛə). [Hawaiian.] A local name for the Pacific golden plover, *Pluvialis dominica fulva*, which is native to the northern parts of North America and eastern Siberia, but winters in Hawaii and other parts of the Pacific.

1887 *Proc. U.S. Nat. Mus.* X. 80 *Charadrius dominicus fulvus* (Gmel.) Pacific Golden Plover, Kolea. **1933** E. H. Bryan *Hawaiian Nature Notes* 256 The golden plover, called kolea by the Hawaiians, is a little larger than the mynah bird but longer in the leg. **1944** G. C. Munro *Birds Hawaii* 56 The kolea is a valuable bird to Hawaii as a destroyer of insects... Yet it has so long been considered a game bird and table delicacy that efforts to obtain the protection it deserves have not been very successful.

koleye, variant of coley *v.*

†**kolfysch**, obs. form of coal-fish.

1338 *Durham Acc. Rolls* (Surtees) 35 In xl kolfysch, 4*s.*

Koli: see Kori[2].

kolibri, var. colibri.

kolier, kolk, obs. ff. collier, colk[2].

kolinsky (kəˈlɪnskɪ). Also **kolinski.** [f. Russ. *Kola*, name of a port in north-west Russia.] A name for the fur of a *Mustela sibirica*, the Japanese mink. Also *attrib.*

1851 *Illustr. Catal. Gt. Exhib.* III. 803 Skins and Furs... Kolinski. **1892** H. Poland *Fur-Bearing Animals in Commerce* p. li, Kolinski, undressed. **1919** *Queen* 5 July 21 (Advt.), Kolinsky coat in the fashionable Sable Colour. **1923** J. C. Sachs *Furs & Fur Trade* 62 The 'sable' brushes, which are in such request by artists, are generally made of kolinski tails. **1928** *Strand Mag.* Aug. 183/2 A Persian lamb coat with a collar of kolinsky. **1968** J. Ironside *Fashion Alphabet* 155 The Siberian China mink is known as Kolinsky.

‖**kolkhoz** (kalˈxos). Also **kolhoz, kolkhos**, etc. Pl. **kolkhoz, kolkhozes, kolkhozy.** [Russ., f. *kol(lektívnoe khoz(yáĭstvo*, collective farm.] A collective farm in the U.S.S.R. Also *transf.*

1921 *Russian Economist* I. II. 389 The 'Kolkhoses' are the means of a guerilla war with the peasants... The measure in which..support is given depends on the degree to which a particular kind of 'Kolkhose' approximates to the ideals of Communism. **1931** *Ann. Reg. 1930* 190 There was a real rush of the peasants to enter the *Kolchosy* (the abbreviated Russian denomination of the collectivised farms). *Ibid.* 191 A sensational article by Stalin entitled, 'Intoxicated by Success'. It dealt with the Kolchos movement, and in it the dictator strongly condemned the forcible methods of collectivisation hitherto used. **1931** H. G. Wells *Work, Wealth & Happiness of Mankind* (1932) iv. 184 The Kolkhoz seems to be the old Tsarist Mir in a state of emotion. *Ibid.* x. 508 The great fields of the Kolkhozy. **1943** E. M. Almedingen *Frossia* viii. 285 He knows Russia... He has seen Sovhozes and Kolhozes. **1946** [see ejido]. **1949** F. Maclean *Eastern Approaches* I. viii. 133 The eating-house ..seemed to be monopolized by the higher *kolkhoz* officials whom I found engaged in preparations for the forthcoming elections to the Supreme Council of the Kazakh S.S.R. **1951, 1952** [see agrogorod]. **1957** *Ann. Reg. 1956* 256 The villages [in Hungary] seem quietly to have dissolved most of their local *kolkhoz* and then returned to work. **1958** *New Statesman* 5 Apr. 423/3 The *kolkhozes*..will now be in a position to introduce certain measures hitherto found only on state farms, including a guaranteed minimum wage. **1968** C. A. Doxiadis *Between Dystopia & Utopia* 46 The Kolkhozes in Russia..are the results of utopian theories. **1972** *Guardian* 4 Aug. 4/4 A kolkhoz, or collective farm, is a symbol of the crude rustic for city dwellers.

Hence ˈ**kolkhoznik** (pl. **-niki**), a member of a *kolkhoz.*

1955 H. Hodgkinson *Doubletalk* 27 Each worker, or *kolkhoznik*, has to give between 100 and 150 work days on the common land. **1964** *Economist* 18 July 255/1 With their dependants the *kolkhozniki* amounted to about 56 million persons.

kolladie, var. korari.

kollergang (ˈkɒləgæŋ). [G., = crushing action.] A crushing machine used in milling paper-pulp.

1890 A. Watt *Art of Paper-Making* 82 For the purpose of crushing the knots of the straw, and other hard particles.. a machine termed the 'kollergang' or 'edge-runner' is

sometimes employed. **1907** G. CLAPPERTON *Pract. Paper-Making* (ed. 2) iv. 38 The ability of the Scandinavian makers to allow a considerable time for milling the pulp in kollergangs or beaters. **1963** [see *edge-runner* s.v. EDGE *sb.* 12 b].

kollow, var. COLLOW *sb.*

kolloxylin (kəˈlɒksɪlɪn). [f. Gr. κολλο-, comb. form of κολλά glue, gum + OXYLIN.] A form of pyroxylin or nitro-cellulose less highly nitrated than common gun-cotton.

1884 EISSLER *Mod. High Explosives* 120 The time necessary for the conversion of cotton into kolloxyline depends on the state of concentration of the nitric acid. *Ibid.*, *Nitro-cellulose* (kolloxyline..). This substance is not to be confounded with gun-cotton, which is not soluble in alcoholic ether.

kollyrite, variant of COLLYRITE.

kolm (kɒlm). *Petrogr.* [Sw.] (See quot. 1954.)

1930 *Jrnl. Amer. Chem. Soc.* LII. 4848 The ash of the kolm constitutes from 20 to 40% of the original, and contains a few hundredths of a per cent. of lead. **1954** S. I. TOMKEIEFF *Coals & Bitumens* 61/1 *Kolm*, variety of cannel coal occurring locally as lenticles in Swedish alum shales, and containing 30% of ash rich in rare metals, including uranium and radium. **1969** M. G. RUTTEN *Geol. W. Europe* iii. 44 Within these black shales lenses may occur of a sort of coal, the 'kolm'. Both shales and kolm have in recent times acquired importance for their uranium content.

Kolmer (ˈkɒlmə(r)). *Med.* The name of John *Kolmer* (1886–1962), U.S. pathologist, used *attrib.* and *absol.* to denote a modification proposed by him of the Wassermann complement fixation test for syphilis using beef heart cardiolipin as the antigen. Also **Kolmer-Wassermann.**

1921 *Med. Clinics N. Amer.* V. 670 We have studied the results of the Kolmer method of performing the Wassermann test in over 2000 tests. **1925** *Jrnl. Laboratory & Clin. Med.* X. 315 (*heading*) Red corpuscle suspension for the Kolmer-Wassermann reaction. **1932** SCHAMBERG & WRIGHT *Treatm. Syphilis* xxxiii. 591 The Kolmer-Wassermann test is not usually positive until the primary lesion has been present for eight days. **1971** S. M. BROOKS *V.D. Story* iv. 60 A positive Kolmer or VDRL.. practically always indicates nervous system involvement. **1971** *Amer. Jrnl. Clin. Path.* LV. 735 The automated Kolmer test appeared less satisfactory than the manual Kolmer test.

Kol Nidre (kɒl ˈniːdreɪ). Also **Kol Nidry.** [Aramaic *kol nidhrē*, all the vows.] A mournful Aramaic prayer, opening with the words *Kol nidhrē*, sung by Jews at the beginning of the service on the eve of Yom Kippur: it asks for annulment of vows made in the previous year and for forgiveness of sins. Also, the service itself or the melody to which the prayer is sung.

1881 M. KEIZER in I. L. Mombach *Sacred Mus. Compositions* p. viii, (*heading*) New Year & Atonement... Ki Vayoum Hazeh.. Kol Nidry.. Mechalkyl. **1891** M. FRIEDLÄNDER *Jewish Relig.* ii. 408 Transgressors.. desirous to pray in the Synagogue on the Day of Atonement, were admitted... Such was the original object of *Kol-nidre.* **1893** I. ZANGWILL *Ghetto Tragedies* 47 It was *Kol Nidré* night, the commencement of.. the Day of Atonement. **1908** *Daily Chron.* 5 Oct. 5/2 All this time services are held wherever a few of the children of the Ghetto are gathered together. The first, held at 6 o'clock on Sunday evening, at the opening of the fast, is called 'Kol-Nidré'. **1922** JOYCE *Ulysses* 470 A.. band is heard.. playing the Kol Nidre. **1932** C. ROTH *Hist. Marranos* 379 The famous ceremony of the Annulment of Vows on the eve of the Day of Atonement, the Kol Nidre service. **1966** H. KEMELMAN *Saturday the Rabbi went Hungry* (1967) i. 7 The chanting of Kol Nidre ushered in the Holy Day. **1973** *Synagogue Light* Sept. 12/1 On Tish B'Av .. we take off our shoes. On Yom Kippur also, commencing before Kol Nidre.

kolo (ˈkəʊləʊ). [Serbo-Croatian, = wheel.] A Yugoslav dance performed in a circle.

1911 E. L. URLIN *Dancing Anc. & Mod.* iii. 45 The Kollo Dance (or Kolo) is seen depicted on very ancient tombs of the Bogomiles in Dalmatia, archaic in type; it must therefore have been of ancient religious origin. **1941** 'R. WEST' *Black Lamb* I. 398 They had our men and women brought in to dance the kolo to them. **1952** L. & D. JANKOVIĆ *Dances Yugoslavia* 21 The kolo usually has many phases and very often works up from a gentle swaying motion to more animated movement, which dies down to a moderate level according to the directions of the musician and the leader. **1963** *Daily Mail* 24 Aug. 2/2 A frolicking Mr. Kruschev... With his holiday host, President Tito, he joined the girls in the kolo, a popular dance performed in a circle to the accompaniment of singing. **1969** *Daily Tel.* 5 Nov. 13/6 The dancers launched themselves on an old Bosnian dance, a silent kolo from Glamotch.

kolong, var. COOLUNG.

kolovratite (kɒləvˈrɑːtaɪt). *Min.* [ad. Russ. *kolovratit* (V. I. Vernadsky 1922, in *Compt. Rend. de l'Acad. d. Sci. de Russie* A. 37), f. the name of L. S. *Kolovrat*-Chervinsky (1884–1921), Russian radiochemist: see -ITE[1].] A greenish-yellow amorphous or finely crystalline mineral that is probably a hydrous vanadate of nickel and zinc.

1925 *Mineral. Mag.* XX. 290 A new mineral, named kolovratite by V. I. Vernadsky, which.. appears to be widely distributed in Fergana... The mineral is a vanadate of nickel. **1927** *Mineral. Abstr.* III. 234 Kolovratite.. from Kara-Chagyr occurs as a fine powder disseminated in carbonaceous quartz-schist. **1962** *Canad. Mineralogist* VII. 314 Our evidence suggests, however, that kolovratite is a hydrous zinc-nickel vanadate, or possibly a silico-vanadate, rather than a nickel vanadate as inferred in the original description.

kolpo-, var. of COLPO-, from Gr. κόλπος bosom, womb, used to form pathological and surgical terms relating to the vagina, as *kolpocele*, COLPOCELE, etc.

† **kolte, kolys**, obs. ff. COLT *sb.*, CULLIS *sb.*[1]

komande, obs. f. COMMAND.

komatik (ˈkɒmətɪk). Also **kamotik, kamootik,** etc. [Eskimo.] A dog-sledge used by the people of Labrador. Also as *v. intr.*, to travel on a komatik.

1824 W. E. PARRY *Jrnl. Second Voy.* 567/1 *Sledge, a*, ka-moo-tik. **1853** *Trans. Lit. & Hist. Soc. Quebec* IV. 337 They .. are so hardy that six or eight of them tackled to a heavily laden sledge or 'commettek' will travel as much as twenty leagues in a day. **1905** N. DUNCAN *Dr. Grenfell's Parish* xi. 133 The sick and starving are sought out by dog-team and komatik. **1919** W. T. GRENFELL *Labrador Doctor* (1920) xi. 199 Sails can sometimes be used with advantage on the komatik as an adjunct. **1921** *Beaver* Jan. 16/1 We had the ordinary length of sled or 'komatik', which is about twelve feet long and weighs about a hundred pounds. We carried a load of about six hundred pounds, which.. is considered light. **1934** G. M. SUTTON *Eskimo Year* xxxvi. 233 Jack and I decided we would *komatik* to the head of the bay to set traps and locate some fox-dens. **1936** *Discovery* Sept. 274/2 An Eskimo *komatik* (sledge) complete with driver and several dogs neatly harnessed. **1940** R. FINNIE *Lure of North* 117 In the dead of winter, however, the native komatik reigns supreme, gliding easily where a basket sled would drag. **1965** *Globe & Mail* (Toronto) 6 Jan. 1/3 The dog sled, or komatik, has replaced the bicycle for northern Cubs. **1973** C. BONINGTON *Next Horizon* xvii. 235 The komatic or sledge... Now I was sitting on the back of a komatic, near the head of Cumberland Sound in Baffin Island.

kombaars (ˈkɒmbɑːs). *S. Afr.* Also **kombers(e.** [Du. *kombaars* coverlet, rug.] A blanket, coverlet, or rug.

1812 W. J. BURCHELL *Jrnl.* 1 May in *Trav. S. Afr.* (1824) II. 175 This *kombaars*, or coverlet, is a genuine South-African manufacture, being nothing more than a Hottentot *karóss* of large dimensions. **1840** B. SHAW *Memorials S. Afr.* i. 28 His *kombaars* tied with leathern strings. **1850** R. G. CUMMING *Five Yrs. Hunter's Life S. Afr.* I. ix. 186 In the evening I took my pillow and 'komberse', or skin blanket, to the margin of a neighbouring vley. **1913** C. PETTMAN *Africanderisms* 274 *Komberse*, a rug, blanket; sometimes a kaross is so styled.

‖ **kombé** (ˈkɒmbiː). [Mang'anja.] The juice obtained from the seeds of *Strophanthus kombe*, a Central African climbing plant of the family Apocynaceæ, which is one of the sources of the drug strophanthin.

1859 J. KIRK *Zambesi Jrnl. & Lett.* (1965) I. 171, I take a walk in the neighbourhood, find the plant used to poison the arrows. It is an arborescent twiner, getting quite to the top of the trees. The juice of the fruit is used... They call it *Kombe.* **1888** *Buck's Handbk. Med. Sci.* VI. 663/1 Strophanthus (Kombé, Arrow Poison). **1934** G. E. TREASE et al. *Text-bk. Pharmacognosy* xx. 512 One of these [species of *Strophanthus*], known to the natives of the Shiré River as *kombi*, was noted by Livingstone in 1861... In 1885 Fraser isolated strophanthin and recommended the use of the seeds in medicine. **1952** *Ibid.* (ed. 6) xviii. 479 The glycosides of *kombé* contain cymarose. **1967** *Martindale's Extra Pharmacopoeia* (ed. 25) 541/2 Strophanthin-K (B.P.C. 1954). Strophanthin; Kombé Strophanthin.

kombu (ˈkɒmbuː). [Jap.] A brown seaweed, one of the local species of *Laminaria*, used as food, esp. as a base for stock.

1884 SATOW & HAWES *Handbk. for Travellers Cent. & N. Japan* (ed. 2) 519 *Kombu*, a broad, thick, and very long species of seaweed, most of which is exported to China. **1905** *Nat. Geogr. Mag.* May 218 Kombu is one of the staple foods of the country [*sc.* Japan], entering into the dietary of almost every family. **1949** *New Biol.* VII. 96 The various preparations of 'kombu' are said to have quite distinctive flavours. **1958** G. MIKES *East is East* 67 *Kombu* (a kind of seaweed) is not less delicious than boiled cabbage. **1969** G. W. PRESCOTT *Algae* x. 350 In Japan, laminarian food (from stipes) is called *kombu*; food from *Alaria* is called *sarumen*. Stipes of some of the larger brown algae are cut, washed in fresh water, boiled and seasoned with preserving fluids.

komfoor (kɒmˈfɔə(r)). *S. Afr.* Also **komvoor, konfoor.** [Afrikaans, f. Picard form of OFr. *chaufoire* kettle for hot water.] A small brazier; a chafing-dish; a foot-stove.

1841 *Cape of Good Hope Almanac* (Advt.), Tools of all descriptions... Brushes, kettles, and komfores. **1844** J. BACKHOUSE *Narr. Visit Mauritius & S. Afr.* v. 84 To preserve warmth, the Dutch women use an apparatus to set their feet upon, called a Komfoor. **1940** 'B. KNIGHT' *Walking the Whirlwind* vii. 144 She signalled to the slave near the door to hand round charcoal from the komfoor to relight some of the pipes. **1951** *Cape Times* 6 Sept. 16/1 Samovars are almost as common in Cape Town as komvoors and spittoons used to be in the salesrooms. **1965** A. GORDON-BROWN *S. Afr. Heritage* II. 21 Brass Coffee Pot under which is the original Konfoor to contain burning charcoal for keeping the coffee hot. **1972** A. A. TELFORD *Yesterday's Dress* 81 She sits drinking coffee with her bare feet upon a 'komfoor' which as its name implies was a wooden 'chaufette' containing a pan of charcoal, a comfortable footwarmer.

Komi (ˈkəʊmɪ). [Native name (see quots. 1800 and 1888).] **a.** A people of northern central U.S.S.R.; a member of this people. **b.** The language of the Komi. Also *attrib.*

[**1800** W. TOOKE *Hist. Russia* I. i. 13 *Komanes.* They were neighbours of the Madshares or Ugres, and migrated in conjunction with them at the close of the eighth century to Pannonia. They dwelt upon the river Kuma, from which they also had their name. On the other side of the Terek is still a people named Kumuiks; perhaps remains of the old Kumanians. *Ibid.* 42 One part of these were called Kumani or Komani, from the river Kuma.] **1888** *Encycl. Brit.* XXIV. 283/1 The Zyrians.. constitute the bulk of the population on the Ural slopes. They formerly inhabited the Kama and Vyatha basins, and call themselves Komi-yurt, or Komi-yas. **1911** *Ibid.* XXVI. 317/2 They [*sc.* the Syrenians] call themselves Komi. **1933** H. KOHN *Nationalism in Soviet Union* 62 These Finnish peoples, the Komi, the Mari, and the Mordvins, were steadily pushed back by the Russians into less fruitful areas with severe climates. **1942** K. W. DEUTSCH in J. A. Fishman *Readings Sociol. of Lang.* (1968) 600 Syryen (Komi). **1959** *Chambers's Encycl.* XIV. 121/1 (table) Komi. **1964** *Language* XL. 906 Komi is today represented by two literary languages, Komi(-Zyryan) and Komi-Permyak. *Ibid.* 98 The semantic functions of the Komi and Udmurt forms.

komita(d)ji, var. COMITADJI.

komli, obs. f. COMELY.

‖ **Kommandatura** (kɒˌmɑːndəˈtʊərə). Also **-antur, -atur.** [ad. G. *Kommandantur* commandant's headquarters, command post.] The centre of operation of a military government.

1937 BLUNDEN *Elegy* II. 31 We met the walls the Roman host Used for their *Kommandantur* post. **1949** *Ann. Reg. 1948* 238 The machinery of four-Power rule set up under the Potsdam Agreement, the Allied Control Council and the Berlin *Kommandatura*, had become more and more an instrument for political propaganda. **1957** H. ROOSENBERG *Walls came Tumbling Down* iii. 65 We saw several people lugging shot-guns and rifles to the new *Kommandatura.* **1958** P. KEMP *No Colours or Crest* x. 220 The miserable Eles .. had been a frequent visitor to the German *Kommandatur* in Peć. **1969** *Listener* 9 Jan. 35/3 The Soviet Kommandatura in the centre of Prague. **1975** *New Yorker* 22 Sept. 78/2 The site of the Russian Kommandatura in Leipzig had been shown on the map of the city.

kommende, obs. f. COMMEND.

‖ **Kommers** (kɒˈmɛrs). Also **commerce, -se, -s.** [G., ad. Fr. *commerce*, L. *commercium* COMMERCE *sb.*] = COMMERS.

1839 LONGFELLOW *Hyperion* I. II. iv. 120 Come in; come in. You shall see some sport. A Fox-Commerce is on foot, and a regular Beer-Scandal. **1841** W. HOWITT *Student-Life Germany* xvi. 315 For these Commerses, the rule is to drink beer, and this is called a Commers in beer. **1908** C. SIDGWICK *Home Life Germany* vi. 56 A *Kommers* is a students' festival in which the professors and other senior members of a university take part. **1960** *Times* 17 Sept. 9/7 One may be fortunate enough to be invited to a *Kommers*, a meeting in which the students settle round tables for the evening, quaffing beer.. and singing.

Komodo (kəʊˈməʊdəʊ). The name of an Indonesian island, used *attrib.* in **Komodo dragon, monitor** to designate a large monitor lizard, *Varanus komodoensis*, native to this island and neighbouring ones.

1927 *Daily Express* 15 June 15 The curator of the reptiles ..introduced me to her latest novelty, a Komodo dragon, seven feet long and as ugly as a bad dream. **1927** *Proc. Zool. Soc.* 256 Lord Rothschild exhibited a mounted specimen of *Varanus komodensis* [*sic*], the so-called 'Dragon' of Komodo Island... The interesting feature of the Komodo Monitor, apart from its bulk, lies in its relationship. **1928** *Ibid.* 1017 (*title*) On a living Komodo Dragon. **1941** J. S. HUXLEY *Uniqueness of Man* viii. 184 The gorilla, the orang-utang, the Komodo dragon, and other creatures are on the margin of this category [of creatures kept from extinction only by rigorous protection]. **1969** A. BELLAIRS *Life of Reptiles* II. xi. 468 The Komodo dragon (*Varanus komodoensis*) has been generally regarded as the largest existing lizard and reaches a length of at least 3 metres (10 ft.) and a weight of 163 kg. (360 lb.). It is found only on the small island of Komodo to the east of Java and on one or two neighbouring islands. **1973** *Nature* 7 Sept. 52/1 There is evidence that the Komodo monitor can take prey as heavy as itself.

kompas, var. KEMPAS.

komˈpology. *rare*[−1]. [ad. late Gr. κομπολογία, f. κόμπος boast + -λογια speaking.] Boasting or vaunting speech.

1854 W. OSBORN *Monum. Hist. Egypt* I. 409 They are mere kompologies; mythic fables, invented by the Alexandrian apologists of Egypt.

Komsomol (ˈkɒmsəmɒl). Also **Comsomol.** [Russ. *komsomól*, short f. *Kommunistícheskiĭ Soyúz Molodëzhi* Communist Union of Youth.] An organization of Communist youth in Russia; a member of this organization. Also *attrib.*

1934 T. S. ELIOT *Rock* i. 39 That's what they do in Russia. Ever 'ear o' the Comsomol? We'll turn all the churches into workers' clubs. **1944** G. B. SHAW *Everybody's Pol. What's What?* x. 82 Comsomols, Ballillas, Leagues of Youth and cognate bodies and movements which are sprouting everywhere. **1948** J. TOWSTER *Political Power in U.S.S.R.* 137 The closest auxiliary of the Party is the Komsomol or Young Communist League. **1949** *Ann. Reg. 1948* 211 Communists and Komsomols had helped to build mosques. **1958** *Listener* 5 June 934/1 Why should Chekhov's

characters proclaim prophetic and optimistic truths about a better future which sounds [*sic*] as if they were gleaned from a Komsomol textbook? **1959** *Ibid.* 3 Dec. 964/2 A Komsomol branch secretary. **1973** *Nat. Geographic* May 606/2 The Komsomol (Communist youth organization) in her district had advertised openings at Togliatti stating that a modern low-rent apartment was part of the employment contract.

komvoor, var. KOMFOOR.

kon, kon(n)e, obs. ff. CAN *v.*, CON *v.*

kona ('kəʊnə). [Hawaiian; orig. the name of the leeward areas of the Hawaiian Islands.] A stormy south-west wind in the Hawaiian Islands.

1864 R. ANDERSON *Hawaiian Islands* i. 28 Occasionally a prolonged gale comes from the south, called a Souther, or 'Kona'. **1866** 'MARK TWAIN' *Lett. from Hawaii* (1967) 23 In the stormy season—in the season of the terrible kona. **1892** STEVENSON & OSBOURNE *Wrecker* 9 It was blowing a kona, hard. **1934** M. D. FREAR *Lowell & Abigail* p. xiv, But by night..how the Kona wind moaned and drove the rain up from the sea. **1967** J. SEVERSON *Great Surfing* Gloss., *Kona wind*, a south wind in the Hawaiian Islands, generally onshore at most of the southern exposure beaches. Occasionally offshore or glassy on the north shore.

konak (kəʊ'nɑːk). [ad. Turk. *qonaq* halting-place, inn.] A large house, palace, or official residence, in Turkey, or in the (former) Ottoman Empire.

[**1675** J. COVEL *Diary* (1893) 175 We..had a man who alwayes went before to every *Conâck*, or stage, and brought in muttons, beafes, veales, and the like.] **1852** C. T. NEWTON *Let.* 30 Sept. in *Trav. & Discov. Levant* (1865) I. vii. 87 We asked for the konak, or official residence of the Aga. **1878** S. L. POOLE *People of Turkey* I. ix. 221 When in the interior I had the opportunity of visiting some Konaks worthy of note. **1897** E. A. BARTLETT *Battlefields Thessaly* iv. 88 The Konak was deserted by all except the Mushir's valet. **1908** tr. *P. Draganof's Macedonia & Reforms* ii. 23 The latter drove them from the konak. **1926** *Spectator* 17 July 88/2 The delicate 'konak' or palace of Prince Milosh Obrenovitch. **1957** L. DURRELL *Bitter Lemons* 163 There is also a wretched Konak and prison.

‖**konaki** ('kɒnəkɪ). *N.Z.* Also **koneka**. [Corruption of Maori *kōneke* sledge.] A horse-drawn wooden sledge.

1914 M. HALL *Woman in Antipodes* I. 86, I also got some insight into up-country life..noting..the primitive Maori 'koneka' or sledge. **1953** J. M. BRIMBLECOMBE in J. Reid *Kiwi Laughs* (1961) 179 He had to go and haul lime tomorrow with the konaki. **1959** M. SHADBOLT *New Zealanders* 15 The trunks were lashed to a konaki, which Mother discovered was the Maori word for a horse-drawn wooden sled. **1961** B. CRUMP *Hang on Minute* 109 Uncle Wally lifted the [cream-]can..out to the old konaki.

Kond, Kondh, varr. KHOND.

‖**konditorei** (ˌkɒndɪtə'raɪ). Pl. **konditorei, konditoreien**. [Ger., f. *konditor* confectioner.] Confectionery; a confectioner's shop, a shop where pastries are sold.

1935 J. BUCHAN *House of Four Winds* iii. 69 He was in the habit of sampling..whatever Unnutz produced in the way of café and konditorei. **1963** N. FREELING *Because of Cats* ii. 35 When she went to a concert it would be to satisfy a need, like women who went to konditoreien to stuff themselves with wonderful cream cakes. **1973** *Times* 30 May (Austria Suppl.) p. iv/6 *Konditorei* abound, and you will find it hard to resist those delectable Viennese pastries bulging with cream.

‖**konfyt** (kɒn'feɪt). *S. Afr.* Also †**comfaat, conf(e)yt**. [Afrikaans, = Du. *konfijt* COMFIT *sb.*] Fruit preserved in sugar; preserve.

1862 LADY DUFF-GORDON *Let.* 15 Apr. (1927) 144, I have bought some Cape 'confeyt'; apricots, salted and then sugared, called 'mebos'—delicious! **1871** *Cape Monthly Mag.* II. 25 Coffee and cakes, tea and '*comfáát*'. **1929** *Daily Tel.* 15 Jan. 9/4 Now that Cape fruits are being sent over to this country in ever-increasing quantities, the word 'konfyt' has come into our vocabulary. 'Konfyts' are delicious preserves made from these exotic fruits. **1939** S. CLOETE *Watch for Dawn* 39 He had konfyt of melon and little oranges. **1947** L. G. GREEN *Tavern of Seas* ix. 87 Malay families sometimes sell these fine eighteenth century saucepans, kettles and konfyt pots. **1950** *Cape Argus* 8 May 4/4 She became particularly famous for her konfyts and jams. **1955** L. G. GREEN *Karoo* xi. 140 White housewives made *konfyt* of it. **1974** D. ROOKE *Margaretha de la Porte* 229 'Konfyt and meerbos, what a typical Dutch spread,' Fanny commented with a patronizing smile; but she was quick enough to help herself to the glazed watermelon and sugary apricots.

kongkang: see KUKANG.

kongoni (kɒŋ'gəʊnɪ). [Swahili.] An alternative name for Coke's hartebeest, *Alcelaphus buselaphus cokei*, found in the plains of East Africa.

[**1889** J. C. WILLOUGHBY *E. Afr. & its Big Game* 54 These hartebeest (*swahili Kongoni*) are of the species known as *Cokii*, and..are very plentiful here. **1905** H. A. BRYDEN in H. G. Hutchinson *Big Game Shooting* II. vi. 114 Coke's hartebeest (*Bubalis cokei*) (*Kongoni* of the Swahilis) is the commonest..of this group in East Africa.] **1908** W. S. CHURCHILL *My Afr. Journey* i. 9 Herds of red kongoni—the hartebeest of South Afica. **1921** *Outward Bound* June 40 Within the noonday shade Of mushroom-headed thorn trees, the great 'Kongoni' wade. **1942** *E. Afr. Ann 1941–2* 127/2 Zebra, kongoni, steinbuck, Thomson's gazelle, and ostrich are numerous on the plains. **1971** *Nature* 24 Dec. 483/2 Eland..and boran..cattle were equal in water demands, while kongoni (*Alcelaphus buselaphus*) and wildebeest..are comparable with sheep.

kongsbergite ('kɒŋzbɜːgaɪt). *Min.* [Named, 1872, from Kongsberg in Norway, where found: see -ITE.] An amalgam of silver and mercury occurring with arquerite.

1880 DANA *Min.* App. ii. 32.

‖**kongsi** ('kɒŋsɪ). [ad. Chin. *kung-ssu* (as pronounced in Hokkien) company, corporation.] In Malaysia, an association or partnership, esp. an association of Chinese people.

1839 T. J. NEWBOLD *Pol. & Statistical Acct. Straits of Malacca* I. i. 14 Their interior affairs..are arranged by the heads of their respective kongsis or fraternities. **1900** W. W. SKEAT *Malay Magic* v. 255 The men of a rival *kongsi* had brought limes. **1964** D. K. BASSETT in Wang Gungwu *Malaysia* II. vii. 122 A *kongsi* is an association of Chinese based on regional, occupational or dialect ties. **1966** D. FORBES *Heart of Malaya* x. 116 Three or four hundred jammed together in a junk chartered by a merchant combine, called a *kongsi*. **1969** J. M. GULLICK *Malaysia* ii. 48 In its primary sense 'kongsi' denotes a Chinese association or secret society. **1972** *Straits Times* (Malaysian ed.) 23 Nov. 11/3 The tin mine kongsi house in which I found her was occupied by the accused's brother.

kongyr, obs. form of CONGER[1].

koniak, koniaku ('kɒnjæk, kɒn'jækuː). Also **konjak, konnyaku**. [ad. Jap. *ko-n-nya-ku, ko-nya-ku.*] A local name for *Amorphophallus rivieri*, a large herb of the family Araceæ, cultivated in Japan for the flour obtained from its roots.

1884 tr. *A. de Candolle's Orig. Cultivated Plants* II. i. 76 The konjak is a tuberous plant of the family Araceæ, extensively cultivated by the Japanese. **1954** J. M. MORRIS *Wise Bamboo* iv. 54 Anything edible can be put into *sukiyaki*. That night we had leeks, *tofu* (beancurd), *konnyaku* (a gelatine-like vegetable which I could not identify), onions and bamboo sprouts. **1965** *This is Japan 1966* 80/3 All the balloons were fashioned of Japanese rice paper and *konnyaku* (devil's-tongue root) which is a chief ingredient in the popular Japanese dish *sukiyaki*. **1970** J. KIRKUP *Japan behind Fan* 4 Lumps of *tofu* (white beancurd) and *konyaku* (devil's tongue jelly). **1972** Y. LOVELOCK *Vegetable Bk.* II. 269 The related giant arum or devil's tongue..known to the Japanese as *koniaku*, is often cultivated for food... Their [*sc.* the tubers'] taste and smell is [*sic*] strong and disagreeable, but this is lost after they have been soaked in whitewash (i.e. milk of lime), crushed and cooked. The resulting flour is used for making a kind of pasta and other dishes.

'konilite. *Min.* [f. Gr. κόνις dust + -LITE.

So named in 1821 by MacCulloch, who had previously (1819) called it CONITE, unaware that this had previously (1795) been applied by Retzius to a variety of dolomite.]

A powdered form of silica found in the cavities of trap.

1821 MACCULLOCH in *Q. Jrnl. Sc.* XI. 219.

konimeter (kə'nɪmɪtə(r)). [f. Gr. κόνις dust: see -METER.] A kind of impinger in which a known volume of air is directed on to a slide coated with a substance to which any dust particles will adhere.

1918 *Jrnl. Chem., Metall. & Mining Soc. S. Afr.* XVIII. 200/1 We are indebted to the perseverance and ingenuity of Mr. R. N. Kotzé, the Union Government Mining Engineer, for a simple solution by means of an instrument he has devised and called a Konimeter. **1937** DRINKER & HATCH *Industr. Dust* vi. 99 The dust-collecting efficiency of the konimeter is admittedly low and is selective with respect to size. **1958** *Ann. Rep. Chief Inspector of Factories on Industr. Health 1957* 17 in *Parl. Papers 1958–9* (Cmnd. 558) XIII. 183 A team..travels to particular factories and takes samples, using..a Kotzé konimeter... Dust samples..are analysed..and the particle size and particle counts recorded. **1965** *Guide to Prevention & Suppression of Dust in Mining* (Internat. Labour Office) xvi. 306 Side-by-side sampling with a thermal precipitator and a konimeter was performed on the dust created by a series of different underground operations.

koninckite ('kəʊnɪŋkaɪt). *Min.* [Named, 1884, after Prof. L. G. de Koninck, of Liège: see -ITE.] Hydrous phosphate of iron, found, at Visé in Belgium, in small globular forms with a radiated structure.

1885 *Amer. Jrnl. Sc.* Ser. III. XXIX. 342 *Koninckite*, a new hydrated phosphate of iron.

konini ('kɔːnini). *N.Z.* [Maori.] A native shrub or small tree, *Fuchsia excorticata*, or its berries.

1867 J. D. HOOKER *Handbk. N.Z. Flora* II. 765/2 Konine. *Fuchsia excorticata*. **1869** T. H. POTTS in *Trans. N.Z. Inst.* II. 48 Beneath, Bell-birds..seek the konini, clinging to its brittle sprays. **1889** T. KIRK *Forest Flora N.Z.* 53 The settlers sometimes term it Kotukutuku or Konini, but more generally fuchsia. **1949** P. BUCK *Coming of Maori* (1950) II. i. 88 The berries of the..konini..are transient and were not important as food. **1960** B. CRUMP *Good Keen Man* 12 When a pigeon shirred up out of a konini I almost dropped by rifle. **1968** M. JOHNSON *N.Z. Flowering Plants* 57 One seldom sees now a rich display of the purple black berries, konini, that delicacy of the Maori palate of former times.

koniscope ('kɒnɪskəʊp). [f. Gr. κόνις dust + -SCOPE.] An instrument for estimating the concentration of dust in the air by observing the depth of colour in a sample of the air when it is expanded into a tube with glass ends and containing moist paper to saturate it with water vapour.

1892 J. AITKEN in *Proc. R. Soc.* LI. 435 This new instrument we intend to call a Koniscope. In its present form this instrument consists of an air-pump and a metal tube with glass ends. **1905** *Westm. Gaz.* 26 Aug. 13/1 Dr. Aitken has invented a very simple instrument for this purpose, which he calls the koniscope, or dust detective. **1925** SHAW & OWENS *Smoke Probl. Gt. Cities* viii. 145 Condensation of water on the dust particles is utilised in Aitken's..koniscope; a fog is produced and compared with a standard.

konite, variant of CONITE.

konjak, var. KONIAK, KONIAKU.

konk, var. CONK *sb.*[1], the nose, and CONK *v.*[2], to break down.

Konkani ('kɒŋkənɪ). [Marathi *Koṅkaṇī*, f. *Koṅkaṇ* Konkan, a coastal region of western India.] **a.** A native or inhabitant of the Konkan. **b.** The Indic language of the Konkani. Also *attrib.* or as *adj.*

1873 *Cycl. India* (ed. 2) III. s.v. *Konkan*, The mixed Konkani tongue, appears to be only Marathi with a large infusion of Tulu and Canarese words... Mr. H. Mogling however mentions that the Konkani-speaking brahmins of Mangalore, consider it quite distinct from, though cognate with, Marathi. **1885** G. C. WHITWORTH *Anglo-Indian Dict.* 169/2 The southern Konkanis..are much more in the habit of seeking their living abroad than other natives. **1905** G. A. GRIERSON *Ling. Survey India* VII. 1 The dialectic differences within the Marāṭhī area are comparatively small, and there is only one real dialect, *viz.*, Kōṅkaṇī. *Ibid.* 17 A Kōṅkaṇī translation of the Bible appeared at Serampore in 1819. **1948** D. DIRINGER *Alphabet* 372 Konkani, one of the most important Marathi forms of speech. **1959** *Chambers's Encycl.* VIII. 354/2 There is a western group composed of Kashmiri, Lahnda.., Sindhi.., Rajasthani,..and Konkani. **1969** *Eve's Weekly* (Bombay) 20 Dec. 55/2 Boy-carollers..singing Christmas carols in Konkani. **1971** *Hindustan Times Weekly Rev.* (New Delhi) 4 Apr. p. iv/5 Konkani has no script, no grammar, no rules.

konne, obs. form of CAN *v.*[1], CON *v.*[1]

konning, -yng, konyng, obs. ff. CUNNING.

Konno(h), varr. KONO[2].

konnyaku, var. KONIAK, KONIAKU.

kono[1] ('kəʊnəʊ). Also **ko-no, Ko-No.** [Korean.] A Korean board game.

1895 S. CULIN *Korean Games* 100 The games played on diagrams, like our game of Merrells, receive the name of *Ko-no* in Korea, a term my informant could not further define. *Ibid.* 101 In all games of *Kono*, as in Pa-tok, the black men move first. **1960** R. C. BELL *Board & Table Games* I. iii. 98 Five Field Kono... The object of the game is to move the pieces across to the other side of the board to occupy the places vacated by the opponent, and the first player to do so wins the game. **1970** *Nature* 19 Sept. 1206/1 Ko-No (Fig. 1) is probably the simplest fully determined board game known.

Kono[2] ('kəʊnəʊ). Also **Konno(h).** [Native name.] **a.** A Mandingo-speaking people of Sierra Leone; a member of this people. **b.** The language of the Kono people, having affinities with Vai. Also *attrib.* or as *adj.*

1909 R. H. K. WILLANS in *Jrnl. R. Afr. Soc.* XXX. 130 The history of the Konnoh people is of great interest... The Konnohs at the present day have degenerated into an almost insignificant tribe. *Ibid.* 145 *Soa*..in Mendi and Konnoh means three. **1916** N. W. THOMAS *Specimens Lang. Sierra Leone* Introd., Kono, Susu and Kisi were recorded from informants with a very moderate knowledge of English. **1925** T. N. GODDARD *Handbk. Sierra Leone* 55 The *Konnos* and *Korankos* are closely connected with the Mandingos. **1925** H. C. LUKE *Bibliogr. Sierra Leone* (ed. 2) 148 Kono Hymns. **1926** F. W. BUTT-THOMPSON *Sierra Leone* vi. 44 The present border of the Kono lands. **1951** K. L. LITTLE *Mende of Sierra Leone* iii. 70 The Kono men, who are mostly labourers in the town, wear European shorts and shirt outside the trousers. *Ibid.* vii. 147 The Mende tend to look down on certain peoples, such as the Kono. **1964** C. FYFE *Sierra Leone Inheritance* 250 During the march to Weeima we were attacked on all sides by the Konnos and several of our people were wounded.

konyne, -yng, obs. forms of CONY *sb.*

konze ('kɒnzɪ). Also **konzi, nkonze.** [Swahili.] A local name for Lichtenstein's hartebeest, *Alcelaphus lichtensteini*, an antelope found in the plains of central and southern Africa.

1877 F. C. SELOUS *Jrnl.* 20 Dec. in *Hunter's Wanderings Afr.* (1881) 303 In the afternoon I went out with my rifle, and shot a konze antelope... The black mark down the front of the face of the hartebeest is..wanting in the konze. **1908** R. LYDEKKER *Game Animals Afr.* 111 The konzi, or Lichtenstein's hartebeest. **1964** E. P. WALKER et al. *Mammals of World* II. 1446/1 Hartebeests; Ngondo, Nkonze, Kondikondi, Sig (native names).

koo, variant of CO[1] *Obs.*, jackdaw.

‖**koochahbee** (kuː'tʃɑːbiː). [American Ind.] The larva of a fly, *Ephydra californica*, found in

enormous quantities in Lake Mono in California.

When dried in the sun and the shell rubbed off these worms form a very important article of food among the Indians.

1885 BREWER in *Stand. Nat. Hist.* II. 432 My guide, an old hunter there, told me that everything fattens in the season of the koo-chah-bee; that ducks get very fat.

koodoo, var. of KUDU.

kooftah, var. KOFTA.

kook (ku:k). *slang.* [prob. abbrev. of CUCKOO *a.* or CUCKOO *sb.* 3.] **1.** A cranky, crazy, or eccentric person. Freq. *attrib.* or as *adj.*

1960 *Daily Mail* 22 Aug. 4/5 A kook, Daddy-O, is a screwball who is 'gone' farther than most. **1963** *Time* 4 Oct. 37 'Don't think that just because he talked about those way-out rockets he's a kook,' cautioned a fellow officer. **1964** *Economist* 28 Nov. 969/2 Thousands of 'beatniks, kooks, and crackpots'. **1965** J. POTTS *Only Good Secretary* (1966) ii. 26 Max is kind of a kook. He paints these kooky pictures. **1968** MRS. L. B. JOHNSON *White House Diary* 18 Jan. (1970) 623 Mrs. Hughes..said..'I think that anybody who takes pot because there is a war on is a kook.' **1968** *N.Y. Times* 26 Mar. 32 'Has it ever occurred to you that the kook market has grown?' said a United States auto executive when asked to explain the growing sales of foreign cars. **1970** E. R. JOHNSON *God Keepers* (1971) xv. 166 It's a kook clique all right. It's..a happy place. That's kooks to you cops. **1971** *Black World* June 67/1 These marchers were all probably a bunch of kooks like Harry always said. **1973** *Publishers Weekly* 25 June 68/1 A bona fide kook who is never quite able to get in gear till he finally dies paddling his canoe across the Atlantic.

2. orig. *U.S.* A novice, or one who is inexpert, in surf-riding. Also *attrib.*

1961 in *Amer. Speech* (1962) XXXVII. 150. **1966** *Surfer* VII. 9 This letter is to protest about dumb kook girls out in the water. *Ibid.* 17 All most of [these surfers] are is a bunch of loud-mouthed kooks who come down here and clutter up the beach. *Ibid.* 39 Malibu..was also the birthplace of the 'kook box', that monstrosity known as the poor man's paddle board. **1971** *Studies in English* (Univ. of Cape Town) II. 25 The reason for this reticence is that surfers wish to differentiate themselves from kooks, who surf badly.

kooka ('kʊkə). *Austral. slang.* = KOOKABURRA.

1933 *Bulletin* (Sydney) 13 Sept. 21/4 An article on upsetting the balance of nature in which one Shepstone quotes the sad case of the kooka. **1949** *Geogr. Mag.* Feb. 374/1 Hence such names for the Kookaburra as..*breakfast bird, kooka* and *ha ha pigeon.* **1964** P. CARLON *Price of Orphan* iv. 44 He was going to be grabbed like a kooka sighting a snake.

‖**kookaburra** ('kʊkəbʌrə). [Native Australian: given as *kūkūburra* by Ridley *Kámilarói*, p. 21.] A large, arboreal, brown kingfisher, *Dacelo novæ-guineæ*, distinguished by its peculiar laughing cry; formerly called the GOBURRA and also called the laughing jackass.

1890 *Argus* (Melbourne) 25 Oct. 4/5 You might hear the last hoot of the kookaburra then. **1899** *Westm. Gaz.* 10 Apr. 8/1 Offers of Australian animals and birds from emus to kookaburras. **1906** *Ibid.* 13 Oct. 16/3 Just before the hour of sunrise the echoes of the Australian bush are awakened by the extraordinary cackling laughter of the great brown kingfisher, or kookaburra, as the aboriginals call it. **1934** *Bulletin* (Sydney) 3 Jan. 31/3 An assembly of kookaburras in the trees close at hand burst into a chorus of derisive laughter. **1936** F. CLUNE *Roaming round Darling* ii. 13 A kookaburra laughed sardonically as we passed the Assembly Hall. **1959** *Guardian* 28 Nov. 5/2 The chortled comments of the kookaburra bird. **1966** G. DURRELL *Two in Bush* iv. 132 The first of these were three fat young Kookaburras, or Laughing Jackasses as these giant kingfishers are called in Australia.

kook-a-vic, var. KOKKEWIET.

kooky ('ku:kɪ), *a. slang.* Also **kookie**. [f. KOOK + -Y[1].] Cranky, crazy, eccentric.

1959 *Motion Pictures* Aug. 32/1 Get set for some far-out talk on teen-age romance by the kookiest cat in town—Edd Byrnes. **1961** *Spectator* 15 Sept. 360 I've got this kooky Aunt who reads novels. **1961** *John o' London's* 30 Nov. 615/4 The dialogue is conscientiously kookie. **1962** *Sunday Express* 21 Jan. 17/1 A Hollywood comedienne noted for her 'kookie' performances. **1963** E. L. WALLANT *Tenants of Moonbloom* (1964) iv. 48, I feel like dropping the Muse and this kooky life and marrying a nice tired businessman. **1965** [see KOOK 1]. **1971** *Daily Tel.* 21 Aug. 16/1 A 'kooky' young American woman: enthusiastic, energetic, enterprising and 'a bit nuts'. **1973** *Nation Rev.* (Melbourne) 31 Aug. 1452/3 (Advt.), 'No Sex Please, We're British!' The funniest, kookiest night of your life.

So **'kookily** *adv.*, in a kooky manner; **'kookiness**, the state of being kooky.

1962 *Sunday Express* 21 Jan. 17/3 Kookiness doesn't go with a kimono. **1968** *Punch* 19 June 899/1 This study of a kooky girl is also..kookily narrated. **1970** *Sudbury* (Ontario) *Daily Star* 26 Feb. 18/4 There's nothing you can do, so accept your mother's kookiness gracefully. Her antics in no way diminish you in the eyes of your friends. **1974** *Observer* 21 Apr. 37/1 'Isadora' kookily takes off on a Freudian odyssey round Europe.

koolack, obs. var. KULAK.

koolah, var. KOALA.

Kooleen, var. KULIN.

koolestocke, obs. f. *cole-stock*: COLE *sb.*[1] 3.

kooliman, var. COOLAMON.

koolookamba (ku:lu:'kæmbə). Also **kulu-kamba** and shortened form **kulu**. [Native name in Gabon.] A West African variety of the chimpanzee, *Pan troglodytes.*

1860 P. B. DU CHAILLU in *Proc. Boston Soc. Nat. Hist.* VII. 360 The cry of the Kooloo-Kamba is very different from that of the *Troglodytes calvus* and chimpanzee. **1896** R. L. GARNER *Gorillas & Chimpanzees* 176 The kulu-kamba is ..by far the finest representative of his genus. *Ibid.*, A young female kulu. **1929** R. M. & A. W. YERKES *Great Apes* xxiv. 302 This observer [*sc.* Du Chaillu] means to imply that the three types of chimpanzee called by him Kooloo-Kamba, *Troglodytes calvus*, and chimpanzee, have distinctive calls or cries.

koomiss, variant of KOUMISS.

koompass, var. KEMPAS.

Koonbee, var. KUNBI.

Kooranko, var. KORANKO.

koorbash, variant of KOURBASH.

koorn kriek, var. KORINGKRIEK.

kooskoosoo, variant of COUSCOUSSOU.

koot, -e, obs. forms of COAT.

kootbah, kootoo, var. KHUTBAH, KOW-TOW.

kootchar ('ku:tʃɑ:(r)). *Austral.* Also **koochee**. [Aboriginal name.] A small stingless bee, *Trigona australis.*

1884 H. J. HOCKINGS in *Trans. Entomol. Soc. London* 149 The second species [of stingless bee] ('Kootchar') is also black in colour but has a fine yellow streak across the upper part of the thorax. *Ibid.* 154 'Kootchar' are only to be found where a sandy soil is present. **1932** Koochee [see KARBI]. **1961** *Amer. Mus. Novitates* No. 2026. 5 It was perhaps by error that Hockings attributes this species (under the aboriginal name of *kootchar*) to the coast.

Kootenai, var. KUTENAI, KUTENAY.

kootie, var. COOTIE *sb.*[2]

‖**kop** (kɒp). [Afrikaans, f. Du. *kop* head, COP *sb.*[2]] **1.** *S. Afr.* A hill. Cf. KOPJE.

1835 C. L. STRETCH *Jrnl.* 1 Apr., The troops..advanced in the direction of T'Slambies Kop, a high point visible from the heights near Graham's Town. **1878** H. A. ROCHE *On Trek in Transvaal* xiv. 303 One fine Kop or Kopje we passed upon which grazed an immense herd of fine oxen and heifers. **1900** A. H. KEANE *Boer States* p. xvii, *Kop*, a crest, an eminence. **1901** L. JAMES in J. Ralph *War's Brighter Side* 347 The three field batteries then came into action against a high tableland *kop* which formed the right of the held position. **1932** C. FULLER *Louis Trigardt's Trek* ii. 26 It is east by north of Taikundo Kop. **1939** *tr. E. N. Marais's My Friends the Baboons* i. 74 On one side the kloof was bordered by a krans, two to three hundred feet high, and on the other by a kop so steep that it could almost be called a krans too. **1971** *Rand Daily Mail* (Home Owner Suppl.) 26 June 5 Two of Johannesburg's most famous 'kops'—Langermann's Kop ..and Pullinger Kop.

2. *Assoc. Football.* (With capital initial.) In full, but now less usu., **Spion Kop** ('spaɪən kɒp). [f. *Spion Kop*, Afrikaans name of a hill near Ladysmith in S. Afr., scene of a battle in the Boer War (1899–1902).] A high bank of terracing for standing spectators, orig. and especially the one at Anfield, home ground of Liverpool Football Club, but now of more general U.K. application (see quot. 1974[2]). Also, the spectators themselves, massed on such terracing, and *attrib.*

1926 *Liverpool Daily Post* 29 May 9/3 At last night's meeting of the Liverpool Football Club an important step was made known... The Club had decided to..concentrate upon improving Spion Kop at the back of the Oakfield-road goal. **1960** B. LIDDELL *My Soccer Story* vi. 43 All they [*sc.* the spectators] wanted was the final whistle, so that they could come swarming over the ground from the Kop..and carry us off the field. *Ibid.* viii. 54 Kicking into our favourite goal, at the Spion Kop end. **1966** P. MOLONEY *Plea for Mersey* 56 There is in Liverpool a school of indigenous verse —known as the Kop choir, which produces, as it were spontaneously, verses to suit every situation that might occur within the game of football. **1966** *Liverpool Echo* (Football ed.) 30 Apr. 1/3 Liverpool went into the lead again in 69 minutes... This set the Kop off again and they gave us pretty well their whole repertoire [of songs and chants]. **1973** B. SHANKLY in *News of the World Football Ann. 1973–74* 4 For a time it seemed as if the Kop would never stop singing. **1973** *Liverpool Echo* (Football ed.) 22 Dec. 1/5 Liverpool immediately resumed the first half pattern of constant attack, this time towards the Kop goal. **1974** *Times* 18 Mar. 10/8 A match of electric energy..ended with the heaving Kop awash with red banners and scarves. **1974** *Sunday Times* 14 Apr. 26/2 What Anfield sings today, other Kops will be singing tomorrow.

So **'Kopite, 'Koppite**, a spectator who frequents the Kop terracing.

1960 B. LIDDELL *My Soccer Story* viii. 53 He got a tremendous ovation from the generous Koppites at the finish. **1966** P. MOLONEY *Plea for Mersey* 58 'You'll never walk alone,' the Koppites sing. **1974** *Liverpool Echo* (Football ed.) 6 Apr. 16/9 The president of the Cambridge University Boat Club who comes from Birkenhead is also a loyal Kopite. **1974** *Sunday Times* 14 Apr. 26/2 It makes Liverpool Kopites smile..to hear other fans singing their songs.

kopasetic, var. COPACETIC *a.*

‖**kopdoek** ('kɒpdʊk). *S. Afr.* [Afrikaans, f. *kop* head, COP *sb.*[2] + DOEK cloth.] A head-cloth.

1911 *State* (Cape Town) Dec. 642/2 He deposited his shapeless hat on the floor, tapped his red kopdoek with a clawlike forefinger, and waited for an inspiration. **1957** *Cape Times Week-end Mag.* 6 Apr. 3/5 The Swazis barter the bones for food and clothing..; half a monkey means a new kopdoek. **1974** *S. Afr. Panorama* Feb. 10 In their bright blue-and-pink 'kopdoeks' (headscarves), they lend a colourful note to an already colourful scene.

kope, obs. form of COPE *sb.*[1]

kopec(k, -peek, -pek, variants of COPECK.

koper, obs. form of COPPER *sb.*[1]

‖**kopi** ('kəʊpɪ). [Austral. Aboriginal word.] Gypsum- or selenite-bearing rock or mud.

1898 D. W. CARNEGIE *Spinifex & Sand* II. ii. 42 We came on a small tract of 'kopi country' (powdered gypsum). *Ibid.* 43 This kopi is peculiar soil to walk over. *Ibid.* III. iii. 91 A sort of powdery gypsum, called 'Kopi' by the natives. **1936** A. RUSSELL *Gone Nomad* ix. 71 The drying bed of the lake was composed of a clinging kopi mud that would have enmeshed a duck. **1957** D. NILAND *Call me when Cross turns Over* i. 8 The lie of all that barren land he knew, the shelves, the pits, the mullock dumps of kopi, every mound and every rise and fall. **1971** J. S. GUNN *Opal Terminol.* 24 *Kopi*, gypsum which sometimes carries good opal. In L. Ridge the kopi is different, being flattish crystals of silenite, rather than the gypsum clay of S. Aust. and Qld.

kopje, var. KOPPIE.

Koplik ('kɒplɪk). *Med.* [The name of Henry *Koplik* (1858–1927), U.S. pædiatrician.] ***Koplik('s) spot***: a small greyish-yellow spot, usually with a red halo, occurring on the bucal mucosa (or sometimes on the intestinal mucosa) in the early stages of measles.

1899 *Med. News* (N.Y.) LXXIV. 734/2 Koplik's spots were seen on the inner surface of the cheeks and under lip. **1939** DUVAL & SCHATTENBERG *Textbk. Path.* ix. 284 Microscopically the macule or Koplik spot is a dense central collection of lymphocytes surrounded by tissue that is edematous and hyperemic. **1948** H. PINKERTON in W. A. D. Anderson *Path.* xv. 359 Koplik spots have been described in fatal cases in the intestinal mucosa. **1970** HORNSTEIN & GORLIN in Gorlin & Goldman *Thoma's Oral Path.* (ed. 6) II. xvii. 756/2 Koplik's spots result from superficial necrosis of the mucosa and disappear after two to six days.

koppa ('kɒpə). A letter (ϙ) standing between π and ρ in the early Greek alphabet (= Heb. *koph* ק, Lat. *q*). It was later displaced by κ, but survived as a numeral = 90.

1870 W. W. GOODWIN *Elem. Greek Gram.* I. 2 Two obsolete letters—*Vau* or *Digamma*..equivalent to F or W, and *Koppa* (ϙ), equivalent to Q..are used as numerals. **1883** I. TAYLOR *Alphabet* II. 138 The letters *vau* and *koppa*, which were discarded in the Eastern alphabets, except as numerals, were retained in Latin. **1888** KING & COOKSON *Princ. Sounds & Inflexion Gr. & Latin* iii. 52 The Phoenician ϙ, *Koppa*, fell into disuse; it survived longest in the alphabet of Chalcis, whence it passed into the Roman alphabet as Q. **1933** C. D. BUCK *Compar. Gram. Gr. & Latin* 73 The *wau*, *koppa*, and *san*, which disappeared from the alphabet, were maintained as numeral signs. **1970** *Oxf. Class. Dict.* (ed. 2) 48/1 K was used originally before *a*, C before *e* and *i*, ϙ (Greek Koppa) before *o* and *u*.

koppel ('kɒpəl). Also **capel, coppel**. [Yiddish.] A skull-cap worn by male Jews.

1892 I. ZANGWILL *Childr. Ghetto* I. 118 Old Hyams..had been sitting quiet with brow corrugated under his black velvet *Koppel.* **1972** *Jewish Chron.* 1 Sept. 22/1 (Advt.), For the high festivals: Machsorim—Tallisim—Kittles—Coppels. Unrivalled selection of New Year cards. **1973** *Ibid.* 9 Feb. 22/5 Some pious Jews..make a point of wearing a hat and not a 'capel' for prayer and some Chasidim wear both a hat and a 'capel' underneath it.

koppie ('kɒpɪ). Also **kopjie, kop(p)je**. [Du. *kopje*, dim. of *kop* head, COP *sb.*[2] (The dim. ending *-je* has usually sunk in colloquial Du. to *-i.*)] In South Africa: A small hill.

1848 R. GRAY *Jrnl.* 14 Nov. (1849) 76 Large dreary plains interrupted by rocky koppies, abounding with the springbok and the gnu. **1850** N. J. MERRIMAN *Cape Jrnls.* (1957) 136 This will account for our retiring behind a koppie to pitch our tent. **1853** *Edin. New Philos. Jrnl.* LV. 79 The bush..covers over all inequalities of ground..and makes almost every kloof and koppie exactly resemble each other. **1881** *Contemp. Rev.* Feb. 226 The insurgents strongly posted in a rocky 'koppie'. **1883** OLIVE SCHREINER *Afr. Farm* viii. (1890) 216 There at the foot of the 'kopje' goes a Kaffir. **1884** E. P. MATHERS *Trip to Moodie's* 143 He was prospecting about and tried the quartz at the bottom of the koppie... The koppie dips into a gully on each side of it. **1899** *Athenæum* 30 Sept. 450/1 The gallant deeds of the kopje and the karroo. **1926** O. SCHREINER *From Man to Man* viii. 290 You will creep on hands and knees over rough koppies. **1957** *Times* 19 Nov. 12/7 In the course of my afternoon walk over the koppies one day I came upon two of my pupils engaged in a strange game. **1966** E. PALMER *Plains of Camdeboo* v. 74 The low ridge of koppies overlooking the gap. **1971** *Rand Daily Mail* (Home Owner) 27 Mar. 9/2 It is a hilly area and there are the Melville koppies to add something extra to the area. **1971** *World Archaeol.* III. 182 With few exceptions, however, smelting sites are not found on the koppies themselves.

Comb. ***koppie-strewn*** *a.*; **koppie** (also **kopje**) **walloper**, a diamond-buyer. *Hist.*

1886 G. A. FARINI *Through Kalahari Desert* ii. 21 The wily Jew was a 'partner' in a 'company' of ten 'Koppje wallopers'. **1897** H. RAYMOND *B. I. Barnato* i. 14 The slang camp term..for this [*sc.* diamond-buyer] was 'kopje

wallopper', derived from the circumstance that in the earliest days the diamonds were obtained from a number of kopjes or small hills in the neighbourhood of the camp, and the dealers travelled on foot from one to the other purchasing the finds as they were turned out at the sorting tables. **1900** *Daily Tel.* 25 Jan. 5/2 A stretch of kopje-strewn, river-cut country. **1947** *Cape Argus* 20 Dec. 2/5 A 'koppie walloper' was a diamond buyer who went from claim to claim buying stones. The name was used in Kimberley in the early days. **1949** K. L. SIMMS *Sun-Drenched Veld* viii. 70 Profits dwindled quickly, especially as native workmen stole many diamonds, which they sold to unscrupulous 'kopje wallopers' who made enormous profits without having done any hard work. **1955** E. ROSENTHAL in Saron & Hotz *Jews in S. Afr.* vi. 114 A 'koppie-walloper', that is one who went from claim to claim buying diamonds as the diggers produced them. **1967** E. M. SLATTER *My Leaves are Green* 38 Now don't sell it to any of these kopje-wallopers.

koppite ('kɒpaɪt). *Min.* [Named, 1875, after Prof. Kopp of Heidelberg: see -ITE.] Columbate of calcium, sodium, and the cerium metals, found in transparent brown crystals.

1880 DANA *Min.* App. ii. 32 Koppite..occurs with apatite and magnoferrite in a granular limestone near Schelingen, Kaiserstuhlgebirge, Baden.

koprolith, variant of COPROLITH.

kopy, obs. form of COPY.

kora[1] ('kɔərə). Also cora, korro. [Native name.] A West African stringed instrument resembling a harp.

1799 M. PARK *Trav. Afr.* xxi. 278, I have now to add a list of their musical instruments, the principal of which are,— the *koonting*, a sort of guitar..; the *korro*, a large harp, with eighteen strings; [etc.]. **1874** C. ENGEL *Descr. Catal. Musical Instruments S. Kensington Museum* (ed. 2) 151 Mungo Park enumerates, among the popular instruments which he saw in Senegambia, the *e-korro*. **1935** G. GORER *Africa Dances* IV. 305 The drums are sometimes supplemented and occasionally supplanted by..the cora, a six-stringed instrument somewhere between a guitar and a harp. **1965** *Economist* 16 Jan. 229/3 The Senegal national anthem.. begins..'Strum your koras, strike the balafous'. **1970** P. OLIVER *Savannah Syncopators* 47 The great harp-lute, called the *kora*.

Kora[2] ('kɔərə). Also Coranna, Koran(n)a, occas. Koraqua. [Of disputed origin.] **a.** Any of a group of Hottentot peoples in southern Africa; also, a member of any of these groups. **b.** The language spoken by them. Also *attrib.* or as *adj.*

1801 J. BARROW *Acct. Trav. S. Afr.* I. vi. 403 The country to the eastward of the Roggeveld, is inhabited by different hordes of Bosjesmans. One of these, called the *Koranas*, dwelling on the right bank of the Orange river, directly east from the Roggeveld, is represented as a very formidable tribe of people. **1806** —— *Voy. Cochinchina* 373 The native inhabitants which are settled on the banks of the Orange river..are a variety of the Hottentot race..called the *Koras*. *Ibid.*, What the Gonaquas were on the eastern coast the *Koras* seem to be to the northward, a mixed breed between the Hottentot and the Kaffer. **1824** W. J. BURCHELL *Trav. S. Afr.* II. 251 The following specimen of the Kora, or Koraqua, dialect, was obtained. **1831** *Graham's Town Jrnl.* 30 Dec. 3 At a Koranna kraal.., the first cases of Small Pox presented themselves. **1871** J. MACKENZIE *Ten Yrs. North of Orange River* 493 A certain word in Koranna, if pronounced in a loud key, means *handkerchief*. *Ibid.* 501 The insecure villages of the pastoral Korannas. **1881** *Encycl. Brit.* XII. 312/2 The Kora dialect, spoken by the Korannas, or Koraquas, dwelling about the middle and upper part of the Orange, Vaal, and Modder Rivers. **1936** J. A. ENGELBRECHT *Korana* I. 2 The history of the origin of the Korana can only be approximately arrived at. *Ibid.* II. 83 Kora tribes..left the Cape to seek new pastures. *Ibid.* III. 197 A complete linguistic survey of all the areas in which Kora..is still spoken at the present day could not be undertaken. **1955** J. H. WELLINGTON *S. Afr.* II. xvi. 234 The tribes occupying the Cape Peninsula and adjacent areas at the time of Van Riebeeck's arrival were the Goringhaiqua and the Kora (later known as the Koranna). **1961** *Encycl. S. Afr.* 278/1 Today pure Koranas are almost extinct. **1968** *Encycl. Brit.* XI. 751/1 Hottentot is the European name for the Nama, Kora and other languages comprising 14 or 15 subdivisions of the main Hottentot speech. **1974** [see HOTTENTOT 1].

kora, var. KOURA.

koraddy, koradi, varr. KORARI.

‖**koradji** ('kɒrədʒɪ). *Austral.* Also 8 carradygan, carrahdy, 9 coradge(e, karaji, kiradjee, korradgee. [Austral. Aboriginal word.] Amongst the Australian Aborigines, a medicine-man.

1793 J. HUNTER *Hist. Jrnl.* xxi. 523 Having taken leave of their new friends the *Car-ra-dy-gans* (doctors), our party set off. **1798** D. COLLINS *Acct. Eng. Colony New South Wales* I. 594, I think I may term the car-rah-dy their high priest of superstition. **1845** J. O. BALFOUR *Sk. New South Wales* 14 The coradgees, who are their wise men, have, they suppose, the power of healing and foretelling. Each tribe possesses one of these learned pundits, and if their wisdom were in proportion to their age, they would indeed be Solons. **1865** W. HOWITT *Hist. Discovery in Austral.* I. 287 One who seemed a coradge, or priest, went through a strange ceremony of singing, and touching his eyebrows, nose and breast, crossing himself, and pointing to the sky like an old Druid. **1867** S. BENNETT *Hist. Austral. Discovery* 250 *Kiradjee*, a doctor. **1885** R. M. PRAED *Austral. Life* 23 The koradgees, or medicine men, are the chief repositories (of the secrets of their religion). **1892** J. FRASER *Aborigines New South Wales* 63 For some diseases, the karāji, or native doctor when he is called in, makes passes with his hand over the sick man, much in the same way as a mesmerist will do. **1966** [see BOYLA].

†**korahl,** obs. form of CORRAL *sb.*

1785 *Europ. Mag.* VIII. 360 A certain korahl,..in which most of the elephants in Ceylon are caught.

korait, variant of KRAIT.

Koran (kɒ'rɑːn, 'kɔəræn). Also 7 core, currawn, 9 coran, kuran. [a. Arab *qurān*, *qorān* recitation, f. *qaraʾa* to read: cf. ALCORAN.] The sacred book of the Muslims, consisting of revelations orally delivered at intervals by Muhammad, and collected in writing after his death: it is in Arabic, and consists of 114 *surahs* or chapters.

1625 PURCHAS *Pilgrims* II. III. v. 264 [Nicetas] Anathematiseth the *Core*, that is, Mahomets Scripture, and all his learning. **1665** SIR T. HERBERT *Trav.* (1677) 271 Gunnet ..imposed that new Currawn as they term it upon the Persian. **1735** BOLLINGBROKE *Lett. Study Hist.* iv. (1777) 97 Maraccio's refutation of the Koran. **1781** GIBBON *Decl. & F.* xxviii. III. 93 *note*, The Moors of Spain, who secretly preserve the Mahometan religion, above a century,.. possessed the Koran, with the peculiar use of the Arabic tongue. **1813** BYRON *Corsair* I. ii, And less to conquest than to Korans trust. **1841** ELPHINSTONE *Hist. Ind.* II. 316 To dispose him to question the infallible authority of the Korán. **1867** LADY HERBERT *Cradle L.* vii. 173 We reached a wall and gateway with inscriptions from the Kurán.

koran, var. KORHAAN.

Koranic (kɒ'rænɪk, -'ɑːnɪk), *a.* Also co-. [f. KORAN + -IC.] Of or pertaining to the Koran.

1811 H. MARTYN *Dairy* in *Mem.* (1825) III. 368, I produced another sentence, and begged to know why it was inferior to the Koranic one. **1858** W. MUIR *Life Mahomet* (1861) I. p. lxxxi, Romantic legends..reared upon the authority of a Coranic basis. **1884** J. PAYNE *Tales fr. Arabic* II. 229 *note*, This belief is summed up in the Koranic saying, 'Verily, the commandment of God is a prevenient decree'.

Koranko (kə'ræŋkəʊ). Also Kooranko. [Native name.] **a.** Name of a West African people; also, a member of this people. **b.** The language of this people.

1825 A. G. LAING *Trav. W. Afr.* iv. 200 The manner of courtship among the Korankos is exactly the same as among the Timannees. *Ibid.* 208 Dancing is a prominent feature among the amusements of the Koorankos. **1883** R. N. CUST *Sk. Mod. Lang. Afr.* I. xi. 184 There appear to be Dialects [of Temne], the Quiah,..and the Koranko. **1957** M. BANTON *W. Afr. City* vii. 127 Koranko is a closely related dialect [to Mandinka]... The Koranko and Kono inhabit the high lands to the north-east and east. **1962** *Times* 3 Mar. 10/6 The man is a Koranko of west Africa.

Koran(n)a, Koraqua: see KORA[2].

korari ('kəʊrɑːrɪ). *N.Z.* Also coorraddie, kauradi, kolladie, koraddy, koradi, kraddy. [Maori.] The flower stalks of the New Zealand flax, *Phormium tenax*; also occasionally used for the plant itself.

1832 G. BENNETT in *London Med. Gaz.* 18 Feb. 750/2 *Phormium Tenax*, or flax plant. *Koradi* of the natives of New Zealand... This valuable plant is indigenous to New Zealand. **1834** E. MARKHAM *N.Z. or Recollections of It* (MS.) 44 Koraddy or Flax undrest split green and worked up. **1840** J. S. POLACK *Manners & Customs New Zealanders* I. xvi. 175 The flax (*Korari*)..is of two or three kinds. **1843** *N.Z. Jrnl.* No. 92 177/2 With a piece of kauradi or flax. **1845** E. J. WAKEFIELD *Adventure N.Z.* I. iii. 63 The plant is called *phormium tenax* by naturalists. The general native name for the plant..was *korari*. **1873** V. PYKE *Story Wild Will Enderby* (ed. 4) III. iii. 115 A 'mohiki' is constructed of 'koradies'—*Anglice*, the flowering stalks of the flax. **1879** J. BARR *Old Identities* 53 A 'kolladie' (the flower-stalk of the flax, about 7 ft long) was carried by each as a balancing pole or staff. **1888** A. H. DUNCAN *Wakatipians* ii. 12 We collected all the dried *coorraddies* (flower stalks of the flax-bush). **1933** *Press* (Christchurch, N.Z.) 19 Oct. 15/7 The individual plants are called *flax bushes* and the dried reed stalks (which Maoris and children tied into bundles to make rafts) are called *flax-sticks*, *koradi sticks*, or *kraddy sticks*. **1949** P. BUCK *Coming of Maori* (1950) II. ix. 238 Children armed with a flax flower stalk (*korari*) were taught to spar by their parents.

korck, korke, korn, var. CORK *v.*[2], CORN.

Kore ('kɔəreɪ). Also 9 Cora, Core. [Gr. κόρη, = maiden.] **1.** In Greek mythology, the daughter of Zeus and Demeter, known as Persephone when she married Hades.

1844 L. SCHMITZ in W. Smith *Dict. Gr. & Roman Biogr. & Mythol.* I. 852/1 Core..the maiden, a name by which Persephone is often called. **1849** *Ibid.* III. 204/2 In the mysteries of Eleusis, the return of Cora from the lower world was regarded as the symbol of immortality. **1885** *Encycl. Brit.* XIX. 824/1 Proserpine herself was commonly known as the daughter (Core). **1916** E. POUND *Lustra* 18 Korè is seen in the North Skirting the blue-gray sea. **1930** —— *XXX Cantos* xvii. 79 Korè through the bright meadow, with green-gray dust in the grass. **1968** *Encycl. Brit.* XVII. 644/2 One of the variants of the name Persephone is..a form with a pre-Hellenic suffix that suggests that she was a pre-Hellenic deity..a goddess of the dead. If this is so, her connection with Demeter came later, when she was identified with Kore (the Greek word for 'maiden').. daughter of Demeter; Demeter and Kore were the leading goddesses in the Eleusinian mysteries.

2. *Gr. Sculpture.* (Often with lower-case initial.) A statue of a draped maiden.

1920 *Q. Rev.* July 28 There are, in our Archaic Room, good examples both of the *Kore* and her male companion the *Kouros*. **1934** *Burlington Mag.* Jan. 46/1 The archaic bronzes include..an Ionian kore..and a warrior. **1950** H. L. LORIMER *Homer & Monuments* vi. 356 This arrangement can be plainly seen on a Kore from the Acropolis. **1971** *Ashmolean Mus. Rep. of Visitors 1970* 18 A terracotta scent vase in the form of a standing kore, Rhodian, late 6th century B.C.

Korean (kə'riːən), *a.* and *sb.* Also 7–9 Corean. [f. *Korea* country in Eastern Asia + -AN.]

A. *adj.* Of or pertaining to Korea, since 1954 divided into the *Republic of Korea* (capital, Seoul) in South Korea and the (Communist) *Korean People's Republic* (capital, Pyongyang) in North Korea (respectively S. and N. of the 38th parallel). **B.** *sb.* **a.** A native or inhabitant of Korea. **b.** The agglutinative language of Korea, which is related to Japanese.

1614 R. COCKS *Let.* 25 Nov. in *Diary* (1883) II. 270 He was prevented by a Corean Noble-man. **1727** J. G. SCHEUCHZER tr. *Kæmpfer's Hist. Japan* I. 63 The Coreans had been subdued. *Ibid.* 76 Encompass'd by the Corean sea. **1813** *Q. Rev.* Oct. 256 Classes and Families of Languages... Tartarian... Corean. **1822** F. SHOBERL tr. *Titsingh's Illustr. Japan* 323 A Corean Fisherman and his Wife. **1885** E. W. HAMILTON *Diary* 11 Apr. (1972) II. 834 The idea was broached in the Cabinet of endeavouring to make arrangements with the Chinese and Japanese Governments for our occupying Port Hamilton in Korean territory in the event of war with Russia. **1899** A. H. KEANE *Man Past & Present* viii. 307 An adaptation of the Chinese symbols to the phonetic expression of the Korean syllables. **1921** [see ANNAMITE *a.* and *sb.*]. **1966** *Listener* 24 Mar. 423/2 The Korean people..are genuine Tartars. *Ibid.*, Korea proves that it is possible for a poor Asian country to hope for both bread and freedom. The Koreans value that freedom. **1967** D. S. PARLETT *Short Dict. Lang.* 70 Agglutinative structure, like Korean, unlike Chinese. **1972** *Korea Times* 19 Nov. 1/6 Written tests in English, Korean and general knowledge will be held.

C. Special collocations. **Korean chrysanthemum**, a late-flowering hybrid chrysanthemum first developed from *Chrysanthemum coreanum* by A. Cumming, American nurseryman, about 1930; also *ellipt.*; **Korean pine**, a slow-growing pine with dark green leaves, *Pinus koraiensis*.

1931 *Horticulture* 15 Sept. 392/1 No list of Fall flowering perennials would be complete if the Korean chrysanthemum were omitted. When the flowers of this splendid novelty open, they are a pure white color with a chrysanthemum gold center, but as the flowers mature they assume a claret pink shade. **1936** K. LUXFORD *Culture of Chrysanthemum* 72 The hardy hybrid Korean chrysanthemum is one of the most notable acquisitions to the border of recent years. **1938** A. E. WRIGHT *Outdoor Chrysanthemums* ix. 87 The Koreans have made a tremendous impression in America. **1961** *Amat. Gardening* 30 Sept. 9/2 Some of the later flowering pompon chrysanthemums and Koreans I am lifting and putting into pots. **1866** 'SENILIS' *Pinaceæ* 115 Pinus Koraiensis: The Corean Pine. **1914** W. J. BEAN *Trees & Shrubs Hardy in Brit. Isles* II. 182 *P*[*inus*] *koraiensis*, Siebold. Corean Pine.. introduced by J. G. Veitch in 1861. **1969** T. H. EVERETT *Living Trees of World* 55/1 The Korean pine (*P. koraiensis*) occurs both in Korea and Japan, and under favorable circumstances it may grow to 150 feet high.

Hence **Ko'reanize** *v. trans.*, to give a Korean character to.

1930 W. F. SANDS *Undiplomatic Memories* (1931) 70 Emily, Koreanized as Lady Om, was now reigning sweetly in Seoul. **1972** *Korea Times* 16 Nov. 1/7 A new turning-point in the realization of a 'Koreanized democracy'.

Koreish (kə'raɪʃ). Also 7–9 Coreis(h), 9– Koreisch, -eysh, Ḳoraish, -aysh, Ḳur-, Quraysh, etc. [Arab. *ḳuraiš* Koreish, *ḳurašī* Koreishite.] An Arabic tribe living around Mecca, to which Muhammad belonged; also, a member of this tribe. Also *attrib.* or as *adj.*

1649 A. ROSS tr. *Alcoran* Introd., He declaimeth against such as worship Idols, particularly against the Inhabitants of the City of Mecca, and against the Coreis, who were enemies to his designe. **1734** G. SALE tr. *Koran* Prelim. Disc. i. 25 There were several dialects of it [*sc.* the Arabic language], very different from each other: the most remarkable were that spoken by the tribe of Hamyar and the other genuine Arabs, and that of the Koreish... The dialect of the Koreish is usually termed the pure Arabic. **1856** R. F. BURTON *Personal Narr. Pilgrimage to El-Medinah* III. xxvi. 157 It was closed by the Kuraysh when they rebuilt the house in Mohammed's day. **1858** W. MUIR *Life of Mahomet* I. I. iii. 197 The likeliest is the meaning '*noble*'; but it is also possible that the Coreish..may have conferred upon the word that meaning... Again, it is derived from a metaphorical resemblance to *Coreish*, the name of a fish which eats up all others; or to *cursh*, a high-bred camel. Others refer it to a root which signifies *to trade*. **1861** J. M. RODWELL tr. *Koran* p. viii, Othman..entrusted the redaction to..Zaid.., with whom he associated as colleagues, three, according to others, twelve of the Koreisch, in order to secure the purity of that Meccan idiom in which Muhammad had spoken. **1871** C. M. YONGE *Pioneers & Founders* iv. 81 Sabat was an Arab of the tribe of Koreish, the same which gave birth to Mahomet himself. **1880** E. H. PALMER in *Sacred Bks. East* VI. p. lix, Zâid.. with three men of the Qurâis (Mohammed's own tribe),..to fix the reading definitely according to the pure Qurâis idiom. **1907** D. S. MARGOLIOUTH tr. *J. Zaydan's Umayyads & Abbásids* 11 The poet Ibn Harmah..was an adoptive member of the clan Khalj which was itself adoptive in the tribe Ḳuraish. *Ibid.* 14 The Ḳuraish dealt in slaves as they did in other merchandise. **1916** J. BUCHAN *Greenmantle* ii. 23 To capture all Islam..the man must be of the Koreish, the tribe of the Prophet himself... There are families..that claim Koreish blood. **1957** *Encycl. Brit.* XV. 646/2 A member of the tribe Koreish.., Mohammed is said to have been a posthumous child. **1959** T. B. IRVING in Kritzeck & Winder *World of Islam* II. 189 The Quraysh, centring

around Makkah, used the purest Arabic of all; the ratio of any tribe's distance from the Quraysh was a good index for ascertaining the purity or corruption of any Arab dialect.

So **Ko'reishite, Qurayshite**, etc., a member of the Koreish tribe.

1708 S. OCKLEY *Conquest Syria, Persia & Ægypt by Saracens* I. sign. DD5 verso, Koreishæ, or Korashites, a noble Tribe among the Arabs, of which Mahomet was. **1734** G. SALE tr. *Koran* Prelim. Disc. vi. 145 The spoil..he bestowed..on the Meccans only.., highly distinguishing the principal Korashites, that he might ingratiate himself with them. **1871** C. M. YONGE *Pioneers & Founders* iv. 81 He formed a close friendship with his colleague, Abdallah, likewise a Koreishite Arab. **1903** D. B. MACDONALD *Devel. Muslim Theol.* App. i. 305 The unlettered Qurayshite prophet, Muhammad. **1968** *New Larousse Encycl. Mythol.* (new ed.) 323/1 The goddess El-'Ozza was also held in high honour among the Koreishites.

koreke (kɒ'reɪkeɪ). *N.Z.* [Maori.] An extinct native quail, *Coturnix novæzealandiæ*.

1871 F. W. HUTTON *Catal. Birds N.Z.* 22 Native Quail. Koreke. Black, streaked with white, and varied with reddish brown on the back. **1882** W. D. HAY *Brighter Britain!* II. 223 The Koreke..the native quail. **1930** W. R. B. OLIVER *N.Z. Birds* 374 New Zealand Quail. Koreke. **1966** R. A. FALLA et al. *Field Guide Birds N.Z.* 100 Galliformes. The only indigenous member of this order, *Coturnix novæzealandiæ*, Koreke of the Maoris, became extinct about 1870.

koren, korn, obs. pa. pple. of CHOOSE *v.*

‖**korero** ('kɔːrerɔ). *N.Z.* Also 9 corero, etc. [Maori.] Talk, conversation, discussion; a conference.

1807 J. SAVAGE *Some Acct. N.Z.* xi. 75 Corero..Speaking. **1834** E. MARKHAM *N.Z. or Recollections of It* (MS.) 4 A grand Corrirow or talk. **1845** E. J. WAKEFIELD *Adventure N.Z.* I. 78 There were about sixty men assembled, and they proceeded to hold a *korero* or 'talk' on the all-important subject. **1855** C. W. RICHMOND *Jrnl.* 20 Aug. in *Richmond-Atkinson Papers* (1960) I. 176 They had a long korero about New Zealand and the Bay, where the Doctor has been quartered for 5 years. **1863** T. MOSER *Mahoe Leaves* 30 He had to pass several pahs on the road, at all of which there would be 'koreros'. **1883** J. P. WARD *Wanderings with Maori Prophets* ii. 13 He was brim full of talk, or *korero*. **1930** B. GUTHRIE *N.Z. Memories* 54 After some *korero* and polite speeches the Maoris stood aside. **1936** 'R. HYDE' *Check to your King* xx. 236 The old and conspicuous means of the *korero* as a call to arms. **1938** R. D. FINLAYSON *Brown Man's Burden* 13 There was to be a korero on politics and the revival of Maori art. **1966** *Weekly News* (Auckland) 22 June 58/3 After New Zealand's first test defeat in South Africa in 1960 by 13-0 all members of the touring team had a korero the next morning. **1971** *N.Z. Listener* 22 Mar. 7/2 The *korero*..would let the Maoris tell the pakehas what they couldn't so easily tell them in a setting shaped by European conventions.

Korewah, var. KORWA.

korfball ('kɔːfbɔːl). Also **korfbal**. [Du. *korfbal*, f. *korf* basket + *bal* ball.] A game of Dutch origin, resembling basketball and netball. Also *attrib.*

1915 J. FEITH *Sport in Netherlands* 27 '*Korfbal*', a game not known in England... The ball, which is as big as that used for football, is thrown.., and the place of the goal is taken by a bottomless basket fastened to a pole. **1960** *Sunday Times* 5 June 40/6 Holland beat England 10-8 in a korfball international at Mitcham, Surrey, yesterday, after leading 7-3 at half-time. **1965** J. B. PICK *Phoenix Dict. Games* (rev. ed.) 89 *Korfball* (24 players)..is a netball-basketball game of Dutch origin..usually played by teams of six ladies and six gentlemen. Starting humbly in 1902..in the Netherlands.., the game was introduced into Britain..in 1946. *Ibid.* 90 There are now ten British korfball clubs. **1969** D. C. JOYNSON *Guide for Games* (ed. 2) vi. 157 Korfball Netball. The court is marked as for Netball. Team—5 players. *Ibid.* viii. 211 *Indoor Korfball.* Two teams of 6 players. The pitch may be (a) a basketball court; (b) a netball court; (c) a rectangular court 60 to 80 ft. by 30 to 40 ft. **1973** *Observer* 7 Oct. 26/1 There is only one mixed team sport in the world: korfball, and the first of its summarised rules is that you can only hinder someone of the same sex.

korhaan (kɒr'hɑːn, kə'rɑːn, kuː'rɑːn). *S. Afr.* Also **knorhaan, knoraan, koerhaan, koorhaan, korhaen, koran**, etc. [ad. S. African Du. *kor-* or *knorhaan*, f. *kor-*, *knor-*, an imitation of the bird's cry (cf. Du. *korren* to coo, *knorren* to grumble, snarl) + *haan* cock. (In Holland *korhaan* is the woodcock; cf. Ger. *kurrhahn* heathcock.)] The name given to certain species of South African bustards, of the family Otididæ.

1731 G. MEDLEY tr. *Kolb's Present State Cape of Good-Hope* II. 139 The Knorhan. Among the Wild Fowls at the Cape, there is a Sort of Birds, a Male of which the Europeans there call Knor-Cock: a Female they call Knor-Hen. **1775** MASSON in *Phil. Trans.* LXVI. 317 The fields abounded also with korhaans (a kind of bustard). **1785** G. FORSTER tr. *Sparrman's Voy. Cape Good Hope* I. iv. 153 *Knorrhane* is the name of a kind of *Otis*. **1786** *Ibid.* (ed. 2) I. iv. 153 *Korr-haen* is the name of a kind of *Otis*. **1801** J. BARROW *Acct. Trav. S. Afr.* I. iv. 264 A new species of Korhaen or bustard was seen here. **1819** STEPHENS *Gen. Zool.* XI. 451 [*Otis afra*] Native of the country north of the Cape of Good Hope, where it is called *Korhane*, or *Knorhaan*, from its cry. **1850** R. G. CUMMING *Hunter's Life S. Afr.* (ed. 2) I. 49, I saw and shot the black koran, an excellent game-bird, allied to the bustards, so abundant throughout South Africa. **1867** E. L. LAYARD *Birds S. Afr.* 287 The Knorhaan (lit. Scolding Cock) is abundant throughout the whole colony, frequenting the open country. **1876** H. BROOKS *Natal* 137 The koraan or knoraan of the Dutch settlers (*Eupodotis scolopacea*). **1880** P. GILLMORE *On Duty* 106, I observed a new variety of 'koran' on these flats..a brown-coloured species. **1896** H. A. BRYDEN *Tales S. Afr.* 250 The bush *koorhaan*..are playing their strange aerial pranks. **1906** W. L. SCLATER *Birds S. Afr.* IV. 291 The Red-crested Knorhaan is found singly or in pairs. **1936** *Blackw. Mag.* Mar. 296/2 The country was still rolling grass, with little game except koerhaan, which were plentiful everywhere. **1936** E. L. GILL *First Guide S. Afr. Birds* 150 The 'Korhaans' are the smaller-sized Bustards. **1964** P. A. CLANCEY *Birds Natal & Zululand* 143 The blue korhaan occurs sparingly in the interior of Natal. **1972** L. G. GREEN *When Journey's Over* (1973) xii. 143 Casserole of guinea fowl, stewed *korhaan* and pigeon and Namaqua partridges were as familiar at Klipfontein as grouse in the Savoy Grill.

kori[1] ('kɔərɪ). *S. Afr.* [Sechuana.] In full, ***kori bustard*** = GOMPAAUW.

1811 W. J. BURCHELL *Jrnl.* 27 Oct. in *Trav. S. Afr.* (1822) I. xvi. 393 We shot a large bird of the bustard kind... The present species, which is called *Kori* in the Sichuana language, measured, in extent of wing, not less than seven feet. *Ibid.*, A representation of the head of the Kori Bustard ..is given at the end of this chapter. **1872** L. LLOYD tr. *Andersson's Notes Birds of Damara Land* 258 Kori Bustard. .. This splendid bird is found throughout the year in Damara. **1889** H. A. BRYDEN *Kloof & Karroo* xvii. 306 Among the bustards stands pre-eminent the great Kori bustard—the gom paauw of the Dutch colonists. **1962** [see GOMPAAUW]. **1966** E. PALMER *Plains of Camdeboo* xii. 209 The Kori bustard, a dweller of the desert or semi-desert, a gigantic creature weighing up to fifty pounds or more, heavier than the great bustard of Eurasia which is usually held to be the heaviest bird of the air. It has a wing span of up to eight feet, and it stands nearly five feet high.

Kori[2] ('kɔərɪ). Also **Koiri, Koli, Koree.** Name of a tribe of low-caste Hindu weavers of northern India; also, a member of this tribe.

1839 J. TOD *Travels in W. India* vii. 143 The chief fragment of this once superb monument is enclosed and half-hidden by the huts of Koli weavers. *Ibid.* xvii. 361 The rest is made up of the agricultural and artizan classes, as Aheers, Kolis, &c. &c. **1868** *Rep. Ethnol. Comm. Specimens Aborig. Tribes Jubbulpore Exhib.* 1866–67 I. 11 The Mahars, Korees, and other weaving clans. **1873** *Cycl. India* (ed. 2) III. s.v. *Kori*, All the weaver caste throughout Hindoostan are stated by Colonel Tod to be Koli. They call themselves Julai, but are sometimes styled Kori. **1885** J. C. NESFIELD *Brief View Caste Syst. N.-W. Prov. & Oudh* xi. 106 The weaver caste is better known to this day by the tribal name of Kori than by the functional names of Bunkar or Joria. **1896** J. N. BHATTACHARYA *Hindu Castes & Sects* XI. ii. 233 The Kori and Koli of Northern India are weavers professing the Hindu faith; but they are very low castes. **1896** W. CROOKE *Tribes & Castes N.-W. Prov. & Oudh* III. 316 Kori, the Hindu weaver caste. *Ibid.* 318 The Koris are all Hindus... The status of the Kori is very low. **1916** R. V. RUSSELL *Tribes & Castes Cent. Prov. India* IV. II. 133 Bodies of the Kori and Katia weaving castes of northern India have been amalgamated with the Mahārs. **1957** G. S. GHURYE *Mahadev Kolis* i. 6 Koris or Koiris are known over a large part of Northern India. I do not know that any responsible student of Indian ethnography has suggested an ethnic connection between Kori and Koli.

Koriac(k), Koriak, varr. KORYAK.

korimako (‖kɔrɪ'makɔ, kɒrɪ'mɑːkəʊ). *N.Z.* [Maori.] A New Zealand honey-eater, the bell-bird, *Anthornis melanura*.

1855 R. TAYLOR *Te Ika a Maui* 75 In the first oven a korimako was cooked. **1863** A. S. ATKINSON *Jrnl.* 29 Sept. in *Richmond-Atkinson Papers* (1960) II. 63, I lay on my back.. listening dreamily to the birds, just waked up. The Korimakos in full chorus in the bush and the larks and matatas in the open land about us. **1873** W. BULLER *Hist. Birds N.Z.* 94 Certain forest-ranges were famed as Korimako preserves. **1888** *Trans. N.Z. Inst.* XXI. 213 In fine weather the bush along the south shores of Lake Brunner re-echoes with the rich notes of the tui and korimako. **1930** W. R. B. OLIVER *N.Z. Birds* 487 Bell Bird. Korimako. *Anthornis melanura*. **1966** *Encycl. N.Z.* I. 193/2 Common Maori names for the species [*sc.* the bellbird] are korimako or makomako.

korin[1] ('kɔərɪn). [Local name.] A small West African gazelle, *Gazella rufifrons*.

[**1846** J. E. GRAY in *Ann. & Mag. Nat. Hist.* XVIII. 214 Senegal Gazelle. *Gazella rufifrons*... The Corinne, F. Cuv[ier]..not of Buffon.] **1852** *Catal. Mammalia Brit. Mus.* III. 60 *Gazella rufifrons*. The Korin. **1893** R. LYDEKKER *Horns & Hoofs* v. 232 The korin (*G. rufifrons*), from Senegal, is a species of fully 24 in. in height, distinguished by the uniformly sandy yellow colour of the central streak on the face, and the absence of any tufts of hair on the knees. *Ibid.* 407/2 (*index*) Korin gazelle. **1962** M. BURTON *Syst. Dict. Mammals of World* 255 Common Gazelles of E. Africa include..Korin or Red-fronted Gazelle (*G. rufifrons*), Senegal to Sudan.

Kōrin[2] ('kɔərɪn). The name of the Japanese artist Ogata *Kōrin* (1658–1716), used *attrib.* in ***Kōrin school, style***, to denote a school of Japanese painting, founded in the Edo period and associated chiefly with Kyoto, of which Kōrin was the greatest exponent.

[**1884** SATOW & HAWES *Handbk. for Travellers Cent. & N. Japan* (ed. 2) 96 The only new school that appeared in the seventeenth century was that of Kōrin, a famous lacquer painter, who appears to have been originally a pupil of the Tosa school.] **1898** M. TOMKINSON *Jap. Collection* II. 113 The Kōrin style was a late offshoot of the Yamato-Tosa school..stamped by a bold flowing line and vigorous composition, and usually by a supreme contempt for naturalistic rules. **1909** L. BINYON *Jap. Art* v. 34 Here we have the first attempts at a fusion of the two styles, Chinese and Japanese, which reached its final development in the Korin school. **1912** E. F. FENOLLOSA *Epochs Chinese & Jap. Art* II. xiv. 129 We can call the chief masters of this Korin school the greatest painters of tree and flower forms that the world has ever seen. **1970** *Oxf. Compan. Art* 632/2 The Kōrin style represented a reversion to classical Japanese tradition.

koringkriek ('kɔərɪŋkriːk). *S. Afr.* Also **koorn kriek.** [Afrikaans, f. Du. *koren* corn + *kriek(en* to chirp.] One of several long-horned grasshoppers of the family Tettigoniidæ.

1913 C. PETTMAN *Africanderisms* 277 *Koorn kriek*,..an insect belonging to the *Locustidæ*; it is very destructive to pumpkins, mealie cobs, etc., and does at times great damage to crops. **1954** S. H. SKAIFE *Afr. Insect Life* ii. 30 Many people in South Africa fear the koringkrieks because they have the reputation of being poisonous. **1955** D. JACOBSON *Trap* iii. 73 The only sound was the shrill call of the koringkrieks, rasping frenziedly in one dry scream. **1966** E. PALMER *Plains of Camdeboo* i. 13 The koringkrieks lurching on immense and crooked legs.

Korku ('kɔːkuː). Also **Korkoo, Kurku. a.** Name of a Kolarian tribe of the Central Provinces of India; also, a member of this tribe. **b.** Their language. Also *attrib.* or as *adj.*

a **1863** S. HISLOP *Papers Aborig. Tribes Cent. Provinces* (1866) App. p. xi, All Kurkus are of one caste. They eat from the hands of Hindus, but not from Gonds or Mahars. **1868** *Rep. Ethnol. Comm. Specimens Aborig. Tribes Jubbulpore Exhib.* 1866–67 III. 17 Vocabulary of Korkoo words. **1874** WATSON & KAYE *People of India* VII. 404 Korkoos are more migratory than Gonds. **1906** G. A. GRIERSON *Ling. Survey India* IV. 167 There is only one sub-dialect of Kūrkū, the so-called Muwāsī... It does not differ much from ordinary Kūrkū. **1908** H. H. RISLEY *People of India* ii. 100 Totems found among sixteen castes and tribes, including..the primitive Gonds, Korkus, and Orāons. **1950** N. S. SAIGAL in A. V. Thakkar *Tribes India* 74 Among Korkus, 3% are Christian converts and 1·5% are Muslim converts. **1961** *Amer. Speech* XXXVI. 223 Korku phonology and morphophonemics... (Analysis of Korku with particular emphasis on low tone-*cum*-aspiration and stress..). **1962** J. J. GUMPERZ in J. A. Fishman *Readings Sociol. of Lang.* (1968) 468 Similarly in India the North Dravidian tribal languages and Munda languages such as Korku are found deep in the Indo-Aryan territory.

†**kornack**, obs. var. CARNAC, elephant-driver.

1785 *Europ. Mag.* VIII. 362 The kornack sits on the tame animal with his sharp-pointed hook. **1785** *Eng. Rev.* VI. 100 These kornacks or huntsmen have a trifling pension.

kornelite ('kɔːnəlaɪt). *Min.* [ad. Hung. *kornelit* (J. Krenner 1888, in *Magyar tudományos akad. értes.* XXII. 131), f. the name of *Kornel* Hlavacsek, who found the original specimen: see -ITE[1].] A violet to pale pink hydrated ferric sulphate, $Fe_2(SO_4)_3.7H_2O$.

1892 E. S. DANA *Dana's Syst. Min.* (ed. 6) 957 Kornelite. .. Stated to be a hydrous ferric sulphate. **1910** *Mineral. Mag.* XV. 429 Rhomboclase..occurring together with szomolnokite..and other iron sulphates (kornelite, copiapite, coquimbite, &c.) at Szomolnok, Hungary. **1937** *Amer. Mineralogist* XXII. 569 The mineral designated as kornelite is a lower hydrate of normal ferric sulphate than coquimbite. **1965** *Mineral. Abstr.* XVII. 180/2 The minerals kornelite..from Tintic Standard mine, Utah.., coquimbite.., and quenstedite.., have been re-examined.

korner, obs. form of CORNER.

korne'rupine. *Min.* [Named, 1884, after A. N. Kornerup, a Danish geologist: see -INE.] A silicate of aluminium and magnesium, somewhat like sillimanite, found in prismatic aggregates.

1892 in DANA *Min.* (ed. 6).

‖**koro** ('koːro). Also **kora.** [Jap. *kōro* incense-pot, censer.] An elaborate Japanese vase, usu. of bronze, jade, or porcelain, in which incense is burned.

1822 F. SHOBERL tr. *Titsingh's Illustr. Japan* II. 234 *Koro*, a fire-terrine. *Ibid.* 228 A..chafing-dish, with its *koro*, or stand, for burning..incense. **1889** M. B. HUISH *Japan & its Art* vii. 89 No notice of the contents of a Japanese house would be complete without some reference to the incense-burners (*ko-ro*) which find a place there, and also in the Buddhist temples. These afforded employment for a large number of artists in bronze. **1891** CHAMBERLAIN & MASON *Handbk. Travellers Japan* (ed. 3) 13 The *Kōro*, or incense-burner, generally in bronze or porcelain. **1959** *Times* 28 Apr. 20/6 A spinach green jade koro and cover. **1974** *Daily Tel.* 4 June 16/6 The koro is carved in archaic style, has large horned dragon handles and is surmounted by a Buddhistic lion and a cub.

‖**koromiko** (kɔrɔ'mikɔ). [Maori name.] A New Zealand shrub, a white-flowered arborescent species of Veronica (*Hebe salicifolia*).

1855 R. TAYLOR *Te Ika a Maui* 454 (Morris) Koromiko.. bears a tapering-shaped flower of a purplish white. **1872** DOMETT *Ranolf* I. i. 2 A ditch, With flowering koromiko rich. **1884** BRACKEN *Lays Maori* 21 The early breeze That played among the koromiko's leaves. **1921** H. GUTHRIE-SMITH *Tutira* iv. 26 Flourished green tutu..and Koromiko (*Veronica salicifolia*). **1933** *Bulletin* (Sydney) 9 Aug. 21/2 The shoots of the koromiko were chewed and swallowed for dysentery. **1963** S. ASHTON-WARNER *Teacher* 76 The idea has its duplicate often enough outdoors—in the right-angled leafing arrangements and the pairs of leaves set exactly opposite each other as in the Koromiko.

koroplast, var. COROPLAST.

korora (ˈkɔrɔra). *N.Z.* [Maori.] The southern blue penguin, *Eudyptula minor.*

1871 F. W. Hutton *Catal. Birds N.Z.* 53 *Eudyptula minor*... Blue Penguin. Korora. **1905** W. B. *Where White Man Treads* 62 A smaller canoe and men..crowding into it ..like 'korora' (penguins) awaiting the tide. **1966** R. A. Falla et al. *Field Guide Birds N.Z.* 22 Southern Blue Penguin. Maori name: Korora.

koroscopy (kɒˈrɒskəpɪ). [f. Gr. κόρη pupil + -σκοπία from -σκοπος watching, observing.] Landolt's name for the 'shadow-test' for the refraction of the eye.

1887 in *Syd. Soc. Lex.*

‖**korowai** (ˈkɔrɔwaɪ). *N.Z.* [Maori.] A cloak or mat made of flax, ornamented with black twisted thrums. Also *attrib.*

1820 *Gram. & Vocab. Lang. N.Z.* (Church Missionary Soc.) 168 *Kóro ai*, a certain garment. **1845** E. J. Wakefield *Adventure N.Z.* I. 244 The *korowai*..is woven of *muka*, or scraped flax, and ornamented with bunches of twisted tags of the same, dyed black. *Ibid.* 245 A great many varieties of the *korowai* are made. **1900** A. Hamilton *Maori Art* (1901) v. 285 The ground-work of a feather cloak is the same as that for a *korowai* mat. *Ibid.* 326 A plain *korowai* mat with the strings arranged in bands. **1921** H. Guthrie-Smith *Tutira* xi. 92 The foe can be seen cloaked in their *korowai* mats. **1938** R. Finlayson *Brown Man's Burden* 10 In the clear space by the flagpole old Tamarua is delivering a speech of welcome, mere in hand, korowai cloak swishing. **1955** W. J. Phillipps *Carved Maori Houses* p. xii, *Korowai*, cloak ornamented with twisted black thrums.

korradgee, var. koradji.

korray, variant of conrey *Obs.*

korrigan (ˈkɒrɪgən). Also corrigan, and with capital initial. [f. Breton (Vannes dial.), fem. of *korrig* gnome, dim. of *korr* dwarf. Cf. Cornish *coryk*.] The name of a fairy or witch in Breton folklore, noted esp. for stealing children.

1855 C. M. Yonge *Hist. Sir Thomas Thumb* 106 She has lost her dear little Louis; the Korrigan has taken him. **1865** T. Taylor tr. *Hersart de la Villemarqué's Ballads & Songs Brittany* p. xiv, Vannes is the home of the legends of gnomes and spirits, of dwarfs and fairies that haunt rocks and woods, streams and fountains, of the *dus* and *mary-morgan*, the *poulpican*, and the *korrigan*. **1883** J. S. Stallybrass tr. *J. Grimm's Teutonic Mythol.* II. xvii. 447 In Bretagne the *korr*, pl. *korred* answers to our elf, the *korrigan* to our elfin. *Ibid.* 469 A Breton story of the *korrigan* changing a child is in Villemarqué. **1949** *Funk's Stand. Dict. Folklore* I. 253/2 *Corrigan*, in the folklore of Brittany, a female fairy: said to have been one of the ancient druidesses, and therefore malicious towards Christian priests. She is fond of pretty human children, and usually gets the blame for all changeling substitutions. **1969** V. Rowe *Loire* i. 43 The sea-cave of the korrigans, a reminder that this is still very much a part of Brittany. The korrigans, in its [*sc.* Brittany's] Celtic folklore, are the pigwidgeons or leprechauns, or hobgoblins, with which most Celtic lands seem always to have been infested.

korrigum (ˈkɒrɪgəm). [f. Kanuri *kargum*.] A West African antelope, *Damaliscus korrigum*; also called the topi.

1826 Denham & Clapperton *Narr. Trav. N. & Cent. Afr.* 192 Senegal Antelope..was found on the plains of central Africa. The natives call this species *Korrigum*. **1836** *Proc. Zool. Soc.* IV. 103 The Korrigum of Denham and Clapperton's Travels..was a very distinct animal from the Koba. **1895** Sclater & Thomas *Bk. Antelopes* I. ii. 61 About the year 1840 Whitfield, a collector employed by Lord Derby..obtained specimens of the korrigum from the vicinity of Macarthy's Island on the River Gambia. **1964** L. S. Crandall *Managem. Wild Mammals in Captivity* 669 The korrigum or Senegal hartebeest (*Damaliscus k. korrigum*), found from Lake Chad to Senegal, was described from an animal living in the Zoological Gardens of London.

korro, var. kora[1].

Korsakoff (ˈkɔəsəkɒf). Also Korsakow, -ov. The name of S. S. *Korsakoff* (1854–1900), Russian physician, used *attrib.* or in the possessive to denote a type of psychosis, namely a syndrome, often the result of chronic alcoholism, which is characterized by disorientation, memory loss for recent events, and consequent confabulation.

1900 Dorland *Med. Dict.* 546/1 *Korsakoff's psychosis*, delirium or insanity associated with polyneuritis. **1903** *Jrnl. Mental Sci.* XLIX. 673 (*heading*) Twelve cases of 'Korsakow's disease' in women. **1924** [see confabulation 2]. **1938** *Arch. Neurol. & Psychiatry* (Chicago) XXXIX. 483 We decided..to study the forces of organization in perception and memory in cases of the Korsakoff syndrome. **1941** *Brit. Jrnl. Psychol.* XXXI. 230 The object of this paper is to describe a variety of paramnesia recently observed in.. Korsakow's psychosis. **1967** *Brit. Jrnl. Psychiatry* CXIII. 619 (*heading*) A case of craniopharyngioma presenting as Korsakov's syndrome. **1968** G. A. Talland *Disorders of Memory & Learning* iii. 63 A Korsakoff patient who, when asked to draw a woman..accurately reproduced the style.. current ten years earlier. **1970** R. M. Suinn *Fund. Behavior Path.* xi. 288/1 The characteristic signs of Korsakoff's psychosis are disorientation of time and place, anterograde amnesia.., and a marked tendency to fabricate answers to fill in the past.

korse, obs. form of corse *sb.*

‖**koru** (ˈkɔrʊ). *N.Z.* [Maori.] A common motif in Maori carving and tattooing, consisting of a spiral pattern terminating in a bulb.

1938 W. J. Phillipps in *Art in N.Z.* X. 205 The *koru*, or *pikopiko*, which today rarely appears in carving, but is used in the construction of composite patterns for rafters. **1946** —— in *Dominion Mus.* (N.Z.) *Rec. Ethnol.* I. 16 In tattoo it was also customary to incise a koru type of design on the centre of the forehead. *Ibid.* 21 Two pairs of koru, large and small. **1964** T. Barrow *Decorative Arts N.Z. Maori* iv. 64 Painted patterns appear on the underside of rafters in ceremonial meeting-houses and superior dwellings. Their elaborate curvilinear designs are usually based on a small bulb-like motif (*koru*) shaped like the looped top of an uncurling fern frond. **1970** *Dominion Mus.* (N.Z.) *Rec. Ethnol.* II. 31 An example of a carved *koru* design in its simplest form. *Ibid.* 34 The *koru* motifs (the curved stalk-like forms that terminate in a bulb).

korue(n, var. *corven*, obs. pa. pple. of carve *v.*

koruna (ˈkɒrʊnə). Also *erron.* korona. Pl. korunas, koruny. [Czech, lit. crown.] The basic monetary unit of Czechoslovakia, introduced as the Czech crown after the 1914–18 war (abbrev. *Kč*), and replaced and revalued after the 1939–45 war as the crown of the Czech and Slovak State (abbrev. *Kčs*); 1 Kčs = 100 hellers (*haléř*, pl. *haléře*). Also, a coin corresponding to this unit. Also *attrib.*

The forms *KC* and *KCS* (for Czech *Kč* and *Kčs*) in quot. 1947 are erroneous.

1920 *Czecho-Slovak Trade Jrnl.* Apr. 9/1 Prices.. between 1100 and 1500 Kč per cwt... Already 3000 to 3200 Kč are being asked for small quantities. **1930** G. Druce *Wanderings Czechoslovakia* i. 29 It may..be taken that 1 crown (*koruna*, abbreviated to Kč, which signifies the Czechoslovak crown) is worth 1½d... These coins are in denominations of 1 and 5 crowns, and also 20 and 50 hellers (halíř, plural haléřů; 100 h. make 1 kč.). **1947** *Whitaker's Almanack* 891/2 Pre-war revenue (1938) in the currency then in use Czechoslovak *Koruna* (Crown) of 100 *heller* was *KC*10,120,000... In October, 1945, currency reform was introduced and a new coinage *KCS* (*Koruna* of Czechs and Slovaks) adopted. **1962** R. A. G. Carson *Coins* 387 The new coinage system took as its unit the korona struck in cupro-nickel. **1967** *Economist* 19 Aug. p. xxvi/3 An annual turnover in the region of 6,000 million koruna (just under £900 million).

‖**korupe** (ˈkɔːrʊpe). *N.Z.* Also korurupe. [Maori *kōrupe, kororupe*.] The outer facing of the lintel of a door, often richly carved.

[**1844** W. Williams *Dict. N.Z. Lang.* 36/2 *Karupe*,.. lintel of a door.] **1897** A. Hamilton *Maori Art* (1901) ii. 84 The front of the doorway was finished off by a carved slab, the *korupe*, or *korurupe*, which rested on the carved edges of the *whakawai*. The *korupe* was not put in its place until the spaces in the walls had been filled in with *raupo*. **1927** T. E. Donne *Maori, Past & Present* xix. 160 The *paré* or *korupe*, which was placed over the outside of the doorway to a house. **1949** P. Buck *Coming of Maori* (1950) ii. ii. 128 A carved lintel (*korupe, pare*) was rested on the upper ends of the forward flanges of the jambs and so completed a doorway that was unique in Polynesian art.

‖**koruru** (ˈkɔrʊrʊ). *N.Z.* [Maori.] **1.** A wooden carving of a man's head, esp. one placed on the gable of a house.

[**1871** W. Williams *Dict. N.Z. Lang.* (ed. 3) 64/2 *Kōrūrū*, ..figure placed on the gable of a house.] **1897** A. Hamilton *Maori Art* (1901) ii. 85 The junction of the barge-boards was covered by a carved flat face, the *koruru*, which was adorned with feathers, and sometimes surmounted by a full-length figure, the *tekoteko*. The *koruru* was kept in place by a boss at the back. **1916** E. Best *Maori Storehouses* i. 3 The carvings thereof were of the *koruru*..type. *Ibid.* 25 Such minor adornments as a carved head (*koruru*) on the gable. **1949** P. Buck *Coming of Maori* (1950) ii. ii. 129 Sometimes a complete human figure (*tekoteko*) was used instead of the *koruru* type and sometimes a combination took place in which the *tekoteko* stood on the head of the *koruru*. **1966** W. J. Phillipps *Maori Life & Custom* xvii. 123 A group of carved heads, koruru, illustrating a variety of presentation.

2. A Maori version of knuckle-bones (see also quot. 1897).

1897 A. Hamilton *Maori Art* (1901) ii. 106 *Koruru*,..2. A toy with two strings, which when played with makes a whizzing or roaring noise. **1924** E. Best *Maori* II. xi. 92 The game of jackstones, or knucklebones..is known as *ruru, koruru*..and *tutukai*.

korvort, repr. an ignorant pronunc. of cavort *v.*

1909 H. G. Wells *Tono-Bungay* iii. iii. 356 She described the knights of the age of chivalry as 'korvorting about on the off-chance of a dragon'.

Korwa (ˈkɔːwə). Also Korewah. **a.** A Kolarian tribe of the Chota Nagpur area of India; also, a member of this tribe. **b.** Their language. Also *attrib.* or as *adj.*

1865 E. T. Dalton in *Jrnl. Asiatic Soc. Bengal* XXXIV. ii. 29 The Khairwars.., Korewahs and Coles number from 5000 to 7000 each. *Ibid.* 18 The Korewah iron..is greatly prized. **1872** —— *Descr. Ethnol. Bengal* v. 125 Not one of them would acknowledge that he could speak a word of Korwa. **1875** Watson & Kaye *People of India* VIII. 424 Korwas..are basket makers by profession... Korwas are evidently descended from an aboriginal stock, and are hardly recognized as Hindoos... Korwa dacoits do not intermarry with Korwa burglars. **1906** G. A. Grierson *Ling. Survey India* IV. 148 The most idiomatic Korwā is spoken in Jashpur and Sarguja, in the south of Palamau, and in Mirzapur. *Ibid.* 149 Remarks on Korwā grammar which follow. **1908** H. H. Risley *People of India* i. 44 Among the large groups..the Korwa (74·4) are just included in the long-headed division. **1923** R. B. Dixon *Racial Hist. Man* iii. i. 259 Groups of 'casteless' aboriginal peoples, such as the Munda, Korwa, Malé. **1950** R. K. Deshpande in A. V. Thakkar *Tribes India* 112 The Korwa Language has much affinity with that of the Korkus of the Mahadoo hills. **1957** G. S. Ghurye *Mahadev Kolis* i. 6 The Korwas and the Korkus..have a better claim to relationship with the Koris. But the Korwa,..and the Korku are..assigned to the Kol or the Kolarian ethnic stock. **1972** W. B. Lockwood *Panorama Indo-Europ. Lang.* 227 The languages in question are.. Koda (35,000) and Korwa (25,000).

Koryak (ˈkɒrjæk). Also Korak, Koriac(k), Koriak. [Russ. *Koryáki* (pl.), the Koryak people.] **a.** A people inhabiting the northern part of the Kamchatka peninsula; also, a member of this people. **b.** The Palæo-Asiatic language of this people. Also *attrib.* or as *adj.*

1780 W. Coxe *Acct. Russ. Discoveries* i. i. 3 The first expedition..was made in 1696, by sixteen Cossacs, under the command of Lucas Semænoff Morosko, who was sent against the Koriacks of the river Opooka. *Ibid.* 5 The peninsula of Kamtchatka..is bounded.. on the North by the country of the Koriacs. *Ibid.* iv. 49 In the autumn of 1754 they were joined by a Kamtchadal, and a Koriac. **1790** tr. *J. B. B. de Lesseps's Trav. in Kamtschatka* II. 105 The idiom of the Koriacs has no affinity to that of the Kamtschadales. *Ibid.* 117, I recognized in his features a Koriac prince... I have long owed the reader a description of a Koriac sledge. **1832** J. Bell *Syst. Geogr.* IV. vi. 74 The Koriaks inhabit the country between the Anadyr and the peninsula of Kamtschatka. **1893** *Funk's Stand. Dict.* I. 989/1 *Koriak*,..a member of a race inhabiting northeast Siberia; also, their language, related to Kamchatkan. *Koryak.* **1898** J. Y. Simpson *Side-Lights on Siberia* i. 12 Of the sub-Arctic races that inhabit the north-east of Siberia, it is sufficient to recall the names of the..Tchuktchi,..the wild Koryaks..and Yukaghirs, all differing in speech and appearance, but still related. **1907** W. Jochelson in *Internat. Congr. Americanists* XV. 121 The subterranean Koryak house is still in use among the maritime Koryak, who are not Russianised. **1910** G. Kennan *Tent Life in Siberia* xx. 203 The Korak numerals are:—Innin, One... Meen-ye-geet-kᵒhin, Ten. *Ibid.* 204 It would be a hard day's work for a boy to explain in Korak one of the.. problems in Ray's Higher Arithmetic. **1917** W. Bogoras *Koryak Texts* 2 The Koryak dialects may be divided into two large groups,—the western branch, which includes the Maritime Koryak of Penshina Bay and also the Reindeer Koryak; and the eastern branch, which includes the Maritime Koryak of Kamchatka. *Ibid.* 3 The Koryak language, in contrast to the Chukchee,..is furthermore divided into several local dialects. **1928** W. Jochelson *Peoples of Asiatic Russ.* ii. 49 The northern Kamchadal dialect..contains a considerable number of Koryak words. **1953** J. Ramsbottom *Mushrooms & Toadstools* v. 45 The Fly Agaric is among the objects believed by the Koryak to be endowed with particular power. **1954** Pei & Gaynor *Dict. Ling.* 116 *Koryak*, a language, spoken by about 1,000 persons in north-eastern Asia; a member of the Chukchi-Kamchadal family of languages, classified in the *Hyperborean* or *Palaeo-Asiatic* group.

kos, koss, var. coss *sb.*[2], a measure of 2 miles.

Kosack, variant of Cossack.

†**kosche**, *a. Sc. Obs. rare*⁻¹. [cf. Gael *còsach* full of holes or crevices, f. *còs* hole, cave.] Hollow.

1513 Douglas *Æneis* v. viii. 55 The mekle kosche fir tre [L. *cava pinus*].

kosen, -in, -yn, obs. forms of cousin.

kosh, var. cosh *sb.*[3]

Koshare (kəʊˈʃɑːriː). [ad. a Keresan word.] A member of a Pueblo Indian clown society representing ancestral spirits in rain and fertility ceremonies.

1890 A. F. Bandelier *Delight Makers* 8 Shyuote, what have you heard about the Koshare? **1924** D. H. Lawrence *Mornings in Mexico* (1927) 123 The intermittent black-and-white fantasy of the hopping Koshare, the jesters, the Delight-Makers. *a* **1956** F. Lawrence *Mem. & Corr.* (1961) 4 These Koshares wore big Spanish hats with plumes. **1959** E. Tunis *Indians* 129/1 Clowns, called Koshare, were provided to lighten the solemnity of the ceremonials.

kosher (ˈkəʊʃə(r)), *a.* (*sb.*) Also coshar, cosher, koscher. [Heb. *kāshēr* right.] **A.** *adj.* **a.** Right, good; applied to meat and other food prepared according to the Jewish law.

1851 Mayhew *Lond. Labour* (1861) II. 121 The meat killed according to the Jewish law is known as 'Coshar'. **1864** *Times* 4 Aug. *Advt.*, They will be supplied with Kosher meat of the best quality. **1892** Zangwill *Childr. Ghetto* vi. (1893) 66 The butter and cheese were equally kosher, coming straight from Hebrew Hollanders. **1892** M. Williams *Round London* (1893) 107 We [Jews] get our kosher meat killed in our own way by our co-religionists according to the law of Moses. **1934** J. Brophy *Waterfront* i. 23 To cook food in the prescribed kosher manner. **1959** *Hotel Managem. & Restaurant Trade Jrnl.* Feb. 28/2 Only kosher meals are served on El Al aircraft. **1971** *Guardian* 14 Oct. 11/2 The artificial meat business has a very good-going trade already in Kosher bacon made from soya beans. **1973** *Jewish Chron.* 19 Jan. 1/5 The Kissingers will also be given kosher food.

b. Hence of shops, houses, etc., where such food is sold or used. Also ***kosher butcher***.

1889 *N. & Q.* 7th Ser. VIII. 85 The defendant kept a 'kosher' shop. **1892** Zangwill *Childr. Ghetto* I. 250, I should have to keep a kosher house, or look how people would talk. **1932** Kipling *Limits & Renewals* 359, I had a

whole tin of salmon once from a kosher butcher. **1973** *Guardian* 16 June 3/6 The last kosher butcher left for Israel.

c. Correct, genuine, legitimate. *colloq.*

1896 FARMER & HENLEY *Slang* IV. 135/1 *Kosh* (or *Kosher*)... Adj. (common).—Fair; square. **1924** *Cosmopolitan* Nov. 104/2 It don't sound kosher to *me!* **1930** D. RUNYON in *Sat. Even. Post* 13 Sept. 7/3 'Everything is very Kosher,' Harry the Horse says. 'You need not be afraid of anything whatever. We have a business proposition.' **1930** *Amer. Mercury* Dec. 456/2 Listen shamus, you got me wrong. I'm strictly kosher. **1953** H. MILLER *Plexus* iv. 164, I made little or no effort to keep up with the others, it being no concern of mine what went on in this realm of make believe. All I felt called upon to do was to keep a straight face and pretend that everything was Kosher. **1959** C. MACINNES *Absolute Beginners* 80 It's so as to play down the queer thing in our country, and hide it behind the kosher game. *Ibid.* 157 It's all very well sneering at universities.. but really and truly, it would be wonderful to have a bit of kosher education. **1961** L. GRIBBLE *Wantons die Hard* iv. 48 'No financial irregularities?' 'Strictly kosher... It's so good it stinks.' **1966** T. PYNCHON *Crying of Lot 49* iii. 60 They got the contracts. All drawn up in most kosher fashion, Manfred. **1973** *Jewish Chron.* 8 June 22/5 As for the children of a couple married in a register office, these are quite kosher.

B. *ellipt.* as *sb.* 'Kosher' food; also, a 'kosher' shop. Also, ***to keep kosher***, to observe the Jewish law regarding diet.

1886 W. J. TUCKER *E. Europe* 125 Would we have to feed her on 'Koscher'? **1889** *N. & Q.* 7th Ser. VIII. 85 The Jews had to buy all the things they required for the Passover from a 'kosher'. **1892** ZANGWILL *Childr. Ghetto* I. xii. (1893) 119 He was almost ashamed to ask whether he could eat *Kosher* there. **1963** 'R. L. PIKE' *Mute Witness* vii. 119, I wouldn't go on the stand and state that my mother kept kosher without a chance to check.

Hence **'kosher** *v.*, to prepare (food) according to Jewish ritual; also **'koshering** *vbl. sb.*; **'kosherness.**

1871 E. LEVY *Jewish Cookery Bk.* 40 Take a fresh tongue, porge and..cosher it. **1892** ZANGWILL *Childr. Ghetto* viii. (1893) 83 She..would never fail to light the Sabbath candles nor to kosher the meat. **1949** KOESTLER *Promise & Fulfilment* III. iii. 317 Kosherness..is only one of the relatively minor rabbinical plagues in the young state. **1950** G. MIKES *Milk & Honey* 117 The Kosherness of a meal depends just as much on the way of cooking as on the raw material bought in the shop. **1960** *Commentary* June 499/2 *Kashrut* has survived in a mangled form... Scarcely anyone *kashered* the meat. **1974** *Times Lit. Suppl.* 31 May 592/3 What Mrs Wahlhaus has tried to do is to bring a new and more interesting approach to many traditional recipes, but without enough style or detail; she does not even explain how to kosher. **1974** W. FOLEY *Child in Forest* II. 218 Meat was meat (until all that Koshering business of soaking it in water and salt had emasculated it).

kosin ('kəʊsɪn). *Chem.* Also †**koussin.** [ad. It. *koussino* (C. Pavesi 1858, in *Giornale di Farm., di Chim.* VII. 49), f. *kouss-o* KOUSSO + *-ino* -IN[1].] Either of two related bicyclic phenols (not orig. differentiated), $C_{25}H_{32}O_8$, which are responsible for the anthelmintic property of kousso and are isolated as pale yellow crystals.

1875 *Pharmaceutical Jrnl. & Trans.* V. 562/2 From the aqueous residue of the alcoholic extract the koussin of Bendall, existing as a calcium compound, is precipitated as a more or less crystalline whitish powder. **1875** *Jrnl. Chem. Soc.* XXVIII. 468 The koso flowers yield about 3 per cent. of kosin. **1911** *Encycl. Brit.* XV. 921/1 *Kousso*... The active principle is koussin or kosin,..which is soluble in alcohol and alkalis, and may be given in doses of thirty grains. **1937** *Jrnl. Chem. Soc.* 563 The pale yellow product was identical with Merck's kosin... By fractional crystallisation we were able to separate this material into two distinct compounds, α-kosin, m.p. 158° (yellow needles), and β-kosin, m.p. 120° (yellow prisms). **1952** *Ibid.* 3103 Extracts of the flowers [sc. *Hagenia abyssinica*] contained large amounts of amorphous material, some of which could be converted into kosins by the action of alkali.

kos-kos, var. KAS-KAS.

‖**koss, kos.** = COSS, COS *sb.*[2]

Kossæan: see KASSITE *sb.* and *a.*

Kossak, var. COSSACK.

kosschen, obs. f. CUSHION.

kosso ('kɒsəʊ), var. KOUSSO.

kost(e, kostome, kostorell, obs. ff. COAST, CUSTOM, COSTREL.

koswite ('kɒzwaɪt). *Petrogr.* Also **kosvite.** [a. F. *koswite* (Duparc & Pearce 1901, in *Compt. Rend.* CXXXII. 892), f. the name of the *Kosw-inski* Mountains, Pawda, in the Middle Urals: see -ITE[1].] A coarse-grained peridotite consisting mainly of diopside, olivine, and magnetite. Hence **ko'switic (kosvitic)** *a.*

1901 *Jrnl. Chem. Soc.* LXXX. II. 398 Associated with olivine-gabbros in the Solimask district, near the source of the Kosswa river, is a new type of basic eruptive rock to which the name koswite is given... As the magnetite decreases in amount and becomes idiomorphic, there is a passage from koswite to ordinary pyroxenite. **1922** *Mineral. Abstr.* I. 327 The mining district around Nikolae-Pavdinsk on the eastern slopes of the northern Urals..consists largely of basic igneous rocks (dunite.., &c., and the local types koswite, tilaite, [etc.]). **1964** *Doklady Earth Sci.* CLIV. 149/2 The exceptionally high contents of volatile components in kosvites (mainly apatite-ore pyroxenites) increase the acidity of the melt. *Ibid.*, In the case of a kosvitic melt, which itself contains a considerable quantity of volatile components.

kot, obs. form of COAT, COT *sb.*[1], CUT *v.*

‖**kotal** ('kəʊtæl). *E. Ind.* [Pushtō *kōtal* mountain pass.] The pass over a mountain; a col; the ridge or summit of a pass.

1880 *Times* 15 Oct. 4/2 The three Afghan guns on the ridge, or *kotal*, as these ascents are called in Afghanistan. **1890** *Ibid.* 31 Jan. 8/3 From the fourth and last of these *kotals* the traveller descends on to a level..plain. **1897** LD. ROBERTS *41 Yrs. India* xxxiv. (1898) 282 By noon the kotal was reached.

kotare ('kɔːtare). *N.Z.* [Maori *kōtare.*] The native kingfisher, *Halcyon sancta.*

1873 W. L. BULLER *Hist. Birds N.Z.* 69 *Halcyon vagans.* (New-Zealand Kingfisher.)..Native names. Kotare and Kotaretare; 'Kingfisher' of the colonists. **1882** W. D. HAY *Brighter Britain!* II. 221 The Kotare..is a kingfisher. **1930** W. R. B. OLIVER *N.Z. Birds* 430 Sacred Kingfisher. Kotare. *Halcyon sanctus.* **1968** *Landfall* XXII. 249 Like worm in kotare's beak my old maori lies limp.

‖**kotatsu** (ko'tatsu). [Jap.] A wooden frame which is placed over the hearth in Japanese houses and covered with a thick quilt to give an enclosed area within which people can warm their hands and feet. Also applied to the hearth and the cover together. Also *attrib.*

1876 W. E. GRIFFIS *Mikado's Empire* II. vii. 416, I got up, entered the best room in the house, and curled up under a kotatsŭ. **1880** I. L. BIRD *Unbeaten Tracks Japan* II. lv. 254 The *kotatsu*..consists of a square, wooden frame, standing over a basin of lighted charcoal, and supporting a large wadded quilt or *futon*, under which you creep... The invitation to creep under the *kotatsu* is as welcome as the 'sit in' of the Scotch Highlands or the 'put your feet in the stove' of Colorado. **1889** M. B. HUISH *Japan & its Art* vii. 86 The only other articles of furniture will be the kotatsu, a square wooden frame, which in winter is placed over the hibachi or stove, and is covered with a large wadded quilt or *futon* (under this the whole family huddle for warmth). **1970** J. KIRKUP *Japan behind Fan* 126 A limited life of kitchen and *kotatsu* gossip in some narrow-minded village.

kote, obs. form of COAT, COTE.

kotla, var. KGOTLA.

†**kotle-loft,** obs. var. COTLOFT, *cockle-loft*, COCK-LOFT.

1661 WOOD *Life* 19 Feb. (O.H.S.) I. 382, I laid up 4 broken fir boxes in the kotleloft.

‖**koto** ('kəʊtəʊ). Also †**kotto.** [Japanese.] A Japanese musical stringed instrument played with both hands.

It has thirteen silk strings stretched over a long box as a resonance chamber, each string having a bridge of its own, by shifting of which it is tuned.

1795 tr. *C. P. Thunberg's Trav. Europe, Afr. & Asia* IV. 58 The *koto* bears a strong resemblance to our dulcimers, having the number of strings, which are struck with sticks. **1822** F. SHOBERL tr. *Titsingh's Illustr. Japan* 234 *Kotto*, a kind of harp. **1864** ENGEL *Mus. Anc. Nations* 46 The strings of the koto are generally twanged with small plectra fastened on the fingers of the performer. **1891** A. M. BACON *Jap. Girls & Women* ii. 42 The *koto* is an embryo piano, a horizontal sounding board, some six feet long, upon which are stretched strings supported by ivory bridges. **1893** F. T. PIGGOTT *Mus. Japan* III. 135 The Koto is the chief of modern Japanese instruments. **1932** F. L. WRIGHT *Autobiogr.* II. 210 A fine lady plays the Koto, its graceful length laid upon the expanse of matting. **1961** A. BAINES *Mus. Instrum.* 208 The *koto*, the national instrument of pre-Westernized Japan. Its six-foot long soundbox is placed on the floor... Along it run thirteen waxed silk strings of equal length and played open, each tuned by its own movable bridge to contribute to a pentatonic scale of the 'major third' type..over two and a half octaves. **1965** W. SWAAN *Jap. Lantern* i. 10 The chief item is a concerto for *koto*, the traditional Japanese harp. **1973** E. T. SITHOLE in T. Kochman *Rappin' & Stylin' Out* 69 You would have expected me to write about the music of Bach..and not about Koto music (Japan).

kotow, var. KOW-TOW *sb.* and *v.*

kotschubeite, var. KOCHUBEÏTE.

kottabos, -bus, variants of COTTABUS.

kotuku ('kɔːtʊkʊ). *N.Z.* Also †**koatuku.** [Maori.] The white heron, *Egretta alba.*

1846 C. HEAPHY *Jrnl.* 23 Apr. in N. M. Taylor *Early Travellers N.Z.* (1959) 218 Shot a very fine *koatuku*, or white heron. **1882** W. L. BULLER *Man. Birds N.Z.* 52 The White Heron occurs so sparingly in most parts of New Zealand that 'rare as the Kotuku' has passed into a proverb among the Maoris. **1949** P. BUCK *Coming of Maori* (1950) II. xii. 284 Feathers of the..heron (*kotuku*) were also valued. **1963** *Evening Post* (Wellington, N.Z.) 26 Oct., In the..action shots..are the..kaka and spectacular kotuku or white heron.

‖**kotwal** ('kɒtwɑːl). *East Ind.* Forms: 6–7 **catual(l, 7 cutwal(l, coute-, cotoval, 8 cautwaul, catwal, 9 cutwahl, -wal, -waul, kat-, cot-, kutwal, kotwal(l.** [Hindī *koṭwāl*, Urdu and Pers. *kotwāl*, *katwāl*, porter or keeper of a castle or fort, magistrate.]

A chief officer of police for a city or town in India; a native town magistrate.

'The office in Western and Southern India, technically speaking, ceased about 1862. In Bengal the term has been long obsolete' (Yule).

1582 N. LICHEFIELD tr. *Castanheda's Conq. E. Ind.* 50 The Catuall sent to the Captaine generall a Horse. **1616** SIR T. ROE in *Pinkerton's Voy.* (1811) VIII. 5, I was conducted by the Cutwall to visit the Prince. **1680** tr. *Trav. Tavernier, etc.* II. 119 The Cotoval, who is, as 'twer, the great Prevost. **1727** A. HAMILTON *New Acc. E. Ind.* I. 197 Mr. Boucher.. presently knew the Poison, and carried it to the Cautwal or Sheriff. **1763** ORME *Hist. Mil. Trans. Ind.* (1803) I. 26 The Catwal is the judge and executor of justice in criminal cases. **1822** *15 Yrs. India* 188 The oldest and most venerable looking man in a village is Cutwal, with a court under him. **1845** STOCQUELER *Handbk. Brit. India* (1854) 410 The Katwal, or chief officer of justice. **1859** LANG *Wand. India* 42, I was enticed away from my home by the Kotwall (native police officer).

Hence ‖**ko'twalee, kotwali,** police station.

1845 STOCQUELER *Handbk. Brit. India* (1854) 227 In the centre of the city is the *cutwallee*, police-office. **1884** MARK THORNHILL *Advent. Ind. Mut.* xvii. 158 We should have to pass the kotwallee to reach the fort. **1964** A. SWINSON *Six Minutes to Sunset* ii. 34 Major MacDonald marched a company of troops down Hall Gate as far as the Kotwali. **1969** *Pioneer* (Lucknow) 13 Aug. 6/7 The kotwali police claim to have arrested last night three of the inter-district gang of burglars operating for several years in Pratapgarh, Sultanpur and Allahabad districts.

kotyle, var. COTYLE (sense 1).

kotyn, obs. form of COTTON *sb.*[1]

kou (kəʊ). [Hawaiian.] A Hawaiian tree, *Cordia subcordata*, of the family Boraginaceæ, or its dark brown wood.

1825 W. ELLIS *Jrnl. Tour Hawaii* i. 27 The houses, which are neat, are generally built on the sea-shore, shaded with cocoanut and *kou* trees. **1866** 'MARK TWAIN' *Lett. from Hawaii* (1967) 128 It [*sc.* the coffin] is made of those two superb species of native wood, kou and koa. The former is nearly as dark as ebony. *Ibid.* 207 Among the varied and handsome foliage of the kou, koa, kukui..its [*sc.* the orange's] dark, rich green cone was sure to arrest the eye. **1913** J. F. ROCK *Indigenous Trees Hawaiian Islands* 415 The Kou, which is indigenous in the Hawaiian Islands,..can only be found along the sea-shore here and there... The wood of the Kou was much sought for. **1969** T. H. EVERETT *Living Trees of World* 292/2 A native of sandy shores of the Indian and the western Pacific oceans, the kou or sea trumpet (*C*[*ordia*] *subcordata*) is an evergreen tree that grows up to 50 feet in height and has a dense, spreading crown.

kou, kouard, kouch, kouckery, obs. ff. COW, COWARD, COUCH, COOKERY.

koude, kouȝde, kouel, kouenand, kouer, obs. ff. COULD, COWL *sb.*[1], COVENANT, COVER.

kouȝe, kouȝhe, kouȝwhe, obs. ff. COUGH.

koukou, var. KUKU 1.

koukri, variant of KUKRI.

Koula(h), varr. KULAH[1].

koulak, var. KULAK.

‖**koulan, kulan** ('kuːlən). [Tartar *kulan.*] A species or sub-species of equine quadruped (*Equus onager*), closely allied to the Dziggetai (with which it is united by some), found in Central and Southern Asia: the wild ass of Mesopotamia, Persia, and the banks of the Indus.

1793 PENNANT *Hist. Quad.* (ed. 3) I. 11 The manners of the *Koulan* or wild ass, are very much the same with those of the wild horse and the Dshikketaei. **1836** *Encycl. Brit.* (ed. 7) XIV. 153/1 The Onager, or wild ass, called *koulan* by many of the tribes of Asia, differs from the domestic breed in its shorter ears, the greater length and finer form of its limbs [etc.]. **1856** KNIGHT *Cycl. Nat. Hist.* I. 327 The Persians and Tartars hold the flesh of the Koulan in high esteem. **1885** *Stand. Nat. Hist.* V. 252 The specific name *hemionus* 'half ass' was given to the kulan by the Greeks, on account of its stature, which is between that of the horse and the ass. *Ibid.* 253 The kulans..migrate in the spring and fall to more suitable pasture grounds.

koule, obs. form of COLE *sb.*[1]

‖**koumiss** ('kuːmɪs). Forms: (6 **cosmos,** 7 **cosmus, cossmos:** see COSMOS[2]), 7 **chumis,** 8 **kumisse, (kumish),** 8– **koumiss, kumiss, kumis,** 9 **koumis, koomiss, kumys(s, (kimmiz, khoumese).** [= F. *koumis*, G. *kumiss*, Pol. *komis*, *kumys*, Russ. *kumys*, a. Tartar *kumiz.*] A fermented liquor prepared from mare's milk, commonly used as a beverage by the Tartars and other Asiatic nomadic tribes; also applied to a spirituous liquor distilled from this.

The fermented beverage is used dietetically and medicinally in various diseases, as phthisis, catarrhal affections, anæmia, chlorosis, etc., and for these purposes imitations are also prepared from asses' milk and cow's milk.

1598–1630 [see COSMOS[2]]. **1607** TOPSELL *Four-f. Beasts* 332 The Tartarians drinke Mares Milke, which they dress like white wine, and call it Chumis. **1723** *Pres. St. Russia* I. 276 [The Kalmucks] drink Kumis, a sort of Brandy drawn off from Mares-milk. **1771** *Gentl. Mag.* XLI. 594 The sour milk which they [the Tartars] drink they call Kumisse. **1839** E. D. CLARKE *Trav. Russia* 52/1 A subsequent process of distillation afterwards obtains an ardent spirit from the koumiss. **1876** BARTHOLOW *Mat. Med.* (1879) 22 By the

fermentation of mare's milk an alcoholic liquor, named koumiss, is prepared in Tartary, and has been introduced into medical practice as a remedy for phthisis. **1892** *Daily News* 28 Dec. 5/4 Mrs. Isabel Hapgood..gives some interesting particulars of koumiss (or 'kumys', as she prefers to spell it).
attrib. **1884** *Pall Mall G.* 15 Sept. 11/2 The koumiss cure is growing greatly in popularity... Sometimes patients spend six or seven summers at the koumiss establishments.

†**koundee**, var. CONDUE *v. Obs.*, to conduct.
c **1450** LONELICH *Grail* xiii. 434 That In theke tyme so wel koundeed & ladde.

koupholite: see COUPHOLITE.

kouprey ('kuːpreɪ). [Cambodian native name.] A large wild ox, *Novibos* (or *Bos*) *sauveli*, first discovered in Cambodia in 1937.
1940 *Mem. Mus. Compar. Zool. Harvard* LIV. 421 On comparing the measurements of the skull and skeleton of the kouprey with those of a gaur and a bantin, the kouprey revealed important differences. **1955** F. BOURLIÈRE *Mammals of World* iii. 131 Mention should also be made here of the curious Kouprey or Cambodian Forest Ox, whose taxonomic status is still rather uncertain. **1970** *New Scientist* 23 July 177/1 The kouprey (*Novibos sauveli*) was.. a large blackish-brown animal, with prominent white legs and a chestnut facial pattern, the bull stands over 6 feet tall. **1971** *Ibid.* 11 Feb. 342/1 The American invasion of Cambodia last year probably put paid to the kouprey *Bos sauveli*, a primitive wild cow.

‖**koura** ('kɔːʊrə). *N.Z.* Also gorau, kora. [Maori.] A small freshwater crayfish, *Paranephrops planifrons*.
1847 J. JOHNSON *Jrnl.* 5 Jan. in N. M. Taylor *Early Travellers N.Z.* (1959) 152 A small settlement, occupied in the summer for the purpose of catching *gorau*, a species of cray-fish, or rather fresh water lobster. **1867** E. SAUTER tr. *F. von Hochstetter's New Zealand* viii. 171 Of the Macrura I may mention especially *Paranephrops tenuicomis Dana*... The natives call it Koura. **1873** J. H. H. ST. JOHN *Pakeha Rambles through Maori Lands* viii. 151 Rotorua has its *kora*, a large prawn, or a diminutive freshwater lobster. **1945** F. SARGESON *When Wind Blows* 92 In the creek they saw the crayfish and Mr Jones said he called them crawlers, but the Maoris called them koura. **1974** *N.Z. Listener* 20 July 13/1 Here we were fed koura and kouras are a real luxury in the North Island.

‖**kourbash, koorbash** ('kʊəbæʃ), *sb.* Also corbage, courbash, -bache, coorbatch, kurbasch, cur-, kur-, korbash. [f. Arabic *qurbāsh*, ad. Turk. *qirbāch* whip: cf. F. *courbache*.] A whip made of hide, esp. that of the hippopotamus; an instrument of punishment in Turkey, Egypt, and the Soudan.
1814 W. BROWN *Hist. Propag. Chr.* II. 40 A Corbage, which consists of a strap of the skin of the hippopotamus, about a yard in length. **1842** R. R. MADDEN *United Irishmen* I. xi. 337 Persons subjected to the torture of the 'courbash', in Damascus. **1866** EMMELINE LOTT *Harem Life Egypt* II. 90, I soon after heard stifled cries, and a cracking of the courbache. **1884** J. COLBORNE *Hicks Pasha* 189 It is the peculiar mission of the hippopotamus to supply Kurbashes for the backs of the natives. **1885** MRS. E. SARTORIUS *In the Soudan* viii. 129 An unlimited application of the koorbash. **1892** *Nation* (N.Y.) 11 Aug. 107/3 To plead urgently for the abolition of the kurbash.

'**kourbash**, '**koorbash**, *v.* [f. prec. sb.] *trans.* To flog with the kourbash.
1850 *Punch's Alm. for 1851.* 7 He [the Persian Prince] had one of his attendants courbashed or flogged yesterday. **1884** CLIFFORD LLOYD in *Times* 30 June 8/2 The Mudir had seized 77 sheikhs and other respectable men,..and had kourbashed and tortured them all.

‖**kouros** ('kuːrɒs). *Gr. Antiq.* Pl. kouroi. [Gr. (Ionic form of κόρος boy).] A sculptured representation of a youth.
1920 [see KORE 2]. **1932** BEAZLEY & ASHMOLE *Greek Sculpture & Painting* vi. 27 For all the beauty and variety of the late archaic kouroi and korai, it is not in these that late archaic sculpture finds its most perfect expression, but in the action-figures—men not being but doing. **1939** *Ann. Brit. Sch. Athens* XXXVI. 2 The Anarysos Kouros is of Parian marble. It has a reddish tint; but in many places..the surface has perished to some extent. **1963** *Listener* 21 Mar. 511/1 The great *Kouroi* at the National Museum in Athens. **1965** D. E. STRONG *Classical World* 58 In figure-sculpture the ideal schemes of the nude *kouros* and the draped female (*kore*) hold the field until the early years of the 5th century.

†**kours**, obs. form of CURSE *sb.* and *v.*
c **1320** *Sir Beues* (MS.A) 2619 Þai hadden mani mannes kours, Whar þourȝ hii ferden wel þe wors. *Ibid.* 3719 Terri ..koursede biter þat while.

kourtepy, kourtt: see COURTEPY, COURT.

kouskous, -koussou, var. COUSCOUS, -SOU.

‖**kousso** ('kʊsəʊ). Also kuosso, cusso, kosso, koso. [Abyssinian.] The dried flowers of an Abyssinian plant, *Hagenia* (*Brayera*) *abyssinica* (N.O. *Rosaceæ*), used as an anthelmintic.
1851 *Illustr. Catal. Gt. Exhib.* 197 Kuosso, from Abyssinia (*Brayera anthelmintica*). The blossom of a tree.. the native remedy..for the removal of tapeworm. **1876** HARLEY *Mat. Med.* (ed. 6) 620 Kousso is an irritant. **1889** WATT *Dict. Econ. Prod. India* I. 534 *Cusso* or *Kousso*..a bazaar commercial article in Bombay; it comes direct from Africa. **1936** E. WAUGH *Waugh in Abyssinia* i. 13 His mother lived by selling *kosso*, a specific against tapeworm, in the streets of Gondar.

koutekite ('kuːtɪkaɪt). *Min.* [f. the name of J. *Koutek* (see quot. 1958) + -ITE[1].] An arsenide of copper, Cu_5As_2, found as bluish-grey microscopic grains with a metallic lustre.
1958 Z. JOHAN in *Nature* 31 May 1554/1 While studying specimens from Černý Důl in Krkonše (Giant Mountains), Bohemia, a new mineral of composition Cu_2As has been found in the bicarbonate gangue... The new mineral has been named koutekite in honour of Academician J. Koutek, professor of economic geology, Charles University, Prague. **1967** *Mineral. Abstr.* XVIII. 281/2 Koutekite, Cu_5As_2.., has been recognized at Daluis in the upper Var Valley, where it occurs with domeykite.

kouth(e, kouþ, obs. pa. t. of CAN *v.*[1]; obs. f. COUTH *a.*

kouuele, obs. form of COWL *sb.*[2]

†**kove.** *Obs. rare.* [a. AF. *couve* for F. *cuve*.] A variant of CUVE, cask, vat.
c **1320** *Sir Beues* (MS.A) 2591 Þe beschop cristnede Iosian. For Ascopard was mad a koue [*MS.M.* a toune; *AFr. text*, un grant couve funt aparailer].

kovsh (kɒvʃ). Pl. kovshi. [Russ.] A ladle or container for drink.
1884 A. MASKELL *Russ. Art* vi. 134 The bowls or ladles termed kovsh. **1935** *Burlington Mag.* June 298/1 The large kovsh, or ladle..follows an interesting evolution. **1949** H. C. BAINBRIDGE *Peter Carl Fabergé* vii. 133 Objects in.. painted enamels in the way of ikons, kovshi, tea sets, [etc.]. **1960** *Harper's Bazaar* Aug. 11/1 A silver-gilt kovsh: used in Russia for drinking vodka. **1966** *Daily Tel.* 18 Oct. 16/5 At Sothebys... A Russian silver and enamel kovsh, a squat wine jug, went to G. Lawrence for £210.

kow, obs. form of COW *sb.* and *v.*

koward, -yse, kowartnes, obs. ff. COWARD, COWARDICE, COWARDNESS.

kowch, obs. form of COUCH *sb.*[1] and *v.*[1]

kowd, obs. pa. t. of CAN *v.*[1]; obs. f. COUTH *a.*

kowdie, obs. var. KAURI.

†**kowe.** *Obs.* [a. OF. *cowe*, *coue*, etc., var. of *queue* tail, QUEUE; cf. CUE *sb.*[3]] A 'tail', tag, or additional short line after a couplet or at the end of a stanza of verse. (Cf. COUWEE.)
c **1330** R. BRUNNE *Chron. Wace* (Rolls) 88 If it were made in ryme couwee,..þat rede Inglis it ere inowe þat couthe not haf coppled a kowe.

kowe, obs. form of COW *sb.*[1] and [2], COUGH *v.*

‖**kowhai** ('kɔːfaɪ, 'kəʊhaɪ). *New Zealand.* Also kowai, kohai, goai. [Maori.] An evergreen shrub or small tree, *Sophora tetraptera*, of the family Leguminosæ, native to New Zealand and bearing racemes of yellow flowers.
1831 G. BENNETT in *London Med. Gaz.* 12 Nov. 182/1 *Sophora tetraptera*... This tree is the Kowhy, or Kongia, of the natives, and attains the height of from forty to fifty feet. **1845** E. J. WAKEFIELD *Adv. N. Zeal.* I. 58 (Morris) The kohai..with bright yellow blossoms. **1860** J. BLAIR *N. Zeal.* (ibid.), The land of the goai tree. **1872** DOMETT *Ranolf* VI. i. 107 Amohia,..scarlet-crowned with Kowhai-flowers. **1883** RENWICK *Betrayed* 42 Gather the kowhai, wet with showers. **1896** R. KIPLING *Seven Seas* 113 Buy the kowhai's gold Flung for gift on Taupo's face. **1897** D. MCK. WRIGHT *Station Ballads* 123 There are dreams in the gold of the kowhai. **1926** *Trans. N.Z. Inst.* LVI. 670 'Kowhai' went through many stages—'goa', 'gohi', etc., before settling to the two forms 'kowhai' in the North and 'gowhai' or 'gowai' in the South. **1947** O. RUHEN in *Coast to Coast 1946* 1 Old gold blossom freckled the untidy lattice of brown boughs that the kowhais threw up on the top of the bank. **1952** 'J. GUTHRIE' *Paradise Bay* i. 12 In a kowhai bush, among the yellow beak-shaped blossom. **1966** *New Statesman* 16 Dec. 915/3 The beach itself is sheltered by..bush patched with yellow and gold kowhai bloom and white clematis.

kowhe, kowke, obs. ff. COUGH, COOK.

‖**kowl**, variant of COWLE (*Anglo-Ind.*), written engagement.
1897 R. KIPLING in *Pearson's Mag.* Dec. 622/1 Things for which we need a kowl.

kowle, kowlt, obs. forms of COWL, COLT.

kownnage, kownsayle, etc., **knownt**, obs. forms of COINAGE, COUNSEL, COUNT.

kowrs, kowschot, obs. ff. COURSE, CUSHAT.

kowse: see COUSE.

kowter, kowth, obs. ff. COULTER, COUTH *a.*

‖**kow-tow** (kaʊ'taʊ), **kotow** (kəʊ'taʊ), *sb.* Also kow-too, ko-too, -tou, ka-tou, koo-too. [Chinese *k'o-t'ou*, f. *k'o* knock + *t'ou* the head.] The Chinese custom of touching the ground with the forehead in the act of prostrating oneself, as an expression of extreme respect, submission, or worship.
1804 BARROW *Trav. China* (1806) 213 The Chinese were determined they should be kept in the constant practice of the koo-too, or ceremony of genuflection and prostration. **1817** ELLIS *Jrnl. Emb. China* 213 Lord Macartney's performance of the ko-tou was asserted. **1845** *Athenæum* 22 Feb. 193 He felt some reluctance when called upon to perform the ko-tow. **1864** D. F. RENNIE *Brit. Arms N. China* 232 *note*, The kowtow is the Chinese obeisance indicating extreme respect. **1898** W. G. GULLAND *Chinese Porc.* I. p. xxiv, Lord Amherst..would not perform the *kow-tow* (kneeling) before the emperor. **1920** *Blackw. Mag.* Aug. 225/1 The conventional bowing or kow-tow position. **1966** *Listener* 29 Sept. 443/2 Not even the emissaries of the Pope could escape the Great Kow-tow—the ceremony involving the three kneelings and nine prostrations before the throne of the Chinese Emperor.
b. *fig.* An act of obsequious respect.
1834 *Fraser's Mag.* X. 230 Thus speaks the high-priest of fashion, and the *beau monde* perform the koo-too with all imaginable submission. **1865** CARLYLE *Fredk. Gt.* (1872) VI. XVI. ix. 235 Voltaire from of old had faithfully done his kowtoos to this King of the Sciences. **1905** [see HEWGAG]. **1972** *Times* 21 Oct. (Hongkong Suppl.) p. i/6 Peking has referred officially to Hongkong's shameful colonial status only once since President Nixon's dignified *kowtow* and the belated entry of the people's republic into the United Nations.

kow-tow (kaʊ'taʊ), **kotow** (kəʊ'taʊ), *v.* [f. prec. sb.] *intr.* To perform the kow-tow. Also *transf.*
1863 *Fraser's Mag.* Dec. 709/2 With one dash of the brush a clever artist at once hits off all the characteristics of his subject, whether it be a bat or moth in the gloaming, or a humble cricket *kow-towing* to a lordly mantis perched on a blade of grass. **1864** D. F. RENNIE *Brit. Arms N. China* 232 He kow-towed to him in proof of his anxiety to follow his advice and give up opium. **1892** *Mission Herald* (Boston) Aug. 326 The literary graduates kneel and kotow before each one of these shrines. *Ibid.*, A *tien*, or cushion, to kneel on in kotowing. **1907** *Westm. Gaz.* 12 Nov. 14/1 The degrading custom of high native Ministers of the Crown kowtowing. **1966** D. FORBES *Heart of Malaya* xi. 129 Miss Khan kowtowed to the laughing monk. **1966** *Listener* 29 Sept. 444/1 An envoy of the Tsar who arrived in Peking in the sixteen-seventies to discuss Russo-Chinese differences refused to kow-tow to the Emperor.
b. *fig.* To act in an obsequious manner.
1826 DISRAELI *Viv. Grey* II. xii, The Marquess kotooed like a first-rate Mandarin, and vowed 'that her will was his conduct'. **1883** *Harper's Mag.* Mar. 578/2 The doctor kowtowed to him.
Hence **kow-'tower**; **kow-'towing** *vbl. sb.* and *ppl. a.* Also **kow-'towism**, the practice of kow-towing.
1836 T. HOOK *G. Gurney* II. 55 Hull, who watched his worship with an almost Koo-too-ing kindness. **1837** —— *Jack Brag* viii, The little group in the full exercise of Koo-too-ism. **1848** THACKERAY *Bk. of Snobs* xxxvi, It was nothing compared to the bowing and kotooing. **1874** A. C. MACLAY *Let.* 1 May (1886) 47 Then followed a tempest of *kow-towing* that beggared description. **1961** *Spectator* 8 Sept. 313 They regard the Russians as..kow-towers to the West.

kowuele, obs. form of COWL *sb.*[2]

koy, koye, obs. forms of COY, QUEY.

‖**koyan** (ko'jan). Also 9 coyan. [Mal. *koyan*.] In Malaysia, a unit of weight equal to 40 *piculs*, equivalent to approximately 5,330 lb. (2·42 tonnes).
1783 W. MARSDEN *Hist. Sumatra* 157 The *coolah* or bamboo, containing very nearly a gallon, is the general standard of measure among the Rejangs: of these eight hundred make a *coyan*. **1820** J. CRAWFURD *Hist. Indian Archipelago* I. III. i. 273 Thirty pikuls [make] one *koyan*. **1839** T. J. NEWBOLD *Pol. & Statistical Acct. Straits of Malacca* I. i. 26 Salt, and..rice, etc. are sold by measure, generally by that of the coyan. **1900** W. W. SKEAT *Malay Magic* v. 228 A field which..produces a *koyan* of rice a year will fetch a rent of about two hundred gallons more or less. **1947** R. O. WINSTEDT *Malays* 125 The produce of rice formerly exceeded the internal consumption by about the annual average of 2,500 *koyan*. **1957** *Federation of Malaya Ann. Rep.* II. iv. 519 The *koyan* (40 *piculs*)..—5,333⅓ lbs.

koyf(e, koyne, koynt(e, koyt, obs. ff. COIF, COIN, QUAINT, QUOIT.

kozack, -ak, variants of COSSACK.

K(-)particle. *Nuclear Physics.* Also †k-particle. = KAON.
1949 *Nature* 15 Jan. 85/2 The agreement between the sets of values for mesons..gives strong support for the assumption of a spontaneous decay of the *k*-particle. **1954** *Proc. R. Soc.* A. CCXXI. 293 Those charged particles more massive than the π-meson which, at the end of their range in the emulsion, transmute with the emission of a singly-charged particle, are referred to as *K*-particles... The charged particles are in some cases μ-mesons, and others π-mesons. **1955** *Sci. News Let.* 19 Feb. 117/2 K particles are mesons of mass intermediate between electrons and protons. **1966** D. L. LIVESEY *Atomic & Nucl. Physics* x. 468 The neutral *K* particle must therefore possess a rest mass greater than 550 m_e, the measured energy release being such that the calculated mass is about 1000 m_e.

kra (krɑː). Also kera. [Mal. *kera*.] The long-tailed or crab-eating macaque, *Macaca fascicularis* (= *M. irus*), native to southern and south-eastern Asia.
1821 T. S. RAFFLES in *Trans. Linnean Soc.* XIII. 247 The Malay name has frequently a close resemblance to the cry of the animal it designates; and this is remarkably the case in the present instance... The Kra is not easily domesticated. **1839** T. J. NEWBOLD *Pol. & Statistical Acct. Straits of Malacca* I. vii. 432 Of the genus Semnopithecus are..the Lotong,..the Kra, or Simia fascicularis. **1911** *Encycl. Brit.* XVII. 472/2 The *lotong*, *kra*, and at least twenty other kinds of monkey. **1932** S. ZUCKERMAN *Social Life Monkeys* ix. 143 No periodicity has been noted in the rarely observed sexual response of bonnet monkeys and adult female kra monkeys

(common macaques). **1969** Ld. Medway *Wild Mammals Malaya* 50/2 Long-tailed or Crab-eating Macaque. Kera. *Macaca fascicularis.*

‖**kraak porselein, kraakporselein** (krɑːk ˈpɔəsɪleɪn). Also (with partial tr.) **kraak porcelain.** [Du.; see quot. 1954.] Blue-and-white Chinese porcelain of the Wan-li period (1573–1619) or later in the seventeenth century, or a European imitation of this.

1954 H. Garner *Oriental Blue & White* v. 37 This type of porcelain is known as *Kraak porselein*, from the Dutch term for the type of Portuguese ship from which the porcelain was first captured in 1603. The ship, the carrack *Catherina*.. was..taken to Amsterdam. *Ibid.*, Kraak porcelain had a great influence on the development of European pottery, being extensively copied at Delft. **1956** J. A. Pope *Chinese Porc. Ardebil Shrine* ii. 137 In terms of general shape the most noticeable difference between these *kraakporseleins* and other sixteenth-century wares is to be found in the dishes. **1961** M. Sullivan *Introd. Chinese Art* ix. 185 Soon after 1600 a particular type of thin, brittle Wan-li export blue-and-white began to reach Europe. This ware, called *kraak* porcelain..caused a sensation when it appeared. **1969** *Times* 25 Mar. 15/5 (Advt.), Kraak porselain [*sic*] dishes.

kraal (krɑːl), *sb.* Also 8 crawl, 8–9 craal, 9 crall, kraul. See also crawl *sb.*[2] [a. Colonial Du. *kraal*, a. Pg. *curral*, *corral*: see corral.]

1. a. A village of Hottentots, Kaffirs, or other South or Central African natives, consisting of a collection of huts surrounded by a fence or stockade, and often having a central space for cattle, etc. Also *transf.* the community of such a village.

1731 Medley *Kolben's Cape G.H.* I. 75 The Kraals, as they call them, or villages, of the Hassaquas are larger. **1771** Sir J. Banks *Jrnl.* (1896) 441 They [the Cape Hottentots] train up bulls, which they place round their crawls or towns in the night. **1785** G. Forster tr. *Sparrman's Voy. Cape G.H.* I. 179 A craal or community of Hottentots, to the amount of about thirty persons. **1836** *Penny Cycl.* V. 229 Kraals of Bosjesmans north of the Orange river who seemed to live in peace under a chief. **1849** E. E. Napier *Excurs. S. Afr.* I. 316 The huts which compose their kraals are of a circular form. **1891** R. W. Murray *S. Africa* 194 A kraal is ..a collection of huts surrounded by mud walls or palisading.

b. Used loosely for a poor hut or hovel.

1832 G. Downes *Lett. Cont. Countries* I. 70 That solitary attraction which the poorest kraals of Ireland possess—hospitality.

2. a. An enclosure for cattle or sheep (esp. in South or Central Africa); a stockade, pen, fold. (Cf. crawl *sb.*[2] 1.) In quot. 1861 applied to an enclosure formed by wagons.

1796 tr. *Thunberg's Cape G.H.* in *Pinkerton's Voy.* (1814) XVI. 23 A place or fold, where sheep as well as horned cattle were inclosed in the open air, was called a Kraal. **1843** Pringle *Afr. Sk.* iv. 180 He led us out towards the kraals or cattle-folds. **1849** E. E. Napier *Excurs. S. Afr.* I. 313 At the door of the Calf kraal. **1861** G. F. Berkeley *Sportsm. W. Prairies* xi. 179 My three waggons could not make a crall or fence around my mules and horses. **1878** H. M. Stanley *Dark Cont.* II. vii. 202 The traveler's first duty in lands infested with lions is to build a safe corral, kraal, or boma, for himself and oxen.

b. In Sri Lanka, an enclosure into which wild elephants are driven; also, the process of capturing elephants in this way. Also *attrib.* So **kraal-town,** a town formed to accommodate the company assembled to view a kraaling of elephants.

1891 *Outing* (U.S.) Dec. 171/1 An elephant kraal is no simple matter, the drive taking possibly a couple of months to accomplish. *Ibid.*, Gradually, slowly but surely, the herds..are driven toward the kraal. *Ibid.* 174/1 In less than a week's time a town springs into existence. 'Kraaltown!' with its clubs, hotels, saloons, cafés, and 'chummeries', to say nothing of suburban villas, etc. **1933** D. E. Blunt *Elephant* ii. 103 Great difficulty was experienced in finding the best way of capturing the young African elephants, the *keddah* or *kraal* method used in Ceylon proving impossible in the Congo. **1956** R. Pieris *Sinhalese Social Organization* v. ii. 185 The *pannikalē* assisted in driving the elephants into the *kraal* or enclosure.

c. An enclosure in water for holding live sponges or turtles; = crawl *sb.*[2] 2.

1939 *Nature* 13 May (Suppl.) 807/2 Inshore waters in close proximity to sponge kraals. **1961** *Encounter* Apr. 18/2 The turtles swim in dense kraals.

3. *attrib.* and *Comb.*

1817 Coleridge *Ess. Own Times* (1850) III. 957 The Kraul-men from whose errors they absterged themselves. **1858** O. W. Holmes *Aut. Breakf.-t.* (1883) 209 The selectmen of an African kraal-village. **1900** *Daily Tel.* 5 June 7/5 The English Yeomanry horses had been kraaled, and, taking fright at the firing, burst through the kraal walls and stampeded.

kraal, *v.* [f. prec. sb.] *trans.* To enclose in a kraal or stockade.

1865 *Pall Mall G.* 16 Oct. 6, 25,000 cattle and 8,000 horses were thus kraaled on the top of a mountain. **1877** T. Baines *Goldfields* 8 The necessity of kraaling the cattle at night within the village. **1891** *Outing* (U.S.) Dec. 174/2 Hurrying them to the kraal we lowered the huge bars and kraaled our first elephant. **1899** Rider Haggard *Swallow* vi, Now I go out to see to the kraaling of the cattle.

krab (kræb), colloq. abbrev. karabiner.

1963 *Oxf. Mountaineering* 8 To add to my worries I found that I was down to my last krab. **1970** *Sunday Mail* (Brisbane) 3 May 7/6 On the way up, the leader puts pitons in the rock, and runs his rope through krabs behind him so he cannot fall far.

krablite (ˈkræblaɪt). *Min.* [Named from Krabla in Iceland (properly *Krafla*), where found: see -ite.] An impure orthoclase, the crystals enclosing quartz and other minerals.

1844 Dana *Min.* 618 Krablite [*printed* Krahlite] is a kind of pearlstone. **1861** Bristow *Gloss.* 204 *Krablite*,..a mineral allied to Spheralite.

kraddy, var. korari.

Kraft (krɑːft). Also **kraft.** [Sw., = strength, in *kraftpapper* kraft paper.] A strong smooth brown paper made from unbleached soda pulp. Also *attrib.* In full, ***kraft paper, kraft brown.***

1907 G. Clapperton *Pract. Paper-Making* (ed. 2) 37 'Kraft' brown papers. *Ibid.*, No Kraft yet produced in this country combines the crispness and elasticity which form so distinctive a feature of the Kraft papers produced by the best Scandinavian mills. **1914** E. A. Dawe *Paper* 56 Kraft browns may be described as glazed browns, as they are sometimes finished with a glazed surface both sides. A special kind of pulp is used for krafts. **1920** *Glasgow Herald* 12 June 5 In the case of sulphite and kraft processes the pulp is prepared by cooking chips of wood under pressure with different liquor solutions. **1930** *Economist* 8 Feb. 303/1 The market for kraft paper must be regarded as declining, but the Swedish newsprint mills are well supplied with orders. **1959** *Gloss. Packaging Terms* (*B.S.I.*) 67 *Kraft liner*, a kraft paper used as the outer or inner facing in the manufacture of solid and corrugated fibreboard, and in the manufacture of fibreboard drums and tubes. **1968** *Economist* 3 Feb. 63/2 Swedish pulps are mainly for kraft, including sack paper, and newsprint. **1969** T. C. Thorstensen *Pract. Leather Technol.* ix. 143 In the manufacture of paper, lignin of the logs of the wood chips is released by cooking the chips with bisulfite in accordance with the Kraft process.

‖**kragdadig** (kraxˈdɑːdɪx), *a.* *S. Afr.* Also **kragdadige.** [Afrikaans, = Du. *krachtdadig.*] Resolute, firm, vigorous. Hence **kragˈdadigheid** (-heɪt), resoluteness, spirit of determination.

1949 *Cape Times* 21 Sept. 8 Where any evidence can be found in this rigamarole of tentativeness for the *kragdadigheid* which is supposed to distinguish Nationalist Ministers we fail to see. **1952** *Ibid.* 21 May 5/3 The Government wanted to make scapegoats of himself and Mr. Carneson so that it could claim *kragdadige* (strong) steps against communism. **1957** *Cape Argus* 11 Feb. 8/8 Signs of that kragdadigheid of which Cabinet spokesmen claim a monopoly. **1958** *Cape Times* 18 Feb. 8/5 Mr. Sauer's answer was that the inquiry was merely United Party propaganda and he was not going to answer it... That is at least a nice *kragdadige* answer. **1963** *Time* 10 May 30/2 Helen Suzman warned that black nationalism as well as white nationalism feeds 'on this type of *kragdadigheid* (toughness)'. **1973** *Sunday Times* (Johannesburg) 15 Apr. 17 Even the Minister of Sport..could not restrain himself from issuing one of those kragdadige statements that get no one anywhere. **1974** *Daily Despatch* (East London) 4 Feb. 8 The new Parliamentary session has barely started and already there are distressingly clear pointers that it will be the season for kragdadigheid.

kragg, obs. form of crag.

Krag-Jørgensen (krægˈjɜːgənsən). The names of O. H. *Krag* (1837–1912) and E. *Jørgensen*, Norwegian firearm designers, used to designate a type of rifle (and carbine) introduced in Denmark and Norway in the late nineteenth century and adopted in U.S.A. Abbrev. (colloq.) **Krag.**

1899 *Scribner's Mag.* XXV. 20/1 Our arms were the regular cavalry carbine, the 'Krag', a splendid weapon, and the revolver. **1901** *Kynoch Jrnl.* Aug.–Sept. 133/2 He has also the latest pattern..Ross straight pull Krag-Jorgensen. **1902** *Encycl. Brit.* XXV. 658/1 The cavalry is armed with the Krag-Jorgensen carbine. *Ibid.*, The infantry and coast artillery have the Krag-Jorgensen rifle. **1910** *Harper's Weekly* 5 Mar. 16/3 Krag-Jorgensen rifles were cracking merrily in their users' pursuit of the wily amigo... Damn, damn, damn the Filipinos, cross-eyed kakiak ladrones. Underneath our starry flag civilize 'em with a Krag, And return us to our own beloved homes. **1964** H. L. Peterson *Encycl. Firearms* 186/1 The bolt-action Krag-Jørgensen.. was developed during the 1880's. *Ibid.* 186/2 The loading gate on the Danish Krag pivots forward, while those of the Norwegian and American Krags pivot horizontally.

krai, var. kray.

‖**krait** (kraɪt). *East Ind.* Also **karait, korait.** [Hindī *karait.*] A venomous snake of the genus *Bungarus*, esp. *B. cæruleus*, common in Bengal.

1874 Fayrer *Venom. Snakes Ind. Penins.* (ed. 2) 14 After a night's dâk in a palanquin, a lady..found a Krait coiled up under her pillow. **1880** *Daily Tel.* 18 Nov. 5/3 His charm against 'the black snake' and the 'korait'. **1887** *Encylc. Brit.* XXII. 196/2 The krait is probably, next to the cobra, the most destructive snake to human life in India. **1898** *Pall Mall Mag.* Christm. No. 583 The snake..was a fine specimen of the karait.

krak, krake, obs. form of crack, crake.

‖**kraken** (ˈkrɑːkən, ˈkreɪkən). Also 8 **craken, cracken, kraaken.** [Norw. *kraken*, *krakjen* (the *-n* being the suffixed definite article), also called *sykraken*, *sjökrakjen* sea-kraken. The name was first brought into general notice by Pontoppidan in his *Förste Forsög paa Norges naturlige Historie* (1752).] A mythical sea-monster of enormous size, said to have been seen at times off the coast of Norway.

1755 tr. *Pontoppidan's Hist. Norway* II. vii. §11. 211 Amongst the many great things which are in the ocean,..is the Kraken. This creature is the largest and most surprizing of all the animal creation. **1770** Douglas in *Phil. Trans.* LX. 41 Enquiry..as to the existence of the aquatic animals, called Kraakens. **1830** Tennyson *Kraken* 4 Far, far beneath the abysmal sea,..The Kraken sleepeth. **1848** Lowell *Ode to France* 30 Ye are mad, ye have taken A slumbering Kraken For firm land of the Past. **1862** Longf. *The Cumberland* vi, Like a kraken huge and black, She crushed our ribs in her iron grasp!

Krakowiak (krəˈkəʊvɪæk). Also **-wyak.** [Polish, f. *Kraków* (Eng. Cracow), a city and region in southern Poland.] = Cracovienne.

1888 F. Niecks *Frederick Chopin* II. xxx. 233 Chopin has only once been inspired by the krakowiak—namely, in his Op. 14, entitled *Krakowiak, Grand Rondeau de Concert.* **1958** P. Kemp *No Colours or Crest* xii. 278 Waltzes and foxtrots were abandoned for the whirling, stamping folk dances of Poland—the Krakowiak, Oberek, and Kujawiak. **1966** *New Statesman* 1 Apr. 465/2 A yellowing piece of paper testifying that in 1952 its bearer danced the Krakowyak satisfactorily before an audience of experts.

kra-kra, kraw-kraw, var. of craw-craw.

1803 Winterbottom *Pres. State Med. Sierra Leone* II. 164 *Kra-kra* is an Ebo word, corrupted from *kra-thra* which signifies the itch. **1897** Mary Kingsley *W. Africa* 438 The kraw-kraw is a frightfully prevalent disease.

Krama, var. Kromo.

kramat (kræˈmɑːt, ˈkrɑːmət). Also 8 **crammat;** 9 **grammat, kramet; karamat, keramat.** [ad. Mal. *keramat* adj., numinous, sacred, holy, unusual, having supernatural qualities; sb., holy place, holy person; ad. Arab. *karāmāt*, pl. of *karāma* miracle worked by a saint other than a prophet.] A Muslim holy place or place of pilgrimage (see also quot. 1833). Also as *adj.*, sacred.

1783 W. Marsden *Hist. Sumatra* 203 The place of greatest solemnity for administering an oath, is the *crammat* or burying ground of their ancestors. **1833** G. Greig *S. Afr. Almanac & Directory* 156 A tomb of a celebrated Malay Priest, near the farm Zandvliet, is frequently visited by the Mahomedans, and where they perform Divine Service, or what is called Grammat. **1839** T. J. Newbold *Pol. & Statistical Acct. Straits of Malacca* I. v. 252 In every part of the country are found tombs of men famed for piety... They call such tombs Kramets. **1900** W. W. Skeat *Malay Magic* 61 There is usually in every small district a holy place known as the *kramat.* **1910** D. Fairbridge *That which hath Been* xxiii. 283 Near the sand hills and the sea lies the kopje on the summit of which is the white mosque, the kramat, which marks to this day the resting place of Sheik Joseph. **1944** I. D. Du Plessis *Cape Malays* iii. 31 From the tomb of Sjech Yussuf a series of *Karamats* stretches in a rough circle round the Peninsula. **1947** L. G. Green *Tavern of Seas* xiv. 136 Followers of the Prophet listening to the reading of the Koran within the 'kramat'. **1947** R. O. Winstedt *Malays* 24 Many sacred (*Keramat*) places are the graves of by-gone shamans. **1964** R. Perry *World of Tiger* xiv. 221 The *kramat* tiger of Malaya..is protected by a guardian spirit and can be driven away from a cattlefold by a child. **1965** R. McKie *Company of Animals* v. 84 He was *kramat* which is as near as any animal can come to being regarded as sacred. **1970** *Straits Times Ann.* 68 Here are three Malay Tombs. They are *keramat*, a sacred or respected place. **1971** *Drum* July 55 As the street fills, there'll be Coons and a band and a jam session, the scene fading out into a shot on Signal Hill, where the Karamat singers will chant the sacred Islamic music.

‖**Krameria** (krəˈmɪərɪə). [Mod.L.; named by Linnæus after J. G. H. Kramer, an Austrian botanist.] **a.** *Bot.* An anomalous genus of *Polygalaceæ* (allied to *Leguminosæ*), comprising branched spreading undershrubs, natives of America, having strongly astringent properties. **b.** *Med.* The root of *K. triandra* (ratany-root), or a drug prepared from this.

1855 in Mayne *Expos. Lex.* **1863–76** Curling *Dis. Rectum* (ed. 4) 115 Vegetable astringents, such as simaruba and krameria. **1866** *Treas. Bot.* 651/2 The infusion of the roots of the *Krameria* is blood-red, on which account advantage is taken of it to adulterate port wine. **1870** L. P. Meredith *Teeth* 214 Tincture of krameria.

krameric (krəˈmɛrɪk), *a.* *Chem.* Also crameric. [f. prec. + -ic.] In ***krameric acid***, a doubtful crystalline substance supposed to have been discovered in the root of *Krameria triandra.*

1838 T. Thomson *Chem. Org. Bodies* 834 The crameric acid discovered by Peschier. **1852** Morfit *Tanning & Currying* (1853) 83 [Decoction of rhatany] is composed of tannin, woody fibre, gum, starch, saccharine matter and krameric acid.

kran (krɑːn). [ad. Pers. *qrān.*] A Persian coin and monetary unit.

1882 E. O'Donovan *Merv Oasis* I. 249 The Turcomans.. will accept only the old-fashioned *kran* and *toman.* **1902** *Encycl. Brit.* XXXIII. 513/2 The Indian rupee and the Persian kran are widely circulated through Mesopotamia. **1920** *Brit. Mus. Return* 75 in *Parl. Papers* XXXVI. 673 A silver kran of Muzaffar al-Din, Shah of Persia. **1922** *Blackw. Mag.* Mar. 393/1 For two krans an Arab will swear a false oath. **1933** V. Sackville-West *Coll. Poems* 178, I bought these beads in Isfahan; I bought a handful for a kran,—That's sixpence—at the motley stall. **1934** F. Stark *Valleys of Assassins* ii. 130 He allowed me to give him two krans with which he wandered off to buy our horses' dinner. **1958** F. Maclean *Person from England* v. 246 O'Donovan had with

him a silver casket,..for which he had paid about six hundred *krans*, or twenty-five pounds sterling.

kranage, krane, obs. ff. CRANAGE, CRANE.

1390 *Earl Derby's Exp.* (Camden) 19 Cum rollagio, kranagio, et conductione unius boot.

krang, variant of KRENG.

‖**krantz** (krænts). *S. Africa.* Also **krans(e, kranz**. Pl. **krantze, krantzes, kranses**. [a. S. African Du., = Du. *krans*, in Kilian *krants*, coronet, chaplet; cf. Ger. *kranz* coronet, garland, circle, ring, encircling horizon of mountains, cornice.] A wall of rock encircling a mountain or summit; hence, more widely, any precipitous or overhanging wall of rocks bordering high ground or hemming in a valley.

1785 G. FORSTER tr. *Sparrman's Voy. Cape Good Hope* II. xi. 48 He looked out for a *klipkrans* (so they generally call a rocky place level and plain at top, and having a perpendicular precipice on one side of it). **1834** PRINGLE *Afr. Sk.* 43 Our Lothian friends with their good Mother dwell Beside yon Kranz. **1849** NAPIER *Excurs. S. Africa* II. 183 'The river', says Farley,..'runs under yon krantz' [*note*, Wooded cragg, or cliff]. **1852** C. BARTER *Dorp & Veld* 93 We had been directed to look out for a white krans in the mountain. **1880** *S. Africa* (ed. 3) 132 The forests are generally situated in kloofs and mountain sides, and in steep krantzes. **1892** *Midl. News & Karroo Farmer* 4 Mar. 6 The krantz that overhangs the Maraisburg road..is in a very dangerous state, and yesterday a large stone..fell into the road. **1903** KIPLING *Five Nations* 196 But 'e wasn't takin' chances in them 'igh an' 'ostile kranzes. **1916** J. BUCHAN *Greenmantle* xxi. 283 A little hill split the valley, and on its top was a *kranz* of rocks. **1924** R. CAMPBELL *Flaming Terrapin* iv. 72 Her pitchy crows..cling with gnarly toes To their steep krantzes. **1927** W. PLOMER *I Speak of Afr.* i. 37 Eddies of sound reaching the nervous leaf-like ears of the krans-coloured sheep in the stones overhead cause them to lift their heads. **1939** tr. *E. N. Marais's My Friends the Baboons* iii. 32 The leopard was still ahead of us in the kloof and unless he had fled up the kranses, it was probable that we would meet him again. **1952** *Cape Times Mag.* 19 July 6/5 Inquisitive baboons often watch the bathers from the krantze above. **1959** G. JENKINS *Twist of Sand* xiv. 301 Peaks and valleys, fretted with razor-like kranzes and unscaleable cliffs. **1961** L. VAN DER POST *Heart of Hunter* xiv. 189 All day long she [*sc.* the rock-rabbit] darts in and out of the shadows and clefts of our Kranses and rocky hill-tops. **1966** E. PALMER *Plains of Camdeboo* v. 89 Koeltas, our guide, led us round the side of a krantz by a pathway as narrow as a bit of string.

krantzite (ˈkræntsaɪt). *Min.* [Named after Dr. Kranz: see -ITE.] A fossil resin allied to amber, occurring near Nienburg in Hanover.

1868 DANA *Min* (ed. 5) 741.

†**krany**, obs. form of CRANNY *v.*

c **1425** LYDG. *Assembly of Gods* 536 A drowthe..That causyd hit [the earth] to chyne & krany more & lesse.

‖**krapfen** (ˈkrapfən). [G.] In Germany and other German-speaking areas: a doughnut (see also quot. 1845).

1845 E. ACTON *Mod. Cookery* (ed. 4) App. 581 *Appel krapfen*... Boil..apples..mix them with..almonds, beaten to a paste,..raisins..cinnamon..roll out some butter-crust ..cut into four-inch squares,..fill them..lay another square on each,..bake them. **1877** E. S. DALLAS *Kettner's Bk. of Table* 156 Beignets à la Dauphine... Throughout Germany they are known as Berliner Pfannkuchen; throughout Austria as Wiener Krapfen. **1966** P. V. PRICE *France: Food & Wine Guide* 151 *Krapfen* (rather like little light doughnuts).

krater, var. CRATER I.

kratogen (ˈkrætədʒɛn). *Geol.* [a. G. *kratogen* (L. Kober *Der Bau der Erde* (1921) i. 21), f. Gr. κράτο-ς strength: see -GEN.] An area of a continent that has resisted deformation over a (geologically) long period of time. Hence **kratoˈgenic** *a.*

1923 *Bull. Geol. Soc. Amer.* XXXIV. 210 The 'Kratogens', once the area of the most ancient geosynclines, may, after they are peneplained, be widely flooded by epeiric seas. **1934** *Geogr. Jrnl.* LXXXIII. 515 After a few preliminary chapters dealing with the evolution of orogenic and kratogenic (continental) areas, he sets forth his views on ..mountain-building. **1939** R. RUEDEMANN in Ruedemann & Balk *Geol. N. Amer.* I. 48 The geosynclines appear to be the compensating areas of subcrustal flowage between the subsiding oceans and the unmoved or horst-like neutral areas or 'kratogens' of the positive elements. **1969** BENNISON & WRIGHT *Geol. Hist. Brit. Isles* v. 91 Certainly, the Midlands of England formed a kratogen which persisted throughout the Ordovician and Silurian. *Ibid.* vi. 129 The marginal facies of south Shropshire and the English Midlands, which were similarly laid down on the margins of the (Midlands) kratogenic block and by shallow seas spreading across it.

kraurosis (krɔːˈrəʊsɪs). *Path.* [mod.L. (A. Breisky 1885, in *Zeitschr. f. Heilkunde* VI. 75), f. Gr. κραῦρ-ος brittle, dry + -OSIS.] Atrophy of the skin of the vulva, by some regarded as a distinct disease.

1888 *Trans. Amer. Dermatol. Assoc.* 64 Under the name 'Kraurosis' Professor Breisky, in his book on gynaecology, describes a disease of the vulva, which he considers a hitherto unknown form... The same disease has been described, fourteen years ago, by Robert F. Weir, of New York, as 'Ichthyosis of the Vulva'. **1901** C. H. ROBERTS *Outl. Gynæcol. Path.* i. 14 In Kraurosis, the tissues of the vulva are smooth and pale, with irritable tender red patches along the margins of the hymen and in the vestibule. **1948** W. SCHILLER in W. A. D. Anderson *Path.* xl. 1167 Kraurosis rarely follows the artificial menopause produced by operative removal of the ovaries. **1973** A. S. WOODCOCK in Fox & Langley *Postgrad. Obstetr. & Gynaecol. Path.* iv. 57 Kraurosis and senile atrophy are generally accepted as synonymous.

Hence **krauˈrotic** *a.*, affected with kraurosis.

1894 *Brit. Med. Jrnl.* 7 Apr. Suppl. 63/1 Carcinomatous nodules were detected in the kraurotic tissue.

Krause (ˈkraʊzə). The name of Wilhelm *Krause* (1833–1909), Ger. anatomist and histologist, used in the possessive and with *of*-adjunct to designate structures in the body which he investigated, as: **a.** A kind of encapsulated plexus of sensory nerve endings found in mucous membranes, the dermis, the conjunctiva, and elsewhere. **b.** (A transverse membrane appearing as) a thin dark line separating adjacent sarcomeres in a striated muscle fibril. **c.** Each of the numerous small accessory lacrimal glands situated under the conjunctiva close to where it joins the eyeball.

a. 1872 H. POWER tr. *Stricker's Man. Human & Compar. Histol.* II. xxix. 317 The nerves of the glans [penis] are very numerous and..end within the papillae in Krause's terminal bulbs. **1875** A. GAMGEE tr. *Hermann's Elem. Human Physiol.* x. 457 Terminal nerve bodies (Krause's corpuscles) are oval, or more or less rounded vesicles of 0·03–0·06 mm, consisting of an areolar sheath, with nuclei and soft homogeneous contents, in which the nerve-fibre runs, terminating in a point. **1888** A. FLINT *Text-bk. Human Physiol.* (ed. 4) xvi. 516 In certain membranes the nerves terminate in end-bulbs, or corpuscles of Krause. **1953** C. E. OSGOOD *Method & Theory Exper. Psychol.* i. 7 Pain is attributed to free nerve endings; cold to Krause's end bulbs. **1960** R. A. WEALE *Eye & its Function* ii. 30 Their shape is reminiscent of one type of pressure receptor, namely Krause's corpuscle. **1972** M. L. BARR *Human Nervous Syst.* iii. 35/2 It was thought at one time that end-bulbs of Krause were receptors for coolness and end-bulbs of Ruffini for warmth, but the evidence that these are special temperature sensors is no longer regarded as conclusive.

b. 1873 *Phil. Trans. R. Soc.* CLXIII. 442 The transverse membrane of Krause and the narrow disk of intermediate substance..of Heppner would seem to be referable to the heads of two contiguous series of muscle-rods, which.. often meet in the middle of the clear stripe. **1887** *Buck's Handbk. Med. Sci.* V. 65/2 Krause's membrane or intermediate disk. **1939** W. E. LE GROS CLARK *Tissues of Body* v. 99 Cutting through the isotropic disc is a thin dark line which is believed by some histologists to mark the position of a membrane (Krause's membrane) separating the length of the fibril into a series of partially isolated segments. **1970** FALLIS & ASHWORTH *Textbk. Human Histol.* viii. 58 The major cross bands of the myofibrils are the A and I bands... In the center of the I band is a thin dark line known as the Z (Zwischenscheibe) band, or intermediate line of Krause; the Z band attaches to the sarcolemma at the periphery of the cell.

c. 1905 *Trans. Ophthalm. Soc.* XXV. 1 (*heading*) Cyst of Krause's gland. **1933** E. WOLFF *Anat. Eye & Orbit* iii. 113 The glands of Krause are accessory lacrimal glands occurring under the conjunctiva from the fornix to the convex border of the tarsus. **1960** R. A. WEALE *Eye & its Function* xii. 185 Accessory lacrimal apparatus is provided by Krause's glands.

krausite (ˈkraʊsaɪt). *Min.* [f. the name of Edward Henry *Kraus* (1875–1973), U.S. mineralogist + -ITE[1].] A pale yellow hydrated sulphate of potassium and iron, $KFe(SO_4)_2 \cdot H_2O$.

1931 W. F. FOSHAG in *Amer. Mineralogist* XVI. 352 In the Calico Hills, San Bernardino County, California, a small deposit of sulfates of iron [was found]. This deposit was found to contain a fair abundance of a new sulfate of iron and potash... For this new mineral species the writer proposes the name *krausite*. *Ibid.*, Krausite occurs in several different forms. That found in the alunite forms comparatively large but rough crystals... The krausite of the transition zone is in lemon yellow crystals, often clear and with brilliant luster. **1935** J. W. MELLOR *Comprehensive Treat. Inorg. & Theoret. Chem.* XIV. 340 Krausite is insoluble in water; and is slowly hydrolyzed when left in contact with water. **1965** *Amer. Mineralogist* L. 1929 This spatial arrangement of the coordination polyhedra accounts for the perfect (001) and good (100) cleavages in krausite.

kraut (kraʊt). [a. G. *kraut* herb, vegetable, cabbage.] **1.** = SAUERKRAUT, SOURCROUT. Also *attrib.* and *Comb.*

[**1845** *Punch* IX. 94/1 Happy midst his native *kraut* [*sc.* cabbage] My princely Albert wanders.] **1855** GEO. ELIOT in *Fraser's Mag.* June 311/1 *Kraut* and *wurst* may be called the solid prose of Thuringian diet. **1895** *Montgomery Ward Catal.* 574/1 Kraut Forks..Combined Clothes Pounder and Kraut Stamper. *Ibid.* 576/2 Kraut Cutters, 8 × 26 inches. 3 cast steel knives. **1937** D. RUNYON in *Collier's* 16 Jan. 47/2 Nicely-Nicely now observes that the very choicest spareribs are on Jake's plate, and also the most kraut. **1950** *Amer. Speech* XXV. 315/1 The recipe for krautfurters..under the title 'Kraut and Frankfurters Team in Delightful Casserole Dishes'. **1961** *John o' London's* 13 July 88/3 Such words as ..turkeyfurter and krautfurter: the last-named being made from *sauerkraut*.

2. (Often with capital initial.) A German, esp. a German soldier. Also *attrib.* and *Comb. Derogatory.*

1918 G. E. GRIFFIN *Ballads of Regiment* 34 But he always loved a soldier, be he..'Krout' or 'Mick'. **1919** C. B. HOYT *Heroes of Argonne* 41 The Frogs and Krauts got it fixed up between 'em. **1926** *Sat. Even. Post* 12 June 148/3 'Wait a while, fellers,' he said. 'The krauts are sockin' the crossroads.' **1929** W. T. SCANLON *God have Mercy on Us!* 4 What gives me a pain in the neck is all the time we wasted up at Verdun in the old trenches when we might have been killing Krautheads. **1936** *Our Army* Feb. 14 We and the kraut-eaters were mixing it up to make the world safe for bigger and better wars. **1938** JOHNSON & PRATT *Lost Battalion* 17 There were 'kraut' machine guns barking at them in the dark. **1945** *Daily Herald* 8 May 4/4 The men just said things like, 'Well, the Krauts are done for.' **1946** J. M. SCOTT *Other Side of Moon* ii. 32 It is the only building left standing in the village. The Krauts blew up the rest. *Ibid.* v. 86 The Kraut will soon have to fall back. **1954** W. FAULKNER *Fable* 376 He's got to be killed from in front, by a Kraut bullet—see? **1957** M. K. JOSEPH *I'll soldier no More* (1958) xiii. 291 I'll fix you, you kraut bastard. **1962** R. COOK *Crust on its Uppers* i. 24 We were doing some biz near Munich..back to this day in krautland. **1966** T. PYNCHON *Crying of Lot 49* i. 15 Maybe..he should have been in a war, Japs in trees, Krauts in Tiger tanks. **1971** J. OSBORNE *West of Suez* I. 27 An odd Kraut or two, bellowing at their Fraus. **1974** *New Society* 21 Feb. 435/2 The Hitler stuff, together with the usual illustrations of inflated multimillion mark notes..looks more like what is inelegantly called 'Kraut-bashing'. **1974** L. DEIGHTON *Spy Story* xviii. 195 'That goddamn Kraut sub,' said the Conning Officer.

†**kravers**, var. *cravas*, *craves*, obs. f. CREVICE.

c **1425** LYDG. *Assembly of Gods* 534 In a krauers forthe he gan hym dresse.

kray (kraɪ). Also **krai**. [Russ.] In the U.S.S.R., a second-order administrative division, a region, a territory.

1938 N. DE BASILY *Russ. under Soviet Rule* iv. 153 Practically each republic is administratively divided into provinces or regions (*oblast* or *krai*). These provinces and regions are in turn divided into districts (*rayon*), towns, and villages. **1951** T. SHABAD *Geogr. U.S.S.R.* ii. 46 An oblast or kray is usually organized in such a manner as to include..a well-coordinated economic region centering on an important industrial and commercial center and specializing in the production of some particular commodity, while striving for regional self-sufficiency in the greatest possible degree. *Ibid.* 47 Krays, which occur only in the Russian SFSR, are identical to the oblasts, but are usually larger in area—the term 'kray' is given to those divisions which contain autonomous oblasts. **1967** J. P. COLE *Geogr. U.S.S.R.* vi. 101 In Siberia some krays and oblasts are enormous, and extend from the Trans-Siberian Railway as far as the Arctic Coast.

kreas, obs. var. *kreese*, KRIS.

kreasote, obs. f. CREOSOTE.

kreat: see CREAGHT.

kreatic, kreatine, etc., var. CREATIC, CREATINE, etc.

Krebs (krɛbz). *Biochem.* The name of Sir Hans Adolf *Krebs* (b. 1900), German-born British biochemist, used *attrib.* (or occas. in the possessive) to designate a circular sequence of enzyme-catalysed reactions occurring in mitochondria as part of cell respiration in aerobic organisms, in which an acetyl group (bound to a coenzyme and produced by glycolysis or other catabolic processes) is combined with oxaloacetic acid and then oxidized by a succession of reactions which produces carbon dioxide, serves to convert adenosine diphosphate to the energy-rich triphosphate (by means of the cytochrome system), and regenerates oxaloacetic acid.

1941 *Jrnl. Biol. Chem.* CXXXIX. 483 Oxidation of pyruvate by the Krebs cycle involves its union with oxalacetate. **1950** *Chem. Abstr.* XLIV. 1552 (*heading*) Final stage in biological oxidation processes: Krebs' tricarboxylic acid cycle. **1955** *New Biol.* XIX. 85 The Krebs cycle is a mechanism through which the various synthetic activities of the cell mutually affect each other. **1969** *New Scientist* 9 Oct. 64/3 Because some of the intermediate compounds in the Krebs cycle need to be bled off for other purposes, the bacillus has a special mechanism for stoking up its level from glucose. **1971** *Sci. Amer.* May 128/2 Next are the tens or hundreds of mitochondria, the enclosures where the complicated biochemical machinery of the Krebs cycle is mounted, producing most of the cell's ATP fuel by the oxidation of small organic molecules. **1971** YUDKIN & OFFORD *Harrison's Guidebk. Biochem.* (new ed.) xi. 101 The Krebs cycle is responsible for the oxidation of the acetyl group of acetyl coenzyme A.

‖**kreˈdemnon**. *Gr. Antiq.* [Gr. κρήδεμνον.] Part of a woman's head-dress; a sort of veil of which the ends hung down on each side.

1850 LEITCH tr. *C. O. Müller's Anc. Art* (ed. 2) 538 Ino-Leucothea has the kredemnon (her regular distinguishing sign..) wound three times round her body. **1865** E. RIMMEL *Bk. Perfumes* v. 94 There were many other modes of wearing the hair, such as the *strophos*, the *nimbo*, the *kredemnon*. **1940** *Times* 19 Mar. 6/3 The captains of two East Coast colliers exchanging views..on the merits of their kredemnons. **1959** E. POUND *Thrones* xcvi. 3 Κρήδεμνον..κρήδεμνον..and the wave concealed her, dark mass of water.

kredill, obs. form of CRADLE *sb.*

kreef (kriːf, kreːf). *S. Afr.* [Afrikaans, f. Du. *kreeft* lobster.] = CRAWFISH *sb.* 1 b.

1863 *Queenstown Free Press* 30 June (Pettman), A new theological schism has sprung up amongst the Malays touching the important question whether *Kreef* or crawfish is to be considered ceremonially unclean or not. **1902** [see *Cape lobster* (CAPE *sb.*[3] 4)]. **1936** *Nature* 11 Jan. 74/1 (*heading*) The natural history and utilisation of the Cape

crawfish, kreef or spiny lobster, *Jasus (Palinurus) lalandii.* **1959** *Cape Argus* 7 Nov. 11/7 The three month open season for kreef fishing..opened last Sunday. **1970** *Cape Times* 28 Oct. (S.A. Fishing Rev.) 5/4 Previously the Government had allowed producers to export 6·9 m. tailweight pounds of kreef. **1970** G. CROUDACE *Scarlet Bikini* vi. 73 'And no *kreef*,' Tony said, referring to the rock lobster.

†**kreeker, kreker.** *Obs.* Also kreekar. [Origin obscure: perh., as stated in quots., for *craker*, f. CRAKE, CRACK *v.*, to boast.] (See quots.)

a **1548** HALL *Chron., Hen. VIII* 119b, Sir Ihon Walop.. had..a M. proper men and hardy..whiche lived alonely on their aventure, wherfore of some they were called adventurers, of some they were called kreekars. *Ibid.* 127 The Frenchmen knewe well their hardines, but yet thei called theim Crakers, whiche by missoundyng, was commonly called Krekers. *Ibid.* 145 All the men of warre.. wer called home, and the shippes brought into the havens, and many a kreker wist not how to lyve. **1674** BLOUNT *Glossogr.* (ed. 4), *Crakers* were a certain choice number of daring English Souldiers, we had in France in the time of H. 8. by some called Kreekers.

KREEP (kriːp). [f. *K*, chem. symbol for potassium + *REE*, abbrev. for *r*are-*e*arth *e*lement + *P*, chem. symbol for phosphorus (in allusion to its unusual composition).] A substance found on the moon as glassy fragments and as a constituent of fines and breccias, characterized by a high content of potassium, phosphorus, and rare-earth elements and unusually little iron.

1971 *Sci. News Let.* 23 Jan. 62 Another Apollo 12 find.. was that of an exotic component called KREEP by some—for high content of potassium, rare earth elements and phosphorus—found in rock 13. **1971** N. J. HUBBARD et al. in *Earth & Planetary Sci. Lett.* X. 343/1 We will refer to this distinctive glass as KREEP glass (from its distinctive potassium, rare-earth element, and phosphorus content). **1971** *Geochim. & Cosmochim. Acta Suppl.* 2 I. 393 Hubbard et al. (1971a) designated this class of material as the KREEP component. *Ibid.* 398 Breccias with glass matrices..are the most abundant form of KREEP in the soil samples. **1973** *McGraw-Hill Yearbk. Sci. & Technol.* 284/2 The activity fell off smoothly in the adjacent regions to the east and west, including the other near-side maria... The localization of the high U-Th regions indicates a restricted distribution of KREEP (a potassium, rare-earth, phosphate-bearing phase), with which the high U-Th component is associated in returned lunar samples.

kreese, var. KRIS, Malay dagger.

kreil, krele, obs. forms of CREEL.

kreittonite ('kraɪtənaɪt). *Min.* [Named, 1848, f. Gr. κρείττων stronger, superior, as being of higher specific gravity than other spinels: see -ITE.] A variety of gahnite or zinc spinel, from Bodenmais in Bavaria, containing a considerable amount of iron.

1850 DANA *Min.* (ed. 3) 371 *Kreittonite*, a black spinel. **1893** CHAPMAN *Blowpipe Pract.* 211 Kreittonite [is] a ferruginous variety.

kreke, obs. f. CREAK.

kreme, obs. f. CREAM; var. CRIM *v. Obs.*

kremele: see CRUMBLE *v.*

kremersite ('krɛməsaɪt). *Min.* [Named, 1853, after Dr. Kremers, who first described it: see -ITE.] Chloride of iron, potassium, and ammonium, occurring as a sublimation product in the fumaroles of Vesuvius.

1854 DANA *Min.* (ed. 4) 90 Kremersite. **1883** *Encycl. Brit.* XVI. 384 *Kremersite*..Cubic. In octahedra.

Kremlin ('krɛmlɪn). Also 7 **cremelina,** 8 **kremelin,** 9 **kremle.** [a. F. *kremlin*, f. Russ. *kreml* citadel, of Tartar origin.] **a.** The citadel or fortifed enclosure within a Russian town or city; *esp.* that of Moscow, which contains the imperial palace and various public buildings. **b.** *The Kremlin* (in Moscow): (used for) the government of the U.S.S.R. Also *transf.* (in trivial use).

1662 J. DAVIES tr. *Olearius' Voy. Ambass.* 57 The Great Duke's Palace, called Cremelena, and which is of greater extent than many other ordinary Cities. **1698** A. BRAND *Emb. Muscovy to China* 5 The Castle, called Cremelina, where the Czars of Muscovy keep their ordinary Residence. **1796** MORSE *Amer. Geog.* II. 91 It stands in the Kremelin, one of the interior circles of the city. **1833** R. PINKERTON *Russia* 227 The inhabitants of Moscow being assembled in the Kremlin. **1839** E. D. CLARKE *Trav. Russia* 38/1 The Kremle is derived from the Tartar word *krim*, or *krem*, which signifies a fortress. **1888** *Century Mag.* May 10 *note*, A Kremlin, or to use the Russian form of the word, a 'Kremle', is merely a walled inclosure with towers at the corners, situated in a commanding position near the center of a city. **1933** H. G. WELLS *Shape of Things to Come* II. §9.211 The Kremlin was content to consolidate the kindred Slav Soviets. **1943** *Sun* (Baltimore) 28 Sept. 12/2 Moscow itself has taken pains to assure us that Mr. Browder has no direct pipeline into the secret councils of the Kremlin. **1961** *Evening Bull.* (Philadelphia) 5 Mar., The Kremlin is the only world capital powerfully arrayed against crossing the new frontier. **1966** [see ELYSÉE]. **1966** H. SHEPPARD *Dict. Railway Slang* (ed. 2) 7 *Kremlin*, British Rail Headquarters. **1973** *Times* 19 Feb. 18/7 People who referred to their head offices as 'the Kremlin'..were somehow lacking in motivation. **1974** *Times* 10 Apr. 18/2 Kremlin-watchers study the pages of *Pravda* for the slight shift in nuance.

So **Kremli'nology,** the study and analysis of the Soviet Government and its policies; **Kremlino'logical** *a.*; **Kremli'nologist,** such an analyst; also *transf.*

1958 *Oxf. Mag.* 13 Feb. 289/1 For all his interest in Kremlinology..the author is not really very good at it. **1960** *Daily Tel.* 7 Dec. 12/2 Kremlinologists, versed in the mysteries of Marx and Lenin, Mao Tse-tung and Mr Khruschev, tell us that the signs are that Mr Khruschev has won yet another battle, at least on points. **1961** *Spectator* 2 June 806 The approach commonly nicknamed 'Kremlinological'. *Ibid.*, Exaggerated claims on behalf of this method by some of its practitioners..who..equate Kremlinology with Soviet studies as a whole. **1968** *Guardian* 2 Apr. 11/5 The 'Kremlinological' expertise which enabled the White House to play the Kremlin power game. **1970** *Ibid.* 1 Oct. 15/4 The question now teasing Labour Kremlinologists is how long Denis [Healey] will be satisfied to remain a mere member of the NEC. **1971** *Times* 22 Jan. 8/8 Kremlinology gone wild. **1972** A. ULAM *Fall of Amer. University* i. 35 The budding Kremlinologists were put in their place, which often and quite properly turned out to be the C.I.A.

Kremnitz, var. CREMNITZ.

Krems (krɛmz). [f. *Krems*, the name of a town of northern Austria.] Used *attrib.* to designate a white lead pigment used as a paint base; the same as Cremnitz white.

1854 F. W. FAIRHOLT *Dict. Terms Art* 256/2 Krems White. A carbonate of lead;...it takes its name from the city where it is manufactured, Krems or Crems, in Austria, and is sometimes termed Vienna white. **1940** *Chambers's Techn. Dict.* 479/2 Krems white.

kreng (krɛŋ). Also **krang,** CRANG. [a. Du. *kreng*, MDu. *crenge* carrion, carcass; of uncertain origin. (See Franck.)] The carcass of a whale from which the blubber has been removed.

[**1821**: see CRANG.] **1835** SIR J. ROSS *Narr. 2nd Voy.* vi. 88 Some of the krang of a whale had been seen in the morning. **1850** W. B. CLARKE *Wreck of Favorite* 39 After the.. blubber, whalebone, and jaw-bones are removed,..the remaining part, called 'the kreng', is left to become the food of sharks and birds. **1851** *Zoologist* IX. 3021 An ivory gull.. stooping down to a piece of 'krang'.

Hence **'krenger,** ? one who strips the blubber from a dead whale; **'krenging-hook,** an instrument for doing this.

1886 *Gd. Words* 83 The krenging hook is used in preparing the kreng for the oil copper. *Ibid., note*, The Closh is a pronged instrument, also used by the Krengers.

krennerite ('krɛnəraɪt). *Min.* [Named, 1877, after Dr. J. A. Krenner, who first described it: see -ITE¹.] A telluride of gold and silver, found in prismatic crystals.

1878 *Amer. Jrnl. Sc.* Ser. III. XVIII. 482 Vom Rath.. proposes the name Krennerite after the discoverer.

kreope(n, early form of CREEP.

kreophagism, -ist, kreosote: see CREO-.

krepe, kreppet, obs. inf. and pa. t. of CREEP *v.*

‖**kreplach** ('krɛplax), *sb. pl.* Also **creplach, -lich.** [Yiddish *kreplech*, pl. of *krepel*, ad. dial. G. *kräppel* fritter, cogn. w. G. KRAPFEN.] Triangular noodles filled with chopped meat or cheese and served with soup.

1892 I. ZANGWILL *Childr. Ghetto* I. 114 *Creplich*, which are triangular meat pasties. **1932** L. GOLDING *Magnolia St.* III. vii. 555 She will also make *knishehs, varennikas, creplach* and *blintsies* for the old-fashioned Jewish people. **1954** *Amer. Speech* XXIX. 104 Though partial to gefilte fish, They scorn the kreplach and the knish, They list pastrami, but evince A total apathy to blintz. **1957** L. STERN *Midas Touch* viii. 66 The thought of *kreplach* and *matzoth* dumplings made his mouth water. **1965** *New Statesman* 20 Aug. 250/1 Kreplach (sing. krepl) are a kind of Jewish dumpling served in hot chicken soup on festive occasions... Chinese serve remarkably good kreplach in..soup... Other close cousins of kreplach are ravioli and especially tortellini. **1972** F. B. MAYNARD *Raisins & Almonds* 89 My mother was making *kreplach*. She placed a dab of cheese on the dough and pinched it in carefully... The *kreplach* dropped into the boiling pot with a sharp plopping noise.

kresol, kresoline, etc., var. CRESOL, etc.

kressibulle, kreste, obs. ff. CRUCIBLE, CREST.

‖**kretek** ('krɛtɛk). [Indonesian *kerétèk*.] In Java, a cigarette containing cloves.

1958 H. FORSTER *Flowering Lotus* i. 6 These were the famous *kretek* cigarettes, in which the tobacco is mixed with cloves; their crackling gives the cigarettes their name. **1966** *Economist* 16 Apr. 235/2 A packet of *kretek*, the clove cigarette smoked by most people, costs almost as much. **1973** *Times* 27 Dec. 10 It also turns out that although Kawung smoking is in general associated with low socio-economic status, and that low status itself affects development of the disease, the relatively small numbers of patients with higher socio-economic status who smoke these cigarettes are also adversely affected, compared with patients of the same status who smoke Kretek or Western cigarettes.

kreton, variant of CRITON *Obs.*

‖**kreutzer** ('krɔɪtsə(r)). Also (6 **crocherd(e),** 7 **creitzer,** 8 **creutzer, crutzer,** 9 **kreuzer.** [Ger. *kreuzer*, f. *kreuz* cross; the coin having been originally stamped with a cross.] A small coin (originally silver, afterwards copper) formerly current in parts of Germany and in Austria.

The value has varied, the most recent being the Bavarian kreutzer = about ⅓ of a penny, and the Austrian = about ⅕*d.*

1547 BOORDE *Introd. Knowl.* xiii. (1870) 157 They [the Dutch] haue crocherdes; iii crocherds is les worth than a styuer. **1617** MORYSON *Itin.* I. 67, I paid for my supper twenty creitzers. **1703** *Lond. Gaz.* No. 3914/5 Worth..16 Creutzers, which is about 8 Pence English. **1756–7** tr. *Keysler's Trav.* (1760) I. 121 This castle was built..in times when artificers worked for a *crutzer* a day. **1822** W. IRVING in *Life & Lett.* (1864) II. 103 The gentlemen..pay each a piece of six kreutzers. **1874** RUSKIN *Fors Clav.* IV. 69 By this time I shouldn't have had a bit of skin left as big as a kreutzer.

krevise, -ys, obs. forms of CRAYFISH *sb.*

krewelle, obs. form of CRUEL.

†**kreyscloth.** *Obs.* A kind of linen fabric.

1507 *Yatton Church-w. Acc.* (Som. Rec. Soc.) 129 Kreyscloth and holland bought for bordclothes and surplices.

kricket(t, obs. forms of CRICKET.

kriegie ('kriːgɪ). *slang.* [Abbrev. of G. *kriegsgefangener* prisoner of war: see -IE.] An Allied prisoner of war in Germany during the war of 1939–45 (see also quot. 1948).

1944 *World's Press News* 31 Aug. 17/1 The *Yorkshire Post* reports receipt of a remarkable publication from Yorkshire prisoners of war in Germany. This takes the form of a special volume called the 'Kriegie Edition' of the *Yorkshire Post. Ibid.* 17/2 Kriegie..is an abbreviation of the German for prisoner of war. **1946** BRICKHILL & NORTON *Escape to Danger* 11 The worn track..which kriegies 'pounded' or 'bashed' (walked) for hours at a time. **1948** *Amer. Speech* XXIII. 217 (*heading*) Kriegie talk. *Ibid.* 218 Ex-prisoners from the E.T.O. speak of Jap kriegies, or, 'If there is another war I'll probably be a Russian kriegie,' and my personal usage would apply it to any prisoner of war from now on. **1956** D. M. DAVIN *Sullen Bell* II. vii. 153 But there I was, a bloody kriegie for the rest of the war.

‖**kriegspiel** ('kriːgspiːl). [Ger., = war-game.] **1.** A game in which blocks representing parts of armies, guns, etc., are moved about on maps: see quot. 1811. Introduced into the English army after the Franco-German War of 1870.

[**1811** *Q. Rev.* May 403 In Switzerland a game has lately been made of war (*Das Kriegspiel*), which is played with figures upon a map, and recommended as exceedingly instructive to military students, because the principles upon which it is constructed are applicable to real operations in the field.] **1878** BESANT & RICE *By Celia's Arbour* xxxiii. (1887) 248 They tell me that the officer of to-day is scientific and plays Kriegspiel. **1887** *Athenæum* 12 Mar. 344/3 As in a game of 'kriegspiel', the onlooker will often find himself wondering what on earth was the object of this or that move.

2. A form of chess invented about 1900 by M. H. Temple. Two players at separate boards play without seeing or being told each other's moves, though they may ask some strictly limited questions of an umpire who conducts the game at a third board.

1903 *Brit. Chess Mag.* Sept. 370 Kriegsspiel..may have merits, but it is not a war game. **1906** H. CAYLEY in *Chess Amat.* Nov. 46 (*heading*) Kriegspiel or the Chess War Game. **1922** *Brit. Chess Mag.* Oct. 375 As a chess-player he.. preferred Kriegspiel, at which he was always the life and soul of the table. **1961** *Times Lit. Suppl.* 1 Dec. 870/5 Kriegspiel itself together with further variations. **1969** A. GLYN *Dragon Variation* viii. 237 There'd be simuls, rapid-transit, five-minute chess, kriegspiels, lectures in the evenings.

So **'kriegspieler, 'kriegsspieler,** one who plays kriegspiel.

1891 *19th Cent.* Feb. 299 Keen Volunteers..are enthusiastic Kriegsspielers. **1916** *Brit. Chess Mag. Chess Ann. 1915* 58 The chartered libertine among P.E.'s, kriegspielers, and chess-players in general.

krieker ('kriːkə(r)). *U.S.* [ad. Ger. *kriecher* creeper.] A name in N. Jersey and Rhode Island of the Pectoral Sandpiper, *Tringa pectoralis.*

1890 in *Cent. Dict.*

kries, variant of KRIS.

krik, krike, obs. forms of CREEK *sb.*¹

Krilium ('krɪlɪəm). [f. *kril-*, altered form of *-cryl-* of *polyacrylonitrile* + *-ium.*] A proprietary name of various mixtures of polyacrylate salts and other carboxylated polymers manufactured as soil conditioners for improving the texture of soil and its ability to resist erosion.

1952 *Sci. News Let.* 5 Jan. 8/2 The soil improvement chemical will come on the market soon under the name of Krilium. **1952** *Official Gaz.* (U.S. Patent Off.) 8 July 226/2 *Krilium* for synthetic resin materials in the form of powders, granules, emulsions, dispersions, and solutions. **1958** TEAKLE & BOYLE *Fertilizers* iv. 116 Krilium is the name given to several compounds selected from over seven hundred chemical synthetics tested by Monsanto. Two of these, VAMA 6— Krilium (6 vinylacetate: maleic acid complex) and HPAN 9— Krilium (9 polyacrylonitrile) have earned good reports. **1967** G. W. COOKE *Control of Soil Fertility* xxix. 458 'Krilium' produced an improvement in the percentage of soil aggregates which were stable in water.

krill (krɪl). Also **kril**. [ad. Norw. *kril* very small fry of fish.] A small, shrimp-like crustacean of the order Euphausiacea, or a large group of these animals, forming food for fishes and whales.

1907 J. G. Millais *Newfoundland* viii. 164 In June.. whales suddenly become extremely scarce, owing..to the trend seawards of the stream of 'kril' or red shrimp, on which the great *Balænoptera* subsist. **1912** *Rep. Brit. Assoc. Adv. Sci.* 178 A small red crustacean...forms the 'krill' of the whalers. **1928** Russell & Yonge *Seas* v. 117 Euphausiids, or 'krill', as they are called by the Norwegians ..are about an inch and a half in length, but are so abundant that they form a large part of the food of many of the northern fishes, and are the chief food of nearly all of the whalebone whales. **1931** *Discovery* XII. 317/1 The catches of plankton show that the shrimp-like crustaceans, or 'kril', on which the whales feed are not..to be found only in local concentrations, but are spread over immense areas in the open ocean. **1959** A. Hardy *Fish & Fisheries* i. 10 The largest of these whales, the rorquals,..specialise in feeding upon the krill (euphausiacean shrimps) which, though large for plankton animals, are but an inch or so in length. **1970** *Sci. Amer.* Dec. 20/3 Perhaps a crop of suitably large zooplankton such as krill—the shrimplike animals that are the principal food of the baleen whales in the Antarctic—could be raised in a fertilized lagoon.

†**krime.** *Obs. rare.* [? ad. Gr. κρῦμός frost.] (See quot.)

1599 T. M[oufet] *Silkwormes* 56 While Scythian krime doth fleete [*marg.* 'Boreas, the north-west wind'].

krimmer (ˈkrɪmə(r)). Also **crimmel, crimmer, krimma.** [G., f. *Krim* (Russ. *Krym*) Crimea (see Crimean *a.*).] A grey or black fur made from the wool of young lambs in or near the Crimea; an imitation of this. Cf. astrakhan b, karakul b.

1834 *Penny Cycl.* II. 519/2 The lamb yields a fine and beautiful fleece, which the dealers call a 'crimmel', the bulk of them being imported from the Crimea. **1892–3** *T. Eaton & Co. Catal.* Fall & Winter 10/2 The same styles of garments trimmed in a hundred different ways with krimmer, imitation lamb, persian-lamb, beaver, otter, nutria, sable, [etc.]. **1904** *Westm. Gaz.* 28 Jan. 4/2 Chinchilla or krimmer. **1906** *Ibid.* 3 Nov. 13/1 Grey krimmer. **1923** *Ibid.* 26 Jan. 11/1 A definition of 'crimmer lamb', as a commodity in the fur trade, was agreed upon at Marlborough-street yesterday. **1929** [see karakul]. **1930** *Economist* 1 Nov. (Russian Suppl.) 37/2 Hare-Peschanik, Persian Lamb, Persian Lamb-Broadtail, Crimmer Lamb. **1949** *Amer. Speech* XXIV. 96 Another common type of Persian lamb is the krimmer.... It is characterized by heavier fur and looser curl. Other strains of lamb can be dyed to simulate krimmer.

Krio (ˈkriːəʊ). [Native name.] An English-based Creole language in Sierra Leone. Also *attrib.* or as *adj.*

1955 P. Strevens *Papers in Lang.* (1965) ix. 116 There is the Freetown Krio, an English-based language, containing many borrowings from Yoruba. **1957** M. Banton *W. Afr. City* i. 6 The Creoles..developed a distinctive dialect version of the English language, known as Krio, which incorporates Portuguese, African, and other loan words, has an African rather than a European syntax, and is incomprehensible to the untrained English ear. Krio is to be distinguished from the native pidgin. *Ibid.* ix. 166 *Geda* is the Krio form of the English 'together'. **1961** *Guardian* 16 Feb. 6/4 Krio, the special Creole patois spoken in Sierra Leone. **1963** *Ann. Reg. 1962* 452 The threat of a collapse into a dialect deriving from English but not easily understood, a dialect less accessible than the base but genuine *lingua franca* of 'Pidgin': Krio, the language spoken at Freetown, was an example. **1972** W. B. Lockwood *Panorama Indo-Europ. Lang.* 119 Creole English has also developed in West Africa. Krio 'Creole', centred on Freetown, Sierra Leone, is of complex origin.

krioboly (kraɪˈɒbəlɪ). *Gr. Antiq.* [f. late Gr. κριοβόλιον, in 4th c. L. *criobolium*, f. κρῑοβόλ-ος ram-slaying.] A sacrifice in which many rams were slaughtered; a bath in the blood of rams.

[**1850** Leitch tr. *C. O. Müller's Anc. Art* (ed. 2) §422 A kriobolion of the Phrygian worship.] **1879** Farrar *St. Paul* (1884) I. xviii. 187 *note.* **1882** —— *Early Chr.* 3 *note*, The taurobolies and kriobolies (baths in the blood of bulls and rams) mark the extreme sensuality of superstition.

krippin, variant of crepine *Obs.*

kris (krɪs), **creese, crease** (kriːs). Forms: 6 crise, (cricke), 6–7 crys, 7 crisse, crize, cryze, (crest, cresset, cric), 8 cris, crice, 8–9 cress, creese, 9 kreese, crese, creeze, crease, kris, kriss, (krist). [a. Malay *kirīs, krīs, kres*, according to Yule and Burnell of Javanese origin: the earliest Eng. uses refer to Java.]

A Malay dagger, with a blade of a wavy form.

1577–80 *Drake's Voy.* in Hakluyt (1600) III. 742 Certaine wordes of the naturall language of Iaua learned and obserued by our men there, *Cricke* [? criche], a dagger. **1586–8** *Candish's Voy.* ibid. 822 Which dagger they [of Java] call a Crise, and is as sharpe as a razor. **1598** tr. *Linschoten's Voy.* 33 (Y.) Manancabo [Sumatra] where they make Poinyards, which in India are called Cryses. **1696** Ovington *Voy. Suratt* 173 (Y.) As the Japanners..rip up their Bowels with a Cric. **1698** W. Chilcot *Evil Thoughts* v. (1851) 53 The Javians, and Sumatrians, by their poisoned crests. **1772–84** Cook *Voy.* (1790) III. 916 A crice or short dagger. **1779** Forrest *Voy. N. Guinea* 332 Sooloos, with drawn cresses, pursued the Buggess. **1789** G. Keate *Pelew Isl.* 143 Snatched Soogle's Malay Creese, and stabbed him. **1847** Tennyson *Princ.* Prol. 21 The cursed Malayan crease. **1857** S. Osborn *Quedah* ii. 33 Standing on the main-hatch, with a long Illanoon creese in his hand. **1883** Mrs. Bishop *Malay Pen.* in *Leisure Ho.* 197/1 Mr. Ferney has..given me a *kris.* **1895** Conrad *Almayer's Folly* xi. 220 With a shout and a leap he would be in the midst of them, kriss in hand, killing, killing, killing. **1927** R. J. H. Sidney *In Brit. Malaya To-Day* 62 She will give Raja Besi a *kris* by means of which he will be able to kill the Jin. **1935** Wodehouse *Blandings Castle* iv. 107 Malays, when pushed past this point, take down the old *kris* from its hook and go out and start carving up the neighbours. **1948** W. S. Maugham *Here & There* 315 He awakened just as he thought a kriss was being drawn across his throat. **1953** *News Chron.* 2 June 7/1 In the first carriage is the Sultan of Kelantan... He carries a kris (a dagger) made from an elephant tusk. **1964** R. Perry *World of Tiger* vii. 106 The bull succumbed to stabs from poisoned *krises* tied to poles. **1965** R. McKie *Company of Animals* i. 16 An ancient Malay kris with ivory scabbard and garuda hilt. **1972** M. Sheppard *Taman Indera* 127 A short beak and a pair of folded arms can be recognized on many Malay kris-hilts to this day.

Krishna (ˈkrɪʃnə). The name of a Hindu deity or hero (see Krishnaism), used *attrib.* to designate Krishnaism or followers of this cult. Cf. Hare Krishna.

1875 Monier Williams *Indian Wisdom* xii. 332 Kṛishṇa-worship is comparatively modern. **1895** E. W. Hopkins *Religions of India* xv. 405 One may represent the attitude of a Krishna-worshipper in the epic somewhat in this way. *Ibid.* 411 The regular Vishnuite laudation affected by the Krishna sect. *Ibid.* xvi. 469 The parallels between the latest Krishna cult and the Biblical narrative are found..in the Puranas. **1958** Gerth & Martindale tr. *Weber's Religion of India* (1960) iv. 138 Vishnu..is honored..as patron of the dance drama and erotic orgies of the Krishna-cult. *Ibid.* v. 188 The ardent love of the redeemer of the later Krishna religion. **1970** J. Needleman *New Religions* (1972) x. 212 Who has walked the streets of any American..cities without encountering the young followers of the Krishna Consciousness movement? **1971** [see Hare Krishna]. **1973** R. Thomas *If You can't be Good* (1974) vi. 44 A fairly old town house..a couple of doors or so down from the Krishna kids.

Krishnaism (ˈkrɪʃnəɪz(ə)m). [f. *Krishna*, name of a great deity or deified hero of later Hinduism, worshipped as an incarnation of Vishnu.] The worship of or belief in Krishna. So **ˈKrishnaist, ˈKrishnaite**, a worshipper of Krishna; also *attrib.*

1885 C. J. Stone *Chr. bef. Christ* 180 The system of philosophy, afterwards adopted in both Krishnaism and Buddhism. **1892** Westcott *Gospel of Life* 156 Krishnaism has been the strength of Hinduism. **1889** J. M. Robertson *Christ & Krishna* x. 47 The other Krishnaist festivals. *Ibid.* xi. 51 The modern discussion of Krishnaite origins.

Kriss Kringle (ˌkrɪs ˈkrɪŋg(ə)l). *U.S.* ? *Obs.* Also **Christ-kinkle, Kriskringel, Krisking'l, Kris Kringle.** [See quot. 1919.] = Santa Claus.

1830 J. F. Watson *Annals of Philadelphia* 242 Every father in his turn remembers the excitements of his youth in Belsh-nichel and Christ-kinkle nights. **1849** J. Rees *Myst. City Life* 93 Do you think Kris Kringle will come down the chimney to-night? **1864** *Sacramento Union* 7 Jan. 5/2, I do not know whether the good Saint Nicholas..answers in those regions to the musical title of Kriss Kringle, as in the Queen City. **1919** H. L. Mencken *Amer. Lang.* iii. 89 Another example of debased German is offered by the American *Kriss Kringle.* It is from *Christkindlein*, or *Christkind'l*, and properly designates, of course, not the patron saint of Christmas, but the child in the manger. A German friend tells me that the form *Kriss Kringle*, which is that given in the Standard Dictionary, and the form *Krisking'l*, which is that most commonly used in the United States, are both quite unknown in Germany. **1928** G. Ade *Let.* 9 Oct. (1973) 136 We really believed that Kris Kringle could..go down chimneys which were not large enough to take care of a nest of barn swallows in the summer time. **1947** *Chicago Tribune* 20 July iv. 3/1 It is the story of an old man whose name was Kris Kringle and who believed he really was Santa Claus.

Kriˈsuvigite. *Min.* [Named, 1842, from Krisuvig in Iceland, where found: see -ite[1].] A synonym of brochantite.

1844 Dana *Min.* (ed. 2) 617 *Krisuvigite* is an emerald green salt of copper, from Krisuvig.

kritarchy (ˈkrɪtɑːkɪ). *nonce-wd.* [f. Gr. κριτής judge + -αρχία rule, after *monarchy*, etc.] The rule, or period of rule, of the Judges in ancient Israel.

1834 Southey *Doctor* (1838) V. Interch. xvii. 337 The Lays of Samson, Jephthah, Gideon, and other heroes of the Kritarchy.

kriti (ˈkrɪtɪ). Also **krithi.** [Skr. *kṛíti* the act of composing.] In the music of southern India, a song, often devotional in character, which is deliberately composed and not an improvisation on a set theme.

1914 A. H. F. Strangways *Mus. Hindostan* iii. 84 In Mudaliar Chinnaswami's *Oriental Music* sixty of his [*sc.* Tyagarāja's] songs (*Kritis*) are printed in staff notation. **1957** O. Gosvami *Story Indian Mus.* xix. 211 The *Kriti* is the most developed type of musical composition in the South. **1969** *Indian Express* (Bombay) 28 July 3/2 The krithi 'Naradamuni' in this raga was extremely pleasing. **1972** P. Halroyde *Indian Mus.* iii. 107 Kritis are sung in all tempos but without the long monosyllabic passages of the alamkaras or ornamentations.

‖**krobylos** (ˈkrɒbɪlɒs). *Gr. Antiq.* [a. Gr. κρωβύλος.] A roll or knot of hair on the crown of the head.

1850 Leitch tr. *C. O. Müller's Anc. Art* (ed. 2) 473 The hair is..knotted together into a krobylos in the undraped statues of Venus produced by later art.

kroci-, krokydolite, *Min.*, var. crocidolite.

1837 Phillips *Min.* 151 Krokydolite.

krocket (ˈkrɒkɪt). *Sc.* A name in Aberdeenshire of the Oyster-catcher (*Hæmatopus ostrilegus*). (Swainson *Prov. Names Birds*, 1885.)

krœhnkite (ˈkrœŋkaɪt). *Min.* [Named, 1876, after B. Kroehnke: see -ite[1].] A hydrous sulphate of copper and sodium, found in blue crystalline masses in Chili.

†**kroket.** *rare*$^{-1}$. [var. crocket[1].] ? A hook.

1426 Lydg. *De Guil. Pilgr.* (E.E.T.S.) 461 A large dyssh ..In hyr hand..she held; And in hyr ffyffthe hand a kroket.

Kromayer lamp (ˈkrəʊmaɪə læmp). *Med.* [f. the name of Ernst *Kromayer* (1862–1933), German dermatologist.] A water-cooled mercury-vapour lamp used therapeutically for local ultra-violet irradiation.

1911 *Allbutt's Syst. Med.* (ed. 2) IX. 480 The comparative value of the Finsen-Reyn and Kromayer lamps has been studied by Maar. **1927** *Observer* 18 Dec. 9/2 We [*sc.* Bermondsey Council] have eight large mercury vapour lamps, two carbon arcs, and one water-cooled Kromayer lamp. **1949** E. B. Clayton *Electrotherapy & Actinotherapy* xx. 342 The Kromayer lamp is designed for local irradiation only. It has the advantages that, being watercooled, it can be held in contact with the skin [etc.].

kromesky, -eski (krəʊˈmɛskɪ, ˈkrɒmɛskɪ). Also **crom-, -esque, -esqui.** [ad. Polish *kroméczka*, little slice.] A croquette made of meat or fish minced, rolled in bacon or calf's udder and fried.

1846 C. E. Francatelli *Mod. Cook* 309 Croquettes of Fowl and Mushrooms. The mince for these is prepared in the same way as for *Kromeskys.* **1861** —— *Cook's Guide* 120 Kromeskys are made with all kinds of croquet preparations, whether of meat, fish, or shell-fish. **1884** *Girl's Own Paper* May 428/1 A dozen oysters will make a moderate sized dish of kromeskies. **1892** *Encycl. Pract. Cookery* I. 478/2 Some authorities spell it Cromesquis, some Kromesquis, and others Kromeskies. **1920** E. Silvester *Sensible Cookery* 54 Kromesques of veal. **1928** *Evening News* 28 Dec. 4/5 Kromeskies of Turkey. **1951** *Good Housek. Home Encycl.* 348/2 A coating batter is used for making fritters, kromeskies, etc.

kromnek disease (ˈkrɒmnɛk). *S. Afr.* [Afrikaans, f. Du. *krom* crooked + *nek* neck.] A local name for the spotted wilt virus disease of tomato; also, a similar disease of tobacco.

1932 *Grocott's Mail* (S. Afr.) 2 Apr. 4 'Kromnek' or Kat River Wilt of tobacco is a disease which is not known anywhere in the world outside the Cape Province. **1933** E. S. Moore in *Sci. Bull. Dept. Agric. Union S. Afr.* No. 123. 1 The disease known locally as 'Kromnek' or 'Kat River Wilt' is by far the most serious of the diseases of tobacco in the Stockviström division. *Ibid.* 15 The evidence indicated not only that the tomato disease is of virus nature but that probably it is caused by the same virus which is responsible for the tobacco kromnek. **1941** *Nature* 19 Apr. 480/2 Control of the Kromnek (Spotted Wilt) Disease of Tomatoes. **1957** K. M. Smith *Textbk. Plant Virus Dis.* (ed. 2) 572 Tomato Spotted Wilt Virus.... Synonyms: T.S.W. Virus; Kromnek or Kat River Disease Virus.

Kromo (ˈkrəʊməʊ). *Indonesia.* Also **Krama.** [ad. Javanese *krama*, Indonesian *keromo.*] The polite form of Javanese, used by those of lower status when addressing social superiors.

1817 T. S. Raffles *Hist. Java* I. viii. 366 Nearly one half of the words in the vernacular language have their corresponding term in the *Bása Kráma* or polite language, without a knowledge of which no one dare address a superior. **1893** W. B. Worsfold *Visit to Java* xiii. 228 Two forms of modern Javanese are employed in everyday speech. First, the language of ceremony, called Krama; and secondly, the common speech, or Ngoko (meaning literally the thou-ing speech). **1925** P. Radin tr. *Vendryès's Lang.* iv. ii. 257 Among the natives of Java, a superior speaks to his inferior in Ngoko, but the inferior answers in Kromo. **1932** W. L. Graff *Lang.* xi. 423 Official Javanese is called *kromo.* **1948** D. Diringer *Alphabet* ii. vii. 424 Modern Javanese gradually breaks up into..Krama Inggil, a form of speech used in addressing gods and the aristocracy, [etc.].

kromogram (ˈkrəʊməgræm). *Photogr. Obs.* exc. *Hist.* Also **Kromogram.** [Altered form of chromogram.] = chromogram.

1897 *Brit. Jrnl. Photogr.* 8 Jan. 18/1 We understand that kromskops and sets of kromograms will shortly be obtainable from the Photo-chromoscope Syndicate Limited. **1898** [see kromskop]. **1969** H. & A. Gernsheim *Hist. Photogr.* (ed. 2) xliii. 523 In his Photochromoscope camera (1893) three separation negatives were taken in succession on one plate by means of a repeating back containing red, green and blue-violet filters. From these, diapositives were made by contact printing. When cut into the three separations and laid on the Kromskop viewing instrument (1892) containing filters of the same colour and mirrors, the optically superimposed Kromograms appear in perfect colour.

kromskop (ˈkrəʊmskəʊp). *Photogr. Obs.* exc. *Hist.* Also **Kromskop.** [f. *krom-*, Ives's altered

form of CHROMO- + *-skop*, altered form of -SCOPE.] A viewer for the three positives of a chromogram, enabling them to be visually combined and seen as a single coloured picture. Freq. *attrib.* (in Ives's use).

1897 *Brit. Jrnl. Photogr.* 8 Jan. 17/2 The Kromskop is the name finally chosen for Mr. Fred. E. Ives's perfected stereo-photo-chromoscope. **1898** F. E. IVES *Krōmskōp Color Photogr.* i. 6 The Kromogram must be placed in the Krōmskōp in order to visually reproduce the object photographed. *Ibid.* xi. 36 It is absolutely necessary to use in any of the Krōmskōp cameras the kind of orthochromatic sensitive plates for which that particular camera has been adjusted. **1928** O. WHEELER *Colour Photogr.* iii. 14 Almost equally obsolete, though still of considerable interest and comparatively practical from the amateur standpoint, is the additive arrangement adopted in an instrument.. variously designated a photochromoscope, chromoscope or kromskop. **1968** E. DE MARÉ *Colour Photogr.* ii. 43 Ives also produced the Lantern Photochromoscope which projected the three pictures first through red, green and blue filters and then through three lenses directed to form a single image on a screen. He improved his camera and a viewer, which in a new form he called the Kromscope [*sic*]. It revealed stereoscopic pictures in full colour and this he demonstrated in 1896.

króna ('krəʊnə). Also **krona**. Pl. **krónur**. [Icel.; cf. KRONE.] The basic monetary unit of Iceland; also a coin representing one króna.

1886 R. SENF *Illustr. Postage Stamp Album* 47 Iceland.. Coinage:.. 100 öre (= aur) = 1 krona. **1922** P. A. ÓLAFSSON *Iceland* 24/2 The coinage is the same as elsewhere in Scandinavia, i.e. 1 króna (pl. krónur) = 100 aurar. **1938** *Encycl. Brit. Bk. of Year* 321/2 Currency unit: *króna* (exchange 22·15 krónur = £1). **1946** K. TRYGGVASON in T. Thorsteinsson *Iceland* (ed. 4) 164 Up to the end of the [1914–18] war there was little or no difficulty in keeping the Icelandic króna at par with the Danish Krone. **1958** *Spectator* 6 June 726/3 The Communists in the Icelandic Government are playing the fishing dispute for all they're worth, and trying to evade collective responsibility for economic measures which will drastically devalue the Kronur. **1970** D. BAGLEY *Running Blind* i. 28 A 100-kronur banknote.

‖**krone** ('kroːnə). [Ger. *krone* (pl. *kronen*), Da. *krone* (pl. *kroner*), Sw. *krona* (pl. *kronor*) crown: cf. CROWN *sb.* 8.]

1. A silver coin of Denmark, Norway, and Sweden, containing 100 öre.

1875 JEVONS *Money* viii. 72 Some merchants [of Sweden] are said already to keep their accounts in kroner and öre. **1884** *Pall Mall G.* 26 Sept. 5/1 For the past business year the Norwegian National Bank shows accounts which leave a balance of 2,232,919 kroner (say £125,000).

2. The 10 mark gold piece of the German Empire.

1898 *Whitaker's Almanac* 695 [*Earlier edd.* 'crown'].

3. A silver coin of the monetary system of the Austrian Empire, = 100 heller.

[**1895**: see HELLER[1].] **1898** *Whitaker's Almanac* 695 [*Earlier edd.* 'crown'].

Kronecker delta ('krəʊnɛkə 'dɛltə). *Math.* [f. the name of Leopold *Kronecker* (1823–91), Ger. mathematician + DELTA.] A function of two integers defined as equal to one if the integers have the same value and zero otherwise; symbol δ_{ij} or δ_j^i. Also (the ***generalized Kronecker delta***), a function of $2k$ integers that takes the values 0 or $\pm$ 1 (see quot. 1927[2]) (*rare*).

1927 O. VEBLEN *Invariants Quadratic Differential Forms* i. 3 The theory of determinants and allied expressions is essentially a theory of alternating sets of quantities, and can be made to depend on certain fundamental alternating sets of quantities which have only the values 0 and + 1 and − 1. These sets of quantities are known as generalized Kronecker deltas because of their analogy with the Kronecker delta which is already well known. *Ibid.*, The generalized Kronecker delta has k superscripts and k subscripts, each running from 1 to n... If the superscripts are distinct from each other and the subscripts are the same set of numbers as the superscripts, the value of the symbol is + 1 or − 1 according as an even or an odd permutation is required to arrange the superscripts in the same order as the subscripts; in all other cases its value is 0. **1937** A. A. ALBERT *Mod. Higher Algebra* (1938) x. 228 Our rule for multiplying matrices implies that $E_{ij}E_{kl} = \delta_{jk}E_{il}$ $(i,j,k,l, = 1,\ldots,s)$ where δ_{jk} is the Kronecker delta. **1961** P. E. PFEIFFER *Linear Systems Analysis* ii. 30 The value Δ of a determinant whose elements are δ_{ik} is unity, where δ_{ik} is the Kronecker delta.

‖**kronia** ('krɒnɪə). *Gr. Antiq.* [Gr. Κρόνια, neuter pl. of Κρόνιος of or pertaining to Kronos or Saturn.] An ancient Greek festival in honour of Kronos, resembling in its features the Roman Saturnalia. It was held at Athens in the month Hecatombæon (corresponding to parts of July and August).

kronk, var. CRONK, cry of wild goose.

kronykele, obs. form of CHRONICLE.

Kroo: var. KRU.

kross, obs. form of KAROSS.

†**krotte**, ? variant of CROT *Obs.*

c **1466** SIR J. PASTON in *P. Lett.* II. 294, I sende yow.. iij tracle pottes.. I mystruste moost the potte that hathe a krotte abovyn in the toppe, lesse that he hathe ben ondoone.

kroude, kroun, obs. ff. CROWD *sb.*[1], CROWN *sb.*

krout: see SOUR-CROUT.

Kru (kruː). Also **Kroo, Krou.** [W. African.] *attrib.* or as *adj.* Of or pertaining to a Negro race so named on the coast of Liberia, very skilful as seamen. Also as *sb.*

1835 MARRYAT *Pirate* vii, These were Kroumen, a race of blacks.. who inhabit the coast near Cape Palmas, and are often employed by our men-of-war. **1883** *Daily News* 12 July 3/1 The Englishmen,.. assisted by Krooboys, sallied out and put their assailants to flight. **1894** AMANDA SMITH *Autobiogr.* xxv. 198 The kroomen.. let a great wave break over us. **1897** MARY KINGSLEY *W. Africa* App. i. 646 The Kruboys, as the natives of the Grain Coast are called, irrespective of the age of the individual, by the white men. *Ibid.* 649 They speak their version of our own—Kru-English, or 'trade English', as it is called. **1957** M. BANTON *W. Afr. City* i. 5 Another important group was that of the Kru. They are members of a sea-faring tribe inhabiting part of what is now the Liberian coast. **1970** P. OLIVER *Savannah Syncopators* 41 The Kru speaking peoples of Liberia. **1973** *Times* 17 Apr. (Liberia Suppl.) p. vi/5 Elizabeth Tonkin has recently been from Birmingham on a study of Kru linguistics.

b. (See quot.)

1884 H. H. JOHNSTON *River Congo* i. 26 There is a subtle distinction between Kru-boy and Kru-man, or, to use its Portuguese form, Krumano... The Kru-man is an artificial name given to the indigenous slaves of the country.. men, for instance, of the lower Congo tribes, that are sold by their chiefs to European merchants.

krug[1] (krʊg). [Ger.] A beer-mug or tankard.

1866 C. M. YONGE *Dove in Eagle's Nest* II. xii. 235 He has .. excused himself from aiding his two gentlemen-squires in consuming their krug of beer. **1963** T. PYNCHON *V.* viii. 203 They seemed to seek some Hofbrauhaus of the spirit like a grail, hold a krug of Munich beer like a chalice.

Krug[2] (kruːg). The proprietary name of a champagne made by the firm of Krug et Cie. of Reims.

1876 *Trade Marks Jrnl.* 6 Sept. 455/1 Krug & Co. Reims. .. Paul Krug, of and on behalf of the firm of Krug and Co., Reims, France; champagne wine merchants. **1891** in C. Ray *Compleat Imbiber* (1967) IX. 122 All Brands of Champagne in stock.. Pol Roger, Krug, Moët et Chandon. **1920** G. SAINTSBURY *Notes on Cellar-Bk.* v. 71 Taking well-known brands.. I do not know that I was more faithful to any than to Krug. **1967** G. SMITH in L. Deighton *London Dossier* 125 The best game pies.. ideal for demolishing with a bottle of Krug in the car park before the Oxford and Cambridge game at Twickenham. **1974** D. MACKENZIE *Zaleski's Percentage* xv. 222 'Champagne for my friend, Inspector-Detective.' It was vintage Krug and perfectly chilled.

Krugerism ('kruːgərɪz(ə)m). *Hist.* [f. the name of Stephanus Johannes Paulus *Kruger* (1825–1904), president of the Transvaal 1883–1901.] The nationalist (pro-Boer) policy of President Kruger. So **Krugerite** ('kruːgəraɪt) *sb.* and *a.*, an adherent of, adhering to President Kruger or his policy.

1896 *Westm. Gaz.* 3 Dec. 5/1 Those who have effusively championed Mr. Chamberlain for what they imagined was his agreement with their Krugerite sympathies. **1897** *Daily News* 25 Jan. 5/6 Krugerites we know, and Rhodesites, but the Schreinerites (politically) all seem to live in London. **1897** *Times* 4 Feb. 3 Pure and unadulterated Krugerism. **1897** *Daily News* 24 Mar. 7/1 The conflict between the two ideals—the Rhodesian or British, and the Krugerite or non-British. **1900** *Pall Mall Gaz.* 29 Mar. 8/1 There are those who suggest that, perhaps, if the scrutineers had not been Krugerites, Joubert would have been found at the head. *Ibid.* 11 June 2/3 In the spring of last year he denounced the corruption of the Krugerite gang. **1902** KIPLING *Traffics & Discov.* (1904) 33 Van Zyl wasn't any Krugerite. **1923** B. RONAN *Forty S. Afr. Yrs.* 183 Rhodes.. was recognised as the only leader capable of checking the spread of Krugerism in South Africa. **1972** *Sunday Times* (Johannesburg) Colour Suppl. 11 June 9 My father was not a Krugerite, he was a follower of Joubert, who would be called a Progressive today, I suppose.

Kruger rand ('kruːgə rænd, rant). Also **Kruger Rand, Krugerrand.** [f. *Kruger* (see prec.) + RAND *sb.*] A South African gold coin bearing a portrait of President Kruger.

1967 *S. Afr. Digest* 14 July 3/3 The first gold Krugerrand coin was struck at the South African Mint in Pretoria last week by the Minister of Finance, Dr. N. Diederichs. *Ibid.*, The Krugerrand is to be minted in limited numbers and is intended for overseas issue. **1971** *Standard Encycl. S. Afr.* III. 313/2 The Krugerrand, a gold coin of 32·7 mm diameter containing 1 troy oz. of fine gold, was first struck in 1967. The obverse shows the bust of Paul Kruger. **1974** *Harpers & Queen* Sept. 33/2 Keep some Kruger rands under your mattress. **1974** *Daily Tel* 14 Dec. 18/3 The South Africans are quickly taking advantage of the price rise by minting Krugerrands (made legal tender to avoid capital gains tax) and Britons have been flocking to buy the coins.

krugite ('kruːgaɪt). *Min.* [Named, 1881, after D. Krug von Nidda: see -ITE[1].] A sulphide of potassium, calcium, and magnesium, akin to Polyhalite. (A. H. Chester *Names of Minerals*, 1896).

Krukenberg ('krʊkənbɜːg). *Med.* The name of Friedrich Ernst *Krukenberg* (1871–1946), Ger. scientist, used *attrib.* to designate a kind of metastatic ovarian carcinoma that is usually secondary to a carcinoma of the stomach or colon (described by Krukenberg in 1896).

1911 *Amer. Jrnl. Obstetr.* LXIV. 930 Among a series of metastatic ovarian carcinomata two.. showed the picture of a Krukenberg tumor. **1934** R. A. WILLIS *Spread of Tumours* xxiii. 312 Gastric carcinomas which yield Krukenberg ovarian growths seldom yield metastases in other tissues. **1961** R. D. BAKER *Essent. Path.* xvii. 464 The most characteristic of the metastatic tumors [of the ovary] comes from the stomach, produces mucous, signet-ring cells, and is called Krukenberg tumor.

krummholz ('krʌmhɒlts). [G. *krummholz* crooked wood, the popular name of a dwarf pine, *Pinus mugo* var. *pumilio*, adopted as the name for a particular type of vegetation by A. Grisebach in *Vegetation der Erde* (1872) II. xxiii. 488.] = *elfin-wood* (ELFIN *sb.* 4).

[**1903** [see ELFIN *sb.* 4].] **1908** *Bot. Gaz.* XLV. 334 The *Krummholz* is composed of two trees only... In its *Krummholz* form it [sc. *Pinus flexilis*] assumes the most fantastic shapes. **1942** R. PEATTIE *Friendly Mountains* 162 The upper part of the spruce slope dwindles to a 'scrub' forest, or 'krummholz'. **1964** GLEASON & CRONQUIST *Nat. Geogr. Plants* ix. 101 (*caption*) Dense, stunted growth of the sort here shown is known as Krummholz. **1967** *Jrnl. Glaciol.* VI. 820 Shading by krummholz spruce and fir, blueberry and willow.

‖**krummhorn** ('krʊmhɔːn, 'krʌm-). *Mus.* Also CRUMHORN, **krumhorn, krum horn.** [Ger., f. *krumm* crooked, curved + *horn* HORN.] **a.** A wind-instrument of a curved form. **b.** An organ reed-stop of 8 ft. pitch, resembling the clarinet in tone; called also CROMORNE, and corruptly CREMONA[2].

1864 WEBSTER, *Krummhorn, Krumhorn*, an instrument of music of the cornet kind, formerly in use. **1880** [see CROMORNE]. **1883** J. W. MOLLETT *Illustr. Dict. Art & Archæol.* 186/2 *Krumhorn*, an old musical instrument of the cornet kind. **1955** AUDEN *Shield of Achilles* iii. 76 There I stand in Eden again, welcomed back By the krumhorns, doppions, sordumes of jolly miners. **1969** *Daily Colonist* (Victoria, B.C.) 6 July 23/1 That's if you call 14th, 15th and 16th century harpsichords, clavichords, recorders, krum horns, citterns, lutes and oboes up to date.

Krupp (krʌp, ‖krup). [Name of Alfred *Krupp* (1812–87), German metallurgist, founder of steel and armament works at Essen in Germany.] A gun made at a Krupp factory.

1883 *Whitaker's Almanack* 445/1 She is a casemate ship.. armed with four 10-in. steel Krupps and one 12-in. Krupp. **1887** *Times* (Weekly ed.) 26 Aug. 8/1 The Krupps.. are mounted on Vavasseur carriages. **1900** *Daily News* 23 July 5/4 The Bogue Forts are being re-armed by the Chinese with quick-firing Krupps. **1916** 'BOYD CABLE' *Action Front* 264 One solitary Krupp dropping in here, and we'd have a pretty-looking mess. **1926** T. E. LAWRENCE *Seven Pillars* (1935) I. xiii. 95 The Arabs rejoiced when they came, and believed they were now equals of the Turk; but the four guns were twenty-year-old Krupps, with a range of only three thousand yards.

Hence **Krupped** (krʌpt), '**Kruppized** *ppl. adjs.*, made or carried out in a manner originated by Krupps.

1899 *Army & Navy Register* (U.S.) 3 June 361/3 The great severity of the ballistic tests.. necessitates the employment of a Kruppized process. **1902** *Encycl. Brit.* XXXI. 355/2 An A.P. shot should perforate two calibres of wrought iron, one calibre of Harveyed steel, or ⅘ calibre of Krupped armour.

Kruschen ('kruːʃən). ***Kruschen salts***, a proprietary aperient; also *ellipt.* As an advertising catch phr. ***that Kruschen feeling***, a feeling of vigorous health.

1925 R. W. G. HINGSTON in E. F. Norton *Fight for Everest, 1924* 350 Kruschen salts, 2 bottles. **1925** R. MACAULAY *Casual Commentary* 131 The happy spring when .. we are full of that Kruschen feeling. **1928** L. C. DUNSTERVILLE *Stalky's Reminisc.* xv. 226 He was very liverish in the early morning and had none of that 'Kruschen feeling' about him. **1936** C. DAY LEWIS *Friendly Tree* xii. 174 That Crane girl acts like a dose of Kruschen on the staff.

kryme, variant of CRIM *v. Obs.*, to crumble.

kryo- (kraɪəʊ), another spelling of CRYO- combining form of Gr. κρύος frost, in various scientific terms: see CRYOGEN, CRYOHYDRATE, CRYOCONITE, CRYOLITE, CRYOSCOPY, etc. **kry'ometer** [Gr. μέτρον measure], a thermometer for measuring very low temperatures.

1877 RAYMOND *Statist. Mines & Mining* 427 Kryolite from spathic iron. **1882** BRANNT tr. *Thausung's Malt & Beer* 38 Alcohol and sulphuret of carbon are used as thermometrical substances for measuring very low temperatures... Thermometers for such low temperatures are called Kryometers [cold meters].

krypto-, variant of CRYPTO-.

krypton ('krɪptən). *Chem.* [f. Gr. κρυπτόν, neuter of κρυπτός hidden, concealed. Discovered by Ramsay in 1898.] A rare inert gaseous element; atomic number 36; symbol Kr.

1898 *Westm. Gaz.* 7 June 4/2 M. Berthelot read a letter from Professor Ramsay,.. giving the first announcement of another discovery... This new gas he proposes to call krypton. **1898** SIR W. CROOKES *Addr. Brit. Assoc.* 19 During the course of the present year he [Prof. Ramsay] has

announced the existence of no fewer than three new gases—krypton, neon, and metargon. **1899** *Hazell's Ann.* 83 Krypton forms a fifth constituent of the atmosphere, but is present in very minute quantities. **1899** L. Dobbin *Ladenburg's Develop. Chem.* xvi. 347 In the case of crypton, the ratio of the specific heats has been ascertained to be 1·66, so that this gas is also a monatomic element.

kryzhanovskite (krɪʒəˈnɒvskaɪt). *Min.* [ad. Russ. *krȳzhanovskit* (A. I. Ginzburg 1950, in *Dokladȳ Akad. nauk SSSR* LXXII. 763), f. the name of V. I. *Krȳzhanovskiĭ* (1881–1947), Russ. mineralogist: see -ite[1].] A greenish-brown hydrated basic phosphate of manganese and ferric iron, $MnFe_2(PO_4)_2(OH)_2·H_2O$, found in Kazakhstan, U.S.S.R.

1951 *Mineral. Abstr.* XI. 189 Kryzhanovskite, a new mineral in the group of phosphates... Rough crystals (2–3 cm.) of prismatic habit occur..in the oxidation zone of pegmatite. **1971** *Amer. Mineralogist* LVI. 5 Since kryzhanovskite is predominantly the ferric equivalent of the phosphoferrite group, the species has valid status and the name is to apply to all members of the phosphoferrite group containing an excess of 50 mol percent Fe^{3+} in the octahedral sites.

ksar, obs. form of tsar.

‖**Kshatriya, Kshatri** (ˈkʃatrija, -triː). *E. Ind.* Also 8 Chittery, 8–9 Cshatriya. [Skr. *kshatriya* a member of the military or reigning order (which in later times constituted the second caste), f. *kshatra* rule, authority.] A member of the military caste, the second of the four great castes or classes among the Hindus (cf. Khatri).

1782 G. Forster *Journ. Bengal* (1798) I. 54 *note*, The Chittery occasionally takes himself to traffic, and the Sooder has become the inheritor of principalities. **1794** Sir W. Jones *Inst. of Menu* i §31 Wks. 1799 III. 69 He [Brahma] caused the Brahmen, the Cshatriya, the Vaisya, and the Súdra..to proceed from his mouth, his arm, his thigh, and his foot. **1834** Caunter *Orient. Ann.* ix. 120 She was the daughter of a wealthy Cshatrya, in the neighbourhood of Delhi. **1849** E. B. Eastwick *Dry Leaves* 7 Here Indra, Rudra, Brimha, and Vishnú are said to have re-produced the warrior caste or Kshatris, who had been extirpated by Parsurám on account of their impiety.

K-shell: see K 3 e.

ktypeite (ˈtɪpəaɪt). *Min.* Also -ïte. [ad. F. *ktypéite* (A. Lacroix 1898, in *Compt. Rend.* CXXVI. 605), f. Gr. κτυπέ-ω crash, resound: see -ite[1].] A form of aragonite, occurring as pisolites under strain, which decrepitates.

1898 *Jrnl. Chem. Soc.* LXXIV. 604 The violent decrepitation, on account of which the name ktypeite is given. **1902** *Ibid.* LXXXII. ii. 89 Conchite..is identical with aragonite, and the same is probably also true of ktypeite. **1951** C. Palache et. al. *Dana's Syst. Min.* (ed. 7) II. 191 Ktypeïte..is a name given to the substance of certain fibrous pisolites in the belief that it represented a new polymorph but which is very probably identical with aragonite. **1962** W. A. Deer et al. *Rock-Forming Min.* V. 312 'Ktypeite', from hot spring pisolites, is almost certainly aragonite.

ku, kuafe, obs. ff. cow *sb.*[1], cue *sb.*[2], coif.

kuaka (ˈkwakə). *N.Z.* [Maori.] The bar-tailed godwit, *Limosa lapponica*.

1873 W. L. Buller *Hist. Birds N.Z.* 198 *Limosa baueri*. (Barred-rumped godwit.)... Native name.—Kuaka. **1882** W. D. Hay *Brighter Britain!* II. 222 The Kuaka..is the bird spoken of as 'curlew' and 'grey snipe' by colonists. **1905** W. B. *Where White Man Treads* 252 These thoughts flow through my brain like a covey of kuaka (snipe). **1966** *Encycl. N.Z.* I. 819/1 In New Zealand the great majority of our migrant birds are waders, and the best known and most abundant of these is the eastern race of the bar-tailed godwit, the kuaka of the Maori (*Limosa lapponica*).

Kuan, Kwan (kwɑːn). [f. Chinese *guān, kuān* official.] Used to denote imperial patronage or official usage in China, as:

1. ***Kuan Hua*** (hwɑː) [language, speech] = mandarin[1] 2.

1814 J. Marshman *Clavis Sinica* ii. 559 The most correct and extensive colloquial dialect is termed..Kwanhwà. **1845** *Encycl. Metrop.* XVI. 583/2 The learned language of the present day (*Kwan-hwa*) or dialect of the Mandarins. **1848** [see *mandarin dialect* (mandarin[1] 4)]. **1889** L. C. Hopkins (*title*) Guide to Kuan Hua. **1932** W. L. Graff *Lang.* xi. 421 The modern Chinese of Pekin, the Mandarin, Kuan Hua, or Guoryu..has become the language of officialdom. **1968** *Encycl. Brit.* V. 634/1 Mandarin... Formerly called variously *kuan-hua* 'official speech', whence the term 'Mandarin', or *p'u-t'ung-hua* 'general (*v.* local) speech'.

2. ***Kuan Yin*** (jɪn) [Lord of Mercy], a goddess of Chinese Buddhism, to whom intercession for aid or protection is made; a representation in sculpture of this deity.

1845 *Encycl. Metrop.* XX. 490/2 The Kwan-yin, or merciful Goddess of the Chinese. **1871** S. Beal *Catena of Buddhist Scriptures* 121 The work known as the Po-kien.. says:... The spirit..gazing on Kwan-Yin, a covenant saviour (a sworn friend). **1906** S. W. Bushell *Chinese Art* II. viii. 7 Large images of Kuan-Yin enamelled with turquoise blue and other soft colours. **1922** E. T. C. Werner *Myths & Legends China* x. 251 As Mary is the guiding spirit of Rome, so is Kuan Yin of the Buddhist faith. **1930** O. Sirén *Hist. Early Chinese Art* III. iv. 47 In the tall eleven-headed Kuan-yins..a suggestion of movement may be observed. **1943** *Burlington Mag.* Dec. 311/2 Kuan yin figures of the Ming and Ch'ing period are represented in great numbers and show the eagerness of the artist to excel in decorative variations and in manual skilfulness. **1963** P. C. Swann *Art of China, Korea & Japan* vi. 142 The best known of Sung Buddhist sculptures are the indolent *Kuan-yin* 'Goddess of Compassion' (the Sanskrit Avalokitésvara) figures with their full, fleshy bodies seated in the *maharaja-lila* or position of royal ease. **1969** R. Quest *Cerberus Murders* v. 35 Some benign deity—Kuan Yin, perhaps.

3. In full, ***Kuan ware, yao*** (jaʊ) [jade]. A type of thickly glazed celadon made in predominantly greyish colours at Hangchow during the Sung dynasty; similar pottery (as the ***Kuan jar***) produced elsewhere in China in later centuries.

1888 F. Hirth *Anc. Porc.* 19 Kuan-yao, or Mandarin Porcelain, is the produce of certain Government factories. **1915** R. L. Hobson *Chinese Pott. & Porc.* I. iv. 48 One of the puzzling features in the study of the Sung wares is the interrelation of the various makes, such as the Ju, Kuan, [etc.]. *Ibid.* v. 59 A new pottery..copied the forms of the older Kuan ware. **1938** *Burlington Mag.* July 37/1 A *Kuan yao* saucer of a delicate bluish grey glaze. **1944** W. E. Cox *Bk. Pott. & Porc.* I. xviii. 426 Neither of the Kuan yao factories so far as we know survived the Mongolian conquest. *Ibid.* II. xx. 592 (*caption*) Bottle vase with glaze of Kuan type of pale blue-green. **1960** *Times* 21 June 22/6 A.. blue and white Kuan or wine jar. **1961** M. Sullivan *Introd. Chinese Art* viii. 158 As soon as Southern Sung had established themselves at Hangchow they naturally sought for factories which could produce a ware fine enough to be classed as *kuan*. **1971** P. David *Chinese Connoisseurship* 139 *Kuan Ware.* This was made on the orders of the Palace Works Department.

ku'anthropy, bad form of kynanthropy.

1865 Baring-Gould *Werewolves* vii. 97 The president went on to say that Lycanthropy and Kuanthropy were mere hallucinations. **1866** *Athenæum* 24 Mar. 393/2 [Review of prec.] Traditions of kuanthropy, and boanthropy.

kub, obs. form of cub *sb.*[2], sheep-pen, crib.

Kuba (kuːˈbɑː). [The name of a town in north-east Azerbaijan, U.S.S.R.] = Kabistan.

1900 J. K. Mumford *Oriental Rugs* viii. 100 *Caucasian*... 'Kabistan' or 'Kuba'. **1931** A. U. Dilley *Oriental Rugs & Carpets* vii. 178 The name Kuba is applied both to the old weavings, allied to dragon rugs, and to semi-antique rugs of a Kabistan character. **1963** *Times* 23 Feb. 4/7 A small Kuba carpet, woven in a pattern of dragons and flowers, fetched £2,000. **1972** P. L. Phillips tr. *Formenton's Oriental Rugs & Carpets* 242 *Kuba or Kabistan*, Caucasian carpets of the Shirvan family. The most common decoration is made up of lines of rectangles or squares one above the other along the central part of the field.

kubong (ˈkuːbɒŋ). Also kubung. [Malay.] The flying lemur, *Cynocephalus variegatus*, a small, south-east Asian mammal of the order Dermoptera, which glides by means of stretching the membranes linking its limbs and tail; also called the colugo.

1821 T. S. Raffles in *Trans. Linn. Soc.* XIII. 248 *Lemur volans* Linn. Kubung of the Malays. **1929** S. S. Flower *List Vertebrated Animals in Gardens Zool. Soc. Lond. 1828–1927* I. 68 The 'Flying Lemurs', 'Kubong' or 'Colugo' of Malaya and the Philippines..not yet alive in the Gardens, 31 Dec. 1927. **1961** *Listener* 2 Nov. 740/1 The flying Kubong as seen in 'Wings in the Malayan Forest'. **1965** C. Shuttleworth *Malayan Safari* vi. 84, I was anxious to trap kubong (flying lemur). **1969** Ld. Medway *Wild Mammals Malaya* 6/1 Malayan Flying-lemur, Kubong... *Cynocephalus variegatus*.

Kuchaean, Kuchean (kʊˈtʃiːən). [ad. F. *koutchéen* (S. Lévi 1913, in *Jrnl. Asiatique* II. 315), f. *Kucha*, the name of a town in Sinkiang, China: see -an.] The western dialect of Tocharian, Tocharian B. Also *attrib.* or as *adj.*

1939 *Cambr. Anc. Hist.* XII. iii. 97 A..language formerly known as Tocharish but now more correctly called the Kuchean or Turfanese language. **1939** L. H. Gray *Foundations of Lang.* 101 Kuchaean *ñäkte* 'god'. *Ibid.* 322 Relatively little of Kuchaean is yet accessible. **1948** D. Diringer *Alphabet* vi. 348 There is..a general agreement to call 'Dialect B' [of Tocharian] *Kuchean*. **1965** *Language* XLI. 108 The Kuchean 3 pl. preterite of *käm* 'come' is *kamem*. **1972** W. B. Lockwood *Panorama Indo-Europ. Lang.* 254 It was subsequently established that Tocharian B was the language proper to Kucha and may therefore be called Kuchean.

‖**Kuchen** (ˈkuːxən). Also kuchen. Pl. Kuchen, Küchen. [G., lit. 'cake'.] (In Germany or among people speaking German or Yiddish) a cake; now freq. a cake taken with coffee.

1854 Geo. Eliot *Let.* 12 Nov. (1954) II. 185 The Germans eat their Bratwurst and Küchen from house to house in gladness of heart. **1855** —— in *Fraser's Mag.* June 706/1 Kuchen (generally a heavy kind of fruit tart). **1858** Mrs. Gaskell *Let.* 1 Oct. (1966) 894 M. Mohl treated us to coffee & kuchen. **1861** —— *Grey Woman* i. in *All Year Round* 5 Jan. 300/1 We had nearly finished our coffee, and our '*kucken*' [sic], and our cinnamon cake. **1894** G. du Maurier *Trilby* I. ii. 164 They will..bring him tea and gin and *küchen* [in *Harper's Mag.* Feb. 348/2 printed kuchen] and *marrons glacés*. **1907** I. Zangwill *Ghetto Comedies* 316 Home-made Kuchen and other dainties. **1972** L. P. Bachmann *Ultimate Act* xxiii. 208 We sat at the kitchen table having coffee and *Kuchen*.

[**kuchiez kote**, erroneous reading of *knauez kote* = servant's cottage.

13.. *E.E. Allit. P.* B. 801 Comez to your kuchiez-kote..; I schal fette yow a fatte your fette for to wasche.]

kuchyn, kuckold, kuckstole, obs. ff. cushion, cuckold, cuckstool.

kud, kudde, pa. t. and pple. of kithe.

kudos (ˈkjuːdɒs). *slang* (orig. *University*) and *colloq.* [a. Gr. κῦδος praise, renown.] Glory, fame, renown.

1831 *Fraser's Mag.* III. 391 He obtained *kudos* immense. **1841** Disraeli 23 Feb. in *Corr. w. Sister* (1886) 171, I am spoken of with great *kudos* in 'Cecil'. **1859** Darwin in *Life & Lett.* (1887) II. 168 Lyell has read about half of the volume in clean sheets, and gives me very great kudos. **1889** *Boy's Own Paper* 17 Aug. 729/1 Our champion was held to have lost no *kudos* in the encounter. **1970** G. F. Newman *Sir, You Bastard* vii. 196 News services buzzed, but George Doodie sought no kudos; his name was mentioned only once. **1972** J. Creasey *Splinter of Glass* vii. 55 He wanted Roger to take the kicks if this failed but was prepared to give him the kudos if the use of the newspapers succeeded.

¶ Sometimes *erron.* treated as *pl.* (ˈkjuːdəʊz); so **ˈkudo** (back-formation) *sing.*, honourable mention, praise for an achievement (see also quot. 1941).

1941 J. Smiley *Hash House Lingo* 34 *Kudo*, good standing with the management. **1950** F. Allen in G. Marx *Groucho Lett.* (1967) 73 A man sitting on a toilet bowl swung open the men's room door and added his kudo to the acclaim. **1961** *Wall Street Jrnl.* (Eastern ed.) 18 Oct. 12/2 This did not win Mr. Eisenhower many kudos in the press. **1963** *Life* 19 Apr. 29/2 A kudo to *Life* for a fine story on baseball's spring training. **1972** *Sunday Mirror* 17 Sept. 47/1 This below-strength Chelsea side captured the few kudos that were going. **1972** *Homes & Gardens* Nov. 60 It seems almost a kudos to have a lady pilot. **1972** *Bankers' Mag.* Winter 23/2 Kudos are expressed to Messrs. Gene Jackson, Joel Anderson, and John Tolford for their aid.

Hence **ˈkudize** *v.*, **ˈkudos** *v.* (*nonce-wds.*), to praise, laud, glorify.

1799 Southey *Eng. Ecl.*, etc., Poet. Wks. III. 57 Lauded in pious Latin to the skies; Kudos'd egregiously in heathen Greek. **1873** M. Collins *Squire Silchester* I. xix. 234 He kudized Louisa, who blushed when he compared her to Penthesilea.

kudu (ˈkuːduː). Also 8- (*S. Afr.*) koedoe, 8–9 coodoo, 9 koodoo, koudou. [Xosa-Kaffir, given as *iqudu* in Davis' *Kaffir Dict.* (1872).] Either of two African antelopes, *Tragelephas strepsiceros*, the greater kudu, or *T. imberbis*, the lesser kudu, which is confined to East Africa; the male of the former has spirally-twisted horns, attaining in full-grown specimens a length of 3 feet or more. Also *attrib.*

1777 G. Forster *Voy. round World* I. 84 The Coodoo, or Kolben's *bock ohne namen* (goat without a name). **1785** —— tr. *Sparrman's Voy. Cape G.H.* II. 213 Koedoe is the name given by the colonists to a beautiful tall gazel with long and slender shanks. **1802** *Sporting Mag.* XX. 141 The n'gou and koudou are also inhabitants of Caffraria. **1866** Livingstone *Last Jrnls.* (1873) I. vii. 161, I got a fine male Kudu. **1879** Atcherley *Trip Boërland* 155 Advancing..with their beautiful spiral horns towering high above them, were two magnificent koodoos. **1901** *Knowledge* July 150/2 The horns take the form of upwardly directed corkscrews, mimicking in fact to a certain degree those of the beautiful African kudu antelope. **1903** J. Y. F. Blake *West Pointer with Boers* xxvii. 367 Where the duiker, spring-bok and koedoe roam. **1931** *Discovery* XII. 61/2, I doubt if the black rhinoceros will long survive, or the sable or the eland or the kudu. **1947** L. Hastings *Dragons are Extra* viii. 176 A Kudu bull with his great spiral horns a good sixty inches long. **1957** *Cape Times* 6 Apr. 5/7 A variety of rhinos, nyalas, koedoe, blou wildebees and other game. **1961** *Guardian* 9 June 9/3 He roused the boys..with a kudu horn he had captured in Matabeleland. **1964** C. Willock *Enormous Zoo* i. 20 Greater kudu..are antelope of scrub-covered mountains. **1971** *Inside Kenya Today* Mar. 52/1 Other craters in Marsabit Forest are frequented by Greater Kudu. **1973** *Nature* 12 Jan. 106/1 The most obvious change has been a decline in woodland-associated species such as lesser kudu, baboon, vervet-monkey, leopard and impala.

kudzu (ˈkʊdzuː). [Jap. *kuzu*.] In full, *kudzu vine*. A perennial climbing plant, *Pueraria thunbergiana* (or *P. lobata*), of the family Leguminosæ, native to China and Japan, and cultivated elsewhere as a fodder plant, an ornamental, or an aid in the prevention of soil erosion.

1893 *Garden & Forest* VI. 504/2 In Japan the Kudzu.. has some economic value. **1901** L. H. Bailey *Cycl. Amer. Hort.* III. 1465/2 Kudzu Vine. Perennial with large tuberous starchy roots..fl[ower]s pea-shaped, purple, in axillary spikes late in the season, not showy: pod large and flat. **1948** *Atlantic Monthly* Nov. 60/1 Kudzu, a coarse, rapidly growing legume of incredible efficiency in checking gullies, restoring drainage, and storing nitrogen, came from Japan. **1951** *Dict. Gardening* (Roy. Hort. Soc.) IV. 1713/2 *P[ueraria] lobata.* Kudzu Vine. Climber with twining, scarcely woody stems growing many feet long in a season; roots thick, fleshy, starchy. **1973** *Daily Colonist* (Victoria, B.C.) 1 Apr. 24/5 The Kudzu vine..is probably the fastest growing of all the perennial vines, making as much as ten feet the first year from seed, and capable of making annual growth of 30 feet or more. **1974** A. Dillard *Pilgrim at Tinker Creek* xii. 212 In summer that path is wrapped past finding in saplings, bushes, kudzu, and poison oak.

kue, obs. f. cue.

kuead, kuel, var. qued(e *Obs.*, quell *v.*

‖**kuei** (kuːeɪ). [Chin.] A Chinese bronze food-vessel.

1935 A. J. KOOP in L. Ashton *Chinese Art* 77 The *fu* is an oblong tray with straight, steeply sloping sides, a dragon-head loop handle at each end, and a spreading hollow foot cut away in the centre of each side... The *kuei* is somewhat similar but has a more rounded form. **1954** H. MUNSTERBERG *Short Hist. Chinese Art* iii. 60 New shapes.. appear, while others like the kuei and the chung, or bell, become very common. **1963** *Times* 23 Jan. 12/7 Aberdeen University paid £580 for a massive bronze *kuei* (food vessel), decorated with vertical ribs between borders of dragon and monster masks. **1963** P. C. SWANN *Art of China, Korea & Japan* i. 26 (*caption*) Chinese ritual bronze food vessel (*kuei*) of about 1000 BC, with dragon-headed handles. **1973** *Oxf. Univ. Gaz.* CIII. Suppl. 5. 55 Two-handled bowl of *Kuei* shape, moulded decoration derived from bronze.

kuen, kuff, obs. ff. QUEEN, CUFF.

Kufic (ˈkjuːfɪk), *a.* Also Cuphic, Cufic. [f. *Kufa* or *Cufa*, an ancient city near Babylon, the residence of the caliphs before the building of Bagdad, and a great seat of Mohammedan learning.] Of or pertaining to Kufa; applied to a variety of Arabic writing, attributed to the scholars of Kufa.

Kufic is found mainly in old copies of the Koran, on coins of the Abbasid and other early dynasties, and in inscriptions. It differs from ordinary Arabic writing (*Naskhī*) in the angular form of many of the letters, and the general rigidity of the strokes, in which it bears a considerable resemblance to the Syriac *Estrangelo*. The name is sometimes loosely applied to old forms of Arabic writing generally; but the opinion once current that the Kufic writing is older than the round characters is now known to be incorrect.

1706 HEARNE *Collect.* 22 June. The Cufic characters. **1792** R. HERON tr. *Niebuhr's Trav. Arabia* I. VIII. vi. 270, I copied here [*sc.* at Beit el Fakih] an ancient *Kusic* [sic] inscription. **1851** D. WILSON *Preh. Ann.* II. IV. iii. 262 Cufic coins inscribed in the old Arabic character. **1879** C. R. CONDER *Tentwork Pal.* 318 Over the outer Arcade of the Dome of the Rock runs the great Cufic inscription, giving the date of the erection of the building in 688 A.D. **1906** *Harmsworth Encycl.* VI. 422/3 The Kufic script was in use for coins from the end of the 7th to the 13th century. **1913** H. J. R. MURRAY *Hist. Chess* 171 The titles being in the Kufic character upon a blue ground. **1931** A. U. DILLEY *Oriental Rugs & Carpets* Pl. 40 (*caption*) Turkish Rug of Arabesque Design and Kufic Border. **1968** G. JONES *Hist. Vikings* III. i. 157 Arabic, German, and Anglo-Saxon coins on Gotland; kufic silver, Arabic and Rhenish glassware.. at Birka. **1971** R. RUSSELL tr. *Ahmad's Shore & Wave* i. 10 He had the name of the house.. written in Kufic script.

kufuffle, var. KERFUFFLE.

‖**Kuge** (ˈkuːge). Also †Cangue; kuge, Kugé. [Jap.] In feudal Japan, the name of the nobility attached to the Imperial Court at Kyoto; a court noble.

1577 R. WILLES in Eden & Willes tr. *Hist. Trauayle W. & E. Indies* f. 255 The heads and beards of his ministers are shauen, they haue name Cangues. **1727** J. G. SCHEUCHZER tr. *Kæmpfer's Hist. Japan* I. II. ii. 152 The whole Ecclesiastical Court in general assumes the title of *Kuge*, which signifies as much as Ecclesiastical Lords, and this they do by way of distinction from the *Gege*. **1871** A. B. MITFORD *Tales Old Japan* I. 71 The cap and robes worn by the Kugé, or nobles of the Mikado's court. **1880** F. V. DICKINS tr. *Chiushingura* (new ed.) 159 They were noble ladies, daughters of *Kugé*, who were peers of the Mikado's creation. **1904** L. HEARN *Japan: Attempt at Interpretation* xii. 265 Next to him stood the kugé, or ancient nobility,—descendants of emperors and of gods. **1957** *Times Lit. Suppl.* 11 Oct. 607/2 The court nobles, almost as useless and cut off from real life by the habits of the Court, of '*ce pays-ci*', as Mme. de Grignan called it, as so many Kuge nobles of old Japan. **1970** [see HININ].

kugel (ˈkuːgəl). Also coogle, kuggol. [Yiddish, lit. ball, f. MHG. *kugel, kugele* ball, globe.] In Jewish cookery, a kind of pudding served as a main course or as a side-dish.

1846 *Jewish Manual, or Pract. Information Jewish & Mod. Cookery* iv. 55 *Kugel and commean*. Soak.. Spanish peas and .. Spanish beans.. take.. fine gravy-beef [etc.]. **1871** E. LEVY *Jewish Cookery Bk.* 58 Coogle, or pudding, and peas and beans. **1892** I. ZANGWILL *Childr. Ghetto* I. 114 Other delicious things there are in Jewish cookery... *Kuggol*, to which pudding has a far-away resemblance. **1914** N. NEWNHAM-DAVIS *Gourmet's Guide to London* 149 In the great earthenware jar which holds the soup is cooked the 'kugel', a kind of pease-pudding. **1958** J. GROSSINGER *Art Jewish Cooking* 115 Vegetables are comparatively unimportant in most Jewish homes. In their place, *kugels* and *charlottes*, resembling puddings or pudding-soufflés, were substituted. They may be served as separate courses, as accompaniments to meat or poultry, or even as dessert if they are sweet. **1972** *Listener* 16 Mar. 341/3 It [*sc.* chollant] was a mélange of meat, potatoes, butter-beans, onions, kishkeh, kugel and hope... The kugel (German for bullet) looked like an anaemic cannonball... The basic formula included fat, flour, grebenes or fried onion.

‖**kugelhupf** (ˈkuːg(ə)lhʊpf). Also kugelhopf, GUGELHUPF. [Ger.] A light Austrian cake baked in a ring-shaped mould.

1886 W. J. TUCKER *E. Europe* 260 There is the eternal 'Kugelhupf' (a genuinely Austrian coffee-cake) centring the table. **1906** *Mrs. Beeton's Bk. Househ. Managem.* lxii. 1656 *Kugelhopf*, a German cake; a kind of rich dough cake. **1961** J. HELLER *Catch-22* (1962) xxiv. 249 Napoleons and *petits fours* from Paris, Reims and Grenoble, *Kugelhopf*, pumpernickel and *Pfefferkuchen* from Berlin. **1966** P. V. PRICE *France: Food & Wine Guide* 148 The traditional *kugelhopf* (a light yeast cake, usually with a hole in the centre).

kuhn-kan, var. COON-CAN.

kuik, kuith, kuiþe, kuitle, obs. forms of COOK, KITH, KITHE, CUITTLE *v.*

kuka (ˈkuːkə). [Native name.] A name used in Ghana for *Khaya senegalensis*; also *kuka-tree*; see KHAYA.

1882 *Encycl. Brit.* XIV. 153/2 Kuka [a Central African town].. received its name from a kuka or monkey bread tree (*Adansonia digitata*), which attracted the attention of the settlers as a rare thing in the district. **1924** *Blackw. Mag.* Sept. 351/1 A kuka-tree is a stumpy smooth, grey-barked thing of enormous girth. **1932** J. CARY *Aissa Saved* xliii. 230 We should go there by the kuka tree. **1961** F. R. IRVINE *Woody Plants of Ghana* 523 *Khaya senegalensis*... Kuka (local name).

kukama (kuːˈkɑːmə). Also kokama, kookaam. [Sechuana.] The southern African antelope, *Oryx gazella*; see ORYX b.

1852 *Catal. Mammalia Brit. Mus.* III. 105 *Oryx gazella*. The Kookaam or Gemsboc. Horns straight, shelving backwards. **1857** D. LIVINGSTONE *Missionary Trav. & Res. S. Afr.* iii. 56 The gemsbuck or kukama. **1888** J. S. KINGSLEY *Riverside Nat. Hist.* V. 326 The *Oryx capensis* of South Africa, or Gemsbok of the Dutch colonists, Kokama of the Bechuanas, is even more striking in its coloring. **1971** R. H. N. SMITHERS *Mammals Botswana* 238/2 *Oryx gazella*. Kukama. Gemsbok.

‖**kukang** (ˈkuːkæŋ). Also kongkang. [Malay *kūkang*.] The slow loris, *Nycticebus coucang*, found in south-east Asia.

1821 T. S. RAFFLES in *Trans. Linn. Soc.* XIII. 247 *Lemur tardigradus* Linn. Kukang (Malay)... Of this the natives distinguish a large and a small variety. **1861** WOOD *Nat. Hist.* I. 107 The Slow-paced Loris, or Kukang, is very similar in its habits to [the Slender Loris]. **1883** *Cassell's Nat. Hist.* I. 245 Naturalists term him the Slow Loris or Kukang. **1900** *Proc. Zool. Soc.* 321 The Slow Loris... 'Kúkang', 'Kongkang', and 'Kongka' of the Malays. *Ibid.*, At one time I used to sleep in a hammock slung in a veranda close to a cage of Kongkangs. **1969** LD. MEDWAY *Wild Mammals Malaya* 47/1 Slow Loris. Kongkang, Kera duku. *Nycticebus coucang*.

kuke, obs. f. COOK.

kukeri, variant of KUKRI.

Kuki[1] (ˈkuːkɪ). [Native name.] Any one of several peoples inhabiting the hills of Manipur and Mizoram, on the Indo-Burmese border; a member of one of these peoples; also, their language. Also *attrib.* and *Comb.*, as *Kuki-Chin* [CHIN *sb.*[2]] (see quot. 1954).

1799 *Asiatick Researches* II. 188 If a *Cúci* assail the house of an enemy.. he acquires honour and celebrity in his tribe. *Ibid.* 193 A party of *Cúcis* visited the late Charles Croftes.. at Jáfarabād, in the spring of 1776, and entertained him with a dance. **1803** *Ibid.* VII. 186 The *Kookies* choose the steepest and most inaccessible hills to build their villages.. which.. are called.. in the *Kookie* language, *K'hooah*. **1871** E. B. TYLOR *Primitive Culture* I. xi. 424 The Kukis of Assam think that the ghost of every animal a Kuki kills in the chase or for the feast will belong to him in the next life. **1872** E. T. DALTON *Descr. Ethnol. Bengal* 75 English.. one.. Kuki khut. **1885** E. BALFOUR *Cycl. India* (ed. 3) II. 618/2 The new Kuki clans are presided over by rajas and muntris. **1927** *Blackw. Mag.* June 816/1 The Kuki alone of all these hill tribes understands the value of combination. *Ibid.* 817/1 Roaring and retaliation keep alive a warlike and truculent spirit among the Kukis. **1939** L. H. GRAY *Found. Lang.* 389 Arakan-Burmese, comprising Kuki-Chin.., Old Kuki (Rānkhōl, Shö or Khyang, Khami, etc.), and Burmese. **1948** D. DIRINGER *Alphabet* vi. 367 Manipuri or Meithei, a Kuki-chin speech. **1954** PEI & GAYNOR *Dict. Ling.* 116 *Kuki-Chin*, a group of dialects (Lai, Lushei, Meithei, Tashon, etc.), constituting a subdivision of the Arakan-Burmese branch of the Tibeto-Burmese sub-family of the Sino-Tibetan family of languages. **1971** B. W. ALDISS *Soldier Erect* 219 But the Assam Battalion kept coming across the road, Kukis, Karsis, and all the other tribesmen. **1972** *Language* XLVIII. 476 The crucially important and ramified group of Tibeto-Burman languages known variously as Kukish, Kuki-Chin, or Kuki-Chin-Naga, spoken in Assam and Western Burma.

‖**kuki**[2] (ˈkuːkɪ). *N.Z. Hist.* Also kooky. [Maori, ad. COOK *sb.*] A slave of a Maori chieftain.

1832 A. EARLE *Narr. Residence N.Z.* (1966) 60 A chief had set one of his kookies (or slaves) to watch a piece of ground planted with the koomera, or sweet potato. **1845** E. J. WAKEFIELD *Adventure N.Z.* I. 230 The alarm had been caused by some *kuki*, or slaves. **1882** W. D. HAY *Brighter Britain!* I. x. 283 Her father and mother were only kukis.

kukkowe, obs. f. CUCKOO.

kuklass, var. KOKLAS(S.

Ku-Klux (ˈkjuːklʌks). More fully Ku-Klux-Klan. [A fantastic name said to be made out of Gr. κύκλος circle + CLAN.]

1. A widespread secret society, which arose in the Southern States of North America after the civil war of 1861–65, beginning with the effort to overawe the Negro population by whipping and arson, and developing a system of political outrage and murder. The original society was finally put down by the U.S. military forces. It was revived in 1915 and spread outside the Southern States, terrorizing various ethnic and religious minorities, and acting violently against white Protestants whom they judged to be opposed to their cause. Later the society fragmented into several State organizations. The Ku-Klux Klan regained strength in the Southern States of the U.S. in the 1950s in opposition to the Civil Rights movement of American Blacks. Also *attrib.* Cf. KLAN, KLUXER.

1867 *Citizen* (Pulaski, Tenn.) 29 Mar. 3/1 The Kuklux Klan will assemble at their usual place of rendezvous.., exactly at the hour of midnight, in costume and bearing the arms of the Klan. **1868** *N.Y. Herald* 1 July 6/4 If the Democratic Convention can only be induced.. at the dictation of the Knights of the Golden Circle and the Ku Klux Klan, to place upon their ticket some copperhead opponent of the war, the radicals will have a clear track next November. **1871** *Illustr. Lond. News* 15 Apr. 359/1 The House of Representatives has passed a bill making Ku-Klux crimes in the south punishable in the Federal Courts. *Ibid.* 29 Apr. 414/3 The Ku-Klux Bill has passed both Houses at Washington with considerable modifications. **1872** WHITTIER *Presid. Elect.* Pr. Wks. 1889 III. 164 Let us not despair of seeing even the Ku-Klux tamed into decency. **1880** E. KIRKE *Garfield* 54 That the horrors of the Ku-klux and the White-Lives should not run riot at the poles. **1884** *Century Mag.* July 398/1 No chapter in American history is more strange than the one which bears for its title: 'Ku Klux Klan'. **1915** *Atlanta* (Ga.) *Jrnl.* 6 Dec. 2/4 (*heading*) Charter is granted for the Ku Klux Klan. *Ibid.*, Secretary of State Philip Cook Monday issued a charter to the Knights of the Ku Klux Klan, a fraternal insurance order which was organized on Stone Mountain a few nights ago with weird and mystic ceremony. **1920** *N.Y. Times* 11 Oct. 1/2 The old Ku Klux Klan has been reorganized and is regularly chartered under the laws of Georgia. **1924** *Imperial Night-Hawk* 10 Sept. 6 The district meeting of the Ku Klux Klan held recently at Twin Lakes, Realm of Iowa, was a huge success. **1944** *Atlanta* (Ga.) *Jrnl.* 4 June 1/1 The Knights of the Ku Klux Klan, Inc. has officially ceased to exist. **1945** *N.Y. Times* 21 Oct. 33/3 The Ku Klux Klan, claiming a membership of more than 20,000 in Georgia, is burning its fiery cross again. **1958** *News & Observer* (Raleigh, N. Carolina) 19 Jan. 1/5 A shouting horde of Robeson County Indians tonight routed the Ku Klux Klan here. **1962** A. S. RICE *Ku Klux Klan in Amer. Politics* ix. 114 [In 1949] the secret order splintered into many rival groups, each considering itself.. the direct spiritual heir of the Invisible Empire, Knights of the Ku Klux Klan founded in 1915. **1970** in J. F. Kirkham et al. *Assassination & Political Violence* iv. A. §3. 216 The first Ku Klux Klan, which lasted from 1865 to 1876, was a principal means of administering this violence in the South. *Ibid.* §4. 218 White Capping seems to have been an important link between the first and second Ku Klux Klans. White Cap methods of punishment and costume seem to have been influenced by the first Klan. *Ibid.* App. D. §1. 364 It was not until 1956 when the efforts .. failed to stem the trend toward integration in the South that the Ku Klux Klans revived... In San Antonio, Tex., a cross was burned.. to 'let the niggers, Jews, and Catholics know we're back in operation'.

b. In extended use, of other vigilante groups. Also *transf.* and *fig.*

1930 W. & E. MUIR tr. *Feuchtwanger's Success* IV. xvi. 539 The Munich Ku Klux Klan.. evidently consisted of young men who did not understand that a match, once it is decided, can't be fought all over again. **1944** A. HUXLEY *Let.* 28 July (1969) 511 You might pass on to your agent these simple talking points, with which to allay the studios' fears of the medical Ku Klux Klan. **1966** A. SACHS *Jail Diary* xxiv. 215 Then he asks me what I know about the local Ku Klux Klan.

2. A member of the Ku-Klux.

1868 in T. D. Clark *Pills, Petticoats & Plows* (1944) 62 We are inclined to think he is somewhat disloyal, and may be in sympathy with the Ku Kluxes. **1877** J. M. BEARD *K.K.K. Sk.* 40 The Ku-Klux themselves were about as intangible examples of ghostliness as were ever wrapped in loose-fitting bombazine. **1884** *Century Mag.* XXVIII. 402 The 'proceedure' was to place the would be Ku Klux in an empty barrel.. and to send him whirling down the hill.

Hence ˈ**Kuklux** *v.*, to outrage, or maltreat in accordance with the methods of the Ku-Klux-Klan; ˈ**Kukluxism**, the system or methods of the Ku-Klux; outrage or murder; **Ku-Klux** ˈ**Klan(n)er**, ˈ**Klanism**, ˈ**Klansman**.

1868 in S. F. Horn *Invisible Empire* (1939) 335 Let every Ku Klux Klansman heed The General Order of General Meade. **1879** *Philadelphia Inquirer* 28 Nov. 1/5 Ten men.. were to-day taken.. on a charge of kukluxing a man named McAlpine, his son and daughter. **1881** *Philadelphia Rec.* No. 3452. 1 A word.. suggestive of kukluxism. **1884** *American* VIII. 72 Not only a Confederate but was sent to the Albany Penitentiary for Ku-Kluxism. **1923** *Nation* (N.Y.) 11 July 35 He will help his fellow Ku Klux Klaners. **1924** H. CRANE *Let.* 5 Mar. (1965) 177 O'Neill's new play.. in which a white woman marries a Negro... He.. receives terrible threats and insults through the mail from the *Ku Klux* Klanners. **1924** J. M. MECKLIN *Ku Klux Klan* 98, I have yet to come in contact with the first trace of Ku Klux Klanism. **1933** H. G. WELLS *Shape of Things to Come* II. §1. 141 They became Ku Klux Klansmen, Nationalists, Nazis. **1948** *Time* 15 Mar. 29/2 Last week Georgia's Grand Dragon Samuel Green carefully explained that Ku Klux Klansmen wore masks to protect themselves against the prejudice of Jews, Catholics and foreigners.

kukow, obs. form of CUCKOO.

‖**kukri** (ˈkʊkrɪ). Also 9 khookheri, kookaree, -eree, -i(e, -y, kookree, -i(e, kukrie, kukeri, kukkri, koukri. [Hindī *kukṛī*.] A curved knife, broader at the point than at the handle, and usually having the keen edge on the concave side, used by the Gorkhas of India.

1811 KIRKPATRICK *Nepaul* v. 118 The dagger, or knife, worn by every Nepaulian, and called Khookheri. **1832** MUNDY *Pen & Pencil Sk.* I. 197 Arming himself with a kookaree or mountain dagger. **1859** LANG *Wand. India* 312 By the side of him knelt the little Goorkha, armed with the

kookeree. **1884** A. Forbes in *Pall Mall G.* 19 Mar. 1/2 The Ghoorka kukrie, the American bowie knife, or any other kindred instrument. **1897** Ld. Roberts 41 *Yrs. India* lxviii. (1898) 538 The Maharaja gave me a gold-mounted kookri.

kukstole, kukwald, -wold(e, obs. forms of CUCKSTOOL, CUCKOLD.

kuku (ˈkuːkuː). *N.Z.* [Maori.] **1.** Also **koukou, kukupa.** = KERERU.

1835 W. Yate *Acct. N.Z.* iii. 53 *Kou-kou*—The bird so-called is a small owl, a native of New Zealand. **1873** [see KERERU]. **1881** J. L. Campbell *Poenamo* vii. 115 The *kukupa* ..was just the bird created expressly for the true cockney sportsman. **1905** W. B. *Where White Man Treads* 19 For food..in his [*sc.* the Maori's] catalogue, for flavour and bulk, the plentiful kereru, or kuku (pigeon) headed the list. **1936** 'R. Hyde' *Check to your King* xiii. 157 Your wild pigeon (*kuku*)..beds itself on the fern. **1949** P. Buck *Coming of Maori* (1950) II. i. 93 The principal forest birds sought for food were the wood pigeon (*kereru, kukupa, kuku*), [etc.].

2. Either of two common mussels *Perna canaliculus* or *Mytilus edulis aoteanus.*

1905 W. B. *Where White Man Treads* 2 White seashore sandhills, representing the accumulated deaths of ages of pipi, pupu, kuku, and other molluscs. **1949** P. Buck *Coming of Maori* (1950) II. i. 106 Shellfish such as..sea mussels (*kuku*)..were cooked..and dried also as reserve food. **1960** N. Hilliard *Maori Girl* 153 Shellfish—*paua, kuku, kina.*

kukui (kuːˈkuːɪ). [Hawaiian.] An evergreen tree, *Aleurites moluccana*, of the family Euphorbiaceæ, native to the Moluccas and south Pacific islands; its large seeds yield an oil used for lighting and other purposes, and the tree is also called the candlenut or candleberry tree.

1825 W. Ellis *Jrnl. Tour Hawaii* vii. 167 Along the narrow and verdant border of the lake at the bottom, the bread-fruit, the *kukui*, and the *ohia* trees, appeared. **1866** "Mark Twain' *Lett. from Hawaii* (1967) 98 These trees were principally of two kinds—the koa and the kukui—the one with a very light green leaf and the other with a dark green. **1890** *Ibis* II. 175 The delicately-indented foliage of the kukui has..a lovely silvery appearance in certain lights. **1913** J. F. Rock *Indigenous Trees Hawaiian Islands* 257 The Kukui is one of the most common of Hawaiian forest trees. .. The nuts contain 50 per cent of oil, which is known as Kekuna in India and Ceylon, and Kukui in Hawaii. **1937** D. & H. Teilhet *Feather Cloak Murders* viii. 143 Silvery Kukui trees draped their clustered pink flowers over old walls. **1967** *Economist* 9 Sept. 892/1 The luau lights outside nearly every [Hawaii] hotel and restaurant may now consist of concealed gas jet instead of kukui nut-meat burning gently in a shell.

kukumakranka (kukumaˈkraŋkə). *S. Afr.* Also **koekmakranka, koekoemakranka.** [Afrikaans, prob. f. Hottentot name for the plant.] A small, bulbous, perennial plant of the genus *Gethyllis*, belonging to the family Amaryllidaceæ, and bearing fragrant white flowers and an underground fruit.

1793 tr. *C. P. Thunberg's Trav. Europe, Afr. & Asia* I. 116 Kukumakranka (*gethyllis*) is the name given to the legumen or pod of a plant, that grew at this time among the sand-hills near the town, without either leaves or flowers. This pod was of the length of one's finger, somewhat wider at top than at bottom, had a pleasant smell, and was held in great esteem by the ladies. The smell of it resembled in some measure that of strawberries, and filled the whole room. **1811** W. J. Burchell *Jrnl.* 31 Jan. in *Trav. S. Afr.* (1822) I. ii. 55 On Green Point on the Flats in the neighbourhood of Cape Town, grows a celebrated little plant, which still preserves its original Hottentot name, being known by no other than that of *Kukumakranki.* **1857** L. Pappe *Floræ Capensis Medicæ Prodromus* (ed. 2) 39 The elongated, club-shaped, orange-coloured fruit of this plant has a peculiar fragrance, and still preserves its old Hottentot name of *Kukumakranka.* **1932** Watt & Breyer-Brandwijk *Medicinal & Poisonous Plants S. Afr.* 28 An alcoholic infusion of the fruit of *Gethyllis spiralis* L.f. (*Gytheilia spiralis*), Koekoemakranka (Bramakranka), Koekmakranka, was taken by the early Cape colonists for the relief of colic and flatulence. **1950** *Cape Times* 15 May 14 Before I found a palate for mushrooms, it was the kukumakranka we used to go seeking in the veld. *Ibid.* 18 May 12/3 Two explanations of how the koekmakranka got its name have reached me. **1973** Y. Burgess *Life to Live* 179 When the drug did not help she asked the old women to gather 'kukumakranka' leaves for her, and she asked Magriet for brandy to steep them in.

kukupa: see KUKU 1.

‖**kula** (ˈkuːlə). Also **Kula.** [Melanesian.] In some Pacific communities, esp. in the Trobriand Islands, an inter-island system of ceremonial exchange of items as a prelude to or concomitant of regular trading.

1920 B. Malinowski in *Man* XX. 97 (*heading*) Kula; the circulating exchange of valuables in the archipelagoes of eastern New Guinea. *Ibid.* 101 Glancing at the map we see a number of circles, each of which represents a certain sociological unit which we shall call a *Kula* community. **1927** —— *Sex & Repression Savage Soc.* II. iii. 93 Those in charge of the overseas expeditions called *Kula* are often supposed to have dreams about the success of their ceremonial trading. **1951** R. Firth *Elem. Social Organiz.* i. 3 The Trobriand islanders of New Guinea exchange in the kula. **1970** *Nature* 12 Dec. 1064/2 The best known exchange mechanism of this kind of recent times is the kula trade of the Trobriand islanders of the western Pacific.

Hence **kula** *v.*, to exchange ceremonial gifts in this manner.

1922 B. Malinowski *Argonauts W. Pacific* iii. 101 Several villages do not kula. *Ibid.* xi. 281 Bokuyoba..gave the pair ..to Kadamwasila..her son..*kula'd* it on to some of his southern partners.

Kula, var. KULLAH. See also next word.

Kulah[1] (ˈkuːlə). Also **Koula(h), Kula.** The name of a town in W. Turkey used *attrib.* or *ellipt.* to denote a rug using the Ghiordes knot made there.

c **1882** *Cardinal & Harford's Price List Oriental Carpets & Rugs* 13 *Koula rugs and mats.* Various qualities, bright colours, Red usually predominant. **1899** *Northern Times* (Golspie, Sutherland) 22 June 1/5 (Advt.), About 600 to 800 Oriental and other Rugs, from 4s 9d upwards, including.. Koula. **1900** J. K. Mumford *Oriental Rugs* x. 150 The narrow stripe with undulating pattern, referred to as a characteristic of all Ghiordes, antique and modern, is rarely found in pure Kulahs. *Ibid.*, In design the modern Kulahs have nothing characteristic. **1904** M. B. Langton *How to Know Oriental Rugs* v. 165 The antique Koulah prayer-rug differs from the Ghiordes in various ways. **1931** A. U. Dilley *Oriental Rugs & Carpets* vi. 164 Ghiordes and Kula prayer rugs were made in adjacent cities. **1962** C. W. Jacobsen *Oriental Rugs* 248 With their close neighbours, Ghiordes, Kulahs share the position of being one of the rarest and most sought after of all Oriental Rugs. **1972** P. L. Phillips tr. *Formenton's Oriental Rugs & Carpets* 94 Kula rugs, like most Anatolian rugs..have no special distinguishing motif and so are difficult to identify.

kulah[2] (ˈkuːlə). Also **kulla, kullah.** [Pers. *kulah* a cap.] (See quot. 1969.)

1920 *Chambers's Jrnl.* 29 May 408/1 Dark-blue *pugris*, with red and white silk stripes, tied round a *kulla* or conical skull-cap of scarlet. **1952** J. Masters *Deceivers* xi. 125 The prisoner second from the left wore a Mohammedan kulla under his turban. **1969** R. T. Wilcox *Dict. Costume* (1970) 189/1 *Kulah*, a conical cap of felt or lamb-skin, the headgear of Middle Eastern monks and dervishes. **1971** R. Dentry *Encounter at Kharmel* iii. 45 The men wore round kullah caps, ragged chogas over long grey tunics, and scarves.

kulak (ˈkuːlæk). Also †**koolack, koulak.** [Russ. *kulák* fist, tight-fisted person, pl. *kulaki*, f. Turki *ḳul* hand.] In pre-Revolution Russia, a well-to-do farmer or trader; in the Soviet Union, a peasant-proprietor working for his own profit. Also *transf.*

1877 D. M. Wallace *Russia* (ed. 2) I. vii. 159 Not a few industrial villages have thus fallen under the power of the *Kulaki*—literally Fists—as these monopolists are called. **1886** *Encycl. Brit.* XXI. 84/1 The enrichment of a few 'kulaks'. **1921** *Contemp. Rev.* Jan. 26 'Kulaks'..a nick-name for the close-fisted village traders, usurers, and rich peasants. **1925** P. Gibbs *Unchanging Quest* xiv. 109 These peasants think the Duma will..kill all the Koulaks, or Jewish moneylenders. **1929** [see COLLECTIVE A. 2 f]. **1931** M. Hindus *Red Bread* iv. 66 Legally, a *koolack* is a man who indulges in some form of exploitation, employs hired help or derives an income from rent or interest or the operation of an agricultural or industrial machine. Actually, however, a *koolack* is a successful farmer as success is measured in Russia. **1934** G. B. Shaw *On Rocks* 164 They [*sc.* the Soviet government] also proscribed the kulak, the able, hardheaded, hardfisted farmer who was richer than his neighbors. **1951** G. Mikes *Down with Everybody* 48 He was a kulak, a spy and an enemy agent, but now he had realised his mistake—namely that it *was* a mistake to be a kulak, a spy and an enemy agent. **1952** R. Campbell *Lorca* 7 Lorca was by birth a landowning 'kulak'. **1957** *Observer* 10 Nov. 5/8 The peasants [in China] have been 'voluntarily' collectivised..but there has been no Russian-style campaign for the 'elimination of the *kulak* as a class'. **1970** *New Scientist* 1 Jan. 15/1 The improved grain husbandry.. may favour the rise of 'kulaks' or 'improving landlord' groups.

kulan, var. form of KOULAN.

kulang: see COOLUNG.

kulchur. ¶ With distortion of spelling to indicate an affected or vulgar pronunciation of CULTURE *sb.* Cf. CULTURE *sb.* after sense 5 a.

1940 E. Pound *Cantos* liv. 43 The 10th a charter of labour And the last on keepin' up kulchur. **1959** *Listener* 4 June 997/3 The famous six essential books, Pound's guide to Kulchur. **1971** *Frenzy* 21 May 3/4 There is a spirit of freedom, solidarity and struggle; an intensity of life worth all the ephemeral fantasies to be offered so far by the Rock/alternative Kulchur.

Kulin (kuːˈliːn). Also **Kooleen, Kulina.** [ad. Skr. *kulīna*, f. *kulin* well-born.] In Bengal, a Brahman of the highest class. Also *attrib.* or as *adj.*

1866 *Atlantic Monthly* Dec. 733/1 The privilege of maintaining a plurality of wives is restricted to a very few.. except in the case of *Kooleen* Brahmins, that superlative aristocracy of caste. **1873** E. Balfour *Cycl. India* (ed. 2) III. 312/1 *Kulin*, a class of brahmans in Bengal, who are deemed by other brahmans to be of very pure descent and in consequence many are anxious to wed their daughters to them. **1911** *Encycl. Brit.* XIII. 511/2 Only an extreme section—the so-called *Kaulas* or *Kulinas*..persist in carrying on the mystic and licentious rites taught in many of the Tantras. **1911** G. B. Shaw *Getting Married* 139 Kulin polygyny, though unlimited, is not really a popular institution. **1932** [see *Kulinism* below]. **1970** N. B. Bonarjee *Under Two Masters* 3 The Kulins became an integral and important part of Bengal's life and culture.

Hence **ˈKulinism,** the polygamous system of the Kulins.

1890 in *Cent. Dict.* **1891** H. H. Risley *Tribes & Castes of Bengal: Ethnogr. Gloss.* I. 146 The Bansajas are those Kulins who lost their distinction on account of..their want of charity, discipline, and due observance of marriage law, three qualities which in later times constituted Kulinism. **1932** L. S. S. O'Malley *Indian Caste Customs* i. 10 A Kulin Brahman who had an embarrassing number of female relatives is known to have had eighteen of them..married in a batch to a boy ten years old—..Kulinism, as the practice is called, has nearly died out. **1968** B. Walker *Hindu World* II. 229 In Bengal..polygamous relationships..were common among certain brāhmin sub-castes, notably the *Kulīn*, 'noble',..and the custom is called kulīnism.

kull, obs. form of CULL *v.*[2], KILL *v.*

Kullah (kəˈlɑː). Also **Kalá, Klá, Kula.** [Pegu *Goḷa* Indian Buddhist immigrant, f. Skr. *Gauḍa* ancient name of N. Bengal (Yule and Burnell).] (See quot. 1886.)

1800 M. Symes *Acct. Embassy to Kingdom of Ava* xii. 290 On being informed that I was 'a Colar', or stranger,..they were reconciled. **1858** H. Yule *Narr. Mission to Court of Ava* i. 5 His private dwelling was a small place on one side of the court, from which the women peeped out at the *Kalás.* **1886** Yule & Burnell *Hobson-Jobson* 378/1 *Kulá* or *Klá*, n.p. Burmese name of a native of Continental India; and hence misapplied also to the English and other Westerns who have come to Burma from India; in fact used generally for a Western foreigner. **1890** Kipling *Departmental Ditties* (ed. 4) 82 For the Burmans said That a kullah's head Must be paid for with heads five score. **1929** F. T. Jesse *Lacquer Lady* I. iii. 21 All foreigners are kalās to the Burmans.

kulla(h), varr. KULAH[2].

kullum, var. COOLUNG.

kullung, var. COOLUNG.

kulne, kulter, obs. ff. KILN, COULTER.

‖**kultur** (kʊlˈtuə(r)). Also **Kultur.** [G., ad. L. *cultūra*, or F. *culture* CULTURE *sb.*] Civilization as conceived by the Germans; esp. used in a derogatory sense during the 1914–18 and 1939–45 wars, as involving notions of racial and cultural arrogance, militarism, and imperialism. Also *attrib.* and *transf.*

1914 *Punch* 16 Sept. 239/1 (*heading*) The Imperial Prussian College of Culture. *Telegrams*: 'Kultur, Berlin'. **1914** *Spectator* 31 Oct. 589/1 The idea that the extension of the *Kultur* of a nation can be effected by the extension by arms of its Empire. **1915** *Times* 30 Mar. 6/4 *Kultur*, in fact, has become the exact opposite of 'culture'. **1915** A. Huxley *Let.* Oct. (1969) 84 We have founded a club, chiefly for the purpose of self protection against Queen's and for the propagation of Kultur. **1916** J. B. Cooper *Coo-oo-ee* xii. 170 People have no time for Germans after their kultur demonstration in Belgium. **1917** A. G. Empey *Over Top* 305 A British rat resembles a bull-dog, while a German one, through a course of Kultur, resembles a dachshund. **1918** Kipling *Kipling's Message*, It is the peculiar essence of German Kultur, which is the German religion, that it is Germany's moral duty to break every tie, every restriction that binds man to fellow-man, if she thinks it will pay. **1926** C. H. Herford *Mind of Post-War Germany* v. 22 The stabilizing forces which post-war Germany derived from her inherited Kultur. **1939** tr. *C. Leiser's Nazi Nuggets* 82 Since the Nazis and the Japanese have been getting cozy and have signed a pact to foster their Kultur. **1973** L. Snelling *Heresy* I. i. 4 How ignorant I am of contemporary Kultur.

Also (with varying degrees of naturalization) **ˈkulturbild** [G. *bild* picture, image], a description of the culture (of a period, etc.); **ˈkulturgeˈschichte** [G. *geschichte* history], the history of the cultural development (of a country, etc.); history of civilization; **ˈkulturgut** [G. *gut* possession], a cultural asset; **ˈkulturhund** [G. *hund* dog], **kultur-hound** = *culture vulture*; **ˈkulturkampf** [G. *kampf* conflict], the conflict between the German government and the Papacy for the control of schools and church appointments (1872–87); also *transf.*; **ˈkulturkreis** [G. *kreis* circle], a cultural group; a cultural complex (the term is associated esp. with the German anthropologists F. Graebner and W. Schmidt); **ˈkulturstaat** [G. *staat* state], a civilized country; **ˈkulturträger** [G. *träger* carrier], an upholder or defender of civilization.

All usu. with capital initial in Eng. as in German.

1961 *Times* 23 Nov. 16/4 This book had to be a *Kulturbild* rather than a biography. **1964** *English Studies* XLV. 91 Professor Schirmer in his *Kulturbild* attempts to relate John Lydgate to his age by means of his poetry. **1876** *Mind* I. 447 The novel facts and attractive generalisations of *Culturgeschichte* are insensibly casting discredit upon the thoughtful introspection of one's own adult experience. **1938** *Year's Work Eng. Stud. 1936* XVII. 29 Brandenstein's little monograph on the first Indo-European migration is a return to the study of comparative vocabulary as a means for re-imagining some aspects of *Kulturgeschichte.* **1968** *Listener* 4 Apr. 448/1 English music historians have, on the whole, concentrated on the chronicling of technical matters and have avoided *Kulturgeschichte*, as it is practised elsewhere. **1952** *Man* June 83 A member of a lower caste tends to imitate the '*kulturgut*' of higher-caste people... At the same time he is attached to his own *kulturgut.* **1966** *Amer. N. & Q.* June 158/1 No effort was made to segregate the demonstrably regional *Kulturgut* from that which is literary, and even worldwide. **1969** *Language* XLV. 235 The later association of the term with the very poor may represent a sort of..Kulturgut. **1946** Mezzrow & Wolfe *Really Blues* (1957) xi. 196 That Kultur-hound didn't know ..that underneath the phony label was a genuine Victor one. **1963** *Listener* 17 Jan. 138/3 So our provincial *Kulturhunde*

had thirty minutes of that Vassar-educated Mona Lisa, Miss Mary McCarthy. **1879** *Dubin Rev.* Oct. 350 History of the Prussian 'Kulturkampf'. **1896** W. MILLER *Balkans* II. v. 205 A regular *Culturkampf* raged for nearly twenty years, in which the Turkish officials were far less adverse than the Greek clergy to the Bulgarian demands. **1902** *Encycl. Brit.* XXXII. 271/2 In Germany, when the Pontificate of Leo XIII. began, a disastrous conflict between the Imperial Government and the Church was in progress. It was called the Kulturkampf, as professing to be undertaken on behalf of civilization and culture. **1926** C. H. HERFORD *Mind of Post-War Germany* i. 6 The Rhinelands, fervently Catholic, and still acutely mindful of Bismarck's *Kulturkampf*. **1936** H. G. WELLS *Anat. Frustration* xiii. 150 A vast Kultur-Kampf lies between mankind and peace. **1966** *New Statesman* 18 Feb. 218/3 The *kulturkampf* between Flemish and Walloon French has now reached the Catholic University of Louvain. [**1897** L. FROBENIUS in *Petermann's Mitteilungen* XLIII. 225 (*title*) Der westafrikanische Kulturkreis. *Ibid.* 225/2 Es mag deshalb die Bezeichnung 'Westafrikanischer Kulturkreis' zunächst beibehalten werden.] **1948** A. L. KROEBER *Anthropol.* (rev. ed.) xvii. 770 Part of a wider theory advanced by the *Kulturkreis* (culture-sphere) movement or school of ethnology in continental Europe is that the Indonesian-Melanesian cultures are also characterized by the same block of culture traits that includes those enumerated for West Africa. **1971** *English Studies* LII. 256 It will have important implications..for the whole theoretical question of genre study in literature and the whole historical one of Anglo-Irish relations in the early middle ages, indeed of all of the early Christian *Kulturkreis*, which included the British Isles, Iceland, Scandinavia, and parts of Germanic Europe. **1925** *Manch. Guardian Weekly* 16 Oct. 311 There is no 'Kulturstaat' (civilised State) that would not punish political crimes. **1936** *Mind* XLV. 295 A state must at least preserve its existence, as a condition of becoming a *Kulturstaat*. **1948** J. TOWSTER *Political Power in U.S.S.R.* I. i. 6 Such conceptions of the state as *Rechtstaat* or *Kulturstaat*. **1920** D. H. LAWRENCE *Women in Love* i. 13 She was a *Kulturträger*, a medium for the culture of ideas. **1962** *N. & Q.* May 190/2 Two types of borrowing situation are envisaged, the bilingual community with oral/aural mediation, and the unilingual community with *Kulturträger* and written mediation.

||**kulturny** (kʊl'tʊrnɪ), *a.* [Russ. *kul'túrnyĭ* civilized.] In the Soviet Union: cultured, civilized.

1955 H. HODGKINSON *Doubletalk* 39 Cultured, or *kulturny* behaviour, is highly esteemed in the Soviet Union. **1959** *New Statesman* 23 May 711/3 Aesthetic considerations never played a part in the previous drives for a more *kulturny* mode of life, which were more concerned with manners than with the cultivation of good taste. **1973** J. SHUB *Moscow by Nightmare* ix. 97 She let the porter take her one small suitcase—it wouldn't be '*kulturny*' to carry it herself.

kulu, kulukamba: see KOOLOOKAMBA.

kum, obs. f. COME.

||'**kumara.** *N. Zeal.* Also **kumera.** [Maori name.] The sweet potato, *Ipomæa batatas*.

1773 S. PARKINSON *Jrnl. S. Seas* in *Trans. N. Zeal. Inst.* X. ix. 124 (Morris) Several canoes came alongside..of whom we got some fish, kumeras or sweet potatoes, and several other things. **1851** H. R. RICHMOND *Jrnl.* 23 Feb. in *Richmond–Atkinson Papers* (1960) I. ii. 88 There was nothing else to help ourselves to except kumara or sweet potato, in appearance like long thin potatoes, in taste like boiled chesnuts. **1884** BRACKEN *Lays of Maori* 18 Some more dainty toothsome dish Than the kumera and fish. **1900** *Blackw. Mag.* Feb. 231 A great pie-dish full of kumaras. **1905** W. B. *Where White Man Treads* 2 Parklands, blurred and dotted with plantations of kumara. **1934** *Bulletin* (Sydney) 26 Sept. 20/1 The supplies of pig, eel, shark and kumara were unlimited. **1936** [see KIT *sb.*[11]]. **1955** *N.Z. Jrnl. Agric.* July 55/1 Most home gardeners purchase their kumara plants from seedsmen. **1971** *N.Z. Listener* 16 Aug. 54/4 Be careful with the kumara... Its energy value is twice that of the potato.

kumbang ('kʊmbæŋ). Also **koembang.** [local Javanese *koembang.*] A föhn wind which blows in Java.

1931 A. A. MILLER *Climatol.* v. 83 These winds have a foehn-like nature, their dry heat doing considerable damage to the more sensitive crops, especially tobacco. Such a wind is the 'Koembang' of Java. **1954** E. D. LABORDE tr. *Robequain's Malaya, Indonesia, Borneo & Philippines* ix. 187 At that time,..the lowlands between Cheribon and Tegal fairly often experience the drying effort of the south-east wind which, after crossing the Pembarisan Hills, becomes a foehn known as the *kumbang*. **1969** M. SUKANTO in H. Arakawa *Climates N. & E. Asia* iv. 222 Tjirebon and Tegal (Central Djawa) are also exposed to such a wind during the dry season. In this case, the wind flows down from the western part of Mount Slamet and blows in a northern and northeastern direction. This wind is called the Kumbang.

kumbecephalic, kumbo-kephalic, bad forms of CYMBOCEPHALIC.

1863 D. WILSON *Preh. Ann.* I. 236, I suggested the term *kumbecephalic*, a boat-shaped,..for this form of skull. **1866** LAING *Prehist. Rem. Caithn.* 64 The kumbo-kephalic, which so many of the best authorities believe to be the primitive British type.

||**kumbuk** ('kʌmbʌk, 'kʊmbʊk). [Sinhala.] A name used in Sri Lanka (Ceylon) for the arjun, *Terminalia arjuna*, an Indian evergreen tree of the family Combretaceæ.

1869 R. H. BEDDOME *Flora Sylvatica* I. 17 It [sc. *Terminalia tomentosa*] is called.. Koombook in Ceylon. **1894** H. TRIMEN *Hand-bk. Flora Ceylon* II. 160 *T*[*erminalia*] *glabra*... Kumbuk. **1923** *Blackw. Mag.* Dec. 860/2 A lovely clear purling stream with the most beautiful Kumbuk trees fringing it on either side. **1971** *Ceylon Observer* (Mag. ed.) 19 Sept. 3/3 She had heard the beast sigh loudly behind the great big *kumbuk* tree.

kumeling, obs. form of COMELING.

kumera, var. KUMARA

kumis, -iss, -ys, variants of KOUMISS.

kum-kat, kumlee, var. KUMQUAT, CUMBLY.

||**kumkum** ('kʊmkʊm). Also **kum-kum, kunku.** [Hindi *kuṅkum* saffron.] A red powder used ceremonially, and by Hindu women to make a small distinctive spot on the forehead; the spot so made. Also *attrib.*

1938 K. VAN A. GATES tr. *Ramabai Ranade's Himself* vii. 57 A pleasant custom..allows a hostess at a ladies' party to apply a dot of red powder (*kunku*) to the forehead of each guest. *Ibid.* xv. 133 Don't you have the custom of wearing ..*kunku* marks, and such things? **1943** MORAES & STIMSON *Introd. India* (ed. 3) 113 Hindu women wear on the forehead a red dot (called *kumkum*, which is also the name of the powder from which it is made). An orthodox Hindu widow does not wear a *kumkum*. **1958** *Times* 15 Oct. 24/5 Mrs. Usha Rajwade, who earlier..rubbed on Kum-Kum powder. **1969** *Commerce* (Bombay) 26 July 149/3 Sometime back there was understandable furore in the city of Bombay when some missionary school asked the girls not to apply *kumkum* which is a sign of good fortune for an Indian girl. **1973** *Guardian* 14 Apr. 11/3 God needs offerings—garlands, coconuts, kum-kum powder, incense.

||**kümmel** ('kʏməl). [G. *kümmel*, repr. MHG. *kümel*, OHG. *kumil*, var. *kumîn* CUMIN.] A liqueur, flavoured with cumin, manufactured in North Germany.

1864 P. MARIÉ *Tribute to Fair* p. x, Our friend here sipping Kümmel. *c* **1870** in H. W. Allen *Number Three St. James Street* (1950) 186/1 Liqueurs. Bottle... Kummel.. 9/-. **1877** E. S. DALLAS *Kettner's Bk. of Table* 269 Caraways in palpable form have now disappeared from our tables, but only to return in the spirit—in Russian bottles labelled Kümmel. **1882** *Encycl. Brit.* XIV. 687/1 In the preparation of *Allasch*—which is a rich *Kummel*. **1897** *Pall Mall G.* 19 May 3/2 Coffee, dry..kummel and good cigars.

Kümmell's disease ('kʏməlz dɪ'zi:z). *Path.* [f. the name of Hermann *Kümmell* (1852–1937), German surgeon.] Delayed collapse of a vertebra after an injury.

1903 *Index-Catal. Library Surg.-General's Office U.S. Army* 2nd Ser. VIII. 874/2 (*heading*) Kümmel's [*sic*] disease. **1923** *Jrnl. Amer. Med. Assoc.* 1 Dec. 1866/1 Kümmell's disease is a distinct clinical entity, having as its basic origin a traumatism to the spine, which may be mild or severe. **1951** *Amer. Jrnl. Surg.* LXXXI. 166/2 The diagnosis of Kümmell's disease is not justified without negative lateral roentgenograms taken in the early postinjury period, with later films showing positive findings of collapse.

kummer, kummerbund: see CUM-.

kummul, var. CUMBLY.

||**kumpit** ('kʊmpɪt). [Native name.] A trading-vessel of the Philippine Islands.

1951 *People* (Austral.) 17 Jan. 48/3 They were finally got away by a Filipino..who paddled over from the Philippines in a 'kumpit' and took them back under a small cargo of rice. **1968** *Economist* 12 Oct. 81/3 There's many a fast kumpit no doubt leaving Sabah bound for the Sulu shores. **1969** R. THOMAS *Singapore Wink* xiii. 138 '..the *Wilfreda Maria.*' 'What's that?' 'A *kumpit.*' 'And a *kumpit* is a what?' 'It's an eight-ton ship. I bought it from a Moro pirate. I'm a smuggler.' **1972** *Sunday Times* (Singapore) 24 Sept. 7/3 Strict watch is maintained on all kumpits (Filipino boats) arriving in Sabah.

kumquat, cumquat ('kʌmkwɒt). Also 7 **camquit,** 9 **cum-, -quot, kum-kat.** [The Cantonese dialectal form of the Chinese name *kin kü* 'gold orange'.]

1. A small, orange-like citrus fruit from a tree of the genus *Fortunella*, native to southern China and Malaysia.

1699 DAMPIER *Voy.* II. i. 23 The Oranges are of divers sorts, and two of them more excellent than the rest. One sort is called Camchain, the other is called Camquit..The Camquit is a very small round Fruit. **1841** SIR J. DAVIS *Sketches China* (1857) II. 302 The Chinese have besides several diminutive species of the genus citrus; one of which, called Kum-kat, makes a good sweetmeat when preserved whole. **1870** *Jrnl. R. Hort. Soc.* II. 46 (*title*) Observations on the kumquat. **1882** *Garden* 7 Jan. 1/2 The Kumquat, or Japanese dwarf Orange. **1892** *Grocer's Catal.* Cumquats (small Oranges in syrup). **1913** E. H. WILSON *Naturalist in W. China* II. iii. 25 The Kumquat (*C. Japonica*) is sparingly cultivated for its fruits, which, preserved with sugar, are an esteemed delicacy. **1968** *Punch* 13 Mar. 402/2 Mr. Adams is ..occasionally affected (a face like 'a hybrid kumquat'). But he's written a master thriller.

2. *Austral.* A very small native citrus fruit, *Eremocitrus glauca*, or the tree producing it.

1889 J. H. MAIDEN *Useful Native Plants of Austral.* 8 *Atalantia glauca*..'Native Kumquat', 'Desert Lemon'... New South Wales and Queensland. **1955** P. WHITE *Tree of Man* (1956) 400 Boys should eat kumquats, the syrup running from the corners of their mouths. **1965** *Austral. Encycl.* IV. 227/2 *Eremocitrus glauca*, native kumquat or wild lime (Rutaceæ): small spiny tree of western New South Wales and Queensland; the globular $\frac{1}{2}$ inch fruits are pleasantly acidic and suitable for preserves, also cool drinks.

kumraid, obs. Sc. pa. t. of CUMBER *v.*

||**kumri** ('kʊmrɪ). [Native term.] A system of shifting cultivation practised in Karnataka, western India (see quot. 1938). Freq. *attrib.*

1904 W. SCHLICH *Man. Forestry* (ed. 3) II. I. iv. 106 The system is still extensively practised in India under a variety of names, as jhooming, dhya, kumri, taungya cultivation, etc. **1938** *Jrnl. Madras Geogr. Assoc.* XIII. 272 These people started what is known as 'Kumri' or 'Podu' cultivation. This is simply clearing the virgin forest, burning the felled trees and sowing rice, ragi, dhall etc., after the fire has died out, without any previous preparation of the soil. As the quantity of the ashes available was considerable, agricultural crop flourished and all that the 'Kumridar' had to do was a little weeding and protection of the crop from wild animals. He then left that area and selected another virgin forest close by. **1954** O. H. K. SPATE *India & Pakistan* xxii. 624 The jungle is largely occupied by tribal remnants practising shifting *kumri* cultivation.

kumshaw, variant of CUMSHAW.

Kumyk ('ku:mɪk). Also 8 **Coumyk;** 20 **Kumik, Kumuk.** [f. *Kumyk* name of a plateau in the Caucasus.] **a.** A Turkish people from the Kumyk plateau; also, a member of this people. **b.** Their language.

1788 G. ELLIS *Mem. Map Countries between Black Sea & Caucasus* 15 The Tartars are of three tribes, viz. 1. Terekemens, Turcomans, or Trukhmenians... 2. Coumyks. These live to the northward of the former, about the lower parts of the rivers Sundsha, Koisu, and Axai. **1902** *Encycl. Brit.* XXX. 81/2 Having long been more civilized than the surrounding Caucasian mountaineers, the Kumyks have always enjoyed some respect among them. **1948** D. DIRINGER *Alphabet* 568 Kumuk Turkish. **1970** *Encycl. Brit.* V. 102/2 Feudal relations developed..in the northern Caucasus among the Kabardians and Kumyk. *Ibid.* XXII. 399/2 Kumyk is also spoken in the Dagestan A.S.S.R.

kun: see CAN *v.*, CON *v.*[1]

Kuna, var. CUNA.

kunai ('ku:naɪ). [Native name in New Guinea.] A large coarse grass, *Imperata cylindrica*, found in tropical Asia, Australia, and the Pacific region; also called *blady grass* (BLADY *a.*) and LALANG. Also *attrib.*

1933 *Bulletin* (Sydney) 6 Sept. 39/4 Soon the weeds will have overrun the scar by the river bank, and a field of lush *kunai* will grow. **1945** *Coast to Coast 1944* 102 A gale..set the tall kunai grass swaying. **1958** *Times* 27 Nov. 12/6 On the waterfront, the buildings were..of native design, thatched with kunai grass. **1962** *Coast to Coast 1961–62* 53 Beyond him was the fantasy of New Guinea green:..in front the kunai plain which reached for five miles to the Finisterre Ranges. **1965** *Austral. Encycl.* IV. 367/1 *Imperata cylindrica* var. *major* (blady grass) is widely spread over eastern and northern Australia, chiefly in coastal districts, and extends through Polynesia and Malaysia to tropical Asia where it is popularly known by other names (kunai, lalang, and kogon).

Kunbi ('ku:nbɪ). Also 6 **Corumbijn,** 9 **Coombie, Koonbee, Kunbee.** [ad. Hindi *kurmī.*] A member of an Indian agricultural caste.

1598 W. PHILLIP tr. *J. H. van Linschoten's Discours Voy. E. & W. Indies* I. xxxix. 73/2 The Canarijns & Corumbjins [*sic*] are the Countrimen. **1808** R. DRUMMOND *Illustr. Gram. Parts Guzerattee, Mahratta & Eng. Lang.*, *Kunbee*, *Koonbee* or *Koolumbee*. (Guz. and Mah.) *Koonbee* is a term, which is given, whatever be his profession or occupation, to the pure *Sooder* or first of the fourth class, who are, in Guzerat for the most part, Cultivators of the Land. This title, in the Deccan distinguishes the Cultivator, from him, who wears arms, and prefers to be called a Mahratta. **1826** W. B. HOCKLEY *Pandurang Hari* I. x. 230, I begged the coombie, or cultivator, to give me some bread and rice. **1845** *Encycl. Metrop.* XX. 33/1 The Kunbí is a pure Súdra. **1875** *Encycl. Brit.* I. 423/2 The bulk of the population [of Ahmadnagar] consists of Marhattás and Kunbís, the latter being the agriculturists. **1923** *United Free Ch. Miss. Rec.* June 250/2 Patils of villages, the kunbi, the cartman, the man on the road with whom I passed the time of day,..all of them were kindly polite and courteous.

kund-: see KIND-.

kundah: see COONDA.

kundit, -ute, obs. forms of CONDUIT *sb.*

kune, obs. Sc. form of CUN *v.*

kunfort, kunger, obs. ff. COMFORT, CONGER.

Kung-fu, kung-fu (kʊŋ'fu:, kʌŋ-). Also without hyphen. [Chinese.] The Chinese form of KARATE. Also *attrib.*

1966 *Punch* 14 Sept. 388/3 Kung-fu is here. **1968** *Clarendonian* XXII. 270 Chinese Kung-fu is still taught today—but only as a Martial Art to a very select, carefully chosen few. **1970** K. PLATT *Pushbutton Butterfly* i. 9 The Chinese now call their form of karate *Kung Fu*... It's mostly leg-fighting. **1971** 'A. HALL' *Warsaw Document* xvii. 213 It was probably *kaminari*, a bastardized form of *kung fu*. **1974** *Listener* 17 Jan. 93/3 The plot..hinges on Lee wiping out an ex-monk, Kung-fu (martial arts) vice chief. **1974** *Bookseller* 13 Apr. 1961/1 There has been a great upsurge of popular interest recently in kung fu, the ancient Chinese art of self-defence, encouraged by the films of Bruce Lee..and the television series Kung Fu.

kungu ('kʌŋgu:). Also **kungo.** [Nyanja *nkungu.*] A small East African gnat, *Chaoborus edulis*.

Hence **kungu cake**, the bodies of large numbers of these gnats, compressed to form a cake.

1865 D. & C. LIVINGSTONE *Narr. Expedition Zambesi* 373 A kungo cake, an inch thick..was offered to us. **1897** H. H. JOHNSTON *Brit. Cent. Afr.* 436 The 'Kungu' fly of Lake Nyasa. **1899** D. SHARP in *Cambr. Nat. Hist.* VI. vii. 467 The kungu cake mentioned by Livingstone as used on Lake Nyassa is made from an Insect which occurs in profusion there, and is compressed into biscuit form. **1902** H. H. JOHNSTON *Uganda Protectorate* I. 413 The kungu fly has a soft little body, scarcely as large as that of a flea, with gauzy wings. **1964** H. OLDROYD *Nat. Hist. Flies* pl. 30 (a) (*caption*) A piece of 'kungu-cake', made up entirely from the bodies of small midges, *Chaoborus edulis*, from an East African lake.

kunku, var. KUMKUM.

‖**kunkur** (ˈkʌŋkə(r)). *E. Ind.* Forms: 8 **konker, concha,** 9 **conca, concher, conker, kankur, -ar, kunkar, -er, -ur.** [Hindī *kankar* = Prakrit *kakkaram*, Skr. *karkaram.*] A coarse kind of limestone found in many parts of India, in large tabular strata, or interspersed throughout the surface soil, in nodules of various sizes; it is burned to lime, and also used for constructing roads, binding to a compact, hard, and even surface.

1793 W. HODGES *Trav. India* 110 The river Jumna, the sides of which consist of what in India is called concha. **1810** WILLIAMSON *Vade M.* II. 13 A weaker kind of lime is obtained by burning a substance called kunkur. **1834** MEDWIN *Angler in Wales* I. 195 A round mass of 'concher'..which he rolled before him. **1859** R. F. BURTON *Centr. Afr.* in *Jrnl. Geog. Soc.* XXIX. 102 Small calcareous nodules of weatherworn 'kunker'. **1879** MEDLICOTT & BLANFORD *Geol. India* I. 397 In places the kankar forms compact beds of earthy limestone.

attrib. **184.** MRS. SHERWOOD *Lady of Manor* III. xxi. 239 The site of his habitation was on a conca rock. **18..** —— in *Life* xxiii. 381 Our long, long voyage terminated under a high conker bank. **1895** MRS. CROKER *Village Tales* (1896) 169 There he sat, on the kunker heap.

kunne(n, obs. inf. of CAN *v.*[1], CON *v.*[1]

kunning(e, kunyng, obs. ff. CUNNING.

kunscence, -sence, kunsent, obs. ff. CONSCIENCE, CONSENT.

‖**Kunst** (kʊnst). [G., = art.] The G. word in Comb. (which are in varying degrees naturalized in Eng. scholarly writings), as **Kunstforscher** (ˈkʊnstfɔrʃər), practitioner of *Kunstforschung*, art historian; also **Kunstforschung**, (scientific) study of fine art, art history; **Kunstgeschichte** (ˈkʊnst,gəˈʃɪçtə), the history of art, art history; **Kunsthistoriker** (ˈkʊnsthɪ,stoːrɪkər), an art-historian; **Kunstlied** (ˈkʊnstliːt) = *art song* (see ART *sb.* 19b); **Kunstprosa** (ˈkʊnstproːzə), literary prose, stylized or highly wrought prose.

1899 R. FRY *Let.* 15 Nov. (1972) I. 175 We are in the thick of a *Kunstforscher* fight. **1923** A. HUXLEY *Antic Hay* vii. 104 As a connoisseur and *kunstforscher*, Mr. Clew was much esteemed. **1933** *Burlington Mag.* Oct. 145/1 It would almost seem as though the Government had never recognized the existence of such a being as the 'Kunstforscher', perhaps because we have no better name for him in English than the clumsy and not altogether accurate 'art historian'. **1959** *Times Lit. Suppl.* 17 July 420/3 The editor, an industrious and knowledgeable *Kunstforscher*, supplies interesting scraps of information concerning the artist and his pictures, his models, his friends, and his methods. **1966** *Punch* 2 Nov. 683/2 There being no formal *Kunstforschung* in his student days. **1892** W. JAMES *Let.* 7 Oct. (1920) I. 328, I have mapped out a profitable course of winter reading, *Naturphilosophie* and *Kunstgeschichte*. **1936** *Mind* XLV. 515 The range of questions that it opens out is exemplified by the two essays in *Kunstgeschichte*. **1937** H. NICOLSON *Diary* 31 Dec. (1966) 315 Ben has been..in Florence preparing himself as a *Kunsthistoriker*. **1971** 'M. INNES' *Awkward Lie* iii. 64 All the professors and judges, the *Kunsthistoriker*, the Ministers of the Crown. **1880** GROVE *Dict. Mus.* II. 133/1 The Volkslied has gradually disappeared, giving place to the Kunstlied, of which the accompaniment is an important feature. **1936** C. S. LEWIS *Allegory of Love* 223 Usk is trying to write prose which shall have wings like verse—coloured and tunable prose—*Kunstprosa* in a word. **1960** K. J. DOVER *Greek Word Order* i. 11, I cannot swear that the decrees of the Ozolian Locrians do not betray the hand of a mute inglorious Gorgias, but I may be allowed to doubt that and to believe that in early documents from the Peloponnese, the North-West and Crete the influence of *Kunstprosa* is minimal. **1965** *Listener* 19 Aug. 281/1 That gigantic waste-paper basket, the Short Story... Straight tales, character-sketches,..experimental *Kunstprosa*, automatic writing, [etc.].

‖**Künstlerroman** (ˈkʏnstləroːˌmaːn). [G.] A BILDUNGSROMAN about an artist.

1941 H. LEVIN *James Joyce* 41 The novel of development ..becomes a novel of the artist, a *Künstlerroman*. **1957** N. FRYE *Anat. Criticism* 307 The confession flows into the novel, and the mixture produces the fictional autobiography, the *Künstler-roman*, and kindred types. **1969** J. GROSS *Rise & Fall Man of Lett.* i. 20 *Pendennis* can be seen as a first faltering step towards the *Künstler-roman*, the novel about the making of a novelist.

kuntenaunce, kunteyne, obs. ff. COUNTENANCE, CONTAIN.

†**kuny**, obs. form of COIN *sb.* Cf. CUNYE.

c **1440** *Promp. Parv.* 282/1 Kuny, or conye of mone.

kunynȝare, variant of CONYGER *Obs.*

kunzite (ˈkʌntsaɪt, ˈkʌnz-). *Min.* [f. the name of George F. *Kunz* (1856–1932), U.S. gemologist; see -ITE[1].] A lilac-coloured variety of spodumene which is valued as a gem and becomes phosphorescent or changes colour when irradiated (see quot. 1962); a gemstone of this mineral.

1903 C. BASKERVILLE in *Science* 4 Sept. 304/2 On account of this unusual and characteristic phosphorescence, as well as the other properties, I propose the name *Kunzite*. **1905** *Westm. Gaz.* 18 Jan. 12/1 To those who love some new thing the latest discovery in precious stones, Kunzite, will..be extremely welcome. **1949** *Rocks & Minerals* Mar.-Apr. 177 Kunzite. A perfect pear shaped stone of good color, 4·70 carats, $50.00. **1962** R. WEBSTER *Gems* I. vii. 129 Kunzite shows a golden-pink or orange glow under long-wave ultra-violet light, and a similar but much weaker effect is seen under the short-wave ultra-violet lamp. Under an x-ray beam kunzite shows a very strong orange fluorescence with a strong and persistent afterglow. When the phosphorescence has died away the stone is found to have changed its colour to a bluish-green; this remains stable provided that the stone is kept away from a stong light. **1973** *Fortnum & Mason Ltd. Christmas Catal.* 23/1 Openwork ring, in 18 ct. gold set with diamonds and one freeform kunzite, £265·00.

Kuomintang (kuːəʊmɪnˈtæŋ, -ˈtɑːŋ). [Chin., lit. 'national people's party'.] A nationalist radical party founded in China under Sun Yat-Sen in 1912, and led, after his death in 1925, by Chiang Kai-Shek, constituting the government before the Communist Party took power in October 1949, and subsequently forming the central administration of Taiwan.

1912 J. O. P. BLAND *Recent Events & Present Policies China* iv. 107 In the beginning of September, an arrangement was effected, by the leaders of the T'ung-Meng-hui, to amalgamate with five minor political groups 'for the sake of harmony' under a new name, the Kuo-Min-tang, or Nationalist party. **1913** W. H. HOSKING *Great Squeeze* iii. 36 The *Kuomintang* is a coalition of parties and is the only one that counts just now. **1928** T. F. MILLARD *China* 39, I remember the assassination of one Sung, a Kuomintang leader. **1941** E. HEMINGWAY *Let.* 30 July in *Morgenthau Diary (China)* (U.S. Senate Committee on Judiciary) (1965) I. 458 The bitterness between the Communists and most of the Kuomintang leaders I talked to including the Generalissimo, can hardly be exaggerated. **1948** J. K. FAIRBANK *U.S. & China* ix. 193 The National Government of China at Nanking in the decade from 1927 to 1937 was the most modern and effective that China had known. It was led by Chiang Kai-shek and controlled by the Kuomintang on the basis of party dictatorship. **1952** C. P. FITZGERALD *Revolution in China* ix. 229 It will be argued that the Kuomintang remnants in Formosa are 'White Chinese', and much Right Wing American misconception of the Chinese Revolution is due to this belief. But..the Nationalists are failed revolutionaires. **1957** *Times Lit. Suppl.* 27 Dec. 782/3 This bitter struggle between Kuomintang and Communists. **1971** K. HOPKINS *Hong Kong* 216 For the present the fifty-year-old struggle between the Communists and the Kuomintang continues, muted, with the British administration holding the ring. **1972** S. L. APPLETON in *Asian Survey* Jan. 35 Kuomintang and government leaders, summoned to an emergency meeting following the U.N. vote, themselves cited the need for political reforms.

‖**Kuo-yü** (kuojy). Also **Guoryu, Kuoyu.** [Chin., lit. 'national language'.] The name given to the Chinese 'national tongue', a form of Mandarin adopted for official use.

1932 Guoryu [see KUAN, KWAN 1]. **1934** in WEBSTER. **1954** PEI & GAYNOR *Dict. Ling.* 116 *Kuo-yü*, the new 'national tongue' of China, based on the Peiping dialect of North Mandarin; now estimated to be used by about 300,000,000 persons. **1957** *B.B.C. Handbook* 132 There were large audiences to the relays by Radio Hong Kong of BBC programmes in Cantonese, English, and Kuoyü. **1964** *New Statesman* 10 Apr. 581/4 (Advt.), Applicants must be native Kuoyu speakers. **1968** D. TORR *Treason Line* 45 He remembered just enough of the *Kuo-yü* he had learnt in Chungking. **1969** J. M. GULLICK *Malaysia* i. 29 The universal teaching in Chinese schools of the national Kuo-Yu dialect should in time provide a *lingua franca*.

‖**kupfernickel** (ˈkʊpfərˌnɪk(ə)l). *Min.* [Ger., f. *kupfer* COPPER + *nickel* NICKEL.] = NICCOLITE. (Cf. *copper-nickel* s.v. COPPER *sb.*[1] 12.)

1796 KIRWAN *Elem. Min.* (ed. 2) II. 271 Found with Native Bismuth, Kupfernickel and Cobaltic efflorescences. **1812** SIR H. DAVY *Chem. Philos.* 421 Nickel exists in an ore called kupfer-nickel, combined chiefly with sulphur. **1879** *Cassell's Techn. Educ.* IV. 226/2 Kupfernickel, which is a compound of this metal [nickel] with arsenic.

Kupferschiefer (ˈkʊpfəʃiːfə(r)). *Petrogr.* Also 9 **Kupfer-schiefer**; and with small **k**. [a. G. *kupferschiefer*, f. *kupfer* COPPER *sb.*[1] + *schiefer* shale, slate.] A bituminous brown or black shale of the Permian series, which is worked in Germany for copper; = *copper schist, -slate* (COPPER *sb.*[1] 11).

1830 H. T. DE LA BECHE *Sections & Views* 47 Professor Sedgwick..considers that he can trace the equivalents of the copper slate (kupfer-schiefer)..of the Thuringerwald, in the magnesian limestone of England. **1831** *Phil. Mag.* X. 46 Those sandstones and conglomerates which surmount the carboniferous series, and separate it from the *kupfer-schiefer* and magnesian limestone. **1879** *Encycl. Brit.* X. 352/1 The Kupfer-schiefer contains numerous fish..and remains of plants. **1886** J. GEIKIE *Outl. Geol.* xxi. 298 The Kupferschiefer (2 feet thick) has long been famous for its ores of copper and other metals. **1921** A. W. GRABAU *Textbk. Geol.* II. xxxviii. 506 At the base of this limestone series lies the important black copper-bearing shale, the Kupferschiefer, which rests upon the red sandstone. **1967** D. H. RAYNER *Stratigr. Brit. Isles* viii. 253 The Hilton Plant Bed..consists of dolomitic sands and silts whose flora includes some species common to the Marl Slate and Kupferschiefer.

Kupffer (ˈkʊpfə(r)). *Histology.* The name of Karl Wilhelm von *Kupffer* (1829–1902), Bavarian anatomist and embryologist, used in **Kupffer('s) cell** (also *cell of Kupffer*), a phagocytic cell that occurs in the lining of the sinusoids of the liver and has long radiating processes of cytoplasm (described by Kupffer in 1876).

1901 tr. *H. Dürck's Atlas & Epitome Special Path. Histol.* II. 18 The so-called stellate cells, or Kupffer's cells,..are faintly visible. **1924** H. E. ROAF *Text-bk. Physiol.* xx. 262 Kupffer cells have been seen containing remnants of red blood corpuscles and they may be instrumental in collecting the hæmoglobin for the formation of bile pigment. **1956** *Nature* 24 Mar. 575/2 Blocking of Kupffer cells interferes with the storage of vitamin A ester in the liver of the rat. **1966** C. R. & T. S. LEESON *Histol.* xiv. 314/1 It is probable ..that the stellate cells of Kupffer are increased in number in time of need by differentiation of the more primitive, endothelial cells.

kupfferite (ˈkʊpfəraɪt). *Min.* [Named, 1862, after Prof. A. T. Kupffer: see -ITE[1].] An emerald-green form of magnesium silicate coloured by chromium.

1868 DANA *Min.* (ed. 5) 231 The original kupfferite, from a graphite mine in the Tunkinsk Mts., is a chromiferous amphibole.

‖**kuphar** (ˈkʊfə(r)). Also **kufa**; properly **kuffah**. [ad. Arab. *quffah*, circular basket or pannier, circular wicker boat.] A circular coracle of wicker-work covered with skins, used on the Euphrates. See Herodotus I. § 194.

1800 J. RENNELL *Geogr. of Herodotus* 264 These [boats] were of a circular form, and composed of willows covered with skins... The same kind of embarkation is now in use in the lower parts of the same river, under the name of kufa, that is, a round vessel. **1827** TENNYSON *Poems by Two Brothers* 65 Where down Euphrates, swift and strong, The shield-like kuphars bound along.

kuple, obs. form of COUPLE *v.*

‖**Kur** (kuːr). [G.] A cure, a taking of the waters (in Germany or another German-speaking country, as at a KURSAAL); a spa.

1885 GEO. ELIOT *Let.* 25 June in J. W. Cross *George Eliot's Life* (1885) II. xiii. 369 It would have marred the Kur for me if I had every day to undergo a *table d'hôte*. **1892** C. M. YONGE *That Stick* I. xx. 238 The end of Constance's holidays was in view, the limit that had been intended for the Kur at Ratzes. **1915** F. M. HUEFFER *Good Soldier* i. 10 The music of the Kur orchestra. **1974** *Country Life* 24 Oct. 1212/1 The Kur park and its monuments are still as the Edwardians knew them.

‖**kura** (ˈkʊrə). [Jap.] In Japan, a fire-proof store-house.

1880 I. L. BIRD *Unbeaten Tracks Japan* I. x. 106 There is a *kura*, or fire proof storehouse, with a tiled roof on the right of the house. **1906** R. A. CRAM *Impressions Jap. Archit.* iii. 63 Every house of any pretension possesses its 'kura', or storehouse, built of wood and bamboo, but covered two feet thick with clay... After a big fire in a Japanese city, nothing is left but fine ashes and the scorched but reliable kura. **1936** K. NOHARA *True Face of Japan* iii. 44 Between the houses of wood, paper and thin plaster, tower the white-washed massive buildings of the kura. **1965** W. SWAAN *Jap. Lantern* v. 58 The works of art may be brought in still packed in the special boxes in which they are stored in the *kura*.

kurakkan (ˈkʊrəkkɑːn). Also 7 **coracan**. The Sinhala name for a type of cereal grass, *Eleusine coracana* (Indian *raggee*), which is extensively grown in chenas in Sri Lanka (Ceylon) where flour from its grain forms a staple food of the poorer villagers.

1681 R. KNOX *Hist. Relation Ceylon* I. iii. 11 There are divers other sorts of Corn, which serve the People for food in the absence of Rice... There is *Coracan*, which is a small seed like Mustard-seed. This they grind to meal or beat in a Mortar, and so make cakes of it. **1824** A. MOON *Catal. Indigenous & Exotic Plants Ceylon* 9 Eleusine... 1 coracana, common,..Kurakkan,..Ceylon, *cult.* **1864** G. H. K. THWAITES *Enumeratio Plantarum Zeylaniæ* v. 371 *E. Coracana*, Gærtn. (nom. vulg. 'Koorakkan'), is extensively cultivated by the Cinghalese as a food grain. **1900** J. D. HOOKER in H. Trimen *Hand-bk. Flora Ceylon* V. 277 The Sinhalese 'Kurrakan'..is a very stout prolific form of this, with the spikelets crowded in many series, and a globose rugose seed. It is extensively cultivated for its grain in Ceylon. **1913** L. WOOLF *Village in Jungle* i. 10 When the rains fall in November the ground is sown broadcast with millet or kurakkan. **1971** *Ceylon Daily News* 18 Sept. 4/6 In the villages around here the traditional food has been kurakkan and curd.

kurbasch, -bash, variants of KOURBASH.

†**kurch(e, -ie,** obs. ff. KERCH, KERCHIEF.

1609 SKENE *Reg. Maj.* 155 (*Treat. Crimes* IV. c. 39) Women suld not come to the kirk..with her face covered,.. vnder the paine of escheit of the kurche. *a* **1700** *Cock Laird* ii. in *Ramsay's Wks.* (1877) II. 222 Kurchis and kirtles Are fitter for thee. *a* **1724** in Ramsay *Tea-t. Misc.* (1733) II. 170

Her kurchy was of holland clear. **1828** Buchan *Ballads* (1875) I. 157 (E.D.D.) She's taen the kurchie frae her head.

kurchatovium (kɜːtʃəˈtəʊvɪəm). *Chem.* [ad. Russ. *kurchátoviĭ* (Flerov & Kuznestov 1967, in *Priroda* Nov. 35), f. the name of Igor *Kurchatov* (1903–60), Russ. nuclear physicist: see -IUM.] (A name proposed for) an artificially produced transuranic element, atomic number 104. Symbol Ku. Cf. RUTHERFORDIUM.

1967 I. Zvára et al. *Joint Inst. Nucl. Res.* (Dubna, U.S.S.R) *Preprint D6-3281* (*title*) Experiments on chemistry of element 104—kurchatovium. **1968** *New Scientist* 11 Jan. 85/1 Scientist working..at Dubna..were last year awarded the Lenin Prize for their work on the synthesis of transuranium elements, in particular element 104. This latter element was named Kurchatovium by the Russians. **1970** *Soviet Radiochem.* XII. 536 It was confirmed..that kurchatovium forms a chloride KuCl4, with properties close to those of the chloride HfCl4, and, consequently, is an analog of hafnium and zirconium, i.e., a member of sub-group IVb. **1971** *Inorg. & Nucl. Chem. Lett.* VII. 1115 The present work shows once again that the doubts expressed by the Berkeley group..concerning the chemical identification of kurchatovium are completely unfounded. *Ibid.* 1119 [*Reply of the 'Berkeley group'.*] We believe that these comments raise some valid questions as to whether or not 'element 104 (kurchatovium—Ku) was chemically isolated and identified'.

Kurd (kɜːd). Also 7 Coord, 8–9 Curd. [Native name.] One of a pastoral and agricultural people of Aryan stock, found in northern Iran and Iraq and eastern Turkey, with the adjacent regions of the U.S.S.R. (the area being collectively known as ***Kurdistan***). Also *attrib.* or as *adj.* So **ˈKurdish** *a.*, of or pertaining to the Kurds or their language, a dialect belonging to the Iranian group; as *sb.*, the language itself; **Kurdiˈstan** *a.* and *sb.*, (of) a Kurdish rug.

1616 T. Roe *Let.* 30 Oct. in *Embassy to Court of Gt. Mogul* (1899) II. 310 The King..tooke occasion to take in by force a reuolted Nation to the East of Babilon. The People are Called Coords. **1776** Gibbon *Decl. & F.* I. xiii. 381 The arrows of the Carduchians... Their posterity, the Curds,..acknowledge the nominal sovereignty of the Turkish sultan. **1813** *Q. Rev.* Oct. 257 Languages and Dialects... Median. Zendish. Pehlvish. Persian. Kurdish. *Ibid.* 267 The Kurds speak a corrupt Persian. **1823** Byron *Don Juan* vi. lxxxvi. 29 Asia, where Kaff looks down upon the Kurds. **1836** T. Skinner *Adventures Journey Overland to India* II. v. 69 The wife of the Kurdish traveller. **1854** J. H. Newman *Lect. Hist. Turks* iv. iii. 265 Saladin was a Curd. **1868** W. D. Whitney *Lang. & Study of Lang.* (ed. 2) v. 192 The Persian ..with its outliers on the north-west and on the east—as the Armenian, the Kurdish, the Ossetic, and the Afghan. **1882** E. O'Donovan *Merv Oasis* I. 325 A Kurd encampment. **1899** Mrs. L. M. Elton tr. *Nazarbek's Through the Storm* 204 About thirty Kurdish brigands rushed out of the forest. **1920** *Glasgow Herald* 12 May 9 Turkey accepts..a scheme of local autonomy for the predominantly Kurdish areas east of the Euphrates, south of the southern frontier of Armenia. *Ibid.*, The Kurds inhabiting that part of Kurdistan which has hitherto been included in the Mosul vilayet are to be allowed..to adhere to the independent Kurdish State. **1924** *Blackw. Mag.* Nov. 583/2 Pursued by a volley of oaths in English, Scots, and Kurdish. **1926** T. E. Lawrence *Seven Pillars* (1935) ii. xix. 124 It was an ordinary bell tent, furnished with..a fairly good Kurd rug, a poor Shirazi, and the delightful old Baluch prayer-carpet on which he prayed. **1931** A. U. Dilley *Oriental Rugs & Carpets* Pl. 22 (*caption*) Kurdistan, Mina Khani Design. **1955** *Times* 21 May 9/6 The Kurds of Iraq live along the frontiers of Turkey and Persia, among the mountains that form Iraq's natural boundaries. They are a hill people, and recognizably related to the Alpine Swiss, the Sherpas, and other mountaineers. **1963** *Times* 12 June 11/1 Kurdish would be the first language in elementary education in Sulaymaniya. **1970** D. M. Lang *Armenia* i. 39 Many of the neighbours of the Armenians in antiquity have vanished from the map, like the Hittites..; relapsed into barbarism, like the Kurds, descendants of the proud Medes; [etc.]. **1970** L. Sanders *Anderson Tapes* lxv. 174 The brothers had taken a very nice Kurdistan [rug] down to the truck. **1971** *Guardian* 3 Dec. 4/4 An unfortunate Pesh Merga (Kurdish soldier). **1973** *Times* 9 Aug. 5/1 Mr Baluk told the court that he was a member of the Kurdish minority in Turkey. **1974** *Evening Standard* 12 Feb. 48/5 (Advt.), Superb oriental carpets & rugs. Including:..outstanding Kurdistan rugs in fascinating geometric designs.

kurdaitcha (kʊəˈdaɪtʃə). *Austral.* Also 9 kooditcha. [Austral. Aboriginal.] (See quot. 1909.) Also, a malignant supernatural being. Also *attrib.*

1886 E. M. Curr *Austral. Race* I. v. 148 It was discovered in 1882..that the Blacks..wear a sort of shoe when they attack their enemies by stealth at night. Some of the tribes call these shoes Kooditcha, their name for an invisible spirit... The soles were made of the feathers of the emu, stuck together with a little human blood... The uppers were nets made of human hair. **1896** *Proc. R. Soc. Victoria* VIII. 66 The wearing of the Urtathurta and going Kŭrdaitcha lŭma appears to have been the medium for a form of vendetta. **1909** *Cent. Dict.* Suppl. I. 693 *Kurdaitcha.* 1. Among the tribes of central Australia, a man chosen to avenge the death of one who had died, every death being supposed to be due to the magic influence of some enemy. 2. A kind of shoe, made of emu-feathers matted together with human blood, worn by the kurdaitcha when on his errand. **1932** *Times Lit. Suppl.* 28 Jan. 52/2 The *Kurdaitcha* among the tribes of Central Australia goes forth against his enemy with a medicine-man skilled in this sinister art. **1940** A. Upfield *Bushranger of Skies* (1963) xvi. 156 You ought to make us Kurdaitcha shoes. *Ibid.* xix. 183 A Kurdaitcha man is an evil spirit—always wandering about the poor blackfellows' camp at night. **1953** —— *Murder must Wait* xxii. 146 All good aborigines should be fast asleep..safe from the dread Kurdaitcha. **1959** S. H. Courtier *Death in Dream Time* ii. 19 The bewildering display of aboriginal weapons and implements...death-bones and kurdaitcha shoes. **1962** A. Upfield *Will of Tribe* vi. 57 The fear of the Kurdaitcha Man and the Great Snake.

kure, obs. f. CURE *v.*[1], to take care.

kure, var. CURE *v.*[2] *Obs.*, to cover.

kurfuffle, var. KERFUFFLE.

kurgan (kʊrˈgɑːn). [Russ. *kur'gan* barrow, tumulus; of Tartar origin.] A prehistoric sepulchral tumulus or barrow in Russia and Tartary.

1889 J. Abercromby *E. Caucasus* 218, I remarked two green basins... They had been found in a kurgan. **1890** Huxley in *19th Cent.* 769 These Tschudish kurgans abound in copper and gold articles..but contain neither bronze nor iron.

‖**Kurhaus** (ˈkuːrhaʊs). [G.] A building at a German health resort where the medicinal water is dispensed for drinking and external use; a pump-room; hence, sometimes, a similar building at a watering-place outside Germany.

1855 Geo. Eliot in *Fraser's Mag.* July 61/2 The white *Kurhaus* glittering on a grassy slope. **1857** C. Kingsley *Two Yrs. Ago* III. ix. 269 He drives up to the handsome old Kurhaus. **1935** J. Buchan *House of Four Winds* 12 Mr. McCunn..accepted the consultant's prescription, and rooms were taken for him at the Rosensee *kurhaus.* **1962** N. Freeling *Love in Amsterdam* i. 38 Tuesday night he was at the Kurhaus in Scheveningen.

‖**kuri** (ˈkʊriː). *N.Z.* [Maori *kurī.*] A Maori dog, long extinct; also, a mongrel. Cf. GOORIE, GOORY.

1838 J. S. Polack *New Zealand* I. ix. 308 The karáráhé, or dog (Canis Australis), which, when young, is known as *kuri*, has been an inhabitant some two or three centuries. **1843** E. Dieffenbach *Trav. N.Z.* II. iv. 46 The New Zealand dog is different from the Australian dingo;..the native name is kuri. **1900** J. Scott *Tales Colonial Turf* 180 It was a sort of poodle..no one would think of asking who owned the kuri. **1930** J. Cowan in J. Reid *Kiwi Laughs* (1961) 97, I wish you'd give it to them hot and strong about the blasted 'kuris' worrying my sheep. **1949** P. Buck *Coming of Maori* (1950) i. iv. 64 The dog (*kuri*) figures a good deal in tradition. **1959** Tindale & Lindsay *Rangatira* 195 *Kuri dog.* The Maori dog was small... It was kept as a pet, it gave some aid in hunting, and it provided..fresh meat... It appears to be a domesticated strain of the feral dog of India..now extinct in New Zealand.

Kurile (ˈkjuːriːl), *sb.* and *a.* [f. the *Kurile islands*, a chain of small islands stretching northwards from Japan to Kamchatka, since 1945 held by the U.S.S.R.] **A.** *sb.* A native or inhabitant of the Kurile islands. **B.** *adj.* Of or pertaining to these islands or this people. Hence **Kuˈrilian** *a.* and *sb.*

1764 J. Grieve tr. *Krasheninnikov's Hist. Kamtschatka* i. i. 19 When the ice is carried thither with the beavers on it, then the Kuriles, who follow the ice along the shore, assemble here in great multitudes. **1819, 1843** [see AINU]. **1845** *Encycl. Metrop.* XXV. 866/2 A small portion of the continent..opposite to the Isle of Sakhalyin..is occupied by the Aïnos or Kurils, whose Isles extend from Japan to the Southern extremity of Kamchatka. **1875** *Encycl. Brit.* I. 426/2 The Ainos..are distinguished by an exuberance of hair on the head and body, a circumstance which has given rise to their name of 'Hairy Kuriles'.

kuriologic, -al, variant of CURIOLOGIC, -AL.

1826 *Edin. Rev.* XLV. 101 The method of Egyptian writing called..the Hieroglyphic,—of which one sort is *kuriologic* (or expressive of objects in a proper, not figurative or metaphorical, manner). **1862** H. Spencer *First Princ.* (1875) 349 The picture-writing of the Mexicans..had been partially differentiated into the kuriological or imitative, and the tropical or symbolic.

kurisee, ? corrupt form of CUIRASSIER.

1649 Cromwell *Lett.* 19 Dec. in *Carlyle*, The horse..took Three-hundred-and-fifty prisoners—amongst whom ..the renegado Wogan, with twenty-four of Ormond's kurisees.

Kurku, var. KORKU.

kurl, obs. form of CURL.

kurl-a-mo, kurl-the-mo: see CURL *v.*[1] 1 c.

kurlu, obs. form of CURLEW.

Kurnai (ˈkʊənaɪ). [Austral. Aboriginal.] **A.** *adj.* Of or pertaining to an Aboriginal tribe of south-eastern Australia. **B.** *sb.* This tribe; a member of this tribe; their language.

1911 J. G. Frazer *Golden Bough: Magic Art* (ed. 3) I. v. 324 The Kurnai tribe of Gippsland in Victoria. **1965** *Austral. Encycl.* I. 72/2 The Kurnai of Gippsland used to cut one or both hands from a corpse. The hand was wrapped in grass and dried, and a possum-fur string attached so that it could be worn about the neck of a near relative. By pushing or pinching the wearer, it was said to give warning of an approaching enemy. **1965** W. E. H. Stanner in R. M. & C. H. Berndt *Aboriginal Man in Austral.* viii. 230 Much mischief has resulted from the supposition that all Aborigines in all important respects resemble the Aranda, Kamilaroi, Kurnai, and Murngin. **1972** *Talanya* I. 29 In Kurnai..he gives the following phrases.

kurnakovite (kɜːnəˈkɒvaɪt). *Min.* [f. the name of N. S. *Kurnakov* (1860–1941), Russian mineralogist: see -ITE[1].] A hydrated borate of magnesium, $Mg_2B_6O_{11}{\cdot}13H_2O$, found as colourless granular aggregates with a vitreous lustre at Inder, Kazakhstan, U.S.S.R.

1940 M. N. Godlevsky in *Compt. Rend.* (*Doklady*) *de l'Acad. des Sci. de l'URSS* XXVIII. 638 During my visit to the Inder deposit in 1938, I found in the dump of one of the pits..a solid colourless mineral which proved to be a borate, of the composition $2MgO.3B_2O_3.13H_2O$. The new mineral was named kurnakovite. **1962** *Amer. Mineralogist* XLVII. 402 In the monoclinic and triclinic dimorphs..inderite and kurnakovite respectively, the asymmetric unit has been found to contain three chemically different boron sites. **1970** *Soviet Physics: Doklady* XIV. 1141/2 In kurnakovite an isolated H_2O particle is bonded to four boroxy rings by a single Mg octahedron.

kurne, kurnel, etc., obs. ff. KERN *v.*[1], KERNEL *sb.*[1], etc.

kurnock, obs. f. CURNOCK, a measure.

‖**Kurort** (ˈkuːrɔrt). Also 9 curort; kurort. [G.] In Germany or other German-speaking countries, a health-resort, a watering-place; also *fig.*

1868 Geo. Eliot *Let.* 27 June (1955) IV. 454 We..daily rejoice that we have found such a Cur-ort, suiting both mind and body. **1926** *Spectator* 21 Aug. 276/1 A company is being formed..to erect a modern thermal *Kurort*, and build an up-to-date hotel. **1930** *Discovery* June 171/2, I had no troubles, except a longing for the mountains..and even the attractions of Prague, the Riesengebirge, and several magnetic *kurorts* failed to hold me back. **1941** V. Nabokov *Real Life S. Knight* xv. 146 She loved inventing some rare illness and going to some famous kurort. **1949** Koestler *Promise & Fulfilment* iii. iv. 325 Others, like Naharia, are German Kurorts grafted on by plastic landscape surgery.

‖**Kuroshiwo** (kuːroˈʃiːwo). Also **Kuroshio**, **Kurosiwo**, and as two words (with or without a hyphen). [Japanese, f. *kuro* black + *shiwo* tide.] The Black Current or Gulf Stream of Japan.

1885 Sir J. Murray in *Encycl. Brit.* XVIII. 118/2 The Kuro-Siwo or Japan current—wholly a warm oceanic river during the S.E. monsoon similar to the Gulf Stream of the Atlantic. **1928** Russell & Yonge *Seas* x. 231 In the Pacific ..there is a system of oceanic currents much after the manner of that in the Atlantic, the Japan Current or 'Kuro Shiwo' corresponding to our Gulf Stream. **1967** *Oceanogr. & Marine Biol.* V. 57 Often compared with the Gulf Stream and Kuroshio, the East Australian Current is essentially different because it does not, as do the other two, make up an eddy system extending towards the east across the ocean. **1969** *Sci. Jrnl.* Jan. 16/1 The Kuroshio..is a swift current that runs along the western edge of the Pacific just as the Gulf Stream does in the North Atlantic.

kurper (ˈkɜːpə(r)). *S. Afr.* Also **karper**, **kerper**, **kurpur**. [Afrikaans, f. Du. *karper* carp.] A name used for several fresh-water fishes resembling carp, esp. *Sandelia capensis*.

1831 *S. Afr. Q. Jrnl.* Oct. 19 Kurper... Inhabits most of the rivers towards the Southern extremity of Africa. **1902** *Trans. S. Afr. Philos. Soc.* XI. 213 In an expedition to the interior, led by Surgeon Pieter van Meerhoff, we are told by him that in the space of 1½ hours they caught 'beautiful Carp (Karper)'... This is undoubtedly the fish (*Spirobranchus capensis*) still called Karper in the Colony by the Dutch. **1913** C. Pettman *Africanderisms* 285 Kurper or Kerper... *Spirobranchus capensis*, a well-known fresh-water fish. See Karper. **1947** K. H. Barnard *Pict. Guide S. Afr. Fishes* 80 The Cape Kurper (*Sandelia capensis*) is a very well-known fish in the rivers and vleis of the south-west Cape... In the Eastern Province a closely allied species known as the Rockey or Bain's Kurper (*Sandelia bainsii*) occurs. **1952** *Cape Times* 31 Jan. 9/8 The casualties include yellow fish..mudfish, carp and kurpur. **1971** *Sunday Times* (Johannesburg) *News Mag.* 28 Mar. 8/5 The big kurper are found much deeper than usual.

‖**ˈkurraˌjong**. *Austral.* Also curra-, curre-, curri-, -gong. A native Australian name for any plant or tree having a tough bark yielding a fibre; hence applied with qualifications to various trees, some called also *cordage-trees*.

black k., *Sterculia diversifolia*, and *S. quadrifida*; **brown k.**, *Commersonia echinata*, and *Brachychiton gregorii*; **green k.**, *Hibiscus heterophyllus*; **Tasmanian k.**, *Plagianthus sidoides*.

1823 Uniacke *Oxley's Exp.* (Morris), The nets..are made ..from the bark of the kurrajong (*Hibiscus heterophyllus*). **1847** L. Leichhardt *Overland Exp.* III. 91 (ibid.) Dillis neatly worked of koorajong bark. **1888** *Cassell's Picturesque Australasia* III. 138 (ibid.) Quaint currajongs..very like in form to the stiff wooden trees we have all played with in childish days. **1890** Lyth *Golden South* ix. 78 Forests of native apple, eucalypti, she oaks, kurragong, cedar, and wattle trees.

kurre, obs. form of CUR.

Kurrichane (kʌrɪˈtʃæneɪ). The name of a place in the western Transvaal, South Africa, used *attrib.* in **Kurrichane thrush** to designate a thrush, several races of which are found in Africa south of the Sahara.

1924 *Ibis* 770 *Turdus libonianus*. Kurrichane Thrush. This thrush is common in Nyasaland. **1936** D. A. Bannerman *Birds Trop. W. Afr.* IV. 314 The Kurrichane Thrush is not unlike a female European Blackbird. **1960** G. Durrell *Zoo in my Luggage* i. 32 A kurrichane thrush treated us to a waterfall of a sweet song.

kurs(e, kurt, obs. ff. CURSE, COURT *sb.*[1]

||**kursaal** ('kuːrzɑːl). [G., f. *kur, cur*, CURE *sb.*[1] + *saal* hall, room.] A public building at a German health resort, provided for the use and entertainment of visitors; hence, sometimes, a similar building at an English watering-place.
1849 THACKERAY *Pendennis* lvi, The resolute old gentleman.. made his appearance in the halls of the Kursaal. *Ibid.*, The Kursaal band at the bath. **1899** *Westm. Gaz.* 14 Sept. 10/2 The Margate and Southend Kursaals, Limited.

||**kurta** ('kɜːtə). *India.* Also **khurta, kurtha.** [Hind.] A loose shirt or tunic worn by men and women.
1913 W. G. LAWRENCE in T. E. Lawrence *Home Lett.* (1954) 485 Me in a dhoti and khurta, white Indian clothes. **1920** *Chambers's Jrnl.* 29 May 408/1 A guard of honour in scarlet *kurtas* (blouse-tunics). **1966** *New Statesman* 2 Sept. 316/3 A painfully thin youth—very Hindu, whose kurtha was always clean. **1968** *Observer* 25 Feb. 3/4 Beatle George Harrison.. dresses in the flowing pyjamas and *kurta* worn by people in North India. **1969** *Femina* (Bombay) 26 Dec. 8/4 Allambana of Delhi, run by Mohini Tandon, held an exhibition of embroidered saris and kurtas at Calcutta's Park Hotel. **1972** *Vogue* May 137 Atlantic and Othello Khanh.. in Indian cotton kurtas and tie-dyed turbans.

kurtosis (kɜː'təʊsɪs). *Statistics.* [mod.L., f. Gr. κύρτωσις a bulging, convexity, f. κυρτός bulging, convex.] A shape characteristic of a frequency distribution that reflects the sharpness of the peak (for a unimodal distribution) and the shortness of the tails, and is generally measured by the quantity $\mu_4/\mu_2{}^2$ or its excess over 3 (μ_4 and μ_2 being the fourth and the second moments about the mean of the distribution).
1905 K. PEARSON in *Biometrika* IV. 181, I have already called $\beta_2 - 3 = \eta$ the degree of kurtosis. **1931** L. H. C. TIPPETT *Methods of Statistics* ii. 28 There are several curves having the same standard deviation but varying kurtosis. **1952** W. L. GORE *Statistical Methods for Chem. Exper.* ii. 16 The kurtosis is useful in determining if a frequency distribution differs from the normal error curve. The kurtosis of a normal distribution is equal to 3; smaller values than 3 indicate a flatter distribution than the normal (a platykurtic distribution), while values above 3 indicate a more sharply peaked distribution than the normal (a leptokurtic distribution). **1968** P. A. P. MORAN *Introd. Probability Theory* vii. 317 Tables of.. the co-efficient of kurtosis $\mu_4\mu_2{}^{-2} - 3$. **1972** P. LASLETT *Household & Family in Past Time* iv. 129 These variables were then summed and averaged: measures of skewness and kurtosis were computed.

kuru ('kʊruː). [Native name.] A progressive and fatal degenerative disease of the brain which is endemic in an area of the Eastern Highlands of New Guinea and is characterized by ataxia and tremor.
1957 *New Eng. Jrnl. Med.* 14 Nov. 974/1 The current report of our preliminary findings is based on the careful study of 114 cases of this new disease, which the local populace know by the name of 'kuru'. **1958** *Times* 9 Jan. 10/1 It is estimated that about 1 per cent. of the population is affected with *kuru*. **1965** *Sunday Mail* (Brisbane) 10 Oct. 2 Outside the Fore region only the adjacent areas where inter-marriage has certainly occurred show cases of kuru. **1967** *New Scientist* 26 Jan. 190/2 A brain disease known as *kuru*.. appeared about 45 years ago in a tribe of cannibals in New Guinea and is now the tribe's most common cause of death. **1971** *Nature* 30 Apr. 589/1 Kuru.. has so far been transmitted from eleven different human patients to eighteen chimpanzees with incubation periods of 14–39 months after intracerebral inoculation. **1973** *Sci. Amer.* Jan. 126/3 The prototype of the slow virus [disease] is probably kuru, that remarkable affliction of the people of the South Fore River of New Guinea, apparently spread by ritual cannibalism of the brain tissue.

||**kuruma** (kʊ'ruːmə). [Jap.] A rickshaw. So **kuru'maya**, one who pulls a rickshaw.
1727 J. G. SCHEUCHZER tr. *Kæmpfer's Hist. Japan* I. II. iv. 180 Sai Sin first obtain'd leave of the Emperor to be carried about in a *khuruma*, or cover'd Chariot, drawn by two Oxen. **1880** I. L. BIRD *Unbeaten Tracks* I. i. 18 From *kuruma* naturally comes *kurumaya* for the *kuruma* runner. **1889** E. ARNOLD *Seas & Lands* (1891) xiv. 188 The Kurumas are wheeled sharply round and brought up with a general shout of arrival in front of a Japanese inn. **1892** —— *Japonica* 44 The *Kuruma*-men can trot in safety round every corner. *Ibid.* 62 The Tokio citizens call their little cab *kuruma*, which means 'a wheel', and the coolie who pulls it is termed *kurumaya*. **1894** L. HEARN *Glimpses Unfamiliar Japan* I. i. 2 The.. charm of Japan.. began for me with my first kuruma-ride... The jinrikisha, or kuruma, is the most cozy little vehicle imaginable. **1898** I. L. BISHOP *Korea & her Neighbours* II. xxiv. 79 Warm winter clothing, a Japanese *kurumaya's* hat.. and Korean string shoes completed my outfit. **1904** R. J. FARRER *Garden of Asia* ii. 12 At dangerous corners the kurumaya howls dolefully to make the people avoid the path. *Ibid.* xxiii. 234 Mr. Desire,.. taking us up in the kuruma, proceeds to whirl us home to our friends. **1909** *Daily Chron.* 21 Oct. 7/2 A couple of stalwart kuruma-ya who do their eight miles an hour with ease.

Kurume (ku'rume). The name of a Japanese town on the island of Kyushu, used *absol.*, or *attrib.* in **Kurume azalea**, to designate one of a group of small, evergreen azaleas developed there from a variety of *Rhododendron obtusum* early in the nineteenth century and introduced to America and Europe by Ernest Henry Wilson (1876–1930) in 1919.
1920 E. H. WILSON in *Garden Mag.* Mar. 38/1 It was during the Arnold Arboretum expedition to Japan in 1914 that I first became acquainted with these Kurume Azaleas. **1924** E. H. M. Cox *Rhododendrons for Amat.* v. 98 Kurume azaleas should be consistently fed to ensure good flowers. **1949** *Jrnl. R. Hort. Soc.* LXXIV. 145 When first introduced the Kurumes were given an undeserved reputation for tenderness. **1964** J. BERRISFORD *Rhododendrons & Azaleas* iii. 41 In the eighteen-twenties a cult arose among the feudal gentlemen of Japan and the dwarf evergreen azaleas were bred privately... Thus arose the two-hundred-and-fifty-odd varieties of Kurume azaleas, so called from the town of Kurume where they were later discovered. **1965** 'M. NEVILLE' *Ladies in Dark* x. 101 I'd taken up two Kurumes that she'd ordered. **1970** S. B. SUTTON *Charles Sprague Sargent & Arnold Arboretum* x. 258 The pilgrimage to the Kurume Azaleas came at the latter part of an expedition which was, as one expected from Wilson, a success both botanically and horticulturally.

||**kurung** (kʊ'rʊŋ), **kurunj** (kʊ'rʊndʒ). *E. Ind.* [Hindī *kurung*, Marhāṭī *kurunj*:—Skr. *kurunja*.] A tree, *Pongamia glabra*, N.O. *Leguminosæ*, widely diffused from India to China and N. Australia; its seeds yield ***Kurung oil***, much used in India for illuminating purposes.
1866 *Treas. Bot.* 919/1 In India, an oil, called Kurunj, or Poonga oil, is expressed from the seeds. **1883–4** *Med. Annual* 48/1 Kurung Oil is obtained from the seeds of a leguminous tree common in most parts of India.

||**kurus** (kə'ruːʃ). Also formerly **ghrush, ghurush, grouch, grush, gurush.** [Turkish *kuruş*.] A Turkish piastre, $\frac{1}{100}$ of the value of a lira; a coin of this value.
1882 *Numismatic Chron.* 3rd Ser. II. 175 Suleyman II. issued his own large silver pieces in 1099, and gave them the name of *ghrúsh*, which recalls the grossi, groschen, and groat of the Western States... Without entering deeply into the question of the exchange value of this Turkish ghrúsh, or piastre, as it was called by travellers—not, however, to be confounded with the small modern piastre—it is interesting to notice that the ghrúsh and the akcheh, which was its lowest 'divisionnaire', were constantly altering their relations. **1906** *N.E.D.* s.v. *Piastre* 2, The English (French, German, etc.) name.. of a small Turkish coin, called in Turkish *ghūrūsh*, $\frac{1}{100}$ of a Turkish pound, having in Turkey, in 1900, a circulating value of about *2d.* **1917** A. R. FREY *Dict. Numismatic Names* 93/1 *Ghrush*,.. The name of the coin is variously written Grush, Gurush,.. etc. **1927** *Weekly Dispatch* 6 Nov. 18 Turkish stamps have a perpetual 'grouch'... There are eleven stamps, values 1, 2, 2½, 3, 5, 6, 10, 15, 25, 50 and 100 *grouch*, which is the current coinage. **1959** E. POUND *Thrones* xcvii. 24 The olde double-ducat, The olde turkish grouch. **1960** M. CASE tr. *Boulanger's Turkey* (Hachette World Guides) p. lxxvi, The monetary unit of Turkey is the Turkish pound (lira), which is made up of 100 kurus. There are metal coins for 1 K.; 2½ K.; 5 K.; 10 K.; 25 K.; 50 K.; 1 T.L. **1971** *Whitaker's Almanack 1972* 954/1 The Turkish *Lira*.. is divided into 100 *Kurus*.

kurvey (kɜː'veɪ), *v. S. Afr.* Also **karwey.** [f. Du. *karwei* hard work, big job (ad. F. *corvée*): see KURVEYOR.] *intr.* To carry goods in an ox wagon. Hence **kur'veying** *vbl. sb.*
1873 *Queenstown Free Press* 8 Aug. (Pettman), For various reasons not a farmer kurveys between either Concordia or Springbok and Port Nolloth. **1876** T. STUBBS *Reminiscences* I. 49, I tryed a trip at Kerveying, I took a load to Fort Wiltshire. **1884** M. A. CAREY-HOBSON *At Home in Transvaal* I. iii. 29 'There will be an end to those visits one of those days,' said the merchant, 'and then good-bye to your karweying, Walters.' **1902** *Encycl. Brit.* XXXI. 81/2 'Kurveying' (the conducting of transport by bullock-waggon) in itself constituted a great industry.

||**kurveyor** (kɜː'veɪə(r)). *S. Africa.* [Anglicized spelling of Du. *karweier*, f. *karwei* job:—MDu. *corweie*, ad. F. *corvée*, CORVEE.] A travelling trader in S. Africa.
1885 W. GRESWELL in *Macm. Mag.* Feb. 285/2 The *kurveyor* or carrier who drags the trade of the country about in his ponderous ox waggon with spans of 16 or 20 oxen. **1896** *Blackw. Mag.* 645 It was a very paying thing for the individual 'transport-rider' or 'Kurveyor' to convey goods to and from Kimberley.

kus, obs. form of KISS.

Kushan ('kʊʃɑːn), *sb.* and *a.* Also **Kushana.**
A. *sb.* A people originating in central Asia who invaded India and established a powerful dynasty (1st–3rd centuries A.D.) in the North-West; also, a member of this people. **B.** *adj.* Of or pertaining to this people, esp. to the dynasty.
1872 *Numismatic Chron.* New Ser. XII. 182 Some time before the Christian era, the chief of the *Kuei-shwang* tribe of the great *Yuchi*.. subjected the other four tribes of the nation, and assuming the title of King of the *Kuei-shwang*, or *Kushân*, conquered.. Ophiana, Kophene, and Parthia. *Ibid.* 183 The *Asiani* are evidently the *Kushân* tribe. **1935** [see *fire-altar* (FIRE *sb.* B. 5)]. **1935** [see HAN]. **1948** D. DIRINGER *Alphabet* vi. 343 More important in the development of Indian writing were the inscriptions of the Kushana kings. **1966** F. STARK *Rome on Euphrates* xi. 261 The Kushans had entered history in the first half of the first century A.D. with their king, Kujula Kadphises. *Ibid.* 262 This expansion of the young Kushan kingdom occurred while the vigorous policy of Nero and his advisers was making itself felt. **1971** *Fashion Panorama* (Ceylon) July–Sept. 25 On the coins of the Kushanas are depicted the portraits of monarchs like Kaniksha, Huvishka, Kadphises etc. The Kushan rulers are depicted in these portraits as wearing trousers and a coat. **1972** *Times* 25 Oct. 21/7 The shrine emerged as a Mazdaean fire-temple dedicated to the memory of Kanishka, legendary emperor of the Kushan dynasty.

kushen, obs. form of CUSHION.

||**kusi'manse.** [Native name.] A small burrowing carnivorous mammal, *Crossarchus obscurus*, of West Africa.
1861 WOOD *Nat. Hist.* I. 242 The food of the Kusimanse consists of the smaller mammalia, of various insects, and some kinds of fruits. **1883** *Cassell's Nat. Hist.* II. 207 The Crossarchus, Mangue, or Kusimanse, presents a good deal of resemblance to the Cynogale.

kuskos, -kus, var. KHUS-KHUS (= CUSCUS[2]).

kus-kus, var. KAS-KAS.

kusshew, obs. form of *cusshewe*, CUISSE.

kusshowne, kussin, obs. ff. CUSHION, COUSIN.

||**kusti** (kʊ'stiː). *E. Ind.* [Pers. *kustī*, girdle, cincture; Gujarātī *kusti, kasti.*] A woollen cord worn round the waist by Parsees, consisting of seventy-two threads to represent the chapters of the Yaśna, a portion of the Zend-Avesta.
1860 J. GARDNER *Faiths World* II. 620/1 The *kusti* is a thin woollen cord. **1885** *Encycl. Brit.* XVIII. 325/1 A long coat or gown is worn over the sadara.. fastened round the waist with the *kustî* or sacred cord, which is carried round three times, and fastened in front with a double knot. *Ibid.*, This cincture is a cord woven by women of the priestly class only. .. The ceremony of the *kustî* or encircling of the girdle.

kustume, kut, obs. forms of CUSTOM, CUT.

kuta ('kʊtə). = KGOTLA.
1943 M. GLUCKMAN *Admin. Organization Barotse Native Authorities* 7 *Kuta* (*khotla*),.. council, court, Native Authority. *Ibid.* 12, I think the kuta would be made more efficient if its numbers were reduced; but this.. can only be discussed after the kuta organisation has been made regular, instead of muddled. **1955** —— *Judicial Process among Barotse* i. 9 Since the council is not only a court, I use the native term *kuta*... Usually the ruler does not attend the hearings of cases, though the kuta's judgment is referred to him for confirmation. Even if the ruler chooses to sit in the kuta while a case is being tried, it proceeds as if he were not there. **1959** G. D. MITCHELL *Sociol.* 83 The council, known as the *kuta*, is both a political and judicial body.

Kutani (ku'tɑːni). [f. the name of the village of *Kutani-mura* in the former province of Kaga, Japan.] Used esp. *attrib.*, as ***Kutani ware***, a kind of gold and dark red Japanese porcelain.
[**1875–80** AUDSLEY & BOWES *Keramic Art Japan* I. 43 Almost all the good and important pieces of Kaga ware which we have seen are marked with the two characters signifying Kutani.] **1880** A. W. FRANKS *Jap. Pott.* 80 The amateur prefers the original Kutani ware of dark-red and greyish-white colour. **1890** B. H. CHAMBERLAIN *Things Japanese* 283 There were two principal varieties of the ware: *Ao-Kutani*, so called because of a green (*ao*) enamel of great brilliancy and beauty.. used in its decoration, and Kutani with painted and enamelled *pâte* varying from hard porcelain to pottery. **1960** B. LEACH *Potter in Japan* vii. 170 Contemporary and old examples of Kutani wares. **1967** *N.Y. Times* 22 Oct. I. 10 The dramatic bronze castings were discovered in Hong Kong, the hand-decorated Kutani porcelains in Japan.

kutch, kutcha, var. CUTCH[2], CUTCHA.

kutchenel, obs. form of COCHINEAL.

kutcheri, -erry: see CUTCHERRY.

||**kuteera** (kə'tɪərə). Also **kutera, katira.** [Hindī *katīrā* (name of the gum).] In ***Kuteera gum***, a kind of gum obtained from an Indian shrub, *Cochlospermum Gossypium* (N.O. *Bixineæ*); also a gum obtained from several species of *Sterculia*.
1838 T. THOMSON *Chem. Org. Bodies* 676 *Gum kuteera.* This gum, according to Dr. Roxburgh, is the produce of the *Sterculia urens*, a tree which grows in Hindostan. **1886** *Guide Museums Kew* No. I. 15 Specimens of Kuteera Gum of the Indian bazaars furnished by *Cochlospermum Gossypium*, DC., used in the North Western Provinces as a substitute for Tragacanth.

Kutenai, Kutenay ('kuːtəneɪ, -nɪ). Also Kootenai and many other variants. [Native name, *Kútonâqa*.] **A.** *sb.* **a.** An Indian people of the Rocky Mountains; also, a member of this people. **b.** Their language. **B.** *adj.* Of or pertaining to this people or their language.
1801 A. MACKENZIE *Voy. from Montreal* (map following pref.) Cattanhowes. **1809** D. THOMPSON *Jrnl.* 9 Sept. in *Washington Hist. Q.* (1920) XI. 99 They all smoked, say 54 Flat Heads, 23 Pointed Hearts & 4 Kootenaes, in all about 80 men. **1831** R. COX *Adventures Columbia River* II. vii. 152 The Cootonais are the remnants of a once brave and powerful tribe. **1838** S. PARKER *Jrnl. Exploring Tour beyond Rocky Mts.* xxiii. 304 The Cootanies inhabit a section of the country to the north of the Ponderas along M'Gillivary's River... They speak a language distinct from all tribes about them, open and sonorous, and free from gutturals. **1846** H. HALE in *U.S. Exploring Expedition 1838–42* VI. 204 (*heading*) Kitunaha, or Coutanies, or Flat Bows. **1877** A. S. GATSCHET in *Mag. Amer. Hist.* I. 111. 170 The Kootenai, Kitunaha, or Flatbow language. **1891** *7th Ann. Rep. U.S. Bureau Amer. Ethnol. 1885–86* 85 (*heading*) Kitunahan Koluschan Families. **1893** *Rep. Brit. Assoc. Adv. Sci.* 575 The Kootenays believe that they came from the East, and one of their myths ascribes to them an origin from a hole in

the ground east of the Rocky Mountains. **1894** *Amer. Anthropologist* Jan. 69 The tomtit, the owl, the robin, and a few other birds are believed [by the Kootenays] to speak Kootenay. **1929** *Amer. Speech* V. 116 Indian tribal names.. were usually transcribed by persons whose ears were unaccustomed to any but European languages... We inherited..corruptions..*Kutenai* from *Kutonaqua*. **1932** D. JENNESS *Indians of Canada* ii. 20 Kootenayan, Siouan, Iroquoian, and Algonkian, are spoken also in the United States. *Ibid.* xxii. 360 In the firm conviction that the dead would one day return to life at lake Pend-d'Oreille, all the Kootenay bands assembled at that lake in certain winters to hold a religious festival. **1955** P. E. BAKER *Forgotten Kutenai* i. 8 The word Kutenai is spelled..Kootenai, Kootenay, Kootenae, Cootanie, and Cootenai as well as Kutenai. **1959** E. TUNIS *Indians* viii. 112/2 One tribe, the Kutenai, made bark canoes with exaggerated back-slanting bows, like the ram bows of 1898 battleships. **1965** *Canad. Jrnl. Linguistics* Spring 78 Kutenai (Powell's 'Kitunahan'), spoken in the eastern Plateau area bordering on the north-western Plains, stands in lonely isolation among a variety of languages of sure affiliation. **1969** O. W. JOHNSON *Flathead & Kootenay* 16 The Kutenais sowed and harvested sacred plants for ceremonial smoking before they ever heard of White men.

kuth, kuthe, obs. ff. COUTH, KITH, KITHE.

kuth, kuyth, var. *cuth*, COOTH, coal-fish.
1884 DAY *Brit. Fishes* I. 295.

kutnahorite (kʊtnəˈhəːraɪt). *Min.* Also kutno-. [ad. G. *kutnohorit* (A. Bukowsky, 1901 (see *Neues Jahrbuch f. Min., Geol. u. Pal.* (1903) II. 338)), f. *Kutná Hora*, name of the town in Czechoslovakia where it was first found: see -ITE[1].] A reddish-white rhombohedral carbonate of calcium, manganese, magnesium, and sometimes iron, belonging to the dolomite group of minerals.
1907 *Mineral. Mag.* XIV. 402 *Kutnohorite*... A rhombohedral carbonate with the atomic ratios Ca:Mn:Fe:Mg = 7:5:1:2 occurring as reddish-white cleavage-masses. **1955** *Amer. Mineralogist* XL. 751 Kutnahorite occurs at Franklin as anhedral masses with curved cleavage surfaces up to three centimeters in size in a small veinlet cutting the normal franklinite ore. It is translucent, with a pale pink color. **1962** W. A. DEER et al. *Rock-Forming Min.* V. 267 Kutnohorites from Franklin containing approximately 10 per cent. excess $CaCO_3$ show some degree of order in their structure. **1967** *Amer. Mineralogist* LII. 1751 Occurrences of kutnahorite have been recorded from Franklin, New Jersey.., Kutná Hora, Czechoslovakia.., Chvaletice, Czechoslovakia..and Providencia, Mexico.

‖**kuttar** (kʌˈtɑː(r)). *E. Ind.* Also 7 catarre, -arry, 8 cuttary. [Hindī *kaṭṭār*:—Skr. *kaṭṭāra*.] A short dagger used in India, having a handle of two parallel bars, joined by a cross-piece which forms the part grasped by the hand.
1696 OVINGTON *Voy. Suratt* 236 With a Catarry or Bagonet in his hand. **1698** FRYER *Acc. E. India & P.* 93 They go rich in Attire, with a Poniard, or Catarre, at their Girdle. **1763** SCRAFTON *Indostan* (1770) 19 A little dagger at their waist, which is called a cuttarry, the principal use of which, is to stab on occasion. **1826** HOCKLEY *Pandurang Hari* xvii, He bore a common kuttar in his girdle.
Comb. **1886** YULE & BURNELL *Hobson-Jobson* 815/2 *Katār*-hilted daggers. *Ibid.*, Blades mounted *katār*-fashion.

kutte, kutteable, obs. ff. CUT, CUTTABLE.

kuttle, var. CUITTLE *v. Sc.*, to wheedle.

kutwal, variant of KOTWAL.

kuuant, kuuele, obs. ff. COVENANT, COWL *sb.*[1]

kuvasz (ˈkuːvæʃ, ˈkuːvæs). Pl. **kuvaszok**. [Hungarian, fr. Turkish *kavas* guard.] A large white long-coated Hungarian breed of dog, used as a guard dog in its native country.
1935 *Working Dogs* (Amer. Kennel Club) 103 Being a working dog of the larger size, the Kuvasz should be sturdily built and impress the eye with its strength and activity. **1947** C. L. B. HUBBARD *Working Dogs of World* II. 100 The Kuvasz is the best-known Hungarian breed of dog... Kuvaszok on 'sentry-go' are most unpleasant if met by strangers. **1971** F. HAMILTON *World Encycl. Dogs* 75 The Kuvasz is spirited, intelligent and courageous.

Kuwaiti (kuːˈweɪtɪ). [Arab. *kuwaytī*, f. *Kuwayt* Kuwait.] A native or inhabitant of Kuwait, a principality on the Persian Gulf; the dialect of Arabic spoken there. Also *attrib.* or as *adj.*, of or pertaining to this country or its inhabitants.
1928 A. RIHANI *Ibn Sa'oud of Arabia* xxviii. 352 The Ikhwan marched on Jahrah, slaughtered five hundred of the *mushrekin*, the infidel Kuwaitis. **1930** —— *Around Coasts Arabia* III. i. 242 The sail—in its shadow and from its bounties, the Kuwaitis live. **1947** *R. Cent. Asian Jrnl.* 271 The Kuwaitis..had invariably used the Turkish flag. **1950** *Middle East Jrnl.* IV. 18 All know the majesty of the Kuwaiti *boom* entering their harbors to exchange cargoes. **1961** *Daily Tel.* 8 July 16/6 The field commander of the Kuwaiti army. **1967** T. M. JOHNSTONE *Eastern Arabian Dial. Studies* 29 The consonant system in Kuwaiti is the same as for the dialect group as a whole. **1970** *Times* 3 Apr. (Arab League Suppl.) p. iii/3 In the field of social affairs and labour, the Public Assistance Law has been issued with special regard to the stipulations of our religion about social welfare as well as the traditions of the Kuwaiti society and in accordance with the constitution. **1971** *Guardian* 30 Aug. 3/2 Kuwaitis can afford a summer-long holiday. Kuwait is the richest country on earth in terms of income per capita. **1972** H. OSBORNE *Pay-Day* I. i. 11 A young Kuwaiti called Rifai. **1975** *Times* 20 Jan. 61/2 Even after the recent Arab purchase by Kuwaiti interests of 14% of Daimler-Benz AG, there seems to be little chance of a change in the laws.

kuy, kuyn, kuynd, obs. ff. KINE *sb.*[1], KIND.

kuyte, kuythe, obs. ff. KITE, KITH, KITHE.

‖**kuzushi** (kʊˈzʊʃɪ). [Jap.] In Judo, a method of unbalancing one's opponent.
1950 E. J. HARRISON *Judo* 103 *Kuzushi*, breaking opponent's posture or balance. **1957** TAKAGAKI & SHARP *Techniques Judo* I. ii. 18 *Kuzushi*, methods of unbalancing the opponent. **1968** P. & K. BUTLER *Judo & Self-Defence for Women & Girls* ii. 36 Do, please, remember that you can break your opponent's balance to *any* angle you wish... *Tsukuri* is the action you take to break your opponent's posture, *kuzushi* is the effect that it has on her.

‖**kvass** (kvas). Forms: 6–9 quass(e, 8 quas, 8–9 quash, 9 kuass, kvass, kvas. [Russ. *kvas* 'leaven, kvass'.] A fermented beverage in general use in Russia, commonly made from an infusion of rye-flour or bread with malt; rye beer.
c **1553** CHANCELOUR *Bk. Emp. Russia* in Hakluyt *Voy.* (1886) III. 51 Their drinke is like our peny Ale, and is called Quass. **1608** HEYWOOD *Rape Lucrece* IV. i. Wks. 1874 V. 216 The Russe drinkes quasses. **1609** *Pimlyco* (N.), The base quasse by peasants drunk. **1753** HANWAY *Trav.* (1762) I. v. lxi. 283 Beer, quash, and bad wine. **1778** *Phil. Trans.* LXVIII. 672 The drink..was quas or sour small beer. **1823** *Mechanics' Mag.* No. 4. 58 The common drink of the Russians is kuass, which is not so good as our small beer. **1863** MRS. ATKINSON *Tartar Steppes* 232 They have bread in unlimited quantity, quass,..farinaceous food. **1894** GARNETT tr. *Turgenev's Ho. Gentlefolk* 121 'Fetch the kvas', repeats the same woman's voice.

kvell (kvɛl), *v. U.S. slang.* [ad. Yiddish *kveln*, ad. G. *quellen* to gush, well up.] *intr.* To boast; to feel proud or happy; to gloat.
1967 *Listener* 28 Dec. 849/3 *The New York Spy* is a useful and terribly bright guide to New York, conscientiously *kvelling* through 'the city's pleasures', charmed alike by brutal manners, as chronicled by Tom Wolfe, and the Jewish takeover (London swings but Jewish New York *kvells*). **1968** L. ROSTEN *Joys of Yiddish* 199 Only from your children can anyone *shep* (derive) such *naches* (prideful pleasure) as makes you *kvell*. **1970** L. M. FEINSILVER *Taste of Yiddish* 364 'You've got reason to kvell'; 'is he kvelling!'

kvetch (kvɛtʃ). *U.S. slang.* Also **kvetsch**. [Yiddish *kvetsh*, ad. G. *quetsche* crusher, presser.] A term of personal abuse: *spec.* a person who complains a great deal, a fault-finder. Also **ˈkvetcher**.
1964 S. BELLOW *Herzog* (1965) 61 She's got a disgusting father and a *kvetsch* of a mother. **1964** W. MARKFIELD *To Early Grave* (1965) xi. 187 There was Ozzie Waldman, Ozzie the *kvetch*. For his favor you could die. He gave away nothing. **1966** *New Society* 12 May 9/2 The idiom of the New Yorker—Gentile or Jew—..has a lot of Yiddish words, like schlepp..shiksa and kvetsch. **1968** L. ROSTEN *Joys of Yiddish* 200 What a congenital kvetcher! *Ibid.*, It will take forever, he's such a kvetch. **1970** S. ELLIN *Man from Nowhere* xix. 94 A bagger [*i.e.* investigator] should not dress so conspicuous that even these old *kvetchers* around here turn and look.
Hence as *v. intr.* [ad. Yiddish *kvetshn*], to complain, to whine; so **ˈkvetching** *vbl. sb.*
1965 *Holiday* July 98 The Beatles..came along in the middle of a wave of *kvetching*—songs constantly stressing the negative. **1968** *Atlantic Monthly* Oct. 70 He is an amiable one, not given to angry kvetching. **1971** *Harper's Mag.* Feb. 111 After listening to Kashouk *kvetch* for a couple of hours, Sol Hurok..put the question direct. 'Tell me, Kashouk,' Hurok wanted to know. 'If you always lose so much money, why do you stay in business?'

kvutza (ˈkvʊtsɑː). Also **kvutzah, kwuza**. Pl. **kvutzot, -oth**. [mod.Heb. *qĕbhūṣāh*, f. Heb., group.] In Israel, a communal and cooperative settlement, which, with others, may form a kibbutz.
1921 H. M. KALLEN *Zionism & World Pol.* xvii. 255 *Kwuzoth* or coöperative workmen's colonies were outfitted. **1929** J. H. HOLMES *Palestine To-Day & To-Morrow* iv. 188 (*heading*) The 'Kvutzoth', or communal colonies. *Ibid.* 195 Most of the settlers in Nahalal, for example, had originally been members of a *Kvutzah*. **1934** *Cook's Traveller's Handbk. Palestine, Syria & Iraq* (ed. 6) 48 The post-war settlements of the Zionist Organisation are all based on co-operative principles, and belong to two classes:—(a) The *Moshav*... (b) The *Kvutzah*, which is more or less communal in character. The entire assets and produce of the village are owned in common... Several of these *kvutzoth* are organised into groups (*kibbutzim*) based on the principle of mutual assistance and exchange of man power. **1944** H. F. INFIELD *Co-operative Living in Palestine* (1946) 6 The Kvutza is well established. The first of these settlements was founded in 1908... A recent census..shows seventy-six Kvutzot. **1967** *Encycl. Brit.* VI. 456 The 'Kibbutz' and 'Kvutza', where all property is collectively owned. **1973** *Times Lit. Suppl.* 23 Feb. 212/5 The burning of the Degania B kvutza by the Arabs.

kw-, a ME. spelling of OE. CW-, mod. QU-, q.v.

Kwa (kwɑː). Also **Kwo, Qua**. [Native name.] A branch of a Niger-Congo language family, including Akan, Ewe, Ibo, and Yoruba. Also applied to a native speaker of one of the languages in this family. Also *attrib.* or as *adj.*
1857 H. GOLDIE *Princ. Efik Gram.* p. viii, If we take Creek Town..as a centre, and describe a circle of one hundred miles radius, we shall either include or touch upon the tribes of Usahadet..Efut..Aqua (Qua), [etc.]. **1883** R. N. CUST *Sk. Mod. Lang. Afr.* xi. 238 Kwa or Qua. Is different from the Efik and is spoken to the South of that Language... It is stated that the Efik are immigrants from the Interior, and that the Qua are the indigenous inhabitants. **1919** [see IBIBIO *sb.* and *a.*]. **1930** A. WERNER *Struct. & Relationship Afr. Lang.* II. 33 Along the coast of the Gulf of Guinea—say from Cape Mount to the Niger mouth—we have what Westermann calls the Kwa group. **1955** [see FANTI *sb.* and *a.*]. **1970** P. OLIVER *Savannah Syncopators* 39 The Kwa group [of tribes] which stretches from Liberia east to Ibo territory in Nigeria. *Ibid.* 42 The Kwa-speaking peoples of the coastal rain forest. **1971** A. KIRK-GREENE in J. Spencer *Eng. Lang. W. Afr.* 128 The Kwa group of languages, of which Yoruba is one.

kwacha (ˈkwɑːtʃə). [Chibemba *kwacha* dawn.] **a.** Used as a Zambian nationalist slogan. **b.** The basic currency unit in Zambia. Also, a banknote of this value.
1962 K. KAUNDA *Zambia shall be Free* xvii. 160 For a long time I have led my people in their shouts of *Kwacha* (the dawn). We have been shouting it in the darkness; now there is the grey light of dawn on the horizon and I know that Zambia will be free. **1966** *Times* 10 Mar. 8/7 Mr. Arthur Wina, Finance Minister, told Parliament today that in 1968 Zambia will have its own decimal currency. The new unit will be the 'Kwacha', worth 10s. and meaning 'Dawn of Freedom'. **1967** D. C. MULFORD *Zambia* v. 198 Speaking to the Conference's 4,000 delegates amid shouts of 'Action Now' and 'Kwacha', Kaunda launched into an impassioned attack. **1971** *Whitaker's Almanack 1972* 775/1 Zambia adopted decimal currency on Jan. 16, 1968, the unit being the *Kwacha*, equivalent to 10s. of the former currency. The *kwacha* = 58 p. sterling. **1972** *Daily Tel.* 18 Sept. 18/8 The company has a fully paid up capital of 2·7 million kwacha, which is to be purchased by Indeco from Unilever of Britain over seven years. **1973** *Guardian* 23 Mar. 14/5 The exchange rate is given as ·7143 kwachas per US dollar.

‖**kwai-lo** (kwailo). Also **kwai-tze** (kwaitsə). [Chinese (Cantonese dial.).] 'Foreign devil', a name given by the Chinese to foreigners.
[**1878** H. A. GILES *Gloss. Far East* 76 *Kwei-tsze* or *Kuei-tzŭ*, devils. A Chinese term for foreigners. **1910** J. S. THOMSON *Chinese* i. 70 Now and then an urchin spits at a foreigner's chair and shouts, *Fan kwei lai* (See, here's a foreign devil). **1944** H. B. RATTENBURY *China, my China* i. 9 On the streets they cursed me for..a '*yang kuei-tze*'—'a foreign devil'.] **1969** *Times* 9 Dec. (Taiwan Suppl.) p. viii/6 To the *kwai-lo's* innocent suggestion that the Foochow or coastal school might be classified under the generic label 'shanghai', Master Wei responded with a sour oath. **1972** *South China Morning Post* (Hong Kong) 4 Dec., *Kwai Lo*, a foreigner (or literally devil man). **1972** *Times* 21 Oct. (Hongkong Suppl.) p. i/4 A discreet variety of Mao-style padded-coat is admirable wear for young and elderly *kwai-lo* (foreign devils) in the Hongkong winter.

Kwakiutl (ˈkwɑːkjʊt(ə)l). Also 9 **Kwahkewlth**, etc. [Native place-name, *Kwá gul*.] **a.** An Indian people of the north-west coast of N. America; also, a member of this people. **b.** Their language. Also *attrib.* or as *adj.*
1848 *Jrnl. Ethnol. Soc. London* I. 233 (*in list*) 7. Quagheuil. Inhabiting Broughton's Archipelago. **1874** *Rep. Indian Branch, Canada Dept. Minister of Interior 1873* 33 Quackewelths with sub-tribes 2,000. **1897** F. BOAS in *Rep. U.S. Nat. Mus. 1895* 311 (*title*) Social organisation and secret societies of the Kwakiutl Indians. *Ibid.* 321 Kwakiutl, Salishan, and Chemakum..show certain similarities in form. **1921** E. SAPIR *Lang.* iv. 81 Causative duplications..as in Kwakiutl *metmat* 'to eat clams' (radical element *met-* 'clam'). **1933** L. BLOOMFIELD *Lang.* xxvi. 470 Thus, Quilleute, Kwakiutl, and Tsimshian all have different articles for common nouns and for names, and distinguish between visibility and invisibility in demonstrative pronouns. **1937** R. H. LOWIE *Hist. Ethnol. Theory* ix. 133 A blue-blood in the caste-ridden Kwakiutl society. **1944** [see DEVIANT *ppl. a.* 1]. **1951** R. FIRTH *Elem. Social Organiz.* i. 3 The Kwakiutl Indians of British Columbia compete in the potlach. **1955** W. GADDIS *Recognitions* I. i. 23 With the loss of Camilla he returned to the times before he had known her, among the Zuñi and Mojave, the Plains Indians and the Kwakiutl. **1959** E. TUNIS *Indians* 136/1 The Kwakiutl and Nootka languages were similar to one another but unlike any other known tongue. **1965** W. P. ALSTON in M. Black *Philos. in Amer.* 24 What in our culture would be a look of contempt would be a look of affection among the Kwakiutl. **1969** *Times* 22 Sept. 14/3 A Kwakiutl door post from Cape Commerell is sculptured in the form of a gigantic bear—a forest spirit—its lips rounded in a mysterious hooting cry.

‖**kwanga** (ˈkwæŋgə). [Native name.] In Zaïre (formerly the Congo), a kind of bread made of manioc.
1907 *Daily Chron.* 28 Oct. 7/3 With the exception of a few people..who supply the State with 'kwanga' (native bread)..all the people I saw are taxed with rubber. **1908** H. H. JOHNSTON *George Grenfell & Congo* II. xxviii. 796 In those happy days ten cakes of kwanga..could be bought for one brass rod. **1971** *Guardian* 31 July 10/6 Kwanga..looks..like..candlewax.

kwashiorkor (kwɒʃɪˈɔːkɔː(r)). [Native name in Ghana (formerly the Gold Coast).] A wasting disease that is caused by an insufficient intake of protein by the body and chiefly affects young children in tropical countries, producing apathy, oedema of the extremities, desquamation, and partial loss of pigmentation (and is generally associated with diarrhoea and stunted growth), and leading in severe cases to death.
1935 C. D. WILLIAMS in *Lancet* 16 Nov. 1151/1 The name 'kwashiorkor' indicates the disease the deposed baby gets when the next one is born, and is the local name in the Gold Coast for a nutritional disease of children, associated with a

maize diet. **1951** G. C. SHATTUCK *Dis. Tropics* lvii. 695 The early stage of kwashiorkor is difficult to recognize. Probably there are many mild cases which never develop the typical syndrome. **1954** *New Biol.* XVII. 20 One of the commonest diseases, called Kwashiorkor, is associated with protein deficiency in the diet when young and especially at the stage when breast-feeding ceases and no very suitable foods to replace it are available. **1959** *Times* 2 Dec. 10/5 Another hospital doctor described the incidence of kwashiorkor as 'needless slaughter' which could easily be prevented by funds for milk and other proper nourishment. **1968** *Observer* (Colour Suppl.) 29 Dec. 18/3 We saw a fretful baby with the unmistakable signs of early *kwashiorkor*, the disease of protein starvation that ravages Africa. **1970** D. B. JELLIFFE *Dis. Children Subtropics & Tropics* (ed. 2) vii. 172 The 'sugar baby' type of child..which conserves his subcutaneous fat, may even be obese and recovers very rapidly on a high-protein diet, is the typical example of kwashiorkor without previous malnutrition. **1971** *Progress* (Cape Town) May 9/1 One of the unit's major achievements was to prove that the cure of kwashiorkor..could be initiated by the administering of a synthetic skimmed milk.

‖**kwedini** (kwiː'dɪnɪ). *S. Afr.* Also **khwedini, khwidini, kweding, kweedini.** [ad. Kaffir *kwenkwendini* vocative form of *kwenkwe* boy (Pettman).] A native boy.

1912 *Queenstown Representative* 27 Jan. 5/1 This '*kween dine*' was walking behind the pole driving the bullocks on. **1946** *Spotlight* (Johannesburg) 23 Aug. 6/1 A twelve-year-old *kwedini* asleep across some sacks. **1949** *Cape Argus Mag.* 12 Nov. 7/5 Uneducated, 'raw' Native kwedinis, aged 15 and upwards. **1955** J. B. SHEPHARD *Land of Tikoloshe* v. 37 A Khwidini is 'not old enough for a man, nor young enough for a boy'. *Ibid.* viii. 59 Abakhweta..do not mix with the younger Khwedinis. **1970** *Daily News* (Durban) 18 Dec. 13 One White trader complained that kwedings (boys) had destroyed more than 1000 white telephone cups.

kweek (kwiːk). *S. Afr.* [Afrikaans. f. Du. *kweek* couch grass.] In full, ***kweek grass***. A local name for several creeping grasses, esp. *Cynodon dactylon.*

1904 *Transvaal Agric. Jrnl.* Oct. 185 The Transvaal kweekgras is shorter and more of a surface grass than the Bermuda grass. **1929** J. W. BEWS *World's Grasses* v. 184 It [sc. *Cynodon dactylon*] is commonly known as 'Bermuda grass' and in S. Africa as 'Kweek grass', though that name is applied to other species of creeping grasses as well. **1937** S. CLOETE *Turning Wheels* xviii. 294 The dark-green rings of kweek grass marking the site of his kraals. **1947** *Cape Times* 2 May 9 Only 342 acres were planted to marram grass and kweek. **1954** C. E. HUBBARD *Grasses* 335 Like other well-known grasses it [sc. *Cynodon dactylon*] has numerous common names, being known as 'Kweek' in S. Africa, 'Doob' in India, 'Couch' in Australia, 'Bermuda Grass' in the United States, and in the British Isles sometimes as 'Creeping Dog's-tooth-grass' or 'Creeping Finger-grass'. **1970** A. FULTON *I swear to Apollo* 4 The redgrass gave way to kweekgrass and steekgrass that grew not in a soft thick carpet but in sparse little tufts dotted here and there amongst the boulders.

kwela ('kweɪlə). [Afrikaans, ? ad. Zulu *khwela* climb, mount.] A popular dance, or its accompanying jazz-like music, of mid- and southern Africa.

1958 *Time* 16 June 37/1 The haunting sound of penny-whistle jazz has become the favorite music of South Africa's slum-caged blacks—and of a great many white hipsters. In the dusty streets, urchins rock to the penny-whistle's fast *kwela* beat; in shabby speakeasies, women shuffle to its slower *marabi* rhythm. **1958** *Gramophone* Dec. 328/2 Those addicted to the shrill squawking of the Kwela flute will have to hear..*Something New From Africa.* **1960** *Guardian* 1 Apr. 10/7 When night falls, she can dance the kwela, mambo, or high-life with any or all of them [*sc.* Nigerians]. **1961** *Sunday Times* 12 Mar. 15/7 One of the tin whistle bands that make kwela music at street corners in Johannesburg. **1969** J. BRUNNER *Plague on Both your Causes* xiii. 96 The music—all local stuff halfway between *kwela* and the long Arab-influenced melodic lines of the Sudan—rose to a pitch of frenzy. **1974** *Sunday Times* (Johannesburg) 13 Oct. 15, I would..listen to kwela music and dance with gouty feet.

†**kwne**, obs. north. form of *cun*, CON *v.*^{1}

a **1400** *Morte Arth.* 1565, I kwne the thanke for thy come.

ky, pl. of COW (now *Sc.* and *north. dial.*).

kya ('kaɪə). Also **kaia, kia.** [ad. Zulu *-khaya* place of abode.] In South Africa and Rhodesia, an African's hut; also, quarters of an African servant.

1909 K. FAIRBRIDGE *Veld Verse* 85 Where the high-veld breaks to valley..Stands a kaia looking Northward through the mountains to the plain. **1910** J. BUCHAN *Prester John* xvi. 257 Inanda's Kraal was a cluster of kyas and rondavels. **1911** *East London* (Cape Province) *Dispatch* 24 Nov. (Pettman), A native living in a kraal at Lydenberg quarrelled with another native, whom he accused of having fired his *kya.* **1935** L. G. GREEN *Great Afr. Mysteries* (1937) xvi. 192 Each house has a separate *kya* in the back garden for the servant. **1950** *Cape Argus* 4 Mar. 9/5 Fowl-pens, temporary tin Native kias and big heaps of rubble. **1956** N. GORDIMER *Six Feet of Country* iii. 38 These two white-washed servants' rooms (some white people called them kyas,..wanting to keep in their minds the now vanished mud huts which the word indicated). **1971** *Guardian* 29 Sept. 19/3 The houseboys' Kias (usually one small room) at the bottom of the garden.

‖**kyabuka, kiabooca** (kaɪə'buːkə). Also **kia-, kyabooca, -buca.** [Malay *kayu-buku* knot-wood, i.e. *kayu* tree + *buku* knot, joint; in Du. spelling *kajoe-boekoe.*] A Malaysian tree (*Pterospermum Indicum*) furnishing an ornamental wood, known also as *Amboyna wood* (q.v.).

1831 TRELAWNEY *Adv. Younger Son* II. 304 A variety of gums and resins, cocoa-nut oil, sandal and kiabouka wood. **1850** WEALE *Dict. Terms* 246/2 *Kiabooca wood*.. imported from Sincapore, is very ornamental, and is used for small boxes and writing-desks. **1861** H. CLEGHORN *Forests S. India* 279 Kiabuca-wood, or Amboyna-wood. **1865** SIR G. BIRDWOOD *Veg. Prod. Bombay* 346 *Pterospermum indicum* is the tree which yields Amboyna or Kyabuca wood.

kyack ('kaɪæk). *U.S.* [Orig. unknown.] 'A form of packsack consisting of two hollow containers swung on either side of a packsaddle' (*Dict. Americanisms*).

1901 *Sunset* Mar. 138/1 Our camp now lay in perfect chaos—blankets, kyacks, saddle-bags, and cooking utensils in a jumble. **1904** *Outing* (U.S.) Oct. 98/2 Exactly the same bitter partisanship obtains in the choice of saddle, in the choice of alforjas or kyacks. **1944** R. F. ADAMS *Western Words* (1945) 88/2 Kyacks might be described as hollow containers, one on each side of the horse, each of sufficient capacity to hold the equal of two five-gallon oil cans placed side by side. **1948** *Sierra Club Bull.* (San Francisco) Dec. 2/2 Stock that..don't mind getting wet up to the kyacks at a stream crossing.

kyack, var. KAYAK^{2}.

kyan, earlier form of CAYENNE.

Kyan, var. KAYAN.

kyang, var. KIANG.

kyanite, variant of CYANITE, now more usual.

kyanize ('kaɪənaɪz), *v.* [f. the name of J. H. Kyan, the inventor of the process (patented in 1832) + -IZE.] *trans.* To impregnate (wood) with a solution of corrosive sublimate, as a preservative against decay. Hence '**kyanized** *ppl. a.*, '**kyanizing** *vbl. sb.*

1837 C. VIGNOLES in *Mech. Mag.* XXVI. 258 A railway bar..to be laid upon half baulks of Kyanized timber. **1843** *Blackw. Mag.* LIII. 417 Let their timbers be Kyanized, their cables of iron. **1871** HARTWIG *Subterr. World* xxiii. 268 Many remedies..among which kyanizing, or saturating the wood with a solution of corrosive sublimate, is one of the most efficacious.

kyano-, var. f. CYANO-: **kyanophyll** (kaɪ'ænəʊfɪl), *Bot.* and *Chem.* [Gr. φύλλον leaf], Kraus's name for a blue-green substance, supposed to be a constituent of chlorophyll.

1885 GRAY *Physiol. Bot.* 291 According to Wiesner kyanophyll is nearly pure chlorophyll freed from its associated yellow pigment xanthophyll.

kyanol ('kaɪənɒl). *Chem.* [f. Gr. κύαν-ος, CYANO- + -OL.] A synonym of ANILINE.

1855 MAYNE *Expos. Lex.*, *Kyanole.* **1865-72** WATTS *Dict. Chem.*, *Kyanol.*

‖**kyat** (kiː'ɑːt). [Burmese.] The basic monetary unit of Burma since 1952.

1952 *Times* 17 June 10/3 It has been announced in Rangoon that the Union Bank of Burma Act, 1952, will become effective on July 1 next, when the new standard unit of monetary value, the *kyat*, comes into force. The kyat will be the exact equivalent of the present Burma rupee and will be divided into 100 units, each of which will be called a *pya.* **1955** E. MANNIN *Land of Crested Lion* xi. 155 We..buy baskets of strawberries from Ghurkas..at half a *kyat* a basket. **1971** *Nat. Geographic* Mar. 361/1 Working seven days a week for nine months of every year, the couple extract an average of 120 pounds of sap from each tree, earning about 7½ *kyats* ($1.56) a day. **1972** *Guardian* 15 Aug. 3/4 Burma's foreign reserves are currently down to..£12 millions... The local currency, the kyat..is worth less than a third its official rate of 14 to the pound sterling.

kyathos, var. CYATHUS, in sense 1 a.

kybe, kybed, kybde, obs. ff. KIBE, KIBED.

kybosh: see KIBOSH *sb.*

kyby, kybill, kyble, obs. ff. KIBY, KIBBLE.

kybyte, obs. var. CUBIT.

c **1440** *Promp. Parv.* 274/1 Kybyte, *cubitus.*

kybzey, kyche, obs. ff. KIPSEY, KEACH.

kyd, kydd(e, kyde, obs. forms of KID.

†**kyd, kydde**, *v. Obs.* (*pseudo-arch.*) [Evolved from ME. *kyd, i-kyd*, pa. pple. of KITHE *v.* misunderstood by Palsgrave, and misused by Spenser.] *trans.* To know.

1530 PALSGR. 598/2, I kydde (Lydgate) I knowe..This terme is nat yet in use. **1579** SPENSER *Sheph. Cal.* Dec. 92, 93 Ah! unwise and witlesse Colin Cloute, That kydst the hidden kinds of many a wede, Yet kydst not ene to cure thy sore hart-roote. [Gloss: *kidst*, knowest.]

kydcote, -cott(e, kyddier, -yer, obs. forms of KIDCOT, KIDDIER.

kydell, kydle, kydenere, -eyre, obs. forms of KIDDLE, KIDNEY.

kydgel, -ell, obs. form of CUDGEL.

kydling, obs. form of KIDLING.

kydne, -neer, -ner(e, -ney, obs. forms of KIDNEY.

kydy: cf. KID *sb.*^{4} 3.

1486 in *Nottingham Rec.* III. 266 Item paid for a spyld to þe kydy þat þe fisshe was in..ij*d.*

kye (kaɪ). *Naut. slang.* [Origin unknown; but cf. E.D.D. *kyish* dirty.] **1.** (See quots.)

1929 F. C. BOWEN *Sea Slang* 80 A kye. A rating who is mean with his money. **1946** J. IRVING *Royal Navalese* 105 *Kye*, a mean, unworthy sort of fellow.

2. Cocoa or chocolate.

1943 HUNT & PRINGLE *Service Slang* 42 *Kie*, seaman's slang for cocoa. **1943** BAKER *Dict. Austral. Slang* (ed. 3) 46 *Kye*, chocolate. (R.A.N. slang.) **1962** GRANVILLE *Dict. Sailor's Slang* 68/2 *Kye*, ship's cocoa which used to be issued in slabs, already sweetened, cut as needed and dissolved in boiling water to the desired consistency. The origin of the word is dialectal, from the adjective *kyish*, muddy-looking, brown. **1968** *Times* 17 Apr. 6/6 Kye, as the service names drinking chocolate, is to end.

kye, kyen, obs. and dial. pl. of COW.

kyebosh, variant of KIBOSH *sb.*

kyestein (kɪ'ɛstiːɪn). *Chem.* Also **kystein, kiestein(e, kiestin(e, kyesteine.** [ad. F. *kiestéine*, the term invented by Nauche (*Journ. de Chimie Médicale*, 2nd Ser. V. 64, 1839), loosely f. Gr. κύησ-ις conception, app. after *protéine* and the like. When spelt as in Fr., often pronounced ('kiːstɪn, -aɪn); but more usually written *ky-* after Gr. κυ-. With more accurate knowledge of the nature of the thing, the name is now little used.] A whitish substance occasionally found as a cloud in or pellicle upon urine; erroneously supposed by Nauche to be diagnostic of pregnancy.

1846 G. E. DAY tr. *Simon's Anim. Chem.* II. 329 Nauche regards kystein as an indubitable sign of pregnancy. **1847-9** TODD *Cycl. Anat.* IV. 461/1 During pregnancy, a substance, kiestein..is eliminated by the urine. **1888** *Syd. Soc. Lex.*, *Kyestein*..is now known to be chiefly composed of ammoniaco-magnesian phosphates, with fat-particles, vibrios, and bacteria, and to be found in putrefying urine other than that of a pregnant woman. It is probably produced by the decomposition of the urea in contact with mucus.

kyeth, kyith, var. KITHE *v.*, to make known.

kyght, kyghth, obs. forms of KITE, KITH.

kyjik, variant of CAIQUE.

1859 *All Year Round* No. 36. 219 To observe the keen swift kyjiks poise and skim over the Bosphorus.

kyke, kyld(e, kylderken, -kin, -kyn, obs. ff. KEEK, KILL *v.*, KILDERKIN.

kyle^{1} (kaɪl). Now *dial.* Also 4-5 **kylle**, 5 **kile**, 7 **keyll.** [a. ON. *kýli* boil, abscess; prob. related to *kúla* ball, knob.] A sore, ulcer, boil.

(Wrongly rendered by Levins, through some confusion.)

1340 HAMPOLE *Pr. Consc.* 2995 Som, for envy, sal haf in þair lyms, Als kylles and felouns and apostyms. **14..** *Rel. Ant.* I. 53 A gude oyntment for kyles, woundes [etc.]. **14..** *MS. Cantab.* Ff. v. 48 lf. 85 (Halliw.) Thai fare as dos a rotyn kile, That rotys and warkys sore. **1483** *Cath. Angl.* 202/2 A Kyle, *vlcus, vlcerosus.* **1570** LEVINS *Manip.* 130 A Kyle, *bilis.* **1579** LANGHAM *Gard. Health* (1633) 314 To breake a botch, byle, or keyll, seethe the roots in water. **1876** *Whitby Gloss.*, *Kyles*, boils on the flesh.

kyle^{2} (kaɪl). *Sc.* [a. Gael. *caol* (kɔːl), gen. *caoil* (kɔː(j)l) 'narrow strait or sound', sb. to *caol* narrow.] A narrow channel between two islands, or an island and the mainland (in the west of Scotland); a sound, a strait.

1549 D. MONRO in P. H. Brown *Scot. bef.* 1700 (1893) 247 Ane right dangerous kyle or stream. **1703** MARTIN *West. Isl.* 205 The Horses and Cows..swim to the Main Land [from Skye] over one of the Ferries or Sounds called Kyles. **1872** BLACKIE *Lays Highl.* 61 Outmost Lewis, Haco, and Skye, with winding kyles. **1900** MACKENZIE *Guide Inverness* 81 The narrow kyle between Rona and Raasay. *Mod.* The steamer passes through the Kyles of Bute to the Crinan Canal.

kyle^{3} (kaɪl). *dial. rare.* [= LG. *kîl*, G. *keil* (MHG. *kîl*), Da. *kile*, Sw. *kil* 'wedge': the precise source is not clear.] A small iron wedge used to fasten the head of a pick, hammer, etc., on the shaft.

1747 HOOSON *Miner's Dict.* E j b, When the Miner haums a Pick..and when he has put in his hard Wood-Wedges and Iron Kyles [etc.]. **1893** *Northumbld. Gloss.*, *Kyle*, a wedge. 'Is thor a kyle i' this mell, Bob?'

kyler, obs. f. KEELER^{2}.

kyles, var. KAYLES, the game.

kylevine, var. of KEELIVINE.

‖**kylie** ('kaɪlɪ). *West Austral.* Also **koilee, kiley.** [Native name.] A boomerang.

1839 N. OGLE *Col. W. Australia* 57 (Morris) In every part of this great continent they have the koilee, or boomerang. **1846** J. L. STOKES *Discov. Australia* I. iv. 72 One of them had a kiley or boomerang. **1885** LADY BARKER *Lett. to Guy* 177 (Morris) The kylie (what is called the boomerang in other

parts of Australia), a curiously curved and flat stick, about a foot long and two or three inches wide.

‖**kylin** ('ki:ˌlɪn). Also **kilin**. [ad. Chinese *ch'i-lin* (Wade), f. *ch'i* male + *lin* female.] A fabulous animal of composite form, commonly figured on Chinese and Japanese pottery.

'According to the *Erh Ya*, it has the body of a deer, the tail of an ox, and a single horn, from which it is often called the *Chinese Unicorn*' (Mayers' *Chinese Reader's Man.*, Shanghai, 1874, 127).

1857 MARRYATT *Pottery & Porcel.* (ed. 2) 217 Dragons, kylins, and all manner of hideous and strange monsters. **1894** *Times* 26 Jan. 11/3 Sale of General Gordon's Chinese objects of art... A vase and cover, of rock crystal, with pierced dragon handles, kylin on the cover.. A small cup, the handle carved as a kylin. **1898** *Daily News* 14 Dec. 8/4 A piece of old Satsuma, representing a kylin playing with a ball and cord.

kylindrite, var. CYLINDRITE.

kylix. Pl. kylikes, kylixes. Variant of CYLIX.

1892 *Times* 7 Feb. 20/1 An Athenian kylix by Sotades. *Ibid.*, These three beautiful kylixes have the ground a pale cream-colour. **1905** H. B. WALTERS *Hist. Anc. Pott.* I. 417 The kylikes of the Epictetan cycle. **1922** *Encycl. Brit.* XXX. 183/2 An Attic *kylix* signed by Pamphaios. **1935** *Antiquity* IX. 508 In the dromoi many kylix fragments were found. **1948** A. LANE *Greek Pott.* iv. 31 About the middle of the sixth century, the pedestal-cup (kylix) became common in East Greece. **1960** [see CYATHUS].

kyll(e, kylne, obs. ff. KILL *v.*, KILN *sb.*

kyloe ('kaɪlə). *Sc.* Also **kylie**. [Origin uncertain. ? Related to *kyle*².] One of a small breed of cattle with long horns reared in the Highlands and Western Islands of Scotland.

1811 AITON *Agric. Ayr.* xiv. 414 Some have imagined that Kyloes, the name given to the Cattle of Argyleshire, is derived from Kyle. **1814** SCOTT *Wav.* xi, Killancureit talked ..of..dinmonts, and stots, and runts, and kyloes. **1861** SMILES *Engineers* II. VIII. viii. 380 Making little or no export from the country beyond the few lean kyloes, which paid the rent. **1882** *Ordnance Gaz. Scot.* I. 71 The cattle are chiefly Kyloes or West Highlanders, a small shaggy race.

kylpe, kylt(e, obs. ff. KILP, KILT.

kylt, obs. pa. pple. of KILL *v.*

‖**kymation** (kaɪ'mætɪən). [ad. Gr. κυμάτιον, dim. of κῦμα wave, billow, CYMA.] = CYMATIUM.

1883 W. G. COLLINGWOOD *Philos. Ornament* iii. 51 Wave-spiral or kymation. *Ibid.* iv. 85 The 'kymation', or rippling line of waves.

kymbe, kyme, obs. ff. KEMB *v.*, KIME.

kymelyn, kymelen, kymnel(l(e, etc.: see KIMNEL.

kymmond, obs. f. CUMMING *Sc.*, brewer's vessel.

kymogram ('kaɪməʊgræm). [f. KYMO(GRAPH + -GRAM.] A recording made with a kymograph (sense 1 or 2). **a.** *Radiology.* (Corresponding to KYMOGRAPH 2.) Also (and orig.) called a ROENTGENKYMOGRAM.

1923 *Proc. R. Soc. Med.* XVI. (Electro-Therapeutics Section) 21 For taking the kymogram a Polyphos universal inductor with a rapid switch was used. **1941** *Jrnl. Amer. Med. Assoc.* 11 Jan. 117/1 Such a paradoxical movement [of the heart] may be recorded in some instances by kymogram, but this affords help only as a permanent record of what can be seen much more satisfactorily by the fluoroscope. **1959** BOONE & NOBLE in A. A. Luisada *Cardiol.* II. IV. viii. 205/1 Roentgen kymography has not become thoroughly established as a mandatory procedure in the examination of the heart. It seems that this is due to the analytical difficulties inherent in the fuzziness, smallness, and brevity of the recorded waves to be examined on the roentgen kymogram,..and the difficulties of simultaneously recording, on the kymogram, curves of other cardiac events.

b. (Corresponding to KYMOGRAPH 1) *Esp.* in *Phonetics*, a recording of pressure variations produced during articulation.

1934 *Amer. Speech* IX. 229/1 Kymograms are obtained from discs by means of an electromagnetic inscriber. **1950** [see CENTISECOND]. **1964** N. C. SCOTT in D. Abercrombie et al. *Daniel Jones* 434 Kymograms for such a word..show wave-forms between the sections for the stops on the mouth tracings.

kymograph ('kaɪməʊgrɑːf, -æ-). [f. Gr. κῦμο-, combining form of κῦμα wave + -GRAPH; in sense 1, ad. G. *kymographion*, the name given by A. W. Volkmann (in *Die Hämodynamik* (1850) iv. 120) to the instrument invented by K. F. W. Ludwig.] **1.** An instrument for graphically recording variations of pressure of a fluid, esp. of blood in the vessels of a living animal; a recording manometer; also called **kymographion**. Later used more widely; the instrument consists of a cylinder rotated by a clockwork or electric motor, together with a stylus designed to trace on a roll of paper wrapped around the cylinder a curve representing pressure variations or motion communicated to the stylus.

1867 C. A. HARRIS *Dict. Med. Terminol.* (ed. 3), *Kymographion*, an instrument which shows the relation between the pulse-wave and the undulations produced by respiration. **1872** *Lancet* I. 675 Fick's spring manometer or spring kymograph..are excellent instruments for registering the pulse-motions. **1897** *Allbutt's Syst. Med.* II. 934 The kymograph registered a very rapid..fall of the arterial pressure. **1901** E. B. TITCHENER *Exper. Psychol.* I. I. viii. 112 *O* fixates the outermost grey ring of the disc... As the grey fades or drops out of view, he presses the bulb... As (or when) the grey returns, he relaxes the pressure. The curve of fluctuation is thus written, above the time line, upon the smoked paper of the kymograph. **1918** A. L. F. SNELL *Pause* 1 The results in this investigation are based upon speech records made with an apparatus such as is used in experimental phonetics... The kymograph used in all the work was the complete Zimmerman pattern, with Herring slide and writing plane. **1928** *Science* 20 July 62/1 When such phenomena as the speed of a nerve impulse or reaction time are to be recorded, a very fast kymograph drum is an absolute necessity. **1938** *Trans. Philol. Soc.* 76 The apparatus used is the physiological kymograph, fitted with three appropriate Marey tambours. The upper bold tracing is that of jaw movement; the second supplies a record of sound obtained..; the third the time-marking inscribed by a tuning-fork. **1949** B. J. UNDERWOOD *Exper. Psychol.* vi. 163 These markers write on a kymograph, a slowly rotating drum covered with waxed or smoked paper. The rat.. bounces the cage on the tambours, thus changing the air pressure which in turn activates the markers which record the animal's activity. **1959** E. PULGRAM *Introd. Spectogr. of Speech* vi. 52 The kymograph produces registrations representing variations in the total amount of pressure during articulation. **1970** REESE & LIPSITT *Exper. Child Psychol.* iii. 83 Head-turning responses were recorded by means of a head harness mechanically attached to a kymograph.

2. *Radiology.* An apparatus for recording the movement of the heart or other internal organs by moving an X-ray plate or film past one or more slits in a screen placed between it and the subject, so that movement of the organ in a direction parallel to a slit is recorded as a curve separating differently exposed portions of the radiograph; = ROENTGENKYMOGRAPH.

1936 P. KERLEY *Rec. Adv. Radiol.* (ed. 2) iv. 69 In its simplest form the X ray kymograph consists of a metal grid with a row of transverse slits of equal width and equidistant from each other. **1938** *Q. Jrnl. Med.* XXXI. 463 In cardiac aneurysm..a paradoxical pulsation—expansion of the sac during ventricular systole—has been recorded by kymograph. **1959** P. CIGNOLINI in A. A. Luisada *Cardiol.* II. IV. viii. 199/1 The RK's of Gott and Rosenthal were recorded through a single slit. Later, Crane (1916) used a kymograph with two overlapping slits.

Hence **kymo'graphic** *a.*, pertaining to or made with a kymograph; hence **kymo'graphically** *adv.*, by means of a kymograph.

1885 *Med. Times* 26 Dec. 888 The new method of writing kymographic curves. **1888** *Encycl. Brit.* XXIV. 106/2 Mercurial kymographic tracing from carotid of a dog. **1930** J. R. FIRTH *Speech* ii. 16 Kymographic speech tracings are invaluable in the study of the length and pitch of vowels.. and other characteristic elements of speech. **1936** P. KERLEY *Rec. Adv. Radiol.* (ed. 2) iv. 70 The kymographic appearance of the right border of the heart is more complicated than that of the left border. **1942** *Biol. Abstr.* XVI. 496/1 The temp. and the specific gravity of the inner soln. were kymographically recorded. **1948** J. W. McLAREN *Mod. Trends Diagn. Radiol.* xiv. 183 Kymographic exposures require much higher loading on an x-ray tube than does ordinary radiography. *Ibid.* 190 Systolic contraction of the ventricle..recorded kymographically. **1963** *Amer. Speech* XXXVIII. 72 Considerable sampling of Hungarian unstressed vowels recorded in natural situations submitted to kymographic analysis. **1964** L. KAISER in D. Abercrombie et al. *Daniel Jones* 106 Rousselot..showed kymographically the large differences in the activity of articulation muscles in stressed and unstressed syllables.

kymography (kaɪ'mɒgrəfɪ). [f. KYMOGRAPH: see -GRAPHY.] The technique or process of using a kymograph (in either sense). (In *Radiology* also known by its orig. name of ROENTGENKYMOGRAPHY.)

1930 J. R. FIRTH *Speech* iii. 24 Phonetic kymography measures phone length to within 0·005 of a second. **1933** H. A. JARRE in O. Glasser *Sci. of Radiol.* xi. 202 We should record here..a publication by T. Gött and J. Rosenthal.. concerning the original method of 'kymography'... It probably will not become very popular anywhere, as it is limited in its application and its evaluation is quite tedious. **1938** *Q. Jrnl. Med.* XXXI. 463 Kymography has been applied to the study of the localized cardiac infarct. **1957** *Times Lit. Suppl.* 8 Nov. 677/1 Some of the papers..are in the first instance 'School' material, being technical in an equipmental, laboratory sort of way like those on Word-palatograms and on Palatology and Kymography. **1959** P. CIGNOLINI in A. A. Luisada *Cardiol.* II. IV. viii. 201/2 In Stumpf's method of kymography, there is regular movement of the film or of the grid in the space between two slits (12 mm.).

Kymric, var. of CYMRIC. Hence '**Kymricize** *v. trans.*, to make Kymric.

1890 *Spectator* 31 May 749 Welsh Disestablishment and Kymric autonomy. **1888** RHYS *Hibbert Lect.* 273 A late Kymricizing of the Latin *Segontium* has yielded a much less correct Welsh form *Seiont*.

kyn, obs. f. KIN; obs. form of *kine*, pl. of COW.

kynanthropy, var. CYNANTHROPY. Hence **kynan'thropic** *a.*, of or pertaining to kynanthropy.

1864 PUSEY *Lect. Daniel* vii. 426 Paulus of Aegina omits only the kynanthropy. *Ibid.*, They who are seized by the kynanthropic or lycanthropic disease, go forth by night imitating in all things wolves or dogs.

kynde, obs. f. KIND; pa. pple. of KEN *v.*²

kynderkyn, kyner-, obs. var. KILDERKIN.

kyne, obs. form of *kine*, pl. of COW.

kyng, kyning, obs. forms of KING.

kynny: see KINLIN *Obs.*

kyntal, kynterkyn, obs. ff. QUINTAL, KILDERKIN.

kynurenic (kɪ-, kaɪnjʊ'rɛnɪk), *a. Biochem.* Also †cyn-. [tr. G. *kynuren-säure* kynurenic acid (J. Liebig 1853, in *Ann. d. Chem.* LXXXVI. 125), f. Gr. κυν-, κύων dog + *-uren-*, irreg. f. οὖρον URINE *sb.*¹: see -IC 1.] ***kynurenic acid***: a crystalline carboxylic acid, $C_{10}H_7NO_3$, that results from the metabolism of tryptophan and is excreted in the urine of man and various animals; 4-hydroxyquinoline-2-carboxylic acid.

1872 *Jrnl. Chem. Soc.* XXV. 1028 When heated by 265° kynurenic acid evolves pure carbon dioxide and melts to a brown liquid. **1889** ROSCOE & SCHORLEMMER *Treat. Chem.* III. v. 226 When..cynurenic acid is heated with zinc dust in a current of hydrogen, it is reduced to quinoline. **1946** W. R. FEARON *Introd. Biochem.* (ed. 3) xvii. 351 Surplus dietary tryptophane is excreted in the urine as kynurenine (in rabbits), and as kynurenic acid (in dogs, rats, foxes and wolves). **1971** *Pediatrics* XLVII. 47/1 This study measured urinary excretion of kynurenic acid..and xanthurenic acid .., two tryptophan metabolites via the kynurenine pathway, in 26 hospitalized children.

kynurenine (kɪ-, kaɪnjʊ'rɛniːn). *Biochem.* [ad. G. *kynurenin* (Kotake & Iwao 1931, in *Zeitschr. f. physiol. Chem.* CXCV. 140), f. *kynuren-säure*, **kynurenic acid*: see -INE⁵.] A crystalline amino-acid, $H_2N{\cdot}C_6H_4{\cdot}COCH_2CH(NH_2)COOH$, that results from the metabolism of tryptophan and is a precursor of kynurenic acid in man and various animals; β-o-aminobenzoylalanine.

1931 *Chem. Abstr.* XXV. 2444 When tryptophan is injected subcutaneously into rabbits whose metabolism has been lowered by a regime of polished rice, a product intermediate between tryptophan and kynurenic acid is excreted in the urine. The name *kynurenine* is proposed for this substance. **1938** H. GILMAN *Orig. Chem.* II. 943 An amino acid, kynurenine, in which the pyrrole ring of tryptophan has ruptured. **1946, 1971** [see KYNURENIC *a.*]. **1972** *Chem. Abstr.* LXXVII. 16364 L-Kynurenine, colorless needles from EtOH, m. 194°, was obtained in a yield of 120 mg from 30 g of rat hair by extn. with hot water and sepn. on a Sephadex column.

kyogen ('kjəʊgɛn). Also **kiogen, kiyogen, kyōgen**. [Jap.] In the Noh theatre of Japan, a comic interlude presented between performances of Noh plays.

1871 A. B. MITFORD *Tales Old Japan* I. 164 The classical severity of the Nô is relieved by the introduction between the pieces of light farces called Kiyôgen. **1899** W. G. ASTON *Hist. Jap Lit.* V. iii. 213 The Kiōgen (madwords) are to the Nō what farce is to the regular drama. They are performed on the same stage in the intervals between the more serious pieces. **1911** *Encycl. Brit.* XV. 170 The Kyōgen needs no elaborate description; it is pure farce, never immodest or vulgar. **1951** *Oxf. Compan. Theatre* 411/2 The language of the *kyōgen* or comic interludes which accompany their performance is the vernacular of the second half of the sixteenth century. **1958** *Spectator* 3 Jan. 24/3 The typical *No* juxtaposition of bleak tragedy and witty comedy (which in the traditional *No* is split into separate but consecutively performed plays—the *No* play proper followed by the *kyogen*). **1964** [see KATSURAMONO]. **1970** *Daily Tel.* 16 May 9/4 The two No pieces were separated by a kyogen (farce) about a melon thief, acted and danced with delightful joviality. **1973** *Times* 5 June 8/8 Following the usual custom, the two main pieces are sandwiched round a kyogen farce; this one about two lords who unload their swords on to a passer-by who then puts them through some undignified games before making off with their weapons and their clothes.

kyoodle (kaɪ'uːd(ə)l), *v. U.S. dial.* and *colloq.* [Imit.] *intr.* To make a loud noise; to bark, to yap. So **ky'oodling** *vbl. sb.*

1922 S. LEWIS *Babbitt* vii. 99 Now I guess the folks in this man's town will quit listening to all this kyoodling from behind the fence. **1935** J. STEINBECK *Tortilla Flat* xv. 263 The dogs..sought out a rabbit and went kyoodling after it.

kyp, kyp-: see KIP, KIP-.

kyped (kaɪpt), *ppl. a. Sc.* [f. KIP *sb.*² + -ED².] = KIPPER *sb.* and *a.* B 1.

1948 *Scots Mag.* Oct. 44 Presently he was lifting the net under a mate for his catch, a deep-bodied kyped male to match his female [see-trout]. **1963** *Times* 9 Mar. 11/5 A spring salmon, long before it grows black and ugly and kyped in the autumn of its fortunes.

kypho-. Another form of CYPHO-, from Gr. κῦφο-ς crooked. Hence **kyphosis, -otic** = CYPHOSIS, -OTIC. Also ˌ**kyphoscoli'osis** (cy-), a

combination of kyphosis and scoliosis; backward and lateral curvature of the spine. Hence ˌkyphoscoli'otic *a.*

1882 *Syd. Soc. Lex.*, *Cyphoscoliosis.* **1898** *Allbutt's Syst. Med.* V. 164 Deformity of the chest—as the result of kyphoscoliosis. **1900** *Brit. Med. Jrnl.* No. 2040. 278 The pelvis was extremely kyphoscoliotic.

† kyr, *v. Obs. rare.* [Cf. Ger. *kehren,* Du. *keeren* to turn (used in same way).] *trans.* To turn.

1448 *Paston Lett.* (1901) IV. 19 As Davy shuld a kyrt the horse, he slenkyd behynd and toke his master on the hepe suyche a stroke that . . brake his hepe.

kyrchef(e, -cheffe, obs. forms of KERCHIEF.

† kyre, var. *kaire,* CAIR *v. Obs.,* to go, proceed.

1515 *Scot. Field* 240 in *Chetham Misc.* (1856) II, Then the mightie lord . . kyred to his king with carefull tithindes.

kyrf(e, obs. form of KERF, cut.

‖ Kyrie ('kaɪrɪ, 'kaɪriː, 'kɪərɪeɪ). Also 6 kirie. [Short for *Kyrie eleison:* see next.]

1. = next, 1. **b.** *esp.* A musical setting of the Kyrie eleison in the Ordinary of the Mass, or of the Response to each of the Commandments in the Anglican Communion Service.

1519 *Churchw. Acc. St. Giles Reading* 6 A Pryk-song boke . . wherin is conteyned iiii masses, iij kyries, iij allohuies and ij exultands. **1597** MORLEY *Introd. Mus.* 153, I remember a peece of composition of four parts of maister Tauernor in one of his kiries. **16 . .** *MS. Music Bk. at Durh. Cath.,* Mr. Brimley his kerrie to Mr. Sheperd's Creede. **1657** SPARROW *Bk. Com. Prayer* (1664) 241 Then follow the Commandments, with a Kyrie, or *Lord have mercy upon us,* after every one of them. **1845** E. HOLMES *Mozart* 41 His first essay in Church Music,—the Kyrie of a mass for four voices and four stringed instruments. **1866** J. H. BLUNT *Annot. Bk. Com. Prayer* 167 The Kyrie thus said appears to represent the ancient Litany element of the Eucharistic Office.

† 2. = next, 2. *Obs.*

15 . . *Jack Jugler* in Grosart *Two Enterludes* (1873) 63 He shoulde haue suche a kyrie, ere he went to bed, As he neuer had before in all his lyfe. **1582** STANYHURST *Æneid* 1. (Arb.) 21 This kyrye sad solfing, thee northern bluster aproching Thee sayls tears tag rag, to the sky thee waues vphoysing.

‖ Kyrie eleison, eleëson ('kɪərɪeɪ ɪ'leɪɪsɒn). Also 4–6 kyrieleyson, 6 Kyrie-eleyson, Kirie-eleeson, 7 (Kerry-Elison). [The Greek words Κύριε ἐλέησον 'Lord, have mercy', occurring in the Gr. text of *Ps.* cxxii. 3, *Matt.* xv. 22, xvii. 15, etc. The Gr. words were written in L. *kyrie* (med.L. also *kirie*), and (by itacism of η) *eleison.* As in other Christian words (e.g. Maria, Sophia, Helena, Jacobus, etc.), the Gr. accent was retained, giving *e'leïson,* later *e'lēïson,* or *e'leïson.* Since the Renascence, some have represented the Gr. more literally and quantitatively by *ele'ēson.* Hence many varieties of pronunciation in Eng., some retaining the med.L. (which is also mod.Gr.) given above, some following the school pronunciation of ancient Gr. or L., or with various Eng. modifications of the vowels, as ('kɪrɪeɪ, 'kaɪrɪː, 'kaɪrɪ, ɪ'liːɪsɒn, ɛlɪ'iːsɒn, ɛlɪ'aɪsɒn, ɪ'laɪsɒn).]

1. *Eccl.* The words of a short petition used in various offices of the Eastern and Roman Churches, esp. at the beginning of the Mass; represented in the Anglican service by the words, 'Lord, have mercy upon us', etc., in the Response to each Commandment in the Communion Service. **b.** A musical setting of these words, esp. as the first movement of a Mass.

[*a* **1225** *Ancr. R.* 30 Hwose wule, mei siggen þesne psalm, 'Ad te levavi' biuoren þe Paternostres, & seoþen 'Kirieleison, Christeleison, Kirieleison'. *Ibid.* 22. *Ibid.* 30 Her also siggeð 'De Profundis' biuore þe Paternoster. Kiriel. Christel. Kiriel. *Ibid.* 36 Beateð on ower breoste . . & siggeð . . Kiriel. Christel. Kiriel.] **13 . .** *St. Alexius* 422 in Horstm. *Altengl. Leg.* (1881) 183 þe folk on knees fell . . And kyrieleyson thries þai sange. **? 14 . .** in *Q. Eliz. Acad.* (1879) 34 Att every Kyrie lyson, one to say with an high voice for yᵉ sowle A Pater noster. **1551** BP. HOOPER *Later Writ.* (Parker Soc. 1852) 145 They were

wont to sit when they said or sang the psalms, kneel at Kyrie-eleyson, and stand up at Magnificat. **1563** PILKINGTON *Confut.* C iv b, Platina . . affirmes, that Pope Sixtus appoynted the Sanctus to be songe, Gregory the Kirie-eleeson. **1678** CUDWORTH *Intell. Syst.* II. iv. §27. 454 That very Form of Prayer . . *Kyrie Eleeson, Lord have mercy upon us,* was anciently part of the Pagans Litany to the Supreme God. **1834** BECKFORD *Italy* II. xiv. 71, I have had pretty nearly my fill of motets, and Kyrie eleisons. **1885** *Catholic Dict.* (ed. 3) s.v., The Second Council of Vaison, . . which met in 529, ordered the Kyrie Eleison to be said at Mass and other services.

† 2. *transf.* A complaint; a scolding. *Obs.*

1528 TINDALE *Obed. Chr. Man* 130 b, He gave me a Kyrieleyson. **1630** J. TAYLOR (Water P.) *Navy Land Ships* Wks. I v b/1, I would . . haue sung him a Kerry-Elison, that should haue made him beene glad to haue promist me a brace of Bucks more, to haue stop'd my mouth withall.

‖ kyrielle (kɪrɪ'ɛl). Also 3 kyriel, 7 kiriele. [a. F. *kyrielle,* OF. (13th c.) *kyriele;* in med.L. *kiriel,* pl. *kyrieles* (Du Cange); so MHG. *kiriel;* shortened from *kyrie eleison:* see prec.]

1. A long rigmarole.

1653 URQUHART *Rabelais* I. xxi, With him he mumbled all his Kiriele and dunsical breborions [*orig.* avecques icelluy marmonnoit toutes ces Kyrielles].

2. A kind of French verse divided into little equal couplets and ending with the same word which serves for the refrain.

1887 *Sat. Rev.* 3 Dec. 770/1 Among the verse-forms . . . The kyrielle, of which we have three specimens, is not a form at all, and ought to have been discarded.

kyrine ('kaɪrɪn). *Biochem.* [a. G. *kyrin* (M. Siegfried 1902, in *Ber. ü. d. Verh. d. k. Sächs. Ges. d. Wissensch. zu Leipzig* (*Math.-phys. Kl.*) LV. 70) f. Gr. κῦρ-ος authority, validity: see -INE⁵.] Any of various basic substances or mixtures obtained by partial hydrolysis of proteins and thought at one time to be the kernel or nucleus of the proteins from which they were derived; also used with prefix indicating the protein, as *glutokyrine.*

1903 *Jrnl. Chem. Soc.* LXXXIV. 1. 587 The protamines of fish spermatozoa are possibly formed by the polymerisation or condensation of kyrine or similar decomposition products of the proteids. **1928** *Physiol. Rev.* VIII. 408 The close resemb[l]ance of these preparations to each other in properties and composition led him [*sc.* Siegfried] to suggest the generic name kyrine for them with the implication that they were the kernel, or nucleus, of the molecular structure of the proteins from which they were derived. This view was founded upon the resistance to hydrolysis of the kyrines under the conditions employed in their preparation. **1953** *Chem. Abstr.* XLVII. 12474 Gelatin was . . hydrolyzed with acid by Grassman's method . . to kyrine sulfate.

kyriolexy ('kaɪrɪəʊˌlɛksɪ). *rare⁻⁰.* [ad. Gr. κυριολεξία, f. κύριος authoritative, authorized, proper + -λεξια speaking (cf. λέξις speech, word).] The use of literal expressions.

1886 in *Cassell's Encycl. Dict.*

kyriologic, variant of CYRIOLOGIC.

Kyrle (kɜːl). The name of John *Kyrle* (1637–1724), English philanthropist, used *attrib.* in *Kyrle Society,* the title of a charitable society concerned with horticulture founded in 1877.

1877 O. HILL *Our Common Land* vi. 142 My sister has founded a society, called, after the Man of Ross, the Kyrle Society, which has for its object to bring beauty into the haunts of the poor. **1888** G. B. SHAW *Let.* 14 Sept. (1965) 195 The books distributed . . by the Kyrle Society. **1913** C. E. MAURICE *Life Octavia Hill* vii. 317 Octavia . . took an active share in the work of the Commons Preservation Society; but she felt that the Kyrle Society had a different function. **1964** D. OWEN *Eng. Philanthropy* III. xvii. 496 The Kyrle Society, of which Octavia Hill's sister Miranda was the principal architect.

kyrlewe, obs. form of CURLEW.

kyrnaill, -ale, -el, etc., obs. forms of KERNEL.

kyrne, obs. form of CHURN.

kyrosite ('kaɪrəsaɪt). *Min.* [ad. Ger. *kyrosit* (Breithaupt, 1843), f. Gr. κύρωσις confirmation,

because its specific character was thought to be confirmed: see -ITE.] A variety of marcasite, containing a small amount of arsenic. (Chester *Names of Minerals,* 1896.)

kyrre, obs. f. QUARRY, beast killed in hunting, etc.

kyrsede, kyrsett(e, obs. ff. CRESSET: see KIRSET².

kyrspe, obs. f. CRISP.

kyrvour, kyrmyry: see KIRVE *v.,* KERIMERY.

kys, kyse, kysse, obs. forms of KISS.

kyst, kyste, obs. pa. t. of CAST *v.,* KISS *v.;* obs. forms of KIST.

kyt, obs. inflexion of CUT *v.;* obs. f. KITE.

kyte (kaɪt). *Sc.* and *north. dial.* Also 7 kyt, 7–9 kite. [Etymology uncertain. Cf. early mod.Du. (Kilian) *kijte, kiete* (mod.W. Flemish *kijte, kiet*), var. of MDu. *cuyte, kuite* a fleshy part of the body, esp. the thigh (Du. *kuit* calf of the leg), = MLG. *kût,* fleshy part, entrails (Lübben). The suggestion of Jamieson, repeated by later dicts., that *kyte* represents OE. *cwið,* ON. *kvið* belly, is inadmissible.] The belly, stomach, paunch.

c **1540** LYNDESAY *Kitteis Confessioun* 140 Thocht Codrus kyte suld cleue and birst. *a* **1585** POLWART *Flyting w. Montgomerie* 754 Misly kyt! **1674** RAY *N.C. Words* 27 A Kite; A Belly, *Cumb.* **1787** BURNS *To a Haggis* iv, Till a' their weel-swall'd kytes belyve Are bent like drums. **1820** SCOTT *Monast.* xxxiii, To dress dainties at dinner-time for his ain kyte. **1855** ROBINSON *Whitby Gloss., Kite,* stomach. **1895** CROCKETT *Men of Moss Hags* xxxvi. 259 His horse . . is now filling his kyte in my stable, as his master is eke doing in hall.

kyte, obs. form of KITE, the bird, etc.

kyth, kyþ, etc., obs. forms of KITH, KITHE.

kythe, another spelling of KITHE *v.,* often used.

kytill, kytlyn, obs. ff. KITTLE, KITLING.

kyton, kytton, obs. forms of KITTEN.

kytt(e, obs. inf., pa. t., and pa. pple. of CUT *v.*

kyttyl, kytylle, etc., obs. forms of KITTLE.

kytylyng, obs. form of KITLING.

‖ kyu (kjuː). [Jap.] In Judo or Karate, the Japanese name for the grade given to the less proficient; such a pupil.

The sixth *kyu* is the lowest grade.

1937 J. KANO *Judo* (*Jujutsu*) iii. 38 The course of Jūdō is divided into two grades or ranks called 'Dan' and 'Kyū'. In the Dan grades, the numbers increase to indicate the higher grade, but in the Kyū grades it is different: thus the first Kyū grade follows the first Dan grade. **1941** M. FELDENKRAIS *Judo* 166 There are two different ranks: Dan and Kyu. A white belt is worn by beginners, corresponding to the sixth kyu. **1954** [see DAN³]. **1960** *Oxf. Mail* 10 Mar. 8/2 Roger Young (Jesus), an American and 3rd kyu (learner grade), beat the Cambridge captain, . . a . . 1st dan (teacher grade) by two and a half points to nil. **1972** *Austin Morris Express* (Oxford) July 8/2 Under the skilful guidance of Maurice King, who is a 2nd Kyu in karate.

kyuer(e, kyver, obs. ff. COVER *v.*¹ and *sb.*¹

kyul, -e, var. CYULE: cf. CHIULE, KEEL *sb.*² 2.

1670 MILTON *Hist. Eng.* Wks. (1847) 507/1 Three long gallies, or kyules.

kyuse, variant of CAYUSE.

† kyvar-knaue *a., nonce-wd.* = Cover-knave, that covers a knave.

1563 STOWE in *Pol., Rel., & L. Poems* Pref. 15 *note,* His [a criminous parson's] gown, and his (kyvar-knaue) hatt, borne after him.

kyx, obs. form of KEX, a dry hollow stalk.

Kyzyl, var. KIZIL *a.* and *sb.*

L

L (ɛl), the twelfth letter of the modern and the eleventh of the ancient Roman alphabet, represents historically the Gr. *lambda* and ultimately the Semitic *lamed*. The earliest known Semitic forms of the character are ℓ and ᒪ; both these occur in early Greek inscriptions; the latter was adopted from the Greek into the Latin alphabet, and is the ancestor of the modern Roman forms, but in Greece itself was superseded by the inverted form ᒥ, which eventually became Λ.

The sound normally expressed by the letter is the 'point-side' consonant, i.e. a sound produced by the emission of breath at the sides, or one side, of the oral passage when it is partially closed by contact of the 'point' of the tongue with the gums or palate.

In phonetic treatises *l* is used as a general name for consonants produced by lateral emission of breath, whether the stoppage is produced (as above) by the 'point', or by some other part of the tongue; thus we speak of a 'guttural *l*' and a 'palatal *l*' as occurring in various foreign languages.

The 'point-side' consonant admits of considerable diversity in mode of articulation and consequently in acoustic quality. The Eng. *l* differs from that of Fr. and Ger. in being uttered with the 'front' of the tongue more concave; hence its sound is 'duller' or 'thicker'. Its precise place of articulation varies according to the nature of the adjacent sounds. In Eng. it is normally voiced; an unvoiced *l* occurring only as a 'glide' connecting the voiced *l* with a preceding or following unvoiced consonant. Like *r* and the nasals, *l* may be used as a sonant or vowel (in the phonetic notation of this Dictionary indicated by ((ə)l)); but this occurs only in unstressed syllables, as in *little* ('lɪt(ə)l), *buckled* ('bʌk(ə)ld).

The mod. Eng. *l* represents not only the OE. *l*, but the OE. *hl* (early ME. *lh*) and *wl*.

In certain combinations an original *l* has regularly become silent, after having modified the sound of the preceding vowel. In most of these cases the *l* is still written, and serves to indicate the pronunciation of the preceding vowel. The following combinations of letters (when occurring in the same syllable, or in derivatives of words in which they were tautosyllabic) may be regarded as compound phonetic symbols of almost unvarying value: *alf* (ɑːf), *alve* (ɑːv), *alm* (ɑːm), *alk*, *aulk* (ɔːk), *aulm* (ɔːm), *olk* (əʊk). In many dialects, esp. in Sc., the instances in which an original *l* regularly disappears are much more numerous than in standard Eng.; cf. Sc. *awfu'*, *fou*, *ca'*, etc.; in Sc. the regular representative of *ol(l* is *ow*, as in *fowk*, *pow*.

I. 1. Illustrations of the literary use of the letter.

c **1000** ÆLFRIC *Gram.* iii. (Z.) 6 *Semivocales* syndon seofan: *f, l, m, n, r, s, x.* **1530** PALSGR. 32 The soundyng of this consonant *L. Ibid.* 46 So often as *l* cometh before *h* havyng his aspiracion . . it is the errour of the printers whiche knowe nat their owne tonge. **1588** SHAKS. *L.L.L.* IV. ii. 60 If Sore be sore, then ell to Sore, makes fiftie sores O sorell: Of one sore I an hundred make by adding but one more L. **1597** A. M. tr. *Guillemeau's Fr. Chirurg.* 24/1 Wordes in the which manye R.R.R. and L.L.L. come. **15..** *Gude & Godl. B.* Calendar (S.T.S.), Where ye shal finde a Capital L there begine for the finding of Lent. **1727–52** CHAMBERS *Cycl.* s.v. *L*, The French louis d'ors have a cross on them consisting of eight L's interwoven, and disposed in form of a cross. **1892** *Daily News* 5 Sept. 5/2 There are pedantic persons who would bid us pronounce the 'l' in 'salmon'. **1897** *Spectator* 2 Jan. 13/1 For the sake of Learning, with a capital 'L'.

2. An object shaped like the letter L. (Also written *ell*.) **a.** An extension of a building at right angles to the main block, giving the whole the shape of the letter L. See also ELL².

1843 'R. CARLTON' *New Purchase* I. xi. 80 On the first floor were two rooms, and connected with a Lilliputian half-story kitchen forming an L—as near as possible. **1873** T. B. ALDRICH *Marj. Daw* etc. 167 Mr. Jaffrey's bedroom was in an L of the building. **1874** *Rep. Vermont Board Agric.* II. 510 To save expense, it is apt to be the case that no cellar is put under the L part of the house. **1879** WEBSTER, Suppl. *s.v.*, L (of a house). **1883** *Harper's Mag.* Feb. 358/2 An L of the house where she was born is still standing.

b. A pipe-joint connecting two pipes at right angles; an elbow-joint (Knight *Dict. Mech.* Suppl. 1884).

3. *attrib.* and *Comb.*, as ***L-shaped*** adj.; **L desk**, a reading-desk of which the ground-plan is of the form of the letter L; **L-head, -headed** *adjs.*, applied to (a reciprocating internal-combustion engine having) L-shaped combustion chambers, in which the valves are situated in a side arm.

1874 MICKLETHWAITE *Mod. Par. Ch.* ix. 57 That glorious compromise called an L desk. **1882** *Macm. Mag.* XLVI. 332/2 It is . . an L-shaped room. **1897** *Allbutt's Syst. Med.* IV. 347 An L-shaped pad. **1916** L. MANTELL *Man. Motor Mech.* iii. 17 One of the most frequent errors made by designers is in attempting to obtain high compression in an L-headed engine with a short stroke. **1920** *Sci. Amer.* 3 Jan. 6/3 The intake manifold of several power plants, both on overhead-valve and L-head types of engine, is cast entirely within the detachable cylinder head. **1922** *Encycl. Brit.* XXX. 37/2 The . . Vee Renault of 1912, . . the . . Vee RAF of 1913–14, and the . . Vee RAF 4a, all of which had cast-iron L-headed cylinders. **1946** R. F. KUNS in Kuns & Plumridge *Automobile Engines* iv. 60 L-head engines are quiet in operation and are long lived. *Ibid.*, The L-head or, as the English call it, the side-valve engine. **1963** BIRD & HUTTON-STOTT *Veteran Motor Car* 98 Their cylinders were L-headed and cast in pairs.

II. Symbolical uses.

4. Used like the other letters of the alphabet to denote serial order; applied e.g. to the twelfth (or more usually the eleventh, either I or J being often omitted) group or section in classification, the eleventh sheet of a book or quire of a MS., etc.

1850 FORSHALL & MADDEN *Wyclif's Bible* Pref. xxxi, [Manuscripts] E, L, and P frequently agree together in differing from the other copies. **1899** *N.B. Daily Mail* 16 Feb. 5, Companies L, D, and H of the Californian Volunteers. **1899** SIR A. WEST *Recoll.* I. iv. 104 He had carefully put it [an umbrella] away under the letter L.

5. In *Cryst.*, *h, k, l* are used to denote the quantities which determine the position of a plane.

1868 DANA *Min.* Introd. 28. **1895** STORY-MASKELYNE *Crystallogr.* ii. 19.

6. The Roman numeral symbol for Fifty.

As in the case of the other Roman numeral symbols, this was originally not the letter, but was identified with it owing to coincidence of form. In the ancient Roman notation L̄ (with a stroke above) represented 50,000.

1484 CAXTON *Fables of Poge* iv, xl or l crownes.

7. Other symbolic uses in science.

a. In *Physics* *L* is used to designate the series of X-ray emission lines of longer wavelength than the *K*-series obtained by exciting the atoms of any particular element (cf. K 3 e); these arise from electron transitions to the atomic orbit of second-lowest energy, with principal quantum number 2, which is thus termed the ***L-shell***, and electrons in this shell ***L-electrons***. **L-capture**, the capture by an atomic nucleus of one of the *L*-electrons.

1911, 1923 [see K 3 e]. **1930** PAULING & GOUDSMIT *Struct. Line Spectra* x. 172 There are three absorption edges corresponding to the removal of an electron from the L shell. **1930** *Phil. Mag.* IX. 205 The K electron distribution in carbon will be determined mainly by the central nucleus, and the influence of the L electrons will be comparatively small. **1934** H. E. WHITE *Introd. Atomic Spectra* xvi. 326 When a *K* electron is missing, . . the binding energy of the *L* electron is approximately that for the corresponding electron in the element with the next higher atomic number. **1956** *Nucl. Sci. Abstr.* X. 1123/2 (*heading*) Effect of the correlations existing between the electron positions on the ratio ρ of the probability of L capture to that of K capture. **1968** *Physical Rev.* CLXVI. 945/1 The exchange correction . . in the case of Be^7 increases the *L*-capture probability by a factor of almost 4. **1970** E. P. BERTIN *Princ. & Pract. X-Ray Spectrometric Analysis* vi. 182 Elements having atomic number 57 (lanthanum) or higher . . are usually determined by measurement of their *L* lines with gas-flow proportional counters. **1972** R. BOLTON *Org. Mechanisms* i. 14 The K-shell is now filled. . . A third electron must . . be placed in the higher-energy L-shell.

b. In *Physics* *l* and *L* denote the quantum numbers of the orbital angular momentum of one electron or a group of electrons, respectively (superseding the k ($= l + 1$) of the old quantum theory).

The use of *l* as a quantum number, and the values assigned to it, varied until shortly after the publication (in 1926) of Schrödinger's theory of the atom.

LS-coupling, an approximation used in the quantum theory of the atom when the spin-orbit interaction of individual electrons is small compared with the remaining electrostatic interaction between one electron and another, so that the orbital angular momenta of the electrons may be coupled to give a resultant L, their spins coupled to give a resultant S, and these resultants coupled in turn to give the total angular momentum J of the electrons. Also called *Russell-Saunders coupling*. Cf. *jj-coupling* (J II. 6 c).

[**1925** RUSSELL & SAUNDERS in *Astrophysical Jrnl.* LXI. 61 Their remaining properties may be explained on the assumption that the two displaced electrons have fixed orbital momenta, L_1, L_2, of the amount indicated by Landé, but that the inclination of their planes is quantized, so that the resultant angular momentum *K* may have any geometrically permissible value in the series 1/2, 3/2, [etc.]. **1926** *Proc. R. Soc.* A. CXI. 84 The spectroscopic nature of each term . . is specified by a quantum number *l* which relates to the whole set of electrons not in complete groups. It . . is taken to be $\frac{1}{2}, \frac{3}{2}, \frac{5}{2}$ . . . for S, P, D terms, so that $l = k_1$ [$\equiv k - \frac{1}{2}$] when there is only one electron in an incomplete group. It may perhaps be thought of as the resultant angular momentum of the incomplete group. **1926** *Ibid.* CXII. 81 Spectral terms are to be designated in the usual way as follows:—S, P, D, F, G, . . . corresponding to the values 1, 2, 3, 4, 5, . . . for a spectral term quantum number denoted by '*l*'.] **1928** H. S. ALLEN *Quantum* iv. 66 The quantum number *ja* is now denoted by *l*, which is called the 'group quantum number'. . . Its value in this case [*sc.* of a single electron] is $l = k - 1$. *Ibid.*, The inner quantum number *j* is compounded vectorially from *s* and *l*. **1934** H. E. WHITE *Introd. Atomic Spectra* xii. 190 These cases are known as *LS*-, or Russell-Saunders, coupling, on the one hand, and *jj*-coupling, on the other. **1934** [see K 3 f]. **1970** G. K. WOODGATE *Elem. Atomic Struct.* vii. 140 Along the sequence $np(n+1)s$ from light to heavy elements, for example C($2p3s$), Si($3p4s$), Ge($4p5s$), Sn($5p6s$), there is a progression from *LS* to *j-j* coupling. Ge($4p5s$) is an example of intermediate coupling for which neither *L*, *S* nor j_1, j_2 are even approximately good quantum numbers.

c. *Bacteriol.* [*L* said to be f. the *L*ister Institute, where Klieneberger worked.] The designation (now usu. as ***L-form***) of an atypical form of certain bacteria which arises from and usually reverts to the normal form but is sometimes stable, and which lacks a cell wall, exhibits a very variable shape, and somewhat resembles a mycoplasma.

1935 E. KLIENEBERGER in *Jrnl. Path. & Bacteriol.* XL. 93 These swollen elements [among the bacillary chains of *Streptobacillus moniliformis*], with an associated fine mycelial system resembling that of pleuropneumonia and agalactia, constitute an independent colonial system containing all strains of *S. moniliformis* so far examined. A delicate streptococcus has also been recovered . . from the nasopharynx of healthy guinea-pigs harbouring a similar pleuropneumonia-like symbiont. These two pleuropneumonia-like organisms in association respectively with *S. moniliformis* and a streptococcus . . will be referred to . . simply as L1 and L2 pending the coining of appropriate generic names. **1950** C. E. CLIFTON *Introd. Bacteria* vi. 132 *Streptobacillus moniliformis* . . resembles the actinomyces in many respects but gives rise after several days' incubation to highly pleomorphic forms characteristic of the pleuropneumonia group. . . Present evidence indicates that there is but one organism involved and that the actinomyces-like form and the L_1 form represent different stages of growth of one organism characterized by a complex reproductive cycle. **1968** *Zinsser Microbiol.* (ed. 14) lii. 794/2 Some L phase mutants revert back to normal size organisms as soon as the penicillin is removed from the medium. Others are stable in the L phase on solid media but revert back when subcultured in broth. **1973** J. LEVY et al. *Introd. Microbiol.* ii. 39 Because they did not have a wall, they were not affected by penicillin or other antibiotics that interfere with cell wall synthesis. The mutation to an L-form is therefore troublesome if the bacterium is a pathogen.

d. ***L-band***: a frequency band of electromagnetic waves used for radar, extending from 390 to 1550 megahertz.

1947 J. S. HALL *Radar Aids to Navigation* vii. 233 A cross-band airborne interrogator-responser recently developed consists of an *L*-band (about 25 cm) transmitter operating on a number of preselected frequency channels and a 10-cm receiver. **1967** *Electronics* 6 Mar. 52/1 Tradex, an adaptation of the radar developed for the ballistic missile early warning system, operates at uhf and L band.

III. 8. a. Abbreviations. (Abbreviations given here with the full stop are frequently found without it.)

L. = various proper names as Lionel, Lucy, etc.; **L.** = †Lord, Lordship (pl. LL.); †lawful (money); in *Bot.*, Linnæus; Latin; in Stage directions, left; in abbreviations of degrees, Licentiate, as L.D.S. = Licentiate of Dental Surgery; (*Chem.*) Lithium; learner; Liberal (in politics); low (on the selector mechanism in a car with automatic transmission); **L** or **l** [L. *libra*] = pound of money (†formerly also in weight, now lb.), now often repr. by the conventional sign £; e.g. 100*l.* or £100; see also L.S.D.; ***the three L's*** (see quot. 1867); **l** = in ship's log-book, lightning; in references, line, as bk. 4, l. 8; in solmization, la; **L.A.**, local authority; **LA, L.A.**, Los Angeles; **L.A.F.T.A.**, Latin-American Free Trade Association; **l.b.w.** (*Cricket*), leg before wicket; **l.c.** (*Printing*), lower case; **L.C.** (**A.**, **I.**, **M.**, **T.**, etc.), landing craft (assault, infantry, mechanized, tank, etc.); **L.C.C.**, London County Council; **LCD** = *liquid crystal display* s.v. LIQUID *a.* 7; freq. *attrib.* (esp. with redundant *display*); **L.C.M.** (*Arith.*), least common multiple; **LD**, lethal dose: used with following numeral, as LD50, LD_{50}, indicating the percentage of a large group of similar animals that is killed by such a dose; **LD** or **L-D (process)**, in steel-making, the Linz-Düsenverfahren (process) or Linz-Donawitz-Verfahren (process); **L.D.C.**, less developed country; **L.D.V.**, Local Defence Volunteers; **L.E.**, **LE** (*Med.*), lupus erythematosus; usu. *attrib.*; **L.E.A.**, Local Education Authority; **L.E.M.**, lunar excursion module; see also LEM; **L.F.**, low frequency; **LH** (*Biochem.*), luteinizing hormone; **L.M.**, (*prosody*) long metre; lunar module; **LMF**, lack of moral fibre; **L.M.S.**, London, Midland, and

Scottish (Railway); **L.N.E.R.** (earlier **L.N.E.**), London and North-Eastern Railway; **LNG**, liquefied natural gas; **LOI**, lunar orbit insertion; **LOS**, loss of signal; **L.P.**, long-playing (record); **LPG**, liquefied petroleum gas; **LRL**, Lunar Receiving Laboratory (building where astronauts and lunar samples are quarantined for a period after returning from the moon); **LRV**, lunar roving vehicle; **L.s.**, letter (not autograph) signed; cf. *A.L.(S.)* s.v. A III; **L.S.** (*Cinemat.*), long shot; **L.S.E.** (occas. **L.S. of E.**), London School of Economics; **LSI**, large-scale integration (of electronic microcircuits); **L.S.T.**, landing ship, tank(s); **LTH** (*Biochem.*), luteotrop(h)ic hormone; **L.V.**, luncheon voucher.

See also LL, LOX *sb.*[1], LSD[2], LXX (as main entries).

1774 *Connect. Col. Rec.* (1887) XIV. 299 To pay said sum of £54 14 0, *L. money. **1936** *Motor Manual* (ed. 29) xiii. 193 '*L' plates must be carried at the front and rear of the car. **1936** *Punch* 26 Feb. 248/1 Ermyntrude, inspired by blind jealousy (and aided by some rather L driving by Rachel), emerged from the garage. **1959** *Manch. Guardian* 27 Aug. 6/3 There are still an unknown number of drivers.. who may have used L-plates for years without even applying for a test. **1963** P. ROBERTS *Know the Law Handbk.* vi. 154 (*caption*) An L driver involved in an accident. **1970** G. S. WILKINSON *Road Traffic Offences* (ed. 6) v. 472 On and from 1st January, 1961, he may drive only as a learner-driver, i.e., with L plates. **1869** *Whitaker's Almanack* 83/1 *Andover*—Hon. D. F. Fortescue, *L. **1908** *Daily Chron.* 16 Dec. 1/2 Mr. Mackarness (L, Newbury) asked whether [etc.]. **1974** *Times* 11 Oct. 4/1 Accrington... Total vote 42,259 (83·8%)—Lab 20,050 (47·4%), C 15,018 (35·5%), L 7,191 (17·0%). **1684** *Acts Tonnage & Poundage* 86 Alabaster the Load.. 02**l.* 00*s.* 00*d.* **1701** DR. WALLIS in *Collect.* (O.H.S.) I. 329 An allowance of 20£ a year. *a* **1715** BURNET *Own Time* (1724) I. 591 An 100000 *l.* was given. **1865** *Derby Mercury* 26 Apr., A.. dividend of 1*s.* in the £. **1865** *Law Jrnl.* 17 Jan. 38/2 A salary of 4*l.* a week. **1684** R. WALLER *Ess. Nat. Exper.* 103 A mass of 500*l.* of Ice. **1858** SIMMONDS *Dict. Trade*, **L.A.C.* an abbreviation used by the dispensing surgeon or chemist, implying that he is a 'licentiate of the Apothecaries Company'. **1870** HOOKER *Stud. Flora* 127 Cratægus, **L.* Hawthorn, Whitethorn. **1527** *Extracts Aberd. Reg.* (1844) I. 117 My lord, we your seruandis.. hes ressauit your *l. guid mynd.. touching your l. brig of Dee. **1554** in W. H. Turner *Select. Rec. Oxford* 218 It was.. ordered by the L.L. **1577** *Ibid.* 389 Appointed by order from their LLs. **1601** R. JOHNSON *Kingd. & Commw.* (1603) Ab, If your L. vouchsafe to receive it. **1637** HEYLYN *Answ. Burton* 61 Your dealing with my LL. the Bishops. **1951** TOBOLDT et al. *Automatic Transmissions* i. 15 The selector may be set in any one of five positions, namely, parking (P), neutral (N), low (*L), drive (D), and reverse (R). **1867** SMYTH *Sailor's Word-bk.*, *L*. The three *L's were formerly vaunted by seamen who despised the use of nautical astronomy; viz. lead, latitude, and look-out... Dr. or Captain Halley added the fourth L—the greatly desired longitude. **1932** J. L. P. W. HEWISON *Local Expenditure: Address E. Sussex Ratepayers' Assoc.* 4 Let every *L.A. be rationed as to the percentage of its income which it may spend on loan charges. **1967** *Punch* 1 Mar. 292/2 The LAs spend between them on nursery schools 0·281 per cent of their total educational expenditure. **1949** H. G. ALSBERG et al. *American Guide* 1199 Los Angeles... Airports: Union Air Terminal, & *L.A. Mun. Airport. **1953** *Amer. Speech* XXVIII. 54 If you're confused—its still L.A... (Native votes on pronunciation of 'Los Angeles'.) **1969** *Daily Tel.* 12 Nov. 20/3 The centre of California is LA, a concrete and glass *mélange* embracing 102 incorporated cities and spread over 4,851 square miles. **1972** B. RODGERS *Queen's Vernacular* 109, I can't walk around LA without gettin' the horns—there's so many pretties. **1973** *Black World* Apr. 96 On a junket to L.A. and New York. **1960** *Times Rev. Industry* July 73/1 In February this year Argentina, Brazil, Mexico, Paraguay, Peru, and Uruguay signed the Montevideo Treaty, setting up the Latin American Free Trade Association... The *L.A.F.T.A. aims at removing customs duties to fellow members in 12 years. **1966** *Economist* 19 Nov. 826/1 As a member of LAFTA, Venezuela hopes not only to increase exports but also to reap economies of scale, especially in the heavier industries. **1972** *Buenos Aires Herald* 2 Feb. 3/3 A large share of the disequilibrium stemmed from trade with LAFTA (Latin American Free Trade Association) nations. **1795** in Lillywhite *Cricket Scores* (1862) I. 190 Hon. J. Tufton, *lbw, b wells... 3. **1891** W. G. GRACE *Cricket* i. in *Out-door Games* 17 You should all know how difficult it is to get any one l.b.w. when [etc.]. **1833** *Penny Mag.* Monthly Suppl. Oct.–Nov. 468 **l.c.*,.. to have words or letters printed in 'lower case', or small letters. **1892** A. POWELL *Southward's Pract. Printing* (ed. 4) xvii. 129 *l.c.*, set the word in lower case letters. **1911** A. E. HOUSMAN *Let.* 28 Aug. (1971) 119 The type-written text contains the letters: J (cap.) j (l.c.). **1973** *Collin's Authors & Printers Dict.* (ed. 11) 244/2 *l.c.*,.. (typ.) lower case, that is *not* caps. **1961** B. FERGUSSON *Watery Maze* i. 42 The mahogany boat.. became the standard Landing Craft Assault, or *LCA. **1967** *Jane's Surface Skimmer Systems 1967–68* 97/2 Current amphibious vehicle programmes being conducted for the Bureau of Ships are: Landing Craft Assault (LCA), [etc.]. **1898** *L.C.C. [see BETTER-TO-DO *adj. phr.*]. **1907** *Daily Chron.* 3 Sept. 4/7 This is one of the little matters that the L.C.C... might well look into. **1970** RUCK & RHODES *Govt. Greater London* iii. 45 The Labour Party Opposition were convinced that a scheme of reform was unnecessary and particularly a scheme which involved the abolition of the L.C.C. **1973** *Electronics* 16 Aug. 33/1 What is claimed to be the first watch using a field-effect *LCD, the Teletime, has been introduced by Gruen Industries. **1979** *Personal Computer World* Nov. 86/4 It's distinguished from an ordinary scientific calculator by its unusually large LCD display. **1980** B. W. ALDISS *Life in West* v. 103 He set the LCD watch down on the step. **1984** *Listener* 5 Apr. 38/3 LCD technology is a 'strategic' one because, at present, any computing device that needs to be light and portable must have an LCD screen. **1985** *Which Computer?* Apr. 28 (Advt.), The Apricot Portable incorporates a unique LCD display. **1943** *Time* 22 Nov. 24/3 The broad wake of a PT, plus the outline of the *LCI, must have looked like bigger game. **1944** *Hutchinson's Pict. Hist. War* 12 Apr.–26 Sept. 344/1 One company of Pioneers, some of whom had spent two hours in the sea, after their L.C.I. had been torpedoed. **1943** *Time* 4 Oct. 63/2 As early as 1936 the Navy experimented with tank lighters, and from these tests emerged the *LCM (Landing Craft, Mechanized), a 50-footer which carries a crew of four and a medium tank. **1943** *Newsweek* 27 Sept. 23/2 The row of *LCT's on the beach belching vehicles looks like a long line of stranded, gasping whales. **1955** 'N. SHUTE' *Requiem for Wren* iii. 79 This was the L.C.T. Mark 4, the standard tank landing craft, British built and the most common of the lot. **1927** J. W. TREVAN in *Proc. R. Soc.* B. CI. 483 Toxicity should be stated primarily in terms of the 'median lethal dose', that is the dose which kills 50 per cent. of a large group of animals. As a convenient abbreviation I would suggest the symbol *LD50... For doses which kill other proportions of large groups of animals it is convenient to use the analogous symbols LD75, LD25, for doses which kill 75 per cent., and 25 per cent., and similarly for doses killing other proportions. **1950** *Proc. Soc. Exper. Biol. & Med.* LXXIII. 497/2 Only 400r of X-irradiation was used. This dose corresponds to $LD_{85\text{-}30}$ for swine. **1958** THOMSON & STRAUBE in W. D. Claus *Radiation Biol. & Med.* iv. 101 Two-thirds of an LD_{50} dose will probably kill less than 1 percent of the animals exposed. **1968** *Observer* 16 June 9/1 Sarin is 30 times more toxic than phosgene, and the amount necessary to achieve what the experts know as 'LD50'.. is 40 drops on the skin. **1954** H. A. TRENKLER in *One Year LD-Oxygen Refining Process* 11/1 Our method of steel refining with pure oxygen by blowing downwards into a bath of metal.. is called '*LD-process' (Linzer Düsenverfahren). **1965** *New Statesman* 7 May 709/3 The building of modern plants, LD converters, bigger blast-furnaces, wider sinter plants, automated soaking pits and rolling mills. **1973** *Times* 30 May (Austria Suppl.) p. iii/7 The Japanese have the highest production of LD steel, and by 1972 51 percent of world steel production was based on the LD process. **1967** *Times* 25 Sept. p. xiv, There is no doubt that the speedy economic advancement of the less developed countries (*L.D.C.s) would benefit the whole world economy. **1973** *Advocate-News* (Barbados) 19 Feb. 9/1 The assembled CARIFTA leadership prepared a package for progress, and the LDCs emerged apparently satisfied that their future was assured. **1940** H. NICOLSON *Diary* 20 July (1967) 104 Opinion slides off into.. rage that the *L.D.V. are not better equipped. **1967** G. F. FIENNES *I tried to run a Railway* iii. 21, I fired this shot without first putting on my L.D.V. armlet. **1948** *Proc. Mayo Clinic* XXIII. 26 The.. cell.. has been called an '*L.E.' cell in our laboratory because of its frequent appearance in bone marrow cases of acute disseminated lupus erythematosus. **1961** R. D. BAKER *Essent. Path.* x. 263 Systemic (disseminated) lupus erythematosus... In the blood are L.E. cells (lupus erythematosus cells), consisting of damaged polymorphonuclear cells or lymphocytes which are surrounded by viable polymorphonuclear leukocytes. **1970** PASSMORE & ROBSON *Compan. Med. Stud.* II. xxv. 26/1 The serum of patients suffering from lupus erythematosus.. contains an abnormal globulin (LE factor) which can exert a uniquely harmful action on nuclei. *a* **1912** W. T. ROGERS *Dict. Abbrev.* (1913) 113/1 **L.E.A.*, (educ.). Local Educational Authority. **1945** [see BURNHAM]. **1966** P. H. J. H. GOSDEN *Devel. Educ. Admin. Eng. & Wales* x. 213 The Inner London Education Area, has a special committee of the G.L.C. to exercise the powers of an L.E.A. **1963** M. CAIDIN *Man-in-Space Dict.* 26 Two astronauts will transfer to the *LEM and descend to the moon. **1969** *Listener* 6 Feb. 162/2 The weakest link is likely to be the LEM or Lunar Excursion Module, which will be the craft used in the actual touch-down of two astronauts. **1969** *Guardian* 22 July 6/1 Armstrong: Going to step off the LEM now... That's one small step for man, one giant leap for mankind. **1922** *Wireless World* 18 Nov. 233 (*heading*) The switching of *L.F. valves. **1923** *Ibid.* 6 Jan. 463/1 Methods of intervalve coupling, namely, 'high frequency transformer',.. and 'low frequency transformer'.. 'H.F. transformer' and 'L.F. transformer'. **1941** *Electronic Engin.* XIV. 404 The L.F. input to the amplifier must be kept at the same voltage for all frequencies. **1971** *Wireless World* Apr. 184/2 It follows that the difference frequency produced when h.f. noise is sampled at a high rate will be l.f. noise. **1936** *Anatomical Rec.* LXV. 267 The *LH produced.. enlargement of the testicles. **1957** [see GONADOTROPHIN, -TROPIN]. **1970** *New Scientist* 29 Jan. 200/2 An important cause of infertility in women is the failure to ovulate because of a lack of FSH or LH (or both). **1969** *L.M. [see *command service module* (COMMAND *sb.* 10)]. **1970** R. TURNILL *Lang. of Space* 73 Because it is not used for re-entry, and the moon has no atmosphere, the LM does not need to be heat-shielded. **1952** M. TRIPP *Faith is Windsock* i. 19 They whose nerves snapped with the prolonged tension of operational flying, who refused to go on with it, were grounded, with the terrible initials *LMF (Lack of Moral Fibre) against their names. **1971** *New Society* 22 July 150 When the second world war began.. the term LMF ('lack of moral fibre') was coined as a pejorative for those pilots who would today be diagnosed and treated as having psychiatric illness. **1923** *Times* 28 Dec. 15/7 (*heading*) *L.M.S. railway's dock charges. **1934** *Discovery* Nov. 314/2 Many expresses on the L.M.S. and G.W.R. now load up to 500 tons or over.. and loads exceeding 600 tons are not unknown on the L.N.E.R. **1967** J. JOYCE *Story Passenger Transport in Brit.* vii. 173 The LMS.. locomotive was also a streamliner,.. of the same wheel arrangement as its LNER counterpart. **1972** 'G. NORTH' *Sgt. Cluff rings True* iv. 30 'You travel much?' 'Not since they did away with the LMS.' **1923** *Times* 6 Dec. 9/4 Alternative routes are wholly within the *L.N.E. system. **1934**, **1967** *L.N.E.R. [see *L.M.S.*]. **1967** *N.Y. Times* 13 Jan. 22 Technology is currently being developed for the use of liquefied natural gas, *LNG, as a motor fuel. **1970** *Sci. Jrnl.* Mar. 39/1 LNG is already widely used wherever natural gas is transported or piped on a large scale. **1972** *Sunday Times* 17 Dec. 55/2 There is still uncertainty about what would happen if an LNG carrier were holed in a collision. **1969** *Radio Times* 10 July 31/4 **LOI*, Lunar orbit insertion. **1970** N. ARMSTRONG et al. *First on Moon* ix. 204 On the first LOI the crew had burned two seconds less than the flight plan called for. **1969** *Times* 22 July (Moon Rep.) p. i/1 Neil Armstrong on the porch of the Eagle at 109 hours 19 minutes and 30 seconds to *L.O.S., all systems go. **1970** N. ARMSTRONG et al. *First on Moon* x. 222 Got about two minutes to LOS here, Mike. **1948** *Musical Amer.* July 19/3 The new disc, called *LP (long playing) Microgroove, requires a new pickup. **1958** *Times* 20 Jan. 10/4 Stereo records will give almost as much playing time as present LPs. **1958** *Spectator* 15 Aug. 220/2 That barbarous invention, the LP song recital. **1967** LP [see ANTHOLOGY 2]. **1961** *New Scientist* 23 Mar. 730/2 The gas used, butane or propane, becomes available as a by-product of oil refining, and is commonly known as *LPG (liquefied petroleum gas). **1974** *BP Shield Internat.* Oct. 26/4 The natural choice for cooking and heating is butane or LPG. **1969** *New Yorker* 12 Apr. 88/2 The *L.R.L. is the building to which the astronauts, the spaceship, and the samples will be brought when the trip is over. **1970** N. ARMSTRONG et al. *First on Moon* xiii. 330 The manager of the LRL, thought the chance of anything harmful coming back with the astronauts was 'probably one in a hundred billion'. **1971** *New Scientist* 3 June 574/1 Design requirements for the *LRV were such that a pneumatic tyre would not be practical. **1894** *Ellis & Elvey's Gen. Catal. Rare Bks. & MSS.* 38 George I. King of England. *L.S. 'George R.', dated St. James, le 1er Octobre, 1715, to Madame de Kameke, congratulating her on the birth of a son. **1971** *Sotheby & Co. Catal. Bks., Autogr. Lett., Hist. Documents* 20 July 104 (*heading*) Tennyson:.. L.s. (text in his wife's hand), acknowledging a gift of *Misunderstood*. **1953** K. REISZ *Technique Film Editing* iii. 71 *Shooting up* subway steps. The blind man stands helpless at the top... **L.S.* Blind man. A small boy is helping him. **1960** C. MORRIS in D. Wilson *Television Playwright* 447 L.S. of a drive in summer along which, walking towards the Camera, are a woman.. and a boy. **1896** B. WEBB *Diary* 16 Sept. in J. Dunbar *Mrs. G. B. S.* (1963) ix. 116 We, knowing she was wealthy, and hearing she was socialistic, interested her in the *LS of E. She subscribed £1,000 to the Library. **1942** PARTRIDGE *Dict. Abbrev.* 58/2 *L.S.E.*, London School of Economics. **1969** G. S. JONES in Cockburn & Blackburn *Student Power* 45 Then, in 1967, mass demonstrations against the raising of overseas student fees and the explosion at the LSE suddenly signalled the beginnings of change. **1973** G. SIMS *Hunters Point* xv. 136, I.. did a course of Political Science at the L.S.E. **1966**, **1967** *LSI [see *large-scale* adj. (LARGE *a.* 15 a)]. **1968** *New Scientist* 7 Mar. 521/2 The very high circuit density possible with LSI means that the time-delays inevitable in the cabled interconnections of present day computers will be greatly reduced. **1971** *Illustr. Weekly India* 18 Apr. 19/1 In 1958, integrated circuits were invented. Since then they have been joined by LSI—large scale integration. **1943** F. D. ROOSEVELT *Let.* 6 Nov. in W. S. Churchill *Second World War* (1952) V. xiv. 222 The Combined Chiefs of Staff to-day authorised Eisenhower to retain until December 15 sixty-eight *L.S.T.s now scheduled for an early departure for the United Kingdom. **1946** T. BLORE *Commissioned Bargees* ii. 21 And by the time victory arrived there had grown.. a great fleet of weird craft, some of American origin, ranging from those quaint sea monsters, the L.S.T., or Landing Ship-Tank, to the Landing Barge. **1973** *Philadelphia Inquirer* 7 Oct. 17/4 The Defense Department.. provides.. elderly LST's. **1961** *Recent Progress Hormone Res.* XVII. 119 The demonstration that a luteotropic hormone (*LTH) causes the maintenance of corpora lutea in rats.. established the concept that the pituitary glands of all mammalian females secrete a luteotropic substance. *Ibid.*, The term 'LTH' will be used in this review (for animals other than rats) with the understanding that it could be an as yet unidentifiable substance, or that it could be LH. **1965** LEE & KNOWLES *Animal Hormones* ii. 20 After ovulation blood levels of LH increase which induce the development of a corpus luteum, but it may be that this will only secrete progesterone if sufficient LTH reaches it. **1955** *Evening Standard* 28 Oct. 15/3 (*heading*) Copy typist with some experience of statement work, required by City firm. Commencing salary.. according to age & ability plus *L.V.'s. **1966** *New Statesman* 4 Mar. 317/1 (Advt.), 32½-hour week (no Sats) LV's and superannuation scheme. **1974** *Times* 2 Oct. 27/1 (Advt.), American law firm.. seeks.. secretary... Own office, IBM Golfball, excellent salary and L.V.s.

b. Alphabetic abbreviation of *elevated*, = Elevated Railroad. Also *attrib. U.S.* (Cf. EL, EL.)

1881 [see ELEVATED *ppl. a.* 1]. **1899** J. L. WILLIAMS *Stolen Story* 23 He was making for the Seventy-second Street 'L' Station. *Ibid.* 189 He took the L train for Cortlandt Street. **1904** *Sun* (N.Y.) 4 Sept. 7 The owners of express wagons are praying that the L strike will come off. **1929** E. L. RICE *Street Scene* I. 5 The noises of the city rise, fall, intermingle: the distant roar of 'L' trains, automobile sirens and the whistles of boats on the river.

c. *Chem.* (i) *l* = lævorotatory.

[**1891** *Jrnl. Chem. Soc.* LX. 1175 Arabinose can be converted into l.-glucose, whilst xylose, under the same conditions, yields l.-gulose.] **1894** *Ibid.* LXVI. I. 487 The cultures have no action on *l*-mannose, *l*-gulose, *l*-arabinose, .. or *a*-glucooctose. **1926** J. READ *Text-bk. Org. Chem.* xvii. 353 Most of the essential oils of plants are also optically active, owing to the presence of such constituents as *d*- and *l*-pinene, *l*-menthone, *l*-menthol, *d*-camphor. **1939** *Jrnl. Amer. Chem. Soc.* LXI. 3201/1 *l*-Propylenediamine was prepared by resolving commercial propylenediamine with tartaric acid. **1971** J. D. ROBERTS et al. *Org. Chem.* xiv. 392 The sign of rotation of an enantiomer, (+) or *d*, (−) or *l*, reveals neither the molecule's absolute configuration nor its configuration relative to some other compound. **1971** L. S. HARRIS in D. H. Clouet *Narcotic Drugs* iii. 93 With pentazocine the *l*-isomer is 20 times more potent than the *d*-isomer.

†(ii) *l* was formerly used to denote configuration (now superseded by L: see (iii)). *Obs.*

1890 *Jrnl. Chem. Soc.* LVIII. I. 466 In view of the fact that the rotation of derivatives of each isomeride is not always in the same direction.. it is necessary to adopt some method of indicating the optical activity of the parent glucose, and the author [*sc.* E. Fischer] proposes to distinguish the derivatives of dextro- and lævo-rotatory, and of inactive mannose, irrespective of their own peculiar rotation, as derivatives of d.-, l.-, and i.-mannose respectively. *Ibid.* 469

The l.-levulose (that is, the dextro-rotatory modification) could not be isolated. **1906** *Jrnl. Amer. Chem. Soc.* XXXVIII. 114 The chemical relationships are indicated by the letters *d* and *l* prefixed to the names of compounds. Thus, ordinary glucose and its corresponding fructose (levulose) are designated, respectively, *d*-glucose and *d*-fructose, notwithstanding the levo-rotation of the latter. **1937** F. C. WHITMORE *Org. Chem.* 481 When the cinchonine salts of racemic acid are crystallized, the *l*-tartrate separates first. **1947** *Jrnl. Biol. Chem.* CLXVIII. 443 *d*-Alanine of previous experiments..is *l*-alanine according to the nomenclature used in the present paper.

(iii) As a small capital L: applied to (a compound having) a configuration about an asymmetric atom analogous to that of an arbitrarily chosen standard compound (now L-glyceraldehyde for organic compounds). When there is more than one asymmetric carbon atom: (*a*) for sugars, the L refers to the configuration about the asymmetric carbon atom most remote from the aldehyde group (in aldoses) or the ketone group (in ketoses); (*b*) for amino-acids, the L refers to the configuration about the carbon atom adjacent to the—COOH group.

When it is desired to indicate the direction of optical rotation in addition to configuration, a + or − (for dextro- and lævo-rotation respectively) are added in parentheses, as D(−).

1947 *Jrnl. Biol. Chem.* CLXIX. 237 Distinction between the stereoisomers of the amino acids is made by a prefixed small capital letter D or L to denote the configurational family to which the *a*-carbon atom belongs. **1951** I. L. FINAR *Org. Chem.* I. xvii. 333 D(−) Ascorbic acid (vitamin C) is more efficient than L(+)-. **1964** *Jrnl. Chem. Soc.* 1370 The most stable isomer of the tris-(−)-*trans*-cyclohexane-1,2-diamineiridium (III) cation will have the L-configuration. **1968** R. F. STEINER *Life Chem.* ii. 26 Only amino acids of the L-configuration occur in natural proteins. **1970** R. W. MCGILVERY *Biochemistry* xxviii. 699 Some L-amino acids cause a rotation of plane polarized light to the left, others to the right.

La, la (la). [Fr. or It., fem. def. art., ad. L. *illa* fem., *ille* that.] Prefixed to a woman's name, ironically as if to that of a prima donna.

In quot. 1869 the reference is to a singer.

1869 [see BLOOD *sb.* 3 e]. **1919** A. HUXLEY *Let.* 5 Jan. (1969) 174 A poem by myself with an outgush of la Whilcox [*i.e.* Ella Wheeler Wilcox]. **1943** N. BALCHIN *Small Back Room* x. 121 What's the time? Four o'clock? Let's go and see if La Susan has rustled up any tea. **1961** *New Statesman* 10 Feb. 210/3 It all began with la Starkie clutching her brandy in front of the Tavern at Lord's with her back to the cricket. **1967** WODEHOUSE *Company for Henry* xi. 197 You can't avoid encountering La Simmons. **1974** E. MCGIRR *Murderous Journey* 78 La Siskin had another woman with her.

la (lɑː), *sb. Mus.* [Orig. the first syllable of L. *labii*: see GAMUT.] The name given by Guido d'Arezzo to the sixth note in his hexachords, and since retained in solmization as the sixth note of the octave; also (now *rarely*) used as in Fr. and It. as a name of the note A, the sixth note of the 'natural' scale of C major.

c **1325** in *Rel. Ant.* I. 292 Sol and ut and la. **1597** MORLEY *Introd. Mus.* (1771) 4 There be in Musicke but vi. Notes, which are called vt, re, mi, fa, sol, la. **1605** SHAKS. *Lear* I. ii. 149 O these Eclipses do portend these diuisions. Fa, Sol, La, Me. *c* **1645** HOWELL *Lett.* (1650) II. lv. 77 The other..will drink often musically a health to every one of these 6 notes, Ut, Re, Mi, Fa, Sol, La; which, with his reason, are all comprehended in this exameter, *Ut Relevet Miserum Fatum Solitosque Labores.* **1811** BUSBY *Dict. Mus.* (ed. 3) s.v. *Solmization*, Of the seven notes in the French scale, only four were for a while used by us, as *mi*, *fa*, *sol*, *la*.

la (lɑː, la), *int.* [Cf. LO (OE. *lá* and early ME. *la*).] An exclamation formerly used to introduce or accompany a conventional phrase or an address, or to call attention to an emphatic statement; †also *la you*. In recent use, a mere expression of surprise. Now only *dial.*, *vulgar*, and *arch.*

1598 SHAKS. *Merry W.* I. i. 86, I thank you alwaies with my heart, la: with my heart. *Ibid.* 324 You doe your selfe wrong indeede—la. **1601** —— *Twel. N.* III. iv. 111 La you, and you speake ill of the diuell, how he takes it at heart. **1694** CONGREVE *Double Dealer* IV. ii, O la now! I swear and declare, it shan't be so. **1749** FIELDING *Tom Jones* IV. xii, La, ma'am, what doth your la'yship think. **1839** DICKENS *Nich. Nick.* x, La, Miss La Creevy, how very smirking. **1844** WILLIS *Lady Jane* II. 311 He'd a caressing way—but, la! you know it's A sort of manner natural to poets! **1881** BESANT & RICE *Chapl. Fleet* III. 239 'La, sir,' she asked, 'Is it the voice of your sweetheart?'

†**b.** Repeated (*a*) as a refrain; (*b*) as an expression of derision. *Obs.* (Hence LA-LA *adj.*, = 'so-so', poor.)

1578 *Gude & Godl. B.* (S.T.S.) 138 Christ..Quhilk meiklie for mankynde, Tholit to be pynde, On Croce Cruellie. La. La. *Ibid.* 83 La Lay La. **1607** SHAKS. *Timon* III. i. 22 [He] hath sent to your Lorship to furnish him: nothing doubting your present assistance therein. *Luc.* La, la, la, la: Nothing doubting sayes hee?

la, obs. form of LAW, LAY *v.*, LO *int.*[1]

laace, obs. form of LACE.

laache, obs. f. LATCH *v.*; var. LASH *Obs.*, lax.

laad, laade, obs. forms of LOAD, LADE.

‖**laager** ('lɑːgə(r)), *sb.* Also **lager**. [S. African Du. *lager* = G. *lager*, Du. *leger* (see LEAGUER).]

a. A camp, encampment; among the S. African Boers, a temporary lodgement in the open marked out by an encircling line of wagons.

1850 R. G. CUMMING *Hunter's Life S. Afr.* (ed. 2) I. 202 Their tents and waggons were drawn up on every side of the farm-house... The Boers informed me that all their countrymen, and also the Griquas, were thus packed together in 'lagers', or encampments. **1883** *Standard* 7 Sept. 5 Captain Mansell, with the native police force, has been obliged to go into laager at Ekowe for safety. **1891** R. W. MURRAY *S. Africa* 177 Laager was formed that same evening about five o'clock. **1899** *Times* 25 Oct. 5/2 Our men dashed forward to carry the laager with bayonets.

b. *transf.* A defensive position in a country other than S. Africa, esp. one protected by armoured vehicles. Also *fig.*, an entrenched policy, viewpoint, etc., under attack from opponents.

1896 G. MEREDITH *Let.* 7 Dec. (1970) III. 1253, I have lowered my health by writing at night..and am now in laager against a host of Matabelly assailants. **1901** *Daily Tel.* 9 Mar. 11/5 It has been the custom of the Secretary of State to lie in laager, surrounded by his civilian secretaries. **1941** *Illustr. London News* CXCIX. 719 According to the dictionary, a *zareba* or *laager* is 'an enclosure against enemies', but now the term is used to describe the protective dispositions of armed and mechanised forces at night. **1946** G. MILLAR *Horned Pigeon* ii. 19 Our close night's formation (called either a 'leaguer' or a 'laager'). **1958** *Times Lit. Suppl.* 14 Feb. 87/4 That the leaders of the Nationalist Party have created a 'laager' mentality and hate all opponents of *apartheid* is a fact. **1960** *Economist* 15 Oct. 216/2 Whether to take Southern Rhodesia into the South African laager for whatever period of time this may buy them. **1968** *Ibid.* 14 Dec. 12/2 It would be disastrous if it showed that members of both faiths [in N. Ireland] have been driven by the atmosphere of crisis back into their laagers. **1971** *Rand Daily Mail* 27 Mar. 12/3 A confrontation which would only drive White South Africa deeper into its laager. **1973** *Times* 1 Oct. (Nigeria Suppl.) p. viii/7 These real or imagined anti-Ibo factors translate themselves inside the state into a kind of laager mentality, 'them' against 'us'. **1975** *Guardian* 11 Jan. 11 What's happening there will only make the Afrikaners withdraw further into their laager.

‖**laager** ('lɑːgə(r)), *v.* [f. LAAGER *sb.*] *trans.* To form (wagons) into a laager; to encamp (persons) in a laager; also with *up* and *fig.* Also *absol.* or *intr.* Hence '**laagered** *ppl. a.*, '**laagering** *vbl. sb.*

1879 *Daily News* 1 Mar., The waggons were not 'laagered' or drawn up so close as to make it difficult to force the camp. **1881** *Contemp. Rev.* Feb. 222 The laagered waggon their sole protection. **1883** *Standard* 17 May 5/4 Four hundred Boers, laagered in Stilleland, have threatened to attack Mankoroane. **1894** *Daily News* 14 Sept. 5/2 The Army Service Corps were drilled in laagering. **1895** *Westm. Gaz.* 28 Aug. 1/2 What, then, can be more absurd, to adopt Mr. Healy's picturesque phrase, than 'to laager the Postmaster-General in the Lords'? **1896** *Tablet* 22 Feb. 290 We stopped firing at about seven o'clock, and laagered up for the night. **1949** *Cape Times* 27 Apr. 10/5 Are we really going to keep ourselves laagered when other countries in Africa get together on economic expansion projects?

laagte ('lɑːxtə). *S. Afr.* Also **leegte**. [Afrikaans, a. Du. *laagte* a valley.] A valley or shallow dip in the veld.

1868 J. CHAPMAN *Trav. S. Afr.* I. 25 We emerged on a sandy elevation or 'buet' [? bult] overlooking an extensive undulation or *leegte*. **1897** SCHULZ & HAMMAR *New Afr.* xv. 188 As far as I could see up the open laagte the ground was teeming with heavy game. **1932** C. FULLER *Louis Trigardt's Trek* 136 Tall grass on the *bults*—not so thick as near the mountain—with the *laagtes* in between, for the most part, wet and boggy. **1944** V. POHL *Adventures Boer Family* 68 Dudley decided that..they should turn left..and take shelter in a *laagte* where they might easily shake off their pursuers in the dark. **1949** M. LEIGH *Cross of Fire* v. 89 On the laagte between ourselves and the main encampment other dim figures moved evenly. **1971** H. C. BOSMAN *Jurie Steyn's Post Office* 155 He emerged from his cottage in the leegte that was all grown about with the thorniest kind of cactus.

laak, obs. form of LACK, LAKE.

laan, laar, obs. forms of LAWN, LORE.

laard, laas, obs. forms of LARD, LACE.

laat, laað, obs. forms of LATE, LOATH.

laavenite, var. LAVENITE.

lab (læb), *sb.*[1] *Obs.* or *dial.* Also 4–5 **labbe**, 8 **labb**. [Belongs to LAB *v.*] A blab, tell-tale.

c **1386** CHAUCER *Miller's T.* 323, I nam no labbe Ne though I seye I am not lief to gabbe. *c* **1422** HOCCLEVE *Jereslaus's Wife* 542, I neuere was yit of my tonge a labbe. *c* **1440** *Promp. Parv.* 282/2 Labbe, or he that can kepe no counsel, *anubicus*. **1746** *Exmoor Scolding* (E.D.S.) 25 Ees dedent thenk tha had'st a be zich a Labb o' tha Tongue. **1847** HALLIWELL, *Lab*, a tittle-tattle; a blab. Also called a lab-o-the-tongue. *West.*

lab (læb), *sb.*[2] *colloq.* [Shortened from LABORATORY.] A laboratory. Also *attrib.* and *Comb.*, as ***lab assistant***, ***boy***, ***coat***, etc.

1895 W. C. GORE in *Inlander* Nov. 64 *Lab*, laboratory. **1900** *Captain* III. 312/1 Permission to footle in the lab. on half-holidays. **1912** *Chums* 5 Oct. 69/3 They walked along the corridor towards the chemistry lab. **1918** P. MAUBYN *Wartime Ballad* 26 Be sure they say the lab's the place For bold experiment. **1937** AUDEN & MACNEICE *Lett. from Iceland* v. 57 A Prince must be anonymous, observant, A kind of lab-boy, or a civil servant. **1949** R. CHANDLER *Let.* 10 Apr. in *R. Chandler Speaking* (1966) 206 There might be excellent reasons for picking up a letter with a handkerchief: ..to avoid putting more prints on it and thus making more work for the lab men. **1951** 'J. WYNDHAM' *Day of Triffids* ii. 50 He..lacked the qualifications for lab work. **1955** *Times* 26 July 10/5 Everyone who did even elementary 'stinks' at school remembers the name of Bunsen and his burner—even if nothing else remains in memory from those hours in the 'labs'. **1957** E. HYAMS *Into Dream* 114 In no time at all he'd be furnace-man, lab-boy. **1961** A. WILSON *Old Men at Zoo* ii. 87, I must also give preliminary seeding out interviews for Beard's four new lab assistants. **1962** L. DEIGHTON *Ipcress File* xviii. 108 Practically all the little countries have got their labs working on this. **1962** 'E. MCBAIN' *Like Love* (1964) xvi. 214 We just got a lab report. .. I'm talking about your fingerprints on the glass. **1964** R. PETRIE *Murder by Precedent* iii. 63 Pollard, covered by a white lab coat. **1967** 'E. PETERS' *Black is Colour* v. 92, I hope to have some specimens for the lab. boys. **1972** *Listener* 6 Apr. 467/1 An honest lab assistant loses his job for refusing to work on a poison gas project. **1972** *Lebende Sprachen* XVII. 72/2 Every hospital approved by the American College of Surgeons has all tissues lab-examined right after their surgical removal.

†**lab** (læb), *v. Obs.* [? Onomatopœic; cf. Du. *labben* = *klappen* 'garrire, blaterare, fabulari' (Kilian).] *trans.* and *intr.* To blab. Hence '**labbing** *ppl. a.*

1377 LANGL. *P. Pl.* B. XI. 102 No þinge þat is pryue publice þow it neuere, Neyther for loue laude [*MS. B.* lab] it nouȝt ne lakke it for enuye. **1393** *Ibid.* C. XIII. 39 Noþer for loue labbe hit out ne lacke hit for non enuye. *c* **1386** CHAUCER *Epil. Merch. T.* 10 Of hir tonge a labbyng shrewe is she. *c* **1475** *Partenay* 3751 By your labbyng tonges ionglin.

Labadist ('læbədɪst). *Eccl. Hist.* [ad. F. *Labadiste*, f. *Labadie*: see -IST.] A follower of Jean de Labadie (1610–74), who seceded from the Roman Church and founded a sect holding Quietist views. So '**Labadism**, the doctrines or practice of Labadists.

1753 CHAMBERS *Cycl. Supp.*, *Labadists*. **1882–3** SCHAFF in *Encycl. Rel. Knowl.* II. 1604.

Laban ('leɪbən). The name of Rudolph *Laban* (1879–1958), Hungarian-born choreographer, used *attrib.* to describe a system of dance notation invented by him. Hence ˌ**Labano'tation**, this system.

1954 R. LABAN *Princ. Dance & Movement Notation* 11/1, I have lived to see several excellent dance creations of our time preserved for coming generations by being written down in my Laban notation. *Ibid.* 19/2 The most active American stage dancers have taken up our notation..and this is largely due to the work of Ann Hutchinson. It may be mentioned here that the American group calls our system 'Labanotation'. **1954** A. HUTCHINSON *Labanotation* 5 Labanotation is a means of recording movement by means of symbols. **1958** *Times* 3 July 14/2 'Labanotation' is now the most widely used of all the notations that have been attempted to set down in score the steps, movements and patterns of the choreographer. **1961** WEBSTER s.v. *Icosahedron*. An imaginary polyhedron in the Laban system of dance notation representing the 20 principal movement directions of a dancer in its center. **1974** *Home & Store News* (Ramsey, New Jersey) 2 Jan. 39 The new typing element, developed by IBM and the Dance Notation Bureau, brings the speed and facility of the electric typewriter to Labanotation, a universally used system of notating movement.

†'**labant**, *a. Obs.*$^{-0}$. [ad. L. *labant-em*, pr. pple. of *labāre*.]

1727 BAILEY vol. II, *Labant*, sliding, falling down, wavering.

labarde, obs. form of LEOPARD.

labaria (læ'bɑːrɪə). Also **labarri**, **labarria**. [Amer. Sp., prob. f. native name.] A name used in Guyana for any of several poisonous coral snakes or pit vipers, esp. the fer-de-lance, *Trimeresurus* (or *Bothrops*) *atrox*, and the bush-master, *Lachesis muta*.

1825 C. WATERTON *Wanderings* I. 12 The Labarri snake is speckled, of a dirty brown colour. *Ibid.* III. 185 One day.. I caught a Labarri alive. **1889** J. RODWAY *In Guiana Wilds* 76 It was a snake, and as its colour could be distinguished, he perceived that it must be the deadly labarria. **1903** *Sci. Amer.* 7 Mar. 176 The Labarri is usually found coiled on the stump of a tree. **1918** W. BEEBE *Jungle Peace* (1919) viii. 188 'Huge labaria, yards long! Big as leg!' The flight of queen bees and their swarms, the call to arms in a sleeping camp creates somewhat the commotion that the news of the bush-master aroused with us. **1956** D. ATTENBOROUGH *Zoo Quest to Guiana* x. 145 Labaria is the local name for the fer-de-lance, one of the most dangerous and venomous of all the South American snakes. **1958** J. CAREW *Wild Coast* vi. 78 Only the small poisonous snakes like the labaria were really dangerous. **1968** *Daily Tel.* 24 July 20/4 The terrain is..full of dangerous snakes including the lethal labaria.

labarinth, obs. form of LABYRINTH.

Labarraque (labarak). The name of Antoine Germain *Labarraque* (1777–1850), Fr. pharmacist, used in the possessive and with *of*-adjunct (also in ***eau de Labarraque***) to denote an aqueous solution of sodium

hypochlorite used as a bleach and disinfectant, also known as *eau de Javelle* (see JAVELLE).

1827 *Q. Jrnl. Sci., Lit. & Art* I. 381 Since the notice which has been taken in this country of Labarraque's liquid, through the public journals, a person has actually forwarded to London the pretended chloride of oxide of sodium in a dry state, so cheap as to undersell the metropolitan chemists. **1863** RICHARDSON & WATTS *Chem. Technol.* (ed. 2) I. III. 393 Chloride of Soda, or Liquid of Labarraque. This solution may be prepared from liquid chloride of lime by double decomposition with carbonate or sulphate of soda, or by passing chlorine into a solution of caustic soda..or into a solution of carbonate of soda. **1875** Labarraque's Liquor [see JAVELLE]. **1886** *Buck's Handbk. Med. Sci.* II. 406/1 In the sick-room, a solution of chloride of lime..is to be recommended, both as a deodorant and as a disinfectant; or Labarraque's solution of hypochlorite of soda..may be substituted for the cheaper preparation. **1939** *Thorpe's Dict. Appl. Chem.* (ed. 4) III. 64/2 Sodium hypochlorite solution (Eau de Labarraque, usually called Eau de Javelle). **1949** KIRK & OTHMER *Encycl. Chem. Technol.* III. 683 Sodium hypochlorite solution U.S.P. 'contains not less than 4 per cent and not more than 6 per cent of NaClO'. This has replaced the former more dilute solution called Labarraque's solution. **1951** Labarraque's solution [see JAVELLE].

‖**labarum** ('læbərəm). [L.; = Gr. λαβαρόν, of unknown origin.] The imperial standard adopted by Constantine the Great (306-337 A.D.), being the Roman military standard of the late Empire modified by the addition of Christian symbols; hence *gen.*, a symbolical standard or banner.

1658 PHILLIPS, *Labarum*, a military streamer, or flag, also a Church Banner, or Ensign. **1682** WHELER *Journ. Greece* II. 189 On the South-side..is the Labarum; which is a Knot, consisting of the first Letters of Χριστὸς, which the Christian Emperours, from Constantine, placed in their Banners. **1835** BROWNING *Paracelsus* 54 A labarum was not deem'd Too much for the old founder of these walls. **1850** SIR J. STEPHEN *Ess. Eccl. Biog.* (ed. 2) I. 347 The Labarum of Luther was a banner inscribed with the legend, 'Justification by Faith'. **1850** LEITCH tr. *C. O. Müller's Anc. Art* §213. 206 Constantine wears the labarum and the phœnix. **1869** FARRAR *Fam. Sp.* (1873) iii. 106 That body of sacred truth..should now be inscribed upon the common labarum.

†**la'bascate**, *v. Obs.*⁻⁰ [erron. f. L. *labascĕre*, inceptive f. *labāre* to totter.] *intr.* 'To begin to fall or slide' (Bailey vol. II, 1727).

†**labascency.** *Obs. rare*⁻¹. [ad. L. **labascentia*, noun of state f. *labascĕre* to totter: see -ENCY.] Tottering state or condition.

a **1657** R. LOVEDAY *Lett.* (1663) 174 He that can take commission from his own sloth, to let fall the thred of a friendly intercourse, betrayes a labascency and a languor in his amicable resentments.

‖**labba** ('læbə). [? Native name.] One of the cavies, *Cœlogenys paca*, native to Guiana.

1825 WATERTON *Wanderings* i. (1879) 92 The Tapir, the Labba, and Deer, afford excellent food. **1876** C. B. BROWN *Brit. Guiana* ii. 25 [He] went..to procure some game for us, and returned with three fine labba (*Cœlogenis paca*).

labbe, obs. form of *let be*: see LET *v.*

labdacism: see LAMBDACISM.

‖**labdanum** ('læbdənəm). Also 6, 8 **lapdanum**. [med.L.; form of L. *lādanum*.] = LADANUM.

[*c* **1400** *Lanfranc's Cirurg.* v. ii. 334 Lapdanum.] **1502** *Arnold's Chron.* (1811) 234 [In list of spices] Lapdanum. **1533** ELYOT *Cast. Helthe* (1541) 11 a, Thinges good for a colde head: Cububes: Galingale: ..Labdanum. **1611** COTGR., *Labdane*, Labdanum; a fat, clammie, transparent, and sweet-smelling Gumme. **1714** *Fr. Bk. of Rates* 93 Lapdanum per 100 Weight 02 60. **1775** R. CHANDLER *Trav. Asia M.* (1825) I. 307 Hills green with flowering shrubs, and in particular with labdanum. **1830** LINDLEY *Nat. Syst. Bot.* 152 The resinous balsamic substance called Labdanum. **1835** BROWNING *Paracelsus* 101 Heap cassia, sandal-buds, and stripes Of labdanum.

la-bee obs. form of *let be*: see LET *v.*

labefact ('læbɪfækt), *ppl. a. rare.* [ad. L. *labefact-us*, pa. pple. of *labefacĕre*: see LABEFY. Cf. It. *labefatto* (Florio).] Shaken, tottering.

1874 BUSHNELL *Forgiveness & Law* i. 86 The integrity of the heathen world in general is just so far labefact, prostitute, and morally rotted away, as it has religiously abounded in expiations.

†'**labefact**, *v. Obs.* [f. ppl. stem of L. *labefacĕre*: see LABEFY.] *trans.* To shake, weaken.

c **1540** ABP. PARKER *Corresp.* (1853) 11 Not with covert inventions to labefact the credence of the people.

†**labe'factate**, *v. Obs. rare.* [f. L. *labefactāt-*, ppl. stem of *labefactāre*, freq. of *labefacĕre*: see LABEFY.] *trans.* To cause to totter or fall.

1657 TOMLINSON tr. *Renou's Disp.* 428 It labefactates houses by its weight.

labefactation (ˌlæbɪfæk'teɪʃən). *rare.* [ad. L. *labefactātiōn-em*, n. of action f. *labefactāre* (see prec.).] = next.

1775 JOHNSON in *Boswell*, There is in it [the 'Beggars' Opera'] such a labefactation of all principles as may be injurious to morality.

labefaction (læbɪ'fækʃən). [n. of action corresp. to LABEFY: see -FACTION.] A shaking, weakening; overthrow, downfall.

1620 VENNER *Via Recta* ii. 41 A suddaine labefaction of the liuer. *Ibid.* vii. 123 It..resisteth the corruption of humors, and labefaction of the vitall and naturall parts. **1793** W. ROBERTS *Looker-on* No. 36 (1794) II. 41 We should.. join them in promoting the labefaction of all human government. **1834** GLADSTONE in Liddon *Life Pusey* (1893) I. xiii. 309 Until the whole body of Churchmen is in such a state that all will be..secure against labefaction. **1878** R. W. DIXON *Hist. Ch. Eng.* I. v. 321 To private difficulties and causes of labefaction such as these, must be added several notable measures of confiscation which took place within the same limits of time.

†'**labefy**, *v. Obs. rare.* [ad. L. *labefacĕre* (f. root of *labāre* to fall, totter + *facĕre* to make): see -FY.] *trans.* To weaken, impair.

1620 VENNER *Via Recta* viii. 178 Not..to oppresse and labefie the digestiue faculty..with too great variety of meats.

label ('leɪbəl), *sb.*¹ Forms: 4 lable, 4-6 labelle, 5-7 labell, 6 labil, 4- label. [a. OF. *label* (also *lablel*) ribbon, fillet, file (in *Her.*); of obscure etymology; by some scholars thought to be of Teut. origin (cf. OHG. *lappa*: see LAP *sb.*¹). The synonymous OF. *lambel*, *lembel* is app. a variant: see LAMBEAU.]

1. A narrow band or strip of linen, cloth, etc.; a fillet, ribbon, tassel; the infula of a mitre.

c **1320** *Sir Beues* 974 King Ermin..ȝaf him a scheld gode & sur wiþ þre eglen of asur, þe champe of gold ful wel i-diȝt Wiþ fif lables [*MS.S.* labelles, *MS.N.* lambels] of seluer briȝt. **1519** HORMAN *Vulg.* 129, I wyll recompense the with a labell, *reponam appendice quadam.* **1530** PALSGR. 237/1 Labell, *houppe.* **1552** HULOET, A labell hanging on each side of a miter, *infula.* Labelles hanging down on garlands, or crownes, *lemnisci.* **1564** tr. *Jewel's Apol. Ch. Eng.* P vj b, Peter..sytting in his Chaire, with his triple Crowne full of labelles. **1577** tr. *Bullinger's Decades* (1592) 335 Broade beneath and sharpe aboue, in fashion somewhat like to the label of a bishops Miter. **1597-8** BP. HALL *Sat.* IV. ii. 24 A knit night-cap..With two long labels button'd to his chin. **1649** JER. TAYLOR *Gt. Exemp.* III. xv. 79 Persons..whose outside seemed to have appropriated religion to the labels of their frontlets. **1872** SHIPLEY *Gloss. Eccl. Terms* 199 s.v. *Fillet*, The labels of a bishop's mitre.

†**2.** A small strip of paper or parchment attached to a document by way of supplement to the matter contained therein; hence, a supplementary note, comment, or clause, a codicil. Also *fig. Obs.*

c **1380** WYCLIF *Wks.* (1880) 331 Certis if þise popis bulles shulen be undurstonden wiþ sich a label, þen-ne þei weren not profitable to þe purchasour ne to þe churche. —— *Sel. Wks.* II. 399 And so sich cursing of popis is tokene of blessing of God. And if þe Chirche were wel enformed of þis sentence, wiþ hise labellis, men shulden not drede feyned cursingis, ne lette for hem to sue Cristis lawe. **1562** *Apol. Priv. Masse* (1850) 39 It is but a very fond dalliance to brawl upon the labels before you agree upon the original verity. The true sense of this little sentence, *This is my body that shall be delivered for you*, is the root and the original of all such labels as we teach. **1592** SHAKS. *Rom. & Jul.* IV. i. 57 Ere this hand by thee to Romeo seal'd, Shall be the Labell to another Deede..this shall slay them both. **1611** —— *Cymb.* V. v. 430 When I wak'd, I found This Labell on my bosome. **1649** JER. TAYLOR *Gt. Exemp.* III. 75 Make us.. read our duty in the pages of revelation, not in the labels of accidentall effects. **1654** H. L'ESTRANGE *Chas. I* 80 It was presented to the King without any such saving label. **1658-1706** PHILLIPS, *Labels*..little pieces of parchment cut out long-wayes, and hanging upon Indentures, or other kinde of writings.

†**3.** *Astron.* and *Surveying.* In an astrolabe or a circumferentor, a narrow thin brass rule used chiefly in taking altitudes. *Obs.*

c **1391** CHAUCER *Astrol.* I. §22 Thanne hastow a label that is schapen lik a rewle, save that it is streit & hath no plates on either ende with holes. **1594** BLUNDEVIL *Exerc.* vi. Introd. (1636) 607 This Labell is divided into 90 degrees twice set doune therein with Arithmeticall figures. **1674** MOXON *Tutor Astron.* (ed. 3) II. xiii. 50 The Astrolabe is a round Instrument flat on either side... Upon the Center is a moveable Label or Ruler..whereupon is placed two Sights. *Ibid.* 51 The degree and part of degree that the Label lies on is the height of the Sun above the Horizon.

†**4.** *gen.* A slip or strip of anything; a narrow piece (of land); a clamp (of iron); etc. *Obs.*

c **1440** *Promp. Parv.* 282/2 Labelle, *labellum.* **1577-87** HARRISON *England* I. x. in *Holinshed* I. 34 By north of the Brier, lieth the Rusco, which hath a Labell or Byland, stretching out towards the southwest. **1649** JER. TAYLOR *Gt. Exemp.* XV. 39 They..'sealed the grave, and rolled a great stone at the mouth of it' and as an ancient tradition says, bound it about with labels of iron. **1650** FULLER *Pisgah* IV. i. 25 Where Balak met Balaam, standing as it were on his tiptoes on the very last labell of his land, to reach forth welcome to that false prophet. **1679** *Hist. of Jetzer* 5 The flesh and skin hung down in long Collops and Labels. **1682** WHELER *Journ. Greece* III. 249 Its Lungs..consisting of a thin, skinny Substance..divided into two Labels, placed on each side, and filled with Air; which being let out, those Labels shrunk together. **1686** PLOT *Staffordsh.* 335 Nine fryingpan-plates..claspt together by turning up 4 Labells which are ordinarily fixt to the lower plate.

5. *Her.* A mark of cadency distinguishing the eldest son of a family and consisting in a band drawn across the upper part of the shield having (usually three) dependent points (*label of three points*); cf. FILE *sb.*² 5. †Also, one of the dependent points (or *lambeaux*).

[**1394** in Rymer *Fœdera* (1709) VII. 763 Habeat justum Titulum hæreditarium ad portandum, pro Cresta sua, unum Leopardum de Auro, cum uno Labello Albo.] ?*a* **1412** LYDG. *Two Merchants* 868 For now of trowthe no man can contryve A verray seel or thenpreent i-grave Withoute a label his armes hool to save. **1463** in *Bury Wills* (Camden) 35 My best herte of gold with aungellys and a ruby with iiij. labellys of white innamyl. **1486** *Bk. St. Albans, Her.* f vii b, Off armys barrit and of labellis borne in armys. *c* **1500** *Sc. poem on Heraldry* 44 in *Q. Eliz. Acad.*, etc. 95 Nobillis bere merkis, to mak be knawin, ther douchtynes ..The fader the hole, the eldas son deffer[e]nt, quhiche a labelle; a cressent the secound. **1562** LEIGH *Armorie* (1597) 107 [see FILE *sb.*² 5]. **1610** GUILLIM *Heraldry* I. vi. (1660) 33 The Labell of the Heire apparent (saith Wyrley) is seldom transferred unto the second brother. **1611** COTGR., *Lambel*, ..a File with three Labels pendant. *Ibid.*, *Pendante*, a labell pendant. *c* **1640**, **1727** [see FILE *sb.*² 5]. **1708** CHAMBERLAYNE *State Gt. Brit.* I. II. v. (1743) 58 The Arms of the Prince of Wales at this Day differ from those of the King only by addition of a Label of three points. **1863** BOUTELL *Heraldry Hist. & Pop.* ix. 46 A Label is sometimes borne as a sole Charge. *Ibid.* xiv. 153 A silver label of five points.

6. A narrow strip of material attached to a document to carry the seal.

1494 FABYAN *Chron.* VII. 344 An instrument or wrytynge, at yᵉ which hynge many labellys with sealys. **1679-88** *Secr. Serv. Money Chas. & Jas.* (Camd.) 64 For writing, flourishing, and embellishing and guilding the subscripc'on and labells of a l're sent to the Czars of Russia. *a* **1680** BUTLER *Licentious Age Chas. II* 142 Until the subtlest of their conjurers Seal'd up the labels to his soul, his ears. **1726** AYLIFFE *Parerg.* 131 On this Label of Lead, the Heads of the two Apostles St. Peter and St. Paul are impressed from the Papal Seal. **1738** BIRCH *App. to Life Milton* M.'s Wks. I. 88 He did stitch the silk Cord or Label of that Seal with silk of the Colours of the said Label, and so fixed the Label and Seal to the said Commission.

7. a. A slip of paper, cardboard, metal, etc. attached or intended to be attached to an object and bearing its name, description, or destination. (The chief current sense.) Also *fig.*

1679 *Roxb. Ball.* (1883) IV. 549 Let several Labels from their mouths proceed, To note the different Tribes o' the Holy Seed: Here, 'Root and Branch'; there, 'Down with Babel, down!' **1680** DRYDEN *Sp. Friar* I. i, About his Neck There hung a Wench; the Label of his Function. **1702** C. MATHER *Magn. Christi* III. III. (1852) 556 A poor Indian having a label going from his mouth, with a *come over and help us.* **1722** DE FOE *Moll Flanders* (1840) 261 The hamper was directed by a lable on the cording. **1765** H. WALPOLE *Vertue's Anecd. Paint.* (1789) IV. 155 Sometimes a short label [in or on Hogarth's figures] is an epigram, and is never introduced without improving the subject. **1773** *Lond. Chron.* 7 Sept. 248/3 Labels for bottles. **1797** GODWIN *Enquirer* I. xv. 129 A collection of books..is viewed through glass doors, their outsides and labels are visible to the child, but the key is carefully kept. **1837** DICKENS *Pickw.* ii, With a brass label and number round his neck. **1841** FORBES *Eleven Yrs. Ceylon* I. 131 'Fine cold-drawn castor-oil' was found printed on the label. **1871** MORLEY *Voltaire* (1886) 4 To the critic of the schools, ever ready with the compendious label, he is the revolutionary destructive. **1888** A. K. GREEN *Behind Closed Doors* vii, Poison that is bought at a drug-store usually has a label on the bottle.

b. An adhesive postage-stamp, bill-stamp, or the like. (Now only in official language.)

1840 in Philbrick & Westoby *Postage Stamps Gt. Brit.* (1881) 46, I beg to enclose you two specimens of the Penny and Twopenny stamped Covers and Envelopes, and two of the Penny adhesive Labels. *Ibid.* 47 Sheets of 1*d.* Labels containing 240 Stamps. **1861** *Brit. Postal Guide* Jan. 14 Postage Stamps. Every Postmaster is required to have on hand a sufficient stock of postage labels and embossed penny envelopes.

c. A circular piece of paper on the centre of a gramophone record on which descriptive details of the record are printed; a recording company, or a section of one, producing records under a distinctive name; a record thus produced.

1907 *Yesterday's Shopping* (1969) 1037/1 Not more than one old 7 in. record will be allowed for against each New Concert Red Label, or 12 in. record. **1929** *Melody Maker* Apr. 369/1 A very fine example of this 'Scat Singing' is in 'Candy Lips' by Louis Armstrong's Washboard Beaters.., the label rightly describing it as 'Scat' chorus by Clarence Williams. **1939** S. W. SMITH in Ramsey & Smith *Jazzmen* 289 There are those who will have nothing but the original label. **1952** B. ULANOV *Hist. Jazz in Amer.* (1958) xviii. 216 The QRS Piano Roll Company was taking a flier in the record business and they invited Earl to record for their new label. **1957** G. EVANS in D. Cerulli et al. *Jazz Word* (1962) 174 A friend of mine..was told by an a&r man at a relatively new major label that if he insisted on charging scale, he'd never be used there again. **1964** *Amer. Folk Music Occasional* I. 16 *R.* A recording company heard of us and wanted to record us. *Q.* What label was that? *R.* That was United. A fellow by the name of Allen was the president of that label. **1970** *Melody Maker* 20 June 27/1 The above could well be the theme song for most record companies today who have finally realised that jazz is a good seller for budget price labels. **1971** *Daily Tel.* 16 Aug. 6/3 Are there precedents for a primadonna appearing on three different labels virtually at the same time?

d. *Biol.* and *Chem.* A substance (as a distinctive isotope, or a dye) used to label another substance (see LABEL *v.* 2).

1935 [see LABEL *v.* 2]. **1939** *Jrnl. Biol. Chem.* CXXVII. 287 The use of two independent isotopic labels (D and N^{15}) in the same amino acid molecule may reveal a more complete picture of its metabolism. **1962** R. C. NAIRN *Fluorescent Protein Tracing* i. 1 The choice of a tracing method with fluorescent rather than radioactive labels is governed by the type of information sought. **1971** *Nature* 23 July 225/3 By allowing the 'toluenized' cells to incorporate the density label bromodeoxyuridine triphosphate and then isolating and characterizing the newly made DNA they have been able to prove that synthesis is semiconservative. **1972**

Science 13 Oct. 185/1 Frogs injected with labeled (radioactive) Na^+ rapidly lose the 'label' to bathing medium containing Na^+.

e. *Computers.* A character or set of characters used as an arbitrary name for a statement in a program so as to facilitate reference to it elsewhere in the program.

1958 *Communications Assoc. Computing Machinery* Dec. 14 A statement may be made identifiable by attaching to it a label L, which is an identifier I, or an integer G (with the meaning of identifier). The label precedes the statement labeled, and is separated from it by the separator colon (:). **1962** B. A. Galler *Lang. Computers* iii. 27 To indicate a transfer to another part of the program, we must be able to label the place to which the transfer is to be made. In other words, we need a way to attach a label such as START to a statement. Let us specify that statement labels must have the same form as names of variables, i.e., up to six letters or digits, the first of which must be a letter. **1969** P. B. Jordain *Condensed Computer Encycl.* 272 The use of labels makes it easier to write programs, for mnemonic names may be used for labels.. and the programmer is relieved of the detail of maintaining the layout of locations assigned in the computer memory. **1970** O. Dopping *Computers & Data Processing* xix. 308 In automatic coding.. each data item receives a name, or symbolic address... Not only data cells need names, but also certain instructions, for example, instructions to which the program has to branch. Names of instructions are often called labels.

f. *Computers.* A set of data recorded on a reel of magnetic tape that is descriptive of its contents and serves for identification by a computer.

1961 L. W. Hein *Introd. Electronic Data Processing* ix. 170 To prevent the incorrect use of tape files, internal labels should be incorporated into every tape. *Ibid.* 171 Wherever possible, the checking of the tape label should be done without operator intervention. **1967** McLachlan & Molsom *Data Processing* xiii. 187 One item usually written in the label is known as a retention period, or purge date... This is to provide on the tape information from which a program can detect whether the data recorded on the tape is out of date and can be overwritten. In addition the name of the file and its generation number are also written in the label... Tape reels are, of course, also labelled externally for visual identification by computer operators.

8. *Arch.* A moulding over a door, window, or other opening; a dripstone.

1823 in Nicholson *Pract. Builder* 587. **1850** *Parker's Gloss. Archit.* (ed. 5) s.v. *Dripstone*, The term *Label* is borrowed from heraldry, and therefore in strictness is only applicable to the straight form which is used in Perpendicular work, which resembles the heraldic label. **1851** *Turner's Dom. Archit.* II. ii. 30 The arches have no projecting label. **1879** Sir G. G. Scott *Lect. Med. Archit.* I. vi. 225 As the junction of the arch with the wall above was but slightly marked a small projecting moulding was introduced which we call the drip-stone or label.

9. *attrib.* and *Comb.*, as (sense 7) ***label-licking***, ***-paster***; **label-cloth**, cloth used for the making of labels for books; **label-ink**, ink used in the marking of labels; †**label-lolling** *a.*, projecting like a label (sense 7); **label-mould**, **-moulding** = sense 8; †**label-seal**, a seal attached to a document by a 'label'; **label-stop** *Arch.*, a boss or corbel supporting the end of a label or dripstone.

1891 *Daily News* 1 Dec. 2/3 The manufacture of book cloth, tracing cloth, *label cloth, and grey cloth. **1863** *Fownes' Man. Elem. Chem.* (ed. 9) III. 683 [It] forms a most excellent *label-ink for the laboratory, as it is unaffected by acid vapours. **1899** *Daily News* 9 Sept. 3/4 *Label-licking, which is practised largely in thread mills and aerated water factories. **1615** Sir E. Hoby *Curry-combe* v. 237 These mushrumps (grounded vpon a lesse motiue) may not bee questioned, though nothing so euident as a blareing *label-lolling tongue, which without the helpe of a Muffler, could not be so well concealed. **1878** McVittie *Ch. Ch. Cath.* 67 Over the large pointed arch is a *label-mould. **1830** Mrs. Bray *Fitz of Fitz-ford* iv. (1884) 33 A well-turned archway, ornamented with the oak-branch and the *label-moulding. **1889** Pask *Eyes Thames* 172 They have been book-binders, boot-closers, *label-pasters, and such like. **1679** Willoughby in *Mansell's Narr. Pop. Plot* 21 A Commission, with thirteen *Label-seals, and as many Names thereto. **1894** C. G. Harper *Marches of Wales* 132 A carefully rendered little head.. carved on the *label-stop of the canopy.

label ('leɪbəl), *sb.*² *Bot.* [ad. L. labellum.] †**a.** ? A segment of a leaf (*obs.*). **b.** The lip of a ringent corolla.

1671 Grew *Anat. Plants* iv. §16 If the Leaves be much indented or jagg'd, now we have the Duplicature; wherein there are divers plaits in one Leaf, or Labels of a Leaf. **1707** Sloane *Jamaica* I. 162 The flower stands on a three inches long foot-stalk, is made like the flowers of the Aristolochia.. the label being covered with a yellowish farina. **1888** *Syd. Soc. Lex.*, *Label*, same as *Labellum*.

label ('leɪbəl), *v.* Also 9 lable. [f. label *sb.*¹]

1. a. *trans.* To affix a label to, mark with a label.

1601 Shaks. *Twel. N.* I. v. 265, I will giue out diuers schedules of my beautie. It shalbe Inuentoried and euery particle and vtensile labell'd to my will: As, Item two lippes indifferent redde [etc.]. **1786** Mad. D'Arblay *Diary* 2 Aug., The Queen.. employed the Princess Royal to label them [books]. **1790** W. Hastings *Let.* 2 Dec. in Boswell *Johnson* (1793) III. 315 A parcel containing other select papers, and labelled with the titles appertaining to them. **1831** Carlyle *Misc.* II. 309 Common ashes are solemnly labelled as fell poison. *c* **1865** J. Wylde in *Circ. Sci.* I. 313/2 This may be labled 'oxygen mixture'. **1885** *Law Times* LXXVIII. 385/2 The due diligence of the consignors in labelling and delivering the goods to the carriers. **1893** Matheson *About Holland* 22 A carriage labelled *Niet rooken*.

b. *fig.* To describe or designate as with a label; to set down in a category (*as* so and so).

a **1853** Robertson *Lect.* ii. (1858) 59 This foolish and wicked system of labelling men with names. **1871** Morley *Voltaire* (1872) 277 We cannot label Voltaire either spiritualist or materialist. **1875** Jowett *Plato* (ed. 2) II. 293 He despatches the bad to Tartarus, labelled either as curable or incurable. **1881** M. Arnold *Byron* in *Macm. Mag.* XLIII. 376 It would be most unjust to label Byron.. as a rhetorician only.

2. *Biol.* and *Chem.* To make (a substance, a molecule, or a constituent atom) experimentally recognizable but essentially unaltered in behaviour, so that its path may be followed (e.g. through chemical reactions) or its distribution ascertained: esp. by replacing an atom in a proportion of the molecules by an atom of another isotope of the same element, identifiable by its radioactivity or its different mass, or by causing a (usu. fluorescent) dye to become attached to a proportion of the molecules. Cf. label *sb.*¹ 7 d.

1935 *Jrnl. Biol. Chem.* CXI. 164 In order successfully to label a physiological substance, it is essential that the chemical and physical properties of the labeled substance be so similar to the unlabeled one that the animal organism will not be able to differentiate between them. The chemist, on the other hand, must be able to distinguish and to estimate them in small quantities and at high dilutions. A possibility for such a label is the use of an isotope. **1949** *Ann. Rep. Progr. Chem.* XLV. 251 Feeding $CH_3{}^{.13}CO_2H$ [to rats] labels the 2 and the 8 carbon atoms of uric acid, but not the 4 carbon atom. $NH_2{}^{.}CH_2{}^{.13}CO_2H$, however, labels carbon atom 4, but not carbon atom 2 or 8. **1951** C. P. Leblond in G. E. W. Wolstenholme *Ciba Foundation Conf. Isotopes in Biochem.* (Ciba Foundation symposia) 5 A number of radioactive steroids have been synthesized: progesterone labelled with ^{14}C in positions 21 or 3; œstrone labelled in position 16; [etc.]. **1951** *Sci. News* XXII. 76 It can be shown that all oxygen evolved by the illuminated chloroplasts comes from water. If some of the molecules of the water in which the chloroplasts are suspended is [*sic*] 'labelled' with isotopic oxygen, i.e. if the water is made to contain an excess of H_2O^*, where O^* is an isotope of oxygen, then the evolved oxygen contains O^*_2, in precisely the same concentration at which H_2O^* is present in the water. **1962** R. C. Nairn *Fluorescent Protein Tracing* i. 1 Proteins, including serum antibodies, can be labelled by chemical combination with fluorescent dyes, without material effect on the biological or immunological properties of the proteins. **1971** J. Z. Young *Introd. Study Man* v. 82 These isotopes can be introduced into the body and used to 'label' a particular compound and discover for how long it remains in the tissues. The isotope differs in nuclear mass from the normally occurring form.. but this does not, in general, make it behave chemically in any markedly different way.

Hence **'labelling** *vbl. sb.* Also **'labeller**.

1871 *Echo* 8 Feb., The public.. condemn us for labelling the Poison... By inserting this in your next issue you will greatly oblige one of the labellers. **1895** *Athenæum* 17 Aug. 219/3 A labelling of Welsh names. **1896** *Westm. Gaz.* 26 Mar. 2/1 Bottle fillers, washers, and labellers.

labellate (lə'bɛlət), *a. Zool.* [f. L. labellum + -ate³.] (See quot.)

1846 Dana *Zooph.* (1848) 432 *Labellate*.. Long-lipped, or in shape nearly like the blade of a shovel.. It passes into the dimidiate form.

labelled ('leɪbəld), *a.* [f. label *sb.*¹ and *v.* + -ed.] **a.** *Her.* Of a mitre: Having labels or infulæ (of a particular tincture). ***labelled line*** (see quot. 1753). **b.** *Arch.* Having a label or dripstone. **c.** Marked with a ticket bearing the name, description of contents, etc. of the article.

1570 Levins *Manip.* 49/37 Labelled, *infulatus*. **1753** Chambers *Cycl. Supp.*, *Labelled line*, in heraldry, a term used by some to express the line in certain old arms, called more usually urdee or champagne. Others apply the same word to express the patee or dovetail line, called also the inclave line by Morgan. **1841** R. P. Ward *De Clifford* II. x. 115 A castle.. with.. its towers, and labelled windows. **1863** Boutell *Heraldry Hist. & Pop.* xxi. 358 Arg., on a cross sa., a mitre labelled or. **1895** *Bookseller's Catal.*, Leech himself in a nightcap sitting by the fire with a labelled bottle on the mantelshelf.

d. *Biol.* and *Chem.* Of an atom: of a different isotope (of the element normally present). Of a molecule or substance: made recognizable by labelling (see sense 2 of the vb.).

1935 [see label *v.* 2]. **1949** *Ann. Rep. Progr. Chem.* XLV. 244 In the acetate, both carbon atoms were derived from the labelled atom in glycine. **1953** *Sci. News* XXIX. 35 If we take a thin sheet of a metal and deposit upon its upper surface a very thin layer of its radioactive isotope.. and heat the sheet to a sufficiently high temperature, self-diffusion will occur, and the labelled atoms will move into, and about, the lattice of atoms in the sheet. **1961** *Lancet* 29 July 258/1 [They] gave ^{131}I-labelled insulin to pregnant rats to study the role of the placenta in the metabolism of carbohydrate. **1962** R. C. Nairn *Fluorescent Protein Tracing* i. 3 Less commonly used is direct fluorescent tracing.. in which labelled proteins are injected into animals and their distribution in the body determined by subsequent microscopy of tissue sections. **1970** *Sci. Amer.* Mar. 92/1 After the hens had been fed the radioactive calcium for a week the skeleton became intensely labeled.

labelloid (lə'bɛlɔɪd), *a. Bot.* [f. next + -oid.] Lip-like, lip-shaped.

1830 Lindley *Nat. Syst. Bot.* 275 Perianthium minute, either a single labelloid lobe, or an urceolate 6-toothed body.

‖**labellum** (lə'bɛləm). [L. 'little lip', dim. of *labrum* lip.]

1. *Bot.* The lower division or 'lip' of an orchidaceous corolla, often enlarged or curiously shaped.

1830 Lindley *Nat. Syst. Bot.* 263 Sometimes it [*sc.* the anther] stands erect, the line of dehiscence of its lobes being turned towards the labellum. **1859** Darwin *Orig. Spec.* vi. (1873) 154 This orchid has part of its labellum or lower lip hollowed out into a great bucket. **1882** Vines *Sachs' Bot.* 882 The labellum of *Megaclinium falcatum*.

2. *Ent.* One of a pair of tumid lobes terminating the proboscis of certain insects.

1826 Kirby & Sp. *Entomol.* III. 361

†**'labent,** *a. Obs.*⁻⁰ [ad. L. *lābent-*, pr. pple. of *lābī* to fall.] 'Falling, sliding, fleeting, running, or passing away' (Bailey 1727 vol. II).

†**labeon, labion.** *Obs. rare.* [ad. L. *labeōn-em*, *labiōn-em*, augmentative, f. *labium* lip.] One who has large lips.

1650 Bulwer *Anthropomet.* (1653) 175 The same or worse must befall these artificiall Labions, for their Lips must need hang in their light, and their words stick in the birth. **1658** Phillips, *Labeons*, blaber-lipped persons.

laberinth, -ynth, obs. forms of labyrinth.

labey ('læbɪ). *Sc.* Also 9 laby, lebbie. [Of obscure origin; cf. Gael. *leòbag* 'little shred or fragment' (McL. & D.); also lap *sb.*¹] A loose garment or wrap; the lappet or skirt of a coat.

a **1597** *Satir. Poems Reform.* xliii. 190 The hirdis and hinde men in their labeis lay. **1811** A. Scott *Poems, Country Smiddy* 68 (Jam.) His new coat labey. **1825–80** Jamieson, *Lebbie*, the lap or fore-skirt of a man's coat. **1890** J. Service *Thir Notandums* iv. 20 The labies o' his Sark.

labia: see labium.

labial ('leɪbɪəl), *a.* and *sb.* [ad. med.L. *labiāl-is*, f. *labi-um* lip. Cf. F. *labial* (1690 in Furetière).]

A. *adj.*

1. Of or pertaining to the lips.

1650 Bulwer *Anthropomet.* xi. 107 Lip-Gallantry, or certain labial Fashions invented by diverse Nations. **1837** Marryat *Dog-Fiend* xix, The olfactory examination was favourable, so he put his mouth to it—the labial essay still more so. **1848** Clough *Amours de Voy.* ii. 157 The labial muscles that swelled with Vehement evolution of yesterday Marseillaises. **1867** Jean Ingelow *Lily & Lute* ii. 108 More than I can make you view, With my paintings labial. **1867** A. J. Ellis *E.E. Pronunc.* I. iii. §3. 161 The volume of the mouth is divided into two bent tubes of which the first may be termed the *lingual* passage as its front extremity is formed by the tongue, and the second, the *labial* passage.

b. *spec.* in *Anat.*, *Zool.*, etc. Pertaining to a lip, lip-like part, or labium; having the character or functions of a lip.

1656 Blount *Glossogr.* s.v. *Vein*, *Labial veins*, the lip veines, whereof there are two on each inner side, both of the upper and under lip. **1722** Quincy *Lex. Physico-Med.* (ed. 2) 227 Labial Glands. **1826** Kirby & Sp. *Entomol.* III. 356 *Palpi Labiales* (the Labial Feelers). **1851–6** Woodward *Mollusca* 211 The lips and labial tentacles of the ordinary bivalves. **1879** T. Bryant *Pract. Surg.* II. 230 Labial cysts are very common, and are usually met with on the inner side of the labia. **1881** Mivart *Cat* 27 The membrane lining the mouth abounds in small glands, those within the cheeks and lips being termed buccal and labial respectively.

c. ***labial pipe***: an organ-pipe furnished with lips, a flue-pipe.

1852 Seidel *Organ* 21 An organ.. which contained the following labial or languet registers. **1863** Tyndall *Heat* viii. App. 280 The flame is also affected by various D's of an adjustable labial pipe. **1876** Hiles *Catech. Organ* iv. (1878) 23 Flue-pipes are also called *Labial*, or lip-pipes.

2. *Phonetics.* The distinctive epithet of those sounds which require complete or partial closure of the lips for their formation, as the consonants p, b, m, f, v, w, and the 'rounded' vowels.

1594 T. B. *La Primaud. Fr. Acad.* II. 87 The Hebrewes name their letters, some gutturall..; others dentall..; & so they call others, labiall, that is letters of the lips. *c* **1620** A. Hume *Brit. Tongue* I. vii, I beginning to lay my grundes of labial, dental, and guttural soundes and symboles. *Ibid.* A labial letter can not symboliz a guttural syllab. **1668** Wilkins *Real Char.* III. xiv. 379 The Vowels, as they are distinguished into *Labial*; being framed by an emission of the Breath through the Lips [etc.]. **1865** Tylor *Hist. Man.* iv. 73 Words containing labial and dental letters.

B. *sb.*

1. A labial sound.

1668 Wilkins *Real Char.* III. xiv. 380 The labials are represented by two curve Figures for the Lips. *a* **1709** W. Baxter *Let.* in *Gloss. Antiq. Rom.* (1731) 409 The third Sort are Labials formed by the Lips alone. **1849–50** Thackeray *Pendennis* xlvi, You have but the same four letters to describe the salute which.. you bestow on the sacred cheek of your mistress—but the same four letters and not one of them a labial. **1864** Max Müller *Sci. Lang.* Ser. II. iv. 162 It is a fact.. that the Mohawks.. have no p, b, m, f, v, w—no labials of any kind.

2. A labial part or organ, e.g. one of the plates or scales which border the mouth of a fish or reptile, one of the labial palpi of insects.

1885 W. K. Parker *Mammalian Desc.* ii. 46 The finished labials (lip-cartilages) of the types just referred to.

labialism (ˈleɪbɪəlɪz(ə)m). *Phonetics.* [f. LABIAL + -ISM.] Tendency to labialize sounds; labial pronounciation.

1881 *Encycl. Brit.* XIII. 810/2 In one set [of cognate words] we see the phenomenon of labialism, in the other assibilation, but no touch of labialism.

labiality (leɪbɪˈælɪtɪ). *Phonetics.* [f. LABIAL *a.* 2 + -ITY.] The quality of being labial; an instance of this.

1893 *Funk's Stand. Dict.* 991/1 *Labiality*, the quality of being labial. **1952** [see ALVEOLARITY]. **1973** *Word 1970* XXVI. 140 A language is modified toward an ideal system, as was Sanskrit in developing voiceless aspirates and losing concomitant labiality.

labialize (ˈleɪbɪəlaɪz), *v. Phonetics.* [f. LABIAL + -IZE.] *trans.* To render (a sound) labial in character; to 'round' (a vowel). Also *absol.* Hence **ˈlabialized** *ppl. a.*

1867 A. J. ELLIS *E.E. Pronunc.* I. iii. §3. 160 Round or Labialised Vowels. *Ibid.* 162 That (u) is almost (ə) labialized or rounded. *Ibid.* 163 By merely neglecting to labialise, (u, *u*) are converted into (*æ*, *ɒ*). **1874** SWEET *Hist. Eng. Sounds* 74 The *i* has been gutturalized and labialized into *u* by *l*. **1876** DOUSE *Grimm's Law* §57. 140 The labialized *K*'s.

Hence **labialiˈzation**, the action of labializing or the condition of being labialized; 'rounding' (of a vowel).

1867 A. J. ELLIS *E.E. Pronunc.* I. iii. 74 The vowels differ by the important distinction of labialisation. **1877** SWEET *Primer Phonetics* §36. 13 Rounding,..a contraction of the mouth cavity by lateral compression of the cheek passage and narrowing of the lip aperture, whence the older name labialization.

ˈlabially, *adv.* [f. LABIAL *a.* + -LY.] **1.** With a labial sound or utterance.

1798 H. T. COLEBROOKE tr. *Dig. Hindu Law* (1801) I xxvii, Sometimes pronounced gutturally, sometimes labially.

2. Toward the lips.

1905 in GOULD *Dict. New Med. Terms* 325/1. **1908** G. V. BLACK *Work on Operative Dentistry* I. 241 The broad cutting edge of the central incisor is that which most frequently pushes the root of the deciduous tooth labially. **1963** C. R. COWELL et al. *Inlays, Crowns & Bridges* iv. 38 The slice is inclined towards the lingual aspect and only extends far enough labially for the margin to reach the embrasure. **1971** *Nature* 30 July 311/1 At the incisor sockets the alveolar margin seems to be preserved lingually but is broken labially.

labiate (ˈleɪbɪət), *a.* and *sb.* [ad. mod.L. *labiāt-us*, f. LABI-UM: see -ATE³.] **A.** *adj.*

1. *Bot.* **a.** Lipped: applied to flowers which have the corolla or calyx divided into two parts opposed in such a way as to suggest lips; bilabiate. **b.** Belonging to the N.O. *Labiatæ*, consisting of herbaceous plants and under-shrubs, characterized by flowers of the form above described, opposite leaves, and usually square stalks, e.g. the mints, ground-ivy, the dead nettles, etc.

1706 PHILLIPS (ed. Kersey), *Labiate Flowers* (among Herbalists) are those that have one or two Lips; some of which represent a kind of Helmet, or Monk's Hood. **1785** MARTYN *Rousseau's Bot.* iv. 46 The white Dead-nettle bears a monopetalous labiate flower. **1835** LINDLEY *Introd. Bot.* (1848) I. 334 When the two lips are separated from each other by a wide regular orifice,..the corolla is said to be labiate or ringent. **1862** BELLEW *Miss. Afghanistan* 451 The greensward..was covered with a variety of labiate herbs, amongst which the wild thyme, mint, basil, sage, and lavender were recognized. **1881** *Sci. Gossip* 254 The black horehound and other labiate plants.

2. a. *Anat.* and *Zool.* Formed like or resembling in shape, function, etc. a lip or labium. **b.** *Ent.* Of an orifice: Having thickened, fleshy margins.

In recent Dicts.

B. *sb. Bot.* A labiate plant.

1845 LINDLEY *Sch. Bot.* vi. (1862) 95 Order XLIV. Lamiaceæ—Labiates. **1861** S. THOMSON *Wild Flowers* III. (ed. 4) 196 The common bugle,..one of the labiates. **1879** LUBBOCK *Sci. Lect.* i. 19 Generally in the Labiates, the corolla has the lower lip adapted as an alighting board for insects.

labiated (ˈleɪbɪeɪtɪd), *a. Bot.* and *Zool.* ? *Obs.* [Formed as prec. + -ED.] Lipped, labiate.

1707 SLOANE *Jamaica* I. 173 Small stalks, having..many white labiated flowers. **1776** WITHERING *Brit. Plants* (1796) III. 26 The labiated shape of the calyx. **1835** KIRBY *Hab. & Inst. Anim.* I. xii. 333 In some [Annelidans] it [the mouth] is simple, orbicular or labiated.

labiatiflorous (ˌleɪbɪeɪtɪˈflɔərəs), *a. Bot.* [f. mod.L. *labiātus* LABIATE + *-flōr-us* (f. *flōr-*, *flōs* FLOWER) + -OUS.] Having a labiate corolla. Also **ˌlabiatiˈfloral** *a.* (in recent Dicts.).

1855 MAYNE *Expos. Lex.*, *Labiatiflorus*..labiatiflorous. **1880** GRAY *Struct. Bot.* 417 Labiatiflorous. Said of certain Compositae with bilabiate corollas.

labidometer (læbɪˈdɒmɪtə(r)). *Surg.* [f. Gr. λαβιδο-, λαβίς forceps + μέτρον -METER. Cf. F. *labidomètre*.] An instrument consisting of a pair of obstetric forceps with a graduated scale attached for measuring the size of the fœtal head.

1853 in DUNGLISON *Med. Lex.* (ed. 9).

†**labies**, *sb. pl. Obs.* [Plural of **labie*, **laby*, ad. LABI-UM. Cf. obs. F. *labie* (Cotgr.).] Lips.

1541 R. COPLAND *Galyen's Therap.* 2 Civ, Yf a shepeherde saw the labies of a sore harde, flynty, wan, and blacke..he wold haue no dowbte for to cut it.

labile (ˈleɪbɪl, -aɪl; formerly also ˈlæbɪl), *a.* Also 5 labyl, 7 labil. [ad. L. *lābil-is*, f. *lābī* to slip, fall, LAPSE: see -ILE. Cf. F. *labile*.]

1. Liable or prone to lapse. †**a.** Prone to fall into error or sin; *Theol.* liable to fall from innocence (*obs.*). **b.** Of a fund, etc.: Lapsable.

1447 BOKENHAM *Seyntys* (Roxb.) 147 My labyl mynde and the dulnesse Of my wyt. **1678** GALE *Crt. Gentiles* III. 199 The supralapsarian Divines, who make man as labile the object of reprobation. **1740** CHEYNE *Regimen* iv. 140 All Creatures being finite and free, must necessarily, by their Nature, be labile, fallible and peccable. **1894** *Forum* June 449 These funds are no more labile than any other form of trust or mortmain.

†**2.** Apt to slip away, slippery. *lit.* and *fig. Obs.*

1623 COCKERAM, *Labile*, slipperie, unstable. **1654** JER. TAYLOR *Real Pres.* 14 Now a man would think we had him sure; but his nature is labile and slippery.

3. Prone to undergo displacement in position or change in nature, form, chemical composition, etc.; unstable. Now only in *Physics* and *Chemistry*.

1603 FLORIO *Montaigne* II. xii. (1632) 340 Pithagoras [said] that each thing or matter was ever gliding and labile. **1654** JER. TAYLOR *Real Pres.* §1 Wood..can..be made thin, labile and inconsistent. **1878** FOSTER *Physic.* II. v. 363 More labile than tissue proteid and yet more stable than the circulating proteid. **1889** BURDON-SANDERSON in *Nature* Sept. 26 Protoplasm..comes to consist of two things..of acting part which lives and is stable, and of acted-on part which has never lived and labile, that is, in a state of metabolism. **1894** LD. SALISBURY in *Pop. Sci. Monthly* Nov. 40 The genius of Lord Kelvin has recently discovered what he terms a labile state of equilibrium. **1947** *New Biol.* VII. 66 In both spring and winter rye the first seven initials to be developed at the growing point give rise to leaves under any combination of environmental factors so far tried. These are followed by about 18 'labile' initials which may give rise either to leaves or flowers according to treatment. **1951** I. L. FINAR *Org. Chem.* I. x. 170 When one tautomer is more stable than the other under ordinary conditions, the former is known as the stable form, and the latter as the labile form. **1970** *Nature* 4 Apr. 25/2 The other component of nitrogenase from the two bacteria has a molecular weight of about 40,000, two iron and two labile sulphide groups.

4. *Electr.* Said of the application of a current by moving an electrode over an affected region instead of holding it firmly at one part.

1888 in *Syd. Soc. Lex.* **1893** A. S. ECCLES *Sciatica* vi. 65 With the anode labile over the foot, leg, and thigh. **1896** *Allbutt's Syst. Med.* I. 369 The battery current labile over the affected muscles.

Hence **laˈbility**, proneness to lapse, instability of form or nature. Now chiefly in scientific use.

1554 in *Maitl. Club Misc.* III. (1855) 65 The labilite and breuitie of tymes maneris and of men in this wale of teiris beand considerit. **1557** R. EDGEWORTH *Sermons* Pref. sig. ✠3, I euer fearinge the labilitie of my remembraunce, vsed to pen my sermons. **1646** GAULE *Cases Consc.* 34 Vanity of Science, error of Conscience, lability of innocence. **1654** JER. TAYLOR *Real Pres.* xi. §32. 247 Consistence or lability, are not essential to wood and water. **1740** CHEYNE *Regimen* v. (1790) 218 But Sensibility and Intelligence, being by their Nature and Essence free must be labile, and by their Lability may actually lapse, degenerat [etc.]. **1810** COLERIDGE *Lit. Remains* (1838) III. 353 To the species water continuity and lability are essential. **1903** A. R. WALLACE *Man's Place in Universe* xi. 207 Those peculiarities which are essential to life—extreme sensitiveness and lability. **1904** *Jrnl. R. Microsc. Soc.* 188 By combining these two methods there is induced a 'nuclear lability', which renders these eggs susceptible to the influence of carbon dioxide as a provocative of cleavage. **1924** J. G. A. SKERL tr. *Wegener's Orig. Continents & Oceans* 154 The frequently described 'lability' of the geosynclinals. **1942** *Jrnl. Immunol.* XLV. 164 The lability in formalin of any antigen studied must thus be determined. **1970** H. C. SHANDS *Semiotic Approaches to Psychiatry* xxiii. 395 Clinical observation often suggests that the emotional lability of the 'schizophrenic' is not only often less than, it is also sometimes greater than, that of the normal. **1973** J. M. ANDERSON *Structural Aspects of Language Change* 143 The holes in the phonological paradigm are characterized by a general condition of lability.

labilize (ˈleɪbɪlaɪz), *v. Chem.* and *Biochem.* [f. LABIL(E *a.* + -IZE.] *trans.* To render labile (esp. a chemical bond). So **ˈlabilizing** *ppl. a.* and *vbl. sb.*

1903 *Nature* 26 Feb. 385/2 The *rôle* of the oxygen must have been that of a labilising agent. **1938** *Jrnl. Biol. Chem.* CXXV. 1 These and other polar groups..may conceivably labilize adjacent carbon-bound hydrogen atoms. **1957** *New Biol.* XXIII. 77 Proteins could also have become radioactive by an exchange reaction in which two peptide bonds in the chain of a protein are labilized, allowing an amino acid held at this point to be exchanged with another molecule of the same amino acid present in the surrounding medium. **1962** *Biochem. Pharmacol.* IX. 113 Stabilization disappears and is replaced by a labilizing influence. **1972** *European Jrnl. Biochem.* XXVI. 540/1 Free lysosome enzymes can labilize lysosomal membrane. **1973** *Chem. Soc. Rev.* II. 177 The factor responsible for a high labilizing ability depends on this mechanism.

Hence **ˌlabiliˈzation**, the process of rendering or becoming labile; **ˈlabilizer**, a labilizing agent.

1938 *Jrnl. Biol. Chem.* CXXV. 19 Stekol and Hamill.. have claimed that proteolytic enzymes can carry out such a labilization. **1956** *Radiation Res.* V. 263 The increased susceptibility of X-irradiated DNP to the action of trypsin is not inconsistent with the concept of a labilization of the DNA-to-protein salt-like secondary linkages. **1965** *Dissertation Abstr.* XXV. 4355/2 It is concluded that the labilization of the carboxyl carbon of glycine is a discrete reaction which can be measured independently of reactions related to further metabolism of the α-carbon. **1967** PIKE & BROWN *Nutrition* vii. 145 Other labilizers of the lysosomal membrane are ultraviolet light and ionizing radiation. **1974** *Nature* 13 Dec. 579/1 The labilisation of the ligand *trans* to an oxo group is a well known effect.

laˈbimeter. *Surg.* [ad. F. *labimètre*, incorrectly f. Gr. λαβίς (nom.): see LABIDOMETER.] = LABIDOMETER.

1853 in DUNGLISON *Med. Lex.* (ed. 9).

labio- (ˈleɪbɪəʊ), taken as comb. form of L. *labium* lip, (*a*) in *Phonetics*, with the sense 'formed with lips and (some other organ)', as ***labio-dental*** adj. and sb., ***labio-guttural***, ***-lingual***, ***-nasal***, ***-palatal*** (hence ***labio-palatalize*** vb.), adjs.; (nonce-wd.) ***labio-palato-nasal*** adj.; **labiovelar** *a.*, formed with the lips and the soft palate; also as *sb.*; hence **labioˈvelarize** *v.*, to pronounce with labiovelar articulation; **ˌlabiovelariˈzation**; (*b*) *Path.*, 'affecting or having to do with the lips and (some other part)', as ***labio-alveolar***, ***labio-glosso-laryngeal***, ***-pharyngeal***, ***labio-mental*** [L. *mentum* chin], etc. (*Syd. Soc. Lex.* 1888); also **labio-lingual** *a.*, pertaining to the lips and the tongue; existing or occurring along a line from the lips to the tongue; hence **ˌlabioˈlingually** *adv.*, in the labiolingual direction; **ˈlabiomancy** [Gr. μαντεία divination], lip-reading.

1669 HOLDER *Elem. Speech* 71 P. and B. are Labial: Ph. and Bh. are *Labio-dental. *Ibid.* 138 The Labiodentals. **1748** *Phil. Trans.* XLV. 405 The labial and labio-dental Consonants. **1887** COOK tr. *Sievers' O.E. Gram.* 100 A sonant spirant, either labial or labio-dental. **1876** *Clin. Soc. Trans.* IX. 82 Progressive *labio-glosso-laryngeal paralysis. **1897** *Allbutt's Syst. Med.* IV. 862 In labio-glosso-laryngeal paralysis anæsthesia of the larynx has been observed. **1879** H. NICOL in *Encycl. Brit.* IX. 632/1 French and Northern Provençal also agree in changing Latin *ū* from a *labio-guttural to a *labio-palatal vowel. **1874** A. J. ELLIS *E.E. Pronunc.* IV. xi. §2 No. 7. 1353 Labials..Labio-dentals ..*Labio-linguals. **1908** G. V. BLACK *Work on Operative Dentistry* II. 15 The axio-bucco-lingual plane, or the bucco-lingual plane,..passes through the tooth bucco-lingually parallel with its long axis. In the incisors and cuspids this is the labio-lingual plane. **1940** O. A. OLIVER et al. *Labio-Lingual Technic* 10 Used jointly, labial and lingual appliances represent the labio-lingual technic. **1972** *Nature* 24 Nov. 236/2 The labiolingual compression of the tooth in hominids. **1949** V. H. SEARS *Princ. & Technics for Compl. Dent. Constr.* xxiii. 284 The upper incising occlusal unit should be narrow *labio-lingually in order to cut through the food with application of little force. **1963** C. R. COWELL et al. *Inlays, Crowns & Bridges* iv. 30 Some anterior teeth are exceptionally thin labiolingually and gold on the lingual aspect may cause the crown..to lose its natural translucence. **1971** *Nature* 23 Apr. 514 The right lateral incisor is represented only by the broken root which measures 4·5 mm mediodistally and 6·0 mm labiolingually. **1686** PLOT *Staffordsh.* 288 So..skill'd was she in this Art (which we may call *Labiomancy)..that..when in bed, if she might lay but her hand on their lipps so as to feel the motion of them, she could perfectly understand what her bedfellows said. **1812** *Europ. Mag.* LXII. 287 [Title of article.] Labiomancy. **1874** A. J. ELLIS *E.E. Pronunc.* IV. xi. §2 No. 7. 1350 Granting that consonants may be labialised, or palatalised, or *labio-palatalised. **1867** O. W. HOLMES *Guardian Angel* ii. (1891) 16 A sort of half-suppressed *labio-palato-nasal utterance. **1894** LINDSAY *Latin Lang.* Index, *Labiovelar Gutt[urals]. **1895** W. M. LINDSAY *Short Hist. Latin Gram.* x. 156 We must distinguish.. Labiovelars,..which become Labials in some languages. **1939** E. PROKOSCH *Compar. Germanic Gram.* 72 The treatment of the labiovelars in Germanic is similar to that in Latin. **1952** A. COHEN *Phonemes of English* 31 *bail*-[beil] v. *wail*-[weil] dist[inguished] by labial v. labiovelar art[iculation]; plosion v. glide. **1968** CHOMSKY & HALLE *Sound Pattern Eng.* 311 An interesting pattern arises with regard to the labiovelars. We may ask whether these are labials with extreme velarization or velars with extreme rounding. **1937** J. R. FIRTH *Papers in Linguistics* (1957) vii. 80 The tonal diacritica and possibly also what we have called yotization and *labio-velarization may be considered as syllabic features. **1953** K. JACKSON *Lang. & Early Brit.* 440 Some degree of labiovelarisation of the ʒ caused by the *u*. **1933** L. BLOOMFIELD *Lang.* 118 These two modifications appear together in *labiovelarized consonants. **1964** E. PALMER tr. *Martinet's Elem. Gen. Ling.* ii. 51 Consonants..which possess the timbre of [u] are called labiovelarized.

labion, variant of LABEON.

labiose (ˈleɪbɪəʊs), *a. Bot.* [f. LABI-ATE, with substitution of suffix.] (See quot.)

1832 LINDLEY *Introd. Bot.* I. ii. §7. 119 If the [polypetalous] corolla..resembles what is called labiate in gamopetalous corollas, it is termed *labiose*.

labirinth, -ynth, obs. forms of LABYRINTH.

‖**labium** (ˈleɪbɪəm). [L. = 'lip'.] A lip or lip-like part. (Cf. LABRUM.)

1. *Anat.* †**a.** One of the sides of the aperture of a vein. *Obs.*

1597 A. M. tr. *Guillemeau's Fr. Chirurg.* 28/4 When we bende the elbowe, both the labia or lippes of the vayn do separate themselves.

b. Chiefly in pl. **labia**, in full *labia pudendi*: The lips of the female pudendum; the folds of integument on either side of the vulva. Now usu. called in full ***labia majora***, and formerly † *labia externa* (or *external labia*). Also (in full ***labia minora***, † *smaller labia*, † *labia interna*, *inner labia*), the two smaller folds of skin situated within the labia majora and extending downwards and backwards from the clitoris: the nymphæ.

The sing. forms *labium majus*, *minus* occas. occur.

1634 A. READ *Man. Anat.* I. vi. 85 In the externall part.. first appeare labia, the lippes which are parted by the magna rima or fossa, the large chinke. **1722** QUINCY *Lex. Physico-Med.* (ed. 2) 174 The *Labia*, or Lips of the great Chink. **1806** *Med. Jrnl.* XV. 21 When the uterus remains within the labia. **1826** J. LIZARS *Syst. Anat. Plates* xi. 82 The mucous surface of the labia externa is the seat of syphilitic ulcers. *Ibid.* 84 The nymphæ, or labia interna. [*Note*] Syn. Labia pudendi minores: Alæ minores. **1838** R. HUNTER *Text Bk. Human Anat.* (ed. 2) ix. 208 Female organs of generation... 1st, the mons veneris—2d, the two labia majora, or labia pudendi—3d, the clitoris, with its prepuce—4th, the two labia minora, or nymphæ—[etc.]. **1845** *Encycl. Metrop.* VII. 493/1 The external or proper labia are thick folds of integument which bound the vulva on either side; and within these are the nymphæ or smaller labia. **1872** THOMAS *Dis. Women* 101 An ichorous, fetid, nauseating fluid bathes the labia majora. **1879** T. BRYANT *Pract. Surg.* II. 229 In women, the labium may be the seat of an inguinal hernia. **1906** H. ELLIS *Stud. Psychol. Sex* V. 134 The inner lips, the nymphæ or labia minora, running parallel with the greater lips which enclose them, embrace the clitoris anteriorly. **1907** W. N. PARKER tr. *R. Wiedersheim's Compar. Anat. Vertebr.* (ed. 3) 483 'Labia minora' also occur in certain other Primates, but in most Monkeys 'labia minora' are alone present bounding the vulva, and these belong morphologically to the clitoris and not to the scrotal folds. **1936** H. M. & A. STONE *Marriage Manual* iii. 89, I have often seen labia barely a quarter of an inch wide and I have examined women whose inner labia measured two and a half inches in width. **1953** A. C. KINSEY et al. *Sexual Behav. Human Female* xiv. 577 As sources of erotic arousal, the labia minora seem to be fully as important as the clitoris. *Ibid.* 578 Sometimes the labia [minora] are rhythmically pulled in masturbation. *Ibid.*, We do not yet have evidence that the labia majora contribute in any important way to the erotic responses of the female. **1962** *Gray's Anat.* (ed. 33) 1547 Anteriorly, each labium minus divides into two portions. **1965** MASTERS & JOHNSON in J. Money *Sex Research* iv. 67 During the excitement phase of the human sexual response cycle, the labia minora (sex-skin) turn bright pink in color and..engorge to approximately twice their previously normal size.

2. a. In insects, crustaceans, etc., the organ which constitutes the lower covering or 'floor' of the mouth and serves as an under lip. (Cf. LABRUM.)

1828 STARK *Elem. Nat. Hist.* II. 209 They [Myriapoda] have..a labium or lip without palpi, formed of united portions. **1862** in *Goldsmith's Nat. Hist.* II. 575 The mouth has usually two mandibles, a labium, or lip below, and from three to five pairs of jaws. **1878** BELL *Gegenbaur's Comp. Anat.* 245 When those gnathites are fused in the middle line the so-called labium is formed.

b. *Conch.* The inner lip of a univalve shell.

1839 SOWERBY *Conch. Man.* 54 *Labium*, or inner lip. Is used to express that side of the aperture which is nearest the axis, and generally contiguous to the body whorl, the lower part of this, when sufficiently distinct from the part which overwraps the body whorl, is called the Columella. **1851** RICHARDSON *Geol.* viii. 240 The *labium*, or columellar lip.

3. *Bot.* The lip, esp. the lower or anterior lip, of a labiate corolla. (Cf. GALEA.)

1823 CRABB *Technol. Dict.*, *Labium*, the Lip, the exterior part of a labiate or ringent corolla. It is distinguished into upper and lower; but sometimes the upper lip is called the *labium*, and the lower *galea*. **1880** GRAY *Struct. Bot.* 419 A bilabiate corolla or calyx..is cleft into an upper (superior or posterior) and a lower (inferior or anterior) portion or lip (labium).

4. The lip of an organ pipe (Stainer & Barrett *Dict. Mus. Terms*).

‖**lablab** ('læblæb). [Arab. *lablāb.*] The Egyptian or black bean, a native of India, but naturalized in most warm countries.

1823 CRABB *Technol. Dict.*, *Lablab*, the *Dolichos Lablab* of Linnæus. **1866** *Treas. Bot.*, *Lablab*, a genus of tropical pulse formerly included in *Dolichos*. The two recognised species are natives of India, but..they are now found naturalised in most tropical countries. **1886** A. H. CHURCH *Food Grains India* 161 Of the numerous forms of Lablab the majority are eaten as a green vegetable.

labor: see LABOUR.

†**laborant.** *Obs.* [ad. L. *labōrant-em*, pr. pple. of *labōrāre* to LABOUR.] A laboratory workman; chemist's assistant; a working chemist.

1665 BOYLE *Occas. Refl.* II. iii. (1848) 105 As I am wont to reverence vulgar Chymists, I then envy'd their Laborants, whose imployment requires them to attend the Fire. **1680** —— *Exper. Chem. Princ.* I. 39 We caused the Laborant with an iron rod dexterously to stirr the kindled part of the Nitre. **1694** *Phil. Trans.* XVIII. 203 Glauber..a very Chymist or Laborant, and nothing at all of a clear Philosopher.

†'**laborate**, *v. Obs. rare.* In 7 labourate. [f. ppl. stem of L. *labōrāre* to LABOUR.] *trans.* To elaborate.

1662 J. CHANDLER tr. *Van Helmont's Oriat.* 298 The transpiring or breathing thorow of Spirits labourated in the heart.

†**labo'ration.** *Obs rare*⁻¹. Also 5 -acion. [ad. L. *labōrātiōn-em*, n. of action f. *labōrāre* to LABOUR.] Working, work, labour.

c **1460** ASHBY *Poems* 77 Wisdam must haue grete applicacion In meche redyng and other laboracion. **1727** BAILEY vol. II, *Laboration*, a labouring.

laboratorial (ˌlæbərə'tɔərɪəl), *a.* [f. LABORATORY + -AL¹.] Pertaining to the laboratory.

1862 H. MARRYAT *Yr. in Sweden* II. 368 A large glass bowl, with a laboratorial spout. **1881** *Nature* XXIII. 509 Their courses of instruction whether lectures or laboratorial.

labora'torian, *a.* and *sb. rare.* [f. LABORATORY + -AN.] **A.** *adj.* = prec. **B.** *sb.* A chemist who works in a laboratory.

1860 PIESSE *Lab. Chem. Wonders* 155 Young laboratorians at home..will not be slow to show their dexterity. *Ibid.* 173 The laboratorian chemists can liquify this metal.

laboratory (lə'bɒrətərɪ, 'læbərətərɪ). Also 7 laboritary, labratory. [ad. med.L. *labōrātōri-um*, f. L. *labōrāre* to LABOUR: see -ORY. Cf. F. *laboratoire*, It., Sp., Pg. *laboratorio*; also ELABORATORY.]

1. a. A building set apart for conducting practical investigations in natural science, orig. and esp. in chemistry, and for the elaboration or manufacture of chemical, medicinal, and like products.

1605 TIMME *Quersit.* III. 191 Wee commonly prouide that they bee prepared in our laboratorie. *a* **1637** B. JONSON *Mercury Vind.* Induction, A Laboratory or Alchemist's work-house. **1683** WILDING in *Collect.* (O.H.S.) I. 258 For seeing yᵉ Labratory..00 00 06. **1691** WOOD *Ath. Oxon.* II. 392 He had a Laboratory to prepare all Medicines that he used on his Patients. **1765** H. WALPOLE *Vertue's Anecd. Paint.* (1786) III. 248 His best pieces were representations of chymists and their laboratories. **1802** *Med. Jrnl.* VIII. 87 To establish in London a laboratory, or manufacture of artificial mineral waters. **1812** SIR H. DAVY *Chem. Philos.* Introd. 9 The greater number of the experiments were made in the laboratory of the Royal Institution. **1881** SIR W. THOMSON in *Nature* 435 The electro-magnetic machine has been brought from the physical laboratory into the province of engineering.

b. *transf.* and *fig.*

1664 POWER *Exper. Philos.* I. 65 The Soul (like an excellent Chymist) in this internal Laboratory of Man, by a fermentation of our nourishment in the Stomach [etc.]. **1794** SULLIVAN *View Nat.* I. 461 Fissures and caverns of rocks are the laboratories, where such operations are carried on. **1814** SIR H. DAVY *Agric. Chem.* 15 The soil is the laboratory in which the food is prepared. **1860** MAURY *Phys. Geog. Sea* xviii. §740 Like the atmosphere it [the sea] is a laboratory in which wonders by processes the most exquisite are continually going on. **1870** J. H. NEWMAN *Gram. Assent* II. viii. 260 A notion neatly turned out of the laboratory of the mind.

2. *Mil.* 'A department of an arsenal for the manufacture and examination of ammunition and combustible stores' (Voyle *Milit. Dict.* 1876).

1716 *Lond. Gaz.* No. 5439/3 The Ammunition Laboratory..was..set on Fire. **1804** WELLINGTON *Let.* in Gurw. *Desp.* (1837) III. 528 The arsenal, the laboratory [etc.]..are under his immediate superintendence. **1846** GREENER *Gunnery* 85 A fuse, invented..by..a person employed in the laboratory at Woolwich.

3. *Metallurgy.* 'The space between the fire and flue-bridges of a reverberatory furnace in which the work is performed; also called the *kitchen* and the *hearth*' (Raymond *Mining Gloss.* 1881).

1839 URE *Dict. Arts*, etc. 822 The flame and the smoke which escape from the sole or laboratory pass into condensing chambers. **1877** RAYMOND *Statist. Mines & Mining* 393 The laboratory is 9 feet long, 6 feet 9 inches wide, and connects with the chimney, 2 feet 6 inches square, by a flue.

4. *attrib.*, as ***laboratory apparatus***, ***chemist***, ***experiment***, ***fire***, ***forge***, ***furnace***, ***machinery***, ***man***, (sense 2) ***stores***, ***work***; **laboratory animal**, any animal (e.g. rat, monkey, mouse) commonly used for experiments in a laboratory; **laboratory-chest**, a chest containing ammunition and explosive stores; **laboratory frame (of reference)** *Nuclear Physics*, the frame of reference in which a laboratory is stationary, and with respect to which measurements of particle energy, velocity, etc., are generally made (see quot. 1958); **laboratory system** *Nuclear Physics* = *laboratory frame*.

1899 *Allbutt's Syst. Med.* VI. 517 The so-called 'irritation contracture' observable in the monkey (but not in other *laboratory animals). **1937** *Nature* 24 July 155/1 Among those using this fish as a 'laboratory animal'. **1860** PIESSE *Lab. Chem. Wonders* 145 As the botanist does with plants so does the *laboratory-chemist with the salts. **1769** FALCONER *Dict. Marine* (1780) Dd, A *laboratory-chest is to be on board each bomb-vessel, in the captain's cabin, in which all the small stores are to be kept. **1898** *Daily News* 8 Feb. 5/2 Most of this evidence has had to be tested by *laboratory experiments. **1870** TYNDALL *Heat* v. §185. 148 My assistant dissolved the substance in a pan over our *laboratory fire. **1958** O. R. FRISCH *Nucl. Handbk.* xix. 22 From a theoretical standpoint it is most convenient to calculate in a frame of reference in which the total linear momentum is zero (centre of mass frame, or..centre of momentum frame..). Experimentally the target particle is usually at rest in the *laboratory frame of reference. **1971** *Sci. Amer.* June 76/3 The theoretical analysis of events in the rapidly moving frame can be made with some degree of confidence and transformed back to the laboratory frame. In this way theory can be compared with experiment. **1866** ODLING *Anim. Chem.* iv. 78 Whether the chemist may not effect in his *laboratory-machinery a similar intercombination of deoxidised carbonic acid and water. **1822–34** *Good's Study Med.* (ed. 4) IV. 449 Coal heavers, dustmen, *laboratory-men, and others who work among dry powdery substances. **1828** SPEARMAN *Brit. Gunner* 8 Ammunition and *Laboratory Stores. **1951** D. BOHM *Quantum Theory* xxi. 525 Collisions usually involve firing particles at other particles that are at rest in the *laboratory system. **1881** LOCKYER in *Nature* 318 Whether we passed from low to high temperatures in *laboratory work.

†**labo'riferous**, *a. Obs. rare*⁻⁰. [f. L. *labōrifer* (f. *labōr(i)-* LABOUR + *-fer* bearing) + -OUS: see -FEROUS.] (See quot.).

1656 BLOUNT *Glossogr.*, *Laboriferous*, that takes pains, that endures labour, painfull, difficult.

laborinth, -ynth, obs. forms of LABYRINTH.

†**laboriose**, *a. Obs.*⁻⁰ [ad. L. *labōriōs-us* (see LABORIOUS).] 'Laborious, pains-taking' (1727 Bailey vol. II).

laboriosity (ləbɔərɪ'ɒsɪtɪ). *rare.* [f. L. *labōriōs-us* (see next) + -ITY. Cf. F. *laboriosité*.] Laboriousness.

1656 BLOUNT *Glossogr.*, *Laboriosity*, painfulness, laboriousness, or laborosity. **1840** *Blackw. Mag.* XLVIII. 132 Numberless folio and quarto dissertations..attest their invincible laboriosity. **1842** BLACKIE in *Tait's Mag.* IX. 749 The lumbering laboriosity of dead grammars and dictionaries.

laborious (lə'bɔərɪəs), *a.* Also 6 -yous(e. [ad. F. *laborieux* (12–13th c. in Hatz.-Darm.) or ad. L. *labōriōs-us*, f. *labor* LABOUR: see -IOUS.]

1. Given to labour or toil; doing much work; assiduous in work, hard-working.

1390 GOWER *Conf.* II. 90 If thou wolt here Of hem that whilom vertuous Were and therto laborious. *c* **1407** SCOGAN *Moral Balade* 69 Therefore laborious Ought ye to be, beseeching god..To yeve you might for to be vertuous. **1555** EDEN *Decades* 318 Thinhabitauntes are men of good corporature..and laborious. **1634** RAINBOW *Labour* (1635) 5 The limbs of your industry are so strong and laborious. *a* **1648** LD. HERBERT *Autobiog.* Life (1886) 192 He..was observed seldom or never..to sweat much, though he were very laborious. **1697** DRYDEN *Virg. Georg.* IV. 242 All.. combine to drive The lazy Drones from the laborious Hive. **1709** STEELE *Tatler* No. 21 ¶5 Laborious Ben's Works will bear this Sort of Inquisition. **1752** HUME *Pol. Disc.* i. 17 Their own steel and iron, in such laborious hands, become equal to the gold and rubies of the Indies. **1857** LD. DUFFERIN *Lett. fr. High Latitudes* (1867) 78 Those calm laborious minds..pursuing day by day with single-minded energy some special object. **1871** MORLEY *Voltaire* (1886) 9 He was always serious in meaning and laborious in matter.

b. = LABOURING *ppl. a.* I.

1777 HUME *Ess. & Treat.* I. 280 By this means..a greater number of laborious men are maintained, who may be diverted to the public service. **1795** BURKE *Th. Scarcity* Wks. VII. 378 The moral or philosophical happiness of the laborious classes.

2. Of actions, conditions, etc.: Characterized by or involving labour or much work; toilsome. †Of wages: Hardly earned. *Obs.*

14.. *Chaucer's Friar's T.* 130 (Corpus MS.) My office [is] ful laborious. **1526** *Pilgr. Perf.* (W. de W. 1531) 83 Nothynge is more..laboryous to kepe, than is virginite. **1549** LELAND (*title*) The laboryouse Journey and Serche of Johan Leylande for Englandes Antiquitees. **1607** TOPSELL *Hist. Four-f. Beasts* (1658) Pref., I have not any accesse of maintenance, but by voluntary benevolence for personal pains, receiving no more but a laborious wages. **1611** BIBLE *Ecclus.* vii. 15 Hate not laborious worke, neither husbandrie. **1637** MILTON *Lycidas* 72 To scorn delights, and live laborious dayes. **1725** POPE *Odyss.* III. 127 Shall I the long laborious scene review, And open all the wounds of Greece anew? **1752** JOHNSON *Rambler* No. 204 ¶11 Forced jests, and laborious laughter. **1781** GIBBON *Decl. & F.* III. 202 The subject of minute and laborious disquisition. **1845** M. PATTISON *Ess.* (1889) I. 7 In a laborious anxiety to be correct, they have evaporated away all the spirit of their book. **1860** TYNDALL *Glac.* I. iv. 33 These days were laborious and instructive. **1878** JEVONS *Primer Pol. Econ.* 43 The great advantage of capital is that it enables us to do work in the least laborious way.

b. Of concrete objects: Entailing labour in construction or execution; involving much elaboration. †Also (*rare*⁻¹), Causing wearisome toil.

1555 EDEN *Decades* To Rdr. (Arb.) 49 The laborious Tabernacle whiche Moises buylded. **1666** PEPYS *Diary* 14 July, Up betimes to the office to write fair a laborious letter. **1705** ADDISON *Italy* (1733) 105 The long laborious Pavement here he treads. **1824** MISS FERRIER *Inher.* xlvii, A most laborious and long-winded letter. **1847** TENNYSON *Princess* Prol. 20 Laborious orient ivory sphere in sphere. **1856** KANE *Arct. Expl.* II. iii. 45 We have a large and laborious outfit to arrange.

3. *Midwifery.* Attended with severe labour.

1637 T. MORTON *New Eng. Canaan* (1883) 148 Very apt are they to be with childe, and very laborious when they beare children. **1753** N. TORRIANO *Gangr. Sore Throat* 23 Labours in such Circumstances are generally laborious. **1754–64** SMELLIE *Midwifery* I. 242 Laborious births. **1855** MAYNE *Expos. Lex.*, *Labour, Laborious*, or *Instrumental*.. that requiring the use of extracting instruments for its completion..also called *Difficult Labour*.

†**4.** Pertaining to labour. *Obs. rare*⁻¹.

1632 QUARLES *Div. Fancies* II. lxxvi. (1660) 89 Me thinks that they should change their trade [*sc.* that of the theatre] for shame Or honour't with a more laborious name.

laboriously (lə'bɔəriəsli), *adv.* [f. prec. + -LY².] In a laborious manner; with labour or assiduous toil.

c **1510** MORE *Picus* Wks. 16 Thei, that..in the space of this temporall death laboriously purchase themself eternall death. **1660** BOYLE *New Exp. Phys. Mech.* viii. 65 The Experiment was laboriously try'd. **1725** POPE *Odyss.* XI. 597, I chuse laboriously to bear A weight of woes. **1828** D'ISRAELI *Chas. I* (1830) III. i. 12 Never was there a Monarch who employed his pen so laboriously. **1856** KANE *Arct. Expl.* II. xvii. 180 The laboriously-earned results of the expedition. **1883** J. HAWTHORNE in *Harper's Mag.* Nov. 934/2 The..beams of the..ceiling..were laboriously carved.

laboriousness (lə'bɔəriəsnis). [f. as prec. + -NESS.] Laborious character or condition; assiduity in work; toilsomeness.

1634 W. TIRWHYT tr. *Balzac's Lett.* (vol. I.) 89 That great laboriousnesse they so much frame to themselves. **1682** SIR T. BROWNE *Chr. Mor.* 38 To strenuous minds there is an inquietude in overquietness, and no laboriousness in labour. **1719** DE FOE *Crusoe* I. 135 The exceeding Laboriousness of my Work. **1818** HALLAM *Middle Ages* (1853) II. 62 Masdeu, in learning and laboriousness, the first Spanish antiquary. **1861** LYTTON & FANE *Tannhäuser* 32 Leaf and stem disintertwined itself With infinite laboriousness.

†**labo'rosity.** *Obs. rare*⁻⁰. [f. L. **labōrōs-us* (see next) + -ITY.] Laboriousness.

1656 [see LABORIOSITY].

†'**laborous**, *a. Obs.* Forms: 4-7 laborous, 5 -ose, 5-8 labourous, 6 -orouse, -orus, 5-6 -erous, *Sc.* laubo(u)r(o)us. [a. OF. *laboros, -us, laboureux*:—L. **labōrōs-us*, f. *labor* LABOUR (cf. *dolōrōsus*, f. *dolor*): see -OUS.] = LABORIOUS.

c **1386** CHAUCER *Friar's T.* 130 Myn offyce is ful laborous [*Corpus MS.* laborious]. *a* **1450** *Fysshynge w. angle* (1883) 4 Huntyng haukyng and fowlyng be so laborous & greuous þat [etc.]. *c* **1450** tr. *De Imitatione* III. lii. 125 Wheþer all laborose þinges be not to be suffrid for euerlasting lif? *c* **1460** ASHBY *Poems* 87 Be ye therin right laberous. *c* **1470** HENRY *Wallace* XI. 958 His laubourous mynd on othir materis wrocht. **1513** DOUGLAS *Æneis* III. vi. 199 Quhow thow may all laubourus pane sustene. **1561** T. NORTON *Calvin's Inst.* II. 72 We nede not a longer or more laborous profe. **1591** SPENSER *M. Hubberd* 266 For husbands life is labourous and hard. **1593** T. HYLL *Gardening* 3 Then must you dig a pit (although yᵉ same wil be very labourous). **1656** EARL MONM. *Advt. fr. Parnass.* 153 Why should we undertake the laborous business of dividing the world into equal partitions? **1704** *Lond. Gaz.* No. 4057/3 After a labourous.. March. **1782** T. VAUGHAN *Fash. Follies* I. 67 Reading and writing..were too laborous [ed. 2 (1810) laborious] for the nerves of a man of fashion.

Hence †'**laborously** *adv.*, †'**laborousness**.

c **1450** tr. *De Imitatione* III. v. 69 Oþir, þat..desiren laborously þinges euerlasting. *Ibid.* III. xxxvi. 106 þat þat is laboresly goten by mannys witte. **1530** PALSGR. 237/1 Labourousnesse, *laboriosité*. **1531** ELYOT *Gov.* III. x. (1880) II. 275 He laborousely and studiousely discussed controuersies.

labour, labor ('leɪbə(r)), *sb.* Forms: 4-5 labore, 4-6 -ur, -oure, 5-6 *Sc.* laubour, 4- labour, 5- labor. [a. OF. *labor, labour* (mod.F. *labeur*), ad. L. *labōrem* labour, toil, distress, trouble. Cf. Pr. *labor, laor*, Sp. *labor*, Pg. *lavor*, It. *labore*.

As in *favour*, etc., the spelling with *-our* is preferred in the British Isles, while in the U.S. *-or* is more common.]

1. a. Exertion of the faculties of the body or mind, esp. when painful or compulsory; bodily or mental toil. ***hard labour***: see HARD *a.* 19 b. †***to do one's labour***: to exert oneself, make efforts (*to* do something).

a **1300** *Cursor M.* 23699 þan sal it [þe erth] blisced be and quit o labur, and o soru, and sit. **13..** *E.E. Allit. P.* A. 633 Why schulde he not her [i.e. innocents'] labour alow? *c* **1386** CHAUCER *Prioress' T.* 11 To telle a storie I wol do my labour. *c* **1400** *Destr. Troy* 10770 Hit were labur to long hir lotis to tell. **1484** CAXTON *Fables of Auian* (1889) 2 He that wylle haue..worship and glorye may not haue hit withoute grete laboure. **1533** GAU *Richt Vay* (1888) 93 O heuinlie fader giff vsz alsua necessar thingis to our corporal sustentatione be our aune richtus laubour. **1535** COVERDALE *Eccl.* ii. 18, I was weery of all my laboure, Which I had taken vnder the Sonne. **1611** BIBLE *Ps.* civ. 23 Man goeth forth vnto his worke: and to his labour, vntill the euening. **1619** DRAYTON *Idea* lix, Labour is light where Loue..doth pay. **1667** MILTON *P.L.* II. 1021 So he with difficulty and labour hard Mov'd on, with difficulty and labour hee. **1752** HUME *Pol. Disc.* i. 12 Everything in the world is purchas'd by labour, and our passions are the only causes of labour. **1781** COWPER *Hope* 20 Pleasure is labour too, and tires as much. **1827** LYTTON *Falkland* 15 Nothing seemed to me worth the labour of success. **1833** TENNYSON *Lotos-Eaters* 87 Ah, why Should life all labour be?

personified. *c* **1400** *Rom. Rose* 4994 With hir Labour and Travaile Logged been. **1764** GOLDSM. *Trav.* 82 Nature.. Still grants her bliss at Labour's earnest call. **1804** GRAHAME *Sabbath* 2 Mute is the voice of rural labour.

transf. **1842** COMBE *Digest.* 267 The stomach, having less labour imposed upon it, will require less blood.

b. Phr. ***labour in vain, lost labour.***

[**1377** LANGL. *P. Pl.* B. Prol. 181 [They] helden hem vnhardy and here conseille feble, And leten here labowre lost & alle here longe studye. **1390** GOWER *Conf.* III. 293 Whan he sigh..that his labour was in veine.] **1500-20** DUNBAR *Poems* lxvi. 13 The leill labour lost, and leill seruice. **1535** COVERDALE *Ps.* cxxvii. 2 It is but lost labour that ye ryse vp early. **1615** T. ADAMS *England's Sickn.* 10 Let Nature doe her best, we dwelt at the Signe of the *Labour-in-vaine*. Onely Christ hath washed vs. *a* **1670** HACKET *Abp. Williams* II. (1693) 67 That Commission ended at *Labour in vain*; not, as the old Emblem is, to go about to make a Black-moor white, but to make him that was White to appear like a Black-moor. **1679** DRYDEN *Tr. & Cr.* II. ii, The sign-post for the *labour in vain*. **1747** WESLEY *Prim. Physick* (1762) p. xviii, Add to the rest (for it is not labour lost) that old unfashionable medicine, Prayer.

†**c.** Bodily exercise. (Cf. Gr. πόνος.)

1584 COGAN *Haven Health* i. (1612) 1 Labour then, or exercise is a vehement moouing, the end whereof is alteration of the breath or winde of man. **1666** HARVEY *Morb. Angl.* x. (1672) 28 Moderate labour of the body is universally experienced to conduce to the preservation of health.

†**d.** An alleged term for a 'company' of moles.

1486 *Bk. St. Albans* f vj b, A Labor of Mollis.

2. a. *spec.* in modern use: Physical exertion directed to the supply of the material wants of the community; the specific service rendered to production by the labourer and artisan.

1776 ADAM SMITH *W.N.* I. Introd. 1 The annual labour of every nation is the fund which originally supplies it with all the necessaries and conveniencies of life, which it annually consumes. *Ibid.* I. I. v. 35 Labour, therefore, is the real measure of the exchangeable value of all commodities. **1798** MALTHUS *Popul.* IV. iv. (1806) II. 348 If the population of this country were better proportioned to its food, the nominal price of labour might be lower than it is now. **1825** *Edin. Rev.* XLIII. 14 The..remedy is to diminish the supply of labour. **1842-59** GWILT *Archit.* Gloss., *Labour*, a term in masonry employed to denote the value of a piece of work in consideration of the time bestowed upon it. **1848** MILL *Pol. Econ.* I. iii. §1 (1876) 28 Labour is indispensable to production, but has not always production for its effect. **1863** BARRY *Dockyard Econ.* 45 The difficulty of organising labour, particularly in masses, is well known. **1885** *Act 48 & 49 Vict.* c. 56 Preamble, Doubts have arisen as to whether or not it be lawful for an employer of labour to permit electors in his regular employ to absent themselves.

b. The general body of labourers and operatives, viewed in its relation to the body of capitalists, or with regard to its political interests and claims. Chiefly *attrib.* (see 8).

1839 J. F. BRAY (*title*) Labour's wrongs and labour's remedy; or, The age of might and the age of right. **1848** *Punch* XV. 261 Thither [*sc.* to Australia] should Labour repair to seek Demand. **1880** S. WALPOLE *Hist. Eng.* III. xiii. 228 Labour..was gradually discovering the truth of the old saying, that God helps those who help themselves. *a* **1901** *Mod.* The parliamentary representation of labour. **1916** A. RICHARDSON *Man-Power of Nation* 55 The time is.. opportune for trade unions to recognise their responsibility for the encouragement of the flow of capital for the benefit of industry... This subject of the relationship of labour to economy of output may be said to be hackneyed. **1940** W. TEMPLE *Hope of New World* 61 If there is to be tension at all, let it be between the financial interests of Shareholders and the productive interests of Management and Labour in co-operation. **1970** *Encycl. Brit.* XXII. 652/2 Until after the turn of the century organized labour seldom gained any measure of public sympathy.

c. (With capital initial.) Short for 'the Labour Party'. Also *attrib.* (see sense 8). Quasi-*adv.* in phr. ***to vote Labour***.

1906 *Times* 19 Jan. 4/3 (*heading*) The Liberals and the Labour men. *Ibid.* 10/1 Just before going to press the news arrived that Lord Stanley..had been defeated..by Mr. W. T. Wilson (Labour). **1918** A. HUXLEY *Let.* 25 Nov. (1969) 171 Tell Brett also to remember to vote, and to vote Labour, our only hope. **1920** *Manch. Guardian* 5 Jan. 6/2 Could any conceivable Labour Government have made blunders so gross? **1924** *Ibid.* 2 May 9/1 The Labour party and Labour leaders have always been divided upon the subject of P.R. [Proportional Representation]. **1932** J. BUCHAN *Gap in Curtain* iii. 149 The younger Tories as a whole were enthusiastic, and, what is more significant, the Left Wing of Labour blessed it cordially. *Ibid.*, Collinson, a young Labour member from the Midlands, declared that Geraldine was the best Socialist of them all. **1945** *Let us face the Future* (Labour Party) x. 10 Labour led the fight against the mean and shabby treatment which was the lot of millions while Conservative Governments were in power. **1949** LEWIS & MAUDE *Eng. Middle Classes* I. iv. 81 Both Conservatives and Labour competed for the middle-class vote. *Ibid.* 82 The new Labour formula was nicely expressed by Philip Snowden. **1956** C. COCKBURN *In Time of Trouble* xix. 244 The Labour people, the 'progressive intellectuals'. **1966** M. EDELMAN *The 'Mirror'* viii. 151 Its brilliance was that at no time did the *Mirror* specifically urge its voters to vote Labour. **1971** B. HINDESS *Decline Working-Class Politics* viii. 173 The teenagers of the 1960s..missed the political experience of their parents, the long identification with and support for Labour.

d. Short for LABOUR EXCHANGE 2.

1935 M. HARRISON *Spring in Tartarus* I. 105 You see, mister, I can't go on the Labour, cause I 'aven't been stood off. I'm on'y ill. **1963** T. PARKER *Unknown Citizen* iii. 88 I'll ring you up Monday to tell you how I went on at the Labour. **1971** R. RENDELL *One Across* iv. 37 Work's not easy to come by when you've no qualifications... Can't they find you anything down at the Labour? **1972** L. HENDERSON *Cage until Tame* vi. 45 I'm going for a job the Labour picked out for me.

3. An instance of bodily or mental exertion; a work or task performed or to be performed. ***a labour of Hercules, a Herculean labour***: a task requiring enormous strength. ***labour of love*** (see LOVE *sb.*¹).

a **1300** *Cursor M.* 2229, I rede we bigin a laboure..and make a toure. **1432-50** tr. *Higden* (Rolls) I. 11 If that a pigmei scholde make him redy to conflicte after the labores of Hercules..plenerly finischede. **1535** COVERDALE *Rev.* xiv. 13 Yee the sprete sayeth, that they rest from their laboures. **1539** TAVERNER *Prov.* 34 Laboures ones done, be swete. **1596** SHAKS. *Tam. Shr.* I. ii. 257. **1599** —— *Much Ado* II. i. 380. **1604** E. G[RIMSTONE] *D'Acosta's Hist. Indies* IV. vii. 226 They are two insupportable labours in searching of the mettall; first to digge and breake the rockes, and then to drawe out the water all together. **1617, 1732** [see HERCULEAN *a.* 3]. **1702** ROWE *Tamerl.* Ded., When they shall reckon up his Labours from the Battle of Seneff. **1732** LAW *Serious C.* iii. (ed. 2) 32 Whose lives have been a careful labour to exercise these virtues. **1835** LYTTON *Rienzi* I. i. 4 My labours of the body, at least, have been light enough. **1871** DAVIES *Metric Syst.* II. 29 The rich treasures of their labors.

4. The outcome, product, or result of toil. Also *pl. Obs.* exc. *arch.* [Cf. L. *hominumque boumque labores*, Virgil.]

a **1300** *Cursor M.* 1986 Ȝeildes til your creatur þe tend part o your labour. **1432-50** tr. *Higden* (Rolls) I. 7 Y..intende to compile a tretys..excerpte of diuerse labores of auctores. **1535** COVERDALE *Ps.* civ. 44 They toke the labours of the people in possession. **1550** CROWLEY *Epigr.* 307 To worke what they can, and lyue on theyr laboures. **1611** BIBLE *Transl. Pref.* 12 Others haue laboured, and you may enter into their labours. **1697** DRYDEN *Virg. Georg.* III. 688 The waxen Labour of the Bees. **1709** SWIFT *Vind. Bickerstaff* Wks. 1755 II. I. 174, I saw my labours, which cost me so much thought and watching, bawled about by common hawkers. **1720** POPE *Iliad* XVIII. 556 Five ample plates the broad expanse [of the shield] compose, And godlike labours on the surface rose. **1736** *Col. Rec. Pennsylv.* IV. 176 The Thing they want is the peaceable Possession of their Labours.

†**5. a.** Trouble or pains taken. (Occas. *pl.*) *Obs.*

14.. *Sir Beues* (MS. O.) 928 ' Haue this', he sayde, 'for thy labour!' **1520** in W. H. Turner *Select. Rec. Oxford* 27 The auditors..be diligent and take labors herapon. **1591** SHAKS. *Two Gent.* II. i. 139 If it please you, take it for your labour; And so good-morrow Seruant. **1611** BIBLE *Transl. Pref.* 2 The Emperour got for his labour the name Pupillus. *a* **1656** USSHER *Power of Princes* II. (1683) 141 He caused the Fellow to be soundly whipped for his labour.

†**b.** *esp.* The exertion of influence in furthering a matter or obtaining a favour. ***to make labour***: = LABOUR *v.* 13. *Obs.*

1454 T. DENYES in *Paston Lett.* No. 199 (1897) I. 274 Aftirward my wif was sum dele easid bi the labour of the Wardeyn of Flete, for the cursid Cardenale had sent hir to Newgate. **1461** J. PASTON *ibid.* No. 408 II. 35, I undirstand ther shall be labour for a coroner that day, for ther is labour made to me for my good wyll here. **1482** CAXTON *Chron. Eng.* ccxlviii. 315 By labour of lordes that wente bytwene ther was a poyntement taken that ther was no harme done. **1491** *Act 7 Hen. VII*, c. 22 Preamble, I pray you make laboure unto my Lady Warwyk to write to the King of Fraunce. **1540** *Act 32 Hen. VIII*, c. 42 §2 Without any further sute or labour to be made to kyngs highnes..for the same. **1542** UDALL in *Lett. Lit. Men* (Camd.) 2 Your labour for my restitution to the roume of Scholemaister in Eton. **1565** STOW in *Three 15th c. Chron.* (Camd.) 136 Yᵉ paryshe of S. Marie Magdalyn in Mylke-stret, makynge labour to yᵉ byshope, had by hym a mynister apoyntyd to serve them with communion that day.

6. a. The pains and efforts of childbirth; travail. Phr. ***in labour***.

1595 SPENSER *Epithal.* 383 Sith of wemens labours thou hast charge, And generation goodly dost enlarge. **1611** BIBLE *Gen.* xxxv. 16 Rachel traueiled, and she had hard labour [COVERDALE: the byrth came harde vpon hir]. **1613** SHAKS. *Hen. VIII*, v. i. 18 The Queens in Labor They say in great Extremity, and fear'd Shee'l with the Labour, end. **1799** *Med. Jrnl.* II. 477 [She] had then been in labour about two hours... Interrogating her afterwards respecting her former labours [etc.]. **1819** SHELLEY in Dowden *Life* (1887) II. 308 She has..brought me a fine little boy, after a labour of the very, very mildest character. **1889** J. M. DUNCAN *Lect. Dis. Women* vi. (ed. 4) 34 In the first labour the woman's power and especially the labour, including the uterine, power is the greatest.

b. *fig.*

1606 SHAKS. *Ant. & Cl.* III. vii. 81 With Newes the times with Labour, And throwes forth each minute, some. **1612** BACON *Ess., Beauty* (Arb.) 208 As if nature were rather busie not to erre, then in labour to produce excellency. **1634** HEYWOOD *Maydenhd. well lost* I. B 3 b, My brain's in labour, and must be deliuered Of some new mischeife. **1665** MANLEY tr. *Grotius' Low C. Warres* 121 And now that sentence is brought forth, wherewith..the Warre had now been in labour for the space of nine years. **1797** T. HOLCROFT tr. *Stolberg's Trav.* (ed. 2) II. lxvi. 29 We beheld ..the mountain incessantly in labour.

†**7.** Eclipse. [A Latinism.] *Obs.*⁻¹

1697 DRYDEN *Virg. Georg.* II. 679 Teach me the various Labours of the Moon, And whence proceed th' Eclipses of the Sun [L. *defectus solis varios, lunæque labores*].

8. *attrib.* and *Comb.*: simple attrib., as ***labour-sphere***; (sense 2) ***labour bank, -bill, bureau, candidate, colony, content, cost, government, law, leader, master, member, movement, party, permit, power, question, song, union***; objective and objective gen., as ***labour-easing, -saving, -worthy*** adjs.; instrumental, as ***labour-bent, coarsened, dimmed, dominated*** adjs.; also **labour book**, a book containing accounts of labour employed; **labour camp**, a penal settlement where the prisoners are obliged to undertake labouring work; **Labour Day** *U.S.*, a legal holiday observed on the first Monday of September; a similar holiday observed in Australia, New Zealand, and elsewhere; †**labour-fellow**, fellow-labourer; **labour force**, (*a*) = *labour power*; (*b*) [cf. FORCE *sb.*¹ 4 d] a body of workmen; workers, as opposed to employers, considered as a single body; †**labour-house**, a laboratory; **labour-intensive** *a.* (see INTENSIVE *a.* (*sb.*) 5 b); **Labour-Liberal** *a.* and *sb.*, (a Member of Parliament) combining Labour and Liberal ideas (in early use a Labour M.P. who accepted the Liberal whip); **labour-market**, the

supply of unemployed labour considered with reference to the demand for it; **labour note**, a note indicating value in terms of work; **labour-only** *a.*, denoting a sub-contractor who, or sub-contracting which, supplies only the labour for a particular piece of work; **labour-pains**, pains of childbirth; **Labour Party**, a political party specially supporting the interests of labour; in the United Kingdom, the organized party formed in 1906 by a federation of trade unions and advanced political bodies to secure the representation of labour in Parliament; **labour relations**, the relations between management and labour; **labour-saving** *a.*, designed to ease or eliminate work; so **labour-saver**; **labour-show** *Obstetrics*, the mucous discharge streaked with blood which immediately precedes the occurrence of labour; **labour-starve** *v. trans.*, to impoverish (land) by expending too little labour upon it; **labour-time** (see quot.); **labour ward** (sense 6), a room in a hospital set aside for childbirth; **labour-yard**, a yard in a workhouse or prison, where enforced labour is done by the inmates.

1832 *Crisis* 28 Apr. 16/1 In Poland-street they had established a *Labour Bank. **1847** *Illustr. Lond. News* 28 Aug. 135/3 The Chartists are raising subscriptions to establish a bank, to be called the 'Labour Bank'. **1883** *Fortn. Rev.* 1 Nov. 609 The..*labour-bent back of the labourer. **1898** *Engineering Mag.* XVI. 26 Every improvement in labour-saving machinery diminishes the proportion which the *labour-bill bears to the cost of the product. **1893** *Jrnl. R. Agric. Soc.* Dec. 665 Taking notes from farmers' *labour-books. **1832** *Crisis* 11 Aug. 90/3 Perhaps the best preliminary mode..will be by the establishment of Equitable Exchange *Labour Bureaus. **1893** *Rep. Agencies & Methods Unemployed* 6 in *Parl. Papers 1893–4* (C. 7182) LXXXII. 377 A detailed account of..labour bureaux and of various organisations dealing with distress. **1908** *New Encycl. Social Reform* 998/2 The recent establishment of a system of public employment bureaux called labor bureaux. **1900** *Jrnl. Soc. Arts* 11 May 510/1 Prisoners..might serve their time in..quarries, which would be turned into *labour camps. **1931** J. S. HUXLEY *What dare I Think?* iii. 88 Infringement of this order could probably be met by a short period of segregation, say in a labour camp. **1958** *Spectator* 6 June 723/3 Recsk, one of the most abominable labour camps in the world. **1974** *Times* 18 Feb. 14/7 Perhaps the conference helped to save Mr Solzhenitsyn from a labour camp. **1893** H. F. MCLELLAND *Jack & Beanstalk* 16 You'd make a good *Labour Candidate. **1921** F. W. P. LAWRENCE *Labour Party* 3 For nearly every seat there is a Labour candidate. **1948** M. PHILLIPS in H. Tracey *Brit. Labour Party* I. 9 Labour candidates are selected by the Constituency Parties in co-operation with the National Executive Council. **1963** J. BLONDEL *Voters, Parties, & Leaders* v. 136 Labour candidates are mainly drawn from the middle and lower middle classes. **1866** HOWELL *Venet. Life* xx. 345 Her *labour-coarsened hands. **1888**, etc. *Labour colony [see COLONY *sb.* 5 c]. **1948** *Spectator* 9 Jan. 38/2 Fine worsteds..have a high '*labour content', and raw material is a low item in the cost of their production. **1896** J. A. HOBSON *Probl. Unemployed* 69 The *labour cost of distributing a given quantity of goods. **1903** *Westm. Gaz.* 9 July 2/1 The imposition of such duties as will equalise our labour-costs with the labour-costs of our foreign competitors. **1914** [see *assembly line* s.v. ASSEMBLY 1 c *attrib.*]. **1966** A. GILPIN *Dict. Econ. Terms* 117 *Labour-costs per unit of output*, the cost of the labour in real terms involved in making each unit of output from a factory. **1886** *N.Y. Times* 7 Sept. 8/1 (*heading*) How *Labor Day was observed by all classes of workmen. **1887** *Westm. Gaz.* 6 Sept. 7/1 An Act passed last winter by the State Legislature, making the first Monday in September a legal holiday, to be called 'Labour Day'. **1910** *World Almanac* (N.Y.) 30 An act [of 1893–4] making Labor Day a public holiday in the District of Columbia. **1931** *Daily Express* 2 Sept. 1/5 The governing committee of the New York Stock Exchange, in response to requests of members, decided to close on Saturday, and also to close on Monday, on account of Labour Day, and to resume on Tuesday. **1963** *Times* 26 Feb. 9/1 The city's [*sc.* Melbourne's] big retail stores invented this affair, which has taken over the traditional public holiday called Labour Day, now in any case a quaint anachronism in a country of trade union strength. **1974** *Anderson* (S. Carolina) *Independent* 23 Apr. 1B/1 This is a drastic change from present and past school calendars which start several days prior to Labor Day and finish earlier in the spring. **1867** M. ARNOLD *Heine's Grave* 89 The weary Titan! with deaf Ears, and *labour-dimm'd eyes. **1959** *Daily Tel.* 19 Aug. 9/2 Nottingham Conservative leaders last night denounced as 'full of inaccuracies and false inferences' a report prepared on behalf of the local Labour party... [The] Conservative vice-Chairman of the *Labour-dominated Watch Committee, said: 'The entire report is..full of inaccuracies and false inferences.' **1974** *Listener* 23 May 650/3 The finished film was shown to the Labour-dominated committee. **1837** WHEELWRIGHT tr. *Aristoph.* I. 196 The fertile vine, whose tendrils bear The *labour-easing grape. **1549** COVERDALE, etc. *Erasm. Par., Phil.* 9 My *labourfelowes in yᵉ gospell. **1557** N. T. (Geneva) *1 Thess.* iii. 2 Timotheus..our labour felowe in the Gospel of Christe. **1885** J. L. JOYNES tr. *Marx's Wage-Labour & Capital* (1886) 8 Capital necessarily presupposes the existence of a class which possesses nothing but *labour-force. **1909** B. WEBB et al. *Socialism & National Minimum* I. 38 The parasitic trades, where the employers are able to exact from their workers more labour-force than they replace. **1911** F. T. CARLTON *Hist. & Probl. Organized Labor* xvi. 431 In times of depression there are unemployed land and capital as well as an unemployed labor force. **1940** *Economist* 11 May 849/2 Men are being tempted away and the labour force is being shifted round without any consideration of the relative urgency or importance or even skill of different jobs. **1969** *Times* 12 Feb. 9/2 They have run a computer model of an underdeveloped country's economy which relates the growth of g.n.p. to the labour force, capital stock and other factors. **1926** *Encycl. Brit.* II. 653/2 In Jan. 1924..the first *Labour Govt. in this country was formed. **1945** *Let us face the Future* (Labour Party) x. 10 A Labour Government will press on rapidly with legislation extending social insurance..to all. **1971** *New Statesman* 9 July 34/2 Aneurin Bevan had a very simple rule about the role of a Foreign Secretary under a Labour Government. **1712** BLACKMORE *Creat.* 169 Did chymic chance the furnaces prepare, Raise all the *labour-houses of the air? **1897** J. BRYCE *Impressions S. Afr.* xxi. 447 There are also certain '*labour laws', applying to natives only, and particularly to those on agricultural locations. **1902** *Ann. Amer. Acad. Pol. & Social Sci.* XX. 240 When a state legislature passes a new labor law, or revises an old one. *Ibid.* 241 Labor laws, however good, cannot enforce themselves. **1967** A. HEPPLE *Verwoerd* ix. 122 With the intensification of race and labour laws, the Non-whites began to resist. **1892** ZANGWILL *Bow Myst.* viii. 113 A hand was laid upon the *labour leader's shoulder. **1920** S. LEWIS *Main St.* xvi. 202 You socialists make me sick! I'm an individualist. I ain't going to be nagged by no bureaus and take orders off labor-leaders. **1972** *N.Y. Times* 3 Nov. 21/8 He is scheduled to meet..labor leaders. **1973** *Times* 16 Nov. 20/8 Labour leaders have been appointed to the boards of nationalized industries..in a personal capacity and not in their own industries. **1902** *Westm. Gaz.* 26 Feb. 6/3 If he could do that when he was returned as a *Labour Liberal member. **1904** *Daily Chron.* 7 Jan. 5/4 Two English Liberal Members (one Liberal and one Labour-Liberal). *a* **1618** SYLVESTER *Spectacles* ix. (Grosart) II. 298 Th' idle Lubber, *labour-loathing. **1834** MILL in *Monthly Repos.* New Ser. VIII. 320 We have to lessen the pressure on the *labour-market. **1861** GEN. P. THOMPSON *Audi Alt.* III. 149 The expenditure consequent on this, is thrown into what people call the labour-market. **1876** H. FAWCETT *Pol. Econ.* II. iv. 146 The home labour-market is relieved by emigration. **1946** *R.A.F. Jrnl.* May 160 There must be many a man..awaiting his release with some trepidation on account of uncertainty about his future in the labour market. **1965** SELDON & PENNANCE *Everyman's Dict. Econ.* 152 It [*sc.* the employment exchange] thus helps to make the labour market work by acting as a clearing-house of information about employment. **1974** *Guardian* 24 Jan. 13/3 Parents are not going to stay at home, and the labour market needs them. **1901** *Daily News* 10 Jan. 9/3 The *labour master..certified him able to do the work. **1921** *Dict. Occup. Terms* (1927) §731 *Labour master*, engages and discharges casual labour..employed by dock or harbour authority [etc.]. **1895** *Whitaker's Almanack* 134 The House of Commons..Liberals, 267 (including 4 *Labour Members). **1870** *Scribner's Monthly* I. 71 The preacher..beats about..in a dissertation on..the '*labor movement'. **1893** L. T. HOBHOUSE (*title*) The Labour Movement. **1944** M. LASKI *Love on Supertax* ix. 88 Her ignorance of Party matters, Labour Movements, working-class life. **1969** A. PLATER *Close Coalhouse Door* III. 66 The Labour movement that was made by the miners out of blood, sweat and tears. **1832** *Crisis* 28 Apr. 12/1 Money was not necessary. *Labour-notes were sufficient. **1894** B. JONES *Co-operative Production* I. 89 These labour notes were to supersede the use of metallic coins and ordinary bank notes, and were to become a superior kind of money. **1967** *Times Rev. Industry* Apr. 64/2 It is partly the search for regular and reasonably high earnings that makes men hire themselves to *labour-only sub-contractors. **1969** M. GAGG in R. Fraser *Work* II. 132 A third system is labour-only sub-contracting in which a bricklayer or a group of bricklayers will undertake to do the brickwork on a job for so much per yard super (98 bricks). *Ibid.* 133 For the past seven years I have been a labour only sub-contractor. **1974** *Shelter News* Easter 3/2 From the trade union point of view, the labour-only sub-contracting practice gives rise to many problems. **1754–64** SMELLIE *Midwifery* I. 197 If it is delivered without any other assistance than that of the *labour-pains the birth ought to be called natural. **1799** ADOLPHUS *Mem. Fr. Rev.* I. 2 The dauphiness..was unexpectedly seized with labour-pains, and delivered. **1886** *Pall Mall G.* 18 May 3/1 The position attained by the new *Labour party. **1892** ROYDHOUSE & TAPERELL (*title*) The Labour Party in New South Wales. **1896** *Labour Annual* 39 This [of 1895] was the first General Election in which an organized Labour party, independent of either Liberal or Tory, and opposing either or both, has taken part in the United Kingdom. **1905** J. R. MACDONALD in W. T. Stead *Coming Men* 222 The Labour Party..will represent trades; it will represent the working class; it will represent a coherent body of fundamental Labour opinion. **1922** *Encycl. Brit.* XXXII. 507/1 The Labour party..included the Independent Labour Party and the Fabian Society and one or two smaller Socialist bodies. Locally it was organized in several hundred Local Labour parties. *Ibid.* 884/2 For many years there was a Labor or Socialist Labor national party, which regularly nominated a candidate for the [U.S.] presidency. **1926** *Daily Chron.* 13 May 2/3 What are we to say of the Trade Union and Labour Party leaders who on Saturday, May 1, agreed to the sending out of the strike instructions? **1945** W. K. RICHMOND *Educ. in England* vi. 116 The generous programme for free secondary education issued..by the Labour Party. **1971** *New Statesman* 9 July 37/1 You could lift almost any quote from the Labour Party's guide for women's sections to illustrate the patronising view they take of us. **1971** *Sunday Australian* 8 Aug. 3/4 The Federal President of the Australian Labor Party..yesterday called on his party to dissociate itself from extremist students. **1927** *Melody Maker* Aug. 777/1 Al Payne should have been leader, but the necessary *labour permits could not be obtained, and the band remains in America. **1943** E. M. ALMEDINGEN *Frossia* ii. 107, I have no right to employ anyone..without a proper labour permit. **1866** *Leisure Hour* 17 Mar. 171/1 The competition of labourers with each other for employment, which, in a country like ours, where there is always a vast reserve of *labour-power, must far more than counterbalance any good to the labourer arising from the competition of the masters for his services. **1896** J. A. HOBSON *Probl. Unemployed* 2 Off-time..implies waste of labour-power. **1959** B. WOOTTON *Social Sci. & Social Path.* ix. 280 He matters in himself, and not merely as a unit of cannon-fodder, labour-power or population. **1888** E. BELLAMY *Looking Backward* v, What solution, if any, have you found for the *labour question? **1943** J. S. HUXLEY *TVA* 116 The TVA's work in making a comparative survey of rates and conditions in all the fertilizer plants of the region, which helped materially in promoting better *labour relations. **1973** *Guardian* 12 Mar. 11/7 Leyland's personnel manager declined to comment... 'I personally am anti-press. I have had too much trouble with you lot buggering up labour relations.' **1902** *Chambers's Jrnl.* Dec. 830/2 The machine appears to be a real *labour and time saver, and is moderate in price. **1929** A. HUXLEY *Do what you Will* 86 The machine..is..a labour-saver. **177.** ADAM SMITH (Worcester), A *labor-saving machine. **1870** LOWELL *Among my Bks.* Ser. I. (1873) 110 Only too thankful for any labor-saving contrivance whatsoever. **1904** *Sci. Amer.* 21 May 404/2 The present enormous industry..was rendered possible only by the introduction of labor-saving machinery. **1932** *Discovery* Jan. 10 Many remarkable labour-saving machines have been evolved in recent years. **1957** *Observer* 11 Aug. 8/4 The old owners have dwindled, departed, and found labour-saving bungalows in quieter spots. **1964** M. MCLUHAN *Understanding Media* xvi. 161 The American farmer, confronted with new tasks and opportunities, and at the same time with a great shortage of human assistance, was goaded into a frenzy of creation of labor-saving devices. **1971** *Engineering* Apr. 92/2 With its time and labour-saving features. **1822–34** *Good's Study Med.* (ed. 4) IV. 60 *Leucorrhea Nabothi*, *Labour-Show. **1888** L. A. SMITH *Music of Waters* 275 Isaac D'Israeli, in his 'Curiosities of Literature', mentions the numerous *labour-songs used by the ancient Greeks. **1921** Labour song [see BLUES]. **1974** *Times* 25 Sept. 14/8 She..sang a labour song about joining the union. **1868** J. H. NEWMAN *Verses Var. Occasions* 140 Severed..From thy loved *labour-sphere. **1891** *Daily News* 28 Mar. 2/6 The land of Lincolnshire..was *labour-starved. **1898** J. ARCH *Story of Life* viii. 183 Hundreds and hundreds of labour-starved acres. **1887** KIRKUP in *Encycl. Brit.* XXII. 212/1 The *labour-time which we take as the measure of value is the time required to produce a commodity under the normal social conditions of production with the average degree of skill and intensity of labour. **1866** in *Documentary Hist. Amer. Industr. Society* (1910) IX. 133 Each member belonging to the National *Labor Union. **1884** J. HAY *Bread-Winners* xi. 183 The labor unions have ordered a general strike. **1944** H. A. WALLACE *Century of Common Man* 25 July 84 The people of America know that the second step towards Nazism is the destruction of labour unions. **1973** *Times* 16 Nov. 20/7 Nationalism has had an important effect on labour union attitudes in Canada. **1933** A. W. BOURNE et al. *Queen Charlotte's Text-bk. Obstetr.* (ed. 3) xiv. 266 No person is allowed in the hospital *labour ward without a mask, which covers both the mouth and nose. **1953** E. SIMON *Past Masters* IV. vi. 260 That first time the baby had been born..at home... Now..I was taken straight to the Labour Ward. **1968** S. BENDER *Obstetr. for Pupil Midwives* xi. 147 The woman admitted to the labour ward and her accompanying relative or friend are greeted cheerfully. **1640** FULLER *Joseph's Coat* ii. (1867) 116 It will be a *labour-worthy discourse. **1856** READE *Never too late* x, He went into the *labor-yard, looked at the cranks [etc.].

labour, labor ('leɪbə(r)), *v.* Forms: 4 **laborie, -y, labre,** 4–5 **labore, -er,** 4–6 **laboure,** 5 **-owre,** *Sc.* **lauber,** 5–6 **labur,** *Sc.* **laubour,** 6 **-or, -ur, -yr,** 4– **labor,** 5– **labour.** [a. F. *labourer* (early *laborer*, 10th c.), ad. L. *labōrāre*, f. *labōr-*, *labor* (see prec.). Cf. It. *lavorare*, Sp. *labrar*, Pg. *lavrar*.

In mod.Fr., Sp., and Pg. the word is chiefly restricted to the specific sense 'to plough', the wider sense having passed to the vb. represented in Eng. by TRAVAIL.]

I. Transitive senses.

1. To spend labour upon (the ground, †vegetable growths, etc.); to till, cultivate. Now *poet.* or *arch.* Also, in recent use, to work (a mine).

13.. *E.E. Allit. P.* A. 503 To labor vyne watz dere þe date. *c* **1470** HENRY *Wallace* VIII. 1607 The abill ground gert laubour thryftely. **1481** CAXTON *Godfrey* viii. (1893) 29 They laboured no londe by eryng. **1523** LD. BERNERS *Froiss.* I. clxxxviii. 223 The landes were voyde and nat laboured. **1549** *Compl. Scot.* xv. 123 The grond that i laubyr. **1596** DALRYMPLE tr. *Leslie's Hist. Scot.* III. 197 He gaue her landes and steddings, with seruandes to labour thame. **1602** CAREW *Cornwall* 82 a, To labor the Lords vineyard. **1667** MILTON *P.L.* XII. 18 Labouring the soile, and reaping plenteous crop. **1696** PHILLIPS (ed. 5) s.v., To Labour the Ground, is to manure the Ground by removing the Earth. **1711** ADDISON *Spect.* No. 115 ¶5 The Earth must be laboured before it gives its Increase. **1792** A. YOUNG *Trav. France* 411 The English labourer..hazards much when he labours land for himself. **1824** SCOTT *St. Ronan's* xxviii, The garden was weeded, and the glebe was regularly laboured. **1833** [see LABOURED *ppl. a.*]. **1876** MORRIS *Sigurd* II. 140 Fair then was the son of Sigmund as he toiled and laboured the ground. **1897** *Westm. Gaz.* 3 Sept. 2/1 A claim must be properly laboured by the owner or by someone paid by him.

2. a. *gen.* To spend labour upon; to work upon; to produce or execute with labour. (Also with cogn. obj.) *Obs.* or *arch.*

c **1430** *Pilgr. Lyf Manhode* II. lx. (1869) 99 Litel rouht hire of spinnynge, or to laboure ooþer labour. **1432–50** tr. *Higden* (Rolls) I. 67 In eny other welle whiche hathe be laborede by diuerse kynges of Egipte. *c* **1440** *Jacob's Well* 4 Now haue I ymagyd and cast all myn hool werk of þis welle; which I schal laboure to ȝou lxxxix. dayes and v., ere it be performyd. **1523** in *10th Rep. Hist. MSS. Comm.* App. v. 328 All manere goods and marchandis as shalbe labored, tracted, and adventured by ony of the inhabitants of this citie. **15..** WITHALS *Dict.* (1568) 11/1 Claye labored to make pottes. **1599** *Broughton's Lett.* vii. 24 With this Rabbinicall rubbish..haue you laboured a lomie and sandie building. **1611** BIBLE *Transl. Pref.* 1 Whether it be by deuising any thing our selues, or reuising that which hath bene laboured by others. **1623** WHITBOURNE *Newfoundland* 82 The other are to labour the fish at land, (of which sixteene) seuen are to be skilfull headders, and splitters of fish. **1697** DRYDEN *Virg. Georg.* IV. 82 They..labour Honey to sustain their Lives. —— *Æneid* VI. 859 Anvils, labour'd by the Cyclops Hands. **1725** POPE *Odyss.* VIII. 317 A wondrous net he labours. **1830** TENNYSON *Poems* 111 Love laboured honey busily. I was the hive and Love the bee. **1832** STANDISH *Maid of Jaen* 8 The diamond labour'd from the mine.

†**b.** *to labour one's needs*: to work for one's livelihood. *Obs.*

c **1400** *Rom. Rose* 6688 A man..That..wol but only bidde his bedis, And never with honde laboure his nedis.

†**3.** To use labour upon in rubbing, pounding, or the like; *hence*, to rub, pound, beat, etc. (Cf. *work* vb.) *Obs.*

1486 *Bk. St. Albans* a v b, Take yᵉ white of an egge, & labur thessame in a sponge. **1544** PHAER *Regim.* (1560) S iij b, Laboure the sope and the rose water wel together. *Ibid.* S vi b, Red coral..hanged about the neck, wherupon the childe should oftentymes labour his gummes. **1569** R. ANDROSE tr. *Alexis' Secr.* IV. III. 25 Boyle them, laboring them with the spatter. **1607** MARKHAM *Caval.* II. (1617) 79 As he trotteth, labour his contrarie side with the calfe of your leg. *a* **1661** FULLER *Worthies* (1840) III. 486 Take to every six gallons of water one gallon of the finest honey, and put into the boorn, and labour it together half an hour.

4. To belabour, ply with blows. *Obs.* exc. *dial.*

1594 CAREW *Huart's Exam. Wits* xiii. (1596) 211 The Asse..if he be laboured with a cudgell, he setteth not by it. **1645** SLINGSBY *Diary* (1836) 177 Our horse did so fast labour yᵐ wᵗʰ their longe tucks yᵗ they could not endure it. **1697** DRYDEN *Virg. Georg.* III. 639 Take a Plant of stubborn Oak; And labour him with many a sturdy Stroak.

mod. Sc. He took a stick an' laubor'd [*or* labber'd] the beast terrible wi'd.

5. a. To work at or treat laboriously; to take great pains with (a matter); to work out in detail, to elaborate. Now almost exclusively in *to labour a point, a question*, and similar expressions.

c **1449** PECOCK *Repr.* I. xvi. 91 So preciose and vnlackeable occupacion to be had and laborid among hem. **1548** UDALL *Erasmus Par.* Pref. 13 b, Verai fewe studentes dooe vse to reade and laboure any one autour in any one particuler facultee or disciplyne. **1605** BACON *Adv. Learn.* II. xxiii. §5. 220 Science of government, which we see is laboured and in some part reduced. *a* **1619** FOTHERBY *Atheomastix* II. xi. §4 (1622) 317 Which point, hee..hath laboured exactly, with much finenesse and subtility. **1691** T. H[ALE] *Acc. New Invent.* p. lii, The Invention of the New-River-Water was much labour'd. **1750** JOHNSON *Rambler* No. 92 ⁋12 These lines, laboured with great attention. *c* **1750** SHENSTONE *Solicitude* 29 How the nightingales labour the strain. **1784** COWPER *Task* III. 787 Th' accomplished plan That he has touch'd, retouch'd, many a long day Labor'd, and many a night pursued in dreams. **1797** BURKE *Regic. Peace* iv. Wks. 1842 II. 357 Though he labours this point, yet he confesses a fact..which renders all his labours utterly fruitless. **1846** ELLIS *Elgin Marbles* II. 225 In a single figure, parts are often highly laboured. **1863** C. CLARKE *Shakesp. Char.* x. 254 The reason why the poet has so laboured the character of his hero. **1892** A. J. BALFOUR *Sp.* in *Standard* 11 Apr. 3/5, I do not desire on the present occasion to labour this proposition.

†**b.** = ELABORATE *v.* 2. *Obs.*

1615 CROOKE *Body of Man* 373 In the cauity of this ventricle the vitall spirits are laboured. **1668** CULPEPPER & COLE *Barthol. Anat.* II. vi. 96 The Heart..is the fountain of Life and labors the vital Spirits.

6. To endeavour to bring about (a state of things); to work for or with a view to (a result); to work hard for (a cause or the like). (Cf. 12.) *Obs.* or *arch.*

In early legal use often associated with *sue*.

1439 *E.E. Wills* (1882) 118 The mater so to be laboryd and sewyd that he be constrayned ther to do hit. **1463** in *Bury Wills* (Camden) 40 If ony wil laboure the contrarye. **1484** *Certificate* in *Surtees Misc.* (1890) 42 þe foresaid forged and untrue testimonyall, shewed [? *read* sewed] & labord by þe said Richard Davis. **1523** in *10th Rep. Hist. MSS. Comm.* App. v. 328 If ony such parson..shall sue or laboure ony such writte. **1611** B. JONSON *Catiline* III. i, Two things I must labour, That neither they upbraid, nor you repent you. **1613** PURCHAS *Pilgrimage, Descr. India* (1864) 28 The Mother of Echebar..laboured a peace, but not preuailing, fell sicke. **1639** FULLER *Holy War* IV. xviii. (1647) 199 [She] laboured his cause day and night. *a* **1661** —— *Worthies* (1840) III. 2 When Shat-over woods..were likely to be cut down, the university by letters labored their preservation. **1678** DRYDEN *Kind Keeper* II. i. Dram. Wks. 1725 IV. 303 Is this a Song to be sung at such a time when I am labouring your Reconcilement? **1742** YOUNG *Nt. Th.* 52 And labour that first palm of noble minds, A manly scorn of terror from the tomb. **1793** BURKE *Observ. Cond. Minority* Wks. 1842 I. 612 How much I wished for, and how earnestly I laboured, that re-union. **1817** JAS. MILL *Brit. India* I. III. iv. 621 In labouring the ruin of Nujeeb ad Dowlah.

†**7. a.** To endeavour to influence or persuade; to urge or entreat. (Cf. 13.) *Obs.*

1461 *Paston Lett.* No. 404 II. 31 Tudynham, Stapylton, and Heydon, with theyr affenyte labur the Kyng and Lords unto my hurt. **1556** J. HEYWOOD *Spider & F.* lv. title, The butterflie..fleeth into the tree: laboring the flies to haue the ant heerd speake ere he die. **1577–87** HOLINSHED *Chron.* III. 1225/2 He was laboured and solicited dailie by wise and learned fathers, to recant his diuelish & erronious opinions. **1598** SPENSER in *Wks.* (ed. Grosart) I. 539 The landlords..began..to labour the Erle of Tireone vnto theire parte. **1603** KNOLLES *Hist. Turks* (1621) 604 Hee began cunningly to labour divers of the noblemen one by one. **1622** BACON *Hen. VII* 119 Yet would not the French King deliver him up to King Henry (as hee was laboured to doe). **1633** CAMPION *Hist. Irel.* II. iii. 75 [He] laboured the King..earnestly for their pardons and obtained it.

†**b.** To advocate strenuously, urge (a matter).

1477 *Paston Lett.* No. 785 III. 172 That ye schuld labur the mater to my maister. **1616** F. COTTINGTON in *Buccleuch MSS.* (Hist. MSS. Comm.) I. 183 Much it is laboured there that he should come as ordinary, and not for a small time.

†**8.** (with *compl.*) To bring into a specified condition or position by strenuous exertion. *Obs.*

c **1485** *Digby Myst.* III. 1823 þer is a woman..þat hether hath laberyd me owt of mercyll. **1550** CROWLEY *Way to Wealth* 171 Loke if thou haue not laboured him oute of his house or ground. **1602** MARSTON *Antonio's Rev.* v. iii. Wks. 1856 I. 134, I have beene labouring generall favour firme. **1611** *Second Maiden's Trag.* v. ii. in Hazl. *Dodsley* X. 465 Our arms and lips Shall labour life into her. Wake, sweet mistress! **1615** T. ADAMS *Spirit. Navigator* 34 Whiles he labours them to Hell, winde and Tide are on his side. *a* **1617** P. BAYNE *Ephes.* (1658) 17 Men must labour their hearts to a sense of the worth of the benefits. **1633** EARL MANCH. *Al Mondo* (1636) 16 To labour the eye to see darknesse. **1655** MOUFET & BENNET *Health's Improv.* (1746) 151 Drink..a good Draught of your strongest Beer..and then labour it out, as Plowmen do. **1697** DRYDEN *Virg. Georg.* III. 65 Sisyphus that labours up the Hill The rowling Rock in vain.

†**9. a.** To impose labour upon; to work (an animal); to use (the body or its parts, *occas.* the mind) in some work. *Obs.* exc. *poet.*

1470–85 MALORY *Arthur* XVIII. xvii, The hors was passynge lusty and fresshe by cause he was not laboured a moneth afore. *c* **1500** *Yng. Children's Bk.* in *Babees Bk.* (1868) 19 A byrde hath wenges forto fle, So man hath Armes laboryd to be. **1526** *Pilgr. Perf.* (W. de W. 1531) 303 b, Thou were so ferre ouer laboured & faynt for payne. **1535** COVERDALE *Deut.* xxi. 3 A yonge cowe which hath not bene laboured, ner hath drawen in the yocke. **1545** ASCHAM *Toxoph.* I. (Arb.) 46 A pastyme..where euery parte of the bodye must be laboured. **1638** *Tarlton's Test.* C j b, My fore-horse..being let bloud and drencht yesterday, I durst not labour him. **1671** MILTON *Samson* 1298 This Idols day..Labouring thy mind More then the working day thy hands. **1872** TENNYSON *Gareth & Lynette* 31 But Kay the seneschal who loved him not Would hustle and harry him, and labour him Beyond his comrade of the hearth.

†**b.** To cause to undergo fatigue. *Obs.*

c **1386** CHAUCER *Shipman's T.* 1298, I trowe..that our gode man Hath yow laboured sith the night bigan. *c* **1400** *Destr. Troy* 13490 A tempest hym toke..þat myche laburt the lede er he lond caght. **1496** *Bk. St. Albans, Fishing* (1810) h v, Yf it fortune you to smyte a grete fysshe wyth a smalle harnays: thenne ye must lede hym in the water and labour him there tyll he be drownyd and ouercome. **1632** J. FEATLY *Hon. Chast.* 25, I will not labour your eares with the many and vulgar arguments to prove a God.

†**10.** To burden, overwhelm, oppress, distress.

1450–1530 *Myrr. Our Ladye* 240 The drede of god, by whiche she was ful sore laboured & troubeled. **1482** *Monk of Evesham* (Arb.) 19 Sore labouryd with gret febulnes and wekenes. **1611** SPEED *Hist. Gt. Brit.* IX. xviii. (1632) 908 Nature being sore laboured, sore wearied and weakned.

II. Intransitive senses.

11. a. To use labour, to exert one's powers of body or mind; in early use chiefly said of physical work, *esp.* performed with the object of gaining a livelihood; to exert oneself, toil; to work, *esp.* to work hard or against difficulties.

1362 LANGL. *P. Pl.* A. VII. 26, I wol helpe þee to labore whil my lyf lastiþ. *Ibid.* 117 We haue no lymes to labore [C. IX. 135 laborie] with. *Ibid.* 259 þat Fisyk schal..beo fayn..his fisyk to lete, And leorne to labre wiþe lond leste lyflode faile. *Ibid.* B. XV. 182þanne wil he some tyme Labory in a lauendrye. *c* **1386** CHAUCER *Merch. T.* 387 He..preyde hem to labouren in this nede, And shapen that he faille nat to spede. **1399** LANGL. *Rich. Redeles* III. 267 Not..to laboure on þe lawe as lewde men on plowes. *c* **1400** MAUNDEV. (1839) vi. 64 Thei tylen not the Lond, ne thei laboure noughte. *c* **1400** *Destr. Troy* 5862 He..Hade laburt so longe, hym list for to rest. *c* **1460** FORTESCUE *Abs. & Lim. Mon.* xiv. (1885) 142 This serche..hath be a digression ffrom the mater in wich we labour. **1542** BRINKLOW *Compl.* xvi. (1874) 40 He that laboryth not, let him not eate. **1611** BIBLE *Isa.* xlix. 4, I have laboured in vain, I have spent my strength for nought. **1651** HOBBES *Leviath.* II. xxx. 181 It is not enough, for a man to labour for the maintenance of his life. **1698** FRYER *East India & P.* 111 Who Run..or else Dance so many hours to a Tune..when they labour as much as a Lancashire man does at Roger of Coverly. **1770** LANGHORNE *Plutarch* (1879) I. 239 Those who laboured at the oars. **1895** *Bookman* Oct. 16/2 [He] labours hard over his proofs of the book.

indirect pass. **1715** DE FOE *Fam. Instruct.* I. i. (1841) I. 22 You must be instructed and laboured with to be a good child.

†**b.** *refl.* in same sense. *Obs.*

c **1374** CHAUCER *Troylus* IV. 981 (1009), I mene as though I laboured me in this, To enqueren which thing cause of which thing be. **1483** CAXTON *Gold. Leg.* C viij b/1 Grete in contemplacion of heuenly thynges and a tylyar in labouryng hymself. **1526** *Pilgr. Perf.* (W. de W. 1531) 171 b, The more yᵘ enforcest & labourest thy selfe in yᵉ begynnynge.

12. To exert oneself, strive (*for* some end); to endeavour strenuously (*to* accomplish or bring about something).

1398 TREVISA *Barth. De P.R.* XVIII. lxxxvii. (1495) 836 They..labouren to helpe eche other wyth all theyr myghte. *c* **1430** LYDG. *Assembly of Gods* 847 Laboryng the Seruyce of God to Multyply. **1500–20** DUNBAR *Poems* lxxi. 10 Is nane of ws..Bot laubouris ay for vthiris distructioun. **1526** *Pilgr. Perf.* (W. de W. 1531) 2 b, They laboured..to knowe the natures of thynges in this worlde. **1535** COVERDALE *Ps.* cxx. 7, I laboured for peace. —— *2 Macc.* iv. 7 Iason the brother of Onias laboured to be hye prest. **1604** E. G[RIMSTONE] *D' Acosta's Hist. Indies* III. iv. 131 They which saile from West to East, labour alwaies to be out of the burning Zone. **1611** BIBLE *Isa.* xxii. 4, I will weepe bitterly, labour not to comfort me. **1613** SHAKS. *Hen. VIII*, III. ii. 191 For your highness' good I ever labour'd More than mine own. **1682** DRYDEN *Mac Flecknoe* 157 When false flowers of rhetoric thou would'st cull, Trust nature, do not labour to be dull. **1711** STEELE *Spect.* No. 95 ⁋4 True Affliction labours to be invisible. **1766** GOLDSM. *Vic. W.* xxv, I laboured to become cheerful. **1796** JANE AUSTEN *Pride & Prej.* vii, Most earnestly did she labour to prove the probability of error. *a* **1862** BUCKLE *Civiliz.* (1873) III. v. 387 Water is constantly labouring to reduce all the inequalities of the earth to a single level. **1874** GREEN *Short Hist.* vii. §3 (1882) 371 Parker was labouring for a uniformity of faith and worship amongst the clergy.

†**13.** To exert one's influence in urging a suit or to obtain something desired. Const. *to* (a person).

?**1475** *Plumpton Corr.* 31, I have receaved from you diverse letters..that I shold labour to Sir John Pilkinton, to labor to my lord of Glocester or to the king. *Ibid.* 51 This day com Wylliam Plompton to labor for Haveray Parke. **1533** MORE *Apol.* viii. Wks. 860/2 If I desired a manne to geue me a thynge, and laboured muche to hym therefore. *c* **1555** HARPSFIELD *Divorce Hen. VIII* (Camden) 236 He laboured to the Pope to have a dispensation. **1577–87** HOLINSHED *Chron.* I. 188/1 His coosen..who was about to labour to the king for his pardon.

14. a. To move or travel, *esp.* with implication of painful exertion or impeded progress. *lit.* and *fig.* Now *rare.*

a **1400–50** *Alexander* 4814 þai labourde vp a-gayn þe lift an elleuen dais. *c* **1450** LONELICH *Grail* xlii. 82 Nasciens that In the se was Abrod, Vpp and down labowred. **1523** LD. BERNERS *Froiss.* I. xxiv. 34 The kynge..retourned agayne into Englande, and laboured so longe that he came to Wyndesor. **1530** PALSGR. 600/2 This horse is nat very fayre, but he laboureth well on the waye,..*il chemine bien.* **1611** BIBLE *Josh.* vii. 3 Let about two or three thousand men goe vp,..and make not all the people to labour thither. **1715–20** POPE *Iliad* XII. 458 He poised, and swung it round; then, toss'd on high, It flew with force and labour'd up the sky. **1877** L. MORRIS *Epic of Hades* I. 3 The stream Which laboured in the distance to the sea.

b. quasi-trans. *to labour one's way*: to pursue it laboriously.

1856 KANE *Arct. Expl.* II. xxiii. 231 Laboring our way with great difficulty upon the ice-belt.

†**c.** To make little progress, suffer impediments.

1736 CHANDLER *Hist. Persec.* 360 The job was labouring for three years space. **1765** T. HUTCHINSON *Hist. Mass.* I. iii. 360 A petition of Capt. Hutchinson and others labored, although their title was originally derived from the Indian sachems and proprietors, and the lands had been long possessed.

15. To be burdened, troubled, or distressed, as by disease, want, etc.; to be trammelled by or suffer from some disadvantage or defect. Const. *under* (also †*of, with, on, in*).

c **1470** HENRY *Wallace* VII. 345 Lawberand [*v.r.* laubourit] in mynd thai had beyne all that day. **1578** BANISTER *Hist. Man* I. 16 No maruaile..if the eye in dolour labouryng, this Muscle sometyme be affected also. **1615** G. SANDYS *Trav.* 106 Whereby vnprofitable marishes were drained..and such places relieued as laboured with the penury of waters. **1641** MILTON *Reform.* II. (1851) 69 This our shaken Monarchy, that now lies labouring under her throwes. **1644** BULWER *Chiron.* 15 Speech labours of a blinde crampe, when it is too concise, confused or obscure. **1662** H. MORE *Philos. Writings* Pref. general xi, Men of very excellent spirits may labour with prejudice against so worthy an Authour. *a* **1677** BARROW *Euclid* (1714) Pref. 3 Seems..to labour under a double Defect. **1697** DRYDEN *Virg. Georg.* III. 746 The wheasing Swine With Coughs is choak'd, and labours from the Chine. **1709** BERKELEY *Ess. Vision* §83 The visive faculty..may be found to labour of two defects. **1712** ADDISON *Spect.* No. 267 ⁋3 Aristotle himself allows, that Homer has nothing to boast of as to the Unity of his Fable ..Some have been of opinion, that the Æneid also labours in this Particular. **1769** WARBURTON *Lett.* (1809) 434, I was then labouring on my old rheumatic disorder. I have not yet got rid of it. **1784** tr. *Beckford's Vathek* (1868) 113 From time to time he laboured with profound sighs. **1839** in *Spirit Metrop. Conserv. Press* (1840) I. 273 Some timid conservatives..labour in the same mistake. **1857** KINGSLEY *Two Y. Ago* (1877) 416 You are labouring under an entire misapprehension. **1862** SIR B. BRODIE *Psychol. Inq.* II. iv. 110 If he laboured under a perpetual toothache.

†**16.** Of women: To suffer the pains of childbirth; to travail. Also *fig. Obs.*

1454 *Paston Lett.* I. 274 Aftir she was arestid she laboured of hir child, that she is with all. **1527** ANDREW *Brunswyke's Distyll. Waters* K iv, Yf a woman dronke it, the chylde sholde dye, and she sholde laboure before her ryght tyme. **1548–9** (Mar.) *Bk. Com. Prayer, Litany*, All women labouryng of chylde. **1588** SHAKS. *L.L.L.* v. ii. 521 When great things labouring perish in their birth. **1604** —— *Oth.* II. i. 128 But my Muse labours, and thus she is deliuer'd. **1653** *Parish Reg. Finghall, Yks.* (MS.), Baptised Elizabeth the daughter of John Parke of Wensley, whose wife laboured at Burton in her journey homeward. **1711** POPE *Temple of Fame* 212 Here, like some furious prophet, Pindar rode, And seem'd to labour with th' inspiring God.

17. Of a ship: To roll or pitch heavily at sea.

1627 CAPT. SMITH *Seaman's Gram.* ix. 40 We say a ship doth Labour much when she doth rowle much any way. **1748** *Anson's Voy.* I. vi. 104 The ship laboured very much in a hollow sea. **1819** BYRON *Juan* II. xli, The ship labour'd so, they scarce could hope To weather out much longer. **1840** R. H. DANA *Bef. Mast* xxv. 82 The ship was labouring hard under her top-gallant sails.

labour-: see LABOR-.

†**'labourable**, *a. Obs.* [a. F. *labourable* (1409 in Hatz.-Darm.) arable, f. *labourer* to LABOUR.] Capable of being laboured or worked.

1481 CAXTON *Godfrey* lxvii. (1893) 112 A londe..ful of..good feldes labourable. **1545** in *Archiv Stud. neu. Spr.* XCIX. 23, I am Sonday moste honorable: That day all thynges laborable Ought for to rest. **1611** COTGR., *Labourable*, labourable, workable, fit to be wrought on; also, nauigable. **1693** EVELYN *De la Quint. Compl. Gard.* I. 21 Three Foot of good Mould, very soft or labourable on the Top. **1738** WARBURTON *Div. Leg.* II. 274 To drain the swampy Marshes of this vast extended Level: and to render the whole Labourable.

labourage ('leɪbərɪdʒ). Also 5 labourrage, 9 laborage. [a. F. *labourage* (12–13th c. in Hatz.-

Darm.), f. *labourer* to LABOUR. In sense 3, f. LABOUR *sb.* + -AGE.]

†1. Ploughing; *concr.* ploughed or cultivated land. *Obs.*

1475 *Bk. Noblesse* 65 Labouragis and approwementis of londes and pastures. *Ibid.* 70 In tilieng, ering, and labourage of his londis to bere corne and fruit. **1502** *Ord. Crysten Men* (W. de W. 1506) IV. xxi. 286 Whiche by huntynges endomageth gretely cornes, grasse, or other labourages.

†2. Labouring, labour, work. *Obs.*

1484 CAXTON *Fables of Æsop* VI. x. (1889) 205 They retorned to theyr labourrage. **1660** HEXHAM *Dutch Dict.*, *Arbeydinge*, labourage, labouring, or taking paines.

3. Payment for labour.

1826 *MS. Bill of John Earle, Hull*, Laborage, Shipping, and Wharfage 4*s.* **1890** *East. Morn. News* 14 Feb. 3/5, I allude specially to the question of labourage, which shows a very great increase.

laboured, labored (ˈleɪbəd), *ppl. a.* [f. LABOUR *v.* + -ED[1].]

1. †Cultivated, tilled, ploughed (*obs.*); also, of a mine, worked.

1579 SPENSER *Sheph. Cal.* Oct. 58 Whereon he earst had taught his flocks to feede, And laboured lands to yield the timely eare. **1697** DRYDEN *Virg. Georg.* II. 414 Root up wild Olives from thy labour'd Lands. **1833** TENNYSON *Œnone* 113 Or laboured mine undrainable of ore.

†2. a. Employed in labour; hard worked; oppressed with labour or toil. *Obs.*

1595 SHAKS. *John* II. i. 232 Your King, whose labour'd spirits Fore-wearied in this action of swift speede. **1634** MILTON *Comus* 291 What time the labour'd Oxe In his loose traces from the furrow came. **1682** DRYDEN *Dk. Guise* I. i, Turn'd out, like labour'd Oxen, after Harvest.

†b. Worn with use. *Obs.*

1535 COVERDALE *1 Sam.* xiii. 21 The edges of the plowshares, and mattockes, & forckes, and axes were laboured, and the poyntes blont.

3. Wrought, produced, or accomplished with labour; highly elaborated; hence in depreciatory sense, performed or accomplished only by the expenditure of excessive toil or tedious elaboration, and consequently showing indications of heaviness or want of spontaneity. Also, of physical action: Heavy, performed with great effort. Also *laboured-at.*

1608 SHAKS. *Per.* II. iii. 17 In framing an Artist, art hath thus decreed, To make some good, but others to exceed, And you are her labourd scholler. *a* **1658** CLEVELAND *Elegy B. Jonson* 65 The marbled Glory of thy labour'd Rhyme. **1703** POPE *Thebais* 202 Labour'd columns in long order plac'd. **1740** PITT *Æneid* x. 759 High in my Dome, are Silver Talents roll'd With Piles of Labour'd and Unlabour'd Gold. **1756** BURKE *Subl. & B.* v. v, There is not perhaps in the whole Eneid a more grand and laboured passage than the description of Vulcan's cavern in Etna. **1826** J. FOSTER in *Life & Corr.* (1846) II. 84 Other writing of a laboured and tedious kind. **1856** OLMSTED *Slave States* 215 A labored investigation of evidence. **1875** JOWETT *Plato* (ed. 2) V. 15 The dialogue is generally weak and laboured. **1876** G. M. HOPKINS *Poems* (1918) 9 And lily-coloured clothes provided Your spouse not laboured-at nor spun. **1897** MARY KINGSLEY *W. Africa* 156 The laboured beat of the engines. **1898** G. MEREDITH *Odes Fr. Hist.* 72 Laboured mounds, that a foot or a wanton stick may subvert.

Hence **ˈlabouredly** *adv.*, **ˈlabouredness**.

1882 *Daily Tel.* 24 Feb. (Cass.), He spoke labouredly and with hesitation. **1930** J. W. MACKAIL *Largeness in Lit.* 6 Largeness is..the opposite..of thinness, of tightness, of labouredness.

labourer, laborer (ˈleɪbərə(r)). [f. LABOUR *v.* + -ER[1].] One who labours.

1. One who performs physical labour as a service or for a livelihood; *spec.* one who does work requiring chiefly bodily strength or aptitude and little skill or training, as distinguished, e.g., from an artisan (often with defining word prefixed, as *agricultural*, *bricklayer's*, *dock*, *farm*, *mason's labourer*, etc.). *Statute of Labourers*: the mod. designation of the statute *De Servientibus* (23 Edw. III), regulating the rate of wages.

c **1325** *Poem temp. Edw. II* (Percy) lxv, A wreched laborer That lyveth by hys hond. **1390** GOWER *Conf.* III. 6 It maketh me drawe out of the way In solein place by my selve, As doth a laborer to delve. **1442-3** *Durham Acc. Rolls* (Surtees) 275 Will'o Harpur laborere laboranti infra Infirmariam, 7*s.* 7*d.* **1470-85** MALORY *Arthur* III. xi. 113 As Kynge Pellinore rode in that valey he mett with a poure man a labourer. **1513** DOUGLAS *Æneis* IV. xi. 91 With fire and swerd to persew and doun thring The laboraris [L. *colonos*] descend from Dardanus. **1543** tr. *Act 23 Edw. III* heading, Here begynnethe the Statute of Labourers. **1548** *Act 2 & 3 Edw. VI*, c. 15 §4 No Person..shall..let or disturb any.. Brickmaker, Tilemaker, Plummer or Labourer. **1590** GREENE *Neuer too late* (1600) 119 The labourer to the fields his plough-swaynes guides. **1769** FALCONER *Dict. Marine* (1780) F ff 4, *Travailleurs*, the ordinary, or labourers, &c. employed to assist in fitting out shipping for the sea. **1799** J. ROBERTSON *Agric. Perth* 342 Common labourers earn between one shilling and one shilling and three pence a-day. **1847** JAMES *Convict* xx, I am a labourer by trade. **1878** JEVONS *Primer Pol. Econ.* 71 Bricklayers' labourers refuse.. to raise bricks to the upper parts of a building by a rope and winch. **1891** *Daily News* 1 Sept. 3/1 An intelligent villager —not a labourer, but a man of the working-class.

†b. *Mil.*

1548 HALL *Chron., Hen. V* 56 b, The pyoners cast trenches and the laborers brought tymber. *Ibid., Hen. VIII* 114 Of bill men five. M. of pioners and laborers .ii. M. .vi. C.

c. *labourer-in-trust*: one of a number of officers (ranking next below the 'clerks of works') who formed part of the staff employed for the repairs of the royal palaces. The office ceased to exist in 1824.

1853 W. JERDAN *Autobiog.* IV. 52 He became what is called a labourer-in-trust on the establishment which has the charge of the Royal palaces. **1884** *Trans. Lond. & Middlesex Archæol. Soc.* VI. 486 Mr. Adam Lee, the Labourer-in-Trust of the Houses of Parliament.

2. *gen.* One who does work of any kind, a worker.

a **1420** HOCCLEVE *De Reg. Princ.* 1348 Swych laborer þe kythe heere in þys lyf, þat god þi soule,.. Reioise may. *c* **1511** *1st Eng. Bk. Amer.* (Arb.) 33/1 They be..great labourers. **1562** *Child Marriages* (1897) 97 The said Ellin was taken for an honest wenche and a good laborer. **1607** TOPSELL *Four-f. Beasts* (1658) 55 Which Kine are of the smallest body, and yet the greatest labourers. **1611** BIBLE *Luke* x. 7 The labourer is worthy of his hire. **1785** PALEY *Mor. Philos.* Wks. 1825 IV. 25 To the labourer, every interruption is a refreshment. **1841** TRENCH *Parables* ix. (1877) 176 In the kingdom of heaven it is God who seeks his labourers, and not they who seek Him.

3. One of the class among colonial insects that performs the work of the community; a 'worker'.

1601 SHAKS. *All's Well* I. ii. 67 Since I nor wax nor honie can bring home, I quickly were dissolued from my hiue To giue some Labourers roome. **1781** SMEATHMAN in *Phil. Trans.* LXXI. 145 The working insects, which, for brevity, I shall generally call labourers. **1834** MCMURTRIE *Cuvier's Anim. Kingd.* 430 The neuters or labourers..as to size, are intermediate between the males and females.

Hence †**labouress**, a female labourer.

1570 in Gutch *Coll. Cur.* II. 10 For Clementes paynes in the kychen a daye, laberess. **1809** *Spirit Publ. Jrnls.* (1810) XIII. 164 Two other fellow-labouresses.

Labour Exchange. Also with lower-case initials. [LABOUR *sb.* 2 + EXCHANGE *sb.*]

1. An establishment for the exchange of the products of labour without the use of money. Also *attrib.* Now only *Hist.*

1832 *Crisis* 28 Apr. 16/1 Mr. B. Warden..stated that they had erected a new school, called a Labour Exchange School. *Ibid.* 25 Aug. 97/3 To investigate the Principles upon which the proposed Equitable Labour Exchange was to be founded. *Ibid.* 6 Oct. 122/1 Labour Exchange notes... Labour Exchange banks. **1894** B. JONES *Co-operative Production* I. 90 The exchange was opened on September 3, 1832, under the title of 'The Equitable Labour Exchange'. **1906** G. J. HOLYOAKE *Hist. Co-operation in Eng.* (rev. ed.) I. 65 The Labour Exchange was not Mr. Owen's idea, but he adopted it.

2. An office serving as a means of connection between workers and employers, esp. one forming part of an organization to assist in the finding of employment. Also *attrib.*

1869 C. L. BRACE *New West* v. 53 One of the remarkable instances of the intelligence and humanity of this new community was the establishment, in 1868, of the 'Labor Exchange'. **1893** *Rep. Agencies & Methods Unemployed* 15 in *Parl. Papers 1893–4* (C. 7182) LXXXII. 377 Registry offices..for shore labourers having the title of the 'British Labour Exchange'. **1896** J. A. HOBSON *Probl. Unemployed* 130 If the Bureaux are to perform effectively the work of Labour Exchanges. **1911** R. BROOKE *Let.* 20 Apr. (1968) 299, I share the Old Vicarage with the Labour Exchange man. **1958** *New Statesman* 22 Feb. 224/3 It hankers after the seaplane factory, the oil refinery, the atomic power station —'better a line of pylons than a line outside the labour exchange'. **1973** [see *job centre* s.v. JOB *sb.*[2] 7].

3. The finding of employment for workers.

1896 J. A. HOBSON *Probl. Unemployed* 128 No system of mere labour-exchange, however well-conducted, would increase the total quantity of employment over a long area of time.

labourhood (ˈleɪbəhʊd). *rare*[−1]. [See -HOOD.] Laborious condition, laboriousness.

1858 BAILEY *Age* 21 A life of most melodious labourhood.

labouring, laboring (ˈleɪbərɪŋ), *vbl. sb.* [f. LABOUR *v.* + -ING[1].] The action of the vb. LABOUR; performance of labour or work; cultivation (of land); †travail of child-bearing; laboured or heavy motion, etc.

c **1400** *Rom. Rose* 6593 That he ne shal..With propre hondis and body also, Gete his fode in laboryng. **1486** *Nav. Acc. Hen. VII* (1896) 23 Marriners reteyned for the.. laboryng in castyng out of the ballast. **1523** LD. BERNERS *Froiss.* I. cxci. 228 There was no labourynge of the yerth. **1524** in *10th Rep. Hist. MSS. Comm.* App. v. 329 The..acte ..made against the laboring of writts. **1596** SHAKS. *1 Hen. IV*, II. i. 57 Thou variest no more from picking of Purses, then giuing direction, doth from labouring. **1597** A. M. tr. *Guillemeau's Fr. Chirurg.* 35 b/2 Some woemen ar as yet not vsed unto the labouringe of childe. **1611** BIBLE *2 Macc.* ii. 31 To vse breuitie, and auoyde much labouring of the worke. **1619** VISCT. DONCASTER *Let.* in *Eng. & Germ.* (Camden) 134 There had beene some..underhand labouring..to promote the Duke of Bavaria. **1644-5** CHAS. I *Let.* Wks. (1662) 332 There were great labourings to that purpose. **1748** *Anson's Voy.* I. v. 56 To render the ships stiffer, and..prevent their labouring in hard gales of wind. **1881** *Daily Tel.* 28 Jan., The heavy labouring of the brig. **1887** HALL CAINE *Deemster* xxiv. 158 He..pressed one hand hard at his breast to quiet the labouring of his heart. **1899** *Westm. Gaz.* 11 Apr. 2/1 Doing a bit of dock-side labouring. *attrib.* **1601** SHAKS. *Jul. C.* I. i. 4 Vpon a labouring day. **1754** ERSKINE *Princ. Sc. Law* (1809) 356 By labouring time is understood, that time, in which that tenant..is ploughing. **1856** OLMSTED *Slave States* 55 A slave woman is commonly esteemed least for her laboring qualities.

b. *concr.* A farm. *Sc.*

1782 SIR J. SINCLAIR *Observ. Scot. Dial.* 181 A labouring, a farm. *a* **1814** J. RAMSAY *Scotl. & Scotsm. in 18th c.* (1888) II. ix. 180 My noble hostess took me then (1792) to see her labouring or farm.

labouring, laboring (ˈleɪbərɪŋ), *ppl. a.* [f. LABOUR *v.* + -ING[2].]

1. That labours or toils; *esp.* (of persons) performing or engaged in unskilled labour, as in ***labouring man, population.***

1398 TREVISA *Barth. De P.R.* IX. xxiv. (1495) 361 In the euentyde labourynge men ben rewarded and payed and goo to reste. **1504** ATKYNSON tr. *De Imitatione* I. ii. 154 A pore homely laborynge man. **1535** COVERDALE *Eccles.* v. 12 A labouringe man slepeth swetely, whether it be litle or moch that he eateth. **1601** SHAKS. *All's Well* XI. i. 121 Labouring Art can neuer ransome nature From her inaydible estate. **1649** BLITHE *Eng. Improv. Impr.* (1653) 8 Labouring Countrie people for the most part brew their own Beer. **1671** MILTON *P.R.* III. 330 Of labouring Pioners A multitude with Spades and Axes arm'd. **1697** DRYDEN *Virg. Georg.* IV. 808 The waxen Work of lab'ring Bees. **1725** POPE *Odyss.* XII. 526, I..oar'd with lab'ring arms along the flood. **1797** BURKE *Reg. Peace* iii. (C.P.S.) 219 We have heard many plans for the relief of the 'Labouring Poor'. **1855** MACAULAY *Hist. Eng.* xx. IV. 421 Other writers did their best to raise riots among the labouring people. **1879** JEFFERIES *Wild Life Southern C.* 194 The labouring lads often amuse themselves searching for these creatures [bats].

b. Of cattle: Engaged in or used for labour.

1523 FITZHERB. *Surv.* xxv. 49 Laborynge horses and mares. **1715** LEONI *Palladio's Archit.* (1742) I. 57 Stables for labouring Cattle, such as Oxen and Horses. **1807** ROBINSON *Archæol. Græca* III. xix. 312 The custom of killing laboring oxen.

†2. Of a woman: Suffering the pangs of childbirth, travailing. Also *transf. Obs.*

1545 RAYNOLD *Byrth Mankynde* (?1564) 61 The midwife shall sit before the labouryng woman. *a* **1700** DRYDEN (Worc.), The laboring mountain must bring forth a mouse. *a* **1704** T. BROWN *Sat. Quack* Wks. 1730 I. 64 Cure hogs of measles, visit labouring swine.

3. Striving or struggling against pressure or some obstacle; that is in trouble or distress; (of the heart, etc.) struggling under emotion or suppressed feeling; also in physical sense, heaving, palpitating; (of a ship) rolling or pitching heavily. (Often with more or less direct reference to 2.)

c **1425** *Found. St. Bartholomew's* (E.E.T.S.) 51 [They] besowght the Apostle that with his woonnte pyte to [? *read* he] wolde succur this laborynge virgyne. **1586** MARLOWE *Jew of Malta* I. ii, I'de passe away my life in penitence,..To make attonement for my labouring soule. **1593** SHAKS. *2 Hen. VI*, III. ii. 163 [The blood] Being all descended to the labouring heart. **1604** —— *Oth.* II. i. 189 Let the labouring Barke climbe hills of Seas Olympus high. **1693** in *Dryden's Juvenal* (1697) 88 When Falern Wines the lab'ring Lungs did fire. **1706** ROWE *Ulyss.* II. i, Her labouring Heart is rent with Anguish. **1738** GLOVER *Leonidas* I. 268 Her lab'ring bosom blotted with her tears. **1814** SCOTT *Lord of Isles* v. xxx, The vest Drawn tightly o'er his labouring breast. **1850** MERIVALE *Rom. Emp.* (1865) III. xxx. 389 The labouring vessel of the state was guided into port by his policy. **1878** WHITE *Life in Christ* III. xvii. 202 The thought of it weighs more and more heavily on the labouring mind.

†b. Of the moon: Eclipsed. (A Latinism.)

1638 WILKINS *New World* I. (1684) 9 She was able to make noise enough to deliver the labouring Moon. **1665** GLANVILL *Scepsis Sci.* xix. 122 Nor do the eager clamors of contending Disputants yield any more relief to eclipsed Truth; then did the sounding Brass of old to the labouring Moon. [**1667** MILTON *P.L.* II. 665 While the labouring Moon Eclipses at thir charms.]

4. ***labouring oar***: the oar which requires the most labour to work it; hence *fig.* esp. in phr. ***to pull, tug, ply the labouring oar***: to take a great or arduous share of the work.

1697 DRYDEN *Æneid* v. 157 Three Trojans tug at ev'ry lab'ring Oar. **1709** STEELE *Tatler* No. 141 ¶ 1, I shall still let the labouring Oar be managed by my Correspondents. **1779** HUME *Dial. conc. Nat. Rel.* XI. (ad fin.) II. 443 Tug the labouring oar. **1894** W. B. CARPENTER *Son of Man among Sons of Men* iv. 106 They vainly ply the labouring oar. **1900** G. C. BRODRICK *Mem. & Impressions* 386 Having found it difficult to pull a labouring oar on the City Council, without neglecting other duties.

Hence **ˈlabouringly** *adv.*, laboriously.

1862 LYTTON *Strange Story* II. 276 Reason is coming back to her—slowly, labouringly.

Labourism (ˈleɪbərɪz(ə)m). [f. LABOUR *sb.* 2 b + -ISM.] The principles or tenets of the Labour Party in politics; the holding or advocacy of these principles.

1903 *Rep. 3rd Ann. Conf. Labour Representative Comm.* 30/1 in *Labour Party Foundation Conf. & Ann. Conf. Rep. 1900–05* (1967) 109 Let them have done with Liberalism and Toryism and every other 'ism' that was not Labourism. **1905** *Westm. Gaz.* 13 May 2/2 Mr. Haldane has plied him with Imperialism, Mr. Keir Hardie with Labourism. **1908** *Ibid.* 4 May 9/2 Two years ago many Liberals coquetted with Labourism, and the result gave them a fright. **1924** J. R. MACDONALD in *Public Opinion* 14 Mar. 248/3 Their Toryisms, Liberalisms and Labourisms. **1975** *Time Out* 8 Aug. 21/1 The play becomes a neat exposition of Labourism over the last 50 years.

Labourist (ˈleɪbərɪst). [f. LABOUR *sb.* 2 b + -IST.] A supporter of the interests of Labour in politics; an advocate of Labourism.

1903 *Handy Notes for Unionist Workers* Aug. 3 The Labourists in Parliament..number over a dozen. **1910** *Daily Chron.* 2 Feb. 1/7 Liberals, Labourists and

Nationalists are solid against the veto of the Lords and against Food-Taxes. **1927** *Observer* 5 June 12/3 Six months ago the five seats concerned were represented by two Conservatives, two Labourists, and one Liberal. **1969** *Guardian* 23 June 4/2 An ideological struggle [in the U.S.] between the Labourists, who favour Maoism.. and the new Leftists.

Labourite (ˈleɪbəraɪt). [f. LABOUR *sb.* 2 b + -ITE¹.] = LABOURIST, often used of members of Parliament representing the Labour Party in Britain, Australia, or other countries.

1903 *Daily Chron.* 19 Dec. 5/5 Free Traders and Free Trade Labourites—40. **1909** T. HODGKIN *Let.* 15 Nov. in L. Creighton *Life & Lett. T. Hodgkin* (1917) xiii. 326 It is this abominable selfishness of men whether Capitalists or Labourites which seems to wreck all forms of government. **1920** *Blackw. Mag.* June 830/1 The moderate Labourites have reason to remember this. **1923** *National Rev.* Jan. 646 The Labourites were led by Mr. Ramsay Macdonald before the war. **1927** [see ANGLO-SAXON IV. A. *adj.*]. **1955** [see DE GAULLIST *a.* and *sb.*]. **1960** *20th Cent.* May 452 He [*sc.* Michael Young] was the first of those Labourites who renounced the tired phrases of inherited socialist doctrine.

labourless, laborless (ˈleɪbəlɪs), *a.* [f. LABOUR *sb.* + -LESS.] Without, devoid of, or unaccompanied by labour; requiring no labour; doing no labour.

1608 SYLVESTER *Du Bartas* II. iv. III. *Schism* 694 There (labour-less) mounts the victorious Palm. **1675** HOBBES *Odyss.* (1677) 225, I doubt thou ne'r wilt labour any more, But rather feed thy carcass labourless. **1854** *Fraser's Mag.* L. 70 This labourless Hercules. **1880** TENNYSON *Voyage of Maeldune* viii, Bread enough for his need till the labourless day dipt under the West. **1888** RHYS *Hibbert Lect.* 643 A fabled age of.. labourless plenty and social equality.

†**b.** Not requiring fatiguing toil. *Obs.*

1630 BREREWOOD *Sabaoth* 48 In forbidding of worke,.. they intend not your precise abstinence from any light and labourlesse worke. **1631** R. BYFIELD *Doctr. Sabb.* 109 Such light and labourlesse workes were no transgressions.

laboursome, laborsome (ˈleɪbəsəm), *a.* [f. LABOUR *sb.* + -SOME.]

†**1.** Given to labour; hard-working; = LABORIOUS I. *Obs.*

1551 EDW. VI *Pol. Ess.* Lit. Rem. (1857) II. 481 So ought ther no part of the commenwealth to be but laborsom in his vocation. **1575–85** ABP. SANDYS *Serm.* iii. 46 The vineyard that shall fructifie must fall into the hands of a skilful and laboursome husbandman. **1607** MARKHAM *Caval.* I. (1617) 79 The braine of a man being a busie and laborsome workmaister. **1620** —— *Farew. Husb.* II. xvii. (1668) 75 Although it [the ant] be but a little creature, yet it is so laboursome, that [etc.].

2. Requiring, entailing, or accompanied by labour; = LABORIOUS 2. Now *rare* or *dial.*

1577–87 HOLINSHED *Chron.* II. 28/1 The painefull diligence, and the laboursome industrie of a famous lettered man M. Peter White. **1594** T. B. *La Primaud. Fr. Acad.* II. 33 Those studies, which seeme laborsome in youthfull yeares, are made right pleasant rest vnto old age. **1602** SHAKS. *Ham.* I. ii. 59 (Qo. 1604), Hath.. wroung from me my slow leaue, By laboursome petition. **1611** CORYAT *Crudities* 350 A way.. very laboursome and painfull to trauell. **1656** EARL MONM. *Advt. fr. Parnass.* 150 The laborsom journey which leads towards the obtaining of Supreme Honors and Dignities. **1855** ROBINSON *Whitby Gloss.* s.v., We have a lang laboursome hill to climm. **1898** TRASK *Norton-sub-Hamdon* 33 Life was laboursome, but not without hope.

†**b.** Of land: Difficult of cultivation. *Obs.*

1604 E. G[RIMSTONE] *D'Acosta's Hist. Indies* IV. ii. 208 The like hath God done for this land so rough and laboursome, giving it great riches in mines.

3. Of a ship: 'Subject to labour or to pitch and roll violently in a heavy sea' (1850 *Rudim. Nav.* 128).

1691 T. H[ALE] *Acc. New Invent.* 127 What makes a Ship Roll and laboursome in the Sea? **1764** *Chron.* in *Ann. Reg.* 80/1 Most.. died in the passage, it beng so very long, and the ship so very laboursome. **1794** *Rigging & Seamanship* II. 336 The.. topsail should be the last.. sail taken in, in a laboursome ship.

Hence ˈ**laboursomely** *adv.*, laboriously; ˈ**laboursomeness**, laboriousness.

1552 EDW. VI *Jrnl.* Lit. Rem. (1857) II. 420 They had.. passed many a strait very painfully and laborsomly. **1561** DAUS tr. *Bullinger on Apoc.* (1573) 68 b, 'And they have no rest, &c.', signifie not any laboursomnes or paynefulnes, but a continual holdyng on and tunable agrement in praysing God. **1592** R. D. *Hypnerot.* 6 b, Which immence.. forme.. mounting up laboursomly foote by foote, conteyned 1410 degrees or steppes. **1880** RHODA BROUGHTON *Second Th.* I. I. ix. 152 It seems as if to each breath a heavy stone were tied, so laboursomely does he drag it up.

Labrador (ˌlæbrəˈdɔː(r)), the name of a large peninsula in Eastern Canada, used *attrib.* in the following specific collocations: **Labrador blue**, the tint of blue reflected from labradorite; **Labrador (dog, retriever)**, a medium-sized, black or yellow, short-coated retriever belonging to a breed originally developed in Newfoundland and Labrador; **Labrador duck**, a sea-duck of the north-east coast of North America, *Camptolæmus labradorius*; **Labrador falcon**, a very dark variety of gerfalcon found in Labrador, *Falco labradorius*; **Labrador feldspar, spar, stone** (also simply *labrador*) = LABRADORITE; **Labrador hornblende** = ENSTATITE (so called because it comes from Labrador and resembles hornblende); **Labrador pine**, the grey or jack pine, *Pinus banksiana*, native to the northern parts of North America; **Labrador tea**, either of the two shrubs of the genus *Ledum* (N.O. *Ericaceæ*) of North America, viz. *L. latifolium* and *L. palustre*, which have evergreen leathery leaves that have been used for tea.

1881 A. LESLIE *Nordenskiöld's Voy. Vega* II. xi. 55 If.. one walks along the beach on the snow which at ebb is dry .. there rises at every step one takes an exceedingly intense, beautiful, bluish-white flash of light, which in the spectroscope gives a one-coloured *labrador-blue spectrum. [**1829** G. HEAD *Forest Scenes* 41 The dog was of the Labrador breed, extremely powerful, and of enormous stature.] **1842** R. H. BONNYCASTLE *Newfoundland in 1842* II. ix. 24 They [*sc.* water-dogs] are of two kinds; the short, wiry-haired *Labrador dog, and the long, curly-haired Newfoundland species. **1921** *Blackw. Mag.* Dec. 794/1 All the guns had dogs—beautifully trained Labradors. **1963** A. SMITH *Throw out Two Hands* xix. 195 John arrived.. with a remarkable collection of people, plus a black labrador who loathed nettles, and a rifle. **1973** *Country Life* 8 Feb. 325/1, I have just chosen a new labrador puppy. **1884–5** *Riverside Nat. Hist.* (1888) IV. 151 The *Labrador duck is now extinct, or at least very nearly so. **1794** KIRWAN *Min.* I. 324 *Labradore Felspar of Werner. **1807** AIKIN *Dict.* I. 428 Labradore Felspar.. is smoak-grey. **1794** KIRWAN *Min.* I. 221 *Labradore Hornblende. **1819** BAKEWELL *Min.* 315 Hypensthene, Labrador Hornblende. **1803** A. B. LAMBERT *Descr. Genus Pinus* I. 7 *Labradore Pine... Habitat in Americâ Septentrionali. **1921** H. KEPHART *Camping & Woodcraft* (new ed.) I. 239 The gray (Labrador) pine or jack pine is considered good fuel in the far North. **1910** *Kennel Encycl.* III. III. 1099 *Labrador Retrievers.. were originally imported from Labrador. **1971** C. FICK *Danziger Transcript* (1973) 155 Finding out.. whether he liked Brahms, silk pajamas, Labrador retrievers and such. **1799** W. TOOKE *View of Russ. Emp.* I. 121 If we except.. window-mica, and a little *labrador spar. **1778** WOULFE in *Phil. Trans.* LXIX. 23 The *Labradore stone is also a Feld spar. **1794** KIRWAN *Min.* I. 324, I conclude Labradore to be specifically different from common felspars. **1834** ALLAN *Min.* 134 A grey felspar totally distinct from the species Labrador. **1784** M. CUTLER in *Life, Jrnls. & Corr.* (1888) I. 103 Large beds of what is called the *Labrador tea, of a very aromatic taste and smell. **1882** *Garden* 29 Apr. 286/2 Labrador Tea.. is really a good and distinct hardy bush.

labradorescence (ˌlæbrədɔːˈrɛsəns). *Min.* [f. LABRADOR(ITE + -ESCENCE.] The brilliant play of colours exhibited by some specimens of feldspars, esp. labradorite.

1911 *Encycl. Brit.* XVI. 30/1 This optical effect, known sometimes as 'labradorescence', seems due in some cases to the presence of minute laminæ of certain minerals.. arranged parallel to the surface which reflects the colour. **1962** W. A. DEER et al. *Rock-Forming Min.* V. 143 The phenomenon of labradorescence, however, has not been conclusively explained. **1966** J. SINKANKAS *Mineral.* viii. 235 Vivid colors also arise from within labradorite feldspar, the effect being known as labradorescence.

Labradorian (ˌlæbrəˈdɔərɪən), *sb.* and *a.* Also -ean. [f. LABRADOR + IAN.] **A.** *sb.* A native or inhabitant of Labrador. **B.** *adj.* Of or pertaining to Labrador.

In quot. 1947 the Labradoreans are Eskimos.

1863 H. Y. HIND *Explor. Labrador Peninsula* II. 135 The residents on the coast, or Labradorians as they may well be termed, frequent the St. Augustine in the winter and travel towards its source. **1888** J. PRESTWICH *Geol.* II. 20 Labradorian or Norian group. **1895** J. D. DANA *Man. Geol.* (ed. 4) 446 C. H. Hitchcock.. adopts the subdivisions, beginning below: Laurentian, Montalban.., Labradorian, and Huronian. **1907** L. MOTT *To Credit of Sea* ii. 43 'An' you a Labradorian!' Johnson said. *Ibid.* iii. 111 The Labradorian.. caught it cleverly. **1909** P. W. BROWNE *Where Fishers Go* 146 Off *Cape Charles* the coast again becomes broken and rugged—'hummocky', as it is termed by Labradorians. **1910** C. W. TOWNSEND *Labrador Spring* 68 Dr. Grenfell's hardest work is to teach the Labradorians the value of fresh air inside their houses. **1947** V. TANNER *Outl. Geogr., Life & Customs Newfoundland-Labrador* II. 527 The heavy, clumsy *tupek* of the Labradoreans, the skin tent, is said to have never given complete protection from rain or wind. **1962** *Encycl. Brit.* XVIII. 74 A, During the Illinoian, the third glacial age, the Labradorean area of radiation was preponderant and the Keewatin played a minor role. **1973** *Town Crier* (St. John's, Newfoundland) May 43/3 The purpose of the club is to provide.. assistance in a practical way to Labradorians living here.

labradorite (læbrəˈdɒraɪt). *Min.* [f. LABRADOR + -ITE. (Named *Labradorstein* by Werner in 1780, because it came from Labrador.)] A kind of feldspar, which shows a brilliant variety of colour when turned in the light.

1814 ALLAN *Min.* 18 Opalescent [felspar], Labradore stone.. Labradorite. **1850** DAUBENY *Atomic Theory* xii. (ed. 2) 417 Recent lavas.. are made up principally, of labradorite, a silicate with 1 atom only of acid, and of hornblende or augite.

Hence **labradoˈritic** *a.*

In mod. Dicts.

labral (ˈleɪbrəl), *a.* [f. LABR-UM + -AL¹.] Pertaining to a labrum or lip-like part.

1877 HUXLEY *Anat. Inv. Anim.* vi. 259 A suture.. connected with the labral suture by one or two sutures.

†**labras.** *Obs. rare*⁻¹. Pistol's blunder for L. *labra*, pl. of *labrum* lip.

1598 SHAKS. *Merry W.* I. i. 166, I combat challenge of this Latine Bilboe: word of denial in thy labras there.

labratory, rare obs. form of LABORATORY.

‖**labrax** (ˈleɪbræks). [mod.L., a. Gr. λάβραξ.] 'A ravenous sea-fish, perh. the *loup de mer*, bass' (Liddell and Scott); *Ichthyol.*, a genus of fishes of the perch family, including the sea-bass.

1854 BADHAM *Halieut.* ii. 19 Oppian.. strongly recommends as bait a living labrax, if you can get one.

labret (ˈleɪbrɪt). [f. LABR-UM + -ET¹.] An ornament consisting of a piece of stone, bone, shell, etc. inserted in the lip.

1857 A. ARMSTRONG *N.W. Passage* vii. 193 In the Esquimaux.. we observed the lower lip perforated in the males, for the admission of labrets or lip ornaments. **1872** R. F. BURTON *Zanzibar* I. iv. 113 As a rule, the South American 'Indians' pierce for their labrets the lower lip. **1884** J. G. BOURKE *Snake Dance of Moquis* xxii. 243 They do not tattoo, do not use nose-rings or labrets.

labretifery (ˌleɪbrɪˈtɪfərɪ). [f. LABRET + L. *fer-*, carrying + -Y³.] The practice of wearing labrets.

1884 *Science* 3 Oct. 345/1 Dr. W. H. Dall then read a paper on the use of labrets, its title being 'The geographical distribution of labretifery'. **1905** C. DAVENPORT *Jewellery* v. 89 In Mexico there was a very remarkable civilisation, and labretifery.. was practised.

labrinth, obs. form of LABYRINTH.

labroid (ˈleɪbrɔɪd), *a.* and *sb.* *Ichthyol.* [ad. mod.L. *Labroidea*, f. *Labrus*, generic name, f. *labrum* lip: see -OID.]

A. *adj.* Pertaining to the family *Labridæ* or superfamily *Labroidea* of acanthopterygian fishes of which the typical genus is *Labrus*.

1839 *Penny Cycl.* XIII. 262/1 Those Labroid fishes which approach the genus *Labrus* in having the lips thick and fleshy. **1864** *Reader* No. 86. 239/3 A new Labroid genus allied to Trochocopus. **1892** *Athenæum* 26 Mar. 407/2 The labroid fishes of America and Europe.

B. *sb.* A labroid fish.

1854 OWEN in *Circ. Sci.* (*c* 1865) II. 96/2 Sparoids, labroids. **1865** *Reader* No. 110. 143/2 Fishes which.. pass to the type of Labroïds and Lophioïds.

labrose (ˈleɪbrəʊs), *a.* [ad. L. *labrōs-us*, f. *labrum* lip.] Having (large) lips; see also quot.

1727 BAILEY vol. II, *Labrose*, that has a Brim, Border, or Bank. Also in recent Dicts.

†ˈ**labrous**, *a.* *Obs. rare*⁻⁰. [f. LABRUM + -OUS, after L. *labrōsus*.] = prec.

1656 BLOUNT *Glossogr.*, *Labrous*, that hath a brim, bank or border. Also that hath great lips.

‖**labrum** (ˈleɪbrəm). Pl. labra. [L., cogn. w. LABIUM.] A lip or lip-like part. (Cf. LABIUM.) **a.** In insects, crustaceans, etc.: A part forming the upper border or covering of the mouth. **b.** *Conch.* The outer lip of a univalve shell.

1816 T. BROWN *Elem. Conchol.* 154 *Labra*, the lip. **1826** KIRBY & SP. *Entomol.* IV. 381 In the *Ephemerina* the parts of the mouth except the labrum and palpi appear to be mere rudiments. **1834** MCMURTRIE *Cuvier's Anim. Kingd.* 301 A mouth composed of a labrum, two mandibles, a ligula, and one or two pairs of jaws, and branchiæ. **1849** MURCHISON *Siluria* x. (1867) 237 [*Pterygotus*] The mouth.. protected by a large heart-shaped labrum. **1851** RICHARDSON *Geol.* viii. 240 The *labrum*, or outer lip.. is the expansion, or continuation of the body of the shell, on the right margin of the aperture. **1880** HUXLEY *Cray-Fish* ii. 51 In front, the mouth is overlapped by a wide shield-shaped plate termed the upper lip or *labrum*.

†**laˈbruscose**, *a.* *Obs. rare*⁻⁰. [f. L. *lābrusca*, *-um* wild vine and its fruit.] (See quot.).

1727 BAILEY vol. II, *Labruscose*, full of or abounding with wild Vine or Briony.

‖**labrys** (ˈlæbrɪs). [a. Gr. λάβρυς, double-headed axe.] The double-headed axe of ancient Crete.

1901 *Jrnl. Hellenic Stud.* XXI. 108 It seems natural to interpret names of Carian sanctuaries like Labranda in the most literal sense as the place of the sacred *labrys*, which was the Lydian (or Carian) name for the Greek πέλεκυς, or double-edged axe. *Ibid.* 109 On Carian coins indeed of quite late date the *labrys*, set up on its long pillar-like handle, with two dependent fillets, has much the appearance of a cult image. **1928** C. DAWSON *Age of Gods* viii. 188 Especially remarkable is the word for the sacred Double Axe—Labrys—which forms the root, not only of the Cretan Labyrinthos.. but also appears in the title of the god of the Double Axe, Zeus Labrandeus, at Mylasa on the mainland of Asia Minor. **1957** A. MACNAB *Bulls of Iberia* i. 6 The emblem which appears on French coins of the Pétain régime.. is precisely the *labrys*, or sacred double-headed axe of Minoan Crete.

laburnum (ləˈbɜːnəm). Also 8 liburnum. [L. (Pliny); adopted as a generic name by P. K. Fabricius (*Enum. Meth. Plant. Hort. Med. Helmstadiensis* (1759) 228).] **a.** A small tree of the genus so called, esp. *L. anagyroides* or *L. alpinum* and their hybrids, belonging to the family Leguminosæ and bearing long pendulous racemes of bright yellow flowers followed by pods of poisonous seeds; also, the dark wood of a tree of this kind.

1578 LYTE *Dodoens* VI. lxvi. 741 Of Anagyris, Laburnum, and Arbor Iuda. Laburnum.. The flowers do grow very thicke togither hanging by a very slender stemme. **1682** WHELER *Journ. Greece* IV. 290 The Flowers [of *Anagyris*

fœtida] also grow out in little bunches, like the other Laburnum but larger. **1754** Dodsley *Agriculture* ii. 387 And pale laburnum's pendent flowers display Their different beauties. **1764** Wesley *Jrnl.* 11 June, We have a tree.., the wood of which is of full as fine a red as mahogany, namely, the Liburnum. **1784** Cowper *Task* vi. 149 Laburnum, rich In streaming gold. **1812** E. Sang *Nicol's Planter's Kalendar* v. 91 The Laburnum timber which brought so high a price was of the variety called the Tree Laburnum. *a* **1821** Keats *Ep.* 271 The dark-leaved laburnum's drooping clusters. **1838** J. C. Loudon *Arboretum et Fruticetum Britannicum* II. xli. 592 Hop-poles ..are said, when formed of laburnum, to be more durable than those of almost any other kind of wood. **1850** Tennyson *In Mem.* lxxxiii, Laburnums, dropping-wells of fire. **1898** Morris *Austral. Eng.*, Laburnum, Native, the Tasmanian Clover-tree, *Goodenia lotifolia*..Laburnum, Sea-coast, also called Golden Chain, *Sophora tomentosa*. **1914** W. J. Bean *Trees & Shrubs Hardy in Brit. Is.* II. 1 Few trees..are so beautiful as the two common laburnums. **1947** A. L. Howard *Trees in Britain* 134 In earlier times.. British-grown laburnum was greatly prized for inlay, turnery and cabinet work... Cut in cross section in the round, it was known by the term 'oyster work'. **1974** W. Condry *Woodlands* xiv. 154 There are long stretches of hedge that are almost purely laburnum which make a marvellous show in June when they are hung with golden chains of blossom. **1975** *Times* 15 Jan. 17/6 An early eighteenth-century oyster walnut and laburnum cabinet.

b. *attrib.*, as ***laburnum chain, gold, yellow.***

1893 N. Gale *Country Muse* Ser. ii. 2 The glory of laburnum-gold. **1899** *Daily News* 23 May 2/3 The laburnum chains are dwarfed. *Ibid.* 27 Feb. 6/6 Rose-pinks, laburnum-yellows, leaf-greens.

labyrinth ('læbɪrɪnθ), *sb.* Forms: 6 **laborynth, lab(e)rinth, -irinth,** 6–7 **-arinth,** 7 **-erinth, -irynth, -orynth,** 7–8 *poet.* **lab'rinth,** 6– **labyrinth.** [ad. L. *labyrinth-us*, a. Gr. λαβύρινθ-ος, of unknown (prob. non-Hellenic) origin. Cf. F. *labyrinthe* (1418 in Hatz.-Darm.).]

1. A structure consisting of a number of intercommunicating passages arranged in bewildering complexity, through which it is difficult or impossible to find one's way without guidance; a maze.

a. With references to the structures so named in classical antiquity.

[**1387** Trevisa *Higden* (Rolls) I. 9 Þis matir, as laborintus, Dedalus hous, haþ many halkes and hurnes..wyndynges and wrynkelynges. **1494** Fabyan *Chron.* vii. ccxxxviii. 277 This house, after some wryters, was named, *labor intus* or Deladus (*v.r.* Labyrinthus or Dedalus) werke.] **1549** *Compl. Scotl.* vi. 64 Dedalus maid the laborynth to keip the monstir minotaurus. **1591** Shaks. *1 Hen. VI*, v. iii. 188 Thou mayest not wander in that Labyrinth, There Minotaurs and vgly Treasons lurke. **1591** Spenser *Ruins of Rome* 22 Crete will boast the Labyrinth. **1601** Holland *Pliny* I. 99 The Labyrinth built vp in the lake of Mœris without any iot of timber to it. *Ibid.* II. 578 This Labyrinth in Crete is counted the second to that of Ægypt: the third is in the Isle Lemnos: the fourth in Italy. **1836** Thirlwall *Greece* II. xii. 112 Theodorus,..the builder of the Lemnian labyrinth.

b. In mod. landscape gardening, a maze formed by paths bordered by high hedges.

1611 Coryat *Crudities* 298, I sawe a fine Labyrinthe made of boxe. **1666** Pepys *Diary* 25 June, Here were also great variety of other exotique plants, and several labyrinths. **1753** Chambers *Cycl. Supp.* s.v., Labyrinths are only proper for large gardens, and the finest in the world is said to be that of Versailles. **1792** A. Young *Trav. France* 7 The labyrinth [at Chantilly] is the only complete one I have seen, and I have no inclination to see another: it is in gardening what a rebus is in poetry.

2. *transf.* An intricate, complicated, or tortuous arrangement (of physical features, buildings, etc.).

1615 Crooke *Body of Man* 465 A mazey laberynth of small veines and arteries. **1634** Milton *Comus* 277 *Co.* What chance good Lady hath bereft you thus? *La.* Dim darknes, and this leafy Labyrinth. **1730–46** Thomson *Autumn* 415 The scented dew Betrays her [*sc.* a hare's] early labyrinth. **1777** Watson *Philip II* (1793) II. xiii. 133 Leyden lies..in the midst of a labyrinth of rivulets and canals. **1778** Robertson *Hist. Amer.* I. ii. 122 He was entangled in a labyrinth, formed by an incredible number of small islands. **1843** Lytton *Last of Barons* I. iv. 56 He suddenly halted..to find himself entangled in a labyrinth of scattered suburbs. **1873** Symonds *Grk. Poets* xii. 400 The labyrinth of peristyles and pediments in which her children dwell.

†**b.** ***rushy labyrinth*** = Gr. ἐκ σχοίνων λαβύρινθος (Theocritus), applied to a bow-net of rushes. *Obs.*$^{-1}$

1658 Sir T. Browne *Gard. Cyrus* ii. 42 The rushy labyrinths of Theocritus.

c. (*a*) *Metallurgy.* A contrivance of winding channels used for distributing and separating the ores in the order of the coarseness of grain. (*b*) A chamber of many turnings for the condensation of fumes arising from dry distillation, etc. (Knight *Dict. Mech.* 1875).

1839 Ure *Dict. Arts*, etc., *Labyrinth*, in metallurgy, means a series of canals distributed in the sequel of a stamping-mill; through which canals a stream of water is transmitted for suspending, carrying off, and depositing, at different distances, the ground ores.

3. *Anat.* A complex cavity hollowed out of the temporal bone consisting of a bony capsule (***osseous labyrinth***) and a delicate membranous apparatus (***membranous labyrinth***) contained by it; the internal ear. In birds, 'the membranous capsule which encloses the end-organs of the auditory nerve' (Newton *Dict. Birds* 1893, 180).

1696 Phillips (ed. 5), *Labyrinth*..In Anatomy, the Third Cavity in the innermost part of the Ear, resembling the Shell of a Snail. **1709** Blair in *Phil. Trans.* XXVII. 125, I search'd for the Labyrinth, or *Lineæ Semilunares*, but could find none. **1722** Quincy *Lex. Physico-Med.* (ed. 2) 126/2 The Labyrinth is made of three Semicircular Pipes, above half a Line wide, excavated in the *Os Petrosum*. **1840** G. V. Ellis *Anat.* 290 There is ..a fluid..contained in the osseous labyrinth, and in it the membranous labyrinth floats. **1873** Mivart *Elem. Anat.* ix. 393 A labyrinth composed of three semicircular canals is also almost universal.

b. Applied to other organs of complex or intricate structure (see quots.).

1774 Goldsm. *Nat. Hist., Birds* I. i. (1824) II. 214 It is some-times also seen that the wind-pipe makes many convolutions within the body of the bird, and it is then called the labyrinth. **1888** *Syd. Soc. Lex.*, *Labyrinth*, a name given to the cells in the lateral masses of the ethmoid bone... *L., ethmoidal*, the irregularly divided space formed by the anterior, middle and posterior cells of the ethmoid bone... *L., olfactory*, the contorted structure formed by the upper end of the middle turbinate bones.

4. *fig.* A tortuous, entangled, or inextricable condition of things, events, ideas, etc.; an entanglement, maze.

1548 Hall *Chron., Rich. III* 47 When the Earle was thus ..escaped all ye daungerous labirinthes and snares that were set for him. **1571** Digges *Pantom.* i. xxx. Kb, The Geometer..without practise..shall fall into manyfoulde errours, or inextricable Laberinthes. **1606** Shaks. *Tr. & Cr.* ii. iii. 2 How now Thersites? what lost in the Labyrinth of thy furie? **1622** Malynes *Anc. Law-Merch.* 211 All will run into a Laborinth and confusion. **1642** Sir E. Dering *Sp. on Relig.* xvi. 74 We shall run our selves into a..Labyrinth of words, and lose the matter. **1756** Burke *Vind. Nat. Soc.* Wks. 1842 I. 17 The more deeply we penetrate into the labyrinth of art, the further we find ourselves from those ends for which we entered it. **1816** T. L. Peacock *Headlong Hall* v, Unravelling the labyrinth of mind. **1818** Scott *Rob Roy* i, He found himself..involved in the labyrinth of mercantile concerns without the clew of knowledge necessary for his extraction. **1823** Lamb *Elia* Ser. i. *South-Sea Ho.*, She traced her descent, by some labyrinth of relationship..to the illustrious, but unfortunate, house of Derwentwater. **1828** Macaulay *Ess., Hallam* (1851) I. 53 In this labyrinth of falsehood and sophistry the guidance of Mr. Hallam is peculiarly valuable. **1876** Mozley *Univ. Serm.* iv. 92 Even in the dark labyrinth of evil there are unexpected outlets. **1885** *Law Times* LXXIX. 130/1 To thread the labyrinth of the statutes under which London is governed.

5. *attrib.* and *Comb.*, as ***labyrinth cave, thread; labyrinth-like, -stemmed*** adjs.; **labyrinth fret** *Arch.* (see quot.); **labyrinth vesicle** *Anat.*, a cavity or furrow in the labyrinth of the ear.

1817 Shelley *Rev. Islam* viii. xi, From slavery and religion's *labyrinth caves Guide us. **1842–59** Gwilt *Archit.* Gloss., **Labyrinth Fret*, a fret, with many turnings, in the form of a labyrinth. **1851** Penrose *Athen. Arch.* 56 The labyrinth fret beneath the mutules. **1622** Drayton *Poly-olb.* xxii. 22 In *Labrinth-like turnes, and twinings intricate. **1855** Richardson *Geol.* 302 The labyrinth-like arrangement of the dentine, from which Professor Owen derived the name Labyrinthodon. **1860** Ruskin *Mod. Paint.* V. ix. iv. 240 Its forests are sombre-leaved, *labyrinth-stemmed. **1823** in Joanna Baillie *Collect. Poems* 210 Life's *labyrinth-thread deceives, and seems but sand. **1878** Bell tr. *Gegenbaur's Comp. Anat.* 44 The *labyrinth-vesicles of the Vertebrata.

'labyrinth, *v.* [f. labyrinth *sb.*] *trans.* To enclose in or as in a labyrinth; to arrange in the form of a labyrinth.

1808 J. Barlow *Columb.* ix. 201 Close labyrinth'd here the feign'd Omniscient dwells. **1820** Keats *Lamia* ii. 53 How to entangle..Your soul in mine and labyrinth you there. **1846** Ruskin *Mod. Paint.* (1851) II. iii. §i. v, The purple clefts of the hill side are labyrinthed in the darkness.

labyrinthal (læbɪ'rɪnθəl), *a. rare.* [f. labyrinth *sb.* + -al[1].] Labyrinthine. Hence **laby'rinthally** *adv.*

1669 *Addr. Hopeful Yng. Gentry Eng.* 42 The soul is.. more labyrinthally and securely imprisoned. **1797** *The College* 42 Each lymphatic fills From myriad springs its labyrinthal rills. **1881** *Arctic Cruise of the Corwin* 30 (Cent.) The labyrinthal ice mazes of the Arctic.

†**'labyrinthed,** *a. Obs. rare*$^{-1}$. [f. as prec. + -ed[2].] Full of labyrinths or complications.

1650 tr. *Caussin's Ang. Peace* 57 Thorow the labyrinthed Successions of so many Ages.

†**laby'rinthial,** *a. Obs.* Also **-all.** [f. as prec. + -ial.] Labyrinthine.

a **1550** *Image Ipocr.* ii. 310 in *Skelton's Wks.* (1843) II. 426 By lawes absynthyall And labirynthyall. *a* **1711** Ken *Hymnarium* Poet. Wks. 1721 II. 34 He o'er the Universe presides, And Labyrinthial Casualties guides.

labyrinthian (læbɪ'rɪnθɪən), *a.* Also 7 **-æan,** 7, 9 **-ean.** [f. labyrinth *sb.* + -ian.] = labyrinthine, in various senses.

1588 J. Harvey *Discoursive Probleme* 42 This intricate Labyrynthian monument. **1597–8** Bp. Hall *Sat.* (1753) 48 His linnen collar labyrinthian set. **1609** Heywood *Brit. Troy* xiii. iii. 332 To guide me through the laborinthean maze In which my brain's intangled. **1614** Raleigh *Hist. World* v. vi. §7. 647 The Labirynthian head of Martius could not allow of such plaine reason. **1615** Crooke *Body of Man* 15 The Labyrinthæan Mazes and web of the small arteries. **1742** Young *Nt. Th.* ix. 1029 The labyrinthian turns they take The circles intricate, and mystic maze. **1837** *Fraser's Mag.* XVI. 71 The labyrinthean mazes of a female heart. **1854** Bakewell *Geol.* 43 This peculiar labyrinthian structure of the teeth. **1864** Hawthorne *Grimshawe* xxi. (1891) 286 It is a labyrinthian house for its size. **1900** H. W. Smyth *Grk. Melic Poets* p. xcii, Clews to guide us through the labyrinthian mazes of the theme.

labyrinthibranch (læbɪ'rɪnθɪbræŋk). *Ichthyol.* [ad. mod.L. *Labyrinthibranchii* (see below), f. Gr. λαβύρινθ-ος labyrinth + βράγχια gills.] One of the *Labyrinthibranchii*, a family or division of acanthopterygian fishes.

So **labyrinthi'branchiate** *a.*, pertaining to the *Labyrinthibranchii*, which have labyrinthine gills.

labyrinthic (læbɪ'rɪnθɪk), *a.* [ad. late L. *labyrinthic-us*, a. Gr. λαβυρινθικ-ός, f. λαβύρινθος labyrinth.] = labyrinthine, in various senses. ***labyrinthic cavity***: the labyrinth of the ear. ***l. teeth*** (see quot. 1888).

1641 Vicars *God in Mount* 20 Its craft and labyrinthick intricacie [*sc.* of an oath]. **1798** W. Taylor in *Monthly Rev.* XXVII. 529 The labyrinthic paths of hypothesis and fiction. **1811** Shelley *St. Irvyne* x, Thence was I led into a train of labyrinthic meditations. **1831** Carlyle *Sart. Res.* (1858) 20 In that labyrinthic combination, each Part overlaps, and indents, and indeed runs quite through the other. **1836–9** Todd *Cycl. Anat.* II. 536/2 In many fishes the labyrinthic cavity forms one with that of the cranium. **1875** Huxley in *Encycl. Brit.* I. 762/2 The complicated or labyrinthic structure exhibited by transverse sections of the teeth of typical Labyrinthodonts. **1888** *Syd. Soc. Lex.*, *Labyrinthic teeth*, teeth which have numerous radiating, sinuous, vertical grooves, which penetrate their substance and interdigitate with similarly shaped processes of the pulp-cavity; as in the Labyrinthodon.

labyrinthical (læbɪ'rɪnθɪkəl), *a. rare.* [Formed as prec. + -al[1].] = prec.

1628 Donne *Serm.* xlviii. 486 Poor intricated Soule! Riddling perplexed labyrinthical Soule. **1670** Swan *Spec. Mundi* 449 The ears be like certain doors, with Labyrinthical entries, and crooked windings. **1681** H. More *Expos. Dan.* Pref. 19, I preferred it before what was more operose, intricate and labyrinthical. **1879** [Lingham] *Sci. of Taste* v. 141 Our laws are a labyrinthical fabric of artificial and incomprehensible complexity.

Hence **laby'rinthically** *adv.*

1849 Carlyle *Irish Journ.* 115 The muddy meanders of Cork harbour labyrinthically indenting it.

labyrinthiform (læbɪ'rɪnθɪfɔːm), *a.* [ad. mod.L. *labyrinthiform-is*, f. *labyrinth-us* labyrinth: see -form.] Having the form of a labyrinth; characterized by sinuous and intricate conformations, markings, etc.; *Ichthyol.* having labyrinthine gills.

1835 Kirby *Hab. & Inst. Anim.* II. xix. 295 Her next labour is to spin a spiral or labyrinthiform line. **1868** *Nat. Encycl.* I. 657 The pharyngeal apparatus being labyrinthiform. **1870** tr. *Pouchet's Universe* 253 The anabas ..fills with water a labyrinthiform cavity which is also situated above its branchiæ. **1883** F. Day *Ind. Fish* 30 The labyrinthiform climbing-perch and its allies.

labyrinthine (læbɪ'rɪnθaɪn, -ɪn), *a.* [f. labyrinth *sb.* + -ine.]

1. Pertaining to, or of the nature or form of, a labyrinth; having or consisting of many intricate turnings or windings.

1632 Lithgow *Trav.* iii. 99 These Laborinthing Seas. **1747** Spence *Polymetis* (L.), She [Ariadne] preserved him in the labyrinthine mazes of Crete. **1817** Shelley *Rev. Islam* i. 53 The long and labyrinthine aisles. **1837** Howitt *Rur. Life* ii. vi. (1862) 163 The midges are celebrating their airy and labyrinthine dances with an amazing adroitness. **1863** N. Hawthorne *Our old Home* 240 The lanes, alleys and strange labyrinthine courts. **1863** H. W. Bates *Naturalist on Amazon* iv. 132 A large flat Helix with a labyrinthine mouth. **1872** Nicholson *Palæont.* 351 The parietes of the teeth are deeply plaited and folded, so as to give rise to a complicated 'labyrinthine' pattern in the transverse section of the tooth. **1876** Ruskin *Arrows of Chace* (1880) I. 172 Your labyrinthine magnificence at Burlington House.

2. *fig.* Intricate, complicated, involved, inextricable.

1840 De Quincey *Style* i. Wks. 1890 X. 158 To follow the discussion through endless and labyrinthine sentences. **1853** F. W. Robertson *Serm.* Ser. iii. iv. (1872) 45 An entangled, labyrinthine enigma. **1865** *Sat. Rev.* 7 Jan. 16/1 [Browning] is apt to entangle the reader in labyrinthine thoughts.

3. Pertaining to the labyrinth of the ear.

1876 *Clin. Soc. Trans.* IX. 101 Labyrinthine disease.

labyrinthitis (læbɪrɪn'θaɪtɪs). *Med.* [f. labyrinth 3 + -itis.] Inflammation of a labyrinth of the internal ear.

1912 Adami & McCrae *Text-bk. Path.* viii. 519 Extension of the disease [*sc.* inflammation of the middle ear]..tends to involve the bone in the direction of least resistance, which may lead to extradural inflammation, labyrinthitis, or infection of the lateral sinus. **1934** *Times Lit. Suppl.* 25 Jan. 56/2 Although..the labyrinthitis from which Swift suffered ..can create an anxiety-complex, it is almost certainly true that any recurrent disability..will induce a similar neurosis. **1939** *Anatomical Rec.* LXXIV. 221 Sporadic cases of labyrinthitis appear at times in strains of rats in which no form of ear disease is commonly found. **1972** *Audiology* XI. 322 Variations occur in..viral labyrinthitis.

labyrinthodon (læbɪ'rɪnθədɒn). *Palæont.* [mod.L. (R. Owen), f. Gr. λαβύρινθος labyrinth + ὀδοντ-, ὀδούς tooth: cf. note s.v. glyptodon.]

Any of the large fossil amphibians of the genus *Labyrinthodon*, characterized by teeth of labyrinthine structure having the enamel folded and sunk inward.

1847 ANSTED *Anc. World* vii. 132 The numerous and gigantic labyrinthodons..as large as rhinoceros. **1854** R. OWEN in *Circ. Sci.* (c 1865) II. 97/2 The extinct gigantic lizard-like toad, called *Labyrinthodon.* **1876** PAGE *Adv. Text-bk. Geol.* xvi. 294 The batrachian or frog-like labyrinthodon.

labyrinthodont (læbɪˈrɪnθədɒnt), *sb.* and *a.* *Palæont.* [Formed as prec.]

A. *sb.* = prec.

1849-52 OWEN in Todd *Cycl. Anat.* IV. 867/2 A singular family of gigantic extinct Batrachians which I have called 'Labyrinthodonts'. **1873** DAWSON *Earth & Man* viii. 201 The crocodilian newts or labyrinthodonts of the Carboniferous.

B. *adj.* Having labyrinthic teeth; *spec.* pertaining to the genus *Labyrinthodon* of fossil amphibians.

1867 SMYTH *Coal* 39 Amphibian Labyrinthodont reptiles. **1876** PAGE *Adv. Text-bk. Geol.* xiv. 254 Those labyrinthodont reptiles that come boldly into force in the Permian and Triassic eras.

lac[1] (læk). Forms: α. (6 lacha, lacta), 6-9 lacca, (7 lacka, 8 laca, lakka). β. 6-8 lack(e, (7 lache, 7-8 lacque, 8 lacc, 8-9 laque), 7- lac. [ad. Hindustani *lākh*:—Prakrit *lakkha*:—Skr. *lākshā*, also *rākshā*. Cf. F. *laque*, Pr., Sp. *laca*, It. *lacca*.]

1. (Also ***gum-lac***.) The dark-red resinous incrustation produced on certain trees by the puncture of an insect (*Coccus* or *Carteria lacca*). It is used in the East as a scarlet dye. The incrusted twigs are called ***stick-lac***; the resin broken off the twigs and triturated with water to remove the colour is called ***seed-lac***; melted, strained, and formed into irregular thin plates, it is known as ***shell-lac*** or SHELLAC *sb.*

α. **1553** EDEN *Treat. Newe Ind.* (Arb.) 21 *marg.*, Lacha, Lacca, or Lacta, is ye gumme of a tree wherewith silke is colored. **1622-62** HEYLIN *Cosmogr.* III. (1682) 217 Lacca (a gum there made by Ants, as here Bees make Wax). **1693** *Phil. Trans.* XVII. 934 Manna and Gum Lacca he clearly shews to be Spontaneous Exudations. **1753** CHAMBERS *Cycl. Supp.* s.v. *Lacca*, A tincture of gum lacc may be thus prepared. **1763** W. LEWIS *Comm. Phil. Techn.* 223 Lacca.. is found incrustated on sticks or branches of trees. **1809** WILFORD in *Asiat. Researches* IX. 65 This Amber of Ctesias is obviously the Indian Lacca, which has many properties of the Amber.

β. **1618** T. BARKER in *St. Papers Col., E. Indies* 1617-21 (1870) 159 Saffron, gumlac, indigo, copper. **1662** J. DAVIES tr. *Mandelslo's Trav.* II. (1669) 122 At Bantam..they sell store of Lacque, whereof they make Spanish wax. **1698** *Phil. Trans.* XX. 273 Gum Lack is the House of a large sort of Ants, which they make on the Boughs of Trees. **1727** BRADLEY *Fam. Dict.* s.v. *Gum*, Powder of Oister-shells, or Gum Lacque in Powder. **1794** PEARSON in *Phil. Trans.* LXXXIV. 385 White lac, in its dry state, has a saltish and bitterish taste. **1838** T. THOMSON *Chem. Org. Bodies* 550 Lac..is deposited in different species of trees in the East Indies, namely, the *ficus indica*, *ficus religiosa*, and *rhamnus jujuba*. **1877** C. W. THOMSON *Voy. Challenger* I. i. 15 The different varnishes and lacs remain soft and sticky.

†**2.** The colour of lac; crimson. Also, a pigment prepared from lac. *Obs.* (Cf. LAKE *sb.*[6])

1677 GREW *Colours Plants* iii. §13 Spirit of Sulphur on a Tincture of Violets turns it from Blew to a true Lacke, or midle Crimson. **1689** MARVELL *Instr. to Painter* 636 Scarce can burnt iv'ry feign a hair so black, Or face so red, thine ocher and thy lack. **1763** *Brit. Mag.* IV. 659 There are three sorts of lacque: the fine Venice lacque, the Columbine lacque, and the Liquid lacque.

†**b.** An extractive pigment; = LAKE *sb.*[6] 3.

1682 *Weekly Memorials* 27 Mar. 74 He also teaches us a way of preparing a sort of *Lacca*, or Paint, out of every Flower, by which it may be drawn or pictur'd in its own.. Native Colour.

†**3.** The varnish made from lac; also applied to various resinous varnishes used for coating wood, etc.; = LACQUER 2 a, 2 b.

1598 W. PHILLIPS tr. *Linschoten* I. lxviii. 117 Desks, Targets, Tables [etc.]..that are all couered and wrought with Lac of all colours and fashions. **1669** *Phil. Trans.* IV. 985 No Arts are to be met amongst them, that are not known in Europe, except that of making Lacca. **1697** DAMPIER *Voy.* (1729) II. I. 24 The Lack with which Cabinets and other fine Things are overlaid. **1727** A. HAMILTON *New Acc. E. Indies* I. ii. 126 The Lack is clear enough, but always clammy.

4. Ware coated with lac or lacquer.

1662 J. DAVIES tr. *Mandelslo's Trav.* I. (1669) 24 Boxes of Lacque or Silver. **1861** C. P. HODGSON *Resid. in Japan* 28 By degrees, the eye becomes accustomed to old laque..Old laque is, like old lace, inimitable. **1888** *Pall Mall G.* 11 Feb. 3/1 The gems of Mr. S.'s unrivalled collection are here to show the supreme masterpieces in 'lac'.

5. *attrib.*, as ***lac-panel***, ***-resin***, ***-tree***, ***-varnish***; **lac-cochineal**, the insect that produces lac (*Coccus lacca*); **lac-dye**, a scarlet dye prepared in India from lac; **lac-lake**, the purple or scarlet pigment obtained from lac.

1813 BINGLEY *Anim. Biog.* III. 191 The *lac cochineal. **1846** *Pope's Jrnl. Trade* p. xxxi, Cochineal, Indigo, *Lac-dye. **1883** *Cassell's Fam. Mag.* Oct. 683/1 Comparatively few people know how the lac-dye they read of in commerce is produced. **1895** *Daily News* 24 May 6/6 A gold box..with old *lac panels. **1876** PREECE & SIVEWRIGHT *Telegraphy* 296 The *gum lac resin is employed to consolidate the carbon-peroxide of manganese mixture. **1763** W. LEWIS *Comm. Phil. Techn.* 331 The species, called by Mr. Miller the true *lac tree, was found to contain, in its bark..a somewhat milky juice. **1688** G. PARKER & J. STALKER *Japaning* 1 The other [strainer] for your *Lacc-varnish. **1799** G. SMITH *Laboratory* I. 178 Make a paste of chalk and lack varnish.

Hence †**lac** *v. trans.*, to cover or varnish with 'lac'; to lacquer.

1698 *Phil. Trans.* XX. 275 And then with a Brush [they] lay it smooth on any thing they design to Lack. **1727** A. HAMILTON *New Acc. E. Indies* I. xi. 125 They make fine Cabinets, both lack'd and inlaid with Ivory. *Ibid.* 126 They lack wooden Dishes and Tables, but not so well as in China.

lac[2] (læk). *Biol.* An abbrev. of LAC(TOSE used (usu. *attrib.*) as a symbol or name (and printed in italics): orig. used to denote the ability (of normal individuals) or inability (of mutants) of the bacterium *Escherichia coli* to metabolize lactose (see quot. 1947), and later to designate (the parts of) the genetic system involved in this ability; as **lac operon**, a group of adjacent genes in the chromosome of *E. coli* which, in the presence of lactose, cause the bacterium to synthesize the enzymes that enable it to metabolize lactose. Also as *sb.*, the (in)ability to metabolize lactose; a lac^{+} bacterium; the *lac* operon.

1947 J. LEDERBERG in *Genetics* XXXII. 505 Particular attention was paid to the isolation of 'lactose-negative' or 'Lac^{-}' mutants [of *E. coli*]. *Ibid.* 506 (Table), Symbols used for various loci... 'Sugar' fermentation. The ability to ferment is designated '+'; the inability '−'. *Lac* lactose. *Gly* glycerol. **1952** *Nature* 24 May 882/2 The number of papillæ forming on surface colonies of lac^{-} bacteria, grown on agar containing lactose and another carbon source, is a reflexion of the number of mutations to the lac^{+} condition. **1961** SAGER & RYAN *Cell Heredity* v. 136 If a cell [of *E. coli*] heterozygous for lac^{+} and lac^{-} is isolated, it produces some progeny still heterozygous and others in which the lac^{-} has segregated from the lac^{+}. **1961** JACOB & MONOD in *Cold Spring Harbor Symp. Quant. Biol.* XXVI. 197 (*caption*) Genetic map of the *Lac* region of *E. coli*... The lower line represents an enlargement of the *Lac* region, with the two structural genes *z* and *y* and the regulator gene *i*. **1961** S. E. LURIA in *Ibid.* 210/1 An altered sensitivity of phage-carried *lac* genes to the specific repressor of the *lac* operon. **1970** J. R. BECKWITH in Beckwith & Zipser *Lactose Operon* ii. 5 (*heading*) *Lac*: the genetic system. *Ibid.*, Strains in which the *lac* genes are fused to other bacterial operons, such as the *trp* operon and *purE* operon... Since, in such strains, the *lac* genes are now part of the other operon, nearly all the methodology used for analysis of *lac* can be used for that operon. *Ibid.*, Most of the major concepts of operon structure, expression and regulation have come out of the work on the *lac* operon of *E. coli*. **1971** *Times Lit. Suppl.* 13 Aug. 958/4 Dr Beckwith..[is] the centre of a political storm-in-a-scientific-teacup following his isolation of the lac operon gene.

lac, obs. form of LACK *sb.*[1] and *v.*[1]; var. LAKH.

laca, lacc, lacca: see LAC[1].

laccage: see LACKAGE.

laccar, obs. form of LACQUER.

laccase (ˈlækeɪz, -s). *Biochem.* [a. F. *laccase* (G. Bertrand 1894, in *Compt. Rend.* CXVIII. 1217), f. mod.L. *lacc-a* LAC[1]: see -ASE.] A copper-containing enzyme which effects the oxidation of hydroquinones to quinones, involved in the setting of lac.

1895 *Jrnl. R. Microsc. Soc.* 649 Laccase resembles the diastatic ferments in its properties, except that, instead of hydrolysing, it incites direct oxidation. **1899** J. R. GREEN *Soluble Ferments* xix. 296 The fungus which yields laccase most readily is *Russula fœtens* Pers., one of the Basidiomycetes, which is fairly common in woods during the summer. **1961** *Jrnl. Biochem.* (Tokyo) L. 264/1 In the present investigation laccases of Japanese and Indo-Chinese lacquer trees have been purified..and their properties compared. **1966** L. I. INGRAHAM in Florkin & Stotz *Comprehensive Biochem.* XIV. 440 Laccase catalyzes the aerobic oxidation of hydroquinones to *p*-quinone. It contains four copper atoms per mole which react with one mole of oxygen. **1971** *European Jrnl. Biochem.* XXIII. 487/2 Whether the unequal load of laccase II with carbohydrate is associated with a fixation of this enzyme to the cell walls, or whether it plays any role in the postulated aggregation of the low molecular weight laccases II and III to the high molecular weight laccase I..must be elucidated by further experiments.

ˈlaccate, *sb. Chem.* [See -ATE[1].] A salt of laccic acid.

1794 PEARSON *Table Chem. Nomencl.* §31.

laccate (ˈlækeɪt), *a. Bot.* [f. mod.L. *lacca* LAC[1] + -ATE[2].] Of leaves: Having the appearance of being lacquered.

In some mod. Dicts.

lacce, lacch(e, obs. forms of LACK *v.*[1], LATCH *v.*

lacchesse, obs. variant of LACHES.

laccic (ˈlæksɪk), *a. Chem.* [f. mod.L. *lacc-a* LAC[1] + -IC. Cf. F. *laccique*.] Only in *laccic acid*, the acid procured from lac.

1794 PEARSON *Table Chem. Nomencl.* §31 Laccic Acid. **1819** J. G. CHILDREN *Chem. Anal.* 277 Laccic acid is obtained from stick-lac.

laccin (ˈlæksɪn). [f. as prec. + -IN. Cf. F. *laccine*.] The colouring principle in lac.

1838 THOMSON *Organic Bodies* 552 A colouring matter, a peculiar body to which he [Dr. John] gave the name of laccin.

laccolite (ˈlækəlaɪt). *Geol.* [f. Gr. λάκκο-ς a reservoir + -LITE. So named by Gilbert in 1877.] A concordant mass of igneous rock thrust up through the sedimentary beds, and giving a dome-like form to the overlying strata.

1877 GILBERT *Rep. Geol. Henry Mts.* ii. 19 For this body the name *laccolite*..will be used. **1896** *Pop. Sci. Jrnl.* L. 241 These are connected..with Plutonic plugs, laccolites. **1937** WOOLDRIDGE & MORGAN *Physical Basis Geogr.* viii. 110 Laccolites are closely related in manner of origin to the stratiform intrusions of igneous rock..termed 'sills'. **1946** L. D. STAMP *Britain's Struct.* ix. 80 A special type of sill is one where the lava swells out to form a lens-shaped mass —which according to its particular form is known as a laccolite (with a flat base) or a phacolite (with a curved base).

Hence **laccoˈlitic** *a.*, pertaining to a laccolite.

1877 DUTTON in Gilbert *Rep. Geol. Henry Mts.* 69 Laccolitic nuclei. **1879** *Nature* XXI. 179 It is not likely that the Henry Mountains are the only ones constructed on the laccolitic type.

laccolith (ˈlækəlɪθ). *Geol.* [f. as prec. + λίθ-ος stone.] = LACCOLITE. (Now commoner in use than *laccolite*.)

1879 DANA *Man. Geol.* (ed. 3) 840 The laccolith, as is seen, rests on horizontal strata. **1944** A. HOLMES *Princ. Physical Geol.* vi. 86 There are few good examples of laccoliths in Britain, though many stocks have been wrongly called laccoliths. Stocks are discordant intrusions, whereas laccoliths, like sills, are concordant. **1960** B. W. SPARKS *Geomorphol.* vii. 151 Laccoliths, which are closely related to sills but which were formed from a magma too viscous to spread far, may form local dome-like features when exposed by erosion.

Hence **laccoˈlithic** *a.*, of, pertaining to, or characteristic of a laccolith.

1896 *Jrnl. Geol.* IV. 741 The hypothesis..that the granites are batholithic, not laccolithic. **1898** *Ibid.* VI. 705 When vertical displacement with faulting is one of the chief characteristics of the intrusion, a distinction from normal laccolithic intrusion should be recognized. **1933** [see BYSMALITHIC *a.*]. **1968** R. W. FAIRBRIDGE *Encycl. Geomorphol.* 281/2 The Devil's Tower of Wyoming is sometimes claimed to be an eroded laccolithic dome.

lace (leɪs), *sb.* Forms: 3-4 las, 4-5 laas, (4 lasse, *Sc.* laise, 5 laace), 5-7 lase, (5 *Sc.* les, 6 laze, *Sc.* lais), 4- lace. [ad. OF. *laz*, *las* (mod.F. *lacs*, with etymologizing spelling), f. popular L. **lacium* (L. *laqueum*) a noose. Cf. It. *laccio*, Sp., Pg. *lazo*.]

†**1.** A net, noose, snare. Chiefly *fig. Obs.*

13.. *K. Alis.* 7698 Woman the haveth bycought: Woman the haveth in hire las! *c* **1386** CHAUCER *Knt.'s T.* 2389 Vulcanus had caught thee in his las. **1430-40** LYDG. *Bochas, Dance Machabree* (1554) 222 Sithens that death me holdeth in his lase. **1491** CAXTON *Vitas Patr.* (W. de W. 1495) I. i. 6 bj, How they myghte eschewe the laces and temptacyons of the deuyll. **1590** GREENE *Never too late* II. (1600) O 3 b, Thus folded in a hard and mournfull laze Distrest sate hee. **1600** FAIRFAX *Tasso* II. xx, The king had snared been in loues strong lace. **1603** HOLLAND *Plutarch's Mor.* 973 And yet if the polype can get and entangle him once within his long laces, hee [the lobster] dies for it.

†**2. a.** A cord, line, string, thread, or tie. *Obs.* exc. *spec.* as in 3 a.

a **1300** *Cursor M.* 15880 (Gött.) Þar he [Iudas] liuerd his maistir up Þai bunden had wid las [*Cott.* laȝas]. *c* **1340** *Ibid.* 22967 (Fairf.), I salle..breke Þaire bandis & Þair lacis. **1390** GOWER *Conf.* III. 237 They taughten him a lace to braide. **1405-6** *Acc. Rolls Durham* (Surtees) 400 Cum..lacez et anulis pro ridellis. **1412-20** LYDG. *Chron. Troy* III. xxii, And hym to treyne [they] layde out hoke & lase. *a* **1425** WYNTOUN *Orig. Cron.* IV. x. 1231 Off gold thrawyn all lyk a les. **1463** in *Bury Wills* (Camden) 42 A stoon and a reed lace with a knoppe. **1484** CAXTON *Fables of Æsop* I. xviii. (1889) 27 The ratte beganne..to byte the lace or cord. **1535** COVERDALE *Eccles.* xii. 6 Or euer the syluer lace be taken awaye. **1639** FULLER *Holy War* III. viii. (1647) 123 Pitie it was that Rahab's red lace was not tied at his window.

†**b.** *transf.* and *fig. Obs.*

a **1547** SURREY in *Tottel's Misc.* (Arb.) 4 To seke the place where I my selfe had lost, That day that I was tangled in the lace. **1555** EDEN *Decades* 200 Abowte whose leaues there growe and creepe certeyne cordes or laces. **1578** LYTE *Dodoens* I. xx. 30 The roote hath many smal strings or threddy laces hanging thereby. **1641** J. JACKSON *True Evang. T.* ii. 143 The red scarlet lace of Christs blood, must be entortled and interwoven into a bracelet, with a white silken thred of holinesse and regeneration. **1650** FULLER *Pisgah* II. iv. 103 Some fancy a small Lace of land (or rather a thread for the narrowness thereof) whereby Naphtali is tyed unto Judah.

3. *spec.* **a.** A string or cord serving to draw together opposite edges (chiefly of articles of clothing, as bodices, stays, boots and shoes) by being passed in and out through eyelet-holes (or over hooks, studs, etc.) and pulled tight. Cf. *boot-*, *shoe-*, *stay-lace*.

†***under lace***: under the bodice; in ME. poetry = 'under gore'.

13.. *Gaw. & Gr. Knt.* 1830, I schal gif yow my girdel, Þat gaynes yow lasse. Ho laȝt a lace lyȝtly, Þat leke vmbe hir sydez. ? *a* **1366** CHAUCER *Rom. Rose* 843 And shod he was with greet maistreye, With shoon decoped, & with laas. *c* **1375** *Sc. Leg. Saints*, *Baptista* 1208 To quham I ame nocht worthi loute na of his schone Þe laise tak oute. *c* **1394** *P. Pl. Crede* 79 To wenen Þat Þe lace of oure ladie smok liȝteÞ hem of children. *c* **1440** *Ipomydon* 326 (Kölbing) He..drew a lace

of sylke full clere, Adowne than felle hys mantylle by. *c* **1440** *Bone Flor.* 1817 They..betoke hur to the marynere, That lovely undur lace. **1534** MORE *Picus* Wks. 30 Ne none so small a trifle or conceyte, Lase, girdle, point, or proper gloue straite. **1593** SHAKS. *2 Hen. VI*, IV. ii. 49 She was indeed a Pedler's daughter, and sold many Laces. **1611** BIBLE *Exod.* xxviii. 28 They shall bind the brestplate..vnto the rings of the Ephod with a lace of blewe. **1625** K. LONG tr. *Barclay's Argenis* I. x. 28 Sprinkling water in her face, and cutting her laces, they made her fit abate. **1676** GREW *Anat. Flowers* i. §3 As Teeming Women, gradually slaken their Laces. **1709** BLAIR in *Phil. Trans.* XXVII. 96 Like so many Thongs or Laces whereinto a piece of Leather had been cut. **1712** tr. *Pomet's Hist. Drugs* I. 193 The Flowers bear a resemblance to tags at the End of long Laces. **1748** RICHARDSON *Clarissa* (1811) I. xvi. 106 When I recovered, [I] found..my laces cut, my linen scented with hartshorn. **1879** BROWNING *Ned Bratts* 133 He taught himself the make Of laces, tagged and tough. **1885** *Law Rep., Q.B.D.* XV. 360 The two ends were rivetted or laced together with metal rivets or leathern laces.

¶ Formerly sometimes used to render L. *fibula* 'brooch'.

1382 WYCLIF *1 Macc.* x. 88 He sente to hym a golden lace [L. *fibulam*]. *c* **1440** *Promp. Parv.* 283/1 Lace, *fibula, laqueum.* **1570** LEVINS *Manip.* 6/35 A lace, *fibula.*

†**b.** A cord used to support something hanging, e.g. a sword; a baldrick, belt. *Obs.*

c **1386** CHAUCER *Can. Yeom. Prol.* 21 His hat heng at his bak doun by a laas. **1490** CAXTON *Eneydos* xvi. 63 Eneas.. had a bystorye..hangynge at a silken lase by his side. *a* **1533** LD. BERNERS *Huon* xxii. 66 He hade about hys necke a ryche horne hangyng by two lases of golde. **1597** MONTGOMERIE *Cherrie & Slae* 115 His quauer by his naked thyis Hang in ane siluer lace.

†**4.** ? *transf.* from 3 a. In building: A tie beam; a brace. Also, a panelled ceiling (= L. *laquear*).

a **1300** *Cursor M.* 1728 Noe..self festnid bath band and lace. *Ibid.* 8778 Quen al was purueid on þe place, And bunden samen balk and lace. *c* **1440** *Promp. Parv.* 283/1 Lace of an howserofe, *laquearea.* **1592** *Nottingham Rec.* IV. 235 Settinge in a lace to Posterne Bridge rayle. **1601** HOLLAND *Pliny* II. 581 A man may..bestow them [beams] againe fast enough without laces to bind them.

5. a. Ornamental braid used for trimming men's coats, etc.; †a trimming of this. Now only in ***gold lace, silver lace***, a braid formerly made of gold or silver wire, now of silk or thread with a thin wrapping of gold or silver.

a **1548** HALL *Chron., Hen. VIII* 239 Flatte golde of Dammaske with small lace myxed betwene of the same golde, and other laces of the same so goyng traverse wyse, that the grounde lytle appered. **1591** GREENE *Disc. Coosnage* III. 36 The Tayler had..so much gold lace, beside spangles, as valued thirteene pound. **1633** G. HERBERT *Temple, Peace* ii, Surely, thought I, This [a rainbow] is the lace of Peaces coat. **1634** PEACHAM *Gentl. Exerc.* 135 Garters deepe fringed with gold lace. **1681** DRYDEN *Prol. to Univ. of Oxford* 16 Tack but a copper lace to drugget suit. **1702** *Lond. Gaz.* No. 3793/4 Mary Presbury..Gold and Silver Lace-seller. **1704** SWIFT *T. Tub* §2. 67 So without more ado they got the largest Gold Lace in the Parish, and walkt about as fine as Lords. **1787** O'KEEFE *Farmer* II. iii, But now a saucy Footman, I strut in worsted Lace. **1791** BOSWELL *Johnson* an. 1749, In a scarlet waistcoat, with rich gold lace, and a gold-lace hat. **1867** SMYTH *Sailor's Word-bk., Lace*, the trimmings of uniforms.

†**b.** *transf.* A streak or band of colour. *Obs. rare*⁻¹. (Cf. LACE *v.* 6.)

1613 [see GUARD *sb.* 11 c].

6. A slender open-work fabric of linen, cotton, silk, woollen, or metal threads, usually ornamented with inwrought or applied patterns. Often called after the place where it is manufactured, e.g. *Brussels lace*. For ***bobbin-, chain-, pillow-, point-***, etc. ***lace***, see the first member. Also BONE-LACE, BRIDE-LACE.

1555 WATREMAN *Fardle Facions* I. v. 50 The men satte at home spinnyng, and woorkyng of Lace. **1613** (*title*) The King's Edict prohibiting all his Subjects from using any Gold or Silver, either fine or counterfeit; all Embroiderie, and all Lace of Millan, or of Millan Fashion. **1715** GAY *Epist. Earl Burlington* 118 The busy town..Where finest lace industrious lasses weave. **1837** GORING *Microg.* 208 Manufactured fabrics, such as lace, blond, muslin, [etc.]. *transf.* **1866** G. MACDONALD *Ann. Q. Neighb.* xi. (1878) 211 In the shadows lay fine webs and laces of ice.

7. A 'dash' of spirits mixed with some beverage, esp. coffee. (Cf. LACE *v.*¹ 9 and LACED *ppl. a.*¹ 6.)

In quot. *c* 1704 the meaning may be 'sugar', as Johnson supposes. (Cf. quot. *a* 1700 s.v. LACED *ppl. a.*¹ 6.)

c **1704** PRIOR *Chameleon* 26 He drinks his coffee without lace. **1712** ADDISON *Spect.* No. 448 ¶1 He is forced every Morning to drink his Dish of Coffee by itself, without the Addition of the *Spectator*, that used to be better than Lace to it. **1755** JOHNSON, *Lace*, sugar. A cant word. [With quot. *c* 1704.]

8. General comb.: **a.** simple attributive, as (sense 3 a) *lace-hole*, (sense 6) *lace-box, -curtain*, (also *fig.* and *attrib.*, middle- or upper-class, 'respectable', having social pretensions), ***-stitch***, *-tracery, -trade, -work, -worker*; *laceless, lace-like* adjs. **b.** objective, as *lace-buyer, -designer, -dresser, -maker, -making, -mender, -seller, -weaver*. **c.** instrumental and parasynthetic, as *lace-covered, -curtained, -edged, -loaded, -trimmed* adjs.

1904 *Lace box [see *Bible-box*]. **1969** E. H. PINTO *Treen* 370 Lace boxes, to stand on chests of drawers..enjoyed their greatest popularity during the second half of the 17th century and during Queen Anne's reign. **1679** *Lond. Gaz.* No. 1391/4 Taken..from two *Lace-buyers..two Geldings. **1883** F. M. CRAWFORD *Dr. Claudius* ii, A dainty *lace-covered parasol fell over the edge. **1895** *Montgomery Ward Catal.* 347/3 *Lace curtains and lambrequins. **1934** J. T. FARRELL *Young Manhood* xviii. 282 They were all trying to put on the dog, show that they were lace-curtain Irish, and lived in steam-heat. **1949** *Sat. Rev. Lit.* (U.S.) 25 June 33/1 Mrs. Ruskay's folks were lace-curtain Jews; they had a piano and a Polish maid. **1960** *Guardian* 8 July 8/4 The Kennedy millions..were..wrested by a lace-curtain Irishman from..the Boston Brahmins. **1964** *Publ. Amer. Dial. Soc.* XLII. 35 The most common-place of these is the distinction between *shanty-* and *lace-curtain Irish*, i.e., those who remain in the lower-class communities near the center of the city..and those who move into lowermiddle-class communities and work hard to approximate the ideals of vulgar respectability. **1965** 'E. QUEEN' *Fourth Side of Triangle* iii. 122 Also, I have the misfortune to be Irish. And not lace-curtain Irish, either! **1970** *Guardian* 5 June 10/2 Britain has a long tradition of what might be called lace-curtain racialism. **1974** J. STUBBS *Painted Face* iii. 56 Every house in the square was veiled in lace curtains. **1891** C. JAMES *Rom. Rigmarole* 128 Dainty, *lace-curtained windows. **1890** *Daily News* 16 Apr. 2/4 Thomas Argyll, ..*lace-designer. **1879** E. JAMES *Ind. Househ. Man.* 31 *Lace-edged antimacassars. **1871** *Figure Training* 34 At the age of fourteen or thereabouts, the front rows of *lace-holes may be omitted. **1901** *Daily News* 4 June 2/6 The shoes, low and *laceless, slip on easily. **1968** R. CLAPPERTON *No News on Monday* xi. 129 His feet were thrust into a pair of laceless tennis shoes. **1833** J. RENNIE *Alph. Angling* 45 All the species of dragon-fly, with the exception of one or two, being characterised by very clear, *lace-like, pellucid wings. **1873** LOWELL *Among my Bks.* Ser. II. 125 Lacelike curves of ever-gaining, ever-receding foam. **1836** T. HOOK *G. Gurney* iii. 86 The strapping, state-fed, *lace-loaded lacqueys of the Mansion-House. **1589** RIDER *Eng.-Lat. Dict.*, A *Lace-maker, *fibularius.* **1611** COTGR., *Passementier*, a Lace-maker. **1848** MILL *Pol. Econ.* I. v. §9. 100 Weavers and lacemakers. **1835-37** SOUTHEY in *Cowper's Wks.* I. 202 *Lace making was the business of the place. **1844** G. DODD *Textile Manuf.* vii. 227 *Lace-menders examine every piece, and mend, with needle and thread, every defect. **1702** *Lond. Gaz.* No. 3793/4 Gold and Silver *Laceseller. **1872** *Young Englishwoman* Dec. 658/2 These medallions are worked in appliqué of muslin or net, in satin stitch, knotted-stitch etc. *Lace stitches fill the centre of the flower. **1961** A. LILEY *Craft of Embroidery* i. 28 (*heading*) Lace stitch filling... This is also a buttonhole stitch variation giving the laciest effect of all the buttonhole fillings. **1890** 'ROLF BOLDREWOOD' *Miner's Right* xliv. 185/1 A faint *lace-tracery of mist. **1819** REES *Cycl.* s.v. *Lace*, The *lace trade of Nottingham. **1835** DICKENS *Sk. Boz* (1836) 1st Ser. I. i. 4 Her previous admiration of 'the board'..fades into nothing before her respect for her *lace-trimmed conductor [*i.e.* the beadle]. **1861** GEO. ELIOT *Silas Marner* xii. 217 A lace-trimmed cradle. **1894** *Daily News* 5 June 8/4 Scarves of crêpon with lace-trimmed ends. **1715** *Lond. Gaz.* No. 5327/2 The Company of *Lace-Weavers at Augsburg. **1802** *Brookes' Gazetteer* (ed. 12) s.v. *Locle*, Famous for watchmakers, laceweavers, goldsmiths. **1849** ALB. SMITH *Pottleton Legacy* xxiv. 242 A white cravat the ends of which were in open *lace-work. **1873** TRISTRAM *Moab* ix. 173 Numbers of stones with very pretty lacework of various patterns. **1896** *Daily News* 1 Oct. 2/2 His sister, another *laceworker, is in charge of the family during their sojourn in London.

9. Special comb.: **lace-bark (tree)**, (*a*) a West Indian shrub (*Lagetta lintearia*), so called from the lace-like layers of its inner bark; (*b*) any of several small New Zealand trees of the family Malvaceæ, including *Plagianthus betulinus* and several species of *Hoheria* (cf. HOUHERE), with toothed leaves and clusters of white flowers; also *attrib.*; **lace-border**, a geometrid moth (*Acidalia ornata*) with a broad lace-like border to the wings; **lace-bug**, an insect of the family Tingidæ, including many species of bugs that feed on plants and sometimes become pests; **lacecap**, a hydrangea whose corymbs are made up of small fertile flowers or a mixture of these with larger sterile ones, giving the effect of lace; also used *attrib.* or as *adj.* to describe flower-heads of this type belonging to hydrangeas or other plants; **lace-coral**, a fossil polyzoan of the family *Fenestellidæ*; **lace-fern**, (*a*) a small elegant fern (*Cheilanthes gracillima*) having the under side of the frond covered with matted wool; (*b*) any of the several species of the genus *Hymenophyllum*; **lace-frame** (see FRAME *sb.* 13 b); **lace-glass**, Venetian glass with lace-like designs; †**lace-head**, a head-dress of lace; **lace-leaf (plant)**, *Ouvirandra fenestralis*, of Madagascar; **lace-lizard**, an Australian lizard (*Hydrosaurus varius*); **lace-man**, a man who manufactures or deals in lace; **lace-paper**, paper cut or stamped in imitation of lace; **lace-pigeon** (see quots.); **lace-pillow**, the pillow or cushion which is laid on the lap of a woman engaged in making pillow-lace; **lace-plant**, ? = *lace-leaf plant*; **lace-runner** (see quot.); †**lace-shade**, a lace veil; **lace-tree**, ? = *lace-bark tree*; **lace-wing (fly)**, a fly with delicate lace-like wings, esp. one of the genus *Chrysopa*; also ***lace-winged fly***; **lace-woman**, a woman who works or deals in lace; **lace-wood**, (*a*) *Austral.* = *lace-bark* (*b*); (*b*) the wood of a plane tree, *Platanus occidentalis* or *P. acerifolia*.

1756 P. BROWNE *Jamaica* 371 The Lagetto or *Lace-bark Tree. The bark is of a fine texture, very tough, and divides into a number of laminæ. **1830** LINDLEY *Nat. Syst. Bot.* 76 In Jamaica a species is found which is called the Lace Bark Tree. **1868** *Trans. N.Z. Inst.* Essays 33 Ribbon Wood, or Lace-bark tree (*Plagianthus Lyalli*). A very ornamental shrub tree, with large leaves and flowers. **1906**, etc. [see HOUHERE]. **1957** *Landfall* XI. 234, I lay in a patch, Of bush —giant manuka, some lace-bark. **1958** S. ASHTON-WARNER *Spinster* 189 Flaring out above the long grass and from beneath the lace-bark tree. **1966** *Weekly News* (Auckland) 6 Apr. 40 The lacebark which is also known as mountain ribbonwood (Hoheria glabrata), grows on the western side of the Southern Alps. **1869** E. NEWMAN *Brit. Moths* 79 The *Lace Border (*Acidalia ornata*). **1895** J. H. & A. COMSTOCK *Man. Study Insects* xiv. 139 The *Lace-bugs. Dainty as fairy brides are these tiny, lace-draped insects. One glance at the fine white meshes that cover the wings and spined thorax is sufficient to distinguish them from all other insects, for these are the only ones that are clothed from head to foot in fine white Brussels net. **1923** E. A. BUTLER *Biol. Brit. Hemiptera-Heteroptera* 196 In the *Tingidae*, or Lace Bugs, we are not rich, for we have but twenty-four in our fauna. **1932** METCALF & FLINT *Fund. Insect Life* viii. 225 Lace bugs look as though they were cut out of fine gauze. **1967** K. M. SMITH *Insect Virol.* xi. 225 The vector in both cases is somewhat unusual, it is not a leafhopper but a 'lace bug'. **1972** SWAN & PAPP *Common Insects N. Amer.* xii. 123 The Tingidæ, or lace bugs, are..small, oval or rectangular in outline, and lacelike in appearance owing to reticulated pattern on the head, thorax, and wings. **1950** W. E. SHEWELL-COOPER *Compl. Gardener* IV. 339 Besides the hortensia type there is another type of *H*[*ydrangea*] *macrophylla*, the *Lacecaps, which have a flat head with small fertile flowers in the centre and a ring round the outside formed by the larger sterile flowers. **1966** J. BERRISFORD *Wild Garden* ii. 29 Hydrangeas will grow extremely well in woodland... Grow the lacecaps too. Their flower-pattern is exquisite... The nearly related *Schizophragma hydrangeoides* is a climbing version of the hydrangea family... Its lacecap flowerheads have a solitary large bract-like sepal. **1967** *Sunday Times* 21 May 14/5 The lovely lacecap hydrangea 'Blue Wave'. **1971** *Guardian* 17 Apr. 7/7 The lacecap-flowered Viburnum mariesii. **1885** LADY BRASSEY *The Trades* 239 The *lace- or fringe-fern.. grew in wild profusion. **1895** *Daily News* 5 Dec. 6/1 Selling a couple of old *lace-frames to some Frenchmen for 200*l.* apiece. **1883** MOLLETT *Dict. Art* 156 There are six kinds of Venetian glass..(6) Reticulated, filigree, or *lace glass. **1884** *Mag. of Art* Feb. 155/2 Briati..was especially celebrated.. for his beautiful work in lace-glass. **1724** RAMSAY *Tea-t. Misc.* (1733) I. 35 Shou'd a..Flanders *lace-head..Gar thee grow forgetfu'. **1809** *Edin. Rev.* XV. 78 He will hear of lace-heads and ruffles. **1866** *Treas. Bot.* (1870), *Lace-leaf plant, *Ouvirandra.* **1880** J. SIBREE Jr. *Gt. African Isl.* iv. 100 This is the Lace-leaf plant, or water-yam; in scientific phraseology, *Ouvirandra fenestralis.* **1881** F. MCCOY *Prodromus Nat. Hist. of Victoria* 4 Dec. (Morris), The present *Lace Lizard is generally arboreal. **1669** PEPYS *Diary* 26 Apr., Calling at the *lace-man's for some lace for my new suit. **1737** FIELDING *Miser* v. vii, The laceman will be here immediately. **1896** *Westm. Gaz.* 5 Dec. 3/1 A laceman of a good many years' standing. **1765** *Treat. Dom. Pigeons* 143 The *Lace Pigeon... They are valued on account of..the peculiarity of their feathers; the fibres, or web of which, appear disunited from each other throughout their whole plumage. **1859** BRENT *Pigeon Bk.* 54 The Lace or Silky Pigeon... The fibres of the feathers are all disunited,..which gives them a lacy or silky appearance. **1793** COWPER *Let.* 9 Jan. in T. Wright *Life* (1892) 260 The *lace pillow is the only thing they dandle. **1865** C. KNIGHT *Passages Work. Life* III. x. 205 The jingling rhymes sung by young girls while engaged at their lace-pillows. **1885** LADY BRASSEY *The Trades* 426 A plant..called the '*lace-plant', from the extreme delicacy and beauty of its foliage. **1844** G. DODD *Textile Manuf.* vii. 225 The term *embroidery* does not seem to be much used in..the Nottingham lace-trade, most of those who work on net with the needle being termed '*lace-runners'. **1803** JANE PORTER *Thaddeus* (1831) 275 Her *lace-shade..half veiled and half revealed her graceful figure. **1887** MOLONEY *Forestry W. Afr.* 460 The public may ..see in our stoves the rare *Lace tree of Jamaica. **1863** WOOD *Nat. Hist.* III. 491 The beautiful *Lace-wing Flies, or Hemerobiidæ... Several species of the Lace-wings are also called..Golden Eyes. **1826** KIRBY & SP. *Entomol.* III. 94 The beautiful *lace-winged flies (*Hemerobius*). **1609** B. JONSON *Silent Wom.* II. iii, Tailors, lineners, *lace-women, embroiderers. **1896** *Daily News* 1 Oct. 2/2 She is a lacewoman in the Exhibition. **1898** MORRIS *Austral Eng.* 258/1 Lace-bark, Lacey-bark, or *Lacewood. **1902** G. S. BOULGER *Wood* v. 101 Very choice ornamental woods are employed mainly as veneers. Such are..those of Walnut; and the beautiful Lacewood or Honeysuckle wood of North America (*Platanus occidentalis*). **1930** *Morning Post* 2 Aug. 12/2 The anomaly that Queensland silky oak should be purchased by the United States..and then shipped to this country where it is sold as lace-wood. **1962** J. C. S. BROUGH *Timbers for Woodwork* (rev. ed.) xvi. 168 Cut upon the quarter, plane-wood shows an exceedingly handsome figure, and American grown wood converted in this fashion was sent over in fairly large quantities some years ago under the name of Lace-wood.

lace (leɪs), *v.* Forms: 4 lacye, 5 lacyn, (lyce), 5–6 lase, 6 *Sc.* laise, 7 ? leese (sense 2 d), 4– lace. *Pa. pple.* 3 i-laced. [ad. OF. *lacier* (F. *lacer*):—popular L. **laciāre* to ensnare, f. **lacium*: see LACE *sb.* Cf. Pr. *lassar*, Sp. *lazar*, Pg. *laçar*, It. *lacciare.*]

†**1.** *trans.* To catch in, or as in, a noose or snare; to entangle, ensnare. *Obs.*

c **1400** *Rom. Rose* 3178, I trowe never man wiste of peyne, But he were laced in Loves cheyne. **1426** LYDG. *De Guil. Pilgr.* (E.E.T.S.) 13,076 Folkys vnder my demeyne, Swych as be lacyd in my cheyne. *c* **1485** *Digby Myst.* v. 580 Fortune in worldes worshepe me doth lace.

2. a. To fasten or tighten with, or as with, a lace or string; to tie on; to fasten the lace of. In mod. use *spec.* to fasten or tighten (boots, stays, etc.) with a lace or laces passed alternately through two rows of eyelets. Also with *down, on, together.*

a **1225** *Ancr. R.* 420 Sum wummon..wereð..þe strapeles adun to hire uet i-laced ful ueste. *a* **1300** *K. Horn* 870 Horn his brunie gan on caste, And laced hit wel faste. *c* **1386**

CHAUCER *Miller's T.* 81 Hir shoes were laced on hir legges hye. *c* **1400** MAUNDEV. (Roxb.) xxvi. 121 þai er..laced togyder with lacez of silke. *c* **1450** *St. Cuthbert* (Surtees) 3933 He kist þe clathes as þai hade bene lasyd And on the saint body brasyd. **1530** PALSGR. 600/2, I wyll lace my doublet first for takyng of colde. **1596** SHAKS. *Tam. Shr.* III. ii. 46 A paire of bootes that haue been candle-cases, one buckled, another lac'd. **1672** WISEMAN *Treat. Wounds* I. iv. 43, I caused a straight stocking to be laced on both legs. **1709** STEELE & ADDISON *Tatler* No. 75 ¶8 To see me often with my Spectacles on lacing her Stays. **1711** W. SUTHERLAND *Shipbuilder's Assist.* 129 Lacing the Mizon. **1748** *Anson's Voy.* III. viii. 380 The galeon was..provided against boarding..by a strong net-work..which was laced over her waist. **1763** *Brit. Mag.* IV. 286, I lace and unlace ladies stays of the first fashion, every day of my life. **1789–96** MORSE *Amer. Geog.* II. 35 They fix the rein-deer to a kind of sledge ..in which the traveller, well secured from cold, is laced down. **1869** FREEMAN *Norm. Conq.* (1876) III. xiii. 259 Ofttimes he laced and ofttimes he unlaced his mantle. **1885** *Law Rep.*, *Q.B.D.* XV. 360 The two ends were..laced together with..leathern laces.

b. *transf.* and *fig.*

13.. *Minor Poems fr. Vernon MS.* xxiii. 466 Heil beo whom þe godhed In vr flesch was laced. *a* **1550** *Christis Kirke Gr.* xviii, Hir glitterand hair that wes full gowdin, Sa hard in lufe him laist. **1576** FLEMING *Panopl. Epist.* 35 When he sawe the perill of us all, lincked and laced to the daunger of hym selfe. **1578** N. BAXTER tr. *Calvin on Jonah* 64 Jonas ..stood harde lased [L. *quasi constrictus*], because [etc.]. **1860** DARWIN in *Life & Lett.* (1887) II. 298 Each series of facts is laced together by a series of assumptions.

c. *intr.* (quasi-*pass.*) To admit of being fastened or tightened with laces.

1792 WOLCOT (P. Pindar) *Wks.* III. 37 She wailing, in most piteous case, Of stubborn stays—that would not lace. **1888** P. FURNIVALL *Phys. Training* 6 Shoes..should..lace from the toe, as high up the foot as is possible.

d. *Naut.* 'To apply (a bonnet) by lacing it to a sail' (Smyth *Sailor's Word-bk.* 1867). Also with *on.* (Cf. F. *lacer.*)

1635 BRERETON *Trav.* (Chetham Soc.) 169 You may take off the main bonnet and top bonnet,..and in a short time you may lace them on again. **1669** STURMY *Mariner's Mag.* i. 16 Leese in [ed. 1684 Lace on] your Boonets.

3. a. To compress the waist of (a person) by drawing the laces tight. With qualifying adv. (*straitly*, *tight*, etc.). Also *fig.* ***to lace in***: to compress the waist of (a person) by lacing. Similarly, ***to lace down.***

a **1566** R. EDWARDS *Damon & Pithias* (1571) B iv, Whiche bothe are in vertue so narrowly laced, That [etc.]. **1599** PORTER *Angry Wom. Abingt.* (Percy Soc.) 107, I do not love to bee last in, when I goe to lase a rascall. **1668** R. STEELE *Husbandm. Call.* x. (1672) 262 They grow crooked by being lac'd too strait. **1700** CONGREVE *Way of World* III. x, Like Mrs. Primly's great Belly; she may lace it down before, but it burnishes on her Hips. **1825** SCOTT *Fam. Let.* 23 Jan. (1894) II. 230 Rather straitly laced in her Presbyterian stays. **1882** *World* 21 June 18/1 The bodice..laced-in a waist of twenty inches.

b. *refl.*, and *intr.* for *refl.*

1650 BULWER *Anthropomet.* 195 Better advised are the Venetian Dames, who never Lace themselves. **1871** *Figure Training* 9 To lace or not to lace. *Ibid.* 99, I can, if disposed, lace in to sixteen inches.

4. a. *trans.* To thread or interlace (a fabric of any kind) *with* a lace, string, or the like; to embroider. Chiefly in *pa. pple.*

1483 *Wardr. Acc.* in *Antiq. Repert.* (1807) I. 30 The foresaide canapies sowed with oon unce of silk, and lyced with 1 lb. xj unces of grene threde. **1576** TURBERV. *Venerie* 21 You shall haue a net made of strong thread laced with a thong. **1630** R. N. *Camden's Eliz.* II. 68 Silkes, glittering with gold and siluer, eyther imbroydered or laced. **1774** WEST *Antiq. Furness* p. xxii, Marle and soil, laced with fibres of vegetables. **1879** H. GEORGE *Progr. & Pov.* VII. v. (1881) 253 We..lace the air with telegraph wires. **1880** *Paper & Print. Trades Jrnl.* No. 32. 38 Oblong vellum binding laced with cat-gut.

b. To pass (a cord, etc.) in and out *through* a fabric by way of ornament, *through* holes, etc. †Also with *in.* Also *fig. spec.* in Bookbinding, to attach the boards to a volume sewn on cords by passing the slips through holes pierced in them; also with *in.*

1638 SANDERSON *Serm.* (1681) II. 108 To lace in a prayer, a blessing, a thanksgiving. **1818** H. PARRY *Art of Bookbinding* 15 Put the paste-boards on each side of the book ..and mark on them, with a bodkin, the places where the bands are to be drawn or laced in. **1835** J. HANNETT *Bibliopegia* 30 One board is then placed on each side of the volume, even at the head, and marked with a bodkin opposite to the slips intended to be laced in. **1871** *Amer. Encycl. Printing* 74 When the boards are affixed to the volume by means of the bands being passed through holes made in the boards, they are said to be laced in. **1880** ZAEHNSDORF *Art Bookbinding* (1890) xiv. 57 The boards having been squared, they are to be attached to the book by lacing the ends of the cord through holes made in the board. **1946** A. J. VAUGHAN in H. Whetton *Pract. Printing & Binding* xxxi. 382/1 The boards are held to the book by three or more cords. These are the cords upon which the sections have been sewn and the boards are said to be 'laced on'. Should these cords not have been laced through the boards the binding is what is known as a cased book, a cheaper style. **1961** [see LACING *vbl. sb.* 3 e].

c. To intertwine, to place together as if interwoven.

1883 HALL CAINE *Cobw. of Crit.* vi. 176 The poet..lacing and interlacing his combinations of thought and measure. **1889** F. M. PEARD *Paul's Sister* I. viii. 218 Lucy..laced her white fingers across her forehead.

†**d.** ? *nonce-use.* To pierce repeatedly with shots.

1622 R. HAWKINS *Voy. S. Sea* x. 21 Wherevpon the Gunner at the next shott, lact the Admirall through and through.

e. *intr.* Of structures that resemble or suggest lacing: to pass *across* a gap or *about* an object. Also *fig.*, to become entwined.

a **1889** G. M. HOPKINS *Poems* (1918) 76 Her dearness.. more and more times laces round and round my heart. **1899** H. G. WELLS *When Sleeper Wakes* x. 103 The cables and bridges that laced across the aisles were empty. *Ibid.* xxii. 288 A flimsy seeming scaffolding that laced about the great mass of the Council House.

f. *trans.* To pass (film or tape) between the guides and other parts of a projector, tape recorder, or the like so that it occupies the path taken from one spool to the other when the machine is running. Usu. with *up.*

1948 C. A. HILL *Cine-Film Projection* v. 54 Unless the film is your own, you must put its care before everything else, even if you have to stop the show, but this should never be necessary if you always lace the film correctly. **1966** G. SINSTADT *Whisper in Lonely Place* vi. 106 A facia panel opened to reveal a tape deck. He removed a spool from the metal container and laced up the tape. **1968** C. N. G. MATTHEWS *Tape Recording* ix. 80 Press the stop button almost at once or you will come to the end of the tape and have the trouble of lacing it up again. **1974** *Some Technical Terms & Slang* (Granada Television), *Lace up*, to thread film through a machine for projection or transmission.

5. To ornament or trim with lace.

1599 SHAKS. *Much Ado* III. iv. 20 Cloth a gold, and cuts, and lac'd with siluer. **1670** LADY M. BERTIE in *12th Rep. Hist. MSS. Comm.* App. v. 21 The under pettycoatt very richly laced with two or three sorts of lace. **1727** SWIFT *Further Acc. E. Curll* Wks. 1755 III. I. 161 Have not I clothed you in double royal,..laced your backs with gold. **1760** tr. *Keysler's Trav.* II. 354 A chair covered with velvet, and laced with gold. **1841** JAMES *Brigand* xxvi, The king was habited..in black velvet richly embroidered and laced with gold.

6. a. To mark as with (gold or silver) lace or embroidery; to diversify with streaks of colour.

1592 SHAKS. *Rom. & Jul.* III. v. 8 Looke Loue what enuious streakes Do lace the seuering Cloudes in yonder East. *c* **1600** —— *Sonn.* lxvii, That sinne by him aduantage should atchiue, And lace it selfe with his societie. **1605** —— *Macb.* II. iii. 118 Here lay Duncan, His Siluer skinne, lac'd with his Golden Blood. **1602** MARSTON *Antonio's Rev.* I. iii. Wks. 1856 I. 81 The verge of heaven Was ringd with flames, and all the upper vault Thick lac't with flakes of fire. **1648** GAGE *West. Ind.* xvii. (1655) 113 A pleasant and goodly valley, laced with a River. **1850** WHIPPLE *Ess. & Rev.* (ed. 3) I. 280 The gloom of his meditations is laced with light in all directions. **1850** *Beck's Florist* 200 Very smooth, stout petal laced with rosy purple. **1860** KINGSLEY *Misc.* II. 259 A Waterfall of foam, lacing the black rocks with a thousand snowy streams. **1861** L. L. NOBLE *After Icebergs* 67 Boats.. freighted with the browner cod, laced occasionally with a salmon. *Ibid.* 139 The ocean with its waves of Tyrian dye laced with silver. **1923** H. G. WELLS *Men like Gods* I. vi. 89 'Tell me', that engaging phrase, laced his conversation. **1971** *Nature* 2 July 70/2 That work led to two by-products: a Beilby award in 1948 and a fund of sea stories with which to lace his general conversation.

†**b.** *Painting. absol.* To insert streaks of any colour, e.g. white. *Obs.*

1634 PEACHAM *Gentl. Exerc.* 74 It is the best white of all others to lace or garnish, being ground with a weak gumme water.

c. *intr.* Of a flower: To acquire the streaks of colour prized by fanciers. (Cf. LACED *ppl. a.* 4.)

1852 *Beck's Florist* 210 The varieties [of pinks] generally laced very well.

7. To lash, beat, thrash.

1599 [see 3]. **1615** *Band, Ruffe & Cuffe* (Halliw.) 10 If I meet thee, I will lace thee roundly. **1618** FLETCHER *Loyal Subj.* v. iv, He was whipt like a top; I never saw a whore so lac'd. **1692** R. L'ESTRANGE *Fables, Life of Æsop* 11 Go your ways..or I'll lace your coat for you. **1783** AINSWORTH *Lat. Dict.* (Morell) 1, To lace,..*cædo, verbero.* **1847** C. BRONTË *J. Eyre* xxi. (1857) 234 A..switch..waiting to leap out imp-like and lace my quivering palm. **1867** SMYTH *Sailor's Word-bk.*, *Lace*, to beat or punish with a rattan or rope's end.

†**8.** *Cookery.* To make a number of incisions in (the breast of a bird). *Obs.*

1658 T. MAYERNE *Archimag. Anglo-Gall.* No. 36. 33 Take a Wigeon..or Mallard..and with your knife lace them down the brest. *a* **1704** *Compleat Servant-Maid* (ed. 7) 33 Lace down the Breast on both sides. **1796** MRS. GLASSE *Cookery* xxvi. 382 Cut off the legs, lace the breast down each side.

9. To put a 'lace' of spirits (or †of sugar) into (a beverage); to mingle or 'dash' (*with* spirits).

[**1677**: see LACED *ppl. a.*[1] 6.] **1687** MIEGE *Gt. Fr. Dict.* II. s.v., To lace Coffee, *mettre un peu de Sucre dans une tasse de Caphé.* **1815** SCOTT *Guy M.* xi, He had his pipe and his tea-cup, the latter being laced with a little spirits. **1852** THACKERAY *Esmond* I. ix. (1878) 84 Polly loves a mug of ale, too, and laced with brandy. **1881** *Blackw. Mag.* CXXIX. 195 Abraham began by lacing his cups for him. **1898** STEVENSON *St. Ives* 53 A jug of milk, which she had handsomely laced with whiskey after the Scottish manner.

10. *Comb.*, as ***lace-boots.***

1827 *Sporting Mag.* XX. 272 Strong lace-boots coming just over the ancle.

Hence **'lacing** *ppl. a. nonce-use* = INTERLACING. Also **'lacer**, one who laces, in comb. ***tight-lacer.***

1871 *Figure Training* 48 So far as I have observed, tight-lacers are, as a rule, active, brisk, healthy young people. **1873** G. C. DAVIES *Mount. & Mere* xiii. 99 We catch glimpses of it sometimes through the lacing branches.

laced (leɪst), *ppl. a.*[1] [f. LACE *v.* + -ED[1].]

†**1.** Of a plant: Entwined with a climbing plant.

1533 ELYOT *Cast. Helth* III. v. (1541) 60 b, Lased sauerie. **1551** TURNER *Herbal* 90 We call in england sauery that hath doder growinge on it, laced sauery: and tyme that hath the same, laced tyme. **1555** EDEN *Decades* 200 The herbe which we caule lased sauery. **1640** PARKINSON *Theat. Bot.* 1740.

2. Of shoes, etc.: Made to be fastened or tightened with laces.

1676 WISEMAN *Chirurg. Treat.* I. xxiii. 124 A pair of laced Stockings. **1697** *Lond. Gaz.* No. 3275/4 One pair of new Laced Shooes. **1813** J. THOMSON *Lect. Inflamm.* 447 The laced stocking was much used, and is particularly recommended by Wiseman. **1874** T. HARDY *Far fr. Madding Crowd* viii, He wore breeches and the laced-up shoes called ankle-jacks.

3. Ornamented or trimmed with lace: **a.** with edgings, trimmings, or lappets of lace. **b.** with braids or cords of gold or silver lace.

a. 1668 DAVENANT *Man's the Master* II. i. Wks. 1874 V. 23, I left your lac'd linen drying on a line. **1673** E. BROWN *Trav. Germ.*, etc. (1677) 112 Two Feather-Beds, with a neat laced sheet spread over. **1720** *Lond. Gaz.* No. 5881/3 A fine Valencia grounded laced Suit of Night Clothes. **1765** H. WALPOLE *Vertue's Anecd. Paint.* (1786) III. 221 They are commonly distinguished by the fashion of that time, laced cravats. **1873** MISS BROUGHTON *Nancy* I. 82 Mother bends her laced and feathered head in distant signal from the table top.

b. 1665 BOYLE *Occas. Refl.* v. v. (1848) 314 A Lac'd, or an Imbroider'd suit..would, now..make a Man look..like..a player. **1786** MAD. D'ARBLAY *Diary* 12 Aug., We met.. such superfine men in laced liveries, that we attempted not to question them. **1841** CATLIN *N. Amer. Indians* (1844) II. lv. 198 His coat..was a laced frock.

4. Diversified with streaks of colour. Of birds: Having on the edge of the feathers a colour different from that of the general surface. Of a flower: Marked with streaks of colour.

1834 MUDIE *Brit. Birds* I. 74 The principal ones [fancy pigeons] are..the Jacobine, the Laced [etc.]. **1867** TEGETMEIER *Pigeons* xxiii. 177 Examples of very good laced Fan-tails. **1882** *Garden* 7 Oct. 312/2 The edged, tipped, or laced Dahlias require a good deal of shading. **1888** *Poultry* 27 July 377 Hen nicely laced on breast.

†**5.** ***laced mutton*** (slang): a strumpet. *Obs.*

Mutton was used alone in the same sense. The adj. may mean 'wearing a bodice', possibly with a pun on the culinary sense LACE *v.* 8, though the latter is not recorded so early.

1578 WHETSTONE *Prom. & Cass.* I. iii. B iij, And I smealt, he lou'd lase mutton well. **1591** SHAKS. *Two Gent.* I. i. 102. **1599** N. BRETON *Phisition's Let.*, You may..eat of a little warm mutton, but take heede it be not Laced, for that is ill for a sicke body. **1607** R. C. tr. *H. Stephen's World of Wonders* 167 The diuell take all those maried villains who are permitted to eate laced mutton their bellies full. **1694** MOTTEUX *Rabelais* iv. Prol. (1737) p. lxxxiii, With several coated Quails, and lac'd Mutton.

6. Of a beverage: Mixed with a small quantity of spirits. (But see quot. *a* 1700; also 1687 in LACE *v.* 9.)

1677 WYCHERLEY *Pl. Dealer* III. i, Prithee, captain, let's go drink a dish of laced coffee, and talk of the times. *a* **1700** B. E. *Dict. Cant. Crew*, *Lac'd Coffee*, Sugar'd. **1712** ADDISON *Spect.* No. 317 ¶39 Mr. Nisby of opinion that laced Coffee is bad for the Head. **1819** *Anderson's Cumberld. Ball.* 108 Set on kettle, Let aw teake six cups o' leac'd tea. **1886** *Illustr. Lond. News* Summer No. 14/2 He took a sip at his laced coffee.

7. Of the spokes of a bicycle: Set so as to cross one another near the hub.

1885 *Cyclist* 19 Aug. 1107/2, 52in. Rudge bicycle No. 1, laced spokes.

†**8.** ***laced stool***: ? one made with a cane or rush seat, or one with a cloth seat stretched by cords.

1649 in *Bury Wills* (Camden) 212, I give vnto my daughter Anna..a greene chaire and foure laced stooles.

9. ***laced valley*** (Building): a valley between the slopes of two adjoining roofs in which the end tile of each row abuts against a tile-and-a-half tile laid diagonally on the valley board.

1931 C. G. DOBSON *Roof Tiling* iii. 39 No lead is required in a laced valley. **1947** R. GREENHALGH *Mod. Building Construction* II. 582/2 Other methods..give swept and laced valleys.

10. *Comb.*, as ***laced-jacketed***, ***-waistcoated*** adjs.

1748 RICHARDSON *Clarissa* Wks. 1883 VII. 495 A couple of brocaded or laced-waistcoated toupets. **1848** THACKERAY *Van. F.* xlviii, The laced-jacketed band of the Life Guards.

†**laced,** *ppl. a.*[2] *Her. Obs.* Also 5 lassed, 6 lased. [more correctly *lassed*, for *lessed*, pa. pple. of LESS *v.*] Lessened, diminished.

1486 *Bk. St. Albans, Her.* b ij b, A lassed cotarmure is on the moderis parte. **1562** LEIGH *Armorie* (1597) 98 A gentlewoman borne, wedded to one, hauing no cote Armour, they hauing issue a sonne,..The same sonne..may beare her cote armour, during his life, with a difference Cynquefoyle, by the curtesie of armes, and this is called a lased cote armour. **1586** FERNE *Blaz. Gentrie* 66 She must be an heire to her auncestour, or els her issue can not beare the Laced coat.

Lacedæmonian (ˌlæsɪdiːˈməʊnɪən), *a.* and *sb.* [f. L. *Lacedæmoni-us*, Gr. *Λακεδαιμόνιος* (f. *Lacedæmōn*, Gr. *Λακεδαίμων*) + -AN.]

A. *adj.* **a.** Of or pertaining to Lacedæmon (Sparta) or its inhabitants. **b.** Of speech or correspondence = LACONIC. **B.** *sb.* A native of Lacedæmon.

1780 COWPER *Let.* 16 Mar., Wks. 1837 XV. 50 Till your letters become truly Lacedæmonian, and are reduced to a single syllable. **1807** ROBINSON *Archæol. Græca* II. xv. 168 Their clothing was so thin that 'a Lacedæmonian vest' became proverbial. **1870** EMERSON *Soc. & Solit.* iv. 87 If any one wishes to converse with the meanest of the Lacedæmonians. **1900** *Daily News* 15 Mar. 6/3 The 46th owed their name of 'The Lacedemonians' to their colonel's stirring speech on the ancient Spartans.

ˈlace-piece. *Shipbuilding.* [? f. LACE *sb.* 4 + PIECE.] The part of the prow of a wooden vessel above the cut-water and behind the figure-head. Also called *lacing* (see LACING *vbl. sb.* 3 d).

1874 THEARLE *Nav. Archit.* 64 The main rails extended generally from the catheads to the lace piece.

lacerability (ˌlæsərəˈbɪlɪtɪ). [f. next: see -ITY.] The condition of being lacerable.

1847-9 TODD *Cycl. Anat.* IV. 713/1 Simple lacerability is frequently set down to softening.

lacerable (ˈlæsərəb(ə)l), *a.* [ad. late L. *lacerābilis*, f. *lacerāre* to LACERATE. Cf. F. *lacérable.*] That may be lacerated, susceptible of laceration.

1656 in BLOUNT *Glossogr.* **1666** HARVEY *Morb. Angl.* xxii. 51 The Lungs..must necessarily lye open to great..dammages..because of their thin, and lacerable composure. **1835-6** TODD *Cycl. Anat.* I. 346/2 The bronchi are..easily lacerable tubes. **1879-89** J. M. DUNCAN *Lect. Dis. Women* vii. (ed. 4) 40 The uterus..may be extremely thinned and easily lacerable.

lacerant (ˈlæsərənt), *a. nonce-wd.* [ad. L. *lacerant-em*, pres. pple. of *lacerāre* to LACERATE.] Of a sound: Tearing, harrowing.

1888 HOWELLS *Annie Kilburn* xxv, The bell..called the members..with the same plangent, lacerant note that summoned them to worship on Sundays.

lacerate (ˈlæsərət), *ppl. a.* [ad. L. *lacerāt-us*, pa. pple. of *lacerāre* to LACERATE.]

1. Mangled, torn, lacerated. Also *fig.* Distracted.

1542 HEN. VIII *Declar.* 205 Our realme hathe ben for a season lacerate and torne by diuersitie of titles. **1660** F. BROOKE tr. *Le Blanc's Trav.* 281 That this town [Alexandria] should now be brought to so lacerate a condition, that was for many ages one of the most ample. **1805** SOUTHEY *Madoc* II. viii, His hands transfix'd, And lacerate with the body's pendent weight. **1878** SYMONDS *Sonn. Campanella* xxviii, Now stays with limbs dispersed and lacerate.

2. *Bot.* and *Zool.* Having the edge or point irregularly cut or cleft as if torn; jagged.

1776 J. LEE *Introd. Bot.* Expl. Terms 384 *Lacerum*, lacerate, where the Margin is variously divided, as if torn. **1794** MARTYN tr. *Rousseau's Bot.* xxvi. 380 Many varieties..with lacerate leaves and simple ones. **1846** DANA *Zooph.* (1848) 324 Folia thin,..sometimes lacerate.

b. In combining form **lacerato-**; as *lacerato-dentate*, *-subdivided*.

1846 DANA *Zooph.* (1848) 225 Lamellæ thin, lacerato-dentate. *Ibid.* 706 Small;..sometimes lacerato-subdivided.

Hence **ˈlacerately** *adv.*, in a lacerated manner, with laceration.

In recent Dicts.

lacerate (ˈlæsəreɪt), *v.* [f. L. *lacerāt-*, ppl. stem of *lacerāre*, f. *lacer* mangled, torn.]

1. *trans.* To rend, tear, mangle; to tear to pieces, tear up. Also, †to separate by violence.

1592 WILMOT, etc. *Tancred & Gism.* v. i. G 3, The dead corps Which rauenous beasts forbeare to lacerate. **1633** BROME *Antipodes* IV. ix, In signe whereof we lacerate these papers. **1713** DERHAM *Phys. Theol.* II. v. 48 If the Heat breaks through the Water with such fury, as to lacerate, and lift up great quantities or bubbles of Water, it causeth what we call Boyling. **1791** COWPER *Iliad* v. 354 He crush'd the socket, lacerated wide Both tendons. **1798** MARSHALL *Garden.* xviii. (ed. 2) 283 So..the fibres will not be lacerated. **1808** J. BARLOW *Columb.* VII. 232 Shells and langrage lacerate the ground. **1868** FARRAR *Silence & V.* VI. (1875) 107 If they could show you how their feet have been lacerated by the thorns. **1880** *Times* 18 Sept. 9/4 Jagged rocks..will rend and lacerate the helpless being.

2. With immaterial objects and *fig.*; esp., to afflict, distress, harrow (the heart).

c **1645** HOWELL *Lett.* (1650) III. 6 The Wars that have lacerated poor Europe. **1773** JOHNSON *Let. to Mrs. Thrale* 17 Mar., Necessity of attention to the present preserves us..from being lacerated..by sorrow for the past. **1780** —— *Let. to Lawrence* 20 Jan. in *Boswell*, The continuity of being is lacerated. **1863** MISS BRADDON *Eleanor's Vict.* I. ii. 33 How cruelly the old heart was lacerated by that bitter letter. **1871** R. W. DALE *Ten Commandm.* ii. 54 The writers of the New Testament make no attempt to lacerate the heart by insisting on the details of our Lord's sufferings.

Hence **ˈlacerating** *vbl. sb.* and *ppl. a.*

1816 BYRON *Parisina* xx, Scars of the lacerating mind Which the Soul's war doth leave behind. **1872** GEO. ELIOT *Middlem.* lxxxi, Will Ladislaw's lacerating words. **1877** BLACK *Green Past.* vii. (1878) 54 The lacerating of a mother's heart. **1893** *Athenæum* 19 Aug. 263/3 The lacerating pangs of neuralgia.

lacerated (ˈlæsəreɪtɪd), *ppl. a.* [f. LACERATE *v.* + -ED[1].] In senses of the vb. *lit.* and *fig.*

1606 WARNER *Alb. Eng.* XIV. lxxxvii. 358 The lacerated Empire of the Romaines, though with griefe, Disclaim'd the Brutaines. **1612** WOODALL *Surg. Mate* Wks. (1653) 304 Observe in great lacerated wounds, as followeth, &c. **1768** STERNE *Sent. Journ.* (1778) II. 183 (*Bourbonnois*) He finds the lacerated lamb of another's flock. **1809** *Med. Jrnl.* XXI. 209 The following Case of lacerated Urethra. **1818** COBBETT *Pol. Reg.* XXXIII. 238-9 To seize hold of..parcels..of the lacerated country. **1849** MACAULAY *Hist. Eng.* v. I. 536 Under the soothing influence of female friendship, his lacerated mind healed fast. **1879** *St. George's Hosp. Rep.* IX. 364 Large lacerated wound 3 inches long.

b. *Bot.* = LACERATE *a.* 2.

1753 CHAMBERS *Cycl. Supp.* s.v. *Leaf*, *Lacerated leaf.* **1830** LINDLEY *Nat. Syst. Bot.* 101 Stigmas..either 2 and lacerated, or discoid and 4-lobed.

laceration (læsəˈreɪʃən). [ad. L. *lacerātiōn-em*, n. of action f. *lacerāre* to LACERATE. Cf. F. *lacération.*] The action or process of lacerating; an instance of this.

1597 A. M. tr. *Guillemeau's Fr. Chirurg.* 5/2 Throughe laceratione of some vayne or arterye. **1615** CROOKE *Body of Man* 344 The orifice..doth..inlarge it selfe without feare of laceration or tearing. *a* **1631** DONNE in *Select.* (1840) 38 Forbearing all lacerations..and woundings of one another. **1646** SIR T. BROWNE *Pseud. Ep.* II. v. 88 The nitrous..exhalations..force out their way, not only with the breaking of the cloud, but the laceration of the ayre about it. **1731** ARBUTHNOT *Aliments* (1735) 167 The Effects are, Extension of the great Vessels, Compression of the lesser, and Lacerations upon small Causes. **1783** P. POTT *Chirurg. Wks.* II. 26 The difference between dilatation and laceration of the peritoneum. **1846** LANDOR *Imag. Convers.* Wks. II. 236/1 The scars and lacerations on your arms. **1862** H. SPENCER *First Princ.* I. v. §32 (1875) 115 No mental revolution can be accomplished without more or less of laceration.

lacerative (ˈlæsərətɪv), *a. rare.* [f. L. type **lacerātīvus*, f. *lacerāre* to LACERATE.] Tending to produce laceration.

1666 HARVEY *Morb. Angl.* xiii. 32 The continual afflux of lacerative humours. **1879-89** J. M. DUNCAN *Lect. Dis. Women* xviii. (ed. 4) 140 This arises from lacerative injury.

†**lacert**[1]. *Obs. rare.* Also 6 laserte. [ad. L. *lacerta* or *lacertus*, in the same sense.] A lizard.

1382 WYCLIF *Levit.* xi. 30 A lacert, that is a serpent that is clepid a liserd. **1578** BANISTER *Hist. Man* IV. 44 A muscle..of the likenes of the little beast called a Laserte. **1585** H. LLOYD *Treas. Health* B ij, Sprynkle it ouer with the Ashes of a grene Lacerte burnt. **1610** J. DENTON *Acc. Estates in Cumberld.* (1887) 128 His seal was a griphon eating a lacert. **1696** PHILLIPS, *Lacert*,..a Lizard.

†**lacert**[2]. *Obs.* [a. OF. *lacerte*, ad. L. *lacert-us* the fleshy part of the arm (? similative use of *lacertus* lizard; cf. *musculus* muscle, lit. 'little mouse').] A muscle.

c **1386** CHAUCER *Knt.'s T.* 1895 Every lacerte in his brest adoun Is schent with venym and corrupcioun. *c* **1400** *Lanfranc's Cirurg.* 292 If þe hole of þe festre..touche þe place of þe lacertis of þe ers. **1541** R. COPLAND *Guydon's Quest. Chirurg.* C iij b, Lyke as those two beestes [the lizard and mouse] are byg in the middle and sclender towarde the tayle so is the muscle or lacerte. **1586** VIGO *Wks.* 287 b, There is a great lacert which hath two heads and keepeth the bone of the adjutorie that it be not displaced on that side. **1696** PHILLIPS, *Lacert*,..the Brawny part of the Arm.

lacertian (ləˈsɜːtɪən, -ʃən), *a.* and *sb.* [f. L. *lacert-a* lizard + -IAN.] **A.** *adj.* Of or pertaining to the lizards or *Lacertilia*; lizard-like, saurian.

1843 in HUMBLE *Dict. Geol.* **1847** ANSTED *Anc. World* viii. 155 The lacertian type—that exhibited in the lizards of the present day. **1877** DAWSON *Orig. World* xv. 338 The lacertian reptiles.

B. *sb.* A lacertilian; a lizard.

1839 *Penny Cycl.* XIII. 265/2 Under the family name of Lacertians Cuvier arranged—1st. The Monitors..2nd. The Lizards properly so called.

lacertid (ləˈsɜːtɪd). [ad. mod.L. *Lacertid-æ*: see -ID[3].] A lizard of the family *Lacertidæ*.

In some mod. Dicts.

lacertiform (ləˈsɜːtɪfɔːm), *a.* [f. L. *lacerta* lizard + -(I)FORM.] Having the form of a lizard; lacertilian.

1855 in MAYNE *Expos. Lex.*

lacertilian (ˌlæsəˈtɪlɪən), *a.* and *sb.* [f. mod.L. *Lacertili-a* pl. the lizard tribe + -AN.]

A. *adj.* Belonging to the *Lacertilia*. **B.** *sb.* An animal of the order *Lacertilia*.

1854 OWEN in *Circ. Sci.* (*c* 1865) II. 63/2 Lacertilian order. **1881** *Nature* XXIII. 551 Its lacertilian affinities are well shown in its long and rat-like tail.

So **lacerˈtilioid** *a.* = prec. A.

In mod. Dicts.

lacertine (ləˈsɜːtaɪn), *a.* [f. L. *lacert-a* lizard + -INE[1].]

1. = LACERTIAN.

1839-47 TODD *Cycl. Anat.* III. 910/2 The Lacertine Sauria are possessed of an inverted intromittent organ. **1863** *Reader* 31 Oct. 502 The lacertine tail curves round again to the level of the forehead. **1882** *Academy* No. 509. 75 The ornament consists chiefly of serpentine and lacertine creatures interlaced.

2. Of ornament: Consisting of intertwined lizard-like figures.

1863 *Sat. Rev.* 448 A lacertine open-work ornament, terminating in a monster's head. **1886** *Quaritch's Catal. MSS.* 3498 Painted in interlacing or lacertine patterns.

lacertoid (ləˈsɜːtɔɪd), *a.* [f. as prec. + -OID.] Lizard-like; pertaining to the super-family *Lacertoidea* of lizards.

1855 in MAYNE *Expos. Lex.*

†**lacertose, lacertous,** *a. Obs.* Also 5 lacertos, 6 lazartus. [ad. L. *lacertōsus* (OF. *lacertos*), f. *lacertus* LACERT[2]: see -OUS.] Consisting of muscles; having large muscles; muscular.

c **1400** *Lanfranc's Cirurg.* 107 (*Ashm. MS.*) Þe skyn þat is aboue þe brayn panne is lacertose [*Add. MS.* lacertos] and ful of þicke fleisch. **1541** R. COPLAND *Guydon's Quest. Chirurg.* C iij, The other is flesshe musculous or lacertous y[t] is harde as bawme styffe of knotty. **1548-77** VICARY *Anat.* iii. (1888) 25 The Skinne of the head is more lazartus, thicker, and more porrus than any other Skinne of any other member of the body. **1727** BAILEY vol. II, *Lacertose*, having great Brawns, brawny, musculous, sinewy. **1855** MAYNE *Expos. Lex.*, *Lacertosus*, having or full of muscle, lacertous.

lacery (ˈleɪsərɪ). [f. LACE *sb.* + -ERY.] Lace-like work.

1893 LADY BURTON *Life Burton* II. 66 The flutings of the open-work are delicate in the extreme, and the general effect is a lacery of stone.

lacet[1] (ləˈsɛt). [f. LACE *sb.* + -ET[1].] (See quots.)

1882 CAULFEILD & SAWARD *Dict. Needlework*, *Lacet stitch*, another term for Half Stitch. *Lacet work*, this work is made with a braid known as Lacet Braid, which is either of silk or cotton, and woven of various widths and descriptions. **1883** *Standard* 26 June 3/3 'Lacet'..in principle is braid or tape shaped into a design, the 'brides' and pattern supplemented with lace stitches. **1883** *Cassell's Fam. Mag.* July 500/2 The lacet point is a needle-made lace.

‖**lacet**[2] (lase). [Fr., 'lace, hairpin bend'.] A hairpin bend in a road.

1895 S. WEYMAN *Red Cockade* vi. 84 The road there descends not in *lacets*, but straight. **1922** *Glasgow Herald* 18 July 9 A series of lacets brings one to the bleak crest of the Col de Cavolles. **1932** KIPLING *Limits & Renewals* 342 The Massif in Spring, the multiplied lacets Hampered by slips or drifts. **1970** 'S. TROY' *Blind Man's Garden* ix. 116 The Route Napoléon with its frequent *corniche* and *lacet*.

lace-up (ˈleɪsʌp), *a.* (and *sb.*). [LACE *v.* 10.] Of boots or shoes: that are fastened with laces. Also *ellipt.* as *sb.*, a lace-up boot or shoe.

1836 DICKENS *Sk. Boz* (1850) 45/2 To fit a pair of lace-up half-boots on an ideal personage. **1841** J. T. HEWLETT *Parish Clerk* I. 22 A stout pair of lace-ups. **1851-61** MAYHEW *Lond. Labour* III. 410 He wore the heavy high lace-up boots, so characteristic of the tribe. **1889** J. K. JEROME *Three Men in Boat* xi. 170 He would have his lace-up boots. **1951** [see *button-up* s.v. BUTTON *v.* 4]. **1964** *Observer* 15 Nov. 14/4 Girls' shoes are much worse for the feet than the usual boys' lace-up. **1972** R. QUILTY *Tenth Session* 20 Her funny old-fashioned lace-up shoes. **1973** *Times* 7 Nov. 18/3 A..quantity surveyor was clumping along in tan three-inch lace-ups.

lacey, variant of LACY.

lach, obs. variant of LASH, LATCH, LAUGH, LAW.

Lach, L'ach, varr. LECH, LEKH *sb.*[5] and *a.*

lacha, obs. form of LAC[1].

†**ˈlachanize,** *v. Obs. rare*$^{-0}$. [ad. Gr. λαχανίζ-εσθαι to gather vegetables.]

1623 in COCKERAM.

†**lachanopolist.** *Obs. rare*$^{-0}$. [f. Gr. λαχανοπώλ-ης a seller of vegetables (f. λάχανον a vegetable + -πώλης a dealer) + -IST.] A greengrocer.

1656 in BLOUNT *Glossogr.* **1727** in BAILEY vol. II.

†**lachanopoll.** *Obs. rare*$^{-0}$. [ad. Gr. λαχανοπώλης (see prec.).] = prec.

1623 in COCKERAM.

†**lache,** *v. Sc.* and *north. Obs. rare.* Also 6 latche. [ad. OF. *lascher* (F. *lâcher*):—popular L. **lascāre* = class.L. *laxāre*, f. *laxus* loose, LAX.]

a. *trans.* To be careless about, to neglect, slight. **b.** *intr.* To be negligent, to lag, loiter.

a **1400** *Relig. Pieces fr. Thornton MS.* (1867) 13 To lache any gude dedis þat we sall do þat may turne vs till helpe. **1513** DOUGLAS *Æneis* XII. x. 146 And mony tymys hym selvyn hes accusyt, That he sa lang had lachit and reffusyt To ressaue glaidly the Troiane Ene. **1530** PALSGR. 604/1, I latche, I lagge, I tary behynde my company, *je tarde*... You ever latche whan you be sente upon an erande. **1607** MARKHAM *Caval.* (1617) iii. 4 If either of the match horses shall latch or linger behind.

lache, early form of LASH *a. Obs.*, slack.

lache, obs. form of LAC[1], LATCH *v.*

lache, var. LETCH *dial.*, wet ditch, bog.

†**ˈlachedness.** *Obs.* In 5 lachednesse, latchednes, -nesse. [f. **lached*, pa. pple. of LACHE *v.* + -NESS. Cf. *lacheness*, LASHNESS.] Laxness or slackness (of mind); remissness.

1484 CAXTON *Royall Bk.* d vj, After [forgetfulness] cometh latchednes, that maketh a man latchous and appayreth fro day to day so moche that he is al recreant and defayllyng. —— *Ordre of Chyualry* 72 Latchednesse and cowardyse. **1491** —— *Vitas Patr.* (W. de W. 1495) I. xxxvi. 36 aa, Feere of dethe folowyth; Desyre of shrewdnes: Lachednesse of vertue; and wekenesse of courage.

lachenalia (læʃəˈneɪlɪə). [mod.L. (N. J. Jacquin 1787, in *Nova Acta Helvetica* I. 39), f. the name of Werner de *la Chenal* (1736-1800), Swiss botanist + -IA[1].] A small, bulbous plant of the genus so called, belonging to the family

Liliaceæ, native to South Africa, and bearing thick, often spotted leaves, and spikes or racemes of tubular or bell-shaped flowers; also called *Cape cowslip*.

1789 *Curtis's Bot. Mag.* III. 82 Like most of the Cape plants, the *Lachenalia* requires to be sheltered in the winter. **1900** L. H. Bailey *Cycl. Amer. Hort.* II. 866/1 Lachenalias are Cape bulbs that are easily flowered in a cool greenhouse in early spring or even in winter. **1923** *Chambers's Jrnl.* Dec. 786/2 A host of delightful, and to us strange, things—..sombre-hued babianas, and the lachenalias with their weird-spotted foliage. **1961** P. White *Riders in Chariot* viii. 236 A plaster pixie..out on the front lawn, beside the golden cypresses, amongst the lachenalia. **1970** *Guardian* 9 May 9/2 It is more than 200 years since the Cape cowslip was first introduced to England... Lachenalias flower in midwinter.

lacheness, var. lashness *Obs.*, slackness.

laches (ˈlætʃɪz), *sb.* Also 4 lacchesse, 5 latches(se, 7 lasches, lachess, 4–7 lachesse. [a. OF. *laschesse*, AF. *lachesse, laches*, f. OF. *lasche*: see lash *a.* and -ess². For the form cf. *riches*.]

† **1.** Slackness, remissness, negligence; also, an act or habit of neglect. *Obs.*

1362 Langl. *P. Pl.* A. ix. 32 Ther weore the monnes lyf i-lost thorw lachesse [**1377** lacchesse] of himselue. **1390** Gower *Conf.* II. 1 The firste point of slouth I calle Lachesse. *c* **1420** *Govt. Lordships* (E.E.T.S.) 82 Some..engendryn sleuthe and lachesse. **1440** *Promp. Parv.* 284 Latchesse [*v. rr.* lahches, lahchesse], or tarryynge, *mora, tarditas*. **1494** *Will Mongomery* (Somerset Ho.), To pardone me of the laches of my prevy tythes.

2. *Law.* Negligence in the performance of any legal duty; delay in asserting a right, claiming a privilege, or making application for redress.

1574 tr. *Littleton's Tenures* 87 a, No laches may be adjudged by the lawe in him yᵗ hath no discrecion. *a* **1626** Bacon *Maxims & Uses Com. Law* iv. (1630) 23 The reason of these cases is the default and laches of the grantor. **1660** R. Sheringham *King's Suprem. Asserted* iv. (1682) 24 No laches, folly, infancy, or corruption of blood can be judged in him. **1741** Robinson *Gavelkind* II. ii. 172 The Laches of the Husband in gaining an actual Seisin by Entry. **1788** J. Powell *Devises* (1827) II. 261 Though there be no default or laches on the part of the devisee himself, the devise fails. **1818** Cruise *Digest* (ed. 2) IV. 493 The right of renewal may be forfeited by the laches of the tenant, in not applying for a renewal within the time mentioned in the lease. **1845** Stephen *Blackstone* II. 304 It is indeed laid down generally as a maxim, that no laches or negligence shall be imputed to an infant. **1894** *Times* 5 Feb. 3/3 To decide whether the party applying has not, by *laches* or misconduct, lost his right to the writ.

b. *transf.* Culpable negligence in general.

1844 Disraeli *Coningsby* II. i. 58 We may visit on the laches of this ministry the introduction of that new principle and power..Agitation. **1872** Geo. Eliot *Middlem.* lii. (1873) 153 His conduct had shown laches which others..were free from. **1890** 'Rolf Boldrewood' *Col. Reformer* I. 146 If he became temporarily abstracted while musing..the dog..would be sent round..to..warn him of his laches.

† **ˈlaches**, *a.* *Obs.* Also 5 lacches, latches. [alteration of *lache*, lash *a.*, influenced by laches *sb.* or lachous.]

a. Loose, lewd, wanton. **b.** Lax, careless, remiss. Hence † **ˈlachesness**.

c **1425** *St. Mary of Oignies* I. x. in *Anglia* VIII. 145/41 Fonned wymmen..þat wiþ hir vntoune and lacches songes kyndeliþ þe fyre of lecchery. *Ibid.* 146/41 Woo to ȝow þat are lacches, slepynge in softe shetys. ? **1461** *Paston Lett.* No. 428 II. 72 For cause ye wer to laches, and cam not in tyme, the mater yede a mys. **1481–4** *Ibid.* No. 859 III. 279 Her mynde hathe ben other weys ocapyed than as to huswyfery, whyche semyth welle by the latchesnes of the tylthe of her landes. **1543–4** *Act 35 Hen. VIII*, c. 11 §1 Some of the said shiriffes..haue ben negligent and laches.

† **ˈlaches, laˈchesse**, *v.* *Obs.* [f. laches *sb.*]

a. *intr.* To be idle, careless. **b.** *trans.* To neglect, slight. Also with *inf.* as object.

1413 *Pilgr. Sowle* I. xxiv. (1859) 29 He, as a fool, hath lachessed, and lost his tyme in veray vanyte. *c* **1425** *Found. St. Bartholomew's* (E.E.T.S.) 6 Tymorosely he dred to laches the preceptis of the Apostle. *Ibid.* 52 Youre Patrone by specyal priuylege grawntid of God to yow ȝe lacches to calle. **1478** *Paston Lett.* No. 811 III. 216 Let it not be lachesyd, but with effect aplyed now.

laches, obs. form of latch.

‖**Lachesis** (ˈlækɪsɪs). *Zool.* [mod.L., a. Gr. Λάχεσις the name of one of the Fates.] A genus of venomous American snakes of the rattlesnake family (*Crotalidæ*).

1872 Darwin *Emotions* iv. 109 In the Lachesis..the tail ends in a single, large, lancet-shaped point or scale. **1887** *Homeopathic World* 1 Nov. 492 The writer speaks of a firm ..using 250 'Lachesis'..tails per annum.

lachet(t(e, obs. form of latchet.

Lachmann (ˈlaxman). [The name of Karl *Lachmann* (1793–1851), German philologist.] *Lachmann's law*: the rule that in Latin, a short root-vowel in the present-tense stem of a verb is lengthened in the past participle if the present-tense stem ends in a voiced plosive.

[**1850** C. Lachmann *In T. Lucretii Cari De Rerum Natura Libros Commentarius* 54 Participia passiva ea quorum in praesenti consonans est aut liquida aut *s* semi-vocalis, quantitatem praesentis secuntur..contra ubi in praesenti media est, participia producuntur.] **1913** *Classical Rev.* XXVII. 122 It is true that 'Lachmann's Law'.., admittedly impossible as originally stated, was revived in a much modified form by Pedersen. **1928** *Language* IV. 181 (*title*) Lachmann's law of vowel lengthening. **1965** W. S. Allen *Vox Latina* 70 The same evidence indicates that Lachmann's Law also applies before *s* in the subjunctive *adāxim*..as against *effĕxim*. **1970** *Harvard Stud. Classical Philol.* LXXIV. 58 Kuryłowicz therefore saw correctly..that a morphophonemic solution was indicated; that Lachmann's law was not a phonetic rule. **1973** W. S. Allen *Accent & Rhythm* 18 Thus, referring to the Latin phenomenon of 'Lachmann's Law' (whereby e.g. *făcio* forms a past participle *fāctus*, but *ăgo* forms *āctus*), Kiparsky ..suggests that it can be accounted for by introducing the presumed Latin vowel-lengthening rule V→long/—*g* before, rather than after, the Indo-European consonant-assimilating rule C→voiceless/—*t*.

† **ˈlachous**, *a.* *Obs.* In 5 lacheous, latchous. [f. *lache*, lash *a.* + -ous.] Negligent. Hence † **ˈlachousness**, remissness, neglect.

1484 Caxton *Royall Bk.* d v, Whan he is slawe, latchous and slowful to do wel. —— *Ordre of Chyualry* 45 In the a squyer whyche arte latchous and slowe to be a knyght. **1496** *Will Huse* (Somerset Ho.), Lacheousnes & slownes of my labours. **1502** *Ord. Crysten Men* (W. de W. 1506) II. vii. 102 Unclennes is a slouth and lachousnes to accomplysshe ye commaundementes of god.

† **lachrymable, lacrymable**, *a.* *Obs.* [ad. L. *lacrimābilis*, f. *lacrimā-re* to shed tears.]

1. Meet for tears or weeping; lamentable.

1490 Caxton *Eneydos* vii. 32 To make hir to ouerthrowe & to brynge hir in-to exyle lacrymable. **1527** *St. Papers Hen. VIII* I. 228 The hevy and lacrymable successe of Rome. **1560** Rolland *Crt. Venus* I. 359 To vthers lufe is richt Lacrymabill. **1594** *2nd Rep. Dr. Faustus* in Thoms *E.E. Prose Rom.* (1858) III. 373 The most lachrimable sight. **1648** J. Quarles *Fons Lachrym.* A 7 Never were.. Lamentations more requisite than in these Lachrymable Times.

2. Expressive of mourning; tearful.

1609 J. Davies (Heref.) *Holy Roode* (Grosart) 28/1 In Grones, and Sighes, and Lachrimable Noise. **1635** Heywood *Hierarchie* III. (1655) 158 Musicke can shew us which are the lacrymable notes.

† **lachrymabund**, *a.* *Obs.*⁻⁰ [ad. L. *lacrimābundus*, f. *lacrimā-re*: see prec.] 'Weeping ripe, big with tears' (Bailey vol. II, 1727).

‖**lachryma Christi** (ˈlækrɪmə ˈkrɪstaɪ). Also 7 lachrymæ Christi, and *simply* 9 lacrima, 8 *pl.* lacrimæ. [L. = It. *lagrima* (or *lagrime*) *di Cristo* Christ's tear (or tears).] A strong and sweet red wine of southern Italy.

[**1611** Coryat *Crudities* (1776) II. 72 Their *Lagryme di Christo*..so toothsome and delectable to the taste.] **1670–81** Blount, *Glossogr.*, *Lachrymæ Christi*. **1731** Fielding *Author's Farce* II. i, Tokay I have drank, and Lacrimæ I have drank. **1820** *Blackw. Mag.* VIII. 44 The Parsons should grow misty On good *Lac Virginis*, or *Lachryma Christi*. **1842** Lytton *Zanoni* I. iii, The old lácrima, a present from the good Cardinal. **1880** *Macm. Mag.* XLI. 237 The 'red fat sweet and gratefully poignant wine'..called Lachryma Christi.

lachrymal (ˈlækrɪməl), *a.* and *sb.* Also 6 lachrimall, 6–7 lachrymall, 8– lacrimal, 8–9 lacrymal. [ad. med.L. *lacrimālis, lachrymālis* (Lanfranc), f. L. *lacrima, lacruma*, OL. *dacruma*, cognate with Gr. δάκρυ a tear. Cf. OF. *lacrimel, lachrymal* (F. *lacrimal*).

The *ch* of the prevailing spelling of this and the related words is due to the med.L. practice of writing *ch* for *c* before Latin *r*; cf. *anchor, pulchritude, sepulchre*. The *y*, in med.L. a mere graphic variant of *i*, has been retained in mod. Eng. orthography from the erroneous notion that *lacrima* is an adoption of Gr. δάκρῡμα. The etymologically correct form *lacrimal* is now usual in scientific use.]

A. *adj.*

1. Of or pertaining to tears; *occas.* characterized by, or indicative of, weeping. Of a vase: Intended to contain tears.

1803 Jane Porter *Thaddeus* (1809) III. iii. 70 A lachrymal scene. **1809** W. Irving *Knickb.* (1861) 149 Collecting the drops of public sorrow into his volume, as into a lachrymal vase. **1809** Syd. Smith *Methodism* Wks. 1854 I. 299 The lachrymal and suspirious clergy. **1837** Marryat *Dog-Fiend* ix, Small-bones made up a lachrymal face. **1855** Bain *Senses & Intell.* II. iv. §22 (1864) 297 The lachrymal effusion is an accompaniment of grief.

2. *Anat.* and *Phys.* Applied to the organs concerned in the secretion of tears, as ***lachrymal canal, duct, gland, sac***, etc., and to structures forming part of these organs, as ***lachrymal bone, sinus***, etc. ***lachrymal fistula***, one situated between the skin of the cheek and the interior of the lachrymal sac.

[*c* **1400** *Lanfranc's Cirurg.* 252 Fistula lacrimalis.] **1597** A. M. tr. *Guillemeau's Fr. Chirurg.* 40/1 Archigenes hath cauterised the lachrimall fistles with liquefacted leade. **1601** Holland *Pliny* II. 367 The fistulaes which are between the lachrymall corners of the eies and the nose. **1696** Phillips, *Lachrymal-Point* [= L. *punctum lachrymale*], a Hole in the Bone of the Nose, by which the matter that makes Tears passes to the Nostrils. **1727** Bradley *Fam. Dict.* I. s.v. *Eye*, It..readily closes up all lacrimal Fistulas. **1780** Blizard in *Phil. Trans.* LXX. 239 The internal surface of the lachrymal sac. **1787** Hunter *Ibid.* LXXVII. 438 The lachrymal gland is small. **1800** *Med. Jrnl.* III. 78 From these lachrymal ducts..the tears flow through the ducts of the nasal bones. **1855** Holden *Human Osteol.* (1878) 101 The lachrymal bone is situated..on the inner wall of the orbit. **1868** *Nat. Encycl.* I. 803 Many antelopes possess lachrymal or sub-orbital sinuses. **1872** Huxley *Physiol.* ix. 235 The secretion of the lachrymal canal is carried away as fast as it forms. **1879** Harlan *Eyesight* ii. 27 The lachrymal apparatus consists of the gland for secreting tears and the passages for draining them off. **1913** *Gray's Anat.* (ed. 18) 960 The lacrimal [*ed. 17 (1909)*: lachrymal] ducts or canals.. commence at minute orifices, termed *puncta lacrimalia*. **1913** *Cunningham's Text-bk. Anat.* (ed. 4) 824 The lacrimal gland..is supplied by the sympathetic and lacrimal nerves. [*Ed. 3 (1909)*: lachrymal.] **1919** *Lancet* 10 May 792/2 During the stage of surgical anæsthesia the lacrymal glands cease to secrete. **1919** *Physiol. Abstr.* IV. 183 [*From abstract of article containing the prec. quot.*] The lacrimal gland in anæsthesia. **1950** D. B. Kirby *Surg. Cataract* xii. 276/1 Care must be exercised to prevent the solution from going through the lacrimal duct to the nose. **1954** S. Duke-Elder *Parsons' Dis. Eye* (ed. 12) xxxiii. 543 The lacrimal apparatus consists of the lacrimal glands and the lacrimal passages. [*Edd. 1 (1907)–11 (1948)*: lacrymal.] **1968** Passmore & Robson *Compan. Med. Stud.* I. xxiv. 54/2 The cornea is continually bathed by the secretion of the lacrimal glands.

3. *nonce-uses.* Resembling a tear or tears.

1607 Brewer *Lingua* IV. i. H, A great quantity of drop shot both round and lachrimall. **1829** Galt in *Blackw. Mag.* XXVI. 143 The milk was pale and lachrymal.

B. *sb.*

1. a. *pl.* The lachrymal organs.

1541 R. Copland *Guydon's Quest. Chirurg.* P j b, Lykewyse they [cauteres] be applyed to yᵉ lachrymalles to consume the superflue flesshe. **1844** [see lachrymatory B. 2].

b. *Anat.* A lachrymal bone.

1872 Mivart *Anat.* 85 The lachrymals are small bones, one of which is placed at the anterior part of the inner wall of each orbit.

2. *pl.* Lachrymal performances; fits of weeping.

1753 Richardson *Grandison* (1781) VI. xlv. 291 Something..that made her laugh in the midst of her *lacrymals*. **1789** Charlotte Smith *Ethelinde* (1814) IV. 28 Do have done with these perpetual lachrymals. **1931** M. Summers *Supernatural Omnibus* 31 What an event [in Dickens] was a funeral from a house! The way to all these sadly sentimental lachrymals had been paved before by the lugubrious cortèges of the time of Anne.

3. = lachrymatory *sb.* 1.

1769 R. Griffith *Gordian Knot* II. 16 Certain urns, stiled Lachrymals. **1839–40** W. Irving *Wolfert's Roost* (1855) 94 His rooms were decorated with..old vases, lachrymals, and sepulchral lamps. **1851** Mrs. Browning *Casa Guidi Wind.* 31, I would but turn these lachrymals to use, Fill them with fresh oil.

lachrymary (ˈlækrɪmərɪ), *a.* and *sb.* [f. L. *lacrim-a* tear + -ary¹ and ².] = lachrymatory.

1705 Addison *Italy* (1733) 188 What a Variety of Shapes in the Ancient Urns, Lamps, Lachrymary Vessels [etc.]. **1854** Lady Lytton *Behind the Scenes* I. II. iv. 242 The aforesaid capacious handkerchief..might have served as the general lachrymary of a joint stock widows' company.

lachrymate (ˈlækrɪmeɪt), *v.* Also lacrimate. [f. L. *lacrimāre* to weep: see -ate³.] (See quots. 1623 and 1656.) Now current chiefly in scientific use (cf. lachrymal *a.* and *sb.*), with the sense: to discharge moisture from the eyes. Hence **ˈlachrymating** *vbl. sb.* and *ppl. a.*

1623 Cockeram, *Lachrymate*, to lament, to bewaile. **1656** Blount *Glossogr.*, *Lachrymate*, to weep, to drop with moisture.

1922 *Encycl. Brit.* XXXII. 110/2 If a sufficient number of lachrymating grenades could be thrown. **1944** *Brit. Jrnl. Ophthalm.* XXVIII. 330 The patient lacrimates when he salivates. **1962** W. K. McEwen in H. Davson *Eye* III. x. 272 In man there is the added ability to weep, or lacrimate, which is an excessive outpouring of the lacrimal gland. **1964** *Amer. Jrnl. Ophthalm.* LVIII. 1056/1 Tension in lacrimating patients is more easily measured with the Schiøtz tonometer.

lachrymation (lækrɪˈmeɪʃən). [ad. L. *lacrimātiōn-em*, n. of action f. *lacrimāre*, f. *lacrima* tear.] The excretion or shedding of tears; weeping.

1572 *Scholeho. Wom.* 767 in Hazl. *E.P.P.* IV. 134 Mighty Sampson two wiues had,..The first him caused by lacrimacion His probleme to hear. **1651** Biggs *New Dispens.* 181 There doth weep forth the lachrymations of an ichorous substance. **1863** R. F. Burton *Abeokuta* I. 204 The priest will squirt capsicum..into the eyes of the accused, and lacrymation proves guilt. **1872** Darwin *Emotions* vi. 171 A strong light acting on the retina, when in a normal condition, has very little tendency to cause lacrymation.

lachrymator (ˈlækrɪmeɪtə(r)). Also lacrimator. [f. *lachrymat-*, *lacrimat-* (in lachrymatory *a.* and *sb.*, etc.) + -or.] Any substance which causes irritation and copious watering of the eyes when it comes into contact with them (in the form of a gas, spray, dust, or the like).

1918 *Jrnl. Amer. Med. Assoc.* 30 Nov. 1823/1 Lacrimators (acetone, xylene or benzene bromid). **1922** *Encycl. Brit.* XXXII. 111/2 Lachrymators, on account of the extreme sensitiveness of the eye, can produce an effect in extraordinarily weak concentrations. **1948** *Biochem. Jrnl.* XLII. p. xxvi, The '—SH' theory provides an explanation for the existence of two main groups of lachrymators: (a) substances containing a halogen atom in some such group as $-CH_2Cl$ together with a neighbouring keto or other group which makes the halogen 'positive', (b) substances containing a $-CH=CH-$ group, also with a neighbouring keto or other group which polarizes the double bond. **1963** *Times* 25 Apr. 6/4 Chloracetophenone, a lacrimator in adequate concentrations, had toxic effects.

lachrymatory ('lækrɪmətərɪ), *a.* and *sb.* [ad. L. type **lacrimātōrius*, f. *lacrimāre*: see LACHRYMATION.]

A. *adj.* Of or pertaining to tears; tending to cause a flow of tears. Of a vase: Intended to contain tears.

a **1849** POE *Loss of Breath* Wks. 1864 IV. 303 A thousand vague and lachrymatory fancies took possession of my soul. **1851** HAWTHORNE *Twice-t. Tales* II. xiii. 210 Drinking out of..a lachrymatory vase, or sepulchral urn. **1873** HERSCHEL *Pop. Lect.* vii. §3. 328 The presence in the lacrymatory secretion of extremely minute globular particles of equal size. **1916** *Yorks. Post* 21 July 5/5 A violent artillery preparation with asphyxiating and lachrymatory shells. **1935** *Brit. Med. Jrnl.* 20 July 133/1 Lachrymatory gases were here and off again unless there was a continual rain of tear-gas shells. **1971** *Agric. & Biol. Chem.* (Tokyo) XXXV. 1831 The lachrymatory character and the pungent flavor [of onions] had been decreased by γ-irradiation.

B. *sb.*

1. A vase intended to hold tears; applied by archæologists, with doubtful correctness, to those small phials of glass, alabaster, etc., which are found in ancient Roman tombs.

1658 SIR T. BROWNE *Hydriot.* 23 No..Lachrymatories, or Tear-Bottles attended these rural Urnes. *a* **1711** KEN *Hymnoth.* Poet. Wks. 1721 III. 72 Magdalen's Tears..her Lachrymatory daily fill'd. **1807** G. CHALMERS *Caledonia* I. I. iv. 147 There have been dug up here..a Roman lachrymatory, and also a pig of lead. **1842** CARLYLE in *Mem. Ld. Tennyson* (1897) I. 214 There is in me what would fill whole Lachrymatories, as I read.

2. *humorously.* A pocket-handkerchief.

1825 *New Monthly Mag.* XIII. 208 Women will be stationed in the pit with white cambric lachrymatories, to exchange for those which have become saturated with the tender tears of sympathy. **1844** *Fraser's Mag.* XXX. 331/1 Our lachrymals were unhumected, our lachrymatories never called into requisition.

†**lachryme.** *Obs. rare*$^{-1}$. In 5 lacryme. [ad. OF. *lacrimer*, ad. L. *lacrimāre*.] *intr.* To weep.

1490 CAXTON *Eneydos* xxvii. 104 Thenne she began somwhat for to lacryme & syghe vpon the bed.

†**lachry'mental,** *a. Obs. rare*$^{-1}$. In 7 -all. [f. L. *lacrima*, after the analogy of adjs. ending in *-mental*.] Mournful, tearful.

1625 A. HOLLAND in J. Davies *Scourge of Folly* (Grosart) 81 Diuers deadly elegies, compil'd..In Lamentable Lachrymentall rimes.

lachrymiform ('lækrɪmɪfɔːm), *a. Bot.* and *Zool.* Also 9 *incorrectly* **lachrymæform**. [f. L. *lacrim-a* tear + -(I)FORM.] Having the form of a tear; tear-shaped.

1866 *Treas. Bot.* 654/1 *Lachrymæform*, tear-shaped; the same as Pear-shaped, except that the sides of the inverted cone are not contracted.

lachrymist ('lækrɪmɪst). [f. L. *lacrima* tear + -IST.] One addicted to tears; a weeper.

1620 J. MELTON *Astrolog.* 18 These Gold-engendring Chymists, are Archymists, rather Lechymists, and make all those that follow them, Lachrymists. **1660** tr. *Paracelsus' Archidoxis* I. x. 135 The Lacrymists, that gape on Gold. **1848** *Blackw. Mag.* LXIV. 229 Yet the man who could move an audience to tears..was any thing but a lachrymist by temperament.

lachrymogenic (ˌlækrɪməʊ'dʒɛnɪk), *a.* [f. LACHRYM(ATION + -O + -GENIC.] Giving rise to lachrymation.

1921 *Chem. Abstr.* XV. 398 (*heading*) Estimation of the lachrymogenic power of irradiating substances by the threshold method. **1971** *Jrnl. Agric. & Food Chem.* XIX. 269/2 Thioethanol, thioacetone, thiobutanal, and thiohexanal *S*-oxides were also synthesized and their lachrymogenic properties were evaluated.

ˌ**lachrymo-'nasal,** *a.* [f. *lachrymo-*, used as comb. form of L. *lacrima* tear + NASAL.] Pertaining both to the lachrymal and the nasal bone.

1883 MARTIN & MOOLE *Verteb. Diss.* 105 Anterior to the orbito-temporal fossa the triangular lachrymo-nasal opening.

lachrymose ('lækrɪməʊs), *a.* [ad. L. *lacrimōsus*, f. *lacrima* tear.]

†**1.** Having the nature of tears; liable to exude in drops. *Obs.*

1661 LOVELL *Hist. Anim. & Min.* 264 As for wax, its begotten of the lachrymose and gummose parts of plants.

b. *Bot.* Bearing tear-like bodies.

1871 M. C. COOKE *Handbk. Brit. Fungi* I. 113 *Agaricus* (*Hebeloma*) *fastibilis*,..gills broad, edges often lachrymose.

2. Given or ready to shed tears. Of the eyes: Suffused with tears.

1727 BAILEY vol. II, *Lacrymose*, full of Tears, sorrowful. **1812** *Examiner* 23 Nov. 737/1 What [is there] in my Lord Eldon but a lachrymose impotence? **1815** T. L. PEACOCK *Nightmare Abb.* (1817) 94 A very lachrymose and morbid gentleman of some note in the literary world. **1858** THACKERAY *Virgin.* lxix. (1878) 565 The eyes that were looking so gentle and lachrymose but now, flame with sudden wrath. **1897** *Allbutt's Syst. Med.* IV. 383 Disease of this nature is sometimes attended with lachrymose depression.

b. Of a tearful character; calculated to provoke tears; mournful.

1822 M. A. KELTY *Osmond* I. 89, I want something now in the way of sentiment; tender, lachrymose. **1858** *Sat. Rev.* VI. 331/2 Lachrymose doggrel. **1884** *Manch. Examiner* 1 Nov. 5/1 Mr. Maciver dealt with the subject in a lachrymose and declamatory fashion.

Hence **'lachrymosely** *adv.*; **lachry'mosity**, the quality or condition of being lachrymose.

1834 CAMPBELL *Mrs. Siddons* II. xiii. 391 As I cannot bear to think of her gloomily, I have not written her life lachrymosely. **1839** LADY LYTTON *Cheveley* (ed. 2) I. i. 3 Those gentlemen who write the most liberally and lachrymosely about the errors of female education. **1880** VERN. LEE *18th C. in Italy* vi. 270 The dullness, the vulgarity, the falseness, the lachrymosity of the *Sposa Persiana*.

lachrymous ('lækrɪməs), *a. rare.* [f. L. *lacrima* tear + -OUS. Cf. OF. *lacrimeus*.] †**a.** Of an ulcer: Exuding drops like tears (*obs.*). **b.** = LACHRYMOSE 2.

1490 CAXTON *Eneydos* viii. 35 Lacrymous and playnynge sorowes. **1612** WOODALL *Surg. Mate* Wks. (1653) 216 An excellent remedy against any lacrimous or weeping ulcers. **1866** J. B. ROSE tr. *Ovid's Fasti* II. 399 Bidding performed by servants lachrymous.

‖**lachsschinken** ('laxsʃɪŋkən). Also erron. lachschinken. [G., f. *lachs* salmon + *schinken* ham.] Cured and smoked loin of pork.

1923 A. WARD *Encycl. Food* 463 *Lachsschinken*, two trimmed, boneless pork-loins, mild sweet-cured, faced and pushed into large beef casings, sixteen inches or so in length, pressed, tied with strings, dried, and lightly smoked. **1937** *Atlantic Monthly* Mar. 267, I burst into enthusiasm on the subject of *Lachs-schinken* (which, as the name indicates, is a sort of ham that both looks and tastes like salmon). **1958** *Catal. County Stores, Taunton* June 5 Continental sausages. .. Lachsschinken, eaten cold, finely sliced—4 ozs. 2/7. **1965** *New Statesman* 11 June 914/2 'Sausages of all kinds not in airtight containers'—which include the mortadella and the salami, the krakauer and lachsschinken. **1971** *Sunday Times* (Colour Suppl.) 27 June 50/3 *Lachschinken*: pork fillet, cured, smoked and rolled in a thin casing of pork back fat. Serve with fresh fruit as an alternative to *prosciutto*.

lacht, Sc. f. LAW, LOW *a.*; pa. t. of LATCH.

'lachter. *Sc.* [? cogn. w. ON. *lagð-r* of the same meaning.] **a.** A flock of wool. **b.** A lock of hair.

1776 *Bothwell* in *Herd's Collect.* I. 84 He gied me..Three lauchters of his yellow hair. **1821** *Blackw. Mag.* Jan. VIII. 402/2 Keeking aye in the maiden's face ilka lauchter he lays down.

lachter, Sc. form of LAUGHTER^{2}.

laciness ('leɪsɪnɪs). [f. LACY *a.* + -NESS.] Lace-like quality or effect.

1903 *Westm. Gaz.* 9 July 4/2 Flowered silk, or embroideries, or chiffon, and laciness.

lacing ('leɪsɪŋ), *vbl. sb.* [f. LACE *v.* + -ING^{1}.]

1. The action of the vb. LACE, in various senses.

c **1386** CHAUCER *Knt.'s T.* 1646 Gigginge of sheeldes, with layneres lacinge. **1577** FENTON *Gold. Ep.* 13 To breake your fast standing and whilest your armour is in laceing. **1599** *Life Sir T. More* in Wordsworth *Eccl. Biog.* (1853) II. 114 What paines she took..with lacinge in of her bodie. **1630** J. TAYLOR (Water P.) *Wks.* II. 248/2 For cutting, edging, stiffning, and for lacing. **1821** BYRON *Juan* IV. lxxxvi. (MS.), To help the ladies in their dress and lacing. **1871** *Figure Training* 75 The lace..at the first lacing was moderately tight. **1888** *Lockwood's Dict. Mech. Engin.*, *Lacing*, the union by means of laces of the ends of leather belting used in driving machines. **1893** H. VIZETELLY *Glances Back* I. ii. 41 The sound lacing which the young rascal should inevitably receive.

2. *concr.* or quasi-*concr.* **a.** That which laces or fastens; a fastening, tie; a shoe-string. **b.** Ornamental braiding for men's clothes (cf. LACE *sb.* 5). **c.** The coloured border on the petal of a flower; also, a similar marking on the feathers of birds. **d.** A small quantity of spirits mingled with some beverage.

a. *a* **1400** *Sir Perc.* 744 He ne couthe never fynd righte The lacynge of his wede. *c* **1400** *Apol. Lollards* 34 Neþer is no man worþi to opun þe lasing of His scho. **1591** R. PERCIVAL *Sp. Dict.*, *Abrochadura*, lacing of a coate, *strictura*. **1860** H. STUART *Seaman's Catech.* 48 Studding sails are generally brought to with a lacing. **1881** *Confess. Frivolous Girl* 120 Canvas shoes with colored lacings.

b. **1593** *Rotherham Feoffee's Acc.* 24 Paid..for fowertene yeardes of lacing,..[etc.] 2*s.* 10*d.* **1611** COTGR., *Passement*, ..a lace, or lacing. **1760–72** H. BROOKE *Fool of Quality* (1808) I. 27 He..began to cut, and rip, and rend away the lacings of his suit, without sparing cloth or seam. **1897** *Westm. Gaz.* 9 Nov. 3/2 The half-state uniforms are made of royal blue cloth, with gold lacings.

c. **1850** *Beck's Florist* 144 Pinks whose delicate lacings are spangled with the early dew. **1882** *Garden* 25 Mar. 202/1 [The] colour and lacing [of a Gold-laced Polyanthus].

d. **1862** *Athenæum* 27 Sept. 396 So long as it [water] be.. united with a proper 'lacing' of wine or brandy.

3. In various technical uses: **a.** *Bridge-building.* (See quot. 1885.) **b.** *Mining.* (See quot. 1883.) **c.** *Math.* A complex of three or more endless cords so arranged that they cannot be separated, though no two are interlinked. **d.** *Naut.* and *Ship-building.* (See quots. *c* 1850 and 1867.) **e.** *Bookbinding* (see quots. *a* 1877 and 1961, and LACE *v.* 4 b).

c **1850** *Rudim. Navig.* (Weale) 128 *Lacing*, one of the principal pieces that compose the knee of the head, which runs up to the top of the hair bracket, and to which the figure and rails of the head are secured. **1867** SMYTH *Sailor's Word-bk.*, *Lacing*, rope or cord used to lace a sail to a gaff, or a bonnet to a sail. *a* **1877** KNIGHT *Dict. Mech.* II. 1244/1 *Lacing*,..securing the book to the sides by carrying the bands or slips through perforations in the boards. **1883** GRESLEY *Gloss. Coal Mining*, *Lacing*, 1. timbers placed across the tops of bars or caps to secure the roof between the gears. 2. Strips or light bars of wrought iron bent over at the ends and wedged in tight between the bars and the roof. **1885** WADDELL *Syst. Iron Railr. Bridges Japan* 246 *Lacing*, a system of bars, not intersecting each other at the middle, used to connect the two channels of a strut in order to make them act as one member. **1961** T. LANDAU *Encycl. Librarianship* (ed. 2) 189/1 *Lacing-in*, in hand-binding, in the 'extra' style, the method of attaching boards to the sewing cords, which are laced through holes in the boards.

4. *attrib.*, as *lacing-bar*, *-silk*; **lacing course** *Building*, a special course built into an arch or wall in order to bond different parts together and give added strength; **lacing-cutter**, **lacing-hook** (see quot. 1884).

1558 *Richmond. Wills & Invent.* (Surtees) 127, iij ounce of lasing silke. **1884** KNIGHT *Dict. Mech.* Suppl., *Lacing Cutter* (Leather), a knife with a gage, to preserve the width of the strip. *Lacing Hook* (Boot), hooks on the margins of the upper, over which a lace is caught side by side alternately to close the opening of the shoe. **1885** WADDELL *Syst. Iron Railr. Bridges Japan* 246 *Lacing Bar*, a bar belonging to a system of lacing. **1886** H. C. SEDDON *Builder's Work* i. 66 It is better..to build the arch in half-brick rings, with a few bonding or lacing courses built in at intervals, to tie the separate rings together. **1899** *Notes on Building Construction* (rev. ed.) I. iii. 46 Walls such as those built with flints, or other small stones,..are frequently strengthened by building in with them lacing courses, consisting of horizontal bands either of ashlar, coursed rubble, or brickwork. **1947** R. GREENHALGH *Mod. Building Construction* I. 229/1 In arches of very wide span, the different rings are sometimes bonded to each other by inserting courses of stretchers in the depth of the arch at intervals. These courses are termed lacing courses.

‖**lacinia** (lə'sɪnɪə). Pl. **laciniæ**. [L. = lappet.]

1. *Bot.* A slash in a leaf, petal, etc.; the slender lobe thus produced.

1699 *Phil. Trans.* XXI. 65 Their..Leaves are..divided into narrower and deeper Laciniae or Jags. **1760** J. LEE *Introd. Bot.* I. xii. (1765) 27 The Variations of the Corolla in respect to Number concern either Petals, or Laciniæ, Segments. **1830** LINDLEY *Nat. Syst. Bot.* 190 Five nerves.. continued through the axes of the laciniæ. **1880** C. R. MARKHAM *Peruv. Bark* 191 Flowers..white, with rose-coloured laciniæ.

2. *Ent.* The apex of the maxilla, esp. when slender.

1826 KIRBY & SP. *Entomol.* III. 446 Slender *laciniæ* or lappets fringed with hairs. **1856–8** W. CLARK *Van der Hoeven's Zool.* I. 161 Proboscis short, with..sulcated lacinia. **1877** HUXLEY *Anat. Inv. Anim.* vii. 402 The galea and lacinia of the maxilla.

laciniate (lə'sɪnɪət), *a. Bot.* and *Zool.* Also 9 *erron.* **lacinate**. [f. prec. + -ATE^{2}.] Cut into deep and narrow irregular segments; jagged, slashed.

1760 J. LEE *Introd. Bot.* III. v. (1765) 179 *Laciniate*, jagged; when they are variously divided into Parts, and those Parts in like manner indeterminately subdivided. **1794** MARTYN tr. *Rousseau's Bot.* xxiv. 337 Five or six lobes, laciniate on their edges. **1816** T. BROWN *Elem. Conchol.* 154 Lacinate. **1849–52** TODD *Cycl. Anat.* IV. 1202/1 Having the branches..finely laciniate. **1856–8** W. CLARK *Van der Hoeven's Zool.* I. 800 Phasianella..Body margined by a laciniate membrane. **1870** HOOKER *Stud. Flora* 16 *Chelidonium majus*..A variety occurs in cultivation with laciniate petals.

b. *Comb.*, as *laciniate-leaved*; also in pseudo-L. combining form, *laciniato-denticulate*, *-palmate*.

1846 DANA *Zooph.* (1848) 322 Lamellæ crowded.. laciniato-denticulate. *Ibid.* 543 Fronds stout, multifid, laciniato-palmate. **1870** HOOKER *Stud. Flora* 174 The 'Cut-leaved Elder', a laciniate-leaved variety.

laciniated (lə'sɪnɪeɪtɪd), *ppl. a.* Also 8 **lacinated**. [f. as prec. + -ED^{1}.] = prec.

1668 WILKINS *Real Char.* II. iv. 118 That [*sc.* Aspin] whose leaves are laciniated. **1734** DERHAM in *Phil. Trans.* XXXVIII. 465 A Bank of Vapours, not curved at Top..but lacinated, or broken. **1748** HILL *Hist. Anim.* 124 The subulated, echinated and laciniated Cochlea. **1806** J. GALPINE *Brit. Bot.* 16 With many-cleft laciniated pencil-form lobes. **1850** *Beck's Florist* 189 The pinnules deeply laciniated and tufted.

lacini'ation. [f. LACINIA: see -ATION.] A cutting into laciniæ or fringes.

1846 DANA *Zooph.* (1848) 196 The slender laciniations of the upper margin of the crest-like folia are half or three-quarters of an inch long.

laciniform (lə'sɪnɪfɔːm), *a. Ent.* [f. LACIN-IA + -(I)FORM.] (See quot.)

1826 KIRBY & SP. *Entomol.* IV. 332 Laciniform..when they [the base-covers] are long, of an irregular shape, and appear like lappets on each side of the trunk.

laciniolate (lə'sɪnɪələt), *a. Bot.* [f. mod.L. **laciniola*, dim. of LACINIA + -ATE^{2}.] Delicately fringed; having minute laciniæ.

In mod. Dicts.

laciniose (lə'sɪnɪəʊs), *a.* [ad. L. *laciniōsus*: see next.] = LACINIOUS 1.

In some recent Dicts.

†**la'cinious,** *a. Obs.* [ad. L. *laciniōsus* (sense 2), f. *lacinia*: see LACINIA and -OUS.]

1. *Bot.* Having many laciniæ.

1657 Tomlinson *Renou's Disp.* 317 The first [Mugwort] is latifolious, lacinious and marginally dissected.

2. *fig.* Full of folds or windings; hence, overloaded, prolix, redundant.

1652 Urquhart *Jewel* 113 The sweet Labyrinth and mellifluent aufractuosities of a Lacinious delectation. **1653** Gataker *Vind. of Annot.* 132 Mr. Swan returns a long lacinious answer, winding and turning to and fro.

‖**lacinula** (lə'sɪnjʊlə). *Bot.* [mod.L., dim. of lacinia.] A diminutive lacinia; the inflexed point of the petals of the *Umbelliferæ*.

1856 in Henslow *Dict. Bot. Terms.*

Hence **la'cinulate** *a.* [-ate [2]], furnished with lacinulæ.

1855 in Mayne *Expos. Lex.*

lacis ('læsɪ). [Fr.] A kind of lace made by darning patterns on net.

1865 F. B. Palliser *Hist. Lace* ii. 14 The volume..is that of the Venetian Vinciolo..dating from 1587... The work is in two books. The first of Point coupé... The second of Lacis, or subjects in squares, Fig. 3, with counted stitches, like the patterns for worsted-work of the present day. **1875** *Encycl. Brit.* XIV. 183/2 The productions of this art, which has some analogy to weaving, in the early part of the 16th century came to be known as..'lacis' in France... With the development of the renaissance of art, free flowing patterns and figure subjects were introduced and worked in lacis. **1953** [see filet 1]. **1963** *Times* 1 June 11/6 One development was the introduction of all-white lacis, such as was recorded in the bed furnishings of Mary Queen of Scots with ornament built up in darning stitches on a basis of open-mesh net.

lack (læk), *sb.*[1] Forms: 3–5 **lac**, 4–6 **lak(e**, (5 **laak**), 5–6 **lakke**, 5–7 **lacke**, 6–8 *Sc.* **laik**, 4– **lack**. [Early ME. *lac* corresponds to MLG. *lak*, MDu. *lac* deficiency, fault, blame (mod.Du. *lak* masc. calumny). Cf. lack *a.*]

†**1.** A defect; failing; a moral delinquency, fault, offence, crime; *rarely*, a natural blemish. ***to give the lack of***: to impute the fault of. *Obs.*

c **1200** *Trin. Coll. Hom.* 258 Fader & sune & holi gost on god in þrimnesse inne þe nis lac ne lest auȝ alle holinesse. *c* **1330** R. Brunne *Chron.* (1810) 29 Constantyn..Brak his feaute sone, of treson it is lak. *c* **1375** *Sc. Leg. Saints, Egipciane* 657 And for my lake be put away. *c* **1386** Chaucer *Merch. T.* 955 If I do that lakke..in the nexte ryuer do me drenche. **1390** Gower *Conf.* I. 99 She hath no lith without a lack. *a* **1400** *Octouian* 1394 And all maner of hors he knew, Bothe the lake and the vertu. *c* **1420** Lydg. *Assembly of Gods* 369 For in hys talkyng no man cowde fynde lak. **1443** *Pol. Poems* (Rolls) II. 213 Esaw wolde have founde a laak, Cause that Jacob was put out of prees. *c* **1450** *Mirour Saluacioun* 2744 That man..to the ordeignaunce of godde of his synne gyves the lakke. **1532** More *Confut. Tindale* Wks. 507/1 Yet haue I before at large opened you yᵉ lackes therof. **1555** Latimer *Serm.* (1584) 294 The lacke is not in the law, but in vs. **1598** Q. Eliz. *Plutarch* ii. 123 The Curius more profit yeldz his foes than good vnto himself; that telleth them ther Lacks.

†**b.** ***without lack***: without defect, flaw, or fault, whether physical or moral; also, without fail. *Obs.*

c **1300** *Havelok* 191 He garte the erl suere, That he sholde yemen hire wel, Withuten lac. *c* **1330** R. Brunne *Chron.* (1810) 95 Fair scho was..& gode withouten lak. *a* **1340** Hampole *Psalter* xvi. 4 þou alowed it as wiþouten lake [*v.r.* lacke]. *c* **1380** *Sir Ferumb.* 1589 A tok a spere wiþ-oute lak. *c* **1400** *Sowdone Bab.* 1185 The botelles of bawme withoute lake. *c* **1440** *York Myst.* xi. 109, I am thy lorde, with-outyn lak. *c* **1460** *Urbanitatis* 86 in *Babees Bk.*, Lette þy Ryȝth sholdur folow his bakke, For nurtur þat ys, with-owten lakke.

†**2.** *Sc.* A fault that brings disgrace; disgrace, reproach, shame. (Often coupled with *shame*.) *Obs.*

c **1375** *Sc. Leg. Saints, Ninian* 644 For thru it haldine wes þar name in gret lak and in schame. *c* **1470** Henry *Wallace* ix. 820 Off us be found no lak eftir to reid. **1513** Douglas *Æneis* ii. x. 46 Schamfull hir to sla, Na victory, bot lak following alswa. **1560** Rolland *Crt. Venus* i. 455 To schame & lak thir twa thair seruand drawis. **1603** *Philotus* lvii, To slay ane taine man, war bot lack allace.

†**b.** Blame, censure for a fault. *Obs.*

14.. *How Good Wife taught Dau.* 230 in *Barbour's Bruce*, The cumpany quhar thai tak Sall neuir chap for-outen lak. **1542** Udall *Erasm. Apoph.* 174 He dyd not stayne ne putte to lacke or rebuke hys royall autoritie in geuynge sentence of iudgement.

3. Deficiency, want, need (*of* something desirable or necessary); also, an instance of this. In early use often *pl.*

c **1398** Chaucer *Fortune* 5 But natheles, the lak of hir favour Ne may nat don me singen [etc.]. *c* **1430** Lydg. *Min. Poems* (Percy Soc.) 158 Lak of discrecioun causeth gret blyndenesse. *c* **1449** Pecock *Repr.* 108 Manye vn-helpis and manye lackis of helpis. **1500–20** Dunbar *Poems* xxi. 13 Lak of spending dois him spur. **1534** More *Comf. agst. Trib.* iii. xxii. (1847) 285 That affection happeth in very few, but that either the cause is lack of faith, or lack of hope, or finally lack of wit. **1549** J. Cheke in *Lett. Lit. Men* (Camden) 8 Among other lacks I lack painted bucrum. **1570–6** Lambarde *Peramb. Kent* (1826) 3 The lacke [of barley] is more commonly supplied with oates. **1588** *Exhort. Subjects* in *Harl. Misc.* (Malh.) II. 105 Remember the remedies, supply the lakes, remove the impediments. **1603** Shaks. *Meas. for M.* v. i. 68 Many that are not mad Haue sure more lacke of reason. **1652** Brome *Mad Couple* iii. Wks. 1873 I. 48 The ablest [servant] that any Lady of your lacks and longings ever bestow'd a favour on. **1663** Butler *Hud.* i. i. 441 We shall not need to say what lack Of Leather was upon his Back. **1753** *Life J. Frith* (1829) 75 He being driven to necessity and lack of money, was forced [etc.]. **1849** Ruskin *Sev. Lamps* i. §11. 21 It is less the mere loss of labour that offends us, than the lack of judgment implied by such loss. **1874** Blackie *Self-Cult.* 64 No genius and no talent can compensate for the lack of obedience.

b. ***no lack*** (***of***): Enough, plenty (of).

c **1305** *Land Cokayne* 29 þer n'is lac of met no cloþ. **1611** Bible *Exod.* xvi. 18 He that gathered litle, had no lacke. **1833** Ht. Martineau *Tale Tyne* vi. 109 There was no lack of loyalty among our people. **1840** Dickens *Barn. Rudge* x, There seems to be no lack in this great mansion. **1870** Max Müller *Sci. Relig.* (1873) 101 There is no lack of materials for the student of the Science of Religion.

c. ***for*** (occas. ***by, from, through***) ***lack of***: for want (*rarely* loss) of.

c **1386** Chaucer *Manciple's Prol.* 48 On the Manciple he gan nodde faste For lakke of speche. —— *Sqr.'s T.* 422 She swowneth now and now for lakke of blood. *c* **1470** Henry *Wallace* v. 827 For lak off blud he mycht no forthir gang. **1526** *Pilgr. Perf.* (W. de W. 1531) 147 b, Yᵉ many for lacke of mortifyenge tasteth not of this feest. *c* **1560** A. Scott *Poems* (S.T.S.) xiii. 16 Throw laik of speich I thoill ryᵗ grit distress. **1674** Playford *Skill Mus.* i. 61 He..slew some of them with his fist for lack of another weapon. **1775** Burke *Sp. Conc. Amer.* Wks. III. 88 By lack whereof they have been oftentimes touched and grieved by subsidies given. **1781** Burns '*Tibbie, I hae seen the day*', For laik o' gear ye lightly me. **1816** Scott *Tales My Landlord* Ser. i. Introd., Those who came to my Landlord for liquor, and went thirsty away for lack of present coin. **1884** Bosanquet *Lotze's Metaph.* 226 A fourth dimension, now unknown to us from lack of incitement to construct it.

d. *Proverb.*

1546 J. Heywood *Prov.* (1867) 8 In loue is no lacke. **1619** Drayton *Idea* lix, In Love there is no lack, thus I begin.

4. The state of being in want; indigence, straitened circumstances. Also, the condition of wanting food; famine, starvation.

1555 L. Digges (*title*) A prognostication of right good effect..contayninge..rules to iudge the wether,..with a brefe iudgement for euer of Plentie, Lacke, Sickenes [etc.]. **1563** *Homilies* ii. *Agst. Gluttony* (1859) 306 Pinched by lacke and poverty. **1568** T. Howell *Newe Sonets* (1879) 156 Where one wee see to be preferde, three liue for lacke as starued. *a* **1605** Polwart *Flyting w. Montgomerie* 737 Woodtyk, hoodpyk, ay like to liue in lacke! **1681** W. Robertson *Phraseol. Gen.* (1693) 797 Lack or want, *indigentia*.

†**5.** The fact that a person or thing is not present; absence. *Obs.*

1548 Udall, etc. *Erasm. Par. Matt.* xviii. 92 So greued with the lack of one lost shepe. **1575** *Laneham's Let.* (1871) 53 Not so goodly az Paradis..yet better a great deel by the lak of so vnhappy a tree. **1596** Lady Pembroke *Lay Clorinda* 89 in Spenser's Wks. (Globe) 563/1 Whilest we here, wretches, waile his private lack. **1605** Verstegan *Dec. Intell.* iv. (1628) 98 Shewing the lacke of the matter or substance which it hath lost.

6. quasi-*concr.* **a.** The thing wanted. *rare.*

1549 Cheke *Hurt Sedit.* (1641) 28 That men..needing divers things, may in litle roome know where to finde their lack. **1599** Hakluyt *Voy.* II. ii. 65 Knowing that out of his countrey the Realme of England might be better serued with lackes, then hee in comparison from vs. **1848** W. H. Bartlett *Egypt to Pal.* vi. (1879) 138 One great lack here and elsewhere is the green sod.

†**b.** The weight deficient in a specified quantity; short weight. *Obs.*

1782 *Phil. Trans.* XCIII. 135 The average of weight hath been only 2 grains 153 decimals lack per lb. which was paid by the moneyers at the scale.

†**lack**, *sb.*[2] *Obs.* [See alack *int.* and good *a.* 6 b.] Only in the exclamation ***good lack!***

1638 [see good *a.* 6 b]. **1672** H. More *Brief Reply* 134 Good lack! **1775** Sheridan *St. Patrick's Day* ii. iii, Good lack, good lack, to think of the instability of human affairs. **1777** —— *Sch. Scandal* iii. ii, Good lack, you surprise me! **1807** Crabbe *Par. Reg.* iii. 822 'Good-lack', quoth James, 'thy sorrows pierce my breast'.

†**lack**, *sb.*[3] *Obs. rare*⁻¹. [ad. F. *lacs*, a special use of *lacs* noose.] An instrument formerly in use for extracting a fœtus; = fillet 2 c.

1754–64 Smellie *Midwif.* I. 250 Different practitioners had recourse to different kinds of fillets or lacks.

†**lack**, *a.* *Obs.* Also 5 **lakk**, 6 **lacks**. [ad. or cogn. with ON. *lak-r*:—OTeut. **lako-*, cogn. with lack *sb.*[1] The mod.Du. *lak* insipid, luxurious, may possibly be connected.]

1. Of a quantity in measurement: Short, wanting.

1479 *Surtees Misc.* (1890) 20, vj yerdes, ane ynche lakk. **1589** *Acc. Bk. W. Wray* in *Antiquary* XXXII. 79 A yeard lacke nale tufte taffete, iijs. iij*d*. **1644** Nye *Gunnery* 2nd Alphab. (1670) 16 Your degree of Random is four and three quarters, or five lack one quarter.

b. ***little lack of***: not far short of (a specified condition).

1579 Spenser *Sheph. Cal.* May 264 Sicke, sicke, alas, and little lack of dead.

2. Missing.

1591 Harington *Orl. Fur.* xvii. xxviii, When he found his wife and men were lack.

3. *Sc.* Deficient in quality, inferior, poor.

14.. *How Good Wife taught Dau.* 56 in *Barbour's Bruce*, And hear honour, bettir thing, And lawar stat, lakar clething. *c* **1470** Henry *Wallace* ix. 98 The lakest ship, that is his flot within, May sayll us doun on to a dulfull ded. **1501** Douglas *Pal. Hon.* i. 534 Diuers vthers..Quhais lakkest weed was silkis ouir brouderit. **1582–8** *Hist. Jas. VI* (1804) 245 As to the laik money printed at his awin comand before he was Regent.

lack (læk), *v.*[1] Forms: 2 **lacen**, 3 **laken**, 4 **lac**, 4–6 **lakyn**, **lake**, **lakke(n**, **-in**, **-yn**, 4–7 **lak**, **lacke**, (6 **lacce**), 6–7 *Sc.* **laik**, 4 **lacky** (*s.w. dial.* 8 **lackee**, 9 **-y**); *pa. pple.* 4 **i-lakked**. [f. lack *sb.*[1] or *a.* Cf. MDu. *laken* to be wanting, to blame (mod.Du. to blame, despise, condemn).]

†**1. a.** *intr.* To be wanting or missing; to be deficient in quantity or degree. In early use const. with dative or *to*. *Obs.* (But ***to be lacking*** is current; see lacking *ppl. a.*)

a **1175** *Cott. Hom.* 233 Wat lacede ȝeu an alle mire rice þat ȝie [etc.]. *c* **1250** *Gen. & Ex.* 1231 Tid-like hem gan ðat water laken. **1362** Langl. *P. Pl.* A. v. 238 And thauh my lyflode lakke letten I nulle That vche mon schal habben his. *c* **1386** Chaucer *Sec. Nun's T.* 498 Ther lakketh no thyng to thyne outter eyen That thou nart blynd. *c* **1430** *Pilgr. Lyf Manhode* iv. ix. (1869) 181 A crooked staf me lakketh for to cholle with. *c* **1460** Fortescue *Abs. & Lim. Mon.* xi. (1885) 137 A subsidie..as shall accomplishe that wich shall lakke hym off such livelod. **1515** More in Grafton *Chron.* (1568) II. 758 His drift covertly conveyed, lacked not in helpyng forth his brother Duke of Clarence to his death. *a* **1548** Hall *Chron., Hen. VI* 154 b, In him lacked neither good will nor courage. **1588** A. King tr. *Canisius' Catech.* 85 Ye..effectual grace of sa gret a sacrament can na wayis laik heirin. **1611** Bible *Gen.* xviii. 28 Peraduenture there shall lacke fiue of the fiftie righteous. **1849** C. Bronte *Shirley* iv. 36 A man in whom awe, imagination and tenderness lack.

†**b.** To be a defaulter, to be absent. *Obs.*

c **1465** *Pol. Rel. & L. Poems* 5 Many yeeris hast þou lakkyd owte of this londe. **1467** *Eng. Gilds* (1870) 386 Yf eny of the xlviij lakke or dissease.

†**c.** To be faulty or defective; to offend; (with *dative*) to offend against. *Obs.*

13.. *E.E. Allit. P.* B. 723 Fyfty..þat neuer lakked þy laue, bot loued ay trauþe. *c* **1450** Holland *Howlat* 994 Bot gif I lak in my leid, that nocht till allow is.

¶**d.** = lag *v.* (Cf. also lache *v.* b.)

1775 S. Thayer *Jrnl.* (1867) 14 The people are very weak and begin to lack in the rear, being so much reduced with hunger and cold.

2. a. *trans.* To be without, not to have; to have too little of; to be destitute of or deficient in.

c **1320** R. Brunne *Medit.* 883 Ful feyn þey wulde Ihesu down taken But strengþe and ynstrumentys bothe þey lakkyn. **1470–84** Malory *Arthur* iv. x, For though I lacke wepen, I shall lacke no worship. **1484** Caxton *Fables of Alfonce* iv, Thow rendrest not to me al my gold..For of hit I lack four hondred pyeces. **1526** *Pilgr. Perf.* (W. de W. 1531) 1 b, Ascrybe it..to my insuffycyency and ignoraunce, whiche lacke both lernynge and eloquence. **1573** *Satir. Poems Reform.* xxxix. 76 Not laiking na thing that belangit to weir. **1588** Udall *Diotrephes* (Arb.) 10 Rather than hee [Judas] woulde lacke money he would sell Iesus Christ himselfe. **1611** Bible *Luke* viii. 6 It withered away, because it lacked moisture. *c* **1680** Beveridge *Serm.* (1729) I. 183 What can they lack who live with him? **1807** Crabbe *Par. Reg.* i. 73 Learning we lack, not books. **1813** Scott *Rokeby* i. xii, I could have laughed—but lacked the time. **1833** Mrs. Browning *Prometh. Bound* Wks. 1850 I. 140, I lack your daring. **1860** Tyndall *Glac.* i. xii. 88 Though not viscous, the ice did not lack the quality of 'adhesiveness'. **1870** Mrs. Riddell *Austin Friars* iv, Luke Ross felt his life lacked something. **1880** Miss Braddon *Just as I am* vii, Dorothy's face lacked colour and brightness.

†**b.** with *cannot*: To do or go without. *Obs.*

1551 Ascham *Let. to E. Raven* 20 Jan., Wks. 1865 I. ii. 256, I was afraid when I came out of England to miss beer; but I am afraid when I shall come into England, that I cannot lack this wine. **1590** Spenser *F.Q.* i. vi. 22 The forlorne mayd did with loves longing burne, And could not lacke her lovers company. **1592** Babington *Notes on Gen.* vii. (1639) 29 The raine from aboue and the fountaines beneath are things wee cannot lacke.

†**c.** To perceive the absence of; to miss. *Obs.*

1604 Shaks. *Oth.* iii. iii. 318 Poore Lady, shee'l run mad When she shall lacke it. **1605** —— *Macb.* iii. iv. 84 My worthy Lord Your Noble Friends do lacke you. **1607** —— *Cor.* iv. i. 15, I shall be lou'd when I am lack'd.

3. To need, stand in need of. †Frequent in the salesman's cry ***what d'ye lack?*** (*obs.*)

1530 Palsgr. 601/1, I lacke, I want a thynge. **1535** Coverdale *James* i. 5 Yf eny of you lacke wyszdome let him axe of God. **1547–8** *Ordre of Commvnion* 7 Lackyng comfort or counsaill. **1614** B. Jonson *Barth. Fair* ii. i, What do you lacke? what is't you buy? what do you lack? rattles, drums, halberts, [etc.]. **1668** Dryden *Evening's Love* v. i. Wks. (1883) III. 363 To draw us in, with a what-do-you-lack, as we passed by.

4. *intr.* To be short *of* something (now *rare*). Also with *for* and †*simply*, to be in want.

1523 Ld. Berners *Froiss.* I. cxviii. 141, I shall go abrode ..and gette vytayle..for within a whyle we shall lacke. **1560** Rolland *Crt. Venus* i. 33, I alone of sic curage did laik. **1599** Marston *Sco. Villanie* ii. v. Wks. 194 Liu'd he now, he should lack, Spight of his farming Oxe-stawles. **1611** Bible *Prov.* xxviii. 27 He that giueth vnto the poore, shall not lacke. **1809** E. S. Barrett *Setting Sun* III. 144 Though individuals may lack of breeches. **1892** 'Mark Twain' *Amer. Claimant* 40 Here's hoping he'll never lack for friends. **1894** *Outing* (U.S.) XXIV. 87/1 Coffee..we were compelled to crush, lacking of a coffee mill. **1898** Skeel & Brearley *King Washington* (1899) 170 He was one of the many who had lacked for partners. **1906** E. Phillpotts *Portreeve* ii. iv. 154 The outward signs that she had marked upon him did not lack for inner causes.

†**5. a.** *trans.* To find 'lacks' or faults in; to find fault with, abuse, blame, reproach, vituperate. Also *absol.* *Obs.* (*Sc.* and *north. dial.*)

1340 Hampole *Pr. Consc.* 797 He loves men þat in ald tyme has bene, He lakes þa men þat now are sene. **1377** Langl. *P. Pl.* B. xi. 2 Thanne Scripture scorned me..And lakked me in Latyne. **1393** *Ibid.* C. xvi. 78 Me is loþ..to lacky eny secte. *a* **1425** Wyntoun *Orig. Cron.* ix. xiii. 1475 Yhe wene to lak, bot yhe commend. *c* **1475** *Rauf Coilȝear* 87 First to lofe, and syne to lak, Peter! it is schame. **1496** *Dives & Paup.* (W. de W.) v. iv. 200/1 The flaterer lacketh and bacbyteth al tho that he hateth. **1535** Stewart *Cron. Scot.*

(1856) II. 102 In euerie land with all leid we are lakkit. **1558** Q. KENNEDY *Compend. Tract.* in *Wodrow Soc. Misc.* (1844) 98 Love or lack, prayse or condempne. *a* **1605** MONTGOMERIE *Misc. Poems* xiii. 17 Thy leiving no man laks.

†**b.** *to lack* (gerundial inf. passing into an adj. phrase): to blame, blameworthy. *Obs.*

Scott seems to have taken the phrase to mean 'wanting', on the analogy of *to seek.*

a **1300** *Cursor M.* 9037 Quilk er to lac, quilk er to luue, þair aun werckes will þam proue. *c* **1330** R. BRUNNE *Chron.* (1810) 194 He sais behind þi bak..Wordes þat er to lak. *c* **1480** *Lytylle Childr. Bk.* 76 in *Babees Bk.*, Ne drynk behynde no mannes bakke, For yf þou do, thow art to lakke. [**1814** SCOTT *Ld. of Isles* II. xxvii, If Bruce shall e'er find friends again..Old Torquil will not be to lack With twice a thousand at his back. **1828** —— *F.M. Perth* xiii, Your house has been seldom to lack, when the crown of Scotland desired ..wise counsel.]

†**6.** In weaker sense: To depreciate, disparage, 'run down'. *Obs.* (Chiefly *Sc.*)

1377 LANGL. *P. Pl.* B. xv. 198 As a lyoun he loketh there men lakketh his werkes. *c* **1400** *Gamelyn* 276 Felaw he seyde why lakkest thou his ware. *c* **1470** HENRY *Wallace* VIII. 906 Thocht he wes best, no nothir lak we nocht. **1513** DOUGLAS *Æneis* I. Pref. 275 Na man wil I lakkin or despyse. **1533** GAU *Richt Vay* 17 Thay that lichtlis and lakkis their nichburs guidis to oders. **1691** in RAY *S. & E.C. Words* 104. **17..** RAMSAY *The Cordial* st. 1 Is that the thing ye're laking?

Proverb. **1546** J. HEYWOOD *Prov.* (1867) 70 Better leaue then lacke. **1598** BARRET *Theor. Warres* VI. i. 224.

7. *Comb.* in various adjs. and sbs. indicating the absence or want of what is signified by the second member, as ***lack-beard***, ***-brain***, ***-grace***, ***-mind***, ***-sense***, sbs.; ***lack-laughter***, ***-life***, ***-linen***, ***-pity***, ***-spittle***, ***-thought*** adjs.; ***lack-learning***, ***-love*** adjs. and sbs.; **lack-all**, one who is in want of everything; hence ***lack-allism*** (nonce-wd.); †**lack-looks**, a woman who is wanting in good looks; **lack-stock** (*nonce-wd.*), one who has no money in stocks. Also LACKLAND, LACK-LATIN, LACK-LUSTRE.

1850 CARLYLE *Latter-d. Pamph.* i. 46 Vagrant *Lackalls, foolish most of you, criminal many of you, miserable all. **1886** W. GRAHAM *Social Problem* 7 Both the labourers and the lack-alls who do not labour. *Ibid.* 8 The great intermediate and most anxious class, whose condition shades into *lack-allism. **1599** SHAKS. *Much Ado* v. i. 196 For my Lord *Lacke-beard there, he and I shall meete. **1596** —— *1 Hen. IV*, II. iii. 17 What a *lacke-braine is this? **1817** COLERIDGE *Biog. Lit.* 277 We should..consider it as a *lack-grace returned from transportation. **1850** BLACKIE *Æschylus* I. 48 Many force *Lack-laughter faces to relax Into the soft lines traced by joy. **1590** DAVIDSON *Reply to Bancroft* in *Wodrow Soc. Misc.* 516 So is there no shaft that oftner flieth out of their bag against others, than the boult of *lack learning. **1602** T. CAMPION *Art Eng. Poesie* in *Ascham's Scholem.* (1863) 261 In those lack-learning times..began that..kind of Poesie..which we abusively call Rime and Meeter. **1765** BLACKSTONE *Comm.* I. 176 The name of *parliamentum indoctum*, or the lack-learning parliament. **1837** SIR F. PALGRAVE *Merch. & Friar* i. (1844) 16 Our common nomenclature still bears testimony to the lack-learning of ancient times. **1889** J. HIRST in *Archæol. Instit. Jrnl.* No. 181. 32 The dreamy, *lack-life, symbolic and ideal creations of the Assyrians. **1597** SHAKS. *2 Hen. IV*, II. iv. 134 You poore, base, rascally, cheating, *lacke-Linnen-Mate. **1861** K. H. DIGBY *Ch. St. John* (1863) 325 The fustian rascal and his poor lack-linen mate. **1618** *Owles Alm.*, Our *lacke-lookes and barren-beauties. **1590** SHAKS. *Mids. N.* II. ii. 77 Pretty soule, she durst not lye Neere this *lacke-loue, this kill-curtesie. **1871** R. ELLIS tr. *Catullus* lxxxi. 3 Only the lack-love signor, a wretch from sickly Pisaurum. **1887** H. KNOLLYS *Life Japan* 17 *Lack-minds..whose stagnant curiosity is satisfied by staring over the ship's side. **1881** CHR. ROSSETTI *Pageant*, etc. 122 Self stabbing self with keen *lack-pity knife. **1881** J. M. BROWN *Stud. Life* 9 Many a *lacksense it has led to waste his patrimony. *a* **1834** COLERIDGE in *Blackw. Mag.* CXXXI. (1882) 123/2, I have not words to express the chopped straw, *lack-spittle, dry-chewing feel I experience in reading them. **1820** SOUTHEY *Lett.* (1856) III. 212 We poor lacklands and *lackstocks who have to earn our livelihood. **1829** —— *Epist. Anniversary* 17 Sauney and sentimental, with an air So *lack-thought and so lack-a-daisycal.

lack (læk), *v.*[2] *Obs.* exc. *dial.* Also 9 **lacky**. *trans.* To beat.

?*c* **1475** *Hunt. Hare* 141 Thei leyd at her with mallus strong As fast as they might lacke. **1847** HALLIWELL, *Lacky*, to beat severely. *Devon.*

[**lack**, *v.*[3], a spurious word explained in some Dicts. 'to pierce the hull of (a vessel) with shot', is evolved from *lact* = 'laced' (in quot. for LACE *v.* 4 d), misunderstood as 'lacked' by Kingsley (*Westward Ho!* xx and xxviii).]

lack, lacka, obs. forms of LAC[1] and LAKH.

lackadaisical (lækə'deɪzɪkəl), *a.* Also 8 **-daysical**, 9 **-daisycal**. [f. LACKADAISY + -IC + -AL[1].] Resembling one who is given to crying 'Lackaday!'; full of vapid feeling or sentiment; affectedly languishing. Said of persons, their behaviour, manners, and utterances.

1768 STERNE *Sent. Journ.* (1775) I. 61 (*Pulse*), Sitting in my black coat, and in my lack-adaysical manner, counting the throbs of it. **1807** ANNA PORTER *Hungar. Bro.* vi. (1832) 77 What do you cast up your lack-a-daisical eyes at, Forshiem? **1818** HAZLITT *Eng. Poets* vi. (1870) 146 No man has written so many lack-a-daisical..verses as he. **1834** BECKFORD *Italy* I. 357 Lackadaisical loitering on the banks of the Arve. **1852** R. S. SURTEES *Sponge's Sp. Tour* lxviii. 384 The..lackadaisical misses whom he could love or not, according to circumstances. **1870** L'ESTRANGE *Miss Mitford* I. v. 149 They [Miss Seward's Letters] are affected, sentimental, and lackadaisical to the highest degree.

Hence ˌ**lackadaisi'cality, lacka'daisicalness**, the quality of being lackadaisical; ˌ**lacka'daisically** *adv.*, in a lackadaisical manner.

1823 *New Monthly Mag.* VII. 169 They conceive the eternal..lackadaisicalities touching the matter of Walter Scott's 'more last dying words'. **1828** MISS MITFORD *Village* Ser. III. (1863) 59 Her father's odd ways..and her mother's odd speeches, and her sister's lack-a-daisicalness. **1829** LYTTON *Devereux* II. iv, 'I think I am', reiterated the dead man, very lackadaisically. **1851** D. JERROLD *St. Giles* xii. 121 He stands..with one leg drawn up, and his ten fingers interlaced lackadaisically. **1887** *Pall Mall G.* 17 Sept. 13/2 If Ministers refuse replies..Don't charge them with.. lackadaisicality.

lackadaisy ('lækəˌdeɪzɪ), *int.* (*sb.*, *a.*) [Extended form of LACKADAY.] = LACK-A-DAY, hence as *sb.* the utterance of the interjection; an instance of this; as *adj.* = LACKADAISICAL.

1748 SMOLLETT *R. Random* I. viii. 56 She exclaimed, 'Good lack-a-daisy! the rogue is fled!' **1792** WOLCOT (P. Pindar) Wks. III. 38 The Swain, in Lack a daisy sort, Held down his head as sorry for't. **1796** M. EDGEWORTH *Parent's Assistant* (ed. 2) I. 164 The carpenter..said '*lack-a-daisy!*' when he saw that the old theatre was pulled down. **1825** R. P. WARD *Tremaine* II. xii. 121 She, with many lack-a-daisies, begged her to come in and dry herself. **1847** HALLIWELL, *Lackadaisy*, alack; alas!

'**lack-a-day**, *int. Obs.* or *arch.* [Aphetized form of ALACK-A-DAY.] = ALACK-A-DAY.

1695 CONGREVE *Love for L.* II. ii, Good lack-a-day, ha, ha, ha. **1728** MORGAN *Algiers* I. vi. 189 Lack-a-Day, Sir, everything will be dwindled away to just nothing. **1719** FIELDING *Tom Jones* x. ix, Good-lack-a-day! why there now, who would have thought it! **1779** MAD. D'ARBLAY *Diary* Nov., I wish all the cloth were like him; but, lackaday! 'tis no such thing. **1820** W. TOOKE tr. *Lucian* I. 455 Lackaday; they are gone every mother's son. **1849** MISS MULOCK *Ogilvies* xvi. (1875) 127 Ah, lack-a-day! it's a troublesome world!

lackage ('lækɪdʒ). In 9 **laccage**. [f. LACK *v.* + -AGE. (Cf. Anglo-Latin *lacta* in Du Cange.)] Deficiency of coins below standard weight.

1840 RUDING *Annals Coinage* I. 283 In his [Edw. IV's] fifth year it was enacted [in the Irish parliament] that the noble of due weight should be of the value of ten shillings.. and that for laccage of weight in such pieces of gold they should be refused. *Ibid.* 284 It was enacted, in his seventh year, that the laccage in weight should not be a cause for refusing the money, but that the value of such laccage should be paid in current silver.

lacke, obs. form of LAC[1], LACK.

lacked (lækt), *ppl. a. rare.* [f. LACK *v.*[1] + -ED[1].] That one has been (long) without.

1590 SPENSER *F.Q.* I. iii. 27 My long lacked Lord.

†'**lacken**, *v. Obs. rare*$^{-1}$. [f. LACK *sb.* + -EN[5].] *trans.* To depreciate, disparage.

1674 N. FAIRFAX *Bulk & Selv.* To Rdr., If I give out I set highly by it, I should lacken it as much by making such a Fondling the Penman of it.

†'**lacker**. *Obs.* [f. LACK *v.*[1] + -ER[1].] One who lacks. **a.** One who blames or disparages. **b.** One who is missing or wanting.

1496 *Dives & Paup.* (W. de W.) v. iv. 200/2 Comonly grete praysers be grete lackers. *a* **1618** J. DAVIES (Heref.) *Wits Pilgr.*, etc. (Grosart) 24/1 The lack of one may cause the wrack of al: Although the lackers were terrestrial gods Yet wil theyr ruling reel, or reeling fall.

lacker, variant of LACQUER *sb.* and *v.*

†**lacket**. *Obs. rare*$^{-1}$. [ad. OF. *laquet*, obs. f. *laquais*.] A lackey.

1523 LD. BERNERS *Froiss.* I. xviii. 26 [They sent back] theyr lackettis, and pagis..in ii. shippes.

lackey, ('lækɪ), *sb.* Forms: α. 6 **lakay, -ey, -ye, lackeie, lacquie**, 6–7 **lackie**, 6–8 **lacky**, 7 **lacquay, -aie, la(ck)quay, lacquy, laquey**, 6– **lackey, lacquey**; *pl.* 6– **lackeys, lacqueys**, etc.; also 6 **lackeis, -yes**, 7 **lack(e)yes**, 7–8 **laquies**, 6–9 **lackies**. β. *Sc.* 6 **alakay, allacay**, 7 **allakey**. [ad. F. *laquais*, in OF. pl. *laquaiz*, *laquetz*, also *alacays*, *(h)alaques* (whence the β. forms), in 15th c. a kind of foot-soldier, subsequently a footman, servant. The etymology is obscure; cf. Sp., Pg. *lacayo*; It. *lacchè* is from Fr.]

1. a. A footman, *esp.* a running footman; a valet.

α. **1529** *Supplic. to King* (E.E.T.S.) 52 His wiffe, her gentle woman or mayde, two yowmen, and one lackey. **1596** MUNDAY *Silvayn's Orator* 354 How manie Noble men doe burst their lacquise legs with running. **1616** R. C. *Times' Whistle* III. 1067 Lackies before her chariot must run. **1642** ROGERS *Naaman* 159 The lackey rides, and the Prince goes on foote. **1709** STEELE *Tatler* No. 44 ¶1 The Coachman with a new Cockade, and the Lacqueys with Insolence..in their Countenances. **1816** BYRON *Ch. Har.* II. *Notes* Wks. I. 160 He was wronged by his lackey, and overcharged by his washerwoman. **1849** COBDEN *Speeches* 10 Popes and potentates have run away in the disguises of lacqueys. **1855** MOTLEY *Dutch Rep.* II. ii. (1866) 146 He was not her lackey, and..she might send some one else with her errands.

β. **1538** *Sc. Ld. Treasurer's Acc.* in Pitcairn *Crimin. Trials* I. 292, ix Pagis, iiij Allacayis, iij Mulitaris. **1560** ROLLAND *Crt. Venus* II. 1035 At ilk bridle ane proper Alakay. **1600** *Sc. Acts Jas. VI* (1816) IV. 212/2 Ane allakey put ane steil bonnet on his heid.

b. *fig.* †A constant follower (*obs.*); one who is servilely obsequious, a toady.

1588 *Marprel. Epist.* (Arb.) 19, I thinke Simonie be the bishops lacky. **1651** BIGGS *New Disp.* §72. 37 There are some flowers that are the Laquies of the sun. **1692** WASHINGTON *Milton's Def. Pop.* iii. (1851) 100 In Politicks no Man more a Lackey and Slave to Tyrants than he. **1880** SPURGEON *J. Ploughm. Pict.* 25 It is right to be obliging, but we are not obliged to be every man's lackey.

c. *spec.* As a term of political abuse: a servile follower.

1939 G. E. R. GEDYE *Fallen Bastions* ii. 37 The Communists did not hesitate to condemn them [*sc.* the Austrian Socialist leaders], as 'Social Fascists' who did 'lackey service' to capitalist reaction. **1941** *Amer. Mercury* Apr. 417/2 American bankers..have already stepped into the role of lackeys of British Imperialism. **1957** C. HUNT *Guide to Communist Jargon* p. xiv, The Soviet Union stands for peace, and the imperialists for war, in which they are once again supported by their socialist 'lackeys'. **1969** *Listener* 27 Apr. 429/3 Whatever else went under the name of socialism was either 'wilful deception by lackeys of the bourgeoisie' or the self-deception of those who hesitated 'between life-and-death struggle and the role of assistants to the expiring bourgeoisie'. **1972** *Sat. Rev.* (U.S.) 24 June 30/2 As any good Maoist..can tell you, Hussein is nothing more than a Western lackey. **1973** *Black Panther* 21 July 10/2 The U.S. government or its lackeys. **1974** A. ROSS *Bradford Business* 129 Bloody fascist lackeys!

2. A hanger-on, a camp follower. *Obs.* or *arch.*

1556 *Acc.* in Sharpe *Cov. Myst.* (1825) 193 Payd to xiiij gonners and a lakye lixs. **1580** NORTH *Plutarch* (1676) 427 Slaues,..Lackies, and other Stragglers that followed the camp. **1600** HOLLAND *Livy* v. viii. 185 Like to lawlesse lackies that follow the campe. **1843** LYTTON *Last Bar.* II. i. 122 The..lackeys and dross of the camp—false alike to Henry and to Edward.

3. = *lackey-moth* (see 4).

1857 STAINTON *Brit. Butterflies & Moths* I. 156 *Clisiocampa castrensis* (Ground Lackey)... *C. neustria* (Lackey). **1869** E. NEWMAN *Brit. Moths* 42 The Lackey (*Bombyx neustria*).

4. *attrib.* and *Comb.*, as ***lackey-boy***, ***-brat***, ***-slave***; also ***lackey-like*** adj. and adv.; **lackey-caterpillar**, the caterpillar from which the lackey-moth is developed; **lackey-moth**, a bombycid moth of the genus *Clisiocampa* (for the origin of the name see quot. 1868).

1575 TURBERVILE *Faulconrie* 371 By misfortune or negligence of your *lackey boyes. **1677** *Lovers Quarrel* 73 in Hazl. *E.P.P.* II. 256 Away this lacky boy he ran. **1599** MARSTON *Sco. Villanie* I. iii. Wks. 180 Shall thy Dads *lacky brat Weare thy Sires halfe-rot finger in his hat? **1603** J. DAVIES (Heref.) *Microcosm.* (Grosart) 37/1 Sweat before Vertue *lacky-like doth rin To ope the gate of Glory sempiterne. **1829** CARLYLE *Misc.* (1857) II. 19 The Sieur Longchamp's..most lackey-like Narrative. **1868** WOOD *Homes without H.* xxx. 577 The *Lackey moths are so called on account of the bright colours of the caterpillars, which are striped and decorated like modern footmen. **1890** ELEANOR ORMEROD *Injur. Insects* (ed. 2) 292 The caterpillars of the Lackey Moth are injurious to the leafage of apples. *a* **1611** CHAPMAN *Iliad* v. 207 Like a *lackey slave.

Hence various nonce-words. †'**lackeyan** *a.*, of or pertaining to a lackey; '**lackeyed** *ppl. a.*, attended by lackeys; '**lackeyism**, the service or attendance of lackeys; '**lackeyship**, the condition or position of lackeys; lackeys collectively.

1620 SHELTON *Quix.* IV. xv. 120 The little blind Boy,.. Love, would not lose the occasion offered to triumph upon a Lackyan Soul. **1762** GOLDSM. *Cit. W.* lxi. [lxiv.] ¶5 For our pleasure the lacquied train..moves in review. **1830** *Examiner* 706/2 Creating a hereditary lackyship in the servant's hall. **1843** LE FEVRE *Life Trav. Phys.* III. II. xiv. 64 As he is awkward in all his operations he cannot enter the ranks of lackeyship. **1843** CARLYLE in Froude *Life Lond.* (1884) I. 312 Sound sleep for a few hours, and a lackey to awaken you at half-past six. It is over now, all that lackeyism, thank God!

lackey ('lækɪ), *v.* Forms: see the sb. [f. LACKEY *sb.*]

†**1.** *intr.* To do service as a lackey, esp. as a running footman; to run on errands, dance attendance, do menial service. Frequently *fig.* of persons and immaterial things. Const. *after*, *by*, *to*, *upon*; also, *to lackey it*. *Obs.*

1568 *Hist. Jacob & Esau* II. iii. C iv, I must lackey and come lugging greyhound and hound. **1592** LYLY *Galathea* IV. ii, Cupid,..you shall..lackie after Diana all day. **1593** MARLOWE *Lust's Dom.* I. iv. (1657) B xj b, *Alv.* Shall they thus tread thee down, which once were glad To Lacquey by thy conquering Chariot wheeles? **1604** DEKKER *King's Entertainm.* 323 The Minutes (that lackey at the heeles of Time) run not faster away then do our joyes. **1613** HEYWOOD *Brazen Age* I. 178 I'le lackey by the wheresoe're thou goest. **1615** CHAPMAN *Odyss.* v. 131 Who would willingly Lackey along so vast a lake of brine? **1633** STAFFORD *Pac. Hib.* II. iii. (1821) 243 Making him lackie it by his horse side on foote like a common Horseboy. **1640** N. FIENNES in Rushw. *Hist. Coll.* III. (1692) I. 181 Let the high and great Censure of the Church no longer lacquy after Fees. **1642** HALES *Tract on Schism* 13 This abuse of Christianity to make it Lacquey to Ambition, is a vice for which [etc.]. **1674** N. FAIRFAX *Bulk & Selv.* 18 The whole of this is eternity,..that share of it that lackies it by the worlds side is time. **1676–7** HALE *Contempl.* II. 73 Intellect, that in the Throne should sit, Must lackie after Lust. *a* **1677** MANTON *Christ's Tempt.* iv. Wks. 1870 I. 295 That his power and goodness should lacquey upon, and be at the beck of, our idle and wanton humours. **1678** CUDWORTH *Intell. Syst.* I. v. 864/1 It being Indecorous that this Divine..

Power should constantly lacquey by and attend upon natural generations. **1697** DRYDEN *Æneid* Ded. e 3, He is a Foot-Poet, he Lacquies by the side of Virgil at the best, but never mounts behind him.

2. *trans.* To wait upon as a lackey; to attend closely upon; to dance attendance upon. Chiefly *transf.* and *fig.*

1599 MARSTON *Sco. Villanie* II. vii. Wks. 203 Note no more, Vnlesse thou spy his faire appendant whore That lackies him. **1612-15** BP. HALL *Contempl. O.T.* XIX. ii, Elijah ..had lacquaied his coach, and tooke a peaceable leaue at this Townes end. **1629** FORD *Lover's Mel.* I. ii, [He] Lackeys his letters, does what service else He would employ his man in. **1646** BOYLE in *Life* Wks. (1772) I. 29, I saw one poor rogue, lacqueyed by his wife. **1649** DRUMM. OF HAWTH. *Fam. Ep.* Wks. (1711) 144 So many dangers and miseries lackeying them. **1764** CHURCHILL *Independence* Poems II. 2, I see Men..lacquey the heels of those Whom Genius ranks amongst her greatest foes. **1801** W. TAYLOR in *Monthly Mag.* II. 505 The syllable *ty*..came over in the suite of the Norman families of words, and lacqueys only its early connexions. **1832** *Fraser's Mag.* V. 671 Why should it lacquey unlearned opinion, and..submit to become the mere registry of popular judgment? **1870** LOWELL *Study Wind.* 402 The artificial method proceeds from a principle the reverse of this, making the spirit lackey the form. **1881** *Q. Rev.* Apr. 319 He had lacqueyed and flattered Walpole.

Hence **'lackeying** *ppl. a.*

1819 KEATS *King Stephen* I. iv. 42 The generous Earl.. with a sort of lackeying friendliness, Takes off the mighty frowning from his brow.

lacking ('lækɪŋ), *vbl. sb.* [f. LACK *v.*[1] + -ING[1].]

1. The condition of being without or in want of (something); deficiency.

1377 LANGL. *P. Pl.* B. XIII. 26 And as low as a lombe for lakkyng of that hym nedeth. **1398** TREVISA *Barth. De P.R.* XIX. xiii. (1495) 872 The body is pale..for scarsytee and lackynge of blood. *c* **1440** HYLTON *Scala Perf.* (W. de W. 1494) I. liii, This nought is no thinge elles but derkenes of conscyence, a lackynge of loue and of lyghte. **1509** HAWES *Past. Pleas.* XXI. (Percy Soc.) 100 Where that is mesure there is no lacking. **1543** tr. *Act I Rich. III*, c. 13 The sellar shall allow or rebate at the same pryce to the Byar..asmoche money as suche lackyng [F. *defaute*] after the rate shall amount to. *a* **1548** HALL *Chron., Edw. IV* 233 At every table were apoynted .v. or .vi. gentelmen..to se them served without lacking. *a* **1851** MOIR *Birth Flowers* iv. Poet. Wks. (1852) I. 133 The Dreamer wist not what might be The thing a-lacking.

†**2.** The action of blaming, the condition of being blamed; blame, censure. *Obs.*

1387-8 T. USK *Test. Love* III. ii. 112 Nothing by reason of that, turneth in-to thy praisinge ne lacking. *c* **1440** HYLTON *Scala Perf.* (W. de W. 1494) II. xxii, To suffre at that may falle, ease or unease: praysyng or lackyng.

lacking ('lækɪŋ), *ppl. a.* [f. LACK *v.*[1] + -ING[2].]

1. Of things: not at hand; missing; also, short in quantity.

1480 *Wardr. Acc. Edw. IV* (1830) 145 Except ij yerdes lakking in alle. **1566** *Eng. Ch. Furniture* (1866) 82 The Rood with a paire of Clappers Lackinge. **1611** BIBLE *Lev.* ii. 13 Neither shalt thou suffer the salt of the Couenant of thy God to bee lacking from thy meat offering. **1879** TYNDALL *Fragm. Sci.* (ed. 6) II. ii. 11 Flour was lacking to make the sacramental bread. **1881** EVANS in *Speaker's Comm. N.T.* III. 241 Historical materials are lacking.

2. Of persons, etc.: Deficient, falling short, in want; also, defaulting. †Of a limb: Crippled. Of a district: Destitute.

1657 REEVE *God's Plea* 18 Clisophus the Sycophant of Philip feigned himself lame, because his Master had through a wound a laking legge. **1805** W. TAYLOR in *Ann. Rev.* III. 310 The lean and lacking corners of the empire produce the most hardy and robust people. **1838** CHALMERS *Wks.* XIII. 186 He may regard God in the light of a jealous exactor and himself in the light of a lacking tributary. **1868** NETTLESHIP *Browning* i. 44 The tree must give me its leaf or I must go lacking. **1868** FREEMAN *Norm. Conq.* (1876) II. vii. 23 In all kingly qualities he was utterly lacking. **1878** BROWNING *La Saisiaz* 61 Grant..This same law found lacking now.

lackland ('læklænd), *sb.* and *a.* [f. LACK *v.*[1] + LAND *sb.*[1]] **A.** *sb.* One who has no landed possessions; one who rules over no territory. **B.** *adj.* Of persons: Having no land.

Used by mod. historians as a rendering of L. *Sine Terra* (*c* 1196 Will. Novoburg. *Hist.* II. xviii.), AF. *Sanz tere* (*c* 1367 *Eulog. Hist.* v. cxii.), the designation of King John. Trevisa tr. *Higden's Polychron.* VII. xxxii. calls him 'Iohn wiþ oute londes'; Grafton and Stowe 'Without land'.

1594 GREENE *Looking Glass* Wks. (Grosart) XIV. 40 How cheere you, gentleman? you crie 'no lands' too; the Judge hath made you a knight for a gentleman, hath dubd you sir John Lack-land. **1610** HOLLAND *Camden's Brit.* 255 Iohn surnamed Sine terra, that is, Without Land [*marg.* Or nick-named Iohn Lack-land]. **1622** ROWLANDS *Good Newes & Bad* 12 What remedy gainst Fortunes raging fits, But liue like other lacklands, by my wits? **1646** BUCK *Rich. III*, I. 6 Sobriquets..Sansterre, Lackland. **1762** HUME *Hist. Eng.* I. ix. 330 John who inherited no territory..was thence commonly denominated Lackland. **1820** [see *lack-stock*, LACK *v.*[1] 7]. **1839** *Penny Cycl.* XIII. 126 John, King of England, surnamed Sansterre or Lackland, a common appellation of younger sons, whose age prevented them from holding fiefs. **1881** *Spectator* 22 Jan. 120 Whatever the lacklands of the League may say to the contrary. **1887** *Pall Mall G.* 21 July 3/2 If they voted for the lackland lawyer they would in the winter starve. **1899** CARDL. VAUGHAN in *Westm. Gaz.* 29 Aug. 2/3 The transference..of the great commons of England to the rich created a lackland and beggared poor.

lack-latin (stress even or variable), *sb.* and *a.* [f. LACK *v.*[1] + LATIN *sb.*] †**A.** *sb.* One who knows little or no Latin; chiefly in ***Sir John Lack-latin***, a name for an ignorant priest. *Obs.* **B.** *adj.* Ignorant of Latin; unlearned.

c **1534** SIR F. BYGOD *Treat. conc. impropriations* C vj, Is it nat great pitye to se a man to haue thre or foure benefyces.. whiche he neuer cometh at, but setteth in euery one of them a syr John lacke laten, that can scarce rede his porteus. **1552** LATIMER *Serm. St. Andrew's Day* (1584) 236 [The patron] will..hyer a Syr Iohn Lacke Latin, whiche shall say seruice. **1608** J. DAY *Law Trickes* I. i. (1881) 11 Your selfe and such lacke-Latin Aduocates Infect the heart. **1614** JACKSON *Creed* III. iii. §5 We are bound to believe the Church's decisions read or explicated unto us (by the pope's messenger though a Sir John Lack-latin). **1649** G. DANIEL *Trinarch., Rich. II* 343 'Tis but in Ayre, as on the Earth, one Cause; Wee haue our Lack-Latins, and They, their Dawes. **1832** J. HODGSON in J. Raine *Mem.* (1858) II. 257 That sad lack-Latin prelate Lewis Beaumont.

†**lackless** ('læklɪs), *a. Obs.* [f. LACK *sb.*[1] + -LESS.] Without fault or blame; faultless, blameless. Const. *of.*

1377 LANGL. *P. Pl.* B. XI. 382 If a man miȝte make hym-self goed to þe poeple, Vch a lif wold be lakles. ? *a* **1500** *Chester Pl.* (E.E.T.S.) VII. 544 He said to me sleeping, that shee lackles was of sinne.

lack-lustre (stress even or variable), *a.* and *sb.* [f. LACK *v.*[1] + LUSTRE.]

A. *adj.* Wanting in lustre or brightness: orig. of the eyes, countenance, etc., after Shakspere.

1600 SHAKS. *A.Y.L.* II. vii. 21 He drew a diall from his poake: And looking on it, with lacke-lustre eye, Sayes [etc.]. **1782** V. KNOX *Ess.* (1819) III. clxxii. 257 With hollow and lack-lustre eye. **1812** BYRON *Ch. Har.* II. vi, Through each lack-lustre, eyeless hole. **1844** DICKENS *Mart. Chuz.* iii, From a gaudy blue to a faint lack-lustre shade of grey. **1883** BLACK *Shandon Bells* xxxi, Existence in these foul-smelling lanes..seemed a lack-lustre kind of thing.

B. *sb.* The absence of lustre or brightness. *rare*[−1].

a **1788** POTT *Chirurg. Wks.* II. 92 The eyes have now a languor and a glassiness, a lack-lustre not easy to be described. **1847** in CRAIG; and in mod. Dicts.

Hence **lack'lustrous** *a.*, wanting in lustre, dull.

1834 *New Monthly Mag.* XL. 80 The most lacklustrous of all games.

lackquaie, -ay, obs. forms of LACKEY.

lack-wit, lackwit ('lækwɪt). [LACK *v.*[1] 7.] A witless or stupid person.

1667 DRYDEN *Sir Martin Mar-all* IV. i. Wks. (1883) III. 53 A conceited lack-wit, a designing ass. **1809** E. S. BARRETT *Setting Sun* I. 40 Alexander, the Lackwit. **1911** H. S. HARRISON *Queed* iv. 42 West..abused himself for a shiftless lackwit who was slated for an unwept grave. **1936** F. CLUNE *Roaming round Darling* xxi. 210, I was embarrassed exceedingly by an inarticulate lack-wit, while I filled the petrol tank.

lacky, dial. f. LACK *v.*; obs. f. LACKEY.

lacmoid ('lækmɔɪd). [f. LACM-US + -OID.] A coal-tar colour used in dyeing.

In some mod. Dicts.

lacmus ('lækməs). [ad. Du. *lakmoes*, f. *lak* LAC *sb.*[1] + *moes* pulp.] = LITMUS.

1794 SULLIVAN *View Nat.* I. 258 The tincture of lacmus. **1812** J. SMYTH *Pract. of Customs* (1821) 150 Litmus, or Lacmus, in the Arts, is a blue pigment, formed from Archil.

Laconian (lə'kəʊnɪən), *a.* and *sb.* [f. L. *Lacōni-a* (f. Gr. *Λάκων* Laconian) + -AN.]

A. *adj.* Of or pertaining to Laconia or its inhabitants; Lacedæmonian, Spartan.

B. *sb.* **1.** An inhabitant of Laconia.

1602 *Metamorph. Tabacco* 41 The rude Laconians, whom Lycurgus care Barr'd from the traffick of exotick ware. **1842** PRICHARD *Nat. Hist. Man* 201 The Laconians differ in manners and address from their neighbours the Arcadians.

Comb. **1580** NORTH *Plutarch* (1676) 44 Some had reason which said heretofore, to speak Laconian-like, was to be Philosopher-like.

2. The dialect of ancient Greek spoken in Laconia (Sparta).

1830 TUFNELL & LEWIS tr. *Müller's Hist. & Antiq. Doric Race* II. App. viii. 502 We have considered the Doric dialect in general, as spoken by the whole race, only marking out the Laconian as its purest variety. **1875** *Encycl. Brit.* XI. 133/2 Three changes characteristic of Laconian came in at a comparatively late date. **1954** PEI & GAYNOR *Dict. Ling.* 118 *Laconian*, one of the Doric dialects of ancient Greek.

laconic (lə'kɒnɪk), *a.* and *sb.* Also 6 -ike, 7 -ique, 7-8 -ick. [ad. Gr. *Λακωνικ-ός* (L. *Lacōnic-us*), f. *Λάκων* Laconian. Cf. F. *laconique.*]

A. *adj.*

1. (With capital initial.) Of or pertaining to Laconia or its inhabitants, made or written in Laconia; Lacedæmonian, Spartan. Now *rare.*

1583 *Exec. for Treason* Pref. (1675) A iij, Plutarch often quotes the Delphick and Laconick Commentaries. **1601** HOLLAND *Pliny* II. 613 There be many other Emeraudes.. taken forth of the mountain Taygetus in Laconia, and those therefore be named Laconick. *a* **1683** SIDNEY *Disc. Govt.* III. vi. (1704) 251 This was not peculiar to the severe Laconic Disciplin. **1807** ROBINSON *Archæol. Græca* II. i. 131 The River Eurotas, which runs into the Laconic Gulf. **1850** CHUBB *Locks & Keys* 5 The Laconic keys consisted of three single teeth, in the figure of the letter E. [Cf. *clavem laconicam*, Plaut. *Most.*]

b. Characteristic of the Laconians; Spartan-like.

1787 J. ADAMS *Def. Constit. Govt.* Pref., Wks. 1851 IV. 287 The latest revolution that we read of, was conducted.. in the Grecian style, with laconic energy.

2. Following the Laconian manner, esp. in speech and writing; brief, concise, sententious. Of persons: Affecting a brief style of speech.

1589 JAS. VI in Ellis *Orig. Lett.* Ser. I. III. 28 To excuis me for this my laconike writting I ame in suche haist. *a* **1625** BEAUM. & FL. *Little Fr. Lawyer* V. i, If thou wilt needs know ..I will discover it..with laconic brevity. **1667** E. CHAMBERLAYNE *St. Gt. Brit.* I. Introd. (1684) 6 Brevity and a Laconick stile is aimed at all along. **1668** DAVENANT *Man's Master* II. 1. Wks. 1874 V. 32 This laconic fool makes brevity ridiculous. **1736** POPE *Let. Swift* 17 Aug., Wks. 1871 VII. 345, I grow laconic even beyond laconicism. **1800** MRS. HERVEY *Mourtray Fam.* I. 149 This cold laconic note..let down all Emma's hopes. **1833** HT. MARTINEAU *Berkeley Banker* I. ii. 29 'None but friends, I see', said the laconic Mr. Williams. **1850** KINGSLEY *Alt. Locke* xxix. (1879) 311 That ..laconic dignity, which is the good side of the English peasants' character. **1888** ANNA GREEN *Behind Closed Doors* iii, 'Trust me' was his laconic rejoinder.

B. *sb.* (The adj. used absolutely.)

†**1.** A laconic speaker. *Obs.*

1628 J. GAULE *Pract. Theor. Paneg.* 22 The most compendious Laconicke with a reinserted Parenthesis of (*vt tribus dicam verbis*) amongst many words, will promise to dispatch in Three. **1692** L'ESTRANGE *Fables* ccccxcii. 467 It was the Ill hap of a Learned Laconique, to make use of Three Words, when two would have done..his business hardly.

2. Laconic or concise speech. *pl.* Brief or concise sentences.

1718 ADDISON *Let. to Swift* in *Swift's Lett.* II. 540 Shall we never again talk together in laconic? **1871** E. F. BURN *Ad Fidem* xvi. 341 A man's hand writes startling laconics on the wall.

†**3.** = LACONICUM. *Obs.*

1715 LEONI *Palladio's Archit.* (1742) II. 55 Laconic, the Sweating Room in the Palestræ.

†**la'conical,** *a. Obs.* [f. LACONIC *a.* + -AL[1].] = LACONIC *a.*

1576 FLEMING *Panopl. Epist.* 236 The Epistles of Nucillus were so Laconicall and shorte. **1586** T. B. *La Primaud. Fr. Acad.* I. (1594) 121 Laconicall sayings, that is, short and sententious. **1603** HOLLAND *Plutarch's Mor.* 338 Proposing forsooth a streight and laconicall manner of life. **1627** BP. HALL *Epist.* I. v. 282 All that Laconicall discipline pleased him well. *a* **1658** CLEVELAND *Poems* (1677) 134 The Spartans ..studying their Laconical Brevity. **1698** FRYER *E. India & P.* 362 Distinctions and Laconical Evasions.

laconically (lə'kɒnɪkəlɪ), *adv.* [f. prec. + -LY[2].] After the manner of the Laconians or Spartans, *esp.* in brevity of speech.

1631 WEEVER *Anc. Funeral Mon.* 572 He..writ thus to the Abbot Laconically..Who answered as briefly. **1631** BRATHWAIT *Eng. Gentlew.* (1641) 298 Farre bee it from me to be so..Laconically severe. **1742** POPE *Let. to Warburton* 28 Dec. Wks. 1751 IX. 254, I write, you know, very laconically. **1823** LINGARD *Hist. Eng.* VI. 32 The king laconically replied, that he should wait for the English..till Friday. **1851** ALFORD in *Life* (1873) 206 The 'Christian Remembrancer'..has taken notice of my answer very laconically. **1873** G. C. DAVIES *Mount. & Mere* xiv. 109 'Donkeys' he answered laconically.

la'conicalness. *rare*[−1]. Laconical quality.

1830-1 BENTHAM *Wks.* (1843) XI. 104/2 The laconicalness of the observation.

laconicism (lə'kɒnɪsɪz(ə)m). [f. LACONIC *a.* + -ISM.] = LACONISM 2 and 2 b.

1656 BLOUNT *Glossogr.*, *Laconicism*, a short speech, containing much matter. **1694** tr. *Gracian's Courtier's Oracle* Pref. A iij[a], This made the learned..Author affect a certain vigorous Laconicism in all his writings. **1736** [see LACONIC 2]. **1789** MRS. PIOZZI *Journ. France* I. 374 Graceful without diffusion, and terse without laconicism. **1801** *Hist. Europe* in *Ann. Reg.* 207 *note*, Highly as the laconicism of Buonaparte has been admired we [etc.]. **1865** R. F. BURTON (*title*) Wit and Wisdom from West Africa, a book of.. Idioms, Enigmas, and Laconicisms.

†**la'conicly,** *adv. Obs. rare.* = LACONICALLY.

1709 *Brit. Apollo* II. No. 53. 3/2 When he Laconicly Harangu'd.

‖**laconicum** (lə'kɒnɪkəm). [L., neuter of *Lacōnicus* LACONIC, sc. *balneum* bath.] The sweating-room in the bath, so called from having been first used by the Spartans.

1696 in PHILLIPS (ed. 5). **1832** GELL *Pompeiana* I. v. 86 The hot air of the laconicum. **1857** BIRCH *Anc. Pottery* (1858) II. 226 The upper floor bricks, or tiles..formed the floor of the laconicum.

laconism ('lækənɪz(ə)m). [ad. Gr. *λακωνισμός*, f. *λακωνίζειν* to LACONIZE. Cf. F. *laconisme.*]

1. (With capital initial.) Partiality for the Lacedæmonians; the practice of favouring the Lacedæmonian interest. *rare.*

1655 STANLEY *Hist. Philos.* III. (1701) 118/2 Xenophon.. was banished for Laconism, upon his going to Agesilaus. **1869** A. W. WARD tr. *Curtius' Hist. Greece* II. III. ii. 375 'Laconism' was with increasing plain-spokenness designated as treason against the national interests of Athens.

2. The habit or practice of imitating the Lacedæmonian manners, esp. in brevity of speech.

1570 LEVINS *Manip.* 146 Laconisme, *laconismus.* **1607** WALKINGTON *Opt. Glass* 31, I doe here passe the limits of

laconisme. **1669** GALE *Crt. Gentiles* I. III. x. 109 Is not Laconisme, or a short stile, provided it be ful and evident, best? **1697** J. COLLIER *Ess.* II. 120 And as the Language of the Face is universal, so 'tis very comprehensive. No Laconism can reach it. **1791–1823** D'ISRAELI *Cur. Lit.* (1866) 205/1 This spiritual laconism invigorated the arm of men. **1836** *Blackw. Mag.* XL. 484 There is a good tone of laconism hit off in that dialogue. **1858** JULIA KAVANAGH *Adèle* I. i. 6 His will was brief to laconism.

b. A laconic speech; a short and pithy sentence.

1682 SIR T. BROWNE *Chr. Mor.* (1756) 35 The hand of Providence writes often by abbreviatures..which like the Laconism on the wall, are not to be made out but by a hint or key. **1791–1823** D'ISRAELI *Cur. Lit.* (1866) 393/1 The 'laconisms' of the Lacedæmonians evidently partook of the proverbial style. **1838** D. JERROLD *Men. Charac., Chr. Snub* iii. Wks. 1864 III. 426 The highway laconism of 'your money or your life'.

† **'Laconist.** *Obs. rare*$^{-0}$. [ad. Gr. λακωνιστής, agent-n. f. λακωνίζειν to LACONIZE.] One who imitates or takes part with the Lacedæmonians.

1570 in LEVINS *Manip.* 147.

Laconize ('lækənaɪz), *v.* [ad. Gr. λακωνίζειν, f. Λάκων LACONIAN: see -IZE.]

1. *intr.* To favour the Lacedæmonians; to imitate their customs or mode of speech; to side with them in politics.

1603 HOLLAND *Plutarch's Mor.* 205 If he be disposed to laconize a little..he would..say: He is not. **1792–1823** D'ISRAELI *Cur. Lit.* (1866) 392/1 The philosopher assures those who in other cities imagined they laconised..that they were grossly deceived.

2. *trans.* To bring under the Lacedæmonian dominion or form of government.

a **1873** LYTTON *Pausanias* II. iii. (1878) 420 We will Laconise all Hellas.

Hence **'Laconizing** *vbl. sb.* and *ppl. a.*

1792–1823 D'ISRAELI *Cur. Lit.* (1866) 393/1 The very instances which Plato supplies of this 'laconising' are two most venerable proverbs. **1869** A. W. WARD tr. *Curtius' Hist. Greece* II. III. ii. 372 The dangerous consequences of his Laconizing tendency. **1875** JOWETT *Plato* (ed. 2) I. 118 The mistake of the Laconizing set in supposing [etc.].

lacque, obs. form of LAC[1].

lacquer ('lækə(r)), *sb.* Also 6 leckar, 6–7 laker, 7 laccar, laquer, 7 lacre, 7–9 lacker. [ad. obs. F. *lacre* (17th c.) a kind of sealing wax = Sp., Pg. *lacre*, 16th c. It. *lacra*, Pg. *alacre*, *laquar* (Yule); an unexplained variant or derivative of Pg. *lacca* LAC. The current form *lacquer* is influenced app. by F. *laque* LAC[1].]

† **1.** = LAC[1] I. *Obs.*

1579 HAKLUYT *Voy.* (1598) I. 432 Enquire of the price of leckar, and all other things belonging to dying. **1582** N. LICHEFIELD tr. *Castanheda's Conq. E. Indies* 33 *marg.*, Laker is a kinde of gum that procedeth of the Ant. **1653** H. COGAN tr. *Pinto's Trav.* xvii. (1663) 58 Oxen..laden with..Ivory, Wax, Lacre, Benjamin, Camphire and Gold in Powder. *Ibid.* lii. 207 They caused..a great deal of Lacre, which is like unto hard Wax, to be dropped scalding hot upon me. **1714** *Fr. Bk. of Rates* 45 Lacker for Paint or Dying.

2. a. A gold-coloured varnish, consisting chiefly of a solution of pale shellac in alcohol, tinged with saffron, anatta, or other colouring matters; used chiefly as a coating for brass.

1673 MARVELL *Reh. Transp.* II. Wks. II. 243 His soul seemed to have set up a gilt vehicle of the new lacker. **1697** EVELYN *Numism.* vi. 215 A sort of fine Varnish or harder Laccar. **1708** *Brit. Apollo* I. No. 2. 3/1 Lacquer [is perform'd] with Leaf Silver, ting'd to a Gold Colour, by a Varnish compos'd of Rectify'd Spirits and Gums. **1773** *Phil. Trans.* LXIII. 326 The best apartments..have usually a broad cornish of lacker, or false gold, round their coved ceilings. **1825** J. NICHOLSON *Operat. Mechanic* 731 To make Lacquer of various Tints. **1855** BROWNING *Old Pictures Florence* xxxii, No civic guards, all plumes and lacquer.

fig. **1681** T. FLATMAN *Heracl. Ridens* (1713) I. No. 37. 241 They have got such a trick of gilding this Pill of Damnation with the spiritual Lacker of a safe Conscience and Protestant. **1863** MRS. OLIPHANT *Salem Ch.* ii. 30 The thin superficial lacker with which Miss Phoebe was coated.

b. Applied to various kinds of resinous varnish, capable of taking a hard polish, used in Japan, China, Burma, and India for coating articles of wood or other materials; chiefly the 'Japanese lacquer', obtained from the *Rhus vernicifera*.

1697 DAMPIER *Voy.* I. (1729) 400 Laquer which is used in Japanning of Cabinets. **1888** *Pall Mall G.* 19 Nov. 2/1 Lacquer is the sap of the lacquer-tree, *Rhus vernicifera*, drawn off by making incisions in the bark during the rainy season. **1889** *Nature* 31 Oct. 655 Japanese lacquer is the product of a tree, the *Rhus vernicifera*.

c. A kind of fixative for a hairstyle, usu. applied as an aerosol spray.

1941 F. E. WALL *Princ. & Pract. Beauty Culture* xii. 454 Many of the coiffures..can be made more lasting through the use of lacquer as a fixative. **1946** *Amer. Hairdresser* Dec. I. 3 (Advt.), Beautician and patron *both* recognize the superiority of Wella, the *original* lacquer. **1966** J. S. COX *Illustr. Dict. Hairdressing* 88/1 Most of the modern lacquers will shampoo out satisfactorily with a soap or soapless shampoo. **1983** P. SPIRES *Boots Bk. Hair Care* iv. 21 During the Fifties and Sixties the *bouffant*, beehive styles led to the over-use and misuse of lacquers.

3. The class of decorative articles made of wood coated with lacquer (sense 2 b), and often inlaid with ornaments of ivory, mother-of-pearl, or metal; chiefly made in Japan, China, and India. Also *pl.* works of art of this kind.

1895 *Daily News* 17 May 6/2 Rare specimens of the finest old lacquers by great masters. *Mod.* Really good Japanese lacquer is not easy to procure.

4. *Comb.*: † **lacquer-hat** (see quot.); **lacquer-tree**, the tree (*Rhus vernicifera*) that yields Japan lacquer; also, a similar tree in S. America; **lacquer-ware** = sense 3; **lacquer-work**, the making of lacquer-ware; also = *lacquer-ware*; **lacquer-wort**, ? = *lacquer-tree*.

1706 PHILLIPS (ed. Kersey), *Lacker-Hat, a Hat made without stiffening. [**1863** BATES *Nat. Amazon* vii. (1864) 175 Its borders were composed in great part of..*Lacre-trees, whose berries exude globules of wax resembling gamboge.] **1884** *Pall Mall G.* 24 Apr. 2/2 The cultivation of the lacquer tree has rapidly declined. **1697** DAMPIER *Voy.* I. (1729) 409 They make very fine *Lacquer-ware. **1705** *Lond. Gaz.* No. 4166/3 Laden with raw Silks, China Lacker-Ware, and Salt-Petre. **1861** C. P. HODGSON *Resid. Japan* 28 It is..disgraceful for a Japanese to part with old lacquer ware. **1669** PEPYS *Diary* 23 Apr., Sir Philip Howard and Watson (the inventors, as they pretend, of the business of varnishing and *lacker-worke). **1878** J. J. YOUNG *Ceram. Art* (1879) 165 In Japan Princes are said to have engaged in lacquer-work. **1659** TORRIANO, *Silphione*, *laker-wort, some say it is an hearb yielding the gum Beniamin.

lacquer ('lækə(r)), *v.* Also 8 laccar, 8–9 lacker. [f. LACQUER *sb.*] *trans.* To cover or coat with lacquer; hence *gen.* to varnish; occas. of the material: To serve as a varnish for. Also with *over*.

1688 G. PARKER & J. STALKER *Japaning* xviii. 56 To lacquer in Oyl, such things as are to be exposed to the Weather. **1692** *Lond. Gaz.* No. 2813/4 The places appointed for receiving Guns, and Pistols.., or other Ironwork to be Lacquer'd..are [etc.]. **1720** DE FOE *Capt. Singleton* xviii. (1840) 315 Her stern..was now all lackered. **1745** J. MASON *Self-Knowl.* III. viii. (1853) 210 A smooth and shining varnish, which may lacker over the basest Metal. **1822** IMISON *Sci. & Art* II. 14 The best material for the lamp furnace is brass lackered. **1830** LINDLEY *Nat. Syst. Bot.* 129 The Black Lac of the Burmah country, with which the natives lacker various kinds of ware. **1859** L. OLIPHANT *China & Japan* II. x. 227 A very handsome china bowl, curiously lacquered inside.

transf. and *fig.* **1705** T. BRADBURY *Serm.* 5 Nov. 101 They may have Names that are laccar'd over with a false Divinity. **1720** GAY *Poems* (1745) II. 22 From patches justly plac'd they borrow graces And with vermilion lacker o'er their faces. **1755** *Connoisseur* No. 65 ¶2 A pretty fellow lacquers his pale face with as many varnishes as a fine lady. **1807** OPIE in *Lect. Paint.* iv. (1848) 336 The knowledge of his principle..served only to lacquer over poverty of thought and feebleness of design. **1831** *Edin. Rev.* LIII. 223 Lackered over with an outer coating of fair-seeming.

lacquered ('lækəd), *ppl. a.* Also lackered. [f. LACQUER *v.* + -ED[1].] Covered or coated with lacquer; varnished.

1687 *Lond. Gaz.* No. 2273/7 Lackered Ware Trunks. **1731** SWIFT *Answ. Simile* 115 Apollo stirs not out of door Without his lacker'd coach and four. **1777** ROBERTSON *Hist. Amer.* (1783) III. 379 They are composed of..lacquered copper-plates. **1838** DICKENS *Nich. Nick.* vi, With spears in their hands like lackered area railings. **1855** THACKERAY *Newcomes* II. 240 The other passed into the club in his lacquered boots. **1859** L. OLIPHANT *China & Japan* II. x. 227 A lacquered cabinet, very highly finished.

transf. and *fig.* **1805** SIR M. A. SHEE *Rhymes on Art* (1806) 42 Life a listless, lacker'd gloom. **1851** D. JERROLD *St. Giles* xxiii. 241 The thief's face..wore the smug, lackered look of a fortunate scoundrel. **1854** THACKERAY *Newcomes* I. 74 His lacquered moustache. **1884** BROWNING *Ferishtah's Fancies* (1885) 94 Knowledge, the golden?—lacquered ignorance!

lacquerer ('lækərə(r)). Also lackerer. [f. LACQUER *v.* + -ER[1].] One who coats with lacquer; one who lacquers. *lit.* and *fig.*

1845 MIALL in *Nonconf.* V. 260 Mr. Macaulay, the best lacquerer of historic ware which modern times have furnished. **1884** *B'ham Daily Post* 24 Jan. 3/4 Lacquerer Wanted, used to Brass Bedstead Work. **1899** C. J. HOLMES *Hokusai* 43 The lacquerer Korin alone seems to have stiffened the sweetness of his country with a proportionate measure of strength.

lacquering ('lækərɪŋ), *vbl. sb.* Also lackering. [f. LACQUER *v.* + -ING[1].] The action or process of coating with lacquer; varnishing. Also quasi-*concr.*, the coat of lacquer laid on.

1688 G. PARKER & J. STALKER *Japaning* xxi. 64 To make Lackering shew like Burnisht Gold. **1822** IMISON *Sci. & Art* II. 314 This is in fact rather lacquering than staining. **1874** MICKLETHWAITE *Mod. Par. Churches* 301 Lacquering, which is the usual method of finishing brass-work. **1877** SIR R. ALCOCK in *Art Jrnl.* June 162/2 In some cases the lacquering is in relief.

b. *attrib.*, as **lacquering-stone** (see quot.).

1854 TOMLINSON *Cycl. Useful Arts* II. 104 In brasswork factories, a lackering-stone, with a broad flat top, is used for holding the articles which are to be heated preparatory to lackering.

lacquey, lacquie, -y: see LACKEY.

lacre, variant of LACQUER.

lacrim-: see LACHRYM-.

‖**lacrimæ rerum** ('lækrɪmaɪ rɛərəm). [L.] With reference to Virgil, *Aeneid* I. 462: the sadness of life; tears shed for the sorrows of men.

[**1841** CARLYLE *Let.* 19 July in R. K. Webb *H. Martineau* (1960) vii. 196 Poor Harriet! She was..almost sublime to me there. *Sunt lachrymae rerum.*] **1929** A. HUXLEY *Do what you Will* 195 Hellenic lovers..may have wept the *lacrimae rerum*. **1951** AUDEN *Nones* (1952) 71 Only the young and the rich Have the nerve or the figure to strike The lacrimae rerum note. **1959** *Times* 19 Mar. 4/1 He [*sc.* Mahler] told in his music truths of humanity, of the *lacrimae rerum*, and of alleviating beauty. **1969** G. SMITH in A. Huxley *Lett.* (1969) 1 Though often tinged with a profound instinct to weep for life, it—and by no means the sadness of *lacrimæ rerum*—is Huxley's hallmark.

lacrimal, lacrimate, -or, see LACHRYMAL *a.* and *sb.*, etc.

lacrosse (lə'krɒs, -ɔː-). [F. *la* the + *crosse* a hooked stick.] A North American game at ball, introduced into England from Canada. In the general arrangements it resembles hockey or football, but the ball is a small one, driven and caught with a CROSSE.

[**1763** A. HENRY *Trav.*, The Indians call the game baggatiway. By the French in Canada it is named 'le jeu de la crosse'. **1805** PIKE *Sources Mississ.* (1810) 18 Passed..a prairie called Le Cross, from a game of ball played frequently on it by the Sioux Indians.] **1867** (*title*) Laws of La Crosse. **1884** S. E. DAWSON *Handbk. Canada* 225 Lacrosse is the national game of Canada, practised by the Indians long previous to the arrival of Europeans.

b. *attrib.*, as *lacrosse-man*; **lacrosse-stick** = CROSSE.

1882 *Sun* 14 May 6/5 The lacrosse men greeted this with hisses and groans.

Hence **la'crosser**, one who plays at lacrosse.

1884 *Sporting Times* 9 June 3/5 The lacrossers of the South [of England].

lacrym-: see LACHRYM-.

lacsamana, var. LAKSAMANA.

lacta: see LAC[1].

† **lac'taceous**, *a.* *Obs. rare*$^{-1}$. [f. L. *lact-*, *lac* milk + -ACEOUS.] Milk-like, milky.

1656 RIDGLEY *Pract. Physick* 18 The cause is a watery, sharp, salt, lactaceous humour.

† **'lactage.** *Obs.* [f. L. *lact-*, *lac* milk + -AGE. Cf. OF. *laictage(s*, F. *laitage*.] Milk produce.

1753 SHUCKFORD *Creation & Fall Man* Pref. 98 Abel did not sacrifice a Lamb; but perhaps only some Wool and Cream, of the Lactage, and Growth of the Firstlings of his Flock.

lactagogue ('læktəgɒg), *a.* [f. L. *lact-*, *lac* milk + Gr. ἀγωγός leading.] Adapted to produce a flow of milk.

1887 MOLONEY *Forestry W. Afr.* 389 Tonic, alterative, aphrodisiac, demulcent, and lactagogue.

lactalbumin (læk'tælbjʊmɪn). *Biochem.* [ad. F. *lactalbumine* (A. Commaille 1866, in *Rec. de Mém. de Méd.* XVII. 155), f. *lact(o-* LACTO- + *albumine* ALBUMIN.] **a.** The fraction of milk proteins which is obtained after the removal of casein and which is soluble in a salt solution such as saturated magnesium sulphate or ammonium sulphate.

1885 [see LACTOGLOBULIN 1]. **1936** *Biochem. Jrnl.* XXX. 956 Probably the so-called lactalbumin is a mixture of the two molecules α and β and the molecule usually referred to as lactoglobulin is γ. **1970** [see b].

b. (Usu. *α-lactalbumin.*) A protein or mixture of closely similar proteins occurring in the lactalbumin fraction of milk and having a molecular weight of about 17,400.

1937 *Nature* 19 Jun. (Suppl.) 1058/2 In cow's milk there are two albumins, the α-lactalbumin, of molecular weight 17,600 and sedimentation constant 1·9 × 10^{-13} and β-lactalbumin (also called Palmer's lactoglobulin) with M = 39,000 and s = 3·12 × 10^{-13}. **1948** [see LACTOGLOBULIN 2]. **1953** *Jrnl. Amer. Chem. Soc.* LXXV. 329/1 It is proposed, therefore, that the protein isolated by the Sørensens also be called α-lactalbumin even though the isoelectric protein is only slightly soluble in water. **1962** *Biochem. Jrnl.* LXXXIII. 271/1 The lactalbumin was prepared from human-milk whey. **1970** R. JENNESS in H. A. McKenzie *Milk Proteins* I. ii. 22 When later the proteins β-lactoglobulin and α-lactalbumin were crystallised from the 'lactalbumin' fraction, the Greek letters used by Pedersen were incorporated into the names... The β-protein was named as a globulin because of its insolubility near the isoelectric point in the absence of salt and the α-protein as an albumin because of its source in the 'lactalbumin' fraction of whey... Two α-lactalbumins, A and B, have been found.

lactam ('læktæm). *Chem.* [a. G. *lactam* (Baeyer & Oekonomides 1882, in *Ber. d. Deut. Chem. Ges.* XV. 2102), f. *lact-on* LACTONE + *am-id* AMIDE.] Any of the class of cyclic amides analogous to the lactones, characterized by the group –NH·CO– as part of a ring (*lactam ring*) and formed by the elimination of a molecule of water from an amino and a carboxyl group of an acid; freq. with prefixed Gr. letter (see LACTONE 2).

1883 *Jrnl. Chem. Soc.* XLIV. 202 The authors propose the name *lactam* for bodies formed like acetylisatin, and *lactim*

for those formed like isatin. **1910** *Encycl. Brit.* VI. 59/1 The internal anhydrides of aminocarboxylic acids (lactams, betaines). **1936** L. J. DESHA *Org. Chem.* xxvi. 522 Lactam-lactim tautomerism involves the shift of a hydrogen atom from nitrogen to oxygen and vice versa. **1949** E. P. ABRAHAM et al. in H. W. Florey et al. *Antibiotics* II. xv. 669 The four-membered lactam ring which was present in this structure [of penicillin] had not previously been found in natural compounds, and the ease with which it could be broken was responsible for the instability of penicillin under a variety of conditions. **1964** ROBERTS & CASERIO *Basic Princ. Org. Chem.* xx. 712 Formation of α- and β-lactams is expected to generate considerable ring strain, and other more favorable reactions usually intervene. **1966** *McGraw-Hill Encycl. Sci. & Technol.* VII. 377/1 Although γ- and δ-amino acids are nontoxic themselves, the corresponding lactams show pronounced strychnine-type toxicity.

lactamase (ˈlæktəmeɪz, -s). *Biochem.* [f. LACTAM + -ASE.] *β-lactamase*: any of the enzymes (produced by certain bacteria) which cause the breaking of the carbon-nitrogen bond in the lactam ring of penicillins and cephalosporins (so rendering them ineffective as antibiotics).

1964 *Jrnl. Gen. Microbiol.* XXXVI. 206 Amidase-forming coliform organisms did not attack the 6-APA nucleus, whereas β-lactamase-forming coliform organisms opened the lactam ring. **1971** N. CITRI in P. D. Boyer et al. *Enzymes* (ed. 3) IV. ii. 24 The role of penicillinase and other β-lactamases in conferring resistance to penicillins and the closely related cephalosporins has been amply demonstrated.

lactamide (ˈlæktəmaɪd). *Chem.* [f. L. *lact-*, *lac* milk + AMIDE.] The amide of lactic acid.

1848 FOWNES *Chem.* (ed. 2) 389 Lactide..combines with ammonia, forming lactamide.

lactant (ˈlæktənt), *a. rare*$^{-0}$. [ad. L. *lactant-em*, pr. pple. of *lactāre* to suckle.] Suckling.

1727 in BAILEY (vol. II).

lactarene, lactarine (ˈlæktəriːn). [f. as next + -ENE, -INE.] A preparation of casein from milk, used in printing calico.

1858 in SIMMONDS *Dict. Trade.* **1860** O'NEILL *Chem. Calico Printing* 166 Lactarine and other preparations of milk ..are..employed for fixing ultramarine and similar colours.

lactarious (lækˈtɛərɪəs), *a. rare*$^{-0}$. [f. L. *lactārius* LACTARY + -OUS.] = LACTARY *a.*; 'applied to some of the agarics which yield a milky juice' (Mayne *Expos. Lex.* 1855). Hence **lacˈtariously** *adv.* (*jocular nonce-wd.*) on milk diet.

1775 C. STURGES in *J. Granger's Lett.* (1805) 167 Her little boy goes on lactariously well.

‖**lactarium** (lækˈtɛərɪəm). [L. neut. of *lactārius* pertaining to milk, f. *lact-*, *lac* milk.] An establishment for the sale of milk; a dairy.

1809 *European Mag.* LX. 22 Our milk houses are called lactariums. **1825** HONE *Every-day Bk.* I. 103 He [S. Crisp, d. 1784] was the institutor of the Lactarium in St. George's Fields.

lactary (ˈlæktərɪ), *a.* and *sb. rare.* [ad. L. *lactārius*, f. *lact-*, *lac* milk.]

A. *adj.* Of or pertaining to milk; concerned with milk. †Of a plant: Yielding a milky juice.

1646 SIR T. BROWNE *Pseud. Ep.* VI. x. 323 Why also from Lactary or milky plants which have a white and lacteous juice dispersed through every part, there arise flowers blue and yellow? **1657** TOMLINSON *Renou's Disp.* 263 A Lactary and a ferulaceous Herb. **1727–51** CHAMBERS *Cycl.* s.v. *Column, Lactary Column*, at Rome [= L. *lactaria columna*]. **1892** LD. LYTTON *King Poppy* I. 381 The Titular Head Of the State's Lactary Department, she.

B. *sb.* †**a.** (See quot. 1623.) *Obs.*$^{-0}$ **b.** A dairy.

1623 COCKERAM, *Lactarie*, She that selleth milke. **1669–81** WORLIDGE *Syst. Agric., Dict. Rust., Lactary*, a Dairy-house. **1755** in JOHNSON. Hence in mod. Dicts.

lactase (ˈlækteɪz, -s). *Biochem.* [a. F. *lactase* (M. W. Beijerinck 1889, in *Arch. néerl. d. Sci. exactes et nat.* XXIII. 434), f. *lact-ose* LACTOSE: see -ASE.] Any enzyme which catalyses the hydrolysis of lactose to glucose and galactose.

1891 *Jrnl. R. Microsc. Soc.* 374 The fermentation [of milk sugar] is effected by a diastase distinct from invertin, which he calls lactase. **1906** *Jrnl. Physiol.* XXXV. 28 The conclusion is from these experiments that lactase is distributed fairly equally through the whole of the mucous membrane of the intestine. **1959** JENNESS & PATTON *Princ. Dairy Chem.* iii. 80 There are at least three significant origins of lactase enzymes which may be used for the hydrolysis of lactose. These are: (a) certain species of yeasts..; (b) the intestinal mucosa of mammals..; and (c) β-galactosidase from almonds.

lactate (ˈlæktət), *sb. Chem.* [f. LACT-IC + -ATE[4].] A salt of lactic acid.

1794 PEARSON *Table Chem. Nomencl.* §24 *Lactates*, compounds of Acid of Milk with different Bases. **1819** J. G. CHILDREN *Chem. Anal.* 317 Lactate of lead..; lactate of iron ..; lactate of copper. **1899** CAGNEY *Jaksch's Clin. Diagn.* vi. (ed. 4) 234 Crystals of lactate of lime occur in the discharges of children.

lactate (lækˈteɪt), *v.* [f. L. *lactāt-*, ppl. stem of *lactāre* to suckle.] *intr.* To secrete or discharge milk. Chiefly as **lacˈtating** *ppl. a.*

1889 in *Cent. Dict.* **1908** *Arch. Middlesex Hosp.* XIII. 59 In the lactating breast the number of acini is very large. **1913** *17th Internat. Congr. Med.* III. II. 173 The pregnant and lactating animals survived the extirpation of the adrenal glands much longer than normal, non-pregnant, or male animals. **1948** *New Biol.* IV. 127 Purified preparations of prolactin were found inferior to more crude pituitary preparations..in their power to increase the milk yield of cows already lactating. **1953** E. GELLHORN *Physiol. Found. Neurol. & Psychiatry* xiii. 305 There is still another function of oxytocin..: the ejection of milk from the lactating mammillary gland. **1956** J. S. FOLLEY *Physiol. & Biochem. Lactation* ii. 28 Mammary tissue from lactating rats.. exhibits much greater respiratory activity *in vitro.* **1956** *Jrnl. Pediatrics* XLIX. 550/2 She had suckled all her daughter's children and lactated freely each time. **1971** J. Z. YOUNG *Introd. Study Man* xxiv. 319 To estimate reliably the number of children born to a group of women under the conditions that their husbands are freely available and that they are not using contraceptives or lactating is nearly impossible.

lacˈtated, *a.* [f. as prec. f. L. *lact-*, *lac* milk.] Combined with a milk-product.

1889 *Buck's Handbk. Med. Sci.* VIII. 100/2 In Horlick's and Mellin's there is said to be no unconverted starch. Hawley's contains eleven per cent.,..as does also the Lactated Food. **1896** *Rep. Vermont Board Agric.* XV. 25 This is used in making..lactated food for infants and invalids. **1907** *Yesterday's Shopping* (1969) 500/2 Lactated Pepsin Tablets.

lactation (lækˈteɪʃən). [n. of action f. L. *lactāre* to suckle. Cf. F. *lactation.*]

1. The action or process of giving suck to an infant; suckling.

1668 WILKINS *Real Char.* II. ix. §2. 233 Lactation, giving suck. **1806** *Med. Jrnl.* XV. 215 The remote causes of nervous diseases, &c. viz. in..Lactation. **1836–7** SIR W. HAMILTON *Metaph.* I. App. 410 By the end of the full period of lactation, it has..reached the full proportion of the adult. **1860** TANNER *Pregnancy* ii. 48 During the periods of lactation and pregnancy. **1879** KHORY *Princ. Med.* 18 Prolonged lactation also causes giddiness.

2. The process of secreting milk from the mammary glands.

1857 J. H. WALSH *Dom. Econ.* 559 The establishment of lactation is the turning-point of the lying-in-room.

lactational (lækˈteɪʃənəl), *a.* [f. LACTATION + -AL[1].] Of or pertaining to lactation.

1903 *Med. Rec.* (N.Y.) 28 Feb. 337/2 Both suicidal and infanticidal promptings are more common in lactational than puerperal cases—that is, in cases in which insanity commenced more than six weeks after confinement. **1970** *Nature* 19 Dec. 1222/2 It has been found that cows excrete less DDT in lactational fluids than human females.

lacteal (ˈlæktiːəl), *a.* and *sb.* Also 7 lacteall. [f. L. *lacte-us* (f. *lact-*, *lac* milk) + -AL[1].]

A. *adj.*

1. Of or pertaining to milk; consisting of milk. ***lacteal fever***, milk fever.

1658 PHILLIPS, *Lacteal*, or *Lacteous*, milky, milk white, or made of milk. **1753** CHAMBERS *Cycl. Supp.*, Lacteal fevers, a term used by medical writers to express what the women call milk fevers. **1802** *Med. Jrnl.* VIII. 443 Restoring a certain degree of order in the process of lacteal secretion. **1854** OWEN *Skel. & Teeth* (1855) 70 The lacteal organs of the dugong are placed on the breast.

jocularly. **1868** *Daily Tel.* 14 Apr., She proceeded very quietly to give him [her infant] a lacteal lunch. **1882** SALA *Amer. Revis.* (1885) 246 The animals [cows]..are driven home, there to yield their lacteal tribute.

b. Resembling milk; milk-white. *rare*$^{-1}$.

1633 P. FLETCHER *Purple Isl.* II. xii, Like the lacteal stones which heaven pave. **1658** [see 1].

2. Of a vessel, etc. in the animal body: Conveying a milky fluid, *sc.* chyle.

1664 POWER *Exp. Philos.* I. 66 The Stomach and guts, and their appendent Vessels, the lacteal Veins. **1691** RAY *Creation* I. (1692) 66 There should have been some lacteal Veins formed. **1813** J. THOMSON *Lect. Inflam.* 357 Substances which..the lacteal absorbents refuse to take up. **1843** J. G. WILKINSON *Swedenborg's Anim. Kingd.* I. v. 144 They have lacteal vessels, or lymphatics.

B. *sb. pl.*

1. *Phys.* The lymphatic vessels of the mesentery, originating in the small intestine, and conveying the chyle from thence to the thoracic duct; chyliferous vessels.

1680 PLOT *Staffordsh.* (1686) 290 How it should pass the Lacteals, or with the blood through the other small capillaries. **1691** RAY *Creation* II. (1692) 63 Driving by their Peristaltick Motion the Chyle into the Lacteals. **1758** JOHNSON *Idler* No. 17 ¶8 [Against vivisection.] He surely buys knowledge dear, who learns the use of the lacteals at the expence of his humanity. **1809** *Med. Jrnl.* XXI. 296 Air will be absorbed from it by the lacteals as well as chyle. **1822–34** *Good's Bk. Nat.* I. 275 The vessels are called lacteals, from the usual milky appearance of the liquid they absorb and contain. **1885–8** FAGGE & PYE-SMITH *Princ. Med.* (ed. 2) 169 The absorption by the lacteals of matters from the affected parts of the intestine.

†**2.** *Bot.* The lactiferous ducts.

1672–3 GREW *Anat. Plants* II. iii. §25 (1682) 68 The Lacteals of Dandelion.

Hence **ˈlacteally** *adv.* (Webster, 1864).

lactean (ˈlæktiːən), *a.* [f. as prec. + -AN.]

†**a.** = LACTEAL *a.* 1 b (*obs.*). **b.** = LACTEAL *a.* 2. (In mod. Dicts.)

1659 MOXON *Tutor Astron.* I. 25 Blaeu saith, This Lactean whiteness and clearness ariseth from a great number of little stars, constipated in that part of Heaven.

lactein (ˈlæktiːɪn). Also -ine. [ad. mod.L. *lacteīna* (F. *lactéine*), f. L. *lacte-us*: see LACTEAL and -IN, -INE.] Solidified milk obtained by evaporation.

1855 in MAYNE *Expos. Lex., Lactein.* **1888** *Syd. Soc. Lex., Lacteine.*

lacteous (ˈlæktiːəs), *a.* [f. L. *lacte-us* (see LACTEAL) + -OUS.]

1. Of the nature of milk; milky.

1646 [see LACTARY *a.*]. **1666** J. SMITH *Old Age* (ed. 2) 174 There is a lacteous, and a caseous part therein. **1696** J. EDWARDS *Demonstr. Existence God* II. 101 Others reckon it to be a lacteous excrement.

fig. **1870** LOWELL *Among my Bks.* Ser. I. (1873) 188 Professors who were forever assiduously browsing in vales of Enna..slowly secreting lacteous facts.

2. Resembling milk; of the colour of milk. †***lacteous circle***: the Milky Way. †***lacteous star***: one belonging to the Milky Way.

1646 SIR T. BROWNE *Pseud. Ep.* IV. xii. 211 Though we leave out the Lacteous circle..yet [etc.]. **1669** W. SIMPSON *Hydrol. Chym.* 278 The lacteous cremor or milky juyce. **1677** PLOT *Oxfordsh.* 48 Two small and very weak springs, of a lacteous colour but no such tast. **1682** SIR T. BROWNE *Chr. Mor.* III. §24 Numerous numbers must be content to stand like lacteous or nebulous Stars. **1826** KIRBY & SP. *Entomol.* IV. 278 Lacteous (*lacteus*), white with a slight tint of blue.

†**3.** = LACTEAL *a.* 2. *Obs.*

1692 BENTLEY *Boyle Lect.* iii. 8 The Lungs are suitable for Respiration,..the Lacteous Vessels for the Reception of the Chyle.

Hence **ˈlacteously** *adv.*, in a lacteous manner (Webster, 1864).

†**lactesce,** *v. Obs. rare*$^{-1}$. In 7 lactess. [ad. L. *lactēsc-ĕre*: see LACTESCENT.] *intr.* To become milky.

1696 W. COWPER in *Phil. Trans.* XIX. 305 By evaporating such Urine by heat, as in a Spoon over a Candle it will lactess and become thick.

lactescence (lækˈtɛsəns). [f. LACTESCENT: see -ENCE.]

1. A milky appearance; milkiness.

1684–5 BOYLE *Hist. Min. Waters* 57 We perceiv'd a light lactescence to be produc'd, and a whitish Precipitate very slowly to subside. **1756** C. LUCAS *Ess. Waters* I. 139 The solution of soap mixes smoothly and causes a slight lactescence. In mod. Dicts.

2. *Bot.* An abundant flow of sap from certain plants when wounded, commonly white, but sometimes red.

1760 LEE *Introd. Bot.* III. xx. (1765) 216 Lactescence, Milkiness, is when a copious Juice flows out on any injury done to the Plant. In mod. Dicts.

†**lacˈtescency.** [f. as prec.: see -ENCY.] = LACTESCENCE 1.

1757 WALKER in *Phil. Trans.* L. 124 A solution of saccharum Saturni..left the upper parts of the water clear and colourless, but formed a lactescency towards the bottom.

lactescent (lækˈtɛsənt), *a.* [ad. L. *lactēscentem*, pres. pple. f. *lactēscĕre*, inchoative vb. f. *lactēre* to be milky, f. *lact-*, *lac* milk.]

1. Becoming milky; having a milky appearance.

1668 *Phil. Trans.* III. 752 Concerning lactescent Bloud in a man..whose Bloud alwayes turn'd into Milk. **1757** WALKER in *Phil. Trans.* L. 135 Saccharum Saturni being added to the solution, precipitated a thick lactescent cloud. **1815** *Sporting Mag.* XLVI. 63 The lactescent juice of the former [lettuce] is powerfully narcotic. **1876** GROSS *Dis. Bladder* 196 The urine assumes a turbid, purulent, or lactescent aspect.

2. Of plants: Yielding a milky juice.

1673 *Phil. Trans.* VIII. 6006 Cheggio, a lactescent plant, found in Cambaja. **1724** SWITZER *Pract. Gard.* VII. lviii. (1727) 308 Common ladies thistle..on account of its lactescent quality. **1830** LINDLEY *Nat. Syst. Bot.* 11 Limnocharis, a genus belonging to Butomeæ, is lactescent. **1880** in GRAY *Struct. Bot.* (ed. 6) 417/2.

¶**3.** Used for: Producing or secreting milk.

1796 DUNCAN *Ann. Med.* I. 236 Tension of the nipples of lactescent women at the sight of a child. **1835** KIRBY *Hab. & Inst. Anim.* II. xxiv. 478 The entire skin of the abdomen forms a pocket, inclosing the lactescent organs.

lactic (ˈlæktɪk), *a. Chem.* [f. L. *lact-*, *lac* milk + -IC.] Of or pertaining to milk. ***lactic acid*** ($C_3H_6O_3$), the acid formed in sour milk. ***lactic fermentation***, the souring of milk, induced by certain bacteria, which decompose the milk sugar.

1790 KERR tr. *Lavoisier's Elem. Chem.* 121 Lactic acid. **1822** IMISON *Sci. & Art* II. 139 The lactic acid is found in sour whey. **1874** ROSCOE *Elem. Chem.* xxxiv. 367 Lactic acid is contained in sour milk, and is formed from sugar by a peculiar change called the lactic fermentation. **1879** *St. George's Hosp. Rep.* IX. 163 Treatment was by port-wine, salicylate of soda, and lactic acid spray.

lactide ('læktaɪd). *Chem.* [f. as prec. + -IDE.] A substance, $C_6H_8O_4$, formed by the decomposition of lactic acid.

1848 FOWNES *Chem.* (ed. 2) 389. **1869** ROSCOE *Elem. Chem.* 368 Lactic acid.. when heated, forms lactide, and dilactic acid.

† **'lactifer.** *Obs. rare*$^{-1}$. [a. late L. *lactifer* milk-bearing, f. *lact(i)-*, *lac* milk + *-fer* bearing.] A lactiferous vessel.

1673-4 GREW *Anat. Plants* III. I. ii. §16 (1682) 109 The outmost which make the other Rings [of the Bark] in Arched Parcels, are the Lactifers.

lactiferous (læk'tɪfərəs), *a.* [f. L. *lactifer* (see prec.) + -OUS.]

1. Of animals and their organs: Producing, secreting, or conveying milk.

1691 RAY *Creation* I. (1692) 144 He makes the Breasts to be.. Glandules.. made up of an infinite number of little Knots or Kernels, each whereof hath its excretory Vessel or lactiferous Duct. **1794-6** E. DARWIN *Zoon.* I. 171 The females of lactiferous animals have another natural inlet of pleasure or pain from the suckling of their offspring. **1802** BINGLEY *Anim. Biog.* (1813) I. 15 The class of animals denominated.. Mammalia, comprehends all those which nourish their offspring by means of lactiferous glands or teats. **1822-34** *Good's Study Med.* (ed. 4) IV. 193 Perfect milk in every separate lactiferous tube.

2. Of plants and their organs: Conveying or yielding a milky fluid.

1673-4 GREW *Anat. Plants* III. II. iv. §10 (1682) 133 The Lactiferous and Resiniferous Vessels of Plants. **1675** *Phil. Trans.* X. 487 He finds sap vessels to be.. Lymphæducts and Lactiferous. **1753** in CHAMBERS *Cycl. Supp.* **1801** *Trans. Soc. Arts* XIX. 198 Lettuces running to seed.. are known to be more particularly lactiferous. **1854** J. HOGG *Microsc.* II. iv. 409 Plants are likewise furnished with lactiferous ducts or tissue.

Hence **lac'tiferousness**, the quality of yielding milk in abundance.

1879 *Punch* 1 Nov. 195/2 The natural lactiferousness of the Alderney.

† **lac'tific,** *a. Obs. rare*$^{-1}$. [f. L. *lact(i)-*, *lac* milk + -FIC. Cf. F. *lactifique*.] Milk-producing.

1657 W. COLES *Adam in Eden* xciv, The lactific vertues which do reside in this herb.

So † **lac'tifical** *a.*, in the same sense.

1656 BLOUNT *Glossogr.*, *Lactifical*, milk-breeding, milk-making, milk-yeelding. **1676** in COLES; **1721** in BAILEY; and in mod. Dicts.

† **lactifi'cation.** *Obs. rare*$^{-1}$. [See prec. and -FICATION.] The making or secreting of milk.

1666 J. SMITH *Old Age* (ed. 2) 106, I shall only mention five;.. Chylification, Sanguification, Assimilation, Lactification, and Spermification.

lactiflorous (ˌlæktɪ'flɔərəs), *a. rare.* [f. L. *lacti-*, *lac* milk + *flōr-em* flower + -OUS.] Having flowers white like milk.

1855 in MAYNE *Expos. Lex.*

lactifluous (læk'tɪflu:əs), *a.* [as if f. L. **lactifluus* (after the analogy of *mellifluus*, f. *lact(i)-*, *lac* milk + *flu-*, stem of *fluĕre* to flow) + -OUS.] Flowing or abounding with milk.

1774 CURTIS *Flora Lond.* (1777) I. xxxv, Most plants of this Genus [*Euphorbia*] contain in them this milky and gummy substance.. and this lactifluous property. **1855** BAILEY *Mystic* 82 And that, lactifluous, from whose flower-tipped stem.. the Caraccan Indian drains, At day-dawn, creamy draughts.

† **'lactiform,** *a. Obs. rare*$^{-1}$. [f. L. *lacti-*, *lac* milk + -FORM.] In the form of milk, like milk.

1681 in tr. *Willis' Rem. Med. Wks.* Vocab.

lactifugal (læk'tɪfjʊgəl), *a. Med.* [f. next + -AL[1].] Acting as a lactifuge.

In mod. Dicts.

lactifuge ('læktɪfju:dʒ). *Med.* [f. L. *lacti-*, *lac* milk + -FUGE.] A medicine which retards the secretion of milk.

1855 in MAYNE *Expos. Lex.*

lactim ('læktɪm). *Chem.* [a. G. *lactim* (Baeyer & Oekonomides 1882, in *Ber. d. Deut. Chem. Ges.* XV. 2102), f. *lact-on* LACTONE + *im-id* IMIDE.] Any of the class of cyclic imines which are isomers of the lactams and characterized by the group $-N{:}C(OH)-$ as part of a ring.

1883, 1936 [see LACTAM]. **1951** I. L. FINAR *Org. Chem.* I. xxx. 619 Isatin exists in two forms, the term *ψ*-isatin being applied to the lactam form I, and isatin to the lactim form II. **1971** *Canad. Jrnl. Chem.* XLIX. 2612 Investigation showed the free lactim ether to be a probable intermediate in this reaction.

lactin ('læktɪn). *Chem.* Also -ine. [f. L. *lact-*, *lac* milk + -IN.] = LACTOSE.

1844 FOWNES *Chem.* 364 Sugar of milk; lactine. **1858** *Ibid.* (ed. 7) 410 Lactin.

lactivorous (læk'tɪvərəs), *a. rare.* [f. L. *lacti-*, *lac* milk + *-vor-us* devouring + -OUS.] Milk-devouring.

1824 *New Monthly Mag.* XI. 314 Babies.—Noisy lactivorous animalculæ. **1855** in MAYNE *Expos. Lex.*

lacto- ('læktəʊ). **1.** Used as combining form of L. *lact-*, *lac* milk: as in ˌ**lactobuty'rometer**, an instrument for estimating the amount of butter in a given quantity of milk; **'lactocele** = GALACTOCELE; **'lactochrome** *Biochem.*, a yellow-orange pigment orig. extracted from milk and now identified with riboflavin; **lacto'flavin** *Biochem.* [a. G. *lactoflavin* (Ellinger & Koschara 1933, in *Ber. d. Deut. Chem. Ges.* LXVI. B. 808)] = RIBOFLAVIN; **'lactogen** *Physiol.*, any lactogenic hormone; *spec.* = PROLACTIN; **lacto'genesis** *Physiol.*, the initiation of milk secretion; **lacto'genic** *Physiol.* [-GENIC], pertaining to or having the ability to initiate the secretion of milk; hence **lacto'genically** *adv.*; ˌ**lacto-'phosphate**, a salt of lactic and phosphoric acids in combination; ˌ**lacto-'protein**, a normal albuminous constituent of milk; **'lactoscope** [see -SCOPE], an instrument for ascertaining the purity of milk from the amount of resistance it offers to the passage of light; ˌ**lacto-thermometer**, an instrument for ascertaining the temperature of milk; **lacto-vege'tarian** *a.*, consisting of milk and vegetables; so **lacto-vege'tarianism.**

1884 *Health Exhib. Catal.* 25/1 Graduated Cream Glasses, *Lactobutyrometer. **1855** MAYNE *Expos. Lex.*, **Lactocele*. **1879** A. W. BLYTH in *Jrnl. Chem. Soc.* XXXV. 532 After the liquid from which the galactin has been removed had been freed from the excess of lead by hydrogen sulphide, an alkaloïdal colouring matter, for which I propose the name of '*lactochrome', may be separated by the addition of nitrate of mercury solution. **1914** *Jrnl. Biol. Chem.* XVII. 261 The facts brought out by this investigation point very clearly to a very close relationship existing between the yellow lactochrome of milk whey and the urochrome of urine. **1936** W. L. DAVIES *Chem. Milk* xi. 218 Milk from other species of mammals also contains lactochrome. It is present in human milk. **1953** FRUTON & SIMMONDS *Gen. Biochem.* xiii. 319 In 1879 Blyth described the isolation from milk of a yellow pigment (named lactochrome) which showed a striking green fluorescence... By 1936 the chemical nature of the yellow pigment of egg yolk and of milk had been established..; it was shown that this pigment, named riboflavin, is identical with vitamin B_2. **1933** *Brit. Chem. Abstr.* A. 847/2 (*heading*) *Lactoflavin, the pigment of milk. **1938** *Encycl. Brit. Bk. of Year* 651/1 Recently it has been found that vitamin B_2 consists of three components, lactoflavin, vitamin B_6.. and pellagrous preventing or p.p. factor. **1943** SUMNER & SOMERS *Chem. & Methods of Enzymes* xiii. 244 Various flavins were described, *e.g.*, lactoflavin of milk, hepatoflavin of liver... The flavin of these workers was the same substance which is called today 'riboflavin', or sometimes, 'lactoflavin'. **1946** J. F. FULTON *Howell's Textbk. Physiol.* (ed. 15) liv. 1209 Both the onset and maintenance of lactation require *lactogen. **1952** S. J. FOLLEY in A. S. Parkes *Marshall's Physiol. Reproduction* (ed. 3) II. xx. 558 When first discovered it [*sc.* an anterior-pituitary protein hormone] was variously named prolactin (Riddle), galactin (Turner) and mammotropin (Lyons). Recent American practice tends to favour the terms lactogen or lactogenic hormone; the name prolactin is adopted in this chapter in accordance with English usage. **1962** *Endocrinology* LXXI. 218/2 The Raben preparation.., although quite potent as a lactogen in the pseudopregnant rabbit,.. has little activity in the local intradermal pigeon crop assay. **1967** *Proc. Nat. Acad. Sci.* LVIII. 2307 The recent indentification of human placental lactogen (HPL), a polypeptide hormone which shares both biological and immunological properties with pituitary growth hormone (HGH). **1939** RIDDLE & BATES in E. Allen *Sex & Internal Secretions* xx. 1089 *Lactogenesis is a *response* to this hormone which excites also—in both sexes—additional responses more ancient phylogenetically and perhaps more significant generally. **1948** Lactogenesis [see *galactopoiesis* (GALACTO-)]. **1969** S. R. WELLINGS in Reynolds & Folley *Lactogenesis* 5 Lactogenesis may be defined as the process by which full lactation is initiated in an already prepared mammary gland. **1933** *Proc. Soc. Exper. Biol. & Med.* XXI. 300 We have never observed milk secretion in normal or ovariectomized virgin guinea pigs uninjected with the *lactogenic hormone. **1946** J. F. FULTON *Howell's Textbk. Physiol.* (ed. 15) liv. 1209 The lactogenic activity of pituitary extracts was first shown by Stricker and Grüter in 1928. **1952** Lactogenic [see *lactogen* above]. **1969** A. T. COWIE in Reynolds & Folley *Lactogenesis* 159, I now turn to the rabbit, the species in which the lactogenic role of the anterior pituitary was first discovered. **1969** R. DENAMUR in *Ibid.* 60 Thus, *lactogenically prolactin modifies the polyribosomes by increasing their number in the cell. **1878** A. HAMILTON *Nerv. Dis.* 335 The syrup of the *lacto-phosphate of lime. **1864** *Reader* No. 86. 239/2 A new albuminoidal substance found in milk.. *lacto-proteine. **1858** SIMMONDS *Dict. Trade*, **Lactoscope*,.. an instrument invented by M. Donne, of Paris, for ascertaining the opacity of milk, and thus estimating the richness of the fluid in cream. **1884** *Health Exhib. Catal.* 25/1 Milk Thermometers.. *Lacto-Thermometer. **1907** *Practitioner* June 845 The *lacto-vegetarian diet.. lessens auto-intoxication. **1929** *Encycl. Brit.* VII. 359/1 A lacto-vegetarian diet which permits the free use of milk and eggs. **1951** *News Chron.* 13 Dec. 3/2 Man was not designed for a purely vegetable diet. There was no objection whatever to lacto-vegetarian diet (this includes milk and eggs). **1940** *Nature* 7 Dec. 726/2 It.. looks as if the Briton's dietary will gradually shift, at least during the war years, towards *lactovegetarianism.

2. Used as comb. form of LACTIC *acid* or LACTOSE: as in **lactobi'onic** *a.*, in ***lactobionic acid*** [tr. G. *lactobionsäure* (Fischer & Meyer 1889, in *Ber. d. Deut. Chem. Ges.* XXII. 362)], 4-(*β*-D-galactosido)-D-gluconic acid, $C_{12}H_{22}O_{11}$: a syrup produced by oxidation of lactose; hence **lacto'bionate**, a salt of lactobionic acid; **lacto'nitrile**, a yellow liquid, $CH_3{\cdot}CH(OH){\cdot}CN$, that is the nitrile of lactic acid and is used in a method of manufacturing acrylonitrile; acetaldehyde cyanohydrin; **lacto-'phenol**, a mixture of approximately equal weights of phenol and lactic acid dissolved in glycerol and distilled water, used for mounting biological specimens.

1927 *Jrnl. Chem. Soc.* 546 Barium lactobionate was methylated in a manner similar to that already mentioned. **1964** *Chem. Abstr.* LXI. 16697 Ca lactobionate.. may be used under the Federal Food, Drug, and Cosmetic Act as a firming agent in dry pudding mixes. **1889** *Jrnl. Chem. Soc.* LVI. 485 Lactobionic acid, $C_{12}H_{22}O_{12}$, is obtained when milk-sugar (1 part) dissolved in water (7 parts) is treated with bromine (1 part). *Ibid.* 486 Lactobionic acid is decomposed into galactose and gluconic acid when warmed with dilute mineral acids. **1967** KIRK & OTHMER *Encycl. Chem. Technol.* (ed. 2) XIII. 571 The sequestrant and emulsifying properties of lactobionic acid suggest a commercial potential, especially in the food industry, for this product. **1898** *Jrnl. Chem. Soc.* LXXIV. II. 509 When silicon tetrachloride is heated with mandelonitrile or lactonitrile, silicic acid and complex tarry products are formed. **1935** *Chem. Abstr.* XXIX. 814 For prepg. an aliphatic cyanohydrin such as lactonitrile, reaction is effected between HCN and an aliphatic aldehyde or ketone such as acetaldehyde. **1961** *Ibid.* LV. 8268 The alkyl and aralkyl *α*-hydroxy nitriles, i.e. lactonitrile, [etc.].., are effective reagents for the extn. of Au and Ag by cyanidation... Crude lactonitrile which is a by-product from the manuf. of acrylonitrile is inexpensive and very efficient. **1896** *Jrnl. R. Microsc. Soc.* 481 M. J. Amann recommends the following fluids for preserving and imbedding mosses.. (1) Lactophenol. **1929** W. R. TAYLOR in C. E. McClung *Handbk. Microsc. Technique* iv. 139 A solution (Lactophenol) composed of lactic acid [etc.].. is very serviceable and may be used for mounting various materials, softening dried material (especially algæ) or decalcifying specimens. **1970** *Watsonia* VIII. 140 Pollen grains stained with cotton blue in lactophenol.

lactobacillus (ˌlæktəʊbə'sɪləs). *Biol.* Pl. -bacilli. [mod.L. (M. W. Beijerinck 1901, in *Arch. néerl. d. Sci. exactes et nat.* VI. 213), f. LACTO- + BACILLUS.] Any bacterium of the genus *Lactobacillus* (family Lactobacillaceæ), which includes microaerophilic or anaerobic, non-motile, Gram-positive rods which convert glucose and related carbohydrates to lactic acid and are found in the intestinal tract and in fermenting plant and animal (esp. dairy) products.

1924 *Jrnl. Bacteriol.* IX. 375 A study of lactobacilli from the intestines. **1928** B. W. HAMMER *Dairy Bacteriol.* xv. 410 The lactobacilli constitute another type of organism bringing about changes that are important in the ripening of cheddar cheese. **1958** W. C. FRAZIER *Food Microbiol.* iii. 51 Characteristics that make the lactobacilli important in foods are (1) their ability to ferment sugars with the production of considerable amounts of lactic acid, enabling their use in the production of fermented plant and dairy products, or the manufacture of industrial lactic acid, but resulting in the deterioration of some products, e.g. wine or beer; (2) production of gas and other volatile products..; (3) their inability to synthesize most of the vitamins they require,.. making them useful in assays for the vitamin content of foods; and (4) the heat resistance.. of most of the high-temperature lactobacilli. **1961** R. D. BAKER *Essent. Path.* ix. 190 Although many microorganisms are observed in association with caries,.. most investigations have centered around the parasitic lactobacilli. These organisms may have a role in the initiation of the process.

lactoglobulin (læktəʊ'glɒbjʊlɪn). *Biochem.* [a. Da. *lactoglobulin* (J. Sebelien 1885, in *Oversigt o. d. K. Danske Viedensk. Selskabs Forhand.* 4), f. *globulin* GLOBULIN: see LACTO-.]

† **1.** The fraction of milk proteins which is obtained after the removal of casein and is precipitated by a salt such as magnesium sulphate or ammonium sulphate. *Obs.*

1885 *Jrnl. Chem. Soc.* XLVIII. 1000 The author has isolated from milk two albuminoïd substances distinct from caseïn. Lactoglobulin, the first of these, is present in minute quantity only... Lactalbumin, the second albuminoïd, is precipitated by acetic acid in the filtrate from the preceding compound. **1936** [see LACTALBUMIN a].

2. (Usu. *β-lactoglobulin.*) A protein or mixture of closely similar proteins occurring in the lactalbumin fraction of milk, insoluble near the isoelectric point in the absence of salt and having a molecular weight of about 40,000.

1936 *Biochem. Jrnl.* XXX. 968 This investigation shows that the lactoglobulin prepared according to the method of Palmer from the lactalbumin fraction of cow's milk is a monodisperse protein. **1945** *Jrnl. Amer. Chem. Soc.* LXVII. 1531/2 *β*-Lactoglobulin consists of 370 amino acid residues with 366 peptide bonds, arranged in 4 sub-units (polypeptide chains). **1948** *New Biol.* IV. 133 The typical milk proteins, casein, lactalbumin and lactoglobulin, are believed to be mainly products of the serum globulin of the blood. **1955** *Nature* 30 July 218/2 Individual cows produce either a mixture of two electrophoretically distinct *β*-lactoglobulins or only one or the other of these. *Ibid.* 219/2 β_1-Lactoglobulin forms rectangular plates indistinguishable from the well-known crystals hitherto prepared from mixed milk.. whereas β_2-lactoglobulin forms diamond-shaped plates. **1961** *Biochim. & Biophys. Acta* XLIX. 591 In cow's milk *β*-lactoglobulin constitutes approx. half of the whey proteins and 7–12% of the total proteins.

lactol ('læktɒl). *Chem.* [a. G. *lactol* (Helferich & Fries 1925, in *Ber. d. Deut. Chem. Ges.* LVIIIB. 1246), f. *lact-on* LACTONE 2 + *-ol* -OL.] Any cyclic compound that is formed by the oxygen atom in a –C(OH)– group (esp. one in a sugar) becoming linked to the carbon atom of a carbonyl group in the same molecule (with the transfer of the hydrogen atom of the former group to the oxygen atom of the latter).

1925 *Chem. Abstr.* XIX. 2931 The name lactol (aldolactol, ketolactol) is proposed for the cyclo-form of hydroxyaldehydes and ketones, the length of the O-bridge being indicated by Greek letters (as for the lactones) or by nos. in brackets (as for the sugars). **1967** [see GLUCOSIDE].

lactometer (læk'tɒmɪtə(r)). [f. LACTO- + -METER.] An instrument for gauging the purity of milk.

1817 *Blackw. Mag.* II. 219 A Lactometer, for ascertaining the comparative value of each cow's milk in a dairy. **1872** *Echo* 8 Oct. 5 Milk which was proved by the lactometer to be more than half water.

lactone ('læktəʊn). *Chem.* [f. L. *lact-*, *lac* milk + -ONE.] **1.** (See quot.)

1848 FOWNES *Chem.* (ed. 2) 389 Another product of the action of heat on lactic acid, is lactone, a colourless volatile liquid.

2. [ad. G. *lacton* (R. Fittig 1880, in *Ann. d. Chem.* CC. 62).] Any of the class of cyclic esters formed (in theory) by the elimination of a molecule of water from a hydroxyl and a carboxyl group of an organic acid, and characterized by the group –O·CO– as part of a ring; freq. with preceding Gr. letter corresponding to the size of the ring (an *α*-lactone having a three-membered ring, a *β*-lactone a four-membered one, etc.).

1880 *Jrnl. Chem. Soc.* XXXVIII. 378 Pyroterebic acid.. is the internal anhydride of hydroxyisocaproic acid... It is the first representative of its class in the lactic series. For this class of anhydrides the author proposes the name 'lactones'. **1929** *Jrnl. Pharmacol. & Exper. Therap.* XXXVI. 355 The pharmacological study of a series of lactones with a view to their possible usefulness as anthelmintics pointed towards beta angelica lactone and the dilactone of the diacetone diacetic acid as the most promising. **1936** L. J. DESHA *Org. Chem.* xxi. 414 All hydroxy acids lose water when heated..: *α*-Hydroxy acids yield lactides; *β*-hydroxy acids are converted into unsaturated acids; *γ*- and *δ*-hydroxy acids form lactones. **1971** G. A. TAYLOR *Org. Chem. for Students Biol. & Med.* xiii. 188 *α*- and *β*-hydroxy-acids cannot be converted directly into the corresponding *α*- and *β*-lactones (three- and four-membered rings).

lactonic (læk'tɒnɪk), *a.* *Chem.* [f. LACTO- (in chem. names: see below).] **1.** ***lactonic acid***: [tr. G. *lactonsäure* (Hlasiwetz & Habermann 1870, in *Ann. d. Chem. u. Pharm.* CLV. 139), f. *lact-ose* LACTOSE + *-on* -ONE: see -IC.] **a.** = *galactonic acid.*

1871 *Jrnl. Chem. Soc.* XXIV. 547 Lactonic acid, which, according to Fittig's views, must also be monobasic.. is found to be really a bibasic acid. **1886** E. F. SMITH tr. *V. von Richter's Chem. Carbon Compounds* 378 Lactonic acid, $C_6H_{10}O_6$, is produced from milk sugar and galactose by the action of bromine water and silver oxide. It is a deliquescent, crystalline mass, melting at 100°.

b. = *lactobionic acid* s.v. LACTO- 2.

1957 *Chem. Abstr.* LI. Subject Index 1358/1 Lactonic acid, calcium salt, calcium gluconate solubilization with. **1964** N. G. CLARK *Mod. Org. Chem.* xvi. 328 Hydrolysis of lactonic acid yields galactose and gluconic acid.

2. [f. LACTON(E + -IC.] Containing the characteristic ring structure of lactones (sense 2).

1885 *Jrnl. Chem. Soc.* XLVIII. 963 (*heading*) Conversion of lactonic acids into lactones. **1888** *Ibid.* LIV. 251 When the lactonic acids, $CHX\left\langle\begin{matrix}CH(COOH)\\O{\cdot}CO{\cdot}CH_2\end{matrix}\right\rangle$, obtained by the union of aldehydes with succinic acid, are boiled.. the greater portion decomposes yielding.. the monobasic unsaturated acids.. together with the lactones. **1924** *Ibid.* CXXVI. I. 45 When it [*sc. iso*campholactone] is oxidised by means of nitric acid, there are formed nitro-*iso*campholactone and a lactonic acid. **1968** *Jrnl. Agric. & Food Chem.* XVI. 252 (*heading*) Lactonic compounds of apricot. **1970** *Acta Chem. Scand.* XXIV. 3428/1 (*heading*) Investigation of lactonic acids in the latex of *Euphorbium canariensis* L. **1971** *Agric. & Biol. Chem.* (Tokyo) XXXV. 27 (*heading*) Studies on the new seventeen member lactonic antibiotics.

lactonization (,læktənaɪ'zeɪʃən). *Chem.* [f. LACTON(E + -IZATION.] Conversion into a lactone.

1909 *Jrnl. Chem. Soc.* XCVI. I. 551 (*heading*) Lactonisation of acid alcohols. **1939** *Jrnl. Amer. Chem. Soc.* LXI. 3198/1 Of the three possible points of lactonization two, C-9 and C-10, should yield secondary hydroxyl groups when the lactone is opened. **1968** R. O. C. NORMAN *Princ. Org. Synthesis* i. 24 Consider the lactonization of *ω*-hydroxybutyric acid in comparison with the esterification of acetic acid by methanol.

lactonize ('læktənaɪz), *v.* *Chem.* [f. LACTON(E + -IZE.] *trans.* and *intr.* To change into a lactone. Hence **'lactonized, -izing** *ppl. adjs.*

1912 *Chem. Abstr.* VI. 1133 The HCl seems to lactonize the Et pyruvate, while on pyruvic acid it acts in 2 ways, either esterifying and then lactonizing, or *vice versa*. **1939** *Jrnl. Amer. Chem. Soc.* LXI. 3198/1 The strong tendency of tetrahydrohydroxyabietic acid.. to lactonize further complicated the oxidation experiments. **1939** *Ibid.* 3199/2 A rapid method for hydrolysis of lactonized dihydroabietic acid by caustic fusion has been developed. **1967** *Jrnl. Bacteriol.* XCIV. 1975/1 The mutation affects the activity of the lactonizing enzyme in one of two possible ways.

[**lactory**, an erroneous form of LACTARY.]

lactose ('læktəʊs). [f. L. *lact-*, *lac* + -OSE². Cf. F. *lactose*.] A saccharine substance present in milk, commonly called sugar of milk.

1858 *Fownes' Chem.* (ed. 7) 410 Sugar of milk; lactin; lactose. **1869** ROSCOE *Elem. Chem.* 369 Lactose, or milk sugar, occurs only in the milk of mammalia.

‖**lactosuria** (læktəʊ'sjʊərɪə). *Path.* [quasi-Latin, f. prec. + Gr. *οὖρ-ον* urine + -IA.] (See quot.)

1866 A. FLINT *Princ. Med.* (1880) 73 Milk-sugar is present in the urine of females during lactation. This condition is lactosuria.

‖**lactucarium** (læktju:'kɛərɪəm). [mod.L., f. L. *lactūca* lettuce.] The inspissated juice of various kinds of lettuce, used as a drug.

1836 J. M. GULLY *Magendie's Formul.* (ed. 2) 165 Dr. Duncan has described the different modes of obtaining lettuce juice, by him called lactucarium. **1876** HARLEY *Mat. Med.* (ed. 6) 541 French lactucarium is formed into circular cakes 1½ inch in diameter.

lactucic (læk'tju:sɪk), *a.* *Chem.* [f. as next + -IC. Cf. F. *lactucique*.] ***lactucic acid***: a crystalline acid found in the juice of the *Lactuca virosa*.

1838 T. THOMSON *Chem. Org. Bodies* 159 Lactucic acid was discovered by Pfaff. **1865-72** in WATTS *Dict. Chem.* III. 465.

lactucin ('læktjʊsɪn). *Chem.* [f. L. *lactūc-a* lettuce + -IN. Cf. F. *lactucine*.] A crystalline bitter substance contained in lactucarium.

1875 H. C. WOOD *Therap.* (1879) 206.

lactyl ('læktɪl). *Chem.* [f. L. *lact-*, *lac* milk + -YL.] An organic radical derived from lactic acid. Also *attrib.*

1868 *Fownes' Chem.* (ed. 10) 764 Lactyl Chloride is a colourless liquid.

lacuna (lə'kju:nə). Pl. **lacunæ**, **lacunas**. [a. L. *lacūna* a hole, pit, f. *lacus* LAKE *sb.*⁴ Cf. LACUNE.]

1. In a manuscript, an inscription, the text of an author: A hiatus, blank, missing portion. Also *transf.*

1663 SIR R. MORAY in *Lauderd. Papers* (Camden) I. 181 You do well to leave no Lacunas in your letters. **1694** GIBSON in *Lett. Lit. Men* (Camden) 228 The lacuna of his behaviour in Holland, Dr. Gregory perhaps may be able to make up. **1851** D. WILSON *Preh. Ann.* IV. v. (1863) II. 326 The context which fills up the numerous lacunae of the time-worn inscription. **1875** MAINE *Hist. Inst.* ix. 256 The description given.. is followed by a lacuna in the manuscript. **1892** ZANGWILL *Bow Myst.* 147 There were various lacunæ and hypotheses in the case for the defence.

2. Chiefly in physical science: A gap, an empty space, spot, or cavity. **a.** *gen.*

1872 PROCTOR *Ess. Astron.* xxiv. 303 The gaps and lacunae are left relatively clear of lucid stars. **1879** RUTLEY *Study Rocks* x. 107 Fluid lacunae.. are of frequent occurrence in nepheline. **1880** *Sat. Rev.* 15 May 637 The curious lacuna in the field of vision, known as the blind spot.

b. *Anat.* 'A mucous follicle; also, a space in the connective tissue giving origin to a lymphatic' (*Syd. Soc. Lex.* 1888).

1706 PHILLIPS (ed. Kersey), *Lacunæ* are certain small Pores or Passages in the Neck of the Womb. **1722** QUINCY *Lex. Physico-Med.* (ed. 2) 175 Between this Muscle [Sphincter] and the inner membrane of the Vagina, there are several little Glands, whose excretory Ducts are called Lacunæ. **1874** VAN BUREN *Dis. Genit. Org.* 77 Inflammation seals the orifice of the follicle and the lacuna is converted into a cyst containing pus.

c. *Anat.* One of the small cavities in the bone substance which contain the bone corpuscles or osteoblasts (*Syd. Soc. Lex.* 1888).

1845 TODD & BOWMAN *Phys. Anat.* I. 109 They [pores] soon arrange themselves in sets, each of which.. discharges itself into a small cavity or lacuna. **1859** [see LACUNAL *a.*]. **1867** J. HOGG *Microsc.* I. ii. 57 The observation of.. the Haversian canals and the lacunæ of bones.

d. *Zool.* One of the spaces left among the tissues of the lower animals, which serve in place of vessels for the circulation of the body fluids.

1867 J. HOGG *Microsc.* II. iii. 566 Minute capillary ramifications [in flukes] terminating in small oval shaped sacs or lacunæ.

e. *Bot.* An air-space in the cellular tissue of plants, an air-cell. Also, a small pit or depression on the upper surface of the thallus of lichens.

1836 LOUDON *Encycl. Plants* 948 [Lichens] *Lacunæ* are small hollows or pits on the upper surface of the frond. **1856** in HENSLOW *Dict. Bot. Terms.* **1874** COOKE *Fungi* 41 In Tuburcinia, the minute cells are compacted into a hollow sphere, having lacunæ communicating with the interior.

lacunal (lə'kju:nəl), *a.* [f. LACUNA + -AL¹.] Of or pertaining to a lacuna, resembling a lacuna.

1846 DANA *Zooph.* iv. (1848) 58 The intermediate lateral pores or lacunal spaces. **1859** J. TOMES *Dental Surg.* 86 A bone lacuna, situated within a semi-circular indentation in the dentine, gives the appearance of a lacunal cell. **1874** VAN BUREN *Dis. Genit. Org.* 77 Another form of lacunal inflammation is where the lacuna magna in the roof of the urethra continues inflamed.

lacunar (lə'kju:nə(r)), *sb.* *Arch.* Pl. **lacunars**, **lacunaria** (lækju:'nɛərɪə). [a. L. *lacūnar*, f. *lacūna*: see LACUNA.] **a.** The ceiling or under surface of any part, when it consists of sunk or hollowed compartments. **b.** *pl.* The sunken panels in such a ceiling.

1696 PHILLIPS, *Lacunar* (in Architect.), the flooring or planking above the Porticoes; a cieled roof arched or fretted. **1727-41** in CHAMBERS *Cycl.* **1727-1800** in BAILEY. **1823** P. NICHOLSON *Pract. Build.* 587 *Lacunariæ*, or *Lacunars*, panels or coffers formed on the ceilings of apartments, and sometimes on the soffits of coronae in the Ionic, Corinthian, and Composite orders. **1845** *Athenæum* 11 Jan. 48 On the grounds of the coffers forming the lacunaria of the ceilings.

lacunar (lə'kju:nə(r)), *a.* [f. LACUNA + -AR.] Of or pertaining to a lacuna or lacunæ; consisting of or characterized by lacunæ.

1870 ROLLESTON *Anim. Life* p. cv, The circulation is always more or less extensively lacunar, even arteries may be wanting. **1871** HUXLEY *Anat. Inv. Anim.* i. (1877) 57 The venous system remains more or less lacunar. **1884** BOWER & SCOTT *De Bary's Phaner.* 430 The zone of lacunar parenchyma.. surrounds the vascular bundles. **1897** *Allbutt's Syst. Med.* IV. 743 The only affection that can be confused with this mycosis is chronic lacunar tonsillitis.

lacunary (lə'kju:nərɪ), *a.* [f. LACUNA + -ARY²; after F. *lacunaire*.]

1. Of or pertaining to a lacuna; consisting of or resembling lacunæ.

1857 E. C. OTTÉ *Quatrefages' Rambles Nat.* II. 289 Lacunary passages connected these two cavities together. **1868** P. M. DUNCAN *Insect World* Introd. 14 On reaching the interior of the head it opens in the lacunary inter-organic system.

2. *Math.* ***lacunary function*** (see quots.). ***lacunary space***: an area in a plane, every point of which is the affix of a value of the variable for which a given function has no determinate values.

1893 CAYLEY in *Q. Jrnl. Math.* May 281 A function such as this, existing only for points within a certain region and not for the whole of the infinite plane, is said to be a lacunary function. **1893** A. R. FORSYTH *Theory Functions* §87. 141 Weierstrass was the first to draw attention to lacunary functions as they may be called. *Ibid.* 143 The first step in the construction of a function which shall have any assigned lacunary space.

†**lacunate**, *v.* *Obs. rare*⁻⁰. [f. L. *lacūnāt-*, ppl. stem of *lacūnāre*, f. *lacūna*.]

1623 COCKERAM, *Lacunate*, to make ditches or holes.

Hence †**lacu'nation**, a making of holes.

1658 in PHILLIPS. **1676** in COLES.

lacune (lə'kju:n). [Anglicized form of LACUNA. Cf. F. *lacune*.]

1. = LACUNA 1. Now *rare*.

1701 BEVERLEY *Apoc. Quest.* 43 Which.. I look upon as a very Great Lacune in his Scheme. **1784** HENLEY in *Beckford's Vathek* (1868) 189 *note*, There being a lacune in his transcript of the original. **1814** W. TAYLOR in Robberd *Mem.* II. 450 He could trust to his extempore eloquence for supplying the lacunes of his text. **1887** *Dublin Rev.* July 213 In the episcopal succession there are some few lacunes which there are no data to fill.

2. = LACUNA 2.

1846 DANA *Zooph.* iv. (1848) 35 The various cavities, lacunes, or pores in the tissues of the animal.

lacune, obs. form of LAGOON.

lacunose (lə'kju:nəʊs), *a.* [ad. L. *lacūnōs-us*, f. *lacūna* LACUNA.] Abounding in lacunæ:

a. Having many cavities or depressions; furrowed, pitted; *spec.* in *Nat. Hist.*

1816 T. BROWN *Elem. Conchol.* 155 *Lacunose*, having the surface covered with small pits. **1826** KIRBY & SP. *Entomol.* IV. 270 Lacunose (*lacunosa*), having a few scattered, irregular, broadish but shallow excavations. **1874** COOKE *Fungi* 56 These latter have either a smooth, warted, spinulose, or lacunose epispore.

b. Of a manuscript: Full of gaps or hiatuses.

1894 R. ELLIS *Fables of Phaedrus* 9 The lacunose condition of both MSS. at this part of Book iv.

¶In combining form *lacunoso-*: **lacu,noso-'fistulose** *a.* *Bot.*, having lacunæ and fistulæ; **lacu,noso-'rugose** *a.* *Bot.*, wrinkled with irregular furrows.

1866 *Treas. Bot.* 655/2 *Lacunoso-rugose*, marked by deep broad irregular wrinkles, as the shell of the walnut, or stone of the peach. **1887** W. PHILLIPS *Brit. Discomycetes* 13 Ribs slender, solid, not lacunoso-fistulose, as in the preceding.

Hence **lacu'nosity**, lacunose quality.

1895 *Athenæum* 31 Aug. 290/2 The vocabulary conveys a general impression of lacunosity and inconsistency.

†**la'cunous**, *a.* *Obs. rare*⁻¹. [f. LACUNA + -OUS.] Resembling a hollow or lacuna.

1653 R. SANDERS *Physiogn.* 272 This lacunous hollow of the upper lip, between the nostrils and the upper lip.

lacunulose (lə'kju:nələʊs), *a.* *Bot.* [f. mod.L. *lacūnula* (dim. of LACUNA) + -OSE.] Minutely lacunose.

1882 TUCKERMAN *N. Amer. Lichens* I. 61 *P*[*armelia*] *lophyrea*. Ach.;.. lobes flattish lacunulose, flexuous.

lacuscular (ləˈkʌskjʊlə(r)), *a.* [f. L. *lacuscul-us* (dim. of *lacus* LAKE *sb.*⁴) + -AR.] Of or pertaining to a small pool; frequenting small pools.

1878 J. COLQUHOUN *Moor & Loch* (1880) I. 266 Perhaps the most lacuscular is the tuft.

lacustral (ləˈkʌstrəl), *a. rare*⁻⁰. [f. as next + -AL¹.] = LACUSTRINE.

1843 in HUMBLE *Dict. Geol.* **1865** in PAGE *Handbk. Geol. T.*

lacustrian (ləˈkʌstrɪən), *a.* and *sb. rare.* [f. as next + -IAN.] **A.** *adj.* = LACUSTRINE 1 b. **B.** *sb.* An inhabitant of a lacustrine dwelling.

1865 *Reader* 8 July 30 The waters of the Lake of Constance have been so low this winter as to allow important researches to be made concerning the lacustrian habitations. **1884** W. WESTALL in *Contemp. Rev.* XLVI. 70 There is ample evidence that the Lacustrians of the Bronze Period had reached a high degree of civilization.

lacustrine (ləˈkʌstrɪn), *a.* [f. as if L. *lacustri- (f. *lacus* LAKE *sb.*⁴, after the analogy of *palūstri-*, *palūster*, f. *palūd-*, *palūs* marsh) + -INE.] Of or pertaining to a lake or lakes. Said *esp.* of plants and animals inhabiting lakes, and *Geol.* of strata, etc., which originated by deposition at the bottom of lakes; also with reference to 'lake-dwellings' such as those of prehistoric Europe. ***lacustrine age, period***: the period when lake-dwellings were common.

1830 LYELL *Princ. Geol.* I. iii. 49 The lacustrine and alluvial deposits of Italy. **1833** *Ibid.* III. 220, I collected six species of lacustrine shells. **1843** PORTLOCK *Geol.* 165 The clays and sands..on Lough Neagh..were of lacustrine origin. **1850** H. MILLER *Footpr. Creat.* i. (1874) 9 Lacustrine plants. **1851** D. WILSON *Preh. Ann.* (1863) I. i. 38 The lacustrine habitations of Switzerland. **1868** PEARD *Water-Farm.* iii. 30 The stream we design to cultivate must possess no lacustrine head. **1869** LUBBOCK *Preh. Times* ix. (ed. 2) 291 The bones generally occur in the lacustrine shell marl. **1875** EMERSON *Lett. & Soc. Aims, Prog. Cult.* Wks. (Bohn) III. 225 Who would live in the stone age..or the lacustrine? **1878** HUXLEY *Physiogr.* 143 *Lacustrine Delta.* The alluvial tract formed by a river at its embouchure into a lake. **1879** RUTLEY *Study Rocks* iii. 15 Identified with a marine or a lacustrine fauna. **1880** HARTING *Brit. Anim. Extinct* 3 Wild boars..wallowing..in lacustrine mire.

‖**lac Virginis.** [L., *lit.* milk of the Virgin.]

†**1.** Some cosmetic. *Obs.*

1477 NORTON *Ordin.* v. in Ashmole *Theat. Chem.* (1652) 77 As Water of Litharge which would not misse With Water of Azot to make *lac virginis.* **1592** NASHE *P. Penilesse* C 2, She should haue noynted your face ouer night with *Lac virginis.* **1641** FRENCH *Distill.* (1651) v. 142 This salt..is as good as any *Lac virginis* to clear, and smooth the face. **1698** SIR R. SOUTHWELL in *Phil. Trans.* XX. 88 This maketh the *Lac Virginis* for the common Wash.

2. A kind of wine; ? = G. *Liebfraumilch.*

1820 *Blackw. Mag.* VIII. 44 The Parsons should grow misty On good *Lac Virginis*, or *Lachryma Christi.*

lacy (ˈleɪsɪ), *a.* Also **lacey.** [f. LACE *sb.* + -Y¹.] Consisting of, or having the appearance of, lace.

1804 in *Charlotte Smith's Convers.* I. 57 Eluding him, on lacey plume The silver moth enjoys the gloom. **1823** GALT *Entail* I. xv. 112 A thin mist, partaking more of the lacy character of a haze than the texture of a vapour. **1848** SARA COLERIDGE in *Q. Rev.* Mar. 439 To display the lacy vein-work of a leaf apart from the cellular tissue. **1883** MISS BROUGHTON *Belinda* I. i. ix. 157 Clad in one of those lawny, lacy gowns.

lacye, -yn, obs. forms of LACE *v.*

lad (læd), *sb.*¹ Forms: 4-6 **ladde,** 6-8 *Sc.* **lawd,** 7 **ladd,** 5- **lad.** [ME. *ladde*, of obscure origin.

Possibly a use of the definite form of the pa. pple. of LEAD *v.*; in ME. *lad* is a dialectal variant of *led* pa. pple. The use might have originated in the application of the plural *ladde* elliptically to the followers of a lord. Actual evidence, however, is wanting. It is noteworthy that a 'Godric *Ladda*' attests a document written 1088-1123 (Earle *Land Charters* 270). If this cognomen be (as is possible) identical with ME. *ladde*, its evidence is unfavourable to the derivation suggested above.

Quite inadmissible, both on the ground of phonology and meaning, is the current statement that the word is cognate with the last syllable of the Goth. *juggalauþs* young man; the ending *-lauþs* (stem *-lauda-* adj., *laudi-* sb.), which does not occur as an independent word, has in compounds the sense 'having (a certain) growth or size', as in *hwēlauþs* how great, *swalauþs* so great, *samalauþs* equally great. The Celtic derivations commonly alleged are also worthless: the Welsh *llawd* is a dictionary figment invented to explain the feminine '*lodes* (in Dictionaries *llodes*), which Prof. Rhys has shown to be shortened from *herlodes*, fem. of *herlawd*, a. ME. *herlot* HARLOT; and the Irish *lath* does not exist in either the earlier or the later sense of 'lad', but means 'hero' or 'champion'.]

†**1.** A serving-man, attendant; a man of low birth and position; a varlet. *Obs.*

c **1300** *Havelok* 1786 'Hwat haue ye seid', quoth a ladde. **13..** *E.E. Allit. P.* C. 154 Mony ladde þer forth-lep to laue & to kest. **1377** LANGL. *P. Pl.* B. XIX. 32 To make lordes of laddes Of lond that he wynneth. *c* **1380** *Sir Ferumb.* 4451 And weþen art þou; þov ladde prout? *c* **1430** *Syr Gener.* (Roxb.) 8280 Whan Serenides the Ring had, Glad she was, and called a lad. *c* **1440** *York Myst.* xxix. 390 þis ladde [Jesus] with his lesyngis has oure lawes lorne. *c* **1485** *Digby Myst.* (1882) III. 43 Lord and lad, to my law doth lowte. **1513** BRADSHAW *St. Werburge* I. 1015 A lad to wedde a lady is an inconuenyent. *c* **1530** L. COX *Rhet.* (1899) 77 He had with hym syngyng laddes and women seruantes. **1530** LYNDESAY *Test. Papyngo* 391 Pandaris, pykthankis, custronis, and clatteraris, Loupis vp frome laddis, sine lychtis amang lardis. **1535** COVERDALE *1 Sam.* ii. 15 Or euer they burned the fatt, the prestes lad [Vulg. *puer*] came, and sayde [etc.]. **1549-50** in Swayne *Churchw. Acc. Sarum* (1896) 277 Smythe the carpenter for j dayes Labor for his servaunte Clerke and his ladde for takyng downe of the tymbre. **1721** KELLY *Scot. Prov.* 240 Lay up like a Laird, and seek like a Lad.

2. a. A boy, youth; a young man, young fellow. Also, in the diction of pastoral poetry, used to denote 'a young shepherd'. In wider sense applied familiarly or endearingly (sometimes ironically) to a male person of any age, esp. in the form of address ***my lad.*** ***lad of wax***: a shoemaker.

[*c* **1440** *Promp. Parv.* 283/1 Ladde, or knave, *garcio.* **1483** *Cath. Angl.* 206/1 A Ladde, *vbi* a knaffe.] **1535** COVERDALE *Prov.* xxii. 15 Foolishnes sticketh in the herte of yᵉ lad, but yᵉ rod of correccion driueth it awaye. **1552** LATIMER *Serm.* (1584) 323 First he is a childe; afterward he becommeth a ladde; then a yong man, and after that a perfect man. **1562** A. SCOTT *Poems* (S.T.S.) i. 53 Lymmer lawdis and litle lassis. **1596** SHAKS. *1 Hen. IV*, I. ii. 112 *Prin.* Where shall we take a purse to morrow, Iacke? *Fal.* Where thou wilt Lad. **1600** DEKKER *Honest Wh.* II. Dram. Wks. II. 115 How now old Lad, what doest cry? **1602** *Narcissus* (1893) 78 Why, well said, my ladds of mettall. **1608** WILLET *Hexapla Exod.* 787 Our blessed Sauiour..said to his disciples, children, or lads, haue ye any meate? *a* **1650** *Captain Carr* 30 in Furnivall *Percy Folio* I. 81 'Ile not giue over my house', shee said, 'neither for Ladds nor man'. **1709** BYROM *Lit. Rem.* (1854) I. i. 6 The other two sizers, one sophister, the other a Lancashire lad of our year. **1717** LADY M. W. MONTAGU *Let. to Pope* 1 Apr., The young lads..divert themselves with making garlands for their favourite lambs. **1724** DE FOE *Mem. Cavalier* (1840) 269 The old lad was not to be caught. **1794** *Sporting Mag.* III. 201 Requesting you as a brother lad of wax to make me some of your tight shoes. **1829** HOOD *Eug. Aram* viii, My gentle lad, what is't you read? **1856** R. M. BALLANTYNE *Snowflakes & Sunbeams* xxviii. 390 What did you say struck you, Harry, my lad? **1871** R. ELLIS tr. *Catullus* lxxviii. 4 Lovely the lady, the lad lovely, a company sweet. **1886** RUSKIN *Præterita* I. v. 140 All handsome lads and pretty lasses.

b. A man of spirit and vigour; used esp. in phrs. ***a bit of a lad, quite a lad.*** Also (*colloq.*), a spirited girl.

a **1553** UDALL *Royster D.* IV. vii. (Arb.) 71, I trowe they shall finde and feele that I am a lad. **1913** [see BIT *sb.*² 4 c]. **1926** T. E. LAWRENCE *Seven Pillars* (1935) v. lxi. 346 He, Rahail, was quite a lad: a free-built, sturdy fellow, too fleshy for the life we were to lead. **1935** G. INGRAM *Cockney Cavalcade* iv. 54 'That matcher of ours is a lad, Mum!' ..'Oh, what's she been up to now?' **1935** *Punch* 13 Mar. 294/1 Women..Describe him freely to my face As quite a lad. **1960** 'H. CARMICHAEL' *Seeds of Hate* xiii. 117 Bit of a lad is Mr. Alan Clark..running round fancy-free for years. **1969** A. CADE *Turn up Stone* iii. 76 Oh dear! The late Clive Neilson was certainly a bit of a lad, wasn't he?

c. A stable-groom of any age; also, a female one.

1848 *Sporting Life* 8 Jan. 242/1 The more important a groom is, the more mysterious, conceited, pedantic he is... The first thing a lad does now-a-days is to set up a watch, after which, if his mind incline towards horses, he buys what he calls a 'printed book' about them. **1862** *Once a Week* 1 Nov. 512/1 Judging..from the quarter in which these betting operations were carried on, they were led to think that the lad who attended to the horse Gosport,..conveyed intelligence to his master. **1894** *Strand Mag.* May 554/1 He was a good lad, tinged with the archaic stable-slang of Thessaly. **1968** D. FRANCIS *Forfeit* iv. 49, I..called on the trainer, whom I saw almost every time I went racing... 'Did you find Sandy Willes?.. She's one of my best lads.' **1971** *Daily Tel.* 5 Apr. 11 (*caption*) A celebration snack for Specify, winner of the Grand National... Celebrating with him are Mr John E. Sutcliffe (left), his trainer, Mr Richard Bullen, his 'lad', and Mrs Sutcliffe. **1971** D. FRANCIS *Bonecrack* 17 The elderly lad who looked after him was standing at the door. *Ibid.* 19 There had been quite a stir in Newmarket when my father had promoted her to head lad. **1972** *Guardian* 6 May 11/3 A famous owner..was watching his horse on the gallops.. 'Who's that lad on 'im?' he said to the trainer. 'Oh,' came the reply, 'that's Cynthia.' **1973** *Daily Tel.* 30 Oct. 9/2 Lads and girls serving their five-year apprenticeship get pocket money..with clothing and keep paid for by the trainer.

3. *Sc.* A sweetheart.

1725 RAMSAY *Gentle Sheph.* v. ii, And am I then a match for my ain lad? **1781** J. MAYNE *Logan Braes* in *Chambers' Cycl. Eng. Lit.* II. 493 While my dear lad maun face his faes Far, frae me. **1786** BURNS *Dream* xiv, Ye royal Lasses dainty, Heav'n..gie you lads a-plenty.

4. *attrib.*, as ***lad-porter***; †**lad-age,** the age of boyhood; **lad-bairn, -wean** *Sc.*, a male child.

1605 SYLVESTER *Du Bartas* II. iii. I. *Vocation* 170 Here have I past my *Lad-age fair and good. **17..** *Herd's Collect. Sc. Songs* (1776) II. 149 This maiden had a braw *lad-bairn. **1821** GALT *Ann. Parish* xix. 180 There was a greater christening of lad bairns than had ever been in any year during my incumbency. **1894** *Daily News* 11 Sept. 5/3 A *lad porter on the..Railway. **1821** HOGG *Jacobite Relics* II. 175 Bonny orphan *lad-weans twa.

Hence the *nonce-wds.* **ˈladdess,** a girl, lass; **ˈladdism,** the condition or character of a lad; **ˈladhood,** the state of being a lad.

1768 H. WALPOLE *Corr.* (1837) II. 407, I know that he is a very amiable lad and I do not know that she is not as amiable a laddess. **1843** *Blackw. Mag.* LIII. 80 They.. emerge..into the full and perfect imago of little lords.. without any of those intermediate conditions of laddism, hobble-de-hoyism [etc.]. **1883** *Spectator* 28 Apr. 543 Youth or ladhood was now protracted further into life. **1891** *Century Mag.* Nov. 61 In this region I grew to ladhood.

†**lad,** *sb.*² *Obs. rare.* A thong. Hence †**ˈladded** *a.*, thonged.

c **1440** *Promp. Parv.* 283/1 Ladde, thwonge (*K.* thounge, *S.* thang), *ligula.* Laddyd, *ligulatus.* **1847** HALLIWELL, *Lad*, a thong of leather; a shoe-latchet.

lad, obs. pa. t. and pple. of LEAD *v.*

Ladakhi (ləˈdɑːkɪ). Also **Ladaki.** [Native name.] **a.** A native or inhabitant of Ladakh, a district of eastern Kashmir. **b.** The language spoken in Ladakh, a dialect of Tibetan. Also *attrib.* or as *adj.*

1893 E. F. KNIGHT *Where Three Empires Meet* viii. 123 A good-natured Ladaki, with a stolid face like that of a Chinese idol, puckered up into an inscrutable and perpetual smile. **1896** *Geogr. Jrnl.* VII. 476 Our Ladakis informed us that this man's predecessor..was promptly put in jail by the Wazir for having defrauded some Ladakis who had been trading in Tibet. **1899** A. H. FRANCKE *Ladakhi Songs* 1st. Ser. 2 The Ladakhi rhyme is, as many examples prove, a rhyme of sentence. *Ibid.* 4 The orthography of the Ladakhi and Purig dialects has always kept as near to that of the book-language as possible. *Ibid.* 5 Silent prefixed letters.. are written with the Ladakhi verb. **1911** *Encycl. Brit.* XVI. 59/1 It [*sc.* Ladakh] was, however, conquered and annexed in 1834-1841 by Gulab Singh of Jammu—the unwarlike Ladakhis, even with nature fighting on their side, and against indifferent generalship, being no match for the Dogra troops. **1939** L. PETECH *Study Chron. Ladakh* 6 There is urgent need of collecting and publishing the most important Ladakhi inscriptions. **1959** *News Chron.* 28 Nov. 4/2 He's a Ladakhi, really. An Indian national, like us. He became a Christian.

‖**ladang** (ləˈdɑːŋ). Also 8 **laddang.** [Malay.] A piece of land under dry cultivation, often a jungle clearing. Also *attrib.*

1783 W. MARSDEN *Hist. Sumatra* 60 *Paddee*, on Sumatra and the Malay islands, is distinguished into two sorts, *Laddang* or up-land paddee, and *Sawoor* or low-land. **1839** T. J. NEWBOLD *Pol. & Statistical Acct. Straits of Malacca* I. iv. 119 A small quantity only is grown on the ladangs, or dry-land plantations. *Ibid.* v. 263 The ladang rice, however, is affirmed by some to be sweeter and whiter, and to keep better than the produce of the sawah. **1906** SKEAT & BLAGDEN *Pagan Races Malay Peninsula* I. i. 119 A blackberry..grows amongst the underwood ('blukar') on the old Sakai clearings ('ladang'). **1935** *Discovery* Sept. 263/1 Nomads of long habit, they [*sc.* the Sakai and the Semang] roam through their territory but no longer from one 'ladang' to another but rather from the borders of kampong to kampong as they lose their..fear of the Malay. **1954** E. D. LABORDE tr. *Robequain's Malaya, Indonesia, Borneo & Philippines* vi. 94 In Indonesia most of the cultivation is done on the *ladang* system. **1958** *Times Lit. Suppl.* 19 Sept. 531/3 Nomads of the deep jungle, they clear and cultivate patches of a few acres, known as *ladangs*..; but in a year or two they move on, clearing new *ladangs* in other parts of the jungle. **1965** C. SHUTTLEWORTH *Malayan Safari* ii. 32 In a number of ladangs..they had planted hill rice.

‖**ladanum** (ˈlædənəm). Also 6 (*anglicized*) **ladane.** [L. *lādanum*, *lēdanum*, a. Gr. λᾱ́δανον, λήδανον, f. λῆδον mastic. Cf. LABDANUM and LAUDANUM.]

1. A gum resin which exudes from plants of the genus CISTUS, esp. *C. ladaniferus* and *C. Creticus*, much used in perfumery and for fumigation.

[*c* **1400** *Lanfranc's Cirurg.* 179 ℞ ladani ʒ j, & resolue it in ʒ iiij of oile of mirtilles. *Ibid.* 188 Olium ladani.] **1551** TURNER *Herbal* I. K vj, Ladanum..hath the propertie to bind to gether to warme, to make softe and to open the mouthes of the veynes. **1568** SKEYNE *The Pest* (1860) 31 Eikand thairtill..sa meikill of ladane as salbe thocht expedient. **1611** COTGR., *Ladane*, the sweet Gumme Ladanum. **1634** PEACHAM *Gentl. Exerc.* I. xii. 40 Sistis (that beareth that excellent gumme Ladanum). **1648** HERRICK *Hesper.* (1869) 194 How can I chuse but kisse her, whence do's come The storax, spiknard, myrrhe and ladanum. **1861** MISS PRATT *Flower. Pl.* I. 161 The balsam called Ladanum ..is produced by the *Cistus Creticus.*

†**2.** = LAUDANUM. *Obs.*

1627 tr. *Bacon's Life & Death* (1651) 29 The compound Opiates are Treacle, Methridate, Ladanum, &c.

ladde-borde: see LARBOARD.

ladden, rare obs. pa. pple. of LADE *v.*

ladder (ˈlædə(r)), *sb.* Forms: 1 **hlǽder, hlǽdder,** 2-4 **leddre,** 4 *Kent.* **lheddre,** 3-5 (6 *Sc.*) **ledder,** 4-5 **leddir(e, leddyr,** 3-4 **laddre,** 4 **laddir,** 6- **ladar,** 6-7 **lather,** 4- **ladder.** [OE. *hlǽd(d)er* str. fem., corresp. to OFris. *hleder, hladder-*, MDu. *lēdere* (Du. *leer*, also *ladder* from Fris.), OHG. *leitara* (MHG., mod.G. *leiter*):—OTeut. **hlaidrjâ*, f. Teut. root **hlī-*: *hlai-* (whence LEAN *v.*):—Aryan **klī-*: cf. Gr. κλῖμαξ ladder.]

1. a. An appliance made of wood, metal, or rope, usually portable, consisting of a series of bars ('rungs') or steps fixed between two supports, by means of which one may ascend to or descend from a height.

971 *Blickl. Hom.* 209 þær wæs ȝewuna þæm folce..þæt hie æfter hlæddrum up to ðæm glæsenum fæte astiȝon. *c* **1000** ÆLFRIC *Gen.* xxviii. 12 þa ȝeseah he on swefne standan ane hlædre fram eorðan to heofenan. *a* **1100** *Gerefa* in *Anglia* (1886) IX. 263 Hlædre, horscamb and sceara. *c* **1250** *Gen. & Ex.* 1607 He..saȝ..fro ðe erðe up til heuene bem, A leddre stonden. **1297** R. GLOUC. (Rolls) 3103 Hii.. cables vette ynowe & laddren & leuours. *c* **1340** *Cursor M.* 3779 (Fairf.) In slepe a ladder him þoȝt he seyghe fra þe

firmament riȝt to his eyghe. **1375** BARBOUR *Bruce* x. 642 Thai set thair ledder to the wall. *c* **1400** *Destr. Troy* 4761 Þai wonyn on the wallis lightly with ladders. **1560** J. DAUS tr. *Sleidane's Chron. our Time* 159 The Emperour goynge forth as farre as the ladder of the shippe to mete him, receaveth him in. **1587** FLEMING *Contn. Holinshed* III. 356/1 A lather of fourteene staves would but reach to the top. **1621** G. SANDYS *Ovid's Met.* XIV. (1626) 298 [He] oft a lather tooke To gather fruit. **1726–7** SWIFT *Gulliver* I. i. 25 That several ladders should be applied to my sides, on which..the inhabitants mounted. **1840** DICKENS *Old C. Shop* xl, Kit mounted half way up a short ladder.

†**b.** *esp.* The steps to a gallows. Chiefly in phr. ***to bring to the ladder***. ***groom of the ladder*** (jocular): a hangman. *Obs.*

a **1533** LD. BERNERS *Huon* lix. 204 [Iuoryn] commaundyd a .xxx. men to lede hym to yᵉ galows &..they causyd the mynstrell to mount vp on yᵉ ladder. **1594** NASHE *Unfort. Trav.* Wks. 1883–4 V. 138, I..should haue been hanged, was brought to the ladder,..and yet for all that scap'd dancing in a hempen circle. *Ibid.* 151 Casting mee off the ladder. *Ibid.* 185 A fidler cannot turne his pin so soone, as he [an executioner] would turn a man of the ladder. **1601** DENT *Path-w. Heaven* 311 Many..haue beene brought to the gallowes, and haue confessed vpon the ladder, that [etc.]. *a* **1640** DAY *Peregr. Schol.* (1881) 72 A kinsman of myne that is grome of the ladder and yeoman of the corde. **1655** GURNALL *Chr. in Arm.* xix. (1669) 233/2 The offer of a pardon comes too late to him that has turn'd himself off the Ladder.

c. *fig.* Also in phr. †***to draw up the ladder after itself*** [cf. F. *après lui il faut tirer l'échelle*]: to be unapproachable. ***to see through a ladder***: to see what is obvious. ***to kick down the ladder***: said of persons who repudiate or ignore the friendships or associations by means of which they have risen in the world.

c **1175** *Lamb. Hom.* 129 Ðis is sunfulla monna leddre. *a* **1225** *Ancr. R.* 354 And forði þet Dauid hefde þeos two stalen of þisse leddre, þauh he king were, he clomb upward. **1340** *Ayenb.* 246 Þis is þe laste stape of þe lheddre of perfeccion. **1377** LANGL. *P. Pl.* B. XVI. 44 The Fende..leith a laddre there-to, of lesynges aren the ronges. **1477** EARL RIVERS (Caxton) *Dictes* 77 Men sette moche store by the foresayde science and was their opynion that it was the laddre to go vp into alle other sciences. **1593** SHAKS. *Rich. II*, v. i. 55 Northumberland, thou Ladder where-withall The mounting Bullingbrooke ascends my Throne. *a* **1625** COPE in Gutch *Coll. Cur.* I. 133 It is not the true way..for men to raise themselves by ladders of detraction. **1670** LASSELS *Voy. Italy* I. 87 After the Domo, I saw the Church of the Annunciata, which draweth up the Ladder after it for neatness. **1794** NELSON in Nicolas *Disp.* (ed. 2) I. 449 Duncan is, I think, a little altered; there is nothing like kicking down the ladder a man rises by. **1843** LE FEVRE *Life Trav. Phys.* I. I. iv. 74 With these two houses alone I have worked up the medical ladder of my life. **1847** DE SMET *Oregon Missions* 31 It was on this occasion he conceived the idea of the Catholic ladder—'a form of instruction which represents on paper the various truths and mysteries of religion in their chronological order'. **1848** THACKERAY *Book of Snobs* vii. (1872) 27 She has struggled so gallantly for polite reputation that she has won it: pitilessly kicking down the ladder as she advanced degree by degree. **1852** MRS. STOWE *Uncle Tom's C.* vi. 37 Can't ye see through a ladder, ye black nigger? **1868** FREEMAN *Norm. Conq.* (1876) II. vii. 73 He now began to climb the ladder of preferment afresh. **1910** *Daily Chron.* 24 Jan. 8/3 Some kind of ladder of subjects..would be a great gain. **1942** *R.A.F. Jrnl.* 18 Apr. 15 Knowledge that would serve as a ladder to further research. **1951** R. FIRTH *Elem. Social Organiz.* i. 29 Special attention was..given to such important matters as the breadth of the educational ladder. **1974** 'W. HAGGARD' *Kinsmen* x. 98 When he'd made a great fortune Duncan Gregg had gone up the ladder a little. But not very much, he was still in trade.

2. With qualifying words indicating its use, construction, position, etc., as ***fire-***, ***extension-***, ***rope-***, ***scaling-***, ***step-ladder***, etc. Also *Naut.*, as ***accommodation***, ***bowsprit***, ***entering***, ***gallery***, ***quarter***, ***stern ladder***. Also JACOB'S LADDER.

1626 CAPT. SMITH *Accid. Yng. Sea-men* 13 An entring ladder or cleats. **1706** PHILLIPS (ed. Kersey) s.v. *Ladders*, the Bolt-sprit-ladder, at the Beak-head, made fast over the Bolt-sprit, to get upon it. **1758** SHARP in *Naval Chron.* VIII. 154 He..got into a boat from the stern ladder. **1769** FALCONER *Dict. Marine* (1780) s.v. *Ladder*, *Accommodation Ladder*, is a sort of light stair-case, occasionally fixed on the gangway of the admiral, or commander in chief, of a fleet. *Ibid.*, *Quarter-Ladders*, two ladders of rope, depending from the right and left side of a ship's stern.

3. a. Applied to things more or less resembling a ladder. Often with qualifying words, as ***cheese***, ***cooper's***, ***paring ladder*** (see quots.); ***fish ladder*** (see FISH *sb.*[1] 7).

1688 R. HOLME *Armoury* III. 318/2 The paring Ladder, or Coopers Ladder..By the help of this all Barrel Staves or Boards are held fast and sure while the Work-man is paring or shaving them. *Ibid.* 335/1 A Cheese Ladder..serveth to lay over the Cheese Tub for the Cheese Fat to rest upon, while the Dairy Woman presseth the Whay out of the Cruds. *Ibid.* 339/2 The Cart Lathers are the Crooked peeces set over the Cart wheels to keepe Hay and Straw loaden off them. **1851** *Catal. Gt. Exhib.* 376 Scotch cart..with ladders complete, so as to be used as a dung or harvest cart. **1875** KNIGHT *Dict. Mech.*, *Ladder*, a notched cleat or stick in a bookcase, for supporting shelves. **1883** *Fisheries Exhib. Catal.* (ed. 4) 90 Two Salmon Ladders, One Jumping Ladder, One Swimming Ladder. **1888** *Lockwood's Dict. Mech. Engin.*, *Ladder*, a series of mud buckets which are carried up and down in an oblique direction, for emptying and refilling in dredging operations. **1890** *Wesleyan Methodist's Mag.* Mar. 162 A woven-ladder tape for Venetian blinds, in lieu of hand-made ladders. **1892** *Daily News* 25 Jan. 3/3 The flowers are formed into ruches, which trim the skirt and are carried up the sides, with a ladder of ribbons between the lines.

b. In knitted garments or stockings: a longitudinal strip of unravelled fabric, so called from the appearance of the threads.

1838 A. MATHEWS *Mem. Charles Mathews* II. xi. 246 He had been diverted by observing a fracture (or what a sempstress would term a *ladder*) in the back part of His Majesty's black-silk stockings. **1875** *Plain Needlework* 10 A crochet needle (to pick up the ladders in stockings). **1908** *Daily Chron.* 31 Dec. 4/6 Silk tights are fragile things, sadly given to 'ladders' on the least provocation. **1919** 'C. DANE' *Legend* 128 Someone ought to see that his socks were mended properly, for there was a great ladder down one ankle. **1957** M. SPARK *Comforters* iv. 76 There was a ladder in her stocking. **1973** J. CLEARY *Ransom* vii. 158 Sylvia looked up from examining the ladders in her stockings.

c. *Naval gunnery.* A series of range-finding shots up to or back from the target.

1922 *Grand Fleet Gunnery & Torpedo Memoranda on Naval Actions 1914–18* (Admiralty) vii. 57 The procedure generally found best by the control officers when the shot should have been straddling but nothing could be seen was to ladder down with a 200 ladder till shorts were clearly seen, and then ladder up till shorts were not seen, when the process was repeated... Although this blind ladder is extravagant in ammunition, it appears that no other course is open under similar conditions of visibility.

4. In names of plants, as ***Christ's ladder*** (see CHRIST 5). ***Ladder to Heaven*** (see quots.). Also JACOB'S LADDER.

1640 PARKINSON *Theat. Bot.* 699 Wee in English [call it] Salomons Seale most usually, but in some countries the people call it Ladder to Heaven,..from the forme of the stalke of leaves, one being set above another. **1760** LEE *Introd. Bot.* App. (1765) 316 Ladder to Heaven, *Convallaria*. **1879** BRITTEN & HOLLAND *Plant-n.*, Ladder to Heaven. (1) *Polemonium cæruleum*, L. (2) *Polygonatum multiflorum*.

5. *attrib.* and *Comb.* **a.** simple attrib., as ***ladder foot***, ***rung***, † ***stale***, ***stave***; **b.** objective, as ***ladder-climber*** (in quot. *fig.*); **c.** instrumental, as ***ladder-travelling***; ***ladder-bridged*** adj.; **d.** similative, as ***ladder-path***, ***road***; ***ladderwise*** adv.

1898 *Westm. Gaz.* 26 Aug. 8/2 The *ladder-bridged crevasse. **1870** *Even. Standard* 17 Sept., The *ladder-climbers, who now direct the affairs of Paris. *c* **1470** HENRYSON *Mor. Fab.* v. (*Parl. Beasts*) xliii, Syne furth him led, and to the gallowis gais, And at the *ledder-fute his leif he tais. **1814** S. ROGERS *Jacquel.* Poems (1839) 26 Up many a *ladder-path he guided. **1828** J. R. BEST *Italy as it is* 30 We had descended many steps of the *ladder-road. **1620** in Swayne *Churchw. Acc. Sarum* (1896) 171 For a peece of Timber to make *Ladder Rungs, 12*d.* *a* **1225** *Ancr. R.* 354 þeos two [þinges] scheome and pine..beoð þe two *leddre stalen þet beoð upriht to þe heouene. *c* **1440** *Promp. Parv.* 293/1 *Leddyr stafe, *scalarium*. **1608** WILLET *Hexapla Exod.* 606 As ladder staues they were equally distant one from another. **1855** *Cornwall* 156 The *ladder-travelling is rendered less fatiguing, by being varied and broken up into short journeys. **1593** Q. ELIZ. *Boethius* I. pr. I. 7 Betwine bothe lettars, *ladarwise, certain steps wer marked.

6. Special comb.: **ladder-back (chair)**, a chair in which the back is formed of horizontal pieces of wood, suggestive of a ladder; **ladder-back(ed) woodpecker** *U.S.*, one of several North American species of woodpecker with black and white, barred markings, esp. *Dendrocopos scalaris*; **ladder-braid**, a kind of braid made on the lace-pillow; **ladder-carriage**, one for conveying fire-ladders (Knight *Dict. Mech.* 1875); **ladder company, detachment** *Mil.* (see quot.); **ladder-dance** (see quot.); hence *ladder-dancer*; **ladder-dredge**, a dredge having buckets carried round on a ladder-like chain (*Cent. Dict.*); **ladder fern**, a fern of the genus *Nephrolepis*, which spreads by creeping rhizomes, producing new crowns; **ladder-like** *a.*, resembling a ladder, gradational; also *adv.*; **ladder-man**, 'in a fire-brigade, a member of a hook-and-ladder company' (*Cent. Dict.*); **ladder network** *Electr.*, a network having two pairs of terminals and consisting of impedances that are alternately in series and in parallel, so that the circuit diagram has the form of a ladder; **ladder party** = *ladder detachment*; **ladder point**, a form of ladder stitch; **ladder polymer**, a polymer in which pairs of long straight-chain molecules are joined by recurring cross-links; **ladder-proof** *a.*, of fabrics: not liable to ladder; **ladder shell**, a marine shell of the genus *Scalaria*, a staircase-shell, wentletrap; **ladder stitch**, a cross-bar stitch in embroidery; **ladder-stop**, at the top and toe of a stocking, a band of open-work designed to prevent a ladder; **ladder-truck**, a vehicle for carrying fire-ladders and hooks; **ladder-walker** = *ladder-dancer*; **ladder way**, a 'way' by which one descends or ascends by means of a ladder, (*a*) in the deck of a ship, (*b*) in the shaft of a mine; **ladder woodpecker** = *ladder-back(ed) woodpecker*; **ladder-work**, work done with the help of a ladder, e.g. house-painting, etc. (Simmonds *Dict. Trade* 1858).

1908 *Daily Report* 24 Aug. 8/3 Three *ladder-back chairs, with cherubs and a crown, brought £46. **1923** *Daily Mail* 11 Jan. 11 Let the table be of the gate-leg variety and the chairs of the style known as ladder-backs. **1966** A. W. LEWIS *Gloss. Woodworking Terms* 51 *Ladder back*, chairs made at the end of the seventeenth century with horizontal slats across the back like a ladder. **1973** J. BURROWS *Like an Evening Gone* i. 14 Greta was sitting on a ladderback chair by the kitchen table. **1884** E. COUES *Key to N. Amer. Birds* (ed. 2) 485 *Picoïdes americanus*..*Ladder-backed Three-toed Woodpecker. **1917** T. G. PEARSON *Birds Amer.* II. 149/1 The Ladder-back Woodpeckers are divisible into three regional varieties, the American, the Alaska.., and the Alpine. **1964** A. WETMORE et al. *Song & Garden Birds N. Amer.* 92/1 Ladder-backed woodpecker. *Dendrocopos scalaris*. Vast stretches of hot, treeless desert seem a curious habitat for a woodpecker. Yet to the ladderback such country is home. **1882** CAULFEILD & SAWARD *Dict. Needlework* 43 **Ladder braid*. **1884** *Mil. Engineering* I. II. 87 The men told off to one ladder (4 files or more, according to length of ladder) form a '*ladder detachment' and the detachments for one line of ladders form a '*ladder company', or 'ladder double company'. **1801** STRUTT *Sports & Past.* III. v. 173 The *Ladder-dance; so called, because the performer stands upon a ladder, which he shifts from place to place, and ascends or descends without losing the equilibrium, or permitting it to fall. **1709** STEELE *Tatler* No. 12 ¶18 *Ladder-dancers, Rope-dancers, Jugglers. **1884** W. MILLER *Dict. Eng. Names Plants* 222/2 *Nephrolepis cordifolia*, *Ladder Fern, of New Zealand. **1893** G. SCHNEIDER *Bk. Choice Ferns* II. xliii. 583 Nephrolepis... Ladder Ferns... This genus..belts the world in the Tropics, passing a little beyond them both north and south. **1951** *Dict. Gardening* (R. Hort. Soc.) III. 1365/2 *Nephrolepis*,.. Ladder fern. A genus of about 35 species of handsome ferns, widely dispersed over the tropics. **1969** *Coast to Coast 1967–68* 49 Beyond that was the swamp—tea-trees, paperbarks, huge ladder ferns. **1859** CORNWALLIS *New World* I. 21 A *ladder-like flight of steps. **1884** BOWER & SCOTT *De Bary's Phaner.* 303 Parallel bundles,.. connected in a ladder-like manner by transverse branches. **1897** MARY KINGSLEY *W. Africa* 565 The great parallel terraces over which, ladderlike, the neighbouring Congo has cut its bed. **1898** P. MANSON *Trop. Diseases* x. 181 A gradual ladder-like rise [of temperature]. **1930** A. C. BARTLETT *Theory Electr. Artificial Lines* iii. 41 The theory of a general *ladder network, in which all the elements may have arbitrary values, will first be considered, and..from it will be derived a class of symmetrical ladder artificial lines, of which the T and Π section lines are but simple cases. **1966** H. J. REICH et al. *Theory & Applications Active Devices* xviii. 543 Ladder-network oscillators..consist of a voltage-inverting amplifier and a ladder-type resistance-capacitance feedback network that usually has three or more similar sections. **1884** *Mil. Engineering* I. II. 98 It is always advisable to have officers and non-commissioned officers.. with *ladder parties. **1891** A. H. CRAWFURD *Gen. Crawfurd & Light Div.* 230 Fleming..fell leading the ladder party.. at Badajoz. **1971** *New Scientist* 24 June 761/2 The use of conventional straight-chain polymers seems to be restricted by an upper temperature limit of about 550°C, but the *ladder polymers (so-called because of their integral cross-linked structure) offer more exciting possibilities. **1974** *Sci. Amer.* Mar. 66/3 Ladder polymers, or double chains, are found in amphibole minerals, such as one form of asbestos. **1927** *Observer* 3 Apr. 25 Celanese cami-bockers... In *Ladder-proof Self Stripe. **1962** *Economist* 2 June 897/1 The new answers to feminine prayer [*sc.* a new type of seamless stockings] are said..to be ladderproof, although not hole-proof. **1882** CAULFEILD & SAWARD *Dict. Needlework* 186 **Ladder stitch*, there are two kinds of this stitch, the open, called *Ladder Point, or Point d'Echelle, in which the bars forming the stitch are taken across an open space, and the closed, known as Jacob, and Ship Ladder, in which the bars are worked on to the material itself. **1931** *Daily Express* 15 Oct. 12/7 (*caption*) Pair of Lady's Artificial Silk Hose with *ladder-stop tops. **1962** *Which?* Apr. 114/1 Most of the leading firms sell a style with a band of open-work knitting at the welt, known as a ladder-stop. **1711** STEELE *Spect.* No. 258 ¶3 Why should not..*Ladder-walkers, and Posture-makers appear again on our Stage? *c* **1850** *Rudim. Navig.* (Weale) 128 **Ladder-ways*, the openings in the decks wherein the ladders are placed. **1875** J. H. COLLINS *Metal Mining* 77 A shaft..large enough to allow of ample pumping space, a good ladder-way [etc.]. **1870** *Amer. Naturalist* III. 474 The resident species not found westward [of the Colorado Valley] were the *Ladder Woodpecker (*Picus scalaris*), the White-bellied Wren, [etc.].

Hence *nonce-wds.* **ˈladderless** *a.*, having no ladder; **ˈladdery** *a.*, resembling a ladder.

1852 *Fraser's Mag.* XLVI. 455 Short flights of abrupt laddery steps. **1897** P. WARUNG *Tales Old Regime* 78 They were separated from the surface by sixty feet of ladderless shaft.

ladder (ˈlædə(r)), *v.* [f. LADDER *sb.*]

1. *trans.* To scale with a ladder; to furnish with a ladder or with ladders. Also *absol.*

a **1578** LINDESAY (Pitscottie) *Chron. Scot.* (1728) 191 His friends came rushing forward to ladder the walls. **1582–8** *Hist. Jas. VI* (1804) 173 The men of Leith..looking for na uther thing bot..to haue ladderit and winn the hous. **1643** *Session Rec.* in *Hist. Brechin* (1867) 232 To Alexander Talbert for laddering the church 3*s.* 4*d.* **1665** J. WEBB *Stone-Heng* (1725) 188 They came from their Stations..by Planks laid from His unto their Stones, and otherwise they could not, without laddring up and down. **1901** J. BLACK *Illustr. Carpenter & Builder Ser.*: *Scaffolding* 67 The stack was laddered from the bottom to the top with a series of ladders. **1901** *Chambers's Jrnl.* Sept. 585/2 When Mr. Grant.. laddered the Moriston falls.., the Crown claimed and gained the new fishings. **1923** *Daily Mail* 22 June 5 Having just laddered the spire of Truro Cathedral, he found every crevice crammed with jackdaws' nests.

2. *intr.* Of garments, esp. stockings: to develop ladders as the result of the breaking of a thread or threads. Also *trans.* Hence **ˈladdering** *vbl. sb.*

1922 *Daily Mail* 14 Nov. 12 (Advt.), Your stockings cannot ladder. Laddering and damage to stockings..are entirely obviated. **1927** W. DEEPING *Doomsday* viii. 78 At the last moment a stocking had 'laddered'. **1963** A. J. HALL *Textile Sci.* iii. 152 The demand for excessive sheerness and transparency in ladies' stockings is the root cause of the

tendency to ladder. **1973** 'S. WOODS' *Enter Corpse* 171 Her dress [was] crumpled, and both her stockings were laddered.

3. *Naval gunnery.* To fire shots in a ladder (sense 3 c).

1922 [see LADDER *sb.* 3 c]. **1959** *Chambers's Encycl.* VI. 662/2 In the case of surface vessels, finding the accurate gun range, which is done by 'laddering' i.e. increasing or decreasing the range of successive salvoes until the target is crossed, is not difficult if the enemy maintains his course and speed.

ladder, obs. form of LATHER.

laddered ('lædəd), *a.* [f. LADDER *sb.* + -ED[2].] Furnished with a ladder; †of a rope, made into a ladder.

1608 MIDDLETON *Fam. Love* I. ii, Attempt not to ascend My chamber-window by a ladder'd rope. **187.** STEVENSON *Child's Gard. Verses* (1895) 81 He [the sun] Into the laddered hayloft smiles. **1892** LD. LYTTON *King Poppy* iv. 83 Their ladder'd scaffolds swarm'd, as high in heaven.

laddic ('lædɪk). *Electronics.* [f. *ladd(er-log)ic.*] A ladder-like device consisting of a rectangular block of a magnetic ferrite containing a line of rectangular apertures, the cross pieces and side pieces being of the same cross-sectional area and having wires passing round them in such a way that the device may be used as a logic element.

1959 GIANOLA & CROWLEY in *Bell Syst. Techn. Jrnl.* XXXVIII. 45 The Laddic is a ladder-like structure cut out of a rectangular hysteresis-loop ferrite. *Ibid.* 46 Any Boolean function can be realized as the output of a single Laddic of suitable length. *Ibid.* 50 The operation of the Laddic as an AND gate. **1963** *Engineering* 25 Jan. 170/3 Logical circuit applications of both toroidal cores and multi-apertured elements—the transfluxor and laddic—are discussed.

laddie ('lædɪ). Formerly chiefly *Sc.* [f. LAD *sb.* + -IE.] A young lad, a lad. (A term of endearment.)

1546 BALE *Eng. Votaries* I. (1550) 16 b, He had a laddy waytynge on hym called Benignus. **1721** RAMSAY (*title*) Yellow Haired Laddie. **1728** —— Soger Laddie. **1789** BURNS *Ep. to Dr. Blacklock* vi, I hae a wife and twa wee laddies. **1865** G. MACDONALD *A. Forbes* 51, I ken naething agen the laddie. **1884** ANNIE SWAN *Dorothea Kirke* xvii. 155 'Aunt Janet?' 'Ay, laddie'. **1919** WODEHOUSE *Damsel in Distress* xv. 171 'I've got a headache.' 'I thought you would have, laddie, when I saw you getting away with the liquid last night.' **1962** *Coast to Coast 1961–62* 66 'Now get yourself a beer,' he said. 'Pour a couple of beers, laddie.' **1973** J. PORTER *It's Murder with Dover* iii. 22 I've been ready for the last bleeding half-hour, laddie!

'laddish, *a.* [f. LAD *sb.*[1] + -ISH[1].] Of or pertaining to a lad or lads; like a lad. Also **'laddishness**.

1841 S. BAMFORD *Passages in Life of Radical* I. xiv. 91 A young officer.. very laddish, and with limbs long enough for windmill arms. **1886** *Wesleyan-Methodist Mag.* 63 Want of sympathy with.. the laddishness of lads. **1907** *Daily Chron.* 24 Oct. 8/3 Missing the laddish laugh, the boisterous gaiety, which they had known aforetime.

laddo ('lædəʊ). *colloq.* (orig. *Ir.*). Also lado. [f. LAD *sb.*[1]] Lad, boy.

1870 [see BOYO]. **1939** JOYCE *Finnegans Wake* 404 Sure, he's lightseyes, the laddo! **1968** J. WAINWRIGHT *Edge of Extinction* 57 She's.. out of range. The laddoes at the Kremlin'll know that. **1970** R. HILL *Clubbable Woman* v. 140 Your intruders'll all turn out to be like that laddo last night. **1973** —— *Ruling Passion* II. vi. 125 You're not seriously suggesting that Lewis wasn't killed by laddo, but by someone else.

†**lade**, *sb.*[1] *Obs.* Also 1 hlæd, 3 ladd. [f. LADE *v.* (OE. *hlæd* is commonly compared with ON. *hlað* stack, pile, and interpreted 'mound', because it renders L. *agger*; but the sense of 'burden' is possible.)] **a.** Draught. **b.** Load, burden, lading.

c **897** K. ÆLFRED *Gregory's Past.* xxi. 160 Besittað hie utan .. & berað hiere hlæd to [L. *comportabis aggerem*]. *c* **1200** ORMIN 19313 We lodenn alle twinne ladd Off hiss godnessess welle. *c* **1435** *Torr. Portugal* 1663 With hym faught a yong knyght Ech on other laid good lade. **1502** ARNOLDE *Chron.* (1811) 229 That they may be in our sayde landis and lordshippys for too bye and gader lade and freith and cary awaye, or doo to bee caryed awey and conueied into the sayde kyngdom of England.

lade (leɪd), *sb.*[2] [app. a variant of LEAD *sb.*[2] (which occurs much earlier in the same sense); perh. confused with *lade*, the regular Sc. and northern form of LODE, OE. *lád*. The synonymous LEAT is not etymologically related.]

1. A channel constructed for leading water to a mill wheel; a mill-race. (Often in comb. ***mill-lade.***) Chiefly *Sc.*

1808–80 JAMIESON, *Lade, lead.* **1862** *Act 25 & 26 Vict.* c. 97 §6 The construction or alteration of mill dams, or lades, or water wheels so as to afford a reasonable means for the passage of salmon. **1864** A. MᶜKAY *Hist. Kilmarnock* (1880) 106 A corn-mill, which was driven by a lade that flowed through the same spot. **1868** *Perthsh. Jrnl.* 18 June, Some fine sport was enjoyed; but the salmon on two or three occasions made a rush into the lade and escaped.

¶**2.** A sb. *lade*, with a sense 'channel, watercourse, mouth of a river', has been evolved by etymologists from place-names in which the last element is *-lade* (OE. *ȝelád* channel, as in *Creccaȝelád* Cricklade); the interpretation has been suggested by LADE *v.* The word was admitted into Bailey's and Johnson's Dicts., and has occasionally been used in literature.

[**1623** LISLE *Ælfric on O. & N. Test.* To Rdr. 34 How many learned men haue mistaken the name of a place neere Oxford called Creklade? as if it sauored of Greeke, when it is but old English, and signifies *Ostium riuuli*, a place where some Creeke or little brooke doth lade or empty it selfe into a greater water.] **1706** PHILLIPS (ed. Kersey), *Lada* (in old Records),.. a Lade, Lading, or Course of Water. **1721–1800** BAILEY, *Lade*, a Passage of Water, the Mouth of a River. **1865** KINGSLEY *Herew.* II. xi. 180 Cotinglade.. seemingly a lade, leat, or canal through Cottenham Fen to the Westwater. **1873** H. KINGSLEY *Oakshott* xxvi. 184 Every trickling tiny lade, every foaming brook, told its own story.

lade (leɪd), *sb.*[3] *local.* [? f. LADE *v.*] A board or rail fixed to the side of a cart or waggon to give greater width.

1686 *Lond. Gaz.* No. 2188/4 Lost.. a short turn Waggon, with two pair of Harness and a Cart Saddle, with Wheel Lades. **1847** in HALLIWELL. **1875** BLACKMORE *A. Lorraine* III. v. 72 The vice-president's cart was in the shed close by, and on the front lade sat Bonny.

lade (leɪd), *v.* Forms: 1 hladan, (ladan), 3 (*Orm.*) ladenn, (4 lhade, 6 laade, 7 laid), ? 3, 4– lade. *Pa. t.* 1 hlód, (*once* ȝehléod), 3–4 lode; *weak* 5– laded. *Pa. pple.* 1 (ȝe)hladen, 4 i-lade, 4–6 (8 *Sc. poet.*) lade, (6 ladden, *Sc.* ladin), 4– laden; *weak* 5 ladyd, 6– laded. [Com. Teut. str. vb.: OE. *hladan* (*hlód*, *ȝehladen*), corresp. to OFris. *hlada*, OS. *hladan* (Du. *laden*), ON. *hlaða* (Sw. *ladda*); with consonant-ablaut the word appears in OHG. *hladan* (G. *laden*), Goth. (*af*)*hlaþan*:—OTeut. **hlaþ-*, *hlað-*:—pre-Teut. **klat-*, parallel with **klad-* in OSl. *klasti* to place. The general Teut. senses are those represented by branch I; branch II is peculiar to Eng., but OS. has the sense 'to put (liquor) into a vessel', as a particular application of a sense similar to 2 below. Another derivative of the root is MHG. *luot* burden, mass, multitude:—OTeut. **hlôþâ*; in the OE. *hlóð* booty, multitude, OLG. *hlótha* booty, this type seems to have coalesced with OTeut. **hlanþâ*.

The pa. t. has from 15th c. been conjugated weak. The pa. pple. is still usually strong when used in the senses of branch I; in those of branch II it is now always weak.]

I. To load.

1. *trans.* To put the cargo on board (a ship). Also (now only in *passive*) to load (a vehicle, a beast of burden).

Beowulf (Z.) 896 Sæbat ȝehleod. *Ibid.* 1897 þa wæs on sande sæȝeap naca hladen herewædum. **13..** *Coer de L.* 1384 Thrittene schyppys i-lade with hyvys Of bees. *Ibid.* 1388 Another schyp was laden.. With an engyne hyghte Robynet. **1387** TREVISA *Higden* (Rolls) IV. 197 A boot þat was so hevy lade wiþ men þat folowede hym þat it sanke doun. *a* **1420** HOCCLEVE *De Reg. Princ.* 983 To lade a cart or fill a barwe. **1513** DOUGLAS *Æneis* III. vi. 211 Our kervalis howis ladis and prymys he With huge charge of siluir. **1535** COVERDALE *Ezek.* xii. 12 The chefest that is amonge you, shall lade his shoulders in the darcke, and get him awaye. **1611** BIBLE *Gen.* xlii. 26 They laded their asses with the corne. **1711** ADDISON *Spect.* No. 69 ⁋5 Our Ships are laden with the Harvest of every Climate. **1830** SCOTT *Demonol.* ix, A foreign ship richly laded with wines. **1853** KANE *Grinnell Exp.* xxxvi. (1856) 325 A sledge.. kept laden to meet emergencies. **1864** TENNYSON *En. Ard.* 817 He.. help'd At lading and unlading the tall barks.

b. To load (a person) *with* gifts, etc., (a tree, branch) *with* fruit; to charge or fill abundantly. Now only in pa. pple. *laden*, loaded, fraught, heavily charged *with*. †Also, *to lade up*.

1481 CAXTON *Godfrey* iv. 22 Whan he myght fynde the messagers of Charlemayn, he charged and laded them alle with richesses of thoryent. **1484** —— *Chivalry* 4 A tree wel laden and charged of fruyte. **1629** CAPT. SMITH *Trav. & Adv.* 9 With every man a bundle of sedge and bavins still throwne before them, so laded up the Lake, as [etc.]. **1674** RAY *Collect. Words, Husb.* 130 Corn.. the earlier it is sown, *cæteris paribus*, the better laden it is. **1693** DRYDEN *Ovid's Met.* XIII. *Acis* 72 Than apples fairer, when the boughs they lade. **1820** SHELLEY *Sensit. Plant* III. 112 A northern whirlwind.. Shook the boughs thus laden. **1847** WILSON *Chr. North* (1857) I. 231 Shores laden with all kinds of beauty. **1849** MURCHISON *Siluria* iv. 67 These.. sandstones are laden with a profusion of fossils. **1865** TROLLOPE *Belton Est.* xxiii. 279 Her eyes were laden with tears. **1878** HUXLEY *Physiogr.* 47 [The air] must have become laden with moisture.

c. To burden, load oppressively; chiefly in immaterial sense. Now only (somewhat *arch.*) in pa. pple., burdened *with* sin, sorrow, etc.

1538 STARKEY *England* I. ii. 28 Yf we be thys lade wyth ignorance. *a* **1553** UDALL *Royster D.* III. ii. (Arb.) 41 Doth not loue lade you? **1555** EDEN *Decades* 159 It is not lawful for any to lade his neighbours waules with rafters. **1602** *Life T. Cromwell* II. iii. 93 Lade him with irons. **1606** SHAKS. *Ant. & Cl.* v. ii. 123, I.. do confesse I haue Bene laden with like frailties. *a* **1618** RALEIGH *Rem.* (1644) 54 To lade no one man with too much preferment. **1655** CULPEPPER & COLE *Riverius* XV. vi. 420 Miserable Woman-Kind is commonly laded with.. manifold Diseases. *a* **1656** BP. HALL *Breath. Devout Soul* 168 Saviour, thy sinner is sufficiently laden, with the burden of his iniquities. **1724** RAMSAY *Health* 143 Phimos, who by his livid colour shews Him lade with vile diseases. **1841** LANE *Arab. Nts.* I. 90 Laden with the sin which they had committed.

2. To put or place as a burden, freight, or cargo; now only, to ship (goods) as cargo.

Beowulf (Z.) 2775 Him on bearm hlodon bunan and discas sylfes dome. *a* **1000** *Riddles* iv. 65 (Gr.) Ic.. me [on] hrycȝ hlade, þæt ic habban sceal. *a* **1000** *Cædmon's Gen.* 2901 (Gr.) Ongan þa ad hladan. *a* **1300** *K. Horn* 1409 Ston he dude lade, And lym therto he made. **1472** *Waterford Arch.* in *10th Rep. Hist. MSS. Comm.* App. v. 309 From the porte that the saide marchandise is lade unto the porte of the said citie. *c* **1489** CAXTON *Sonnes of Aymon* xxviii. 580 Thenne fet he stones & morter in grete plente.. and I promyse you that reynawd laded more atones than xv. other dyde. **1542–3** *Act 34 & 35 Hen. VIII*, c. 9 §3 No person.. shall enbote or lade .. anie wheate.. in anie picard. **1665** *Lond. Gaz.* No. 16/2 A Legorn ship.. bound to Tunis with moneys to lade Corn. **1799** NELSON in Nicolas *Disp.* (1845) III. 347 He had his Vessel seized by the Genoese, when lading wine for our Fleet. **1800** COLQUHOUN *Comm. Thames* viii. 261 It is impossible to lade or deliver Cargoes. **1888** BRYCE *Amer. Commw.* III. VI. cxiv. 641 The surplus products.. must be laden on board the vessels.

b. *absol.* or *intr.*

c **1470** HENRY *Wallace* IX. 704 Quhen thai off hay was ladand most bysse. **1611** BIBLE *Neh.* iv. 17 They that bare burdens, with those that laded. **1667** *Lond. Gaz.* No. 202/1 As many light ships come in the last evening Tyde to lade. **1712** E. COOKE *Voy. S. Sea* 179 At this High-land of Ariquipa, is good anchoring, where Vessels use to lade. **1796** MORSE *Amer. Geog.* I. 450 A pier.. at which vessels.. lade and unlade.

†**3.** To lay a burden of (guilt) *upon*. Also *absol.*

1535 COVERDALE *Deut.* xxii. 8 Make a battlement aboute thy rofe, that thou lade not bloude vpon thine house yf eny man fall therof. *a* **1541** WYATT *Poet. Wks.* (1861) 196 Him seemeth that the shade Of his offence again his force assays By violent despair on him to lade.

†**4.** To load or charge (a gun); also, to load (cartridges) in a gun. *Obs.*

1633 T. STAFFORD *Pac. Hib.* III. viii. (1810) 569 Going to lade her againe, their Gunner was slaine at his Peece. **1635** LD. LINDSEY in Sir W. Monson *Naval Tracts* III. (1704) 335/1 To command the Gunners to laid Cartrages. **1690** *Mor. Ess. Present Times* vii. 129 Cannon-like, will discharge but once till they are new Laden.

II. To draw water.

5. *trans.* To draw (water); to take up or remove (water or other fluids) from a river, a vessel, etc., with a ladle, scoop, or by similar means; to bale. †*occas.* with cogn. obj. (Now chiefly *techn.* and *dial.*)

c **950** *Lindisf. Gosp.* John iv. 7 Cuom uif of ðær byriȝ to ladanne [*Rushw.* hladanne] uæter. *c* **1000** *Ags. Gosp.* John ii. 9 þa þenas soðlice wiston þe þæt wæter hlodon. *c* **1000** ÆLFRIC *Hom.* II. 180 Ænne ealdne munuc wæter hladende. *c* **1200** ORMIN 14044 Gaþ.. and ladeþþ upp & bereþþ itt Till þallderrmann onn hæfedd. *Ibid.* 19313 We lodenn alle twinne ladd Off hiss godnessess welle. *c* **1330** *Arth. & Merl.* 1475 (Kölbing) þai.. þe water vp loden þo, Al way bi to & to. **1340** *Ayenb.* 178 Alsuo ase hit behoueþ ofte þet ssip lhade out þet weter þet alneway geþ in. *c* **1440** *Promp. Parv.* 283/2 Ladyn or lay water.. *vatilo.* *c* **1450** *Merlin* 37 Thei hadde a-wey the erthe, and fonde the water, and dede it to laden oute. **1530** PALSGR. 600/1, I laade water with a scoup or any other thyng out of a dytche or pytte. *a* **1648** DIGBY *Closet Open.* (1677) 8 Then lade forth your liquor and set it a cooling. **1674** RAY *Collect. Words, Smelting Silver* 114 It is laded out and cast into long square bars. **1725** BRADLEY *Fam. Dict.* s.v. *Brewery*, The first Wort.. must be pumped or laded off into one or more Coolers. **1784** TWAMLEY *Dairying* 47 To lade off the Whey clear from Curd. **1839** URE *Dict. Arts* 585 By lading the glass out of one pot into another.. with copper ladles. **1842** J. AITON *Domest. Econ.* 332 Out of this underbuck you must lade the ale-wort into the tun-tub.

b. *absol.* or *intr.*

1612–15 BP. HALL *Contempl., N.T.* II. v, She did not think best to lade at the shallow channel, but runs rather to the well-head. **1613–16** W. BROWNE *Brit. Past.* I. v. (1772) I. 142 Or with their hats lade [for fish] in a brooke. **1741** *Compl. Fam.-Piece* I. vi. 279 You must gradually lade out of the second Copper.

†**6.** To empty by 'lading'. *Obs.*

c **1532** DU WES *Introd. Fr.* in *Palsgr.* 1020 Whan a man doth come to the great see for to lade [F. *espuisér*] it. **1593** SHAKS. *3 Hen. VI*, III. ii. 139 Like one that.. chides the Sea .. Saying hee'le lade it dry. **1628** BP. HALL *Old Relig.* (1686) 73 We are not they who think to lade the sea with an egg-shell.

†**7.** *trans.* Of a ship: To let in (water). *Obs.*

1412–20 LYDG. *Chron. Troy* I. iii, The shyp.. was so staunche it myht no water lade. **1530** PALSGR. 601/1, I lade, I take in water, as a shyp or bote that is nat staunched... This bote ladeth in water a pace.

8. *Comb.* The verb stem used in comb. with names of vessels used in lading, as ***lade-†bowl***, ***-bucket***, ***-gallon*** (dial. ***gawn***, ***gorn***), †***-mele*** [? ME. MELE, bowl], ***-pail***.

1420 *Inv.* in *Linc. Chaper Acc. Bk.* A. 2. 30 lf. 69, 1 *ladebolle.. 6*d.* **1891** *Hartland Gloss.*, **Lade-bucket*, a small dipping-bucket, used in brewing, &c. *c* **1575** *Balfour's Practicks* (1754) 234 The air sall haue.. the best brewing leid, the mask fat, with tub, barrellis, and *laid-gallon. **1881** *Leicester Gloss.*, **Lade-gawn*,.. any vessel for lading out liquid. **1847** HALLIWELL, **Lade-gorn*, a pail with a long handle to lade water out with. *Derb.* Also called a *lade-pail.* **1579** in W. H. Turner *Select. Rec. Oxford* 401 Bruers measures, as barrells, kilderkins, firkins, runletts, *lademeales, gallons. **1558** *Ludlow Churchw. Acc.* (Camden) 87 Paid for a vesselle and a *lad payle to putt in lyme. **1886** ELWORTHY *W. Somerset Word-bk.*, *Late pail*.. A late-pail (or lade-pail) is commonly used for dipping hot water from a copper, or for making cider.

lade, Sc. and north. form of LOAD *sb.*

ladeborde: see LARBOARD.

†**'laded**, *ppl. a.* [f. LADE *v.* + -ED[1].] = LADEN.
1630 DRAYTON *Descr. Elysium* 3 Pomegranates..Their laded branches bow. **1697** DRYDEN *Virg. Georg.* II. 752 The laded Boughs their Fruits in Autumn bear. **1708** *Rhode Island Col. Rec.* (1859) IV. 58 Very few of the enemy's privateers..will..outsail one of our laded vessels.

†**'ladel**. *Obs. rare*$^{-1}$. [f. *lade* LODE *sb.* + -EL[1].] ? A little path, by-path.
1387-8 T. USK *Test. Love* I. iii. (Skeat) l. 42 By smale pathes, that swyne and hogges hadden made, as lanes with ladels their maste to seche.

laden ('leɪd(ə)n), *v.* Also 6 *Sc.* **ladin, ladne, laiden**, 7 **laidin**. [f. LADE *v.* + -EN; but perh. partly a Sc. var. of LOADEN *v.*] *trans.* = LADE *v.*
1514 *Extracts Aberd. Reg.* (1844) I. 89 The..gudis that happinnis to be input and ladnyt in the samyn schippis. **1531** *Ibid.* 142 The losing and laidnyng of schippis. **1579** MUNDAY in Hakluyt *Voy.* (1589) 151 Euery prisoner being most grieuously ladened with yrons on their legges. **1596** DALRYMPLE tr. *Leslie's Hist. Scot.* x. 356 To ladne him with deceitful leisingis, criminable crymes, and tailes vntrue. **1607** WALKINGTON *Opt. Glass* 147 Trees..ladened with..fruits. **1652** GAULE *Magastrom.* 303 They..used him with all curtesie, and ladened him with gifts. **1746** W. HORSLEY *Fool* (1748) II. No. 63. 94 Let each Mule carry his own Burthen, and not laden him further. **1808-18** JAMIESON, *Ladenin time*, the time of laying in winter provisions. **1885** MRS. C. L. PIRKIS *Lady Lovelace* I. i. 19 He ladened himself obediently with Edie's belongings. **1890** CUSHING *Bull i' th' Thorn* II. xiii. 243 The air was ladened with the fragrance of jasmine.

laden ('leɪd(ə)n), *ppl. a.* [str. pa. pple. of LADE *v.*] Burdened, loaded, weighed down (*lit.* and *fig.*). Often in comb. with sbs., as *sorrow-laden*; also HEAVY-LADEN.
1595 MAYNARDE *Drake's Voy.* (Hakl. Soc.) 3 A man entering into matters with so laden a foote, that the other's meat would be eaten before his spit could come to the fire. **1693** DRYDEN *Ovid's Met.* XIII. *Acis* 118 The laden boughs for you alone shall bear. *a* **1790** T. WARTON *Eclog.* iii. 94 Where..clust'ring nuts their laden branches bend. **1850** ROBERTSON *Serm.* Ser. III. v. 70 The better..impulses of a laden spirit. **1867** SMYTH *Sailor's Word-bk.*, *Laden*, the state of a ship when charged with materials equal to her capacity. **1868** LYNCH *Rivulet* CLXII. ii, Now mount the laden clouds, Now flames the darkening sky. **1897** *Daily News* 13 Sept. 7/1 The laden trains start hence.

laden, obs. form of LATTEN, brass.

lader ('leɪdə(r)). ? *Obs.* [f. LADE *v.* + -ER[1].] One who lades; *esp.* one who freights a ship.
1542-3 *Act 34 & 35 Hen. VIII*, c. 9 §3 The said owner or lader of the said picard bote or other vessel. **1552** *Act 5 & 6 Edw. VI*, c. 14 §7 The Buying of any Corn..by any such Badger, Lader, Kidder or Carrier. **1626** *Impeachm. Dk. Buckhm.* (Camden) 42 The name of the lader of the fore-said hides. **1697** *View Penal Laws* 9 A Lader of Corn or Grain. **1755** MAGENS *Insurances* I. 494 The Goods..appear to have been..restored..to the Masters of the Ships in which they were laden; and, by the Customs of the Sea, the Master is in the Place of the Lader, and answerable to him.

lade sterne, obs. form of LODESTAR.

la-di-da (lɑːdɪ'dɑː), *sb. slang.* [Onomatopœic, in ridicule of 'swell' modes of utterance. Cf. HAW-HAW.] A derisive term for one who affects gentility; a 'swell'. Also *attrib.* or *adj.* = LARDY-DARDY.
c **1883** in Atkin *House Scraps* (1887) 166 The young 'un goes to music-halls And does the la-di-da. **1893** GUNTER *Baron Montez* III. viii. 77 That French brother of his, Frank, the Parisian la-de-da. **1895** *Westm. Gaz.* 31 Jan. 3/2, I may tell you we are all homely girls. We don't want any la-di-da members.

la-di-da, *v.* Also **lah-de-dah**. [Cf. the sb.] *intr.* To use affected manners or speech.
1901 *N. & Q.* 6 July 20/2, I like to la-di-da with the ladies. **1930** *John o' London's* 15 Mar. 907/3 There is perhaps too much 'lah-de-dahing about' when royalty is concerned.

†**'ladied**, *a. Obs. rare*$^{-1}$. [f. LADY *sb.* + -ED.] Lady-like; soft, gentle.
1628 FELTHAM *Resolves* II. [I.] viii. 20 Sores are not to bee anguish't with a rusticke pressure; but gently stroaked with a Ladyed hand.

ladify: see LADYFY.

Ladik (læ'diːk). The name of a village in Turkey, formerly Laodicea, used *attrib.* to describe a type of prayer rug made in the district. Also *ellipt.*
1900 J. K. MUMFORD *Oriental Rugs* x. 155 Ladik rugs resemble..those of Kulah... The Kulah small stripes, however, are not often found in the Ladiks. **1931** A. U. DILLEY *Oriental Rugs & Carpets* vi. 165 Among later weavings Ladik prayer rugs display a versatile art that ranges in architectural pattern from impressive columns to dwarf apexes. **1972** *Country Life* 23 Nov. 1412/2 Antique Turkish Ghiordes and Ladik prayer rugs.

Ladin (lə'diːn). [L. *Latīn-us, -um.*] The Rhæto-Romanic dialect spoken in the Engadine in Switzerland, closely related to Romansh.
1877 A. H. KEANE tr. *Hovelacque's Sci. of Lang.* v. 238 Known also as the language of the Grisons, the Rheto-Romance, the Rumonsh, and Rumansh. But it seems best to call it simply *Ladin*, with Ascoli, who has recently devoted an important work to its elucidation. **1879** *Encycl. Brit.* VIII. 213/2 The language [in the Engadine] is a dialect known as 'Ladin'. **1880** *Ibid.* XI. 205/1 The remainder [of the inhabitants of the Grisons] use the Romansch or the Ladin dialect. **1969** *Daily Tel.* 29 Jan. 16/5 The first book to be translated into English from Ladin, one of the Romansh group of languages which is spoken in the canton of Grisons, Switzerland, will be published..tomorrow.

ladin, obs. Sc. f. LADEN *v.*; obs. Sc. pa. pple. of LADE *v.*

lading ('leɪdɪŋ), *vbl. sb.* [f. LADE *v.* + -ING[1].]
1. The action of the verb LADE; the loading of a ship with its cargo; the bailing or ladling out of water, etc. ***bill of lading*** (see BILL *sb.*[3] 10).
1500 *Galway Arch.* in *10th Rep. Hist. MSS. Comm.* App. v. 391 In lading and discharging of his goodes..into forayn realmis. **1661** FELTHAM *Resolves, Lusoria* xxxv. (1677) 32 Must we haue fire still glowing under us, Only that we with constant Lading may Keep our selues cool? **1743** *Lond. & Country Brew.* II. (ed. 2) 121 Where the Water is put over by the Hand-bowl, or what is called Lading over. **1839** URE *Dict. Arts* 589 The transfer of the glass into the cuvettes, is called lading.
2. *concr.* That with which a ship is laded; freight, cargo. †Also *transf.* (see quots. 1611, 1621).
1526 TINDALE *Acts* xxvii. 10 Syrs, I perceave that thys vyage wilbe with hurte and domage, not off the ladynge and shippe only: but also off oure lyues. **1611** COTGR., *Prendre son sel*, to swill, quaffe, caroose; to take in his lading, or his liquor, to the full. **1621** MOLLE *Camerar. Liv. Libr.* v. xiii. 369 Drunkards..when they haue their lading of wine. **1669** NARBOROUGH *Jrnl.* in *Acc. Sev. Late Voy.* I. (1694) 7 With much ado I got off a boats lading of Water. **1670** *Ibid.* (1711) 91, I was bound for China, and..had rich Lading for that Country. **1709** *Lond. Gaz.* No. 4598/4 Two Ships lading of ..Russia Rhine Hemp. **1834** H. MILLER *Scenes & Leg.* xxi. (1857) 303 A small sloop..entered the frith, to take in a lading of meal. **1836** W. IRVING *Astoria* II. 169 The crews were saved, but much of the lading was lost or damaged. **1870** MORRIS *Earthly Par.* III. IV. 184 A lading of great rarities.
fig. **1850** TENNYSON *In Mem.* xxv, When mighty Love would cleave in twain The lading of a single pain.
†**3.** A place where cargoes are laded. *Obs.*
1594 NORDEN *Spec. Brit., Essex* (Camden) 10 It is inuironed with creekes, which leade to certayne ladinges, as to Landymer lading..wher they take in wood.
4. *attrib.* and *Comb.*, as *lading-can* (*dial.*), †***gin, hole, utensil, well***.
1886 *Cheshire Gloss.*, *Lading can, a small tin can, containing two or three quarts, used for taking hot water out of a boiler. [Common in the north midlands and Yorkshire.] **1497** *Nav. Acc. Hen. VII* (1896) 103 *Lading gynne..j. *Ibid.* 104 Lading gynnes..iij. **1839** URE *Dict. Arts* 589 *Glass-making*, In this operation ['lading'] ladles of wrought iron are employed, which are plunged into the pots through the upper openings or *lading holes. **1872** HARDWICK *Trad. Lanc.* 189 The only *lading or baling utensil employed by the miserable sinner should be a limpet shell. **1769** JOHNSON *Let. to Mrs. Thrale* 14 Aug., The *lading-well in this ill-fated George Lane lies shamefully neglected.

ladino[1] (læ'diːnəʊ). [Sp.] **1.** A vicious or unmanageable horse, steer, etc.; a stray animal. Also as *adj.*, wild, vicious, cunning.
1863 H. W. BATES *Naturalist on River Amazons* II. iv. 265 The old Indians told us..the turtles were 'ladino' (cunning), and would take no notice of the beating a second day. **1891** *Dialect Notes* I. 191 *Ladino*, in Spanish, learned, knowing Latin; then crafty, cunning. In Texas as a noun, a vicious, unmanageable horse, full of cunning and tricks. **1929** J. F. DOBIE *Vaquero of Brush Country* ii. 14 They were all outlaws, *ladinos*, wild as bucks, cunning and ready to fight anything that got in front of them... Among them were wrinkled-necked maverick cows and bulls that had never had a loop tossed over their heads. **1942** BERREY & VAN DEN BARK *Amer. Thes. Slang* §916/2 *Ladinos, outlaw cattle*, unbranded strays.
2. In Central America, a mestizo or a white person. Also *attrib.* or as *adj.*
1877 *Encycl. Brit.* VI. 682/2 The inhabitants of Cuba are divided into four classes..; those under servitude, constituting the fourth class, divided into the *bozales*, those recently brought from Africa,—the *ladinos*, those imported before the law of 1821 prohibiting the slave trade,—and the *criollos*, those born on the island. **1902** *Ibid.* XXXII. 395/1 The number of Ladinos (whites and persons of mixed blood) [in Salvador in 1887] was returned at 772,200, and of Indians at 234,648. **1934** A. HUXLEY *Beyond Mexique Bay* 69 Whites and *ladinos* were conspicuously absent from the ranks. *Ibid.*, These Quichés and Cakchiquels from the hills are as foreign in the white and *ladino* capital as Nepalese in the Punjab. *Ibid.* 70 *Ladino* housewives stood bargaining at the stalls. **1959** *Times* 17 Jan. 7/7 The basic division in Chiapas is that between Indian and *ladino*, the *ladino* being a white or a *mestizo*, who follows the customs of the *patrón* and of western civilization. **1973** 'F. CLIFFORD' *Amigo, Amigo* v. 46 She was dressed *ladino* style, blouse and skirt, and was lighter skinned than pure Indian.
3. (Usu. with capital initial.) A language based on Old Spanish and written in modified Hebrew characters, used by some Sephardic Jews, esp. in Mediterranean countries. Also *attrib.* and *Comb.*
1889 in *Cent. Dict.* **1932** C. ROTH *Hist. Marranos* xiii. 324 A few works..were printed..in Ladino (or Spanish in Hebrew characters) in the Levant, at Smyrna or at Salonica. **1948** [see JUDÆO-]. **1949** *Spectator* 4 Nov. 595/2 A dialect of Hebrew-cum-Spanish called Ladino is still spoken by many Sephardic Jews everywhere; it is common at the Holland Park synagogue in London..whose members mostly come from the Middle East. **1959** *Israel Digest* 23 Jan 6/3 Another important project..is the preparation of a Ladino dictionary. **1965** *Listener* 30 Sept. 490/2 He records a meeting with three Ladino-speaking Jews in the railway station in Sofia. **1972** O. SELA *Bearer Plot* xvi. 101 Ashraf and I are both Sephardic. We both speak Ladino which is very close to Spanish.

ladino[2] (lə'diːnəʊ). [It.] In full, *ladino clover*. A large fast-growing variety of white clover (*Trifolium repens*), native to northern Italy and cultivated elsewhere, esp. in the U.S.A., as a fodder crop.
1924 A. G. ERITH *White Clover* xii. 139 In Italy white clover is named Trifoglio ladino or Ladino clover. **1931** *N.Z. Jrnl. Agric.* XLII. 83 In many ways the Italian Ladino type seems to be related to the large-leaved New Zealand Wild White No. 1... The New Zealand form is..altogether the more valuable pasture type. **1937** COX & JACKSON *Crop Managem. & Soil Conservation* xxiv. 385 *Ladino* is a large-growing type of white clover that provides much more pasture per acre and is of value for hay. Ladino is a native of northern Italy and is established in importance in Idaho, Oregon, and Washington and is gaining in importance in New England. **1950** CARROLL & KRIDER *Swine Production* xviii. 367 Ladino clover hay contains 19 per cent protein. **1956** GILLESPIE & HATHAWAY *Textbk. Gen. Agric.* viii. 151 *Ladino* or *Giant White Clover*, also called Lodi, is Italian in origin and has all the appearance of a giant form of the other white clovers... Its demerit is that it is not frost-hardy and so cannot stand British winters. **1969** J. JANICK et al. *Plant Sci.* xix. 381/1 White clover..includes the robust ladino variety from Italy.

ladiship, variant of LADYSHIP.

ladisman, variant of LODESMAN.

'ladkin. [f. LAD *sb.* + -KIN.] A young lad.
1642 H. MORE *Song of Soul* I. III. xxxi, Tharrhon that young ladkin hight.

ladle ('leɪd(ə)l), *sb.* Forms: 1-2 **hlædel**, 3 **ladele**, 4-5 **ladel**, 5 **laddil, ladill, ladyl, ladyll(e**, 5-7 **ladell(e**, 6 **ladil**, 7 **ladul**, 5- **ladle**. [OE. *hlædel*, f. *hladan* LADE *v.*: see -EL.]
1. a. A large spoon with a long handle and cup-shaped bowl, used chiefly for lading liquids.
a **1000** *OE. Gloss.* in Haupt's *Zeitschrift* IX. 418 *Antlia*, mid hlædele. *a* **1100** *Gerefa* in *Anglia* (1886) IX. 264 Cytel, hlædel, pannan. *c* **1290** *S. Eng. Leg.* I. 187/94 Sethþe salt heo nome And Mid ladeles on is wondene it casten. **1377** LANGL. *P. Pl.* B. XIX. 274 A ladel bugge with a longe stele, That cast for to kepe a crokke to saue the fatte abouen. *c* **1386** CHAUCER *Knt.'s T.* 1162 The cook yscalded, for al his longe ladel. *c* **1440** *Promp. Parv.* 283/2 Ladylle, pot spone, *concus*. **1468-9** *Durham Acc. Rolls* (Surtees) I. 92, 2 laddils et 1 scomer de cupro pro coquina, 23d. **1590** SPENSER *F.Q.* II. vii. 36 Some stird the molten owre with ladles great. **1602** PLAT *Delightes for Ladies* Recipe liv, You must haue a fine brason ladle to let run the sugar vppon the seedes. **1680** BOYLE *Exper. Produc. Chym. Princ.* I. iv. 48 The materials of Glass..having been..kept long in fusion, the mixture casts up the superfluous salt, which the work-men take off with Ladles. *c* **1718** PRIOR *Ladle* 135 A ladle for our silver dish Is what I want. **1744** BERKELEY *Let. Tar Water* §2 Wks. 1871 III. 462 Stir..with a wooden ladle, or flat stick. **1773** *Lond. Chron.* 7 Sept. 248/3 Punch ladles. **1844** *Mem. Babylonian P'cess* II. 54 Jaffa contains some fine marble fountains, to which ladles are attached by chains, for the convenience of the stranger who is athirst. **1867** SMYTH *Sailor's Word-bk.*, *Paying-ladle*, an iron ladle with a long channelled spout opposite to the handle; it is used to pour melted pitch into the seams. **1895** *Daily News* 12 Sept. 3/5 An egg-and-ladle race.
b. In Scottish churches: a similar instrument consisting of a wooden box at the end of a long wooden handle used for taking up the collection and communion tokens.
1813 W. LESLIE *Gen. View Agric. Nairn & Moray* 412 The elders make these collections by going round to each with a ladle or small box with a handle to it, when the public worship is concluded. **1830** *2nd Rep. Evidence Sel. Comm. State of Poor in Ireland* §3369 in *Parl. Papers* VII. 459 The elders carrying about what they call a ladle. **1871** W. ALEXANDER *Johnny Gibb* xi. 81 The elders seized the ladles ..and perambulated the kirk. **1929** *Life & Work* Oct. 232/2 A ladle preserved in the parish church of Foulis Easter. **1960** *Press & Jrnl.* (Aberdeen) 26 Apr., Long may they continue to use the ladle and metal communion tokens.
2. In various technical applications.
a. *Gunnery.* 'An instrument for charging with loose powder; formed of a cylindrical sheet of copper-tube fitted to the end of a long staff' (Smyth *Sailor's Word-bk.* 1867). Also a similar instrument for removing the shot from a cannon.
1497 *Nav. Acc. Hen. VII* (1896) 85 Charging ladells..ij, Rammers..ij. **1622** R. HAWKINS *Voy. S. Sea* (1847) 185 We ..could not avoyd the danger, to charge and discharge with the ladell, especially in so hotte a fight. **1627** CAPT. SMITH *Seaman's Gram.* viii. 34 The Master Gunner hath the charge of the ordnance, and shot, powder, match, ladles [etc.]. **1769** FALCONER *Dict. Marine* (1780) I 4 b, Cannon are charged.. with an instrument..termed a ladle. **1851** DOUGLAS *Nav. Gunnery* (ed. 3) 518 To practise with the Eprouvette, charge it with a small quantity of loose powder, by means of a ladle.
b. *Founding.* A pan with a handle, to hold molten metal for pouring. Also in *Glass-making*, a similar instrument used to convey molten glass from the pot to the cuvette.
1483 *Cath. Angl.* 206/2 A Ladylle for yettynge, *fusorium*. **1495** *Nav. Acc. Hen. VII* (1896) 195 Ladylles of iron to melt lede. **1823** P. NICHOLSON *Pract. Build.* 404 Ladles are of three or four different sizes, and are used for melting the solder. **1839** [see LADING *vbl. sb.* 4]. **1881** RAYMOND *Mining Gloss.*, *Ladle*, a vessel into which molten metal is conveyed from the furnace or crucible, and from which it is poured into the moulds.
†**3.** Applied to the cup of an acorn. *Obs.*

1599 A. M. tr. *Gabelhouer's Bk. Physicke* 172/1 Take of the best Aquavitæ a quarte..and Akorne dishes or Ladles.

4. One of the float-boards of a water-wheel.

1611 COTGR., *Aubes*, the short boordes which are set into th' outside of a water-mills wheele; we call them, ladles, or aue-boords. **1673-4** GREW *Anat. Plants* III. vii. §6 (1682) 138 The Ladles and soles of a Mill-wheel are always made of Elm. **1731** BEIGHTON in *Phil. Trans.* XXXVII. 11 The Ladles or Paddles 14 Foot long. **1875** in KNIGHT *Dict. Mech.*

†**5.** *Sc.* 'A burghal duty charged on grain, meal, and flour, brought to market for sale; also, the proceeds or income obtained from that duty'. Also, 'The dish or vessel used as the measure in exacting this duty' (Jam. *Suppl.*). *Obs.*

1574 *Burgh Rec. Glasgow* (1876) I. 14 The casualiteis of the mercat callit the Ladill is sett to Robert Millare, meleman, quhill Whitsone tysday nixtocum.

6. *attrib.* and *Comb.*, as ***ladle-staff***, ***-washer***; ***ladle-shaped*** adj.; **ladle-board** = LADLE 4; **ladle-dues** *Sc.* (see sense 5); **ladle-furnace**, a gas furnace in which the metal to be melted is contained in a ladle; **ladle-man**, †(*a*) (see quot. 1750); (*b*) a workman who uses a ladle (sense 2 b); **ladle-shell** (*local U.S.*), a name for certain large shells (*Fulgur*, *Sycotypus*, etc.), which are or may be used as ladles in baling out boats, etc. (*Cent. Dict.*); **ladle-wood** *Bot.*, the wood of a S. African tree (*Cassine Colpoon*), used for carving (*Treas. Bot.* 1866).

1744 DESAGULIERS *Exper. Philos.* II. 92 Therefore the *Ladle-Board is struck by twice the Matter. **1793** SMEATON *Edystone L.* §197 To knock off the Floats or Ladle-boards from the wheels. **1853** GLYNN *Power Water* App. 148 The floats or ladle-boards. **1832-53** *Whistle-Binkie* (Scot. Songs) Ser. II. 120 *note*, Farmer of *ladle-dues. **1880** *Cooley's Cycl. Pract. Receipts* (ed. 6) I. 772 *Ladle furnace. This takes ladles up to 6½ inches diameter, and will melt 6 to 8 lbs. of zinc in about 15 minutes. **1750** W. ELLIS *Mod. Husbandm.* III. I. 184 An Insect seldom, or never, misses attacking our green Cherries with so much Diligence and Fury, as to spoil great Numbers of them, by eating into their very Stone; and, because of this hollow Operation, we call them *Ladlemen, or the Green Fly, or Bug. **1884** *St. James's Gaz.* 13 June 11/1 Thomas Green, a ladleman..was fearfully scalded all over the body. **1885** *Census Instructions* 93 *Bessemer Steel Manufacture*..Ladle Man. **1877** RAYMOND *Statist. Mines & Mining* 384 [The clay] is beaten in with a *ladle-shaped instrument attached to a long handle. **1669** STURMY *Mariner's Mag.* v. 68 Put the Ladle home to the Chamber stedily holding your Thumb upon the upper part of the *Ladle-staff. **1470-85** MALORY *Arthur* VII. v. 219 What arte thou but a luske and a torner of broches and a *ladyl wessher.

ladle ('leɪd(ə)l), *v.* [f. LADLE *sb.*] *trans.*

a. To fit up (a water-mill) with ladle-boards. Also const. *up*. **b.** To lift out with a ladle. Also with *out* and *fig.*

1525 in W. H. Turner *Select. Rec. Oxford* 55 Ladillyng of myll, makyng of the flodde yates. *c* **1532** DU WES *Introd. Fr.* in *Palsgr.* 945 To ladle, *espuiser*. **1851** H. MELVILLE *Moby Dick* III. xlviii. 287 Stubb was lustily singing out for some one to ladle him up. **1858** LYTTON *What Will He do* I. iv, Vance ladled out the toddy. **1872** W. H. G. KINGSTON *On Banks Amazon* iii. 93 Wooden spoons were served to enable us to ladle up the soup. **1873** G. C. DAVIES *Mount. & Mere* xiii. 102 Insinuate your fingers softly under him and ladle him out. **1913** R. BROOKE *Let.* 8 Sept. (1968) 508 But it's absurd to ladle out indiscriminate praise, as most people do. **1969** *Listener* 27 Feb. 278/2, I..was concerned at the way the present system..ladles out routine scientific and technological qualifications which one in five graduates later find are not useful to them.

ladleful ('leɪd(ə)lfʊl). [f. LADLE *sb.* + -FUL 2.] As much as fills a ladle.

c **1430** *Two Cookery-bks.* 8 Þan caste a ladel-ful, or more or lasse, of boter þer-to. **1589** R. HARVEY *Pl. Perc.* A ij b, The first ladlefull had a smacke as soft as pap. **1700** TYRRELL *Hist. Eng.* II. 900 The..Cook..cast a Ladle-full of Boiling Water in his Face. **1727** SWIFT *Wonder of all W.* Wks. 1755 II. II. 56 He takes a pot of scalding oyl and throws it by great ladlesfull directly at the ladies. **1871** C. GIBBON *Lack of Gold* vi, He raised the ladleful of the liquid and allowed its contents to drip into the glass.

ladler ('leɪdlə(r)). [f. LADLE *v.* + -ER[1].]

1. One who ladles.

1875 WHYTE MELVILLE *Katerfelto* i. (1876) 4 'A fine!' objected the punch-ladler, judicially. **1885** *Census Instructions* 89 *Rolled Plate Glass Making*: Ladler.

2. *Sc.* 'The customer of the ladle in the grain market' (Jam. *Suppl.*).

1643 *Burgh Rec. Glasgow* (1881) II. 57 It is to be remembred that the ladlearis hes receavit seavine ladils. **1644** *Ibid.* 71 The ladillars hes gottin seavin ladils.

'ladlike, *a.* [f. LAD[1] + -LIKE.] Resembling a lad; in quots. †churlish, unknightly (cf. LAD[1] 1).

1450-70 *Golagros & Gaw.* 95 Yhit ar thi latis vnlufsum and ladlike. *Ibid.* 160 He was ladlike of laitis.

ladne, obs. Sc. form of LADEN *v.*

ladner, var. LARDINER *Obs.*

ladrone. Also 8 *Sc.* ladren, laydron, latherin, 7, 9 ladron, 9 lath(e)ron. [a. early OF. *ladron* (see LAROUN):—L. *latrōn-em* robber. In mod. use ad. Sp. *ladrón*:—L. *latrōn-em*.]

1. *Sc.* (Stressed '*ladron*.) Used as a vague term of reproach: Rogue, blackguard.

a **1557** LYNDESAY in *Pinkerton's Sc. Poems* (1792) II. 8 Quhair hes thow bene, fals ladrone lown? **1706** *J. Watson's Collect. Poems* I. 11 But when Indemnity came down, The Laydron caught me by the Thraple. **1718** RAMSAY *Christ's Kirk Gr.* III. xv, Whisht, ladren. **1789** D. DAVIDSON *Seasons* 90 Maggy wha fu' well did ken, The lurking Latherin's meaning. **1887** SERVICE *Dr. Duguid*, Thou impiddent latheron!

attrib. **1811** GALT *Ann. Parish* xxiv. 159 She..would not let me..mess or mell with the lathron lasses of the clachan.

2. (lə'drəʊn.) Used *occas.* in books on Spain or Spanish America for: A highwayman. Also *attrib.* (see quot. 1867).

[**1626** SHIRLEY *Brothers* v. iii. (1652) 62 *Ped.* I am become the talk Of every *Picaro* and *Ladron*.] **1832** W. IRVING *Alhambra* I. 17 With the protection of our redoubtable Squire, Sancho, we were not afraid of all the ladrones of Andalusia. **1851** MAYNE REID *Scalp Hunt.* ix. 74 There are other ladrones besides the Indians. **1867** SMYTH *Sailor's Word-bk.*, *Ladrone ship*, literally a pirate, but it is the usual epithet applied by the Chinese to a man-of-war. **1883** LD. SALTOUN *Scraps* I. ii. 189 They would have been bold ladrones that molested any travellers conducted by him.

la'dronism. *Hist.* [f. Sp. *ladrón* (see LADRONE), a hostile Filipino, an insurgent + -ISM.] In the Philippine Islands, organized resistance to law or authority among the native population.

1902 *Outlook* (N.Y.) LXXII. 298/1 A local police and an insular constabulary system have been created, and ladronism, or organized robbery and brigandage,..has almost disappeared. **1903** *Daily Chron.* 26 Dec 5/6 Ladronism had also been successfully treated by the Courts.

†**'ladry.** *Sc. Obs.* [a. F. *ladrerie*, lit. leprosy, f. *ladre* (see LAZAR).] Impure discourse.

14.. *How Good Wife taught Dau.* 86 in *Barbour's Bruce*, Thoill thaim nocht rage with rybaldry, Na mengill thame with neuir vith ladry. *a* **1491** *Priests of Peblis* 17 Thay lufit nocht with ladry, nor with lown, Nor with trumpours to travel throw the town. *a* **1500** *Ratis Raving* III. 184 Luf nocht raginge na rebaldry, Na our loud lauchtyr na ladry, For maner makis man of valour.

'lad's love. *dial.* [Cf. BOY'S LOVE.] The Southern-wood (*Artemisia Abrotanum*).

a **1825** FORBY *Voc. E. Anglia*, *Lad's-love*, the herb southern-wood. **1827** CLARE *Sheph. Cal.* 58 Sprigs of lad's-love. **1851** MAYHEW *Lond. Labour* I. 137 Southernwood (called 'lad's love' or 'old man' by some). **1884** J. HATTON in *Harper's Mag.* July 234/2 Roses, and 'lad's-love', or 'old-man'.

lady ('leɪdɪ), *sb.* Forms: 1 **hlǽfdíȝe, hlǽfdí, hlǽf-, hléfdíȝe,** *Northumb.* **hláfdía,** *Mercian* **hláfdíe,** 2-4 **lefdi,** 3 **læfdi, lævedi, laf(e)di(e, lafvedi, leafdi, leivedi, leofdi, levede,** *Orm.* **laffdiȝ,** 3-4 **lavedi, levedi, -y,** 4 **laidi, -y, lavede, laydy, ledy, lefdye, levdi, -y, levedie, levidi, lhevedi, -y, livedi,** 4-5 **lavedy, lefdy, lade,** 4-7 **ladi(e, -ye,** (*pl.* **ladise**), 6, 9 *Sc.* **leddy,** 9 *arch.* **ladye,** 4- **lady.** [OE. *hlǽfdíȝe* wk. fem.; f. *hláf* bread, LOAF + root *dig-* to knead: see DOUGH.

Like the corresponding masc. designation *hláford*, LORD, the word is not found outside Eng. (the Icel. *lafði* is adopted from ME.). The etym. above stated is not very plausible with regard to sense; but the attempts to explain *hlǽfdíȝe* as a deriv. of *hláford* are unsatisfactory: the fem. suffix in OE. is *-icȝe*, not *-iȝe*, and the umlaut in the first syllable is difficult to explain on this supposition.

The OE. *ǽ*, being regularly shortened in ME. before two consonants, yielded regularly *ă* and *ĕ* according to dialect. The ME. *lĕfdi*, *lĕvdi*, is represented by Sc. *leddy*. The other form *lăfdi* (= **lavdi*) became *lăvedi* (3 syllables), and by regular development *lāvedi*; afterwards the *e* became silent and the *v* was dropped; hence the mod.Eng. form.

The genitive sing. (OE. *hlǽfdiȝan*) became by regular phonetic change in ME. coincident in form with the nom.; hence certain syntactical combs. have the appearance of proper compounds, as *lady-bird*, *Lady-day*, *Lady-chapel*.]

I. As a designation for a woman.

†**1.** A mistress in relation to servants or slaves; the female head of a household. *Obs.*

The 18th c. instances in brackets seem to represent a redevelopment of this sense from sense 6 a.

c **825** *Vesp. Psalter* cxxii[i]. 2 Swe swe eȝan menenes hondum hlafdian hire. *a* **1000** *Laws of Penitents* ii. §4 in Thorpe *Anc. Laws* II. 184 Ðif hwylc wif..hire wifman swingð & heo þurh þa swingle wyrð dead..fæste seo hlæfdiȝe .vii. ȝear. *a* **1100** *Ags. Voc.* in Wr.-Wülcker 310/26 *Materfamilias*, hiredes moder oððe hlæfdiȝe. *a* **1225** *Ancr. R.* 4 Ant þeos riwle nis bute vorto serui þe oðer. Þe oðer is ase lefdi: þeos is ase þuften. *c* **1250** *Gen. & Ex.* 967 Forð siðen ȝhe bi abram slep. Of hire leuedi nam ȝhe no kep. **1382** WYCLIF *Ps.* cxxii[i]. 2 As the eȝen of the hondmaide, in the hondis of hir ladi. —— *Prov.* xxx. 23 Bi an hand womman, whan she were eir of hir ladi. [**1718** *Freethinker* No. 17. 116 Her Maid..lisps out to me that her Lady is gone to Bed. *a* **1745** SWIFT *Direct. Servants* iii. (1745) 50 When you are sent on a Message, deliver it in your own Words..not in the Words of your Master or Lady.]

2. a. A woman who rules over subjects, or to whom obedience or feudal homage is due; the feminine designation corresponding to *lord*. Now *poet.* or *rhetorical*, exc. in ***lady of the manor***. †In OE. used *spec.* (instead of *cwén*, QUEEN) as the title of the consort of the king of Wessex (afterwards of England).

a **1000** *O.E. Chron.* an. 918 Her Æðelflæd forðferde Myrcena hlæfdiȝe. **1038-44** *Charter of Ælfwine* in Kemble *Cod. Dipl.* IV. 76 Eadweard cinge and Ælfȝyfu seo hlefdiȝe, and Eadsiȝe arcebisceop. *c* **1205** LAY. 6310 Bruttes nemnede þa laȝen æfter þar lafuedi. **1382** WYCLIF *Isa.* xlvii. 7 Thou agreggedist the ȝoc gretli, and seidest, In to euermor I shal ben a ladi. **1387** TREVISA *Higden* (Rolls) IV. 129 Þe laste lady of Cartage hadde riȝt suche a manere ende as Dydo þe firste lady hadde. *c* **1450** *Merlin* 362 'And also', quod she, 'I am lady of the reame cleped the londe susteyne'. **1481** CAXTON *Myrr.* II. ii. 65 Asia the grete..taketh the name of a quene that somtyme was lady of this regyon and was callid Asia. **1562** WINȜET *Cert. Tractates* i. Wks. 1888 I. 10 We suspect nocht zoure gentle humanitie,..to be offendit with vs zour pure anis, bot our Souerane Ladyis fre liegis. **1590** SPENSER *F.Q.* I. Introd. 4 Great Ladie of the greatest Isle. *c* **1630** RISDON *Surv. Devon* §43 (1810) 50 Beatrix de Vallibus was lady of this land. **1633** MILTON *Arcades* 105 Bring your Flocks, and live with us, Here ye shall have greater grace, To serve the Lady of this place. **1711** *Act 9 Anne* in *Lond. Gaz.* No. 4870/1 Any Lord or Lady of a Manor might appoint several Game-keepers. **1832** TENNYSON *Dream Fair Wom.* 97 No marvel, sovereign lady: in fair field Myself for such a face had boldly died.

†**b.** *transf.* and *fig.* *Obs.*

a **1225** *Ancr. R.* 176 Þet fleschs wolde awiligen & bicomen to ful itowen touward hire lefdi, ȝif hit nere ibeaten. **1382** WYCLIF *Isa.* xlvii. 5 Thou shalt no more be clepid the ladi of reumes [**1611** the Ladie of kingdomes]. **1565** COOPER *Thesaurus* s.v. *Auspex*, *Musa auspice*..the ladie of learnyng beyng our guide. **1587** GOLDING *De Mornay* xvi. 265 The Spirit of ours..was free of it selfe, and Ladie of the bodie, and therefore could not receyue her first corruption from the bodie. **1591** SPARRY tr. *Cattan's Geomancie* B 2 b, By the influence of the Sunne she [the Eagle] hath a marueilous property, which is, to be Lady of all other birdes. **1601** R. JOHNSON *Kingd. & Commw.* (1603) 107 Rome, once the Lady of the world. *a* **1610** HEALEY *Epictetus* (1636) 79 Beware that thou hurt not thy minde, the Lady of thy workes, and thine actions governesse.

c. A woman who is the object of chivalrous devotion; a mistress, 'lady-love'.

c **1374** CHAUCER *Troylus* I. 811 Many a man hath love ful dere y-bought, Twenty winter that his lady wiste, That never yet his lady mouth he kiste. **1509** HAWES *Past. Pleas.* XVIII. (Percy Soc.) 83 You are my lady, you are my masteres, Whome I shall serve with all my gentylnes. *a* **1547** SURREY in *Tottel's Misc.* (Arb.) 20 A praise of his loue: wherein he reproueth them that compare their Ladies with his. **1588** SHAKS. *L.L.L.* v. ii. 436. **1633** T. JAMES *Voy.* 71 This euening being May euen; we..chose Ladies, and did ceremoniously weare their names in our Caps. **1867** TENNYSON *Window* 120 Never a line from my lady yet! Is it ay or no? *a* **1881** ROSSETTI *House of Life* viii, My lady only loves the heart of Love.

3. *spec.* **a.** The Virgin Mary. (Usually ***Our Lady*** = L. *Domina Nostra*, and equivalents in all mod. European langs.) †***Our Lady's bands***: pregnancy.

a **900** CYNEWULF *Crist* 284 Cristes þeȝnas cweþað ond singað þæt þu sie hlæfdiȝe halȝum meahtum wuldorweorudes. *c* **1175** *Lamb. Hom.* 17 He wes iboren of ure lefdi Zeinte Marie. *c* **1200** *Trin. Coll. Hom.* 161 Maidene maide and heuene quen and englene lafdi. *c* **1200** ORMIN 2127 Ure deore laffdiȝ wass þurrh Drihhten nemmnedd Marȝe. *c* **1325** *Metr. Hom.* 160 Ilke day deuotely Herd scho messe of our Lefdye. *c* **1410** LOVE *Bonavent. Mirr.* ii. 28 (Gibbs MS.) Þan come þei forþermore to þe house of oure lady cosyn Elizabeth. **1513** MORE in Grafton *Chron.* (1568) II. 761 By Gods blessed Ladie (that was euer his othe). **1553** BECON *Reliques of Rome* (1563) 233* Ye shall also praye..for the women that bene in our Ladyes bandes and with childe. *a* **1555** *Articles imputed to Latimer* in Foxe *A. & M.* (1563) 1309/2 No doubt our lady was, through the goodnes of God, a good & a gratious creature. **1592** SHAKS. *Rom. & Jul.* II. v. 63 O Gods Lady deare, Are yow so hot? marrie come vp I trow. **1797** MRS. RADCLIFFE *Italian* xi, On the morning of our high festival, our Lady's day, it is usual for such as devote themselves to heaven to receive the veil. **1832** TENNYSON *Mariana* iii, Low on her knees herself she cast, Before Our Lady murmur'd she.

†**b.** ***Our, the Lady in March,*** or ***Lent***: the Annunciation, Mar. 25. ***Our Lady in Harvest***: the Assumption, Aug. 15. ***Our Lady in December***: the Conception, Dec. 8. (See LADY-DAY.)

c **1297** R. GLOUC. (Rolls) 9080 Vr leuedy [*v. rr.* leuedi dai, lefdi day] in decembre. *c* **1483** CAXTON *Dialogues* (E.E.T.S.) 28/21 Our ladye in marche. *Ibid.* 28/23 Our lady in heruest. **1608** *Acc. Bk. W. Wray* in *Antiquary* XXXII. 213 A great frost from Martinmas till almost y[e] Lady in lent.

†**c.** An image of the Virgin Mary. *Obs.*

1563 *Homilies* II. *Agst. Idolatry* III. (1859) 225 Christophers, Ladies, and Mary Magdalenes, and other Saints. **1606** *Arraignm. late Traitors* D 1 b, Their [Papists'] kissing of babies, their kneeling to wodden Ladies.

4. a. A woman of superior position in society, or to whom such a position is conventionally or by courtesy attributed. Originally, the word connoted a degree equal to that expressed by *lord*; but it was (like its synonyms in all European langs.) early widened in application, while the corresponding masc. term retained its restricted comprehension. In mod. use *lady* is the recognized fem. analogue of *gentleman*, and is applied to all women above a loosely-defined and variable, but usually not very elevated standard of social position. Often used (*esp.* in 'this lady') as a more courteous synonym for 'woman', without reference to the status of the person spoken of. See also FINE LADY, YOUNG LADY.

As the traditional association of *lady* with *lord* still survives, the former is a title of ostensibly higher dignity than *gentleman*. Hence, and not directly as the result of the sentiment of gallantry, the customary order of words in 'ladies and gentlemen'.

c **1205** LAY. 24715 Alle þa lafdies leoneden ȝeond walles to bihalden þa duȝoðen. *c* **1230** *Hali Meid.* 9 Aske þes cwenes, þes riche cuntasses, þes modie lafdis. **1297** R. GLOUC. (Rolls) 3280 Mony was þe vayre leuedi þat icome was þer to.

1340 *Ayenb.* 215 þe greate lhordes and þe greate lheuedyes. *c* 1350 *Will. Palerne* 2968 Whan þat loveli ladi hade listened his wordes..for ioye sche wept. 1377 LANGL. *P. Pl.* B. XVIII. 335 Ylyke a lusarde with a lady visage. *c* 1386 CHAUCER *Knt.'s T.* 898 A companye of ladies..clad in clothes blake. 1486 *Bk. St. Albans* F vj, A Beuy of Ladies. 1526 *Pilgr. Perf.* (W. de W. 1531) 268 Labouryng & seruyng for these two ladyes, Lya & Rachel. *c* 1560 A. SCOTT *Poems* (S.T.S.) vi. 27 A lord to lufe a silly lass, A leddy als, for luf, to tak Ane propir page. 1588 SHAKS. *L.L.L.* II. i. 192 What Lady is that same? 1589 PUTTENHAM *Eng. Poesie* III. xxiv. (Arb.) 296 For Ladies and women to weepe..it is nothing vncomely. 1611 BEAUM. & FL. *Knt. Burn. Pestle* III. iv, To punish all the sad enormities Thou hast committed against ladies gent. 1664 EVELYN *Kal. Hort.* in *Sylva*, etc. (1729) 190 Keep your Wall and Palisade-Trees..sharp'd like a Lady's Fan. 1674 DRYDEN *Epil.* Misc. (1685) 289 A Country Lip may have the Velvet touch, Tho' She's no Lady, you may think her such. 1702 ADDISON *Dial. Medals* i. Wks. 1721 I. 438 We find too on Medals the representations of Ladies that have given occasion to whole volumes on the account only of a face. 1768–74 TUCKER *Lt. Nat.* (1834) I. 246 This is giving the ladies' reason, 'It is so because it is'. 1791 COWPER *Retired Cat* 38 Linen..such as merchants introduce From India, for the ladies' use. 1807–8 W. IRVING *Salmag.* xviii. (1860) 414 It appears to be an established maxim..that a lady loses her dignity when she condescends to be useful. 1886 MISS MULOCK *K. Arthur* i. 11 Poor lady!.. But if she were a real lady she would never be an opera-singer. 1888 *Harper's Mag.* Nov. 960/1 She was born, in our familiar phrase, a lady, and..throughout a long life, she was surrounded with perfect ease of circumstance.

b. *vocatively.* (*a*) In the *singular* (not now in standard use). (*b*) In the *plural*, the ordinary term of oral address to a number of women, without reference to their rank; corresponding to 'Madam' in the singular.

The uneducated, esp. in London, still often use 'Lady' in the sing. as a term of address for 'Madam' or 'Ma'am'.

c 1384 CHAUCER *H. Fame* III. 519 Lady, graunte us now good fame. *c* 1400 *Sowdone Bab.* 1889 Noe, certes, lady, it is not I. 1599 SHAKS. *Much Ado* II. i. 285 *Pedr.* Come Lady, come, you haue lost the heart of Signior Benedicke. 1634 MILTON *Comus* 277 What chance, good Lady, hath bereft you thus? *Ibid.* 319, I can conduct you, Lady, to a low But loyal cottage. 1808 [see GENTLEMAN 4 b]. 1819 SHELLEY *Cenci* v. ii. 172 Know you this paper, Lady? 1914 G. B. SHAW *Pygmalion* (1916) I. 107 *The Flower Girl.* Thank you kindly, lady. 1924 I. GERSHWIN (*song title*) Lady, be good. 1953 *Manch. Guardian Weekly* 10 Sept. 7 Why, lady, take route 128. 1972 P. RUELL *Red Christmas* xiv. 148 'Lady,' he said, 'you talk sense. Just remember, it's guns that count.' 1974 M. BABSON *Stalking Lamb* xxiii. 176, I *know* it can, lady. It won't be the first time.

†**c.** ***lady errant***: a humorous feminine analogue of 'knight errant'.

a 1643 CARTWRIGHT (*title*) The Lady Errant. 1655 FULLER *Ch. Hist.* VI. vii. 364 Conscientious Catholicks conceived these Lady Errants so much to deviate from feminine..modesty..that they zealously decried their practice.

d. Applied to fairies.

1628 MILTON *Vacation Exerc.* 60 At thy birth The Faiery Ladies daunc't upon the hearth. *a* 1650 *K. Arthur's Death* 235 in Furnivall *Percy Folio* I. 506 He see a barge from the land goe, & hearde Ladyes houle & cry.

e. Phraseological expressions. ***lady of the lake***, (*a*) the designation of a personage in the Arthurian legends, Nimue or Vivien; †(*b*) a nymph; †(*c*) a kept mistress. ***lady of pleasure***, a courtesan, whore. ***lady of easy virtue***, a woman whose chastity is easily assailable. ***lady of the frying-pan***, a jocular term for a cook. ***lady of Babylon, of Rome***, abusive terms for the Roman Catholic Church, with reference to the 'scarlet woman' of the Apocalypse. †***lady of honour***, †***lady of presence***, a lady who holds the position of attendant to a queen or princess (cf. *maid of honour*); similarly ***lady of the bedchamber, lady-in-waiting***. ***Lady Bountiful*** (see BOUNTIFUL *a.* 1). ***a lady in the case***, indicating that the key to the problem is a lady (cf. CHERCHEZ LA FEMME). ***the Old Lady*** (***in*** or) ***of Threadneedle Street***, the Bank of England. ***the lady of the house***, the mistress of a household; a housewife.

1470–85 MALORY *Arthur* I. xxv. 73 What damoysel is that? said Arthur. That is the lady of the lake, said Merlyn. 1530 PALSGR. 237/1 Lady of presence, *damoiselle dhonneur*. 1536 HEN. VIII *Let.* 10 Jan. in Halliwell *Lett. Eng. Kings* (1846) I. 352 At the interment [of Katharine of Arragon] it is requisite to have the presence of a good many ladies of honour. 1579 SPENSER *Sheph. Cal.* Apr. 120 They bene all Ladyes of the lake behight [E. K. *Gloss*, Ladyes of the lake be Nymphes]. 1625 MASSINGER *New Way* II. i, Thou shalt dine..With me, and with a lady. *Marrall.* Lady? What lady? With the Lady of the Lake, or Queen of Fairies? 1631 *High Commission Cases* (Camden) 187 The Lady Willoughby..now one of the Ladyes of Honour attendant upon the Queene. 1637 SHIRLEY (*title*) The Lady of Pleasure. *c* 1645 HOWELL *Lett.* (1650) I. 447 He hath no such cloisters or houses for ladies of pleasure. 1678 BUTLER *Hud.* III. i. 869 The difference Marriage makes 'Twixt Wives, and Ladies of the Lakes. 1708 MOTTEUX *Rabelais* (1737) V. 217 Kept-Wenches, Kind-hearted-Things, Ladies of Pleasure, by what..Names soever dignified. 1727 J. GAY *Fables* I. l. 172 And when a lady's in the case, You know, all other things give place. 1785 GROSE *Dict. Vulg. Tongue*, *Lady of easy virtue*, a woman of the town, a prostitute. *c* 1793 JANE AUSTEN *Volume Second* in *Minor Works* (1954) 136 We had scarcely paid our Compliments to the Lady of the House. 1797 J. GILLRAY *Caricature* 22 May, Political Ravishment, or The Old Lady of Threadneedle-Street in danger! 1809 MALKIN *Gil Blas* III. x. ¶4 The lady of the frying-pan..was assisted in her cookery by the coachman. 1809 [see EASY *a.* 12]. 1816 JANE AUSTEN *Emma* III. xiv. 254 It was with difficulty that she could summon enough of her usual self to be the attentive lady of the house, or even the attentive daughter. 1820 *Black Dwarf* IV. 36 Van went to wheedle—the street of Threadneedle, To get him, poor dog, a loan;..He ask'd the old lady to cash him a bill. 1821 BYRON *Don Juan* v. xix. 243 'Ay,' quoth his friend, 'I thought it would appear That there had been a lady in the case.' 1850 *Househ. Words* 6 July 337 (*heading*) The Old Lady of Threadneedle Street. 1858 TROLLOPE *Barchester T.* xx. 150 The ordeal through which he had gone, in resisting the blandishments of the lady of Rome. 1860 —— *Castle Richmond* I. v. 83 The pope, with his lady of Babylon, his college of cardinals [etc.]. 1861 MRS. BEETON *Bk. Househ. Managem.* 9 The more usual plan is for the lady of the house to have the joint brought to her table, and afterwards carried to the nursery. 1862 MRS. H. WOOD *Mrs. Hallib.* II. xii. 205 Making the avowal as freely as though he had proclaimed that his mother was lady-in-waiting to the Queen. 1863 A. TROLLOPE *Rachel Ray* I. xiii. 260 Luke, is there no young lady in the case? 1884 *Peel City Guardian* No. 26. 2/1 The rest of the 'Old Lady in Threadneedle-street' remained unbroken. 1909 W. S. GILBERT *Fallen Fairies* II. 37 In all the woes that curse our race There is a lady in the case. 1958 R. GENDERS *Pansies, Violas & Violets* x. 100 Those who have retired will be able to give the plants their full attention, whilst those who have to go out to work each day may have to entrust the care of the plants to the lady of the house. 1971 *Guardian* 19 Aug. 9/3 Door-to-door sales people were asked why the opening question is always, 'Is the lady of the house home?' 1974 G. VAIZEY *Tangled Web* ii. 26 He..is highly respected by the Old Lady of Threadneedle Street.

f. *pl.* Designation of a public convenience for females. Freq. ***ladies'***, and with capital initial.

1918 'K. MANSFIELD' *Jrnl.* (1954) 140 Also, when she goes to the 'Ladies', for some obscure reason she wears a little shawl. 1936 R. CAMPBELL *Mithraic Emblems* 120 No 'Ladies' here or 'Gentlemens' are seen For most of you to hesitate between. 1938 G. GREENE *Brighton Rock* III. i. 98 The white steps down to the ladies'. 1939 C. MORLEY *Kitty Foyle* 36 How to get undressed in a Pullman berth, how to find the Ladies. 1944 T. RATTIGAN *While Sun Shines* I. 190, I lost the plans of the Station Defence... We found them again all right. I'd only left them in the Ladies. 1965 G. MELLY *Owning-Up* vi. 64 'They're no good,' he'd tell us as two of them swayed past on their way to the ladies. 1974 D. MEIRING *President Plan* vi. 42 Comunicado Number Two ..was found, as anonymously advised, in the Ladies' of a San Agustín restaurant.

5. A woman whose manners, habits, and sentiments have the refinement characteristic of the higher ranks of society.

1861 GEO. ELIOT *Silas M.* I. xi. 185 She had the essential attributes of a lady—high veracity, delicate honour in her dealings, deference to others, and refined personal habits. 1880 C. E. NORTON *Ch.-building Mid. Ages* ii. 40 Her [Venice's] gentlemen were the first in Europe, and the first modern ladies were Venetian.

6. As an honorific title.

a. A prefix forming part of the customary designation of a woman of rank. Also in ***my lady***, an appellation used (chiefly by inferiors) in speaking to or of those who are designated by this prefix.

In the 15–16th c., *The* (or *My*) *Lady* was prefixed to the Christian name of a female member of the royal family, as 'Princess' is now. With regard to the use of the prefix in the titles of the nobility of the British Isles, usage has varied greatly at different times, but the following rules are now established: (1) In speaking of a marchioness, countess, viscountess, or baroness (whether she be such in her own right, by marriage, or by courtesy), the prefix *Lady* is a less formal substitute for the specific designation of rank, which is not used in conversational address: thus 'the Marchioness (of) A.' is spoken to, and informally spoken of, as 'Lady A.' (2) The daughters of dukes, marquises, and earls have *Lady* (more formally, e.g. on a superscription, *The Lady*) prefixed to their Christian names. (3) The wife of the holder of a courtesy title in which *Lord* is prefixed to a Christian name is known as '(The) Lady John B.' (4) The wife of a baronet or other knight ('Sir John C.') is commonly spoken of as 'Lady C.', the strictly correct appellation 'Dame Mary C.' being confined to legal documents, sepulchral monuments, and the like.

c 1489 CAXTON *Blanchardyn* Ded. 1 Unto the right noble puyssant & excellent pryncesse, my redoubted lady, my lady Margarete, duchesse of Somercete. 1509 in *Fisher's Wks.* (1876) 288 The moost excellent pryncesse my lady the kynges graundame. *a* 1548 HALL *Chron.*, *Hen. VIII* 238 b, The Ladye Marques Dorset. 1555 GRIMALD in *Tottel's Misc.* (Arb.) 113 An Epitaph of the ladye Margaret Lee. 1594 SHAKS. *Rich. III*, I. ii. *Stage direct.*, Enter the Coarse of Henrie the sixt..Lady Anne being the Mourner. 1599 *Broughton's Lett.* vii. 21 Who selected him..to bee the Lady Margarets Reader. *a* 1674 CLARENDON *Hist. Reb.* XI. §235 The general's wife, the lady Fayrefax. 1694 CONGREVE *Double Dealer* Dram. Pers., Lord Touchwood,..Sir Paul Plyant..Knight..Lady Touchwood..Lady Plyant. *a* 1715 BURNET *Own Time* I. (1724) I. 19 Lady Margaret Dowglas was the child so provided for. *Ibid.* III. 353 The Lady Bellasis, the widow of the Lord Bellasis's son. 1719 PRIOR (*title*) Verses spoken to Lady Henrietta Cavendish-Holles Harley, Countess of Oxford. 1766 *Gentl. Mag.* XXXVI. 103/1 Lady North,—of a son. *Ibid.*, Lady Anne Conway, eldest daughter to the Earl of Hertford. 1833 TENNYSON (*title*) Lady Clara Vere de Vere. 1864 —— *Aylmer's F.* 190 My lady's Indian kinsman. 1870 DISRAELI *Lothair* II. xiv. 148 Lothair danced with Lady Flora Falkirk, and her sister, Lady Grizell, was in the same quadrille.

b. Prefixed to the names of goddesses, allegorical personages, personifications, etc. Now *arch.* exc. in ***Lady Luck*** = FORTUNE *sb.* 1.

c 1205 LAY. 1198 Leafdi Diana: leoue Diana heȝe Diana, help me to neode. *c* 1425 LYDG. *Assembly of Gods* 239 My lady Diane, the goddesse. 1508 DUNBAR *Gold. Targe* 74 Thare saw I..The fresch Aurora, and lady Flora schene. *Ibid.* 210 A wofull prisonnere To lady Beautee. 1551 ROBINSON tr. *More's Utop.* II. (Arb.) 160 If that same worthye princesse lady money did not alone stop up the waye betwene vs and our lyuing. 1566 DRANT *Horace's Sat.* I. iii. B vj, Thus graunte you must, that feare of wronge set ladye lawe in forte. 1597 J. PAYNE *Royal Exch.* 20 [Those] that make so small accowmpt of religion and good lyfe, otherwyse then of there belly God and ladie pleasure. *a* 1625 BOYS *Wks.* (1629) 487 Ladie Venus dwels at the signe of the Iuie bush. 1932 M. SHORT (*title*) Lady Luck in 1941. 1936 C. SANDBURG *People, Yes* 165 Yes, get Lady Luck with you and you're made. 1961 T. HENROT *Belgium* 119 A thousand ways of flirting with Lady Luck.

c. Prefixed to titles of honour or designations of dignified office, as an added mark of respect. *Obs.* or *arch.* ***Lady Mayoress***: see MAYORESS.

c 1386 CHAUCER *Prioress' Prol.* 13 My lady Prioresse. 1530 PALSGR. 237/1 Lady maystres, *dame dhonnevr*; *gouvernante*. 1613 SHAKS. *Hen. VIII*, v. iii. 169 You shall haue two noble Partners with you: the old Duchesse of Norfolke, and Lady Marquess Dorset. 1638 FORD *Fancies* IV. ii, Are you not enthroned The lady-regent? 1710 SHAFTESB. *Adv. Author* III. ii. 167 The Method of expostulating with his Lady-Governess. 1721 STRYPE *Eccl. Mem.* II. i. 3 The Lady Mary, the Kings daughter, appointed for the lady godmother. 1771 SMOLLETT *Humph. Cl.* 8 Aug., The lady-directress of the ball..had her conveyed to another room. 1820 SCOTT *Abbot* xii, 'They call me Lady Abbess, or Mother at the least, who address me', said Dame Bridget.

d. Prefixed to designations of relationship, by way of respectful address or reference, as ***lady wife***, etc. (Cf. F. *Madame votre mère*, etc.) *arch.* or *genteel.*

15.. *Roberte the Deuyll* 522 in Hazlitt *E.P.P.* I. 239 And when he sawe hys mother goynge, He sayde, alas, Lady mother, speake with me. 1528 MORE *Dial.* III. xii. Wks. 227/2 But were I Pope. By my soule quod he, I would ye wer, & my lady your wife Popesse too. 1602 *2nd Pt. Return fr. Parnass.* II. vi. 983 A Turkey Pye, or a piece of Venison, which my Lady Grand-mother sent me. 1628 FORD *Lover's Mel.* IV. ii, Your business with my lady-daughter toss-pot? 1655 DRYDEN (*title*) Lines in a Letter to his Lady Cousin Honor Driden. 1749 FIELDING *Tom Jones* XV. v, Answer for yourself, lady cousin. 1805 SCOTT *Last Minstr.* VI. xxiii, But that my ladye-mother there Sits lonely in her castle-hall. 1820 W. TOOKE tr. *Lucian* I. 730 As to your lady-bride, I envy not her beauty. 1840 DICKENS *Lett.* (1969) II. 7, I wish I could send you some autographs..but I find..that my lady wife has been bestowing them upon her friends. 1855 TENNYSON *Maud* I. iv. 15, I bow'd to his lady-sister as she rode by. 1895 C. M. YONGE *Long Vacation* xxviii. 292 Mr. White, in his joy at possessing his graceful lady wife, had spared no expense. 1969 *Listener* 27 Mar. 417/3 We don't think you've laid enough emphasis on the colonel's foresight, courage, and heroic lady wife. 1971 'A. GILBERT' *Tenant for Tomb* viii. 142, I don't know how far your lady wife's in your confidence.

e. ***Lady Macbeth***, with allusion to the character in Shakespeare's play *Macbeth*: a remorseless or melodramatic woman, usu. leading or assisting a weak man.

1876 TROLLOPE *Prime Minister* I. xi. 169, I feel myself to be a Lady Macbeth, prepared for the murder of any Duncan or any Daubeny who may stand in my lord's way. 1919 KIPLING *Years Between* 92 A boy drowning kittens Winced at the business; whereupon his sister (Lady Macbeth aged seven) thrust 'em under. 1969 M. PUGH *Last Place Left* iv. 26 'I know you're up to something,' Nell repeated. 'You're taking all this far too calmly.' 'All right, Lady Macbeth.' 1974 J. MANN *Sticking Place* x. 153 Hasn't there been enough killing? I am no Lady Macbeth.

7. Wife, consort. Now, as in the original use, chiefly restricted to instances in which the formal title of 'Lady' is involved in the relationship. In the 18th and the former half of the 19th c. the wider use was prevalent in polite society, but is now regarded as vulgar, esp. in the phrase ***your good lady***.

c 1205 LAY. 2864 Swa þe king haihte, to wrðscipe his læfdi. *a* 1400–50 *Alexander* 517 Sire þere sall borne be a barne of þi blithe lady. 1483 CAXTON *G. de la Tour* cxxxv. M v b, A grete lady, whiche was lady to a baron. 1613 *Organ Specif. Worcester Cathedral*, Sr Jo Packinton & his Lady. 1686 S. SEWALL *Diary* 23 Sept., Gov. Bradstreet is gone with his lady to Salem. *a* 1715 BURNET *Own Time* II. (1724) I. 338 About the end of May, Duke Lauderdale came down with his Lady in great pomp. 1756–7 tr. *Keysler's Trav.* (1760) IV. 7 The lady of a noble Venetian..is indulged with greater freedom in this respect. 1768 STERNE *Sent. Journ.* (1775) II. 98 (*Sword*) The Marquis..supported his lady. *c* 1796 T. TWINING *Trav. Amer.* (1894) 87 She was granddaughter of Mrs. Washington, the President's lady. 1796 LAMB *Let. to Coleridge* Corr. & Wks. 1868 I. 11 It has endeared us more than any thing to your good lady. 1796 JANE AUSTEN *Pride & Prej.* (1833) 1 'My dear Mr. Bennet', said his lady to him one day, 'have you heard' [etc.]. —— *Sense & Sens.* (1879) 1 By a former marriage, Mr. Dashwood had one son; by his present lady, three daughters. 1825 WATERTON *Wand. S. Amer.* IV. ii. 313 The unfortunate governor and his lady lost their lives. 1841 *L'pool Mercury* 11 June 195/4 On Thursday, the 3d instant, the lady of Thomas William Phillips, Esq...of a daughter... On Monday last, at Everton, the lady of Thomas Shaw, Esq., of a daughter. 1841 C. ANDERSON *Anc. Models* 101 An organ was lately given by the estimable lady of the Rev. J. B. Stonehouse.. to the church of Owston. 1845 STEPHEN *Comm. Laws Eng.* (1874) II. 608 As where it [i.e. a peerage] is limited to a man and the heirs male of his body by Elizabeth, his present lady. 1860 O. W. HOLMES *Elsie V.* vii. (1861) 71 'How's your health, Colonel Sprowle'. 'Very well, much obleeged to you. Hope you and your good lady are well'.

II. In transferred applications.

†**8.** A queen at chess. *Obs.*

c 1489 CAXTON *Sons of Aymon* xxii. 478 The duk rycharde ..helde in his hande a lady of yvery, wherwyth he wolde have gyven a mate to yonnet.

9. A kind of butterfly; now ***painted lady***.

1611 FLORIO, *Papiglione*, any kind of Ladie or butter-flie. **1846** EMBLETON in *Proc. Berw. Nat. Club* II. 171 Not a single specimen has been observed of the Peacock, Wood Lady, Wall Brown, or the Dark Green Aglaia. **1893** EARL DUNMORE *Pamirs* I. 197 This 'painted lady' was the name by which a certain gaudy butterfly was known.

10. The calcareous structure in the stomach of a lobster, serving for the trituration of its food; fancifully supposed to resemble the outline of a seated female figure.

1704 SWIFT *Batt. Bks.* Misc. (1711) 253 Like the Lady in a Lobster. **1796** J. ADAMS *Diary* 28 July Wks. 1851 III. 421 To-day, at dinner, seeing lobsters at table, I inquired after the Lady, and Mrs. B. rose and went into the kitchen to her husband, who sent in the little lady herself, in the cradle in which she resides. **1804** FARLEY *Lond. Art Cookery* (ed. 10) 47 Take out their bodies, and what is called the lady.

11. The smallest size of Welsh (and Cornish) roofing slates. (Cf. COUNTESS, DUCHESS.)

1803 *Sporting Mag.* XX. 109 He had delivered to the defendant eight thousand Countesses and eleven thousand Ladies. **1859** GWILT *Archit.* II. ii. (ed. 4) 501 Ladies are generally about 15 in. long, and about 8 in. wide. **1893** BROWN *Opening Rly. to Delabole* xxiii, We've countess, duchess..doubles, ladies, slabs, and flags.

12. A female hound. (Cf. 15 b, and *lady pack* in 17.)

1861 WHYTE MELVILLE *Mkt. Harb.* x. 80 Nineteen couple are they of ladies, with the cleanest of heads and necks.

13. *Naut.* (See quots.)

1711 W. SUTHERLAND *Shipbuild. Assist.* 43 A Lady's Hole, or Place for the Gunner's small stores, which Stores are looked after by one they call a Lady, who is put in by turns to keep the Gun-room clean. **1867** SMYTH *Sailor's Word-bk., Lady of the Gun-room*, a gunner's mate, who takes charge of the after-scuttle, where gunners' stores are kept.

14. *N. Amer.* A female harlequin duck, *Histrionicus histrionicus*. See ***lord and lady (duck)*** (LORD *sb.* 16).

1792 G. CARTWRIGHT *Jrnl.* I. p. xii, *Lady*, a water-fowl of the duck genus, and the hen of the lord.

III. In Combination.

15. appositively (quasi-*adj.*). **a.** Prefixed, with the sense 'female', to designations of employment, office, function, etc., which are ordinarily applied to men, as in ***lady actor, citizen, clerk, critic, doctor, farmer, friend, guest, novelist, page, president, reader, singer, superintendent, tyrant***, etc.

1684 OTWAY *Atheist* II. i. Wks. 1728 II. 29 The Lady-Tyrant of your Enchanted Castle. *a* **1687** WALLER *Wks.* (1729) 222 Prologue for the Lady-Actors. **1694** CONGREVE *Double Dealer* Epil., The Lady Criticks who are better Read, Enquire if Characters are nicely bred. **1775** MAD. D'ARBLAY *Early Diary* (1889) II. 109 She has a fine voice, and has great merit, for a lady singer. **1784** R. BAGE *Barham Downs* I. 9 Instead of hunting for..a wealthy widow, or a rich lady citizen, he retired to his country seat. **1818** SHELLEY *Rosalind & Helen* 91 Bring home with you That sweet strange lady-friend. **1826** MISS MITFORD *Village* Ser. II. (1863) 428 A good sort of lady-farmer. **1827** G. DARLEY *Sylvia* 110 Or any lady-page that soothes A steed whose neck she hardly smoothes. **1837** DICKENS *Pickw.* xxx, If our observant lady readers can deduce any satisfactory inferences from these facts, we beg them by all means to do so. **1848** *Blackw. Mag.* Aug. 186 Miss Martineau is lady-president of the gossip school. **1858** *English Woman's Jrnl.* I. 90 As she went through the streets,..rude cries of 'Come on, Bill! let's have a good look at the lady-doctor!' would meet her ears. **1860** G. H. K. in *Vac. Tour.* 137 These hinds ..are the lady-superintendents of an educational institution for young stags. **1873** C. M. YONGE *Pillars of House* IV. xlii. 219 To be a lady-doctor was surely her vocation! **1879** GEO. ELIOT *Let.* 18 Mar. (1956) VII. 117 This week for the first time I am going to see a lady friend. **1890** 'ROLF BOLDREWOOD' *Col. Reformer* (1891) 333 The first lady-guest ever seen at Rainbar. **1891** *Argus* (Melbourne) 7 Nov. 9/2 The 'lady doctor' has become an institution in Victoria. **1894** *Daily News* 28 Mar. 3/2 To the lady clerks is allotted half the ledger keeping. **1895** HARDY *Jude* v. iii. 343, I couldn't very well tell it to your lady friend. **1912** A. BRAZIL *New Girl at St. Chad's* iv. 69 'We have a lady doctor, you see,' said Ruth, 'and she's so jolly.' **1923** Lady-novelist [see APOLLINE *a.*]. **1928** R. CAMPBELL *Wayzgoose* ii. 35 And still new-comers to the Wayzgoose throng And lady-novelists a thousand strong. **1931** *Weekend Rev.* 17 Oct. 496/1 The night-watchman, after taunting Larry with his inexperience in affairs of the heart, is obliged to stand by and see the youngster making rapid headway in the affections of his own lady-friend. **1961** *Listener* 30 Mar. 574/3 If 'women novelists' are to become 'lady novelists' as a matter of course, I give notice..that in future, when reviewing the novels of male writers of fiction, I shall make a point of referring to these writers as 'gentlemen novelists'. **1975** C. AIRD *Slight Mourning* vi. 58 The lady doctor had arrived.

b. Used jocularly for 'female' with names of animals.

1820 SHELLEY *Œdipus* II. i. 157 Gentlemen swine, and gentle lady-pigs. **1832** IRVING *Alhambra* II. 33 The very beetle woos its lady-beetle in the dust. **1887** G. R. SIMS *Mary Jane's Mem.* 37 The dog..had five beautiful puppies afterwards, it being a lady-dog. **1894** G. R. O'REILLY in *Pop. Sci. Monthly* Nov. 77 One..night an old lady cobra surprised me by depositing a number of living young ones.

c. Prefixed to designations of employment usually associated with inferiority of social rank, to denote that the person is or claims to be regarded as a lady. Cf. *lady-help* (see 16 below).

1811 L. M. HAWKINS *C'tess & Gertr.* I. 94 Some lady-nurses..forego not an hour's amusement. **1873** *St. Paul's Mag.* II. 233 He, a dignified ecclesiastic butler, with a perfect palate for port, to be levelled with a pert little chit of a 'lady-housekeeper'. **1898** *Advt.* in *Westm. Gaz.* 11 July 2/3 Lady-Cook, also Lady-Parlourmaid wanted..lady-nurse and man kept.

16. Obvious combinations: **a.** attributive (pertaining to a lady or ladies), as ***lady-bower, -chamber***; (characteristic of or befitting a lady), as ***lady-air, -fingers, -look, -slang, -trifle***; (consisting of ladies), as ***lady portion, train, world***. **b.** similative, as ***lady-clad, -faced, -handed, -looking, -soft*** adjs. **c.** instrumental, as ***lady-laden*** adj.

a **1637** B. JONSON *Underwoods, Eupheme* ix, She had a mind as calm as she was fair, Not lost or troubled with light *lady-air. **1741** RICHARDSON *Pamela* (1824) I. xv. 253 What, I say, had I to do, to take upon me lady-airs, and resent? **1832** J. BREE *St. Herbert's Isle* 19 The burly thane..oft in *lady-bower would long remain. **1853** MERIVALE *Rom. Rep.* xi. (1867) 323 This tender nursling of a patrician *lady-chamber was climbing mountains on foot. **1847** TENNYSON *Princess* Prol. 119 But while they talk'd, above their heads I saw The feudal warrior *lady-clad. *c* **1610** SIR J. MELVIL *Mem.* (Bannatyne) 120 He wes very lusty, berdles, and *lady facit. **1831** HOWITT *Seasons* (1837) 317 Rose-wood desks, where *lady-fingers pen lady-lays. **1728** RAMSAY *Archers diverting themselves* 28 The *lady-handed lad. **1870** TENNYSON *Holy Grail* 54 Where the long Rich galleries, *lady-laden, weigh'd the necks Of dragons clinging to the crazy walls. **1887** *Times* (weekly ed.) 24 June 4/4 Every balcony..was 'lady-laden'. **1824** MISS MITFORD *Village* Ser. I. (1863) 4, I have never seen any one in her station who possessed so thoroughly that undefinable charm, the *lady-look. **1834** H. MILLER *Scenes & Leg.* xx. (1857) 291 So *lady-looking a person, and an heiress to boot. **1866** WHITTIER *Marg. Smith's Jrnl.* Prose Wks. 1889 I. 11 His daughter, Rebecca, is just about my age, very tall and lady-looking. **1890** 'ROLF BOLDREWOOD' *Col. Reformer* (1891) 165 The *lady portion of the guests. **1821** 'P. ATALL' (*title*) The Hermit in Philadelphia, Second Series, containing some Account of Young Belles and Coquettes..Dandy-Slang and *Lady-Slang. **1607** MARKHAM *Caval.* II. (1617) 15 This Cauezan I haue seen very good hors-men vse, but with such a temperate and *Lady-soft a hand, that [etc.]. **1717** E. FENTON *Poems* 111 The *Lady-Train dispers'd, the pensive Form Of Agamemnon came. **1606** SHAKS. *Ant. & Cl.* v. ii. 165, I some *Lady trifles haue reseru'd Immoment toyes. **1775** MAD. D'ARBLAY *Early Diary* 21 Nov., Being herself a performer of reputation in the *lady world, she [etc.].

17. a. Special comb. (in many cases orig. syntactical uses of *lady* genitive, in sense 3): **Lady-altar**, an altar in a Lady-chapel; **lady-apple**, a kind of small apple, with a red waxy-looking skin; valued chiefly for its ornamental appearance; also *attrib.*; **Lady-bell** (also ***Our Lady bell***), a bell for ringing the Angelus; **lady-chair**, a seat formed by the hands of two persons standing facing each other: each person grasping his own left wrist with his right hand, and the right wrist of the opposite person with his left hand, or *vice versa*; **lady-clock** = LADY-BIRD; **lady-court**, the court of a lady of a manor (in mod. Dicts.); **lady-crab**, a name given variously to certain species of crabs remarkable for elegance of colouring or form; **(Our) Lady eve, even**, the day before a Lady-day; **lady-fluke** (see quot.); **lady-fly** = LADY-BIRD; **lady-fowl**, a name for the smew or the widgeon; **lady-help**, a woman engaged to perform domestic service on the understanding that she is to be considered and treated by her employers as a lady; **lady-killer** *humorous*, a man who is credited with dangerous power of fascination over women; so ***lady-killing*** sb. and adj.; **Lady-meat** (also ***Lady's meat***), alms given in Our Lady's honour *arch.*; **lady-monger** *contemptuous*, a 'lady's man'; **lady-pack**, a pack of female hounds; †**lady-pear**, some variety of pear; **(Our) Lady-psalter**, the 'PSALTER of the Blessed Virgin Mary'; **Lady-quarter**, the quarter in which Lady-day occurs; **Lady-tide**, the time of the year about Lady-day; †**lady-wit**, an effeminate pretender to culture; **Lady-worshipper**, one who worships the Virgin Mary. Also LADY-BIRD, LADY-COW, etc.

1898 *Weekly Reg.* 16 July 68 Mrs. Franks..presented a carved oak *lady-altar in memory of her late father. **1860** O. W. HOLMES *Prof. Breakf.-t.* iii. (Paterson) 50 Joe, with his cheeks like *lady-apples. **1876** T. HARDY *Ethelberta* (1890) 24 The girl with the lady-apple cheeks. **1541** *Ludlow Churchw. Acc.* (Camden) 8 For mendynge of the whele of our *Lady belle. **1872** ELLACOMBE *Bells of Ch.* viii. in *Ch. Bells Devon* 395 Six other bells from the rood tower, called the Lady Bells. **1869** MRS. STOWE *Oldtown Folks* xxvi. 298 Tina..insisted upon it that we should occasionally carry her in a *lady-chair over to this island. **1848** C. BRONTË *J. Eyre* (1857) 255 That was only a *lady-clock, child, 'flying away home'. **1894** HALL CAINE *Manxman* 113 A lady-clock settled on her wrist. **1882** *Cassell's Nat. Hist.* VI. 200 The Velvet Fiddler Crab..in the Channel Islands is known as the *Lady Crab, from its velvet coat. **1884** *Stand. Nat. Hist.* (1888) II. 63 *Platyonichus ocellatus*, lady crab. **1885** C. F. HOLDER *Marvels Anim. Life* 171 Their motions..resembling those of our common lady-crab. **1306** *Pol. Songs* (Camden) 219 This wes on oure *Levedy even. *a* **1548** HALL *Chron., Hen. VIII* 255 The Quene his wife was delivered of a daughter, on our lady Even before Christmas. **1603** OWEN *Pembrokesh.* (1891) 191 At vsuall feastes that ys the one on our ladie Eve in March, the other at Maye Eve. **1836** YARRELL *Brit. Fishes* II. 323 *Lady fluke. The Holibut, *Hippoglossus vulgaris*. **1714** GAY *Sheph. Week* Thursday 83 This *lady-fly I take from off the grass. **1821** CLARE *Vill. Minstr.* I. 209 Lady-fly with freckled wings, Watch her up the tall bent climb. **1772** RUTTY *Nat. Hist. Dublin* I. 335 The *Lady-Fowl..is much esteemed in the London market..the Male being distinguished by the name of Easterling, and the female strictly called the Lady-fowl. *Ibid.* 336 The cock Lady-fowl is entirely distinct from the cock Widgeon. **1893** NEWTON *Dict. Birds, Lady-fowl*, said to be a name of the Wigeon. **1875** *Punch* 11 Sept. 98/1 In poor genteel families, *lady-helps could hardly expect any wages. **1881** MISS BRADDON *One Thing Needful* ix, I suppose we must call this paragon of yours a lady-help. **1811** *Ora & Juliet* II. 197 Upwards of twenty sat down at table, amongst whom was the *lady killer, or Colonel Sackville. **1884** *Graphic* 4 Oct. 362/1 He had been a lady-killer in his day, and was by no means out of the hunt yet. **1825** C. M. WESTMACOTT *Eng. Spy* I. 192 *Ladykilling coterie. **1837** MARRYAT *Dog-fiend* li, 'Pretty lady-killing', muttered the sergeant. **1858** R. S. SURTEES *Ask Mamma* i. 2 Nature had favoured Billy's pretensions in the lady-killing way. **1849** ROCK *Ch. of Fathers* III. ix. 284 Many an alms was given for Mary's sake, and the food, so set aside, went by the name of '*Lady-meat'. **1879** E. WATERTON *Pietas Mariana* 115 Bread and meat given in our Ladye's love were called Saint Marye's loaf, and Ladymeat. **1597** *1st Pt. Return fr. Parnass.* IV. i. 1236 This haberdasher of lyes, this bracchidochio, this *ladyemunger. **1678** BUTLER *Hud.* III. i. 378 He serv'd two Prentiships and longer I' th' Myst'ry of a Lady-Monger. **1861** WHYTE MELVILLE *Mkt. Harb.* 10 He did not quite fancy making one of that crowd of irregular-horse who appear on a Wednesday at Crick or Misterton, to the unspeakable dismay of the Pytchley *lady pack. **1896** *Westm. Gaz.* 18 Dec. 4/1 Crossing the Swift brook the lady pack made play across the meadows beyond at a rare pace. **1664** EVELYN *Kal. Hort.* in *Sylva* etc. (1729) 223 Sugar-Pear, *Lady-Pear, Amadot, Ambret. *c* **1380** WYCLIF *Sel. Wks.* III. 113 Te seie eche day our *Ladi sauter. **1547** *Homilies* I. *Good Wks.* III. (1859) 61 Papistical superstitions and abuses..Lady Psalters and Rosaries. **1803** in *Naval Chron.* XV. 217 The men working in *Lady Quarter, 1802. **1888** *Bill-heading at Maidstone*, *Ladytide. **1894** *Athenæum* 17 Mar. 341/1 The practice of sending sheep to be kept in the Weald districts from Michaelmas to Ladytide is not wholly abandoned. **1647** H. MORE *Song of Soul* To Rdr. 6/1 Some *Lady-wits that can like nothing that is not as compos'd as their own hair, or as smooth as their Mistresses Looking-glasse. **1579** TOMSON *Calvin's Serm. Tim.* 893/2 If God do make men that haue some deuotion, whiche are *Ladie worshippers [etc.].

b. In names of plants: **lady-bracken**, the brake, *Pteris aquilina*; **lady-fern**, an elegant fern, *Athyrium Filix-femina*; **lady-key(s**, *(a)* the primrose, *Primula veris* (Britten and Holland *Plant-n.* 1879); *(b)* (see quot.); **lady-lords** (see quot.); **lady-of-the-night**, an evergreen shrub, *Brunfelsia americana*, native to the West Indies and bearing white and yellow flowers which are particularly fragrant at night; **lady orchid, orchis**, *Orchis purpurea*, a European and Western Asian orchid with white and reddish-purple flowers.

1820 *Blackw. Mag.* June 278/1 Having removed the heather and decayed leafs of *lady-bracken which covered the inscription. **1825–80** JAMIESON, *Lady-bracken*, the female fern. **1825** J. WILSON *Noct. Ambr.* Wks. 1855 I. 73 Groves o' the *ladyfern embowering the sleeping roe. **1859** CAPERN *Ball. & Songs* 137 A crown of lady-fern she wore. **1863** KINGSLEY *Water-Bab.* 14 The great tuft of lady ferns. **1887** *Kent. Gloss.*, **Lady-keys*, same as *Lady-lords*. **Lady-lords*, lords and ladies; the name given by children to the wild arum. **1924** L. H. BAILEY *Man. Cultivated Plants* 667 *B[runfelsia] americana*, L. *Lady-of-the-Night. **1959** M. M. KAYE *House of Shade* xiii. 167 Lash..had taken her down into the garden—ostensibly to look at the nocturnal flowering Lady-of-the-Night which grew in profusion in a bed some distance from the house. **1960** *Harper's Bazaar* July 80/2 The scent of frangipane and lady of the night. **1933** M. J. GODFERY *Monogr. & Iconogr. Native Brit. Orchidaceæ* 171 *Orchis purpurea* Huds. Brown-winged Orchid, Maids of Kent, *Lady Orchid. **1951** V. S. SUMMERHAYES *Wild Orchids Brit.* xiii. 251 (*heading*) Brown-winged or lady orchid (*Orchis purpurea*). *Ibid.* 252 The lady orchid belongs to the Southern Eurasian Element of the British orchid flora. **1855** A. PRATT *Flowering Plants & Ferns Gt. Brit.* V. 208 Kentish country people call it [sc. *O. fusca*] the *Lady Orchis; and..though its form is not very suggestive of its name, yet..there exists some slight similarity in each blossom to a lady attired in wide-spread gown and close bonnet.

18. a. Specialized collocations with the genitive *lady's* (occas. *ladies'*): **Ladies' Aid (Society)**, † *(a)* *U.S.* (*Obs.*) during the American Civil War, a women's organization devoted to sending garments, bandages, etc., to the soldiers; *(b)* *N. Amer.*, an organization of women who support the work of a church by fund-raising, arranging social activities, etc.; **ladies' cabin, car, carriage**, on public transport, a compartment, etc., reserved for ladies; **ladies' cloakroom**, a cloakroom or lavatory for ladies; **lady's companion**, a small case or bag arranged to hold implements for needlework, etc.; **ladies' fair** ? *nonce-wd.*, a bazaar; **ladies' gallery**, a gallery in the House of Commons reserved for ladies; **lady's gown**, 'a gift made by a purchaser to the vendor's wife on her renouncing her life-rent in her husband's estate' (Cassell); **lady's hole**, *(a)* *Naut.* (see quot.); *(b)* a card game (also ***my lady's hole***); **lady's hood** *Sc.*, the omentum of a pig; **lady's horse**, a horse trained to carry a lady riding side-saddle; similarly **lady's hunter**; **lady's ladder**, 'shrouds rattled too closely' (Smyth *Sailor's Word-bk.* 1867); **lady's loaf** = *lady meat* (sense 17); **lady's maid**, a woman servant whose special

duty it is to attend to the toilet of a lady; **lady's** or **ladies' man**, a man who is devoted to the society of women and is assiduous in paying them small attentions; **ladies' night**, a function at a men's club, etc., to which ladies are invited; **ladies' room** = *ladies' cloakroom*; **ladies' school**, a school for the education of 'young ladies'; **lady's waist** *Austral. colloq.*, a small gracefully-shaped glass; a drink served in such a glass; **lady's wind** *Naut.* (see quot.); † **lady's woman**, (*a*) ? one who professes devotion to Our Lady; (*b*) a lady's maid.

1866 F. MOORE *Women of War* 214 Mrs. Wittenmeyer, as president of the *Ladies' Aid Society of Iowa. **1873** *Sentinel* (Woodstock, Ont.) 5 Dec. 3/1 The Ladies' Aid Society in connection with the Baptist Church in this Town will hold a social this evening. **1893** 'O. THANET' *Stories Western Town* 185 The furnishing of the church.. is in charge of the Ladies' Aid Society. **1895** *Times* (Niagara-on-the-Lake, Ont.) 4 Apr. 1/2 The Social [was] under the auspices of the Ladies Aid of the Methodist Church. **1908** L. M. MONTGOMERY *Anne of Green Gables* xiv. 143 She had taken it off.. when returning from the Ladies' Aid. **1913** E. H. PORTER *Pollyanna* iii. 21 Part of the Ladies' Aid wanted to buy me a black dress and hat, but the other part thought the money ought to go toward the red carpet they're trying to get,—for the church, you know. **1964** *Calgary Herald Mag.* 21 Mar. 8/9 The 'Apron Social' and tea given in the basement of the Knox Church last evening under the auspices of the Ladies' Aid Society of the congregation. **1832** E. GROSVENOR *Diary* July in G. Huxley *Lady Elizabeth & Grosvenors* (1965) vi. 124 There were 20 fellow-passengers, so that the *Lady's cabin was utterly untenable. **1925** E. H. YOUNG *William* iv. 42 She sat down on a velvet-covered couch in the ladies' cabin. **1842** DICKENS *Amer. Notes* I. iv. 145 There are no first and second class carriages .. but there is a gentlemen's car and a *ladies' car. **1847** F. A. KEMBLE *Let.* 29 May in *Rec. Later Life* (1882) III. 183 From Liverpool to Crewe I had companions in the *ladies' carriage in which I was. **1860** E. HALL *Diary* 30 July in O. A. Sherrard *Two Victorian Girls* (1966) 263, I am thankful today that 'Ladies' carriages have been given up in *our* country! **1922** E. H. YOUNG *Bridge Dividing* III. ix. 289 'I have to catch a train.'.. 'Be careful to get into a ladies' carriage, Henrietta.' **1918** A. BENNETT *Pretty Lady* xxiii. 157 She hurried.. to the *ladies' cloakroom, got her wraps. **1844** MARG. FULLER *Wom. 19th C.* (1862) 35 Governors of *ladies' fairs are no less engrossed by such a charge, than the governor of a state by his. **1897** OUIDA *Massarenes* xvii, The speaker's box.. is much more comfortable than the *Lady's Gallery. **1711** W. SUTHERLAND *Shipbuild. Assist.* 43 A *Lady's Hole, or Place for the Gunner's small Stores, which Stores are looked after by one they call a Lady. **1732** MRS. PENDARVES *Let. to Mrs. A. Granville* in *Mrs. Delany's Life & Corr.* 385 We got early into our inn, played at my lady's hole, supped, and went early to bed. **1813** *Sporting Mag.* XLII. 273 From whist, that charms the noble's soul, To kitchen putt and lady's hole. **1826** J. WILSON *Noct. Ambr.* Wks. 1855 I. 133 What black puddins!—and oh what tripe! Only think o' the *leddy's hood and monyplies!—Then the marrowbanes. **1814** JANE AUSTEN *Mansf. Park* I. iv. 71 Fanny should have a regular *lady's horse of her own. **1894** KIPLING *Day's Work* (1898) 46 An absolutely steady lady's horse—proof against steam-rollers, grade-crossings, and street processions. **1938** D. A. HOUBLON *Side-Saddle* vii. 64 In Victorian days and even later a lady's horse to be perfect had always to canter with the off fore leading. **1948** *Horseman's Year* 172 (*heading*) Royal Welsh Agricultural Society show... Hunters... *Ladies' Hunters. To be ridden side-saddle. **1955** *Horse & Pony Ann. Illustr. 1954–55* iii. 101 The leading ladies' hunters were Cufflink, Earmark,.. Mighty Grand. **1875** T. E. BRIDGETT *Our Lady's Dowry* 242 Alms, which naturally accompanied fasting, were also given in our Lady's honour. Indeed this was so constant a practice, that it acquired a peculiar name as Lady's meat or *Lady's loaf. **1808** *Ann. Reg.* 71 Elizabeth Daniels, *lady's maid, said Sir A. Paget always visited at the house. **1840** DICKENS *Old C. Shop* xxxix, The man who sang the song with the lady's-maid. **1863** MISS BRADDON *Eleanor's Vict.* (1878) I. iii. 23 The German governess and the Parisian lady's-maid still attended upon Vane's daughters. **1784** COWPER *Tiroc.* 423 A slave at court, elsewhere a *lady's man. **1809** MALKIN *Gil Blas* VII. vii. (Rtldg.) 23, I should have chosen the youngest, and the most of a lady's man. **1842** THACKERAY *Fitz-Boodle Pap.* Pref. (1887) 10, I am not.. a ladies' man. **1891** N. GOULD *Double Event* 149 They told me you were not a ladies' man, Mr. Smirke. **1889** G. B. SHAW *London Music 1888–89* (1937) 266 An invitation from the Grosvenor Club to their '*ladies' night' at the Grosvenor Gallery. **1970** K. GILES *Death in Church* i. 18 The atmosphere of a Masonic ladies' night. **1970** G. GREER *Female Eunuch* 142 On ladies' nights.. men embrace and fool about. **1880** 'E. LEATHES' *Actor Abroad* xviii. 226 Many of them retire to the *ladies' room, and changing their costume for evening dress reappear in the ball-room. **1927** D. L. SAYERS *Unnatural Death* xi. 120 The attendant in the Ladies' Room. **1948** G. VIDAL *City & Pillar* (1949) iii. 64 'I think,' said Emily, when she came back from the ladies' room, 'I think that we should go over to that room on the left and get a drink.' **1971** D. EDEN *Afternoon Walk* ix. 124 I'll go to the ladies' room while you do. **1865** DICKENS *Mut. Fr.* I. iv, He had an order for another *Ladies' School.. door-plate. **1934** *Bulletin* (Sydney) 4 Apr. 20/1 But a daintier goblet I never fingered than the hour-glass shape of a *lady's waist. **1963** A. LUBBOCK *Austral. Roundabout* 59 A pony is drunk out of a small glass called a lady's waist. **1886** *Century Mag.* XXXII. 700/2 A gentle breeze blew from the Shore.. a '*lady's wind', sailors would call it. **1579** TOMSON *Calvin's Serm. Tim.* 885/2 Hee [St. Paul] saith not women but simple women, as if he said, these little *Ladies women [orig. *ces petites bigotes*], that woulde eat the crucifix (as we say) which make a shewe of great devotion. **1748** SMOLLETT *Rod. Rand.* xi, The deplorable vanity and secondhand airs of a lady's woman.

b. In names of plants.

Lady's here is in origin a shortening of *Our Lady's*, and became familiar through the 16th c. herbalists; in more recent times *ladies'* has in some cases been substituted, the change being perhaps assisted by the old spelling *ladies* of the possessive singular. The designation is usually given to plants of a more than usual beauty or delicacy. (Cf. G. *Marien-*, *frauen-*, and F. *de notre Dame*.)

lady's bedstraw (see BEDSTRAW); **lady's bower**, clematis; **lady's comb**, the Shepherd's Needle, *Scandix Pecten*; **lady's delight**, the violet; **lady's ear-drop**, the common fuchsia; **lady's foxglove**, the Great Mullein, *Verbascum Thapsus*; **lady's glass, looking-glass**, *Campanula Speculum*; **(Our) Lady's hair**, (*a*) the grass *Briza media*; (*b*) *Adiantum Capillus-veneris*, also called Venus' hair; † **lady's linen**, ? = LADY-SMOCK; † **(Our) Lady's milkwort**, a name for Lungwort, *Pulmonaria officinalis*; † **(Our) Lady's mint**, *Mentha viridis*; **lady's navel** [adaptation of L. *umbilicus Veneris*], a name for Navelwort, *Cotyledon Umbilicus*; † **(Our) Lady's signet** = LADY'S SEAL; **lady's thimble**, (*a*) the Heath Bell, *Campanula rotundifolia*; (*b*) the Foxglove, *Digitalis purpurea* (*Syd. Soc. Lex.* 1888); **lady's thumb** *U.S.*, *Polygonum Persicaria*; † **(Our) Lady's tree** (see quot.). See also LADY'S FINGER, LADY'S GLOVE, LADY'S LACES, etc.

1597 GERARDE *Herbal* II. cccxxvi. (1633) 887 *Ladies Bower is called in Latine *Ambuxum*. **1696** PHILLIPS (ed. 5), *Ladies Bower*, (*Clematis*), a Plant, which.. is fit to make Bowers and Arbors, even for Ladies. **1760** J. LEE *Introd. Bot.* App., Lady's Bower, *Clematis*. **1597** GERARDE *Herbal* II. cccc. 884 The Latines call it *Scandix*.. of others *Acus Veneris*, and *Acus Pastoris*, or Shepheards Needle, wilde Cheruill, and *Ladies Combe. **1783** AINSWORTH *Lat. Dict.* (Morell) I. s.v. *Comb*, Lady's comb, *Pecten Veneris*. **1843** L. M. CHILD *Lett. from N.Y.* i. 2, I am like the *Lady's Delight, ever prone to take root. **1860** O. W. HOLMES *Elsie V.* v. (1861) 46 Flower-de-luces, and lady's-delights. **1829** A. H. LINCOLN *Familiar Lect. Bot.* xxv. 145 The *Ladies'-ear-drop (*Fuchsia*,) is a beautiful exotic. It has a funnel-form calyx of a brilliant red colour... This plant is a native of Mexico, except one species brought from the island of New Zealand. Ten species are said by horticulturists to be cultivated. **1882** H. FRIEND *Gloss. Devon. Plant Names* 33 Lady's Eardrops. The common garden Fuchsia. Still employed by the older people, but not so commonly as of yore. **1887** M. E. WILKINS *Humble Romance* 195 He cut lavishly sprays of dioletra, or lady's ear-drop, snow-balls, daffodils. **1908** L. M. MONTGOMERY *Anne of Green Gables* i. 1 A little hollow, fringed with alders and ladies' eardrops. **1967** D. G. HESSAYON *Be your own House Plant Expert* (ed. 2) 18/2 Fuchsia (Lady's Eardrops). Spring and summer flowering plant with pendant blooms. **1776–96** WITHERING *Brit. Plants* (ed. 3) II. 248 Great White Mullein.. *Ladies Foxglove. **1597** GERARDE *Herbal* II. civ. §4. 356 It is called .. Venus looking glasse, *Speculum Veneris*, or *Ladies glasse. **1551** *Ladyes heyre [see HAIR *sb.* 4 b]. **1597** GERARDE *Herbal* II. ccccliii. 983 In English black Maiden haire and Venus haire, and may be called our Ladies haire. **1794** MARTYN *Rousseau's Bot.* xiii. 135 Briza or ladies' hair. **1761** W. STUKELEY *Palæogr. Sacra* (1763) 25 Botanists.. show a very particular regard to the fair sex.. as we may well conclude from so many names they give to plants; ladys fingers, ladys traces, *ladys linen,.. ladys slipper, etc. **1640** PARKINSON *Theat. Bot.* 1740 *Ladies, or Venus looking-glasse. **1677** GREW *Anat. Plants, Colours Plants* i. §15 (1682) 271 The youngest Buds of Ladys-Lookinglass. **1879** BRITTEN & HOLLAND *Plant-n.*, *Lady's (Our) Milkwort, *Pulmonaria officinalis*. **1597** GERARDE *Herbal* II. ccxv. 553 In English Speare Mint, common Garden Mint, *our Ladies Mint [etc.]. *Ibid.* cxliii. §3. 424 Nauelwoort is called.. in English Pennywoort, Wall Pennywoort, *Ladies nauell, and Hipwoort. **1611** COTGR., *Escueller*, Hipwort, Wall-penniewort, Ladies-nauell (an hearbe). **1657** W. COLES *Adam in Eden* cxci. 299 The black Bryony is called Sigillum Sanctæ Mariæ, our *Ladies Signet. **1853** G. JOHNSTON *Nat. Hist. E. Bord.* I. 134 *Campanula rotundiflora*. Blue-Bells: *Ladies' Thimbles. *Ibid.* 158 Our little girls glove their fingers with them [*Digitalis purpurea*] and call them Ladies' thimbles. **1608** TOPSELL *Serpents* (1658) 601 In ancient time, the ignorant multitude, seeing a Birch tree with green leaves in the Winter, did call it our *Ladies Tree, or a holy tree, attributing that greenness to miracle.

Hence **'ladydom**, the realm of ladies. **'ladyish** *a.*, resembling a lady, having the objectionable characteristics of a 'fine lady'. **'ladyism**, the manners or behaviour of a lady (cf. *young-ladyism*). **'ladyness**, (*a*) cf. quot. 1538; (*b*) effeminacy.

1538 LATIMER *Serm. & Rem.* (Parker Soc.) 403 By reason of their lady [a wooden image of Our Lady] they have been given to much idleness; but now that she is gone, they be turned to laboriousness, and so from ladyness to godliness. **1785** [E. PERRONET] *Occas. Verses, Who & What is a Man?* 135 Powder'd fops of ladyness. **1830** *Examiner* 773/1 The whining of an artificial and lady-ish City Miss. **1843** *Fraser's Mag.* XXVIII. 568 Accustomed to the atmosphere and language of Ladydom. **1856** WHYTE MELVILLE *Kate Cov.* xxi, Miss Molasses, the pink of propriety and 'what-would-mamma-say' ladyism.

lady ('leɪdɪ), *v.* [f. LADY *sb.*]

† **1.** *trans.* To make a lady of; to raise to the rank of a lady; to address as 'lady'. *Obs.*

1607 MARSTON *What you will* I. i. Wks. 1887 II. 337 *Iaco.* Nay, sir, her estimation's mounted up. She shall be ladied and sweet-madam'd now. *Ran.* Be ladied? Ha! ha! **1614** W. B. *Philosopher's Banquet* (ed. 2) A iij b, Widowes with their heapes of hourded gold, That would be Ladied though a month to hold.

† **b.** To render lady-like or feminine. *Obs.*

1656 W. MONTAGUE *Accompl. Wom.* 121 It is to be feared that Ladies too Chevaliere, are beyond modesty: Men too much Ladyed, are short of Manhood.

2. *intr.* *to lady it*: to play the lady or mistress. (Cf. *to lord it*, *queen it*.) *rare.*

1600 BRETON *Pasquil's Mad-cappe* 27 A Iacke will be a Gentleman And mistris Needens Lady it at least. *a* **1638** MEDE *Wks.* I. (1672) 140 That great seven-hilled City still Ladies it over the Nations of the Earth. **1868** W. CORY *Lett. & Jrnls.* (1897) 252 My lawn with a single harebell ladying it over the grass.

lady-bird ('leɪdɪbɜːd). [In sense 1, f. LADY *sb.* 3 (genitive, as in LADY-DAY). Cf. G. *Marienhuhn*, *Marienkäfer*, *Marienwürmchen*.]

1. The common name for the coleopterous insects belonging to the genus *Coccinella*.

1704 A. VAN LEUWENHOEK in *Phil. Trans.* XXV. 1615 Flies, in likeness to Cow-ladies or Lady-birds, as some call 'em. **1816** KIRBY & SP. *Entomol.* II. 9 Many years ago, those [*sc.* the banks] of the Humber were so thickly strewed with the common Lady-bird (*C. Septempunctata*, L.) that [etc.]. **1861** DELAMER *Fl. Gard.* 169 Encourage lady-birds.. which eat or rather suck the aphides.

2. A sweetheart. (Often used as a term of endearment.)

1592 SHAKS. *Rom. & Jul.* I. iii. 3 What Lamb: what Lady-bird.. Where's this Girle? **1599** B. JONSON *Cynthia's Rev.* II. i, Is that your new ruffe, sweet lady-bird? **1656** R. FLETCHER *Poems* 176 A cast of Lacquyes, and a Lady-bird. *a* **1700** B. E. *Dict. Cant. Crew*, *Lady-birds*, Light or Lewd Women. **1858** LYTTON *What will he do* I. xiv, Let us come into the town, lady bird, and choose a doll.

3. The pintail duck, *Anas acuta*.

1885 C. SWAINSON *Provincial Names & Folklore Brit. Birds* 155 Pintail (*Dafila acuta*)... Also called Cracker, Winter duck, Lady bird (Dublin Bay). From its grace of form. **1917** T. G. PEARSON *Birds Amer.* I. 128 Pintail. *Dafila acuta*... Winter Duck; Lady-bird; Long-necked Cracker. **1968** C. E. JACKSON *Brit. Names of Birds* 61 Pintail .. lady bird Ire[land].

lady-bug. *dial.* and *U.S.* = LADY-BIRD.

1699 *Phil. Trans. R. Soc.* XXI. 50, I have happened upon .. three or four sorts of Lady-Bugs. **1787** GROSE *Pop. Superstit.* in *Provinc. Gloss.*, etc. 64 It is held extremely unlucky to kill a cricket, a lady-bug, a swallow [etc.]. **1844** 'J. SLICK' *High Life N.Y.* II. 30 Like lady bugs round a full blown rose. **1886** *Harper's Mag.* June 45/2 We may discover lady-bugs—small red or yellow and black beetles—among our vines. **1889** M. E. BAMFORD *Up & Down Brooks* 49 Very frequently one will find a lady-bug with the spider. **1910** *N.Y. Even. Post* 4 Apr. (Th.), Los Angeles, April 1... Millions of ladybugs are receiving free transportation.. to the melon fields of the Imperial valley. **1972** SWAN & PAPP *Common Insects N. Amer.* xx. 403 Lady Beetles (Coccinellidae). The common British name for these beetles, 'ladybird', is still used to some extent in America; 'ladybug' is probably the most familiar name.

Lady chapel. Orig. **Our Lady** (or **Lady's**) **chapel.** A chapel dedicated to the Virgin, attached to large churches, generally situated eastward of the high altar.

1439 in *E. Eng. Wills* 114 A C lb wex to mynystere and to serue to the vse of the Salue of oure lady chapell yn the said chirch of seynt Austyns. **1553** T. ROSE in Foxe *A. & M.* (1583) II. 2084/2, I was called agayne into Christes church within their Ladies chapell (as they termed it). *a* **1562** G. CAVENDISH *Wolsey* (1893) 78 And there.. in our Lady Chappell he sayd his servyce & masse. **1710** HEARNE *Collect.* (O.H.S.) II. 339 Queen Katherin.. was buried at Westminster, in our Ladies Chapell. **1718** B. WILLIS *Mitred Abbeys* I. Index 2 The Lady Chapel [*in text* our Ladys Chapel] adorn'd and other parts of the Church improved. **1880** *Times* 8 June 4/1 There was a chancel at the east end, and at the side a 'Lady chapel'—each with its altar.

lady-cow ('leɪdɪkaʊ). [f. LADY *sb.* 3 (genitive, as in next). Cf. G. *Marienkuh*.]

1. = LADY-BIRD. (Cf. COW-LADY.)

1606 SYLVESTER *Du Bartas* II. iv. I. *Trophies* 274 [Goliath says to David:] O Lady-cow [Fr. *Ha petit Damereau!*], Thou shalt no more be-star thy wanton brow With thine eyes rayes. **1630** DRAYTON *Muses Eliz.* viii. 70 The Lady-Cow: The dainty shell vpon her backe Of Crimson strew'd with spots of blacke. **1713** DERHAM *Phys. Theol.* 8 note, Wasps, Bees,.. and Lady-Cows. **1868** *Daily News* 15 Aug., The earth for several miles adjoining the river Severn.. was thickly covered with insects commonly called 'lady cows'.

2. *nonce-use.* A term of mock dignity for a cow.

1649 LOVELACE *Poems* (1864) 63 A rev'rend lady-cow drawes neere.

Lady day ('leɪdɪ deɪ). Orig. **Our Lady day.** [f. LADY *sb.* 3 (genitive: see the etymological note on the word).] A day kept in celebration of some event in the life of the Virgin Mary. Now only March 25th, the Feast of the Annunciation; formerly also Dec. 8th, the Conception of the Virgin, Sep. 8th, the Nativity, and Aug. 15th, the Assumption.

1297 [see LADY *sb.* 3 b]. *a* **1300** *Cursor M.* 17288 + 65 On our laidy day als-soo, þe syn was first wroght. *a* **1450** *Knt. de la Tour* (1868) 37 It happed that oure lady day felle on the sonday. *c* **1450** *Merlin* 120 This was on oure lady day in septembre. **1556** *Chron. Gr. Friars* (Camden) 2 Then was a grete wynter of frost and colde that lastyd from new-yeres daye unto our lady day the Annunciacion. **1578** *Scotter Manor Roll* (N.W. Linc. Gloss.), Euery one shall take vppe ther tuppes or rammes before the first ladie daye. **1611** COTGR. s.v. *Dame*, *L'assumption notre Dame*, Our Ladie day in Haruest. **1665** WOOD *Life* 15 May, Rent which was due the last Our Lady day. **1888** M. ARNOLD in *19th Cent.* Jan. 27 On Lady Day he [Shelley] was summoned before the authorities of his College.

lady-fish ('leɪdɪfɪʃ). A name applied in various parts of the world to many different species of

fish, as *Albula vulpes*, *Harpe rufa*, *Scomberesox saurus*, *Sillago domina*.

1712 E. COOKE *Voy. S. Sea* 341 The Lady-Fish, being a very small Sort taken off Cape St. Lucas. **1884-5** *Stand. Nat. Hist.* (1888) III. 137 A single species (*Albula vulpes*) the bone-fish or lady-fish of our Atlantic coasts. **1885** *Daily Tel.* 25 Sept. 2/2 The dainty, long-jawed beings which in the Soudan were called 'lady-fish'.

ladyfy, ladify ('leɪdɪfaɪ), *v.* [f. LADY *sb.* + -FY.] *trans.* To make a lady of; to give the title of 'Lady' to. Hence **'ladyfied** *ppl. a.* (*colloq.*), having the airs of a fine lady.

1602 DEKKER *Satiromastix* Wks. 1873 I. 221 Ile enter into bond to be dub'd by what day thou wilt, when the next action is layde upon me thou shalt be Ladified. **1622** ROWLANDS *Good Newes & B.* 7 She..would be Madam'd, Worship'd, Ladifide. **1632** MASSINGER *City Madam* IV. iv, He made a knight, And your sweet mistress-ship ladyfied. **1682** MRS. BEHN *City-Heiress* 61 How, Mrs. Dy Ladyfi'd! This is an excellent way of disposing an old cast-off Mistriss. **1881** *Oxfordsh. Gloss.*, *Ladyfied*, lady-like. [**1883** D. C. MURRAY *Hearts* III. xxxiii. 229 Azubah had certainly grown wonderfully fine ladyfied in the last year or two.] **1885** T. MOZLEY *Remin. Towns*, etc. II. 222 They could hardly be restrained from ladifying every plain Mrs. who came near them.

†**'ladyhead.** *Obs. rare*⁻¹. In 4 **ladyhede.** [f. LADY *sb.* + -HEAD.] = LADYSHIP.

1390 GOWER *Conf.* II. 40 Whan she goth to here masse That time shall nought overpasse, That I napproche her ladyhede.

ladyhood ('leɪdɪhʊd). [f. LADY *sb.* + -HOOD.]

1. The state or condition of being a lady; the qualities pertaining to a lady.

1820 COLERIDGE *Lett., Convers.*, etc. I. 42 She often represents to my mind the best parts of the Spanish Santa Teresa ladyhood by nature. **1878** BESANT & RICE *Celia's Arb.* xli, A lady about five-and-forty..with delicate features and an air of perfect ladyhood.

2. Ladies collectively; the realm of ladies.

1821 *Blackw. Mag.* X. 63 The gallantry of ladyhood is abroad. **1879** F. HARRISON *Choice Bks.* (1886) 46 That wonderful storehouse..preserves for us an inimitable picture of the knighthood, ladyhood, and yeomanry of the Middle Ages.

ladykin ('leɪdɪkɪn). [f. LADY *sb.* + -KIN.] A little lady; *occas.* used as a term of endearment.

1853 MISS SHEPPARD *Ch. Auchester* I. 321, I had missed it in my room—that baby of mine, that doll, that ladykin. **1876** T. HARDY *Ethelberta* (1890) 315 The young ladykin whom the solemn vowing concerned had lingered round the choir screen. **1884** BROWNING *Ferishtah, Camel-driver* 46 'Ha, Ladykin, Still at thy frolics, girl of gold?' laughed he.

'ladykind. *rare.* [f. LADY *sb.* + KIND, after *womankind.*] The lady or female portion of a party; also *loosely*, a woman.

1829 SCOTT *Jrnl.* 24 Mar., This morning our sportsmen took leave, and their ladykind..followed after breakfast. **1878** E. J. TRELAWNY *Shelley, etc.* (1887) 107 An ordinary lady-kind would have screamed.

ladyless ('leɪdɪlɪs), *a.* [f. LADY *sb.* + -LESS.] Having no lady; unaccompanied by a lady.

1470-85 MALORY *Arthur* VIII. xxvi, Sythen I am lady les I wil wyn thy lady. **1858** MORRIS *K. Arthur's Tomb* 37 Perchance, indeed, quite ladyless were best. **1888** BRYCE *Amer. Commw.* III. VI. cv. 518 At hotels their [women's] sitting-room is..sometimes the only available public room, ladyless guests being driven to the bar or the hall.

ladylike ('leɪdɪlaɪk), *a.* and *adv.* [f. LADY *sb.* + -LIKE.] **A.** *adj.*

1. Of a woman: Having the distinctive appearance or manner of a lady. Also (in early use chiefly) said *sarcastically* of men: Effeminately delicate or solicitous about elegance or propriety. †In a personification: Comparable to a lady; queenly.

1601 R. JOHNSON *Kingd. & Commw.* (1603) 30 And Madera, famous for the Wines which grow therin, and the lady-like Iland of all the Atlantique sea. **1656** *Artif. Handsom.* 179 Some of these so rigid, yet very spruce and Ladylike preachers, think fit to gratifie as their own persons, so their kind hearers and spectators. **1756** COWPER *Let. to Town* Wks. (1837) XV. 262 Those lady-like gentlemen, whom we may distinguish by the title of their mother's own sons. **1813** *Examiner* 8 Mar. 156/2 Miss Smith is a very lady-like actress. **1818** HAZLITT *Eng. Poets* viii. (1870) 196 He is a very lady-like poet. **1828** SCOTT *F.M. Perth* xxxi, Tell me now, how look I, thus disposed on the couch—languishing and ladylike, ha? **1852** MRS. CARLYLE *Lett.* II. 199 A pretty, ladylike, rather silly young woman.

2. Befitting a lady; resembling what pertains to a lady; sometimes with depreciatory sense, effeminately delicate or graceful.

1586 WARNER *Alb. Eng.* II. ix. (1592) 37 With fingers Ladie-like. **1687** DRYDEN *Hind & P.* II. 686 The dew-drops on her silken hide Her tender constitution did declare Too lady-like a long fatigue to bear. **1698** CROWNE *Caligula* I. Dram. Wks. 1874 IV. 358 A manly daring soul lurks deep, Under this gentle lady-like outside. **1739** CIBBER *Apol.* (1756) II. 31 After a few days of these coy lady-like compliances on his side, we grew into a more conversable temper. **1754** RICHARDSON *Grandison* (1781) III. xvii. 137 Perhaps you mean no more than to give a little specimen of Lady-like pride in those words. **1816** SCOTT *Antiq.* xi, The controversy began in smooth, oily, lady-like terms, but is now waxing more sour and eager as we get on. **1824** MISS MITFORD *Village* Ser. I. (1863) 216 Her lady-like spirit would have scorned the idea of selling them. **1877** MRS. FORRESTER *Mignon* I. 53 You have not a very lady-like way of expressing yourself. **1890** L. FALCONER *Mlle. Ixe* i. (1891) 20, 'I hope you will teach Evelyn some of these pretty things', said Mrs. Merrington. 'There is something so ladylike about them'. **1900** SKEAT *Chaucer Canon* 139 Both [poems]..are wholly lacking in interesting touches of personal character. Whatever opinions they express are of a highly genteel and ladylike order.

Hence **'ladylikeness.**

1875 HOWELLS *Foregone Concl.* (1882) 305 He remembered the charm of her perfect ladylikeness.

†**B.** *adv.* As a lady does; in the guise of a lady. *Obs.*

a **1635** CORBET *Poems* (1807) 126 Nor didst thou two years after talk of force, Or, lady-like, make suit for a divorce. *c* **1650** *Roxburgh Ballads* (1888) VI. 544 Achilles he was in disguise, When first he heard of this enterprize, He Lady-like with a Lady lay.

ladyling ('leɪdɪlɪŋ). *rare.* [f. LADY *sb.* + -LING.] A little lady.

1855 BAILEY *Mystic* 137 Ladylings and lordlings dancing, piping, harping. **1895** F. THOMPSON *Sister Songs* 5, I bid them dance, I bid them sing, For the limpid glance Of my ladyling.

'lady-love. Also pseudo-*arch.* **ladye-love.** [f. LADY *sb.* (in sense 1 *appositive*; in sense 2 *attrib.*).]

1. A lady who is loved; a sweetheart.

A supposed example quoted from R. Wilson's *Coblers Prophesie* (1594) is not to the point; Venus is called 'Lady Love' by more than one of the dramatis personæ.

1733 *Theobald's Shaks. Rom. & Jul.* I. ii. 102 Your Lady-love [1623 Ladies loue]. **1805** SCOTT *Last Minstr.* IV. xix, With favour in his crest, or glove, Memorial of his ladye-love. **1841** JAMES *Brigand* ii, What man is there without a lady-love. **1871** MISS YONGE *Cameos* II. xxxii. 331 She begged the King to consent to his..marriage with his lady-love.

2. Love for ladies.

1818 BYRON *Ch. Har.* IV. xl, The minstrel who..Sang ladye-love and war.

'ladyly, *a. Obs.* exc. as *nonce-wd.* Also 5 **ladily.** [f. LADY *sb.* + -LY¹.] Befitting or characteristic of a lady, ladylike.

13.. *E.E. Allit. P.* A. 773 Ouer alle oþer so hyȝ þou clambe, To lede with hym so ladyly lyf. ? *a* **1400** *Morte Arth.* 3254 In a surcott of sylke..with ladily lappes the lenghe of a ȝerde. *c* **1477** CAXTON *Jason* 12 b, He brought to his mynde her fair and fresshe colour—her ladyly maytiene and her noble facoun and corpulence. **1840** *Tait's Mag.* VII. 385 We do not refer to the fashionable annuals, those very ineffable bulletins of lordly and ladyly inanity.

†**'ladyly,** *adv. Obs.* [f. as prec. + -LY².] In a manner befitting a lady; as a lady.

c **1450** LONELICH *Grail* xxvi. 129 This duchesse..nolde therto assente..and excused here ful ladyly.

lady's cushion. Also 6 **Our Lady's cushion.**

†**a.** The plant Thrift, *Armeria maritima*. *Obs.*

b. The Mossy Saxifrage, *Saxifraga hypnoides*.

1578 LYTE *Dodoens* IV. l. 509 That kinde of grasse whiche groweth by the sea syde, is called..in Englishe our Ladies quishion. **1597** GERARDE *Herbal* II. clxxvii. 483 In English Thrift, Sea grasse, and our Ladies Cushion. **1794** MARTYN *Rousseau's Bot.* xix. 271 From the manner of its growth in a thick tuft, it [mossy Saxifrage] has acquired the English name of Ladies Cushion. **1854** S. THOMSON *Wild Fl.* III. (ed. 4) 201 The Lady's cushion—mossy saxifrage.

lady's finger, lady-finger. *Pl. occas.* **ladies' fingers.**

1. *sing.* and *pl.* The plant *Anthyllis vulneraria*, the Kidney Vetch.

Also applied dial. to various other plants, as *Lotus corniculatus* (formerly called ***lady-finger grass***): see Britten and Holland *Plant-n.*

1670 RAY *Catal. Plant. Angl.* 24 *Anthyllis leguminosa*... Kidney-vetch, Ladies finger. **1743** in W. Ellis *Mod. Husbandm.* (1750) II. I. xv. 148 Your Lady-finger-grass (or Birds-foot Trefoil..which is the Botanical Name). **1756** WATSON in *Phil. Trans.* XLIX. 842 Kidney Vetch, or Ladies Finger. **1848** C. A. JOHNS *Week at Lizard* 306 *Anthyllis vulneraria*, variety *Dillenii*, Lady's-fingers, occurs..all along the coast.

2. Applied to various objects of long and slender form. **a.** A kind of cake (cf. *finger-biscuit*).

1820 KEATS *Cap & Bells* xlviii, Steep Some lady's-fingers nice in Candy wine. **1828** *Lights & Shades* II. 196 Honey and ladies' fingers for tea. **1864** 'MARK TWAIN' in Harte & 'Twain' *Sk. Sixties* (1926) 138 'Lady-fingers'..suggestive of..soft dalliance with pastry, ices, and sparkling Moselle. **1906** *Westm. Gaz.* 30 Apr. 10/1 Lady-fingers and ice-cream. *a* **1938** T. WOLFE *Web & Rock* (1939) I. ii. 22 Was.. President Taft the easy prey of lady fingers? **1942** C. BARRETT *On Wallaby* iii. 39 'Nana' nibbled at a sponge 'lady's finger'. **1974** H. MCCLOY *Sleepwalker* vi. 108 We adjourned for tea and ladyfingers at quarter of six.

b. *Austral.* A kind of grape. Also, a banana.

1892 E. REEVES *Homeward Bound* 90 The very finest ladies'-fingers, sweet-waters, and muscatels. **1893** MRS. C. PRAED *Outlaw & Lawmaker* II. 91 They were sitting..in the banana grove, whither Elsie had gone on pretext of finding some still ungathered 'Lady's fingers'.

c. *U.S.* (*a*) A variety of the potato; (*b*) One of the branchiæ of the lobster; (*c*) A variety of apple. (*Cent. Dict.*)

1876 J. BURROUGHS *Winter Sunshine* VII. 154 Others are indeed lady apples..like the egg-drop and lady-finger.

d. = OKRA.

1905 W. R. BEATTIE in *U.S. Dept. Agric. Farmers' Bull.* no. 232. 12 There are three general types of okra, viz., tall green, dwarf green, and lady finger. **1935** M. MORPHY *Recipes of all Nations* 771 Chicken with 'Ladysfingers'... Put in..a few *bamies*, or 'ladysfingers'. This vegetable..is a variety of okra, or *gombo* [*sic*], but smaller than the okra of the Southern United States. **1972** Y. LOVELOCK *Vegetable Bk.* 147 Indians call it [*sc.* okra] *bhindi* and, in their restaurants, *ladies' fingers*, although this is a name applied to many other plants, including grapes, bananas and a kidney vetch.

lady's glove. Also 6-7 **Our Ladies,** 7-8 **ladies' gloves,** 9 **lady glove.** [Orig. LADY *sb.* 3.] The foxglove, *Digitalis purpurea*. The name has been applied to several other plants, e.g. †Lungwort, *Pulmonaria officinalis*; Fleawort, *Inula Conyza*; the Bird's-foot Trefoil, *Lotus corniculatus* (dial.).

1538 ELYOT *Dict.* Addit., *Bacchar*..an herbe..some do call it..our ladies gloues. **1611** COTGR., *Gantelée*, the hearbe called Fox-gloues, our Ladies gloues. **1621** BEAUM. & FL. *Pilgrim* v. vi, Full of pincks, and Ladies gloves [*mod. edd.* lady-gloves], Of hartes-ease too. **1668** WILKINS *Real Char.* II. iv. §3. 80 Sage of Jerusalem, Ladies-glove [marg. *Pulmonaria*]. **1736** BAILEY *Househ. Dict.* 369 *Ladies Gloves.* The vertues of this plant [fleawort] are to warm and dry; but it is also an opener. **1879** BRITTEN & HOLLAND *Plant-n.*, Lady glove, *Digitalis purpurea*. *Ibid.*, Lady's glove, *Lotus corniculatus*.

ladyship ('leɪdɪʃɪp), *sb.* Forms: see LADY and -SHIP. Also 7-8 *colloq.* **la'ship.**

1. The condition of being a lady; rank as a lady.

a **1225** *Ancr. R.* 100 ȝif þu hauest uorȝiten nu þi wurðfule lefdischipe,—go & folewe þeos geat. *c* **1230** *Hali Meid.* 7 And trukie for a mon of lam þe heuenliche lauerd & lutlin her lafdischipe. **13..** *E.E. Allit. P.* A. 577 More haf I of ioye & blysse here-inne, Of ladyschyp gret & lyuez blom. **1623** MASSINGER *Bondman* III. iii, How dost thou like Thy ladyship, Zanthia? **1771** *Contempl. Man* II. 152 This Lady did not enjoy her Title long—she died in the fifth Year of her Ladyship. **1856** EMERSON *Eng. Traits* Wks. 1874 II. 134 What facility and plenteousness of knighthood, lordship, ladyship, royalty, loyalty! **1874** TROLLOPE *Lady Anna* iv. 26 He hated the countess-ship of the countess, and the ladyship of the Lady Anna.

2. The personality of a lady. In ***her, your ladyship***, a respectful substitute for *she*, *you*, referring to a lady; in mod. use only to one whose rank is designated by the titular prefix 'Lady'. Also used *sarcastically*.

c **1374** CHAUCER *Anel. & Arc.* 191 She..drof hym forthe, vnnethe list her knowe That he was servaunt vn to hir ladishippe. *c* **1400** *Destr. Troy* 3352 Ne trawes not, tru lady, þat I take wolde Thy ladyship to losse, ne in lust holde. *a* **1400-50** *Alexander* 3715, I leue it to ȝour ladyschip þis lange noȝt vnknawen. *a* **1500** *Flower & Leaf* lxxi, Yet I would pray Your ladiship..That I might knowe..What that these knightes be in rich armour. **1551** CROWLEY *Pleas. & Pain* Ded., I thought it my duty to dedicate the same vnto youre Ladishyppes name. **1600** SHAKS. *A.Y.L.* I. ii. 120 If it please your Ladiships, you may see the end. **1650** *Nicholas Papers* (Camden) 174 Lord Jermyn in a jeering manner, as her ladyshipp conceaved, told her he hoped now shortly Sir Edward Herbert would returne to Paris. **1700** CONGREVE *Way of World* II. v, O Mem, your Laship staid to peruse a Pecquet of Letters. **1711** ADDISON *Spect.* No. 37 ¶1, I waited upon her Ladyship pretty early in the morning. *a* **1839** PRAED *Poems* (1865) II. 34 Her ladyship is in a huff.

fig. **1595** SHAKS. *John* III. i. 119 Thou Fortunes Champion, that do'st neuer fight But when her humorous Ladiship is by To teach thee safety.

†**b.** *concr.* = LADY. *Obs.*

1390 GOWER *Conf.* II. 301 My sone, of that unkindship, The which toward thy ladiship, Thou pleignest, for she woll the nought, Thou art to blamen of thy thought.

c. *nonce-use.* One who is called 'her ladyship'.

1784 COWPER *Task* II. 386 Constant at routs, familiar with a round Of ladyships, a stranger to the poor.

†**3.** Kindness or beneficence befitting a mistress.

1390 GOWER *Conf.* I. 128 This maide..To whom this lady hath behote Of ladiship all that she can To vengen her upon this man. *Ibid.* III. 66 Tho quod the quene..I wol do the such ladiship, Wherof thou shalt for evermo Be riche.

4. A district governed by a lady. *nonce-use.*

1709 STEELE *Tatler* No. 46 ¶3 All that long Course of Building is under particular Districts or Ladiships, after the Manner of Lordships in other Parts.

Hence **'ladyship** *v.* (*nonce-wd.*) *trans.*, to give the title of 'Your Ladyship' to. Also ***to ladyship it.***

1813 E. S. BARRETT *Heroine* (1815) III. 9 'Ladyship! Oh, her ladyship!' and away he cantered, ladyshipping it, till he was out of hearing. **1820** *Hermit in London* IV. 165 He so ladyshiped Lady —— what's her ugly name, that it was quite disgusting.

†**lady-silver.** *Obs.* Also 5 **ladesilver.** [? f. LADY: possibly because payable at Lady-day.]

1425-6 *Durh. MS. Burs. Roll*, vjs. viijd. rec. pro ladesilver ejusdem ville per annum. **1536-7** *Durham Acc. Rolls* (Surtees) 672 Et de 6s. 8d. rec. de eodem Coll. pro ladysiluer debit. tenentibus ibidem.

lady's laces. †Also **lady-laces.** The striped garden variety of *Phalaris arundinacea*.

1597 GERARDE *Herbal* I. iv. 5 The grasse called in Latine *Gramen sulcatum*, or *Pictum*: and by our English women, Ladies Laces, because it is stript or furrowed with white and greene strakes, like silke laces. **1611** COTGR., *Aiguillettes d'armes*, the hearbe, or grasse, called Ladies laces, white Cameleon grasse, painted, or furrowed grasse. **1706** PHILLIPS (ed. Kersey), *Lady-laces*, a sort of striped Grass. **1713** J. PETIVER in *Phil. Trans.* XXVIII. 179 Painted Grass, or Ladies Laces. **1821** CLARE *Vill. Minstr.* II. 97, I..Tried through the pales to get the tempting flowers, As lady's laces, everlasting peas.

† **lady's longing.** *Obs.* In 7 ladies longing; also 6 lady longing. A variety of apple.

1591 LYLY *Endym.* III. iii. 38 For fruit these, fritters, medlers, hartichokes and ladylongings. **1664** EVELYN *Kal. Hort.* in *Sylva*, etc. (1729) 213 Apples. The Ladies Longing, the Kirkham Apple, John Apple [etc.]. **1676** WORLIDGE *Cyder* (1691) 211 There is a curious apple newly propagated, called Pome-appease... I suppose this is that which is called the Ladies Longing.

lady's-maid, *v.* [See LADY *sb.* 18.] *trans.* To wait on (one) as a lady's maid. Also **lady's-maiding** *vbl. sb.*

1914 W. DE MORGAN *When Ghost meets Ghost* I. xxxii. 392 Maggie goes with her, to lady's-maid her. **1923** U. L. SILBERRAD *Lett. J. Armiter* v. 115 It prevents her suffering under his lady's maiding.

lady's mantle. Also 6 Our Ladies, 6-8 ladies. [LADY *sb.* 3; cf. G. *Frauen-, Marienmantel.*] A common name for the rosaceous herb *Alchemilla vulgaris.* Also applied, with qualification, to other species (see quot. 1864).

1548 TURNER *Names of Herbes* 82 *Alchimilla*.. is called in english our Ladies Mantel or syndow. **1578** LYTE *Dodoens* I. xcviii. 140 Great Sanicle or Ladies Mantell, groweth in some places of this countrey. **1611** COTGR., *Alchimille*, Lions foot, Ladies mantle, great Sanicle. **1794** MARTYN *Rousseau's Bot.* xv. 167 Ladies mantle has a calyx of one permanent leaf divided into eight segments. **1864** SOWERBY *Brit. Bot.* (ed. 3) III. 140 Silvery Lady's-Mantle. *Ibid.* 141 Alpine Lady's Mantle. **1882** *Gd. Words* 673 Silken Alpine lady's mantle rare.

lady-smock. Also lady's, ladies' smock. A common name for the Cuckoo-flower, *Cardamine pratensis.* (Applied locally also to *Convolvulus sepium.*)

1588 SHAKS. *L.L.L.* v. ii. 905 Ladie-smockes all siluer white. **1597** GERARDE *Herbal* II. xviii. 203 They are commonly called in Latine, *Flos Cuculi*; in English Cuckowe flowers.. at the Namptwich in Cheshire.. Ladie smockes. **1648** HERRICK *Hesper.* (1869) 121 Dispose That lady-smock, that pansie, and that rose Neatly apart. **1794** MARTYN *Rousseau's Bot.* xxiii. 325 Ladies Smock, (forgive the vulgar name) has the calyx gaping a little. **1796** H. HUNTER tr. *St. Pierre's Stud. Nat.* (1799) I. 83 Some of the convolvuluses, vulgarly called lady's-smock. **1874** T. HARDY *Far fr. Madding Crowd* I. 239 Clear white ladies' smocks. **1878** BROWNING *Poets Croisic* 96 Chains of lady's-smock.

lady's seal. ? *Obs.* Also 6 Our Ladies seale. **1.** The plant Solomon's Seal, *Polygonatum multiflorum.*

?**1516** *Grete Herball* Z iij, Sigillum sancte marye or sigillum Salamonis is al one herbe that is called Salomons seale or our ladies seale. **1870** *Treas. Bot.*, Lady's seal, *Convallaria Polygonatum.*

2. The Black Bryony, *Tamus communis.*

1578 LYTE *Dodoens* III. xlvii. 383 Our Ladies Seale hath long branches, flexible, of a wooddishe substance. **1597** GERARDE *Herbal* II. cccvii. 722 Called.. in English blacke Bryonie, wilde Vine, and our Ladies Seale. **1712** tr. *Pomet's Hist. Drugs* I. 30 The Black Vine, which some have given the name of our Lady's Seal.

lady's slipper. Also 6 Our Ladies slipper, 8-9 ladies', lady slipper.

1. A common book-name for the orchidaceous plant *Cypripedium Calceolus.* Also applied occas. to the cultivated calceolaria, and the Bird's-foot Trefoil, *Lotus corniculatus.*

1597 GERARDE *Herbal* II. cvii. 359 Ovr Ladies Shooe or Slipper, hath a thicke knobbed roote. **1794** MARTYN *Rousseau's Bot.* xxvii. 422 The Ladies Slipper.. its singular, large hollow inflated nectary. **1861** MISS PRATT *Flower. Pl.* II. 116 *Lotus corniculatus*.. commonly called Lady's Slipper. **1872** OLIVER *Elem. Bot.* II. 266 One extremely rare British species, the Lady's Slipper (*Cypripedium Calceolus*). **1894** WILKINS & VIVIAN *Green bay tree* II. 161 The boxes of geranium and lady-slipper in the window.

2. ? *U.S.* The garden-balsam, *Impatiens balsamina* (*Cent. Dict.*).

1836 A. H. LINCOLN *Familiar Lect. Bot.* (ed. 5) xv. 101 The Impatiens of the garden is sometimes called Ladies'-slipper, sometimes Balsamine. **1874** B. F. TAYLOR *World on Wheels* II. iv. 220 The lady-slippers dance upon the air, while wild Sweet Williams stand admiring by.

lady's thistle. Also 6 Our ladies, 6-7 lady, 8-9 ladies' thistle. [Cf. G. *Frauendistel*, Du. *Vrouwendistel.*] The thistle *Carduus Marianus.*

1552 ELYOT *Dict.* s.v. *Spina, Spina alba*, Our ladies Thistle. **1578** LYTE *Dodoens* IV. lxii. 525 Our Ladyes Thistel groweth.. in rough untoyled places. **1579** LANGHAM *Gard. Health* (1633) 634 Lady Thistles. **1688** R. HOLME *Armoury* II. 63/2 The Lady-Thistle is our common Thistle. **1776-96** WITHERING *Brit. Plants* (ed. 3) III. 190 Milk Thistle. Ladies Thistle. **1831** J. DAVIES *Manual Mat. Med.* 436 Ladies' thistle. *Carduus marianus.*

lady's traces, tresses. Also 6-9 lady, ladies' traces, lady's traces. Name for the plants of the genus *Spiranthes* (N.O. *Orchidaceæ*); also locally applied to grasses of the genus *Briza.*

1548 TURNER *Names of Herbes* 70 Satyrion.. bryngeth furth whyte floures in the ende of harueste, and it is called Lady traces. **1578** LYTE *Dodoens* II. lvi. 222 The sweete Orchis, or Ladie traces and moste commonly to be found in high, untilled, and dry places. **1597** GERARDE *Herbal* I. cii. 168 Friezland Ladie traces hath two small round stones or bulbes. **1611** COTGR., *Satyrion à trois couillons*, Triple Orchis, or triple Ladies traces. **1794** MARTYN *Rousseau's Bot.* xxvii. 419 The spiral Ophrys commonly called Triple Ladies' Traces. **1842** C. W. JOHNSON *Farmer's Encycl.*, *Briza media*, common quaking grass; ladies' tresses. **1848** C. A. JOHNS *Week at Lizard* 310 *Neottia spiralis*, Lady's tresses, an orchideous plant about six inches high.

‖ **læn** (leɪn). *O.E. Law.* [OE. *lǽn*: see LOAN.] An estate held as a benefice.

a **988** in Birch *Cart. Sax.* III. 329 þa ȝewat Eadric ær Ælfheh cwideleas & Ælfeh feng to his læne. *a* **1000** ÆLFRIC *Voc.* in Wr.-Wülcker 115/36 *Precarium*, landeslæn. **1844** LINGARD *Anglo-Sax. Ch.* (1858) I. App. K. 371 National property at the disposal of the king, to be distributed by him as laens (loans) or benefices. **1876** DIGBY *Real Prop.* I. i. §2. 17 The person having the 'laen' possessing only the usufructuary enjoyment to a greater or less extent.

b. *Comb.*: **læn-land**, land held as 'læn'; **læn-right**, beneficiary right.

985 in Kemble *Codex Dipl.* III. 217 Fif hida ðe Oswald.. bocaþ Eadrice.. swa swa he hit ær hæfde to lænlande. **1872** E. W. ROBERTSON *Hist. Ess.* 117 Laenlands, or benefices. *Ibid.* 153 In property held by Læn-right possessions, privileges and obligations devolved upon the eldest born. **1874-5** STUBBS *Const. Hist.* I. v. 77 Either bookland or folkland could be,.. under the name of *lænland*, held by free cultivators.

læotropic (liːəʊˈtrɒpɪk), *a.* Also *erron.* leio-. [f. Gr. λαιό-ς left + τροπικ-ός turning, f. τροπή a turn.] Turned or turning to the left: said of the whorls of a shell; opposed to *dexiotropic.*

1883 [see DEXIOTROPIC].

læsed, læsion, variants of LESED, LESION.

‖ **læt** (lɛːt). *Hist.* [OE. *lǽt* (found only once) = OHG. *lâz* (? descendant of a freedman; glossed *libertinus*):—OTeut. **lǣto-z*, app. related to OE. *lǣtan* LET *v.*[1]] The Old English designation for a person of status intermediate between that of a freeman and a slave.

a **1000** *Laws Æthelb.* (Liebermann) §26 Gif læt of slæhð, þone selestan xxx scll. forȝelde; ȝif þane oþerne of slæhð, lx. scillingum forȝelde; ðam þriddan xl scillingum forȝelden. **1875** STUBBS *Const. Hist.* I. iv. 64 The three ranks of men, the noble, the freeman, and the læt.

† **ˈlætable,** *a. Obs. rare*—⁰. [ad. L. *lætābilis*, f. *lætārī* to rejoice, f. *lætus* joyful.] 'Worthy to bee reioyced at' (Cockeram, 1623).

Lætare (liːˈtɛərɪ, laɪˈtɑːrɪ). [L., imper. sing. of *lætārī* to rejoice: see quot. 1921.] *attrib.* (with *Sunday*) or *ellipt.* Mid-Lent Sunday.

1870 BREWER *Dict. Phr. & Fable* 491/1 *Lætare Sunday.* The fourth Sunday in Lent is so called from the first word of the Introit. **1886** E. L. DORSEY *Midshipman Bob* 6 We would notify the Catholic neighbours the day before 'Lætare-Sunday' (as we called our Mass-day). **1921** *Spectator* 19 Feb. 243/2 The Fourth Sunday of Lent or Mothering Sunday, called 'Laetare' from the opening word of the Introit. **1951** R. KNOX *Stimuli* III. vi. 100 The Church gives us Laetare Sunday in the middle of Lent. **1974** *Oxf. Dict. Chr. Ch.* (ed. 2) 792/2 Laetare Sunday.. is also known as Mothering Sunday and Refreshment Sunday.

† **læˈtation.** *Obs.* Also 7 letation. [ad. L. *lætātiōn-em*, f. late L. *lætāre* to render fertile, f. *læt-us* fertile, joyful.] A manuring; also quasi-*concr.* manure.

(Frequent in Evelyn; in the Advertisement prefixed to ed. 3 of *Sylva*, 1679 he says that 'the meaner capacities' among his readers may 'read for letation, dung'.)

1664 EVELYN *Sylva* I. ii. (1670) 11 Meliorating barren-ground with sweet and comminuted lætations.

lætic (ˈliːtɪk), *a. Hist.* [ad. late L. *lætic-us*, f. *lætus* (see below); the word is usually viewed as adopted from Teut. **lǣto-z* (see LÆT).] Of or pertaining to the *læti*, a class of non-Roman cultivators under the later Roman empire, who occupied lands for which they paid tribute.

1839 KEIGHTLEY *Hist. Eng.* I. 129 At a subsequent period [in Roman history] lands denominated Lætic were given in the interior of the provinces to larger bodies of the Barbarians on similar condition. **1874** STUBBS *Const. Hist.* I. vi. 161 As the freemen were mingled more or less with lætic or native races. **1892** C. M. ANDREWS *Old Eng. Manor* Introd. 39 Portions of the Teutonic laetic organization may have lingered in Kent.

læˈtificant, *a. rare*—¹. [ad. L. *lætificant-em*, pres. pple. of *lætificāre* to make glad, f. *lætificus* gladdening, f. *læt-us* joyful.] Of a medicine: Cheering, stimulating.

1627 tr. *Bacon's Life & Death* (1651) 28 Vapours work powerfully upon the Spirits.. by lætificant Medecines, ..&c. **1855** MAYNE *Expos. Lex.*, *Lætificans*,.. letificant.

† **læˈtificate,** *v. Obs. rare*—⁰. [f. L. *lætificāt-*, ppl. stem of *lætificā-re* (see prec.).] *trans.* To make joyful, cheer, revive.

1623 in COCKERAM.

Hence † **lætifiˈcation**, rejoicing; also, a making joyful. † **læˈtificative** *a.*, adapted to cheer.

c **1485** *Digby Myst.* (1882) I. 26 The shepherdes of Cristes birthe made letificacion. **1623** COCKERAM II, *Reioycing*,.. Lætification. **1657** TOMLINSON *Renou's Disp.* 386* Storax is a good ingredient for cordial and lætificative antidotes.

Laetrile (ˈleɪtraɪl, -rɪl). Also laetrile. [f. *læ(vo-rotatory* adj. s.v. LÆVO-, LEVO- + NI)TRILE.] A proprietary name for a substance that has been used in the treatment of cancer with controversial results and is identical with or related to amygdalin.

No longer proprietary in the U.S.

1953 *Official Gaz.* (U.S. Patent Office) 31 Mar. 1159/1 John Beard Memorial Foundation, San Francisco, Calif. Filed July 8, 1952. *Laetrile.* For treatment of disorders from intestinal fermentation. Claims use since June 2, 1952. **1953** *Calif. Med.* Apr. 320/1 The term Laetrile is derived from the fact that the chemical is a laevo-rotary-nitrile. It is claimed that this type of therapy was first used in human cancer by Ernst T. Krebs, Sr.,.. when 'substantial clinical results' were obtained from the use of a beta-cyanogenetic glucoside named amygdalin. *Ibid.* 326/1 In two independent studies.. Laetrile has been completely ineffective.. on cancer in laboratory animals. **1957** *Jrnl. Philippine Med. Assoc.* XXXIII. 18/1 We instituted Laetrile therapy... After the first injection of Laetrile the patient slept better. **1963** *Rep. Calif. Cancer Advisory Council: Beta-Cyanogenetic Glucosides (Laetriles)* 1 As used in this report Laetrile refers solely to amygdalin, a beta-cyanogenetic (cyanogenic) glucoside, commonly extracted from apricot pits, with or without the addition of dispropyl ammonium iodide. **1967** *Los Angeles Times* 11 Dec. 3/2 She first began taking Laetrile injections in Montreal in 1962... 'It was Laetrile that saved my life.' **1976** *Jrnl. Amer. Med. Assoc.* 13 Sept. 1286/3 Laetrile, no longer claimed to be a 'magic bullet' that destroys cancer cells with cyanide, has become transmuted into the fake 'vitamin B_{17}'. **1977** C. MCFADDEN *Serial* (1978) xxiv. 54/2, I haven't got cancer. So never mind the Laetrile, okay? **1981** M. C. GERALD *Pharmacol.* (ed. 2) xxx. 590 The FDA.. continues to oppose laetrile legalization because, contrary to the claims of its proponents: it is not completely nontoxic; it has not been proven to be effective in preventing or treating cancer; and there is no basis for the claim that it is a vitamin that plays an essential role in human nutrition. **1983** *Trade Marks Jrnl.* 27 Apr. 764/2 *Laetrile*... Pharmaceutical substances. Dipix Distributions Limited, Gusta Lodge, Worth, Deal, Kent.

lævigate, obs. form of LEVIGATE.

lævo-, levo- (ˈliːvəʊ), used as combining form of L. *lævus*, in the sense '(turning or turned) to the left', in physical and chemical terms, chiefly having reference to the property possessed by certain substances of causing the plane of a ray of polarized light to rotate to the left (cf. DEXTRO-). Among these are: **a. lævoˈgyrate, lævoˈgyrous** *adjs.*, characterized by turning the plane of polarization to the left. **lævo-roˈtation**, rotation to the left. **lævo-ˈrotatory** *a.*, = LÆVOGYRATE. **b. lævo-ˈcompound**, a chemical compound which causes lævo-rotation. **lævo-ˈglucose** = LÆVULOSE. **lævo-raˈcemic, lævo-tarˈtaric acid**, the modifications of racemic and tartaric acid which are lævo-rotatory. Hence **lævo-ˈracemate, -ˈtartrate**, the salts of these.

a **1856** HAYDN (Cent. s.v. *Levogyrate*), If the analyser has to be turned from right to left to obtain the natural order of colours, the quartz is called left-handed or *levogyrate. **1853** *Levoracemic acid [see DEXTRO- b]. **1882** *Nature* XXV. 283 With each electrode, diverging currents produce dextro- and converging ones *lævo-rotation. **1873** *Fownes' Chem.* (ed. 11) 779 Both are *levorotatory. **1897** *Allbutt's Syst. Med.* III. 216 When the urine is lævo-rotatory after trituration with Fehling. **1876** tr. *Schützenberger's Ferment.* 6 Paratartaric acid easily splits up.. into dextro-tartaric and *lævo-tartaric acid.

lævodopa, var. LEVODOPA.

lævulin, levulin (ˈliːvjʊlɪn). *Chem.* [f. LÆVUL-OSE + -IN.] A substance resembling dextrin, obtained from the roots of certain composite plants. Hence **lævulinic**, only in *l. acid* (see quot. 1888).

1888 *Syd. Soc. Lex.*, *Lævulin*, $C_6H_{10}O_5$.. *Lævulinic acid*.. $C_5H_8O_3$. **1897** *Naturalist* 44 The root contains.. also sugar, levulin, while its juice exposed to the air ferments.

lævulosan, levulosan (ˈliːvjʊləsæn). *Chem.* Also **-ane** (see next). [ad. F. *lévulosane* (A. Gélis 1860, in *Compt. Rend.* LI. 333), f. *lévulose* LÆVULOSE, LEVULOSE.] **a.** An anhydride, $C_6H_{10}O_5$, of lævulose. ? *Obs.*

1862 H. WATTS tr. *Gmelin's Hand-bk. Chem.* XV. 338 Cane-sugar quickly heated to 160°, and kept in the melted state at that temperature for a moderate time, is converted into.. lævulosan and dextro-glucose. **1887** *Encycl. Brit.* XXII. 624/1 It [*sc.* lævulose] fuses at 95° C.; at 170° it passes into lævulosan, $C_6H_{10}O_5$, analogous to glucosan.

b. Any polysaccharide composed chiefly of lævulose residues. Cf. LEVAN.

1913 *Chem. Abstr.* VII. 3511 (*heading*) Hydrolysis of levulosans and application to vegetable analysis. **1931** [see FRUCTOSAN]. **1966** NOWAKOWSKI & CLARKE tr. *Kretovich's Princ. Plant Biochem.* ix. 295 Higher plants also contain enzymes which catalyse the conversion of sucrose into a variety of polyglucosides and polyfructosides. In some plants (members of the Graminae and Liliaceae) levulosans .. function as transport carbohydrates.

lævulose, levulose (ˈliːvjʊləʊs). *Chem.* [f. L. *læv-us* left + -ULE + -OSE.] Formerly, the form of GLUCOSE which is lævo-rotatory to polarized light; now, the naturally occurring (lævo-rotatory) form of fructose, D(—)-fructose. (Cf. DEXTROSE.)

1871 ROSCOE *Elem. Chem.* 396 In manna and honey mixed with levulose, or left-handed glucose. **1878** KINGZETT *Anim. Chem.* 404 Cane sugar is first resolved into dextrose and

lævulose before it ferments. **1897** *Allbutt's Syst. Med.* III. 386 Cane sugar is partly left unchanged, partly converted into glucose and lævulose. **1902** *Encycl. Brit.* XXII. 721/1 Glucose and fructose (lævulose)—the two isomeric hexases of the formula $C_6H_{12}O_6$ which are formed on hydrolysing cane sugar. **1948** W. PIGMAN *Chem. Carbohydrates* xv. 605 Hydrolysis of inulin by enzymes leads to a practically quantitative yield of levulose (D-fructose). **1974** *Nature* 10 May 194/3 Although it is true that some bacteriologists are extremely conservative in the names they use for carbohydrates, surely nobody now uses 'levulose'.. in preference to 'fructose' these days.

Hence **lævulosane** [+ -ANE] obs. var. LÆVULOSAN, LEVULOSAN *a.*

1876 HARLEY *Mat. Med.* (ed. 6) 792 Heated to 338° lævulose loses water and is converted into lævulosane.

laf(e, obs. f. LAVE *sb.*; obs. Sc. f. LOAF *sb.*

Lafayette (læfeɪ'jɛt). *U.S.* [f. the name of the French general Lafayette.]

1. A sciænoid fish of the Northern United States (*Liostomus xanthurus*).

1859 BARTLETT *Dict. Amer.*, Lafayette fish (*Leiostomus obliquus*), a delicious sea-fish, which appears in the summer in great abundance at Cape Island on the Jersey coast... The name Lafayette..was given it on account of its appearance one summer coinciding with the last visit of General Lafayette to America.

2. A stromateoid fish (*Stromateus triacanthus*).

1884-5 *Stand. Nat. Hist.* (1888) III. 215 A much smaller species..otherwise known as 'Lafayette' or 'Cape May goodie'.

laferk, obs. Sc. form of LARK.

laff, laffe, obs. forms of LAUGH, LAVE *sb.*

lafful, obs. form of LAWFUL.

Lafite (læ'fiːt). Also (now considered erron.) Lafitte. [Fr., place-name.] Used as the designation of the claret produced and bottled at Château Lafite, in the Médoc district of the Gironde, France.

1707 [see CLARET *sb.*[2] (*a.*) 1 b]. **1792** [see HAUT-BRION]. *a* **1845** BARHAM *Ingol. Leg.* (1847) 3rd Ser. 186 Chambertin, Chateau Margaux, La Rose, and Lafitte. **1871** M. COLLINS *Marquis & Merchant* II. viii. 237 We'll have some Lafitte. **1888** *Athenæum* 21 Apr. 499/1 Your noble magnum of *Lafitte* E'en Rothschild would have deem'd a treat. **1920** G. SAINTSBURY *Notes on Cellar-Bk.* iv. 48 A '71 Lafite which hailed from Pall Mall. **1931** S. JAMESON *Richer Dust* iv. 77 His glass about to be filled for the third time with an excellent Lafitte. **1963** A. L. SIMON *Guide Good Food & Wines* 732/1 The spelling of *Lafite* with two *f*'s and two *t*'s instead of one occurs in old records and even on old labels, but all forms are now obsolete other than *Lafite*. There are other Châteaux in the Gironde, however, bearing the same name with different spelling. **1973** *Country Life* 19 Apr. 1052/2 Similar bottles of '66 of Lafite and Latour brought £360 and £300 respectively.

La France (la frɑ̃s). [Fr.] An early type of hybrid tea rose, introduced in 1867, and bearing large, pink, scented flowers. Also *attrib.*

1868 *Floral Mag.* VII. 399 La France has evidently a mixture of Tea and Bourbon blood in it. **1906** *Westm. Gaz.* 11 Aug. 2/3 Roses red, roses yellow, roses white, roses of all known shades and varieties—fragrant La Frances, flaunting Jacqueminots, stately American Beauties. **1928** [see GLOIRE DE DIJON]. **1937** F. B. YOUNG *Portrait of Village* vi. 119 Its flowers are all old-fashioned and mostly sweet-scented:.. moss-roses and silvery-pink *La France*. **1952** 'M. COST' *Hour Awaits* 78 Fanchon, lovely as a La France rose, but English as Mayfair, was also leaning from her window. **1969** V. C. CLINTON-BADDELEY *Only Matter of Time* 48 He wished so many of the old roses had not disappeared. When did you last see La France? **1973** [see HYBRID B. 1 b].

laft, Sc. form of LOFT.

laft(e, obs. pa. t. and pa. pple. of LEAVE.

lafter, dial. form of LAUGHTER.

lafully, obs. form of LAWFULLY.

lag (læg), *sb.*[1] and *a.* [Belongs to LAG *v.*[2]; the origin and mutual relation of the words are obscure.

In some parts of England *fog, seg, lag,* or *foggie, seggie, laggie*, are used in children's games as substitutes for 'first, second, last' (see *Eng. Dial. Dict.* s.v. *Fog*). This suggests the possibility that *lag* may have originated in the language of sports as an arbitrary distortion of *last*; but even in that case the word may have coalesced with a homophone of independent origin. The current hypothesis that the adj. is a. Welsh *llag* (earlier *llac*), Ir. and Gael. *lag*, slack, weak, is highly improbable. There is some affinity of sense between *lag* and LACK *a.* and *v.* (cf. *to come lag* and *to come lack*); the former might conceivably be an alteration of the latter under the influence of words like FLAG *v.*[1], FAG *sb.*[2] Cf. further MDa. *lakke* to go slowly (Kalkar).]

A. *sb.* **1. a.** The last or hindmost person (in a race, game, sequence of any kind). Now *rare* exc. in schoolboy use.

1514 BARCLAY *1st Eclogue* in *Cyt. & Uplondyshm.* (Percy Soc.) p. xii, In the tavern remayne they last for lag. **1567** DRANT *Horace's Ep.* B vj, Since eche man bragges, the lagge of vs A shendefull shame him take. **1611** COTGR. s.v. *Dernier, Le dernier le loup le mange*,..lags come to the lash. **1641** M. FRANK *Serm.* vii. (1672) 112 The *novissimus virorum*, the lag and fag of all a very scum of men. **1687** MIEGE *Gt. Fr. Dict.* II, *Lag*, a School-Word that signifies the last, *le dernier*. As the Lag of a Form, *le dernier d'une Classe.* **1700** DRYDEN *Iliad* I. 337 In threats the foremost, but the lag in fight. **1776** JEFFERSON *Writ.* (ed. Ford) II. 39 The omission of H—— and B—— and my being next to the lag [in the nomination of delegates] give me some alarm. **1777** JOHNSON *Let. to Mrs. Thrale* 25 Oct., How long do you stay at Brighthelmstone? Now the company is gone, why should you be the lag? **1825** *Sporting Mag.* XVI. 310 Ward first mounted the stage and Cannon was no lag. **1859** FARRAR *J. Home* iv. 38, I say, Julian, I vote we both try for lag next trials. It'd save lots of grind. **1890** A. LANG *Sir S. Northcote* I. I. 15 Stafford Northcote occupied the undistinguished place of 'lag' in his form.

b. *Comb.*: **lag-out** (= 'last out'), the name of a boys' game.

1845 in *Brasenose Ale* 76 No marble in circles on the hall-step rolls, We cannot play lag-out, nor yet three-holes.

†**2.** *pl.* What remains in a vessel after the liquor is drawn off; dregs, lees. *Obs.*

15.. *Regul. Househ. Earl Northumb.* (1770) 57 That Vinacre be made of the brokyn Wynes..And that the Laggs be provide by the Clerks of the Hous and markid after thei be past drawing that thei can be set no more of broche. **1594** PLAT *Jewell-ho.* III. 65 Transmutations..of old lags of Sacks or Malmesies..into Muskadels. **1615** MARKHAM *Eng. Housew.* II. iv. (1668) 116 Laggs of Claret and Sack. **1703** *Art & Myst. Vintners* 21 Muskadel is sophisticated with the Lags of Sack.

†**3.** The lowest class. (Cf. *lag-end.*) *Obs.*[−1]

1607 SHAKS. *Timon* III. vi. 90 The Senators of Athens, together with the common legge [*Rowe* (1709) *and later editors* lag] of People.

4. [from the vb.] **a.** The condition of lagging.

1837 *Fraser's Mag.* XVI. 114 When Spaniard meets Spaniard, then comes, not the tug, but the lag, of war.

b. in *Physics*: the retardation in a current or movement of any kind; the amount of this retardation; more widely in general use: a period of time separating any phenomenon or event from an earlier one to which it is related (causally or in some other way); = *time-lag* (TIME *sb.* 60). ***angle of lag*** (Electr.), the fraction of a complete cycle, multiplied by 360° or 2π radians, by which a sinusoidal current lags behind the associated sinusoidal voltage; ***lag of the tide***: the interval by which the tide-wave falls behind the mean time in the first and third quarters of the moon. See also *jet lag* (JET *sb.*[3] 11).

1855 OGILVIE Suppl. s.v., The lag of the tide... The lag of the steam-valve of a steam-engine. **1881** CHAMBERS in *Nature* XXIII. 399 The remarkable lag which takes place in the occurrence of the critical barometric epochs at the more easterly stations. **1886** S. P. THOMPSON *Dynamo-Electr. Machinery* (ed. 2) xviii. 330, ϕ is called the retardation or angle of lag. *Ibid.* 331 The retardation will increase with increased speed... There will be less lag therefore if the machine is so designed that it can be driven at a slow speed. **1892** *Electrical Engineer* 16 Sept. 287/1 It is obvious that at the point where B cuts the axis the induction is a maximum; hence if there were no 'magnetic lag' and no currents in the iron, this point should occur at the same time as that at which the current is a maximum. **1902** *Encycl. Brit.* XXVIII. 42/1 [His] method consisted in measuring the interval which elapses between the application of a potential difference..and the passage of the spark. This lag of the spark, as we may call it, is a very important quantity. **1909** *Jrnl. Hygiene* IX. 240 He found that there is an initial period after inoculation during which growth is almost absent: the length of time of this 'lag' varies with the age of the culture used for inoculation and with the species of the bacillus. **1923** *Glasgow Herald* 2 Nov. 12/4 The operation of the 'lag' of two months between the period of ascertainment and the months when the wages based on such ascertainment are paid. **1934** L. T. AGGER *Alternating Currents* iii. 38 The current goes through all the events in its cycle one-quarter of a period, or 90°, later than the P.D. For this reason it is said to lag behind the P.D. by 90°; or, expressed in another way, the angle of lag of the current is 90°. **1934** Cultural lag [see CULTURAL *a.* 3]. **1940** *Economist* 7 Dec. 707/1 It must not be forgotten that a very considerable lag must occur between the dates when insured losses are incurred and compensation is paid. In the case of certain shipping losses, ..this lag may extend for the duration of the war. **1962** J. THEWLIS et al. *Encycl. Dict. Physics* VII. 190/1 Lag in a control system may be defined briefly as delayed response of the output to changes of input. **1966** *McGraw-Hill Encycl. Sci. & Technol.* VII. 153/2 No instrument responds instantaneously to a change in the measurand; the lag is dependent on the natural frequency of the instrument system and its degree of damping.

c. *Comb.* **lag fault** *Geol.*, a type of overthrust formed when the uppermost of a series of rocks moves more slowly than the lower ones; **lag phase** *Biol.*, the period elapsing between the introduction of an inoculum of bacteria into a culture medium (or other new environment) and the commencement of its exponential growth; **lag time**, the period of time elapsing between one event and a later, related, event, esp. between a cause and its effect; (the extent of) a lag.

1900 J. E. MARR in *Proc. Geologists' Assoc.* XVI. 461 These fissures..would have an outcrop similar to those of thrust-planes or over-faults which approached the horizontal; but they would differ from these, inasmuch as no inversion on a large scale would accompany them. We shall speak of them here as 'lag' faults. **1947** *Q. Jrnl. Geol. Soc.* CIII. 100 There are several lag-faults in the district, but.. only in the case of the Tirbach lag-faults is the evidence considered to be conclusive. **1963** E. S. HILLS *Elem. Struct. Geol.* vii. 191 Lag faults.—These are low angle faults with normal fault displacement, that originate from the upward movement of the footwall block in a region of general thrusting. The hanging-wall block appears to have lagged behind in the regional movements. **1914** *Jrnl. Hygiene* XIV. 260 A seeding taken during the lag-phase grows with diminished lag. **1944** L. E. H. WHITBY *Med. Bacteriol.* (ed. 4) i. 6 Multiplication [of bacteria] passes through four phases: (1) Lag phase—lasting from half an hour to eight hours, during which time there is no increase in numbers..; during this time the organism adjusts itself to its new environment. **1972** *Biochim. & Biophys. Acta* CCLXX. 41 When *E. coli* cells are exposed to low temperatures, they enter a prolonged lag phase. **1956** *Nature* 24 Mar. 579/1 Fragments of chorioallantoic membrane..support the growth of hæmagglutinating particles, but there is a lag-time of about ten hours. **1962** F. I. ORDWAY et al. *Basic Astronautics* xiii. 530 (*table*) Equipment lagtime before response. **1972** *Times* 26 June 12/4 The typical lag times for technological and cultural change. **1973** *Nature* 7 Dec. 327/1 The lag time of four years has been reduced to two at the behest of the governing council.

B. *adj.*

1. a. †Last, hindmost (*obs.*); belated, lingering behind, lagging, tardy (now *rare*). (In early instances only *absol.* or *predicative*, and hence hardly distinguishable from the sb.) † (*to come*) ***lag of***: short of, too late for, or in arrear of.

1552 HULOET, Lagge and last. **1568** *Hist. Jacob & Esau* v. v. F iv b, Haue not we well hunted, of blessing to come lagge? **1589** R. HARVEY *Pl. Perc.* 22 Beshrow him that comes lagge in so good a course. **1594** SHAKS. *Rich. III*, II. i. 90 Some tardie Cripple..That came too lagge to see him buried. **1605** —— *Lear* I. ii. 6, I am some twelue, or fourteene Moonshines Lag of a Brother. **1612** *Two Noble K.* V. iv. 8 Beguile The gout and rheum, that in lag hours attend For grey approachers. **1624** SIR C. MOUNTAGU in *Buccleuch MSS.* (Hist. MSS. Comm.) I. 260 Your neighbour will struggle so long for place as he will be cast lagg. *a* **1639** T. CAREW *To Mistresse in Absence* 31 There seated in those heavenly bowers, Wee'le cheat the lag and lingring hours. **1678-9** DRYDEN & LEE *Œdipus* III. i, Then hell has been among ye, And some lag fiend yet lingers in the grove. **1691** WOOD *Ath. Oxon.* I. 594 A fourth person, who comes lagg, as having lately appeared in print..tells us..he died. **1742** R. BLAIR *Grave* 731 Even the lag flesh Rests. **1785** BURNS *Address Deil* iii, An' faith! thou's neither lag nor lame. **1832-53** *Whistle-Binkie* (Scot. Songs) Ser. II. 100 Lauchie had looms, but was lag at the weaving.

b. as an exclamation at play (see quot. 1869).

1609 ARMIN *Maids of More-Cl.* C 3 *Boy.* Now Iohn, i'le cry first. *Ioh.* And i'le cry lagge. I was in hoblies hole. **1869** *Lonsdale Gloss.*, *Lag* or *Lag last* is said by boys when playing at pitch and toss, or other games, in order that they may bespeak the last pitch.

2. Special collocations (sometimes hyphened): **lag-end**, the hinder or latter part, the fag end (now *rare*); †**lag-man**, the last man, the one who brings up the rear; †**lag-tooth**, a wisdom tooth (from its late appearance). Also *Comb.*: **lag-bellied** *a.*, ? slow-paced, tardy.

1596 SHAKS. *1 Hen. IV*, v. i. 24, I could be well content To entertaine the Lagge-end of my life With quiet hours. **1599** NASHE *Lenten Stuffe* 37 The Essex calfe or lagman, who had lost the calues of his legs by gnawing on the horslegs. **1611** FLORIO, *Sophronisteri*, the two teeth which grow last when a man is about twentie yeares ould, lag-teeth. **1624** HEYWOOD *Gunaik.* I. 17 In the lagge end of the same troope were driven a certaine number of faire and goodlie oxen. **1822** HOOD *Lycus the Centaur* 62 From the lag-bellied toad To the mammoth. **1857** MRS. MATHEWS *Tea-Table T.* I. 204 A shelter..where they may..wear away the lag-end of their madness.

lag (læg), *sb.*[2] Also 7 lagg. [app. a. ON. *lǫgg*, recorded only in the sense 'rim of a barrel' (cf. 1 b); but the Sw. *lagg* means also 'stave', whence *laggkärl* vessel composed of staves, cask.]

1. A stave of a barrel. Now *dial.*

1672 HOOLE *Comenius' Vis. World* 165 The Cooper.. maketh Hoops of Hassel-rods..and Lags of Timber. **1676** *Burgery of Sheffield* 209 For mendyng the church yatis and barrell laggs and nayles 4*s.* 4*d.* **1869** in *Lonsdale Gloss.*

†**b.** (See quot.) *Obs. rare*[−0].

1688 R. HOLME *Armoury* III. 108/1 *Lag*, is a piece put into the top of a Barrel staff that is broken off at the Grooping.

2. One of the staves or laths forming the covering of a band-drum or a steam boiler or cylinder, or the upper casing of a carding machine.

1847 *Specif. Sykes' & Ogden's Patent* No. 11798 On these bands [in a carding engine] we fix a continued series of lags or small blocks of wood. **1875** in KNIGHT *Dict. Mech.*

3. *Comb.*: **lag-link**, a link for holding a lag or bar (*Cent. Dict.*); **lag-machine**, a machine for shaping wooden lags (see sense 2); **lag-screw**, (*a*) a flat-headed screw used to secure lags to cylinders or drums; (*b*) U.S. = *coach-screw*.

1873 J. RICHARDS *Wood-working Factories* 26 Almost any kind of shafting can be hung with safety on wood screws, or lag screws. **1875** KNIGHT *Dict. Mech.*, *Lag-machine*.

†**lag**, *sb.*[3] *Obs.* [Of unknown origin; cf. G. *lache* cleft or mark in a tree. Cf. LAG *v.*[5]] A cleft or rift in timber. Also *Comb.*, as *lag-clift* (unless *lagge* in quot. 1579 be the adj.).

1579 HYLL *Ord. Bees* (1608) 24 The stocke thus cut asunder at both the ends, couer with a faire sheete, lest any lagge clifts appeare after the cutting. **1790** W. MARSHALL *Midl. Counties* II. 333 The 'lag'..is a cleft, or rift, reaching sometimes from the top to the bottom of the stem, and, perhaps, to near its center.

†**lag**, *sb.*[4] *Cant. Obs.* Also 6 lagge. [Possibly f. *lag*, LAGE *v.* to wash.] ***lag of duds***: a 'buck' or 'wash' of clothes.

1567 HARMAN *Caveat* 86 We wyll fylche some duddes of the Ruffemans, or myll the ken for a lagge of dudes. **1622**

BEAUM. & FL. *Beggar's Bush* v. i, If it be milling of a lag of duds. *a* **1700** B. E. *Dict. Cant. Crew, Lag-a dudds*, a Buck of Cloths. *As we cloy the Lag of Dudds*, come let us Steal that Buck of Cloths. **1725** in *New Cant. Dict.*

lag (læg), *sb.*[5] *Cant.* [f. LAG *v.*[3]]

1. A convict who has been transported or sentenced to penal servitude.

1812 J. H. VAUX *Flash Dict., Lag*, a convict under sentence of transportation. **1828** 'JON BEE' *Living Pict. Lond.* 39 A few are 'returned lags'. **1887** *Westm. Rev.* June 383 It was no uncommon thing to see an old 'lag' enlarged for good conduct. **1894** H. NISBET *Bush Girl's Rom.* 232 As Wildrake was walking along the beach, he met a lag who had got his ticket-of-leave.

2. A term of transportation or penal servitude.

1821 HAGGART *Life* 84 Another prisoner.. under sentence of lag for fourteen stretch. **1896** *Daily News* 13 May 9/5, I have had a look round with another man who did a lag with me.

3. *Comb.*: **lag-fever, -ship** (see quots.).

1811 *Lex. Balatron., Lag-fever*, a term of ridicule applied to men who being under sentence of transportation, pretend illness, to avoid being sent from gaol to the hulks. **1812** J. H. VAUX *Flash Dict., Lag ship*, a transport chartered by government for the conveyance of convicts to New South Wales; also a hulk or floating prison.

†**lag**, *sb.*[6] *Obs. rare.* ? A flock (of geese).

1624 MOUNTAGUE *New Gagg*, To Rdr., Hee hath stopped the mouths of all Protestants for euer; the proudest of them dare not *hiscere* hereafter against Himselfe, or any one of his Lagg. *Ibid.* 180 This Goose the Gagger may put his Gag into the Bils of many of his owne Gaggle, as well as into others Lagges. [**1896** *Eng. Dial. Dict., A-lag*, Cum., the sporting term for a flock of geese.]

†**lag**, *v.*[1] *Obs.* [Of obscure origin; cf. DAG *v.*[1], CLAG *v.*]

1. *trans.* To daggle, render wet or muddy.

[*a* **1300** ? Implied in BELAG *v.*] *c* **1440** *Promp. Parv.* 283 Laggyd, or bedrabelyd, *labefactus, paludosus*. Laggyn, or drablyn, *palustro*.

2. *intr.* To daggle, become wet or muddy.

1682 BUNYAN *Holy War* 230 Let them [your new garments] not lag with dust and dirt.

lag (læg), *v.*[2] Also 6-7 lagg, 6-8 lagge. [See LAG *sb.*[1] and *a.*]

1. a. *intr.* To fail to maintain the desired speed of progress; to slacken one's pace, as from weakness or sloth; to fail to keep pace with others; to hang back, fall behind, remain in the rear. Often with *behind* adv. or const. *after, behind* preps.; also with *on.*

1530 PALSGR. 601/1, I lagge behynde my felowes, *je trayne*... Why lagge you ever behynde on this facion? **1570** LEVINS *Manip.* 10/23 To Lag, *fatigare, fatiscere*. **1607** TOURNEUR *Rev. Trag.* II. E 1 b, To prison with the Villaine. Death shall not long lag after him. **1622** R. HAWKINS *Voy. S. Sea* (1847) 173 The admirall.. began to lagge a sterne, and with him other two shippes. **1651** DAVENANT *Gondibert* III. III. xxvi, And lagg'd like Baggage Treasure in the Wars. **1667** MILTON *P.L.* x. 266, I shall not lag behinde, nor erre The way, thou leading. **1697** DRYDEN *Æneid* XII. 379 He lags and labours in his flight. **1711** STEELE *Spect.* No. 137 ¶4 His Master.. wondered what made the lazy young Dog lag behind. **1748** JOHNSON *Van. Hum. Wishes* 313 Superfluous 'lags' the vet'ran on the stage. **1800** WORDSW. *Brothers* 363 He, at length Through weariness,.. lagged behind. **1801** MAR. EDGEWORTH *Knapsack* (1832) 298 My poor fellows, how they lag! **1824** W. IRVING *Trav.* II. 107 Suffering them [his mules] to lag on at a snail's pace. **1837** —— *Capt. Bonneville* II. 46 He grew silent and gloomy, and lagged behind the rest. **1857** HUGHES *Tom Brown* II. iii. (1871) 260 When they had crossed three or four fields without a check, Arthur began to lag. **1897** *Allbutt's Syst. Med.* IV. 492 If the sign is present, the upper eyelids lag, not closely following the movements of the eyeballs.

b. of immaterial things and *fig.*

1591 SHAKS. *1 Hen. VI*, III. iii. 34 Fortune, in fauor makes him lagge behinde. *a* **1661** FULLER *Worthies* (1840) III. 498 And this our Gildas [the Fourth]; who laggeth last in the team of his name sakes. **1703** J. SAVAGE *Lett. Antients* vi. 40 We lagg in the care of Things of no kin to us. **1713** SWIFT *Cadenus & Vanessa* 355 Ideas came into her mind So fast, his lessons lagg'd behind. **1762** FOOTE *Lyar* III. Wks. 1799 I. 322 Think how the tedious time has lagg'd along. **1775** BURKE *Sp. Conc. Amer.* Wks. III. 44 When we speak of the commerce with our colonies, fiction lags after truth. **1820** W. IRVING *Sketch Bk.* II. 94 The vocal parts generally lagging a little behind the instrumental. **1833** HT. MARTINEAU *Fr. Wines & Pol.* vi. 84 Business lagged in every department of the administration. **1865** CARLYLE *Fredk. Gt.* XVII. ii. (1872) VII. 14 Military preparation does lag at a shameful rate. **1874** GREEN *Short Hist.* vi. §6. 332 The work lagged for five years in the hands of the bishops. **1892** *Electrical Engineer* 16 Sept. 287/2 The maximum induction lags behind the maximum magnetising force.

2. *trans.* To cause to lag; to retard, to tire. *Obs.* exc. *dial.*

1570 [see 1]. **1632** HEYWOOD *1st Pt. Iron Age* v. Wks. 1874 III. 338 The weight would lagge thee that art wont to flye. **1638** R. BRATHWAIT *Psalm* cli. 298 Thine Armours load, but laggs faint heart, for flight the more unfit. **1876** *Whitby Gloss., Lagg'd*, tired as with carrying a load.

†**3.** *trans.* To drag after one.

1530 PALSGR. 601/1 He laggeth the dogge at his horse tayle: *il trayne le chien a la queue de son cheual.*

4. *trans.* To lag behind.

1930 M. G. MALTI *Electr. Circuit Analysis* iii. 26 A curve lags the origin if its zero value.. occurs after the point $x = 0$. **1966** L. A. MANNING *Electr. Circuits* iv. 56 The current function lags the voltage by 90 degrees; that is, the current rises to a maximum value a quarter of a cycle later than does the voltage. **1973** *Nature* 21/28 Dec. 444/1 After the time step, Atomic Time will lag UT by 0·7 s.

Hence †**lagged** *ppl. a.*, delayed, tardy.

1602 MARSTON *Antonio's Rev.* I. i. Wks. 1856 I. 75 O, I could eate Thy fumbling throat, for thy lagd censure.

lag (læg), *v.*[3]

†**1.** *trans.* To carry off, steal. *Obs.*

1573 TUSSER *Husb.* xx. (1878) 54 Some corne away lag in bottle and bag. Some steales, for a iest, egges out of the nest. *Ibid.* xxxvi. 86 Poore cunnie, so bagged, is soone ouer lagged.

2. a. To transport or send to penal servitude.

1812 J. H. VAUX *Flash Dict., Lag*, to transport for seven years or upwards. **1838** DICKENS *O. Twist* xvi, They'll ask no questions after him, fear they should be obliged to prosecute, and so get him lagged. **1870** READE *Put Yourself in His Place* II. 288 Let Little alone, or the trade will make it their job to lag you.

b. To catch, apprehend.

1847 DE QUINCEY *Schlosser's Lit. Hist.* Wks. 1858 VIII. 58 Aladdin himself only escaped being lagged for a rogue and a conjurer by a flying jump after his palace. **1858** A. MAYHEW *Paved w. Gold* III. i. 252 They tell him adventures of how they were nearly 'lagged by the constables'. **1891** NAT GOULD *Double Event* xxxiv, I'm a dead un. You'll never lag me alive, you cur!

lag (læg), *v.*[4] [f. LAG *sb.*[2]] *trans.* To cover (a boiler, etc.) with wooden 'lags', strips of felt, etc.

1887 EWING in *Encycl. Brit.* XXII. 488/1 The loss of efficiency due to this cause will therefore be greater in an unprotected cylinder than in one which is well lagged or covered with non-conducting material. **1888** in *Sheffield Gloss.* **1891** *Labour Commission* Gloss., *Lagging a boiler*, covering a boiler in a steamship with some material to keep in the heat. **1898** *Dublin Rev.* Apr. 423 Lagged outside with layers of felt two centimetres thick.

lag, *v.*[5] *dial.* [Cf. LAG *sb.*[3]] (See quot.)

[**1570**: LEVINS renders *lag* v. by *fatiscere*, which it is barely possible may be meant to express the sense of this vb. along with that of LAG *v.*[1]] **1881** *Leicestersh. Gloss., Lag*, to crack or split from the centre like wood from heat or hasty drying. **1888** in *Sheffield Gloss.*

lag: see LAGE *Cant.* (*sb.* and *v.*).

lagan ('lægən). *Law.* Also 6 lagen, 7, 8 lagon, ligan, 9 lagend. [a. OF. *lagan, laguen, lagand* (whence med.L. *laganum*); perh. of Scandinavian origin, from the root of LIE, LAY *vbs.* Cf. ON. *lǫgn*, pl. *lagnir*, 'a net laid in the sea' (Vigf.). The spelling *ligan* seems to be due to pseudo-etymology.] Goods or wreckage lying on the bed of the sea. Cf. FLOTSAM and JETSAM.

[**1200** *Carta de Dunewic* in Stubbs *Sel. Charters* (1895) 311 De ewagio de wrec et lagan.] **1531** *Charterparty* in R. G. Marsden *Sel. Pl. Crt. Adm.* (1894) 37 Yff the sayd shype take any pryse purchase any flotson or lagen. **1533** *Ibid.*, Flotezon or lagason. **1591** *Articles conc. Admiralty* 21 July §6 Any ship, yron, leade, or other goods floating or lying under the water or in the depth, of which there is no possessor or owner, which commonly are called Flotzon, Jetson, and Lagan. **1605** COKE *Rep.* v. (1624) 106 b Lagan (vel potius *ligan*) est quand [etc.; translated in quot. 1641]. **1622** CALLIS *Stat. Sewers* (1647) 18 [citing Coke] Flotsan, Jetsan and Lagan are goods on or in the Sea, and.. they belong to the King. **1641** *Termes de la Ley* 193 Lagan is such a parcell of goods as the Mariners in a danger of shipwracke cast out.. and fasten to them a boigh or corke, that so they may finde them... These goods are called Lagan or Ligan *à ligando*. **1707** J. CHAMBERLAYNE *St. Gt. Brit.* I. II. x. 143 To the Lord High Admiral belongs.. a Share of all lawful Prizes, Lagon ..that is, goods lying in the Sea, on Ground. **1865** KINGSLEY *Herew.* I. vi. 171 Prowling about the shore after the waifs of the storm, deserted jetsom and lagend. **1894** *Act 57-8 Vict.* c. 60 §510 In this Part of this Act..'wreck' includes jetsam, flotsam, lagan, and derelict found in or on the shores of the sea or any tidal water. **1906** *Westm. Gaz.* 13 June 4/2 These are, says Mr. Clifford, the 'ligan' of history. **1909** *Daily Chron.* 20 Mar. 5/5 The custody of flotsam, jetsam, and ligan. **1952** *Brewer's Dict. Phr. & Fable* 534/2 *Lagan*, or *Ligan*, goods thrown overboard, but marked by a buoy in order to be found again.

Hence †'**lagander**, an officer (at Calais) who takes charge of lagan or wreckage.

1526 in Dillon *Customs of Pale* (1892) 86 If ther be anie manner of Wracke found by the sea coste, it muste be presented to the Lagander or to the Sergeante.. broughte to the foresaide Lagander's hous.

‖**la'garto.** *Obs.* [Sp. *lagarto*: see ALLIGATOR[2].] An alligator.

1577 FRAMPTON *Joyful News* II. 73 b, Pimple stones.. whiche are founde in greate quantitie in the mawes of Caimanes, y[t] are called Lagartos. **1596** RALEIGH *Discov. Guiana* 48 We saw in it [the Orenoque] diuers sorts of strange fishes, & of marvellous bignes, but for Lagartos it exceeded, for there were thousands of those vglie serpents. **1600** HAKLUYT *Voy.* III. 489 In this riuer we killed a monstrous Lagarto or Crocodile.

†**lage, lag**, *sb. Cant. Obs.* Also 7 lagge. [Origin and phonetic form uncertain.] Water; urine.

1567 HARMAN *Caveat* 83 *Lage*, water. **1610** ROWLANDS *Martin Mark-all* E 3, *Lagge*, water or pisse. **1641** BROME *Joviall Crew* II. Wks. 1873 III. 391, I bowse no Lage, but a whole Gage Of this I'll bowse to you. **1665** R. HEAD *Eng. Rogue* I. v. (1680) 46 Lage, water. **1676-1708** COLES *Lage*. **1859** MATSELL *Voc.* (Farmer), *Lag*.

Hence †**lag(e** *v.* **a.** *intr.* To make water. **b.** *trans.* To water (spirits). Also, to wash *off.*

1567 HARMAN *Caveat* 85, I will lage it of with a gage of benebouse... I wull washe it of with a quart of good drynke. **1812** J. H. VAUX *Flash Dict., Lag*, to make water. To *lag* spirits, wine, &c., is to adulterate them with water.

'**lagen.** *Obs.* exc. *Hist.* Also 6 laggon, 7, 9 lagan. [ad. L. *lagōna, lagēna*, flagon, ad. Gr. λάγυνος.] A liquid measure (see quots.).

1570 LEVINS *Manip.* 163/44 A Laggon, *lagena*. **1607** COWELL *Interpr., Clerk of the market*.. is an officer.. whose dutie is to take charge of the kings measures..: as of elns, yards, lagens. **1676** COLES, *Lagen*.. a measure of six Sextaries. **1841** TYTLER *Hist. Scot.* (1879) I. 237 With an obligation to sell their ale to the abbott at the rate of a lagen and a half for a penny. **1891** J. TAIT *Two Cent. Border Ch. Life* II. 218 The lagan was equal to 7 quarts.

lagen, variant of LAGGIN.

†**lage'narious**, *a. Obs. rare*[−1]. [f. L. *lagēna* a flagon + -ARIOUS.] Flagon-shaped.

1657 TOMLINSON *Renou's Disp.* 241 Four sorts of Cucurbites, the greater, the lesser, or the lagenarious.

lagend, lagene, obs. ff. LAGAN, LAGGIN.

lagenian (lə'dʒiːnɪən), *a. Zool.* [f. L. *lagēna* + -IAN.] Like or pertaining to the genus *Lagena* of *Foraminifera*, having a straight chambered shell.

1890 in WEBSTER.

lageniform (lə'dʒiːnɪfɔːm), *a. Zool.* and *Bot.* [f. as prec. + -(I)FORM.] (See quot.)

1826 KIRBY & SP. *Entomol.* IV. 268 Lageniform.. bellying out and then ending in a narrow neck, something like a bottle. **1862** M. C. COOKE *Man. Bot. Terms, Lageniform*, shaped like a Florence flask. **1868** W. B. CARPENTER *Microscope* (ed. 4) §382. 500 The shell of *Nodosaria* is obviously made up of a succession of Lageniform chambers.

lager ('lɑːgə(r)), *v.* [ad. G. *lagern* to store.] To store (beer) (see quots.). Hence '**lagering** *vbl. sb.*

1946 A. SIMON *Conc. Encycl. Gastron.* VIII. 98/2 *Lager beer*, a light type of beer which is brewed from malt, with hops and water, fermented, and then stored (*lagered*). **1962** *Economist* 10 Feb. 543/1 A continuous fermentation process can eliminate the 'lagering' time. **1965** O. A. MENDELSOHN *Dict. Drink* 193 *Lagering*, the almost obsolete process of aging beer by holding it in large tanks, where it clarifies naturally.

lager beer ('lɑːgə 'bɪə(r)). Also simply **lager.** [ad. G. *lager-bier* beer brewed for keeping, f. *lager* a store + *bier* beer.] A light beer, consumed largely in Germany and America, and to some extent in England.

1853 URE *Dict. Arts* (ed. 4) I. 153 Beers at present brewed in Germany... 11. Wheat *Lager*-beer (slowly fermented). **1858** *N.Y. Express* June (Bartlett), The German drinks his lager, and drinks it apparently in indefinite quantities. **1863** DICEY *Federal St.* II. 80 Neither for love nor money could a stranger obtain a drink more intoxicating than lager beer.

attrib. **1882** SALA *Amer. Revis.* (1885) 401 Tinware shops, butchers', bakers' and lager beer Saloons.

‖**la'getta, la'getto.** [West Indian.] A genus of dicotyledonous trees of the W. Indies (N.O. *Thymelæaceæ*); also called *lace-bark.*

1756 P. BROWNE *Jamaica* 371 The Lagetto or Lace-Bark tree. **1773** *Phil. Trans.* LXIII. 492 Specimen of the Lagetta Tree, and its lace-like Bark, from Jamaica. **1871** C. KINGSLEY *At Last* II. xiii. 196 A bit of veritable natural lace, similar to.. the famous lace-bark of the Lagetta-tree.

‖**lagg** (læg). [a. Sw. dial. *lagg* edge of a bog or marshland, bank of a stream or river (see LAG *sb.*[2]).] A natural ditch along the edge of a raised bog.

1939 A. G. TANSLEY *Brit. Islands & their Vegetation* xxxiv. 675 The marginal watercourses from the *lagg* (a Swedish term) of raised bog. **1968** R. F. DAUBENMIRE *Plant Communities* iii. 149 Raised bog.. is a type confined to the area of a wet basin... The surface becomes convex so that the feeble drainage channels (*lagg*) that run across the basin are pushed to one or both sides of the peat dome.

laggard ('lægəd), *a.* and *sb.* Also 9 laggart. [f. LAG *v.*[1] + -ARD.]

A. *adj.* Lagging, hanging back, loitering, slow. Chiefly of living things, their actions, and attributes. Occas. of days, time, etc.

1702 ROWE *Tamerlane* IV. i, Tho' Laggard in the Race.. I will pursue the shining Path thou tread'st. **1706** [WARD] *Wooden World Dissected* (1708) 31 [The press-gang lieutenant] beats up all Quarters.. and drives the laggard Dog along the Streets, with as much noise and Bustle as Butchers do Swine to Smithfield. **1713** J. HUGHES *Ode to Creator World* 4 Decrepit Winter, laggard in the Dance.. A heavy Season does maintain. **1747** COLLINS *Passions* 112 Than all which charms this laggard age. **1814** SCOTT *Lord of Isles* IV. xviii, And Lennox cheer'd the laggard hounds. **1842** MANNING *Serm.* xvi. (1848) I. 235 Ours is a.. laggard obedience at the best. **1871** PALGRAVE *Lyr. Poems* 91 My heart outruns these laggart limbs. **1889** JESSOPP *Coming of Friars* iv. 183 The Angel of Death moves at no laggard pace.

B. *sb.* One who lags behind; a lingerer, loiterer.

1808 SCOTT *Marm.* v. xii, A laggard in love, and a dastard in war. **1836** W. IRVING *Astoria* I. 89 He meant to let the laggards off for a long pull and a hearty fright. **1860** RAWLINSON *Herodotus* IV. IX. lxxvii. 449 They declared themselves to deserve a fine, as laggarts. **1876** TAIT *Rec. Adv. Phys. Sci.* x. (ed. 2) 259 Formed of the laggards, as it were, which have been thrown out of the race.

Hence '**laggard** *v.*, to play the laggard. Also '**laggardism**, '**laggardly** *adv.*, '**laggardness.**

1835 PUSEY *Let. to Newman* in Liddon, etc. *Life Pusey* (1893) II. i. 8 [It] hardly seems to come heartily, because it

has not come before, but comes laggardly. **1865** CARLYLE *Fredk. Gt.* xv. viii. (1872) VI. 40 Austrians mainly are gone laggarding with D'Ahremberg up the Rhine. **1865** *Sat. Rev.* XIX. 756/1 The insolent contempt of labour on the one hand, and the petty aping of laggardism and polite inanity on the other. **1869** GOULBURN *Purs. Holiness* i. 10 That laggardness of will.

laggen, variant of LAGGIN.

lagger (ˈlægə(r)), *sb.*[1] [f. LAG *v.*[2] + -ER[1].]

1. One who lags or hangs back; a lingerer, loiterer.

1523 LD. BERNERS *Froiss.* I. xvii. 18 Theyr hole host..are all a horsebacke..without it be the traundals and laggers of the oost, who folow after a foote. **1682** DRYDEN *Duke of Guise* IV. ii, The guard is mine, to..lash the laggers from the sight of day. **1789** MRS. PIOZZI *Journ. France* I. 286 The mob..lash the laggers along with great indignation. **1844** STANLEY *Arnold* I. iv. 235 Himself always keeping with the laggers, that none might strain their strength by trying to be in front with him. **1852** R. S. SURTEES *Sponge's Sp. Tour* li. 291 The laggers were stealing quietly up the lanes and by-roads. **1878** FR. A. KEMBLE *Record Girlhood* II. iv. 131 The laggers who would fain have fallen a few paces out of the sound of the dreary parrotry of her inventory.

2. *slang.* A sailor. [? A distinct word: cf. LAGE.]

1812 J. H. VAUX *Flash Dict.*, *Lagger*, a sailor.

lagger (ˈlægə(r)), *sb.*[2] *Cant.* [f. LAG *v.*[3] or *sb.*[5]] A convict undergoing or having undergone penal servitude.

1819 *Sporting Mag.* III. 230/2 The laggers had an interest as to the result. **1880** S. LAKEMAN *Kaffir-Land* 19 Many of them were what they termed at the Cape, laggers..men who, having got away from Norfolk Island, or other penfolds for black sheep, lag behind, under the guardianship of Dutch laws.

†**ˈlagger**, *v. Obs.* [? f. LAG *v.*[2] + -ER[2]; but cf. Icel. *lakra* to loiter.] *intr.* To lag, linger, loiter.

c **1620** A. HUME *Brit. Tongue* Ded. (1865) 2 Heere my harte laggared on the hope of your Majestie's judgement. **1622** R. PRESTON *Godly Man's Inquis.* ii. 49 They shall neuer come to the Lord, that lagger by the way.

laggin (ˈlægɪn). *Sc.* and *north.* Also 6 **laggyne**, **lagene**, 8 **legen**, 8–9 **laggen**, 9 **lagen**. [f. ON. *logg* of the same meaning: see LAG *sb.*[2] The identification of the suffix is uncertain; it may be -ING[2] (cf. LAGGING *vbl. sb.*[3]).]

1. The projecting part of the staves at the bottom part of a cask or other hooped vessel.

1587 *Sc. Acts Jas. VI* (1814) III. 522/1 That..þe edge of þe bottom, entring within the laggyne be pairit outwith, toward þe nethir syde. **1893** in *Northumbld. Gloss.*

b. = LAG *sb.*[2] 1. ? *Obs.*

1825 BROCKETT *N.C. Words*, *Laggins*, staves.

2. The inner angle of a wooden dish, between the sides and the bottom.

1786 BURNS *Dream* xv, But or the day was done, I trow, The laggen they hae clautet Fu' clean that day. **1802** R. ANDERSON *Cumberld. Ball.* 24 When on the teable furst they set The butter'd sops, sec greasy chops, 'Tween lug and laggen! oh what fun, To see them girn and eat!

transf. **1842** *Chr. Jrnl.* 309 The 'laggin' of the Sowen-pot.

3. *Comb.*: **laggen-gird**, a hoop securing the bottom of a tub or wooden vessel. Phr. ***to cast a laggen-gird***: to have an illegitimate child.

1718 RAMSAY *Christis Kirke Gr.* III. ix, I..coost a Legen-girth my sell, Lang or I married Tammie. **1821** *Blackw. Mag.* Jan. 406/2 Ye'll souk the laggin-gird off the quaigh, and mar yere minstrelsy and our mirth.

lagging (ˈlægɪŋ), *vbl. sb.*[1] [f. LAG *v.*[2] + -ING[1].] The action or condition of LAG *v.*[2]

1600 HOLLAND *Livy* VI. vii. 221 What meanes this strange and unwonted lagging behind? **1862** DANA *Man. Geol.* 41 The westward tropical flow is due simply to a slight lagging of the waters. **1867** DENISON *Astron. without Math.* 123 This is called the priming and lagging of the tides. **1897** *Allbutt's Syst. Med.* II. 915 Cardiac irregularity is a frequent consequence of tobacco-smoking, lagging and intermission being the earlier forms of it.

lagging (ˈlægɪŋ), *vbl. sb.*[2] [f. LAG *v.*[3] + -ING[1].] A sentence or term of imprisonment or penal servitude. Also *attrib.* (see quot. 1812).

1812 J. H. VAUX *Flash Dict.*, *Lagging matter*, any species of crime for which a person is liable on conviction to be transported... Speaking of a person likely to be transported they say lagging dues will be concerned. **1838** DICKENS *O. Twist* xliii, If they do [get fresh evidence], it's a case of lagging. **1844** *Port Phillip Patriot* 22 July 2/6, I remained with him five years after I served my 'lagging'.

lagging (ˈlægɪŋ), *vbl. sb.*[3] [f. LAG *v.*[4] + -ING[1].] The action of the vb. LAG[4].

1. The action of covering a boiler, an arch, a wall, etc., with strips of wood or felt.

1870 *Eng. Mech.* 11 Feb. 516/1 This may be..prevented by careful 'lagging' with non-conductors of heat. **1895** HATCH & CHALMERS *Gold Mines of Rand* vi. 121 Side lagging is seldom necessary after the first 50 to 100 feet.

attrib. **1884** *Leisure Hour* Sept. 531/2 The old engine-house was exchanged for part of the old lagging-shop.

2. *pl.* and *collect. sing.* The material with which this is done. Also *attrib.*

1851 *Pract. Mech. Jrnl.* III. 242 The boiler is covered with lagging and Russia sheet iron. **1867** 'BEN BRIERLEY' *Marlocks Merriton* 68 The fence (his own making) was but a rickety fabric of 'laggins', worn-out treadles [etc.]. **1869** *Lonsdale Gloss.*, *Laggins*, the part of the wooden frame work upon which the stones are laid when building an arch. **1870** *Spon's Dict. Engineering* II. 479 The term bolster has also been applied to the pieces of timber placed across the ribs of the centering of an arch to support the voussoirs; but these are more generally known by the name of laggings. **1881** RAYMOND *Mining Gloss.*, *Lagging*, planks, slabs, or small timber placed over the caps or behind the posts of the timbering.

lagging (ˈlægɪŋ), *ppl. a.* [f. LAG *v.*[2] + -ING[2].] That lags; behindhand, lingering, loitering, tardy.

1593 SHAKS. *Rich. II*, I. iii. 214 Foure lagging Winters, and foure wanton springs End in a word. **1655** FULLER *Ch. Hist.* v. i. §4 The lagging money which was last sent thither. **1697** DRYDEN *Virg. Past.* VIII. 25 Come, Lucifer, drive on the lagging Day. **1735** SOMERVILLE *Chase* I. 280 A lagging Line Of babling Curs [shall] disgrace thy broken Pack. **1813** SCOTT *Trierm.* III. xxxiii, A lofty lay Seem'd thus to chide his lagging way. **1832** HT. MARTINEAU *Demerara* i. 6 The slaves came with a lagging step. **1859** G. MEREDITH *R. Feverel* xxxiii, The eager woman hastened his lagging mouth.

Hence **ˈlaggingly** *adv.*

c **1817** HOGG *Tales & Sk.* III. 50 Moves heavily and laggingly along. **1872** LEVER *Ld. Kilgobbin* xxxvi. (1875) 210 Thoughts that came laggingly.

laggon, variant of LAGEN.

laggoose (ˈlæggu:s). **a.** (See GREY LAG GOOSE.) †**b.** ***Gill laggoose***: a personification of sloth.

1573 TUSSER *Husb.* lxxxv. (1878) 174 Beware of Gill laggoose, disordring thy house.

lagh(e, **laȝhe**, obs. forms of LAUGH, LAW, LOW.

laght, **laȝt**, obs. pa. t. of LATCH *v.*[1]

laghter, **-ir**, etc., obs. forms of LAUGHTER.

laghtnes, obs. form of LOWNESS.

ˈlag-ˌlast. [f. LAG *v.*[2] + LAST *adv.*] One who lags or lingers to the very last. Also *attrib.*

1830 JAMES *Darnley* ix. 41 He'll be lag last. **1851** *Fraser's Mag.* XLIII. 634 The laglasts, springing simultaneously out of bed, turned the late quiet dormitory into a very noisy assembly-room. **1862** CHR. ROSSETTI *Goblin Market*, etc. (1884) 84 One day in the country Is worth a day and a year Of the dusty, musty, lag-last fashion That days drone elsewhere. **1869** [see LAG *a.* 1 b].

†**ˈlagly**, *adv. Obs. rare*⁻⁰. [f. LAG *a.* + -LY[2].]

1611 FLORIO, 149 *Diretanamente*, lastly, lagly, behind all.

lagniappe (læˈnjæp). *U.S.* Also **lagnappe**, **lanyap**, **-yappe**. [Louisiana Fr., ad. Sp. *la ñapa*, in the same sense.] Something given over and above what is purchased, earned, etc., to make good measure or by way of gratuity.

1849 *Knickerbocker* XXXIV. 407/1 Ime sum pumpkins in that line; but he's a huckleberry above my persimmon, and right smart lanyope too, as them creole darkies say. **1883** 'MARK TWAIN' *Life on Mississippi* xliv. 402 We picked up one excellent word—a word worth travelling to New Orleans to get; a nice limber, expressive, handy word—'lagniappe'. They pronounce it lanny-*yap*. It is Spanish—so they said. **1884** G. W. CABLE *Creoles of Louisiana* xvi. (1885) 114 The pleasant institution of *ñapa*—the petty gratuity added, by the retailer, to anything bought—grew the pleasanter, drawn out into Gallicized *lagnappe*. **1936** W. FAULKNER *Absalom, Absalom!* viii. 338 As lagniappe to the revenge as it were. **1947** S. J. PERELMAN *Westward Ha!* (1949) vii. 84 Since the ship was calling there anyway, the trip would be pure lagniappe, an extra dash of stardust unforeseen in our program. **1958** M. MAYER *Madison Ave.* xiv. 217 Finally, as lagniappe, Nielsen told the company the extent of 'dealer push'. **1966** *New Yorker* 1 Oct. 186 This amusing architectural lagniappe. **1971** *N.Y. Times Bk. Rev.* 7/4 And, as lagniappe, they threw in a list of 'spurious words' the scholars had come upon in dictionaries. **1972** *New Yorker* 7 Oct. 15/2 (Advt.), 64 pieces of exquisite Limoges porcelain sculpture..with superb porcelain tiles to play on as lagniappe.

lagomorph (ˈlægəmɔ:f). *Zool.* [f. Gr. λαγώ-ς hare + μορφή form.] One of the *Lagomorpha*, a group of rodents of which the hares form one family. Hence **lagoˈmorphic** *a.*, having the form and structure of a hare.

1882 *Pop. Sci. Monthly* XX. 423 The lagomorphs (hares), almost exclusively of the northern hemisphere.

‖**lagomys** (ˈlægəmɪs). *Zool.* [mod.L., f. Gr. λαγώ-ς hare + μῦς mouse.] The tailless hare, the typical genus of the group *Lagomyidæ* of rodents.

1869 LUBBOCK *Preh. Times* ix. 297 The lagomys, or tailless hare,..had been identified by Prof. Owen among the bones from Kents Cavern.

lagon, obs. form of LAGAN.

lagonite (ˈlægənaɪt). *Min.* [f. It. *lagone* LAGOON *sb.*[2]; named by Huot, 1841: see -ITE.] A hydrous borate of iron from the Tuscan lagoons.

1850 DANA *Min.* 446 Lagonite. An earthy mineral of an ochreous yellow color. **1868** *Ibid.* (ed. 5) 600 Lagonite.. occurs as an incrustation.

lagoon (ləˈgu:n), *sb.*[1] Also 7–9 **lagune**, and 7–9 in It. form **laguna**, pl. **lagune**. [ad. F. *lagune*, ad. It. and Sp. *laguna* :—L. *lacūna* pool.]

1. An area of salt or brackish water separated from the sea by low sand-banks or a similar barrier, *esp.* one of those in the neighbourhood of Venice.

1612 in *Crt. & Times Jas. I* (1848) I. 184 He was observed that day to row to and fro in the laguna towards Murano, to see what show his house made. **1673** RAY *Journ. Low C.* 8 The *Lagune* or Flats about Venice. **1697** DAMPIER *Voyages* I. 241 They went into a Lagune, or Lake of Salt-water [on the Mexican coast]. The mouth of this Lagune is not Pistol-shot wide. **1716** *Lond. Gaz.* No. 5407/2 People..have come over the Lagune on the Ice. **1763** W. ROBERTS *Nat. Hist. Florida* 8 This river..forms a lagune at the mouth. **1789** MRS. PIOZZI *Journ. France* I. 187 Covering the lagoons with gaiety and splendour. **1803** W. TAYLOR in *Ann. Rev.* I. 32 The ornithorhynchus,..an animal peculiar to the lagoons in New South Wales. **1818** SHELLEY *Lett.* Pr. Wks. 1888 II. 237 He took me in his gondola across the laguna to a long sandy island. **1856** MRS. BROWNING *Aur. Leigh* VII. 715 God alone above each, as the sun O'er level lagunes. **1874** LYELL *Elem. Geol.* i. 4 'Lagoons' nearly separated by sand bars from the ocean. **1877** A. GEIKIE *Elem. Lessons Physical Geogr.* iv. 271 Lagoons along the sea-margin are for the most part shallow and narrow, running parallel with the coast, from which they are separated by a strip of low land formed of sand, gravel, or other loose material. **1883** F. M. PEARD *Contrad.* I. 1 Behind them and beyond the lagoons lay the tossing and flying waves of the Adriatic. **1939** W. H. TWENHOFEL *Princ. Sedimentation* xii. 455 The barrier separating a lagoon from its parent body may result from many causes, but under most conditions it is thrown up by the waves. **1952** W. SHEPHERD *Living Landscape Brit.* iii. 50 Two bays have been cut off from the sea by shingle. These now form a salt-water lagoon, and may slowly silt up to form a marsh. *Ibid.* 53 A line of rocks across the bay encloses a 'lagoon'. **1968** R. W. FAIRBRIDGE *Encycl. Geomorphol.* 590/2 The entrance of a lagoon is restricted by the narrow tidal inlets through the barrier islands and the complex of sand bars which form on both the lagoonal and seaward side of the inlet.

2. The lake-like stretch of water enclosed in an atoll. Also, the stretch of water inside a barrier reef.

1769 COOK *Jrnl.* 4 Apr. (1893) 55 Found it to be an Island ..of an Oval form, with a Lagoon in the Middle, for which I named it Lagoon Island. **1842** PRICHARD *Nat. Hist. Man* 326 Reefs of coral rock, generally disposed in a circular form, and enclosing a lagoon. **1848** M. SOMERVILLE *Physical Geogr.* I. xiv. 215 Encircling reefs differ in no respect from atoll reefs except that they have one or more islands in their lagoon. **1863** J. B. JUKES *School Man. Geol.* vi. 67 There are ..many islands in tropical seas in front of which coral reefs are found at a distance of many miles from the beach of the dry land, their outer edge being nearly dry at low tide, but plunging steeply down into fathomless water, while a broad navigable channel or lagoon..extends between this outer edge and the shore. These are called Barrier reefs. **1878** HUXLEY *Physiogr.* xv. (ed. 2) 254 Inside the rim of land, there is a shallow lake, or lagoon, of clear green water. **1928** W. M. DAVIS *Coral Reef Probl.* xi. 271, I made a circuit of the island on trading steamers, following the lagoon for the greater part of the way. **1959** *Chambers's Encycl.* IV. 121/1 Barrier reefs surround islands or lie off the mainland, with an intervening navigable channel or lagoon, the width of which may be many miles.

3. *Austral.* and *N.Z.* (See quots. 1849 and 1933.)

Adopted from Amer. Eng.: 1766– examples in *D.A.E.* in sense 'a shallow, fresh-water pond or lake, sometimes artificially formed and usually located near or connected with a lake, river, etc.'

1838 W. C. SYMONDS in *Jrnl. R. Geogr. Soc.* VIII. 422 On the S.E. coast at this island [*sc.* South Island] are several immense lagoons, into which flow rivers. **1844** *Nelson* (N.Z.) *Examiner* 7 Sept. 108/1 A lagoon..quite a lake in fact. **1849** F. WAKEFIELD *Colonial Surveying* II. 59 Lagoons differ from lakes in being generally formed by surface water gathering in low grounds during the winter, from which there is no outlet. **1927** M. M. BENNETT *Christison* iii. 37 At the back was a shallow lagoon. **1933** *Press* (Christchurch, N.Z.) 4 Nov. 15/7 *Lagoon*, any tarn, pond, or open water too small to be called a lake.

4. An artificial shallow pool used in the treatment and concentration of sewage and slurry.

1909 E. C. S. MOORE *Sanitary Engin.* (ed. 3) II. xviii. 691 Drying in lagoons is the system which is often adopted at works where sufficient land is available, and it is without doubt the least satisfactory method. **1926** G. M. FLOOD *Sewage Treatment & Disposal* x. 106 The sludge produced by any method of treatment may be pumped into lagoons in almost every case. **1975** *Daily Tel.* 9 Jan. 16/6 Sometimes 7,000 or 8,000 wading birds came..to the ash lagoons of West Thurrock power station.

5. *attrib.* and *Comb.*, as ***lagoon-channel***; **lagoon-island**, an atoll; **lagoon-whaling**, the occupation of hunting the grey-whale in the Californian lagoons (*Cent. Dict.*).

1845 DARWIN *Voy. Nat.* xx. (1852) 452 This is one of the lagoon-islands (or atolls) of coral formation. *Ibid.* 469 The depth within the Lagoon-channel..varies much.

Hence **laˈgoonish** *a.*, characterized by the presence of lagoons; **laˈgoonless** *a.*, having no lagoon.

1841 *Tait's Mag.* VIII. 348 The numerous creeks, islands, and inlets in this lagoonish..coast are minutely described. **1877** LE CONTE *Elem. Geol.* ii. (1879) 142 Sometimes the lagoon closes up, and a lagoonless island is the result.

lagoon (ləˈgu:n), *sb.*[2] *rare.* [Anglicized form (after LAGOON *sb.*[1]) of It. *lagone*, augmentative of *lago*:—L. *lacus* LAKE *sb.*[4]] In Tuscany, the basin of a hot spring from which borax is obtained.

1868 DANA *Min.* (ed. 5) 882 Larderellite..Occurs at the Tuscan lagoons. **1885** GEIKIE *Text-bk. Geol.* III. i. §2 (ed. 2) 218 The lagoons of Tuscany.

lagoon (ləˈgu:n), *v.* [f. the sb.] *trans.* To treat (by oxidation) in lagoons. So **laˈgooning** *vbl. sb.*

1911 G. B. KERSHAW *Mod. Methods Sewage Purification* xi. 155 (*heading*) Lagooning. **1922** H. E. BABBITT *Sewerage*

& *Sewage Treatment* xx. 495 The results of lagooning at Philadelphia are given in Table 103. **1935** METCALF & EDDY *Amer. Sewerage Pract.* (ed. 3) III. ii. 23 Odors from sludge lagooned at Houston were so objectionable that another method of sludge disposal was required. **1969** J. G. BRENNAN et al. *Food Engineering Operations* xvii. 380 Lagooning is extensively used for the treatment of cannery wastes. **1972** J. SKITT *Disposal of Refuse & Other Wastes* iii. 36 Do not lagoon the top layer.

lagoonal (lə'gu:nəl), *a.* [f. LAGOON *sb.*[1] + -AL.] Of or characteristic of a lagoon or lagoons.

1910 *Encycl. Brit.* IX. 663/2 Of the Gasteropod genera *Cerithium* with its estuarine and lagoonal forms *Potamides, Potamidopsis*, &c., is very characteristic. **1950** *New Biol.* VIII. 92 The earliest known birds were quite small, about the size of a crow, and are known from only two specimens ..; even these were preserved in an unique lagoonal environment. **1956** *Nature* 31 Mar. 607/2 The coral reef was not bottomed, the strata penetrated consisting entirely of fine detrital limestones.. originally deposited in lagoonal waters not less than 30 fathoms in depth. **1963** D. W. & E. E. HUMPHRIES tr. *Termier's Erosion & Sedimentation* ix. 192 The marine and lagoonal faunas of the Cretaceous in the Gulf of Guinea. **1971** I. G. GASS et al. *Understanding Earth* xii. 158/2 The reefs and lagoonal sediments which flourished during the Mesozoic and Tertiary periods. *Ibid.* 159/1 For the past 50 million years reefs have been very efficient structures leading to the formation of vast lagoonal areas.

‖**lagophthalmus** (,lægəf'θælməs). *Path.* [mod.L., ad. Gr. λαγώφθαλμος adj. 'hare-eyed' (i.e. unable to close the eyes, as the hare was supposed to be), f. λαγώς hare + ὀφθαλμός eye. The disease is called by Galen τὸ λαγώφθαλμον.] A morbid condition, in which the eye remains wide open. Also called ‖**lagoph'thalmia**, and in anglicized form † **lagoph'thalmy**.

Hence **lagoph'thalmic** *a.*, pertaining to, or affected with, lagophthalmus.

1657 *Physical Dict., Lagophthalmus.* **1656** BLOUNT, *Lagophthalmy.* **1676** COLES, *Lagophthalmia.* **1888** *Syd. Soc. Lex., Lagophthalmia, Lagophthalmic, Lagophthalmus.*

lagopode ('lægəpəud). [ad. Gr. λαγώποδ-, λαγώπους, f. λαγώ-ς hare + ποδ-, πούς foot.] A ptarmigan. (Cf. LAGOPUS.)

In some mod. Dicts.

lagopodous (lə'gɒpədəs), *a. Zool.* [f. as prec. + -OUS.] Having feet like those of a hare; having the foot thickly covered with feathers or fur.

1855 in MAYNE *Expos. Lex.*

lagopous (lə'gəupəs), *a. Bot.* [f. mod.L. *lagōp-us* (see LAGOPUS) + -OUS.] Of certain plants: Having rhizomes resembling a hare's foot.

In some mod. Dicts.

† **la'gopus.** *Obs.* [a. L. *lagōpūs*, Gr. λαγώπους, f. λαγώς hare + πούς foot.] A bird with a foot resembling that of a hare; the ptarmigan.

1693 SIR T. P. BLOUNT *Nat. Hist.* 385 Some.. Birds.. live upon the highest tops of the Alps, and that all the winter too .. as.. the Lagopus among birds. **1773** BARRINGTON in *Phil. Trans.* LXIII. 224 The Lagopus, of which M. de Buffon gives an engraving, is in its winter plumage.

lagotic (lə'gəutɪk), *a.* [f. Gr. λαγώ-ς hare + ὠτ-, οὖς ear + -IC.] Having ears like a hare's.

In some mod. Dicts.

Lagrange (‖lagrɑ̃ʒ, lə'grɒndʒ). The name of Joseph Louis *Lagrange* (1736–1813), the Italian-born mathematician who worked in Prussia and France, used *attrib.* and in the possessive to designate various concepts introduced by him or arising out of his work, as **Lagrange('s) equation**, each of a set of equations of motion in classical dynamics relating the total kinetic energy T of a system to a set of generalized co-ordinates q_r and forces Q_r, and to the time t, and having the form $d(\partial T/\partial \dot{q}_r)/dt - \partial T/\partial q_r = Q_r$. (In many contexts interchangeable with *Lagrangian.*)

1858 *Rep. Brit. Assoc. Adv. Sci. 1857* I. 12 The force function U is independent of the differential coefficients η', .. and, consequently, of the variables ω,.., hence, writing H = T − U, the equations take the form $d\eta/dt = d\mathrm{H}/d\omega$, $d\omega/dt = -d\mathrm{H}/d\eta$,.. which correspond to the condensed form obtained by writing T − V = R in Lagrange's equations. **1902** *Encycl. Brit.* XXVII. 568/1 Hence the typical Lagrange's equation may be now written in the form $d(\partial\mathrm{T}/\partial\dot{q}_r)/dt - \partial\mathrm{T}/\partial q_r = -\partial\mathrm{V}/\partial q_r$, or, again, $\dot{p}_r = -\partial(\mathrm{V} - \mathrm{T})/\partial q_r$. *Ibid.*, A classical example of the application of Lagrange's equations is to the motion of a top. **1942** SYNGE & GRIFFITH *Princ. Mech.* xv. 453 Two features of Lagrange's equations should be emphasized. First, there is no unique set of generalized coordinates; however we choose them, the equations of motion always have the form (15.215). Secondly, since only working forces contribute to δW, reactions of constraint are automatically eliminated. [*Note*] Except where forces of friction do work. **1958** CONDON & ODISHAW *Handbk. Physics* v. ii. 18/1 If the total number of systems is N, $\Sigma n_j = N$ $\Sigma n_j E_j = E$... Using the method of Lagrange multipliers, introduce multipliers β and λ and find the set of n_j's which make $\delta[\log P - \lambda(N - \Sigma n_j) + \beta(E - \Sigma n_j E_j)] = 0$. **1962** J. RIORDAN *Stochastic Service Syst.* iv. 66, $g(y)e^{-g(y)} = y$. The solution of this, obtained by Lagrange expansion, is $g(y) = \sum_{n=1} (n^{n-1}y^n)/n!$ **1967** M. G. SMITH *Introd. Theory Partial Differential Equations* i. 3 Comparing (1.2.8) and (1.2.9) we have the Lagrange equations $\dot{p}_k = \partial L/\partial q_k$ and $p_k = \partial L/\partial \dot{q}_k$.

Lagrangian (‖lagrɑ̃ʒɪən, lə'grɒndʒɪən), *a.* and *sb. Math.* Also **lagrangian, Lagrangean.** [f. prec. + -IAN, -AN.]

A. *adj.* Of or pertaining to the work of J. L. Lagrange (see prec.); of the kind introduced by Lagrange or associated with his work; *spec.* applied to (*a*) *Lagrange('s) equation*; (*b*) the difference between the kinetic energy and the potential energy of a system expressed as a function of generalized co-ordinates, their time derivatives, and time. (In many contexts interchangeable with *Lagrange('s)*.)

1858 A. CAYLEY in *Rep. Brit. Assoc. Adv. Sci. 1857* I. 2 The above-mentioned form is *par excellence* the Lagrangian form of the equations of motion, and the one which has given rise to almost all the ulterior developments of the theory. *Ibid.* 15 When there is no force function.. the forms corresponding to the untransformed forms in T and U are as follows, viz. the Lagrangian form is $dq/dt = q'$, $d(d\mathrm{T}/dq')/dt - d\mathrm{T}/dq = \mathrm{Q}$, and the Hamiltonian form is $dq/dt = d\mathrm{T}/dp$, $dp/dt = -d\mathrm{T}/dq + \mathrm{Q}$. **1870** *Rep. Brit. Assoc. Adv. Sci. 1869* II. 10 Equations of motion in the Lagrangean form. **1882** Lagrangian method [see EULERIAN *a.*]. **1904** E. T. WHITTAKER *Treat. Analytical Dynamics* ii. 38 If we introduce a new function L of the variables $q_1, q_2, \ldots q_n, \dot{q}_1, \ldots \dot{q}_n$, t, defined by the equation $L = T - V$, then Lagrange's equations can be written $d(\partial L/\partial \dot{q}_r)/dt - \partial L/\partial q_r = 0$ $(r = 1, 2, \ldots n)$. The function L is called the Kinetic Potential, or Lagrangian function; this single function completely specifies, so far as dynamical investigations are concerned, a holonomic system for which the forces are conservative. **1908** J. H. JEANS *Math. Theory Electr. & Magn.* xvi. 484 The Lagrangian equation corresponding to the coordinate r is found to be.. $d(\partial T/\partial \dot{r})/dt - \partial(T - w)/\partial r = R$. *Ibid.* 486 Let Q be the charge on the positive plate at any instant, and let this be taken as a Lagrangian coordinate. **1949** *Math. Tables & Other Aids to Computation* III. 466 Tables of 4-point and 6-point Lagrangean interpolation coefficients. **1954** D. TER HAAR *Elem. Statistical Mech.* 445 The values of the x_i for which f is [an] extremum while equations (MA4.01) are satisfied can be determined from the equations

$$\frac{\partial f}{\partial x_i} + \sum_{j=1}^{p} \lambda_i \frac{\partial g_j}{\partial x_i} = 0, \quad i = 1, \ldots, n.$$

The x_i are now functions of the λ_j, but these quantities, which are called the undetermined multipliers or the Lagrangian multipliers, can be eliminated by substituting for the x_i into equations (MA4.01) and solving for the λ_j. **1957** L. FOX *Numerical Solution Two-Point Boundary Probl.* ii. 31 Lagrangian [interpolation] formulae.. may be defined as formulae in which all significant differences have been replaced by pivotal values. **1964** *Oceanogr. & Marine Biol.* II. 14 The velocity along a particular trajectory varied more slowly than one would expect from the variability between one trajectory and another, suggesting that the Lagrangian scale of motion was noticeably larger than the Eulerian scale.

B. *sb.* The Lagrangian function (see (*b*) above).

1938 R. C. TOLMAN *Princ. Statistical Mech.* ii. 22 For more complicated mechanical systems, or even non-mechanical ones, suitable choices of the Lagrangian may be possible which will make Hamilton's principle still applicable. **1961** J. THEWLIS et al. *Encycl. Dict. Physics* II. 99/2 This function, called the Lagrangian of the given mechanical system, contains everything for the unique determination of the motion of the system, provided that we know its initial position and velocity. **1964** E. A. POWER *Introd. Quantum Electrodynamics* ix. 129 Then for the interaction with the electromagnetic field the substitution **p** → **p** − (*e*/*c*)**A**, $i\hbar\partial/\partial t \to i\hbar\partial/\partial t - e\phi$ is made in the Lagrangian of the free electron according to the principle of minimal electromagnetic coupling. **1973** *Physics Bull.* Mar. 183/3 Nonlinear lagrangians.

‖**lagre** (lɑgr). [Fr.] In sheet-glass making: A sheet of perfectly smooth glass, placed between the flattening stone and the cylinder to be flattened.

1883 H. CHANCE *Princ. Glassmaking* 129 The flattening-stone, from the slight irregularities of whose surface it is protected by a lagre or sheet of glass laid upon the stone. **1890** W. J. GORDON *Foundry* 148 In his furnace is a stone with a piece of glass on it; upon this so-called 'lagre' the cylinder lies with its split side uppermost.

lagting ('lɑ:gtɪŋ). Also **lagthing.** [Norw. Cf. LAWTING.] **1.** A functional division of the Norwegian Parliament, operating primarily for law-making purposes.

1836 S. LAING *Jrnl. Residence Norway* xi. 456 The Storthing then proceeds to elect what is equivalent to our House of Peers, the Lagthing, or division in which the deliberative functions of the legislative body are invested. *Ibid.*, The functions of the Lagthing are not exactly the same as those of our House of Lords... It can only receive bills from the other house, the Odelsthing; deliberate.. and approve or reject. **1927** *Glasgow Herald* 21 Mar. 13 The Bill is now going up to the Lagting. **1957** *Encycl. Brit.* XVI. 556/1 After the opening, parliament divides itself into two sections, the *lagting* consisting of 38 members and the *odelsting* of the remainder. **1974** *Whitaker's Almanack 1975* 918/1 The *Storting* (Parliament) itself elects one-quarter of its members to constitute the *Lagting* (Upper Chamber).

2. Also **Løgting.** [Faroese *Løgting.*] The Provincial Parliament of the Faeröe Isles.

1948 K. WILLIAMSON *Atlantic Islands* iv. 104 The Løgting imposes a small money tax on every whale.. caught. **1961** *Denmark* (Danish Ministry for Foreign Affairs) 136 Under the Home Rule Act of March 27, 1948, the publicly elected Faroese assembly, the Lagting or Løgting, has legislative powers in various fields. **1972** J. F. WEST *Faroe* x. 199 The members of the government may address the Løgting, but they may not vote unless they are elected members.

lagune, variant of LAGOON *sb.*[1]

lagwort ('lægwɜ:t). [f. LAG *v.*[2] + WORT.] The plant *Petasites Vulgaris* (Britten & Holland).

1702 in J. K. *Dict.* **1725** BRADLEY *Fam. Dict.* s.v. *Syrup*, The Roots of Lagwort, Elicampane, Smallage and Fennel.

lahar ('lɑ:hɑ:(r)). [Javanese.] A mud-flow of volcanic ash mixed with water.

1929 *Geol. Mag.* LXVI. 433 (*heading*) The mudstreams ('lahars') of Gunong Keloet in Java. **1944** C. A. COTTON *Volcanoes* xiii. 247 Lahars follow mainly channels already existing, filling them temporarily to the brim with rushing torrents but leaving them empty again and eventually depositing their loads of debris on low ground many miles beyond. **1954** W. D. THORNBURY *Princ. Geomorphol.* xix. 497 A lahar that accompanied an eruption of the volcano Galunggung, in Java, in 1822, spread over 114 villages. **1972** *Science* 9 June 1119/1 The site of the eastern spillway is now covered by lahar deposits.

Hence **laharic** (lɑ:'hɑ:rɪk) *a.*, of or pertaining to a lahar.

1968 *Mem. Geol. Soc. Amer.* CXVI. 472 Approximately 300 cubic miles of laharic debris came from the source areas.

lahe(n, lahȝenn, obs. forms of LAUGH *v.*

Lahnda ('lɑ:ndə). Also **Lahndi.** [Punjabi, 'western' (see quot. 1907).] An Indo-Aryan language spoken in the western Punjab. Also *attrib.* or as *adj.*

1903 RISLEY & GAIT *Rep. Census India 1901* I. 311 Lahndā is a language the existence of which has long been recognized, but under many names. In the last Census Report it was called Jatkī... I therefore think it best to give it the name which is indicated by the natives of the Punjab themselves, i.e. Lahndā or the Language of the West (Panjabi *Lahndē-di Bōlī*). **1907** G. A. GRIERSON in *Imperial Gazetteer India* I. vii. 371 Lahndā or Western Panjābī is a language which appears under many names, such as Pothwārī, Chibhālī, Jatkī, Mūltānī, or Hindko... Lahndā, i.e. 'Western', has been lately suggested, and has been tentatively adopted, although it.. is far from satisfactory. **1911** *Encycl. Brit.* XVI. 80/2 *Lahnda* (properly *Lahndā* or *Lahindā*, western, or *Lahndē-dī bōlī*, the language of the West), an Indo-Aryan language spoken in the western Punjab... Lahnda is also known as Western Panjabi and as Jatki, or the language of the Jats, who form the bulk of the population whose mother-tongue it is. **1948** D. DIRINGER *Alphabet* vi. 376 Kashtawari, which is a dialect of Kashmiri .., but is much influenced by the Pahari and Lahnda languages, spoken by its southern and south-eastern neighbours. **1967** D. S. PARLETT *Short Dict. Lang.* 76 *Lahnda*... Closely related to Punjabi proper, with some features associated with the contiguous Dardic dialects.

laht, pa. t. and pa. pple. of LATCH *v.*[1]

† **lahter.** *Obs.* Forms: 1 leahter, 2 lehter, 3 leihter. [OE. *leahter*, f. OTeut. **lahan* (OE. *léan*) to blame.] A vice, sin, crime.

*c***900** tr. *Bæda's Hist.* III. xi. [xiii.] (1890) 190 Ic ma synnum & leahtrum þeowde, þonne Godes bebodum. **971** *Blickl. Hom.* 163 Ne hie nænіȝ leahter ne drefde. *a***1175** *Cott. Hom.* 243 In þes deofles heriscole fihteð agen us his iferred ȝewerȝed gastes, and unþeawes and unwraste lahtres. *c***1200** *Trin. Coll. Hom.* 79 Ðe fule lehtres him holden bunden on here þralshipe. *a***1225** *Ancr. R.* 156 Non empti stude iðe heorte to underuongen flesliche leihtren.

lahter, obs. form of LAUGHTER.

lai[1] (leɪ). [OFr. (see LAY *sb.*[4]).] **a.** One of a number of short narrative poems written either in French or in English in England between the twelfth and the fifteenth centuries, of a Celtic type and concerned with love, magic, and music. Often called ***Breton lais.*** **b.** A medieval French lyric associated with the *trouvères* of Northern France.

1774 T. WARTON *Hist. Eng. Poetry* I. Diss. I. sig. a2 At the conclusion of most of the tales it is said that these Lais were made by the poets of Bretaigne. **1824** R. PRICE in T. Warton *Hist. Eng. Poetry* II. 430 But Marie's was not the only Collection of British Lais, in French. **1838** E. GUEST *Hist. Eng. Rhythms* II. 103 The 'short measures' of Skelton.. may perhaps be looked upon as the *direct* descendants of the Anglo-Saxon rhythms, though it must be confessed they much resemble, in their flow, the *lais* and *virelais* of the fifteenth century. **1855** H. H. MILMAN *Hist. Latin Christianity* VI. vii. 547 Slighter pieces which may call to mind the Lais and Serventes of the South. **1865** T. TAYLOR tr. *Hersart de la Villemarqué's Ballads & Songs of Brittany* 125 A *lai* by a northern *trouvère* on the same subject was discovered by M. de Fréminville, in the Bibliothèque du Roi. **1883** H. KENNEDY tr. *B. ten Brink's Hist. Eng. Lit.* I. II. 179 The Breton *lais* retain most fully their native fragrance. They are usually romantic even when the topic is comic... The poem is often pervaded by a tone of elegiac longing. **1905** E. RICKERT in *Mod. Philol.* II. 376 The fresh literary impulse that came with the Normans found little to do with the old Saxon heroes. A few tales were transformed into the *lai* or *chanson de geste* or *roman d'aventure*—*Havelock, Horn, Guy of Warwick, Bevis of Hampton.* **1906** [see CONTE b]. **1907** ST. J. LUCAS in *Oxf. Bk. French Verse* p. vii, Various other kinds of lyric poetry begin to appear at the end of the twelfth century, *motets*,.. *rondeaux*, *lais*, *ballettes* and *virelais.* **1923** J. VISING *Anglo-Norman Lang. & Lit.* 47 Breton lais in England are mentioned in *Roman de Renard.* **1925** A. BELL *Le Lai d'Haveloc* 26 There is, however, not only a general connection with the 'lais' but also a special one with those of Marie. **1929** [see CONTE b]. **1932** *Oxf. Hist. Music* (ed. 2) II. II. v. 285 The initial stanzas of two trouvères *lais* are written on the melody of 'Ave gloriosa virginum regina'. *Ibid.* 286 On the other side the *lai* is

related to the *chanson de geste* and to the other popular songs of the time, to which many of the anonymous *lais* show some resemblance. **1940** *Grove's Dict. Mus.* (ed. 4) III. 269/1 The *lais* (long lyrical poems written in twelve pairs of stanzas, each pair having a different metrical form and a different melody from the rest, except the last pair, which repeats metre and melody of the first) are all set to one musical part only. **1954** [see CONTE b]. **1965** R. S. LOOMIS in Bessinger & Creed *Medieval & Ling. Stud.* 237 We possess three Breton *lais*: *Doon*, *Desiré*, and *Gurun*..which evince some knowledge of Scottish geography.

Lai^2 (laɪ). [Local name.] A Mongoloid people living in the Chin hills of Burma; a member of this people; also, the language spoken by this people. Also *attrib.* or as *adj.*

1896 CAREY & TUCK *Chin Hills* I. I. i. 3 The Northern Chins call themselves Yo, the Tashons, Haka, and more southern tribes Lai. *Ibid.* iii. 23 The Hakas call themselves Lai, and Yo is the general name by which the Chins call their race. *Ibid.* xiv. 152 The clans which claim the title of Lais are the Hakas, Klang-klangs, Yokwas... The first two are universally acknowledged as Lais, and refuse to admit that the others belong to their race. **1897** A. G. E. NEWLAND *Pract. Hand-bk. Lang. Lais* 1 The *Lais* are the great tribe and its offshoots that occupy the Chin Hills... The language of these people is the *Lai* language, called by the Burmese *Baungshè*, by which term we have hitherto known it. Dialects of it are spoken by all the surrounding tribes, but nearly all understand the *Lai* tongue. *Ibid.* 3 Unlike the Southern Chin language, it will be found that the consonants 'f' and 'r' are both used in the *Lai* speech. **1906** J. G. SCOTT *Burma* I. 106 The Tashôn tribe is..the most numerous, and next to them come the Hakas, also called the Lai... Lai is said to be likely to become the *lingua franca* of the Chin Hills. **1924** C. M. ENRIQUEZ *Races Burma* iii. 15 The Haka (a group of about ten villages including the parent village) claim to be the only true Lai. *Ibid.* vii. 43 The Lai tribes are controlled..by Chiefs. **1963** F. K. LEHMAN *Struct. Chin Soc.* i. 30 The Haka villagers call themselves *lai*, thinking of themselves as better than their cultural near relations to the South.

lai, obs. f. LAY *sb.* and *v.*, and of *lay*, pa. t. LIE.

laic (ˈleɪɪk), *a.* and *sb.* Forms: 6–7 laik(e, (7 laycke), 7–8 layick(e, 7–9 laick(e, 6– laic. [ad. late L. *lāicus*, Gr. λᾱϊκός, f. λᾱός the people. Cf. OF. *laic*, *laique*.]

A. *adj.* Of or pertaining to a layman or the laity; non-clerical, secular, temporal; = LAY *a.*

1562 WINȜET (*title*) The last Blast of the Trompet of Godis worde..Put furth..At the desyre of ye inferiour ordoure of Clergie, and laic men. **1596** DALRYMPLE tr. *Leslie's Hist. Scot.* I. 105 *marg.*, Thrie ordouris of the Realme, Ecclesiastik, Nobilitie, and the laik sorte. **1626** MEADE in Ellis *Orig. Lett.* Ser. I. III. 220 It understands the King not to be merely laic, but a mixed person. **1634** SIR T. HERBERT *Trav.* 86 A well voiced boy from the..top of their Churches sings Eulogies to Mahomet..and then each Laycke Pagan fals to devotion. **1662** J. BARGRAVE *Pope Alex. VII* (1867) 38 To avoid the appearance at a laic King's court. **1736** CHANDLER *Hist. Persec.* 10 The prosecution [of Socrates] was truly laick. **1821** LAMB *Elia* Ser. I. *Imperf. Sympathies*, A kind of secondary or laic-truth is tolerated, where clergy-truth—oath-truth, by the nature of the circumstances, is not required. **1861** TULLOCH *Eng. Purit.* ii. 291 The common life, clerical and laic, is of a very coarse kind.

B. *sb.* One of the laity; a layman or lay person; one who is not an ecclesiastic.

1596 DALRYMPLE tr. *Leslie's Hist. Scot.* x. 297 He sendis messingeris..with the fyre crose in thair handes,..sulde shaw it out to al man baith laikis and kirkmen. **1609** BP. HALL *Disswas. fr. Poperie* Wks. (1627) 642 How wretchedly and fearefully must their poore layicks needs die! **1660** R. COKE *Power & Subj.* 167 If he be a Laick, he shall be excommunicated from every Christian thing. **1739** J. TRAPP *Right. overmuch* 10 For unletter'd Laics to take upon them to expound or interpret the Scriptures. **1787** SIR J. HAWKINS *Johnson* 261 The clergyman was now become an amphibious being, that is to say, both an ecclesiastic and a laic. **1823** LINGARD *Hist. Eng.* VI. 245 A committee of thirty-two members, half laics and half clergymen. **1847** BUSHNELL *Chr. Nurt.* iv. (1861) 114 No person, whether laic or priest. **1884** TENNYSON *Becket* I. i, Laics and barons, thro' The random gifts of careless kings, have graspt Her livings.

laic, variant of LAKE *sb.*^{2} *Obs.*, play.

laical (ˈleɪɪkəl), *a.* Also 6 lai-, laycall. [f. as prec. + -AL^1.] = prec. Also *occas.*, non-professional.

[**1290** *Rolls of Parlt.* I. 60/2 Exactionibus..per quas plus extorquent de populo quam omnes Cur' laycales.] **1563–87** FOXE *A. & M.* (1596) 1050/1 The distinction used to be made betweene the priestes communion and the laicall communion. **1596** BELL *Surv. Popery* III. x. 408 The faithful laycall people. **1656** in BLOUNT *Glossogr.* **1704** NELSON *Fest. & Fasts* x. (1739) 603 The Canon Law..declares that every Laical Person who..shall take a Bribe for a Presentation..shall be excommunicated. **1818** LADY MORGAN *Autobiog.* (1859) 106 This religious house..is almost laical. **1822–34** *Good's Study Med.* (ed. 4) I. 557 No complaint is so common as fever; none in which mankind, whether professional or laical, are so little likely to be mistaken. **1864** LOWELL *Fireside Trav.* 175 A phrase commonly indicated in laical literature by the same sign which serves for Doctorate in Divinity. **1886** *Athenæum* 17 July 79/2 The special circumstances of Dulwich make its headmastership one more laical..than that of other leading schools.

absol. **1605** CAMDEN *Rem.*, *Wise Sp.* 180 In all ages the Clericall will flatter, as well [as] the Laicall.

Hence **laiˈcality**, the state or condition of a layman; **ˈlaically** *adv.*, in a laical manner; after the manner of a layman.

In mod. dicts.

laicity (leɪˈɪsɪtɪ). [f. LAIC *a.* and *sb.* + -ITY.] The principles of the laity; the rule or influence of the laity; the fact of being lay; also *attrib.*

1909 WEBSTER, *Laicity*, laicality. **1925** *Brit. Weekly* 19 Mar. 587/3 The text of the document, which is directed against the 'laicity laws', lies before us. **1928** *Daily Tel.* 30 Oct. 12/3 Accused by his own hotheads of betraying the cause of 'laicity' by acquiescing in these details of the Budget. **1939** A. TOYNBEE *Study of Hist.* VI. 20 This laicity of the Gods was taken so much in earnest that in a Mahayanian sutra a chapter..is formally addressed to the Gods, as a hint that it is an *œuvre de vulgarisation.*

laicization (ˌleɪɪsaɪˈzeɪʃən). [f. next + -ATION. Cf. F. *laïcisation.*] The action or process of rendering lay or subjecting to lay control.

1881 *Sat. Rev.* 9 July 37/2 The example of England was frequently quoted in support of this process of 'laicization'. **1884** *Ch. Times* 13 June 445/3 There is one reform which we desire to see carried out..that is what we may call the laicisation of the parish churches. **1889** *Times* 5 Jan. 5/3 The laicization of the hospitals has provoked, and still provokes, extreme irritation. **1896** *Speaker* 25 July 102/2 The laicisation of elementary education may easily be exaggerated.

laicize (ˈleɪɪsaɪz), *v.* Also -ise. [f. LAIC *a.* + -IZE. Cf. F. *laïciser.*] *trans.* To make lay; to deprive of a clerical character; to secularize, *esp.* to commit (a school, etc.) to the direction of laymen; to make (an office) tenable by laymen.

1870 *Nonconformist* 30 Nov. 1133 A measure tending..to laicise..the constitution and government of the Universities. **1882** *Q. Rev.* Oct. 491 Clerical fellowships have been extinguished, and the Headships of Houses laicised. **1885** *Pall Mall G.* 16 June 3/2 The proposal to laicize the names of the Paris streets, and banish therefrom the word 'Sainte'. **1896** *Edin. Rev.* July 211 It is competent for the authority to laicise a public school.

Hence **ˈlaicizing** *vbl. sb.* and *ppl. a.* Also **ˈlaicizer**, one who laicizes. **ˈlaicism** (see quot. 1796).

1796 *Hist.* in *Ann. Reg.* 185 This occasional exercise of the priestly function was denominated laicism, and represented as sacrilegious usurpation of the sacerdotal rights. **1884** *Athenæum* 19 July 79/3 The laicizing of the staff of masters. **1890** *Ch. Rev.* 22 Aug., First we had the laicising of the dons, then the marrying of the fellows. **1891** *Tablet* 2 May 691 In five years the laicisers have squandered 15 millions of francs. **1893** *Nation* (N.Y.) 24 Aug. 133/3 Certain laicizing Catholics. **1897** DOWDEN *Fr. Lit.* 73 Whether it had its origin in a laicising of the irreverent celebration of the Feast of Fools. **1931** *Economist* 4 July 13/1 The political antagonisms which the Spanish Revolution has let loose: the issues of Republicanism versus Monarchism, Syndicalism versus Capitalism, and Laicism versus Clericalism. **1966** *Ibid.* 11 June 1178/2 Their priests, many of whom equate laicism with socialism, have been outraged by its [*sc.* the government's] plans to modify the present confessional structure of education.

laid (leɪd), *ppl. a.* [pa. pple. of LAY *v.*]

a. In various senses of the vb. †Of a design: Deliberately framed. **laid drain** (see quot. 1811); **laid paper** (see quot. 1839); **laid wool**, tarry wool; **laid-work** (see COUCHING *vbl. sb.* 2, quot. 1884). (Cf. *best-laid*, NEW-LAID.)

a **1547** SURREY *Æn.* II. 954 My shoulders broad, and laied neck [L. *subjectaque colla*] with garments gan I spread. **1634** J. TAYLOR *Needles Excellency* (ed. 10) sig. A2 For Tent-worke, Raisd-worke, Laid-worke, Frost-worke. **1697** in Perry *Hist. Coll. Amer. Col. Ch.* I. 46 A laid designe to obstruct..the business..of the College. **1720** OZELL tr. *Vertot's Rom. Rep.* I. III. 169 There seemed to be a laid Design of making away with all the Senators. **1733** BERKELEY *Vind. Theory Vision* § 5 Wks. 1871 I. 374, I think one may observe a laid design gradually to undermine the belief of the Divine Attributes and Natural Religion. **1790** GROSE *Prov. Gloss.* (ed. 2), *Laid*, just frozen. When water is slightly frozen, it is said to be *laid.* Norf. **1805** SOUTHEY *Ballads*, etc. Poet. Wks. VI. 266 The Old Dragon's own laid egg was this. **1805** FORSYTH *Beauties Scotl.* II. 127, 25½ lb. of what is called *laid* wool to the stone. **1811** G. S. KEITH *Agric. Surv. Aberd.* 426 It is generally found advisable to use a *laid drain*, i.e. a row of stones laid on each side,..and a course of flat stones laid above these. **1818** J. HASSELL *Rides & Walks* II. 106 Mr. Staines manufactures wove drawing papers and laid writing ones. **1825** J. NICHOLSON *Operat. Mechanic* 373 Observing that the laid wires should be parallel with the axis. **1839** URE *Dict. Arts* 927 A strong raised wire is laid along each of the cross bars [of the mould] to which the other wires are fastened; this gives the laid paper its ribbed appearance. **1860** GEO. ELIOT *Let.* 27–28 Aug. (1954) III. 337 It is piteous to see the laid corn, and then hear the rain pouring in the still night! **1865** F. B. PALLISER *Hist. Lace* xxiii. 275 Then there is..true stitch, laid-work,..and cut-work. **1880** *Paper & Printing Trades Jrnl.* xxx. 8 The thick cream laid paper on which this work is printed. **1886** *Pall Mall G.* 28 July 6/1 There are many good standing pieces [of wheat]..A laid crop being quite a rarity, except in some of the fens. **1900** *Westm. Gaz.* 10 July 10/1 Harvest labour..is..much greater for laid fields than for good standing crops. **1960** [see *brick-stitch* (BRICK *sb.*^{1} 10)]. **1971** *Country Life* 10 June 1440/2 Reaping a small field of badly laid corn with sickles and reaping hooks.

b. of rope, with some defining word prefixed, as *cable-*, *hawser-*, *short-*, *slack-*, *soft-*, *twice-laid*, for which see the first member.

c. with adverbs, as *by* (cf. LAY *v.*^{1} 50 f), *down*, *off* (cf. LAY *v.*^{1} 54 f), *on*, *out*, *up*; † *laid in* = 'inlaid'. Also, *laid-back*, inclined backwards; as *fig.*, relaxed.

1598 *Inv.* in Willis & Clark *Cambridge* (1886) III. 325 A..bedsteade of walnuttree varnished vpon layd in woorke. **1769** FALCONER *Dict. Marine* (1780), *Laid-up*, the situation of a ship when she is either moored in a harbour during the winter-season, or laid by, for want of employment: or when by age and craziness she is rendered incapable of further service. **1827** STEUART *Planter's G.* (1828) 390 An ill laid-out place..is, generally speaking, the work of the owner. **1851** GREENWELL *Coal-trade Terms Northumb. & Durh.* 34 A laid out tub of coals is a tub of coals containing stones or foul coal beyond a certain specified quantity, usually one quart. **1852** C. W. H[OSKINS] *Talpa* 60 However good in their way broad principles, and laid down courses of cropping or of treatment may be. **1868** Laid-off [see LAY *v.*^{1} 54 f]. *a* **1877** KNIGHT *Dict. Mech.* II. 1246/1 *Laid-on* (Joinery), a term applied to moldings which are got out in strips and nailed on to the surface of the object. **1882** DE WINDT *Equator* 22 In the midst of beautifully laid-out gardens, is the..Palace of the Raja. **1906** *Westm. Gaz.* 9 June 16/3 The Valenciennes running around the laid-on tucks surrounding the skirt. **1908** *Ibid.* 23 Dec. 4/1 To get in under the ball you must have a shallow head..or else a very much laid-back face. **1909** *Ibid.* 30 Apr. 4/2 You can take a laid-back club and loft right over it. **1932** W. FAULKNER *Light in August* xviii. 394 Any man could look at him and perhaps recognise him: Byron Bunch, that weeded another man's laidby crop, without any halvers. **1934** *Archit. Rev.* LXXVI. 13 Central heating, lighting, cooking, vacuum cleaning, laid-on water and drainage. **1943** HUNT & PRINGLE *Service Slang* 43 *Laid on*, confirming that transport and supplies are available, that men are on the spot, and, in short, that everything is ready for action. **1955** *Times* 31 May 5/3 The union proposed that the guaranteed level of pay for 'laid off', meaning temporarily unemployed, workers, should be 80 per cent. of gross pay rather than 100 per cent. of take-home pay as originally proposed. **1960** *Farmer & Stockbreeder* 15 Mar. 75/3 The appeal of zero-grazing is that it requires no fencing, no laid-on water, but maintains fertility. **1967** *Guardian* 26 July 10/7 A group of laid-on Turkish peasants in costume, dancing a jig. **1970** *Daily Tel.* 11 Sept. 6/2 Laid-off workers at Coventry are receiving..£5 unemployment benefit. **1973** *Melody Maker* 28 July 36/2 This hit-writer of the early 60s came out with a highly contemporary style which fitted the fashionable term 'laid-back', and her 'Tapestry' album zoomed up to become one of the three biggest-selling LPs of all time. **1974** *New Society* 7 Mar. 589/3 It's all cheerfully grotty and relaxed in the usual laid-back Montreal style.

laid(e, Sc. and north. form of LOAD *sb.*

laidly (ˈleɪdlɪ), *a.* Now *Sc.* and *arch.* (with allusion to ballad use). Also 4 laithly, 5 lathely, 6 laithlie, 7, 9 laidlie, 8 laily. [Northern var. of LOATHLY.] Offensive, hideous, repulsive.

a **1300** *Cursor M.* 2406 (Gött.) Sore i me drede, þar we wend bi þis laithly lede. *a* **1400–50** *Alexander* 491 He..Lete sa lathely a late. **1513** DOUGLAS *Æneis* IV. viii. 100 Wynis gude Anon returnit into laithlie blude. **1567** *Gude & Godly Ball.* (S.T.S.) 40 Lickand the fylth furth of his laithlie flesche. *a* **1605** POLWART *Flyting w. Montgomerie* 132 With laidlie language, loud and large. *a* **1800** *Laily Worm & Machrel* ii. in Child *Ballads* (1884) I. 316/1 She has made me the laily worm, That lies at the fit o the Tree. **1843** *Blackw. Mag.* LIII. 177 When first the destrier eyed The laidly thing, it swerved aside. **1849** LYTTON *K. Arthur* VI. lxvi, The laidliest widows find consoling mates. **1878** *19th Cent.* 992 Her laidly wooer, whose income was better than his looks. **1884** *Q. Rev.* Apr. 326 Long black boats, outriggered, and manned, as one might think, by a lot of overgrown black spiders, so long, so lank, so 'laidlie' are the crew.

laid-sterne, obs. form of LOADSTAR.

†**laidure.** *Obs.* [a. F. *laideur*, f. *laid* ugly.] Ugliness, deformity.

1483 CAXTON *Gold. Leg.* 431 b/1, I wold fayne susteyn on my lyppes suche laydure or shame as long as I shal lyue soo that alle the euyl vyce of sweryng were lefte and caste out from alle our royame.

laier, laiety, obs. ff. LAIR *sb.*, LAYER, LAITY.

laife(o, obs. form of LAY FEE.

laigh (lɛːx), *a.*, *adv.*, and *sb.* *Sc.* Also 4–9 laich(e, 5 laych, 4 lawch, 5 lauch. [See LOW *a.*]

A. *adj.* = LOW *a.* in various senses: Near the ground, not elevated; †inferior in rank or quality; not loud.

1375 BARBOUR *Bruce* XIII. 651 And it, that wondir lawch wer ere, Mon lowp on loft in the contrere. *c* **1375** *Sc. Troy-bk.* II. 1719 Now as hillis hie yt schauris Now set laich with ane noþir skift. *c* **1470** HENRY *Wallace* x. 622 The lauch way till Enrawyn thai ryd. **1581** *Satir. Poems Reform.* xliv. 119 Go hence then, lounis! the laich vay in Abyssis. **1582–8** *Hist. Jas. VI* (1804) 75 Finding the lentell stane of the bak zet to be sumquhat laiche. **1693** *Scot. Presbyt. Eloq.* (1738) 124 Christ..rode upon an Ass, which is a Laigh Beast. **1728** RAMSAY *Last Sp. Miser* xxv, Sic are but very laigh concerns, Compar'd with thee. **1753** *Scots Mag.* Apr. 162/2 The commissioners..shall meet in the laigh council-house, Edinburgh. **1816** SCOTT *Antiq.* i, A sharp-looking old dame..who inhabited a 'laigh shop', *anglicè*, a cellar. **1881** STEVENSON *Thrawn Janet* Wks. 1895 III. 253 It's a lang, laigh, mirk chalmer. *Ibid.* 257 When a' of a sudden he heard a laigh, uncanny steer upstairs. **1894** CROCKETT *Lilac Sunbonnet* 74 One of the farms at the 'laigh' end of the parish.

B. *adv.* In a low position; to a low point; in a low tone.

1583 *Satir. Poems Reform.* xlv. 349 Laich in a lymbus, whair they lay. **1596** DALRYMPLE tr. *Leslie's Hist. Scot.* VII. 2 Quhen he saw the vertues of the Bruse..and how laich [he] was brocht. **1792** BURNS *Bessy & Spinnin Wheel* i, I'll set me down and sing and spin, While laigh descends the simmer sun. **1868** G. MACDONALD *R. Falconer* I. 18 Speyk laicher, man; she'll maybe hear ye. **1893** STEVENSON *Catriona* 20 But—laigh in your ear, man—I'm maybe no very keen on the other side.

C. *sb.* **a.** A hollow. **b.** A low-lying ground.

1... *Chart. Aberbrothok* (Advoc. Libr. MS.) 79 Passand eist downwart to the greyn laigh to Gemylis myr. **1768** Ross *Helenore* (1789) 47 A burn ran in the laigh, ayont there lay As many feeding on the other brae. **1798** *Statist. Acc. Scot.* XX. 232 The whole laigh of Moray had been covered with the sea in the year 1010. **1811** G. S. KEITH *Agric. Surv. Aberd.* 172 Low wet lands, called *laighs*.

laik, Sc. form of LACK; variant of LAKE.

-laik, *suffix*, in the Ormulum written -leȝȝc, in northern and north-midland texts usually -laik, -layk(e, in the Ancren Riwle (MS. Nero) and a few other 13th c. texts -leic, -lec, -leik; appended in ME. to adjs. to form sbs. of quality, none of which have survived into mod.Eng. Etymologically it represents the ON. *-leik-r* str. masc. which (with a parallel form *-leike* wk. masc.) is the ordinary suffix in ON. corresponding functionally to the Eng. *-ness*; its use in Eng. must have originated in words adopted from Scandinavian, as *godleȝȝc* (Orm.) from ON. *góðleikr*; but already in the Ormulum (*c* 1200) it is added freely to native English adjs., as in *clænleȝȝc* cleanness, *grediȝleȝȝc* greediness. Ormin has in all 28 words of this formation; in some instances he originally wrote *-nesse*, but *-leȝȝc* has been substituted 'in a ruder but apparently contemporary hand' (editorial note in *Orm.* II. 349); the reason was perh. metrical, as *-leȝȝc* and *-nesse* were in Ormin's prosody equivalent only before a vowel. Except in the Ormulum the suffix is somewhat rare, and no instance is known of its being appended to an adj. of Romanic origin.

The ON. *-leik-r* corresponds in form with the OE. suffix *-lác* (usually neut., rarely masc.), now -LOCK (q.v. for the etymology); but in function the two are distinct, the ON. suffix being appended only to adjs., and the OE. suffix only to sbs. or verb-stems to form sbs. expressive of action. Occasionally the suffix representing OE. *-lác* was in northern or north midland texts written *-laik*, so that it became coincident in form with the Scandinavian suffix, e.g. in *dwimerlaik* (Alex.), *wedlaik* (R. Brunne).

laika ('laɪkə). Pl. laiki. [Russ. *laĭka*, f. *laĭ* bark.] A dog belonging to a group of Asiatic breeds of the spitz type, characterized by a pointed muzzle, pricked ears, a stocky body with a thick, rough, grey, fawn, white, or black coat and a tail curled over the back.

1905 H. DE BYLANDT *Dogs All Nations* I. 576 Samoyed dog. (Laika or Siberian dog)... Dog of medium size, well built and cobby, covered with a thick fur. **1928** *Daily Sketch* 7 Aug. 4/3 The Elkhound is of similar type to the Russian Laïka (barking) dog, so-called because, unlike others of the lupine group, its tongue is a bark and not a howl. **1948** C. L. B. HUBBARD in B. Vesey-Fitzgerald *Bk. Dog* II. 517 The Spitz of the Asiatic sphere shew considerable variation, and are consequently divided into many well-defined breeds. These are collectively known as Laiki, and each Laika is called (in most cases) after its province or its people. **1971** F. HAMILTON *World Encycl. Dogs* 599 Laiki are seen all over Northern Russia... When a Laika, out hunting, sees a bird in a tree or bush, it barks ceaselessly.

laike, variant of LAKE *v.*[1], *sb.*[2], *sb.*[3]

laill, variant of LEAL.

laily, variant of LAIDLY *a.*

†**lain**, *sb.*[1] *Obs.* Also 5-6 layn(e, 6 lane. [f. LAIN *v.*; cf. ON. *leyni* neut., hiding-place, *í leyni* in secret.] Concealment; chiefly in ***without*** (or ***but***) ***lain***, without concealment or disguise.

a **1300** *Cursor M.* 13966 (Cott.), I sal spek of his sisters tua, þat was martha, wit-vten lain, and als sua mari magdalain. *c* **1460** *Towneley Myst.* xvi. 146, I kepe not layn, truly Syn thay cam by you last, An othere way in hy thay soght. **1535** STEWART *Cron. Scot.* I. 306 To say the suith but lane. **1560** ROLLAND *Crt. Venus* III. 760 The fourt I can find ȝit withoutin lane. **1575** *Wyfe Lapped in Morrelles Skin* 83 in Hazl. *E.P.P.* IV. 184 Her mother doth teach her, withouten layne To be mayster of her husband another day.

†**lain**, *sb.*[2] *Obs.* Also 6 laine, 6-7 lane. [? f. *lain* pa. pple. of LIE *v.*[1]] A layer, a stratum.

1577 HARRISON *England* II. xii. (1877) I. 235 In plastering ..of our fairest houses ouer our heads, we vse to laie first a laine or two of white morter tempered with haire, vpon laths. **1584** R. SCOT *Discov. Witchcr.* XIII. xxx. 279 The bottome being no deeper than as it may conteine one lane of corne or pepper glewed thereupon. **1677** PLOT *Oxfordsh.* 260 After every six inches thickness of Corn, a stratum of Pebbles,..then Corn again to the same thickness, and so SSS [i.e. *stratum super stratum*] to ten lains apiece. *c* **1682** J. COLLINS *Making of Salt in Engl.* 121 The Meat..is pack'd ..with Salt betwixt every Lane or Lay. **1706** PHILLIPS (ed. Kersey), *Laines* (in Masonry), Courses or Ranks laid in the building of Stone or Brick-walls.

lain, *v. Obs.* exc. *Sc.* Forms: 4, 6 leyn(e, (6-7 lean(e, 7 lene), 4-5 (9 *Sc.*) layn(e, 4-6 lane, lain(e. [a. ON. *løyna* to conceal, corresponding to OE. *lí(e)ᵹnan* to deny, OS. *lôgnian* (Du. *loochenen*), OHG. *loug(i)nen* (MHG. *lögenen*, G. *läugnen*, *leugnen*), Goth. (and OTeut.) *laugnjan*; f. OTeut. **laugnâ* str. fem. represented by OHG. *lougna* denial, ON. *laun* (Sw., Da. *lön*) secrecy, concealment; f. Teut. root **laug-* (: *leug-* : *lug-*): see LIE *sb.*[1], *v.*[2]

Phonologically some of the forms might descend from OE. (Anglian) **léᵹnan*; but the examples seem to show the specially ON. development of sense.]

trans. To conceal, hide; to be silent about, disguise (a fact). Also *absol.* ***not to*** (or ***at***) ***lain***: not to be concealed. Hence **laining**, *vbl. sb.*

a **1300** *Cursor M.* 1549 (Cott.) In sua lang time, es noght to lain, þe planetes all ar went again. *Ibid.* 2738 (Gött.) Abraham..fra þe wil i noght leyne mi priuite. *c* **1350** *Will. Palerne* 906, I wol it nouȝt layne. *c* **1375** *Sc. Leg. Saints, Symon & Iudas* 162 Of our kine gyf þou wil frane, we are hebreis, nocht to layne. ? *a* **1400** *Morte Arth.* 419 Gret wele Lucius, thi lorde, and layne noghte þise wordes. *c* **1400** *Ywaine & Gaw.* 703 Thou mon be ded, es noght at laine, For my lord that thou has slayne. *c* **1400** tr. *Secreta Secret.*, *Gov. Lordsh.* 100 But þai layned it to his ffader. *c* **1420** *Avow. Arth.* xxxiii, Hit is atte the quene wille Qwi schuld I layne? *c* **1440** *York Myst.* xxv. 101 This tydyngis schall haue no laynyng. **1535** STEWART *Cron. Scot.* (1858) II. 648 Makdufe ..in nothing wald lane, How Makcobey bayth wyfe and barnis had slane. **1598** R. BERNARD tr. *Terence, Adelphi* III. iii, He lained nothing [L. *nihil reticuit*]. **1638** BRATHWAIT *Bessie Bell* iv, 'Las, maidens must faine it; I love though I laine it. *a* **1650** *Earle Westmorld.* 120 in Furnivall *Percy Folio* I. 305 Duke Iohn of Austria is my Masters name, he will neuer Lene it vpon the sea. *a* **1802** *Jamie Telfer* xxx. in Child *Ballads* (1890) IV. 7/1, I winna layne my name for thee. **1862** HISLOP *Prov. Scot.* 212 Women and bairns layne what they ken na.

lain, pa. pple. of LIE.

laine (leɪn). *local.* A name given to certain tracts of arable land at the foot of the Sussex Downs.

1794 *Ann. Agric.* XXII. 219 Rent of the arable, including the laines, is 15*s.* per acre. *Ibid.* 230 The laines or bottoms ..Laine land or arable. **1797** *Ibid.* XXVIII. 124 His course is what is called in Sussex three laines, that is, wheat once in three years. **1881** SAWYER *Land Tenure Brighton* in *Proc. Incorp. Land Soc.* 95 [Outside the boundaries of Brighton] were five large tracts of land, known as the Tenantry Laines, and called the East Laine, Little Laine, Hilly Laine, North Laine, and West Laine... These Laines were again divided into furlongs... The 'Tenantry flock' was..when taken from the Down, invariably kept in the fallow lands or grattens in the 'Tenantry Laines'. **18..** *Spectator* No. 2137. 574 (Cent.; reference erroneous) Light falls the rain on link and laine.

lainer ('leɪnə(r)). *Obs.* in literary use. Also 4-7 layner, 5-7 laner, 5 lanyr. [a. F. *lanière*; afterwards re-adopted as *lanyer*, corrupted into LANYARD.] A lace, strap, thong, lash.

c **1386** CHAUCER *Knt.'s T.* 1646 Gigginge of sheeldes, with layneres [*Camb. MS.* lanyerys] lacinge. **1387** TREVISA *Higden* (Rolls) V. 369 Hire hosen..i-teyed wiþ layners al aboute. **14..** *Sir Beues* 2753 + 85 (MS. E.) Hese laynerys [*printed* layuerys] he took anon And fastenyd hys hawberk hym vpon. *c* **1440** *Promp. Parv.* 286/1 Lanere, *ligula*. *c* **1450** *Merlin* 697 A-noon brake the layners that he had bounden vp his hosen of stiell. **1483** CAXTON *Gold. Leg.* 338/1 Layners or lachettes of theyre skynne were cutte oute of theyr back. —— *G. de la Tour* C j b, Yf I shold sytte lowe I myght breke my poyntes or layners. **1485** *Naval Acc. Hen. VII* (1896) 37 Layners for the truss perell..j. **1610** HOLLAND *Camden's Brit.* I. 542 An oxe hide cut out into very small laners, that we call Thongs. **1616** BULLOKAR, *Layners* [*printed* Layuers], thongs of lether. *Mod.* (Essex) This whip wants a new lainer.

laing, Sc. form of LONG.

Laingian ('læŋɪən), *a.* [-IAN.] Of or pertaining to the theories of the British psychologist R. D. Laing (1927-), esp. that a disintegrative mental illness such as schizophrenia is due to 'normal' social or family pressures which are intolerable to the self, and that re-integrative therapy is therefore possible only when such conventionally accepted pressures are removed. Hence as *sb.*, one who adheres to Laing's theories or practises his method of therapy.

1971 *New Statesman* 16 Apr. 535/1 A Laingian stereotype has blossomed. **1972** *Listener* 20 Jan. 95/3 Her psychiatrist ..a 'Laingian' who wants to treat the underlying cause.. and not the symptoms. **1973** E. Z. FRIEDENBERG *Laing* (1974) i. 27 Edward Chamberlayne, an archetypical victim ..of a Laingian entrapment. **1973** *Listener* 10 May 623/2 The now-familiar Laingian argument that language is the first and strongest of the prison-houses with which our civilisation enslaves the free self.

laip, obs. Sc. form of LAP *v.*[1]

lair (lɛə(r)), *sb.*[1] Forms: 1 leᵹer, 3-6 leir, 5 layere, 5-7 lare, layre, 5-7 leyre, 6-7 lear(e, laire, laier, (lieare), 6-9 layer, 9 *Sc.* layre, *dial.* lear, 4- lair. See also LAYER. [OE. *leᵹer* str. neut., corresponding to OFris. *legor* lying, situation, OS. *legar* neut., bed, bed of sickness (Du. *leger* bed, camp), OHG. *leger* masc., bed, camp (mod.G. *lager*, influenced by *lage*, lying, situation), ON. *legr* neut., seduction, Goth. *ligr-s* masc., bed:—OTeut. **legro-*, f. root **leg-*: see LIE *v.*[1]]

†**1.** The action or fact of lying. *Obs.*

Beowulf (Gr.) 3043 Se [*sc.* se draca] wæs fiftiᵹes fotᵹemearces lang on leᵹere. *c* **893** ÆLFRED *Oros.* I. i. §23 Mid þan langan leᵹere þæs deadan mannes inne. **1513** DOUGLAS *Æneis* VIII. iv. 70 All the beistis war Repaterit weyll eftyr thair nychtis lair. **1631** MARKHAM *Way to Get Wealth* V. II. xviii. (1668) 87 Touching the keeping of Corn after it is thrasht and drest, it is divers wayes to be done, as by stowage or place of lear.

†**b.** A lying with a person; fornication. *Obs.*

1296 *Durham Halmote Rolls* (Surtees) 1 Eda filia Pater Noster pro leyr, 6*d.* **1332-3** *Ibid.* 13 De Ivetta Horner, pro leyr in adulterio, 2*s.* **1361** *Ibid.* 27 De Christiana ancilla Willelmi capellani pro leyr cum capellano, 2*s.*

†**c.** Of land: The state of lying fallow. *Obs.*

1602 CAREW *Cornwall* 20 a, The Tiller..is driuen to giue it at least seuen or eight yeres leyre.

2. The resting place of a corpse; a grave, tomb. Now only *Sc.*, a plot in a graveyard.

c **1000** *Laws Northumbr. Priests* §62 in Schmid *Gesetze* 370 þoliᵹe he clænes leᵹeres. *c* **1000** *Sax. Leechd.* III. 288 Unsac he wæs on life beo on leᵹere swa swa he mote. ? *a* **1400** *Morte Arth.* 2293 Sir Arthure..ledde hyme to the layere thare the kyng lygges. *c* **1425** WYNTOUN *Cron.* VII. x. 3243 He chesyd his layre in till Kelsew. *c* **1470** HARDING *Chron.* LXXXIV. iii, The mynster churche..Of Glastonbury, where nowe he hath his leyre. **1535** STEWART *Cron. Scot.* (1858) I. 118 Ane feild full fair, Quhair that him self befoir chesit his lair. *a* **1578** LINDESAY (Pitscottie) *Chron. Scot.* (S.T.S.) I. 154 Sanct Salvatouris colledge quhairin he maid his lair verri cureouslie and costlie. **1882** MCQUEEN in *Macm. Mag.* XLVI. 162 Some of the inhabitants..had their family 'lair' or burying-place in the graveyard of a village. **1890** [Notice in Stromness Ch.-yard] The Committee appointed by the Heritors to take charge of the new Burial Ground have had before them alternative plans for placing of lairs.

3. That whereon one lies down to sleep; a bed, couch. † ***at*** or ***to lair***: in or to bed. † ***to take one's lair***: to take to one's bed. Now chiefly with some reference to sense 5 b.

a **1000** *Wife's Compl.* 34 Frynd leᵹer weardiaþ þonne ic on uhtan ana gonge. *c* **1200** *Trin. Coll. Hom.* 103 He beð neðer þanne he er was, alse fro sete to leire. *a* **1300** *Cursor M.* 29091 In askes and in hare, and weping and vneses lair. *c* **1425** *Dispute Mary & Cross* 96 in *Leg. Rood* (1871) App. 200 My love I lulled vppe in hys leir. **1494** *Acta Dom. Conc.* (1739) 372/2 His wiff wes liand in cheld bed lare. **1619** H. HUTTON *Follies Anat.* (Percy Soc.) 35 Robin has for tobacco sold his chaire, Reserving nothing but a stoole for's lare. **1633** T. ADAMS *Comm. 2 Pet.* i. 9 (1865) 107 The physician coming to his patient inquires the time when he took his layre. **1821** CLARE *Vill. Minstr.* II. 24 The shepherd ..on the sloping pond-head lies at lair. **1831** CARLYLE *Sart. Res.* (1858) 13 Wretchedness..shivers hunger-stricken into its lair of straw. **1851** MAYNE REID *Scalp Hunt.* xx. 139 There were 'lairs' among the underwood, constructed of branches. **1899** F. T. BULLEN *Log of a Sea-waif* 160 The villainous den beneath the top-gallant-forecastle, far in the fore-part of the ship, which is the lair of seamen in most English ships.

transf. and *fig.* **1814** SCOTT *Ld. of Isles* IV. iv, Till stretch'd upon the bloody lair Each rebel corpse was laid! **1821** SHELLEY *Prometh. Unb.* I. 687 We make there our liquid lair.

4. A place for animals to lie down in. **a.** for domestic animals. †Also, a haunt or range. Now *spec.* an enclosure or large shed for cattle on the way to market.

By Spenser, if the reading be correct, used pseudo-*arch.* for 'pasture'.

c **1420** *Pallad. on Husb.* I. 52 Take heede ek if the dwellers in that leir Her wombis sidis, reynys swelle or ake. **1513** DOUGLAS *Æneis* XIII. Prol. 44 All stoyr and catall seysit in thar lair. **1573** TUSSER *Husb.* cxiii. (1878) 206 Borne I was.. In Essex laier, in village faier, that Riuenhall hight. **1596** SPENSER *F.Q.* IV. viii. 29 More hard for hungry steed t' abstaine from pleasant lare. *a* **1605** MONTGOMERIE *Mindes Mel.*, Ps. xxiii. 5 He makes my leare In feelds so fare. **1649** BLITHE *Eng. Improv. Impr.* (1653) 110 The Warmest parts of many Pastures, which Sheep and Cattell chuse alway for their Lieare. **1697** DRYDEN *Virg. Georg.* III. 233 Nature shall provide..Mossy Caverns for their Evening lare. **1725** BRADLEY *Fam. Dict.* s.v. *Cow*, You must..fill up the Holes carefully that are in the Cowhouse-yard or Layer. **1810** in *Risdon's Surv. Devon* 406 Each flock of sheep has its particular range,..These places are called lears. **1821** CLARE *Vill. Minstr.* II. 105 Low of distant cattle..dropping down to lair. **1865** *Daily Tel.* 22 Aug. 5/5 These lairs..are tolerably comfortable places, and the cattle have food and water while staying there. **1887** *Times* 27 Aug. 11/4 Hay, straw, and forage for use in the lairs.

b. for beasts of chase or of prey. Phr. ***at lair***: in his or their lair.

1576 TURBERV. *Venerie* 115. **1592** NASHE *P. Penilesse* (ed. 2) 31 b, All the nimble Citizens of the wood betooke them to their Laire. **1626** BRETON *Fantasticks, Summer* (1857) 324 The stately Hart is at Layre in the high wood. **1667** MILTON *P.L.* VII. 457 Out of the ground up rose, As from his laire the wilde Beast. **1735** SOMERVILLE *Chase* III. 294 Fierce from his Lair springs forth the speckled Pard. **1840** THIRLWALL *Greece* VII. lv. 96 They were hunted like wild beasts into their lairs. **1870** MORRIS *Earthly Par.* I. II. 535 In that forest was the lair Of a great boar.

transf. and *fig.* **1814** BYRON *Lara* II. ix, He had hoped quiet in his sullen lair. **1860** W. COLLINS *Wom. White* III. viii. 383, I had stirred in its lair the serpent-hatred of years. **1870** SPURGEON *Treas. Dav.* Ps. xxxii. 6 Before the great devouring floods leap forth from their lairs.

c. of other animals.

1841 BROWNING *Pippa* 167 That mossy lair of lizards. **1860** EMERSON *Cond. Life, Fate* Wks. (Bohn) II. 324 Every creature,—wren or dragon,—shall make its own lair. **1867** F. FRANCIS *Angling* v. (1880) 182 A fish feeding in his lair.

5. *Agric.* Nature or kind of soil, with reference to its effect on the quality of crops, or of the animals pastured upon it.

1519 HORMAN *Vulg.* 178 The tyllar wyll..shone it as poysonde leyre. **1530** PALSGR. 237/2 Layre of a grounde, *terroy[r]*. **1573** TUSSER *Husb.* (1878) 141 What laier much better then there, or cheaper (thereon to doo well?) **1610** FOLKINGHAM *Art of Survey* I. viii. 15 Virgill infers the best layer for Tillage to be an Earth which is blackish and darke. **1616** SURFLET & MARKH. *Countrey Farme* 117 Sheepe bred either of a fruitfull ground, and rich leare, or vpon barren ground, and poore leare. **1623** MARKHAM *Cheape & Good*

Husb. (ed. 3) 104 Leare, which is the earth on which a Sheepe lyeth, and giueth him his colour, is much to be respected; the red Leare is held the best. **1655** MOFFET & BENNET *Health's Improv.* (1746) 158 Chuse the Female before the Male [rabbit],..and both from out a chalky Ground and a sweet Layer. **1688** R. HOLME *Armoury* II. 135/2 Sheep at their Lear. Some say, Feeding or Grasing. **1799** A. YOUNG *Agric. Lincs.* 211 Where the soil is so good as to run well to grass good layers are easily formed. **1847** *Jrnl. R. Agric. Soc.* VIII. I. 64 Manure is used heavily on clover-layers.

fig. **1565** JEWEL *Repl. Harding* (1611) 355 Lacke of Deuotion both in the people and in the Priest, is a good leare to breed Masses. **1602** BRETON *Wonders worth hearing* (Grosart) 8/1 His Bride and hee were both Rabbets of one Laier.

6. *Comb.*: **lair-holder** *Sc.*, the owner of a grave; †**lair-stall**, †**-stead**, a grave within a church; †**lair-stone**, a gravestone; †**lair-stow**, a burial-place.

1864 *N.B. Mail* 2 Nov., The subcommittee of the *lair-holders thought it would [etc.]. **1541** *Mem. Ripon* (Surtees) III. 195 Pro denariis debitis pro le *layrestall infra ecclesiam. **1672** *Vestry Bks.* (Surtees) 338 For laying downe layerstalls, 5*s.* **1559** *Richmond. Wills* (Surtees 1853) 130, I gyue for my *lare stede in the churche iij[s]. iiij[d]. **1538** *Invent.* in *Archæologia* LI. 71 Itm the laton on the *larestones, *vd.* **1565** *Wills & Inv. N.C.* (Surtees 1835) 247 For his lairstone in ye church iij[s]. iiij[d]. *c* **1632** in Brand *Hist. Newcastle* (1789) I. 370 *note*, One swea tree with two rolles for taking and laying down lairstones. *c* **1000** ÆLFRIC *Hom.* (Th.) I. 430 Ypolitus ðа bebyrigde ðone halȝan lichaman on ðære wudewan *leȝer-stowe. *c* **1205** LAY. 22874 Me nom alle þa dede & to leirstowe heom ladden.

lair (lɛə(r)), *sb.*² Now *dial.* Also 4, 8 lare, 4–5 layre, 4–5, 9 laire, 8 laier. [a. ON. *leir* (Sw. *ler*, Da. *leer*):—OTeut. type **laizo-n*, ? cogn. w. *laimo-* LOAM.] Clay, mire, mud. †*under lair*: under the ground.

a **1300** *Cursor M.* 519 O watur his blod, his fless o lair, His hete o fir, hijs and of air. *a* **1340** HAMPOLE *Psalter* lxviii. 18 Out take me of the lare that .i. be not infestid. *a* **1400–50** *Alexander* 4445 All sall leue ȝow at þe laste and in-to laire worth. *c* **1440** *York Myst.* xxxi. 213 One Lazar.. Lay loken vndir layre fro lymme and fro light. **1637** RUTHERFORD *Lett.* (1862) I. 276 My short legs could not step ouer this lair or sinking mire. **1787** GROSE *Prov. Gloss.*, *Laier*, soil, dung. Ess. and Suff. *Lare*, a quagmire. N. **1803** W. S. ROSE *Amadis* 76 He sees two damsels o'er the laire advance. **1825** BROCKETT *N.C. Words*, *Lair*, mire, dirt. **1893** *Northumbld. Gloss.*, *Lair*, mud, 'sleck', quicksand, or any soft yielding surface. **1895** CROCKETT *Men of Moss Hags* 31 He was covered with the lair of the moss-hags.

†**lair**, *sb.*³ *Obs.* Also 5–6 layer, 6 leyar, leire, laire. A ewer.

1491 *Will of Vaughan* (Somerset Ho.), A layer of siluer ouer gilt. **1508** *Sponselles L. Marye* 25 in *Camden Misc.* (1895), No salte, cuppe, or layer..set on the borde. **1565** in *Leland's Collect.* (1770) I. II. 691 The Communion Table was richly furnished with Plate..viz... Two great Leires, garnished with stones. **1576** in H. Walpole *Vertue's Anecd. Paint.* (1786) I. 287 A fair bason and lair guilt.

lair (lɛə(r)), *sb.*⁴ *Austral. slang.* Also lare. [Back-formation from LAIRY *a.*²] A flashily dressed man, one who 'shows off'. Also (*rare*) 'lairize *v. intr.*, to act like a lair, to show off.

1935 K. TENNANT *Tiburon* ix. 106 He was also considered something of a lare among the girls. **1941** BAKER *Dict. Austral. Slang* 42 *Lair*, a flashily-dressed man. **1941** K. TENNANT *Battlers* iii. 29 But a brainy young lare called 'the mob' together on the pavement outside the shop. 'This can be worked, can't it?' he asked, displaying his slip. **1953** —— *Joyful Condemned* iii. 22 You came lairizing round at our place like you owned it. **1955** H. DRAKE-BROCKMAN *Men without Wives* 83 A flash young man. What they call on the goldfields 'a regular lare'. Hair much slicked, double-breasted coat, patent leather shoes. **1956** J. WRIGHT in *Coast to Coast 1955–56* 168 But he was what they called a bit of a lair; he couldn't keep a job and had run through three already. **1956** K. TENNANT *Honey Flow* xvi. 188 When they dressed in their best, they looked cheap lares, the type you see leaning against the hotel or the general store. **1973** A. BROINOWSKI *Take One Ambassador* iii. 31 Two young lairs from the surf club carried their boards down..and tossed them onto the sea. With insolent grace they hopped on.

lair (lɛə(r)), *v.*¹ Also 2 leire. [f. LAIR *sb.*¹]

†**1.** *trans.* To prostrate, lay on the ground.

c **1200** *Trin. Coll. Hom.* 103 þe rihte bileue and þe soðe luue..ben leirede and slaine on his heorte.

2. a. *intr.* To lie, repose (*on* a bed). **b.** Of cattle: To go to their lair. **c.** *trans.* To place in a lair. Also *refl.* To find one's lair. **d.** To serve as a lair for; in quot. 1870 *fig.*

1607 TOPSELL *Serpents* (1658) 766 Vnder this herb a Snake full cold doth lear [= L. *latet anguis sub herba*]. **1662** G. SWINNOCK *Life of Christ* Pref., O how sad is it that so many precious souls should be laring on their beds of security and idleness. **1821** CLARE *Vill. Minstr.* II. 74 The berries of the brambly wood..Which, when his cattle lair, he runs to get. **1851** MAYNE REID *Rifle Rangers* i. 13 The jaguar is not far distant, 'laired' in the secret depths of the impenetrable jungle. **1853** ALEX. SMITH *Life Drama* x. 183 I'd rather lair me with a fiend in fire Than look on such a face as hers to-night. **1870** LOWELL *Cathedral* Poet. Wks. (1879) 453 As a mountain seems To dwellers round its bases but a heap Of barren obstacle that lairs the storm. **1890** *Daily Tel.* 22 May 5/6 At this moment there are over 7,000 beasts laired in Deptford Market.

lair (lɛə(r)), *v.*² Also 6 lare. [f. LAIR *sb.*²]

1. *intr.* To stick or sink in mire or bog.

a **1572** KNOX *Hist. Ref.* Wks. (1846) I. 86 Some Scottismen..not knowing the ground lared, and lost thair horse. *a* **1575** *Diurn. Occurr.* (Bannatyne Club) 252 In the quhilk passage ane of thair greit peices of ordinance larit. **1785** BURNS *Winter Nt.* iii, Silly sheep, wha..thro' the drift, deep-lairing, sprattle. **1805** *State, Leslie of Powis* 74 (Jam.) His cattle sometimes laired in the waggle. **1880** in *Antrim & Down Gloss.* **1897** CROCKETT *Lads' Love* xxix. 290, I feared o' lairin' in the moss mysel'.

fig. **1859** CAIRNS in *Life* (1895) 438 The subject [origin of Evil] is the deepest bog in which the human mind can lair.

2. *trans.* To cause or allow to sink in mire or a morass. Also *refl.*

c **1560** A. SCOTT *Poems* (S.T.S.) xx. 46 Thow wald no[t] rest but raik, And lair thee in þe myre. *a* **1578** LINDESAY (Pitscottie) *Chron. Scot.* (S.T.S.) I. 405 They come to ane place callit the Solloun mose..and thair in lairit and mischeiffit thair horse. **1722** RAMSAY *Three Bonnets* IV. 76 But past relief lar'd in a midding, He's now oblig'd to do her bidding. **1830** LYELL *Princ. Geol.* (1875) II. III. xliv. 510 In Scotland..Cattle venturing on a 'quaking moss', are often mired or 'laired'. **1875** W. MCILWRAITH *Guide Wigtownshire* 76 Watery flows, in which sheep and cattle sometimes lair themselves. **1894** CROCKETT *Raiders* (ed. 3) 213 They say that King Robert..laired and bogged a hale army o' the English there.

fig. *a* **1810** TANNAHILL *Poems* (1846) 83 Some..polemic wight..Wha lairs himself in controversy.

lair (lɛə(r)), *v.*³ *Austral. slang.* Also lare. [f. LAIR *sb.*⁴ or LAIRY *a.*²] To dress flashily, to dress *up*; to act in a lairy manner. Freq. in pa. pple. (*all*) *laired up*.

1941 BAKER *Dict. Austral. Slang* 42 *Lair up*, to dress, esp. to don one's best clothes for a festive occasion. **1945** —— *Austral. Lang.* vi. 119 *All laired up* and its synonym *all mockered up* may also be noted. **1955** H. DRAKE-BROCKMAN *Men without Wives* 83 It's that Rienzi. He's a trimmer. Always laring round. No good to girls. **1962** S. GORE *Down Golden Mile* 64 He climbs out of the cockpit, all laired up in this red rig-out.

lair, obs. f. LAYER; Sc. f. LORE, learning.

lairage ('lɛərɪdʒ). [f. LAIR *sb.*¹ or *v.*¹ + -AGE.]

1. The placing of cattle in a lair or lairs.

1881 *Daily News* 31 Jan. 2/6 The lands and buildings at Birkenhead approved by the Privy Council for the landing or lairage of foreign animals. **1881** *Cork Constitution* 12 Apr., The housing and lairage of stall-fed cattle.

2. *collect.* **a.** Space where cattle may lie down and rest. **b.** An establishment where cattle are placed in lairs.

1883 *Summary* 26 July 6/4 Cattle lairage will be provided. **1887** *L'pool Daily Post* 14 Feb. 3/7 He visited the lairages and found several oxen suffering from suppurating wounds on the head. **1893** *Standard* 15 Aug. 5/1 The butchers..prefer to attend the lairages at Birkenhead.

3. *attrib.* and *Comb.*

1871 *Daily News* 16 Sept., His duty being to collect the outdoor lairage accounts. **1882** *Pall Mall G.* 26 July 7/2 Increasing the lairage accommodation at Deptford Cattle Market. **1883** ROSHER *Princ. Rating* 25 Lairage dues, levied on the consignees of foreign cattle. **1896** *Times* (weekly ed.) 599/2 Lairage-slaughtered beef and mutton.

lairbar: see LARBAR.

laird (lɛəd). *Sc.* Also 5–7 lard(e. [The regular Sc. form of LORD (repr. northern ME. *laverd*), surviving only in a special sense.

The southern form *lord* was as early as the 14th c. introduced into Scottish use in the English senses of the word. The native form *lard* appears occasionally in the 15th c. instead of *lord*: for examples see LORD *sb.*]

A landed proprietor. In ancient times limited to those who held immediately from the king.

c **1450** HOLLAND *Howlat* 193 Pure freris..That, with the leif of the lard, Will cum to the corne ȝard At ewyn and at morn. **1508** KENNEDIE *Flyting w. Dunbar* 515, I sall ger bake the to the lard of Hillhouse. **1535** STEWART *Cron. Scot.* (1858) I. 65 Ouir all the land lord or laird wes nane, Bot he tuke part at that tyme witht the tane. **1596** DALRYMPLE tr. *Leslie's Hist. Scot.* IX. 177 The lard of Cesfurde..meites him. **1647** CLARENDON *Hist. Reb.* II. §19 A petition drawn up in the names of the nobility, lairds, clergy and burgesses, to the King. **1716** *Lond. Gaz.* No. 5424/2 Our Detachment burnt the Laird's House. **1721** RAMSAY *Whin-Bush Club* i, Tho', to my loss, I am nae laird, By birth, my title's fair. **1786** BURNS *Twa Dogs* 51 Our Laird gets in his racked rents. **1846** MCCULLOCH *Acc. Brit. Emp.* (1854) II. 205 By the lesser barons were meant the proprietors of the smaller class of estates, provincially called lairds. **1872** E. W. ROBERTSON *Hist. Ess.* 138 *note*, In Scotland every tenant in capite, holding in Ward and Blench, continued to be reckoned as a Baron and was known as the Laird.

Hence (chiefly *nonce-wds.*) 'lairdess, a laird's wife; 'lairdie, a petty laird; 'lairdly *a.*, having the rank or quality of lairds; lair'docracy [after *aristocracy*], lairds as forming a ruling class.

17.. in Hogg *Jacob. Relics* (1819) I. 83 Wha the deil hae we gotten for a king But a wee wee German lairdie? **1819** *Metropolis* III. 83 The Highland and Border Lairdies. **1848** *Tait's Mag.* XV. 123 The Scotch lairdocracy may take it into their heads. **1857** AITON *Domest. Econ.* 51 The Court of Teinds,..by their cruel bias to the lairdocracy, starve the ministers of the kirk. **1863** BURTON *Book Hunter* 10 Her sister lairdesses were enriching the tea-table conversation with broad descriptions of the abominable vices of their several spouses. **1877** *Tinsley's Mag.* XXI. 46 He yet was descended from an ancient lairdly stock in that northern county.

lairdship ('lɛədʃɪp). [f. LAIRD + -SHIP.]

1. The condition or dignity of a laird. Also quasi-*concr.* Lairds as a whole.

1854 H. MILLER *Sch. & Schm.* (1858) 395 The august shadow of lairdship lay heavy on society. **1870** RAMSAY *Remin.* (ed. 18) p. xxviii, The annals of 'Forfarshire Lairdship'.

2. The estate of a laird.

1649 BP. GUTHRIE *Mem.* (1702) 91 Mr. A. M...having been..preferr'd to the Lairdship of Balvaird. *a* **1693** *Urquhart's Rabelais* III. ii. 26 He wasted..the..Revenue of his Lairdship. **1725** DE FOE *Journey thro' Scotl.* (1729) 4 (Jam.) A lairdship is a tract of land with a mansion house upon it, where a gentleman hath his residence. **1816** SCOTT *Old Mort.* xl, When ye tak up the lairdship, ye maun tak the auld name and designation again. **1864** BURTON *Scot Abr.* II. ii. 182 An estate held directly of the crown was a lairdship.

fig. **1794** BURNS *Contented wi' Little* ii, My Freedom's my lairdship nae monarch dare touch.

lairg(e, obs. Sc. form of LARGE.

lairock, obs. form of LARK.

†**lairwite.** *Old Law.* Also 1 leȝerwite, 3 learwite, 4 leyrewite. [OE. *leȝerwíte*, f. *leȝer* lying, LAIR *sb.*¹ + *wíte* fine.] A fine for fornication or adultery, esp. with a bondwoman.

[*a* **1135** *Laws of Hen. I*, xxiii. §23 in Schmid *Gesetze* 447 Si quis blodwitam, fightwitam, legerwitam et hujusmodi forisfaciat.] *c* **1230** *Hali Meid.* 47 þu..waldes warpe me as wrecche iþi learwite. **1387** TREVISA *Higden* (Rolls) II. 97 Leyrewite, amendes for liggynge by a bond womman. **1670** BLOUNT *Law Dict.* s.v. *Adultery*, The penalty of this sin was called Lairwite by our Saxons.

†'**lairy**, *sb.* *Obs. rare*⁻⁰. In 6 layrie, 7 lairie.

1598 FLORIO, *Couata*,..any birds hatching or sitting, a nestfull, a layrie [**1611** lairie], an eyas.

lairy ('lɛərɪ), *a.*¹ Also 4 lay(e)ry. [f. LAIR *sb.*² + -Y¹.] †**a.** Earthly, filthy (*obs.*). **b.** Boggy, miry, swampy.

a **1340** HAMPOLE *Psalter* xvii[i]. 36 [32], I lepe ouer all þe thorny and þe lairy besynes of þis warld. *c* **1340** —— *Prose Tr.* (1866) 13 All þat it duellis in it lyftes abowne layery lustes and vile couaytes. **17..** *Donald & Flora* 19 (Jam.) Did ony [ewes]..Come near the lairy springs. **1855** MORTON *Cycl. Agric.* II. 724 *Lairy* (Scot.) wet, swampy. **1897** CROCKETT *Lads' Love* xxix. 290 Wallowing mid-thigh in the lairy depths of the Muckle Flowe.

lairy ('lɛərɪ), *a.*² Also lary. [ad. LEERY *a.*²]

1. *Cockney slang.* Knowing, 'fly', conceited.

1846 *Swell's Night Guide* 78 Lairy and cautious to the green ones, never too fast. **1933** J. MASEFIELD *Conway* 211 *Lairy*, slow, slack; also cunning. **1945** B. NAUGHTON in C. Madge *Pilot Papers* 99 We'll have to keep an eye on him. Spivs are lary perishers. Anything goes wrong they'll never risk their own skin. *Ibid.* 108 They appear to be mentally quicker than most young men: ('Lary' is the word they use for it). **1958** *News Chron.* 23 May 4/7 If someone..is conceited he's lairy. **1967** *Spectator* 4 Aug. 130/3 What I was getting at—before that lairy loon butted in about his thumb—was this. Down the East End we're overcrowded an' we're bleedin' poor.

2. Also leary, leery. Flashily dressed; vulgar. *Austral. slang.*

In quot. 1906 used as quasi-*adv.*

1906 E. DYSON *Fact'ry 'Ands* xii. 160 Found drownded with a bloke what done-up 'is 'air dead leary. **1916** C. J. DENNIS *Songs Sentimental Bloke* 125 *Leery*, vulgar; low. **1936** F. CLUNE *Roaming round Darling* xxiv. 258 Then climbed..Jack the Ripper on to Tugboat Annie, his hat at a leery angle, and the pommel leerier still. **1941** BAKER *Dict. Austral. Slang* 42 *Lairy*, vulgar, flashily or showily dressed. **1966** B. BEAVER *You can't come Back* (1968) 146, I just stood still under the big lairy neon, chuckling a bit and trying to roll a smoke.

lais, obs. Sc. form of LACE.

laisar, -er, obs. forms of LEISURE *sb.*

laise: see LEESE *v.*

‖**laisse** (lɛs). [Fr.] In Old French verse, = TIRADE *sb.* 2.

1872 [see CHANSON 2]. **1879** [see TIRADE *sb.* 2]. **1929** *Encycl. Brit.* II. 567/2 All the lines in a *laisse* or stanza close with the same vowel-sound. **1955** J. T. SHIPLEY *Dict. World Lit. Terms* 246/1 *Laisse*; tirade. Fr. Pros. Running lines (of 8 or 10 syllables) assonanced; later, rhymed; the verse form of the *chanson de geste*.

‖**laissez-aller** ('leɪseɪ 'æleɪ; Fr. lese ale). Also laisser-aller. [Fr.; as next + *aller* to go, i.e. let (persons or things) go.] Absence of restraint; unconstrained ease and freedom.

1842 THACKERAY *Miss Löwe* Misc. Ess. (1885) 310 As Wilder said with some justice, though with a good deal too much *laisser-aller* of tongue. **1862** —— *Philip* II. xxi, Sir John..was constrained to confess that this young man's conduct showed a great deal too much *laissez aller*.

attrib. **1818** LADY S. MORGAN *Flor. Macarthy* II. iii. 178 He..found or fancied in her what he called the 'delicious *laissez aller* ease of a charming French woman'. **1832** LD. LYTTON *Godolphin* xx, Those well-chosen *laissez aller* feasts. **1839** DICKENS *Nich. Nick.* Pref., A magnificent high-handed *laissez-aller* neglect. **1871** [see *fatigue man*]. **1923** [see DOZY *a.*¹ 2].

‖**laissez-faire** ('leɪseɪ fɛə(r); Fr. lese fɛr). Also laisser-faire. [Fr.; *laissez* imp. of *laisser* to let + *faire* to do, i.e. let (people) do (as they think best).

Laissez faire et laissez passer was the maxim of the French free-trade economists of the 18th c.; it is usually attributed to Gournay (Littré s.v. *laisser*).]

A phrase expressive of the principle that government should not interfere with the action

of individuals, esp. in industrial affairs and in trade. Also *attrib.* Hence **laissez-faireism**; **laissez-'fair(e)ist**, one who believes in a doctrine of *laissez-faire*.

1825 [MARQ. NORMANBY] *Eng. in Italy* I. 296 The *laissez faire* system of apathy. **1848** *Simmonds's Colon. Mag.* Aug. 338 Mammonism, laissez-faireism, Chartism, currency-restriction [etc.]. **1873** H. SPENCER *Stud. Sociol.* xiv. 352 Shall we not call that also a *laissez-faire* that is almost wicked in its indifference. **1887** *Contemp. Rev.* May 696 The 'orthodox' *laissez-faire* political economy. **1891** S. C. SCRIVENER *Our Fields & Cities* 168 *Laissez-faire* is the motto, the gospel, of the person who lives upon the work of another. **1932** G. B. SHAW *Platform & Pulpit* (1962) 252 A Cabinet of talkers and Laisser-fairists. **1944** A. JONES *Right & Left* 16 The Conservative is neither a planner nor a laisser-faire-ist. **1966** *Guardian* 1 Dec. 8/6 Professor Peacock.. isn't too keen on being cast as a 'relentless laisser-fairist'.

‖**laissez-passer** (lese pɑse). Also **laisser-passer**. [Fr., lit. 'allow to pass'.] A permit, a pass.

1914 T. A. BAGGS *Back from Front* xx. 94 You must first pass grim Charon and his watchdogs at the entrance, where your passports, laisser-passers, sauf-conduits, are inspected. **1928** *Sunday Express* 1 July 5 The Ballet was given a laissez-passer and were allowed to come to England through Paris. **1936** E. WAUGH *Waugh in Abyssinia* 77 Many writers have left accounts of the intricate system of tolls and hospitality by which the traveller was passed on from one chief to another and of the indifference with which the Emperor's *laissez-passer* was treated within a few miles of the capital. **1951** J. B. PRIESTLEY *Festival at Farbridge* I. i. 34 He handed over an Order to View as if it were a *laissez-passer* for the captain of the Swiss Guard at Versailles. **1955** *Times* 28 July 8/4 He has been granted by the Greek Foreign Ministry a laisser-passer to the Greek military zone of the Greek-Bulgarian frontier. **1970** R. G. FELTHAM *Diplomatic Handbk.* 178 *Laissez-passer*, a permit to travel or to enter a particular area.

laist, Sc. form of *laced* pa. pple. of LACE *v.*

laistoff, -stowe, variants of LAYSTOW.

†**lait**, *sb.*¹ *Obs.* Forms: 1 **léȝet(u, líȝet(u, -yt, léȝeð**, 2–4 **leit**, 2, 4 **leyt**, 3 **liȝt**, 4 **laite, layt(e, leyȝt**, 4–5 **leate, late**, 6 **layth**. [OE. *léȝet, líȝet* masc. and neut., *líȝetu* fem., f. *léȝ, líeȝ* flame. Cf. LAIT *v.*¹] Lightning; *occas.* flash of fire.

c **900** tr. *Bæda's Hist.* IV. iii. (1890) 268 Drihten.. leȝetas sceotað of heofonum. **971** *Blickl. Hom.* 91 Æfter þæm wolcne cymeþ leȝetu. *c* **1000** *Ags. Gosp.* Matt. xxviii. 3 Hys ansyn wæs swylce liȝyt [*c* **1160** *Hatton*, leyt]. *c* **1175** *Lamb. Hom.* 43 Heore eþem scean swa deð þe leit a-monge þunre. *c* **1205** LAY. 25599 Me þuhte.. þat þa sæ gon to berne of leite & of fure. **1297** R. GLOUC. (Rolls) 6283 Ech dunt þoȝte liȝt [*MS. B* leyȝt] as it were and þondring. **13..** *Gaw. & Gr. Knt.* 199 He loked as layt so lyȝt. **1340** *Ayenb.* 66 Lhapþ þet smeþ efter þe layt. **1382** WYCLIF *Exod.* ix. 23 The Lord ȝaf .. dyversly rennynge leytis upon the erthe. *c* **1449** PECOCK *Repr.* 482 Leit gooth out of the eest and apperith into the west. **1470–85** MALORY *Arthur* XVII. xi, Ther felle a sodeyne tempest and thonder layte and rayne. ? *a* **1500** *Chester Pl.* II. 85 Leate, thounder, and eirth beganne to quake, Therof I am adreade. **1513** BRADSHAW *St. Werburge* II. 121 Thondryng and layth, erth-quake moost terrible.

†**lait**, *sb.*² *Obs.* In 5 **laytt**. [f. LAIT *v.*²] Searching, search.

c **1460** *Towneley Myst.* xxiv. 238 Lefe syrs, let be youre laytt and loke that ye layn.

†**lait**, *v.*¹ *Obs.* Forms: 3–4 **leite(n**, 5 **layt**, *pa. t.* 3 **leited**, 5 **layt, laytid**. [? OE. ****légettan***, f. *léȝ, líeȝ* (:—**laugi-z*) flame; cognate and parallel formations are Goth. *lauhatjan*, OHG. *lohazzan, lohezên, -ôn, lougazzan.*] *intr.* To flash, gleam, lighten. Hence †**leitende** (= **laiting*) *ppl. a.*

c **1205** LAY. 18539 Ofte he hire lokede on & leitede mid eȝene. *a* **1225** *Leg. Kath.* 1370 Iþe leitende fur, het warpen euch fot. *a* **1225** *St. Marher.* 13 Ich loki ne mei, swa þæt liht leomeð ant leiteð. *a* **1225** *Ancr. R.* 356 Ne kumeð non into Parais bute þuruh þisse leitende sweorde. **1390** GOWER *Conf.* III. 95 The thunder-stroke smit, er it leite. *c* **1425** *Seven Sag.* (P.) 2228 Hyt laytyd, thondred, and reynned among. *Ibid.* 2234 Hyt raynyd ne thondryd ne layt nout Sythen thou wentyst out of thys toune.

lait (leɪt), *v.*² *Obs.* exc. *dial.* Forms: 4 **latt**, 4–5 **layte, lait(e**, 5–9 **late**, 9 **lait**. [a. ON. *leita*, corresponding to OE. *wlátian* to behold, Goth. *wlaitôn* (περιβλέπεσθαι); related by ablaut to ON. *lit-r*, OE. *wlite* aspect, appearance, OS. *wliti* face, form, Goth. *wlit-s* face, and ON. *líta*, OE. *wlítan* to look.]

1. *trans.* To look or search for; to seek, try to find. Also with *inf.* or *clause* as object.

a **1300** *Cursor M.* 7323 Omang þir puple sal þou latt A stalworth man þat saul haitt. **13..** *E.E. Allit. P.* C. 277 He lurkkes & laytes where watz le best. *a* **1350** *St. James* 305 in Horstm. *Altengl. Leg.* (1881) 101 Graithly up he laites and lukes All his bagges and all his bokes. *a* **1400** *Sir Perc.* 255 The grete Godd for to layte Fynde hyme whenne he may. *c* **1400** *Ywaine & Gaw.* 237 Aventures for to layt in land. *a* **1400–1450** *Alexander* 2341 (Dubl.) Lates ane oþer lodesman, alosed more of strenth. *c* **1440** *York Myst.* xvii. 111 Vn-witty men ȝe werre To lepe ouere lande to late a ladde. **1674–91** RAY *N.C. Words*, To *Late*, Cumb. to seek. **1787** GROSE *Prov. Gloss.*, *Lait*, to seek any thing hidden. N. **1864** ATKINSON *Stanton Grange* 122 Now, all you can do is to late her poor little body. **1891** —— *Moorland Par.* 136 Are you laiting goud?

†**b.** To search or look through; to examine.

13.. *St. Erkenwolde* 155 in Horstm. *Altengl. Leg.* (1881) 269 We haue oure librarie laitid þes longe seuene dayes.

2. *absol.* or *intr.* To look, search. Also *dial.* To look for a word; to hesitate in speech.

c **1300** *Cursor M.* 5975 Quar-to suld yee ferrer lait. **13..** *E.E. Allit. P.* B. 97 Sayde þe lorde to þo ledez, laytez ȝet ferre. *c* **1400** *Destr. Troy* 7669 All.. laited aftur þe lede with a light wille. *c* **1460** *Towneley Myst.* x. 137 And this is, who wyll late, The sext moneth of hyr conceytate, That geld is cald. *Ibid.* xviii. 180 Thise ar the commaundmentys ten, who so will lely layt. **1804** R. ANDERSON *Cumberld. Ball.* 87 He ne'er hes a teale widout laitin.

lait, Sc. and north. form of LATE.

laitakarite (laɪtəˈkɑːraɪt). *Min.* [ad. Finn. *laitakariittii* (A. Vorma 1959, in *Geologi* (Helsinki) III. XI. 11), f. the name of Aarne *Laitakari* (b. 1890), director of the Geological Survey of Finland (see quot. 1959): see -ITE¹.] A white rhombohedral selenide and sulphide of bismuth, Bi_4Se_2S.

1959 *Mineral. Abstr.* XIV. 139/2 The new mineral was named, in the honour of the discoverer of the material from which it was disclosed, laitakarite, and it is supposed to be isomorphous with joseite. **1963** *Canad. Mineralogist* VII. 678 The data given in Table 1 show the probable identity of laitakarite and selenjoseite. **1968** I. KOSTOV *Mineral.* II. ii. 164 Additional minerals are laitakarite (Bi_4Se_2S) and paraguanajuatite ($Bi_2(Se,S)_3$), which are isostructural with the minerals of the tetradymite group.

laitance (ˈleɪtəns). Also (*erron.*) **laitence**. [Fr.] A milky scum appearing on the surface of freshly laid cement.

1909 TAYLOR & THOMPSON *Treat. Concrete* (ed. 2) xv. 303 The milky laitance which appears on concrete laid under water represents an actual loss of cement. **1930** *Engineering* 23 May 677/3 The value of carefully providing for the adequate junction between successive layers and the elimination of laitance. **1939** *Archit. Rev.* LXXXV. 267 First is the way in which the tile is fixed to its backing, due to insufficient soaking of both the tile and the rendering, robbing the cement of the water necessary for proper hydration; 'killing' the cement by re-mixing new and old compo that has already started to set; 'laitence', a white scum of water and cement which forms on the surface of the bed of floor tiles, if it is pressed up and down too much while the tiles are being levelled. **1968** D. C. TIBBETTS in E. G. Swenson *Performance of Concrete* (1969) x. 168 Laitance was removed and necessary holes cut in the sides of the cylinders for the setting of the low water ends of the concrete braces.

laiter, obs. variant of LAUGHTER².

laith, laith-: see LOATH, LOATH-.

laithly, obs. form of LAIDLY *a. dial.*

†ˈ**laiting.** *Obs.* Also 4 **leityng(e.** [f. LAIT *v.*¹ + -ING¹.] Lightning.

c **1340** *Cursor M.* 533 (Trin.) þonder & leitynge [*Cott.* leuening]. **1388** WYCLIF *Ecclus.* xxxii. 14 Leityng schal go bifore hail. **1422** tr. *Secreta Secret., Priv. Priv.* 141 Of the Reyne also comyth.. many harmes, As thondyr, laitynge.

laity (ˈleɪɪtɪ). Forms: 6 **layetie**, 6–7 **lai-, laytie**, 6–8 **laiety**, 7 **lay(e)ty**, 7– **laity**. [f. *lai*, LAY *a.* + -(I)TY. An AF. *laité* occurs, with the sense of 'lay property' (cf. *realty, spiritualty*), in *Year-bk. 33 Ed. I* (1864) 411.]

1. The condition or state of a layman; the not being in orders.

1616 BULLOKAR, *Laitie*, the estate or degree of a lay man. **1726** AYLIFFE *Parergon* 208 The more usual Causes of this Deprivation are such as these, viz. a mere Laity, or want of Holy Orders [etc.]. **1831** MANNING *Let.* in *Life* (1895) I. x. 72 The objection against my laity has been strongly urged.

2. The body of the people not in orders as opposed to the clergy; laymen collectively. (The older term for 'the laity' was LAY-FEE. In 1548 a synonymous *lealty* occurs app. as a nonce-wd.)

? **1541** *Constitutio T. Cranmeri et aliorum* in Wilkins *Concilia* (1737) III. 862/2 In the yere of our Lord MDXLI it was agreed.. that if any of the inferiour degree dyd receave at their table any Arch-bishop, Bishop,.. or any of the laitie of lyke degree, as Duke, Marquess [etc.]. **1546** LANGLEY tr. *Pol. Verg. De Invent.* IV. iii. 85 In the Christen common welthe there bee two sortes of menne one called the laytie. **1579** FENTON *Guicciard.* III. (1599) 143 The diuision being no lesse amongst the spiritualtie then the layetie. **1660** R. COKE *Power & Subj.* 82 Both of them have power to consecrate the Sacrament of our Lord's Supper, and give it to the laity. **1710** PRIDEAUX *Orig. Tithes* iii. 162 The Alienations.. of Tithes which gave unto the Laiety in France a civil Right to them. **1780** W. COLE in Willis & Clark *Cambridge* (1886) III. 68 Most of the Clerical Subscribers, and possibly many of the Layity. **1837–9** HALLAM *Hist. Lit.* I. I. iii. §42 The clergy were now retrograding, while the laity were advancing. **1870** DICKENS *E. Drood* ii, You may offer bad grammar to the laity, or the humbler clergy, but not to the Dean.

3. Unprofessional people, as opposed to those who follow some learned profession, to artists, etc.

1832 AUSTIN *Jurispr.* xxxviii, The laity (or non-lawyer part of the community) are competent to conceive the more general rules. **1875** HELPS *Ess., Organiz. Daily Life* 107 Artists are wont to think the criticisms of the laity rather weak and superfluous. **1880** H. QUILTER in *Macm. Mag.* Sept. 393 Most of the laity still connect the word pre-Raphaelitism with visions of gaunt melancholy women. **1898** *Allbutt's Syst. Med.* V. 281 The disease being one of the existence of which the laity may be said to be ignorant.

Hence ˈ**laityship** *nonce-wd.*, the position or personality of one of the laity; in quot. a jocular title.

1670 EACHARD *Cont. Clergy* 128 Should I make thy laityship heir of such an estate.. thou wouldest count me the wisest man that ever was since the creation.

laizer, obs. form of LAZAR.

lak¹ (lak). Repr. *U.S. dial.* (esp. *Black English*) pronunc. of LIKE *a.*, *adv.*, and *v.*¹

1881 J. C. HARRIS *Nights with Uncle Remus* (1884) xvi. 80 He'd skuze hisse'f, he would, en gallop down de big road a piece, en paw up de san' same lak dat ar ball-faced steer w'at tuck'n tuck off yo' pa' coat-tail las' Feberwary. **1901** F. L. STANTON (*song-title*) Mighty lak' a rose. **1936** M. MITCHELL *Gone with Wind* v. 78 Ain' nobody got a wais' lak mah lamb. **1949** *Crisis* (N.Y.) Nov. 303/1 Would you lak t'go t' the sto' ..lak a darlin' li'l boy. **1973** B. GATES in S. Henderson *Understanding New Black Poetry* 310 Now, you gon' stop Yo ackin lak a fool!

Lak² (læk). The name of a Caucasian language (see quot. 1954).

1954 PEI & GAYNOR *Dict. Ling.* 118 *Lak*, a language.. spoken in the Caucasus; a member of the Eastern Caucasian group of the North Caucasian family of languages. **1971** *Language* XLVII. 233 The West Caucasian languages, where.. Lak has forty cases and Tabassaran forty-eight. **1972** *Ibid.* XLVIII. 845 Hockett exemplifies 3a with 'Arunta.. Lak and Wishram'.

lak, obs. form of LACK; var. LATCH.

‖**lakatoi** (ˈlækətɔɪ). [Papuan.] In New Guinea, a native dug-out canoe, with two or more hulls.

1885 W. W. GILL in Chalmers & Gill *Work & Adventures New Guinea* II. i. 258 We were fortunate in seeing two *lakatoi* or Gulf-going crafts; the larger one consisted of fourteen immense canoes lashed firmly together and decked. *Ibid.* 259 Each *lakatoi* starting for the Gulf is filled with earthenware pots. **1911** *Encycl. Brit.* XX. 742/2 The Papuans build excellent canoes and other boats... The most remarkable of their vessels is the 'lakatoi', composed of several capacious dug-outs, each nearly 50 ft. long, which are strongly lashed together. **1926** *Mariner's Mirror* XII. 216/2 Fig. 2 is a *lakatoi* of Port Moresby, S.E. New Guinea. **1964** *Sunday Truth* (Brisbane) 9 Aug. 20/5 Some of them have purchased £400 outboard motors which they fit to lakatois—generally two hollowed out logs with a connecting wooden decking. **1964** *Punch* 26 Aug. 319/2 How will the *lakatoi* run before the wind of change? **1968** *Mariner's Mirror* LIV. 348 Today the sails used on lakatoi are rectangular, with the peak held by a sprit.

lakay, laka(y)n, obs. ff. LACKEY, LAKIN¹.

†**lake**, *sb.*¹ *Obs.* Forms: 1 **lác**, 2–3 **lac, (lak-)**, 3 **loc, (lok-), loac**. [OE. *lác* (:—prehistoric **laikom*, **laikâ*) neut. and fem.; not found with the same meaning in any other Teut. lang., but usually identified with the Com. Teut. **laiko-* 'play', LAKE *sb.*² With regard to the sense, it may be compared with OE. *lícian* to please, LIKE *v.*, from another grade of the same root.] An offering, sacrifice; also, a gift. Only OE. and early ME. ***to lake*** (dat.), as a gift.

Beowulf (Z.) 1584 He.. oðer swylc ut of-ferede lað-licu lac. *c* **1000** *Ags. Gosp.* Matt. viii. 4 Ac gang æt-eowe þe þam sacerde and bring hym þa lac þe moyses bebead on hyra ȝecyðnesse. *c* **1175** *Lamb. Hom.* 39 Ne con him crist na mare þong þene þah he sloȝe þin child and bere þe his heaued to lake. *c* **1200** *Trin. Coll. Hom.* 45 þe þre loc þe ich er nemde þat is gold, and recheles and mirre. *a* **1225** *Leg. Kath.* 63 Ðe riche reoðeren.. brohten to lake. *a* **1225** *Ancr. R.* 152 þe þreo kinges.. offren Jesu Crist þeo deorewurðe þreo lokes. *c* **1250** *Gen. & Ex.* 1798 And iacob sente fer bi-foren him riche loac, and sundri boren.

†**lake**, *sb.*² *Obs.* Forms: 2 *Orm.* **leȝȝk**, 3 **leyk**, 4 **laic**, 4–6 **laik(e, layk(e**, 5 **lak(e.** [a. ON. *leik-r* play, corresp. to OE. *lác* neut. or masc. warlike activity (once only; but see LAKE *sb.*¹), OHG. *leich* masc. and neut. song, melody, Goth. *laik-s* dance:—OTeut. **laiko-*, a verbal sb. from **laikan* to play, LAKE *v.*¹]

1. Play, sport, fun, glee. In *pl.* games, tricks, goings on.

c **1200** ORMIN 2166 Inn ægæde and in leȝȝkess. *c* **1300** *Havelok* 1021 For it ne was non horse-knaue.. That he ne kam thider, the leyk to se. **13..** *E.E. Allit. P.* B. 274 þat for her lodlych laykez alosed þay were. **1340–70** *Alex. & Dind.* 465 We ne louen in our land no laik nor no mirthe. *a* **1400** *Sir Perc.* 1704 The childe hadd no powste His laykes to lett. *a* **1400–50** *Alexander* 4685 þe cursed laike o couatis ware clene with it drenchid. *c* **1460** *Towneley Myst.* xvi. 66 Welcom hym worshipfully laghyng with lake. **1570** LEVINS *Manip.* 198/15 A layke, play, *ludus*.

b. A stake at play.

1597 MONTGOMERIE *Cherrie & Slae* 1109, I pledge, or all the play be playd That sum sall lose a laike.

2. A fight, contest.

[*a* **1000** *Guthlac* 1007 Wiȝa nealæceð unlæt laces.] *c* **1400** *Destr. Troy* 10408 þe lyght wex lasse, and þe laik endit. *c* **1420** *Anturs of Arth.* 538 (Douce MS.) Lordes and ladies of þat laike likes. *c* **1470** *Golagros & Gaw.* 832 Thus may ye lippin on the lake, throu lair that I leir. **1515** *Scot. Field* 569 in *Chetham Misc.* (1856) II, This layke lasted on the lande, the lengthe of fower howers.

lake (leɪk), *sb.*³ *Obs.* exc. *dial.* [OE. *lacu* str. fem.; the sense shows that it is not ad. L. *lacus* (see next) but a native word, from a Teut. root

**lak-* denoting moisture; cf. OE. *lęccan* to moisten, LEACH *v.*[2], also LEAK *sb.* and *v.* The OHG. *lahha* (G. *lache*) pond, bog, is formally coincident, but is perh. of Latin origin.]

A small stream of running water; also, a channel for water. *Obs.* exc. *dial.*

955 *Charter of Edred* in Earle *Charters* 382 Ðæt to Mæȝðe forda andlang lace ut on Temese. **1235–52** *Rentalia Glaston.* (Somerset Rec. Soc.) 35 Pro decem acris inter Lak. *c* **1450** HOLLAND *Howlat* 19 This riche Revir dovn ran.. Throwe ane forest.. And for to lende by that laike thocht me levar. **1559** MORWYNG *Evonym.* 346 The matter must.. be by and by tied and pressed in a little presse of wood, with a little lake or gutter of wood. *c* **1630** RISDON *Surv. Devon* §341 (1810) 351 Lyn, a pretty lake, streameth out of the Exmoor hills. **1630** T. WESTCOTE *Devon.* (1845) 265 We shall find him [Taw] a very small lake at his birth in Dartmoor. **1842–71** PULMAN *Rustic Sk.* 6 Vrem rise to mouth there's lots o' lakes, —An rivers zum—that into 'n fall. **1880** *E. Cornw. Gloss.*, *Lake*, a small stream of running water. **1885** *Pall Mall G.* 11 June 4/1 Each tiny drain, called locally a 'lake', was edged broadly by a band of great saffron-hued king cups.

b. *Comb.*: †**lake-frith**, the close-time for fishing in a stream; †**lake-rift**, a gully made by a stream.

1235–52 *Rentalia Glaston.* (Somerset Rec. Soc.) 141 Et debet servare Lakefrithe. **13..** *E.E. Allit. P.* B. 536 And lyonnez and lebardez to þe lake ryftes.

lake (leɪk), *sb.*[4] Forms: 3, 5 lac, 3, 4 lak, 4–5 laake, leke, 4–6 lacke, 5–7 *Sc.* laik(e, 6 *Sc.* layk, 7 laque, 3– lake. [Early ME. *lac*, a. OF. *lac*, ad. L. *lacus* basin, tub, tank, lake, pond; the popular form of the word in OF. was *lai*. The present Eng. form *lake* (recorded from the 14th c.) may be due to confusion with prec., or perh. rather to independent adoption of L. *lacus*.]

1. a. A large body of water entirely surrounded by land; *properly*, one sufficiently large to form a geographical feature, but in recent use often applied to an ornamental water in a park, etc.

c **1205** LAY. 1279–80 Ouer þen lac of Siluius & ouer þen lac [*c* **1275** lake] of Philisteus. *a* **1300** *Cursor M.* 2863 A stinkand see, þat semes als a lake of hell. **13..** *E.E. Allit. P.* B. 438 Þenne lasned þe llak þat large watz are. *c* **1375** *Sc. Leg. Saints* xx. (*Blasius*) 226 Quhy thole ȝe þame oure godis tak, & þis to kast þame in þe lak? *c* **1400** MAUNDEV. (Roxb.) xxi. 98 In þe grund of þat lac er funden faire precious stanes. *c* **1450** *St. Cuthbert* (Surtees) 799 Þar is a grete lake nere hand. **1513** DOUGLAS *Æneis* VII. xii. 150 Of thair bruyt resoundis the river And all the layk of Asia fer and neyr. **1520** *Caxton's Chron. Eng., Descr. Irel.* 5/1 The ryver Ban renneth out of the leke into the north ocean. **1657** HOWELL *Londinop.* 382 Being built on the South side of a large Laque. **1696** WHISTON *Theory Earth* IV. (1722) 362 There were only smaller Lakes and Seas, but no great Ocean before the Deluge. **1774** GOLDSM. *Nat. Hist.* (1776) I. 84 Nothing can exceed the beauty of the landscape which this lake affords. **1813** BYRON *Let.* 5 Sept., in Moore *Lett. & Jrnls.* (1830) I. 426 Rogers wants me to go with him on a crusade to the Lakes. **1835** WORDSWORTH (*title*) A Guide through the District of the Lakes. **1836** W. IRVING *Astoria* I. 210 The navigation of the lakes is carried on by steamboats. **1853** M. ARNOLD *Sohrab & Rustum* Poems 1877 I. 108 Never more Shall the lake glass her, flying over it.

b. *transf.* and *fig.* (perh. in some instances from sense 2).

a **1225** *St. Marher.* 14 Ich leade ham.. iþe ladliche lake of the suti sunne. **1526** TINDALE *Rev.* xx. 14 Deth and hell were cast into the lake of fyre. **1669** STURMY *Mariner's Mag.* Verses a4 Over the Ocean's Universal Lake. **1866** G. MACDONALD *Ann. Q. Neighb.* ii. (1878) 21 Close by the vestry-door, there was this little billowy lake of grass. **1890** W. J. GORDON *Foundry* 109 We can see the wide lake of liquid metal simmering and spurting like porridge. **1974** *Daily Tel.* 30 July 17/1 The Common Market has a 'wine lake' estimated at 8 million litres..—and yesterday a Labour MP called for some of it to be brought to Britain. **1975** *Times* 9 Apr. 15/3 Butter mountains and wine lakes are part of the price which Europe pays for a common agricultural policy.

c. *the Great Lake* (a phrase borrowed from the North American Indians): the Atlantic ocean. *the Great Lakes*: the five lakes Superior, Huron, Michigan, Erie, and Ontario, which form the boundary between Canada and the U.S. (In earlier use freq. without the adjective.)

c **1665** P. E. RADISSON *Voyages* (1885) 187 Those great lakes had not so soone comed to our knowledge if it had not ben for those brutish people. **1727** C. COLDEN *Hist. Five Indian Nations* 64 We have put ourselves under the great Sachem Charles, that lives on the other side of the great Lake. **1748** H. ELLIS *Voyage to Hudson's-Bay* 151 A Communication with the great Lakes behind Canada. **1759** P. COLLINSON in W. Darlington *Memorials J. Bartram & H. Marshall* (1849) 217, I don't remember ever reading of any [goats] in the country about the lakes. **1803** W. B. GROVE *Let.* 25 Feb. in J. Steele *Papers* (1924) I. 367 The Ocean, the Mexican Gulf, the Mississippi & the Lakes must be our boundaries. **1813** *Niles' Reg.* V. 65/1 The position of the great lakes is.. well known to the people of the United States. **1840** J. F. COOPER *Pathfinder* I. p. v, Incidents that might be supposed characteristic of the Great Lakes. **1857** G. LAWRENCE *Guy Liv.* xxxi. 308 The most terrible tempest that ever desolated the shores of the Great Lake. **1902** *Encycl. Brit.* XXXII. 551/1 Plan of Great Lake steamer. **1904** N. S. SHALER *Citizen* 77 Where the territory borders on the sea or the Great Lakes, the authorities have charge of such harbours as are not in the control of the federal authority. **1966** *Canadian Geogr. Jrnl.* Apr. 113/2 The abnormally low water levels on the Great Lakes.

d. *to jump* (or *go* (*and*) *jump*) *in the lake*: see JUMP *v.* 1 d.

†**2.** A pond, a pool. *Obs.*

a **1000** *O.E. Chron.* an. 656 (Laud MS.) Þurh ælle þa meres and feonnes þa liggen toward Huntendune porte and þas meres and laces. *a* **1300** *Cursor M.* 11934 Þarbi satt iesus on his plai, And lakes seuen he made o clai. *c* **1325** *Song Mercy* 162 in *E.E.P.* (1862) 123 We slepe a[s] swolle swyn in lake. *c* **1386** CHAUCER *Wife's Prol.* 269 Ne noon so grey goos gooth in the lake. *a* **1400** *Pistill of Susan* 229 He lyft vp þe lach and leop ouer þe lake, þat 3outhe. ? *a* **1500** *Chester Pl.* (E.E.T.S.) vii. 291 Lye there, lydder, in the lake. **1609** *Sc. Acts Jas. VI* (1816) IV. 432/1 All vtheris, garthis, pullis, haldis, Laikis and nettis.

†**3. a.** [after Vulg. *lacus*.] A pit; a den (of lions); *occas.* a grave. *Obs.*

c **1320** R. BRUNNE *Medit.* 347 For þey to my soule deluyn a lake. *a* **1340** HAMPOLE *Psalter* vii. 16 Þe lake he oppynd and vp grofe it. **1382** WYCLIF *Isa.* xxxviii. 18 Thei shul not abyden thi treuthe, that gon doun in to the lake. *a* **1450** *Cov. Myst.* (Shaks. Soc.) 350 Whan he dede ryse out of his lake Than was ther suche an erthe quake That [etc.]. **1506** GUYLFORDE *Pilgr.* (Camden) 35 And set hym in ye lake of lyons where Danyell the prophete was.

fig. *a* **1400** *Prymer* (1891) 83 He ladde me out of þe laake of wrechchednesse.

†**b.** An underground dungeon; a prison. *Obs.*

1382 WYCLIF *Jer.* xxxviii. 6 Thei putte doun Jeremye in cordis and in to the lake. **1447** BOKENHAM *Seyntys* (Roxb.) 73 Cristyn thus entryd was In to that horribyl and lothful lake.

†**4.** Used after L. *lacus* = a wine-vat. *Obs.*

1382 WYCLIF *Rev.* xiv. 20 And the lake is defoulid with oute the citee, and the blood wente out of the lake vn to the brijdels of horsis. **1657** G. THORNLEY *Daphnis & Chloe* 48 Daphnis cast them [*sc.* grapes] into the presse, and trod them there; and then anon, out of the Lake, tunn'd the Wine into the Butts.

5. *attrib.* and *Comb.*: **a.** simple attrib., as *lake-bed*, *-fishery*, *-fowl*, *-front*, *-island*, *-isle*, *-level*, *-shore*, *-side*, *-steamer*, *-system*, *-water*; also *lakeward* adj. and adv. Also in the names of fishes, as *lake-bass*, *-herring*, *-shad*, *-sturgeon*, *-trout*, *-whiting*, for which see the second member.

1795 J. SCOTT *U.S. Gazetteer* s.v. *Vermont*, A species of fish called *lake bass. **1884** G. B. GOODE *Fisheries U.S.: Nat. Hist. Aquatic Animals* 424 The White Bass or Striped Lake Bass, *Roccus chrysops*. **1973** R. LOCKRIDGE *Not I, said the Sparrow* (1974) vi. 87 There was only one right way to cook lake bass. **1906** *Yorks. N. & Q.* July 100 Their position on the edge of the old *lake-bed. **1937** *Discovery* Jan. 24/1 The bones [of the shovel-tusked Mastodon] lay embedded in the hardened mud deposit of an ancient lake-bed in Mongolia. **1883** F. A. SMITH *Swedish Fisheries* 13 (Fish. Exh. Publ.) It is scarcely possible to find the approximate value of the *lake fisheries of Sweden by the official returns. **1813** HOGG *Queen's Wake, Nt. Second* Wks. (1876) 26 The *lake-fowl's wake was heard no more. **1880** 'MARK TWAIN' *Tramp Abroad* 245 The *lake-front is walled with masonry like a pier. **1968** *Economist* 13 July 38/3 A lakefront site that would be better as a park. **1842** J. E. DEKAY *Zool. N.Y.* IV. 267 The Lake Moon-eye, *Hyodon clodalis*,.. is common in Lake Erie. At Buffalo and Barcelona, it is called Moon-eye, Shiner, and *Lake Herring. **1875** *Amer. Naturalist* IX. 135, I received.. a collection of deep water 'Siscoes'... Compared with Coregonus most of the species have a more slender form; hence their popular name of 'lake herrings', although their resemblance to the sea herring is quite superficial. **1955** *Arctic Terms* 48/1 *Lake herring*, any of various whitefish of the genus *Leucichthys*, caught in great numbers in circumpolar fresh waters. Also called 'cisco'. **1893** W. B. YEATS in *Bookman* May 43/1 It is said that an enchanted tree once grew on the little *lake-island of Innisfree. **1890** —— *Countess Kathleen* (1892) 121 (*title*) The *Lake Isle of Innisfree. **1917** E. POUND *Lustra* 61 (*title*) The lake isle. **1860** MAURY *Phys. Geog. Sea* (Low) xii. §538 A lowering of the *lake-level. **1798** I. ALLEN *Nat. & Pol. Hist. Vermont* 61 The two Frenchmen were landed.. with instructions to follow the *lake shore. **1813** *Niles' Reg.* IV. 159/1 Previous to this period, a great deal of prejudice existed against the lake *shore*, as unhealthy. **1849** *Ex. Doc. 31st U.S. Congress 1 Sess. House* No. 5. II. 731 The sandstone on the lake-shore is.. covered by fifteen.. feet of sand and clay. **1851** C. CIST *Sk. Cincinnati in 1851* 319 Hence [arise] their efforts to reach Chicago, by way of the Erie lake shore. **1896** HOWELLS *Impressions & Exp.* 7 In that cold lake-shore country the people dwelt in wooden structures. **1973** *Tucson* (Arizona) *Daily Citizen* 22 Aug. 1/1 The 15½-foot-deep lake gives Tucson the appearance of being a major lakeshore metropolis. **1560** J. DAUS tr. *Sleidane's Comm.* 323 After they couche them selues in a pece of grounde, by the *lake side. **1727** *Philip Quarll* (1816) 31 He attended me to the lake side. **1871** W. MORRIS in Mackail *Life* (1899) I. 258 A swan rose trumpeting from the lakeside. **1847** *Knickerbocker* XXX. 456 He has been inspired by looking down through the iron foot-grating of a great *lake-steamer. **1888** C. D. FERGUSON *Experiences Forty-Niner* i. 11 It was in the month of September, 1849, when.. I embarked on the lake-steamer, A. D. Patchen for Chicago. **1861** *Times* 22 Oct., Canada and the *lake system ..cut into the States on the north. **1871** W. MORRIS in Mackail *Life* (1899) I. 270 The slope on the *lakeward side. **1890** W. B. YEATS *Countess Kathleen* (1892) 121, I hear *lake water lapping with low sounds. **1906** *Westm. Gaz.* Oct. 6 6/2 And far below the blue lake-waters shine. **1920** JOYCE *Let.* 5 June (1966) II. 469 It should be read in the evening when the lakewater is lapping.

b. instrumental, as *lake-girt*, *-moated*, *-reflected*, *-surrounded* adjs. **c.** locative, as *lake-diver*; *lake-resounding* adj. Also *lake-like* adj.

1657 REEVE *God's Plea* 23 What art thou?.. Adam's Ulcer,.. the *lake-diver, the furnace brand, the brimstone-match of that cursed man. **1878** H. M. STANLEY *Through Dark Continent* I. x. 222 From the summit of this *lake-girt isle. **1908** *Daily Chron.* 4 Aug. 3/1 The *noche triste* when the Spaniards found themselves surrounded in the lake-girt capital of the Aztecs. **1843** RUSKIN *Mod. Paint.* I. II. III. iv. 251 White and *lake-like fields [of mist]. **1820** SCOTT *Abbot* xxxviii, The locked, guarded, and *lake-moated Castle of Lochleven. **1821** SHELLEY *Prometh. Unb.* I. i. 744 He will watch.. the *lake-reflected sun illume the yellow bees. **1717** PARNELL *Homer's Batt. Frogs & Mice* 5 The *Lake-resounding Frogs selected Fare. **1821** SHELLEY *Prometh. Unb.* II. ii. 38 Like many a *lake-surrounded flute, Sounds overflow the listener's brain.

6. a. Special comb.: **lake-basin**, a depression which contains, or has contained, a lake; also, the area drained by all the streams entering a lake; **lake country** = LAKE-LAND; **lake-crater**, a crater which contains or has contained a lake; **Lake District** = LAKE-LAND; **lake-fever** *U.S. local*, malaria; **lake-fly** *U.S.*, an ephemerid (*Ephemera simulans*), which swarms in the Great Lakes late in July (*Cent. Dict.*); **Lakehead** *Canad.*, (*a*) *Hist.*, the western end of Lake Ontario (quot. 1827); (*b*) the city of Thunder Bay, Ontario, and the surrounding region on the north-west shore of Lake Superior; **lake-lawyer** *U.S.*, a jocular name given to two different fishes, the bow-fin and the burbot, in allusion to their voracity; **lake-lodge**, **-ore** (see quots); **lake rampart**, **ridge** = *ice-rampart* (ICE *sb.* 8); **lake-weed**, water-pepper (*Polygonum hydropiper*). Also LAKE-LAND.

1833 LYELL *Princ. Geol.* III. 9 The whole assemblage must terminate somewhere:.. where they reach the boundary of the original *lake-basin. **1865** D. PAGE *Handbk. Geol. Terms* (ed. 2) 272 *Lake-basin*, in geography, the depressed area which contains the waters of a lake; also the entire area drained by the streams that fall into a lake. In geology, the concavity.. in which the waters of a lake rest. **1882** *Proc. Boston Soc. Nat. Hist.* XXI. 326 In the Himalaya, the valleys of Nepal and Kashmir are old orographic lake basins. **1965** W. D. THORNBURY *Regional Geomorphol. U.S.* xxiv. 494/2 Fish can be carried by birds from one lake basin into another. **1967** JENNINGS & MABBUTT *Landform Stud. Austral. & New Guinea* vi. 111 Such an argument would explain why well formed alluvial fans survive outside the catchment of Lake Torrens and why they are absent or present in only a degraded form within the lake basin. **1842** *Amer. Pioneer* I. 211 No where was the pressure or want of money more sensibly felt than in the *lake country. **1875** LOWELL *Wks.* (1890) IV. 363 The greater part of Wordsworth's vacations was spent in his native Lake-country. **1833** LYELL *Princ. Geol.* III. 197 If we pass from the Upper to the Lower Eifel we find the celebrated *lake-crater of Laach. **1835** WORDSWORTH *Yarrow Revisited* 241 *Force* is the word used in the *Lake District for Water-fall. **1851** *Art Jrnl.* 1 May 132/2 The scale upon which the scenery of the English Lake district is laid out. **1886** J. PRESTWICH *Geol.* I. 267 In the Lake District the planes of cleavage also usually strike about E.N.E. **1936** *Discovery* May 150/2 Lovers of the Lake District.. feel that the peculiar wild beauty of the innermost fells will be destroyed by the introduction of large acreages of larch and spruce planted in small rows on the hillsides. **1957** G. E. HUTCHINSON *Treat. Limnol.* I. i. 1 Lakes therefore tend to be grouped together in *lake districts*. *Ibid.*, The whole group of lakes of a given lake district may be compared with another group. **1827** *Gore Gaz.* (Ancaster, Ont.) 25 May 50/4 It appeared, that a person at the *Lake Head, had furnished the York Garrison with 800 bbls. of Flour last year. **1955** *Beaver* Summer 37 From the deck of the loaded freighter, bound for the Sault and Welland Canals, the grain strongholds of the lakehead stand like castles against the sunset. **1968** *Globe & Mail* (Toronto) 13 Feb. B7/2 One of the world's largest multiple-line insurance companies requires a sales oriented management man to establish a sales force in the lakehead. **1859** BARTLETT *Dict. Amer.*, **Lake lawyer*, the Western Mud-fish.. Dr. Kirtland says it is.. called the lake lawyer, from its 'ferocious looks and voracious habits'. **1884** *Evangelical Mag.* May 212 [Beavers'] Lodges are built sometimes on the shores of lakes ..These are called '*lake-lodges'. **1864** T. L. PHIPSON *Utiliz. Minute Life* x. 256 In the lakes of Sweden there are vast layers of iron oxide almost exclusively built up by animalcules. This kind of iron-stone is called *lake-ore. **1860** C. H. HITCHCOCK in *Proc. Amer. Assoc. Adv. Sci.* XIII. 335 We have discovered similar walls of stone in Vermont, and venture to describe this form of drift under the name of *Lake Ramparts. **1870** *Amer. Naturalist* IV. 199 Above all these Drift deposits.. are the '*lake ridges'—embankments of sand, gravel, sticks, leaves, etc., which run imperfectly parallel with the present outlines of the lake margins. **1693** *Phil. Trans.* XVII. 876 'Tis branched and seeded something like Spinage or Mercury, but leaved rather like *Lakeweed. **1760** J. LEE *Introd. Bot.* App. 316 Lakeweed, *Polygonum*.

b. Lake poets, **school**, terms casually applied to the three poets, Coleridge, Southey, and Wordsworth, who resided in the region of the English Lakes; **Lake poetry**, the poetry written by them.

1816 *Edin. Rev.* XXVII. 66 Other productions of the Lake School. *Ibid.* XXVII. 278 His [*sc.* Byron's] views fell more in with those of the Lake poets, than of any other party in the poetical commonwealth. **1817** *Edin. Rev.* Aug. 509 When we have occasion to consider any new publication from the Lake school. **1824** MILL in *Westm. Rev.* I. 516 Mr. Southey ..and the other Lake poets.. commenced writing with higher objects. **1837** *Penny Cycl.* VII. 343/2 The appellation of Lake-poets, given to these three individuals after the publication of the 'Lyrical Ballads.' **1843** H. N. COLERIDGE in Stanley *Life Arnold* (1884) I. i. 16 What has been somewhat unreasonably called the Lake Poetry. **1874** L. STEPHEN *Hours in Library* II. 307 To the whole Lake school his [Hazlitt's] attitude is always the same—justice done grudgingly.

c. lake-dweller, one who in pre-historic times lived in a **lake-dwelling** or **lake-habitation**, i.e. one built upon piles driven into the bed of a lake; **lake-hamlet**, **-settlement**, **-village**, a collection of such dwellings; **lake-man** = *lake-dweller*.

1863 LYELL *Antiq. Man* 21 In the stone period the *lake-dwellers cultivated all these cereals. *Ibid.* 18 The Swiss *lake-dwellings seem first to have attracted attention during the dry winter of 1853–4. **1884** *Times* (weekly ed.) 19 Sept. 12 Researches into the lake-dwellings of West Scotland. **1865** LUBBOCK *Preh. Times* 69 The piles used in the Swiss Stone age *Lake-habitations were evidently..prepared with the help of stone axes. *Ibid.* (1878) 54 A..piece of pottery apparently intended to represent a *Lake-hamlet. **1884** W. WESTALL *Contemp. Rev.* July 70 The brain of the *lake-man was equal to that of the men of our own time. **1863** LYELL *Antiq. Man* 23 The reindeer is missing in the Swiss *lake-settlements. **1865** LUBBOCK *Preh. Times* 126 The *Lake-villages of the Bronze age were contemporaneous.

†**lake**, *sb.*⁵ *Obs.* Also 6 *Sc.* **laik**, 7 **layke**. [First found in Chaucer; prob. a. Du. *laken*, corresp. to OE. *lachen* 'clamidem' (Wr.-Wülcker 377/22), OFris. *leken*, OS. *lakan* mantle (*chlamys*), veil of the temple, OHG. *lahhan* (MHG. *lachen*), mod.G. *lakan* from LG.] Fine linen.

c **1386** CHAUCER *Sir Thopas* 147 He dide next his white leere Of clooth of lake fyn and cleere. **1447** BOKENHAM *Seyntys* (Roxb.) 73 Bryngyng hir brede als whyt as lake. **1501** DOUGLAS *Pal. Hon.* I. lii, Thir fair ladyis in silk and claith of laik. **1535** STEWART *Cron. Scot.* III. 234 Quhilk causit hes to lurk wnder the laik Richt mony cowart durst nocht cum to straik. **1603** *Philotus* lx, The quhytest layke bot with the blackest asse.

lake (leɪk), *sb.*⁶ [Orig. a variant of LAC¹.]

1. A pigment of a reddish hue, originally obtained from lac (cf. LAC¹ 2), and now from cochineal treated as in 3.

1616 BULLOKAR, *Lake*, a faire red colour vsed by painters. **1622** PEACHAM *Compl. Gent.* xiii. (1634) 130 Lay your colours upon your Pallet thus: first your white lead, then Lake. **1674** *Beale's Pocket Bk.* in H. Walpole *Vertue's Anecd. Paint.* (1786) III. 131 Several parcells of Lake of my own makeing. **1728** DESAGULIERS in *Phil. Trans.* XXXV. 608 Instead of Vermilion the red Paper may be painted with Carmine or Lake. **1816** J. SMITH *Panorama Sci. & Art* II. 751 Deep Prussian blue and lake..form a purple of the next degree of excellence. **1859** GULLICK & TIMBS *Paint.* 224 The common lake is prepared from Brazil wood.

2. *transf.* as the name of a colour.

1660 *Albert Durer Revived* 11 Lake..is an excellent Crimson-colour. **1686** AGLIONBY *Painting Illustr.* I. 23 In imploying of fine Colours, as fine lacks Ultra Marine Green, &c. **1882** *Garden* 7 Oct. 312/3 Of new flowers there are.. Constancy, yellow, deeply edged with lake.

3. In extended sense: A pigment obtained by the combination of animal, vegetable, or coal-tar colouring matter with some metallic oxide or earth. Often preceded by some qualifying word, as *crimson*, *Florence*, *green*, *madder*, *yellow*, etc. *lake*. ***Indian lake***: a crimson pigment prepared from stick-lac treated with alum and alkali.

1684 R. WALLER *Nat. Exper.* 137 How to take the Lake of any Flower. **1791** HAMILTON *Berthollet's Dyeing* I. I. I. ii. 37 If a solution of a colouring substance be mixed with a solution of alum..[and] if..we add an alkali..the colouring particles are then precipitated, combined with the alumine ..this compound has got the name of Lake. **1812** SIR H. DAVY *Chem. Philos.* 430 The red juices of fruits were fixed by it [tungsten] so as to make permanent and beautiful lakes. **1822** IMISON *Sci. & Art* II. 410 The lakes chiefly used are red colours, and these are of different qualities. **1853** W. GREGORY *Inorg. Chem.* (ed. 3) 204 Carmine is a lake of cochineal. **1866** ROSCOE *Elem. Chem.* xx. 180 Alumina..has the power of forming insoluble compounds called lakes with vegetable colouring matter. **1877** O'NEILL in *Encycl. Brit.* VII. 573/1 The precipitate is usually called the 'lake' of the particular metal and colouring matter.

4. *Comb.*, as ***lake-red***, ***vermilion*** sbs. and adjs.; ***lake-coloured*** adj.

1764 *Mus. Rust.* I. 166 *note*, The lake-red used by the painters in enamel is composed of fine gold dissolved in aqua regia, with sal armoniac. **1796** WITHERING *Brit. Plants* (ed. 3) IV. 214 Pileus fine lake red, changing with age to a rich orange and buff. **1882** *Garden* 25 Mar. 196/2 A leafy cluster of blossoms..of a brilliant lake-vermillion hue. **1898** P. MANSON *Trop. Diseases* i. 25 The black pigment shews up very distinctly in the homogeneous lake-coloured sheet of free hæmoglobin.

lake (leɪk), *v.*¹ Now chiefly *dial.* Forms: 1 **lácan**, 4 **leyke, laiky**, 4–6 **laike, layke**, 6, 9 **laak**, 8–9 **laik**, 4– **lake**. [A Com. Teut. reduplicative str. vb., OE. *lácan*, pa. t. *léolc*, *léc* = ON. *leika*, pa. t. *lék* (Sw. *leka*, Da. *lege*), Goth. *laikan*, pa. t. *lailaik*, MHG. *leichen*, pa. t. *leichte*, pa. pple. *geleichen*. The word seems in ME. to have been re-adopted in the Scandinavian form. Its currency is almost entirely northern, no forms with *o* being known. The inflexion has been weak since the 13th c.]

†**1.** *intr.* To exert oneself, move quickly, leap, spring; hence, to fight. *Obs.*

Beowulf (Z.) 2848 Ða ne dorston ær dareðum lacan on hyra man-dryhtnes miclan þearfe. *a* **1000** *Juliana* 674 Heliseus..leolc ofer laȝuflod longe hwile on swonrade. *c* **1205** LAY. 21270 Arður him læc to swa hit a liun weoren. *Ibid.* 28522 Hit læc toward hirede folc vnimete. *c* **1400** *Destr. Troy* 9997 Thus þai laiket o þe laund the long day ouer.

†**b.** *trans.* To move quickly.

c **1205** LAY. 29662 Up he læc þene staf þat water þer after leop.

2. *intr.* To play, sport; *occas.* in amorous or obscene sense; *dial.* to take a holiday from work; to be out of work. Also with *about*, *away*.

c **1300** *Havelok* 950 The children..with him leykeden here fille. **13..** *E.E. Allit. P.* B. 872 Laykez wyth hem as yow lyst & letez my gestes one. **1393** LANGL. *P. Pl.* C. I. 187 And yf hym luste for to layke þanne loke we mowe. *c* **1400** *Destr. Troy* 12734 This Clunestra..For lacke of hir lord laiked besyde. *c* **1440** *York Myst.* xxvi. 238 How þis losell laykis with his lorde. **1570** LEVINS *Manip.* 198/15. **1599** T. CUTWODE *Caltha Poet.* Pref. (1815) A v, Let the lasses giue over laaking in the greene. **1674** RAY *N.C. Words* 28 To Lake: to Play, a word common to all the North Country. **1803** R. ANDERSON *Cumberld. Ball.* 62 The peat-stack we us'd to lake roun'll be brunt ere this! *a* **1804** J. MATHER *Songs* (1862) 91 (Sheffield Gloss.) Why don't these play-acting foak lake away? **1818** SCOTT *Hrt. Midl.* xxxiii, Any tidy lass..that..would not go laiking about to wakes and fairs. **1859** MRS. GASKELL *Round the Sofa* II. 101 The men [in Westmoreland] occasionally going off laking..that is, drinking, for days together. **1892** *Spectator* 16 Apr. 529/1 The Yorkshire word to signify playing, as generally understood, is 'laking'.

†**b.** quasi-*trans.* To sport with, mock. *Obs.*

13.. *Seuyn Sag.* (W.) 1212 A! hou wimmen conne hit make Whan thai wil ani man lake!

†**3.** *refl.* To amuse oneself, play. *Obs.*

c **1350** *Will. Palerne* 31 [He] layked him long while to lesten þat merþe. *c* **1380** *Sir Ferumb.* 3356 Þai hadden.. burdes briȝte & bolde..to layky hem wan þay wolde. *a* **1400–50** *Alexander* 1770 Se quat I send to þe, son þi-selfe with to laike. *c* **1425** WYNTOUN *Cron.* II. xiv. 1271 As this Queyne apon a day Hyr laykand in a medow lay.

†**lake**, *v.*² *Obs.* [f. LAKE *sb.*¹] *trans.* To present an offering or sacrifice to.

c **1200** ORMIN 1172 Þa lakesst tu Drihhtin wiþþ shep Gast-like i þine þæwess. *Ibid.* 7430 Þa þre kingess lakedenn Crist Wiþþ þrinne kinne lakess.

lake (leɪk), *v.*³ [f. LAKE *sb.*⁶] *trans.* To make lake-coloured; *spec.* by causing the hæmoglobin in red blood cells to pass out into the plasma. Hence **laked** *ppl. a.*

1898 *Allbutt's Syst. Med.* V. 446 This difficulty [number of chromocytes obscuring leucocytes] may be overcome by using Thomas' 0·3 acetic acid solution for diluting the blood, this having the effect of 'laking' the chromocytes. **1903** *Science* 6 Mar. 369 For the preparation of hæmoglobin the blood was collected in ammonium oxalate, washed, laked with distilled water [etc.]. **1912** GULLAND & GOODALL *Blood* vi. 48 Dilution of the plasma causes the corpuscles to swell up and become rounded, and if the dilution be carried too far the corpuscle ruptures and the hæmoglobin passes into solution. The blood is then said to be 'laked'. **1925** C. H. BROWNING *Bacteriol.* vi. 122 If now tetanus toxin is added the suspension soon becomes transparent, *i.e.* it is laked or lysed, owing to the hæmoglobin diffusing out of the red cells. **1946** *Nature* 28 Dec. 953/1 This is..far from reaching the refractive index level of the red cells (which would have resulted in producing 'laked blood' without hæmolysis).

lake, obs. form of LAC *sb.*¹, LACK.

lakeism: see LAKISM.

'lake-land, 'lakeland. Also with capital initial. [f. LAKE *sb.*⁴ + LAND.]

1. The land of lakes; *spec.* the region of the English lakes, consisting of parts of Cumbria and Lancashire. Also *attrib.*

1829 SOUTHEY *Sir T. More* II. 150 Those contests were carried on at a distance from our Lake-land. **1883** *Spectator* 21 July 928/1 Lovers of English lakeland. **1884** *Illustr. Lond. News* 22 Nov. 491 Will you enlighten us lakeland folk? **1895** *Daily News* 19 Aug. 3/1 How delicious are these lakeland gardens.

2. Lakeland terrier, a rough-coated, red or black and tan terrier with a stocky body and a broad muzzle, belonging to a breed developed in Lakeland; also *ellipt.*

1928 *Kennel Gaz.* Dec. 1294/1 (*heading*) Any other breed or variety of British, Colonial or foreign dogs not classified. .. Lakeland terriers. **1931** *Times Lit. Suppl.* 13 Aug. 620/4 Others [*sc.* terriers] in favour are the Border, the Lakeland, the Fox, the Sealyham. **1960** *Guardian* 18 Nov. 12/6 Two Lakeland Terriers were lost for four days in a disused mine. **1971** F. HAMILTON *World Encycl. Dogs* 457 It is doubtful if anyone knows exactly how the Lakeland Terrier was developed but it is generally thought the Border Terrier, the Bedlington and the Fox Terrier were used in its formation. *Ibid.* 458 The trimming of the Lakeland for the show ring has reached a high peak of perfection.

Hence **'lakelander**, a dweller in lakeland.

1895 *Daily News* 19 Aug. 3/1 As to the rain, Lakelanders seemed to think their district is greatly maligned.

lakeless ('leɪklɪs), *a.* [f. LAKE *sb.*⁴ + -LESS.] Having no lakes.

1882 G. ALLEN *Colin Clout's Cal.* (1883) 216 Relatively hilly and lakeless Europe. **1893** *Daily News* 17 Nov. 5/4 In respect of equability of flow..the Thames is probably superior to all other lakeless rivers in this country.

lakelet ('leɪklɪt). [f. LAKE *sb.*⁴ + -LET.] A small lake. Also *transf.*

1796 W. MARSHALL *W. England* I. 13 Dosmary Pool, a small lakelet..lies among the mountains. **1865** LIVINGSTONE *Zambesi* xix. 393 The fine fish which abound in the lakelet. **1883** STEVENSON *Silverado Sq.* (1886) 81 A little white lakelet of fog would be seen far down in Napa Valley.

laken, obs. f. LACK *v.*¹; variant of LAKIN.

laker¹. ('leɪkə(r)). [f. LAKE *sb.*³ + -ER¹.]

†**1.** A visitor to the English lakes. [A pun: see quot. 1805.] *Obs.*

1798 [J. PLUMPTRE] (*title*) The Lakers; a Comic Opera in Three Acts. **1805** BP. WATSON in R. Watson *Life* (1818) II. 269 *Lakers* (such is the denomination by which we distinguish those who come to see our country, intimating thereby not only that they are persons of taste who wish to view our lakes, but idle persons who love *laking*: the old Saxon word to lake, or play, being of common use among schoolboys in these parts). **1806** SOUTHEY in C. C. Southey *Life* III. 41 You would come as a mere laker and pay a guide for telling you what to admire. **1829** —— *Sir T. More* (1831) I. 42 A stepping-stile has been placed to accommodate Lakers with an easier access.

2. One of the 'Lake poets'.

1814 *Edin. Rev.* XXIV. 1 Imitations of Cowper, and even of Milton.., engrafted on the natural drawl of the Lakers. **1819** MISS MITFORD in L'Estrange *Life* (1870) II. 73 *Apropos* to Mr. Jeffrey and Mr. Wordsworth, I want you to read one fair specimen of the great Laker. **1876** E. FITZGERALD *Lett.* (1889) I. 381 The Lakers all..first despised, and then patronised 'Walter Scott'.

3. (*U.S. local.*) A fish living in or taken from a lake, *spec.* the lake-trout of N. America.

1823 J. F. COOPER *Pioneers* II. xxiv. 261, I see a laker there, that has run out of the school. It's seldom one finds such a creater in the shallow waters. **1846** J. WILSON *Let.* in Hamilton *Mem.* vii. (1859) 234 Fresh-water ones [trout] found in the river, but more like lakers. **1876** *Forest & Stream* 13 July 368/2 He pulls like a laker, and you'll think you've got a whale.

4. A boat constructed for sailing on the great lakes of America.

1887 *Century Mag.* Aug. 484/2 A twenty-foot laker can slip through any lock without scratching her paint. **1945** *Seafarers' Log* 27 Apr. 6/3 She is a small laker but generally has more beefs than would the SS Queen Elizabeth. **1961** *Guardian* 15 June 1/2 Until the Seaway opened in April, 1959, the 'freshwater' trade was carried in specially-designed lakers and smaller canallers... New 20,000-ton lakers..are coming into service. **1970** *Daily Colonist* (Victoria, B.C.) 23 Sept. 26/1 The 5,300-ton laker Orefax ran aground..off Battery Island in the St. Lawrence River. **1974** *Globe & Mail* (Toronto) 11 Sept. 8/9 The Canadian pilots will continue to serve ocean vessels downbound through the canal and take U.S. lakers west-bound.

5. One accustomed to sailing on a lake.

1838 J. F. COOPER *Home as Found* II. 75 After fishing a few hours, the old laker [*sc.* Captain Truck] pulled the skiff up to the Point. **1910** *Blackw. Mag.* Aug. 173/1 He was an experienced 'Laker', but the scene..had completely unmanned him. **1936** K. MACKENZIE *Living Rough* 274 When the deep-water sailor goes on the lakes, he has a tendency to..refer to the lakers as farmers, niggerhead sailors, and other salt-water jokes.

'laker². [f. LAKE *v.*¹ + -ER¹.] One who 'lakes'.

1805 [see LAKER¹ 1]. **1876** in *Whitby Gloss.*, s.v. *Lake.*

lake-wake, erroneous form of LYKE-WAKE.

lakey, obs. form of LACKEY; var. LAKY *a.*²

lakh (læk). *Anglo-Indian.* Forms: 7 **laches, le(c)k, leake, lacque, laquesaa** (? from Skr.), 7–9 **lak, lack**, 9 **lac**. [ad. Hindustani *lākh*:—Skr. *laksha* masc. and neut., *lakshā* fem.] One hundred thousand: **a.** of things in general; *occas.* used for an indefinite number; **b.** *spec.* of coins, esp. in ***a lac of rupees***.

a. 1613 PURCHAS *Pilgrimage* V. vi. (1614) 478 Euery Laches containeth an hundred thousand yeares. **1653** H. COGAN tr. *Pinto's Trav.* lvii. 225 There was slain..sixteen Laquesaas of men, each of which an hundred thousand. **1698** J. FRYER *E. India & P.* 104 With Lamps to the Number of two or three Lacques, which is so many Hundred thousand on our Account. **1800** *Asiat. Ann. Reg.* 62/2 The troops of that country [China] were upwards of three lacks of horsemen. **1804** MRQ. WELLESLEY in Owen *Desp.* (1877) 454 Calamities would fall on lacs of human beings. **1820** T. MAURICE *Hist. Hindostan* I. I. iv. 126 Four Yugs, or forty-three lacks and twenty thousand years. **1881** LUBBOCK in *Nature* No. 618. 407 The Laccadives..meaning literally the 'lac of islands'. **1964** E. HUXLEY *Back Street New Worlds* x. 100 Plenty of Pakistanis are here already—the High Commissioner's estimate is one *lakh*, or 100,000. **1969** *National Herald* (New Delhi) 29 July 6/5 The labour acts which relate to factories, mines, plantation, transport, shops and establishments, wages, safety and welfare, industrial relations and protection of children are expected to benefit lakhs of workers and wage-earners in the state. **1969** *Hindu* (Madras) 3 Aug. 6/4 The area worst hit by the recent floods in the Brahmaputra Valley is the Sibsagar district where about two lakhs of people have been affected, with thousands rendered homeless.

b. 1613 PURCHAS *Pilgrimage* V. xvii. (1614) 544 Euery Crou is a hundred Leckes, and euery Lecke a hundred thousand thousand [*sic*] Rupias. **1615** CORYAT *Lett. fr. India* in *Crudities* (1776) III. L 6, The whole Present was worth ten of their Leakes, as they call them; a Leak being ten thousand pound sterling. **1687** A. LOVELL tr. *Thevenot's Trav.* III. I. ix. 18 Great sums of money are reckoned by Leks, Crouls. **1692** in J. T. Wheeler *Madras in Old. Time* (1861) I. 262 A lak of Pagodas. **1773** *Gentl. Mag.* XLIII. 145 Whilst Patriots of presented lacks complain, And Courtiers brib'ry to excess arraign. **1802** WOLCOT (P. Pindar) *Great Cry & Little Wool* Wks. 1812 V. 175 The lacks are not easily got Nor honestly made in a hurry. **1859** THACKERAY *Virgin.* xliii, Making rather too free with jaghires, lakhs, gold mohurs. **1871** MATEER *Travancore* 72 The annual revenue of the Travancore State amounts..to about forty lacs of rupees. **1955** *Times* 3 Aug. 2/6 Detailed prospecting, which has so far cost 19·80 lakhs of rupees, led to the location of iron ore in Kalabagh and its suburbs in the Punjab. **1971** *Weekend* (Ceylon) 12 Sept. 3/2 The project would cost four lakhs of rupees. **1972** *Times of India* 28 Nov. 5/3 The parcel actually contained 900 Japanese-made wrist watches worth Rs. 2 lakhs. **1975** *Bangladesh Times* 18 July 1/3 The Finance Minister said that the Government had already increased the ceiling of private investment for setting up industries from Tk 25 lakh to Taka three crore.

lakie ('leɪkɪ). *Sc.* Also 8 **leaky**. An irregularity in the tides observed in the Firth of Forth (see quot. 1795). Also *lakie-tide*.

1710 SIBBALD *Hist. Fife* (1803) 87 There are lakies in the river of Forth, which are in no other river in Scotland. **1795** SINCLAIR *Statist. Acc. Scot.* XIV. 612 The tides in the river Forth.. exhibit a phenomenon not to be found (it is said) in any other part of the globe. This is what the sailors call a leaky tide... When the water has flowed for 3 hours, it then runs back for about an hour and a half;.. it returns immediately, and flows during another hour and a half to the same height it was at before, and this change takes place both in the flood and ebb tides. **1885** D. BEVERIDGE *Culross & Tulliallan* I. i. 35 The lakie tide never recedes much more than two feet before returning on its regular course... When the lakie has run its course, the tide flows or recedes, as the case may be, to the proper limit of high or low water.

lakin[1] ('leɪkɪn). *Obs.* exc. *dial.* Also 5 **lakan, lakayn**, 5–6 **laykin, -yn**, 8 **laken, laking**, 9 (in glossaries) **lairkin**. [app. connected with LAKE *v.*[1]; cf. ON. *leika* plaything.] A plaything, toy; in quots. 1440, 1460 said of a baby.

Bp. Kennet (*c* 1700), quoted in *Promp. Parv.*, gives 'Leikin, a sweetheart. *Northumb.*'
c **1440** *Gesta Rom.* xxxii. 123 (Harl. MS.) He putt vp in his bosom þes iij. lakayns. *c* **1460** *Towneley Myst.* xiii. 242 Ilk yere that commys to man She bryngys furth a lakan. **1570** LEVINS *Manip.* 134/5 A Laykin, babie, *crepundia*. **1790** GROSE *Prov. Gloss.* (ed. 2) Suppl., *Lakings*, playthings for children. North. **1790** MRS. WHEELER *Westmld. Dial.* (1821) 87, I brout her a Lunnon laken, a conny bab. **1855** ROBINSON *Whitby Gloss.*, *Lairkins*, children's toys; trinkets in general.

†**lakin**[2]. *Obs.* Also 5, 7 **laken**, 6 **lakens**. See also BYRLAKIN. [Contracted f. LADY + -KIN; cf. *bodikins, pittikins.*] Only in *by (our) lakin*, a trivial form of *by Our Lady*.

1496 *Dives & Paup.* (W. de W.) II. xii. 121/2 Some [swere] by laken, some by our lady. **1533** MORE *Apol.* iv. Wks. 849/2 By our lakens brother husband.. yet woulde I rather abyde the perill of breding wormes in my bely. **1610** SHAKS. *Temp.* III. iii. 1 By'r lakin, I can goe no further, Sir, My old bones akes. **1616** [W. HAUGHTON] *English-men for my Money* C 4, Bir laken sirs, I thinks tis one a clocke. *a* **1625** [see BYRLAKIN].

laking ('leɪkɪŋ), *vbl. sb.*[1] Now *dial.* [f. LAKE *v.*[1] + -ING[1].] Playing, amusement. Also *attrib.*

1340 HAMPOLE *Pr. Consc.* 594 When he es yhung and luffes laykyng. *c* **1425** WYNTOUN *Cron.* VIII. xxxv. 5188 Than he Sayd.. God mot at yhoure laykyng be! *a* **1816** [see LAKER]. **1857** E. WAUGH *Lanc. Life* 216 They were used to call this pastime.. 'laking wi't' Boggart'; that is, playing with the Boggart. **1884** H. SEEBOHM *Brit. Birds* II. 436 These 'laking'-places, as they are locally termed, are frequented by a great number of males, who fight for possession of the females.

laking ('leɪkɪŋ), *vbl. sb.*[2] [f. LAKE *sb.*[4] + -ING[1].] **a.** Visiting the English lakes. **b.** Writing poetry in the style of the Lake school.

1822 J. WILSON *Lakes* Note, Wks. 1856 VI. 105 We should suppose that Spring was a season by no means amiss for Laking. **1837** *Foreign Q. Rev.* XIX. 301 German romanticism and English laking are one.

lakish ('leɪkɪʃ), *a.* [f. LAKE *sb.*[4] + -ISH[1].]
1. †**a.** Abounding in lakes or pools. †**b.** Inhabiting a lake. **c.** Like a lake.

1590 GREENE *Orl. Fur.* (1599) F 3, I know he knowes that watrie lakish hill. **1661** LOVELL *Hist. Anim. & Min.* Introd., Fishes which are.. lakish, as the Umbla, trout, carp [etc.]. **1681** CHETHAM *Angler's Vade-m.* xi. §1 (1689) 110 All Fishes, whether Marine, Fluviatile, or Lakish. **1872** G. M. HOPKINS *Jrnls. & Papers* (1959) 222 The broad smooth fall of a lakish apron of water.

2. Of or pertaining to the Lake poets; resembling the productions of those poets. *rare.*

1819 *Abelard & Heloisa* 222 Oh! that we had the Lakish pow'r To dwell on owls!—for half an hour. **1822** *Blackw. Mag.* XI. 478 The Edinburgh Reviewers would say it was a Lakish rant. **1831** *Ibid.* XXIX. 218 This couplet.. was pronounced 'lakish'. **1946** *Mod. Lang. Q.* Dec. 497 Bitterly as he attacked Southey for his faults, Jeffrey did not accuse him of the 'Lakish' fault of 'mysticism'.

Hence '**lakishness**.

1831 *Blackw. Mag.* XXIX. 218 Talking of lakishness—the Southrons.. have a strange idea of the Lakes.

Lakist ('leɪkɪst). [f. LAKE *sb.*[4] + -IST. Adopted in Fr. as *lakiste*.] A member or adherent of the 'Lake School' of poetry; a Lake poet.

1822 *New Monthly Mag.* V. 546 Voted at last a rhymer and a pedant by the lakists and cockneys. *a* **1849** POE *Cockton* Wks. 1864 III. 462 The cant of the Lakists would establish the exact converse. **1883** *B'ham Daily Post* 2 Apr. 5/1 The last surviving son of another 'Lakist' has followed him.

So '**Lakism**, affectation of the style of the Lake poets.

1822 *Blackw. Mag.* XI. 462 The third canto of Childe Harold.. which from beginning to end is Lakeism—rank Lakeism.

lakka, lakke, obs. forms of LAC[1], LACK.

Lakoda (lə'kəʊdə). [Name of an area in the Pribilof Islands in the Bering Sea.] Used *attrib.* or *absol.*: a type of sealskin used as a material for coats.

1969 *New Yorker* 8 Nov. 179 A midicoat of Lakoda in its natural caramel uses black beaver for the collar and cuffs. **1975** *Ibid.* 7 Apr. 118/2 On the Atlanta trip, he wore a Lakoda-sealskin coat.

‖**laksamana** (ˌlæksə'mɑːnə). Also 7 **laxaman**, 9 **lacsamana**. [Malay, ad. Skr. *lakshmaṇa* 'having fortunate tokens' (the name of a mythical hero, Rama's half-brother).] The title formerly given to a high dignitary or admiral in Malaya.

1615 in Danvers & Foster *Lett. received by E. India Co.* (1900) IV. 6 On the morrow I went to take my leave of Laxaman, to whom all strangers' business are resigned. **1821** J. LEYDEN tr. *Malay Annals* xi. 96 Whoever bears the title of sangcuan may succeed to the rank of lacsamana. **1839** T. J. NEWBOLD *Pol. & Statistical Acct. Straits of Malacca* II. iii. 46 Paul de Gama attacked Johore, but was defeated and slain by the Lacsamana. **1969** J. M. GULLICK *Malaysia* ii. 40 Command of the navy rested with the Laksamana.

laky ('leɪkɪ), *a.*[1] [f. LAKE *sb.*[4] + -Y[1].] Of or pertaining to a lake; lake-like.

1611 COTGR., *Lacustre*, lakie, belonging to a lake. **1808** SCOTT *Marm.* v. Introd., By.. flanking towers, and laky flood, Guarded and garrison'd she stood. **1826** W. ELLIOTT *Nun* 43 And all the Italian glory of the day, seems sweetly sleeping in each laky ray.

laky ('leɪkɪ), *a.*[2] Also 9 **lakey**. [f. LAKE *sb.*[6] + -Y[1].] Of or pertaining to lake; of the colour of lake; *spec.* of the blood, when the red corpuscles are acted upon by some solvent.

1849 *Blackw. Mag.* LXVI. 420 The gray stones.. are of a delicate hue, blue intermingling with pale greenish and lakey tints. **1898** P. MANSON *Trop. Diseases* xxxi. 457 *note*, The hæmoglobin has become diffused and the blood lakey.

lakye, obs. form of LACKEY.

la-la ('lɑː'lɑː), *a.* [adj. use of *la la* interj.: see LA *int.* b.] 'So-so', not so good as it might be, poor.

1800 in *Spirit Publ. Jrnls.* (1801) IV. 253 Finding my appetite very la, la, took two glasses of bitters. **1806** SURR *Winter in London* I. 240 As to his singing, it is but la la. *a* **1849** HARTLEY COLERIDGE *Ess.* (1851) II. 94 A species of composition so la-la and lackadaisacal.

la-la ('lɑː'lɑː), *v.* [Redupl. LA *int.*] *intr.* To sing or say the syllable *la* repeatedly, esp. in place of the words or notes of a tune. Also *trans.*, to sing (a song) in this way.

1906 *Daily Chron.* 19 Sept. 9/6 Miss Neale.. 'la la'-ed a simple tune. **1908** *Ibid.* 18 Aug. 7/1 They search out the secret places of past grandeur, la-la-ing as they issue from court and passage. **1974** *Listener* 17 Jan. 84/1 Those boys who couldn't sing didn't just 'la-la': they said the words, and they were called 'Talking Josephs'. The boys who really could sing were called 'Canaries'.

lala, var. ILALA.

lalang ('lɑːlaŋ). Also **lallang**. [Malay.] A local name for *Imperata cylindrica*, a large coarse grass, widespread in tropical countries.

1779 T. FORREST *Voy. New Guinea* II. iii. 192 The country hereabouts is now covered with long grass, called lalang. **1887** H. W. DALY *Digging, Squatting, & Pioneering Life S. Austral.* 158 A shake-down.. made up of dried lallang—the thick strong grass of the country. **1887** *Encycl. Brit.* XXII. 93/1 There are waste spaces.. covered with coarse lalang grass. **1912** *Chambers's Jrnl.* Feb. 98/1 As I stood in the lalang patch.. there passed over my head.. all the turmoil of a great city. **1918** [see BLADY *a.*]. **1925** *Chambers's Jrnl.* June 408/2 The manager.. contracted with a Chinese to eradicate some four hundred acres of lalang grass on his estate. **1933** L. AINSWORTH *Confessions Planter in Malaya* 190 It was decided to tackle all 'lallang' land (areas that in the past had been cleared of virgin jungle by the Chinese, but which subsequently had been.. allowed to become overgrown with lallang weed). **1969** J. M. GULLICK *Malaysia* ii. 67 Lallang is the Malay name for *Imperata cylindrica*, a coarse grass which grows freely on untended land in Malaya. **1972** *Malay Mail* (Kuala Lumpur) 25 May 6/3 Poisons to kill weeds and lallang.. could have been absorbed by the jering tree.

†**lale**, *v. Obs. rare.* [Cf. Da. *lalle* to prattle.] *intr.* To speak.

13.. *E.E. Allit. P.* B. 153 Þen þe lorde wonder loude laled & cryed. *Ibid.* B. 913 Þen laled Loth, 'lorde what is best?' [**1877** *N.W. Linc. Gloss.*, *Lall*, to cry out.]

-lalia, a terminal element repr. Gr. λαλιά speech, chatter, used in forming words denoting various disorders or unusual faculties of speech; as in *dyslalia* (s.v. DYS-), ECHOLALIA, GLOSSOLALIA, *idiolalia* (s.v. IDIO-).

Lalique (læ'liːk). [f. the name of René *Lalique* (1860–1945), French designer of jewels and glassware.] Used *attrib.* and *ellipt.* to designate jewellery and decorative glassware by or after the manner of Lalique.

1902 *Daily Chron.* 31 May 2/3 Any jewel of uncommon design is modish, but prominently a Lalique, strung upon an imperceptible platinum chain. **1927** *Daily Express* 28 Oct. 5/3 Both tray and stopper are decorated in the Lalique manner. **1936** O. LANCASTER *Progress at Pelvis Bay* 67 Its modernistic sofas, lalique panels and cleverly concealed lighting. **1939** A. KEITH *Land below Wind* xiii. 224 Like figures on a Lalique vase. **1970** G. SAVAGE *Dict. Antiques* 232/2 A good deal of Lalique glass deserves to be classified as 'antiques of the future'. **1972** *Vogue* 15 Mar. (*inside front cover*) Pair of 'Lalique' glass doves—£65·00.

lall (læl), *v.* [Echoic, after L. *lallāre*.] *intr.* To say 'lal, lal'; to speak childishly. Hence '**lalling** *vbl. sb.* Also *attrib.*

1878 tr. *Ziemssen's Cycl. Med.* XIV. xxxv. 844 When stammering attains such a grade that the speech is thereby rendered very indistinct or entirely unintelligible, it is called lalling (*lallatio*). *Ibid.*, When the attendants are silly enough to imitate this lalling,.. the speech may retain a childish, lalling character.

Lallan ('lælən), *a.* and *sb. Sc.* [variant of LOWLAND.] **A.** *adj.* Belonging to the Lowlands of Scotland. **B.** *sb.* (Now usu. *Lallans.*) The Lowland Scotch dialect; esp., in modern use, a revived and modifed form of the spoken dialect as a literary language.

1785 BURNS *Addr. to Deil* xix, But a' your doings to rehearse.. Wad ding a' Lallan tongue, or Erse, In prose or rhyme. —— *To W. Simpson*, Postscr. ii, They.. spak their thoughts in plain, braid Lallans. **1791** A. WILSON *Laurel Disputed* Poems (1816) 40 (Jam.) Far aff our gentles for their poets flew, And scorn'd to own that Lallan songs they knew. **1887** R. L. STEVENSON *Mem. & Portraits, Pastoral*, 99, I translate John's Lallan, for I cannot do it justice, being born *Britannis in montibus*. **1946** M. LINDSAY *Mod. Scottish Poetry* 18 It is largely under MacDiarmid's influence.. that the younger poets, especially those who use Gaelic and Scots (or Lallans, as I prefer to call their Scots, drawing more, as it does, upon middle Scots) have developed. **1947** D. YOUNG *Plastic Scots* 3 As it is convenient to have some term of distinction for that part of Scottish literature which is written in Braid Scots or Anglic, to refer to it separately from Scots literature written in Gaelic, English, Latin, or any other tongue, I suggest '*Lallans*', adopting the term of Robert Burns. **1959** *Glasgow Herald* 29 May 8 Lallans is an artificial plaything of frustrated xenophobes. **1974** *Encycl. Brit. Macropædia* XVI. 410/1 Hugh MacDiarmid,.. the most prominent exponent of Lallans, achieved an international reputation, but the Lallans revival has faded.

lallang, var. LALANG.

lallapaloosa (ˌlæləpə'luːsə,-zə). *U.S. slang.* Also **lala-, lolla-, -palooser, -paloozer**, etc. [Fanciful formation.] Something outstandingly good of its kind.

1904 'H. MCHUGH' *I'm from Missouri* vi. 89 Saturday night we had our final parade with the fireworks finish, and it was a lallapalootza! **1909** F. B. CALHOUN *Miss Minerva* xxvi. 204 You sho' is genoowine corn-fed, sterlin' silver, all-wool-an'-a-yard-wide, pure-leaf, Green-River Lollapaloosas. **1911** *Dialect Notes* III. 545 A second word-list from Nebraska... *Lallapaloosa*, something fine or grand; a term of approbation. 'You have a lallapaloosa of a hat', 'That's a lallapaloosa.' **1926** WODEHOUSE *Heart of Goof* i. 40 To-day he had been so preoccupied with his broken heart that he had made his shots absently, almost carelessly, with the result that at least one in every three had been a lallapaloosa. **1933** A. MERRITT *Burn Witch Burn!* (1934) x. 135 She thinks this doll woman a lallapaloozer. Yeah, a lallapaloozer, a corker! **1947** W. STEVENS *Let.* 28 Feb. (1967) 547, I think that the book, as a book, is a lollapalooza. **1951** *New Yorker* 20 Oct. 28/3 Though I had long ago forgotten the background, characters, and plot, I distinctly remembered it as a lollapaloosa. **1966** *Listener* 2 June 811/1 What is the tone of lalapalooza, since Hector was a pup, bumbershoot, hornswoggle, Milwaukee tumour, benzine buggy—or lalapalooza's equivalent, époustouflante? **1970** S. J. PERELMAN *Baby, it's Cold Inside* 172 All agreed that Luba Pneumatiç was a lollapaloosa, the Eighth Wonder of the World.

†'**lallate**, *v. Obs. rare*—[0]. [f. ppl. stem of L. *lallāre*: see next.] 'To speake baby-like' (Cockeram, 1623).

lallation (læ'leɪʃən). [n. of action f. L. *lallāre* to 'sing lalla or lullaby' (Lewis & Sh.). Cf. F. *lallation*.] †**a.** Childish utterance (*obs.*). **b.** An imperfect pronunciation of *r*, by which the sound of that letter is confused with that of *l*; lambdacism.

1647 R. BARON *Cyprian Acad.* A ij b, This makes me hope that you will dispence with the Lallation and Low dialect of this babe [*sc.* a book], whose tone is rude. **1864** R. F. BURTON *Dahome* I. 158 The Popos and Dahomans have the same lallation as the Chinese, who call rum 'lum'.

lallygag ('lælɪgæg), *v. U.S. slang.* Also **lollygag**. [Origin unknown.] *intr.* To fool around; to 'neck'; to dawdle, to dally. Also as *sb.*, fooling around. Hence '**lallygagging** *vbl. sb.* and *ppl. a.*

1862 *Harper's Mag.* Aug. 324/1 Mr. Biggs paused and turned the flesh of the succulent lobster over with his finger. The gentleman inside addressed him: '..Try er lobstaw, bossy?' 'Ain't got no money,' said Mr. Biggs, still fingering the morsels. 'Oh, come now, none o' that ere lallygag,' responded the gentleman. **1868** *Northern Vindicator* (Estherville, Iowa) 30 Dec., The lascivious lolly-gagging lumps of licentiousness who disgrace the common decencies of life by their love-sick fawnings at our public dances. **1869** *Tidal Wave* (Silver City, Idaho) 15 Jan. 3/2 They are too pious to encourage dicing, and the feature of their entertainments may be what the boys call 'lally-gagging'. **1870** *Northern Vindicator* (Estherville, Iowa) 19 Feb., The weather once more is 'salubrious' and balmy, and indicates that winter will not lollygag in the lap of spring. **1880** E. L. WHEELER *Boss Bob, King of Bootblacks* vii. 9/1, I kin get lots o' jobs, if I'd take my pay in friendship an' all sech lollygag. **1910** *Sat. Even. Post* 30 July 19/1 Frank lally-gagged through his first term and came back for the second. **1927** D. RUNYON *Trials & Other Tribulations* (1947) 112 When your correspondent was a 'necker' of no mean standing back in the dim and misty past, they called it 'lally-gagging'. **1949** *Jrnl. Amer. Folk-Lore* Jan.—Mar. 63 'Lally-gaggin' was Grandmother's word for love-making. **1965** 'E. QUEEN' *Fourth Side of Triangle* i. 2 Lallygagging around under the awning away from the gassy streets. **1969** S. GREENLEE *Spook who sat by Door* xi. 95 We lolly-gag, maybe turn on, or cook up some soul food. **1971** D. BAGLEY *Freedom Trap* iii. 20, I said there was to be no lally-gagging around with the staff, Rearden; you just stick to doing your job. **1973**

Springfield (Mass.) *Union* 25 Sept. 14/1 The Dow Jones average of 30 industrials, which lollygagged most of the day, gained strongly in afternoon trading.

lam (læm), *sb.*[1] [? f. LAM *v.* (sense 2 b).] A kind of fishing net. Also ***lam-net***. (Cf. LAMMET.)

1626 SPELMAN *Gloss.* s.v. *Lama*, Sed nos hodie retis genus quo vtuntur piscatores, *a lam* vocamus. **1895** *E. Angl. Gloss.*, *Lam net*, a net into which fish are driven by beating the water.

lam (læm), *sb.*[2] *Weaving.* [ad. F. *lame* (lit. 'blade') in the same sense.] (See quot. 1883.)

1801 J. BUTTERWORTH in A. Barlow *Weaving* (1878) 317 The generality of weavers couple the first and third healds or shafts, and so are enabled to weave it with only two lams. **1883** *Almondb. & Huddersf. Gloss.*, *Lams*, pieces of wood in a loom, connected with the treadles by strings, which are connected also with the jacks (above) in a similar way, and work the yelds.

lam (læm), *sb.*[3] *U.S. slang.* [f. LAM *v.* 3.] Escape, flight. Esp. in phr. ***on the lam***, on the run; ***take it on the*** (or ***a***) ***lam*** (see quot. 1935).

1897 *Appleton's Pop. Sci. Monthly* Apr. 832 *To do a lam*, meaning to run. **1904** 'No. 1500' *Life in Sing Sing* xiii. 263 He plugged the main guy for keeps and I took it on a lam for mine. **1931** [see *area-way* s.v. AREA 2 b]. **1935** A. J. POLLOCK *Underworld Speaks* 118/2 *Take it on the lam*, to run away; escape. **1953** W. R. BURNETT *Vanity Row* xiii. 94 The dolly was on the lam. **1959** *John o' London's* 10 Dec. 322/3 A young man stops the car, points a gun at them, and orders them to drive him to the border. He is a juvenile delinquent, 'on the lam' after a robbery. **1968** *Washington Post* 5 July A20/1 What useful public purpose is served by making it easy for convicts on the lam from a state penitentiary to acquire an arsenal? **1972** G. BAXT *Burning Sappho* ix. 158 Were you stalling for time while your Brunhilde takes it on the lam?

lam (læm), *v.* Forms: 6–8 **lamme, lamb,** 7 **lambe,** 8 **lamm,** 6– **lam.** [Cf. ON. *lęmja* (pa. t. *lamða*), lit. 'to lame' (= OE. *lęmian*, f. *lama* LAME), but chiefly used with reference to beating.]

1. *trans.* To beat soundly; to thrash; to 'whack'. Now *colloq.* or *vulgar.*

1595 [implied in BELAM]. **1596** THOMAS *Dict.* (1606), *Defusto*, to lamme or bumbast with strokes. **1631** *Celestina* IX. 111 They will not sticke to strip them and lamme them soundly. **1719** OZELL tr. *Misson's Mem.* 306 A Fellow, whom he lamb'd most horribly. **1783** AINSWORTH *Lat. Dict.* (Morell) I, Lammed, *Verberatus*. **1812** H. & J. SMITH *Rej. Addr., G. Barnwell*, Quoth he, I would pummel and lam her well. **1869** F. H. LUDLOW *Little Bro.* 16, I wish I'd been there; I'd ha' lammed him, I would!

transf. **1898** *Westm. Gaz.* 20 July 7/2 The Lancashire amateur.. woke up in astonishing fashion and lammed the ball in every direction to the delight of all beholders.

2. a. *intr.* Chiefly school-boy slang, as ***to lam (it) into one, to lam out.***

1875 A. R. HOPE *My Schoolboy Fr.* 179 'I had six cuts.. and Vialls did lam into me.' **1882** 'F. ANSTEY' *Vice Versâ* (ed. 19) 84 'Let him undress now, and we can lam it into him afterwards with slippers.' **1894** CONAN DOYLE *Round Red Lamp* 276 'Lam out with your whip as hard as you can lick.'

b. *dial.* (See quot.) Cf. LAM *sb.*[1]

1895 *E. Angl. Gloss.*, *Lamming for eels*, thrashing the water to make the eels go into a net.

3. *intr.* To run off, to escape, to 'beat it'. *U.S. slang.*

1886 A. PINKERTON *Thirty Yrs. a Detective* 41 After he [*sc.* a pickpocket] has secured the wallet he will.. utter the word 'lam!' This means to let the man go, and to get out of the way as soon as possible. **1901** *Smart Set* Oct. 3/2 Well, when he [*sc.* Uncle Remus] was just driven to desperation he 'lammed aloose', and so shall I. **1932** *Evening Sun* (Baltimore) 9 Dec. 31/5 *Lam*, run away from the police. **1935** R. E. SHERWOOD *Petrified Forest* II. 124 Say, boss—we better lam out of here. *Ibid.* 158, I hear a car coming, boss. We better lam. *Ibid.* 162 When they get around there, we'll lam. **1946** 'P. QUENTIN' *Puzzle for Fiends* (1947) xvi. 111 When I get my share, I'll lam out of this place so fast you won't see me for dust. **1959** P. TOWNEND *Died o' Wednesday* iv. 61 What was it they always did in any self-respecting cowboy film?—lammed out.. and took to the hills. **1973** M. MACKINTOSH *King & Two Queens* xii. 171 The time of death ..[was] four days before Fisher lammed out.

Hence **'lamming** *vbl. sb.*, a beating, a thrashing; **'lamster, 'lammister,** a fugitive, a person on the run.

1611 BEAUM. & FL. *King & no K.* v. iii, One whose dull body will require a lamming. **1611** COTGR., *Gaulée*,.. a cudgelling, basting, thwacking, lamming. **1883** *Almondb. & Huddersf. Gloss.*, *Lammin*, i.e. lamming, a beating. **1904** 'No. 1500' *Life in Sing Sing* 250 *Lamaster*, fugitive from justice; one who forfeits bail-bonds. **1926** *Clues* Nov. 161/2 *Lamster*, fugitive. Also a member of a pickpocket gang that leaves with the loot. **1948** E. L. IREY *Tax Dodgers* (1949) 47 'My line,' he said, 'is keeping quiet.' With that he had told Kelly that he was a lammister, in other words fleeing justice. **1953** W. BURROUGHS *Junkie* (1972) ix. 81 Gamblers, perverts, drifters, and lamsters from every state in the Union. **1962** K. ORVIS *Damned & Destroyed* xii. 81 Smuggling American lamsters into Canada.

lam, obs. form of LAMB, LAME, LOAM.

lama[1] ('lɑːmə). Also 9 *erron.* **llama.** [Tibetan *blama*, the *b* being silent.] The title given to the Buddhist priests of Mongolia and Tibet. The chief Lamas of Tibet and Mongolia are called respectively ***Dalai*** (***dalae*** or ***delli***)***-lama***, or simply *Dalai*, and ***Tesho-*** or ***Teshu-lama***; the former is the higher in dignity, and was also known to Europeans as the 'Grand Lama'.

The Dalai Lama lives in the strictest seclusion, and is worshipped with almost divine honours. When he dies, the lamas profess to search for a child who gives evidence that the soul of the deceased pontiff has entered into him; when found, the child succeeds to the office.

1654 tr. *Martini's Conq. China* 13 This Letter.. he sent by one of their Indian Priests (whom they call Lama). **1698** J. CRULL *Muscovy* 64 A certain High Priest, whom they call Dalae-Lama, or Lamalamalow. **1753** HANWAY *Trav.* (1762) I. II. xvi. 68 Their supreme deity is the delli lama. **1807** W. IRVING *Life & Lett.* (1864) I. 199 When surrounded like the grand Lama.. by a crowd of humble adorers. **1876** *Times* 15 May 5/2 The greater in this last respect.. is the Dalai (or 'Ocean') Lama or Lhasa; the other is the Panchen Rinbochê ('Jewel Doctor'), or Teshu Lama of Tashi-lunpo. **1881** *Ch. Bells* 10 Dec. 24/1 In spite of the determined antagonism of the preaching of the Shamans and Lamas from Mongolia. **1895** WADDELL *Buddhism of Tibet* 1 Tibet, the mystic Land of the Grand Lama, joint God and King of many millions.

attrib. **1799** W. TOOKE *View Russian Emp.* II. 119 We find in the russian empire.. the lama, and the schamane religions. **1861** SWINHOE *N. China Camp.* 366 The majority of the llama temples were situated outside the wall.

Hence **'lamaic** *a.*, of or pertaining to the lamas; believed or taught by the lamas. **'lamaism** (also **lamism**), the system of doctrine and observances inculcated and maintained by the lamas. **'lamaist,** one who professes lamaism; also *attrib.* **lama'istic** *a.*, of or pertaining to the lamaists. **'lamaite** = LAMAIST. **lama'itic** *a.* = LAMAISTIC.

1814 tr. *Klaproth's Trav.* 115 This is the greatest festival of the Lamaites. **1817** *Edin. Rev.* XXVIII. 313 Prayer is one of the principal duties enjoined by Lamaism. **1827** H. E. LLOYD tr. *Timbowski's Trav.* II. 207 Before the introduction of the Lamaic religion among them [the Mongols]. **1834** *Good's Study Med.* (ed. 4) III. 108 The cruel and senseless penances and punishments sustained in many of the convents and nunneries of Lamism. **1840** CARLYLE *Heroes* (1858) 188, I find Grand Lamaism itself to have a kind of truth in it. **1852** *Blackw. Mag.* LXXI. 347 The Lamaitic worship. **1883** *Athenæum* 24 Feb. 242/1 The Lamaistic deviations from the simplicity of Gautama's teaching. **1889** *Century Mag.* Mar. 657/2 The great annual festival of the lamaists in July. **1895** WADDELL *Buddhism of Tibet* 287 The Lamaist temple is called 'God's house'. *Ibid.* 298 The Lamaist sceptre or *Dorje*.

‖**lama**[2] ('lɑːmə). [Sp.; lit. 'plate'.] Gold or silver cloth, originally made in Spain.

1818 *La Belle Assemblée* XVII. 133/2 A gold embroidered lama drapery.. Borders of silver lama on crimson satin. **1821** in Mrs. Armytage *Old Crt. Customs* (1883) 36 A dress of silver lama over French lilac.

lama, erroneous form of LLAMA.

†**'lamanism.** *Obs.* [After F. *lamanisme* (Huc).] = LAMAISM. So **la'manical** *a.* = LAMAIC.

1852 *Blackw. Mag.* LXXI. 339 The Tibetan portion.. is inhabited by a rough race,.. retaining many primitive superstitions beneath the engrafted Lamanism. **1867** M. JONES *Huc's Tartary* 243 The foundation of the lamanical hierarchy, framed in imitation of the pontifical court. *Ibid.* 252 It is with this view [of enfeebling the strength of the Mongol princes] that the Emperors patronise lamanism.

lamantin (lə'mæntɪn). Also 8–9 **lamentine, lamentin,** 9 **lamantine.** [a. F. *lamantin, lamentin.*] The manatee.

1666 J. DAVIES tr. *Rochefort's Caribby Isl.* I. xvii. 103 A certain fish by the French called Lamantin, by the Spaniards Namantin and Manaty. *Ibid.* 300 Their not eating of salt, Swines-flesh, Tortoises, and Lamantin. **1706** PHILLIPS (ed. Kersey), *Lamentine*. **1762** *Gentl. Mag.* 208 Tortoises also and lamantins are found here in great plenty [in Granada]. **1797** *Naval Chron.* VII. 333 The lamentin (sea-cow or manattee). **1827** G. HIGGINS *Celtic Druids* 138 The bones of mammiferous sea animals namely, of the Lamentin and of seals. **1865** LUBBOCK *Preh. Times* viii. (1869) 250 The Manatee or Lamantin.

lamar, variant of LAMBER[1], amber.

Lamarckian (lə'mɑːkɪən), *a.* and *sb.* [f. *Lamarck*, the name of a French botanist and zoologist (1744–1829) + -IAN.]

A. *adj.* Of or pertaining to Lamarck or to his theory respecting the cause of organic evolution, which he ascribed to inheritable modifications produced in the individual by habit, appetency, and the direct action of the environment. **B.** *sb.* One who holds Lamarckian views.

1846 DANA *Zooph.* vii. §106 (1848) 107 These remarks are intended to support no monad or Lamarckian theory. **1858** DARWIN *Life & Lett.* II. 121 To talk of climate or Lamarckian habit producing such adaptations to other organic beings, is futile. **1893** *Athenæum* 12 Aug. 220/2 Hegel was a keen enough scientific critic to see the defects of the Lamarckian theory. **1928** G. H. CARPENTER *Biol. Insects* xii. 365 To sum up this brief discussion on the Lamarckian factor in evolution, it must be admitted that belief in it is encouraged on account of the simple manner in which it explains—if it be a true cause—many observed facts of life. **1953** E. MAYR et al. *Methods & Princ. Syst. Zool.* i. 11 Most of them [*sc.* late nineteenth-century taxonomists].. were Lamarckians. **1972** *Science* 12 May 623/1 The Lamarckian postulate that characters acquired by parents during their own lives can be passed on to their offspring. **1972** *National Observer* (U.S.) 27 May 21/3 The controversy between Darwinians and Lamarckians has raged for nearly a century.

So **La'marckianism, La'marckism,** the doctrine of the origin of species as laid down by Lamarck. **La'marckite** = LAMARCKIAN *sb.*

1884 *Stand. Nat. Hist.* (1888) I. p. lvi, These views essentially agree with what is known as Lamarckianism. **1884** RAY LANKESTER in *Athenæum* 29 Mar. 412/2 Lamarckism looks very well on paper, but.. when put to the test of observation and experiment it collapses absolutely. **1890** *Times* (weekly ed.) 10 Jan. 7/3 There are [in biology] pure Darwinists, Wallaceists, Weissmannists, Lamarckites, and Romanesists.

Lamarque (lə'mɑːk). [Prob. a. the name of Comte Maximilien *Lamarque* (1770–1832), French general and politician.] A variety of noisette rose first introduced in 1830, bearing large, fragrant, white flowers with a yellow centre. Also *attrib.*

1837 T. RIVERS *Rose Amateur's Guide* II. 82 Lamarque is another hybrid Noisette, approaching to the tea-scented rose, in the size and fragrance of its flowers. **1869** S. R. HOLE *Bk. about Roses* viii. 122 Lamarque, the parent of Cloth-of-gold, well deserves a place on some sunny wall.. with its refined and graceful flowers. These are large and full, the outer petals of a soft pure white, the inner of a pale straw colour. **1885** C. M. YONGE *Nuttie's Father* II. viii. 101 She came in leading her little son.. carrying a little bouquet for the guest of one La Marque rosebud and three lilies of the valley. **1965** G. S. THOMAS *Climbing Roses* vi. 99 'Lamarque' .. is a plant only for the warmer west outdoors.

lamasery (lə'mɑːsərɪ). Also **lamasary, lamaserai, lamassery, lamastery, lamestery.** [a. F. *lamaserie*, app. formed irreg. by Huc from *lama*: see LAMA[1].

The spelling *lamaserai* indicates that the word has been supposed to be a compound of Pers. *sarāī* inn (see SERAI).]

A Thibetan or Mongolian monastery of lamas.

1867 M. JONES *Huc's Tartary* 36 During our stay at Tolon Noor, we had frequent occasion to visit the Lamaseries, or Lama Monasteries. **1870** *Pall Mall G.* 23 Nov. 11, I was for seven years steward of the grand lamasary of Ga-den. **1882** BABER in *R. Geog. Soc. Suppl. Papers* I. I. 96 It contains many lamaserais of 200 or 300 monks, some indeed of 2000 or 3000.

Lamasse, obs. form of LAMMAS.

lamb (læm), *sb.* Forms: α. 1 **lam(b, lamp, lęmb,** 2, 4–6 **lam,** 4–6 **lame,** 4–7 **lambe,** 5–6 **lamme,** 7 **lamm,** 2– **lamb.** *Pl.* 1 **lamb,** 3 **lambre,** *Orm.* **lammbre,** 3–5 **lambren,** 4 **lamberne,** 4–5 **lambryn,** 5 **lamber, lamborn, lambres, lambron,** 6 **lambes,** (**lames,** *Sc.* **lammis**), 6– **lambs.** β. 1–5 **lomb, lombor,** 2–5 **lombe,** 3 **lombbe,** 4 **lome, loombe,** (**lowmpe**), 4–5 **loomb,** 5 **loom.** *Pl.* 1 **lomber, lombern, lombor, lombro, lombur,** 3 **lombren.** [Com. Teut.: OE. *lamb, lambor* (*lǫmb, lǫmbor*), *lęmb* str. neut., corresponds to OS. *lamb* (Du., MLG. *lam*), OHG. *lamb* (MHG. *lam(b, lamp*, mod.G. *lamm*), ON. *lamb* (Sw. *lamm*, Da. *lam*), Goth. *lamb*:—OTeut. **lamboz-*, **lambiz-*; no certain extra-Teut. affinities have been found.

The regular pl. form in OE. was *lǫmberu* (**lamberu*):—OTeut. **lambozâ*; there were disyllabic forms produced by omission of the final or syncopation of the middle vowel; the occasional form *lamb* is due to the analogy of animal names of the *o* declension. In ME. the plural was assimilated to that of the *-n* declension (cf. *children, calveren, brethren*).]

1. a. The young of the sheep.

c **725** *Corpus Gloss.* (Hessels) E 216 *Enixa est genuit agnam idest* ceolbor lomb. *c* **825** *Vesp. Psalter* cxiii. 6 Muntas for hwon uphofun ȝe swe swe rommas & hyllas swe swe lomberu scepa. **858** *Charter of Æthelberht* in *O.E. Texts* 438, xx lamba & xx fehta. *a* **900** *Kent. Glosses* in Wr.-Wülcker 61/29 *Et quasi agnus lasciuiens*, and swa pleȝende lamp. *c* **950** *Lindisf. Gosp.* Luke x. 3 Ic sendo iuih sua lombro bi-tuih ulfum. *c* **1000** ÆLFRIC *Exod.* xii. 5 Witodlice þæt lamb sceal beon anwintre þur lamb clæne and unwemme. *c* **1175** *Lamb. Hom.* 87 þet i-offrede lomb þet þe engel het offrian bitacneð cristes deðþe. *a* **1225** *Ancr. R.* 66 Monie cumeð to ou ischrud mid lombes fleose, & beoð wode wulues. **1297** R. GLOUC. (Rolls) 7609 Wolues dede hii nimeþ vorþ, þat er dude as lombe. *a* **1300** *Cursor M.* 11302 Wit hir child suld offer þare, A lamb if sco sua riche ware. **1387** TREVISA *Higden* (Rolls) II. 229, Iabel.. departide kydes from lambren. *c* **1425** LYDG. *Assembly of Gods* 801 Humylyte was the furst: a lambe he bestrode. *c* **1440** *Jacob's Well* 38 þe tythe owyth to be payed of lambryn. **1486** *Bk. St. Albans* C vij b, Take pressure made of a lombe that was borne in vntyme. **1500–20** DUNBAR *Poems* xxxviii. 18 He for our saik that sufferit to be slane, And lyk a lamb in sacrifice wes dicht, Is lyk a lyone rissin vp agane. **1535** COVERDALE *Is.* lxv. 25 The wolff and the lambe shal fede together. *a* **1550** *Christis Kirke Gr.* xx, Bludy berkit wes thair baird, As thay had worriet lammis. **1586** *Vestry Bks.* (Surtees) 21 Item receaved of Nicolas Newbye for twoe lames.. ijs. vjd. **1621** MIDDLETON *Sun in Aries* Wks. (Bullen) VII. 348 Illustrated by proper emblems.. as.. Sincerity by a Lamb. **1667** MILTON *P.L.* XI. 645 Ewes and thir bleating Lambs. **1735** SOMERVILLE *Chase* III. 26 The poor defenceless Lamb,.. Supplies a rich Repast. **1784** COWPER *Task* VI. 111 Sheepwalks populous with bleating lambs. **1813** SHELLEY *Q. Mab* viii. 128 His teeth are harmless, custom's force has made His nature as the nature of a lamb. **1884** RUSKIN *Pleas. Eng.* (1885) 133 A Lamb means an Apostle, a Lion an Evangelist.

transf. and *fig.* **1450–1530** *Myrr. our Ladye* 87 Yf we be hys trew shepe, fruytfull in wolle of verteues.. and in lambren of good dedes. **1591** SHAKS. *Two Gent.* IV. iv. 97 Alas poor Proteus, thou hast entertain'd A Foxe, to be the Shepheard of thy Lambs.

b. Proverbs.

1620 SHELTON *Quix.* II. vii. 40 As soone goes the yong lambe to the roste, as the olde sheepe. **1748** RICHARDSON *Clarissa* I. x. 60 In for the lamb, as the saying is, in for the sheep. **1768** [see GOD 5 b]. *Mod.* As well be hanged for a sheep as a lamb.

2. *fig.* Applied to persons. **a.** A young member of a flock, esp. of the church.

c **1000** *Ags. Gosp.* John xxi. 15 He cwæð to him heald mine lamb [*c* **950** *Lindisf.*, *c* **1160** *Hatton* lombor]. *c* **1200** ORMIN 13329 To standdenn gæn þe laþe gast, To werenn hise lammbre. *a* **1225** *St. Marher.* 12 Icham mi lauerdes lomb, ant he is min hirde. *c* **1386** CHAUCER *Pars. T.* ¶718 Therfore shul they neuere han part of the pasture of lambes, that is the blisse of heuene. **1526** *Pilgr. Perf.* (W. de W. 1531) 2 To shewe the waye of vertue to his yonge pilgrymes & tender lambes. **1761** WESLEY *Jrnl.* 21 Jan. (1827) III. 38, I spent a hour with one who was as hot as any of the lambs at the tabernacle; but she is now a calm, reasonable woman. **1864** TENNYSON *Aylmer's F.* 361 Leolin, I almost sin in envying you: The very whitest lamb in all my fold Loves you.

b. One who is as meek, gentle, innocent, or weak as a lamb.

c **1000** ÆLFRIC *Hom.* I. 390 He ʒefullode ðone wulf and ʒeworhte to lambe. **13..** *Cursor M.* 20010 + 671 (B.M. Add. MS.) Iesu crist, godes sone, of a wilde hounde haþ made a lomb. *c* **1460** *Towneley Myst.* xxiii. 391 *Maria.* Alas, my lam so mylde, whi wille thou fare me fro Emang thise wulfes wylde. **1500–20** DUNBAR *Poems* lii. 4 He is na Dog; he is a Lam. **1589** PUTTENHAM *Eng. Poesie* III. xxiv. (Arb.) 299 It is comely for a man to be a lambe in the house, and a Lyon in the field. **1819** SHELLEY *Cenci* II. i. 136 Innocent lambs! They thought not any ill. **1858** LYTTON *What will he do* I. xiv, The Baron was a lamb compared to a fine lady.

c. used as a term of endearment.

a **1553** UDALL *Royster D.* I. iv. (Arb.) 27 Ah sir, be good to hir, she is but as gristle, Ah sweete lambe and coney. **1673** KIRKMAN *Unlucky Cit.* 165 But Lamb [*sc.* his wife], you mistake the matter quite. **1715** DE FOE *Fam. Instruct.* I. iii. (1841) I. 59 To hear the dear lamb ask me, Father, will not God be angry with me. **1820** SHELLEY *Fiordispina* 76 And say, sweet lamb, would you not learn [etc.]?

d. A simpleton; one who is cheated; esp. one who speculates and loses his money.

1668 *Leathermore's Adv. conc. Gaming* (ed. 2) 5 When a young Gentleman or Prentice comes into this School of Vertue unskil'd in the quibbles and devices there practiced, they call him a Lamb. **1680** COTTON *Compl. Gamester* (ed. 2) 5 And then the Rooks.. laugh and grin, saying the Lamb is bitten. **1881** J. MILLS *Too fast to last* III. x. 127 'In order —That we may not be among the skinned lambs', interrupted William Bottles. **1884** *Chicago Tribune* Feb., 'Lamb' is an outsider who goes into the market and leaves his money. **1886** GLADDEN *Applied Chr.* 204 A recent estimate.. puts the amount of which the 'lambs' are shorn in this New York stock market alone at eight hundred million dollars a year.

3. a. *the Lamb*, † *God's Lamb*, *the Lamb of God.* (After John i. 29, Rev. xvii. 14, etc.)

a **1000** *Guthlac* 1015 (Gr.) Ic siððan mot.. godes lomber in sindreamum siððan awo forð folʒian. *c* **1000** *Ags. Gosp.* John i. 29 Her is godes lamb, her is se þe deð aweʒ middaneardes synnæ. *c* **1200** ORMIN 12649 Crist Wass Godess Lamb ʒehatten. **13..** *E.E. Allit. P.* A. 413 My lorde þe lombe, þurʒ hys god-hede, He toke my self to hys maryage. **1340** *Ayenb.* 232 Volʒeþ þet lamb of mildenesse þet is Iesu crist. *a* **1400** *Prymer* (1891) 68 Loomb of god.. haue mercy on us. *c* **1430** *Hymns Virg.* 53 þis lomb, y spak of him þat al þe worldis synne a-batys. **1567** *Gude & Godlie Ball.* (S.T.S.) 43 That Lamb for sober summe was sauld. **1611** BIBLE *Rev.* xxii. 1 A pure riuer of water of life.. proceeding out of the throne of God, and of the Lambe. **1784** COWPER *Task* VI. 792 One song employs all nations, and all cry, 'Worthy the Lamb, for He was slain for us!' **1842** TENNYSON *St. Agnes' Eve* 17 So shows my soul before the Lamb, My spirit before Thee.

b. *Her.* **Holy Lamb** = AGNUS DEI b.

1823 in CRABB *Technol. Dict.* **1843** FOSBROKE *Cycl. Antiq.* 815 *Holy-Lamb.* This was anciently a lamb with St. John pointing to him, and was ordered to be changed into the human form by the Trullan canons made in 653. **1882** CUSSANS *Her.* vi. (ed. 3) 100 The Paschal or Holy Lamb is a Lamb passant supporting with its dexter fore-leg a staff, usually in bend-sinister, from which depends a Banner, charged with a Cross of St. George.

4. *pl.* **a.** The name given to the proverbially cruel and rapacious soldiers of Col. Kirke's regiment in 1684–6, in ironical allusion to the device of the Paschal Lamb on their flag. **b.** The name given to bodies of 'roughs' hired to commit acts of violence at elections. (The 'Nottingham Lambs' were notorious about 1860–1870.)

1744 RALPH *Hist. Eng.* I. 888 So infamous was the Behaviour of his own particular Corps, that he [Kirke] himself, by way of Irony, call'd them his Lambs; an appellation which was adopted by the whole West of England. **1757** HUME *Hist.* II. 387. **1844** *Times* 4 Nov. 5/2 Upwards of 200 'lambs' were employed by the same political party to carry off voters. *Note.* 'Lambs'.. means ruffians employed at elections to impress upon the persons and property of the peaceable inhabitants the 'physical force' doctrine. **1849** MACAULAY *Hist. Eng.* iii. I. 334 As they had been levied for the purpose of waging war on an infidel nation, they bore on their flag a Christian emblem, the Paschal Lamb... These men, the rudest and most ferocious in the English army, were called Kirke's Lambs. **1869** *Latest News* 17 Oct., Samuel Dawson was examined at some length in reference to the employment of a number of 'lambs', or roughs, in Stracey's interest at the last election.

5. In various applications. **a.** The flesh of the lamb used as food.

1620 VENNER *Via Recta* iii. 50 Lambe of two or three moneths old is the best. **1683** TRYON *Way to Health* 92 There is no flesh either more healthy or grateful than Lamb. **1841** LANE *Arab. Nts.* I. 123 Lamb or Mutton cut into small pieces.

fig. **1809** MALKIN *Gil Blas* x. xii. (Rtldg.) 384 The happy man.. seemed to be very little less happy than his partner..; and one would have sworn.. that he liked mutton better than lamb. [Said of a bridegroom and his elderly bride.]

b. short for LAMBSKIN.

1527 *Lanc. Wills* (Chetham Soc.) I. 6 My gowne furrett wt whyte lambe. **1567** R. MULCASTER *Fortescue's De Laud. Leg.* (1672) 123 b, The Serjeants Cape is ever Furred with white Lambe. **1889** *Daily News* 24 Dec. 2/7 Allow me to state what means are employed to procure the Persian lamb or Astrakhan.

c. *vegetable lamb*: = BAROMETZ.

1698 A. BRAND *Emb. Muscovy to China* 125, I am not very apt to give credit to the Relations of the vulgar sort in Muscovy, among which, that of the Vegetable Lamm is a general received Fable.

6. *attrib.* and *Comb.*: **a.** simple attributive, as ***lamb-chop*** [CHOP *sb.*[1] 2 b] (also *fig.*), ***-cote***, † ***-fell***, ***-flesh***, ***-fold***, ***-glove***, ***-hurdle***, ***-meadow***, ***-shepherd***, ***-trade***. **b.** objective, as ***lamb-hymning***, ***-shearing***. **c.** instrumental (sense 5 b) as ***lamb-lined***.

c **1838** C. MATHEWS in M. R. Booth *Eng. Plays of 19th Cent.* (1973) IV. 136 He ate three pounds and a half of *lamb chops. **1865** MRS. STOWE *House & Home Papers* 248 All the edible matters.. would form those delicate dishes of lamb-chop. **1962** E. LUCIA *Klondike Kate* ii. 40 Mrs Bettis was persistent and her daughter was quite a lamb chop, so he finally agreed. **1963** R. CARRIER *Great Dishes of World* 145 Place lamb chops in a flat dish just large enough to hold them and pour marinade mixture over them. **1974** 'E. LATHEN' *Sweet & Low* xvii. 165 Deep in a choice between lamb chops and pork chops. **1459–60** *Durham Acc. Rolls* (Surtees) 320 Pro tectura apud le *lambecote. *c* **1500** in Arnold *Chron.* (1811) 75 *Lambefelle for the C... i. d. *c* **1400** tr. *Secreta Secret., Gov. Lordsh.* 78 Meene metys engendrys noght bolnynges ne superfluytes, as *lombe ffless h, motoun and Capouns. **1884** GILMOUR *Mongols* 91 Most of the west side [of the tent] was taken up by a *lamb-fold. **1811** *Self Instructor* 121, 3 pair of fine *lamb gloves. **1805** R. W. DICKSON *Pract. Agric.* (1807) I. 160 Fig. 7 represents a *lamb-hurdle. *a* **1711** KEN *Edmund* Poet. Wks. 1721 II. 366 As we wander o're the blissful Plains, You daily shall compose *Lamb-hymning strains. **1591** SYLVESTER *Du Bartas* I. iv. 706 A payr of *Lamb-lyn'd buskins on her feet. **1459–60** *Durham Acc. Rolls* (Surtees) 320 Pro falcacione de le *Lammedowe. **1774** *Lamb-shearing [see *lamb-ale* in 7 below]. **1886** C. SCOTT *Sheep-Farming* 139 Lamb-shearing has long been an established practice in East Cornwall and other parts. *a* **1711** KEN *Sion* Poet. Wks. 1721 IV. 331 May I, like you, sing the *Lamb-Shepherd's Love. **1895** *Daily News* 31 May 8/7 *Lamb trade firm.

7. a. Special Comb.: **lamb-ale** (see quot.); **lambs'-cage** (see quot.); **lamb-creep**, a hole in a hedge or hurdle just large enough for lambs to get in and out of the fold (see CREEP *sb.* 4); **lamb-emptied** *a.*, emptied of lambs; **lamb-fashion**, after the fashion of a lamb; used in prov. phr. ***mutton dressed lamb-fashion***, applied to an old woman dressed in youthful style; **lamb-florin** *Hist.*, a florin stamped with the 'Agnus Dei'; **lamb's fry** (in U.S. also **lamb fries**) [cf. FRY *sb.*[2] 2 b], in the U.K. and U.S., lamb's offal, esp. testicles; in Austral. and N.Z., lamb's liver; **lamb-hog**, a lamb of the second year; **lamb-house** (see quot.); † **lamb's-lease**, a meadow in which lambs are reared; † **lamb's leather**, lambskin; **lamb-ram**, a ram under two years old; **lamb-stones**, the testicles of a lamb; **lamb-suckler**, **lamb-suckling** (see quots.).

1774 WARTON *Hist. Eng. Poetry* (1840) III. 119 *Lamb-ale is still used at the village of Kirtlington in Oxfordshire, for an annual feast or celebrity at lamb-shearing. **1857** TOULMIN SMITH *Parish* 503 The 'Ales' were numerous. Brand mentions.. Lamb-Ales, Leet-Ales, [etc.]. **1813** T. DAVIS *Agric. Wilts* 264 *Lambs'-Cages, cribs for foddering sheep in fold; they are usually made semi-cylindrical, with cleft Ash-rods about six to seven feet long and about one foot diameter. **1886** C. SCOTT *Sheep-Farming* 167 If the ewes and lambs are folded, *lamb creeps can be brought into use. **1898** 'ROLF BOLDREWOOD' *Rom. Canvass Town* 96 The ewes of the *lamb-emptied small yard are then carefully counted out. **1810** *Splendid Follies* I. 131 Ewe mutton without garnish is a tough bite, to be sure; but methinks she's dished herself off to day, *lamb-fashion. **1885** R. SHARPE *Cal. City Letters* 107 The 170 *lamb-florins in their keeping. **1822** W. KITCHINER *Cook's Oracle* (ed. 4) 492 **Lamb's fry.* Fry it plain.. garnish with crisp parsley. **1861** MRS. BEETON *Bk. Househ. Managem.* 353, 1 lb. of lamb's fry. **1888** ELWORTHY *W. Somerset Word-bk.* s.v., The product of lambs' castration are called lamb's-fries. **1891** HARDY *Tess* (1900) 8/2, I should like for supper,—well, lamb's fry. **1894** [see FRY *sb.*[2] 2 b]. **1936** S. E. NASH *Cooking Craft* (ed. 3) xii. 106 Lamb's fry consists of the liver, sweet-bread, heart, and some of the inside fat. **1944** H. WENTWORTH *Amer. Dial. Dict.* 345 *Lamb fries*, lamb's testicles. **1951** *Good Housek. Home Encycl.* 530 *Lamb's fry*, sliced lamb's offal, cooked as a rich stew. **1963** ROMBAUER & BECKER *Joy of Cooking* (ed. 4) 449/1 Skin, cut into quarters: 4 medium lamb fries. **1966** BAKER *Austral. Lang.* (ed. 2) iv. 83 We could pause to consider *lambs' fry*, as a euphemism for testicles from *marked* or castrated lambs... Our later use of *lamb's fry* for lamb liver is one of our most 'refined' additions. **1969** R. & D. DE SOLA *Dict. Cooking* 138 *Lamb fries*, lamb testicles. **1607** TOPSELL *Four-f. Beasts* (1658) 495 As, the first year, we call it in English a Lamb, so, the second year, a Hog, *Lam-hog, or Teg if it be a female. **1891** *Times* 28 Sept. 4/1 Lamb-hogs, 18*s.* to 28*s.* per head. **1819** REES *Cycl.* XX, **Lamb-house*,.. the place where lambs are fattened. **1609** BP. W. BARLOW *Answ. Nameless Cath.* 58 Wherein, if the Reader obserue (as if he had beene brought vp in *Lambs-lease) he seemes for the most part very tenderly affected. **1607** T. COCKS *Acc.* 27 Apr. (*Canterb. Cath. Libr.* MS. E. 31) *Lambes lether gloves 6*d.* **1886** C. SCOTT *Sheep Farming* 74 A good strong *lamb ram will serve as many as twenty-five ewes without hurt. *a* **1613** OVERBURY *Charac., Ordinarie Fencer* Wks. (1856) 112 For an inward bruise, *lambstones and sweet-breads are his onely sperma ceti which he eats at night. **1677** *Compleat Servant-Maid* 87 Put in Lamb-stones and sweetbreads. **1819** REES *Cycl.* XX, **Lamb-suckler*,.. a person who.. carries on the business of fattening house-lamb. *Ibid.*, **Lamb-suckling*,.. the art of fattening house-lamb.

b. In various plant names, as **lamb's cress**, *Cardamine hirsuta*; **lamb's lettuce** = CORN-SALAD (*Valerianella olitoria*); **lamb's quarter(s**, (*a*) *Atriplex hastata* or *patula*; (*b*) *Chenopodium album*; **lamb's tails**, the catkins of the hazel, *Corylus Avellana*; **lamb('s toe(s**, a name for *Lotus corniculatus*, *Anthyllis Vulneraria*, and *Medicago lupulina*. Also LAMB'S TONGUE.

c **1000** *Sax. Leechd.* II. 24 Cersan sædes, sume men hatað *lambes cersan. *a* **1100** *Voc.* in Wr.-Wülcker 300/14 *Thiaspis*, lambescerse. **1882** in FRIEND *Devonshire Plant-n.* **1597** GERARDE *Herbal* II. xxxv. §1. 242 *Lambes Lettuce. **1830** LINDLEY *Nat. Syst. Bot.* 197 The young leaves of the species of Valerianella are eaten as salad, under the French name of Mâche, or the English one of Lamb's Lettuce. **1872** OLIVER *Elem. Bot.* II. 192 Corn-salad, or Lamb's-lettuce.. is eaten as a salad. **1773** HAWKESWORTH *Voy.* III. 442 We also once or twice met with a plant like what the country people in England call *Lamb's quarters, or Fat-hen. **1869** E. A. PARKES *Pract. Hygiene* (ed. 3) 233 A salad made of the 'lamb's quarter' (*Chenopodium album*), was found very useful. **1882** *Garden* 4 Feb. 77/1 That modest kind of beauty which these catkins, 'pussies', and '*lambs'-tails', as the country people call them, suggest. **1896** *Warwicksh. Gloss.*, *Lambs'-tails*, the male catkins of hazel and filbert trees. **1821** CLARE *Vill. Minstr.* II. 94 Handfuls.. of rose and *lambtoe sweet.

lamb (læm), *v.* [f. LAMB *sb.*]

1. *trans.* (*passive only.*) To bear or bring forth; to 'drop' (a lamb).

1641 BEST *Farm. Bks.* (Surtees) 5 It.. inableth the lambe to seeke after a livinge soe soone as it is lambed. **1725** BRADLEY *Fam. Dict.* s.v. *Lamb*, If he be like to dye when first Lambed, it is usual to open his Mouth and blow therein. **1793** *Hollym Inclos. Act* 13 A modus of one shilling a score of all lambs lambed and living at Midsummer. *c* **1817** HOGG *Tales & Sk.* IV. 199 The.. shepherd.. found her with a new-yeaned lamb on the very gair of the Crawmel Craig, where she was lambed herself. **1829** *Glover's Hist. Derby* I. 214 Not one of these [rams] was lambed before Feb. 6, 1828.

2. *intr.* To bring forth a lamb; to yean.

1611 COTGR., *Agneler*, to lambe. **1641** BEST *Farm. Bks.* (Surtees) 5 An ewe putt into a goode pasture three weekes afore shee lambe, is as goode as to lett her goe in a goode pasture three weekes after. **1701** J. BRAND *Zetland* (1703) 75 As for the sheep,.. they Lamb not so soon as with us. **1846** J. BAXTER *Libr. Pract. Agric.* (ed. 4) II. p. xxii, Each ewe.. lambing at two, three, and four years old.

3. Of a shepherd: To tend (ewes) at lambing-time. Also, *to lamb down.*

1850 *Jrnl. R. Agric. Soc.* XI. I. 76 The flocks are usually lambed down about the latter end of March. **1851** *Ibid.* XII. II. 574 Every shepherd considers himself an adept at lambing his ewes. *Mod. Advt.*, Wanted, a Cowman, one used to lamb-down a few Ewes preferred.

4. lamb down. *Austral.* [? a transferred use of sense 3.] *trans.* **a.** To part with, pay down (money), *esp.* recklessly. Also *absol.*

1890 *Melbourne Argus* 7 June 4/2 The paying off of drovers, the selling off of horses, the 'lambing down' of cheques. *Ibid.* 9 Aug. 4/5 The old woman, of course, thought that we were on gold, and would lamb down at the finish in her shanty.

b. To induce (a person) to get rid of his money; to 'clean out'. Also *absol.*

1873 M. CLARKE *Holiday Peak*, etc. 21 Trowbridge's did not 'lamb down' so well as the Three Posts. **1890** *Melbourne Argus* 16 Aug. 4/7 One used to serve drinks in the bar, the other kept the billiard-table. Between them they lambed down more shearers and drovers than all the rest on the river.

Hence **lambed** *ppl. a.*, **'lambing** (*down*) *vbl. sb.*

1611 COTGR., *Agnelé*, lambed. **1844** STEPHENS *Bk. Farm* II. 599 Of the lambing of ewes. *Ibid.* 601 Think also what sort of care is bestowed on a newly lambed flock. **1850** *Jrnl. R. Agric. Soc.* XI. I. 76, I have kept 500 ewes in lamb this way.. and had them in very high condition.. on their lambing down. **1867** *Gainsborough News* 23 Mar., 200 lambed and in-lamb ewes and gimmers. **1873** J. B. STEPHENS *Black Gin* 51 It is the Bushman come to town.. Come to do his 'lambing down'. **1880** G. WALCH *Victoria in 1880.* 130 The operation—combining equal parts of hocussing, over-charging, and direct robbery.. and facetiously christened by bush landlords 'lambing down'.

lamb, obs. form of LAM *v.*

lamba[1] ('læmbə). [Malagasy.] A large cloak worn by the natives of Madagascar.

1729 DRURY *Madagascar* 234 The Corps being.. wrapped up in a Lamber, or perhaps two Lambers. **1880** J. SIBREE *Gt. Afr. Island* xvi. 326 The specially national article of dress is the lamba, a piece of cloth about three yards long and two wide. **1895** *Daily News* 21 Nov. 5/3 The natives in their white lambas.

Lamba ('læmbə), *sb.*[2] and *a.* Also **Ilamba.** [African name.] **A.** *sb.* **a.** An African of a Bantu people in Northern Zambia and Zaïre; also used as collect. sing. = this people. **b.** The language of this people. **B.** *adj.* Of or pertaining to this people or their language.

1908 A. C. MADAN *Lala-Lamba Handbk.* p. iii, The Lala and Lamba dialects are so nearly identical, and both so closely allied to the Wisa, that knowledge of either is a sufficient introduction to the other. **1919** H. H. JOHNSTON *Compar. Study Bantu & Semi-Bantu Lang.* I. iii. 207 Lala-Lamba is spoken.. east and north of the Kafue watershed. **1937** I. SCHAPERA *Bantu-Speaking Tribes S. Afr.* xiv. 314 In

Lamba (Central Bantu) the word is *umusi*. **1948** M. GUTHRIE *Classification Bantu Lang.* 78 Nįlamba, iki—(Ilamba). **1949** E. A. NIDA *Morphol.* (ed. 2) 51 Ilamba, a language of Tanganyika. **1950** RADCLIFFE-BROWN & FORDE *Afr. Syst. Kinship & Marriage* 221 The Lamba on the Kafue river seem to have a very similar family system. **1956** W. V. BRELSFORD *Tribes N. Rhodesia* vi. 46 Lamba area as a whole, because of its proximity to the copperbelt, is the most mixed area in the territory. **1956** J. LOTZ in Saporta & Bastian *Psycholinguistics* (1961) 9/2 In certain languages the whole sentence is constructed in a single syntactic key..as in Ilamba of Northern Rhodesia. **1957** W. M. HAILEY *Afr. Survey* (rev. ed.) iii. 113 Studies made..of the Zulu, Shona, and Lamba languages. **1957** V. W. TURNER *Schism & Continuity in Afr. Soc.* viii. 255 Among the Lamba of the Ndola District of Northern Rhodesia..traceable cross-cousin marriages formed an extremely low proportion of the total marriages recorded.

† **lamback**, *v. Obs.* Also 6 lambacke, lambeak(e. [? f. LAM *v.* + BACK *sb.*] *trans.* To beat, thrash. Also *fig.*

1589 *Rare Triumphs Love & Fort.* IV. in *Five Old Plays* (Roxb.) 122 You are no devill; mas, and I wist you were, I would lamback the devill out of you. **1591** NASHE *Prognostication* 17 Sundrie tall fellowes..armed with good cudgels, shall so lambeake these stubborne hus-wiues. **1592** G. HARVEY *Four Lett.* iii. 21 That brauely threatned to coniure-vpp one, which should massacre Martins witt, or should bee lambackd himself with ten yeares prouision. **1601** MUNDAY *Death Earl Huntington* v. i. R I a, With this dagger lustilie lambackt.

Hence † **lamback** *sb.*, a whack, a heavy blow. Also † **lambacker**, one who beats or drubs.

1591 GREENE *Disc. Coosnage* (1592) 25 Fiue or sixe wiues ..gaue him a score of sound lambeakes with their cudgels. **1592** G. HARVEY *Pierce's Super.* 131 Out upon thee for a cowardly lambacker.

‖ **lambardar** (læmbə'dɑː(r)). Also **lambadar**, **lumberdar**, etc. [Urdū *lambardār*, f. Eng. NUMBER + Urdū (Pers.) *-dār* suffix.] The registered head-man of an Indian village.

1855 H. H. WILSON *Gloss. Judic. & Rev. Terms*, *Lambardar, Lumburdar*, The cultivator who,..pays the government dues and is registered in the collector's roll according to his number. **1858** J. B. NORTON *Topics* 193 The moral control of head men and lumberdars is destroyed. **1900** MARY CARUS WILSON *Irene Petrie* xii. 284 The doctors operated successfully on the wife of the lumbardar—that is the hereditary taxgatherer, the headman of the village. **1908** *New Reformer* (Madras) II. 68 Securing the co-operation of the literate among them and the Lambardars to bring about sanitary reforms, etc. **1920** *Glasgow Herald* 12 Jan. 9/6 At one village the Lambardar was obstructive, would give no information, and refused to accompany him. **1960** J. MASTERS *Venus of Konpara* xxiii. 177 Our lambardar thinks she [*sc.* a tigress] has not started to eat yet. **1971** R. DENTRY *Encounter at Kharmel* iii. 46, I am not the Wazir... I am only the Lambadar, Raza Khan. *Ibid.* 48 Lambadar is honorific. I am Mayor, you see?

lambaste (læm'beɪst), *v.* Also 9 lambust, lambast. [? f. LAM *v.* + BASTE *v.*] **a.** *trans.* To beat, thrash. *colloq.*

1637 I. JONES & DAVENANT *Brit. Tri.* 18 Stand off a while and see how Ile lambaste him. **1678** J. PHILLIPS *Tavernier's Trav.* I. viii. 52 Otherwise they would be fin'd, and lambasted with a good Cudgel. **1837** HALIBURTON *Clockm.* I. xxiii, I am six foot six in my stockin feet, by gum, and can lambaste any two of you in no time. **1877** *N.W. Linc. Gloss.*, *Lambaste*, to beat.

b. *fig.* To scold, castigate.

1886 *Harper's Mag.* July 321/2 With an avalanche of facts, sarcasm and ridicule..a more complete lambasting and more vigorous and thorough roasting than Wise gave Bontelle was never known. **1891** KIPLING *Light that Failed* viii. 151, I only gave him his riding-orders to—to lambast you on general principles for not producing work that will last. **1930** *Times* 13 Jan. 14/4 Mr. Maxton was heard to say, 'Mr. Chairman... It has been said that you were going to "lambast" me at this conference.' **1938** J. RICE *Somers Inheritance* I. iv. 29 His sermons got down to the bed-rock.. even if they..failed to lambaste wickedness with quite the fury it deserved. **1947** *People* 22 June 4/2 So he has castigated America for daring to interfere in Palestine, and now he lambasts Russia for meddling in the affairs of the little countries. **1951** *Oxf. Dict. Nursery Rhymes* 28 Halliwell struck a saner note (1842) but greedily copied down as facts any theories related to him, and though he lambasted Ker, he was not above speculation himself. **1956** *Jrnl. Educ.* July 304 Having myself been lambasted more than once by the Italicists because I dared to qualify my praise of their handwriting. **1958** *Times* 16 Oct. 8/5 To this lambasting Dr. Rowse was all smiles and soothing words. **1967** *Boston Globe* 20 May 2/2 He lambasted teaching techniques, saying they have become 'a disciplinary practice'. **1969** N. HARE in A. Chapman *New Black Voices* (1972) 428 They lambasted the ultradevotion of many black intellectuals to jazz music. **1972** *Newsweek* 10 Jan. 19/1 If the economy should stay sour, the alternative script called for Mr. Nixon to lambaste the labour bosses.

Hence **lam'basting** *vbl. sb.*

1694 MOTTEUX *Rabelais* IV. xii. 48 If they were long without a tight Lambasting. **1867** SMYTH *Sailor's Word-bk.*, *Lambusting*, a starting with a rope's end.

lambative, variant of LAMBITIVE *Obs.*

lambda ('læmdə). Also 7 lamda. [Gr. λάμβδα (or λάβδα).]

1. The 11th letter of the Greek alphabet, Λ, λ.

c **1400** MAUNDEV. (1839) iii. 20 Thei clepen hem..α Alpha ..κ Kappa, λ Lambda. **1603** HOLLAND *Plutarch's Mor.* 1324 Whether in the Future tense it [the verb βάλλω] should lose one of the two Lamdaes? **1799** KIRWAN *Geol. Ess.* 285 The calcareous mountains of Savoy are often arched like a lambda.

2. *Anat.* 'The point of junction of the sagittal and lambdoidal sutures' (*Syd. Soc. Lex.* 1888).

[*c* **1400** *Lanfranc's Cirurg.* 109 A boon þe which is clepid alauda. (The Latin has: ad modum literæ laudæ grecæ.)]

3. *lambda moth*, a moth so called from a mark on its wings, resembling the letter (Webster 1890).

1798 NEMNICH *Polyglot Lex. Nat. Hist., Eng.*, Lambda moth, *Phalaena gamma*.

4. *Physics.* **lambda point**, the temperature (approximately 2·18°K) below which liquid helium in equilibrium with its vapour exhibits superfluidity, and at which there is a sharp maximum and apparent discontinuity in its specific heat; *transf.*, any temperature at which the specific heat of a substance exhibits similar behaviour, increasing at an increasing rate as the temperature is raised to this value and then dropping abruptly; hence ***lambda curve***, ***line*** (on a phase diagram), ***transition***. Freq. written as *λ point*, etc.

1932 W. H. & A. P. KEESOM in *Proc. Sect. Sci. Kon. Akad. Wetensch. Amsterdam* XXXV. 742 The specific heat of liquid helium at about 2·19°K falls from a value of 3·0 to a value of about 1·1 certainly within 0·02 degree... For convenience sake it is desirable to introduce a name for the point at which this jump occurs. According to a suggestion made by Prof. Ehrenfest we propose to call that point, considering the resemblance of the specific heat curve with the Greek letter λ, the lambda-point. **1933** W. H. KEESOM in *Ibid.* XXXVI. 149 It is in this sense that..we speak of the lambda-point..and of the lambda-curve. **1940** *Physical Rev.* LVII. 417 Measurements of the temperature variation of the adiabatic and isothermal Young's and rigidity moduli and of the coefficient of thermal expansion of pressed specimens of ammonium chloride in the neighbourhood of the λ-point transition at 242·8°K are reported. **1952** J. F. ALLEN in F. E. Simon et al. *Low Temperature Physics* iii. 73 The phase diagram of liquid helium..is crossed by a line which has been called the λ-line. **1958** CONDON & ODISHAW *Handbk. Physics* v. xi. 159/2 The λ transition involves no detectable change in spatial structure. **1964** *Physical Rev.* CXXXV. A1696/1 One would expect that the elastic properties of β brass near its lambda point should strongly resemble those of other solids which undergo cooperative order-disorder transitions. **1966** K. MENDELSSOHN *Quest for Absolute Zero* x. 234 The characteristic feature of superflow ..was transport completely free of friction, taking place at a 'critical velocity' which only depended on temperature and vanished at the lambda-point.

5. a. *Chem.* A millionth of a litre; usu. denoted by λ.

1934 P. L. KIRK in *Mikrochemie* XIV. 13 It seems logical to use the designations mm³ = μ l = λ. Such a procedure could simplify discussion considerably if the letter lambda were used with this significance, and we shall in future adhere to this usage. *Ibid.*, Since 1 l. of normal solution contains 1 equivalent..1 λ contains 1 micro-equivalent. **1939** *Mikrochemie* XXVI. 32 All the drops should have the same volume, 1 λ. **1939** E. J. CONWAY *Micro-diffusion Anal.* i. 4 For the actual designation of the minute quantities or volumes..we have the milligramme (mg.), and the gamma (γ or 0·001 mg.), also termed the microgramme (μg) and the lambda (λ or 0·001 ml.—introduced by Kirk). **1961** A. STEYERMARK *Quantitative Org. Microanalysis* (ed. 2) i. 2 The terms gamma (γ), and lambda (λ) are to be substituted with microgram (μg.) and microliter (μl.) respectively. **1974** *Nature* 15 Nov. p. xi (Advt.), Corning disposable micro-sampling pipettes are made from 'Pyrex' brand borosilicate glass... The accuracy of the graduated 5 Lambda (λ) is ±1%.

b. *Nuclear Physics.* Used, usu. *attrib.*, to denote a neutral hyperon (and its anti-particle) which has a mass 2183 times that of the electron, a spin of ½, and zero isospin, and on decaying usually produces a nucleon and a pion; †orig. applied to other hyperons also. Freq. written as Λ.

1954 *Physical Rev.* XCIII. 861/1 We have reported two examples of Λ^0 particles produced in hydrogen by negative pions (π^-) of 1·5-Bev kinetic energy. *Ibid.*, We are using here the nomenclature suggested for *V* events at the International Congress on Cosmic Radiation, Bagnères-de-Bigorre, France. Accordingly $\Lambda^{0,+,-} \rightarrow$ nucleon + pion + Q_Λ. *Ibid.* XCVI. 543/1 The known hyperons, Λ^-, Ω^-, have masses equivalent to 1200 and 1320 Mev, respectively. **1963** *Sci. Amer.* Jan. 40/2 When a $\bar{K}^-$ meson struck a proton (p), a small fraction of the collisions produced a neutral lambda particle (Λ^0) and a negative and a positive pi meson. **1963** K. W. FORD *World of Elem. Particles* vi. 179 The sigma particle lives too short a time to move a measurable distance.., decaying almost at once into a lambda and a photon ($\Sigma^0 \rightarrow \Lambda^0 + \gamma$). **1968** M. S. LIVINGSTON *Particle Physics* iv. 80 This evidence was the observation of V tracks consisting of two charged-particle tracks coming from a common origin, of which one was identified as a proton and the other as a negative pion. The neutral particle which decayed to give these products, now called the lambda-zero, (Λ^0), must have had a mass greater than the sum of proton and pion masses.

lambdacism ('læmdəsɪz(ə)m), **labdacism** ('læbd-). [ad. L. *lambdacismus*, *labdacismus*, a. Gr. λα(μ)βδακισμός, f. λά(μ)βδα LAMBDA.]

1. A too frequent repetition of the letter *l* in speaking or writing.

1658 PHILLIPS, *Labdacisme, Lambdacisme*. **1676** COLES, *Lambdacism*. **1753** CHAMBERS *Cycl. Supp.*, *Labdacism*, Λαβδακισμός, in rhetoric, the too frequent repetition of the letter L.

2. A faulty pronunciation of the letter *r*, making it sound like *l*; lallation.

1864 R. F. BURTON *Dahome* I. 158 Allada is called by older authors Ardrah, another instance of lambdacism, confusing the L and the R.

† **'lambdal**, *a. Obs. rare*⁻¹. [f. LAMBDA + -AL¹.] = LAMBDOIDAL.

1634 T. JOHNSON tr. *Parey's Chirurg.* x. viii. (1678) 234 If that part of one of the bones of the Bregma, which is next to the Lambdal suture [orig. *suture lambdoide*] be smitten.

lambdoid ('læmdɔɪd), *a.* [a. F. *lambdoïde*, ad. mod.L. *lambdoīdēs*, ad. Gr. λαμβδοειδ-ής: see LAMBDA and -OID.] = LAMBDOIDAL 1.

1597 A. M. tr. *Guillemeau's Fr. Chirurg.* 42/2 In the end of the suture lamdoid, behind vnder the eare. **1741** MONRO *Anat.* (ed. 3) 70 The old Anatomists reckoned the proper Lambdoid Suture to terminate at the Squamous Sutures. **1866** HUXLEY *Preh. Rem. Caithn.* 88 There is a large Wormian bone in the right crus of the lambdoid suture.

lambdoidal (læm'dɔɪdəl), *a.* Also 7-9 lamdoidal. [f. prec. + -AL¹.] Resembling the Greek letter lambda (Λ) in form.

1. *Anat.* ***lambdoidal suture*** (†***commissure***), the suture connecting the two parietal bones with the occipital. Also ***lambdoidal ridge*** (see quot. 1888).

1653 URQUHART *Rabelais* I. xxvii, If any thought by flight to escape, he made his head to flie in pieces by the Lamdoidal commissure, which is a seame in the hinder part of the scull. **1698** TYSON in *Phil. Trans.* XX. 148 The Lambdoidal Suture. **1741** MONRO *Anat.* (ed. 3) 70 The Lambdoidal Suture, begins some way below, and farther back than the Vertex or Crown of the Head, whence its two Legs are stretched obliquely down and to each Side, in Form of the Greek Letter Λ. **1866** HUXLEY *Preh. Rem. Caithn.* 86 The coronal suture is traceable throughout; the sagittal and the middle part of the lambdoidal are almost completely obliterated. **1888** *Syd. Soc. Lex.*, *Lambdoidal ridge*, the edge of the occipital bone forming the lambdoid suture, which in some animals, as the cat, forms a salient ridge for the attachment of muscles.

2. *nonce-use.* Resembling the shape of the small Greek letter lambda λ.

1818 J. BROWN *Psyche* 189 Bid her forbear when males are by, To stand like an inverted Y. Since modesty and sense avoid all Postures and attitudes lamdoidal.

lambe, obs. form of LAM *v.*

lambeak(e, variant of LAMBACK *v. Obs.*

‖ **lambeau.** *Obs.* Also 6 lambewe. Pl. **lambeaux** (also erroneously used as sing.). [Fr.: see LABEL.] A strip or fillet hanging from a head-dress or garment. In *Her.*, one of the dependent points of a label (see LABEL 5); *occas.* the label itself.

1562 LEIGH *Armorie* (1597) 107 He beareth Argent, a fyle with iij Lambeaux Azure, for a difference. Some will call them a Labell of three pointes... The field Argent, a File, and one Lambewe Vert. **1599** HAKLUYT *Voy.* II. II. 81 At his cappe hang certaine Lambeaux much like vnto a Bishops Miter. **1610** GUILLIM *Heraldry* I. vi. (1611) 22 Some other authors call them files, and others Lambeaux or labels. **1688** R. HOLME *Armoury* I. 108/2 Lambeaux, Plaits of a Garment. **1828-40** BERRY *Encycl. Herald.* I, Cross lambeaux is the bearing of a cross upon a lambeaux or label.

Hence † **'lambeauxed** *a.*, 'dovetailed' (*Gloss. Her.* 1847).

Lambeg ('læmbɛg). The name of a village near Belfast, N. Ireland, used *attrib.* of the large drums traditionally beaten there on ceremonial occasions; also *absol.* Hence **'Lambegger**, one who beats such a drum.

1932 *Sun* (Baltimore) 18 Nov. 3/6 The booming 'lam-legs' [*sic*], huge goatskin drums which are an important part of this kind of celebration. **1938** R. HAYWARD *In Praise of Ulster* 23 Of all the bands the Lambeggers alone are of the real vintage. *Ibid.* 24 Nothing in the world is quite like a Lambeg Band... The combination is usually composed of four or six gigantic drums. **1949** H. SHEARMAN *Ulster* xxxiii. 299 Not far from Lisburn, on the Belfast side, is Lambeg, a place traditionally famous for drums, for it used to be a great centre for..the drumming parties which used to be so characteristic of the Orange organization. The largest type of Orange drum used to be referred to as a Lambeg drum, and when one beat a tattoo on it one was said to beat Lambeg. **1952** D. O'D. HANNA *Face of Ulster* x. 112 Slowly and inexorably the drumming parties creep past, for the Lambeggars do not march. **1966** S. HEANEY in *Listener* 29 Sept. 475/3 Orange drums, Tyrone 1966. The lambeg balloons at his belly, weighs Him back on his haunches. **1970** *Guardian* 8 Aug. 1/5 The Lambeg drums, the noisiest and most fervent symbol of Protestant supremacy in Northern Ireland, will not be beaten in Londonderry next Wednesday.

‖ **lambel** ('læmbɛl). *Her.* [Fr.; older form of LAMBEAU (see LAMBEAU).] In Fr. Heraldry, a file used as a mark of cadency.

1847 *Gloss. Her.*, *Lambel*, see *Label*. **1896** *Daily News* 7 Apr. 5/4 Before the death of the Comte de Chambord, the Comte de Paris had a horizontal bar or lambel on his shield. This showed that he belonged to a younger branch of the Royal family.

lambency ('læmbənsɪ). [f. next: see -ENCY.]

1. The state or quality of being lambent or shining with a clear soft light like a flame. Also (with *pl.*) an instance or occurrence of such shining.

1817 L. HUNT *Day by the Fire* in *Hazlitt's Round Table* II 146 Sometimes a little flame appears at the corner of the grate like a quivering spangle; sometimes it swells out at top into a restless and brief lambency. **1835** *New Monthly Mag.* XLIII. 305 The morning star, melting into the east with its transcendent lambency and whiteness. **1845** DE QUINCEY *Suspiria de Profundis* I. in *Blackw. Mag.* LVII. 279 The fitful gloom and sudden lambencies of the room by fire-light suited our evening state of feelings. **1856** RUSKIN *Mod. Paint.* IV. v. viii. §9 The soft lambency of the streamlet. *fig.* **1866** CARLYLE *Remin.* (1881) I. 86 But there were sacred lambencies, tongues of authentic flame from heaven which kindled what was best in one. **1873** SYMONDS *Grk. Poets* viii. 250 So that his [Aristophanes'] splendour is like that of northern streamers in its lambency, though swift and piercing as forked lightnings in its intensity.

b. *transf.* Brilliance and delicate play of wit or fancy.

1871 CARLYLE in *Mrs. Carlyle's Lett.* I. 153 Thought, flowing out in lambencies of beautiful spontaneous wit and fancy. **1871** MORLEY *Vauvenargues* in *Crit. Misc.* I. (1878) 14 The presence of a certain lambency and play even in the exposition of truths of perfect assurance. **1886** STEVENSON *Pr. Otto* I. iv. 51 A man of great erudition and some lambencies of wit.

¶**2.** In etymological sense: The action of licking.

1834 *Oxf. Univ. Mag.* I. 176 The mother's tongue..with assiduous lambency has licked the unsightly cubs into shape.

lambent ('læmbənt), *a.* [ad. L. *lambent-em*, pr. pple. of *lambĕre* to lick.]

1. Of a flame (fire, light): Playing lightly upon or gliding over a surface without burning it, like a 'tongue of fire'; shining with a soft clear light and without fierce heat.

1647 COWLEY *Mistress, Answ. Platonicks*, As useless to despairing Lovers grown, As Lambent flames, to men i' th' Frigid Zone. **1656** —— *Pindar. Odes, Destinie* iv, The Star that did my Being frame, Was but a Lambent Flame, And some small Light it did dispence, But neither Heat nor Influence. **1697** DRYDEN *Æneid* VII. 114 Lambent Glories danc'd about her Head. **1781** CAVALLO in *Phil. Trans.* LXXI. 330 Because its light..was stationary and not lambent. **1834** MRS. SOMERVILLE *Connex. Phys. Sci.* xxviii. (1849) 323 Those lambent, diffuse flashes of lightning without thunder, so frequent in warm summer evenings. **1854** THACKERAY *Newcomes* I. 284 The lambent lights of the starry host of heaven. **1871** ROSCOE *Elem. Chem.* 13 Sulphur, which in the air burns with a pale lambent flame.

b. *transf.* and *fig.*

1682 DRYDEN *Mac Flecknoe* 111 His brows thick fogs instead of glories grace, And lambent dulness played around his face. **1748** RICHARDSON *Clarissa* (1811) III. xxxi. 187 My next point will be to make her acknowledge a lambent flame, a preference of me to all other men at least. **1841** MYERS *Cath. Th.* IV. xxxiii. 340 A mild and lambent light of Prophecy may be considered as encircling their [the Jews'] whole constitution. **1866** G. MACDONALD *Ann. Q. Neighb.* xii. (1878) 235 His intellect was rather a lambent flame than a genial warmth.

c. By extension, of eyes, the sky, etc.: Emitting, or suffused with, a soft clear light; softly radiant.

1717 POPE *Eloisa* 64 Those smiling eyes, attemp'ring ev'ry ray, Shone sweetly lambent with celestial day. **1808** J. BARLOW *Columb.* v. 304 A general jubilee, o'er earth and heaven, Leads the gay morn and lights the lambent even. **1867** LYDIA M. CHILD *Rom. Repub.* i. 3 Her large brown eyes were..lambent with interior light. **1873** BLACK *Pr. Thule* vi. 94 The strange lambent darkness..of those northern twilights. **1877** —— *Green Past.* iv. (1878) 29 The great acacia spread its feathery branches into a cloudless and lambent sky. **1887** RUSKIN *Præterita* II. 159 The Rhone flows like one lambent jewel.

d. *fig.* Of wit, style, etc.: Playing lightly and brilliantly over its subjects; gracefully sportive.

1871 MORLEY *J. de Maistre* in *Crit. Misc.* I. (1878) 112 A humour now and then a little sardonic, but more often genial and lambent. **1879** O. W. HOLMES *Motley* viii. 59 Lambent phrases in stately articles. **1880** DISRAELI *Endym.* lxxvii, The style so picturesque and lambent!

2. In etymological sense: Licking, that licks. †Also = LAMBITIVE *a. rare.*

1706 PHILLIPS (ed. Kersey), *Lambent*, licking with the Tongue; as, *Lambent Medicines*, i.e. such as are taken by licking off from the end of a Stick of Licorish, &c. **1784** COWPER *Task* VI. 782 To dally with the crested worm..or to receive The lambent homage of his arrowy tongue. **1826** KIRBY & SP. *Entomol.* (1828) IV. 492 The Hymenoptera generally lap their food with their tongue and may be called lambent insects.

lambently ('læmbəntlɪ), *adv.* [f. prec. + -LY².] In a lambent manner.

1819 SHELLEY *P. Bell 3rd* VI. xxvi, In the death hues of agony Lambently flashing from a fish. **1883** F. M. CRAWFORD *Mr. Isaacs* xiii. 289 The blazing eyes flamed, lambently under the black brows. **1889** *Universal Rev.* III. 143 Its wit played lambently over the doings of Society.

†**'lamber¹**. *Obs.* Chiefly *north. dial.* Also 4-6 **lambre**, 5 **laumb(e)re**, **lambur**, **lawmer**, 6, 9 **lammer**, 9 **lamar**, **-er**, **-our**. [a. F. *l'ambre*, applied esp. to *ambre jaune* 'yellow amber', i.e. amber as distinguished from *ambre gris* or AMBERGRIS.] Amber. Also *attrib.*, as ***lamber beads***, ***colour***.

a **1387** *Sinon. Barthol.* (Anecd. Oxon.) 26 *Kacabre*, i. lambre. *c* **1400** MAUNDEV. (Roxb.) xxi. 97 Bedes of laumbre. **1429** *Test. Ebor.* (Surtees) I. 417 A pare of lambre bedes. *c* **1430** *Two Cookery-bks.* 26 Take..Safron, þat it haue a fayre Laumbere coloure. *c* **1450** *Bk. Curtasye* 480 in *Babees Bk.*, Bedys of coralle and lambur. **1550** LYNDESAY *Sqr. Meldrum* 1008 Than scho passit vnto hir Chalmer, And fand hir madinnis, sweit as Lammer, Sleipand full sound. **1552** HULOET, Ambre called lambre or yelow Ambre. **1603** E. FAIRFAX *Eclog.* iv. in Eliz. Cooper *Muses Libr.* (1737) I. 368 Crown thy Lamber Horns with Corall Roses. **1610** MARKHAM *Masterp.* I. xiv. 38 If the vrine..be..high-coloured, bright and cleare like lamber and not like amber. **1724** RAMSAY *Tea-t. Misc.* (1733) I. 107 Her locks that shin'd like lammer. **1806** R. JAMIESON *Pop. Ballads* I. 181 It is your lady's heart's blood; 'Tis as clear as the lamer. **1818** SCOTT *Hrt. Midl.* xiii, Dinna ye think poor Jeanie's een wi' the tears in them glanced like lamour beads, Mr. Saddletree? —— *Br. Lamm.* xii, A grogram gown, lammer beads, and a clean cockernony.

lamber² ('læmə(r)). [f. LAMB *v.* + -ER¹.]

1. One who tends ewes when lambing.

1809 D. PRICE in Spurgeon *Treas. Dav. Ps.* lxxviii. 71 Many lambs may be lost without its being possible to charge the lamber with neglect or ignorance. *Ibid.* in H. Stephens *Bk. Farm* (1849) I. 591/1 Lambing presents a scene of confusion..which it is the lamber's business to rectify.

2. A lambing ewe.

1886 C. SCOTT *Sheep Farming* 80 At the end of the first week the second lot of lambers may be brought in.

lamber(ne, obs. pl. form of LAMB.

Lambert ('læmbət). [The name of Johann Heinrich *Lambert* (1728-77), German mathematician.]

1. a. In *Cartography* used *attrib.* and in the possessive to designate certain map projections devised by Lambert, *spec.* a conical conformal projection having two standard parallels along which the scale is true. Also *ellipt.* as *Lambert*.

1879 *Encycl. Brit.* X. 207/2 A translation of this essay [of Gauss's] is to be found in the Philosophical Magazine for 1828.., where Lambert's projection comes out as a particular solution of the general problem. **1912** A. R. HINKS *Map Projections* ii. 18 When the conical orthomorphic projection is used, it is always that with two standard parallels, which is Lambert's second, or Gauss'. **1953** A. H. ROBINSON *Elem. Cartogr.* iii. 43 The Lambert conic projection..has concentric parallels and equally spaced straight meridians that meet the parallels at right angles... It has two standard parallels, but the spacing of the other parallels on the Lambert increases away from the standard parallels. *Ibid.* iv. 74 The Lambert azimuthal equal-area projection is most useful when centered in the area of interest. **1971** I. G. GASS et al. *Understanding Earth* xv. 224 *(caption)* A possible geometrical fit of the southern continents at the 500-fathom..contour... Lambert equal area projection.

b. In *Physics* used in the possessive to designate two laws enunciated by Lambert: (*a*) the intensity of the light emitted by an element of area of a perfectly diffusing surface is proportional to the cosine of the angle between the direction of emission and the normal to the surface; (*b*) (see quots. 1911, 1966).

1895 *Electrician* 20 Sept. 672/2 The diffused reflection practically follows Lambert's cosine law. **1911** R. W. WOOD *Physical Optics* (rev. ed.) xv. 437 Lambert's law states that each layer of equal thickness absorbs an equal fraction of the light which traverses it. **1952** R. W. DITCHBURN *Light* xv. 441 Experimental observations on the transmission in a homogeneous medium which absorbs, but does not scatter, the light are summarized in Lambert's law, which may be written $L(z) = L_0e^{-2az}$. The constant $2a$ is called the absorption coefficient. **1966** D. G. BRANDON *Mod. Techniques Metallogr.* ii. 65 The fraction of the incident intensity transmitted through a thin slice, of thickness t, can be calculated from Lambert's law: $I/I_0 = \exp(-\mu t)$, where μ is the absorption coefficient.

2. (Written **lambert.**) A unit of luminance equal to one lumen per square centimetre (equivalent to approximately 3180 candelas per square metre).

1915 P. G. NUTTING in *Electr. World* 6 Feb. 333/1, I prefer to speak of a brightness of so many 'lamberts'. This term is now well understood in our laboratory. Where required it is easily translated into lumens and any desired units of area. **1915** H. E. IVES in *Ibid.* 20 Feb. 460/1 Dr. Nutting..comes forward with an excellent name,..the 'lambert'. But he applies it, in my opinion, to the wrong unit... Let us say that a surface has a brightness of one 'lambert' if it is as bright as a 'Lambert's law' white surface under unit illumination. **1923** L. C. MARTIN *Colour* 178 The normal radiation corresponds to $1/\pi$ candles per square centimetre when the brightness is 1 lambert. **1953** AMOS & BIRKINSHAW *Television Engin.* I. 280, 1 lambert = 1 lumen per square centimetre = 0·3183 candle per square centimetre = 2·054 candles per square inch = 929 foot-lamberts. **1962** F. I. ORDWAY et al. *Basic Astronautics* iii. 37 *(table)* Sun... Surface brightness, lamberts... $6{\cdot}24 \times 10^5$. **1966** D. G. BRANDON *Mod. Techniques Metallogr.* i. 58 Haine gives the minimum practical screen brightness [of an electron microscope] as 3×10^{-4} lamberts.

Lambeth ('læmbəθ). [The name of a South London borough.] **1.** Used allusively (chiefly *attrib.*) to refer to the Archbishop of Canterbury, whose palace is at Lambeth, or to the Church of England; esp. in **Lambeth Conference**, an assembly of the Anglican bishops, usu. held decennially at Lambeth Palace; **Lambeth degree**, a degree *honoris causa* conferred by the Archbishop of Canterbury.

1859 W. F. HOOK *Church Dict.* (ed. 8) 429/2 *Lambeth degrees*, the popular designation given to degrees conferred by the Archbishop of Canterbury, who has the power of giving degrees in any of the faculties. **1867** *Times* 10 Dec. 7/3 The Bishops..complain that the necessary work of their dioceses is too much for them, and demand an addition to their numbers. That demand is not likely to be listened to while they can find time and thought for a Lambeth Conference. **1875** *Encycl. Brit.* II. 369/2 The archbishop also continues to grant degrees in the faculties of theology and law, which are known as Lambeth Degrees. *Ibid.* 654/2 In 1595,..the Primate, Whitgift, accepted a series of articles proposed by Dr Whitaker of Cambridge. These, generally known as the Lambeth Articles, were strongly Calvinistic in tone. **1902** *Ibid.* XXX. 120/2 The resolutions of the Lambeth Conferences have never been regarded as synodical decrees, but their weight has increased with each conference; and in particular the 'Lambeth Quadrilateral' of 1888 has already had a great effect as a plan of reunion. **1941** W. TEMPLE *Citizen & Churchman* iv. 70 It is the duty of Lambeth to remind Westminster of its responsibility to God; but this does not mean that Westminster is responsible to Lambeth. **1958** E. L. MASCALL *Recovery of Unity* vii. 153 The often-quoted statement of the Lambeth Conference Committee. **1974** J. MELVILLE *Nun's Castle* iii. 62 She kept to a set of religious observances which..would have caused raised eyebrows in both the Vatican and Lambeth Palace.

2. Used *attrib.* or *absol.* to designate a kind of glazed and painted earthenware manufactured in Lambeth from the 17th to the 19th century.

[**1863** W. CHAFFERS *Marks Pott. & Porc.* 131 *Lambeth.* About 1640 some Dutch potters established themselves here, and by degrees the manufacture of earthenware became important... The ware made here was a sort of Delft, with landscapes and figures painted in blue.] **1884** C. SCHREIBER *Jrnl.* 23 Sept. (1911) II. 440 One of the Lambeth Wine bottles. *Ibid.* 17 Nov. 456 A cat..which he pronounced to be Lambeth (dated 1676). **1900** [see DOULTON]. **1948** F. H. GARNER *Eng. Delftware* iv. 29 A Lambeth brick is illustrated. **1961** L. G. G. RAMSEY *Connoisseur New Guide Antique Eng. Pott., Porc. & Glass* 27 'Lambeth' and 'Bristol' polychrome 'delftwares' of the second half of the seventeenth century. **1974** *Times* 26 Oct. 13/3 Immigrant Dutch potters had come to set up there [*sc.* in Lambeth], bringing with them the techniques for tin-plating earthenware which had been associated with Delft. The English products of these potters and their successors are called English Delftware, and that made in Lambeth is called Lambeth Delftware.

3. Lambeth Walk, the name of a street in Lambeth, used as the title of a Cockney song and dance first performed by Lupino Lane in the revue *Me and my Gal* in 1937.

1937 FURBER & GAY *(song-title)* Lambeth Walk. **1939** *Times* 23 Mar. 14/4 The 'Lambeth Walk' and its successors have destroyed the tyranny of the foxtrot which for 20 years has made the ball-room an unsociable place. **1942** J. W. DRAWBELL *Dorothy Thompson's Eng. Journey* ix. 83 She can hardly pull herself away from that cheerful, excited London throng—from the people who have fought fires while the bombs fell and can still sing and dance the Lambeth Walk. **1962** *Guardian* 31 Dec. 5/1 The Lambeth Walk, invented in the thirties..to publicize 'Me and My Girl'.

lambetive, variant of LAMBITIVE *Obs.*

lambewe, variant of LAMBEAU *Obs.*

lambhood ('læmhʊd). [f. LAMB *sb.* + -HOOD.] The state of being a lamb; the youth of a sheep.

1853 LD. COCKBURN *Circuit Journeys* (1888) 397 It was a leg which told how it had strayed among mountains from its lambhood to its death. **1891** E. & D. GERARD *Sensit. Plant* I. II. vii. 279 They themselves will have left their lambhood behind them for ever.

‖**Lambic** (lɑ̃bik). Also **Lambick**. [Fr.; cf. *alambic* a still.] A strong beer brewed in Belgium.

1889 *Cent. Dict.*, *Lambick*, a kind of strong beer made in Belgium by the process called the self-fermentation of worts. **1908** *Daily Chron.* 2 Mar. 5/6 On being offered a glass of champagne he refused it, asking for some 'Lambic', a popular beverage in Belgium. **1952** G. GORDON in E. Fodor *Benelux in 1952* 69 The high-density drink..is *Geuze* (so called when it is bottled, and *Lambic* when it is on tap). **1956** A. CAMPBELL *Bk. Beer* vi. 95 In Belgium there is a beer known as *Lambic*,..left to stand and mature for about two years in granaries, fermenting slowly in wooden casks. **1960** [see FARO²]. **1964** L. BREWER *A to Z of Holidays Abroad* 107 A wheat-and-barley based beer is made, draught called *Lambic*, bottled *Geuze*.

lambie ('læmɪ). orig. *Sc.* Also **lammie**, **lammy**. [See -IE, -Y.] A term of endearment for a lamb and hence for a child or young person.

1718 RAMSAY *Christ's Kirk Gr.* III. xx, She her man like a lammy led Hame. **1768** ROSS *Helenor* (1789) 14 For tweesh twa hillocks the poor lambie lies. **1785** BURNS *Holy Fair* iii, The third cam up, hap-step-an'-lowp, As light as ony lambie. **1801** MACNEILL *Poems* II. 84, I held her to my beating heart, My young, my smiling Lammie! **1879** C. M. YONGE *Burnt Out* ix. 149 Is he hurt? Is my little lambie hurt? **1935** N. MITCHISON *We have been Warned* IV. 357 Oh, Lilias, what have you got, Lambie—oh, a *lovely* stone.

lambiness ('læmɪnɪs). *nonce-wd.* [f. LAMB *sb.* + -Y (adj. suffix) + -NESS] Lamb-like quality.

1886 STEVENSON *Pr. Otto* II. iv. 105, I have always abominated the lamb, and nourished a romantic feeling for the wolf. O, be done with lambiness!

lambing ('læmɪŋ), *vbl. sb.* Also 6 **lamming**. [f. LAMB *v.* + -ING¹.] The parturition or yeaning of lambs; (of a lamb) birth, time of birth. Also *attrib.*, as ***lambing fold***, ***season***, ***time***.

1573 TUSSER *Husb.* xxxv. (1878) 80 Now therefore thine ewe, vpon lamming so neere, desireth in pasture that all may be cleere. **1611** COTGR. s.v. *Agneler*, At lambing time we find what Ewes were full. **1616** SURFL. & MARKH. *Country Farme* 111 When the Ewe is in Lambing. **1797** *Monthly Mag.* III. 486 A premium of five guineas to the owner of the best South-down wether, to be two years old last lambing-time. **1813** *Examiner* 3 May 279/2 The lambing has been.. successful. **1861** PEARSON *Early & Mid. Ages Eng.* 141 The

tithes..were due three times a year,—at the lambing season, at harvest-time, and at Martinmas. **1881** A. C. GRANT *Bush Life Queensland* xxxii. (1882) 328 Stone had also done very well; his lambings had been good. **1886** C. SCOTT *Sheep-Farming* 79 Admirable lambing folds can be constructed very readily..with no other materials than wattled hurdles and straw.

'lambing, *ppl. a.* [f. LAMB *v.* + -ING².] Of a ewe: Breeding, with young.

1861 *Times* 24 Sept., The roots are..carted to lambing ewes on the pastures. **1883** *Pall Mall G.* 17 Mar. 4/1 They smash the farmer's gates, level his fences..frighten the lambing ewes.

lambish ('læmɪʃ), *a. rare.* [f. LAMB *sb.* + -ISH. Cf. *sheepish.*] Lamb-like, meek as a lamb.

c **1374** CHAUCER *Former Age* 50 The lambisshe pepyl voyd of all vice, Hadden noo fantasye to debate. *c* **1470** HARDING *Chron.* LXII. ii, He had also a lambish patience To here all pleyntes mekely with sobernes.

†**'lambitate,** *v. Obs. rare*⁻⁰. [f. L. *lambitāt-*, ppl. stem of *lambitāre*, frequentative of *lambĕre* to lick.] 'To lick or lap' (Cockeram, 1623).

†**lam'bition.** *Obs. rare*⁻⁰. [n. of action f. L. *lambĕre* to lick.] (See quots.)

1658 PHILLIPS, *Lambition*, a licking, or lapping with the tongue, also a going over a thing with a soft touch. **1676** in COLES. **1721–1800** BAILEY, *Lambition*, a Licking.

†**'lambitive,** *a.* and *sb. Obs.* Also 7–8 **lambative, lambetive.** [ad. mod.L. *lambitīv-um* (= B. below), f. *lambĕre* to lick: see -IVE.]

A. *adj.* Of medicines: Taken by licking up with the tongue. **B.** *sb.* A medicine so taken.

1646 SIR T. BROWNE *Pseud. Ep.* IV. viii. 198 In affections both of Lungs and weazon, Physitians make use of syrupes, and lambitive medicines. **1656** W. D. tr. *Comenius' Gate Lat. Unl.* §818. 255 Lambatives, or medicines to be lickt in. **1671** BLAGRAVE *Astrol. Physic* 87 These lambetives are usually taken with a liquorish stick. **1684** tr. *Bonet's Merc. Compit.* XIV. 479 Some Physicians do ill in prescribing Lambitives at the first visit. **1696** J. EDWARDS *Demonstr. Exist. God* II. 44 Lohocs and the like lambitive medicines for distempers in the lungs. **1710** STEELE *Tatler* No. 266 ¶3 Upon the Mantle Tree..stood a Pot of Lambetive Electuary. **1710** T. FULLER *Pharm. Extemp.* 273, I have utterly denied the immediate descent of Lambatives into the Lungs.

'lambkill. *N. Amer.* **a.** *Andromeda mariana* (*Syd. Soc. Lex.* 1888); **b.** the sheep-laurel, *Kalmia angustifolia.*

1790 L. CASTIGLIONI *Viaggio negli Stati Uniti dell' America* II. 271 *K[almia] Angustifolia*... Sheep poison, Ivy, Dwarf-Laurell, Lamb-kill. **1814** J. BIGELOW *Florula Bostoniensis* 103 *Kalmia angustifolia*,..a low shrub with rose coloured flowers, very common in low grounds, and known by the names *sheep poison, lambkill, low laurel*, &c. **1851** S. JUDD *Margaret* xiv. (1871) 90 Cymes of viburnums, rose-blooming lambkill. **1898** C. A. CREEVEY *Flowers of Field* 515 Lambkill..is a low shrub..with narrow, evergreen leaves in whorls of three. **1939** *Nat. Geogr. Mag.* Aug. 255/1 Other poisonous members of the heath family are the kalmias, frequently called 'lamb-kill' from the effect they have on grazing animals. **1954** C. J. HYLANDER *Macmillan Wild Flower Bk.* 281 Sheep laurel..is also known as lambkill because of the severely toxic substance in the leaves. **1965** E. RICHARDSON *Living Island* 120 Not yet completely grown up in lambkill, wild-roses and blueberry bushes. **1974** A. HUXLEY *Plant & Planet* xxv. 283 In North America species of *Kalmia*..are known as Sheep-kill or Lamb-kill.

lambkin ('læmkɪn). [f. LAMB *sb.* + -KIN.]

1. A little lamb, young lamb.

1579 SPENSER *Sheph. Cal.* Dec. 8 O soveraigne Pan!.. Which of our tender Lambkins takest keepe. **1613–16** W. BROWNE *Brit. Past.* I. iii, Doridon..Goes sadly forth..To ope his fold and let his Lamkins out. **1693** DRYDEN tr. *Ovid's Met.* xiii. *Acis* 129 In their warm folds their tender lambkins lie. **1725** POPE *Odyss.* IX. 160 The kid distinguish'd from the lambkin lies. **1870** J. H. NEWMAN *Gram. Assent* I. v. 108 The new-dropped lamb recognizes each of his fellow-lambkins as a whole.

2. *transf.* A young tender person; chiefly used as a term of endearment.

1597 SHAKS. *2 Hen. IV*, v. iii. 121 Sir John, thy tender Lamb-kinne now is King. **1599** —— *Hen. V*, II. i. 133 Let vs condole the knight, for (Lambekins) we will liue. **1681** OTWAY *Soldier's Fort.* III. i. Wks. 1728 I. 370 Poor Fool! poor Birdsnies! poor Lambkin! **1741** RICHARDSON *Pamela* I. 162 Well, well, Lambkin (which the Foolish often calls me). **1812** SHELLEY *Devil's Walk* vii. 3 One would think that the innocents fair, Poor lambkins! were just doing nothing at all. **1860** READE *Cloister & H.* lxxviii, We will pray for her, won't we, my lambkin; when we are old enough? **1889** H. F. WOOD *Eng. Rue Cain* ii, It staggered me, and I'm no lambkin.

lamb-like, lamblike ('læmlaɪk), *a.* Like a lamb, or that of a lamb; gentle, meek.

1599 ? KYD *Soliman & Perseda* I. A 4 Put Lambe-like mildenes to your Lyons strength. **1616** R. SHELDON *Surv. Miracles Ch. Rome* 161 What else doth the beast..portend by his lambe-like hornes but Anti-christ? **1621** QUARLES *Esther* (1638) 105 Thy Lamb-like Countenance so faire, so meeke. *a* **1711** KEN *Sion* Poet. Wks. 1721 IV. 334 With nerves of Lambs, Soul, string your Lute, They'll best with Lamb-like Agnes sute. **1840** MRS. CARLYLE *Lett.* I. 119, I am very lamb-like to-day. **1843** CARLYLE *Past & Pr.* I. iii. (1845) 19 What a lamblike Insurrection!

lambling ('læmlɪŋ). *rare.* [See -LING.] A young or little lamb, a lambkin.

1591 SYLVESTER *Du Bartas* I. ii. 181 The Lambling tender. **1839** BAILEY *Festus* (1840) 77 Like lambling strayed from some gold-fleecy flock. **1857** THACKERAY *Virgin.* (1858) I. v. 36 It was over the black sheep [negroes] of the Castlewood flock that Mr. Ward somehow had the most influence. These woolly lamblings were immensely affected by his exhortations.

lambly ('læmlɪ), *a. nonce-wd.* [See -LY¹.] Resembling (that of) a lamb, lamb-like.

1868 BUSHNELL *Serm. Living Subj.* 437 Yet in Christ there is a godly or rather lambly sorrow.

Lambmass, -mes(se, obs. ff. LAMMAS.

lamborn, obs. pl. form of LAMB.

lamboys ('læmbɔɪz). *Antiq.* [In quot. *a* 1548 (the source from which the word is derived) the meaning is obscure, and it has been suspected that *lamboys* is a mistake for some form of JAMBERS or JAMBEAUX.] The name given by mod. antiquaries to: An imitation in steel of the 'bases' or skirt, reaching from the waist to the knee; occasionally found in armour of the Tudor period.

If the word meant what Meyrick supposes, there is an anachronism in Hall's use of it.

a **1548** HALL *Chron., Hen. IV* 12 The tasses, the lamboys, the backpece. **1824** MEYRICK *Anc. Armour* II. 220 The large puckered plates of steel, which cover each thigh to the knee, and continue behind, except where hollowed out for the saddle. These plates are..in imitation of cloth, and called lamboys. **1834** PLANCHE *Brit. Costume* 225 The lamboys,.. a sort of petticoat of steel in imitation of the puckered skirts or petticoat of cloth or velvet worn at this time. **1841** J. HEWITT *Tower* 66 On the edge of the lamboys or skirts are the initials of the royal pair. **1863** THORNBURY *True as Steel* I. 132 The spreading lamboys or steel skirts of the period.

lamb-pie.

1. *lit.* A pie made of lamb; †*fig.* applied to a young woman.

a **1625** BEAUM. & FL. *Custom Country* I. i, A Surgeon, I must confesse an excellent descetor; One that has cut up more young tender Lamb-pies—.

2. *punningly.* (Cf. LAM *v.*, LAMBSKIN.)

1607 MARKHAM *Caval.* VIII. (1617) 6 This beating of horses thus amongst Horse-coursers is called giuing them Lambe-pye, from a knauish iest of a horse-coursers Boy. **1609** DEKKER *Lanthorne & Candle-light* x. Wks. (Grosart) III. 280 How a Horse-courser makes a Iade that has no stomach to eate Lamb-pye. *a* **1700** B. E. *Dict. Cant. Crew*, *Lamb-pye*, Beating or Drubbing. **1791** PEGGE *Derbicisms* Ser. II. 109 *Lam*, to beat; hence *Lamb-pye*, a drubbing. *a* **1825** FORBY *Voc. E. Anglia.*

lambre(n, obs. pl. forms of LAMB.

lambrequin ('læmbrɪkɪn). Also 8 ? **lamequin,** 9 **lambrikin.** [a. F. *lambrequin.*]

1. A scarf or piece of stuff worn over the helmet as a covering. In *Her.* represented with one end (which is cut or jagged) pendant or floating. (In 18th c. works explained as = LABEL or LAMBEAU.)

1725 J. COATS *Dict. Heraldry, Lambrequin*, the Point of a Label; or Label of a File. **1780** EDMONDSON *Heraldry* II. Gloss., *Lambrequin*, or *Lamequin*. *a* **1843** SOUTHEY *Comm.-pl. Bk.* (1851) IV. 202 Lambrequins, ribbands embroidered with silver and gold, which hung from the armets of the knights. **1869** CUSSANS *Her.* (1893) 190 The Mantling, Lambrequin or Cointise is the ornamental accessory which generally appears behind and around the Escutcheon. It was probably devised to protect the Helmet from the rain and sun, in the same manner that the Surcoat protected the armour. **1891** *Cornh. Mag.* May 456, I might bear it as a token or lambrequin upon my helm.

2. *U.S.* A cornice with a valance of pendent labels or pointed pieces, placed over a door or window; a short curtain or piece of drapery (with the lower edge either scalloped or straight) suspended for ornament from a mantel-shelf. Also *transf.* and *attrib.*

1883 F. M. CRAWFORD *Dr. Claudius* iii, Mr. Barker smiled under the lambrikin of his moustache. **1885** HOWELLS *Silas Lapham* (1891) II. 55 Heavy curtains..hung from gilt lambrequin frames at the window. **1885** *Century Mag.* Aug. 581 At dull times it is usual to renovate an entire floor [of a Hotel] with carpets, curtains and lambrequins. **1888** T. W. HIGGINSON *Women & Men* 162 The carved marble mantle-piece was concealed by a lambrequin.

3. *Ceramics.* Ornamentation consisting of solid colour with a lower edge of jagged or scalloped outline. Also *attrib.*

1873 MRS. PALLISER tr. *Jacquemart's Ceram. Art* 362 Let us explain what we understand by lambrequins, dentelles and style rayonnant. **1878** J. J. YOUNG *Ceram. Art* (1879) 127 On others are..lace or lambrequin patterns.

lambres, -ron, -ryn, obs. pl. forms of LAMB.

Lamb shift (læm ʃɪft). *Physics.* [f. the name of Willis E. *Lamb* (b. 1913), U.S. physicist (who with R. C. Retherford demonstrated the effect in 1947) + SHIFT *sb.*] A displacement of energy levels in hydrogen and hydrogen-like atoms such that those with the same values of the quantum numbers n and j but different values of l are not coincident, as predicted by Dirac's theory, but separated by a very small amount (the level with the lower value of l being the higher).

1948 *Physical Rev.* LXXIV. 1157 The effects treated are the Lamb shift, the correction of the *g*-factor..and the correction of the Compton scattering cross section. **1950** *Ibid.* LXXVII. 745 (*heading*) Departure of the Lamb shift from the h^{-3} law in He^+. **1958** CONDON & ODISHAW *Handbk. Physics* VII. iv. 63/1 The Lamb shift has been interpreted..as resulting from changes in the electron self-energy which results from its interactions with the electromagnetic and electron-positron fields. **1964** E. A. POWER *Introd. Quantum Electrodynamics* i. 7 The modern versions of quantum electrodynamics have enabled a very accurate comparison to be made between theory and experiment. Well-known examples are the Lamb shift energy splitting of the $2S_{\frac{1}{2}}$ and $2P_{\frac{1}{2}}$ levels in hydrogen and the radiative corrections to the magnetic moment of the electron. **1970** G. K. WOODGATE *Elem. Atomic Struct.* iv. 69 Figure 4.3 shows the fine structure of the $n = 2$ and $n = 3$ levels of hydrogen, modified to take account of the Lamb shift. **1973** *McGraw-Hill Yearbk. Sci. & Technol.* 111/1 Experimental programs to measure heavy-ion Lamb shifts are now in progress.

lambskin ('læmskɪn), *sb.* Also **lamb's skin.**

1. a. The skin or hide of a lamb with the wool on. Proverbial phr. ***a wolf*** (or ***fox***) ***in a lamb's skin.*** **b.** The same dressed and used for clothing, for ornamentation of dress, for mats, etc. Often in *collect. sing.*, denoting the material or fur so prepared.

? *a* **1366** CHAUCER *Rom. Rose* 229 A burnet cote..Furred with no menivere, But with a furre rough of here, Of lambe-skinnes hevy and blake. *c* **1375** *Sc. Leg. Saints* xxv. (*Julian*) 506 For he resemblyt fore to be worthy and gud; bot ȝet he wykyt wolfe wes withine, & heylyt in a lame-skine. *Ibid.* xxxi. (*Eugenia*) 378 He is wolf in lamskine hyd, & ful verray ypocrite. **1492** *Ld. Treas. Acc. Scotl.* I. 202 Item, for quhyte smal cotton lamskynnis to lyne this gowne. **1500–20** DUNBAR *Poems* xiii. 37 Sum in ane lamb skin is ane tod. **1562** *Act 5 Eliz.* c. 22 §1 Yt shall not bee lawful..to pull, sheare, clippe, or take away the wool of anie sheepe skinne or lambe skinne. **1571** *Satir. Poems Reform.* xxix. 45 Schawing quhow, wolfis in lam skynis! þe puire scheip ȝe misgyde. *a* **1586** SIDNEY *Arcadia* II. (1622) 115 Like rich Tissew furd with Lambe-skins. **1603** SHAKS. *Meas. for M.* III. ii. 9 A fur'd gowne to keepe him warme; and furd with Foxe and Lamb-skins too. **1682** OTWAY *Venice Preserved* I. i. Wks. 1727 II. 276 A Rogue that uses Beauty like a Lamb-skin, Barely to keep him warm. **1834** L. RITCHIE *Wand. by Seine* 139 A kind of cloak..furred with lambskin.

2. Leather prepared from the skin of lambs.

1745 *De Foe's Eng. Tradesman* xxvi. (1841) I. 266 Her gloves, lambskin, from Berwick and Northumberland, or Scotland. **1899** *Westm. Gaz.* 1 June 3/2 The volumes..are bound in limp lambskin, gilt lettered.

3. Woollen cloth made to resemble lambskin (Ogilvie).

†**4.** *punningly.* A heavy blow. *Obs.* (Cf. LAMBSKIN *v.*, LAM *v.*)

[**1546** J. HEYWOOD *Prov.* (1867) 62 She must obey those lambs, or els a lambs skyn, Ye will prouyde for hir, to lap her in.] **1573** G. HARVEY *Letter-bk.* (Camden) 14 Les if you get ous within the half swurd you chaunc to give us the lamskin. **1600** S. FORMAN *Autobiog.* (1849) 7, I did give her three or four lambskines with the yerd. **1622** R. HAWKINS *Voy. S. Sea* xli. 97 I discovered their slynesse, and with a truncheon, which I had in mine hand, gaue the Indians three or foure good lamskinnes.

5. *Mining.* Anthracite slack, culm.

1873 *Weale's Dict. Terms* (ed. 4), *Lamb-skin*, a name given to a variety of anthracite coal sold at Swansea.

6. *attrib.*: †**lamb-skin-man** (see quot.).

a **1700** B. E. *Dict. Cant. Crew*, *Lamb-skin-men*, the Judges of the several Courts.

†**lambskin,** *v. Obs.* [f. LAMBSKIN *sb.*] *trans.* To beat, to thrash.

1589 *Marprel. Epit.* B, He hath giuen the cause sicken a wipe in his bricke, and so lambskinned the same, that the cause will be the warmer..for it. **1592** G. HARVEY *Pierce's Super.* 131 To lamback him with ten yeares preparation, that can lamskin thee with a dayes warning. **1635** BROME *Sparagus Gard.* IV. v. Wks. 1873 III. 185 Or if I baste you not well a fine, and Lambe-skinne your jackets till your bones rattle i' your hides.

lambskin-it: see LANSQUENET.

lamb's tongue.

1. A name given to species of plantain (tr. med.L. *arnoglossa*, Gr. ἀρνόγλωσσον), and other plants.

1578 LYTE *Dodoens* I. lxiii. 92 Plantayne is called in Greeke ἀρνογλωσσος that is *Lingua Agnina*, Lammes tungue. **1597** GERARDE *Herbal* II. xcii. §6. 340. **1688** R. HOLME *Armoury* II. 64/2 A bunch of Plantan Leaves..some call it Lambs Tongue. **1803** *Trans. Soc. Arts* XXI. 171 A sort of weed provincially termed Lamb's Tongue (somewhat resembling the *sweet gale* in appearance, but not in smell).

2. A sort of plane (see quot.); also the moulding shaped by this plane.

1858 *Skyring's Builder's Prices* (ed. 48) 36 If astragal and hollow, lamb's tongue or other modern bar, add 1½*d.* **1875** KNIGHT *Dict. Mech., Lamb's-tongue*, a plane with a deep, narrow bit for making quirks.

lamb's-wool ('læmzwʊl).

1. The wool of lambs; soft fine wool used for hosiery and other clothing; clothing-material made of this wool.

1552 *Act 5 & 6 Edw. VI*, c. 6 §1 Some by myngelinge Fell Wooll and Lambes Wool..withe the Fleese Wooll. **1631** *Star Chamb. Cases* (Camden) 13 They changed the markes of the sheepe, and deteyned the lambes wooll, and when it was demanded it was denyed as if it were upon the sheepes

backes. **1830** MISS MITFORD *Village* Ser. IV. (1863) 163 The poor little creatures, shivering tho' wrapt in lamb's-wool and swan's-down. **1854** EMERSON *Lett. & Soc. Aims, Resources* Wks. (Bohn) III. 199 The invalid sits shivering in lambs-wool and furs.

fig. **1869** TROLLOPE *He knew* iv. (1878) 19 Wrapping himself up for life in the scanty lambswool of a fellowship.

b. *attrib.*

1836 E. HOWARD *R. Reefer* xxiii, White lamb's-wool stockings. **1837** J. F. PALMER *Devonsh. Gloss., Lambs-wool-sky*, a collection of white orbicular masses of cloud (cirrostratus). **1886** *Fortn. Rev.* Feb. 179 The sponges are sorted..into glove, reef, lamb's wool, grass, &c.

2. A drink consisting of hot ale mixed with the pulp of roasted apples, and sugared and spiced.

1592 G. HARVEY *Pierce's Super.* 33 Drinking a Cupp of Lammeswool. **1595** PEELE *Old Wives T.* Wks. (Rtldg.) 446/1 Lay a crab in the fire to roast for lamb's-wool. **1621** BURTON *Anat. Mel.* II. v. III. i. (1651) 399, I finde those that commend use of Apples in Splenatick and this kinde of Melancholy (Lambswooll some call it). **1666** PEPYS *Diary* 9 Nov., We to cards till two in the morning, and drinking lamb's-wool. **1725** SLOANE *Jamaica* II. 147 They roast a ripe plantain and mix it with a pint and half of water, and it is like Lamb's Wool. **1766** GOLDSM. *Vic. W.* xi, The lamb's wool, even in the opinion of my wife, who was a connoisseur, was excellent. **1839** MRS. PALMER *Devon. Dial.* iv. 59 'There is two special stubberd trees, vor making squab pies and lambs wool.'

lambur, variant of LAMBER[1] *Obs.*, amber.

lamda, lamdoidal: see LAMBDA, -DOIDAL.

‖**lamdan** (læm'dɑːn). [Heb. *lamdān*, lit. one who has learned, f. *lāmadh* to learn.] A person learned in Jewish law; a Talmudic scholar.

1907 I. ZANGWILL *Ghetto Comedies* 124, I am enough of a *Lamdan* (pundit) to answer it. **1925** 'R. LEARSI' *Kasriel the Watchman* 98 Some asserted that Getzel was a learned man, a *lamdan*. **1948** M. SAMUEL *Prince of Ghetto* xvii. 251 In Radziwill there lived a *lamdan*, a scholarly Jew... All day long he studied, while his wife attended to the shop. **1970** *New Stand. Jewish Encycl.* 1174/1 *Lamdan*,..a person steeped in talmudic learning. **1973** *Jewish Chron.* 16 Mar. 18/3 He lives in the ideal Jewish world, where the rabbi is the lamdan.

lame (leɪm), *sb.*[1] ? *Obs.* Also 6–7 lamm, 7– lame. [a. F. *lame*:—L. *lām(m)ina, lāmna* thin piece or plate.] A thin plate, esp. of metal; a thin piece of any substance, a lamina; *spec.* applied to the small overlapping steel plates used in old armour.

a **1586** SIDNEY *Arcadia* III. (1590) 288 He strake Phalantus iust vpon the gorget, so as he battred the lamms thereof. **1611** FLORIO, *Ali*, wings. Also among armorers called lamms. **1633** J. DONE *Hist. Septuagint* 47 Thinke not it was couered with Plates or Lames of Gold superficially but was made all of solide, massie, pure and fine Gold. **1725** BRADLEY *Fam. Dict.* s.v. *Nose*, It has a great Extent in a small Space, because it wraps up all the bony Lames that stick to the cribrous Bone. **1834** PLANCHÉ *Brit. Costume* 223 The helmet assumes the form of the head, having moveable lames or plates at the back to guard the neck. **1869** BOUTELL *Arms & Arm.* viii. 147 To the lower part of this demi-cuirass there was attached a system of articulated lames, or narrow plates, in their contour adapted to cover the figure. **1894** *Antiquary* Jan. 26 The most curious part of the present suit is the tonlet, a system of lames or half-hoops of steel, which, supported by leather straps inside, descend nearly to the knees in form of a short petticoat.

lame, *sb.*[2] [f. LAME *a.*] †**1.** Lameness; infirmity. *Obs.*

a **1300** *Cursor M.* 22323 (Cott.) A mikel man.. Luued wel wit-vten lame, wit-vten last al his licam. *c* **1340** *Ibid.* 5153 (Trin.), I may not rise he seide for lame. *c* **1425** WYNTOUN *Cron.* VIII. xxxv. 5243 He sayd, that he wald [ayl] na-thyng. .. Thus hapnyd till hym off this lame. **1500–20** DUNBAR *Poems* xxviii. 34 Off God grit kyndness may ȝe clame, That helpis his peple fra cruke and lame.

2. *U.S. slang.* A socially unsophisticated person; one who is not skilled in the behaviour patterns of a particular group.

Freq. in Black English.

1959 *Esquire* Nov. 70 J *A lame*, one who doesn't know what's happening. A square. **1967** *Trans-action: Social Sci. & Community* Apr. 5/2 One either knows 'what's happening' on the street, or he is a 'lame'... Negroes..have contributed much to the street tongue... Such expressions as 'a lame', 'taking care of righteous business'..and 'soul' can be retraced to Negro street life. **1968** in A. Dundes *Mother Wit* (1973) 331/1 Who's the lame who says he knows the game And where did he learn to play? **1971** *Black Scholar* Sept. 39/2 'You owe me some buns, lame!' teased a tall, lanky, yellow young man. **1972** J. WAMBAUGH *Blue Knight* (1973) vi. 93 They're a couple of lames trying to groove with the Kids. They're nothing.

lamé ('lɑːmeɪ), *sb.*[3] [Fr., f. *lame* LAME *sb.*[1]] A material consisting of silk or other yarns interwoven with metallic threads.

1922 *Daily Mail* 16 Dec. 15/3 Fur panels trim evening gowns of lamé. **1930** *Times* 13 Mar. 11/6 The collection included some beautiful Court gowns, one in pink marquisette embroidered in silk for a débutante had a silver lamé train. **1950** P. BOTTOME *Under Skin* xii. 106 The Paris doll, splendid in turquoise-blue taffeta under a golden lamé coatee, was poised within reach of Henriette's hand. **1968** J. IRONSIDE *Fashion Alphabet* 235 Synthetic metal yarns are now used in lamés. **1973** *Fortnum & Mason Christmas Catal.* 41/1 Gold..light-weight lamé jersey turban. Also available in silver. £27.50.

lame (leɪm), *a.* Forms: 1 lama, (lame), loma, 3 lomme, 3–4 lome, 4 lam, 2– lame. [OE. *lama*, *lǫma* (the wk. declension is, from some unexplained cause, used in indefinite as well as definite context, the form in *-a* being, moreover, commonly used for all genders), corresponding to OFris. *lam, lom*, OS. *lamo* (Du. *lam*), OHG. *lam* (MHG. *lam*, mod.G. *lahm*), ON. *lame* (wk.):—OTeut. **lamo-*; an ablaut-variant is **lômjo-* in OHG. *luomi*, MHG. *lüeme* dull, slack, gentle, early mod.G. *lumm*, whence *lümmel* blockhead. From the same root is OSl. *lomitĭ* to break.]

1. Of a person or animal: **a.** Crippled or impaired in any way; weak, infirm; paralysed; unable to move. Const. *on*, *of* (cf. 1 c). *Obs.* exc. *arch.*

c **725** *Corpus Gloss.* 815 *Conclamatus, commotus* loma. *c* **900** tr. *Bæda's Hist.* v. v. (1890) 396 He wæs loma & ealra his lioma þegnunga benumen. *c* **1000** *Ags. Gosp.* Matt. ix. 2 Ða brohton hiȝ hym ænne laman [L. *paralyticum*] on bedde licȝende. *c* **1000** ÆLFRIC *Gloss.* in Wr.-Wülcker 112/32 *Pleuriticus*, on sidan lama, *uel* sidadl. *Ibid.* 162/1 *Debilis, uel eneruatus*, lame. *a* **1250** *Owl & Night.* 363 Ȝet þu me seist on oþer schome þat ich am on mine eȝen lome. *a* **1300** *Cursor M.* 5153 (Gött.), I may noght rise, i am sua lame. **1530** PALSGR. 317/1 Lame of all ones lymmes, *perclus*. **1581** MULCASTER *Positions* xxii. (1887) 94 They did thinke the childe lame of the one side. **1604** E. GRIMSTONE *Hist. Siege Ostend* 63 A Germaine..who was lame of halfe his body, and simple. **1878** B. TAYLOR *Deukalion* I. iv. 37 One gets old and lame, And then the Gods themselves forget their words.

b. Crippled through injury to, or defect in, a limb; *spec.* disabled in the foot or leg, so as to walk haltingly or be unable to walk.

Proverb. *to help a lame dog over a stile*: see DOG *sb.* 17 f.

c **1000** ÆLFRIC *Saints' Lives* (1885) I. 220 þa læȝ þær sum creopare lama fram cild-hade. *c* **1205** LAY. 19479 Under þe lome [*c* **1275** lame] mon. *a* **1300** *Cursor M.* 8136 An heremite þar þai fand at ham, In þat montan, was halt and lam. **1388** WYCLIF *2 Sam.* v. 8 A blynde man and lame schulen not entre in to the temple. *a* **1529** SKELTON *E. Rummyng* 512 Up she stert, halfe lame, And skantly could go For payne and for wo. **1611** BIBLE *2 Sam.* xix. 26 Thy seruant sayd, I will saddle me an asse that I may ride thereon,..because thy seruant is lame. **1762–71** H. WALPOLE *Vertue's Anecd. Paint.* (1786) III. 76 He hurt his hip at the fire of London and went lame for the rest of his life. **1871** MISS YONGE *Cameos* II. xxx. 314 He kicked her downstairs, so that she broke her leg, and went lame ever after. **1875** JOWETT *Plato* (ed. 2) V. 364 In the use of the hands we are in a manner lame. **1880** *Times* 18 Sept. 9/5 Lame men might be illustrious warriors like Agesilaus, bold horsemen like Scott, extraordinary swimmers like Byron.

c. Const. *of*, *in*, †*on*, †*with* (the crippled part).

a **1300** *Cursor M.* 12260 þat þe poueral get sum bote, And ganging þat ar lame o fote. *c* **1460** *Play Sacram.* 768 Jonathas on thyn hand thow art but lame. **1581** SAVILE *Tacitus' Hist.* IV. lxxxi. (1591) 232 Another lame of a hande [L. *manum æger*]. *c* **1645** T. TULLY *Siege of Carlisle* (1840) 36 Hinks,.. being lame in that hand he was shot in. **1646** SIR J. TEMPLE *Irish Rebell.* (1746) 206 Her hand grew black and blew, rankled, and she was extreme lame with it. **1676** HOBBES *Iliad* II. 193 Lame of one Leg he was. **1685** *Lond. Gaz.* No. 2072/4 A Man,..ruddy Countenance,..and lame of one of his little fingers. **1766** ENTICK *London* IV. 285 If they were lame in their arms. **1870** L'ESTRANGE *Miss Mitford* I. v. 132 Poor Marmion is lame in one of his hind legs.

d. *absol.*

a **1000** *Elene* 1214 (Gr.) Oft him feorran to Laman, limseoce, lefe cwomon. *a* **1300** *Cursor M.* 19096 þe oncall of his hali nam, has lent us hele nu to þis lame. **1377** LANGL. *P. Pl.* B. XIX. 120 He made lame to lepe. **1484** CAXTON *Fables of Alfonce* vii. (1889) 272 Of euery lame scabbed and of alle suche that had ony counterfaytour on theyr bodyes he tooke a peny. **1500–20** DUNBAR *Poems* lxxxii. 53 Through streittis nane may mak progres, For cry of cruikit, blind, and lame. **1535** COVERDALE *Job* xxix. 15, I was an eye unto the blynde, and a fote to the lame. *a* **1619** DANIEL (J.), Who reproves the lame, must go upright. **1715** GAY *Trivia* II. 51 But above all, the groping blind direct, And from the pressing throng, the lame protect.

e. said of the limb; also of footsteps, etc.

a **1300** *Cursor M.* 17950 His lymmes..ȝit are lame. **1592** DAVIES *Immort. Soul* XXX. xii. (1714) 93 Most Legs can nimbly run, tho' some be lame. *a* **1656** BP. HALL *Soliloq.* 26 What have I got by it but a lame shoulder and a galled back? **1675** W. HARBORD *Let. to Earl Essex* in *Essex Papers* (Camden) I. 318 Had not my lame foote compelled me to make use of my Coache. **1710** *Lond. Gaz.* No. 4784/4 The Thumb on his Right Hand is Lame. **1775** JOHNSON *Let. to Mrs. Thrale* 17 June, Her present qualifications for the niceties of needlework being dim eyes and lame fingers. **1840** R. H. DANA *Bef. Mast* xxix. 99 Tossing..from eight to ten thousand hides, until my wrists became so lame that I gave in. **1859** TENNYSON *Enid* 628 Myself would work eye dim, and finger lame. **1885** R. BRIDGES *Eros & Psych, Apr.* 24 With footsteps slow and lame They gather'd up their lagging company.

†**f.** *transf.* of trees. *Obs.*

1600 SURFLET *Country Farm* III. xlvii. 522 Trees become lame when they be planted in too drie a place. *Ibid.* (*margin*) Lame trees.

2. *fig.* **a.** Maimed, halting; imperfect or defective, unsatisfactory as wanting a part or parts. Said esp. of an argument, excuse, account, narrative, or the like. †Phr. ***lame to the ground*** (cf. *Antrim & Down Gloss.* s.v. *Lame* 'A stab of a bayonet which has lamed me to the ground.').

c **1374** CHAUCER *Troylus* II. Prol. 17 Disblameth my yf ony word be lame. For as myn auctor seyde so sey I. **1390** GOWER *Conf.* II. 218 The gold hath made his wittes lame. **1531** ELYOT *Gov.* I. xxv, That the knowlege and contemplation of Natures operations were lame and.. imperfecte, if there followed none actuall experience. **1581** J. BELL *Haddon's Answ. Osor.* 164b, Let us yet helpe his lame Logicke as well as we may. **1604** SHAKS. *Oth.* II. i. 162 Oh most lame and impotent conclusion. **1634** CANNE *Necess. Separation* (1849) 287, I will not contend much with him about the proposition, which is lame to the ground. **1668** HALE *Pref. to Rolle's Abridgm.* 9 Tables, or other Repertories..are oftentimes short, and give a lame account of the Subject sought for. **1670** TEMPLE *Let. to Sir J. Temple* Wks. 1731 II. 245, I found the Business of admitting the Emperor into the Guarantee, went downright lame. *a* **1677** BARROW *Serm.* Wks. 1686 III. 208 Nothing of worth or weight can be atchieved..with a faint heart, with a lame endeavour. **1699** BENTLEY *Phal.* 259 Our Argument from the Date of Phrynichus's *Phœnissæ* will be very lame and precarious. **1703** MOXON *Mech. Exerc.* 253 Alterations, or Tearing and pulling the Building to pieces after it is begun ..makes the Building lame and Deficient. **1726** SWIFT *Gulliver* III. iii. 197 The theory of comets, which at present is very lame and defective. **1800** MRS. HERVEY *Mourtray Fam.* II. 104 Her account was so lame and imperfect, that Mrs. Mourtray lost all patience. **1818** HAZLITT *Eng. Poets* iv. (1870) 100 His grammatical construction is often lame and imperfect. **1867** FREEMAN *Norm. Conq.* (1876) I. iv. 218 This certainly seems a very lame story.

b. Const. *of*, *in* (the defective part): cf. 1 c. Also with *to* and *inf.*

c **1366** CHAUCER *A.B.C.* 76 And who so goth to you þe rihte wey Him thar not drede in soule to be lame. *a* **1420** HOCCLEVE *De Reg. Princ.* 2797 Swich vnbuxumnesse Suffred, vs make wol of seuerte lame. **1578** BANISTER *Hist. Man* VIII. 99 Idiotes and foolish bodyes, who hauyng defect in this [reason], are lame in all the rest. *c* **1586** C'TESS PEMBROKE *Ps.* CIII. i, What gratious he..hath done for thee, Be quick to mind, to utter be not lame. **1604** SHAKS. *Oth.* I. iii. 63 Being not deficient, blind, or lame of sense. *a* **1656** BP. HALL *Soliloq.* 35 Alas, we cannot be but lame in all our obediences. **1819** SHELLEY *Peter Bell 3rd* VI. xxi. 4 His thoughts grew weak, drowsy, and lame Of their intelligence. **1860** MOTLEY *Netherl.* (1868) I. iii. 77 This course seemed to be lame in many parts.

c. Said of metrical 'feet' or the verses composed of them: Halting, metrically defective.

1600 SHAKS. *A.Y.L.* III. ii. 178 *Cel.* That's no matter: the feet might beare yͤ verses. *Ros.* I, but the feet were lame and could not beare themselues without the verse. **1608** —— *Per.* IV. Prol. 48 The lame feete of my rime. **1693** DRYDEN *Persius, Sat.* i. (1697) 406 The Prose is Fustian, and the Numbers lame. **1751** CHATHAM *Lett. Nephew* i. 1 Your translation..is very close to the sense of the original..the numbers not lame, or rough.

3. ***lame duck***, (*a*) (see DUCK *sb.*[1] 9); (*b*) *U.S. Politics*, an office-holder who is not, or cannot be, re-elected; *spec.* (before 1933), a defeated member in the short session of Congress after a November election; also *attrib.*; (*c*) a ship that is damaged, esp. one left without a means of propulsion; (*d*) an industry, commercial firm, etc., that cannot survive without financial help, esp. by means of a government subsidy; hence as *v. trans.* (*rare*), to help (a disabled person); ***to lame-duck it***: to travel with difficulty; †***to come by the lame post***: (of news, etc.) to be behind time.

1658 OSBORN *Jas. I* iii. Wks. (1673) 469 Till by a lamer Post he was advertised of his being joyfully Proclaimed in London by the Lord Mayor and Aldermen. **1701** MOTT in Sir J. Floyer *Hot & Cold Bath.* II. 240 Yours of the 24ᵗʰ of May I received, but it had the misfortune to come by the Lame Post, or else you had sooner received an Answer. **1761**, etc. [see DUCK *sb.*[1] 9]. **1863** *Congress. Globe* 14 Jan. 307/1 In no event..could it [*sc.* the Court of Claims] be justly obnoxious to the charge of being a receptacle of 'lame ducks' or broken down politicians. **1876** C. CHAPMAN *First Ten Yrs. Sailor's Life at Sea* x. 411 A lame duck on the sea means a ship which has been more or less damaged while crossing the perilous ocean. **1910** *N.Y. Even. Post* 8 Dec. 8 'Lame Duck Alley'..is the name they [*sc.* reporters] have given to a screened-off corridor in the White House offices, where statesmen who went down in the recent electoral combat may meet. **1922** *N.Y. Times* 6 Dec. 18/2 Senator Norris is all for the plan 'to have the convening of Congress moved up to avoid lame-duck Congresses'. **1925** *Independent* (Boston, Mass.) 21 Feb. 213/1 The proposed Constitutional amendment..has been usually designated as the 'lame-duck' amendment. **1932** *Times* 14 Dec. 13/2 A 'lame duck' Administration was in power, and a 'lame duck' Congress still in being. **1933** P. A. EADDY *Hull Down* xiv. 256 Our old 'lame duck' had not done so badly after all. **1943** N. BALCHIN *Small Back Room* 70 It's so bloody *dangerous* lame-ducking it home by yourself. **1963** J. FOWLES *Collector* II. 213, I want to be his friend and lameduck him in London. **1970** *New Yorker* 14 Nov. 175/3 My father, with his predilection for lame ducks, was the natural person to try to rescue it. **1972** *Economist* 26 Aug. 8 The *Economist* calls lame ducks those industries whose survival is claimed to depend on government subsidy. In the United States a lame duck is a politician whose current term is his last, owing to defeat in a primary or general election, or other reasons. **1973** *Times* 5 June 22/6 The Government, being at that stage still keen on its lame duck policy, refused to help, and the board went away to have a further think. **1973** *Listener* 29 Nov. 741/1 It is now the Congress..which will be disposing what a lame duck President may propose.

4. *Comb.*, as ***lame-born***, ***-footed***, ***-horsed***, ***-legged***, †***-limb*** adjs.

1823 BENTHAM *Not Paul* 306 The *lame-born cripple. **1614** RALEIGH *Hist. World* III. (1634) 67 Seldome the villaine though much haste he make *Lame-footed Vengeance failes to overtake. **1881** BLACKMORE *Christowell* xl, Labouring along with the *lame-horsed guns. **1610** HOLLAND *Camden's Brit.* I. 515 Being skornfully rejected by Judith the mother for that he was *lame-legged. **1583** T. WATSON *Centurie of Loue* xcviii. Poems (Arb.) 134 Loue is.. A *Lamelimme Lust.

lame (leɪm), *v.* [f. LAME *a.*; OE. had *lęmian* of equivalent formation (= ON. *lęmja*) which did not survive into ME.] *trans.* To make lame; to cripple.

c **1300** *Havelok* 2755 Hwan he hauede him so shamed, His hand of plat, and yuele lamed. *c* **1330** R. BRUNNE *Chron. Wace* (Rolls) 1836 þen was Coryneus a-schamed þat he was for þe geaunt lamed. **1375** BARBOUR *Bruce* IV. 284 The kyng, throu his cheuelry, Wes laid at erd and lamyt bath. *c* **1440** *Promp. Parv.* 286/1 Lamyn, or make lame, *acclaudico* (MS. K. *claudico*). **1460** *Lybeaus Disc.* 1917 Hys stede was lamed. **1607** SHAKS. *Cor.* IV. vii. 7, I cannot helpe it now, Vnlesse by vsing meanes I lame the foote Of our designe. **1650** W. BROUGH *Sacr. Princ.* (1659) 219 Covetousness..lames the hand to good works. **1700** DRYDEN *Fables, Cock & Fox* 644 The son and heir Affronted once a cock of noble kind, And either lam'd his legs, or struck him blind. **1725** DE FOE *Voy. round World* (1840) 338 They killed eleven or twelve..and lamed as many. **1859** TENNYSON *Elaine* 487 A spear Down-glancing lamed the charger.

b. *transf.* and *fig.* To cripple, maim, disable.

1568 *Satir. Poems Reform.* xlvii. 51 Now ȝe ar lamit fra labour, I lament it. **1611** SHAKS. *Wint. T.* v. ii. 62, I neuer heard of such another Encounter; which lames Report to follow it. —— *Cymb.* v. v. 163 For Feature, laming The shrine of Venus, or straight-pight Minerva. **1699** DAMPIER *Voy.* II. II. 129 We kept firing at her, in hopes to have lamed either Mast or Yard. **1865** CARLYLE *Fredk. Gt.* IV. x. (1872) II. 37 The Spanish Navy got well lamed in the business. **1868** TENNYSON *Lucretius* 123 My mind Stumbles, and all my faculties are lamed. **1878** E. JENKINS *Haverholme* 45 Lamed by the reticence imposed on him as a condition of his office, he had made a halting explanation.

Hence **lamed** (leɪmd), *ppl. a.*

a **1586** SIDNEY *Arcadia* III. (1590) 293 b, His minde was euill wayted on by his lamed force, so as he receyued still more and more woundes. **1602** F. HERING *Anat.* 4 One-eyed or lamed Fencers. **1839** CARLYLE *Chartism* iii. (1858) 15 That was a broken reed to lean on..and did but run into his lamed right-hand.

absol. **1567** *Gude & Godly Ball.* (S.T.S.) 67 He haillit the seik, sair, lamit, and blinde.

lame, obs. f. LAMB; Sc. and north. dial. f. LOAM.

'lame-brain. *colloq.* [f. LAME *a.* + BRAIN *sb.*] A dull-witted or stupid person. Also **'lame-brained** *a.*

1929 WODEHOUSE *Mr. Mulliner Speaking* i. 16 A girl with an aunt who knew all about Shakespeare and Bacon must of necessity live in a mental atmosphere into which a lame-brained bird like himself could scarcely hope to soar. **1945** S. J. PERELMAN *Crazy like Fox* 82 'Well, Miss "Lame Brain",' he retorted sardonically, 'maybe you had better stop galvanizing around nights and pay attention!' **1948** G. H. JOHNSTON *Death takes Small Bites* vii. 163 But it's the same bunch of lame-brains kiddin' themselves they're master minds of crime. **1962** K. ORVIS *Damned & Destroyed* xix. 142 Not like the usual lame-brained addict. **1968** *New Yorker* 14 Sept. 58 None of your lame-brain philosophers ever cut any ice with me. **1972** *Times Lit. Suppl.* 24 Nov. 1426/3 We have finished feeling indulgent towards the disaffected lamebrains who turn this kind of stuff out.

lamel ('læməl). Now *rare.* [ad. L. *lāmella* (see next).] = LAMELLA.

1676 COLES, *Lamel*, a little thin plate. **1677** GREW *Anat. Plants* IV. III. i. §8 (1682) 180 From this utmost Parenchyma Nine or Ten Insertions or Lamells are produced. **1681** H. MORE *Postscr. to Glanvill's Sadducismus* 39 By vertue of any Lamels or Plates of Metal. **1848** in CRAIG. **1871** MISS YONGE *Cameos* (1877) II. xiv. 159 Every mottoed lamel, so tersely and correctly sculptured, associated also so closely with his historical and English recollections.

‖**lamella** (lə'mɛlə). Pl. **lamellæ** (læ'mɛliː). [L. *lāmella*, dim. of LAMINA.] A thin plate, scale, layer, or film, esp. of bone or tissue; e.g. one of the thin scales or plates which compose some shells, one of the gills forming the hymenium of a mushroom, one of the erect scales appended to the corollas of some flowers.

1678 *Phil. Trans.* XII. 977 These Lamellæ, wherewith the said Tunick is roll'd up in so many more folds. **1741** MONRO *Anat. Bones* (ed. 3) 87 The nasal Lamella of the ethmoid Bone. **1777** G. FORSTER *Voy. round World* I. 502 A talcous stone, which when exposed to the sun and air..dissolves into lamellæ. **1830** LINDLEY *Nat. Syst. Bot.* 244 Corolla monopetalous..5-lobed, with 2 lamellæ at the base of each lobe. **1841–71** T. R. JONES *Anim. Kingd.* (ed. 4) 428 The ventral surface of the central lamella of the terminal fin. **1879** RUTLEY *Study Rocks* x. 87 More than fifty lamellae have been noted, under the microscope, in a single crystal.

lamellar (lə'mɛlə(r)), *a.* Chiefly *scientific.* [f. prec. + -AR. Cf. F. *lamellaire.*] **1.** Consisting of, characterized by, or arranged in, lamellæ or thin plates or scales.

1794 SULLIVAN *View Nat.* I. 439 Its texture, lamellar or scaly. **1796** KIRWAN *Elem. Min.* (ed. 2) I. 244 Lamellar, by some called foliated, or sparry quartz. **1849** DANA *Geol.* iii. (1850) 274 The lava is lamellar in structure. **1870** HOOKER *Stud. Flora* 244 Convolvulaceæ..Stigmas capitate linear or lamellar. **1881** MAXWELL *Electr. & Magn.* II. 34 If a magnet can be divided into simple magnetic shells, either closed or having their edges on the surface of the magnet, the distribution of magnetism is called Lamellar.

2. *Physics.* = LAMINAR *a.* 2 (in the broader sense).

1931 W. WILSON *Theoret. Physics* I. viii. 190 Problems of lamellar flow in an incompressible fluid are mathematically identical with electrostatic problems in regions free from electric charges. **1942** M. P. BILLINGS *Struct. Geol.* xvi. 299 In lamellar flow..the individual particles move in parallel sheets which slide over one another like the cards in a sheared playing pack. In such a viscous substance as magma beneath the surface of the earth, the flow is lamellar. **1966** *McGraw-Hill Encycl. Sci. & Technol.* XIII. 175/1 In some instances, streamline flow can best be depicted as formed from thin layers of fluid which slip past each other (lamellar flow).

Hence **la'mellarly** *adv.*, in thin plates or scales (Webster, 1828).

lamellate ('læmɛlət), *a.* [ad. mod.L. *lāmellātus*: see LAMELLA and -ATE².] Furnished with or arranged in lamellæ; lamellar.

1826 KIRBY & SP. *Entomol.* IV. 311 Lamellate (*Lamellati*), when the last joint is divided into transverse lamellæ. **1846** DANA *Zooph.* (1848) 359 Cones acervate and proceeding from lamellate cells.

Hence **la'mellately** *adv.*

1846 DANA *Zooph.* iv. §48 (1848) 54 The lamellæ of the stars in an Astræa..extend throughout the interstitial spaces between the cells, striating lamellately the surface.

lamellated ('læmɛleɪtɪd), *a.* [formed as LAMELLATE + -ED².] = LAMELLATE.

1713 DERHAM *Phys.-Theol.* VIII. iv. 402 The lamellated Antennæ of some, the Clavellated of others. **1780** J. T. DILLON *Trav. Spain* (1781) 211 This lamellated metal is composed of various plates. **1831** R. KNOX *Cloquet's Anat.* 413 A true lamellated lobule, composed of a great number of parallel transverse laminæ. **1851–6** WOODWARD *Mollusca* 24 The lamellated tentacles of the nudibranchs.

lamellibranch (lə'mɛlɪbræŋk), *sb.* (*a.*) *Zool.* [ad. mod.L. *lāmellibranchia* pl., f. L. LAMELLA + Gr. βράγχια gills.] A lamellibranchiate or bivalve mollusc; one of the *Lamellibranchiata.*

1855 H. SPENCER *Princ. Psychol.* (1872) I. I. ii. 15 In the Lamellibranchs several such..ganglia are distributed..in different parts of the body. **1872** NICHOLSON *Palæont.* 188 No Lamellibranch is destitute of a shell.

b. *attrib.* or *adj.* = LAMELLIBRANCHIATE *a.*

1867 J. HOGG *Microsc.* II. ii. 377 The contents of the stomachs of most Lamellibranch molluscs..exhibit a considerable admixture of the minute calcareous Foraminifera.

lamellibranchiate (ləmɛlɪ'bræŋkɪət), *a.* (*sb.*) *Zool.* [ad. mod.L. *lāmellibranchiātus* (implied in *-āta* sb. pl.): see prec. + -ATE³.] Belonging to the group *Lamellibranchiata* of molluscs (so called as having lamellate gills) of which the ordinary bivalves (oysters, mussels, etc.) are typical.

1855 OGILVIE, Suppl., *Lamellibranchiate*, relating to the lamellibranchiata. **1863** LYELL *Antiq. Man* xx. 404 The existing lamellibranchiate bivalves. **1880** HUXLEY *Crayfish* 356 The little lamellibranchiate mollusk, *Cyclas fontinalis.*

b. *sb.* A lamellibranch; a bivalve mollusc.

1842 BRANDE *Dict. Sci.* etc., *Lamellibranchiates, Lamellibranchiata*, an order of Acephalous Mollusks.

lamellicorn (lə'mɛlɪkɔːn), *a.* and *sb. Ent.* [ad. mod.L. *lāmellicornis*, f. L. *lāmella* thin plate + *cornū* horn.] **A.** *adj.* Belonging to the *Lamellicornes* of Latreille's system or the modern group *Lamellicornia* of beetles, having antennæ characterized by a lamelliform club. **B.** *sb.* A lamellicorn bettle, as the dung-beetle, cockchafer, etc.

1842 BRANDE *Dict. Sci.* etc. *Lamellicorns.* **1843** KIRBY & SP. *Entomol.* II. 314 The dung-chafers..and others of the lamellicorn beetles. **1871** DARWIN *Desc. Man* I. xi. 399 We know that ants and certain lamellicorn beetles are capable of feeling an attachment for each other.

So **lamelli'cornate, -'cornous** *adjs.* = prec. *adj.*

1852 TH. ROSS *Humboldt's Trav.* I. vii. 257 The Indians assured us that the guachara does not pursue..the lamellicornous insects. **1855** MAYNE *Expos. Lex.*, *Lamellicornis*..lamellicornate.

lamelliferous (læmə'lɪfərəs), *a.* [f. LAMELLA + -(I)FEROUS.] Having a lamellate structure.

1832 LYELL *Princ. Geol.* II. 111 The madrepores, or lamelliferous polyparia. **1876** PAGE *Adv. Text-Bk. Geol.* xiv. 245 Lamelliferous corals.

lamelliform (lə'mɛlɪfɔːm), *a.* [f. LAMELLA + -(I)FORM.] Having the form or structure of a lamella or thin plate.

1819 G. SAMOUELLE *Entomol. Compend.* 233 Antennæ lamelliform, small, [etc.]. **1869** GILLMORE tr. *Figuier's Rept. & Birds* ii. 253 The Scoters have the bill broad, with dilated margins, and coarse lamelliform teeth. **1882** VINES *Sachs' Bot.* 338 The hymenium..covers the surface of the lamelliform, peg-shaped, or tubular projections of the under-side of the pileus.

lamelliped (lə'mɛlɪpɛd), *a.* and *sb. Zool.* [ad. mod.L. *lāmellipedia* (pl.), f. L. *lāmella* thin plate + *ped-*, *pēs*, foot.] **A.** *adj.* Belonging to the *Lamellipedia*, a division of conchiferous molluscs, having a flattened lamelliform foot. **B.** *sb.* One of the *Lamellipedia.*

1855 OGILVIE, Suppl., *Lamellipeds*, a section of conchifers containing bivalves with the foot broad and thin, as in Cardiaceæ, &c. **1888** *Syd. Soc. Lex.*, *Lamellipede*, having flattened and lamelliform feet.

lamellirostral (ləmɛlɪ'rɒstrəl), *a.* and *sb. Ornith.* [f. mod.L. *lāmellirostris*, f. LAMELLA + L. *rostr-um* beak + -AL¹.] **A.** *adj.* Belonging to the *Lamellirostres*, the fourth family of Cuvier's sixth order (*Palmipedes*) of birds, so called as having lamellose bills. **B.** *sb.* A lamellirostral bird.

1835–6 TODD *Cycl. Anat.* I. 277/2 The lamellirostral Palmipedes. **1839–47** *Ibid.* III. 387/1 The flat and sensitive bill of a lamellirostral bird. **1842** BRANDE *Dict. Sci.* etc., *Lamellirostrals, Lamellirostres*, a tribe of swimming birds.. comprehending those in which the margin of the beaks are furnished with numerous lamellæ or dental plates, arranged in a regular series, as in the swan, goose, and duck.

Also **lamelli'rostrate** *a.* = prec. *adj.* (Mayne *Expos. Lex.* 1855); **lamelliroster** = prec. *sb.* (*Cent. Dict.*).

lamelloid (lə'mɛl-, 'læməlɔɪd), *a. rare.* [f. LAMELL(A + -OID.] Resembling a lamella.

1866 *Mem. Boston Soc. Nat. Hist.* I. 141 These transverse processes..possess regular lamelloid walls, so as to form rather canals than simple foramina for the artery.

lamellose (lə'mɛləʊs), *a. scientific.* [f. LAMELLA + -OSE.] Arranged in or composed of lamellæ.

1752 SIR J. HILL *Hist. Anim.* 418 The beak of the Anas is convex..the whole verge is furnished with transverse, lamellose teeth. **1846** DANA *Zooph.* (1848) 571 Glomerate or lamellose. **1854** WOODWARD *Mollusca* II. 237 Upper valve limpet-like, smooth or concentrically lamellose. **1875** BLAKE *Zool.* 266 The branchiæ are at the sides of the body,..mostly lamellose.

b. *Comb.* **lamellose-** (also quasi-L. **lamelloso-**) **dentate** *a.*, having lamelliform teeth, as the bill of a duck; **lamellose-stellate** *a.*, having lamellæ arranged in star-shaped groups.

1855 MAYNE *Expos. Lex.*, *Lamellosodentatus*..lamelloso-dentate. **1856–8** W. CLARK *Van der Hoeven's Zool.* I. 88 Polypary conical, with base acuminate, cell single, terminal, lamellose-stellate. *Ibid.* II. 383 Bill with margins lamellose-dentate internally.

lamellous (lə'mɛləs), *a. rare.* [f. LAMELLA + -OUS.] = LAMELLOSE.

1803 *Med. Jrnl.* x. 43 A lamellous, or fibrous matter.

lamellule (lə'mɛljuːl). [f. LAMELLA + -ULE.] A small lamella.

1888 in *Syd. Soc. Lex.*

lamely ('leɪmlɪ), *adv.* [f. LAME *a.* + -LY².] In a lame manner; with halting steps or limbs; haltingly; imperfectly, defectively, inefficiently.

1591 SHAKS. *Two Gent.* II. i. 97 *Val.* She enjoin'd me, To write some lines to one she loves... *Speed.* Are they not lamely writt? **1594** —— *Rich. III*, I. i. 22 Deform'd, vnfinish'd..scarse halfe made vp, And that so lamely and vnfashionable, That dogges barke at me, as I halt by them. **1599** *Life More* in Wordsw. *Eccl. Biog.* (1853) II. 94 This booke..is translated..into English absurdly and lamely. **1614** T. ADAMS in Spurgeon *Treas. Dav.* lxxi. 18 A comedy that..goes lamely off in the last act, finds no applause. **1679** DRYDEN *Troylus & Cr.* Pref., So lamely is it left to us, that it is not divided into Acts. **1709** STEELE & SWIFT *Tatler* No. 66 ¶1 They who speak gracefully, are very lamely represented in having their Speeches read or repeated by unskilful People. **1739** HUME *Hum. Nature* (1874) I. Introd. 305 Principles taken upon trust, consequences lamely deduced from them. **1837** CARLYLE *Fr. Rev.* I. IV. iv, Halting lamely along, thou noticest next Bishop Talleyrand-Perigord. **1885** R. W. DIXON *Hist. Ch. Eng.* III. 201 Cardwell lamely tries to screen Ridley.

lamen, variant of LAMIN.

lameness ('leɪmnɪs). [f. LAME *a.* + -NESS.] The condition or quality of being lame; unsoundness of a limb causing halting movement; *fig.* imperfectness, defectiveness.

1530 PALSGR. 237/1 Lamenesse, *mehaygneté.* **1597** A. M. tr. *Guillemeau's Fr. Chirurg.* 31/1 The patient is wholye cured, without retayninge any lamnes in his arm. **1658** A. FOX *Wurtz' Surg.* II. ix. 78 On the Temple is a sinew, which if that be cut, it causeth lameness in the jaw bone. **1658–9** *Burton's Diary* (1828) III. 18, I love not to hear it, that there is a lameness in this House. **1670** DRYDEN *2nd Pt. Conq. Granada* 163 The lameness of their plots. **1723** S. MORLAND *Spec. Lat. Dict.* 9 As for the Law, care has been taken to help the Lameness of their Latin. **1782** WILSON in *Phil. Trans.* LXXIII. 161 The lameness of the views..may..proceed.. from our..imperfect knowledge. **1841** CATLIN *N. Amer. Ind.* (1844) II. xl. 50 Complaining of the lameness of our bones from the chase on the former day. **1846** GROTE *Greece* (1862) II. vii. 189 Respecting the lameness of Tyrtæus, we can say nothing.

lamenrie, -y, variants of LEMANRY.

lament (lə'mɛnt), *sb.* [ad. L. *lāment-um* wailing, weeping, lamentation.]

1. An act of lamenting, a passionate or demonstrative expression of grief. Also *poet.* the action of lamenting, lamentation.

1591 SHAKS. *1 Hen. VI*, I. i. 103 To add to your laments ..I must informe you of a dismall fight, Betwixt the stout Lord Talbot, and the French. *c* **1592** MARLOWE *Jew of Malta* I. ii, Why stand you thus, unmoved with my laments? **1629** MILTON *Christ's Nativity* 183 A voice of weeping heard, and loud lament. **1697** DRYDEN *Virg. Georg.* IV. 666 All her fellow Nymphs the Mountains tear With loud Laments. **1715–20** POPE *Iliad* XXIII. 17 The troops..thrice in order led..their coursers round the dead; And thrice their sorrows and laments renew. **1768** BEATTIE *Minstr.* I. xxxiv, When the long-sounding curfew from afar Loaded with loud lament the lonely gale. **1821** SHELLEY *Hellas* 868 Voices Of strange lament soothe my supreme repose. **1869** J. MARTINEAU *Ess.* II. 283 What is this but the morbid lament of scepticism? **1870** BRYANT *Iliad* I. v. 136 On his knees With sad lament he fell.

2. A set or conventional form of mourning; a song of grief, an elegy; *esp.* a dirge performed at a death or burial; also, the air to which such a lamentation is sung or played.

1698 M. MARTIN *Voy. St. Kilda* (1749) 57 Upon those Occasions [they] make doleful Songs, which they call Laments. **1791** BURNS (*title*) Lament for James, Earl of Glencairn. **1814** SCOTT *Lord of Isles* v. xxvii, Soon as the dire lament was play'd. **1882** D. STEWART *Sk. Highlanders* I. 81 Solemn and melancholy airs or Laments (as they call them) for their deceased friends. **1882** OUIDA *In Maremma* I. 154 It was rarely that she chose other themes than the passionate laments of the provincial *canzoni*.

lament (lə'mɛnt), *v.* [ad. L. *lāment-ārī*, f. *lāment-um* LAMENT *sb.* Cf. F. *lamenter.*]

1. *trans.* To express profound sorrow for or concerning; also, in mod. use, to feel sorrow for; to mourn for the loss of (a person); to bewail (an occurrence, etc.: with *simple obj.* or *clause*).

1535 COVERDALE *Luke* xxiii. 37 There folowed him a greate multitude of people and of wemen, which bewayled and lamented him. **1548-9** (Mar.) *Bk. Com. Prayer* Collect Ash-Wednesday, Wee worthely lamentyng oure synnes. **1611** BIBLE *1 Sam.* xxv. 1 Samuel died, and all the Israelites ..lamented him. **1667** MILTON *P.L.* I. 448 Thammuz came next behind, Whose annual wound in Lebanon allur'd The Syrian Damsels to lament his fate In amorous dittyes all a Summers day. **1712** HEARNE *Collect.* (O.H.S.) III. 453 He died in the 32^d Year of his Age, and is much lamented. **1756-7** tr. *Keysler's Trav.* (1760) IV. 94 This stone laments the death of Andrea Pisano. **1794** MRS. RADCLIFFE *Myst. Udolpho* xxx, For your own sake I lament this. **1801** *Med. Jrnl.* V. 559 As she was thus lamenting her situation, she was seized by a very violent convulsive fit. **1856** FROUDE *Hist. Eng.* (1858) II. vi. 12 The parliament had lamented that the duties of the religious houses were left unfulfilled.

2. a. *intr.* To express (also, simply, to feel) profound grief; to mourn passionately. Const. *for*, *over*, rarely *after*; also with indirect pass.

1530 PALSGR. 603/2, I lamente, I make mone for a losse, *je lamente.* *a* **1533** LD. BERNERS *Huon* lxxxii. 256 It wolde haue made a hard herte to lament. **1595** *Locrine* III. i. 160 He loves not most that doth lament the most. **1603** KNOLLES *Hist. Turks* (1638) 106 Greatly lamented for by all the Christians in Syria. **1611** BIBLE *1 Sam.* vii. 2 All the house of Israel lamented after the Lord. **1667** MILTON *P.L.* XI. 671 Adam was all in tears, and to his guide Lamenting turnd full sad. **1697** DRYDEN *Virg. Georg.* IV. 743 Her Children gone, The Mother Nightingale laments alone. **1738** GLOVER *Leonidas* I. 245 Forget not her, who now for thee laments. **1830** TENNYSON *Dying Swan* 7 With an inner voice the river ran, Adown it floated a dying swan, And loudly did lament. **1831** T. L. PEACOCK *Crotchet Castle* v. 85 He laments bitterly over the inventions of gunpowder, steam, and gas. **1853** C. KINGSLEY *Hypatia* I. xiii. 271 Why should they lament over other things?

b. *refl.* in the same sense. *arch.*

1749 FIELDING *Tom Jones* II. vii, Because he does not cry out and lament himself, like those of a childish or effeminate temper. **1768** STERNE *Sent. Journ.* (1775) 124 (*Fragment*) The poor notary..lamented himself as he walk'd along in this manner. **1788** CHARLOTTE SMITH *Emmeline* (1816) IV. 178 She..bursts into tears, and laments herself over him. **1850** MRS. JAMESON *Leg. Monast. Ord.* (1863) 99 When Hugolin returned, he began to lament himself because of the robbery.

†**3.** *causative.* To cause grief to, distress. *Obs.*

1580 LUPTON *Sivqila* I. 131 What paines he hath put me to euer since, bothe nighte and day, it would lament you if you knewe it. **1583** STOCKER tr. *Civ. Warres Lowe C.* I. 113 a, It greatly lamenteth, and maruellously amazeth vs. **1704** in Ashton *Social Life Q. Anne* (1882) I. 124 He lay much Lamented and wonderfully affrighted with the Old Woman coming to afflict him.

lamentable ('læməntəb(ə)l), *a.* (*sb.*) [a. F. *lamentable* or ad. L. *lāmentābil-is*, f. *lāmentā-rī* to LAMENT: see -ABLE.]

1. Of persons, their appearance, actions, voice, song, etc.: Full of or expressing sorrow or grief; mournful, doleful. Now *rare* or *arch.*

1432-50 tr. *Higden* (Rolls) I. 317 In whiche place.. lamentable voices be herde ofte tymes. **1494** FABYAN *Chron.* IV. lxxv. 53 The lamentable request made vnto hym by the sayde Ambassade. **1502** *Will of Auncell* (Somerset Ho.), An Image of o^r blessid lady of grace as lamentable as can be devised. **1513** DOUGLAS *Æneis* II. vi. [v.] 38, I see stand me befor,..maist lamentable [L. *mæstissimus*] Hector, With large fluide of teris. **1529** *Acts 21 Hen. VIII*, c. 16 §11 Our true and faithful Subjects..exhibited unto us a lamentable Bill of Complaint. *a* **1548** HALL *Chron., Hen. IV* 9 With a lamentable voyce and a sorowfull countenance. **1600** HAKLUYT *Voy.* (1810) III. 380 Dancing and singing in a lamentable tune. **1656** BLOUNT *Glossogr., Elegiographer*, a writer of Elegies, or lamentable verses. **1725** POPE *Odyss.* x. 611 Where..Cocytus' lamentable waters spread. **1739** LD. CASTLEDURROW in *Swift's Lett.* (1766) II. 261 A lamentable Hymn to Death, from a lover, ascribed to his mistress. **1848** C. BRONTE *J. Eyre* (1873) 2 With ceaseless rain sweeping away wildly before a long and lamentable blast. **1851** HAWTHORNE *Snow Image, Old News.* (1879) 154 The lamentable friends, trailing their long black garments. **1873** SYMONDS *Grk. Poets* xi. 370 With this wail the thin lamentable voice of the desiccated rhetorician ceases.

2. That is to be lamented; such as to call for lamentation, sorrow, or grief; pitiable, deplorable.

c **1430** LYDG. *Minor P.* 145 That owgly careyn lamentable. **1490** CAXTON *Eneydos* ii. 16 It is a greuous thyng to me to passe ouer so lyghtly the lamentable circumstaunces..in soo fewe wordis. *a* **1500** *Assembly of Ladies* 686 The case itself is inly lamentable. **1545** BRINKLOW *Compl.* xxiii. (1874) 58 What a lamentable thing is this, that men shuld be dryuyn from the Gospel of Christ. **1587** COLLINGWOOD in *Border Papers* (1894) I. 259 The..lamentable estayt of this ruinose and waysted cuntre. **1590** SPENSER *F.Q.* III. iv. 42 They.. strowe with flowres the lamentable beare. **1639** WOODALL *Wks.* Pref. (1653) 18 The most lamentable diseases of poor men require the most care of the Surgeon. **1667** MILTON *P.L.* II. 617 Thir lamentable lot. **1712** STEELE *Spect.* No. 509 ¶2 A lamentable change from that simplicity of manners. **1855** MACAULAY *Hist. Eng.* xiii. III. 331 Another Macdonald, destined to a lamentable and horrible end.

b. In jocular or trivial use: 'Pitiful, despicable' (J.); wretchedly bad. Cf. *deplorable.*

a **1699** STILLINGFL. (J.), This bishop, to make out the disparity between the heathens and them, flies to this lamentable refuge. **1876** STEDMAN *Victorian Poets* iii. 65 But when he [Landor]..attempted to regulate the orthography of our language the result was something lamentable.

†**B.** *sb. pl.* Laments, complainings. *Obs.*

1748 RICHARDSON *Clarissa* (1811) VIII. 5 Come, come, good Norton,..you are up again with your lamentables!

Hence **'lamentableness**.

1589 RIDER *Eng.-Lat. Dict.*, Lamentablenes, *elegia.* **1727** BAILEY vol. II, *Lamentableness*, wofulness, pitiableness.

lamentably ('læməntəblı), *adv.* Also 6 lamentablely. [f. LAMENTABLE + -LY^{2}.]

1. With lamentation or passionate expression of sorrow; mournfully, dolefully. Now *rare.*

1470-85 MALORY *Arthur* v. v, They lefte her shryking and cryenge lamentably. **1523** LD. BERNERS *Froiss.* I. vii. 5 She ..lamentably recounted to hym all the felonyes and iniuries done to her by Syr Hewe Spencer. **1534** MORE *Comf. agst. Trib.* II. Wks. 1201/2 Lette him lamentablye beseche God of hys gracyous ayde and helpe, to strength hys infyrmitie. **1575-85** ABP. SANDYS *Serm.* xv. 260 Of this his great miserie he complaineth him lamentably in diuerse of his Psalmes. **1611** SHAKS. *Wint. T.* IV. iv. 190, I loue a ballad but euen too well, if it be dolefule matter merrily set downe: or a very pleasant thing indeede, and sung lamentably. **1679** *Hist. Jetzer* a 2/1 She complains Lamentably of the affront done her. **1783** WOLCOT (P. Pindar) *Odes to R.A.'s* vi. Wks. 1812 I. 64 Pity it is! 'tis true 'tis pity. As Shakspeare lamentably says. **1847** JAMES *J. Marston Hall* xii, He spoke learnedly and lamentably upon the evils and inconveniences of his own profession.

2. So as to call for lamentation or mourning; pitiably, deplorably; hence (with weakened meaning), woefully, grievously.

1577-87 HOLINSHED *Chron.* III. 355/2 A hundred and twentie temporall men with diuerse preests and manie women were drowned and lamentablie perished. **1585** J. NORDEN *Sinf. Man's Solace* i. 13 b, Lazarus, who lamentably oppressed with hunger..begged at his gate. **1606** SHAKS. *Ant. & Cl.* III. x. 26 Our Fortune on the Sea is out of breath, And sinkes most lamentably. **1671** GLANVILL *Disc. M. Stubbe* 23 What you add..is lamentably impertinent. **1678** WANLEY *Wond. Lit. World* v. ii. §78. 472/1 The miserable Emperour being lamentably trod to death in the Throng. **1816** T. L. PEACOCK *Headlong Hall* ii, It will grow small by degrees and lamentably less. **1849** MACAULAY *Hist. Eng.* ii. I. 212 He had a strong though a lamentably perverted sense of duty and honor. **1885** *Leeds Mercury* 24 June 4/4 The new Government will be so lamentably weak in debating power.

†**lamen'tado.** *Obs.* *rare*$^{-1}$. [quasi-Sp. f. LAMENT.] Lament, lamentation.

1618 LITHGOW (*title*) The Pilgrimes Farewell to his native Country..with his Lamentado in his second Travels, his Passionado on the Rhyne, &c.

lamentation (læmən'teıʃən). [a. F. *lamentation* or ad. L. *lāmentātiōn-em*, n. of action f. *lāmentārī* to LAMENT.] The action of lamenting; the passionate or demonstrative expression of grief; mourning; in weakened sense, regret.

1375 BARBOUR *Bruce* xx. 282 The lamentacioune..That thai folk for thair lord maid. **1382** WYCLIF *Luke* vii. 32 We han maad lamentacioun, and ȝe han not wept. *c* **1400** *Destr. Troy* 7156 Myche weping & wo,..And lamentacioun full long for loue of hym one. *a* **1533** LD. BERNERS *Huon* xxxv. 110 They all made gret lamentasyon for his departyng. **1535** COVERDALE *Ps.* lxxvii. 64 Their prestes were slayne..and there were no wyddowes to make lamentacion. **1601** SHAKS. *All's Well* I. i. 64 Moderate lamentation is the right of the dead, excessiue greefe the enemie to the liuing. **1667** MILTON *P.L.* II. 579 Cocytus, nam'd of lamentation loud Heard on the ruful stream. **1819** SHELLEY *Cenci* IV. i. 185 There shall be lamentation heard in Heaven As o'er an angel fallen. **1850** M^cCOSH *Div. Govt.* III. iii. (1874) 435 Another subject of general lamentation is the evil produced by party spirit.

attrib. **1817** COBBETT *Pol. Reg.* XXXII. 122 The Morning Chronicle..treated the town with some neat lamentation puffs.

b. An instance of this; a lament. *the Lamentations of Jeremiah*, or, shortly, *Lamentations* [Vulg. *Lamentationes*, LXX. Θρῆνοι]: the title of one of the poetical books of the Old Testament, traditionally ascribed to the prophet Jeremiah, and having for its subject the destruction of Jerusalem by the Chaldeans.

1382 WYCLIF *2 Chron.* xxxv. 25 As lawe it is hadde in Israel, Loo! it is told writen in the Lamentaciouns. *a* **1533** LD. BERNERS *Huon* lv. 189 He caused his Nephew to be buryed with sore wepynges and lamentacyons. **1535** COVERDALE *Jer.* xlviii. 5 At the goinge vp vnto Luhith there shall arise a lamentacion. **1611** BIBLE *Ezek.* xix. 1 Take thou vp a lamentation for the princes of Israel. **1725** DE FOE *Voy. round World* (1840) 87 A sad lamentation and howling. **1836** W. IRVING *Astoria* II. 45 The lamentations of women who had lost some relative in the foray. **1841** LANE *Arab. Nts.* I. 110, I will call it the House of Lamentations. **1855** KINGSLEY *Heroes, Theseus* II. 237 A great lamentation arose throughout the city.

c. *Eccl.* One of the lessons (taken from *Lamentations*) in the office of Tenebræ.

1853 DALE tr. *Baldeschi's Ceremonial* 185 The latter having made a genuflection to the Altar, and a reverence to the choir, sings the Lamentation, without asking the Benediction.

Hence **lamen'tational** *a.*

1827 BENTHAM *Wks.* (1838-43) X. 61 Half lamentational, half congratulational, rhythmical commonplaces.

†**lamen'tatious,** *a.* *Obs.* *rare*$^{-1}$. In 4 lamentacious. [f. LAMENTATION: see -OUS.] Marked by lamentation.

1387-8 T. USK *Test. Love* I. i. (Skeat) l. 128 The soune of my lamentacious wepyng.

†**lamentatory,** *a.* *Obs.* *rare*$^{-1}$. [f. L. *lāmentārī* to LAMENT: see -ORY.] = prec.

1576 FLEMING *Panopl. Epist.* To Rdr. ¶5 b *note*, Nunciatorie, Lamentatorie, Mandatorie, Laudatorie.

lamented (lə'mɛntıd), *ppl. a.* (and *sb.*) [f. LAMENT *v.* + -ED^{1}.] Mourned for; bewailed; regretted. Also *absol.* or as *sb.*, esp. in phr. ***the late lamented***, someone recently dead.

1611 COTGR., *Regretté*,..bewayled, lamented. **1667** FLAVEL *Saint Indeed* (1754) 73 Involuntary and lamented distractions. **1709** POPE *Ess. Crit.* 733 This humble praise, lamented shade! receive. **1784** COWPER *Task* IV. 576 Lamented change! **1859** M. THOMSON *Cawnpore* 83 We thought it a more savoury meal than any of the *recherché* culinary curiosities of the lamented Soyer. **1864** LE FANU *Uncle Silas* I. xxiv. 297 Your late lamented father. **1864** C. M. YONGE *Trial* I. ix. 172 Depend upon it, the late lamented will remain in the ascendant till there are no breakers ahead. **1908** *Daily Chron.* 28 Sept. 4/7 An alternative in the Greek language was 'the blessed', but English can get no farther in the way of euphemism than 'the late lamented'. **1952** D. AMES *Murder, Maestro, Please* xvi. 111 You're the one whose husband identified the late lamented, aren't you? **1972** A. HUNTER *Vivienne* ix. 113 He wouldn't happen to be the late lamented's husband?

Hence †**la'mentedly** *adv.*

1645 MILTON *Colast.* 24 Somtimes they are not both actors, but the one of them most lamentedly passive.

lamenter (lə'mɛntə(r)). [f. LAMENT *v.* + -ER^{1}.] One who laments or mourns.

1589 RIDER *Eng.-Lat. Dict.*, A Lamentour, *lamentator.* **1607** HIERON *Wks.* I. 362 The renued spirit..for sinnes past and committed is an vnfained lamenter. *c* **1610** *Women Saints* 206 This spake I with as highe a voice as I coulde, to the end that I might drowne the sounde of the lamenters. **1742** RICHARDSON *Pamela* IV. 405, I might have continu'd on in the Words of the Royal Lamenter. **1748** —— *Clarissa* (1811) IV. 7 What a cruelty in my fate! said the sweet lamenter. **1861** TULLOCH *Eng. Purit.* iii. 366 He was a great lamenter of the extremities of the times.

lamentful (lə'mɛntfʊl), *a.* *rare*$^{-1}$. [f. LAMENT *sb.* + -FUL.] Charged with lament; mournful.

1876 DOWDEN *Poems* 82 But thou art terrible, with the unrevealed Burden of dim lamentful prophecies.

lamentin(e, variant of LAMANTIN.

lamenting (lə'mɛntıŋ), *vbl. sb.* [-ING^{1}.] The action of the verb LAMENT; lamentation.

1513 DOUGLAS *Æneis* XI. ii. 7 To be present at the lamentyng Of his fadir, to confort his murnyng. **1530** PALSGR. 237/1 Lamentyng, *regret.* **1605** SHAKS. *Macb.* II. iii. 61 Our Chimneys were blowne downe, And (as they say) lamentings heard i' th' Ayre. **1680** OTWAY *Orphan* IV. vi. 1562 Should'st thou know the cause of my lamenting. **1819** SHELLEY *Julian & Maddalo* 216 Fierce yells, and howlings, and lamentings keen.

lamenting (lə'mɛntıŋ), *ppl. a.* [-ING^{2}.] That laments or mourns.

1581 SIDNEY *Apol. Poetrie* (Arb.) 28 The..lamenting looke of Lucrecia. *Ibid.* 44 The lamenting Elegiack. **1593** SHAKS. *Lucr.* 1079 By this, lamenting Philomel had ended The well-tuned warble of her nightly sorrow. **1674** R. GODFREY *Inj. & Ab. Physic* 122 He domineering through deficiency in Medicine, causeth the lamenting Patient to cry out..Give me a Medicine or else I die. *a* **1822** SHELLEY *Dante's Convito* 10 How the lamenting spirit moans in it. **1857** RUSKIN *Pol. Econ. Art* i. (1868) 4 They saw kings and rich men coming down to the shore of Acheron, in lamenting and lamentable crowds.

Hence **la'mentingly** *adv.*

c **1610** SIR J. MELVIL *Mem.* (1735) 10 Then said the Treasurer lamentingly, 'My Life or Warding is a small Matter'. **1655** SIMEON ASHE *Funeral Serm. R. Robinson* 18 June 7 Laying lamentingly to heart the death of righteous and mercifull ones. **1804** J. GRAHAME *Sabbath* (1839) 25/2 When sad the voice of Cona, in the gale, Lamentingly the song of Selma sang. **1831** *Fraser's Mag.* III. 435 He informs [them], very lamentingly, that they must grow old.

‖**lamentoso** (lamen'toso). *Mus.* [It.] A direction indicating that a passage is to be played in a mournful style.

1876 STAINER & BARRETT *Dict. Mus. Terms* 251/1 *Lamentoso*,..mournfully, plaintively. **1959** D. COOKE *Lang. Mus.* iii. 137 The *lamentoso* opening of the finale of Tchaikovsky's *Pathétique* Symphony. **1967** *Listener* 2 Feb. 177/3 This serene opening is followed by a striking fugue, in five parts, marked *lamentoso.*

lamer, variant of LAMBER^{1}, amber.

Lamesse, obs. form of LAMMAS.

lamester ('leımstə(r)). [See -STER.] = next.

1639 W. SCLATER *Worthy Communicant Rewarded* 19 As those Lamesters at the poole of Bethesda. **1850** JAMES *Old Oak Chest* III. 12 A rude man..who would not even ask an old lamester like mysel' to sit down.

lameter, lamiter ('leɪmɪtə(r)). *Sc.* and *dial.* Also 9 **lametar, laimeter.** [f. LAME *a.*; the formation is obscure.] A lame person; a cripple.

1804 J. STRUTHERS *Poor Man's Sabbath* Wks. 1850 I. 43 A lisping lamiter, of feeble frame. *c* **1817** HOGG *Tales & Sk.* V. 358 He proved a lametar to the day of his death. **1848** C. BRONTË *J. Eyre* xxxvi. (1857) 448 You have..friends who will..not suffer you to devote yourself to a blind lameter like me. **1884** J. PAYNE *1001 Nts.* VIII. 119 The king..sent after her that one-eyed lameter, for that he was his chief vizier. **1896** CROCKETT *Men of Moss Hags* xliii. 307 A foot..came into the passage, dunt-duntin' like a lameter hirplin' on two staves.

attrib. **1822** GALT *Entail* I. xiii. 95 Jenny Hirple, a lameter woman, who went round among the houses of the heritors of the parish with a stilt.

‖**lametta** (læ'mɛtə). [It., dim. of *lama* = LAME *sb.*[1]] Brass, silver, or gold foil or wire.

1858 SIMMONDS *Dict. Trade.*

‖**lamia** ('leɪmɪə). Forms: 4 **lamya,** 4- **lamia.** *Pl.* 4 **lamie,** 7, 9 **lamiæ,** 9 **lamias.** Also (*anglicized*) 4 **lamȝe,** 4, 6 **lamye,** 8 **lamie.** [L. *lamia* a witch who was supposed to suck children's blood, a sorceress, also, a kind of flatfish, a species of owl, a. Gr. *λάμια* a fabulous monster, also, a fish of prey. Cf. F. *lamie.*]

1. A fabulous monster supposed to have the body of a woman, and to prey upon human beings and suck the blood of children. Also, a witch, she-demon.

The word is used in early translations of the Bible in *Isa.* xxxiv. 15 and *Lam.* iv. 3, where the A.V. has respectively 'shrichowle', marg. 'Or, night-monster', and 'sea monsters', marg. 'Or, sea calues'.

1382 WYCLIF *Isa.* xxxiv. 15 There shal lyn lamya..and he fyndeth to himself reste. —— *Lam.* iv. 3 The cruel beestis clepid lamya, nakeden ther tetes, ȝeeuen ther whelpus souken. **1398** TREVISA *Barth. De P.R.* XVIII. xlviii. (1495) 809 In Sicia ben beestys wyth shape of men and fete of horses: and suche wonderfull beestys ben callyd Lamie amonge many men. **1621** BURTON *Anat. Mel.* III. ii. I. i. (1660) 438 Apollonius..by some probable conjectures, found her out to be a Serpent, a Lamia. [Hence **1820** KEATS (*title*) Lamia.] **1622** MASSINGER *Virg. Mart.* IV. i, Where's the lamia That tears my entrails? **1674** COTTON *Compl. Gamester* (1680) 13 For here you shall be quickly destroy'd under pretence of kindness, as Men were by the Lamiæ of old. **1757** E. PERRONET *Mitre* I. xi, As plump as Lamies fed with fawn. **1865** BARING-GOULD *Werewolves* xv. 255 Troops of lamias, female evil spirits. **1871** B. TAYLOR *Faust* (1875) II. II. iii. 113 They are the Lamiæ, wenches vile, With brazen brows and lips that smile.

†**2.** *Ichth.* In Willoughby's and some later classifications, a genus of sharks. *Obs.*

1727-41 CHAMBERS *Cycl.* s.v. *Fish,* The *canis carcharias,* or *lamia,* the white shark. **1776** J. NEILL *Serm.* 214 Whatever kind of fish it was, whether it was a whale or a lamia,..where is the occasion for..condemning this passage of Holy Writ as fabulous?

3. *Ent.* A genus of longicorn beetles (J. C. Fabricius, 1775).

In recent Dicts.

lamiger ('læmɪdʒə(r)). *dial.* Also **lammiger.** [Cf. LAMETER.] A lame person, a cripple.

1847 HALLIWELL, *Lameter,* a cripple. *North.* In the West of England a *lamiger.* **1886** T. HARDY *Mayor of Casterbr.* II. 220 What can we two poor lammigers do against such a multitude!

lamin ('læmɪn). Forms: 5-6 **lamyn(e,** 6-7 **lamine,** 6- **lamin,** 7- **lamen.** [Anglicized form of next. Cf. F. *lamine.*] A lamina; a thin plate or layer (of metal, etc.); a plate of metal used as an astrological instrument or as a charm.

1489 CAXTON *Faytes of A.* II. xxxv. 147 Thys engyn is called Towre. It behoueth hym to be couered that may with lamynes of yron lest fyre sholde be caste or sette therin. **1576** BAKER *Jewell of Health* 42b, Spreade that sediment on a Lamyne of Iron polyshed and burning, or redde hote. **1647** LILLY *Chr. Astrol.* xcvii. 485 Without exact knowledge of the Astrologicall planetary hour, no worthy work can be done, with it wonders, either in collecting Hearbs, framing Sigils, Images, Lamens, &c. **1678** *Phil. Trans.* XII. 976 The cavities hereof [the Nose] are fill'd with many Cartilaginous Lamines distinct one from another. **1682** *Phil. Collect.* XII. No. 5. 159 The increase of the Oyster shell is caused by the addition of a new lamen or plate in the shell. **1783** W. F. MARTYN *Geog. Mag.* II. 508 An exfoliated circular lamen of the green part of the tree. **1816** SCOTT *Antiq.* xxiii, You have used neither charm, lamen, sigil, talisman, spell, crystal, pentacle..nor geomantic figure. **1875** BLACKMORE *A. Lorraine* III. xxvii. 340 Its lustre and versatile radiance flow from innumerable lamins, united by fusion in the endless flux of years.

‖**lamina** ('læmɪnə). Pl. **laminæ** ('læmɪniː). Chiefly *scientific.* [L. *lām(m)ina.* Cf. LAME *sb.*[1]] A thin plate, scale, layer, or flake (of metal, etc.).

1656 BLOUNT *Glossogr., Lamina,* a thin plate of any mettal, most commonly such as Sculpters use to engrave upon. **1670** J. BEALE in *Phil. Trans.* V. 1159 'Tis..full of very small and thin Laminæ, seeming to be Metalline, and bright like the purest Silver. **1674** PETTY *Disc. Dupl. Proportion* 122, I think it easiest to consider Elastic, Springing, or Resilient Bodies, as Laminæ, Laths, or Lines. **1709** F. HAUKSBEE *Phys. Mech. Exper.* Suppl. (1719) 329 Pieces of Brass Laminæ, whose Thickness when laid one upon another,..made a Distance between the Planes equal to $\frac{1}{18}$ of an inch. **1792** BELKNAP *Hist. New-Hampsh.* III. 98 This bark is composed of several laminæ. **1797** M. BAILLIE *Morb. Anat.* (1807) 51 Many small broken laminæ of the coagulable lymph. **1800** tr. *Lagrange's Chem.* II. 63 Lead..may be reduced into laminæ and plates thinner than paper. **1832** GELL *Pompeiana* II. xiii. 22 The chamber was covered with laminæ of rare marbles. **1860** TYNDALL *Glac.* I. xxi. 148 At some places the ice had been weathered into laminæ not more than a line in thickness.

b. *Anat.,* etc. A thin layer of bone, membrane, or other structure.

1706 PHILLIPS (ed. Kersey) s.v., In Anatomy, *Laminæ* are the Plates or Tables of the Scull, two in number. **1815** W. PHILLIPS *Outl. Min. & Geol.* (1818) 105 These shells..are ..extremely brittle, and readily separate into laminæ. **1843** YOUATT *Horse* 375 The Horny Laminæ [of the foot]. **1859** DARWIN *Orig. Spec.* vii. (1872) 183 The middle and longest lamina in the Greenland whale is ten, twelve, or even 15 feet in length. **1864** MAYHEW *Illustr. Horse Managemt.* 95 The laminæ, or the highly-sensitive covering of the internal foot, secrete the inward layer of horn. **1881** MIVART *Cat* 35 A superior broad and flat portion called the neural lamina.

c. *Geol.* The thinnest separable layer in stratified rock deposits.

1794 SULLIVAN *View Nat.* I. 421 In caverns and fissures laminæ of spar..crystallize in various forms. **1849** MURCHISON *Siluria* vii. 129 The laminæ of deposit being marked by layers of shells and corals. **1872** NICHOLSON *Palæont.* 6 The finer beds of clay or sand will all be arranged in thicker or thinner layers or laminæ.

d. *Bot.* (*a*) A thin 'plate' of tissue, as in the 'gill' of a mushroom. (*b*) The blade, 'limb', or expanded portion of a leaf. (*c*) The (usually widened) upper part or 'limb' of a petal. (*d*) The expanded part of the thallus or frond in algæ, etc.

1760 J. LEE *Introd. Bot.* I. iii. (1765) 7 Lamina, a thin Plate, which is the upper Part, and usually spreading. **1776-96** WITHERING *Brit. Plants* (ed. 3) I. 393 The 2 lamina [*sic*] or plates which constitute each gill. **1830** LINDLEY *Nat. Syst. Bot.* 153 Leaves radical, with a hollow urn-shaped petiole, at the apex of which is articulated the lamina. **1861** COOKE *Man. Struct. Bot.* (1893) 63 The upper or free portion [of a petal] is called the lamina or limb. **1875** BENNETT & DYER *Sachs' Bot.* 296 A cellular lamina or a mass of tissue which fixes itself by root-hairs and produces the thallus by growth at its apex.

e. *Kinematics.*

1837 WHEWELL *Hist. Induct. Sci.* VIII. vi. II. 331 Any combination of rods, strings, and laminæ. **1878** WOLSTENHOLME *Math. Probl.* (ed. 2) 416 A lamina moves in its own plane so that two fixed points of it describe straight lines with accelerations f, f'. **1882** MINCHIN *Unipl. Kinemat.* 39 The locus traced out in the body..is a circle concentric with the lamina.

laminable ('læmɪnəb(ə)l), *a.* [f. L. **lāmināre* (see LAMINATE *v.*) + -ABLE.] Capable of being formed into thin plates or layers.

1796 KIRWAN *Elem. Min.* (ed. 2) II. 103 Laminable as Gold. **1856** *Leisure Hour* V. 268/1 Beautiful white metal,.. ductile, laminable, fusible, and tough.

Hence **lamina'bility,** laminable quality.

1839 URE *Dict. Arts* s.v. *Laminable,* A table of the relative laminability of metals. **1881** *Nature* No. 627. 14 Iron.. combines the qualities of tenacity and laminability, with a greater sensitiveness in its electric resistance to temperature changes than either gold, platinum, or silver.

laminagraph ('læmɪnəgrɑːf, -æ-). *Radiology.* Also **lamino-.** [f. LAMINA + -GRAPH.] = TOMOGRAPH. (Originally a particular design of tomograph.)

1938 J. KIEFFER in *Amer. Jrnl. Roentgenol.* XXXIX. 497/1 The laminagraph is a device embodying the principle of roentgenographic body sectioning, or planigraphy... It was built at the instigation of, and in co-operation with, the director, Dr. Sherwood Moore, who named it (lamina: a thin layer). **1942** *Surg., Gynecol. & Obstetr.* LXXV. 508/2 The last case..demonstrates the increase of bone detail by laminagraph as compared to the usual x-ray examination. **1960** *Jrnl. Speech & Hearing Disorders* XXV. 137/2 With a multilayer laminagraph cassette or film-holder, it is possible to record simultaneously a number of adjacent planes or body sections with a single exposure.

Hence ˌ**lamina'graphic** *a.,* of or pertaining to laminagraphy; '**laminagram,** a radiograph taken using a laminagraph; **lami'nagraphy** = TOMOGRAPHY.

1938 *Amer. Jrnl. Roentgenol.* XXXIX. 507/2 The extent of the layer sharply rendered during laminagraphic motion is limited only by the size of the object roentgenographed and by the size of the film used. *Ibid.* 503/2 Satisfactory chest laminagrams can be made in one second. **1939** *Radiology* XXXIII. 560/1 The last method has also been spelled 'laminography' by various authors. *Ibid.* 560/2 Laminagraphy—a method whereby body-section roentgenography is accomplished by motion of the tube and film in planes parallel to one another and at any angle to the film surface. **1942** *Urologic & Cutaneous Rev.* XLVI. 706/1 Laminography permits the roentgenographic delineation of structures at different levels.... Laminograms are made by synchronously moving the X-ray film and the tube carrier in opposite directions. **1960** *Jrnl. Speech & Hearing Disorders* XXV. 137/2 Laminagraphy is used most advantageously when skeletal structures are not clearly visualized with standard techniques. **1966** *Amer. Speech* XLI. 229 Clear images of vocal fold cross-sections during actual phonation by laminagraphic X-ray photographs. **1968** H. O. ANGER in Gottschalk & Beck *Fund. Probl. in Scanning* xiv. 195 A tomographic or laminographic series will be obtained from a single rectilinear scan. **1969** R. & E. BRECHER *Rays* xix. 258 The modern technique, known generally as body-section radiography but also as laminography, stratigraphy, tomography, and planigraphy, depends upon imparting a reciprocal motion to the X-ray tube and film. **1971** *Jrnl. Amer. Med. Assoc.* 16 Aug. 927/2 The ability to record both dynamic studies and 'thick' laminagrams..reduces the time necessary for the physician to view the films. **1971** *Radiology* CI. 617/1 A rounded soft-tissue mass was seen near the canal of the infraorbital nerve at laminagraphy.

laminal ('læmɪnəl), *a.* [f. LAMINA + -AL[1].]

a. Formed into laminæ; laminar.

1825 J. NICHOLSON *Operat. Mechanic* 727 Until the whole be precipitated upon the zinc, which will assume the form of a tree or bush, whose leaves and branches are laminal, or plates of a metallic lustre.

b. *Phonetics.* Produced by the blade of the tongue.

1956 C. F. HOCKETT in *Internat. Jrnl. Amer. Ling.* XXII. 202/1 In all the Central Algonquian dialects..there is..an apical or laminal affricate /c/. The affricate is laminal, with hushing offglide, in those languages..which distinguish two spirants. **1964** P. LADEFOGED *Phonetic Study W. Afr. Lang.* iv. 19 There are clear differences in the formant transitions which are due to using the blade as opposed to the tip of the tongue in the (laminal) denti-alveolar as opposed to the apical alveolar articulations. **1966** M. PEI *Gloss. Ling. Terminol.* 141 *Laminal,* pertaining to the blade (upper front surface) of the tongue; sometimes applied to palatal phonemes ([ʃ], [ʒ], [č] or [tʃ], [ǧ] or [dʒ], [j]). **1968** CHOMSKY & HALLE *Sound Pattern Eng.* vii. 313 The difference characterized by distributed versus nondistributed does not correspond precisely to the distinction between laminal and apical.

laminar ('læmɪnə(r)), *a.* [f. LAMINA + -AR. Cf. F. *laminaire.*] **1.** Consisting of or arranged in laminæ, thin plates, or layers.

1811 PINKERTON *Petral.* I. 220 Laminar pitch-stone, in thin horizontal layers. **1845** PETRIE *Round Towers Irel.* II. iii. 210 Bracteati—by which is understood, thin laminar pieces, usually of silver. **1854** WOODWARD *Mollusca* II. 214 Discina and Lingula consist almost entirely of a horny animal substance, which is laminar. **1875** BLAKE *Zool.* 202 Gills laminar, with a small proportion of the border free. **1876** HARLEY *Mat. Med.* (ed. 6) 75 Soft laminar crystals.

2. a. *Physics.* Of the flow of a fluid: smooth and regular, the direction of motion at any point remaining constant as if the fluid were moving in a series of layers sliding over one another without mixing; *occas.* restricted to the case in which the layers are plane (cf. LAMELLAR *a.* 2).

1895 H. LAMB *Hydrodynamics* iii. 34 This analysis may be illustrated by the so-called 'laminar' motion of a liquid. **1949** H. F. P. PURDAY *Streamline Flow* i. 6 In laminar flow in the strict use of the term, the fluid moves in a system of parallel planes, the velocity having everywhere the same direction, but the magnitude of the velocity is a function of the distance from some fixed plane of the system. The motion is not necessarily steady; it may, for instance, be periodic. **1965** D. A. GILBRECH *Fluid Mech.* (1966) vi. 265 In general, laminar flow occurs at low velocities, between close boundaries, when the fluid is very viscous, and when the fluid is of low density. **1968** PASSMORE & ROBSON *Compan. Med. Stud.* I. xxix. 8/2 Flow of gas through tubes is laminar at slow speeds, but at faster rates of flow molecular collisions set up eddies and the flow is then turbulent.

b. *transf.* Applied to a body whose shape is such as to produce a laminar flow of fluid in the boundary layer round it (at normal speeds).

1955 J. KESTIN tr. *Schlichting's Boundary Layer Theory* xiii. 229 The prevention of transition on laminar aerofoils. **1963** *Ann. Reg. 1962* 390 Handley Page continued the development of their laminar wing project, in which hundreds of small slits in an aircraft wing were used to suck air away from the so-called boundary layer around the wing and thus to reduce friction and hence fuel costs.

laminaria (læmɪ'nɛərɪə). [mod.L. (J. V. F. Lamouroux *Essai sur les genres de la famille des Thalassiophytes non articulées* (1813) 20), f. L. *lamina* thin plate or leaf.] A thin, flat, brown seaweed of the genus so called; also known as oar-weed or kelp. Also *attrib.*

1848 A. HENFREY tr. *Schleiden's Plant* xiv. 399 For its [*sc.* the sea's] trees stand the Laminarias, often 30 feet long, waving their broad bands. **1857** GEO. ELIOT *Jrnl.* 28 June in *Lett.* (1954) II. 356 A long stretch of fine pale sand where the large roots of the *laminaria* were thrown up in abundance. **1883** [see LAMINARIAN *a.*]. **1935** J. E. TILDEN *Algae* vi. 269 Yendo, a Japanese phycologist, gives a recipe for making *kombu-mati,* or '*Laminaria* roll'. **1963** C. I. DICKINSON *Brit. Seaweeds* 82 The Laminarias are closely related to *Macrocystis* and *Lessonia.*

laminarian (læmɪ'nɛərɪən), *a.* [f. mod.L. *Laminaria* name of a genus of seaweeds (see quot. 1883), f. L. *lāmina* thin plate.] *laminarian zone*: the zone of the sea, extending from low-water mark to a depth of ninety feet, in which seaweeds of the genus *Laminaria* are found.

1851-6 WOODWARD *Mollusca* 149 The key-hole limpets.. chiefly inhabit the laminarian zone. **1883** *Good Words* Aug. 530/1 Below the littoral we come upon the great laminarian zone, the region of waving laminaria, or sea-tangle.

laminarite ('læmɪnəraɪt). *Geol.* [f. as prec. + -ITE.] A broad-leaved fossil seaweed supposed to be allied to the genus *Laminaria.*

1839 *Penny Cycl.* XIII. 283/2 *Laminarites.* Brongniart, classing fossil fuci according to the analogy they offer to recent tribes, uses this term for one species found in the secondary strata of Aix, near La Rochelle.

laminarize ('læmɪnəraɪz), *v.* *Aeronaut.* [f. LAMINAR *a.* + -IZE.] *trans.* To design (an aircraft surface) so as to maximize the area over

which the flow in the boundary layer is laminar. So 'laminarized *ppl. a.*

1960 *Times* 2 Sept. 6/3 Handley Page are about to test in flight a complete laminarized wing. **1961** *Aeroplane* CI. 428/1 This has been achieved by 'laminarizing' nearly half the metal skin of the airframe, including the fuselage forward of the cabin, and the leading-edges back to half-chord on the tailplane and fin. These surfaces are free from protruding rivet heads or skin overlap. **1966** D. STINTON *Anat. Aeroplane* 265 The most promising technique is to laminarize a large part of the surface of an aeroplane—70 per cent or more—to bring about greatly improved lift/drag ratios.

Also ˌ**laminari'zation**, the design or use of laminarized surfaces.

1960 *Times* 2 Sept. 6/3 The airliner would cruise at high subsonic speed, although laminarization was still effective above sonic speed. **1964** *New Scientist* 6 Feb. 329/3 Beyond the first generation supersonic airliner, which is already half-way towards being an all-lifting surface, the next step might be laminarisation..in combination with an all-wing design. **1966** D. STINTON *Anat. Aeroplane* 265 The conclusion is that laminarization leads to huge savings in fuel weight.

laminary ('læmɪnərɪ), *a.* [f. LAMINA + -ARY. Cf. F. *laminaire*.] Laminar.

1830 MAUNDER *Treas. Knowl.* I., *Laminary*, composed of layers. **1853** TH. ROSS *Humboldt's Trav.* III. xxxii. 381 Pegmatite, composed of laminary felspar.

laminate ('læmɪnət), *a.* [ad. mod.L. *lāmināt-us*: see next and -ATE².] Having the form of or consisting of a lamina or thin plate; furnished with a lamina or laminæ.

1668 WILKINS *Real Char.* II. v. §6. 128 Exanguious animals..having a broad head with two short, broad, laminate prominencies from it. **1826** KIRBY & SP. *Entomol.* IV. 300 Laminate Horn (*Cornu laminatum*), a horn dilated at its base into a flat plate. *Ibid.* 346 Laminate (*laminatæ*), when the posterior coxæ form a broad thin plate which covers the trochanter and the base of the thighs. **1852** DANA *Crust.* I. 316 Upper finger laminate.

laminate ('læmɪneɪt), *v.* [f. L. **lāmināt-*, ppl. stem of **lāmināre*, f. LAMINA: see -ATE³. Cf. F. *laminer*, It. *laminare*.]

1. *trans.* To beat or roll (metal) into thin plates.

1666 BOYLE *Orig. Formes & Qual.* 370 We take then the finest Gold we can procure, and having either Granulated it, or Laminated it, we dissolve it. **1684** —— *Porousn. Anim. & Solid Bod.* vii. 108 We took good Copper laminated to the thickness of a shilling or thereabouts. **1825** J. NICHOLSON *Operat. Mechanic* 633 Milled lead is laminated..by means of a roller or flatting-mill. **1831** J. HOLLAND *Manuf. Metal* I. 122 The art of laminating ductile metal by passing it between a pair of rollers.

2. To separate or split into layers or leaves. Also *intr.* for *refl.*

1668 *Phil. Trans.* III. 783 Very many *vasa lacrymalia* of Glass, which by length of time were become laminated into divers leaves. **1864** *Jrnl. R. Agric. Soc.* XXV. II. 373 When dried by exposure, it laminates like thin slate. **1866** ROGERS *Agric. & Prices* I. ii. 19 Where stone was easily laminated, a rude drain was formed by laying large stones in the course.

3. To cover or overlay with plates (of metal).

1697 EVELYN *Numism.* vi. 213 Laminated only with a thin Foil..of..Metal. **1869** *Latest News* 3 Oct. 15 Gold richly laminated with flowers or texts from the Alcoran.

4. To manufacture by placing layer upon layer of material.

1858 GREENER *Gunnery* 224 My method of laminating steel. **1888** *Scribner's Mag.* Aug. 180/2 'Laminating the armature core', that is, making it up out of a great number of thin sheets of iron.

5. To unite so as to form a laminated material.

1945 H. BARRON *Mod. Plastics* xi. 238 Latterly there has been a trend to use plastic fibres for weaving into fabrics which are then laminated in the usual way. **1949** B. L. DAVIES *Technol. Plastics* xiii. 238 The technique of laminating wood veneers using synthetic adhesives was developed to the stage when the very high strength bonds were sufficiently good for the manufacture of airscrews. **1955** KIRK & OTHMER *Encycl. Chem. Technol.* XIV. 696 These adhesives are much used for laminating metal foils to paper. **1973** *Daily Tel.* 6 Nov. 3/6 It [*sc.* the glue] is used in laminating and veneering wood.

Hence '**laminating** *vbl. sb.*

1823 P. NICHOLSON *Pract. Build.* 406 In the operation of making it [milled lead], a laminating-roller is used. **1875** KNIGHT *Dict. Mech.*, *Laminating-machine*, a gold-beater's rolling-mill for reducing the ingot of gold to such a thickness that a square inch will weigh 6½ grains. **1939** H. R. SIMONDS *Industr. Plastics* (1940) v. 115 The paper or other laminating material is impregnated with the varnish. **1965** *Guardian* 31 Mar. 16/2 The British laminating trade is respected even as far away as North America for the severity of its standards.

laminate ('læmɪnət), *sb.* [Substantival use of the adj.] **1.** A manufactured laminated structure or material, as: **a.** = *laminated plastic*; **b.** a fabric or a flexible packaging material consisting of two or more layers held together by an adhesive.

1939 H. R. SIMONDS *Industr. Plastics* (1940) v. 118 Care must be taken to keep the steel platens free from scratches and dents, for even the most minute defect on the platen will repeat itself on the surface of the laminate. **1952** KIRK & OTHMER *Encycl. Chem. Technol.* VIII. 189 Paper- and fabric-base laminates have now been generally accepted as an engineering material. **1964** *McCall's Sewing* iv. 57/2 *Laminate*, a layer of fabric which has been fused with a layer of foam; currently the term is widely used for fabrics fused with foam rubber. **1967** *Times Rev. Industry* May 84/3 A host of combinations of film, foil and paper can provide the correct balance of product resistance, strength and light, vapour and moisture barrier. Such combinations, or laminates, are made possible by the availability of modern two-part adhesives. **1969** W. R. R. PARK *Plastics Film Technol.* vi. 148 For purposes of clarity, a laminate is defined as any combination of distinctly different plastic film materials or plastic plus nonplastic materials. **1970** *Financial Times* 13 Apr. 13/8 A layer of plastic is sandwiched between thin strips of steel. This has advantages in weight and strength and can compete with other types of laminates in office partitions, gearbox casings and building cladding. **1970** O. DOPPING *Computers & Data Processing* x. 138 Another static magnetic memory is the laminated ferrite memory which consists of a laminate of a number of thin sheets. **1973** *Sci. Amer.* July 39/1 Sandwich materials (such as plaster-board) and metal laminates (such as the active element of a thermostat) are constructed entirely of laminae, or layers, which taken together give the composite its form.

2. = LAMINATION 3.

1968 W. E. WILLIS *Timber* v. 100 Laminated timber can be made with the laminates either vertical or horizontal.

laminated ('læmɪneɪtɪd), *ppl. a.* [f. LAMINATE *v.* + -ED¹.] Consisting of, arranged in, or furnished with laminæ; formed or manufactured in a succession of layers of material, as some metallic objects, etc. ***laminated tubercle***: the nodule of the cerebellum (*Syd. Soc. Lex.* 1888). In armour (see quot. 1869). Now common as a designation of various manufactured materials made by lamination, as ***laminated glass***, a material consisting of two outer layers of plate or sheet glass attached to an inner layer of transparent plastic; ***laminated plastic***, a more or less rigid material made by bonding together, usu. by means of heat and pressure, layers of cloth, paper, or the like that have been impregnated or coated with a synthetic resin; ***laminated wood***, layers of wood bonded together with the grain in adjacent layers parallel (in contrast to plywood); also ***laminated spring***, a leaf spring.

1665 HOOKE *Microgr.* 209 Each of them consisting of an infinite number of very thin shells or laminated orbiculations. **1668** WILKINS *Real Char.* II. iii. §2. 61 [Stones] of a laminated figure, either natural, or factitious. **1677** PLOT *Oxfordsh.* 71 Those [lumps of pyrites] from Clifton aforesaid seem to be laminated. **1768** PENNANT *Zool.* I. Pref. 4 The laminated lead ore of Lord Hoptoun's mines. **1794** SULLIVAN *View Nat.* II. 332 Crystals and gems..are all found to be of a foliated or laminated structure. **1833** LYELL *Princ. Geol.* III. 78 Volcanic tuff thinly laminated. **1851** *Illustr. Catal. Gt. Exhib.* 311 Section of rail and laminated beam. **1851** RICHARDSON *Geol.* viii. 230 They respire by laminated branchiæ. **1858** GREENER *Gunnery* 222 A laminated steel barrel has never been known to burst. **1869** BOUTELL *Arms & Arm.* iii. 51 Laminated corslets..of iron or steel—corslets, that is, formed of rows of metal scales sewn upon garments of leather or linen, in such a manner that the scales in each row would overlap those in the row below them. **1872** HUXLEY *Phys.* xi. 262 Overhanging the fourth ventricle is a great laminated mass, the cerebellum. **1875** KNIGHT *Dict. Mech.*, *Laminated Arch*, a timber arch made of successive thicknesses of planking bent on to a centreing and secured together by tree-nails. **1888** *Lockwood's Dict. Mech. Engin.* 202 *Laminated spring*, a curved spring composed of thin plates superimposed one over the other, as distinguished from helical and coiled springs. **1912** *Automobile Engineer* Feb. 63/3 The main laminated springs are lighter than usual. **1930** *Engineering* 3 Jan. 26/1 The experience of the war showed unexpected weakness in the laminated springs of motor vehicles. **1930** *Canad. Patent Office Rec.* 12 Aug. 2145/1 (*title*) Laminated glass. **1931** *Official Gaz.* (U.S. Patent Office) 1 Dec. 270/2 The process of making a low moisture absorption laminated wood product which comprises..impregnating the dried wood under pressure with a phenolic resin,..covering a plurality of laminations of the impregnated wood with a surface coating of powdered phenolic resin and molding the laminations into a homogeneous solid mass. **1933** *Product Engineering* Dec. 456/2 Laminated plastics, for example, can be given any of the usual machining operations. **1936** Laminated board [see *block-board* (BLOCK *sb.* 23)]. **1937** R. S. MORRELL et al. *Synthetic Resins* iv. 125 Laminated material can also be made in the form of blocks, bars, rods, and tubes, by rolling the paper in special machines to the cross-section required, and then moulding them in the hydraulic press. **1938** *Encycl. Brit. Bk. of Year* 147/2 Translucent laminated plastic..made its appearance for use in instrument dials and lighting fixtures. **1939** *Chem. Abstr.* XXXIII. 3209 A pressed board consisting of 2 layers of asbestos stone bound together under pressure by a layer of resin-impregnated hard paper board has outstanding chem. resistance... This laminated board is especially well suited as the top for lab. benches. **1947** W. J. BROWN in P. I. Smith *Pract. Plastics* xxi. 281/2 Modern laminated plywoods can also be considered as belonging to the plastics group of materials because the plies are bonded together by means of synthetic resins. **1953** KIRK & OTHMER *Encycl. Chem. Technol.* X. 860 If the direction of the grain in adjacent layers is parallel, the product is called laminated wood and is not considered to be a type of plywood. **1957** *N.Z. Timber Jrnl.* Sept. 61/2 *Laminated board*, a number of veneers about ¼in. thick placed edge on between an upper and a lower sheet of veneer or ply. **1958** BROWN & BETHEL *Lumber* (ed. 2) x. 293 Glued laminated timber structures are prepared by gluing together relatively small pieces of wood into a large timber member or structure..in such a manner that the grain of each of the small pieces or laminations is parallel to the length of the member. *Ibid.*, Laminated arches have been erected that provide buildings with clear spans up to 170 feet. **1962** *Which? Car Suppl.* Oct. 131/1 The windscreens in the Fiat 1500, Ford Taunus and Riley 4/72 were made of laminated glass. The windscreens in the other cars were made of toughened glass. **1965** R. B. ORAM *Cargo Handling* v. 84 Parcels of plywood, laminated boards, block boards, box-boards. **1965** *Guardian* 31 Mar. 16/1 Quantities of laminated fabric were imported from the United States to bridge the temporary gap between fashion demand and the setting up of domestic facilities. **1968** J. IRONSIDE *Fashion Alphabet* 235 Laminated fabric is one where two or more layers have been fused together by the use of an adhesive... Originally the idea was to provide the fabric either with a built-in lining or to make it reversible, but developments have proved that almost any two fabrics can be bonded together, and the desirable characteristics of both are retained. **1974** *Daily Tel.* 12 Jan. 5 (Advt.), Non-shrinking laminated curtains with the look of velvet.

lamination (læmɪ'neɪʃən). [f. LAMINATE *v.*: see -ATION.]

1. a. The action of laminating or beating metal into thin plates. *rare*⁻⁰. **b.** 'In Midwifery, applied to the method of reducing the size of the skull in embryotomy by cutting it into slices' (*Syd. Soc. Lex.* 1888).

1676 COLES, *Lamination*, a beating into a *Lamina*.

c. The process of uniting two or more layers of material so as to form a laminated material or object; the manufacture of laminates.

1945 H. BARRON *Mod. Plastics* xii. 259 Low pressure lamination is now a very popular technique. *Ibid.* 269 The continuous lamination of veneers into tubing and ducts by the winding method. **1952** J. P. CASEY *Pulp & Paper* II. xx. 1211 The lamination of metal foil to sulfite paper in the manufacture of candy or gum wrappers. **1967** *Times Rev. Industry* May 84/3 No plastic film is outstanding for all requirements but the lamination of, say, cellulose film and polypropylene provides a combination of properties not otherwise attainable. **1968** J. ARNOLD *Shell Bk. Country Crafts* xvii. 219 As far back as the sixteenth century..a Manchester bowyer, one Kelsall, laid a strip of ash along the belly of his bows and so became a pioneer of lamination.

2. The condition of being laminated; arrangement in laminæ; laminated structure.

1830 LYELL *Princ. Geol.* I. 205 The lamination of some of the concentric masses of San Filippo is so minute, that sixty may be counted in the thickness of an inch. **1845** TODD & BOWMAN *Phys. Anat.* I. 120 The lamination of bone. **1860** TYNDALL *Glac.* I. xxi. 148 Near to the moraine..a magnificent lamination was developed. **1870** ROLLESTON *Anim. Life* Introd. 53 Its grey matter however is considerable in quantity, owing to its transverse lamination.

3. Any of the layers of a laminated material or object.

1858 GEIKIE *Hist. Boulder* xi. 226 A few thin laminations of coal. **1905** S. P. THOMPSON *Dynamo-Electr. Machinery* (ed. 7) II. iii. 173 A laminated ring core built up of segmental laminations. **1920** *Whittaker's Electr. Engineer's Pocket-Bk.* (ed. 4) 241 Many [transformer] makers prefer laminating the conductor, and, of course, insulating each lamination. **1940** 'PLASTES' *Plastics in Industry* v. 59 Another form of laminated product, that made up of laminations of wood, should be especially attractive to the engineering world. **1968** J. ARNOLD *Shell Bk. Country Crafts* xvii. 218 The bows are built up with laminations of various woods and glass-fibre. **1971** I. G. GASS et al. *Understanding Earth* xiii. 171/1 [Sedimentary] laminations are defined as layers less than 1 cm in thickness.

laminator ('læmɪneɪtə(r)). [f. LAMINAT(E *v.* + -OR.] A person or organization that makes laminates, esp. plastic laminates.

1941 *Modern Plastics* Oct. 31 (Advt.), Complete lists of molders, fabricators, laminators, material manufacturers, press and equipment manufacturers. **1952** KIRK & OTHMER *Encycl. Chem. Technol.* VIII. 185 With the advent of World War II, a tremendous amount of development and testing work was instituted and carried on, not only by laminators, but by suppliers, fabricators, [etc.]. **1965** *Guardian* 31 Mar. 16/1 Some laminators tried to help manufacturers to move fabrics which had been gathering dust on warehouse shelves, producing laminated fabrics entirely unsuited for the applications they were used for.

laminboard ('læmɪnbɔəd). [f. *lamin*(*ated*) *board*.] (A) composite board consisting of numerous thin strips of wood glued face to face between two facing sheets of wood (or laminated plastic).

1927 S. B. WAINWRIGHT *Mod. Plywood* iii. 15 The newer forms of laminated wood,..generally known as laminboards. *Ibid.* vi. 24 Laminboards, ⅜" thick or more, may be used..for ceilings or walls. *Ibid.* viii. 44 There is no risk of the joints opening, as the laminboards cannot shrink. **1938** *Archit. Rev.* LXXXIV. 219 (*caption*) Veneered laminboard doors. **1965** MALLINSON & LEIGH *Timber Trade Pract.* (ed. 3) xxi. 286 In 1961 out of the total import of all these materials, plywood counted for 80%, blockboard, laminboard and battenboard accounted for 20% and of this the bulk was blockboard. **1971** *Cabinet Maker & Retail Furnisher* 24 Sept. 531/2 Work-tops are of laminboard which is bought in faced with Warerite.

laminectomy (læmɪ'nɛktəmɪ). *Surg.* [f. LAMIN(A + -ECTOMY.] Excision of one or more of the posterior arches of the vertebræ (each arch being formed by the junction of two laminæ), esp. as a method of access to the spinal canal.

1892 *Med. Ann.* 458 Formerly the operation was called 'trephining'.., but the trephine is now seldom used, and the term 'laminectomy' has been substituted. **1921** J. S. HORSLEY *Operative Surg.* xvi. 290 The operation by which tumors or other lesions of the spinal cord are approached is laminectomy. **1962** *Punch* 24 Oct. 598/1 That was the worst laminectomy I've seen for months! **1971** *Canad. Jrnl. Surg.* XIV. 229 The spinal cord was decompressed by laminectomy from T3 to T6.

'laming, *sb. dial.* ? *Obs.* [? f. LAME *sb.*[1] + -ING[1]; or var. LAMIN.] (See quots.)

1686 PLOT *Staffordsh.* 131 The partings or lamings which the coal has in it self;..all coale-Mines..haveing divers partitions in the body of the coal it self, made by thin substances called partings or lamings. *Ibid.* 141 The Laming (that lyes between the measures of the coal). **1847** HALLIWELL, *Lamings*, the partings of coal. *Staff.*

laming ('leɪmɪŋ), *vbl. sb.* [f. LAME *v.* + -ING[1].] The action of the verb LAME; rendering lame, halting, or defective.

1583 BABINGTON *Commandm.* vi. (1637) 49 Hurting and laming of our brethren in fight. **1599** *Life More* in Wordsw. *Eccl. Biog.* (1853) II. 118 To the laming and blemishing of a most notable sentence. **1849** GROTE *Greece* II. lxi. (1862) 311 The laming of their horses on the hard and stony soil. **1863** MRS. CARLYLE *Lett.* III. 181, I have given myself a bad headache in addition to my other lamings.

lamington ('læmɪŋtən). *Austral.* and *N.Z.* [app. f. name of Lord *Lamington*, Governor of Queensland, 1895–1901.] A square of sponge cake dipped in melted chocolate and grated coconut.

1929 *Kookaburra Cookery Bk.* (ed. 2) 242 (*heading*) Lamington cake. **1944** J. K. EWERS in *Coast to Coast 1943* 61 Mrs. Whiskers making scones; even Filthy Kate enlisted to turn out lamingtons by the score, because they were her specialty. **1952** *P.W.M.U. Cookery Bk.* (9th impr.) 132 Lamingtons..spread icing on all sides of cake..roll cakes in desiccated coconut. **1969** *Southerly* XXIX. 4 They had the innocence of oatmeal porridge, the sweetness of lamingtons.

lamini- ('læmɪnɪ), comb. form of LAMINA, as in **lami'niferous** *a.*, 'having a structure consisting of laminæ or layers' (Ogilvie 1851). **la'miniform** *a.*, laminar in form or structure. **lamini'plantar** *a. Ornith.* [L. *planta* sole], having laminate tarsi; pertaining to the *Laminiplantares* of Sundevall's classification. **laminiplan'tation**, the quality or condition of being laminiplantar.

1834 MCMURTRIE *Cuvier's Anim. Kingd.* 345 The four last [feet] are compressed, ciliated, or laminiform. **1872** COUES *Key N. Amer. Birds* (1884) 126 This results from the laminiplantation..and is equally well exhibited by most passerine birds, whether they have booted or anteriorly scutellate tarsi. **1888** *Syd. Soc. Lex.*, *Laminiplantar*, applied to the metatarsus of birds when the integument forms a continuous horny sheath along its anterior and lateral surfaces, as in thrushes.

‖**laminitis** (læmɪ'naɪtɪs). [f. LAMINA + -ITIS.] Inflammation of the sensitive laminæ of a horse's hoof.

1843 YOUATT *Horse* 382 Chronic laminitis..is a species of founder.

'lamino-. Combining form of LAMINAL *a.* b used in *Phonetics*, as **lamino-dental** *a.*, produced by pressing the blade of the tongue against the front upper teeth; **lamino-palatal** *a.*, produced by pressing the blade of the tongue against the palate.

1968 P. M. POSTAL *Aspects Phonol. Theory* iv. 82 Hence there are few languages with lamino-dental consonants. **1966** *Publ. Amer. Dial. Soc.* XLVI. 34 Aspirated, voiceless, lamino-palatal stop. **1968** P. M. POSTAL *Aspects Phonol. Theory* iv. 82 But apico-dental and lamino-palatal segments are found almost everywhere.

laminograph, laminographic, etc.: varr. LAMINAGRAPH, etc.

laminose ('læmɪnəʊs), *a.* [f. LAMINA + -OSE.] Consisting of or having the form of laminæ.

1826 KIRBY & SP. *Entomol.* IV. xxxviii. 57 Laminose or foliaceous respiratory appendages distinguish the sides of the larvae..of the Ephemeræ. **1871** COOKE *Brit. Fungi* I. 314 *Thelephora fastidiosa*..Effused, soft, amorphous, incrusting, white, passing into laminose branches.

laminous ('læmɪnəs), *a.* [f. LAMINA + -OUS.] = prec.

1798 LANDOR *Gebir* II. 9 Wks. 1846 II. 490/1 Some raise the painted pavement, some on wheels Draw slow its laminous length. **1800** *Asiat. Ann. Reg.* 276/1 Leaves opposite,..fruit laminous. **1807** VANCOUVER *Agric. Devon* (1813) 11 The whole of this rock is of a laminous character.

lamish ('leɪmɪʃ), *a.* [f. LAME *a.* + -ISH.] Somewhat lame.

1592 NASHE *P. Penilesse* Wks. (Grosart) II. 68, I could no refraine but bequeath it to the Priuie, leafe by leafe as I read it, it was so vgly, dorbellicall, and lamish. **1689** *Lond. Gaz.* No. 2448/4 One Grey Gelding about 14 hands and a halfe high, goes lamish behind. **1711** *Ibid.* No. 4895/3 Trots lamish with his off Leg behind. **1881** CARLYLE in *Remin.* I. 164 Something lamish about one of the knees or ankles. **1887** JESSOPP *Arcady* ii. 41 He was lamish and walked with a stick.

lamism: see under LAMA.

lamkin, obs. form of LAMBKIN.

lamm, obs. form of LAM *v.*, LAMB, LAME *sb.*[1]

Lammas ('læməs), *sb.* Forms: 1 Hláf-, Hlámmæsse, -messe, 2–7 Lammasse, 3 Lanmasse, 3–4 Lamasse, 3–5 Lam(m)es(s)e, 6–7 Lambmes(se, Lammes, 7 Lamas, 8 Lambmass, 5– Lammas. [OE. *hláfmæsse*, f. *hláf* bread, LOAF + *mæsse* MASS; afterwards popularly apprehended as if f. LAMB + MASS.]

1. The 1st of August (Festum Sancti Petri ad Vincula in the Roman calendar; see also GULE), in the early English church observed as a harvest festival, at which loaves of bread were consecrated, made from the first ripe corn. (In Scotland, one of the usual quarter-days.) Also, the part of the year marked by this festival.

c **893** K. ÆLFRED *Oros.* v. xiii. §2 þæt (wæs) on þære tide calendas Agustus, & on þæm dæʒe þe we hatað 'hlaf-mæsse'. **1154** *O.E. Chron.* an. 1135 (Laud MS.) On þis ʒære for se king..ouer sæ æt te Lammasse. *c* **1290** *S. Eng. Leg.* I. 37/124 Bi-fore lamasse seueniʒht. ? *a* **1400** *Morte Arth.* 421, I salle at Lammese take leue. *c* **1440** *Promp. Parv.* 286/1 Lammesse, *festum agnorum, vel Festum ad Vincula Sancti Petri.* **1480** CAXTON *Chron. Eng.* ccxliv. (1482) 296 To mete at southampton by lammasse next sewyng without ony delay. **1570** *Reg. Ministers* in *Lauder's Tractate* (1864) Pref. 10 William Lauder, Minister of Forgondynye (in 1567), [his stipend] iiijxxli. [£80], and xxli. mair sen Lambmes, 1569. *a* **1651** CALDERWOOD *Hist. Kirk* (1843) II. 393 Adam, called Bishop of Orkney, was delated for not visiting the kirks of his countrie, from Lambmesse to Allhallowmesse. **1716** ADDISON *Drummer* v. i, Six years old last Lammas. **1833** TENNYSON in *Mem.* (1897) I. 112 A voice ran round the hills When corny Lammas bound the sheaves.

†**2.** Short for *Lammas-wheat*. *Obs.*

1677 PLOT *Oxfordsh.* 151 The white Lammas has both ears and grain white, and the red Lammas both red.

3. *latter Lammas* (†*day*), a day that will never come. *at latter Lammas*: humorously for 'never'.

1567 GASCOIGNE *Instruct. Making Verse* Posies (1575) U ij, Many writers..draw their sentences in length, & make an ende at latter Lammas. **1576** —— *Steele Gl.* (Arb.) 55 This is the cause (beleue me now my Lorde)..That courtiers thriue, at latter Lammas day. **1642** FULLER *Holy & Prof. St.* IV. xv. 316 This your will At latter lammas wee'l fulfill. *a* **1734** NORTH *Lives* (1826) I. 4 The very expectation of them puts me in mind of latter Lammas. **1805** W. TAYLOR in *Ann. Rev.* III. 244 This convocation was some-what unbecomingly postponed to latter Lammas. **1857** KINGSLEY *Two Y. Ago* vii, A treatise..which will be published probably..in the season of Latter Lammas, and the Greek Kalends.

4. *attrib.* and *Comb.*: chiefly with the sense of 'occurring' or (of fruits) 'ripening at Lammas,' as ***Lammas-apple, -assize, -eve, -feast, -month, -night, -tide, -time***; **Lammas-day**, August 1; **Lammas growth** *Forestry* [equivalent of G. *Johannestrieb* St. John's shoot, in allusion to St. John the Baptist's day, 24 June], a shoot produced by a tree in summer, after a pause in growth; **Lammas-land** (see quot. 1870); similarly ***Lammas-field, -mead, -meadow-ground, -rights***; **Lammas shoot** = *Lammas growth*; **Lammas-tower** (see quot. 1792); **Lammas-wheat** = *winter wheat*.

1886 ELWORTHY *W. Somerset Word-bk.*, **Lammas-apple*. *c* **1605** *Acc. Bk. W. Wray* in *Antiquary* XXXII. 213 This yeare (1604) was *lammasse sysies holden at Rippo'. *c* **1000** *Sax. Leechd.* III. 290 Nim of ðam ʒehalʒedan hlafe þe man haliʒe on *hlafmæsse dæʒ. **1297** R. GLOUC. (Rolls) 8669 In a þoresdai it was & þe morwe al so After lammasse day þat þis dede was ydo. **1387** TREVISA *Higden* (Rolls) V. 239 Of hem is þe feste [of] Lammesse day, þey Peter were brouʒt out of prisoun aboute Ester tyme. *a* **1557** *Diurn. Occurr.* (Bannatyne Club) 9 Wpoun the Lambes day, the king desyrit fra all his officiaris renunciatioun of thair offices. **1677** W. HUGHES *Man of Sin* II. viii. 122 On the first of August (Lammas Day; that the Reader may not forget it). **1592** SHAKS. *Rom. & Jul.* I. iii. 17 Of all daies in the yeare come *Lammas Eue at night shall she be fourteene. **1820** COMBE *Consol.* I. 132 I'm sure he'll grieve From Midsummer to Lammas Eve. **1721** RAMSAY *Richy & Sandy* 40 We'll meikle miss his blyth and witty jest, At spaining time, or at our *Lambmass feast. **1872** E. W. ROBERTSON *Hist. Ess.* 246 The Roman tribesman..would probably have followed the early custom retained in the regulations of the '*Lammas fields' in England, his arable resuming the character of common pasturage as soon as the crops were off the ground. **1950** F. S. BAKER *Princ. Silviculture* xv. 302 So-called '*lammas growth' is common in some species... In vigorous young oak trees the lammas shoot formation may be repeated three or four times a season. **1971** T. T. KOZLOWSKI *Growth & Devel. Trees* I. v. 204 Lammas growth often causes profuse branching and knotty lumber. **1787** MRS. TRIMMER *Œconomy Charity* 113 The privilege of the people to turn in on the *Lammas lands is insensibly sliding away. **1870** LUBBOCK *Orig. Civiliz.* x. (1875) 445 Thus our 'Lammas Lands' were so called, because they were private property until Lammas Day (Aug. 1) after which period they were subject to common rights of pasturage till the spring. **1826** *Sunday Times* 27 Aug. 3/3 To enquire to whom the right of hiring, mowing or feeding-off the crops on King's or *Lammas Meads vested. **1694** *Lond. Gaz.* No. 2989/4 [It] has the benefit of a good Common, and several Acres of *Lammas Meadow-Ground. **1387** TREVISA *Higden* (Rolls) IV. 369 Claudius bygan to regne in *Lammesse monþe [L. mense Augusto]. **1297** R. GLOUC. (Rolls) 11650 In a *lammasse niʒt..Out of Wurcetre he wende. **1892** *Law Rep.* Weekly Notes 165/1 Lands which were subject to *lammas rights had been acquired by the Ealing Local Board. **1929** T. THOMSON tr. *Büsgen's Struct. & Life Forest Trees* i. 10 The part of the annual shoot formed after the pause..appears as a new growth to which the name of *Lammas Shoot has been given in view of the approximate date of its appearance... The lammas shoots of the oak are very vigorous. **1971** T. T. KOZLOWSKI *Growth & Devel. Trees* I. v. 202 Lammas shoots often form in response to abundance of available water. *c* **1330** R. BRUNNE *Chron.* (1810) 221 þe fift day it was after *Lammesse tide, & writen is in þat pas, at Euesham gan þei ride. **1592** SHAKS. *Rom. & Jul.* I. iii. 15 How long is it now to Lammas tide? **1362** LANGL. *P. Pl.* A. IX. 314 Bi this lyflode we mot lyue till *Lammasse tyme. **1792** *Archæol. Scot.* I. [194 Each of these communities agreed to build a tower in some conspicuous place..which was to serve as the place of their rendezvous on Lammas day. *Ibid.*] 198 The name of *Lammas towers will remain..after the celebration of the festival has ceased. **1594** CAREW *Huarte's Exam. Wits* (1616) 6 Some bring a plentifull encrease of good *Lammas Wheat. **1832** *Veg. Subst. Food* 31 Winter, or Lammas Wheat—*Triticum hybernum*.

lammbre, obs. pl. form of LAMB.

lamme, obs. form of LAM *v.*, LAMB.

lammer, variant of LAMBER[1] *Obs.*, amber.

lammergeyer ('læməgaɪə(r)). Also **lammergeier**. [a. G. *lämmergeier*, f. *lämmer*, pl. of *lamm* lamb + *geier* vulture, GEIR, hence lit. 'lamb-vulture'.] The Bearded Vulture, *Gypaetus barbatus*; it is the largest European bird of prey, and inhabits lofty mountains in Southern Europe, Asia, and Northern Africa.

1817 L. SIMOND *Switzerland* (1822) I. 239 An inaccessible shelf of rock,..upon which a lammergeyer..once alighted with an infant it had carried away. **18..** MRS. HEMANS *Cavern Three Tells* Poems (1875) 341 They start not at..the Lammer-geyer's cry. **1867** A. L. ADAMS *Wand. Nat. India* 78 The Lammergeyer is easily distinguished from the other vultures by its pointed wings and wedge-shaped tail.

‖**lammervanger** ('laməfaŋə(r)). *S. Afr.* Also **laemer-vanger, lamvanger**. [Afrikaans, f. *lam* lamb + *vanger* catcher.] The martial eagle, *Polemaetus bellicosus*, or the African lammergeyer or bearded vulture, *Gypaetus barbatus meridionalis*.

1830 *S. Afr. Q. Jrnl.* Jan./Apr. 105 *Gypaetus Barbatus*, Cuv.—Arend and Lammervanger of the Colonists. **1835** A. STEEDMAN *Wanderings S. Afr.* II. i. 7 Others [*sc.* jackals] had been destroyed by the *Læmer-vanger*, or bearded vulture. **1846** J. C. BROWN tr. *Arbousset & Daumas's Narr. Tour N.-E. of Cape Good Hope* xxi. 220 The English of the Cape call it the *golden eagle*.., and the Dutch farmers, *lamvanger*, or *lamb seizer*, because it is accustomed to seize, and carry off to its aerie, a lamb or kid. **1920** F. C. CORNELL *Glamour of Prospecting* xii. 205, I had wasted a shot on a splendid *lammer-vanger*, a fine specimen of an eagle. **1944** V. POHL *Adventures Boer Family* xiii. 79 The *lammervanger* is one of the wariest, shyest and most keen-eyed of all birds. **1959** *Cape Times* 20 June 2/3 Mr. Sonny Waks..saw an eagle—commonly known as a *lammer-vanger*—catching one of his young lambs. **1970** *Daily News* (Durban) 4 June 21 A 13-year-old White youth captured a long taloned golden eagle (lammer-vanger) with his bare hands.

†**lammet**. *Obs.*[−1] [Cf. LAM *sb.*[1]] A kind of fishing-net.

1558 *Act 1 Eliz.* c. 17 §1 No Person..with..Weblister, Seur, Lammet, or with any Device or Engine..shall take..Spawn or Fry of Eels, Salmon, Pike or Pikerel.

lammie, lammy ('læmɪ). Also **lamby**. [Perh. a particular use of *lammie*, LAMBIE.] A thick quilted woollen over-garment worn by sailors in cold weather. Also ***lammy coat, suit***.

1886 *Gentl. Mag.* Oct. 390 The look-out, who, wrapped in his lammy suit, was stationed in the bows. **1903** G. S. BOWLES *Stretch off Land* 268 The 'lammy-suit' known aboard Torpedo-Boats and Destroyers. **1915** KIPLING *Fringes of Fleet* 64, I loathe destroyers,..the smell of the wet 'lammies' and damp wardroom cushions. **1916** 'TAFFRAIL' *Pincher Martin* xi. 191 He undid the toggles of his lammy coat, and gave the muffler another turn round his neck. **1920** *Blackw. Mag.* Jan. 7/2 North Sea fishermen, fully accoutred in their thick 'lamby' suits. **1931** 'TAFFRAIL' *Endless Story* xxiii. 357, I arrayed myself in a tolerably dry 'lammy coat'. **1948** PARTRIDGE *Dict. Forces' Slang* 108 *Lammies*, hooded coats of lamb's wool worn by officers and men in severe weather. Also known as 'duffle coats'.

lammie, -y, variants of LAMBIE.

lammister: see LAM *v.*

lamnoid ('læmnɔɪd), *a.* and *sb. Zool.* [f. mod.L. *Lamna* (a genus of sharks; a. Gr. λάμνα some kind of fish of prey) + -OID.] **A.** *adj.* Resembling a mackerel-shark of the genus *Lamna*.

1898 D. S. JORDAN *Descr. Species of Fish from Japan* title-page, The Type of a Distinct Family of Lamnoid Sharks. *Ibid.* 199 A remarkably distinct new genus of lamnoid affinities. **1925** —— *Fishes* (rev. ed.) xiv. 190 The most active and most ferocious of the sharks, as well as the largest and some of the most sluggish, belong to a group of families known collectively as Lamnoid, because of a general resemblance to the mackerel-shark or *Lamna*.

B. *sb.* One of the *Lamnidæ*.

In some recent Dicts.

Lamoot, Lamout, varr. LAMUT.

lamour, variant of LAMBER[1] *Obs.*, amber.

lamp (læmp), *sb.*[1] Forms: 2–7 lampe, 3–6 laumpe, (4 lompe, 5 lawmp(e), 4– lamp. [ad. F. *lampe* (recorded from 12th c.) = Pr. and It. *lampa*, ad. L. *lampas*, Gr. λαμπάς, f. λάμπειν to shine.]

1. a. A vessel containing oil, which is burnt at a wick, for the purpose of illumination. Now also a vessel of glass or some similar material, enclosing the source of illumination, whether a

candle, oil, gas-jet, or incandescent wire. Often preceded by some defining word, as *arc*, *Argand*, *Davy*, *electric*, *gas*, *spirit*, *sun*, *Vesta lamp*.

c **1200** *Vices & Virtues* 33 Hit wile on lampe bernen brihte. c **1230** *Hali Meid.* 45 As is wiðute lihte oile in a laumpe. **13..** *K. Alis.* 5253 Tofore the kyng honge..two thousande laumpes of gold. **1393** LANGL. *P. Pl.* C. II. 186 Hit is as lewede as a lamp þat no lyght ys ynne. c **1449** PECOCK *Repr.* II. xviii. 258 A laumpe hangith bifore Seint Kateryn. **1477** EARL RIVERS (Caxton) *Dictes* 70, I haue putte more oille in my lampe to studie by. **1526** *Pilgr. Perf.* (W. de W. 1531) 128 b, Apperynge to hym..in yͤ similitude of the good aungell, with great lyghtes and lampes. **1584** R. SCOT *Discov. Witchcr.* XIV. i. (1886) 295 Also their lamps,.. alembicks, viols, croslets, cucurbits, [etc.]. **1605** SHAKS. *Macb.* II. iv. 7 Darke Night strangles the trauailing Lampe. **1685** *Lond. Gaz.* No. 2092/4 A Patent..for enlightening the Streets, by a new sort of Lantern with Lamps. **1756–7** tr. *Keysler's Trav.* (1760) III. 186 Seven golden lamps are continually burning before the image. **1806** A. DUNCAN *Nelson's Funeral* 13 Lamps, having two candles in each. **1829** *Nat. Philos., Heat* ix. 47 (U.K.S.) A quantity of the liquid..was..rapidly distilled into the globe, by the heat of an Argand lamp. **1850** L. HUNT *Autobiog.* III. 251 Their [actors'] only one object in life is to keep themselves, as they phrase it, 'before the lamps'; that is to say, in the eyes of the audience, and in the receipt of personal applause. c **1865** LETHEBY in *Circ. Sci.* I. 113/1 Among the disadvantages of the Vesta lamp, are its liability to smoke, and its disagreeable smell. **1892** *Electrical Engineer* 16 Sept. 283/1 Forked terminals fixed on the ends of the connecting wires serve to complete the circuit between lamp and battery.

b. (Said of a literary composition). ***to smell of*** (or †***taste***) ***the lamp***: to be the manifest product of nocturnal or laborious study.

1579 NORTH *Plutarch, Demosthenes* (1595) 889 Pytheas.. taunting him on a time, tolde him, his reasons smelled of the lampe. Yea, replied Demosthenes sharply againe: so is there great difference, Pytheas, betwixt thy labor and myne by lampelight. **1615** in *Breton's Charac. Essaies* (Grosart) 4/1 He that shall read thy characters..must say they are well written. They taste the lampe. **1732** BERKELEY *Alciphr.* v. §20 That dry..pedantic..style, which smells of the lamp and college. **1768** CHESTERF. *Lett.* 268 But they [Familiar Letters] should seem easy and natural, and not smell of the lamp. **1887** SAINTSBURY *Elizabethan Lit.* iv. 91 Hardly any poet smells of the lamp less disagreeably than Spenser.

c. Used for *torch*; (in quots. 1722 and 1848–9 with allusion, after Plato *Legg.* 776 B and Lucret. II. 79, to the Grecian torch-race: see LAMPADEDROMY).

1382 WYCLIF *Song Sol.* viii. 6 The laumpis of it the laumpes of fir, and of flaumes. **1610** SHAKS. *Temp.* IV. i. 23 Therefore take heede, As Hymens Lamps shall light you. **1722** WOLLASTON *Relig. Nat.* vi. 136 Or death extinguishes him and his title together, and he delivers the lamp to his next man. **1848–9** KINGSLEY *Poems, World's Age* ii, Still the race of Hero-spirits Pass the lamp from hand to hand.

d. = *safety-lamp*.

1839 URE *Dict. Arts, Lamp of Davy.* **1883** in GRESLEY *Gloss. Coal Mining.*

2. *transf.* **a.** *sing.* One of the heavenly bodies, the sun, moon, a star or meteor; also, a flash (of lightning). *pl.* The stars or heavenly bodies in general. Also ***lamp(s of the night, the world.***

1423 JAS. I, *Kingis Q.* lxxii, Esperus his lampis gan to light. **15..** in *Dunbar's Poems* (1893) 329 The Sterne of glory is rissyn ws to gyd,..Abone Phebus, the radius lamp divrn. **1591** HARINGTON *Orl. Fur.* IX. lxix, Straight like a lampe of lightning out it flies. **1601** HOLLAND *Pliny* I. 17 Those lampes or torches make long traines. **1613** PURCHAS *Pilgrimage* (1614) 13 It is high time for me to descend from these measures of time; the lampes of the world. **1665** SIR T. HERBERT *Trav.* (1677) 5 When they see Sun, we see the Lamps of night. **1792** WOLCOT (P. Pindar) *Wks.* III. 198 Mild and placid as the light Shed by the Worm, the lamp of dewy night. **1813** SCOTT *Trierm.* III. ii, Thus as he lay the lamp of night Was quivering on his armour bright. **1821** SHELLEY *Prometh. Unb.* I. i. 362 Yon clear lamps that measure and divide the weary years. **1830** HOGG in *Blackw. Mag.* XXVII. 767 Lamps of glory begemm'd the sky.

b. *pl.* The eyes (formerly *poet.*; now *slang*).

1590 SHAKS. *Com. Err.* V. i. 315 My wasting lampes some fading glimmer left. **1647** FANSHAWE *Faithf. Sheph.* (1676) 77 Behold that proud one on me turn Her sparkling lamps. **1812** J. H. VAUX *Flash Dict., Lamps*, the eyes; to have *queer lamps*, is to have sore or weak eyes. **1899** C. ROOK *Hooligan Nights* iv. 63 Ole ruby boko put 'is lamps over me, wiv no error, an' he says, 'Why you're the youngster as come in 'ere afore.' **1901** 'H. MCHUGH' *John Henry* 90 The old hen with the languishing lamps was still on my trail. **1928** *Daily Express* 29 Aug. 7/4 Woman in an assault case at Weymouth: I said I would fill her lamps for her. Clerk: What does that mean? Woman: Blacken her eyes. **1938** F. D. SHARPE *Sharpe of Flying Squad* 331 He had his lamps on the copper.

3. *fig.* A source or centre of light, spiritual or intellectual. Also, ***lamp of beauty, joy, life***, etc.

'Seven lamps' are freq. mentioned in Biblical passages either as part of the Temple furniture or in symbolic references (e.g. Ex. xxv. 37, Zech. iv. 2, Rev. iv. 5); hence allusive uses as in quots. 1582, 1849.

1500–20 DUNBAR *Poems* lxxvii. 2 Blyth Aberdein,..The lamp of bewtie, bountie, and blythnes. *Ibid.* lxxxvi. 13 O lamp lemand befoir the trone devyne!..O mater Jhesu, salue Maria! **1567** *Gude & Godlie Ball.* (S.T.S.) 162 Go, hart, vnto the lampe of lycht,..Go, hart, vnto thy Sauiour. **1576** FLEMING *Panopl. Ep.* 434 *note*, Cambridge and Oxenford the twoe lampes of England, for learning, knowledge, etc. **1582** BENTLEY (*title*) The Monument of Matrons; conteining seven severall Lamps of Virginity. a **1626** BACON *New Atl.* (1650) 33 We have Three that take care..to Direct New Experiments, of a Higher Light,.. These we call Lamps. **1633** BP. HALL *Medit. & Vows* (1851) 78 Blessed be God, that hath set up so many clear lamps in his Church. **1635** R. BOLTON *Comf. Affl. Consc.* xviii. (ed. 2) 331 Hold out a lamp of goodly profession to the eye of the world. **1717** L. HOWEL *Desiderius* (ed. 3) 86 This Lamp is called by the Name of Good Conscience. **1719** DE FOE *Crusoe* I. xiv. (1840) 249 The great lamp of instruction, the Spirit of God. **1742** YOUNG *Nt. Th.* III. 2 Reason, that heav'nlighted lamp in man. **1780** COWPER *Table T.* 556 Ages elapsed ere Homer's lamp appeared. **1814** SCOTT *Ld. of Isles* IV. xi, Quench'd is his lamp of varied lore. **1828** CARLYLE *Misc.* (1857) I. 218 Quesnay's lamp..kindled the lamp of Adam Smith. **1849** RUSKIN (*title*) The Seven Lamps of Architecture. **1878** J. P. HOPPS *Jesus* ii. 11 Whoever despaired of the world, he, at least, kept the lamp of hope burning brightly in his soul.

4. *attrib.* and *Comb.*: **a.** simple attributive, as ***lamp accident***, † ***basin, -bracket, -bulb, -burner, -chimney, -cotton, -fête, -fire, -flame, -glass, -globe, -glow, -house***, †***-micrometer, -room, -scissors, -sconce, -shade, -shine, -soot, -stand, -stead, -stove, -student, -worm.***

1895 *Daily News* 17 Oct. 6/6 Switzerland appears to share with Germany practical immunity from *lamp accidents. **1531** *MS. Acc. St. John's Hosp., Canterb.*, Paid for mendyng of the *lamp basyn viijd. **1552** *Inv.* in *Archæol. Cant.* VIII. 101 Item an old lampe-bason of laten. **1875** KNIGHT *Dict. Mech.*, **Lamp-bracket.* **1911** *Chambers's Jrnl.* Jan. 78/1 If a thin gold film is deposited on the lower half of the *lamp-bulb. **1851** *Illustr. Catal. Gt. Exhib.* 1106 *Lamp-burners in different numbers. **1847** *Rep. Comm. Patents 1846* (U.S.) 276, I also claim the *lamp chimney, formed of glass, with two contractions. **1870** A. S. STEPHENS *Married in Haste* xv. 85 She unscrewed the lamp-chimney..and polished off a stain of black smoke. **1906** JOYCE *Let.* 6 Nov. (1966) II. 186 A lamp chimney here costs one lira! **1782** HERSCHEL in *Phil. Trans.* LXXII. 167 The wick of the flame consists only of a single very thin *lamp-cotton thread. **1899** WATTS-DUNTON *Aylwin* (1900) 82/2 It is one of the great *lamp-fêtes of Sais. **1707** *Curios. in Husb. & Gard.* 344 Make a *Lamp Fire under it. **1904** *Westm. Gaz.* 13 Aug. 6/2 Not a single *lamp-flame stirs or quivers. **1920** J. MASEFIELD *Enslaved* 52 The lamp-flame purred from want of oil. **1521** *MS. Acc. St. John's Hosp., Canterb.*, Paied for a *lampe glasse jd. **1914** D. H. LAWRENCE *Widowing of Mrs. Holroyd* I. i. 7 She has been lighting the lamp and holds the lamp-glass. **1974** G. JENKINS *Bridge of Magpies* vii. 99 The condensation dripped from the lamp-glass. **1922** JOYCE *Ulysses* 423 Their tunics bloodbright in a *lampglow. **1849** F. B. HEAD *Stokers & Pokers* vii. 63 The driver..then takes his lamps to the *lamp-house to be cleaned and trimmed by workmen solely employed to do so. **1782** HERSCHEL in *Phil. Trans.* LXXII. 165 The instrument I am going to describe, which I call a *Lamp-Micrometer, is free from all these defects. **1895** *Daily News* 25 Sept. 7/2 The boatswain was in charge of the *lamp-room, but did not trim the lamp. **1766** AMORY *J. Buncle* (1825) II. 82 The golden *lamp-sconce of seven golden candlesticks. **1913** C. MACKENZIE *Sinister St.* II. xviii. 449 The uneasy warmth of the overarching trees would draw them very close, while hushed endearments took them slowly into *lamp-shine. **1938** W. DE LA MARE *Memory* 90 He shook his rascal head, Its curls by the lamp-shine gilt. **1853** KANE *Grinnell Exp.* xxxix. (1856) 355 Our clothing..was black with *lamp-soot. **1893** *Funk's Stand. Dict.*, *Lamp-stand. **1909** H. G. WELLS *Tono-Bungay* II. iv. 235, I found her in our drawing-room, standing beside the tall lamp-stand that half filled the bay. **1961** NEW ENG. BIBLE *Hebr.* ix. 2 For a tent was prepared—the first tent—in which was the lamp-stand, and the table with the bread of the Presence. **1965** M. SPARK *Mandelbaum Gate* vii. 223 He then unscrewed the base of the mosaic lampstand. **1897** MICKLETHWAITE *Ornaments Rubric* 30 We find a *lamp-stead in a wall in the form of a niche. **1875** KNIGHT *Dict. Mech.*, **Lamp-stove.* **1681** W. ROBERTSON *Phraseol. Gen.* (1693) 798 *Lamp-students, that study by the lamp, or candle. **1917** HARDY *Moments of Vision* 61 As delicate as *lamp-worm's lucency.

b. objective, as ***lamp-bearer, -bearing, -cleaner, -maker, -trimmer***, †***-waster***; ***lamp-lighting*** adj. and sb. **lamp-locking** (see quots.).

1849 JAMES *Woodman* xiv, You must be my *lamp-bearer. **1824** J. SYMMONS *Æschylus' Agam.* 31 Such is the course of the *lamp-bearing games. **1898** *Daily News* 17 Nov. 5/4 He gossiped with the *lamp-cleaner and the porter. **1823** BYRON *Juan* XI. xxvi, The French were not yet a *lamp-lighting nation. **1872** 'MARK TWAIN' *Innoc. Abr.* xii. 82 We went out to a restaurant, just after lamp-lighting. **1894** *Gloss. Terms Evidence R. Comm. Labour* 51/2 in *Parl. Papers 1893–4* (C. 7063) XXXVIII. 411 **Lamp-locking station*, the place in a mine where the safety-lamps of all the miners are examined and locked by an official. **1905** *Westm. Gaz.* 12 July 7/1, I was in the lamp-locking cabin, which is a short distance from the bottom of the shaft. **1598** FLORIO, *Lamparo*, a *lampe-maker. **1875** *Carpentry & Join.* 100 A disc of talc, to be had of any lampmaker, will answer even better than tin. **1882** *Navy List* July 466 *Lamptrimmer.. in 1st Class Ships. **1641** MARMION *Antiquary* III. i. F 3 b, Head-scratchers, thumb-biters, *lamp-wasters.

c. instrumental, as ***lamp-decked, -heated, -lighted***, †***-lined, -lit, -warmed*** adjs. Also ***lamp-like*** adj.

1826 MILMAN *A. Boleyn* (1827) 33 Around the *lamp-deck'd altar high and dim. **1875** *Carpentry & Join.* 95 We will now describe a better class of *lamp-heated case. **1844** DICKENS *Mart. Chuz.* v, The now *lamp-lighted streets. **1674** PETTY *Disc. Dupl. Proportion* 95 Let there be a *Lamplike Vessel of common Aquavitæ. **1819** SHELLEY *Cyclops* 615 Fire will burn his lamp-like eyes. **1913** D. H. LAWRENCE *Love Poems* 17 But the Moon..unfurled Her white, her lamp-like shape. **1650** FULLER *Pisgah* II. viii. 174 Gedeons men by order from him brake their *lamp-lined pitchers. **1835** *Court Mag.* VI. 82 In *lamplit vistas cold and grey, The streets deserted stretch away. **1847** TENNYSON *Princess* IV. 8 No bigger than a glow-worm shone the tent Lamp-lit from the inner. **1852** R. S. SURTEES *Sponge's Sp. Tour* (1893) 286 Sundry *lamp-warmed dishes of savoury grills.

5. Special comb.: †**lamp-beam**, ? a chandelier; **lamp-cap**, the base of an electric light bulb or lamp into which are sealed the terminals and the neck of the glass globe; **lamp-fish** (see quot.); **lamp-fly**, ? a glow-worm; **lamp-furnace**, a furnace in which a lamp was used as the means of heating; **lamp-hole**, a hole or opening to receive a lamp; in sewers, a hole to admit of the passage of a lamp; **lamp-house**, the part of a photographic enlarger or projector which houses the light-source; †**lamp-iron**, a projecting iron rod from which a lamp was suspended; in the French Revolution sometimes used as a gallows; **lamp-jack** *U.S.* (see quot.); **lamp-man**, (*a*) a manufacturer of or dealer in lamps; (*b*) one who has charge of or tends lamps; **lamp-mat**, a mat on which a table-lamp is placed; **lamp-moss**, moss used as material for lamp-wicks; **lamp-shell**, a brachiopod, esp. one of the genus *Terebratula* or family *Terebratulidæ*; **lamp-socket**, = LAMP-HOLDER; **lamp-standard**, a post or other strong support for a lamp; **lamp-wick**, (*a*) the wick of a lamp; (*b*) the labiate plant *Phlomis Lychnites*; **lamp-worker** (see quot. 1962).

1565 GOLDING *Ovid's Met.* XII. (1567) 151 b, He ran And pulled downe a *Lampbeame [L. *funale*] full of lyghtes. **1899** W. P. MAYCOCK *Electr. Wiring* iii. 324 The *lamp caps are fitted with a central plunger contact. **1971** L. E. VRENKEN in W. Elenbaas *Fluorescent Lamps* (ed. 2) v. 60 To connect a lamp to the electrical circuit a number of different lamp caps have been designed. **1883** C. F. HOLDER in *Harper's Mag.* Jan. 186/1 The *Scopelus resplendens*..is called the brilliant *lamp-fish..from the fact that it has upon its head at night a glowing light. **1840** BROWNING *Sordello* III. 105 Thorn-rows Alive with *lamp-flies. **1641** FRENCH *Distill.* v. (1651) 153 There is another sort of *Lamp furnaces with three candles. **1669** WORLIDGE *Syst. Agric.* (1681) 195 Therefore may you with much facility hatch three or four dozen of Eggs in a Lamp-furnace made of a few Boards, only by the heat of a Candle or Lamp. **1770** HEWSON in *Phil. Trans.* LX. 385, I therefore prepared a lamp-furnace with a small vessel of water upon it. **1884** *Health Exhib. Catal.* 55/2 Ventilator with Dirt Boxes and *Lamphole Cover combined. **1890** W. J. GORDON *Foundry* 151 The second-class passengers..drenched by the rain pouring through the lamp-hole! **1912** J. F. HODGES *Opening & Operating Motion Pict. Theatre* 49 (*caption*) *Lamp house. **1916** R. E. WELSH *A-B-C of Motion Pict.* 17 In the first place, there is a 'lamp-house', a small cabinet which contains the light. **1933** *Discovery* Mar. 90/1 The illuminant itself [is] enclosed in a lamp house which is glazed with a filter of the same type as that used in the camera. **1971** L. B. HAPPÉ *Basic Motion Pict. Technol.* x. 306 A xenon arc lamp can be substituted for a carbon arc in an existing lamphouse optical system but it is preferable to have a complete lamphouse designed around the new source. **1790** BURKE *Fr. Rev.* Wks. V. 171 Though the latter should act with the libel and the *lamp-iron. **1831** *Soc. Life Eng. & Fr.* 411 The lamp-iron yet remains at the corner of the Place de Greve, to which Foulon..was suspended in July 1790. **1849** MISS WARNER *Wide wide World* i, As he hooked his ladder on the lamp-irons, ran up and lit the lamp. **1884** KNIGHT *Dict. Mech.* Suppl., **Lamp jack* (Railway), a hood over a lamp chimney on the roof of a car. **1842** *Spirit of Times* 15 Oct. 389/2 (Weingarten), Also to Miss Waterman..[a diploma] for various specimens of her exquisite work of *lamp mats. **1856** *Trans. Mich. Agric. Soc.* VII. 700 Some beautiful lamp-mats and other worsted and crochet work. **1873** *Young Englishwoman* June 302/1 Embroidered border for lamp-mat. **1883** 'MARK TWAIN' *Life on Mississippi* xxxviii. 400 Lamp..standing on a gridiron, so to speak, made of high-colored yarns, by the young ladies of the house, and called a lamp-mat. **1704** *Lond. Gaz.* No. 4060/6 *Lamp-men, Ironmongers, Brasiers. **1797** MRS. A. M. BENNETT *Beggar Girl* (1813) V. 240 Fiddlers, tailors, lampmen, and all sorts of trades. **1876** F. S. WILLIAMS *Midl. Railw.* 655 The driver..now takes his lamps to the lamphouse to be cleaned and trimmed by the lamp-men. **1892** *Daily News* 3 Mar. 5/6 The lamp man inside..hands out the check and a lamp to collier No. 46. **1865** LUBBOCK *Preh. Times* 401 The women have lamps and stone-kettles, *lamp-moss [etc.]. **1854** WOODWARD *Mollusca* I. 209 The Brachiopoda are bivalve shell-fish... Their forms are symmetrical, and so commonly resemble antique lamps that they were called *lampades* or '*lamp-shells' by the old naturalists. **1876** HUXLEY *Amer. Addresses* ii. (1877) 36 One of the cretaceous lamp-shells (*Terebratula*). **1908** *Westm. Gaz.* 27 Oct. 6/1 A small transformer can be placed in the *lamp-socket. **1968** *Lighting Equipment News* Mar. 23/1 The adaptor fits into the existing lamp socket. **1908** *Daily Chron.* 5 Aug. 3/5 A motor fire engine..collided with a *lamp standard. **1967** *Lighting Equipment News* Jan. 26/3 The complete lamps and lamp standard are constructed on zinc coated sheet metal and painted. **1845** C. M. KIRKLAND *Western Clearings* 135 Miss Teeny had picked up the *lamp-wick with a pin several times. **1863** BERKELEY *Brit. Mosses* ix. 39 One species [of moss] affords a substitute for lampwicks to the Esquimaux. **1665** HOOKE *Micrographia* 209 The blowing of Glass into exceeding thin shells, and then breaking them into scales, which any *lamp-worker will presently do. **1962** *Gloss. Terms Glass Industry (B.S.I.)* 46 *Lamp worker*, a worker who forms glassware from tubing or rod by heating in an oxy-gas or air-gas flame at a work bench. **1970** *Canad. Antiques Collector* Apr. 26/2 He may.. watch a lampworker forming ornaments from glass softened over a gas torch.

†**lamp**, *sb.*² *Obs. rare*⁻¹. [? for **lampne*, ad. L. *lāmina* (cf. LAME *sb.*¹).] ? A plate.

c **1386** CHAUCER *Can. Yeom. Prol. & T.* 211 And in an erthen potte how put is al..And wel y-covered with a lampe [*v.r.* lamp, laumpe] of glas.

lamp (læmp), *v.*¹ [f. LAMP *sb.*¹]

1. *intr.* To shine. Also *fig.*

1609 DANIEL *Civ. Wars* VIII. lxiv, A cheerliness did with her hopes arise That lamped cleerer then it did before. **1820** L. HUNT *Indicator* No. 22 (1822) I. 175 An evil fire out of their eyes came lamping. **1827–35** WILLIS *Scholar of Thebet Ben Khorat* 37 White-brow'd Vesta, lamping on her path

Lonely and planet-calm. **1875** BROWNING *Aristoph. Apol.* 5345 Fire—with smoke—All night went lamping on!

2. *trans.* To supply with lamps.

?*c* **1600** *Distracted Emp.* I. i. in Bullen *O. Pl.* III. 172 To play with Luna or newe lampe the starres. **1602** MARSTON *Antonio's Rev.* III. i. Wks. 1856 I. 105 Set tapers to the toumbe, and lampe the church. **1889** G. FINDLAY *Eng. Railway* 128 Men engaged at out stations in cleaning, lamping, and examining carriages.

3. *transf.* To light as with a lamp.

1808 J. BARLOW *Columb.* IX. 5 Like one surrounding sky Lamp'd with reverberant fires. **1839** BAILEY *Festus* xxxi. (1852) 515 Falling stars.. Lamping the red horizon fitfully. **1868** BROWNING *Ring & Bk.* VI. 1173 Scattered lights Lamping the rush and roll of the abyss.

fig. **1890** E. GOSSE in *Athenæum* 10 May 605/2 A star to lamp Man's heart to heaven.

4. *slang* (orig. *U.S.*). To see, look at, recognize, watch. Cf. LAMP *sb.*[1] 2 b.

1916 H. L. WILSON *Somewhere in Red Gap* v. 198 Stella.. was standing on the centre table by now, so she could lamp herself in the glass over the mantel. **1921** *Adventure* (U.S.) 18 July 42/2 But she lamps me auburn mug all to oncet an' draws back sudden, like I was a rattler. **1923** L. J. VANCE *Baroque* viii. 50 Nobody even lamped its number. **1928** E. WALLACE *Again Sanders* x. 259 These niggers have lamped the gats. **1938** G. GREENE *Brighton Rock* III. ii. 113 Afraid we'd lamp you if you didn't change your mug? *Ibid.* v. i. 190 Come an' lamp the bathing belles. **1953** K. TENNANT *Joyful Condemned* xi. 96 One of the fellows from Central has only to lamp you coming in here, and we all go up. **1962** R. COOK *Crust on its Uppers* ii. 34 We were dying to have a butchers and lamp all the new bird. **1969** R. BUSBY *Robbery Blue* iii. 26 I'd like to know how the coppers got on to us. They couldn't have lamped us on the road.

Hence **lamped** *ppl. a.*

1822 B. W. PROCTER *Let. of Boccaccio* iv, Some lampèd feast.

lamp (læmp), *v.*[2] *Sc.* [? An onomatopœic formation suggested by LIMP *v.* Cf. LAMPER *v.*] *intr.* 'To go quickly by taking long steps' (Jam.).

a **1605** MONTGOMERIE *Misc. Poems* xli. 39 The stoned steed stampis Throu curage and crampis, Syn on the land lampis. **1819** W. TENNANT *Papistry Storm'd* (1827) 3 Lampin' alang in joyous glee Frae jaw to jaw athort the sea. **1820** SCOTT *Monastery* xxxiii, It was all her father's own fault, that let her run lamping about the country, riding on bare-backed nags. **1884** T. SPEEDY *Sport* xvi. 278 Those who.. shoot down the hares as they come unsuspectingly 'lamping' forward.

lampad ('læmpæd). *poet. rare.* [ad. Gr. λαμπαδ-, λαμπάς, LAMP *sb.*[1]] In *pl.*, the seven 'lamps of fire' burning before the throne of God (Rev. iv. 5).

1796 COLERIDGE *Ode Departing Year* v. 76 Till wheeling round the throne the Lampads seven, (The mystic Words of Heaven) Permissive signal make. **1862** TRENCH *Poems* 132 Now I know To what was likened the large utterance sent By Him who mid the golden lampads went.

lampadary ('læmpədərɪ). [ad. L. *lampadārius*, Byzantine Gr. λαμπαδάριος, f. λαμπάς (see LAMP *sb.*[1]); in sense 2 as if ad. L. **lampadārium*. Cf. F. *lampadaire*.]

1. *Hist.* An officer in the church of Constantinople, whose duty it was to provide for the lighting of the church, and to bear a taper before the emperor and the patriarch in processions.

1727–41 in CHAMBERS *Cycl.* **1731** in BAILEY vol. II.

2. A cluster of lamps; a candelabrum. *rare.*

1885 *Pall Mall G.* 1 June 7/1 At nightfall thirty-two lampadaries were lighted, the lamps in the Champs Elysées and the streets being covered with crape.

lampadedromy (ˌlæmpə'dɛdrəmɪ). *Gr. Antiq.* [ad. Gr. λαμπαδηδρομία, f. λαμπαδ-, λαμπάς torch + -δρομία running.] A torch-race; a race (on foot or horseback) in which a lighted torch was passed from hand to hand.

1848 CRAIG has the incorrect form *Lampadrome.* So in many later Dicts. **1889** *Century Dict.*, *Lampadedromy.*

lampadephore ('læmpədiːfɔə(r)). *Gr. Antiq.* [ad. Gr. λαμπαδηφόρος, f. λαμπαδ-, λαμπάς torch + φορ-, φερ-, stem of φέρειν to bear.] A torch-bearer; *spec.* a competitor in a torch-race.

‖**lampadephoria, lampadophoria** (ˌlæmp ədiː-, ˌlæmpədəʊ'fɒrɪə). *Gr. Antiq.* [a. Gr. λαμπαδηφορία, λαμπαδοφοία, f. as prec.] = LAMPADEDROMY.

1848 CRAIG, *Lampadephoria.* **1850** LEITCH tr. *C. O. Müller's Anc. Art* §423 (ed. 2) 608 On a vase found at Kertsch.. the beginning of a lampadophoria.

lampadist ('læmpədɪst). *Gr. Antiq.* [ad. Gr. λαμπαδιστής, agent-n. f. λαμπαδίζειν to run a torch-race, λαμπαδ-, λαμπάς torch, LAMP.] A competitor in a torch-race.

1838 *Fraser's Mag.* XVIII. 512 As amid the race of torches one Succeeds another Lampadist in the course. **1848** in CRAIG; and in later Dicts.

lampadite ('læmpədaɪt). *Min.* [Named by Huot in 1841, after Prof. W. A. *Lampadius*, who first described it: see -ITE.] A cupriferous variety of wad.

1850 DANA *Min.* 461 Wad, Earthy cobalt,.. Lampadite. **1892** *Ibid.* 258 Lampadite is found at Schlackenwald.

lampadomancy ('læmpədəmænsɪ). [ad. med.L. **lampadomantīa*, f. Gr. λαμπαδ-, λαμπάς LAMP *sb.*[1] + μαντεία divination.] (See quots.)

1652 GAULE *Magastrom.* xix. 166 Lampadomancy, [divining] by candles and lamps. **1888** *Syd. Soc. Lex.*, *Lampadomancy*, a mode of divination by the observation of substances burned in a lamp.

lampas ('læmpəs), *sb.*[1] Forms: 6 lampysse, 6–7 lampasse, 7 *vulg.* lamprey(e)s, 8 lampars, lampra(y)s, lampus, 8–9 lampers, 6– lampas. [a. F. *lampas* (in 16th c. also *lampast*), in 12–15th c. *gen.*, a disease producing intense thirst (e.g. attributed to 'Dives' in hell), later only a disease of horses.

The origin is obscure. The primary sense may be 'inside of the mouth'; this is not proved by the existence of the phrase *humecter le lampas* 'to wet one's whistle', but cf. *lampassé* (Her.) 'langued' (see LAMPASSING); some Fr. dialect glossaries, also, have the word with the sense 'uvula'. Florio has It. *lampasco* as the name of the disease, and Littré cites a Fr. dial. form *empas*, which is due to mistake of the initial *l* for the article.]

A disease incident to horses, consisting in a swelling of the fleshy lining of the roof of the mouth behind the front teeth.

1523 FITZHERB. *Husb.* §81 In the mouthe is the lampas, & is a thycke skyn full of bloude, hangynge ouer his tethe aboue, that he may not eate. **1547** SALESBURY *Welsh Dict.* *Mintag*, Lampysse. **1596** SHAKS. *Tam. Shr.* III. ii. 52 His horse.. troubled with the Lampasse. **1607** TOPSELL *Four-f. Beasts* (1658) 282 The Lampass, called of the Italians, *Lampascus*, proceedeth of the abundance of bloud. **1702** *Lond. Gaz.* No. 3868/4 A Strawberry Gelding with a bald Face,.. newly burnt of the Lampus. **1741** *Compl. Fam.-Piece* III. 446 Let a Smith burn it down with a hot Iron; this is a compleat Cure for the Lampars. **1772** NUGENT tr. *Hist. Fr. Gerund* II. 418 My girl thy cuzzen Isidora first of all had the lamprays or soare mouth, then she had the small-pox. **1828** *Sporting Mag.* XXIII. 127 The Lampas is.. a swelling .. of some of the lowermost ridges or bars of the palate. **1884** *Bradford Observer* 15 May, He mentioned.. that the horse did not eat well, and said it was suffering from 'lampas'.

lampas ('læmpəs), *sb.*[2] Also 4 lawmpas, 6 lampors. [The combination *lampas douck* (Du. *doek* cloth) in the second quot. suggests that the word may be adopted from Du.; the recorded form in MDu. and early mod.Du. is *lampers* (cf. the Eng. form *lampors*); mod.Du. has *lamfer* (the MDu. *lamfeter*, denoting some appurtenance of a hawk, is identified with this by Verwijs and Verdam, but with doubtful correctness). The etymology is quite obscure; derivation from Gr. λαμπρός, shining, was suggested in the 16th c. In sense 2 the Eng. word is a. F. *lampas*, recorded only from the 18th c., and possibly a different word.]

†**1.** A kind of glossy crape. *Obs.*

1390 *Test. Ebor.* (Surtees) I. 130 Half a pes of lawmpas.. A volet of lawmpas neu. *a* **1548** HALL *Chron., Hen. VIII* (1809) 519 Ye orrelettes were of rolles wrethed on Lampas douck holow so that the Golde shewed thorow the Lampas douck. **1559** *Letter* (N.), Before the stoole of estate satt another mayde, all clothyd in white, and her face coveryd with white lampors.

2. A kind of flowered silk, originally imported from China.

1851 *Illustr. Catal. Gt. Exhib.* 1262 Piece of figured lampas, in Algerian silk, crop of 1850, manufactured at Lyons. **1889** *Pall Mall G.* 17 Apr. 2/1 The new-made Countess, who is in white lampas, with spotless ermine and yellow for relief. **1894** *Daily News* 11 Apr. 3/1 The over-dress is in rich lampas of the same period.

†**'lampas,** *v. Obs. rare*[−1]. [f. LAMPAS *sb.*[1]] *trans.* To cure a horse of the lampas.

1536 *MS. Acc. St. John's Hosp., Canterb.*, Payd for lampasyng off owre mare *jd.*

†**'lampassing,** *vbl. sb. Obs. rare*[−1]. *Her.* [f. F. *lampassé* langued, f. *lampas*: see LAMPAS *sb.*[1]] The manner in which an animal is langued.

1586 FERNE *Blaz. Gentrie* 306 The difference of the cullors, in their attyring arming lampassing or membring, will so differ and make diuers the sayde armes.

†**'lampate.** *Chem. Obs.* [f. LAMP-IC + -ATE.] A salt of 'lampic' acid; an aldehydate.

1819 J. G. CHILDREN *Chem. Anal.* 282 Lampate of magnesia. **1839** URE *Dict. Arts* s.v.

†**lampatram.** *Obs. rare*[−1].

a **1529** SKELTON *E. Rummyng* 506 Quake, quake, sayd the duck In that lampatrams lap.

lamp-black ('læmpˌblæk, ˌlæmp'blæk). Also 7–8 (and 9 *dial.*) lam-black. A pigment consisting of almost pure carbon in a state of fine division; made by collecting the soot produced by burning oil or (now usually) gas. Also *attrib.*, as in *lamp-black-ink*; **lamp-black furnace**, an apparatus for making lamp-black.

1598 HAYDOCKE tr. *Lomazzo* III. iv. 99 The shels of almondes burnt, ball blacke, Lampe-blacke. **1612** PEACHAM *Gent. Exerc.* I. 76 The making of ordinary lamp blacke. Take a torch or linke, and hold it vnder the bottome of a latten basen, and as it groweth to be furd and blacke within, strike it with a feather into some shell or other, and grind it with gumme water. **1723** J. SMITH *Art Paint. in Oyl* (ed. 5) 29 *Lam-black*, a Colour of so greasy a nature. **1772** VAN HAAKE in *Abridg. Specif. Ship Building* (1862) 23 [To the deposit on the interior of a vessel held over the cylinder in which the mineral is heated so as to receive the smoke] I give the name of lamp black. **1799** G. SMITH *Laboratory* II. 37 Draw with the lamp-black-ink lines from one side to the other. **1879** PRESCOTT *Sp. Telephone* 38 The best substance for these disks is lamp-black, such as is produced by the burning of any of the lighter hydrocarbons.

lamp-black (læmp'blæk), *v. trans.* To paint, smear, or coat with lampblack.

1676 WYCHERLEY *Pl. Dealer* III. i, The Clerks Ink is scarce off of your fingers, you that newly come from Lamblacking the Judges shooes, and are not fit to wipe mine! *a* **1704** T. BROWN *Praise Poverty* Wks. 1730 I. 98 A.. scoundrel who knows no pleasure beyond.. lampblacking signs.

Hence **lamp-'blacked** *ppl. a.*

1864 *Morning Star* 25 May 4 The lamp-blacked nigger melodists. **1889** *Lond. & Edinb. Philos. Mag.* Ser. v. XXVII. 2 A thickly lampblacked thermometric apparatus. **1899** WATTS-DUNTON *Aylwin* (1900) 132/2 Piles of lamp-blacked coffins.

lampbrush ('læmpbrʌʃ). *Cytology.* Also (with hyphen) lamp-brush. [repr. G. *lampen-cylinderputzer* lit. 'lamp-glass cleaner', to which lampbrush chromosomes were likened by J. Rückert (in *Anat. Anzeiger* (1892) VII. 115): see LAMP *sb.*[1] and BRUSH *sb.*[2]] Used *attrib.* to designate chromosomes having numerous paired lateral projections or loops, which loops are usu. apparent only during diplotene in a few groups of animals and give the whole chromosome the appearance of a bottle-brush.

[**1901** *Jrnl. R. Microsc. Soc.* 135 This large nucleolus then breaks up.. with the production of 'bottle-brush' and plumose figures in the caryoplasm.] **1911** *Ibid.* 456 The formation of the curious 'lamp-brush' chromosomes. **1925** E. B. WILSON *Cell* (ed. 3) iv. 350 Thus are the very loose so-called 'lamp-brush' chromosomes.., characteristic of the middle growth-period in large, yolk-bearing eggs. **1940** *Proc. Nat. Acad. Sci.* XXVI. 344 The typical lamp-brush chromosomes of the ovocytes of lower vertebrates. **1965** PEACOCKE & DRYSDALE *Molecular Basis Heredity* vii. 72 In the newt, *Triturus cristatus*, large diplotene chromosomes may be isolated from oocytes and maintained for several days in buffer. These 'lampbrush chromosomes' are sufficiently large for the action of enzymes on the chromosomes to be studied microscopically. Evidence obtained from this material supports the conclusion that chromosomes contain protein, RNA and DNA.

lamper ('læmpə(r)), *sb. U.S. colloq.* [f. LAMP *sb.*[1] + -ER[1].] (See quot.)

1886 *Pall Mall G.* 23 Sept. 12/1 In Philadelphia, women make a good living as professional 'lampers'. They contract to call each day, and trim and keep in perfect order the lamps of the household.

lamper ('læmpə(r)), *v. dial.* [? freq. of LAMP *v.*[2]; see -ER[5].] *intr.* (See quot. 1895.)

1727 BRADLEY *Fam. Dict.* s.v. *Hart*, Now there are three ways to know when a Hart is spent. 1. He will run stiff, high and lampering. **1895** *E. Angl. Gloss.*, *To lamper along*, to take big strides.

lamper-eel. [? f. *lampre*, var. of LAMPREY + EEL *sb.* But cf. LAMPREL.]

1. = LAMPREY.

1824 MACTAGGART *Gallovid. Encycl.*, *Lamper eels*,.. common in spring wells during summer. *a* **1825** FORBY *Voc. E. Anglia*, *Lamper-eel*, the lamprey. **1885** *Harper's Mag.* Mar. 659/1 Lamper-eels ascended the river. **1897** *Outing* (U.S.) XXX. 440/1 The lamprey, or lamper-eel, may once have been considered a delicacy.

2. *U.S.* The mutton-fish or eel-pout (*Zoarces anguillaris*) of N. America.

1885 *Stand. Nat. Hist.* (1888) III. 259 Mutton-fish,.. eel-pout, and lamper-eel are names bestowed on the *Zoarces anguillaris.*

lampern ('læmpən). Forms: 4–5 laumprun, lamproun, 4–8 lampron, 5 lampren, lamprone, lamprun(e, 5–6 laumpron, lawmpron, lawmperowne, 5–7 lampurne, 7 lamperne, lamproon, 7– lampern. [a. OF. *lamproyon*, *lamprion*, *lampreon*, dim. of *lampreie* LAMPREY.] The river lamprey (*Petromyzon fluviatilis*).

1324–5 *Durham Acc. Rolls* (Surtees) 14, 60 Lamprouns. **1382** WYCLIF *Job* Prol. 671 As if thou woldest an eel or a laumprun holde with streite hondis. *c* **1460** J. RUSSELL *Bk. Nurture* 588 Elis & lampurnes rosted. **1589** COGAN *Haven of Health* (1636) clxxx. 165 Lamprayes or Lampurnes bee partly of the nature of Eeles. **1655** MOUFET & BENNET *Health's Improv.* (1746) 277 The little ones called Lamprons are best broil'd, but the great ones called Lampreys are best baked. **1730** MRS. DELANY in *Life & Corr.* (1861) I. 265 Many thanks for the lamperns. **1838** JOHNSTON in *Proc. Berw. Nat. Club* I. No. 6. 176 The Lampern or River Lamprey. **1883** *Fisheries Exhib. Catal.* (ed. 4) 125 Weels used on the Apron of Weirs for taking Lamperns.

attrib. **1565** *Richmond. Wills* (Surtees 1853) 178 Fyve long spets, j lampron spet. **1688** R. HOLME *Armoury* II. 325/2 A Lampron-Grigg, then a Lampret, then a Lamprell, then a Lamprey. **1883** *Fisheries Exhib. Catal.* 57 Eel Wheels or Traps. Lampern Spurts as used in Thames Fishery.

lampers, variant of LAMPAS *sb.*[1]

lampert, obs. form of LIMPET.

lampful ('læmpfʊl), *a. poet.* [f. LAMP *sb.*[1] + -FUL.] Of the sky: Full of 'lamps', starry.

1598 SYLVESTER *Du Bartas* II. ii. I. *Ark* 500 A temporal beauty of the lampfull skies. **1866** W. STOKES *Goidelica*

(1872) 125 Let lampful heaven's Sovran spare us from our misery.

lamp-holder. Also lampholder. [LAMP *sb.*[1] 4 b.] A device for securing an electric lamp, a lamp-socket.

1885 *Electrician* XIV. 416/1 Fig. 1 is the lamp-holder as fitted at the Royal Courts of Justice. **1907** *Installation News* Sept. 14/2 In wiring Electroliers.. it is generally found to be impracticable to group wires into the lamp-holders. **1935** *Discovery* June 183/2 An operation which is typical of a vast number of manipulative jobs in industry—the assembly of an ordinary electric lampholder consisting of eighteen parts. **1963** *Times* 6 May p. vii/5 Similarly, when in the interests of safety the traditional brass lampholder was replaced by its plastics successor, this was more or less a slavish imitation of the metal one.

† **'lampic,** *a. Chem. Obs.* [f. LAMP *sb.* + -IC. (The name was proposed by Daniell; the substance was first prepared by burning ether in a lamp with a platinum wire twisted round the wick.)]

In *lampic acid*: an earlier name of aldehyde.

1819 J. F. DANIELL in *Jrnl. Sci. & Arts* VI. 320 After much consideration, it is but with diffidence that I venture to propose for it the appellation of *Lampic acid*. **1819** J. G. CHILDREN *Chem. Anal.* 282 *Lampic acid* formed from ether is a colourless fluid, with an intensely sour taste, and pungent odour. **1839** URE *Dict. Arts* 738.

lamping ('læmpɪŋ), *vbl. sb.* [f. LAMP *v.*[1] + -ING[1].] A sudden blaze of light.

1814 CARY *Dante, Par.* xxv. 80 A lamping [It. *lampo*], as of quick and vollied lightning, Within the bosom of that mighty sheen, Play'd tremulous.

lamping ('læmpɪŋ), *ppl. a.* [f. LAMP *v.*[1] + -ING[2]. Perh. suggested by It. *lampante.*] Flashing, beaming, resplendent.

1590 SPENSER *F.Q.* III. iii. 1 Most sacred fyre,..ykindled first above Emongst th' eternall spheres and lamping sky. **1610** G. FLETCHER *Christ's Vict.* I. x, Her eye with heav'ns, so, and more brightly shin'd Her lamping sight. **1828** *Blackw. Mag.* XXIII. 688 His bright forehead..and his large lamping eyes. **1859** LD. LYTTON *Wanderer* 8 Hot oleanders in a rosy vale Searched by the lamping fly. **1885** R. F. BURTON *Arab. Nts.* V. 353 She flew off, like the wafts of the wind or the lamping leven.

lampion ('læmpɪən). [a. F. *lampion*, ad. It. *lampione* carriage or street lamp, augmentative of *lampa* LAMP *sb.*] A pot or cup, often of coloured glass, containing oil or grease with a wick, used in illuminations.

1848 THACKERAY *Van. Fair* lxiii, At the French Chancellerie they had six more lampions in their illumination than ours had. **1855** BROWNING *Men & Wom., Respectability* iii, Eh! down in the Court three lampions flare —Put forward your best foot! **1889** G. W. CABLE *Stories of Louisiana* 110 Hidden among the leaves were millions of fantastically colored lampions seeming like so many glow-worms.

lampist ('læmpɪst). [ad. F. *lampiste*, f. *lampe*: see LAMP *sb.*[1] and -IST.]

1. One skilled in, or employed in, the construction or management of lamps.

1839 URE *Dict. Arts*, etc. 735 The operations of the lampist..belong to a treatise upon handicraft trades. **1855** SILLIMAN in Cone & Johns *Petrolia* iv. (1870) 64, I have submitted the lamp burning Petroleum to the inspection of the most experienced lampists who were accessible. **1858** LARDNER *Hand-bk. Nat. Phil.* 124 One of the difficulties with which lampists have had to struggle was, to [etc.].

2. *nonce-use.* (See quot.)

1887 RIBTON-TURNER *Vagrants & Vagrancy* xxvii. 559 *Allampadati*, or Lampists, who during Passion Week and at the great festivals begged oil for the lamps which are lighted in front of the host, or the images of the virgin.

lampistry ('læmpɪstrɪ). *rare.* [ad. F. *lampisterie*, f. *lampiste*: see prec. and -ERY.] The kind of plastic art appropriate to the decoration of lamps.

1874 *Edin. Rev.* July 199 We may observe the difference between lampistry and sculpture.

lampit, Sc. form of LIMPET.

lampless ('læmplɪs), *a.* [f. LAMP *sb.*[1] + -LESS.] Destitute of lamps.

a **1625** FLETCHER *Mad Lover* II. i, Your Ladies eyes are lamplesse to that vertue. **1819** SHELLEY *Cenci* v. iv. 59 The wide, grey, lampless, deep, unpeopled world! **1849** J. STERLING in *Fraser's Mag.* XXXIX. 411 A lampless archway. **1884** A. J. BUTLER *Anc. Coptic Ch.* I. i. 36 More often in the present day they are uncoloured and lampless.

lamplet ('læmplɪt). [f. LAMP *sb.*[1] + -LET.] A small lamp.

1621 QUARLES *Argalus & P.* (1678) 97 Enter you Lamplets of Terrestrial fire. **1855** BAILEY *Mystic* 141 Emerald lamplets ranked around it, tempered this with cooler ray. **1884** *Chr. Commw.* 11 Dec. 119/5 Electricians will probably have invented a lamplet which will last for months.

lamplight ('læmplaɪt). [f. LAMP *sb.*[1] + LIGHT.] The light afforded by a lamp or lamps.

1579 [see LAMP *sb.*[1] 1 b]. **1705** HICKERINGILL *Priest-cr.* I. (1721) 53 Juglers play their Tricks..by Candle-light, or dim Lamp-light. **1822** BYRON *Werner* III. iii. 23 A distant lamp-light is an incident. **1832** G. DOWNES *Lett. Cont. Countries* I. 397 We descended by lamp-light to a considerable depth. **1884** ROE *Nat. Ser. Story* iii. in *Harper's Mag.* Feb. 457/1 Lamp-light and fire-light revealed a group.

lamplighter ('læmplaɪtə(r)). [f. LAMP *sb.*[1] + LIGHTER.]

1. One who lights lamps; one whose business it is to light the street lamps.

like a lamplighter: said with allusion to the rapidity with which the lamplighter ran on his rounds, or climbed the ladders formerly used to reach the street lamps.

1750 BAKER in *Phil. Trans.* XLVI. 601 A Lamp-lighter was giving an Account, that [etc.]. **1776** *Court & City Reg.* 167/2 John Bird, master lamp lighter. *a* **1813** A. WILSON *Hogmenae* Poet. Wks. (1846) 293 So Dempster, and Brodie, in Co., Like lamplighters ran to the baker's. **1830** MARRYAT *King's Own* xxxiii, Skim up the rigging like a lamplighter. **1843** BETHUNE *Sc. Fireside Stor.* 68 That's Lucifer, flying about like a lamplighter. **1874** BURNAND *My time* ii. 12 The arrival of the lamplighter in the winter-time was quite the event of the day.

2. *U.S.* A contrivance for lighting lamps; e.g. a spill of paper, a torch, or an electric appliance.

1859 EMILY DICKINSON *Lett.* (1894) I. 194 Please, now I write so often, make lamplighter of me.

3. *local U.S.* The calico bass.

In recent (American) Dicts.

4. A North American freshwater sunfish of the genus *Pomoxis*, esp. the white crappie, *P. annularis*.

1877 *1st Ann. Rep. Ohio State Fish Comm.* 77 *P[omoxys] hexacanthus*... Strawberry Bass;..Lamp-lighter, of Portsmouth. **1892** C. F. LUMMIS *Tramp across Continent* 33 For three years I had been fairly starving for a bout with these beauties—a hunger which the catfish and 'lamplighters' of Ohio had utterly failed to satisfy. **1947** B. W. DALRYMPLE *Panfish* 84 Here, my friend, are the various names by which you would address that little gamester, the Crappie, depending on where you happened to be at the moment: Bachelor,..Lake Bass, Lake Erie Bass, Lamplighter.

lamp oil. Oil used for burning in a lamp; also *fig.* nocturnal labour or study.

1581 SIDNEY *Apol. Poetrie* (1595) H b, Some of my Maisters the Phylosophers, spent a good deale of theyr Lamp-oyle, in setting foorth the excellencie of it. **1598** BARRET *Theor. Warres* 135 Common lampe oyle. **1657** W. COLES *Adam in Eden* cli. 231 The Countrey-man..that had eaten Fish fryed with Lamp-Oyl. **1842** S. LOVER *Handy Andy* iii, Andy..returned with a can of lamp-oil to Dick. **1895** *Daily News* 17 Oct. 6/7 The question of the safety of the lamp oils that are now finding their way into the English market.

attrib. **1888** *Syd. Soc. Lex.*, *Lamp-oil seeds*, the seeds of *Ricinus viridis*.

lampoon (læm'puːn), *sb.* [a. F. *lampon*, recorded from 17th c.; the vb. †*lamponner*, to ridicule, is cited from Brantôme (died 1614).

The Fr. etymologists regard the sb. as f. *lampons* 'let us drink', imperative of *lamper* (slang) to booze, guzzle.]

A virulent or scurrilous satire upon an individual.

1645 EVELYN *Mem.* (1857) I. 174 Here they still paste up their drolling lampoons and scurrilous papers. **1689** SHADWELL *Bury F.* I. i, I pepper'd the Court with libels and Lampoons. *a* **1704** T. BROWN *Pindar. Petit. Lds. Council* Wks. 1730 I. 61 Should you order Tho. Brown, To be whipp'd thro' the town, For scurvy lampoon. **1779–81** JOHNSON *L.P.*, *Pope* Wks. IV. 3 On his master at Twyford he had already exercised his poetry in a lampoon. **1830** D'ISRAELI *Chas I*, III. vii. 153 This circumstance only appeared by two bitter lampoons in the works of Jonson. **1842** DE QUINCEY *Pagan Oracles* Wks. 1858 VIII. 172 The rancorous lampoons of Gregory Nazianzen against his sovereign. **1872** MINTO *Eng. Prose Lit.* I. ii. 145 Taking the lampoons of the time as documents of literal fidelity.

Comb. **1721** STRYPE *Eccl. Mem.* II. vii. 54 Among the rest [of the ballads] there was published a very unlucky one, lampoon-wise..pretending to take the part of the papists against the preachers.

lampoon (læm'puːn), *v.* [f. LAMPOON *sb.*] *trans.* To make the subject of a lampoon; to abuse or satirize virulently in writing.

a **1657** LOVELACE *Poems* (1864) 233 The noblest matrons of the isle lampoon. **1706** FARQUHAR *Recruiting Officer* I. i. Wks. 1892 II. 131 Suppose we lampooned all the pretty women in town, and left her out? **1768–74** TUCKER *Lt. Nat.* (1834) II. 362 Thwarted in the cabinet, baited in parliament, and lampooned in public. **1822** HAZLITT *Table-t.* I. vi. 125 He lampooned the French Revolution when it was hailed as the dawn of liberty by millions. **1878** MACLEAR *Celts* vii. 115 The bards..did not scruple to defame or lampoon any who annoyed them.

lampooner (læm'puːnə(r)). [f. LAMPOON *v.* + -ER[1].] One who lampoons.

1693 DRYDEN *Juvenal* (1697) p. lix, How few Lampooners are there now living, who are capable of this Duty. **1779–81** JOHNSON *L.P.*, *Pope* Wks. IV. 77 A lampooner, who scattered his ink without fear or decency. **1862** MERIVALE *Rom. Emp.* (1865) IV. xxxiii. 103 Augustus had the good sense to bear with temper the virulence of clandestine lampooners. **1879** SALA *Paris herself again* (1880) II. xxv. 359 The stern Republican, the unsparing lampooner of Louis Philippe.

lampoonery (læm'puːnərɪ). [f. LAMPOON *sb.* + -ERY.] The practice of writing lampoons; lampooning quality or spirit.

1715 *Key to Lock* (1718) 21 A very artful Pun to conceal his wicked Lampoonery. **1889** *Voice* (N.Y.) 12 Dec., We do not complain of the lampoonery and ferocity of the expressions.

lampoonist (læm'puːnɪst). [f. LAMPOON *sb.* + -IST.] A writer of lampoons.

1880 *Standard* 12 July 4/8 The shafts of that lively lampoonist [M. Rochefort] will now be directed against the Republic.

lampors, obs. form of LAMPAS *sb.*[2]

lamp-post ('læmp,pəʊst). [f. LAMP *sb.* + POST.] A post, usually of iron, used to support a street-lamp. Sometimes with allusion to its use during the French Revolution for hanging a victim of popular fury.

1790 ROY in *Phil. Trans.* LXXX. 164 The same socket that fitted the top of the flag-staff, or lamp-post, could be applied to the tripod. **1790** BURKE *Fr. Rev.* Wks. V. 109 This sort of discourse does well enough with the lamp-post for its second. **1865** DICKENS *Mut. Fr.* I. v, He contrived a back to his wooden stool by placing it against the lamp-post. **1880** L. WALLACE *Ben-Hur* 295 A platform garnished by some lamp-posts.

lampras, -ays, obs. forms of LAMPAS *sb.*[1]

† **lamprel.** *Obs.* Forms: 6 lawmprell, lamprile, 6–7 lamprel(l, 7 lampreel, -pril(l. [? f. *lampre* LAMPREY + -EL[1]. Cf. F. *lamprillon.*] Some fish resembling the lamprey; according to R. Holme the lamprey at a certain stage of growth.

1526 *Househ. Exp. Sir T. Le Strange* (B.M. Add. MS. 27448. lf. 30 b), Item..ij lawmprells and a counger, iijd. **1561** HOLLYBUSH *Hom. Apoth.* 38 b, Such diseased must beware of smouth fishes, as Iles, Lampriles, Barbels, Tenches. **1601** HOLLAND *Pliny* I. 246 The table is serued with a kinde of Lamprels or Elepouts like to sea Lampreis. **1653** WALTON *Angler* xiii. 165 Fish, whose shape and nature are much like the Eel..namely, the Lamprel, the Lamprey, and the Lamperne. **1688** [see LAMPRET].

lampren, obs. form of LAMPERN.

† **lampret.** *Obs.* Also 7 lamprete, -prid. [Orig. a mere var. of LAMPREY; but the ending was apprehended as the dim. suffix -ET[1].] A lamprey at a certain stage of growth.

1656 W. D. tr. *Comenius' Gate Lat. Unl.* §153. 45 Others are smooth, slippery, long, as the Eel, the Conger, the Lamprey, the Lamprete. **1688** R. HOLME *Armoury* II. 325/2 How several sorts of Fish are named according to their Age, or Growth... A *Lamprey*, first a *Lampron*—Grigg, then a *Lampret*, then a *Lamprell*, then a *Lamprey*. A *Lampron*, first a Barle, then a Barling, then a *Lamprell*, and then a *Lamprey* or *Lampron*.

lamprey ('læmprɪ). Forms: 3, 6–7 lamprei(e, -ye, 4–7 lampray(e, laumpray, -ee, -ey, 5 laumperey, lawmpery, 5–7 lampre, 6–7 lampry, lamprie, 4– lamprey. [a. OF. *lampreie (OF. and mod.F. *lamproie*) = Pr. *lampreza*, *lamprea*, *lamprada*, It. *lampreda* (the Sp., Pg. *lamprea* seem to be from Fr.):—med.L. *lamprēda* (glossed *murœna c* 1050 in Wr.-Wülcker 180/28); the word was adopted into the Teut. langs.: OE. *lamprede* (also *lęmpedu* LIMPET), OHG. *lampreta* (mod.G. *lamprete*, whence Sw., Da. *lampret*), MDu. *lampreide*. The ulterior etymology is uncertain.

The med.L. *lamprēda* is usually believed to be an alteration of the synonymous *lampetra* (recorded earlier, viz. in the Glossary of Philoxenus, ? 4–5th c.), which is explained as f. L. *lambere* to lick + *petra* stone, in allusion to the fact that the lamprey attaches itself by a sucker to stones. The use of med.L. *lamprēda* for the LIMPET as well as the lamprey gives some plausibility to this; but possibly *lampetra* may be merely an etymologizing perversion.]

a. A fish of the genus *Petromyzon*, resembling an eel in shape and in having no scales. It has a mouth like a sucker, pouch-like gills, seven spiracles or apertures on each side of the head, and a fistula or opening on the top of the head.

1297 R. GLOUC. (Rolls) 9114–17 Þo he com he willede of an lampreye to ete..& et as in luþer cas, vor þulke lampreie him slou. **1333–4** *Durham Acc. Rolls* (Surtees) 21 In xij Laumprays. *c* **1400** *Rom. Rose* 7038 They defende hem with lamprey, With luce, with elis, with samons. *a* **1400–50** *Alexander* 5473 Lamprays of weȝt Twa hundreth pond ay a pece. **1444** *Pol. Poems* (Rolls) II. 218 Withoute avys make no comparysoun Atween a laumperey and a shynyng snake. **1531** TINDALE *Exp. 1 John* Prol., Wks. (1573) 388/2 The boy ..would fayne haue eaten of the pastie of lamprese. **1634** R. H. *Salernes Regim.* 88 Although Lampreyes be a little wholesommmer then Eeles, and lesse jeopardous. **1672–3** MARVELL *Reh. Transp.* Wks. 1776 II. 61 He hath been fed all his life with vipers insteed of lampres, and scorpions for cray fish. **1720** GAY *Poems* (1745) II. 122 Why then send lampreys? fy, for shame 'Twill set a virgins blood on flame. **1837** M. DONOVAN *Dom. Econ.* II. 201 The Lamprey, like the eel..is remarkably tenacious of life. **1870** YEATS *Nat. Hist. Comm.* 324 Lampreys reach this country packed in jars with vinegar,..and bay leaves.

b. *attrib.* and *Comb.*, as *lamprey-pie*, *-weel*; **lamprey bake** = *lamprey-pie*; **lamprey-eel,** the Sea-lamprey (*Petromyzon marinus*); **lamprey-stock** (see quot.).

c **1440** *Douce MS.* 55 lf. 31 b, *Lampray bake. *c* **1460** J. RUSSELL *Bk. Nurture* 630 Fresche lamprey bake þus it must be dight. **1726** S. PENHALLOW in *Coll. New Hampsh. Hist. Soc.* (1824) I. 31 Next day, they kill'd Edward Taylor near *Lamprey-Eel River. **1831** R. COX *Adventures Columbia River* I. vii. 149 We got plenty of salmon while we remained here, and some lamprey eels, the latter of which were oily and very strong. **1883** C. F. HOLDER in *Harper's Mag.* Dec. 102/1 Very similar in its habit of erecting a nest is the

lamprey-eel (*Petromyzon marinus*). **1885** *Amer. Naturalist* XIX. 922 The lamprey eel of Kansas.. proves to be usually the *chestnut* lamprey. **1599** H. BUTTES *Dyets drie Dinner* M 3 Many in England have surfetted of *Lampry pies, as our Chronicles will tell us. **1599** MASSINGER, etc. *Old Law* II. i. (1656) 22 Backe Snakes for Lamprie Pies, and Cats for Cunnies. **1883** *Fisheries Exhib. Catal.* 365 *Lamprey 'Stock'.—A wooden Cylinder for catching Lampreys. *Ibid.* 366 *Lamprey-Weel.

lamprey(e)s, obs. form of LAMPAS *sb.*[1]

lampro- (ˈlæmprəʊ), repr. Gr. λαμπρο-, combining form of Gr. λαμπρός bright, shining, as in: **ˈlamprophane** [Gr. φαν-, φαίνειν to show] *Min.*, a mineral occurring in long, thin, cleavable folia at Longban, Wermland, Sweden (Cassell, 1885); **ˈlamproˌphoner** [Gr. φωνή + -ER], an instrument for increasing the intensity of sound; so **ˌlamproˈphony**, a term for a clear and sonorous state of the voice (Mayne *Expos. Lex.* 1855); **lamproˈphyllite** *Min.* [ad. G. *lamprophyllit* (V. Hackman 1894, in *Fennia* XI. 119): see PHYLLO-], a silicate of sodium, strontium, and titanium, $Na_2SrTiSi_2O_8$, found as golden-brown prisms; **lamprophyre** [a. G. *lamprophyr* (C. W. Gümbel *Die paläolith. Eruptivgesteine des Fichtelgebirges* (1874) 36, f. Gr. (πορ)φύρεος purple: see PORPHYRY], the name given by Gümbel to rocks, considerably varied in lithological character, occurring in dikes in strata of palæozoic age; hence **ˌlamproˈphyric** *a.*, of or pertaining to lamprophyre (*Cent. Dict.*); **lamprotype** [Gr. τύπος type] *Photogr.*, a paper print glazed with collodion and gelatine (*Cent. Dict.*).

1897 *Amer. Ann. Deaf* June 265 In the Indiana Institution experiments are in progress with the 'lamprophoner', an instrument which.. increases the intensity of sound. **1899** E. S. DANA *Dana's Syst. Min.* (ed. 6) 1st App. 40 *Lamprophyllite*... A mineral related to astrophyllite in form and cleavage. **1942** *Amer. Mineralogist* XXVII. 416 The Bearpaw and Kola lamprophyllite are almost identical in refringence, habit, and orientation. **1965** *Scientia Sinica* (Peking) XIV. 1839 The lamprophyllite in general belongs to the monoclinic system and the orthorhombic lamprophyllite exists as a submicroscopic crystallite in the polysynthetic twin of monoclinic lamprophyllite. **1890** *Mineral Mag.* IX. 43 The rock.. is most closely paralleled by the olivine-bearing lamprophyres. **1923** *Geol. Mag.* LX. 553 The potash series of lamprophyres, in which orthoclase and abundance of biotite form the expression of excess of potash over soda, is not so complex a group as that of the soda-lamprophyres. **1959** W. W. MOORHOUSE *Study of Rocks in Thin Section* xvii. 325 Lamprophyres.. are for the most part melanocratic to mesotype rocks... Nearly all.. of the true lamprophyres are characterized by a definitely alkaline aspect, indicated by the presence of abundant biotite, alkali feldspar, soda pyriboles, nepheline, or analcite, combined with a low silica content. **1966** *Jrnl. & Proc. R. Soc. New South Wales* XCIX. 38/1 Many of the common lamprophyres, such as minettes, vogesites, kersantites and spessartites are almost chemically identical. **1892** *Geol. Mag.* IX. 201 An intermixture of the acid and lamprophyric magmas took place during the injection. **1965** G. J. WILLIAMS *Econ. Geol. N.Z.* xiii. 205/1 Narrow lamprophyric dykes and sills cut granite, Ohika beds and the Breccia. **1875** KNIGHT *Dict. Mech.*, *Lamprotype* (Photography), a polished collodion picture.

lampron, -roon, etc., obs. ff. of LAMPERN.

lamp-shade, lampshade. [LAMP *sb.*[1] 4 a.] A shade placed over a lamp to diffuse or direct the light. Also *attrib.* and *fig.*

1850 GEO. ELIOT *Let.* 30 Nov. (1954) I. 337, I have bought the Lucifers and done my duty about the Lamp shade. *a* **1877** KNIGHT *Dict. Mech.* II. 1248/1 *Lamp-shade*, a screen placed above the light to intercept or mellow it. It may have a dark exterior and reflecting interior surface. **1899** A. WERNER *Captain of Locusts* 212 He removed the burnt matches, set the lamp-shade straight. **1908** *Stratford-upon-Avon Herald* 24 July 7/2 Lamp-shade-like protectors are obtainable cheaply. **1908** *Daily Chron.* 2 Oct. 4/4 There were the young ladies of gay Bohemia in Directoire dresses and lamp-shade hats. **1953** R. MACAULAY *Last Lett. to Friend* (1962) 107 It didn't really *destroy* very much, except some pictures (which I mourn) and curtains and covers and a few books and lamp-shades, etc. **1960** J. BROPHY *Front Door Key* 179 She had compromised with the present, babyish neo-1920's fashion, refusing to wear, along with bows and tiers and lampshade hems, very short and very tight skirts. **1967** E. SHORT *Embroidery & Fabric Collage* iii. 83 Care should be taken with lampshades to avoid fancy shapes and over-fussy trimmings. **1971** *Shankar's Weekly* (Delhi) 18 Apr. 18/4 He pointed to two burly figures who came out of the nearby tea-shop, one of them wiping his lampshade moustaches.

lampuki (ˈlæmpʊkɪ). Also **lampuca, lampuka.** [Maltese.] A large marine food fish, *Coryphæna hippurus* or *C. equisetis*; = DOLPHIN 2.

1925 J. A. HAMMERTON *Countries of World* IV. 2673/1 The lampuca, a migratory fish which comes to the islands in autumn, is caught in considerable quantities and is eaten by all classes of the people. **1958** G. G. LANFRANCO *Compl. Guide Fishes Malta* 28 *Coryphaena hippurus*, Linn... Lampuka; easily distinguished.. much valued as food. **1964** G. BUTLER *Coffin in Malta* iii. 80 The smell of calamari and *lampuki* mingling beautifully with onion and tomato grew stronger. **1969** *Vogue* Nov. 68/2 Lampuki is a delicious fish. **1975** *Times* 11 Jan. 11/6 The greatest [Maltese] delicacy is *lampuki*, which is a fish similar in size to seabass.. usually grilled.

lampus, obs. form of LAMPAS *sb.*[1]

lampyrid (ˈlæmpɪrɪd). [f. mod.L. family name Lampyridæ: see LAMPYRINE *a.* and *sb.*] An insect belonging to the Lampyridæ, a family of Coleoptera which includes the glow-worms and fire-flies.

[**1841** E. NEWMAN *Familiar Introd. Hist. Insects* v. 249 Glow-worms or *Lampyrites*.] **1895** J. H. & A. B. COMSTOCK *Man. Study Insects* xxi. 550 (*heading*) The Firefly Family or Lampyrids. *Ibid.* 551 Another common diurnal Lampyrid is *Calopteron reticulatum*. **1899** D. SHARP in *Cambr. Nat. Hist.* VI. II. v. 248 The Lampyrides, or glow-worms, are of special interest, as most of their members give off a phosphorescent light when alive. **1916** *Jrnl. Morphol.* XXVIII. 145 (*title*) Photogenic organs and embryology of Lampyrids. **1961** *New Scientist* 16 Nov. 664/1 They [*sc.* the Cantharids] include.. the photogenic Lampyrids.

lampyrine (ˈlæmpɪrɪn), *a.* and *sb.* [f. L. *lampyris* glowworm (adopted in mod. Latin as the name of the glowworm genus), a. Gr. λαμπυρίς, f. λάμπειν to shine. See -INE.]

A. *adj.* Of or pertaining to the *Lampyrinæ* or fire-flies. **B.** *sb.* One of the *Lampyrinæ*.

1842 BRANDE *Dict. Sci.* etc. s.v. *Lampyrinæ*, The females of some of the Lampyrine tribe are apterous.. and are luminous. All the Lampyrines, when seized, press their feet and antennæ against their body, and remain as motionless as if they were dead.

lampysse, obs. form of LAMPAS *sb.*[1]

lamsiekte (ˈlamˌsɪktə). *S. Afr.* Also **lamziekte.** [Afrikaans, f. *lam* lame, paralysed + *siekte* disease.] A cattle disease, usually fatal, found on land deficient in phosphorus, caused by the bacterium *Clostridium botulinum* and characterized by paralysis or muscular weakness; bovine botulism. Also *attrib.*

1790 E. HELME tr. *Le Vaillant's Trav. Afr.* II. v. 92 The first [disease], called at the Cape *Lam-Sikte*, is a sudden paralitic stroke. **1798** S. H. WILCOCKE tr. *Stavorinus's Voy. E. Indies* II. 64 The *lamziekte*, is when the cattle are not able to stand; it comes on gradually, and is slow in its progress. **1896** R. WALLACE *Farming Industries Cape Colony* xiv. 286 Stiff-sickness or 'stijf-ziekte' and 'lam-ziekte' or paralysis, would appear to be two forms of the same disease. **1946** *Nature* 17 Aug. 239/1 In practice, 0·5–1 unit of circulating antitoxin adequately protects a bovine against natural botulism (lamsiekte). **1948** *Cape Argus* 6 Nov. 1/9 The Division of Veterinary Services.. will shortly make available a new, improved and concentrated lamsiekte vaccine. **1974** *Eastern Province Herald* (S. Afr.) 15 Nov. 15 A young couple.. who lost about 70 per cent. of their income when 34 of their dairy cows died of botulism (lamsiekte), have been given three cows and lent four.

lamster: see LAM *v.*

Lamut (læˈmuːt). Also **Lamoot, Lamout. a.** A branch of the Tungus people living on the shores of the Sea of Okhotsk. **b.** The language spoken by this people, belonging to the Tunguso-Manchurian group of the Altaic language family. Also *attrib.* or as *adj.* Also **Laˈmutic** *sb.*

1764 J. GRIEVE tr. *Krasheninnikov's Hist. Kamtschatka* III. xxi. 223 The people that they [*sc.* the Koreki] border upon are the Kamtschadales, the Tchukotskoi,.. and the Tungusi or Lamuti. **1790** tr. *J. B. B. de Lesseps's Trav. Kamtschatka* II. 383 Vocabulary of the Kamtschadale, Koriac, Tchouktchi, and Lamout languages. *Ibid.*, (*heading*) Koriac... Tchouktchi... Lamout. **1830** P. DOBELL *Trav. Kamtchatka & Siberia* I. ix. 189 Lamoots are the Wild Reindeer Tongusees, who seldom inhabit one spot more than a month or two at a time. **1880** A. H. SAYCE *Introd. Sci. of Lang.* II. viii. 201 To find them we must look to the ruder Lamutic and Tungusian. **1888** *Encycl. Brit.* XXIII. 608/2 On the Pacific the chief subdivisions of the race are the Lamuts, or 'sea people', grouped in small isolated hunting communities round the west coast of the Sea of Okhotsk. **1927** F. WHYTE tr. *Bergman's Through Kamchatka* xii. 196 One of the older men.. was.. chanting monotonous Lamut melodies... The Lamuts.. are nominally Christians. *Ibid.* xiii. 215 So ended the Lamut winter festival. **1957** G. CLARK *Archaeol. & Soc.* (ed. 3) iii. 94 The best preserved.. of the Siberian mammoths was found at Beresovka by a Lamut tribesman. **1964** tr. *Levin & Potapov's Peoples of Siberia* 670 The Evens, who were formerly known as Lamuts,.. border in the north and northeast with the Yukagirs, Koryaks and Chukchi.

lamyn(e, variant of LAMIN.

lan, variant of LOAN *sb.*[1], reward, recompense.

lan, pa. t. of LIN *Obs.*, to cease.

‖**lana** (ˈleɪnə). [S. American.] (See quot.)

1858 SIMMONDS *Dict. Trade*, *Lana*, a close grained wood obtained in Demerara from *Genipa Americana*... The fruit yields the pigment known as Lana dye, with which the Indians stain their faces and persons.

lanai (‖lana-i, ləˈnaɪ). Also 9 **ranai.** [Hawaiian.] In Hawaii (and by imitation elsewhere), a porch or veranda; a roofed structure with open sides near a house. Also *attrib.*

1823 C. S. STEWART *Jrnl.* 28 Apr. (1828) v. 97 The chiefs were all under one *ranai*, or rude bower. **1826** W. ELLIS *Narr. Tour Hawaii* xiv. 387 At half-past ten, the bell rung for public worship, and about 800 people.. assembled under a large *ranai* (a placed sheltered from the sun) formed by two large canvass awnings, and a number of platted cocoa-nut leaves, spread over the place from posts fixed in the fence which enclosed the court-yard around the house of the governor's wife. *a* **1869** L. SMITH in M. D. Frear *Lowell & Abigail* (1934) 124 We soon found that the school house did not accomodate one half of the congregation; and we built a large *lanai* in the front yard and covered it with rushes for them to sit upon, a la Hawaii. **1897** 'MARK TWAIN' *Following Equator* iii. 61 Nearly every house [in Honolulu] has what is called a *lanai*. It is a large apartment, roofed, floored, open on three sides, with a door or a draped archway opening into the drawing-room. **1898** M. H. KROUT *Hawaii* v. 93 On these verandahs or in the *lanai* the family practically lives. **1937** D. & H. TEILHET *Feather Cloak Murders* x. 174 The wide windows opening upon an immense lanai, or porch, with cool overhanging eaves. **1945** L. MUMFORD *City Devel.* (1946) 81 Without it, adequate gardens are impossible and the private lanai, even when provided, is stuffy. **1947** M. LOWRY *Under Volcano* ix. 272 He sat on the lanai sipping okoolihao and singing plaintive Hawaiian songs. **1963** D. B. HUGHES *Expendable Man* (1964) ii. 31 Sliding glass lanai doors opened to a vast expanse of close-cropped green. **1964** D. TEILHET *Big Runaround* ii. 30 She hadn't ever seen a couch this wide, she said; and I explained that it was called a lanai-couch. **1969** *New Yorker* 31 May 95/2 (Advt.), 1000 air-conditioned rooms, tower suites and lanais surrounding the.. swimming pool.

lanar, obs. form of LANNER.

†**laˈnarious**, *a.* *Obs. rare*$^{-0}$. [f. L. *lānāri-us* (f. *lāna* wool) + -OUS.] 'Of or belonging to wool' (Blount *Glossogr.* 1656–81).

lanarkite (ˈlænəkaɪt). *Min.* [Named by Beudant, 1832, from Lanarkshire, where it was first found. See -ITE.] Sulphocarbonate of lead, found in greenish-white, grey, or yellowish crystals.

1835 SHEPARD *Min.* II. I. 300 *Lanarkite*. **1868** DANA *Min.* (ed. 5) 628 Lanarkite, Sulphato-Carbonate of Lead.

†**ˈlanary.** *Obs. rare*$^{-0}$. [ad. L. *lānāria* (? sc. *fabrica*) fem. of *lānārius*: see LANARIOUS.] 'A wool-house, a warehouse or storehouse for wool' (1727 Bailey vol. II).

lanate (ˈleɪnət), *a.* *Bot.* and *Ent.* [ad. L. *lānāt-us*, f. *lāna* wool: see -ATE[2].] Having a woolly covering or surface.

1760 J. LEE *Introd. Bot.* III. v. (1765) 182 *Lanate*, woolly, when they are covered as it were with a spider's web. **1826** KIRBY & SP. *Entomol.* IV. 275 Lanate (*Lanata*), covered with fine, very long, flexible and rather curling hairs like wool.

So **lanated** *a.*, in the same sense.

1828–32 in WEBSTER.

Lancashire (ˈlæŋkəʃə(r)). [f. *Lancaster* the name of the county town + SHIRE, with contraction.] The name of one of the northern counties of England, used *attrib.* in ***Lancashire boiler*** (see quot. 1888); ***Lancashire cheese***, a white semi-hard cheese made in Lancashire (also *ellipt.*); also (in quots. *ellipt.* as *sb.*) as the designation of a breed of cattle; also, of a breed of canary.

1834 YOUATT *Cattle* vi. 203 The dairy-farmers.. if they permit any admixture of short-horn blood.. are anxious that that of the old Lancashire's shall decidedly prevail. **1888** *Lockwood's Dict. Mech. Engin.*, *Lancashire Boiler*, a horizontal, cylindrical, internally fired boiler, having two flues. **1896** J. T. LAW *Grocer's Manual* 811/1 The peculiarity and distinctive mark of Lancashire, as distinct from Cheshire and Cheddar, is that it is a softer cheese, a good toaster, mellower, and very palatable when ripe. **1898** *Daily News* 28 Nov. 3/3 Slim and sprightly Yorkshires.. contrast strongly with the equally esteemed Lancashires of pale yellow plumage. **1910** *Encycl. Brit.* VII. 749/2 Lancashire cheese, when well made and ripe, is loose in texture and is mellow; it has a piquant flavour. As a rule it ripens early and does not keep long. **1937** 'G. ORWELL' *Road to Wigan Pier* I. i. 15 For supper there was the pale flabby Lancashire cheese and biscuits. **1955** J. G. DAVIS *Dict. Dairying* (ed. 2) 195 *Lancashire cheese.* Although not well known outside the county of its origin, it is in great demand in Lancashire, especially in the industrial areas of the south, and is reckoned an excellent cheese for toasting. **1960** S. FRASER *Cheeses Old Eng.* 29 It was dark when I arrived in Preston in search of Lancashire cheese. **1971** *Sunday Times* (Colour Suppl.) 28 Mar. 36/1 *Lancashire.* When young it is slightly sharp and soft enough to spread, but it mellows with age.

Lancaster[1] (ˈlæŋkæstə(r)). [f. the name of the inventor, C. W. *Lancaster* (died 1878).] In full ***Lancaster gun, rifle***, the name of a cannon and rifle (respectively) having a slightly oval bore.

1857 G. LAWRENCE *Guy Liv.* iv. 49 Guy's great Lancaster rang out with the roar of a small field-piece. **1858** GREENER *Gunnery* 121 Wrought iron shells have already been thoroughly tried in the Lancaster oval gun. **1860** *All Year Round* No. 73. 545 As for the Lancaster guns, how they burst!

Lancaster[2] (ˈlæŋkæstə(r)). [Name of the county town of Lancashire.] Used *attrib.* in ***Lancaster cloth*** (see quot. 1950). Cf. *American cloth* (AMERICAN *a.* 3).

1939 *Archit. Rev.* LXXXVI. 258/1 *Lancaster cloth.* This is a muslin base impregnated with a linseed oil compound. **1950** '*Mercury*' *Dict. Textile Terms* 312/2 *Lancaster cloth*, a light, washable oilcloth used on shelves, tables, round wash basins, etc. Made with a cotton back and with a face dressing of linseed oil, etc. compound. **1951** *Good Housek. Home Encycl.* 166/2 A less expensive covering is provided.. by

Lancaster (or American) cloth. **1960** *Design* Sept. 71/2 The indicator boards..are faced with Lancaster cloth in red, grey-green and yellow.

Lancasterian (læŋkæ'stɪərɪən), *a.* Also (early in 9) **Lancastrian.** [f. the proper name *Lancaster* + -IAN.] Of or pertaining to Joseph Lancaster (1778–1838) and the monitorial form of instruction which he established in schools.

1807 G. W. MARRIOT in Southey *Life A. Bell* (1844) II. 200 He praises Lancaster as the founder of the Lancasterian System. **1812** SOUTHEY *Lett.* (1856) II. 255 The Lancastrian scheme must needs operate to undermine the Church Establishment. **1813** L. HUNT in *Examiner* 17 May 305/2 The Church is against the Lancasterian system. **1832** G. DOWNES *Lett. Cont. Countries* I. 465 He has founded a Lancasterian School for boys. **1870** ANDERSON *Missions Amer. Bd.* III. vii. 95 He established several Greek Lancasterian schools, with the New Testament for a class-book.

Lancastrian (læŋ'kæstrɪən), *a.* and *sb.* [f. *Lancaster* + -IAN. Cf. YORKIST.]

A. *adj.* Pertaining to the English royal family which based its title on its descent from John of Gaunt Duke of Lancaster (died 1399), or to the party (whose emblem was the Red Rose) that supported this family in the Wars of the Roses.

1828–40 TYTLER *Hist. Scot.* (1864) I. 145 For his good service in the destruction of the Lancastrian faction. **1861** *Sat. Rev.* 21 Dec. 643 The deaths of the Lancastrian Princes did not..open to him a near propsect of the crown.

B. *sb.*

1. An adherent of the house of Lancaster; one of the Lancastrian faction in the Wars of the Roses.

1838 *Penny Cycl.* XII. 129/1 Henry VI was after his death revered as a martyr by the Lancastrians.

2. A native of Lancashire.

1888 BRYCE *Amer. Commw.* III. VI. cxiii. 627 The difference between a Yorkshireman and a Lancastrian.

Also †**Lan'castrist** = prec. B. 1.

1654 VILVAIN *Epit. Ess.* IV. 66 Yorkists and Lancastrists on English land Darraind twelv cruel conflicts.

lance (lɑːns, -æ-), *sb.*[1] Forms: 3–8 **launce,** (4 **lancie**), 5 **lans, launse, lence,** 6 **lanse, (launch), lawnce,** 8 *Sc.* **lanss,** 4– **lance.** See also LAUNCE. [a. F. *lance* = Pr. *lansa*, Catal. *llansa*, Sp. *lanza*, Pg. *lança*, It. *lancia*:—L. *lancea.* The F. word has been adopted in all the Teut. langs.: MDu. *lanse, lancie* (Du. *lans*), MHG., mod.G. *lanze*, Da. *landse*, Sw. *lans.*

According to Varro the L. word was from a Spanish (? Iberian) source. Connexion with the synonymous Gr. λόγχη is phonologically improbable.]

1. a. A weapon, consisting of a long wooden shaft and an iron or steel head, held by a horseman in charging at full speed, and sustained formerly by a rest, now by a strap, through which the arm is passed. ***to break a lance*** (see BREAK *v.* 3). ***lance in rest*** (see REST).

c **1290** *S. Eng. Leg.* I. 281/118 Þreo launcene he heold in is hond. **1377** LANGL. *P. Pl.* B. III. 303 Alle that bereth baslarde, brode swerde or launce..Shal be demed to the deth. *c* **1473** G. ASHBY *Active Policy Prince* 541 Youre Comyns shude nat bere dagger, ne Lance, Ne noon other wepins defensife. **1580** SIDNEY *Ps.* XXXV. i, O Lord..take thy launce, and stoppe the way of those That seeke my bane. **1604** E. G[RIMSTONE] *D'Acosta's Hist. Indies* IV. 303 The Indians kil them with launces and crossebowes. **1673** RAY *Journ. Low C.* 234 The combatants being mounted on horseback with Launces in their hands, run one at another a full gallop. **1777** WATSON *Philip II* (1839) 43 The count's lance broke on Henry's corslet. **1781** GIBBON *Decl. & F.* lviii. III. 434 The lance was the..peculiar weapon of the knight. **1815** ELPHINSTONE *Acc. Caubul* (1842) II. 193 Their arms are a long and heavy lance and a shield.

b. *transf.* and *fig.*

1390 GOWER *Conf.* III. 351 And in his hond with many a firy launce He [Cupid] woundeth ofte. **1430–40** LYDG. *Bochas* I. iv. (1494) b ij b/1 Tyme..all consumith with his sherpe launce. **1713** YOUNG *Last Day* I. 128 And death might shake his threat'ning launce in vain. **1825** LONGF. *Sunrise on Hills* 10 Many a pinnacle Through the gray mist thrust up its shattered lance. **1880** C. & F. DARWIN *Movem. Pl.* 79 Their [the leaves] laminæ were..pressed against each other, forming a lance or wedge by which means they had broken through the ground. **1887** MRS. BURNETT *Little Ld. Fauntleroy* v. 86 He liked the big broad-branched trees, with the late afternoon sunlight striking golden lances through them.

†c. *fig.* Career as a soldier. *Obs. rare*⁻¹.

a **1635** NAUNTON *Fragm. Reg.* (Arb.) 29 Hitherto I have only touch'd him in his Courtship. I conclude him in his Lance.

†d. As a unit of measurement. *Obs. rare*⁻¹.

1604 E. G[RIMSTONE] *D'Acosta's Hist. Indies* IV. xxxvii. 311 It riseth many elles, yea, many launces in height.

2. A similar weapon, used for various purposes, e.g. for spearing fish; also in the whale-fishery, with modifying prefixes, as ***bomb-, gun-, hand-lance***, an instrument for killing the whale, after he has been harpooned and wearied out.

1727–41 CHAMBERS *Cycl.* s.v. *Fishery*, [Whale-Fishery.] Thrusting a long steeled lance under his gills into his breast. **1790** *Asiatic Res.* II. 342 When a man dies, all his live stock, cloth, hatchets, fishing lances, and in short every moveable thing he possessed is buried with him. **1883** *Fisheries Exhib. Catal.* 199 Earliest types of the hand-lances, formerly..used for killing whales..the old-fashioned, non-explosive gun-lance, and the bomb-lance.

3. = LANCET. Now *rare.*

1575 TURBERV. *Faulconrie* 346 If the pin open not of it selfe, slit it and open it with a little sharp launce of steele made whot. **1576** NEWTON *Lemnie's Complex.* I. x. 83 The veynes..swel out..offfering themselues to the Launce, by incision hansomly to be cut. **1681** GLANVILL *Sadducismus* II. 181 [He] took a Launce and launc't one of her hands. **1769** R. GRIFFITH *Gordian Knot* II. 122 By..the surgeon's lance I was dragged back to life and wretchedness again. **1878** L. P. MEREDITH *Teeth* 180 If the lance is sharp, it generally does not hurt at all.

4. a. A horse-soldier armed with a lance; a lancer.

1602 SEGAR *Hon. Mil. & Civ.* IV. xiv. 224 Esquires..able at the Musters to present a Launce or light horse, for the Prince's seruice. **1633** T. STAFFORD *Pac. Hib.* II. xxvi. (1810) 467 There is now in readinesse 150 Launces, which shall be presently embarqued. **1724** DE FOE *Mem. Cavalier* (1840) 227 Those lances..were brave fellows. **1831** SCOTT *Cast. Dang.* ii, A lance, in other words, a belted knight, commands this party.

b. *Hist.* A man-at-arms with his attendant archers, foot-soldiers, etc. Cf. F. *lance fournie.*

1818 HALLAM *Mid. Ages* (1872) I. 468 A lance in the technical language of those ages included the lighter cavalry attached to the man at arms, as well as himself. **1864** KIRK *Chas. Bold* II. IV. iii. 413 The 'lance' was simply the feudal family—the baron, or knight, with his wonted retinue of kinsmen and dependents.

†5. A branch of a tree, a shoot. *Obs.*

13.. *E.E. Allit. P.* A. 977 Lurked by launcez so lufly leued. **1523** FITZHERB. *Husb.* §138 Thou muste get thy graffes of the fayrest lanses, that thou canste fynde on the tree. **1669** WORLIDGE *Syst. Agric.* (1681) 132 Those [Graffs] you find to shoot up in one Lance, pinch off their tender tops.

6. In technical uses: a. *Carpentry.* 'A pointed blade, usually employed to sever the grain on each side of the intended path of a chipping-bit or router' (Knight *Dict. Mech.* 1875).

b. *Mil.* (*a*) 'An iron rod which is fixed across the earthen mould of a shell, and which keeps it suspended in the air when it is cast'. (*b*) 'An instrument which conveys the charge of a piece of ordnance and forces it home into the bore' (James *Milit. Dict.* 1802).

c. *Pyrotechny.* (See quots.) [F. *lance à feu.*]

1878 KENTISH *Pyrotechn. Treas.* 112 Lances. These are little cases charged with white or coloured star composition. **1879** W. H. BROWNE *Pyrotechny* vii. 81 Lances are..small, thin cases, containing compositions which burn with a white or coloured flame.

7. = *lance-corporal* (LANCE *sb.*[1] 10). *colloq.*

1888 KIPLING *Wee Willie Winkie* (1889) 74 The reg'ment don't go 'ome for another seven years. I'll be a Lance then or near to. **1961** PARTRIDGE *Dict. Slang* Suppl. 1164/1 *Lance*, lance-corporal: coll. late C. 19–20.

8. In full, ***oxygen lance.*** a. A thin metal pipe through which oxygen under pressure may be passed in order to burn away metal, concrete, or the like using heat generated by the burning of either the metal to be cut or the pipe itself.

1925 *Iron Trade Rev.* 24 Sept. 749/1 The oxygen lance is a means of burning a hole quickly through steel, slag or brick. Essentially it is nothing but a stream of pure oxygen flowing through a small iron pipe. If the oxygen strikes hot iron or steel, the metal burns rapidly... If the oxygen strikes non-metallic substances, like firebrick or slag, the lance pipe itself burns, produces the necessary heat and flux to melt the way through. **1926** *Blast Furnace & Steel Plant* XIV. 19/1 If a layer of slag is encountered, the lance pipe itself burns. **1944** *Ibid*, XXXII. 1077/1 The oxygen lance..has been used..for opening tap holes in blast furnaces and open-hearth furnaces, for tapping slag from soaking pits, for cutting up spills and skulls, and for..piercing or severing..heavy masses of iron and steel. **1945** *Machinery* (N.Y.) Nov. 156/1 Since the oxygen lance can sever metal of practically any thickness, it is an effective 'trouble-shooter' for metal-disposal problems.

b. A metal pipe, often water-cooled, through which oxygen under pressure may be injected into molten metal or directed on to its surface.

1948 *Jrnl. Iron & Steel Inst.* CLX. 221/1 Oxygen can be used in the basic electric-arc furnace for decarburization, either by means of the 'oxygen lance' or by direction of a strong blast of the gas through the slag cover. **1950** *Ibid.* CLXV. 411/1 The use of the oxygen lance for refining a high-chromium steel..enables the heat to be worked at a temperature some 200°C higher than normal. **1959** *New Scientist* 30 Apr. 965/2 Oxygen for the refining action is injected into the through metal water-cooled jets or 'lances'. **1971** *Engineering Index 1970* 3426/2 Effect of blowing practices in the LD converter on oxygen content of steel... Statistical methods were employed to study this influence, with particular reference to the effect of..the height of the lance on the bath.

9. *attrib.* and *Comb.*: a. simple attributive, as ***lance-blade, -bucket, -butt, -game, -head, -rest, -shaft, -throw, -thrust***; b. objective, as ***lance-breaking***; c. instrumental, as ***lance-pierced, -worn*** adjs.; d. similative, as ***lance-acuminated, -leaved, -like, -shaped*** adjs.

1800 *Asiatic Ann. Reg., Misc. Tracts* 271/1 Ovate, *lance-acuminated, entire towards the base. **1849** STOVEL *Canne's Necess.* Introd. 9 Truths in his hand were like *lance-blades in a cupping instrument, they entered the whole length of their steel. **1829** SCOTT *Ho. of Aspen* I. i, Neither hunting, nor feasting, nor *lance-breaking for me! **1876** JAS. GRANT *One of the '600'* i. 5 Captains of troops will report to Lieutenant..on the state of the saddlery, holsters, and *lance-buckets. **1865** KINGSLEY *Herew.* i. (1877) 36 When he came to the abbey-gate, he smote thereon with his *lance-butt. **1801** STRUTT *Sports & Past.* III. i. 108 The Just or *lance-game..differed materially from the tournament. **1851** D. WILSON *Preh. Ann.* (1863) I. vi. 173 The arrow and *lance heads, constructed from the amorphous masses of native flint. **1811** A. T. THOMSON *Lond. Disp.* (1818) 609 Take of *lance-leaved cinchona bark bruised, an ounce. **1579** J. JONES *Preserv. Bodie & Soule* I. xl. 87 Blasing Starres..as berdelike, *launcelike, swordlike [etc.]. **1868** LYNCH *Rivulet* CLXIII. ii, The lance-like rain, the darting hail. **1897** *Dublin Rev.* Apr. 375 The *lance-pierced side of Christ. **1855** OGILVIE, Suppl., **Lance-rest.* **1869** BOUTELL *Arms & Arm.* x. 206 At this period [*c* 1450–1500] a lance-rest was fixed to the upper part of the breast-plate on the right side. **1868** G. STEPHENS *Runic Mon.* I. 314 It is not..likely that all the long and round and straight poles found in the Danish Mosses..have always been *Lance-shafts. **1776** J. LEE *Introd. Bot.* Explan. Terms. 389 *Lanceolatæ*, *lance-shaped. **1864** T. MOORE *Brit. Ferns* 26 The leafy part of the frond is lance-shaped. **1856** KANE *Arct. Expl.* II. xxviii. 282 On two occasions we came upon the walrus sleeping,—once within actual *lance-thrust. **1842** FABER *Styrian Lake* 269 Like bruised embossing on a *lance-worn shield.

10. Special comb.: **lance-bombardier**, the rank in the Royal Artillery corresponding to lance-corporal in the infantry; **lance-corporal** [after LANCEPESADE] (see quot. 1802); †**lance-egged** *a. Bot.* = *lance-ovate*; **lance-famed** *a.*, famed for prowess with the lance; **lance-fish** = LAUNCE; **lance-head** = *lance-snake*; **lance-jack** *Army slang*, lance-corporal, lance-bombardier; **lance-knife**, ? = LANCET; **lance-linear** *a. Bot.*, narrowly lanceolate, almost linear; **lance-man**, †(*a*) a highwayman; (*b*) a warrior armed with a lance; **lance-oblong** *a. Bot.*, narrowly oblong; **lance-oval** *a. Bot.*, narrowly oval; **lance-ovate** *a.* = prec.; **lance-sergeant** [on analogy of *lance-corporal*], a corporal acting as sergeant; **lance-snake**, a venomous snake of the American genus *Bothrops* (or *Craspedocephalus*), esp. *B. lanceolatus*, of the W. Indies; = FER-DE-LANCE 2.

1935 A. H. BURNE *Royal Artillery Mess, Woolwich* xi. 230 In 1901 Driver Homewood was appointed kennel-huntsman. He has since received well merited, if not exactly rapid, promotion to the rank of *Lance-Bombardier. **1943** HUNT & PRINGLE *Service Slang* 43 *Lancejack.* Army for Lance-Corporal or Lance-Bombardier. **1960** D. A. CAMPBELL *Dress R. Artillery* ix. 47 In 1920 the rank of bombardier was upgraded to replace that of corporal, the latter rank being abolished in the Regiment... In the same year the appointment of acting bombardier was changed to that of lance bombardier, both these appointments wear a single chevron. **1968** *Listener* 22 Aug. 252/3 Tempting to identify with the lance-bombardier in charge of this guard squad. **1786** GROSE *Milit. Antiq.* I. 311 The lancepesata, anspesade, or as the present term is, *lance corporal. **1802** C. JAMES *Milit. Dict.* s.v. *Corporal*, Lance-Corporal, one who acts as corporal, receiving pay as a private. **1844** *Regul. & Ord. Army* 133 Corporals may be appointed to act as Lance-Serjeants, and the most approved Private Soldiers as Lance-Corporals. **1787** *Fam. Plants* I. 242 Divisions of the Border *lance-egg'd. **1718** POPE *Iliad* xiii. 278 The *Lance-fam'd [δουρικλυτός] Idomen of Crete. **1859–62** SIR J. RICHARDSON, etc. *Museum Nat. Hist.* (1868) II. 40/2 Amongst the former, or spine-tailed species [of Crotalidæ], are the *Lance-heads (*Craspedocephalina*) of the New World. *Ibid.* 41/1 The Lance-head is the most abundant of all serpents in the islands of Martinique and St. Lucia. **1912** H. WYNDHAM *Following the Drum* vii. 80 A junior corporal is a '*lance-jack'. **1937** D. JONES *In Parenthesis* III. 28 Tin soldiers, toy soldiers, militarymen in rows—you somehow suffer the pain of loss—it's an ungracious way of life—buttocked lance-jacks crawling for the second chevron. **1953** A. BARON *Human Kind* ix. 68 Foller the Salvation Corporal an' 'is Saintly Lance-Jack. **1971** L. DEIGHTON *Declarations of War* 11 Lance-jack at the time, actually. *Ibid.*, You're not looking too good, Colonel, if you don't mind an ex-lance-jack saying so. **1610** MARKHAM *Masterp.* II. cxi. 396 Others take a sharpe *launce-knife, and [etc.]. **1787** *Fam. Plants* I. 30 Petals..*lance-linear. **1589** RIDER *Eng.-Lat. Dict.*, A *Launce man, *hastiger.* **1592** GREENE *Conny Catching* II. A 3 b, The Priggar is he that steales the horse... The Priggar if he be a Launce man, that is, one that is already horst, then [etc.]. **1598** FLORIO, *Lanciatore*..a lance-man, a pike-man. **1808** PIKE *Sources Mississ.* III. App. (1810) 11 The lancemen are always mounted. **1787** *Fam. Plants* I. 285 Germ *lance-oblong, compress'd. *a* **1794** SIR W. JONES in *Asiatic Res.* (1795) IV. 262 Leaves opposite, *lance-oval, pointed at both ends. **1889** in *Lancet* 27 Apr. I. 866/2 The cocci, as found in the blood of an inoculated animal, are, as a rule, oval or lance-oval in form. **1799** *Asiatic Res.* VI. 349 Leaflets..*lance-ovate, entire, smooth. **1815** WELLINGTON in Gurw. *Desp.* (1838) XII. 617, I now beg leave to recommend to you *Lance Sergeant Graham of the Coldstream regiment of Guards. **1880** *Cassell's Nat. Hist.* IV. 319 The last group of the American Pit Vipers is that of the *Lance Snakes. One of these is the Yellow Viper, of Martinique, called Fer-de-lance there.

†**lance,** *sb.*[2] *Obs.* In 4 (5) **launce, lanss.** [f. LANCE *v.*]

1. A leap, bound, dash. (Cf. LAUNCH *sb.*)

1375 BARBOUR *Bruce* x. 414 And he that was in iuperdy Till de, a lanss [*MS. E.* launce] till him he maid.

2. A cut, incision, slit.

1669 WORLIDGE *Syst. Agric.* vii. §10 (1681) 132 It [Pinching] gives not that wound to Trees that Incisions or Lances usually do... Giving the Lance close behind a Bud, a thing to be especially observed in Pruning. *Ibid.* 133 When you cut any Pithy Tree..make your Lance under, or on one side.

lance (lɑːns, -æ-), *v.* Forms: 4–8 **launce,** 4 *Sc.* **launss,** 4–6 chiefly *Sc.* **lans(s,** 5 **lawnce,** 5–6 **launse,** 4– **lance.** [a. OF. *lancier* (F. *lancer*):—L.

lanceāre, f. *lancea* LANCE *sb.*[1]; the ONF. form *lanchier* was adopted as LAUNCH *v.* In branch II f. LANCE *sb.*[1]]

I. 1. a. *trans.* To fling, hurl, launch, throw (a dart, also fire, lightning, smoke); to shoot out (the tongue); to put forth (blossoms). Also with *forth, out, up.* Now *rare* (chiefly *poet.*).

13.. *Guy Warw.* (A.) 2394 To him þai launced boþe spere and swerd. **1393** LANGL. *P. Pl.* C. XIX. 10 The tree hihte trewe-loue..launceþ vp blossemes. *c* **1394** *P. Pl. Crede* 551 þei [friars]..launceþ heiȝe her hemmes wiþ babelyng in stretes. *c* **1532** DU WES *Introd. Fr.* in Palsgr. 949 To lance, *lancer.* **1598** BARRET *Theor. Warres* III. i. 32 A lauelin..they did lance or dart at the enemie. **1663** SIR G. MACKENZIE *Relig. Stoic* iii. (1685) 28 As beams are lanced out from the body of the Sun. **1710** *Lond. Gaz.* No. 4653/1 A spread Eagle, representing his Majesty's Arms, lanced a Rocket. **1795–7** SOUTHEY *Juvenile & Minor Poems* Poet. Wks. II. 210 The lightning is lanced at our sires. **1801** —— *Thalaba* v. xi, The adder in her haunts disturbed Lanced at the intruding staff her arrowy tongue. **1827** I. TAYLOR *Transm. Anc. Bks.* xvii. 279 He affirms [Xerxes] to have lanced darts at the sun. **1834** M. SCOTT *Cruise Midge* (1859) 488 Rolling in smoaky wreaths and lancing out ragged shreds from their lower edges. **1898** M. P. SHIEL *Yellow Danger* 136 The torpedo-boat lances one of her horrid needles of steel.

b. with immaterial obj., *e.g.* a look; †also with *forth.*

13.. *E.E. Allit. P.* C. 350 Lo! my lore is in þe loke, lance hit þerinne. **1635** PERSON *Varieties* I. 15 The Stars, and these celestiall bodies..doe lance forth their power upon the Earth also. **1752** CARTE *Hist. Eng.* III. 9 The pope was to lance his censures against the common enemy. **1765** H. WALPOLE *Otranto* iv. (1798) 76 Here I lance her anathema at thy head. **1832** *Examiner* 436/1 He lances one of his droll looks. **1855** M. ARNOLD *The Voice* 3 As the kindling glances..Which the bright moon lances From her tranquil sphere. **1898** M. P. SHIEL *Yellow Danger* 157 Suddenly he lanced a horrid shriek.

†c. *refl.* To hurl oneself, to spring, shoot. *Obs.*

c **1530** LD. BERNERS *Arth. Lyt. Bryt.* (1814) 183 He launced hymselfe [from the ship] & lepte into the myddes of the prease wyth his good swerde in his hande. **1658** R. WHITE tr. *Digby's Powd. Symp.* (1660) 20 The light..lancing herself by a marvellous celerity on all sides by streight lines.

2. a. *int.* for *refl.* To bound, spring, move quickly, rush. Also with *forth, out.* Const. *on. Obs.* exc. *dial.*

c **1330** R. BRUNNE *Chron.* (1810) 94 With a herde þei mette, a herte þerof gan lance. **1375** BARBOUR *Bruce* III. 122 He..strak with spurs the stede in hy, And he lansyt furth delyvirly. *c* **1470** *Golagros & Gaw.* 901 He lansit out our ane land, and drew noght ane lyte. *c* **1470** HENRYSON *Mor. Fab.* v. (*Parl. Beasts*) vii, Ane vnicorne come lansand ouer ane law. **1481** CAXTON *Godfrey* xliii. 82 The conestables..launced on this partye of thoost whiche was not yet passed. **1513** DOUGLAS *Æneis* IX. ix. 74 Turnus, lanssand lychtly our the landis. **1530** LYNDESAY *Test. Papyngo* 353 Ȝe, that now bene lansyng vpe the ledder, Tak tent in tyme. **1840** *Evidence Hull Docks Comm.* 74 When there is no wind, we lance along with poles. **1883** *Hampsh. Gloss.*, *Lance*, to leap, bound; the deer are said 'to lance over the turf'.

†b. *transf.* and *fig.* Of leaves, fire: To spring, spring forth, shoot up. Of pain: To shoot. *Obs.*

13.. *Gaw. & Gr. Knt.* 526 þe leuez lancen fro þe lynde, & lyȝten on þe grounde. **13..** *E.E. Allit. P.* B. 966 As lance leuez of þe boke þat lepes in twynne. **1393** LANGL. *P. Pl.* C. XIII. 185 Of greyn ded in erthe Atte laste launceth vp wher-by we lyuen alle. *a* **1400** *Pistill of Susan* 109 þe Lilye, þe louache, launsyng wiþ leue. *c* **1470** HENRY *Wallace* VII. 429 The lemand low sone lanssyt apon hycht. **1756** MOUNSEY in *Phil. Trans.* L. 21 The pain on the stomach returned, which lanced to the left side, with dartings inwardly.

†3. a. *trans.* To launch (a boat).

c **1515** *Cocke Lorell's B.* 12 Some ye longe bote dyde launce, some mende y[e] corse.

b. *intr.* To launch forth, push *out.*

1526 *Pilgr. Perf.* (W. de W. 1531) 141 b, Now hath y[e] patriarke Noe all his chyldren..in his shyp, & is launced from the lande. **1581** STUDLEY tr. *Seneca's Agamem.* I. Chorus 61 Nor launcing to the depe where bottom none is found. **1595** MAYNARDE *Drake's Voy.* (Hakl. Soc.) 7 Had wee lanced under the forte at our first cominge to anchor, we had [etc.].

†4. To throw out (a tale, words, etc.); to utter.

13.. *Gaw. & Gr. Knt.* 1212 Al laȝande þe lady lanced þo bourdez. *Ibid.* 2124 þat I schal lelly yow layne, & lance neuer tale.

†5. *intr.* To make a dash or stroke with a pen.

1588 J. MELLIS *Briefe Instruct.* E iij, When yee haue thus entered it into Journall, then presently after in the memoriall..yee shall launce or make a stroke.

II. 6. a. To pierce with or as with a lance or a lancet; to cut, gash, slit. Also, to slit open; to open. *Obs.* exc. *poet.*

13.. *E.E. Allit. P.* B. 1428 [He] comaundes hym cofly coferes to lance. *c* **1440** *Promp. Parv.* 290 Lawncyn [*v.r.* lawnchyn], or stynge wythe a spere, or blode yryne, *lanceo.* **1586** MARLOWE *1st Pt. Tamburl.* I. ii, We will lift our swords, And..lance his greedy thirsting throat. **1615** G. SANDYS *Trav.* 12 In the Summer they lanced the rine with a stone. **1638** *Penit. Conf.* vii. (1657) 155 Baals Priests, lancing themselves to procure audience. **1678** BUNYAN *Pilgr.* I. 167 Then they Lanced his flesh with Knives. **1713** TICKELL *Guardian* No. 125 ¶9 Bold Nimrod first..lanc'd the bristling boar. **1728** MORGAN *Algiers* II. iii. 253 They lanced the Ravisher, and every one of the Turks. **1783** *Phil. Trans.* LXXIII. 241 On the brain being lanced, the..whale died immediately.

fig. **1494** FABYAN *Chron.* VII. 431 Many with great honours I dyd whylom auaunce, That nowe with dyshonoure doon me stynge and launce. **1828** *Blackw. Mag.* XXIV. 716 The jagged lightning lanced the forest-gulfs with its swift and perilous beauty.

b. *intr.* To pierce.

a **1400** *Leg. Rood* (1871) 142 þe swerd of loue þorw hire gan launce.

c. *trans.* To wound or kill with a lance.

1898 *Westm. Gaz.* 6 Apr. 6/3 The troopers lancing and sabring, and the officers pistolling the Dervishes.

7. *Surg.* **a.** To make an incision in (the gums, a sore, a tumour) with a lancet; to cut open. Occas. with a person as object. Also, to fetch *out* or let out by lancing.

1474 CAXTON *Chesse* III. v. h j b, The surgyens..ought not to be hasty to launce and cutte aposthumes & soores. **1526** *Pilgr. Perf.* (W. de W. 1531) 278 O blessed lorde, here in this lyfe, cutte me, burne me, launce me, that fynally thou mayst haue mercy on me. **1575** TURBERV. *Faulconrie* 257 The way to cure it, is to give the humor a vent by launsing it. **1578** T. WILCOCKS *Serm. Pawles* 93 Thrust diligently your sword of iustice in, to launce out all corruption and bagage which is gathered in the bowels. **1615** LATHAM *Falconry* (1633) 132 You must haue care to launce it long wayes as the sinews do run. **1654** TRAPP *Comm. Job* v. 18 He is both a Father and a physitian, hee lanceth us not unlesse need be. **1722** DE FOE *Plague* (1884) 268 To lance and dress the..Tumours. **1725** POPE *Odyss.* XIV. 87 Of two [porkers] his cutlass lanced the spouting blood. **1878** L. P. MEREDITH *Teeth* 36 The dentist ..sees the immediate beneficial results of lancing hot, congested gums.

fig. **1561** DAUS tr. *Bullinger on Apoc.* (1573) 38 We are many tymes launced and cut with the worde of God, to our great profit and discipline. **1621** QUARLES *Esther* xii. I 2 b, When Haman then had lanc'd his rip'ned griefe, In bloody tearmes, they thus appli'd reliefe. **1665** BOYLE *Occas. Refl.* III. vi, The Orator..is more sollicitous to tickle their Ears, than..to launce their Consciences. **1705** HICKERINGILL *Priest-cr.* II. viii. 90 Some Inconveniencies in Church-Government, are better palliated, then lanced to the bottom.

b. *absol.* or *intr.* To make an incision.

1646 J. HALL *Horae Vac.* 48 They doe better Launce into secret humours.

8. *trans.* To cut (a hole) or inject (oxygen) by means of an oxygen lance.

1945 *Machinery* (N.Y.) Nov. 156/1 After a hole had been lanced completely through, the cut was continued to the bottom of the casting. **1946** *Steel* 11 Feb. 114/2 It was planned..to drain the salamander..by drilling and lancing a hole below the taphole in the base of the furnace. **1963** *Times* 22 Apr. p. viii/6 Oxygen is lanced into the furnace as it is being tapped. This causes the slag and lead to run.

Hence **lanced** *ppl. a.*

1607 TOPSELL *Four-f. Beasts* 516 To..spread them vpon the aforesaid eaten or launced woundes.

lanced (lɑːnst, -æ-), *a.* [f. LANCE *sb.*[1] + -ED[2].] Having a lance or point; pointed or shaped like a lance.

1787 *Fam. Plants* I. 32 The leaflets lanced. **1815** KIRBY & SP. *Entomol.* I. 391 The bloodthirsty gnat has five [suckers], some acutely lanced at the extremity. **1894** BLACKMORE *Perlycross* 23 The delicate bells of sky-blue flax quivering on lanced foliage.

lancegay ('lɑːnsgeɪ, -æ-). *Obs.* exc. *Hist.* Also 4–8 **launcegay(e**, 5 **lawncegay**, 6 **launcezagaye, launsgay**, 7 *erron.* **lance de gay**. [a. OF. *lancegaye*, f. (with contraction) *lance*, LANCE *sb.*[1] + *zagaye* (see ZAGAIE, ASSAGAI *sb.*).] A kind of lance.

[**1383** *Act 7 Rich. II*, c. 13 §1 Le Roi defende que desoremes null homme chivache deinz le Roialme armez.. ovesque lancegay.] *c* **1386** CHAUCER *Sir Thopas* 41 In his hand a launcegay A long swerd by his side. **1390** GOWER *Conf.* III. 369 A firy lancegay, Which whilom through my hert he cast. **1467** in *Eng. Gilds* (1870) 388 That no man go armed, to bere launcegayes, Gleyves, Speres, and other wepyn. *c* **1500** *Robin Hood* (Ritson) 18 He bare a launsgay in his honde. **1591** SIR J. SMYTH *Instruct. Milit.* 199, I would wish them to have Launces commonly called Launceza-gayas of good, tite, and stiffe ash. **1605** CAMDEN *Rem.* (1657) 209 To speak of lesser weapons, both defensive and offensive of our nation, as their granad, baselard, launce-gay, &c. would be endless. **1614** RALEIGH *Hist. World* v. iii. §1. 359 These carrying a kinde of Lance de gay, sharpe at both ends, which they held in the middest of the staffe. **1799** SCOTT *Sheph. Tale*, A launcegay strong, full twelve ells long, By every warrior hung.

attrib. **1436** *Nottingham Rec.* II. 158 Duorum garmentorum, unius clocher, et unius launcegaysshaft.

'lance-knight. *Hist.* Forms: see LANCE *sb.* and KNIGHT. Also 6 **lance-kneyght**, 9 **lance-knecht**; and see LANSQUENET. [ad. G. *lanzknecht* (*lanz* = LANCE *sb.*[1]), an etymologizing perversion of *landsknecht*, f. *lands*, genitive of *land* LAND *sb.*[1] + *knecht* servant.

Originally the G. word denoted the mercenary foot-soldiers belonging to the imperial territory, in contradistinction to the Swiss; but it was very early applied in a wider sense; afterwards the etymological association with *lance* caused it to be restricted to men armed with a lance or similar weapon.]

A mercenary foot-soldier, esp. one armed with a lance or pike.

1530 PALSGR. 237/1 Lansknyght, *lancequenet.* **1550** W. LYNNE *Carion's Cron.* 248 Many Launceknyghtes of the Germayne nation sawe with their eyes that [etc.]. **1552** HULOET, Men bearyng shyldes of siluer, called launce knyghtes, *argyraspidæ.* **1579** DIGGES *Stratiot.* 120 The Lance Kneyghts also encamp always in the fielde very stronglye. **1581** J. BELL *Haddon's Answ. Osor.* 463 b, Although λογχαιος be nothing els then a greeke word, signifiyng a launceknight. **1598** B. JONSON *Ev. Man in Hum.* II. i, Well, now must I practise to get the true garbe of one of these Launce-knights. **1606** BRYSKETT *Civ. Life* 145 The Lansknight and the Switzer vse also the fife at this day with the drum. **1825** SCOTT *Talism.* vi, Give him a flagon of Rhenish to drink with his besmirched baaren-hauters and lance-knechts.

attrib. **1653** URQUHART *Rabelais* I. xxxv, Tripet would have traiterously cleft his head with his horsemans sword, or lanse-knight fauchion.

transf. *c* **1626** *Dick of Devon* IV. i. in Bullen *O. Pl.* II. 63 The needle lance knights..put so many hookes and eyes to every hose and dubblet.

lancelet ('lɑːnslɪt, -æ-). Also 6 **lancelette, launcelet, -lot**, 9 **lancelot**. [f. LANCE *sb.*[1] + -LET.]

†1. A lancet. *Obs.*

1573 BARET *Alv.* L 77 A Lancelette or like instrument, *scalprum chirurgicum.* **1589** RIDER *Eng.-Lat. Dict.* s.v. *Launce*, A Launcelot to cut wounds, *smilium.* **1593** G. HARVEY *New Letter* 12 Pierces Supererogation..is lest beholding to the penknife: Nashes S. Fame hath somewhat more of the launcelet. **1656** BLOUNT *Glossogr.*, *Launcelot*, or *Lancelot.*

2. *Zool.* A small fish-like animal; = AMPHIOXUS.

1836 YARRELL *Brit. Fishes* II. 468 The Lancelet, *Amphioxus lanceolatus.* **1846** CARPENTER *Physiol.* 382 The Amphioxus or Lancelot. **1847–9** TODD *Cycl. Anat.* IV. 450/2 In the..lancelet the only vestige of a distinct hepatic organ is a large cœcum. **1859** DARWIN *Orig. Spec.* iv. (1873) 99 Members of the shark family would not tend to supplant the lancelet.

†lancell. *Obs.* Also 4 **launsele**. [a. OF. *lancele*, dim. of *lance* LANCE *sb.*[1]] A herb (*Plantago lanceolata*).

a **1400** *Med. MS.* in *Archæologia* XXX. 356 Take jws of launsele I seye W[t] ye whyte of tweyne eyre. **1538** TURNER *Libellus*, Lancell, *Plantago.*

†'lancely, *a. Obs.* In 6 **launcely**. [f. LANCE *sb.*[1] + -LY[1].] Proper to a lance; lance-like.

a **1586** SIDNEY *Arcadia* II. (1622) 179 His Lances..strong to giue a launcely blow indeede.

†'lancement. *Obs. rare*[−1]. [f. LANCE *v.* + -MENT. Cf. F. *lancement.*] The action of lancing or cutting; an incision.

1658 SIR T. MAYERNE *Archimag. Anglo-Gall.* xix. 15 You must make some Lancements or inlets [in the fowl]..that your said spices may the better hold or fasten.

†'lancent, *a.* and *sb. Obs.* Also 5 **lanceaunt, lawncent**. [a. F. *lançant*, pres. pple. of *lancer* LANCE *v.*] **A.** *adj.* That lances, adapted for lancing. **B.** *sb.* = LANCET (if not a scribal error).

c **1400** tr. *Secreta Secret., Gov. Lordsh.* 111 Oper Instrumentȝ perceaunt & lanceaunt. *c* **1440** *Promp. Parv.* 290 Lawncent [*v.r.* lawnset], or blode yryne, *lanceola.* **1622** MABBE tr. *Aleman's Guzman d'Alf.* II. 142 It is now a great while agoe since I finger'd my fleame or lancent.

lanceolar ('lɑːnsiːələ(r), -æ-), *a.* [f. L. *lanceola* (see next) + -AR.] = next.

1810 *Asiatic Res.* XI. 165 Leaves broad, lanceolar, subsessile on their sheath.

lanceolate ('lɑːnsiːələt, -æ-), *a.* Chiefly in scientific use. [ad. L. *lanceolātus*, f. *lanceola* small lance; in med.L. *lancet*, dim. of *lancea* LANCE *sb.*[1]] Resembling a spear-head in shape; narrow and tapering to each end.

1760 J. LEE *Introd. Bot.* III. v. (1765) 176 *Lanceolate, Spear-shaped*; when the Figure is oblong, narrowing gradually at each End towards the Extremity. **1794** MARTYN *Rousseau's Bot.* xxii. 313 Toadflax has linear leaves inclining to lanceolate. **1845** LINDLEY *Sch. Bot.* iv. (1858) 26 *Wood Anemone*... Leaflets lanceolate, lobed, and cut. **1851–6** WOODWARD *Mollusca* 69 *Loligo vulgaris*:..Pen lanceolate, with the shaft produced in front. **1869** GILLMORE tr. *Figuier's Reptiles & Birds* ii. 46 The broad, flat, and lanceolate form of head is exemplified in certain Tree Snakes.

¶ **b.** Used for 'lancet-shaped'.

1883 *Century Mag.* Apr. 821/1 The long, shapeless splits in the walls became the delicate lanceolate windows.

c. *Comb.*, signifying 'lanceolate and...', 'between lanceolate and...', as ***lanceolate-acute, -linear, -subulate*** adjs.; also in quasi-Lat. form **lanceolato-**, as ***lanceolato-hastate, -subulate*** adjs.

1806 GALPINE *Brit. Bot.* 184 L[eaves] lanceolato-hastate. **1836** LOUDON *Encycl. Plants* 897 *Sphagnum cuspidatum*.. Leaves lanceolato-subulate lax. **1845** LINDLEY *Sch. Bot.* vi. (1858) 82 Leaves green, smooth, lanceolate-linear. **1847** W. E. STEELE *Field Bot.* 73 Sep[als] lanceolate-acute. **1870** HOOKER *Stud. Flora* 240 Sepals slender lanceolate-subulate.

Hence **'lanceolately** *adv.*, in a lanceolate shape. Also **lanceo'lation**, the property of being lanceolate (in recent Dicts.).

1872 H. C. WOOD *Fresh-Water Algæ* 109 [*Closterium*] Narrowly lanceolately-fusiform.

lanceolated ('lɑːnsiːəˌleɪtɪd, -æ-), *a.* [formed as LANCEOLATE + -ED.] = LANCEOLATE.

1752 SIR J. HILL *Hist. Anim.* 78 The sharp-horned Phalæna..with white lanceolated wings. **1753** CHAMBERS *Cycl. Supp.* s.v. *Leaf*, Lanceolated Leaf. **1769** PENNANT *Zool.* III. 62 The tail is lanceolated and sharp at the end. **1782** MARSHALL in *Phil. Trans.* LXXIII. 220 A delicate point or sting..which on a cursory view appears to be a simple lanceolated instrument. **1821** SCOTT *Pirate* xxv, The votary dropped his offering..through the mullions of a lanceolated window. **1901** *Chambers's Jrnl.* May 348/2 The under side [of the *phiale*] is occupied by narrow lanceolated leaves.

lancepesade, lanceprisado (lɑːnspɪ'zɑːd, -æ-, ˌlænsprɪ'zɑːdəʊ). *Hist.* Forms: α. 6 **lancepezzade**, 7 **lance-, lans(e)pesade, -ado, lanspasata**, 8

lancepesata, lanspessade. Cf. ANSPESSADE. *β.* 7 lancepers-, -pres-, -prez-, -pris, -prizade, -ado, lans-, launcepres-, -prisade, -ado, 9 lanceprisade. [a. F. *lancepessade* (now *anspessade*) 'lancepesado, the meanest officer in a foot-company' (Cotgr.), ad. It. *lancia spezzata*, lit. 'broken lance' (*spezzare* to break in pieces, 'dispiece', f. *s-* = *dis-* + *pezza* piece). For the quasi-Sp. ending of some forms see -ADO; the forms with *r* are due to association with Sp. *presa* grip, clutch.

The It. word is recorded only in the senses 'one of a prince's bodyguard' and (in *pl.*) 'soldiers of a superior class not included in the ordinary companies'; Florio (s.v. *Spezzato*) renders it 'a demi-lance, light horseman'; Italian etymologists suggest that the primary sense was 'one whose lance has often been shivered in warfare, one who has seen much service' (Tommaseo s.v. *Spezzato*). The peculiar Fr. and Eng. sense (= lance-corporal) can be accounted for only conjecturally, but it may have arisen from the practice of appointing specially experienced privates, in emergencies, to act as officers of the lowest rank.]

a. (See quot. 1578.) **b.** A non-commissioned officer of the lowest grade; a lance-corporal.

1578 FENTON *Guicciard.* II. 104 The Marquis..being followed with a valiant companye of younge gentlemen and Lancepezzades (these are braue and proued souldiers interteyned aboue the ordinary companies). **1605** *Tryall Chev.* III. i. in Bullen *O. Pl.* III. 305 The tother Launcepresado. [Applied derisively by a soldier to an officer of high rank.] **1611** CHAPMAN *May Day* Plays 1873 II. 390 Serjeant Piemeat, Corporall Conny, Lanceprizado Larke. **1617** MIDDLETON & ROWLEY *Fair Quarrel* IV. iv, I will learne to roare, and still maintain the name of captaine over these Launcepresadoes. **1625** MARKHAM *Soldier's Accid.* 7 The Lanspresado..in the Corporalls absence, as vpon a guard or otherwise, doth all the Corporalls duties. **1708** *Lond. Gaz.* No. 4420/7, 10 Serjeants, 10 Corporals, 10 Lanspessades. **1758** J. WATSON *Milit. Dict.* (ed. 5) *Lancepesade*, an inferior Officer, subordinate to the Corporal, to assist him in his Duty, and supply his Place in his Absence. **1826** SCOTT *Woodst.* xxxiv, Thou, Zerubbabel Robins, I know wilt be their lance-prisade.

c. *transf.*

a **1605** POLWART *Flyting w. Montgomerie* 795 Beld bisset! marmissed! lansprezed to the lownes! **1622** MASSINGER *Virg. Mart.* II. i, This Bacchus, who is..lanceprezade to red noses. *a* **1700** B. E. *Dict. Cant. Crew, Lanspresado*, he that comes into Company with but Two pence in his Pocket.

¶ In the Italian sense (see above) with corrupt It. form.

1687 *Lond. Gaz.* No. 2250/3 His Eminencies own Equipage consisted of..12 Pages, as many Lanspasatas or Gentlemen, walking on foot by him, 12 more on Horse-back [etc.].

lancequenet, obs. variant of LANSQUENET.

† **'lancer**[1]. *Obs.* Forms: 5 lanceour, 6-7 launcer, 7 lancer. [ad. OF. *lanceor, lanceur*, f. *lancer* to lance, throw, or f. LANCE *v.* + -ER[1].] One who, or that which lances, in senses of the vb.

1. One who lances or throws (a dart).

1422 tr. *Secreta Secret., Priv. Priv.* 215 Archeris, abblastres, and Lanceouris of Dartes brandynge.

2. = LANCET.

1537 *Matthew's Bible, 1 Kings* xviii. 28 They..cut them selues as their maner was with knyues and launcers [**1611** lancers]. **1587** MASCALL *Gov. Cattle* (1627) 177 Raze him with a crooked launcer, from the heele to the toe. **1611** FLORIO, *Lanciatore*, a launcer. **1614** T. WHITE *Martyrd. St. George* C b, The Pincers, Lancers, Hunger, Thirst did tyre His holy bodie. *a* **1625** BOYS *Wks.* (1629-30) 39 They did see him whetting his lancer to cut the throat of the disease. **1688** R. HOLME *Armoury* III. 324/2 Another [Farriers Instrument] with a sharp point, called a Lancer.

'lancer[2] ('lɑːnsə(r), -æ-). Forms: 6 lancere, 6-7 launcier, 6-8 lancier, 7 lanceer(e, launceer, launcer, 7- lancer. [a. or ad. F. *lancier*, f. *lance* LANCE *sb.*[1] Cf. late L. *lanceārius* or *lanciārius*.]

1. A (cavalry) soldier armed with a lance; now only, a soldier belonging to one of certain regiments officially called Lancers.

In the British army there were, in 1901, six regiments of Lancers, the 5th, 9th, 12th, 16th, 17th, and 21st. They were armed with carbine (formerly sword) and pistol as well as lance. They have since been reorganized as three regiments of the Royal Armoured Corps, the 16th/5th, 9th/12th, and 17th/21st Lancers.

1590 MARLOWE *2nd Pt. Tamburl.* I. ii. F 5 b, Backt by stout Lanceres of Germany. **1611** SPEED *Hist. Gt. Brit.* IX. xiii. §107. 740 In his Company were..not aboue fifteene Lanciers. **1611** FLORIO, *Lanciere*, a launcier. **1648** *Lanc. Tracts* (Chetham Soc.) 263 Collonal Thornhaugh..was slaine, being ran into the body, and thigh, and head, by the enemies Launcers. **1712** *Perquisite Monger* 14 Invested with the Command of a Regiment of Horse and a Troop of Lanciers. **1833** *Regul. Instr. Cavalry* I. 159 The lancer is to have his lance near the right foot. **1879** *Cassell's Techn. Educ.* III. 362 The lancer has sword and pistol besides his lance.

transf. *a* **1657** LOVELACE *Poems* (1864) 177 The heron mounted doth appear On his own Peg'sus a lanceer.

2. *pl.* The name of a species of quadrille. Also the music proper to this dance.

1862 *Athenæum* 25 Jan. 111 The 'Lancers', now so fashionable, was introduced by Laborde in 1836. **1868** B. HARTE *Arctic Vision*, Trip it all ye merry dancers In the airiest of lancers. **1870** H. SMART *Race for Wife* i, As she whirls by in the Valse, or glides in front of them in the Lancers.

3. *attrib.* and *Comb.*, as ***lancer-braiding, -cap, -regiment***; also ***lancer-like*** adj.

1897 *Daily News* 16 Mar. 6/4 Bolero white cloth is arranged under the *lancer braiding. **1844** W. H. MAXWELL *Sports & Adv. Scotl.* iii. (1855) 45 The *lancer cap and green habit of the Honourable Juliana Beningfield! **1892** E. REEVES *Homeward Bound* 248 Making..quadrille and *lancer-like figures with sudden turns on the toes. **1868** *Regul. & Ord. Army* ¶ 1146 In a *lancer Regiment, the Men who collected the lances, are to be marched to the baggage waggons.

lancet ('lɑːnsɪt, -æ-). Forms: 5 lan-, lawncette, lawnset, 6 launcette, 6-8 launcet, 6- lancet. [ad. OF. F. *lancette*, dim. of *lance* LANCE *sb.*[1] Cf. It. *lancetta*.]

† **1. a.** ? A small lance, a dart. **b.** In whale-fishery = LANCE *sb.*[1] 2. *Obs.*

c **1420** *Siege Rouen* in *Archæologia* XXI. 52 And also lawnsetys were leyde on hey, For to schete both ferre an ney. **1752** BOND in *Phil. Trans.* XLVII. 430 Which the fishers observing, row up and dispatch the whale with long lancets.

2. a. A surgical instrument of various forms usually with two edges and a point like a lance, used for bleeding, opening abscesses, etc.

c **1440** [see LANCENT]. **1474** CAXTON *Chesse* 86 He dyd his vysage to be kutte wyth a knyf and lancettis endlong and overthwart. **1530** PALSGR. 237/1 Lancet, an instrument, *lancette*. **1543** TRAHERON *Vigo's Chirurg.* (1586) 64 Cut the Scrophule..with a sharpe instrument, as with a launcet. **1612** WOODALL *Surg. Mate* Wks. (1653) 18 Without question each Surgeons Mate knoweth a Launcet as well as myself. **1665** BOYLE *Occas. Refl.* II. iv, And calls for a Lancet, rather than a Julep. **1775** SHERIDAN *St. Patr. Day* I. i, Such an arm for a bandage, veins that seemed to invite the Lancet. **1837** W. IRVING *Capt. Bonneville* III. 146 When they underwent the operation of the lancet, the doctor's wife and another lady were present. **1856** DRUITT *Surgeon's Vade mecum* 631 The operator..pushes the lancet obliquely into the vein.

b. *Ent.* (See quot.)

1826 KIRBY & SP. *Entomol.* III. 362 *Scalpella* (the Lancets), a pair of instruments, usually more slender than the Cultelli, which probably enter the veins or sap-vessels, and together with them form a tube for suction.

3. Short for *lancet-arch, -light, -window*.

1848 B. WEBB *Continent. Ecclesiol.* 45 Two stages of tall Pointed arches, and a huge lancet within each. **1864** TENNYSON *Aylmer's F.* 622 Greenish glimmerings through the lancets. **1879** SIR G. SCOTT *Lect. Archit.* I. 296 Some gable-end with its lofty lancets shows the noble scale of the ancient church.

4. *attrib.* and *Comb.* **a.** ***lancet edge, †-ichthyodont; lancet-shaped, lancet-pointed*** (cf. 4 b) adjs.; **lancet-fish**, the doctor-fish (*Acanthurus*); † **lancet-loupe**, a loophole for throwing darts (cf. 1 a).

1875 *Carpentry & Join.* 52 A side filister..having a second point or *lancet edge to cut the fibres across as the work proceeds. **1840** MUDIE *Cuvier's Anim. Kingd.* (1849) 303 *Acanthurus*, *Lancet-fishes, have..a strong spine on each side of the tail, as sharp as a lancet, with which they inflict severe wounds. **1708** *Phil. Trans.* XXVI. 78 The *Lancet or Mucronated Ichthyodont. **1562** PHAER *Æneid* IX. C cj, The Troyans..through their *launcet loupes their whirling darts do thick bestowe. **1888** *Century Mag.* Aug. 585/1 These parts..are all in the *Lancet-Pointed (Early English) style. **1956** *Nature* 10 Mar. 484/1 This is then crushed to a very fine paste by means of a lancet-pointed dissecting needle. **1899** CAGNEY tr. *Jaksch's Clin. Diagn.* vi. (ed. 4) 232 Certain *lancet-shaped bodies.

b. *Arch.*, as **lancet arch**, one with an acutely-pointed head resembling the blade of a lancet; **lancet window** a high and narrow window terminating in a lancet arch; similarly, ***lancet Gothic, lancet light, lancet style***.

1823 P. NICHOLSON *Pract. Build.* 587 *Lancet-arch. **1848** RICKMAN *Archit.* 50 Lancet arches..have a radius longer than the breadth of the arch. **1836** *Gentl. Mag.* Feb. 164/2 A chapel..The style is the *lancet Gothic. **1874** PARKER *Goth. Archit.* I. iv. 131 In the transept of Salisbury Cathedral..is a good example of a window of four *lancet-lights. **1849** FREEMAN *Archit.* 352 The details lose the great distinctness of the *Lancet style. **1781** J. WARTON *Kiddington* (1783) 17 Mouldings of *lancet windows. **1866** G. MACDONALD *Ann. Q. Neighb.* ii. (1878) 20 The dusky light that came through a small lancet window.

Hence **lance'teer**, one who uses a lancet; a surgeon. **lan'ceted** *a.*, (of a window) having a lancet arch; (of a church) having lancet-windows.

1824 *Examiner* 8/2 A person named Mort-r, a lanceteer, residing in the same place. **1855** WHEWELL in Mrs. S. Douglas *Life* (1881) 562 Where, rich-glowing, the light streams through the lanceted window. **1864** CROWDY *Ch. Choirmaster* 27 A little lancetted church.

lancewood ('lɑːnswʊd, -æ-). [f. LANCE *sb.*[1] + WOOD *sb.*] **1. a.** A tough elastic wood imported chiefly from the West Indies, used for carriage-shafts, fishing-rods, cabinet-work, etc. Also, a fishing-rod made of this wood. **b.** A tree yielding this wood; the best known are *Duguetia quitarensis* from Cuba and Guiana and *Oxandra virgata* from Jamaica.

'The name in Australia is given to *Backhousia myrtifolia* and in New Zealand to *Panax crassifolium*' (Morris *Austral Eng.* 1898).

1697 DAMPIER *Voy.* I. 118 The Lancewood grows strait like our young Ashes; it is very hard, tough and heavy. **1756** P. BROWNE *Jamaica* 177 The aculeated *Lycium* or Lance-wood. This shrub is common in most parts of the island. **1858** O. W. HOLMES *Aut. Breakf.* (1883) 221 He sent for lancewood to make the thills. **1879** *Cassell's Techn. Educ.* IV. 160/2 The very best ash..is greatly inferior to lance-wood both in strength and elasticity. **1895** *Outing* (U.S.) XXVI. 376/1 We put the little lancewoods together and started out.

2. = HOROEKA.

1910 L. COCKAYNE *N.Z. Plants* viii. 120 The lancewood is neither *Pseudopanax crassifolium* nor *P. ferox*—it is *P. chathamica*. **1966** *Encycl. N.Z.* II. 258/2 Lancewood, Horoeka (*Pseudopanax crassifolium*). *Ibid.* 259/1 *P. ferox*, a rather rare and local tree occurring from about latitude 35° southwards, has the same juvenile form as that of lancewood.

lanch, obs. form of LAUNCH *sb.* and *v.*

† **lanchara.** *Obs.* Also 7 lanchare, 9 LANTCHA. [a. Pg. *lanchara*, ad. Malay *lancharan* (Kinkert), f. *lanchār* quick, nimble.] 'A kind of small vessel often mentioned in the Portuguese histories of the 16th and 17th centuries' (Yule).

1653 H. COGAN tr. *Pinto's Trav.* ix. 27 These things being laden aboard a Lanchara with oars. *Ibid.* vii. 18 Five Lanchares.

lanchet: see LANDSHARD.

† **lan'ciferous**, *a.* *Obs.* *rare*[−0]. [f. med.L. *lancifer* (f. *lanc-ea* lance + *-(i)fer* bearing) + -OUS.] Bearing a lance.

1656 in BLOUNT *Glossogr.* **1676** in COLES.

lanciform ('lɑːnsɪfɔːm, -æ-), *a.* [f. LANCE *sb.* + -(I)FORM.] Lance or lancet-shaped.

1855 in MAYNE *Expos. Lex.* **1861** *Sat. Rev.* 27 July 102 These humble buildings have sometimes no east window at all: at other times only a single narrow lanciform light.

lancinate ('lɑːnsɪneɪt, -æ-), *v.* *rare.* [f. L. *lancināt-*, ppl. stem of *lancināre* to rend, tear to pieces (rendered 'to strike, thrust through' in Cooper *Thesaurus* 1565).] *trans.* To pierce, tear.

1603 HARSNET *Pop. Impost.* 91 Blacke hel-mettal..to excoriat and lancinate a deuil. **1623** COCKERAM, *Lancinate*, to thrust through. **1876** *Overmatched* I. vii. 117 How had she lancinated the wound, already, as she could see, quick and bleeding!

lancinating ('lɑːnsɪneɪtɪŋ, -æ-), *ppl. a.* [f. prec. + -ING[2].] Chiefly of pain: Acute, darting, piercing.

1762 R. GUY *Pract. Obs. Cancers* 77 She complained of frequent lancinating Pains. **1804** ABERNETHY *Surg. Obs.* 39 The pain is lancinating. **1813** J. THOMSON *Lect. Inflam.* 473 A burning and lancinating sensation. **1861** F. H. RAMADGE *Curabil. Consumption* 71 Lancinating pains shooting in the direction of the ear.

fig. **1814** *Sporting Mag.* XLIV. 147 He inflicts, without mercy, the most ingenious, home-directed and most lancinating cuts. **1894** *Westm. Gaz.* 12 Feb. 3/2 Simplicity in recounting his own exploits excuses lancinating criticisms about other people.

lancination (lɑːnsɪ'neɪʃən, -æ-). [as if ad. L. **lancinātiōn-em*, n. of action f. *lancināre* to LANCINATE.] The action of lancinating; cutting, lancing.

1630 DONNE *Serm.* xiii. 132 Every Sin is an Incision of the Soule, a Lancination, a Phlebotomy. *a* **1670** HACKET *Cent. Serm.* 241 He took upon him to cure us..by cutting and lancination.

b. *transf.* A cutting *into*, an indentation.

1650 FULLER *Pisgah* II. v. xii. 164 Undoubtedly Judah his portion made many incisures and lancinations into the Tribe of Simeon, hindering the entireness thereof.

c. *fig.* Piercing pain; acute agony.

1649 JER. TAYLOR *Gt. Exemp.* I. Exhortation §15 With what affections and lancinations of spirit, with what effusions of love, Jesus prayed. **1669** *Addr. Hopeful Young Gentry* 62 [Love] breaks in upon you withal the noise, tumult and lancination of distracted passions.

lancing ('lɑːnsɪŋ, -æ-), *vbl. sb.* [f. LANCE *v.* + -ING[1].]

1. The action of the vb. LANCE in various senses: e.g. † **a.** Launching (of boats). † **b.** Piercing, pricking. **c.** Cutting with a lancet.

1470-85 MALORY *Arthur* XXI. ii, Thenne there was launcynge of grete botes and smal. **1592** DAVIES *Immort. Soul* II. vii. (1714) 28 The cruel Lancing of the knotty Gout. **1638** BAKER tr. *Balzac's Lett.* (vol. II) 202 You make with it [syllogisme] a wholesome and delightful lancing. **1645** MILTON *Tetrach.* Introd., Wks. 1851 IV. 140 The launcing of that old apostemated error. **1655** WOOD *Life* 17 Dec., Which caused a swelling in his cheek..and that a lancing thereof, which made him unfit to appeare in public. **1677** GALE *Crt. Gentiles* III. 105 God forbids his people this funeral rite of cutting and lancing because abused to Demon-idolatrie. **1945** *Machinery* (N.Y.) Nov. 156/1 It was decided that oxygen lancing was the only feasible means of cutting the huge piece. **1955** *Jrnl. Iron & Steel Inst.* CLXXX. 74/1 A new development is the small-scale intermittent process to convert iron in the ladle directly into steel by oxygen lancing.

attrib. **1530** PALSGR. 604/2, I launce a sore, as a cyrurgien dothe with a launsyng yron. **1859** SALA *Gas-light & D.* x. 119 He has curiously a dominant passion for leaping, darting the lancing pole..and other feats of strength and agility.

2. Acting as a lancer.

1838-9 THACKERAY *Major Gahagan* iii, A ball..put a stop to his lancing.

lancing ('lɑːnsɪŋ, -æ-), *ppl. a.* [f. LANCE *v.* + -ING[2].] That lances: **a.** Darting forward; *fig.* ?

bold, dashing. **b.** Of a ship: Launching, putting forth. **c.** Cutting, piercing.

1573 L. Lloid *Pilgr. Princes* (1586) 6 b, Hercules..hearde the offers of these two launcing Ladies. **1635** Person *Varieties* I. 12 The Comets, and these lancing Dragons, and falling Stars, &c...we visibly see. **1647** Stanley *Preti's Oronta* (1650) 5 Along the shore the wretched mothers stray ..The lancing ships beholding from on high. **1697** Dryden *Virg. Georg.* III. 695 When the launcing knife requires his hands. **1756** Mounsey in *Phil. Trans.* I. 20 But the scene soon began again with lancing pain in the left eye.

land (lænd), *sb.*[1] Forms: 1- land; also 1, 3-5 7 lond, 4-6 londe, 4-7 lande, (3 loande, 4 loond, lont, 5 lonnde, lannde, 8-9 *Sc.* lan, lan'). [Com. Teut.: OE. *land, lǫnd* str. neut. = OFris. *land, lond*, OS. (Du., LG.) *land*, OHG. *lant* (MHG. *lant, land-*, mod.G. *land*), ON. (Sw., Da.) and Goth. *land*:—OTeut. **lando*m, cogn. w. OCeltic **landā* fem. (Irish *land, lann* enclosure, Welsh *llan* enclosure, church, Cornish *lan*, Breton *lann* heath), whence the F. *lande*, heath, moor. The pre-Teut. **londh-* is not evidenced in the other Aryan langs., but an ablaut-variant **lendh-* appears in OSl. *lędina* heath, desert (Russian *lyada, lyadina*), and in MSw., mod.Sw. *linda* waste or fallow land.]

I. The simple word.

1. a. The solid portion of the earth's surface, as opposed to *sea, water*. Cf. *firm land* (see firm *a.* 8), dry land. †*Occas.* classed as one of the 'elements' = earth *sb.*[1] 14. Often in phr. ***to land, on land*** (cf. aland), ***by land*** (in quot. 1841 *transf.*); also † ***at land*** = on land, ashore.

Beowulf 1623 Com þa to lande lidmanna helm swiðmod swymman. *c* **900** tr. *Bæda's Hist.* II. iii. (1890) 104 Seo is monigra folca ceapstow of londe & of sæ cumendra. *c* **1205** Lay. 117 On Italiȝe he com on lond. *c* **1250** *Gen. & Ex.* 103 It hiled al ðis werldes drof, And fier, and walkne, and water, and lond. *c* **1300** *Havelok* 721 Fro londe woren he bote a mile. **13..** *E.E. Allit. P.* C. 322 Þe barrez of vche a bonk ful bigly me haldes, þat I may lachche no lont. *c* **1330** R. Brunne *Chron.* (1810) 266 Nouþer suld werri bi lond, no in water bi schip. *c* **1386** Chaucer *Man of Law's Prol.* 29 Ye seken lond and see for yowre wynnynges. *c* **1400** Maundev. (1839) i. 6 He may go by many Weyes, bothe on See and Londe. **1539** Taverner *Erasm. Prov.* (1552) 13 It is most pleasaunte rowynge nere the land, and walkynge nere the sea. **1590** Spenser *F.Q.* III. ii. 7 To hunt out perilles..By sea, by land, where so they may be mett. **1604** E. G[rimstone] *D'Acosta's Hist. Indies* II. xi. 107 We feele greater heat at land then at sea. *Ibid.* III. ii. 118 It behooves vs now to treate of the three elements, aire, water and land. **1610** Shaks. *Temp.* II. i. 122, I not doubt He came aliue to Land. **1667** Milton *P.L.* XI. 337 His Omnipresence fills Land, Sea, and Aire. **1675** tr. *Machiavelli's Prince* xii. (1883) 82 They began to enterprise at land. **1719** De Foe *Crusoe* I. viii, I fairly descry'd Land, whether an Island or a Continent, I could not tell. **1798** Coleridge *Anc. Mar.* VII. xiii, And now, all in my own countree, I stood on the firm land! **1841** Fr. A. Kemble *Rec. Later Life* (1882) II. 142 At the beginning of railroad travelling, persons who preferred posting on the high road were said to go by land. **1849-50** Alison *Hist. Europe* VIII. 628 All the great defeats of France at land have come from England. **1865** Kingsley *Herew.* i. (1877) 44, I was never afraid..to speak my mind to them, by sea or land.

b. Nautical phrases. † ***to take land***: to come to land; to land, go ashore. ***land to***: just within sight of land, when at sea. † ***to raise land***: to sail with the land just within sight. ***to lay the land***: to lose sight of land. † ***to set (the) land***: to take the bearings of land. ***land ho!*** a cry of sailors when first sighting land. ***land shut in*** (see quot. 1753).

c **1330** R. Brunne *Chron.* (1810) 59 Whan þe kyng wist, þat þei had taken land. *c* **1375** Barbour *Bruce* XVI. 551 Quhill thai..On vest half, toward Dunfermlyne, Tuk land. *a* **1533** Ld. Berners *Huon* xlii. 528 They..aryuyd at the porte of Marseyle there they toke londe. **1611** Cotgr., *Surgir*, to arriue, take land, goe ashore. **1627** Capt. Smith *Seaman's Gram.* ix. 43 One to the top to looke out for land, the man cries out Land to; which is iust so farre as a kenning, or a man may see the land. And to lay a land is to saile from it iust so farre as you can see it. **1633** T. James *Voy.* 28 We hull'd off, North North-East, but still raised land. **1669** Sturmy *Mariner's Mag.* I. 21 When we set Land, some this, some that do guess. **1753** Chambers *Cycl. Supp.* s.v., *Land shut in*, at sea. When another point of land hinders the sight of that which a ship came from, then they say the land is shut in. *Setting the Land*, at sea, is observing by the compass how it bears. **1769** Falconer *Dict. Marine* (1780), *Terre qui fuit*, double-land, or land shut in behind a cape or promontory. **1840** R. H. Dana *Bef. Mast* iv. 8 A man on the forecastle called out 'Land ho!'

c. Phr. ***how the land lies***: primarily *Naut.* (see quot. *a* 1700); now chiefly *fig.* = what is the state of affairs.

a **1700** B. E. *Dict. Cant. Crew, How lies the Land?* How stands the Reckoning? **1809** Malkin *Gil Blas* VII. vii. (Rtldg.) 14 Several gentlemen..had a mind to feel how the land lay. **1870** Miss Bridgman *Ro. Lynne* I. vii. 99 Uncle Charles's eyes had discovered how the land lay as regarded Rose and himself.

†**d.** A tract of land. Also *transf.* of ice. *Obs.*

1604 E. G[rimstone] *D'Acosta's Hist. Indies* III. x. 153 There is a straight and a long and stretched out land on eyther side. **1652** Needham tr. *Selden's Mare Cl.* To Rdr., A large Bay or inlet of the Sea,..entering in betwixt two lands. **1669** Sturmy *Mariner's Mag.* IV. 139 Captain Luke Fox in his North-West Discoveries..complained fearfully of the fast Lands of Ice upon those Coasts.

2. a. Ground or soil, esp. as having a particular use or particular properties. Often with defining word, as ***arable land, corn-land, plough-land, stubble land***.

c **825** *Vesp. Psalter* cvii. 37 And seowun lond & plantadon wingeardas. *a* **1050** *Liber Scintill.* x. (1889) 51 Færlic & swiðlic storm on hryre landu [L. *arua*] forhwyrfð. *c* **1050** *Supp. Ælfric's Voc.* in Wr.-Wülcker 177/11 *Seges*, ȝesawen æcer *vel* land. *c* **1380** Wyclif *Serm.* Sel. Wks. II. 35 Lond wel eerid and wel dungid. *c* **1420** *Pallad. on Husb.* I. 8 Tilynge is vs to write of euery londe. *c* **1475** *Pict. Voc.* in Wr.-Wülcker 796 *Hec bovata*, a hoxgangyn lond... *Hec virgata*, a eryd lond. *Hic selis*, a ryggyd lond. **1632** Milton *L'Allegro* 64 While the Plowman neer at hand, Whistles ore the Furrow'd Land. **1697** Dryden *Virg. Georg.* III. 605 And from the marshy Land Salt Herbage for the fodd'ring Rack provide. **1727-52** Chambers *Cycl.* s.v. *Mushroom*, They are never found but on burnt lands. **1752** Hume *Ess. & Treat.* (1777) I. 283 In England, the land is rich, but coarse. **1813** Shelley *Q. Mab* v. 8 Loading with loathsome rottenness the land. **1849** Macaulay *Hist. Eng.* v. I. 593 The land to a great extent round his pleasure grounds was in his own hands. **1856** Olmsted *Slave States* 616 The conversation was almost exclusively confined to the topics of steam-boats, ..black-land, red-land, bottom-land, timber-land [etc.].

†**b.** *poet.* = ground in various senses. *Obs.*

a **1000** *Cædmon's Gen.* 203 (Gr.) Inc is..wilde deor on ȝeweald ȝeseald & lifiȝende, ða ðe land tredað. **14..** *Fencing w. Two Handed Sword* in *Rel. Ant.* I. 309 Fresly smyte thy strokis by dene, And hold wel thy lond that hyt may be sene. **1596** Spenser *F.Q.* V. vii. 7 Her selfe uppon the land She did prostrate. **1716** Pope *Iliad* VII. 18 He..roll'd, with Limbs relax'd, along the Land.

3. a. A part of the earth's surface marked off by natural or political boundaries or considered as an integral section of the globe; a country, territory. Also put for the people of a country.

(Sometimes defined by a phrase containing the name of the country or stating one of its prominent characteristics or products, as *the land of Egypt, the land of the midnight sun, the land of the chrysanthemum*, etc. Cf. b and c.)

c **725** *Corpus Gloss.* 1995 *Territorium*, lond. *a* **900** *O.E. Chron.* an. 787 (Parker MS.) Þæt wæron þa ærestan scipu Deniscra monna þe Angel cynnes lond ȝesohton. **971** *Blickl. Hom.* 197 Þonne is seo cirice on Campania þæs landes ȝemæro. **1154** *O.E. Chron.* an. 1132 (Laud MS.) Ðis ȝear com Henri king to þis land. *c* **1205** Lay. 1244 Albion hatte þat lond. **1297** *R. Glouc.* (Rolls) 10154 He sende to alle þe bissopes of þis lond is sonde. *a* **1300** *Cursor M.* 3766 Þis esau ..Oute o þe land did iacob chace. **13..** *E.E. Allit. P.* A. 936 In Iudy londe. **1382** Wyclif *Gen.* xxi. 33 Abymalech..and Phicol..turneden aȝen into the loond of Palestynes. *c* **1400** *Destr. Troy* 13932, I haue faryn out of fere lannd my fader to seche. **14..** *Sir Beues* 2327 (MS. M.) All the lond after hem drowȝe Armyd with good harnes inouȝe. **14..** *Dyal. Gent. & Husb.* in *Rede me*, etc. (Arb.) 148 God left neuer lande yet vnpunished which agaynst his worde made resistence. *c* **1450** *Merlin* 26 Vortiger..often tyme faught so with them that he drof hem oute of hys londe. **1535** Coverdale *Exod.* iii. 8 To carye them out of that londe, in to a good and wyde londe, euen in to a londe that floweth with mylke and hony. **1611** Bible *Josh.* ii. 1 Go, view the land, euen Iericho. —— *Isa.* ix. 1 When at the first he lightly afflicted the land of Zebulun and the land of Naphtali. **1629** Milton *Hymn Nativity* 221 He feels from Juda's Land The dredded Infants hand. **1697** Dryden *Æneis* VII. 148 These Answers in the silent Night receiv'd The King himself divulg'd, the Land believ'd. **1770** Goldsm. *Des. Village* 51 Ill fares the land, to hastening ills a prey, Where wealth accumulates, and men decay. **1819** Shelley *Peter Bell* v. xv, He made songs for all the land Sweet both to feel and understand. **1849** Macaulay *Hist. Eng.* iii. I. 279 In our own land, the national wealth has, during at least six centuries, been almost uninterruptedly increasing.

fig. **1593** Shaks. *Lucr.* 439 Her bare brest, the heart of all her land. **1595** —— *John* IV. ii. 245 In the body of this fleshly Land, This kingdome, this Confine of blood, and breathe.

b. Phrases. ***law of the land*** († ***land's law***: see land-law 1): see law *sb.*[1] ***land of promise*** (†***promission***, †***repromission***, †***behest***), ***promised land***: see promise *sb.*, etc. ***land of cakes*** (Sc.): see cake *sb.* 1 b. See also Holy Land.

c **1300** [see behest *sb.* 1]. *c* **1400** Maundev. (Roxb.) Pref. 1 Þe land of repromission, þat men calles þe Haly Land. **1513** Bradshaw *St. Werburge* I. 1612 Duke Iosue..Ledynge the Isrehelytes to the lande of promyssyon. *c* **1730** Burt *Lett. N. Scotl.* (1760) II. xxiv. 271 The Lowlanders call their part of the Country the Land of Cakes. *a* **1846** J. Imlah *Song, Land o' Cakes*, An' fill ye up and toast the cup, The land o' cakes for ever.

c. *fig.* = Realm, domain. ***land of the leal*** (Sc.): the realm of the blessed departed, heaven. ***land of the living*** (a Hebraism): the present life. ***in the land of the living*** (a Hebraism): alive. ***land of Nod***: see nod.

c **825** *Vesp. Psalter* cxiv. 9 In londe lifȝendra. *c* **1230** *Hali Meid.* 13 Þis world þat is icleopet lond of unlicnesse. **13..** *Minor Poems fr. Vernon MS.* (E.E.T.S.) 637/22 Ye shal not with-outen Strif fro this world passe to þe lond of lyf. **1611** Bible *Jer.* xi. 19 Let vs cut him off from the land of the liuing. **1671** Milton *Samson* 99 As in the land of darkness yet in light, To live a life half dead, a living death. **1707** *Curios. in Husb. & Gard.* 313 In the Land of Nature we are often out of our Knowledge. **1798** Lady Nairne *Song, The Land o' the Leal*, I'm wearin' awa' John,..To the land o' the leal. **1806-7** J. Beresford *Miseries Hum. Life* (1826) VI. Introd. 116 You'd better have sent out Jedidiah Buxton if he is still in the land of the living. **1819** J. Hodgson in Raine *Mem.* (1857) I. 223, I was frequently travelling in the Land of Nod. **1836** Irving *Astoria* I. 129 They dug a grave..in which they deposited the corpse, with a biscuit..and a small quantity of tobacco, as provisions for its journey in the land of spirits. **1871** Morley *Voltaire* (1886) 10 There are unseen lands of knowledge and truth beyond the present.

†**d.** In ME. poetry used vaguely in certain expletive phrases: ***on*** or ***in land, to come to land***. Cf. similar uses of town. *Obs.*

c **1175** *Lamb. Hom.* 65 To eni monne þet is on londe. *c* **1300** *Harrow. Hell* 46 Þritti winter and þridde half ȝer, Haui woned in londe her. *c* **1320** *Cast. Love* 551 Maken I chulle Pees to londe come,..And sauen al þe folk in londe. *c* **1380** *Sir Ferumb.* 2793 Welawo to longe y lyue in londe. *c* **1386** Chaucer *Sir Thopas* 176 His steede..gooth an Ambil in the way Ful softely and rounde In londe.

¶**e.** *U.S.* Substituted euphemistically for Lord, in phrases ***the land knows, Good land!*** Also, ***(for the) land's sake, land sakes, my land(s)***.

1846 *Knickerbocker* XXVII. 18 (Th.), Jedediah, for the land's sake, does my mouth blaze? **1848** J. F. Cooper *Oak Openings* I. v. 82 Land's sake! I've forgotten all about them barrels! **1849** Miss Warner *Wide wide World* xiv, 'But what are they called turnpikes for?' 'The land knows—I don't'. **1854** M. J. Holmes *Tempest & Sunshine* xvi. 223 For land's sake dont tell Tempest. **1863** A. D. Whitney *Faith Gartney's Girlhood* ii. 12 Land sakes, Miss Faith! I don't know what you mean. **1889** 'Mark Twain' *Yankee Crt. K. Arthur* xi. 110 Good land! a man can't keep his functions regular on spring chickens thirteen hundred years old. **1894** 'Mark Twain' in *Century Mag.* XLVII. 337/2 My lan', what de reason 't ain't enough? **1908** L. M. Montgomery *Anne of Green Gables* xiv. 141 'For the land's sake!' gasped Marilla... 'I believe the child is crazy.' **1913** A. Huxley *Let.* 30 July (1969) 51 The Americans..say Gee, whiz, bully, my lands, my soul, [etc.]. **1916** A. Bennett *Lion's Share* xlv. 350 'My land!' exclaimed Nick. 'If he sees me here he'll think I've come on purpose to talk about him.' **1930** J. Dos Passos *42nd Parallel* 50 Land sakes, it gives me the creeps to think of it. **1952** V. Wilkins *King Reluctant* I. iii. 45 But land's sake, how did he get into dat ole lonesome graveyard? **1974** K. Benton *Craig & Tunisian Tangle* xiii. 180 We've only got another week, for land's sake.

4. a. Ground or territory as owned by a person or viewed as public or private property; landed property. ***(common, concealed, copyhold, debatable, demesne, fabric, fiscal land*** or ***lands***: see the defining words. Also bond-land, crown-land 1.)

971 *Blickl. Hom.* 51 Þa teoþan sceattas..ȝe on lande, ȝe on oþrum þingum. *c* **1205** Lay. 3914 His lond he huld half ȝer. *a* **1300** *Cursor M.* 4033 To dele þair landes þam betuixs þat aiþer might þam ald wit his. **1362** Langl. *P. Pl.* A. VII. 295 Laborers that haue no lond to liuen on bote heore honden. *c* **1386** Chaucer *Prol.* 579 Worthy to been stywardes of rente and lond Of any lord that is in Engelond. **1509** Hawes *Past. Pleas.* XVI. (Percy Soc.) 72 Borne to great land, treasure, and substaunce. **1587** Lady Stafford in *Collect.* (O.H.S.) I. 209 They have recovered their land, with the Arrerages. **1602** Shaks. *Ham.* V. i. 113 This fellow might be in's time a great buyer of Land. **1611** Bible *2 Kings* viii. 3 She went foorth to crie vnto the king for her house, and for her land. **1732** Berkeley *Alciphr.* I. §1 A convenient house with a hundred acres of land adjoining to it. **1849** Macaulay *Hist. Eng.* vi. II. 142 He had no intention of depriving the English colonists of their land. **1878** Jevons *Prim. Pol. Econ.* 12 Some one will say that he is beyond question rich, who owns a great deal of land.

b. *pl.* Territorial possessions. †Also *rarely* in sing., a piece of landed property, an estate in land.

c **1000** Ælfric *Saints' Lives* (1885) I. 192 Feower land he forȝeaf forð In mid him æþeodiȝum to andfencge and to ælmes-dædum. *c* **1250** *Gen. & Ex.* 1843 Ðor him solde an lond kinge emor. *c* **1330** *Spec. Gy Warw.* 163 Þouh man haue muche katel As londes, rentes, and oþer god. *a* **1450** *Knt. de la Tour* (1868) 86 [He] became..riche..and purchased londes and possessiones. **1560** Daus tr. *Sleidane's Comm.* 423 b *note*, John Frederick demaundeth his landes and dignities. **1599** Shaks. *Hen. V*, I. i. 9 All the Temporall Lands which men deuout By Testament haue giuen to the Church. *a* **1656** Bp. Hall *Rem. Wks.* (1660) 143 Who should have your Lands but your heirs? **1787** Burns *Poems* (1809) II. 101 *note*, The Earl gave him a four merk land near the castle. **1827** Jarman *Powell's Devises* II. 135 All his messuages, lands, and tenements. **1841** W. Spalding *Italy & It. Isl.* I. 84 Considering this grievance more tolerable than..the loss of the public lands. **1849** Macaulay *Hist. Eng.* vi. II. 130 Their lands had been divided by Cromwell among his followers.

c. *Law.* (See quots.)

1628 Coke *On Litt.* 4 Land in the legall signification comprehendeth any ground, soile or earth whatsoeuer, as meadowes, pastures, woods, moores, waters marishes, furses and heath,..It legally includeth also all castles, houses, and other buildings. **1767** Blackstone *Comm.* II. 18 Land hath also, in its legal signification, an indefinite extent, upwards as well as downwards. **1839** *Penny Cycl.* XIII. 300/1 Land in its most restricted legal signification is confined to arable ground... In its more wide legal signification land extends also to meadow, pasture, woods, moors, waters, &c.

d. *S. Afr.* An area of ground under cultivation; = field *sb.* 4 a. Freq. in *pl.*

1731 G. Medley tr. *Kolb's Present State Cape Good-Hope* I. xxviii. 357 The Value of the Tenth of the Produce of Lands is computed at 14000 Florins yearly. *Ibid.* 358 The Colonies are encreasing daily, and daily taking in new Lands for Tillage. **1806** J. Barrow *Trav. S. Afr.* (ed. 2) I. i. 5 At the feet of the hills..are several pleasant farms, having gardens well stored with vegetables for the table, vineyards, and extensive corn lands. **1896** H. A. Bryden *Tales S. Afr.* 248 She had..some good tobacco 'lands', which yielded no mean profit each year. **1926** O. Schreiner *From Man to Man* 23 They burnt harpuis bushes on the lands. **1939** tr. *E. N. Marais's My Friends the Baboons* ix. 112 If he raids a land..he will..hand over to her a share of the mealies or fruit. **1941** S. Cloete *Hill of Doves* (1942) xxviii. 398 They were riding through a mealie land. **1966** E. Palmer *Plains of Camdeboo* xviii. 297 Dust enveloped the world. Maurice and Sita could not even see where the lands had been.

†**5.** The country, as opposed to *the town*. *on* (*in*, †Sc. *to*) *land*: in the country; also, into the country; hence, to distant parts. *Obs.*

c 900 tr. *Bæda's Hist.* III. xx. [xxviii.] (1890) 246 Byriȝ & lond & ceastre & tunas & hus. *c* 1000 ÆLFRIC *Gram.* xxxviii. (Z.) 234 *Ruri*, on lande. *c* 1386 CHAUCER *Prol.* 702 A poure person dwellynge vpon lond. —— *Nun's Pr. T.* 4069 Swiche a ioye was it to here hem synge,.. In sweete accord, My lief is faren in londe. ? *a* 1400 *Plowman's T.* 1138 Thou.. livest in londe, as a lorell. 1425 *Sc. Acts Jas. I* (1814) II. 11/2 Ande at þis be done als wele in borowis as to lande throu al þe realme. *c* 1470 HENRYSON *Tale of Dog* 123 [He] dytis all the pure men up-on-land. 1491 *Sc. Acts Jas. IV* (1814) II. 226/2 The aulde statutis and ordinances maid of before baith to burghe and to lande. 1513–75–1818 [see BURGH b]. *a* 1800 *Jock the Leg* in Child *Ballads* (1894) V. 128 In brough or land.

6. Expanse of country of undefined extent; = COUNTRY 1 b. *rare* exc. with qualifying word, as *down-land*, HIGHLAND, LOWLAND, *mountain-land*, etc.

1610 SHAKS. *Temp.* IV. i. 130 Leaue your crispe channels, and on this greene-Land Answere your summons. 1784 COWPER *Task* I. 323 The Ouse, dividing the well-watered land, Now glitters in the sun, and now retires. 1833 TENNYSON *May Queen* III. 7 And sweet is all the land about, and all the flowers that blow.

7. One of the strips into which a corn-field, or a pasture-field that has been ploughed, is divided by water-furrows. Often taken as a measure of land-area and of length, of value varying according to local custom.

1377 LANGL. *P. Pl.* B. XVII. 58 Feith had first siȝte of hym ..And nolde nouȝt neighen hym by nyne londes lengthe. 1522 *Will* in *Market Harboro' Rec.* (1890) 211 A lond of barly next the whet lond. 1523 FITZHERB. *Husb.* §2 In Kente they haue other maner of plowes, some wyll tourne the sheldbredth at euery landes ende, and plowe all one waye. —— *Surv.* 38b, A furlong called Dale furlong ye whiche furlong conteyneth .xxx. landes and two heed landes. *a* 1550 *Merry Jest Mylner Abyngton* 77 in Hazl. *E.P.P.* III. 103 The mylners house is nere, Not the length of a lande. 1565 COOPER *Thesaurus*, *Arepennem*, a measure of ground as much as our lande or halfe aker. 1641 BEST *Farm. Bks.* (Surtees) 5 To putt ewes into the Carre three weekes before Lady-day, allowing five ewes for a lande. 1679 BLOUNT *Anc. Tenures* 21 To cut down one Land of Corn. 1688 R. HOLME *Armoury* III. 137/1 Land, or Lond, or Launde, in some places called a Loone, it is as much as two large Buts. 1767 *Cries of Blood* 7 He went down Campden field..about a land's length. 1786 *The Har'st Rig* xxv. (1801) 12 O' Gath'rers next, unruly-bands Do spread themsel's athwart the Lands. 1791 COWPER *Retirement* 421 Green balks and furrowed lands. 1793 *Trans. Soc. Arts* V. 83 The produce of one land or ridge of each crop. 1817–18 COBBETT *Resid. U.S.* (1822) 114, I made a sort of land with the plough, and made it pretty level at top. 1861 *Times* 4 Oct. 7/4 Fields laid out in six-yard lands with deep water-furrows for the sake of drainage.

8. *Sc.* A building divided into flats or tenements for different households, each tenement being called a 'house'.

1456 *Extracts Burgh Rec. Peebles* (1872) 111 A land liand of this side the Hau. 1457 *Ibid.* 116 A land was his faderis liand in the burgh Peblis. 1466 *Extracts Aberd. Reg.* (1844) I. 26 He conquest a lande within your saide burgh. 1482 *Act. Audit.* (1839) 107/2 Diuerss housis..lying in the brugh of Edinburgh, on þe north side of þe strete..betuix þe land of Johne patonsone & þe land of Nicol spedy on þe est & west partes. 1555 *Sc. Acts Mary* (1814) II. 490/2 The annuellar hauand the grownd annuell vpone ony brint land quhilk is or beis reparellit. 1753 W. MAITLAND *Hist. Edin.* II. 140 The Buildings here, elsewhere called Houses, are denominated Lands. 1776 E. TOPHAM *Lett. Edin.* 27 These buildings are divided by extremely thick partition walls, into large houses, which are called lands, and each story of a land is called a house. Every land has a common stair-case. 1780 ARNOT *Hist. Edin.* II. i. (1816) 185 The houses were piled to an enormous height, some of them amounting to twelve stories. These were called lands. *c* 1817 HOGG *Tales & Sk.* V. 68, I showed him down stairs; and just as he turned the corner of the next land, a man came rushing violently by him. 1858 MRS. OLIPHANT *Laird of Norlaw* I. 308 The 'land', or block of buildings in which it was placed, formed one side of a little street. 1864 BURTON *Scot Abr.* II. i. 117, I remember an old 'land' in the High Street of Edinburgh. 1893 STEVENSON *Catriona* 238 A certain frail old gentlewoman..who dwelt in the top of a tall land on a strait close.

9. Technical uses. **a.** [*transf.* from 7.] The space between the grooves of a rifle bore; also, the space between the furrows of a mill-stone. In wider use, esp. in *Engin.*: an area left between adjacent grooves, holes, or the like in any surface; e.g. that between the flutes of a twist drill or the grooves of a gramophone record, or the top of a tooth on various metal-cutting tools immediately behind the cutting edge. **b.** In a steam-engine, 'the unperforated portion of the face-plate of a slide-valve' (Knight *Dict. Mech.* 1875). **c.** 'The lap of the strakes in a clincher-built boat. Also called *landing*' (*Ibid.*).

1854 *Chamb. Jrnl.* II. 202 These furrows and belts [in the bore of a cannon], technically called *lands*. 1857 SIR P. DE COLQUHOUN *Compan. Oarsman's Guide* 28 The *lans* are where one straik overlaps another. 1864 *Daily Tel.* 15 June, Some of the 'lands' being slightly injured, as might..have been expected with so delicate a system of rifling. 1881 *Metal World* No. 9. 131 The circular or angular lands and furrows [of a mill-stone]. 1907 J. V. WOODWORTH *Grinding & Lapping* II. 62 The flutes [of the reamers] were milled sharp—without land. *Ibid.* 63 Cutting the reamer sharp with no lands on the teeth. 1935 H. C. BRYSON *Gramophone Record* iv. 81 The engineer has a table showing the widths and depths of the grooves and the amount of land for various cuts per inch. 1949 BAKER & KOZACKA *Carbide Cutting Tools* x. 213 The land is that portion of the tooth which is just behind the cutting edge. 1958 *Proc. IRE* XLVI. 1063/2 The diffusion regions in the lands of the grooved surface [of the silicon] are then removed in a second step of lapping. 1962 A. NISBETT *Technique Sound Studio* 255 The groove normally used for 78 rpm recordings... About 4 mils land between grooves, and a pitch of the order of 100–150 grooves per inch. 1964 S. CRAWFORD *Basic Engin. Processes* ix. 228 The lands run along the leading edge of the flutes and act as a guide in the hole already drilled. 1971 B. SCHARF *Engin. & its Lang.* xi. 97 Studs. These are very useful headless fastening devices which are threaded on both ends, with an unthreaded section (land) in the middle.

II. Attributive uses and Combinations.

10. General relations. **a.** simple attrib., as ***land-belt, -boom,*** †***-cape, certificate, claim, classification, -crescent, deal, -development, distribution, -estate,*** †***-ground, improvement, -labour, market, -mass,*** †***-people, -price, question, reclamation, reform, -rent, -revenue, room, -sculpture, -security, speculation, -spit, -strip, taxation, -tenant, -tenure, title, use, utilization, -wave, -wealth, work.***

1856 KANE *Arct. Expl.* I. viii. 78, I am obliged to follow the tortuous *land-belt. 1891 STEVENSON & L. OSBOURNE *Wrecker* (1892) 288 There was some rumour of a Napa *land-boom. 1656 BLOUNT *Glossogr.*, **Landcape*, an end of land that stretcheth further into the Sea then other parts of the Continent thereabouts. 1838 in *Indiana Mag. Hist.* (1926) XXII. 451 Gentle had settled that he was to pay in land and made an assignment on a *land certificate. 1967 E. RUDINGER *Wills & Probate* 97 A week or so later he receives from the registry the land certificate, which is substantially the same as the charge certificate, but with the very important difference of having had the details of the mortgage removed from it. 1812 J. MCDONOGH *Papers* (1898) 12 They therefore, sir, look forward to you, knowing ..your knowledge of their *land claims, to have those claims before Congress. 1949 *Minnesota Hist.* Mar. 30 The Sioux disputed the German colonists' right to establish land claims on the site. 1930 *U.S. Dept. Agric. Yearbk.* *1929* 39 These considerations point to the need for a public policy of economic *land classificaton. 1970 *Toronto Daily Star* 24 Sept. 27/7 The report's principal authors were Angus Hill, a specialist in land classification, Professor David Love and Professor Douglas Lacate. 1875 W. MCILWRAITH *Guide Wigtownshire* 48 The *land-crescent that forms the bay. 1974 *Guardian* 11 Apr. 1 Mrs Marcia Williams, Mr Wilson's private secretary, said last night she would not resign over the *land deals affair. 1895 *Law Times* 13 July 254 If the Company is a *Land-development one. 1965 L. CHEVALIER in Glass & Eversley *Population in Hist.* iii. 75, I have myself tried to study the evolution of the population in three cantons of Vendée..in terms of *land-distribution and the social and religious structure. 1968 R. A. LYTTLETON *Mysteries Solar Syst.* vi. 213 The configuration of the land-distribution could also have been somewhat different at the time of fall. 1690 *Mor. Ess. relat. Pres. Times* iii. 41 The Enjoyment of *Land Estates. 1575 LANEHAM *Let.* (1871) 4 *Londground by pool or riuer. 1849 *Hansard Commons* 4 May 1266 An advance of money..under the *Land Improvement Act. 1902 *Encycl. Brit.* XXIX. 554/2 The number and amount of loans..under the Land Improvement Acts from 1847 to 1900. 1909 *Daily Chron.* 14 Sept. 5/6 The other kind of banks are rent charge and land-improvement banks. 1776 BURKE *Let.* 14 Aug., Condemned to *Land Labour at the last Assizes for this County. 1845 C. M. KIRKLAND *Western Clearings* 5 *Standing round*; i.e., watching the *land market for values. 1962 H. R. LOYN *Anglo-Saxon Eng.* iv. 171 There is evidence indeed for something approaching a land-market in late Anglo-Saxon England. 1856 KANE *Arct. Expl.* I. i. 16 The probable extension of the *land-masses of Greenland to the Far North. 1881 JUDD *Volcanoes* 287 The land-masses of the globe. *c* 1440 *Eng. Conq. Irel.* xxxvii. 91 The *londe-Pepill that crystyn shold be. 1898 *Atlantic Monthly* Apr. 498/2 Immigrants were pouring into the state, and *land-prices were rising. 1830 *Deb. Congress U.S.* 26 Feb. 210/1 The final adjustment of the *land question. 1962 H. R. LOYN *Anglo-Saxon Eng.* viii. 329 In connection with the land-question, the situation is more complicated. 1881 W. D. SEYMOUR (*title*) Waste *land reclamation and peasant proprietorship with practical suggestions for the establishment of a land bank in Ireland. 1939 *U.S. Dept. Agric. Yearbk.* *1938* 1171 *Land reclamation*, making land capable of more intensive use by changing its character, environment, or both through operations requiring collective effort. 1955 Land reclamation [see CON AMORE]. 1940 *Economist* 6 July 12/2 The *land reform [in Transylvania] which had aroused such bitter protest was admittedly more severe..than in the Old Kingdom. 1955 *Times* 4 July 8/4 His post in the Tokyo Embassy as an expert on land reform. 1706 in *Arbuthnot's Misc. Wks.* (1751) II. 192 Paying high Interest for Money, which *Land-rents cannot discharge. 1733 SWIFT *Reasons agst. Settling Tithe of Hemp*, etc. Wks. 1761 III. 313 The land-rents of Ireland are computed to about two millions. 1689 *Lond. Gaz.* No. 2472/4 The Office of Receiver of the *Land-Revenues for the Counties of Suffolk and Cambridge. 1800 *Asiat. Ann. Reg.*, *Proc. Parl.* 15/2 Land revenues to the amount of 191,042*l.* 1871 *Leisure Hour* 8 Apr. 223/1 An aeronaut cannot get far enough from the sea in England, and requires all the *land-room of a continent to make his voyage. 1960 *Tamarack Rev.* XIV. 6 The rough half-moon of islands on the western periphery of the North Atlantic contains under 8,000 square miles of landroom for three and a half million people. 1882 GEIKIE *Text-bk. Geol.* VII. 922 A chief element in the progress of *land-sculpture, is geological structure. 1677 YARRANTON *Eng. Improv.* 17 The *Land Security was so uncertain and bad, and it was so troublesome and chargeable getting their Moneys again when they had occasion to use it. 1807 *Deb. Congress U.S.* 6 Oct. (1852) 605 We made a purchase of a single tract of land together. Perhaps you call that *land speculations. 1848 'D. KNICKERBOCKER' *Hist. N.Y.* (1850) II. vii. 121 He was soon permitted to land, and a great land-speculation ensued. 1885 W. D. HOWELLS *Rise S. Lapham* xx. 366 He's been dabbling in..patent-rights, land speculations. 1974 D. FRANCIS *Knock Down* xiv. 172 It was like property development and land speculation. You could make a great deal of money without breaking the law. 1865 *Sat. Rev.* 5 Aug. 182 Two *landspits and three bays are ignored by Van de Velde. 1878 BROWNING *Poets Croisic* 10 To that *land-strip waters wash. 1794 D. ROBERTSON *Tour through Isle of Man* v. 37 Here the oppression of game-laws, *land-taxation, and excise-establishment are utterly unknown. 1883 *Peel City Guardian* 8 Dec. 4/1 Land Taxation. 1909 *Westm. Gaz.* 19 May 2/1 The land-taxation proposals of the Budget would affect them. 1543 tr. *Act 14 Edw. III*, stat. i. c. 3 The heyres executours, and *lande tenauntes of suche ministers and receyuours. 1607 COWELL *Interpr.*, Land tenent. 1876 DIGBY *Real Prop.* I. i. §1. 2 The main features of *land-tenure. 1812 J. MCDONOGH *Papers* (1898) 11 The people..of Florida are..in a dissatisfied state, arising from this uncertainty in which their *land titles are placed. 1936 *Discovery* May 131/2 Land titles have taken nearly 20 years or more to prepare. 1935 *Ibid.* Aug. 223/1 A careful *land use survey. 1961 *Listener* 7 Sept. 347/2 Recent scientific advance in land-use policy in Africa. 1971 *New Scientist* 21 Jan. 134/2 We are ahead of most countries in democratic land-use planning. 1935 *Discovery* Aug. 220/1 *Land Utilisation is the problem of the moment. 1936 *Archit. Rev.* LXXX. 1 (*title*) The Land Utilization Survey of Britain: the first part of the report. 1864 R. F. BURTON *Dahome* 35 Gentle ridges..not unlike the wrinkles or *land waves behind S. Paul de Loanda. 1845 DARWIN in *Life & Lett.* (1887) I. 343 *note*, So as to lessen the difference in *land-wealth. 1945 R. M. LOCKLEY *Islands round Brit.* 47 Much of the *landwork is done by hand with rude implements. 1971 *Daily Tel.* 19 Nov. 13/1 By 1942, the NUS had 1,000 students in its summer landwork camps.

b. objective and objective genitive, as ***land-buyer, -catcher, -ditching, -hirer, -hunter, -locator, -monger, -monopolist, -nationalization, -nationalizer, -occupier, -planning, -proprietor, -roller, -seeker, -speculator,*** †***-tilie, -tiller, -tilling, -worker; land-devouring, -eating, -scourging, -tilling, -visiting,*** adjs.

1362 LANGL. *P. Pl.* A. XI. 209 A ledere of louedayes and a *lond biggere. 1598 R. BERNARD *Terence, Hecyra* III. v, They..are no great land-biers. *a* 1625 BEAUM. & FL. *Wit without M.* V. ii, Thou most reverent *land-catcher. 1641 VICARS *God in Mount* 12 These and such like *Land-devouring enormities. 1806–7 A. YOUNG *Agric. Essex* (1813) I. 116 *Land-ditching is done at different prices. 1883 G. C. DAVIES *Norfolk Broads* xl. (1884) 315 Walberswick is a decayed port, a victim of the *land-eating sea. 1552 HULOET, *Lande hyrer, *redemptor*. 1894 *Outing* (U.S.) June 172 Four or five rough-looking men—evidently *land-hunters. 1816 U. BROWN *Jrnl.* in *Maryland Hist. Mag.* (1915) X. 364 Those present *Land Locaters Surveys will hold good until the former can be Established. 1971 *Islander* (Victoria, B.C.) 30 May 5/1 The tragedy..occurred..when two land locators..came to grief on the Bear River glacier. 1647 HARVEY *Schola Cordis* vii. 7 The greedy *landmunger. 1798 I. ALLEN *Hist. Vermont* 21 The persecutions of the settlers were carried on by the Governor and his *land-monopolists. 1882 A. R. WALLACE (*title*) *Land Nationalization. Its necessity and its aims. 1884 *Pall Mall G.* 5 Mar. 3/1 One point..will..be seized upon by the *land nationalizers. 1576 *Act 18 Eliz.* c. 10 §10 All the Inhabitants and *Land-occupiers within the whole Isle. 1829 SOUTHEY *Sir T. More* (1831) II. 135 The relation between land-owner and land-occupier has undergone an unkindly alteration. 1936 *Discovery* Feb. 49/1 There has been a certain amount of '*land-planning', though not on the scale undertaken in the United States. 1961 E. A. POWDRILL *Vocab. Land Planning* ii. 22 Thus, in administering the same aims of land planning, the instrument used for expressing them differs in the fundamental aspect of policymaking. 1815 L. SIMOND *Tour Gt. Brit.* I. 172 The *land-proprietor does not get more than three per cent. 1875 KNIGHT *Dict. Mech.*, **Land-roller*, one for leveling ground and mashing clods in getting land into tilth for crops. 1641 VICARS *God in Mount* 48 Such a *Land-scourging rod. 1845 J. J. HOOPER *Some Adventures Simon Suggs* iii. 37 By the time he had ridden half a mile, he overtook the *land-seeker. 1946 C. MCWILLIAMS *Southern California Country* 126 They sold prospective settlers so-called 'land-seekers' tickets', under an arrangement whereby the fare could later be applied on the purchase of railroad land. 1798 I. ALLEN *Nat. & Pol. Hist. Vermont* 24 Lawyers and *land speculators called on Mr. Allen. 1873 'MARK TWAIN' & WARNER *Gilded Age* I. 456 He might have been a 'railroad man', or a politician, or a land-speculator. 1948 *Reader's Digest* May 124/1 He was ill-educated, selfmade, an incurable land speculator. *c* 1205 LAY. 14847 We scullen.. wurðen mils liðe wið þa *lond-tilien. 1387–8 T. USK *Test. Love* I. iii. (Skeat) l. 32 Than good *lond-tillers ginne shape for the erthe..to bringe forth more corn. *c* 1475 *Pict. Voc.* in Wr.-Wülcker 804/34 *Hic cultor*, a londtyllere. 1895 *Q. Rev.* Apr. 555 The interests of the landowner and the land-tiller became antagonistic. *c* 1420 *Pallad. on Husb.* I. 528 Donge of fowlis is ful necessary To *londtiling. 1393 LANGL. *P. Pl.* C. IX. 140 Ȝe ben wastours..that deuouren That leel *land-tylynge men leelliche byswynken. 1883 C. F. HOLDER in *Harper's Mag.* Dec. 107/2 Jumping and *land-visiting fishes. 1887 *Andover* (Mass.) *Rev.* VIII. 154 Only the tradesworkers and the *landworkers are specially considered. 1960 *Farmer & Stockbreeder* 15 Mar. 72/3 Land-workers in the Thirsk and Easingwold districts of Yorkshire.

c. instrumental, as ***land-penned, sheltered, surrounded*** adjs.; similative, as ***land-like*** adj.

1804 COLERIDGE *Lett.* (1895) 470 This [the green on the water], though occasioned by the impurity of the nigh shore ..forms a home scene: it is warm and *landlike. 1850 TENNYSON *In Mem.* cii. 56 We steer'd her toward a crimson cloud That landlike slept along the deep. 1883 *Harper's Mag.* Aug. 453/1 *Land-penned rivers. 1883 MOLONEY *W. African Fisheries* (Fish. Exhib. Publ.) 27 Grassy banks of *land-sheltered waters. 1776 MICKLE tr. *Camoens' Lusiad* 479 *Land-surrounded waves.

11. a. *attrib.*, passing into *adj.*, with the sense: Belonging or attached to, or characteristic of, the land; living, situated, taking place, or performed upon land (as opposed to *water* or

sea); terrestrial: as in ***land-admiral***, ***-army***, ***-battery***, ***-battle***, ***-communication***, ***-company***, ***-engine***, ***-fight***, ***-goods***, ***-gunner***, **†*-herd***, ***-journey***, ***-life***, ***-monster***, ***-passage***, ***-pilot***, ***-plant***, ***-power***, ***-prospect***, ***-siren***, ***-soldier***, ***-spout***, ***-trade***, ***-travel***, ***-wages***, ***-war***, ***warfare***, etc.

1490 *Act 7 Hen. VII*, c. 1. §1 If any Captain..give them not their full Wages..except for Jackets for them that receive Land-wages. **1595** SPENSER *Col. Clout* 278 The fields In which dame Cynthia her landheards fed. **1618** BOLTON *Florus* III. vi. (1636) 191 Impatient of land-life, they launcht againe into their water. **1625** *Queries agst. Dk. Buckhm.* in Rushw. *Hist. Coll.* (1659) I. 217 Admiral and General in the Fleet of the Sea, and Land-Army. **1625** PURCHAS (*title*) Purchas his Pilgrimes contayning a History of the World in Sea Voyages and Lande Travells. **1630** WADSWORTH *Pilgr.* vi. 51, I intreated him for a commission and patent for a land company in Flanders. **1634** MILTON *Comus* 307 To find out that..Would overtask the best Land-Pilots art. **1667** *Phil. Trans.* II. 488 Their Land-voyage from Pekin to Goa. **1667** PEPYS *Diary* 4 Apr., I made Sir G. Carteret merry with telling him how many Land-admirals we are to have this year. **1669** STURMY *Mariner's Mag.* To Rdr., A most useful Instrument for all Land and Sea Gunners. **1682** SOUTHERNE *Loyal Bro.* III. Wks. 1721 I. 44 Curse on these land-syrens! **1694** *Lond. Gaz.* No. 3023/3 They..are to be provided for in their way as Land-Soldiers are in their march. **1695** PRIOR *Taking Namur* 86 The water-nymphs are too unkind To Villeroy; are the land-nymphs so? **1711** SHAFTESB. *Charac.* (1737) II. 289 Anchoring at sea, remote from all land-prospect. **1774** GOLDSM. *Nat. Hist.* I. 395 The nature..of these land spouts. **1785** J. PHILLIPS *Treat. Inland Navig.* p. vi, Roads for land-communication and carriage. **1817** *Parl. Deb.* 316 Of the lords of the Admiralty, three of the sea officers, and one of the land lords, were efficient officers. **1822** *Specif. Brunel's Patent* No. 4683. 3 The common governor usually applied to land engines cannot act regularly at sea. **1844** H. H. WILSON *Brit. India* I. 335 Being exposed to the fire of the land-batteries as well as of the shipping. **1852** GROTE *Greece* II. lxxxii. X. 665 If the preparations for land-warfare were thus stupendous, those for sea-warfare were fully equal if not superior. **1884** BOWER & SCOTT *De Bary's Phaner.* 300 The foliage of land-plants. **1928** *Observer* 1 Apr. 14/3 Sea-power took the place of land-power in the sixteenth century. **1957** [see *geostrategy* (GEO-)]. **1962** *Listener* 29 Mar. 543/1 A world which, seen from Moscow, is divided into three or four land masses, and a number of similar areas which can be dominated by land power.

b. Prefixed to names of animals to indicate that they are terrestrial in their habits, and esp. to distinguish them from aquatic animals of the same name; as ***land-animal***, ***-beast***, ***-bird***, **†*-cormorant***, ***-dog***, **†*-dove***, ***-dragon***, **†*-eft***, ***-fowl***, ***-mammifera***, ***-mouse***, ***-mollusca*** (hence ***land-molluscan*** adj.), **†*-pullen***, ***-reptile***, ***-scorpion***, ***-spaniel*** (also fig.), ***-toad***; **land-beetle**, a terrestrial predatory beetle, one of the group *Geadephaga*; **land-bug**, a bug of the group *Geocores*; **land chelonian**, a tortoise; **land-cod**, a kind of catfish, the mathemeg, *Amiurus borealis* (Cent. Dict.); **land-crocodile**, †(*a*) ? meant to designate the CAYMAN; (*b*) the sand-monitor, *Psammosaurus arenarius* (Cent. Dict.); **land-leech**, a leech of the genus *Hæmodipsa*, abounding in Ceylon; **land-lobster**, **†-martin** (see quots.); **land moccasin** (see MOCCASIN 3); **land otter**, 'any ordinary otter of the subfamily *Lutrinæ*, inhabiting rivers and lakes, as distinguished from the sea-otter, *Enhydris marina*' (Cent. Dict.); **land pike**, (*a*) = HELL-BENDER 1; (*b*) an inferior type of pig; **land-shell**, a terrestrial mollusk or its shell; **land-slater**, a terrestrial isopod crustacean, a wood-louse; **land-snail**, a snail of the family *Helicidæ*; **land-sole**, the common red slug, *Arion rufus*; **land-tortoise**, **-turtle**, any tortoise or turtle of terrestrial habits; **†land-urchin**, the hedgehog; **†land-winkle**, a snail.

1691 RAY *Creation* (1692) 62 So necessary is it [air] for us and other *Land-Animals. **1748** *Anson's Voy.* II. viii. 217 Besides these mischievous land-animals, the sea..is infested with great numbers of alligators. **1601** HOLLAND *Pliny* I. 191 Let vs returne now to discourse of other liuing creatures; and first of *land-beasts. **1836–9** TODD *Cycl. Anat.* II. 888/1 This division into lobes occurs in most of the *land-beetles. **1570** *Order for Swans* in Hone *Every-day Bk.* (1827) II. 959 The..custome of this Realme..dothe allow to every Owner of such ground..to take one *Land-bird. **1863** KINGSLEY *Water-Bab.* vii. 343 The sea-birds sang as they streamed out into the ocean, and the land-birds as they built among the boughs. *c* **1865** *Circ. Sci.* (ed. Wylde) II. 184/1 The Geocores or *Land-bugs. **1880** *Cassell's Nat. Hist.* IV. 249 The *Land Chelonians. *a* **1653** G. DANIEL *Idyll* iv. 4 *Land-Cormorants may Challeng them for food. **1688** R. HOLME *Armoury* II. 159/2 He beareth Azure, the Bresilian *Land Crocodile, proper. **1664** COTTON *Scarron.* IV. (1715) 69 Curs, Spaniels, Water-dogs, Bandogs, and *Land-dogs. **1712** E. COOKE *Voy. S. Sea* 319 Saw some Widgeons, and many *Land-Doves. **1894** MIVART in *Cosmopolitan* XVI. 344 The enormous *land-dragons that lived by rapine. **1768** G. WHITE *Selborne* xvii. 49 The water-eft or newt is only the larva of the *land-eft. **1669** WORLIDGE *Syst. Agric.* (1681) 304 If *Land-Fowl gather towards the Water. **1859** TENNENT *Ceylon* I. 302 Of all the plagues which beset the traveller in the rising grounds of Ceylon, the most detested are the *land leeches. **1897** *Westm. Gaz.* 20 Aug. 2/1 Huge '*land lobsters'—the 'robber crab' of the Pacific Islands. **1830** LYELL *Princ. Geol.* I. 96 The annihilation of certain genera of *land-mammifera. **1674** RAY *Collect. Words, Eng. Birds* 86 The *Land-martin or Shore-bird: *Hirundo riparia.* **1601** HOLLAND *Pliny* II. 403 A certain wel, wherein there keep ordinarily *land-mice. **1836** M. HOLLEY *Texas* v. 104 *Land and water moccasin..are the only venomous snakes, besides the rattlers, found in Texas. **1881** *Nature* XXIV. 84 The *land-molluscan fauna of Socotra. **1844** LEE & FROST *Ten Yrs. in Oregon* vi. 71 Beaver was valued at two dollars per skin,..*land otter at fifty cents. **1947** V. H. CAHALANE *Mammals N. Amer.* 200 The river or land otter has the outline of a small seal or a very big weasel. **1687** R. BLOME *Present State Isles & Territories in Amer.* 56 A *Land-Pike is another strange Reptile, so called from its likeness to that Fish; but instead of Fins, it hath four Feet. **1706** PHILLIPS (ed. Kersey), *Land-Pike*, a Creature in America, like the Fish of the same Name, but having Legs instead of Fins. **1841** *Cultivator* VIII. 152, I am anxious that he should soon get rid of his land-pikes and alligators. **1842** *Ibid.* X. 37 Hogs, landpike variety, are so cheap. **1856** *Trans. Mich. Agric. Soc.* VII. 716 The Suffolk swine..are of the same descent as the long-nosed, slabsided land pike, so often seen in the highways. **1890** *Amer. N. & Q.* V. 21/2, I think the term *land-pike* more frequently designates a thin, lank, half-wild swine. **1601** HOLLAND *Pliny* I. 507 Hens, and other *land pullen. **1796** STEDMAN *Surinam* II. xxviii. 315, I narrowly escaped being bitten by a *land-scorpion. This insect is of the size of a small cray-fish. **1853** *Zoologist* XI. 4127 In *land-shells..the locality would not be easily surpassed. **1880** A. R. WALLACE *Isl. Life* v. 76 The air-breathing mollusca, commonly called land-shells. **1863** WOOD *Nat. Hist.* III. 632 The *Land-slater (*Oniscus asellus*). **1729** WOODWARD *Nat. Hist. Fossils* I. I. 151 A *Land-Snail, incrusted over with..fine Stoney Matter. **1854** WOODWARD *Mollusca* II. 168 The *land-soles occasionally devour animal substances. **1576** FLEMING tr. *Caius' Eng. Dogs* §2 (end) *Land spaniels. **1616** *Rich Cabinet* 55 b, He would proue..a good land-spaniel or setter for a hungry Courtier, to smell him out a thousand pound sute, for a hundred pound profit. **1624** HEYWOOD *Captives* IV. i. in Bullen *O. Pl.* IV, Proceed sea-gull. Thus land-spaniell; no man can say this is my fishe till he finde it in his nett. **1774** GOLDSM. *Nat. Hist.* (1776) VII. 105 It is only the Rubeth, the *land toad, which has the property of sucking. *Ibid.* VI. 380 The *land tortoise will live in the water, and..the sea turtle can be fed upon land. **1850** LYELL *2nd Visit U.S.* II. 293 In Mr. Clark's garden were several land-tortoises (*Testudo clausa*, Say). **1697** DAMPIER *Voy.* I. 109 We refresht our selves very well, both with *Land and Sea Turtles. **1796** STEDMAN *Surinam* II. xxiii. 163 The land-turtle of Surinam is not more than eighteen or twenty inches in length. **1603** HOLLAND *Plutarch's Mor.* 973 The hedgehoge, or *land urchin. **1601** —— *Pliny* I. 218 Of the Viper, *Land-winkles or Snailes, and Lizards.

12. Special combinations: **land abutment**, the terminal pier at the landward end of a bridge; **land-agency**, the occupation or profession of a land-agent; **land-agent**, a steward or manager of landed property; also, an agent for the sale of land, an estate agent; **land-arch**, an arch or bridge which spans dry land; **land army**, (*a*) (see sense 11 a); (*b*) a corps of women established in 1917 for work on the land in wartime (in full ***Women's Land Army***); also *attrib.*; **land-base**, **-based** *a.*, operating from a base on land, as opp. to one on a ship or water; **†land-bat**, a measure of land of varying length; **land-berg** ? *nonce-wd.* (after *iceberg*), an 'ice-mountain' on land; **land-blink**, an atmospheric glow seen from a distance over snow-covered land in the arctic regions; **†land-board** ? *nonce-wd.* (after *seaboard*), the borders of a country; **†land-born** *a.*, native; **land-borne**, *a.*, carried by land, effected over land; **land-breast**, the whole frontage formed by the abutment and wing-walls or retaining walls of a bridge; **land-bred**, *a.*, brought up on land (as distinguished from on sea); also, native, indigenous; **land-bridge**, (*a*) a connection (usu. prehistoric) between two land masses; (*b*) an overland route linking countries more directly than previously, esp. one used by containerized freight; **†land-carrack**, (*a*) ? a coasting vessel; (*b*) = *land-frigate*; **land-cast**, an orientation; **land-chain**, a surveyor's chain (Simmonds); **†land-coal**, coal transported by land; **land-community**, joint or common ownership of land; **land-company**, a commercial company formed for the exploitation of land; **land-connection** = *land-bridge* a; **land-cook**, *U.S.*, one who 'cooks' land for the market; **land cress**, a biennial herb of the family Cruciferæ, *Barbarea verna*; also, occasionally used for *B. vulgaris*; **land district** *U.S.*, one of the districts into which a state or territory is divided for matters connected with land; **land-drain** (see quot. 1967); also as *vb.*; hence **land-draining** *vbl. sb.*, **land-drainage**; **land-dummier** *Austral.* (see DUMMY *v.* 1); so **land-dummying**; **†land-evil**, (*a*) an epidemic; (*b*) ? the falling sickness, epilepsy; **†landfang**, holding-ground for an anchor; **land-fast**, an attachment on the land for a vessel; *a.*, firmly attached to the shore; **†land-feather**, a bay or inlet; **land fever** *N. Amer.*, eager desire for, or excitement about, securing land (cf. *gold-fever*); **landfill** orig. *U.S.*, the disposal of refuse by burying it under layers of earth; the refuse so disposed of; also *fig.*; **†land-fish**, (*a*) ? fresh-water fish; (*b*) a fish that lives on land; hence, an unnatural creature; **land-floe**, a sheet of sea-ice extending from the land; **†land-frigate**, a harlot, strumpet; **land-fyrd** *OE.* and *Hist.*, the land force; **land-gift** = BHOODAN; **land girl**, a member of the Women's Land Army (see *land army* (*b*) above); **†land-good** [ad. Du. *landgoed*], a landed estate; **land grant**, a grant of land; *spec.* attrib. in **land-grant-college** *U.S.*, a college set up orig. under the Morrill Land Grant Act of 1862, which donated public lands to certain States for the establishment of colleges of agriculture, etc.; **land-honour** (see HONOUR *sb.* 7); **land-horse**, the horse on the land-side of a plough; **land-hunger**, keen desire for the acquisition of land; hence **land-hungry** *a.*; **land-ice**, ice attached to the shore, as distinguished from floe; **†land-ill**, an epidemic (cf. *land-evil*); **land-jobber**, one who makes a business of buying and selling land on speculation; so **land-jobbing**; **land-lead**, a navigable opening in the ice along the shore; **†land-leak**, ? a leak produced in a vessel before starting on a voyage; **land legs**, [cf. SEA LEGS *pl.*], used to designate the ability to walk comfortably on land after being at sea, in a train, etc.; **land-looker** *U.S.* (see quot.); also (*obs.*), a person claiming to have appraised the land in a given area; **†land-lurch** *v.*, to rob of land (see LURCH *v.*); **†land-male**, 'a reserved rent charged upon a piece of land by the chief lord of the fee, or a subsequent mesne owner' (Wright *Provinc. Dict.* 1857); also attrib. *land-male-book*; **†land-march**, territory bordering on another country; **land-marker**, 'a machine for laying out rows for planting' (Knight *Dict. Mech.* 1875); **†land-mate** (see quot.); **†land-mead**, a tract of meadow land; **land-mine**, (*a*) an explosive mine used on land; (*b*) a bomb dropped by parachute from an aircraft; **land-mistress** = LANDLADY 1; ‖**landnám** [ON. *land-nám* f. *land* land, territory + *nám*, f. *nema* to take] = *land-take*; **†land-neck**, an isthmus; **†land-oath** (see quot.); **land-office**, *U.S.* and *Colonial* (see quot. 1855); hence **land-office business**, a thriving business, like that done in a land-office in boom times; a 'roaring trade'; **land-packet** *U.S.* (see quot.); **land-passage**, †(*a*) an isthmus; (*b*) passage by land; **†land-peerage** (see quot.); **land-pirate**, one who robs on land, a highwayman; †also, a literary pirate; **landplane**, an aircraft which can only operate from land (opp. SEAPLANE); **land-plaster**, 'rock-gypsum ground to a powder for use as a fertilizer' (*Cent. Dict.*); **†land-pole**, the pole or perch; **land-poor** *a.* (*U.S.*), poor through owning much land and being unable easily to support the burden of taxation; **land-presser**, an apparatus for pressing down the soil; **land-province**, 'a province of the land distinct from others in the assemblage of plants or animals which it contains, or in their distribution' (Cassell, 1884); **†land-raker** (see *foot-land-raker*, s.v. FOOT *sb.* 35); **land-reeve** (see quot.); **Land Registry**, a government department with which titles to or charges upon land must be registered; the building or office in which this department is housed; **land-roll** (see quot.); **Land-Rover**, **Landrover** [trade name], a sturdy, four-wheel-drive motor vehicle designed esp. for work in rough or agricultural country; **†land-rush**, a landslip; **land sale**, (*a*) a sale of land; (*b*) applied *attrib.* to collieries which are worked on a small scale and from which coal is supplied only to the country round; *pl.* the coal so disposed of; **land-score**, *Hist.*, a division of land [repr. OE. *landscoru*]; **†land-scot**, a tax on land formerly levied in some parishes for the maintenance of the church; **land-scrip** *U.S.*, a negotiable certificate, issued by the U.S. government or by corporate bodies holding donations of land therefrom, entitling the holder to the possession of certain portions of public land (Webster, 1864); **land-scurvy**, scurvy occurring on land, as amongst inmates of workhouses, armies, etc.; **land-sealing**, hunting seals on land; **land-sergeant** (see quot. 1893); also, the steward of an estate; **land-shark**, (*a*) one who makes a livelihood by preying upon seamen when ashore; (*b*) a land-grabber; **† land-sharking** *vbl. sb. N.Z.* (see quot. 1840) *Obs.*; **land-sick** *a.*, (*a*) sick for the sight of land; (*b*) *Naut.*, (of a ship) impeded in its movements by being close to land; (*c*) sick of being on the land; (*d*) sick as a result of being on land again after a long sea voyage; **land-slide** = LANDSLIP; also *fig.* (cf. *avalanche*), esp. with

reference to a sweeping electoral victory; †**land-speech**, a language, tongue; **land-speed**, (*a*) speed (of an aircraft) relative to the ground; (*b*) speed on the ground (e.g. in a motor vehicle); †**land-stall**, a staith or landing-place; †**land-stead** *a. Colonial*, provided with landed property; **land-steward**, one who manages a landed estate for the owner; **land-stone**, a stone turned up in digging; **land-stool**, ? *Sc.* = *land-stall*; †**land-strait**, an isthmus; **land-stream**, a current in the sea due to river waters; †**land-strife**, strife with respect to land, agrarian contention; **land-swarmer**, app. a kind of rocket; **land-swell**, the roll of the water near the shore; **land-take** [ON. *land-taka*], the action of taking land; *spec.* with reference to the Norse colonization of Iceland, the land taken by a chief as his province; **land-taxer**, one who believes in, or advocates, the taxing of land-values; **land-thief**, (*a*) one who robs on land or ashore; (*b*) a robber of land; **land-tide** *Sc.*, 'the undulating motion of the air, as perceived on a droughty day' (Jam.); **land-trash**, broken ice near the shore; †**land-turn**, a land-breeze; **land-value**, the economic value of land in all respects, especially as a basis for rating or taxation; hence ***land-valuation***; **land-valuer**, one whose profession is to examine and declare the value of land or landed estates; **land-waiter** = *landing-waiter* (see LANDING *vbl. sb.*); **land-war**, (*a*) a war waged on land, opposed to a *naval war*; (*b*) a 'war' or contention with respect to land or landed property; **land-warrant** *U.S.* (see quot. 1858); **land-wash**, the wash of the tide near the shore; †**land-water** *a.*, amphibious, nondescript; **land wheel**, the wheel of a plough that runs on the unploughed land; †**land-wine** [cf. Du. *landwijn*, G. *landwein*], wine of native or home growth; **land wire** = LAND-LINE 2; **land-worthiness** *nonce-wd.*, fitness to travel over land; **land-yacht**, a land vehicle similar to a yacht; **land-yard** *local* (see quot. 1828). Also LAND FORM, LAND-SHIP.

1776 G. SEMPLE *Building in Water* 7 It was composed of twenty Arches, nineteen Piers, and two *Land Abutments. **1868** M. PATTISON *Academ. Org.* iv. 110 The requirement that he should be experienced in *land-agency, may seem in itself not unreasonable. **1846** COBDEN *Sp.* (1870) I. 354 We know right well that their [landlords'] *land agents are their electioneering agents. **1805** FORSYTH *Beauties Scotl.* IV. 274 The bridge consists of ten arches, one of which is a *land-arch. **1917** *Times* 4 Aug. 5/4 The work of appealing for the *Women's Land Army will be carried on by the Board of Agriculture. **1918** *Times* 6 Feb. 3/5 The conditions under which the land army women are recruited have recently been changed. **1940** *Punch* 19 June 660/1 As soon as you join the Land Army you will find..that you are in the thick of a whole lot of live stock. **1943** K. TENNANT *Ride on Stranger* xxv. 275, I could always sack you, George,..and get some of these land army girls. **1974** *Country Life* 26 Sept. 829/1 One looks..at a model wearing Land Army uniform, or stoops..to peer into an Anderson shelter. **1962** *Listener* 29 Mar. 540/1 *Land-base missiles and sea-going missiles. **1933** *Land-based [see BASED *pa. pple.*]. **1941** *Air News* May 9 The intrinsic disparity between carrier- and land-based planes. **1960** *Times* 11 Feb. 11/6 Though land-based missiles can be 'hardened'..they are still vulnerable to a fairly accurate nuclear attack. **1973** *Sci. Amer.* May 42/3, 2,500 [nuclear warheads] in land-based missiles. **1603** OWEN *Pembrokeshire* xvii. (1891) 135 The *lande batte or pole of Penbrokshire is in Kemes xij foote..Penbrokshire xj foote. **1853** KANE *Grinnell Exp.* xlv. (1856) 420 When first the mass separates from the *land-berg or glacier. **1835** SIR J. ROSS *Narr. 2nd Voy.* iii. 41 The *landblink was now very perceptible; and in the evening we discerned the land itself. **1790** JEFFERSON *Writ.* (ed. Ford) V. 229 If Great Britain establishes herself on our whole *land-board [*i.e.* along the Mississippi]. **1796** —— in Pickering *Vocab. U.S.* (1816) 170 The position and circumstances of the United States leave them nothing to fear on their land-board. **1589** PUTTENHAM *Eng. Poesie* III. xix. (Arb.) 215 The *land-borne liues safe, the forreine at his ease. **1888** *Pall Mall Gaz.* 30 Oct. 12/1 Another class of coal—best selected brights—which are landborne, fetch at the pit mouth 10*s.* **1934** J. L. MYERS in E. Eyre *European Civilization* I. 156 The profoundly different qualities of sea-borne and land-borne cultures. **1957** *Economist* 5 Oct. 19/2 Few [Arab states] fear Russian imperialism because, unlike Turkey or Iran, they have never felt the dead-weight of landborne pressure. **1739** LABELYE *Short Acc. Piers Westm. Bridge* 70 Each of the *Land Breasts are to spread about 25 Feet on each Side of the Bridge. **1591** SYLVESTER *Du Bartas* I. iv. 160 We resemble *Land-bred Novices New brought aboord to venture on the Seas. **1596** SPENSER *State Irel.* Wks. (Globe) 627/2 Whatsoever relickes there were left of the land-bredd people. **1887** F. M. CRAWFORD *Paul Patoff* I. viii. 273 Till one day the land-bred boaster puts to sea in a Channel steamer. **1897** W. B. SCOTT *Introd. Geol.* xx. 353 Fossils of land animals may demonstrate the former existence of *land bridges between regions which have long been separated by water. **1898** W. TURNER in *Nature* 13 Jan. 259/1 A 'Neolithic land bridge' was produced..and a free immigration of Neolithic man with his domestic animals became possible. **1911** J. L. MYRES *Dawn of Hist.* vii. 138 Some think..that the Hyksos conquest of Egypt may have been a further adventure along this southern land-bridge. **1941** *Manch. Guardian Weekly* 26 Sept. 194/4 There is now also a land bridge to Russia through Iran, and the Government is certain to consider whether and when we can give any military aid to Russia by that route. **1950** A. L. ROWSE *England of Elizabeth* ii. 39 He cites the opinion of Master Twyne that a land-bridge once existed between Dover and Calais. **1969** *Jane's Freight Containers 1968–69* 28/1 The Port of Vancouver..put into operation the concept of the 'Land-Bridge'. *Ibid.* 32/2 The land bridge concept which foresees Canada being used as a rail-link for containers moving between Europe and the Orient. **1970** *Times* 2 June (Container Suppl.) p. ii/2 What is this concept, land-bridge? The term refers to the part of a movement from one place to another..consisting of an overland haul between ports. **1973** A. QUINTON *Nature of Things* x. 301 It is generally believed that Britain was connected to the continent of Europe by a land-bridge at some time in the fairly remote past. **1604** SHAKS. *Oth.* I. ii. 50 Faith, he to night hath boarded a *Land Carract. **1629** DAVENANT *Albovine* III. i, *Grim.* I must be furnish'd too. *Cuny.* With a Mistresse? *Grim.* Yes, inquire me out some old Land-Carack. **1881** BLACKMORE *Christowell* I, He turned upon his track..and making a correct *landcast this time, found his way to the fountains of the Taw. *a* **1661** FULLER *Worthies, Shropsh.* (1662) II. 1 One may observe a threefold difference in our English-Coale. 1 Sea-coale..2 *Land-coale, at Mendip, Bedworth, &c. and carted into other Counties. 3 What one may call River or Fresh-water-Coale. **1874** STUBBS *Const. Hist.* I. v. 85 The historical township is the body of alodial owners who have advanced beyond the stage of *land-community. **1805** *Deb. Congress U.S.* 30 Jan. (1852) 1044 Having never thought of purchasing any land from the Georgia *land companies. **1833** *Knickerbocker* I. 283 'Look,' said an old man..to the agent of the land company. **1854** LOWELL *Jrnl. in Italy* Prose Wks. 1890 I. 172 Nothing else but an American land-company ever managed to induce settlers upon territory of such uninhabitable quality. **1876** A. R. WALLACE *Geogr. Distribution Animals* I. III. xiii. 402 There is no evidence of a former *land-connection between the Australian and Neotropical regions. **1924** J. G. A. SKERL tr. *Wegener's Orig. Continents & Oceans* ii. 19 The former existence of broad land connections between continents which are widely separated at the present day can scarcely be doubted. **1957** J. K. CHARLESWORTH *Quaternary Era* II. xxxii. 696 Glaciation seems irreconcilable with a land-connexion, so often suggested, between Australia and South America during Tertiary time. **1807** *Edin. Rev.* X. 112 How comes it to pass that the American *land-cook is cunning enough to carry on his trick. **1856** W. A. BROMFIELD *Flora Vectensis* 33 Mr R. Loe of Newchurch tells me it [sc. *Barbarea verna*] is often substituted by the people of this island [*sc.* the Isle of Wight] for the common Water Cress, being known by the opposite cognomen of *Land Cress. **1878** BRITTEN & HOLLAND *Dict. Eng. Plant-Names* 129 Cress, Land. (1) *Barbarea præcox*, Br... (2) *Cardamine hirsuta*, L. **1944** W. J. STOKOE *Caterpillars Brit. Butterflies* 179 Wintercress *Barbarea vulgaris*..is also known as Yellow Rocket and Land Cress, to distinguish it from Watercress, which, in general appearance, it closely resembles. **1946** *Nature* 21 Dec. 920/1 Investigations under the Dairy Research Institute have included landcress taint in cream and butter. **1969** *Oxf. Bk. Food Plants* 152/2 Winter Cress or Land Cress (*Barbarea verna*), is a useful but rarely-grown salad plant. **1812** *Deb. Congress U.S.* 9 Dec. (1853) 28 The Board of Commissioners for the western *land district, in the State of Louisiana. **1831** J. M. PECK *Guide for Emigrants* 257 The State is divided into land districts, which are designated by Congress. **1883** *Rep. Indian Affairs* (U.S.) 187 An Act to create three additional land districts in the territory of Dakota. **1767** A. YOUNG *Farmer's Lett.* 245 When the ditching is done, the next work is to *land-drain the whole fields in such a manner that every part of them may be laid dry. *Ibid.* 251 In some fields..it is very difficult to tell exactly where to make the land-drains. **1841** J. F. BURKE *On Land-Drainage* 4 Remains have been found of some very ancient land-drains. **1932** BLUNDEN *Fall in, Ghosts* 9 The trickling land-drain under the culvert did not report the imminence of an enemy. **1967** *Gloss. Sanitation Terms* (*B.S.I.*) 6 *Land drain*, a drain, composed of porous or perforated pipes, laid in a trench filled with gravel, broken stone, or the like, for sub-soil drainage. **1841** J. F. BURKE (*title*) On *land-drainage, subsoil-ploughing and irrigation. **1950** *Engineering* CLXIX. 143/3 The book should be of great value also to designers of..land-drainage, irrigation and water-supply works. **1841** J. F. BURKE *On Land-Drainage* 35 *Land-draining..should never be undertaken but with a determination to do it effectually. **1880** *Gentl. Mag.* CCXLVI. 77 The successes and failures of Australian *land-dummiers. *Ibid.* 76 The fraudulent transaction known as *land-dummying. *a* **1225** *Ancr. R.* 360 þet *lond vuel þat alle londes leien on, & liggeð ȝet monie. *c* **1440** *Promp. Parv.* 312/1 Lond ivyl, sekenesse (*P.* londe euyll), *epilencia*. **1557** BURROUGH in *Hakluyt* (1886) III. 153 Where a ship may ride..in 4 fadome..of water, and haue *Landfange for a North and by West winde. **1703** W. DAMPIER *Voy.* III. 36 There is not clean Ground enough for above 3 Ships..One even of these must lie close to the Shore, with a *Land-fast there. **1926** *Daily Colonist* (Victoria, B.C.) 24 Jan. 6/4 Amundsen's experience in the Arctic has been on shipboard, on land, and on *landfast polar ice. **1973** *Nat. Geographic* Mar. 350 Anchoring block and tackle to land-fast ice, all strain together to haul the bowhead out of the water. *c* **1582** DIGGES in *Archæologia* XI. 236 The south baye or *landfether of the great sluce. **1839** *Picayune* (New Orleans) 23 Apr. 2/2 Then came the *land *fever*, which swept over the country like a pestilence. **1845** C. M. KIRKLAND *Western Clearings* 4 In the days of the land-fever. **1900** E. B. OSBORN *Greater Canada* 60 Many years passed before the North-West recovered from the commercial lethargy which followed this attack of land-fever. **1946** E. HODGINS *Mr. Blandings builds his Dream House* 16 Then, suddenly the land fever seized them. **1972** J. MINIFIE *Homesteader* vi. 40 Many of the harvesters were bitten by the land fever, and filed on land for themselves once the harvest was over. **1942** in *Sun* (Baltimore) (1944) 10 Feb. 8/1 The so-called sanitary or *land fill [system]. **1953** *Richmond* (Va.) *News Leader* 2 Sept. 21 A bulldozer struck water in the landfill dump area. **1967** *Boston Sunday Globe* 23 Apr. 20/3 By 1970, it is expected that the majority of the area's dumps and landfill sites will be filled to capacity. **1969** *New Yorker* 17 May 131/2 We intend to put a lot of landfill in the Credibility Gap. **1971** *Pollution: a Review* (Greater London Council) 8 The Greater London Council..operates a code of practice for good management of landfill sites under its own control. **1971** *Guardian* 11 Oct. 3/6 Land-fill is considered one of the most economical ways to dispose of refuse. **1419** *Liber Albus* 221 (Rolls) I. 376 Qui ducit *landfisshe post prandium, bene licet ei hospitari piscem suum, et in crastino ponere piscem suum in foro Domini Regis. **1606** SHAKS. *Tr. & Cr.* III. iii. 264 Hee's growne a very land-fish, languagelesse, a monster. **1823** W. SCORESBY *Jrnl. Voy. Northern Whale-Fishery* iv. 101 The drift of the ice towards the south-west,..for three weeks preceding our entrance amid the *land floes, had averaged seven or eight miles a-day. **1866** C. E. SMITH *Diary* 20 July in *Listener* (1969) 17 Apr. 525/2 We are unable to stir, with a tremendous land-floe on one side of us and, on the other side, a body of ice extending as far as we can see from the mast-head. **1939** *Beaver* June 31 By May literally hundreds of thousands [of eider ducks] have arrived to feed in the sea and rest idly on the edge of land-floe and ice-pan. **1611** L. WHITAKER in Coryat *Crudities* Introd. Verses, Here to this *Land-Friggat he's ferried by Charon, He bords her; a seruice a hot and a rare one. **11..** *O.E. Chron.* an. 1001 (Laud MS.), Ne him to ne dorste scip here on sæ, ne *land-fyrd. **1874** GREEN *Short Hist.* ii. §4. 75 The Land-Fyrd, or general levy of fighting men. **1953** *Land-gift [see BHOODAN]. **1957** *Listener* 30 May 889/3 The Land Gifts Movement..aims at persuading landowners large and small to surrender voluntarily a sixth of their land for distribution to the poor. **1964** T. ZINKIN *India* vi. 125 Vinoba Bhave..managed to create such a response for his 'Bhoodan'—land-gift—that the bitterness on which the communists had thrived in Telengana vanished. **1918** *Times* 20 Mar. 9/4 The *land girls [had] little felt hats and smocks and their red badges of service. **1919** 'I. HAY' *Last Million* 81 We have consorted with..Farmers, Hedgers, and Land Girls. **1928** 'R. CROMPTON' *William—the Good* iv. 103 He found his sister Ethel wearing a neat land girl's costume and weeding a bed. **1940** *Manch. Guardian Weekly* 8 Nov. 325 One German pilot even turned his guns against land girls working in the fields. **1958** *Times Lit. Suppl.* 11 July 399/5 A young Tunisian land-girl and youth leader. **1974** M. CECIL *Heroines in Love* vii. 175 Down on the farm the Land Girl was swept off her feet by the farmer. **1591** HORSEY *Trav.* (Hakl. Soc.) 246 Purchasing..howses and *landgoods upon which they did inhabite. **1862** *N.Y. Tribune* 21 Mar., Some years since, the movement for a Pacific Railroad, attended by an enormous *land-grant, assumed proportions that indicated the probable success of the movement. **1869** *Bradshaw's Railway Manual* XXI. 431 Expended..Land grant expenses—$7,205. **1889** *Century Mag.* Jan. 404/2 The land-grant colleges graduate men fitted to superintend farms and workshops. **1900** *Daily Chron.* 28 Aug. 5/1 At the present time no land-grants to emigrants are being made by the Natal Government. **1943** J. S. HUXLEY *TVA* vi. 30 In 1862..Land Grant Colleges were established—so called because in every State lands were granted from the public domain to endow a College for the teaching of 'Agriculture and the Mechanic Arts'. **1944** F. CLUNE *Red Heart* 5 He was..a hander-out of liberal land-grants to sycophantic favourites. **1962** H. R. LOYN *Anglo-Saxon Eng.* iv. 158 If arable is at the centre of the land-grant, connected rights in meadow, pasture..and wood were closely associated with it. **1967** MRS. L. B. JOHNSON *White House Diary* 14 Mar. (1970) 498 Federal participation in education is not exactly new, going back as far as 1785 in the Land Ordinance, the land grant colleges of the 1860's [etc.]. **1671** MADOX (*title*) Baronia Anglica, a History of *Land-Honours and Baronies, and of Feudal Tenure in capite. *a* **1848** FINLAYSON in *Chambers's Inform.* I. 486/2 The..most forward horse, should be put in the furrow, and only bound back to the right or off theet of the *land-horse. **1862** J. M. LUDLOW *Hist. U.S.* vi. 221 The *land-hunger of the South now outstripped even the ambition of conquest of Mr. Polk. **1889** *Century Mag.* Jan. 369/2 When the *land-hungry band of Welsh and Norman barons entered Ireland. **1820** SCORESBY in *Ann. Reg.* II. 1324 *Land-ice consists of drift-ice attached to the shore; or drift-ice, which, by being covered with mud or gravel, appears to have recently been in contact with the shore; or the flat-ice, resting on the land, not having the appearance or elevation of ice-bergs. **1856** KANE *Arct. Expl.* I. xxiii. 281 Crossing the land-ices by portage. **1873** J. GEIKIE *Gt. Ice Age* (1894) 547 These boulders could not have been carried by land-ice. *c* **1500** *Addic. Scot. Cron.* (1819) 4 The *land Ill..was so violent þ^t^ þar deit ma þ^t^ yere than euir þar deit ouder in pestilens [etc.]. *a* **1745** SWIFT *Direct. Servants* vii. 74 Let him be at Home to none but..a *Land-Jobber, or his Inventor of new Funds. **1876** BANCROFT *Hist. U.S.* IV. xv. 419 A physician, land-jobber, and subservient political intriguer. **1781** in *Mass. Hist. Soc. Coll.* (1814) 2nd. Ser. I. 186 Toryism, British interest, and *Land-jobbing views, combine numbers without and within doors. **1885** *Century Mag.* Apr. 826 When the bill to establish a State park at Niagara was on its passage,..the great majority of the country members were opposed to it, fearing that it might conceal some land-jobbing scheme. **1856** KANE *Arct. Expl.* II. xxviii. 278 Here the *land-leads ceased, with the exception of some small and scarcely practicable openings near the shore. **1649** G. DANIEL *Trin-arch., Hen. V*, xcii, What horror stops my Quill? ere yet aboard Wee see the Royall Fraught, a *Land-Leake Springs. **1871** *City-Road Mag.* I. 242/1 If Mr. Goschen has had to get his sea-legs on, Jack finds it as difficult to put on his *land-legs. **1927** *Sunday Times* 6 Mar. 23/4 The tourists will disembark..and proceed to Teignmouth to spend eighteen days recovering their 'land legs' and developing combination. **1938** H. NICOLSON *Let.* 17 Apr. (1966) 337 Have you..recovered your landlegs as yet? After three days in the train one feels the room rocking like after three days at sea. **1840** *Knickerbocker* XVI. 206 Another class of operators..became popularly known as '*land-lookers'. These met you at every turn, ready to furnish 'water power', 'pine-lots', 'choice farming tracts' or any thing else, at a moment's notice. **1845** C. M. KIRKLAND *Western Clearings* 6 These blunders called into action another class of operators, who became popularly known as 'land-lookers'. **1891** R. A. ALGER in *Voice* (N.Y.) 15 Oct., What woodsmen call a 'land-looker', i.e. a timber expert whose business it is to locate pine timber land in Michigan. **1893, 1900** Landlooker [see CRUISER 3]. **1902** S. E. WHITE *Blazed Trail* xvi. 116 This is the usual method of procedure adopted by land-lookers everywhere. **1602** WARNER *Alb. Eng.* IX. xlvi. 217 Hence countrie Loutes *land lurch their Lords. **1390–91** *Durham Acc. Rolls* (Surtees) 392 Pro *landmale, 9*d.* **1416–17** *Ibid.* 614 Pro ligatura cujusdam libri vocati le landmalebok, 16*d.* **1429** *Ibid.* 60 In laynd-mayle solut. sacristæ Dunelm., 9½*d.* **1577** in Balfour *Oppressions in Orkn. & Shetl.* (1859) 18 Ane dewitie thai pay to the Kingis Maiestie for thair scat and landmales zeirlie. **1665** *Vestry*

Bks. (Surtees) 218, 15 August, Paid for Land Male, 1s. 9d. 1614 Selden Titles Hon. 212 Many of the Imperial Marquisats..had their names from being *Land-marches of the State, and not from their maritime situation. 1670 Blount Glossogr., *Land-mate, in Herefordshire he that in Harvest-time reaps on the same ridge of ground, or Land, with another, they call Land-mates, that is fellow Laborers on the same land. 1577–87 Harrison England I. xviii. (1877) III. 132 Our medowes, are either bottomes..or else such as we call *land meads, and borrowed from the best and fattest pasturages. 1890 Electrician 16 Mar. 502/1 *Land Mines. These mines..are intended to be placed a few inches below the surface of the ground, and are so constructed that they..fire themselves electrically or mechanically when the measure of the weight of a man is brought to bear upon them. 1915 R. W. Campbell Private Spud Tamson xix. 288 A terrific explosion of land mines, which burst beneath the feet of the enemy. a1917 E. A. Mackintosh War, the Liberator (1918) 134 Two sappers brought up land mines and laid them. 1940 N. & Q. 21 Dec. 440/2 Up to September of this year a land-mine..signified a receptacle filled with explosive and concealed immediately below the surface of the ground... In popular parlance it has come to mean a mine, that is to say a thin metal container holding a large quantity of explosive, dropped from an enemy aeroplane upon the land. 1959 Chambers's Encycl. II. 413/1 The effectiveness of the 'land-mines' dropped by the Luftwaffe on Britain. 1968 M. Richler in R. Weaver Canad. Short Stories 2nd Ser. 183 Had a little disagreement with a land mine, son. 1973 'R. MacLeod' Nest of Vultures vi. 129 British antipersonnel Claymore land-mines. 1860 Gen. P. Thompson Audi Alt. III. cxxxiv. 102 If our Welsh *land-mistress said, 'Here are Martin and John making me fair offers for the farm' [etc.]. 1858 G. W. Dasent in Oxford Ess. 185 Chief after chief coming out [to Iceland]..settling himself on some great chief's lot or *landnám, who allotted him a portion on condition of the acknowledgement of his supremacy. 1877 C. A. V. Conybeare Place of Iceland in Hist. European Inst. 28 The Goðorð was no doubt intimately connected with the landnám of the most powerful of the immigrants. 1915 K. Gjerset Hist. Norwegian People (1932) xxv. 140 The chieftains..claimed large tracts of land by right of settlement and occupation..while the freemen.. with their consent, settled in their landnám. 1618 Bolton Florus II. xvi. (1636) 140 At the very entrance of the Isthmus or *Land-neck. 1672 Petty Pol. Anat. xii. Tracts (1769) 364 Of all oaths they [the Irish] think themselves at much liberty to take a *land-oath, as they call it: Which is an oath to prove a forged deed, a possession, livery or seisin, payment of rent, &c. in order to recover for their countrymen the lands which they forfeited. 1790 A. Hamilton Wks. (1886) VII. 48 It seems requisite that the general *land-office should be established at the seat of government. 1855 Ogilvie, Suppl., Land-office, in most colonies there are land-offices, in which the sales of new land are registered, and warrants issued for the location of land, and other business respecting unsettled land is transacted. 1839 Picayune (New Orleans) 2 Apr. 2/3 A practical printer..could do a *land-office business here. 1877 'Mark Twain' in Atlantic Monthly Nov. 590/1 Naturally, the prophets of Baal took all the trade. Isaac..went a-prophesying around, letting on to be doing a land-office business, but 't wa'n't any use. 1882 Rep. to Ho. Repr. Prec. Met. U.S. 153 It is owned by the Union Mill and Mining Company, which once did a land-office business in ore crushing. 1935 M. M. Atwater Murder in Midsummer v. 51 He was doing a land-office business in gas and pop and candy. 1951 E. Paul Springtime in Paris xi. 203 American students..used to do a land-office business in contraband cigarettes. 1972 New York 12 June 35/2 Allen & Co... was doing a land-office business touting Planet Oil. 1847 W. T. Porter Quarter Race 115 Known as the Captain of a '*land-packet'—in plain terms, the driver of an ox-team. 1601 Holland Pliny I. 78 Another *land passage or Isthmus there is of like streightnesse..and of equall breadth with that of Corinth. 1642 Declar. Chas. I to Parlt. in Rushw. Hist. Coll. III. (1692) I. 602 He hath..cut the Banks, and let in the Waters to drown the Land-passages, and to make the Town inaccessable by that way. a1677 Hale Prim. Orig. Man. II. vii. 190 There is no Land-passage from this Elder World unto that of America. 1741 T. Robinson Gavelkind II. viii. 273 A Custom..is set up at present in most Manors of..the ..Weald under the Name of *Landpeerage; whereby the Owners of the Lands, on each side the Highways, claim to exclude the Lord from the Property of the Soil of the Way, and of the Trees growing thereon. 1609 Dekker Lanth. & Candle-l. viii. Wks. (Grosart) III. 262 The Cabbines where these *Land-pyrates lodge in the night, are the Out-barnes of Farmers. c1670 in T. Brooks Wks. (1867) VI. 388 Some dishonest booksellers, called land-pirates, who make it their practice to steal impressions of other men's copies. a1700 B. E. Dict. Cant. Crew, Land-pirates, Highwaymen or any other Robbers. 1890 'Rolf Boldrewood' Miner's Right (1899) 148/1 A bloody murdering land-pirate that ought to be hung at the yard-arm. 1923 Daily Mail 23 June 5 Among *landplanes there are huge new troop-carriers. 1932 19th Cent. Feb. 205 One squadron of flying-boats and one of torpedo-bomber landplanes. 1941 E. C. Shepherd Military Aeroplane 27 The Coastal Command..has..landplane reconnaissance craft which can also carry bombs. 1942 Tee Emm (Air Ministry) II. 61 Land planes are not designed for alighting on the sea. 1969 K. Munson Pioneer Aircraft 1903–14 152/2 Unlike Fabre's seaplane, however, this was both a landplane and a biplane, with a twin-girder 'fuselage' on which was lightly attached an aluminium nacelle encompassing side-by-side seats for pilot and passenger. 1603 Owen Pembrokesh. xvi. (1891) 133 The vsuall measure of land vsed in this shire much differeth from the statute acre, for yt differeth all together in summinge vp, as allso in the *land pole. 1873 J. H. Beadle Undevel. West 781 In the country, the old settlers are '*land-poor'—so rich that they can not pay their taxes. 1914 Collier's Mag. 31 Jan. 22/2 The land-poor farmer is a well-known institution in the Middle West. a1953 E. O'Neill Long Day's Journey (1956) IV. 125 All I told them was I couldn't afford any millionaire's sanatorium because I was land poor. 1834 Penny Cycl. II. 224/2 In such soils an artificial pan may be formed by the *land-presser or press-drill. 1842 Brande Dict. Sci. etc., *Land-reeve, a subordinate officer on an extensive estate, who acts as an assistant to the land steward. 1862 Act 25 & 26 Vict. c. 53 s. 108 An Office, to be called the Office of *Land Registry, shall be established. 1974 J. M. Brownjohn tr. H. H. Kirst's Time for Truth iii. 73 The information does seem to be genuine... I took the liberty of running a preliminary check at the Land Registry. 1986 Homes & Savings Winter 46/1 The Land Registry issues a land certificate..to the owner. 1858 Simmonds Dict. Trade, *Land-roll, a clod-crusher and seam-presser. 1948 Trade Marks Jrnl. 29 Sept. 786/2 Land-rover... Land motor-vehicles and parts thereof... The Rover Company Limited. 1948 Motor 3 Nov. 381/1 Also exhibited is the Land Rover, as a closed estate car with seven-seat capacity, a go-anywhere, four-wheel-drive model powered by the '60' engine. 1953 New Statesman 13 June 696/3 Commuting barristers and stockbrokers in their shooting brakes and land-rovers. 1959 Times Lit. Suppl. 24 Apr. 243/4 It is one of the few recent books about the Sahara desert in which there is no mention of a Land-Rover. 1960 Times 5 July (Agric. Suppl.) p. iv/1 The Land-Rover is as much part of the farming scene as the cattle or the sheep. 1971 Country Life 25 Feb. 436/2 Then came the Landrover, also a multi-purpose, cross-country vehicle. 1549 Compl. Scot. vi. 39 Mony hurlis of stannirs & stanis that tumlit doune vitht the *land rusche. 1708 J. C. Compl. Collier (1845) 47 *Land-Sale Collieries. 1848 Simmond's Colon. Mag. May 63 The whole sum realised by land sales. 1860 Eng. & For. Mining Gloss., Newcastle Terms, Landsale, coals sold to the country in the neighbourhood of the pit. 1886 J. Boyd Bewick Gleanings 2 His father and grandfather before him, had.. held a small 'landsale' colliery near their home at Cherryburn. 1828 N. Carlisle Acc. Charities 295 Anciently the greatest part of the Country lay in common, only some parcels about the villages being inclosed, and a small quantity in *Land-Scores allotted out for tillage. 1617 in G. W. Hill & W. H. Frere Mem. Stepney Parish (1891) 77 There shalbe a generall *Landskot and assessemt made of all the inhabitants of the parish..toward the necessarie repayre of the Church. 1875 Parish Sussex Gloss., Lanscot or Landscote. 1834 A. Jackson in Messages & Papers of Presidents (1896) III. 52 Mr. St. Clair..had permitted the clerk in his office to be the agent of speculations in *land scrip. 1848 Indiana Gen. Assembly Doc. (1849) I. 181 Such land Scrip as had been issued on the Wabash and Erie Canal. 1862 Congress. Globe 10 June 2628/1 There is no railroad company..that has the right to locate land scrip. 1943 L. V. Hamner Short Grass 174 Surveyors..bought up a lot of land scrip for almost nothing. 1789 W. Buchan Dom. Med. (1790) 397 Harrowgate-water is certainly an excellent medicine in the *land scurvy. 1891 C. Creighton Hist. Epidemics 605 note, At one time land-scurvy was detected (under the influence of theory) in many forms. 1911 Chambers's Jrnl. July 475/2 In the *land-sealing..thousands of fur-seals are driven and forced onwards. a1775 Hobie Noble ix. in Child Ballads (1890) IV. 2/2, I dare not with you into England ride, The *land-sergeant has me at feid. 1893 Northumbld. Gloss., Land-serjeant, one of the officers of the Border watch, under the Warden of the March. 1894 R. S. Ferguson Hist. Westmorland 197 The steward or land-sergeant of their barony or manor. 1769 Wesley Jrnl. 30 Mar., Let all beware of these *land-sharks. 1815 Scott Guy M. xxxiv, Lieutenant Brown..told him some goose's gazette about his being taken in a skirmish with the landsharks. 1829 in Ohio Archaeol. & Hist. Q. (1939) XLVIII. 331 The Counsel is sure to be supported by the presiding Judges..& thus the Property of Society is Confiscated Legally between these Land Sharks. 1839 J. D. Lang N.Z. in 1839 i. 14 A class of persons in that Colony [sc. New South Wales] who were known by the name of Land Sharks..have turned their eyes all at once to New Zealand. 1857 Kingsley Two Y. Ago iv, Can't trust these landsharks; they'll plunder even the rings off a corpse's fingers. They think every wreck a god-send. 1865 C. F. Hursthouse Lett. on N.Z. Subjects 89 'Land Sharks', twenty years ago this was a term rife in Australia and New Zealand. a1910 'O. Henry' Rolling Stones (1915) 218 A class of land speculators commonly called land sharks, unscrupulous and greedy. 1935 A. Sullivan Great Divide 342 The Metis are being stirred up by the land sharks to demand their scrip, then the sharks will swallow them. 1839 Colonial Gaz. 28 Aug. 627/2 *Land-sharking means pretending to purchase, but really obtaining somehow, land from the natives. 1840 N.Z. Company Rep. I. 31 The practice of land-sharking, or the acquisition of land from the barbarous natives by private persons, without any reserves for the use of the natives, or indeed any sort of regard for their just rights. 1855 C. W. Richmond Let. 28 Apr. in Richmond-Atkinson Papers (1960) I. 162 Such agreements favor landsharking and tend to produce strife and contention. 1846 H. Melville Typee i. (heading) A *land-sick ship. 1888 L. A. Smith Music of Waters 219, I could understand any land-sick lad longing for a sea-life if he once heard this ballast-throwing song. 1908 Westm. Gaz. 13 Feb. 2/1 The joy of the land-sick sailors who cried, 'The sea, the sea!' 1908 Daily Chron. 10 June 4/4 It was very curious, that first step ashore... I was thoroughly land-sick. 1922 D. H. Lawrence Let. 5 Sept. (1962) II. 714 We were twenty-five days at sea and are still landsick—the floor ought to go up and down, the room ought to tremble from the engines, the water ought to swish around but doesn't, so one is landsick. The solid ground almost hurts. 1924 —— & Skinner Boy in Bush 19 Jack was a little tired and a little land-sick, after the long voyage. 1856 Emerson Eng. Traits iv. 65 Slain by a *land-slide, like the agricultural King Onund. 1870 Lowell Study Wind. 240 The Roman road, which linked them with the only past they knew, had been buried under the great barbarian land-slide. 1870 Anderson Missions Amer. Bd. II. xxxiv. 308 A terrible landslide occurred, an eruption of mud, earth, and rocks. 1888 N.Y. Times 4 Nov. 5/1 A veritable landslide in Mr. Hewitt's favor. 1895 Century Mag. Mar. 734 There was then a great landslide of votes for McClellan. 1896 Westm. Gaz. 6 Nov. 7/1 We were justified in urging our readers yesterday to accept with caution the earlier views of the extent of McKinley's majority. It is not a 'land-slide'. 1936 Punch 23 Sept. 362/1 The first volume of the long expected biography of Arthur James Balfour (which takes us as far as the Conservative landslide in 1906). 1946 Ann. Reg. 1945 239 Another undoubted shock was the Labour landslide in the British general elections. 1955 Times 9 May 11/4 The electoral landslide which swept into power the hastily organized Labour Front. 1974 Times 27 Feb. 18/5 Modern Toryism..wants a land-slide victory. c1250 Gen. & Ex. 669 Sexti *lond-speches and .xii. mo, weren delt ðane in werlde ðo. 1910 R. Ferris How it Flies xx. 464 *Land-speed, the speed of aircraft as related to objects on the ground. 1935 Eyston & Lyndon Motor Racing & Record Breaking vi. 56 Record breaking can be somewhat grim, as is shown by the land-speed attempts at Daytona. 1963 Times 2 May 11/2 Donald Campbell reached 110 miles an hour on the salt flats here today when his turbo-jet car Bluebird made a first trial run for his world landspeed record bid. 1971 Guinness Bk. Records (ed. 18) xi. 160 The highest land speed recorded by a woman is 335·070 m.p.h. by Mrs. Lee Ann Breedlove. 1739 N. Riding Rec. VIII. 227 Money laid out in repairing the *land stall leading to Burn and Masham Bridges. 1688 New Jersey Archives (1881) II. 31 There is a gushet of about 2000 acres..which I design to take vp for you, being good land; so I think by farr you will be the best *land-stead of any concerned in the province. c1701 Ibid. II. 34 He says I was in 1688, the best Land-stead of any concern'd in the Province. 1535 Stewart Cron. Scot. II. 679 His *land-stewart in the tyme he maid Ouir all Scotland. 1701 Steele Funeral v. i. (1702) 72 He is not now with his Land-steward. 1899 Crockett Kit Kennedy xiv. 100 'My Lord', answered the land steward, meekly, 'were it a thing' [etc.]. 1796 Capt. Haig Diary in J. Russell Haigs (1881) 482 Many *land stones, some whin ones, but mostly all fine quarried stones. 1813 R. Kerr Agric. Berw. 35 In all free soils, numerous stones, provincially termed land-stones, are found. 1886 Cheshire Gloss., Land stones, the name given..to the pebbles and boulders turned up in digging and draining. 1873 W. McDowell Hist. Dumfries I. 584 The pier or *landstool was commenced. 1601 R. Johnson Kingd. & Commw. (1603) 11 Peruana is..enuironed on al sides with the sea, saue wheras the forsaid *Land-streight doth ioyn the same to Mexicana. 1625 Bp. Mountagu App. Cæsar II. v. 158 In a Foreland or Landstreight where two Seas meet. 1868 Swinburne Poems & Ballads (ed. 3) 73 The *land-stream and the tide-stream in the sea. 1553 Grimalde Cicero's Offices II. (1558) 109 Did not *land striues bring them to distruction? 1799 G. Smith Laboratory I. 10 Charge for *land swarmers, or small rockets. 1812 J. Wilson Isle of Palms IV. 552 As her gilded prow is dancing Through the *landswell. 1906 Ann. Rep. Board of Regents Smithsonian Inst. 287 Until a Parliament for Iceland was established in 930 these chieftains were the rulers of the island, each in his district or *land-take (land-nám), as it was called. 1908 W. G. Collingwood Scandinavian Brit. 193 In each landtake the bóndi fixed his homestead, neither on the exposed hill-top, nor on the marshy flat. 1927 E. V. Gordon Introd. Old Norse 235 The method of land-take used by settlers in Iceland; they carried fire through the land they were to occupy, and around its limits. 1905 Westm. Gaz. 13 Apr. 4/1 The *land taxers have an idea that valuable sites are being held back by grasping ground landlords. 1909 Daily Chron. 30 Apr. 1/6 As land-taxers, we are thoroughly satisfied that we have got a complete system of land valuation. 1928 Daily Express 6 June 2/4 Colonel Wedgwood, the famous Socialist land-taxer. 1596 Shaks. Merch. V. I. iii. 24 There be land rats, and water rats, water theeues, and *land theeues. 1865 Kingsley Herew. I. x. 229, I am Hereward the Berserker, the land-thief, the sea-thief. 1894 H. Spencer in Westm. Gaz. 29 Aug. 8/2 The stronger peoples have been land-thieves from the beginning, and have remained land-thieves down to the present hour. 1818 Edin. Mag. Oct. 328/2 Whar the dew neer scanc't, nor the *landtide danc't Nor rain had ever fawn. 1856 Kane Arct. Expl. I. xxvi. 341 The *land-trash is cemented by young ice. 1676 Coles, *Land-turn, the same from off the land by night, as a Brieze is off the Sea by day. 1851 Fraser's Mag. XLIII. 117 Luckily..for railway companies,..*land-valuation is a remarkably elastic art. 1908 Daily Chron. 6 Aug. 8/3 The land-valuation proposals of the Government. 1880 H. George Progress & Poverty VIII. ii. 365 To abolish all taxation save that upon *land values. 1900 W. Smart Taxation of Land Values 38 Of late years we have heard much of a proposal called the taxation of land values. 1908 Westm. Gaz. 20 Feb. 2/2 The rates charged on the land-value basis. 1962 H. R. Loyn Anglo-Saxon Eng. viii. 319 Considerable variation in land-values.. occurred between 1066 and 1086. 1844 Cobden Sp. (1870) I. 127 They are all auctioneers and *land-valuers. 1711 Swift Examiner No. 28 ⁋4 Give a Guinea to a Knavish *Land-Waiter, and he shall connive at the Merchant for cheating the Queen of an Hundred. 1809 R. Langford Introd. Trade 132 Land waiter or searcher, a Custom-House officer who enters goods imported. 1714 Q. Anne in Lond. Gaz. No. 5204/2 They are Delivered from a Consuming *Land-War. 1870 Emerson Soc. & Solit. x. 204 Who, sitting in his closet, can lay out the plans of a campaign,—sea-war and land-war. 1873 J. Godkin (title) The Land-War in Ireland. 1787 Jefferson Writ. (1859) II. 334 Sharpers had duped so many with their unlocated *land-warrants. 1858 Simmonds Dict. Trade, Land-warrant, a title to a lot of public land; an American security or official document for entering or settling upon government land, much dealt in among jobbers. 1557 W. Towrson in Hakluyt Voy. (1589) 114 The *land wash went so sore, that it overthrew his boate, and one of the men was drowned. 1891 Blizzard of 1891 ii. 26 Breakers fell with great force close to the landwash and over the promenade. 1721 De Foe Moll Flanders (ed. 3) 58 This amphibious Creature, this *Land-water-thing, call'd, a Gentleman-Tradesman. 1743 W. Ellis Mod. Husbandman Sept. iv. 27 The *Land Wheel being obliged to go on the Turf its Share is kept too high. 1960 Farmer & Stockbreeder 15 Mar. 102/3 For a one-man unit the spreader should be land-wheel-driven for ease of hitching on and off. 1970 G. E. Evans Where Beards wag All ii. 46 A two-horse iron plough with round coulter,..land and furrow wheel. 1972 Country Life 10 Feb. 321/3 It [sc. a plough] had no land wheel, so that depth had to be kept by bearing on the stilts. 1390–1 Earl Derby's Exped. (Camden) 47 Lautre barell continente xxix stopas de *lande-wyn. 1573 Baret Alv. L 80 Land wine, or of our owne countrie growing, vinum indigena. 1876 Preece & Sivewright Telegraphy v. 128 Between London and Amsterdam there are 130 miles of *land wire over the Great Eastern Railway, then a cable 120 miles long, and then 20 more miles of land wire. 1908 Westm. Gaz. 24 Feb. 4/1 The..cable from Ascension touches land in Cornwall.., whence a land-wire passed the signals on to Greenwich. 1930 Aberdeen Press & Jrnl. 23 Jan. 7/6 A microphone was installed at 10 Downing Street, and the Premier's words were carried by land wire to Chelmsford. 1782 Pownall Antiq. 140 The..state..of the *land-worker. 1827 G. Higgins Celtic Druids 192 When the borders of Europe began to be settled and cultivated by the land-workers. 1794–1811 Ld. Ellenborough in Espinasse Rep. III. 259 He would expect a clear *landworthiness in the carriage itself to be established. 1928 Daily Express 26 May 9/3 There was shown at Olympia last year a '*land-yacht' that was palatial in its appointments. 1967 Times 23 Jan. 9 A school that has its own land yacht, wind tunnel, go-kart

and canoeing clubs. **1828** N. CARLISLE *Acc. Charities* 295 Two staves or 18 feet, in..Cornwall, are a *Land Yard, and 160 Land Yards are an English acre. **1869** BLACKMORE *Lorna D.* xii, I could smell supper, when hungry, through a hundred landyards of bog.

‖**Land** (lant), *sb.*² Pl. Länder ('lɛndər), Laender, Lands. [G.] A semi-autonomous unit of local government in Germany and Austria.

[**1920** G. YOUNG *New Germany* 321 The transformation of this Constitution from a centralised republic..back to a federation has been reviewed already. The word 'lander' is literally translated for this and other reasons.] **1920** H. W. V. TEMPERLEY *Hist. Peace Conf. Paris* III. 347 The word *Länder*..has been deliberately used instead of the word *Staaten*... The word *States* for the members of a federal Constitution seems therefore to be misleading as expressly repudiated and 'Lands' is used, a new word coined by Professor Young. *Ibid.* 348 Article 5. Constitutional power is exercised..in matters pertaining to the Lands, by the Constitutional bodies of those Lands within the lines laid down by the constitutions of those Lands. **1950** THEIMER & CAMPBELL *Encycl. World Politics* 42 Austria became a federal republic, consisting of eight *Lands.* **1955** *Times* 26 Aug. 7/2 Many wage agreements are settled on a Land and not a federal basis. **1958** *Listener* 9 Oct. 571/1 In the Laender under its sway..it [*sc.* Austria] produced the nearest approach to the Welfare State that existed before its establishment in the United Kingdom. **1966** *Economist* 13 Aug. 633/1 The ambitious and consequently hard-pressed *Länder* are demanding that..Bonn's share of the tax-collectors' booty should be no more than 35 per cent. **1969** *Nature* 15 Nov. 633/2 The German universities are at present the responsibility of the Länder. **1973** *Times* 30 Jan. 4/6 The four *Länder*—Hamburg, Bremen, Lower Saxony and Schleswig-Holstein—have asked the Bonn Government to sanction a boycott.

land (lænd), *v.* [f. LAND *sb.*¹ (OE. had *lęndan* of similar formation: see LEND *v.*)]

I. Transitive senses.

1. a. To bring to land; to set on shore; to disembark.

a **1300** *K. Horn* 779 A gode schup he hurede, þat him scholde londe In Westene londe. **1508** KENNEDIE *Flyting w. Dunbar* 461 The skippar bad ger land the at the Bas. **1665** BOYLE *Occas. Refl.* IV. xii. (1848) 246, I see the Water-man prepare to Land us. **1678** WANLEY *Wond. Lit. World* v. ii. §79. 472/1 He Landed an Army in Apulia. **1748** *Anson's Voy.* II. xiv. 286 Our ships, when we should land our men, would keep at..a distance. **1838** THIRLWALL *Greece* III. xx. 149 The troops, having been landed in Cephallenia. **1842** CAMPBELL *Napoleon & Brit. Sailor* 64 He should be shipped to England Old And safely landed. **1894** HALL CAINE *Manxman* v. iii. 288 Four hundred boats were coming..to land their cargoes.

b. To bring to the surface (from a mine). ? *Obs.*

1603 OWEN *Pembrokeshire* xi. (1891) 91 These persons will Lande about..hundred barells of coale in a daye.

c. *pass.* In Canada, to be given the status of a landed immigrant (see LANDED *ppl. a.* 3).

1910 [see LANDED *ppl. a.* 3]. **1962** *Canada Month* Aug. 16/3 They arrived from an Italian refugee camp in three groups around mid-month, were duly 'landed' by immigration officials. **1974** *Globe & Mail* (Toronto) 16 May 3/3 So far 22,905 have actually been 'landed'—given legal status as landed immigrants—and it's just a matter of time before most of the others achieve the same goal.

2. To bring into a specified place, e.g. as a stage in or termination of a journey; to bring into a certain position: usually with advb. phr. Also *fig.* to bring into a certain position or to a particular point in a course or process. (Cf. 8.)

1649 JER. TAYLOR *Gt. Exemp.* Ep. Ded. a 3 b, It is onely a holy life that lands us there [*sc.* in heaven]. **1649** BLITHE *Eng. Improv. Impr.* (1653) 57 This drain to be continued to that place where you have most conveniencie to land your water. **1850** MCCOSH *Div. Govt.* II. ii. (1874) 212 The pantheist, when compelled to explain himself, is landed in Atheism. **1856** WHYTE MELVILLE *Kate Cov.* xix, Now then, give us your hand; one foot on the box, one on the roller-bolt, and now you're landed. **1859** THACKERAY *Virgin.* II. i. 4 Poor Harry's fine folks have been too fine for him, and have ended by landing him here. **1874** BURNAND *My time* xxviii. 271 A jerk that nearly landed me on his [the horse's] back. **1878** BOSW. SMITH *Carthage* 200 The pass over the Cottian Alps ..would have landed Hannibal in the territory of the Taurini. **1882** BESANT *Revolt of Man* vi. (1883) 126 Such a sermon..would infallibly land its composer..in a prison. **1892** *Bookman* Oct. 29/2 His wife, his temperament, his philanthropy contrive to land him in fraudulent bankruptcy.

b. To set down from a vehicle. (Cf. 8 b.)

1851 THACKERAY *Eng. Hum.* iii. (1853) 108 The Exeter Fly..having..landed its passengers for supper and sleep. **1859** —— *Virgin.* I. xxvii. 213 One chair after another landed ladies at the Baroness's door. **1894** MRS. H. WARD *Marcella* II. 267 His hansom landed him at the door of a great mansion.

c. *slang.* To set (a person) 'on his feet'.

1868 YATES *Rock Ahead* II. vi, Lord Ticehurst, having done his duty in landing Gilbert [viz. by giving him an introduction], had strolled away. **1876** HINDLEY *Adv. Cheap Jack* 33, I bought a big covered cart and a good strong horse. And I was landed! **1879** '*Autobiog. of a Thief*' in *Macm. Mag.* XL. 502, I was landed (was all right) this time without them getting me up a lead (a collection).

d. *Naut.* To lower on to the deck or elsewhere by a rope or tackle.

1867 SMYTH *Sailor's Work-bk., To land on deck.* A nautical anomaly, meaning to lower casks or weighty goods on deck from the tackles. **1882** NARES *Seamanship* (ed. 6) 61 Land them on the taffrail.

e. *slang.* To get (a blow) home. Also *intr.* with *out.*

1886 H. BAUMANN *Londinismen* 93/1 He landed him a little one on his left ogle. **1888** RUNCIMAN *Chequers* 93 Their object is to land one cunning blow. **1891** *Gentl. Mag.* Aug. 110 That's right, Captain Kitty!..Land him [*sc.* the Devil] one in the eye. **1898** J. D. BRAYSHAW *Slum Silhouettes* 2 That on'y made Bill madder 'n ever, an' 'e lands aht wiv 'is right, but the Gent. jest ketched 'is arm. **1912** *Chambers's Jrnl.* June 395/2 After sparring for five minutes, and frustrating every attempt you made to 'land' on him, he would sit down. **1928** *Manch. Guardian Weekly* 5 Oct. 274/3 Why didn't his man 'land out' at the insulting blighter?

f. *Sporting colloq.* (with and without compl.) To bring (a horse) 'home', i.e. to the winning post; to place first in a race. Also *intr.* to get in first, win.

1853 WHYTE MELVILLE *Digby Grand* I. vi. 151 St. Agatha ..after one of the finest races on record, is landed a winner by a neck. **1890** 'ROLF BOLDREWOOD' *Col. Reformer* (1891) 291 A shower of flukes at the latter end landed him the winner. **1891** *Licensed Victualler's Gaz.* 20 Mar. (Farmer), Had the French filly landed, what a shout would have arisen from the ring! **1898** *Daily News* 28 May 8/3 The Prince's colours were landed amid enthusiastic cheering.

g. *Machine knitting.* To secure (a loop) on the closed beard of a needle.

1885 [see KNOCK *v.* 15 c]. **1926** J. CHAMBERLAIN *Knitting Math. & Mech.* v. 98 Using different lengths of beards in the same machine may result in certain loops not being landed, and consequently not cast off. **1952** D. F. PALING *Warp Knitting Technol.* i. 6 The old fabric loops on their upward movement pass over the tips of the beards which are embedded in the needle eyes, and the old loops are landed on to the closed beards.

h. To bring (an aircraft) to earth from the air; to place (an aircraft or spacecraft, or its contents) on the ground or some other surface after a flight.

1916 H. BARBER *Aeroplane Speaks* 49 I'll guarantee to safely land the fastest machine in a five-acre field. **1926** *Encycl. Brit.* I. 65/2 Attempts were later made to land machines on this forward deck [of the aircraft carrier]. **1931** *Times* 19 Feb. 17/2 There was a difference of opinion as to who should land the flying boat?—Very definitely. **1932** W. E. JOHNS *Camels are Coming* ii. 35 Agents..are usually taken over by aircraft; sometimes they drop by parachute and sometimes we land them. **1948** GREGORY & ALLAN *Helicopter* xvi. 190 There are a lot of things that we have to do to this machine before you can take off and land it. **1952** K. W. GATLAND *Devel. Guided Missile* vi. 103 (*caption*) Instead of landing the entire space-ship, a secondary rocket will descend to the surface. **1962** *Times* 30 Apr. 12/7 Russia's latest earth satellite has been successfully landed in a predetermined area. **1967** J. ROWLAND *Jet Man* vi. 59 Now Whittle's experience of aerobatics came in useful, for he had to 'land' the machine in the water. **1968** *Ann. Reg. 1967* 178 The two accidents were a severe setback to American plans to land a man on the moon before 1970. **1972** *Nature* 3 Mar. 3/1 It is simply too dangerous to attempt to land a manned spacecraft in the lunar mountains.

3. *Angling.* To bring (a fish) to land, esp. by means of a gaff, hook, or net. Also, ***to land the net.***

1613 J. DENNYS *Secrets Angling* II. xxi, Then with a net, see how at last he lands A mighty carp. **1653** WALTON *Compl. Angler* iv. 105 Help me to land this as you did the other. **1787** [see LANDING-NET]. **1867** F. FRANCIS *Angling* viii. (1880) 297 When you have hooked a grayling your next job is to land him. **1873** *Act 36 & 37 Vict.* c. lxxi. §14 Any person who shall..work any seine or draft net for salmon.. within one hundred yards from..any other seine or draft net ..before such last-mentioned net is fully drawn in and landed, shall..be liable [etc.]. **1883** *Manch. Exam.* 30 Oct. 8/4, I will not trouble you with an account of the trout and grayling we landed during the first two or three days of our visit. **1884** PAE *Eustace* 62 They were pretty constantly engaged in shooting and landing the net.

b. *fig.* To catch or 'get hold of' (a person); to secure or win (a sum of money, esp. in betting or horse-racing). Also, to obtain (employment). Also *absol.*

1854 WHYTE MELVILLE *Gen. Bounce* II. xx. 114, I landed a hundred gold mohrs by backing his new lot for the Governor-General's Cup. **1857** HUGHES *Tom Brown* II. vii, You must be gentle with me if you want to land me. **1876** OUIDA *Winter City* vi. 143 So that they land their bets, what do they care? **1884** BLACK in *Harper's Mag.* Dec. 24/1, I can't say I've landed a fortune over its tips. **1926** WHITEMAN & MCBRIDE *Jazz* viii. 167 That is another reason why the outsider fails to land. He doesn't know about these rogues. **1946** E. O'NEILL *Iceman Cometh* (1947) III. 152 I'll bet you tink yuh're goin' out and land a job, too. **1952** GRANVILLE *Dict. Theatr. Terms* 108 *Land a spot*, obtain an engagement.

†**4.** To throw (a bridge) across a river. *Obs.*

1637 *Petit. to Chas. I* in Willis & Clark *Cambridge* (1886) I. 91 They may be suffered at their owne chardge to land a bridge over yᵉ river. **1638** CHAS. I. *Let. to King's College, ibid.*, To permitt them at their owne charge to land a bridge from the middest of yᵗ oʳ Colledge.

†**5.** To bestow land upon. *Obs. nonce-use.*

1624 HEYWOOD *Captives* I. i. in Bullen *O. Pl.* IV, Thou hast monied me in this, Nay landed me..And putt mee in a large possession.

6. a. *to land up*: to fill or block up (a watercourse, pond, etc.) partially or wholly with earth; to silt up.

1605 WILLET *Hexapla Gen.* 30 Gobaris caused the naturall current, landed vp, to be opened and enlarged. **1682** BUNYAN *Holy War* 307 Diabolus sought to land up Mouthgate with dirt. **1793** R. MYLNE *Rep. Thames & Isis* 16 These lands have a very imperfect drainage at present, by the water-courses and ditches being landed up. **1815** W. MARRATT *Hist. Lincolnsh.* III. 243 A serpentine fish pond.. partly landed up. **1851** *Jrnl. R. Agric. Soc.* XII. II. 300 The river became landed up by the sediment of the tides.

b. To earth up (celery). Also with *up.*

a **1806** ABERCROMBIE in Loudon *Gardening* III. i. (1822) 723 Repeat this..till by degrees they are landed up from twelve inches to two feet. **1856** [see LANDING *vbl. sb.* 2].

II. Intransitive senses.

7. To come to land; to go ashore from a ship or boat; to disembark. Of a ship, etc.: To touch at a place in order to set down passengers.

In early use occas. conjugated with the verb *to be.*

1382 WYCLIF *1 Macc.* iii. 42 The oost appliede, or londide, at the coostis of hem. **1387** TREVISA *Higden* (Rolls) II. 151 Irisch Scottes londede at Argoyl. *c* **1400** *Sir Beues* p. 24 (MS. S.) With her ship þere gon þey lond. *a* **1450** *Le Morte Arth.* 3054 He wende to haue landyd..At Dower. **1470–85** MALORY *Arthur* I. xvii, The Sarasyns ar londed in their countreyes mo than xl M. *a* **1548** HALL *Chron., Hen. VIII* 259 b, He had knowledge..that the Frenche army entended to land in the Isle of Wight. **1611** BIBLE *Acts* xxi. 3 We.. sailed into Syria, and landed at Tyre. **1661** DRYDEN *To his Sacred Majesty* 9 Thus, royal Sir, to see you landed here Was cause enough of triumph for a year. **1725** POPE *Odyss.* XIII. 156 Behold him landed, careless and asleep, From all th' eluded dangers of the deep! **1748** *Anson's Voy.* II. xiii. 276 No place where it was possible for a boat to land. **1837** MARRYAT *Dog-fiend* xxii, The dog..landed at the same stairs where the boats land. **1882** MRS. B. M. CROKER *Proper Pride* I. ii. 11 Among the passengers who landed at Southampton from the Peninsular and Oriental *Rosetta.*

8. *lit.* and *fig.* To arrive at a place, a stage in a journey, or the like; to come to a stage in a progression; to end *in* something. Also with *up.* (Cf. 2.)

1679 MOXON *Mech. Exerc.* 153 Landing by the first pair of Stairs with your Face towards the East. **1721** RAMSAY *Elegy Patie Birnie* iii, When strangers landed. **1726** *Wodrow Corr.* (1843) III. 243 Thus this matter is entered on; where it will land, the Lord himself direct. **1727** *Ibid.* 304 If any subordination and dependence [of the Persons of the Trinity]..were asserted, he could not but think it would land in a dependent and independent God. **1927** H. CRANE *Let.* 19 Mar. (1965) 291, I had just landed in town after three months with the bossy cows. **1958** *Listener* 30 Oct. 694/3 They [*sc.* migrants] land up, exhausted, on islands and headlands. **1965** *Ibid.* 2 Sept. 351/2 After unspecified work in a map shop he landed up, furnished with a testimonial from Charles Graves, in the publishing house of Novello.

b. To alight upon the ground, *e.g.* from a vehicle, after a leap, etc. Esp. of an aircraft or spacecraft, or a person in one: to alight upon or reach the ground, or some other surface, after a flight. (Cf. 2 b.)

1693 SOUTHERNE *Maid's Last Prayer* III. ii, *Lady Susan.* There's a Coach stopt, I hope 'tis hers. *Jano.* 'Tis my Lady Trickit's; she's just Landed. **1708** *Lond. Gaz.* No. 4427/14 To receive them as they Landed out of their Coaches. **1784** V. LUNARDI *Acct. First Aërial Voy. in Eng.* 37 My principal care was to avoid a violent concussion at landing, and in this my good fortune was my friend. At twenty minutes past four I descended in a spacious meadow. **1814** *Sporting Mag.* XLIII. 287 The spot where the horse took off to where he landed is above eighteen feet. **1837** MARRYAT *Dog-fiend* xxxvii, It landed among some cabbage-leaves. **1899** H. G. WELLS *When Sleeper Wakes* xxiv. 326 On Blackheath no aëroplane had landed. **1908** —— *War in Air* ii. 60 The balloon was bumping as though its occupants were trying to land. **1911** W. KAEMPFFERT *New Art of Flying* xiv. 238 Ely's remarkable feat in landing on the deck of a warship in the harbour of San Francisco. **1917** [see FLATTEN *v.* 2 b]. **1917** 'CONTACT' *Airman's Outings* ii. 45 The machine in question was probably hit, however, for it did not return, and I saw it begin a glide as though the pilot meant to land. **1930** *Times* 11 Nov. 16/4 She [*sc.* a flying boat] circled the station and then landed in comparatively calm water. **1952** *Oxf. Jun. Encycl.* X. 7/2 When landing, the pilot is guided on to the deck by the Deck Control Officer who signals with 'bats'. **1953** LESLIE & ADAMSKI (*title*) Flying saucers have landed. **1969** *Times* 21 July 1/1 The first word from man on the moon came from Aldrin: 'Tranquillity base. The Eagle has landed.' **1973** *Sci. Amer.* Dec. 102/1 If the birds are pursued, they take off, but they do not fly far before they land again.

†**c.** *fig.* To fall, light (*upon*). *Obs.*

a **1670** HACKET *2nd Serm. on Incarnat.* (1675) 11 Each parcel of comfort landed jump..in the same model of Ground. **1727** *Wodrow Corr.* (1843) III. 304 We inquired into the reports, found them all land on Mr. Simson.

d. With *on.* Of an aircraft: to land on the deck of an aircraft carrier. Hence **landing-on** *vbl. sb.*

1937 *Aeroplane* 9 June 691/1 The ship was headed into wind and permission to land-on was given to the first Nimrod. *Ibid.* 16 June 724/1 The landing-on is organised similarly to the flying-off. **1939** *Nature* CXLIII. 592/2 'Landing on' had proved safer than driving a car on an English road. **1954** P. K. KEMP *Fleet Air Arm* 95 They took off and landed on without difficulty, completely independent of the sea.

land, obs. f. LANT *sb.*¹, urine; var. LAUND *Obs.*

Landabrides, erron. f. LINDABRIDES *Obs.*

†'**landage.** *Obs.* In 5 londage. [f. LAND *v.* + -AGE.] Landing, coming ashore.

1470–85 MALORY *Arthur* XXI. ii, There was syr Mordred redy awaytynge vpon his londage to lette his owne fader to lande vp the lande that he was kyng ouer.

‖**landamman(n** ('landaman). [Swiss Ger.; f. *land* LAND *sb.*¹ + *amman(n* = G. *amtmann*, f. *amt* office, magistracy + *mann* man.] In Switzerland, the title applied to the chief magistrate in certain cantons, and formerly also to the chief officer in certain smaller administrative districts.

1796 MORSE *Amer. Geog.* II. 308 The village of Gersaw.. has its land amman, its council of regency. **1822** L. SIMOND *Switzerland* I. 438 All the landammanns and statthalters. **1868** KIRK *Chas. Bold* III. v. iii. 435 The old landamman of Schwytz, Ulrich Kätzy, gave wiser counsel.

landar, obs. variant of LAUNDER.

landart, Sc. form of LANDWARD.

landau ('lændɔː). Also 8 **landeau**, **lando**. [f. *Landau*, the name of a town in Germany, where the vehicle was first made. The Ger. name is *landauer*, short for *landauer wagen*.] A four-wheeled carriage, the top of which, being made in two parts, may be closed or thrown open, When open, the rear part is folded back, and the front part entirely removed. Also ***landau carriage***.

1743 in J. Strang *Glasgow* (1856) 17 The coach or lando to contain six passengers. **1748** *St. James's Even. Post* No. 5982 Three Landaus with six Horses each..waited his coming. **1753** SHENSTONE *Wks. & Lett.* III. 218 There were near 200 people gathered round Lady Luxborough's landeau at Birmingham. **1786** WESLEY *Wks.* (1872) XI. 322 The Pope was in an open landau. **1794** W. FELTON *Carriages* (1801) I. 22 The body of a landau carriage differs nothing in shape from a Coach. The landau is the Coach form, the landaulet the Chariot form. **1879** *Cassell's Techn. Educ.* IV. 306/1 The landau..combines more than the advantages of three distinct vehicles—a close carriage, a barouche or half-headed carriage, and one entirely open.

landaulet (,lændɔː'lɛt). Also **-ette**. [f. prec. + -LET.] **a.** A small landau; a coupé with a folding top like a landau. Also called ***demi-landau***.

1771 *Patent Specif.* No. 997 The fore part of the head of a landawlet is constructed with a hinge [etc.]. **1794** [see LANDAU]. **1799** *Gentl. Mag.* I. 449 A vehicle with a bow-window, that is not a coach, or landau, or chariot, or landaulet, or sociable. *c* **1815** JANE AUSTEN *Persuas.* (1833) II. xii. 438 The mistress of a very pretty landaulette. **1880** TENNYSON *Sisters* 84 An open landaulet Whirled by.

b. In form ***landaulette***. A type of motor car with a leather hood above the rear seats. Also *attrib.*

1901 *Autocar* 17 Aug. 153 (*heading*) The Peugeot landaulette. *Ibid.*, Mr. C. Friswell's Peugeot landaulette... The vehicle may be stated to be of the standard Peugeot type, but with only such alterations made as are necessary for the accommodation of the landau body. **1905** *Daily Chron.* 17 Nov. 8/4 Now the 'landaulette' is the popular car of the moment. **1906** *Ibid.* 15 Sept. 6/2 The cabs would be of the landaulette type. **1922** A. HADDON *Green Room Gossip* viii. 172 The other evening I rolled up to the Palladium in a big landaulette that carries seven persons. The chauffeur and I had it to ourselves. **1968** G. N. GEORGANO *Complete Encycl. Motorcars* 175 (*caption*) 1912 *Dennis* 24 hp landaulette. **1973** *Country Life* 18 Oct. 1190/3 It was not until 1909 that..I hired a cumbersome Astor landaulette from the Oxford garage. **1974** *Daily Tel.* 19 Oct. 17/2 Rolls-Royce's most expensive current car is the open landaulette, made in very limited numbers for heads of State at a cost of about £36,000.

'land-,bank. A banking institution which issues notes on the security of landed property.

1696 (*title*) Remarks on the proceedings of the Commissioners for putting in Execution the Act past last Session for establishing a Land-Bank. **1711** SHAFTESB. *Charac.* (1737) III. 45 In Egypt, the generation or tribe, being once set apart as sacred, wou'd..be able..to establish themselves a plentiful and growing fund, or religious land-bank. **1790** BURKE *Fr. Rev.* Wks. V. 416 To establish a current circulating credit upon any Land-bank..has hitherto proved difficult. **1900** *Pilot* 19 May 351/1 A gentleman energetic in promoting the spread of landbanks (perhaps the best of several good things which Mr. Plunkett has introduced in Ireland).

'land-boc (-bəʊk). *Hist.* [OE. *landbóc*, f. *land* LAND *sb.*[1] + *bóc* BOOK *sb.*] A charter or deed by which land is granted.

961 in Earle *Land Charters* (1888) 199 þis is þæra feower hyda land boc æt wiþiȝlea þe eadgar cing hæfð ȝebocod cenulfe on ece yrfe. *a* **1000** *Voc.* in Wr.-Wülcker 225/2 *Donatio*, landbec. *a* **1207** GERVASE (of Canterbury) *Gesta Regum* Wks. (Rolls) II. 59 Has scedulas tunc temporis 'land-bokes', id est libros terrarum, Angli vocabant. **1676** COLES, *Landboc*, a Deed whereby lands are holden. **1839** KEIGHTLEY *Hist. Eng.* I. 78 Landbocs or grants and charters were there [*i.e.* in the Hundred mote] read out and published.

'land-breeze. A breeze blowing from the land seawards.

1667 H. STUBBE in *Phil. Trans.* II. 499 There is little of Land-brise, because the Mountain is remote from thence. **1698** FRYER *Acc. E. India & P.* 55 The Land-Breezes brought a poysonous Smell on board Ship. **1783** COWPER *Loss R. George* 9 A land-breeze shook the shrouds, And she was overset. **1846** GROTE *Greece* II. xlix. (1862) IV. 316 The strong land-breeze out of the Gulf of Corinth.

†**land-brist.** *Sc. Obs.* Also **byrst**, **birst**. [Cf. ON. *brest-r* outburst, crash.] Surf.

1375 BARBOUR *Bruce* IV. 444 Bot the vynde wes thame agayn, That it gert sa the land-brist [*v.r.* byrst] ryss, That thai mycht weld the se na viss. **1513** DOUGLAS *Æneis* VII. Prol. 21 Landbrist rumland rudely. *Ibid.* x. vi. 11 Na land brist [*ed.* 1553 birst] lyppering on the wallis.

'land-,carriage. [See LAND *sb.*[1] 11.] Carriage, conveyance, or transport by land; also, the cost of such carriage.

1613 PURCHAS *Pilgrimage* (1864) 63 Spices are deere in Persia by reason of the long land-carriage from Masulapatan this way. **1726** LEONI *Alberti's Archit.* I. 4/2 The easy bringing in..of Necessaries, both by Land Carriage and Water Carriage. **1825** J. NICHOLSON *Operat. Mechanic* 526 The expense of quarrying, land-carriage to the place where it is to be used [etc.]. *c* **1850** *Arab. Nts.* (Rtldg.) 120, I..sent it by land-carriage to the nearest seaport.

'land-cheap. *Obs.* exc. *Hist.* [OE. *landcéap*, f. *land* LAND *sb.*[1] + *céap* CHEAP *sb.* Cf. ON. *landkaup*.] A customary fine paid to the lord upon the alienation of land.

c **848** in Birch *Cartul. Sax.* (1887) II. 35 Ego Berchtwulf cyning sile Forðrede minum ðeȝne niȝen hiȝida lond..he salde to lond ceape xxx mancessan & niȝen hund scillinga wið ðæm londe. **1670** BLOUNT *Law Dict.*, *Land cheap*, a certain ancient customary Fine, paid either in Mony or Cattel, at every alienation of land lying within some Mannor, or within the liberty of some Borough.

landchet, variant of LANDSHARD.

'land-crab. [See LAND *sb.*[1] 11.] Any of the various species of crabs that live mostly on land but resort to the sea for breeding.

1638 T. VERNEY *To Sir E. Verney* in *Verney Papers* (1853) 195 Thees land-crabs are innumerable,..they are very like our sea-crabs, but nothing att all soe good, becaus most of them are poysonous. **1779** FORREST *Voy. N. Guinea* 74 Some Papua people brought me land crabs, shaped like lobsters. **1871** MATEER *Travancore* 92 Landcrabs burrow in the rice fields, and are used as food by the slave castes.

transf. **1665** HOOKE *Microgr.* 178 The little Mite-worm, which I call a Land-crab.

†**land-damn**, *v. Obs. rare*[−1]. *trans.* ? To make a hell on earth for (a person).

The sense is uncertain; the text may be corrupt. The alleged survival of the word in dialects, with the sense 'to abuse with rancour' (E.D.D.), appears to be imperfectly authenticated.

1611 SHAKS. *Wint. T.* II. i. 143 You are abus'd, and by some putter on, That will be damn'd for't; would I knew the Villaine, I would Land-damne him.

‖**landdrost** ('lænddrəʊst). Also *erron.* landro(o)st. [S. African Du.; f. *land* LAND *sb.*[1] + *drost* (see DROSSARD).] A kind of magistrate in South Africa. (Under British administration, the office was abolished.)

1731 MEDLEY *Kolben's Cape G. Hope* II. 10 He gave this Land-Drost the powers of a Fiscal..to seize and prosecute all criminals, vagabonds, and disorderly persons. **1801**, etc. [see HEEMRAD]. **1888** *Times* (weekly ed.) 25 May 7/3 President Kruger appointed as landroost an Austrian gentleman. **1895** C. S. HORNE *Story of the L.M.S.* 64 The local magistrate, or landdrost. **1947** L. HASTINGS *Dragons are Extra* ii. 35 Any old leader or *landrost* of the Free State or Transvaal had just Botha's sort of serenity. **1952** E. H. BURROWS *Overberg Outspan* i. 16 Outwardly the old Dutch form persisted until 1827 when the *Collegies* were abolished, and the *landdrosts* replaced by Resident Magistrates and Civil Commissioners.

‖**lande** (lɑ̃d). [Fr. See LAUND, LAWN.] A tract of wild land, a moor. Used by Eng. writers chiefly with reference to S. W. France.

1792 A. YOUNG *Trav. France* 43 These *landes* are sandy tracts covered with pine trees. **1883** OUIDA *Wanda* II. 19 Out on the *landes* some cows were driven through the heather and broom.

lande, landeau, obs. ff. LAUND, LANDAU.

landed ('lændɪd), *a.* [f. LAND *sb.*[1] + -ED[2].

The OE. *ȝelandod* (= MHG. *gelandet*), which occurs once in the sense 1 below, is of different formation, the pple. of a vb. **landian* (cf. *gódian* to endow with goods). It is possible that the mod. word may partly represent this.]

1. Possessed of land; having an estate in land.

Formerly often qualified by advs.; as ***most, well, best landed***; also in parasynthetic comb., as ***great-landed***. The collocation ***landed man*** was not uncommonly written with a hyphen and occas. as a single word.

c **1000** *Laws of Æthelstan* § 11 in Schmid *Gesetze* 26 Ælc minra þeȝna þe ȝelandod sy. *c* **1440** *Promp. Parv.* 312/1 Londyd, or indwyd wythe lond, *terradotatus*. *c* **1470** HENRY *Wallace* IX. 1810 Na landyt man chapyt with him bot ane. **1500–20** DUNBAR *Poems* xxii. 76 How suld I leif that is not landit? **1579** J. STUBBES *Gaping Gulf* D iij, Noble men and other great landed ones. **1595** SHAKS. *John* I. i. 177 A landlesse Knight, makes thee a landed Squire. **1605** CAMDEN *Rem.* (1637) 212 Descended from an Ancestor well landed in Kent. **1647** N. BACON *Disc. Govt. Eng.* I. xxii. (1739) 40 In such case a Country-Gentleman should be fined one hundred and twenty shillings if he were landed. *a* **1661** FULLER *Worthies* (1840) II. 454 Sir Oliver Hingham was born, richly landed, and buried in Hingham. **1691** LOCKE *Consid. Lower. Interest* (1692) 16 The Landed man who thinks perhaps by the fall of Interest to raise the Value of his Land. **1714** SWIFT *Pres. State Affairs* Wks. 1755 II. I. 202 The majority of landed-men. **1778** BOSWELL *Johnson* (1831) IV. 104 That a landed gentleman is not under any obligation to reside upon his estate. **1849–50** ALISON *Hist. Europe* XIV. xcv. §96. 190 The gradual extinction of the old landed aristocracy.

b. *transf.* (*humorous*). Characteristic of, or giving the impression of, a landed man.

1826 SYD. SMITH *Wks.* (1859) II. 88/2 A large man, with a large head, and very landed manner.

2. ***landed interest***: interest or concern in land as a possession; the class having such interest.

1711 ADDISON *Spect.* No. 126 ¶8 The first of them inclined to the landed and the other to the monied Interest. **1719** W. WOOD *Surv. Trade* 76, I have shewn, how much it concerns the Landed and Trading Interests to be Friends to each other. **1842** BISCHOFF *Woollen Manuf.* II. 265 It became evident that the landed interest were mistaken in the views they entertained. *a* **1859** MACAULAY *Hist. Eng.* xxiv. (1861) V. 126 The old landed interest, the old Cavalier interest, had now no share in the favours of the Crown. **1880** DISRAELI *Endym.* I. i. 7 There are other interests old landed besides the landed interest now.

3. Consisting of land; consisting in the possession of land; (of revenue) derived from land.

1711 ADDISON *Spect.* No. 69 ¶7 It has multiplied the Number of the Rich, made our Landed Estates infinitely more Valuable than they were formerly. **1796** LD. SHEFFIELD in *Ld. Auckland's Corr.* III. 357 Not because they had..talents.., but because they have landed property. **1800** STUART in Owen *Wellesley's Desp.* 575 The landed revenues of Guzerat are also very considerable. **1809–10** COLERIDGE *Friend* (1865) 126 Those tribes..which possess individual landed property. **1862** TROLLOPE *Orley F.* i, A landed estate in Yorkshire of considerable extent and value. **1896** *Law Times* CII. 124/2 Could the coroner himself be removed for want of the landed qualification?

landed ('lændɪd), *ppl. a.* [f. LAND *v.* + -ED[1].] **1.** That has landed or gone ashore: in comb. as ***new-***, ***newly landed***.

1835 *Court Mag.* VI. 235/2 The new-landed throng Find no lodging at hand. **1890** 'ROLF BOLDREWOOD' *Miner's Right* (1899) 76/1 For a newly-landed official, I don't recollect seeing your equal.

2. Caught, stuck, encumbered *with*.

In some of the examples a use of the pa. pple. of *land* v. rather than a ppl. adj.

1866 W. GREGOR *Dial. Banffshire* 100 A'm fairly lantit wee the aul' coo. **1900** G. B. SHAW *Press Cuttings* 34 Sometimes ..they get an idea of their own; and then of course youre landed. **1910** A. BENNETT *Clayhanger* IV. vi. 508 The right sort of women don't get landed as the wives of convicts. **1943** J. B. PRIESTLEY *Daylight on Saturday* xxii. 171 One thing leads to another..an' then, before you know where you are, you're landed. **1947** 'G. ORWELL' *Let.* 23 Oct. in *Coll. Ess.* (1968) IV. 382 I've been landed with another long article which I can't dodge out of. **1960** 'N. SHUTE' *Trustee from Toolroom* i. 7 You'll be landed with a cat for the rest of your lives. **1974** K. ROYCE *Trap Spider* i. 27, I told you that I'd speak to your son and I'm landed with it.

3. ***landed immigrant***: an immigrant to Canada, admitted for permanent residence; so ***landed*** (***immigrant***) ***status***.

1910 *Statutes of Canada* c. 27, s. 2 (p), 'Land', 'landed' or 'landing', as applied to passengers or immigrants, means their lawful admission into Canada by an officer under this Act, otherwise than for inspection or treatment or other temporary purpose provided for by this Act. **1963** *Maclean's Mag.* 20 Apr. 18/3 The only black people freely admitted to Canada as landed immigrants are a limited number of women. **1964** *Calgary Herald* 4 May 25/3 If he is to see his child, he will have to..be accepted as a landed immigrant. **1968** *Globe & Mail* (Toronto) 2 May 2/4 Brooks..was granted landed immigrant status but Stonehill was refused. *Ibid.*, Stonehill's bid to obtain landed status had strong political repercussions in Ottawa. **1973** *Ibid.* 27 Dec. 2/2 Most Canadians don't realize it but any visitor or landed immigrant with less than five years residence can be deported, together with his entire family, for any criminal code offence, including impaired driving or shoplifting. **1975** *Canadian Mag.* (Toronto) 8 Mar. 6/4 [Some] East Indians who have obtained citizenship or landed immigrant status have been involved in illegal immigration rackets.

land-end. Now *dial.* A piece of ground at the end of a 'land' in a ploughed field. (See also quots. 1877, 1893.)

1555 *Stanford Churchw. Acc.*, *Antiquary* XVII. 119/2 For Reping doune ye corne yt growyde at mens landds endds y[e] wich was sooyd to farre upon the comon viij[d]. **1610** *Quarter Sess. Rec.* in *N.R. Record Soc.* I. 202 (N.W. Linc. Gloss.) Tho. Skelton..tooke vj[d] a daie..and a land end of grass besides, of Geo. Osborne of the same. **1624** *Rental* in *Sheffield Gloss.*, Rich. Shirtclyffe had 8 land ends at will vijs. **1870** in E. Peacock *Ralf Skirl.* III. xv. 240 An' the eller tree blossoms like snaw was besprent On the land ends 'at ligs by the side o' the Trent. **1877** *N.W. Linc. Gloss.*, *Land-ends*, (1) small portions of cultivated land between the Trent bank and the road, at the ends of the lands in the open fields, more commonly called groves. **1893** *Northumbld. Gloss.*, *Landin*, *Land-end*, the end of a ridge or of a furrow in ploughing, or of a drill in drilling..where it meets the heedrig. **1899** DICKINSON & PREVOST *Cumberld. Gloss.*, *Heedlin'*... *Land end*, head rig or head-land, or those butts in a ploughed field which lie at right angles to the general direction of the others.

Landenian (læn'dɛnɪən), *a. Geol.* [a. F. *Landenien* (A. Dumont 1839, in *Bull. de l'Acad. R. des Sci.*, etc., *de Bruxelles* VI. II. 466), f. *Landen*, name of a town near Liège in Belgium: see -IAN.] Of, pertaining to, or designating a stratigraphic stage at the top of the Palæocene series (or the bottom of the Eocene), lying above the Montian. Also *absol.*

1852 *Q. Jrnl. Geol. Soc.* VIII. 254 In his visit to this country..he [sc. Dumont] pointed out to me the many characters common to these Thanet sands and his 'Landenian System', which occupies the same position in the Belgian series. **1902** A. J. JUKES-BROWNE *Student's Handbk. Stratigr. Geol.* xvi. 485 In Belgium the Montian limestone..is overlain by glauconitic sands which are known as the Lower Landenian and unquestionably correspond to our Thanet Beds. **1923** L. D. STAMP *Introd. Stratigr.* xvi. 274 Upper or Continental Landenian strata succeed [the lower or Marine Landenian] conformably, and are known as the Woolwich and Reading Beds. **1955** G. G. WOODFORD tr. *M. Gignoux's Stratigraphic Geol.* ix. 485 The English Tertiary begins with the transgressive Landenian. **1969** BENNISON & WRIGHT *Geol. Hist. Brit. Isles* xv. 336 Sedimentation commenced with the inundation by the sea of the eastern part of the London Basin in Landenian times, depositing the Thanet Beds. *Ibid.*, The marine facies may not have persisted throughout the Landenian even in the east of the London Basin.

lander ('lændə(r)). [f. LAND *v.* + -ER[1].]

1. a. One who lands or goes ashore.

1859 TENNYSON *Enid* 330 The sweet voice of a bird, Heard by the lander in a lonely isle. **1890** C. MARTYN *W. Phillips* 16 The famous landers on Plymouth Rock.

b. A spacecraft, or a part of one, which is designed to land on the surface of a planet or of the moon.

1961 *Astronautica Acta* VII. 130 The rotary drill..is designed to penetrate 1·5 ft or more into the lunar surface and bring samples into the lander for chemical analysis. **1962** F. I. ORDWAY et al. *Basic Astronautics* v. 176 Hard landers contain retrorockets to reduce the terminal velocity to between 100 and 300 m.p.h... Soft landers..are built to descend gently onto the surface. **1967** *Technology Week* 23 Jan. 61/1 (Advt.), This calls for a varied series of probes, orbiters and hard and soft landers. **1971** *Listener* 7 Oct. 476/3 Each vehicle consists of two main parts: an orbiter and a lander.

2. *Mining.* The man who 'lands' the kibble at the mouth of the shaft.

1847 in HALLIWELL. **1865** J. T. F. TURNER *Slate Quarries* 8 Wagons..are filled by a party of men..called 'fillers', while a similar number of 'landers' and 'emptiers', at the surface, receive and dispose of their freight.

lander, -erer, variants of LAUNDER, -ERER.

landert, Sc. form of LANDWARD.

landesite (ˈlændiːzaɪt). *Min.* [f. the name of K. K. *Landes* (b. 1899), American geologist + -ITE[1].] A brown hydrated phosphate of manganese and ferric iron, occurring as an alteration product of reddingite at Berry Quarry, Poland, Maine, U.S.A.

1930 BERMAN & GONYER in *Amer. Mineralogist* XV. 385 This mineral seems to represent a new species for which the name landesite is here proposed in honor of Professor Kenneth K. Landes who has done much work on the pegmatites of Maine. **1964** *Ibid.* XLIX. 1123 The landesite formula is better expressed in the following manner... $[Mn^{2+}{}_{1-x}(Fe^{3+}OH)_x]_3\ [(3-3x)H_2O]\ (PO_4)_2$ in which, for type landesite, *x* is approximately 0·25.

landfall (ˈlændfɔːl).

1. a. *Naut.* An approach to or sighting of land, esp. for the first time on a sea-voyage. ***to make a good*** (or ***bad***) ***landfall***: to meet with land in accordance with (or contrary to) one's reckoning.

1627 CAPT. SMITH *Seaman's Gram.* ix. 43 A good Land fall is when we fall iust with our reckoning, if otherwise a bad Land fall. **1670** NARBOROUGH in *Acc. Sev. Late Voy.* I. (1711) 79 The best Land-fall in my Opinion, is to make the face of Cape Desseada for to come out of the South Sea to go into the Streight of Magellan. **1706** [E. WARD] *Wooden World* (1708) 89 If his Reckoning in a long Voyage, jump with his Land-fall, he's as exalted [etc.]. **1850** SCORESBY *Cheever's Whalem. Adv.* xviii. (1859) 281 It is not until a captain has made three or four good landfalls..just according to his calculations that the living by faith in..the results upon his slate begin[s] to come easy. **1891** WINSOR *Columbus* ix. 214 Las Casas reports the journal of Columbus unabridged for a period after the landfall.

b. *concr.* The first land 'made' on a sea-voyage.

1883 T. W. HIGGINSON in *Harper's Mag.* Jan. 218/2 His 'Prima Vista', or point first seen—what sailors call landfall —was..Cape Breton. **1884** SIR T. BRASSEY in *19th Cent.* May 833 The Bahamas will be for ever memorable as the landfall of Columbus.

c. Arrival at land after a flight over the sea; also, = LANDING *vbl. sb.* 1 d.

1908 H. G. WELLS *War in Air* vi. 194 New York had risen out of the blue indistinctness of the landfall. **1909** —— *Tono-Bungay* IV. i. 449, I remember our prolonged dragging landfall. **1928** C. F. S. GAMBLE *Story N. Sea Air Station* ix. 121 The airship L.3..made her 'landfall' off Ingham. **1942** *R.A.F. Jrnl.* 3 Oct. 31 You get a feeling of warming pride as a good landfall is made. Once round the beacon and down you come. **1954** 'J. CHRISTOPHER' *22nd Cent.* 86 They check you each landfall. Hans got his final warning at Luna City. **1959** *Listener* 22 Jan. 160/1 The average drift-migrants [*sc.* birds] that make a landfall are not necessarily lost.

d. The place where an undersea pipeline reaches land.

1974 *People's Jrnl.* (Inverness & Northern Counties ed.) 7 Sept. 2/6 Burmah and British Petroleum..have..approached Zetland County Council about the possibility of a pipeline landfall in Shetland. **1975** *Petroleum Rev.* XXIX. 387/2 It took twelve months..to select Flotta..as the landfall for the oil pipeline from the Piper field.

2. 'A sudden translation of property in land by the death of a rich man' (J.).

1876 *Whitby Gloss.* s.v., 'They've got a bonny land-fall', a large amount of property bequeathed.

3. A landslip. (Ogilvie, 1882.)

†**landfall**, *v. Naut. Obs. rare*[−0]. [f. prec.] *intr.* To make a 'landfall'.

1727 BOYER *Eng.-Fr. Dict.*, To land fall (a Sea-term), *atterrer*.

ˈ**land-flood.** Overflowing of land by water from a swollen river or other inland water.

1390 GOWER *Conf.* III. 126 Februar, which..with londflodes in his rage At fordes letteth the passage. **1523** FITZHERB. *Husb.* §54 Grasse, that the lande-floudde renneth ouer, is verye ylle for shepe, bycause of the sande and fylthe that stycketh vppon it. **1646** FULLER *Wounded Consc.* (1841) 303 Like a land-flood, quickly come, quickly gone. **1720** DE FOE *Capt. Singleton* ix. (1840) 166 The rivers were..swelled with the landfloods. **1833** LYELL *Princ. Geol.* III. 181 The land-floods which accompany earthquakes.

attrib. **1852** WIGGINS *Embanking* 69 Any..rush of tidal or land-flood waters against the bank.

b. *fig.*

1579 FENTON *Guicciard.* VII. (1599) 296 The furie of Almaines entring Italie as a landflood. *a* **1628** PRESTON *New Covt.* (1630) 83 It is but a Pond, it is but a land-floud, the spring of comfort belongs only to the Saints. **1830** SCOTT *Demonol.* viii. 242 Some of the country clergy were carried away by the landflood of superstition.

landfolk (ˈlændfəʊk). ? *Obs.* Also 9 **landsfolk.** [OE. *landfolc*, f. *land* LAND *sb.*[1] + *folc* FOLK. Cf. MHG. *lantvolc*, G. *landvolk.*] The people of a land or country.

c **1000** ÆLFRIC *Saints' Lives* (E.E.T.S.) II. 324 þa..com þæt land-folc to þe þær to lafe wæs þa. *c* **1205** LAY. 30930 þat lond-folc wes bliðe for heore leod-kinge. *a* **1250** *Owl & Night.* 1156 That lond-folc wurth i-dorve. *a* **1300** *Cursor M.* 9752, I sal..saue þi land folk al fra wa. *c* **1425** *Eng. Conq. Irel.* xxxvii. 90 (Dubl. MS.) þe lond-folke, that crysten shold be. **1865** KINGSLEY *Herew.* I. xvii. 304 Tosti..went off to the Isle of Wight and forced the landsfolk to give him money.

ˈ**land-force.** A force serving on land; a military as opposed to a naval force. Also *pl.* the troops or soldiers composing such a force.

1614 RALEIGH *Hist. World* III. (1634) 73 The Navie of Athens..over-threw the fleet of Xerxes, whose Land-forces were soone after discomfited by them. **1790** BEATSON *Nav. & Mil. Mem.* II. 191 Having on board..near 3,000 land-forces. **1849** GROTE *Greece* II. xxxviii. V. 38 He surveyed..his masses of land-force covering the shore.

ˈ**land form.** Also land-form, landform. [LAND *sb.* 10 a.] **1. a.** A physical feature of the earth's surface such as a hill, plain, cirque, or alluvial fan.

1893 Land form [see GEOMORPHOLOGY]. **1910** *Encycl. Brit.* XI. 633/2 Thus new land forms are created—valleys of curious complexity, for example—by the 'capture' and diversion of the water of one river by another. **1938** L. D. STAMP *Physical Geogr. & Geol.* ix. 142 The land forms in deserts developed in sedimentary rocks are similar to those in damper temperate climates except that slopes are usually sharper and steeper. **1970** R. J. SMALL *Study of Landforms* i. 8 Classification can be attempted not only of individual kinds of landform (such as slopes, cliffs, terraces, beaches, lakes, volcanoes, planation surfaces and so on) or types of process.., but of landform assemblages.

†**b.** A landscape of any particular kind. *Obs.*

1893 W. M. DAVIS in *Nat. Geogr. Mag.* 10 July 73 Every land-form passes through a systematic series of changes from its youth, when its form is defined chiefly by constructional processes, past its maturity, when the processes of sub-aerial sculpture have carved a variety of mouldings and channellings, to its old age in which..denudation reduces the mass to base-level. **1899** —— in *Geogr. Jrnl.* XIV. 485 Where the forces of uplift or deformation have lately..initiated a cycle of changes, the destructive forces can have accomplished but little work, and the land-form is 'young'.

2. A kind (of living organism) found on land.

1897 WILLIS *Flower. Pl.* I. 169 All the Water-plants that are here dealt with are undoubtedly descended from land forms. **1926** J. S. HUXLEY *Ess. Pop. Sci.* 93 There are three or four other species of animals, such as Proteus,..which..are not known in a land-form at all.

†**land-gate.** *Obs.* [See GATE *sb.*[1]]

1. *Sc.* Way or passage over land; also used *advb.* = by land. Also †**landgates** *adv.*, ? landward, away from the sea.

1536 BELLENDEN *Cron. Scot.* (1821) I. 143 He began to..come landgait ouir the riveir of Levin. **1637** RUTHERFORD *Lett.* (1862) I. 456 If ye..w[d] have only summer weather and a land-gate not a sea-way, to heaven. **1765** ROSS *Helenore* (1789) 95 Land-gates unto the hills she took the gate.

2. (See quot.)

1726 KERSEY, *Landgate*, a long and narrow Piece of Land.

land-gavel (ˈlændˌgævəl). *Hist.* Forms: 1 **landgafol**, 3 **lond-gavel, lon-ȝavel**, 4 **lond-gov(e)l**, 5 **langable**, 7 **languable**, 7, 9 **land-gable**, 9 **-gavel.** [OE. *landgafol*, f. *land* LAND *sb.*[1] + *gafol* GAVEL *sb.*[1]] Land-tribute, land-tax; rent for land, ground-rent. Also *attrib.*

c **1000** *Rect. Sing. Pers.* c. 2 in Schmid *Gesetze* 372 He sceal land-gafol syllan. *c* **1205** LAY. 7465 Fehten he wold wið Cezar þe axede lon-ȝauel her. *Ibid.* 7789 Ȝeond al he sette reuwen..þo fengen þa lond-gauel. **1308** *Cal. Close Rolls* (1892) 59 [There are delivered to him 2*s.* 11*d.* of rent called] Londgovl [to be received in New Bukenham from the following tenants]. **1478** R. RICART *Mayor of Bristol's Cal.* (Camden) 9 This Toune of Bristowe is holde of oure souueraigne Lorde the Kinge in frank burgage and with-out meane by reason of his langable of the same. *c* **1640** J. SMYTH *Lives Berkeleys* (1883) I. 338 Out of his landgable rents of Bristoll, he gave yearly 3[li.] 6[s.] 8[d.] to a preist. **1670** in BLOUNT *Law Dict.* **1676** *Wood's Life*, etc. (Oxf. Hist. Soc.) II. 340 The townsmen would have the college pay for it as a languable. **1882** BRAMSTON & LEROY *Historic Winchester* 69 The King's lands in Winton rendering Land-gable and Burgage. **1897** MAITLAND *Domesday & Beyond* 182, 310 tenements paying landgavel to the king's farmers.

ˈ**land-ˌgrabber.** One who grabs or seizes upon land (landed property or territory), esp. in an unfair or underhand manner; *spec.* in reference to Irish agrarian agitation, a man who takes a farm from which a tenant has been evicted.

1872 GOLDW. SMITH in *Fortn. Rev.* Mar. 254 The great Elizabethan mansions..are the graceful monuments of the Tudor land-grabbers. **1880** *Times* 24 Nov. 6/1 The holding had been taken by a land-grabber. **1883** *Nonconf. & Indep.* 28 Dec. 1176/2 Filibustering operations of 'land-grabbers' in New Guinea.

So ˈ**land-ˌgrabbing** *vbl. sb.*, the action or practice of a land-grabber; ˈ**land-ˌgrabbing** *ppl. a.*

1880 *Daily Tel.* 27 Oct., To protest against land grabbing. **1884** MARY HICKSON *Ireland in 17th C.* I. Introd. 6 That selfish, land grabbing spirit. **1887** *Spectator* 3 Sept. 1169 'Land-grabbing' as it is called,—i.e., the taking of land from which another has been evicted.

landgravate (ˈlændgrəvət). [f. next + -ATE[1].] = LANDGRAVIATE.

1761 *Brit. Mag.* II. 162 By accounts from Turingia, we learn that his Prussian Majesty..has already entered that landgravate. **1802** *Brookes' Gazetteer* (ed. 12), *Leuchtenberg*, a town of Bavaria, in a landgravate of the same name. **1865** *Cornh. Mag.* Aug. 221 Hesse-Homburg..is a Landgravate ..and its capital is Homburg.

landgrave (ˈlændgreɪv). Also 6 **langrave**, 6–7 **lantgrave**, 7 **landtgrave.** *β.* 6 **lan(t)z-, landisgrave**, 7 **lants-, landsgrave.** [a. MHG. *lantgrâve* (G. *landgraf*) = MLG. *landgrave* (Du. *landgraaf*): see LAND *sb.*[1] and GRAVE *sb.*[4]] In Germany, a count having jurisdiction over a territory, and having under him several inferior counts; later, the title of certain German princes.

1516 *Fabyan's Chron.* (1811) II. VII. 328 After the deth of hir husbonde, Langraue, duke of Thorynge in Almayne. **1560** DAUS tr. *Sleidane's Comm.* 57 b, Then was he led to Duke George of Saxonie, and to the Lantzgrave. **1616** J. WHELER in *Buccleuch MSS.* (Hist. MSS. Comm.) I. 179 A daughter of the Lantsgrave of Hessen. **1656** BLOUNT *Glossogr.*, *Landgrave*, or *Landsgrave*. **1673** RAY *Journ. Low C.* 78 The Lantgrave of Darmstadt. **1756** NUGENT *Gr. Tour* II. 421 Hanau had formerly counts of its own, but the last of them dying in 1736 without issue, it devolved to the landgrave of Hesse Cassel. **1839** *Penny Cycl.* XI. 192/1 The Temporal princes were:—the archduke of Austria..the landgraves of Hessen-Cassel and Hessen-Darmstadt..the landgrave of Leuchtenburg [etc.].

†**b.** In the colony of Carolina (see quots.). *Obs.*

1702 *S. Carolina Stat.* (1836) I. 42 The upper house, consisting of the Landgraves and Casiques..are..a middle state between Lords and Commons. **1707** J. ARCHDALE *Carolina* 13 They are there by Patent, under the Great Seal of the Provinces, call'd Landgraves and Cassocks, in lieu of Earls and Lords.

Hence ˈ**landgraveship** = LANDGRAVIATE. ˈ**landgravess** = LANDGRAVINE.

1669 LOCKE *Dft. Constit. Carolina* xii. in *33rd D. K. R.* 259 Upon y[e] devolution of any landgraveship or cassiqueship. **1716** M. DAVIES *Athen. Brit.* III. *Crit. Hist.* 107 At Jena in the Landgraveship of Thuring. **1762** tr. *Busching's Syst. Geog.* IV. 429 Caroline Christina, who had been espoused Landgravess of Hesse-Philipsthal. *Ibid.* V. 504 Christina Magdalena, Landgravess-dowager to Hesse-Homburg. **1809** SOUTHEY *Q. Rev.* II. 329 The Landgraveship with which Locke had been requited for his legislative labours.

landgraviate (lændˈgreɪvɪət). [ad. med.L. *landgrāviāt-us*, f. LANDGRAVE (med.L. *-grāvio*): see -ATE[1]. Cf. F. *landgraviat.*] The office, jurisdiction, or province of a landgrave.

1656 in BLOUNT *Glossogr.* **1709** *Lond. Gaz.* No. 4542/1 His Imperial Majesty..has been pleased..to grant him the Landgraviate of Leuchtenberg, an immediate Fee of the Empire. **1836** *Penny Cycl.* V. 290 Charles managed to acquire the landgraviate of Alsace.

landgravine (ˈlændgrəviːn). Also 7 **-inne.** [ad. G. *landgräfin*, Du. *landgravin.*] The wife of a landgrave; a female ruler of a landgraviate.

1682 *Lond. Gaz.* No. 1744/2 The Landgravinne of Hesse. **1779** J. MOORE *View Soc. Fr.* II. liii. 33 The Landgravine plays at Quadrille, and chooses her own party every night. **1882–3** SCHAFF *Encycl. Relig. Knowl.* II. 1261 The widowed landgravine Elizabeth.

ˈ**landˌholder.** A holder, proprietor, or occupier of land; in mod. use sometimes (opposed to *land-owner*), a tenant holding land from a proprietor.

1414 *Rolls Parlt.* IV. 58 They have cleymed..the Kynges trew lieges, that ben his fre tenentz annexed to his Coroune, as for her bonde bore men, and her bonde lond holderes. **1662** DUGDALE *Imbanking* 51 The Land-holders in the said Marsh. **1691** LOCKE *Consid. Lower. Interest* (1692) 88 Here is one fourth part of his yearly Income goes immediately out of the Landlords and Landholders Pocket. **1741** TAILFER (*title*) A..Narrative of the Colony of Georgia in America.. By Pat. Tailfer, M.D...and others, Land-holders in Georgia. **1800** *Asiat. Ann. Reg.*, *Chron.* 28/1 The great body of the land-holders appear fully impressed with a sense of the superior comforts they enjoy. **1874** GREEN *Short Hist.* i. §1. 3 In the very earliest glimpse we get of the German race we see them a race of land-holders and land-tillers. **1880** M[c]CARTHY in *19th Cent.* Aug. 310 A combination of all the great interests concerned, the landowner as well as the landholder; the peer as well as the peasant.

So ˈ**landˌholding** *a.*

1876 DIGBY *Real. Prop.* I. i. §1. 8 The assembly of landholding inhabitants considered as tenants of a lord.

†**landier.** *Sc. Obs.* Also **laundier.** [a. F. *landier*: see ANDIRON, LANDIRON.] An andiron.

1457 *Extracts Burgh Recs. Peebles* (1872) 119 A spet and lantter, a peudar chader, a dis [etc.]. **1612** *Sc. Bk. Rates* in *Halyburton's Ledger* (1867) 292 Brassin wark sic as landiers, chandlers, baissones [etc.]. *Ibid.* 317 Laundiers, of latten.. of irne.

landimere (ˈlændɪmɪə(r)). *Obs.* exc. *Sc.* Also 9 **landimar, lanimer.** [OE. *landȝemǽre*, f. *land* LAND *sb.*[1] + *ȝe-mǽre* boundary, MERE.] Boundary of land. **Landimere's** or **Lanimer**

day, the day on which the annual perambulation of the boundaries is made in Lanarkshire and Aberdeen.

944 in Earle *Land Charters* (1888) 178 Ðis sint þa land ȝemæra & se embegang þara landa to baddan byriȝ & to doddan forda & to eter dune. **1825–80** JAMIESON, *Landimar*, ..2. A march or boundary of landed property, Aberd. *To ride the Landimeres*, to examine the marches, ibid., Lanarks. .. The day in which the procession is made is called Landimere's day. **1864** *Edin. Daily Rev.* 11 June, Lanimer Day at Lanark. **1888** *Scott. Leader* 16 May 5 Lanark Landimeres.

¶ 'A land-measurer... This word is here [*viz.* in Skene] used improperly' (Jam.).

1597 SKENE *De Verb. Sign.* s.v. *Particata*, The measurers of land, called Landimers, in Latine, *Agrimensores*. **1670** BLOUNT *Law Dict.*, *Landimers*, measurers of Land, anciently so called. **1825–80** JAMIESON, *Lannimor*, a person employed by conterminous proprietors to adjust marches between their lands, Ayrsh.

landing ('lændɪŋ), *vbl. sb.* [f. LAND *v.* + -ING[1].]

I. The action of the verb LAND.

1. a. The action of coming to land or putting ashore; disembarkation.

c **1440** *Promp. Parv.* 312/1 Londynge fro schyppe and watur, *applicacio*. **1577–87** HOLINSHED *Chron.* I. 9/2 They take landing within the dominion of king Goffarus. **1655** *Nicholas Papers* (Camden) II. 308 Att his landing att Towre wharfe. **1697** DAMPIER *Voy.* I. 264 There is Water enough for Boats and Canoes to enter, and smooth landing after you are in. **1748** *Anson's Voy.* III. vii. 355 The Commodore.. was saluted at his landing by eleven guns. **1798** DK. CLARENCE in Nicolas *Disp.* (1845) III. 10 *note*, The French cannot effect a landing in Ireland. **1855** STANLEY *Mem. Canterb.* i. (1857) 3 There are five great landings in English history, each of vast importance.

b. Arrival at a stage or place of landing, e.g. on a staircase.

1705 ADDISON *Trav. Italy* 433 A Stair-Case..where..the Disposition of the Lights, and the convenient Landing are admirably well contriv'd.

c. Coming to ground at the end of a leap.

1881 *Times* 14 Feb. 4/2 The taking off at the jumps was awkward, and the landing more ugly still.

d. The (or an) action of approaching and alighting on the ground or some other surface after a flight. ***happy landings!***: see HAPPY *a.* 3.

1784 [see LAND *v.* 8 b]. **1909** *Flight* 13 Feb. 93/1 (*heading*) Flight 'landings'. **1912** *Aeroplane* 19 Dec. 621/2 Major Cameron and Capt. Salmon with Mr. Barnwell and, later, Mr. Knight up behind, put in large number [*sic*] of straights each making very good flights and landings. **1916** H. BARBER *Aeroplane Speaks* 49 You can..imagine what a difference that would make where forced landings are concerned! **1923** H. G. WELLS *Men like Gods* I. iii. 37 The aeroplanes made an easy landing. **1927** G. ASTON *Navy of To-Day* v. 31 The airman, and the airman's home, the aircraft carrier, must steam head to wind..when the airmen want to accomplish 'landings' on her deck. **1936** *Discovery* Aug. 238/1 The camera is raised during take-offs and landings. **1956** [see EMERGENCY 5 b]. **1967** D. P. DAVIES *Handling Big Jets* iii. 30 For take-off and landing the weight should be known to within 5,000 lb. **1969** *Times* 21 July 1/1 The landing, in the Sea of Tranquillity, was near perfect and the two astronauts on board Eagle reported that it had not tilted too far to prevent take-off. **1974** *Daily Tel.* 21 Feb. 17/7 He [*sc.* a balloonist] has food and water for 10 days and the gondola is equipped with floatation devices to keep it upright if he is forced to make a water landing.

2. a. ***landing up***: blocking up of a watercourse by earth or mud. **b.** Earthing up of plants.

1692 RAY *Dissol. World* III. v. (1732) 352 This Landing up and Atterration of the Skirts of the Sea. *a* **1806** ABERCROMBIE in Loudon *Gardening* III. i. (1822) 723 Give them [celery-plants] a final landing-up near the tops. **1856** LEVER *Martins of Cro' M.* 4 Celery, that wanted landing.

3. *Angling.* (See LAND *v.* 3.)

1884 *Public Opinion* 5 Sept. 302/1 His attention is fixed upon..the skilful 'landing' of his fish.

4. *Mining.* (See quot. 1860 and LAND *v.* 1 b.)

1860 *Eng. & For. Mining Gloss., S. Staffs. Terms*, *Landing*, the banksman receiving the loaded skip at surface.

II. Concrete senses.

5. a. A place for disembarking passengers or unlading goods; a landing-place.

1609 DANIEL *Civ. Wars* VII. xxxvi, Defend all landings, barre all passages. **1793** SMEATON *Edystone L.* §100 Amending the landing at the Edystone. *Ibid.*, As my proposed materials would not swim, a safe landing became a still more important object. **1832** S. CUMINGS *Western Pilot* 49 There is a pretty good landing at the upper end of the town. **1867** J. N. EDWARDS *Shelby* xx. 366 The next day the brigade moved to the river near Gaines Landing. **1895** M. A. JACKSON *Mem. Stonewall Jackson* (ed. 2) xii. 211 Just before reaching the landing I stopped to look back.

b. 'The platform of a railway station' (Simmonds *Dict. Trade* 1858). ? *Obs.*

6. a. A platform in which a flight of stairs terminates; a resting-place between two flights of stairs.

1789 P. SMYTH tr. *Aldrich's Archit.* (1818) 122 A resting-place, or landing, should be contrived after 9, 11, or at the utmost 13 steps. **1836–9** DICKENS *Sk. Boz* ii, He took to pieces the eight day clock on the front Landing. **1869** E. A. PARKES *Pract. Hygiene* (ed. 3) 308 The ablution rooms.. must be placed on the landings. **1882** *Macm. Mag.* XLVI. 441 The five bedrooms all opened on a square landing.

b. Stone used in or suitable for the construction of staircase landings.

1847 SMEATON *Builder's Man.* 190, 6-in. rubbed York landing. **1858** *Skyring's Builders' Prices* (ed. 48) 84, 3 inch Portland balcony bottoms, or landings. **1886** *Mod. Newspaper Advt.*, All kinds of flags, steps, landings, ..&c.

7. Various technical senses (chiefly *U.S.*). **a.** (See quot. 1844.) **b.** *Lumbering.* A place where logs are landed and stored. **c.** 'A platform of a furnace at the charging height' (Knight *Dict. Mech.* 1875). **d.** *Boat-building.* = LAND *sb.*[1] 9 c (q.v.). **e.** *Mining.* A place at the mouth of a shaft for the landing of kibbles or other receptacles (*Cent. Dict.*). **f.** *Fortif.* 'The horizontal space at the entrance of a gallery or return' (*Ibid.*).

1844 GOSSE in *Zoologist* II. 706 Every extensive planter, whose estate borders on the river [Alabama], has what is called a landing; that is a large building to contain bales of cotton. **1868** *Harper's Mag.* XXXVI. 420 We emerged from the thick timber into an opening through which ran Tibbett's Brook. Here was what is called the landing..we could see thousands of logs that had been hauled. **1883** GRESLEY *Gloss. Coal Mining*, *Landing*, a level stage for loading or unloading coals upon.

8. *attrib.* and *Comb.*, as (sense 1) ***landing area, fee, field, ground, -leg, -pier, -quay, site, -stairs, -steps, -tower, vehicle***; (sense 3) ***landing-gaff, -hook, -ring***; **landing beam** *Aeronaut.*, a radio beam to guide aircraft when landing; **landing card**, a card issued to a passenger on an international flight or voyage, which is surrendered on arrival; **landing charges, rates** (Ogilvie), 'charges or fees paid on goods unloaded from a vessel' (Webster, 1864); **landing craft**, a naval vessel with a shallow draught designed for landing troops, tanks, etc., in an amphibious assault; hence *transf.* in *Astronaut.*, the section of a spacecraft which is used for the final descent to the surface of a planet or moon; **landing flap** *Aeronaut.*, a flap that can be lowered to increase the lift and the drag and so make possible lower speeds for take-off and landing; **landing floor** = sense 6; **landing gear**, (*a*) *Aeronaut.*, the structure underneath an aircraft that is designed to support it on the ground and to absorb the shock of landing (in modern aircraft made to be retracted in flight); (*b*) the retractable support at the front of a semi-trailer that supports it when not attached to the tractor; **landing light**, (*a*) a light on the runway of an aerodrome to guide an aircraft in a night landing; (*b*) a light attached to an aircraft to illuminate the ground for a night landing; **landing pad**, (*a*) a small area of an aerodrome or heliport, used for the landing and taking off of helicopters; (*b*) a cushioned or strengthened foot which supports a hovercraft, spacecraft, or the like when stationary on the ground; **landing ship (tank(s))**, a large landing craft for the transport of tanks and other vehicles; **landing speed**, the speed at which an aircraft lands (see also quot. 1911); **landing-stage**, a platform, often a floating one, for the landing of passengers and goods from sea-vessels; **landing-strake** *Boat-building*, 'the upper strake but one' (Weale's *Rudim. Nav.* 128); **landing strip** = *air-strip* (AIR *sb.*[1] B. III. 7); **landing-surveyor**, a customs officer who appoints and superintends the landing waiters; **landing ticket** = *landing card*; **landing-waiter**, a customs officer whose duty is to superintend the landing of goods and to examine them; **landing wire**, *Aeronaut.*, a wire on a biplane or light monoplane that is designed to take the weight of a wing when the aircraft is on the ground. Also LANDING-NET, -PLACE.

1910 R. FERRIS *How it Flies* xx. 464 **Landing area*, a piece of land specially prepared for the alighting of aeroplanes without risk of injury. **1951** *Gloss. Aeronaut. Terms* (*B.S.I.*) III. 23 *Landing area*, the part of the movement area primarily intended for the take-off and landing of aircraft. **1974** G. MITCHELL *Javelin for Jonah* ix. 115 You may go ahead with the new landing-areas for jump and pole. **1929** *Landing beam [see BEAM *sb.*[1] 24 b]. **1933** *Flight* 1 June 524 A pointer on a simple instrument showed him any deviation from the landing beam. **1945** *Aeronautics* Feb. 30 (*heading*) Diagram showing the aircraft..entering the landing beam. **1932** G. GREENE *Stamboul Train* I. i. 3 The purser took the last *landing card..and watched the passengers cross the grey wet quay. **1950** P. BOTTOME *Under Skin* ii. 18 Got your landing card ready, and your passport? **1966** 'W. HAGGARD' *Power House* vi. 58 He could be asked for a landing card and as a through-booking he didn't have one. **1973** *Times* 13 Dec. 11/2 He included landing cards among the paraphernalia of controls. **1940** W. S. CHURCHILL *Second World War* (1949) II. 593 Great efforts should be made to produce the *landing-craft as soon as possible. **1942** *R.A.F. Jrnl.* 18 Apr. 32 Two landing craft were sent ashore with reconnaissance parties. **1943** Landing craft [see ASSAULT *sb.* 8]. **1953** *Jrnl. Brit. Interplanetary Soc.* XII. 275 The landing craft (a small supplementary vehicle designed for vertical descent with rocket braking, carried to the destinaton by the parent spaceship). **1957** P. WORSLEY *Trumpet shall Sound* vii. 144 Landing-craft of all kinds poured out their cargo upon the beaches. **1966** D. HOLBROOK *Flesh Wounds* 93 Three thousand landing craft were ready to move out of all the ports all along the coast, from Falmouth to Harwich. **1969** *Times* 21 July 8/2 At 1,500 ft., the astronauts slowed the landing craft and brought it gently down four miles off the scheduled target in the Sea of Tranquillity. **1922** *Flight* XIV. 660/1 No extra *landing fee will be charged in respect of test flights before departure. **1972** *Times* 11 Feb. 1/1 Strong opposition has come from the airlines to a new system of landing fees which is to be introduced at Heathrow. **1921** *Aeronautics* 13 Jan. 26/1 The improvement of *landing fields and equipment. **1959** *Chambers's Encycl.* I. 97 The emergency landing fields, which were set aside by the Royal Air Force for special purposes, were usually grass covered. **1936** *Technical Rep. Aeronaut. Res. Comm. 1934–35* I. 30 Now that so many aeroplanes are being fitted with *landing flaps it is important to permit the flap to extend along the whole span. **1940** *War Illustr.* 19 Jan. 620 With wheels and landing flaps lowered, the pilot makes his approach. **1966** *McGraw-Hill Encycl. Sci. & Technol.* XIV. 517/1 Structurally, the aileron is similar to the landing flap. **1856** CAPERN *Poems* (ed. 2) 143 A cautious footfall stealing Gently o'er the *landing-floor. **1911** *Rep. & Mem. Advisory Comm. Aeronaut.* No. 59. Nov. 103 The efficiency of *landing gear on various sorts of ground may be tried. **1931** *Flight* 9 Jan. 30/1 The landing gear is designed to give very smooth landing and taxying characteristics. **1931** J. E. YOUNGER *Airplane Construction & Repair* iii. 48 Some airplanes are designed with landing gears which fold up into the fuselage and hence offer no direct wind resistance. **1951** *Amer. Speech* XXVI. 308/2 *Landing gear*, a strong support that holds up the front end of a semi-trailer when it is not attached to a tractor. **1971** M. TAK *Truck Talk* 97 *Landing gear*, the retractable supports on a trailer that prop up the front end when the trailer is unhitched from the tractor. **1971** *Physics Bull.* Apr. 217/1 Steels with improved fracture properties needed in nuclear submarines and aircraft landing gear are also under development. **1912** *Aeroplane* 12 Dec. 584/1 The great deterrent at present is the lack of proper *landing grounds. **1920** Landing ground [see *flying school* (FLYING *vbl. sb.* 3)]. **1943** T. S. ELIOT in Ld. Sempill et al. *Friendship, Progress, Civilisation* 20 To descend from this flight into generalities on to the particular landing-ground of the present occasion. **1961** L. VAN DER POST *Heart of Hunter* I. v. 80 The great pan..had a floor so wide, level and firm that..the biggest aircraft could land on it. I myself had used it as a landing-ground many times. **1741** *Compl. Fam.-Piece* II. ii. 330 A young Angler should be furnished.. with..*Landing-Hook,..Shot and Floats of divers Sorts. **1951** *Jrnl. Brit. Interplanetary Soc.* X. 101 In the case of a Moonflight..this means a vertical descent using reverse rocket braking in conjunction with a radar-altimeter and *landing-legs. **1969** *Sun* 22 July 1/2 The Eagle, leaving its spidery landing-legs behind, soared away. **1917** *Flight* 4 Jan. 18/1 A new system, called 'Triplex glass *landing lights', proved to be inferior to petrol flares. **1920** *Proc. Air Conf., London* 11 Aerodromes will be equipped..as night flying is practicable. Permanent electric landing lights..are being installed. **1922** *Flight* XIV. 519/2 Lighting Set (including navigation lights, landing lights and illumination of instruments). **1937** *Times* 16 Apr. 9/3 They see no reason why they should confuse coloured Véry lights or landing lights in the air. **1942** *R.A.F. Jrnl.* 3 Oct. 7 From beneath him a landing light groped downwards. **1969** I. KEMP *Brit. G.I. in Vietnam* iii. 69 He..switched on his landing light, illuminating three paratroopers standing on the landing zone signalling us in. **1973** *Times* 11 Apr. 3/7 They used landing lights to make three trips and everyone on board was winched to safety. **1958** *World Helicopter* Apr. 6/1 Our cover picture shows one of Sabena's fleet of 12-passenger Sikorsky S.58's making a landing at the heliport on the strip between the two 80 ft. diameter *landing pads. **1961** *New Scientist* 2 Mar. 528/3 The actual landing pad need still be no more than 150 ft square. **1967** *Gloss. Terms Air-Cushion Vehicles* (*B.S.I.*) 6 *Landing pads*, strong points, protruding below the rigid bottom of an ACV, which support the vehicle when at rest on land. **1969** *Islander* (Victoria, B.C.) 23 Mar. 10/1 The first landing pad for the young [helicopter] company was a patch of open land way down Shelbourne Street, at that time the outskirts of Victoria. **1969** *Times* 17 May 8/5 Its landing pads are 37 in. across, each of them fitted with a probe which can sense the surface. **1858** SIMMONDS *Dict. Trade*, **Landing-pier*, *Landing-stage*. **1861** M. PATTISON *Ess.* (1889) I. 45 Broad *landing quays covered with cranes lined the river bank. **1883** *Fisheries Exhib. Catal.* 51 *Landing Rings, Gaffs, Nets, &c. **1943** *Life* 11 Oct. 34/2 The first is the LST (*Landing Ship, Tank), 327 ft. long and displacing 5,500 tons. **1944** *Hutchinson's Pict. Hist. War* 27 Oct. 1943–11 Apr. 1944. 166 (*caption*) Landing Ship Tanks. These two landing ships tanks close inshore at Bougainville are unloading supplies and equipment for the U.S. Marines and army troops. **1944** *Daily Tel.* 11 July, It [*sc.* the port of Cherbourg] will be open shortly for craft of the L.S.T. type (landing ship tanks). **1945** T. BLORE *Turning Point—1943* vi. 51 Cedric and I put off in a motor fishing vessel to find our Tank Landing Ship. **1951** W. S. CHURCHILL *Second World War* (1952) V. ii. 26 The 'landing-ship, tank'..had first been conceived and developed in Britain in 1940. **1961** B. FERGUSSON *Watery Maze* iv. 106 Rear-Admiral Burrough, with the cruiser *Kenya* and four destroyers, was to escort the two landing ships. **1966** D. HOLBROOK *Flesh Wounds* 93 Paul's Squadron embarked on its Landing Ship Tank late on the 3rd June. **1969** *Times* 4 Feb. 13/4 The eastern end of the planned Apollo *landing site. **1972** *Nature* 3 Mar. 3/1 The landing site of Luna 20 was some 120 km north of the region from which Luna 16 recovered specimens. **1911** R. M. PIERCE *Dict. Aviation* 144 **Landing-speed*.., the speed with which a landing or descent to the earth is made, as by a man falling from a height. **1937** *New Republic* 19 May 35/1 The modern air liner's landing speed has gone up as designers have boosted its top speed by refining line and form. **1961** P. W. BROOKS *Mod. Airliner* iii. 75 Wheel brakes..now became a necessity because of the increased take-off and landing speeds of the more heavily loaded monoplanes. **1858** *Landing-stage [see *landing-pier* above]. **1861** DICKENS *Gt. Expect.* liv, An old landing-stage. **1868** *Less. Mid. Age* 269 On Monday morning, in a thick white fog, I entered a little steamer at the landing-stage at Liverpool. **1838** DICKENS *O. Twist* viii, The steps..form a *landing-stairs from the river. **1887** *Spectator* 21 May 692/1 Jack is going to sea, and his friends are on the landing-stairs to take leave of him. **1838** THIRLWALL *Greece* III. xxii. 239 He..advanced foremost on the *landing-steps. **1864** MRS. LLOYD *Ladies Polc.* 28 A little natural pier, in which landing-steps had been cut. **1930** *Aircraft Engineering* Jan. 16/1 The standard intermediate field in low altitudes provides two *landing strips or runways. **1944** *Times* 1 July 4/3 Squadrons flying from landing strips in Normandy are taking advantage of every break in the clouds. **1956** W. GRAHAM *Sleeping Partner* 62

Llanveryan had been an aerodrome—a glorified landing strip—in the first place. **1973** G. GREENE *Honorary Consul* IV. iii. 218 Señor Escobar has a landing strip on his *estancia*. **1812** J. SMYTH *Pract. of Customs* (1821) 144 Sail-cloth and Sails are required to be stamped in the presence of a *Landing-Surveyor and Landing-waiter, on the common quay. **1925** E. GELLIBRAND *Travelling Do's & Don'ts* v. 19 While the cool, collected person gets things done without unnecessary waste of energy, the flustered one.. not having his *landing ticket ready.. is hustled by the impatient ones. **1930** A. BENNETT *Imperial Palace* li. 382 The hand of the official at the bottom of the gangway was full of landing tickets. **1912** KIPLING *Divers. Creatures* (1917) 23 They began turning out traffic-lights and locking up *landing-towers. **1967** *Jane's Surface Skimmer Systems 1967–68* 97/2 Landing Vehicle Hydrofoil. **1969** *Observer* 20 July 7/1 The astronauts crawl into the landing vehicle.. and spend three hours checking it. **1797** *Monthly Mag.* III. 480 Mr. J. Brook, *landing waiter of the custom-house. **1917** 'CONTACT' *Airman's Outings* 46 Something sang to the right, and I found that part of a *landing-wire was dangling helplessly from its socket. **1942** C. C. REDMAN in R. A. Beaumont *Aeronaut. Engin.* xvii. 482/1 Landing wires support the wings on the ground, but when the aircraft becomes airborne, the stresses are transferred to the flying wires, as the wings tend to lift upwards. **1952** A. Y. BRAMBLE *Air-Plane Flight* vii. 100 Those above [the wings of the glider] are obviously supporting the weight of the wings when the machine is on the ground. They are called 'landing wires'. Those below the wing.. are called the 'flying wires'.

'landing, *ppl. a.* [-ING².] That lands; in *Mil.* phr. ***landing force, party.***

1884 *Pall Mall G.* 8 Sept. 8/1 This was due to the French having no landing force. **1894** LD. WOLSELEY *Life Marlborough* II. 175 Sending three armed boats ashore, a landing party took the battery.

'landing-net. A net for landing large fish.

1653 WALTON *Angler* ii. 60 Reach me that Landing net. **1787** BEST *Angling* (ed. 2) 15 *A landing net*, to land large fish with, and which are made with joints to fold up in a small compass. **1848** THACKERAY *Bk. Snobs* xxvi, Fishing-rods, and landing-nets. **1885** *Athenæum* 1 Aug. 136/3 Mr. Webster does not appear to use any landing-net, which increases the difficulty of capturing fish.

b. *transf.* 'A pair of forceps with a small net attached to the blade, devised by A. Buchanan, for the removal of the calculus from the bladder in lithotomy' (*Syd. Soc. Lex.* 1888).

'landing-place.

1. a. A place where passengers and goods are or can be landed or disembarked.

1512 *Act 4 Hen. VIII*, c. 1 §1 The Frenchemen.. knowe aswell every haven and creke within the sayde Countie as every landyng place. **1620–55** I. JONES *Stone-Heng* (1725) 13 They were imbarked, dis-imbarked, and brought from their Landing Place to Salisbury Plain. **1687** *Lond. Gaz.* No. 2221/8 Lost.., between Richmond and Putney Landing-place, a Point Crevat and Cuffs. **1748** *Anson's Voy.* II. vi. 191 Pilots were ordered to.. conduct him to the most convenient landing-place. **1840** R. H. DANA *Bef. Mast* vii. 15 Waiting at the landing place for our boat to come ashore.

b. A platform at a railway station.

1882 in OGILVIE.

c. A place where a bird, insect, aircraft, etc., can or does land.

1776 T. PENNANT *Tour in Scotl. & Voy. Hebrides 1772* II. 24 Woodcocks... Their first landing-places are in the eastern counties. **1889** *Leisure Hour* 642/2 Insect 'landing-places' would thus, according to the theory, acquire considerable importance in affecting the structure of the flower. **1899** *Strand Mag.* Aug. 183/1 Captain Spelterini's sharp eye had quickly chosen an advantageous landing-place, and the anchor was thrown [from the balloon]. **1909** *Flying: the Why & Wherefore* v. 33 Another advantage of flying high is that in case of an engine stoppage the aeronaut will have time to look round and choose a landing place. **1935** C. DAY LEWIS *Time to Dance* 35 The oil ran out and cursing they turned about Losing a hundred miles to find a landing-place. **1962** K. W. GATLAND *Astronautics in Sixties* xi. 338 After reconnaissance spacecraft and soft-landing probes had given information concerning a suitable landing place, a Surveyor-type probe would be put down close to the desired landing point.

2. = LANDING *vbl. sb.* 6 (now the usual word).

1611 COTGR., *Aire*,.. the halfe-pace, or landing place of a half-pace staire. **1625** BACON *Ess., Building* (Arb.) 550 The Staires likewise.. let them bee vpon a Faire open Newell, and finely raild in.. And a very Faire Landing Place at the Top. **1765** FOOTE *Commissary* I. Wks. 1799 II. 7 Simon.. flew up stairs, fell over the landing-place, and quite barr'd up the way. **1840** DICKENS *Barn. Rudge* ix, His stealthy footsteps on the landing-place outside. **1849** MACAULAY *Hist. Eng.* iii. I. 352 The staircases and landing places are not wanting in grandeur.

attrib. **1852** R. S. SURTEES *Sponge's Sp. Tour* xxxiv. (1893) 193 The dinner and ball invitations gradually dwindled away, till he became a mere stop-gap at the one, and a landing-place appendage at the other.

3. *transf.* and *fig.* (in prec. senses). A place at which one arrives; a stopping- or resting-place.

1727 ARBUTHNOT *Tables Anc. Coins*, etc. vii. 151 What the Romans called Vestibulum was no part of the House, but the Court or Landing-place between it and the Street. **1850** TENNYSON *In Mem.* xlvii, He seeks at least Upon the last and sharpest height.. Some landing-place, to clasp and say, 'Farewell! We lose ourselves in light'. **1861** HUGHES *Tom Brown at Oxf.* I. Introd. 2 Tom was.. beginning to feel that it was high time for him to be getting to regular work again.. A landing place is a famous thing, but it is only enjoyable for a time by any mortal who deserves one at all. **1884** J. TAIT *Mind in Matter* (1892) 245 When the conscience-troubles.. lead to scepticism, the ultimate landing-place.. is superstition.

†landiron¹. *Obs.* Also 5 laundyren, 6 lawndyrne, laund(e iron, 6–7 landyron, 7 -iyron. [An alteration (influenced by IRON, as in ANDIRON) of LANDIER *a.*, F. *landier* = def. article *l'* + OF. *andier* andiron.] An andiron, fire-dog.

1459–60 *Durham Acc. Rolls* (Surtees) 89 It. ij cobertez alias laundyrens, ij rostyngyrens. **1511** *Nottingham Rec.* No. 1384. 42 Unum lawndyrne, pretii xviijd. **1541** in *Lanc. Wills & Invent.* I. 128, ij. old great laund irons, vs. **1590** *Inv. Linc.* in *Midl. Co. Hist. Coll.* II. 31 Item.. ij landyrons, one fire shovell. **1640** BRATHWAIT *Boulster Lect.* 304 Her Pots, Pipkings, Kettles, Land-irons with all her other Utensiles. **1685** *Inv. Ch. Wetherill of Keadby* 15 May (N. W. Linc. Gloss.), One iyron potte and one land iyron with spitts and racks and crookes.

†landiron². *Obs.* [? f. LAND *sb.*¹ + IRON *sb.*] A kind of iron.

1428 in *Surtees Misc.* (1888) 2 Sent hym with hys awen cariage iijᶜ & di. of landyren. *Ibid.* 3 He had mykyll with in him of dross and landiren.

†'landish, *a. Obs.* Also 3 londisse, 5 landysshe. [f. LAND *sb.*¹ + -ISH.] **a.** Belonging to the land or country; native. **b.** Of the commons or common people.

a **1300** *K. Horn* 634 Al wiþ sarazines kyn, And none londisse Men [*Ritson* Mid unlondisshe menne, Of Sarazynes kenne]. **1489** CAXTON *Faytes of A.* I. x. 26 They putte no dyfference betwene them [*sc.* the noblemen] & the landish-men. *Ibid.* xxiv. 76 The.. alarme that the landysshe peple or commons maken.

‖land-junker (-'jʊŋkə(r)). Also *anglicized* -younker. [Ger.] A country-squire.

1840 THACKERAY *Catherine* ii, I.. eased a great fat-headed Warwickshire land-junker.. of forty pieces. **1860** MOTLEY *Netherlands* II. 548 Land-younkers.. paid their black-mail.

landlady ('lændleɪdɪ). [f. LAND *sb.*¹ + LADY *sb.* Cf. *landlord*.]

1. 'A woman who has tenants holding from her' (J.); †*fig.* a mistress. *rare.*

a **1536** TINDALE *Expos. Matt.* v. Wks. (1573) 210/1 Let thy wife visit thy Landladye three or four tymes in a yeare, wyth spised cakes.. and such like. **1600** DEKKER *Fortunatus* Wks. 1873 I. 84 Great landlady of hearts pardon me. **1687** MIEGE *Gt. Fr. Dict.* II, s.v. *Landlady*, I am the Tenant, and she is my Landlady. *Mod.* Our landlady lives next door.

2. The hostess of an inn; the mistress of a lodging- or boarding-house.

1654 *Nicholas Papers* (Camden) II. 56 She called for the Landlord and Landlady of the Lodging. **1667** PEPYS *Diary* 7 Oct., There was so much tearing company in the house that we could not see the landlady. **1734** BERKELEY *Let. to T. Prior* 30 Apr., Wks. 1871 IV. 227 The landlady of the lodging must.. be obliged to furnish linen. **1824** SCOTT *Redgauntlet* let. xii, We soon reached the Shepherd's Bush, where the old landlady was sitting up waiting for us. **1857** DICKENS *Lett.* (1880) II. 30 We have a very obliging and comfortable landlady. **1886** RUSKIN *Præterita* I. vii. 209 The early widowed landlady of the King's Head Inn.

3. *Sc.* One's hostess, the wife of one's host or entertainer. ? *Obs.*

1815 SCOTT *Guy M.* iii, The circumstances of the landlady [Mrs. Bertram, wife of the laird] were pleaded to Mannering.. as an apology for her not appearing to welcome her guest.

Hence (*nonce-wds.*) **'landladydom,** the realm of landladies. **'landladyhood, -ship,** the position or dignity of a landlady. **'landladyish** *a.*, resembling or characteristic of a landlady.

1854 *Tait's Mag.* XXI. 349 The end of my landladyship is drawing nigh. **1862** J. SKINNER *Let.* 12 July in *Life* xi. (1884) 209 Maggie was in all the dignity of landladyhood. **1864** *Realm* 30 Mar. 8 Mrs. Falconer as Dame Quickly displayed a proper amount of landladyish indignation at her corpulent customer's misdeeds. **1890** BARING-GOULD *Pennycomequicks* 194 When I come to landladydom.

land-law. [In sense 1 repr. OE. *landlaȝu*, f. *land* LAND *sb.*¹ + *laȝu* LAW *sb.*¹; otherwise a modern formation. Cf. ON. *lands lǫg*.]

1. (Also †*land's law*.) The law of a land or country; the 'law of the land'.

c **1000** *Rect. Sing. Pers.* c. 4 in Schmid *Gesetze* 376 Ðeos landlaȝu stænt on suman lande. *Ibid.* c. 21 *ibid.* 382 Landlaȝa syn mistlice, swa ic ær.. sæde. *a* **1300** *Cursor M.* 12095 þat he yu ne luue mare þan lands lau. *c* **1380** WYCLIF *Wks.* (1880) 132 To stryue and plede for worldly possessions by londis lawe. **1818** SCOTT *Hrt. Midl.* xxviii, 'It's the fashion here for decent bodies, and ilka land has its ain land-law'.

2. Law, or a law, relating to land considered as property.

1878 *N. Amer. Rev.* CXXVII. 253 The land-laws of that country. **1894** *Daily News* 20 Apr. 4/7 Mr. John Stuart Mill pointed out that the English land law system was peculiar, and even was alone, among the land law systems of Europe. **1894** F. N. THORPE *Govt. U.S.* 9 Land-laws originate in the use of the land for grazing.

Land league. An association of Irish tenant farmers and others, organized in 1879 by Charles Stewart Parnell under the name of 'The Irish National Land League' (and suppressed by the Government in 1881), having for its object primarily the reduction of rent, and ultimately the carrying out of radical changes in the Irish land-laws, e.g. by the substitution of peasant proprietors for landlords. Hence **'Land-league** *v. trans.*, to treat according to the principles of the Land League. **'Land-leaguer,** a member of or sympathizer with the Land League. **'Land-leaguism,** the principles or practice of the Land League.

1880 *Libr. Univ. Knowl.* (N.Y.) VIII. 136 The incendiary speeches of the Land Leaguers. **1881** *Times* 17 Jan. 12/2 The Land League strikes at the root of Irish misery. **1881** C. GIBBON *Heart's Problem* iv. (1884) 56 He could quite believe that the old tailor and his family had gone to America on some Land League commission. **1881** SULLIVAN in *Macm. Mag.* XLIV. 343 The Land League and Land Leaguism have kept the peace in Ulster on this occasion. **1886** *Sat. Rev.* 6 Mar. 315/2 A Welsh Parliament, in which they might disestablish the hated Church, land-league the landlords.

†'land-leaper. *Obs.* Also 4–6 -leper(e, 5 -lepar, 7 *Sc.* -leiper. [f. LAND *sb.*¹ + LEAP *v.* (in the sense 'to run') + -ER¹.] = LAND-LOPER.

[**1362** LANGL. *P. Pl.* A. v. 258 þat Penitencia is pike he schulde polissche newe, And lepe with him ouerlond al his lyf tyme.] **1377** *Ibid.* B. xv. 207 He ne is nouȝte in lolleres, ne in lande-leperes [*v.r.* land-lepynge] hermytes. **14..** *Voc.* in Wr.-Wülcker 565/46 *Arvambulus*, a londlepar. *c* **1460** *Towneley Myst.* xvi. 166 Gett I those land lepars I breke ilka bone. **1560–77** *Misogonus* IV. ii. 11 (Brandl) Thou landleper, thou runagat roge. **1565** CALFHILL *Answ. Treat. Crosse* 51 b, Then eyther was your author a lyer, or a leude byshop: to forsake hys charge and be such a land-leaper. **1621** BURTON *Anat. Mel.* I. ii. III. xv. (1676) 83/2 Let Marriners learn Astronomy.. Landleapers Geography. *Ibid.* II. iii. IV. 212/2 Alexander, Cæsar, Trajan, Adrian, were as so many land-leapers, now in the East, now in the West, little at home. *a* **1670** HACKET *Abp. Williams* II. (1692) 111 As Budæus says proverbially of a Land-leaper, that makes himself a Cripple and cries out for help, *Tolle eum qui non novit.* **1706** PHILLIPS (ed. Kersey), *Land-leaper's-spurge*, a kind of Herb.

Hence †**landleapt** *a.*, ? vagabond, runaway; **land-leaping** *sb.* (*arch.*), ? vagabond style of living; †*a.*, vagabond.

1377 Land-lepynge [see above]. **1602** WARNER *Alb. Eng.* x. lv. (1612) 245 With her, Mendoza, Papists here, forren, and Land-leapt Foes. **1886** M. K. MACMILLAN *Dagonet the Jester* iii. 135 In good sooth your learning and land-leaping is nought but a kind of fooling.

†land-leave. *Obs.* ? A fee paid for permission to convey goods over certain land.

?*c* **1357** *Durham Acc. Rolls* (Surtees) 560 Pro 3 par. Molarum lucrand... præter Landleve et cariag. eorundem, xiijs. iiijd. **1664** in Hargreave *Coll. Tracts* (1787) I. 57 The defendants pretended title to it as parcell of the town of Plymouth, and shewed usage to have had certain customs called land-leave, terrage, &c. **1669** in *4th Rep. Hist. MSS. Comm.* (1874) 405/2 Penrose.. said.. that he had always received a 15ᵗʰ part of all goods cast on shore upon his ground for Landleave.

‖ländler ('lɛndlər). Also *erron.* landler. [G.] An Austrian peasant dance, similar to a slow waltz; the music for such a dance.

1876 STAINER & BARRETT *Dict. Mus. Terms* 251 *Ländler*, the name given to a dance popular among the Styrian peasants. **1934** C. LAMBERT *Music Ho!* I. 58 The romantic orchestration, the solid hymn-tune harmonies, the *Landler* rhythms, [etc.]. **1961** *Times* 21 Oct. 11/3 The humorous ländler that forms the second movement. **1964** *Listener* 6 Feb. 250/2 If the trio-section is taken at the same speed, it may sound unnaturally hurried, since its *Ländler*-like characteristics justify a more leisurely pace.

landless ('lændlɪs), *a.* [f. LAND *sb.*¹ + -LESS.]

1. Not possessing land; having no landed property.

c **1000** *Laws of Æthelstan* II. c. 8 in Schmid *Gesetze* 136 Be landleasum mannum.. ȝif hwylc landleas man folȝode on oðre scire. **1540–1** ELYOT *Image Gov.* 115 We shall neither haue usurour dwell in this citee, nor gentilmen landlesse. **1602** SHAKS. *Ham.* I. i. 98 Young Fortinbras.. Hath.. Shark'd vp a List of Landlesse Resolutes. **1638** BROME *Antipodes* I. i. Wks. 1873 III. 234 As mad as landlesse Squire could bee. **1814** SCOTT *Ld. of Isles* III. xxxi, A landless prince, whose wandering life Is but one scene of blood and strife. **1865** *Edin. Rev.* CXXI. 36 Turned adrift landless and homeless. **1878** *N. Amer. Rev.* CXXVII. 102 The negro, poor, landless, and deserted by the North.

2. Without land, void of land.

1605 SYLVESTER *Du Bartas* II. iii. III. *Law* 1197 A Fruitless, Flood-less, yea a Land-less Land. **1868** MORRIS *Earthly Par.* (1870) I. 16 Risk dying in an unknown landless sea. *Ibid.*, Within the landless waters of the west.

Hence **'landlessness.**

1851 H. MELVILLE *Whale* xxiii. 118 In landlessness alone resides the highest truth.

'land-line. Also landline and as two words.

1. The outline of the land against sky and sea.

1875 W. McILWRAITH *Guide Wigtownshire* 50 Ross Isle terminates the land-line of the view.

2. A telegraphic line running overland, as opposed to a cable. Also, an overland (or underground) line for telecommunication by other means.

1865 *Phil. Mag.* XXIX. 409 (*heading*) On the retardation of electrical signals on land lines. **1869** *Bradshaw's Railway Manual* XXI. 454 Telegraph to India... A provisional agreement entered into for leasing the land line in Egypt to the proposed British-Indian Submarine. **1884** S. E. DAWSON *Handbk. Canada* 21 The [telegraphic] cables and the land-lines in British Columbia. **1887** *Pall Mall G.* 9 Dec. 8/1 The Western Union now controls the land-line system of the United States. **1927** *Observer* 12 June 20 Last Sunday I had the curiosity to listen to the Eastbourne programme... There were obvious defects in the landline, which made the general effect thin and poor. **1930** *Bell Syst. Techn. Jrnl.* IX. 408 The linking of ships at sea with the land line telephone network. **1962** *B.B.C. Handbook* 109 A separate receiving station where broadcasts are intercepted and fed to the monitors by land line. **1970** 'J. EARL' *Tuners &*

Amplifiers iv. 77 It sometimes 'filters' the signal so as to rid it of certain shortcomings that could have been picked up during its transmission through the ether (radio waves) and studio landlines.

3. *Fishing.* Line passing from the end of the seine to the shore (Knight *Dict. Mech.* Suppl. 1884).

Hence **ˈlandline** *v. trans.*, to transmit over a land-line.

1966 *Times Lit. Suppl.* 24 Mar. 248 This Crusade is going to be landlined to most major cities in the United Kingdom. **1969** J. BENNETT *Dragon* iii. 43 That at least means no radio pictures to Peking... They'll probably take us ashore tomorrow and landline our pictures to Canton. **1974** J. DRUMMOND *Boon Companions* xxxi. 98 That first story's been land-lined and it's going to hit nine o'clock television all over the country.

land-lock (ˈlændlɒk), *sb. rare.* [? Back-formation from next.]

†**1.** The condition of being landlocked.

1627 CAPT. SMITH *Seaman's Gram.* ix. 45 Land locked. Land locke, is when the land is round about you.

attrib. *a* **1661** FULLER *Worthies, Shropsh.* III. (1662) 1, I behold it [*sc.* Shropshire] really (though not so Reputed) the biggest Land-lock-shire in England.

2. Landlocked country.

1895 *Outing* (U.S.) XXVII. 239/2 From Prospect Hill is had a delightful view of the Devonshire Valley, one of those many deceptive land locks, which [etc.].

landlocked (ˈlændlɒkt), *pa. pple.* and *ppl. a.* [See LOCK *v.*] Shut in or enclosed by land; almost entirely surrounded by land, as a harbour, etc. Also *transf.* of fish: Living in land-locked waters so as to be shut off from the sea.

1622 R. HAWKINS *Voy. S. Sea* (1847) 92 In the lesser of these ilands, is a cave for a small ship to ryde in, land-lockt. **1697** DRYDEN *Virg., Georg.* Ded. (1721) I. 194 A good Conscience is a Port which is Land-lock'd on every side. **1740** WOODROOFE in *Hanway's Trav.* (1762) I. IV. lix. 275 Twelve or fifteen sail of ships might lie land-locked, with the utmost security. **1779** FORREST *Voy. N. Guinea* 253 Went farther round into a land-locked bay, and moored the vessel. **1840** R. H. DANA *Bef. Mast* xiv. 36 Decidedly the best harbour on the coast, being completely land-locked. **1868** *Rep. U.S. Commissioner Agric.* 324 The taking of..land-locked salmon by any other means than by hook and hand-line is prohibited. **1876** PAGE *Adv. Text-bk. Geol.* ii. 44 The shores of the land-locked Baltic.

b. Hemmed in, limited, or hindered from movement by surrounding land.

1770 BARETTI *Journ. Lond. to Genoa* I. xiv. 88 Our land-lock'd Ladies on the other side the Alps. **1847** DISRAELI *Tancred* III. vii, The little caravan was apparently land-locked. **1855** KINGSLEY *Glaucus* (1878) 62 Along a pleasant road, with land-locked glimpses of the bay.

land-loper, land-louper (ˈlændˌləʊpə(r), -ˌlaʊpə(r)). Now chiefly *Sc.* Also 7 -lowper, 8 -looper. [ad. Du. *landlooper* (= MHG. *lantloufære*, G. *landläufer*), f. *land* LAND *sb.*¹ + *loopen* to run: see LEAP *v.* Cf. LANDLEAPER.]

1. One who runs up and down the land; a vagabond; *fig.* †a renegade; an adventurer.

15.. tr. *Bull Pope Martin* (*c* 1417) in Foxe *A. & M.* (1583) 648/2 Certaine Archhereticks haue risen and sprong vp.. being landlopers, schismatikes, and seditious persons. **1580** HOLLYBAND *Treas. Fr. Tong*, *Vn villotier*, a lande loper, a runnagate. *a* **1605** POLWART *Flyting w. Montgomerie* 757 Land lowper, light skowper, ragged rowper like a raven. **1622** BACON *Hen. VII* 114 Hee [Perkin Warbeck] had beene from his Child-hood such a Wanderer, or (as the King called him) such a Land-loper. **1642** HOWELL *For. Trav.* (Arb.) 57 Such Travellers as these may bee termed Land-lopers, as the Dutchman saith, rather than Travellers. **1681** W. ROBERTSON *Phraseol. Gen.* (1693) 799 A Land-loper, *prædo.* **1701** C. WOLLEY *Jrnl. New York* (1860) 19 The materials of this Journal have laid by me several years expecting that some Landlooper or other in those parts would have done it more methodically. **1816** SCOTT *Antiq.* xiii, This High-German land-louper, Dousterswivel. **1855** MOTLEY *Dutch Rep.* IV. iii. (1866) 596 Bands of land-loupers had been employed..to set fire to villages and towns in every direction.

Comb. **1787** BURNS *Let. to W. Nicol* 1 June, My land-lowper-like stravaguin.

†**2.** = LAND-LUBBER. *Obs.*

1694 MOTTEUX *Rabelais* V. xviii, We lay by and run adrift, that is in a Landlopers phrase, we temporis'd it. *a* **1700** B. E. *Dict. Cant. Crew*, *Land-lopers* or *Land-lubbers*, Fresh-water Seamen so called by the true Tarrs. **1725** in *New Cant. Dict.*

ˈland-ˌloping, -ˌlouping, *ppl. a.* Now *Sc.* [Back-formation from prec. + -ING².] Wandering, roving, vagabond. Also *fig.*

1577 HOLINSHED *Chron.* (1807–8) II. 401 These his land-loping legats and Nuncios have their manifold collusions to cousen christian kingdoms of their revenues. **1694** S. JOHNSON *Notes Past Let. Bp. Burnet* I. 32 It is a Lond-loping Argument. **1816** SCOTT *Antiq.* xxvi, I canna think it an unlawfu' thing to pit a bit trick on sic a land-louping scoundrel, that just lives by tricking honester folk. **1828** —— *F.M. Perth* iv, These land-louping Highland scoundrels.

landlord (ˈlændlɔːd), *sb.* Also 6 land(i)slord. [f. LAND *sb.*¹ + LORD *sb.* OE. had *landhláford*, but the mod. word is a new formation.]

1. a. Originally, a lord or owner of land; in recorded use applied only *spec.* to the person who lets land to a tenant. Hence (perh. already in 16th c.) in widened sense (as the correlative of *tenant*): A person of whom another person holds any tenement, whether a piece of land, a building or part of a building.

a **1000** in Earle *Land Charters* (1888) 376 Æt ælcum were ðe binnan ðam .xxx. hidan is ȝebyreð æfre se oðer fisc ðam landhlaforde. *c* **1000** *Laws of Edgar* Suppl. c. 11 in Schmid *Gesetze* 196 Healde se land-hlaford þæt forstolene orf..oð þæt se aȝenfriȝea þæt ȝeacsiȝe. **1419** *Liber Albus* 192 b (Rolls) I. 221 Le lessour, appelle 'landlorde'. **1455–6** GREGORY *Chron.* (Camden) 199 The Lombardys..toke grete old mancyons in Wynchester..and causyd the londe lordys to do grete coste in reparacyons. **1552** in *Vicary's Anat.* (1888) App. III. ii. 152 Suche rate as thei paye in yerely rent..to the landelordes therof. **1553** T. WILSON *Rhet.* 15 Would servauntes obey their masters..the tenaunt his landlorde. **1557** F. SEAGER *Sch. Virtue* 1071 in *Babees Bk.*, Ye that be landlordes and haue housen to let. **1587** *Sc. Acts Jas. VI* (1814) III. 462/1 þe landislordes and baillies vpoun quhais landis and in quhais Jurisdictioun þai duell. *c* **1590** GREENE *Fr. Bacon* x. 11, I am the lands-lord keeper of thy holds. **1593** SHAKS. *Rich. II*, II. i. 113 Landlord of England art thou, and not King. **1662** STILLINGFL. *Orig. Sacr.* III. iii. §1 His Landlord may dispossess him of all he hath upon displeasure. **1701** DE FOE *Orig. Power People* Misc. (1703) 157 If the King was universal Landlord, he ought to be universal Governor of Right. **1809** LAMB *Let. to Coleridge* 7 June, I have been turned out of my chambers in the Temple by a landlord who wanted them for himself. **1818** CRUISE *Digest* (ed. 2) I. 282 Six months notice to quit must be given by a landlord to his tenant at will. **1876** FREEMAN *Norm. Conq.* V. xxiv. 381 The doctrine was established that the King was the supreme landlord. **1878** JEVONS *Prim. Pol. Econ.* 92 The laws concerning landlord and tenant have been made by landlords.

b. *fig.* (said of God.)

a **1635** CORBET *Poems* (1807) 6 It wounded me the Land-lord of all times Should let long lives and leases to their crimes. **1676** W. HUBBARD *Happiness of People* 59 It is no wonder if God our great Land-lord, layes his arrest upon our tillage.

2. a. In extended sense: The person in whose house one lodges or boards for payment; one's 'host'. **b.** The master of an inn, an innkeeper.

a **1674** CLARENDON *Hist. Reb.* XIII. §86 He new dressed himself, changing clothes with his landlord. **1692** LUTTRELL *Brief Rel.* (1857) II. 411 His landlords daughter testified that [etc.]. **1724** SWIFT *Drapier's Lett.* i. Wks. 1761 III. 21 Suppose you go to an alehouse with that base money and the landlord gives you a quart for four of those half-pence. **1774** GOLDSM. *Retal.* 3 If our landlord supplies us with beef and with fish. **1777** SHERIDAN *Trip Scarb.* I. i, I suppose, sir, I must charge the landlord to be very particular where he stows this? **1870** *Daily News* 16 Apr., The word landlord is never used here [*sc.* New England] in its primary or English signification, and is applied only to the keeper of a tavern or boarding house.

3. A host or entertainer (in private). Chiefly *Sc.*

1725 DE FOE *Voy. round World* (1840) 65 Which their new landlords took very kindly. **1858** RAMSAY *Remin.* Ser. I. (1860) 256 Persons still persist among us in calling the head of the family, or the host, the landlord. **1864** BURTON *Scot. Abr.* I. i. 26 Not so satisfactory..as the confiding landlord expects it to be.

4. *attrib.* and *Comb.*

1845 *Douglas Jerrold's Shilling Mag.* I. 515 Judge-made law may be bad, but landlord-made law is worse. **1880** 'MARK TWAIN' *Tramp Abroad* 586 The landlord-apprentice serves as call-boy, then as under-waiter. **1908** *Daily Chron.* 26 June 5/7 With an air of detachment, as though he were not addressing a landlord-ridden assembly. **1924** R. GRAVES *Mock Beggar Hall* 72 Waiting the landlord-absentee's return. **1959** *Good Food Guide* 383 Both landlord-chef and waiter are Spanish. **1963** *Times Lit. Suppl.* 17 May 350/5 The parasitic landlord-usurers had to be destroyed as a class.

landlordism (ˈlændlɔːdɪz(ə)m). [f. prec. sb. + -ISM.] The principles or practice of landlords; the system according to which land is owned by landlords to whom tenants pay a fixed rent (chiefly used with reference to Ireland); advocacy or practice of such a system.

1844 MARY HENNELL *Soc. Systems* 82 The Mail, the recognized organ of Irish landlordism. **1849** COBDEN *Speeches* 87 If it is the spirit of landlordism that stands in the way of improvement in Ireland. **1880** MCCARTHY *Own Times* IV. 281 The landlordism of Ireland was, compared with most European institutions, a thing of the day before yesterday.

ˈlandlordly, *a.* [-LY¹.] Belonging to or characteristic of a landlord or landlords.

1853 LOWELL *Moorehead Jrnl.* Prose Wks. 1890 I. 18 He waits upon it himself in the good old landlordly fashion. **1866** *Daily Tel.* 8 Jan. 4/6 Landlordly coercion. **1897** MAITLAND *Domesday & Beyond* 199 As far as landlordly rights are concerned.

†**ˈlandlordry.** *Obs. rare*⁻¹. [-RY.] Landlords as a class.

1597–8 BP. HALL *Sat.* V. i. 98 Such pilfring slips of Pety land-lordrye.

ˈlandlordship. [-SHIP.] The position or condition of a landlord; the tenure of such a position. Also, with poss. pron., used as a title.

[**1824** *Blackw. Mag.* XV. 15 The evil system of middle-landlordship.] **1828** MISS MITFORD *Village* Ser. III. 44 [He] did not intend to retire yet awhile to the landlordship of the Bell. **1874** RUSKIN *Fors Clav.* IV. 199 Neither British constitution nor British law..can keep your landlordships safe. **1897** MAITLAND *Domesday & Beyond* 172 Lordship in becoming landlordship begins to lose its most dangerous element.

land-lubber (ˈlændˌlʌbə(r)). [LUBBER occurs in the 16th c. in this sense.] A sailor's term of contempt for a landsman.

a **1700** [see LAND-LOPER 2]. **1752** JOHNSON *Rambler* No. 198 ¶ 11 My Uncle..bid me prepare myself against next year for no land lubber should touch his money. **1824** W. IRVING *T. Trav.* (1849) 417 There was many a land-lubber looked on that might much better have swung in his stead. **1875** R. F. BURTON *Gorilla L.* II. 15 The philosophic landlubber often wonders at the eternal restlessness of his naval brother-man. **1884** PAE *Eustace* 130 The service is not intended to pamper landlubbers, but to make smart seamen.

Hence **ˈlandlubberish**, **ˈlandlubberly** *adjs.*

1829 J. WILSON in *Blackw. Mag.* XXXVI. 912 Land-lubberish terms. **1860** DICKENS *Lett.* 4 Sept. (1880) II. 119 The costermongers in the street outside..have an earthy, and, as I may say, a landlubberly aspect. **1893** VIZETELLY *Glances Back* I. viii. 166 My land-lubberly intelligence failed to grasp the proper meaning.

land-lubbing, *a.* [Irreg. f. LAND-LUBBER.] Land-lubberly.

1885 *Punch* 29 Aug. 100/2 The Judge, a land-lubbing chap in a wig. **1927** *Daily Express* 4 Oct. 3/3 We land-lubbing civilians know less about the Navy than our maiden aunts might be expected to know about alimony. **1960** *House & Garden* Aug. 31/2 Judged by sea-going or land-lubbing standards. **1966** *Economist* 21 May 799/2 Many..seamen are obeying their union's strike call with more enthusiasm than some landlubbing trade unionists would. **1974** *Sci. Amer.* June 132/2 The line-of-sight land-lubbing microwave relay networks are too expensive. What can the engineers do in orbit?

landman (ˈlændmən). [OE. *landmann*, f. *land* LAND *sb.*¹ + *mann* MAN *sb.* Cf. MHG. *lantman* native, mod.G. *landmann*, Du. *landman* countryman, peasant, farmer. Cf. LANDSMAN.]

†**1.** A man of a (specified or indicated) country. = COUNTRYMAN 1. *Obs. rare.*

a **1000** *Cædmon's Exod.* 179 (Gr.) Feond onseȝon laðum eaȝan landmanna cyme. *c* **1000** *Ordin. Dunsæte* c. 6 in Schmid *Gesetze* 360. **1641** MILTON *Ch. Govt.* I. vii. 29 The Englishman of many other nations is least atheisticall..; but ..he may fall not unlikely sometimes as any other land man into an uncouth opinion.

2. A countryman, peasant.

(In Carlyle, after G. *landmann*.)

a **1300** *Cursor M.* 28072 Nu sal i tell þe..Hu þu sal sceu þi scrift to preist,..þat landmen mai sumquat lere, To scape þair scrift wit þis samplere. *Ibid.* 29411 Quen he [a clerk] chaunges crun or wede, And funden [es] in land mans dede. **1497** *Extracts Aberd. Reg.* (1844) I. 60 That euere burges sal inbring certaine landmen, out duellaris..to remane within the tone. **1543** *Ibid.* 191 The toune is hauely murmurit be the landmen. **1825** CARLYLE *Schiller* III. (1845) 215 They are no philosophers or tribunes, but frank, stalwart landmen.

3. = LANDSMAN 2. Now *rare* or *Obs.*

1480 *Howard Househ. Bks.* (Roxb.) 9, iij. M. men, lande men and maryners..arrayed for the werre. **1606** SHAKS. *Ant. & Cl.* IV. iii. 11 If tomorrow Our Nauie thriue, I haue an absolute hope Our Landmen will stand vp. **1664** J. KEYMOR *Dutch Fish.* 6 Thus they make their Landmen Seamen, their Seamen Fishermen, their Fishermen Mariners. **1752** FIELDING *Amelia* III. iv, What inspires a landman with the highest apprehension of danger gives not the least concern to a sailor. **1769** *De Foe's Tour Gt. Brit.* (ed. 7) II. 129 The Distinction between Landmen and Seamen on board, which used to create Animosity, and subject the Landmen to some Hardships. **1808** G. EDWARDS *Pract. Plan* i. 7 The facility with which these convert landmen into sailors. **1846** WHATELY *Addit. Elem. Rhet.* 3 Nautical terms..it is little loss to a landman to be ignorant of.

†**4.** A man having landed property. *Obs.*

1562 A. SCOTT *Poems* (S.T.S.) i. 156 But kirkmennis cursit substance semis sweit Till landmen, wᵗ þat leud burd lyme are lyttit. **1670** BLOUNT *Law Dict.* (1691), *Landman*, the Terre-tenant. **1708** J. CHAMBERLAYNE *St. Gt. Brit.* II. III. iii. (1737) 405 A Gentleman of three Generations claims Precedency from any ordinary Land-man, who has but newly acquired his Lands.

landmark (ˈlændmɑːk), *sb.* [OE. *landmearc* fem.: see LAND *sb.*¹ and MARK *sb.* (Cf. G. *landmark* boundary, *landmarke* sailor's landmark.)]

1. The boundary of a country, estate, etc.; an object set up to mark a boundary line.

982 in Kemble *Cod. Dipl.* III. 189 Seo landmearce lið of Terstan upp be Hohtuninga mearce. *a* **1000** *Juliana* 635 Ða wæs ȝelæded lond-mearce neah. **1535** COVERDALE *Job* xxiv. 2 Some men there be, that remoue other mens londe markes. **1611** BIBLE *Deut.* xxvii. 17 Cursed be he that remooueth his neighbours land-marke [COVERDALE mark]. **1791** BURKE *Corr.* (1844) III. 211 When..he returned to the possession of his estates,..he found none of the ancient landmarks removed. **1838** THIRLWALL *Greece* II. xiv. 235 The landmarks of Platæa..were carried forward to the Asopus. *Ibid.* IV. xxxvi. 416 The landmarks which separated the two states had been removed.

fig. *a* **1652** J. SMITH *Sel. Disc.* iv. 126 May we not too hastily displace the ancient termini, and remove the land-marks of virtue and vice? **1771** *Junius' Lett.* lxi. 319 He has introduced new law, and removed the landmarks established by former decisions. **1858** BRIGHT *Sp., Reforms* 27 Oct. (1876) 284, I do not wish to endanger or remove any of the ancient landmarks of our Constitution.

†**b.** ? A district. *Obs.* [So formerly G. *landmark.*]

1550 W. LYNNE *Carion's Cron.* 255 He wrought much wo to the citie of Brunswike, roauing and burnyng in her suburbes, villages, landmarkes, and iurisdictions.

2. An object in the landscape, which, by its conspicuousness, serves as a guide in the direction of one's course (*orig.* and *esp.* as a

guide to sailors in navigation); hence, any conspicuous object which characterizes a neighbourhood or district.

1570 Dee *Math. Pref.* 18 Hydrographie, requireth a particular Register of certaine Landmarkes..from the sea. **1627** Capt. Smith *Seaman's Gram.* ix. 43 A Land marke, is any Mountaine, Rocke, Church, Wind-mill or the like, that the Pilot can know by comparing one by another how they beare by the compasse. **1667** Milton *P.L.* xi. 432 Ith' midst an Altar as the Land-mark stood. **1719** De Foe *Crusoe* ii. ii. (1840) 34 Having no chart for the coast, nor any land-mark. **1856** Froude *Hist. Eng.* (1858) II. vii. 183 Like unskilful sailors who have lost the landmarks of their course. **1859** Dickens *Lett.* (1880) II. 91 The house altogether is the great landmark of the whole neighbourhood.

fig. **1712** Hughes *Spect.* No. 316 ¶2 Now one Face of Indolence overspreads the whole, and I have no Land-mark to direct my self by. **1880** *Times* 18 Sept. 9/3 Two or three land-marks, however, in the dreary waste [of evidence] attract attention.

3. (In mod. use.) An object which marks or is associated with some event or stage in a process; *esp.* a characteristic, a modification, etc., or an event, which marks a period or turning-point in the history of a thing.

1859 C. Barker *Assoc. Princ.* ii. 46 This important landmark in our social history. **1862** Mill *Utilit.* 5 This..man, whose system of thought will long remain one of the landmarks in the history of philosophical speculation. **1870** Rolleston *Anim. Life* 127 The black pigment specks which are seen in this variety [of leech]..seem..to point in the same direction as those more constant land-marks just specified. **1884** W. K. Parker *Mammal. Descent* vii. (1885) 177 In these skulls the landmarks are all gone, except the holes for the vessels and nerves [etc.].

landmark, *v.* [f. the sb.] *trans.* To be or act as a landmark to; to provide with a landmark.

1921 J. F. Porte *Sir E. Elgar* 8 It is not necessary here to landmark further successes. **1928** *Sunday Dispatch* 9 Dec. 2/2 Her mother, perhaps the only disinterested figure of all the many who landmarked those ten years, had died.

ˈland-marshal. *Hist.* [ad. Sw. *landtmarskalk*, G. *landmarschall.*]

a. In Sweden, the speaker or president of the assembly of the first estate. **b.** In Prussia, Austria, etc., the marshal of a province.

1682 *Lond. Gaz.* No. 1767/1 His Majesty has named Baron Fabian Wrede, to be Land-Marshal, that is, Speaker, or President, in the Assembly of the Nobility and Gentry. **1711** *Ibid.* No. 4808/1 His Majesty has..conferr'd the Employment of Land-Marshal of Prussia upon his Chamberlain. **1862** H. Marryat *Year in Sweden* I. 408 No member was allowed to leave the chamber during the transaction of business without permission of the landmarshal. **1898** *Daily News* 29 Jan. 7/3 The Moravian Diet at Brünn... The Landmarshal, who was presiding, asked them to leave the Diet.

ˈland-measure. †**a.** Measurement of land (*obs.*). **b.** Any of the denominations of measurement used in stating the area of land (e.g. the acre, the rood, etc.); also applied as a name for the system of such denominations in current use.

1611 Cotgr., *Latte*..a Land-measure..in some places longer then in other. **1662** Atwell *Faithf. Surveyor* i. 1 Of errours in Land-measure. **1857** Boucher *Mensuration* 5 Land Measure by Gunter's Chain. 100 linear links = 1 linear chain. **1900** Addy in *N. & Q.* 20 Oct. 303/1 (heading) English and Roman Land Measures.

So **ˈland-measuring, -measurement**, the art or process of determining by measurement the area of lands, fields, farms, etc.: properly a subordinate branch of land-surveying, but the terms are often used synonymously.

1570 Dee *Math. Pref.* 14 Other Philosophers, writing Rules for land measuring. **1849** *Chambers' Inform.* II. 624/1 The principle of throwing the area of any given field or set of fields into triangular spaces, is that pursued in all processes of land-measurement. *Ibid.* 624/2 In land-measuring, the scale of operations is ordinarily too limited to require any such allowance for difference of levels.

ˈland-measurer.

1. One whose occupation is land-measuring.

1632 *MS. Acc. St. John's Hosp., Canterb.*, Layd out on our selues and the landmeasurer when we went to..laye out our land. **1828** Miss Mitford *Village* Ser. iii. 232 A staid, thick, sober, silent, middle-aged personage, who united the offices of schoolmaster and land-measurer.

2. [tr. mod.L. *geometra.*] A geometer moth.

188. *Cassell's Nat. Hist.* VI. 66 The Geometræ (or Land Measurers).

ˈland-mere. ? *Obs.* In 7 -meare, 9 -meer. [f. land *sb.*[1] + mere *sb.* (OE. *mǽre*). Cf. landimere.] A boundary of land.

1603 Owen *Pembrokeshire* (1891) 5 And then by land-meares from Kilhredyn to Cronmere Water. **1884** C. Rogers *Soc. Life Scotl.* II. xiv. 333 Land Meer Processions, or Riding of the Marches.

†**ˈland-meter.** *Obs.* In 6–7 -meater, 7 -meeter. [f. land *sb.*[1] + meter, agent-n. f. mete *v.*, to measure.] A land-measurer or surveyor.

1582 E. Worsop (*title*) A Discoverie of Sundrie errours and faults daily committed by Landemeaters to the damage of her Maiesties subiects. **1608** Norton *Stevin's Disme* D 2 The greater number of Land-meaters vse not the Pole, but a chayne line of 3, 4 or 5 Perch long. *c* **1613** *Soc. Cond. People Anglesey* (1860) 32 The English yard..is used by..masons, carpenters, land-meeters and others. **1636** Bedwell (*title*) The Way to Geometry, being necessary..for Astronomers, Geographers, Land-meaters [etc.], by Peter Ramus.

So †**land-mete**, a measurement of land; †**land-meting**, land-measuring.

1608 Norton *Stevin's Disme* D 1 b, Of the Computations of Land-meating. *Ibid.* D 4 b, The like is sufficiently manifest amongst Land-meats in surfaces.

ˈland-metster. *Sc.* [See metster (f. mete *v.* + -ster).] = land-meter.

1726 *Minutes Presbytery* in Sage *Memorab. Domestica* (1889) I. 7 Cite masons, wrights, and land metters [? *read* -metsters]. The said..land-melsters [*read* metsters] being duly sworn. **1822** *Law Case, Rev. D. Macarthur* (Jam.), John Currie, land-metster.

lando, obs. form of landau.

landocracy (lænˈdɒkrəsɪ). *jocular.* [f. land *sb.*[1]: see -cracy.] The class of people which owes its controlling position in the country to its possession of landed property. So **ˈlandocrat**, a member of this class.

1848 *Simmonds's Colon. Mag.* Aug. 343 The Landocracy—in which term we comprehend all landowners great and small. *a* **1865** Cobden in *Daily News* (1869) 16 Jan., The aristocracy and landocracy and moneyocracy who govern our elections. **1882** T. Mozley *Remin.* II. xcviii. 173 [I felt] a deep grievance with the British landocracy. **1893** *Nat. Observer* 23 Sept. 484/1 The wail of the landocrat is heard in the land.

landolphia (lænˈdɒlfɪə). [mod.L. (A. M. F. J. Palisot de Beauvois *Flore d'Oware* (1804) I. 55), f. the name of M. *Landolphe* (1765–1825), commander of the expedition on which the genus was first discovered + -ia[1].] A tropical African climbing plant of the genus so called, belonging to the family Apocynaceæ and yielding a latex formerly used as a source of rubber.

1887 *Curtis's Bot. Mag.* CXIII. 6963 The first notice of the *Landolphia* yielding India-rubber..is by Col. now Sir J. A. Grant, in the appendix to Speke's Journal. **1910** *Westm. Gaz.* 20 Apr. 4/1 Landolphias, woody climbers,..yield the African rubbers. **1951** *Dict. Gardening* (R. Hort. Soc.) III. 1125/1 Landolphias are an important source of caoutchouc.

landowner (ˈlændəʊnə(r)). [f. land *sb.*[1] + owner.] An owner or proprietor of land. Hence **ˈlandownership**.

a **1733** North *Ld. Kpr. North* (1742) 137 Any Land Owner may make that which they call a Key, next to the River. **1845** Darwin *Voy. Nat.* xii. (1879) 255 Each landowner in the valley possesses a certain portion of hill-country. **1849** Macaulay *Hist. Eng.* vi. II. 141 Landowners hastened to sell their estates for whatever could be got. **1867** Musgrave *Nooks Old France* II. 334 England's landownership will never be without the representatives and reflected honours of her ancient Aristocracy. **1878** Jevons *Prim. Pol. Econ.* 91 Many large land-owners in England refuse to let their land for long periods.

So **ˈlandowning** *sb.* and *a.*

1845 Miall in *Nonconf.* V. 149 The landowning majority contemplate no concessions. **1881** *Macm. Mag.* XLIV. 127 Landowning and farming are as much businesses as cotton-spinning. **1894** Mrs. H. Ward *Marcella* I. 280, I..have no landowning relations.

landrace (ˈlændreɪs). [Da.] A large white pig of the variety so called, originally developed in Denmark, now used elsewhere to produce bacon. Also *attrib.*

1935 Layley & Malden *Evolution Brit. Pig* 98 (*heading*) Landrace. The modern model. *Ibid.*, The Danish Landrace ..is the model set up to which it is the ambition of our state to mould all British pigs. **1937** G. R. H. Bishop *Improvement of Bacon Pigs* ii. 27 The contented Landrace sows were hardy and prolific. **1948** H. R. Davidson *Production & Marketing Pigs* ix. 126 There [*sc.* in Denmark], in 1895, were set up the first breeding centres to maintain and improve the breed type of the native Landrace. **1958** 'R. Crompton' *William's Television Show* viii. 253 'A Landrace pedigree, that pig is,' said the farmer. **1971** *Country Life* 2 Dec. 1588/1 Our breeders [of pigs].. readily accept Large White, Landrace, or crosses of these breeds.

landrail (ˈlændreɪl). [See rail *sb.*; cf. *water-rail.* So G. *landralle.*] The corn-crake, *Crex pratensis.*

1766 Pennant *Zool.* (1768) II. 387 The land rail lays from twelve to twenty eggs, of a dull white color, marked with a few yellow spots. **1828** Stark *Elem. Nat. Hist.* I. 302 The Land-Rail is a migratory species, appearing in Britain about the latter end of April, and departing about the middle or close of September. **1877** L. Morris *Epic Hades* i. 3 Through the dew The landrail brushed.

ˈland-rat. [Cf. G. *landratte, -ratze* land-rat, land-lubber.] A rat that lives on land. †Also used as a term of abuse.

1596 Shaks. *Merch. V.* i. iii. 24 There be land rats, and water rats, water theeues, and land theeues—I mean, pirates. **1609** Dekker *Gul's Horne-bk.* Wks. (Grosart) II. 233 The Duke's Tomb is a Sanctuary, and will keepe you alive from wormes and land-rattes, that long to be feeding on your carkas. **1632** Shirley *Ball* iv. ii, *Lo.* Will you not draw? *Bo.* Not against your honour, but you shall see. *Lo.* And vex my eyes to look on such a Land-rat. **1860** Wynter *Curios. Civilizat.* 129 There are in England two kinds of land-rats,—the old English black rat, and the Norwegian or brown rat.

landress, landrie, obs. ff. laundress, -ry.

ˈland-right. *OE.* and *Hist.* [OE. *landriht* (see land *sb.*[1] and right *sb.*): cf. OS. *landreht*, OFris. *landriucht*, OHG. *lantreht*, G. *landrecht.*] 'Law of the land; legal rights of natives of the country; legal obligation connected with land or estate' (Sweet *Ags. Dict.*).

Beowulf (Gr.) 2886 Londrihtes mot þære mæȝburȝe monna æȝhwylc idel hweorfan. *a* **1000** *Cædmon's Gen.* 1911 (Gr.) Unc modiȝe ymb mearce sittað..ne willað rumor unc land-riht heora. —— *Exod.* 354 Landriht ȝeþah. **1872** E. W. Robertson *Hist. Ess.* 236 *note*, In later days it was a principle of Land-right that no freeman should be amerced 'above his wer'. **1892** Stopford A. Brooke *E.E. Lit.* i. 6 He received money and landright from the King.

Landsborough (ˈlændzbərə). *Austral.* The name of a small town in Queensland, used *attrib.* in **Landsborough grass**, a pasture grass, *Iseilema membranaceum*, found in the area, and better known as small Flinders grass.

1883 F. M. Bailey *Synopsis Queensland Flora* 646 The Landsborough grass. A weak, very leafy, brittle grass of a reddish color, one of the most valuable for fodder. **1889** [see Barcoo]. **1891** R. Wallace *Rural Econ. Austral. & N.Z.* xxii. 294 *Anthistiria membranacea*, Lindl.—Barcoo grass of Queensland; also called Landsborough grass. West and South Australia, New South Wales and Queensland. **1927** M. M. Bennett *Christison* v. 55 Landsborough grass.. shimmered gold and silver. **1929** J. W. Bews *World's Grasses* vi. 253 'Barcoo', 'Landsborough' or 'Red Gulf grass', covers large tracts of the north and interior of Australia.

landscape (ˈlændskeɪp), *sb.* Forms: α. 7 lan(d)-, landtschap, lantschape, landt-shape, landscap, -skap, (lantskop, land-scept), 7–8 landskape, -schape, -shape, -chape, 7– landscape. β. 6–8 (9 *arch.*) landskip; also 6 launce-skippe, 7 lan(d)tskip, lantsc(h)ip, lanscippe, land-, lantskipp. [a. Du. *landschap* (= OE. *landscipe* masc., OS. *landscepi* neut., OHG. *lantscaf*, mod.G. *landschaft* fem., ON. *landskap-r* masc.), f. *land* land *sb.*[1] + *-schap* (see -ship). The word was introduced as a technical term of painters; the corrupt form in *-skip* was according to our quots. a few years earlier than the more correct form.]

1. a. A picture representing natural inland scenery, as distinguished from a sea picture, a portrait, etc.

α. **1603** Sylvester *Du Bartas* i. vii. 13 The cunning Painter..Limning a Land-scape, various, rich, and rare. **1605** B. Jonson *Masque Blackness* Wks. (1616) 893 First, for the Scene, was drawne a *Landtschap*, consisting of small woods. **16..** A. Gibson *L'Envoy* in *Guillim's Heraldry* (1660), As in a curious Lant-schape, oft we see Nature, so follow'd, as we think it's she. **1683** Dryden *Life Plutarch* Ded. 18 Let this part of the landschape be cast into shadows that the heightnings of the other may appear more beautiful. **1821** Craig *Lect. Drawing* v. 271 If..you paint your landscapes in oil-colours. **1841–4** Emerson *Ess.*, *Art* Wks. (Bohn) I. 145 In landscapes, the painter should give the suggestion of a fairer creation than we know. **1899** L. Cust in *Nat. Gallery Brit. Art* 8 The landscapes exhibited on this occasion by Constable.

β. **1598** R. Haydocke tr. *Lomazzo* iii. i. 94 In a table donne by Cæsar Sestius where hee had painted Landskipes. **1615** G. Sandys *Trav.* 154 Vallies such as are figured in the most beautifull land-skips. **1648** *Bury Wills* (Camden) 216, I give alsoe vnto her Lapp, the landskipp inamiled vpon gold which is in the Dutch cabinett in my closett. **1698** Fryer *Acc. E. India & P.* 83 Such a Troop as went to apprehend our Saviour, dressed after the same manner we find them on old Landskips. **1702** *Eng. Theophrast.* 116 The perfections of a fine Landskip decrease, when you behold it at a close view. **1718** J. Chamberlayne *Relig. Philos.* (1730) III. xxv. §29 A noble Landskip of Men, Trees, Flowers..and such like. **1725** Watts *Logic* ii. iv, As a Painter who professes to draw a fair and distinct Landskip in the Twilight, when he can hardly distinguish a House from a Tree.

†**b.** *spec.* The background of scenery in a portrait or figure-painting. *Obs.*

1656 Blount *Glossogr.*, *Landskip*, Parergon, Paisage or By-work, which is an expressing of the Land, by Hills, Woods, Castles, Valleys, Rivers, Cities, &c. as far as may be shewed in our Horizon. All that which in a Picture is not of the body or argument thereof is Landskip, Parergon, or by-work. **1676** Beale *Pocket-bk.* in H. Walpole *Vertue's Anecd. Paint.* (1786) III. 134, I gave Mr. Manby two ounces of very good lake..in consideration of the landskip he did in the Countess of Clare's picture.

c. As *adj.* = oblong *a.* 1 c. Also as *adv.*

1932 Sayers & Smart in W. Atkins *Art & Pract. Printing* I. xii. 139 The frontispiece..may be printed either upright (termed portrait) or broad way (termed landscape). If a full-page illustration be printed landscape, the inscription or caption beneath must read from foot to head. **1951** D. Bland *Illustration of Books* ix. 146 The landscape plate is always a problem. It is unfortunate that the tall narrow format which is so suitable for a page of type does not lend itself to the average photograph. **1956** H. Williamson *Methods Bk. Design* iii. 16 The same formats can..be used for landscape or oblong books. **1966** G. Hamilton-Edwards *In Search Ancestry* ii. 24 This can be done by buying the full quarto size exercise book..and asking a printer to cut it in half, wide-ways, or 'landscape'... This gives you two booklets of 8″ × 5″.

2. a. A view or prospect of natural inland scenery, such as can be taken in at a glance from one point of view; a piece of country scenery.

α. **1725** Pope *Odyss.* iii. 630 O'er the shaded landscape rush'd the night. **1742** Young *Nt. Th.* vi. 773 Sumptuous Cities..gild our Landschape with their glitt'ring Spires.

1750 GRAY *Elegy* 5 Now fades the glimmering landscape on the sight. **1876** MOZLEY *Univ. Serm.* v. 99 There are no two more different landscapes than the same under altered skies. **1877** BLACK *Green Past.* ii. (1878) 11 What could be a fitter surrounding for this young English girl than this English-looking landscape?

β. **1632** MILTON *L'Allegro* 70 Streit mine eye has caught new pleasures Whilst the Lantskip round it measures. **1635** A. STAFFORD *Fem. Glory* (1869) 86 As terrible to them as a Lanscippe with a May-pole in it. **1697** ADDISON *Ess. Georg.* in Dryden's *Virg.* sig. ¶4 It raises in our Minds a pleasing variety of Scenes and Landskips. **1712** —— *Spect.* No. 411 ¶2 Scenes and Landskips more beautiful than any that can be found in the whole Compass of Nature. **1748** *Anson's Voy.* II. i. 111 Thus we coasted the shore, fully employed in the contemplation of this diversified landskip. **1855** BAILEY *Mystic* 107 Where bright Herat, city of roses, lights With dome and minaret the landskip green. **1894** CROCKETT *Raiders* (ed. 3) 29 The hues of the landskip and the sea.

b. A tract of land with its distinguishing characteristics and features, esp. considered as a product of modifying or shaping processes and agents (usually natural).

1886 A. GEIKIE *Class-Bk. Geol.* i. 2 The surface of a country is not now exactly as it used to be. We notice various changes of its topography going on now,.. the accumulated effect of which may ultimately transform altogether the character of landscapes. **1896** *Rep. 6th Internat. Geogr. Congr. 1895* 749 We thus have six ranks of units: (1) The form-element. (2) The fundamental form [*sc.* land form]. (3) The group of forms or landscape. [Etc.]. **1922** L. MUMFORD in H. E. Stearns *Civilisation in U.S.* 4 West of the Alleghanies, the common, with its church and school, was not destined to dominate the urban landscape. **1925** *Univ. Calif. Geogr.* II. 37 The works of man express themselves in the cultural landscape. There may be a succession of these landscapes with a succession of cultures. They are derived in each case from the natural landscape, man expressing his place in nature as a distinct agent of modification. **1937** WOOLDRIDGE & MORGAN *Physical Basis Geogr.* p. ix, Geography cannot dispense with geomorphology, for a real understanding of the characters and development of the physical landscape is an indispensable preliminary to the study of the cultural landscape and of regions. **1944** A. HOLMES *Princ. Physical Geol.* xi. 191 In the Grampian Highlands an old peneplain, now dissected into a landscape of late youth or early maturity (though modified by glaciation), is easily recognised by the even skyline. **1954** W. D. THORNBURY *Princ. Geomorphol.* xiv. 364 Two contrasting ideas have developed regarding the ability of glaciers to modify by erosion the landscapes over which they move. **1971** I. G. GASS et al. *Understanding Earth* vii. 100/1 (*caption*) Two photographs of the lunar crater Tycho.., whose ramparts rise 5 400 m above the level of its floor, though only 1 600 m above the level of the surrounding landscape. **1974** H. F. GARNER (*title*) The origin of landscapes: a synthesis of geomorphology.

3. In generalized sense (from 1 and 2): Inland natural scenery, or its representation in painting.

α. **1606** DEKKER *Sev. Sinnes* Ded., A Drollerie (or Dutch peece of *Lantskop*). **1747** HOARE in *Phil. Trans.* XLIV. 570 These Pictures shew, that the Antients understood Perspective and Landschape. **1795** COLERIDGE *Lines on Climbing Brockley Coomb*, What a luxury of landscape meets My gaze! **1844** RUSKIN *Mod. Paint.* (1851) I. Pref. to ed. 2. 25 The true ideal of landscape is precisely the same as that of the human form. **1873** PATER *Renaissance* 142 The feeling for landscape is often described as a modern one.

β. **1602** DEKKER *Satiromastix* C 2, Good peeces of lantskip, shew best a far off. *a* **1649** DRUMM. OF HAWTH. *Poems* 104 Like imagin'd Landskip in the Aire. **1667** MILTON *P.L.* v. 142 The Sun.. Discovering in wide Lant-skip all the East Of Paradise and Edens happie Plains. **1678** CUDWORTH *Intell. Syst.* I. v. 855 Landskip in Picture.

4. In various transf. and fig. uses.

†**a.** A view, prospect *of* something.

1612 W. PARKES *Curtaine-Dr.* (1876) 22 In my mentall and priuate Peregrinations, taking a view and land-scape.. of all the famous Courts and Cities of the world. **1658** R. FRANCK *North. Mem.* (1821) 195 Come, then, let us break the heart of these hills, and bless our eyes with a landskip of the Lowlands. **1698** FRYER *Acc. E. India & P.* 3 Too great a distance to take a perfect Landschap, it being only discernible to be Land. *a* **1711** KEN *Serm.* Wks. (1838) 155 The Love of God.. presented Daniel with a clearer landscape of the Gospel than any other prophet ever had.

†**b.** A distant prospect: a vista. (Cf. 2 b.)

1599 NASHE *Lenten Stuff* Wks. (Grosart) V. 204, I care not, if in a dimme farre of launce-skippe, I take the paines to describe this.. Metropolis of the redde Fish. *a* **1613** OVERBURY *Charac., Whore* (1616), The sins of other women shew in Landscip, far off and full of shadow; hers in Statue, neere hand, and bigger in the life. **1643** T. FULLER *Serm. Reform.* (1875) 6 The Jewes.. saw Christ presented in a land-scept, and beheld him through the perspective of faith. **1654** H. L'ESTRANGE *Chas. I* (1655) 62 These storms appeared as Land-skaps and aloof. **1698** NORRIS *Pract. Disc.* IV. 221 Nothing which this visible World can set before us is worthy our regard, especially when at the End of the Landskip the Invisible Glories of Heaven Solicit and Court our Love.

†**c.** The object of one's gaze.

1659 *Lady Alimony* II. v. C 4, There is a Caranto-man with all my heart! must Beauty be his Land-skip on the seat of Justice? **1664** LD. FALKLAND *Marriage Nt.* I. i. 4 At distances she is a Goodly Landskip.

†**d.** A sketch, adumbration, outline; *occas.* a faint or shadowy representation.

a **1649** DRUMM. OF HAWTH. *Irene* Wks. (1711) 168 Imaginary and fantastical councils, landskips of commonwealths. **1650** CHARLETON *Paradoxes* 69 Every single entity containes.. an adumbration or landskip of the whole Vniverse. *a* **1680** CHARNOCK *Attrib. God* (1682) 420 This is but a small Landskip of some of his Works of Power, the outsides or extremities of it. **1692** BENTLEY *Boyle Lect.* x. (1715) 366 This short but true Sketch and faithful Landskip of Popery. **1709** MRS. MANLEY *New Atal.* (ed. 2) II. 57 A Feint, a distant Landshape of immortal joys.

†**e.** A compendium, epitome.

1656 in Clarendon *Hist. Reb.* xv. §113 That Landskip [*MS.* lantskipp] of iniquity, that Sink of Sin, and that Compendium of baseness, who now calls himself our Protector. *a* **1670** HACKET *Abp. Williams* II. (1693) 59 London.. is.. our England of England, and our Landskip and Representation of the whole Island. **1679** C. NESSE *Antid. agst. Popery* 104 To give but a scantling and landskip of some of them. *Ibid* 197 This scantling landskip or compendium. [**1826** SCOTT *Woodst.* xxv, That landscape of iniquity, that sink of sin,.. Oliver Cromwell.]

†**f.** A bird's-eye view; a plan, sketch, map.

1642 HOWELL *For. Trav.* (Arb.) 21 Some have used to get on the top of the highest Steeple, where one may view.. all the Countrey circumjacent.. and so take a Landskip of it. *c* **1645** —— *Lett.* (1726) 87 If you saw the Landskip of it [*viz.* a house] you would be mightily taken with it. **1657** R. LIGON *Barbadoes* (1673) 2 The weather clearing up, the Master and Mates drew out several plots and Landscapes: which they had formerly taken upon the Coast of France and England. ? *a* **1700** *Frost of 1683-4* (Percy Soc.) p. xiv, There was first a map, or landskip, cut in copper, representing all the manner of the camp. **1723** *Pres. State Russia* I. 306 It rather resembles a Landskip of many Boroughs than a City.

†**g.** The depiction or description of something in words.

1681-6 J. SCOTT *Chr. Life* (1747) III. 119 Precepts and Discourses of Virtue are only the dead Pictures and artificial Landskips and Descriptions of it. **1689** BURNET *Tracts* I. 5, I will not describe the Valley of Dauphine, all to Chambery, nor entertain you with a Landskip of the Country, which deserves a better Pencil than mine. **1704** ADDISON *Italy* Pref. (1733) 12 To compare the Natural Face of the Country with the Landskips that the Poets have given us of it. **1712** —— *Spect.* No. 416 ¶5 In this case the Poet seems to get the better of Nature; he takes indeed the Landskip after her, but gives it more vigorous Touches.

h. Other *transf.* and *fig.* uses.

1952 G. SARTON *Hist. Sci.* I. x. 256 Let us return again to Athens and try to consider the intellectual landscape from the point of view of a well-educated man. **1953** A. HUXLEY *Let.* 31 Oct. (1969) 687 The jewelled palaces.. may.. be actual *choses vues*—items in the ordinary landscape of certain kinds of people. **1963** *Listener* 7 Mar. 405/1 The landscape of international politics is now very different from what it was only two or three years ago.

5. *attrib.* and *Comb.*, as ***landscape art, book-plate, draughtsman, -lover, -work***; **landscape architect**, a practitioner of landscape architecture; **landscape architecture**, the planning of parks or gardens to form an attractive landscape, often in association with the design of buildings, roads, etc.; **landscape-gardening**, the art of laying out grounds so as to produce the effect of natural scenery; so ***landscape-garden***, (also as vb.) ***-gardener***; **landscape lens**, a lens used in photographing landscape; **landscape marble**, a variety of marble which shows dendritic markings resembling shrubbery or trees; **landscape mirror**, = CLAUDE LORRAINE GLASS (*Cent. Dict.*); **landscape-painter**, one who paints landscapes, a landscapist; so ***landscape-painting***; †**landscape-worker**, a landscapist.

1874 R. TYRWHITT *Sketch. Club* p. vii, A series of papers on *Landscape Art—that is to say on all works of art in which landscape is concerned. **1863** *6th Ann. Rep. Board of Commissioners Central Park* (N.Y.) *1862* between pp. 60–61 (Map), Olmsted and Vaux, *Landscape Architects. **1879** *Chicago Tribune* 3 May 1/3 (Advt.), H. W. S. Cleveland, Landscape Architect. **1890** C. ELIOT *Let.* 3 Dec. in *C. Eliot: Landscape Architect* (1924) xv. 273 Landscape gardening is that part of the landscape architect's labor which is directed to the development of formal or natural beauty by means of removing or setting out plants. **1927** T. H. MAWSON *Life & Work Eng. Landscape Architect* xiv. 160 A young and able landscape architect.. had heard me lecture in England. **1967** G. COLLENS in A. E. Weddle *Techniques Landscape Archit.* ii. 33/1 The employer should start by setting out his requirements as a basis for discussion with the landscape architect. **1972** *Times* 15 Sept. 2/1 For decades.. landscape architects' services were not sufficiently appreciated. **1840** J. C. LOUDON in H. Repton *Landscape Gardening & Landscape Archit. of H. Repton* (new ed.) p. vii, These writings [*sc.* of Gilpin and Price] are full of the most valuable instruction for the gardener, relative to the general composition of landscape scenery, and *landscape architecture. **1865** F. L. OLMSTED *Let.* 1 Aug. in *F. L. Olmsted: Landscape Architect* (1928) II. vi. 74, I am all the time bothered with the miserable nomenclature of L.A. *Landscape* is not a good word, *Architecture* is not; the combination is not—*Gardening* is worse. **1891** C. ELIOT in *C. Eliot: Landscape Architect* (1924) xx. 366 We cannot avoid seeing behind the fair figures of Gardening and Building a third figure of still nobler aspect.. the art which, for want of a better name, is sometimes called Landscape Architecture. **1915** S. PARSONS *Art of Landscape Archit.* p. vi, The study of nature assisted by the best examples is the proper field for the study of landscape architecture. **1967** A. E. WEDDLE (*title*) Techniques in landscape architecture. **1880** WARREN *Book-plates* vi. 52 The *landscape book-plate.. was rather the lineal descendant of the Chippendale than of the Jacobean style. **1861** THORNBURY *Turner* I. 50 Dayes, the *landscape-draftsman and geographical artist. **1806** J. DALLAWAY *Observ. Eng. Archit.* 245 Detached pieces of architecture are essential in creating a *landscape garden. **1836** F. A. KEMBLE *Let.* 1 Mar. in *Rec. Later Life* (1882) I. 45 Adam and Eve landscape-gardened in Paradise, you know. **1891** W. MORRIS *News from Nowhere* iii. 17 The other day we heard that the philistines were going to landscape-garden it [*sc.* the place]. **1941** E. WILSON *Wound & Bow* ii. 119 When the transfer [of the land] had been effected, Mrs. Kipling set out to landscape-garden it. **1974** 'M. INNES' *Appleby's Other Story* i. 5 You don't care, Tommy, for wild nature tamed and landscape-gardened? *a* **1763** W. SHENSTONE *Works* (1764) II. 139, I have used the word *landskip-gardiners; because in pursuance of our present taste in gardening, every good painter of landskip appears to me the most proper designer. **1788** A. SEWARD *Let.* 14 Oct. (1811) II. 172, I should suppose nobody has ever been so well qualified as yourself [*sc.* H. Repton] for the profession you purpose to assume, that of landscape gardener. **1827** STEUART *Planter's G.* (1828) 386 Useful to the General Planter, as well as to the Landscape Gardener. **1870** LOWELL *Study Wind.* (1886) 333 The landscape-gardeners of literature give to a paltry half-acre the air of a park. *a* **1763** W. SHENSTONE *Works* (1764) II. 125 Gardening may be divided into three species —kitchen-gardening—parterre gardening—and *landskip, or picturesque-gardening: which latter.. consists in pleasing the imagination by scenes of grandeur, beauty, or variety. **1788** H. REPTON in D. Stroud *Humphry Repton* (1962) ii. 37, I mean in this place to keep an account of the time employed and expenses incurr'd in this service at the same rate as if employ'd in my profession of Landscape Gardening. **1805** H. REPTON (*title*) Observations on the Theory and Practice of Landscape Gardening. **1861** DELAMER *Fl. Gard.* 5 A park in the Brownean style of landscape-gardening. **1938** *New Statesman* 8 Jan. 56/2 In Andrew Young there are touches of a lesser, a more landscape-gardening Frost. **1946** R. MACAULAY *They went to Portugal* 137 Landscape gardening always showed him [*sc.* William Beckford] at his most likeable. **1975** *Garden History* III. II. 1 Mavis Batey's essay on Goldsmith, 'An Indictment of Landscape Gardening', is the clearest and best exposition we have had of that frequent eighteenth-century occurrence, the destruction of villages and hamlets to further the creation of landscape gardens. **1890** *Anthony's Photogr. Bull.* III. 179 A fairly good camera and a single *landscape lens. **1882** TENNYSON *To Virgil* ii, *Landscape-lover, lord of language. **1816** R. JAMESON *Min.* II. 196 It resembles in many respects the *landscape marble. **1883** *Encycl. Brit.* XV. 529 The well-known landscape marble or Cotham stone. *a* **1763** W. SHENSTONE *Works* (1764) II. 129 The *landskip painter is the gardiner's best designer. **1779** T. BLAIKIE *Diary Scotch Gardener* (1931) 159 Those Gardens are Layd out under the Derections of Mr Robert one of the first Landskape painters in France. **1793** A. MURPHY *Tacitus* (1811) I. p. lxii, What landskip painter can equal the description [etc.]. **1842** TENNYSON *Ld. of Burleigh* 7 He is but a landscape-painter, And a village maiden she. **1861** THORNBURY *Turner* I. 22 Most true, yet most poetic of landscape-painters. **1937** *Discovery* July 211 The greatest of English landscape painters. **1974** B. MASSINGHAM *Turn on Fountains* iv. 65 They met a landscape painter.. who confessed that he 'could do nothing with Connemara'. **1706** *Art of Painting* (1744) 406 He understood *landskip-painting and perform'd in it to perfection. **1841** W. SPALDING *Italy & It. Isl.* II. 402 Landscape-painting.. may be said to have owed its origin to Titian. **1632** SHERWOOD, **Landskip worke* (in painting), *païsage, grotesques.* **1598** R. HAYDOCKE tr. *Lomazzo* III. i. 94 Barnazano, an excellent *Landskip-worker.

landscape, *v.* [f. the sb.] **1.** *trans.* To represent as a landscape; to picture, depict.

1661 HOLYDAY *Surv. World* To Rdr., As weary travelour ..oft.. Landskippes the Vale, with pencil; placing here Medow, there Arable [etc.]. **1868** BROWNING *Ring & Bk.* I. 1352 Putting solely that On panel somewhere in the House of Fame, Landscaping what I saved, not what I saw.

2. To lay out (a garden, etc.) as a landscape; to conceal or embellish (a building, road, etc.) by making it part of a continuous and harmonious landscape. Also *transf.* So **'landscaping** *vbl. sb.*

1927 [implied by LANDSCAPED *ppl. a.*]. **1930** *N.Y. Times* 9 Feb. XI. 2/1 Suburban developers and home owners are paying more attention to landscaping today. **1930** *Publishers' Weekly* 15 Feb. 858/2 Landscaping is about to become the topic of smart conversation, with the result that garden books should sell as never before. **1943** FORSHAW & ABERCROMBIE *County of London Plan* vii. 103 Landscaping must play an important part in the layout of these open spaces particularly those which provide a setting for the houses and blocks of flats. **1957** *Listener* 13 June 949 The planners intend to plant trees round the perimeter and generally landscape the whole area. **1959** *Motor* 22 Apr. 410/1 New Roads.. are 'landscaped into the countryside and not stuck on it'. **1962** *Daily Tel.* 23 May 21/1 Some aspects of road landscaping were still not fully accepted in Britain. **1966** MRS. L. B. JOHNSON *White House Diary* 11 Jan. (1970) 350 The check would be given to landscape the new automobile entrance of the National Zoo. **1974** *Country Life* 17 Oct. 1095/1 The National Trust has landscaped the island.

landscaped ('lændskeɪpt), *ppl. a.* [f. prec.] Laid out as a landscape; embellished by landscaping. Also *transf.*, of an office.

1927 *Brit. Weekly* 15 Dec. 283/2 Even factories.. frequently have lovely landscaped grounds. **1957** V. NABOKOV *Pnin* 9 An artificial lake in the middle of a landscaped campus. **1959** A. HARRINGTON *Life in 'Crystal Palace'* (1960) viii. 112 Our landscaped grounds.. will flower. **1968** *Guardian* 17 June 8/3 The open 'landscaped' office, or *burolandschaft* as it is called by its German inventors. **1968** *Daily Tel.* (Colour Suppl.) 29 Nov. 56/2 The American reaction now is for open-plan 'landscaped' offices where all workers, regardless of status, are visually connected in one low horizontal block. **1970** *Times* 9 Feb. 13/2 It will be an eight-storey block with about 60,000 sq. ft. in a landscaped site. **1974** *Daily Tel.* (Colour Suppl.) 8 Mar. 18/2 The initial impression one gets of a landscaped office is often one of irregularity and informality.

landscapist ('lændskeɪpɪst). [f. LANDSCAPE *sb.* + -IST.] **1.** A painter of landscape, landscape-painter.

1843 RUSKIN *Mod. Paint.* II. I. vii. §16 (1851) I. 90 The professed landscapists of the Dutch school. **1869** —— *Q. of Air* 199 If you are a landscapist, Turner must be your only guide. **1880** *Athenæum* 29 May 700/2 For the greater number of our landscapists Girtin and Turner have lived in vain. **1881** GRANT WHITE *Eng. Without & Within* 455 Like the ideal composition of an imaginative landscapist.

2. A landscape-gardener; one skilled in landscaping roads, offices, etc. Also **'landscaper**.

1936 T. Sharp *Eng. Panorama* iii. 48 The activities of the landscapists became founded on a realization and acceptance of natural informality. **1963** *Times* 4 June 12/5 Whereas seventeenth-century landscapers might have moved a tree across an estate, we now move them 30–50 miles. **1963** *New Society* 20 June 26/1 The British method of inviting a landscape committee (few of them landscapists) to study the landscaping of the road. **1965** I. Fleming *Man with Golden Gun* vii. 101 He soon came to the end of the young shrubs and guinea grass the landscaper had laid on. **1967** *House & Garden* Mar. 68/1 Several famous landscapists, including Bridgeman. **1974** *Daily Tel.* (Colour Suppl.) 8 Mar. 18/1 Open plan, say many landscapers, was ..only too often a mere space-saving exercise.

Landseer ('lændsɪə(r)). The name of the English painter Sir Edwin *Landseer* (1802–73) used *attrib.* in **Landseer Newfoundland** to designate a black and white Newfoundland dog of a type once painted by him. Also *absol.*

1877 G. Stables *Pract. Kennel Guide* ix. 98 The black-and-white, or Landseer Newfoundland. This is quite a distinct breed, not as yet properly recognised at shows. *Ibid.* x. 113 A white chest in a Newfoundland or Retriever, indicates a cross with the Landseer or Setter. **1927** W. A. Wetwan in C. C. Sanderson *Pedigree Dogs* 281 In 1836 Sir Edwin Landseer painted a white and black Newfoundland ..imbuing the mind of the great British public with the idea that black and white was the only correct Newfoundland wear... 'Landseers', which are true to type, are a very beautiful dog. **1971** F. Hamilton *World Encycl. Dogs* 164 In 1779 a well-known English naturalist described a very fine specimen in Northumberland, England, and this dog was later identified as a Landseer. *Ibid.* 165 (*caption*) Taaran Taru..is a typical example of the Landseer Newfoundland.

Land's end.

†**1.** = land-end. *Obs.*

c **1394** *P. Pl. Crede* 437 And at þe londes ende laye a litell crom-bolle. **15..** *Wife of Auchtermuchty* (Bann. MS.) 9 He lowsit the pluche at the landis end, And draif his oxin hame at evin. **1562** J. Heywood *Prov. & Epigr.* (1867) 68 Thou gossepst at home, to meete me at landis ende.

2. The extremity or furthest projecting point of a country. Now only as the proper name of the most westerly point of Great Britain.

14.. *Sailing Directions Circumnavig. Eng.* (Hakluyt Soc. 1889) 17 A newe cours and tide betwene Englonde and Irlonde and the Londis end. *Ibid.* 18 The Londes end of Irlonde. **1604** E. G[rimstone] *D'Acosta's Hist. Indies* iii. xi. 156 They passed on no further, neyther could they discover the lands end (which some holde to be there). **1793** *Phil. Trans.* LXXXIII. 190 We..were barely able to lay a course through the passage between those islands and the Land's End.

'land-,service. Service performed on land; military, as opposed to naval, service.

a **1586** Sidney *Arcadia* (1622) 123 Seeing wherein the Sea-discipline differed from Land-service. **1597** Shaks. *2 Hen. IV*, i. ii. 154 As I was then aduised by my learned Councel, in the lawes of this Land-seruice, I did not come. **1697** Dryden *Æneis* Ded. f3, I Writ not always in the proper terms of Navigation, Land-Service, or in the Cant of any Profession. **1725** De Foe *Voy. round World* (1840) 57 A good army for land-service. **1801** T. S. Surr *Splendid Misery* II. 194 Salano, a Neapolitan pirate originally..took to the land service afterwards, and committed murders out of number. **1819** Byron *Juan* i. iv, The prince is all for the land-service, Forgetting Duncan, Nelson, Howe, and Jervis.

landsfolk: see landfolk.

landsgrave: see landgrave.

landshard ('læn(d)ʃəd). *dial.* Also **landsherd, landchet, lanchet, lanshet, langet.** [f. land *sb.*[1] + shard *sb.* The forms show contamination with the synonymous *lynchet.*] = lynchet.

1813 T. Davis *Agric. Wilts* App. 259 Linch, Linchet, or *Landshard*, the mere green-sward dividing two pieces of arable in a common-field called in Hants, a lay bank. **1847** Halliwell, *Langet*, a strip of ground. *West.* **1886** W. *Somerset Gloss.*, *Landsherd*, a ridge or strip of land left unploughed or untilled. **1891** T. Hardy *Tess* (1900) 104/2 A stretch of a hundred odd acres..rising above stony lanchets or lynchets. **1893** H. J. Moule *Old Dorset* 81 The terraces called landchets or linchets.

land-ship. [land *sb.* 11.] **a.** A wagon or other vehicle serving the same purpose on land as a ship on the sea; *spec.* = tank *sb.*[7] **b.** A ship erected and kept on land for training purposes.

[**1627** J. Taylor *Armado* sig. B1[v], (*heading*) A Navy of Land Ships.] **1837** *Penny Mag.* 22 July 276/1 The ox-carts of the Pampas..are quaintly termed by the natives, *barcos de tierra*, i.e., 'land-ships'. **1869** *Cassell's Mag.* Jan. 156/2 In some of the best schools of France and Belgium, it has long been a custom to erect a dry land-ship in the playground. **1907** L. Osbourne *Adventurer* xiii. 159 The land-ship..was hardly more than an aluminium shell..requiring weeks of labor, possibly months, to make her habitable and ready. Ready? For what? To sail those vast and billowy plains? **1916** *Daily News* 19 Sept. 1/2 The new land-ships or tanks did invaluable work. **1916** *Daily Mirror* 22 Nov. 1/1 (*caption*) To-day we are able to publish the first photograph of one of his Majesty's land ships which have been making such successful cruises on the sea of mud on the Somme. **1934** W. S. Churchill *Gt. War* II. xxxv. 519/1 The next day, the 20th [February 1915], I sent for Mr. Tennyson-d'Eyncourt..and convened a conference... As the result of it the Landships Committee of the Admiralty was formed. **1972** *Times Lit. Suppl.* 4 Feb. 113/4 The original initiative in tank development, the so-called 'landships', was naval rather than military.

'land-side.

†**1.** The shore. *Obs.*

a **1533** Ld. Berners *Huon* cxxiii. 443 He caste his ancre nere to the land syde. *Ibid.* clxi. 623 And then the waues brought me to the lond syde.

2. The side towards the land or on which there is land (not water).

1840 Thirlwall *Greece* VII. 343 To assault the city on the land-side. **1852** C. W. Hoskyns *Talpa* 181 Playing upon the edge, or land-side of the trench as it advances. **1875** W. McIlwraith *Guide Wigtownshire* 51 On the accessible land-side a double line of protection was thus formed.

3. The flat side of a plough which is turned towards the unploughed land.

1765 A. Dickson *Treat. Agric.* (ed. 2) 239 The plough being confined on the land-side, and at liberty on the fur-side, which naturally gives it less land. **1875** in Knight *Dict. Mech.*

landsknecht: see lansquenet.

landslip ('lændslɪp). The sliding down of a mass of land on a mountain or cliff side; land which has so fallen. Also *fig.* and *attrib.*

1679 *Roxb. Ballads* IV. 549 Paint dismal Ruin stalking in the rear, Than Landslip Desolation far and near. **1774** Goldsm. *Nat. Hist.* (1776) I. 158 Those disruptions of hills, which are known by the name of land-slips. **1830** Lyell *Princ. Geol.* I. 276 There was an immense land-slip from this cliff, by which Dover was shaken as if by an earthquake. **1872** Baker *Nile Tribut.* iv. 62 The valley was a succession of landslips and watercourses. **1894** *Pop. Sci. Monthly* June 281 Landslip lakes have been noticed by Lyell, and Gilbert records the formation of small lakes behind landslip terraces.

Hence **'landslipped, 'landslippy** *adjs.*, characterized by landslips.

1885 H. O. Forbes *Nat. Wand. E. Archip.* 474 An eerie and dangerous path, dilapidated and often landslipped. **1893** G. Allen *Scallywag* I. 49 Where the rocks towards the slope were loosest and most landslippy.

‖**Landsmål** ('lantsmɔːl). Also **Landsmaal.** [Norw., f. *land* country + *mål* language.] A literary form of Norwegian devised by the Norwegian philologist Ivar Aasen (1813–1896) from the country dialects most closely descended from Old Norse, and considered to be a 'purer' form of the Norwegian language than the official Riksmål or Dano-Norwegian.

The *Landsmål* controversy followed the appearance of Aasen's grammar and dictionary (1848 and 1850); in 1885 *Landsmål* was given equal status with Dano-Norwegian.

1886 *Encycl. Brit.* XXI. 374/1 By the study of the Modern Norwegian dialects and the mother language, Old Norwegian, the eminent philologist J. Aasen was led to undertake the bold project of constructing ..a Norwegian-Norwegian..language, the so-called 'Landsmål'. **1906** *Westm. Gaz.* 10 Aug. 2/3 The party programmes are said to lack definiteness, but that of the Liberals comprises..the official recognition of the 'Landsmal', or Norwegian of Norway as against the Dano-Norwegian, which is at present the language of the Government. **1911** [see Dano-]. **1924** *Glasgow Herald* 14 Nov. 7 Let him perpend the circumstances of the Czech revival or of the Norwegian landsmaal movement. **1927** *Observer* 6 Nov. 12 Now Norway has a linguistic national movement, called the Landsmaal or Real Norwegian Language-movement, which holds that the language generally used in Norway is not Norwegian but a Danish dialect, and their aim is to root out that dialect and make the Landsmaal compulsory. **1933** [see Dano-]. **1957** T. K. Derry *Short Hist. Norway* ix. 190 For the peasantry, in the west at least, *landsmaal* had become a shibboleth by which to distinguish the true democrat from the adherents of the language of foreign snobbery. **1961** L. F. Brosnahan *Sounds of Lang.* ix. 205 The Landsmål, a somewhat more artificial creation based on the main dialects of the west of the country.

landsman ('lændzmən). Pl. **landsmen.** [f. genit. of land *sb.*[1] + man *sb.* Cf. landman.]

1. †**a.** A native of a particular country. *Obs.*

c **1000** Ælfric *Hom.* II. 26 Twegen landes menn and an ælþeodiȝ. **11..** *O.E. Chron.* an. 1068 (Laud MS.) Ða comon ða landes menn toȝeanes him & hine ofsloȝon. *c* **1200** *Trin. Coll. Hom.* 197 Oðer kinnes neddre is ut in oðer londe..and te londes men hire bigaleð oðer wile and swo lacheð and doð of liue. **1387** Trevisa *Higden* (Rolls) VII. 33 It were a wrecched schame þat a newe comynge schulde putte olde londesmen [L. *veteres incolas*] out of here place.

b. One's fellow-countryman.

1598 Sylvester *Du Bartas* ii. i. iii. *Furies* 806 If (brave Lands-men) your war-thirst be such [orig. *Que si tant, ô Francois, vous cerchez les batailles*]..What holds you here? **1823** Scott *Quentin D.* vi, I am innocent—I am your own native landsman. **1882–3** *Schaff's Encycl. Relig. Knowl.* I. 319/2 [He] boldly dissuaded his landsmen from idolatry. **1950** B. Malamud in *Partisan Rev.* Sept.–Oct. 664 With, after all, a *landsman*, he would have less to fear than with a complete stranger. **1971** *Islander* (Victoria, B.C.) 3 Jan. 10/3, I found out the mate was a landsman of mine who came from Helsingfors. **1973** *Listener* 20 Sept. 377/1 You put on your Shabbat suit..and descended on a nearby relative or *landsman*.

2. a. One who lives or has his business on land: opposed to *seaman*. **b.** *Naut.* 'The rating formerly of those on board a ship who had never been to sea, and who were usually stationed among the waisters or after-guard' (Adm. Smyth).

1666–7 Pepys *Diary* 2 Jan., The French..have certainly shipped landsmen, great numbers, at Brest. **1788** Burns *1st Ep. to R. Graham* 50 Weak, timid landsmen on life's stormy main. **1830** Marryat *King's Own* i, Employed, as a landsman usually is, in the afterguard, or waist, of the ship. **1845** Darwin *Voy. Nat.* x. (1879) 208 Sailors..can make out a distant object much better than a landsman. **1883** Stevenson *Treas. Isl.* iv. xviii, Thomas Redruth.. landsman, shot by the mutineers.

'land-spring. 'A spring which comes into action only after heavy rains' (Webster). Also *fig.*

1642 Rogers *Naaman* To Rdr., All he hath is drawn from a land-spring of naturall parts and gifts. **1675** E. Wilson *Spadacr. Dunelm.* 15 Such are only Land-springs, and in no sort to be called perpetual Springs. **1774** G. White *Selborne* 14 Feb., Landsprings, which we call levants. **1824** Miss Mitford *Village* Ser. i. (1863) 37 Our land-springs were dried up: our wells were exhausted. **1898** Watts-Dunton *Aylwin* (1900) 109/1 Enormous masses of the cliff newly disintegrated by the landsprings.

Hence **'land-,springy** *a.*, full of land-springs.

1767 Bush *Hibernia Cur.* (1769) 80 In very moist, land-springy grounds.

landsquenet, obs. form of lansquenet.

‖**landsturm** ('lant-ʃtʊrm). [Ger. = lit. 'landstorm'.]

In Germany, Switzerland, etc., a general levy in time of war; the forces so called out; the militia force consisting of those men not serving in the army or navy or in the *landwehr*.

1814 *Alpine Sk.* i. 20 Some skirmishing between about sixty Cossacks..and a strong party of the *landstrum* [*sic*]. **1866** *Cornh. Mag.* Nov. 553 The 'Landsturm'..should only be employed in the home districts. **1874** Miss R. H. Busk *Tirol* ix. 288 The *Landsturm* was out.

'land-sur,veying. The process, art, or profession of measuring, and making plans of, landed property.

1771 Breaks (*title*) A complete system of Land-Surveying. **1849** *Chambers Inform.* II. 623/1 Trigonometry ..is of great importance..in land-surveying. *Ibid.* 624/1 A principle of measuring by triangles, which is common alike to land-surveying and the trigonometrical surveys of engineers. **1858** Simmonds *Dict. Trade*, *Land-surveying Chain-maker*, a manufacturer of the chain-links used by surveyors.

'land-sur,veyor.

†**1.** = *landing-surveyor* (see landing *vbl. sb.* 8).

1755 Chamberlayne *State Gt. Brit.* ii. iii. 58 Port of Leith..William Towrie..Land-Surveyor. **1776** *Addit. to Pope* I. 2 *note*, When George I. made him [Rowe] one of the land surveyors of the port of London.

2. One whose professional occupation is to measure land, draw up plans of estates, and the like.

1792 B. Marston in *N.E. Hist. & Gen. Register* (1873) XXVII. 399, I am engaged to go out with a large Company who are going to make a Settlement on the Iland Bulam.. as their Land Surveyor General. *a* **1815** G. Rose *Diaries* (1860) II. 443 Mr. Wakefield, the land-surveyor, was at Cuffnells. **1853** Herschel *Pop. Lect. Sci.* ii. vii. (1873) 54 The triangle in question is always what a land surveyor would call a favourable one for calculation.

landswoman. [After landsman.] A woman accustomed to live mainly or entirely on the land; one skilled in land-work.

1837 *Penny Mag.* 14 Oct. 398/1 The scene is presented exactly as it appeared to the eye and imagination of a landswoman. **1891** H. S. Merriman *Prisoners & Capt.* III. viii. 144 The strangeness of a landswoman to all things maritime. **1923** *Weekly Dispatch* 1 Apr. 7 Miss Ford might be described as 'the complete landswoman'. She can milk, do anything with horses, and do field tasks.

‖**land-tag** ('lanttɑːx). Also 6 **landtaye**, 7 **landt-tag**; (*anglicized*) **land-day.** [Ger. (MHG. *lanttac*) = lit. 'land-day'.] In Germany, the diet or legislative body of a state; formerly, the Diet of Empire or of the German Confederation.

1591 Wotton *Let.* 27 Feb. in *Reliq. W.* (1685) 628 Of our Landtaye we hear nothing yet, but the necessity is such as it must be shortly. **1665** *Lond. Gaz.* No. 11/1 It's now determined *in Concilio Senatorum*, at Warsaw, that the Parliament shall begin the 17th of March, and the Landt-tag the third of February. **1668** *Ibid.* No. 225/2 The Land-day for Prussia is to begin the third day of the next month at Marienburgh, in Order to the General Diet. **1684** *Scanderberg Rediv.* ii. 22 They have a Convention held in each County, call'd The Landt-Tag, six weeks before the Session of the Diet.

'land-tax. A tax assessed upon landed property.

1689 Bp. G. Hooper (*title*) The Parsons Case under the Present Land-Tax. **1690** *Consid. Raising Money* 34 There will be nothing..so much for the good of the Nation, as a Land-Tax. **1709** *Royal Proclam.* in *Lond. Gaz.* No. 4510/1 Receivers or Collectors of the Land-Taxes for the years 1708 and 1709. **1827** Hallam *Const. Hist.* (1876) III. xv. 135 The first land-tax was imposed in 1690, at the rate of three shillings in the pound on the rental. **1858** J. B. Norton *Topics* 82 Pitt's scheme of the year 1798 for the redemption of the land-tax. **1882** *Macm. Mag.* XLVI. 366 The old military tenures were abolished and the land-tax was imposed by way of compensation to the Crown for the dues which it thereby lost.

attrib. and *Comb.* **1740** Lady Hartford *Corr.* (1805) II. 92 The land-tax gatherers. **1765–93** Blackstone *Comm.*

(ed. 12) 174 The land-tax and malt-tax acts are passed for one year only. **1858** LD. ST. LEONARDS *Handy-Bk. Prop. Law* ix. 62 The Clerk of the Land-tax Commissioners.

land-tie ('lændtaɪ). A rod, beam, piece of masonry, etc. imbedded in the earth at one end, and connected at the other end with a wall or other building in order to secure it in position, or to relieve it from the pressure of a bank, etc.

1715 LEONI *Palladio's Archit.* (1742) I. 82 The Banks are exposed to be wash'd away by the Waters, whence the Bridge in such a case would become destitute of Land-tyes, and remain an Island. *Ibid.* II. 27 Another Wall with Stone Land-ties, that enter'd into the Hill. **1874** THEARLE *Naval Archit.* 9 In the Royal dockyards, where the ground of the building slip is paved with hewn stone, it is customary to alternate with the latter transverse baulks of timber, termed 'land ties'. **1875** KNIGHT *Dict. Mech.*, *Land-tie*, a rod securing a face-wall to a bank.

landward ('lændwəd), *adv.* and *a.* Also 6 landewarde, *Sc.* 5–8 landwart, 8 landart, 9 -ert. [f. LAND *sb.*[1]: see -WARD.]

A. *adv.*

1. In phrases with preps.

†a. *to landward, in (the) landward*: in the country, as opposed to the town. *Sc.*

1424 *Sc. Acts Jas. I*, c. 21 (1814) II. 8/1 Þai..sall haue a certane takyn to landwart of þe schireff & in burowis of þe aldermen & þe bal3eis. **1457** *Ibid.* 49/1 Within burowis and commonys to landwart. **1536** BELLENDEN *Cron. Scot.* XII. v. (1821) II. 264 Ane vailyeant and lusty man, of greter curage and spreit than ony man that was nurist in landwart, as he was. *a* **1572** KNOX *Hist. Ref.* Wks. 1846 I. 276 Als-weill within townes as to landwarte. **1753** *Scots Mag.* Apr. 203/1 No part of the parish is to landward.

b. *to (the) landward*: towards or in the direction of the land; on or to the land side (*of*).

c **1450** *St. Cuthbert* (Surtees) 631 Whils þai wer þus to landward boune. **1500–20** DUNBAR *Poems* xxxix. 17 In burghis, to landwart and to sie. **1555** EDEN *Decades* 352 Vppon the innermoste necke to the landewarde is a tufte of trees. **1625** K. LONG tr. *Barclay's Argenis* II. i. 68 Where the mountaine looks to landward of the ile. *a* **1674** MILTON *Hist. Mosc.* Wks. 1738 II. 129 To the Land-ward [stand] Mezen and Slobotca..: To Seaward lies the Cape of Candinos. **1725** DE FOE *Voy. round World* (1840) 65 As for fortifications to the landward, they had none. **1853** KANE *Grinnell Exp.* xii. (1856) 86 Except to landward, there is nothing to arrest the eye. **1876** T. HARDY *Ethelberta* (1890) 26 On the broad moor to landward of the town.

2. Towards the land; = 1 b.

1610 HOLLAND *Camden's Brit.* I. 318 Couched betweene a high cliffe sea-ward and as high an hill land-ward. **1816** WORDSW. *Ode, 'Imagination—ne'er before content'* 13 A sudden shower That land-ward stretches from the sea. **1868–70** MORRIS *Earthly Par.* I. 237 Landward she saw the low green meadows lie. **1873** BLACK *Pr. Thule* vi. 90 Deep and narrow valleys that ran landward.

3. *Sc.* In the country; = 1 a. *rare.*

1827 SCOTT *Surg. Dau.* i, Within burgh, and not landward.

B. *adj.*

1. *Sc.* Belonging to, inhabiting the country; country-, rustic.

1533 BELLENDEN *Livy* I. (1822) 5 It wes callit eftir Pagus, that is to say, ane landwart towne. **1585** JAS. I *Ess. Poesie* (Arb.) 63 Gif zour purpose be of landwart effairis, To vse corruptit and vplandis wordis. **1596** DALRYMPLE tr. *Leslie's Hist. Scot.* x. 344 The burgessis, and landwart men. **1637–50** ROW *Hist. Kirk* (Wodrow Soc.) 24 The communion to be celebrated within burghs four times in the yeare, in landwart twise. **1649** BP. GUTHRIE *Mem.* (1702) 54 A Landward Kirk in Galloway. **1676** W. ROW *Contn. Blair's Autobiog.* x. (1848) 168 The common people in the landward round about the town. **17..** RAMSAY *Birth of Drumlanrig* ii, Some landart lass. **1725** —— *Gent. Sheph.* IV. ii, I've shook off my landwart cast In foreign cities. **1816** SCOTT *Old Mort.* viii, The door was locked, as is usual in landward towns in this country. *Note*, A landward town is a dwelling situated in the country. **1854** H. MILLER *Sch. & Schm.* (1858) 362 The landward contemporaries of my grandfather. **1876** GRANT *Burgh Sch. Scot.* II. ii. 127 The town councils generally took more interest in the welfare of a school..than the landward heritors.

2. Lying or situated towards the land (as opposed to the sea); *occas.* belonging to the land.

1845 STOCQUELER *Handbk. Brit. India* (1854) 129 The Upper and Lower Circular Roads, which nearly encompass the city on its eastern or landward side. **1859** R. F. BURTON *Centr. Afr.* in *Jrnl. Geogr. Soc.* XXIX. 436 The tree..ceases to be found at any distance beyond the landward counterslope, and it is unknown in the interior. **1865** *Reader* 2 Sept. 253/2 This barbarian innocency on the part of our landward population as to the teeming plenty of the deep. **1881** J. GRANT *Cameronians* I. i. 16 On the landward side the view was different.

3. *Comb.* **landward-bred** *a.* (*Sc.*), country-bred.

1816 SCOTT *Old Mort.* xiv, I am landward-bred. **1893** STEVENSON *Catriona* 7 If you are landward bred it will be different.

Hence **'landwardness** (*landertness*) *Sc.*, rusticity.

1882 STEVENSON *Fam. Stud.* 61 He [*sc.* Burns] affected a rusticity or landertness.

landwards ('lændwədz), *adv.* [f. LAND *sb.*[1]: see -WARDS.] = prec. A 2. †Also *to the landwards.*

1574 W. BOURNE *Regt. for Sea* xiv. (1577) 41 a, If you come directly to the landwardes. **1833** HT. MARTINEAU *Tale of Tyne* v. 82 Not only was there this treacherous Cut to beguile them landwards..but there was a labyrinth at sea. **1885** *Law Times* LXXIX. 317/2 The soil as far landwards as where the ordinary high-water mark was before the construction of the pier.

'land-,water. a. Water that flows through or over land, as opposed to sea water. b. A land-flood. c. Water free from ice along a frozen shore.

1531–2 *Act 23 Hen. VIII* c. 5 ¶, Lande waters, and other outragious springes in and upon medowes, pastures, and other lowe groundes. **1598** W. PHILLIPS *Linschoten* (1864) 192 The land-waters that by the continuall raine falleth from the Hills. **1604** E. G[RIMSTONE] *D'Acosta's Hist. Indies* II. vi. 91 Land-waters, as rivers, fountaines, brookes, springs, floods, and lakes. *a* **1631** DONNE *Serm.* li. 520 Sudden riches come like a Landwater and bring much foulnesse with them. **1725** DE FOE *Voy. round World* (1840) 335 Which river they supposed to be..swelled with a land-water. **1807** VANCOUVER *Agric. Devon* (1813) 297 No springs or land-waters are to be found here. **1856** KANE *Arct. Expl.* II. xxvi. 264 We..found ourselves in a stretch of the land-water wide enough to give us rowing-room.

'land-way.

†1. A way or path over land. Also *advb.* = by land. *Obs.*

c **1250** *Gen. & Ex.* 2681 Bi a lond wei3e he wente ri3t. *c* **1470** HARDING *Chron.* CLXXVIII. xv, Thei tooke none hede of shippes home again But landeway ride for all the Scottes dain.

†2. *local.* A path by which coal is landed. *Obs.*

1603 OWEN *Pembrokesh.* xi. (1891) 89 The people carried the coales vppon their backes alonge stayres which they called lande wayes.

3. *U.S.* A road giving access to land.

1899 D. P. COREY *Hist. Nalden* 90 The land-way and drift-way along the five acre lots ended at the head of the North River.

So **'landways** *adv.*, by land, overland.

a **1670** SPALDING *Troub. Chas. I* (1829) 14 He has them landways to London, and from thence transported them by sea over into France. **1804** SOUTHEY in *Ann. Rev.* II. 63 It is remarkable that Newcastle coal should be cheaper than coal carried landways.

‖**landwehr** ('landveːr). [Ger. = 'land-defence'.] In Germany and some other countries, that part of the organized land forces (corresponding to the militia of Great Britain) of which continuous service is required only in time of war. Also *transf.* (quot. 1855).

1815 HEL. M. WILLIAMS *Pres. St. France* xiv. 313 A great part of these troops were of the landwehr, or Prussian levy in mass. **1855** GROTE *Greece* II. xcii. (1856) XII. 77 The poor and hardy Landwehr of Macedonia, constantly on the defensive against predatory neighbours. **1866** *Cornh. Mag.* Nov. 552 To every district was assigned a detachment of the Landwehr proportionate to its population. **1878** SEELEY *Stein* II. 130 The Prussian Landwehr dates..from 1813.

b. *attrib.*, as *landwehr man.*

1866 *Cornh. Mag.* Nov. 553 The Landwehrmen were to provide their own uniforms.

'land-wind. A wind blowing from the land seawards. Also *attrib.* (Cf. LAND-BREEZE.)

1598 W. PHILLIPS *Linschoten* (1864) 192 The East windes beginne to blowe from off the Land into the Seas, whereby they are called Terreinhos, that is to say, the Land windes. **1604** E. G[RIMSTONE] *D'Acosta's Hist. Indies* III. viii. 142 There be foraine or land windes which come from the land. **1793** SMEATON *Edystone L.* §12 Being a Land-wind, it must blow hard before it raises any considerable sea at the rock. **1804** *Med. Jrnl.* XII. 538 It is not uncommon, during the land-wind, for the thermometer to stand at upwards of 100° in the shade. **1848** LONGF. *Sir H. Gilbert* v, Alas! the land-wind failed. **1862** MRS. SPEID *Last Years Ind.* 44 In the land-wind season.

†**'land-wrack, -wreck.** *Obs.* A wreck on land; the destruction of some object on land; the object so destroyed.

1649 G. DANIEL *Trinarch., Hen. IV*, xxiii, Thus Land-wraks Cædars lye, Or Cockle Shells vpon the Shores are drye. **1667** WATERHOUSE *Fire Lond.* 32 What they took being in a kind of Land-wreck, wherein no body owned goods. *a* **1707** BP. PATRICK *Autobiog.* (1839) 12 Mr. Fuller..was mistaken in saying this College was like a landwrack,..in which there was one left to keep possession.

lane (leɪn), *sb.*[1] Also 5 laane, 6 laine, layne. See also LOAN *sb.*[2] [OE. *lane*, *lǫne* wk. fem. = OFris. *lana*, *lona*, *laen* (North Fris. *lana*, *lona*), Du. *laan* (16th c. *laen*).]

I. 1. a. A narrow way between hedges or banks; a narrow road or street between houses or walls; a bye-way. *blind lane*, † *turn-again lane*: a cul-de-sac (see also quot. 1725).

971 *Blickl. Hom.* 237 Forþon þe..þinne lichoman 3eond þisse ceastre lanan hie tostenceað. **13..** *Sir Beues* (A.) 4439 Þe cri aros be ech a side Boþe of lane and of strete. *c* **1386** CHAUCER *Can. Yeom. Prol. & T.* 105 In the suburbes of a toun..Lurkynge in hernes and in lanes blynde. **1478** BOTONER *Itin.* (Nasmith 1778) 177 A laane goyng yn the south syde of Seynt Stevyn church. **1480** CAXTON *Chron. Eng.* ccxlii. (1482) 278 Euery strete and lane in london and in the subarbes. **1511** *Nottingham Rec.* III. 338 Clensyng of the lanys at the comyng in off the towne. **1531** TINDALE *Expos. 1 John* Prol. *Wks.* (1573) 388/1 It is becomme a turnagaine lane vnto them, which they can not goe thorough. **1611** BIBLE *Luke* xiv. 21 Goe..into the streetes and lanes of the city, and bring in hither the poore. **1611** SHAKS. *Cymb.* v. iii. 13 *Lo.* Where was this Lane? *Post.* Close by the battell, ditch'd, and wall'd with turph. **1698** J. FRYER *Acc. E. India & P.* 105 The Hedges and Lanes are chiefly set with two sorts of Bushes. **1725** *New Cant. Dict.*, *Blind Lane*, a Lane fit to run down to avoid Pursuers, after a Villainy committed. **1794** *Act Inclos. S. Kelsey* 12 Any of the Roads or Ways within the Manor..which shall be made into Lanes, or fenced on both Sides. **1828** MISS MITFORD *Village* Ser. III. 148 Their way..leading through cross country lanes. **1832** TENNYSON *Miller's Dau.* 130 The lanes were white with May. **1837** DICKENS *Pickw.* vii, Their walk lay through shady lanes.

fig. *a* **1625** BEAUM. & FL. *Laws of Candy* I. ii, The man That had a heart to think he could but follow..through the lanes Of danger and amazement.

b. *Proverb.* Also *allusively.*

1778 FOOTE *Trip Calais* II. Wks. 1799 II. 355 It is a long lane that has no turning. **1890** W. E. NORRIS *Misadventure* xvii, The longest lane, however, has a turning. **1893** MISS HARRADEN *Ships that pass*, etc. 158 The lane had come to an ending at last, and Mr. Reffold was dead.

II. Transferred senses.

2. a. A narrow or comparatively narrow passage or way, or something resembling this; *esp.* a channel of water in an ice-field (also called a *vein*); the course prescribed for ocean steamers; a route prescribed for aircraft.

c **1420** *Pallad. on Husb.* IX. 170 And yf hit happe an hil thi water mete, Let make a lane & thorgh thi licour hale. **1714** GAY *Trivia* III. 25 Forth issuing from steep lanes, the colliers' steeds Drag the black load. **1835** SIR J. ROSS *Narr. 2nd Voy.* Explan. Terms 15 *A lane or vein*, a narrow channel between two floes or fields, or between the ice and the shore. **1842** TENNYSON *Gold. Year* 50 And like a lane of beams athwart the sea. **1847** —— *Princess* v. 6 By glimmering lanes and walls of canvas led Threading the soldier-city. **1853** KANE *Grinnell Exp.* xxviii. (1856) 228 A black lane of open water stopped our progress. **1862** SIR H. HOLLAND *Ess., Atlantic Ocean* 223 It is proposed to mark off lanes, 20 or 25 miles in width..as the routes..to be followed and adhered to, by all steam vessels. **1911** [see *air lane* s.v. AIR *sb.*[1] III. 8]. **1929** *Encycl. Brit.* I. 231/1 Neon lighting is particularly suitable for landing in fog owing to its distinctive colour, and to the fact that long 'lanes' of illumination can be provided. **1941** A. O. POLLARD *Bombers over Reich* 105 The clouds parted a little, and the approaching raiders found enemy fighters collected in the open 'lanes' like soldiers guarding breaches in a fortification. **1956** J. C. SWAYNE *Conc. Gloss. Geogr. Terms* 86 *Lane*, a much used ocean or air route. **1971** E. C. B. & K. LEE *Safety & Survival at Sea* i. 8 Safety sea-lanes, consisting of a series of two-way lanes with a safety buffer zone separating the inward and outward bound traffic, are used in the approaches to New York harbour and other seaports. **1971** *Sci. Amer.* July 1/1 [An automatic weather information station] was moored in the middle of the Gulf Stream, off the Florida Coast, in a hurricane lane. **1974** L. DEIGHTON *Spy Story* xv. 146 The pilot..climbed again, now that he was no longer forced down under the lanes.

b. A passage between two lines of persons; a way to pass through a crowd.

1525 LD. BERNERS *Froiss.* II. ccxvii. [ccxiii.] 672 The people..made a lane for hym to passe thorough. **1587** FLEMING *Contn. Holinshed* III. 1996/1 A double canon..shooting off, made..a lane among the Frenchmen. **1677** *Lond. Gaz.* No. 1206/1 The Magistrates did..pass through a Lane of their own guards. **1701** W. WOTTON *Hist. Rome* 395 The People made a Lane for him and the Chariot to pass. **1806** *Naval Chron.* XV. 141 The 7th Royal Veteran battalion..formed a lane two deep. **1860** O. W. HOLMES *Prof. Breakf.-t.* v. (Paterson) 109 The fire-buckets passed along a 'lane' at a fire. **1867** MORRIS *Jason* II. 287 Then moved the princes..Between a lane of men. **1875** TENNYSON *Q. Mary* I. i, Stand back, keep a clear lane! **1893** FORBES-MITCHELL *Remin. Gt. Mutiny* 145 Every charge [of grape-shot]..leaving a lane of dead from four to five yards wide.

fig. **1641** MILTON *Ch. Govt.* vii. (1851) 132 Passe on..to establish the truth though it were through a lane of sects and heresies on each side.

c. In *Athletics*, a course for a runner marked out by broad chalk-lines (orig. strings). Hence also in *Swimming*, such a course marked out by ropes buoyed up by cork floats.

1909 in *Cent. Dict.* Suppl. **1911** *Encycl. Brit.* XXIII. 853/2 The course for sprinting races..is marked off in lanes for the individual runners by means of cords stretched upon short iron rods. **1927** *Daily Express* 23 Mar. 13/5 Sprint-racing in 'lanes' instead of in strings will be in force at the next Olympic Games... The 'lanes' are marked by chalk lines, and have been used in America for some time. **1955** R. BANNISTER *First Four Minutes* 21, I moved out into the second lane so that I could..avoid the danger of being boxed in. **1960** J. GRINHAM *Water Babe* xiv. 158 Suddenly the roar in the pool turned to a gasp—Di swam on to the lane ropes. **1970** MCGREGOR & STILL *Bobby McGregor Story* ix. 77, I stepped on to the poolside of the magnificent Olympic swimming stadium. I took up my position behind lane 2, officially the position for the fifth fastest qualifier. **1971** D. EMERY *Lillian* vii. 75 The bends were tighter on the inside lane and therefore harder to round at full speed.

d. A part of a road, wide enough for one file of vehicles, which is marked out by painted lines and is used to segregate traffic according to speed, intended direction, etc. Also *attrib.* and *Comb.*

1926 *Amer. City* Apr. 358/1 One of the most recent developments in highway design is the so-called super-highway where eight or more traffic lanes are provided for on the same right of way. **1933** *Evening Standard* 19 Apr. 7/2 Roads..would carry any volume of traffic, divided into slow, medium and fast 'lanes'. **1951** *Economist* 22 Sept. 685/3 Super-highways; with at least four lanes. **1959** *Times* 31 Mar. 15/6 The motorist who elects to park his car on a main road reduces the width of the road for a complete traffic lane for what may be hundreds of yards. **1960** *Guardian* 21 Nov. 2/4 Where there is good lane discipline, traffic should be able to pass on the near side. **1962** *Economist* 27 Jan. 327/1 Mr Barnes is a great believer in lane-painting to increase the capacity of streets. **1966** [see *fast lane* s.v. FAST *a.* 11]. **1968** *Autocar* 7 Mar. 61/3 The first week's working of the London experiments with bus lanes in Park Lane and on Vauxhall Bridge. **1970** *Guardian* 4 Aug. 15/2 Lane-changing, the constant pressure to keep up speeds. **1971** *Daily Tel.* (Colour Suppl.) 22 Oct. 25/4 In

town traffic, lane discipline is more a matter of cunning than of boldness. **1972** *Police Rev.* 8 Dec. 1597/2 Failure to judge distance at speed and bad lane drill accounted for most of the accidents. **1973** D. WESTHEIMER *Going Public* ix. 127 Drivers on the inbound lane slowed to a crawl.

e. In ten-pin bowling, etc.: = ALLEY 4.

1960 D. TAYLOR *Secret of Bowling Strikes* 125 Most old-fashioned lanes have a center peg in the center of the alley. **1964** F. BRUNDLE *Tenpin Bowling Tips* 79 In some localities a lane which allows the ball to take a wide hook is termed fast... Some authorities.. speak of lanes as either 'holding' or 'running'. **1970** C. SCHUNK *Bowling* i. 4 When alleys were first built in the Southern United States, three-fourths of the lanes were constructed for duck pins. **1974** *Plain Dealer* (Cleveland, Ohio) 26 Oct. 5-D/5 Likewise, the lanes can also be too slick or too dry.

3. *Austral.* A long narrow yard leading into the final yard in a kangaroo drive.

1866 *Cornh. Mag.* Dec. 741 Longer enclosures, called 'lanes', led in circuitous fashion to this *oubliette*. **1890** 'ROLF BOLDREWOOD' *Col. Reformer* xviii. 226 About fifty head have been run into the drafting lane... The 'lane' is a long narrow yard about three panels wide and eight in length—a panel of fencing is not quite nine feet in length—immediately connected with the pound or final yard.

4. a. *slang.* The throat; chiefly in ***the lane, the narrow, red lane***, etc.

1542 UDALL *Erasm. Apoph.* 119 Whole mainour places.. thei make no bones ne sticke not, quite and clene to swallowe down the narrowe lane, and the same to spue vp again. *a* **1553** —— *Royster D.* I. iii. (Arb.) 20 Good ale for the nones, Whiche will slide downe the lane without any bones. **1812** G. COLMAN *Poet. Vagaries* (1818) 75 O butter'd egg!.. I bid your yelk glide down my throat's red lane. **1865** *Lond. Soc.* Jan. 13, I eat the macaroon. You see it's all gone down Red Lion Lane.

b. ***the lane***: short for various 'lanes' in the City or for buildings situated there, *e.g. Chancery Lane, Drury Lane (Theatre), Mincing Lane, Petticoat Lane*, etc.: see quots.

1831 P. EGAN *Show Folks* 29 The *swell* performers.. who proudly observe, 'I am engaged at the Lane.'.. But the 'Lane', alluded to in this instance, is Horsemonger Lane; where a number of engagements are suffered to *expire*. **1856** MAYHEW *Gt. World Lond.* 82 *note*, Horsemonger Lane Jail —The lane. **1865** *Chambers's Jrnl.* 18 Feb. 106/1 The 'Lane' (as Chancery Lane is familiarly called). **1872** B. JERROLD *London* viii. 77 When on a certain Sunday we turned into Petticoat Lane, we had the key to the activity of the clothes market of Lazarus. The Lane clothes thousands at Epsom. **1879** '*Autobiog. of a thief*' in *Macm. Mag.* XL. 500 We used to.. sell it.. to a fence.. down the Lane (Petticoat Lane). **1880** G. R. SIMS *Ballads Babylon, Forgotten* 9 Whenever the Lane tried Shakespeare, I was one of the leading men. **1899** *Westm. Gaz.* 24 Apr. 2/3 When people who know that district [Drury-lane] hear it said that there has been 'another murder in the lane', they have no need to ask what particular lane is referred to. **1909** *Westm. Gaz.* 6 Aug. 11/4 'The Lane', as that of Mincing is fondly known among the wholesale grocery crowd. **1926** F. M. FORD *Man could Stand Up* II. iii. 138 He had lately promised [them] tickets for Drury Lane... The Lane was the *locus classicus* of the race. **1959** B. KOPS *Hamlet of Stepney Green* I. 24, I also stand down the Lane [*sc.* Petticoat Lane] on Sundays now and again. I'm what you might call a purveyor of bad taste. **1974** M. BIRMINGHAM *You can help Me* i. 11 Wentworth Street, down which the stalls of Petticoat Lane market spill. .. We never say 'Wentworth Street'; it's 'The Lane' to us. *Ibid.* ii. 29 Friday is the day for buying flowers in the Lane.

5. *Sc.* A sluggish stream of water; also the smooth part of a stream. (Perh. a different word.)

1825–80 in JAMIESON. **1891** *Daily News* 2 July 4/8 Vast pastoral expanses, with here a loch, and there a 'lane' or sullen deep stream threading the wilderness. **1897** CROCKETT *Lads' Love* xxv. 253 The still, black pools of the lazy, sluggish, peaty 'lane'.

6. *Astr.* A narrow band or strip in the sky that differs markedly from its immediate surroundings (e.g. in containing no observable stars or in emitting strong radio signals).

1899 *Astrophysical Jrnl.* IX. 157 The wonderful nebulous region about Rho Ophiuchi.. and.. the great vacant lanes near that star. **1917** *Proc. Nat. Acad. Sci.* III. 678 A study of the negatives of spiral nebulae obtained with the Crossley Reflector has shown that the phenomenon of dark lanes caused by occulting or absorbing matter is much more frequent than had.. been supposed. **1964** R. H. BAKER *Astron.* (ed. 8) xvii. 506 The hydrogen lanes traced by Dutch radio observers.. in longitudes available to them are shown in Fig. 17·22... In a direction 80° from the sun we note three hydrogen lanes, which trace three spiral arms. **1970** *Nature* 12 Dec. 1077/1 This is identified with NGC 1579 which is a small, irregular, diffuse nebulosity.. with a prominent dark lane. **1971** *Ibid.* 21 May 197/3 The underlying common feature of spiral galaxies is the existence of elongated spiral arms traced out by gaseous material (neutral hydrogen lanes; ionized HII regions and dust).

III. 7. *attrib.* and *Comb.*, as ***lane-end, -side, -way***; ***lane-filling*** adj.; **lane-born** *a.*, country-born, rustic; **lane-galloper** *hunting*, one who keeps to the lanes in preference to riding across country; **lane-route**, a route laid out for ocean steamers.

1834 LANDOR *Exam. Shaks.* Wks. 1846 II. 279/2 *Lane born boys.. embezzling hazel-nuts in a woollen cap. **1898** *Westm. Gaz.* 12 Mar. 2/1 A proclamation.. was.. posted at every *lane-end throughout his dominions. **1831** HOWITT *Seasons* (1837) 13 Deep, *lane-filling, hedge-burying snows. **1826** *Sporting Mag.* XVII. 361 That when the select few have got well away with the hounds.. they should be stopped, to enable tailers, *lane-gallopers, and all the οἱ πολλοὶ of the field to come up. **1895** *Funk's Stand. Dict.* 1000/1 **Lane-route*, or *ocean-l. route*, one of the routes prescribed for transatlantic steamers in Northern waters, being different for eastward- and westward-bound vessels, to avoid collisions. **1950** *Ocean Passages for World* (Admiralty, Hydrographic Dept.) (ed. 2) B. I. ii. 41/1 The large number of steam vessels crossing the Atlantic.. has necessitated the adoption of clearly defined separate routes to be followed by outward and homeward bound ships... These are known as the *North Atlantic Lane Routes*. *Ibid.*, Masters of all ships.. who do not.. make use of the 'lane routes', should make themselves acquainted with them, for their own safety. **1463** *Bury Wills* (Camden) 22 Yᵉ doore be the *lane syde. **1899** H. T. TIMMINS *Nooks & Corners Shropshire* ix. 167 An old country woman tending her cow by the laneside. **1923** *Daily Mail* 2 Apr. 6 To see the lanesides in this delicate livery of verdure and bloom. **1882** *Standard* 8 Dec. 3/4 There was a border, or *laneway, near the house of the Prisoner. **1914** JOYCE *Dubliners* 185 A crowd which had followed him down the laneway collected outside the door. **1933** L. A. G. STRONG *Sea Wall* 258 He charged like a bull across the open space and disappeared into the human laneway.

Lane, *sb.*[2] The name of John *Lane*, 19th-c. English horticulturalist, used in the possessive in **Lane's Prince Albert** to designate a large, green cooking apple of a variety introduced by him in 1857.

1875 *Florist & Pomologist* 233 Lane's Prince Albert.. is remarkable both for its excellent quality as a culinary apple and for its prodigious bearing qualities. **1902** [see BRAMLEY]. **1933** HALL & CRANE *Apple* xii. 200 Lane's Prince Albert.. is a mid-Victorian introduction. **1962** *Listener* 27 Sept. 495/1, I am thinking of cooking apples like Bramleys and Lane's Prince Albert.

†**lane,** *v. dial. Obs. rare.* [f. LANE *sb.*[1]] *trans.* ***to lane off***: To mark the course of (intended roads); to mark the roads on (land).

1772 *Welton Inclos. Act* 13 After the same [roads] shall be laned-off. **1773** *Harpham Inclos. Act* 15 At all times after the same [lands] shall be laned off.

lane, Sc. form of LOAN *sb.* and *v.*, LONE *a.*

lane, var. LAIN *sb.*, concealment; *v.*, to conceal.

lane, variant of LAIN *sb.*[2], stratum.

lane, obs. form of LAWN, linen.

laneing, var. LOANING *Sc.* and *north.*, a lane.

†**laneous,** *a. Obs. rare*⁻⁰. [f. L. *lāne-us* (f. *lāna* wool) + -OUS.] Of or pertaining to wool.

1676 in COLES. **1727** in BAILEY vol. II.

laner(e, variant of LAINER, lash, thong.

laner, laneret(te: see LANNER, -ET[1], falcon.

lanesome, Sc. form of LONESOME.

laney ('leɪnɪ), *a. nonce-wd.* [f. LANE *sb.*[1] + -Y[1].] Of or pertaining to a lane.

1876 W. MARSTON *Dram. & Poet. Wks.* II. 345 Whether they rise by grey-walled Towns.. Or bend from laney nooks that skirt the bay.

Lang (læŋ). Also **lang**. The name of John *Lang*, used *attrib.* and in the possessive (esp. in ***Lang('s) lay***) to designate a lay (LAY *sb.*[7] 7 b) used for wire ropes and patented by him in 1879, in which the strands forming the rope are twisted in the same direction as the wires forming each strand.

1883 *Engineering* 14 Dec. 537/1 In the Lang method the strands and the rope are laid in the same direction. **1887** J. B. SMITH *Treat. Cable or Rope Traction* viii. 156 (*heading*) The 'Lang lay', or construction of wire ropes. **1896** W. E. HIPKINS *Wire Rope* 52 Ropes on the lang principle. **1930** *Engineering* 1 Aug. 135/1 The hauling rope is of the Lang-lay type, built up of six three-cornered strands and a hemp core. **1959** *B.S. Handbk. No. 4: Lifting Tackle (B.S.I.)* I. 90 Ropes made Lang's lay require careful handling to ensure that the rope's end does not twist, and so allow 'turn' to come out of the rope. **1966** *McGraw-Hill Encycl. Sci. & Technol.* XI. 627/1 In lang lay, wires in the strand and the strands themselves are laid in the same direction. This type rope wears better, is more flexible, and lasts longer.

lang, lang-: see LANGUE I, LONG, LONG-.

langage, -ed, obs. forms of LANGUAGE, -ED.

langald, langate: see LANGLE *sb.*, LANGUET.

langaon, variant of LONGANON *Obs.*, rectum.

långbanite ('lɔːŋbənaɪt). *Min.* [ad. G. *långbanit* (G. Flink 1887, in *Zeitschr. f. Kryst. und Min.* XIII. 1), f. *Långban*, the name of its original locality in Wermland, Sweden + *-it* -ITE[1].] A black silicate and oxide of antimony, iron, and manganese, near $(Mn^{II}, Sb)_4(Mn^{IV}, Fe^{III})_3SiO_{12}$, with a brilliant metallic lustre.

1887 *Jrnl. Chem. Soc.* LII. 782 (*heading*) Långbanite, a new Swedish mineral. **1949** *Mineral. Abstr.* X. 542 Tetragonal braunite with a cubic pseudo-cell can be fitted into the hexagonal structure of långbanite. **1968** *Arkiv för Mineral. & Geol.* IV. 456 Since the original discovery of långbanite, so many specimens have been identified that it may be considered a moderately abundant mineral.

langbeinite ('læŋbaɪnaɪt). *Min.* [ad. G. *langbeinit* (S. Zuckschwerdt 1891, in *Zeitschr. f. angew. Chem.* 356/2), f. the name of A. *Langbein*, 19th-cent. German chemist + *-it* -ITE[1].] A sulphate of potassium and magnesium, $K_2Mg_2(SO_4)_3$, colourless when pure, which is known only in salt deposits of marine origin and as a synthetic product, and is used in the production of fertilizers.

1898 *Jrnl. Chem. Soc.* LXXIV. II. 169 The crystals of langbeinite are optically inactive. **1932** *Bull. U.S. Geol. Survey* No. 833. 41 Most of the langbeinite.. has a distinctive pink color. It is the 'hardest looking' of the saline minerals and has a conchoidal or irregular fracture with no cleavage. **1951** *Mineral. Abstr.* XI. 247 Langbeinite.. on exposure to air falls to powder consisting of picromerite.. and epsomite. **1960** R. A. MACDONALD in V. Sauchelli *Chem. & Technol. Fertilizers* xv. 387 Langbeinite.. is mined and processed by International Mineral & Chemical Corporation in the Carlsbad basin... The product is marketed at a purity in excess of 95 per cent langbeinite.

langdebeef, -befe, etc.: see LANGUE DE BŒUF.

lange, obs. variant of LANGUE, LAUNCH *v.*

†**langel(l.** *dial. Obs.* Also **laungell.** [? a. OF. *langeul*:—popular L. **lāneolum*, dim. of *lāneum* something woollen, f. *lāna* wool.] A woollen rug or blanket.

1324–5 *Durham Acc. Rolls* (Surtees) 165, vˣˣ iiijᵒʳ uln. panni pro lanugells [*read* laungells] et pro cooperturis, 105*s.* 9*d.* **1366–7** in *Charters*, etc. *Priory Finchale* (Surtees) lxxii, xxviij ulnis pro saccis, et blanketts pro langells. **1383–4** *Durham Acc. Rolls* (Surtees) 390 In 14 uln. de blanket empt. pro langels.. 4*s.* 4*d.*

langel(l, variant of LANGLE.

‖**langeleik** ('laŋəlaɪk). Also **langleik.** [Norw.] An early Norwegian stringed instrument, resembling the zither.

1907 *Westm. Gaz.* 10/1 Ancient music of the Vikings was played.. on the 'langleik', the crude guitar of the Norsemen, by an aged minstrel.. who is a direct descendant of King Harald Haarfager. **1938** *Oxf. Compan. Mus.* 839/2 Norway possesses several distinctive instruments. The Langleik.., used until near the end of the eighteenth century, was a sort of developed monochord. **1961** A. BAINES *Mus. Instruments* 210 A tuning given by Panum for the slightly more advanced Norwegian langeleik. **1970** *Daily Tel.* (Colour Suppl.) 13 Nov. 47 The fjord-loving fiddle is the offspring of a local zither-like instrument called the *langeleik*, whose strings were struck with a plectrum.

†**langer,** *adv. north.* and *Sc. Obs.* Also **langare, -ayr, -eir.** [f. *lang* LONG *adv.* + ERE *adv.*] Long ere, long since.

1303 R. BRUNNE *Handl. Synne* 10660 But, langer þat y sykerde þe, Shalt þou haue no skaþe for me. *a* **1375** *Lay Folks Mass Bk.* App. IV. 338 Two wyues sat ȝonder, langare. **1513** DOUGLAS *Æneis* v. Prol. 35 Langer in murning, now in melody. *Ibid.* XII. xi. 40, I knew full weill at it was thou, langere, That [etc.].

Langerhans ('læŋəhænz). *Histology.* The name of Paul *Langerhans* (1847–88), German anatomist, used *attrib.*, in the possessive, and with *of*-adjunct to designate a kind of dendritic or stellate cell found in the epidermis and characterized by the presence of cytoplasmic granules (***Langerhans granules***). (See also *islet of Langerhans* s.v. ISLET 2 b).

1890 BILLINGS *Med. Dict.* II. 32/1 *Langerhans' cells*, stellate cells found in deeper layers of epidermis, apparently related to nerve terminations. **1934** E. V. COWDRY *Textbk. Histol.* xxix. 449 Cells of the third category are called melanoblasts (Langerhans, stellate or dendritic cells) because they are supposed to form melanin. **1953** *Phil. Trans. R. Soc.* B. CCXXXVII. 162 This technique.. led to the erroneous conclusion that the cells of Langerhans occur in the basal layer. *Ibid.*, Langerhans' cells are invariably unpigmented. **1965** *Jrnl. Investigative Dermatol.* XLIV. 202/2 The characteristic granules within the Langerhans cell are shaped like a tennis racket... The number, as well as the size, of the Langerhans granules is.. variable. **1965** *Ibid.* XLV. 403/1 The capability of Langerhans cells to synthesize melanin remains to be proven. **1969** S. BRADBURY *Hewer's Textbk. Histol.* (ed. 9) xvii. 237 It was at one time thought that the Langerhans cells were effete melanocytes, but they have been shown to be active in the uptake of tritiated thymidine and their E/M appearance suggests also that they are active cells. Their function is still unknown.

†**'langern,** *v. Obs. rare*⁻¹. [? f. LANGUOR + -EN[5].] *intr.* To languish, lie sick.

c **1440** HYLTON *Scala Perf.* (W. de W. 1494) II. xvii, He shall langern [**1533** linger] a grete whyle or that he be fully hole.

langet, variant of LANDSHARD, LANGUET.

†**langfad.** *Sc. Obs.*, original form (a. Gaelic *langfhada*, f. *lang* ship + *fhada* long) of LYMPHAD, q.v.

1536 BELLENDEN *Cron. Scot.* (1821) I. 43 With mony galyouns and lang faddis. **1641** in Rushw. *Hist. Coll.* III. (1692) I. [407] The numbre of Bottis or Lime Faddis.

langhalde, -hold: see LANGLE *sb.*

Langhans ('læŋhænz). *Histology.* The name of Theodor *Langhans* (1839–1915), German pathologist, used *attrib.*, in the possessive, and with *of*-adjunct to designate: (*a*) (a cell of) an inner layer of large cuboidal cells, one cell thick, that covers chorionic villi and lies beneath the syncytial layer; (*b*) a distinctive kind of giant cell

which has many nuclei, arranged in a ring around the periphery or clustered together at one end of the cell, and is observed esp. in tuberculosis and related granulomatous conditions.

1886 *Buck's Handbk. Med. Sci.* II. 146/2 (*heading*) Langhans' cellular layer. **1900** DUNGLISON *Dict. Med. Sci.* (ed. 22) App. 1276/2 *Langhans's giant cell*, giant-cell of tubercular granulation-tumor. **1906** *Practitioner* Nov. 663 A teratoma is defined as a growth that consists of elements represented in the developing ovum, whether at an early (e.g. syncytia, Langhans' cells, large mono-nuclear cells), or, at a later date (e.g. neuro-epithelial cutaneous, or other elements). **1937** E. E. HEWER *Textbk. Histol.* xxxii. 280 (*heading*) Layer of Langhans. *Ibid.*, The villi during early pregnancy are covered by an inner layer of cubical cells (Langhans' layer) and an outer syncytial layer. **1939** G. G. KAYNE et al. *Pulmonary Tuberculosis* I. iii. 38 Granulomata consisting of epithelioid and Langhans giant cells may be seen as early as the third to sixth day. **1968** H. HARRIS *Nucleus & Cytoplasm* v. 97 This peripheral distribution of nuclei in certain types of multi-nucleate cell was first discussed by Langhans, and when such cells are found in pathological conditions they are commonly referred to as 'Langhans' giant cells. **1972** EBE & KOBAYASHI *Fine Struct. Human Cells & Tissues* 226 Cytotrophoblasts or Langhans cells of the chorionic villus are thought to be the site of production of a proteinic hormone, chorionic gonadotrophin.

langing, obs. form of LONGING.

langite ('læŋgaɪt). *Min.* [Named by Maskelyne, 1864, after V. von Lang: see -ITE.] A hydrous oxy-sulphate of copper, resembling brochantite.

1865 *Reader* No. 114. 259/1 Langite and gypsum. **1867** READWIN *Index Min.* 21. **1868** DANA *Min.* (ed. 5) 665.

lang-kail. *Sc.* [f. *lang* LONG *a.* + *kail* KALE.] A variety of borecole; sometimes called 'Scotch kale'. Also *attrib.*

1724 RAMSAY *Tea-t. Misc.* (1733) I. 89 And there will be lang-kail and pottage And bannocks of barley-meal. **1789** BURNS *Capt. Grose's Peregrin.* viii, The knife that nicket Abel's craig..was a faulding jocteleg, Or lang-kail gullie. **1820** SCOTT *Monast.* i, The ill-cultivated garden afforded 'lang-cale', and the river gave salmon.

‖**langlauf** ('laŋlaʊf). [G.] Cross-country skiing; a cross-country skiing race. Hence '**langlaufer**, a competitor in such a race.

1927 A. LUNN *Hist. Ski-ing* xvii. 223 The *Langlauf* was the logical development of Norwegian ski-ing. **1929** *Times* 6 Dec. 6/4 They [*sc.* the British] could not hope to compete against foreign Langlaufers and jumpers. **1963** I. FLEMING *On H.M. Secret Service* xvii. 191 Bond..somehow stayed upright on the two miles of treacherous Langlauf down the gentle slope to Samaden. **1968** *Punch* 28 Feb. 293/2 And not only did he win the jumping, but also the downhill, the slalom, and the langlauf. It was a great day for Britain! **1970** *Country Life* 17–24 Dec. 1214/3 The young and energetic have turned ski-loping into a competitive sport. The 30 and 50 km langlauf races are included in the Winter Olympics.

Lang lay: see LANG.

langle ('læŋg(ə)l), *sb. Obs.* exc. *dial.* Forms: 4 **langald, langhalde,** 6 **langhold,** 8 **langel(l,** 8, 9 *dial.* **langle.** [Of obscure origin; both form and sense appear to point to an OF. **langle*, **lengle*:—L. *lingula* thong, strap, dim. of *lingua* tongue; but the word is app. not recorded in French. Cf. LINGEL.] A thong, rope, or other contrivance used to confine the legs of an animal in order to prevent its straying; a hobble. Also *fig.*

1394–5 *Durham Acc. Rolls* (Surtees) 599 In 3 Tethirs cum paribus de langalds 22*d.* **1398** TREVISA *Barth. De P.R.* XVIII. xiv. (1495) 774 An oxe herde fedeth and nourysseth oxen: and byndeth their fete with a langhaldes. **1609** J. PORY tr. *Leo's Africa* III. 137 Certaine langols or withs, which the Africans put upon their horses feete. **1737** RAMSAY *Sc. Prov.* (1797) 95 Ye ha'e ay a foot out o' the langle. **1880** *Antrim & Down Gloss.* s.v., A 'sheep's langle' is a short piece of any kind of rope, with a slip knot at each end. The loops are passed over the fore and hind leg of a sheep.

langle ('læŋg(ə)l), *v. Obs.* exc. *dial.* In 5, 8 **langel,** 7 **langol.** [f. prec. sb.] *trans.* To fasten with a thong; to confine (the legs of an animal) with a thong, rope, or the like. Hence **langled** *ppl. a.*

c **1440** *Promp. Parv.* 286/2 Langelyd, or teyyn to-gedyr, *colligatus. Ibid.*, Langelyn or byynd to-geder, *colligo* (*P. compedio*). **1647** TRAPP *Comm. Rom.* vii. 24 This carcase of sin to which I am tied and lungold [*sic*]. **1650** —— *Comm. Gen.* iv. 12 He was langold to it, and must abide by it. **1755** FORBES *Ajax' Sp.* 25 This..your sma banes wou'd langel sair. *Ibid.*, Key, *Langel*, entangle. **1790** GROSE *Prov. Gloss.* (ed. 2), *Langled*, having the legs coupled together at a small distance, North. **1880** *Antrim & Down Gloss.*, *Langle*, to tie the hind foot and the fore foot of an animal together, to prevent it straying far.

langley ('læŋlɪ). *Meteorol.* [f. the name of Samuel P. *Langley* (1834–1906), U.S. astronomer. Orig. proposed (in G.) by F. Linke 1942, in *Handbuch d. Geophysik* VIII. 30, as a unit of solar energy flux, equal to one gramme-calorie per sq. cm. per minute.] A unit of solar energy per unit area, equal to one gramme-calorie per square centimetre (approximately 41,900 joules per square metre).

1947 *Nature* 6 Sept. 327/1 It is herewith proposed that the 'langley' be defined as the gm. cal./cm.^{2}, where 'gm. cal.' denotes the 15°C. gm. cal. It is also proposed that the written abbreviation of 'langley' be 'ly'. **1954** J. C. JOHNSON *Physical Meteorol.* iv. 108 $\sigma = ..8{\cdot}22 \times 10^{-11}$ langley minute^{-1}. σ is called the Stefan-Boltzmann constant. **1970** DAY & STERNES *Climate & Weather* v. 145 The solar constant..is alternatively expressed as nearly 2·0 langleys per minute. **1974** *Nature* 15 Nov. 217/1 For the point of equilibrium I take 17 langley per day (1 langley = 1 calorie cm^{-2}) above the 1950 value of 847 langley per day.

Langobard ('læŋgəbɑːd). Also **Longobard.** [see LOMBARD *sb.*[1] and *a.*] = LOMBARD *sb.*[1] 1 a. Also as *adj.* Hence **Lango'bardian** *a.*

1788 GIBBON *Decl. & F.* IV. xlii. 216 The original name of Langobards is expressive only of the peculiar length and fashion of their beards. **1902** L. VILLARI tr. *P. Villari's Barbarian Invasions Italy* II. III. i. 279 As usual the Longobard host comprised a motley throng of Bavarians, Bulgarians, Gepidæ,..and more especially Saxons. *Ibid.* 280 The beginning of the Longobard rule may be said to date from this event. **1925** *Contemp. Rev.* Aug. 212 The people are of Langobardian, French, or even Gothic origin. **1952** E. HYAMS *Soil & Civilization* iv. 30 The first we hear of the buffalo, as a domestic animal, in Europe, is as a gift to the Langobard Court, in Italy, about A.D. 600. **1974** R. A. HALL *External Hist. of Romance Lang.* v. 86 The Langobards' linguistic influence was exerted chiefly in Italy.

Langobardic (læŋgə'bɑːdɪk), *a.* [ad. late L. *Langobardic-us*, f. *Langobardī* the Lombards.] = LOMBARDIC.

1724 WATERLAND *Athan. Creed* 50 The character of the manuscript is Langobardick. *Ibid.* vi. 86 The manuscript of Bobio, in Langobardick character. **1839** K. H. DIGBY *Mores Catholici* IX. viii. 260 These fragments of Langobardic inscriptions. **1895** T. HODGKIN *Italy & her Invaders* V. iii. 140 Vast stores of wealth, taken from the Gepid dwellings, enriched the Langobardic homes. **1960** W. D. ELCOCK *Romance Lang.* iii. 228 Words of Langobardic origin having undergone certain sound-shifts characteristic of High German. *Ibid.* 259 A Langobardic king, Liutprand,..saw the possibility of exploiting the political situation.

†**Lan'goon.** *Obs.* [ad. F. *Langon*, name of a town on the Garonne.] A kind of white wine.

1674 *Gallantry à la Mode* 15 Suspition then I washt away With old Langoon and cleansing Whey. **1680** SHADWELL *Wom. Captain* I. 5 He us'd to let him have very good Langoon and Burdeaux. **1693** *Content. Liquors* 7 (Stanf.) The White Wines..And Trusty Langoon. **1750** E. SMITH *Compl. Housew.* (ed. 14) 116 The best langoon white wine.

‖**langooty, lungooty** (lʌŋ'guːtɪ). Also **langotee, -ty.** [Hindī *langotī.*] (See quots.)

1816 'QUIZ' *Grand Master* II. 43 *note*, The hamauls, or bearers of India, are literally naked, with the exception of an article of dress called a langooty..which I cannot describe better to my female readers, than substituting a pocket-handkerchief for Eve's fig-leaf. **1826** J. LEYDEN & W. ERSKINE tr. *Mem. Baber* 333 A langoti..is a piece of clout that hangs down two spans from the navel. **1889** *Blackw. Mag.* Aug. 242 He ordered the natives to muffle the cubs in their turbans or langooties.

langorius, obs. Sc. form of LANGUOROUS.

‖**langostino** (lango'stino). [Sp.] = *Dublin (Bay) prawn* (DUBLIN). Cf. LANGOUSTINE.

1915 E. R. LANKESTER *Diversions of Naturalist* xii. 100 A very large Mediterranean prawn..is called 'Barcelona prawn' and 'Langostino'. **1967** [see CAMARON]. **1970** 'D. HALLIDAY' *Dolly & Cookie Bird* ii. 20 A plate of fat pink *langostinas* [sic].

langot, obs. form of LANGUET.

‖**langouste** (lɑ̃gust). [Fr.] A crawfish, *Palinurus vulgaris*, and related species; = CRAYFISH B. 3 b.

1832 W. MACGILLIVRAY *Trav. & Res. A. von Humboldt* xxi. 306 The sailors had been searching for *langoustes.* [**1835** W. KIRBY *On Power of God in Creation of Animals* II. xv. 49 There is one of a most ferocious aspect..called in the London market the *Thorny lobster*..: it is also called..by the French, who esteem it highly, the *Langouste.*] **1917** N. DOUGLAS *South Wind* xix. 232 Those succulent *langoustes* for which the coastal waters of the island are renowned. **1924** *Blackw. Mag.* Sept. 409/1 The fishwives..spread out before them all varieties of fish and shell-fish from langoustes to cockles. **1942** 'R. WEST' *Black Lamb* I. 23 In Nice, as I sat eating langouste outside a little restaurant down by the harbour. **1949** A. WILSON *Wrong Set* 171 The champagne, the langouste, the pine-scented air..were making of this dinner one of those..never to be forgotten hours of happiness. **1951** E. DAVID *French Country Cooking* 53 Put in the cut-up pieces of *langouste* and let the pan simmer. **1960** I. FLEMING *For your Eyes Only* 230 The blue and yellow langouste came a few steps out from under the rock.

‖**langoustine** (lɑ̃gustin). [Fr.] = *Dublin (Bay) prawn* (DUBLIN). Cf. LANGOSTINO.

1946 G. MILLAR *Horned Pigeon* xiv. 192 Langoustines in the Union Bar at Alexandria. **1949** [see DUBLIN]. **1951** E. DAVID *French Country Cooking* 35 *Langoustines* are the small ..shell fish about three inches long, delicate pink, with a very thin shell, resembling Dublin Bay Prawns. **1965** M. WALLENSTEIN *Merlin's Forest* vii. 86 He began to plan their dinner; beginning with crab or *langoustine.* **1966** P. V. PRICE *France: Food & Wine Guide* 41 The *langoustine* is like a giant prawn or little langouste. **1974** J. STUBBS *Painted Face* xi. 151 You must try the *langoustine.* It is very good.

langrage ('læŋgrɪdʒ). *Naut.* and *Mil.* Also **langridge.** [Of unknown origin.] Case-shot loaded with pieces of iron of irregular shape, formerly used in naval warfare to damage the rigging and sails of the enemy.

1769 FALCONER *Dict. Marine* (1780), *Langrel*, or *langrage*, a particular kind of shot, formed of bolts, nails, bars, or other pieces of iron tied together, and forming a sort of cylinder, which corresponds with the bore of the cannon. **1796** NELSON in Nicolas *Disp.* (1845) II. 146 It is well known that English ships of war are furnished with no such ammunition as langrage. **1839** W. O. MANNING *Law Nations* IV. vi. (1875) 203 Except the use of langridge (*mitraille*). **1862** BEVERIDGE *Hist. India* I. III. xi. 637 A twenty-four pounder, double loaded with langrage.

attrib. **1781** JUSTAMOND *Priv. Life Lewis XV*, III. 385 The gunners..could not stand the langrage-shot. **1813** SOUTHEY *Nelson* v. (Rtldg.) 128 Nelson received a severe wound on the head from a piece of langridge shot.

†**langrel**, *sb. Naut. Obs.* Also 7 **-rill.** = prec.

1627 CAPT. SMITH *Seaman's Gram.* xiv. 67 *Langrill shot.* Langrell shot runnes loose with a shackell, to be shortened when you put it into the Peece. **1669** STURMY *Mariner's Mag.* I. 19 Be sure to load our Guns with Cross-bar and Langrel. **1769** [see LANGRAGE]. **1867** SMYTH *Sailor's Word-bk.*, *Langrel*, or *Langrage.*

langrel, *a. Obs.* exc. *dial.* [? f. *lang* LONG *a.*; cf. *gangrel.*] Tall, 'lanky'.

1608 TOPSELL *Serpents* (1658) 810 The wary Bird soared so high above his reach, that the langrel Serpent could not catch him. **1847** HALLIWELL, *Langrel*, very tall..lanky.

†'**langret.** *Obs.* A kind of false die.

c **1550** *Dice-Play* A j b, A bale of Langretes contrary to the vantage. *Ibid.* C j, A well fauored die that semeth good & square: yet is the forhed longer on the cater and tray, then any other way, and therfore holdeth the name of a langret. **1591** GREENE *Disc. Coosnage* (1859) 11 The Chetor with a langret, cut contrarie to the vantage, wil cros-bite a bard cater tray. **1600** ROWLANDS *Lett. Humours Blood* iii. 59 His Langrets, with his Hie men, and his low, Are ready what his pleasure is to throw.

langridge, variant of LANGRAGE.

langsat ('læŋsæt). Also **langseh, lansat,** etc. [Malay.] The edible fruit of *Lansium domesticum*, a tree of the family Meliaceæ, native to Indonesia and Malaysia; also, the tree itself.

1783 W. MARSDEN *Hist. Sumatra* 83 *Lansai.* The tree which bears this fruit is large; the leaves are of a lightish green and somewhat pointed. [**1795** tr. *C. P. Thunberg's Trav. Europe, Afr. & Asia* (ed. 2) II. 276 *Boa lansay* is the Malay name for the fruit of a tree..which is yet unknown to botanists.] **1839** T. J. NEWBOLD *Pol. & Statistical Acct. Straits of Malacca* I. ii. 53 In the valley grow various fruit-trees, such as..the langseh. **1869** A. R. WALLACE *Malay Archipelago* I. v. 132 The Dyaks brought us daily heaped-up baskets of Mangustans and Lansats, two of the most delicious of the subacid tropical fruits. **1911** *Encycl. Brit.* XVII. 472/2 The principal fruit trees are the..*langsat, rambai*, jack-fruit, etc. **1920** W. POPENOE *Man. Tropical & Subtropical Fruits* xvi. 427 The langsat has not yet become generally cultivated outside of the Asiatic tropics. **1938** *Nature* 14 May 866/2 Many of the fruits and vegetables.. have been but names, if that, to dwellers in the temperate zones so far;..the mangosteen and the langsat are still awaited. **1940** E. J. H. CORNER *Wayside Trees Malaya* I. 463 The Langsat has an oblong fruit (about 1½ × 1") with thin, pale greyish-buff rind containing much white latex. **1963** J. KIRKUP *Tropic Temper* 115, I had some chicken..followed by sour-sweet langsat fruit.

langsettle ('læŋsɛt(ə)l). *north. dial.* Forms: 4 **langsedil,** 5 **-sedylle, -cetel, longsetylle,** 6 **langsaddil, -saild, -settell,** 7 **long settle,** (9 *dial.* **lang-, long-saddle**), 8–9 **lang-settle.** [f. *lang* LONG *a.* + SETTLE *sb.*] A long bench or 'settle', usually with arms and a high back.

1352–3 *Durham Acc. Rolls* (Surtees) 208, 1 langsedil. *c* **1425** *Voc.* in Wr.-Wülcker 657/9 *Hoc sedile*, langsedylle. **14..** *Nom.* ibid. 723/37 *Hoc sedile*, a longsetylle. **1571** *Wills & Inv. N.C.* (Surtees 1835) 366 A langsettell, a round dyssenge table. **1622** *N. Riding Rec.* IV. 156 Conveyance of a cottage house and heirloomes (one long settle onelie excepted). **1790** GROSE *Prov. Gloss.* (ed. 2), *Lang-settle*, a bench like a settee. North. **1841** C. ANDERSON *Anc. Models* 128 What is vulgarly called the long saddle in an ale-house. **1855** ROBINSON *Whitby Gloss.*, *Lang settle*, a long seat or form with a back-rail and arms; in some cases, however, the back, &c., is an entire boarded surface.

b. *attrib.*, as ***langsettle-bed, -end, -form.***

1566 *Inv. R. Wardr.* (1815) 173 Item, ane langsaddil-bed. **15..** *Aberd. Reg.* XVI. (Jam.), Ane langsaild bed. *Ibid.*, XVII. (*ibid.*), Ane langsadill form of fyr worcht iiij *sh.* **1785** HUTTON *Bran New Wark* 137 (E.D.S.) Bibles and testaments were formerly seen on the sconce or lang-settle end.

Langshan ('læŋʃæn). [Name of a locality about fifty miles from Shanghai; in Chinese = 'wolf hill'.] A breed of domestic fowl, introduced from China (see quots.).

1871 in A.C.C. & C.W.G. *Langshan Fowls* ii. 11, I send you some fowls by S. S. Achilles..they are black, and are called Langshans. **1884–5** L. WRIGHT *Poultry* 227 About the year 1872..a fresh importation of black Chinese fowls was shown... At first shown as Cochins, they were very soon shown by their admirers as 'Langshans', which was alleged to be their native name in North China.

langspiel ('læŋspiːl). [a. Norw. *langspil*, f. *lang* long + *spil* play.] A kind of harp formerly used in Shetland.

1822 SCOTT *Pirate* xv, The sound of the Gue, and the Langspiel.

langsuir (ˈlæŋsjʊə(r)). Also **langsuyar**. [Malay.] A female vampire with a whinnying cry, that preys on newborn children. Cf. PENANGGALAN.

1881 *Jrnl. R. Asiatic Soc., Straits Branch* June 28 If a woman dies in child-birth..she is popularly supposed to become a *langsuyar*, a flying demon of the nature of the 'white lady' or '*banshee*'. **1900** W. W. SKEAT *Malay Magic* vi. 320 The Langsuir..takes the form of an owl. **1972** *Daily Tel.* (Colour Suppl.) 12 May 58/3 The Malayan vampire family includes..the Langsuir, the spirit of a woman who died after hearing that her child was stillborn, known by her green robe, her tapering nails of amazing length and her long black hair which conceals a hole in the back of her neck through which she sucks the blood of children.

langsyne (ˌlæŋˈsaɪn), *adv.* (*sb.*) *Sc.* [Properly two words: see LONG *adv.* and SYNE *adv.*] Long since, long ago. Also *sb.* esp. in ***auld lang syne***. (Somewhat common in English use with allusion to Burns's song.)

1500–20 DUNBAR *Poems* xxiv. 34, I had bene deid langsyne, dowtless. **1570** *Satir. Poems Reform.* xvii. 3 In eirth lang syne yair had been nothing than, Saif only vice. *a* **1774** FERGUSSON *Poems* (1807) 309 Hame-o'er langsyne you hae been blithe to pack. **1788** BURNS *Auld Lang Syne*, For auld lang syne, my dear, For auld lang syne, We'll tak a cup o' kindness yet, For auld lang syne. **1820** SCOTT *Monast.* iv, Like what I hae seen langsyne, when we dwelt at Avenel. **1841** LYTTON *Nt. & Morn.* II. vii, A friend..of the happy lang syne. **1870** H. SMART *Race for Wife* ii, In days lang syne.

langteraloo, -trilloo, var. ff. LANTERLOO *Obs.*

†**langtra.** *dial. Obs.* ? = LANTERLOO.

1796 PEGGE *Anonym.* (1809) 245 Langtra, as they pronounce it, is a game at cards much played in Derbyshire and Staffordshire.

languable, obs. form of LAND-GAVEL.

language (ˈlæŋgwɪdʒ), *sb.*[1] Forms: 3–6 **langage**, (3 **langag**, 4 **longage**, **langwag**, 5 **langwache**, **langegage**), 3, 5– **language**. [a. F. *langage* (recorded from 12th c.) = Pr. *leng(u)atge*, *lengage*, Sp. *lenguaje*, Pg. *linguage(m*, It. *linguaggio*:—pop.L. type **linguāticum*, f. *lingua* tongue, language (F. *langue*: see LANGUE).

The form with *u*, due to assimilation with the F. *langue*, occurs in AF. writings of the 12th c., and in Eng. from about 1300.]

1. a. The whole body of words and of methods of combination of words used by a nation, people, or race; a 'tongue'. ***dead language***: a language no longer in vernacular use. ***first language***: one's native language. ***second language***: a language spoken in addition to one's native language; the first foreign language one learns.

c **1290** *S.E. Leg.* I. 108/55 With men þat onder-stoden hire langage. **1297** R. GLOUC. (Rolls) 1569 Vor in þe langage of rome rane a frogge is. *a* **1300** *Cursor M.* 247 (Gött.) Seldom was for ani chance Englis tong preched in france, Gif we þaim ilkan þair langage [*MS. Cott.* langage], And þan do we na vtetrage. *Ibid.*, 6384 (Gött.) þis mete..þai called it in þair langag man. **1387** TREVISA *Higden* (Rolls) II. 157 Walsche men and Scottes, þat beeþ nouȝt i-medled wiþ oþer nacions, holdeþ wel nyh hir firste longage and speche. *c* **1400** *Apol. Loll.* 32 In a langwag vnknowun ilk man and womman mai rede. *c* **1449** PECOCK *Repr.* I. xii. 66 Thei..han vsid the hool Bible..in her modris langage. *c* **1450** *Mirour Saluacioun* 3650 Wymmen spak these diuerse langegages. **1588** SHAKS. *L.L.L.* v. i. 40 They haue beene at a great feast of Languages, and stolne the scraps. **1589** PUTTENHAM *Eng. Poesie* III. iv. (Arb.) 156 After a speach is fully fashioned to the common vnderstanding, and accepted by consent of a whole countrey and nation, it is called a language. **1699** BENTLEY *Phal.* xiii. 392 Every living Language..is in perpetual motion and alteration. **1769** *De Foe's Tour Gt. Brit.* (ed. 7) IV. 303 It is called in the Irish Language, I-colm-kill; some call it Iona. **1779–81** JOHNSON *L.P.*, *Addison* Wks. III. 44 A dead language, in which nothing is mean because nothing is familiar. **1823** DE QUINCEY *Lett. Yng. Man* Wks. 1860 XIV. 37 On this Babel of an earth..there are said to be about three thousand languages and jargons. **1845** M. PATTISON *Ess.* (1889) I. 13 In fact, Bede is writing in a dead language, Gregory in a living. **1875** STUBBS *Const. Hist.* II. 414 The use of the English language in the Courts of law was ordered in 1362. **1875** W. D. WHITNEY *Life & Growth of Language* ii. 25 We realize better in the case of a second or 'foreign', than in that of a first or 'native' language, that the process of acquisition is a never-ending one. **1876** C. M. YONGE *Womankind* vi. 40 The second language has been really and grammatically learnt. **1943** I. A. RICHARDS *Basic Eng. & its Uses* 14 The history of the nationalist movement in India is an instructive instance. Its leaders and its chief supporters are speakers of English and sometimes use it rather as their first than as their second language. **1962** R. QUIRK *Use of English* i. 6 Something like 250 million people for whom English is the mother-tongue or 'first language'. **1971** *Guardian* 23 June 7/3 Indians and Pakistanis..using a second language at school and their first language for many home activities.

fig. **1720** GAY *Prol. Dione* 4 Love, devoid of art, Spoke the consenting language of the heart. **1812** W. C. BRYANT *Thanatopsis* 3 To him who in the love of Nature holds Communion with her visible forms, she speaks A various language.

b. *transf.* Applied to methods of expressing the thoughts, feelings, wants, etc., otherwise than by words. ***finger language*** = DACTYLOLOGY. ***language of flowers***: a method of expressing sentiments by means of flowers. .

1606 SHAKS. *Tr. & Cr.* IV. v. 55 Ther's a language in her eye, her cheeke, her lip. **1697** COLLIER *Ess. Mor. Subj.* II. 120 As the language of the Face is universal so 'tis very comprehensive. **1711** STEELE *Spect.* No. 66 ⁋2 She is utterly a Foreigner to the Language of Looks and Glances. **1827** WHATELY *Logic* (1850) Introd. §6 A Deaf-mute, before he has been taught a Language, either the Finger-language, or Reading, cannot carry on a train of Reasoning. **1834** tr. *C. de la Tour's Lang. Flowers* 95 It is more especially by.. modifications that the Language of Flowers becomes the interpretation of our thoughts. **1837** *Penny Cycl.* VIII. 282/2 Dactylology must not be confounded with the natural language of the deaf and dumb, which is purely a language of mimic signs. **1847** THACKERAY *Van. Fair* (1848) iv. 31 Perhaps she just looked first into the bouquet, to see whether there was a *billet-doux* hidden... 'Do they talk the language of flowers at Boggley Wollah, Sedley?' asked Osborne, laughing. **1876** MOZLEY *Univ. Serm.* vi. 134 All action is.. besides being action, language. **1880** *Times* 23 June 9/5 Teaching the deaf by signs and by finger language. **1894** H. DRUMMOND *Ascent Man* 212 A sign Language is of no use when one savage is at one end of a wood and his wife at the other. **1949** *Enquire within upon Everything* (ed. 122) 462 *Language of Flowers.* The symbolism of flowers has always possessed a certain fascination, especially for the young person of either sex.

c. *transf.* Applied to the inarticulate sounds used by the lower animals, birds, etc.

1601 SHAKS. *All's Well* IV. i. 22 Choughs language, gabble enough, and good enough. **1667** MILTON *P.L.* VIII. 373 Is not the Earth With various living creatures, and the Aire Replenisht,..know'st thou not Thir language and thir wayes? **1797** BEWICK *Brit. Birds* (1847) I. p. xxvii, The notes, or as it may with more propriety be called, the language of birds.

d. *Computers.* Any of numerous systems of precisely defined symbols and rules for using them that have been devised for writing programs or representing instructions and data.

1949 E. C. BERKELEY *Giant Brains* iii. 29 We must translate into machine language, in this case punched holes in the program tape. **1956** *Jrnl. Assoc. Computing Machinery* III. 272 In the development of an automatic coding system, two major problems arise. The first is to develop a coding language which permits a programmer to specify the computation he wants the machine to perform. Once this has been done, there remains the task of coding a compiler for a particular high speed calculator which will translate the language into actual machine instructions... The language described here is the one translated by the PACT I Compiling Routine into instructions for the IBM Type 701. **1959** E. M. GRABBE et al. *Handbk. Automation, Computation, & Control* II. ii. 186 The purpose of these activities has been to..set up a class of languages that will be easily translatable by machine from one to another, and also easily recognizable to the ordinary human user... Such languages form the input to a class of automatic computer programs called translators, which perform a translation.. into a second or target language. The latter may be either (1) an assembly language such as SOAP, SAP, or MAGIC.., or (2) a straight machine language, in pure decimal, binary (or in some cases such as the Univac I and II), alphanumeric. **1961** LEEDS & WEINBERG *Computer Programming Fund.* ii. 46 The best way of writing down operations is to write them in alphabetical format. A format used for writing down these alphabetical instructions is called the programming language or paper language, to distinguish it from the machine language..acceptable to the machine circuitry. **1964** F. L. WESTWATER *Electronic Computers* ix. 145 As the benefits of these codes were realised, each manufacturer produced different 'languages'. **1966** A. BATTERSBY *Math. in Managem.* viii. 206 If each manufacturer prepares a compiler routine which will translate instructions in some universal 'language' into a program in his own code, then programs written in the universal language can be run on any machine. **1967** A. HASSITT *Computer Programming* i. 1 An efficient way of learning to use a computing machine utilizes one of the problem oriented languages such as Fortran, Algol, or PL/1. **1970** A. CAMERON et al. *Computers & Old Eng. Concordances* 27 If we program in so-called higher-languages, like Fortran, conceivably PLI,..I myself will be very surprised if the next generation of machines will not accept Fortran programming and probably Cobol, Algol, and PLI programming.

2. a. In generalized sense: Words and the methods of combining them for the expression of thought.

1599 SHAKS. *Much Ado* IV. i. 98 There is not chastitie enough in language, Without offence to vtter them. **1644** MILTON *Educ.* Wks. (1847) 98/2 Language is but the instrument conveying to us things useful to be known. **1781** COWPER *Conversat.* 15 So language in the mouths of the adult,..Too often proves an implement of play. **1841** TRENCH *Parables* ii. (1877) 25 Language is ever needing to be recalled, minted and issued anew. **1862** J. MARTINEAU *Ess.* (1891) IV. 104 Language, that wonderful crystallization of the very flow and spray of thought. **1882** WESTCOTT *Gospel of Life* 186 Language must be to the last inadequate to express the results of perfect observation.

b. Power or faculty of speech; ability to speak a foreign tongue. Now *rare*.

1526 WOLSEY *Let. to Tayler* in Strype *Eccl. Mem.* I. v. 66 A gentleman..who had knowledge of the country and good language to pass. **1601** SHAKS. *All's Well* IV. i. 77, I shall loose my life for want of language. If there be heere German or Dane, Low Dutch, Italian, or French, let him speake to me. **1610** —— *Temp.* II. ii. 86 Here is that which will giue language to you Cat; open your mouth. **1790** COWPER *Receipt Mother's Pict.* 1 Oh that those lips had language!

3. a. The form of words in which a person expresses himself; manner or style of expression. ***bad language***: coarse or vulgar expressions. ***strong language***: expressions indicative of violent or excited feeling.

a **1300** *Cursor M.* 3743 Iacob..þat es to sai wit right langage, Supplanter als of heritage. *c* **1384** CHAUCER *H. Fame* II. 353 With-outen any subtilite Of speche..For harde langage and hard matere Is encombrouse for to here Attones. *c* **1425** LYDG. *Assembly Gods* 368 In eloquence of langage he passyd all the pak. **1430–40** —— *Bochas* II. xiii. (1554) 53 a, Though some folke wer large of their langage Amisse to expoune by report. *c* **1489** CAXTON *Blanchardyn* i. 14 For it is sayde in comyn langage, that the good byrde affeyteth hirself. *a* **1533** LD. BERNERS *Huon* lxix. 236 Come to yᵉ poynt, and vse no more such langage nor suche serymonyes. **1593** SHAKS. *2 Hen. VI*, IV. ix. 45 Be not to rough in termes, For he is fierce, and cannot brooke hard Language. **1611** BIBLE *Ecclus.* vi. 5 Sweet language will multiply friends. **1643** SIR T. BROWNE *Relig. Med.* I. §5 By his sentence I stand excommunicated: Heretick is the best language he affords me. **1694** PENN *Pref. to G. Fox's Jrnl.* (1827) I. 15 They also used the plain language of Thou and Thee. [**1759** BURKE *Philos. Enquiry Sublime & Beautiful* (ed. 2) v. vii. 338 We do not sufficiently distinguish, in our observations upon language, between a clear expression, and a strong expression.] **1770** *Junius Lett.* 187 They suggest to him a language full of severity and reproach. **1809–10** COLERIDGE *Friend* (1865) 135 These pretended constitutionalists recurred to the language of insult. **1849** MACAULAY *Hist. Eng.* vi. II. 118 He lived and died, in the significant language of one of his countrymen, a bad Christian, but a good Protestant. **1855** MOTLEY *Dutch Rep.* II. ii. (1856) 155 In all these interviews he had uniformly used one language: his future wife was to 'live as a Catholic'. *c* **1863** T. TAYLOR in M. R. Booth *Eng. Plays of 19th Cent.* (1969) II. 109 Come, cheeky! Don't you use bad language. **1875** JOWETT *Plato* (ed. 2) V. 348 The language used to a servant ought always to be that of a command. *a* **1910** 'MARK TWAIN' *Autobiogr.* (1924) II. 88 She made a guarded remark which censured strong language. **1934** R. MACAULAY *Milton* vi. 100 Milton's familiarity with the tradition [of scurrility] may account for much of his strong language, even when reviling in English.

b. The phraseology or terms of a science, art, profession, etc., or of a class of persons.

1502 *Ord. Crysten Men* (W. de W. 1506) Prol. 4 The swete and fayre langage of theyr phylosophy. **1596** SHAKS. *1 Hen. IV*, II. iv. 21, I can drinke with any Tinker in his owne Language. **1611** —— *Cymb.* III. iii. 74 This is not Hunters Language. **1651** HOBBES *Leviath.* III. xxxiv. 207 The words Body, and Spirit, which in the language of the Schools are termed Substances, Corporeall and Incorporeall. **1747** SPENCE *Polymetis* VIII. xv. 243 Those attributes of the Sword, Victory, and Globe, say very plainly (in the language of the statuaries) that [etc.]. **1841** J. R. YOUNG *Math. Dissert.* i. 10 Thus can be expressed in the language of algebra, not only distance but position. **1891** *Speaker* 2 May 532/1 In it metaphysics have again condescended to speak the language of polite letters.

c. The style (of a literary composition); also, the wording (of a document, statute, etc.).

1712 ADDISON *Spect.* No. 285 ⁋6 It is not therefore sufficient that the Language of an Epic Poem be Perspicuous, unless it be also Sublime. **1781** COWPER *Conversat.* 236 A tale should be judicious, clear, succinct, The language plain. **1886** SIR J. STIRLING in *Law Times Rep.* LV. 283/2 There are two remarks which I desire to make on the language of the Act.

d. ***long language***: †(*a*) verbosity (tr. Gr. *μακρολογία*; (*b*) language composed of words written in full, as opposed to cipher.

1589 PUTTENHAM *Eng. Poesie* III. xxii. (Arb.) 264 *Macrologia*, or long language, when we vse large clauses or sentences more than is requisite to the matter. **1823** J. BADCOCK *Dom. Amusem.* 34 Those Greeks did not use cypher, but the long language of the country.

e. *vulgar.* Short for *bad language* (see above).

1860 DICKENS *Uncomm. Trav.* (1861) v. 65 Mr. Victualler's assurance that he 'never allowed any language, and never suffered any disturbance'. **1865** —— *Dr. Marigold's Prescriptions* i, in *All Year Round* Extra Christmas No., 7 Dec. 4/1 But have a temper in the cart, flinging language and the hardest goods in stock at you, and where are you then? **1886** BESANT *Childr. Gibeon* II. xxv, That rude eloquence which is known in Ivy Lane as 'language'. **1893** SELOUS *Trav. S.E. Africa* 3 The sailor.. had never ceased to pour out a continuous flood of 'language' all the time. **1929** C. C. MARTINDALE *Risen Sun* 173, I have heard more 'language' in a 'gentleman's' club in ten minutes than in all that evening in the Melbourne Stadium. **1974** 'M. INNES' *Mysterious Commission* vii. 75 'You behave like bloody fools.' 'Language, now, Mr Honeybath, language.'

f. Phr. ***to speak*** (***talk***) ***someone's language***, ***to speak*** (***talk***) ***the same language***: to have an understanding with someone through similarity of outlook and expression, to get on well with someone; ***to speak a different language*** (***from someone***): to have little in common (with someone).

1893 'S. GRAND' *Heavenly Twins* I. II. vi. 256 What could Evadne have in common with these flippant people..? They did not even speak the same language. (To their insidious slang she opposed a smooth current of perfect English.) **1904** H. JAMES *Golden Bowl* I. xvii. 297 They hung together, they passed each other the word, they spoke each other's language, they did each other 'turns'. **1915** CONRAD *Victory* IV. xi. 391 You seem to be a morbid, senseless sort of bandit. We don't speak the same language. **1923** H. CRANE *Let.* 13 Apr. (1965) 131 The older poets and writers down here..don't talk the same language as we do. **1930** A. HUXLEY *Brief Candles* viii. 284 You'll perceive that he speaks your language, that he inhabits your world of thought and feeling. **1938** F. SCOTT FITZGERALD *Let.* 7 July (1964) 33, I want my energies and my earnings for people who talk my language. **1957** J. OSBORNE *Look Back in Anger* II. ii. 64 As for Jimmy—he just speaks a different language from any of us. **1961** A. WILSON *Old Men at Zoo* i. 25 Bobby..had presumed that since he and I 'spoke the same language', I should naturally dislike the Director as much as he did. **1971** R. RENDELL *No More Dying Then* xix. 166 She really didn't understand him at all, his need to be respectable... They didn't speak the same language.

†**4. a.** The act of speaking or talking; the use of speech. ***by language***: so to speak. ***in language***

with: in conversation with. ***without language***: not to make many words. *Obs.*

a **1400** *Cov. Myst.* iv. *Noah's Flood* ii, Afftyr Adam withoutyn langage, The secunde fadyr am I [Noe] in fay. *a* **1450** *Knt. de la Tour* (1868) 18 My fader sette me in langage with her. **1461** *Paston Lett.* No. 393 II. 17, I said I dwelled uppon the cost of the see here, and be langage hit were more necessare to with hold men here than take from hit. **1477** EARL RIVERS (Caxton) *Dictes* 57 One was surer in keping his tunge, than in moche speking, for in moche langage one may lightly erre. **1490** CAXTON *Eneydos* xxviii. 107 Wythout eny more langage dydo..seased thenne the swerde. **1514** BARCLAY *Cyt. & Uplondyshm.* (Percy Soc.) p. xviii, To morowe of court we may have more language.

†**b.** That which is said, words, talk, report; *esp.* words expressive of censure or opprobrium. Also *pl.* reports, sayings. ***to say language against***: to talk against, speak opprobriously of. *Obs.*

a **1450** *Knt. de la Tour* (1868) 2 And so thei dede bothe deseiue ladies and gentilwomen, and bere forthe diuerse langages on hem. **1465** MARG. PASTON in *P. Lett.* No. 502 II. 188, I hyre moch langage of the demenyng betwene you and herre. **1467** *Mann. & Househ. Exp.* (Roxb.) 172 ȝe haue mekel on setenge langwache aȝenste me, were of I mervel gretely for I have ȝeffen ȝowe no schwsche kawse. **1470–85** MALORY *Arthur* II. xl, Euery daye syre Palomydes brauled and sayd langage ageynst syr Tristram. **1485** CAXTON *Chas. Gt.* 225 Feragus said in this manere... The valyaunt Rolland was contente ryght wel, & accepted hys langage. **1636** SIR H. BLUNT *Voy. Levant* 33 A Turke..gave such a Language of our Nation, and threatning to all whom they should light upon, as made me upon all demands professe my selfe a Scotchman.

5. a. A community of people having the same form of speech, a nation. *arch.* [A literalism of translation.]

1388 WYCLIF *Dan.* v. 19 Alle puplis, lynagis, and langagis [**1382** tungis]. **1611** BIBLE *Ibid.* **1653** URQUHART *Rabelais* I. x, All people, and all languages and nations.

b. A national division or branch of a religious and military Order, *e.g.* of the Hospitallers.

1727–52 CHAMBERS *Cycl.*, *Language* is also used, in the order of Malta, for *nation*. **1728** MORGAN *Algiers* I. v. 314 Don Raimond Perellos de Roccapoul, of the Language of Aragon,..was elected Grand Master. **1885** *Catholic Dict.* (ed. 3) 413/2 The order [of Hospitallers]..was divided into eight 'languages', Provence, Auvergne, France, Aragon, Castile, England, Germany, and Italy.

6. *attrib.* and *Comb.* **a.** simple attributive, as ***language acquisition***, ***-capacity***, ***change***, ***course***, ***description***, ***engineering***, ***event***, ***-family***, ***-form***, ***-group***, ***-history***, ***-pattern***, ***sign***, ***structure***, ***-study***, ***-system***, ***-turn***, ***-use***. **b.** objective, as ***language-learner***, ***-learning***, ***-maker***, ***-teacher***, ***-teaching***, ***-user***, ***-using***; **language area**, (*a*) an area of the cerebral cortex regarded as especially concerned with the use of language; (*b*) a region where a particular language is spoken; **language barrier**, a barrier to communication between people which results from their speaking or writing different languages; **language-contact** *Linguistics* (see quot. 1964); **language-game** *Philos.*, a speech-activity or limited system of communication and action, complete in itself, which may or may not form a part of our existing use of language; **language laboratory** (*colloq.* **language lab**), a classroom, equipped with tape recorders, etc., where foreign languages are learnt by means of repeated oral practice; **language-master**, a teacher of language or languages; **language-particular** *a.*, = *language-specific* adj.; **language-specific** *a. Linguistics*, distinctive to a specified language.

1921 H. E. PALMER *Princ. Lang.-Study* 14 In addition to certain *spontaneous* capacities, we possess what we may term 'studial' capacities for *language-acquisition. **1965** N. CHOMSKY *Aspects of Theory of Syntax* i. 52 The innate structure of a language-acquisition device. **1971** D. CRYSTAL *Ling.* 257 Alternative theories of language acquisition are much needed. **1937** *Bull. Los Angeles Neurol. Soc.* II. 36 (*heading*) Case illustrating capacity for use of symbols after destruction of the major (left) *language area. **1939** L. H. GRAY *Foundations of Lang.* ii. 25 One may frequently say that such-and-such an individual is from such-and-such a district within the language-area. **1961** *Lancet* 12 Aug. 361/2 The insistence that the degree of disability—e.g., in aphasia—was proportional to the amount of 'language area' destroyed. **1933** *Discovery* Sept. 281/2 Science itself..might go forward with greatly increased efficiency if the *language barrier were removed by the adoption of Basic for Abstracts and Congresses. **1961** *Guardian* 18 May 8/2 A German girl tries to talk to him, but the language barrier is impenetrable. **1971** *Physics Bull.* Sept. 514/2 Important work in a number of countries may be missed because of the language barrier. **1875** WHITNEY *Life Lang.* xiv. 281 Every division of the human race has been long enough in existence for its *language-capacities to work themselves out. **1912** L. BLOOMFIELD in C. F. Hockett *Leonard Bloomfield Anthol.* (1970) 37 A suggestion of 'concerted effort to shape usage' is ..hitched on to a discussion of the universal unconscious processes of *language-change. **1968** J. LYONS *Introd. Theoret. Ling.* i. 22 To have developed a general theory of language change and linguistic relationship was the most significant achievement of nineteenth-century linguistic scholarship. **1954** U. WEINREICH in Saporta & Bastian *Psycholinguistics* (1961) 378/1 A full account of interference in a *language-contact situation..is possible only if the extra-linguistic factors are considered. **1964** M. A. K. HALLIDAY et al. *Ling. Sci.* 77 Situations in which one language community impinges on another have been called 'language contact' situations. **1966** *Amer. Speech* XLI. 39 A name in a language-contact situation is sometimes the only element which survives the impact of another language. **1921** H. E. PALMER *Princ. Lang.-Study* 54 Most *language-courses must necessarily be *corrective courses*. **1973** A. PRICE *October Men* xi. 155 [He] had been sent on a language course at a provincial English university. **1963** J. LYONS *Structural Semantics* ii. 36 The distinction between language-operation and *language-description. **1971** D. CRYSTAL *Ling.* 54 It proved necessary to..redefine many of the catagories,..to make them applicable to the task of language description. **1953** J. B. CARROLL *Study of Lang.* iv. 113 Linguistics may play a part in the solution of certain social problems. If so, a new kind of applied science—'*language engineering' as it has recently been termed—may come into being. **1957** *Economist* 7 Sept. 851/2 An electronic data-processing machine..is breaking new ground in 'language engineering' by providing words—as many as five consecutive ones—which are missing from the Dead Sea Scrolls. **1964** *English Studies* XLV. 21 This admits under the label of 'English' a great range of different kinds of '*language event'. **1965** R. M. W. DIXON *What is Lang.?* 93 The data to be accounted for are observed language events. **1891** *Tablet* 29 Aug. 331 The rank it holds among the *language-families of the world. **1901** H. OERTEL *Lect. Study of Lang.* ii. 102 The results of all higher classification beyond these, such as *language-forms, are ideal types. **1932** A. H. GARDINER *Theory of Speech & Lang.* iv. 207 Jespersen..points out that particular phrases used in this way have become so stereotyped as to be real language-forms, e.g. *Well, I never! I must say!* Most curious of all is *I say!* with nothing following. **1934** R. BENEDICT *Patterns of Culture* (1935) iii. 48 When we describe the process [of the evolution of Gothic architecture] historically, we inevitably use animistic forms of expression as if there were choice and purpose in the growth of this great art-form. But this is due to the difficulty in our language-forms. **1971** D. CRYSTAL *Ling.* 71 The philosophical search for laws of thought underlying language forms. **1921** H. E. PALMER *Princ. Lang.-Study* 145 *Language-games may not further the student sufficiently in the habit-forming process. **1933–4** WITTGENSTEIN *Blue & Brown Bks.* (1958) 17, I shall in the future again and again draw your attention to what I shall call language games. These are ways of using signs simpler than those in which we use the signs of our highly complicated everyday language. Language games are the forms of language with which a child begins to make use of words. **1970** A. MACINTYRE *Marcuse* vii. 80 Wittgenstein tries to construct language games. **1970** *Times Lit. Suppl.* 23 July 787/1 In this country it was a dominant caste of philosophers..who seemed to be most gainfully preoccupied with the verbal manifestations of mind, having been coached at 'language-games' by Wittgenstein. **1927** PEAKE & FLEURE *Peasants & Potters* 121 A group with common speech, that is to say a *language-group. **1964** *English Studies* XLV. Suppl. 11 His systematic sub-division of the principal language-groups.. represents an astonishing linguistic perception. **1875** WHITNEY *Life Lang.* Pref. 5 Scholars..versed in the facts of *language-history. **1963** *Guardian* 4 Oct. 4/3 In a '*language lab' each student has his own booth and a tape-recorder which guides his speaking in French, Russian, or in any other language. **1968** A. DIMENT *Bang Bang Birds* ii. 18 There was my speech training. Usually a couple of hours a day down in the language labs. **1931** R. H. WALTZ in *Mod. Lang. Jrnl.* XVI. 217 (*title*) *Language laboratory administration. **1946** *French Rev.* XX. 19 A large Language Laboratory was installed... Phonographs and records were available at all times of the day. **1963** *Listener* 14 Nov. 791/1 In 1942..my ideas were referred to as the 'language laboratory', a name that has stuck..to this day. **1969** *Ibid.* 3 July 8/2 I've done most through the Language Laboratory. I think it's a marvellous idea to start off a language by listening to what people say in the language. **1973** *Jrnl. Genetic Psychol.* CXXIII. 7 The *S*s were brought in groups of 20 to 30 students each, to a language laboratory where they were seated at individual carrels. **1921** H. E. PALMER *Princ. Lang.-Study* 14 Most *language-learners at the present day are found to make an almost exclusive use of their studial capacities. **1965** N. CHOMSKY *Aspects of Theory of Syntax* i. 43 Cyclic regularities..are much more difficult for the language-learner to construct. **1697** J. SERGEANT *Solid Philos. Asserted* Pref. §10 Perhaps there is not one Evident Truth in it..but only such a way of Plausible Discourse or *Language-Learning, as may serve equally and indifferently to maintain either side of the Contradiction? **1964** *Language* XL. 134 Chomsky's hypothesis is that the child is innately equipped with a language-learning device. **1607** BREWER *Lingua* III. v. F 2, These same *language makers haue the very quality of colde in their wit, that freezeth all Hetero-geneall languages together. **1867** W. D. WHITNEY *Lang. & Study of Lang.* v. 197 Language-makers in different parts of the earth. **1952** H. READ in B. Hepworth *Carvings & Drawings* p. ix/1 In this situation the artists of a period are the language-makers, inventing visual symbols. **1712** ADDISON *Spect.* No. 305 ¶11 The Third is a sort of *Language-Master, who is to instruct them in the Style proper for a Foreign Minister in his ordinary Discourse. **1831** T. MOORE *Mem.* (1854) VI. 190 It turned out that what his friend, the language-master, had ..been teaching him was Bas-Breton! **1968** P. M. POSTAL *Aspects Phonol. Theory* viii. 164 The function of morpheme structure rules was to represent those *language-particular predictable constraints on the possible combinations of feature specifications both within a segment and sequentially. **1970** *Language* XLVI. 377 It is a possible language-particular constraint on pronominalization in complex structures that a pronoun and its antecedent must lie within the same 'chain of command'. **1935** G. K. ZIPF *Psycho-Biol. of Lang.* (1936) 19 Conditions present in all speech-elements or *language-patterns. **1961** J. B. WILSON *Reason & Morals* iii. 178 Accepted language-patterns..act primarily as conservative forces both in the individual and in society. **1946** C. MORRIS *Signs, Lang. & Behavior* 350 In this book '*language sign' is often used in place of 'lansign'. **1970** Language sign [see LANSIGN]. **1972** *Language* XLVIII. 431 The post-Saussurean debate on the arbitrary nature of the language sign. **1965** N. CHOMSKY *Aspects of Theory of Syntax* iv. 166 However, there are also many *language-specific redundancies. **1969** *Computers & Humanities* III. 258 Studies of..relative frequencies of language-specific syllabic patterns. **1970** *Language* XLVI. 784 It is non-language-specific in that it is empirically based on studies in English, some ten Meso-American languages, some twenty-four Philippine languages, and a few scattered languages from other areas. **1933** L. BLOOMFIELD *Lang.* i. 18 H. Steinthal..published in 1861 a treatise on the principal types of *language structure. **1971** D. CRYSTAL *Ling.* 59 Areas of language structure other than grammar were disregarded in most traditional accounts. **1921** H. E. PALMER (*title*) The principles of *language-study. **1933** L. BLOOMFIELD *Lang.* i. 1 Many people have difficulty at the beginning of language study. **1964** C. BARBER *Ling. Change Present-Day Eng.* vii. 149 Your own speech..is always the right place to begin language-study. **1940** A. H. GARDINER *Theory of Proper Names* 67 Regardless of the *language-system as a whole. **1946** *Mind* LV. 339 This task should be approached by construction of consistent language-systems. **1966** *English Studies* XLVII. 193 An item in a highly personal language-system. **1826** PUSEY *Let. to Lloyd* in *Life* (1893) I. v. 97 A *language-teacher gives me lectures..five times a week. **1921** H. E. PALMER *Princ. Lang.-Study* 58 The language-teacher must possess a considerable knowledge of phonetic theory. *Ibid.* 15 The *language-teaching forces of nature. **1964** W. R. LEE in D. Abercrombie et al. *Daniel Jones* 291 The clear purpose is to see in what manner aids can subserve language-teaching. **1803** SOUTHEY *Let. to C. W. W. Wynn* 9 June, In all these modern ballads there is a modernism of thought and *language-turns to me very perceptible. **1956** J. HOLLOWAY in A. Pryce-Jones *New Outl. Mod. Knowl.* viii. 42 Discoveries about *language-use which are in themselves not necessarily connected at all with metaphysics. **1963** J. LYONS *Structural Semantics* i. 7 The known or apparent facts of language-learning and language-use. **1965** N. CHOMSKY *Aspects of Theory of Syntax* 6 The grammar of a particular language..is to be supplemented by a universal grammar that accommodates the creative aspect of language use. **1953** *Mind* LXII. 332 The sentence.. mentions neither linguistic expressions nor *language users. **1959** *Brno Studies in English* I. 29 The consciousness in language-users of the existing quasi-ideographic trends of the written norm. **1961** *Encounter* Mar. 60/1 Intentional action is characteristic of human beings..as language-users. **1971** D. CRYSTAL *Ling.* 85 We must..start with the study of individual language users. **1921** H. E. PALMER *Princ. Lang.-Study* 96 These then are the chief things to be done once we have decided to enlist on our behalf the universal and natural powers of *language-using. **1954** U. WEINREICH in Saporta & Bastian *Psycholinguistics* (1961) 376/1 The language-using individuals are thus the locus of the contact.

language (ˈlæŋgwɪdʒ), *v.* [f. LANGUAGE *sb.*] *trans.* To express in language, put into words.

1636 ABP. WILLIAMS *Holy Table* (1637) 95 Learn, Doctour, learn to language this Sacrament from a Prelate of this Church. *a* **1652** J. SMITH *Sel. Disc.* VI. xiii. (1821) 294 The style and manner of languaging all pieces of prophecy. **1655** FULLER *Ch. Hist.* VI. v. False Miracles §11 Predictions ..were languaged in such doubtfull Expressions, that they bare a double sense. **1667** WATERHOUSE *Fire Lond.* 185 Seneca has languaged this appositely to us.

b. *transf.* To express (by gesture).

1824 *New Monthly Mag.* X. 196 'Twas languaged by the tell-tale eye.

Hence **ˈlanguaging** *vbl. sb.* In quot. *attrib.*

1875 LOWELL in *N. Amer. Rev.* CXX. 395 It is very likely that Daniel had only the thinking and languaging parts of a poet's outfit.

language, variant of LANGUID *sb.* (sense 2).

languaged (ˈlæŋgwɪdʒd), *ppl. a.* [f. LANGUAGE *sb.* + -ED².]

1. Skilled *in* a language or languages. Also ***well languaged***.

1303 R. BRUNNE *Handl. Synne* 8095 Þoghe he were wyser þan Salamon And bettyr langagede þan was Mercyon. **1513** EARL WORCESTER, etc. *Let. to Hen. VIII* in Strype *Eccl. Mem.* (1721) I. 6 If any Doctors of Civil Law and Languaged might be found in England. **1589** PUTTENHAM *Eng. Poesie* III. xxiii. (Arb.) 278, I maruell your Noblemen of England doe not desire to be better languaged in forraine languages. **1593** T. MATHEWS *Let. to Burghley* 2 Aug. in Tytler *Hist. Scot.* (1864) IV. 200 Well languaged in the French and Italian. **1605** B. JONSON *Volpone* II. ii, Great generall schollers,..The onely languag'd-men, of all the world! **1627–77** FELTHAM *Resolves* I. lxxxvii. 135 Well uersed in the World, languaged and well read in men. **1628** EARLE *Microcosm., Meere Dull Phisitian* (Arb.) 25 He is indeed only languag'd in diseases, and speakes Greeke many times when he knows not. **1671** F. PHILLIPS *Reg. Necess.* 222 The six Gentlemen of the Privy Chamber should be well languaged.

b. Provided with or having a language. Chiefly with qualifying word prefixed: Characterized by the use of or expressed in (such or such) a language, or (many, etc.) languages.

1605 VERSTEGAN *Dec. Intell.* i. (1628) 5 This towre by these new languaged Masons thus left vnfinished. **1628** BP. HALL *Old Relig.* xii. §2. 121 How doth hee tell vs that in a strange languaged prayer the vnderstanding is vnfruitfull. **1725** POPE *Odyss.* III. 408 He..many languag'd nations has survey'd. **1798** CANNING *New Morality* 46 in *Anti-Jacobin* 9 July, The stream of verse and many-languaged prose. **1865** D'A. W. THOMPSON *Wayside Th. of Asophophilos.* I. 5 The many-languaged harbour. **1870** LOWELL *Among my Bks.* Ser. I. 151 That tree which Father Huc saw in Tartary, whose leaves were languaged. **1871** G. MACDONALD *Sonnets concerning Jesus* v, How had we read, as in new-languaged books, Clear love of God.

2. With qualifying word prefixed: Having (good, etc.) speech, (well or fair) -spoken. ? *Obs.*

1470–85 MALORY *Arthur* VII. xxxvi, This syr Gareth was a noble knyghte and a wel rulyd and fayr langaged. **1523** LD. BERNERS *Froiss.* I. ccxxxi. 316 These two sage and well languaged knightes. **1561** T. HOBY tr. *Castiglione's Courtyer* Y yiv, To be well spoken and faire languaged. **1613–16** W. BROWNE *Brit. Past.* II. 303 Well-languag'd Daniel. **1633** HEYWOOD *Eng. Trav.* III. Wks. 1874 IV. 43 Pray be more open languag'd. **1652** KIRKMAN *Clerio & Lozia* 44 Her gently languag'd mouth opened it self to disclose the dream to Vincia.

3. Expressed in language, worded. Also with qualifying word, as *well*.
1646 S. BOLTON *Arraignm. Err.* 236 Because an opinion comes languaged under the most receptible termes. **1691** WOOD *Ath. Oxon.* II. 169 His..well-languag'd Sermons speak him eminent in his generation.

languageless ('læŋgwɪdʒlɪs), *a.* [f. LANGUAGE *sb.* + -LESS.] Without language.
1606 SHAKS. *Tr. & Cr.* III. iii. 264 Hee's growne a very land-fish, languagelesse, a monster. **1848** LYTTON *Harold* VII. v, They understand me not, poor languageless savages. **1863** HAWTHORNE *Our Old Home* (1883) I. 37 Tool-less, houseless, languageless, except for a few guttural sounds.

†**languager.** *Obs. rare.* Also 5 langageur. [a. OF. *langageur* 'a prater...babler' (Cotgr.), f. *langagier* to talk abundantly, f. *langage* LANGUAGE.] **a.** A verbose person. **b.** One versed in languages.
1483 CAXTON *G. de la Tour* B viij b, We ought not to stryue ayenst them that ben langageurs and full of wordes. *c* **1570** *Pride & Lowl.* (1841) 30 Travayled he had, and was a languager.

‖**langue** (lɑ̃g). In 4 lange, 7 lang. [Fr.]
†**1.** A tongue or language. *Obs. rare.*
c **1330** R. BRUNNE *Chron. Wace* (Rolls) 125 And þerfore for þe comonalte þat blythely wild listen to me, On lighte lange I it began. **1388** WYCLIF *Gen.* xi. 1 The lond was of o langage [2 *MSS.* lange]. —— *Esther* i. 22 In dyuerse langagis [*MS. C.* langis] and lettris. *c* **1665** R. CARPENTER *Pragm. Jesuit* Epil. 66 If your lang be scanty, Th' Italian Tongue welcoms you *tuttie quanti*.
2. = LANGUAGE *sb.* 5 b.
1799 NELSON in Nicolas *Disp.* (1845) III. 313 If it is in my power, you shall be elected a Chevalier of the Order. I find the Russian Langue has the privilege of admitting married men. **1802** *Naval Chron.* VIII. 124 There shall be no English nor French Langues. **1888** *Ch. Times* 13 July 613 There is no reason why each nation or langue should not maintain at Rome a sort of embassy, with its chapel at St. Peter's.
3. *Linguistics.* A language viewed as an abstract system, accepted universally within a speech-community, in contrast to the actual linguistic behaviour of individuals (opp. PAROLE *sb.*).
1924 L. BLOOMFIELD in *Mod. Lang. Jrnl.* VIII. 318 This rigid system, the subject-matter of 'descriptive linguistics', as we should say, is *la langue*, the language. **1947** *Word* III. 16 Langue, tho described as a repository, is not to be thought of simply as a pile of words. **1953** W. J. ENTWISTLE *Aspects of Lang.* i. 26 One may..treat language (*langue*) as a generalization which becomes concrete and individual in speech (*parole*). **1957** [see *diachronistically* adv. s.v. DIACHRONISM]. **1964** *Language* XL. 214 Current theorizing about the acquisition and functioning of the speaker's langue. **1965** N. CHOMSKY *Aspects of Theory of Syntax* i. 4 The distinction..is related to the *langue-parole* distinction of Saussure; but it is necessary to reject his concept of *langue* as merely a systematic inventory of items. **1968** *Word* XXIV. 56 Accent, viewed dynamically, constitutes the *parole* which manifests the pattern or *langue*.

langued (læŋgd), *a. Her.* [f. F. *langue* tongue + -ED[2]: cf. F. *langué*.] Of a charge: Represented with a tongue of a specified tincture.
1572 BOSSEWELL *Armorie* II. 37 One Lyon Saliant d'Azure, armed, langued, and crowned Gules. **1610** GUILLIM *Heraldry* VI. vii. (1611) 276 A lion Rampand Pearle, armed and langued saphire. **1663** BUTLER *Hud.* I. ii. 259 Armed, as Heraulds cant, and langued Or, as the Vulgar say, sharp-fanged. **1792** *Statist. Acc. Scot.* V. 497 On a branch in the sinister side a bell langued or. **1870** ROCK *Text. Fabr.* I. 49 A hound, green, collared, armed, and langued white.

†**langue de bœuf.** *Obs.* Forms: 5-6 lang(e)debefe, -beefe, -boef, -beafe, -biefe, 5 landebeffe, long debefe, long debeof, 6 languedebiefe, -beuf, lang du beaffe, landebeuf, 7 langdebeef, -beuf, landebeef, (8 Langley beef). [Fr.; lit. 'ox tongue'.]
1. A name variously applied to certain boragineous and other plants with rough leaves, as *Echium vulgare*, *Helminthia echiodes*, *Borrago officinalis*, etc., for most of which the etymologically synonymous name BUGLOSS has been applied.
c **1400** *Secreta Secret., Gov. Lordsh.* 84 Of water of lange de boef, a Rote. *c* **1440** *Anc. Cookery* in *Househ. Ord.* (1790) 426 Take cole, and borage, and lang de beeff, and parsell. [*c* **1450** *Alphita* (Anecd. Oxon.) 24 *Buglossa*..(gall. lange de beof), anglice oxtunge.] **1551** TURNER *Herbal* I. G iv b, Dioscorides..saythe that Cirsion (whyche I take to be oure langdebefe) hath longer leues than buglossum. **1573** TUSSER *Husb.* xxxix. (1878) 93 Seedes and herbes for the Kitchen.. Langdebiefe. **1597** GERARDE *Herbal* II. cclxx. §2. 654 Lang de Beefe is a kinde heereof, altogither lesser. *Ibid.* cclxxi. 656 Landebeuf. **1601** HOLLAND *Pliny* II. 279 The leaves [of Cirsion] in forme resemble an ox tongue or the hearbe Langue-de-bœufe. **1615** MARKHAM *Eng. Housew.* II. i. (1668) 14 To quicken a mans wits, spirit and memory, let him take Langdebeef, which is gathered in June or July. **1620** VENNER *Via Recta* vii. 146 Lang de beuf is..of like operation with Borage and Buglosse. **1732** ELLIS *Pract. Farmer* (ed. 2) 47 That called here Langley-Beef.
2. A kind of spike or halbert, with a head shaped like an ox tongue.
1450 *Rolls of Parlt.* V. 212 Arraied in fourme of werre, with Jakkes Salettez, longe Swerdes, long Debeofs, Boresperes, and all other unmerciable forbodon wepons. **1453** *Nottingham Rec.* II. 216 Cum uno langdebefe et dagario. **1487** *Will of J. Cooke* (Somerset Ho.), A jak, a salett & a long debefe. **1488** *Will of Shamebourne* (ibid.), viij saletty & iiij landebeffe & pollax. **1885** FAIRHOLT *Costume* II. 271.

‖**langue de chat** (lɑ̃g də ʃa). [Fr., lit. cat's tongue.] A long thin piece of chocolate; a crisp biscuit of the same shape.
1907 *Yesterday's Shopping* (1969) 48/2 Chocolate for dessert... Langues de Chat. **1926-7** *Army & Navy Stores Catal.* 54/1 Chocolate... Langues de Chat—box 2/6. **1931** R. H. HEATON *Perfect Hostess* 111 Hand round any Biscuits you prefer. Langue de Chat are popular. **1945** A. HUXLEY *Time must have a Stop* i. 2 It was French chocolate... Those delicious *langues de chat*. **1964** J. FLEMING *The Chill & the Kill* ii. 26 The Christmas Hamper..included..Elvas plums, Turkish Delight,..Cape gooseberries, and Langues de Chat. **1970** SIMON & HOWE *Dict. Gastron.* 239/1 *Langue de chat*, a type of biscuit (cookie) which derives its name from its shape; thin, long and flat like a cat's tongue.

‖**Languedoc** (lɑ̃gdɔk). **1.** Wine produced in the old province of Languedoc, in the south of France.
1709 ADDISON *Tatler* No. 131 ¶7 Two more [drops].. heightened it into a perfect Languedoc. **1755** *Gentl. Mag.* XXV. 326 Much lov'd Languedoc that guggles forth From mouth of long-neck'd bottle.
2. **langue d'oc**, the language spoken in mediæval France in areas roughly south of the Loire, where the use of *oc* [f. L. *hoc*] for *yes* was characteristic of many phonetic variations; opp. **langue d'oïl, d'oui**, the language spoken in areas north of the Loire, where *oïl* [f. L. *hoc ille*] (mod.Fr. *oui*) was used for *yes*, and which has developed into standard modern French.
1703 *Acct. Theatre of War in France, being a Geogr. & Hist. Descr. Languedoc* 3, I more approve of the Etymology of those who observe, that, time out of mind, the French have been distinguish'd into *Langue d'Ouy*, and *Langue d'Oc*, that is, into such as say *Ouy*, and such as say *Oc* for *Yes*; the first living on this, and the other on that side the River Loire. [**1819** SCOTT *Ivanhoe* II. iii. 42 The knight.. asked..whether he would choose a *sirvente* in the language of *oc*, or a *lai* in the language of *oui*.. 'A ballad, a ballad,' said the hermit, 'against all the *ocs* and *ouis* of France.'] **1854** C. M. YONGE *Little Duke* i. 8 The Normans..had taken up what was then called the Languéd'oui, a language between German and Latin, which was the beginning of French. **1866** —— *Prince & Page* iv. 53 My own children..scarce knew whether they spoke English, Languédoc, or Languéd'oui. **1885** H. JAMES *Little Tour in France* xx. 134 Meetings at which poems in the fine old *langue d'oc* are declaimed. **1903** G. E. C. CASEY *Riviera Nature Notes* (ed. 2) liii. 377 The various *Provençal Dialects* are..remnants of the old 'Langue d'Oc'... The 'Langue d'Oil', or northern French was spoken by men more warlike and more barbarous. **1931** G. J. RENIER *The English* viii. 156 The Kings of France did what they could to extirpate the *Langue d'Oc* as soon as they had conquered the southern half of France. **1934** M. K. POPE *From Latin to Mod. French* ii. 17 In the twelfth century the vernaculars of the south and the north (the *Langue d'Oc* and the *Langue d'Oïl*, as they were called after their particles of affirmation) were held to be distinct languages. **1961** P. GREEN tr. *Oldenbourg's Massacre at Montségur* i. 8 The great barons of the North, the land of the *langue d'oïl*,..were by no means all loyal to the French King.

Languedocian (ˌlæŋgə'dəʊʃ(ɪ)ən), *a.* and *sb.* [f. *Languedoc* (see LANGUEDOC).] **A.** *adj.* Of or pertaining to Languedoc, its inhabitants, or their language. **B.** *sb.* **a.** An inhabitant of Languedoc. **b.** The language spoken there, a dialect of Provençal.
1736 [see UNSTAINED *ppl. a.* 1]. **1765** STERNE *Tr. Shandy* VII. xliv. 154 That sprightly frankness which at once unpins every plait of a Languedocian's dress. **1771** C. BURNEY *Present State of Mus. France & Italy* 391 Agreeable Provençale and Languedocian melodies. **1792** A. YOUNG *Trav. France* I. 32 Languedocian bishops are certainly not English ones. **1823** A. THIERS *Pyrenees* v. 66 The old Romance language, which mixed with..the Spanish in Languedoc, forms..the Languedocian. **1908** *Daily Chron.* 25 May 6/4 He has..found time to write poems in the Languedocian language. **1927** A. L. MAYCOCK *Inquisition* 178 The records of the Languedocian tribunals. **1936** A. W. CLAPHAM *Romanesque Archit.* iv. 100 A series of apostles.. typical of later Languedocian sculpture. **1960** *20th Cent.* Sept. 209 We have used the words *Languedoc* and *Languedocian* in some places where *land of Oc* and *occitanian* would be the literal translation. **1972** J. AVIAS in Herak & Stringfield *Karst* v. 131 Epeirogenic movements (on the Languedocian coast for example) together with climatic changes caused variations in the relative basal marine or oceanic level.

langue d'oïl, d'oui: see LANGUEDOC 2.

†'**languefy**, *v. Obs. rare.* Also -ify. [Formed to represent L. *languefacĕre*, f. *languēre*: see LANGUISH *v.* and -FY.]
1. *trans.* To make faint or languid.
1607 *Schol. Disc. agst. Antichr.* II. vi. 59 By the clamour whereof how many..were couched and languefied?
2. *intr.* To become weak or languid.
a **1734** NORTH *Exam.* I. iii. §110 (1740) 197 The Plot.. began to languify, and must haue gone out, like a Snuff, if this Murder had not happened.
Hence †'**languefying** *ppl. a.*
1651 BIGGS *New Disp.* ¶207 Physitians may deservedly suffer the lash and feel compunction for their inhumane languifying practises.

languell, variant of LANGEL *Obs.*

'**languent**, *a.* [ad. L. *languent-em*, pr. pple. of *languēre*: see LANGUISH *v.*] †**1.** That is sick; in quot. *absol. Obs.*
c **1510** BARCLAY *Mirr. Gd. Manners* (1570) F ij, Geue nowe to poore languent spirituall medicine.
2. Languid. *poet. rare*[−1].
1862 G. M. HOPKINS *Vision of Mermaids* (1929), Some would plash The languent smooth with dimpling drops.

languescent (læŋ'gwɛsənt), *a. rare.* [ad. L. *languēscent-em*, pr. pple. of *languēscĕre* to become faint, f. *languēre*: see LANGUISH *v.*] Growing faint or languid.
1837 CARLYLE *Fr. Rev.* II. I. xi, Scarcely have the languescent mercenary Fifteen Thousand laid down their tools. **1855** BAILEY *Mystic* 18 In massive ease and power Languescent.

languet ('læŋgwɪt), *sb.* Also 5-7 langett(e, 5-8 langet, 6, 9 languette, 7 langate, langot. [a. F. *languette*, dim. of *langue* tongue.] Anything shaped like a little tongue.
†**1.** The tongue of a balance. *Obs.*
1413 *Pilgr. Sowle* (Caxton) I. xiv. (1859) 11 Pledours in worldly courtes hauen tonges lyke to the languet of the balaunce that draweth hym..to the more peysaunt party.
†**2.** A tongue-shaped ornament; *esp.* a 'drop' of amber, jet, etc. *Obs.*
1430 *Will of Grymston* (Somerset Ho.), J par precum de jete langettes. **1451** *Will of Halle* (ibid.), Par precum de Aumbre voc. langetes. **1538** ELYOT *Dict.*, *Langurium*, langettes of aumbre, lyke to longe beadestones. *a* **1548** HALL *Chron.*, *Hen. VIII* (1809) 791 A clothe of estate of the same worke, valanced with frettes knotted and langettes tassaled with Venice golde and siluer.
†**3.** The thong used for tying a shoe, a latchet.
c **1460** *Towneley Myst.* iii. 224 Take the ther a langett To tye vp thi hose. **1674** RAY *N.C. Words* 28 The Langot of the Shooe; The latchet of the shooe. **1688** R. HOLME *Armoury* III. 291/2 The Punching Lead is for the Punching of Holes in the instep and Langetts of a Shooe for the ties to go through. **1787** GROSE *Prov. Gloss.*, *Langot.*
4. Applied to tongue-shaped parts of various implements; e.g. a narrow blade projecting at the edge of a spade.
1611 FLORIO, *Lingula*..Also that parte of the barre which is put vnder the weight, and sticketh in the roller, the point, end or languet. **1649** BLITHE *Eng. Improv. Impr.* (1653) 68 Which Spade shoo must be made with two sides, or Langets, up from the end of the bit, like as if you would plant two broad Knife Blades to look upwards with their points upon a common Spade. **1659** TORRIANO, *Stile*, a languet or pin of a pair of writing-tables. **1669** WORLIDGE *Syst. Agric.* (1681) 231 For the cutting Trenches in Watery, Clayie, or Morish Lands, they usually use a Spade, with a Langet or Fin like a knife, turned up by the side of the Spade, and sometimes on both sides. **1677** PLOT *Oxfordsh.* 238 [A pipe] terminated in a very small Cistern of water behind a stone of the rock, and having a mouth and Languet just above its surface. **1727** BRADLEY *Fam. Dict.* s.v. *Chimney*, If the Funnel is loose, you must have Languets or Tenons at the Sides. **1875** KNIGHT *Dict. Mech.*, *Languet, Languette*..2. A thin tongue of metal placed between the blades of a comb-cutter's saw, to preserve their distance. 3. A small piece of metal on a sword-hilt which overhangs the scabbard.
5. *Organ-building.* In a flue-pipe: A flat plate or tongue fastened by its edge to the top of the foot, and opposite the mouth. Also LANGUID *sb.*
1852 SEIDEL *Organ* 21 An organ..which contained the following labial or languet registers. **1875** KNIGHT *Dict. Mech.* s.v. *Mouth-pipe*, At a point opposite the mouth..a languette, or plate, is placed, nearly closing the interior area of the pipe.
†**6. a.** A spatula. **b.** (See quot. 1656.) *Obs.*
1580 HOLLYBAND *Treas. Fr. Tong*, *Magdaleons*, a langate, or roller, little round stones like a roller. **1611** COTGR. s.v. *Magdaleon*. **1611** FLORIO, *Lingua*..Also a little spatle or languet to take salues out of a boxe. **1656** BLOUNT *Glossogr.*, *Magdaleon*, a Langate or long plaister like a Rowler. Dr. Br[owne]. **1823** CRABB *Technol. Dict.*, *Langate*, a linen roller for a wound.
7. A 'tongue' or narrow projecting piece of land.
1610 HOLLAND *Camden's Brit.* I. 606 From the Citie, Northwestward, there Shooteth out a languet of land or promontorie of the maine-land into the Sea. **1652-62** HEYLIN *Cosmogr.* IV. (1682) 40 At the point of a long Languet, or tongue of Rock. **1670** BLOUNT *Glossogr.*, *Langate* or *Languet*, a long and narrow peece of land or other thing. **1673** RAY *Journ. Low C.* (1738) I. 239 The haven of Messina is..compassed almost round with the city on one side, and a narrow languet or neck of land on the other.
†**8.** *gen.* A tongue-shaped piece of anything. *Obs.*
1686 PLOT *Staffordsh.* 266 A true Hippomanes, or Languet of flesh of a dark purple colour near four inches long, that dropt from the forehead of a Colt newly foled.
9. *Zool.* One of the row of little tongue-like or tentacular processes along the dorsal edge of the branchial sac of an ascidian.
1849-52 TODD *Cycl. Anat.* IV. 1219/2 The branchial sac of the *Botryllidæ* is very similar to that of the *Clavellinidæ*. .. The crest or fold corresponding to the anterior border of the branchial sinus has no membraneous languet. **1870** ROLLESTON *Anim. Life* 67 Along the opposite side of the branchial sac there runs the 'oral lamina' which in other species, such as *Ascidia Intestinalis*, may be represented by a row of 'languettes'. **1878** BELL *Gegenbaur's Comp. Anat.* 401 The tongue-like appendages ('languets') found in Ascidians..form a long row along the dorsal surface.

† **languet**, *v.* *Obs.* *rare*⁻¹. [a. OF. *languet-er* to wag the tongue, chatter.] *intr.* To chatter, talk idly. Hence † **langueting** *vbl. sb.*

c **1430** *Pilgr. Lyf Manhode* III. xxxii. (1869) 153 So michel haue j gabbed and forsworn, and so falsliche languetted, that j shal neuere be bileeued. *Ibid.*, And for the brennynge that she hath, to assemble ootheres goodes bi false languetinges and vntrewe sweringes.

languid (ˈlæŋgwɪd), *sb.* Also (in sense 2) language. [Corruption of LANGUET.]

† **1.** = LANGUET 3. *Obs.*

1688 R. HOLME *Armoury* III. 14/2 Close Shooes, are such as have no open in the sides of the Latchets or Languides.

2. = LANGUET 5. (Also *attrib.*)

1852 SEIDEL *Organ* 78 The language, just above the foot to which it is soldered on. **1855** HOPKINS *Organ* 360 The language or languid is the flat plate of metal that lies horizontally over the top of the foot, just inside the mouth. *Ibid.* 375 Languid Wood Pipes are sometimes made. **1876** HILES *Catech. Organ* iv. (1878) 24 A flat piece of metal called the language, or languid.

languid (ˈlæŋgwɪd), *a.* [a. F. *languide* or ad. L. *languid-us*, f. *languēre* to LANGUISH.]

1. Of persons or animals, the body, etc.: Faint, weak; inert from fatigue or weakness; wanting in vigour or vitality.

1597 A. M. tr. *Guillemeau's Fr. Chirurg.* 50 b/2 The natural caliditye being in these partes feeble and languide. **1615** CROOKE *Body of Man* 338 The first births in the beginning of the seauenth moneth are..verie languid and weake. **1707** FLOYER *Physic. Pulse-Watch* 33 A languid Pulse depends on languid Spirits. **1744** ARMSTRONG *Preserv. Health* III. 381 Happy he whose toil Has o'er his languid powerless limbs diffus'd A pleasing lassitude. **1774** GOLDSM. *Nat. Hist.* (1776) VII. 168 (*Serpents*) Their lungs ..are long and large, and doubtless are necessary to promote their languid circulation. **1816** J. WILSON *City Plague* II. ii, How pale you look! Wearied, and pale, and languid. **1857** MRS. GATTY *Parables fr. Nat.* Ser. II. (1868) 144 Languid, indeed, was the voice, and languid were the movements of the grub. **1876** J. SAUNDERS *Lion in Path* xi, This recent illness had still left him languid.

transf. **1764** GOLDSM. *Trav.* 218 Unknown to them when sensual pleasures cloy, To fill the languid pause with finer joy. **1832** TENNYSON *Lotos-eaters* 5 All round the coast the languid air did swoon. **1871** MISS YONGE *Cameos* II. xxxii. 333 No doubt he had longed for her in the weary languid hours before Meaux.

b. Of persons and their deportment: Slow in movement; showing an indisposition (natural or affected) to physical exertion.

1728 YOUNG *Love Fame* v, The languid lady next appears in state, Who was not born to carry her own weight. **1863** FR. A. KEMBLE *Resid. in Georgia* 67 They are languid in their deportment.

2. Of persons, their character, feelings, actions, etc.: Not easily roused to emotion, exhibiting only faint interest or concern; spiritless, apathetic. Of interest, impressions: Faint, weak.

1713 ADDISON *Cato* I. v, I'll hasten to my troops, And fire their languid souls with Cato's virtue. **1713** STEELE *Guardian* No. 18 ¶ 1 [Death] which, by reason of its seeming distance makes but languid impressions upon the mind. **1742** POPE *Dunc.* IV. 46 With mincing step, small voice, and languid eye. **1751** BUTLER *Charge Clergy Durham* Wks. 1874 II. 331 Without somewhat of this nature, piety will grow languid even among the better sort of men. **1774** BURKE *Amer. Tax.* Wks. 1842 I. 169, I never heard a more languid debate in this house. **1791** MRS. RADCLIFFE *Rom. Forest* i, Madame gazed with concern upon her languid countenance. **1849** LYTTON *Caxtons* 12 He was too lazy or too languid where only his own interests were at stake. **1849** MACAULAY *Hist. Eng.* ii. I. 177 In him dislike was a languid feeling. *Ibid.* v. 570 A war of which the theatre was so distant..excited only a languid interest in London. *Ibid.* xvii. IV. 90 An appeal which might have moved the most languid and effeminate natures to heroic exertion. **1870** HOWSON *Metaph. St. Paul* iv. 153 What a contrast this is to our dull and languid Christianity!

b. Of ideas, style, language: Wanting in force, vividness, or interest. Said also of a writer.

a **1677** BARROW *Serm.* Wks. 1686 III. xxxvi. 404 Methinks the highest expressions that language..can afford, are very languid and faint in comparison of what they strain to represent, when [etc.]. *a* **1704** T. BROWN *Sat. Antients* Wks. 1730 I. 24 To hear Homer call'd dull and heavy..and Horace an Author unpolished languid and without force. **1864** BURTON *Scot. Abr.* II. ii. 179 They sent me two inscriptions but they were long and languid. **1865** CARLYLE *Fredk. Gt.* xx. vi. (1872) IX. 108 He had written certain thin Books, all of a thin languid nature. **1865** SEELEY *Ecce Homo* iii. (ed. 8) 25 The languid dreams of commentators.

3. Of business, trade, or other activity viewed externally to persons: Sluggish, dull, not brisk or lively.

1832 DIBDIN (*title*) Bibliophobia. Remarks on the present languid and depressed state of Literature and the Book Trade. **1833** HT. MARTINEAU *Vanderput & S.* iv. 64 The business has been very languid. **1866** CRUMP *Banking* viii. 169 On account of the circulation of their currencies being more languid. **1866** ROGERS *Agric. & Prices* I. xviii. 406 The market for exports was exceedingly languid. **1887** *Daily News* 20 June 2/5 A languid tone has been observed in many quarters.

4. Of inanimate things, physical motion, etc.: Weak, wanting in force; slow of movement.

1646 SIR T. BROWNE *Pseud. Ep.* III. xxv. 176 A languid and dumbe allision upon the parts. **1692** BENTLEY *Boyle Lect.* 190 No motion so swift or languid, but a greater velocity or slowness may still be conceived. **1715–20** POPE *Iliad* IX. 279 When the languid flames at length subside. **1748** SHENSTONE *Odes, Verses to W. Lyttleton* iv, When languid suns are taking leave Of every drooping tree. **1830** LYELL *Princ. Geol.* I. 199 That the same power..should even in it's more languid state be capable of raising to the surface considerable quantities of water from the interior. **1834** MACAULAY *Pitt* Ess. (1854) 302 Two rivers met, the one gentle, languid, and though languid, yet of no depth.

b. Of colour: Faint, not vivid.

1747 GOULD *Eng. Ants* 3 The first are of a languid Red; the second extremely black and shining. **1764** REID *Inquiry* vi. §22 The colours of objects, according as they are more distant, become more faint and languid.

languidly (ˈlæŋgwɪdlɪ), *adv.* [f. LANGUID *a.* + -LY².] In a languid manner.

1660 BOYLE *New Exp. Phys. Mech.* xlii. 386 The Menstruum also working as languidly upon the coral, as it did before they were put into the Receiver. **1729** BUTLER *Serm.* Wks. 1874 II. 99 Peevishness..languidly discharges itself upon every thing which comes in its way. **1747** WESLEY *Prim. Physic* (1762) 86 When the Nerves perform their Office too languidly. **1798** MALTHUS *Popul.* (1817) I. 247 With a population nearly stationary, or at most increasing very languidly. **1849** MACAULAY *Hist. Eng.* v. I. 548 They either neglected it altogether, or executed it languidly and tardily.

languidness (ˈlæŋgwɪdnɪs). [f. LANGUID *a.* + -NESS.] The quality or condition of being languid; languor.

1665 BOYLE *Exp. Hist. Cold* xiii. (1683) 132 This languidness of operation may perhaps proceed in great part from the smalness of the Pieces of Ice that were imploy'd. **1678** WOOD *Life* 8 Jan., Colds without coffing or running at the nose, onlie a languedness and faintness. **1744** WALL in *Phil. Trans.* XLIII. 224 The Operation of Musk much resembles that of Opium; but..it leaves not behind it any Stupor or Languidness. **1762** R. GUY *Pract. Obs. Cancers* 32 The seeming Languidness and Inactivity of the contained Humour.

† **lan'guific**, *a.* *Obs.* *rare*⁻⁰. [ad. late L. *languific-us*, f. *languēre*: see LANGUISH *v.* and -FIC.] = next. (Bailey vol. II. 1727.)

† **lan'guifical**, *a.* *Obs.* *rare*⁻⁰. [f. as prec. + -AL¹.] (See quots.)

1656 BLOUNT *Glossogr.*, *Languifical*, that makes faint or weak. **1676** COLES, *Languifical*, causing languor.

languish (ˈlæŋgwɪʃ), *sb.* [f. the verb.]

1. The action or state of languishing.

c **1380** WYCLIF *Serm.* Sel. Wks. I. 198 Crist was.. occupied in heeling of syke men and men þat were in languishe. **1382** —— *Luke* iv. 40 Sike men with dyuerse langwischingis [*v.r.* languyschis, languisches]. **1485** CAXTON *Chas. Gt.* 233 Of the languysshe that was comynge to Charles, he wyste not, how sone it was comyng. **1562** PHAER *Æneid* IX. B b iij b, The purple floure that..In languish withering dies. **1592** SHAKS. *Rom. & Jul.* I. ii. 49 One desparate greefe cures with anothers languish. **1613–16** W. BROWNE *Brit. Past.* I. i. 11 Faire Nymph, surcease this death-alluring languish. **1682** T. A. *Carolina* 19 It..being ..admirable in the languishes of the Spirit Faintings. **1718** *Entertainer* xix. 129 Religion is upon the Languish, and only the Ghost of Godliness remains. **1833** HARTLEY COLERIDGE *Poems* I. 118 A long record of perishable languish.

2. A tender look or glance.

1715–20 POPE *Iliad* XVIII. 50 The blue languish of soft Alia's eye. **1728–46** THOMSON *Spring* 949 Then forth he walks, Beneath the trembling languish of her beam. **1802** W. IRVING *Lett. J. Oldstyle* (1824) 19 An arch glance in one box was rivalled by a smile in another;..and in a fourth a most bewitching languish carried all before it.

† **'languish**, *a.* *Obs.* *rare*⁻⁰. [? f. the vb.] Languishing, sickly.

1552 HULOET, Languyshe to be, *langueo*. **1660** HEXHAM, *een Vlockaert*, a Pyning or a Languish man.

languish (ˈlæŋgwɪʃ), *v.* Forms: 4 languis, -uysce, 4–5 -uess(e, -uysh(e, -uysch(e, -wiss(e, -wys(se, -wisch(e, -wis(s)h(e, -usch(e, -ussh(e, 4–6 -uiss(e, -uissh(e, (6 language), 4– languish. [a. F. *languiss-*, *languir*, = Pr., Sp., Pg. *languir*, It. *languire*:—popular L. **languire* for class. L. *languē-re* (inchoative *languēscĕre*); perh. cogn. w. L. *lax-us* (see LAX *a.*) and Teut. **slako-* SLACK *a.*]

1. *intr.* Of living beings (also of plants or vegetation): To grow weak, faint, or feeble: to lose health, have one's vitality impaired; to continue in a state of feebleness and suffering. †In early use often: To be sick (const. *of*).

a **1300** *Cursor M.* 14138 In his sekenes he languist sua, þat he na fote had might to ga. *c* **1330** R. BRUNNE *Chron. Wace* (Rolls) 9550 Bedrede doun ful longe he lay, & languissed so forþ fro day to day. **1382** WYCLIF *Dan.* viii. 27 And Y, Danyel, languyshide, and was seeke by ful manye days. **1494** FABYAN *Chron.* 651 He lastly fell in a greuouse sykenesse.. And so languysshynge by the space of thre yeres more before he dyed. **1601** SHAKS. *All's Well* I. i. 37 What is it..the King languishes of? *Laf.* A Fistula, my Lord. **1635** R. BOLTON *Comf. Affl. Consc.* v. (ed. 2) 202 Some for the losse of an over-loved child have languished, fallen into a consumption and lost their owne lives. **1744** BERKELEY *Siris* §77 Those who had been cured by evacuations often languished long. **1759** tr. *Duhamel's Husb.* II. i. (1762) 123 Observing one day a tuft of wheat which languished. **1783** CRABBE *Village* I. 141 Health, Labour's fair child, that languishes with wealth. **1798** FERRIAR *Illustr. Sterne* ii. 24 He wrote for the recreation of persons languishing in sickness. **1850** MRS. JAMESON *Leg. Monast. Ord.* (1863) 197 It was said of him that he did not live, but languished through life. **1865** KINGSLEY *Herew.* xiv. 180 He lies languishing of wounds.

fig. **1652–62** HEYLIN *Cosmogr.* IV. (1682) 26 It began to languish, and was at last reduced to nothing but a few scattered Houses. **1882** PEBODY *Eng. Journalism* xviii. 134 The *Morning Chronicle*..languished and died.

b. To live under conditions which lower the vitality or depress the spirits.

1489 CAXTON *Faytes of A.* III. xxiii. 223 To..make hys prysonners to langwysshe in pryson. **1592** tr. *Junius on Rev.* ix. 4 The miserable world languishing in so great calamities. **1711** ADDISON *Spect.* No. 181 ¶ 2, I..have ever since languished under the Displeasure of an inexorable Father. **1797** MRS. RADCLIFFE *Italian* xi, The unfortunate captive is left to languish in chains and darkness. **1828** CARLYLE *Misc.* (1857) I. 195 The street where he languished in poverty is called by his name. **1879** FARRAR *St. Paul* (1883) 329 Peoples languishing under the withering atrophy of Turkish rule.

2. Of appetites or activities: To grow slack, lose vigour or intensity. †Of light, colour, sound, etc.: To become faint.

1626 BACON *Sylva* §255 Visibles and Audibles..doe languish and lessen by degrees, according to the Distance of the Obiects from the Sensories. **1635** R. BOLTON *Comf. Affl. Consc.* xii. (ed. 2) 509 The brightness of lamps languish in the light. **1707** WATTS *Hymn, 'Come holy Spirit, heavenly Dove'* iii, Hosannas languish on our Tongues, And our Devotion dies. **1855** MACAULAY *Hist. Eng.* xx. IV. 516 Along the eastern frontier of France the war during this year seemed to languish. **1871** NAPHEYS *Prev. & Cure Dis.* II. i. 414 The appetite languishes.

† **b.** Of health: To fall *off*.

1729 SAVAGE *Wanderer* v. 670 Late months, that made the vernal season gay, Saw my health languish off in pale decay.

3. To droop in spirits; to pine with love, grief, or the like.

a **1300** *Cursor M.* 24646, I languis al for þe. **1382** WYCLIF *Song Sol.* v. 8, I languysshe for looue. *c* **1386** CHAUCER *Frankl. T.* 222 He dorste nat his sorwe telle But langwissheth as a furye dooth in helle. *c* **1400** *Destr. Troy* 9154 Made hym langwys in Loue & Longynges grete. **1483** CAXTON *Cato* G ij b, Whan the courage languyssheth &..is abandonned to slouthfulnesse. **1509** HAWES *Past. Pleas.* XVI. (Percy Soc.) 72 Languysshe no more, but plucke up thyne herte. **1562** EDEN *Let. to Sir W. Cecil* 1 Aug. in *1st 3 Eng. Bks. Amer.* (Arb.) p. xliij, My spirites heretofore no lesse languysshed for lacke of suche a Patrone. **1590** SHAKS. *Mids. N.* II. i. 29 Loue and languish for his sake. **1604** —— *Oth.* III. iii. 43 A man that languishes in your displeasure. **1697** DRYDEN *Virg. Georg.* III. 334 With two fair Eyes his Mistress burns his Breast; He looks, and languishes, and leaves his Rest. **1791** BURNS *Bonie Wee Thing*, Wishfully I look and languish In that bonie face o' thine. **1844** THIRLWALL *Greece* VIII. lxii. 134 The spirit languished as the body decayed. **1871** R. ELLIS tr. *Catullus* xxxii. 11 A lover Here I languish alone.

b. To waste away with desire or longing *for*, to pine *for*. Also const. with *infinitive*.

[**1611**: see 4 a.] **1699** *Relat. Sir T. Morgan's Progr.* in Somers *Tracts* Ser. IV. (1751) III. 160 Major-general Morgan desired the Marshal not to let him languish for Orders. **1720** OZELL *Vertot's Rom. Rep.* I. v. 282 The People languished for the Restoration of their Tribunes. **1738** WESLEY *Psalms* VI. iv, Yet still with never-ceasing Moans I languish for Relief. **1791** COWPER *Iliad* II. 430 What soldier languishes and sighs To leave us? **1847** DE QUINCEY *Sp. Mil. Nun* i, The poor nuns, who..were languishing for some amusement. **1870** BRYANT *Iliad* I. II. 49 All give way to grief And languish to return.

c. To assume a languid look or expression, as an indication of sorrowful or tender emotion. Also quasi-*trans.*

1714 MRS. MANLEY *Adv. Rivella* 71, I saw his Eyes always fix'd on her with unspeakable Delight, whilst hers languish'd him some returns. **1849** THACKERAY *Pendennis* lx, When a visitor comes in, she smiles and languishes, you'd think that butter wouldn't melt in her mouth.

4. a. quasi-*trans.* (usually with *out*): To pass (a period of time) in languishing.

1611 SHAKS. *Cymb.* I. vi. 72 To think that man..will's free houres languish For assured bondage. **1683** TEMPLE *Mem.* Wks. 1731 I. 449 He languish'd out the rest of the Summer, and died. **1713** ADDISON *Cato* II. v, But whilst I live I must not hold my tongue, And languish out old age in his displeasure. **1734** tr. *Rollin's Anc. Hist.* XVI. ii. §8. VII. 302 Those who chose rather to destroy one another, than languish out their lives in that miserable manner.

† **b.** *causal.* To make to languish. *Obs. rare.*

1575 FENTON *Gold. Epist.* (1582) 222 The displeasures passing in our house pearce deeper, and as a martyr languishe the heart euen vnto death. **1603** FLORIO *Montaigne* III. v. 529 Least by that jouissance he might or quench, or satisfie, or languish [F. *allanguir*] that burning flame..wherewith he gloryed.

† **languishant**, *a.* *Obs.* *rare*⁻¹. [partial anglicizing of F. *languissant*, pres. pple. of *languir* to LANGUISH.] Languishing, suffering from languor.

[**1673** DRYDEN *Marr. à la Mode* III. i. 37 *Mel.* That glance, how sutes it with my face? *Phil.* 'Tis so *languissant*! *Mel. Languissant*! that word shall be mine too.] **1674** T. TURNOR *Case Bankers & Creditors* Introd. 4 The whole body in fine becomes Feavourish and Languishant.

languished (ˈlæŋgwɪʃt), *ppl. a.* *Poet.* [f. LANGUISH *v.* + -ED¹.] Reduced to languor, that is made or has become languid.

1621 G. SANDYS *Ovid's Met.* I. (1632) 16 Cyllenius spyes How leaden sleep had seal'd vp all his eyes; Then, silent, with his Magick rod he strokes Their languisht lights, which sounder sleep prouokes. **1634** MILTON *Epit. March. Winchester* 33 And the languisht Mothers Womb Was not long a living Tomb. **1667** —— *P.L.* VI. 497. **1671** —— *Samson* 119 With languish't head unpropt. **1693** WATTS *Death Mrs. M. W.* Wks. 1813 IX. 298/1 Groaning and panting on the bed, With ghastly air, and languish'd head. **1697** DRYDEN *Æneid* x. 1013 The Troops..Their Darts with

Clamour at a distance drive: And only keep the languish'd War alive.

languisher ('læŋgwɪʃə(r)). [f. LANGUISH *v.* + -ER[1].] One who languishes or pines; also, one who assumes languid looks, or casts glances expressive of amorous languor.

1599 NASHE *Lenten Stuffe* 37 Our moderne phisitions, that to any sicke languishers if they be able to waggle their chaps, propound veale for one of the highest nourishers. **1713** STEELE *Guardian* No. 87 ⁋1 The very servants are bent upon delights, and commence oglers and languishers. **1751** MRS. E. CARTER in *Rambler* No. 100 ⁋2 These unhappy languishers in obscurity. **1759** MASON *Caractacus* 77 Mingle the potion so, that it may kill me Just at the instant, this poor languisher Heaves his last sigh. **1896** *Godey's Mag.* Feb. 193/2 A few silly languishers flutter and simper, 'How nice! how lovely!'

languishing ('læŋgwɪʃɪŋ), *vbl. sb.* [f. LANGUISH *v.* + -ING[1].] The action of the verb LANGUISH; languor. With *a* and *pl.*: An attack of languor or faintness, esp. such as proceeds from disease.

c **1374** CHAUCER *Troylus* I. 529 Then were I quyt of langwysshyng yn drede. **1382** WYCLIF *Luke* iv. 40 Sike men with dyuerse langwischingis. *c* **1477** CAXTON *Jason* 8 b, Feling also the languisshing and smarting of their woundes. **1500–20** DUNBAR *Poems* lxxxv. 23 Bricht sygn, gladyng our languissing. **1601** SHAKS. *All's Well* I. iii. 235 A remedie.. To cure the desperate languishings whereof The King is render'd lost. **1611** BIBLE *Ps.* xli. 3 The Lord will strengthen him vpon the bed of languishing. *a* **1688** CUDWORTH *Immut. Mor.* (1731) 161 If this Harmonical Temperature of the whole Body be disturbed.. Weakness and Languishing will immediately seize upon it. **1711** STEELE *Spect.* No. 140 ⁋2 He.. speaks of Flames, Tortures, Languishings and Ecstasies. *a* **1715** BURNET *Own Time* (1724) I. 391 He fell into a languishing, which, after some months carried him off. **1816** CHALMERS *Let.* in *Life* (1851) II. 53 To sustain you under all the sickenings, and faintings, and languishings of your earthly disease.

languishing ('læŋgwɪʃɪŋ), *ppl. a.* [f. LANGUISH *v.* + -ING[2].] That languishes.

1. Declining in health, pining away, drooping. Now *rare*. †In early use: Suffering from sickness or disease.

c **1340** HAMPOLE *Prose Tr.* (1866) 2 Shewe þe to þis languessande, be þou leche vn-to þis woundyde! **1382** WYCLIF *John* v. 3 A greet multitude of langwischinge men. **1683** TRYON *Way to Health* vi. (1697) 100 The gasping parched Earth and languishing Nature. *a* **1715** BURNET *Own Time* (1724) I. 585 He was now in so languishing a state,.. that.. his death.. seemed to be very near. **1719** LONDON & WISE *Compl. Gard.* 112 The weaker and more languishing a Tree is, the sooner it ought to be prun'd. **1777** JOHNSON *Let. to Mrs. Thrale* 27 Aug., The poor languishing Lady is glad to see me. **1858** BRYANT *Rain-dream* ii, A thousand languishing fields, A thousand fainting gardens, are refreshed.

b. Said of a sickness, a death: Lingering. ? *Obs.*

1611 SHAKS. *Cymb.* I. v. 9 These most poysonous Compounds, Which are the moouers of a languishing death. **1612** WOODALL *Surg. Mate* Wks. (1653) 185 A Flux drawing to a languishing dropsie is mortal. **1683** TRYON *Way to Health* xix. (1697) 424 Consumptions, and other languishing Diseases. **1709** STEELE *Tatler* No. 78 ⁋8, I am just recovered out of a languishing Sickness. **1768** H. WALPOLE *Hist. Doubts* 129 His wife, who died of a languishing distemper.

c. *fig.* of immaterial things.

1382 WYCLIF *Wisd.* xvii. 8 Fro the languysshende soule. **1661** (*title*) An Humble Representation of the Sad Condition Of many of the Kings Party, Who since His Majesties Happy Restauration have no Relief, and but Languishing Hopes. **1697** JOS. WOODWARD *Rel. Soc. London* Ded. (1701) 6 Do all that you regularly can, toward.. the revival of languishing religion. *a* **1711** KEN *Divine Love* Wks. (1838) 327 My weak and languishing soul.

2. a. Pining with love or grief. **b.** With reference to looks or behaviour: Expressive of sentimental emotion (now used in ridicule).

? *a* **1400** *Morte Arth.* 4339 Ladys languessande and lowrande to schewe. **1657** G. THORNLEY *Daphnis & Chloe* 61 They [lovers] are languishing and carelesse to other things. **1683** D'URFEY *New Collect. Songs* 9 Possess the pleasing toil of languishing Embraces! **1683** TRYON *Way to Health* xix. (1697) 428 Whether they look Soberly, or Merry, Languishing, or with Wide Mouths. **1748** SMOLLETT *Rod. Rand.* lxii. (1804) 445 Looking at me with a languishing eye, he said [etc.].

3. Suffering from, or exhibiting, weariness or ennui; acting in a slow or tardy fashion. Of a narrative, etc.: Failing to excite interest.

1655 EARL ORRERY *Parthen.* (1676) 1 With so languishing and careless a pace. *a* **1693** DRYDEN *Juvenal* Ded. (1697) 7 Mr. Smith, and Mr. Johnson.. were two such languishing Gentlemen in their Conversation. **1711** ADDISON *Spect.* No. 255 ⁋1 The soul.. is.. slow in its resolves, and languishing in its executions. **1741** tr. *D'Argens' Chinese Lett.* xxiii. 162 Our Poets deprive themselves of a great Advantage, by rejecting almost all Narratives as languishing, and putting the most simple and most cruel Things equally into Dialogue and Action.

languishingly ('læŋgwɪʃɪŋlɪ), *adv.* [-LY[2].] In a languishing manner. Now chiefly, in a manner expressive of sentimental tenderness.

1579 TWYNE *Phisicke agst. Fort.* II. xlix. 225 a, *Sorowe.* My chylde is dead of a fal from an hygh. *Reason.* Vnto them that dye languishingly, death often times seemeth the sharper. *a* **1586** SIDNEY *Arcadia* III. (1622) 291 Howsoeuer the dulnesse of Melancholy would haue languishingly yeelded therunto. **1657** R. MOSSOM in Spurgeon *Treas. Dav.* Ps. xxx. 7 The soul becomes languishingly afflicted, even with all variety of disquietments. **1668** DRYDEN *All for Love* III. i. (1678) 35 She.. cast a look so languishingly sweet, As if, secure of all beholders hearts, Neglecting she could take 'em. **1733** CHEYNE *Eng. Malady* I. xi. §13 (1734) 107 The Digestions and Secretions must be weaker and more languishingly perform'd than they ought to be. **1761** J. HAWKESWORTH *Edgar & Emm.* II. i. 21 Edgar, being fir'd with the charms of Emmeline, first gaz'd languishingly upon her. **1813** BYRON *Giaour* xviii, Her eye's dark charm 'twere vain to tell, But gaze on that of the Gazelle, It will assist thy fancy well; As large, as languishingly dark. **1850** KINGSLEY *Alt. Locke* xxxvi. (1879) 380 Their long arms and golden tresses waved languishingly downward in the breeze. **1856** *Chamb. Jrnl.* V. 157 A fat, fair.. creature, shutting one eye languishingly.

languishment ('læŋgwɪʃmənt). [f. LANGUISH *v.* + -MENT.]

1. Sickness, illness; physical weakness, faintness, pining, or suffering. ? *Obs.*

1596 SPENSER *F.Q.* IV. xii. 23 Who now was falne into new languishment Of his old hurt, which was not throughly cured. **1609** J. DAVIES (Heref.) *Holy Roode* F 3 b, That in the Lab'rinth of his Languishment [*sc.* Christ's passion] We may, though lost therein, find solagement. **1625** JACKSON *Creed* V. viii. 73 The languishment of a certain friend.. hath taught me of late, that we are best men when we are sickly. **1646** SIR T. BROWNE *Pseud. Ep.* VII. xiii. 364 He dyed at Chalcis of a naturall death and languishment of stomack. **1742** YOUNG *Nt. Th.* v. 496 When by the bed of Languishment we sit. **1809** KENDALL *Trav.* II. lii. 211 Pulmonary consumption... This disease, which, after the country-people among the whites, they call a languishment, is equally fatal to the Indians. **1831** J. WILSON in *Blackw. Mag.* XXIX. 289 A hue foreboding languishment and decay. **1845** WORDSW. *Love Lies Bleeding* 8 Thus leans.. Earthward in uncomplaining languishment, The dying Gladiator.

b. *pl.* Sufferings, fits of weakness or illness.

1665 BOYLE *Occas. Refl.* II. iii. (1848) 107 If it [a Disease] tire out the Patient with tedious Languishments. **1674** T. TURNOR *Case Bankers & Creditors* Concl. 33 The Law.. acquits the person that steals viands to pacify the present Languishments of nature. **1685** EVELYN *Mrs. Godolphin* 150 Thus ended this incomparable Lady:.. leaving.. a disconsolate Husband, whose vnexpressible griefe.. would hardly suffer him to be spectator of her languishments. **1702** C. MATHER *Magn. Chr.* III. III. (1852) 577 He fell into some languishments attended with a fever.

c. Weariness, lassitude, languor; listlessness, inertness.

c **1620** T. ROBINSON *Mary Magd.* 388 Parte of her time in idle languishement.. shee spent. *a* **1680** CHARNOCK *Attrib. God* (1834) II. 23 God can produce more worlds than the sun doth plants every year, without weariness, without languishment. **1748** THOMSON *Cast. Indol.* I. 39 Each sound, too, here to languishment inclined, Lulled the weak bosom, and inducèd ease.

d. *fig.* Of things: Decline, decay, loss of activity.

1617 HIERON *Wks.* (1619–20) II. 252 The graces of regeneration and sanctification, when they are abused and brought to a kinde of languishment. **1626** T. H[AWKINS] *Caussin's Holy Crt.* 117 The first is a certaine languishment, and debility of Fayth. **1821** *Examiner* 546/2 There is a languishment here for want of persecution.

2. Mental pain, distress or pining; sorrow, trouble, grief; depression or affliction of spirits, sadness.

1591 SPENSER *Ruins Time* 159 Yet it is comfort in great languishment, To be bemoned with compassion kinde. **1591** *Troub. Raigne K. John* (1611) 38 Madame good cheere, these drouping languishments Add no redresse to salue our awkward haps. **1626** T. H[AWKINS] *Caussin's Holy Crt.* 427 Mariamne resisted the dull languishments of this captiuity with a generous constancy. **1681** GLANVILL *Sadducismus* II. 206 He would put him in a course to rid his Wife of this languishment and trouble. **1751** JOHNSON *Rambler* No. 159 ⁋11 Who can wonder that the mind.. quickly sinks into languishment and despondency.

3. *esp.* Sorrow caused by love or by longing of any kind; amorous grief or pain.

a **1541** WYATT *Compl. Love* in *Tottel's Misc.* (Arb.) 48 Thence came the tears, and thence the bitter torment, The sighs, the words, and eke the languishment. **1594** SPENSER *Amoretti* lx, The spheare of Cupid fourty yeares containes: Which I have wasted in long languishment. **1596** *Edw. III*, II. i. 14 How heart-sick and how full of languishment Her beauty makes me. *a* **1711** KEN *Hymnotheo* Poet. Wks. 1721 III. 237 As a chast Dove.. For her dead Mate a lively Love retains, And in continued Languishment remains. **1712** STEELE *Spect.* No. 423 ⁋5 The Comparison of Strephon's Gayety to Damon's Languishment. **1819** KEATS *Sonn.*, '*Happy is England*', Yet do I sometimes feel a languishment For skies Italian. **1822** B. W. PROCTER *Scenes Julian Apostate* ii, That inward languishment of mind, which dreams Of some remote and high accomplishment. **1877** MRS. OLIPHANT *Makers Flor.* i. 21 Love-agonies and languishments beyond the reach of words.

b. Expression of longing or tenderness.

1709 W. KING *Art of Love* IV. 19 Whilst sinking eyes with languishment profess Follies his tongue refuses to confess. **1717** LADY M. W. MONTAGU *Let. to C'tess Mar* 18 Apr., Her eyes!—large and black, with all the soft languishment of the blue. **1748** SMOLLETT *Rod. Rand.* (1812) I. 361 A look full of languishment. **1814** SCOTT *Wav.* ii, The sighs and languishments of the fair tell-tale. **1876** GEO. ELIOT *Dan. Der.* v. xxxv, Adorers who might hover around her with languishment.

† **'languishness.** *Obs. rare*$^{-1}$. [f. LANGUISH *a.* + -NESS.] Languor, languid condition.

1540 HYRDE tr. *Vives' Instr. Chr. Wom.* (1592) Rj, That languishnes should be avoided and put from the body.

languister, obs. var. LINGUISTER.

languor ('læŋgə(r), 'læŋgwə(r)), *sb.* Forms: 4–5 **langur(e, langoure, 4–6 langor(e, 4, 6, 8 languour,** (6 *Sc.* **langre**), 4–7 (8–9) **langour,** 4– **languor.** [a. OF. *languor, lango(u)r* (mod.F. *langueur*), ad. L. *languōr-em*, f. *langu-ēre*: see LANGUISH *v.* Cf. Pr. *languor-s*, Sp., Pg. *langor*, It. *languore* of the same meaning; Roumanian *lăngoare* 'nervous fever'.]

† **1.** Disease, sickness, illness. *Obs.*

a **1300** *Cursor M.* 3596 Sua has eild now þis ysaac ledd þat he in langur lijs in bedd. *Ibid.* 14179 To ded sal noght his langur turn. *c* **1330** R. BRUNNE *Chron. Wace* (Rolls) 16675 In langour lay he many a day, & deyde þe twelfte kalende of May. **1393** LANGL. *P. Pl.* C. XIX. 142 He lechede hem of here langoure lazars and blynde bothe. *c* **1425** LYDG. *Assembly of Gods* 1853 In hele and in langoure. **1544** PHAER *Pestilence* (1553) K iv b, [He] curethe.. all theyre gryeuous soores, languoures and dyseases. **1590** SPENSER *F.Q.* III. xii. 16 From thenceforth a wretched life they ladd, In wilfull languor and consuming smart. **1593** NASHE *Christ's T.* 86 a, Hee will.. heale euery disease and languor amongst you. **1609** SKENE *Reg. Maj.* 9 Gif they.. verifies in the court, the infirmitie to be ane langour (or ane vehement seiknes of bodie or of minde). [*a* **1850** ROSSETTI *Dante & Circ.* I. (1874) 136 Over the curse of blindness she prevails, And heals sick languors in the public squares.]

† **2.** Distressed condition, sad case, woeful plight. *Obs.*

a **1300** *Cursor M.* 4499 Bot ioseph in þat prisun lai, Wit langor lengand and with care. **1377** LANGL. *P. Pl.* B. XIV. 117 Beggeres.. That al her lyf han lyued in langour and in defaute. *c* **1386** CHAUCER *Monk's T.* 417 Off the Erl Hugelyn of Pyze the langour Ther may no tonge telle for pitee. *c* **1450** LONELICH *Grail* xxxvii. 606 ȝif it so be that I from ȝow go, Neuere geten ȝe helpe ne Socour ȝow to bryngen owt of this langour. **1462** *Pol. Poems* (Rolls) II. 267 In whos tyme ther was habundaunce with plentee of welthe and erthely joye, withouȝt langoure. **1513** BRADSHAW *St. Werburge* I. 68 And how this lyfe is of no suerte Now in great languor now in prosperyte. **1590** SPENSER *F.Q.* III. iii. 35 Whiles thus thy Britons doe in langouur pine.

† **3.** Mental suffering or distress, pining, sorrow, affliction of spirit. ***to make languor***: to mourn, make lament. *Obs.*

a **1300** *Cursor M.* 24603 Mi sorful scurs þat þai sagh ledd wit sli langurs. *c* **1350** *Will. Palerne* 986 His liif nel nouȝt for langour last til to-morwe. *c* **1386** CHAUCER *Pars. T.* ⁋649 [He] hath swich langour in soule, that he may neither rede ne singe in hooly chirche. *c* **1450** *Mirour Saluacioun* 3769 In whas absence alwaye sho brent in swilk langoure. *c* **1470** HENRY *Wallace* I. 270 For dreid thar of in gret languor he grew. **1470–85** MALORY *Arthur* X. viii, There he made grete langour and dole. **1483** CAXTON *Gold. Leg.* 58 b/1, I shal not brynge none of the langours no sorowes upon the. **1588** SHAKS. *Tit. A.* III. i. 13 My harts deepe languor, and my soules sad teares. **1593** T. WATSON *Tears Fancie* iii. Poems (Arb.) 180 That she would worke my dollor, And by her meanes procure my endles langor. **1614** RALEIGH *Hist. World* II. xxii. §5 (1634) 465 The text.. saith, they exercised upon Joas ignominious judgements and that departing from him, they dismissed him in great languor.

b. *Sc.* [? associated with *lang*, LONG *a.* and *v.*] † (*a*) Longing for some object (*obs.*). (*b*) Ennui. ***to hold out of langer***: to amuse.

1596 DALRYMPLE tr. *Leslie's Hist. Scot.* x. 457 To recreat the quene and hald her out of Langre. **1616** ROLLOCK *On the Passion* 383 If thou hast not a desire, but art afraid to flit, it is a token that thou hast no langour of God.

4. Faintness, weariness, lassitude, fatigue (of the body or faculties).

1656 BLOUNT *Glossogr.*, *Languor*, faintness, feebleness, want of spirit. **1707** FLOYER *Physic. Pulse-Watch* 34 Great Evacuations produces Languor of Spirits. **1751** JOHNSON *Rambler* No. 90 ⁋2 That can hardly fail to relieve the languors of attention. **1762** GOLDSM. *Cit. W.* xliv, All the senses seem so combined, as to be soon tired into languor by the gratification of any one of them. **1789** W. BUCHAN *Dom. Med.* (1790) 141 When the fever comes on gradually, the patient generally complains first of languor or listlessness. **1818** MRS. SHELLEY *Frankenst.* iv. (1865) 68, I nearly sank to the ground through languor and extreme weakness. **1874** BLACKIE *Self-Cult.* 50 The feverishness and the languor that are the necessary consequences of prolonged artificial wakefulness. **1878** C. STANFORD *Symb. Christ* i. 31 In the midst of the languor or pains of death.

b. Expression or indication of lassitude, in the voice, features, etc.

1760–72 tr. *Juan & Ulloa's Voy.* (ed. 3) I. 122 Here their pronunciation has a faintness and languor. **1783** POTT *Chirurg. Wks.* II. 92 The eyes have now a languor and glassiness.

c. Habitual lassitude and inertia in one's movements and behaviour, want of energy and alertness (whether as a natural quality or an affectation).

1825 LYTTON *Falkland* 30 There was spread over his countenance an expression of mingled energy and languor. **1852** MRS. STOWE *Uncle Tom's C.* xvi, She now opened her eyes, and seemed quite to forget her languor. **1863** MRS. OLIPHANT *Salem Ch.* x. 171 That stick over which his tall person swayed with fashionable languor.

d. Tenderness or softness (of mood, feeling, etc.); lassitude of spirit caused by sorrow, amorous longing, or the like. Said also of a melody.

1751 JOHNSON *Rambler* No. 94 ⁋2 The same languor of melody will suit an absent lover. **1791** MRS. RADCLIFFE *Rom. Forest* i, The languor of sorrow threw a melancholy grace upon her features. **1792** S. ROGERS *Pleas. Mem.* II. 170 A softer tone of light pervades the whole And steals a pensive languor o'er the soul. **1819** BYRON *Juan* I. cxiv, The silver light.. Breathes also to the heart, and o'er it throws A loving languor, which is not repose. **1832** TENNYSON *Eleanore* 77 Whene'er The languors of thy love-deep eyes Float on to me. **1865** SWINBURNE *Poems & Ball.*, *Dolores* 67 The lilies and languors of virtue.

5. Of immaterial things: Depressed or drooping condition, want of activity or interest; slackness, dullness.

a **1748** WATTS *Improv. Mind* I. xiii. (1868) 114 Academical disputation..relieves the languor of private study and meditation. **1751** JOHNSON *Rambler* No. 153 ¶18, I had formerly been celebrated as a wit, and not perceiving any languor in my imagination, I essayed to revive that gaiety. **1752** HUME *Ess. & Treat.* (1777) I. 348 The arts must fall into a state of languor, and lose emulation and novelty. **1769** BURKE *Late St. Nat.* Wks. 1842 I. 89 Possibly some parts of the kingdom may have felt something like a languor in business. **1786** W. THOMSON *Philip III*, v. 329 A place.. where she would be freed from the languor of her present solitude. *Ibid.* 353 Since that time, it [that monarchy] had exhibited a striking token of improvidence and langour. *Ibid.* 402 A manifest langour and irresolution appeared in her [Spain's] counsels. **1838** THIRLWALL *Greece* III. xxii. 218 Athens discovered none of the langour of recent convalescence. **1895** *Daily News* 18 June 2/6 Extreme languor now characterizes the trade for field seeds.

b. Of the air, sky, etc.: Heaviness, absence of life and motion, oppressive stillness.

1728-46 THOMSON *Spring* 442 When the sun Shakes from his noonday throne the scattering clouds, Even shooting listless languor thro' the deeps. **1742** POPE *Dunc.* IV. 304 Lily-silver'd vales, Diffusing languor in the panting gales. **1762** FALCONER *Shipwr.* I. 332 A sullen langour still the skies oppress, And held th' unwilling ship in strong arrest. **1772-84** COOK *Voy.* (1790) IV. 1245 The sky became serene; but with a haziness and languor, as if the current of air, like water upon an equipoise, moved only by its own impulse. **1858** HAWTHORNE *Fr. & It. Jrnls.* II. 220 The languor of Rome,—its weary pavements, its little life.

ˈlanguor, (ˈlæŋgə(r).) *v.* Forms: 4-5 langor(e, langur(e, 5 languowr(e, -uyre, -wyre, langer, 5-6 langour, 6 languer. [a. OF. *langorer*, also *langorir*, f. *langor* sb.: see prec.] = LANGUISH *v.* (in various senses).

c **1350** *Will. Palerne* 983 He has langured for ȝour loue a ful long while. *c* **1386** CHAUCER *Merch. T.* 623 (Corpus MS.) Now wol I speke of woful dauyan þat langureþ [*v.r.* langwissheth] for loue as ȝe schullen heere. *c* **1400** *Lanfranc's Cirurg.* 73 Þei ben so feble þat þei dien, or ellis þei languren [*v.r.* langoren] longe tyme. **14..** *Circumcision* in *Tundale's Vis.* (1843) 95 Salue unto hem that langor in sekenes. *c* **1440** *Gesta Rom.* II. xxiv. 342 (Add. MS.) The lady for love be-gan to langour. **1470-85** MALORY *Arthur* IX. xx, He came to the herd men wandryng and langerynge. **1526** *Pilgr. Perf.* (W. de W. 1531) 255 b, Our blessed sauyour..so thyrsted and langoured for the saluacyon of mankynd, that [etc.]. **1891** A. BEARDSLEY *Let.* July (1971) 24 'I should like,' he [*sc.* Burne-Jones] says, 'to see your work from time to time... I know you will not fear work, nor let disheartenment languor you.' **1969** *Harper's Mag.* June 37 America languors with an illness of euphoria brought on by our leaders. **1975** *N.Y. Times* 11 May 73/2 It embraces contemporary English aristocracy at upper-crust social functions,..hedonistic Romans languoring in ancient cities, [etc.].

Hence †ˈ**langouring** *vbl. sb.* and *ppl. a.*

c **1330** R. BRUNNE *Chron. Wace* (Rolls) 9565 Our kyng þat lay in langoryng. **1387-8** T. USK *Test. Love* II. xiv. (Skeat) l. 59 Thus as an oxe to thy langoryng deth wer thou drawen. **1450-1530** *Myrr. our Ladye* 111 To vysyte the langurynge poure. **1552** HULOET, Languerynge in care, sorowe or thought, *languidus*.

†languorment. *Obs.* [f. LANGUOR *v.* + -MENT.] A state of languishing.

1593 NASHE *Christ's T.* (1613) 54 With a hoarse sound, (such as fitteth farre-spent languorment).

languorous (ˈlæŋgwərəs), *a.* Also 5 langorous, 6 *Sc.* langorius. [ad. OF. *lango(u)reux*, f. *langor* LANGUOR *sb.*]

†**1.** Distressful, sorrowful, mournful. *Obs.*

1490 CAXTON *Eneydos* iv. 20 Durynge the langorous tyme that polidorus tolde this vysion myserable. **1549** *Compl. Scot.* Epist. 1 Ane..medicyne..to cure.. al the langorius desolat & affligit pepil. *Ibid.* vii. 70 Quhen this lady persauit hyr thre sonnis in that langorius stait. **1590** SPENSER *F.Q.* II. i. 9 Deare lady! how shall I declare thy cace, Whom late I left in languorous constraynt? **1834** BECKFORD *Italy* II. 295 Then succeeded some languorous tirannas.

2. Full of, characterized by, or suggestive of, languor (see LANGUOR *sb.* 4-5).

a **1821** KEATS *Sonn.*, *The day is gone*, Bright eyes, accomplish'd shape, and lang'rous waist. **1847** TENNYSON *Princess* VII. 48 A medicine in themselves To wile the length from languorous hours, and draw The sting from pain. **1879** MRS. PATTISON *Renaissance Art Fr.* viii, The languorous sentiment of the Italian model was dispelled by the liveliness native to the French character. **1882** J. PAYNE *1001 Nts.* I. 155 Slender and sleepy-eyed, and languorous of gait. **1883** LADY VIOLET GREVILLE *Keith's Wife* II. 95 She threw killing glances from her languorous black eyes. **1886** SYMONDS *Renaiss. It., Cath. React.* (1898) VII. xii. 200 The devotion of the cloister was becoming languorous and soft. **1887** *Old Man's Favour* II. 286 The atmosphere was..languorous and heavy with the rich scent of flowers.

Hence ˈ**languorously** *adv.*

1875 HOWELLS *Foregone Concl.* 25 The air..was here almost languorously warm. **1879** *Athenæum* 24 May 671 A portrait..of a young mother..languorously reposing in a crimson chair.

‖**langur** (ˈlʌŋgʊə(r)). Also lungoor, lungar, langour. [Hindi *langūr*, cogn. w. Skr. *lāngūlin*, having a tail.] The name applied in India to certain species of monkeys of the genus *Semnopithecus*, esp. *S. entellus* (see ENTELLUS) and *S. schistaceus*.

a **1826** HEBER *Journ. Upper Prov. Ind.* (1844) II. 85 Why do you challenge the lungoor? he cannot answer you! **1842** *Penny Cycl.* XXI. 223 Lungar. **1860** RUSSELL *Diary India* I. 249 The trees..affording..cover to innumerable langours. **1880** V. BALL *Jungle Life India* i. 3 Troops of long-tailed monkeys called Langurs. **1895** *Pall Mall G.* 10 Jan. 3/2 Leafy green trees..were continually shaken by the antics of the lungoors.

†languste. *Obs. rare.* [a. OF. *languste* (cf. F. *langouste* crayfish), repr. L. *locusta*.] = LOCUST.

c **1200** *Trin. Coll. Hom.* 127 Weste was his wunienge and stark haire of oluente his wede, wilde hunie and languste his mete and water was his drinke.

†lanhure, *adv. Obs.* [A comb. of the synonymous HURE *adv.*; the prefixed element seems connected with OE. *lá* LO *int.*[1]] At least.

a **1225** *Leg. Kath.* 557 Ich mihte..wel, habben awealt hire, ȝif ha nalde wið luue, wið luðer eie, lanhure. *a* **1225** *St. Marher.* 12 Swic nuthe lanhure swikele swarte deouel. *c* **1230** *Hali Meid.* 21 Þat he greiðede ham lanhure þa ha walden of meidenes hehscipe.

laniard, variant of LANYARD.

laniariform (lænɪˈærɪfɔːm), *a.* [f. L. *laniāri-us* LANIARY *a.* + -FORM.] Shaped like laniary teeth.

1847-52 TODD *Cycl. Anat.* IV. 881/2 The office of the two laniariform teeth is to pierce and retain the prey. **1881** OWEN in *Nature* XXIII. 523 The molars probably..all more or less laniariform.

†laniˈarious, *a. Obs. rare.* [f. as prec. + -OUS.] Butcher-like.

1651 BIGGS *New Disp.* ¶236 They have a trick of paring away, (palpably laniarious) and wounding the membrane.

†laniary, *sb.*[1] *Obs.*—[0] In 7 laniarie. [ad. L. *laniārium*, f. *lanius* butcher.] A shambles (Cockeram, 1623).

laniary (ˈlænɪərɪ), *a.* and *sb.*[2] [ad. L. *laniārius* pertaining to a butcher, f. *lanius* butcher, f. *laniāre* to tear.] **A.** *adj.* Of teeth: Adapted for tearing; canine. **B.** *sb.* A laniary or canine tooth.

1826 KIRBY & SP. *Entomol.* III. 445 These are principally their claws or laniary teeth. **1839-47** TODD *Cycl. Anat.* III. 242/1 The laniaries [of Insectivora] small. **1854** R. OWEN *Skel. & Teeth* in *Circ. Sci., Organ. Nat.* I. 270 The laniary or canine teeth of carnivorous quadrupeds. *Ibid.* 271 Some [teeth] present the laniary type. **1888** *Syd. Soc. Lex.*, *Laniary teeth.*

laniate (ˈlænɪeɪt), *v. rare*—[1]. [f. L. *laniāt-*, ppl. stem of *laniāre* to tear.] *trans.* To tear to pieces. So ˈ**laniated** *ppl. a.* (Cockeram, 1623).

1721 BAILEY, *Laniate*, to butcher, to cut up, to quarter, to tear in Pieces. (Hence in JOHNSON 1755; and in later Dicts.) **1886** BURTON *Arab. Nts.* I. 115 Bedded on new made scones and cakes in piles to laniate.

†laniˈation. *Obs.*—[0] [ad. L. *laniātiōn-em*, n. of action f. *laniāre* to tear.] 'A tearing like a butcher' (Cockeram, 1623).

lanier, obs. form of LANNER.

laniferous (leɪˈnɪfərəs), *a.* [f. L. *lānifer* (f. *lāna* wool + *-fer* bearing) + -OUS.] Wool-bearing.

1656 in BLOUNT *Glossogr.* **1676** in COLES. **1794** MRS. PIOZZI *Synon.* I. 353 Care and cultivation..in laniferous animals is of apparent use. **1805** LUCCOCK *Nat. Wool* 28 The laniferous animals were very early diffused over the western parts of Asia.

lanific (leɪˈnɪfɪk), *a. rare.* [ad. L. *lānific-us*, f. *lāna* wool + *-ficus* making: see -FIC.] **a.** Wool-bearing. **b.** Busied in spinning wool.

a **1693** *Urquhart's Rabelais* III. li. (1737) 353 All the Lanific Trees of *Seres*. **1806** W. TAYLOR in *Ann. Rev.* IV. 772 The distinct offices of the lanific sisters, as Catullus calls them, were afterwards transferred to the distaff and the rock.

So †**laˈnifical,** *a.* (1656 in Blount *Glossogr.*), †**laˈnificous,** *a.* (1721 in Bailey).

†ˈlanifice. *Obs. rare.* [a. obs. F. *lanifice*, ad. L. *lānificium*, f. *lānificus*: see prec.] A spinning or weaving of wool; also *concr.* wool-work.

1626 BACON *Sylva* §696 The Moath breedeth vpon Cloth, and other Lanifices. **1633** PRYNNE *Histriom.* 21 Or use any spelles or ceremonies..in their lanifices.

laniflorous (ˌleɪnɪˈflɔərəs), *a.* [f. L. *lāna* wool + *flōr-*, *flōs* flower + -OUS.] (See quot.)

1855 MAYNE *Expos. Lex.*, *Laniflorus*, having woolly flowers, as the incisions or divisions of the limb of the corol of *Asclepias laniflora*: laniflorous.

lanigerous (leɪˈnɪdʒərəs), *a.* [f. L. *lāniger* (f. *lāna* wool + *ger-* carrying) + -OUS.] Wool-bearing; woolly.

1608 TOPSELL *Serpents* (1658) 784 Whether there be within them [spiders] a certain lanigerous fertility..as in silk-worms. **1706** PHILLIPS (ed. Kersey) *Lanigerous Trees*, those sort of Trees that bear a woolly, downy Substance; as ..Poplars, Willows, and Osiers. **1786-7** tr. *Savary's Lett. fr. Egypt* I. 316 This triangular rush [the papyrus]..bears a lanigerous tuft. **1839** G. RAYMOND in *New Monthly Mag.* LVII. 408 He had a bushy, lanigerous head. **1841** T. SOUTHEY (*title*) A Treatise on Sheep:..suggesting ideas for the Introduction of other Lanigerous Animals suited to the Climate. **1881** *Academy* No. 491. 252 To him the republic is a..lanigerous and pelliferous region.

ˈlanikin, *a. rare*—[1]. [Cf. Cheshire dial. *lankin* and *lanniky*.] Lanky.

1862 BORROW *Wild Wales* II. xxvi. 295 He was a tall lanikin figure with a pair of..staring eyes.

lanimer: see LANDIMERE.

†ˈlaning. *Obs. rare*—[1]. [f. LANE *sb.* + -ING[1].] = LOANING.

c **1648-50** BRATHWAIT *Barnabees Jrnl.* III. P 4 Singing along down Sautry laning, I saw a Tombe one had beene laine in.

†laniˈonious, *a. Obs. rare*—[0]. [f. L. *laniōni-us* (f. *laniōn-em* = *lanius* butcher) + -OUS.] Of or pertaining to a butcher.

1656 in BLOUNT *Glossogr.*

†laniˈpendious, *a. Obs. rare*—[0]. [f. L. *lānipendi-us* (f. *lāna* wool + *pend-ĕre* to weigh) + -OUS.] Engaged in weighing or spinning wool.

1656 in BLOUNT *Glossogr.* **1676** in COLES.

‖**lanista** (ləˈnɪstə). *Rom. Antiq.* [L.] A trainer of gladiators.

1834 LYTTON *Pompeii* II. i, Our lanista would tell a different story.

Comb. **1880** L. WALLACE *Ben-Hur* 432, I did not tell thee that I am lanista-taught. Defend thyself!

lank (læŋk), *a.* (*sb.*) Also 6-7 lanck(e, lanke. [OE. *hlanc*; not found in other Teut. langs.; a primary sense 'flexible' may be inferred from the factitive vb. (OTeut. **hlankjan*) which appears in Ger. *lenken* to bend, turn aside. Other cognates are ME. LONKE = OHG. *lancha* (whence Rom. **flanco* FLANK); see also LINK *sb.*]

A. *adj.*

1. Loose from emptiness; not filled out or plump; shrunken, spare; flabby, hollow.

a. of the animal body or its parts.

a **1000** *Judith* 205 (Gr.) Þæs se hlanca ȝefeah wulf in walde. **1556** WITHALS *Dict.* (1568) 80 b/1 Lanke or thinne in the bodie, as they that be leane, *strigosus, macilentus*. **1576** TURBERV. *Venerie* 362 And that oftentimes is the foulest and worst favourd by cause he is overwearied and lankest. **1583** STANYHURST *Æneis* III. (Arb.) 89 With lanck wan visadge. **1603** DEKKER *Grissil* (Shaks. Soc.) 10 In the lean arms of lank necessity. **1633** P. FLETCHER *Purple Isl.* XII. xxxii, Long sootie hair Fill'd up his lank cheeks. **1648** *Hunting of Fox* 21 They must looke to goe out as lank and lean as they came in. **1649** G. DANIEL *Trinarch., Hen. V*, cci, A Tiger, (whom lanke Ravin fires To sett vpon the Herds). **1668** CULPEPPER & COLE *Barthol. Anat.* I. xiv. 37 Because any Artery being tied, is full, and swells towards the Heart, but is empty, and lank towards the Veins. **1709** STEELE *Tatler* No. 28 ¶6 The Men of the Service look like Spectres, with long Sides, and lank Cheeks. **1713** —— *Englishm.* No. 40. 261 A lank Monsieur with a huge Fruz Wigg,..is France in little. **1726** GAY *Fables* I. xxiii. 20 Cats, who lank with hunger mew'd. **1791** BOSWELL *Johnson* 15 Mar. an. 1779, The bard was a lank bony figure, with short black hair. **1820** W. IRVING *Sketch Bk.* II. 354 He was a huge feeder, and though lank, had the dilating powers of an Anaconda. **1848** MRS. JAMESON *Sacr. & Leg. Art* (1850) 45 This lank, formal angel is from the Greco-Italian school of the eleventh century.

b. of vegetable growth. Of grass: Long and flaccid. †Of a harvest: Meagre, scanty.

1634-5 BRERETON *Trav.* (Chetham Soc.) 36 Here is barren dry sandy land as in Sherwood Forest, like Bowden Downs, save longer lank grass. **1645** QUARLES *Sol. Recant.* xi. 75 Cast not lank grain upon too lean a ground. **1658** *Whole Duty Man* xvii. §11 If by the sparingness of our alms, we make ourselves a lank harvest hereafter. **1697** DRYDEN *Virg. Georg.* II. 342 Lest the lank Ears in length of Stem be lost. **1884** MRS. C. PRAED *Zero* ii, These lank, sickly gum-trees make me feel quite sentimental.

c. of inanimate things, esp. of a bag, bladder or purse. ? *Obs.*

c **1000** *Ags. Ps.* (Gr.) cxviii. 83 Ic eom nu ȝeworden werum anlicast, swa þu on hrime setest hlance cylle. **1571** CAMPION *Hist. Irel.* II. x. (1633) 138 If your bagges bee full where theirs were lancke. **1593** SHAKS. *2 Hen. VI*, I. iii. 132 The Commons hast thou rackt, the Clergies Bags Are lanke and leane with thy Extortions. **1602** *2nd Pt. Return fr. Parnass.* IV. iii 1934 Drinking a long lank watching candles smoake. **1660** BOYLE *New Exp. Phys. Mech.* xiii. 84 A great Bladder well tyed at the Neck, but very lank. **1719** D'URFEY *Pills* I. 272 My Purse..is but lank. **1830** GALT *Lawrie T.* II. x. (1849) 73 A day at this time was precious to my light and lank purse.

†**d.** of immaterial things. Also *fig. Obs.*

1607 WALKINGTON *Opt. Glass* 27 His conceit is as lancke as a shotten Herrin. **1615** T. ADAMS *White Devil* 26 That subtle winnower..w[d] keep the soule..lanke with ignorance. **1622** in *Reliq. Wott.* (1685) 248 The Empire grew lank and the Popedom tumorous. **1638** BP. REYNOLDS *Serm. July 12th* 43 Men of greene heads, of crude and lanke abilities. *a* **1650** *Scot. Field* 269 in Furnivall *Percy Folio* I. 226 Now lanke is their losse: our lord itt amend! **1663** J. SPENCER *Prodigies* (1665) 111 Tempted to blow out with their quills a lean and lank occurrence. **1664** H. MORE *Myst. Iniq.* 360 It is but a lank business to take notice of one single Statue for Idolatry. **1729** YOUNG *Imperium Pelagi* Pref., Lank writing is what I think ought most to be declined. **1780** COWPER *Table T.* 532 From him who rears a poem lank and long.

2. Of hair: Without curl or wave, straight and flat.

1690 SHADWELL *Am. Bigot* III. i, Thick lips and lank flaxen hair. **1727** BRADLEY *Fam. Dict.* s.v. *Hair*, To make that which curls too much, lanker, anoint it thoroughly..with Oil of Lillies. **1776** MAD. D'ARBLAY *Early Diary* 5 Apr., Two of her curls came quite unpinned, and fell lank on one of her shoulders. **1835** WILLIS *Pencillings* I. xxiv. 168 High

cheek bones, lank hair, and heavy shoulders. **1849** MACAULAY *Hist. Eng.* i. I. 82 The extreme Puritan was at once known..by..his lank hair.

†**3.** Drooping, languid. *Obs. rare*$^{-1}$.

1634 MILTON *Comus* 835 Nereus,..piteous of her woes, rear'd her lank head.

4. *Comb.*, chiefly parasynthetic, as ***lank-bellied, -cheeked, -eared, -haired, -jawed, -legged, -sided, -winged*** adjs.; also ***lank-blown, -lean*** adjs.

1691 *Lond. Gaz.* No. 2559/4 Stoln.., a black Gelding ..*lank Belly'd, and a switch Tail. **1785** FRANKLIN *Lett.* Wks. 1840 VI. 507 A *lank blown bladder laid before a fire will soon swell, grow tight, and burst. **1838** JAS. GRANT *Sk. Lond.* 184 A little, *lank-cheeked, sharp-eyed man. **1820** KEATS *Hyperion* I. 230 O *lank-ear'd Phantoms of black-weeded pools! **1687** *Lond. Gaz.* No. 2207/4 T.L. and C.L., middle-sized men..*lank-hair'd. **1849** MACAULAY *Hist. Eng.* iii. I. 370 Puritan coffee houses..where lankhaired men discussed election and reprobation through their noses. **1778** MISS BURNEY *Evelina* (1787) III. xxi. 233 Is he as *lank-jawed as ever? **1843** LYTTON *Last Bar.* II. i, Our red-faced yeomen, alas, are fast sinking into lank-jawed mechanics. **1599** SHAKS. *Hen. V*, IV. Prol. 26 Their gesture sad Inuesting *lanke-leane Cheekes. **1906** E. DYSON *Fact'ry 'Ands* xiii. 172 Levi Goss..a *lank-legged, ungainly object. **1921** W. DE LA MARE *Veil* 56 Like lank-legged grasshoppers in June-tide meadows. **1937** —— *This Year, Next Year*, And out of window gaze At lank-legged Peggy. **1743** R. BLAIR *Grave* 337 The *lank-sided Miser..meanly stole.. From Back and Belly too, their proper Cheer. **1649** G. DANIEL *Trinarch., Hen. V*, lxviii, Where *lanke-wing'd Puttocks hope to catch their Prey.

B. *sb.*

†**1.** Leanness, scarcity, thinness. *Obs.*

Only in proverbial phrase. (See quots.)

1655 FULLER *Hist. Camb.* iii. §16. 47 *margin*, A Bank and a Lank of Charitie. *a* **1661** —— *Worthies, Shropsh.* III. (1662) 10 This Ioseph collected from the present plenty, that a future famine would follow, as in this kind, a Lank constantly attendeth a Bank. **1727** BOYER *Eng.-Fr. Dict.* s.v., A Lank makes a Bank. *Ce Proverbe s'applique aux Femmes qui déchéent dès le moment qu'elles sont enceintes jusqu'à ce que leur ventre commence à lever.*

2. A lanky or lean person.

1881 MRS. LYNN LINTON *My Love* III. 212 You are not such a peaky lank as you were.

Hence †**'lankish** *a.*, somewhat lank; **'lankly** *adv.*, in a lank manner; **'lankness**, the condition of being lank.

1611 COTGR., *Maigrement*, Meagerly,.. lankly, slenderly. *Ibid.*, *Maigreté*, Meagarnesse, leannesse, thinnesse, lankenesse. **1627–77** FELTHAM *Resolves* II. xxiv. 209 She, like the humble one, falls flat, and lankly lies upon the earth. *a* **1643** W. CARTWRIGHT *Ordinary* III. v, Hungry Notes are fit for Knels: May lankenes be No Quest to me. *a* **1648** DIGBY *Closet Open.* (1677) 160 They [the guts] are to be cleansed in the ordinary manner and filled very lankly. **1689** *Lond. Gaz.* No. 2483/4 A Tall fresh coloured Fellow, with lankish white Hair. **1774** GOLDSM. *Nat. Hist.* (1776) I. 317 Being thus compelled to open its jaws, it [a viper] once more resumed its former lankness. **1824** *Examiner* 23/2 There was a haggardness and lankness about his cheeks. **1840** DICKENS *Barn. Rudge* xxxv, A certain lankness of cheek..added nearly ten years to his age. **1924** C. MACKENZIE *Old Men of Sea* xi. 182 Mrs. Ringshaw used to stand beside him, her grey hair wet with spray and lankly waving.

†**lank**, *v. Obs.* [f. LANK *a.*]

1. *trans.* To make lank.

1519 HORMAN *Vulg.* 39 b, As soone as thou arte vp lanke thy bely [L. *levato alvum*] and spett out rotten fleme. **1562** LEIGH *Armorie* (1597) 44 b, The Lion..(if he be in daunger to bee chased)..vomiteth at his will, and lanketh himselfe. **1604** *Meeting of Gallants* 7, I rack the vaines and Sinewes, lancke the lungs. **1610** G. FLETCHER *Christ's Vict.* I. xiii, Greefes companie..lankes the cheekes.

2. *intr.* To become lank or shrunken.

1606 SHAKS. *Ant. & Cl.* I. iv. 71 And all this..Was borne so like a Soldiour, that thy cheeke So much as lank'd not.

lanket ('læŋkɪt), *v. dial.* [f. *lanket*, dial. form of LANGET.] *trans.* In the Isle of Man: To tie the legs of an ox, a horse, etc. together, as a restriction on its movements; to hobble.

1894 HALL CAINE *Manxman* v. x. 313 There were a few oxen also, tethered and lanketted.

'lankily, *adv.* [f. LANKY *a.*] In a lanky fashion.

1903 CONRAD & HUEFFER *Romance* i. 37 The second mate was lankily stalking the deck. **1926** A. BENNETT *Lord Raingo* I. xlviii. 215 'Yes, Raingo,' said the tall, gaunt old man, striding lankily into the presence [of the minister]. **1937** A. WAUGH *Eight Short Stories* viii. 253 He was lankily overgrown, with a sallow complexion and a pimply chin.

lanktraloo, variant of LANTERLOO *Obs.*

lanky ('læŋkɪ), *a.* (and *sb.*) [f. LANK *a.* + -Y[1].]

1. a. Awkwardly or ungracefully lean and long. †Also (of hair) somewhat lank (*obs.*).

1670 *Lond. Gaz.* No. 437/4 He is..of a tall Stature, with fair lanky hair. **1818** TODD, *Lanky* adj., a vulgar expression to denote a tall thin person. **1833** HT. MARTINEAU *Cinnamon & Pearls* v. 82 Their worn and lanky frames. **1847–8** H. MILLER *First Impr.* i. (1861) 3 A tall lanky Northumbrian. **1860** *All Year Round* No. 72. 509, I pass by many a church, ..with their tall hulking fronts and lanky pillars. **1861** W. H. RUSSELL in *Times* 12 July, A sharp-looking Creole, on a lanky pony,..superintended their labours. **1874** BURNAND *My time* ii. 21 The lanky Charles..did something with a chorus to it. **1892** BARING-GOULD *Str. Survivals* v. 112 The spiral coil would prevent the lanky rushlight from falling over.

b. *Comb.*, as ***lanky-eared, -legged, -limbed, -looking*** adjs.

1815 W. H. IRELAND *Scribbleomania* 82 The station of groom to a lanky-ear'd Neddy. **1932** AUDEN *Orators* III. 90 Lanky-legged Lloyd, and Morgan from Aberdovey, Peacock and long-skulled Cornish Davy. **1896** MARY BEAUMONT *Joan Seton* 170 A schoolboy, bright-eyed and lanky-limbed. **1922** JOYCE *Ulysses* 108 Now who is that lankylooking galoot over there.

2. Used as *sb.*, as a nickname or form of address for a lanky person.

c **1863** T. TAYLOR in M. R. Booth *Eng. Plays of 19th Cent.* (1969) II. 109 Just you try it, lanky! Yah! Hit one of your own size—do. **1942** BERREY & VAN DEN BARK *Amer. Thes. Slang* §184/7 Nicknames for a tall, lanky person... Harry Longlegs, Lanky, Legs, Lengthy. **1948** D. BALLANTYNE *Cunninghams* 212 Hiya, Lanky! **1959** I. & P. OPIE *Lore & Lang. Schoolch.* ix. 169 *Lankies.* Inevitably there is a fusion of terms between those for the thin and lanky lad and those for the overgrown.

†**'lannard.** *Obs.* Also 6–7 lanard(e. [variant of LANNER, ? after *haggard* sb.] = next.

1530 PALSGR. 237/2 Lanarde a hauke, *lanier.* **1598** FLORIO, *Lainero*, a kind of hauke called a lanard or a lanaret. **1607** BREWER *Lingua* II. vi. E 2 A wondrous flight Of Falcons, Haggards, Hobbies, Terselets, Lanards and Goshaukes. *a* **1627** MIDDLETON & ROWLEY *Sp. Gipsy* IV. iii, That young lannard..if you can whistle her To come to fist, make trial.

lanner ('lænə(r)). Forms: 5–7 laner(e, -yer(e, (5 lanare, 6 lanor), 6–7 lanier, 6 lanar, 7 lannar, 6– lanner. [ad. F. *lanier*, app. a subst. use of the OF. *lanier* cowardly.

Cf. the med.L. synonym *tardarius*, and the description 'le lannier..est mol et sans courage', quoted by Godef. s.v.]

A species of falcon, found in countries bordering on the Mediterranean, *Falco lanarius* or *F. feldeggi.* In *Falconry*, the female of this species.

c **1400** MAUNDEV. (Roxb.) xxv. 117 Gentill fawcouns, laneres, sagres, sperhawkes. **1486** [see LANNERET]. **1575** TURBERV. *Faulconrie* 114 You muste haue a gentle Lanner. **1598** SYLVESTER *Du Bartas* I. v. 720 The Marlin, Lanar, and the gentle Tercell. **1637** T. MORTON *New Eng. Canaan* (1883) 198 The use whereof in other parts makes the Lannars there more bussardly then they be in New England. **1676** *Lond. Gaz.* No. 1127/4 Lost Aug. 27. at night, a young Lanner Nyes Hawk without Bells or Jesses. **1766** PENNANT *Zool.* (1768) I. 134 Except the Lanner none seem to have been noted among the British birds by any of our countrymen. **1834** R. MUDIE *Brit. Birds* (1841) I. 87 The Lanner (*Falco Lanarius*) bears some resemblance to the peregrine, but it is smaller. **1852** R. F. BURTON *Falconry Indus* ii. 18 The female was called a Lanner, the male a Lanneret. **1860** LONGF. *Wayside Inn, Crew Long Serpent* i, Downward fluttered sail and banner as alights the screaming lanner.

attrib. **1686** tr. *Chardin's Trav. Persia* I. 82 Lanner-Hawks, Gos-Hawks, Hobbies. **1873** TRISTRAM *Moab* ii. 32 A pair of lanner falcons.

lanneret ('lænərɪt). Forms: 5 lanret(t, 5–6 lanerette, 6 lanaret, 6–9 laneret, (6 -at), 7 lannaret, 7– lanneret. [ad. OF. and F. *laneret* in same sense.] The male of the lanner.

1432–50 tr. *Higden* (Rolls) I. 339 Hawkes that be called lanerettes [*printed* lauerettes]. *c* **1440** *Promp. Parv.* 286/2 Lanret, hauke, *tardarius.* **1486** *Bk. St. Albans* D iv, Ther is a Lanare and a Lanrell [? *read* Lanrett]. And theys belong to a Squyer. **1495** *Act 11 Hen. VII* c. 17 Laner lanerette or fawcon. **1575** TURBERV. *Faulconrie* 125 The myllane and the lanerette. **1637** T. MORTON *New Eng. Canaan* (1883) 196 At my first arrivall in those parts [I] practised to take a Lannaret, which I reclaimed. **1838** J. P. KENNEDY *Rob of Bowl* xiv. 151 The falcone [was] bent to fly the cast of lanerets.

lanolin ('lænəlɪn). *Chem.* Also **lanoline.** [f. L. *lāna* wool + *ol-eum* oil + -IN[1]. Named by O. Liebreich.] The cholesterin-fatty matter extracted from sheep's wool, used as a basis for ointments.

1885 *Brit. Med. Jrnl.* 5 Dec. II. 1075/1 Dr. Oscar Liebreich read a paper on Lanolin before the Berlin Medical Society, on October 28th. **1894** *Brit. Jrnl. Photogr.* XLI. 16 First grease their hands with lanoline or vaseline.

lanose ('leɪnəʊs), *a. scientific.* [ad. L. *lānōs-us*, f. *lāna* wool.] Of the nature of wool; woolly. Hence **la'nosity**, woolliness (*Syd. Soc. Lex.* 1888).

1852 DANA *Crust.* I. 335 Hand naked and smooth without, ..within over a spot lanose. **1871** COOKE *Fungi* 786 Mycelium forming white lanose patches.

lanosterol (læ'nɒstərɒl). *Biochem.* [f. L. *lān-a* wool + -O + -STEROL.] An unsaturated sterol, $C_{30}H_{50}O$, which occurs in wool fat.

1929 DRUMMOND & BAKER in *Jrnl. Soc. Chem. Industry* 9 Aug. 238T/2 We recommend that the misleading name *iso*cholesterol be replaced by the less committal lanosterol. **1955** *Soap, Perfumery & Cosmetics* XXVIII. 1262/2 Lanosterol. This lanolin derivative is the newest to arouse interest in the cosmetic and related fields... Pure lanosterol is a light-coloured, free-flowing amorphous powder. **1964** *New Scientist* 22 Oct. 220/1 No fewer than thirteen distinct enzymic reactions are required to build up the sterol prototype, lanosterol, from acetic acid, and about as many to modify lanosterol into cholesterol, the characteristic animal sterol.

lanret(t, obs. form of LANNERET.

lansfordite ('lænsfədaɪt). *Min.* [Named by Genth, 1888, from *Lansford* in Pennsylvania, where it was found: see -ITE.] Hydrous carbonate of magnesium, resembling paraffin when first found.

1888 in *Amer. Jrnl. Sci.* Ser. III. XXXVI. 156. **1892** in DANA *Min.* 305.

lanshet, variant of LANDSHARD.

lansign ('lænsaɪn). Short for *language sign.*

1946 C. MORRIS *Signs, Lang. & Behavior* 36 We propose therefore to call sign-sets of the kind in question lansign-systems, and the individual members of these systems lansigns. **1970** *Sci. Jrnl.* Jan. 57 In the 1930s C. K. Ogden, I. A. Richards and A. Korzybski, and more recently C. E. Osgood, D. H. Mowrer and others, tried to show how language symbols and signs (lansigns, as they are sometimes called) are associated with their referents in much the same way as conditioned stimulus becomes associated with an unconditioned stimulus, as in the classical conditioning theory of Pavlov.

†**'lansket.** *Obs. rare*$^{-1}$.

a **1625** FLETCHER *Woman's Prize* II. vi, How knowst thou? *Jaq.* I peep't in At a loose lansket.

lansquenet ('lɑːnskənɛt, 'læns-). Forms: 7 lancequene(n)t, lansquenight, 7–8 lanskenet, 8 landsquenet, (sense 2 only, **lamb-skin-it, lambskinnet**), 7, 9 lansquenett(e, 9 (sense 2) lansquinnet, 7– lansquenet. *β.* (sense 1 only) 9– (now usual) landsknecht, 9 lanzknecht. See also LANCE-KNIGHT. [a. F. *lansquenet*, ad. G. *landsknecht* lit. servant of the country, f. *lands* (gen.) country + *knecht* servant. The Ger. word was at an early date miswritten *lanzknecht*, as if f. *lanz* lance.]

1. *Hist.* One of a class of mercenary soldiers in the German and other continental armies in the 16th and 17th centuries.

Originally applied to the serfs brought into the field by the nobles within the territories of the Empire, in contra-distinction to the Swiss mercenaries. Subsequently this distinction became obsolete, and the designation seems to have connoted a particular kind of equipment, of which a lance was part.

1607 DEKKER *Knight's Conjuring* (Percy) 59 Our lansquenight of Lowe-Germanie. **1608** E. GRIMSTONE *Hist. France* (1611) 662 Christopher..brought ten thousand Lansquenets to passe the Alpes. **1622** A. COURT *Constancie* I. 8 Certaine Women..cryed out,..That the Lanskenets had eaten vp Children. **1726–31** TINDAL *Rapin's Hist. Eng.* XVII. (1743) II. 138 Ten thousand Switzers, two thousand Landsquenets. **1824** BYRON *Deformed Transf.* I. ii, From some Stray bullet of our lansquenets. **1845** S. AUSTIN tr. *Ranke's Hist. Ref.* I. 235 In the year 1513, the authorities hesitated to punish some deserters from the Landsknechts. **1855** MOTLEY *Dutch Rep.* II. ii. (1866) 163 Some were disguised as hussars, some as miners, some as lansquenettes. **1884** *Contemp. Rev.* June 818 He gave up entire communes to be pillaged by the lansquenets. **1911** *Encycl. Brit.* XIV. 521/1 The Landsknecht was the prototype of the infantryman of the 16th and 17th centuries. **1936** *Burlington Mag.* June 294/1 Among the daggers is an elaborate landsknecht one in its sheath. **1944** AUDEN *Sea & Mirror* in *For Time Being* iii. 56 Our moth-eaten..stock costumes which with only a change of hat and re-arrangement of safety-pins, had to do for the *landsknecht* and the Parisian art-student. **1959** *Chambers's Encycl.* I. 610 (*caption*) Landsknecht sword, first half 16th century.

β. In the incorrect Ger. form *lanzknecht.*

1856 FROUDE *Hist. Eng.* I. 240 If..his German lanzknechts had stormed the Holy City.

2. A game at cards, of German origin.

1687 *Lond. Gaz.* No. 2263/3 Strictly forbidding all Persons..to use or allow any Gaming in their Houses, more particularly the Games of Hoca, Bassett, or Lansquenett. **1707** J. STEVENS *Quevedo's Com. Wks.* (1709) 204 We play'd at Lanskenet. **1735** BAILEY, *Lamb Skin-it*, a certain Game at Cards. **1766** ANSTEY *Bath Guide* ix. (1804) 72 And to play I bid adieu, Hazard, lansquenet, and loo, Fairest nymph, to dance with you. **1859** THACKERAY *Virgin.* xli, He dines at White's ordinary, and sits down to Macco and lansquenet afterwards. **1885** MABEL COLLINS *Prettiest Woman* vi, Each day she dreaded to hear that he had lost everything at lansquenet. **1917** 'H. H. RICHARDSON' *Fortunes Richard Mahony* 9 Even the 'shepherds' beguiled the time with euchre and 'lambskinnet'.

lanss, obs. Sc. form of LANCE.

lant (lænt), *sb.*[1] Now *rare.* Forms: 1 hland, hlǫnd, 7–8 land, 7– lant. [OE. *hland, hlǫnd* = ON. *hland.* (The form *lant* seems to belong to n.w. dialects; cf. Lancashire *bant* for *band.*)] Urine, *esp.* stale urine used for various industrial purposes, chamber-lye.

c **1000** *Sax. Leechd.* I. 362 Wearras & weartan on weȝ to donne nim wulle & wæt mid biccean hlonde. *Ibid.* II. 40 Wið earena deafe ȝenim hryþeres ȝeallan wiþ gæten hland ȝemenȝed. **1611** COTGR., *Vrine*, vrine, lant, stale, chamber-lye. **1634–5** BRERETON *Trav.* (Chetham Soc.) 106 The linen do so strongly taste and smell of lant and other noisome savours, as that [etc.]. **1640** GLAPTHORNE *Wit in Constable* II. Wks. 1874 I. 191 Your nose by its complexion does betray Your frequent drinking country Ale with lant in't. **1787** GROSE *Prov. Gloss., Land*, or *Lant*, urine. **1859** *Autobiog. Beggar boy* 105 Twice a-week I had to collect stale lant (urine), from a number of places where it was preserved for me.

attrib. **1870** tr. *Erckmann-Chatrian's Blockade Phalsburg* 139 A lane..full of dungheaps and lant-holes.

lant (lænt), *sb.*[2] A fish = LAUNCE.

1620 J. MASON *Newfound-land* (1887) 151 May hath cods and lants in good quantity. **1880–4** DAY *Brit. Fishes* I. 332 *Ammodytes tobianus*..Lesser launce..lant, Cornwall.

lant, *sb.*³ *dial.* Short for LANTERLOO.

1706 *Acc. Bk. Sir J. Foulis* (1894) 422 Lost at lant with L. Col. his lady &c. £0 10. 2. **1899** PREVOST *Cumberld. Gloss.*, *Lant, Lanter*, the game of Loo. A distinction is made between *Lant*, and *Lanter*, five cards being required for the latter. The proper designation may be three-card and five-card loo.

† **lant**, *v. Obs.* Also 7–8 leint. [f. LANT *sb.*¹] *trans.* To mingle with 'lant'.

1630 *Tinker of Turvey* Ded. Ep. 5, I have drunke double-lanted Ale, and single-lanted, but never gulped downe such Hypocrenian liquor in all my life. **1662** M. W. *Marriage Broker* v. i. 73 My Hostess takings will be very small, Although her lanted ale be nere so strong. **1674** J. WRIGHT *Mock-Thyestes* 134 Dead drunk with double lanted Ale. **1674–91** RAY *N.C. Words* 42 To Leint Ale, to put Urine into it to make it strong. **1787** in GROSE *Prov. Gloss.* s.v. *Land.* *transf.* **1656** [S. HOLLAND] *Wit & Fancy in a Maze* I. vi. 58 They found their eares unguented with warm water, well lanted with a viscuous Ingredient.

lant, obs. pa. t. of LEND.

lan'tado, lan'tedo. Short for ADELANTADO.

1602 MIDDLETON *Blurt* IV. iii. G 1 b, Your Lantedoes nor your Lanteeroes cannot serue your turne. **1633** T. STAFFORD *Pac. Hib.* II. iii. (1810) 255 They reported that the Lantado wished rather his person then the Ship.

lantana (læn'tɑːnə). [mod.L. (Linnæus *Hortus Cliffortianus* (1737) 349), f. an earlier Latin name for *Viburnum*, to which its foliage bears a slight resemblance.] An evergreen herb or shrub of the genus so called, belonging to the family Verbenaceæ, often a native of sub-tropical America, and bearing heads of red, yellow, or white flowers.

1791 W. BARTRAM *Carolina* 103 There grows on this island, many curious shrubs, particularly a beautiful species of Lantana. **1882** *Cornh. Mag.* Jan. 24 Fritz Müller noticed a lantana in South America which changes colour as its flowering advances. **1893** *Daily News* 26 July 7/4 That showy flower, the Lantana. **1917** *Nature* 20 Sept. 57/2 Two introduced shrubs, Guava and Lantana, now occupy extensive areas [of Hawaii], and have become great pests. **1933** *Times Lit. Suppl.* 9 Nov. 776/4 The scene is the Tweed River district of New South Wales, where banana plantations compete with the lantana creeper for a foothold. **1947** K. TENNANT *Lost Haven* (1968) Prologue 3 The loveliness of the place is a faint, sweet corruption; old, grey, wooden wharves..heaps of coal overgrown with wild convolvulus and lantana. **1961** *Amat. Gardening* 21 Oct. Suppl. 31/1 Most of the lantanas form small shrub-like plants with roundish heads of small flowers. **1969** *New Scientist* 20 Feb. 385/1 The world's worst weeds..include purple nut-sedge, Bermuda grass..cogon grass, and lantana.

lantane, obs. form of LANTERN.

lantanium, variant of LANTHANUM.

lantanuric (læntə'njʊərɪk), *a. Chem.* [f. LANTANA + URIC.] ***lantanuric acid*** (see quot.).

1866 ODLING *Anim. Chem.* 135 Lantanuric acid is probably identical with the allanturic acid of Pelouze.

lantarne, lanter(e, obs. ff. LANTERN.

‖**lantcha** ('læntʃə). [Shortened from LANCHARA.] = LANCHARA. In some recent Dicts.

'lanterloo ('læntəluː) Forms: 7 lanter(e)loo, (langtrilloo, lanktraloo), 8 lan(g)teraloo, lanctrelooe, lantreloo. [ad. F. *lantur(e)lu*, orig. the unmeaning refrain of a song popular in the 17th c. (cf. the earlier *laturelure*). Cf. Du. *lanterlu.*] † **1.** The older form of the game now called LOO. (The knave of clubs, called 'Pam', was the highest card.) *Obs.*

1668 ETHEREDGE *She Would if She Could* v. i. Wks. (1888) 213 They are..playing at lanterloo with my old Lady Loveyouth and her daughter. **1679** SHADWELL *True Widow* IV. 49 Let's send for some Cards, and play at Lang-trilloo in the Box. **1685** CROWNE *Sir Courtly Nice* III. 22 Thou art..the very Pam at Lantereloo, the knave that picks up all. **1710** STEELE *Tatler* No. 245 ¶2 An old Ninepence bent both Ways by Lilly, the Almanack-maker for Luck at Langteraloo. **1711** PUCKLE *Club* §123. 23 Guess then the numbers of frauds there are at..Lantreloo.

2. Used as a meaningless refrain (cf. etym.).

1951 AUDEN & KALLMAN *Rake's Progress* I. 17 The sun is bright, the grass is green: *Lanterloo, lanterloo.* The King is courting his young Queen. *Lanterloo, my lady.* **1951** AUDEN *Nones* (1952) 54 Turning his barrel-organ, playing *Lanterloo, my lovely*, my *First-of-May*.

lantern ('læntən), *sb.* Forms: 3–4 lanter(e, 4–6 launtern(e, 4–7 lanterne, (4 -tirne, 4–5 -tyrne, 5 -tarne, laterne), 5 lantane, lawnterne, -tryn, 5–6 lantron, 6 lantren, -trin, -turne, 6–7 lanthorne, 8–9 lanthern, 6–9 lanthorn, 4– lantern. [ad. F. *lanterne*, ad. L. *lanterna*, also *lāterna*, believed to be ad. Gr. λαμπτήρ (f. λάμπ-ειν to shine, cf. LAMP *sb.*), with ending after L. *lūcerna*.

The form *lanthorn* is prob. due to popular etymology, lanterns having formerly been almost always made of horn.]

1. a. A transparent case, e.g. of glass, horn, talc, containing and protecting a light. For *blind, bull's eye, Chinese, friar's lantern*, see those words. Also DARK LANTERN, MAGIC LANTERN.

a **1300** *Cursor M.* 12910 He þe chess als his lanter Be-for his face þe light to bere [*Gött.* lantern: bern]. *Ibid.* 15847 Quarfor haf yee taken me, And als a theif vm-soght Wit lantern. *c* **1385** CHAUCER *L.G.W.* 926 *Dido*, I shal as I can ffolwe thyn lanterne as thow gost byforn. *a* **1400–50** *Alexander* 5398 Li3t lemand e3en as lanterns he had. *c* **1470** HENRY *Wallace* XI. 1255 Lyk till lawntryns it illuminyt so cler. **1587** FLEMING *Contn. Holinshed* III. 376/2 The said lanthorne to be mainteined by those two widowes that shall haue the hanging of them out. **1615** CROOKE *Body of Man* 460 It is like a sliuer of the Muscouy glasse whereof we vse to make Lanthorns. **1635** QUARLES *Embl.* v. xii. 289 Alas, what serves our reason, But, like dark lanthornes, to accomplish Treason With greater closenesse? **1755** JOHNSON, *Lantern*..it is by mistake often written lanthorn. **1756** NUGENT *Gr. Tour* II. 238 The streets are..well furnished with lanthorns for the winter nights. **1816** C. WOLFE *Burial of Sir J. Moore* 8 By the struggling moonbeam's misty light And the lantern dimly burning. **1840** MARRYAT *Poor Jack* xiii, Our poop lanterns were so large that the men used to get inside them to clean them. **1873** G. C. DAVIES *Mount. & Mere* xvi. 140 Fishing up a lanthorn he turned the light on her face.

b. † ***lantern and candle-light***: the old cry of the London bellman at night. Hence † ***lantern and candle man***: a bellman.

1592 NASHE *P. Penilesse* C 2, It is said, Lawrence Lucifer, that you went vp and downe London crying then like a lanterne and candle man. **1600** HEYWOOD *Edw. IV*, I. (1613) C, No more calling of lanthorne and candle light. **1602** DEKKER *Satiromastix* I 2 b, Dost roare, bulchin, dost roare? th'ast a good rounciuall voice to cry Lanthorne & Candle-light.

c. Proverbs. † ***to bear the lantern***: to show the way as a leader.

a **1483** *Pol. Poems* (Rolls) II. 283 Of alle the remes in the worlde this beryth the lanterne. **1562** J. HEYWOOD *Prov. & Epigr.* (1867) 205 A Lanthorne and a light mayde: manerly sayde. **1683** BURNET *More's Utopia* 2 They need not my Commendations, unless I would, according to the Proverb, Shew the Sun with a Lanthorn. **1827** CARLYLE in Froude *Life* (1882) I. 374 To prove the existence of God, as Paley has attempted to do, is like lighting a lantern to seek for the sun.

d. *spec.* = MAGIC LANTERN. Chiefly *attrib.* (see 8).

2. a. *transf.* Now *rare.*

c **1374** CHAUCER *Troylus* v. 543 O lanterne, of which queint is þi light. **1398** TREVISA *Barth. De P.R.* XVI. xii. (Tollem. MS.) In a temple of Venus is made a candelstik, on þe whiche was a lantarne so brennynge þat [etc.]. **1513** DOUGLAS *Æneis* III. ix. 91 Lyk onto the lantrin of the mone. **1536** BELLENDEN *Cron. Scot.* (1821) I. 52 Utheris..belevit ..that the..lanternis of the hevin, war verray Goddis. **1641** J. JACKSON *True Evang. T.* I. 25 Others [Nero] staked through, rosined and waxened over their bodies, and so set them lighted up, as torches and lanthornes to passengers. **1664** POWER *Exp. Philos.* I. 24 The Gloworm..This is that Night Animal with its Lanthorn in its tail. **1880** W. WATSON *Prince's Quest* (1892) 92 And now the Moon her lanthorn had withdrawn.

b. *fig.* Applied to things metaphorically giving light. †Formerly often of persons.

13.. *E.E. Allit. P.* A. 1046 Þe lombe her lantyrne withouten drede. **1382** WYCLIF *Ps.* cxviii[i]. 105 Lanterne to my feet thi woord, and li3 t to myn pathis. **1387** TREVISA *Higden* (Rolls) VII. 171 Two lanternes of þe world..Lanfranc, and Anselme. ? *a* **1412** LYDG. *Two Merch.* 454 His lives lanterne, staff of his crokyd age. **1423** JAS. I *Kingis Q.* lxxi, And [Muses] with 3our bryght lanternis conuoye My pen, to write my turment and my Ioye. **1503** HAWES *Examp. Virt.* XIV. (Arb.) 66 O geme of gentylnes and lanterne of plasure. **1548** VICARY *Anat.* To Brethren (1888) 11 Galen, the Lanterne of all Chirurgions. **1558** KNOX *First Blast* (Arb.) 31 Those that shuld haue bene the lanterns to others. **1577–87** HOLINSHED *Scot. Chron.* (1805) II. 42 The cathedrell church of Murrey, the lantren and ornament of all the north part of Scotland. **1591** SPENSER *Ruins Time* 169 Camden!..lanterne unto late succeeding age. **1627–77** FELTHAM *Resolves* I. xviii. 31 Extreme poverty one calls a Lanthorn, that lights us to all miseries. **1766** SMOLLETT *Trav.* 99 This great lanthorn of medicine is become very rich. **1874** BANCROFT *Footpr. Time* i. 38 The lantern of science has guided us on the track of time.

3. † **a.** A lighthouse. **b.** The chamber at the top of a lighthouse, in which the light is placed. † **c.** Some part of a ship.

a. 1601 HOLLAND *Pliny* I. 110 In truth it [a watch-tower] serueth in right good stead as a Lanthorne. **1615** G. SANDYS *Trav.* 40 Vpon the shore there is an high Lanterne, large enough at the top to containe about threescore persons, which by night directeth the sailer into the entrance of the Bosphorus. **1705** ADDISON *Italy* 258 Caprea, where the Lanthorn fix'd on high, Shines like a Moon through the benighted Sky, While by its Beams the wary Sailor steers.

b. 1796 MORSE *Amer. Geog.* I. 440 Within that stands the lanthorn. **1809** KENDALL *Trav.* II. xxxv. 9 The height.. measured from its base to the top of the lanthorn, is sixty-nine feet. **1851** *Illustr. Catal. Gt. Exhib.* 320 The bird..was carried against the lantern in a gale. **1882** *Standard* 23 May, The height of the new tower above high water to the middle of the lanthorne is 130 feet.

c. 1661 PEPYS *Diary* 17 Jan., The 'Soverayne'..is a most noble ship:..all went into the lanthorne together.

4. *Arch.* An erection, either square, circular, elliptical, or polygonal, on the top either of a dome or of an apartment, having the sides pierced, and the apertures glazed, to admit light; a similar structure serving as a means of ventilation, or for any other purpose. In quots. 1600 used to translate L. *culmen* and *fastigium.*

c **1406** *Scriptores tres* (Surtees) 144 Hic etiam magnam partem campanilis, vulgo lantern, minsterii Eboracensis construxit. **1547** BOORDE *Introd. Knowl.* x. (1870) 151 The spyre of the church is a curyous and a right goodly lantren. **1600** HOLLAND *Livy* x. xxiii. 368 The image of Iupiter himselfe in the lanterne or frontispice of the Capitoll. *Ibid.* XXXVII. iii. 946 Both the lanterne, yea and the leaved dores thereof, were foully disfigured. **1634–5** BRERETON *Trav.* (Chetham Soc.) 174 A tower-like building, almost like your lanthorns in college halls. **1766** ENTICK *London* IV. 291 Upon which tower a short spire rises, with its base fixed on a broad lanthern. *a* **1817** T. DWIGHT *Trav. New Eng.* (1821) I. 521 The prospect of this town, and its environs, is taken completely from the lantern of the State-House. **1831** LYTTON *Godolph.* lx, Lady Erpingham was in the lantern of the House of Commons.

5. A name of certain fishes (cf. *lantern-fish* in 9). **a.** The whiff, *Arnoglossus megastomus.* **b.** ? *U.S.* A species of gurnard, *Trigla obscura.*

1674 RAY *Collect. Words, Sea Fishes* 100 *Lanterns*: Lug aleth Cornubiensibus. **1686** —— *Willughby's Ichthyogr.* IV. 102 Arnoglossus..species illa quam piscatores nostri Cornubienses à pelluciditate sua *a Lantern*..vocant. **1880–4** F. DAY *Brit. Fishes* II. 22 *Arnoglossus megastoma*,..Names, ..*lantern*, referring to its semi-transparency when held up against the light.

6. a. The luminous appendage of the lantern-fly.

1750 G. EDWARDS *Birds* III. 120 The Fly, I take to be a Kind of Fire-Fly, and that part on his Head, the Lanthorn. **1810** A. v. SACK *Voy. Surinam* 279 From the head rises a large proboscis of an oval form, but tapering most towards the head, and making one third of the whole size of the insect, which is vulgarly called the lantern, emitting a bright light.

b. ***lantern of Aristotle*** (see quots.).

[This is derived from Arist. *Hist. Anim.* IV. v. (Bekker p. 531) where the body of the echinus is said to be shaped like the frame of a lantern (λαμπτήρ).]

1841–71 T. R. JONES *Anim. Kingd.* (ed. 4) 216 Dental system of Echinus. 1. Represents three of the pyramidal pieces forming the 'lantern of Aristotle' *in situ.* **1870** NICHOLSON *Man. Zool.* xvii. (1880) 198 In *Echinus* this [masticating apparatus] consists of five long calcareous rod-like teeth, which perforate five triangular pyramids, the whole forming a singular structure known as 'Aristotle's Lantern'.

7. Technical uses. **a.** *Calico-printing*, etc. A steam chamber in which the colours of printed fabrics are fixed.

1839 in URE *Dict. Arts* 233.

b. *Electricity.* The part of the case of the quadrant electrometer which surrounds the mirror and suspension-fibres.

1872 SIR W. THOMSON *Electrostatics & Magn.* 263 Plate I fig. 1 represents the front elevation of the instrument, of which the chief bulk consists of a jar of white glass.. supported on three legs by a brass mounting, cemented round the outside of its mouth, which is closed by a plate of stout sheet-brass, with a lantern-shaped cover standing over a wide aperture in its centre. For brevity, in what follows these three parts will be called the jar, the main cover, and the lantern. **1889** in *Century Dict.*

c. *Founding.* 'A perforated barrel to form a core upon' (W.).

1839 URE *Dict. Arts* 519 The lantern is a cylinder or a truncated hollow cone of cast iron, about half an inch thick; and differently shaped for every different core.

d. *Mech.* A form of cog-wheel (see quot. 1812–16). Also ***lantern-wheel.***

1659 LEAK *Waterwks.* 18 Near the end, there is..a Lanthorn or Pinion of 12. Staves. **1709** F. HAUKSBEE *Phys.-Mech. Exp.* 1 The Winch is fasten'd to a Spindle, that passes thro' a Lanthorn, whose Pins perform the Office of Cogs. **1805** BREWSTER in J. Ferguson *Lect.* I. 82 *note*, A lantern. **1812–16** PLAYFAIR *Nat. Phil.* (1819) I. 79 Sometimes the smaller wheel is a cylinder, in which the top and bottom are formed by circular plates or boards, connected by staves inserted at equal distances along their circumferences, serving as teeth; this is called a lantern. **1829** *Nat. Philos., Mech.* II. vii. 30 (U.K.S.), The teeth of the wheel, instead of working in the leaves of a pinion, are made to act upon a form of wheel called a lantern. **1884** F. J. BRITTEN *Watch & Clockm.* 208 The screw is slipped into a hole in a narrow-faced 'lantern'.

8. *attrib.* and *Comb.*: **a.** simple attributive, as ***lantern fruitage, -glass, -horn, -post***; also (sense 1 d) ***lantern entertainment, lecture, -photograph, -plate, -size, slide***; (sense 4) ***lantern roof, tower, turret.*** **b.** objective, as ***lantern-bearer, -carrier, -maker.*** **c.** instrumental, as ***lantern-fruited, -led, -lighted, -lit*** adjs.

1565 COOPER *Thesaurus, Laternarius*, a *lanterne bearer. **1883** STEVENSON *Treas. Isl.* I. v, A rush was made upon the 'Admiral Benbow', the lantern-bearer following. **1611** COTGR., *Lanternier*, a *Lanterne-carrier. **1890** *Anthony's Photogr. Bull.* III. 37 *Lantern entertainments. **1920** A. HUXLEY *Leda* 7 Moons of many-coloured light That swing their *lantern-fruitage in the night. **1912** W. DE LA MARE *Listeners* 53 She rested her old eyes From the *lantern-fruited yew trees. **1897** MARY KINGSLEY *W. Africa* 590, I see he has smashed the *lantern glass again. **1543** tr. *Act 1 Rich. III*, c. 12 No merchaunt Straungier [shall]..brynge into this Realme of England to be sold any maner..*lantern hornes. **1820** SCORESBY *Acc. Arctic Reg.* I. 486 It is..semi-transparent, almost like lantern-horns. **1912** W. OWEN *Let.* 6 Feb. (1967) 114 Miss Lingley, brother, & friend, who are giving a *Lantern Lecture on their tour among Korean Missions. **1938** L. MACNEICE *I crossed Minch* II. viii. 119 At the end of the service a lantern lecture was announced, which reminded me pleasantly of my childhood. **1808** SCOTT *Marm.* IV. i, Better we had through mire and bush Been *lanthorn-led by Friar Rush [cf. Milton *L'Allegro* 104]. **1871** M. S. JEUNE *My School Days in Paris* vii. 92 At midnight a procession, *lantern-lighted, wound slowly through the garden-walks. **1906** *Westm. Gaz.* 14 July 2/3 And to our fog-bound window came A lantern-lighted ancient dame. **1942** *R.A.F. Jrnl.* 13 June 3 In caves and cellars,..lantern-lighted, a multitude of people endure. **1884** J. COLBORNE *Hicks Pasha* 218 We enjoyed our coffee *al fresco* in the cool *lantern-lit garden. **1598** FLORIO, *Lanternaro*, a *lanterne maker. **1668** H. MORE *Div. Dial.* II. 193 To prevent the Art of the Lantern-maker. **1884** *B'ham*

Daily Post 3 Nov. 7/3 Three of the members will demonstrate the processes of photography, by *lantern-photographs..taken during the conversazione. **1889** *Anthony's Photogr. Bull.* II. 291 Placing the negative in a printing frame, the *lantern plate was laid upon it, film to film. **1871** MORELY *Condorcet* in *Crit. Misc.* Ser. I. (1878) 53 Summary hangings at the nearest *lantern-post. **1882** MISS BRADDON *Mt. Royal* I. ii. 46 Its wide shallow staircase, curiously carved balustrades, and *lantern roof. **1967** *Gloss. Caravan Terms (B.S.I.)* 2 *Lantern roof*, a roof with raised centre portion usually throughout its length, the side walls of which are provided with windows and ventilators. **1969** *Canad. Antiques Collector* May 16/2 The Great Kitchen.. has a lantern roof supported on four cast-iron columns. **1889** *Anthony's Photogr. Bull.* II. 66 Carriers, to carry quarter plates or *lantern-size plates. **1871** G. FOX in *English Mechanic* 13 Jan. 405/3 (*heading*) *Lantern slides. **1896** *Westm. Gaz.* 8 Sept. 3/3 Amateur photographers are learning to make lantern slides from their own negatives. **1909** W. OWEN *Let.* 4 Jan. (1967) 49 There was a Church Army Mission with lantern slides. *a* **1930** D. H. LAWRENCE *Phoenix II* (1968) 115 Gilbert's lectures..with lantern-slides, thrilled Woodhouse to the marrow. **1615** G. SANDYS *Trav.* 40 *fig.*, F. the foote of the *Lanterne Tower. **1762** H. WALPOLE *Vertue's Anecd. Paint.* (1765) I. 121 *note*, The Lantern-tower in the same cathedral [Ely]. **1879** SIR G. SCOTT *Lect. Archit.* II. 262 The dome [of the Baptistery at Florence] had formerly an eye, like the Pantheon, but has now a *lantern turret.

9. Special combs.: **lantern-bellows**, a kind of bellows resembling in structure a Chinese lantern; **lantern-braces** (see quot.); **lantern bug** = *lantern-fly*; also *fig.* (see quot. 1774); **lantern-carrier** (also **-bearer**) = *lantern-fly*; **lantern clock**, a 17th-century bracket clock worked by weights and surmounted by a bell in a frame; **lantern-face**, ? = LANTERN-JAWS; **lantern-fish**, the smooth sole; **lantern-fly**, one of several species of insects of the family *Fulgoridæ* (see quots.); † **lantern-leaves**, thin sheets of horn for lanterns; † **lantern-lerry**, 'some trick of producing artificial light' (Nares); **lantern-light**, (*a*) the light from a lantern; (*b*) a 'light' (i.e. a glazed frame or sash) in the side of a lantern (sense 4); (*c*) an arrangement for giving light through the roof of an apartment; **lantern-man**, one who carries a lantern, †*spec.* one who empties privies by lantern-light, a nightman; **lantern-pier**, ? a pier supporting a lantern (sense 4); **lantern-pinion** = *lantern-wheel*; **lantern-pump** (see quot.); **lantern-service**, a religious service during which magic-lantern slides are employed to furnish illustrations; **lantern-shell**, the bivalve genus *Anatina*, with a translucent shell; **lantern-spar** (see quot.); **lantern-sprat**, a sprat infested by a Lernæan parasite (see quot.); † **lantern-stairs** (see quot.); **lantern test** *Ophthalm.*, a test for colour-blindness in which the subject is asked to name or match colours shown by a lantern; **lantern-wheel** = sense 7 d. Also LANTERN-JAWS.

1875 KNIGHT *Dict. Mech.*, **Lantern-bellows*, so called from its resemblance to a paper lantern. **1867** SMYTH *Sailor's Word-bk.*, **Lantern-braces*, iron bars to secure the lanterns. **1810** A. V. SACK *Voy. Surinam* 279 The *Lantern Carrier..The *Lantern Bearer. **1774** J. BURGOYNE *Maid of Oaks* I. ii. 14, I would have put out Mr. *Lanternbug's stars with one dash of my pincil. **1847** G. A. F. RUXTON *Adventures Mexico & Rocky Mts.* xix. 156 Of bugs and beetles there is endless variety—including the cocuyo or lantern-bug, and the tarantula. **1927** HALDANE & HUXLEY *Animal Biol.* xi. 228 Many lantern bugs have this anterior prolongation of the head. **1913** L. V. LOCKWOOD *Furnit. Collectors' Gloss.* 18/1 Clock..Chamber... These clocks are intended to hang high on the wall on brackets. Called also *Lantern and Bird Cage clocks. **1960** H. HAYWARD *Antique Coll.* 161/2 *Lantern clock*: a clock of typically English design evolved in the early part of the 17th cent., and persisting, especially in the provinces, until well into the 18th cent... All original lantern clocks are weight driven. **1970** *Canad. Antiques Collector* Dec. 12/1 Lantern clocks..were designed to hang on the wall, and were weight driven and regulated by a balance wheel. **1795** J. WOLCOT (P. Pindar) *Royal Tour* 10 Lo, Pitt arrives! alas with *lantern face! **1753** CHAMBERS *Cycl. Supp.*, **Lantern fish.* **1769** PENNANT *Zool.* III. 191 It [the smooth sole] is a scarce species, but is found in Cornwall, where from its transparency, it is called the Lantern Fish. **1822** COUCH in *Linnæan Trans.* XIV. 78 Carter, or Lanternfish, *Pleuronectes megastoma*..It is also called Marysole. **1880** *W. Cornwall Gloss.*, *Lanthorn fish*, a smooth sole. **1753** CHAMBERS *Cycl. Supp.*, **Lantern fly.* **1780** J. T. DILLON *Trav. Spain* (1781) 474 Those harmless insects called lanthorn flies. **1802** BINGLEY *Anim. Biog.* (1813) III. 172 The Great Lantern Fly. **1883** C. F. HOLDER in *Harper's Mag.* Jan. 191/1 The Chinese have the curious lantern-fly (*Fulgora candelaria*), with its long cylindrical proboscis, from the transparent sides of which a brilliant light appears. **1714** *Fr. Bk. of Rates* 44 *Lanthorn-Leaves, as mercery, per 100 Weight, 03 00. **1721** C. KING *Brit. Merch.* I. 294 Lanthorn Leaves. *c* **1630** B. JONSON *Expost. Inigo Jones* 72 Smiling at his feat Of *lantern-lerry. *c* **1400** MAUNDEV. (Roxb.) xii. 50 If men caste in to it a *lanterne-light, it fletez abouen. **1814** SOUTHEY *Roderick* XXI. 139 Why 'twas in quest of such a man as this That the old Grecian searched by lanthorn light. **1823** P. NICHOLSON *Pract. Build.* 188 With regard to the lighting of a grand stair-case, a lantern-light is the most appropriate. **1897** HALL CAINE *Christian* x, There was a refreshment-room with its lantern lights pulled open. **1599** NASHE *Lenten Stuffe* 57 Wee will make him..tell what *Lanterneman or groome of Hecates close stoole hee is. **1813** *Sporting Mag.* XLII. 4 The lanthorn-man should be silent, nor show the light till at the place of sport. **1889** P. H. EMERSON *Eng. Idyls* 89 Now he felt sure a lantern-man was approaching him. **1848** B. WEBB *Continent. Ecclesiol.* 98 The four evangelists are in niches over the *lantern-piers. **1884** F. J. BRITTEN *Watch & Clockm.* 140 *Lantern pinions answer admirably as followers, but are not suited for driving. **1875** KNIGHT *Dict. Mech.*, **Lantern-pump*, one having a pair of disks at the end of a flexible cylinder, like a Chinese lantern. **1897** *Ch. Times* 20 Aug. 187/1 The *lantern services, especially that on the 'Life of Christ', proved most helpful to the people. **1851-6** S. P. WOODWARD *Mollusca* II. 321 *Anatina*, Lamarck. *Lantern-shell. **1777** WATSON in *Phil. Trans.* LXVIII. 867 A piece of rhomboidal, otherwise called refracting or *lantern spar, was broken into four smaller pieces. **1880-4** F. DAY *Brit. Fishes* II. 233 This Lernea is luminous at night-time, and fishermen assert that shoals of sprats are often preceded by several of these fishes infested by parasites and which have occasioned their being termed '*lanthorn sprats'. **1653** URQUHART *Rabelais* I. liii, Between every tower, in the midst of the said body of building, there was a paire of winding (such as we now call *lantern) staires. **1890** *Brit. Med. Jrnl.* 11 Jan. 73/2 The *Lantern Test is the one which I recommend for the testing of sailors and railway *employés*. **1966** K. WYBAR *Ophthalm.* ii. 26 The Ishihara or Stilling Test... The tests are more subtle than the lantern tests and are of value in identifying the anomalous trichromats (of the protanomalous or deuteranomalous types) who are often able to pass the lantern tests successfully. **1792** YOUNG *Trav. France* (1889) 17 The stone drawn up by *lanthorn-wheels of a great diameter. **1831** G. R. PORTER *Silk Manuf.* 199 These parallel spokes are then connected together by bands of string, thus forming a kind of lantern-wheel.

Hence † **'lanterner**, a maker of lanterns.

c **1515** *Cocke Lorell's B.* 10 Lanterners, stryngers, grynders.

lantern ('læntən), *v.* Also 8-9 **lanthorn**. [f. the sb.]

1. a. *trans.* To enclose as in a lantern. **b.** To furnish with a lantern; to light with a lantern.

1789 E. DARWIN *Bot. Gard.* II. (1791) 112 Prometheus.. lantern'd in his breast,..Bore the bright treasure to his Man of Clay. **1799** SOUTHEY *Nondescripts* iii. 24 Were it midnight, I should walk Self-lanthorn'd, saturate with sunbeams. **1832** LAMB *Let. to Cary* in Talfourd *Final Mem.* xviii. 174, I dreaded that Argus Portitor who doubtless lanterned me out, on that prodigious night. **1846** C. MAITLAND *Ch. Catacombs* 227 If a Christian woman marries a Pagan..she must go in and out of a gate laurelled and lanterned.

2. To put to death by hanging upon a lamp-post. (= F. *lanterner*.)

1815 *Paris Chit-Chat* (1816) II. 184 He was himself very near being lanterned in the streets of Paris by a group of the *fauxbourg Saint Antoine*. **1855** in WRIGHT. **1860** in WORCESTER; and in later Dicts.

Hence **'lanterned** *ppl. a.*, furnished with a lantern.

1800-24 CAMPBELL *Grave of Suicide* 6 Nor will the lantern'd fisherman at eve Launch on that water.

lantern, variant of LENTREN *Sc.*, Lent.

lanternist ('læntənɪst). [f. LANTERN *sb.* + -IST.] One who uses a magic lantern.

1880 *Ch. Times* 12 Nov. 744 Photographs of the persecuted clergy, with their churches, &c., would be of great use to 'lanternists' this winter. **1891** *Anthony's Photogr. Bull.* IV. 336 A bad lot of slides..or a bungling lanternist.

lantern-jaws. Long thin jaws, giving a hollow appearance to the cheek. Hence **lantern-jawed** *a.*, having lantern-jaws.

[**1362** LANGL. *P. Pl.* A. VII. 163 Hongur..buffetede the Brutiner aboute bothe his chekes; He lokede lyk a lanterne al his lyf after.] *a* **1700** B. E. *Dict. Cant. Crew*, *Lantern jaw'd*, a very lean, thin faced Fellow. **1707** J. STEVENS *Quevedo's Com. Wks.* (1709) 372 A Lanthorn-Jaw'd Woman, with a Hatchet-Face. **1711** ADDISON *Spect.* No. 173 ¶5 A Ploughman..being very lucky in a Pair of long Lanthorn-Jaws, wrung his face into..a hideous Grimace. **1778** WOLCOT (P. Pindar) *Poetic Ep. Reviewers* Wks. 1812 I. 3 The censure dire my lantern jaws will rue. **1818** SCOTT *Rob Roy* vi, His lantern jaws and long chin assumed the appearance of a pair of nut-crackers. **1848** THACKERAY *Van. Fair* xxix, Drink yourself, and light up your lantern jaws, old boy. **1865** TYLOR *Early Hist. Man.* ii. 30 To give himself a lantern-jawed look.

lantgrave, obs. form of LANDGRAVE.

lanthana ('lænθənə). *Chem.* [f. LANTHAN(UM + *-a*, after *alumina*, *magnesia*, *thoria*, etc.] Lanthanum oxide, La_2O_3, a white powder.

1887 *Chem. News* 12 Aug. 62/1 A specimen of white lanthana prepared by myself some years ago..on being strongly calcined, became of a fawn colour. **1917** H. F. V. LITTLE in J. N. Friend *Text-bk. Inorg. Chem.* IV. 406 Lanthanum sesquioxide or lanthana, La_2O_3, is obtained as a white powder by the ignition of the hydroxide, carbonate, nitrate, oxalate, etc. **1961** W. K. ANDERSON in Spedding & Daane *Rare Earths* xxii. 565 Use of ceria, yttria, and lanthana as diluents for oxide fuel bodies is a promising developmental area.

† **lanthanate** ('lænθəneɪt). *Chem. Obs.* [f. LANTHAN(UM + -ATE[1].] = LANTHANIDE.

1946 *Nature* 27 July 134/2 Actually, however, samarium has an abnormally large atomic volume, a peculiarity which it shares with the other two lanthanates having bivalent properties. **1953** [see LANTHANOID].

lanthanide ('lænθənaɪd). *Chem.* [ad. G. *lanthanid* (V. M. Goldschmidt et al. 1925, in *Skrifter Norske Vidensk-Akad.* (*Mat.-nat. Kl.*) v. 6), f. *lanthan* LANTHANUM: see -IDE 2.] **1.** Any of the series of elements with an atomic number between 57 (lanthanum) and 71 (lutetium) inclusive, or (following the later definition by Goldschmidt et al., on the suggestion of A. Sommerfeld, in *loc. cit.* VII. 10), between 58 (cerium) and 71; all these elements occupy a single position in group IIIA of the periodic table, are predominantly trivalent electropositive metals with similar chemical properties, and occur together in monazite, gadolinite, and certain other minerals. Cf. *rare earth.*

1926 *Chem. Abstr.* XX. 1969 (*heading*) Synthetic pyromorphites, vanadinites and mimetites in which lead is partially substituted by lanthanides. **1937** *Jrnl. Chem. Soc.* 662 A large rather coherent group is furnished by the rare-earth elements, comprising the lanthanide family (elements of atomic number from 57 to 71) and yttrium. **1946** J. R. PARTINGTON *Gen. & Inorg. Chem.* x. 262 The rare-earth elements in this period (sometimes called lanthanides, to distinguish them from the total number of rare-earth elements which includes scandium and yttrium in earlier periods). **1950** N. V. SIDGWICK *Chem. Elements* I. 444 Two of the lanthanides, samarium and lutecium, have been found to be radioactive. **1957** *Sci. News* XLV. 95 In the conventional periodic table..the pigeon-hole allotted to the element lanthanum..contains fourteen additional elements, formerly called the 'Rare Earths', but now usually called the 'Lanthanons' or 'Lanthanides'. **1965** [see F III. 1 j]. **1973** J. J. LAGOWSKI *Mod. Inorg. Chem.* xvi. 616 The trivalent lanthanide cations also exhibit striking colors in their crystalline salts and in aqueous solution. **1973** *Chem. Soc. Rev.* II. 49 The most common practice is to successively add known amounts of the lanthanide shift reagent..to the compound under study..and record the n.m.r. spectrum after each addition.

2. *Comb.*: **lanthanide contraction** [tr. G. *lanthanidenkontraktion* (V. M. Goldschmidt et al. 1925, in *Skrifter Norske Vidensk.-Akad.* (*Mat.-nat. Kl.*) VII. 13)], the decrease in atomic and ionic radii with increasing atomic number observed in the lanthanide series; **lanthanide series**, the series of elements from lanthanum (or cerium) to lutetium.

1926 *Chem. Abstr.* XX. 131 'Lanthanide contraction' is the term applied to the volume contraction of the atoms in the rare earth series Ce-Cu [*sic*]. This contraction opposes the progressive increase of at. vol. in each vertical column of the periodic table. **1945** A. F. WELLS *Structural Inorg. Chem.* iii. 94 As a result of this 'lanthanide contraction', so called because it is observed in the elements following lanthanum, certain pairs of elements in the same Periodic Group have practically identical ionic (and atomic) radii. **1971** *Jrnl. Inorg. & Nucl. Chem.* XXXIII. 385 The lanthanide contraction as reflected in certain properties of the lanthanide compounds is not a smooth function of *Z*. **1945**, **1958** Lanthanide series [see ACTINIDE]. **1965** B. G. WYBOURNE *Spectroscopic Properties Rare Earths* i. 2 As we proceed through the lanthanide series, the nuclear charge, together with the number of 4*f*-electrons, increases by one at each step.

lanthanite ('lænθənaɪt). *Min.* [f. LANTHANUM + -ITE. Named by Haidinger, 1845.] Hydrous carbonate of lanthanum, found in white tabular crystals.

1849 J. NICOL *Min.* 344 Lanthanite..is found in the emerald mines of the Musso Valley. **1868** DANA *Min.* (ed. 5) 709 Lanthanite..Effervesces in the acids.

lanthanoid ('lænθənɔɪd). *Chem.* [f. LANTHAN(IDE + -OID.] Any element of the lanthanide series (including lanthanum).

1953 BARNETT & WILSON *Inorg. Chem.* xii. 135 In modern nomenclature the term 'lanthanons', with variations such as 'lanthanides', 'lanthanates', 'lanthanoids' and 'lanthans' is replacing 'rare earths'. **1969** H. T. EVANS tr. *Hägg's Gen. & Inorg. Chem.* xxviii. 681 The colored lanthanoid ions are used in many ways in the glass industry. **1971** *Nomencl. Inorg. Chem.* (I.U.P.A.C.) (ed. 2) 11 The name lanthanoids for the elements 57-71 (La to Lu inclusive) is recommended.

lanthanon ('lænθənɒn). *Chem.* [f. LANTHAN(IDE + *-on*, prob. to avoid confusion with the systematic use of *-ide* (-IDE).] (See quot. 1947.)

1947 J. K. MARSH in *Q. Rev. Chem. Soc.* I. 126 The term 'lanthanon' (Ln) is proposed to denote any element of the group from lanthanum to lutecium inclusive and to replace such objectionable terms as 'lanthanate' or 'lanthanide' which have recently had some currency. **1951** *Nature* 31 Mar. 526/1 An analysis of the lanthanon (rare earth) fraction from davidite..has revealed an unusual variation in the abundance of the lanthanons. **1961** W. K. ANDERSON in Spedding & Daane *Rare Earths* xxii. 522 Advances in the technology and availability of the lanthanons..have brought about an upsurge of interest among nuclear technologists. **1973** *Jrnl. Chromatogr.* LXXVI. 459 *Sym.-*EDDA was studied..as a complexant for the trivalent lanthanons and yttrium.

lanthanum ('lænθənəm). *Chem.* Also 9 **lant(h)anium**. [f. Gr. λανθάν-ειν to escape notice (see quot. 1841).] A rare element belonging to the group of earth metals, found in certain rare minerals, e.g. cerite; it was discovered by Mosander 1839-41. Symbol Ln. Also *attrib.*

1841 BRANDE *Man. Chem.* (ed. 5) 877 Another metallic oxide, which, as it has hitherto lain concealed in oxide of cerium, he [Mosander] designates Lantanum (λανθανειν, to lurk). **1842** PARNELL *Chem. Anal.* (1845) 338 Oxide of lantanium. **1849** D. CAMPBELL *Inorg. Chem.* 167 Lanthanum. **1863** *Fownes' Chem.* (ed. 9) 320 Metallic

lanthanium is prepared like cerium. *Ibid.*, A tolerably pure lanthanium salt may be obtained by [etc.]. **1873** *Ibid.* (ed. 11) 381 Lanthanum Sulphate forms small prismatic crystals.

lanthern, variant of LANTERN.

lanthopine ('lænθəpɪn). *Chem.* [f. Gr. λανθάνειν (see prec.) + OP-IUM + -INE: see -INE.] An alkaloid found in opium.
1888 *Syd. Soc. Lex.*, *Lanthopin*, $C_{23}H_{25}NO_4$.

lanthorn, variant of LANTERN.

† **'lantify**, *v. Obs. rare*⁻¹. [f. LANT *sb.*[1] + -(I)FY.] *trans.* To wet with urine.
a **1652** A. WILSON *Inconst. Lady* II. ii. (1814) 37 A goodly peece of puff pac't, A little lantified, to hold the gilding.

lantirne, obs. form of LANTERN.

† **lantone**. *Obs. rare*⁻¹. [Anglicized form of LANTANA.] The wayfaring tree, *Viburnum Lantana*.
1733-7 MILLER *Gard. Dict.* (ed. 3) s.v. *Viscum*, The Bark of our Lantone or Way-faring Shrub.

lantreloo, variant of LANTERLOO *Obs.*

lantren, -in, -on, obs. forms of LANTERN.

lants-, lantzgrave, obs. forms of LANDGRAVE.

'lantum ('læntəm). [prob. merely echoic.] A kind of accordion or concertina, shaped and played like a hurdy-gurdy.
1876 STAINER & BARRETT *Dict. Mus. Terms.*

lanturne, -yrne, obs. forms of LANTERN.

† **la'nuge**. *Obs. rare*⁻⁰. [ad. L. *lānūgo*, f. *lāna* wool.] (See quot.)
1623 COCKERAM, *Lanuge*, Downe, or the beard when it first appeares to grow.

lanuginic (lænju:'dʒɪnɪk), *a. Chem.* [f. L. *lanūgin-* (see next) + -IC.] *lanuginic acid* (see quot.).
1888 *Syd. Soc. Lex.*, Lanuginic acid, an acid obtained by boiling wool in potash.

lanuginose (lə'nju:dʒɪnəʊs), *a. scientific.* [ad. L. *lānūginōs-us*, f. *lānūgin-* (*lānūgo*) down, f. *lāna* wool: see -OSE.] = next.
1693 *Phil. Trans.* XVII. 684 The Stone is oblong flattish, and lanuginose. **1731** MASSEY *ibid.* XXXVII. 218 These.. soon became covered with an exceeding white fine lanuginose Substance. **1826** in KIRBY & SP. *Entomol.* IV. 275.

lanuginous (lə'nju:dʒɪnəs), *a.* Chiefly *scientific.* [ad. L. *lānūginōs-us*: see prec. and -OUS.] Covered with down or fine soft hair; having a surface resembling down; of the nature of down; downy.
1575 LANEHAM *Let.* (1871) 56 Lanuginoous az a lad of eyghteen yee[r]z. **1608** TOPSELL *Serpents* (1658) 670 Hairy or lanuginous Caterpillers. **1671** *Phil. Trans.* VI. 2167 That Lanuginous Stone, called *Amianthus.* **1684** *Ibid.* XIV. 823 A lanuginous matter exactly resembling that of pappous Plants. **1706** BAYNARD in Sir J. Floyer *Hot & Cold Bath.* II. 236 The Mouth and Tongue.. by reason of its downy and lanuginous Membrane. **1762** *Nat. Hist.* in *Ann. Reg.* 76/1 Clothed with a lanuginous skin. **1796** KIRWAN *Elem. Min.* (ed. 2) II. 28 Found in Lanuginous Crystals on the walls of an old cellar. **1877** COUES & ALLEN *N. Amer. Rod.* 46 Lanuginous tufts of hair.
Hence **la'nuginousness**. (Bailey, vol. II. 1727.)

‖**lanugo** (lə'nju:gəʊ). *scientific.* [L f. *lāna* wool.] Fine soft hair or down, or a surface resembling this; *spec.* that covering the human fœtus.
1677 *Phil. Trans.* XII. 904 The lanugo seen upon a Peach, Quince, or the like. **1766** *Misc. Ess.* in *Ann. Reg.* 192/1 A Monchinel-apple falling into the sea and lying in the water will contract a lanugo of salt-petre. **1871** DARWIN *Desc. Man* I. i. 25 The.. so-called lanugo, with which the human foetus during the sixth month is thickly covered. **1876** DUHRING *Dis. Skin* 33 Very fine, soft hair, called lanugo, found upon the face, trunk, and other regions.
attrib. and *Comb.* **1891** W. A. JAMIESON *Dis. Skin* i. (ed. 3) 4 The small lanugo hairs seem as if dependents of the sebaceous glands. **1897** *Allbutt's Syst. Med.* III. 686 A tuft of delicate lanugo-like hairs.

‖**lanx** (læŋks). *Antiq.* [L.] A large dish.
1857 BIRCH *Anc. Pottery* (1858) II. 317 The *catinus* was large enough to hold the tail of a tunny, the *lanx* could hold a crab. **1864** *Q. Rev.* July 235 The magnificent silver 'lanx' or dish, weighing 150 ounces, which was found in 1734 at Corstopitum.

lanyard ('lænjəd). Forms: α. 5 lanȝer, 5-6, 9 *dial.* lanyer, 7 lannier, 9 *dial.* lanner. β. 7 lanyeard, lennerd, 7-9 lan(n)iard, 8 *erron.* land yard, 8- lanyard. [A re-adoption of F. *lanière* (see LAINER).]
† **1.** = LAINER. *Obs.*
1483 *Cath. Angl.* 208/1 A lanȝer, *ligula.* **1530** PALSGR. 237/2 Lanyer of lether, *lasniere.* **1787** MARSHALL *Norfolk* (1795) II. 383 *Lanniard*, the thong of a whip. *a* **1825** FORBY *Voc. E. Anglia*, *Lanner, Lanyer*, the lash of a whip.

2. *Naut.* 'A short piece of rope or line made fast to anything to secure it, or as a handle' (Smyth *Sailor's Word-bk.*).
a. Used to secure the shrouds and stays.
1626 CAPT. SMITH *Accid. Yng. Sea-men* 15 They haue all of them pullies,.. Lanyeards, caskets, and crowes feete. **1627** —— *Seaman's Gram.* v. 19 Those Lanniers are many small Ropes reeued into the dead mens eyes of all shrouds. **1709** *Lond. Gaz.* No. 4543/1 Having.. cut all the Land yards of the Falmouth's Fore and Mizen-shrowds. **1748** *Anson's Voy.* I. x. 104 We exerted ourselves the best we could.. to reeve new lanyards. **1833** M. SCOTT *Tom Cringle* (1862) 347 A hammock, slung.. by two lanyards fastened to rings. **1840** R. H. DANA *Bef. Mast* Gloss., *Lanyards*, ropes rove through the dead-eyes, for setting up rigging. **1881** SIR T. MARTIN *Horace* I. xiv, Dost thou not.. hear thy lanyards moan and shriek?
b. Used for firing a gun.
1825 H. B. GASCOIGNE *Nav. Fame* 95 Captains of the guns their Laniards bear. **1836** MARRYAT *Midsh. Easy* xxx, The captains of the guns had dropped their lanyards in disappointment. **1861** W. H. RUSSELL in *Times* 10 July, The gunner pulled the lanyard hard, but the tube did not explode. **1876** *Daily News* 30 Sept. 2/2 The artillerymen would.. have no objection to firing the gun themselves with a lanyard.
c. Used for various other purposes.
1669 STURMY *Mariner's Mag.* I. 17 Stand by to hawl off above the Lennerd of the Whipstaff. **1797** NELSON in Nicolas *Disp.* (1845) II. 417 Four ladders, (each of which to have a lanyard four fathoms long). **1864** *Reader* 8 Oct. 454 A small knife lashed with a lanyard to the wrist. **1883** STEVENSON *Treas. Isl.* II. x, He carried his crutch by a lanyard round his neck. **1897** R. KIPLING *Captains Courageous* 76 The lanyard of a bell that hung just behind the windlass.
d. The material of which lanyards are made.
1862 *Times* 7 Mar., A packing of lanyard [was] put between the armour plates and screw nuts. **1883** *Fisheries Exhib. Catal.* 24 Tarred Russian Hemp Laniard.

† **'lanyer**, *v. Obs.* [f. *lanyer* (see prec.).] *trans.* To bind with a thong.
1483 *Cath. Angl.* 208/1 To lanȝere, *ligulare.*

lanzknecht (Ger.): see LANSQUENET.

Lao (laʊ), *sb.* and *a.* [Native name.] **A.** *sb.* **a.** A branch of the Thai people (see quot. 1949) in South-East Asia; also, a member of this people.
1882 *Encycl. Brit.* XIV. 294/2 The Laos are closely related in physique and speech to the Siamese proper. **1885** T. DE LACOUPERIE in A. R. Colquhoun *Amongst Shans* p. lii, We know more of the original seat of the *Lao* or *Ngai Lao*, than of the others. **1915** W. W. COCHRANE *Shans* I. 198 The teaching that God is more powerful than all the hosts of evil spirits.. ought to be attractive.. particularly to the Laos among whom the demons seem to be uncommonly active. **1949** *Jrnl. Amer. Oriental Soc.* LXIX. 63/1 The use of *Lao* is confusing because, while it is now specifically applied to a specific Tai people—called Laotians by the French—another branch, not especially close to the Laotian, has been called Ngai-lao, or Ai-lao; while the name has also been sometimes used as synonymous with *Tai.* **1961** P. KEMP *Alms for Oblivion* ii. 22 The majority of Laos stood by the French, whereas the Annamites detested them. **1969** I. KEMP *Brit. G.I. in Vietnam* iv. 78 The Lao also look down on them [*sc.* montagnards], calling them *kha*, meaning 'slaves'.
b. A group of dialects (see quot. 1954) spoken in Laos and neighbouring areas.
1939 L. H. GRAY *Found. Lang.* 390 To the south-eastern division belong Siamese, Lao, Lü, and Khün. **1948** D. DIRINGER *Alphabet* 414 Lao is nowadays widely spoken in northern Siam. **1954** PEI & GAYNOR *Dict. Ling.* 120 *Lao*, a group of vernaculars spoken in Siam and in parts of Burma, classified as Shan dialects. **1961** *Times* 23 Jan. 13/6 One of the Lao-speaking provinces. **1966** *Economist* 6 Aug. 536/1 The Americans are beginning to bring in a flood of school textbooks in Lao.
B. *adj.* Of, concerning, or pertaining to the Lao or their language.
1882 *Encycl. Brit.* XIV. 294/2 The last surviving descendant of the ancient Lao dynasty. **1915** W. W. COCHRANE *Shans* I. 155 The Lao alphabet.. has 45 consonants. **1970** *Times* 26 Feb. 11/2 Somehow a Laos for the Lao people will have to be conserved.

Laocoön (leɪ'ɒkəʊɒn). Also **Lacoon, Laocoon, Laokoon.** [ad. Gr. Λαοκόων.] The name of a legendary Trojan priest who, with his two sons, was crushed to death by two sea-serpents (Virgil *Aeneid* II. 40-56, 199-231), used allusively, esp. with reference to statues representing him and his sons in their death-struggle. Freq. *attrib.*
1601 P. HOLLAND tr. *Pliny's Hist. World* XXXVI. v. 569 This may be seene in the image of Laocoon.. a peece of worke to be preferred.. before all pictures or cast images. *a* **1666** EVELYN *Diary* an. 1644 (1955) II. 107 Above all that fountaine of the Laocoon.. is a most glorious & surprizing object. **1699** M. LISTER *Journey to Paris* 143 The Atteliers or Work-houses of Two of the famous Sculptures Tuby; in which was a Lacoon Copied in White Marble. **1811** B. R. HAYDON *Jrnl.* 12 Jan. in *Autobiogr.* (1853) I. ix. 150 Went to the Academy in the evening, and saw the Laocoon placed out as it was four years ago. **1843** DICKENS *Christmas Carol* v. 153 Scrooge.. making a perfect Laocoön of himself with his stockings. **1910** H. G. WELLS *Hist. Mr. Polly* i. 11 If Mr. Polly.. had been transparent.. he might have realized, from the Laocoon struggle he would have glimpsed, that.. he was not so much a human being as a civil war. *a* **1930** D. H. LAWRENCE *Last Poems* (1932) 172 Leave the fearful Laocoön of his fellow-man entangled in iron To its fearful fate. *Ibid.* 282 We have become.. fatally entangled in the Laocoön coils of our conceit. **1938** L. MACNEICE *I crossed Minch* II. viii. 108 The usual Chirico nightmare of marble Fathers of the City and laocoons in plaster. **1967** I. MARDER *Paris Bit* 84 She was draped like a female Laocoön in yards of inky black silk. **1970** *Sunday Times* 18 Jan. 56/4 The old flexibility and flair may become Laocoön to the computers.

Laodicean (ˌleɪədɪ'si:ən), *a.* and *sb.* [f. L. *Laodicē-a* (a. Gr. Λαοδίκεια) a city in Asia Minor + -AN.]
A. *adj.* **a.** Of or pertaining to Laodicea. **b.** Having the fault for which the Church of Laodicea is reproached in Rev. iii. 15, 16; hence, 'lukewarm, neither cold nor hot', indifferent in religion, politics, etc.
1633 EARL MANCH. *Al Mondo* (1636) 127 Worse.. is profane Newtralitie, or Laodicean coldnesse. **1642** ROGERS *Naaman* 24 Lazy, Laodicean temper of a fulsome, carelesse, surfeted spirit. **1877** L. TOLLEMACHE in *Fortn. Rev.* Dec. 857 Laodicean liberals sometimes boast that [etc.]. **1888** MRS. H. WARD *R. Elsmere* 165 You will loathe all this Laodicean cant of tolerance as I do. **1889** *Times* 12 Sept. 7/1 A force of which Englishmen in these somewhat Laodicean days may easily fail to take proper account.
B. *sb.* **a.** An inhabitant of Laodicea. **b.** One who is lukewarm or indifferent in religion, politics, etc.
1611 BIBLE *Rev.* iii. 14 And vnto the Angel of the Church of the Laodiceans, write. **1646** P. BULKELEY *Gospel Covt.* III. 239 These are.. Laodiceans, who are poore, and blind and naked. **1772** FLETCHER *Appeal* Wks. 1795 I. 230 Antinomian Laodiceans, and Antichristian Pharisees, are equally blameable. **1849** MACAULAY *Hist. Eng.* vii. II. 233 Two years earlier he would have been pronounced by numerous bigots on both sides a mere Laodicean. **1881** T. HARDY (*title*) A Laodicean.
Hence **Laodi'ceanism**, lukewarmness, indifference.
1774 J. ADAMS *Lett.* Wks. 1850 II. 340 There is, in this town and county, a Laodiceanism that I have not found in any other place. **1856** SPURGEON *New Park St. Pulpit* I. 204 Let not Laodiceanism get into Southwark.

Laotian ('laʊʃən, lɑ:'əʊʃən), *a.* and *sb.* Also **Laosian.** [f. *Laos*, name of a country in South-East Asia: see -IAN, LAO.] **A.** *adj.* Of or pertaining to the country of Laos. **B.** *sb.* A native or inhabitant of Laos; also the language of the Laotian people.
a **1861** H. MOUHOT *Trav. Indo-China* (1864) II. xviii. 154 The Laotian priests.. make a frightful noise, chanting from morning to night. **1890** J. G. FRAZER *Golden Bough* I. i. 42 Before beginning to work at the salt-pans in a Laosian village, the workmen offer sacrifice to a local divinity. **1911** *Encycl. Brit.* XVI. 190/2 Laos is inhabited by a mixed population falling into three main groups—the Thais (including the Laotians..); various aboriginal peoples classed as Khas; and the inhabitants of neighbouring countries. **1931** *Times Lit. Suppl.* 12 Nov. 880/4 A Laotian festival. **1949** *Jrnl. Amer. Oriental Soc.* LXIX. 63/2 The Southern group of Tai in Indo-China includes the Siamese and the Laotians. **1954** PEI & GAYNOR *Dict. Ling.* 120 Thai Lao or Eastern Laotian.. and Tai Yüan or Western Laotian. **1967** D. S. PARLETT *Short Dict. Lang.* 122 Siamese and Laotian boast literature from comparatively ancient times. **1968** *Guardian* 1 May 9/1 The American.. was having an argument with four Laotian officials... Suddenly the American threw the contents of his glass at one of the Laotians. **1971** *Ibid.* 8 Apr. 2/1 The writer is an American freelance who speaks fluent Laotian. **1972** *Mainichi Daily News* (Japan) 6 Nov. 19/4 (*caption*) Japanese 'peace corps' members.. teach Laotian farmers how to operate a tractor.

lap (læp), *sb.*[1] Forms: 1 læppa, 3-7 lappe, 6 lapp, 4- lap. [OE. *lappa, læppa* wk. masc. = OFris. *lappa*, OS. *lappo* (Essen gloss.), MDu. *lappe* (Du. *lap*), OHG. (with unexplained *pp* instead of *pf*) *lappa* fem. (MHG. *lappe* masc. and fem., mod.G. *lappen* masc.); cf. ON. *lepp-r* clout, rag, lock of hair.
App. the OTeut. type would be **lappon-* with *pp* for earlier *pn*; the pre-Teut. root might be either **lop-*, **lob-*, or **lobh-*. Scholars have variously suggested connexion with Gr. λόβος LOBE (see sense 2 a below), with Skr. *ramb-, lamb-*, to hang loose, or with Lith. *lópas* patch.]
1. a. A part (of a garment or the like) either hanging down or projecting so as to admit of being folded over; a flap, lappet. In later use chiefly, a piece that hangs down at the bottom of a garment, one of the skirts of a coat, a portion of the skirt of a robe. Hence *pl.* (*colloq.*) a tail-coat.
c **897** K. ÆLFRED *Gregory's Past.* xxviii. 197 [Dauid] forcearf his mentles ænne læppan [L. *oram chlamydis*]. *c* **1290** *S. Eng. Leg.* I. 101/29 And cam ant touchede þe lappe of ore louerdes cloþes ene. **13..** *E.E. Allit. P.* A. 201 Wyth lappez large. **13..** *Gaw. & Gr. Knt.* 1356 Bi þe byȝt al of þe þyȝes, þe lappez þay lance bi-hynde. *c* **1374** CHAUCER *Troylus* II. 399 (448) She hym a-gayn by þe lappe caughte. *a* **1400** *Sir Beues* 2456 (MS. S.) þe Lyoun.. with his teeþ.. kitte a pece of his lappe. ? *a* **1400** *Morte Arth.* 3255 And with ladily lappes the lenghe of a ȝerde. *c* **1430** *Pilgr. Lyf Manhode* II. li. (1869) 200 And hadde trussed hire lappes in hire girdel, redy.. for to wrastle. *c* **1460** *Emare* 654 Her vysage she gan hyde, With the hynther lappes [of her surkote]. **1502** *Ord. Crysten Men* II. v. (W. de W. 1506) 95 Pryde is shewed in gownes, in furres, with sleues with syde lappes or plyted. **1530** PALSGR. 237/2 Lappe or skyrt, *gyron.* **1535** COVERDALE *Ezek.* v. 3 Take a little off the same & bynde it in thy cote lappe. **1555** W. WATREMAN *Fardle Facions* II. xi. 258 Their women.. vpon their heades do vse a certeine attire,.. wherof the one lappe so rangeth vpon whiche side semeth her good. **1583** *Satir. Poems Reform.* xlv. 870 Who tuke him by the lap and lewch. **1608** WILLET *Hexapla Exod.* 638 The Ephod.. had foure laps or wings. **1620** in Gutch *Coll. Cur.* I. 172 They were never able to cut so much as the lap of her coat. **1637** RUTHERFORD *Lett.* (1862) I. 200 Let me beseech your

Lordship to draw by the lap of time's curtain and to look in thro' the window to great and endless eternity. *a* **1656** HALES *Gold. Rem.* (1688) 262 When David had cut off the lap of Saul's Garment. **17..** *Mary Myle* xii. in Child *Ballads* (1889) III. 386 The lap cam aff her shoe. *c* **1817** HOGG *Tales & Sk.* III. 259 Wiped his eyes..with the lap of his plaid. **1824** SCOTT *Redgauntlet* xi, With the lap of my cloak cast over my face. **1828** —— *F.M. Perth* viii, The..horseman's feet did not by any means come beneath the laps of the saddle. **1876** *Whitby Gloss.*, *Laps*, the skirts of a coat. **1878** *Mozley's Ess.* I. Introd. 16 A little fellow in a jacket, which had to be exchanged for 'laps' before the examination.

fig. **1651** *Coronat. Chas. II at Scoone* 7 That we may be far from cutting of a lap of that just power..which God hath allowed to the King.

†**b.** *transf.* The outlying part (of an army). Cf. the use of 'skirt'. *Obs.*

a **1578** LINDESAY (Pitscottie) *Chron. Scot.* (S.T.S.) I. 314 The laird of Cesfurde..sett on fercelie wpoun the lape and winge of the laird of Balcluchеis feild.

2. Applied to certain parts of the body:

a. of the ear, liver, lungs: = LOBE. *Obs.* exc. in *ear-lap*. [A Com. Teut. sense.]

c **1000** *Sax. Leechd.* II. 198 Sio [lifer] biþ on þa swiþran sidan aþened oþ þone neweseoþan sio hæfð fif læppan. **14..** *Voc.* in Wr.-Wülcker 631/8 Lap of þe ere. **1538** ELYOT *Dict.*, *Fibræ*, are the extreme partes of the liuer, the hart, or the lunges, or of other thinges wherin is any diuysyon, they maye be called lappes, brymmes. **1573** BARET *Alv.* L 86 The lappes of the lights or lunges, *fibræ pulmonis*. **1607** TOPSELL *Four-f. Beasts* (1658) 402 The laps or fillets of the liver of a Mouse. **1647** N. BACON *Disc. Govt. Eng.* I. lix. (1739) 117 The Synod..decreed that men should cut their Hair so as their Eyes and laps of their Ears might be seen. **1658** ROWLANDS *Moufet's Theat. Ins.* 912 The convulsion of the laps of the lungs (which useth to be a deadly disease). **1681** W. ROBERTSON *Phraseol. Gen.* (1693) 799 The lap of the ear, *lobus*. **1722** RAMSAY *Three Bonnets* II. 52 Require a thing I'll part wi' never! She's get as soon a lap o' my liver.

†**b.** A fold of flesh or skin; *occas.* the female pudendum. *Obs.*

1398 TREVISA *Barth. De P.R.* XVIII. xiii. (*MS. Bodl.* 3738) In Siria beþ oxen þat haue no dewe lappis nother fresche lappes vnder þrote [L. *palearia sub gutture*]. *c* **1420** [see DEWLAP]. **1553** EDEN *Treat. Newe Ind.* (Arb.) 16 The two great tuskes..hauinge on euerye syde lappes hanging downe of the bignes of two hand brea[d]th. **1605** TIMME *Quersit.* I. xiii. 60 By reason of his soliditie and hardness inconcocted..it doth fret and teare the laps of the stomach. **1607** TOPSELL *Four-f. Beasts* (1658) 74 The female [is gelded] by searing her privy parts within the brim and laps thereof with a hot iron. **1615** CROOKE *Body of Man* 250 The *Clitoris* is a small body, not continuated at all with the bladder, but placed in the height of the lap.

†**3.** A piece of cloth, a cloth, clout. *Obs.*

c **1386** CHAUCER *Clerk's T.* 529 That he pryuely Sholde this child..winde and wrappe And carie it in a cofre or in a lappe. ? *a* **1400** *Morte Arth.* 3286 Nowe es lefte me no lappe my lygham to hele. *c* **1460** *Towneley Myst.* xxiv. 265 A lap..ffor-tatyrd and torne. **14..** *Pol. Rel. & L. Poems* 227 For ich nabbe clout ne lappe.

4. The 'lap' (sense 1) of a garment used as a receptacle. †**a.** The fold of a robe (e.g. the toga) over the breast, which served as a pocket or pouch; hence, the bosom.

In figurative use this sense is sometimes hardly to be distinguished from sense 5.

c **1290** *S. Eng. Leg.* I. 284/229 In heore lappen huy brouȝten mete. **1393** LANGL. *P. Pl.* C. XIX. 273 In hus bosom he bar a thyng and that he blessede ofte. And ich loked in hus lappe, a lazar lay ther-ynne. *c* **1400** *Sowdone Bab.* 1800 Thai smyten of here hedes alle, Eche man toke one in his lappe. *c* **1440** *Gesta Rom.* lxix. 321 (Harl. MS.) Suche ben to be put out of þe lappe of holy chirche. **1484** CAXTON *Chivalry* i. 6 He beganne to rede in a lytyl book that he had in his lappe. **1513** DOUGLAS *Æneis* XI. xv. 19 Hys rych mantill, of quham the forbreist lappis..was buklit wyth a knot. *c* **1586** C'TESS PEMBROKE *Ps.* CXXIX. iv,[Your harvest] Filling neither reapers hand Nor the binders inbow'd lapp. **1600** HOLLAND *Livy* XXI. xviii. 403 Having made a hollow lap within the plait and fold of his side gowne. **1605** BACON *Adv. Learn.* I. vi. §14. 31 It was the Christian Church which..did preserve in the sacred lappe and bosome thereof, the pretious Reliques even of Heathen learning. **1643** *Myst. Iniq.* 3 He desires that the Prince of Wales might be brought backe againe into the lap of the Romish Church.

b. The front portion of a skirt when held up to contain or catch something.

13.. *Seuyn Sag.* (W.) 901 Ful he gaderede his barm, In his other lappe he gaderede some. *c* **1386** CHAUCER *Sqr.'s T.* 433 She..heeld hir lappe abrood, for wel sche wiste The ffaukon moste fallen fro the twist. **1636** HEYWOOD *Love's Mistress* II. i. Wks. 1874 V. 109 Hold up your lapps; tho' them you cannot see That bring this gold. **1848** LYTTON *Harold* I. i, Followed by girls with laps full of flowers. **1848** MRS. JAMESON *Sacr. & Leg. Art* (1850) 41 Some come dancing forward with flowers in their hands or in the lap of their robe.

c. A form of loin-cloth worn by Indians in Guyana.

1769 E. BANCROFT *Ess. Nat. Hist. Guiana* 273 This is called a lap, and is the ordinary covering of the Negroes also. **1876** C. B. BROWN *Canoe & Camp Life Brit. Guiana* 34 There were two Indians,..dressed in nature's garb, barring the 'lap'. **1899** J. RODWAY *In Guiana Wilds* 254 A party of Indians in nothing but their laps. **1924** *38th Ann. Rep. U.S. Bureau Amer. Ethnol.* xxi. 439 To this belt or girdle..the apron or lap may be attached. *Ibid.* 443 Among the Wapishana, the length of the bark 'lap' (tururi) was..a guide to the importance of the wearer. **1958** M. SWAN *Marches of El Dorado* I. 56 An Indian in these parts would be ashamed to wear the bead apron or the red cotton lap of his parents; he cleans his teeth and brilliantines his hair.

5. a. The front portion of the body from the waist to the knees of a person seated, considered with its covering garments as the place *in* or *on* which a child is nursed or any object held.

c **1275** LAY. 30261 Com þar a bour-cniht and sat adun forþ riht..he nam þan kynges hefd and leyde vppe his lappe [*earlier text* in his bærm]. **1340** HAMPOLE *Pr. Consc.* 6766 Als a childe þat sittes in þe moder lappe. *c* **1386** CHAUCER *Prol.* 686 His walet lay biforn hym in his lappe. **1393** LANGL. *P. Pl.* C. IX. 283 Ich sauh hym [Lazarus] sitte..in Abraham's lappe. *c* **1422** HOCCLEVE *Min. Poems* (1892) 231 Streeche out anoon thy lappe, In which wole I myn heed doun leye and reste. *c* **1440** *Gesta Rom.* lxv. 286 (Harl. MS.) She late hit [a stone] fall in þe lappe of gwido. **1535** COVERDALE *Prov.* xvi. 34 The lottes are cast in to the lappe, but their fall stondeth in the Lord. **1605** SHAKS. *Macb.* I. iii. 3 A Saylors Wife had Chestnuts in her Lappe. **1667** MILTON *P.L.* IX. 1060 So rose..Herculean Samson from the Harlot-lap Of Philistean Dalilah. **1709** STEELE *Tatler* No. 15 ⁋2 She lays me upon my Face in her Lap. **1768–74** TUCKER *Lt. Nat.* (1834) II. 387 A child will never grow to vigorous manhood, who is kept always in his mother's lap. **1792** CHARLOTTE SMITH *Desmond* III. 125 Of those six [persons], three were infants in lap. **1832** HT. MARTINEAU *Ireland* iii. 43 Dora had sunk down at her mother's feet, hiding her face in her lap. **1894** HALL CAINE *Manxman* VI. iii, The child lay outstretched on Grannie's lap.

b. *transf.* A hollow among hills.

1745 WARTON *Pleas. Melanch.* 253 Sunny vales In prospect vast their level laps expand. **1820** W. IRVING *Sketch Bk.*, *Leg. Sleepy Hollow* (1865) 416 A little valley, or rather lap of land, among high hills. **1847** LE FANU *T. O'Brien* 312 A little village lay in the lap of a hill. **1870** F. R. WILSON *Ch. Lindisf.* 126 Edlingham church stands in a green lap of a vale. **1883** *Harper's Mag.* Aug. 327/1 Two hundred miles west..lies Altoona, in the lap of the..Mountains.

c. *fig.* Freq. in such expressions as ***in fortune's, nature's, pleasure's lap; bred up, nursed,*** etc. ***in the lap of*** (luxury, etc.). †***to lay in (a person's) lap***: to thrust upon his notice. For ***in the lap of Providence, the future, the gods***, cf. Gr. *θεῶν ἐν γούνασι*.

1531 ELYOT *Gov.* II. iv, Lete yonge gentilmen haue often times tolde to them, and (as it is vulgarely spoken) layde in their lappes, how [etc.]. **1593** SHAKS. *Rich. II*, v. ii. 47 Who are the Violets now, That strew the greene lap of the new-come Spring? **1598** SPENSER *Wks.* (Grosart) I. 544 A Countrie of yoʳ owne dominion, lying hard vnder the lapp of England. **1616** R. C. *Times' Whistle* v. 2125, I luld a sleep in pleasures lap. **1617** HIERON *Wks.* II. 266 He would..sleepe securely vpon the lap of Gods protection. **1646** *Hamilton Papers* (Camden) 124 When they finde these wishes throwne in their lap, [they] will be apt enough to turne their sailes another way. **1667** MILTON *P.L.* IX. 1041 Flowers were the couch..Earth's freshest softest lap. **1712** PRIDEAUX *Direct. Ch.-wardens* (ed. 4) 105 There is in the Lap of Providence an appointed Time yet to come. **1726–46** THOMSON *Winter* 593 They pine beneath the brightest skies, In Nature's richest lap. **1742** YOUNG *Nt. Th.* I. 259 What Numbers, once in Fortune's Lap high-fed, Solicit the cold Hand of Charity! **1764** GOLDSM. *Trav.* 172 But winter lingering chills the lap of May. **1796** MORSE *Amer. Geog.* I. 30 Nursed in the lap of indolence. **1797** GODWIN *Enquirer* II. xii. 402 Bred up..in the lap of republican freedom. **1802** MAR. EDGEWORTH *Moral T.* (1816) I. vi. 36 Brought up in the lap of luxury. **1803** R. HALL *Wks.* (1833) I. 190 Freedom poured into our lap opulence and arts. **1806** A. DUNCAN *Nelson* 317 A thorough seaman..nursed in the lap of hardship. **1818** JAS. MILL *Brit. India* II. IV. v. 217 The current of presents..flowed very naturally, and very copiously, into the lap of the strangers. **1820** KEATS *Eve St. Agnes* xv, Madeline asleep in lap of legends old. **1822** BYRON *Werner* II. ii. 103 Rash, new to life, and rear'd in luxury's lap. **1884** *Pall Mall G.* 10 May 1/2 These things, however, lie in the lap of the future. **1920** 'SAPPER' *Bull-Dog Drummond* 23 Perhaps a year—perhaps six months... It is in the lap of the gods. **1965** *New Statesman* 30 Apr. 674/3 Almost all power lies in the laps of the different Laender [in Germany]. **1971** *Guardian* 27 Feb. 5/5 Lord Justice Davies said it was in the 'lap of the gods' what would be the effect on the younger children if they were ordered to go to their mother's home.

6. †**a.** ***to fall into the lap*** or ***laps of***: to come within the reach, or into the power, of. ***to be left in the laps***: to be left in difficulties, 'in the lurch'. (*Lapse* is sometimes written for *laps*, by confusion with LAPSE *sb.*)

The origin of this use is somewhat obscure; it may be from sense 5; but cf. G. *durch die lappen gehen*, to escape, get clear off, where *lappen* means literally a contrivance for catching deer.

1558 in Strype *Ann. Ref.* I. App. iv. 5 Clemency to be extended not before they do..acknowledge themselves to have fallen in the Lapse of the Law. **1560** DAUS tr. *Sleidane's Comm.* 153 b, In the retire they fel into the lappes of their ennemies. **1598** R. BERNARD *Terence, Andria* III. v, Dost thou not see me left in the lapps thro' thy device and counsaile? **1602** WARNER *Alb. Eng.* IX. li. (1612) 230 They will exact by Torture what thou thinkest,..till in the Lapse thou fall. *a* **1618** RALEIGH *Rem.* (1644) 122 Let them blame their own folly if they..fall head-long into the lap of endless perdition. *a* **1642** SIR W. MONSON *Naval Tracts* v. (1704) 463/1 They cannot avoid falling into the lap of one of the other two [ships].

b. ***to drop, throw,*** etc., (something) ***in someone's lap***: to shift a burden to (someone). Also (*intr.*) ***to drop into the lap of***.

1962 B. KNOX *Little Drops of Blood* ii. 35 'And Sammy Bell's gear?' 'We'll dump that one in the lap of the Scientific boys.' **1964** MRS. L. B. JOHNSON *White House Diary* 7 May (1970) 134, I showed Mr. Fosburgh the Winslow Homer painting and I think he was as amazed as I am that it should have so precipitously and happily dropped into our laps. **1970** 'M. HEBDEN' *Mask of Violence* (1971) xx. 187 I'll throw this into Pinow's lap. It's German and high-level, and I don't want to be mixed up in it. **1972** V. CANNING *Rainbird Pattern* ii. 33 Quite simply—and this is for you, Bush, because I'm dropping it in your lap—Trader has got to be scotched. **1973** M. WOODHOUSE *Blue Bone* ii. 12, I went..to meet some people who had a development problem they wanted to drop in our laps.

7. *attrib.* and *Comb.*, as (sense 5) †***lap-child***, ***-cloth***, †***-mantle***, ***-spaniel*** (cf. LAPDOG), ***-thing***; **lap belt**, a safety belt across the lap; **lap-board**, a board to lay on the lap, as a substitute for a table; **lap-cock** (see quot. 1848); **lap-held** *a.* = *lap-top* adj. below; also *ellipt.* as *sb.*; **lap-iron**, a piece of iron used as a lapstone; †**lap-lettuce**, ? curly lettuce; †**lap-lock** = DEWLAP; **lap-robe**, a rug or cloth to cover the lap of a person seated in a vehicle; **lap-shaver** (see quot.); **lap strap**, a safety strap across the lap; **lap-table** = *lap-board*; **lap-tea** (*U.S. local*), a tea at which the guests take refreshments in their laps, not at a table; **lap-top** *a.* [after DESK-TOP], (of a computer) small and light enough to be used on one's lap; = *lap-held* adj. above; also *ellipt.* as *sb.* Also LAP-DOG, LAPSTONE.

1952 *Los Angeles Examiner* 21 Mar., Wider '*lap belts' than those now used. **1959** *Sunday Graphic* 25 Jan. 4/5 The easy-to-fit and unobtrusive 'lap-belts' which give 65 per cent of the protection afforded by the full harness. **1961** *B.S.I. News* Mar. 7/1 Car safety belts,..three types..lap belt, diagonal strap and full harness. **1962** A. SHEPARD in *Into Orbit* 114, I took off my lap belt and loosened my helmet. **1973** *Sci. Amer.* Feb. 81/3 In the Utah statistics (from 1969) only 16.5 percent were wearing the seat belts; the estimate at present is that, notwithstanding all the urgings by authorities, only about 25 to 35 percent use the lap belt and only about 5 percent the lap-and-shoulder combination. **1974** *Country Life* 31 Jan. 191/2 The cab..has a bench seat with diagonal belts for two and a further lap belt for a third occupant. **1840** *Picayune* (New Orleans) 18 Sept. 2/3 Ashamed! why, I feel as flat as my own *lapboard. **1867** A. D. WHITNEY *Summer in L. Goldthwaite's Life* vi. 125 On the lap-board across her knees lies her work. **1875** KNIGHT *Dict. Mech.*, *Lap-board*, a board resting on the lap and hollowed out on the side next the user. Employed by tailors and seamstresses to cut out work upon. **1655** FULLER *Ch. Hist.* III. iii. §3 Canterbury his servants dandled this *lap-childe with a witness. **1849** ROCK *Ch. of Fathers* I. v. 409 The *lap-cloth, under the name of 'gremiale', is still employed in our ritual. **1880** L. WALLACE *Ben-Hur* IV. xiv. (1884) 223 They laved their hands again, had their lapcloths shaken out. **1802** DUBOURDIEU *Statist. Surv. Down* 125 It [grass] is made into small cocks called *lap-cocks. **1848** *Jrnl. R. Agric. Soc.* IX. II. 515 Lap-cocks, i.e...small heaps of the dimensions just capable of being taken up in the arms. **1984** *Sunday Times* 26 Aug. 49/3 (*heading*) *Lapheld contend with luggables. **1985** *Daily Tel.* 29 July 14/2 Then came the desk-top computer..and then..the lapheld micro. **1986** *What Micro?* Nov. 101/1 Multi-user systems and lap-helds are listed separately. **1962** *Westm. Gaz.* 8 Oct. 6/2 The lapstone and the *lap-iron have gone out of existence. **1796** C. MARSHALL *Garden.* xx. (1813) 425 Small sallading and *lap lettuce..on a little heat. **1660** HEXHAM *Dutch Dict.*, *Vaen*, the Bullocks, or *Laplock of Oxen. **1603** *Q. Eliz. Wardr.* in *Leisure Hour* (1884) 673/2, 18 *lappe mantles. **1875** MRS. STOWE *We & Neighbors* xxxix. 373 He took her to ride in such a stylish carriage, white lynx *lap-robe, and all! **1914** G. ATHERTON *Perch of Devil* I. 121 He smiled..into her..eyes and tucked the lap-robe about her. **1948** *Chicago Tribune* 15 Jan. 3/2, I loved the sleighrides too—snuggled under great buffalo hide lap robes. **1955** W. GADDIS *Recognitions* III. iv. 846 Engulfed in the flow of a tartan lap robe..he stared fixedly at an open book. **1974** 'I. DRUMMOND' *Power of Bug* xvi. 220 The thin cotton lap-robe which protected the passenger's legs and feet from the dust. **1875** KNIGHT *Dict. Mech.*, **Lap-shaver*, a machine for shaving leather to a thickness... The term is derived from the old practice of shaving away inequalities by means of a knife while the leather is laid upon a board in the lap. **1705** *Lond. Gaz.* No. 4144/4 A *Lap Spaniel..Bitch. **1960** *Guardian* 22 July 20/2 For rear seat passengers a *lap strap is probably sufficient. **1961** *Times* 10 Jan. 6/6 If the ordinary lap strap..is used, an occupant of the car will tend to 'jack knife' forward. **1968** A. DIMENT *Gt. Spy Race* ix. 165, I did up the lap strap [on a seat in a passenger aircraft] and went straight to sleep. **1884** KNIGHT *Dict. Mech.* Suppl., **Lap table*, a sewing or cutting-out table, supported in or over the lap. **1866** LOWELL *Biglow P.* Introd., Poems 1890 II. 197 **Lap-tea*: where the guests are too many to sit at table. **1740** J. MILLER *Mahomet* II. ii, Shall enervating contagious love..make a *lapthing of me? **1984** *Fortune* 28 May 75/1 Led by Tandy's four-pound Radio Shack Model 100..the *lap-tops are selling briskly. **1984** *Byte* Nov. 105/1 Laptop portables such as Gavilan were stealing the show. **1986** *Guardian* 14 Apr. 22/5 Laptops are battery-powered micros about the size of a telephone book, with small LCD screens and typewriter-style keyboards. **1986** *What Micro?* Nov. 6/3 Unusually for a laptop machine, provision is made to add an 8087 maths co-processor.

lap (læp), *sb.*² Also 4 lappe. [f. LAP *v.*¹]

1. Something that is lapped.

a. Liquid food for dogs. Also *slang* and *dial.*, any weak beverage or thin liquid food (cf. CATLAP). **b.** *slang*. Drink, liquor in general.

a. **1567** HARMAN *Caveat* 83 Lap, butter milke or whey. *a* **1700** B. E. *Dict. Cant. Crew*, *Lap*, Pottage, Butter-milk, or Whey. *c* **1700** *Street Robberies Consider'd*, *Lap*, Spoon-meat. *a* **1754** FIELDING *Jon. Wild* I. xiv, As when their lap is finished, the cautious huntsman to their kennel gathers the nimble-footed hounds. **1781** P. BECKFORD *Hunting* (1802) 50* If your hounds are low in flesh, and have far to go to cover, they may all have a little thin lap again in the evening. *a* **1825** FORBY *Voc. E. Anglia*, *Lap*, thin broth or porridge; weak tea, &c. **1886** ELWORTHY *W. Somerset Word-bk.* s.v., 'Call this here tay! I calls it lap'.

b. **1618** HORNBY *Scourge Dronk.* (1859) 17 Hee which will not take his lap downe free, Lap, so they terme it, such as dogs do vse. **1623** J. TAYLOR (Water P.) *Wks.* (1630) II. 29 They will..inforce mee to drinke..with such a deale of complementall oratory, as *off with your Lap, Wind vp your Bottome* [etc.]. *a* **1625** BEAUM & FL. *Bonduca* I. ii, A pretty valiant fellow, Die for a little lap and lechery? **1641** BROME *Jovial Crew* II. Wks. 1873 III. 388 Here's Pannum and Lap.

1725 *New Cant. Dict.*, *Lap*..also strong Drink of any Sort. **1815** SCOTT *Guy Mann.* xxviii, The gentry..would have given baith lap and pannel to ony poor gypsey. **1865** *Slang Dict.*, *Lap*, liquor, drink.

2. The action or an act of lapping; so much as may be taken up thus; a lick, smack, taste. Also *fig.*

1393 LANGL. *P. Pl.* C. III. 37 What man þat loueþ mede.. He shal lese for hure loue a lappe of trewe charite. **1820** MRS. PIOZZI *Let.* 9 June, Mr. Iveson will have a Lap of the Pellegrini Picture. *a* **1837** BEDDOES *Sec. Brother* I. i, These veiny pipes hold a dog's lap of blood. **1860** HOLME LEE *Leg. Fairy Land* 77 He persuaded them [two puppies] to take a lap at his breakfast.

3. A sound resembling that of lapping; e.g. that produced by wavelets on the beach.

1884 W. C. SMITH *Kildrostan* 43 Only the lap of the rippling wave Broke on the hush of their solitude. **1889** AMELIA BARR *Feet of Clay* iv. 64 The lazy whish and lap of the ocean.

lap (læp), *sb.*³ [f. LAP *v.*²]

†**1.** ? Something wrapped up; a bundle. *Obs.*

1673 *New Jersey Archives* (1880) I. 132 In token whereof they presented about 20 deer skins, 2 @ 3 laps of Beaver, and 1 string of Wampum.

2. a. The amount by which one thing overlaps or covers a part of another; hence *concr.* the overlapping part.

1800 *Trans. Soc. Arts* XVIII. 377 Stopping the apertures between the laps of glass with putty. **1808** PIKE *Sources Mississ.* II. (1810) 194 *note*, Those logs were joined together by a lap of about two feet at each end. **1823** P. NICHOLSON *Pract. Build.* 399 All kinds of slate have a lap of each joint, generally equal to one-third of the length of the slate. *c* **1850** *Rudim. Navig.* (Weale) 128 *Laps*, the remaining part of the ends of carlings, &c. which are to bear a great weight or pressure, such as the capstan-step. **1869** SIR E. REED *Shipbuild.* ii. 39 The laps of the outer keel-plate and garboard..require the usual double row [of rivets]. **1895** *Jrnl. R. Inst. Brit. Archit.* 14 Mar. 351 The roof should.. have a lap of at least 3½ inches of tiles. **1897** *Daily News* 10 May 5/5 The hand-made cigarette..having a smaller 'lap'.

b. *half-lap*: an arrangement for the joining of rails, shafts, etc., consisting in cutting away half the thickness of each of the two ends to be joined, and fitting them together. Also *attrib.*

1816 *Specif. Losh & Stephenson's Patent* No. 4067. 6 The half lap joinings of the rails. **1825** N. WOOD *Railroads* (1838) 42 [The rails] are now formed with a half-lap. **1875** *Carpentry & Join.* 71 The half lap dovetail..has this one advantage, that [etc.].

c. *Steam-engine.* The distance traversed by a slide-valve beyond what is needed to close the passage of steam to or from the cylinder.

1869 E. MALBON in *Eng. Mech.* 3 Dec. 282/2 Ascertain if they have had equal lap on the steam and exhaust side. **1881** J. W. ASTON in *Metal World* No. 18. 274 The amount that these faces overlap the steam-ports being termed the *lap* of the valve. **1895** *Mod. Steam Eng.* 38 The lap of the slide being equally divided.

d. *U.S.* 'Any portion of a railroad track used in common by the trains of more than one system' (Funk's *Stand. Dict.* 1893).

e. *Metallurgy.* A kind of defect that results when a projecting part is folded over against the surface of the metal and pressed in (e.g. during rolling or forging), so that a seam is produced on the surface.

1914 W. ROSENHAIN *Introd. Study Physical Metall.* xiv. 324 'Laps', 'rokes', etc.,..result from the partial welding up of fissures or of portions of metal which have become accidentally overlapped. **1939** E. C. ROLLASON *Metall. for Engineers* iv. 55 A defect, somewhat similar to a roke, is caused by poor roll design or by rolling at too low a temperature. The metal spreads to an extent greater than the designed pass and forms fins on opposite sides of the bar, which in subsequent passes are lapped over to give the lap illustrated. **1967** E. BISHOP tr. *M. van Lancker's Metall. Aluminium Alloys* viii. 238 Working may scratch the metal and result in corrosion damage.., or form laps..tears..and excessive work-hardening.

3. *Euchre.* (See quot.)

1886 *Euchre: how to play it* iii. 40 The Lap game may be played by two, three, or four persons, when they agree to play a series of games, so that the *lap* may be applied, which is simply counting upon the score of the ensuing game all the points made over and above the five of which the game consists.

4. a. A layer or sheet (usually wound upon a bobbin or roller) into which cotton, wool, or flax is formed in certain stages of its manufacture.

1825 J. NICHOLSON *Operat. Mechanic* 381 The cotton is in this state called a lap. **1888** J. PATON *Wool* in *Encycl. Brit.* XXIV. 658 The wool [for felted cloth] is scribbled or carded out into a uniform lap of extreme thinness. **1890** W. J. GORDON *Foundry* 163 The scutcher turns out the fibre in a thick fleecy mat, or 'lap', which is wound round a roller.

b. *Warp Knitting.* A loop of yarn on a needle.

1884 W. T. ROWLETT tr. *Willkomm's Technol. Framework Knitting* I. i. 41 Each warp thread is also laid *over* a needle and forms the 'lap' over one. **1884**, etc. [see KNOCK-OFF *sb.* and *a.* B. 2 a]. **1926** J. CHAMBERLAIN *Hosiery, Yarns & Fabrics* vii. 173 The knock-off stitch is often used to produce pure longitudinal stripes on warp knitted fabrics in which case the pressed lap is always made on the same needle and only the knock-off lap..is traversed to effect a lateral joining. **1952** D. F. PALING *Warp Knitting Technol.* i. 5 Assuming that two fully threaded guide bars are used, then each needle will be provided with two threads across its beard. These laps may be in similar directions or in opposite directions according to the relative directions of the overlaps. **1964** H. WIGNALL *Knitting* ii. 44 The needles are then raised to move the laps below the beards.

5. a. The act of encircling, or the length of rope required to encircle, a drum or wheel. Also, enough of silk, thread, etc., to go once round something.

1867 W. W. SMYTH *Coal & Coal-mining* 163 A large vertical cylinder..16, 18, or even 20 feet in diameter at the first lap of the rope. **1867** F. FRANCIS *Angling* iv. (1880) 134 It should be tied by a lap or two of silk. **1888** *Lockwood's Dict. Mech. Engin.*, *Lap*..(4) a single turn of a rope or chain around a barrel.

b. *Racing.* One of the number of turns round the track, that are required to complete the course.

1861 *Chamb. Jrnl.* 23 Nov. 333 They had gone fourteen 'laps' (as these circuits are technically called). **1870** R. BURN *Rome* 297 The number of laps was usually seven. **1884** *Dickens' Dict. Lond.* 27/2 A running track, three laps to the mile. **1894** ASTLEY *50 Years Life* II. 155 Having measured off the requisite number of laps to the mile on the gravel walks in our kitchen-garden.

6. *attrib.* and *Comb.*, as (sense 2) *lap-boarded*, *-butt*, *-carling*, *-dovetail*, *-dovetailing*, *-jointed*, *-seam*; *lap-weld* sb. and vb.; (sense 4) *lap-bobbin*, *-cylinder*, *-drum*, *-head*, *-machine*, *-roller*, *-tenter*; (sense 5 b) *lap-scorer*, *-sprint*, *time*. Also **lap-dissolve** *v.*, = DISSOLVE *v.* 7 b; **lap-joint** (see quot. 1847); hence **lap-join** *v. trans.*, to join by means of a lap joint; **lap-system** (see quot.); **lap winding** *Electr. Engin.*, a kind of armature winding in which the two ends of each coil are connected to adjacent commutator segments, so that each coil overlaps the next; †**lap-yard**, the part of a roll of cloth which forms the outside wrapper. Also LAP-STREAK.

1927 *Chambers's Jrnl.* Sept. 597/2 *Lap-boarded houses which overhang the sea. **1892** *Daily News* 9 Sept. 6/1 The shell plating..is fitted on the *lap-butt principle. **1874** THEARLE *Naval Archit.* 47 When these carlings are required to resist an upward instead of the ordinary downward thrust, they..lap over the under side of the beams, in which case they are termed *lap carlings. **1851** *Illustr. Catal. Gt. Exhib.* 263 This felt or lap is delivered to a wooden *lap-cylinder. **1927** *Observer* 17 Apr. 3 No sooner has it [*sc.* the title] been read than it *lap-dissolves into the director's name... It should be lap-dissolved in for a mere flash. [**1934** H. M. HARWOOD *Old Folks at Home* I. i. 21 Sometimes the next picture's on before the last one's gone...lap...dissolve ...isn't it?] **1962** *Sunday Times* 5 Aug. 20/4 *The Stranger*: All right, pardon me for living, it's just you looked so much like this very attractive party I met down here last year. (*Lap dissolve to what may be the following day.*) **1847** SMEATON *Builder's Man.* 89 Fig. 24 represents the pin part of a *lap-dovetail. **1825** J. NICHOLSON *Operat. Mechanic* 588 *Lap dovetailing conceals the dovetail, but shews the thickness of the lap on the return side. **1902** T. THORNLEY *Cotton Combing Machines* 17 The six webs are..drawn by frequent pairs of press rollers to the *lap-head, consisting of two pairs of heavily weighted press rollers..and of the lap drums. **1968** J. ARNOLD *Shell Bk. Country Crafts* vi. 116 The arrangement is to have a 'V' on one side and an inverted 'V' on the other, the apex of which is *lap-joined flush with the top rail. **1823** P. NICHOLSON *Pract. Build.* 164 Folding doors, which meet together upon a *lap-joint. **1847** SMEATON *Builder's Man.* 93 In a lap-joint, that is, in lapping two pieces together, supposing them of equal thickness, half the substance of each should be cut away. **1874** THEARLE *Naval Archit.* 113 The bulkheads..are connected by single-riveted lap joints and butts. *Ibid.*, Liners are required behind the stiffeners by the *lap-jointed system. **1879** *Cassell's Techn. Educ.* IV. 209/1 Carding engines, *lap-machines or doublers [etc.]. **1850** *Rep. Comm. Patents 1850* (U.S.) 160, I also claim the combination of burring apparatus..with the calender and *lap rollers. **1896** *Westm. Gaz.* 25 July 5/2 At one corner outside the track a little shed is filled with the '*lap-scorers'. **1905** *Westm. Gaz.* 21 Mar. 5/1 He says the explosion was caused by a crack in the *lap-seam [of the boiler]. **1964** H. HODGES *Artifacts* iv. 77 Bronze vessels of (riveted) sheet metal could be made perfectly watertight, even when the edges were joined by a simple lap seam. **1886** *Cyclist* 25 Aug. 1174/1 Fenlon, by a fine *lap sprint, landed a winner by five yards. **1894** *Gloss. Terms Evidence R. Comm. Labour* 51/2 in *Parl. Papers 1893–4* (C. 7063) XXXVIII. 411 **Lap System*, also called 'trip system', is a system (in the carter's industry) of piece-work, *e.g.*, a driver taking loads of coal a given distance for a stated sum, works under the lap system. **1881** *Instructions to Census Clerks* (1885) 68 *Lap Tenter. **1921** *Dict. Occup. Terms* (1927) 164/2 Lap tenter (cotton). **1909** *Westm. Gaz.* 7 Dec. 5/1 The net *lap times of the Auvergne races of 1905. **1973** *Times* 28 Apr. 7/2 Both he and his team-mate, François Cevert, were later able to equal Regazzoni's lap time. **1875** KNIGHT *Dict. Mech.*, **Lap-weld* (*Forging*), a weld in which the welding edges are thinned down, lapped, and welded. *a* **1901** *Mod. Catal.*, The tubes are *lapwelded. **1892** S. P. THOMPSON *Dynamo-Electr. Machinery* (ed. 4) xii. 311 When we go on to those cases in which the winding is entirely exterior to the core, as for drum armatures, or to those in which there is no core at all, namely for disk armatures, we find that there are two distinct modes of procedure, which we may respectively denote as *lap-winding and wave-winding. **1937** A. S. LANGSDORF *Theory Alternating-Current Machinery* v. 295 The end connections of a distributed winding may be arranged in several ways, all electrically identical... The order of grouping and the resultant shape of the coils give rise to the respective designations of spiral, lap, and wave windings. **1966** *McGraw-Hill Encycl. Sci. & Technol.* XIV. 505/2 Lap windings are adapted to high-current machines because they may have more than two parallel paths, whereas the wave windings are adapted to small-capacity machines and high-voltage machines because of the series connection of the coils. **1733** P. LINDSAY *Interest Scot.* 93 No Part of it [Linen Cloth] worse than the *Lap-yard or outside Cover.

lap (læp), *sb.*⁴ [Of obscure etymology; perh. a use of prec., as the original tool may have been a 'lap' or wrapping of cloth or leather.] **a.** A rotating disk of soft metal or wood, used to hold polishing powder in cutting or polishing gems or metal.

1812–16 J. SMITH *Panorama Sci. & Art* I. 35 In the manufacture of cutlery, the use of the stone is followed by that of the lap or glazor. **1833** J. HOLLAND *Manuf. Metal* II. 29 The blade being properly ground, is then glazed..by applying it to the lap. **1884** F. J. BRITTEN *Watch & Clockm.* 212 A soft steel lap at first and afterwards a zinc one are generally used. **1888** *Sheffield Gloss.*, *Lap*, a wooden wheel with a leaden surface used to glaze razors.

b. A polishing tool of some relatively soft material (as lead or cast iron) made to a special shape for use in lapping (see LAP *v.*⁴).

1881 GREENER *Gun* 238 The lap is fixed into a head revolving 650 times a minute. The barrel is moved backwards and forwards upon the lap. **1886** WALSINGHAM & PAYNE-GALLWEY *Shooting* I. 71 The polisher, or 'lap', as it is called, consists of an iron rod round which is secured a leaden plug the exact size of the tube. **1905** W. S. LEONARD *Machine-Shop Tools & Methods* (ed. 3) xxxi. 506 The laps described above are of the simplest and cheapest forms, namely, a plain shaft for the internal, and a collar for the external, lap. **1920** OBERG & JONES *Gage Design* vii. 191 Laps for Ring Gages.—Three laps are shown in Fig. 15 for lapping ring gages... They are made of cast iron and are ground to fit the ring gage to be lapped. Grinding the thread on a lap will insure accuracy. **1932** HARDY & PERRIN *Princ. Optics* xvi. 338 The exposed surface of the blank is then ground by holding it against another tool, called a lap, which has previously been given the proper radius of curvature. The lap is rotated at a moderate speed on a vertical shaft and is fed with a mixture of coarse emery and water. **1942** A. F. COLLINS *Greatest Eye in World* ii. 43 A concave iron lap is then placed over the lenses on the head and the spindle is rotated by an electric motor.

lap (læp), *v.*¹ Forms: α. 1 lapian, 4–6, 8 *Sc.* lape, 5–6 *Sc.* laip, 9 *Sc.* lepe. β. 4–6 lappe, 4– lap. [OE. *lapian* = MLG. and MDu. *lapen*, OHG. *laffan*; cf. Icel. *lepja*; the OTeut. root **lap-* (cogn. w. L. *lambĕre*, Gr. λάπτειν to lick, lap) is represented also by OHG. *leffil*, mod.G. *löffel* spoon. The normal representative of the OE. word is the obsolete *lape*; the form *lappe*, *lap* may be due to the influence of F. *laper* (an adoption of the Teut. word).]

†**1.** *intr.* To take up liquid with the tongue. In OE. const. *on*, in early mod.Eng. *in*. *Obs.*

c **1000** *Sax. Leechd.* II. 184 Gebeorh þæt hie..neaht nestiȝe lapien on huniȝ. **13..** *E.E. Allit. P.* B. 1434 Let þise ladyes of hem lape. **1390** GOWER *Conf.* III. 215 What man that hath the water nome Up in his hande and lappeth so, To thy part chese out alle tho. *c* **1470** HENRYSON *Mor. Fab.* XII. (*Wolf & Lamb*) i, [The lamb] In the streme laipit to cuill his thrist. *c* **1570** *Marr. Wit & Science* IV. iii. D iij, Alas why hath she this delite to lap in giltles blode? **1607** SHAKS. *Timon* III. vi. 95 Vncouer Dogges, and lap. *c* **1630** RISDON *Surv. Devon* §286 (1810) 296 Cattle accustomed to drink or lap. **1721** RAMSAY *On a Punch-bowl* 7 Take up my Ladle, fill, and lape. **1731** MORTIMER in *Phil. Trans.* XXXVII. 172 And then he lapped again, but could not stand on his Legs.

2. a. *trans.* Of animals, *rarely* of human beings: To take up (liquid, *rarely* food) with the tongue; to drink greedily up (like an animal). Also with *up*.

a **1340** HAMPOLE *Psalter* lxvii. 25 Berkand agayn wickidnes & lapand watire of grace. **1382** WYCLIF *Judg.* vii. 5 Thilk that with hoond and with tonge lapen the watris. **1481** CAXTON *Reynard* xvi. (Arb.) 34 There lerned I fyrst to lapen of the bloode. **1513** DOUGLAS *Æneis* x. x. 44 Thyr sey monstreis..[sal] lape thy blude thar hungeir to asswage. **1610** SHAKS. *Temp.* II. i. 288 They'l take suggestion, as a Cat laps milke. **1681** W. ROBERTSON *Phraseol. Gen.* (1693) 799 They lap up their meat, what they eat. **1709** STEELE *Tatler* No. 40 ¶9 He had the Cholick last Week with lapping sour Milk. **1735** SOMERVILLE *Chase* I. 155 Soon as the growling Pack..Have lapp'd their smoaking Viands. **1813** HOGG *Queen's Wake* 177 He baitit the lyon to diedis of weir, Quhill he lepit the blude to the kyngdome deire. **1819** MOORE *Tom Crib* (ed. 3) 21 Up he rose in a funk, lapp'd a toothful of brandy, And to it again. **1849** MACAULAY *Hist. Eng.* viii. II. 384 Some basons of water for washing were suffered to pass. .. The jurymen, raging with thirst, soon lapped up the whole. **1871** ROSSETTI *Poems, Eden Bower* xlix, The soul of one shall be made thy brother, And thy tongue shall lap the blood of the other.

b. *U.S.* Of a bear: to gather and eat fruits or nuts. Hence *lapping-season*.

1868 *Amer. Naturalist* May 122 They climb in order to 'lap', as the hunter says. *Ibid.*, When mast is not plenty, they lap black-gum berries. **1881** *Scribner's Mag.* Oct. 858/2 This is called the lapping season, as he ensconces himself in a tree lap and breaks the limbs to pieces, in gathering nuts and fruits.

c. *to lap up*: (*fig.*) to receive (praise, news, etc.) eagerly.

1890 A. JAMES *Diary* 20 May (1964) 119 Where do you suppose they have discovered Self-Sacrifice now? In the heroic bosom of Stanley! who on his own showing laps up the *agréments* of African travel as I do my afternoon tea. **1922** S. LEWIS *Babbitt* xxx. 359, I was simply astonished, the way those women lapped it up! **1930** D. H. LAWRENCE *Phoenix II* (1968) 493 People wallow in emotion: counterfeit emotion. They lap it up: they live in it and on it. **1931** G. ATHERTON *Sophisticates* II. xix. 210 'Polly, of all women, to start such a thing!' muttered Emerey. 'Or Toddles, for that matter. I've found out it was she who fed Polly with the idea of doing something new and strange. Of course she lapped it up.' **1958** *Listener* 20 Nov. 815/1 The Indian Embassy in Bonn will lap up information about Eastern Germany. **1972**

Times 20 Apr. 25/1 Americans have lapped the book up, already getting through Dell's first order of 100,000.

†**3.** To suck (a teat). *Obs. rare*$^{-1}$.

1562 Phaer *Æneid* viii. C cj b, Their mammies teats thei lap wᵗ hungrie lipps.

4. *intr.* Of water: To move with a rippling sound like that made in lapping. Also with *in, up*.

1823 Scott *Peveril* xxxvi, Flinty steps,..against which the tide lapped fitfully with small successive waves. **1840** Marryat *Poor Jack* xxii, You'd think that the water was lapping in right among us. **1842** Tennyson *Morte d'Arthur* 116, I heard the water lapping on the crag. **1873** Black *Pr. Thule* xxiii. 384 The sea lapped around the boat. **1887** Ruskin *Præterita* II. 152 The water..lapping up, or lashing, under breeze, against the terrace wall.

5. *trans.* To beat upon (the shore, etc.) with a lapping sound.

1854 Mrs. Gaskell *North & S.* vii, The distant sea, lapping the sandy shore with measured sound. **1874** Longf. *Cadenabbia* iv, I..hear the water..lapping the steps beneath my feet. **1883** Mrs. Rollins *New Eng. Bygones* 59 Where was a rotting old boat, which the waves lapped lazily.

lap (læp), *v.*[2] Forms: 4–6 **lappe**, 4–5 **wlappe**, 5–6 **lape**, 4– **lap**. [Not in OE. or in any other Teut. lang.; first recorded *c* 1200–1225 in the compound *bi-lappe, bi-leppe*. Prob. f. lap *sb.*[1] in the sense 'fold' or 'piece of cloth'. The perplexing form *wlappe* (Wyclif, Pecock) is prob. not original, but due to the influence of the synonymous wrap *v.*; it is hardly likely that OF. *voloper, veloper, voloper* can have contributed to the change of form.]

1. a. *trans.* To coil, fold, wrap (a garment, or anything supple). Const. *about, in,* †*on,* †*over, round,* †*to,* †*until*; also with *about, round* advs.

a **1300** *Sarmun* xxxix. in *E.E.P.* (1862) 5 In to þis world.. he broȝte a stinkind felle i-lappid þer an. *a* **1350** *St. Laurence* 194 in Horstm. *Altengl. Leg.* (1881) 110 Iren plates he gert þam glew And lap until his sides ay new. **1390** Gower *Conf.* II. 268 That yonge fresshe quene That mantel lapped her aboute. *c* **1440** *Gesta Rom.* vii. 17 (Harl. MS.) She lappid hire taile aboute þe corde of the belle. **1501** Douglas *Pal. Hon.* Prol. 3 Paill Aurora..Her russat mantill..Lappit about the heuinly circumstance. **1569** Newton *Cicero's Olde Age* 38 a, The vine..lappeth it selfe fast, to what soever it commeth neare. **1578** Banister *Hist. Man* i. 19 Nature hath in such wise lapped, and fastened to the tooth [of the Vertebra] a solid Ligament. **1600** Hakluyt *Voy.* (1810) III. 497 The frier lapping a garmente about his arme [etc.]. **1677** Moxon *Mech. Exerc.* 18 Hammer the Plate that is lap'd over the wyre close to the wyre. **1704** Swift *T. Tub* xi, He would lap a Piece of it about a Sore Toe. **1774** Goldsm. *Nat. Hist.* (1776) IV. 121 This is lapped round the rest of the body. **1832** *Blackw. Mag.* XXXI. 625 Lapping the skirts..about the little feet. **1839** Ure *Dict. Arts* 215 After they are bleached..they are lapped round in great lengths of several pieces. **1849** Rock *Ch. of Fathers* II. 140 Its upper roll, instead of being lapped about, was kept fastened in its place ..by a golden pin. **1859** Tennent *Ceylon* II. viii. v. 363 They..mutually entwined their trunks, lapped them round their limbs and neck.

transf. c **1470** Henry *Wallace* ix. 146 The wer schippis was lappyt thaim about. **1513** Douglas *Æneis* ii. x. 201 About my feit My spous lappit fell doun into the ȝet.

b. *intr.* for *refl.* Const. *about, round.* Now *rare* exc. *dial.*

1563 *Homilies* ii. *Agst. Disobedience & Rebel.* iv. (1859) 577 A great tree..caught him by..his goodly hair, lapping about it as he fled. **1680** *Vind. Reforming Clergy* (ed. 2) 16 This is a fine pliable principle..'twill lap about your finger like Barbary Gold. **1717** Lady M. W. Montagu *Let. to C'tess Mar* 1 Apr., This [dress]..laps all round them, not unlike a riding-hood. **1845** Sir W. Napier *Conq. Scinde* ii. vi. 387 The two regiments thus opposed, lapped round the nearest point of the houses. **1883** *Almondbury Gloss.*, *Lap*, the end of a piece of cloth, which in weaving laps round the low beam.

†**2.** To fold, fold *up, together*; to roll *up* in successive layers. Const. *into. Obs.* or *dial.*

1390 Gower *Conf.* II. 320 She wafe a cloth of silke all white..And lapped it together. **1398** Trevisa *Barth. De P.R.* xvii. xciv. (1495) 661 The leues of Lappates ben.. wonderly wrallyd and lappyd. *a* **1400–50** *Wars Alex.* 4568 Quen he had lokid on þe lyne he lappid it to-gedire. **1548–77** Vicary *Anat.* iv. (1888) 30 This Piamater deuideth the substaunce of the Brayne, and lappeth it into certen selles or diuisions. **1561** Daus tr. *Bullinger on Apoc.* (1573) 95 As a booke lapped vp together. *a* **1568** Ascham *Let. to E. Raven*, That he may both see news &c. largely told, and also learn to lap up a letter. **1641** H. Best *Farm. Bks.* (Surtees) 22 To give charge that in lapping up a fleece, they allwayes putte the inne side of the fleece outwardes. **1678** Duchess of Newcastle in *Buccleuch MSS.* (Hist. MSS. Comm.) I. 330 Since I lapt up my letter I writ this. **1725** De Foe *Voy. round World* (1840) 347 Bulls' hides joined, and lapped and rolled one over another. *c* **1790** Imison *Sch. Art* II. 80 A..clean linen rag lapped up.

fig. **1577–87** Holinshed *Chron.* (1807–8) IV. 401 Lapping up (among a bundle of other misfortunes) this evill chance.

3. a. To enfold in a wrap or wraps, to enwrap, swathe; hence, to clothe, to bind up, tie round. Const. *in,* †*with,* †*within*. Also with †*in, over, round, up*. ***to lap on***: to attach or fix on with a lapping of thread or the like. †***to lap in lead***: to place in a leaden coffin; hence, to entomb.

13.. *E.E. Allit. P.* B. 175 Alle þyn oþer lymez lapped ful clene, Þenne may þou se þy sauior. *c* **1325** *Kyng & Hermyt* 289 in Hazl. *E.P.P.* I. 24 Go to slepe, And I schall lape thee with my cope. *c* **1340** Hampole *Prose Tr.* (1866) 5 Laid in a crib and lappid in clathis. **1382** Wyclif *Matt.* xxvii. 59 The body taken, Ioseph wlappide [**1388** lappide] it in a clene sendel. ? *a* **1400** *Morte Arth.* 2300 They..bawmede þaire honourliche kynges,..Lappede them in lede. *c* **1450** *ME. Med. Bk.* (Heinrich) 170 Lappe hem [warts] in wort leues. **1530** *Test. Ebor.* (Surtees) V. 292 Unto every ij or iij gud and discreit women that wyndes and lappis my body in one sheit ..iiijd. **1578** Lyte *Dodoens* iii. iii. 317 The seede, lapped as it were in a certaine white wooll. **1601** Dent *Pathw. Heaven* 376 Christ Iesus..will swaddle you, and lappe you. **1608** Middleton *Mad World* ii. ii. 44 Let him trap me in gold, and I'll lap him in lead. **1627** Capt. Smith *Seaman's Gram.* xiii. 60 With a malet in the one hand, & a plug lapped in Okum..in the other. **1685** R. Burton *Eng. Emp. Amer.* iv. 83, I shewed the Captain and his Wife my Fingers, who.. bid me lap it up again. **1727** Swift *Gulliver* ii. i, I..laid myself at full length upon the handkerchief, with the remainder of which he lapped me up to the head. **1780** *Phil. Trans.* LXX. App. 3 This brush is again lapped round with thread. **1817** Scott *Harold* i. xx, The good old Prelate lies lapp'd in lead. **1821** Clare *Vill. Minstr.* II. 31 The mower too lapt up his scythe from our sight. **1832** *Blackw. Mag.* XXXI. 624, I had fished..; but having broken my top in an unlucky leap, was..lapping the fracture. **1861** Reade *Cloister & H.* lv. (1896) 154 A good dozen of spices lapped in flax paper. **1867** F. Francis *Angling* xiii. (1880) 467 Lay the tail to the hook..and lap it on securely. **1876** Preece & Sivewright *Telegraphy* 233 The ends are lapped over with tape and yarn to prevent abrasion of the gutta percha.

transf. **1388** Wyclif *Exod.* xiv. 27 The Lord wlappide hem in the myddis of the floodis. **1587** Golding *De Mornay* ii. (1617) 16 The Sea and Earth together are lapped vp in the Ayre. **1602** Marston *Antonio's Rev.* iii. iii. Wks. 1856 I. 111 Were thy heart lapt up In any flesh but in Piero's bloode, I would thus kisse it. *a* **1628** Preston *New Covt.* (1634) 96 Who lookes upon him as lapping the waters as in a garment. **1657** W. Morice *Coena quasi Κοινή* Pref. 2 The reasons thereof in writing..I lapt up in one sheet, and transmitted to him. **1860** Ruskin *Mod. Paint.* V. ix. ii. §19. 216 Lapped in pale Elysian mist.

†**b.** To hem in, press close upon with a hostile force, or with something noxious. Also with *about, in. Obs.* (in later use only *Sc.*)

c **1330** R. Brunne *Chron.* (1810) 276 Lap þam bituex ȝow. *c* **1430** *Syr Tryam.* 1057 They lapped hym in on every syde. **14..** *Pol. Rel. & L. Poems* 94 Thus ame I lappyd al a-boute; With todys and snaks. *c* **1470** Henry *Wallace* ix. 1843 Thiddyr he past, and lappyt it [Dunde] about. **1552** Lyndesay *Monarche* 3974 The Romanis lappit thame about, That be no waye thay mycht wyn out.

†**c.** To fold (*in the arms*); to clasp, embrace.

c **1350** *Parlt. Three Ages* (text B) 247 With ladis full lufly lapped yn armes. *c* **1374** Chaucer *Compl. Mars* 76 This worthi Mars that is of knyghthode wel The flour of feyrenesse lappeth in his armes. *c* **1440** *Bone Flor.* 113 Sche schall..in hur lovely armes me lappe. *c* **1470** Henry *Wallace* vi. 54 He at will may lap hyr in his armys. **1513** Douglas *Æneis* iii. ix. 38 Gruling on his kneis, He lappit me fast by baith the theis.

†**d.** Proverb. ***to be lapped in one's mother's smock***: to be born to fortune. *Obs.*

1690 W. Walker *Idiomat. Anglo-Lat.* 262 He was lapt in his mother's smock, (*plane fortunæ filius*).

4. In immaterial senses. †**a.** To involve; to imply, include; to implicate, entangle; to wrap *up* in a disguise. *Obs.*

a **1340** Hampole *Psalter* xlviii. 1 Rightwismen þat ere not ..lappid in errours of þe warld. **1395** Purvey *Remonstr.* (1851) 3 No preest or dekene wlappith hymself in seculer officis. *c* **1425** Lydg. *Assembly of Gods* 126 And..er they coude beware, With a sodeyn pyry, he lappyd hem in care. *c* **1440** *Gesta Rom.* xxvii. 103 (Harl. MS.), I am a thef, *scil.* lappid with swiche a synne. *c* **1460** *Towneley Myst.* xiii. 4, I am al lappyd In sorow. *c* **1540** tr. *Pol. Verg. Eng. Hist.* (Camden No. 29) 112 Howsooer the matter was lapped up, it is apparent. **1549** [see lapping *vbl. sb.*[2] 1 c]. **1552** Latimer *Serm. Gosp.* i. 150 He lappeth up all thynges in Loue. —— *5th Serm. Lord's Prayer* (1562) 37 This Vs lappeth in al other men with my prayer. **1589** R. Robinson *Gold. Mirr.* (Chetham Soc.) 25 No..secret shift so closely lapt, but Time the trueth shall trie. **1594** Carew *Huarte's Exam. Wits* xi. (1596) 172 Herein is lapped vp a very great secret. **1627–77** Feltham *Resolves* ii. xxix. 218 You shall..whether you will or no..be lapp'd in some drunken fray.

b. Of conditions or influences: To enfold, surround, *esp.* with soothing, stupefying, or seductive effect. Often with *round*.

c **1350** *Will. Palerne* 740 Swiche listes of loue hadde lapped his hert. *c* **1400** *Destr. Troy* 465 Soche likyng of loue lappit hir within. *c* **1450** *Cov. Myst.* (Shaks. Soc.) 125 The plage of dompnesse his leppis lappyd. **1632** Milton *L'Allegro* 136 And ever against eating Cares Lap me in soft Lydian Aires, Married to immortal verse. **1745** Warton *Pleas. Melanch.* 201 Till all my soul is..lapp'd in Paradise. **1806** Moore *Genius Harmony* i. 19 Such downy dreams, As lap the spirit of the seventh sphere. **1819** S. Rogers *Hum. Life* 757 Lapping the soul in sweetest melancholy! **1821** Joanna Baillie *Metr. Leg., Ghost of Fadon* liv, A spell of horror lapped him round. **1853** M. Arnold *Requiescat* 12 For peace her soul was yearning, And now peace laps her round. **1871** L. Stephen *Playgr. Europe* viii. (1894) 174, I was..lapped in some dim consciousness that I had still an hour and a half before..starting. **1877** L. Morris *Epic Hades* i. 13, I who was..Only a careless boy lapt round with ease. **1880** Swinburne *Songs Springtides* 17 The joy that like a garment..lapped him over and under.

5. With allusion to lap *sb.* 5: To enfold caressingly like a child in its mother's lap; to nurse, fondle, caress; to surround with soothing and shielding care. Now chiefly *pass.*, to be nursed *in* luxury, etc.

c **1430** *Hymns Virg.* 3 Þou..þat lappid me loueli with liking song. *c* **1430** *Syr Tryam.* 417 Sche toke up hur sone to hur And lapped hyt fulle lythe. **1556** J. Heywood *Spider & F.* ii. 16 Who all my life haue beene Lapped in lap of thy fayre flattering flowres. *a* **1649** Drumm. of Hawth. *Poems* Wks. (1711) 18 It is his hap To lie lap'd in her lap. **1811** W. R. Spencer *Nursing True Love* 1 Lapt on Cythera's golden sands. **1822** Hazlitt *Table-t.* Ser. ii. xvi. (1869) 323 We grow fastidious, effeminate, lapped in idle luxury. **1847** Bushnell *Chr. Nurt.* ii. ii. (1861) 259 The child that is.. lovingly lapped in the peaceful trust of Providence, is born to a glorious heritage. **1862** Goulburn *Pers. Relig.* II. iii. viii. 202 Moses has been lapped in royal luxury from his infancy. **1865** Carlyle *Fredk. Gt.* xii. ix. (1872) IV. 210 Beautiful blue world of Hills..fruitful valleys lapped in them. **1870** Bryant *Iliad* I. vi. 189 There is a town Lapped in the pasture-grounds.

6. *trans.* **a.** To lay (something) *on, over* (another thing) so as partly to cover it. **b.** Of a slide-valve: To pass over and close (a port). Also, to cause (a slide-valve) to overlap the port. **c.** ? *U.S.* Of a boat, in racing: To come partly alongside (another).

1607 Markham *Caval.* ii. (1617) 175 Till you perceiue at last he lap and throw his outmost leg ouer his inmost. **1676** Grew *Anat. Plants* iv. ii. ii. §2 (1682) 164 The Leaves of the Flower of Blattaria..are so lapped one over another, as to make an Equilateral Pentangle. **1678** Moxon *Mech. Exerc.* 67 Two Boards are thus lapped on the edges over one another. **1748** Richardson *Clarissa* (1811) IV. 157 [She] Lapped one horse-lip over the other and was silent. **1825** J. Nicholson *Operat. Mechanic* 626 When laid on the roof, they [slates] are bonded and lapped as in common slating. **1869** E. Malbon in *Eng. Mech.* 3 Dec. 282/3 Lapping the high pressure valves will greatly raise the exhaust side. **1879** *Cassell's Techn. Educ.* IV. 79/1 The edge-joints, as well as the butts, are generally lapped.

b. 1870 *Eng. Mech.* 28 Jan. 482/3 The steam-valve.. commences to lap its port by the motion of the eccentric.

c. 1897 Webster s.v. *Lap*, The hinder boat lapped the foremost one.

7. *intr.* †**a.** ***to lap on to, over, upon*** (something): to lie upon, so as to cover partially; also, to lie upon and project over, overlap. **b.** To project *into* (something).

1677 Moxon *Mech. Exerc.* 18 Double the end of the Plate ..over the wyre to lap over it. **1774** Goldsm. *Nat. Hist.* (1776) IV. 120 One edge sticks in the skin, while the other laps over that immediately behind it. **1776–96** Withering *Brit. Plants* (ed. 3) II. 399 Calyx segments lapping over each other. **1779** *Projects* in *Ann. Reg.* 103/2 When either of the ends of any of the laths laps over other laths. **1843** *Jrnl. R. Agric. Soc.* IV. i. 34 They should be laid as regularly as possible—one part lapping on to the next layer. **1846** *Ibid.* VII. i. 51 The four furrows..then lie two furrows right and left, lapping on to the furrow-slices thrown out of the old furrows. *c* **1850** *Rudim. Navig.* (Weale) 128 The mast-carlings are said to lap upon the beams by reason of their great depth; and head-ledges at the ends lap over the coamings. **1853** G. Johnston *Nat. Hist. E. Bord.* I. 263 They lap over rocks and shelving banks. **1854** Kelly & Tomlinson tr. *Arago's Astron.* 57 If the two images of the sun be made to lap over each other. **1856** Kane *Arct. Expl.* I. xxiii. 286 One end lapped into the west side a considerable distance.

8. With *over* adv.: To project beyond something else, forming a lap or flap; *fig.* to extend beyond some limit.

1631 R. Byfield *Doctr. Sabb.* 102 The..end..lapped over, and strucke the childe. *a* **1661** Fuller *Worthies* (1840) I. 343 Worldly wealth he cared not for, desiring only to make both ends meet; and as for that little that lapped over he gave it to pious uses. **1681** Grew *Musæum* 171 The upper Wings .., at their hinder ends, where they lap over, transparent.. like the Wing of a Fly. **1895** Mackail *Latin Lit.* 135 He outlived Augustus by three years, and so laps over into the sombre period of the Julio-Claudian dynasty.

9. a. *Euchre.* [Cf. lap *sb.*[3] 3.] *intr.* (See quot.) **b.** *Horse-* and *Motor Racing.* [Cf. lap *sb.*[3] 5 b.] *trans.* To get one or more laps ahead of (a competitor). Also *fig.*

1847 W. T. Porter *Quarter Race Kentucky* 50, I told you the brown horse was a mighty fast one... But soon I lapped him. **1857** *Lawrence* (Kansas) *Republ.* 11 June 3 This..was a killing pace, but Mahen lapped him inside the first quarter. **1890** 'Cavendish' *Pocket Guide to Euchre* 9 If the score of a game laps (that is, if more points are made than are necessary to win a game), the surplus is carried to the next game. **1890** *Illustr. Sporting & Dram. News* 26 Apr. 210/1 He lapped most of his opponents before half the distance was covered. **1897** *Daily News* 30 Aug. 3/3 Stocks started well, and lapped his opponents in the first 20 miles. **1961** J. S. Salak *Dict. Amer. Sports* 259 *Lap*, pass another car for the second or third time. **1966** *Publ. Amer. Dial. Soc. 1964* xlii. 6 'To be lapped', to be passed by a car the race distance for which already exceeds the car being overtaken by the length of a complete lap. **1969** 'D. Rutherford' *Gilt-Edged Cockpit* i. 18 The leading Ferrari..was in fourth place and about to be lapped by the Mascot. **1973** *Times* 9 Feb. 15/5 We are constantly being lapped in the wages race.

c. *trans.* and *intr.* Of persons engaged in a race, or their vehicles: to travel over (a distance) as a lap; also simply, to traverse.

1923 *Daily Mail* 24 May 10 The course, 37⅜ miles in length, has to be lapped six times. *Ibid.* 4 June 13 The Leyland expert put up the highest speed of the day when he lapped the 2⅜ miles at an average of 117 miles an hour. **1927** *Daily Express* 2 June 12/4 Major Segrave hopes..to lap the course at a fair speed. **1928** *Ibid.* 26 May 9/2 There are many machines entered which could lap all day at sixty-five miles an hour. **1973** P. Evans *Bodyguard Man* xiii. 93 Just lapping the track gently. Nothing too strenuous.

10. [Properly another word, f. lap *sb.*[3] sense 4.] *trans.* To reduce raw cotton to a lap.

1851 *Art Jrnl. Illustr. Catal.* p. iv**/1 This cylinder is cleaned of the teazed cotton by means of brushes, which deliver the cotton on to fluted rollers so regularly, that it comes out of the machine lapped into the form of a broad, felt-like web of cleaned cotton. **1879** Escott *England* I. 150 The various rooms for scutching, lapping, carding and roving the raw fibre [cotton].

11. *Comb.*, as **lap-band, -bander**, *dial.* (see quots.); **lap-work**, work in which one part is interchangeably lapped over another.

1681 GREW *Musæum* 373 The Ground is a Packthred-Caule; not Netted, but Woven. Into which by the Indian-Women are wrought, by a kind of Lap-Work, the Quills of Porcupines. **1829** BROCKETT *N.C. Words*, *Lapbander*, that which binds closely one thing to another... A tremendous oath is frequently called a lap-bander. **1868** ATKINSON *Cleveland Gloss.*, *Lap-band*, hoop-iron.

lap (læp), *v.*[3] [back-formation from *lapcock*: see LAP *sb.*[1] 9.] *trans.* To put up (hay) in small cocks.

1839 W. CARLETON *Fardorougha* (ed. 2) 57 We'd get this hay lapp'd in half the time.

lap (læp), *v.*[4] [f. LAP *sb.*[4]] *trans.* To rub or abrade so as to make a surface smooth (and often correctly shaped) to a high degree of precision, usually by the use of a rotating lap of suitable shape coated or impregnated with an abrasive dust, paste, or liquid.

1881 GREENER *Gun* 238 Most of the barrels are lapped or polished with a lead and emery upon another bench. **1888** *Sheffield Gloss.*, *Lap*, to polish steel on a wood or lead surface prepared with flint stone, thus giving it a beautiful opalescence. **1905** W. S. LEONARD *Machine-Shop Tools & Methods* (ed. 3) xxxi. 506 We sometimes lap a machine-shaft which is required to run at an extremely high speed... Other machine details may be lapped when an exceptionally high degree of refinement is required, but the process is more commonly applied to measuring-tools, such as the collar- and plug-gages, etc. **1928** E. BUCKINGHAM *Spur Gears* xii. 444 Hardened gears are sometimes run together under load with some form of abrasive introduced with the lubricant.. to smooth the surfaces and correct some of the errors. This process, however, does more grinding or crushing of the abrasive than it does to polish or lap the gear-tooth profiles. **1958** *Proc. IRE* XLVI. 1063/1 Wafers, of dimensions 1 × ½ inch, of this material are lapped to a thickness of 10 mils. **1973** *Physics Bull.* July 427/2 The techniques devised for lapping and polishing x ray reflectors have been modified to allow the same basic principles to be employed in lapping and polishing surfaces more complex than the plane, sphere or cylinder.

lap, obs. and *Sc.* pa. t. of LEAP.

†**la'pactic**, *a.* and *sb.* *Med. Obs.* [ad. Gr. λαπακτικ-ός purgative, f. λαπάσσειν to evacuate.] **A.** *adj.* Purgative, laxative. (Mayne *Expos. Lex.* 1855.) **B.** *sb.* in *pl.* (See quot.)

1753 CHAMBERS *Cycl. Supp.*, *Lapactics*, a term used by the old writers in medicine to express such things as purged by stool, or at least gently loosened the belly.

lapadary, obs. form of LAPIDARY.

lapageria (læpə'dʒɪərɪə). [mod.L. (Ruiz & Pavon *Flora Peruviana* (1802) III. 64), f. the name of Joséphine Tascher de *la Pagerie* (1763–1814), Empress of France + -IA[1].] A climbing shrub of the monotypic genus so named, belonging to the family Liliaceæ, native to Chile, and bearing large, bell-shaped, pendulous, red or white flowers.

1849 *Curtis's Bot. Mag.* LXXV. 4447 (*heading*) Rose-coloured Lapageria. **1886** G. NICHOLSON *Dict. Gardening* II. 234/2 Lapagerias rank amongst the most beautiful greenhouse climbing plants in existence. **1929** *Times* 1 Nov. 19/6 A tiny, pillared stone temple of exquisite proportions bowered in clematis, lapageria, and a climbing yellow rose. **1971** *Country Life* 8 Apr. 820/2 This is one of the finest outdoor specimens of lapageria I have seen in the British Isles.

laparo- ('læpərəʊ), rarely before a vowel **lapar-**, combining form of Gr. λαπάρᾱ flank, f. λαπαρός soft, in mod. terms of *Anat.*, *Surg.*, etc. **lapa'rectomy** [Gr. ἐκτομ-, ἐκτέμνειν to cut out], 'an excision or cutting out of a portion of the intestine at the side' (*Syd. Soc. Lex.* 1888). **'laparocele** [Gr. κήλη tumour], †(*a*) ventral hernia at the flank or side of the belly; (*b*) lumbar hernia. **'laparotome** [Gr. -τόμος cutter], an instrument for performing laparotomy (1855 in Mayne *Expos. Lex.* s.v. *Laparotomus*). **lapa'rotomy** [Gr. -τομία cutting], a cutting through the abdominal walls into the cavity of the abdomen; hence (in some recent Dicts.) **ˌlaparo'tomic** *a.*, pertaining to laparotomy; **lapa'rotomist**, one who performs laparotomy; **lapa'rotomize** *v. trans.*, to perform laparotomy upon. Also prefixed to the names of various surgical operations to denote that they are performed by cutting through the abdominal wall, as in *ˌlaparoco'lotomy*, *-ente'rotomy*, *-hyste'rectomy*: for these and many similar terms see Mayne *Expos. Lex.* (1855) and *Syd. Soc. Lex.* (1888).

1802–19 REES *Cycl.*, *Laparocele*, a term, in Surgery, denoting a swelling, or hernia, at the side of the belly. **1878** T. BRYANT *Pract. Surg.* I. 630 In Laparotomy the abdomen should be opened in the median line below the umbilicus. **1879** J. M. DUNCAN *Lect. Dis. Wom.* viii. (1889) 49 The laparotomy enthusiasm of recent times. **1885** *Lancet* 26 Sept. 566 It indicates the real value of laparotomy as an aid to herniotomy.

laparoscope ('læpərəʊskəʊp). *Med.* [f. LAPARO- + -SCOPE.] Any instrument used in examining the abdomen; now *spec.* one in the form of a tube for insertion into the peritoneal cavity in laparoscopy, having a source of light at the inserted end and an optical system for forming at the other end an image of the illuminated region.

1855 R. G. MAYNE *Expos. Lex. Med. Sci.* (1860) 571/2 *Laparoscopium*, name of an instrument for ascertaining the condition of the abdomen under disease; applicable to the stethoscope and the plessimeter: a laparoscope. **1941** DORLAND & MILLER *Med. Dict.* (ed. 19) 776/2 *Laparoscope*, a special form of trocar bearing a light by means of which the peritoneal cavity, especially the surface of the liver and the peritoneum, can be inspected. **1967** P. C. STEPTOE *Laparoscopy in Gynaecol.* ii. 11 A cold-light projector.. is used with a fibre glass cable for transmission of light to a quartz rod incorporated in the laparoscope. *Ibid.* iii. 22 The laparoscope is introduced through the vaginal fornix into the pouch of Douglas. **1970** *Sci. Jrnl.* June 57/1 Human ovaries may be inspected by inserting a tube (laparoscope) through to body wall which both illuminates the internal organs and transmits an image back to the observer.

laparoscopy (læpə'rɒskəpɪ). *Med.* [f. LAPARO- + -SCOPY.] Examination of the loins or abdomen; now *spec.* [ad. G. *laparoskopie* (H. C. Jacobaeus 1910, in *Münchener Med. Wochenschr.* 4 Oct. 2091/1)], visual examination of the interior of the peritoneal cavity by means of a laparoscope inserted into it through the abdominal wall or the vagina.

1855 R. G. MAYNE *Expos. Lex. Med. Sci.* (1860) 571/2 *Laparoscopia*, a term for the examination of the loins, by means of the stethoscope, plessimeter, etc.: laparoscopy. **1890** BILLINGS *Med. Dict.* II. 33/1 *Laparoscopy*, examination of the abdomen. **1916** *Jrnl. Amer. Med. Assoc.* 23 Sept. 982/2 Laparoscopy and Thoroscopy.—Johnsson has been applying the cystoscope in investigation of the interior of the abdomen and thorax. **1937** *Surg., Gynecol. & Obstetr.* LXIV. Internat. Abstr. Surg. Suppl. 560/1 By means of laparoscopy almost the same observations may be made as when the anterior wall of the abdominal cavity of a cadaver is removed. **1967** P. C. STEPTOE *Laparoscopy in Gynaecol.* viii. 42 An ovarian cyst is readily recognised by laparoscopy. **1969** *Nature* 15 Feb. 635/2 Work using laparoscopy has shown that oocytes can be recovered from ovaries by puncturing ripening follicles *in vivo*. **1970** M. R. COHEN *Laparoscopy, Culdoscopy & Gynecogr.* i. 3 By means of laparoscopy the gynecologist can obtain the same view of the pelvic organs as is seen in laparotomy.

Hence **laparo'scopic** *a.*, pertaining to or obtained by laparoscopy; **lapa'roscopist**, one who uses the laparoscope.

1967 P. C. STEPTOE *Laparoscopy in Gynaecol.* iii. 25 It is.. possible to present laparoscopic views direct to a large audience. *Ibid.* vi. 30 The experienced laparoscopist can offer sound advice about the technical errors. **1969** *Proc. R. Soc. Med.* LXII. 440/1 Interpretation of laparoscopic findings depends on..examination of the site, size and development of the ovary, the appearance of the surface and the presence of follicles or corpora lutea. *Ibid.* 441/2 The proper use of laparoscopic techniques is one of the most valuable advances..in gynæcology in the last twenty years. **1970** M. R. COHEN *Laparoscopy, Culdoscopy & Gynecogr.* xvii. 111 It is possible for the gynecologic laparoscopist to view upper abdominal organs as well.

laparostict ('læpərəʊstɪkt), *a.* and *sb.* *Ent.* [f. LAPARO- + Gr. στικτ-ός spotted, vbl. adj. f. στίζειν to prick.] **A.** *adj.* Of scarabæid beetles: Having abdominal spiracles in the membrane connecting the dorsal and ventral corneous plates. **B.** *sb.* A laparostict beetle.

1882 *Amer. Nat.* XXII. 951 This genus [*Pleocoma*], which he insisted was a Laparostict, and not a Pleurostict Lamellicorn.

lapdanum, obs. form of LABDANUM.

'lap-dog. [f. LAP *sb.*[1] 5 + DOG.] A small dog, such as is allowed to lie in a lady's lap.

1645 EVELYN *Diary* May, The lap-dogs which the ladies are so fond of. **1709** PRIOR *When Cat is Away* 56 Nor rats nor mice the lap-dog fear. **1774** GOLDSM. *Nat. Hist.* II. 168 The lapdog at the time of Dr. Caius was of Maltese breed. **1802** WOLCOT (P. Pindar) *Ld. Belgrave* Wks. 1812 IV. 516 A poor tame thing Just like a Lap-dog in a string. **1881** BESANT & RICE *Chapl. of Fleet* I. x, The pet and plaything..a sort of lapdog to be carried in..coaches.

attrib. **1810** *Sporting Mag.* XXXVI. 71 Lap-dog beagles. **1838** LYTTON *Alice* VI. iii, Had I not fed his lap-dog vanity ..you would be Caroline Merton still. **1905** *Dial* (Chicago) 16 Feb. 114/2 Lap-dog poets. **1963** *Times Lit. Suppl.* 22 Feb. 132/4 A lap-dog lover.

lape, obs. form of LAP *v.*[1], *v.*[2]

lap-eared: see LOP-EARED.

lapel (læ'pɛl). Also 9 **lapell(e**, **lappel**. [f. LAP *sb.*[1] + -EL.] That part of the front of a coat which is folded over towards either shoulder.

1789 MRS. PIOZZI *Journ. France* I. 340 A stiff brocaded silk, and green lapels. **1803** JANE PORTER *Thaddeus* xiv. (1831) 128 The sleet falling on his dress, lodged in its embroidered lappels. **1838** DICKENS *Nich. Nick.* xiv, Laying his hand upon the lappel of his threadbare coat. **1876** GEO. ELIOT *Dan. Der.* v. xxxvi, He..held the lapels of his coat with his thumbs under the collar as his manner was.

b. *attrib.*

1824 in S. B. WEEKS *South. Quakers & Slavery* 131 [In 1824 Friends in Southern U.S. record their condemnation of] such articles of dress as lapell coats. **1849** ALB. SMITH *Pottleton Leg.* xxv. 261 With inches of ribbon in their lappel button-holes. **1895** *Montgomery Ward Catal.* 180 Lapel Buttons, Enameled. **1940** *Chambers's Techn. Dict.* 486/2 *Lapel microphone*, a small microphone, worn on the lapel; suitable for use when the speaker is addressing an audience, or when he cannot remain in a stable position. **1967** *Observer* 26 Mar. 9 The hippies themselves do not need to pin on the lapel buttons they sell. **1969** *New Scientist* 16 Oct. 109/2 The indignity of wearing a lapel badge displaying their name, rank and work-place to the world at large. **1972** *Times* 7 Feb. 1/3 They were issued with lapel badges depicting a black coffin on a white background. **1973** *Country Life* 31 May 56/1 For the sportsman's wife... Lapel brooches in three colours of gold.

lapelled (læ'pɛld), *pa. pple.* and *ppl. a.* [f. LAPEL *sb.* (as if through **lapel* vb.) + -ED.]

1. Furnished with a lapel, or with one of a specified kind.

1751 SMOLLETT *Per. Pic.* (1779) I. viii. 68 His waistcoat was of red plush lapelled with green velvet. **1766** in W. Smith *Bouquet's Exped.* (1868) 111 A short coat of brown cloth, lapelled, and without plaits. **1848** J. GRANT *Adv. of Aide-de-C.* iv, A scarlet uniform, lapelled and faced with black velvet. **1861** THORNBURY *Turner* I. 65, I see, again, his frilled shirt,..his lapelled waistcoat, and his Michael Angelo watch-seal.

2. Folded over so as to form a lapel.

1789 E. DARWIN *Bot. Gard.* II. (1791) 148 With net-wove sash and glittering gorget dress'd, And scarlet robe lapell'd upon her breast, Stern Ara frowns. **1829** MRS. SOUTHEY *Churchyards* I. 290 A..coat, of dark blue broad cloth, lapelled back with two rows of..buttons.

lapful ('læpfʊl), *sb.* and *a.* [f. LAP *sb.*[1] + -FUL.]

A. *sb.* So much as will fill a person's lap.

[**1611** BIBLE *2 Kings* iv. 39 One..found a wild vine, and gathered thereof wilde gourds his lap full.] **1611** COTGR., *Gironnée*, a lapfull, or bosomefull of. **1648** WARD (*title*) The Simple Cobbler's Boy, with a Lapful of Caveats. **1710** SWIFT *Tatler* No. 230 ¶2 They are handed about from Lapfulls in every Coffee-house to Persons of Quality. **1850** MRS. JAMESON *Leg. Monast. Ord.* (1863) 313 Her proper attribute is the lapful of roses. **1887** BARING-GOULD *Gaverocks* xiii, I have got a lap-full of chestnuts.

B. *adj.* Having the lap full. *rare.*

1884 SYMONDS *Shaks. Predecessors* vii. §3. 264 Lap-full of flowers..the country lass of English art returns from those excursions.

lapicide ('læpɪsaɪd). [ad. L. *lapicīda*, contraction for *lapidicīda*. f. *lapid-*, *lapis* stone: see -CIDE 1.] One who cuts stones, or inscriptions on stone.

1656 BLOUNT *Glossogr.*, *Lapicide*, a digger, or hewer of stones; a Stone-cutter or Free-Mason. **1736** in BAILEY (fol.). **1831** M. RUSSELL *Egypt* iv. (1853) 107 The Master Mohammed Ahmed, lapicide, has opened them. **1889** D. G. HOGARTH *Devia Cypria* 9 The cognomina of the three brothers being identical, the lapicide has not repeated them.

Hence †**lapici'darial** *a.*, of or pertaining to the work of a lapicide; †**lapi'cidary**, one who is engaged in stone-cutting; a lapidary.

1592 R. D. *Hypnerotomachia* 23 b, The workemanship.. seemed to excell the cunning of any humaine Lapicidarie. *Ibid.* 90 The hollowed and bending leaves with all the other lapicidariall lineaments, were performed with such an emulation of nature as was woonderfull.

†**'lapidable**, *a.* *Obs. rare*[—0]. [as if ad. L. **lapidābilis*, f. *lapidāre* to stone, from *lapid-*, *lapis* stone.] That may be stoned.

1656 in BLOUNT *Glossogr.* **1706** PHILLIPS (ed. Kersey), *Lapidable*, marriageable, fit for a husband. [This strange mistake is copied in some later Dicts.]

lapidaire, obs. form of LAPIDARY.

†**'lapidar**, *a.* *Obs. rare*[—1]. [ad. L. *lapidāris*, f. *lapid-*, *lapis* stone.] Of the nature of stone.

1767 BUSH *Hibernia Cur.* (1769) 61 A similar natural process with many sparry or lapidar productions.

lapidar(e, obs. form of LAPIDARY.

lapidarian (læpɪ'dɛərɪən), *a.* *rare.* [f. L. *lapidāri-us* + -AN.] **a.** Versed in the knowledge of stones. **b.** Executed in, or inscribed on, stone.

1683 PETTUS *Fleta Min.* II. 4 Our Author..was not a Sophisticating Alchimist, nor a Lapidarian Philosopher. **1864** WEBSTER s.v., A lapidarian record. **1882** RAU (*title*) Observations on Cup-shaped and other Lapidarian Sculpture.

†**lapi'darious**, *a.* *Obs. rare*[—0]. [f. as prec. + -OUS.] Consisting of stones: stony.

1656 in BLOUNT *Glossogr.* Hence in mod. Dicts.

'lapidarist ('læpɪdərɪst.) [f. next + -IST.] = LAPIDARY B 1 a, b; also *fig.*

1607 TOPSELL *Four-f. Beasts* (1658) 340 The skilful lapidarists of Germany affirm that this beast hath a stone in his eyes. **1620** SHELTON *Quix.* IV. vi. II. 70 A most precious Diamond, of whose Goodness and Quality all the Lapidarists that had view'd the same, would rest satisfied. **1886** *Sci. Amer.* 7 Aug. 84/2 The stone called sapphire by Pliny is now known to lapidarists as lapis lazuli. **1926** C. L. WARR *Principal Caird* iv. 135 He was a slow-working lapidarist, polishing every literary pebble. **1967** *Sat. Rev.* 13 May 31 Limited editions presses are the lapidarists of the publishing world.

lapidary ('læpɪdərɪ), *a.* and *sb.* Forms: 4–5 **lapidaire**, 4–6 *Sc.* **lapidar**, 4–7 **lapidarie**, **-ye**, (5 **lapadary**, **lipidarye**), 7 **lapidare**, **-ery**, 6– **lapidary**. [ad. L. *lapidārius*, f. *lapid-*, *lapis* stone. Cf. F. *lapidaire*. In B. 2 and 3 ad. L. *lapidārium* or L. type **lapidāria*.]

A. *adj.*

1. Concerned with stones. *rare* exc. in ***lapidary bee*** (see quots. 1854–68).

1831–57 De Quincey *Dr. Parr* Wks. VI. 164 That lapidary style of retort in which their wrath has been trained to express itself. **1835** *Court Mag.* VI. 166/2 An Irish pavior expressed an anxiety to enter into partnership with a friend, who likewise followed the same lapidary profession. **1854** H. Miller *Sch. & Schm.* (1858) 68 The lapidary red-tipped bees, that built amid the recesses of ancient cairns, and in old dry stone walls. **1868** Wood *Homes without H.* vii. 138 The Lapidary Bee (*Bombus lapidarius*).

2. a. Of an inscription, etc.: Engraved on stone, esp. monumental stones. **b.** Of style, etc.: Characteristic of or suitable for monumental inscriptions.

1724 *Life of Dr. Barwick* 40 *note*, See a farther Account of him.. in Dr. Jenkins's Lapidary Verses prefix'd to those Sermons. **1730** A. Gordon *Maffei's Amphith.* 147 These Words.. expressed, in the Lapidary Stile, that it was built from its very Foundation. **1775** Johnson in *Boswell* Dec., In lapidary inscriptions a man is not upon oath. **1817** Lamb *Let. to Ayrton* in Talfourd *Final Mem.* x. 101 Tell me candidly how you relish This, which they call The lapidary style. **1822** Byron *Vis. Judgm.* xii, He's buried; save the undertaker's bill, Or lapidary scrawl. **1838–9** Hallam *Hist. Lit.* II. viii. ii. §63. 361 They were the encouragers of a numismatic and lapidary erudition. **1873** Tristram *Moab* vii. 135 If the new-comers had had any reverence for the lapidary records of their predecessors. **1899** *Academy* 18 Feb. 210/2 A stanza [which] has a lapidary dignity, as of some thing carved in stone.

B. *sb.*

1. One busied about or concerned with stones. **a.** An artificer who cuts, polishes, or engraves gems or precious stones.

1382 Wyclif *Ecclus.* xlv. 13 With werk of the lapidarie grauun. **1500–20** Dunbar *Poems* lxiii. 15 Glasing wrichtis, goldsmythis, and lapidaris. **1555** Eden *Decades* 233 The region of Malabar where are many cunnynge Lapidaries. **1624** Fletcher *Rule a Wife* v. ii, An excellent lapidary set those stones sure. **1684** Winstanley in *Shaks. C. Praise* 401 Cornish Diamonds are not Polished by any Lapidary. **1753** Smollett *Ct. Fathom* (1784) 92/2 Ratchkali, who was an exquisite lapidary, had set it in such a manner, as would have imposed upon any ordinary jeweller. **1860** Tyndall *Glac.* i. xx. 141 Portions of the vertical walls.. are polished.. as if they had come from the hands of a lapidary. **1869** Boutell *Arms & Arm.* v. (1874) 81 The productions of the sculptor and the lapidary.

†**b.** One who is skilled in the nature and kinds of gems or precious stones; a connoisseur of lapidary work. *Obs.*

c **1440** *Gesta Rom.* xxiv. 89 (Harl. MS.) He went to a lapadary, that was expert in the vertue of stonys. **1577** Stanyhurst *Descr. Irel.* Ep. Ded. in *Holinshed*, If it shall stand with your honor his pleasure (whom I take to be an expert lapidarie). **1639** G. Daniel *Ecclus.* xxxii. 14 The bright Carbuncle (whose wondrous flame Pussles the skillfull Lapidare to Name). *a* **1658** Cleveland *Gen. Poems* (1677) 166 The Lapidary tells you how the Compassionate Turcoise confesseth the Sickness of his Wearer by changing colour. **1750** tr. *Leonardus' Mirr. Stones* 145 (225), I find twelve species of the emerald described by lapidaries. **1796** Kirwan *Elem. Min.* (ed. 2) I. 361 This name [Pudding stone] was invented by English Lapidaries.

2. A treatise on (precious) stones. *Obs.* exc. *Hist.*

c **1375** *Sc. Leg. Saints, Margaret* 2 Qwa wil þe vertu wyt of stanis In þe lapidar ma fynd ane is [etc.]. *c* **1384** Chaucer *H. Fame* iii. 262 The fynest stones faire That men reden in the lapidaire. *c* **1440** Lydg. *Secrees* 539, I dar seyn breffly, and nat tarye, Is noon suych stoon ffound in the lapydarye. **1652** Ashmole *Theat. Chem.* 221 Alle Stonys in the lapidery. **1884** Symonds *Shaks. Predecessors* xiii. 512 The Bestiaries and Lapidaries of the Middle Ages.

†**3.** *collect.* [after sbs. in -ery.] Precious stones in general; jewellery. *Obs.*

1509 Barclay *Shyp of Folys* (1570) 43 There is no.. Carbuncle, Rubie,.. Nor other lapidary comparable to me. **1609** Armin *Maids of More-Cl.* F 4 A iewell.. Whose liuing beauty staind all lapidary.

4. *attrib.*, as **lapidary('s-mill, -wheel**, the grinding and polishing apparatus of the lapidary.

1839 Ure *Dict. Arts* 738 The lapidary's mill, or wheel. **1875** Knight *Dict. Mech.*, *Lapidary-mill*, *Lapidary-wheel.* **1878** Huxley *Physiogr.* 58 As though they [the crystals] had just been polished at the lapidary's wheel.

lapidate (ˈlæpɪdeɪt), *v.* [f. L. *lapidāt-*, ppl. stem of *lapidāre*, in same sense, f. *lapid-*, *lapis* a stone. Cf. F. *lapider.*] *trans.* To throw stones at, to pelt with stones; also, to stone to death.

1623 in Cockeram. **1816** Byron *To Moore* 24 Dec., Whom the.. mob quartered and lapidated. **1824** Scott *St. Ronan's* xxxi, We were lapidated by the natives, pebbled to some purpose, I give you my word. **1837** *Fraser's Mag.* XVI. 666 They may go on lapidating him.. with paving-stones. **1876** G. Meredith *Beauch. Career* II. x. 185 It is better they be roused to lapidate us than soused in their sty.

lapidation (læpɪˈdeɪʃən). [ad. L. *lapidātiōn-em*, n. of action f. *lapidāre*: see prec.]

1. *spec.* The punishment of stoning to death.

1611 Florio, *Lapidatione*, a Lapidation, a stoning. **1662** Stillingfl. *Orig. Sacr.* ii. v. §3 Gods own messengers [were] punished with the death of seducers, which was lapidation. **1796** Morse *Amer. Geog.* II. 628 Punishments.. flaying alive, lapidation, plucking out the eyes. **1830** D'Israeli *Chas. I*, III. xv. 328 A man gathering faggots in a wood was condemned to the punishment of lapidation. **1855** R. F. Burton *El-Medinah* II. xxi. 281 Adultery, if detected, would be punished by lapidation, according to the rigour of the Koranic law.

2. *gen.* The action or process of throwing stones; pelting with stones.

1802 A. Ranken *Hist. France* II. iv. ii. 291 He was invulnerable by either fire or lions, or popular lapidation. **1844** *For. Q. Rev.* XXXIII. 94 The people.. treated them to a taste of lapidation. **1879** *Temple Bar* LVI. 497 The tenants are too hungry to take interest in the lapidation of the devoted animal [a donkey].

fig. **1864** *Sat. Rev.* 24 Dec. 766/2 Quite content to await the lapidation that is in store for us from Chairmen and Secretaries.

lapidator (ˈlæpɪdeɪtə(r)). [a. L. *lapidātor*, agent-n. f. *lapidāre*: see lapidate *v.*] One who stones.

18.. in Ogilvie (citing *Scotsman*).

†**laˈpidement.** *Obs. rare*⁻¹. [a. F. *lapidement*, f. *lapider*, ad. L. *lapidāre* to lapidate.] = lapidation.

1483 Caxton *Gold. Leg.* 123 b/2, I may not bere.. the lapydementis that the fendes don to me.

lapideous (ləˈpɪdɪəs), *a.* Now *rare.* Also 7 -ious. [f. L. *lapide-us*, f. *lapid-*, *lapis* stone.]

1. Of the nature of stone, stony.

1646 Sir T. Browne *Pseud. Ep.* ii. v. 91 The.. lapidificall juyce of the sea.. entring the parts of that plant.. converts it into a lapideous substance. **1694** *Phil. Trans.* XVIII. 112 This Lapidious Concretion took up the whole Cavity of the Bladder. **1758** Borlase *Nat. Hist. Cornwall* xv. §7. 164 From malleable and metallic they become lapideous. **1865** A. S. Herschel in *Intell. Observ.* No. 39. 220 The lapideous morsels.

†**2.** Consisting of or inscribed on stone. *Obs.*

1807 G. Chalmers *Caledonia* I. Pref. 7 Camden, by throwing his antiquarian eye on the lapideous records, which had been dug from its foundations, ascertained that.. fact.

lapidery, obs. form of lapidary.

†**lapiˈdescence.** *Obs.* [f. lapidescent *a.*: see -ence.] Lapidescent condition; petrifaction. So †**lapiˈdescency**, in quot. quasi-*concr.*, a result of petrifaction.

1646 Sir T. Browne *Pseud. Ep.* iii. xxiii. 167 Those fragments and pieces of *Lapis Ceratites*, commonly termed *Cornu fossile*.. are but the Lapidescencies and petrifactive mutations of hard bodies. **1650** Charleton *Paradoxes* Prol. 23 A.. laborious exploration of the Causes of Coagulation, conductive to Lapidescence or Petrifaction. **1799** Kirwan *Geol. Ess.* 125 Some proportion of water is always necessary to promote this lapidescence.

lapidescent (læpɪˈdɛsənt), *a.* and *sb.* ? *Obs.* [ad. L. *lapidescent-em*, pres. pple. of *lapidescĕre* to become stony, f. *lapid-*, *lapis* stone.] **A.** *adj.* That is in process of becoming stone; having a tendency to solidify into stone. Said chiefly of 'petrifying' waters and the salts dissolved or suspended in them. **B.** *sb.* A 'lapidescent' substance.

1644 Evelyn *Mem.* (1857) I. 77 The drops meeting with some lapidescent matter, it converts them into a hard stone. **1675** —— *Terra* (1676) 42 Worm-casts hardened by the air and a certain lapidescent succus, or spirit, which it meets with. **1694** Salmon *Bate's Dispens.* (1713) 62/2 Whence the Stone and Gravel, and the lapidescent Concretions in the Gout are produc'd. **1727–41** Chambers *Cycl.*, Lapidescent Waters or Springs. **176.** Ellis in *Phil. Trans.* LVII. 406 All of them are very distinct.. from all vegetables, on account of their lapidescent substance. **1811** K. Macleay *Spar Cave* 62 This lapidescent process is perpetually going forward. **1828–97** Webster, *Lapidescent*, sb., Any substance which has the quality of petrifying a body.

†**laˈpidial,** *a. Obs. rare*⁻¹. [f. L. *lapid-*, *lapis* stone + -al¹.] Resembling stone; stony. So †**laˈpidian** *a.*, concerned with stones; working on stones.

1599 A. M. tr. *Gabelhouer's Bk. Physicke* 71/2 Till such time the Vinegar be evaporated, and the Alumme agayne of a lapidialle obduratnes. **1600** E. Blount *Garzoni's Hosp. Incur. Fooles* 21 If thou beest the Lapidian Iupiter [orig. *se tu sei quel Gioue Lapideo*], which workest wonders in stones.

lapidicolous (læpɪˈdɪkələs), *a.* [f. L. *lapid-*, *lapis* stone + *col-us* inhabiting + -ous.] Of beetles: living under stones or similar objects. Hence **laˈpidicole** *sb.*, a beetle living in this kind of habitat.

1899 D. Sharp in *Cambr. Nat. Hist.* VI. ii. v. 205 These blind lapidicolous Carabidæ are of extremely minute size, and of most sluggish habits. **1948** J. R. Dibb *Field Bk. Beetles* p. xiii, Habitat-group 4. Under Stones. Logs, timber, sacking, old metal objects and discarded material which has been thrown down in the open. Lapidicoles. **1959** E. F. Linssen *Beetles Brit. Isles* I. 57 Beetles found under stones are Lapidicoles. **1965** B. E. Freeman tr. *Vandel's Biospeleol.* ii. 20 Thousands of.. lapidicoles.. have been recorded.

†**lapidiˈfactory,** *a. Obs. rare*⁻¹. [f. lapidify, after the analogy of calefactory, etc.] Of or pertaining to the making of stones.

1650 Charleton *Paradoxes* Prol. 23 The.. Lapidifactory Principle, to which all Concreted substances owe their Coagulation.

lapidific (læpɪˈdɪfɪk), *a.* ? *Obs.* [f. L. *lapid-*, *lapis* stone + -(i)fic. Cf. F. *lapidifique.*] Adapted to or concerned with the making of stones.

1693 Sir T. P. Blount *Nat. Hist.* 35 In the Kidneys.. that part which.. is the most Lapidifick of the whole Body. **1746** Simon in *Phil. Trans.* XLIV. 317 The finer the lapidific Particles are, the more beautiful and natural the Petrifaction will appear. **1786** Jefferson *Writ.* (1859) I. 516 Have we any better proof of such an effort of nature, than of her shooting a lapidific juice into the form of a shell. **1802** Playfair *Illustr. Hutton. Theory* 373 Carrying some cementing substance along with it, or some lapidific juice, as it is called.

So †**lapiˈdifical** *a.* = lapidific.

1646 Sir T. Browne *Pseud. Ep.* ii. i. 50 Crystall.. is.. concreted by.. lapidificall principles of its owne. **1675** E. Wilson *Spadacrene Dunelm.* 46 The Seeds of Petrifaction, or lapidifical Principle, which converts all materials it meets withall into a stony concrete.

lapidification (ləˌpɪdɪfɪˈkeɪʃən). [f. lapidify: see -fication.] The action or process of converting or being converted into stone.

1626 Bacon *Sylva* §82 Lapidification of Substances more soft, is likewise another degree of Condensation. **1727–52** Chambers *Cycl.*, *Lapidification*, in chemistry, an operation whereby any substance is converted into a sort of stone. **1774** *Projects* in *Ann. Reg.* 110/1 It.. turned out a kind of instantaneous lapidification. **1851** Richardson *Geol.* (1855) 31 Cesalpini.. ascribing them [fossils].. to 'the retiring of the sea and the lapidification of the soil'. **1875** Lyell *Princ. Geol.* I. ii. xviii. 426 We shall feel no surprise at the lapidification of the newly deposited sediment in this Delta.

lapidify (ləˈpɪdɪfaɪ), *v.* [ad. F. *lapidifier*, ad. med.L. *lapidificāre*, f. *lapid-*, *lapis* stone: see -fy.] †**a.** *intr.* To become stone. **b.** *trans.* To make or turn into stone.

1657 Tomlinson *Renou's Disp.* 422 Where this Chrystalline humour.. lapidifies. **1816** W. Smith *Strata Ident.* 31 The Fuller's Earth Rock.. in many places is so soft and imperfectly lapidified as scarcely to deserve the name of stone. **1860** *Macm. Mag.* I. 410 Layers of coloured clayey sand, in the lowest parts almost lapidified. **1874** Lyell *Elem. Geol.* iv. 45 Yet when the whole is 'lapidified' it may not form one homogeneous mass.

Hence **laˈpidified** *ppl. a.*; **laˈpidifying** *vbl. sb.* and *ppl. a.*

1669 W. Simpson *Hydrol. Chym.* 266 From which lapidifying juyce [etc.]. **1830** Lyell *Princ. Geol.* I. 25 Porous bodies.. might be converted into stone, as being permeable to what he [Mattioli] termed the 'lapidifying juice'. **1832** *Ibid.* II. 257 Lapidified plants. **1832** De la Beche *Geol. Man.* (ed. 2) 145 A.. struggle between the destructive power of the Nera, and the lapidifying power of the Velino. **1835** Kirby *Hab. & Inst. Anim.* I. viii. 260 They [pearls] are produced by the extravasation of a lapidifying fluid.

lapidious, obs. form of lapideous.

†**ˈlapidist.** *Obs. rare.* [f. L. *lapid-*, *lapis* + -ist.] = lapidary *sb.* 1 a or b.

1647 Trapp *Comm. Mark* vii. 33 The wise lapidist brings not his softer stones to the stithy. **1691** Ray *Creation* i. (1692) 81 The factitious Stones of Chymists in imitation being easily detected by an ordinary Lapidist.

laˈpidity. [ad. med.L. *lapiditās*, f. L. *lapid-*, *lapis* stone: see -ity.] The quality of being stone.

1750 tr. *Leonardus' Mirr. Stones* 84 Others say, crystal acquires its lapidity from earthiness and not from coldness. **1847** [see aureity].

lapidose (ˈlæpɪdəʊs), *a.* [ad. L. *lapidōsus*, f. *lapid-*, *lapis* stone.]

1. Abounding in stones. Also, of stony nature.

c **1420** *Pallad. on Husb.* xii. 225 Ther cleyi londis are and lapidose, With donge is good to helpe hem. **1807** G. Chalmers *Caledonia* I. i. ii. 83 Carns.. are more numerous in North, than in South Britain, from its abounding more with lapidose substances.

2. Growing in stony ground.

1866 in *Treas. Bot.*

†**ˈlapidous,** *a. Obs. rare*⁻¹. [f. L. *lapid-*, *lapis* + -ous. Cf. F. *lapideux.*] Full of stones.

1610 Barrough *Meth. Physick* v. xxv. (1639) 352 Commit the cure of a Scirrhus spleene and a lapidous liver, to the wisedome of the Physician.

lapiés (ˈlæpjeɪz, ˈlæpɪeɪz), *sb. pl. Geomorphol.* Also **lapiaz, lapies, lapiez.** [a. F. dial. *lapiaz*, *lapiés* pl. (used in the Jura), f. pop.L. **lapida* f. L. *lapis* stone.] **a.** (Const. as *pl.*) = karren, Karren *sb. pl.*; also (const. as *sing.*), a *karrenfeld.*

1902, etc. [see karren, Karren]. **1903** *Geogr. Jrnl.* XXI. 328 The surface formation met with most commonly in limestone districts, which is usually known by the German term *Karren*, or the French *Lapiaz.* **1921** *Geogr. Rev.* XI. 594 The identification of 'karren' and 'lapiez' is taken from Eugène Renevier's 'Monographie des Hautes Alpes Vaudoises' (Matériaux pour la carte géol. Suisse), p. 499. *Ibid.* 598 The name adopted by Professor Cvijič is 'lapiez', which is the term used in the French Jura. **1924** J. Cvijič in *Geogr. Rev.* XIV. 27 Lapiés are found at all altitudes from sea level to lofty mountain summits. They were first observed and described in the limestone alps of Switzerland, where in the cantons of German speech they are called *Karren* or *Schratten* and in districts of French speech *lapiéz* or *lapiaz* or *lapiés. Ibid.* 40 Lapiés are formed principally by chemical erosion of limestone surfaces by meteoric water. *Ibid.* 44 Typical lapiés occur chiefly on moderately steep slopes. *Ibid.*, Scattered limestone monoliths are rapidly formed out of the lapiés ridges. **1954** W. D. Thornbury

Princ. Geomorphol. xiii. 319 Where relief is considerable, limestone surfaces are bare of terra rossa and there is exposed an etched, pitted, grooved, fluted and otherwise rugged surface to which the name *lapiés* is most commonly applied. Cvijić (1924) has described .. the amazing diversity of surface and form which lapiés exhibits in the Dalmatian karst region. He maintained that lapiés is found chiefly on outcrops of naked rock. **1968** R. W. FAIRBRIDGE *Encycl. Geomorphol.* 645/1 Well developed lapiés with pinnacles standing up to 5 meters high are common in emerged limestone reefs, particularly in the South Pacific. **1972** BAUER & ZÖTL in Herak & Stringfield *Karst* vii. 236 At these altitudes [in Austria] lapies are dominant karst phenomena, covering wide areas. *Ibid.* 237 Where the surface of limestones is exposed by recent soil erosion, irregularly shaped, more or less rounded rills and lapies of different depth are found.

b. Used in the *sing.* form **lapié**. *rare.*

1968 R. W. FAIRBRIDGE *Encycl. Geomorphol.* 644/2 (*caption*) Lapiés formed in limestone covered by residual clay... When the lapié ridges are destroyed, a dolina will be formed, filled with clay.

†**lapillation** (læpɪˈleɪʃən). *Obs.* [f. L. *lapillus*, dim. of *lapis* stone + -ATION.] (See quot. 1722.)

1722 QUINCY *Lex. Physico-Med.* (ed. 2) 229 Paracelsus calls the same Faculty [of turning any Bodies into a stony Nature] in an human Body Lapillation. **1724** in BAILEY.

‖**lapilli** (ləˈpɪlaɪ), *pl.* [L., pl. of *lapillus*, dim. of *lapis* stone. In the specific sense orig. the plural of It. LAPILLO.] Small stones or pebbles; now only *spec.* of the fragments of stone ejected from volcanoes.

1747 *Gentl. Mag.* 523 Most of their lapilli are a fluor of the stalactite kind. **1833** LYELL *Princ. Geol.* III. Gloss., *Lapilli*, small volcanic cinders. **1858** GEIKIE *Hist. Boulder* xii. 237 Ashes and lapilli, ejected from some submarine orifice. **1875** LYELL *Princ. Geol.* II. II. xxvi. 18 Ashes and lapilli of the size of nuts [were projected] as far as 40 miles. **1883** R. A. PROCTOR in *Contemp. Rev.* Oct. 567 A heavy rain of cinders and lapilli.

Hence **laˈpilliform** *a.*, pebble-shaped.

1836–9 TODD *Cycl. Anat.* II. 537/1 A small pouch containing .. a lapilliform body.

‖**lapillo** (laˈpillo). [It.; ad. L. *lapillus*: see LAPILLI.] Matter ejected from volcanoes in the form of lapilli.

1811 PINKERTON *Petral.* I. 48 Mountains .. formed of heaps of scoriæ, fragments of lava and of lapillo. **1862** G. P. SCROPE *Volcanos* 57 The lapillo is generally of a deep-black colour.

‖**lapis** (ˈlæpɪs). The Latin word for 'stone'.

1. Used with qualification in several med.L. names of minerals and gems: **lapis Armenus**, Armenian stone, a blue carbonate of copper; **lapis calaminaris**, calamine; **lapis causticus**, caustic potash; **lapis divinus**, a preparation consisting of copper sulphate, potassium nitrate, alum, and camphor; **lapis granatus**, garnet; **lapis hæmatites**, hæmatite; **lapis hibernicus** (see quot.); **lapis infernalis**, lunar caustic (cf. INFERNAL A. 4 a); **lapis judaicus** = JEWS' STONE 1; **lapis Lydius**, basanite; **lapis ollaris**, potstone, or soapstone.

1641 FRENCH *Distill.* iii. (1651) 82 Take of *Lapis Armenus .. as much as you please. **1796** KIRWAN *Elem. Min.* (ed. 2) II. 153 Lapis Armenus is Chalk or Gypsum impregnated with the blue Calx of Copper. **1696** PHILLIPS (ed. 5), *Cadmia*, Brass Oar or Stone out of which Brass is tryed or molten, called by divers *Lapis Calaminaris. **1799** G. SMITH *Laboratory* I. 108 Add to it a third part of powdered lapis calaminaris. **1822** IMISON *Sci. & Art* II. 228 Brass is made by fusing together lapis calaminaris (which is an ore of zinc) and copper. **1657** *Physical Dict.*, *Lapis *Granatus*, the Granate stone. **1741** *Compl. Fam.-Piece* I. i. 76 Take the fine Powder of *Lapis Hæmatites. **1778** WOULFE in *Phil. Trans.* LXIX. 25 The Irish slate, *lapis Hybernicus of the druggists. **1741** *Compl. Fam.-Piece* I. i. 40 Take of *Lapis Infernalis one Ounce. [*c* **1400** *Lanfranc's Cirurg.* 278 ℞, cineris vitris .. lapidis spongie, *lapidis iudaici .. ana .ʒ. j.] **1646** SIR T. BROWNE *Pseud. Ep.* II. v. 92 Bezoar is Antidotall, Lapis Judaicus diureticall. **1772–84** COOK *Voy.* (1790) V. 1722 Besides the *lapis lydius, we found a species of cream-coloured whetstone. **1696** PHILLIPS (ed. 5), **Lapis Nephriticus*, a Stone of great Efficacy against the Stone in the Kidneys. **1753** HANWAY *Trav.* (1762) I. VII. xcv. 437 A cup of lapis nephriticus. **1796** KIRWAN *Elem. Min.* (ed. 2) I. 155 Pot-stone, *Lapis Ollaris. **1865** LUBBOCK *Preh. Times* xiv. (1869) 482 A .. lamp or shallow vessel of lapis ollaris.

2. Short for: **a.** med.L. *lapis philosophicus*, philosophers' stone; **b.** LAPIS LAZULI.

1666–7 LOCKE *Let. to Boyle* 24 Feb. in B.'s Wks. 1772 VI. 537 He and I are now upon a new sort of chemistry, i.e. extracting money out of the scholars pockets; and if we can do that, you need not fear but in time we shall have the lapis. **1811** PINKERTON *Petral.* II. 89 At Ekaterinburg in Siberia .. I inquired .. concerning the nature of the mountains whence the Lapis is brought. **1861** *All Year Round* V. 14 Basalt, lapis, syenite.

†**lapise**, *v. Obs.* Also 6 lapyse, -yst, 6–7 lappise, 8 lapist. [Cf. F. *glapiss-*, *glapir* (also *clapir*, said of a rabbit) to yelp.] (See quots.)

1576 TURBERV. *Venerie* 86 Never fearyng to make him lappise or call on. *Ibid.* 240 When they [Hounds] open in the string (or a Greyhounde in his course) we say *They lapyse.* **1686** BLOME *Gentl. Recr.* II. 82 If the Hound stick well upon the Scent, then let him hold him short for fear lest he Lapist (that is open).

‖**lapis lazuli, lapis-lazuli** (ˈlæpɪs ˈlæzjʊlaɪ). *Min.* Also 6–7 lapis lazari, 7 lazarilli. Also shortened LAZULI. [L. *lapis* + med.L. *lazuli* gen. of *lazulum*: see AZURE.] A complex silicate containing sulphur, of bright blue colour, used as a pigment (see ULTRAMARINE). Also, the colour of this mineral.

1398 TREVISA *Barth. De P.R.* XVI. cii. (1495) 588 Zineth is a stone other a veyne of erthe wherof lapis Lazuli is made. **1460–70** *Bk. Quintessence* II. 18 Poudre of lapis lasuly. *c* **1530** in Gutch *Coll. Cur.* II. 341 A peyre of Beydes of Lapis Lazary. **1641** FRENCH *Distill.* v. (1651) 168 It will become full of golden veins very like true lapis lazuli. **1692** SETTLE *Tri. Lond.* 9 On the Right and Left of these Columns, stand four Pilasters of Lapis Lazari. **1740** THOMPSON & HOGG in *Hanway's Trav.* (1762) I. IV. lii. 243 Formerly they received lapis-lazuli, and other precious stones, from Biddukshan. **1823** P. NICHOLSON *Pract. Build.* 414 Ultramarine is a preparation of calcined lapis-lazuli. **1870** DISRAELI *Lothair* lxxi, The terrace .. looked upon a sea of lapis lazuli.

attrib. **1881** E. COXON *Basil Pl.* II. 78 The splendour of the wrinkled lapis lazuli sea. **1896** G. M. STISTED *Life R. F. Burton* xi. 169 The water .. was of a deep lapis lazuli blue.

lapist, variant of LAPISE *v. Obs.*

Lapith (ˈlæpɪθ). *Gr. Mythol.* Pl. **Lapithæ, Lapiths.** [f. L. *Lapithæ*, ad. Gr. Λαπίθαι.] One of the Lapithæ, a people of Thessaly, celebrated for their wars with the Centaurs.

1607 TOPSELL *Foure-f. Beasts* 504 The fight betwixt the Lapithæ and the Centaurs. **1611** CORYAT *Crudities* sig. C8 Amongst the woers of Penelope themselues, amongst the huge bolles of the Lapithæ. *a* **1846** [see HELLENIAN *sb.*]. **1874** *Guide Græco-Roman Sculptures Dept. Greek & Roman Antiquities Brit. Mus.* I. 57 One of the Centaurs .. attacked by Lapiths while carrying off Greek women. **1883** A. S. MURRAY *Hist. Greek Sculpture* II. 55 The Lapiths are youthful, beardless, slim, but firmly knit. **1886** *Guide Exhib. Galleries Brit. Mus.* 77 Sepulchral urn. On the front a Centaur carrying off a female Lapith. **1949** *Oxf. Classical Dict.* 179/2 The fight [*sc.* of the Centaurs] with the Lapiths occurs on the famous François vase and in sculpture on the pediment of the temple of Zeus in Olympia. **1968** *New Larousse Encycl. Mythol.* (new ed.) 169/2 (*caption*) A Centaur struggles with a Lapith at the wedding feast of King Peirithous.

Laplace (laplas). The name of Pierre Simon, Marquis de *Laplace* (1749–1827), French astronomer and mathematician. **a.** Used *attrib.* and in the possessive to designate various concepts and mathematical expressions devised by him or arising out of his work, as †**Laplace's coefficient**, a Legendre polynomial; **Laplace's equation**, the equation $\nabla^2 V = 0$, esp. its representation in Cartesian co-ordinates,

$$\frac{\partial^2 V}{\partial x^2} + \frac{\partial^2 V}{\partial y^2} + \frac{\partial^2 V}{\partial z^2} = 0,$$

where V is a function of x, y, and z; **Laplace('s) operator** = LAPLACIAN *sb.*; **Laplace transform**, a function $f(x)$ related to a given function $g(t)$ by the equation $f(x) = \int_0^\infty \exp(-xt)\, g(t)dt$; so **Laplace transformation**, the transformation by which $f(x)$ is obtained from $g(t)$.

1845 F. LUNN in *Encycl. Metrop.* IV. 144 If f be the distance of the differential particle dm from the attracted particle V = $\int dm/f$. We have now to find the quantity V; this we shall do by expanding it into a series, the coefficients of which have peculiar properties, depending upon a partial differential equation to which they are subject... We shall .. distinguish them by that [*sc.* name] of their illustrious inventor, calling the differential equation and the coefficients .. Laplace's equation, and Laplace's coefficients. **1873** J. C. MAXWELL *Treat. Electr. & Magn.* II. I. ix. 162 The theory of spherical harmonics was first given by Laplace in the third book of his *Mécanique Celeste.* The harmonics themselves are therefore often called Laplace's Coefficients. *Ibid.* 164 It is shewn in treatises on Laplace's Coefficients that Q_i is the coefficient of h^i in the expansion of $(1 - 2\mu h + h^2)^{-1/2}$. **1812** *Phil. Trans. R. Soc.* CII. 31 It is exclusively confined to that class of spheroids which, while they differ from spheres, likewise have their radii expressed by rational and integral functions of a point in the surface of a sphere: in this hypothesis Laplace's equation has been rigorously demonstrated. **1813** *Phil. Mag.* XLI. 9 In Laplace's equation $(d^2V/dx^2) + (d^2V/dy^2) + (d^2V/dz^2) = 0$, .. V is a function of x, y, and z. **1962** CORSON & LORRAIN *Introd. Electromagn. Fields* ii. 36 If we introduce into Eq. 2–23 the electrostatic potential V, .. $\nabla^2 V = -\rho/\epsilon_0$. This is Poisson's equation. In a region of the field where the charge density ρ is zero, $\nabla^2 V = 0$, which is Laplace's equation. *Ibid.* iv. 154 Certain cases of symmetry are best treated in spherical polar coordinates. Laplace's equation then takes the form

$$\nabla^2 V = \frac{1}{r^2}\frac{\partial}{\partial r}\left(r^2 \frac{\partial V}{\partial r}\right) + \frac{1}{r^2 \sin\theta}\frac{\partial}{\partial\theta}\left(\sin\theta \frac{\partial V}{\partial\theta}\right) + \frac{1}{r^2 \sin\theta}\frac{\partial^2 V}{\partial\phi^2} = 0.$$

1873 J. C. MAXWELL *Treat. Electr. & Magn.* I. 29 One of the most remarkable properties of the operator ∇ is that when repeated it becomes $\nabla^2 = -(d^2/dx^2 + d^2/dy^2 + d^2/dz^2)$, an operator occurring in all parts of Physics, which we may refer to as Laplace's Operator. **1935**, **1936** Laplace operator [see LAPLACIAN *sb.*]. **1944** T. H. TURNEY *Heaviside's Operational Calculus made Easy* vii. 84 (*heading*) The Laplace transform method of circuit analysis. **1962** D. R. COX *Renewal Theory* i. 3 One of the main mathematical tools used in renewal theory is the Laplace transform. **1949** S. GOLDMAN *Transformation Calculus* iii. 57 The Laplace transformation transforms $f(t)$, a function of t, into $F(s)$, a function of some new variable s. **1956** *Nature* 21 Jan. 106/2 The approach is mathematical and based throughout on the use of the Laplace transformation. The book is .. intended .. as a supplement to introductory text-books on feedback systems and on the functions of a complex variable.

b. *Philos.* Used in the possessive to designate an imaginary intelligence described by him which, given the values at any instant of certain physical quantities for all the particles in the universe, could predict in detail the whole of the future from the laws of physics.

1911 J. WARD *Realm of Ends* i. 17 The omniscience of Laplace's imaginary spirit with its completed world-formula. **1947** H. REICHENBACH *Elem. Symbolic Logic* viii. 390 Such verification may be technically impossible, although in principle it should be possible to foretell the results of a throw of a die from the initial conditions, given the position of the die, the physiological status of the person considered, and other factors. Let us say that Laplace's superman could do it. **1965** P. CAWS *Philos. of Sci.* xxxix. 300 This intelligence has been called 'Laplace's demon', and it has become the patron saint of determinism.

Laplacian (laˈplasɪən), *a.* and *sb.* Also **Laplacean** (*rare* in the physical sciences). [f. LAPLACE + -IAN.] **A.** *adj.* Of or pertaining to Laplace; originating with Laplace.

1836 *Rep. Brit. Assoc. Adv. Sci. 1835* 27 M. Poisson, indeed, carries much further than Laplace himself the Laplacian views of molecular action. **1852** *Cambr. & Dublin Math. Jrnl.* VII. 127 The class of partial differential equations to which the Laplacian equation belongs. **1881** MAXWELL *Electr. & Magn.* I. 117 When we have to specify a distribution [of electricity] which is at once irrotational and solenoidal, we shall call it a Laplacian distribution; Laplace having pointed out some of the most important properties of such a distribution. **1908** *Westm. Gaz.* 21 Feb. 2/1 According to the Laplacian hypothesis no 'month' can be shorter than the corresponding day [of the parent planet]. **1911** J. WARD *Realm of Ends* i. 15 Laplace, brushing aside freewill as a palpable illusion, proclaimed the implicit omniscience of the mechanical theory. [*Note*] It was reserved for Clerk Maxwell to point out clearly the inevitable limitation of the Laplacean data. **1920** S. ALEXANDER *Space, Time, & Deity* II. 328 The famous puzzle of the Laplacean calculator is full of confusions but contains a truth. A person who knows the whole state of the universe at any moment can calculate, so it urges, the whole future. **1929** V. BUSH *Operational Circuit Analysis* x. 184

$$f(\omega)/\omega = \int_0^\infty e^{-\omega\lambda} A(\lambda)d\lambda.$$

.. In an expression of this sort $f(\omega)/\omega$ is called the Laplacian transform of A. **1936** P. M. MORSE *Vibration & Sound* v. 136 Writing the wave equation as $\nabla^2\eta = (\partial^2\eta/\partial t^2)/c^2$ where the symbol ∇^2 is called the Laplacian operator, or simply the Laplacian. It stands for the operation of finding the bulginess of the surface at some point. **1962** SIMPSON & RICHARDS *Physical Princ. Junction Transistors* 468 In these [equations] ∇, $\nabla.$, and ∇^2 are symbols for the gradient, divergence, and Laplacian operators. **1971** I. G. GASS et al. *Understanding Earth* iii. 64/2 The planets have only 0·1% of the mass of the solar system, but 98% of .. the energy of angular momentum. From the Laplacian hypothesis [of their origin] the Sun would be expected to have much more angular momentum. **1972** J. RAWLS *Theory of Justice* §28. 171 They must follow what some may have called the Laplacean rule for choice under uncertainty. The possibilities are identified in some natural way and each assigned the same likelihood.

B. *sb.* The Laplacian operator, i.e. the differential operator ∇^2 ('del squared') that occurs in Laplace's equation.

1935 PAULING & WILSON *Introd. Quantum Mech.* iv. 85 This [Schrödinger] equation is often written as

$$\frac{-h^2}{8\pi^2}\sum_{i=1}^{N}\frac{1}{m_i}\nabla_i^2\Psi + V\Psi = -\frac{h}{2\pi i}\frac{\partial\Psi}{\partial t},$$

in which ∇_i^2 is the Laplace operator or Laplacian for the ith particle. **1936** P. M. MORSE *Vibration & Sound* vii. 232 We can write the wave equation as $\nabla^2 p = (\partial^2 p/\partial t^2)/c^2$... The operator ∇^2 is called the Laplace operator, or the Laplacian: it measures the concentration of a quantity (or, rather, the negative of the concentration). The value of $\nabla^2 p$ at a point is proportional to the difference between the average pressure near a point and the pressure right at the point. **1962** CORSON & LORRAIN *Introd. Electromagn. Fields* i. 17 The product $\nabla.\nabla f$ is commonly abbreviated to $\nabla^2 f$, and the operator ∇^2 is called the Laplacian.

Lapland (ˈlæplənd, -lænd). [a. Sw. *Lappland*: see LAPP and LAND.] **1. a.** The region which forms the most northerly portion of the Scandinavian peninsula, now divided politically between Finland, Norway, Sweden, and the Soviet Union.

Formerly, the fabled home of witches and magicians, who had power to send winds and tempests. Freq. *attrib.*, as ***Lapland witch, giant***, etc.

c **1590** MARLOWE *Faustus* I. i, Like .. Lapland Gyants, trotting by our sides. **1621** BURTON *Anat. Mel.* I. ii. I. ii. 63 And nothing so familiar .. as for Witches and Sorcerers, in Lapland, Lituania, and all ouer Scandia, to sell winds to Marriners, and cause tempests. **1636** SHIRLEY *Duke's Mistr.* II. i. (1638) C 4 b, I .. dare Encounter with an armie out of Lapland. **1640** HABINGTON *Q. of Arragon* I. i, Your Lordship then Shall walke as safe, as if a Lapland witch .. preserv'd you shot-free. **1668** DRYDEN *Even. Love* II. (1671) 26 Not a Ship shall pass out from any Port, but shall ask thee for a wind; thou shalt have all the trade of Lapland within a month. **1679** OLDHAM *Sat. Jesuits* III. (1685) 55 How travelling Saints, well mounted on a Switch, Ride Journeys thro' the Air, like Lapland Witch. **1695** CONGREVE *Love for love* III. 42 Marry thee! Oons I'll Marry a Lapland Witch as

soon, and live upon selling of contrary Winds, and Wrack'd Vessels. **1725** RAMSAY *Gent. Sheph.* II. ii, Lapland clay, Mixt with the venom of black taids and snakes. **1802** WORDSW. '*Dear Child of Nature*', An old age, serene and bright And lovely as a Lapland night.

†**b.** A native of this region; a Lapland witch.

1634 T. HEYWOOD *Lanc. Witches* v. K, Then to work, to work my pretty Laplands: Pinch, here, scratch. **1635** —— *Hierarch.* VIII. 506 The Finnes and Laplands are acquainted well With such like Sp'rits, and Windes to Merchants sell.

2. **Lapland bunting**, a northern species of bunting, *Calcarius lapponicus*.

1862 [see LARK *sb.*[1] 2]. **1912** W. E. CLARKE *Stud. Bird Migration* II. xxiv. 268 Lapland bunting, *Calcarius lapponicus.*—Since our discovery of this species, Eilean Mor has been visited annually. **1953** D. A. BANNERMAN *Birds Brit. Isles* I. 313 The Lapland bunting was added to the British list in 1826, when Selby described an example sent from Cambridgeshire to Leadenhall Market. **1971** *Country Life* 9 Sept. 616/2 Rare visitors [in Yorkshire]..such as.. Lapland Bunting.

Laplander (ˈlæpləndə(r), -lændə(r)). [f. prec. + -ER[1].] An inhabitant of Lapland; a Lapp.

1637 SHIRLEY *Yng. Admirall* IV. G 2 Great Lady of the Laplanders. **1647** *Case Kingd.* 10 As if they ment to imprison Æolus..in a bagge (as tis said of the Laplanders). **1712** SWIFT *Jrnl. to Stella* 17 June, Can I help wind and weather? am I a Laplander? am I a witch? **1778** ABIGAIL ADAMS in *J. Adams' Fam. Lett.* (1876) 343 By Heaven, if you could, you have changed hearts with some frozen Laplander. **1839** E. D. CLARKE *Trav. Russia* 52/1 Others.. were smoking..much after the manner of Laplanders.

So **Lapˈlandian, Lapˈlandic, ˈLaplandish** *adjs.*, of or pertaining to Lapland, its people, or their language.

a **1711** KEN *Edmund* I. Wks. 1721 II. 10 To a delusive Banquet, I last Night Sent, the Laplandian Witches to invite. **1796** MORSE *Amer. Geog.* II. 54 The Laplandic grammar of Mr. Lindahl. **1881** *Med. Temp. Jrnl.* XLVII. 167 A steady diminution of the population of the Laplandish part of Norrland commenced in 1825.

lap-lap (ˈlæpˈlæp), *sb.* [Echoic reduplication of LAP *sb.*[2] 3.] A frequently reiterated sound of lapping. Also *attrib.* Hence **lap-lap** *v. intr.*

1834 M. SCOTT *Cruise Midge* (1863) 60 The rushing water ..lap-lapping against our bows. **18..** *Cornh. Mag.* (Ogilv.), There was nothing to be heard but the faint lap-lap of the water against the pier. **1890** W. J. GORDON *Foundry* 164 Yarn is being rinsed on square spindles that jerk it with a curious lap-lap motion as they turn it round and round, sunk to half its length in the water.

‖**laplap, lap-lap** (ˈlæplæp), *sb.*[2] [Local word.] In New Guinea, a loin-cloth.

1930 M. MEAD *Growing up in New Guinea* xi. 191 A gorgeous new *laplap* proclaims his special state. **1957** O. RUHEN in B. James *Austral. Short Stories* (1963) 197 They were not bush natives, because all three wore cloth lap-laps. **1967** 'E. LINDALL' *Time too Soon* i. 3 A couple of policemen, militarily smart in their new uniforms... Earlier they had worn dark blue *laplaps.* **1973** *Sunday Times* (Colour Suppl.) 10 June 51/3 When Michael Somare walked through the bar of a Bougainville motel..he heard himself described as a 'bush kanaka in a lap-lap'.

†ˈ**lapling.** *Obs.* [f. LAP *sb.*[1] + -LING.] One who loves to lie on a (lady's) lap.

1627–77 FELTHAM *Resolves* I. lviii. 90 He might have swam in Gold, and liv'd a lapling to the silk and dainties. **1658** HEWYTT *Last Serm.* 7 You must not stream out your Youth in Wine and live a Lapling to the Silk and Dainties.

laplolly, obs. form of LOBLOLLY.

Laponian, variant of LAPPONIAN.

Lapp (læp), *sb.* and *a.* [a. Sw. *Lapp*, possibly in origin a term of contempt: cf. MHG. *lappe* simpleton. In med.L. the name was *Lap(p)o* (pl. *Lap(p)ones*), whence F. *Lapon*; see LAPPONIC.] **A.** *sb.* One of a nomadic people (called by themselves *Sabme*), inhabiting the north of Scandinavia. **B.** *adj.* Pertaining to this race, Lappish; also *absol.* the Lappish language.

1859 T. S. HENDERSON *Mem. E. Henderson* II. 64 The huts where a party of Lapps were located. **1879** J. A. H. MURRAY *Addr. Philol. Soc.* 46 Used in several cases as a supine in Finn and Lapp.

‖**lappa** (ˈlæpə). *W. Afr.* [Hausa.] A woman's shawl or skirt.

1954 E. WARNER *Trial by Sasswood* (1955) iv. 68 Gloriously decked out from the waist down in a bright new golden wrap-around *lappa*. **1957** M. BANTON *W. Afr. City* ix. 173 A woman may dance with two or three trilby hats on her head and a man with a woman's *lappa* or shawl, round his shoulders. **1966** C. ACHEBE *Man of People* ix. 100 She rubbed her eyes with a corner of her lappa and blew her nose into it.

†**laˈppacean**, *a. Obs. rare*[−0]. [f. L. *lappāce-us* (f. *lappa* a bur) + -AN.] = next.

1656 BLOUNT *Glossogr.*, Lappacean, of or like a bur.

lappaceous (læˈpeɪʃəs), *a. Bot.* [f. as prec. + -OUS.] Of, pertaining to, or resembling a bur.

1707 SLOANE *Jamaica* 38 To which follows several large rough lappaceous or echinated seeds. **1866** *Treas. Bot.* 660/1 *Lappaceous*, having the appearance of a *lappa* or bur; that is to say, of a round body covered with small hooks.

lapped (læpt), *ppl. a.* [f. LAP *v.*[2] + -ED[1].] In senses of the vb. †**a.** Wrapped up, disguised. **b.** *fig.* Lulled. **c.** Formed with, or arranged so as to form a lap or laps.

1637 GILLESPIE *Eng. Pop. Cerem.* Ep. A ij b, The lapped Nicodemite, holdes it enough to yeeld some secret assent to the trueth. **1825** J. NICHOLSON *Operat. Mechanic* 589 Fig. 602, lapped and tongued mitre. **1850** S. DOBELL *Roman* viii. Poet. Wks. 1875 I. 161/2 The lapp'd sense in soft confusion own'd Redolent light. **1869** SIR E. REED *Shipbuild.* i. §7 The plating of the bottom was made flush from this point to above the turn of the bilge, by plates worked between the lapped edges of the outer over-lapping plates of the bottom. **1894** J. E. DAVIS *Elem. Mod. Dressmaking* iv. 83 Where the back basque of the bodice is box-pleated, full in any way, or has a lapped centre seam, and is not sewn together much below the waist. **1964** *McCall's Sewing* ix. 130/2 *Single lapped seam.* This seam is used for joining seams in interfacings and interlinings because it gives the least possible bulk.

lappel, variant of LAPEL.

lapper[1] (ˈlæpə(r)). [f. LAP *v.*[1] + -ER[1].] One who laps, or takes up (liquid) with the tongue.

1606 J. CARPENTER *Solomon's Solace* vii. 28 Those doggish lappers, and those faint hearted dastardes. **1826** KIRBY & SP. *Entomol.* III. 418 The great majority of the Hymenoptera order..though furnished with mandibles and maxillæ, never use them for mastication, but really lap their food with their tongue: these therefore might be denominated *lappers.* **1827** *Blackw. Mag.* XXII. 470 The pupils of the modern school discover in him but the crafty, cruel, and cowardly lapper of blood.

lapper[2] (ˈlæpə(r)). [f. LAP *v.*[2] + -ER[1].]

1. One who laps or folds up (linen).

1732 SWIFT *Consid. Two Bills* Pr. Wks. 1898 III. 269 They may be lappers of linen, bailiffs of the manor, they may let blood [etc.]. **1891** *Labour Commission* Gloss., *Lappers*, male operatives who fold into shape for the market the various fabrics that are manufactured in the textile industry. **1893** *Star* 29 Apr. 2/6 The trade of the linen lapper consists in measuring the goods and folding them for the different markets.

2. = *lapping-machine* (see LAPPING *vbl. sb.*[2] 3). In some mod. Dicts.

lapper[3] (ˈlæpə(r)). [f. LAP *v.*[4] + -ER[1].] One who uses a lap or lapidary's wheel.

1877 GEE *Pract. Gold-worker* 178 The lapper produces the plain and diamond-shaped surfaces by the rotary action of the lapidary's wheel. **1896** *Mod. Advt.*, Lapper wanted, to fill in spare time with polishing.

lapper: see LOPPER.

lappet (ˈlæpɪt), *sb.* Also 7–8 lappit. [f. LAP *sb.*[1] + -ET[1].]

1. a. A loose or overlapping part of a garment, forming a flap or fold.

1573 TWYNE *Æneid* XI. Kk j b, The yelowish silken weed, ..Whose lappets ratling large in knot of costly gold were tyde. **1676** GREW *Anat. Flowers* i. §3 (1682) 164 Or as Taylors use to split their Stomachers into several Lappets, to spread. **1734** tr. *Rollin's Anc. Hist.* (1827) II. II. 85 He threw out of the lappet of his robe, in the midst of the senate, some African figs. **1866** J. G. MURPHY *Comm. Ex.* xxviii. 8 It was a shoulder-piece..or single lappet covering the back and reaching under the arm.

b. *gen.* A part of anything that hangs loose; a flap; a key-hole guard.

1677 *Lond. Gaz.* No. 1215/4 Lost in Easter Term 1676, an Almanack bound with red Leather with a Lappet tyed over with a red Ribon. **1780** *Phil. Trans.* LXX. App. 32, I.. covered everything well with the lappets of the rag. **1867** J. HOGG *Microsc.* I. iii. 174 The little lappet of tin-foil can be so doubled as to shorten the aperture. **1885** C. GIBBON *Hard Knot* I. xv. 212 He closed the door,..bolted it, and drew the porcelain 'lappet' over the key-hole.

2. a. A fold or pendent piece of flesh, skin, membrane, etc. (cf. LAP *sb.*[1] 2).

1605 TIMME *Quersit.* I. xiii. 66 The salts of mynt and worme-wood are good to purge the lappets and tunicles of the stomach. **1705** PETIVER in *Phil. Trans.* XXV. 1955 A thin furrowed lappet exerts itself near ½ of an inch from the side of the Shell. **1826** KIRBY & SP. *Entomol.* III. 446 Slender *laciniæ* or lappets fringed with hair. **1861** J. R. GREENE *Man. Anim. Kingd., Cælent.* 218 The apical appendages, or lappets, of some *Beroidæ*. **1865** JEFFREYS *Brit. Conchol.* III. 320 Mantle thin and semitransparent,..lappets large in proportion, forming two saucer-shaped lobes, one on each side of the tentacles. **1871** DARWIN *Desc. Man* II. viii. 72 The fleshy appendages about the head of the male Tragopan pheasant swell into a large lappet on the throat.

b. A lobe of the ear, liver, lungs, etc.

1609 HOLLAND *Amm. Marcell.* XXV. iii. 264 An horsemans jauelin..stucke fast in the neather lappet or fillet of his liuer. **1628** LE GRYS tr. *Barclay's Argenis* 91 The naturall order being broken the lappets of it [the liuer] did appeare out of their owne place. **1650** BULWER *Anthropomet.* 95 The Malabars both men and women, the lappets of their Eares are open. *a* **1693** *Urquhart's Rabelais* III. iv. 49 The Lights never cease with its Lappets and Bellows to cool and refresh it [the Blood]. **1727** A. HAMILTON *New Acc. E. Ind.* II. xxxvii. 56 Their Ears large, and the Lappets very thick. **1870** ROLLESTON *Anim. Life* 52 A triangular lappet, the so-called 'columellar lobule'.

3. The flap or skirt (of a coat). Also, the lapel.

1726 SWIFT *Gulliver* II. i. 100 Lifting up the lappet of his coat. **1812** J. HENRY *Camp. agst. Quebec* 142 He had no pockets to this coat, unless you may call the flannel such which interiorly lined the lappets. **1843** BORROW *Bible in Spain* 324 A grey kerseymere coat with short lappets. **1883** D. C. MURRAY *Hearts* I. 3 Laying hold of him by the lappet of the coat.

4. An appendage or pendant to head-gear of any kind; esp. one of the streamers attached to a lady's head-dress. Also, in clerical attire, = BAND *sb.*[3] 4 b.

c **1720** DUKE OF MONTAGU in *Buccleuch MSS.* (Hist. MSS. Comm.) I. 367 Four pinners with..eight lappets hanging down behind. **1781** GIBBON *Decl. & F.* III. liii. 297 Two strings or lappets of pearl depended on either cheek. **1787** J. KING *Bath Rules* in *Guide Water. Places* (1806) 30, 3dly, That ladies who intend dancing minuets do wear lappets. **1851** LAYARD *Pop. Acc. Discov. Nineveh* xiii. 324 With the addition of lappets falling over the ears. **1863** GEO. ELIOT *Romola* x, The black cloth berretta, or simple cap with upturned lappet. **1869** E. A. PARKES *Pract. Hygiene* (ed. 3) 401 A sealskin cap with ear lappets. **1869** *Daily News* 30 Jan., He wore the black gown and white lappets of the church of England. **1876** HUMPHREYS *Coin Coll. Man.* xii. 147 A kind of tiara, with a singular striped or plaited lappet falling down at the back. **1879** 'HESBA STRETTON' *Thro. Needle's Eye* I. 151 Mrs. H...tossed the long lappets of her lace cap behind her shoulders.

transf. **1601** HOLLAND *Pliny* I. 229 They [goats] have two lappets, locks or plaits as it were of haire, hanging downe along their bodie on either side from their neck.

5. Short for *lappet-moth*.

1857 STAINTON *Brit. Butterflies & Moths* I. 157 *Gastropacha quercifolia* (Lappet). **1862** E. NEWMAN *Brit. Moths* (1869) 45 The Lappet (*Lasiocampa quercifolia*). *Ibid.* 46 The Small Lappet (*Lasiocampa ilicifolia*).

6. *Weaving.* **a.** A figure produced on cloth during lappet-weaving; also, cloth bearing such figures, lappet-cloth.

1863 J. WATSON *Theory & Pract. Art of Weaving* vi. 207 The framing of a power-loom for weaving Lappets is nearly the same as the framing of one for plain cloth. *Ibid.* 227 In working lappets with the jacquard machine, the length of the figure will depend upon the number of cards used. **1884** *Encycl. Brit.* XVII. 109/2 For window-curtains, hangings, &c., there are manufactured harness and book muslins, lenos, sprigs, spots, and lappets. **1920** R. BEAUMONT *Union Textile Fabrication* ix. 304 Combinations of Lappet and Gauze.—Pattern origination in gauze, lappet, and plain or straight weaving, provides for additional changes in the materials of which the yarns are spun. The lappet (dark sections in Fig. 187) being a surface warp yarn is quite a supplementary element. **1957** *Encycl. Brit.* XXIII. 460/2 Crossed Weaving.—This group includes all fabrics, such as gauzes, in which the warp threads intertwist amongst themselves to give intermediate effects between ordinary weaving and lace. Also those, such as Lappets, in which some warp threads are laid transversely..to imitate embroidery.

b. A mechanism for producing the figures in lappet-weaving.

1894 T. W. FOX *Mechanism of Weaving* IX. 250 Elaborate figures are beyond the range of lappets, still there are many small effects that can be economically woven by them. **1924** W. P. CRANKSHAW *Weaving* xi. 121 Lappets, Swivels, Smallwares and Warp Piles... Lappet and swivel mechanisms are used to produce effects which resemble those obtained by embroidery. **1927** T. THORNLEY *Cotton Spinning* (ed. 4) ix. 311 (*heading*) The lappets or thread boards and wires. *Ibid.*, During recent years metal thread lappets have become very largely used, being much less likely to warp, become damaged or to lose concentricity with the spindles although the first cost of metal lappets is greater than wood ones.

7. *attrib.* and *Comb.* in words denoting products of or appliances for *lappet-weaving* (see below), as ***lappet-cloth, -frame, -lay, -loom, -muslin, -needle, -wheel.*** Also **lappet-end**, the free end of a lappet of lace, etc., often highly ornamented; †**lappet-head**, a head-dress provided with lappets (see LAPPETED *ppl. a.*); **lappet-moth**, one of several species of bombycid moths; **lappet-weaving**, a method of weaving by which figures are produced on the surface of cloth by means of needles placed in a sliding frame.

1863 J. WATSON *Art Weaving* 206 The ground of *lappet cloth may be either plain texture or gauze. **1880** *Art Jrnl.* Jan. 8/2 Designs..for Lace *Lappet Ends. **1878** A. BARLOW *Weaving* xvi. 189 Fig. 193..represents..the *lappet frame with four needles only fitted to a loom. **1759** GOLDSM. *Mem. Voltaire* (Globe) 500/1 He beheld his ugly friend, dressed up in a *lappet-head and petticoat, approach to salute him. **1781** COWPER *Truth* 139 She sails with lappet-head and mincing airs Duly at chink of bell to morning prayers. **1863** J. WATSON *Art Weaving* 211 The *Lappet Lay for a power-loom is similar in many respects to a common lay. *Ibid.* 215 *Lappet looms. **1816** KIRBY & SP. *Entomol.* (1818) II. xxi. 222 One of our largest moths—called by collectors the *Lappet-moth. **1882** *Cassell's Nat. Hist.* VI. 62 The Lappet Moth (*Gastropacha quercifolia*)..may be known by its reddish-brown dentated wings. **1858** SIMMONDS *Dict. Trade.*, **Lappet-muslin*, a white or coloured, sprigged or striped muslin for dresses, &c. **1863** J. WATSON *Art Weaving* 211 *Lappet needles are made from brass or iron wire. *Ibid.* 205 So *lappet weaving is just to make representations of different kinds of flowers, birds, and other things, on the surface of woven cloth. *Ibid.* 218 The *lappet wheel requires to be moved one tooth every second shot.

lappet (ˈlæpɪt), *v.* [f. prec. sb.] *trans.* To cover with, or as with a lappet.

1864 WEBSTER (citing LANDOR). Hence in mod. Dicts.

lappeted (ˈlæpɪtɪd), *ppl. a.* [f. LAPPET *sb.* + -ED[2].] Of a person: Wearing lappets. Of a head-dress: Provided with lappets.

1797–1805 S. & HT. LEE *Canterb. T.* V. 177 Her defection was lamented by her lappetted, rouged and titled friends. **1804** *Europ. Mag.* XLV. 330/1 The Lady had on..a double lappetted head. **1824** MISS MITFORD *Village* Ser. I. 37 The towering lappeted cap. **1884** *Mag. Art* Jan. 104 A well-dressed woman, in..a lappeted head-dress.

lappewincke, -winke, etc. obs. ff. LAPWING.

†**Lappian.** *Obs.* [f. LAPP + -IAN.] A Lapp or Laplander.
1599 ABBOT *Descr. World* (1634) 61 Damianus a Goes hath written a pretty Treatise describing the manners of those Lappians.

Lappic ('læpɪk), *a.* (*sb.*) [f. LAPP + -IC.] Pertaining to the Lapps. Also *absol.* the Lappic language. (Ogilvie.)

lappie ('læpɪ). *S. Afr.* Also formerly **lapje.** [Afrikaans *lappie* (formerly *lapje*).] A dishcloth, a small rag.
1892 J. WIDDICOMBE *Fourteen Yrs. in Basutoland* vi. 106, I kept them rolled up in a *lappie* (old piece of rag). **1900** B. M. HICKS *Cape as I found It* x. 179 The dish-cloth is a great institution in the Boer household. A dirty bit of 'lapje' (rag) it is. **1926** E. LEWIS *Mantis* IV. xiv. 208 Pouring out a saucerful of water and using his handkerchief for a 'lappie' as he called it, he cleaned the cup. **1939** S. CLOETE *Watch for Dawn* 325 It was a beautiful little dress..and Kaspar never gave back the lappie in which it was wrapped. **1970** *Cape Times* 16 Sept. 7/6 There had been 'dramatic evidence about the finding of the *lappie* and the hair stuck in the middle'.

lapping ('læpɪŋ), *vbl. sb.*^{1} [f. LAP *v.*^{1} + -ING^{1}.] The action of LAP *v.*^{1} in various senses.
1. Taking up liquid with the tongue.
? *a* **1400** *Morte Arth.* 3236 Alle fore lapynge of blude of my lele knyghtez. *c* **1440** *Promp. Parv.* 287/2 Lappynge of howndys, *lambitus.* **1611** COTGR., *Lappement*, a lapping, or licking vp.
2. Of water: Breaking gently against a solid body.
1855 LONGF. *Hiaw.* III. 100 The little Hiawatha..heard the lapping of the water. **1867** SMYTH *Sailor's Word-bk.*, *Lapping*, the undulations occasioned in the waves by the paddle-wheels of a steam-boat. **1876** MISS BRADDON *J. Haggard's Dau.* III. 19 The gentle lapping of summer waves upon the pebbly beach. **1884** *Harper's Mag.* Aug. 392/2 The gentle lapping of the wavelets.

lapping ('læpɪŋ), *vbl. sb.*^{2} [f. LAP *v.*^{2} + -ING^{1}.] The action of LAP *v.*^{2} in various senses.
†**1.** The action of wrapping up in something; in quots. *concr.* A wrapping; trappings, wraps. **b.** Folding (in the arms); embracing; also caressing, fondling. **c.** Winding *up* (of a matter). *Obs.*
c **1380** WYCLIF *Sel. Wks.* III. 28 þou reftist him al þe lappinge of pride and ipocrisie. *c* **1400** *Destr. Troy* 476 So luffly, so lykyng with lapping in armys. *c* **1440** *Promp. Parv.* 515/2 Wappynge, happynge or hyllynge (*S.* lappynge). **1549** LATIMER *4th Serm. bef. Edw. VI* (Arb.) 122 There is not a more comfortable lesson in all the scripture, then here now in the lappyng vp of the matter. **1627–77** FELTHAM *Resolves* I. xxxi. 54 The loving part in her, wanted an object; so play, and lapping of it [her dog], made her place it there. **1762–71** H. WALPOLE *Vertue's Anecd. Paint.* (1786) IV. 3 As those casual lappings and flowing streamers were imitated from nothing.
d. *concr.* (See quot.)
1858 SIMMONDS *Dict. Trade*, *Lapping*, a kind of machine blanket or wrapping material, used by calico-printers, &c., and made either plain, twilled, or fine.
2. The action of causing one thing to lap *over* another; the condition of being so placed. Also *concr.* the part that laps over.
1607 MARKHAM *Caval.* II. (1617) 173 Which indeede importes a lapping or folding ouer of the outmost legge ouer the inmost. **1678** MOXON *Mech. Exerc.* 67 Two Boards are thus lapped on the edges over one another, this lapping over is called Rabbetting. **1703** T. N. *City & C. Purchaser* 146 Gain..is..us'd for the lapping of the end of the Joyst, &c. upon a Trimmer or Girder. **1867** SMYTH *Sailor's Word-bk.*, s.v., In the polar seas, lapping applies to the young or thin ice, one plate overlapping another.
3. The process of forming into laps; *attrib.* in ***lapping cylinder, machine*** (cf. LAP *sb.*^{3} 6).
1825 J. NICHOLSON *Operat. Mechanic* 381 The doffing-plate continually strips the doffer cylinder of the carded cotton, which it delivers upon the lapping cylinder in one continuous web of about 18 inches wide. **1851** L. D. B. GORDON in *Art Jrnl. Illustr. Catal.* p. iv**/1 The web of cleaned cotton..is passed through a lapping machine.

lapping ('læpɪŋ), *vbl. sb.*^{3} [f. LAP *v.*^{4}] **a.** The action or process of grinding or polishing on a 'lap'. Also *attrib.*, as ***lapping machine, plate.***
1877 GEE *Pract. Gold-worker* 178 Lapping..is a distinct process of finishing jewellery. **1879** *Cassell's Techn. Educ.* IV. 350/2 'Lapping'..consists in grinding small facets such as those cut on a diamond to bring up its lustre, and which are cut on the gold for the same reason. **1886** WALSINGHAM & PAYNE-GALLWEY *Shooting* I. iv. 69 A barrel..undergoes three distinct stages, viz.: rough-boring; fine-boring; and polishing or lapping. **1907** J. V. WOODWORTH *Grinding & Lapping* II. 65 (*caption*) Flat cast iron lapping plate. *Ibid.* 68 For lapping small thread gages a lapping machine was constructed. **1935** H. J. DAVIES *Precision Workshop Methods* xiii. 242 The general effect produced by lapping is to remove the crests of a ground surface down to the bases of the intervening hollows. **1950** C. R. HINE *Machine Tools for Engineers* xii. 241 Rough lapping may remove as much as 0·003 in., and finish-lapping as little as 0·0001 in... Commercial lapping operations can produce parts to limits of 0·000025 in. **1950** W. COOPER in A. W. Judge *Grinding, Lapping & Polishing* II. vi. 201 The Newall 10U Universal Lapping Machine..is a type employed..for lapping anvils and parts of gauges and the locating rollers of their jig-borers and measuring machines. **1971** B. SCHARF *Engin. & its Lang.* x. 94 Lapping is regularly used in order to finish gear teeth, plug gauges,..straight surfaces, etc.
b. lapping in, the action of grinding in a valve (see GRIND *v.*^{1} 5 b).
1921 *Daily Colonist* (Victoria, B.C.) 12 Oct. 6/1 (Advt.), The quick-seating feature of 'Burd's' Piston Rings enables them to be perfectly and quickly fitted to the engine wall. No slow, laborious 'lapping-in' is necessary. **1950** W. COOPER in A. W. Judge *Grinding, Lapping & Polishing* II. vi. 188 It has long been recognized by bearing and lubrication engineers that the 'lapping-in' method of bearing conditioning, by abrasive means, is the only sure and certain way to obtain best bearing performance and life.

lapping ('læpɪŋ), *ppl. a.*^{1} [f. LAP *v.*^{1} + -ING^{2}.]
1. That laps or takes up liquid with the tongue.
1398 TREVISA *Barth. De P.R.* XVIII. i. (1495) 742 Kynde ordenyth wysely in houndes and in other lappynge beestes tendre tonge longe and plyaunt.
transf. and *fig.* **1865** SWINBURNE *Ilicet* 80 Roses whose lips the flame has deadened Drink till the lapping leaves are reddened. **1871** ROSSETTI *Last Confess.* 349 The..flame.. has come to be The lapping blaze of hell's environment Whose tongues all bid the molten heart despair.
2. Of water, waves: Breaking gently on the shore, etc.; plashing softly.
1862 M. HOPKINS *Hawaii* 355 This Aphrodite stepping on shore from the lapping waters was instantly recognized as superlatively beautiful. **1873** BLACK *Pr. Thule* xxvii. 454 The yacht..was cutting her placid way through the lapping waves. **1894** GLADSTONE *Horace, Odes* III. xvii, Where lapping Liris pours His current on Marica's shores.

lapping ('læpɪŋ), *ppl. a.*^{2} [f. LAP *v.*^{2} + -ING^{2}.] In senses of the vb.
1703 T. N. *City & C. Purchaser* 195 He Soddereth the Lapping-sheet down to the other. **1839** URE *Dict. Arts* 215 To spread out the web as it is drawn over it by the rotation of the lapping roller. **1876** PREECE & SIVEWRIGHT *Telegraphy* 222 The lapping wire was destroyed.

lappise, variant of LAPISE *v. Obs.*

Lappish ('læpɪʃ), *a.* and *sb.* [f. LAPP + -ISH.] **A.** *adj.* Of or pertaining to the Lapps or their language. **B.** *sb.* The language of the Lapps.
1875 JEVONS *Money* iv. 20 Its equivalent in the kindred Lappish tongue. **1877** DAWSON *Orig. World* xiv. 299 The smaller or Lappish race. **1882–3** SCHAFF *Encycl. Relig. Knowl.* III. 2498/1 He..translated Luther's catechism into Lappish; wrote..a Lappish spelling-book [etc.]. **1897** *Saga-Bk. Viking Club* Jan. 344 Peter being a Finnish Lap spoke Kvænsk as well as Lappish.

lappit, obs. form of LAPPET.

†**lappoint.** *Obs. rare.* [Corruption of LAPWING. Minsheu (*Ductor in Ling.* 1617) gives *lapouin* as the Fr. name of the bird.] = LAPWING.
1584 R. SCOT *Discov. Witchcr.* XII. xviii. 268 The smoke of a lappoints fethers [renders *pennæ upupæ* in Wier] drieuth spirits awaie.

Lapponian (læ'pəʊnɪən), *a.* and *sb.* Also 8–9 **Laponian.** [ad. med.L. *Lap(p)ōn-em* (see LAPP) + -IAN.] **A.** *adj.* Of or pertaining to the Lapps, or their language. **B.** *sb.* A Lapp.
1607 TOPSELL *Four-f. Beasts* (1658) 459 There was a Lapponian which brought one of these into Germany. **1768** BEATTIE *Ministr.* I. lix, The chill Lapponian's dreary land. **1854** MACAULAY in Trevelyan *Life* (1876) II. 377, I amused myself with making out a Laponian New Testament by the help of a Norwegian Dictionary.
So **La'pponic,** *a.* [cf. F. *laponique.*] = prec. A.
1890 in WEBSTER.

Lapponoid ('læpənɔɪd), *a.* [ad. med.L. *Lap(p)ōn-em* (see LAPP *sb.* and *a.*) + -OID.] Descriptive of racial, particularly cranial, features associated with the early Lapp peoples.
[**1882** QUATREFAGES & HAMY *Crania Ethnica* I. iv. 142 Ce type *Laponoïde*, si l'on peut s'exprimer ainsi,.. se confond, suivant nous, avec celui qu'Eschricht, Masch et Nilsson ont les premiers fait connaître.] **1939** C. S. COON *Races of Europe* viii. 288 Czekanowski defines his Lapponoid in such a way as to include the Alpine of Ripley, as well as the Lapps proper. **1948** A. L. KROEBER *Anthropol.* (rev. ed.) iv. §71. 151 *Yellow Race.* Lapponoid: Enters into several European crossed races. **1957** V. G. CHILDE *Dawn European Civilization* (ed. 6) xi. 209 Most of the skulls from sites in North and Central Russia are described as Lapponoid.

†'**lappy,** *a. Obs. rare*$^{-1}$. [f. LAP *sb.*^{1} + -Y^{1}.] Resembling a lap or lobe.
1611 COTGR., *Lobeau*, a little lobe, lap, or lappie peece of.

†'**lapron.** *Sc. Obs.* Also 6 **laproun.** [ad. F. *lapereau, lapreau*, dim. of *lapin* rabbit.] A young rabbit.
1547 *Prices Provis.* in Maitland *Hist. Edin.* I. i. (1753) 13 The best Lapron 2^{d}. **1551** *Sc. Acts Mary* (1814) II. 484/1 Item the laproun .ij.*d. Ibid.* 486/2 That na maner of persoun tak vpone hand to slay ony Lapronis.

laps, obs. form of LAPSE.

lapsa'bility, lapsi'bility. ? *Obs.* [f. next: see -ITY.] Liability to err or fall.
1661 RUST *Let. conc. Origen* 48 Though they should through the lapsability of their nature fall from this eminent pitch of primitive felicity. **1678** CUDWORTH *Intell. Syst.* I. iv. §36. 565 It implieth imperfection—that is, peccability and lapsibility. **1682** H. MORE *Annot. Glanvill's Lux O.* 80 His humane nature being ever void of that lapsabilitie which is essential to humanitie.

lapsable, lapsible ('læpsəb(ə)l, -ɪb(ə)l), *a.* [f. L. types **lapsābilis*, **lapsibilis*, f. L. *lapsāre* (see LAPSE *v.*) or *laps-*, ppl. stem of *lābī* to fall, slip.]
1. Liable to pass or change; liable to err or fall. Const. *into.* ? *Obs.*
1678 CUDWORTH *Intell. Syst.* I. iv. §36. 565 No particular Created Spirits [are] absolutely in their own nature impeccable, but lapsible into vitious habits. *Ibid.* v. 793 The Former [Demons] are Lapsable, into Aereal Bodies only, and no further. **1702** *Pres. State Jacobitism* 26 Arguments for Compassion may be drawn from the lapsable Estate of Mankind.
2. *Law.* Liable to lapse or become forfeited.
1751 *Laws N. Carolina* (1791) 147 Which said Lots, by Reason of the Proviso in the said Deed mentioned, will soon become lapsable.

Lapsang Souchong ('læpsæŋ suː'ʃɒŋ). [Cf. SOUCHONG.] A variety of Souchong China tea with a smoky flavour. Also *ellipt.* **Lapsang.**
Lapsang is a 'market name'. In quot. 1942 the spelling *Lapseng* is erron.
1883 *Junior Army & Navy Stores* 71 China Lapsang Souchong. **1935** M. MORPHY *Recipes of all Nations* 726 Among the most popular for exportation are the different grades of Lapsang Souchong. **1938** S. BECKETT *Murphy* v. 68 'I hope you like the aroma,' said Miss Carridge. 'Choicest Lapsang Souchong.' **1942** G. MITCHELL *Laurels are Poison* xvii. 184 Jonathan..took the lid off the teapot, sniffed, said: 'Lapseng? All right, I'll have some.' **1946** *Aristotelian Soc. Suppl. Vol.* XX. 167 X may *think*, without much confidence, that it tastes to him like Lapsang. **1947** A. HUXLEY *Let.* 8 Jan. (1969) 562 We have taken to drinking maté, to which a smoky flavour as of Lapsang Soochong has been imparted. **1962** I. MURDOCH *Unofficial Rose* vii. 69 He took a sip of the sweet Lapsang Suchong. **1966** *Punch* 28 Sept. 476/1 Both knees free for the Lapsang and seedcake. **1973** G. BUTLER *Coffin for Pandora* ii. 71, I drank my favourite Lapsang Souchong tea.

lapsarian (læp'sɛərɪən), *sb.* and *a.* [f. L. *laps-us* fall + -ARIAN, or as back-formation from *infralapsarian*, etc.] **A.** *sb.* (See quot. 1928.) **B.** *adj.* Of or pertaining to the fall of man. Also *transf.*
1928 *Funk's Stand. Dict.*, *Lapsarian*, one who believes in the doctrine of the fall of man from innocence. **1954** DILLENBERGER & WELCH *Protestant Christianity* 91 The holders of lapsarian theories..attempted to safeguard the priority of God's activity by ascribing all events and all happenings to him. **1969** A. RICHARDSON *Dict. Chr. Theol.* 189/2 (*heading*) Lapsarian controversy. **1970** K. MILLETT *Sexual Politics* (1971) 181 The awesome lapsarian moment when the female discovers her inferiority.

lapse (læps), *sb.* Also 7 **lap(p)s.** [ad. L. *lapsus* (*u-* stem), a slip or fall, f. *lābī* to glide, slip, fall. Cf. F. *laps.* In Eng. the physical senses are of late appearance, though earlier than in the vb.]
1. A 'slip' of the memory, the tongue, the pen, or †the understanding; a slight error, a mistake.
1526 *Pilgr. Perf.* (W. de W. 1531) 100 Anone by lapse of tonge they ronne in to inconuenyentes. **1610** GUILLIM *Heraldry* II. viii. (1611) 76 Lest they fall into the Laps of the iteration or doubling of any prohibited words. **1643** SIR T. BROWNE *Relig. Med.* I. §7 Not Heresies in me, but bare Errors, and single Lapses of my understanding. **1665** STILLINGFL. *Acc. Protest. Relig.* 198 Those very words which his Lordship, by a lapse of memory, attributes to Occham. **1674** DRYDEN *State Innoc., Author's Apol. Heroic Poet.* (1692) B 1 b, 'Tis..unmanly to snarl at the little lapses of a Pen, from which Virgil himself stands not exempted. **1706** [WARD] *Wooden World* (1708) 18 Sometimes their villanous Reflexions take Wind, and then ten to one but their Bullet-heads compound for the Lapses of their Tongue. **1885** W. H. THOMPSON in *Athenæum* 23 May 662/1 A further lapse of memory in the venerable astronomer's letter is the statement [etc.].
2. a. A falling from rectitude, imputable to weakness or lack of precaution: a moral 'slip'.
1582 EARL ESSEX in Ellis *Orig. Lett.* Ser. II. III. 80, I do beseache your good Lordship, notwithstanding the lapse of my youth, still to continue a loving frende unto me. **1601** SHAKS. *All's Well* II. iii. 170, I will throw thee..Into the staggers, and the carelesse lapse Of youth and ignorance. **1672** WILKINS *Nat. Relig.* 225 The fear of God..must fortifie us in our temptations, and restore us in our lapses. **1712** STEELE *Spect.* No. 276 ¶1 To..abruptly inform a virtuous Woman of the Lapse of one who till then was in the same Degree of Esteem with her self. **1838** PRESCOTT *Ferd. & Is.* (1846) II. v. 362 The severe training which he had undergone made him less charitable for the lapses of others.
†**b.** *Theol.* The 'Fall' (of Adam). *Obs.*
1659 PEARSON *Creed* x. 729 The first affection we can conceive in him upon the lapse of man, is wrath and indignation. *a* **1711** KEN *Psyche* Poet. Wks. 1721 IV. 217 To heav'nly Truths my Mind Is by the Lapse, born Blind. **1768–74** TUCKER *Lt. Nat.* (1834) II. 375 Evil is represented to have been brought upon the human race by the lapse of Adam.
c. A lapsing or apostatizing *from* the faith, a falling *into* heresy. Also, in weaker sense, an involuntary deviation *from* one's principles or rule of action.
1660 H. MORE *Myst. Godl.* v. xvii. 206 Suspecting our selves not to have emerged quite out of this General Apostasy of the Church, into which the Spirit of God has foretold she would be lapsed for 1260 years; let us see if we can find out what Remainders of this Lapse are still upon us. **1753** *Scots Mag.* July 315/1 Of our lapses and relapses since, I may perhaps treat. **1796** BURKE *Regic. Peace* iv. Wks. IX. 66 It is from their lapses and deviations from their principle, that alone we have any thing to hope. **1828** D'ISRAELI *Chas. I*, I. iii. 43 Laud..read a list of persons whom he had recovered from their lapses into Papistry. **1873** DIXON *Two*

Queens I. I. ii. 9 Domingo heard of men being stabbed and hung for lapse of faith.

3. A decline to a lower state or degree; †a fall (in temperature).

1533 ELYOT *Cast. Helthe* (1541) 8a, Accordynge to the lapse or decaye of the temperatures of the sayd humours. **1620** VENNER *Via Recta* viii. 170 If.. the lapse be in heat, meates and drinkes of colde quality agreeable to the lapse.. are to be vsed. **1680** BURNET *Rochester* (1692) 85 So that it is plain there is a Lapse of the high powers of the Soul. **1855** MACAULAY *Hist. Eng.* xiv. III. 434 The hero sank again into a voluptuary; and the lapse was deep and hopeless. **1875** POSTE *Gaius* I. (ed. 2) 125 A lapse from liber to servus was a dissolution of marriage, for servus was incapable of matrimony. **1883** H. SPENCER in *Contemp. Rev.* XLIII. 5 All these lapses from higher to lower forms begin in trifling ways.

4. a. *Law.* The termination of a right or privilege through neglect to exercise it within the limited time, or through failure of some contingency. In early use only with reference to ecclesiastical patronage.

1570 *Act 13 Eliz.* c. 12 §7 No Title to confer or present by Lapse, shall accrue upon any Depryvation, ipso facto. **1615** JAS. I in *Buccleuch MSS.* (Hist. MSS. Comm.) I. 171 Spiritual livings do often fall void either by lapse or by the death of the incumbent. **1642** tr. *Perkins' Prof. Bk.* i. §15 8 After the five moneths past the Ordinary shall present for Lapps. **1654** BRAMHALL *Just Vind.* iv. (1661) 69 The King only could incurr no lapse, *Nullum tempus occurrit Regi.* **1726** AYLIFFE *Parergon* 117 A Layman ought to Present within four Months, and a Clergyman within six, otherwise a Devolution or Lapse of Right happens. **1767** BLACKSTONE *Comm.* II. 276 The law has therefore given this right of lapse, in order to quicken the patron. **1788** H. WALPOLE *Remin.* vii. 53 By the lapse of some annuities on lives not so prolonged as her own, she found herself straitened. **1827** JARMAN *Powell's Devises* (ed. 3) II. 51 The destination of sums, given out of the produce of land devised to be sold, failing by lapse. **1844** WILLIAMS *Real Prop.* (1877) 210 The failure of a devise by the decease of the devisee in the testator's lifetime, is called a lapse. **1875** STUBBS *Const. Hist.* II. xvii. 621 The Presentation to vacant churches after lapse.

b. *gen.* A falling into disuse; an intermission.

1838 PRESCOTT *Ferd. & Is.* (1846) II. xiv. 41 Restoring the authority of the law, which was exposed to such perpetual lapses. **1847–9** HELPS *Friends in C.* Ser. I. (1851) 7 A casual function which may be fulfilled at once after any lapse of exercise.

5. A falling into ruin. *rare.*

1605 BACON *Adv. Learn.* I. vii. §6. 35 His [Adrian's] whole time was a very restauration of all the lapses and decayes of former times. **1894** BLACKMORE *Perlycross* 7 The vaults of the Waldron race lay at the bottom of half the lapse [of a church].

6. a. A gliding, flow (of water); quasi-*concr.* a gliding flood. Also *occas.* a gentle downward motion.

1667 MILTON *P.L.* VIII. 263 Sunny Plaines, And liquid Lapse of murmuring Streams. **1725** POPE *Odyss.* XVII. 232 From the rock, with liquid lapse distills A limpid fount. **1784** COWPER *Task* IV. 326 The downy flakes Descending, and, with never-ceasing lapse Softly alighting upon all below, Assimilate all objects. **1794** HURDIS *Tears Affect.* 22 The liquid lapse Of Rother gliding o'er some pebbly shoal. **1822** T. TAYLOR *Apuleius* 98 Near the lapse of the fountain there was a royal house. **1825** LONGF. *Burial of Minnisink* 4 With soft and silent lapse came down The glory, that the wood receives, At sunset, in its golden leaves. **1850** MRS. BROWNING *My Doves* vi, They listen.. For lapse of water, swell of breeze. **1856** AIRD *Poet. Wks.* 27 Down comes the stream, a lapse of living amethyst. **1879** TRENCH *Poems* 52 With lapse just audible, From font to font the waters fell. *fig.* **1800** MOORE *Remarks on Anacreon* 5 The sweetest lapses of the cygnet's song. *c* **1800** K. WHITE *Poems* (1837) 138 And laugh, and seize the glittering lapse of joy.

b. Of life, time, etc.: The gliding or passing away, passage; a period or interval elapsed.

1758 JOHNSON *Idler* No. 13 ⁋3 During this gentle lapse of life. **1790** GIBBON *Misc. Wks.* (1814) III. 416 The term of his mortal existence was almost commensurate with the lapse of the eleventh century. **1818** JAS. MILL *Brit. India* II. v. v. 484 Troops.. could not.. be collected without a lapse of time. **1853** M. ARNOLD *Scholar-Gipsy* xv, No, no, thou hast not felt the lapse of hours. **1877** MRS. OLIPHANT *Makers Flor.* v. 124 A lapse of a hundred years is not much in the story of such a city as Florence. **1898** J. T. FOWLER *Durham Cathedral* 62 Old inhabitants, after a lapse of nearly three centuries and a half, still speak of 'The Abbey'.

¶ 7. Confused with *laps*, pl. of LAP *sb.*

1558, 1602 [see LAP *sb.*[1] 6].

8. Special Comb. **lapse rate** *Meteorol.*, the rate of fall of temperature with height; also *transf.*

1918 *Meteorol. Gloss.* (Meteorol. Office) 183 *Lapse*,.. a word suggested for use instead of gradient.. to denote the loss of temperature or pressure of the atmosphere with height. So that *lapse-rate*, or *lapse-ratio*, for temperature will be the fall of temperature per kilometre of height. **1928** D. BRUNT *Meteorol.* vi. 46 The average conditions in the troposphere are specified by a lapse-rate of 3°F. per 1,000 feet. **1957** HALTINER & MARTIN *Dynamical & Physical Meteorol.* xiii. 210 The local increase in lapse rate was due to a combination of low-level warming and high-level cooling by horizontal advection. **1972** *Biol. Abstr.* LIV. 1081/2 The lapse rate of soil temperature indicates a large value in summer and a small one in winter.

lapse (læps), *v.* [ad. L. *lapsāre* to slip, stumble, fall, f. *laps-*, ppl. stem of *lābī* to glide, slip, fall. In some senses, prob. a new formation on LAPSE *sb.* (The physical applications, though etymologically primary, are of late appearance in Eng.)]

I. Intransitive senses.

1. a. To fall away by slow degrees; to pass or sink gradually through absence of effort or sustaining influence. Also with *away*, *back*, *out*. Constr. *from*, *into*.

1641 J. JACKSON *True Evang. T.* I. 39 Many lapsed and apostatized from the faith. **1654** H. L'ESTRANGE *Chas. I* (1655) 124 So ill are even the best actions relisht of men lapsed into common disdain. **1691** NORRIS *Pract. Disc.* 169 Man is deeply lapsed and degenerated from a state of Excellency. **1704** NELSON *Fest. & Fasts* vi. (1739) 79 Their Fathers lapsed into Idolatry. **1798** MALTHUS *Popul.* (1817) III. 151 Should the British constitution ultimately lapse into a despotism. **1804** KNOX & JEBB *Corr.* I. 121 Those that are lapsed into some wounding sin. **1851** *Illustr. Catal. Gt. Exhib.* 205 Hybrids.. gradually lapse into the one or the other of the originals. **18..** DICKENS *Repr. Pieces* (1866) 128 They seemed to lapse away, of mere imbecility. **1862** GOULBURN *Pers. Relig.* III. ii. (1873) 164 Take away the variety of vocations.. and.. society lapses again into barbarism. **1872** BLACK *Adv. Phaeton* xxx. 407 The road itself seems lapsing back into moorland. **1873** BURTON *Hist. Scot.* VI. lxviii. 131 In his account of this copy of the book, Prynne lapses from his usual exactness. **1891** E. PEACOCK *N. Brendon* I. 25 Joel lapsed into thought. **1920** D. H. LAWRENCE *Women in Love* xxiii. 351 She possessed him so utterly and intolerably that she herself lapsed out. **1928** —— *Phoenix II* (1968) 525 If I could dance all day as well, I might keep going. It's this leaving off that does me in.—And she lapsed out.

†b. *simply.* To fall into error, heresy, or sin. *Obs.*

1611 SHAKS. *Cymb.* III. vi. 12 To lapse in Fulnesse Is sorer, then to lye for Neede. **1649** ROBERTS *Clavis Bibl.* 368 That highest wisdome cannot secure us from lapsing, if the Lord a little leave us to ourselves. **1667** MILTON *P.L.* x. 574 Oft they fell Into the same illusion, not as Man Whom they triumph'd once lapst.

c. *nonce-use.* To pass out of existence; to become eliminated.

1884 tr. *Lotze's Logic* 322 The case ($C - a = E + a$). The part *a* disappears in our observation from *C* or is by experimental means made to lapse.

†2. To fall into decay. *Obs.*

1620 VENNER *Via Recta* viii. 170 The like respect also, in reducing a constitution lapsed, is to bee had of the age. **1654** H. L'ESTRANGE *Chas. I* (1655) 167 Having appointed the.. Governour of the Castle, to take order for the re-edification of what was lapsed.

3. *Law.* Of a benefice, an estate, a right, etc.: To fall in, pass away, revert (*to* some one) owing to non-fulfilment of conditions or failure of persons entitled to possession. Of a devise or grant: To become void. (Quot. 1726 may be pass. of 7.)

1726 AYLIFFE *Parergon* 333 Such Benefices as are lapsed unto the Bishop. **1767** BLACKSTONE *Comm.* II. 183 If they do not both agree within six months, the right of presentation shall lapse. **1806** SURR *Winter in Lond.* (ed. 3) III. 44 There must be an heir to the Beauchamp estates, or they will lapse into possession of the crown. **1827** JARMAN *Powell's Devises* (ed. 3) II. 327 If.. the gift were to testator's children.. by name,.. the share of one of the objects subsequently dying in his lifetime would, if the gift were joint, survive to the others; but, if it were several, lapse. **1845** STEPHEN *Comm. Laws Eng.* (1874) I. 177 The estate which was lapsed or fallen in by the death of the last tenant. **1852** HOOK *Ch. Dict.* (1871) 430 When a patron neglects to present a clergyman to a benefice in his gift within six months after its vacancy, the benefice lapses to the bishop; and if he does not collate within six months, it lapses to the archbishop; and if he neglects to collate within six months, it lapses to the Crown. **1874** GREEN *Short Hist.* iv. §2. 168 The bulk of the earldoms had already lapsed to the Crown. **1876** DIGBY *Real Prop.* viii. 351 If a devisee dies in the lifetime of the testator, though the devise may have been expressed to be made to him and his heirs,.. the devise lapses, or fails to take effect. **1879** *Cassell's Techn. Educ.* IV. 90/2 For the whole of fourteen years it lay unused, the consequence was that the patent altogether lapsed. **1884** *Law Times Rep.* 12 Apr. 202/1 The income.. lapses and goes to the testator's widow and grandson, as next of kin.

transf. **1882** J. H. BLUNT *Ref. Ch. Eng.* II. 2 The government lapsed into the hands of a few working members of the Privy Council.

4. a. To glide, pass with an effortless motion; also, to descend gradually, to sink, subside.

1798 LANDOR *Gebir* Wks. 1846 II. 491 And now one arm Fell, and her other lapsing o'er the neck Of Gebir, swung against his back incurved. **1858** HAWTHORNE *Fr. & It. Jrnls.* II. 127 Where angels might alight, lapsing downward from heaven. **1867** HOWELLS *Ital. Journ.* 317 They rise and lapse [*sc.* in intonation] several times in each sentence. **1889** *The County* ix, I manage a cool 'How do you do, Mr. Vaudrey?' and lapse into a low chair.

b. Of a stream: To glide, flow; app. used by many writers with a reminiscence or echo of LAP *v.*[1] (sense 4). Also with *along*. Occas. of a person, a vessel: To float, glide gently over the water.

1832 L. HUNT *Sonnets Poems* 211 Hear the fruitful stream lapsing along 'Twixt villages. —— *Sir R. Esher* (1850) 255, I lapsed about the Isis in a boat. **1852** HAWTHORNE *Blithedale Rom.* I. xii. 220, I saw the river lapsing calmly onward. **1859** DICKENS *Haunted Ho.* IV. 19 Of rippling waves, that lapsed in silver hush Upon the beach. **1863** COWDEN CLARKE *Shaks. Char.* vi. 142 And, with this, come thronging visions of the 'silver Thames'.. and barges lapsing on its tranquil tide. **1865** *Cornh. Mag.* Oct. 447 The murmurous water lapses against the far-off sea-wall with a sound as of a distant hum of bees. **1880** W. WATSON *Prince's Quest, River* (1892) 132 My soul is such a stream as thou Lapsing along it knows not how.

c. Of time: To glide past, pass *away*.

1702 C. MATHER *Magn. Chr.* IV. iv. (1852) 77 Sixteen years will this summer be lapsed since [etc.]. **1860** HAWTHORNE *Marb. Faun* (1878) II. xvi. 118 She knew that the moments were fleetly lapsing away.

II. Transitive (causative) senses.

†5. To cause to slip or fall, to draw down. Const. *into*. *Obs.*

1664 H. MORE *Myst. Iniq.* 250 That notorious serpentine shape which deceived Adam and Eve and Lapsed them into rebellion. **1681** —— *Exp. Dan.* App. i. 258 In lapsing and keeping down the Empire in Superstition and Idolatry.

†6. To let slip (time, a term); to let pass without being turned to account. *Obs.*

1667 *Decay Chr. Piety* vi. ⁋17 We know the danger of lapsing time in case of mortgage, but here our danger is greater. **1680** MORDEN *Geog. Rect.* (1685) 127 Erick the Fifth.. lapsed his time of demanding the Investiture of the Electorship. **1683** CAVE *Ecclesiastici, Chrysostom* 528 He would many times lapse the usual times of dining, and eat nothing till the evening. **1726** AYLIFFE *Parergon* 81 An Appeal may be deserted by the Appellants lapsing the Term of Law.

†7. To allow (a right) to lapse; to suffer the lapse of (a living); to forfeit, lose. *Obs.*

1642 LAUD *Diary* Wks. 1853 III. 249 Tuesday I received a letter, dated Jan. 17, from His Majesty, to give Chartham to Mr. Reddinge, or lapse it to him. **1660** *Plea for Ministers in Sequestration* 4 The complainants have lapsed their Livings. **1687** in *Magd. Coll. & Jas. II* (O.H.S.) 45 Q. Eliz: did jure suo make Dr Bond præs: ye Coll. hauing lapsd yr election. **1697** *Confer. Lambeth* in W. S. Perry *Hist. Coll. Amer. Col. Ch.* I. 47 A Vestry cannot lapse their right of presentation as a patron may.

¶ 8. ? Associated with *lapse* = *laps* pl. (LAP *sb.*[1] 8): ? To pounce upon as an offender, apprehend. *Obs.*

1601 SHAKS. *Twel. N.* III. iii. 36 For which if I be lapsed in this place I shall pay deere.

lapsed (læpst), *ppl. a.* [f. LAPSE *v.* + -ED[1].]

1. That has glided away, dropped out of use, disappeared from sight, or fallen into decay.

1667 MILTON *P.L.* III. 176 Once more I will renew His lapsed powers, though forfeit and enthrall'd By sin to foul exorbitant desires. **1823** BYRON *Juan* XVI. xxi, A monk.. appear'd, Now in the moonlight, and now lapsed in shade. **1854** H. MILLER *Sch. & Schm.* iv. (1857) 66 During the lapsed century the waves had largely encroached on the low flat shores. **1881** *Times* 2 Feb. 9/2 The House of Commons must recover its lapsed authority. **1890** *John Bull* 5 Apr. 231/1 It is probable that the Lapsed custom of an annual dinner will be revived.

†b. That has been let slip incautiously. *Obs.*

1741 WATTS *Improv. Mind* ix. (1801) 80 Let there be.. no sudden seizure of a lapsed syllable to play upon it.

2. Of a person: Fallen or sunk into a lower grade, or a depraved condition; esp. fallen into sin, or from the faith (cf. COLLAPSED 3); applied *Hist.* to Christians who denied the faith during persecution. ***lapsed classes, masses***: those who have dropped out of social standing. Also *absol.*

1638 *Penit. Conf.* iii. (1657) 36 Such a lapsed sinner may not be incapable of pardon. **1664** H. MORE *Myst. Iniq.* xiv. 48 But this plea is in common with the Heathens and lapsed Christians. **1668** —— *Div. Dial.* I. xvi. (1713) 35 That the standing Spirits hugely exceed the number of the lapsed. **1677** HORNECK *Gt. Law Consid.* iv. (1704) 98 Free you from the rubbish the lapsed posterity of Adam lies groaning under. **1702** ECHARD *Eccl. Hist.* III. v. 406 His greatest Concern was for the Case of the Lapsed. **1706** STANHOPE *Paraphr.* III. 294 The Author of all Goodness to lapsed Man. **1754** RICHARDSON *Grandison* (ed. 6) II. 231 May not virtue itself pity the lapsed? **1822** LAMB *Elia* Ser. I. *Praise Chimneysw.*, Good blood and gentle conditions, derived from lost ancestry and a lapsed pedigree. **1831–3** E. BURTON *Eccl. Hist.* xxv. (1845) 532 These lapsed Christians, as they were called.. retained their belief in Christ. **1854** H. MILLER *Sch. & Schm.* xvi. (1857) 367 It almost necessarily takes its place among the lapsed classes. **1865** PUSEY *Truth Eng. Ch.* 198 The lapsed were restored under the prospect of renewed persecution. **1887** *Pall Mall G.* 8 Mar. 2/2 To facilitate the elevation of the lapsed masses.

3. Said of a fief, devise, or legacy, the right to which has passed from the original holder, devisee, or legatee.

1617 MINSHEU *Ductor*, s.v. *Lapse*, That Benefice is in lapse or lapsed, whereunto he that ought to present, hath omitted or slipped his opportunities. **1767** BLACKSTONE *Comm.* II. 513 If the legatee dies before the testator, the legacy is a lost or lapsed legacy, and shall sink into the residuum. **1816** SCOTT *Antiq.* xviii, His lands.. were reassumed by the emperor as a lapsed fief. **1818** CRUISE *Digest* (ed. 2) VI. 195 The devise was lapsed and void. **1896** T. F. TOUT *Edw. I*, i. 16 The bestowal of lapsed fiefs was among the most important of the prerogatives of the Crown.

lapser ('læpsə(r)). [f. LAPSE *v.* + -ER[1].] One who lapses or falls away *from* (something, †esp. from the Christian faith).

1695 J. SAGE *Cyprianic Age* Wks. 1847 II. 9 Such as.. absolved the lapsers. **1718** HICKES & NELSON *J. Kettlewell* III. lv. 330 With regard to any.. who were looked upon by him as Lapsers. **1899** *19th Cent.* Sept. 451 These lapsers from sobriety.

lapsibility, -ible: see LAPSA-.

lapsided, variant of LOPSIDED.

lapsing ('læpsɪŋ), *vbl. sb.* [f. LAPSE *v.* + -ING[1].] The action of the vb. LAPSE. a. Gliding or dropping of water. b. In immaterial sense: The action or process of sinking or dropping; also, of falling *to* (a public body) as an acquisition.

1663 J. SPENCER *Prodigies* (1665) 145 The lapsing of that People to the grossest ignorance. **1820** L. HUNT *Indicator* No. 24 (1822) I. 187 In the notes of the birds and the lapsing of the water-fall. **1862** GOULBURN *Pers. Relig.* I. I. iv. 64 To

reduce prayer to a form..But how to prevent..its lapsing into a form? **1884** H. SPENCER in *Pop. Sci. Monthly* XXIV. 727 The law-makers who provided for the ultimate lapsing of French railways to the state.

ˈlapsing, *ppl. a.* [f. LAPSE *v.* + -ING².]

1. a. Of water: Gliding, dropping. **b.** Of time: Gliding or passing away.

a **1771** SMOLLETT (Worc.), To magic murmur of lapsing streams. **1794** MRS. RADCLIFFE *Myst. Udolpho* xv, At twilight hour, with tritons gay I dance upon the lapsing tides. **1827** in Hone *Every-day Bk.* II. 893 We pass near some gently lapsing water. **1841** LADY FLORA HASTINGS *Poems* 11 Though many a lapsing year hath intervened. **1862** W. STORY *Roba di R.* xvii. (1864) 352 Rome is the city of fountains. Wherever one goes he hears the pleasant sound of lapsing water. **1862** S. LUCAS *Secularia* 381 Test the growth of enlightenment by lapsing centuries.

2. Sinking (into decay or depravity); failing, flagging.

1667 *Decay Chr. Piety* vii. 146 The lapsing state of human corruption. **1668** HOWE *Bless. Righteous* (1825) 90 It is the peculiar honor and prerogative of a Deity..to be the fulcrum, the centre of a lapsing creation. **1867** G. MACDONALD *Poems* 67 O lapsing heart! thy feeble strain Sends up the blood so spare.

Hence **ˈlapsingly** *adv.*, in a lapsing manner.

1848 *Blackw. Mag.* LXIV. 291 The soft moan Of billows that shoreward Are lapsingly thrown.

lapstar, Sc. f. LOBSTER.

ˈlapstone. [f. LAP *sb.*¹ + STONE.] A stone that shoemakers lay in their laps to beat their leather upon.

1778 *Love Feast* 18 Next, black-thumb'd Jobson..throws his Lap-Stone down. **1794** WOLCOT (P. Pindar) *Ode For. Soldiers*, Behold his pretty fingers wax the thread, And now the leather on the lap-stone hole. *a* **1810** TANNAHILL *Come hame to Lingels* Poems (1846) 143 Come hame to your lap-stane, come hame to your last, It's a bonny affair that your family maun fast. **1852** HAWTHORNE *Blithedale Rom.* I. v. 68 A lapstone, a hammer, a piece of sole-leather, and some waxed ends.

ˈlap-streak. Also lapstrake. [f. LAP *sb.*³ or *v.*³ + STREAK.] A boat in which each streak overlaps the one below; a clinker-built boat.

1771 *Boston Gaz.* 11 Mar. (Advt.) (Th.), Whale-boats and all sorts of Lapstreak Boats. **1860** *All Year Round* No. 75. 587 Two boats... Long graceful lapstreaks, roomy and stiff, yet so light that [etc.]. **1873** *Forest & Stream* 25 Sept. 108/2 Five six-oared shells, two six-oared lapstreaks. **1959** *Times Lit. Suppl.* 9 Jan. 22/4 How to fit clinker (or lapstreake) planking on a hull. **1971** *Islander* (Victoria, B.C.) 10 Oct. 2/1 His 25-foot lapstrake boat was built by Vancouver shipbuilders.

attrib. **1895** *Outing* (U.S.) XXVI. 488/2 Their boat is of lap-streak construction.

Hence **ˈlapstreaked** *a.*, (of a boat) built in this fashion. **ˈlap-streaker** (*U.S.*), one who uses such a boat.

1883 *Pall Mall G.* 30 Aug. 11/1 The owner's gig..will be of cedar, lapstreaked. **1961** F. H. BURGESS *Dict. Sailing* 130 *Lap jointed, lap straked.* Describes the system of planking as used in clinker-built boats.

‖**lapsus** (ˈlæpsəs). [L.; see LAPSE *sb.*] A lapse, slip, or error. Chiefly in the L. phrases **lapsus linguæ**, a slip of the tongue, and **lapsus calami**, a slip of the pen.

1667 DRYDEN *Mart. Mar-all* III. (1668) 28 What have I done besides a little lapsus linguæ? **1713** ADDISON *Guardian* No. 121 ⁋3 He..was unfortunately betrayed into a lapsus linguæ. **1822** J. FLINT *Lett. Amer.* 109 The people committed the lapsus, when they [etc.]. **1893** *Nation* (N.Y.) 2 Mar. 165/2 The following..is a lapsus calami whose occurrence it is quite impossible to understand.

Laputan (ləˈpjuːtən), *a.* and *sb.* In Swift Laputian. [f. *Laputa*, the flying island in *Gulliver's Travels*, whose inhabitants were addicted to visionary projects: see -AN, -IAN.]

A. *adj.* Of or pertaining to Laputa; hence, chimerical, visionary, absurd. **B.** *sb.* An inhabitant of Laputa.

1726 SWIFT *Gulliver* III ii. (*heading*), The Humours and Dispositions of the Laputians described. **1866** HERSCHEL *Fam. Lect.* ii. 62 After all, Swift's idea of extracting sunbeams out of cucumbers, which he attributes to his Laputan philosophers, may not be so very absurd. **1870** O. W. HOLMES *Mechanism in Th. & Mor.* in *Old Vol. of Life* (1891) 293 *note*, It is curious to compare the Laputan idea of extracting sunbeams from cucumbers with George Stephenson's famous saying about coal.

So **Laˈputically** *adv.* (*nonce-wd.*), after the fashion of the Laputans.

a **1849** POE *R. H. Horne* Wks. 1864 III. 426 Occupied, Laputically, in their great work of a progress that never progresses.

lapwing (ˈlæpwɪŋ). Forms: 1 hléapewince, 4 lhapwynche, 4–7 lapwinge, -wynge, lap-, lappewin(c)ke, -wynke, (4 leepwynke, 5 lapwinch, -wynche, 7 -winc(k)le), 4– -lapwing. Also 6 LAPPOINT. [OE. *hléapewince*, str. fem., f. *hléapan* to leap + **winc-* to totter, waver (so OHG. *winkan*, MHG. *winken*, also to wink; cf. OE. *wincian* to wink. The bird was named from the manner of its flight. The current form is in part due to popular etymology, which connected the word with LAP *v.*² and WING *sb.* (see quot. 1617).] A well-known bird of the plover family, *Vanellus vulgaris* or *cristatus*, common in the temperate parts of the Old World. Called also PEWIT, from its peculiar cry. Its eggs were the 'plovers' eggs' of the London markets. Allusions are frequent to its crested head, to its wily method of drawing away a visitor from its nest, and to the notion that the newly hatched lapwing runs about with its head in the shell.

c **1050** *Ags. Voc.* in Wr.-Wülcker 260/2 *Cucu*, hleapewince. **1340** *Ayenb.* 61 Hy byeþ ase þe lhapwynche þet ine velþe of man makeþ his nest. **1390** GOWER *Conf.* II. 329 A lappewinke has lost his feith And is the brid falsest of alle. *c* **1430** LYDG. *Temple of Glass* 495 + 21 Had In dispit, ryght as a-mong foulys Ben Iayis, Pyis, Lapwyngis & these Oulys. *a* **1529** SKELTON *P. Sparowe* 430 [They] With puwyt the lapwyng, The versycles shall syng. *c* **1532** DU WES *Introd. Fr.* in *Palsgr.* 911 The lapwyng, *le uaniau.* **1569** J. SANFORD tr. *Agrippa's Van. Arts* 137 b, The Lapwinke.. seemeth to haue some royall thinge, and weareth a crowne. **1592** GREENE *Art Conny Catching* II. 4 Who..cry with the Lapwing farthest from their nest. **1602** SHAKS. *Ham.* v. ii. 192 This Lapwing runs away with the shell on his head. **1606** *Sir G. Goosecappe* I. i. in Bullen *O. Pl.* III. 9 As fearefull as a Haire, and will lye like a Lapwing. **1617** MINSHEU *Ductor*, a *Lappe-wing*, *q.* leapwing, because he lappes or clappes the wings so often. *a* **1628** F. GREVILLE *Sidney* (1652) 204 Like Lapwings with the shels of authority about their necks. **1633** T. STAFFORD *Pac. Hib.* II. iii. (1810) 239 And left the Wood with the Lapwings policie; that they being busied in pursuite of them, the other might remaine secure within that Fastnesse. **1786** BURNS *Afton Water* ii, Thou green-crested lapwing, thy screaming forbear. **1842** TENNYSON *Locksley Hall* 18 In the Spring the wanton lapwing gets himself another crest. **1876** SMILES *Sc. Natur.* xiii. (ed. 4) 260 You could now hear..the pleasant peewit of the Lapwing.

b. *attrib.* and *Comb.*, as in ***lapwing stratagem***, ***lapwing-like*** adv.; **lapwing-gull** (see quot. 1844).

1638 BRATHWAIT *Spir. Spicerie* 406 Lapwing-like, with shell on head, I begun to write, before my yeares could well make mee an Author. **1669** DRYDEN *Tyrannic Love* IV. i, Your guilt dares not approach what it would hide; But draws me off, and (lapwing-like) flies wide. **1676** in *Hist. Northfield* (Mass.) (1875) 86 Be careful not to be deceived by their lapwing stratagems, by drawing you off from the rest to follow some men. **1844** W. H. MAXWELL *Sports & Adv. Scotl.* (1855) 326 The Laughing Gull..or Black Head..has been called 'peewit' or 'lapwing gull'.

lapyst, variant of LAPISE *v.* *Obs.*

laquais, -ay, obs. forms of LACKEY.

laque, obs. form of LAC *sb.*¹ and ³.

‖**laquear** (ˈlækwiːɑː(r)). [L. f. *laque-us* noose, band: see LACE *sb.*]

a. *Arch.* (See quots.)

1706 PHILLIPS (ed. Kersey), *Laquear* (in *Archit.*), a Roof, the inward Roof of a House; the Roof of a Chamber embowed, channelled, and done with Fret-work. **1859** GWILT *Archit.* (ed. 4) Gloss., s.v. *Lacunar*, The ceiling of any part in architecture receives the name of lacunar only when it consists of compartments sunk or hollowed, without spaces or bands, between the panels; if it is with bands, it is called *laquear*.

b. *Anat.* (See quot. 1888.)

1888 *Syd. Soc. Lex.*, *Laquear*, the roof of a part. **1889** J. M. DUNCAN *Lect. Dis. Women* xxii. (ed. 4) 172 Where the disease attacks only parts of the passage, as the laquear.

laquearia (lækwiːˈɛərɪə). *rare*⁻¹. [L., pl. of *laqueāre* a panelled ceiling.] A ceiling, roof. Cf. LAQUEAR, LAQUEARY.

1922 T. S. ELIOT *Waste Land* ii. 18 Odours..ascended In fattening the prolonged candle-flames, Fling their smoke into the laquearia.

laquearian (lækwiːˈɛərɪən), *a.* [f. L. *laqueāri-us* (see next) + -AN.] Of a gladiator: Armed with a noose to entangle his antagonist.

1818 BYRON *Ch. Har.* IV. cxlii. *note*, Whether the wonderful statue which suggested this image be a laquearian gladiator.

†**ˈlaqueary**, *sb.* *Obs.* *rare*⁻⁰. [app. ad. L. *laqueāria* (pl. of LAQUEAR), treated as sing.] = LAQUEAR.

1656–81 BLOUNT *Glossogr.*, *Laqueary*, the roof of a chamber. **1658–96** in PHILLIPS.

†**ˈlaqueary**, *a.* *Obs.* *rare*⁻¹. [ad. L. *laqueārius*, f. *laqueus* noose.] = LAQUEARIAN.

1682 SIR T. BROWNE *Chr. Mor.* I. §24 Our inward Antagonists..like Retiary and Laqueary Combatants, with Nets, Frauds and Entanglements fall upon us.

†**ˈlaqueat**, *pa. pple.* *Sc.* *Obs.* [ad. L. *laqueāt-us*, pa. pple. of *laqueāre* to ensnare, f. *laqueus* noose: see LACE *sb.*] Ensnared.

1560 ROLLAND *Crt. Venus* III. 375 With lust of luif ȝit he was laqueat.

†**laqueˈation.** *Obs.* [n. of action f. L. *laqueāre*: see prec.] (See quot.)

1638 A. READ *Chirurg.* vii. 50 So much I have thought good to deliver unto you concerning laqueation or dry stitching.

laquer, obs. form of LACQUER.

laquesaa: see LATCH.

‖**lar** (lɑː(r)). Pl. ‖lares (ˈlɛəriːz), lars (lɑːz). Also 7 larre. [L. *lār*, pl. *larēs*, earlier *lasēs*.]

1. *Roman Myth.* **a.** *pl.* (Freq. with capital initial.) The tutelary deities of a house; household gods; hence, the home. Often coupled with *penates*. **b.** *sing.* A household or ancestral deity; also *transf.* and *fig.*

1586 T. B. *La Primaud, Fr. Acad.* I. (1594) 473 The ancients had a private and houshold god, whom they called lar, which we may translate into our language, the god of the harth. **1600** HOLLAND *Livy* VIII. ix. 287 O yee Lares and domestical gods. **1629** MILTON *Christ's Nativity* 191 In consecrated Earth, And on the holy Hearth, The Lars, and Lemures moan with midnight plaint. **1647** R. STAPYLTON *Juvenal* 278 Build houses; joyne to ours anothers lares; Sleepe safe, confiding in our neighbours cares. **1648** HERRICK *Hesper.*, *Pan. to Sir L. Pemberton* 4 To thee, thy lady, younglings and as farre As to thy genius and thy larre. **1742** POPE *Dunc.* IV. 366 So shall each youth..keep his Lares, tho' his house be sold. **1775** H. WALPOLE *Lett.* (1857) VI. 270, I am returned to my own Lares and Penates—to my dogs and cats. **1832** L. HUNT *Poems* 239 So shall no disease or jar Hurt thy house, or chill thy Lar. **1889** LOWELL *Oracle of Goldfishes* Last Poems (1895) 14 You were my wonders, you my Lars, In darkling days my sun and stars. **1889** *Athenæum* 20 July 88/3 Thomas Pitt..through his sons and daughters, the great *lar* of not fewer than five families in the English peerage.

†**c.** A sprite, hobgoblin. *Obs.*

1598 FLORIO, *Mazzaruolo*, a sprite..a hodgpoker, a lar in the chimney.

2. *Zool.* The white-handed gibbon of Burmah, *Hylobates lar*.

1819 REES *Cycl.* s.v., The lar, or, as it is sometimes denominated the gibbon. **1859** WOOD *Nat. Hist.* I. 34 The Lar, or White-handed Gibbon.

larach (ˈlɑːrəx). *Sc.* Also lerroch. [Gael. *làrach* site of a building, habitation. = OIrish *láthrach* (mod.Ir. *laithreach*), f. OCeltic **lā* to extend.] The site of a building or habitation.

1705 *Court Bk. Barony of Urie* (1892) 113[That] ilke tennant keepe ther owen larache. *a* **1774** FERGUSSON *Farmer's Ingle* Poems (1845) 38 In its auld lerroch yet the deas remains. **1794** *Statist. Acc. Scot.* XII. 273 *note*, Amidst the various changes..of..proprietors they have continued in the same possession, and on the self-same Larach.

‖**lararium** (ləˈrɛərɪəm). [L. *larārium*, f. *lar-ēs* (see LAR).] The part of a Roman house where the images of Lares or household gods were kept; hence, a private shrine or chapel.

1706 in PHILLIPS (ed. Kersey). **1816** J. DALLAWAY *Statuary & Sculpt.* iii. 165 The Penates..were deposited in the Lararium or wardrobe which stood in some secret apartment, the sleeping room or library. **1848** LYTTON *Harold* I. i, The old lararium, stripped of its ancient images of ancestor and god. **1871** FARRAR *Witn. Hist.* iii. 98 *note*, The Emperor Alexander Severus admitted an image of Christ into his lararium.

†**ˈlarbar**, *a.* and *sb.* Chiefly *Sc.* In 5 larbre, 6 larbar, la(i)rbair. [Of obscure origin: cf. LEER *a.*, empty.] **A.** *adj.* Lean; exhausted, worn out. **B.** *sb.* A lean, withered, or worn out person.

1486 *Bk. St. Albans* E viij b, He is meegre larbre and leene. **1508** DUNBAR *Flyting w. Kennedie* 121 Lene larbar, loungeour, baith lowsy in lisk and lonȝe. *Ibid.* 169 The larbar lukis of thy lang lene craig. —— *Tua mariit wemen* 175 His lwme is vaxit larbar, and lyis into swonne. **1603** *Philotus* xxxv, With ane lairbair for to ly, Ane auld deid stock, baith cauld and dry.

Comb. **1603** *Philotus* cxii, Sa larbair-lyke lo as scho lyis.

larboard (ˈlɑːbɔəd, -bəd), *sb.* (*a.*) *Naut.* Forms: α. 4 ladde-borde, 5 ladeborde, latheborde, latebord. β. 6 larborde, lerbord, leereboord, 6–7 larbo(o)rd, 7 lubbord, 7– larboard. [ME. *lad(d)eborde*, *latheborde*, altered in the 16th c. into *ler-*, *leere-*, *larbord*, by form-association with the contemporary *ster-*, *-steere-*, *starbord*. The second component is OE. *bord*, ON. *borðe*, ship's side (BOARD *sb.* 12); the origin of the first component, which appears as *ladde-*, *lade*, *lathe-*, *late-*, has not been determined.

Some would connect it with LADE *v.*, taking it to mean 'the side on which cargo was received', or on which deck cargo was placed.

In OE. the corresponding term was *bæcbord*; this did not survive into ME., though its etymological equivalent still remains in all the mod. continental Teut. tongues, and was adopted into Rom. (F. *bâbord*). The word seems to have meant 'the side at the *back* of the steersman'; the rudder or steering-paddle of early Germanic ships having been worked over the right side, whence the name *stéorbord* 'steering-side', STARBOARD.]

The side of a ship which is to the left hand of a person looking from the stern towards the bows. Opposed to *starboard*. (Freq. in phr. without the article, as †*on*, †*by*, †*a*, *to larboard*.)

The term has now been discarded in the navy and supplanted by *port*, to avoid confusion with the similar-sounding *starboard*.

α. **13..** *E.E. Allit. P.* C. 106 Þay layden in on laddeborde & þe lofe wynnes. **1495** *Naval Acc. Hen. VII* (1896) 203 Devettes..j a sterbord an other a latebord.

β. **15..** *Sir A. Barton* in *Surtees Misc.* (1888) 68 Ethere bye lerbord or by lowe That Scootte would overcome yowe. *Ibid.* 69 A larborde wher Sir Andrewe lay. **1583** STANYHURST *Æneis* I. (Arb.) 21 Theire ships too larboord doo nod. **1591** RALEIGH *Last Fight Rev.* (Arb.) 19 Two on her larboord, and two on her starboord. **1598** HAKLUYT *Voy.*

I. 4 Vpon his steereboord alwayes the desert land, and vpon the leereboord the maine Ocean. **1667** MILTON *P.L.* II. 1019 When Ulysses on the Larbord shunnd Charybdis. **1698** FROGER *Voy.* 171 We saw five ships, three to the Star-board, and two to the Lar-board. **1707** *Lond. Gaz.* No. 4380/2 In firing along our Larboard, we saw he had a Design to board us on the Bow. **1853** HERSCHEL *Pop. Lect. Sci.* i. §17 (1873) 11 She will heel over to larboard.

†**b.** as *adv.* = To larboard; formerly used as a nautical command. *Obs.*

1634-5 BRERETON *Trav.* (Chetham Soc.) 169 Larboard, that is, to the left hand. **1647** R. STAPYLTON *Juvenal* 224 Larboard now The reeling tree, then starboard, forc't to bow. **1663** GERBIER *Counsel* 32 As well understood..as one at Sea among Mariners; saying, Steere, or Lar-board. **1667** DRYDEN *Tempest* I. i, You Dogs, is this a time to sleep? Lubbord. Heave together, Lads.

B. *attrib.* passing into *adj.* Belonging to or situated on the left or port side of a vessel.

1495 *Naval Acc. Hen. VII* (1896) 192 Latheborde Bowers ..Sterborde destrelles..Ladeborde destrelles. *a* **1613** OVERBURY *A Wife, Saylor,* In a storme tis disputable..on which side of the ship he may be saued best, whether his faith bee starre-bord faith or lar-bord. **1613** PURCHAS *Pilgrimage* IX. vii. 862 The Land on Larbord side (saith Sir R. Hawkins) is without doubt Ilands. **1627** CAPT. SMITH *Seaman's Gram.* ix. 39 His Mate with his Larboord men.. releeues them till foure in the morning. **1669** STURMY *Mariner's Mag.* I. 18 Cast off your Larboard-Braces. **1748** *Anson's Voy.* I. vi. 59 A signal was made..to bring to with the lar-board tacks. *Ibid.* II. v. 177 About four points on the larboard-bow. **1762** FALCONER *Shipwr.* I. 282 On the larboard quarter. **1833** MARRYAT *P. Simple* viii, Ease off the larboard hawser. **1867** SMYTH *Sailor's Word-bk., Larboard-watch,* the old term for port-watch.

b. *humorously* used for: Left.

1781 COWPER *Let. to J. Newton* 18 Mar., Wks. 1837 XV. 75 A slight disorder in my larboard eye may possibly prevent my writing you a long letter.

larboarder. *rare.* [f. LARBOARD *sb.*] One who is on the larboard side of a boat.

1846 H. MELVILLE *Typee* vi. 44 The poor larboarders shipped their oars, and commenced pulling us ashore.

ˈlarbolins, -ians, *sb. pl. Naut.* [Short f. LARBOARD + ? -LING. Cf. STARBOLINS.] (See quot.)

1867 SMYTH *Sailor's Word-bk., Larbolins,* or *Larbolians,* a cant term implying the larboard-watch.

larcener (ˈlɑːsənə(r)). Also 7 lassoner. [f. LARCENY + -ER¹. Cf. OF. *larcineur.*] One who commits larceny; chiefly ***petty larcener***, one who commits petty larceny. Also *fig.*

1634-5 BRERETON *Trav.* (Chetham Soc.) 20 As a punishment..upon whores, petty larceners, shippers that exact. **1640** FULLER *Joseph's Coat* I Cor. xi. 30 The whip for the petty lassoner. **1642** —— *Holy & Prof. St.* II. xxiv. 152 Thus petty Larceners are encouraged into Felons. **1839** *Fraser's Mag.* XIX. 91 Bother about perjurers, robbers, larceners. **1854** LADY LYTTON *Behind Scenes* I. iv, That great petty larcener of sentiment, Lawrence Sterne. **1864** SIR F. PALGRAVE *Norm. & Eng.* III. 373 How it was possible ..to imprison the petty larcener unless the offence was duly laid in the indictment.

ˈlarcenish (ˈlɑːsənɪʃ), *a.* [f. LARCENY + -ISH.] Disposed to larceny or small thefts.

1862 BURTON *Bk. Hunter* 50 A tendency to be larcenish.

larcenist (ˈlɑːsənɪst). [f. LARCENY + -IST.] = LARCENER.

1803 SYD. SMITH *Wks.* (1869) 30 The injuries which have been inflicted on society by pickpockets, larcenists and petty felons. **1882** *Macm. Mag.* XLV. 379 These have also suffered by the predatory fingers of petty larcenists.

larcenous (ˈlɑːsənəs), *a.* [f. LARCEN-Y + -OUS. Cf. OF. *larcineux, larrecinos.*] Pertaining to or characterized by larceny; thievish.

1742 FIELDING *J. Andrews* IV. v, 'Ay' says the Justice, 'a kind of felonious larcenous Thing'. **1807** SYD. SMITH *P. Plymley's Lett.* iv. Wks. 1840 III. 403 The acquittal of any noble and official thief would not fail to diffuse the most heartfelt satisfaction over the larcenous and burglarious world. **1861** DICKENS *Gt. Expect.* ii, I knew..that my larcenous researches might find nothing available in the safe. **1880** SWINBURNE *Stud. Shaks.* 63 In all the larcenous little bundle of verse. **1888** GLADSTONE in *19th Cent.* XXIII. 783 A huge larcenous appropriation..of goods which do not belong to them.

Hence **ˈlarcenously** *adv.*, thievishly.

1864 in WEBSTER. **1882** *Daily News* 3 Jan. 5/4 Molière was accused..of larcenously conveying the ideas of *Les Précieuses Ridicules* from a piece acted two years before.

larceny (ˈlɑːsənɪ). *Law.* Also 6 larcenie, larsonie, 8 larciny. [app. f. AF. *larcin* (see LARCIN) + -Y, perh. with a recollection of L. *latrōcinium.*] The felonious taking and carrying away of the personal goods of another with intent to convert them to the taker's use. Also *gen.* theft.

Distinction was formerly made between ***grand*** and ***petty larceny***, the former being the larceny of property having a value of more, the latter of less, than 12 pence. ***simple, mixed,*** or ***compound larceny*** (see quot. 1769).

c **1460** FORTESCUE *Abs. & Lim. Mon.* xiii. (1885) 142 There is no man hangyd in Scotlande in vij. yere to gedur ffor robbery. And yet thai ben often tymes hanged ffor larceny [*ed.* 1714 lacenye, *MS. Digby* larcerye]. **1581** LAMBARDE *Eiren.* II. vii. (1602) 272 All manner of theft, whether it were robberie it selfe, or great or petite Larcenie. **1596** BP. W. BARLOW *Three Serm.* i. 126 Egging men on to Larsonies, Thefts. **1764** BURN *Poor Laws* 137 Picking of pockets, and such other larcenies. **1769** BLACKSTONE *Comm.* IV. 229 Larciny..is distinguished by the law into two sorts; the one called simple larciny, or plain theft unaccompanied with any other atrocious circumstance; and mixt or compound larciny, which also includes in it the aggravation of a taking from one's house or person. **1818** SCOTT *Rob Roy* vi, You are not charged with any petty larceny, or vulgar felony. **1850** BLACKIE *Æschylus* II. 17 This god..wilt thou Not hate, thou, whom his impious larceny Did chiefly injure? **1871** SMILES *Charac.* vi. (1876) 184 It is said that Lord Chatham was the first to set the example of disdaining to govern by petty larceny. **1875** POSTE *Gaius* III. (ed. 2) 462 By English law, to take a man's own goods out of the hands of a bailee, if the taking have the effect of charging the bailee, is larceny.

†**ˈlarcery.** *Obs.* Also 7 lasserie. [Cf. LARCENY and LARCINRY.] Larceny.

? *a* **1500** [see *c* 1460 in prec.] **1611** FLORIO, *Latrocinatione,* larcerie. **1613** R. CAWDREY *Table Alph.* (ed. 3), *Pettilasserie,* stealing of things of no great value.

larch (lɑːtʃ). Also 6 larche, larshe. *β.* 8 larich, larinch. [Introduced by Turner (see quot. 1548 in 3), ad. G. *lärche*:—MHG. *lerche, larche*:—OHG. **lerihha,* **larihha,* an early adoption (prior to the assibilation of *c* in Latin) of L. *laricem, larix* (whence late Gr. λάριξ): corresponding phonetically to OCeltic **darik-* (Irish *dair*, genitive *darach*, Welsh *dar*) oak. Other Eng. writers in the 16th. c. adopted the word in the L. form (see LARIX), sometimes corrupted into *larinx*; hence app. some of the dialectal forms given above. Cf. further Du. *lariks*, and the unexplained forms G. *lorche*, Du. *lorke(boom)*; also It. *larice*, Sp. *lárice*, Pg. *larico*, F. (Cotgr.) *larege, lareze*, med.L. *laresus.*]

1. a. A well-known coniferous tree; *Abies Larix* or *Larix europæa*, a native of the Alps, which is largely cultivated in this country. Its timber is tough and durable. It yields Venetian turpentine, and the bark is used in tanning. **b.** Any tree of the genus *Larix*, e.g. the American Larch, *L. americana.*

1548, etc. [see *larch-tree* in 3]. **1576** NEWTON *Lemnie's Complex.* I. 72 Yᵉ best is that, which issueth out of yᵉ Larch, the Pyne, or the Firre tree. **1794** MRS. RADCLIFFE *Myst. Udolpho* iii, The scene of barrenness was here and there interrupted by the spreading branches of the larch and cedar. **1827-35** WILLIS *May* 15 The larch stands green and beautiful Amid the sombre firs. **1832** *Planting* 33 (L.U.K.) *Pinus pendula*, black larch. —— *microcarpa*, red larch. —— *larix*, common larch. **1850** TENNYSON *In Mem.* xci, When rosy plumelets tuft the larch. **1866** *Treas. Bot.* s.v. *Larix*, The American Larch, *Abies* or *Larix pendula*, is the tree known to the Canadians as the Tamarack.

2. The wood of this tree.

1867 W. W. SMYTH *Coal* 141 The props are usually of larch, or, in low seams, of oak.

3. *attrib.*, as ***larch-plank, -plant, -tree, -turpentine***; **larch-bark**, the bark of the larch-tree; the *laricis cortex* of the British Pharmacopœia; **larch blister, canker**, a disease caused by the fungus *Trichoscyphella willkommii*, which causes cankers on the bark of larch trees; **larch needle cast**, a disease caused by the fungus *Meria laricis*, which attacks and kills the foliage of larch trees; **larch red**, a substance obtained by boiling extract of larch-bark with dilute sulphuric acid (Cassell); **larch-scale**, a scale-like insect which infests larch trees; **larch-wood**, (*a*) the wood of the larch tree; (*b*) a wood consisting of larch trees.

1827 STEUART *Planter's G.* (1828) 489 The present Mr. White, had often drawn more than £400 a year for his *Larch-bark only. **1895** W. R. FISHER *Schlich's Man. Forestry* IV. 402 The *larch-blister or canker..is most prevalent in damp places with moist air and in frosty and cloudy localities. [**1891** *Jrnl. R. Agric. Soc.* II. 300 In the course of last summer's visit of inspection..the Consulting Botanist found cases of canker in larch plantations all over England and Wales.] **1895** *Larch canker [see *larch blister*, above]. **1919** W. E. HILEY *Fungal Dis. Common Larch* ii. 19 At present larch canker is prevalent only in Europe. **1968** F. G. BROWNE *Pests & Dis. Forest Plantation Trees* II. 990 *Trichoscyphella willkommii* (Hartig) Nannf. Fungi, Ascomycotina Helotiales. Synonym: *Dasyscypha willkommii* (Hartig) Rehm. Larch canker. Europe, including Britain and Northern Ireland, and also in the north-eastern United States of America. **1921** *Q. Jrnl. Forestry* XV. 61 The *larch needle-cast appears to be very widespread in Britain. **1968** F. G. BROWNE *Pests & Dis. Forest Plantation Trees* II. 877 Larch leaf blight, Larch needle cast. Widely distributed in north western Asia and northern Europe..and also recorded in New Zealand and the United States of America. **1847** SMEATON *Builder's Man.* 43 Tiberius caused the Naumachiarian bridge..to be rebuilt of *larch planks. **1871** PALGRAVE *Lyr. Poems* 30 The young *larch-plant upon Pelion's side. **1832** *Planting* 72 (L.U.K.) *Coccus lariceo* [sic], *larch scale. **1548** TURNER *Names of Herbes* 46 Larix or larex groweth on the highest toppes of the Alpes..frenche men cal it Dularge. It maye be called in englishe a *Larche tree. **1578** [see LARIX]. **1601** HOLLAND *Pliny* II. 182 From the Larch tree there issueth a subtill and thin liquor. **1706** PHILLIPS (ed. Kersey), *Larix*, the Larinch-tree, or Larch-Tree. **1712** tr. *Pomet's Hist. Drugs* I. 66 *Cedrus Magna*..is a Species of the Larch Tree. **1728** KERSEY, *Larix*, the Larich-tree, or Larch-tree. **1855** LONGF. *Hiaw.* VII. 49 Give me..of your fibrous roots, O Larch-Tree! **1616** BULLOKAR, **Larch Turpentine*, a kind of Turpentine or rosen growing vpon the Larch tree in Italie, vsed often in oyntments and emplaisters. **1780** COXE *Russ. Disc.* 46 Another ship built of *larch-wood. **1856** MISS MULOCK *J. Halifax* xxv, It was lovely to see the morning sun climbing over One-Tree Hill, catching the larchwood [etc.].

larchen (ˈlɑːtʃən), *a.* [f. LARCH + -EN⁴.] Consisting of larches, larch-.

1818 KEATS *Meg Merrilies* 10 Her Brothers were the craggy hills, Her Sisters larchen trees. *a* **1851** MOIR *Poems, To Wounded Ptarmigan* vii, From larchen grove to grove.

†**ˈlarcin.** *Obs.* Also 5 larson, 6 larcyne, -ine, larrecine, 7 larzon, larçon. [a. AF. and F. *larcin*, OF. *larrecin* (also *larcine* fem.):—L. *latrōcinium* robbery, f. *latro* robber.]

1. = LARCENY.

[**1292** BRITTON I xxv. §115 De Apels de Robberies et de Larcins.] *c* **1400** *Plowman's T.* 323 Tything of bribry and larson Will make falshed full foul fall! *c* **1530** L. COX *Rhet.* (1899) 75 To Brytayns, Gascoignes, and Polones, [is attributed] larcyne [*v.r.* larrecine]. **1598** FLORIO, *Furto*, a theevery, a larcine, a burglarie. **1658** tr. *Bergerac's Satyr. Char.* Pref. 2 Others content them selves with petty Larcins. **1679** BLOUNT *Anc. Tenures* 119 If he be condemned for a common Larcin, he ought to be hanged.

2. One who commits larceny; a larcener.

1596 in Tytler *Hist. Scot.* (1864) IV. 350 Shall any castle or habytacle of mine be assailed by a night larcin. **1624** BP. HALL *Trve Peace-Maker* Wks. (1627) 540 Whips for harlots, brands for petty larzons, ropes for felons. *a* **1656** —— *Rem. Wks.* (1660) 11 Some poor petty-larçons and pilferers.

†**ˈlarcinry.** *Obs.* Also 7 larcenary. [f. LARCIN + -RY.] Larceny.

a **1639** CAREW *Coelum Brit.* (1640) 214 The god of petty Larcinry. **1656** EARL MONM. *Advt. fr. Parnass.* 183 Having committed many larcenaries.

lard (lɑːd), *sb.* Forms: 4-6 larde, 5 laard, 5 laurde, 4- lard. [a. OF. (mod.F.) *lard* bacon (= It., Sp., Pg. *lardo*):—L. *lārdum, lāridum*, usually believed to be cogn. w. Gr. λᾱρ-ινός fat, λᾱρ-ός pleasant to the taste.]

†**1.** The fat of a swine; (fat) bacon or pork; *rarely*, other fat meat used for larding. *Obs.*

c **1420** *Liber Cocorum* (1862) 12 Take larde of porke, wele soþyn. *Ibid.* 26 Take tho ox tonge..Sethe hit, broche hit in lard yche dele. *c* **1440** *Promp. Parv.* 288/1 Larde of fleshe, *Larda*. *c* **1460** FORTESCUE *Abs. & Lim. Mon.* iii. (1885) 114 Thai eyten no flesshe but yf it be right seldon a litle larde. **1552** HULOET, Larde, *succidia*. **1607** TOPSELL *Four-f. Beasts* (1658) 532 The fat of Swine they commonly call Lard which groweth betwixt the skin and the flesh. **1615** [see LARD *v.* 1]. **1626** BACON *Sylva* §997 She got a Peece of Lard with the Skin on, and rubbed the Warts all ouer with the Fat Side. **1693** DRYDEN *Ovid's Met.* VIII. *Baucis & P.* 107 By this the boiling kettle had prepar'd And to the table sent the smoaking lard. **1725** BRADLEY *Fam. Dict.* s.v. *Swine*, Feeding a Hog for Lard or Boar for brawn.

fig. *a* **1613** OVERBURY *A Wife* (1638) 290 Patience is the lard of the leane meat of adversitie.

†**b.** ? A slice of fat. *Obs.*

c **1430** *Two Cookery-bks.* 49 Take lardez of Venysoun.

2. a. (Often *hog's lard.*) The internal fat of the abdomen of a swine, esp. when rendered and clarified, much used in cooking, and in pharmacy as the basis of unguents. Also, in mod. use, any edible pig-fat, and (in commercial use) a fatty preparation containing or resembling lard.

c **1420** *Pallad. on Husb.* I. 433 Frote hit wel with larde ffaat & decoct. **1556** WITHALS *Dict.* (1568) 18b/1 *Axungia propriæ*, is larde or hogges greace. **1704** *Lond. Gaz.* No. 4026/3 Lading, consisting of..Dry Codfish, Dry Jack, Hogslard. **1707** MORTIMER *Husb.* (1708) 189 If Hogs get a Swelling on the side of their Throat..anoint it with Hog's Lard. **1811** A. T. THOMSON *Lond. Disp.* (1818) 728 The addition of the metallic solution to the melted mixture of lard and oil. **1825** J. NEAL *Bro. Jonathan* I. 76 A kind of sweet cake fried in lard. **1836-9** TODD *Cycl. Anat.* II. 232/2 When hog's-lard becomes rancid, a peculiar volatile acid forms in it. **1873** E. SMITH *Foods* 139 Lard is derived from the loose fat of the pig, and is a very pure fat. **1881** *Analyst* VI. 233 Watered lard being now used extensively, owing to the high price of the pure quality, we are giving our special attention to its manufacture. **1887** *Buck's Hand-bk. Med. Sci.* IV. 380/2 Commercial lard is so universally impure, either being mixed with water or salt, or having a portion of its liquid oil removed, that it is in general unfit for medicinal use. **1906** L. L. LAMBORN *Mod. Soaps* iii. 44 Two grades of neutral lard are made—one from the leaf, the other from the back fat of the hog. **1913** BOLTON & REVIS *Fatty Foods* iv. 100 Lard is often adulterated with a judicious mixture of beef fat and vegetable oils. **1944** H. G. KIRSCHENBAUER *Fats & Oils* vi. 63 After a Congressional investigation the compounded products which up to then had been sold as 'pure lard', 'refined lard', etc., were required to be labelled 'lard compounds'. **1974** *Guardian* 27 Dec. 9/2 Rub 4 oz butter and 2½ oz lard into 10 oz flour sifted with a pinch of salt.

b. *transf.*

1486 *Bk. St. Albans* C v b, Yeue hir larde of a gote. **1835** W. IRVING *Tour Prairies* 306 Fritters of flour fried in bear's lard. **1849** *Sk. Nat. Hist., Mammalia* III. 162 In the Greenland whale the layer of this subcutaneous lard varies from eight or ten to 20 inches in depth.

c. ***earth lard*** (see quot.).

1801 *Trans. Soc. Arts* XIX. 175 The Grubs of the Cock-chafer..appear like lumps of white fat. Hence the British name 'Earth-Lard'.

3. *attrib.*, as ***lard-cake, -pail, -slice***; **lard-bladder** *colloq.*, a fat person; **lard-butter, -cheese**, substitutes for butter and cheese made from lard; **lard compound**, a substitute for lard made from lard stearin, oleostearin, or esp.

cottonseed oil; †**lard-house** = LARDER; **lard oil**, 'a valuable oil made from lard, used for burning, and for lubricating machinery' (Ogilvie, 1882); **lard stearin(e**, the solid residue left after the expression of lard oil from lard, used for stiffening soft lard, as an ingredient of some lard substitutes and margarines, and in the manufacture of some soaps; **lard-stone**, a kind of soft stone found in China; cf. *agalmatolite*.

1891 KIPLING *Life's Handicap* 195 Mulcahy confused the causes of things, and when a very muzzy Maverick smote a sergeant on the nose or called his commanding officer a bald-headed old *lard-bladder.. he fancied that rebellion and not liquor was at the bottom of the outbreak. **1928** W. GIBSON *Between Fairs* 19 Ay, but I'd have you know there is offence, when an old lard-bladder of a circus-clown, the likes of you, tries to teach her own business to Nanny Ragtag. **1881** *Chicago Times* 16 Apr., Very little *lard-butter is now sold in Chicago. **1858** C. M. YONGE *Christmas Mummers* v. 59 Mrs. Harper was..preparing a *lard cake for tea. **1861** GEO. ELIOT *Silas Marner* x. 160 Some small lard-cakes, flat paste-like articles. **1881** *Chicago Times* 16 Apr., Large amounts of butterine and *lard-cheese were sold here as the genuine article. **1904** L. L. LAMBORN *Cottonseed Products* ix. 172 The ingredients of *lard-compound are summer white cottonseed-oil and oleo-stearin. **1913** BOLTON & REVIS *Fatty Foods* iv. 103 We have found products described as 'lard compounds' in which no lard was present at all. **1946** *Thorpe's Dict. Appl. Chem.* (ed. 4) VII. 189/1 Under pressure of reformative legislation..the term 'refined lard' was replaced by the expressions 'compound lard' or 'lard compound'..; later the term 'lard compound' was still further restricted to products containing more than 50% of genuine lard. **1555** *Richmond. Wills* (Surtees) 85 All the salting vessell in the *lardhouse. **1599** MINSHEU, A Lardary, or lard-house. **1843** *Rep. Comm. Patents 1842* (U.S.) 82 The article of lard offered for sale in the market for domestic use, and now about to be so much in demand as material for the manufacture of *lard oil and candles, is prepared from the adipose matter of the omentum and mesentery of the hog. **1920** OBERG & JONES *Gage Design* vii. 198 When a very slow cutting abrasive is required and the amount to be removed by lapping is small, rouge and lard oil may be used. **1957** *Encycl. Brit.* XIII. 723/2 Lard oil is the limpid, clear, colourless oil expressed by hydraulic pressure from pure lard after it has been 'grained' by storage at a temperature of 45°F. **1891** *Fur, Fin & Feather* Mar. 195 Two empty *lard pails with their covers..will complete the culinary outfit. **1968** R. M. PATTERSON *Finlay's River* 178 Soon the tea-pail—an old lard-pail, smoked and blackened by hundreds of camp fires—was singing, swaying a little over the flames. *a* **1693** *Urquhart's Rabelais* III. xxiii. 193 Some Lackey, snatching at the *Lard-slices. **1885** W. L. CARPENTER *Treat. Manuf. Soap* ii. 26 The so-called '*lard-stearin' left in the presses is frequently used as a substitute for tallow in the soap-pan, when the price of it is suitable. **1906** L. L. LAMBORN *Mod. Soaps* iii. 46 Lard-stearin of non-edible quality is a soap-stock for certain grades of soap. **1944** H. G. KIRSCHENBAUER *Fats & Oils* vii. 109 Lard stearine and lard oil for edible purposes are obtained from lard by graining and pressing. **1811** PINKERTON *Petrol.* I. 374 The rock called *lard-stone, used by the Chinese.

lard (lɑːd), *v.* [ad. F. *lard-er*, f. *lard* (see LARD *sb.*).]

1. *Cookery.* (*trans.*) To insert small strips of bacon (†or of other fat meat) in the substance of (meat, poultry, etc.) before cooking. Also *absol.* (Cf. INTERLARD *v.* 1.)

c **1330** R. BRUNNE *Chron. Wace* (Rolls) 15756 He schar a pece out of his þe, & lardid & rostoid. *c* **1420** *Liber Cocorum* (1862) 21 Perboyle the hare and larde hit wele, Sethyn loke thou rost hir everydele. *c* **1430** *Two Cookery-bks.* 18 Take Conyngys..& sethe hem, oþer larde hem & Rost hem. **1615** MARKHAM *Eng. Housew.* II. ii. (1664) 73 If you will Roast any Venison,..if it be lean, you shall either lard it with Mutton lard, or Pork lard. **1661** LOVELL *Hist. Anim. & Min.* 73 The skinn being pulled off, the flesh larded, & stuck with cloves, may be rosted. **1741** *Compl. Fam.-Piece* I. ii. 136 Flea your Hare, and lard it with Bacon. **1769** MRS. RAFFALD *Eng. Housekpr.* (1778) 127 Take three young ducks, lard them down each side the breast. **1884** *Girl's Own Paper* June 491/1 Nearly all lean meat may be larded with advantage.

†**2.** To enrich with or as with fat; to fatten. (Cf. ENLARD.) *Obs.*

1579 SPENSER *Sheph. Cal.* Feb. 110 A goodly Oake.. Whilome had bene the King of the field,..And with his nuts larded many swine. **1596** SHAKS. *1 Hen. IV*, II. ii. 116 Falstaffe sweates to death, and Lards the lean earth as he walkes along. **1607** —— *Timon* IV. iii. 12 It is the Pastour Lards the Brothers sides, The want that makes him leane. **1607** DEKKER *Whore Babylon* Wks. 1873 II. 221 This lards me fat with laughter. **1621** BURTON *Anat. Mel.* Democr. to Rdr. (1651) 7 They lard their lean books with the fat of others works. **1624** SANDERSON *Serm.* I. 184 Thou hast larded thy leaner revenues with fat collops sacrilegiously cut out of the sides or flanks of the church. *a* **1661** FULLER *Worthies* (1840) III. 240 [Wheat-ears] Naturally larded with lumps of fat. *a* **1687** COTTON *Noon Quatrains* Poems (1689) 235 The lagging Ox is now unbound, From larding the new turn'd-up ground.

†**b.** *intr.* for *refl.* or *pass.*

1612 [see LARDING *ppl. a.*].

3. *transf.* To stick all over *with*; to cover, line, or strew *with*. *Obs.* or *arch.*

1543 SIR J. WALLOP in *State Papers* IX. 457 Divers of the Frenchemen's horse killed, and well larded with arrows. **1590** MARLOWE *Edw. II*, I. iv, He weares a short Italian hooded cloake, Larded with pearle. **1602** SHAKS. *Ham.* IV. v. 37 White his Shrow'd as the Mountaine Snow..Larded with sweet flowers. **1611** SPEED *Hist. Gt. Brit.* IX. xv. §55 Their sides were altogether larded with arrowes. **1631** H. SHIRLEY *Mart. Souldier* II. i. in Bullen *O. Pl.* I. 190 A Soldado Cassacke of Scarlet, larded thicke with Gold Lace. **1641** MILTON *Reform.* II. (1851) 70 His Navall ruines that have larded our Seas. *a* **1658** CLEVELAND *Times* 13 A Land ..Larded with Springs, and fring'd with curled Woods. **1843** LYTTON *Last Bar.* I. ii, Larding himself with sharp knives and bodkins.

†**b.** *fig.*

1565 JEWEL *Def. Apol.* (1611) 407 Yee thought it good, thus to lard the same, by a proper Parenthesis. **1660** tr. *Amyraldus' Treat. conc. Relig.* III. iii. 362 His gross follies wherewith he hath larded and strewed it. **1687** SETTLE *Refl. Dryden* 81 But to lard his gross oversights with some more pardonable mistakes.

4. To intersperse or garnish (speech or writing) with particular words, expressions, ideas, etc.; to interlard.

1549 *Compl. Scot.* Prol. to Rdr. 16, I thocht it nocht necessair til hef fardit ande lardit this tracteit vitht exquisite termis. **1581** SIDNEY *Apol. Poetrie* (Arb.) 53 They say, the Lirick, is larded with passionate Sonnets. **1598** SHAKS. *Merry W.* IV. vi. 14 The mirth whereof, so larded with my matter, That neither (singly) can be manifested Without the shew of both. **1602** —— *Ham.* V. ii. 20 An exact command, Larded with many seuerall sorts of reason. *a* **1661** FULLER *Worthies* xxiv, Monkes began to lard the lives of their Saints with lies. *a* **1677** BARROW *Serm.* Wks. 1716 I. 158 How mean a skill to lard every sentence with an oath. **1702** *Eng. Theophrast.* 52 A few modish lewd words to lard his Discourse with. *a* **1797** H. WALPOLE *Mem. Geo. II* (1847) I. xii. 404 Lord Egmont..always larded..his speeches with speculative topics of government. **1823** SCOTT *Quentin D.* x, Unable to refrain from larding them with interjections of surprise. **1837** HOWITT *Rur. Life* (1862) I. iv. 39 Their conversation was larded and illustrated with the phraseology of their own favourite pursuit.

5. To smear or cover with lard or fat; to grease. *rare.*

c **1420** *Pallad. on Husb.* I. 436 Vp walle hit euery side In lyke maner, eek larde it. **1740** SOMERVILLE *Hobbinol* II. 306 His Buff Doublet, larded o'er with Fat Of slaughter'd Brutes. **1842** TENNYSON *Will Waterproof* xxviii, Old boxes, larded with the steam Of thirty thousand dinners.

†**6.** *intr.* To ooze with lard or fat. *Obs. rare.*

1577 HANMER *Anc. Eccl. Hist.* (1650) 161 His whole body larded and distilled much like unto..melting wax.

7. *trans.* To adulterate with lard.

1886 *Pall Mall G.* 20 Sept. 3/1 The Mahommedans fear that their ghee may be larded.

lard, obs. form of LAIRD, LORD.

lardacein (lɑːˈdeɪsiːɪn). *Chem.* [f. as next + -IN.] A nitrogenous substance found deposited under morbid conditions in certain minute arteries and tissues of the body.

1873 RALFE *Phys. Chem.* 10 The so called amyloid substance or lardacein. **1890** *Athenæum* 15 Mar. 344/1 The substance..may perhaps be allied to lardacein.

lardaceous (lɑːˈdeɪʃəs), *a. Med.* [f. LARD *sb.* + -ACEOUS.] Of the nature of or resembling lard; containing lardacein; *spec.* applied to a form of degeneration characterized by the formation of lardacein; also said of the patient.

1822 *Blackw. Mag.* XII. 526 The body when choked and obstructed by this lardaceous incumbrance. **1873** T. H. GREEN *Introd. Pathol.* (ed. 2) 59 Amyloid degeneration..is often known as the lardaceous, or waxy change. **1876** DUHRING *Dis. Skin* 434 A solid, fatty, lardaceous deposit beneath the epidermis. **1897** *Allbutt's Syst. Med.* IV. 409 It was not known when he began to be lardaceous.

larˈdacity. *rare.* Lardaceous condition.

1897 *Allbutt's Syst. Med.* III. 276, I have often thought that temporary suppuration may produce temporary lardacity.

lardarie, -ary, var. LARDRY *Obs.*

larded (ˈlɑːdɪd), *ppl. a.* [f. LARD *v.* + -ED[1].] Stuffed with fat bacon; smeared with lard, greased.

c **1440** *Promp. Parv.* 288/1 Laardyd, *lardatus.* **1570** LEVINS *Manip.* 49/25 Larded, *lardo adipatus.* *a* **1700** DRYDEN *Iliad* I. Fables (1700) 191 Larded Thighs on loaded Alters laid. **1709** ADDISON *Tatler* No. 148 ¶9 A larded Turkey. **1724** RAMSAY *Health* 67 The larded peacock, and the tarts *de moy*. **1784** COWPER *Task* IV. 642 As smart above As meal and larded locks can make him. **1821** CLARE *Vill. Minstr.* I. 43 To hunt the pig, As soapt and larded through the crowd he flies. **1837** DICKENS *Pickw.* xiv, There's a very nice ham..and a beautiful cold larded fowl. **1862** *Fraser's Mag.* July 42 The application of a hot iron to his 'larded' feet.

lardeous (ˈlɑːdiːəs), *a.* *rare*⁻⁰. [f. mod.L. *lardeus*, f. *lardum* LARD: see -OUS.] Lardaceous.

1855 in MAYNE *Expos. Lex.*

larder (ˈlɑːdə(r)), *sb.*[1] Forms: 4, 7 lardere, 5, 7 lardre, 5 lardar, -yr(e, -ure, laardere, lardder, larddre, (6 lawder), 7 *Sc.* lairder, 4– larder. [a. OF. *lardier*, AF. *larder*:—med.L. *lardārium*, f. *lardum* LARD *sb.* Cf. OF. *lardoir*, *lardouer* 'garde-manger'.]

1. a. A room or closet in which meat (? orig. bacon) and other provisions are stored.

c **1305** *St. Kenelm* 236 in *E.E.P.* (1862) 54 Þeȝ his larder were neȝ ido & his somer lese lene. *c* **1330** R. BRUNNE *Chron.* (1810) 28 Alle Northwales he set to treuage hie. Tuenti pounde of gold be ȝere..& þer to fyue hundreth kie ilk ȝere to his lardere. *c* **1340** *Cursor M.* 4688 (Trin.) Moo þen a þousande seleres Filled he wiþ wynes..And larderes [*Gött.* lardineris] wiþ salt flesshe. **1390–1** *Earl Derby's Exped.* (Camden) 60 Pro ligno et clauis per ipsum emptis ibidem pro la lardre. *c* **1440** *Promp. Parv.* 288/1 Laardere, *lardarium*. **1468–9** *Durham Acc. Rolls* (Surtees) 92, 1 axe pro le lardar. **1541** *Act 33 Hen. VIII* c. 12 §13 The serieant of the larder for the time being of the same household. **1567** MAPLET *Gr. Forest* 105 Espying hir time when and how she may come to the Lawder or Vittailehouse. **1613** SHAKS. *Hen VIII*, V. iv. 5 Good M. Porter I belong to th' Larder. **1644** D. HUME *Hist. Douglas* 28 This Cellar is called yet the Douglas Lairder [cf. LARDINER 1. 1375]. **1768–74** TUCKER *Lt. Nat.* (1834) I. 378 The hen gratifies her desires in hatching and breeding up chickens for the larder. **1784** COWPER *Task* II. 615 Dress drains our cellar dry, And keeps our larder lean. **1838** PRESCOTT *Ferd. & Is.* (1846) III. xx. 266 The larders of Savona were filled with the choicest game. **1858** R. S. SURTEES *Ask Mamma* lxx. 311 The whole repast bespoke the exhausted larder peculiar to the end of the week. **1877** MRS. FORRESTER *Mignon* I. 50 Utterly unmindful of the probable condition of the larder at home.

b. *transf.* and *fig.* Something serving as a storehouse.

1623 LISLE *Ælfric on O. & N. Test.* Ded. 34 Forth, Taw, Cluyd, Tems, Severne, Humber, Trent, And foure great Seas, your Larders be for Lent. **1864** J. S. HARFORD *Recoll. W. Wilberforce* 195 It [the antediluvian mammoth] had only been hanging in Nature's larder for the last five thousand years. **1877** MRS. OLIPHANT *Makers Flor.* viii. 220 His table became the larder and patrimony of the poor.

c. The collection of prey formed by a butcher-bird or shrike.

1919 H. F. WITHERBY *Pract. Handbk. Brit. Birds* (1920) I. 277 J. H. Gurnsey also records a shrew impaled in a 'larder' and Oldham a young bank-vole. **1964** A. L. THOMSON *New Dict. Birds* 733/1 Many species [of shrike] have the habit of impaling their prey on thorns..or of hanging it from the fork of a branch... This provision of a 'larder' is responsible for the English popular name 'butcher bird'.

†**2.** *fig.* Chiefly in phr. ***to make larder of***: to turn into meat for the larder; to bring to the slaughter-house, hence, to slaughter; ***to larder***, to the slaughter-house. Also *occas.* simply = slaughter. *Obs.*

a **1330** *Otuel* 1129 Al the Kinges ost..maden a foul larder. *a* **1340** HAMPOLE *Psalter* lxxxii. 10 Zebee, that is, swilke þat þe deuyl makis his lardere of. *c* **1380** WYCLIF *Eng. Wks.* (1880) 251 Prelatis courtis þat ben dennys of þeues & larderis of helle. **1387–8** T. USK *Test. Love* II. xiv. (Skeat) l. 13 Thus drawen was this innocente, as an oxe to the larder. **1390** GOWER *Conf.* III. 124 Than [in November] is the larder of the swine. *c* **1430** *Syr Gener.* (Roxb.) 7228 Of oon he hoped larder to make. *c* **1450** *Merlin* 337 The knyghtes of the rounde table made soche lardure thourgh the felde as it hadde ben shepe strangeled with wolves.

3. *attrib.* and *Comb.*: **larder beetle**, an insect which devours stored animal foods, *Dermestes lardarius* (Cent. Dict.); **larder bird** = BUTCHER-BIRD; **larder-fly**, ? = *larder beetle*; †**larder-house** = sense 1; †**larder-silver**, some kind of manorial dues (cf. *larding money*).

1895 J. H. & A. COMSTOCK *Man. Study Insects* xxi. 539 The *Larder Beetle, *Dermestes lardarius*..is the most common of the larger members of this family. **1942** E. O. ESSIG *College Entomol.* xxxii. 559 Small convex scaly beetles usually feeding on dead or dry animal matter. (Skin or Larder Beetles.) Dermestidæ. **1974** *Times* 16 Apr. 12/7 The larder beetle has been left on the shelf, but a related species ..is piling up its numbers. **1948** *Brit. Birds* XLI. 200 Because of the habit of pinning up spare food on thorns the Red-backed Shrike (*Lanius c. collurio*) was far better known in Essex when I lived there, as the *Larder Bird. **1836–9** TODD *Cycl. Anat.* II. 872/2 In the maggot of the *larder-flies ..the mouth is formed..differently. **1390–1** *Earl Derby's Exped.* (Camden) 24 Duobus valettis pro mundacione le *larderhous, vj d. **1460–1** *Durham Acc. Rolls* (Surtees) 90 Pro le pavyng in le larderhouse. *c* **1540** BOORDE *The boke for to Lerne* B j b, The celler, the kytchyn, the larderhowse with al other howses of offices. *a* **1568** ASCHAM *Scholem.* I. (Arb.) 45 This similitude is not rude, nor borowed of the larder house. **1486–7** *Bailiff's MS. Acc. Dunster Boro'*, De iiij[s] vj[d] de proficuis cujusdam consuetudinis vocati *Larder sylver.

Hence ˈ**larderless** *a.*, without a larder.

1852 FORD in *Q. Rev.* Mar. 436 The barren larderless venta..without shelter or food for man or beast.

larder, *sb.*[2] [f. LARD *v.* + -ER[1].] One who lards.

1598 FLORIO, *Lardatore*, a larder, one that lardes meate.

ˈ**larder**, *v. rare.* [f. LARDER *sb.*[1]] *trans.* To store up as in a larder.

1904 RIDER HAGGARD *Gardener's Year* (1905) July 251 The first wasp which came into being must have paralysed caterpillars and lardered them in key-holes. **1948** *Brit. Birds* XLI. 200 The male bird..is much more given to lardering than the hen.

larderellite (lɑːdəˈrɛlaɪt). *Min.* [Named by Bechi, 1854, after Count F. de *Larderel*, who owned the fumaroles where it was found.] Hydrous borate of ammonium, occurring as a white powder.

1854 *Amer. Jrnl. Sci.* XVII. 129 Larderellite..dissolves in hot water. **1868** DANA *Min.* (ed. 5) 882 Larderellite.. Occurs at the Tuscan lagoons.

larderer (ˈlɑːdərə(r)). [f. LARDER + -ER[1], ? after CELLARER.] One who has charge of a larder.

1483 *Cath. Angl.* 208/2 A larderere, *lardarius*. **15..** *Regul. Househ. Earl Northumb.* (1770) 165 That the saide Clarks of the Kechinge..faile not appoint the Larderer ande Cooks. **1550** BALE *Eng. Votaries* II. 64 b, The Kynge had made..an other Roger whyche was hys larderer, the byshop of Herforde. **1577–87** HOLINSHED *Chron.* III. 930/1 The lord Aburgauennie to be chiefe larderer. **1611** SPEED *Hist. Gt. Brit.* IX. xiii. §2 The Mannour of S. in Norfolke was holden of the King by the seruice of Chiefe Larderer at his Coronation. **1745** tr. *Columella's Husb.* XII. iii, Such things as we make use of upon holidays..these we delivered to the Larderer.

larderie, -ery, var. LARDRY *Obs.*

† **'lardet**. *Obs. rare*⁻⁰. [f. LARD *sb.* + -ET[1].] A small piece of bacon for larding meat.
1598 FLORIO, *Lardegli, Lardelli*, the pieces of larde, or lardet that they put into rostemeate.

lardiform ('lɑːdɪfɔːm), *a. Med.* [f. LARD *sb.* + -(I)FORM.] Resembling lard, lardaceous.
1860 in FOWLER *Med. Voc.* **1888** *Syd. Soc. Lex., Lardiform tissue*, a term applied to a variety of scirrhous cancer having the appearance of lard.

lardine ('lɑːdiːn). [f. LARD *sb.* + -INE.] A commercial name for an inferior substitute for lard.
1888 *Grocer* 20 Oct., 'Lardine', which is made from the refuse of lard. **1895** *Daily News* 8 May 8/6 Lardine consisted of lard and cotton seed oil.

lardiner ('lɑːdɪnə(r)). Forms: 4-5 lardener(e, 4, 7, 9 lardiner, 5 -yner, lardnir, lardnare, 6 *Sc.* ladinar, ladner, laidner, 7 *Sc.* lairner. [a. AF. *lardiner*, an altered form (? after *gardiner* GARDENER; for the form cf. *vintner*) of *larder*, OF. *lardier*, f. *lard*: see LARD *sb.*]
†**1.** = LARDER 1. *north.* and *Sc. Obs.*
a **1300** *Cursor M.* 4688 (Gött.) Ma þan a thousand celers Fild he wid wines..And lardineris wid saltid fless. **1375** BARBOUR *Bruce* v. 410 Tharfor the men of that cuntre, For sic thingis thar mellit were, Callit it 'the Douglas lardenere'. *c* **1450** HOLLAND *Howlat* 217 Quhill the lardnir [MS. B. lardun] was laid, held he na houss. **14..** *Chalmerlan Ayr* c. 20 (*Sc. Stat.* I.), Item quhen þai opyn fische þai luke nocht quheder þai be mesale fische or wane, þat js þe cause quhy na fischar suld mak lardnare. **1663** *Inv. Ld. J. Gordon's Furniture*, Item, in the lairner, ane mat and ane pair of blankets. **1710** COLVIL *Whig Supplic.* II. (1741) 94 His Wardrobe and his Buttery; His Lardner and his Bibliotheck.
2. An official who has charge of a larder. *Obs.* exc. as the title of an honorary office (see quot. 1887).
[**13..** *Liber Custumarum* (1860) 474 Tenuȝ..par le service destre Chief Lardiner al Coronement nostre dit Seignur le Roy.] *c* **1400** *Dogg Lardyner* in *Babees Bk.* 358 Hoo so makyȝt at Crystysmas a dogge lardyner and yn March a sowe gardyner,..he schall neuer haue good larder ne fayre gardyn. **1469** *Househ. Ord.* (1790) 93 To see the remaines hadde into the lardre, and the lardener to be charged with it. **1507** *Extracts Aberd. Reg.* (1844) I. 437 The fleschouris, baxteris, brousteris, ladinaris. **1601** F. TATE *Househ. Ord. Edw. II* §50 (1876) 34 Vsher of the larder, under the lardiner. **1610** HOLLAND *Camden's Brit.* I. 473 Sculton..was held by this tenure, that the Lord thereof on the Coronation daie of the Kings of England, should bee chiefe Lardiner. **1679** BLOUNT *Anc. Tenures* 10. **1887** *St. James's Gaz.* 25 Aug. 5/1 To the manor of Scoulton, in the county of Norfolk, is attached the office of Chief Lardiner, whose duty it is on the coronation day to attend to the provisions in the royal larder.
†**3.** *attrib.* in **ladner time**, the time when cattle were slaughtered; also (confused with LADE *v.*), in †**ladner ship**, a freight or transport ship. *Sc.*
1596 DALRYMPLE tr. *Leslie's Hist. Scot.* II. VIII. 96 With a ladner schip [L. *navi oneraria*] standeng thair be chance. *Ibid.* II. IX. 237 Certane shipis callet ladner. **1805** in Ramsay *Scotl. & Scotsmen in 18th Cent.* (1888) II. ii. 69 The laidner or slaughtering time was therefore an occasion of much festivity. **1861** SMILES *Lives Engineers* II. 97 Salted beef and mutton, which was stored up at ladner time, betwixt Michaelmas and Martinmas, for the year's consumption.

larding ('lɑːdɪŋ), *vbl. sb.* [f. LARD *v.* + -ING[1].]
a. The action of the verb LARD; the preparation of meat for cooking by inserting pieces of fat bacon. †Rarely *concr.* Fat, grease, unguent.
c **1440** *Promp. Parv.* 288/1 Laardynge, *lardacio.* **1583** STANYHURST *Æneis* III. (Arb.) 79 Soom feloes naked with larding smearye bebasted. *c* **1645** HOWELL *Lett.* (1650) I. v. xxxviii. 174 He is also good at Larding of meat after the mode of France. **1736** BAILEY *Housh. Dict.* 376 Larding is done with slips of bacon which must be cut small and of a convenient length according to the meat or fowl that you would lard. **1884** *Girls' Own Paper* June 491/1 Larding is one of the advanced operations in cookery.
b. *fig.* (See LARD *v.*)
1674 N. FAIRFAX *Bulk & Selv.* To Rdr., The Larding of Latine with High Dutch. **1687** SETTLE *Refl. Dryden* 22 I'le ..with Larding of part Quibble, and part Sophistry imitate his way of arguing.
c. *attrib.* and *Comb.*, **larding-bacon**, bacon used in the culinary operation of larding; †**larding money** (see quot.); **larding-needle**, **-pin**, †**-prick**, †**-stick**, pointed instruments with which the meat is pierced and the bacon inserted in the process of larding meat.
1884 *Girls' Own Paper* June 491/1 *Larding bacon is sold by many dealers. **1670** BLOUNT *Law Dict.* (1691), **Larding-money*, in the Manour of Bradford in Com. Wilts. the Tenants pay to the Marquis of Winchester, their Land-lord, a small yearly Rent by this Name. **1675** S. FELL *Let.* 4 Mar. in *Househ. Acct. Bk. 1673-78* (1920) p. xvii, Two *larding needles. **1855** E. ACTON *Mod. Cookery* (rev. ed.) ix. 181 Secure one end of the bacon in a slight larding-needle. **1870** *Warne's Every-day Cookery* 23 *Larding needle*, made with split ends, like a cleft stick, to receive strips of fat bacon. **1958** *House & Garden* Feb. 85/1 A larding needle... With this,..you can thread strips of bacon fat through the breast of a chicken. **1970** SIMON & HOWE *Dict. Gastron.* 239/1 *Larding needle*, a long steel needle with a large eye into which narrow strips of pork fat or larding bacon are threaded. **1598** FLORIO, *Lardaruola*, a lardrie, a larder, a *larding pinne. **1693** *Lond. Gaz.* No. 2853/4, 1 Orange Strainer, 1 Larding Pin. **1697** tr. *C'tess D'Aunoy's Trav.* (1706) 201 Don Augustin intreated me also, to let him have some of my Larding-Pins. **1796** MRS. GLASSE *Cookery* v. 60 Put the bacon through and through the beef with the larding-pin. **1845** [see LARDON]. **1611** COTGR., *Larder*,..to pricke, or pierce, as with a *larding pricke. **1580** HOLLYBAND *Treas. Fr. Tong*, *Vne Lardoire*, a *larding sticke. **1611** COTGR., *Lardoire*, a larding sticke, or pricke. **1694** MOTTEUX *Rabelais* IV. xxix. (1737) 120 He's the most industrious Larding-stick and Skewer-maker.

'larding, *ppl. a.* [f. LARD *v.* + -ING[2].] Fattening (in trans. and intr. senses).
1612 DRAYTON *Poly-olb.* xiv. 108 Th' unweldy larding swine his mawe then having fild. *c* **1630** in Risdon *Surv. Devon* §308 (1810) 315 Our lofty tower'd trees..Did to the savage swine let fall their larding mast.

lardite ('lɑːdaɪt). *Min.* [ad. mod.L. *lardītēs* (Wallerius, 1778), f. *lardum* (see LARD *sb.*); its earlier Fr. name was 'pierre de lard'.] †**a.** A synonym of STEATITE. **b.** A synonym of PAGODITE.
1796 KIRWAN *Elem. Min.* (ed. 2) I. 153 Indurated Steatites. Lardites of Wallerius. **1814** ALLAN *Min. Nomen.* 46 Steatite..Lardite. **1868** DANA *Min.* (ed. 5) Gen. Index 817/2 Lardite, *v.* pagodite.

† **'lardlet**. *Obs. rare*⁻⁰. [f. LARD *sb.* + -LET.] A small piece of bacon for larding meat.
1659 TORRIANO, *Spioccare*, to lard birds with lardlets.

lardon ('lɑːdən), **lardoon** (lɑː'duːn). *Cookery.* Also 5 lardun. [a. F. *lardon* (= It. *lardone*), f. *lard*: see LARD *sb.*] One of the pieces of bacon or pork which are inserted in meat in the process of larding.
c **1450** [see LARDINER 1]. **1653** URQUHART *Rabelais* II. xiv, The lardons or little slices of bacon, wherewith I was stuck, kept off the blow. **1658** tr. *Bergerac's Satyr. Char.* xxv. 92 A lumpe of Veale that struts about upon its lardons. **1747** MRS. GLASSE *Cookery* To Rdr., When I bid them lard a Fowl, if I should bid them lard with large Lardoons, they would not know what I meant: But when I say they must lard with little Pieces of Bacon, they know what I mean. **1845** ELIZA ACTON *Mod. Cookery* (ed. 2) 167 The lardoons..must be drawn through with a large larding-pin. **1884** *Girls' Own Paper* June 491/1 The process of inserting slips of bacon, called lardons, into lean meat by means of a larding-needle.

lardose ('lɑːdəʊs). *Obs.* exc. *Hist.* Also 6 laordose. [? a. F. *l'ardoise* (*ardoise* slate, with prefixed article).] The name given to the screen at the back of the high altar of Durham cathedral.
1593 *Anc. Mon. Rites, etc. Durham* (Surtees) 6 Betwixt the said High Altar and St. Cuthbert's Feriture is all of French Peere..with faire Images of alabaster being most finely gilted, beinge called in the antient history the Laordose [*ed.* 1672 Lardose], the said curious workmanshipp of French Peere or Laordose reachinge in hight almost to the middle vault. **1838** BRITTON *Dict. Archit.*, *Lardose*, a corruption of the French term *l'arrière dos*, employed to designate the high altar-screen of Durham Cathedral. **1850** in PARKER *Gloss. Terms Archit.*

† **'lardry**. *Obs.* Forms: 6-7 lardery, -erie, lardarie, -y, lardrie, -y. [ad. OF. *larderie*, f. *lard*: see LARD *sb.* and -ERY.] = LARDER *sb.*[1] 1.
1538 LELAND *Itin.* I. 55 The 4 [Tower] conteinith the Botery, Pantery, Pastery, Lardery, and Kechyn. **1594** BARNFIELD *Aff. Sheph.* II. xiv, Then will I lay out all my Lardarie (Of Cheese, of Cracknells, Curds and Clowted-creame). **1598** FLORIO, *Carnaio*, *Carnario*, a lardrie or place to hang and keepe meate in. **1631** WEEVER *Anc. Funeral Mon.* 630 Clarke of the Kings Kitchin, and keeper of his Lardarie. **1661** COWLEY *Adv. Exper. Philos.* in *Verses & Ess.* (1669) 45 That it contain the Kitchin, Butteries, Brew-house, Bakehouse, Dairy, Lardry, Stables, &c.
attrib. **1649** in E. B. Chancellor *Hist. Richmond* (1885) 91 One little Gallery above-stayrs, used for the Pantry and Larderie men.

lardy ('lɑːdɪ), *a.* [f. LARD *sb.* + -Y.] Full of or containing lard; fat.
1879 C. M. YONGE *Magnum Bonum* I. xiv. 261 Hot tea and 'lardy cake' tendered for his refreshment. **1881** *Oxfordsh. Gloss.* Suppl., *Lardy cake*, lard cake. Also *Fatty-cake.* **1888** R. DOWLING *Miracle Gold* I. v. 98 The pallid, lardy, stolid face of the publican. **1892** *Daily News* 23 Dec. 5/6 A quality of lean and nutritious flesh much superior to the lardy bacons which come from foreign countries. **1933** W. DE LA MARE *Lord Fish* 64 She had brought Griselda not only a pitcher of new milk..but some lardy-cakes and a jar of honey. **1970** SIMON & HOWE *Dict. Gastron.* 239/2 *Lardy cake*, country-style bread-dough cakes which appear in several English counties: Sussex, Wiltshire, Oxfordshire and Cambridgeshire.

lardy-dardy ('lɑːdɪ'dɑːdɪ), *a. slang.* [Cf. LA-DI-DA *sb.*] Characteristic of an affected swell; languidly foppish.
1861 MISS BRADDON *Trail Serpent* IV. vi. 227 You're not much good, my friend, says I, with your lardy-dardy ways, and your cold-blooded words, whoever you are. **1874** *Punch* 14 Mar. 109/1 This only when the lardy-dardy swells are present. **1887** *Illustr. Lond. News* 15 Oct. 448 The modern 'lardy-dardy' school [of acting].
Hence **lardy-dardy** *v. intr.*, to act the swell, to 'do the la-di-da'.
1887 SIMS *Mary Jane's Mem.* 58 Other men were lardy-dardying about..enjoying themselves.

† **lare**[1]. *Obs. rare*⁻¹. [ad. L. *larus.*] ? A seagull.
1388 WYCLIF *Lev.* xi. 16 A strucioun, and nyȝt crowe, a lare, and an hauke bi his kinde.

† **lare**[2]. *Obs.* [Of obscure origin: ? connected with LATHE *sb.*[3]] A turner's lathe.
1611 COTGR., *Tournoir*, a Turne, turning wheele, or Turners wheele, called a Lathe or Lare. **1684** R. WALLER *Nat. Exper.* 75 To take the Lump of Ice out whole, we made a small crease round it, where by putting it again in the Lare, it might be cut in two in the midst. *Ibid.* 77.

lare: see LAIR, LAYER, LORE.

laree: see LARIN.

larel, obs. form of LAUREL.

lares: see LAR.

† **larew**. *Obs.* Also 1 láréow, (lárow, láruu), 2 lareaw. [OE. *láréow*, for **lár-þéow* (whence ME. LORTHEW).] A teacher.
c **900** tr. *Bæda's Hist.* III. xviii. [xxiv.] (1890) 240 He hæfde ærest Trumhære biscop him to lareowe. *c* **950** *Lindisf. Gosp.* John iii. 2 La laruu ue uuton þætte from Gode ðu ȝecuome laruu. *c* **1050** *Voc.* in Wr.-Wülcker 390/35 *Dogmatista*, lareow. *a* **1175** *Cott. Hom.* 241 Ur hlaford sanctus paulus.. is þeoden lareaw. *c* **1200** ORMIN 7233 Bisskopess & larewess.

larf. ¶. Jocular spelling of LAUGH *sb.* and *v.*, esp. representing Cockney speech.
1847 *Punch* XII. 2/1 She is so innocent..a half-larfin, and a half-poutin. **1851** MRS. STOWE *Uncle Tom's Cabin* (1852) I. iv. 45 'And what did mother say?' said George. 'Say?—why, she kinder larfed in her eyes—dem great handsome eyes o' hern...' **1894** KIPLING *Day's Work* (1898) 62 The folks..larfed—why, they all but lay down themselves with larfin'. **1901** M. FRANKLIN *My Brilliant Career* (1966) xxxi. 196 A sorrowful lookin' delicate creetur', that couldn't larf to save her life. **1965** L. DEIGHTON *Horse under Water* iii. 19 'I'll larf, sir, that's what I will do; larf.' The Chief gave no sign of laughing either now or at any future time: I thought for a moment that LARF was some strange nautical verb. **1968** —— (*title*) Only when I larf. **1971** *Guardian* 8 Apr. 10/2 Give us a larf, pass the time.

‖**larga** ('lɑːgə). [Sp.] In bull-fighting, a pass using the cape (see quots.).
1932 E. HEMINGWAY *Death in Afternoon* xv. 170 Quites were made..by the use of largas. In these the cape was fully extended and one end offered to the bull who was drawn away following the extended cape and then turned on himself to fix him in place by a movement made by the matador who would swing the cape over his shoulder and walk away. **1957** A. MACNAB *Bulls of Iberia* v. 52 It is now the job of the peones to 'run' it, *correr al toro.* That means, to wave capes at it, get it to charge the capes, and give it long-distance passes. These are called *largas*, the big cape being held by one tip and sent flying out at full length. **1967** MCCORMICK & MASCAREÑAS *Compl. Aficionado* ii. 61 He works the toro with *largas. Ibid.*, In the larga, the cape is trailed in the sand with one hand as the torero runs (bregar) the toro.

Largactil (lɑː'gæktɪl). *Pharm.* Also **largactil**. A proprietary name of chlorpromazine hydrochloride, $C_{17}H_{19}ClN_2S{\cdot}HCl$, the form in which chlorpromazine is usually administered.
1953 *Trade Marks Jrnl.* 20 May 430/1 Largactil... May & Baker Limited, Dagenham, Essex; manufacturing chemists. **1965** J. POLLITT *Depression & its Treatment* iv. 56 In uncomplicated cases, the intramuscular injection of chlorpromazine (Largactil) 100 mg. is helpful. **1966** *New Statesman* 4 Feb. 168/1 Others might use a quarter grain of Largactil to take the edge off life in London or the Midlands. **1970** G. GREER *Female Eunuch* 90 If all else fails largactil.. and other forms of 'therapy' will buttress the claim of society.

‖**largamente** (larga'mente, ˌlɑːgə'mɛnteɪ), *adv. Mus.* [It.] (See quots.)
1876 STAINER & BARRETT *Dict. Mus. Terms* 252/1 *Largamente (It.)*, slowly, widely, freely, fully. **1880** GROVE *Dict. Mus.* II. 92/1 (s.v. *largo*), The term *Largamente* has recently come into use to denote breadth of style without change of *tempo.* **1958** *Times* 27 Nov. 6/6 He did cause just one raised eyebrow with the very much slower tempo he adopted for the *largamente* second subject tune in the finale.

‖**largando** (lar'gando, lɑː'gændəʊ), *adv. Mus.* [It.] = ALLARGANDO.
1893 J. S. SHEDLOCK tr. *Riemann's Dict. Mus.* 429/1 *Largando* (*slargando, allargando*) Ital., 'broadening'; as a rule it is united with *crescendo.* **1972** *Harper's Dict. Mus.* 178/1 *Largando*..Italian, another spelling of *allargando.*

large (lɑːdʒ), *a.*, *adv.*, and *sb.* Forms: 4-7 larg, 6 largue, *Sc.* lairg, lairge, lerge, 6-7 lardg(e, 2- large. [a. F. *large*, now chiefly in the sense 'broad, wide':—L. *larga*, fem. of *largus* abundant, copious, bountiful, profuse. The masc. *largus* gave OF. *larc*, *larg* (whence ME. *larg*, *largue*), but these forms were ultimately supplanted by the fem. form *large*; though in nautical senses mod.F. has *largue* masc. and fem., adopted from southern dialects. Cf. Pr. *larg*, *largue*, broad, Sp., Pg. *largo* long, It. *largo* wide.]
A. *adj.*
†**I. 1.** Liberal in giving; generous; bountiful, munificent; open-handed. Also, liberal in expenditure, prodigal, lavish. (Cf. FOOL-LARGE.) Const. *of*, *in*. *Obs.*
c **1175** *Lamb. Hom.* 143 Þe large Men and þe milde Men.. sculen beon icleoped on þe fader riht halue. *a* **1225** *Ancr. R.* 430 Se uorð ase ȝe muwen of drunch and of mete and of cloð, ..beoð large touward ham [servants], þauh ȝe þe neruwure beon and te herdure to ou suluen. **13..** *Guy Warw.* (A.)

1265 He was large, curteys, and fre. **1375** BARBOUR *Bruce* XI. 148 The landis of Scotland delt he then Of othir mennis landis large wes he. *c* **1386** CHAUCER *Pars. T.* ₱391 To be liberal, that is to seyn, large by mesure. *a* **1420** HOCCLEVE *De Reg. Princ.* 1393 She [Fortune] lovethe yonge folk and large of despence. *c* **1450** *Merlin* 150 Yef euer ye haue be large of yeftes here before, loke now that ye be larger hensforth. **1470–85** MALORY *Arthur* VII. vii, Syre knyghte thou art ful large of my hors and my harneys, I lete the wete it coste the noughte. *c* **1500** *Lancelot* 1765 Beith larg and iffis frely of thi thing. **1530** PALSGR. 317/1 Large in expence, *prodigue*. **1553** GRIMALDE *Cicero's Offices* II. (1558) 99 That other kinde of largegiuing whiche proceedes of liberalitie. **1593** SHAKS. *2 Hen. VI*, I. i. 11 The poore King Reignier, whose large style Agrees not with the leannesse of his purse. **1664** J. WILSON *Cheats* V. iii. Dram. Wks. (1874) 93 Indeed I won't! You have been large to me already. [Jolly *would press money upon him.*] **1688** DRYDEN *Britannia Rediv.* 86 Large of his treasures.

absol. **13..** *K. Alis.* 2054 Theo large geveth; the nythyng lourith. **1484** CAXTON *Fables of Æsop* V. xii. (1889) 170 And therefore more despendeth the nygard than the large.

II. Ample, wide, great.

†**2.** Ample in quantity; copious, abundant. *Obs.*; merged in sense 8.

The early instances referring to gifts or alms may belong to sense 1.

a **1225** *Ancr. R.* 168 Noble men & wummen makieð large relef. *a* **1240** *Ureisun* in *Cott. Hom.* 187 Hwet deþ þenne þi blod isched on þe rode, hwet deþ þenne þe large broc of þi softe side. *a* **1300** *Cursor M.* 3964 Iacob þan sent him of his aght Giftes large. *a* **1400–50** *Alexander* 602 Large lyons lockis þat lange ere and scharpe. *c* **1425** LYDG. *Assembly of Gods* 2067 That to dysceme I purpose nat to deele So large by my wyll hit longeth nat to me. **1552** HULOET, Large, aboundaunt or plentyfull, *affluens*. **1578** TIMME *Calvin on Gen.* 161 This.. offereth unto us, large matter of bewailing our misery. **1582** N. T. (Rhem.) *Mark.* xii. 40 These shall receive larger judgement [Vulg. *prolixius judicium*; 1611 greater damnation]. **1599** HAKLUYT *Voy.* II. I. 31 The kings of France and England gaue large money towards the maintenance of the army. **1635** R. N. *Camden's Hist. Eliz.* I. an. 9. 67 She gave them large thanks. **1667** MILTON *P.L.* V. 558 And we have yet large day, for scarce the Sun Hath finisht half his journey.

3. † **a.** Ample in spatial extent; allowing plenty of room; spacious, roomy, capacious. *Obs.*; merged in sense 8.

a **1225** *Ancr. R.* 18 Makieð on ower muþe mit te þume a creoiz, & et ' Deus in adjutorium', a large creoiz mit þe þreo vingres vrom abuue þe vorheaued dun to þe breoste. *c* **1330** R. BRUNNE *Chron.* (1810) I. 144 Large er þo landes, þat his eldres wonnen. **1382** WYCLIF *Heb.* ix. 11 Forsoth Crist beynge a bischop of goodis to comynge [entride] bi a larger and perfiter tabernacle [L. *amplius et perfectius*]. **1390** GOWER *Conf.* III. 27 He seeth her front is large and pleine Withoute frounce of any greine. *c* **1400** *Destr. Troy* 10389 Olofte for to lenge in his large sete. **1526** *Pilgr. Perf.* (W. de W. 1531) 2 b, The byrde in a cage, be the cage.. neuer so large and hye, can not be contented or quyete. **1530** PALSGR. 237/2 Large grounde, *covrtil*. *Ibid.* 317/1 Large wyde and brode, *spacieux*, *ample*. **1604** E. G[RIMSTONE] *D' Acosta's Hist. Indies* V. xvii. 373 They retired themselves into a large place, where there were many lights. **1697** DRYDEN *Virg. Georg.* IV. 531 Two Golden Horns on his large Front he wears.

† **b.** Const. *of*.

c **1340** *Cursor M.* 22322 (Fairf.) A mikil man of stature heye & large of face. *c* **1400** MAUNDEV. (1839) V. 43 So is the Contree large of Lengthe. **1535** COVERDALE *Neh.* vii. 4 As for yᵉ cite, it was large of rowme, and greate.

c. *fig.* Of the 'heart': Capacious. Cf. 6.

In the earliest instances the expression is a literal translation from the Heb., where 'heart' means intellect.

1535 COVERDALE *1 Kings* iv. 29 God gaue Salomon maruelous greate wyszdome and vnderstondinge, and a large hert. **1667** MILTON *P.L.* I. 444 That uxorius King, whose heart though large, Beguil'd by fair Idolatresses, fell To Idols foul. **1686** WALLER *H.R.H. Mother to Pr. Orange* Poems 244 Tho streighter Bounds your Fortune did confine, In your large Heart was found a wealthy Mine. **1876** BLACKIE *Songs Relig. & Life* 228 The brain by knowledge grows, the heart Is larger made by loving.

†**4.** Extensive in transverse dimension; = BROAD *a.* 1, 1 b. [The usual sense in mod.Fr.] Often in phrase ***long and large***, for which ***wide and large*** sometimes occurs. *Obs.*

1377 LANGL. *P. Pl.* B. XVIII. 45 Bothe as longe and as large bi loft and by grounde. *c* **1400** MAUNDEV. (Roxb.) V. 16 It es nere hand a c. cubites large. **1500–20** DUNBAR *Poems* lxxii. 49 Ane croce that was baith large and lang, To beir thai gaif that blessit Lord. **1578** LYTE *Dodoens* I. viii. 15 The great Clote hath leaves very large and long. **1599** ABP. ABBOT *Descr. World* (1634) 281 The Spaniards.. entered Florida.. and there conquered a thousand miles wide and large. **1653** H. COGAN tr. *Pinto's Trav.* xxxviii. 152 Three hundred ladders made, very strong, and so large, that three men might easily mount up on them a front. **1667** MILTON *P.L.* I. 195 His other Parts.. extended long and large Lay floating many a rood. *Ibid.* IV. 223 Southward through Eden went a River large. **1709** BLAIR in *Phil. Trans.* XXVII. 141 Two Tusks 2½ Spans large, and 8 foot long. **1715** LEONI *Palladio's Archit.* (1742) I. 78 The Ways ought to be.. so large, that Carriages and Horses be no hindrance to each other when they meet.

†**5.** **a.** With definite measures of space and time, indicating the full or rather more than the full quantity: = GOOD A. 20. *Obs.*

1377 LANGL. *P. Pl.* B. x. 162 Leue him on thi left halue a large myle or more. **1529** *Malory's Arthur* x. lxiv, They fought.. two large houres and neuer brethed them. **1678** *Lond. Gaz.* No. 1315/1 At Bucken, a large League from Friburg. **1707** *Ibid.* 4336/7 As to the Breadth of the Chanel, it is a large half Mile. **1737** tr. *Le Comte's Mem. & Rem. China* iii. 79 The steps.. being almost all 10 large inches high.

† **b.** Of the time of day: Fully come, full. *Obs.*

c **1386** CHAUCER *Sqr.'s T.* 352 They slepen til that it was pryme large. *c* **1470** HENRY *Wallace* IV. 223 Thir men went furth as it was large mydnycht.

6. **a.** Of immaterial things: Wide in range or capacity; comprehensive, extensive, capacious.

a **1300** *Cursor M.* 93 Mater fynd ȝe large and brade? **1340** HAMPOLE *Pr. Consc.* 3915 Bot alle þis dett may þar be qwytt Thurgh large pardon, wha-swa has itt. *c* **1400** *Apol. Loll.* 8 A feiþful curat owiþ to notify to his sugets, were is pardoun, sikirar, largar, & for les price, to be bout to his sogets. **1500** *Galway Arch.* in *10th Rep. Hist. MSS. Comm.* App. v. 391 In as ampull and lardg manner as we grauntid to anny other ffreman. *a* **1548** HALL *Chron.*, *Hen. IV* 15 b, Exhortyng them with large promisses and flatteryng wordes. **1560** DAUS tr. *Sleidane's Comm.* 239 b, I wyll sende Ambassadours to the assemblye with large commission. **1595** SHAKS. *John* I. i. 88 Doe you not read some tokens of my sonne In the large composition of this man? **1606** —— *Tr. & Cr.* I. iii. 223 Fair leaue and large security. **1667** MILTON *P.L.* XII. 305 From imposition of strict Laws, to free Acceptance of large Grace. **1704** SWIFT *Mechan. Operat. Spir.* Misc. (1711) 296 A large Memory, plentifully fraught with Theological Polysyllables. *a* **1715** BURNET *Own Time* (1724) I. 179 It was resolved, that whatever should be granted.. should go in so large a manner, that Papists should be comprehended within it. **1730–46** THOMSON *Autumn* 280 Vernal suns and showers Diffuse their warmest, largest influence. **1738** WESLEY *Ps.* CXVI. v, How good Thou art, How large thy Grace! **1778** SIR J. REYNOLDS *Disc.* viii. (1876) 450 Notions large, liberal and complete. **1779–81** JOHNSON *L.P.*, *Smith*, His memory was large and tenacious. **1784** COWPER *Task* III. 423 No portion left That may disgrace his art, or disappoint Large expectation. **1793** BURKE *Policy Allies* Wks. VII. 176, I speak of policy too in a large light; in which large light, policy too is a sacred thing. **1842** TENNYSON *Locksley Hall* 111 Yearning for the large excitement that the coming years would yield. **1849** MACAULAY *Hist. Eng.* i. I. 106 A good reason for giving large powers to a trustworthy magistrate. *a* **1859** *Ibid.* xxiii. (1861) V. 91 The English Government.. had been willing to make large allowance for Berwick's peculiar position. **1885** SIR N. LINDLEY in *Law Times Rep.* LII. 319/2, I think the language is large enough to include them. **1886** *Law Times* LXXXI. 172/1 The court had a large discretion as to the joinder of parties.

b. Of persons, with reference to some specified attribute or action. Const. *in*, *of*. Cf. sense 1.

c **1375** *Sc. Leg. Saints*, *Theodera* 220 þu art larg of cheryte. **1574** HELLOWES *Gueuara's Fam. Ep.* (1577) 63 It is not a iust thing to be large in sinning, and short in praying. **1612** T. TAYLOR *Comm. Titus* iii. 1 When Paul would be large in commending the Church of the Romanes, he affirmeth they were full of goodnesse. **1672** WILKINS *Nat. Relig.* 326 To be generous and large in their well-wishing and their well-doing. **1883** F. M. PEARD *Contrad.* xxvi, He was large in his offers of friendship towards a young nephew of Mr. Pritchard's.

c. With reference to artistic treatment: Broad.

1782 SIR J. REYNOLDS *Disc.* xi. (1876) 28 In his colouring he was large and general.

7. **a.** Of discourse, narrative, or literary treatment: Ample, copious, lengthy. Now *rare*.

1477 MARG. PASTON in *P. Lett.* No. 799 III. 193 The large comunycacyon that dyvers tymes hathe ben had towchyng the maryage of my cosyn Margery.. and my son Iohn. **1526** TINDALE *Acts* xx. 2 When he had gone over those parties, and geven them large exhortacions. **1577** FRAMPTON *Joyful News* II. (1596) 80 Of many others which shoulde bee verie large to speake of. **1622** R. HAWKINS *Voy. S. Sea* 131 It were large to recount the voyages and worthy enterprises overthrowne by this pollicie. **1655** STANLEY *Hist. Philos.* II. (1701) 65/1 Plutarch, hath this large Discourse upon it. **1675** TEMPLE *Let. to Chas. II* Wks. 1731 II. 344 Since the Prince's Return, I have had two large Discourses with his Highness. **1685** WOOD *Life* 13 Apr., Mr. Wyatt spake a large speech by hart. **1705** HEARNE *Collect.* 23 July (O.H.S.) I. 13 Mr. Milles writ a large reply. **1756–82** J. WARTON *Ess. Pope* (ed. 4) I. ii. 49 These observations on Thomson.. would not have been so large if there had been already any considerable criticism on his Character. **1860** MOTLEY *Netherl.* (1868) I. v. 273 He fell into large and particular discourse with the deputies.

† **b.** Of persons: Copious in writing or speech; diffuse, lengthy, prolix. *Obs.*

1605 BACON *Adv. Learn.* II. xviii. §8 (1873) 181 *Antitheta* are theses argued *pro et contra*; wherein men may be more large and laborious. **1613** PURCHAS *Pilgrimage* (1614) 108 My intent is to bee largest in relation of those things which are not in the Scriptures. **1618** BOLTON *Florus* (1636) Ded., He held it more honorable to be.. the first among briefe writers than one among few in the large ones. **1668** TEMPLE *Let. to Ld. Arlington* Wks. 1731 II. 82 The Marquis is large in arguing to me, that our Interest lies in a joint War. **1679** PENN *Addr. Prot.* II. App. (1692) 240, I could be very large upon this point. **1711** HEARNE *Collect.* (O.H.S.) III. 136, I am afraid he will be much too large, tho' 'tis certain wᵗ he shall do will be very curious and learned. **1737** WHISTON *Josephus*, *Antiq.* XII. vi. §3 He was very large in his encomiums upon the young man. **1763** J. BROWN *Poetry & Mus.* vi. 111 Homer is equal, large, flowing and harmonious; Eschylus is uneven, concise, abrupt and rugged. **1788** PRIESTLEY *Lect. Hist.* IV. xxiii. 179 His work is an epitome of the Roman History to his own times, upon which he is more large.

8. In mod.Eng., a general designation for considerable magnitude, used instead of *great* when it is not intended to convey the emotional implication now belonging to that word. (See GREAT *a.* 6.) The more colloquial or less refined synonym is *big*.

a. Of material objects. Also in phrases like ***large of limb*** = 'having large limbs'.

Not ordinarily said of persons; the occasional use of expressions like 'a large man' is somewhat playful, the notion being 'taking up a great deal of room'. To say 'the larger (= 'bigger') children' is admissible, if perh. somewhat unusual, but the positive (and, indeed, the comparative in the singular) could not be similarly used.

In the earlier examples there may be some notion of the sense 'ample'.

c **1440** *Promp. Parv.* 288/1 Large, hey, longe, and semely, *procerus*. **1526** TINDALE *Gal.* vi. 11 Beholde how large a letter I have written vnto you with myne awne honde. *c* **1560** A. SCOTT *Poems* (S.T.S.) ii. 135 Thow art moir lerge of lyth and lym Nor I am, be sic thre. **1590** SHAKS. *Mids. N.* IV. i. 4 While I.. kisse thy faire large eares. **1596** DALRYMPLE tr. *Leslie's Hist. Scot.* I. 46 In this toune is the Kingis castel baith lairge and stark. **1611** BIBLE *Mark* xiv. 15 He will shew you a large [Gr. μέγα : earlier versions 'great'] vpper roome furnished. **1667** MILTON *P.L.* x. 529 Now Dragon grown, larger than whom the Sun Ingenderd in the Pythian Vale on slime. **1697** DRYDEN *Virg. Georg.* IV. 805 A large Cluster of black Grapes. —— *Æneid* x. 432 Great Theron, large of Limb, of Gyant height. **1751** *Affect. Narr. Wager* 89 One of us killed a large Seal.. Such Hits as these were but rare, and very far from affording Supplies. **1791** W. BARTRAM *Carolina* 10 These swamps are daily clearing and improving into large fruitful rice plantations. **1803** RAPTON *Landsc. Gard.* (1805) 21 We generally pronounce that object large, the whole of which the eye cannot at once comprehend. **1816** J. SMITH *Panorama Sci. & Art* I. 14 The large vice must be firmly fixed to the side of the work-bench. **1837** DICKENS *Pickw.* ii, A large lady in blue satin. **1837** MRS. SHERWOOD *H. Milner* III. xvi. 323 An infant, and three or four larger children. **1840** MARRYAT *Poor Jack* i, He was a very large man, standing six feet high. **1868** LOCKYER *Elem. Astron.* iii. §16 (1879) 91 At rising or setting, the Moon sometimes appears to be larger than it does when high up in the sky. **1870** DICKENS *E. Drood* vi, 'Is he a large man, Ma?' 'I should call him a large man, my dear.. but that his voice is so much larger'. **1895** *Bookman* Oct. 26/2 Plans.. should not be large folded sheets, but single page plans of small districts.. with a key-map. **1896** *Law Times Rep.* LXXIII. 615/1 There were two gates, one large one for carriages and the other a small one for foot passengers.

absol. **1595** SHAKS. *John* II. i. 101 This little abstract doth containe that large, Which died in Geffrey.

b. Used in the specific names of objects, esp. plants and animals, to distinguish a kind or variety of greater size than the ordinary; also used similarly (chiefly *pred.*) as the trade term for a size of clothing, packet, etc. **Large Black (pig)**, a pig belonging to the variety so called, developed late in the 19th century and formerly called the Devonshire Black; **large-paper**, a size of paper used for a special or limited edition of a book, having wider margins than that of the ordinary edition; also *attrib.*; **Large White (pig)**, a heavy bacon pig of the variety so called, first introduced in Yorkshire about 1850 and formerly called the Yorkshire pig.

The compar. *larger* and superl. *largest* are also used in specific names, as ***larger cabinet beetle, larger red-crested woodpecker, largest red oak***.

1714 *Lond. Gaz.* No. 5225/3 The Price of the few large Paper that are printed [will be] 40*s.* per Book in Sheets. **1727** CHAMBERS *Cycl.* s.v. *Minion*, The large Minion, or one of the largest size, has its bore 3¼ inch diameter, and is 1000 pounds weight. **1787** W. SARGENT in *Mem. Amer. Acad. Arts & Sci.* (1793) II. 159 Large Laurel. **1802** DIBDIN *Introd. Classics* 11 *note*, The large paper edition of this work is chiefly sought after. **1810** F. A. MICHAUX *Hist. Arbres Forestiers de l' Amérique Septentrionale* I. 39 American large aspen.. nom donné par moi. **1813** H. MUHLENBERG *Catal. Plant.* 92 Large aspen (*Populus trepida* or *grandidentata*). **1832** D. J. BROWNE *Sylva Amer.* 255 As it surpasses the aspen in height, we have given it the name of Large Aspen. **1832** J. RENNIE *Conspectus Butterflies & Moths Brit.* 259/1 Large Blue.. Large Copper. **1832** T. BROWN *Bk. Butterflies, Sphinxes & Moths* I. 18 (*heading*) The large white cabbage butterfly. **1837** MACGILLIVRAY *Withering's Brit. Plants* (ed. 4) 334 Large White Helleborine. **1837** *Southern Lit. Messenger* III. 660 There are for sale hats, boots and shoes, India rubber articles,.. large bread,.. everything on earth. **1845** C. M. KIRKLAND *Western Clearings* 154 'You'd ought to begin with large-hand, Joshuay,' said Master Horner to this youth [instructing him in penmanship]. **1857** H. T. STAINTON *Man. Brit. Butterflies & Moths* I. 11 The Swallow-tail and the Large Copper are only to be obtained in the fens of Cambridgeshire and Huntingdonshire. **1859** STAINTON *Brit. Butterflies & Moths* II. 34 *Geometra papilionaria* (Large Emerald). **1859** BAGEHOT *Coll. Works* (1965) II. 190 A large-hand copy of life. **1862** E. NEWMAN *Brit. Moths* (1869) 299 The Large Nutmeg (*Mamestra anceps*). **1867** *Jrnl. R. Agric. Soc.* III. 633 Some of the classes, the large white breed and those not qualified for the specified classes were only scantily filled. **1876** H. E. SCUDDER *Dwellers in Five-Sisters Court* i. 7 There was a large-bread bakery at Skōlas. **1878** *Print. Trades Jrnl.* xxv. 20 Large post folio size. **1883** WALLEM *Fish. Supply Norway* 16 (Fish. Exhib. Publ.) 'Large' or North-herring. **1896** W. J. MALDEN *Pig Keeping for Profit* i. 12 The Large White started with a strong frame. **1896** *Allbutt's Syst. Med.* I. 192 Fatty changes in the kidneys.. Large white, and small white kidneys. **1897** *Sears, Roebuck Catal.* (1968) 29/1 Bromo-Caffeine, large. *a* **1902** *Mod.* The second edition of the book is a large octavo. **1906** J. LONG *Bk. Pig* (ed. 2) xii. 156 The Large Blacks are regarded as being of gentle disposition... The chief counties in which the Large Black pig is bred are Cornwall and Devon. **1909** *T. Eaton & Co. Catal.* Fall & Winter 84/2 Men's heavy ribbed red wool undershirt.. sizes small, medium and large. **1947** J. STEVENSON-HAMILTON *Wild Life S. Afr.* xxv. 205 The large grey mongoose (*Herpestes caffer*).—Colour, grizzled grey, limbs darker. A black brush at the end of the tail. Length over all, about 45 inches. This animal is spread throughout the Ethiopian region. **1961** J. FITZHUGH *Pig Breeding* xiv. 160 The National Pig Breeders' Association caters for the Large Blacks, Large Whites, [etc.]. **1966** [see *economy-size* s.v. ECONOMY 9.] **1966** E. PALMER *Plains of Camdeboo* x. 181 The large grey mongoose is nocturnal and rarely seen. **1970** *Times* 19 Aug. 9/7 There are five or six species (e.g. the Large Blue or Glanville Fritillary) which ought to be protected. **1971** *Farmers Weekly* (Extra) 19 Mar. 37/2 The Farnsworths fatten all progeny from a herd of 60 Welsh sows, put to the Large White boar. **1973** T. G. HOWARTH

South's Brit. Butterflies 51 The tiny parasitic wasp, *Apanteles glomeratus* Linnaeus.. normally acts as a control to the common Large White caterpillar. **1974** *Times* 26 Apr. 7/7 The tights..are in three sizes—Petite, Medium or Large... The large size will not be ready until July. **1985** R. Lourie *First Loyalty* xiv. 92 'How about the size?' 'Size?' 'Sweater size. Small, medium, large.'

c. Of collective unities, quantities, dimensions, or any immaterial entity of which extensive as distinct from intensive magnitude can be predicated.

1526 Tindale *Rev.* xxi. 16 The length was as large as the bredth of hitt. **1679** Penn *Addr. Prot.* ii. v. (1692) 135 [It] is..in a large Degree true among us. **1751** Labelye *Westm. Br.* 72 At the Commissioners Desire, and before a very large Board, I had the Honour of explaining..my Method. **1823** De Quincey *Lett. Educ.* ii. Wks. (1860) XIV. 26 Forty years are not too large a period for such a work. **1849** Macaulay *Hist. Eng.* iii. I. 325 It is certainly now more than seven times as great as the larger of these two sums. *Ibid.* vii. II. 216 That party was not large; but the..virtues of those who belonged to it made it respectable. **1881** Jowett *Thucyd.* I. 224 The simplicity which is so large an element in a noble nature was laughed to scorn and disappeared. **1895** R. L. Douglas in *Bookman* Oct. 22/2 Louis [XIV] was in a large measure responsible for the horrors of the Revolution. *Mod.* He made large profits on some articles, but his business did not pay on the whole.

d. Of a movement, pace, etc.: Covering a good extent of ground at a step. (Cf. B. 6.)

c **1400** tr. *Secreta Secret., Gov. Lordsh.* 117 He, þat yn goynge, hauys his paas large and latly, welfare shall folwe him yn all his werkys. **1719** De Foe *Crusoe* I. xx. (1840) 358 As fast as we could make our horses go, which..was only a good large trot. **17..** in 'J. Larwood' (L. R. Sadler) *Bk. Cleric. Anecd.* (1871) 229 [A contemporary journalist describes Orator Henley as entering like a harlequin by a door behind the pulpit, and] at one large leap jumping into it, and falling to work.

†**e.** *rarely* of actions or processes, with reference to degree.

1660–1 Marvell *Corr.* xviii. Wks. 1872–5 II. 50 As I shall haue more busynesse or more news, I shall giue you a larger trouble. **1748** *Anson's Voy.* II. xiii. 276 They..found every where so large a surf, that there was not the least possibility of their landing.

f. Of a meal: Heavy, abundant (cf. 2). ? *rare.*

1748 *Anson's Voy.* III. ii. 313 Having..made a large beef breakfast. **1890** Kipling *Light that failed* vi, After a large lunch they went down to the beach.

g. Of sounds heard in auscultation: Full, sonorous. Also of the pulse: Full.

1822–34 *Good's Study Med.* (ed. 4) I. 544 *note*, If a pulse be both hard and large, it is a strong pulse also. **1898** *Allbutt's Syst. Med.* V. 10 To the first [class] belong the large or sonorous, the small or sibilant, and the intermediate or subsibilant rhonchi. *Ibid.* 142 The large, coarse, toneless rattles produced by mucus and air in the trachea and larger bronchi.

h. With an agent-noun or its equivalent: That is engaged in the occupation or business implied on a large scale.

1883 *Manch. Exam.* 29 Oct. 5/4 The largest calico printer in the world. **1891** J. G. Paton *Autobiog.* 4 Large farmers and small farmers. **1892** *Law Times* XCII. 177/2 A very large oyster planter.

i. *law of large numbers* [tr. F. *loi des grands nombres* (S. D. Poisson 1835, in *Compt. Rend.* I. 478)]: a statistical law which states that if a series of independent trials or observations is made, in each of which there is the same probability of a particular outcome, then as the number of trials is made larger the chance that the observed proportion of such outcomes differs from the probability by less than any given number, however small, approaches a certainty (or, in stronger terms, the observed proportion approaches the probability).

[**1921** J. M. Keynes *Treat. Probability* xxviii. 336 The 'Law of Great Numbers' is not at all a good name for the principle which underlies Statistical Induction. The 'Stability of Statistical Frequencies' would be a much better name for it. The former suggests, as perhaps Poisson intended.., what is certainly false, that every class of event shows statistical regularity of occurrence if only one takes a sufficient number of instances of it. It..encourages the method..by which it is thought legitimate to take an observed degree of frequency or association, which is shown in a fairly numerous set of statistics, and to assume..that, because the statistics are numerous, the observed degree of frequency is therefore stable.] **1937** J. V. Uspensky *Introd. Math. Probability* x. 182 A far reaching generalization of Bernoulli's theorem, known under the name of the 'law of large numbers'. **1949** W. Kneale *Probability & Induction* III. 139 Many people who have heard of it under the name of the law of large numbers..suppose it to be a mysterious law of nature which guarantees that in a sufficiently large number of trials a probability will be 'realized as a frequency'. *Ibid.* 141 As an illustration of the importance of the law of large numbers in practical affairs it will be sufficient to mention the business of insurance... The greater the number of persons insuring with the company, the greater the probability that the company's finances will remain sound. **1960** S. Goldberg *Probability* iv. 227 The law of large numbers can be used to supply a theoretical counterpart to our intuitive feeling that if an event *A* occurs *f* times in *n* identical trials and if *n* is large, then *f/n*, the proportion of times *A* occurs, should be near the probability *P*(*A*) of the event *A*.

j. larger-than-life *attrib. phr.* Cf. LIFE *sb.* 7 a.

1950 *New Yorker* 23 Dec. 42 Inviting Mr. Churchill..as the living, larger-than-life embodiment of the British people's opposition to appeasement. **1967** *Sunday Times* 23 Apr. 49 The larger-than-life political figures thunder their dogmas through the act. **1972** D. Francis *Smokescreen* ii. 27, I had very little in common with the sort of larger-than-life action man I played in film after film. **1972** *Jazz & Blues* Oct. 22/1 For many years Mezzrow was an almost larger than life personality.

9. Of speech or manner: Pompous, imposing, assuming airs of grandeur, 'big'.

1605 Shaks. *Lear* I. i. 187 Your large speeches, may your deeds approue. **1818** Hallam *Mid. Ages* (1872) III. 153 The prerogative was always named in large and pompous expressions. **1894** Hall Caine *Manxman* III. xx. 192 Cæsar made a prolonged A-hm! and said in a large way, 'Has the carriage arrived?'

III. Not rigorous or restricted: lax, free. [Developed from sense 3.]

†**10.** Indulgent, lax; not strict or rigorous. *Obs.*

c **1440** *Jacob's Well* xvi. 108 Takyng non hede of þi wycked suspectys..ne of þi consentyng to euyll, ne of þi large conscyence. **1594** *Mirr. Policy* (1599) Nij, Kings..ought..to be carefull, that they put not couetous men & such as haue a large conscience in publick offices & authority. **1604** Parsons *3rd Pt. Three Convers. Eng.* 374 The King, vpon his first breach with the Pope, was somewhat carelesse & large towards the protestants. **1609** Bible (Douay) *1 Sam.* xxiv. Comm., A large conscience sticketh at nothing. **1694** Strype *Mem. Cranmer* III. xxxvi. 456 When King Henry was large towards the Protestants, Cranmer was so also. **1733** Neal *Hist. Purit.* II. 245 If the Puritans were too strict in keeping Holy the Sabbath, his Grace [Laud] was too large in his indulgence.

†**11. a.** Having few or no restrictions or limitations; allowing considerable freedom. Also said of persons with respect to their thought or action.

c **1510** *Lytell geste Robyn hode* (W. de W.) VII. 108 Smyte on boldely sayd Robyn I gyue the large leue. *a* **1548** Hall *Chron., Hen. IV* 10 It was concluded, that kyng Richard should continew in a large prisone. **1635** R. N. *Camden's Hist. Eliz.* III. an. 27. 267 Shee besought that she might be kept in larger custody. **1671** Milton *P.R.* I. 365 Leaving my dolorous Prison I enjoy Large liberty to round this Globe of Earth. **1680** *Connect. Col. Rec.* (1859) III. 299 Our people in this Colony are, some strict Congregationall men, others more large Congregationall men, and some moderate Presbeterians. **1793** in Morse *Amer. Geog.* (1796) I. 274 General Baptists..who hold Large Communion.

b. Liberated, free. Const. *of. Obs. rare.*

1600 Fairfax *Tasso* I. lxxxiv. 18 Of burdens all he set the Paynims large.

c. Of 'circumstances': Easy. *Obs.*

1738 Neal *Hist. Purit.* IV. 404 Many families who the last week were in large circumstances, were now reduced to beggary.

†**12.** Of language: Used in a wide sense, loose, inaccurate. *Obs. rare.*

c **1400** *Lanfranc's Cirurg.* 305 Cauterium is seid in ij. maners, þat is to seie large & streit [L. *cauterium dicitur duobus modis, large & stricte*]. *c* **1449** Pecock *Repr.* I. xix. 116 In thilk maner of vnpropre and large speche, in which it may thouȝ vnpropirli be seid that [etc.].

†**13.** Of speech, etc.: Free, unrestrained; (in bad sense) lax, licentious, improper, gross. *Obs.*

c **1374** Chaucer *Troylus* v. 804 Som men seyn he [Diomede] was of tunge large. *c* **1380** Wyclif *Serm.* Sel. Wks. I. 73 þei seien þat Baptist was to harde, and Cristis lyfe was to large, but þei have founden a good mene. *c* **1400** *Rom. Rose* 4144 On me he leyeth a pitous charge, Bicause his tunge was to large. *c* **1401** Lydg. *Flour Curtesye* 157 Dredful also of tonges that ben large. **1553** Grimalde *Cicero's Offices* I. (1558) 46 The very maner of our iesting muste not be to large nor unsober. **1599** Shaks. *Much Ado* II. iii. 206 The man doth fear God, howsoeuer it seemes not in him, by some large ieasts hee will make. *Ibid.* IV. i. 53, I neuer tempted her with word too large.

14. *Naut.* Said of a wind that crosses the line of the ship's course in a favourable direction, esp. on the beam or quarter. (Cf. F. *vent largue*; also FREE *a.* 13 b.)

1591 in *Hakluyt's Voy.* (1600) III. 491 When the wind came larger we waied anchor and set saile. **1627** Capt. Smith *Seaman's Gram.* ix. 44 When a ship sailes with a large wind towards the land. **1669** Narborough in *Acc. Sev. Late Voy.* I. (1694) 8 As we got Southerly and the Wind grew large, we might alter our Course when we would. **1748** *Anson's Voy.* II. vii. 215 As we had the wind large, we kept in a good depth of water. **1769** Falconer *Dict. Marine* (1780) K k 3 b, The ships..have the wind six points large, or more properly on the quarter; which is considered as the most favourable manner of sailing, because all the sails co-operate to increase the ship's velocity. **1851** in Kipping *Sailmaking* (ed. 2) 185.

IV. 15. *Comb.* **a.** Parasynthetic combinations, unlimited in number, as ***large-acred, -bayed, -berried, -billed, -bodied, -boned, -brained, -browed, -celled, -dugged, -featured, -finned, -flewed, -flowered, -framed, -fronded, -fruited, -grained, -headed, -ideaed, -leaved, -limbed, -looked, -lugged, -moulded, -mouthed, -natured, -quartered, -scaled, -sized, -souled, -spaced, -thoughted, -utteranced, -viewed, -wheeled*** adjs.; also ***large-angle, -aperture, -bore, -calibre, -denomination, -scale, -signal, -size, -type*** adjs. **b.** Combinations with pa. pples., in which *large* is used as a complement, as ***large-drawn, -grown, -made*** adjs. **c.** Special comb.: **large calorie** = CALORIE a; **large-eyed** *a.*, having a large eye or large eyes; characterized by wide open eyes; **large-greaved** *a.*, the specific epithet of the S. American tortoise *Podocnemis expansa*, having the legs protected by large greave-like plates; **large-lung** *a. Path.* = *large-lunged* adj.; **large-lunged** *a. Path.*, characterized by enlargement of the lungs; **large-minded** *a.*, having a liberal or generous mind; marked by breadth of ideas; taking a large view of things; hence ***large-mindedness*** (in recent Dicts.); **large-mouth (bass)**, a variety of the black bass, *Micropterus salmoides*; also **large-mouthed bass**; † **large-parted** *a.*, of great parts or talents; **large-scale** *a.*, drawn to a large scale, on a large scale, extensive, widespread, relating to large numbers; so **large-scale integration** *Electronics*, the development or use of integrated circuits that each contain a large number of components. Also LARGE-HANDED, LARGE-HEARTED.

1737 Pope *Hor. Epist.* II. ii. 240 Heathcote himself, and such *large-acred men. **1956** *Nature* 3 Mar. 413/1 *Large-angle scatters of cosmic-ray particles. **1966** D. G. Brandon *Mod. Techniques Metallogr.* iii. 138 Few electrons are backscattered out of the target, and those which do escape do so principally by large-angle Rutherford collisions. **1935** *Discovery* Jan. 25/1 The picture was taken on sensitised paper, probably with a small short-focus camera having a *large-aperture lens. **1966** D. G. Brandon *Mod. Techniques Metallogr.* i. 10 Using a large-aperture reflecting surface to give good resolution and a reflecting plate to project the reflected image into the microscope column. **1612** Drayton *Poly-olb.* iii. 115 The *large-bay'd Barne. **1785** G. Washington *Diary* 2 Mar. (1925) II. 346 Planted..all the *large berried thorns. **1835** J. J. Audubon *Ornith. Biogr.* III. 599 The birds observed were *Large-billed Puffins. **1908** E. J. Banfield *Confessions of Beachcomber* I. iii. 123 Many of the birds are..named in accordance with their notes... 'Piln-piln' the large-billed shore plover. **1954** Fisher & Lockley *Sea-Birds* 294 *Phaëtusa simplex*, large-billed tern. **1693** Dryden *Persius* (1697) 500 Such as were to pass for Germans:..*Large Body'd Men. **1702** *Lond. Gaz.* No. 3849/4 A roan Gelding,..large Body'd. **1854** H. Miller *Sch. & Schm.* (1858) 320 A tall, large-bodied, small-headed man. **1741** Richardson *Pamela* (1824) I. 84 A giant of a man..*large-boned and scraggy. **1859** Geo. Eliot *A. Bede* i, A large-boned muscular man nearly six feet high. **1898** *Daily News* 1 Mar. 5/4 The old *large bore pistols. **1874** Carpenter *Ment. Phys.* I. ii. §88 (1879) 98 *Large-brained persons, of strong Intellectual and Volitional powers. **1832** Tennyson *Pal. Art* xli, Plato the wise, and *large-brow'd Verulam. **1897** *Westm. Gaz.* 28 Apr. 7/2 Nine *large-calibre cannon. **1927** Haldane & Huxley *Animal Biol.* iii. 88 The kilocalorie of 1,000 calories is the unit of energy which is most useful in human physiology. It is sometimes called the '*Large calorie'. **1875** Bennett & Dyer *Sachs' Bot.* 440 Smaller cells enclosing a *larger-celled tissue. **1973** P. Evans *Bodyguard Man* ii. 19 A wallet thick with *large-denomination banknotes. **1974** J. Cleary *Peter's Pence* viii. 237 The large-denomination notes would be distributed by those banks. **1844** Mrs. Browning *Lay Brown Rosary* II. 112 The great willow, her lattice before, *Large-drawn in the moon, lieth calm on the floor. **1853** G. Johnston *Nat. Hist. E. Bord.* I. 105 The *large-dugged sow. **1818** Shelley *Homer's Hymn to Sun* 4 Euryphaessa, *large-eyed nymph. **1861** J. Brent in *Archæol. Cant.* IV. 28 A large-eyed needle or bodkin. **1876** Geo. Eliot *Dan. Der.* II. xxix. 234 A large-eyed gravity. **1847** Thoreau *Let.* 29 Dec. in *Corr.* (1958) 200 He is *large featured. **1963** J. Fountain in B. James *Austral. Short Stories* 269 His face, large-featured, serious and brown. *a* **1661** Holyday *Juvenal* 91 The fair trout and *larg-fin'd barbel. **1565** Golding *Ovid's Met.* III. (1593) 62 Tone of them cald jolliboy a great And *largeflewd hound. **1813** H. Muhlenberg *Catal. Plant.* 53 *Large-flowered Custard Apple. **1846** D. J. Browne *Trees Amer.* 2 The Large-flowered Magnolia is most remarkable. **1952** A. G. L. Hellyer *Sanders' Encycl. Gardening* (ed. 22) 142 There are many large-flowered hybrid strains [of cyclamen] in cultivation. **1971** J. Raven *Botanist's Garden* iv. 84 Our native large-flowered Geraniums..afford excellent illustrations..of the second type of plant distribution. **1869** *Rep. Comm. Agric. 1868* (U.S. Dept. Agric.) 438 *Large-framed, wide and straight-backed, and deep-bodied, short-horn cows. **1890** 'Rolf Boldrewood' *Col. Reformer* (1891) 311 Large-framed healthy wethers. **1897** Mary Kingsley *W. Africa* 570 The most exquisite dark-green, *large-fronded moss. **1813** H. Muhlenberg *Catal. Plant.* 48 *Large fruited Hawthorn. *Ibid.* 88 Large-fruited Shellbark hickory. **1952** A. G. L. Hellyer *Sanders' Encycl. Gardening* (ed. 22) 198 Large-fruited varieties [of strawberry] now in cultivation are all hybrids. **1772–84** Cook *Voy.* (1790) I. 15 Corn which is *large grained and fine. **1816** W. Phillips *Min.* 129 Of a large-grained and soft calcareous stone. **1858** Greener *Gunnery* 39 Large-grained gunpowder. **1880** *Cassell's Nat. Hist.* IV. 255 These *Large Grieved Tortoises line the shallow water in great rows. **1603** Drayton *Barons Wars* VI. xxviii. 131 The tree..Whose *large growne body doth repulse the wind. **1828** Miss Mitford *Village* Ser. III. 75 That stunted and *large-headed appearance which betokens a dwarf. **1883** P. Brooks *Serm.* 279 *Large-ideaд, or small-ideaд, appreciative or unappreciative. **1785** H. Marshall *Arbustrum Americanum* 93 *Large-leaved Virginian Mulberry Tree. **1832** D. J. Browne *Sylva Amer.* 212 We have given it the specific name of Large-Leaved Umbrella Tree. **1891** T. Hardy *Tess* xxvii, The large-leaved rhubarb and cabbage plants. **1957** M. Hadfield *Brit. Trees* 399 Large-leaved Lime-tree... This species varies a good deal, and has for long been extensively planted as an ornamental tree. **1974** *Country Life* 28 Nov. 1639/3 The large-leaved rhododendrons..will grow only on acid soils. **1612** Drayton *Poly-olb.* v. 238 Where once the portly Oke, and *large-limb'd Popler stood. **1623** Milton *Ps.* cxxxvi. 69 Large-lim'd Og he did subdue. **1647** Crashaw *Poems* 105 These curtained windows, this self-prison'd eye Out-stares the lids of *large-look'd tyranny. **1661** K. W. *Conf. Charac., Informer* (1860) 47 A..*large lugg'd eagle ey'd hircocervus. **1961** R. D. Baker *Essent. Path.* xv. 372 Hypertrophic, or '*large lung' emphysema, is seen at autopsy as voluminous lungs which do not collapse when the pleural cavities are opened. **1896** *Allbutt's Syst. Med.* I. 315 Emphysema, in the tense or *large-lunged form. **1824** Miss Mitford *Village* Ser. I. 221 A *large-made though meagre woman. **1725**

YOUNG *Sat.* iv. 11 *Large-minded men. **1833** J. H. NEWMAN *Arians* III. i. (1876) 247 A generous and large-minded prince. **1847** TENNYSON *Princess* v. 509 That *large-moulded man, His visage all agrin as at a wake. **1884** G. B. GOODE *Fisheries U.S.: Nat. Hist. Aquatic Animals* 401 The *Large-mouth is known in the Great Lake region.. as the 'Oswego Bass'. **1893** *Outing* (U.S.) XXII. 94/1 In the fresh pond above Nag's Head.. are found the large-mouth black-bass [etc.]. **1897** *Ibid.* XXX. 219/2 Florida large-mouths weighing well up in the 'teens'. **1973** *Sat. Rev. World* (U.S.) 4 Dec. 47/3 Fresh-water fishermen.. can try for.. large-mouth bass. **1878** C. HALLOCK *Sportsman's Gazetteer* 679 *Large mouthed bass. **1883** 'MARK TWAIN' *Life on Mississippi* 264 Every detail of the pilot-house was familiar to me, with one exception—a large-mouthed tube under the breast-board. **1883** *Century Mag.* July 376/2 There are but two well-defined species, the large-mouthed bass and the small-mouthed bass. **1919** E. POUND *Quia Pauper Amavi* 39 Oh august Pierides! Now for a large-mouthed product. **1956** *Nature* 3 Mar. 413/2 The fish is related to the freshwater large-mouthed bass of the eastern United States. **1856** EMERSON *Eng. Traits, Char.* Wks. (Bohn) II. 57 They are *large-natured, and not so easily amused as the southerners. *a* **1659** BP. BROWNING *Serm.* (1674) II. xviii. 234 Quick and *large-parted men. **1689** *Lond. Gaz.* No. 2432/4 A *large Quartered brown Gelding. **1887** *Large scale [see SCALE *sb.*[3] 11 a]. **1897** *Westm. Gaz.* 14 Apr. 1/3 The large-scale maps of Essex and Norfolk. **1907** *Daily Chron.* 9 Dec. 3/3 Schumann is a minor poet among musicians. We remember his lesser things.. and remain cold to his large-scale pieces. **1920** T. P. NUNN *Education* ix. 114 This large-scale experiment. **1934** *Discovery* Oct. 303/2 We do not all realise that the first large-scale (6-inch) survey of these islands was made in Ireland. *a* **1942** B. MALINOWSKI *Sci. Theory of Culture* (1944) vii. 72 Every army must get along on its stomach and.. also most large-scale organizations. **1952** V. A. DEMANT *Relig. & the Decline of Capitalism* i. 21 A period which preceded the appearance of large-scale manufacturing industry. **1957** L. F. R. WILLIAMS *State of Israel* 33 The Security Council's action brought large-scale fighting in Palestine to an end. **1966** *AFIPS Conference Proceedings* XXIX. (1966 Fall Jt. Computer Conf.) 65/1 We are now entering another phase of the expansion of materials technology, in which complete equipment components will be processed on slices of semiconductor... This phase has already been given several names, some of which are 'large-scale integration' (LSI), 'computer on a slice', and 'array technology'. The term 'large-scale integration' is close to being the most descriptive, although at times the syntax is awkward. A somewhat more precise term is 'large-scale integrated electronics'. We will use LSI to abbreviate both 'large-scale integrated electronics' and 'large-scale integration'. **1967** *Proc. IEEE* LV. 1988/2 Large scale integration (LSI) presents an opportunity to exploit many of the concepts of design automation. **1968** *Times* 24 Oct. 7/7 The permissible number of large-scale accidents in nuclear reactors should be about one every 100 million years. **1970** *Sci. Amer.* Feb. 22/1 The technology that produces such high-density electronic circuits is called large-scale integration, or LSI. Although the term has no precise definition, it is usually reserved for integrated circuits that comprise 100 or more 'gates', or individual circuit functions, laid down with a density of 50,000 to 100,000 components per square inch. **1973** A. BEHREND *Samarai Affair* iii. 30 The large-scale model which occupied the centre of the big oval table.. was made of painted wood and represented the approaches to the Port of Liverpool. **1869** *Large-scaled [see *brown-banded snake*]. **1936** J. T. JENKINS *Fishes Brit. Isles* (ed. 2) 157 The Hake is a large-scaled member of the cod family. **1955** COBLENZ & OWENS *Transistors* xi. 146 No truly *large-signal theory for transistors exists today that can be applied directly by the design engineer. **1962** SIMPSON & RICHARDS *Physical Princ. Junction Transistors* vii. 139 Other applications in which transistors are used to a considerable extent include the following: 1. Large-signal steady-state amplification. [Etc.] **1904** *Westm. Gaz.* 30 Mar. 2/1 A reason for utilising the gas-engine as a *large-size power unit for central engine work. **1960** E. DELAVENAY *Introd. Machine Transl.* 93 A large-size dictionary. *a* **1678** MARVELL *Poems, Appleton Ho.*, When *larger-sized men did stoop To enter at a narrow loop. **1765** A. DICKSON *Treat. Agric.* II. (ed. 2) 256 The largest-sized cattle should be placed next the plough. **1853** SIR H. DOUGLAS *Milit. Bridges* (ed. 3) 271 Two or three large-sized pickaxes. **1715** TICKELL *Iliad* 10 The *Large-soul'd Greeks consent. **1856** R. A. VAUGHAN *Mystics* (1860) I. 108 How much we owe still to that large-souled Augustine. **1866** GEO. ELIOT *F. Holt* Introd., The *large-spaced, slow-moving life of homesteads and far-away cottages. **1871** E. F. BURR *Ad Fidem* viii. 139 *Large-thoughted policy. **1899** *Westm. Gaz.* 2 Feb. 2/3 The *large-type letters. **1870** LOWELL *Among my Bks.* Ser. I. (1873) 153 His *large-utteranced genius. **1892** *Fortn. Rev.* LI. 741 A clear-headed and *large-viewed student of architecture. **1860** W. G. CLARK in *Vac. Tour* 49 A *large-wheeled single-horse vehicle.

B. *adv.*

†**1.** Amply; fully, quite, by a great deal; abundantly. Chiefly *north.* and *Sc. Obs.*

a **1300** *Cursor M.* 8812 (Cott.) It wanted large an eln on lenght. *c* **1340** *Ibid.* 7332 (Fairf.) Saul.. was heyer þen any man large bi a meten span. *c* **1470** HENRY *Wallace* v. 204 Xv fute large he lap out of that in. **1530** PALSGR. 317/2 Large open, *patent.* **1587** FLEMING *Contn. Holinshed* III. 1327/1 Garded with such a sufficient companie as might expresse the honor of iustice the larger in that behalfe. **1637–50** ROW *Hist. Kirk* (Wodrow Soc.) 281 It is a question if *papatus politicus* be not large worse nor *papatus ecclesiasticus.* **1666** J. LIVINGSTONE in *Life* (1845) I. 163 There was large more of that sort the year before. **1667** MILTON *P.L.* XI. 728 A Vessel of huge bulk.. and in the side a dore Contriv'd, and of provisions laid in large For Man and Beast.

†**2.** Liberally, generously. *Obs.*

1477 MARG. PASTON in *P. Lett.* No. 801 III. 197 That I dele not evenly with theym to geve Iohn Paston so large, and theym so lytyll. **1596** DALRYMPLE tr. *Leslie's Hist. Scot.* I. 63 Mair bountiful and large thay lyue, than evin thair. **1667** MILTON *P.L.* v. 317 Well we may afford Our givers thir own gifts, and large bestow From large bestowd.

3. Freely, unrestrainedly, boldly.

? *a* **1400** *Morte Arth.* 1784 Ȝone kynge.. karpes fulle large Be-cause he killyd this kene. *c* **1440** *York Myst.* xx. 118 But ȝitt, sone, schulde þou lette Here for to speke ouere large. [Cf. *in large*, C. 8 a.] *c* **1500** *Notbrowne Maid* 167 in Hazl. *E.P.P.* II. 279 Theirs be the charge That speke so large In hurting of my name. **1834** S. SMITH *Sel. Lett. J. Downing* 149 Other folks may talk larger and bluster more. **1872** in A. W. Tourgée *Fool's Errand* (1880) II. v. 411 He had just talked large about the Ku-Klux.

†**4.** Of speech and writing: At length, fully. *Obs.*

1501 *Plumpton Corr.* (Camden) 154 As for all other causes, this bringer can shew to you by mouth, as larg as I can wryte. **1554** LATIMER in Foxe *A. & M.* (1563) 982, I cannot speake Latin, so longe and so large. **1633** T. STAFFORD *Pac. Hib.* I. xv. (1810) 172 As I need not larger to expresse it. *c* **1645** MILTON *Sonn., On the new forcers of Conscience* 20 New *Presbyter* is but *Old Priest* writ Large. **1676** I. MATHER *K. Philip's War* (1862) 83, I thought to have written some-what more large with respect to Reformation.

†**5.** ? Far and wide. *Obs.*

c **1400** *Destr. Troy* 741 Þow loket not large, for lust þat þe blyndit.

†**6.** With big steps; with ample gait. *Obs.*

1642 FULLER *Holy & Prof. St.* IV. iv. 254 Quick and large-striding minds loving to walk together. **1695** *Lond. Gaz.* No. 3065/4 A black Gelding, above 14 hands,.. Trotts large.

7. *Naut.* **a.** With a 'large' wind; with the wind on the quarter or abaft the beam; 'with the wind free when studding sails will draw' (Smyth); off the wind: chiefly in ***to sail, go large.*** (Cf. FREE *adv.* c.)

[**1513** DOUGLAS *Æneis* VI. i. 1 Thus wepand said, and leit his flot go large (L. *classique immittit habenas*).] **1627** CAPT. SMITH *Seaman's Gram.* xii. 57 If you weather him,.. he will laske, or goe large. *a* **1688** DK. BUCKHM. *Cabin-Boy* Wks. 1705 II. 101 He could Sail a Yatcht both nigh and large. **1748** *Anson's Voy.* III. v. 342 The proas.. lying much nearer the wind than any other vessel.. have an advantage, which no vessels that go large can ever pretend to. **1789** *Trans. Soc. Arts* VII. 210 It can only operate to steer a ship large (and that but very wildly). **1793** SMEATON *Edystone L.* §159 Two points behind the beam (or large). **1794** *Rigging & Seamanship* II. 265 The ship runs.. large. *a* **1845** HOOD *Pain in Pleasure-Boat* 16 Nothing, Ma'am, but a little slop! go large, Bill! keep her full!

b. ***by and large***: see BY AND LARGE *adv.* †Also *fig.* In one direction and another, all ways.

1669 [see BY AND LARGE *adv.*]. **1706** [WARD] *Wooden World Dissected* (1708) 35 Tho' he tries every Way, both by and large, to keep up with his Leader. *Ibid.* 106 Take this same plain blunt Sea-Animal, by and large,.. and you'll find him of more intrinsick Value.

c. ? Wide of a particular course, whether one's own or another's.

1670 *Lond. Gaz.* No. 519/2 The Sally man got large from him. **1726** SHELVOCKE *Voy. round World* 232 She kept away large, and at too great a distance to perceive any thing of us. **1816** 'QUIZ' *Grand Master* I. 15 Why are you blind? d——n you, steer large, You'll get aboard of that coal barge.

d. *Naut.* and *Mil.* ***to go*** or ***lead large***: in a manœuvre, to break off at a particular point from the course marked out, and proceed straight ahead.

1749 CAPT. INNES in *Naval Chron.* III. 93 Did not the Strafford.. obey the Signal for leading large. **1797** NELSON in Nicolas *Disp.* (1845) II. 341 Perceiving the Spanish Ships all to bear up before the Wind,.. evidently with an intention of forming their Line going large, joining their separated Division,.. or flying from us—to prevent either of their schemes from taking effect, I ordered the ship to be wore. **1833** *Regul. Instr. Cavalry* I. plate 1, 3 Leading File circle. 4 Go large.

C. *sb.*

I. The simple word.

†**1.** Liberality, bounty; ? also = LARGESS 2 c. *Obs.*

a **1300** *Cursor M.* 27861 Frenes of hert and large of gift. **1377** LANGL. *P. Pl.* B. XIX. 43 It bicometh to a kynge to kepe and to defende, And conquerour of conquest his lawes and his large. **1426** LYDG. *De Guil. Pilgr.* 451 To be Conservyd ffro dampnacion vnder the large off thy Charyte. **1537** in Strype *Eccl. Mem.* II. i. 3 When the prince was christened .. Garter.. proclaimed his name in the form following 'God .. grant good life and long to the.. Prince Edward.. Large, Large'.

†**2.** Extent, size. *Obs.*

c **1470** *Golagros & Gaw.* 241 The land wes likand in large and lufsum to call.

†**3.** ? Freedom. *Obs.* (Cf. 6, 9 below.)

1526 SKELTON *Magnyf.* 182 So that welthe with measure shalbe conbyned, And lyberte his large with measure shall make.

4. *Mus.* The longest note recognized in the early notation, equivalent to two or three 'longs', according to the rhythm employed; also, the character by which it was denoted, viz. ▬ or ▭.

a **1547** *Prov.* in *Antiq. Rep.* (1809) IV. 406 He may not make his brevys to short, nor his largs to longe. **1594** BARNFIELD *Sheph. Cont.* iii, My Prick-Song's alwayes full of Largues and Longs. **1597** MORLEY *Introd. Mus.* 9. **1603** J. DAVIES *Microcosm.* (1878) 81 O let the longest Largs be shortest Briefes In this discordant Note. **1609** DOULAND *Ornith. Microl.* 39 A Large is a figure, whose length is thrise as much as his breadth, hauing on the part toward your right hand a small tayle. **1706** A. BEDFORD *Temple Mus.* xi. 227 In Process of Time, they added a longer Note,.. which they called a Large. **1727–41** CHAMBERS *Cycl.* s.v. *Note.* **1876** STAINER & BARRETT *Dict. Mus. Terms.*

II. Phrases.

5. at large. a. At liberty, free, without restraint. † ***at more large***: at greater liberty.

1399 *Pol. Poems* (Rolls) I. 396 He.. lete him go at large to lepe where he wolde. *a* **1420** HOCCLEVE *De Reg. Princ.* 277 Hy tyme it is to.. walke at large out of þi prisoun. **1470–85** MALORY *Arthur* v. lx, I wille slee the and euer I maye gete the at large. **1523** LD. BERNERS *Froiss.* I. cccxxxix. 533 Thare king determyned to departe, and go and lye in garysons, to be at more large. **1579** SPENSER *Sheph. Cal.* May 40 Letting their sheepe runne at large. **1667** MILTON *P.L.* I. 213 Left him at large to his own dark designs. *Ibid.* III. 430 Here walk'd the Fiend at large in spacious field. **1711** STEELE *Spect.* No. 154 ¶2, I always kept Company with those who lived most at large. **1724** DE FOE *Mem. Cavalier* (1840) 196 The enemy.. lived a little at large, too much for good soldiers, about Cirencester. **1727** POPE, etc. *Art of Sinking* 76 Small beer, which is indeed vapid and insipid, if left at large and let abroad. **1833** HT. MARTINEAU *Briery Creek* iv. 93 Whether appropriated, or left at large because they cannot be appropriated. **1837** CARLYLE *Fr. Rev.* I. VII. i, The King is conquered; going at large on his parole. **1878** BOSW. SMITH *Carthage* 353 They felt also that Hannibal was still at large, and it might not be well to drive him to despair.

b. In an unsettled or unfixed state; not limited or confined one way or another. ? *Obs.*

1611 SPEED *Theat. Gt. Brit.* i. (1614) 1/2 Which as a matter merely conjecturall.. I leave at large. *a* **1715** BURNET *Own Time* (1724) I. 183 Another point was fixed by the Act of Uniformity, which was more at large formerly. **1782** COWPER *Friendship* 136 On points which God has left at large, How fiercely will they meet and charge! **1833** I. TAYLOR *Fanat.* vi. 169 The tremendous doctrine of eternal perdition.. will remain at large.. to be drawn on this side or that as may best subserve the purposes of intimidation.

c. Of speech or writing: At length, in full, fully.

1472–3 *Rot. Parl.* 12 & 13 *Edw. IV* §36 As in the said your Letters Patentes therof is conteyned more at large. **1587** MASCALL *Govt. Cattle* (1627) 158 There he shall finde written all things more at lardge. **1596** DALRYMPLE tr. *Leslie's Hist. Scot.* I. 8, I.. will explicat mair at lairge quhilkes to Scotland ar proper. **1628** EARLE *Microcosm.*, *Yng. Raw Preacher* (Arb.) 22 His prayer is conceited, and no man remembers his Colledge more at large. **1660** *Trial Regic.* 23 If you plead Not guilty; you shall be heard at large. **1668** DRYDEN *Evening's Love* II. i. Wks. 1883 III. 287 I'll wait on you some other time, to discourse more at large of astrology. **1719** DE FOE *Crusoe* II. xi. (1840) 237, I.. told him the story at large. **1845** STEPHEN *Comm. Laws Eng.* (1874) II. 295 As was explained at large in a former chapter. **1890** *Spectator* 1 Nov. 590/2 The Oxford speech, which Mr. Froude quotes at large.

†**d.** In full size: said e.g. in contrast with the smaller scale of a model or abridgement. (Cf. 8 b.)

1600 SHAKS. *A.Y.L.* IV. iv. 175 A land it selfe at large, a potent Dukedome. **1606** —— *Tr. & Cr.* I. iii. 346 There is seene The baby figure of the Gyant-masse Of things to come at large. **1793** SMEATON *Edystone L.* §128 The design for the Lighthouse.. was subject to some change in entering on the detail of the work at large. **1799** HAN. MORE *Fem. Educ.* (ed. 4) I. 181 Abridgments.. are put.. into the hands of youth, who have, or ought to have, leisure for the works at large.

e. As a whole, as a body; in general; (taken) altogether.

1588 SHAKS. *L.L.L.* I. i. 156 So to the Lawes at large I write my name. **1645** FULLER *Good Th. in Bad T.* (1841) 14 Not only of the commission at large but so of the quorum. **1766** GOLDSM. *Vic. W.* xx, I now therefore was left once more upon the world at large. **1790** BURKE *Fr. Rev.* Wks. V. 179 All punishments are for example towards the conservation of the people at large. **1833** HT. MARTINEAU *Brooke Farm* viii. 102 He would be serving me and society at large. **1862** H. SPENCER *First Princ.* II. i. §36 (1875) 130 Moral Philosophy and Political Philosophy, agree with Philosophy at large in the comprehensiveness of their reasonings and conclusions. **1868** *Pref. to Digby's Voy. Medit.* 36 The credit which they obtained him with the people at large. **1874** GREEN *Short Hist.* vii. §7. 415 In his own day he was the poet of England at large.

f. In a general way; in a general sense; without particularizing. ***gentleman-at-large***: see GENTLEMAN 2 c. Now *rare.*

1625 BACON *Ess., Stud.* (Arb.) 9 And Studies themselues doe giue forth Directions too much at Large, except they be bounded in by experience. **1640** FULLER *Joseph's Coat* vi. (1867) 165 And be not only their acquaintance at large, but in ordinary. **1667** MILTON *P.L.* VIII. 191 Not to know at large of things remote From use,.. but to know That which before us lies in daily life. **1670** R. MONTAGU in *Buccleuch MSS.* (Hist. MSS. Comm.) I. 485 Promises made at large. **1718** ATTERBURY *Serm.* (1734) I. 181 Whether these were of the Number of the Eleven, or only Disciples at large. **1896** *Law Q. Rev.* July 199 The Official Receiver must find fraud, not at large, but against the particular examinee.

†**g.** To the open; away, off. *Obs.*

1546 J. HEYWOOD *Prov.* (1867) 35 If this nightes lodgeyng and bordyng Maie ease the,.. Then welcome, or els get the streight at large.

h. In the open sea. *rare.*

1643 SIR T. BROWNE *Relig. Med.* I. §3 Who had rather venture at large their decayed bottome then bring her in to be new trim'd in the dock.

†**i.** Over a large surface or area; abroad. *Obs.*

1579 SPENSER *Sheph. Cal.* Oct. 44 There may thy Muse display her fluttryng wing, And stretch her selfe at large from East to West. **1613** PURCHAS *Pilgrimage* (1614) 300 The first thing hee doth is to stretch out his handes at large. **1675** *Lond. Gaz.* No. 1029/3 We hear that he has quartered his Cavalry at large, for their better refreshment in several neighbouring Villages. **1715** LEONI *Palladio's Archit.* (1742) I. 101 Seeing that the.. legions were so close and crouded, he commanded them to set themselves more at large.. so they might have room to handle their Weapons. **1722** DE FOE *Plague* (1756) 229 They would by their living so much at large, be much better prepared.. than if the same Number of People lived close together.

j. *Naut.* = 'going large' (see B. 7 a).

1757 CAPT. RANDALL in *Naval Chron.* XIV. 98 We.. tried them before the Wind—then at large.

k. *Law.* (See quot.) ***verdict at large***: see verdict *sb.* 1 c.

1767 Blackstone *Comm.* II. iii. 34 Common in gross or at large, is such as is neither appendant nor appurtenant to land, but is annexed to a man's person; being granted to him and to his heirs by deed; or [etc.].

l. *U.S.* Said of electors or elected who represent the whole of a State and not merely a district of it.

1741 B. Lynde *Diary* (1880) 161, I was again chose a Counsellor in ye 1st 18, and my Coz. Wm. Browne chose a Counsellor at Large. **1864** Webster s.v., *Electors at large*, electors chosen to represent the whole of a State, in distinction from those chosen to represent one of the districts in a State. **1888** Bryce *Amer. Commw.* I. xiii. 166 The additional member or members are elected by the voters of the whole State on a general ticket, and are called 'representatives at large'.

m. Without definite aim or specific application.

1863 H. Cox *Instit.* II. xi. 569 The pleadings are at large ..and do not tend to definite issues. **1891** *Edin. Rev.* July (*Tales R. Kipling*), He knows that a single stroke well aimed returns a better result than a score which are delivered at large.

†**6. at one's large**: at liberty. *Obs.*

c **1384** Chaucer *H. Fame* II. 237 While eche of hem is at his large, Lyght thinge vpwarde and downwarde charge. *a* **1420** Hoccleve *De Reg. Princ.* 1455 It sore me agaste To bynde me, where I was at my large. *c* **1450** *St. Cuthbert* (Surtees) 1176 þan myght we leue all at oure large. **1479** *Plumpton Corr.* (Camden) 34, I will that ye suffer him to be at his larg without longer enpresonment. **1502** Arnolde *Chron.* (1811) 114 Thei..may..at ther large and libartie.. goo and come.

†**7. at the large**: at the utmost. *Obs.*

? *a* **1400** *Morte Arth.* 447 Seuene dayes to Sandewyche, I sette at the large, Sexty myle on a daye.

8. in large. †**a.** In a free, unrestrained, or bold manner. *Obs.*

c **1460** *Towneley Myst.* xviii. 90 Neuer the les, son, yit shuld thou lett her for to speke in large. [Cf. *York Myst.* xx. 118 Here for to speke ouere large.]

b. On a large scale: opposed to *in little.* ***in the large***: = *in large*; also, in general, as a whole.

1614 Sylvester *Little Bartas* 12 To do, in Little, what in Large was done. **1662** J. Bargrave *Pope Alex. VII* (1867) 138 The copies of which [picture] in large I gave, one to his Matie..another..to my patron. **1712** J. James tr. *Le Blond's Gardening* 36 The..Plates represent, in large, the same Designs..as those described in little. **1793** Smeaton *Edystone L.* §219 *note*, I have made trial of this method, both in small and in large. **1840** Arnold *Let.* in *Life & Corr.* (1844) II. ix. 200 Viewed in the large, as they are seen in India. **1855** Browning *Old Pict. Florence* xxi, Where the strong and the weak, this world's congeries, Repeat in large what they practised in small. **1943** *Sun* (Baltimore) 24 Aug. 2/6 In the large, there is something else to be said for this recent destruction of more than one hundred of the enemy's fighter planes. **1961** A. J. Deutsch in 'E. Crispin' *Best SF Four* 75 The missing persons did not return. In the large, they were no longer missed. **1968** *Times* 15 Oct. 16/7 Much of the information needed to produce a uniformly precise map therefore will be missing. However, it is only the picture in the large that will suffer.

†**9. to the** (or **one's**) **large**: to or into a state of freedom. *Obs.*

13.. *Evang. Nicoa.* 1032 in *Archiv. Stud. neu. Spr.* LIII. 410 How þat he wan o way ffro presoune vn to þe large. *c* **1400** *Destr. Troy* 10996 Philmen the fre kyng..He lete to þe large. *c* **1500** *Melusine* xxxvi. 255 He was out of the lane & came to his large.

†**10. with the largest**: in the most liberal fashion. *Obs.*

1525 Ld. Berners *Froiss.* II. cxviii. [cxiv.] 339 They.. payed euery thynge with the largeste [Fr. *bien & largement*], so that euery man was contente.

large (lɑːdʒ), *v.* [f. large *a.* Cf. OF. *largir* and (with sense 3) F. *larguer.*]

†**1.** *trans.* To enlarge, increase, widen. *Obs.*

a **1340** Hampole *Psalter* cxlii[i]. 6, I largid my willys and my werkis. *Ibid.* Cant. 499 Largid is my mouth abouen my enmys. *c* **1380** Wyclif *Serm.* Sel. Wks. II. 248 For his propre or pryvy avauntage shulde not man lette to large þis love. **1382** —— *1 Chron.* xviii. 3 Whanne he wente for to largen his empyre vnto the flode of Eufraten. *c* **1440** *Promp. Parv.* 288/1 Largyn, or make large, *amplio, amplifico.* **1647** H. More *Song of Soul* II. i. I. viii, To large their spirit By vaster cups of Bacchus.

†**b.** *intr.* ? To increase (*in* something).

c **1380** Wyclif *Wks.* (1880) 341 þus we largen in sacramentis, for iche good sensible dede þat we don, or þat springith of mannes charite, may be called a sacrament.

†**2.** *intr.* To get or keep away *from* or wide (of).

1506 Guylforde *Pilgr.* (Camden) 60 With mervayllous dyffycultie we larged frome the shore.

3. *Naut.* Of the wind: To become 'large'.

1622 R. Hawkins *Voy. S. Sea* (1847) 116 Thwart Cape Froward, the wind larged with us. **1633** T. James *Voy.* 18 The winde larged, and wee stowed away S.S.W. **1890** Hall Caine *Bondman* xxiv. III. 4 Suddenly the wind larged again.

†**larged,** *ppl. a. Obs. rare.* [f. prec. + -ed¹.] Enlarged, unconstrained, slack.

1382 Wyclif *Ecclus.* xxxiii. 26 He werketh in disciplyne, and the largid [*v.r.* large, Vulgate *laxa*] hond to hym secheth to resten, and secheth fredam.

large-handed, *a.* (Stress variable.)

†**1.** *fig.* Grasping, rapacious. *Obs.*

1607 Shaks. *Timon* IV. i. 11 Large-handed Robbers your graue Masters are.

2. *fig.* Generous, liberal, open-handed.

a **1628** [implied in large-handedness]. **1885** *Cassell's Encycl. Dict.* s.v., Large-handed charity.

3. *lit.* Having large hands.

1896 O. Schreiner in *Fortnightly Rev.* Aug. 233 They [Boers] are generally large-limbed, large-handed men.

Hence **large-'handedness** (in quot. ? lavishness, or ? rapacity).

a **1628** F. Greville *Sidney* xvi. (1652) 208 Shee watched over the nimble Spirits, selfe-seeking or large handednesse of her active Secretaries.

large-hearted, *a.* (Stress variable) Having a large heart (see large *a.* 3 c); magnanimous, generous; having wide sympathies.

1645 Waller *C'tess Carlisle in Mourning* 32 Such as made Sheba's curious Queen resort To the large-hearted Hebrews famous Court. **1842** Manning *Serm.* ii. (1848) I. 22 We see some men large-hearted and generous, denying themselves, almost above measure. **1865** Pusey *Truth Eng. Ch.* 17 It is strange to contrast his niggard concessions with the large-hearted statements of Roman Catholics of other days. **1888** Burgon *Lives 12 Gd. Men* I. Pref. 27 Large-hearted and open-handed too he was, when a real case was brought before him.

Hence **large-'heartedness**, magnanimity, generosity.

1640 Bp. Reynolds *Passions* xvii. (1647) 452 In regard of Reasonable and Spiritual Desires, The effects of this affection are: Large-heartedness and Liberality. **1851** D. Jerrold *St. Giles* xxiii. 241 The cobbler..being mightily touched by the large-heartedness of Blast. **1876** Mozley *Univ. Serm.* iv. (1877) 87 Suddenly endowed with a new large-heartedness and benevolence.

largely ('lɑːdʒlɪ), *adv.* Also 3–4 largeliche, 4–6 largly, -lie, 5 largele, 6 *Sc.* lairglie. [f. large *a.* + -ly².] In a large manner.

1. Liberally, generously, bountifully. Now *arch.* and with mixture of sense 2.

c **1230** *Hali Meid.* 29 þat he nule gladluche ifinde þe largeliche al þat te biheoued. **1297** R. Glouc. (Rolls) 7869 He ȝef ..To abbeys and to priories largeliche of is golde. *a* **1300** *Cursor M.* 27873 He may..largely do almus dede. *c* **1491** *Chast. Goddes Chyld.* viii. 22 Some tyme they wyll yeue largely. **1568** Grafton *Chron.* II. 258 Take with you Gold and Silver..and depart largely thereof unto your men of warre. **1583** Golding *Calvin on Deut.* lxix. 421 Wee haue gods grace much largelier towardes vs. **1827** Keble *Chr. Y.* Sund. after Ascension, Largely Thou givest, gracious Lord, Largely Thy gifts should be restor'd. **1879** Browning *Pheidippides* 48 Too rash Love in its choice, paid you so largely service so slack!

2. Copiously, abundantly; in a large measure; to a great extent; extensively, greatly, considerably, much.

a **1225** *Ancr. R.* 112 So largeliche ant so swuðe vleau þet ilke blodi swot of his blisfule bodie. **1393** Langl. *P. Pl.* C. III. 138 For thorw lesynges ȝe lacchen largeliche mede. **1469** *Plumpton Corr.* (Camden) 23 For and it go to matter in law, it will cost mony largely. *c* **1470** Henry *Wallace* XI. 879 He ..Send to the Erll, and thankit him largele. **1529** More *Dyaloge* I. Wks. 139/2 What so euer fashion of worshipping of Latria be, the same is as largely done to saintes and ymages as to god. **1580** Sidney *Ps.* XVIII. vi, He lifted me, unto a largly noble place. **1594** Bacon *Let. to A. Bacon* in Spedding *Lett.* (1861) I. 349 There is a collection of Dr. James, of foreign states, largeliest of Flanders, which [etc.]. **1611** Bible *1 Macc.* xvi. 16 When Simon and his sonnes had drunke largely. **1613** Purchas *Pilgrimage* (1614) 210 They sup largely. **1697** Dryden *Virg. Georg.* III. 482 The salacious Goat encreases more; And twice as largely yields her milky Store. **1747** Wesley *Prim. Physic* (1762) 114 Drink largely of warm Lemonade. **1849** Macaulay *Hist. Eng.* iv. I. 432 The patient was bled largely. **1880** Geikie *Phys. Geog.* iv. §24. 228 Water enters largely into the composition of the bodies both of plants and animals. **1887** Lightfoot *Leaders North. Ch.* (1891) 3 The prosperity of a Church, as of a Nation, depends largely on its connexion with the past. **1891** Freeman *Sk. Fr. Trav.* 120 These surrounding hills are largely rocky.

†**b.** With words expressive of quantity or extent: Fully, quite. *Obs.*

1297 R. Glouc. (Rolls) 10528 Al a ȝer largeliche this wrechede ilaste. **1377** Langl. *P. Pl.* B. xx. 86 That largelich a legioun lese her lyf. *c* **1386** Chaucer *Knt.'s T.* 1908 Another, That coste largely of gold a fother. *c* **1400** *Ywaine & Gaw.* 423, I wate that he was largely By the shuldres mare than i.

†**3.** Of discourse: At (great) length, in full, fully. *Obs.* or *arch.*

1483 Caxton *G. de la Tour* D v, Gretter boldnesse to speke to her more largely. *a* **1533** Frith *Disput. Purgat.* (1829) 121 Which point I will touch more largely anon. **1551** Turner *Herbal* I B vij, This herbe is so well knowen in all contrees, that I nede not largelyer to describe it. **1655** Stanley *Hist. Philos.* I. (1701) 55/1 The Feast is largely described by Plutarch. **1782** Priestley *Corrupt. Chr.* I. Pref. 19, I have written..largely on the subject of the soul. **1801** Strutt *Sports & Past.* III. iii. 160 We shall have occasion farther on to speak more largely concerning all these kinds. **1831** *Society* I. 154 The girls had written so largely to their friend, she would not repeat news.

4. Generally; with a wide or general application or comprehension; in a wide sense. *rare* or *arch.*

c **1380** Wyclif *Sel. Wks.* III. 344 Ʒif men speken largeli, many men ben here more blessid þan þe pope. **1533** Frith *Mirr. Sacrm. Bapt.* (1829) 287, I take the congregation of God in this place even somewhat largely, this is, for all them that are thought or counted to be the members of Christ. **1570** *Act 13 Eliz.* c. 8 §6 The sayde Statute..shalbe most largely and strongly construed for the repressing of Usurie. **1613** Purchas *Pilgrimage* (1614) 228 This name Æthiopia sometimes taken more largely, otherwhiles more straitned. **1646** Sir T. Browne *Pseud. Ep.* I. iii. (1686) 6 Error, to speak largely, is a false judgement. **1774** Burke *Amer. Tax.* Wks. 1842 I. 155 He was certainly in the right when he took the matter largely. **1868** Gladstone *Juv. Mundi* ii. (1869) 43 His [Proitos'] subjects may have been Argives of Argolis, taken largely.

†**b.** Loosely, inaccurately. *Obs.*

c **1449** Pecock *Repr.* I. xix. 116 Ech of the xj. gouernauncis, which y schal..menteyne and defende is groundid in Holi Scripture largeli and vnpropirli forto speke of grounding. **1654** Bramhall *Just Vind.* ii. (1661) 17 In all Sacraments improperly and largely so called.

†**5.** Freely, without restraint. *Obs.*

c **1425** Lydg. *Assembly of Gods* 1637 Wantons..Oft sythe bryng hem sylf in dystresse, Because they somtyme to largely deele. *c* **1440** *York Myst.* xxx. 493 Me likes noȝt [t]his langage so largely for to lye. *c* **1530** Ld. Berners *Arth. Lyt. Bryt.* (1814) 396 Ye saye not wysely to call the archebysshop traitour..it is to largely sayde. **1564** J. Rastell *Confut. Jewell's Serm.* 73 It ys largelye and lowdelye spoken.

†**6.** For a large sum; at a high price. *Obs. rare.*

1611 Coryat *Crudities* 216 Certaine prisoners being largely hired by the King of Spaine conspired together.

†**7.** Widely. *Obs.*

1551 Recorde *Pathw. Knowl.* I. iii, Open your compasse as largely as you can.

8. In large characters, letters, or outlines; on a large scale (of drawing). Now *rare.*

1624 Bedell *Lett.* iv. 78 On the top of this Tower, was this representation curiously and largely cut. **1680** Moxon *Mech. Exerc.* 237 The Fore-Puppet is more largely delineated in Plate 18. **1887** Sir G. Trevelyan in *Standard* 27 Aug. 2/3 You could almost read them across the floor of the House, they are so largely printed.

9. With lofty demeanour; loftily, pompously.

1857 Trollope *Barchester T.* xlvi. (1858) 389 He, therefore, walked rather largely upon the earth. **1887** Hall Caine *Deemster* xviii. 107 'Do you know, my good people', he said largely, 'I'm at a loss to understand what you mean'.

†'**largemost,** *adv. Obs. rare.* [f. large *a.* + -most.] Most largely or considerably; most.

1666 J. Livingstone in *Life* (1845) I. 132 That year was to me the largemost profitable year I had in the schools.

largen ('lɑːdʒ(ə)n), *v. poet.* [f. large *a.* + -en⁵.]

1. *intr.* To grow large or larger.

1844 Patmore *Poems* 145 Eyes, large always, slowly largen. **1889** Lowell in *Atlantic Monthly* LXIV. 148 The one eye that meets my view, Lidless and strangely largening.

2. *trans.* To make large or larger, enlarge.

1869 Lowell *Pict. fr. Appledore* vi. 51 No more a vision, reddened, largened, The moon dips toward her mountain nest. **1881** Emily Dickinson *Lett.* (1894) I. 186 Each new width of love largens all the rest.

largeness ('lɑːdʒnɪs). [f. large *a.* + -ness.]

†**1.** Liberality, open-handedness; freedom in giving or spending. *Obs.*

a **1300** *Cursor M.* 27404 Largenes [es] sett again couetteis. *c* **1380** Wyclif *Wks.* (1880) 174 Prestis weiward of lif.. colouren..glotonye bi largenesse & fedynge of pore men. *a* **1400–50** *Alexander* 3404 Syn it lokid has þe largenes of þe lord of heuen, þat me þis diademe of Dary demed is & graunted. **1500–20** Dunbar *Poems* xlvi. 84 Luve makis wreches full of lergeness. *a* **1540** Barnes *Wks.* (1573) 362/1 The grace, which is geuen of the largenes of God. **1598** Grenewey *Tacitus' Ann.* I. xi. (1622) 21 That Germanicus had purchased the souldiers fauour by largenesse. *a* **1626** Bp. Andrewes *Serm.* vii. (1661) 436 His largenesse or bounty, as it were..the casting abroad of His new coine. *personified.* **1377** Langl. *P. Pl.* B. v. 632 Largenesse the lady heo let in ful manye. *c* **1430** *Hymns Virg.* 63 Quod largenes in almesse dede. **1627** Donne *Serm.* clvii. VI. 274 Alacrity married with a Thoughtfulness and Largeness married with a Providence.

†**2.** Lengthiness or prolixity (of discourse or writing). *Obs.*

1561 T. Norton *Calvin's Inst.* III. 221 Ye stile runneth of it selfe into such largenesse with plentie of matter, yt [etc.]. **1597** Hooker *Eccl. Pol.* v. l. §3 In other things we may be more briefe, but the waight of these requireth largenes. **1655** Fuller *Ch. Hist.* IV. ii. §5 The Reader I presume will pardon our largeness..in relating the proceedings against this first Martyr. **1655** Stanley *Hist. Philos.* I. (1701) 46/2 By reason of the largness of the Discourse. **1664–94** South *Serm.* II. 192 If the Matter of our Prayers lies within so narrow a compass, why should the Dress and Out-side of them spread..into so wide and disproportioned a largeness?

3. Amplitude of dimension; great size, volume, or bulk; bigness. †Also, magnitude or size in the abstract (*obs.*).

1303 R. Brunne *Handl. Synne* 7024 Myȝte no man ayme þe largenesse [F. *grandur*]. *c* **1430** *Syr Gener.* (Roxb.) 794 In a twelmonth he waxed more Of largenes..Than any othir in yeres thre. **1448** Hen. VI *Will* in Willis & Clark *Cambridge* (1886) I. 370 Ouer the said librarie an hows of the same largenesse. *a* **1400–50** *Alexander* 68 For all þe largenes of lenth at he luke myȝt. **1523** *Act 14 & 15 Hen. VIII* c. 6 One other way..of as greate largenesse in bredeth or larger than the said olde way. **1568** Grafton *Chron.* II. 85 The bones of a great..man, among the which bones, the huckle bone.. was of such largenesse, as..did declare the man to be .xiiii. foote. **1603** Owen *Pembrokeshire* (1891) 2 Other sheres in Wales of farre more lardgnes. **1653–4** Whitelocke *Jrnl. Swed. Emb.* (1772) I. 111 By reason of the largenes, and roughnes of the water. **1661** Lovell *Hist. Anim. & Min.* Introd. b 6, Their motion is slow, by reason of their largenesse. **1708** J. Chamberlayne *St. Gt. Brit.* II. I. ii. (1737) 305 Glasgow..in respect of Largeness, Building, [etc.]..is the chief city in the Kingdom next to Edinburgh. **1726** Swift *Gulliver* II. i. 98 Each hook about the largeness of six scythes. **1785** Sarah Fielding *Ophelia* I. xix, The largeness of the assembly. **1807** G. Chalmers *Caledonia* I. III. x. 458 They were similar, in the largeness of their joints, and in the likeness of their hair.

b. semi-*concr.*

c **1611** CHAPMAN *Iliad* XVIII. 314 Then wrapt the body round In largenesse of a fine white sheete. **1871** R. ELLIS tr. *Catullus* lxxxvi. 3 In all that bodily largeness Lives not a grain of salt, breathes not a charm anywhere.

4. Of immaterial things: Amplitude; (large) size or extent; extensiveness.

1526 *Pilgr. Perf.* (W. de W. 1531) 220 Of suche largenes it may of ryght be sayd and called catholicall. **1605** BACON *Adv. Learn.* I. Ded., I..wonder at..the largenesse of your capacitie. **1606** SHAKS. *Tr. & Cr.* I. iii. 5 The ample proposition that hope makes..Fayles in the promist largeness. **1651** FULLER *Abel Rediv.*, *Fox* (1867) II. 85 Considering the height of his friends and largeness of his deserts. **1832** HT. MARTINEAU *Each & All* viii. 109 Complaints were made against the largeness of their profits. **1856** FROUDE *Hist. Eng.* (1858) I. i. 57 The largeness of the power..committed to the councils was at once a temptation ..to abuse those powers. **1864** BOWEN *Logic* xiii. (1870) 428 The largeness of his information. **1886** *Manch. Exam.* 9 June 5/3 The unexpected largeness of the majority.

†**5.** Breadth, width. *Obs.*

c **1400** MAUNDEV. (1839) xxv. 258 It..strecchethe toward the West in lengthe..in largenesse, it durethe to the Cytee of Alizandre. **1597** A. M. tr. *Guillemeau's Fr. Chirurg.* 14/2 Consideringe the largenes and length of the wounde. **1607** MARKHAM *Caval.* VI. (1617) 19 Lay ouer it two or three other Blankets at their vttermost largenesse. **1747** CARTE *Hist. Eng.* I. 11 The largeness, depth or rapidity of the stream of rivers, which they had occasion to pass.

6. The attribute or quality of not being circumscribed or limited in scope, range, or capacity; the reverse of *narrowness*.

1382 WYCLIF *1 Kings* iv. 29 God ȝaf wisdam to Salomon, and myche prudence.., and laargenesse of herte. **1551** T. WILSON *Logike* (1580) 8 b, If any worde be used that hath a double meanyng, restrain the largenesse thereof, and declare how you will have it taken. **1690** LOCKE *Hum. Und.* IV. xvii. (1695) 388 Some Men of that Strength of Judgment, and Largeness of Comprehension, that [etc]. **1692** L'ESTRANGE *Fables* viii. (1708) 10 If the Largeness of his Heart shall carry him beyond the Line of Necessary Prudence. *a* **1715** BURNET *Own Time* (1724) I. 589 A man of his temper, and of his largeness in point of opinion. **1845–6** TRENCH *Huls. Lect.* Ser. I. iii. 36 One who..in the largeness of his love would send none empty away. **1855** MACAULAY *Hist. Eng.* xx. IV. 492 A man..distinguished..by the largeness of his views and by his superiority to vulgar prejudices. **1874** GREEN *Short Hist.* viii. §1. 456 The largeness of temper which characterized all the nobler minds of his day.

b. Of artistic treatment: Breadth.

1885 *Manch. Exam.* 21 May 5/4 A frequent largeness of phrase, with quaintness of response. **1885** *Athenæum* 23 May 669/3 This picture..may be mentioned as a true illustration of breadth and largeness of style.

†**7.** Freedom, scope, opportunity. *Obs. rare.*

a **1631** DONNE *Lett.* lxxx. Serm. etc. (Alford) VI. 397 Your man brought me your letter of the 8th of December this 21st of the same, to Chelsey and gives me the largeness, till Friday, to send a letter to Paul's house.

8. Lofty bearing, pomposity.

1887 HALL CAINE *Deemster* xxvii. 175 The perspiration started from his temples, but his dignity and his largeness did not desert him.

†**largeour.** *Obs. rare*$^{-1}$. In 6 largeouer. [a. F. *largeur*, f. *large* LARGE *a.*] Width, girth.

1545 RAYNOLD *Byrth Mankynde* I. iv. 23 A certaine thinne ..skinne..which compasseth round the amplitude and largeouer of the belly.

†**largeous,** *a. Obs. rare*$^{-1}$. [f. LARGE *a.* + -OUS.] Liberal, bountiful.

1583 STUBBES *Anat. Abus.* I ij b, But as some be over largeous, so some are spare enough.

†**largerly,** *adv. Obs. rare.* [irreg. f. *larger*, comp. of LARGE *a.* + -LY^{2}. Cf. *largierly*, *bloodierly*.] More largely.

c **1380** WYCLIF *Serm.* Sel. Wks. I. 176 Lest þer falshede growide more and largerli [*v.r.* largerely] envenymede þe Chirche. **1632** SPELMAN *Hist. Sacrilege* (1846) 121 Largerly.

largess, largesse (lɑːˈdʒɛs, ˈlɑː-). *arch.* and *literary.* Forms: 3–4 largesce, 4–7 **larges**, (5 -eys, -is, 7 lardges), 3– **largesse**, 6– **largess**. [a. F. *largesse* = Pr., Sp. *largueza*, It. *larghezza*:—late L. **largitia*, f. *largus* (see LARGE *a.*).]

†**1.** Liberality, bountifulness, munificence. *Obs.*

a **1225** *Ancr. R.* 416 Of ancre kurtesie, and of ancre largesse, is i-kumen ofte sunne. *c* **1340** *Cursor M.* 27404 (Fairf.) Largesse gaine couaitise is sette. *c* **1386** CHAUCER *Pars. T.* ⁋210 Jhesu Crist yeueth us thise yiftes of his largesse and of his souereyn bountee. **1477** EARL RIVERS (Caxton) *Dictes* 8 Largesse and liberalite is knowen whan a man is in necessite and pourete. **1549** COVERDALE, etc. *Erasm. Par. Tim.* 12 Himnes wherwith the larges of god is praysed before meate. **1589** PUTTENHAM *Eng. Poesie* I. xx. (Arb.) 58 The Prince hauing all plentie to vse largesse by. **1623** COCKERAM, *Largesse*, Liberalitie.

personified. **1362** LANGL. *P. Pl.* A. VI. 112 Largesse the ladi ledeth in ful monye. ? *a* **1366** CHAUCER *Rom. Rose* 1157 Not Avarice, the foule caytyf, Was half to grype so ententyf, As Largesse is to yeve and spende. *a* **1420** HOCCLEVE *De Reg. Princ.* 4119 Of myne helply lady souereyne Largesse, my lady, now wil I ryme.

2. Liberal or bountiful bestowal of gifts; *occas.* †lavish expenditure; *concr.* money or other gifts freely bestowed, e.g. by a sovereign upon some special occasion of rejoicing or the like.

a **1340** HAMPOLE *Psalter* Cant. 505 Worshipful he is in larges of giftys. *c* **1470** *Golagros & Gaw.* 423 For na largese my lord noght wil he neuer let. **1484** CAXTON *Chivalry* 67 Whan it shal be tyme of necessite to make largesse his hondes must gyue and dispende. **1561** T. NORTON *Calvin's Inst.* III. xx. (1634) 431 So great and so plenteous largesse of his benefits doth in a manner overwhelme us. **1593** SHAKS. *Rich. II*, I. iv. 44 Our Coffers, with too great a Court, And liberall Largesse, are growne somewhat light. **1614** LODGE *Seneca* 3 Neither can the prodigalitie and largesse of anything bee honest. **1622** HAKEWILL *David's Vow* ii. 86 The widowes..heart being put to her mite, gave it weight aboue the greater..largess of the Pharisee. **1698** FRYER *Acc. E. India & P.* 107 The Governor goes in Procession, and bestows his Largess. **1864** BURTON *Scot Abr.* I. v. 302 The handsel-day belongs to the New Year itself. It is still in full practice in Scotland as a day of largess. **1870** DICKENS *E. Drood* xiii, Largess, in the form of odds and ends of cold cream and pomatum,..was freely distributed among the attendants. **1873** BROWNING *Red Cott. Nt.-cap* 256 Your planned benevolence To man, your proposed largess to the Church. **1887** BOWEN *Virg. Æneid* v. 248 Æneas..then gives to the crews Largess noble of three steers each.

b. In particularized sense: A free gift or dole of money, etc.

1561 DAUS tr. *Bullinger on Apoc.* (1573) 187 Least any man shoulde vnthankfully and uniustly take away this larges of the French Kyng. **1600** HOLLAND *Livy* XXIV. xxi. 522 There was good hope that the souldiours should haue a largesse dealt amongst them out of the kings treasure. **1611** HEYWOOD *Gold. Age* III. i. Wks. 1874 III. 52 Let all raryeties Showre downe from heauen a lardges. **1655** STANLEY *Hist. Philos.* III. (1701) 101/2 Courting vulgar Applause with Largesses and Feasts. **1725** DE FOE *Voy. round World* (1840) 103, I gave a largess or bounty of five dollars a man. **1814** SCOTT *Chivalry* (1874) 38 Largesses to the heralds and minstrels..were necessary accompaniments to the investiture of a person of rank. **1840** ARNOLD *Hist. Rome* (1846) II. ix. 54 His triumphs were followed by various largesses of provisions and money to the populace.

c. *largess!* or †*a largess!*: a call for a gift of money, addressed to a person of relatively high position on some special occasion. (Still in use locally at 'harvest home'; otherwise *Hist.*)

1377 LANGL. *P. Pl.* B XIII. 449 A blynd man..To crie a largesse by-for oure lorde. *c* **1384** CHAUCER *H. Fame* III. 219 Ther mette I cryinge many oon A larges larges. *c* **1485** *Digby Myst.* (1882) III. 261 A largeys, ȝe lord, I crye þis day. **1573** TUSSER *Husb.* (1878) 129 Giue gloues to thy reapers, a larges to crie. **1587** FLEMING *Contn. Holinshed* III. 1342/2 Then the heralds cried A larges, and the trumpets and drums were sounded euerie where. **1674–91** RAY *S. & E. C. Words* 104 A *Largess*,..a Gift to Harvest-men particularly, who cry a Largess so many times as there are pence given. **1688** R. HOLME *Armoury* I. 3/2 Herաulds have a right three several times to cry Largesse. **1787** GROSE *Prov. Gloss.* s.v., The reapers in Essex and Suffolk ask all passengers for a largess, and when any money is given to them, all shout together largess, largess. **1808** SCOTT *Marm.* I. xi, Now largesse, largesse, Lord Marmion. *a* **1825** FORBY *Voc. E. Anglia*, *Largess*, a gift to reapers in harvest. When they have received it, they shout thrice, the words 'halloo largess'.

3. *transf.* and *fig.* (from 2). A generous or plentiful bestowal; something freely bestowed.

a **1533** LD. BERNERS *Gold. Bk. M. Aurel.* (1546) E vij b, The greateste vyllany in a villayne is to be gyuen in largesse of lyes. **1682** DRYDEN *Relig. Laici* 364 The Book's a common largess to mankind. **1688** CROWNE *Darius* I. Dram. Wks. 1874 III. 382 He's like the sun, a largesse to the world. **1785** COWPER *Needless Alarm* 62 How glad they catch the largess of the skies. **1832** TENNYSON '*All good things have not kept aloof*' 4, I have not lacked thy mild reproof, Nor golden largess of thy praise. **1888** LOWELL *Protest* 2, I could not bear to see those eyes On all with wasteful largess shine.

†**4.** Freedom, liberty. ***at his largesse***, at liberty (cf. *at one's large*), at one's own discretion. *Obs.*

1375 BARBOUR *Bruce* v. 427 Quhar he mycht at his largess be. *c* **1425** LYDG. *Assembly of Gods* 1327 There to haue.. largesse to stryke as longeth to thy cure. *c* **1470** HENRY *Wallace* IX. 524 Thai..maid thaim fre, at their largis [*v.r.* at larges] to pass. **1547** *Act 1 Edw. VI*, c. 3 §4 He shall not goe abroad, and at larges. **1594** CAREW *Huarte's Exam. Wits* (1596) 225 Discoursing of the largesse and liberty which souldiers enioy in Italie.

5. *attrib.* (dial.)

1827 HONE *Every-day Bk.* II. 1047 The 'Largess'-cry, the 'Harvest-home!' **1856** *Farmer's Mag.* Jan. 79 Two especial seasons of jollity among them generally occur in each year —the harvest-home,..and the largess feast.

larget (ˈlɑːdʒɪt). [Fr.; f. *large* LARGE *a.*] 'A piece of bar-iron, cut off to a length..forming a blank to be heated and rolled into a sheet of iron' (1875 Knight *Dict. Mech.*).

larghetto (‖larˈgetto, lɑːˈgɛtəʊ). *Mus.* [It., dim. of LARGO.] A term indicating that a passage is to be played slowly; also, a movement or passage played in this way.

1724 *Short Explication Foreign Words in Musick Bks.* 40 *Largetto, or Larghetto* denotes a Movement a little quicker than *Largo.* **1801** BUSBY *Dict. Mus.*, *Larghetto*... A word specifying a time not quite so slow as that denoted by *Largo*, of which word it is the diminutive. **1877** G. B. SHAW *How to become Mus. Critic.* (1960) 28 The overture was taken too rapidly at the *larghetto.* **1958** *Listener* 4 Dec. 964/3 The beautiful *larghetto* from the E minor *sinfonia.* **1959** *Times* 2 Feb. 12/4 In Haydn's F major sonata..there was finesse in his phrasing of its central larghetto. **1970** *Oxf. Compan. Mus.* (ed. 10) 566/1 *Larghetto*,..slow and dignified.

largier, comp. of LARGY *a. Obs.*

†**largierly,** *adv. Obs. rare*$^{-1}$. In 6 largyorly. [irreg. f. *largier*, comp. of LARGY *a.* + -LY^{2}.] More fully, at greater length.

1536 R. BEERLEY in *Four C. Eng. Lett.* 34 Wych fault he shall know of me heyrafter more largyorly.

†**larˈgifical,** *a. Obs. rare.* [f. L. *largific-us* (f. *largus*: see LARGE *a.*) + -AL^{1}.] Liberal, bountiful.

1656 in BLOUNT *Glossogr.* **1708** *Brit. Apollo* I. No. 33. 2/1 The Benignity of our Largifical Essence. **1709** *Ibid.* II. No. 64. 2/2 Largifical Redundances.

†**larˈgifluent,** *a. Obs. rare*$^{-1}$. In 5 largy-. [f. L. *largiflu-us* (Lucretius) + -ENT.]

c **1460** *Play Sacram.* 824 O thu largyfluent lord most of lyghtnesse.

†**larˈgiloquent,** *a. Obs. rare*$^{-0}$. [f. L. *largiloqu-us*, f. *largus* (see LARGE *a.*) + *loquī* to speak: see -ENT.] 'Full of words, that is liberal of his tongue' (Blount *Glossogr.* 1656).

†**ˈlarging,** *vbl. sb. Obs.* [f. LARGE *v.* + -ING^{1}.] Enlargement.

1510 *Acc.* in Willis & Clark *Cambridge* (1886) II. 200 The largienge of the vestrie dore.

largish (ˈlɑːdʒɪʃ), *a.* [f. LARGE *a.* + ISH.] Somewhat large.

1787 *Fam. Plants* I. 90 The divisions roundish, concave, expanding, largish. **1807–26** S. COOPER *Surg.* 108 The largish ligatures used in Mr. Warner's time. **1872** BESANT & RICE *Ready Money M.* v, He carried about with him a largish sum in valuables and money.

Comb. **1831** A. HEADLEY in J. Raine *Mem. J. Hodgson* (1858) II. 208 A largish sized box.

largition (lɑːˈdʒɪʃən). Now *rare.* [ad. L. *largītiōn-em*, n. of action f. *largīrī* to be liberal or bountiful, f. *largus* (see LARGE *a.*). Cf. obs. F. *largition.*] The bestowal of gifts or largess; bountiful giving. Also an instance of this.

1533 BELLENDEN *Livy* II. (1822) 169 The Faderis.. dredand Cassius, be thir largiciouns, to conques sic favoure and riches that micht be noysum to thair liberte. **1570–6** LAMBARDE *Peramb. Kent* (1826) 456 He had, by great largition and briberie, prevailed at Rome. *a* **1670** HACKET *Abp. Williams* I. (1692) 225 Necessity is the companion of immoderate largition. **1781** S. PETERS *Hist. Connect.* 318 The largition enabled them to build a meeting and settle a minister. **1854** CARDL. WISEMAN *Fabiola* II. xxviii. (1855) 307 The separate cell, which Agnes had obtained..backed by her parents' handsome largitions.

Hence **larˈgitional** *a.*, of the nature of largess.

1656 in BLOUNT *Glossogr.*

†**largitude.** *Obs. rare*$^{-1}$. [ad. late L. *largitūdo*, f. *largus* (see LARGE *a.*); see -ITUDE.] Breadth, width.

1599 A. M. tr. *Gabelhouer's Bk. Physicke* 112/1 Cut the same of such a largitude as you desire to have it.

‖**largo** (ˈlargo, ˈlɑːgəʊ). *Mus.* [It. = broad.] A term indicating that a passage is to be rendered in slow time and with a broad, dignified treatment. Also *transf.*

1683 PURCELL *3-Pt. Sonnatas* To Rdr. (1893), Presto Largo, Poco Largo, or Largo by it self. **1724** [see GRAVE *a.*^{2}]. **1753** CHAMBERS *Cycl. Supp.*, *Largo*, in the Italian music, a slow movement, one degree quicker than *grave* and two than *adagio.* **1866** GEO. ELIOT *F. Holt* I. xiii. 279 The gathering excitement of speech gave more and more energy to his manner..he..ended with his deepest-toned largo, keeping his hands clasped behind him.

†**largy,** *a.*, *adv.*, and *sb. Obs.* [f. LARGE *a.* + -Y.] **A.** *adj.* Large. **B.** *adv.* Largely. **C.** *sb.* ***at the largiest***: in the fullest manner.

1395 PURVEY *Remonstr.* (1851) 154 Of this abhominacoun it is seid largiere bifore in the ij. article. *c* **1400** *Destr. Troy* 4961 Largior þen a lawriall & lengur with all. **1535** COVERDALE *2 Macc.* ii. 32 He..vseth few wordes, and toucheth not the matter at the largiest. **1555–8** PHAER *Æneid* I. B iij, Largy streames out from his eies he shed. **1567** TURBERV. *Ovid's Ep.* 143 b, In largie seas..Aye fleeting to and fro. **1594** CAREW *Tasso* (1881) 102 Who open..saw this largy gate.

lariat (ˈlærɪət), *sb.* Also **lariette, larriet.** [a. Sp. *la reata* (see RIATA).] A rope used for picketing horses or mules; a cord or rope with a noose used in catching wild cattle; the lasso of Mexico and South America.

1835 W. IRVING *Tour Prairies* 26 Lariats, or noosed cords, used in catching the wild horse. **1859** MARCY *Prairie Trav.* i. 41 Lariats made of hemp are the best. **1861** G. F. BERKELEY *Sportsm. W. Prairies* xv. 250 Two mules put so near together that they had got their larriets entangled. **1876** BESANT & RICE *Gold. Butterfly* (1877) 3 The horsehair lariette, which serves the Western Nimrod for lassoing by day and for keeping off snakes at night.

Hence **ˈlariat** *v. trans.*, to secure with a lariat.

1850 B. TAYLOR *Eldorado* xi. (1862) 104 My mules had already been caught and lariated.

lariat, obs. form of LORIOT, golden oriole.

larick (ˈlærɪk). *Sc.* and *north.* Also **lerrick.** [sing. f. LARIX taken as a pl.] = LARCH.

1805 A. SCOTT *Poems* 197 (Jam.) A planting..Where pilches an' laricks were seen. **1893** *Northumbld. Gloss.*, *Larick*, larch fir. **1896** LUMSDEN *Poems* 160 Lang tail an' swirlin' Twinklin' on the lerrick taps.

larid (ˈlærɪd). *Ornith.* [ad. mod.L. *Larid-æ*, f. *larus* gull.] A bird of the *Laridæ* or gull family.

In recent Dicts.

Hence **laridine** *a.*, having the characters of the gull family.

1877 COUES *Birds N.-W.* 589 Various classifications of the Laridine birds.. have been proposed.

larie, larielle, vars. LAURY, LAUREL.

lariette, variant of LARIAT.

larigot ('lærɪgɒt). *Mus.* [ad. F. *larigot*, OF. *larigau* 'a Flute or Pipe..called so by the clownes in some parts of France' (Cotgr.), of unknown origin.] An organ-stop; see quot.

1876 HILES *Catech. Organ* ix. (1878) 69 *Larigot*, Nineteenth, Octave Twelfth, a small metal Mutation stop. .. The Larigot sounds a perfect fifth above the Fifteenth, and consequently a Nineteenth above the Diapasons.

larikin, variant of LARRIKIN.

‖**larin** ('lærɪn). Also 6 larine, (larijn), 8 laryn; 7 lari-, lar(r)ee, lawree. [Pers. *lārī*, ? f. *Lār* name of a territory on the north of the Persian Gulf (Yule).] A kind of Persian and Arabic money formerly in use, consisting of a strip of metal bent over in the form of a hook.

1588 HICKOCKE tr. *Frederick's Voy. Ind.* 35b, I bought many salted kine there..for halfe a Larine a peece, which Larine may be twelue shillinges sixe pence. **1616** N. WHITHINGTON in Purchas *Pilgrims* (1625) I. 484 We agreed with one of the Ragies or Governours kinred for twenty Laries (twenty shillings) to conduct vs. **1623** *Docum. Impeachm. Buckhm.* (Camden) 77 Lawrees, beinge peeces of silver..worthe aboute tenne pence. **1634** SIR T. HERBERT *Trav.* 151 Larrees fashioned like point-aglets, and are worth ten pence. **1681** R. KNOX *Hist. Relat.* IV. vi. 144 Five and twenty Larees, that is, five dollars. **1704** *Collect. Voy.* (Churchill) III. 822/2 The most current coin here are the Silver *Laryns*, each whereof is worth about 10*d.*

larine ('lærɪn), *a. Ornith.* [ad. mod.L. *Larin-æ*, f. *larus* gull.] Pertaining to the *Larinæ*, a sub-family of the *Laridæ*.

In recent Dicts.

la'rinoid, *a. rare.* [f. Gr. λᾱρῑν-ός fatted + -OID.]

1860 FOWLER *Med. Voc. Larinoid*, syn. of *lardaceous*. **1888** in *Syd. Soc. Lex.*

larix ('lærɪks). Also 8 laryx. *β.* 6 larnix, 7 larinx, 8 -ynx. [L. (see LARCH).]

1. a. = LARCH. Also *attrib.*, as ***larix tree, wood.*** (Now only *Sc.*: cf. LARICK.)

1572 J. JONES *Bathes of Bath* II. 12b, The oke trees, pyne trees, larnix [*sic*] trees, fir trees, ash trees. **1578** LYTE *Dodoens* VI. xcii. 775 Of the larche or larix tree. **1611** COTGR., *Larege*, the Larch, or Larinx tree. **1626** BACON *Sylva* §642 The Mosse of the Larix Tree burneth also sweet, and sparkleth in the Burning. **1744** DRUMMOND *Trav.* i. (1754) 16 The larynx is as frequent upon the mountains in this country, as the white pine, or common Scotch fir. **1770-4** A. HUNTER *Georg. Ess.* (1803) I. 515 A small summer-house finished with Larix wood. **1791** NEWTE *Tour Eng. & Scot.* 240 Plane trees, poplars, birches, limes, larixes. **1805** FORSYTH *Beauties Scotl.* I. 429 They [squirrels] attack the young Scotch firs, but more particularly the larix and elm. **1842** J. AITON *Domest. Econ.* (1857) 163 Gates should be made of..Larix wood.

‖**b.** *Bot.* The genus of coniferous trees to which the larches belong.

†**2.** The herb *Camphorosma monspeliacum. Obs.*

1548 TURNER *Names of Herbes* 26 Chamepeuce is a very rare herbe..it may be called in Englishe Alpeare or Petie Larix. **1624-61** DAVENPORT *City Nightcap* I. 2 Beauty, like the Herb Larix, is cool i' th' water, But hot i' th' stomack.

lark (lɑːk), *sb.*¹, **laverock** ('lævərək, *Sc.* 'levrək). Forms: *α.* 1 láferce, láw-, láu(w)erce, lǽwerce, láuricæ, -e, 3-4 laverke, 5 laveroc, -k(ke, (lavercok, lawrok), 6 laverok(e, lavorocke, *Sc.* laferok, 7 laveracke, lavroc, levero(c)k, -ucke, 9 *dial.* lair-, layrock, 5- chiefly *Sc.* lav(e)rock, lav'rock. *β.* 4-7 larke, 4- lark. [OE. *láferce*, older *lǽwerce, láuricæ*, wk. fem., corresponding to Du. *leeuwerik*, OHG. *lêrahha* (MHG. and mod.G. *lerche*), ON. *lǽvirke* (masc.), MSw. *lærikia* (Sw. *lärka*, Da. *lerke*); not found in Goth.

The ulterior etymology is unknown; some of the OE. forms, and the ON. *lǽvirke* (only in the Edda Gloss., and perh. from Eng.) lend themselves to the interpretation 'treason-worker' (OE. *lǽw*, ON. *lǽ*, treason; cf. ON. *illvirke* worker of ill); but, apart from the fact that nothing is known in folklore to account for such a designation, the Teut. forms generally seem to point to some such OTeut. type as **laiwirakjôn*-.]

1. a. A name used generally for any bird of the family *Alaudidæ*, but usually signifying, when used without a prefix, the SKYLARK (*Alauda arvensis*). The lark has a sandy-brown plumage, and remarkably long hind-claws (cf. LARKSPUR).

α. *c* **725** *Corpus Gloss.* (Hessels) 71/2 *Laudae*, laurice. *c* **1000** ÆLFRIC *Gloss.* in Wr.-Wülcker 131/28 *Alauda*, lauerce. *c* **1290** *S. Eng. Leg.* I. 67/455 A gret hep of lauerkene opon þe churche a-liȝhte. *a* **1310** in Wright *Lyric P.* xi. 40 Ich wold ich were a threstelcok, A bountyng other a lavercok, Swete bryd! ? *a* **1366** CHAUCER *Rom. Rose* 662 Ther mighte men see many flokkes Of turtles and laverokkes. *c* **1420** *Liber Cocorum* (1862) 36 Other smalle bryddes..As osel, smityng, laveroc gray, Pertryk, werkock. **1438** *Bk. Alexander Gt.* (Bannatyne) 12 It semis thay sparhalkis war And we lawrokis that durst bot dar. *a* **1650** *Eger & Grine* 922 in Furnivall *Percy Folio* I. 383 The throstlecocke, the Nightingale, the laueracke, & the wild woodhall. **1725** RAMSAY *Gent. Sheph.* II. iv, Hark how the lav'rocks chant aboon our heads. *a* **1810** TANNAHILL *Winter wi' his cloudy brow* Poems (1846) 112 Now lavrocks sing to hail the spring, And nature all is cheery. **1837** R. NICOLL *Poems* (1842) 77 Where laverocks lilting sing Is the place that I love best. **1897** *Outing* (U.S.) XXIX. 595/1 A colony of tuneful lavrocks darted their almost perpendicular flight above our heads.

β. ? *a* **1366** CHAUCER *Rom. Rose* 915 With fynche, with lark, and with archaungelle. *c* **1380** *Sir Ferumb.* 1498 On þe morwe wan it was day, & þe larke by-gan to synge, þys messegers come in god aray. *c* **1450** HOLLAND *Howlat* 714 The blyth Lark that begynnis. **1588** SHAKS. *Tit. A.* III. i. 158 Did euer Rauen sing so like a Larke? **1620** VENNER *Via Recta* iii. 63 Larkes are of a delicate taste in eating. **1774** GOLDSM. *Nat. Hist.* (1776) V. 10 An hawk..perceives a lark at a distance which neither men nor dogs could spy. **1828** WORDSW. *Morn. Exerc.* iv, Ne'er could Fancy bend the buoyant Lark To melancholy service. **1876** SMILES *Sc. Natur.* xiii. (ed. 4) 260 You could now hear the..bright carol of the Lark.

b. With allusion to the lark's habits; *e.g.* its early song, and the height it attains in contrast with the low position of its nest.

1580 LYLY *Euphues* (Arb.) 229 Goe to bed with the Lambe, and rise with the Larke. **1594** SHAKS. *Rich. III*, v. iii. 56 Stir with the Larke to morrow, gentle Norfolk. **1613** —— *Hen. VIII*, II. iii. 94 With your Theame, I could O're-mount the Larke. **1607** DEKKER *Westw. Hoe* Wks. 1873 II. 295 We..must be vp with the lark. **1798** COLERIDGE *Anc. Mar.* v. xv, Sometimes a dropping from the sky I heard the Lavrock sing. **1822** B. W. PROCTER *Lysander & Ione* i, Be constant..As larks are to the morn or bats to eve. **1826** J. WILSON *Noct. Ambr.* Wks. 1855 I. 131 Nae lively lilting awa like a rising laverock. **1865** WAUGH *Lanc. Songs* 26 Though we livin' o' th' floor same as layrocks We'n go up like layrocks to sing.

c. *Proverbs.*

c **1530** R. HILLES *Common-Pl. Bk.* (1858) 140 And hevyn fell we shall have meny larkys. **1546** J. HEYWOOD *Prov.* (1867) 9 A leg of a larke Is better than is the body of a kyght. *Ibid.* 20 Louers liue by loue, ye as larkes liue by leekes. **1589** GREENE *Menaphon* (Arb.) 48 Men..die for loue, when larkes die with leekes. **1711** *Brit. Apollo* III. No. 153. 3/2 When the sky falls, we shall catch Larks.

d. With some defining prefix, or qualifying adjective, denoting some member of the genus or family, as ***crested lark, horned lark, red lark, shore-lark***; also SKYLARK, WOODLARK.

1766 PENNANT *Zool.* (1768) II. 239 Red-lark. **1784-5** —— *Arct. Zool.* (1792) II. 84 Shore Lark..*Alauda alpestris.* **1837** GOULD *Birds Europe* III. 165 Crested Lark, *Alauda cristata.* **1894** R. B. SHARPE *Handbk. Birds Gt. Brit.* (1896) 80 The Horned Larks are principally northern birds, occurring throughout the greater part of North America..more than one form of Horned Lark is found in the higher ranges of the Himalayas. *Ibid.* 89 The Wood-Lark..agrees with the Crested Lark,..in having the first primary quill well developed.

2. Applied with defining prefix to birds resembling the lark, but not belonging to the *Alaudidæ*; e.g. to certain buntings and pipits. Also TITLARK.

1766 PENNANT *Zool.* (1768) II. 238 It is larger than the tit-lark. **1848** *Zoologist* VI. 2290 The meadow pipet is the 'twit lark'. **1849** *Ibid.* VII. 2354 The tree pipet is the 'tree-lark'. **1862** WOOD *Nat. Hist.* II. 484 The Lapland Bunting, Snow Bunting... In some places it is called the..White Lark. **1893** NEWTON *Dict. Birds* 512 The Mud-Lark, Rock-Lark, Titlark, and Tree-Lark are Pipits. The Grasshopper-Lark is one of the aquatic Warblers, while the Meadow-Lark of America..is an *Icterus*. Sand-Lark and Sea-Lark are.. names often given to some of the smaller members of the *Limicolæ*. **1894** R. B. SHARPE *Handbk. Birds Gt. Brit.* (1896) 70 From the curious 'scribbling' on the eggs the Yellow Bunting..is in many places known as the 'Writing Lark'.

3. *attrib.* and *Comb.*, as ***lark-catcher, -note, -pie, pudding, -song; lark-awakened, -charmed, -crested, -footed, -high*** adjs.; also ***lark-like*** adj.; **lark bunting**, the prairie bobolink, *Calamospiza melanocorys*, a bird found on the plains of central North America; **lark-call** (see quot.); †**lark's-claw**, the wild larkspur; **lark-finch, -sparrow**, a bird of the western U.S., *Chondestes grammacus*; †**lark-fish** (= L. *alauda*) a name given to certain species of Blenny; **lark's-foot** = LARKSPUR; **lark's-head** *Naut.*, a form of bend (Knight *Dict. Mech.*); **lavrock-height** (*nonce wd.*), the height that the lark rises to; **lark-silver**, an annual payment due to the Crown from tenants of the Honour of Clare; **lark's toes** = LARKSPUR; **lark-worm**, a kind of tape-worm (see quot.). Also LARK('S)-HEEL.

1835 *Edin. Rev.* LX. 324 The tell-tale smoke of *lark-awakened cottages. **1869** *Amer. Naturalist* III. 296 That pretty and musical bird of the high plains, the *Lark Bunting (*Calamospiza bicolor*), also occurred [along the Upper Missouri River]. **1963** R. D. SYMONS *Many Trails* iii. 30 Small black ones [*sc.* birds] with white wing patches, which the children at once called white wings, not knowing that they were lark buntings. **1791** E. DARWIN *Bot. Gard.* I. Notes 89 There is a whistle, termed a *lark-call, which consists of a hollow cylinder of tin-plate, closed at both ends. **1881** *Macm. Mag.* XLV. 42 A *lark-catcher will catch and slaughter ignominiously in a single night more skylarks than a falconer can hope to catch with one hawk in a year. **1879** G. M. HOPKINS *Poems* (1918) 41 Cuckoo-echoing, bell-swarmèd, *lark-charmèd. **1578** LYTE *Dodoens* II. xv. 165 The wilde [Lark's spur] is called..in English..*Larckes Claw. **1776-96** WITHERING *Brit. Plants* (ed. 3) II. 494 Larks-claw. **1848** E. S. DIXON *Ornamental & Domestic Poultry* 319 *Lark-crested Fowls are of various colours; pure snow-white, brown with yellow hackles, and black. **1831** A. WILSON & BONAPARTE *Amer. Ornith.* IV. 126 *Fringilla grammaca*—*Lark Finch. **1898** *Burrough's Riverby* Index, Lark finch or lark sparrow, *Chondestes grammacus.* **1661** LOVELL *Hist. Anim. & Min.* Introd. a6b, Fishes.. smooth, as the *Larkfish cristate and not cristate. **1573** TUSSER *Husb.* xliii. (1878) 96 Herbes, branches, and flowers, for windowes and pots,..*Larkes foot. **1626** BACON *Sylva* §510 This Experiment of severall Colours, comming up from one seed, would be tried also in Larkes-Fott. **1607** TOPSELL *Four-f. Beasts* (1658) 253 The Epithets of a swift running courser are these, winged or wing-bearing, *Lark-footed. **1785** BURNS *Halloween* xxvi, Poor Lizzie's heart maist lap the hool; Near *lav'rock height she jumpit. **1909** *Westm. Gaz.* 29 Dec. 8/3 Sometimes he wings straight up, *lark-high, into the blue. **1946** DYLAN THOMAS *Deaths & Entrances* 22 A stone lies lost and locked in the lark-high hill. **1742** YOUNG *Nt. Th.* v. 20 Pleasure, *Lark-like, nests upon the Ground. **1894** R. B. SHARPE *Handbk. Birds Gt. Brit.* (1896) 79 The Meadow-Pipit having a Lark-like hind claw. **1866** R. LEIGHTON in *Westm. Gaz.* (1909) 6 Mar. 6/3 Deep in my soul the throbbing *lark-notes lie. **1906** *Westm. Gaz.* 14 Apr. 6/2 Yet hear the lark-note piercing the grey morn. **1723** J. NOTT *Cook's & Confectioner's Dict.* sig. R6 (*heading*) To make a *Lark Pye. **1861** MRS. BEETON *Bk. Househ. Managem.* 479 (*heading*) Lark Pie (an Entree). **1910** W. DE LA MARE *Three Mulla-Mulgars* xii. 166 What's lark-pie to a hungry sailor? **1963** T. FITZGIBBON *Game Cooking* 96 Lark pie. **1863** G. MEREDITH *Let.* 1 Feb. (1970) I. 189 A new Receipt:—I try it at Orridge's tonight. '**Lark Pood'n*'. **1877** E. S. DALLAS *Kettner's Bk. of Table* 272 *Lark Pudding or Pie.* —For the perfection of a lark pudding, go to the Cheshire Cheese, in Fleet Street. **1934** J. J. WILLIAMS *Seasonal Cook. Bk.* 263 Lark pudding... Grease a pudding basin... Clean and bone the larks. **1635** J. LAYER in *N. & Q.* 9th Ser. V. (1900) 376 The lete is of Clare, of fee, and ye townsmen paid ..3*s.* per annum for *larkesilver, but what the meaning of it is, I know not. **1900** *Ibid.*, The term larkesilver first occurs in the reign of Richard II. The Court Leet at Meldreth has not been held for centuries, but the 'larksilver' [etc.] are still paid by the parish constable to the Commissioners of Woods and Forests. **1880** G. MEREDITH *Tragic Com.* (1881) 193 He ..had within the month received her *lark-song of her betrothal. **1597** *Larkes Toes [see LARK-HEEL 1]. **1863** WOOD *Nat. Hist.* III. 713 *Lark worm, *Tænia platycephala.*

lark (lɑːk), *sb.*² *colloq.* [Belongs to LARK *v.*²]

1. A frolicsome adventure, a spree. Also ***to go on, have, take a lark; to make a lark of*** = 'to make game of'.

1811 *Lex. Balatronicum, Lark*, a piece of merriment. People playing together jocosely. **1812** J. H. VAUX *Flash Dict., Lark*, fun or sport of any kind, to create which is termed *knocking up a lark.* **1813** BYRON *Let.* 27 Sept. in Moore *Lett. & Jrnls.* (1830) I. 428 You must and shall meet me..and take what, in flash dialect, is poetically termed 'a lark' with Rogers and me for accomplices. **1835** MARRYAT *Jac. Faithf.* xxxviii, Tom was..always..ready for any lark or nonsense. **1837** DICKENS *Pickw.* ii, 'Here's a lark', shouted half a dozen hackney-coachmen. **1850** THACKERAY *Pendennis* xxxix. (1885) 385 Don't make a lark of me, hang it! **1857** MRS. CARLYLE *Lett.* II. 321 My mother..once by way of a lark, invited her to tea. **1873** HOLLAND *A. Bonnic.* xvi. 254 'It's a lark, fellows', said Mullens from behind his handkercheif. **1884** *Punch* 1 Mar. 108/1 Bradlaugh only having a lark with the Hon. Gentlemen.

2. *transf.* An affair, line of business, etc. *colloq.*

1934 P. ALLINGHAM *Cheapjack* xiii. 167 There are many Jews among the grafters, but they usually stick to the chocolate 'lark'—or auction. **1936** [see CON c]. **1961** *New Statesman* 22 Sept. 376/3 Exhibitionists they may be but they mean business. This wet sitting for hours on end is not my lark. **1964** J. PORTER *Dover One* i. 11 There's an outbreak of fowl pest..or something and, naturally, that's far more up his street than one of these vanishing-lady larks. **1967** G. F. FIENNES *I tried to run a Railway* iii. 28 Jeremy came in one day while this lark was going on. *Ibid.* vii. 86, I am up to my ears in this bloody diesel lark.

lark (lɑːk), *sb.*³ *Naut.* A small boat (Smyth *Sailor's Word-bk.* 1867).

1796 *Grose's Dict. Vulg. Tongue, Lark*, a boat.

lark (lɑːk), *v.*¹ [f. LARK *sb.*¹] *intr.* To catch larks.

In mod. Dicts.

lark (lɑːk), *v.*² *colloq.* (orig. *slang*). [Belongs to LARK *sb.*²; the sb. and vb. appear first in 1811-3. The origin is somewhat uncertain.

Possibly it may represent the northern LAKE *v.*, as heard by sporting men from Yorkshire jockeys or grooms; the sound (lɛək, læək), which is written *lairk* in Robinson's *Whitby Glossary* and in dialect books, would to a southern hearer more naturally suggest 'lark' than 'lake' as its equivalent in educated pronunciation. On the other hand, it is quite as likely that the word may have originated in some allusion to LARK *sb.*¹; cf. the similar use of *skylark* vb., which is found a few years earlier (1809).]

1. *intr.* To play tricks, frolic; to ride in a frolicsome manner; to ride across country. Also with *about.*

1813 COL. HAWKER *Diary* (1893) I. 68 Having larked all the way down the road. **1835** *Nimrod's Hunting Tour* 227 There is another way of making use of horse-flesh..and that is,..what in the language of the day is called 'larking'. One of the party holds up his hat which is a signal for the start; and, putting their horses' heads in a direction for Melton, away they go, and stop at nothing till they get there. **1842** BARHAM *Ingol. Leg.* Ser. II. *St. Cuthbert*, Don't 'lark' with the watch, or annoy the police! **1846-57** DE QUINCEY *Keats* Wks. VI. 276 *note*, It is a ticklish thing to lark with honest men's names. **1848** THACKERAY *Van. Fair* lxv. 496 Jumping the widest brooks, and larking over the newest gates in the country. **1857** HUGHES *Tom Brown* I. v, Larking about at leap-frog to keep themselves warm. **1861** WHYTE MELVILLE *Mkt. Harb.* 56 If we are to lark home..I may as well ride a nag I can trust. **1871** 'M. LEGRAND' *Cambr. Freshm.* 261 These..expert riders..set off to 'lark' it home. **1889** H. O'REILLY *50 Years on Trail* 3, I was always larking about and playing pranks on my schoolfellows.

2. *trans.* To make fun of, tease sportively (a person); to ride (a horse) across country.

1848 THACKERAY *Van. Fair* lxvi. 603 A staid English maid ..whom Georgy used to 'lark' dreadfully, with accounts of German robbers and ghosts. **1861** WHYTE MELVILLE *Mkt. Harb.* 21 'May I lark him?' said he, pulling up after a short canter to and fro on the turf by the wayside.

3. To clear (a fence) with a flying leap.

1834 AINSWORTH *Rookwood* IV. vii, Bess was neither strained by her gliding passage down the slippery hill side, nor shaken by *larking* the fence in the meadow.

larked (lɑːkt), *a. poet. nonce-wd.* [f. LARK *sb.*¹ + -ED².] With larks overhead, noisy with the song of larks.

1952 DYLAN THOMAS *Coll. Poems* 173, I hear the bouncing hills Grow larked.

larker¹ ('lɑːkə(r)). [f. LARK *sb.*¹ + -ER¹.] One whose occupation it is to catch larks.

1634 A. WARWICK *Spare Min.* (1637) 68 When I see the Larker's day net spread out in a faire morning. **1766** PENNANT *Zool.* (1768) II. 235 When the weather grows gloomy the larker changes his engine. **1789** G. WHITE *Selborne* xxvii. (1853) 108 The larkers in dragging their nets by night frequently catch them [fieldfares] in the wheat-stubbles.

larker² ('lɑːkə(r)). *colloq.* [f. LARK *v.*² + -ER¹.] One given to 'larking' or sporting.

1826 *Sporting Mag.* XVIII. 285 He has been a bit of a larker in his time. **1896** *Westm. Gaz.* 3 July 1/3 He was conveyed by the 'larkers', who were medical students, to the statue of William III.

larker³ ('lɑːkə(r)). [Cf. LARK *sb.*³] (See quot.)

1888 *Argosy* XIX. 278 Seine fishing is carried on by companies, each company owning 3 boats—the 'seine boat' ..the 'vollier'..and another small boat called a larker.

lark-heel, lark's-heel.

1. a. = LARKSPUR. **b.** Indian cress or garden nasturtium (*Tropæolum*).

1597 GERARDE *Herbal* II. ccccxxvi. 923 *Flos Regius*..in English Larkes spur, Larkes heele, Larkes toes, Larkes clawe and Munkes hoode. **1612** *Two Noble K.* I. i. *Song*, Mary-golds, on death beds blowing, Larkes-heeles trymme. **1669** WORLIDGE *Syst. Agric.* (1681) 280 Now sow Larks-heels, Canditufts, Columbines, &c. **1695** TATE tr. *Cowley's Plants* IV. C.'s Wks. 1721 III. 360 The Indian-Cress our Climate now does bear, Call'd Larks-heel, 'cause he wears a Horsemans Spur. **1706** J. GARDINER *Rapin's Gard.* (1728) 18 The Larkheel train, And Lychnis famous for her scarlet stain. **1760** J. LEE *Introd. Bot.* App. (1765) 316 Lark's Heel, *Delphinium*. **1827** CLARE *Sheph. Cal.* 58 The tall topp'd lark-heels, feather'd thick with flowers.

2. The elongated heel, common among Negroes.

1865 LIVINGSTONE *Zambesi* 501 Nor do we meet what is termed the lark-heel any oftener here than among the civilized races of Europe. **1872** —— in *Daily News* 29 July, Prognathous jaws, lark heels, and other physical peculiarities common among slaves and West Coast negroes.

Hence **lark-heeled** *a.* (See quots.)

1837 GOULD *Birds Europe* III. 169 Lark-heeled Bunting, *Plectrophanes Lapponica*, Selby. **1855** ROBINSON *Whitby Gloss.*, *Lairock-heel'd*, having an uncommon projection of heel. **1862** WOOD *Nat. Hist.* II. 567 The Coccyginæ, or Lark-heeled Cuckoos, so called from their long hind toe.

larkiness ('lɑːkɪnɪs). [f. LARKY *a.* + -NESS.] The quality of being larky; sportiveness.

1896 *Columbus* (Ohio) *Dispatch* 22 Aug., In reality he [*sc.* a choirboy] is the incarnation of all that is mischievous; and ..if he sings at a cathedral or important church, the more 'larkiness' is found in his composition. **1905** CHESTERTON *Heretics* 90 It is hard to see at first sight why so human a thing as leisure and larkiness should always have a religious origin. **1924** R. HICHENS *After Verdict* II. xx. 303 The ball-boys stood ready, looking alert and full of suppressed larkiness. **1928** *Observer* 26 Feb. 15/3 Miss Helen Gilliland ..has great quality.., but she needs the supreme gift for this work, of larkiness. **1973** *Times Lit. Suppl.* 30 Nov. 1466/4 Wastage or mere larkiness is fatal both to its intention and execution.

larking ('lɑːkɪŋ), *vbl. sb.*¹ [f. LARK *v.*¹ + -ING¹.] The action or process of catching larks. *attrib.* in **larking-glass**, a machine with mirrors, used to attract larks to the net.

1826 S. R. JACKSON in Hone *Every-day Bk.* II. 118 Persons go out with what is called a larking glass.

larking ('lɑːkɪŋ), *vbl. sb.*² *colloq.* [f. LARK *v.*² + -ING¹.] The action of LARK *v.*²; fun, frolic.

1813 COL. HAWKER *Diary* (1893) I. 68 Much as larking was in force, there had been no spree to top this. **1825** BEDDOES *Let.* 19 July in *Poems* p. xlvii, Two Oxford men, professors of genteel larking. **1838** LADY GRANVILLE *Lett.* 14 July, He..like me, shuns actual practical larking.

larking ('lɑːkɪŋ), *ppl. a. colloq.* [f. LARK *v.*² + -ING².] That larks; frolicsome, sportive.

1828 J. H. NEWMAN *Lett.* (1891) I. 182, I have learned to leap..which is a larking thing for a don. **1848** THACKERAY *Bk. Snobs* x, The 'larking' or raffish Military Snob. **1889** 'ROLF BOLDREWOOD' *Robbery under Arms* (1890) 330 Maddie was in one of her larking humours.

Hence 'larkingly *adv.*

1896 H. W. WOLF in *Contemp. Rev.* Aug. 204 Larkingly engaging in acrobatics.

larkish ('lɑːkɪʃ), *a. colloq.* [f. LARK *sb.*² + ISH.] Of the nature of a 'lark'; frolicsome.

1823 *Spirit of Public Jrnls. M.DCCC.XXIII* (1825) I. 75 She went to see the lamplighter's burying, and the folks were all very merry 'and quite *larkish*, in a manner'. **1882** *Echo* 29 Aug. 1/5 Foote lost his leg owing to amputation caused by a larkish exploit with the Duke of York. **1926** F. M. FORD *Man could stand Up* I. ii. 32 The larkish freak of a school-girl.

Hence 'larkishness.

a **1893** SIR A. BLACKWOOD *Records Life* (1896) 14 One other exploit was the result of West's and my larkishness that half.

larksome ('lɑːksəm), *a. colloq.* [f. LARK *sb.*² + -SOME.] Given to 'larking', sportive.

1871 *Daily News* 11 Sept., Hinting..that the melodrama had not been produced for larksome purposes. **1890** *Longm. Mag.* Sept. 574 Obstreperous and larksome ghosts.

larkspur ('lɑːkspɜː(r)). *Bot.* [f. LARK *sb.*² + SPUR.] **a.** Any plant of the genus *Delphinium*; so called from the spur-shaped calyx. The common larkspur is *D. Consolida.*

1578 LYTE *Dodoens* II. xv. 165 The garden Larkes Spurre floureth all the Somer long. **1597** GERARDE *Herbal* II. ccccxxvi. 922 The garden Larkes spur hath a rounde stem full of branches. *Ibid.* 923 The wilde Larkes spur hath most fine iagged leaues. **1664** EVELYN *Kal. Hort.* Feb. (1679) 11 Sow also Lark-spurs, &c. **1769** *De Foe's Tour Gt. Brit.* (ed. 7) I. 89 In the Ground between these Hills and Cambridge grows naturally abundance of Larkspur. **1856** MISS MULOCK *F. Halifax* xxi, Sweet-Williams and white-Nancies, and larkspur and London-pride. **1882** *Garden* 11 Feb. 91/2 Larkspurs are exceedingly showy annuals.

b. The blue colour characteristic of the larkspur.

1927 *Sunday Express* 27 Feb., Newest Season's colours including..Grey, Cocoa, Larkspur, Fawn. **1927** *Daily Express* 12 Mar. 3/5 Larkspur, a pastel blue slightly inclining to the mauve.

lark-spurred, *a.* (See quot.)

1805 J. LAWRENCE *Cattle* (1809) 531 The old shepherds had a comical notion, that sheep blind in the summer were *lark-spurred*; that the sheep having trod upon a lark's nest, the old one..had spurred the intruder in the eye. **1837** YOUATT *Sheep* x. 406.

larky ('lɑːkɪ), *a. colloq.* [f. LARK *sb.*² + -Y.]

a. Inclined or ready for a lark; frolicsome, sportive.

1841 *Punch* 25 Dec. 278/2 The old girl has her two nieces home for the holidays—devilish handsome, larky girls. **1851** H. MAYO *Pop. Superst.* (ed. 2) 133 When the Devil is larky, he solicits the witches to dance round him. **1866** *Spectator* 24 Nov. 1301/1 An under-bred, ignorant, larky young naval lieutenant. **1885** 'F. ANSTEY' *Tinted Venus* 24, 'I look larky, don't I', said poor Tweddle, dolefully. **1909** [see BUCK *v.*⁷ 2a]. **1911** E. M. CLOWES *On Wallaby* ii. 35 The young people..are loud and larky and irreverent. **1912** D. H. LAWRENCE *Lett.* (1932) 28 Every blessed place was full of men, in the larkiest of spirits. **1958** *Vogue* July 57 Osborne has shocked the stage with a real-life genus of larky lower-middle class humanists and given them the heroic status of being worried. **1967** *Listener* 8 June 747/2 A character in whom humility and submissiveness are combined with a larky humour. **1974** *Ibid.* 21 Nov. 673/1 The only disk jockey who sounds genuinely happy... Larky, insouciant and very funny.

b. *transf.*

1925 *Blackw. Mag.* July 80/2 (*Rugby School*) The 'swells' were allowed to wear 'larky' waistcoats, *i.e.*, waistcoats of various hues often with flowery designs embroidered on them.

†**larm,** *sb. Obs.* Also 6–7 **larme.** [Aphetic form of ALARM *sb.* Cf. LARUM and G. *lärm* noise.] = ALARM *sb.* 4. Also ***to blow, ring a larm.***

1530 PALSGR. 237/2 Larme in a felde, *alarme.* **1557** *Tottel's Misc.* (Arb.) 198 Then come they to the larme, then shew they in the fielde. **1560** DAUS tr. *Sleidane's Comm.* 65 Therfore he ryngeth a larme and admonysheth all men to [etc.]. **1565** COOPER *Thesaurus* s.v. *Cano, Bellicum canere*,.. to blowe a larme. **1581** STUDLEY *Seneca's Hercules Œtæus* 216 To thumpe vppon thy sounding breast thy griefe with doleful larmes. **1633** P. FLETCHER *Purple Isl.* xi. 2 To change my oaten quill For trumpet 'larms.

†**b.** *attrib.* **larm-list**, ? a body of firemen or militia. *U.S. Obs.*

1779 *Hist. Pelham, Mass.* (1898) 133 Voted that the Arms ..be sold at Public Vendue to the Highest Bidder, None to bide But the training band and Larm list.

larm, *v. Obs. rare*⁻¹. [Aphetic form of ALARM *v.*] *trans.* To alarm.

1758 S. THOMPSON *Diary* 20 July (1896) 11 In the morning 10 men in a scout waylaid by the Indians, and shot at and larmed the Fort.

larmier ('lɑːmiːeɪ). Also 7 **larmer.** [a. F. *larmier* in same sense, f. *larme* a tear.]

1. *Arch.* = CORONA 4, DRIP *sb.*¹ 4a.

1696 PHILLIPS (ed. 5), *Larmer.* **1723** CHAMBERS tr. *Le Clerc's Treat. Archit.* I. 25 Corona with its Larmier or Drip underneath. **1727–41** CHAMBERS *Cycl.*, The Larmier is also called *corona*, and in English the *drip.* **1875** in KNIGHT *Dict. Mech.*

2. *Anat.* (See quot.)

1848 in CRAIG. **1893** LYDEKKER *Horns & Hoofs* 64 The lachrymal fossa—in which rests the gland termed the crumen, larmier, or 'tear-bag'.

Larmor ('lɑːmə(r)). *Physics.* The name of Sir Joseph *Larmor* (1857–1942), Irish-born physicist, used *attrib.* and in the possessive with reference to a theorem enunciated by him in 1897, according to which the effect of a uniform magnetic field on a rotating particle is (to a first approximation) to cause the frame of reference in which the particle is rotating to rotate in turn about the direction of the magnetic flux with a frequency $\gamma B/2\pi$ (where γ is the magneto-mechanical ratio and B the magnetic induction), which for an orbital electron in a monatomic molecule represents a precessional frequency of $eB/4\pi m$ (e and m being the charge and mass of the electron); so ***Larmor frequency, precession; Larmor's theorem***; also **Larmor radius**, the radius of the helical path of a free charged particle spiralling about magnetic field lines.

1923 Larmor's theorem [see CORIOLIS]. **1926** E. C. STONER *Magnetism & Atomic Struct.* iv. 68 The Larmor precession is of great importance in the treatment of the Zeeman effect, this and diamagnetism being different aspects of the same phenomenon. **1951** *Physical Rev.* LXXXIII. 1000/2 The Larmor frequency, $\omega_p = 2\mu_p H/h$, of a sample of protons in the magnetic field is measured by the resonance absorption method. **1957** B. I. & B. BLEANEY *Electr. & Magn.* viii. 186 As a consequence of the Larmor precession, each electron acquires a component of angular momentum about the direction of [the magnetic induction] B. **1962** W. B. THOMPSON *Introd. Plasma Physics* vii. 151 In a magnetic field a second length becomes important, the Larmor radius, r_L, i.e. the radius of the circle formed by the particle orbit about the magnetic field lines. **1971** D. W. SCIAMA *Mod. Cosmol.* ii. 36 The galactic magnetic field thus has an important effect on the motion of cosmic rays if their Larmor radius is substantially less than the size of the Galaxy.

larmoyant (lɑː'mɔɪənt), *a.* [ad. F. *larmoyant*, pres. pple. of *larmoyer* to be tearful, f. *larme* tear.] Given to tears, lachrymose.

[**1813** BYRON *Let.* 2 Oct. in Moore *Life* (1830) II. 430 But thou know'st I can be a right merry and conceited fellow, and rarely 'larmoyant'.] **1824** MISS MITFORD *Village* Ser. I. (1863) 81 Ellen and I, although not at all larmoyante sort of people, had much ado not to cry. **1897** *Naturalist* 270 Another strange face, though not so larmoyant, provocative of laughter unto tears.

larn (lɑːn), *v. colloq.* [f. dial. form of LEARN *v.* 4; see *E.D.D.* for further examples.] *trans.* To teach; to give (a person) a lesson; freq. used ironically as a threat of punishment.

1790 T. WILKINSON *Mem.* I. 117 You are unfit for the stage, Muster Whittington, and I won't larn you—you may go, Muster Whittington. **1851** [see JES, JES']. **1899** *Manch. Guardian* 13 Mar. 10/1 Said Mr. Dooley, '..we'll larn thim a lesson.' **1902** E. NESBIT *Five Children & It* viii. 204 I'll larn you, you young varmint! **1928** 'BRENT OF BIN BIN' *Up Country* xiii. 228 The taller ruffian put a bullet in the wall above his head just to larn him, and his companions advised him to be still. **1931** W. HOLTBY *Poor Caroline* v. 180 'I'll larn her,' swore he to himself. **1949** 'J. TEY' *Brat Farrar* xvii. 183 Bee took him to call on the tenants... 'Gates last; just to larn him,' Bee said. **1956** C. BLACKSTOCK *Dewey Death* ix. 216 That'll larn you, you so-and-sos.

larnax ('lɑːnæks). *Gr. Antiq.* Pl. **larnakes** ('lɑːnəkiːz). [Gr. λάρναξ chest, urn.] A chest, ossuary, urn, or coffin, usually of terra cotta, frequently ornamented with designs.

1870 *Catal. Greek & Etruscan Vases Brit. Mus.* II. 191 In the centre Aphroditê seated on a chest, *larnax*, and looking back at a youthful male figure. **1901** A. J. EVANS *Mycenaean Tree & Pillar Cult* 77 In a chambered tomb at Milato..was a painted clay ossuary chest or larnax of the usual Cretan type. **1901** *Rep. Brit. Assoc. Adv. Sci.* 444 The one [tomb], a square chamber with a dromos, yielded parts of two painted *larnakes*, thoroughly Mycenean in design. **1904** *Westm. Gaz.* 24 Aug. 7/3 A later cemetery, containing larnax burials, yielded bronze implements, beads, and vases like those in the palace magazines. **1910** *Encycl. Brit.* I. 248/2 The Cretan 'larnax ' coffins..have no parallels outside the Aegean. **1939** V. G. CHILDE *Dawn European Civilization* (ed. 3) ii. 24 Individual burial..in clay coffins (larnakes). *Ibid.* 27 Larnax burials.

larnite ('lɑːnaɪt). *Min.* [f. *Larne*, the name of a town in Co. Antrim, N. Ireland + -ITE¹.] A mineral consisting of a metastable monoclinic phase of dicalcium silicate, Ca_2SiO_4.

1929 C. E. TILLEY in *Mineral. Mag.* XXII. 79 Next in importance to spurrite comes a mineral consisting of calcium orthosilicate. As this is the first recorded natural occurrence of this compound it is proposed to designate it as larnite, from Larne, in the vicinity of which these contact minerals occur. **1950** *Ibid.* XXIX. 182 Both the nagelschmidtite and larnite phases have been seen in slags. **1957** *Amer. Mineralogist* XLII. 384 The larnite zone is very prominent, forming a band about thirty inches thick, dark grey to almost black in color, hard, flinty, and very tough. The dark color is..due to..the presence of a small amount of very fine-grained magnetite. Pure larnite is presumably white. **1966** [see BREDIGITE].

larom(e, -owme, obs. forms of LARUM.

†**laron.** *Obs.* Also 4 laroun, 6 la-roone, 7 lar(r)one, larroone. [ad. OF. *laron* (F. *larron*):—L. *latrōn-em*. Cf. LADRONE.] A robber.

13.. *K. Alis.* 4209 Of thefthe Y wol me defende, Ageyn knyght, swayn, and baroun, That Y no am no laroun. **1598** SHAKS. *Merry W.* I. iv. 71 O Diable, Diable: vat is in my Closset? Villanie, La-roone: Rugby, my Rapier. **1631** H. SHIRLEY *Mart. Souldier* II. iii, I am Prince over those Publicans, Lord over these Larroones, Regent of these Rugs. *a* **1656** USSHER *Ann.* VI. (1658) 358 But like a very Laron, sought to strip his brother of all that he had in his necessity.

Larose (læ'rəʊz). [Name of some vineyards in the Bordeaux area of France.] A type of claret; the vineyard or area itself.

1841 THACKERAY in *Fraser's Mag.* June 720/1 It is my firm opinion that a third-rate Burgundy, and a third-rate claret—Beaune and Larose for instance, are *better* than the best. **1863** G. MEREDITH *Let.* 3 Feb. (1970) I. 190 Vins.. Claret—Larose. **1920** G. SAINTSBURY *Notes on Cellar-Bk.* iv. 66 It is true that some of the very best vineyards (Léoville, Larose, Ducru-Beau-Caillou..) are situated there [*sc.* at Saint-Julien]. **1958** A. L. SIMON *Dict. Wines* 99/2 Larose, Château. There are several wine-producing estates in the Gironde bearing this name, mostly hyphenated with the name or names of present or past owners.

larrecine, variant of LARCIN *Obs.*

larree: see LARIN.

larriet, variant of LARIAT.

larrigan ('lærɪgən). *N. Amer.* Also 9 **larigan, larrigin.** [Of unknown origin.] A long boot made of undressed leather.

1886 *Engineering News* XVI. 99/1 And the ordinary footgear is a pair of cow-hide moccasins (called shoe-packs or larrigans). **1889** *Amer. N. & Q.* III. 308 A *larigan*, or *larrigin*, in Maine and New Brunswick, is a kind of boot or moccasin of yellow leather, having a long leg reaching above the knee. It is worn by lumbermen in the deep snows of winter. **1915** *Outing* (U.S.) Oct. 27/2 A 'shoe-pac' or 'larrigan' is a beef-hide moccasin with eight to ten-inch top, and with or without a light, flexible sole. **1922** *Short Stories* (U.S.) Feb. 128/2 Over six feet in his larrigans. **1931** 'GREY OWL' *Men of Last Frontier* 180, I was much hampered by a pair of still hard-soled larrigans which I had donned. **1961** *Saturday Night* (Toronto) 23 Dec. 18/1 After breakfast that day I rode to school..wearing a pair of cowhide larrigans greasy with linseed oil. **1968** E. R. BUCKLER *Ox Bells & Fireflies* ii. 25 Little Tim was six foot seven..who could yet sew a larrigan together with the waxed end neater than a woman could hem-stitch.

Hence **'larriganed** *a.*, wearing larrigans.

1904 C. G. D. ROBERTS *Watchers of Trails* 287 Then, turning on his larriganed heels, he strode up the trail. **1922** *Short Stories* Feb. 129/1 [The dogs] clipped fangs at Cherriman's larriganed legs.

larrikin ('lærɪkɪn). Chiefly *Austral.* Also **larikin.** [Of uncertain origin; possibly f. *Larry* (a nickname for Lawrence, common in Ireland) + -KIN.

The word seems to have originated in Melbourne not long before 1870; but the story that it was evolved by a reporter from an Irish policeman's pronunciation of *larking*, heard in a Melbourne police-court in 1869, appears to be a figment, no trace of the incident being found in the local papers of the time. (See Morris, *Austral Eng.*, s.v.) A guess that has been proposed is that it is short for Eng. slang *leary kinchen.* Wright, Suppl. to *E.D.D.*, cites *larrikin* 'a mischievous or frolicsome youth' from informants in Warwickshire and Worcestershire; see also quot. 1882. Cf. *E.D.D.*, *Larack* (*larack about*, to 'lark' about), cited from C. C. Robinson's *Dial. of Leeds* (1861).]

a. A (usually juvenile) street rowdy; the Australian equivalent of the 'hoodlum' or 'hooligan'. Also *transf.* and *attrib.*

1868 H. W. HARPER *Lett. from N.Z.* (1914) vii. 123 We are beset with larrikins, who lurk about in the darkness and deliver every sort of attack on the walls and roof with stones and sticks. **1870** *Melbourne Herald* 4 Apr. 3/2 Three larikins ..had behaved in a very disorderly manner in Little Latrobe-street. **1871** *Evening Post* (Wellington, N.Z.) 27 Apr. 2/4 Such rowdyism I never saw before, even in Melbourne and San Francisco, the hotbeds of larrikins. **1882** F. W. P. JAGO *Anc. Lang. & Dial. Cornwall* 205 *Larrikins*, mischievious young fellows, larkers. 'Mischievious larrikins who pull the young trees down.' *The Cornishman.* **1886-7** BURTON *Arab. Nts.* I. 4 Story of the Larrikin and the Cook. **1890** *Melbourne Argus* 26 May 6/7 He was set upon by a gang of larrikins, who tried to rescue his prisoner. **1898** G. W. STEEVENS *With Kitchener to Khartum* 142 Lord and larrikin, Balliol and the Board School, the Sirdar's brain and the camel's back—all welded into one. **1901** *Daily Tel.* 8 Mar. 8/7 The larrikins of the Legislature..could not be visited retrospectively with an adequate punishment. **1925** E. WALLACE *King by Night* xlix. 224 The desire of the larrikin for closer association with his social superiors. **1943** D. STEWART in *Coast to Coast 1942* 204 For all his larrikin assurance, Les was afraid to put his feeling for Leila into words. **1966** 'J. HACKSTON' *Father clears Out* 26 It had headed straight for the sturdiest, roughest, most larrikin-looking mob of cattle. **1972** *Southerly* XXXII. 199 He had come around a corner in a corridor to find her confronting a larrikin from 2D.

b. *attrib.* passing into *adj.*

1870 M. CLARKE *Goody Two Shoes* 26 He's a lively little Larrikin Lad, and his name is Little Boy Blue. **1884** *Lit. Era* II. 165 Such a larrikin phrase as 'O crimini' is to be found ..in his writings. **1891** E. KINGLAKE *Australian at H.* 108 The larrikin hordes of the cities of Australia.

Hence **larrikiness**, a female larrikin; **larrikinism**, the habits and practices of larrikins.

1870 *Australian* (Richmond, Vict.) 10 Sept. 3/3 (Morris) A slight attempt at 'larrikinism' was manifested. **1871** *Collingwood Advertiser* (Austral.) 22 June 3/5 (ibid.) Evidence was tendered as to the manner of life led by these larikinesses. **1871** *Evening Post* (Wellington, N.Z.) 27 Apr. 2/4 (*heading*) Larrikinism v. Public Entertainments. **1879** C. L. INNES *Canterbury Sk.* v. 39 We had not then [*sc.* in 1852-3] the pestilential element of 'larrikinism' which is so rife now, and which makes many public meetings so objectionable. **1891** E. KINGLAKE *Australian at H.* 106 Larrikinism confines itself to no particular class. **1892** G. PARKER *Round Compass Austral.* xii. 224 Nor does the young larrikiness..exist as a class. **1927** M. M. BENNETT *Christison* xxviii. 264 This last piece of larrikinism took Mimi so completely by surprise that she could not think of anything to say.

larrom, -um, obs. forms of LARUM.

larrup ('lærəp), *v.* and *intr. dial.* and *colloq.* Also **larrop, lirrop.** *trans.* To beat, flog, thrash. Hence **'larruping** *vbl. sb.*

1823 MOOR *Suffolk Wds.* 208 *Larrup*, to beat—similar to lace, lather [etc.]. **1824** PEAKE *Amer. Abr.* I. i, I'll larrup you till you can't stand. *a* **1825** JENNINGS *Observ. Dial. W. Eng.* 53 To *Lirrop*, to beat. This is said to be a corruption of the sea term, *lee-rope.* *a* **1825** FORBY *Voc. E. Anglia*, *Larrup.* **1829** FONBLANQUE *Eng. under 7 Administr.* (1837) I. 246 Is this a land of liberty, where a man can't larrop his own nigger? **1833-4** *Jack Giant K.* v. xiv. in *Comic Nursery T.* (1846) v. 44 Drinking success to the hero stout Who larruped the Giants out-and-out. **1874** M. COLLINS *Transmigr.* I. xii. 221 He larruped me once when I was a boy for throwing stones at a cat. **1889** 'ROLF BOLDREWOOD' *Robbery under Arms* (1890) 156 'Your father'll give you a fine larrupin' if he comes home and there's that cow lost'. **1893** ZINCKE *Wherstead* 261 Here [in East Anglia] the farmer used in old times to 'larrup' his idle disorderly boys. **1922** JOYCE *Ulysses* 498, I let him larrup it into me for the fun of it. **1939** C. FRY *Boy with Cart* 26 Heard the first spatter of drops, the outriders Larruping on the road. **1953** DYLAN THOMAS *Under Milk Wood* (1954) 81 From the larrupped waves the lights of the lamps in the windows call back the day. **1970** [see CRUELTY 1 b.].

larry ('lærɪ), *sb.*[1] *dial.*

1. Confusion, excitement.

1876 T. HARDY *Ethelberta* (1890) 358 'My brain is all in a spin, wi' being rafted up in such a larry!' **1886** —— *Mayor of Casterbr.* xxxvi, 'The worst larry for me was that pleasant business at Horewood'.

2. (See quot.)

1883 *Nature* XXVII. 452 The 'Larry' is a dense mass of rolling white land fog, and is confined to the bottom of the Teign valley.

larry ('lærɪ), *sb.*[2] *dial.* **a.** (See quot. 185.). **b.** Liquid mortar, grout. Hence **'larry** *v. dial.* (see quot. 1890).

185. *Dict. Archit.* (Arch. Publ. Soc.), *Larry*, a kind of long handled iron hoe with holes in it, used by bricklayers in making mortar; and to rake backwards and forwards the mortar laid on walls when mixing it with water to form grout. **1890** *Gloucester Gloss.*, *Larry*, liquid mortar, growt. Hence 'to larry it in' means to flush up well with growt.

Larry ('lærɪ), *sb.*[3] [Etym. uncertain.] Phr. ***happy as Larry***, extremely happy.

1905 T. COLLINS in *Barrier Truth* (Broken Hill) 29 Dec. 1 Now that the adventure was drawing to an end, I found a peace of mind that all the old fogies on the river couldn't disturb. I was as happy as Larry. **1915** L. STONE *Betty Wayside* xix. 254 If it hadn't been for that busybody we'd have been as happy as Larry. **1934** T. WOOD *Cobbers* iii. 25 He said he was as happy as Larry to see a fresh face. **1938** S. BECKETT *Murphy* ix. 180 Kept in peace they would have been as happy as Larry, short for Lazarus. **1946** F. SARGESON *That Summer* 32 Then he'd hop round happy as Larry. **1966** BAKER *Austral. Lang.* (ed. 2) xii. 271 *Happy as Larry*, extremely happy. Possibly but not certainly commemorating the noted Australian pugilist Larry Foley (1847-1917). **1966** B. KENNELLY *Collection One: Getting Up Early* 26 The Knockanore woman was happy as Larry. **1967** *Daily Mail* 18 Jan. 12/3 The tobacco and pipe trade..are as happy as Larry that Dr. Cameron..has won the award.

larry, variant of LORRY *sb.*

larson, larsonie: See LARCIN, LARCENY.

larthew, variant of LORTHEW *Obs.*, teacher.

larum ('lɛərəm, 'lærəm), *sb.* Forms: 6 **larom(e, larowme,** 8 **larrom, -um,** 6- **larum.** [Aphetic form of ALARUM.]

1. A call to arms, a battle-cry; news of an enemy's approach; any sound to warn of danger. †Hence (*rarely*) a sudden attack.

1549 COVERDALE, etc. *Erasm. Par. Eph.* p. xiv, What larum so euer happeneth, with this buckeler it shalbe vaynquished. **1555** EDEN *Decades* 56 They fiercely assayled theyr enemyes with a larome. **1555** PROCTOR *Wyat's Rebell.* D iij b, In the night..there happened a larom, sundrie criinge: treason, Treason. **1559** *Fabyan's Chron.* VII. 707 Sir Thomas Poinynges..cried a newe larum, and sette on the Frenchmen. **1607** SHAKS. *Cor.* I. iv. 9 Then shall we heare their Larum, & they Ours. **1755** in G. Sheldon *Hist. Deerfield, Mass.* (1895) I. 638 We fired several larrums and the great gun at Fort Dummer was shot. **1784** COWPER *Task* IV. 569 The first larum of the cock's shrill throat May prove a trumpet, summoning your ear To horrid sounds of hostile feet. **1812** BYRON *Ch. Har.* II. 72. **1833** HT. MARTINEAU *Fr. Wines & Pol.* vii. 100 The drums and larums which kept all Paris awake. **1847** LYTTON *Lucretia* (1853) 185 A larum [of a door-bell] loud enough to startle the whole court.

fig. **1650** R. STAPYLTON *Strada's Low C. Warres* I. 7 Warned by his disease, that still rung the larum of death.

b. In wider sense: A tumultuous noise; a hubbub, uproar.

a **1533** LD. BERNERS *Huon* cxxix. 472 Then the crye and larum began. **1588** SHAKS. *Tit. A.* I. i. 147 Remaineth nought but..with low'd Larums [to] welcome them to Rome. **1596** DALRYMPLE tr. *Leslie's Hist. Scot.* II. VII. 5 Thay crie a larum, that [etc.]. **1800** COLERIDGE *Wallenst.* I. vii, But whence arose this larum in the camp? **1840** THACKERAY *Paris Sk.-bk.* (1869) 151 His invention has not made so much noise and larum in the world as some others. **1858** G. MACDONALD *Phantastes* xix. in *Wks. Fancy & Imag.* (1871) VI. 96 The continually renewed larum of a landrail.

fig. **1593** R. HARVEY *Philad.* I, I will be so bold as answere your larum, touching the history of mighty Brute.

†**c.** An uneasy condition. = ALARM 12. *Obs.*

1598 SHAKS. *Merry W.* III. v. 73 The peaking Curnuto her husband..dwelling in a continual larum of ielousie.

†**2.** An apparatus attached to a clock or watch, to produce a ringing sound at any fixed hour. *Obs.*

1586 BRIGHT *Melanc.* xiii. 66 Automaticall instruments as clockes, watches, & larums. **1607** DEKKER *Whore Babylon* Wks. 1873 II. 264 What houre is this? does not my larum strike? This watch goes false. **1648** BP. WILKINS *Math. Magick, Dædalus* iii. 171 That larum..which..would both wake a man, and of it self light a candle for him at any set hower of the night. **1692** LOCKE *Educ.* xiv. Wks. 1727 III. 6 Others..have set their Stomachs by a constant usage, like Larums to call on them for four or five. **1807** SOUTHEY in *Rem. H. K. White* (1819) I. 34 He would..rise again to his work at five, at the call of a *larum*, which he had fixed to a Dutch clock in his chamber.

transf. and *fig.* **1661** COWLEY *Disc. Govt. O. Cromwell* in *Verses & Ess.* (1687) 70 There needs no Noise at all t' awaken Sin Th' Adulterer and the Thief his Larum has within. **1691** SHADWELL *Scourers* I. ii. Dram. Wks. (1720) 326 Will the larum of your tongue never lie down. **1711** STEELE *Spect.* No. 11 ¶1 She had often an Inclination to interrupt him, but could find no Opportunity 'till the Larum ceased of its self. **1778** G. WHITE *Selbourne* 9 Sept., By this [crowing] he has been distinguished in all ages as the countryman's clock or larum.

3. *attrib.* and *Comb.*, as ***larum-call, -clock, -watch.*** Also LARUM-BELL.

1683 *Lond. Gaz.* No. 1846/4 A large Silver Larum Watch with a Chain. **1697** *Ibid.* No. 3251/4 Lost..a Larum Clock in a little Box. **1821** JOANNA BAILLIE *Metr. Leg., Ghost Fadon* xxii, Till they heard a bugle's larum call.

larum ('lærəm), *v.* *Obs.* exc. *dial.* Also 8 **larom.** [f. LARUM *sb.*]

†**1.** *trans.* **a.** To sound *forth* loudly. **b.** To alarm. *Obs.*

1595 P. T. G. tr. *Blanchardine* II. Ded., Hauing presumed to tune my rustic stringes to larum foorth my simple musicke. **1758** S. THOMPSON *Diary* 21 July (1896) 12 At prayer this evening we were Laromed by a false outcry.

2. *intr.* †**a.** To rush *down* with loud cries (*obs.*). **b.** 'To talk incessantly' (*Holderness Gloss.* 1877).

1728 POPE *Dunc.* III. 158 Down, down they larum, with impetuous whirl, The Pindars and the Miltons of a Curl.

'larum-bell. *Obs.* exc. *poet.* [f. LARUM *sb.* + BELL.] = ALARM-BELL.

1568 T. HOWELL *Arb. Amitie* (1879) 57 Lest by the way some watchman lay, to ring the larome bell. **1590** SPENSER *F.Q.* II. ix. 25. **1597** SHAKS. *2 Hen. IV*, III. i. 17. **1609** HEYWOOD *Brit. Troy* xv. lxxi, The Larum Bels of death on all sides ringing. *a* **1634** CHAPMAN *Alphonsus* Plays 1873 III. 248 Run to the Tow'r and Ring the Larum Bell. **1813** SCOTT *Rokeby* II. xxv, Ring out the castle larum bell!

larva ('lɑːvə). *Pl.* **larvæ.** [L. *larva* a ghost, spectre, hobgoblin; also, a mask.]

1. A disembodied spirit; a ghost, hobgoblin, spectre. *Obs.* exc. *Hist.*

1651 BAXTER *Inf. Bapt.* 273, I live almost perpetually in my bed or chair or pulpit; as Calvin said of Cassander; such a *larva* I am that here am called up. **1882** *Encycl. Brit.* XIV. 313/2 The dead..were..spirits of terror..: in this fearful sense the names *Lemures* and still more *Larvæ* were appropriated to them.

fig. **1827** SYD. SMITH in *Edin. Rev.* Mar. 429 There is the larva of tyranny, and the skeleton of malice.

2. a. An insect in the grub state, i.e. from the time of its leaving the egg till its transformation into a pupa. **b.** Applied to the early immature form of animals of other classes, when the development to maturity involves some sort of metamorphosis.

In the first quot. the word is used in a general sense = 'mask', 'guise': the technical restricted use is due to Linnæus. In the larva the perfect form, or *imago*, of the insect is unrecognizable.

[**1691** RAY *Creation* I. (1692) 7 We exclude both these from the degree of *Species*, making them to be the same Insect under a different *Larva* or Habit.] **1768** G. WHITE *Selborne* xviii. (1789) 54 The *larvæ* of insects are full of eggs. **1770** PENNANT *Zool.* IV. 37 The two small ones [*sc.* lizards] are *Larvæ*, with their branchial fins, which drop off when they quit the water. **1815** KIRBY & SP. *Entomol.* I. 67 This Linné called the *larva* state, and an insect when in it a *larva.* **1837** GORING & PRITCHARD *Microgr.* 212 Among aquatic larvæ, the most beautiful and delicate are those of the numerous species of gnat. **1849** MURCHISON *Siluria* App. D. 539 They are larvæ of Echinoderms. **1859** DARWIN *Orig. Spec.* xiii. 440 Cuvier did not perceive that a barnacle was.. a crustacean; but a glance at the larva shows this to be the case. **1874** BREWER in Coues *Birds N.W.* 65 Collecting flies and larvae among a clump of locust trees. **1897** *Daily News* 23 Jan. 6/1 This plaice larva has no mouth, at least no open mouth.

fig. **1854** H. ROGERS *Ess.* II. i. 32 He is sure to deposit in his own writings the larvæ of future controversies.

c. *attrib.*, as ***larva-case, -form, -stage, -state.***

1791 E. DARWIN *Bot. Gard.* I. 197 So in his silken sepulchre the worm, Warm'd with new life, unfolds his larva-form. **1855** J. PHILLIPS *Man. Geol.* 459 Thin tufaceous limestones, sometimes full of the larva-cases of phryganidae. **1874** CARPENTER *Ment. Phys.* I. ii. §59 (1879) 58 The change from the larva to the perfect or *imago* state of the Insect. **1893** J. TUCKEY tr. *Hatschek's Amphioxus* 159 Those stages which form the transition from the development of the embryo..to the larvae stages which are self-nourishing.

larval ('lɑːvəl), *a.* [ad. L. *larvāl-is* pertaining to larvæ, or ghosts.]

†**1.** (See quot.) *Obs.*

1656 BLOUNT *Glossogr.*, *Larval*, belonging to a night-spirit, goblin or masker, haggish, ghastly, dreadful.

2. Of or pertaining to a larva or grub; characteristic of a larva.

1848 in MAUNDER *Treas. Nat. Hist.* 791. **1851-6** WOODWARD *Mollusca* iv. 21 The young [of mollusca] generally pass through one preparatory, or larval, stage. **1859** DARWIN *Orig. Spec.* ii. (1878) 35 The immature and larval states of many of the lower animals. **1894** H. DRUMMOND *Ascent Man* 352 The larval forms of the Star-fish or the Sea Urchin.. are disguised past all recognition.

b. Of an animal: In the condition of a larva.

1864 *Reader* IV. 669/1 The mode in which the larval flukes found in the molluscs re-enter the sheep. **1866** DK. ARGYLL *Reign Law* iv. (ed. 4) 197 The eating of some larval parasite into the tissue of the wing.

3. *Path.* Of a disease: Latent, undeveloped. Also, 'applied to certain diseases in which the skin of the face is disfigured as if covered by a mask' (Mayne *Expos. Lex.* 1855).

1897 *Allbutt's Syst. Med.* III. 172 Certain irritations in the various organs, such as characterize irregular or larval gout. **1898** P. MANSON *Trop. Dis.* vi. 105 The quinine test is generally conclusive in.. the various larval forms of malaria. *Ibid.* viii. 159 Abortive or larval plague.

larvate ('lɑːveɪt), *a.* [ad. mod.L. *larvāt-us*, f. *larva* a mask: see -ATE[2] 2. Cf. F. *larvé*.] Masked, covered as by a mask.

1846 BUCHANAN *Technol. Dict.*, *Larvate*, masked; applied in entomology. **1848** MAUNDER *Treas. Nat. Hist.* 791 *Larvate*, masked, as a larva or caterpillar. **1888** *Syd. Soc. Lex.*

larvated ('lɑːveɪtɪd), *a.* [f. prec. + -ED[1].] †**a.** Provided with a mask (*obs.*). **b.** *transf.* Masked, concealed. In *Path.* (see quot. 1888).

1623 COCKERAM, *Laruated*, masqued. **1658** PHILLIPS, *Larvated*, masqued or visarded for the representing some Gobling or dreadful Spirit. **1727** in BAILEY vol. II. **1832** W. STEPHENSON *Gateshead Poems* 39 He.. can place his soul at stake, With sanctity larvated. **1888** *Syd. Soc. Lex.*, *Larvated*, applied to diseases whose ordinary symptoms are hidden.

†**lar'vation.** *Obs.* [f. as prec. + -ATION.] A discoloration of the face in a fever-patient, producing a resemblance to a mask; a masking.

1651 BIGGS *New Disp.* ¶ 234 These larvations vanish, the feaver being taken away.

larve (lɑːv). [a. F. *larve*, ad. L. *larva*.]

1. = LARVA 1.

1603 FLORIO *Montaigne* I. xvii. (1632) 27 Larves, Hob-goblins, Robbin-good-fellowes, and such other Bug-beares. **1822** W. IRVING *Braceb. Hall* (1823) I. 174 The opinions of the ancient philosophers about larves, or nocturnal phantoms. **1863** *Veronia* III. 147 Elementary spirits.. for which a later philosophy has furnished the designation of larves.

†**2.** A mask; *lit.* and *fig. Obs.*

a **1656** HALES *Gold. Rem.* (1688) 423 Under this larve, this whifling suit of Toleration, there lay personated more dangerous designs. **1677** GALE *Crt. Gentiles* II. IV. 365 *Πρόσωπον* signifies.. the face, that part.. which was covered.. with the larve or visard.

3. = LARVA 2.

1769 PENNANT *Zool.* III. 15 We.. are uncertain whether we ever met with it [a lizard] under the form of a *larve*. **1822-34** *Good's Study Med.* (ed. 4) IV. 353 Sometimes resembling the larves of insects. **1852** DANA *Crust.* II. 1594 The animal is probably the larve of some Penæidean.

†**larved,** *a. Obs. rare*[−1]. [f. L. *larva* mask + -ED.] Masked, concealed.

1654 VILVAIN *Theol. Treat.* vi. 174 That grand general Apostasy into Analogical larved Idolatry.

larvi- ('lɑːvɪ), combining form of L. *larva*, LARVA. **'larvicide** [-CIDE 1], a preparation adapted to kill larvæ; also *attrib.* or *adj.*; so **larvicidal** *a.* **lar'vicolous** *a.* [L. *col-ĕre* to inhabit: see -OUS], living in the body of larvæ (Mayne *Expos. Lex.* 1855). **larviform** *a.* [-FORM], having the form of a larva. **lar'vigerous** *a.* [-GEROUS], bearing or containing larvæ. **lar'viparous** *a.* [L. *par-ĕre* to bring forth: see -OUS], (*a*) producing young in the condition of larvæ, (*b*) produced in the form of larvæ.

1900 *Brit. Med. Jrnl.* No. 2041. 305 A cheap *larvicidal substance.. not injurious to the growth of the rice plants. *Ibid.* 325 The *larvicides are intended to be used for the destruction of mosquito larvæ and pupæ in pools and ditches. *Ibid.*, Professor Celli showed experiments at the Institute of Hygiene with certain insecticide and larvicide substances. **1848** MAUNDER *Treas. Nat. Hist.* 791 **Larviform*, shaped like a larva. **1891** C. L. MORGAN *Anim. Life* 223 The females of certain beetles.. are described by Professor Riley as larviform. **1884** *Stand. Nat. Hist.* (1888) II. 428 When ready to change into the *larvigerous pupæ they [the maggots of the bot-fly] dislodge themselves. **1815** KIRBY & SP. *Entomol.* I. 103 So Aristotle employs it, when he says that all insects produce a *Scolex*, or are *larviparous. **1826** *Ibid.* III. 65 *Larviparous*, coming forth from the matrix in the state of larvæ. **1858** LEWES *Sea-side Stud.* 285 The viviparous or larviparous generation effects a multiplication of the plant-lice adequate to keep pace with the rapid growth and increase of the vegetable kingdom in spring and summer.

larvikite ('lɑːvɪkaɪt). *Petrogr.* Also **laurvikite**, †**-vigite** ('laʊə-). [ad. G. *laurvikit* (W. C. Brögger 1890, in *Zeitschr. f. Kryst.* XVI. 29), f. *Laurvik* (now *Larvik*), name of a Norwegian seaport: see -ITE[1].] A kind of syenite that has a characteristic coarse texture dominated by rhombs of soda or soda-lime feldspar, with augite as the chief mafic mineral, and is used as a decorative stone.

1895 A. HARKER *Petrol.* 304 (Index), Laurvikite. **1911** *Encycl. Brit.* XVI. 30/1 The ornamental stone from south Norway, now largely used as a decorative material in architecture, owes its beauty to a felspar with a blue opalescence.. which Professor W. C. Brögger has termed cryptoperthite, whilst the rock in which it occurs is an augite-syenite called by him laurvigite, from its chief locality, Laurvik in Norway. **1962** R. WEBSTER *Gems* I. ix. 157 The Norwegian rock known as laurvikite.. is a material extensively used for building façades. **1965** *Norsk Geol. Tidsskr.* XLV. 69 The two monsonitic syenites from the Oslo area, larvikite and tönsbergite, differ mainly in the colour of the feldspar minerals. The blue schiller which is so predominant in the larvikite varieties is normally completely masked by the red colour of the tönsbergite varieties. **1971** *Country Life* 16 Sept. 683/1 By the date of the opening of Highgate [Cemetery].. the Victorians had become eclectic in their choice, employing all manner of stones, often of distant source, simply on account of their pleasing colour or texture. So we find the iridescent Larvikite from Norway together with all colour tones of granite-type rock from Finland or Sweden.

lary, variant of LAURY *Obs.*, laurel.

laryngal (lə'rɪŋgəl), *a.* [f. mod.L. *laryng-* LARYNX + -AL[1].] Produced in the larynx. Also *absol.*

1818-60 WHATELY *Commpl. Bk.* (1864) 168, B, D, &c. are sounded in the larynx.. so that they might be called.. the laryngal.. letters. **1883** *Scotsman* 9 May 6/4 That the only service of praise acceptable to the Deity consists in human laryngal sounds. **1922** D. JONES *Outl. Eng. Phonetics* (ed. 2) vi. 14 Glottal or laryngal sounds, viz. sounds articulated in the glottis. **1933** L. BLOOMFIELD *Lang.* vii. 99 A glottal or laryngal stop is produced by bringing the vocal chords tightly together and then letting them spring apart under the pressure of the breath. **1939** L. H. GRAY *Foundations of Lang.* iii. 49 Two other glottal (or laryngal) sounds of importance are represented by the *h*'s of English *how*, *ahoy*.., unvoiced and voiced respectively. **1958** PRIEBSCH & COLLINSON *German Lang.* (ed. 4) 6 It [*sc.* Hittite] has 'laryngeal' sounds—not identical with the Semitic 'laryngals'.

laryngeal (lə'rɪndʒɪəl), *a.* and *sb. Anat.* and *Surg.* Also 9 **laringeal.** [f. mod.L. *larynge-us* (f. *laryng-*, LARYNX) + -AL[1].]

A. *adj.* **1.** Of or pertaining to the larynx; *e.g.* ***laryngeal muscle, nerve***. Of a disease: Affecting or seated in the larynx. Of an instrument: Used in treating or examining the larynx.

1795 HAIGHTON in *Phil. Trans.* LXXXV. 198 The eighth pair of nerves communicates energy to the larynx by means of the laryngeal branch. **1854** BUSHMAN in *Circ. Sci.* (*c* 1865) I. 282/1 The superior laryngeal nerve. **1861** T. J. GRAHAM *Pract. Med.* 179 Constituting what.. is frequently spoken of as laringeal phthisis. **1871** DARWIN *Desc. Man* II. xviii. 276 The male gorilla.. when adult is furnished with a laryngeal sack. **1880** M. MACKENZIE *Dis. Throat & Nose* I. 235 The patient may be directed to practise on himself.. with the laryngeal mirror. **1881** MIVART *Cat* 229 There are no less than eight pairs of laryngeal muscles. **1897** *Allbutt's Syst. Med.* IV. 791 The chief remedy is the application of astringents to the cords by means of the laryngeal brush.

2. Of a sound: produced in or modified by the larynx; = LARYNGAL *a.* Also *absol.*

1921 E. SAPIR *Lang.* 249 Articulations, laryngeal. **1927** R. BRIDGES in *S.P.E. Tract* XXVI. 177 The method is that in singing the mouth is fixed in the position that gives the required vowel resonance.. and that the laringeal note is as it were forced through it. **1932** W. L. GRAFF *Lang.* 28 *Laryngeals* or *glottals*, produced by a narrowing or closure of the vocal cords.

3. Corresponding to sense B. 2 below.

1952 *Bull. Board Celtic Stud.* XIV. 296, I reconstruct in terms of the so-called 'laryngeal theory', here, however, without committing myself to the number of laryngeals necessarily to be assumed at a given time. **1958** [see LARYNGAL *a.*]. **1958** A. S. C. ROSS *Etym.* 7 It is certainly quite impossible for anyone to understand Laryngeal Theory without being thoroughly familiar with junggrammatisch Ablaut.

B. *sb.* **1.** A laryngeal nerve or artery.

In some Dicts.

2. *Philol.* A hypothetical phonetic element with a laryngeal quality supposed to have existed, spec. in Proto-Indo-European, and to have left traces in the vocalic features of extant Indo-European languages.

1942 E. H. STURTEVANT *Indo-Hittite Laryngeals* 15 In this book the word *laryngeals* designates certain consonants of Proto-Indo-Hittite. The name is historically a translation of German *Laryngale*, which term was borrowed from Semitic grammar by Hermann Möller to designate five phonemes of his Proto-Indo-European-Semitic. **1951** *Trans. Philol. Soc.* 88 (*title*) A reconsideration of the Hittite evidence for the existence of 'Laryngeals' in Primitive Indo-European. **1963** *Language* XXXIX. 252 It is intrinsically implausible that a presumably nonsyllabic laryngeal next to a syllabic resonant should vocalize. **1969** *Ibid.* XLV. 260 Plain stops immediately followed by a laryngeal became aspirated stops in Indo-Iranian. **1971** F. R. ADRADOS in *Archivum Linguisticum* II. 95, I refer particularly to those stems in which the presence of laryngeals gives rise to diverging interpretations.

So **la'ryngean** *a.* [see -AN] = LARYNGEAL; **la'ryngealist**, an adherent of a laryngeal theory; also *attrib.* or as *adj.*; **la,ryngeali'zation**, the action or fact of being laryngealized; **la'ryngealized** *a.*, of a sound produced in or affected by the larynx.

1828 WEBSTER, Laryngean. [Hence in mod. Dicts.] **1943** K. L. PIKE *Phonetics* vii. 127 Laryngealization may conveniently be said to be trillization with superimposed voice. *Ibid.*, In English one often hears laryngealized vowels. **1964** O'CONNOR & TOOLEY in D. Abercrombie et al. *Daniel Jones* 176 Glottal stop and laryngealization before word-initial vowel were accepted. **1964** *Language* XL. 138 The laryngealist will retort that another.. problem.. is also solved by applying a laryngeal solution. *Ibid.* 140 A typical phonemic analysis of the PIE vowels in laryngealist terms. **1968** *Ibid.* XLIV. 529 Much is made of the fact that only one laryngealized stop (i.e. glottalized or aspirated) occurs per word in Quechua. **1968** CHOMSKY & HALLE *Sound Pattern Eng.* 315 Several African and Caucasian languages exhibit the so-called laryngealized or 'creaky' voice. **1971** *Canad. Jrnl. Ling.* Fall 70 He rejects phonemic /ə/.. thus discomfiting the more elderly laryngealists.

laryngectomy (lærɪn'dʒɛktəmɪ). *Surg.* [f. Gr. *λαρυγγ-*, LARYNX + *ἐκ* out + *-τομία* a cutting.] The excision of the larynx.

1888 in *Syd. Soc. Lex.* **1897** *Allbutt's Syst. Med.* IV. 840 Thyrotomy, or subhyoid pharyngotomy, with removal of the growth by excision and partial laryngectomy, offers the best chance of getting rid of the whole disease.

Hence **laryngec'tomic** *a.*

In some mod. Dicts.

laryngic (lə'rɪndʒɪk), *a.* [f. as prec. + -IC.] = LARYNGEAL.

1822-34 *Good's Study Med.* (ed. 4) I. 459 *Laryngismus.* Laryngic suffocation. **1887** *Pall Mall G.* 3 Sept. 7/1 The disposition to laryngic catarrh is also much less marked.

‖**laryngismus** (lærɪn'dʒɪzməs). *Path.* [mod.L. *laryngismus*, f. *laryng-*, LARYNX. Gr. *λαρυγγισμός* had the sense of shouting, f. *λαρυγγίζειν* (f. *λάρυγξ* larynx) to shout.] Spasm of the muscles closing the larynx; laryngic suffocation.

1822-34 *Good's Study Med.* (ed. 4) I. 460 In spasmodic laryngismus the constriction commences in the larynx. **1897** *Allbutt's Syst. Med.* III. 111 In these cases laryngismus is a constant accompaniment.

Hence **laryn'gismal** *a.*, of or pertaining to laryngismus.

1880 *Encycl. Brit.* XI. 390/2 Tracheotomy in laryngismal epilepsy.

‖**laryngitis** (,lærɪn'dʒaɪtɪs). *Path.* [mod.L., f. as prec. + -ITIS.] Inflammation of the lining membrane of the larynx.

1822-34 *Good's Study Med.* (ed. 4) I. 460 Laryngitis or inflammation of the larynx. **1879** *St. George's Hosp. Rep.* IX. 555 The treatment of the earlier stages of catarrhal laryngitis.

Hence **laryn'gitic** *a.*, pertaining to or of the nature of laryngitis. (In recent Dicts.)

laryngo- (lə'rɪŋgəʊ), before a vowel **laryng-**, combining form of LARYNX, chiefly in anatomical, pathological and surgical terms. **la'ryngo-ca'tarrh**, catarrh of the larynx (Mayne *Expos. Lex.* 1885). **la,ryngo-'fissure**, the division of the thyroid cartilage (*Syd. Soc. Lex.* 1888). **laryngography** (-'gɒgrəfɪ) [-GRAPHY], a description of the larynx (Mayne). **la,ryngo'logical** *a.*, pertaining to laryngology. **laryn'gologist**, one who is versed in laryngology. **laryngology** (-'gɒlədʒɪ) [-LOGY], that branch of medical science which treats of the larynx and its diseases. **la,ryngo-pha'ryngeal** *a.*, pertaining both to the larynx and to the pharynx. **laryngo-'pharynx**, = HYPOPHARYNX 2. **la'ryngophone**, a microphone designed to be placed or attached to the throat so as to pick up the voice directly with little intrusion of other sounds. **laryngophony** (-'gɒfənɪ) [Gr. *-φωνία* sounding], 'the sound of the voice as heard through the stethoscope applied over the larynx' (Grant *Hooper's Lex. Med.* 1839). **la,ryngo'phthisical** *a.*, pertaining to laryngophthisis (Mayne). **laryn,gophthisis**, consumption of the larynx (Mayne). **la,ryngo'rrhœa** [Gr. *ῥοία* a flowing], 'a pituitous or serous flow from the larynx' (Mayne). **la'ryngo,spasm**, spasm or convulsion of the larynx (Mayne). **la,ryngoste'nosis** [Gr. *στένωσις* a being straitened], contraction of the larynx (Mayne). **laryngostro'boscopy** [Gr. *στρόβο-ς* a whirling + -SCOPY] (see quot.). **la,ryngo'tracheal** *a.*, pertaining to both the larynx and the trachea or windpipe. **la,ryngo,tracheobron'chitis** *Path.*, inflammation of the larynx, trachea, and bronchi; *spec.* an acute febrile disease (a form of croup) that exhibits these symptoms and occurs chiefly in young children, in which excessive secretion of mucus causes obstruction of the larynx and sometimes the bronchi. **la,ryngotra'cheotomy**, **la,ryngo-'typhoid**, **la,ryngo-'typhus** (see quots.).

1888 M. MACKENZIE *Fredk. the Noble* i. 11, I had never seen him mentioned in *laryngological literature. **1871** —— *Growths in Larynx* iii. 18 From the varying.. character of

the voice..the presence of a growth may be occasionally inferred by the experienced *laryngologist. **1842** DUNGLISON *Med. Lex.*, **Laryngology*. **1887** (*title*), Journal of Laryngology and Rhinology. **1892** *Pall Mall G.* 4 Feb. 6/2 Laryngology being his almost invariable subject. **1872** COHEN *Dis. Throat* 10 The *laryngo-pharyngeal sinuses. **1893** A. W. MACCOY in C. H. Burnett *Syst. Dis. Ear, Nose, & Throat* II. 195 The *laryngo-pharynx..is chiefly interesting because of its relationship to the epiglottis and the superior margin of the larynx, which is situated in front of it. **1897** *Allbutt's Syst. Med.* IV. 754 When the laryngo-pharynx and œsophagus are the primary seat [of cancer], the cervical glands are not so rapidly implicated. **1960** Laryngopharynx [see INLET *sb.* 5]. **1927** *Observer* 6 Nov. 19/3 We have a special instrument, the *laryngophone, by means of which we can speak to each other in flight. **1941** *Jrnl. R. Aeronaut. Soc.* XLV. 402 The picking up of the throat vibrations is done with a laryngophone. **1862** H. W. FULLER *Dis. Lungs* 105 In *laryngophony..the voice seems not only to be produced but to be concentrated immediately beneath the stethoscope. **1880** M. MACKENZIE *Dis. Throat & Nose* I. 289 Excessive secretion from the larynx (*laryngorrhoea). **1878** *Cassell's Fam. Mag.* 574/2 *Laryngostroboscopy..a method of examining the vibrations of the vocal chords during the production of sounds. **1880** M. MACKENZIE *Dis. Throat & Nose* I. 559 Contraction of the *laryngo-tracheal canal. **1897** *Allbutt's Syst. Med.* IV. 764 The front part of the neck corresponding to the larynx and upper part of the trachea, the laryngo-tracheal region. **1932** DORLAND & MILLER *Med. Dict.* (ed. 16) 685/2 *Laryngotracheobronchitis. **1956** HINSHAW & GARLAND *Dis. Chest* xi. 183 Among the most serious and difficult ailments affecting small children are a group of diseases variously called acute laryngotracheobronchitis, bronchiolitis, fibrinous bronchitis or 'croup'. These are characterized by violent cough, often associated with laryngospasm and bronchospasm and appear to be of infectious origin. **1972** *Daily Tel.* 2 Feb. 13/5 Two American pathologists have been claiming that laryngotracheobronchitis is frequently responsible for cot deaths, since they have found signs of inflammation in the larynxes, windpipes and bronchial tubes of babies who died. **1879** *St. George's Hosp. Rep.* IX. 587 *Laryngotracheotomy was therefore performed. **1888** *Syd. Soc. Lex.*, *Laryngotracheotomy*, the operation of opening the larynx by division of the crico-thyroid membrane, the cricoid cartilage, the crico-tracheal membrane, and some of the upper rings of the trachea also. **1896** *Allbutt's Syst. Med.* I. 812 In very rare cases [typhoid fever commences with] laryngeal symptoms (*laryngo-typhoid). *Ibid.* 818 Ulcerations, which according to some observers are due to the typhoid bacillus, and may thus be looked upon as a typical form of typhoid, 'laryngo-typhoid'. **1888** *Syd. Soc. Lex.*, **Laryngotyphus*, a form of typhus fever in which there is secondary ulceration of the larynx and necrosis of its cartilages. **1897** *Allbutt's Syst. Med.* II. 364 Its occurrence [*sc.* laryngitis in typhus] led Rokitansky to give to this variety the name of Laryngo-typhus.

laryngoscope (ləˈrɪŋgəskəʊp). [f. LARYNGO- + -SCOPE.] An apparatus which by a combination of mirrors enables an observer to inspect a patient's larynx.

1860 *Med. Times & Gaz.* I. 453 The highly practical results obtained on the Continent by the use of the Laryngoscope. **1864** MAX MÜLLER *Sci. Lang.* Ser. II. iii. (1868) 109 The newly-invented laryngoscope (a small looking-glass, which enables the observer to see as far as the bifurcation of the windpipe and the bronchial tubes). **1880** M. MACKENZIE *Dis. Throat & Nose* I. 213 There is no trace of a laryngoscope before the middle of the eighteenth century.

laryngoscopic (ləˌrɪŋgəˈskɒpɪk), *a.* [f. as prec.: see -SCOPIC.] Of or pertaining to the laryngoscope, or to inspection of the larynx.

1861 tr. *Czermak's Uses of Laryngoscope* i. 1 My laryngoscopic studies. **1864** T. HOLMES *Syst. Surg.* (1870) IV. 518 Mackenzie's 'rack movement laryngoscopic lamp'.. is admirably adapted for use in the consulting room. **1872** COHEN *Dis. Throat* 11 A good light is an indispensable prerequisite to a laryngoscopic examination. **1896** *Allbutt's Syst. Med.* I. 287 There is slight hoarseness with the laryngoscopic appearances of laryngeal catarrh.

So **laˌryngoˈscopical** *a.* = prec.; whence **laˌryngoˈscopically** *adv.*, with respect to, or by the use of the laryngoscope.

1861 tr. *Czermak's Uses of Laryngoscope* i. 6 On the manner of obtaining the laryngoscopical image enlarged. **1864** T. HOLMES *Syst. Surg.* (1870) IV. 519 Laryngoscopical and other examinations. **1879** *Sat. Rev.* 13 Sept. 322 A Committee so laryngoscopically learned. **1880** M. MACKENZIE *Dis. Throat & Nose* I. 558 That this condition ..arises after tracheotomy has been proved laryngoscopically by Gerhardt.

laryngoscopist (lærɪŋˈgɒskəpɪst). [f. LARYNGOSCOPE + -IST.] One who uses, or is skilled in using, the laryngoscope.

1864 T. HOLMES *Syst. Surg.* (1870) IV. 514 Dr. B. G. Babington appears to have just claims to be considered the first successful laryngoscopist. **1880** M. MACKENZIE *Dis. Throat & Nose* I. 221 Various lamps..recommended by different laryngoscopists.

laryngoscopy (lærɪŋˈgɒskəpɪ). [f. LARYNGO- + Gr. -σκοπία inspection.] Inspection of the larynx; the use of the laryngoscope.

1861 *Braithwaite's Retrosp. Med.* XLII. 90 Those who wish to occupy themselves with laryngoscopy will do well to follow Türck's advice. **1897** *Allbutt's Syst. Med.* IV. 672 For rhinoscopy the same reflector and source of illumination are employed as for laryngoscopy.

laryngotome (ləˈrɪŋgəʊtəʊm). *Surg.* [f. LARYNGO- + Gr. -τόμος cutter.] An instrument for performing laryngotomy (Mayne *Expos. Lex.* 1855).

laryngotomy (lærɪŋˈgɒtəmɪ). *Surg.* [ad. Gr. λαρυγγοτομία, f. λαρυγγο- LARYNX + -τομία cutting.] The operation of cutting into the larynx from without, esp. in order to provide an aperture for respiration.

1661 LOVELL *Hist. Anim. & Min.* 354 The quinzey..; it's cured, by..laryngotomy, and thin diet. **1684** tr. *Bonet's Merc. Compit.* I. 13 Breath may be restored to the Choaking Patient, by the help of Laryngotomy. **1725** N. ROBINSON *Theory of Physick* 273 In this Case, Laryngotomy is the last Refuge the miserable Patient has for his Life. **1872** COHEN *Dis. Throat* 43 The wound left after laryngotomy or tracheotomy.

Hence **laˌryngoˈtomic** *a.*, pertaining to or of the nature of laryngotomy.

In some mod. Dicts.

larynx (ˈlærɪŋks). *Anat.* Pl. larynges (ləˈrɪndʒiːz). Also 6–7 **larinx**, 6 **laringa**. [a. Gr. λάρυγξ, mod.L. *larynx*.] A cavity in the throat with cartilaginous walls, containing the vocal cords, by means of which sounds are produced. In man and most animals this cavity forms the upper part of the trachea or wind-pipe. In birds there are two larynges, one at each end of the trachea; the lower of these, called SYRINX, is the true organ of sound.

1578 BANISTER *Hist. Man* I. 16 b, This Larinx is the Organ, by which we receiue and put forth breath; as also of makyng and fourmyng voyce. **1597** A. M. tr. *Guillemeau's Fr. Chirurg.* 19/2 Muscles situated aboute the Laringa. **1633** P. FLETCHER *Purple Isl.* IV. 45 *note*, The Larynx, or coveryng of the winde-pipe is a grisly substance. **1732** ARBUTHNOT *Rules of Diet* 387 The Ulcer may break suddenly into the Larynx with the danger of Suffocation. **1802** PALEY *Nat. Theol.* x. §5 The larynx..besides its other uses, is also a musical instrument. **1881** MIVART *Cat* 223 At its front end the trachea expands into a membranous and cartilaginous box-like structure called the larynx. **1900** *Westm. Gaz.* 20 June 1/2 Splendid lungs and larynges which had never known a London fog.

attrib. **1861** *Braithwaite's Retrosp. Med.* XLII. 88 The observer..introduces the larynx-speculum.

larzon, variant of LARCIN *Obs.*

las (lɑːs, læs), *int.* [aphetic form of ALAS.] = ALAS.

1604 DEKKER *Honest Wh.* I. x. G, Las! now I see The reason why fond women loue to buy Adulterate complexion. **1694** CONGREVE *Double Dealer* IV. iii, O las! no indeed, Sir Paul. **1844** MRS. BROWNING *House of Clouds* xii, Poet's thought,—not poet's sigh. 'Las, they come together!

las, obs. form of LACE, LASS, LESS.

lasagne (‖laˈzaɲɲe, ləˈzænjə, -zɑːnjə, -s-). In sing. **lasagna**. [It.] An Italian dish: a variety of pasta cut in long wide strips.

[**1760** BARETTI *Dict. Eng. & Ital. Lang.* I, *Lasagna*, a kind of thin paste cut into slices and dry'd, boiled in water or broth, [etc.].] **1846** E. ACTON *Mod. Cookery* (ed. 5) 579 The ribbon maccaroni (or lasagnes). **1849** BROWNING *Englishman in Italy* in *Poems* II. 333 We shall feast our grape-gleaners..With lasagne so tempting to swallow In slippery ropes. **1960** *News Chron.* 17 Feb. 6/2 Excellent ravioli and lasagne (soft ribbon noodles)..at 2s. 6d. a pound. **1961** *Listener* 20 Apr. 719/1 To make *lasagne verdi* (green *lasagne*)..you will need [etc.]. **1966** T. PYNCHON *Crying of Lot 49* i. 10 The layering of a lasagna, garlicking of a bread. **1972** *Guardian* 18 Aug. 11/3 Lasagne..perhaps the finest of all pasta dishes. **1974** *Times* 7 Feb. 16/7 To assemble the lasagne, spoon a little of the meat sauce into the base of a large shallow baking dish. Cover with a layer of lasagne, spoon over a layer of cottage cheese and sprinkle with Parmesan.

lasar, variant of LAZAR.

lasar(e, obs. Sc. form of LEISURE *sb.*

†**lasard**. *Obs. rare*⁻¹. [? a. F. *lézard*, lit. 'lizard', in 17th c. the name of some kind of firearm.] A kind of musket.

1641 EARL CORK *Diary* in *Lismore Papers* Ser. I. (1886) V. 201 Paid Tho. Badnedg for five new lasard muskets.

lascar (ˈlæskə(r), læˈskɑː(r)). Also 7 **laskayre**, (**luscar**), 7–8 **lascarr**. [Either an erroneous European use of Urdu *lashkar* army, camp (see LASHKAR), or a shortened form of its derivative *lashkarī* (see LASCARINE). In Pg. *c* 1600 *laschar* occurs in the same sense as *lasquarim*, i.e. native soldier; this use, from which the current applications are derived, is not recorded in Eng. (but see quot. 1698 in 1).]

1. (Freq. with capital initial.) An East Indian sailor.

1625 PURCHAS *Pilgrims* I. v. 650, I caused all my Laskayres to remaine aboord the Vnicorne. **1696** OVINGTON *Voy. Surratt* 464 The English Sailers..perceiv'd the softness of the Indian Lascarrs; how tame they were [etc.]. **1698** FRYER *Acc. E. India & P.* 107 The Seamen and Soldiers differ only in a Vowel, the one being pronounced with an *u*, the other with an *a*; as *Luscar* is a Soldier; *Lascar*, a Seaman. **1712** W. ROGERS *Voy.* (1718) 311, 36 Manila Indians, call'd Lascarrs. **1777** MILLER in *Phil. Trans.* LXVIII. 172 Besides the four lascars that rowed the boat. **1800** *Asiatic Ann. Reg., Chron.* 46/1 There were only the captain and three officers, with 13 lascars, able to do duty. **1832** MARRYAT *N. Forster* xli, If we only had all English seamen on board, instead of these Lascars and Chinamen. **1849** LONGF. *Building of Ship* 161 Where the tumbling surf, O'er the coral reefs of Madagascar, Washes the feet of the swarthy Lascar.

attrib. and *Comb.* **1887** *Pall Mall G.* 3 Aug. 2/2 The second mate of a Lascar-manned ship is on watch until four o'clock. **1900** *Daily News* 20 Sept. 9/4 Sickness broke out among the Lascar crew.

2. *Anglo-Indian.* 'A tent-pitcher'; also, an inferior class of artilleryman (more fully ***gun-lascar***).

1798 WEBBE in Owen *Wellesley's Desp.* 7 A body of about 14,000 men can be drawn together, including Lascars and pioneers. **1799** BAIRD *ibid.* 126 One hundred artillerymen with a proportion of gun lascars. **1800** WELLINGTON in Gurw. *Desp.* (1837) I. 125 We can get neither recruits, servants, lascars, coolies, or bullock drivers. **1870** J. W. KAYE *Hist. Sepoy War* II. IV. iii. 89 All the natives in the Magazine, the gun-lascars, the artificers and others.

lascaree (læskəˈriː). Also 8 **lascari**. [a. Urdu (Pers.) *lashkarī*: see next.]

†**1.** = LASCAR 1. *Obs.*

1712 E. COOKE *Voy. S. Sea* 354 All the Prisoners were put Aboard the Bark, except about 30 Lascaris.

2. 'A short spear used in the East Indies as a hunting-spear, or more rarely as a javelin for throwing' (*Cent. Dict.*).

†**lascaˈrine**. *Indian. Obs.* Also 6 **lascariin**, 8 **-yn**, 9 **lascoreen**. [ad. Pg. *lasquarin*, *-im*, a. Urdu (Pers.) *lashkarī* (adj., military; hence as sb., a soldier), f. *lashkar* army: see LASHKAR.] An East Indian soldier; also, one of the native police.

1598 W. PHILLIPS *Linschoten* I. xxxix. 74 The soldier of Ballagate, which is called Lascariin. **1704** *Collect. Voy.* (Churchill) III. 706/2 A Convoy of 20 Lascaryns, under the Command of a Colonel. **1807** CORDINER *Ceylon* I. 170 A large open boat formed the van, containing his excellency's guard or lascoreens. **1825** HEBER *Jrnl.* xxvii. (ed. 2) 140 Attended by some lascarines, who answer in some respects to our peons in Calcutta.

lasce, obs. form of LASS.

†**lasch**. *Obs.* In 5 **lassche**. [The *rede lassche* of the quot. represents OE. *réadlęsc* 'pellis rubricata' (Napier *Gll.* no. 5324); cf. OHG. *loski* (MHG. *lösche*, early mod.G. *lasch*, *lösch*).] A fine kind of red leather; ? morocco.

14.. *E.E. Misc.* (Warton Club) 86 To make rede lassche, take [etc.].

lasche, obs. form of LASH *sb.*¹, *a.*, and *v.*¹

†**laschety**. *Obs. rare.* Also 8 **laschete**. [ad. F. *lascheté*, now *lâcheté*: see LASH *a.* and -TY.] Laxity, carelessness.

1673 O. WALKER *Educ.* II. iv. (ed. 2) 263 The general defect being negligence, laschety, and love of ease. **1702** C. MATHER *Magn. Chr.* IV. iv. (1852) 83 He had a certain discretion, without any childish laschete or levity in his behavior.

lascitt, variant of LASSET *Obs.*

†**laˈscive**, *a. Obs. rare*⁻¹. [a. F. *lascive*, ad. L. *lascīvus*.] Lascivious, wanton.

1647 LILLY *Chr. Astrol.* cvii. 537 Lyra..inclines to gravity and sobriety, yet but with outward pretences, for usually the person is lascive.

†**laˈsciviate**, *v. Obs. rare.* [erroneously ad. L. *lascīvīre*, after verbs in *-iate*: see -ATE³.] *intr.* To sport wantonly; to indulge in unseemly jesting.

1627–77 FELTHAM *Resolves* I. xx. 36 Divinity should not lasciviate [*ed.* 1709 *has* be wanton... Gravity becomes the pulpit. **1656** in BLOUNT *Glossogr.* **1721** in BAILEY.

Hence **laˈsciviating** *ppl. a.*

1660 *Charac. Italy* To Rdr. A iij, He will..say these Whimsies are but *Ingenii lascivientis flosculi*, the superfluous Excrescencies of lasciviating wit.

†**laˈsciviency**. *Obs. rare.* [f. next: see -ENCY.] Lasciviousness, wantonness.

1664 H. MORE *Myst. Iniq.* xii. 153 Any villanies..that the lasciviency of their own lawless phancy shall suggest. **1681** HALLYWELL *Melampr.* 9 Men,..through the..lasciviency of the bodily life, quite lose the..sense of true Goodness.

†**laˈscivient**, *a. Obs.* [ad. L. *lascīvient-em*, pres. pple. of *lascīvīre* to be wanton, f. *lascīvus* wanton.] Wantoning, lascivious.

1653 H. MORE *Conject. Cabbal.* (1713) 21 Set upon doing things..according as the various toyings and titillations of the lascivient Life of the Vehicle suggested to him [Adam]. *a* **1703** BURKITT *On N.T.* 1 Cor. v. 5 For the destruction of the flesh, so lascivient in him.

Hence †**laˈsciviently** *adv.*

1664 H. MORE *Myst. Iniq.* 331 Men ran up and down in Vizards madly and lasciviently.

†**lasciviˈosity**. *Obs. rare*⁻⁰. [f. next + -ITY.] Lasciviousness.

1727 in BAILEY vol. II.

lascivious (ləˈsɪvɪəs), *a.* Also 5 **lassivyous**, 6 **lacivious**. [ad. late L. *lascīviōs-us* (Isidore), f. L. *lascīvi-a* (n. of quality f. *lascīvus* sportive, in bad sense lustful, licentious): see -OUS.]

1. Inclined to lust, lewd, wanton.

c **1425** LYDG. *Assembly of Gods* 686 Lastyuyous [*read* lascyuyous] lurdeyns, & pykers of males. **1494** FABYAN *Chron.* VII. 402 Yᵉ lassiuyous and wanton disposicions of the sayd Pyers of Gaueston. **1555** EDEN *Decades* 141 He

chaunced to lyue in those lasciuious and wanton dayes. **1567** Maplet *Gr. Forest* 88 The Gotebucke is verie wanton or lasciuious. **1601** Shaks. *All's Well* iv. iii. 248, I knew the young Count to be a dangerous and lasciuious boy. **1601** Holland *Pliny* II. 544 One picture there is of his doing, wherein he would seeme to depaint Lascivious [quoted in mod. Dicts. as 'lascious'] wantonnesse. **1667** Milton *P.L.* ix. 1014 Hee on Eve Began to cast lascivious Eyes. **1781** Cowper *Anti-Thelyphthora* 199 The Fauns and Satyrs, a lascivious race, Shrieked at the sight. **1856** Mrs. Browning *Aur. Leigh* iii. 767 Thin dangling locks, and flat lascivious mouth.

Comb. **1586** W. Webbe *Eng. Poetrie* D iiij, He.. is wholy to bee reputed a laciuious disposed personne.

b. Inciting to lust or wantonness. †Also in milder sense, voluptuous, luxurious. *Obs.*

1589 Puttenham *Eng. Poesie* ii. ix. [x.] (Arb.) 97 Carols and rounds and such light or lasciuious Poemes. **1594** Shaks. *Rich. III*, i. i. 13 He capers nimbly in a ladies Chamber, To the lasciuious pleasing of a Lute. **1602** T. Fitzherbert *Apol.* 36 b, How many are there.. that.. make no scruple to keep lasciuious pictures to prouoke themselues to lust? **1621** Burton *Anat. Mel.* ii. ii. ii. (1651) 240 By Philters and such kinde of lascivious meats. **1660** F. Brooke tr. *Le Blanc's Trav.* 155 Their garments are something lascivious, for being cut and open their skin is seen. **1671** L. Addison *W. Barbary* 150 That they should have Chaires there to sit in with as much lascivious ease, as at home. **1780** Cowper *Table T.* 462 To the lascivious pipe and wanton song, That charm down fear, they frolic it along. **1838** Lytton *Leila* i. iv, Not thine the lascivious arts of the Moorish maidens.

¶ **2.** Used for: Rank, luxuriant.

1698 Fryer *Acc. E. India & P.* 243 Forded several Plashes where flourished lascivious Shrubs.

lasciviously (lə'sɪvɪəslɪ), *adv.* [f. prec. + -ly².]

1. In a lascivious manner, lewdly.

1546 Langley *Pol. Verg. De Invent.* iii. ix. 76 b, Menne & Women were permitted moste lasciuiously to bath together. **1611** Beaum. & Fl. *King & No K.* iii. iii, I would desire her loue Lasciuiouslie, leudlie, incestuouslie. **1624** Wotton *Archit.* i. 37 The Corinthian, is a Columne, lasciuiously decked like a Curtezane. **1786** tr. *Beckford's Vathek* (1868) 110 A throng of Genii and other fantastic spirits of each sex danced lasciviously in troops.

†**2.** (In sense of L. *lascīvē*.) Sportively. *Obs.*

1607 Topsell *Four-f. Beasts* (1658) 32 A young maid, playing with the bear lasciviously, did so provoke it that he tore her in pieces.

lasciviousness (lə'sɪvɪəsnɪs). [f. as prec. + -ness.] The quality of being lascivious.

1596 Spenser *F.Q.* Ded. Verses to Raleigh, The vertuousnes of Belphœbe, the lasciviousnes of Hellenora, and many the like. **1611** Bible *Eph.* iv. 19. **1680** Dryden *Ovid's Epist.* Pref., The lasciviousness of his Elegies. **1796** Morse *Amer. Geog.* II. 546 They acquire, as they grow warm in the dance, a frantic lasciviousness. **1900** Kipling in *Westm. Gaz.* 14 May 5/3 If, through any intellectual lasciviousness, we.. prefer to tickle our emotions by being generous.. at other people's expense.

†**la'scivity.** *Obs.* [ad. F. *lascivité*, ad. L. *lascīvitāt-em*, f. *lascīvus*.] = prec.

1490 Caxton *Eneydos* ix. 37 To rendre theym from theyr lacyuyte in-to.. shamefaste chastyte. **1513** Bradshaw *St. Werburge* i. 1923 The naturall mocyon of his lascyuyte Was shortly slaked.

†**lascivy.** *Obs. rare*⁻⁰. [ad. L. *lascīvia*: see lascivious *a.*] Lasciviousness.

1727 in Bailey vol. II.

lase (leɪz), *v.* [Back-formation from laser², the ending *-er* being treated as the ending -er¹ of agent nouns.] *intr.* Of a substance, or an atom or molecule: to undergo the physical processes (of excitation and stimulated emission) employed in the laser; to function as the working substance of a laser. Of a device: to operate as a laser.

1962 *New Scientist* 1 Feb. 270/3 This is well illustrated by the uses now being made of the entirely novel verb 'to lase'... It is common currency among those.. whose lives are given to the search for materials that will emit light in coherent and narrow-pencilled beams. **1963** *Ibid.* 10 Jan. 65/3 Hitherto, only certain ionic crystals (notably ruby), some gas mixtures and.. one or two liquids, had been persuaded to 'lase'; that is, to emit coherent infrared or visible light of a single wavelength. **1963** *Ibid.* 7 Feb. 293/2 Scientists at Standard Telecommunications Laboratories.. last week persuaded their version of the gallium arsenide laser to 'lase'. **1963** *Monsanto Mag.* Mar. 10/2 Calculations.. indicated that gallium arsenide would 'lase', or amplify light, if suitably stimulated. **1967** *Guardian* 11 Feb. 1/1 Can X-ray lasers be made? There is no problem in getting substances to lase at the right frequency. **1969** *Sci. Jrnl.* Apr. 55/2 The term 'dye laser' is generally used. Different dyes lase at different wavelengths and.. it has been possible to span without a break the range 700–1000 nm by using some 20 different dyes. **1970** *Daily Tel.* (Colour Suppl.) 28 Aug. 16/2 Not all atoms can be made to 'lase'. **1971** *Sci. Amer.* July 37/2 When the injection current becomes high enough so that the light in the crystal making a round trip along the junction plane is amplified enough to offset losses due to absorption, to scattering, to leakage out of the mirrors and so on, the diode is said to be lasing.

Hence '**lasing** *ppl. a.* and *vbl. sb.*

1963 *Monsanto Mag.* Mar. 9/3 Many variations have been produced since then, employing other solids, as well as gases and liquids, as 'lasing' materials. **1966** Smith & Sorokin *Laser* vii. 369 The characteristics of these lasing diodes.. differ considerably from those of other lasers. **1973** *Physics Bull.* Dec. 723/1 Lasing at 145 nm in high pressure krypton has also been achieved.. with intense electron beam pumping.

lase, obs. form of lace; obs. Sc. form of lass.

laser¹ ('leɪsə(r)). *Hist.* Also 6 lasser, 7 lazer. [a. L. *lāser*.] A gum-resin mentioned by Roman writers; obtained from an umbelliferous plant called *lāserpīcium* or *silphium* (σίλφιον).

[*c* **1420** *Pallad. on Husb.* iv. 326 Stampe a quantite of laseris with wyne.] **1578** Lyte *Dodoens* iii. cxii. 303 From out of the rootes and stalkes being scarified and cut floweth a certayne strong liquor,.. called Laser. **1579** Langham *Gard. Health* (1633) 411 The hearbe being rubbed, smelleth like vnto Laser. **1591** Percivall *Sp. Dict.*, *Benjuy*, herbe laser.

b. *Comb.*: †**laser-tree**, the tree yielding laser; **laser-wort**, any plant of the genus *Laserpitium*, esp. *L. latifolium*.

1626 Bacon *Sylva* §555 A Kind of Spongie Excrescence, which groweth chiefly upon the Roots of the *Laser-Tree. **1597** Gerarde *Herbal* ii. cccxci. (1633) 1007 Laserpitium called in English *Laserwort. **1658** J. R. tr. *Mouffet's Theat. Insects* 1057 Take Castoreum, Lazerwort, Pepper, of each four drams. **1760** J. Lee *Introd. Bot.* App. 316 Laser-wort, *Laserpitium*. **1796** Morse *Amer. Geog.* I. 188 Great laserwort, and Wild Angelica. **1870** *Treas. Bot.*, Laserwort, *Laserpitium*; also *Thapsia Laserpitii*.

laser² ('leɪzə(r)). [f. the initial letters of '*l*ight *a*mplification by the *s*timulated *e*mission of *r*adiation', after the earlier maser.] **1.** Any device that is capable of emitting a very intense, narrow, parallel beam of highly monochromatic and coherent light (or other electromagnetic radiation), either continuously or in pulses, and operates by using light to stimulate the emission of more light of the same wavelength and phase by atoms or molecules that have been excited by some means.

Orig. treated as the name of a particular kind of maser (*optical maser*) emitting visible light, *laser* is now the general term for all devices of this kind, whatever the wavelength of the emitted radiation.

1960 *N.Y. Times* 8 July 7/6 The Hughes device is an optical maser, or 'laser', (the 'l' standing for 'light'). **1960** *Aviation Week* 18 July 97/2 The optical Maser is also referred to by the term Laser. **1960** *Daily Tel.* 29 Dec. 9/4 The laser, a device for amplifying light which could conceivably be developed to produce a searchlight beam that would reach the moon, is still a paper project as far as British scientists are concerned. **1961** *Jrnl. Appl. Physics* XXXII. 178 [*Paper received 13 June 1960.*] The Fabry-Perot interferometer has been suggested for use as a high-mode LASER (light amplification by stimulated emission of radiation) resonator. **1961** *Observer* 19 Feb. 5/2 The new 'laser', as it is called, uses a mixture of helium and neon gas to produce a continuous beam of infra-red radiation... Previous devices have produced only brief pulses of light. **1962** *Science Survey* III. 27 The principle of the maser has been extended also to solid materials and, in addition, it has been found possible to make a light maser (or 'laser') that produces, not microwaves, but visible light. **1963** *Electronics Weekly* 2 Jan. 1/4 The new high-power laser uses a six-inch by half-inch ruby. **1963** *Monsanto Mag.* Mar. 9/2 Early lasers absorbed energy from a strong burst of ordinary white light, organized it, then expelled a powerful beam of a different kind of light. **1963** *Daily Tel.* 24 Oct. 19/4 Already in metal working the term 'Gillette power' is used as a measure of the laser's metal-vaporising capabilities. It represents the number of stacked razor blades through which a beam can bore its way. **1964**, **1966** [see hologram]. **1969** *Sci. Jrnl.* Apr. 53/1 Lasers have been operated which produce visible radiation, ultraviolet, infrared and even submillimetre radiation. **1970** [see holograph *v.*]. **1971** *Sci. Amer.* June 21/3 A laser is a device for generating or amplifying a beam of light whose waves are both monochromatic (all the same wavelength) and coherent (all in step). The light beam emitted by a laser can be made almost perfectly parallel, its divergence angle being theoretically limited only by diffraction effects. **1972** *McGraw-Hill Yearbk. Sci. & Technol.* 266/2 The first purely chemical lasers requiring no external source of energy to initiate or sustain laser excitation have been operated successfully.

2. *attrib.* and *Comb.*, as ***laser beam***, ***bomb***, ***light***, ***reflector***; ***laser-guided***, ***-ignited*** ppl. adjs.; ***laser-heat*** vb.; **laser disc**, a disc on which signals or data are recorded to be reproduced by directing a laser beam on to its surface and detecting the light reflected or transmitted by it; **laser-driven** *ppl. a.*, powered by a laser beam; **laser printer**, a non-impact printer in which a laser is used to form a pattern of dots on a photosensitive drum corresponding to the pattern of print required on a page.

1963 *Monsanto Mag.* Mar. 10/3 A *laser beam can generate intense heat—10,000°F. or higher—in a small area. **1970** *Daily Tel.* (Colour Suppl.) 28 Aug. 17/1 A laser beam, focused through the lens of the eye, can weld a detached retina back into place by creating scar tissue. **1970** *Daily Tel.* 31 Jan. 4/2 Scientists.. maintain that the *laser bomb.. is a theoretical possibility. **1972** *Guardian* 29 June 4/3 The drawback to the laser bomb is that the plane producing the beam must keep it on target until the bomb's impact. [**1978** *Electronics & Communications in Japan* LXI. 97/1 The signal is read from the laser video disc by detecting either the transmitted or reflected light when a laser beam is incident at the recorded signal track.] **1980** C. S. French *Computer Sci.* vii. 32 *Laser disc units. Development is going ahead on disc units which use optical methods requiring lasers. **1982** *World Bk. Sci. Ann. 1983* 131 Today's videodiscs differ radically.. from one another. The most sophisticated is the optical disc, or laser disc. **1985** *Sunday Times* 20 Jan. 72/7 Laser disc technology is about to make the filing cabinet obsolete. **1976** *Jrnl. Physical Soc. Japan* XL. 867/2 In order to pull out thermonuclear fusion energy from a *laser-driven pellet, the implosion must take place in a stable manner. **1984** *Progress Optics* XXI. 355 (*heading*) Fluctuations, instabilities and chaos in the laser-driven nonlinear ring cavity. **1967** *New Scientist* 11 May 326/2 With the *laser-guided bomb, the large bombers might be able to drop their loads over the target area from high altitudes with greater assurance of putting them on target. **1972** *Science* 9 June 1108/3 The laser-guided bombs now being used are mostly in the 2000 to 3000-pound range. **1971** *Sci. Amer.* June 27/1 The second question—regarding the feasibility of *laser-heating a small dense plasma to thermonuclear conditions without the necessity of a confining magnetic field—is receiving increased attention. *Ibid.* 29/1 A method for converting the fusion energy from laser-ignited deuterium-tritium pellets into electrical power was evolved.. early in 1969. **1966** *Listener* 28 July 129/3 The editor.. will brandish a *laser-light pen to indicate alterations which a computer will make. **1971** B. de Ferranti *Living with Computer* ix. 83 In laser light the waves are all in the same plane and in phase. **1979** *Product Engin.* May 16 (*heading*) *Laser printer is crucial to office machine that does just about everything. **1985** *Personal Computer World* Feb. 13/3 (Advt.), Laser Jet is a quiet, eight page-per-minute tabletop laser printer. **1969** *New Scientist* 9 Oct. 81/1 The first men on the Moon have.. already placed one *laser-reflector on the lunar surface.

laser, var. lazar; obs. form of leisure *sb.*

laserte, variant of lacert¹ *Obs.*

laset, variant of lasset *Obs.*

lash (læʃ), *sb.*¹ Also 4–6 lasshe, 5 las(c)he. [? f. lash *v.*¹]

1. † **a.** *gen.* A sudden or violent blow; a dashing or sweeping stroke (*obs.*). **b.** *spec.* A stroke with a thong or whip.

c **1330** *Arth. & Merl.* 9375 (Kölbing) Kehenans com wiþ gret rape & ȝaf king Arthour swiche a las, þat Arthour al astoned was. *c* **1374** Chaucer *Troylus* i. 220 Proude bayard gynneth for to skyppe.. Til he a lassh haue of þe long whippe. **1387** Trevisa *Higden* (Rolls) VI. 31 Foure score lasshes [L. *octoginta verbera*]. *c* **1460** *Play Sacram.* 468 On lashe I shalle hyme lende or yt be long. **1549** Coverdale, etc. *Erasm. Par. Heb.* 23 Oure parentes.. dyd wyth.. lashes teach vs the commen behauiour of this lyfe. **1604** E. G[rimstone] *D'Acosta's Hist. Indies* v. xvii. 374 Therewith they whipped themselves, giving great lashes over their shoulders. **1639** Fuller *Holy War* ii. xi. (1840) 64 All desiring to have a lash at the dog in the manger. **1661** T. Lye in *Morn. Exerc. Cripplegate* xviii. 459, I that have deserved the blow of an Executioners Axe, am sent away with the Lash only of a Fathers Rod. **1735** Somerville *Chase* ii. 116 Let each Lash Bite to the Quick, till howling he return. **1769** *Junius Lett.* xxxv. 165 The private men have.. five hundred lashes if they desert. **1791** Mrs. Radcliffe *Rom. Forest* ii, I gave my horse a lash that sounded through the forest. **1844** *Regul. & Ord. Army* 230 The Mutiny Act restricts the award of Corporal Punishment by a General Court-Martial to 200 Lashes. **1880** Mrs. Forrester *Roy & Viola* I. 175 The first lash brought the colour to her cheeks.

transf. and *fig.* **1526** *Pilgr. Perf.* (W. de W. 1531) 159 Moost domage of all and perylous lasshe they procure to themselfe. **1599** Marston *Sco. Villanie* i. Proem., Skud from the lashes of my yerking rime. **1602** Shaks. *Ham.* iii. i. 50 How smart a lash that speech doth giue my Conscience. **1693** in *Dryden's Juvenal* iv. Argt., The Poet.. brings in Crispinus, whom he had a lash at in his first Satyr. **1697** Bentley *Phal.* Pref. (1699) 3 This was meant as a lash for me. **1710** Addison *Whig Exam.* No. 2 ⁋5 The first lash of his Satyr falls upon the Censor of Great Britain.

2. a. The flexible part of a whip; now sometimes in narrower sense, the piece of whipcord or the like forming the extremity of this. Cf. lash *sb.*²

c **1381** Chaucer *Parl. Foules* 178 The boxtre pipere, holm to whippis lasch. **1592** Shaks. *Rom. & Jul.* i. iv. 63 Her Whip of Crickets bone, the Lash of Philome. **1711** Addison *Spect.* No. 108 ⁋2, I observed.. that your Whip wanted a Lash to it. *a* **1800** Cowper *Morning Dream* 30 In his hand.. A scourge hung with lashes he bore. **1819** Shelley *Cenci* iv. i. 69 He will not ask it of me till the lash Be broken in its last and deepest wound. **1859** Jephson *Brittany* vii. 94 Employing himself in plaiting fresh pieces [of whipcord].. on the lash of his whip.

b. Used *poet.* and *rhetorically* = 'whip, scourge'. *lit.* and *fig.* Also in phrase, † *out of* (a person's) *lash*: out of danger from (his) attacks.

1586 J. Hooker *Hist. Irel.* in *Holinshed* II. 98/1 He was out of his lash that minded to haue betraied him. *a* **1656** Bp. Hall *Rem. Wks.* (1660) 209 The slave fears the lash of his cruell Master. **1659** Bp. Walton *Consid. Considered* 197 The Vulgar Latin scapes the lash pretty well. **1715–20** Pope *Iliad* v. 457 The lash resounds, the rapid chariot flies. **1732** Swift *Corr.* Wks. 1841 II. 671 Lest they should fall under the lash of the penal laws. **1786** Mad. D'Arblay *Diary* 28 Nov., With all this.. she has not escaped the lash of scandal. **1820** Shelley *Hymn to Mercury* lxxxv, Apollo.. gave him in return the glittering lash, Installing him as herdsman. **1838** Thirlwall *Greece* II. 288 The Persians.. were driven on to the conflict by the lash of their commanders. **1887** Bowen *Virg. Æneid* vi. 571 Tisiphone.. Scourges the trembling sinners, her fierce lash arming her hands. **1891** S. C. Scrivener *Our Fields & Cities* 117 Hunger is as keen a lash as the whip of the overseer of slaves.

c. *the lash*: the punishment of flogging.

1694 F. Bragge *Disc. Parables* (1706) I. vii. 238 Such Vagabonds.. would.. look upon honest Industry as more eligible than the Lash. **1711** Steele *Spect.* No. 157 ⁋6 This Custom of educating by the Lash. **1781** Gibbon *Decl. & F.* xxxi. III. 126 He expired under the lash. **1860** *Knight's Eng. Cycl., Arts & Sci.* V. 654 Serious breaches of discipline are still punished with the lash. **1881** *Times* 29 Mar. 9/3 There is throughout these kingdoms a strong instinctive dislike of the lash.

†**d.** ? The next place to the front in a team of four horses. Cf. *lash-horse* in 5. *Obs. rare*⁻¹.

1607 Markham *Caval.* v. (1617) 56 Cause him to be put vnto the Cart, placing him in that place which the Carters

call the Lash, so that hee may haue two Horses to follow behinde him, whome together with the loade.. he cannot draw away.

¶**e.** An alleged name for a 'company' of carters. *Obs. rare*—[1].

1486 *Bk. St. Albans* F vij.

3. Short for EYE-LASH.

1796 BROUGHAM in *Phil. Trans.* LXXXVI. 267 Priestley [makes them arise] from inflection through the lashes. **1797** COLERIDGE *Christabel* I. 316 Tears she sheds—Large tears that leave the lashes bright! **1840** DICKENS *Barn. Rudge* i, Long dark lashes.. concealed his downcast eyes.

†**4.** Phrases of obscure origin in which the identity of the word is doubtful. ***to leave in the lash*** = to leave in the lurch. ***to lie in the lash***: to be left in the lurch. ***to run in*** or ***upon the lash***: to incur more debts than one can pay. *Obs.*

[Possibly we should compare *in the lash* with *out of his lash* (quot. 1586 in 2 b). The passage from Tusser (quot. 1573 below) is given by Johnson as his only example of the sense 'a leash or string in which an animal is held, a snare' (cf. LASH *sb.*[2]). Some have assigned to the sb. in these phrases a sense 'mire'.]

1573 TUSSER *Husb.* lxiii. (1878) 144 The fermer they leaue in the lash, with losses on euerie side. **1575** GASCOIGNE *Fable Ferd. Ieron.* Posies 228 My Nell hath stolne thy finest stuffe and left thee in the lash. **1576** WOOLTON *Chr. Manual* I iij, The wyse and welmeaning debtour who, goeth eyther vppon the score, or booke, hath oftentymes an eye vnto the score; least he be ouerreckoned and runne in the lashe. **1584** R. WILSON *Three Ladies Lond.* II. A iij, I will flaunt it and braue it after the lusty swash: Ile deceiue thousandes, what care I who lye in the lashe? **1607** HIERON *Wks.* I. 436 We runne on still vpon the lash, and neuer looke on the score. *a* **1624** BP. M. SMITH *Serm.* (1632) 110 When we lost Callis in his quarrell, he left vs in the lash, and gaue vs the slip.

5. An attempt; esp. in phr. ***to have a lash (at)***, to make an attempt, to 'have a go at'. *Austral.* and *N.Z.*

1941 BAKER *Dict. Austral. Slang* 42 *Lash at, have a*, to make an attempt at (something). **1945** J. PASCOE *Canterbury High Country* 28 A few may spend their cheque in a glorious lash at the beer. **1948** D. BALLANTYNE *Cunninghams* (1963) vii. 38 Hoping to get a lash at the Huns. **1949** R. PARK *Poor Man's Orange* (1950) 193 The blithe pipings of old men who, safe [from the fight] up on their balconies, leaned over rails and exhorted everyone to 'ave a lash. **1971** *Sunday Sun* (Brisbane) 17 Oct. 14/2, I am a natural sportsman. Only last week I donkey licked the local kindy kids at drop the hankie. So I went out to Surfers Paradise course to have a lash.

6. *attrib.* and *Comb.*, as (sense 1) ***lash-free***; (sense 3) ***lash-shaded***, ***-shadowed***, ***-tender*** adjs.; **lash-horse** (see quot.); **lash rope** *N. Amer.*, a rope used for lashing a pack or load on a horse or vehicle; **lash-whip**, a whip with a lash, opposed to a 'crop' (see CROP *sb.* 7 c).

1623 B. JONSON *Masques, Time Vind.*, I with this whipp you see Doe lash the Time, and am my selfe *lash-free. **1887** *Kentish Gloss.*, **Lash-horse*, the third horse from the plough or wagon, or horse before a pin-horse in the team. **1806** LEWIS & CLARK *Orig. Jrnls. Lewis & Clark Expedition* (1905) V. 114 Sergt. Gass, McNeal, Whitehouse and Goodrich accompanyed them [*sc.* Indians] with a view to procure some pack or *lash ropes. **1822** J. FOWLER *Jrnl.* 18 June (1898) 159 We then took the lash Roaps and tyed up the Horses. **1843** *Amer. Pioneer* II. 162 Each horse was provided with.. a lash rope to secure the load. **1888** LEES & CLUTTERBUCK *Ramble in Brit. Columbia* 229 The lash rope is from thirty to forty feet long. **1929** *Collier's* 5 Jan. 33/3 'Wait until I get my lash rope' (i.e., the rope with which he bound his load on his sledge). **1963** R. SYMONS *Many Trails* vii. 77 Lash ropes were tightened till the pack animals grunted. **1872** J. H. INGRAHAM *Pillar of Fire* 111 The aquiline nose and the *lash-shaded dark, bright eye. **1891** T. HARDY *Tess* (1900) 115/2 Her..*lash-shadowed eyes. *a* **1889** G. M. HOPKINS *Poems* (1918) 74 Whether.. furled Fast ór they [*sc.* ash-boughs] in clammyish *lashtender combs creep Apart wide. **1787** 'G. GAMBADO' *Acad. Horsemen* (1809) 35, I would advise you always to ride with a *lash whip; it shews the sportsman.

lash (læʃ), *sb.*[2] [Perh. var. of LATCH *sb.*, a. OF. *lache* vbl. sb., f. *lachier*, dial. variant of *lacier*: see LACE *v.* Cf. Swiss Ger. *laschen* shoe-lace.

It is possible that the three senses below have arisen from the substitution of LASH *sb.*[1] for other words of somewhat similar sound and meaning.]

†**1.** A string, cord, thong. Cf. LACE *sb.*[2], LATCH *sb.*[1] 1. *Obs.* (Quot. *c* 1440 is somewhat doubtful; *throat-lash* is current as a var. of *throat-latch.*)

c **1440** *Promp. Parv.* 288/1 Lasche, stroke [*sic*], *ligula*.

†**2.** = LASSO 1. *Obs. rare.*

1748 *Anson's Voy.* I. vi. 65 A machine, which the English .. at Buenos Ayres, generally denominate a lash. It is made of a thong of several fathoms in length.. with a running noose at one end of it. *Ibid.* 66 The address both of the Spaniards and Indians in.. the use of this lash or noose.

3. *Weaving.* = LEASE or LEASH.

1731 MORTIMER in *Phil. Trans.* XXXVII. 106. **1831** G. R. PORTER *Silk Manuf.* 246 Eight rows, forming as many leases or lashes in the warp. **1857** PARKHILL *Hist. Paisley* xiv. 113 In the shawl manufacture the lashes have to be drawn twice. **1875** KNIGHT *Dict. Mech.*, *Lash* (*Weaving*), a thong formed of the combined ends of the cords by which a certain set of yarns are raised in the process of weaving Brussels carpet.

LASH, Lash, lash (læʃ), *sb.*[3] The initials of *lighter aboard ship*, used, freq. *attrib.*, to denote a ship, or system of shipping, in which loaded barges are placed directly on board the ship.

1965 *Maritime Reporter* 1 Nov. 21 (Advt.), The LASH System combines an ultra-simple, fast, automated ship with a large number of low-cost lighters. **1967** *Economist* 7 Jan. 51/2 This is the LASH shipping system (Lighter Aboard Ship Inc.) which both the Americans and Germans are now building. A LASH ship is designed to pick up and carry 250-ton lighters, which are towed to and from the ship regardless of tides or port labour schedules. **1969** *Jane's Freight Containers 1968–69* 378/2 No container ships, but 5 Lash vessels.. are under construction. **1970** *Times* 12 Aug. 18 Shipowners also hastened the introduction of.. lash vessels in which laden barges are floated directly into a large hull.

lash (læʃ), *a. Obs.* exc. *dial.* Also 4–5 **lache**, 5 **laach, lacche**, 5–7 **lasch(e**, 6 **lashe**. [a. OF. *lasche* (F. *lâche*) vbl. adj., f. OF. *lascher* (F. *lâcher*): see LACHE *v.* With sense 3, cf. LUSH *a.*]

†**1.** Culpably negligent or remiss. *Obs.*

c **1374** CHAUCER *Boeth.* IV. pr. iii. 122 Yif he be slowe and astoned and lache he lyueþ as an asse. *c* **1422** HOCCLEVE *Learn to Die* 267 How laach and negligent Haue y been. **1549** *Compl. Scot.* xvii. 146 Thai that var lasche couuardis gat nothing. **1567** *Satir. Poems Reform.* v. 64 Sen God hes to ȝow power lent, Gif ye be lashe ye ar to blame. **1673** O. WALKER *Educ.* v. 39 Immoderate praise makes him.. lasch and negligent. **1694** L'ESTRANGE *Fables* 385 A lasche demission of Sovereign authority.

†**2.** In physical sense: Loose, lax, relaxed. *Obs.*

1513 DOUGLAS *Æneis* IX. xiii. 81 Hys wery breist and lymmys lasch. **1530** PALSGR. 317/1 Lashe nat fast, *lache*. **1546** PHAYER *Regim. Lyfe* L iij, Goute, which procedeth som time of debility of the synowes being lashe.

3. a. Of food, fruits, grass, etc.: Soft, watery. **b.** Of weather: Raw, wet. **c.** Of a hide: Tender. **d.** ***lash egg*** (see quot. *a* 1825). *Obs.* exc. *dial.*

c **1440** *Promp. Parv.* 288/1 Lasche, or to fresche, and vnsavery. **1599** H. BUTTES *Dyets drie Dinner* I, Not so good for the weake.. stomackes, for it is of a lash and yet grosse substance. **1658** SIR T. BROWNE *Gard. Cyrus* v. 71 Fruits being unwholsome and lash, before the fourth, or fifth Yeare. **1787** W. MARSHALL *Norfolk* (1795) II. 383 *Lash*, or *Lashy*, very wet; as 'cold lashy weather'. **1798** *Ann. Agric.* XXX. 314 A thick hide is bad, and a very thin one too lash. *a* **1825** FORBY *Voc. E. Anglia*, *Lash-egg*, an egg without a full formed shell; covered only with a tough film. **1857** BORROW *Romany Rye* (1858) I. 299 'After September the grass is good for little, lash and sour at best.'

Hence †'**lashly** *adv.*

1694 SIR W. HOPE *Sword-man's Vade-m.* 12 That he may not by being advised to play calmly, fall into the other extreme of playing too carelessly, lashly, and perhaps timerously.

lash (læʃ), *v.*[1] Forms: (*pa. t.* 4 **last, laiste**), 4–6 **las(s)ch(e, lasshe**, 5 **lasschyn**, 5–6 **lashe**, 6– **lash**. [Of difficult etymology. The quots. seem to show that in branch I. the vb. is the source, not the derivative, of LASH *sb.*[1] An onomatopœic origin is possible, and is favoured by the early appearance of the parallel and nearly synonymous LUSH *v.*; cf. *dash, dush, flash, flush, mash, mush, smash, smush*, etc. Some uses resemble those of F. *lâcher* (OF. *lascher*) to loose, let go (*lâcher un coup* to 'let fly'). The senses in branch II. are from the sb., and in mod. use have coloured the other senses.]

I. To move swiftly and suddenly.

1. *intr.* To make a sudden movement; to dash, fly, rush, spring, start. Of light: To flash. Of tears, water: To pour, rush. Occas. with allusion to LASH *sb.*[1] 2. Also with *about*, †*asunder*, *away*, *back*, *down*, *out*, †*together*. Const. *at*, *from*, *into*, †*on*, *out of*, *to*.

c **1330** *Arth. & Merl.* 9263 (Kölbing) Mani geauntes.. þat on Arthour at ones last & wiþ his hors to grounde him dast. **13..** *S. Erkenwolde* 334 in Horstm. *Altengl. Leg.* (1881) 273 Liȝtly lasshit þer a leme loghe in þe abyme. **13..** *Minor Poems fr. Vernon MS.* (E.E.T.S.) 502/346 Wiþ his teth anon He logged, þat al in-synder gon lasch. ? *a* **1400** *Morte Arth.* 2801 Whene ledys with longe speris Lasschene to gedyrs. *a* **1400–50** *Alexander* 553 Þe liȝt lemand late laschis fra þe heuyn. *c* **1460** *Emare* 298 The teres lasshed out of his yyen. **1470–85** MALORY *Arthur* VI. xi. 200 Al thre lasshed on hym at ones with swerdes. *Ibid.* xii. 203 Thenne they drewe her swerdes and lasshyd to gyder egerly. **1627** FELTHAM *Resolves* II. [I.] xl[iii.] (1628) 39 Thou knowest not.. what ioyes thou losest, when thou fondly lashest into new offences. **1633** QUARLES *Ded. to P. Fletcher's Poet. Misc.*, I .. Past on my way; I lasht through thick and thinne. **1670** COTTON *Espernon* III. xi. 562 To keep them.. from lashing into those extremes, whereinto [etc.]. *a* **1716** SOUTH *Serm.* (1744) XI. 249 When it [sin] finds the least vent, it lashes out to the purpose. **1820** *Edin. Mag.* May 423 Wi' swash an' swow, the angry jow Cam lashan' down the braes. **1851** RUSKIN *Stones Ven.* (1874) I. xxv. 283 A lizard [in stone] pausing and curling himself round a little in the angle; one expects him the next instant to lash round the shaft and vanish. **1883** ANNIE THOMAS *Mod. Housewife* 124 The rain was still lashing down furiously. **1897** *Allbutt's Syst. Med.* II. 1065 The *Filariæ sanguinis*.. wriggling and lashing about .. among the corpuscles.

2. To let fly *at*, make a dash or rush *at*, aim a blow *at*. †Also with *at* used adverbially. In later use, with mixture of sense 6.

a **1400–50** *Alexander* 1392 Archars.. Lasch [*Dublin MS.* lashe] at þam of loft. **1470–85** MALORY *Arthur* VI. x, The chorle.. lasshyd at hym with a grete clubbe. **1513** DOUGLAS *Æneis* XII. ix. 67 Now lasch thai at with bludy swerdis brycht. **1596** SPENSER *F.Q.* IV. vi. 16 Lashing dreadfully at every part. *Ibid.* v. v. 6 She hewd, she foynd, she lasht, she laid on every side. **1693** DRYDEN *Persius' Sat.* v. (1697) 471 To laugh at Follies, or to lash at Vice. **1728** T. SHERIDAN *Persius* Prol. (1739) 4 He rather lashes at those Poetasters. **1859** TENNYSON *Enid* 563 Each.. lash'd at each.. with such blows, that [etc.].

b. ***to lash out***: to strike out violently, to lay about one vigorously; (of a horse) to kick out. Also *fig.* †Also ***to lash it out.***

1567 *Triall Treas.* (1850) 42 Yet will I.. repugne, lashe out, and kicke. **1587** FLEMING *Contn. Holinshed* III. 321/2 After that to the barriers, where they lashed it out lustilie, and fought couragiouslie. **1852** SMEDLEY *L. Arundel* xxxv. 269 Lewis.. lashed out too, when he was first put in harness. **1884** *Truth* 4 Sept. 369/2 He.. 'revived pamphleteering' only to lash out at a famous Quarterly Reviewer for the great Tory historian's vilification of Carlyle. **1900** F. ANSTEY *Brass Bottle* xiv. 222 He might.. be lashing out with his hind legs and kicking everything to pieces.

†**c.** *trans.* To assail, attack.

c **1330** *Arth. & Merl.* 9783 (Kölbing), Bohort als a geaunt laiste & þe heued al todaiste.

3. *trans.* To dash, throw, or move violently. *Obs.* exc. in technical use. †Also with *forth*, *out*, *up*. ***to lash off***, to strike off.

c **1330** *Arth. & Merl.* 7584 (Kölbing) Among þe ribaus anon he dast & sum þe heued of he laist. *a* **1400–50** *Alexander* 1325 He laschis out a lange swerde quen his launce failes. *c* **1430** *Chev. Assigne* 323 Feraunce launces vp his fete & lasschethe out his yen. **1519** HORMAN *Vulg.* 54 He lasshed ageynst the grounde the cuppe that I loued beste. **1542** *Lam. & Piteous Treat.* in *Harl. Misc.* (Malh.) I. 241 Lashinge oute, and shotynge of, in all the haste theyr greate gownes and harquebusshes. **1693** DRYDEN *Ovid's Met.* XII. 472 He falls; and lashing up his Heels, his Rider throws. **1879** *Cassell's Techn. Educ.* IV. 378/1 The wool-comber.. throws or 'lashes' a handful of wool.. over the points of the teeth.

†**4.** To lavish, squander. Chiefly with *out*. *Obs.*

1513 MORE *Rich. III*, Wks. 62/1 There was dayly pilled fro good men & honest, gret substaunce of goodes to be lashed oute among vnthriftes. **1539** TAVERNER *Erasm. Prov.* (1552) 11 They had leuer lash out theyr wicked Mammon on the dead than on the quicke. **1573** TUSSER *Husb.* xxiii. (1878) 64 Some horsekeeper lasheth out prouender so.. that corne loft is empted er chapman hath his. **1586** J. HOOKER *Hist. Irel.* in *Holinshed* II. 30/1 Then would he lash & powre all that euer he had in store or treasurie. **1603** H. CROSSE *Vertues Commw.* (1878) 64 [He] must instantly.. lash out that riotously, that his father got miserly. **1609** W. M. *Man in Moone* C 3 b, You suppose it a great glory to lash your coyne, you care not where, nor vppon whom. **1630** BRATHWAIT *Eng. Gentlem.* (1641) 88 Neither to hoard up niggardly nor lash out all lavishly. **1657** S. PURCHAS *Pol. Flying-Ins.* II. 327 A wicked man doth prodigally lash out all his joyes in the time of his prosperitie. **1922** JOYCE *Ulysses* 736 You cant get on in this world without style all going in food and rent when I get it Ill lash it around I tell you in fine style.

†**b.** To pour *out* or *forth* impetuously (words, etc.).

1529 MORE *Dyaloge* IV. Wks. 287/1 Colis.. lasheth out scripture in bedelem as fast as they bothe in Almayn. *c* **1555** HARPSFIELD *Divorce Hen. VIII* (Camden) 232 Then lasheth he forth many authorities and examples. **1556** J. HEYWOOD *Spider & F.* ii. 56 Hate, lashth out trewth, foes to displease. **1577** tr. *Bullinger's Decades* (1592) 129 Som men lash out cursings and othes of God, thereby prouoking him to anger. **1653** H. COGAN tr. *Pinto's Trav.* v. 13 Lashing out some words, that were a little more harsher than was requisite.

5. *intr.* Of persons. With *out*: To rush, launch out, into excess of any kind; to break out into violent language; to squander one's substance, be lavish. (In some quots. = *absol.* use of 4.)

a **1560** BECON *Sick Man's Salve* (1572) 145 Then lash they out, & liberally geue unto the poore, because they can keepe it no longer. **1592** GREENE *Def. Conny Catch.* (1859) 13 A yoong youthful Gentleman, given a little to lash out liberally. **1594** T. B. *La Primaud. Fr. Acad.* II. 287 So that hee.. fall into no excesse, neither lash out beyond all reason and measure. **1629** Z. BOYD *Last Battell* 826 That I lash not out into the excesse of supperfluitie of wickednesse. **1664** *Floddan F.* III. 22 Alas too lewdly he lashed out And foolishly his Ordnance spend. **1670** COTTON *Espernon* III. ix. 470 Yet could not the Duke.. sometimes forbear lashing out into very free expressions. **1709** STRYPE *Ann. Ref.* I. xiv. (1824) 281 It consisted not with the gravity.. of a nation professing true religion, to lash out so excessively that way [in dress]. **1959** G. FREEMAN *Jack would be Gent.* I. 10 He'd never had the money to lash out properly. **1973** 'M. YORKE' *Grave Matters* I. vi. 35 He must have paid plenty for the place, besides what they're going to lash out in alterations.

II. Senses referring to LASH *sb.*[1]

6. *trans.* To beat, strike with a lash, whip, †rod, etc.; to flog, scourge.

1398 TREVISA *Barth. de P.R.* VI. xii. (Tollem. MS.), A bonde seruaunt.. is bete and lasshid with ȝerdis. *c* **1440** *Promp. Parv.* 288/1 Lasschyn.. *verbero*. **1500–20** DUNBAR *Poems* xxvi. 75 Belliall, with a brydill renȝie, Evir lascht thame on the lunȝie. **1605** SHAKS. *Lear* IV. vi. 165 Why dost thou lash that Whore? **1660** F. BROOKE tr. *Le Blanc's Trav.* 363 Some.. furiously lash their bare shoulders with thorns. **1725** DE FOE *Voy. round World* (1840) 89 What became of the fellow that was lashed we knew not. **1839** DICKENS *Nich. Nick.* vii, Lashing the pony until they reached their journey's end. **1858** MRS. CARLYLE *Lett.* II. 361 The lady lashed her horse and set off in pursuit. **1887** BOWEN *Virg. Æneid* v. 147 The charioteer as he speeds Tosses his flowing reins, and arising, lashes his steeds.

absol. *a* **1684** T. LYE in Spurgeon *Treas. Dav.* Ps. lxxxix. 30–4 He lashes in love, in measure, in pity, and compassion. **1697** DRYDEN *Virg. Georg.* III. 169 The Youthful Charioteers.. Stoop to the Reins, and lash with all their Force. **1876** G. M. HOPKINS *Wreck of Deutschland* viii, in *Poems* (1967) 54 Oh, We lash with the best or worst Word last! **1877** A. SEWELL *Black Beauty* (*c* 1878, ed. 5) xx. 93 The man, fiercely pulling at the head of the forehorse, swore and lashed most brutally. **1892** A. CONAN DOYLE *Adventures Sherlock Holmes* viii. 205 The sudden glare.. made it impossible for me to tell what it was at which my friend lashed so savagely.

b. *transf.*, esp. of the action of waves upon the shore, etc. Occas. *intr.* To fall with a lashing movement *on* the shore.

c **1694** PRIOR *Lady's Looking Glass* 16 Big waves lash the frighten'd shores. **1735** SOMERVILLE *Chase* III. 255 Ah! what avail[s]..thy length of Tail, That lashes thy broad Sides. **1762** FALCONER *Shipwr.* Proem 52 From where th' Atlantic lashes Labrador. **1818** SHELLEY *Lines Euganean Hills* 186 Poesy's unfailing river..Lashing with melodious wave Many a sacred poet's grave. **1837** APPERLEY *Chase, Road & Turf* (1898) 48 Another hound slips out of cover..with his nose to the ground and his stern lashing his side. *a* **1851** MOIR *Poems, Starlight Refl.*, Lash the hoarse billows on the shore. **1853** C. BRONTË *Villette* i. (1876) 3 It was a wet night; the rain lashed the panes. **1887** BOWEN *Virg. Æneid* IV. 249 Atlas the rude..lashed by the wind and the rain evermore.

c. *fig.*; esp. 'To scourge with satire' (J.); to castigate in words, rebuke, satirize, vituperate.

1590 SHAKS. *Com. Err.* II. i. 15 Why, headstrong liberty is lasht with woe. **1621** BURTON *Anat. Mel.* II. i. I. i. (1651) 221 He calls a Magician Gods Minister and his Vicar..for which he is lashed by T. Erastus. **1661** T. LYE in *Morn. Exerc. Cripplegate* xviii. 436 It is true God may frown on, yea, and severely lash a Solomon, a Jedidiah, when they break his Statutes. *a* **1704** T. BROWN *Persius' Sat.* I. Wks. 1730 I. 53, I must..Lash the vile town with my satirick rhime. **1801** STRUTT *Sports & Past.* I. ii. 27 They [the hunting clergy] were severely lashed by the poets and moralists. **1837–9** HALLAM *Hist. Lit.* I. vii. I. 391 He does not fail to lash the schoolmen directly. **1859** TENNYSON *Pelleas & Ettarre* 581 A scourge am I To lash the treasons of the Table Round. **1877** BLACK *Green Past.* xxv. 203 Balfour..found himself lashed and torn to pieces every morning by the 'Englebury Mercury'.

7. With *adv.* or phrase as *complement*: To urge or drive by, or as by, lashes.

1594 SHAKS. *Rich. III*, V. iii. 328 Let's whip these straglers o're the Seas againe, Lash hence these ouer-weening Ragges of France. **1666** DRYDEN *Ann. Mirab.* cclxxii, Those that disobey'd He lash'd to duty with his sword of light. **1715–20** POPE *Iliad* x. 584 These [steeds], with his bow unbent, he lash'd along. **1729** T. COOKE *Tales, Proposals*, etc. 182 He does not threaten to disarm him, but..to lash him from the Assembly. **1737** BRACKEN *Farriery Impr.* (1757) II. 132 The passionate pedantic Schoolmaster, that lashes his Disciples into Learning. **1781** COWPER *Truth* 260 A glassy lake..Lashed into foaming waves. **1838** DICKENS *Nich. Nick.* xxviii, The excitement into which she had been lashed. **1864** TENNYSON *Aylmer's F.* 325 Should I find you by my doors again, My men shall lash you from them like a dog. **1871** MISS YONGE *Cameos* II. xvii. 188 The violence of a weak nature lashed up to rage. **1884** W. C. SMITH *Kildrostan* 89 Then I see..the waves Lashed into madness. **1893** SELOUS *Trav. S.E. Africa* 307 A strong head wind lashed the river into waves.

absol. *a* **1716** SOUTH *Serm.* (J.), Let men out of their way lash on ever so fast, they are not at all the nearer their journey's end.

†**b.** To force *out* by a lash or stroke. *Obs.*

1642 ROGERS *Naaman* 23 Others have their eie lasht out by a twig in their travaile.

lash (læʃ), *v.*² [Perh. f. LASH *sb.*², or a. OF. *lachier*, dialectal var. of *lacier*: see LACE *v.*

Words of similar sound, and somewhat approximating in sense, are Du. *lasschen*, to patch, sew together, to scarf (timber); G. *laschen* to fit with a gusset, to scarf; from M.Du. *lasche* (mod. *lasch*) rag, patch, gusset; G. *lasch*, *lasche* flap, lappet, gusset, scarf-joint. But it does not appear probable that these have any connexion with the Eng. word.]

†**1.** *trans.* To lace (a garment). *Obs.*

c **1440** *Promp. Parv.* 288/1 Lasschyn, *ligulo.* **1602** MIDDLETON *Blurt* II. ii. D i b, An Eele-skin sleeue lasht heere and there with lace, Hye coller, lasht agen; breeche lasht also. **1611** COTGR., *Aiguilletter*, to whip, or lash, with points.

2. Chiefly *Naut.* To fasten or make fast with a cord, rope, thong, piece of twine, etc.; †to truss (clothes); to fasten *to* (something). Also with *down*, *on*, *together*; †*refl.* of a plant. ***lash away***, ***lash and carry*** (see quots. 1867).

1624 CAPT. SMITH *Virginia* v. 194 Her Ordnance being lashed so fast they could not be vnloosed. **1692** *Capt. Smith's Seaman's Gram.* I. xvi. 79 Lash the Fish on to the Mast. **1711** W. SUTHERLAND *Shipbuild. Assist.* 37 Bolts to lash the Boats on the upper Deck. **1712** tr. *Pomet's Hist. Drugs* I. 31 This Plant..lashes itself round any tree that is near it. **1748** *Anson's Voy.* III. iv. 330 We had not a gun on board lashed. **1772–84** COOK *Voy.* (1790) VI. 1956 A child ..had been lashed under the thwarts of the canoe. **1793** SMEATON *Edystone L.* §97, *note*, The rods were here lashed together by a packthread. **1829** LONGF. *Wreck Hesperus* xx, A maiden fair, Lashed close to a drifting mast. **1836** W. IRVING *Astoria* II. 257 The Indians had lashed their canoes to the ship. **1840** R. H. DANA *Bef. Mast* xxix. 105 All our spare spars were taken on board and lashed. **1853** SIR R. DOUGLAS *Milit. Bridges* (ed. 3) 66 *marg.*, Lashdown Pontoons. **1867** F. FRANCIS *Angling* xiii. (1880) 461 This process of lashing on a hook. **1867** SMYTH *Sailor's Word-bk.*, *Lash and carry*, the order given by the boatswain and his mates on piping up the hammocks, to accelerate the duty. *Ibid.*, *Lash away*, a phrase to hasten the lashing of hammocks. **1879** LADY BRASSEY *Sunshine & Storm* 26 Our chairs were lashed. **1889** *Anthony's Photogr. Bull.* II. 55 Lash all together by passing a string several times round each end of the package.

3. *Comb.* **lash-up**, (*a*) a makeshift or hastily contrived improvisation; also *attrib.*; (*b*) (see quot. 1925). Hence **lashed-up** *a.*, improvised.

1898 W. P. DRURY *Tadpole of an Archangel* 86 Such a godforsaken lash-up of a bridge you never clapped eyes on! **1907** J. MASEFIELD *Tarpaulin Muster* viii. 102 And down they all go—ship, and tea, and mate, and bishop, and general, and Jimmy and the whole lash-up. **1920** *Blackw. Mag.* Feb. 154/1 By 'lashed up' means—(that is to say, 'improvised')—and with a makeshift staff of assistants, a tolerable chart was produced. *Ibid.* 158/1 We..had been obliged to make 'lash-up' (*i.e.*, makeshift) arrangements. **1924** P. P. ECKERSLEY *Captain Eckersley Explains* i. 5 A 'lash-up' or experimental station was erected at the Marconi Works. **1925** FRASER & GIBBONS *Soldier & Sailor Words* 140 *Lash-up*, a failure. A fiasco. The break-down of anything. **1929** O. HARLAND *Golden Plough* iv. 97 Until we come to the present Imbroglio, the Glorious Lash-up of this very age. **1936** 'TAFFRAIL' *Mystery at Milford Haven* 281 The boat.. was what a blue-jacket would have called a 'lash-up', a thing of bits and pieces. **1958** *Economist* 13 Sept. 869/2 Black Knight is essentially a lash-up on which to test various designs of nose cone for the 2,500 mile ballistic weapon Blue Streak that should be ready for test in the early 1960s. **1962** W. SCHIRRA in *Into Orbit* 46 It [*sc.* the couch] was a simple bit of furniture compared to the lashup of tubing, fans, filters and tanks which was built around it. **1966** M. WOODHOUSE *Tree Frog* xxv. 182 We didn't have time for an instrument check. It's just a lash-up really. **1974** *Exchange & Mart* (South) 27 June 53M/3 Rebuilt motor, not a lash-up.

lash (læʃ), *v.*³ *dial. trans.* To comb (the hair). Also with *out*.

1863 MRS. TOOGOOD *Yorks. Dial.*, Go and lash thee hair out, child. **1886** ALICE REA *Beckside Boggle* 9 I's just wesh me and lash me hair. **1894** HALL CAINE *Manxman* III. xii. 170 Take the redyng comb and lash your hair out.

b. *Comb.*: **lash-comb**, a wide-toothed comb (*Lonsdale Gloss.* 1869).

1887 HALL CAINE *Deemster* vi. 38 When the lash comb had tossed back his long hair. **1894** —— *Manxman* 108.

lashed (læʃt), *ppl. a.*¹ [f. LASH *v.*¹ + -ED¹.] Beaten with or as with a whip.

1611 COTGR., *Foüetté*, whipped, lashed, scourged. *a* **1625** FLETCHER *Love's Cure* II. i, Your lashed shoulders [covered] with a Velvet Pee. **1818** SHELLEY *Rev. Islam* I. iii. 3 And the lashed deeps Glitter and boil beneath.

lashed (læʃt), *ppl. a.*² [f. LASH *v.*² + -ED¹.] Fastened with a lash or cord.

1897 R. KIPLING *Captains Courageous* 53 The lashed wheel groaned and kicked softly.

lashed (læʃt), *ppl. a.*³ [f. LASH *sb.*¹ + -ED².] Furnished with lashes. Chiefly with qualifying word prefixed, as ***black-***, ***dark-***, ***long-lashed***.

1776 J. LEE *Introd. Bot.* Explan. Terms 389, *Ciliatæ*, lashed like the eye. **1854** WHITTIER *Maud Muller* 32 A pleased surprise Looked from her long-lashed hazel eyes.

lasher (ˈlæʃə(r)). [f. LASH *v.*¹, ² + -ER¹.] One who or that which lashes.

†**1.** One who beats or whips. Also *fig.*

1602 B. JONSON *Poetaster* Apol. Dial., Wks. (1616) 352 Or I could doe worse, Arm'd with Archilochvs fury, write Iambicks, Should make the desperate lashers hang themselues. **1611** COTGR., *Foüetteur*, a whipper, scourger.. lasher.

2. In the names of fishes, e.g. ***lasher bull-head***. Also FATHER-LASHER.

1867 SMYTH *Sailor's Word-bk.*, *Lasher bull-head*, a name for the fish *Cottus scorpius*.

3. *Naut.* (See quot. 1848.) = LASHING *vbl. sb.*²

1669 STURMY *Mariner's Mag.* I. 20 Make ready to board him; Have your Lashers clear, and able men with them. **1711** W. SUTHERLAND *Shipbuild. Assist.* 143 Lashers for the Yards as big as the Lanyards of the Shrowds. **1848** BIDDLECOMBE *Art of Rigging* 20, Lashers.—The ropes employed to lash or secure particular objects; as jeers, etc.

4. Chiefly *local* (on the Thames). The body of water that lashes or rushes over an opening in a barrier or weir; hence the opening itself, and by extension, a weir.

1677 PLOT *Oxfordsh.* 185 Our Mills and Locks have most of them back streams and lashers to carry off the water when it is too plentiful. **1800** HURDIS *Fav. Village* 96 Not louder falls The foamy lasher's cataract superb In fullest flood-time. **1840** *Ann. Reg.* 15 The lasher is an opening to let off the water when too high. **1858** HUGHES *Scouring White Horse* 16 The great lasher at Pangbourn, where the water was rushing and dancing through in the sunlight. **1884** *Blackw. Mag.* 342 The huge rafts of silver-fir..shoot the lashers in safety.

b. The pool into which the water of the lasher falls.

1851 G. BUTLER *Let.* in *Recoll.* (1892) 70, I bathed in a lasher about four miles from Oxford. **1853** M. ARNOLD *Scholar-Gipsy* x, Men who through these wide fields of breezy grass..To bathe in the abandon'd lasher pass. **1861** HUGHES *Tom Brown at Oxf.* II. xii. 232 He sculled down to Sandford, bathed in the lasher, and returned in time for chapel. **1872** *Daily News* 3 May 5/3 If the..Board can prevent bathing in these dangerous lashers it ought to do so without delay.

lashing (ˈlæʃɪŋ), *vbl. sb.*¹ [f. LASH *v.*¹ + -ING¹.]

a. The action of LASH *v.*¹ in various senses; beating, flogging; an instance of this. †***lashing out***, lavishing, squandering.

c **1400** *Destr. Troy.* 6789 Mony lyue of lept with lasshyng of swerdis. *c* **1440** *Promp. Parv.* 288/2 Laschynge, or betynge. **1553** GRIMALDE *Cicero's Offices* (1556) 85 These lasshinges oute of money which bee done to clawe the multitude. **1651–3** JER. TAYLOR *Serm. for Year* (1678) 344 Those secret lashings and whips of the exterminating Angel. **1791** BURKE *Th. Fr. Affairs* Wks. (1808) VII. 41 The king [of Sweden]..keeps up the top with continual agitation and lashing. **1801** T. MILNER in *Life* xiii. (1842) 246 He said some things which..called for a fresh lashing. **1900** *Daily News* 19 Feb. 2/5 As a rule the natives took their lashings quietly.

b. *pl.* (orig. *Anglo-Irish*). 'Floods', abundance.

1829 SCOTT *Jrnl.* 18 Mar., Cigars in loads, whisky in lashings. **1841** S. C. HALL *Ireland* (1843) III. 334 There's lashins of holy water, and blessed palm. **1856** LEVER *Martins of Cro' M.* 84 A good dinner, some excellent port wine, and 'lashings' of whiskey-punch. **1883** LD. SALTOUN *Scraps* I. 116 There's plenty of sport to be had, an' lashins of parties, an' balls, an' picnics. **1884** *Illustr. Lond. News* 24 May 510/3 'There's lashins of room', said the driver. **1901** E. W. HORNUNG *Black Mask* v. 74 There were lashings of sound wine for one and all. **1927** D. L. SAYERS *Unnatural Death* xxiii. 278 Nice little dinner—lashings of champagne. **1942** *R.A.F. Jrnl.* 3 Oct. 30 We fought through lashings of rain and mud to our billets. **1962** J. WAIN *Strike Father Dead* 164 Real comfort. And plenty of money. Lashings! She earned a good solid packet at this job. **1966** *Lancet* 2 Apr. 765/1 The crusty wholemeal bread..eaten with lashings of butter. **1975** *Country Life* 6 Feb. 336/3 Chicory..requires lashings of water.

lashing (ˈlæʃɪŋ), *vbl. sb.*² Chiefly *Naut.* [f. LASH *v.*² + -ING¹.] The action of LASH *v.*²; the action of fastening any movable body with a cord. Hence *concr.* the cord used for this purpose.

1669 STURMY *Mariner's Mag.* I. ii. 20 Loose the Lachings, we will sheer off our Ship. **1729** CAPT. W. WRIGLESWORTH *MS. Log-bk. of the 'Lyell'* 20 Oct., At 8 cast off our Lashings and made Sail. **1758** J. BLAKE *Plan Mar. Syst.* 6 A hammock, with a lashing, shall be delivered him, and a birth assigned to hang it in. **1789** G. KEATE *Pelew Isl.* 4 In the afternoon the lashings of the booms broke. **1834–47** J. S. MACAULAY *Field Fortif.* (1851) 139 The..side rails are secured with rack lashings to the extreme balks. **1836** W. IRVING *Astoria* III. 220 It was impossible to stand at the helm without the assistance of lashings. **1869** TROYTE *Change Ringing* 5 It is well to keep lashings ready for all the bells in a tower. **1872–6** VOYLE & STEVENSON *Milit. Dict.*, Lashings used in mounting and dismounting guns are of different dimensions.

Comb. **1828** J. M. SPEARMAN *Brit. Gunner* (ed. 2) 19 Lashing Rope. **1867** SMYTH *Sailor's Word-bk.*, *Lashing-eyes*, fittings for lower stays, block-strops, &c., by loops made in the ends of ropes, for a lashing to be rove through to secure them. **1884** KNIGHT *Dict. Mech.*, *Suppl.*, *Lashing knot*, A form of bend.

lashing (ˈlæʃɪŋ), *ppl. a.* [f. LASH *v.*¹ + -ING².] That lashes.

14.. *Siege Jerusalem* 17/304 Was noȝt bot..red laschyng lye [*i.e.* flame] alle þe londe ouer. *c* **1645** HOWELL *Lett.* I. 2 Under a learned (though lashing) Master. **1693** DRYDEN *Juvenal* I. (1697) 11 The Lady, next, requires a lashing Line, Who squeez'd a Toad into her Husband's Wine. **1714** GAY *Trivia* II. 231 The lashing whip resounds. **1812** BYRON *Ch. Har.* I. lxxv, Bounds with one lashing spring the mighty brute. **1820** SHELLEY *Cloud* 9, I wield the flail of the lashing hail. **1827–44** WILLIS *Elms New Haven* 129 The air Below the lashing tree-tops was all black. **1885** STEVENSON *Dynamiter* 198 A certain day of lashing rain in December. **1900** *Edinb. Rev.* Oct. 379 This lashing sarcasm was undeserved.

Hence **ˈlashingly** *adv.*, in a lashing manner; †(*a*) lavishly; (*b*) by means of the lash or whip.

1573 TUSSER *Husb.* ix. (1878) 17 To lash not out too lashinglie, for feare of pinching penurie. **1839** *New Monthly Mag.* LVI. 358 Tripes bawled out, 'Wo-ho!'—a sound Woodpecker and old Peter willingly obeyed, in spite of Dick's persuasions lashingly applied.

la'ship, obs. colloquial form of LADYSHIP.

‖**lashkar** (ˈlæʃkɑːr). *Indian.* Also 7 lescar, leskar. [Urdu (Pers.) *lashkar* army, camp. See LASCAR.]

†**a.** A camp of native Indian soldiers (*obs.*). **b.** A body of Afridi soldiers.

1616 SIR T. ROE in Purchas *Pilgrims* (1625) I. 559, I tooke horse to auoyd presse and other inconuenience and crossed out of the Leskar before him. **1625** TERRY *ibid.* II. IX. vi. 1481 There being no lesse then two hundred thousand men, women, and children in this Leskar, or Campe. **1634** SIR T. HERBERT *Trav.* 32 Normall his Queene..had passed safely ouer the Riuer, with most part of the Lescar, or Army, which shee immediately put into Battaglia. **1897** *Times* 6 Oct. 3/1 The lashkar is prepared to offer terms on behalf of the Afridi, Mamund, and Malakand tribesmen. **1908** *Daily Chron.* 27 Apr. 1/7 General Willcock's columns yesterday searched out the enemy's lashkars. **1924** *Glasgow Her.* 14 May 8 The rebel lashkars are melting away. **1955** *Times* 31 May 7/6 Inside this frame, lashkars, or tribal columns, are still raised occasionally. **1973** *Times* 22 Mar. (Pakistan Suppl.) p. ii/3 Baluchistan..is led largely by tribes amenable only to the jurisdiction of their own *sardars*..who often command sizeable *lashkars*, or private levies.

lashless (ˈlæʃlɪs), *a.* [f. LASH *sb.*¹ (sense 3) + -LESS.] Devoid of (eye-)lashes.

1812 KEATS *Lamia* II. 288 His lashless eyelids stretch around his demon eyes. **1840** BROWNING *Sordello* III. 350 Tiring suitors out With..lashless eyes Inveterately tearshot. **1879** DOWDEN *Southey* i. 5 Ma'am Powell..with her lashless eyes gorgonized the new pupil.

†**ˈlashlite, lashlight.** *Obs.* Also 7 laghslite, 8 lagslite. [Blundered form of OE. *lahslit*, f. *lah* law + *slit* tear, breach.] The fine imposed for breach of (Danish) law.

c **1030** *Laws of Cnut* II. c. 15 (Liebermann) 318 Beo se wið þone cinge cxx scyll' scyldiȝ on Engla laȝe..and on Dena laȝe lahslites scyldiȝ. **11..** *Laws of Will. I* c. 39 (Schmid) 345 In Danelahe erit foris factura de suo laslite [AF. *laxlite*]. **11..** *Laws of Hen. I* c. 11 §11 (Schmid) 443 Si quis Dei rectitudines per vim teneat, solvat lashlite cum Dacis plenam witam cum Anglis. **1607** COWEL *Interpr.*, *Laghslite*. **1647** N. BACON *Disc. Govt. Eng.* I. xl. 99 Even in Germany they had learned the trick to set a price upon that crime; and this they afterward called..lashlight. **1721** BAILEY, *Lagslite*, a Breach of the Law. **1862** MIALL *Title Deeds Ch. Eng.* 21 *note*, Lashlite denoted a common forfeiture among the Danes.

† 'lashness. *Obs.* Also 5-6 **lachenes,** 6 **lasshnesse,** 7 **lasch(e)nes(s.** [f. LASH *a.* + -NESS.] Slackness (of body or mind); remissness; also, cowardice.

*c***1477** CAXTON *Jason* 15, I cannot haue meruaille ynough of the grete slouthe and lachenes of your men. **1484 ——** *Ordre of Chyualry* 77 Gloutonye.. engendreth slouthe and lachenes of body. **1530** PALSGR. 237/2 Lasshnesse, *lascheté.* **1533** *St. Papers Hen. VIII,* II. 162 The great lachenes my Lord of Ossory hath imputed to me. **1591** R. BRUCE *Serm.* vi. O v b, Let it not come to passe be 3our misbehaueour and lashnes, that the glorie of God.. be impared in any waies. **1641** R. BAILLIE *Lett. & Jrnls.* (1841) I. 347 In the end, after some lashness and fagging, he made.. ane pathetick oration. **1673** O. WALKER *Educ.* I. v. (ed. 2) 36 Not to.. degenerate into softnes and laschenes.

lash-up: see LASH *v.*² 3.

lasiocampid (leɪsɪəʊ'kæmpɪd), *sb.* and *a.* [f. mod.L. family name *Lasiocampidæ,* f. the generic name *Lasiocampa* (N. Contarini *Catal. Uccelli e Insetti Padova* (1843) 37), f. Gk. λάσιος hairy, shaggy + κάμπη caterpillar.] A member of the family Lasiocampidæ, a group of large moths also known as eggars or lappet-moths, including some species whose larvae are called tent-caterpillars; of or pertaining to an insect of this kind.

1895 J. H. & A. B. COMSTOCK *Man. Study Insects* 360 The larvæ of the Lasiocampids feed upon the foliage of trees, and are frequently very destructive. **1912** *Proc. Entomol. Soc. London* p. iv, Prof. Poulton exhibited specimens of the Lasiocampid moth *Mimopacha gerstaeckeri,* Dewitz. **1934** *Discovery* XVII. 98/1 Sometimes the hairs and spines are.. exhibited in an ostentatious manner whenever an enemy appears. This is well illustrated in Lasiocampids. **1964** V. B. WIGGLESWORTH *Life of Insects* vii. 112 The male.. may be specially modified for the recognition and location of these scents. That is most evident in the Saturniid, Bombycid, and Lasiocampid moths, in most of which the female is sluggish and sedentary.

lasionite ('læzɪənaɪt). *Min.* [Named by Fuchs 1816; irregularly f. Gr. λάσιον, neut. of λάσιος hairy (in allusion to its fibrous structure and capillary crystals) + -ITE.] A synonym of WAVELLITE.

1819 *Ann. Philos.* XIX. 281 Lasionite must be ranked among the salts. **1861** BRISTOW *Gloss. Min.* 209 Lasionite, Fuchs. A var. of wavellite. **1868** DANA *Min.* (ed. 5) 576.

lask (lɑːsk, læsk), *sb.*¹ Also 6-7 **laske.** [a ONF. **lasque* = Central OF. *lasche* loosening, relaxation, f. *lasker* = *lascher* (mod.F. *lâcher*) to loosen.]

1. Looseness of the bowels, diarrhœa; an attack of this; = LAX *sb.*² 1. Now only in veterinary use.

1542 *Fabyan's Chron.* VII. 701 Many honeste persones died of yᵉ hote agues, and of a greate laske. **1574** NEWTON *Health Mag.* 16 Meate excessively ingurgitate and eaten.. engendreth.. laskes and vomit. **1601** HOLLAND *Pliny* II. 93 The Cornell tree.. is not good for bees, for if they chance to tast the floure therof, they fal presently into a vehement lask. **1671** SALMON *Syn. Med.* III. xxii. 433 Flixweed, the seed stops laskes, and issues of blood. **1727** BRADLEY *Fam. Dict., Aniseed,* has the Virtue to appease Belly-Rumblings and Gripes, Lask, Vomiting, and the Hiccup. **1803** MACNAB in *Prize Ess. Highl. Soc.* II. 208 The Lask or Scour.. generally originates from feebleness, cold, or grazing on a soft rich pasture, without a mixture of hard grass.

† 2. A laxative, aperient; = LAX *sb.*² 2.

*a***1550** *Image Ipocr.* in *Skelton's Wks.* (1843) II. 433 They gave ther lorde a laske for purge withall his caske.

3. *Comb.:* **laskwort,** a herb supposed to be a remedy for 'lask' or diarrhœa.

1647 LILLY *Chr. Astrol.* ix. 64 Violets, Laskwort [etc.].

lask (lɑːsk, læsk), *sb.*² [? a. MDu. *lasche,* (prob. pronounced (lasxə)); mod.Du. *lasch,* pronounced (las) piece cut out, flap.] (See quots.)

1864 COUCH *Brit. Fishes* II. 125 A hook baited with a slice (termed a lask) from the side of a mackarel. **1874** WOOD *Nat. Hist.* 581 To pass the hook through the thicker end of the strip—technically called a 'lask'.

† lask, *a. Obs.* Also 5 **laske.** [? a. ONF. **lasque* = Central OF. *lasche:* see LASH *a.*] Loose (in the bowels); relaxed, weak. Cf. LASH *a.* 2.

*c***1460** J. RUSSELL *Bk. Nurture* 91 He [buttir] norishethe a man to be laske. **1721** BAILEY, *Lask,* loose in the Belly. **1727** BRADLEY *Fam. Dict.* s.v. *Fever,* His [horse's] lips and all his body grows lask and feeble.

lask (lɑːsk, læsk), *v.* Also 4-7 **laske,** 5 **leske.** [? a. ONF. **lasquer* = Central OF. *lascher* (mod.F. *lâcher*) to loosen, relax:—popular L. **lascāre* = class. L. *laxāre,* f. *lax-us* LAX *a.*]

† 1. *trans.* To lower in quality, quantity, or strength, relax; to thin (the blood); to shorten (life); to alleviate (pain). *Obs.*

*c***1350** *Will. Palerne* 570 Heiȝh hevene king to gode havene me sende oþer laske mi liif daywes wiþ inne a litel terme. *Ibid.* 950, I wol a litel and litel laskit [*i.e.* lask it] in hast. *c***1400** *Lanfranc's Cirurg.* 280 Summen seien þat olde men ben able to be kutt, for her blood is miche laskid & her hete. *Ibid.* 296 þou schalt laske his greet blood wiþ blood-letyngis. *c***1440** *Jacob's Well* 196 For þis superfluyte mayst þou neuere ben heyl in soule, tyl þis blood be leskyd in blood-letyng. *a***1450** MYRC 1736 Laske hys peynes or cese hys synne.

† 2. *intr.* To become loose in the bowels; to purge.

1552 [see LAX *v.*]. **1598** SYLVESTER *Du Bartas* II. I. III. *Furies* 529 Soft Child-hood puling.. Are apt to Laske through much humidity. **1618** *Owles Almanack* 43 Then will they untrusse a hoope and laske like a squirt. **1634** R. H. *Salernes Regim.* 23 Goates milk.. maketh a man to laske.

3. *Naut.* To 'go large'; to sail neither 'by the wind' nor 'before the wind'.

1622 R. HAWKINS *Voy. S. Sea* (1847) 40 When we cast about, shee beganne to vere shete, and to goe away lasking. **1626** CAPT. SMITH *Accid. Yng. Sea-men* 29 Goe large, laske, ware yawning. **1684** *Bucaniers Amer.* II. (1698) 138 We bore up one point of the compass thereby to hinder her lasking away. **1726** G. ROBERTS *Four Years Voy.* 378 You must put the Ship away lasking, or afore the Wind. **1756** *Gentl. Mag.* XXVI. 602 The admiral.. kept lasking away, angling from the enemy. **1867** SMYTH *Sailor's Word-bk., Lasking along,* sailing away with a quartering wind.

† 4. *Mining.* (App. used as a word of command: see quot.) *Obs.*

1747 HOOSON *Miner's Dict.* L iij, Lask [is] a word used in drawing Shafts, Sumps, &c. for Spare Rope, or not enough; as *Lask,* the Drawer understands he must let down more Rope; and *no Lask* is that the Rope is too short to hang on the Corfe.

Hence **† 'lasking** *vbl. sb.,* purging, diarrhœa; **'lasking** *vbl. sb.* and *ppl. a. Naut.,* '(going) large'.

1527 ANDREW *Brunswyke's Distyll. Waters* B iv, The same water.. stopped all maner of laskynge. **1706** PHILLIPS (ed. Kersey), *Lasking* (Sea-Term), when a Ship sails neither by a Wind, nor directly before the Wind,.. she is said *To go lasking.* **1882** T. ROOSEVELT *Naval War 1812* (1883) 120 The Java.. came down in a lasking course on her adversary's weather quarter.

lask, laskayre, obs. ff. LASQUE, LASCAR.

lask(e, variant of LESK, flank, groin.

lasket ('lɑːskɪt, 'læs-). *Naut.* [Perh. an alteration, after GASKET, of F. *lacet* (see LATCHET) which is used in the same sense.] One of the loops or rings of cord by which a bonnet is attached to the foot of a sail.

1704 J. HARRIS *Lex. Techn., Laskets* or *Latches,* are small Lines like Loops, fastned by sowing into the Bonnets and Drablers of a Ship; in order to lace the Bonnets to the Courses, or the Drablers to the Bonnets. **1721** in BAILEY. **1867** in SMYTH *Sailor's Word-bk.*

† 'lasky, *a. Obs.*—⁰. [f. LASK *a.* + -Y.] = LASK *a.*

1552 HULOET, Laskie and laxatiue.

laso, variant of LASSO.

† 'laspick. *Obs. rare*—¹. [a. F. *l'aspic* (= ASPIC³ with prefixed article).] = ASPIC³.

1761 *Bill of Fare* in Pennant *London* (1813) 563 Garnished round with Plates of sorts, as Laspicks, Rolards, &c.

'laspring. [Perh. a corruption of *lax-pink* (see LAX *sb.*¹ b); interpreted as a contraction for *last spring*; cf. *last brood* in quot. 1861.] One of the many names for the young salmon. Also *gravel laspring.*

1760 HAWKINS in *Walton's Angler* I. vi. 143 *note,* A small but excellent fish of the Trout kind, called a Last-spring. *Ibid.* vii. 153 *note.* **1836** YARRELL *Brit. Fishes* II. 50 Brandling, Fingerling, Skirling, Gravelling, Laspring, Sparling, &c. **1861** *Act* 24-5 *Vict.* c. 109 §4 'Young of Salmon' shall include.. Par, Spawn, Pink, Last Spring, Hepper, Last Brood, Gravelling [etc.]. **1881** *19th Cent. Apr.* 693 It is.. unlawful for me.. to catch a small samlet or laspring as long as my finger, although there are thousands on the streams below my house. **1889** 'J. BICKERDYKE' *Bk. All-round Angler* III. 7 Gravel laspring, same as par.

lasque (lɑːsk, læsk). Also 7 **laske,** 8 **lask.** [? a. Pers. *lashk,* bit, piece.] (See quots.) Also *lasque diamond.*

1678 *Lond. Gaz.* No. 1330/4 A Laske, Indian-cut,.. weighing 6. carrets ½ full. **1751** D. JEFFRIES *Diamonds* 115 Lasks.. are in general ill shaped, or irregular in their form at the girdle. **1813** MAWE *Diamonds* (1823) 81 Lasques are formed from flat or veiny diamonds. **1874** WESTROPP *Precious Stones* 4 Lasque diamonds are the flat thin stones used much in native Indian work, in neck and head-bands, bangles, rings, &c.

lass (læs). Forms: 4 **las, lasce,** 4-7 **lasse,** 6 *Sc.* **lase,** 6- **lass.** [ME. *lasce, las(se;* perh. a. prehistoric ON. **lasqa,* wk. fem. of **lasqar* unmarried: cf. MSw. *lösk kona* unmarried woman.

The adj. means primarily 'free from ties'; hence the above sense and those of 'unoccupied', 'having no fixed abode', which are also recorded in MSw. The Icel. *løsk-r* occurs only in the sense 'idle, weak'.

The phonology of the Eng. word, according to the above conjecture, is somewhat difficult; but the same sound-change occurs in other northern forms, as *ass* for **ask* (ashes), *ass* for *ask v., buss* for *busk.*]

1. a. A girl.

In northern and north midland dialects the ordinary word; in the southern counties it has little or no popular currency.

*a***1300** *Cursor M.* 2608 Til abram þan dame sare said, 'Yone lasce.. For-þi þat sco has barn o þe, Als in despit sco haldes me'. *c***1325** *Metr. Hom.* 39 Bifor him com a fair yong lasce That Herodias dohter was. *c***1375** *Sc. Leg. Saints, Baptista* 632 Medyature als here he, betwene ws & þe trinite. ȝet he, þat of sic uertu wes, wes gefine til a lurdan las. *a***1400-50** *Alexander* 3746 If any consaue þe knaf þan

lasice, *laska*, Russian *lastka*, F. *lasquette*.] Also ***lasset-mouse***, ***-weasel***, a fur-bearing animal; the ermine or miniver.

1591 G. FLETCHER *Russe Commw.* (Hakl. Soc.) 14 Their beasts of strange kinds are the losh..the gurnstale, the laset or minever. **1607** TOPSELL *Four-f. Beasts* (1658) 424 There is no difference between the Lascitt mouse and the Lascitt weesill. **1611** COTGR., *Rat de Lasse*, the Lasset Mouse; a beast that beares the Furre which we call Mineuar.

lassie ('læsɪ). Chiefly *Sc.* Also 9 **lassy**. [f. LASS + dimin. suffix -IE (-Y).] **a.** A lass, girl.

1725 RAMSAY *Gentle Sheph.* I. song vi, I yield, dear lassie, ye hae won. **1792** BURNS '*What can a young lassie*' i, What can a young lassie do wi' an auld man? **1802** MAR. EDGEWORTH *Moral T.* (1816) I. ix. 74 What sort of a lassy is the cobbler's daughter? **1889** BARRIE *Window in Thrums* 169 Na, it's other lassies' brothers they like as a rule.

b. = LASS 1 d.

1906 'O. HENRY' *Four Million* 84 A Salvation lassie shook her contribution receptacle. **1970** *Guardian* 12 May 10/5 Such items as whether Army lassies should wear lipstick in uniform.

Hence **'lassiehood**, girlhood. **'lassieish** *a.*, young-womanish.

1857 A. WALLACE *Gloaming of Life* ii. 28 Where Robin.. has to make the important transition from the equivocal garb of lassie-hood into his first 'corduroys'. **1882** J. BROWN *Horæ Subs.*, *J. Leech*, etc. 307 There is a somewhat vulgar and lassieish objection to Landseer's subjects, that they are painful.

lassitude ('læsɪtju:d). [a. F. *lassitude*, ad. L. *lassitūdo* f. *lassus* weary.] The condition of being weary whether in body or mind; a flagging of the bodily or mental powers; indifference to exertion; weariness; an instance of this.

1533 ELYOT *Cast. Helthe* (1541) 84b, Lassitude is a disposition towarde syckenesse, wherin a man feleth a soorenesse, a swellinge or an inflammation. **1581** MULCASTER *Positions* xxxiii. (1887) 119 Though they faint, and feele some little lassitude and wearines. **1626** BACON *Sylva* §730 Lassitude is remedied by bathing or anointing with oil and warm water. **1647** TRAPP *Comm. Matt.* ix. 37 Such as will labour to lassitude. **1653** H. MORE *Conject. Cabbal.* (1713) 19 Lassitude of Contemplation, and of Affectation of Immateriality..brought upon him remisness and drowsiness to such like exercises. **1711** SHAFTESB. *Charac.* (1737) II. II. II. i. 115 Ordinary Lassitudes, Uneasinesses, and Defects of Disposition. **1756** BURKE *Subl. & B.* IV. vi, A long exercise of the mental powers induces a remarkable lassitude of the whole body. **1863** GEO. ELIOT *Romola* xvi, The feverish excitement..had given place to a dull, regretful lassitude. **1886** RUSKIN *Præterita* I. 307 Periods of renewed enthusiasm after intervals of lassitude.

lasso (lə'su:, 'læsəʊ), *sb.* Also 9 **laso**, **lazie**, **lazo**. [Sp. *lazo* (in America pronounced 'laso) = OF. *laz*: see LACE *sb.*]

Fowler remarked (*Mod. Eng. Usage*, 1926, p. 315) '*lasso* is pronounced *lasoo'* by those who use it; but the English pronunciation is *lă'sō*.' In ed. 2 (1965) Sir E. Gowers changed this to '*lasso* is pronounced *lăsoo'* by those who use it, and by most English people too'.

1. A long rope of untanned hide, from 10 to 30 yards in length, having at the end a noose to catch cattle and wild horses; used chiefly in Spanish America.

[**1768** J. BYRON *Narr. Patagonia* (ed. 2) 221 The laço is a long thong of leather, at the end of which they made a sliding noose.] **1808** *Narr. Exped. Gen. Craufurd* II. viii. 189 Numbers of these fellows, with the lazie, hovered about us. **1824** W. BULLOCK *Six Months' Residence Mexico* 179 It requires the use of a lasso to catch them. This is thrown with great dexterity by every hostler or servant. **1835** W. IRVING *Tour Prairies* xix, The coil of cordage..is called a lariat, and answers to the laso of South America. **1837** W. IRVING *Capt. Bonneville* III. vi. 86 The California horsemen seldom ride out without the laso; that is to say, a long coil of cord, with a slip noose, with which they are expert, amost to a miracle. **1860** O. W. HOLMES *Elsie V.* xxv. (1891) 356 Measuring his distance..as nicely as if he were throwing his lasso. **1879** BEERBOHM *Patagonia* v. 66 Before it could recover Garcia's lasso whizzed through the air and lighted on its neck. **1940** H. L. MENCKEN *Happy Days* 284 They lay in wait in dark Greene street with their..lassos, and knives. **1966** H. MARRIOTT *Cariboo Cowboy* v. 53 Al was sure a good man with a lasso rope.

fig. **1922** JOYCE *Ulysses* 50 In long lassoes..the water flowed full. **1924** R. CAMPBELL *Flaming Terrapin* i. 15 He.. hurled Lassoes of dismal smoke around the world.

2. *Mil.* = *lasso-harness*.

1847 F. A. GRIFFITHS *Artil. Man.* (ed. 4) 167 The first time they were required to draw by means of the Lasso. **1868** *Regul. & Ord. Army* §614 Ten men per Troop..are to be equipped with the tackle of the Lasso.

3. *attrib.* and *Comb.*, as ***lasso-man***, ***-throw***; ***lasso-like***, ***-throwing*** adjs.; **lasso-cell**, one of the urticating cells of the *Cœlenterata*, which eject the contained thread in the manner of a lasso; **lasso-harness**, a kind of girth placed round a cavalry horse, with a lasso or long rope attached, for use in drawing guns, etc., as an assistance to the draught-horses.

1865 AGASSIZ *Seaside Stud. Nat. Hist.* 18 The *lasso-cells are very formidable weapons. **1885** C. F. HOLDER *Marvels Anim. Life* 25 The beautiful sea-anemone..covered in many parts by lasso-cells that hurl out sharp, poisonous darts. **1847** F. A. GRIFFITHS *Artil. Man.* (ed. 4) 166 *Lasso Harness consists of a brown leather circingle, and one trace. **1841–71** T. R. JONES *Anim. Kingd.* (ed. 4) 58 The inner wall [of the thread-cell] is much stronger, having one extremity open and prolonged into a stout rather fusiform sheath which terminates in a long *lasso-like filament. **1808** BRIG.-GEN. CRAUFURD in *Trial of Lieut.-Gen. J. Whitelocke* I. 196 *Lasso men employed in killing cattle for the troops. **1841** G. CATLIN *Lett. on N. Amer. Indians* II. 152 A line, with a sort of '*lasso throw', came from an awkward hand on the deck. *a* **1861** T. WINTHROP *John Brent* (1883) ii. 11 Man to them was power, and nothing else,—a lasso-throwing machine.

lasso (lə'su:, 'læsəʊ), *v.* Also **lazo**. [f. LASSO *sb.*]

1. *trans.* To catch with a lasso. Also *fig.*

1807 *Exped. to Buenos Ayres* 6 Here and there they 'lassoed' the stragglers. **1831** TRELAWNY *Adv. Younger Son* xxv. (1890) 116 Like the wild horse..lazoed by the South American Gauchoes. **1881** P. B. DU CHAILLU *Land Midn. Sun* II. 80 A man went into the wood and returned with a deer he had lassoed. **1891** SMILES *J. Murray* II. xxviii. 252 He..crossed the Pampas, catching and lassoing wild horses. **1965** V. BONHAM CARTER *Winston Churchill* xviii. 253 Fisher happened to be at Naples and it seemed a heaven-sent opportunity for lassoing him there and roping him in again.

2. *Mil.* To draw (guns, etc.) with lasso-harness.

1864 *Daily Tel.* 14 Mar., The mode of lassoing guns, as practised by the mounted troop of the Royal Engineers.

Hence **la'ssoed** *ppl. a.*, **la'ssoing** *vbl. sb.* Also **la'ssoer**, **la'ssoist**, one who lassoes.

1838 'TEXIAN' *Mexico v. Texas* 48 The men were collecting the mules, and when these were driven together, the lassoing began. **1864** SALA in *Daily Tel.* 5 May, Called in to treat cases of private shooting, stabbing, and lassoing. **1881** DARWIN in *Life & Lett.* III. 245 A struggling and lassoed cow. **1882** SALA *Amer. Revis.* (1885) 413 The.. neighing of our lassoed horses. **1883** SWEET & KNOX *On Mexican Mustang through Texas* xli. 584 Juan Gonzales..is said to be the champion lassoer in the world. **1884** W. SHEPHERD *Prairie Experiences* 40 The lassoer picks out the unbranded calves, and drags them off to the fire. **1896** *Chamb. Jrnl.* XIII. 16/2 The lassoers often manage to take two or three [horses] per man. **1906** *Daily Chron.* 16 May 5/7 There have been lassoists before, but never, perhaps, such a master of the art as Will Rogers.

lassock ('læsək). *Sc.* [f. LASS + diminutive suffix -OCK.] A little girl.

1816 SCOTT *Old Mort.* v, I mind, when I was a gilpy of a lassock, seeing the Duke. **1818** —— *Rob Roy* xxxvi, I wadna for ever sa muckle that even the lassock Mattie kenn'd ony thing about it. **1887** R. BUCHANAN *Heir of Linne* i, A young lassock's petticoat from the linen-press.

lassu ('lɑ:ʃu:). [Hung. *lassú*.] The slow part of a Hungarian csardas (opp. *friss*).

1880 GROVE *Dict. Mus.* II. 198/2 Every Csárdás consists of two movements,—a 'Lassu', or slow movement, andante maestoso, and a 'Friss', or 'quickstep', allegro vivace. **1944** [see CSARDAS]. **1961** *Times* 13 May 5/1 A Haydnish *lassu*.

lassy me, *int. vulgar.* Also **lausy me**. [? Contraction of *Lord save me!*] Used to express surprise.

1840 BARHAM *Ingol. Leg.* Ser. I. *Spectre Tappington*, 'Lassy me!' said Miss Julia. **1890** W. A. WALLACE *Only a Sister* 338 Lausy me! what's in the taking now, dearie.

last (lɑ:st, læst), *sb.*¹ Forms: 1 **lást**, **lǽst**, **lǽste**, 4–8 **laste**, 4–5 **lest(e**, 4– **last**. [OE. *lást* masc., footstep, *lǽst* fem., boot, *lǽste* fem., shoemaker's last, cogn. w. Du. *leest* masc., OHG. *leist* (MHG. *leist*, mod.G. *leiste(n* masc.), last, ON. *leist-r* foot, sock (Sw., Da. *läst* last), Goth. *laist-s* footstep, track (ἴχνος), cogn. w. OHG. (*wagan*) *-leisa* track, rut (MHG. *leis(e* fem., *geleis* truckway, mod.G. *geleise*, *gleise* rut); by most recent scholars referred to a Teut. root **lais-* (:*līs-*) to follow a track (whence in immaterial sense Goth. *lais* pret.-pres., I know, and the related words: see LEARN *v.*, LORE), cogn. w. L. *līra* furrow. Some, however, would connect it with the Teut. **laip-*, *laid-* (: OE. *līðan* to go); see LOAD *sb.*]

†**1.** A footstep, track, trace. After OE. only in Sc. phrase ***not a last***: nothing, not at all.

Beowulf (Z.) 132 Hie þæs laðan last sceawedon. **971** *Blickl. Hom.* 127 Man dæghwamlice þa moldan nimeþ on þæm lastum. *c* **1375** *Sc. Leg. Saints* xxxiv. (*Pelagia*) 102 Oure verray spouse, rekis nocht a laste how foule ore vnfaire we be. *Ibid.* xliii. (*Cecile*) 580 þu ma with þi handis taste, þo þu ma nocht se a laste. *a* **1500** *Ratis Raving* I. 2339 That louit neuer his lord a last.

2. A wooden model of the foot, on which shoemakers shape boots and shoes.

c **1000** ÆLFRIC *Gloss.* in Wr.-Wülcker 125/32 *Calopodium uel mustricula*, læste. *a* **1300** *Sat. People Kildare* xiii. in *E.E.P.* (1862) 154 Hail be ȝe sutlers [? *read* sutars] wiþ ȝour mani lestes. *c* **1440** *Promp. Parv.* 298/2 Leste, sowtarys forme, *formula*. **1483** *Cath. Angl.* 209/1 A Laste of a sowter, *formula*. **1589** GREENE *Menaphon* (Arb.) 54 That as he were a Coblers eldest sonne, would by the laste tell where anothers shooe wrings. **1644** JESSOP *Angel of Eph.* 6 These Lawyers..stretch Scripture as they please, just as the Shoemaker doth his leather with his teeth, to fit it to his Laste. **1714** GAY *Trivia* I. 35 Should the big Laste extend the shoe too wide. **1810** *Sporting Mag.* XXXV. 192 [A prize-fight] between two brethren of the last. **1842** DICKENS *Amer. Notes* (1850) 69/2 Occasionally there is a drowsy sound from some lone weaver's shuttle, or shoemaker's last.

b. *transf.* and *fig.* ? *Obs.*

a **1592** H. SMITH *Wks.* (1866–7) I. 391 All three are of one last. **1604** DEKKER *Honest Wh.* Wks. 1873 II. 138, I set my braines vpon an vpright Last. **1607** MIDDLETON *Michaelm. Term* I. i, Here's gallants of all sizes, of all lasts. **1613** PURCHAS *Pilgrimage* (1614) 372 Lesse matters set on the Friers lasts, make seely Papists beleeve [etc.]. **1625** FLETCHER *Noble Gent.* III. ii, As though his spirit were a last or two Above his veines and stretcht his noble hide. **1647** N. BACON *Disc. Govt. Eng.* I. liii. (1739) 94 The Normans had reduced the Saxon law..unto their own Last, which stretched their desire as far as the estate would bear.

c. With allusion to the proverb ***Let the cobbler stick to his last*** ('Ne sutor ultra crepidam').

1592 SHAKS. *Rom. & Jul.* I. ii. 40 Heere it is written, that the Shoo-maker should meddle with his Yard, and the Tayler with his Last. **1605** HEYWOOD *If you know not me* Wks. 1874 I. 210 Shoomaker, you goe a little beyond your last. **1692–4** R. L'ESTRANGE *Fables* ccxxv. (1708) 245 The Cobler is not to go beyond his Last. **1768–74** TUCKER *Lt. Nat.* (1834) II. 330 To enter upon these discussions would be carrying the shoemaker beyond his last. **1875** JOWETT *Plato* (ed. 2) III. 53 Great evil may arise from the cobbler leaving his last and turning into..a legislator.

3. *Comb.*, as ***last-maker***.

1583 *Faversham Par. Reg.* (MS.), John Wythers, an olde man, a lastmaker. **1825** J. NICHOLSON *Operat. Mechanic* 8 The second sort of lever is presented to us in the cutting-knives used by last-makers.

last (lɑ:st, læst), *sb.*² Forms: 1 **hlæst**, 4–6 **laste**, **lest(e**, (6 **lasse**), 4– **last**. [OE. *hlæst* neut., corresp. to OFris. *hlest*, MLG., MDu., Du. *last* masc. and fem., OHG. *hlast*, *last* masc. and fem. (MHG., mod.G. *last* fem.); according to the now prevailing view repr. a pre-Teut. type **klat-sto-* (*-sti-*), parallel with **klat-to-* represented by ON. *hlass* neut., load; f. **klat-* root of LADE *v.*

Some scholars still adhere to the older view that WGer. **hlast-* and ON. *hlass* both represent a pre-Teut. **klatt-*, the divergence being conjectured to be due to difference of accentual conditions.]

†**1.** A load, burden, weight carried. *Obs.*

Beowulf (Z.) 52 Men ne cunnon secgan..hwa þæm hlæste on-feng. *c* **1000** *Riddles* ii. 15 (Gr.) Saȝa, hwa mec þecce oþþe hu ic hatte, þe þa hlæst bere. **1399** LANGL. *Rich. Redeles* IV. 74 Than lay the lordis a-lee with laste and with charge, And bare aboute the barge and blamed the maister.

2. A commercial denomination of weight, capacity, or quantity, varying for different kinds of goods and in different localities. Cf. G. *last*.

Originally the 'last' must have been the quantity carried at one time by the vehicle (boat, wagon, etc.) ordinarily used for the particular kind of merchandise. As a weight, it is often stated to be (like the Ger. weight of the same name) nominally equivalent either to 2 tons or to 4,000 lbs. In wool weight it is 4368 lbs. (= 12 sacks). A last of gunpowder is said to be 2,400 lbs. (= 24 barrels), and of feathers or flax 1,700 lbs.

The equivalence of the last of wool with 12 sacks seems to have led to an association of the word with the number twelve. Thus a last of hides was formerly 12 dozen (also 20 dickers of 10 hides each); of beer 12 barrels; of pitch 12 (sometimes 14) barrels; of cod and herrings 12 barrels (but of red herrings and pilchards 10,000 to 13,200 fish).

As a measure for grain and malt, the last was in the 16th c. 12 quarters, but is now 10 quarters = 80 bushels.

[**1314–5** *Rolls of Parlt.* I. 312/2, IIII. lest' & dim' de quyre.] **1333–4** *Durham Acc. Rolls* (Surtees) 30 In uno last et ix M[l] allec. melioribus emp...vjli. vjs. viijd. **1390–1** *Earl Derby's Exped.* (Camden) 58 Et pro j laste de beer..Et pro j laste de vino de Ryne. **1396–7** *Durham Acc. Rolls* (Surtees) 600 In j last bituminis, 34s. **1428** in *Surtees Misc.* (1888) 2 John Bower proferd to sell hym a laste of osmundes. **1469** *Househ. Ord.* (1790) 102 White Herringes a laste, that is to say, xij barrelles. *c* **1483** CAXTON *Dialogues* vi. 21 Men selle the goodes,.. By sackes or by lastes. **1486** *Naval Acc. Hen. VII* (1896) 15 A last of pitch and Tarre. **1509–10** *Act 1 Hen. VIII*, c. 20 §1 For the Subsidie..of every laste of hydes lxvjs. viijd. **1540** *Act 32 Hen. VIII*, c. 14 For every laste of whete and rye xxvis. viiid. **1548** *Privy Council Acts* (1890) II. 174 Serpentyne pouldre, iij lestes. **1583** *Satir. Poems Reform.* xlv. 882 To get a licence..For fortie last of Inglis beir. **1597** SKENE *De Verb. Sign.* s.v. *Serplaith*, Item 24 meales makis ane Last. Item, of meille and malt called *coist*, ane *last* makis ane Scottish chalder. **1599** NASHE *Lenten Stuffe* Ep. Ded. (end), For a whole laste of redde Herrings. **1612** HOPTON *Conserv. Yeares* 164 A Last of Wooll is 4368 pounds, or 12 Sackes. **1640** in Entick *London* II. 170 Quernstones, the last. **1665** *Lond. Gaz.* No, 8/1 Sixteen Lasts of Gunpowder, and Four thousand Musquets are brought in hither. **1725** BRADLEY *Fam. Dict.*, s.v., A Last of Cod Fish is twelve Barrels; a Last of Herrings is twenty Cades, or ten Thousand. **1727** *Ibid.* s.v. *Ale*, Twelve Ale-Barrels making a Last. **1750** CARTE *Hist. Eng.* II. 418 An extraordinary duty of ten shillings on a sack of wool, and a last of leather for one year. **1753** HANWAY *Trav.* (1762) I. VII. lxxxvi. 401 They have..exported fourteen thousand lasts. or twenty-eight thousand tuns English of all sorts of grain. **1875** STUBBS *Const. Hist.* II. xvi. 412 A grant of..forty shillings on the last of leather. **1884** *Brit. Almanac & Companion* 33 A Yarmouth last of herrings is supposed to count 13,200 fish. **1893** LANG *Red Fairy Bk.* 318 Someone who could brew a hundred lasts of malt at one brewing. **1894** R. LEIGHTON *Wreck Golden Fleece* 143 A single 'last' [of herrings] being equal to ten thousand fish.

†**b.** *transf.* A huge indefinite number. *Obs.*

c **1386** CHAUCER *Prioress' Prol.* 4 God yeve this Monk a thousand last quade yeer. **1581** RICH *Farew. Milit. Profess.* Tj, Goyng his waie to his sweete harte, tellyng her the whole discourse..with a whole laste of kisses. **1712** ARBUTHNOT *John Bull* III. ix, Ten thousand last of devils haul me, if I don't love thee as I love my life.

†**3.** A unit in the measurement of a ship's burden = 2 tons (occas. 1 ton). *Obs.*

1643 *Declar. Lords & Comm., Reb. Irel.* 46 The ship called Saint Michaell the Archangell of burden an hundred and twentie Lasts or Tuns. **1722** *Lond. Gaz.* No. 6096/3 The.. Snow..is of the Burthen of 50 or 60 Tons or 25 or 30 Lasts. **1796** in Morse *Amer. Geog.* II. 52 The Swedish vessels which perform the voyage to China, are generally of four hundred lasts burden.

†**4.** ? A dozen (of hawks). *Obs.*

162. HORSEY *Trav.* (Hakl. Soc.) 234 Two white garr-faulkens, a last of girckens and a last of sloght faulcons and two gashaukes.

†5. Shetland. *last of land*: a quantity of land = 18 merks. *Obs.*

1605 *Feu Contract* in Mill *Diary* (1889) 193 The said twa last of land in Sandwick. *a* 1733 *Shetland Acts* 36 in *Proc. Soc. Ant. Scot.* (1892) XXVI. 201 That none have more swine than four upon a last of land over winter.

†last, *sb.*³ *Obs.* Also 3–4 lest. [a. ON. *lǫst-r* (genit. *lastar*, dat. *lesti*):—OTeut. **lahst-uz*, f. **lah-*, whence OHG. *lahan*, OE. *léan* to blame. Cf. LAHTER.] A fault, vice, sin; blame; also, a physical blemish.

c 1175 *Lamb. Hom.* 145 Summe men luuieð..galiche lectres and luðere lastes. *c* 1200 ORMIN 4522 Forr gredi3nesse iss hefi3 lasst Biforenn Godess e3hne. *c* 1205 LAY. 22974 Þe mon þe him weore lað him cuðe last finde. *c* 1300 *Cursor M.* 22324 (Edin.) Wiþoutin laste al his liccame. *a* 1310 in Wright *Lyric P.* x. 37 Betere is were thunne boute laste, then syde robes ant synke into synne. *c* 1380 *Sir Ferumb.* 459 For þo3 y ben in batail schent it ys no lest for hem.

last (lɑːst, læst), *sb.*⁴ Also 5 lest. [f. LAST *v.*¹]

1. Continuance, duration. Now *rare.*

a 1300 *Cursor M.* 19562 In last o cristen mans lijf. *c* 1470 HENRY *Wallace* VI. 90 Fy on fortoun, fy on thi frewall quheyll; Fy on thi traist, for her it has no lest. 1587 FLEMING *Contn. Holinshed* III. 1549/2 Things memorable, of perpetuitie, fame, and last. *a* 1626 BACON *New Atl.* (1650) 29 These Drinks are of Severall Ages, some to the Age or Last of forty yeares. 1884 *Pall Mall G.* 12 Jan. 4/2 Another omission, and a more important one, from the point of view of the literary *last* of the book, is [etc.].

2. Power of holding on or out; 'staying' power.

1857 HUGHES *Tom Brown* II. vii, It's a fair trial of skill and last between us and them [the masters]. 1865 *Pall Mall G.* 16 May 10 His [a waterman's] 'last' is not in the same proportion to his pace as that of the amateur.

last (lɑːst, læst), *sb.*⁵ *Obs. exc. Hist.* [ad. Anglo-Latin *lastum, lestum* (Domesday Book *lest*), used as the regular equivalent of late OE. *læþ* LATHE *sb.*¹

The etymology is obscure: it is difficult on the ground of sense to suppose the word to be connected with LAST *sb.*², or with the OF. *lest* loading of a ship. It is also difficult on the ground of form to connect the word with OE. *læþ*; it is conceivable that the Norman *lest* might represent this by sound-substitution, but no analogous instance is known.]

= LATHE *sb.*¹ Also as the designation of an administrative assembly (see quot. 1670); more fully ***last-court***.

1086 *Domesday Bk.* I. 1/3 Has..leges regis concordant hostes de quatuor Lestis, hoc est Boruuar Lest, & Estrelest & Linuuartlest & Wiuuartlest. *c* 1120 *Rochester Bridge-bote Charter* in Birch *Cart. Sax.* III. 658 (*Latin text*), Postea sexta pera debet fieri de holingeburna et de toto illo lesto quæ [*sic*] ad hoc pertinet. *Ibid.* (*O.E. text*) þonne is syo syoxte per to holingan burnan & to eallan þam læþe. *a* 1272 *Charter Romney Marsh* (1597) 73 Si aliquis..conuincatur per testimonium Balliui et Iuratorum in communi lasto, amercietur [etc.]. *c* 1380 W. THORN *Chron.* in Twysden *Hist. Angl. Scriptores decem* (1652) 1777 Hic [*sc.* Elfredus] constituit Hundred & Lestes. 1570–6 LAMBARDE *Peramb. Kent* (1826) 165 Of this place the whole Last of Shipwey (conteining twelve Hundrethes) at the first tooke, and yet continueth, the name. 1662 DUGDALE *Imbanking* 54 Also it was decreed and ordained that twice every year, for ever, there should be held a principal and general Last, within the said Land and Marsh. 1670 BLOUNT *Law Dict.*, *Last* also, in the Marshes of East Kent, signifies a Court held by Twenty four Jurats, and summoned by the two Bailiffs thereof, wherein they make Orders, lay and levy Taxes, impose Penalties, &c. For preservation of the said Marshes. 1729 in JACOB *Law Dict.* 1753 in CHAMBERS *Cycl. Supp.*

last (lɑːst, læst), *a.*, *adv.*, and *sb.*⁶ Forms: 1 latost, (lætest), 2–3 latest, latst, (3 *Ormin* lattst), 3 least, 3, 4–5 (*Sc.*) lest(e, 4–6 laste, 6 *Sc.* laist, 4– last. [OE. *latost*, Northumb. *lætest*, superl. of *læt* adj., *late* adv. Cf. OFris. *letast, lest*, OS. *latst, last, lętist* (MLG. *lest*, Du. *laatst, lest*), OHG. *lazzôst, lęzist* (MHG. *letzest, letzst, letst*, mod.G. *letzt*), ON. *latast-r*. The syncopation of the vowel before *-st* must have originated in the inflected forms; for the subsequent dropping of the *t* cf. BEST. The mod. LATEST does not descend from early ME. *latest*, but is a new-formation on the positive.]

A. *adj.* Following all others; coming at the end.

I. As simple adjective.

1. a. Following all the others in a series, succession, order, or enumeration; subsequent to all others in occurrence, existence, etc. *spec.* in *Cricket*, (*the*) ***last man*** (*in*): the batsman who is not out at the end of an innings; the man who goes in to bat last; hence ***the last pair, wicket.***

For the syntactical relation involved in *last comer* and the like, cf. *early riser*, etc. (See EARLY *a.* 1 a *note.*)

c 1200 ORMIN 4168 Þe sefennde, þe lattste da3, He sette þe33m to resste. *a* 1300 *Cursor M.* 1492 Þe formast werld adam be-gan, þar-of lameth [*i.e.* Lamech] þe last man. 1340 *Ayenb.* 245 Þe laste yefþe and þe meste and þe he3este is þe yefþe of wysdom. *c* 1400 *Lanfranc's Cirurg.* 58 In þe laste chapitle of þe firste book. *c* 1440 *Promp. Parv.* 288/2 Laste, save one, *penultimus.* *a* 1548 HALL *Chron., Hen. VIII* 244 She was the last of the right lyne and name, of Plantagenet. *c* 1560 A. SCOTT *Poems* (S.T.S.) xii. 51 It is bot waist Mo wirde to taist, 3e haif my laist. 1560 DAUS tr. *Sleidane's Comm.* 12 b, A prophete that sayd Maximilian should be the last Germaine Emperour. 1604 E. G[RIMSTONE] *D'Acosta's Hist. Indies* v. xxviii. 415 The twelfth and last month was called *Aymara.* 1611 COTGR. s.v. *Dernier*, The last commers get the maisterie. 1613 PURCHAS *Pilgrimage* (1614) 223 This last clause..is added by the Talmudists. 1667 MILTON *P.L.* v. 166 Fairest of Starrs, last in the train of Night, If better thou belong not to the dawn. *Ibid.* XII. 330 Of Kings The Last. 1724 DE FOE *Mem. Cavalier* (1840) 275 This was the last day of May. 1794 MRS. RADCLIFFE *Myst. Udolpho* iv, The sun now gave his last light. 1800 WORDSW. *Waterfall & Eglantine*, The Briar quaked—and much I fear Those accents were his last. 1842 TENNYSON *Love & Duty* 65 A hundred times In that last kiss, which never was the last, Farewell, like endless welcome, lived and died. 1864 —— *En. Ard.* 217 When the last of those last moments came. 1864 LE FANU *Uncle Silas* II. v. 70 So the morning came—my last for many a day at Knowl.

Cricket. 1773 *Kentish Gaz.* 24 July, Surry. Yaldin, Last man in, 17. Kent. Mr. Hussey, Last man in, 0. 1833 J. NYREN *Young Cricketer's Tutor* 113 Small went in the last man for fourteen runs, and fetched them. 1870 *Times* 20 July 10/3 Southerton appeared as 'last man'. 1897 H. NEWBOLT *Vitaï Lampada* in *Admirals All* 21 An hour to play and the last man in. 1953 R. WEBBER *Australians in Eng.* 155 Oldfield (123) and Mailey (46 not out) added 124 for the last wicket in only 40 minutes. 1957 R. CAMPBELL *Coll. Poems* II. 101 No last-man-in has ever batted With a more desperate intent. 1963 A. ROSS *Australia 63* iii. 88 The last pair, perched not uncomfortably for forty-nine minutes, had put on 20 runs.

b. With a cardinal numeral. In this combination two varieties of word-order are commonly used. (*a*) The more frequent form till the 17th c. appears to be ***the two*** (***three***, etc.) ***last*** (= F. *les deux derniers*, G. *die zwei letzten*); the variant ***seven the last*** appears in one example. (*b*) The form ***the last two*** (***three***, etc.) is now the more frequent of the two, exc. where *last* is equivalent to 'last-mentioned'; see also 3. Also preceded by an ordinal number, to denote how many places from the end of a series an object, name of a person, etc., occurs.

(*a*) 1382 WYCLIF *Rev.* xv. i, Seuen aungels hauinge seuen the laste plages [so 1388, with *v.rr.* the laste seuene, the seuene laste; *later versions* the seven last(e]. *c* 1450 *ME. Med. Bk.* (Heinrich) 144 A veyne by twene two laste fyngeres. 1526 *Pilgr. Perf.* (W. de W. 1531) 1 b, The two last dayes [perteyneth] to the contemplatyue lyfe. 1710 C. WHEATLY *Ch. Eng. Man's Companion* 51 The two last of these versicles. *a* 1715 BURNET *Own Time* (1724) I. 591 Three parliaments had sat. The two last had not mentioned him. 1779–81 JOHNSON *L.P.*, *Young* Wks. IV. 242 The three last stanzas are not more remarkable for just rhymes. 1818 HAZLITT *Lect. Eng. Poets* iii, Chaucer, Spenser, Shakespeare, and Milton... The two last have had justice done them by the voice of common fame.

(*b*) 1388 [see (*a*)]. 1669 STURMY *Mariner's Mag.* IV. 205, In the 12th and 13th, or last two Columns of your Journal. 1805 *Johnson's Dict.* s.v. *Disloyal*, The last three [*ed.* 1755 three latter] senses are now obsolete. 1833 *Regul. Instr. Cavalry* I. 98 Place the last three fingers behind the steel. 1898 *Daily News* 8 Aug. 6/5 The last two volumes (fifth and sixth) of their new edition of Macaulay's History.

1880 W. F. SKENE *Celtic Scotl.* III. 122 Dathi the second last of the pagan monarchs of Ireland. 1938 I. GOLDBERG *Wonder of Words* ix. 186 There are technical names for words having accented last, second-last, and third-last syllables. 1963 J. LUSBY in B. James *Austral. Short Stories* 235 Before breakfast on our second-last day the Eccentric stood facing Mooney on the sand.

c. Coupled with *least.*

a 1586 SIDNEY *Arcadia* I. (1633) 14 Among many strange conceits you told me..truely even the last..would not seem the least unto me. 1589 NASHE *Pref. to Greene's Menaphon* (Arb.) 17 For the last, though not the least of them all. 1595 SPENSER *Col. Clout* 444 And there, though last, not least, is Aetion. 1599 H. BUTTES *Dyets drie Dinner* C iij, Both these, are of last and least request. 1601 SHAKS. *Jul. C.* III. i. 189 Though last, not least in loue. 1852 DICKENS *Bleak Ho.* lviii, Volumnia..is a prey to horrors of many kinds. Not last nor least among them, possibly, is a horror of what may befall her little income.

d. *ellipt.* The last day (of a month). Also more generally, the final portion of a period of time, esp. in ***the last of pea-time***; also *fig.* Now *N. Amer.*

1560 DAUS tr. *Sleidane's Comm.* 110 The last of June. 1596 *Acc. Bk. W. Wray* in *Antiquary* XXXII. 119 This laste of octobʳ. 1630 WADSWORTH *Pilgr.* vi. 52 He..dyed, Nouember the last, 1623. 1683 TRYON *Way to Health* v. (1697) 86 From the midle of June to the last of October. 1834 W. A. CARUTHERS *Kentuckian in N.Y.* I. 190 Our parson whines it out like an old woman in the last of pea-time. 1883 *Century Mag.* Oct. 921/2 The snipe usually makes its appearance in New Jersey and New York about the last of March or the first of April. 1904 E. ROBINS *Magnetic North* I. 63 Things looked pretty much like the last of pea time. 1908 L. M. MONTGOMERY *Anne of Green Gables* xxxvi. 405 There is a distinguished oculist coming to the Island the last of June. 1931 A. E. MARTIN *Hist. U.S.* II. ii. 24 By the last of May he had formulated his plan and on the twenty-ninth he issued two proclamations.

e. In spatial sense: Utmost, extreme, remotest (*rare*). †Also, hindmost, rearmost.

a 1225 *Leg. Kath.* 586 Clerkes..of alle clergies ut of Alixandres lond þe alre leste ende [*v.rr.* laste, leaste]. *a* 1548 HALL *Chron., Hen. VIII*, 239 The kyng rode to the last ende of the ranke where the Speares or Pencyoners stoode. 1549 in Strype *Eccl. Mem.* II. App. DD. 104 The L. Gray was fain..to retyre to our last horsemen and footmen. 1871 R. ELLIS tr. *Catullus* lxviii. 102 The land's last verge Holds him.

f. ***last across*** (***the road***): a children's game in which each tries to be the last to cross a road (or railway) safely in front of an approaching vehicle (or train). Also *fig.*

1904 A. B. F. YOUNG *Compl. Motorist* ix. 230 If it seems good to them [*sc.* children] to play at 'last across', you had better go very gingerly in their neighbourhood. 1914 'I. HAY' *Knight on Wheels* xi. 108 A frisky calf, encountered by the way, almost wrecked its own prospects of ever becoming veal by an untimely indulgence in the game of 'Come to Mother, or Last Across the Road'. 1928 *Sunday Dispatch* 15 July 11/3 Socialist back-benchers are playing a dangerous game of 'last across' with Mr. Speaker—just seeing how far they can go at question time without being 'named'. 1957 *Times* 12 Mar. 4/6 Engine drivers are threatening to refuse to drive trains over a section of track..because children are using it for a game of 'last across'. 1958 R. LIDDELL *Morea* II. iv. 103 Chickens seemed to be playing 'last across the road';..dogs tried to meet us head on. 1969 'A. HALL' *Striker Portfolio* v. 45 We finished up playing 'Last Across' and he cut it too fine.

2. a. Belonging to the end or final stage, *esp.* belonging to the end of life or the end of the world. (In some applications only a contextual use of sense 1.) †***last age***: the closing years of life, old age. ***the*** (***four***) ***last things*** (Theol.; = L. *quatuor novissima*): Death, Judgement, Heaven, and Hell. ***last words***, a person's dying words.

c 1200 *Vices & Virtues* (1888) 19 Ðes wer3inge nis bute erres of ðare laczste [? = latste *or* lasste]. *c* 1200 *Trin. Coll. Hom.* 5 Of ðe lateste to-cume of ure louerd specð þe holie boc on oðer stede. 1382 WYCLIF *Wisd.* iv. 8 The laste age [1388 eelde, Vulg. *senectus*] forsothe wrshipeful is not longe durende. 1382 —— *1 Cor.* xv. 52 In a moment, in the smytinge of an y3e, in the laste trumpe. 1440 J. SHIRLEY *Dethe K. James* 29 Translated..bi youre symple subget John Shirley, in his laste age. 1479 EARL RIVERS (*title*) The book named Cordyal which treteth of the four last and final thinges. 1522 MORE *De Quat. Noviss.* in *Works* (1557) 76/2 The busi minding of thy .iiii. last things, and the depe consideracion therof, is the thyng that shal kepe thee fro synne. 1560 DAUS tr. *Sleidane's Comm.* 216 b, He confessed his doctryne constantlye even to the laste breathe. 1606 (*title*) Foure-fould Meditation, of the foure last things: viz. ..of the Houre of Death. Day of Iudgement. Paines of Hell. Ioyes of Heauen. *a* 1621 BEAUM. & FL. *Thierry & Theod.* v. ii, Bear vm vnto their last beds. 1638 BAKER tr. *Balzac's Lett.* (vol. II.) 59 Having performed to him the last duties. 1697 DRYDEN *Virg. Georg.* IV. 763 With his last Voice, Eurydice, he cry'd. 1709 POPE *Ess. Crit.* 403 That sun..Which from the first has shone on ages past, Enlights the present, and shall warm the last. 1734 J. TRAPP (*title*) Thoughts upon the four last things... A poem in four parts. 1781 COWPER *Truth* 564 'Twas the last trumpet—see the Judge enthroned. 1808 SCOTT *Marmion* VI. xxxiii. 366 'Charge, Chester, charge! On, Stanley, on!'..Were the last words of Marmion. 1833 J. H. NEWMAN *Arians* IV. iii. (1876) 326 Hosius..with his last breath, abjured the heresy. 1845 G. BUSH *Anastasis* p. v, The great scheme of Scriptural Eschatology, or the doctrine of the last things. 1864 C. M. YONGE *Trial* II. xi. 189 Come, come,..there must be some last words. 1897 J. A. BEET *Last Things* xix. 231 This vision of glory..will be the closing scene of our study of the Last Things. *a* 1916 H. JAMES *Middle Years* (1917) iv. 49 Those 'last words' of the *raffiné* that were chanted and crooned in the damask-hung temple of the Grosvenor Gallery. 1945 E. WAUGH *Brideshead Revisited* I. vii. 173, I can't remember all he told me..plenary indulgences, four last things. 1948, etc. [see FAMOUS *a.* 1 c]. 1975 J. AIKEN *Voices in Empty House* viii. 190 The four last things are death, judgement, heaven and hell. 1975 R. PLAYER *Let's talk of graves* i. 31 Languishing in the Condemned Cell, contemplating the Last Things.

b. †(***one's***) ***last day***: the day of one's death (*obs.*). ***the last day***: the Day of Judgement, the end of the world. ***the last days***: the concluding period in the life or history *of* (a person, etc.); also the period including and immediately preceding the Last Judgement. Similarly ***the last time, times.***

a 1300 *Cursor M.* 5458 Thinges..þat..suld in last dais bi-tidd. *Ibid.* 23928 On min aun last dai. 1340 HAMPOLE *Pr. Consc.* 1986 Þe last day of man is hyd. *Ibid.* 2596 Swilk als his last day fyndes a man..Swilk mon he be demed at þe ende. 1388 WYCLIF *Isa.* ii. 2 And in the laste daies the hil of the hous of the Lord schal be maad redi in the cop of hillis. 1560 DAUS tr. *Sleidane's Comm.* 189 b, Before the laste daye of judgement. 1611 BIBLE *John* vi. 39, I should lose nothing, but should raise it vp againe at the last day. —— *1 Pet.* i. 5 Ready to be reuealed in the last time [ἐν καιρῷ ἐσχάτῳ]. *Ibid.* 20 Who..was manifest in these last times [ἐπ' ἐσχάτων τῶν χρόνων] for you. 1613 PURCHAS *Pilgrimage* (1614) 548 Our English first had Trade heere in the last times of Queene Elizabeth. 1651 HOBBES *Leviath.* III. xli. 262 The day of Judgment, (which is therefore also called, the last day). 1834 LYTTON (*title*) The Last Days of Pompeii. 1883 R. W. DIXON *Mano* I. iv. 10 Wherefore the last days seem to be begun.

c. ***last end***: the very end, †the utmost extremity or limit; *esp.* the end of life, death. (Cf. MHG. *das letzte ende*; OE. had *se ýtemesta ende.*) *arch.* and *dial.*

1377 LANGL. *P. Pl.* B. XIV. 133 Allas! þat ricchesse shal reue and robbe mannes soule Fram þe loue of owre lorde at his laste ende! *c* 1425 WYNTOUN *Cron.* IX. Prol. 31 Off this Tretys the last end Tyl bettyr than I am, I commend. 1450–1530 *Myrr. our Ladye* 260 This I haue writen vpon this antempne for the laste ende semeth darckely spoken. 1611 COTGR. s.v. *Final, Fin finale*, the last end of all. 1611 BIBLE *Num.* xxiii. 10 Let mee die the death of the righteous, and let my last end be like his. *c* 1625 MILTON *Death Fair Infant* 77 Till the worlds last-end shall make thy name to live. 1637 *Sc. Bk. Com. Prayer, Public Baptism* (Rubric), At the last end, the Presbyter..shall say this exhortation following. 1889 *N.W. Linc. Gloss.*, I caame at th' start, an' I've seed th' last end on it [a sale]... She's been aailin' a long time, poor thing, bud her last end's cum'd at last.

d. Phr. ***if it's the last thing I*** (etc.) ***do***: used to indicate a very strong desire to do something.

1921 E. O'NEILL *Emperor Jones* 180, I kills you, you white debil, if it's de last thing I evah does! **1938** M. ALLINGHAM *Fashion in Shrouds* ix. 146 He's got to go on that plane. If it's the last thing he does he's got to go back today. **1971** 'D. CORY' *Sunburst* iii. 44, I want to kill him if it's the last thing I do. **1972** P. NEWTON *Sheep Thief* xv. 119 I'll get that bloke if it's the last thing I do.

3. a. Occurring or presenting itself next before a point of time expressed or implied in the sentence; the present time, or next before; most recent, latest. † ***the last age***: recent times.

With a cardinal numeral the order is now always *the last two* (*three*, etc.).

1377 LANGL. *P. Pl.* B. XVIII. 311 And now for thi last lesynge ylore we haue Adam, And al owre lordeship. **1411** *Rolls of Parlt.* III. 650/1 The last Parlement of oure sayd liege Lord. *a* **1548** HALL *Chron.*, *Hen. IV*, 18 So muche was their courages abated..with the remembraunce of the last conflicte and batail. **1562** WINȜET *Cert. Tractates* i. Wks. 1888 I. 7 Ȝour eldaris in the last aige foresaid. **1598** SHAKS. *Merry W.* IV. ii. 98 To meete him at the doore with it, as they did last time. **1610** —— *Temp.* V. i. 153 When did you lose your daughter? In this last Tempest. **1660** F. BROOKE tr. *Le Blanc's Trav.* 246 For those three or four last Ages. **1669** MARVELL *Corr.* cxxx. Wks. 1872–5 II. 294 Having writ to you last post saves me the labor of a long letter this. **1678** T. RYMER (*title*) The Tragedies of the last Age consider'd. **1750** JOHNSON *Rambler* No. 71 ¶11 Among the improvements made by the last centuries in human knowledge. **1797–1805** S. & HT. LEE *Canterb. T.* V. 292 He wore his best Brutus wig, which was curled in the last new taste. **1804** *Med. Jrnl.* XII. 166 In the last fortnight, a number of subjects..have been submitted to the test. **1843** H. MILLER in J. L. Watson *Life R. S. Candlish* vi. (1882) 78 The events of the last twelve days. **1885** J. PAYN *Talk of Town* I. 168, 'I say, my astute young friend..where have you been to these last three hours?' *a* **1902** *Mod.* We have been having bad weather these last few weeks.

b. Said *esp.* of the period, season, etc., occurring next before the time of writing or speaking, as *last Wednesday*, *last Christmas*. ***last day*** (now *dial.*), yesterday; † ***last morning***, yesterday morning; ***last evening***, yesterday evening. Cf. equivalent phrases in B. 2 b.

(Orig. used with a demonstrative, *this* or *the*, and still sometimes with the former when a very recent date is indicated; with the names of days and months, the adj. may precede or follow the sb., as *last Tuesday* or *Tuesday last*, *last January* or *January last*.)

c **1340** *Cursor M.* 16122 (Trin.) A siȝt þat she in hir slepyng say þis ilke laste nyȝt. *a* **1400–50** *Alexander* 2785 Two..þat lost wer nowe þe last day. **1502** *Privy Purse Exp. Eliz. of York* (1830) 110 Tharrerags of the last yere. *a* **1553** UDALL *Royster D.* II. i. (Arb.) 33 Loe yond the olde nourse that was wyth vs last day. **1560** DAUS tr. *Sleidane's Comm.* 201 b, Commyng thither the laste yere in Decembre. **1591** SHAKS. *Two Gent.* II. i. 86 Last morning You could not see to wipe my shooes. **1613** PURCHAS *Pilgrimage* (1614) 96 On Bartholmew day last 1613. **1677** E. SMITH in *12th Rep. Hist. MSS. Comm.* App. v. 37 His Majesty..went on Munday last to Windsor to see his workemen. **1711** STEELE *Spect.* No. 53 ¶4 Yours of Saturday last. **1712** ADDISON *Spect.* No. 305 ¶1 In the *Daily Courant* of last Friday. **1784** COWPER *Tiroc.* 834 Their breath a sample of last night's regale. **1787** BURNS *Humble Petit. Bruar Water* iii, Last day I grat wi' spite and teen, As Poet Burns came by. **1795** COWPER *Pairing Time Anticipated* 28 A Finch..With golden wing and satin poll, A last year's bird. **1816** BYRON *Ch. Har.* III. xxviii, Last noon beheld them full of lusty life, Last eve in Beauty's circle proudly gay. **1847** HALLIWELL, *Last-day*, yesterday. *West.* **1872** RAYMOND *Statist. Mines & Mining* 185 Last fall a Chicago merchant shipped a fair stock of merchandise to Eldorado.

c. With ellipsis of *letter*. Now chiefly in commercial use.

1638 WOTTON *Let. to Dr. C.* in *Reliq.* (1651) 501, I find in the bowels of your last..much harsh and stiffe matter from Scotland. *c* **1645** HOWELL *Lett.* I. VI. xv. (1650) 202 Your last unto me was in French of the first current. **1749** FIELDING *Tom Jones* XVIII. iv, My worthy friend, I informed you in my last.

d. ellipt. (*colloq.*) (A person's) latest joke, freak, characteristic action or utterance.

a **1902** *Mod.* Have you heard Professor X.'s last?

4. That comes at the end of a series arranged in order of rank or estimation; lowest. Chiefly *ellipt.*

1382 WYCLIF *Mark* ix. 34 If any man wole be the first among ȝou, he schal be the laste, and mynystre of alle. **1601** CHESTER in *Shaks. C. Praise* 43 King Arthur the last of the nine Worthies. **1709** POPE *Ess. Crit.* 196 Oh may some spark of your celestial fire, The last, the meanest of your sons inspire. **1774** GOLDSM. *Nat. Hist.* (1776) IV. 183 [The manati] may be indiscriminately called the last of beasts, or the first of fishes. **1781** COWPER *Expost.* 242 The last of nations now, though once the first. **1871** R. ELLIS tr. *Catullus* xlix. 6 He as easily last among the poets As thou surely the first among the pleaders.

5. a. Remaining or arrived at after others have disappeared, have been removed, exhausted, or spent; the only remaining; ***last lap*** [LAP *sb.*³ 5 b]: the final circuit of a track, course, etc.; also *fig.*

1382 WYCLIF *Luke* xii. 59 Thou schalt not go thennis, til thou ȝelde also the last ferthing. **1388** —— *Amos* ix. 1, Y schal sle bi swerd the laste of hem. **1560** DAUS tr. *Sleidane's Comm.* 120 Than flye they unto her, as unto the laste ancker. *Ibid.* 216 They of necessitie doe flee to the laste remedye. **1596** SPENSER *State Irel.* Wks. (Globe) 682/2 Such an one I could name, upon whom..our last hopes now rest. **1597** SHAKS. *2 Hen. IV*, IV. ii. 44 Wee readie are to tryе our fortunes, To the last man. **1613** —— *Hen. VIII*, III. ii. 453 Take an Inuentary of all I haue, To the last peny. **1637** MILTON *Lycidas* 71 That last infirmity of Noble mind. **1697** DRYDEN *Virg. Georg.* IV. 274 Having spent the last Remains of Light. **1697** DAMPIER *Voy.* I. 20 This night our last Slave run away. **1742** LADY M. W. MONTAGU *Let. to Mr. Wortley* 10 June, Being always at his last shirt and last guinea. **1781** COWPER *Hope* 378 Mercy, fled to as the last resort. *a* **1836** O. W. HOLMES *Last Leaf* viii, If I should live to be The last leaf upon the tree. **1857** BUCKLE *Civiliz.* I. xii. 686 There can be no doubt that rebellion is the last remedy against tyranny. **1885** *Daily News* 1 Sept. 2/5 At half-distance the positions remained unaltered, and, as they began the last lap, it appeared to be any one's race. **1908** *Daily Chron.* 7 Mar. 7/5 Such an event [*sc.* a cycling race]..is declared to have been won on the last-lap sprint. **1922** JOYCE *Ulysses* 234 Bang of the lastlap bell spurred the halfmile wheelmen to their sprint. **1926** O. BARFIELD *Hist. in Eng. Words* 56 There is a ..tendency to transmute..[modern sports] terms into lively idiom. In this way we can use..the *last lap.* **1932** *Discovery* Dec. 393/1 We learned that weather conditions there had improved and that, for the last lap, we might expect better flying conditions.

b. With the application defined by a relative clause or *to* with *infin.* Often with idiomatic force = 'most unlikely', 'most unwilling', 'most unsuitable'.

a **1450** *Knt. de la Tour.* (1868) 61 The .ix. foly, and the last, that Eue dede was the grettest. **1513** MORE in Grafton *Chron.* (1568) II. 757 In the Sommer last that ever he sawe. **1535** COVERDALE *2 Sam.* xix. 11 Why wyl ye be the last to fetch the kynge agayne vnto his house? *a* **1548** HALL *Chron.*, *Hen. VIII*, 243 b, This was the last Monke that was seen in his clothyng in Englande. **1588** SHAKS. *L.L.L.* I. i. 161, I am the last that will last keepe his oath. **1659** B. HARRIS *Parival's Iron Age* 138 This was the last favour Fortune did this Darling of hers. **1751** FIELDING *Amelia* IV. x. vii. 74 This was indeed almost the last man in the World, whose company he wished for. **1790** COWPER *Catharina* 9 The last evening ramble we made,—Catharina, Maria, and I. **1832** HT. MARTINEAU *Life in Wilds* iv. 53 One of the last men we could spare. **1838** PRESCOTT *Ferd. & Is.* II. xvi. III. 251 She was the last person to be approached with undue familiarity. **1840** H. REEVE tr. *A. de Tocqueville's Democracy in Amer.* IV. IV. iii. 269, I am the last man to contend that these propensities are unconquerable. **1852** MRS. STOWE *Uncle Tom's C.* xxx. 279 It's the last night we may be together. **1861** GEN. P. THOMPSON *Audi Alt.* (ed. 2) III. clxxvii. 213 Bellona is the last of the goddesses to be flirted with. **1967** *Listener* 28 Sept. 395/3 Degas was the last man to believe in untutored brilliance.

6. a. After which there is nothing to be done or said; final, conclusive, definitive. ? Now only in the collocation ***last word.***

1654 BRAMHALL *Just Vind.* vii. (1661) 228 All Christian Nations do challenge this right..to be the last Judges of their own liberties and priviledges. *Ibid.* viii. 232 The Catholick Church..is the last visible Judg of controversies, and the supream Ecclesiastical Court. **1678** BUTLER *Hud.* III. ii. 1330 Money that like the Sword of Kings, Is the last Reason of all things. **1751** JOHNSON *Rambler* No. 142 ¶8 Whatever shall be the last decision of the law. **1881** S. COLVIN *Pref. to Select. Landor's Writings* (1882) 6 Concerning this part of Landor's work,..Mr. Swinburne has in those two felicitous lines said the last word. **1891** CHURCH *Oxford Movement* x. 167 It [Evangelical theology] regarded the Epistles of St. Paul as the last word of the Gospel message. **1933** *Punch* 17 May 543/3 Although to my mind the Inverness alterations are absolutely the last word [in modernity], opinions are bound to differ. **1936** *Discovery* Apr. 130/1 The book cannot be the last word on M. Coué. **1966** *Listener* 6 Jan. 12/2 The Trombay establishment is the last word in nuclear sophistication. **1973** *Archivum Linguisticum* IV. 12 Perhaps it is most reasonable to leave the last word to Pidgin.

† **b.** ***last hand***: the final or finishing stroke or touch.

1614 SELDEN *Titles Hon.* Ded. a iij, Some yeer since it was finish't, wanting, only in some parts, my last hand. **1648–1865** [see HAND *sb.* 13 b]. **1676** DRYDEN *Dram. Wks.* (1725) IV. 81 To recommend it to the King's perusal, before the last Hand was added to it. **1704** *Swift's T. Tub* To Rdr., Whether the work received his last hand or whether he intended to fill up defective places. **1715–20** POPE *Iliad* XVIII. 702 Thus the broad shield complete the artist crown'd With his last hand.

7. Reaching its ultimate limit; attaining a degree beyond which one cannot go; utmost, extreme. Now chiefly in phr. ***of the last importance.*** (Cf. F. *dernier.*) Also ***last cry*** [tr. Fr. *le dernier cri*]: something in the newest fashion. Cf. DERNIER *a.* c.

a **1674** CLARENDON *Hist. Reb.* XIV. §139 He told the earl that he would impart a secret to him of the last importance. **1693** DRYDEN *Lucretius* II. 13 Their last endeavours bend To outshine each other. **1705** STANHOPE *Paraphr.* II. 424 One of the last Affronts, capable of being passed upon any Man. **1711** *Light to Blind* in *10th Rep. Hist. MSS. Comm.* App. v. 110 A Prince, who with the last zeal is desir'd by suffering nations. **1775** HARRIS *Philos. Arrangem.* (1841) 348 Demosthenes, in whom rhetoric attained its last perfection. **1827** SCOTT *Napoleon* xxxvi, Territory of the last and most important consequence. **1849** MACAULAY *Hist. Eng.* ix. II. 395 Their Church was suffering the last excess of injury and insult. **1875** E. WHITE *Life in Christ* III. xxii. (1878) 325 The citation of these words..in order to support the speculation ..seems to the last degree perverse. **1881** MAHAFFY *Old Greek Educ.* iii. 26 Rowing..was of the last importance in their naval warfare. **1916** W. J. LOCKE *Wonderful Year* x. 133 A morning coat (last cry of Bond Street).

ellipt. **1667** MILTON *P.L.* IX. 1079 Even shame, the last of evils. **1727** FIELDING *Love in Sev. Masques* I. v, Well, positively, going into a bookseller's shop is to me the last of fatigues.

8. Special collocations. **last brood, last spring** (see LASPRING), terms denoting a young salmon at a certain stage of growth.

1861 *Act 24–5 Vict.* c. 109 §4.

¶ For *last cast*, *l. ditch*, *l. extremity*, *l. gasp*, *l. heir*, *l. honour(s*, *l. legs*, *l. multiplier*, *l. name*, *l. post*, *l. straw*, *l. will*, see the sbs.

II. *absol.* (quasi-*sb.*)

9. In certain absolute uses.

a. With a demonstrative or relative adj.: The last-mentioned person or thing.

1560 DAUS tr. *Sleidane's Comm.* 44 b, Which two last were not agreed upon. **1640** BP. HALL *Chr. Moder.* (Ward) 33/2 These two last will teach him to acknowledge and admire other men's better faculties. **1697** DAMPIER *Voy.* I. 215 With a Fireship and 3 Tenders, which last had not a constant crew. **1796** H. HUNTER tr. *St.-Pierre's Stud. Nat.* (1799) I. 418 It..contains, as it ought, the history of the knowledge, and of the errors of his time. These last are sometimes imputed to him very unjustly. **1864** MISS BRADDON *H. Dunbar* II. iii. 43 To this last, love is faith.

† **b.** ***the last*** (advb.): at last, finally. *Sc. Obs.*

c **1340** *Cursor M.* 6818 (Trin.) Þe flesshe þat beest bifore haþ tast Ete ȝe not þerof þe last [*Cott.*, *Fairf.* a last(e)]. *a* **1578** LINDESAY (Pitscottie) *Chron. Scot.* (S.T.S.) I. 35 [They] maid greit lauboris and trawellis to bring them to peace and concord whill the last they brocht them togither in S. Geillis kirk.

c. The latest or most recent part; conclusion, end.

1607 SHAKS. *Temp.* I. ii. 107 Sit still, and heare the last of our sea-sorrow. **1669** STURMY *Mariner's Mag.* I. 18 We will draw to the last with a Man of War in Chase and taking of her Prize. **1918** GALSWORTHY *Five Tales* 308 The last of daylight from without mingled with faint intrusion from the lamp within. **1943** K. O'BRIEN (*title*) The last of summer.

† **d.** The last time. *Obs. rare.*

1601 SHAKS. *All's Well* V. iii. 79 The last that ere I tooke her leaue at Court.

e. The last day or last moments (of a life); the end of life, death. Chiefly with a possessive.

1382 WYCLIF *Ecclus.* xxx. 1 That he glade in his laste [Vulg. *ut lætetur in novissimo suo*]. **1618** BOLTON *Florus* IV. vi. (1636) 303 Who would not wonder that those most wise men used not their own hands at their last? *a* **1635** NAUNTON *Fragm. Reg.* (Arb.) 44 The haughtinesse of his spirit, which accompanied him to his last. **1671** MILTON *Samson* 1426 The last of me or no I cannot warrant. **1748** RICHARDSON *Clarissa* VII. 418 She regrets to this hour, and declares that she shall to the last of her life, her cruel treatment of that sister. **1817** BYRON *Manfred* III. i. 88 When Rome's sixth Emperor was near his last. **1860** LEVER *One of them* xlvi, As he drew nigh his last his sufferings gave little intervals of rest. *a* **1902** *Mod.* Towards the last the pain seemed to leave him, and his end was very peaceful.

f. ***one's last***: the last thing a person does or can do; used *esp.* with certain verbs, the sb. implied by them being understood, e.g. ***to breathe one's last*** (sc. ***breath***), ***to look one's last*** (sc. ***look***).

1592 SHAKS. *Rom. & Jul.* V. iii. 112 Eyes looke your last. Armes take your last embrace. **1593**, **1651**, **1714** [see BREATHE *v.* 10 c]. **1597** SHAKS. *Lover's Compl.* 168 The one a palate hath that needs will taste, Though Reason weep, and cry 'It is thy last'. **1607** —— *Timon* III. vi. 100 This is Timons last. *a* **1711** KEN *Hymnotheo* Poet. Wks. 1721 III. 68 On his Cross breathing his painful last. **1717** ADDISON *Ovid's Met.* II. Poems (1790) 118 The swans..now sung their last, and dy'd. **1790** BURNS *Tam o' Shanter* 73 The wind blew as 'twad blawn its last. **1864** LE FANU *Uncle Silas* II. v. 71, I was looking my last..on the old house, and lingered.

† **g.** The utmost, the extremity. *Obs.*

1633 T. STAFFORD *Pac. Hib.* II. xxiii. (1810) 433 Hee and all his would rather endure the last of misery, then bee found guilty of so fowle a treason.

h. *colloq.* The end of one's dealings with something.

1816 SCOTT *Old Mortality* in *Tales my Landlord* 1st Ser. II. x. 241 'Ye hae seen the last o' me, and o' this bonny dye too,' said Jenny, holding between her finger and thumb a silver dollar. **1854** DICKENS *Hard T.* I. viii, If it was ever to reach your father's ears I should never hear the last of it. **1862** MRS. H. WOOD *Mrs. Halliburton's Troubles* III. xvii. 218 Dick little thought the manufactory had seen the last of him [*sc.* Cyril]. **1889** 'MARK TWAIN' *Connecticut Yankee* 280 That is the last you are going to see of him till he emerges on the other side. **1910** 'M. RUTHERFORD' *More Pages from Jrnl.* 22, I shall be thankful to see the last of you! **1924** G. B. SHAW *St. Joan* vi. 97 Her heart would not burn, my lord; but everything that was left is at the bottom of the river. You have heard the last of her.

10. In phrases formed with prepositions.

a. at last, ***at the last*** (ME. *at* or *a þan laste*, *atte laste*; also *alast(e*, *o least*, ALAST *adv.*; in Ormin ***att tallre lattste*** = at the last of all): at the end, in the end, finally, ultimately. In ME. poetry often = 'in fine', 'after all'.

c **1200** ORMIN 13319 Te Laferrd Jesu Crist Himm seȝȝde att tallre lattste, Nu shallt tu nemmnedd ben Cefas. *c* **1205** LAY. 26785 A þan laste [*c* **1275** at þan laste] ne mihte mon wite wha oðerne smite. *a* **1225** *Leg. Kath.* 41 O least wið stronge tintreohen & licomliche pinen. *c* **1340** *Cursor M.* 4274 (Trin.) At þe laste hit most be kidde. **1362** LANGL. *P. Pl.* A. II. 110 Hit schal bi-sitten oure soules sore atte laste. *c* **1374** CHAUCER *Boeth.* II. pr. vi. 54 And at þe laste I may conclude þe same þinge of al þe ȝiftes of fortune. *c* **1386** —— *Prol.* 707 Trewely to tellen atte laste, He was in chirche a noble ecclesiaste. *a* **1400–50** *Alexander* 1007 Be þe floure neuer sa fresche it fadis at þe last. *a* **1450** *Knt. de la Tour* (1868) 18 Atte the laste she waxe right familier with me. **1535** COVERDALE *Ps.* lxxxix. 13 Turne the agayne (o Lorde) at the last, and be gracious vnto thy seruauntes. **1596** SHAKS. *Tam. Shr.* V. i. 130 Happilie I haue arriued at the last Vnto the wished hauen of my blisse. **1620** SKELTON *Quix.* II. IV. iv. 46 It is not lost, that comes at last. **1668** DRYDEN *Even. Love* Prol. 28 But at the last you threw them off with scorn. **1681** FLAVEL *Meth. Grace* v. 67 Nothing can comfort a man that must to hell at last. **1711** STEELE *Spect.* No. 2 ¶1 His Temper being jovial, he at last got over it. **1819** SHELLEY *Cenci* II. i. 57 O! before worse comes of it 'Twere wise to die: it ends in that at last. **1821** KEATS *Isabella* xxii, And at the last, these men of cruel clay Cut Mercy..to the bone. **1868** DICKENS *Uncomm. Trav.* xxviii, At last to my great joy, I received notice of his safe arrival. **1886** RUSKIN *Præterita* I.

268 Here at last I had found a man who spoke only of what he had seen, and known.

b. ***at*** **(†** ***the*****)** ***long last***: at the end of all; finally, ultimately. [Perh. associated with LAST *sb.*[4]]

1523 SKELTON *Garl. Laurel* 1398 How than lyke a man he wan the barbican With a sawte of solace at the longe last. **1692** R. L'ESTRANGE *Fables* cxcviii. 168 This Woman, I say ..was at the Long-Last prevail'd upon to hear the Will read. **1864** CARLYLE *Fredk. Gt.* IV. 211 At long last, on Sunday. **1870** LOWELL *Study Wind.* 131 We can find a useful and instructive solace in a hearty abuse of human nature, which at the long last is always to blame. **1923** W. DE LA MARE *Private View* (1953) 244 And at long last the acquisition of a technical mastery in any art..is by no means nothing but a gain. **1926** *Manch. Guardian Weekly* Feb. 104/1 The Government followed up the references to agriculture..by launching at long last its land policy. **1936** KING EDWARD VIII in *Times* 12 Dec. 14/4 (*abdication speech*) At long last I am able to say a few words of my own. *a* **1936** KIPLING *Something of Myself* (1937) vi. 159 At long last we were left apologising to a deeply-indignant people. **1971** J. AIKEN *Nightly Deadshade* ii. 21 Someone answers the phone at long last, making me jump.

†**c. by the last**: at the latest. *Obs.*

a **1175** *Cott. Hom.* 231 He..sette ænne deȝie þat hi alle be þe latst to þa deȝie þer were. *Ibid.* 235. *c* **1330** *Arth. & Merl.* 4786 (Kölbing) And that strengþe him last Fort arne-morwe bi þe last.

†**d. in the last**: in the end, finally. *Obs. rare.*

1607 SHAKS. *Cor.* v. vi. 42 And in the last, When he had carried Rome, and that we look'd For no lesse Spoile, then Glory.

e. to the last: † (*a*) to the utmost; (*b*) up to or until the end, *esp.* up to the last moment of life, to the point of death; also ***till the last***.

c **1400** *Destr. Troy* 12015 When the Cité was sesit & serchet to the last. **1602** SHAKS. *Ham.* II. i. 100 He seem'd to finde his way without his eyes, For out adores he went..And to the last, bended their light on me. **1719** DE FOE *Crusoe* II. xvi. (1840) 326 He was always the same to the last. *c* **1730** *Moribundus* in *Buccleuch MSS.* (Hist. MSS. Comm.) I. 380 This fate must necessarily attend the honestest who pays to the last. **1780** COWPER *Progr. Err.* 107 It..brands him to the last What atheists call him—a designing knave. **1849** MACAULAY *Hist. Eng.* v. I. 665 To the last she preserved a tranquil courage. **1855** *Ibid.* xii. III. 196 The men who guarded these walls..were determined to resist to the last. **1864** TENNYSON *Aylmer's F.* 714 And these had been together from the first; They might have been together till the last. **1878** F. HALL in *Nation* (N.Y.) XXVI. 422/1 Almost from his boyhood, and to the very last, his thoughts were well-nigh engrossed by the radical problems of mind and matter. **1885** *Manch. Exam.* 23 May 5/4 He refused to the last the religious consolations which the Archbishop of Paris was wishful to offer him.

B. *adv.*

1. After all others; at the latest time; at the end. *Occas.* coupled with *least.*

c **888** K. ÆLFRED *Boeth.* (Sedgefield) xxxiv. § 10 þær þær.. hit hraðost weaxan mæȝ & latost wealowian. *c* **975** *Rushw. Gosp.* Matt. xxii. 27 þe lætest [*Lindisf.* ðe læt-mesta] þonne ealra & þæt wif ek a-swalt. **1382** WYCLIF *2 Sam.* xix. 11 Whi ben ȝe comen last to brynge aȝen the kyng into his hows? *c* **1420** *Pallad. on Husb.* x. 155 Gith is last eke in this mone ysowe. *c* **1450** *ME. Med. Bk.* (Heinrich) 145 Geue þe seek to drinke last, when he gos to bedde. **1526** TINDALE *Matt.* xxii. 27 Laste of all the woman dyed also. **1562** J. HEYWOOD *Prov. & Epigr.* (1867) 160 He that cumth last make all fast. *c* **1600** SHAKS. *Sonn.* xc. 9 If thou wilt leave me, do not leave me last. **1613** —— *Hen. VIII*, III. ii. 444 Love thy selfe last. **1667** MILTON *P.L.* III. 278 Nor man the least Though last created. **1715–20** POPE *Iliad* XXIII. 607 Last came Admetus, thy unhappy son. **1808** SCOTT *Marm.* I. viii, Last, twenty yeomen two and two.

2. a. On the occasion next before the present; in the last instance; most lately; latest.

a **1300** *Cursor M.* 3989 Vte-ouer þis flum, last quen i ferd. *c* **1300** *Havelok* 678 Þanne i last[e] spak with þe. **1526** *Pilgr. Perf.* (W. de W. 1531) 307 Those seuen wordes..whiche thou spake last before thy moost precyous deth. **1591** SHAKS. *Two Gent.* II. i. 12, I was last chidden for being too slow. **1613** PURCHAS *Pilgrimage* (1614) 632 Since I last published these Relations, certaine Letters have beene printed. **1719** DE FOE *Crusoe* II. xiii. (1840) 280 He came last from Astracan. **1818** CRUISE *Digest* (ed. 2) III. 408 The paternal grandmother of the person last seised. **1819** SHELLEY *Cenci* v. ii. 22 When did you see him last? **1822** —— *Hellas* 209 The robes they last On Death's bare ribs had cast.

†**b.** ***last past***, also Sc. ***last by past***, ***last was***: (with dates) = LAST *a.* 3 b; also (of a period of time) extending to the present, (the) past (year, etc.). *Obs.*

1411 *Rolls of Parlt.* III. 650/1 The Saterday neghst after the fest of Seint Michael last passed. **1461** *Paston Lett.* No. 368 I. 543 The Bysshop of Norwich sente us on Thrusday laste paste to gader the dymes. **1484** CAXTON *Fables of Æsop* IV. xvii, What hast thou done al the somer last passed. **1549** LATIMER *1st Serm. bef. Edw. VI* (Arb.) 19 Sermons.. preached in Lente last past. *a* **1557** *Diurn. Occurr.* (Bannatyne) 123 Vpoun the xxv day of August last by past. **1559** KENNEDY *Let.* in *Wodr. Soc. Misc.* (1844) 266 The day ..(quhilk wes Sounday last wes). **1711** STEELE *Spect.* No. 48 ¶2 The Beau has varied his Dress every Day of his Life for these thirty Years last past. *Ibid.* No. 53 ¶7, I am a Gentleman who for many Years last past have been well known to be truly Splenetick.

3. As the last thing to be mentioned or considered; in the last place, lastly.

1560 DAUS tr. *Sleidane's Comm.* 114 b, Belmen are hyred ..to declare the name..also wher and whan they shal be buried, and last to exhorte the people to praye for the dead. **1597** SHAKS. *2 Hen. IV*, v. v. Epil., First, my Feare: then, my Curtsie: last, my Speech. **1613** —— *Hen. VIII*, III. ii. 403 Last, that the Lady Anne, Whom the King hath in secrecie long married, This day was view'd in open. **1819** SHELLEY *Cenci* III. i. 354 You may Conceive such half conjectures as I do, From her fixed paleness, and the lofty grief Of her stern brow..and last From this. **1851** KINGSLEY *Yeast* xvii, Last, but not least, is it not the very property of man that he is a spirit invested with flesh and blood?

4. In the end, finally.

1667 MILTON *P.L.* VI. 797 By force or fraud Weening to prosper, and at length prevaile Against God and Messiah, or to fall In universal ruin last. *Ibid.* XI. 542 In thy blood will reigne A melancholly damp of cold and dry To waigh thy spirits down, and last consume The Balme of Life. *a* **1700** DRYDEN *Ovid's Met.* x. *Pygmal.* 12 Pleas'd with his Idol, he commends, admires, Adores; and last, the Thing ador'd, desires. **1859** TENNYSON *Enid* 42 The King Mused for a little on his plea, but, last, Allowing it, the prince and Enid rode..to the shores of Severn. **1871** R. ELLIS tr. *Catullus* lxiv. 239 So for a while that charge did Theseus faithfully cherish. Last, it melted away.

C. Combinations.

Comb. **1.** Chiefly of the adv. with ppl. adjs., as ***last-born***, ***-cited***, ***-erected***, ***-made***, ***-mentioned***, ***-named***.

1868 MILMAN *St. Paul's* 230 And, *last-born, Christian tolerance and charity. **1659** PEARSON *Creed* (1859) 164 If then we consider the two *last-cited verses by themselves. **1863** H. COX *Instit.* I. viii. 129 The last cited statute. **1807** VANCOUVER *Agric. Devon* (1813) 97 In the *last-erected cottages, I..have made a double roof. **1626** JACKSON *Creed* VIII. I. v. §1 The new and *last-made visible creature man. **1863** LYELL *Antiq. Man* 25 This *last-mentioned race. **1838** DICKENS *O. Twist* xlii, The *last-named apartment. **1869** DUNKIN *Midn. Sky* 59 The last-named being near the horizon.

2. *occas.* of the adj. qualifying a sb., the whole being used attrib., as ***last-century***, ***-chance***, ***-gasp***, ***-resort***, ***-time***, ***-war***, ***-wicket***; **last-minute**, (given, done, made, etc.) at the latest possible time.

1876 GEO. ELIOT *Dan. Der.* II. xx. 12 Last-century children. **1962** *Aeroplane* CIV. 18/1 Carbon deposits had clogged the 'last chance' filter, causing the oil starvation of No. 2 bearing in the JT3D-1 turbofan. **1963** J. LUSBY in B. James *Austral. Short Stories* 234 He was giving the Eccentric a last-chance test in individual combat. **1974** G. JENKINS *Bridge of Magpies* xvi. 239 It was a desperate last-chance throw. **1921** D. H. LAWRENCE *Let.* 2 Mar. (1962) II. 643 K.—who is doing the last-gasp touch. **1971** R. THOMAS *Backup Men* xxii. 191 All last-gasp businesses with no need for much of a front. **1972** *Sat. Rev.* (U.S.) 6 May 34/3 Our strategists have spoken too often of 'last-gasp' offensives for us to believe that this one will be any different. **1920** *Ladies' Home Jrnl.* May 140/2 Last-minute sketches from Paris. **1929** J. B. PRIESTLEY *Good Companions* II. iii. 329 Jimmy had a last-minute inspiration. **1931** E. LINKLATER *Juan in Amer.* III. i. 204 I've been doing some last-minute Christmas shopping. **1948** 'J. TEY' *Franchise Affair* xix. 227 A last-minute reprieve with the rope round the hero's neck? **1974** M. YORKE *Mortal Remains* II. i. 39 People were trying to buy last-minute tickets for the day's excursions. **1950** J. DEMPSEY *Championship Fighting* 170 The pull-away should only be used as a last-resort defence. **1965** H. KAHN *On Escalation* i. 10 The threat of a strike or a lockout is ever present as a last-resort pressure for compromise. **1894** W. C. SIMPSON in *Mem.* (1899) 132 The votes are to be given to the most pressing last-time case. **1942** S. SPENDER *Ruins & Visions* 42 The ghastly last-war voices. **1959** *Encounter* July 29/2 The plan..envisaged the defence of Western Europe almost completely in last-war terms. **1909** *Westm. Gaz.* 1 June 12/2 A great last-wicket stand might once in a way occur. **1975** *Times* 6. Jan. 7/7 A last-wicket partnership of 37 between Mallett and Thomson.

last (lɑːst, læst), *v.*[1] Forms: 1 **lǽstan, léstan**, 2–4 **lasten, lesten**, 3 **læsten, leasten**, *Orm.* **lasstenn**, 4–5 **laste, -in, leste, -yn, lesst**, 5–6 *Sc.* **lest**, 4– **last**; also YLAST. *pa. t.* 1 **lǽste**, 2 **lastede**, 3 **læste, leaste**, 4–5 **last(e, leste**, 4 **lasted(e, -et, -id(e, lested(e**, 4, 6 **lastit**, 5– **lasted**. *pres. pple.* 4 **lastand(e, -onde**. *pa. pple.* 4 **last**, 5 *Sc.* **lestyd**. See also YLAST. [OE. *lǽstan* wk. vb., corresponds to OFris. *lâsta*, *lêsta* to fulfil, to pay (duties), OS. *lêstian* to execute, OHG. (MHG., mod.G.) *leisten* to afford, yield, Goth. *laistjan* to follow, f. OTeut. *laisti-* (*-to-*): see LAST *sb.*[1]]

†**1.** *trans.* **a.** In OE. only: To follow (a leader; with *dative*), to follow, pursue (a course, a practice; with *accusative*). **b.** To accomplish, carry out, execute (a command), perform (a promise); to pay (tribute), to abide by, maintain (peace). *Obs.*

Beowulf (Gr.) 2663 Leofa biowulf læst eall tela. **837** *Charter of Badanoð* in *O.E. Texts* 450 Ic biddo..ðæt se monn se hiȝon londes unnen to brucanne ða ilcan wisan leste on swæsendum to minre tide. **971** *Blickl. Hom.* 185 Gif þu wilt his wordum hyran & his bebodu læstan, þu forleosest þin rice. *a* **1000** *Boeth. Metr.* i. 27 (Sedgefield) Þeah wæs maȝorinca mod mid Crecum, ȝif hi leodfruman læstan dorsten. *c* **1200** *Trin. Coll. Hom.* 189 He him seluen com and lestede his bihese. *c* **1205** LAY. 9848 Þu mine fader swore to lasten alche ȝere..gauel in to Rome. *c* **1250** *Gen. & Ex.* 2906 Ðat ic ðe haue hoten wel, Ic it sal lesten euerilc del. *c* **1315** SHOREHAM 65 To leste Of chaste professioun Hys solempne by-heste. **1387** TREVISA *Higden* (Rolls) III. 383 [Philip] wolde by-hote more þan he wolde laste. *a* **1420** HOCCLEVE *De Reg. Princ.* 2218 Hym oghte..heete naght a deel By word ne bond, but if he wole it laste. **1480** CAXTON *Chron. Eng.* ccxvii. 204 This pees for to holde and last.

2. a. *intr.* Of a state of things, a process, period of time: To continue, endure, go on.

a **900** CYNEWULF *Crist* 1288 Þonne him daȝas læstun. **1154** *O.E. Chron.* an. 1137 (Laud MS.) And ðet lastede þa xix wintre wile Stephne was King. *c* **1200** ORMIN 2228 And tatt himm shollde hiss kinedom A lasstenn butenn ende. *a* **1225** *Ancr. R.* 20 Siggeð non efter mete..þe hwule þet sumer lested. *c* **1250** *Gen. & Ex.* 2952 Ðis wreche, in al egypte riȝt, Lestede fulle seuene niȝt. **13..** *Sir Beues* 2789 (MS. A.) So be-twene hem leste þat fiȝt, Til it was þe þerke niȝt. *c* **1430** *Hymns Virg.* 87 It is likened to a schadewe þat may not longe leste. *a* **1500** *Flower & Leaf* 288 The justes last an houre and more. **1535** STEWART *Cron. Scot.* XXI. 96 This seige lastit langer nor the seigeris thairof luikit ffor. **1580** SIDNEY *Ps.* IX. iii, Their renown, which seem'd so like to last, Thou dost put out. **1611** BIBLE *Judg.* xiv. 17 Shee wept before him the seuen dayes, while the feast lasted. **1697** DRYDEN *Virg. Georg.* II. 405 For length of Ages lasts his happy Reign. **1781** COWPER *Hope* 746 These shall last when night has quenched the pole. **1806** *Med. Jrnl.* XV. 507 The pain returned about eleven, and lasted till one. **1855** MACAULAY *Hist. Eng.* xviii. IV. 190 While the civil war lasted, his vassals could not tend their herds..in peace. **1895** *Law Times* XCIX. 499/2 Even if fine weather lasts, days are considerably shorter at this time of year.

†**b.** With complement or prepositional phrase: To continue in a specified condition, course of action, etc.; to remain or dwell *in* (*at*, etc.) a place. Also, ***to last long that...not***, to be a long time before doing so-and-so. *Obs.*

c **1250** *Gen. & Ex.* 4147 And ðoȝ him [Moyses] lestede hise siȝte briȝt. *c* **1340** *Cursor M.* 2479 (Trin.) Abraham last & his þan Bisyde þe lond of canaan. **1375** BARBOUR *Bruce* XX. 272 In liff quhill he lestit ay, With all our fais dred war we. *c* **1380** WYCLIF *Wks.* (1880) 71 Graunte þi seruauntes grace to laste trewe in þe gospel. **1382** —— *Acts* xii. 16 Forsoth Petre lastide knockynge. *c* **1385** CHAUCER *L.G.W.* 791 *Cleopatra*, And longe hym thoughte that the sunne laste That it nere gon vndyr the se a doun. *c* **1400** *Apol. Loll.* 38 If þei last in þer synne,..þer blessing is turnid in to cursing. *c* **1470** HENRY *Wallace* I. 412 On athir side full fast on him thai dange; Gret perell was giff thai had lestyt lang. **1513** DOUGLAS *Æneis* X. v. 51 Amangis the fludis for to leyf and lest. **1667** MILTON *P.L.* VI. 693 Whence in perpetual fight they needs must last Endless, and no solution will be found.

3. a. To hold out, continue fresh, unbroken, undecayed, unexhausted. Also (now *rarely*) of persons: To continue in life. Also with *out*.

a **1300** *Cursor M.* 12764 Ferli þam thoght hu he moght last, Wit sua gret trauail and fast. **1390** GOWER *Conf.* II. 195 While thilke mirrour last, Ther was no lond, which [etc.]. *c* **1400** MAUNDEV. (Roxb.) ii. 5 Þai trowed þat he schuld hafe bene hingand apon þat crosse als lang as þat crosse myght last. *a* **1400–50** *Alexander* 989 Aires for nane alyens quils Alexander lastis. **1486** *Bk. St. Albans* E v, While that frute may last his time is neuer past. **1596** SHAKS. *Merch. V.* III. ii. 207 At last, if promise last, I got a promise of this faire one heere To haue her loue. **1602** —— *Ham.* v. i. 183 A Tanner will last you nine year. **1631** GOUGE *God's Arrows* III. §65. 304 To annoint their rolles..with a liquour..which kept them from rotting, and made them last the longer. **1703** MOXON *Mech. Exerc.* 239 Those..Bricks..will last to Eternity. **1715–20** POPE *Iliad* XXIV. 779 The rock for ever lasts, the tears for ever flow. **1849** RUSKIN *Sev. Lamps* vi. §6. 168, I would have, then, our ordinary dwelling-houses built to last. **1874** HELPS *Soc. Press.* ii. 17 The cows do not last a third part of the time that they would last in the country. **1881** MRS. J. H. RIDDELL *Senior Partner* III. 56 What would hinder him lasting out to ninety [years] or a hundred even? **1884** *Spectator* 4 Oct. 1286/1 He was able by rationing the townsmen as well as his troops to make this supply last to the present time. **1921** G. B. SHAW *Back to Methuselah* IV. II. 194 You people lived on the assumption that you were going to last out for ever and ever and ever.

b. With indirect obj.: To suffice for a person's (or animal's) requirements for a specified time.

1530 PALSGR. 604/1 This gowne hath lasted him longe. **1698** FRYER *Acc. E. India & P.* 263 A stock of Hard Eggs.. which will last them from Spahaun to the Port. **1719** DE FOE *Crusoe* II. iv. (1840) 71 They should have a proportion of corn given them to last them eight months. **1856** KANE *Arct. Expl.* I. vi. 56 Our two bears lasted the cormorants but eight days. **1893** EARL DUNMORE *Pamirs* II. 112 As much corn.. as will last us a month.

c. quasi-*trans.* (*a*) To continue in vigour as long as or longer than (something else). Now only with *out*. † (*b*) To sustain, hold out under or against.

c **1500** *Lancelot* 811 Bot al to few thei war, and mycht nocht lest This gret Rout that cummyth one so fast. **1603** SHAKS. *Meas. for M.* II. i. 139 This will last out a night in Russia When nights are longest there. *a* **1611** BEAUM. & FL. *Maid's Trag.* III. ii, I pray, my legges Will last that pace that I will carrie them. **1658** SIR T. BROWNE *Hydriot.* v. 27 Old Families last not three Oakes. **1875** JOWETT *Plato* (ed. 2) IV. 290 He who lasts out his competitors in the game without missing, shall be our King. **1878** SPURGEON *Treas. Dav.* Ps. civ. 23 If labour lasts out the average daylight it is certainly all that any man ought to expect of another.

†**4.** To extend in space; to reach, stretch. *Obs.*

c **1205** LAY. 5819 Ne leaste hit [a ditch] na wiht ane mile. **13..** *K. Alis.* 2596 Of his people theo grete pray Laste twenty myle way. *c* **1315** SHOREHAM 3 Thy laddre nys nauȝt of wode That may to hevene leste. *c* **1386** CHAUCER *Clerk's T.* 266 Ther..deynteuous vitaille..may be founde as fer as last ytaille. *c* **1400** *Lanfranc's Cirurg.* 108 Þe firste boon.. lastiþ to þe seem þat departiþ þe heed quarter. *c* **1450** *Merlin* 274 More than a myle lasted the route. **1470–85** MALORY *Arthur* XVII. iv, He hunted in a woode of his whiche lasted vnto the see. **1493** *Festivall* (W. de W. 1515) 53 b, Than he was ware of a pyller of fyre that lasted from erth to heuen. **1577** HELLOWES *Gueuara's Chron.* 29 A broad high waye that lasted two leagues and halfe.

†**last**, *v.*[2] *Obs. rare*$^{-1}$. [OE. (*ȝe*)*hlæstan*, f. *hlæst* LAST *sb.*[2]] *trans.* To load, burden.

[*c* **900** tr. *Bæda's Hist.* v. ix. (1890) 412 Mid þy heo ða þæt scip ȝehlested hefdan mid þæm þingum.] **13..** *E.E. Allit. P.* A. 1145, I loked among his meyny schene, How þay wyth lyf wern laste & lade.

†**last**, *v.*[3] [ON. *lasta*, f. *last-*, *lǫstr* blame.] *trans.* To blaspheme, blame.

a **1225** *Juliana* 70 And feng to fiten his mawmez and lasten his lauerd. *a* **1225** *Ancr. R.* 352 Preise him, laste him,..al him is iliche leof. *c* **1300** *Thrush & Night.* 107 in Hazl. *E.P.P.* I. 52 Thou lastest hem, thou hauest wou.

last (lɑːst, læst), *v.*⁴ [f. LAST *sb.*¹] *trans.* To put (a boot or shoe) on the last.

1880 *Times* 21 Sept. 4/4 Light boots..are lasted inside out, sewed by machine as by hand, and then turned.

lastage (ˈlɑːstɪdʒ, ˈlæst-). Also 4–5, 8 **lestage**, 7 **lastidge**. [a. AF. and F. *lestage* (med.L. *lestagium*), f. *lest* = LAST *sb.*²]

1. A toll payable by traders attending fairs and markets. *Obs.* exc. *Hist.*

[**1290** *Rolls of Parlt.* I. 60/1 Thomas de Hamull' recepit lestagium..de omnibus Mercandisis. **1292** BRITTON I. xx. §1 De pleder en sa court pletz de vee de naam, ou de aver lestage, ou amerciement de ses tenauntz.] **1387** TREVISA *Higden* (Rolls) II. 97 Lestage, custom i-chalanged in chepynges and in feyres. **1502** ARNOLDE *Chron.* (1811) 17 That alle the citezens of London be quyt off toll and lastage. **1616** BULLOKAR, *Lastage*, a terme in the common law, which signifieth to be quite of a certaine payment in faires and markets, for carrying of things where a man will.

†**2.** The ballast of a ship. *Obs.*

[**1397–8** *Act 21 Rich. II*, c. 18 Toutz maneres dez Niefs au dit porte..portent ovesq eux tout lour lastage des bones piers covenables pur lestuffure de les Beeknes susditz.] *c* **1440** *Promp. Parv.* 299/1 Lestage of a shyppe, *saburra*. **1543** tr. *Act 21 Rich. II*, c. 18 All maner of shyppes..shall brynge with them all theyr lastage of good stones. **1736** AINSWORTH *Lat. Dict.* II, *Săburra*..Ballast, or lastage.

3. A payment for liberty to load a ship; a port duty levied at so much per 'last'.

1592 in Picton *L'pool Munic. Rec.* (1883) I. 70 [the various heads under which dues were claimed are set forth as follows:—] Daiage; Lastage; Wharfage [etc.]. **1603** OWEN *Pembrokeshire* (1891) 164 Anchorage, lastage, and balast. **1706** in Picton *L'pool Munic. Rec.* (1886) II. 21 Free from all Toll, Passage, Lastage. **1759** *Chron.* in *Ann. Reg.* 97/2 The better regulation of lastage and ballastage in the Thames. **1789** BRAND *Hist. Newcastle* II. 714 Lastage is three-pence per last [of goods on board ships piloted]. **1865** C. R. MANNING in *Norfolk Archæology* VII. 4 Sir William Gerberge was possessed of a moiety of the lastage at Yarmouth.

4. An impost levied on the catch of herrings at so much per last.

1601 J. KEYMOR *Dutch Fish.* (1664) 4 There was paid above 300000*l.* 14 years past..for Exizes, Licences, Wastage, and Lastage. **1641** S. SMITH *Herring Buss Trade* 2 In the Lastidge where the nets are haild in.

5. = TONNAGE. Cf. LAST *sb.*² 2.

1858 *Merc. Marine Mag.* V. 247 The Tonnage or Lastage of Ships.

†**6.** Garbage, rubbish. *Obs. rare*⁻⁰.

1691 BLOUNT *Law Dict.*, *Lastage*, was also used for Garbage, Rubbidge, or such like Filth.

7. *Comb.* **lastage-free** *a.*, free of lastage (sense 3).

1395 in *Rolls Parlt.* V. 405/1 Quod sint Wrecfry & Witefry, Lestagefry & Lunatofry.

†**lastage**, *v. Obs.* [f. the sb.] *trans.* To supply with lastage or ballast.

1552 HULOET, Lastaged or balased, *saburratus*. **1599** MINSHEU *Sp. Dict.*, To lastage, or balasse, *lastrar*.

last-ditch, *a.* [See DITCH *sb.*¹ 5.] Of opposition, resistance, etc.: maintained to the end. Of an effort, etc.: made at the last minute in an attempt to avert disaster. Also **last-'ditcher**, one who fights to the last ditch; **last-'ditchery**.

1909 *Westm. Gaz.* 30 Jan. 2/1 The only part he is likely to take in the Social Revolution is to be what may be called a last-ditcher in the attempt to resist it. **1927** *Daily Express* 19 Nov. 3/1 A constituency which is to be congratulated on a true last ditcher. **1928** *Daily Tel.* 17 July 18/3 There are few performers who have decided not to broadcast. Almost the 'last-ditcher' is perhaps Harry Tate. **1932** *Mind* XLI. 53 Formal Logic dies hard. It still commands the services of numbers of 'last ditchers'. **1936** 'J. TEY' *Shilling for Candles* i. 6 'Might have walked into the water till she drowned,' said Bill, who was a last-ditcher by nature. *Ibid.*, 'Might have died of an overdose of bulls-eyes,' said Potticary, who approved of last ditchery in Arabia but found it boring to live with. **1951** KOESTLER *Age of Longing* II. i. 205, I would rather have been one of the last-ditchers at Thermopylae. **1951** M. MCLUHAN *Mech. Bride* 44/1 A last-ditch stand of denuded minds. **1955** *Bull. Atomic Sci.* Feb. 54/2 If the French in their last ditch stand at Dien Bien Phu had appealed for U.S. nuclear aid, there would have been similar reactions. **1961** W. VAUGHAN-THOMAS *Anzio* viii. 171 Some got as far as the Loyals manning their last-ditch line on the Lateral Road. **1961** M. BEADLE *These Ruins are Inhabited* (1963) vi. 76 All that defeated them was a last-ditch appeal. **1971** *Times* 27 Apr. 9/5 Charlton himself surely was offside before McNab made his last ditch effort to recover the situation. **1973** *Times* 27 Aug. 3/1 Colonel Gaddafi, the Libyan leader, today began a last-ditch attempt to forge a full union with Egypt after his unexpected arrival in Cairo.

laster (ˈlɑːstə(r), ˈlæst-), *sb.*¹ [f. LAST *sb.*¹ + -ER¹.] In *Bootmaking*, a workman who shapes a boot or shoe, by fixing the parts smoothly on a last.

1878 *Ure's Dict. Arts* IV. 121 The sole..is now taken in hand by the laster, who secures it by a few tacks to the upper [etc.]. **1885** *Harper's Mag.* Jan. 282/2 The laster is about the only shoemaker left who can still talk..of his 'kit'.

laster (ˈlɑːstə(r), ˈlæst-), *sb.*² [f. LAST *v.*¹ + -ER¹.] One who or that which lasts. **a.** Of a person: One who has staying power. **b.** Of a fruit: That continues fresh and sound.

1719 LONDON & WISE *Compl. Gard.* IV. 56 The Russellet. It's no long laster, but soon grows soft and pappy. **1861** HUGHES *Tom Brown at Oxf.* xvi. (1889) 152, I put him down as a laster, and he has trained well.

[**lastery**, spurious word in Dicts., is from the early edd. of Spenser *F.Q.* II. ix. st. 41; but in the 'Faults escap'd in the Printing' the word is corrected to CASTORY, q.v.]

Lastex (ˈlæstɛks). Also **lastex**. The proprietary name of an elastic yarn formed from a combination of rubber (see also quot. 1968) with silk, cotton, or rayon, used in the manufacture of corsetry, etc.

1934 *Trade Marks Jrnl.* 17 Jan. 70/1 *Lastex*. Yarns and threads composed of a mixture of india-rubber and silk, the silk predominating. Dunlop-Revere Thread Co., Ltd.,.. Birmingham. **1935** *Times* 12 June 15/6 Bathing suits are of woollen fabrics woven with lastex yarn. **1946** 'G. ORWELL' in *Tribune* 8 Nov. 12/2 Someone has just sent me a copy of an American fashion magazine... Here are a few sample sentences..'Gentle discipline for curves in lacy lastex pantie-girdle'. **1951** J. D. SALINGER *Catcher in Rye* xviii. 161 He wore those white lastex kind of swimming trunks. **1955** *Punch* 16 Mar. 348/3 Beautifully less! The ideal is now achieved with a caress of nylon, lastex, and lace. **1968** J. IRONSIDE *Fashion Alphabet* 236 Lastex yarns... The rubber is now being replaced by synthetic elastomeric fibres, which are easier to wash and quicker to dry.

†**'lastful**, *a. Obs. rare.* Also 1 **ȝelástful**. [f. OE. *ȝe-lást* duty + -FUL.] Helpful, serviceable.

c **1000** *Laws of Æthelstan* VI. c. 4 (Schmid) 160 Ðæt ælc man wære oðrum ȝelastfull. *c* **1200** *Trin. Coll. Hom.* 183 Þu ware me lastful on alle þo þe ich wolde we ware onmode godes wille to done.

lasting (ˈlɑːstɪŋ, ˈlæst-), *sb.* [Elliptical use of LASTING *ppl. a.*] A durable kind of cloth; = EVERLASTING B. 3.

1782 PENNANT *Journ. Chester to Lond.* 141 The making and sale of shags, camblets, lastings, tammies, &c. **1844** G. DODD *Textile Manuf.* iv. 113, 3–4 Lastings, 3–4 Fancy Lastings. **1857** JAMES *Hist. Worsted Manuf.* x. 362 There were different sorts of lastings as prunelles wrought with three healds. Also serge de Berry. **1871** *Echo* 14 Jan., Other branches of trade,..such as damask and lastings, have much benefitted by the war. **1878** A. BARLOW *Weaving* 440 Lastings, a strong cloth used for ladies' boots and made of hard twisted yarn. **1895** *Strand Mag.* Mar. 311 The man is clothed in a suit of 'lasting'—that curious leathery material affected by the London apprentices in the days of Queen Elizabeth.

b. *attrib.*

1872–6 VOYLE & STEVENSON *Milit. Dict.*, *Lasting Cloth*, a material similar to prunella cloth... It has the property of not readily catching fire. **1892** *Labour Commission* Gloss., *Lasting-shoes*, shoes of which the tops or upper parts are made from lasting.

lasting (ˈlɑːstɪŋ, ˈlæst-), *vbl. sb.*¹ Also 4–5 **lesting**. [f. LAST *v.*¹ + -ING¹.] The action of LAST *v.*¹; continuance, duration, permanence.

c **1340** *Cursor M.* 19562 (Fairf.) In lasting of cristen mannis life. **1375** BARBOUR *Bruce* IX. 283 Thai had bath bot schort lesting, For thai deit soyn eftir syne. *c* **1400** tr. *Secreta Secret., Gov. Lordsh.* 108 After þe quantyte of þy tresour is þe lastyng and þe defens, of þy kyngdom. *c* **1440** *Promp. Parv.* 299/1 Lestynge, or yndurynge, *perduracio*. **1580** HOLLYBAND *Treas. Fr. Tong*, *Longue durée*, of long during or lasting. **1597** BACON *Ess.*, *Reg. Health* (Arb.) 58 To be free minded, and chearefully disposed at howers of meate, and of sleepe, and of exercise, is the best precept of long lasting. **1609** B. JONSON *Sil. Wom.* II. iii, Thou art made for euer.. if this felicitie haue lasting. **1715** LEONI *Palladio's Archit.* (1742) I. 30 To prevent the Doors and Windows from being press'd with too much weight..is of no little importance for the lasting of the Building. **1765** A. DICKSON *Treat. Agric.* II. (ed. 2) 230 The lasting of the iron plough, and the value of the iron.

b. Staying power; = LAST *sb.*⁴ 2. Also *attrib.*

1860 RUSSELL *Diary India* II. 346 Essentials to develope a man in stature, or strength, or 'lasting'. **1898** *St. James's Gaz.* 12 Nov. 4/1 That mysterious thing known as 'lasting power', or 'staying quality'.

†**'lasting**, *vbl. sb.*² *Obs.* Also 3 **lastung**. [f. LAST *v.*³ + -ING¹.] Abuse, blame, reproach.

a **1225** *Ancr. R.* 66 Vor heo hunteð efter pris, & kecceð lastunge. *Ibid.* 212 Þuruh more lastunge heo wrencheð hit to wurse. *c* **1380** WYCLIF *Wks.* (1880) 270 A þef is more worþi to be suffrid þan þe lastynge of a lesyngmongere.

lasting (ˈlɑːstɪŋ, ˈlæst-), *vbl. sb.*³ [f. LAST *v.*⁴ + -ING¹.] The action of shaping a boot or shoe on the last: chiefly *attrib.*, as ***lasting-awl***, ***-machine***, †***-stick***; **lasting-jack**, **-pincers** (see quots.).

1719 D'URFEY *Pills* VI. 92 My Lasts..and my lasting Sticks. **1875** KNIGHT *Dict. Mech.*, *Lasting-jack*, an implement to hold the last while straining and securing the upper thereon. *Ibid.* *Lasting-pincers* (*Shoemaking*), a tool to grip the edges of the upper leather of a boot and draw it over the last. **1880** *Encycl. Brit.* XXI. 830/2 Lasting is a crucial operation, for, unless the upper is drawn smoothly and equally over the last, leaving neither crease nor wrinkle, the form of the boot will be bad. **1895** *Daily News* 13 Mar. 3/2 There is a magnetic lasting machine which takes up the tacks and presses them into a boot when it is on the last. **1907** *Westm. Gaz.* 4 Nov. 8/4 This method of 'lasting' is new. **1968** J. IRONSIDE *Fashion Alphabet* 126 The lasting, i.e. the making of the upper on the last.

lasting (ˈlɑːstɪŋ, ˈlæst-), *ppl. a.* and *adj.* Forms: 2–3 **lestend**, **-inde**, 3 **leastinde**, 4–5 **lastand**, **-end**, **-ond**, 4–6 *Sc.* and *north.* **lestand**, 4– **lasting**. [f. LAST *v.*¹ + -ING².]

1. Continuing, enduring; also of long continuance, permanent. (In early use often contextually = 'everlasting'.) †***always*** (or †***ay***) ***lasting*** = EVERLASTING.

c **1175** *Lamb. Hom.* 159 Eche hele, lestende liht, and endeles lif. *a* **1225** *Leg. Kath.* 2294 To arisen from ream to aa lestinde lahtre. **1258** *Charter Hen. III* in Tyrrell *Hist. Eng.* (1700) II. App. 25 We willen thet this beo stede-fæst and lestinde. *c* **1330** R. BRUNNE *Chron.* (1810) 221 Stoutly was þat stoure, long lastand þat fight. **1375** BARBOUR *Bruce* XX. 620 God..Bryng ws hye till hevynnis bliss, Quhar allwayis lestand liking is. *c* **1440** *York Myst.* i. 46 In blys for to byde in hys blyssyng, Ay lastande. *c* **1470** HENRY *Wallace* VII. 104 To thi reward thou sall haiff lestand blyss. ? *a* **1550** in *Dunbar's Poems* (1893) 328 Fall on kneis doun Befoir the king of lestand lyfe and lycht. *a* **1586** SIDNEY *Arcadia* III. (1590) 337 b, The strongest building, and lastingest monarchies are subiect to end. **1603** B. JONSON *K. Jas.' Entertainm. Coronation* Wks. (1616) 862 That did auspicate So lasting glory to Avgvstvs state. **1651** HOBBES *Leviath.* II. xvii. 87 Somwhat else required to make their Agreement constant and lasting. **1682** SIR T. BROWNE *Let.* Wks. (1836) I. 346 Retarded by the lasting south-west wind. **1738** G. LILLO *Marina* III. ii. 47 The lasting'st peace is death. **1776** GIBBON *Decl. & F.* xii. I. 346 A lasting deliverance from the inroads of the Scythian nations. **1809** *Med. Jrnl.* XXI. 312 It is not..from a vast variety of external applications..that we are to expect lasting or even temporary benefit. **1855** MACAULAY *Hist. Eng.* xv. III. 506 The husband of that Alice Lisle whose death has left a lasting stain on the memory of James the Second. **1875** JOWETT *Plato* (ed. 2) V. 363 All these things are only lasting when they depend upon one another.

2. Of material substances: Durable. †Of provisions, fruit, etc.: Keeping well; continuing fresh and undecayed (*obs.*).

c **1350** *Will. Palerne* 1736 [She] laced wel eche leme wiþ lastend þonges. **1599** H. BUTTES *Dyets drie Dinner* N v, Creame..neither is it so lasting as butter. **1602** SHAKS. *Ham.* I. iii. 8 A Violet..Forward, not permanent; sweet, not lasting. **1604** E. G[RIMSTONE] *D'Acosta's Hist. Indies* III. xvii. 173 This stone..is light and lasting. **1660** F. BROOKE tr. *Le Blanc's Trav.* 55 A sort of good lasting fish. **1669** STURMY *Mariner's Mag.* VII. 50 And Spanish Brown will make a lasting Colour for course Work. **1721** BERKELEY *Prev. Ruin Gt. Brit.* Wks. III. 199 Our black cloth is neither so lasting, nor of so good a dye as the Dutch.

3. *Sporting slang.* Of a horse: Able to 'stay'; possessed of staying power. (Cf. LAST *sb.*⁴)

1811 *Sporting Mag.* XXXVII. 135 To get not only speedy but lasting racers. **1821** *Ibid.* New Ser. VIII. 88 How much a..lasting English racer, is capable of performing.

lastingly (ˈlɑːstɪŋlɪ, ˈlæst-), *adv.* Forms: 4 **lastenlyche**, **lestendliche**, 4–5 **lastandly**, 5 *Sc.* **lestandly**, 4– **lastingly**. [f. LASTING *a.* + -LY².] In a lasting manner; continually, enduringly, permanently, perpetually, persistently.

a **1340** HAMPOLE *Psalter* xxvi. 13, I sall seke þi face lastandly til my ded. **1389** in *Eng. Gilds* (1870) 45 Lestenliche for to fyndyn..on candelle. *c* **1400** tr. *Secreta Secret., Gov. Lordsh.* 60 Wynter and somer þat God hauys lastandly stabyled of cold and hete. *c* **1470** HENRY *Wallace* VIII. 659 Thocht he refusyt it [the croun] lestandly to ber. *a* **1682** SIR T. BROWNE *Tracts* 15 So to incorporate wine and oil that they may lastingly hold together. **1749** WESLEY *Jrnl.* 14 Apr., Some..were deeply and lastingly affected. **1798** MAD. D'ARBLAY *Let.* Mar., I have escaped offending lastingly the Royal Mistress I love and honour. **1856** MISS BIRD *Englishw. in Amer.* 273 Kindness which should make my recollections of Quebec lastingly agreeable. **1860** J. F. THRUPP *Introd. to Ps.* II. 65 As though in them were lastingly perpetuated that olden hatred wherewith their forefather Esau had hated Jacob.

lastingness (ˈlɑːstɪŋnɪs, ˈlæst-). [f. as prec. + -NESS.] The quality of being lasting; continuance, duration, permanence. Also, durability, †constancy, perseverance.

a **1340** HAMPOLE *Psalter* ii. 7 Þe lastandnes of god euermare is all at ans. *c* **1440** *Jacob's Well* 289 Lastyngnes fayleth noȝt in wele ne wo tyl þe lyues ende. *c* **1470** HENRY *Wallace* VIII. 1319 Pees is in hewyn, with blyss and lestandnas. *a* **1586** SIDNEY *Arcadia* I. (1590) 8 The consideration of the exceeding lastingnesse. *c* **1645** HOWELL *Lett.* (1650) II. 36 Though the heart be the box of love, the memory is the box of lastingnes. **1670** CLARENDON *Contempl. Ps.* in *Tracts* (1727) 621 The lastingness of anything adds very much to the esteem of it. **1704** NEWTON *Optics* III. i. (1721) 322 The lastingness of the Motions excited in the bottom of the Eye by Light. **1715** LEONI *Palladio's Archit.* (1742) I. 10 The solidity and lastingness of the Work. **1820** *Examiner* No. 650. 609/1 It was all over with them, as to any real tenure of empire, any lastingness of dictation. **1851** CAROLINE FOX *Jrnl.* (1882) II. 160 The lastingness of an individual conviction is with him a pledge of its truth. **1885** PATER *Marius* II. 19 Anxious to try the lastingness of his own Epicurean rose-garden.

†**'lastless**, *a. Obs.* Also 3 **leasteless**. [ad. ON. *lastalauss*, f. *last-*, *lǫstr* (see LAST *sb.*³) + *-lauss*, -LESS.] Blameless.

a **1225** *St. Marher.* 12 Ah leaf me gan lefdi leasteles ich þe bidde. *a* **1225** *Juliana* 44 Godes licome þat he nom on þe lastelese meiden. *c* **1250** *Compassio Mariæ* v. in *Holy Rood* (1894) 79 Þine loates weren lasteles. *a* **1310** in Wright *Lyric P.* xvi. 52 A lussum ledy lasteles.

lastly (ˈlɑːstlɪ, ˈlæst-), *adv.* Also 4 *Sc.* **lestely**. [f. LAST *a.* + -LY².]

1. At the end; in the last instance; ultimately. *Obs.* or *arch.* exc. as used to indicate the last point or conclusion of a discourse or the like: In the last place, finally.

c **1375** *Sc. Leg. Saints, Paulus* 187 Wit þu þat schorte tyme I sall tholl now, bot lestely I sall luf sine with my lord Ihesu withowtyn fyne. *c* **1586** C'TESS PEMBROKE *Ps.* LI. viii, Lastly, O Lord, how soe I stand or fall, Leave not thy loved Sion to

embrace. **1588** Shaks. *Tit. A.* v. iii. 104 Our Brothers were beheaded, Our Fathers teares despis'd,.. Lastly, my selfe vnkindly banished. **1598** —— *Merry W.* i. i. 142 There is three Vmpires in this matter,.. that is, Master Page.. and there is my selfe.. and.. (lastly, and finally) mine Host. **1605** Willet *Hexapla Gen.* 386 Lastely he made him ruler of his house. **1611** Bible *Transl. Pref.* 1 And lastly, that the Church be sufficiently provided for. **1631** Weever *Anc. Funeral Mon.* 697 Alice his wife (who lastly married one William Ramsey). **1641** J. Jackson *True Evang. T.* ii. 115 S. Peter.. lastly was crucified under Nero. **1667** Milton *P.L.* iii. 240, I for his sake will leave Thy bosom,.. and for him lastly die Well pleased. **1749** Bracken *Farriery* (ed. 6) 20 Fourthly, and Lastly; I recommend Purging as usefull in gross Habits. **1783** Hailes *Antiq. Chr. Ch.* ii. 44 And lastly, that the arguments of the Apostle satisfied some of the Jews. **1861** Lytton & Fane *Tannhäuser* 113 With the strength that lastly comes to break All bonds. **1875** Lightfoot *Comm. Col.* (1886) 218 Lastly of all, show your gratitude by your thanksgiving.

†**2.** Conclusively, finally. *Obs.*

1612 Drayton *Poly-olb.* v. 79 Then take my finall doome pronounced lastlie this. **1637** Milton *Lycidas* 83 As he pronounces lastly on each deed.

†**3.** Very lately, recently. *Obs.*

1592 Greene *Groat's W. Wit* (1617) 36 Young Iuuenall, that byting Satyrist, that lastly with mee together writ a Comedie. **1641** J. Jackson *True Evang. T.* i. 50 The blood of him.. who lastly suffered, it may be yesterday, or to day.

'lastness. *rare.* [f. last *a.* + -ness.] The condition of being last or of there being a last one.

1625 Gill *Sacr. Philos.* i. 89 If the world be eternall, then neither was there any first man, neither can there be any last: without which lastnesse there cannot be any generall resurrection of men. *a* **1665** J. Goodwin *Filled with Spirit* (1867) 92 Lastness or worstness in estate or condition. **1927** 'E. Bramah' *Max Carrados Myst.* 72 Your account.. is entirely based on the fact that you were the last... There stands the man we want,.. only you and your lastness get between.

lasya ('lɑːsjə). [Skr. *lāsya.*] A graceful style of female dancing in India.

1937 Subrahmaṇya Śāstrī & Śrīnivāsa Ayyaṅgār in Śaṅkara Ācārya *Saundarya-Laharī* 160 The Lāsya or female-dance and the Tāndava or male-dance, both being types of the same Nṛtya. **1967** Singha & Massey *Indian Dances* 23 Lasya is that element of the dance which is graceful and delicate and expresses emotions on a gentle level... Krishna's dance with the *gopees* (milkmaids) is in lasya. **1973** *Daily Tel.* 28 Mar. 15/1 What was most striking was her combination of the tandava (masculine) and lasya (feminine) in a way unique to her.

‖**lat**[1] (lɑːt). [Hindī *lāṭ, lāṭh.*] **a.** A staff, pole (*rare* in Eng. use). **b.** *Antiq.* 'An obelisk or columnar monument; specifically used for the ancient Buddhist columns of Eastern India' (Yule).

1800 *Asiatic Ann. Reg., Misc. Tracts* 313/2 A high pillar of stone called Bheem-lat, or the Tealee, or oilman's lat or staff. **1876** J. Fergusson *Hist. Ind. & East. Archit.* i. ii. 52 The oldest authentic examples of these lâts that we are acquainted with are those which King Asoka set up. **1899** *Westm. Gaz.* 18 Aug. 2/1 A bamboo lat descended on his skull.

lat[2]. [f. the first syllable of *Latvija* Latvia.] A unit of gold currency established by the state of Latvia in August 1922, with a par value of about 25 to the pound sterling, and discontinued in 1941.

1923 *Glasgow Herald* 23 June 10 The last Budget year was closed with a surplus of over 18,000,000 lats gold. **1928** *Daily Express* 29 Aug. 2/5 The Latvian Ministry of Finance has decided to place an order for five-lat silver pieces.. with the Royal Mint, London. **1942** *Statesman's Year-Bk.* 1261 Latvia... The U.S.S.R. authorities abolished the lat currency on April 10, 1941.

lat[3]. (Usu. in pl. *lats.*) Slang abbrev. of latrine.

1927 W. E. Collinson *Contemp. Eng.* 92 At Salisbury Plain and Camberley in 1909/10 I learnt a number of camping expressions like.. lats (*latrines*). **1940** M. Marples *Public School Slang* 112 Other synonyms [for lavatories] are rears, lats.. and dubs. **1957** J. I. M. Stewart *Use of Riches* i. ii. 25 Turk says that conscientious objectors have to clean out the lats in lunatic asylums.

lat, obs. and dial. f. late, lath.

lat, obs. form of let *v.*

‖**lata** ('lɑːtə). Also **latah**. The Malay name under which a form of religious hysteria is known in Java. It is characterized by a rapid ejaculation of inarticulate sounds, and a succession of involuntary movements, with temporary loss of consciousness (*Syd. Soc. Lex.* 1888).

1884 *Western Daily Press* 25 June 7/5 This disease has been met with in Java, where it is known as Lata. **1895** W. G. Ellis in *Jrnl. Ment. Sci.* (1897) 32 (heading) Latah. A Mental Malady of the Malays. *Ibid.* 33 Under the name 'Latah' the Malays describe a variety of peculiar nervous conditions of a transitory character.

Latakia (lætə'kiːə). [Short for *Latakia tobacco.*] A fine kind of Turkish tobacco produced near and shipped from Latakia (the ancient Laodicea), a seaport of Syria.

1833 Disraeli *Corr. w. Sister* 19 Jan., Smoking Latakia. **1849** Thackeray *Pendennis* xxxix, Enveloped in fragrant clouds of Latakia.

latania (lə'teɪnɪə, lə'tænɪə).

1. *U.S.* [Amer. Sp.] = latanier 1.

1799 in F. Cuming *Sk. Tour Western Country* (1810) 336 Some.. cabins [were] covered over with a shrub like a large fan, called latania. **1819** E. Dana *Geogr. Sk. Western Country* 238 On the.. outer margin of the cane, the palmetto, or latania, fill the slope between the cane and the inundated lands.

2. [mod.L. (P. Commerson in A. L. de Jussieu *Genera Plantarum* (1789) 39), f. F. *latanier* the name used in Mauritius.] A fan palm of the genus so called, native to Mauritius and neighbouring islands.

1856 B. Seemann *Pop. Hist. Palms* 229 The Latanias are middle-sized trees. **1900** L. H. Bailey *Cycl. Amer. Hort.* II. 887/1 Latanias are tall, spineless palms. *Ibid.* 887/2 Latanias are essentially warmhouse palms. **1910** [see geonoma]. **1966** E. J. H. Corner *Nat. Hist. Palms* vii. 162 (*caption*) The Borassoid *Latania*; male inflorescence.

latanier (‖latanje, lə'tænɪə(r)). [Fr.]

1. *U.S.* [See quot. 1939.] One of several fan palms found in the southern United States and central America, esp. the cabbage palmetto, *Sabal palmetto.*

[**1719** tr. *H. Joutel's Jrnl. Voy. Mexico* 14, I could see from the Ships.. [an] Abundance of that Sort of Palm-Trees, in French call'd *Lataniers.*] **1827** *Western Monthly Rev.* I. 315 Palmetto, or latanier, peet, and long moss, add an aspect of novelty to the view. **1868** *Putnam's Mag.* I. 594/1 Here and there.. is a 'latanier-hut' with adobe walls and a roof thatched with.. palmetto. [**1939** W. A. Read in *Zeitschrift für franz. Sprache* LXIII. i-ii. 46 The usual term in Louisiana-French for this palmetto is *latanier*, m., a derivative of Carib *aláttani*, a name recorded by Breton for a West Indian palm with fan-shaped leaves.]

2. The Mauritian name for several fan palms, esp. = latania 2.

1929 *Encycl. Brit.* XV. 108/1 The coco-nut palm, an importation [to Mauritius], the palmiste (*Palma dactylifera latifolia*), the latanier (*Corypha umbraculifera*) and the date-palm.

latch (lætʃ), *sb.*[1] Forms: 4-5 **lach, lacch(e,** 5-6 (7) **lache,** 5-6 **latche,** 6- **latch.** [The equivalence of sense 1 with lace *sb.* suggests that the word (in that sense at least) may be a. OF. *lache* lace, a vbl. noun f. *lachier* (= Central OF. *lacier*):—popular L. **laciāre*, f. **lacium* lace *sb.* Sense 2 is prob. a development of this; on the other hand, the analogy of *catch* sb. gives some support to the view that it may be f. latch *v.*[1]]

1. A loop or noose; a gin, snare; a 'tangle'; a latchet, thong. ***a latch of links***: (*dial.*) a string of sausages. *Obs.* exc. *dial.* and *techn.*

?*a* **1366** Chaucer *Rom. Rose* 1624 Love wil noon other bridde cacche Though he sette either net or lacche. **1624** Capt. Smith *Virginia* iv. 129 She [the ship] was fast in the latch of our cable, which in haste of weighing our anchor hung aloofe. **1653** H. Cogan tr. *Pinto's Trav.* xxii. 79 All Scepters do serve but as latches to his most rich sandals. **1840** Spurdens *Suppl. to Forby* (E.D.S.), *Latch*,.. As a *sb.*, it means a thong of leather. **1895** *E. Angl. Gloss., Latch of Links*, a string of sausages.

2. A fastening for a door or gate, so contrived as to admit of its being opened from the outside. It now usually consists of a small bar which falls or slides into a catch, and is lifted or drawn by means of a thumb-lever, string, etc. passed through the door. Now also, a small kind of spring-lock for a front-door (more fully ***night-latch***) which is opened from the outside by means of a key. ***on the latch***: (said of a door) fastened with a latch only; so ***off the latch***, unlatched, ajar. Also with qualifying word, as *dead-, night-, spring-*, q.v.

1331 [?implied by draw-latch 2]. **1382** Wyclif *Song Sol.* v. 6 The lach of my dore I openede to my lemman. *a* **1400** *Pistill of Susan* 229 To þe ȝate ȝapely they ȝedyn.. And he left up þe lacche. *c* **1420** *Chron. Vilod.* st. 732 And breke up bothe lok and lache. *c* **1440** *Partonope* 5440 Vp she nome The lacch of the dore and in she come. **1520** [see catch *sb.*[1] 10]. **1575** *Gamm. Gurton* iii. iii, Take heede, Cocke, pull in the latche! **1611** Shaks. *Wint. T.* iv. iv. 449 If euer henceforth, thou These rurall Latches, to his entrance open. **1624-5** in Swayne *Churchw. Acc. Sarum* (1896) 180 A cache and a Lache for the Church gate. **1637** Heywood *Royall King* iii. vii. Wks. 1874 VI. 47 Pray draw the latch, sir. **1765** Wesley *Jrnl.* 25 May, The door [is] only on the latch. **1833** Ht. Martineau *Briery Creek* iii. 54 For want of a latch, the gate.. was tied. **1842** Tennyson *Dora* 127 The door was off the latch: they peep'd and saw The boy set up betwixt his grandsire's knees. **1851** Longf. *Gold. Leg.* ii. *In the Garden*, To thee it [the thought of death] is not So much even as the lifting of a latch. **1885** Black *Wh. Heather* ii, The outer door is on the latch, thieves being unheard of in this remote neighbourhood.

3. *techn.* **a.** † (*a*) The click of the ratchet-wheel of a loom (*obs.*). † (*b*) See quot. 1704 (*obs.*). (*c*) *Naut.* = lasket. (*d*) 'A cord clamp which holds the in-board end of a mackerel-line' (Knight *Dict. Mech.* 1875). (*e*) The part of a knitting-machine needle which closes the hook to allow the loop to pass over its head (= fly *sb.*[2] 5 f).

1688 R. Holme *Armoury* iii. 107/2 The Latch [of a Loome] is an Iron or peece of Wood that falls into the Catch of the Wheel aforesaid, which holds the Yarn Beam from turning. **1704** J. Harris *Lex. Techn.* I, *Latches* are those Parts of a Clock which [wind] up, and unlock the Work. **1710** *Ibid.* II, *Latches*, in a Ship, are the same with Laskets. **1875** Knight *Dict. Mech.* 1238/2 Two positions of the latch-needle: one with the latch lying back,.. the other showing the hook closed by the latch.

b. *Electronics.* A logic circuit which retains whatever output state results from a momentary input signal until the application of a different signal to the same input point or the same signal to a different point. Also ***latch circuit.***

1959 E. M. Grabbe et al. *Handbk. Automation, Computation, & Control* II. xvii. 6 A delay element is provided with external gating which enables it to hold information provided on the 'set' input until a 'reset' input of 1 occurs. This configuration.. is sometimes referred to as a latch. **1962** Simpson & Richards *Physical Princ. Junction Transistors* xvi. 403 A variant of it [*sc.* the 'flip-flop'], known as the latch, is an asymmetric bistable multivibrator. **1971** J. H. Smith *Digital Logic* iv. 54 A push button might be pressed and at a certain time in a machine sequence the fact that the button was pressed may be needed to change the sequence. The latch circuit is therefore used to 'remember' that a push button has been pressed. *Ibid.*, A *1* signal applied momentarily to the set input of NOR 1 will make O/P_1 a *0* signal... To reset the latch a *1* signal is fed to the reset input which makes O/P_2 fall to *0*. As NOR 1 no longer has a *1* input, O/P_1 changes to *1*, thereby holding O/P_2 at the *0* level.

†**4.** *Mil. Antiq.* (See quots.) *Obs.*

1547-8 in Meyrick *Ant. Arm.* (1824) III. 10 Crosse-bowes called latches, windlasses for them. **1786** Grose *Armour & Weapons* 59 There were two sorts of English cross bows, one called Latches, the other Prodds.

5. *attrib.* and *Comb.*, as ***latch-hole***; ***latch-like*** adj.; **latch bolt** (see quots.); **latch-closer, -lifter, -opener,** devices for closing and opening the latch of a knitting-machine needle (Knight *Dict. Mech.* 1875); †**latch-drawer,** one who draws or lifts the latch to enter for an unlawful purpose: = draw-latch 2; **latch-needle,** a kind of knitting-machine needle, the hook of which is closed by a latch (see 3 e). Also latch-key, latch-string.

1909 *Cent. Dict.* Suppl., **Latch-bolt*, any latch or door-bolt, controlled by a spring and having a beveled head which, when the door is closed, is pressed back by meeting the strike and is thrown out again when the door is shut: the common form of self-locking bolt. **1958** *Encycl. Locks* (J. Parkes & Sons Ltd.) 247 A spring bolt, called also a latch bolt, of a lock or latch is one which having been drawn in shoots out automatically as soon as the handle or key is released. **1393** Langl. *P. Pl.* C. ix. 288 Lyers and *lacche-drawers. *c* **1440** *Jacob's Well* 134 Lacche-drawerys, þat vndon mennys dorys. **1861** Geo. Eliot *Silas M.* iv, Dunstan.. pushed his fingers through the *latch-hole. **1894** Crockett *Raiders* 246 One that came to the door and spied upon me through the latch-hole. **1875** *Latch-needle [see 3].

†**latch,** *sb.*[2] *Naut. Obs.* [? cf. lurch *sb.*] ? = lurch. (See also *lee-latch*, lee *sb.*)

a **1687** Petty *Pol. Arith.* iii. (1691) 51 Such [Ships] as draw much Water, and have a deep Latch in the Sea.

latch (lætʃ), *v.*[1] Forms: 1 **læcc(e)an, ȝelæcc(e)an,** *Northumb.* **læcca,** 3 *Orm.* **lacchenn,** 3-4 (6) **lache,** 3-4 **lacche,** 4 **lach, (lachche, laache, lachi),** 4-5 **lachen,** 6 **latche,** (*Sc.* **lauch),** 6- **latch.** *Pa. t.* α. 1 **(ȝe)læht(e,** *Northumb.* **(ȝe)lahte,** 3 **laht(e,** 3-4 **laght, lauȝt(e,** (3 **lahut,** 4 **laught, lauȝtte, lauht, laute, lawte, lawght, leȝte),** 4-5 **laȝt.** β. 4 **lached,** *Sc.* **lacht,** 7 **latcht,** 7- **latched.** *Pa. pple.* α. 1 **(ȝe-)læht,** 3 **lah(h)t, laȝt,** 4 **lauht, laught(e,** 4-5 **lauȝte,** 5 **laȝt, laght(e, y-lauȝthe.** β. 4 **lachched, lached,** 6 *Sc.* **lachit,** 4, 7- **latched.** [OE. *læcc(e)an* (Northumb. *læcca*) wk. vb.; not found in the other Teut. langs.; the OTeut. type **lakk-* may represent either pre-Teut. **laqn-* cogn. w. L. *laqueus* (see lace *sb.*), OSl. *lęca* to catch, ensnare, *po-lęčĭ* snare, or **lagn-* cogn. w. Gr. λάζεσθαι (:—**lagy-*) to take.]

1. a. *trans.* To take hold of, grasp, seize (esp. with the hand or claws); to clasp, embrace (with the arms); to grasp with the mind, to comprehend. Now only *intr.* or *absol.* with *on*, †*at*, †*till.*

c **1000** Ælfric *Gram.* viii. (Z.) 23 Ðis þing ic ȝelæhte. *c* **1000** Ælfric *Hom.* II. 122 Germanus ȝelæhte ðone pistol æt Gregories ærendracan, and hine totær. *c* **1160** *Hatton Gosp.* Mark ix. 18 Se swa hwær he hine læcd [*Ags. Gosp.* ȝelæcð] forgnit hine. *a* **1225** *Ancr. R.* 102 Hweðer þe cat of helle claurede.., & cauhte [*v. rr.* lahte, lachte], mid his cleafres, hir heorte heaued? *a* **1225** *Juliana* 38 þis eadie meiden.. þen engel leop to ant lahte him. *c* **1250** *Gen. & Ex.* 2621 A fostre wimman, On was tette he sone aueð laȝt. *a* **1300** *K. Horn* 243 Horn in herte laȝte Al þat he him taȝte. *a* **1300** *Cursor M.* 7240 Quils sampson slepped, sco laght a schere, His hare sco kerf. **13..** *Parlt. thre Ages* 52 Bot at the laste he loutted doun & laughte till his mete. **13..** *Gaw. & Gr. Knt.* 328 Lyȝtly lepez he hym to, & laȝt at his honde. *c* **1375** *Sc. Leg. Saints, Barnabas* 140 And fra Barnabas had tauchte þe trewcht to hyme, he it sone lacht. **1387-8** T. Usk *Test. Love* i. iii. (Skeat) l. 51 Then were there inowe to lache myne handes, and drawe me to shippe. *c* **1400** *St. Alexius* (Laud 622) 219 And whan he [Alexius] seide had al his wille þe holy gost hir lauȝtte. *a* **1440** *Sir Degrev.* 827 And I in armus had y-lauȝthe That commely and swete.

1937 *Esquire* Jan. 146/2 Dar's uh green sedan up front, uh fo' do' job. Latch on it 'n earn dis dime. **1940** *Sat. Even. Post* 13 Jan. 17/3, I latched onto a shark and killed it. **1946** B. Treadwell *Big. Bk. of Swing* 125/1 *Latch on*, grab on to. **1951** I. Shaw *Troubled Air* viii. 144 They're out for something of their own and they latch on to us. **1954** D.

RIESMAN *Individualism Reconsidered* xiv. 220 [He] has latched on to American consumption know-how at its most garish. **1957** *New Yorker* 29 June 68/2 Mr. Kelly has latched on to a sound (indeed, indestructible) idea for keeping a film in motion. **1959** C. MACINNES *Absolute Beginners* 58 Hundreds of pure pink numbers..who've latched on to the Welfare thing, but don't belong here. **1962** J. WAIN *Strike Father Dead* 107 It was a long time before I could latch on to what was happening. Then I got it. **1968** *Listener* 27 June 837/1 When the doctor said, 'You're going to die, you'd better come back into hospital,' I said: 'Thanks for telling me. I'm going to latch on to life and I'm not coming back to hospital.' **1971** *Engineering* Apr. 41/3 The astute entrepreneurs are latching on to the idea. **1972** C. DRUMMOND *Death at Bar* i. 36 Jarvis soon latched on to two portly dowagers—relatives of his hostess.

†**b.** To put or strike swiftly *off*, *out*, *up*; to dart *out* (the tongue). Also *fig.* *Obs.*

a **1225** *St. Marher.* 9 Lahte ut his tunge swa long þat he swong hire al abuten his swire, ant semde as þa ha scharp sweord of his muð lahte. **13..** *E.E. Allit. P.* C. 425 Now lorde lach out my lyf, hit lastes to longe. *c* **1350** *Will. Palerne* 1244 þanne li3tly lep he a-doun & lau3t out his brond. *Ibid.* 2308 Our wurþi werwolf..lau3t vp þe 3ong lyoun li3tly in his mouþe. ?*a* **1400** *Morte Arth.* 1515 Þay ledde hym furthe in þe rowte, and lached ofe his wedes. *c* **1430** *Hymns Virg.* 76 For deeþ his swerd out haþ lau3te. **1535** STEWART *Cron. Scot.* (1858) I. 383 Helme and hewmont wer hewin in schunder, Lymnis war lachit hard of be the kne.

†**2. a.** To take with force; to capture, seize upon (a person or his goods). *Obs.*

c **950** *Lindisf. Gosp.* Mark xiv. 48 Allsuæ to ðeafe ȝie foerdon mið suordum et stengum..to læccane mec. *c* **1000** *Ags. Laws, Instit. Polity* §19 (Th.) II. 328 Hi..læccað of manna beȝeatum hwæt hi ȝefon maȝan. *a* **1300** *Cursor M.* 6766 If I giue þe for to kepe Ox or ass..And it wit wiþerwin be laght. *Ibid.* 7928 For to spar his aun aght þis pouer mans scep he laght. **1393** LANGL. *P. Pl.* C. III. 215 And if 3e lacche lyere let hym nat a-skapie. **1399** —— *Rich. Redeles* II. 159 The knyttis..That rentis and robis with raveyn evere lau3te. **1535** STEWART *Cron. Scot.* (1858) I. 277 The Romanis fled..thai war lachit at the last.

†**b.** To catch (with a snare, net, etc.). *Obs.*

c **1200** ORMIN 13474 To lacchenn him wiþþ spelless nett To brinngenn himm to Criste. *a* **1250** *Owl & Night.* 1057 Lim and grinei..Sette and lede the for to lacche. *a* **1300** *Cursor M.* 29532 Ar þou be laght in findes snarr. *c* **1350** *Leg. Cathol., Pope Gregory* 17 Out of an abbay thai weren ysent With nettes..To lache fische.

3. To catch (something falling); to catch or receive *in* (a receptacle). *Obs.* exc. *dial.*

1530 PALSGR. 604/1, I latche, I catche a thyng that is throwen to me in my handes..*je happe*. If I had latched the potte betyme, it had nat fallen to the grounde. **1579** SPENSER *Sheph. Cal.* Mar. 94 Tho pumie stones I hastly hent And threwe; but nought availed: He..oft the pumies latched. **1600** HOLLAND *Livy* 161 Some latch the firebrands as they flew. **1601** —— *Pliny* I. 301 Vnlesse there be good heed taken that the eggs be latched in some soft bed vnder-neath, they are soone broken. **1639** HORN & ROB. *Gate Lang. Unl.* xxxv. §415 A dairy-maid milketh out milk latching it in a milk-paile. *Ibid.* xli. §445 The droppings, or any thing else spilt by chance, is latcht in a latch-pan. **1787** W. MARSHALL *Norfolk* (1795) II. 383 To *Latch*, to catch as water, &c. *a* **1825** FORBY *Voc. E. Anglia, Latch*, to catch what falls.

4. a. To be the recipient of, to get; to receive (a name, gift; a blow, injury); to catch, take (a disease). *Obs.* exc. *dial.*

a **1300** *Cursor M.* 19038 Þai þat had hus or ani aght þai sald þam and þe pris laght, Be-for þe apostels fete it broght. *c* **1300** *Havelok* 744 The stede of Grim the name laute. *c* **1330** R. BRUNNE *Chron.* (1810) 94 Þe kyng stode ouer nehi, þe stroke he lauht so smerte. *Ibid.* 332 Þe erle of Arundelle his londes lauht he þan. —— *Chron. Wace* (Rolls) 8813 Þo þat were seke, or had laught skaþes. **1340–70** *Alex. & Dind.* 40 For we ben hid in oure holis or we harm laache. **1340–70** *Alisaunder* 4 Lordes, and ooþer..þat boldely thinken..For to lachen hem loose. **1393** LANGL. *P. Pl.* C. II. 101 Thei shoulde..neuere leue for loue in hope to lacche seluer. *c* **1400** *Ywaine & Gaw.* 3230 For nowther of tham na woundes laght. **1513** DOUGLAS *Æneis* VIII. Prol. 27 All leidis langis in land to lauch quhat thaim leif is. *c* **1600** SHAKS. *Sonn.* cxiii, Mine eye..no forme deliuers to the heart Of bird, of flowre, or shape which it doth latch. *a* **1603** T. CARTWRIGHT *Confut. Rhem. N.T.* (1618) 306 They should haue warded and latched the enemies strokes. **1605** SHAKS. *Macb.* IV. iii. 192, I haue words That would be howl'd out in the desert ayre Where hearing should not latch them. **1633** P. FLETCHER *Purple Isl.* IX. i, The Bridegroom Sunne..Leaves his star-chamber..His shines the Earth soon latcht to gild her flowers. **1649** BP. HALL *Cases Consc.* II. x. (1650) 155 A man that latches the weapon in his own body to save his Prince. *c* **1655** LOVEDAY *Lett.* (1659) 47 My first request then is, that if you latch any news that [etc.]..you will not grudge to send it me. **1875** *Lanc. Gloss.* s.v., To latch a distemper.

†**b.** In ME. poetry often used (esp. for alliteration) in various senses of TAKE; e.g. in phrases ***to latch delight, to latch one's ease, one's leave***. *Obs.*

a **1300** *Cursor M.* 2445 To pastur commun þai laght þe land þe quilk þam neiest lay to hand. *Ibid.* 4999 Þair leue þai laght. *Ibid.* 10778 Þan was þe mai ioseph bi-taght, And he has hir in spusail laght. **13..** *Gaw. & Gr. Knt.* 1676 For-þy þow lye in þy loft, & lach þyn ese. **13..** *E.E. Allit. P.* A. 1128 To loue þe lombe his meyny in melle, I-wysse I la3t a gret delyt. **1377** LANGL. *P. Pl.* B. XVII. 148 The sone that sent was til erthe..and mankynde lau3te. *Ibid.* C. IV. 26 Whenne thei had lauht here leue at þys lady mede. *c* **1400** *Destr. Troy* 13360 Euery lede to the lond laghtyn þere gayre. *a* **1400–50** *Alexander* 3861 He..þo3t þare a longe quile to lie & lachen his esee.

†**5.** To reach, get to (land, a destination); to take, 'get on' (the water, way). *Obs.*

c **1330** R. BRUNNE *Chron.* (1810) 120 With hors & herneis Bristow has scho latched. ?*a* **1400** *Morte Arth.* 750 Launchez lede apone lufe, lacchene þer depez. *c* **1400** *Destr. Troy* 5702 And who þat lacchit the lond with the lyf þen, Were..tyrnet to dethe. *Ibid.* 12483 Thus the lordes in hor longyng laghton þe watur. *c* **1400** *Ywaine & Gaw.* 2025 Fra his lord the way he laght.

6. *intr.* To alight, settle. *dial.*

a **1825** FORBY *Voc. E. Anglia, Latch*,..to alight. Ex. 'He will always latch on his legs.' **1847** HALLIWELL, *Latch*, to light or fall. *Suffolk.* Kennet gives these meanings as current in Durham. **1871** *East Anglian* IV. 111 The Golden crested Wren, often caught by the hand while 'latching' in the rigging.

latch (lætʃ), *v.*[2] [f. LATCH *sb.*[1]] *trans.* To fasten or secure with a latch.

1530 PALSGR. 604/1, I latche a doore, I shytte it by the latche. **1556** J. HEYWOOD *Spider & F.* lvii. 89 The very locke and key, That lacheth and lockth vs all, from quiet stey. **1579** SPENSER *Sheph. Cal.* May 291 He popt him in, and his basket did latch. **1865** DICKENS *Mut. Fr.* IV. xv, He latched the garden-gate. **1882** J. HAWTHORNE *Fort. Fool* I. xxxi, The street door was to be latched, but not bolted.

b. *slang.* (See quot.)

c **1700** in *Street Robberies Consider'd.* **1725** *New Cant. Dict., Latch*, let in.

†**latch**, *v.*[3] *Building. Obs. rare.* [? a. ONF. *lachier* = Central OF. *lacier* LACE *v.*] *trans.* To cover with interlaced work. (Cf. LACE *sb.* 4.)

1598 in Willis & Clark *Cambridge* (1886) II. 252 The particions betwixt euery fellowes chamber on both sides of the same to be double latched with good lath lyme and hare. **1625** PURCHAS *Pilgrims* II. 1369 Rampiers made of that woodden walled fashion, double, and betwixt them Earth and Stones, but so latched with crosse Timber, they are very strong.

latch, latche, variants of LEACH *v.*, LACHE *v.*

latch, var. LETCH *sb.*[1]

latched (lætʃt), *ppl. a.* [f. LATCH *v.*[2] and *sb.*[1] + -ED.] Fastened with or having a latch.

c **1440** *Promp. Parv.* 284/1 Latchyd, or speryd wythe a leche, *pessulatus*. **1693** LOCKE *Educ.* §131. 161 The Door was only latch'd, and when he had the Latch in his Hand, he turn'd about his Head [etc.]. **1722** DE FOE *Plague* (1840) 118 He had left the Door open, or only latched.

latchednes, -nesse, vars. LACHEDNESS *Obs.*

latches(se, obs. forms of LACHES.

latchet ('lætʃɪt). Forms: 4–6 **lachet**, 4–5 **lacchet**, 5 **lachett**, 6 **latchett**, 6– **latchet**. [ad. OF. *lachet*, dial. var. of *lacet*, dim. of *laz*, *las*, LACE *sb.*]

†**1.** A loop; a narrow strip of anything, a thong. *Obs.* exc. as in c.

c **1350** *Ipomadon* 4458 (Kölbing) He gaff hym suche a spetuous falle, In sunder brast the lachettes all, That shuld his helme socoure. **13..** *Gaw. & Gr. Knt.* 591 His harnays watz ryche, þe lest lachet ou[þ]er loupe lemed of golde. **14..** *Siege Jerusalem* 42/748 A grete girdel of gold..Layþ vmbe his lendis, with lacchetes ynow. **1483** CAXTON *Gold. Leg.* 338/1 Layners or lachettes of theyre skynne were cutte oute of theyr back. **1660** HEXHAM *Dutch Dict., Een Klinck-snoer*, a Latchet, Thong, or Cord that Rings the bell in a house. **1676** HOBBES *Iliad* (1677) 45 And Paris then was mightily distrest, Choakt by the latchet underneath his chin. **1709** BLAIR in *Phil. Trans.* XXVII. 145 There were two Latchets, or Foldings of Wire plac'd in the inner side.

†**b.** *Naut.* = LASKET. *Obs.*

1497 *Naval Acc. Hen. VII* (1896) 321, iiij Smale lynes for lachetes & Robyns to the seid Ship. **1611** COTGR., *Les nervins des bonnettes*, the latchets wherewith bonnets be fastened to a sayle. **1627** CAPT. SMITH *Seaman's Gram.* v. 24 Latchets are small lines sowed in the Bonnets and Drablers like loops to lash..the Bonnet to the course, or the course to the Drabler.

c. A thong used to fasten a shoe; a (shoe-)lace. Now only *dial.* exc. in Biblical allusions.

c **1440** *Promp. Parv.* 284/1 Lachet of a schoo, *tenea*. **1483** CAXTON *Gold. Leg.* 166 b/1 They of the towne within had so grete defaulte that they ete theyr shoys and lachettis. **1526** TINDALE *Mark* i. 7 Whos shue latchett I am not worthy to stoupe doune and vnlose. **1535** COVERDALE *Isa.* v. 27. **1555** EDEN *Decades* 298 Patentes of woodde whiche they make faste to theyr feete with latchettes. **1688** CAPT. J. S. *Art of War* 16 Keeping..the but-end near the Latchet of your shoe. **1785** BOSWELL *Tour to Hebrides* 11 Aug. an. 1773, Dr. Adam Smith..told us he was glad to know that Milton wore latchets in his shoes instead of buckles. **1827** SCOTT *Two Drovers* ii, I would not kiss any man's dirty latchets for leave to bake in his oven. **1839** LONGF. *Hyperion* IV. v, Day, like a weary pilgrim, had reached the western gate of heaven, and Evening stooped down to unloose the latchets of his sandal-shoon. **1859** J. BROWN *Rab & F.* (1862) 27 He..put them [shoes] on, breaking one of the leather latchets.

†**d.** Phrases. ***to go above*** or ***beyond one's latchet***: to meddle with what does not concern one. (Cf. LAST *sb.*[1] 2 c.) ***a lie with a latchet***: a great lie.

1580 LYLY *Euphues* (Arb.) 475 And yet in that goe not aboue thy latchet. **1603** H. CROSSE *Vertues Commw.* (1878) 61 The shomaker must not goe beyond his latchet. **1610** A. COOKE *Pope Joane* 20 He writes, that, in as much as she was a Germaine, no Germaine could euer since be chosen Pope. Which is a lie with a latchet. **1612** WOODALL *Surg. Mate* Wks. (1653) 263, I to my Latchet will return, and rest me in a mean. **1647** WARD *Simp. Cobler* 49 You will say I am now beyond my latchet; but you would not say so, if you knew how high my latchet will stretch, when I heare a lye with a latchet, that reaches up to his throat that first forged it. **1694** MOTTEUX *Rabelais* v. xxx. 152 That's a Lye with a Latchet: Tho 'twere Ælian that Long-Bow-man that told you so, never believe him.

2. A catch or fastening for a shutter-bar. [? Another word, f. LATCH *sb.*[1] + -ET.]

1842–59 GWILT *Archit.* II. iii. §2263. 593 Door springs..door chains..bars with latchets, shelf brackets [etc.].

†**3.** *Comb.*: **latchet-line**, cord for latchets.

1468 in *Mann. & Househ. Exp.* (Roxb.) 347 Paid for ij. pertz lachet lyne and halff..xij*d.* ob.

latchett ('lætʃɪt). Also **latchet**. A name applied to the gurnard, *Trigla cuculus*.

1882 W. HOUGHTON in *Academy* 14 Oct. 280 Latchett.—This name..is used to designate one of the gurnards or gurnets. It is well known in the Grimsby fish-market. **1889** *Catholic News* 1 June 8/4 Latchets 8*s.* to 11*s.* per box.

latching ('lætʃɪŋ), *vbl. sb.* [f. LATCH *v.*[1] + -ING[1].]

†**1.** The action of the vb. LATCH. *Obs.*

1362 LANGL. *P. Pl.* A. I. 101 And leuen for no loue ne lacching of 3iftus. *a* **1400–50** *Alexander* 1835 For þe lachynge of your Lorde sall noght a lede weynde.

2. *Naut.* = LASKET. Also ***latchings keys***.

1794 *Rigging & Seamanship* 84 A bonnet..has latchings in the upper part..to go through holes in the foot of the sail. **1851** KIPPING *Sailmaking* (ed. 2) 37 The additional parts of sails, made to fasten with latchings to the foot of the sails. **1867** SMYTH *Sailor's Word-bk., Latchings keys*, loops on the head-rope of a bonnet, by which it is laced to the foot of the sail.

latch-key ('lætʃkiː). Orig., a key used to draw back the night-latch of a door. Now usu., the key of a spring door-lock. Freq. allusive and *attrib.*, with reference to the use of a latch-key by a younger member of a household (esp. one who comes home from school when his parents are still at work) or a lodger.

1825 C. MATHEWS *Memorandum-Bk.* (ed. 2) 19 At last he recollected he had a latch key in his pocket. **1836** DICKENS *Pickw.* (1837) xx. 199, I couldn't find the place where the latch-key went in. **1839** DICKENS *Nich. Nick.* xvi, Here, at all hours of the night, may be heard the rattling of latch-keys in their respective keyholes. **1856** MRS. CARLYLE *Lett.* II. 270 He opened the door with his latch-key. **1950** T. S. ELIOT *Cocktail Party* I. iii. 70 Lavinia lets herself in with a latch-key.

attrib. **1892** ZANGWILL *Bow Mystery* 37 The front door..is guarded by the latchkey lock and the big lock. **1902** *Daily Chron.* 22 Aug. 3/6 At the beginning of the latchkey life everything looks delightful. **1905** *Ibid.* 17 Nov. 1/7 The names of 2,596 workmen in Devonport, known as latch-key voters,..were restored to the occupiers' list. **1944** in *Amer. Speech* (1965) XL. 145 Latchkey children. **1945** BAKER *Austral. Lang.* 158 The arrival of American servicemen in Australia produced..*latch-key kids* for children left at home on their own by mothers engaged in war industry. **1946** *Life* 8 Apr. 90/2 His was a latchkey existence. **1960** *Guardian* 23 Nov. 8/5 What happens to the 'latch-key children' in Germany? **1974** *Courier-Mail* (Brisbane) 14 June 11/5 One in every four school children was a latch-key child.

Also as *v.*, to open with a latch-key; to let oneself into (a house, etc.) by means of a latch-key.

1939 E. S. GARDNER *Case of Rolling Bones* (1940) v. 60 Mason latch-keyed the office door to find Gertrude down on hands and knees scrubbing at the charred carpet. **1961** WODEHOUSE *Ice in Bedroom* xv. 119 As he latchkeyed himself into Peacehaven..there was a song on his lips.

latchous, var. LACHOUS *a. Obs.*, negligent.

'**latch-pan.** *dial.* [See LATCH *v.*[1]] (See quots.)

1639 HORN & ROB. *Gate Lang. Unl.* xli. §445 The droppings, or any thing else spilt by chance, is latcht in a latch-pan. *a* **1825** FORBY *Voc. E. Anglia, Latch-pan*, the pan placed under the joint while it is roasting, to latch the dripping.

'**latch-string.** A string passed through a hole in a door so that the latch may be raised from the outside. Hence *fig.* in *U.S.* colloq. phrases.

1791 in W. R. Jillson *Tales Dark & Bloody Ground* (1930) 109 The doors and the window shutters are..secured by stout bars on the inside with a latch-string of leather hanging out. **1859** *Trans. Illinois Agric. Soc.* III. 342 It is but another proof of the well known characteristics of the people of the west, that they are always to be found with 'their latch strings out'. **1861** GEO. ELIOT *Silas M.* iv, Intending to shake the door and pull the latch-string up and down, not doubting that the door was fastened. **1887** E. EGGLESTON *Graysons* xxiv. (1888) 254 Zeke impatiently rattled the door of the cabin, the latch-string of which had been drawn in to lock it. **1887** *Pall Mall. G.* 8 Jan. 6/2 We have..hung our latch-string out to you and yours. **1889** in *Times* 5 Mar. 9/2 Her [the United States'] free latchstring never was drawn in Against the meanest child of Adam's kin. **1893** *Advance* (Chicago) 16 Mar. 209 'Our latch string is out', has become a classic expression of cordial hospitality. **1895** *Daily News* 19 Apr. 4/7 The latch-string of English society hangs outside the door for an American. **1937** V. D. SCUDDER *On Journey* III. ii. 298 Especially at Commencement time, when the latch-string hangs out for returning alumnae.

†**late**, *sb.*[1] *Obs.* Forms: α. 3–5 **late**, 4 **lat**, 5–8 *Sc.* **lait**, (6 **laitt, laytt**). β. 3–5 **lote**, 4 **lot**. γ. 2–4 **lete**, 3 **læte**. [a. ON. (1) *lát* let, letting (as in *blóð-lát* blood-letting), loss, in pl. manners, sounds; (2) *læte* (only in nom. and acc.) manner, sound; f. root of LET *v.*[1]]

1. Look; appearance, aspect; outward manner or bearing.

α. *c* **1200** ORMIN 1213 3iff þu..hafesst 3et, tohh þu be 3ung, Elldernemanness late. *a* **1225** *Ancr. R.* 90 ȝif þu makest..eni luue lates touward unðeauwes. *c* **1320** *Sir Tristr.* 2097 It semeþ by his lat As he hir neuer had sene Wiþ si3t. *c* **1375** *Sc. Leg. Saints* ix. (*Bartholomaeus*) 235 With gret noyse & il-mowtht late. **1375** BARBOUR *Bruce* VII. 127 Thai changit contenanss and late. *c* **1470** *Golagros & Gaw.* 746 Lufsum of lait.

β. *c* **1250** *Gen. & Ex.* 2328 Wid reweli lote, and sorwe, and wep. **13..** *E.E. Allit. P.* A. 895 Lyk to himself of lote & hwe. *γ.* *c* **1175** *Lamb. Hom.* 69 Habben [we] feir lete and ec skil. *c* **1200** *Trin. Coll. Hom.* 79 He makeð lete of þole-burdnesse and neðeles ne haueð non. *c* **1205** LAY. 18543 Ofte he hire loh to & makede hire letes. *a* **1250** *Owl & Night.* 35 For þine vule lete. *c* **1340** *Cursor M.* 14053 (Trin.) Ihesu þo bihelde hir lete.

b. *pl.* Looks, manners, behaviour; *hence*, actions, goings-on.

α. *c* **1205** LAY. 1196 Ofte he custe þat weofed mid wnsume lates. *a* **1225** *Leg. Kath.* 105 þeos lufsume lafdi wið laste-lese lates. *a* **1400** *Isumbras* 180 So come a lyonne with latys unmylde. ? *a* **1400** *Morte Arth.* 248 Lughe one hyme luffly with lykande lates. *a* **1400–50** *Alexander* 3998 Porrus, as a prince suld, persayued þar latis. *c* **1470** *Golagros & Gaw.* 160 He wes ladlike of laitis, and light of his fere. **1501** DOUGLAS *Pal. Hon.* III. 302 Men that callis ladyis lidder, And licht of laitis. *c* **1560** A. SCOTT *Poems* xxxiv. 84 Auldit rubiatouris To hant the laittis of lawdis. **1590** A. HUME *Hymns*, etc. (1832) 2 Alace, how lang haue I delayed To leaue the laits of youth? **1728** RAMSAY *Monk & Miller's Wife.* 215 Sic laits appear to us sae awfu', We hardly think your learning lawfu'.

β. *c* **1205** LAY. 14321 Freond sæiðe to freonde mid fæire loten hende Leofue freond wæs hail. *c* **1400** *Destr. Troy* 10770 Hit were labur to long hir lotis to tell.

γ. *c* **1205** LAY. 15661 Vortigerne..þa læuedi aueng mid swiðe uæire læten. *a* **1300** *Cursor M.* 3285 Ne was sco not o letes [*Fairf.* lates] light.

2. Voice, sound.

a **1300** *Cursor M.* 12496 Quen iesus herd þis quaining gret þe late þai thoru þe cite let, He had þar-for wel gret pite. *c* **1325** *Metr. Hom.* 123 Hir lufli lat [*MS. C.* voice] es win gastlye, That Iesus drinkes ful gladlye. **13..** *E.E. Allit. P.* C. 161 þe lot of þe wyndes. **13..** *Gaw. & Gr. Knt.* 1398 Wyth lotez þat were to lowe. *a* **1400–50** *Alexander* 4384 þan we haue liking to lithe þe late of þe foules.

late (leɪt), *a.*[1] (*sb.*[2]) Forms: 1 læt, (lat-), 3 let, 3–7 *chiefly Sc. and north.* lat, (4 latt, 5 laat), 3– late; *Sc.* (*and north.*) 4–5 layt, 4–6 lait, 5 layte, 5–7 laite, 6 lett. For the comparative and superlative see LATER, LATTER, and LATEST, LAST. [Com. Teut.: OE. *læt* = OFris. *let*, OS. *lat*, LG. *lât* (Du. *laat*), OHG., MHG. *laz* (G. *lass*), ON. *lat-r* (Sw. *lat*, Du. *lad*), Goth. *lats*, all in the sense of 'slow, sluggish, lazy':—OTeut. **lato-*; f. **lat-* (:— pre-Teut. **lad-*, cf. L. *lassus* weary = **lad-tus*) ablaut-var. of **lēt-*: see LET *v.*[1]]

A. *adj.* **1.** Slow, tardy; *dial.* slow in progress, tedious. Const. *to* with *inf.*; also with gen. or *of*. Now *dial.*

Beowulf 1529 Eft wæs unræd, nalas elnes læt. *c* **897** K. ÆLFRED *Gregory's Past.* xxxviii. 281 Swiðe ȝeornfull to ȝehieranne, & swiðe læt to sprecanne. **971** *Blickl. Hom.* 43 Se mæsse-preost se þe bið to læt þæt he þæt deofol of men adrife. *c* **1000** *Sax. Leechd.* II. 238 Be latre meltunge innan. *c* **1200** *Trin. Coll. Hom.* 183 To gode þu ware slau & let, & to euele spac & hwat. *c* **1230** *Hali Meid.* 37 His wax-unge se lat & se slaw his thrifti. *a* **1300** *Cursor M.* 17288 + 374 'A! foyls', quod our lord, 'ful latt are ȝe to traw'. **13..** *E.E. Allit. P.* B. 1172 Of leaute he watz lat to his lorde hende. *a* **1375** *Joseph Arim.* 695 Ioseph..Called him Mordreyns 'a lat mon' in troupe. **1422** tr. *Secreta Secret., Priv. Priv.* 223 Laat of mevynge, and Slow to take nedys but yf thay bene grete. **1674–91** RAY *N.C. Words* 42 Lat, late, slow, tedious... Lat week. **1826** WILBRAHAM *Gloss. Cheshire* 53 *Lat-a-foot*, slow in moving. **1887** *S. Cheshire Gloss.*, *Lat*..(4) tedious. 'A lat job'.

2. a. Occurring, coming, or being after the due or customary time; delayed or deferred in time. Const. *to* with *inf.*, and *for*. Frequently in the impers. phrase *it is* (*too*) *late to* do something.

c **1000** *Ags. Gosp.* Luke i. 21 þæt folc wæs zachariam ȝeanbidiende & wundredon þæt he on þam temple læt wæs. **1297** R. GLOUC. (Rolls) 7824 It was þo to late ynou. *c* **1375** *Sc. Leg. Saints* xxix. (*Placidas*) 2 Lat penance is rycht perolouse. *Ibid.* xxxviii. (*Adrian*) 77 ȝet wil I, þo it lat be, to criste and his treutht tak me. **1560** DAUS tr. *Sleidane's Comm.* 113 b, She aunswereth that it is to late nowe to examyne the licence, whiche so longe synce they had allowed. *a* **1572** KNOX *Hist. Ref.* Wks. 1846 I. 116 Thei begane to suspect, (albeit it was to lett). **1588** SHAKS. *L.L.L.* I. i. 108 So you to studie now it is too late. **1676** LADY CHAWORTH in *12th Rep. Hist. MSS. Comm.* App. v. 33 A great snow with us makes the post so late that [etc.]. **1779–81** JOHNSON *L.P., Prior* Wks. III. 144 Of his behaviour in the lighter parts of life, it is too late to get much intelligence. **1816** A. C. HUTCHISON *Pract. Obs. Surg.* (1826) 206 'Ah Pat, my boy, you are just in time to be too late'. **1855** MACAULAY *Hist. Eng.* xiii. III. 349 Their late repentance might perhaps give them a fair claim to pardon. **1862** MRS. H. WOOD *Channings* I. iv. 58 The head-master..is waiting for you; marking you all late, of course. **1884** MAY CROMMELIN *Brown-Eyes* x. 102 The cab is at the door; don't be late for the train.

b. Of plants, fruit, etc.: Flowering or ripening at an advanced season of the year.

c **1440** *Promp. Parv.* 288/2 Late frute, *sirotinus*. **1697** DRYDEN *Virg. Georg.* IV. 184 The late Narcissus. **1727–51** CHAMBERS *Cycl.* s.v. *Flower*, Autumnal or late Flowers, denotes those of September and October. **1796** C. MARSHALL *Gardening* (1813) 405 Sow annuals of all sorts for a late blow. **1837** MACGILLIVRAY *Withering's Brit. Plants* (ed. 4) 332 Late Spider Orchis..Early Spider Orchis.

c. Of fruit, etc.: Backward in ripening. Of seasons: Prolonged or deferred beyond their due time. †*dial.* Of weather: Unseasonable.

1631 MILTON *Sonn., Arriv. Age Twenty-three* 3 My late spring no bud or blossom shew'th. **1674–91** RAY *N.C. Words* s.v. *Lat*, Lat weather; wet or otherwise unseasonable weather. **1886** *Cheshire Gloss.*, *Lat*,..(2) backward; 'A lat spring'. **1887** *S. Cheshire Gloss.* s.v. *Lat*, 'My wuts bin very lat this 'ear'.

d. With agent-nouns and vbl. sbs. (For the syntactical relation, cf. EARLY *a.* 1 a *note.*)

late comers in *Fr. Hist.* (transl. of F. *tard-venus*), the name given to troops of soldiers, who were disbanded after the treaty of Bretigny (1374) and overran and ravaged France (see quot. 1869). *late developer*: see DEVELOPER e.

c **1430** *How Wise Man taught Son* 69 in *Babees Bk.*, Of late walking, comeþ debate. **1598** SHAKS. *Merry W.* V. v. 153 This is enough to be the decay of lust and late-walking through the Realme. **1612** BACON *Ess.*, *Custom*, For it is true that late learners cannot so well take the plie. **1869** W. LONGMAN *Hist. Edw. III*, II. iv. 63 A cloud of Lorrainers, Brabanters, and Germans spread themselves over Champagne and the countries of the Upper Meuse, and these called themselves the 'Tard venus', or late comers, 'because they had not as yet much pillaged the kingdom of France'. **1873** HAMERTON *Intell. Life* x. x. 387 The late-risers are rebels and sinners—in this respect—to a man. **1891** *Cornh. Mag.* Oct. 416 His whole life was spent in raids ..upon the Brabanters, late-comers, flayers, [etc.]. **1892** J. S. FLETCHER *When Chas. I was K.* (1896) 18 Then did late-comers, hearing the solitary bell, hurry their movements.

e. *late cut* (*Cricket*): a cut, but with the actual stroke delayed until after the usual moment. Hence also as vb. Cf. CUT *sb.*[2] 10 a and CUT *v.* 31 a.

1887 F. GALE *Game of Cricket* 263 A splendid bat, back player, and great at a late 'cut'. **1906** [see *square-cut* s.v. SQUARE *a.* 15]. **1912** J. B. HOBBS *Recovering the Ashes* 124 An off ball gave Mr. Trumper a chance to late cut one nicely to the cycle path. **1960** *Times* 3 June 21/2 He will..late cut another in a way possible to few. **1963** *Times* 7 June 4/5 Padgett, after a delicate late cut for four.., was bowled off his pads. **1974** *Observer* 9 June 24/7 When Underwood came on, Gavaskar danced out to drive him straight, then lay back to late cut through the slips.

f. *late-tackle v. trans.*: in *Rugby* and *Assoc. Football*, to tackle (an opponent) illegally, when he is no longer in possession of the ball. Also as *sb.* So *late-tackling* vbl. sb.

1957 Late-tackling [see BLATANT *a.* 2 c]. **1960** T. MCLEAN *Kings of Rugby* xi. 198 Raureti for the second time in the match palpably late-tackled Young. **1962** *Times* 26 June 3/6 People who have seen the film are now satisfied that he was not late-tackled at Pretoria. **1971** J. B. G. THOMAS *Roaring Lions* vi. 117 McNaughton swung him round to the ground without malice, but it was a late tackle, and Referee Pring.. had no alternative but to award a penalty. **1974** *Times* 22 Nov. 11/1 England got bogged down..against a defence.. in which a combination of offside tactics, obstruction and the cynical late tackle played a major role. This is what has come to be expected from visitors to Wembley.

g. Applied to a woman whose menstrual period has failed to occur at the expected time. *colloq.*

1962 J. LUDWIG in R. Weaver *Canad. Short Stories* (1968) 2nd Ser. 255 Shirley, maybe you're late this month, eh, dollie? **1969** 'V. PACKER' *Don't rely on Gemini* (1970) xiv. 119 Penny was two weeks late... There was a very good possibility that she was carrying Neal Dana's child. **1974** D. FLETCHER *Lovable Man* i. 21 Linda realised that she was late. .. It was impossible to consult her family doctor.

3. a. Advanced in point of time in the course of the day or night; so *late in the day* (also *fig.*). (Frequent in the impers. phrase *it is late* = the time is advanced.) Phr. *late hours*: hours which encroach on the proper time for sleep; so *late-houred a.* Hence *colloq.* of persons, in the sense 'keeping late hours, rising or going to bed late'; so *late bird*. Also *late-afternoon*, *late-night*, used attrib.

a **1000** *Andreas* 1210 (Gr.) Nis seo stund latu. **1340** HAMPOLE *Pr. Consc.* 1433 Now es arly, now es late, Now es day, now es nyght. **1375** BARBOUR *Bruce* VII. 236 It wes weill lat of nycht be then. *a* **1400–50** *Alexander* 5051 þar logis he fra þe late niȝt till efte þe liȝt schewis. *c* **1470** HENRY *Wallace* v. 244 'Quhat art thow walkis that gait?' 'A trew man, Schyr, thocht my wiagis be layt'. **1513** DOUGLAS *Æneis* VII. i. 34 In silence, al the lait nycht [L. *sera sub nocte*] rummesand. *a* **1548** HALL *Chron.*, *Hen. VIII*, 240 To se..how late it was in the nyght yer the footemen coulde get ouer London brydge. **1634** MILTON *Comus* 179 The rudenesse, and swill'd insolence Of such late Wassailers. **1732** BERKELEY *Alciphr.* II. §13 Without love, and wine, and play, and late hours we hold life not to be worth living. **1776** *Trial of Nundocomar* 2/1 It being late, the Court adjourned till the next morning at seven o'clock. **1842** TENNYSON *Vision Sin* I, I had a vision when the night was late. **1870** SWINBURNE *Ess. & Stud.* 367 The stunted brushwood, the late and pale sky. **1884** *Bread Winners* 76 Drunkenness, late hours, and botchy work. **1888** E. BELLAMY *Looking Backward* v. 64 If I was inclined to wakefulness nothing would please him better than to bear me company. 'I am a late bird, myself,' he said. **1897** OUIDA *Massarenes* xiv, We are all of us very late people. **1898** *Daily News* 30 June 6/3 His friend was what might be called a late man. The Duke [of Wellington], as everybody knew, was quite the reverse. The appointment was for eight o'clock in the morning... 'How can you manage to keep it?' 'Oh,' he replied, 'it's the easiest thing in the world. I shall take it the last thing before going to bed.' **1908** *Daily Chron.* 10 Jan. 4/6 The pantomime crowd is a very good crowd after all, late-houred and not without failings, perhaps, but generous..to a fault. **1969** V. C. CLINTON-BADDELEY *Only Matter of Time* 9 He had never been a late bird... He was seldom out after twelve.

fig. phrase. **1797** WASHINGTON *Let.* Writ. 1892 XIII. 411 It is too late in the day for me to see the result. **1816** JANE AUSTEN *Emma* I. xvii. 303 It was rather too late in the day to set about being simple-minded and ignorant. **1824** BYRON *Def. Transf.* II. iii. 155 A sage reflection, But somewhat late i' the day. **1861** C. J. LEVER *Day's Ride* xlvii. in *All Year Round* 23 Mar. 568/1 Rather late in the day, I take it, to ask who Bob Rogers is! **1912** A. HUXLEY *Let.* 16 June (1969) 44 They are also on the point of putting up a war memorial, though none of the people who were in the war want it and it is now a little late in the day. **1965** *Listener* 16 Dec. 1012/1 Just when the smoke..has cleared..Mr Roger Pemberton [tells]..why he hates the views of Miss Laski... Surely this is a bit late in the day? **1972** P. A. WHITNEY *Listen for Whisperer* ii. 22. 'I've brought her something from my father.'..'It's a bit late in the day for such a message.'

attrib. **1885** 'MARK TWAIN' in *Century Mag.* Dec. 202/2 The damp, earthy, late-night smells. **1944** D. EDWARDS in *Austral. Short Stories* (1951) 338 The street that glows with late-afternoon sun. **1956** B. HOLIDAY *Lady sings Blues* (1973) xv. 124 If you're an American citizen and unless you go to bed early these nights, you're liable to see me on the late-late show. **1957** J. OSBORNE *Entertainer* iii. 31 He plays the piano in one of these late-night drinking places. **1968** *Listner* 5 Sept. 306/2 For thousands of young people Peel has the only late-night show worth turning on. **1971** *Black Scholar* Apr.–May 47/1 Some are sleeping because they're the late late TV show viewers. **1971** P. PURSER *Holy Father's Navy* xxii. 109 We got them on to the late-afternoon plane to Zagreb. **1973** *Amer. Speech 1969* XLIV. 277 An unusual example evolved on a late-night television talk show.

b. *late dinner*: esp. in Victorian society, the main evening meal, held later than the children's dinner.

1838 MRS. GASKELL *Let.* 2 Dec. (1966) 38 Mr Bradford coming home to late dinner and so agreeable. **1873** L. TROUBRIDGE *Life amongst Troubridges* (1966) 11 Mrs Quick is the cook... She makes very good things for late dinner but not for our [*sc.* the children's] dinner. **1885** A. EDWARDES *Girton Girl* I. vi. 136 The dinner-hour at Tintajeux was five, the 'late dinner' of Andros Bartrand's youth. **1941** MRS. BELLOC LOWNDES *I, too, have lived in Arcadia* xviii. 350 Even now the presence of a child at late dinner would certainly occasion surprise, to almost any guest of that child's parents.

4. Belonging to an advanced stage in a period, the development of something, the history of a science, language, etc. Also *occas.* in partitive concord, the late portion of (a period, season). spec. *late-Victorian* adj.; **late blight**, a disease of potatoes caused by the fungus *Phytophthora infestans*; = *potato blight* (POTATO *sb.* 7); **late wood**, a denser section of the annual ring of a tree, formed late in the growing season.

c **1380** WYCLIF *Wks.* (1879) 332 What meued þis late popes to make furst þis lawe..and god meued not crist ne hise vikers to sue it. **1583** FULKE *Defence* iii. 114 The late pettie Prelates of the seconde Nicene Councell. **1777** SIR W. JONES *Turkish Ode* x. Poems 93 Late gloomy winter chill'd the sullen air. **1781** COWPER *Retirement* 31 Looked for at so late a day, In the last scene of such a senseless play. **1784** —— *Tiroc.* 143 E'en in transitory life's late day. **1842** PRICHARD *Nat. Hist. Man* 141 The Chaldee of the late Scriptures of the Old Testament. **1849–52** ROCK *Ch. of Fathers* III. i. 194 *note*, The 'Dome', or last judgment, is shown in late but beautiful Flemish stained glass at Fairford. **1868** W. K. PARKER *Shoulder-girdle & Sternum Vertebr.* 185 The ossification of the sternum in the Hemipods is very late, as compared with the Fowl. **1888** SWEET *Hist. Eng. Sounds* §609. 164 The late Latin hymn metres. *Ibid.* §756. 200, 1800–1850 Early Living English. 1850–1900 Late Living English. **1905** *28th Ann. Rep. Connecticut Agric. Exper. Station* 379 Spraying will be of greater value, especially if early blight has been injurious or the late blight appears before the end of their season. **1909** B. M. DUGGAR *Fungous Diseases of Plants* x. 165 The late blight and rot of the potato is so generally known that frequently this malady is simply called the 'potato disease'. **1913** W. J. LOCKE *Stella Maris* iii. 26 Risca's room was transformed from late-Victorian solidity into early-Georgian elegance. **1918** E. J. BUTLER *Fungi & Dis. in Plants* viii. 277 The potato disease known as 'blight', 'late blight' or 'Irish blight' first attracted general attention in Europe in 1845. **1920** BEERBOHM *And Even Now* 3 A tired suit of Late Victorian pattern. **1929** T. THOMSON tr. *Büsgen's Struct. & Life Forest Trees* vi. 178 The difference between early and late wood consists in the former appearing more porous and open than the latter and often differently coloured. **1933** F. D. HEALD *Man. Plant Dis.* (ed. 2) xvi. 419 The late-blight attacks and kills the tops of the potato plant and invades the tubers, causing either a *dry* or a *wet rot*. **1955** *Sci. News Let.* 11 June 381/1 In an effort to find clues that might help clear up the mystery surrounding late blight..plant pathologists..have surveyed the world. **1969** J. MANDER *Static Soc.* vi. 175 Teasingly sexless in the late-Victorian manner. **1972** *Sci. Amer.* May 92/1 Effect of smog on a Jeffrey pine that was growing in a forest near Los Angeles may be indicated by the narrowed rings and a reduced amount of latewood in the last nine years of the tree's life. **1975** *Nature* 10 Apr. 507/1 Whatever the cause, there is no indication that the width of the subsequent latewood was significantly altered.

5. a. Of a person: That was alive not long ago, but is not now; recently deceased.

1490 CAXTON *Eneydos* vi. 28 Her swete and late amyable husbonde. *a* **1548** HALL *Chron.*, *Hen. IV*, 10 b, The homecide of Thomas his uncle late duke of Glocester. **1570** BUCHANAN *Admonitioun* Wks. (S.T.S.) 22 Ye murthour of ye lait King Henry. **1662** STILLINGFL. *Orig. Sacr.* II. vii. §7 The late learned Rabbi Manasse Ben Israel. **1727** DE FOE *Syst. Magic* I. iii. (1840) 84 Our late friend Jonathan. **1794** MRS. RADCLIFFE *Myst. Udolpho* xxv, I did nothing but dream I saw my late lady's ghost. **1838** LYTTON *Alice* 23, I always call the late Lord Vargrave my father. **1884** *Times* (weekly ed.) 5 Sept. 1/1 The remains of the late Lord Ampthill.

b. That was recently (what is implied by the sb.) but is not now. [App. developed from the use of LATE *adv.* 4 b.]

a **1548** HALL *Chron.*, *Hen. IV*, 19 b, [He] maried Jane Duches of Britaine late wife to Jhon duke of Britaine. *Ibid.*, *Hen. VIII*, 240 At the late Freers walle all men alyghted savyng the Kyng. **1689** WOOD *Life* 7 Nov., A late Roman Catholic schoolmaster..hath embraced his former persuasion, viz. protestancy. **1766** GOLDSM. *Vic. W.* xxv, Our late dwelling. **1820** W. IRVING *Sketch Bk.* I. 48 All the splendid furniture of his late residence. **1842** MACAULAY *Ess.*, *Fred. Gt.* (1887) 717 He conceived himself secure from the power of his late master.

6. Recent in date; that has recently happened or occurred; recently made, performed,

completed; of recent times; belonging to a recent period. Now *Obs.* of persons, and chiefly in phr. ***of late years***; also ***late model***, a recent model of a motor vehicle (usu., with hyphen, *attrib.*); ***the late unpleasantness*** (*U.S.*), the American Civil War (see UNPLEASANTNESS).

1513 MORE in Grafton *Chron.* (1568) II. 803 All things were in late dayes so covertly demeaned. **1560** DAUS tr. *Sleidane's Comm.* 168b, The kynge..was than scarcely amended of a late disease. **1573** *Satir. Poems Reform.* xl. 210 Of lat ȝeiris. **1599** SHAKS. *Hen. V*, II. ii. 61 Who are the late Commissioners? **1667** MILTON *P.L.* v. 113 Ill matching words and deeds long past or late. **1685** BAXTER *Paraphr. N.T.*, 1 Tim. iii. 6 Not a late young Convert. **1711** BUDGELL *Spect.* No. 161 ¶1 My late going into the Country has encreased the Number of my Correspondents. **1817** COLERIDGE *Biogr. Lit.* 103 The late war, was a war produced by the Morning Post. **1838** MACAULAY *Let. to Napier* in Trevelyan *Life* (1876) II. vii. 10 His late articles, particularly the long one in the April number, have very high merit. **1849** —— *Hist. Eng.* vi. II. 104 During the late reign Johnson had published a book entitled Julian the Apostate. **1893** W. P. COURTNEY in *Academy* 13 May 412/3 The public appetite for the consumption of memoirs has been wonderfully sharpened of late years. **1917** G. ADE *Let.* 26 Apr. (1973) 63 Our own majestic work of art..has more late-model cars parked around it. **1973** R. BUSBY *Pattern of Violence* i. 15 They had found a late-model Ford Cortina XL unmistakably tooled up for violent crime.

7. *colloq.* Having to do with persons or things that arrive late.

late mark, a mark indicating that a scholar is late for school; so ***late book***, a book to contain such marks. ***late fee***, an increased fee paid in order to secure the dispatch of a letter posted after the advertised time of collection (earlier ***late-letter fee***).

1862 MRS. H. WOOD *Channings* I. xv. 237 They escaped the 'late' mark. **1864** *Brit. Postal Guide* Jan. 16 Upon payment of a late fee of fourpence. **1889** SKRINE *Mem. E. Thring* i. 9 Excluded wretches..entered, and..wrote their names in the late-book.

B. *absol.* or quasi-*sb.*

†**1.** Lateness, tardiness. *Obs. rare.*

a **1400** *Destr. Troy* 9679 The store was full stith, þen stynt þai for late. *Ibid.* 10913 All left þai for late & lackyng of Sun.

2. of late: during a comparatively short time extending to the present; recently, lately.

c **1470** HENRY *Wallace* v. 757 Sen I off laitt now come owt off the west In this cuntre. **1500–20** DUNBAR *Poems* xiv. 46 Sa mony jugeis and lordis now maid of lait. *a* **1533** LD. BERNERS *Huon* li. 172 Of late I haue lost my goode lorde and mayster. **1611** BIBLE *John* xi. 8 Master, the Iewes of late sought to stone thee, and goest thou thither againe? **1644** EVELYN *Mem.* (1857) I. 121 Till of late that some of the stones were carried away to repair the city walls. **1716** ADDISON *Freeholder* No. 32 ¶2 Great Numbers of them [women] have of late eloped from their Allegiance. **1827** STEUART *Planter's G.* (1828) 14 Since the Ladies of late have become students of Chemistry. **1845** STEPHEN *Comm. Laws Eng.* (1874) II. 744 In modern times, and particularly of late, various alterations have been introduced.

†**late**, *a.*² *Obs. rare*⁻¹. [ad. L. *lāt-us* broad.] Broad, wide.

1657 TOMLINSON *Renou's Disp.* 297 Leaves..long, late, mucronated, hispid.

late (leɪt), *adv.* Forms: 1 late; the rest as in LATE *a.*¹ [OE. *late* = OHG. *laz*, *lazzo* slowly, lazily (comp. *lazzôr*); f. *læt*, *lat-* LATE *a.*¹]

†**1.** Slowly. (Only OE.)

c **1000** *Sax. Leechd.* II. 196 Late mylt gæten flæsc. *c* **1050** *Voc.* in Wr.-Wülcker 430/15 *Lento*, late.

2. a. After the proper or usual time; at an advanced or deferred period; after delay; at a late stage or season.

a **1000** *O.E. Chron.* an. 867 (Parker MS.) Late on ȝeare. *c* **1000** *Juliana* 444 Ic þæt sylf ȝecneow to late micles. *a* **1200** *Moral Ode* 128 Wel late he latheð uuel werc þe ne mei hit don ne mare. *c* **1200** ORMIN 753 Þatt teȝȝ swa late mihhtenn child I mikell elde streonenn. *c* **1320** *Sir Tristr.* 695 Fair his tale bi gan Rohand, þei he com late. *c* **1375** *Sc. Leg. Saints* xviii. (*Egipciane*) 1483 Þocht at I lat turne me to þe, dere laydy, ȝet þu succure me. *c* **1386** CHAUCER *Pars. T.* ¶300 Whan he comth by thilke encheson to late to chirche. **1483** *Cath. Angl.* 209/2 Late ripe, *serotinus, tardus.* **1560** DAUS tr. *Sleidane's Comm.* 13 Then shal we bewaile our bondage all to late. **1598** SHAKS. *Merry W.* II. ii. 328 Better three houres too soone, then a mynute too late. *a* **1657** SIR W. MURE *Misc. Poems* i. 127 In tyme tak heid thairof then, least too lait thou mourne. **1766** GOLDSM. *Vic. W.* ii, But not till too late I discovered that he was violently attached to the contrary opinion. **1862** THACKERAY *Philip* xxxv, Philip had come late to dinner.

transf. **1897** W. C. HAZLITT *4 Gen. Lit. Fam.* II. 155 Byron said, her costume began too late, and ended too soon.

Proverb. c **1386** CHAUCER *Can. Yeom. Prol.* & *T.* 857 For bet than never is late. *c* **1425** LYDG. *Assembly of Gods* 1204 He seyde Vyce to forsake ys bettyr late then neuer. **1529** MORE *Suppl. Soulys* Wks. 336/2 Sith that late is better then neuer. **1708** OCKLEY *Saracens* (1848) 222 Whilst he was murdering the unhappy Aleppians, Kaled (better late than never) came to their relief. **1852** C. M. YONGE *Two Guardians* xviii. 364 She obtained from Agnes some admiration for Caroline's conduct, though in somewhat of the 'better late than never style'. **1876** G. H. LEWES *Let.* 10 Jan. in Geo. Eliot *Lett.* VI. (1956) 211, I think that in the next number at any rate a bill might be inserted with effect—better late than never! **1950** G. GREENE *Third Man* ix. 77 Oh, Mr. Dexter, we have been so anxious, but better late than never. **1954** A. HUXLEY *Let.* 16 Sept. (1969) 711, I am sorry your holiday will have to be postponed so long; but better late than never.

b. Coupled with *early*, (†*ere*), *soon*, (†*rathe*).

c **1200** ORMIN 6242 Beon ar & late o ȝunkerr weorrc. *a* **1225** *Ancr. R.* 338 Oðer ich hit do ungledliche oðer to er oðer to leate. *a* **1310** in Wright *Lyric P.* xxxvi. 99 Er ant late y be thy foo. *c* **1340** *Cursor M.* 1318 (Trin.) Fison, gison, tigre, & eufrate Al erþe þese weten erly & late. **1362** LANGL. *P. Pl.* A. x. 13 Dobet..serueþ þat ladi lelly boþe late and raþe. *c* **1425** [see ERE A 1]. **1430–40** LYDG. *Bochas* III. i. (1554) 69b, Glad Pouert, late nother sone, With thy riches hath nothing to done. **1578**, **1795** [see ERE A 1]. **1818** BYRON *Ch. Har.* IV. clxxi, A weight..which crushes soon or late.

3. Of the time of day: At or till a late hour.

c **1400** *Lanfranc's Cirurg.* 189 Herwiþ þou schalt anoynte hir face at euen late. *c* **1475** *Rauf Coilȝear* 40 Euill lykand was the King it nichtit him sa lait. **1500–20** DUNBAR *Poems* lvii. 8 Sum lait at evin bringis in the moreis. **1540** BIBLE (Great) *Ps.* cxxvii. 2 It is but loste laboure that ye haste to ryse up early, and so late take reste [**1611** to sit vp late]. **1613** PURCHAS *Pilgrimage* (1614) 210 They continue singing till late in the night. **1697** DRYDEN *Virg. Georg.* IV. 197 Late returning home he supp'd at Ease. **1698** FRYER *Acc. E. India & P.* 74 It is dangerous to walk late for fear of falling into the Hands of those..Rascals. **1716** ADDISON *Freeholder* No. 22 ¶3 We sat pretty late over our punch. **1794** MRS. RADCLIFFE *Myst. Udolpho* xv, After supper, her aunt sat late. **1837** DICKENS *Pickwick* xxxvii, I was up very late last night.

4. a. Recently, of late, lately; in recent times; not long since; but now; †not long (*ago, before*). Now only *poet.*

c **1330** R. BRUNNE *Chron.* (1810) 149 He regnes after him, and late had þe coroune. *c* **1340** *Cursor M.* 7917 (Trin.) Twey men were late in londe A pore and a riche wononde. **1362** LANGL. *P. Pl.* A. III. 105 Ichaue a Kniht hette Conscience com late from bi-ȝonde. **1377** *Ibid.* B. XVI. 249, I herde seyne late Of a barne þat [etc.]. *c* **1400** *Destr. Troy* 4887 Noght leng sithen but late. **1470–85** MALORY *Arthur* XIV. viii, She asked hym yf he had ete ony mete late. Nay madame truly I ete no mete nyghe this thre dayes. **1490** CAXTON *Eneydos* Prol. 1 A lytyl booke in frenshe, whiche late was translated oute of latyn. **1513** MORE in Grafton *Chron.* (1568) II. 767 The great obloquy that he was in so late before. **1530** PALSGR. 143 *Naguayres*, lately or late a go. **1592** SHAKS. *Ven. & Ad.* 1131 Their vertue lost, wherein they late exceld. **1665** MANLEY *Grotius' Low C. Warres* 625 The Castle..which he had late before rendred to the people of Cleves. **1677** W. MOUNTAGU in *Buccleuch MSS.* (Hist. MSS. Comm.) I. 325 The sickness late upon her. **1769** SIR W. JONES *Pal. Fortune* Poems (1777) 17 The bower, which late outshone the rosy morn. **1812** BYRON *Ch. Har.* To Ianthe i, Those climes where I have late been straying. **1820** KEATS *St. Agnes* xii, He had a fever late. **1883** R. W. DIXON *Mano* I. viii. 20 Gazing the sky which late thou seemedst to shun.

b. Not long since (but not now); recently (but no longer). (Cf. LATE *a.* 5 b.)

1474 CAXTON *Chesse* 57 John the monke late cardynal of Rome. **1491** *Act 7 Hen. VII*, c. 15 John Mountagu late Erle of Sarum. **1512** *Act 4 Hen. VIII*, c. 10 The Domynyons..that late were to Edwarde Courteney. **1590** SPENSER *F.Q.* III. iii. 42 Late king, now captive; late lord, now forlorne. **1593** SHAKS. *Rich. II*, II. i. 282 His brother Archbishop, late of Canterbury. **1605** —— *Ham.* II. ii. 530 A clout about that head, Where late the Diadem stood. **1669** (*title*) The mute Christian under the Smarting Rod..By Thomas Brooks late Preacher of the Word at St. Margarets New Fish-street, London. **1706** *Lond. Gaz.* No. 4249/4 John Barton, late of London, Clothdrawer. **1852** THACKERAY *Esmond* I. xiv, As Esmond crossed over to his own room, late the chaplain's.

†**5.** Behind the others; in the rear. *rare.*

1697 DRYDEN *Virg. Georg.* III. 708 Where..thou seest a single Sheep..Listlessly to crop the tender Grass, Or late to lag behind.

6. Relatively near the end of a historical period or of the history of a nation, etc.

1849 MACAULAY *Hist. Eng.* i. I. 22 Some faint traces of the institution of villenage were detected by the curious so late as the days of the Stuarts.

7. *Comb.* When qualifying a following ppl. adj., the word, like most other advs., is commonly hyphened, forming innumerable quasi-compounds, as (sense 2) ***late-begun***, ***-blowing***, ***-born***, ***-coming***, ***-flowering***, ***-lamented***, ***-lingering***, ***-protracted***, etc.; (sense 4) ***late-betrayed***, ***-built***, ***-coined***, ***-come***, ***-disturbed***, ***-embarked***, ***-filled***, ***-found***, ***-imprisoned***, ***-kissed***, ***-lost***, ***-met***, ***-raised***, ***-sacked***, ***-taken***, ***-transformed***, etc. adjs.

1933 *Mind* XLII. 279 The physiological and psychological processes which *cause* it to be given may be as complex and as *late-acquired as you please. **1651** JER. TAYLOR *Serm. for Year* I. vi. 75 A..*late-begun repentance. **1591** SHAKS. *1 Hen. VI*, III. ii. 82 As sure as in this *late betrayed Towne, Great Cordelions Heart was buryed. *a* **1800** COWPER *Winter Nosegay* iii, The charms of the *late-blowing rose. **1881** M. ARNOLD *Westminster Abb.* 8 Hither he came, *late-born and long-desired. **1709** *Lond. Gaz.* No. 4535/3 An excellent *late-built dwelling House. **1613** T. GODWIN *Rom. Antiq.* (1625) 29 *Novi, id est*, *late-coyned Nobles or vpstarts. **1639** FULLER *Holy War* II. xxix. (1647) 81 The *late-come Pilgrims. **1626** BACON *Sylva* §421 A *Late-Comming Fruit. **1923** BLUNDEN *To Nature* 10 *Late-departing yelps the fox. **1932** —— *Halfway House* 72, I have contrived that some most secret treasures Shall lie an age untouched, and *late-discovered Shall be the source of hope and peace. **1596** SHAKS. *1 Hen. IV*, II. iii. 62 Like bubbles in a *late-disturbed Streame. **1592** —— *Ven. & Ad.* cxxxvi, As one on shore Gazing upon a *late-embarked friend. **1923** D. H. LAWRENCE *Birds, Beasts & Flowers* 57 About your feet spontaneous aconite..and purple husband-tyranny Enveloping your *late-enfranchised plains. **1884** W. C. SMITH *Kildrostan* 43 At the head of a *late filled Grave. **1814** WORDSW. *White Doe Ryl.* IV. 86 *Late-flowering woodbine. **1855** MOTLEY *Dutch Rep.* (1861) I. 12 That noble Language which her late-flowering literature has rendered so illustrious. **1559** W. CUNNINGHAM *Cosmogr. Glasse* 169 The *late founde Ilandes. **1883** R. W. DIXON *Mano* I. iv. 8 Whilst our late found advantage all is ceased. **1937** BLUNDEN *Elegy* 30 Child of *late-gone gale. **1906** *Westm. Gaz.* 16 Oct. 10/1 Only a few stragglers—most of them birds with their *late-hatched broods—are left. **1725** POPE *Odyss.* x. 488 Around them throng With leaps and bounds their *late-imprison'd young. **1599** MARSTON *Sco. Villanie* II. vi, Mato ..with his *late kist-hand my booke doth grace. **1819** SHELLEY *Prometh. Unb.* I. 608 An early-chosen, *late-lamented home. **1865** G. M. HOPKINS *Poems* (1948) 36 That yield That I may win with *late-learnt skill uncouth. **1859** LD. LYTTON *Wanderer* (ed. 2) 297 The maid, *Late-lingering in her lover's arm. **1850** TENNYSON *In Mem.* xiii. 2 A *late-lost form that sleep reveals. **1936** AUDEN *Look, Stranger!* 29 On their behalf guard all the more This *late-maturing Northern shore. **1631** CHAPMAN *Cæsar & Pompey* Plays 1873 III. 152 In our *late-met Senate. **1790** HAN. MORE *Relig. Fash. World* (1791) 211 The frequent and *late-protracted ball. **1711** *Light to Blind* in *10th Rep. Hist. MSS. Comm.* App. v. 126 Many regiments of his *late raysed army. **1593** SHAKS. *Lucr.* ccxlix, Who like a *late-sacked island vastly stood. *a* **1586** SIDNEY *Arcadia* I. (1622) 42 Remembering that it was *late-taken loue, which had wrought this new course. **1725** POPE *Odyss.* x. 532 Meanwhile the Goddess, with indulgent cares And social joys, the *late-transform'd repairs.

late, var. LAIT; obs. f. LATH; see LET *v.*

latebord, obs. form of LARBOARD.

‖**latebra** (ˈlætɪbrə). *Embryology.* [L., = 'hiding-place', f. *latē-re* to be hid.] 'A small spherical mass of white yolk in the centre of the yellow yolk of a fowl's egg' (*Syd. Soc. Lex.* 1888).

latebricole, *a. rare*⁻⁰. [ad. mod.L. *latebricola*, f. L. *latebra* (see prec.) + *col-ĕre* to inhabit.] (See quot.)

1889 in *Century Dict.* **1894** GOULD *Illustr. Dict. Med.*, *Latebricole*, in biology, inhabiting a hiding-place, as certain spiders, crabs, etc.

†**latebrous**, *a. Obs. rare*⁻⁰. [ad. L. *latebrōs-us*, f. *latebra*: see prec.] 'That is full of holes, and dens to hide in' (Blount *Glossogr.* 1656).

lated (ˈleɪtɪd), *ppl. a. poet.* [as if f. *late vb. (f. LATE *a.*¹) + -ED¹.] = BELATED.

a **1592** GREENE *Orpharion* Wks. (Grosart) XII. 73 Cvpid abroade was lated in the night. **1592** WARNER *Alb. Eng.* VIII. xli. (1612) 198 If, perhaps, he lated weare. **1605** SHAKS. *Macb.* III. iii. 6 Now spurs the lated traveller apace. **1606** —— *Ant. & Cl.* III. xi. 3, I am so lated in the world, that I Haue lost my way for euer. **1697** DRYDEN *Virg. Past.* VII. 56 Come when my lated Sheep at Night return. **1812** BYRON *Ch. Har.* I. lxxii, Ne vacant space for lated wight is found. **1813** SCOTT *Rokeby* II. x, The lated peasant shunned the dell. **1829** —— *Doom Devorgoil* II. ii, Some hedge-inn, the haunt of lated drunkards. **1867** G. MACDONALD *Poems* 67 High sails the lated crow. **1898** T. HARDY *Wessex Poems* 80 Albeit therein—as lated tongues bespoke—Brunswick's high heart was drained.

lateen (læˈtiːn), *a.* (*sb.*) Also 8 latin, 8–9 latine, 9 lattine, latteen. [A phonetic spelling of F. *latine* (in *voile latine*, 'Latin sail', in allusion to its use in the Mediterranean), fem. of *latin* LATIN *a.* Cf. It. *latina* (Florio).] ***lateen sail***: a triangular sail suspended by a long yard at an angle of about 45 degrees to the mast. Hence, belonging to or having such a rig, as ***lateen mizzen***, ***vessel***, ***yard***.

1727–41 CHAMBERS *Cycl.* s.v. *Sail*, Others are triangular, called..by some Latin-sails, because chiefly used in Italy. **1769** FALCONER *Dict. Marine* (1780), *Lateen-sail*,.. frequently used by xebecs, polacres, settees, and other vessels..in the Mediterranean sea. *Ibid.* Tt 4, All yards are either square or lateen. **1777** FORSTER *Voy. round World* I. 462 Their sails, which are latine, are made of strong mats. **1779** FORREST *Voy. N. Guinea* 10, I..gave her a lateen mizen. **1836** MARRYAT *Midsh. Easy* xiii, The white latteen sails of the gun-boat. **1836** E. HOWARD *R. Reefer* xl, There was a spanking felucca, with her long lateen sails brailed up. **1842** E. NAPIER *Mediterranean* I. 312 These Latine vessels, or 'misticos' and 'feluccas', as they are generally termed, are fine boats. **1848** W. IRVING *Columbus* I. 130 The latine sails of the Niña were also altered into square sails, that she might work more steadily and securely. **1883** G. C. DAVIES *Norfolk Broads* ix. 67 In the old times the almost universal rig was the lateen, the most picturesque of all rigs.

Comb. **1880** *Daily Tel.* 17 Sept., Lateen-rigged feluccas.

b. A lateener.

1836 MARRYAT *Midsh. Easy* (1863) 275 Only three men were left in the latteens, and four in the galliot.

Hence **laˈteener**, a vessel with a lateen rig.

1873 *Young Englishwoman* Oct. 515/2 'Here comes a lateener,' says the captain, as a light vessel rigged in the style familiar to mariners of the Mediterranean,..takes a flight up the Broad. **1882** G. C. DAVIES *Riv. & Broads Norf. & Suff.* viii. 49 An eight-ton lateener. **1883** —— *Norfolk Broads* ix. 68 One or two ancient craft at Norwich, are the only survivors of the old lateeners. **1953** C. S. FORESTER *Hornblower & Atropos* 245 The lateener's heading this way.

†**ˈlateful**, *a. Obs.* [f. LATE *a.*¹ + -FUL.] Late in season.

1382 WYCLIF *Jas.* v. 7 An erthe tilyer abijdith precious fruyt of the erthe, pacientli suffringe, til he receyue tymeful and lateful [so **1388**]. **1388** —— *Hos.* vi. 3 He schal come as a reyn to vs which is timeful and lateful [**1382** late].

lateis, obs. form of LATTICE.

†**ˈlateliness.** *Obs. rare.* Also 4 latlynes. [f. next + -NESS.] **a.** Tardiness. **b.** Recency.

a **1340** HAMPOLE *Psalter* xxxix. 24 Þat hulynes [*MS. S.* latlynes] þat he will not bifell. **1605** RALEIGH *Introd. Hist. Eng.* (1693) 2 A Work difficult, as well for the Antiquity, as the Lateliness of things done. **1610** HEALEY *St. Aug. Citie of God* XV. xx. 557 The latelinesse of maturity, whereby they

were not enabled to generation vntill they were aboue one hundred yeares old.

†ˈ**lately**, *a. Obs.* [f. LATE *a.*¹ + -LY¹.]

1. Slow.

c **1400** tr. *Secreta Secret., Gov. Lordsh.* 117 He, þat yn goynge, hauys his paas large and latly, welfare shall folwe him yn all his werkys.

2. Recent, late.

1581 STUBBES *Two Wunderf. Examples* in *Shaks. Soc. Papers* (1849) IV. 85 Remember thou thy lately plague, of blayne, of botche, and bile.

lately (ˈleɪtlɪ), *adv.* [OE. *lætlíce* (= ON. *latliga*), f. *læt-* LATE *a.*¹ + *-líce* -LY²; but mostly a mod. formation. (The inflected comparative and superlative are obs.)]

†**1.** Slowly, tardily, sluggishly; reluctantly, sparingly. *Obs.*

c **1000** *Life of Guthlac* xx. (1848) 80/12 Ða andswarode he him lætlice. *a* **1340** HAMPOLE *Psalter* lxxi. 15 Wise men of werldes witte wenes þat þai be rightwis..& forthy þai are latlier turned till shrift. *a* **1400** *Relig. Pieces fr. Thornton MS.* 17 Þou ȝernys ilke a daye þat at noghte avayles the, and euer mare ouer lattly þat it may availe the. *c* **1400** tr. *Secreta Secret., Gov. Lordsh.* 55 Do he hit noght ouer latly ne ouer hastly. *Ibid.* 73 Sterynge of body, ne bathes vse but latly. *Ibid.* 114 Of a meene heued bytwen greet and lytill, latly spekyng but mystere be.

†**2.** After or beyond the usual or proper time; behind time; at a late hour, late. *Obs.*

1515 BARCLAY *Egloges* II. (1570) A v b/1 That hath me caused so lately to be here. **1589** R. HARVEY *Pl. Perc.* (1590) 2 A policie..which they put in practise too lately. **1614** LODGE *Seneca* 1 Being badly lent, they are worse satisfied, and being unrestored are too lately complained of.

3. Not long since; within a short time past; within recent times; recently, of late.

1483 *Cath. Angl.* 210/1 Latly, *nuper*. **1494** FABYAN *Chron.* I. iv. 11 There to buylde a Cytie in the remembraunce of the Cytie of Troye lately subuerted. **1500–20** DUNBAR *Poems* xiii. 6 Bot laitly lichtit of my meir, I come of Edinburch fra the Sessioun. **1526** TINDALE *Acts* xviii. 2 A..iewe named Aquila,..latly come from Itali. **1533** GAU *Richt Vay* (S.T.S.) 104 The sekkis..quhilk ar rissine laitlie in the kirk. **1581** SAVILE *Tacitus' Hist.* II. liii. (1591) 85 To enquire newes of the passengers which latelyest came from those quarters. **1591** SYLVESTER *Du Bartas* I. vi. 1131 'T was first a green Tree, then a gallant Hull, Lately a Mushroom, now a flying Gull. **1645** MILTON *Tetrach.* Wks. 1851 IV. 167 They were suspected of pollution by some sects of Philosophy and Religions of old, and latelier among the Papists. **1670** LADY MARY BERTIE in *12th Rep. Hist. MSS. Comm.* App. v. 22 There is letely come out a new play by Mr. Dreyden. *a* **1758** RAMSAY *Vision* vi, Thy graneing, and maneing, Have laitlie reich'd myne eir. **1766** GOLDSM. *Vic. W.* xvi, One of your tenants, whose mother is lately dead. **1849** MACAULAY *Hist. Eng.* ix. I. 469 The Exclusionists, lately so powerful, might rise in arms against him.

b. In comb. with ppl. adjs.

1607 HIERON *Wks.* I. 230 Some vnexperienced & lately-pressed souldiers. **1612** DRAYTON *Polyolb.* xvii. 267 The lately-passed times denominate the new. **1619** —— *Leg. Robt. Dk. Normandy* cxxi, Dealing abroad his lately-purchas'd Prey. **1848** BUCKLEY *Iliad* 239 With lately-whetted axes.

¶**4.** At a later time, subsequently. *Obs. rare*⁻¹.

1673 WOOD *Life* 14 July, He said that he would leave it (being too long to recite) to a book that would lately come forth.

†ˈ**latemost**, *a. Obs.* Forms: 1 læt(e)mest, (hlætmest), 3 latemist, -mest, 7 latmost. [OE. *læt(e)mest*, f. *læt* LATE *a.*¹ + superl. suffix *-mest*.] Last.

c **950** *Lindisf. Gosp.* Luke xii. 59 Ne gæs ðu ðona oðð uutedlice ðone hlætmesto [*Rushw.* lætemestu, *Ags. Gosp.* ytemystan] pricclu ðu forȝelde. *c* **975** *Rushw. Gosp.* John vi. 40 Aweco ic hine on ðæm lætemesta dæȝe. *c* **1275** LAY. 11080 þat was þe latemiste [*earlier text* utemesten] read þat Custance iwarþ dead. ? *a* **1300** *Death* 49 in *O.E. Misc.* 171 þe latemest dai deþ haueð ibrouhit. *a* **1638** MEDE *Wks.* (1672) III. 597 The latmost Head is counted both a Seventh and an Eighth, though in truth it be but the Seventh according to the Vision. *Ibid.* 609 The latter times of the Fourth Kingdom..are the latmost times of the last times, or last times in special.

laten (ˈleɪt(ə)n), *v.* [f. LATE *a.*¹ + -EN.] **a.** *intr.* To become or grow late. **b.** *trans.* To make late. Hence ˈ**latening** *vbl. sb.* and *ppl. a.*

1880 MISS BROUGHTON *Sec. Th.* III. v, Meanwhile the rich summer latens. **1887** *Athenæum* 19 Feb. 252/2 The..calculation of fifty minutes' latening [of the moon] every day. **1889** *Pall Mall G.* 14 Nov. 2/1 The first numbers of the new daily will have to go to press as early as 11 p.m., latening the hour by degrees. **1890** *Temple Bar* Aug. 474 At this latening season.

laten, obs. f. LATIN; var. LATTEN; obs. inf. LET.

latence (ˈleɪtəns). *rare.* [f. LATENT *a.*: see -ENCE.] = next.

1794 COLERIDGE *Destiny Nations* iii, Infinite Love Whose latence is the plentitude of all.

latency (ˈleɪtənsɪ). [f. LATENT *a.*: see -ENCY.]

1. a. The condition or quality of being latent; concealed condition, nature, or existence; *spec.* in *Biol.* (see quot. 1888).

a **1638** MEDE *Wks.* (1672) v. 921 By the Woman in the Wilderness, I understand the condition of the true Church in respect of her Latency and Invisibility to the eyes of man. **1794** PALEY *Evid.* (1800) II. II. vii. 195 Which undesignedness is gathered from their latency, their minuteness, their obliquity [etc.]. **1817** CHALMERS *Astron. Disc.* iv. (1852) 93 Beneath the surface of all that the eye can rest upon, there lies the profoundness of a most unsearchable latency. **1883** TYNDALL in *Times* 28 May 5 Every great scientific generalisation..is preceded by a period of latency, to use a medical term. **1883** *Proc. Roy. Soc. Lond.* XXXV. 281 On the Variations of Latency in certain Skeletal Muscles of some different Animals. **1888** *Syd. Soc. Lex.*, *Latency*, a term applied to certain dispositions, powers, capabilities, or faculties, which may lie concealed in a plant, an animal, or a race, and only become manifest when the necessary conditions for their development are supplied. **1890** *Nature* 11 Dec. 123 The transfer and latency of heat. **1898** *Allbutt's Syst. Med.* V. 173 The extreme latency of the tubercle bacillus postulated by some writers.

b. *Psychoanalysis.* (See quot. 1934.) Freq. *attrib.*, esp. in ***latency period***.

1910 A. A. BRILL tr. *Freud's Three Contrib. to Sexual Theory* ii. 38 It is during this period of total or at least partial latency that the psychic forces develop which later act as inhibitions on the sexual life. *Ibid.* ii. 39 Sexual activity remains throughout the whole duration of the latency period until the reinforced breaking through of the sexual impulse in puberty. **1913** E. JONES *Papers on Psycho-Anal.* ii. 26 A period of latency follows, usually from the fifth to the tenth years, when the process of sublimation is at its highest activity. **1934** H. C. WARREN *Dict. Psychol.* 150/1 *Latency period*, the period of life between the ages of 4 or 5 and ca. 12 years, which separates the infantile or pregenital sexuality from the beginning of puberty or genital sexuality and in which the sexual manifestations are as a rule less prominent. **1949** J. STRACHEY tr. *Freud's Three Ess. Theory of Sexuality* ii. 57 It is from Fliess that I have borrowed the term 'period of sexual latency'. **1960** *Encounter* Jan. 80/2 The life of latency groups in Britain. *Ibid.* 81/1 These beliefs and customs are passed on entirely within the latency world without any intervention of adults. **1967** B. RUSSELL *Autobiogr.* I. ii. 38, I remember a very definite change when I reached what in modern child psychology is called the 'latency period'. **1968** E. ERIKSON *Identity: Youth & Crisis* iv. 156 In postulating a 'latency period' which precedes puberty, psychoanalysis has given recognition to some kind of psychosexual moratorium in human development.

2. a. Delay between a stimulus and a response, esp. in muscle; a latent period.

1882 *Proc. R. Soc.* XXXIII. 463 If, after a muscle has been powerfully extended, and while it is returning, by reason of its elasticity, towards its normal condition, a stimulation be applied, the latency may become as short as the 1/200–1/400 second. **1932** *Jrnl. Physiol.* LXXIV. 17 The general interest in the problem of latency increased when it was found, that while recording the action current of the muscle the latent period was absent, or seemed to be absent. **1951** H. DAVSON *Textbk. Gen. Physiol.* xvii. 483 The latency, as ordinarily recorded, is thus of the order of 3·5 msec. at 23°C; if, however, we take as a measure of the mechanical latent period the time between the stimulus and the moment when the tension [in the muscle] begins to rise from its minimum value, the period is 3·0 msec. **1963** *Jrnl. Pediatrics* LXII. 724 Cry latency is defined as the time which elapses between the moment of painful stimulation and the onset of crying. **1973** *Jrnl. Genetic Psychol.* CXXII. 177 The child was presented with a standard stimulus along with a number of comparison stimuli and told to point to the one that was the same as the standard... *E* recorded, to the nearest half-second, latency to the first response.

b. *Computers.* More fully ***latency time***. The delay before a transfer of data begins following an instruction for its transfer, esp. to or from a rotating storage device.

1954 *First Gloss. Programming Terminol.* (Assoc. Computing Machinery) 11 *Latency*, in a serial storage system, the access time less the word time, e.g. the time spent waiting for the desired location to appear under the drum heads or at the end of an acoustic tank. **1961** P. SIEGEL *Understanding Digital Computers* xii. 258 The access time consists of the latency time plus the transfer time. The latency represents the amount of time it takes to find the chosen address. **1970** O. DOPPING *Computers & Data Processing* x. 145 If the drum makes 3,000 revolutions per minute, each revolution takes 20 milliseconds, and the average latency time becomes 10 milliseconds.

La Tène (la'tɛn). The name of a district at the east end of Lake Neuchâtel, Switzerland, where archæological finds were made, used esp. *attrib.* to denote a culture (fl. *c* 3rd century B.C.) of the second Iron Age of central and west Europe, and objects found there.

[**1866** J. E. LEE tr. *Keller's Lake Dwellings* 239 A La Tène, Near Marin (Lake of Neuchâtel). This station was known and mentioned in my first report on the lake dwellings to the Society of Antiquaries at Zürich, in 1858. *Note.* The terms Tène (shallow) and Ténevière (submerged hillock) are provincialisms of the fishermen in the lake of Neuchâtel, and Professor Desor in his late work 'Les Palafittes', derives them from the Latin '*tenuis*'.] **1890** R. MUNRO *Lake-Dwellings of Europe* iv. 278 In making a section through the La Tène elevation there is first encountered a bed of water-worn gravel and sand. **1905** H. B. WALTERS *Hist. Anc. Pott.* II. xxiii. 502 It is interesting for its close relation to the older La Tène pottery. **1917** [see BEADED *ppl. a.* 4 b]. **1932** *Antiquity* VI. 198 *La Tène*. A trading post on Lake Neuchâtel gives its name to certain cultures of the *Second Iron Age*. **1935** *Discovery* Apr. 102/1 The three tumuli..proved to be Early Iron Age in date, one of them yielding a small bone plaque with advanced La Tène ornament. **1943** J. & C. HAWKES *Prehist. Brit.* v. 94 Already when the first Hallstatt settlers were arriving in this country their kinsfolk in eastern France and south Germany were building up a new culture, that known as La Tène, which came to represent the height of early Celtic achievement. **1961** *Antiquaries Jrnl.* XLI. 44 Barrows, or burials, within square-ditched inclosures have recently been recognized as characteristic of the La Tène cultures both in the Rhineland and in France. **1962** *Times* 29 Mar. 15/5 The British Celts had evolved..their own superb, non-naturalistic late-La Tène art. **1970** BRAY & TRUMP *Dict. Archaeol.* 130/2 An art style with La Tène elements persisted into the Early Christian period.

lateness (ˈleɪtnɪs). Also 1 lætnys, 4–5 latnes(se. [OE. *lætnes*, f. *læt* LATE *a.*¹ + *-nes* -NESS.] The quality or condition of being late. **a.** Slowness. (Now *dial.*) **b.** The being advanced in some period of time. **c.** The being behind usual or proper time. **d.** Recency.

c **1050** *Byrhtferth's Handboc* in *Anglia* (1885) VIII. 308 Eall swa þære sunnan lætnys binnan feower ȝeara fæce. *c* **1375** *Sc. Leg. Saints* xviii. (*Egipciane*) 19 þe latnes of þe houre. *c* **1400** tr. *Secreta Secret., Gov. Lordsh.* 89 þe soueravn vertu maynteignes alle þinges, ffor it geues latnesse, and it makys swyftnesse. **1587** GOLDING *De Mornay* viii. (1617) 112 Thus do ye see the latenesse of the Westerne Nations. **1727** SWIFT *Let. to Gay* 23 Nov., Wks. 1841 II. 610 Your lateness in life..might be improper to begin the world with, but almost the eldest men may hope to see changes in a court. **1750** COSTARD *Dissert. Kesitah* 29 A farther proof of the lateness of that Composition [*sc.* the Book of Job]. **1840** THIRLWALL *Greece* VII. 311 The lateness of the season. **1874** SAYCE *Compar. Philol.* vi. 216 The existence of compounds in a language may be considered a mark of lateness. **1881** FITCH *Lect. Teaching* 74 A systematic record for each pupil of these particulars:..(3) absence; (4) lateness. **1885** *Bookseller* May 454/2 Its palpable lateness of date. **1887** *S. Cheshire Gloss.*, *Latn'ss*, delay, slowness.

latensification (leɪˌtɛnsɪfɪˈkeɪʃən). *Photogr.* [f. LATEN(T *a.* + INTEN)SIFICATION.]

Intensification of an existing latent image on a photographic film or plate by treatment with a chemical, prolonged exposure to light, or other means. Cf. HYPERSENSITIZATION b.

1940 *Amer. Cinematographer* XXI. 499/2 With no more equipment than a panchromatic safelight, any photographer can increase the speed of a film from two to four times right in his own darkroom. 'Latensification', the name describing this new process, is an outgrowth of the research being done by Du Pont Film Manufacturing Corporation on high speed 35 mm. films. **1948** *PSA Jrnl.* XIV. 675 (*heading*) Latensification studies with sodium perborate. **1956** [see HYPERSENSITIZATION b]. **1973** H. W. CLEVELAND in W. Thomas *SPSE Handbk. Photogr. Sci. & Engin.* vi. 417 Latensification is primarily an increase in the rate of development and therefore more effective with development well below γ_∞.

latent (ˈleɪtənt), *a.* [ad. L. *latent-em*, pres. pple. of *latēre* to be hidden. Cf. F. *latent*.] **a.** Hidden, concealed (†*rarely* const. *from*); present or existing, but not manifest, exhibited, or developed. (The opposite of ***patent***.)

latent ambiguity: in *Law*, a doubt as to the meaning of a document, not patent from the document itself, but raised by the evidence of some extrinsic and collateral matter (Wharton *Law Lex.* 1848). ***latent partner***, one whose name does not appear as a member of a firm or company.

1616 BULLOKAR, *Latent*, hiden, or secret. **1624** GATAKER *Transubst.*, etc. 197 The pretence of a Church and Religion like to theirs in former ages canot..be defended... Some will haue it to haue beene latent and invisible for 800..yeers. **1651** BAXTER *Inf. Bapt.* 241 Though the Historicall part have some latent corruption in it. **1671** J. WEBSTER *Metallogr.* iii. 55 A metalline plastick principle latent in it. **1689** T. PLUNKET *Char. Good Commander* Prol., New Necessities Will things produce, now latent from the wise. **1736** BUTLER *Anal.* I. i. Wks. 1874 I. 26 We know not what latent powers and capacities they [brutes] may be endued with. **1757** BURKE *Abridgm. Eng. Hist.* Wks. 1842 II. 530 An exertion of a latent genius. **1849** MACAULAY *Hist. Eng.* i. I. 100 Under this apparent concord a great schism was latent. *Ibid.* v. 568 The meaning latent under this specious phrase. **1873** BLACK *Pr. Thule* xv. 241 The latent force of character that underlay all her submissive gentleness. **1879** HADDAN *Apost. Succ.* iv. 80 Döllinger's expression, that the Episcopate was from the first latent in the Apostolate. **1913** *Act 3 & 4 Geo. V* c. 20 §90 Any latent partner of a company whose estates have been sequestrated.

b. Of material things. ? *Obs.*

1646 SIR T. BROWNE *Pseud. Ep.* IV. xiii. 223 That most insects are latent, from the setting of the 7 Starres. *a* **1661** FULLER *Worthies* (1840) III. 138 His admirable writings of mathematics are latent with some private possessors. *c* **1690** SCOTTOW in *Harper's Mag.* Mar. (1883) 591/2 A snake which Lay Latent in the Tender Grass. **1700** DRYDEN *Ajax & Ulysses* 172 The glitt'ring helm by moonlight will proclaim The latent robber. **1769** GRAY *Ode for Music* 3rd Air, Thy liberal heart..Shall raise from earth the latent gem To glitter on the diadem.

c. That is really but not evidently what is implied by the sb.; disguised. *rare.*

1662 J. BARGRAVE *Pope Alex. VII* (1867) 19 This latent nuntio gave over his fruitless design. **1725** POPE *Odyss.* III. 54 Then first approaching to the elder guest, The latent goddess in these words addrest. **1892** STEVENSON *Across the Plains* i. 26, I had been but a latent emigrant, now I was to be branded once more, and put apart with my fellows.

d. *Med.* and *Biol.* 'Applied to diseases, the usual symptoms of which are not manifest, and to symptoms which do not appear under conditions in which they are natural' (*Syd. Soc. Lex.* 1888); ***latent period***, the period during which a disease lurks in the system before manifesting its presence; ***latent virus***, a virus causing no apparent disease in a plant or animal, but capable of producing disease in another to which it is transmitted.

1684 [see LATIC]. **1706** PHILLIPS (ed. Kersey) s.v. *Cancer*, *Primitive Cancer*, is that which comes of it self, and appears at first about the bigness of a Pea or Bean, causing an inward continual and pricking Pain; during which time it is call'd an Occult, Latent, or Blind Cancer. **1834** J. FORBES *Laennec's*

Dis. Chest (ed. 4) 97 The constant presence of a catarrhal affection of the lungs, either latent or manifest. **1837** M. HALL *Med.* 143 Rubeola is unequivocally contagious. A latent period of from ten to fourteen days intervenes between exposure and the development of the febrile symptoms. **1886** *N.Y. Med. Jrnl.* 4 Dec. 626/2 Heterophoria may, like hypermetropia, be partly or entirely latent. **1897** *Allbutt's Syst. Med.* IV. 9 The foregoing train of symptoms being..known as those of 'gouty dyspepsia' or as 'suppressed', 'anomalous' or latent gout. **1931** *Phytopathology* XXI. 593 A virus remaining latent or producing a mosaic in some varieties may cause a well-defined necrotic effect in others. **1937** *Science* 20 Aug. 179 (*title*) A latent virus of lily. **1950** K. M. SMITH *Introd. Study of Viruses* ii. 17 We have seen already a good example of the 'lighting up' of a latent virus when discussing swine influenza... The virus is latent in its intermediate host, the swine lungworm, and to induce infection in the pig it must be rendered active by the application of a provocative stimulus. **1951** *Nature* 30 June 1061/1 The presence of latent or 'silent' viruses in plants and other organisms is not, of course, new. **1954** S. DUKE-ELDER *Parsons' Dis. Eye* (ed. 12) xxix. 483 In all types [of squint] if the fusion mechanism is well-developed and the defect slight, visual alignment may be maintained in normal circumstances by a continued effort of fusion: the squint is then latent and can only be made manifest when fusion is impossible (as by covering up one eye). **1962** W. CARTER *Insects in Relation to Plant Dis.* viii. 329 Latent viruses are often important components of virus complexes.

e. *Physics. latent electricity*: see quot. **1885**. *latent heat*: see HEAT *sb.* 2 c; so † *latent caloric*.

1816 J. SMITH *Panorama Sci. & Art* II. 334 Latent caloric may become sensible in a variety of ways. **1885** WATSON & BURBURY *Math. Theory Electr. & Magn.* I. 83 The fluid of either kind in any electrified body in excess of that of the opposite kind is called the Free Electricity of the body, and the remaining fluids of the body, consisting of equal amounts of fluids of opposite kinds, together constitute what is called the Latent, Combined or Fixed Electricity of the body.

f. *Bot.* and *Zool.*

1787 *Families of Plants* I. 263 The rudiments of eight anthers latent in the bottom of the flower. **1826** KIRBY & SPENCE *Entom.* IV. 348 Latent (*Latens*) when it [the post dorsolum] is covered by the mesothorax. **1856** HENSLOW *Dict. Bot. Terms, Latent*, lying dormant till excited by some particular stimulus; as the adventitious buds occasionally developed in trees.

g. *Photogr.*

c **1865** J. WYLDE in *Circ. Sci.* I. 157/2 The latent picture becomes developed. **1878** ABNEY *Treat. Photogr.* iii. 18 The invisible image is frequently termed latent, an appellation which, though convenient, is yet open to some criticism.

h. *Biol. latent period*: a period between a stimulus and a response, esp. in a muscle or an irradiated individual. (See also sense d and LATENCY 2 a.)

1877 M. FOSTER *Text Bk. Physiol.* I. ii. 37 A phase antecedent to any visible alteration in the muscle..during which invisible preparatory changes are taking place in the nerve and muscle, is often called the 'latent period'. **1926** L. HOGBEN *Compar. Physiol.* viii. 140 The rate of conduction can be determined directly by observing the difference in the latent period of muscular contraction, when a nerve-muscle preparation is stimulated at points along the nerve separated by a measured distance apart. **1933** O. GLASSER *Sci. of Radiol.* xviii. 319 Should the criterion be the first reaction which can be observed under the microscope in the living cell, the latent period will be very short. **1947** *Radiology* XLIX. 361/2 The incidence of bone tumors was approximately proportional to the dose administered, and the latent period—in no case less than about 200 days—increased gradually with decreasing dose. **1966** *McGraw-Hill Encycl. Sci. & Technol.* VIII. 638/1 Between the stimulus and the first tension development there is a brief latent period of a few thousandths of the twitch duration.

i. *Math. latent root*: a scalar quantity λ which, when subtracted from each of the elements in the principal diagonal of a square matrix A, makes the determinant of the resulting matrix equal to zero (and so is a solution of the equation $Ax = \lambda x$, where x is a column vector).

1883 J. J. SYLVESTER in *Phil. Mag.* XVI. 267 It will be convenient to introduce here a notion (which plays a conspicuous part in my new theory of multiple algebra), viz. that of the latent roots of a matrix—latent in a somewhat similar sense as vapour may be said to be latent in water or smoke in a tobacco-leaf. If from each term in the diagonal of a given matrix, λ be subtracted, the determinant to the matrix so modified will be a rational integer function of λ; the roots of that function are the latent roots of the matrix; and there results the important theorem that the latent roots of any function of a matrix are respectively the same functions of the latent roots of the matrix itself: *ex. gr.* the latent roots of the square of a matrix are the squares of its latent roots. **1958** R. V. ANDREE *Sel. Mod. Abstract Algebra* ix. 195 In quantum mechanics and elsewhere, the terms latent roots, proper value, eigenvalue, and eigenwerte are often used in place of characteristic root. **1968** E. T. COPSON *Metric Spaces* viii. 117 The condition..is known to imply that all the latent roots of A lie in $|z| < 1$. Hence the latent roots of $I - A$ lie in $|z - 1| < 1$. Thus $z = 0$ is not a latent root of $I - A$, so that $I - A$ is non-singular.

j. *latent* (*finger-*)*print* = LATENT *sb.*

1923 J. A. LARSON *Single Fingerprint Syst.* i. 8 Take to your office all removable objects with visible or latent prints. *Ibid.* 9 Various powders, fumes, and solutions are recommended and have been used for the development and preservation of latent prints. **1937** *Discovery* Feb. 56/2 When a latent print is discovered, the area can receive a more liberal fuming to yield the maximum contrast. The amount of time required for fuming a single latent image is variable. **1956** 'E. McBAIN' *Cop Hater* (1963) xix. 145 The tech crew dusted the latent fingerprints. **1962** M. PROCTOR *Devil in Moonlight* x. 102 'What's he expert on?' 'Latent fingerprints.' *Ibid.* xiv. 145 What they call latent prints, not visible to the human eye. **1974** G. F. NEWMAN *Price* viii. 242

Latent prints brought out on the non-absorbent surfaces with grey powder for photographing.

k. *Psychol. latent learning*, learning that has taken place without conscious purpose and that is not manifested until there is a goal to be achieved.

1929 H. C. BLODGETT in *Univ. Calif. Publ. Psychol.* IV. 122 Do these drops in errors which come after the introduction of reward indicate that something to be called a latent learning developed during the non-reward period —a latent learning which made itself manifest after the reward had been presented? *Ibid.* 133 During the non-reward period, the rats were developing a *latent* learning of the maze which they were able to utilize as soon as reward was introduced. **1938** R. S. WOODWORTH *Exper. Psychol.* vi. 137 'Latent learning', i.e., learning that is not revealed by the animal's path through the maze, until food has been found in the food box. **1956** E. R. HILGARD *Theories of Learning* (ed. 2) vi. 214 This second phase demonstrates genuine latent learning of the true path. **1957** *New Biol.* XXIV. 123 If rats, not deprived of any primary bodily needs, are put in a maze, they explore it... If such rats are later trained to run from one part of the maze to another to get food, they learn this task more quickly than similar rats which have not previously experienced the maze. This consequence of exploration is called latent learning. **1968** CHAPLIN & KRAWIEC *Syst. & Theories Psychol.* (ed. 2) vii. 277 Latent learning is hidden learning which goes on unobserved but which, under certain conditions, can be revealed in performance.

l. *Sociol. latent function*, a function which exists unrecognized within a social attitude or action and which will produce results that have not been foreseen.

1949 R. K. MERTON *Social Theory* i. 51 Latent functions ..being those which are neither intended nor recognized. **1961** M. SPIRO in B. Kaplan *Studying Personality* ii. 108 Latent functions are those consequences which—whether intended or unintended—are not recognized by them [*sc.* members of a society].

m. *Sociol.* and *Statistics.* Applied to certain attributes, structures of relations, and the like (see quots. 1957).

1950 P. F. LAZARSFELD in S. A. Stouffer *Measurement & Prediction* x. 362 (*heading*) The logical and mathematical foundation of latent structure analysis. *Ibid.*, The latent structure approach to the treatment of itemized tests. **1952** GOODE & HATT *Methods in Social Res.* xvii. 286 One alternative..was to abandon the factorial approach and in doing so abandon the concept of a latent-attitude continuum. *Ibid.* 295 Another problem posed by latent-structure analysis..is the fact that its computations are both arduous and complex. **1957** KENDALL & BUCKLAND *Dict. Statistical Terms* 158 *Latent structure,..* a structure expressed in terms of variates or variables which are 'latent' in the sense of not being directly observable. Certain econometric relations (e.g. in terms of 'utility') are of this type. *Ibid., Latent variable*, a variable which is unobservable but is supposed to enter into the structure of a system under study, such as demand in economics or the 'general' factor in psychology. Unobservable quantities such as errors are not usually described as latent. **1961** J. ROTHENBERG *Measurement Social Welfare* iv. xi. 290 The spatial arrangement of alternatives is a uni-dimensional scale of some single 'latent attribute' calibrated by the particular alternatives. **1966** B. S. PHILLIPS *Social Res.* xi. 176 Latent structure analysis may prove to be of particular value in bringing to light a systematic set of assumptions or propositions about the probabilistic relationships between manifest data and latent structures. **1968** LAZARSFELD & HENRY *Latent Structure Analysis* ii. 15 It is necessary to make some assumptions about the nature of what we called the 'latent variable'. *Ibid.* iii. 47 Once a latent structure model has been specified, with accounting equations.. relating the latent probabilities to the manifest probabilities, we must ask whether those equations can be solved uniquely.

Hence **'latently** *adv.*, in a latent manner, so as to be hidden or invisible; **'latentness**, latency.

1651 *Raleigh's Ghost* 103 Who would not affirm that a certain understanding..were invisibly and latently in the said things? **1660** J. DURHAM *Comm. Rev.* xii. 531 Her latentnesse and inconspicuousnesse. **1684** T. BURNET *Theory Earth* I. 285 Neither can we..judge..of what things the memory may be still latently conserv'd. **1837** WHEWELL *Hist. Induct. Sci.* IV. v. I. 343 The lateral support..was supplied latently.

latent ('leɪtənt), *sb.* [f. the adj.] A kind of fingerprint, invisible to the naked eye.

1923 J. A. LARSON *Single Fingerprint Syst.* ix. 186 Several latents were left at the house which had been burglarized. **1937** *Discovery* 57/2 This method [of fingerprint detection] does not result in the destruction of the latent. **1939** E. S. GARDNER *D.A. draws Circle* (1940) iv. 48 'Any latents, Bob?' the sheriff asked. **1973** A. HUNTER *Gently French* iii. 23 The recognisable latents were either Quarles' or off-record, probably innocent.

later ('leɪtə(r)), *a.* and *adv.* Also 6 *Sc.* laitter. [f. LATE *a.*[1] + -ER[3]. (The OE. comparative *lator* is represented by LATTER *a.*; the modern word is a new formation.)]

A. *adj.* More late; coming at a longer interval after the usual or proper time; further advanced in a period; more recent.

1559 W. CUNNINGHAM *Cosmogr. Glasse* 119, I have folowed Ptolomæus in certaine pointes..In th' other, I have used later writers travelles. **1596** DALRYMPLE tr. *Leslie's Hist. Scot.* I. 5 The laitter historiographers. **1632** MILTON *Penseroso* 101 Or what (though rare) of later age, Ennobled hath the Buskind stage. **1698** FRYER *Acc. E. India & P.* 75 This seems to be of later date than that of Canorein. **1784** COWPER *Tiroc.* 110 In early days the conscience has in most A quickness, which in later life is lost. **1871** MORLEY *Voltaire* (1886) 8 The strange and sinister method of assault upon religion which we of a later day watch with wondering

eyes. **1878** R. H. HUTTON *Scott* ii. 19 The later border songs of his own country.

B. *adv.* At a later time or period; subsequently. *later on*: subsequently. Also (*U.S. slang*) used as a farewell, representing *I'll see you later*.

1548 UDALL, etc. *Erasm. Par. Matt.* ii. 1-2 Christe is no where knowen later or with more difficultie, than in.. princes courtes. **1660** F. BROOKE tr. *Le Blanc's Trav.* 393 The Tide and Ebbe coming sooner or later. **1667** MILTON *P.L.* x. 613 To destroy, or unimmortal make All kinds, and for destruction to mature Sooner or later. **1849** MACAULAY *Hist. Eng.* iv. I. 518 Three days later the King informed the House that [etc.]. **1868** FREEMAN *Norm. Conq.* (1876) II. vii. 127 A foretaste of what was to come fifteen years later. **1882** *Times* 12 July 5 The Admiral ran up the signal ..and later on sent the Bittern and Beacon to assist in the work. **1954** *Time* 8 Nov. 42 Later, catchall word for 'I'll be seeing you'; also used at the end of letters. **1955** L. FEATHER *Encycl. Jazz* x. 346 Later, parting phrase, short for 'I'll see you later'. **1972** J. MARYLAND in T. Kochman *Rappin' & Stylin' Out* 214 The players all started heading for the door, stating, 'Peace,' 'Later,' 'Hat Time,' 'I'm in the wind,' etc.

Comb. **1823** JOANNA BAILLIE *Collect. Poems* 273 Leave we the clouds of ancient story, For scenes of later-parted glory.

later, obs. form of LATTER *a.*

laterad ('lætəræd), *adv. Anat.* [f. L. *later-, latus* side + -*ad* (see DEXTRAD).] Towards the side.

1814 WISHART *Scarpa's Hernia* I. 79 *note*, More dorsad and laterad and yet more to the dermal aspect. **1888** *Amer. Jrnl. Psychol.* I. 492 Caudad the cells were connected with the postero-lateral column, while cephalad and laterad they could be seen to be connected with the direct cerebellar tract.

lateral ('lætərəl), *a.* and *sb.* [ad. L. *laterālis*, f. *later-, latus* side. Cf. F. *latéral*.] **A.** *adj.*

1. a. Of or pertaining to the side; situated at or issuing from the side; side-. †In quot. 1600, of a look: Directed sideways.

lateral branch (of a family): a branch descended from a brother or sister of a person in the direct line of descent. *lateral moraine*: see the *sb.* †*judge lateral*: an assessor; cf. *side judge*.

1600 B. JONSON *Underwoods* xxiii. (*In Authorem*), One coming with a lateral view, Unto a cunning piece wrought perspective, Wants faculty to make a censure true. **1611** FLORIO, *Laterale*, laterall, of one or some side, belonging to a side. **1681** W. ROBERTSON *Phraseol. Gen.* (1693) 779 A Judge-lateral, *adsessor*. **1706** PHILLIPS (ed. Kersey) s.v., *Judge Lateral*, one that assists and sits on the Bench with another Judge; an Assessour. **1730** A. GORDON *Maffei's Amphith.* 287 The four lateral Arches at the two greatest Gates. **1787** M. CUTLER in *Life*, etc. (1888) I. 289 He has but one son, whose name is Jesse, which has been much of a family name in the lateral branches. **1820** W. IRVING *Sketch Bk.* II. 200, I..found my way to a lateral portal which was the every-day entrance to the mansion. **1831** BREWSTER *Optics* xxxi. 261 There is produced the appearance of two persons moving in opposite directions, constituting what has been termed a lateral mirage. **1850** MERIVALE *Rom. Emp.* (1865) I. vii. 284 By a lateral movement they reached the banks of the river. **1860** TYNDALL *Glac.* II. xviii. 325 In virtue of the quicker central flow the lateral ice is subject to an oblique strain. **1867** F. FRANCIS *Angling* i. (1880) 14 He should..let his motions be as little lateral as possible. **1874** MICKLETHWAITE *Mod. Par. Churches* 23 All the main entrances, whether western or lateral. **1878** HUXLEY *Physiogr.* 118 The river and its lateral streams.

b. *lateral thinking*: a way of thinking which seeks the solution to intractable problems through unorthodox methods, or elements which would normally be ignored by logical thinking.

1966 *London Life* 22 Oct. 20/3 He [*sc.* Dr. Edward De Bono] divides thinking into two methods. One he calls 'vertical thinking'—that is, using the processes of logic, the traditional-historical method... The other type he calls 'lateral thinking', which involves disrupting an apparent sequence and arriving at the solution from another angle. **1967** E. DE BONO *Use of Lateral Thinking* 5 Some people are aware of another sort of thinking which..leads to those simple ideas that are obvious only after they have been thought of. This book is an attempt to look at this sort of thinking... For the sake of convenience, the term 'lateral thinking' has been coined to describe this other sort of thinking; 'vertical thinking' is used to denote the conventional logical process. **1972** *Observer* 5 Nov. 20/6 Don't trade on the argument that women have special qualities (intuition, perception, lateral thinking, or what have you) which are denied to men.

†2. Existing or moving side by side. Of winds: Coming from the same half (eastern or western) of the horizon. Also in comb. *lateral-sited* adj.

c **1611** CHAPMAN *Iliad* IX. 4 As two lateral-sited winds (the West wind and the North) Meete at the Thracian seas blacke breast. **1635** SWAN *Spec. M.* (1670) 145 Eurus on the one side and Cæcias on the other, being..lateral winds pertinent to the East. **1654** H. L'ESTRANGE *Chas. I* (1655) 221 The Commons Charge and the Earls Defence run lateral and in pale each with other. **1662** HOBBES *Seven Prob.* Wks. 1845 VII. 42 It must needs move the air before it, even to the earth, and the earth repel it, and so make lateral winds every way. **1667** MILTON *P.L.* x. 705 Eurus and Zephir, with thir lateral noise, Sirocco and Libecchio.

3. Specific scientific uses.

a. *Anat.* and *Zool.* Situated on one side or other of the mesial plane; also const. *to*. So *lateral eye, fin, lobe, ventricle;* **lateral line**, in fishes and certain amphibia, a system of organs of sensory perception, arranged in a row along the sides of the body; also *attrib.;* **lateral plate**, in the early stages of vertebrate embryos, the

ventral part of the mesoderm, from which certain internal organs develop.

1722 QUINCY *Lex. Physico-Med.* (ed. 2) 50 This Plexus reaches from one lateral Ventricle to the other, passing under the Fornix, above the third Ventricle. **1826** KIRBY & SP. *Entomol.* IV. 314 Lateral.. when they [eyes] are placed in the side of the head. **1830** R. KNOX *Béclard's Anat.* 232 The external ligaments are.. placed at the two sides of the articulation, and for this reason are called lateral ligaments. **1840** E. WILSON *Anat. Vade M.* (1842) 340 The lateral sinuses are often unequal in size. **1870** ROLLESTON *Anim. Life* Introd. 62 The sensory organs developed in Fish, in connection with the 'lateral line'. **1874** FOSTER & BALFOUR *Elem. Embryol.* iii. 54 A transparent longitudinal line makes its appearance on either side of the notochord along the line of junction of the lateral with the vertical plate. **1880** GÜNTHER *Fishes* 68 The articulation with the vertebral column is effected by a pair of lateral condyles. **1913** *Gray's Anat.* (ed. 18) 242 Lateral to the foramen ovale is the foramen spinosum. **1914** W. E. KELLICOTT *Outl. Chordate Devel.* iv. 278 The lateral plate [of the chick] is separated into somatic and splanchnic layers by the extra-embryonic cœlom. **1926** J. S. HUXLEY *Ess. Pop. Sci.* xvii. 191 The special sense-organs for perceiving low-frequency vibrations in water which, like a herring or any other fish, it [*sc.* the tadpole] carries on a 'lateral line' along its flank. **1959** A. HARDY *Fish & Fisheries* ii. 24 We may not yet know all the functions of the lateral line system. **1964** H. W. MANNER *Elem. Compar. Vertebr. Embryol.* ix. 150 The mesoderm.. was in three distinct, potentially different, portions: a medially located somite, an intermediate mesoderm, and a lateral plate mesoderm. **1968** C. OSBORNE tr. *Stenuit's Dolphin* (1969) v. 91 Fish perceive the variations in water pressure through a biological system known as the lateral line. **1972** *Nature* 31 Mar. 233/1 Electrodes.. were placed at bilaterally symmetrical points over the left and right hemispheres,.. 2 mm lateral to the sagittal suture and 1 mm posterior to bregma.

b. *Bot.* Belonging to, situated or borne upon the side of an organ, as ***lateral bud, flower, petal.***

1776–96 WITHERING *Brit. Plants* (ed. 3) II. 306 Umbels on fruit-stalks, both lateral, and terminating. **1787** *Families of Plants* I. 5 The lateral divisions of the exterior corol. **1830** LINDLEY *Nat. Syst. Bot.* 216 The two carpellary leaves of which the fruit is formed are lateral, or right and left with respect to the common axis of the inflorescence. **1837** MACGILLIVRAY *Withering's Brit. Plants* (ed. 4) 88 Lateral flowers destitute of germen. **1875** BENNETT & DYER *Sachs' Bot.* 155 Lateral shoots arise far most frequently at a greater distance from the apex of the stem than the youngest leaves.

c. *Path.* Of diseases: (*a*) Affecting the side or sides of the body; (*b*) confined to one side of the body (see quots.); (*c*) (of curvature of the spine) directed sideways.

1724 BAILEY, Lateral Disease [tr. L. *morbus lateralis*], the Pleurisy. **1727–41** CHAMBERS *Cycl.* s.v. *Palsy, Lateral Palsy*, called also Hemiplegia, is the same disease with the paraplegia; only that it affects but one side of the body. **1852** MILLER *Practice Surg.* (ed. 2) xxiv. 303 Lateral curvature of the spine. **1878** tr. *Ziemssen's Cycl. Med.* XIII. 453 That form of chronic myelitis called lateral sclerosis.

d. *Surg.* ***lateral operation***: a mode of cutting for the stone, in which the prostate gland and neck of the bladder are divided laterally. Also ***lateral lithotomy***.

1727–41 CHAMBERS *Cycl.* s.v. *Lithotomy*, The lateral operation, invented by Frere Jacques.. of the third order of S. Francis. **1730** *Hist. Litteraria* I. 416 The lateral Operation for the Extraction of the Stone. **1870** T. HOLMES *Syst. Surgery* (ed. 2) IV. 1059 The causes of death after lateral lithotomy are the following.

e. *Conch.* Situated on one side or other of the hinge, as ***lateral tooth***.

1816 T. BROWN *Elem. Conchol.* 20 Lateral Teeth are teeth which diverge from the umbo. **1828** STARK *Elem. Nat. Hist.* II. 106 Shell regular, inequivalve, inequilateral; a single primary tooth in each valve.. no lateral teeth.

†**f.** *Math.* Of a quantity: Of the first power. Of equations: Linear. *Obs.*

1674 S. JEAKE *Arith.* (1701) IV. iv. iv. 645 If 170 304 782 be divided.. by 1250, the Quotient shall be Quadratical, and if by 6480, the Quotient shall be Lateral. *Ibid.*, If then the lateral Coefficient 15, and √ 9160, and √ c1250, and √ qq 6480 be made Sursolids, they shall produce four Homogeneal Species of Affections. **1706** PHILLIPS (ed. Kersey), *Lateral Equation* (in Algebra), such an Equation as has but one Root.

g. *Cryst.* Applied to those axes of a crystal or crystalline form which are inclined to the main or 'vertical' axis; also to edges, faces, or angles, connected with such axes.

1805–17 R. JAMESON *Char. Min.* (ed. 3) 104 Lateral edges are the edges of the lateral faces of the table, so that there are eight lateral edges in a four-sided table. **1823** H. J. BROOKE *Introd. Crystallogr.* 207 Class *g.* Lateral solid angles replaced by single planes inclining on the superior edges. **1851** RICHARDSON *Geol.* v. (1855) 86 The edges produced by the meeting of the lateral planes, are termed lateral edges. **1868** DANA *Min.* Introd. 21 [The Hexagonal] system differs from the Tetragonal in having three equal lateral axes.. instead of two; the vertical.. is at right angles to the lateral.

h. *Physics* and *Mechanics.* Acting or placed at right angles to the line of motion or of strain.

lateral pressure or ***stress***, a pressure or stress at right angles to the length, as of a beam or bridge.

lateral strength, strength which resists a tendency to fracture arising from lateral pressure. (Webster, 1864.)

1803 J. WOOD *Princ. Mech.* vii. 154 When the lateral motion is entirely prevented by the adhesion of the body to the plane. **1881** YOUNG *Every Man his own Mechanic* §441. 193 We must now proceed to the method of forming lateral joints. **1885** J. A. L. WADDELL *Syst. Iron Railr. Bridges Japan* 246 Lateral Rod.. Lateral Strut.. Lateral System.

i. *Phonetics.* Of a consonant: formed by partial closure of the air-passage by the tongue, which is so placed as to allow the breath to escape at one or both sides of the point of contact (e.g. English *l*).

1891 L. SOAMES *Introd. Phonetics* 34 Some persons.. let the breath escape on one side only, so it seems better to call it [*l*] a *lateral* or *side* consonant. **1899** W. RIPPMANN *Elem. Phonetics* §91. 72 For the *l* sounds the narrowing is between the side rim or rims of the tongue and the side teeth (*lateral* formation). **1903** SCHOLLE & SMITH *Elem. Phonetics* 75. §148 In the articulation of 'l' both sides (or only one side) of the tongue form a narrow passage with the molars and side gums, hence the term *lateral* articulation. **1957** *Essays in Crit.* VII. 128 'Woolly' is composed of two vowels, a semi-vowel and a voiced lateral consonant.

j. Applied (orig. in ***lateral cut***) to (the cutting of) gramophone records in which the undulations are cut in the plane of the record by the side-to-side movement of the recording stylus, and hence to equipment and techniques involved in this. Opp. ***hill and dale*** (HILL *sb.* 1 b).

1917 *Sci. Amer.* 27 Oct. 307 While many of these patents are more in the nature of slight refinements, particularly means of twisting the mounting of the reproducer so that it can be used for hill-and-dale and for lateral cut records at will, a few of them represent a genuine effort to improve the tonal qualities of the conventional disk phonograph. **1934** *Amer. Speech* IX. 312/2 The records will be.. both of the ordinary lateral-cut type and of the new and superior hill-and-dale, long-playing, unbreakable kind. **1935** H. C. BRYSON *Gramophone Record* i. 16 From 1900 onwards there existed three types of record: (*a*) Discs with hill and dale cut. .. (*b*) Discs with a lateral cut... (*c*) Wax cylinders with hill and dale cut. **1942** *Proc. IRE* XXX. 356/2 (*heading*) Frequency characteristics for lateral recording. **1966** *McGraw-Hill Encycl. Sci. & Technol.* IV. 240/1 Modern lateral pickups are of the crystal, ceramic, magnetic, or dynamic type. *Ibid.* 241/2 A lateral disk record. **1968** *Times* 29 Nov. 11/5 A decade later Emil Berliner saw the advantages of a flat disc and also developed the technique of the lateral cut disc. **1975** *Hi-Fi Answers* Feb. 58/2 Test records used.. were those by EMI.. and Decca's own lateral cut record, LXT 5346. *Ibid.* 59/2 Modulation levels .. which upset it at 8 kHz (for both vertical and lateral cuts) and 18 kHz (for lateral cuts only).

B. *sb.*

1. A lateral or side part, member, or object; †a wind that is 'lateral' (see A. 2) to another (*obs.*); a lateral shoot, tooth, branch, etc.

1635 SWAN *Spec. M.* (1670) 145 These winds.. if at any time they blow up rain.. then continue it by the space of a whole day. The reason of which I take to be, because.. their laterals, not being absolutely of the same quality, may arise together with them and so bring Rain. **1730** A. GORDON *Maffei's Amphith.* 298 In the Walls of these Laterals are two Hollows. **1851** *Beck's Florist* 107 As laterals are produced, I pinch them off; but I never stop the main stem. **1851–6** WOODWARD *Mollusca* 157 Chiton Squamosus.. lingual teeth 3; median small, laterals large. **1856** OLMSTED *Slave States* 366 From this trunk [road] there are many laterals. **1860** DELAMER *Kitch. Gard.* (1861) 177 Look over tomatoes, and suppress all useless laterals. **1866** TATE *Brit. Mollusks* iii. 50 The term laterals is employed.. to designate a series of teeth between the rachidian and the uncini. **1887** *Pall Mall G.* 22 June 5/2 Ilissus.. would not make a lateral for an irrigating ditch in Colorado.

†**2.** One of a series of numbers in arithmetical progression from which a series of 'triangular' numbers are formed by the summation of each successive term and all those preceding it. See FIGURATE *a.* *Obs.*

1706 W. JONES *Syn. Palmar. Matheseos* 162.

3. *Phonetics.* A lateral consonant: see sense 3 a of the adj.

1933 L. BLOOMFIELD *Lang.* vi. 97 In some of these the tongue actually touches the roof of the mouth, but leaves enough room at one or both sides for the breath to escape without serious friction-noise; such sounds are *laterals*, of the type of our [l]... In unvoiced laterals, which occur in Welsh and in many American languages, the friction-noise of the breath-stream is more audible than in unvoiced nasals.

4. *N. Amer. Football.* (See quot. 1971.) Also as vb., to make such a pass.

1934 WEBSTER, *Lateral*, a lateral pass. **1949** *Richmond* (Va.) *Times-Despatch* 10 Oct. 13/2 The last carried 27 yards as Quarterback Ben Raimondi threw a lateral to his left to End Cotton Howell. **1961** WEBSTER, *Lateral*, to throw a lateral pass. **1970** *Globe & Mail* (Toronto) 28 Sept. 18/4 He lateralled to Joe Hernandez, who ran the last 45 yards of a 59-yard touchdown play. **1971** L. KOPPETT *N.Y. Times Guide Spectator Sports* ii. 69 *Lateral*, a pass to a teammate that does not travel forward. **1972** J. MOSEDALE *Football* iii. 40 The Bronk passed to Bill Hewitt who lateraled to Bill Karr for a 36-yard score. **1974** *Los Angeles Times* 13 Oct. III. 7/1 Greene ran 11 yards to the Badgers' 5-yard line and lateraled to Baschnagel, who sped into the end zone.

laterality (lætəˈrælɪtɪ). [f. prec. + -ITY.] **a.** The quality of having (distinct) sides; (right- or left-) sidedness; *spec.* the dominance of the right- or the left-hand member of a pair of bodily organs as regards a particular activity or function (such as the hands in writing, or the cerebral hemispheres in controlling speech). Also, the condition of being sideways. **b.** (See quot. 1894.)

1646 SIR T. BROWNE *Pseud. Ep.* IV. v. 187 This prevalency is uncertainly placed in the laterallity, or custom determines its indifferency. *Ibid.* 191 These lateralities in man are not only fallible, if relatively determined unto each other, but made in reference unto the heavens and quarters of the Globe. *Ibid.* 192 We may as reasonably conclude a right and left laterallity in the Ark or navall edifice of Noah. **1656** BLOUNT *Glossogr.*, *Laterality*, the side-being, or being sideways of a thing. **1894** GOULD *Illustr. Dict. Med.*, *Laterality*, excessive development on one side. **1926** *Brit. Jrnl. Exper. Biol.* III. 317 The symmetry of right or left limbs will depend on the direction of growth.., and from a proximal cut surface an appendage of reversed laterality may thus originate. **1927** *Biometrika* XIX. 181 There is no evidence whatever of even a correlation between ocular and manual lateralities to say nothing of a master eye determining which is the master hand. **1937** S. T. ORTON *Reading, Writing & Speech Probl. in Children* i. 48 We have no guide.. as to which is the dominant hemisphere except the 'laterality' of the individual, that is, his handedness, eyedness and footedness. **1950** *Brain* LXXIII. 168 In a systematic study of 100 cases of brain injury, these authors report varying degrees of deformation of the [visual] coordinates in patients with unilateral lesions of either hemisphere. They state that the direction and extent of deformation varied simply with the laterality of the lesion; deviations in right-sided cases were in an anti-clockwise direction..; in cases with left-sided lesions, they were in the opposite direction. **1964** *Dissertation Abstr.* XXIV. 3423/2 Predictions of laterality of cerebral hemisphere lesions can be made with a fairly high degree of confidence for those patients with well-lateralized, rapidly expanding lesions. **1964** M. CRITCHLEY *Developmental Dyslexia* viii. 51 Mixed laterality was then imagined to be a factor of special importance in dyslexics who might, for example, prove to be left-eyed, right-handed and left-footed. **1967** *Biol. Abstr.* XLVIII. 8522/2 (*heading*) Laterality in the use of the forepaws in cat. **1971** *Nature* 23 Apr. 524/1 Although usually used when speech dominance is questionable, amobarbital testing is also indicated in persons with apparently well established laterality when they are to undergo commissural section.

c. *Phonetics.* Lateral articulation (cf. LATERAL *a.* 3 i).

1953 C. E. BAZELL *Ling. Form* 41 A voiced (or voiceless) character of *l* is not regarded as relevant even in languages in which voice is functionally discrete, on the grounds that it is not of functional relevance in combination with laterality.

lateralization (ˌlætərəlaɪˈzeɪʃən). [f. LATERALIZ(E *v.* + -ATION (or LATERAL *a.* and *sb.* + -IZATION).] Laterality, esp. of cerebral activity; the property of being lateralized.

1950 PENFIELD & RASMUSSEN *Cerebral Cortex of Man* ii. 42 (*heading*) Table showing lateralization of sensory responses .. in the face area. **1954** *Brain* LXXVII. 526 It is hardly possible to trace familial tendencies in the cerebral lateralization of language function. **1960** O. L. ZANGWILL *Cerebral Dominance* ii. 5 Conrad.. regards left-handedness as in itself bound up with incomplete lateralization of higher cerebral function. **1964** *Dissertation Abstr.* XXIV. 3423/1 (*heading*) Lateralization of lesions of the cerebral hemispheres. **1971** *Nature* 23 Apr. 524/1 When brain surgery which may affect language mechanisms is being contemplated, lateralization of speech is sometimes ascertained before operation. **1973** *Sci. Amer.* Apr. 76/3 Although the relation between speech lateralization and hand preference is not perfect, the high incidence of both left-hemisphere control of speech and right-hand preference is probably not coincidental.

lateralize (ˈlætərəlaɪz), *v.* [f. LATERAL *a.* + -IZE.] **1.** *trans.* To move or displace to the side; to render lateral. *rare*$^{-1}$.

1903 *Therapeutic Gaz.* 15 Feb. 74/2 The woven coudé catheter or soft-rubber catheter should be chosen to measure the urethral length,.. since the bend.. enables it more readily to surmount or pass projections on the floor,.. providing the elbow tip is lateralized.

2. *pass.* To be largely under the control of the left- or the right-hand side of the brain.

1954 *Brain* LXXVII. 533 Milner reports visual-spatial defects consistently more severe in right temporal lobe excisions than left. She suggests that this is a function which is usually lateralized on the right. **1970** M. S. GAZZANIGA *Bisected Brain* vi. 116 The neural organization required for spoken language is usually lateralized to one cerebral hemisphere. *Ibid.* 85 Position sense is.. crisply lateralized.

lateralized (ˈlætərəlaɪzd), *ppl. a.* [f. LATERAL *a.* + -IZE + -ED^{1}.] **a.** Rendered lateral in position; placed at the side. ***lateralized operation*** = lateral operation.

1835–6 TODD *Cycl. Anat.* I. 400 The lateralised.. operation for stone. **1891** SIR D. WILSON *Right Hand* 198 The viscera of the quadruped have the same general lateralised position as in man.

b. Of consonants (cf. LATERAL *a.* 3 i).

1968 P. M. POSTAL *Aspects Phonol. Theory* iv. 82 There are no languages with only Lateralized consonants, although languages with no Lateralized consonants are not uncommon. **1969** *Word* XXV. 19 It would seem to be a simple solution to interpret these Yakur sounds as lateralized plosives.

laterally (ˈlætərəlɪ), *adv.* [f. LATERAL *a.* + -LY^{2}.] At the side; to or from the side; in a side direction; sideways.

1561 EDEN tr. *Cortez' Arte Nauig.* I. viii. 10 The inferior parte is moued.. laterally. **1646** SIR T. BROWNE *Pseud. Ep.* IV. i, 181 Pectinals, or such as have their bones made laterally like a comb. **1694** W. HOLDER *Disc. conc. Time* 89 The Days whereof are set Laterally after and against the Columns of [the] Golden Number. **1797** HOLCROFT tr. *Stolberg's Trav.* (ed. 2) III. lxxx. 259 A rope.. was fastened laterally to a wall. **1857** C. BRONTE *Professor* I. x. 160 [She] turned her eye laterally on me. **1860** TYNDALL *Glac.* I. v. 38 The greater portion of it [the water] escaping laterally from the glacier. **1861** HULME tr. *Moquin-Tandon* II. III. iii. 96 The rostrum [of the Crayfish] is dentated laterally. **1866** HOWELLS *Venet. Life* 128 They.. abandoned the main subject of dispute and took up the quarrel laterally.

lateralward(s ('lætərəlwəd, -wədz), *adv. Anat.* [f. LATERAL *a.* + -WARD, -WARDS.] Laterally; to or from the mesial plane of the body.

1913 *Gray's Anat.* (ed. 18) 236 Extending lateralwards.. on either side is the superior nuchal line. **1967** Lateralward [see GENICULUM].

Lateran ('lætərən). [ad. L. *Laterān-a, Laterān-um.*] The name of a locality in Rome, originally the site of the palace belonging to the family of the Plautii Laterani, afterwards of the palace of the popes of the same name, and the cathedral church known as St. John Lateran [L. *Sancti Joannis in Laterano*]. Also *attrib.* or as *adj.* (= Eccl. L. *Lateranensis*), esp. with reference to the five general councils of the Western Church held in the church of St. John Lateran.

1297 R. GLOUC. (Rolls) 1568 [Nero] let hit rere a noble court..& clupede laterane [*v.r.* þe court laterane]. *Ibid.* 1573 þe verste churche þat me let in þe world rere, Seint Jones de lateran. **1560** DAUS tr. *Sleidane's Comm.* 18 b, The decrees of the last counsel of Laterane. *Ibid.* 19 Then called he a Counsell agaynste the nexte yeare, to begynne at Rome ..in the Churche Laterane. **1692** BURNET *Past. Care* v. 92 The Thirteenth Canon of the Third Lateran Council, runs thus. **1727–52** CHAMBERS *Cycl.* s.v., A church called S. John of Lateran. *Ibid.*, Canons Regular of the Congregation of the Lateran. **1845** S. AUSTIN *Ranke's Hist. Ref.* I. 333 The decision of the Lateran council. **1896** *Ch. Times* 1 May 505/4 The Lateran and Tridentine dogma of Transubstantiation.

lateran, Sc. form of LATRINE and LECTERN.

lateratour, obs. form of LITERATURE.

lateri- ('lætərɪ), combining form of L. *later-, latus* side, in scientific terms: cf. LATERO-. **ˌlateri-'cumbent** (-'kʌmbənt) *a.* [L. *cumbent-em*, pr. pple. of *cumbĕre* to lie], lying on the side. **lateri-'flexion** [cf. F. *lateriflexion*], a flexion or bending sideways; lateral curvature (*Cent. Dict.*). **laterifloral, -florous** (-'flɔərəl, -'flɔərəs) *adjs. Bot.* [L. *flōr-, flōs* flower], having lateral flowers. **laterifolious** (-'fəʊlɪəs) *a. Bot.* [L. *folium* leaf], of flowers: see quot. **'laterigrade** (-greɪd) *a. Zool.* [L. *-grad-us* walking], belonging to the group *Laterigradæ* of spiders, which run sideways; *sb.* a spider of this group; so **late'rigradous** *a.* (Mayne *Expos. Lex.* 1855). **'laterinerved** (-nɜːvd), **-'nervous** *a.*, (of leaves) having lateral nerves. **lateri'version**, a turning or deviation to one side.

1883 WILDER & GAGE *Anat. Technol.* (Cent.), **Lateri-cumbent*, with a block transversely under the neck. **1888** *Syd. Soc. Lex.*, **Laterifloral*, having at the side flowers. **1855** MAYNE *Expos. Lex.*, *Lateriflorus*..*laterifiorous. **1760** J. LEE *Introd. Bot.* III. xxi. (1765) 218 **Laterifolious*, such as come out at the Side of the Base of the Leaf. **1887** *Amer. Nat.* XXI. 966 The Thomisidæ, or *laterigrade spiders. **1866** *Treas. Bot.*, **Laterinerved*, straight-veined, like the leaves of grasses. **1898** G. E. HERMAN *Dis. Women* x. 103 *Lateriversion is either normal..or results from the uterus being pulled aside by adhesions, or pushed aside by a swelling.

laterite ('lætəraɪt). *Min.* [f. L. *later* brick + -ITE[1].] **a.** A red, porous, ferruginous clayey substance, forming the surface covering in some parts of India, south-western Asia, and other tropical and sub-tropical regions, which is soft when first dug but hardens irreversibly to the consistency of rock when exposed to the air. **b.** Applied *loosely* to various reddish or iron-rich surface materials in the tropics and sub-tropics. **c.** *Soil Science.* Any soil or soil horizon characterized by a high proportion of sesquioxides, esp. of aluminium and iron, and an unusually low proportion of alkali metals, alkaline earths, and combined silica, such as occurs as a product of chemical weathering in hot climates with periods of abundant rain; *esp.* one which hardens on exposure to air or is derived from one already exposed.

The use and proper application of the word have been the subject of much debate.

1807 F. BUCHANAN *Journey from Madras* II. xii. 441 What I have called indurated clay is not the mineral so called by Mr. Kirwan. It..is one of the most valuable materials for building. It is diffused in immense masses, without any appearance of stratification, and is placed over the granite that forms the basis of Malayala... As it is usually cut into the form of bricks.., in several of the native dialects, it is called the brick-stone (*Itica cullu*). Where, however, by the washing away of the soil, part of it has been exposed to the air, and has hardened into a rock, its colour becomes black, and its pores and inequalities give it a kind of resemblance to the skin of a person affected with cutaneous disorders; hence in the Tamul language it is called *Shuri cull*, or itch-stone. The most proper English name would be *Laterite*. *Ibid.*, 460 In general, the Laterite, or brick-stone, comes very near the surface. **1871** TYLOR *Prim. Cult.* I. 53 In the gravel-beds of Europe, the laterite of India, and other more superficial localities. **1893** R. D. OLDHAM *Man. Geol. India* (ed. 2) xv. 385 The origin of laterite is still wrapt in obscurity. *Ibid.*, According to some geologists this laterite [of Buchanan] is in reality a soil and formed by the direct decomposition *in situ* of the underlying rock. **1898** *Agric. Ledger* (Calcutta) V. II. 34 If..it is difficult for the Geologist to decide what is 'laterite', it becomes practically impossible for the agriculturist to say what is a 'laterite soil'. Those 'laterite soils', that is, soils lying on or adjacent to what had every appearance of being laterite rock, which I have seen, had all a bright red appearance when dry; but as will be seen when discussing the analyses of the samples.., some at least of these are probably not true laterite. **1909** *Geol. Mag.* Decade V. VI. 431 The term 'laterite' has been used, in the Malay Peninsula at least, for many years by a large body of engineers for what are essentially masses of iron oxide replacing portions of weathered rock and filling fissures in such rocks near the surface. This (Malayan) laterite..is largely used for public works. **1910** *Ibid.* VII. 444 The foregoing representatives of the class of more or less ferruginous and aluminous deposits which in the Guianas.. have been termed 'laterite' do not possess, except in the case of the concretionary ironstones, the property..of 'setting' or hardening on exposure to the atmosphere. Parts of them agree to some extent with what has been laid down as the modern scientific qualification for a rock to be termed 'laterite'—the fact that they are 'essentially characterized by the presence of free hydrate of alumina'. **1911** *Ibid.* VIII. 565 Laterite (or rather some varieties of it) is formed by a process..by which certain rocks undergo superficial decomposition, with the removal in solution of combined silica, lime, magnesia, soda, and potash, and with the residual accumulation..of a hydrated mixture of oxides of iron, aluminium, and titanium, with, more rarely, manganese. *Ibid.*, The property of hardening on exposure to the air is characteristic of many varieties of laterite, but it is not essential property. **1927** *Jrnl. Agric. Sci.* XVII. 546 It is ..suggested that where the silica/alumina ratio in the clay fraction [of a soil] falls below 2·0 the soil should be described as 'lateritic', and where this ratio falls below 1·33 the soil should be described as laterite. **1932** G. W. ROBINSON *Soils* xiii. 279 Many of the descriptions of the supposed laterites merely relate to red soils... It is now generally agreed that the terms laterite and lateritic should be restricted to materials characterised by excess of sesquioxides. **1949** *Publ. Inst. Nat. pour l'Étude Agron. du Congo Belge* Sér. Sci. No. 46. 7 The word 'laterite' is used by us for the sesquioxide-rich, highly weathered clayey materials that change irreversibly to concretions, hardpans, or crusts, when dehydrated, and for the hardened relicts of such materials, more or less mixed with entrapped quartz and other materials. **1966** D. FORBES *Heart of Malaya* iii. 35 It [*sc.* a bungalow] was set on a hillside..at the end of a three-mile estate road of red laterite. **1967** *Nat. Geographic* July 110/2 [Thailand.] A foreman said this was laterite, a low-grade iron ore, good for making roads and filling land. **1970** E. M. BRIDGES *World Soils* ix. 72/1 Laterite..is formed by an accumulation in the soil of sesquioxidic material.

attrib. **1851** R. F. BURTON *Goa* 176 A pile of laterite rock rising abruptly from a level expanse of sand. **1886** GUILLEMARD *Cruise Marchesa* II. 327 The red laterite roads. **1898** [see above]. **1906** *Daily Chron.* 24 Aug. 6/5 The soil and the climate of Seychelles are evidently favourable to the growth of Para rubber, which thrives even in laterite soils where no other plants are at present growing.

lateritic (lætə'rɪtɪk), *a.* [f. prec. + -IC.] Resembling or of the nature of laterite; in *Soil Science*, applied to a soil that is not regarded as laterite but approaches it in composition.

1847 CAPT. NEWBOLD in *Jrnl. Asiatic Soc. Bengal* XIV. 305 Lateritic sandstone. **1880** V. BALL *Jungle Life Ind.* i. 4 A very notable change..from a swampy alluvium into a lateritic gravel. **1927, 1932** [see LATERITE]. **1938** *U.S. Dept. Agric. Year-bk.* 974 Soils in which the laterization process has become markedly evident but has not reached completion are known as lateritic soils... They are very important in the West Indies... These soils are characterized by a colloidal fraction whose molecular ratio of silica to alumina is approximately 2. **1946** LUTZ & CHANDLER *Forest Soils* xi. 403 The laterization process, in conjunction with podzolization, has resulted in the development of six zonal soils in the forested warm-temperature and tropical regions: (1) laterites, (2) reddish-brown lateritic soils, (3) yellowish-brown lateritic soils, (4) red podzolic soils, (5) yellow podzolic soils, and (6) terra rossa. **1952** L. M. THOMPSON *Soils & Soil Fertility* xvii. 285 The clay soils which he studied..were lateritic in nature (high percentage of kaolinite or high in hydrated oxides of iron and aluminum), and it is now recognized that lateritic or kaolinitic materials are resistant to erosion. **1970** *Toronto Daily Star* 24 Sept. 14/7 He pointed to the lateritic, or oxide, ores of the tropics and subtropics as an area where future major expansion in the industry will occur.

lateritious (lætə'rɪʃ(ɪ)əs), *a.* Also **latericeous** (in mod. American Dicts.). [f. L. *laterītius, -īcius*, f. *later* brick: see -ITIOUS[1].] Pertaining to or resembling brick; of the colour of brick, brick-red: said chiefly of urinary deposits.

1656 BLOUNT *Glossogr.*, *Lateritious*, made of brick, or like brick. **1658** PHILLIPS, *Latericious.* **1733** CHEYNE *Eng. Malady* II. xi. §2 (1734) 229 The Water..never with a gross or full lateritious Sediment. **1763** E. STONE in *Phil. Trans.* LIII. 200 The longer they are kept the more they incline to a cinnamon or lateritious colour. **1875** H. C. WOOD *Therap.* (1879) 418 A secretion of thick lateritious urine.

lateritization (ˌlætərɪtaɪ'zeɪʃən). [f. LATERIT(E + -IZATION, rendering G. *lateritisirung* (now *-ierung*) (M. Bauer 1898, in *Neues Jahrb. f. Min., Geol. u. Paläont.* II. 203).] = LATERIZATION.

1903 *Geol. Mag.* Decade IV. X. 62 That the formation of laterite is a mere question of average temperature seems unlikely, for lateritization is very prominent at elevations of 6,000–7,000 feet..in South India, where the temperature varies very little above or below 60° F. **1920** *Geol. Mag.* LVII. 212 The depth of lateritization was so great on the right bank of the Congo at a height of about 500 O.D. that [etc.] . **1934** *Discovery* July 202/1 Lateritization (silica leaching) may be considered as the reverse of podsolization (iron and aluminium leaching). **1966** *McGraw-Hill Encycl. Sci. & Technol.* VII. 406/2 The resulting concentrations of iron and aluminum oxides sharply differentiate lateritization from temperate-climate weathering in which the end product is largely clay minerals (hydrous aluminum silicates).

Hence (as a back-formation, or after G. *lateritisi(e)ren*) **'lateritize** *v. trans.*, to convert into laterite; **'lateritized** *ppl. a.*, **-itizing** *vbl. sb.*

1911 *Geol. Mag.* Decade V. VIII. 509 These five rocks.. were probably formed in situ under conditions in which the lateritizing processes were not pushed to a finish. **1920** *Geol. Mag.* LVII. 214 Certain inclined bands in the norite have been thoroughly lateritized for many yards along their outcrop, and seams of magnetite in them..run practically unaltered from norite into laterite. *Ibid.* 212 The lateritized portion was more readily removed by erosive agencies, and the masses of unaltered rock were left standing in relief. **1970** *Nature* 23 May 693/2 The southern half of Western Australia is an old, slightly dissected, lateritized land surface dating from the middle or late Tertiary. *Ibid.*, The Giles Complex of mafic and ultramafic igneous rocks..has been lateritized.

laterization (ˌlætəraɪ'zeɪʃən). [f. LATER(ITE + -IZATION, rendering G. *lateritisirung* (see prec.).] The alteration of rock to laterite; the kind of weathering or soil-forming process that results in laterite and lateritic soils.

1903 A. GEIKIE *Text-bk. Geol.* (ed. 4) I. 169 Laterite... The peculiar kind of alteration exemplified by this rock and by Bauxite has been termed 'Laterisation' [by Bauer]. **1917** *Mining Mag.* XVII. 74/2 A very definite line must be drawn ..between live laterite or that in process of formation, and dead laterite or that in which laterization is no longer actively operative. **1936** *U.S. Dept. Agric. Misc. Publ.* No. 229.22 The laterization process is, perhaps, more strictly a geological process than one of soil building. **1938** *U.S. Dept. Agric. Yearbk.* 973 The soil-forming process called laterization is essentially the progressive hydrolysis of rock minerals, and its full development results in their conversion to silicic acid, aluminum hydroxide, and iron hydroxide or their more or less complete dehydration products—the Laterites. **1952** P. W. RICHARDS *Trop. Rain Forest* ix. 209 This preferential leaching of silica from a soil is called laterization. **1967** M. J. COE *Ecol. Alpine Zone Mt. Kenya* 76 The clays show a certain number of darker stratifications but, due to the low temperatures, there are no signs of laterisation.

Hence (as back-formations) **'laterized** *ppl. a.*, converted into laterite; **'laterizing** *vbl. sb.* and *ppl. a.*

1917 *Mining Mag.* XVII. 67/2 Water from the laterizing zone when exposed to the air deposits ferric and aluminium hydrates with hydrous silicate of alumina. *Ibid.* 74/2 The upper portion of the laterite..is detrital, the lower part laterized and partly laterized schist merging gradually into altered schist. **1932** *Technical Communications Imperial Bureau Soil Sci.* No. 24. 19 Soils formed under laterising conditions. **1964** *Sci. Amer.* Nov. 97/2 Laterized soils occur most commonly in the tropical belt between the latitudes of 30 degrees North and 30 degrees South.

† **'latermore**, *a. Obs.* [A double comp. f. LATER + -MORE.] Later, last.

1548 UDALL, etc. *Erasm. Par. Mark* i. 12–15 Is it meete that the carnall be fyrste, and that latermore, whiche is spirituall and gostely.

laterne, obs. form of LANTERN.

latero- ('lætərəʊ), taken as combining form of L. *later-, latus* side: cf. LATERI-. Prefixed to Eng. words, forming compounds, usually hyphened (*a*) in sense 'pertaining to the side (and another part)', 'pertaining to the side of (a specified structure)', e.g. ***latero-anterior, -caudal, -cervical, -dorsal, -marginal, -nuchal, -posterior, -ventral*** adjs.; (*b*) 'on or towards the side', e.g. ***latero-flexion, -prone*** adj., ***-pulsion, -version***.

1848 JOHNSTON in *Proc. Berw. Nat. Club* II. No. 6. 296 There are four eyes in two *latero-anterior groups. **1852** DANA *Crust.* I. 625 Latero-anterior spines large. **1888** COMSTOCK *Introd. Entomol.* I. ix. 219 *Latero-caudal angles of the head unarmed. **1888** *Syd. Soc. Lex.*, **Latero-cervical*, relating to a side and a neck, or to the side of the neck. **Latero-dorsal*, situated on the side of the back. **1857** BULLOCK *Cazeaux' Midwif.* 54 This inflexion may take place anteriorly, posteriorly, or laterally, and has been styled accordingly anteflexion, retroflexion, and *latero-flexion. **1869** T. H. TANNER *Pract. Med.* (ed. 6) II. 349 Where the uterus is bent and its fundus fixed to the right or left side, the cervix remaining in the median line (latero-flexion) this deviation from the natural position will [etc.]. **1881–2** W. S. KENT *Man. Infusoria* II. 792 A few postero-marginal or caudal, but never a continuous series of *latero-marginal setæ. **1872** COUES *Key N. Amer. Birds* (1884) 734 *Latero-nuchal feathers elongated. **1852** DANA *Crust.* I. 217 The *latero-posterior margin is somewhat less oblique. **1856** WOODWARD *Mollusca* 446 The latero-posterior margins of the body. **1897** *Albutt's Syst. Med.* IV. 340 The patient being placed on the back, or else in the *latero-prone position. **1888** *Syd. Soc. Lex.*, **Latero-pulsion*, an involuntary impulse towards one or other side. **1881–2** W. S. KENT *Man. Infusoria* II. 790 The composition of each of the *latero-ventral rows. **1869** T. H. TANNER *Pract. Med.* (ed. 6) II. 351 Supposing the fundus to be inclined to one side of the body while the os uteri looks towards the opposite side (*lateroversion), there will [etc.].

lates ('leɪtiːz). [mod.L. (Cuvier & Valenciennes *Histoire naturelle des Poissons* (1828) II. 88), f. Gr. λάτος Nile perch.] A large fish of the genus so called, esp. the *Nile perch* (NILE), *Lates niloticus*; = LATUS[2].

1920 *Blackw. Mag.* May 655/1 Playing a giant lates is no joke. **1921** W. RADCLIFFE *Fishing from Earliest Times* xxv. 326 A picture of a bronze mummy-case containing remains of a small *Lates*.

lates, obs. form of LATTICE.

latescent (leɪˈtɛsənt), *a.* [ad. L. *latēscent-em*, pr. pple. of *latēscĕre*, inceptive of *latēre* to be hid.] Becoming latent, hidden, or obscure. So **laˈtescence**, latescent condition or quality.

1836-7 Sir W. Hamilton *Metaph.* xxx. (1859) II. 215 This obscuration can be conceived in every infinite degree, between incipient latescence and irrecoverable latency. *Ibid.* xxxii. II. 251 The under play of the latescent activities.

†**lateship.** *Obs. rare*⁻¹. In 4 latschipe. [f. Late *a.*¹ + -ship.] Slowness, sluggishness.

13.. *Minor Poems fr. Vernon MS.* (E.E.T.S.) 523/26 þorw bi-ginnyng vertu encresceþ, And þorw latschipe hit is wiþ-drawe & ceseþ.

latesome (ˈleɪtsəm), *a.* (and *adv.*) *Obs.* exc. *dial.* Also 4 **latsom, -sum.** [OE. *lætsum*, f. *læt* Late *a.*¹ + -some.] Backward; slow, sluggish; late.

11.. *O.E. Chron.* an. 1089 (Laud MS.) Wæs swiðe lætsum ȝear on corne. **1340** Hampole *Pr. Consc.* 793 He es swyft to spek.. And latsom and slaw for to here. **1382** Wyclif *Exod.* iv. 10 Y am of more latsum and of more slow tongue. *c* **1450** *Mirour Saluacioun* 1142 And broght hym precioue gifftes and latsomest to fynd. **1469** *Plumpton Corr.* (Camden) 21 Whether is so latesum in this cuntrey, that men can neither well gett corne nor hay. **1847** *Whistle-Binkie* (Scot. Songs) (1890) II. 200 We've dandered baith latesome and early. **1877-89** in *N.W. Linc. Gloss.*

Hence †ˈ**latesomeness.**

a **1340** Hampole *Psalter* xxiii. 3 Wha is sett here for latsumnes. **1357** *Lay Folks Catech.* 528 Of this syn [slauthe] comes.. latsumnesse or lite to draw opon lenthe Any gode dede that we sal do.

latesse, obs. form of Lattice.

latest (ˈleɪtɪst), *a.*¹ (*adv.*, *sb.*) Also 5 **lattest.** [A mod. superlative f. Late *a.*¹ + -est, the connexion of Last *a.* (repr. OE. *latost*, *latst*), with the positive having been obscured by its change of form and its independent sense-development.]

1. = Last. Now *arch.* and *poet.*

[*c* **1420** *Pallad. on Husb.* i. 363 The see grauel is lattest for to drye, And lattest may thow therwith edifie.] **1588** Shaks. *L.L.L.* v. ii. 797 Now at the latest minute of the houre, Grant vs your loues. **1591** *Troub. Raigne K. John* (1611) 29 Ile fight it out unto the latest man. **1604** Shaks. *Oth.* i. iii. 28 To leaue that latest, which concernes him first. **1607** Topsell *Four-f. Beasts* (1658) 337 The thinnest or latest part of the milk of a Mare. **1619** Drayton *Idea* No. 61 Now at the last gaspe of Loues latest Breath. **1669** Dryden *Tyr. Love* v. i 'Tis done, tyrant, this is thy latest hour. **1795** Southey *Joan of Arc* i. 320, I had her latest look of earthly love, I felt her hand's last pressure. **1821** Keats *Isabella* xliii, How she might.. sing to it one latest lullaby. **1864** Tennyson *Enoch A.* 728 For Phillip's dwelling fronted on the street, The latest house to landward. **1883** R. W. Dixon *Mano* i. i. 1, I, Fergant, living now my latest days.

absol. *c* **1440** *Girald. Hist. Irel.* 26 Thay wer fyrst y-sete yn þe latest of þe host.

2. a. Most late; most recent. Also *ellipt.* as *sb.* in ***the latest***: the most recent story, piece of news, fashion, etc.

1593 Shaks. *Rich. II*, v. vi. 1 The latest newes we heare, Is that [etc.]. **1825** Southey *T. Paraguay* Ded. viii, Take therefore now thy Father's latest lay,.. Perhaps his last. **1884** *Times* (weekly ed.) 17 Oct. 3/2 The latest.. of these speeches. **1884** *Graphic* 23 Aug. 198/1 The passengers in all except the latest trains are as a rule orderly enough. **1886** H. Baumann *Londinismen* 94/1 What's the latest: was gibt's Neues? **1889** *Kansas City* (Missouri) *Times & Star* 25 June, The latest the dear girls hereabouts are singing.. is, Will he love you as today? **1900** F. Anstey *Brass Bottle* i. 5 Let's have a look at Beevor's latest performance. **1911** A. Bennett *Card* v. 128 This was Denry's 'latest', and it employed the conversation of the borough for I don't know how long. **1916** G. B. Shaw *Matter with Ireland* (1962) 95 If you want to dine in evening dress confronted with a bediamonded wife and flanked by daughters in the very latest,.. you will be unhappy in Ireland. **1922** Joyce *Ulysses* 319 Well, says the citizen, what's the latest from the scene of action? **1940** *War Illustr.* 19 Jan. 623 The newsvendor who still stands shivering at his wintry pitch, lustily shouting 'the latest' when you can only discern him dimly by the glow of his cigarette. **1961** Wodehouse *Service with Smile* (1962) iv. 58 'I say,' he said.. 'have you heard the latest?'

b. Phr. ***at (the) latest***: at the most advanced hour, at the most distant date (cf. At *prep.* 25 c).

1884 *Times* 30 Jan. 9/3 Between February, or March at latest, and May.

3. quasi-*adv.* (e.g. in *Comb.* with ppl. adjs.: cf. Late *adv.* 7).

1667 Milton *P.L.* v. 18 My fairest, my espous'd, my latest found. **1864** Tennyson *Enoch A.* 150 Nursing the sickly babe, her latest-born.

late-wake, corrupt form of Lykewake.

1771 Pennant *Tour Scotl. in 1769*, 112 The Late-wake is a ceremony used at funerals. **1814** Scott *Ld. of Isles* vi. xxxiv, Bid Ninian's convent light their shrine, For late-wake of De Argentine. **1821** Galt *Ann. Parish* xxiv. 222 The body was.. removed to Mr. Mutchkin's brew-house, where the lads and lassies kept the late wake.

latewar, variant of Lectuary.

†ˈ**lateward**, *a.* and *adv.* *Obs.* Also 5-6 **latward.** [f. Late *a.*¹ + -ward.] **A.** *adj.*

1. Late, slow, backward: said mostly of fruit and crops ripening, and seasons of the year.

1538 Elyot *Dict.*, *Cordum fœnum*, latewarde haye. *Cordi agni*, latewarde lambes. **1546** *Supplic. Poore Commons* (E.E.T.S.) 71 They mighte not gather their grapes nor frutes twyse, but must leue the latward fruit. **1587** Golding *De Mornay* viii. 93 If Greece were to lateward therein [the studie of wisedome], where shall the antiquitie thereof be found among the Gentiles? **1589** Fleming *Virg. Georg.* i. 9 There Vesper or th' euening doth kindle lateward lights. **1601** Holland *Pliny* I. 501 Trees which be late-ward and keep their fruit long ere they ripen. **1611** Cotgr., *Arriere-saison*,.. a late harvest, a lateward yeare. *a* **1659** Osborn *Ess.* iii. Wks. (1673) 568 The Garden having not yet produced any Fruit so lateward. **1719** London & Wise *Compl. Gard.* 273 We sow our last Cucumbers about the tenth or twelfth of this Month, to have some lateward ones. **1745** tr. *Columella's Husb.* xi. ii, Now it is time to have finished the digging and dressing of your lateward rosebeds.

2. Pertaining to a late period. *rare.*

1577 Harrison *England* ii. ix. (1877) i. 190 Such also was the lateward estimation of them [the old laws] that [etc.].

B. *adv.*

1. Of late, recently.

1471 Sir J. Paston in *P. Lett.* No. 670 III. 6 As myche plesyer and hertys ease as I have latward causyd you to have trowbyll and thowght. **1649** Bp. Hall *Confirm.* (1651) 28 Deducing it self through all the ages of the Church, (though lateward not without some taint of superstitious interspersions).

2. Late, after the due time or season.

1572 Mascall *Plant. & Graff.* v. 24 Whether the tree be forwarde or not, or to be graffed soone or latewarde. **1573** Tusser *Husb.* xlvi. (1878) 101 Who soweth too lateward, hath seldome good seed. **1609** Bible (Douay) *Jer.* ii. 31 Am I become a wildernes to Israel, or a lateward springing land? **1620** Bp. Hall *Hon. Mar. Clergy* iii. §13 The cited clergy and laity doe now thus late-ward discusse *de iure.* **1659** Torriano, *Sèro*, late, or lateward.

3. ? Towards the last.

1494 Fabyan *Chron.* vii. 622 The most losse turned euer latewarde vpon yᵉ Englysh partie.

Also †ˈ**latewards** *adv.*, lately, recently.

1483 *Act. 1 Rich. III*, c. 13 The Butts of Malmseys latewards brought into this.. Realm.

†ˈ**latewardly**, *a.* *Obs. rare.* [f. Lateward + -ly¹.] = Lateward *a.* 1.

1573 Tusser *Husb.* xxi. (1878) 56 Leaue latewardly rering.

†ˈ**latewardly**, *adv.* *Obs.* [f. as prec. + -ly².]

a. Of late, lately. **b.** At a late date.

1720 Strype *Stow's Surv. Lond.* I. 6 This our City of London was also walled with Stone in the Time of the Roman Government here; but yet very latewardly [*edd.* 1598-1633 lately]. For it seemeth not to have been walled in the Year of our Lord ccxcvi. **1721** —— *Eccl. Mem.* II. i. 9 His tutors were latewardly much detained at court. *Ibid.* III. xviii. 147 Here latewardly also were J. Pilkington [etc.].

latewes, obs. form of Lettuce.

late-while(s, *adv.* [f. Late *a.*¹ + While *sb.*, with and without genitival *s.*] Of late, recently.

1839 Bailey *Festus* xix. (1848) 227 Hast met that anger late-while? **1887** *S. Cheshire Gloss.*, *Late-wheiles*, of late.. 'I hanna seyn nowt on her late-wheiles'.

‖**latex** (ˈleɪtɛks). Pl. (see sense 3) ˈ**latexes, latices** (ˈleɪtɪsiːz). [L., = liquid, fluid.]

†**1.** *Old Phys.* The name given to juice of any sort in the body; esp. the watery part of the blood and other secretions.

1662 J. Chandler *Van Helmont's Oriat.* 115 Religion is amazed.. at the finding of a latex or liquor, which being reduced to the least Atomes possible to nature, as loving a single life, would despise the Wedlocks of every ferment. *Ibid.* 194 Seperation of the Liquor Latex, Urine, and Sweat doth employ the Liver. **1669** W. Simpson *Hydrol. Chym.* 31 The exorbitant latex, which before was extravasated runs in its own chanels again. **1766** Spry in *Phil. Trans.* LVII. 91 Her blood appeared of a good texture, otherwise than giving off a little more than its due proportion of latex.

2. *Bot.* A milky liquid found in many plants (in special vessels called *laticiferous*), which exudes when the plant is wounded, and coagulates on exposure to the air; *spec.* that of *Hevea brasiliensis* or other plants used to produce rubber. Also *attrib.*

1835 Lindley *Introd. Bot.* (1848) II. 338 Many plants.. when old, have a milky latex. **1858** Carpenter *Veg. Phys.* §58 Destined for the conveyance of the latex or prepared juice of the plant. **1885** Goodale *Physiol. Bot.* 96 Upon exposure to the air latex coagulates, and forms upon drying a sticky, elastic mass. **1922** *Glasgow Herald* 4 Dec. 11 Rubber latex is a limpid liquid which is mixable with water. **1937** *Archit. Rev.* LXXXII. 57/3 The hearth-scene surround is constructed of re-inforced concrete, rendered in a mix of latex-rubber and *ciment fondu.* **1951** M. Abercrombie et al. *Dict. Biol.* 125 Latex of a number of species is collected and used in manufacture of several commercial products, most important being rubber. **1955** *Times* 14 June 11/1 Almost the entire production of the estates is in the form of latex.. as distinct from sheet rubber. **1960** G. Lewis *Handbk. Crafts* 237 Latex Foam Cushion. In many of the modern suites of furniture latex foam or some other kind of rubber stuffing is used. **1966** L. Cohen *Beautiful Losers* (1970) ii. 177 Several comfortable Latex cups assumed exciting holds here and there.

attrib. **1874** Cooke *Fungi* 23 True latex vessels occur occasionally in Agaricus. **1885** Goodale *Physiol. Bot.* 95 Latex-cells are not restricted to any one organ of the plant.

3. Any dispersion in water of particles of a polymer (originally synthetic rubber) that is formed in a polymerization process, such as is used as a binder in paints or for coating paper and leather.

1937 W. J. S. Naunton *Synthetic Rubber* viii. 140 'Rubber dispersions' should be divided into two groups: (1) Latices produced *in situ* by emulsion polymerisation... (2) Dispersed rubbers produced by the dispersion of pre-formed solid rubbers. *Ibid.* 150 This synthetic latex forms a good cement for assembling the numerous pieces of natural and artificial leather which constitute the modern mass-produced shoe. **1952** J. P. Casey *Pulp & Paper* II. xxi. 1247 Pulp treated with small amounts of elastomer latices has improved strength properties and increased wet strength. **1954** H. F. Payne *Organic Coating Technol.* I. ix. 372 During the past few years stabilized latexes of a variety of polymeric film-formers have been made available to the paint industry. **1969** T. C. Thorstensen *Pract. Leather Technol.* xiv. 226 In a latex system the binder is emulsified in water. When the latex is applied the water evaporates, or sinks into the leather, and eventually a phase inversion takes place.

4. Special Comb. **latex paint**, a paint having a latex as its binding medium.

1954 H. F. Payne *Organic Coating Technol.* I. ix. 372 Another advantage of latex paints is their very fast drying property. **1965** D. H. Parker *Princ. Surface Coating Technol.* xliv. 724 Exterior latex paints should not be applied directly to unpainted wood, for poor adhesion may result.

lateys(e, obs. form of Lattice.

lath (lɑːθ, læθ), *sb.* Forms: α. 1 lætt, (*pl.* lætta, latta), 5-8 latt, 6-7 latte, 5, 7-9 *dial.* lat; *pl.* 4-6 **lattes, -is,** 5 **lattys, lates, latez,** 6 **layttes,** 6- **latts,** 8- **lats.** β. 4-6 **lathe,** (4 **laþþe, latthe**), 6- **lath.** [OE. *lætt* sb. fem. (whence mod. dial. *lat*) corresponds to MDu. *latte* (Du. *lat*), HG. dial. *latz*, Da. (16th c.) *latte, lætte, lecthe* (now *lægte*, which is phonetically difficult). The ME. *laþþe*, from which the modern standard Eng. form descends, prob. represents an OE. **læþþ-*, as this would correspond to the synonymous OHG. *lat(t)a, ladda* (MHG., mod.G. *latte*); but the mutual relation of the two types is obscure, and the occurrence of a geminated *þ* in OTeut. has no known parallel or explanation. Some scholars think that the substitution of *þ* for *t* was due to the influence of the synonymous (and perh. cognate) Welsh *llath* = Irish *slat*:—OCeltic **slattā*. The Teut. word has passed into the Rom. langs. (cf. It. *latta*, Sp. *lata*, F. *latte*); it is usu. regarded as cogn. w. MHG. *lade* plank (mod.G. *laden* counter, shop).]

1. a. A thin narrow strip of wood used to form a groundwork upon which to fasten the slates or tiles of a roof or the plaster of a wall or ceiling, and in the construction of lattice or trellis work and Venetian blinds. ***double, single, pantile lath***: see quots. 1825, 1842-59.

a. *c* **1000** Ælfric *Gloss.* in Wr.-Wülcker 126 *Asseres*, lætta. *c* **1050** *Suppl. Ælfric's Gloss.*, ibid. 185 *Asseres*, latta, *uel* reafteres. **1361-2** *Durham Acc. Rolls* (Surtees) 385 Cum calce, lattes, et sclatstan. *a* **1400-50** *Alexander* 756* [He] stighillys hym in som stede, a stable by hym one, With lang lates of yren, þat he might lig in. *c* **1425** *St. Mary of Oignies* i. ii. in *Anglia* VIII. 136/1 She slepte but litil & þat vpon a fewe lattys. *c* **1450** *St. Cuthbert* (Surtees) 642 Be þe lattis it toke festnyng. **1483-4** in Swayne *Churchw. Acc. Sarum* (1896) 33 For v bondellez of latez. **1515-16** *Durham Acc. Rolls* (Surtees) 253 In le Storehouse.. ccc layttes. **1578** *Richmond. Wills* (Surtees 1853) 282 Woodd and bords.. with stangs, hots, and cares, and spelks, and latts, xxs. **1641** Best *Farm. Bks.* (Surtees) 148 They will sowe downe theire thatch in fower places.. allsoe sowinge once aboute a latte, ever betwixt sparre and sparre. **1662** J. Davies tr. *Olearius' Voy. Amb.* 395 The houses of this Village were very wretched ones, as being built only with lats nail'd across, and plaister'd over with clay. **1674** Ray *N.C. Words* 29 A Lath is also called a Lat in the Northern Dialect. **1779** Mann in *Phil. Trans.* LXIX. 626 Latts.. were nailed against each end. **1878** *Cumbld. Gloss.*, *Lat*, lath.. 'As thin as a lat'. **1886** *S.W. Linc. Gloss.*, *Lat*, a lath.

β. **1330** *Kenfig Ord.* in Gross *Gild Merch.* II. 134 Noe burgess shall buy.. boards, lathes, tyles. *c* **1380** Wyclif *Serm.* Sel. Wks. II. 167 Bi þe laþþis þei senten him doun, wiþ his bed. **1398** Trevisa *Barth. De P.R.* xvii. clxvii. (1495) 711 The lathe is longe and somwhat brode and playne and thyn and is naylled thwart ouer to the rafterers and theron hangyth slattes, tyle and shyngles. **1523** Fitzherb. *Husb.* §15 They [harowe bulles].. haue shotes of wode put through theym lyke lathes. **1563** Hyll *Art Garden.* (1593) 7 The Romans vsed to inclose and fence their gardens with stakes and laths. **1703** Moxon *Mech. Exerc.* 244 Laths.. are made of heart of Oak, for outside Work..; and of Fir for inside Plastering. **1725** Bradley *Fam. Dict.* s.v., A Bundle of Laths is generally call'd a Hundred of Laths. **1825** J. Nicholson *Operat. Mechanic* 611 The single are the thinnest.. those called *lath and half*, are supposed to be one third thicker than the single; and the double laths are twice that thickness. **1842-59** Gwilt *Archit.* Gloss. s.v. *Lath*, *Pantile laths* are long square pieces of fir, on which the pantiles hang. **1866** Rogers *Agric. & Prices* I. xx. 487 Stout oak laths rent from heart timber. **1881** Young *Every Man his own Mechanic* §175 Specialities in Venetian blind laths. *Ibid.* §445 In planing.. laths for trellis-work.

b. *collect.* Laths as a material used in building (chiefly as a groundwork for a coating of plaster) to form a wall or partition. Freq. in ***lath and plaster*** (often written with hyphens, esp. when used *attrib.* or quasi-*adj.*); rarely ***lath and clay.***

1573 Tusser *Husb.* xvii. (1878) 36 A frower of iron, for cleaning of lath. **1663** Gerbier *Counsel* 79 Ruff cast upon Lath.. is worth eighteen pence the yard. **1715** Prior *Down-Hall* 152 A house should be built, or with brick, or with stone. Why 'tis plaster and lath. **1719** De Foe *Crusoe* ii. xiv. (1840) 285 It was.. a house built, as we call it in England, with lath and plaster. **1765** Griffith in *Phil. Trans.* LV. 274 A lath and plaister wall. **1807** Crabbe *Par. Reg.* i. Wks. 1834 II. 150 A paltry screen Of paper'd lath. **1839** Carlyle

Chartism viii. 158 Dons, Tons..not a few..of burnt brick, of timber, of lath-and-clay. **1859** JEPHSON *Brittany* xvi. 269 Buildings of lath and plaster. **1866** ROGERS *Agric. & Prices* I. xx. 496 Lath-and-plaster work.

c. lath and plaster: rhyming slang for 'master'.

1857 'DUCANGE ANGLICUS' *Vulgar Tongue* 11 Lath-and-plaster, master.

2. a. In wider application: A thin, narrow, flat piece of wood used for any purpose. Also, as the material of a counterfeit weapon, as ***bow***, ***sword of lath***. † ***dagger of lath***: see DAGGER 1 b.

1592 SHAKS. *Rom. & Jul.* I. iv. 5 No Cupid..Bearing a Tartar's painted Bow of lath. **1616** SURFL. & MARKH. *Country Farm* 35 Hee shall cut the roots of the Vines, and set square Laths or Props for the defending of them. **1658** A. FOX *Wurtz' Surg.* II. xvii. 124 One lath or splinter will serve the turn here. And apply the lath either above or below the great sinew on the Arm. **1796** J. OWEN *Trav. Europe* II. 504 An old woman..holding a lath lighted at one end. **1820** SCOTT *Ivanhoe* i, A sword of lath.

b. *transf.*, applied to what is slender or fragile.

1633 QUARLES *Prelim. Verses to Fletcher's Purple Isl.*, His ribs are laths, daub'd o're Plaister'd with flesh, and bloud. **1748** SMOLLETT *Rod. Rand* (1812) I. 59 You man of lath. **1799** MAD. D'ARBLAY *Lett to Dr. Burney*, July, 'You used to be as thin as Dr. Lind', says the King. Lind was then in sight —a mere lath. **1814** SCOTT *Ld. of Isles* II. i. Interl., Some phantom, fashionably thin, With limb of lath. **1922** A. BENNETT *Lilian* II. iii, The entire office, thanks to that lath, Millicent, was disorganised.

c. *Min.* and *Petrol.* A mineral crystal that is thin, narrow, and elongated.

[**1908** L. V. PIRSSON *Rocks & Rock Minerals* iv. 36 In some rocks, such..as the syenites, which are mainly composed of feldspar..they have more or less perfectly the shape of flat tables or rude laths.] **1916** A. JOHANNSEN tr. *Weinschenk's Fund. Princ. Petrol.* x. 199 In this [intersertal] texture the interstices between the feldspar laths are filled with glass. **1941** *Proc. Prehist. Soc.* VII. 65 The rock is a strongly ophitic dolerite with..plates of fresh augite and laths of plagioclase. **1959** W. W. MOORHOUSE *Study of Rocks in Thin Section* v. 160 Intersertal includes diabasic and ophitic textures, in which the feldspar laths are enclosed with large grains of pyroxene.

3. The bending part of an arbalest or cross-bow.

1545 *Rates Custom ho.* a vii, Crosbowe lathes the pounde iiii*d.* **1685** BOYLE *Effects of Mot.* viii. 91 When the Lath of a Cross-bow stands bent.

4. *attrib.* and *Comb.* **a.** simple attributive, as ***lath-hammer***, ***-wood***; **b.** quasi-*adj.* (in sense of 'made of a lath or of laths'), as ***lath-house***, ***partition***, ***sword***, ***wall***, ***-work***; **c.** objective, as ***lath-cleaver***, ***-cutting***, ***-maker***, ***-render***, ***-river***, ***-splitter***, ***-splitting***; **d.** parasynthetic and similative, as ***lath-backed***, ***-legged***, ***-like***, ***-shaped*** adjs. **e.** Special combinations, as **lath-bedstead**, a bedstead with laths to support the bedding; **lath-brick**, a long narrow brick used for the floors of grain-kilns; †**lath-brod**, ? a small lath-nail; **lath-coop**, **-pot** *U.S.* (see quot. for *lath-pot*). Also LATH-NAIL.

1676 WYCHERLEY *Pl. Dealer* II. i, Thou pitiful, paltry, *lath-back'd Fellow. **1830** R. B. PEAKE *Crt. & City* I. iii, Brother, observe his make—none of your lath-backed wishy-washy breed. **1806** *Med. Jrnl.* XV. 11 A *lath bedstead. **1677** PLOT *Oxfordsh.* 251 *Lath-bricks..are put in the place of the Laths or Spars (supported by Pillars) in Oasts for drying mault. **1823** P. NICHOLSON *Pract. Build.* 587 Lath-bricks..used for drying malt upon. **1536–7** *Durham Acc. Rolls* (Surtees) 698, 2000 *latbroddes ad 2s. 1d. **1620** *Naworth Househ. Bks.* (Surtees) 132, c. of late broades, iij*d.* **1622** *Canterb. Marriage Licences* (MS.), Will'm Paine of the Citty of Cant. *latcleaver. **1825** J. NICHOLSON *Operat. Mechanic* 612 The lath-cleavers having cut their timber.. cleave each piece with wedges. **1887** *Lath-coop [see *lath-pot* below]. **1827** *Western Monthly Rev.* I. 80 A *lath-cutting machine..cuts them with great rapidity. **1847** *Rep. Comm. Patents 1846* (U.S.) 91 One patent has been granted for improvements in lath-cutting machines. **1573** TUSSER *Husb.* xvii. (1878) 37 A *lath hammer. **1901** J. BLACK *Illustr. Carpenter & Builder Ser.: Home Handicrafts* 35 The laths are nailed to each stud, or joist... For this purpose the best tool to employ is the..lath-hammer. **1964** J. S. SCOTT *Dict. Building* 188 *Lath hammer*.., a plasterer's hammer for nailing laths. **1882** *Garden* 7 Jan. 1/2 Azaleas, &c. are kept under a *lath-house shelter through the summer months. **1523** FITZHERB. *Husb.* §78 The .ix. propertyes of an asse.. the syxte, to be *lathe-legged. **1611** COTGR., *Tringle*, a ..*lath-like peece of wood. **1674** MOXON *Tutor Astron.* (ed. 3) 201 A sphear is complicated only of Lath-like Circles to represent each Orb. **1530** PALSGR. 237/2 *Lathe maker, *faiseur de lattes.* **1533** *MS. Acc. St. John's Hosp., Canterb.*, To the lathe maker..xvij*d.* **1607** *Canterb. Marriage Licences* (MS.), Abraham Garke of Marden, latmaker. **1886** RUSKIN *Præterita* I. 286 Separated only by a *lath partition. **1887** G. B. GOODE, etc. *Fisheries of U.S.* II. 666 The term *lath-pot is almost universally employed to designate the common forms of closed lobster traps,..providing they are constructed of laths or of any narrow strips of wood. Other names..are 'box-traps', 'house-pots', 'stick-pots', 'lath-coops'. **1688** *Lond. Gaz.* No. 2318/4 A Man..by Trade a Hoopshaver, or *Lathrender. **1610** in *Eng. Hist. Rev.* (1898) XIII. 524 A *lath Ryver. **1876** *Whitby Gloss.*, *Lat-river*, one who splits laths for the plasterers. **1888** J. J. H. TEALL *Brit. Petrogr.* 435 This [interstitial] substance occurs in irregular masses wedged in between the *lath-shaped felspathic constituent. **1973** *Nature* 9 Feb. 374/1 Lath-shaped crystals also occur and their size is about 0·15 × 0·05 mm². **1858** *Simmonds Dict. Trade*, *Lath-splitter. **1882** OGILVIE, *Lath-splitting. **1697** DRYDEN *Virg. Georg.* IV. 168 The God obscene, who frights away, With his *Lath Sword, the Thiefs and Birds of Prey. **1940** BLUNDEN *Poems 1930–40* 250 While with a half-triumphant mind you crost Lath-swords of words on some uncertain matter. **1756** BP. POCOCKE *Trav.* (1889) II. 228 Outhouses..built..with what they call *lath walls. **1641** BEST *Farm. Bks.* (Surtees) 16 Ashen barres ..very streight and riven very thinne allmost like unto *latte-wood. **1887** MOLONEY *Forestry W. Afr.* 3 Foreign and Colonial Timber used for..lath-wood, shingles for roofs, &c. **1611** COTGR., *Latage*,..*lath-worke. **1663** GERBIER *Counsel* 79 Ruff cast upon Lath-work, the owner finding all, is worth eight pence a yard. **1863** R. B. PEACOCK *S. Lonsdale Dial.* in *Trans. Philol. Soc.* 262 He's gloorin out a 't winda, èn shewin' hissel through 't lat-wark.

lath (lɑːθ, læθ), *v.* Also 6 lathe, 7–9 *dial.* lat. [f. LATH *sb.*] ***trans.*** To cover or furnish (a wall or ceiling) with laths for plastering. Also with *over*.

c **1532** DU WES *Introd. Fr.* in *Palsgr.* 949 To lathe with lathes, *latter.* **1575** *Churchw. Acc. Stanford* in *Antiquary* XVII. 171/1 It. for lathing & mending the churche howse mounds v*d.* **1600** SURFLET *Countrie Farme* I. xviii. 113 [The feasant] house shall be..thicke latted and of clouen boardes. **1641** BEST *Farm. Bks.* (Surtees) 148 After that an house is latted, the first thatch that is layd on woulde bee of rye-strawe. **1725** BRADLEY *Fam. Dict.* s.v. *Walls*, Walls..being quarter'd and lath'd between the Timber, or sometimes lathed all over, they are plaister'd with Lome. **1823** P. NICHOLSON *Pract. Build.* 110 When lathed over, the lath may be equally stiff to sustain the plaster. **1869** *Daily News* 10 Sept., The dining-rooms..in the sixteenth century were neither lathed nor plastered. **1886** *S.W. Linc. Gloss.*, *Latted, part.*, covered with laths: as 'I'll have it studded and latted'.

absol. **1663** GERBIER *Counsel* 79 To Lath and lay with Lime and haire. **1703** MOXON *Mech. Exerc.* 250 A Budget.. to put their Nails in when they Lath.

Hence **lathed** *ppl. a.* Also **'lather**, one who fixes laths or makes lath-work.

1578 BANISTER *Hist. Man* v. 65 Like the plaster, or dawbe vnto the latted house. **1897** *Daily News* 8 Dec. 4/4 By employing lathers to do the lathing work instead of plasterers.

lath, obs. form of LOATH.

lathe (leɪð), *sb.*[1] [Late OE. *læð* str. neut., corresponding to ON. *láð* (poet.) landed possession, land:—OTeut. **læþom*; according to some scholars cogn. w. *-lǣd-* in Goth. *un-lēds* poor (? lit. without landed possessions), OE. *unlǣd(e* wretched.

The form *lathe* (recorded from 14th c.) would, if it represented a pronunciation handed down by oral tradition, imply that the OE. word had a short vowel, and connexion with *laðian*, to summon, would then be possible. Probably, however, the word had little oral currency, so that its form may have been influenced by the spelling of early documents. The identity of the word with ON. *láð* (which involves the conclusion that the OE. form was *lǣð*) is rendered almost certain by the following facts. (1) The OE. word is in one instance recorded in the sense of the ON. word, viz., in the legal formula 'ne ȝyrne ic þines ne lǽðes ne landes ne sace ne sócne' (Schmid, *Gesetze der Angelsachsen*, app. xi), where it has the same alliterative association as in the frequent ON. phrase 'land ok láð'. (2) This alliterative association recurs in our first quotation, where the word has its specific Kentish application. (3) Our second quotation implies that 'the lathe of Aylesford' was the territory that was under a jurisdiction attached to the *manor* of Aylesford, so that the development of the special Kentish use from the general sense of 'landed possession' presents no difficulty.

The possibility is not excluded that the Kentish term may represent a coalescence of the original OE. *lǣð*, territory, with other words of similar form: cf. ON. *leið* fem. a court or judicial assembly, and OE. *-lǣð* or *-lǽðe* in *mótlǽðu* pl., attendances at a 'moot' or assembly (? related to ON. *líða*, OE. *líðan*, to go); also mod.Da. *lægd* 'division of a parish for military purposes' (f. root of LIE, LAY *vbs.*).

The latinized *leidegrevei* (see b) may, as is commonly assumed, represent an OE. **læðȝeréfan* 'lathe-reeves'; but the text is of little authority.]

One of the administrative districts (most recently five in number) into which Kent was divided, each comprising several hundreds.

? *a* **1100** *Charter* in Birch *Cart. Sax.* III. 162 Seo duȝuð folces on westan Cænt, þær þæt land and þæt læð to lið. *c* **1120** *Rochester Bridge-bote Charter* ibid. 659 Of æȝlesforda & of ellan þam læþe þe þær to liþ. [*Latin text:* De Æilesforda et de toto illo lesto quod ad illud manerium pertinet. (See LAST *sb.*[5])] *c* **1150** in *Laws of Edw. Conf.* c. 31 (interpolation) in Schmid *Gesetze* 508 *note* 5, In quibusdam vero provinciis Anglice vocantur leð [*v.r.* vocabatur led], quod isti dicunt tithinge [*v.r.* trihinge]. **1392–3** *Rolls Parlt.* III. 305/1 Certains Wapentakes, Hundredes, Rapes, Lathes, Baillies..& Villes, queux furent grant parcelle del Ferme des corps des Countees. **1545** *Act 37 Hen. VIII*, c. 25 §9 In every such Shire Riding Lathe Wapentake Rape Citie Towne Borough Isle. **1570–6** LAMBARDE *Peramb. Kent* (1826) 3 The whole Shyre hath long been divided into five partes communly called Lathes. **1670** BLOUNT *Law Dict.*, *Lathe* or *Leth*,..is a great part of a County, sometimes containing three or more Hundreds or Wapentakes; as it is used in Kent and Sussex. **1765** BLACKSTONE *Comm.* I. 116 In some counties there is an intermediate division between the shire and the hundreds, as lathes in Kent, and rapes in Sussex. **1832** *Act 2 & 3 Will. IV*, c. 64 §9 Such Eastern Division shall include the whole of the respective lathes of St. Augustine and Shepway. **1875** STUBBS *Const. Hist.* I. v. 100 In Kent..the hundreds are arranged in Lathes or Lests.

b. *Comb.*: †**lathe reeve**, the official charged with the administration of a lathe; †**lathe silver** (see quot. 1778).

c **1200** *London interpolation* in *Leges Hen. I*, c. 7 §2 (MS. *c* 1310) in Schmid *Gesetze* 440 *note* 4, Leidegrevei, vicarii. **1765** BLACKSTONE *Comm.* I. 116 These had..their lathe-reeves and rape-reeves, acting in subordination to the shire-reeve. **1778** HASTED *Kent* I. 124 The chief-rent payable to the crown, called lath or tythe silver,..was 8*s.* as was returned by the survey taken in 1650.

lathe (leɪð), *sb.*[2] Now only *dial.* Also 6 laythe, 6–7 lath, 7, 8 *dial.* leath, 9 *dial.* leathe, laith(e. [a. ON. *hlaða* (Sw. *lada*, Da. *lade*), connected with *hlaða* LADE *v.*] A barn.

c **1250** *Gen. & Ex.* 2134 To maken laðes and gaderen coren. *a* **1300** *Cursor M.* 4681 (Gött.) Wid win and corn, fless and mele, And [? *read* þai] fild þe lathes here and þar. *c* **1384** CHAUCER *H. Fame* III. 1050 For alle mote oute other late or rathe, Alle the sheves in the lathe. *c* **1425** *Voc.* in Wr.-Wülcker 670 *Hoc orreum*, lathe. *Hoc granarium, idem est.* *c* **1450** *St. Cuthbert* (Surtees) 7643 He gart bigg thaim in house and lathe. *c* **1550** *Plumpton Corr.* (Camden) 257 They ar threshing in the one lath beanes and barley both. **1605** CAMDEN *Rem.* 101 *Lath*, a Barne among them of Lincolnshire. **1781** J. HUTTON *Tour to Caves* Gloss. 92 *Leath*, barn. **1847** E. BRONTE *Wuthering Heights* I. ii. 16 'Goa rahnd by th' end ut' laith'. **1893** PEEL *Spen Valley* 293 Garside's old laithe stood about where Mr. Dawson's shops now are.

b. *attrib.*, as ***lathe-door***, ***-yard***.

c **1746** J. COLLIER (Tim Bobbin) *View Lanc. Dial.* Wks. (1862) 67 Just as i'r gett'n to th' Leath Dur. **1891** ATKINSON *Last of Giant Killers* 214 The fowls of the lathe-yards even had not been spared.

lathe (leɪð), *sb.*[3] Also 5, 7 **lath**. [Of obscure history; prob. cognate with Da. *lad*, in *drejelad* turning-lathe, also in other compounds in which it has the general sense of 'stand, supporting framework', e.g. *savelad* saw-bench, *sengelad* bedstead, *tøndelad* gantry, *væverlad* loom. The Da. word is prob. a special use of *lad* pile, heap regularly built up:—ON. *hlað*, related to *hlaða* to LADE.

If the coincidence in form and meaning with Da. *lad* be not purely accidental, the Eng. word must, not withstanding its late occurrence, have come down from the time of the Danish settlements in England. (A native OE. cognate is out of the question, as it would have had *d*, not *ð*.) The Da. word, in compounds, is cited by Kalkar from the 15–16th c.

As the older form of turning-lathe, used as late as the 19th century, was worked by means of a spring-lath overhead (see drawing in *Encycl. Brit.* ed. 9, XIV. 323), it is not wholly impossible that the word may be a modification of LATH *sb.*; but against this is the occurrence of the word in the wider Danish sense (see sense 1).

The ON. *lauð* (in Dicts. miswritten *löð*, and explained 'smith's lathe') is commonly given as the etymon, but erroneously. All that is known of the word is that it was used in composition to form poetic synonyms for gold.]

†**1.** ?*gen.* A supporting structure, stand, scaffold.

1476 *Record St. Mary's Ratcliffe* in *Antiq. Sarisb.* (1771) 209 A new Sepulchre..with all the ordinance that longeth thereto; that is to say, A lath made of timber and iron work thereto; Item, thereto longeth Heven, made of timber.. Item Hell made of timber and iron-work with Devils.

2. *spec.* (More fully ***turning-lathe***.) A machine for turning wood, metal, ivory, etc., in which the article to be turned is held in a horizontal position by means of adjustable centres and rotated against the tools with which it is cut to the required shape.

The lathe is used chiefly for turning circular and oval work, but it is also used for turning irregular forms and in engraving figure-work and geometrical designs on metal.

1611 [see LARE[2]]. **1659** LEAK *Waterwks.* 25 As in a Turners Lathe. **1678** BUTLER *Hud.* III. ii. 376 Could turn his Word and Oath and Faith As many ways as in a Lath. **1753** HOGARTH *Anal. Beauty* x. 58 A turner, in his lathe, might turn a much finer neck. **1812–16** J. SMITH *Panorama Sci. & Art* I. 31 A file..to smooth wood or metal revolving in the lathe. **1875** JOWETT *Plato* (ed. 2) III. 616 In the form of a globe, round as from a lathe.

b. With qualifying words indicating: (*a*) the source of driving power, as ***engine-***, ***foot-***, ***hand-***, etc.; (*b*) a special form of construction, as ***centre-***, ***chuck-***, ***duplex-***, ***mandrel-***, ***pole-***, etc.; (*c*) the kind of work done with it, as ***chasing-***, ***fluting-***, ***oval-***, ***screw-cutting-***, etc.; for which see those words.

c. A machine for 'throwing' and turning potteryware, the article being placed upon a revolving horizontal disc. (More explicitly ***potter's lathe***.)

1773 *Encycl. Brit.* III. 506/2 The wheel and lathe are the chief..instruments in pottery; the first for large works, and the last for small... The potter's lathe is also a kind of wheel, but more simple and slight than the former. **1839** URE *Dict. Arts* 1012 In large potteries, the whole of the lathes, both for throwing and turning, are put in motion by a steam engine.

3. *attrib.* and *Comb.*, as ***lathe-chuck***, ***-drill***, ***-frame***, ***-mark***, ***-work***; ***lathe-turned*** adj.; **lathe-bearer**, **-carrier**, **-dog**, various names for the appliance which connects the object to be turned with the centres of the lathe; **lathe-bed**, the lower framework of a lathe, having a slot from end to end in which one or both of the heads may be moved backwards or forwards; **lathe-frame**, the frame upon which the lathe stands; **lathe-head**, (*a*) the head-stock of a lathe; (*b*) 'a small dental or laboratory lathe that may be fitted to a bench' (*Cent. Dict.*); **lathe-man** (see quot.); **lathe-treader**, a man or boy employed to turn the potter's lathe.

1853 O. BYRNE *Handbk. Artisan* 146 Sometimes..the grinder is laid upon the *lathe-bearers or other support. **1849** WEALE *Dict. Terms* 253/1 A long frame, called the *lathe-bed..is fixed at each end upon two short standards. **1879** *Cassell's Techn. Educ.* IV. 266/1 The slide-rest will.. move along the lathe-bed. **1873** J. RICHARDS *Wood-working Factories* 160 The shear, or *lathe frame..can be made of

wood. **1893** *Labour Commission* Gloss., **Lath Men*, brass-finishers employed solely in turning at the lathe and not engaged in fitting at the bench or vice. **1868** G. STEPHENS *Runic Mon.* I. 287 On the battered and broken metal we can still see traces of the *lathe-mark. **1865** ELIZA METEYARD *Life J. Wedgwood* I. 338 This branch of the trade employed a skilled body of men..and the boys called *lathe-treaders who made the necessary movements for them. **1868** G. STEPHENS *Runic Mon.* I. 286 'Barbarian' work of this period was as often *lathe-turned as Roman. **1875** *Carpentry & Join.* 146 For *lathe work I have pursued a different course.

lathe (leɪð), *sb.*^{4} In 7 lath, 7–8 leath. [Cogn. w. Sw. *lad*, G. *lade*, of the same meaning; cf. prec. and LAY *sb.*] The movable swing-frame or batten of a loom.

a **1633** AUSTIN *Medit.* (1635) 281 At every change the Shittle flyes thorow and thorow it [the web]; and ever and anone the Lath thumps and smites it. **1688** R. HOLME *Armoury* III. 107/2 The Leath, that is a moving Frame in which the reed is placed by which the Woof is knockt or beaten into the Warp. **1743** MAXWELL *Sel. Trans.* 342 The Weaver should..likewise be careful each time he throws the Shuttle, that he draws the Thread straight and light to the Cloth, before he strikes with the Leath. **1889** POSSELT *Techn. Textile Design* 123 Lay, Lathe or Batten, a part of a loom. To it are secured the shuttle-boxes and the reed.

lathe, *v. Obs.* exc. *dial.* Also 9 *dial.* laith(e. [OE. *laðian* = OFris. *lathia, ladia*, OS. *laðian*, OHG. *ladôn* (MHG., mod.G. *laden*), ON. *laða*, Goth. *laþôn*; cogn. w. Goth. *laþaleikô* willingly.] *trans.* To invite, call.

c **900** tr. *Bæda's Hist.* III. iii. [v.] (1890) 160 þonne laþode he hi þæt hi onfengan þam ȝeryne Cristes ȝeleafan. *c* **1050** *Voc.* in Wr.-Wülcker 429 *Inuitat me*, he me lathath. *c* **1175** *Lamb. Hom.* 145 Ach him is wel þet is ilaðed from lutel weole to muchele. *a* **1225** *Ancr. R.* 144 Eihte þinges nomeliche muneȝeð & laðieð us to wakien i sume gode. **13..** *E.E. Allit. P.* B. 163 To þis frelych feste þat fele arn to called, For alle arn laþed luflyly. **1432–50** tr. *Higden* (Rolls) V. 275 Hengistus callede or lathede by treason the kynge of Briteyne. **1859** WAUGH *Poems & Lanc. Songs* II. (1870) 82 Aw'll laithe a rook o' neighbour lads.

Hence †**lather**, one who invites or summons.

a **1175** *Cott. Hom.* 235 An þesser laȝe of þe witȝin wer laðieres moche. *Ibid.* 237 An þisser beoð bedeles and laðieres. [Cf. *laver, lavier* (Pembrokesh.): see E.D.D.]

lathe, obs. form of LOATH, LOATHE.

latheborde, obs. form of LARBOARD.

lathee, var. LATHI.

lathen ('lɑːθ(ə)n, 'læθ-), *a. rare.* [f. LATH *sb.* + -EN^4.] Made of lath.

1843 H. AINSWORTH *Windsor C.* IV. v, Settle the grievance with thy [a jester's] lathen dagger. **1868** BROWNING *Ring & Bk.* I. 1239 In the plain closet..With..one stool One table and one lathen crucifix There sits the Pope. *Ibid.* v. 849 My poor lathen dagger puts aside Each pass o' the Bilboa.

lather ('læðə(r), 'lɑːðə(r)), *sb.* Also 1 léaðor, 7 ladder, lavour. [OE. *léaðor* str. neut. = ON. *lauðr* washing soda, foam (Sw. *lodder* soap):—OTeut. type **lauþro*^{m}:—pre-Teut. **loutrom* (= Gr. λοετρόν, λουτρόν bath, Irish *loathar* washing vessel), f. root **lou-* to wash (= L. *lavāre*) + *-tro-* instrumental suffix.]

1. †**a.** (OE. only.) Washing soda. **b.** A froth or foam made by the agitation of a mixture of soap and water.

c **1000** *Sax. Leechd.* III. 2 Leȝe on clað gnid in wæter gnid swiðe þæt heo sy eall ȝeleðred þweah mid þy leaðre þæt heafod ȝelome. *c* **1050** *Voc.* in Wr.-Wülcker 455/8 *Nitria*, þæt is of leaðre. *Ibid.* 456/14 *Nitrum*, leaðor. **1583** STUBBES *Anat. Abus.* II. (1882) 50 Then shall your mouth be bossed with the lather..(for they haue their sweete balles wherewith-all they vse to washe). **1669** W. SIMPSON *Hydrol. Chym.* 335, I ordered the maid to put some of the usual soap thereto..and it made a very good lather (as they call it). **1677** *Compl. Servant Maid* 64 Wash them very well in three Ladders. **1799** G. SMITH *Laboratory* I. 392 Take scalding hot water, and..with Newcastle soap beat and work up a clear lather. **1815** SCOTT *Let. to Dk. Buccleuch* Dec. in *Lockhart*, It looked like a shaving-brush, and the goblet might be intended to make the lather. **1873** E. SMITH *Foods* 279 Hard water..prevents the formation of a lather, until a large quantity of soap has been added. **1926** FOWLER *Mod. Eng. Usage* 315/2 Though lah'dher is often heard, *lather* apparently does not belong to the class of words in which ah & ă are merely southern & northern variants (*pass* &c.). **1968** *New Society* 22 Aug. 266/1 *Lather*: non-U to rhyme with 'father' (invariable in television advertisements)/U to rhyme with 'gather'.

fig. **1725** BAILEY *Erasm. Colloq.* 570 Such as by the Lather of Tears, and Soap of Repentance..have washed away their Pollutions. **1940** L. MACNEICE *Last Ditch* 10 The sky is a lather of stars.

c. *transf.* Violent perspiration, esp. the frothy sweat of a horse.

1660 F. BROOKE tr. *Le Blanc's Trav.* 143, I could not possibly bring forth a word..being all in a lavour with agony and distresse. **1828** in WEBSTER. **1837** MRS. SHERWOOD *H. Milner* III. v, Miss Bell had already exercised her [a mare] so well, that, to use a jockey term, she was all in a lather. **1883** E. PENNELL-ELMHIRST *Cream Leicestersh.* 238 The mare..was covered with lather.

d. *transf.* A state of agitation, anxiety, irritation, or the like, such as induces sweat. (Cf. quot. 1660 in sense c.)

1839 F. TROLLOPE *Fragment* in *Dom. Manners Amer.* (ed. 5) 271 Don't be in a lather, father, before you are shaved. I'll do your job, I expect, if you won't be in such a tarnation fuss. **1892** KIPLING *Lett. of Travel* (1920) 99 Forced inaction frets the man to a lather. **1931** V. WOOLF *Waves* 273, I arrived all in a lather at her house..but did not marry her, being..unripe for that intensity. **1945** E. S. GARDNER *Case of Gold-Digger's Purse* (1949) v. 44 You're standing there in a lather of indecision. **1948** 'J. TEY' *Franchise Affair* xvi. 181, I suppose Christina is in the usual lather of sentiment? **1970** *Daily Tel.* 24 Sept. 4/8, I can't work myself up into a middle aged lather over long hair.

2. The action of lathering or applying lather to.

1626 MIDDLETON *Women Beware W.* II. ii, She'd..sponge up herself, And give her neck three lathers.

3. *attrib.* and *Comb.*, as *lather-bowl*; *lather-dried, -making* adjs.; **lather-boy**, a boy employed in a barber's shop to lather the chins of customers.

1856 R. W. PROCTER *Barber's Shop* xxi. (1883) 216 A *lather bowl. **1898** *Daily News* 9 Dec. 5/7 They were '*lather boys to a barber'. **1852** R. S. SURTEES *Sponge's Sp. Tour* (1893) 294 Reining in the now *lather-dried brown. *c* **1611** CHAPMAN *Iliad* XI. 370 His *lather-making jaws.

lather ('læðə(r), 'lɑːðə(r)), *v.* Forms: 1 (ȝe)léðran, líðrian, 3 leþere, liðere, 5 lathere, 6– lather, 7 ladder, laver (in *lavering* ppl. adj.). [OE. **líeðran, léðran*, corresponds to ON. *løyðra*:—OTeut. **lauþrjan*, f. **lauþro*^{m}: see LATHER *sb.*^{1} From the 16th c. the word has been assimilated in form to the sb.; cf. Icel. *lauðra*.]

1. a. *trans.* To cover with or as with a lather; to wash in or with a lather. Also *fig.*

c **950** *Lindisf. Gosp.* John xi. 2 Maria uutudlice wæs ðio ȝeðuoȝ *vel* smiride *vel* leðrede ðone drihten mið smirinise. *c* **1000** *Sax. Leechd.* II. 124 Lyþre mid sapan. *Ibid.* III. 2 [see LATHER *sb.* 1 a]. **1654** GAYTON *Pleas. Notes* II. i. 33 Their Horses..by excessive heats, continuall evaporations, and sweats..were laundred and ladder'd. **1713** ADDISON *Guardian* No. 71 ¶4 He would rub and lather a man's head, till he had got out every thing that was in it. **1715** tr. *Pancirollus' Rerum Mem.* I. I. iv. 12 Cleaner and brighter, than if it had been..lather'd with a Wash-ball. **1748** SMOLLETT *Rod. Rand.* viii. (1804) 36 He lathered my face. **1851** D. JERROLD *St. Giles* xxiii. 235 The self-same brush that had lathered the beard of that very vulgar man. **1862** GEO. ELIOT *Romola* xvi, Nello skipped round him, lathered him, seized him by the nose, and scraped him. **1917** P. GIBBS *Battles of Somme* 171 The enemy was 'lathering' the field of observation with every kind of 'crump' and shell.

Proverb. **1860** HUGHES *Tom Brown at Oxf.* xxiii, 'Twas waste of soap to lather an ass.

†**b.** *absol.* or *intr. Obs. rare.*

c **1430** *Pilgr. Lyf Manhode* I. liii. (1869) 32 And for that j kan so wel wasshe, so wel lathere..hath god maad me his chambrere. **1630** J. TAYLOR (Water P.) *Praise Cleane Linnen* Wks. II. 169/1 For Laundresses are testy..When they are lathering in their bumble broth.

†**c.** *intr.* in quasi-passive sense.

1691 *Phil. Trans.* XVII. 532 [They] put them over a Fire till they are more than Blood-warm; which will make them [skins] ladder and scour perfectly clean.

2. *intr.* To become covered with foam; now chiefly of a horse.

a **1225** *Juliana* 16 And beten hire swa luðere þat hire leofliche lich liðeri al oblode. [Similarly *a* **1225** *Leg. Kath.* 1554.] *a* **1225** *St. Marher.* 5 Hit brek oueral ant litherde o blode. *c* **1275** LAY. 7489 He swang in þan fihte þat he leþerede [*c* **1205** lauede] a swote. **1884** *St. James's Gaz.* 1 May 7/1 Harvester..lathered a good deal before being saddled.

3. To produce and form a lather or froth. Said *esp.* of water when mixed with soap; also of soap.

1608 ARMIN *Nest Ninn.* (1842) 21 The trotting of this mule made the mingled confection lather. **1677** PLOT *Oxfordsh.* 36 Water..such as..would lather well. **1715** GAY *Ep. to Earl Burlington* 106 Our shirts her busy fingers rub, While the sope lathers oer the foaming tub. **1789** G. WHITE *Selborne* i. 3 A fine limpid water..but which does not lather well with soap. **1796** KIRWAN *Elem. Min.* (ed. 2) I. 189 It [indurated lithomarga] does not lather, yet is detersive.

4. *trans.* To spread *on* like lather.

1885 *Manch. Exam.* 10 Feb. 5/3 In other pictures coarse yellow paint appears to have been lathered on with a trowel.

5. To beat, thrash. Also *intr.* with *into*. Also *fig.*

1797 *Sporting Mag.* X. 320 He was so well lathered that he was near his end. **1850** P. CROOK *War of Hats* 54 The uxorious cleric too was..lathered with a cane. **1886** MAXWELL GRAY *Silence Dean Maitland* I. v. 129 He was a latherin' into Hotspur [a horse] like mad.

Hence '**lathered** *ppl. a.*, '**lathering** *ppl. a.* Also '**latherer**.

1630 J. TAYLOR (Water P.) *Praise Cleane Linnen* Ded., Wks. II. 164 Not doubting but the lathering suds of your lennitie will wash away all such faults. **1647** H. MORE *Insomn. Philos.* i. 178 Her curbed steeds foaming out lavering tarre. **1814** SOUTHEY *Carmina Aulica* Poet. Wks. III. 315 When at the looking-glass with lather'd chin..I sit. **1863** GEO. ELIOT *Romola* xvi, The doctor had his lathered face turned towards the group. **1899** *Westm. Gaz.* 18 May 2/3 Boys employed as latherers in barbers' shops.

lather, obs. form of LEATHER.

latherin, -on, obs. Sc. forms of LADRONE.

lathering ('læðərɪŋ, 'lɑː-), *vbl. sb.* [f. LATHER *v.* + -ING^1.] The action or an act of lathering; *fig.* (*slang*) a beating.

1598 FLORIO, *Saponata*, a soping, a lathring. **1836** E. HOWARD *R. Reefer* lvi, A stubble of your growth..requires a double lathering. **1865** CARLYLE *Fredk. Gt.* XVIII. x. (1872) VII. 283 Such a pell-mell..our King must have given them a dreadful lathering. **1835** J. P. KENNEDY *Horse-Shoe Robinson* I. ii. 25 He shut that up..by giving Huger a most tremenjious lathering. **1843** 'R. CARLTON' *New Purchase* I. xix. 169 Vain all pelting with clods and stones—all latherings with long bean poles! **1954** WEINGARTEN *Amer. Dict. Slang* 222/2 *Lathering*, a scolding; a beating, a thrashing.

lathery ('læðərɪ, 'lɑː-), *a.* [f. LATHER *sb.* + -Y^1.] Consisting of or covered with, or as with, lather. Also of a horse: Covered with foam. Chiefly *fig.*, 'frothy', unsubstantial.

1803 W. TAYLOR in *Ann. Rev.* I. 399 A certain lathery tautology which makes a mouthful of breath into a cisternful of sud. **1819** SOUTHEY *Lett.* (1856) III. 150 Having set aside a paper..to substitute a lathery composition of his own. **1880** BLACKMORE *M. Anerley* I. xvii. 273 Sluicing, and wringing, and rinsing went on, over the bubbled and lathery turf. **1890** B. PERRY *Broughton Ho.* xiii. 271 (Funk) The horse was lathery from his ten miles of uphill work.

‖**lathi** (lʌ'tiː). *Anglo-Indian.* Also lathee, lattee, latti. [Hindi *lāṭhī*.] A long heavy stick, usually of bamboo and bound with iron. Also *attrib.*

1850 FANNY PARKES *Wand. Pilgrim* I. xiv. 132 A very heavy lāthī, a solid male bamboo, five feet five inches long, headed with iron in a most formidable manner. **1860** RUSSELL *Diary India* II. 317 Sometimes a peasant runs away with a long lathee or stick over his shoulder. **1864** G. O. TREVELYAN *Competition Wallah* 170 Placing a lattee, which is the name for the quarter-staff carried by all Indian peasants, under the defaulter's knee. **1878** *Life in Mofussil* I. 114 We came upon about a hundred men..all with latties..in their hands. **1895** MRS. B. M. CROKER *Village Tales* (1896) 187 A man's body found in a nullah, killed by a sickle or a lathi (heavy stick). **1920** *Glasgow Herald* 31 Dec. 7 Some disturbance..in which lathis were used. **1924** R. GRAVES *Mock Beggar Hall* 64 Then the new power, foreseeing grave events Calls out the lathi-wallahs to line the streets. **1930** *Daily Express* 6 Nov. 3/6 The police made a number of lathi charges to disperse the crowd. **1936** J. NEHRU *Autobiogr.* 177 My body felt the baton and *lathi* blows of the police. **1972** *Times of India* 28 Nov. 11/2 A judicial inquiry was demanded into the lathi-charge at Gulbarga.

lathing ('lɑːθɪŋ, 'læ-), *vbl. sb.*^{1} Also 8 latting. [f. LATH *v.* + -ING^1.]

1. The action of the vb. LATH.

1544 *Churchw. Acc. St. Giles, Reading* 70 To a mason for lathyng [an]d dawbyng iiijd. **1663** GERBIER *Counsel* (1664) 78 Lathing is worth six pence the yard. **1823** P. NICHOLSON *Pract. Build.* 372 By lathing is meant the nailing up laths..on the ceiling and partitions.

2. *concr.* Lath-work.

1756 P. BROWNE *Jamaica* 342 The outward part of the trunk [of Cocoa Nut] is made into lattings. **1825** J. NICHOLSON *Operat. Mechanic* 612 Lathing, laying, and set..is, when the work, after being lathed, is covered with one coat of lime and hair, and afterwards..a thin and smooth coat spread over it, consisting of lime only, or, as the workmen call it, putty, or set... Lathing, floating, and set..differs from the foregoing, in having the first coat pricked up to receive the set, which is here called the floating. **1858** SIMMONDS *Dict. Trade*, *Lathing*, small wooden bars to fix mortar in; bed staves for the centre-frame of a bedstead, to rest the bedding on. **1889** *Anthony's Photogr. Bull.* II. 9 Thin lathing should be tacked on over the paper joints. **1891** *Pall Mall G.* 14 May 1/3 The plaster..is spread upon expanded metal lathing.

3. *Comb.*: **lathing hammer**, †**hatchet**, a lather's hammer with a cutting peen for shortening laths; **lathing saw**, a saw for cutting iron laths; **lathing staff** (see quot. 1703).

1703 MOXON *Mech. Exerc.* 249 A *Lathing Hammer..with which the Laths are nailed on with its head, and with its Edge they cut them to any length. **1797** *Trial of J. Dobbins, at Worcester*, 3 A *lathing hatchet. **1890** W. J. GORDON *Foundry* 223 *Lathing saws. **1577–87** HOLINSHED *Chron.* (1807–8) II. 736 Hir husband [Iohn Tiler]..came running home with his *lathing staffe in his hand. **1703** MOXON *Mech. Exerc.* 248 A Lathing Staff of Iron, in the form of a Cross, to stay the cross Laths while they are nailed to the long Laths, and also to clinch the Nails.

lathing ('leɪðɪŋ), *vbl. sb.*^{2} *Obs.* exc. *dial.* Also 1–3 laðung(e. [f. LATHE *v.* + -ING^1.] An invitation; a calling together. Also, a congregation.

c **897** K. ÆLFRED *Gregory's Past.* lii. 405 Be ðære miltsunga æfter ðære laðunga is swiðe wel ȝesæd ðurh Essaias ðone witȝan. *c* **1175** *Lamb. Hom.* 93 And alle þeo ileafulle laðunge him ihersummede. *c* **1205** LAY. 5115 þa makeden heo ane laðunge [*c* **1275** laþinge] of heore leoue folke. **1547** SALESBURY *Welsh Dict.*, *Gwys gwahadd*, lathyng, byddyng. **1611** COTGR., *Semonce*, a bidding, lathing, inuiting. **1674** RAY *N.C. Words* 29 *Lathing*, entreaty or invitation: You need no lathing: You need no invitation or urging. **1746** *Exmoor Scolding* l. 189 (E.D.S.) Tha wut net look vor Lathing, chell warndy. **1857** WAUGH *Lanc. Life* 54 'Come, poo a cheer up', said he, 'an' need no moor lathein'.

'**lath-nail.** A nail for fixing laths upon battens.

1388–9 *Abingdon Acc.* (Camden) 54 In latthes et latthe nayl vjs. **1422–3** *Ibid.* 97 In lathnail et bordnail emptis iijs. **1483–4** in Swayne *Churchw. Acc. Sarum* (1896) 33 For iiij ml. latez nayllez. **1509–10** *Durh. Acc. Rolls* (Surtees) 105 Pro v^{xx} lattnalis. **1540** *Ludlow Churchw. Acc.* (Camden) 3 Payd for borde nayle and lathe neale for the same cofer. **1667** H. STUBBE in *Phil. Trans.* II. 502, I heated a Lath-nail glowing hot. **1881** YOUNG *Every Man his own Mechanic* §330 The lath nail..used for nailing laths to quartering.

lathy ('lɑːθɪ, 'læ-), *a.* [f. LATH *sb.* + -Y^1.]

1. Resembling a lath; thin or long and thin like a lath. Said *esp.* of a very thin person.

1672 WOOD *Life* (O.H.S.) II. 239 Duns Scotus his picture—a leane lathie man. *a* **1756** G. WEST *Abuse Trav.* xx, He..eft his lathy falchion brandished. **1784** J. BARRY in *Lect. Paint.* iii. (1848) 148 In some parts of the profile view it is too lathy and slender. **1828** SCOTT *F.M. Perth* ii, His figure was gaunt and lathy. **1851** *Fraser's Mag.* XLIII. 167/1 From the hips downwards he was remarkably well made, straight, and lathy. **1881** GRANT WHITE *Eng. Without & W.* ix. 201 The

elder daughter was, I will not say a lathy girl, but very slim. **1893** E. H. BARKER *Wand. S. Waters* 265 The lathy poplars leaning in every direction.

2. Made of lath (and plaster).

1804 COLLINS *Scripscarf* 12 One of John Bull's True Breed, overhearing, by chance, Through a lathy partition, those good friends to France. **1855** *Househ. Words* XII. 215 We are divided only by a lathy partition.

lathyric (lə'θɪrɪk), *a. Path.* [f. LATHYR-US + -IC.] Produced by the use of the seeds of a plant of the genus *Lathyrus*; causing lathyrism.

1897 *Allbutt's Syst. Med.* II. 806 This.. would suggest a similarity of action between the lathyric and the ergotic poisoning.

lathyrin ('læθɪrɪn). *Chem.* [f. as prec. + -IN.] An amorphous, yellow, bitter substance obtained by Reinsch from the species of the genus *Lathyrus* (*Syd. Soc. Lex.* 1888).

lathyrism ('læθɪrɪz(ə)m). *Path.* [f. LATHYR-US, + -ISM.] A condition produced by the use as food of the seeds of some species of the genus *Lathyrus*. It is characterized by formication, tremors, convulsive movements, and paraplegia.

1888 in *Syd. Soc. Lex.* **1897** *Allbutt's Syst. Med.* II. 461 A paralytic affection called lathyrism, resulting from the use of a dal prepared from a lentil—*Lathyrus sativus*, prevails extensively in upper and Central India.

‖**lathyrus** ('læθɪrəs). [mod.L., a. Gr. λάθυρος a kind of vetch.] The name of a genus of plants (N.O. *Leguminosæ*), comprising the 'everlasting pea' (*L. latifolius*) and other species.

1741 *Compl. Fam. Piece* II. iii. 386 Blue flower'd Lathyrus. **1778** G. WHITE *Selborne* xli. (1789) 236 *Lathyrus sylvestris*, narrow-leaved or wild lathyrus.

lati- (leɪtɪ, lætɪ), combining form of L. *lātus* broad, as **lati'costate** *a. Zool.* [COSTATE], having broad ribs (Mayne *Expos. Lex.* 1855; and in later Dicts.). **lati'dentate** *a. Zool.* [DENTATE], having broad teeth (Mayne *Expos. Lex.* 1855; and in later Dicts.). **lati'foliate** *a. Bot.* [FOLIATE] = next (Ogilvie *Suppl.* 1855; and in recent Dicts.). **lati'folious** *a.* [f. L. *lātifoli-us* (f. *lātus* broad + *folium* leaf) + -OUS], having broad leaves. **lati'pennate** *a. Ornith.* [PENNATE], having broad wings (Mayne *Expos. Lex.* 1855); so **lati'pennine** *a.* (in recent Dicts.). †**lati'rostrous** *a. Ornith.* [L. *rostr-um* beak + -OUS], having a broad beak; so **lati'rostral**, **lati'rostrate** *adjs.* (in recent Dicts.). **'latisept** *a. Bot.* [SEPTUM], having a broad septum. **lati'septate** *a. Bot.* = *latisept* adj. **lati'sternal** *a.* [STERNUM], having a broad breast-bone.

1656 BLOUNT *Glossogr.*, *Latifolious. **1797** *Encycl. Brit.* IX. 581/1 The latifolious, or everlasting pea. **1646** SIR T. BROWNE *Pseud. Ep.* III. xxv. 172 Yet have they a knowne and open disadvantage from an other, which is not common unto any singing bird wee know, that is a flat bill: For no *Latirostrous animal.. were ever commended for their note. **1650** *Ibid.* v. i. 234 Latirostrous or flat bild birdes. **1877** A. W. BENNETT tr. *Thomé's Bot.* 413 The silicula is said to be angustisept.. or *latisept. **1959** A. R. CLAPHAM et al. *Excursion Flora Brit. Isles* 555 *Latiseptate. Of a fr[uit] with the septum across the widest diameter. **1880** *Libr. Univ. Knowl.* (N.Y.) XII. 324 They [anthropoid apes] have a sternum, and are therefore sometimes called *latisternal apes.

latialite ('leɪʃəlaɪt). *Min.* [f. L. *Latiāl-is* of or belonging to Latium + -ITE.] = HAÜYNE.

1868 DANA *Min.* 332. **1869** PHILLIPS *Vesuv.* x. 293 Haüyne, or Latialite occurs disseminated and in cavities of gray micaceous or augitic lava.

Latian ('leɪʃ(ɪ)ən), *a.* [f. L. *Lati-um* (see LATIN) + -AN.] Of or belonging to Latium; Latin.

1598 GRENEWEY *Tacitus' Ann.* II. viii. (1622) 149 What.. if any of the Latian Senators fall to decay? **1631** MASSINGER *Believe as you List* I. ii, All rich ornaments of your Latian dames. **1849** MACAULAY *Hist. Eng.* i. (1874) 4 No magnificent remains of Latian porches.. are to be found in Britain. **1879** M. PATTISON *Milton* iii. (1880) 42 [In the Epitaphium Damonis] Milton takes a formal farewell of the Latian muse.

†**la'tibulate**, *v. Obs. rare*$^{-0}$. [f. ppl. stem of L. *latibulāri*, f. *latibulum*: see next.]

1623 COCKERAM, *Latibulate*, privily to hide ones selfe in a corner.

†**latibule.** *Obs. rare.* Also 7 latible. [ad. L. *latibul-um*, f. *latēre*: see LATENT.] A hiding-place.

1623 COCKERAM, *Latibule*, a denne or lurking place. **1658** PHILLIPS, *Latible*, a hiding or lurking place. [**1691** RAY *Creation* I. (1692) 114 One great Mother-wasp.. lying hid in some hollow tree or other latibulum.]

latibulize (lə'tɪbjuːlaɪz), *v. rare.* [f. L. *latibul-um* a hiding-place + -IZE.] *intr.* To retire into a hiding-place or retreat (for the winter).

1802 SHAW *Gen. Zool.* III. I. 11 *note*, When kept in gardens in Italy and Germany, it [the Tortoise] is observed to latibulize in October, and to reappear in April.

†**latic**, *a. Obs. rare.* In 7 latick. [ad. mod.L. *latic-a*, a. Arab. *laþiqaʰ* (Avicenna *Qānūn* IV. fen 1, treat. ii. p. 23).] A quotidian fever, or phlegmatic fever, in which there are no symptoms of apyrexy or intermission (Mayne *Expos. Lex.* 1855).

1684 tr. *Bonet's Merc. Compit.* VI. 226 In a Phlegmatick Ague, which the Arabians call Latick, or Latent. *Ibid.*, In a Latick Ague we must have a care of Purges.

laticiferous (lætɪ'sɪfərəs), *a. Bot.* [f. L. *latic-*, LATEX + -(I)FEROUS. Cf. F. *laticifère*.] Bearing or containing latex. ***laticiferous tissue***, tissue containing laticiferous tubes or vessels.

1835 LINDLEY *Introd. Bot.* (1848) II. 392 A portion of cinenchyma, or laticiferous tissue. **1861** H. MACMILLAN *Footn. Page Nat.* 257 Like the milk in the laticiferous vessels of.. lettuce. **1884** BOWER & SCOTT *De Bary's Phaner.* 432 The laticiferous tubes.. traverse the entire body of the plant as a continuous system.

laticlave ('lætɪkleɪv). *Rom. Antiq.* [ad. late L. *lāticlāvium, lāticlāvus*, f. *lātus* broad + *clāvus* purple stripe. (In cl.L. the term was *latus clavus*.)] A badge consisting of two broad purple stripes on the edge of the tunic, worn by senators and certain other classes of persons of high rank.

1658 in PHILLIPS. **1739** MELMOTH *Fitzosb. Lett.* (1749) II. 125 When I was first invested with the laticlave. **1781** GIBBON *Decl. & F.* xvii. II. 30 The Roman knights who were distinguished by the permission of wearing the laticlave. **1793** A. MURPHY *Tacitus* (1805) VIII. 11 Pliny the younger shews, that the laticlave was a favour granted by the emperor on particular occasions. **1871** FARRAR *Witn. Hist.* iii. 100 A symbol more glorious than the laticlave of consuls or the diadem of kings.

transf. **1848** B. WEBB *Continental Ecclesiol.* 433 Angels who are in white, with laticlaves of gold.

‖**latifundia** (leɪtɪ'fʌndɪə), *sb. pl.* Also 7 anglicized **latifunds**; in Italian form **lati'fondi** (sing. **latifondo**). [L. pl. of *lātifundium*, f. *lātus* broad + *fundus* estate.] Large estates; large plantations in Latin America.

1630 T. WETCOTE *Devon.* (1845) 242 Each of them having their parks and large lati-funds. **1869** ROGERS *Hist. Gleanings* Ser. I. 66 The latifundia of our time had hardly begun to exist. [**1874** MAHAFFY *Soc. Life Greece* xii. 375 The Roman *latifundia*.] **1902** *Encycl. Brit.* XXIX. 612/2 Special contracts.. are applied to the *latifondi* or huge estates [in Italy]. **1930** C. F. JONES *S. Amer.* xxi. 310 The establishment of the *latifundia* first began on a large scale during Rosas' first campaign. *Ibid.* 447 The *latifundia* system. **1937** F. BORKENAU *Spanish Cockpit* i. 48 Abolition of *de facto* serfdom, splitting up of the *latifundia* in the South and the Centre. **1954** KOESTLER *Invis. Writing* xxiv. 263 The ruin of farmers and the growth of large latifundia. **1961** *Listener* 24 Aug. 266/2 The actual state farms [in Cuba] have been set up on what were almost uncultivated latifundia. **1964** *Punch* 26 Aug. 291/1 The tired and near-forsaken *latifundia* in the main [W. Indies] sugar-producing islands. **1967** C. SETON-WATSON *Italy from Liberalism to Fascism* viii. 312 Most of the proprietors of the *latifondi* were absentees. **1974** *Times Lit. Suppl.* 8 Feb. 124/2 The 25,000 or so medium farmers [in Chile] whose holdings were below the minimum legally classified as *latifundia*.

Hence **lati'fundian** *a.*, *nonce-wd.*, possessing large estates. **lati'fundiarist** *a.* = LATIFUNDIAN *a.* **latifun'dista** [Sp.], the owner of a *latifundium* (Sp. *latifundio*) in Spain or Latin America; also in anglicized form **lati'fundist**.

a **1734** NORTH *Exam.* II. v. §156 (1740) 414 Although the Interest of a very latifundian Faction was concerned. **1962** *Economist* 27 Jan. 333/2 There is no *latifundista* class [in the Dominican Republic] to prevent effective land reform. **1963** *Ibid.* 2 Nov. 461/2 The *latifundistas*, local dignitaries and conservative Catholics [in Spain]. **1964** GOULD & KOLB *Dict. Social Sci.* 268/1 A polity dominated by the owners of large estates. As this type of society has been called latifundiarist, there is no point in wasting the word *feudal* on it. **1970** *Time* 2 Nov. 20 He is determined to expropriate the wealth of the big capitalists, the latifundists and the imperialists.

‖**latigo** ('lætɪgo). *U.S.* [Sp.] A strap for tightening a cinch. Also *attrib.*, as *latigo strap*.

1873 A. S. EVANS *À la California* 331 The wide band of woven horsehair, known as the cinch, is drawn up by the powerful purchase on the *latigo* strap until it deeply imbeds itself in the animal's belly. **1894** *Dialect Notes* I. VII. 325 Látigo: a thong... The two ends of the cinch terminate in long, narrow strips of leather—*látigos*—which connect the cinch with the saddle and are run through an iron ring called *larigo*. **1952** J. STEINBECK *East of Eden* 149 He was lacing the latigo through the cinch rings. **1962** W. STEGNER *Wolf Willow* III. ii. 155 He picked at the latigo with one freezing unmittened hand. **1968** R. M. PATTERSON *Finlay's River* 237 The latigo laces are long, finely cut leather thongs, taken from a big hide.

latijs, obs. form of LATTICE.

†**'latimer.** *Obs.* Also 4-5 latymer, 4 ? latynier, latynere. [a. OF. *latim(m)ier*, a corruption (perh. orig. graphic, but adopted in oral use) of *latinier*, f. *Latin*: see LATIN *sb.*] An interpreter.

c **1205** LAY. 14319 He wes þe bezste latimer þat ær com her. *a* **1310** in Wright *Lyric P.* xv. 49 Lyare wes mi latymer. **13..** *K. Alis.* 7089 Ther he fond latimeris, That ladde him to hyghe rocheris. *c* **1330** R. BRUNNE *Chron. Wace* (Rolls) 7573 Þys Breþ was þe kynges latynier. *c* **1400** MAUNDEV. (1839) v. 58 And alle weys fynden Men Latyneres to go with hem. **1480** CAXTON *Chron. Eng.* lvii. 41 A latymer told the kyng the full understondyng ther of wassaylle.

latimeria (lætɪ'mɪərɪə). [mod.L. (J. L. B. Smith 1939, in *Nature* 18 Mar. 456/2), f. name of Marjorie E. D. Courtenay-*Latimer* (b. 1907), director of the East London Museum at the time of the discovery + -IA[1].] A large marine fish of the genus so called, the only living representative of the order of crossopterygian fishes Actinistia, which was discovered in deep water off the south-east coast of Africa in 1938; = CŒLACANTH.

1940 *Nature* 13 July 53/1 The exceptionally oily nature of Latimeria.. is interesting geologically. **1953** J. S. HUXLEY *Evolution in Action* v. 128 Latimeria is the name of a rather primitive kind of fish, more nearly related to lung-fish than to modern Teleosts, one single specimen of which was recently brought up alive by a fishing vessel off the coast of South Africa. **1956** J. L. B. SMITH *Old Fourlegs: Story of Coelacanth* 236 All [cœlacanths] have been large fishes.. with fins like *Latimeria*. **1968** A. S. ROMER *Procession of Life* viii. 166 (*caption*) *Latimeria*, about five feet long, is the last surviving coelacanth.

Latin ('lætɪn), *a.* and *sb.* Forms: 3-6 **Latyn**, 3-7 **Latine**, 5-6 **Latyne**, **Laten**, 6 **Latten**, (**Lattin**, *Sc.* **Latyng**), 3- **Latin.** [a. L. *Latīn-us* adj., f. *Latium*, the portion of Italy which included Rome. Cf. F. *latin*. The word (as sb. denoting the language) was adopted in OE. as *læden* (see LEDEN).]

A. *adj.*

1. Of or pertaining to Latium or the ancient Latins (or Romans).

c **1391** CHAUCER *Astrol.* Prol. 2 As wel as suffyseth to thise noble clerkes Grekes thise same conclusiouns in Greek.. and to the Latin folk in Latin. **1552** *Bk. Com. Prayer* Ordin. Pref., Learned in the Latyne tongue. **1557** GRIMALD in *Tottel's Misc.* (Arb.) 116 Caiet the Phrygian.. who gaue to Latine stronds the name. **1644** MILTON *Areop.* (Arb.) 37 Nævius and Plautus the first Latine comedians. **1670–98** LASSELS *Voy. Italy* Pref. 3, I am writing of the Latin country. **1882** OUIDA *Maremma* I. 149 The ruins of Roman roads, of Latin castles.

2. a. Pertaining to, characteristic of, or composed in the language of the ancient Latins or Romans. Of a writer, scholar, etc: Versed in the Latin language. ***Latin letter***, a letter of the Latin alphabet.

c **950** *Lindisf. Gosp.* Matt. Prol., *Latinis exemplaribus*, latinum bisenum. *c* **1470** HENRY *Wallace* XI. 1413 Eftyr the pruff geyffyn fra the Latyn buk. **1535** STEWART *Cron. Scot.* II. 356 In Latyng letteris and in dowbill forme Tha wrait it. **1588** SHAKS. *L.L.L.* III. i. 138 Remuneration, O, that's the Latine word for three-farthings. *a* **1614** DONNE Βιαθανατος (1644) 160 The Latine Text is thus cited. **1668** WILKINS *Real Char.* IV. vi. 453 Latin Grammer. **1712** in Picton *L'pool Munic. Rec.* (1886) II. 6 In the Chancery of England in the Petty Bag Office or Latin side. **1774** J. BRYANT *Mythol.* I. 110 He sometimes subjoins the Latine termination. **1777** ROBERTSON *Hist. Amer.* (1783) II. 451 A Latin translation of them appeared in Germany. **1845** STODDART *Gram.* in *Encycl. Metrop.* (1847) I. 163/1 Adelung.. is of opinion that the Latin *et*, and Greek ἔτι are identical in origin with the Teutonic *enti, unte*, &c. **1953** K. JACKSON *Lang. & Hist. Early Brit.* 179 Latin-letter inscriptions. **1965** *Language* XLI. 238 All Serbo-Croatian examples.. are cited in conventional Latin-letter orthography.

b. *transf.* (*jocular*).

1598 SHAKS. *Merry W.* IV. i. 50 Hang-hog is latten for Bacon. **1599** H. BUTTES *Dyets drie Dinner* K iv, So these two words, Eate it, are the unlettered mans latine for any good meate. **1738** SWIFT *Pol. Convers.* II. 157 Brandy is Latin for a Goose, and Tace is Latin for a Candle.

3. The distinctive epithet of that branch of the Catholic Church which acknowledges the primacy of the Bishop of Rome, and uses the Latin tongue in its rites and formularies. Also applied to its rites, clergy, etc.

1560, *a* **1600** [see GREEK *a.* 3]. **1654** JER. TAYLOR *Real Pres.* 67 These words.. are usually called the words of Consecration in the Latine Church. **1796** H. HUNTER *St. Pierre's Stud. Nat.* (1799) III. 689 To have the Latin offices of our churches chanted in French. **1845** S. AUSTIN *Ranke's Hist. Ref.* I. 483 He wished to break up the unity of Latin Christendom. **1869** H. VAUGHAN *Year of Preparation* I. xii. 113 The Easterns deliberated among themselves without the presence of any Latin bishops. **1899** J. STALKER *Christol. Jesus* ii. 47 The Greek and Latin Fathers, from Irenaeus downwards, thus employ it.

4. a. *Hist.* Applied (in opposition to *Greek*) to what pertains to the peoples of Western Europe, viewed in their relations with the Eastern Empire and with the Saracens and Turks. **b.** Used as a designation for the European peoples which speak languages descended from Latin; often with implication of the erroneous notion that these peoples are of Roman descent. ***Latin-American*** *a.*, of or belonging to those countries in Central and South America in which Spanish or Portuguese is the dominant language (and which are often referred to collectively as ***Latin America***); also *sb.*, an inhabitant of one of these countries. Also (*ellipt.*) *Latin*.

Latin League: a proposed association of Latin nations, advocated by the Spanish minister Castelar in 1884, to restore the balance of power in Europe, and check the increasing influence of Germany. *Latin Union*: the monetary alliance formed in 1865 by France, Belgium, Italy

and Switzerland, and afterwards joined by Greece, its object being the adoption and maintenance of a uniform system of bimetallic coinage in each of these states, and the recognition by each state of the coins of the others as legal tender.

1788 GIBBON *Decl. & F.* lviii. *heading* VI. 1 Characters of the Latin princes.—.. Godfrey of Bouillon, first King of Jerusalem.—Institutions of the French or Latin Kingdom. *Ibid.* lxi. *heading* VI. 174 Partition of the Empire by the French and Venetians.—Five Latin Emperors of the Houses of Flanders and Courtenay [1204–1261]. **1821** BYRON '*The isles of Greece*' xiv. (*Don Juan* III.), But Turkish force, and Latin fraud, Would break your shield, however broad. **1856** EMERSON *Eng. Traits, Truth* Wks. (Bohn) II. 51 The Teutonic tribes have a national singleness of heart, which contrasts with the Latin races. **1882** *Sat. Rev.* 18 Mar. 323/1 One of Señor Castelar's tirades on the Latin League. **1893** *Funk's Stand. Dict.*, Latin American. **1903** *Westm. Gaz.* 22 June 11/1 Mexico..the richest district in the richest of the Latin-American countries. **1906** *Ibid.* 17 Apr. 9/1 Colombia ..is taking her place with those Latin-American countries [etc.]. **1911** *Q. Rev.* Oct. 456 Serious competition for British merchants doing trade with the Latin-American States. **1912** *Chambers's Jrnl.* June 358/2 The amount of British capital invested in the countries of Latin-America is very great. *Ibid.* Nov. 720/2 An Englishman..soon wishes himself well rid of the..Latin-American. **1936** *Discovery* Dec. 365/1 An issue [of *Discovery*] devoted to Latin America. **1955** L. FEATHER *Encycl. Jazz* i. 30 The wedding of jazz with Latin-American rhythms. **1962** K. ORVIS *Damned & Destroyed* iv. 30 The pianos segued smoothly into Latin rhythms. **1962** S. DE MADARIAGA (*title*) Latin-America between the Eagle and the Bear. **1965** *Crescendo* Dec. 14/3 The arrangements are all in the Latin idiom and all of well-known tunes, getting off to a really swinging start with a L-A 'Peter Gunn' you *must* hear. **1966** *Ibid.* Nov. 6/1 All the side one tracks have this straight eight-to-the-bar or Latin feel about them. **1973** 'D. JORDAN' *Nile Green* xxxi. 145 It's oil sheiks and Latin American generals and Lebanese rentiers who are going to buy your bonds. **1973** A. MANN *Tiara* i. 4 In the Philippines, some crazy Latin American got near enough to Paul VI to attack him with a knife. **1973** D. ROBINSON *Rotten with Honour* 8 He stood for a moment in the sunshine, snapping his fingers to a Latin beat. **1974** *Radio Times* 14 Sept. 26/3 Let's Go Latin..a fiesta of Latin-American music.

†**5.** Of a kind of printing type = ROMAN. *Obs.*

1709 TANNER 3 Oct. in *Ballard MSS.* IV. 53 Their Latin Small-Letter being worn out.

6. Phrases. ***Latin cross***: see CROSS *sb.* 18. ***Latin square*** [named (as F. *quarré* (now *carré*) *latin*) by Euler 1782, in *Verh. uitgegeven door het Zeeuwsch Genootschap d. Wetensch. te Vlissingen* IX. 90, from the fact that letters of the Latin alphabet were used in forming it] (see quot. 1890); used as the basis of experimental procedures in which it is desired to control or allow for two sources of variability while investigating a third; hence used *attrib.* (also *absol.*) to designate such a procedure.

1797 Latin cross [see CROSS *sb.* 18]. **1936** A. W. CLAPHAM *Romanesque Archit.* ii. 25 Although occasionally..the transept is of the T-form of the earlier ages, more generally the arrangement takes the Latin-cross form distinctive of the full Romanesque style. **1966** *Listener* 9 June 835/2 It is a Latin-cross church. *Ibid.*, A Latin cross is a more obviously Christian symbol than a regular geometric figure. **1890** CAYLEY *Coll. Math. Papers* (1897) XIII. 55 If in each line of a square of n^2 compartments the same *n* letters *a, b, c*, .. are arranged so that no letter occurs twice in the same column, we have what was termed by Euler 'a Latin square.' **1925** R. A. FISHER *Statistical Methods Res. Workers* viii. 229 (*heading*) The Latin square. **1926** —— in *Jrnl. Ministry of Agric.* XXXIII. 510 For the purpose of variety trials, and of those simple types of manurial trial in which every possible comparison is of equal importance, the problem of designing economical and effective field experiments, reduces to two main principles..[of which the second is] the use of arrangements which eliminate a maximum fraction of the soil heterogeneity, and yet provide a valid estimate of the residual errors. Of these arrangements, by far the most efficient..is that which the writer has named the Latin Square. *Ibid.*, The term Latin Square should only be applied to a process of randomization by which one is selected at random out of the total number of Latin Squares possible. **1935** —— *Design of Exper.* v. 80 The object of arranging plots in a Latin square is to eliminate from the experimental comparisons possible differences in fertility which may exist between whole rows of plots, and between whole columns of plots, as they stand in the field. **1960** D. J. FINNEY *Introd. Theory Exper. Design* iii. 30 Four different doses of insulin..were tested on rabbits and compared in terms of the subsequent sugar contents in the rabbits' blood. .. There is..a strong case for using rabbits as blocks and testing each dose, on different occasions on every rabbit. In addition, however, a block constraint based upon day of injection, so that on each day every dose is tested, is a useful precaution against the possibility that laboratory conditions on a particular day may tend to affect all animals in the same direction. A 4 × 4 Latin square with columns corresponding to different rabbits and rows corresponding to different days, enables both constraints to be incorporated. **1971** *Nature* 13 Aug. 499/1 On drug weeks each of six rats received one of six doses, each in a different order (latin-square design). *Ibid.*, An additional 6·0 mg/kg dose was administered to all subjects during the week after the completion of the latin-square.

B. *absol.* and as *sb.*

1. a. The language of the Latins or people of ancient Rome; the Latin language.

c **950** *Lindisf. Gosp.* Mark v. 41 *Interpraetatum*, ȝetrahtad in latin. *c* **1275** *Passion our Lord* 470 in *O.E. Misc.* 50 Hit wes iwryten on ebreu on gryv and latyn. *c* **1290** *S. Eng. Leg.* I. 143/1305 þat ne connen latin non. *c* **1391** CHAUCER *Astrol.* Prol. 2 For latyn ne kanstow yit but smal, my lite sone. *a* **1420** HOCCLEVE *De Reg. Princ.* 1854 Endite in frensch or latyn þi greef clere. **1553** EDEN *Treat. Newe Ind.* title-p., Translated out of Latyne into Englishe. **1623** B. JONSON in *Shaks. Wks.* (1st Fo.) Pref. verses, And though thou hadst small Latine, and lesse Greeke. **1678** CUDWORTH *Intell. Syst.* I. v. 894 When a man speaking Latin, observes not the laws of grammar. **1712** STEELE *Spec.* No. 296 ¶1 They adore and honour the Sound of Latin as it is old Italian. **1845** M. PATTISON *Ess.* (1889) I. 13 The Latin which Gregory writes is, with little difference, his native tongue. **1847** JAMES *J. Marston Hall* vii, I was filled with a great deal more Latin than I ever knew what to do with.

b. with qualifying words, as *good, bad*, etc. ***dog Latin***: see DOG *sb.* 19 e. ***false Latin***: Latin which is faulty in construction; hence *transf.*, a breach of manners.

1551 T. WILSON *Logike* (1580) 3 A Grammarian is better liked, that speaketh true & good Latine, than he y^t speaketh false. **1588** SHAKS. *L.L.L.* v. i. 83 Oh I smell false Latine, *dunghel* for *ungnem*. *a* **1626** BACON *New Atl.* (1900) 2 Written ..in Ancient Greeke, and in good Latine of the Schoole, and in Spanish. **1665** G. HAVERS *P. della Valle's Trav. E. India* 186 He (the King) bid us several times put on our Hats; but our Captain..answer'd that he would not, that they should not cause him to commit that false Latine.

c. ***thieves' Latin***, the secret language or 'cant' of thieves.

1821 SCOTT *Kenilw.* xxix, A very learned man..and can vent Greek and Hebrew as fast as I can Thieves' Latin. **1824** —— *Redgauntlet* ch. xiii, The thieves-Latin called slang.

2. An inhabitant or native of Latium; one who possessed the 'Latin right' of citizenship. †Also, one who spoke or wrote the Latin language; a Latin writer or author (*obs.*).

1398 TREVISA *Barth. De P.R.* XVII. cviii. (1495) 670 Many Latines calle the notte tre Iouilanus. *a* **1400–50** *Alexander* 5652 Sum in latens lare sum langage of grece. **1594** BLUNDEVIL *Exerc.* III. I. xxxvi. (1636) 351 Time consisteth of two parts..knit together by a common band, called of the Latines Nunc, that is to say, now. **1615** BEDWELL *Moham. Imp.* I. §15 The languages of..the Syrians, Greekes, and Latines. **1644** DIGBY *Bodies* xxxii. (1645) 336 So that to exercise sense (which the Latines doe call *sentire*..) is [etc.]. **1841** W. SPALDING *Italy & It. Isl.* I. 326 The Sabines and Latins worshipped the powers of external nature. **1880** MUIRHEAD *Gaius* I. §28 Latins may attain to Roman citizenship in many ways.

3. (Chiefly in *pl.*) **a.** *Hist.* The designation given at the period of the Crusades to persons belonging to any of the Western nations of Europe, in contradistinction to the 'Greeks'; = FRANK *sb.*[1] (Cf. A 4 a.) **b.** A member or adherent of the Latin or Western Church; now *rare* or *obs.* exc. *Hist.* with reference to subjects of the Turkish Empire.

c **1400** MAUNDEV. (1839) iii. 19 [Men of Grece] suffre not the Latynes to syngen at here Awteres. **1547** [see GREEK *sb.* 2]. **1682** O. N. tr. *Boileau's Lutrin* IV. 296 Why vex we then Dead Fathers, Greeks and Lattins? Our Mother Tongue will serve to Mumble Mattins. **1788** GIBBON *Decl. & F.* liii. V. 510 After the restoration of the Western empire by Charlemagne and the Othos, the names of Franks and Latins acquired an equal signification and extent. **1867** LADY HERBERT *Cradle L.* iii. 76 It was only intended for the Catholics (here [at Jerusalem] called 'Latins'). **1881** CONDER in *Encycl. Brit.* XIII. 644/1 The Latins in Palestine are not numerous, the country villages, when Christian, belonging generally to the Greek Church.

c. A member of any of the various communities in Europe (France, Italy, Spain, etc.) and Latin America whose language is derived from Latin.

1876 R. BROWN *Races of Mankind* IV. xvii. 292 The Aryans of Europe are the Skipitar, Celts, Greeks, Latins, Germans of all branches, Lithuanians, or Letts and Slavs. **1908** BEERBOHM *Lett. to R. Turner* (1964) 180 And then, of course, there is the pendant-fact that the Latins are born actors. **1936** J. CURTIS *Gilt Kid* iii. 35 A kind of wooden.. expression had come over her as it does over all Latins when they're scared of having to give something for nothing. **1949** H. VAN ZELLER *We live with our Eyes Open* 65 A Latin loves differently from a Saxon for instance. **1955** *Publ. Amer. Dial. Soc.* XXIV. 44 Most of these Latins [*sc.* immigrants from Cuba etc.] congregate on the East Coast. **1963** *Times* 2 Mar. 4/5 The Latins are said to be less susceptible to these emotions than we are.

†**4.** A translation into Latin, as a school exercise. Chiefly *pl.*

c **1500** *Song* in *Rel. Ant.* I. 117 Latens for to make. **1552** HULOET N n iij, With all the Lattens to the sayde nombres. *a* **1568** ASCHAM *Scholem.* (Arb.) 88 The hard pointes of Grammar..which scholers in common scholes, by making of Latines, be groping at. **1607** *Statutes* in *Hist. Wakefield Gram. Sch.* (1892) 68 Makinge of translations or Latins. **1679** W. WALKER *Eng. Particles* Pref., The first column contains some Englishes, the second such childish and bald Latines as we often find them turned into.

5. *Comb.*: ***Latin-based, -derived*** adjs.; **Latin-Greek,** of or pertaining to both Latin and Greek; †**Latin-maker,** a writer of Latin, a Latinist; †**Latin making,** Latin composition; **Latin Quarter** (F. *Quartier latin*; cf. QUARTER *sb.* 14), the district of Paris on the left or south bank of the Seine, where Latin was spoken in the Middle Ages, and where students and artists live and the principal university buildings are situated; also *transf.*; **Latin school** (also **Latin grammar school**) *U.S.*, a school offering Latin (and sometimes Greek) as part of the syllabus; cf. G. *Lateinschule*, Da. *Latinskole*, Du. *Latijnsche school*; †**Latin-wit,** wit that depends for its quality on being expressed in Latin.

1964 M. A. K. HALLIDAY et al. *Ling. Sci.* I. 121 Old-fashioned *Latin-based grammars. **1964** *Language* XL. 93 The inherited tradition of Latin- and Romance-based usage. **1946** H. JACOB *On Choice of Common Lang.* 38 A *Latin-derived constructed language. **1965** W. S. ALLEN *Vox Latina* 109 As early as the fourteenth century one finds spellings with *ngn* for Latin-derived words. **1942** PARTRIDGE *Usage & Abusage* (1947) 290/2 Slang tends to be 'Saxon' rather than '*Latin-Greek'. **1960** *Amer. Speech* XXXV. 233 Unvoicing originated mainly in Latin- Greek bilingualism. **14..** *Nom* in Wr.-Wülcker 682 *Hic latinista*, a *Latyn-maker. *a* **1568** ASCHAM *Scholem.* (Arb.) 102 Though ye say well, in a *latin making, .. yet you being but in do[u]bte..ye gather and lay vp in memorie, no sure frute of learning.. But if ye fault in translation, ye ar[e] easelie taught, how..to amende it. **1869** 'MARK TWAIN' *Innocents Abroad* xv. 150 The *grisettes*!..so devoted to their poverty-stricken students of the *Latin Quarter. **1878** R. L. STEVENSON *New Arabian Nights* (1882) I. 55 He had chosen to study the attractions of Paris from..a furnished hotel, in the Latin Quarter. **1904** J. T. GREIN *Dramatic Crit.* IV. 175 It was a generous mixture of the Latin Quarter and the various queer streets where London minor poetry flourishes. **1904** *Daily Chron.* 12 Dec. 4/4 They are good English garden-party hats, but they don't do for midi on an autumn day in the Latin Quarter. **1922** JOYCE *Ulysses* 18 And there's your Latin quarter hat, he said. **1930** E. B. CHANCELLOR (*title*) London's old Latin Quarter, being an account of Tottenham Court Road and its immediate surroundings. **1961** M. BEADLE *These Ruins are Inhabited* (1963) iv. 54 There is good reason now for wags to call the university 'the Latin Quarter of Oxford'. **1968** *Listener* 4 July 5/2, I left my friends in the Latin Quarter three weeks ago in a mood of exhausted elation. **1651** *Mass. Bay Rec.* (1854) III. 242 Whosoeuer shall..cause Schollers belonginge to the Colledge or any other *Latine Schoole.. to spend any of theire time [etc.]. **1680** in C. W. Manwaring *Digest of Early Connecticut Probate Rec.* (1904) I. 355, I give to the lattin Schoole in Hartford £50. **1685** *New Plymouth Laws* (1836) 300 That every County Town shall have and maintain a Latine School. **1781** S. PETERS *Gen. Hist. Connecticut* 185 Elms..surround the center square, wherein are..the jail, and Latin school. **1856** B. H. HALL *Collection of College Words & Customs* (rev. ed.) 124 [A young man from the country] shall be examined and 'conditioned' in everything, and yet he shall come out far ahead of his city Latin-school class-mate. **1959** C. V. GOOD *Dict. Educ.* (ed. 2) 311/2 *Latin grammar school*, a secondary school, emphasizing Latin and usually Greek, the purpose of which was to prepare youths for the universities. **1966** *Oxf. Compan. Amer. Hist.* 462/2 *Latin grammar schools*, the earliest type of college preparatory schools in the colonies, were established on the English model. The first, the Boston Latin School (1635), is still one of the principal schools in that city. *Ibid.* 463/1 By mid 18th century Latin schools were supplanted by academies. **1670** EACHARD *Cont. Clergy* 36 Such things as these go for wit so long as they continue in Latin; but what dismally shrim'd things would they appear, if turn'd into English? And..we shall find the advantages of *Latin-wit to be very small and slender, when it comes into the world.

†**ˈLatin,** *v. Obs.* [f. LATIN *sb.*]

1. *trans.* To render or turn into Latin.

1563 L. HUMFREY (*title*) The Nobles or of Nobilitye... Whereto for the readers commoditye, .. is coupled the small treatyse of Philo a Jewe. By the same Author out of the Greeke Latined. **1584** R. SCOT *Discov. Witchcr.* VI. i. (1886) 89 Chasaph, being an Hebrue word, is Latined *Veneficium.* **1670** EACHARD *Cont. Clergy* 31 He hales in all proverbs, .. tales..ready latin'd to his hand out of Licosthenes. **1678** CUDWORTH *Intell. Syst.* I. i. §3. 5 That of the Greek Poet, Latin'd by Cicero.

b. ***to Latin it***: to speak or write Latin.

1581 MULCASTER *Positions* i. (1887) 3 Though he thinke he haue the habite and can Latin it exceeding well.

2. To interlard with Latin. *rare*$^{-1}$.

1553 T. WILSON *Rhet.* 86 b, The..foolishe phantasticall that smelles but of learnyng..will so latine their tongues, that the simple cannot but wonder at their talke.

Hence **ˈLatined** *ppl. a.*, versed in Latin; **ˈLatining** *vbl. sb.*

1579 FULKE *Confut. Sanders* 626 He chargeth the bishop with false Latining and worse Englishing of this greeke. **1591** PERCIVALL *Sp. Dict.* E ij, That the Latined Reader, may be the sooner acquainted with this toong..let him marke this table following, which I set downe in Latine. **1893** F. J. FURNIVALL in J. Capgrave *Life St. Katherine* p. xxiv, I don't think *Prata* above can be a latining of *Akker*, acre, field.

latin(e, obs. form of LATEEN, LATTEN.

Latinate (ˈlætɪnət), *a.* Also **latinate.** [f. LATIN *a.* and *sb.* + -ATE[2] 2.] Of, pertaining to, or derived from Latin; having a Latin character. Also, occas., resembling an inhabitant of a Latin country.

1904 *Atlantic Monthly* Nov. 690/2 Cranmer transferred to the English..the rich sound and rhythm of the mediæval Latin; and that without the use of Latinate words. **1952** D. DAVIE *Purity of Diction in Eng. Verse* iv. 67 With intent Of being officious, grow impertinent... 'Officious' (in its Latinate sense, as in Johnson's 'Elegy on Robert Levett') defines and is defined by 'impertinent'. **1956** *Essays in Crit.* VI. 260 An anxious, questioning, excited passage, more latinate in diction. **1960** *Times* 16 Mar. 16/7 Miss Miranda, flamboyant and Latinate in temperament, is given..the part. **1962** W. NOWOTTNY *Lang. Poets Use* i. 23 Latinate syntax is important to Milton because it provides him with more ways..of devising contrasts. **1971** D. CRYSTAL *Ling.* 143 The distortions which..Latinate descriptions could impose.

Latiner (ˈlætɪnə(r)). *colloq.* [f. LATIN *sb.* or *v.* + -ER[1]. Cf. F. *latineur*, G. *Lateiner*. (Distinct from *latynere* LATIMER.)] A Latin scholar; one who speaks Latin.

a **1691** in *E. Pocock's Life* §3 (1816) 95 'Our parson is one Mr. Pocock, a plain honest man; but master', said they, 'he is no Latiner'. **1727** W. MATHER *Yng. Man's Comp.* 17 K is not heard in Back..for the Latiners made the same sound

with c alone. **1752** FOOTE *Taste* I. Wks. 1799 I. 13 The children are all wonderful latiners. **1834–43** SOUTHEY *Doctor* xxiii. (1862) 55 Rowland Dixon is no Latiner... Schools are the proper place for representing such pieces, and if I had but Latiners enough we would have them ourselves. **1857** BORROW *Rom. Rye* xlii, The chap that I'm talking about..came out first-rate Latiner.

Latinesque (lætɪˈnɛsk), *a.* [f. LATIN *a.* and *sb.* + -ESQUE.] Resembling Latin; having a Latin character.

1887 E. C. STEDMAN *Victorian Poets* (ed. 13) 448 Its atmosphere, landscape, and notes of sympathy..are so unEnglish that one must possess the author's latinesque training to feel them adequately. **1903** *Westm. Gaz.* 8 Apr. 2/3 A new language, or a Latinesque language. **1960** *Times* 13 Jan. 6/4 Here the dances are lighter and predominantly Latinesque.

Latinic (ləˈtɪnɪk), *a.* [f. LATIN + -IC.] Of or pertaining to the ancient Latins or to the modern Latin nations.

1875 WHITNEY *Life Lang.* vii. 116 A nearly pure Latinic dialect. **1894** *Review of Rev.* (Amer. ed.) Aug. 166/1 France and the Latinic countries.

Latinical (ləˈtɪnɪkəl), *a.* [f. LATINIC *a.* + -AL.] = LATINIC *a.*

1892 *Forum* (N.Y.) July 585 He [*sc.* Hardy] is, in point of diction, the most Latinical writer we have had since Dryden and Milton. **1919** [see AUREATE *a.* 2].

ˈ**Latinish**, *a. rare.* [f. LATIN + -ISH.] Of the nature of Latin.

a **1603** T. CARTWRIGHT *Confut. Rhem. N.T.* (1618) 632 Avoyding the word dedicated as forraine and Latinish. **1920** H. G. WELLS *Outl. Hist.* 340/2 Neustria, the nucleus of France, speaking a Latinish speech.

Latinism (ˈlætɪnɪz(ə)m). [f. LATIN + -ISM. Cf. F. *latinisme.*] An idiom or form of expression characteristic of the Latin language, esp. one used by a writer in another language; conformity in style to Latin models; the influence or authority of the Latin Church (see LATIN *a.* 3). Also, *rarely*, the modes of thought characteristic of the ancient Romans.

1570 LEVINS *Manip.* 146 Latinisme, *latinismus.* **1612** BRINSLEY *Lud. Lit.* 98 That the Latinismes bee obserued.. and to expresse them by as elegant and fit phrases as we can in our tongue. **1642** MILTON *Apol. Smect.* (1851) 310 Preferring the gay ranknesse of..any moderne fustianist before the native Latinisms of Cicero. **1712** ADDISON *Spect.* No. 285 ⁋9 Milton..has infused a great many Latinisms, as well as Græcisms..into the language of his poem. **1837** THACKERAY *Carlyle's Fr. Rev.*, It abounds with Germanisms and Latinisms. **1849** *Fraser's Mag.* XXXIX. 394 He is so imbued with Latinism that the whole beautiful Hellenic manifestation seems..an impertinence to his eyes. **1855** MILMAN *Lat. Chr.* XIV. vii. (1864) IX. 238 His Latinisms, and words of Latin descent, might seem drawn directly from the Vulgate. **1875** STEDMAN *Victorian Poets* (1887) 161 Milton's Latinism is so pronounced as to be un-English. **1920** *Contemp. Rev.* Oct. 495 The Spanish Court ladies were sheltered..under the vaulted roof of Latinism. **1970** H. BRAUN *Parish Churches* iii. 32 In Rome itself, Ravenna, and other towns of Latinism the basilican halls continued to be built out of the ruins of paganism.

Latinist (ˈlætɪnɪst). Also 6 **Latenyste**, 7 **Lattinist.** [f. LATIN + -IST. Cf. med.L. *Latīnista*, F. *latiniste.*]

1. One who is versed in the Latin language; a Latin scholar; †*occas.* a writer of Latin.

1538 COVERDALE *Let. to Ld. Crumwell* Wks. (Parker Soc.) II. 494 There is diversity of reading among the Hebrews, Chaldees, and Greeks, and Latinists. **1547** BOORDE *Brev. Health* lxxx. 33 Some grekes with the latenystes doth name it Cholera... In Englyshe it is named the belly ache. **1583** STANYHURST *Æneis* Ded. (Arb.) 4, I heeld no Latinist so fit ..as Virgil. **1612** BRINSLEY *Lud. Lit.* 158 For..placing the words after the manner of the purest Latinists. **1660** PEPYS *Diary* 29 June, My Lord must have some good Latinist to make the preamble to his Patent. **1784** COWPER *Tiroc.* 382 Church-ladders are not always mounted best By learned Clerks and Latinists profess'd. **1821** JEFFERSON *Autobiog.* Writ. 1892 I. 3 My teacher..was but a superficial Latinist. **1882** MASSON *Edin. Sketches* 230 The worst Latinist in the whole school.

attrib. **1602** *2nd Pt. Return fr. Parnass.* IV. ii. 1677 (Arb.) 54, I am stil haunted with these needy Lattinist fellowes.

2. A theologian of the Latin Church.

a **1568** COVERDALE *Hope Faithf.* xviii. (1574) 140 Among the Greekes also and Latinistes there wer excellent men. **1964** *Catholic Herald* 4 Dec. 13/2 (*heading*) The conversion of a convinced Latinist. **1965** *Ibid.* 29 Jan. 1/8 (*heading*) Latinists ask for prayers.

Latinistic (lætɪˈnɪstɪk), *a.* [f. LATINIST + -IC.] Pertaining to or characterized by Latinism; characteristic of a Latinist.

1804 COLERIDGE *Let.* 10 Mar. in *Lit. Rem.* (1836) II. 413 [Sir T. Browne's diction is] hyperlatinistic. **1886** SYMONDS *Renaiss. It., Catholic React.* (1898) VII. viii. 23 The classical enthusiasm of the Renaissance is on the point of expiring in those Latinistic artifices.

So **Latiˈnistical** *a.*

1723 MATHER *Vind. Bible* 45 Latinistical words are to be found in the New Testament.

latinitaster. *rare*⁻⁰. [irreg. f. next + -ASTER.] A petty Latinist.

1836 SMART *Walker remodelled* p. l, [Examples of suffix *-aster*] grammaticaster, latinitaster. Hence in mod. Dicts.

Latinity (ləˈtɪnɪtɪ). [ad. L. *latīnitātem*, f. *Latīnus*: see LATIN and -ITY.]

1. The manner of speaking or writing Latin; Latin (with reference to its construction or style).

In the first quot. the sense of the word is doubtful, and the text insecure.

1619 in *Crt. & Times Jas. I* (1848) II. 172 One Shingleton ..who preaching in Pauls..glanced, they say, scandalously at him [Bacon], and his Latinities, as he called them. *a* **1656** HALL *Rem. Wks.* (1660) 241 The Romans expressed the womans marriage by, *nubere*, which signifies to vail... Neither doubt I but before all latinity was hatched this was alluded to by Abimelech, Genes. 20. 16. **1661** BOYLE *Style of Script.* (1675) 148 That cardinal..that said, that once indeed he had read the Bible, but if he were to do it again, 'twould lose him all his Latinity. **1781** GIBBON *Decl. & F.* xlvii. II. 738 His latinity is pure. **1826** MISS MITFORD *Village* Ser. III. (1863) 519 [He] used to..growl as he compounded the medicines over the bad latinity of the prescriptions. **1831** CARLYLE *Sart. Res.* (1858) 81, I undertook to compose his Epitaph..which, however, for an alleged defect of Latinity..still remains unengraven. **1865** MERIVALE *Rom. Emp.* VIII. lxiv. 100 The last remains we possess of classical Latinity are the biographies of the later emperors.

2. *Roman Law.* The status of a Latin citizen.

1880 MUIRHEAD *Gaius* I. §22 note 1 On the nature of colonial latinity see Savigny. *Ibid.* §96 Latinity is either the greater or the lesser. There is the greater latinity when those who..fill some high office or magistracy, acquire Roman citizenship along with their parents, wives, and children; the lesser, when those who..hold a magisterial or other high office, themselves alone attain to citizenship.

3. Latin character.

1915 M. C. FRASER *More Italian Yesterdays* x. 191 True to their Latinity, they gave their victim no chance of testing it [*sc.* their mistrust]. **1934** G. B. SHAW *Prefaces* 740/1 By the end of the nineteenth century the press and the theatre had lost all their Latinity.

Latinization (ˌlætɪnaɪˈzeɪʃən). [f. next + -ATION.] The action of Latinizing or making Latin in form; the rendering or turning into Latin.

1830 DE QUINCEY in *Blackw. Mag.* XXVIII. 646 The Latinization of Grecian proper names. **1837** T. HOOK *Jack Brag* xiv, Andrew Borde, or according to his own absurd latinisation of his name, Andreas Perforatus. **1861** J. G. SHEPPARD *Fall Rome* viii. 409 From that invasion we may date the era of its complete Latinization. **1861** M. ARNOLD *Pop. Educ. France* 172 By the mixture of our race, by the Latinisation of our language. **1898** *Trans. Amer. Philol. Soc.* XXVIII. 49 A Latinization of the speculative and didactic poem of Empedocles.

Latinize (ˈlætɪnaɪz), *v.* [ad. L. *latīnizāre*, f. *Latīnus* Latin: see -IZE.]

1. *trans.* To turn into Latin, to write in Latin, to give a Latin form to (a word, etc., of another language).

1589 NASHE *Pref. to Greene's Menaphon* (Arb.) 9 That could scarcelie latinize their necke-verse. **1603** FLORIO *Montaigne* (1634) 555 To vtter this verse, latinized by Cicero. *a* **1682** SIR T. BROWNE *Tracts* 86 Pliny hath latinized that word into Æra. **1691** WOOD *Ath. Oxon.* II. 10 He had a hand in latinizing that..book. **1728** N. SALMON in *Lett. Lit. Men* (Camden) 361 They took the antient names of Rivers and Provinces, only latinizing them. **1855** TRENCH *Eng. Past & Pres.* iii. 107 The tendency to latinize our speech received a new impulse from the revival of learning. **1881** *Athenæum* 26 Feb. 294/1 That island..which for ages our geographers have insisted on Latinizing from the Russian Novaya Zemlya into Nova Zembla.

2. To make Latin or Latin-like; to make conformable to the ideas, customs, etc. of the Latins, or to the rites, etc. of the Latin Church.

1603 FLORIO *Montaigne* I. xxv. (1632) 84 My Father and my Mother learned so much Latine..To be short, we were all so Latinized, that [etc.]. **1682** WHELER *Journ. Greece* I. 31 They make profession of the Greek Religion; but are in most things Latinized, except in Obedience to the Sea of Rome. **1699** WANLEY in *Lett. Lit. Men* (Camden) 273 The help of many such at Rome (being Latiniz'd), father Kircher could not want. **1866** *Cornhill Mag.* May 539 Gaul was Latinized in language, manners, and laws, and yet her people remained essentially Celtic. **1882–3** G. WASHBURN in Schaff *Encycl. Relig. Knowl.* 549 The Roman Catholic Church has ..made great efforts to Latinize its Oriental branches.

3. To transcribe in Latin characters.

1837–9 HALLAM *Hist. Lit.* ii. I. §7 These sprinklings of Greek in mediæval writings, whether in their proper characters or latinised.

4. *intr.* To use Latin forms, idioms, etc.

1642, 1724 [see LATINIZING *ppl. a.*]. **1646** SIR T. BROWNE *Pseud. Ep.* V. vii. 246 Marke who writ his Gospell at Rome did Latinize and wrote it Ναζαρήνος. **1697** DRYDEN *Ded. Æneis* (near end), I will not excuse but justify myself for one pretended crime..that I latinize too much. **1849** TICKNOR *Sp. Lit.* II. 485 *note*, He Latinizes less in the poems that follow, because it is more difficult to do it in verse. **1892** *Guardian* 18 May 743/2 Some of the correctors Latinise strongly. *Ibid.* 743/3 The MS. quite certainly does not Latinise but Graecises.

Hence ˈ**Latinized** *ppl. a.*; ˈ**Latinizing** *vbl. sb.* and *ppl. a.*

1642 MILTON *Apol. Smect.* Wks. 1738 I. 127 The lofty nakedness of your latinizing Barbarian. **1724** WATERLAND *Athan. Creed* 96 It is plain from the copy it self, that it was no Latinizing Greek that made it. **1807** G. CHALMERS *Caledonia* I. I. i. 16 *note*, *Durius* is merely the latinized *Dur.* **1837–9** HALLAM *Hist. Lit.* vii. II. §9 A Latinised phraseology. **1849** TICKNOR *Sp. Lit.* III. 350 They had fled from the ruins of the Latinized kingdom of the Goths. **1853** KINGSLEY *Hypatia* ix. 109 They spoke with sneers of Augustine's Latinizing tendencies. **1870** LOWELL *Study Wind.* (1886) 329 It was of Latinising in this sense that Dryden was guilty. **1896** *Tablet* 9 May 725 The outcry against Latinizing is a favourite battle-cry.

Latinizer (ˈlætɪnaɪzə(r)). [f. LATINIZE *v.* + -ER¹. Cf. F. *latiniseur.*] One who Latinizes; a Latinist.

1603 FLORIO *Montaigne* I. xxv. (1632) 81 These collegiall Latinizers. **1885** *Homilet. Rev.* Feb. 98 Half-educated men who can beat him as latinizers.

Latinless (ˈlætɪnlɪs), *a.* [f. LATIN *sb.* + -LESS.] Without Latin; ignorant of Latin.

1599 NASHE *Lenten Stuffe* 64 Latinless dolts. **1615** tr. *Brightman's Revelation* 144 There is no Castle so defenced, which a latinlesse Asse laden with golden metall may not scale and conquerre. **1848** LYTTON *Harold* VI. vi, An example of learning to our Latinless nobles. **1906** *Athenæum* 21 July 71/3 The Latinless enthusiast who is curious to explore Propertius. **1958** *Duckett's Reg.* Apr. 44/2 The most Latinless lout cannot fail to understand what the monks are doing at Solesmes.

†**Latinly** (ˈlætɪnlɪ), *adv. Obs.* [f. LATIN *a.* + -LY².] In Latin; in good or pure Latin.

1388 WYCLIF *Ps.* Prol., A Sauter..that..Latinli is seid an orgne. **1548** Q. KATH. PARR *Let. to University Cambr.* in Strype *Eccl. Mem.* II. App. K. 39 Your letters..be Latynely wrytten. **1559** MORWYNG *Evonym.* 67 They which speake not very aptly nor latinly. *a* **1577** SIR T. SMITH *Commw. Eng.* III. x. 128 *Fidei commissum*, or more latinely, *fidei committere.* **1606** WARNER *Alb. Eng.* XV. xciii. 374 Rome heere prevailing, latenlie, old Britons, Picts, were said Of their self-painting. **1656** HEYLIN *Surv. France* III. iii 150 You shall hardly finde a man amongst them [the French] which cannot make a shift to expresse himself in that language [*sc.* Latin]; nor one amongst an hundred that can do it Latinly.

Latino (ləˈtiːnəʊ). *U.S.* [Amer. Sp., f. **Latin-American* + Spanish ending *-o.*] A Latin-American inhabitant of the United States. Also *attrib.* or as *adj.*

1946 G. PEYTON *San Antonio* xxi. 232 The first program on the University's list is an exchange of students with Latin America. That in itself would be a fresh intellectual experience for Texas, where Latinos are usually looked on as sinister specimens of an inferior race. **1966** MRS L. B. JOHNSON *White House Diary* 2 Apr. (1970) 377 Six young girls, all Latinos, had encased themselves in cardboard boxes. **1972** *Listener* 9 Mar. 310/1 America..is meant to be a great melting-pot... Its racial components—Blacks, Latinos, Chinese, Japanese, [etc.]. **1973** *Black Panther* 17 Mar. 5/3 A program was drawn up..by an..action group composed of Blacks, Latinos, and Whites. **1974** *Ibid.* 19 Jan. 5/1 Mr. Rhodes' home was broken into..by a man who appeared to be of Latino origin.

Latino- (ˈlætɪnəʊ), used as combining form of LATIN *a.* 2 and 4 b, as in ***Latino-Faliscan, -Jazz, -Sabellian.*** Also (with *Latino* = abl. of L. *Latīnus*) ***Latino sine flexione***, the basis for the international language *Interlingua.*

1939 L. H. GRAY *Found. Lang.* 332 The Italic dialects fall into three groups: Latino-Faliscan, Osco-Umbrian, and Sabellian. **1954** PEI & GAYNOR *Dict. Ling.* 121 *Latino-Faliscan*, a branch of the Italic group of the Indo-European family of languages, consisting of the extinct languages Latin, Faliscan, Hernician and Praenestinian. **1958** P. GAMMOND *Decca Bk. Jazz* xxi. 265 It is worth remembering, when the history of the Latino-Jazz movement is written, that Kenton and the West Coast boys were years ahead of the boppers and the East Coast 'cool' men in hitching their wagon to the Latin star. **1880** A. H. SAYCE *Introd. Sci. of Lang.* II. vii. 110 We find in Italy two great stocks, the Iapygian and the Latino-Sabellian. **1928** O. JESPERSEN *Internat. Lang.* I. 45 In 1903 the famous Italian mathematician G. Peano started his *Latino sine flexione*... The idea is to take the ablative of each Latin noun and one simple form of each verb to be used practically everywhere. **1939** L. H. GRAY *Found. Lang.* 35 Esperanto, Ido, Latino sine flexione. **1946** H. JACOB *On Choice of Common Lang.* 16 *Latino sine flexione*, or Interlingua, as Peano called his system.

†**lation.** *Astrol. Obs.* [a. L. *lātiōn-em*, n. of action f. *lāt-*, ppl. stem of *ferre* to bear, carry.] The action of moving, or the motion of a body from one place to another; motion of translation.

1603 SIR C. HEYDON *Jud. Astrol.* xii. 290 Then Lation or locall permutation should not be the first of all motions. *a* **1619** FOTHERBY *Atheom.* II. i. §4. 177, I meane Lation, or local-motion from one place to another. **1648** HERRICK *Hesper.* (1869) 64 Make me the straight and oblique lines, The motions, lations, and the signes. **1655** STANLEY *Hist. Philos.* I. (1701) 7/1 The four kinds of motion (viz. Lation, Alteration, Diminution, Accretion). **1690** LEYBOURN *Curs. Math.* 431 The Mundane System is consider'd..having the Sun in the Centre, exempt from any motion of Lation.

latipennate, -rostrous, -sept, etc.: see LATI-.

latish (ˈleɪtɪʃ), *a.* Also lateish. [f. LATE *a.* + -ISH.] Somewhat late. Also quasi *adv.*

1611 COTGR., *Tardelet*, latish; or, somewhat tardie. **1741** RICHARDSON *Pamela* II. 172 It will be a little latish today. **1817** R. B. HAYDON *Let.* in *Keats' Wks.* (1889) III. 49 I'll be at Reynolds tonight but latish. **1837** T. HOOK *Jack Brag* xiv, It was lateish in the evening when he reached Hastings. **1865** CARLYLE *Fredk. Gt.* VIII. iii. (1872) III. 14 It is Sunday 27th of May, latish. **1892** STEVENSON *Across the Plains* 204 Latish at night.

latitancy (ˈlætɪtənsɪ). [f. next: see -ANCY.] The state of lying concealed or hid; *spec.* in *Phys.* and *Path* (see quots.). Of an animal: Hibernation.

1646 SIR T. BROWNE *Pseud. Ep.* III. xxi. 163 [The Cameleon] by reason of its..latitancy in the winter..will long subsist without a visible sustentation. *Ibid.* IV. xiii. 223

By this way Aristotle through all his books of Animals, distinguisheth their times of generation, latitancy, migration, sanity, and venation. **1701** BEVERLEY *Apoc. Quest.* 37 If we can find according to Prophecy there ought to be such a Latitancy, or Secrecy of the Papacy. **1888** *Syd. Soc. Lex.*, *Latitancy*, .. A term expressive of the hypothesis that the ovum and the spermatozoa lie in wait for each other, as it were, after insemination. **1890** BILLINGS *Nat. Med. Dict.*, *Latitancy*, the condition of lying in wait, of waiting for development under favorable circumstances.

latitant ('lætɪtənt), *a.* (*sb.*) [ad. L. *latitant-em*, pr. pple. of *latitāre* to lie hid.] That lies concealed or hid; lurking; latent; (of an animal) hibernating.

1646 SIR T. BROWNE *Pseud. Ep.* III. xxi. 163 Lizards, Snails, and divers other insects latitant many moneths in the yeare. **1650** CHARLETON *Paradoxes* 77 In the outward man ..the Magicall power is latitant. **1650** BULWER *Anthropomet.* (1653) 264 The Latitant effect is supposed greater than indeed it is, which had not been so much suspected had she not painted her selfe. **1660** BOYLE *New Exp. Phys. Mech.* xvii. 128 By forcing the small latitant bubbles of Air to disclose themselves and break. **1660** H. MORE *Myst. Godl.* To Rdr. 20 Some latitant averseness or enmity to Religion it self. **1682** —— *Annot. Glanvill's Lux O.* 81 That facultie or measure of it in their Plastick, essentially latitant there.

b. *sb.* One who is in hiding. (Cf. next word.)

1887 *Edin. Rev.* July 146 Leaving him in the position of a latitant from justice.

latitat ('lætɪtæt). *Law. Obs.* exc. *Hist.* [a. L. *latitat*, 3rd pers. sing. ind. pres. of *latitāre* to lie concealed.] A writ which supposed the defendant to lie concealed and which summoned him to answer in the King's Bench.

1565 COOPER *Thesaurus, Annotare reos absentes*, when the iudge ordeineth persons accused in their absence to be sought for: as to send out a latitat. *c* **1570** *Pride & Lowl.* (1841) 75 Then ryseth quarrell:..out gon sub penes, out flaien latitattes. **1620** MELTON *Astrolog.* 67 Writs, Latitats, and Procidendos. **1647** WARD *Simp. Cobler* 66, I desire him also to conceale himself as deeply as he can, if he cannot get a speciall pardon, to weare a Latitat about his neck. **1768** BLACKSTONE *Comm.* III. 236 There issues out a writ of latitat, to the sheriff of another county. **1796** J. ANSTEY *Pleader's Guide* (1803) 55 If haply John-a-Stile provoke The legal fight 'gainst John-a-Noke, The Latitat the foe besieges And baffles him in Banco Regis. **1843** LEVER *J. Hinton* v. (1878) 32 You may laugh at a latitat,..and snap your fingers at any process-server. **1848** STEWART *Mem. A. Averell* xviii. 375 Having bailiffs serving him with latitats.

†**b.** *transf.* = LATITATION. *Obs. rare*$^{-1}$.

1647 R. STAPYLTON *Juvenal* 248 In which his flight..he was a while in Latium, which took the name from his latitat.

†'**latitate**, *v. Obs. rare*$^{-0}$. [f. L. *latitāt-*, ppl. stem of *latitāre* to lie hid.] *intr.* 'To lurke' (Cockeram 1623).

latitation (lætɪ'teɪʃən). [ad. L *latitātiōn-em*, f. *latitāre* to lie hid.] The fact of lying concealed; hiding, lurking.

1623 COCKERAM, *Latitation*, a lurking. **1629** JACKSON *Creed* VI. II. xxxviii. §6 The women of Hungary..buried their children alive lest their timorous outcries might bewray the place of their abode or latitation. **1875** POSTE *Gaius* IV. Comm. (ed. 2) 510 Avoidance of in jus vocatio by latitation or keeping house rendered a defendant liable to manus injectio.

latitude ('lætɪtjuːd). [ad. L. *lātitūd-o*, f. *lātus* broad, wide: see -TUDE. Cf. F. *latitude*.]

I. Breadth, width.

1. a. Transverse dimension; extent as measured from side to side; breadth, width of a surface, as opposed to length; also *occas.* spaciousness. Now only *jocular*.

c **1391** CHAUCER *Astrol.* II. §39 þe latitude of a climat is a lyne ymagined from north to south þe space of the erthe, fro the byginnyng of the firste clymat vnto the verrey ende of the same climat. **1398** TREVISA *Barth. De P.R.* VIII. xxiv. (1495) 335 Orion..his lengthe and longitude stretchyth nyghe to the brede and latitude of thre sygnes. **1412-20** LYDG. *Chron. Troy* III. xxvi, Twenty pase was the latytude. **1471** RIPLEY *Comp. Alch.* II. xi. in Ashm. (1652) 137 Altytude, Latytude, and Profundyte. **1559** W. CUNNINGHAM *Cosmogr. Glasse* 25 The latitude and bredth of the Zodiack is .xij. degrees. **1571** DIGGES *Pantom.* I. xxv. Hb, The square of yᵉ ditches latitude. **1615** G. SANDYS *Trav.* 2 The Gulph of Venice..being seuen hundred miles in length, and seuen score in latitude. **1650** FULLER *Pisgah* 364 The great latitude and capacity of the Temple consisted in the outward Courts. *a* **1677** HALE *Prim. Orig. Man.* I. ii. 64 Though his [*sc.* man's] Feet, the Basis of the Pillar of his Body, be much narrower than the latitude of his Body. **1692-4** L'ESTRANGE *Fables* ccclvii. (1708) 375 'Tis a Field of a Huge Latitude that the Devil has to Dance..in. **1713** POPE *Frenzy J. Dennis* Miscell. (1732) III. 4 The Latitude of whose Countenance was not a little eclips'd by the Fullness of his Peruke. **1739** NEVE *Builder's Dict.* (ed. 3) s.v. *Building*, The Longitude, Latitude and Crassitude of Ground-plates. **1830** T. HAMILTON *C. Thornton* (1845) 99 His beaver was.. distinguished by an unusual latitude of brim.

†**b.** A tract or area as defined by its breadth; a wide compass or extent. *Obs.*

1432-50 tr. *Higden* (Rolls) I. 81 Mony multitudes of peple may sytte vnder the latitude of oon figge tre. **1605** BACON *Adv. Learn.* I. vii. §1 (1873) 52 Fruitful showers..serve but for that season, and for a latitude of ground where they fall. **1650** FULLER *Pisgah* II. iii. 95 A chace with a vengeance all the latitude of the land, the Canaanites flying as far as sea or mountains would give them leave. **1675** BROOKS *Gold. Key* Wks. 1867 V. 59 What a vast distance is there betwixt the east and west! of all visible latitudes, this is the greatest. **1791** COWPER *Yardley Oak* 21 Thy yet close-folded latitude of boughs.

2. a. Extent, range, scope. Also, great or full extent. Now *rare*.

1605 BACON *Adv. Learn.* II. xxv. §9 (1873) 258 It is a thing of great use well to define what, and of what latitude those points are. **1625** BACON *Ess.*, *Atheism* (Arb.) 337 Even those Barbarous People, have the Notion, though they have not the Latitude, and Extent of it. **1646** SIR T. BROWNE *Pseud. Ep.* I. viii. 33 For his great learning and latitude of knowledge sirnamed Magnus. **1655** FULLER *Ch. Hist.* II. ii. §77 Grant this Miracle of Oswald's Hand literally true in the Latitude thereof. **1674** PLAYFORD *Skill Mus.* III. 16 They have assumed the nature of some part for a Note or two, and so want the full latitude of a Bass in those Notes. *a* **1677** BARROW *Serm.* Wks. 1716 II. 123 The Greek word in the latitude of its signification..comprehendeth all these senses. **1691** RAY *Creation* I. (1692) 167 To compass and comprehend the whole Latitude of Learning. **1751** JOHNSON *Rambler* No. 105 ¶1 The latitude to which this design may be extended. **1776** R. KING in *Life & Corr.* (1894) I. 22 Had the scheme been executed with success, in its greatest latitude. **1801** STRUTT *Sports & Past.* I. i. 16 If this record be taken in its full latitude. **1851** MANSEL *Prol. Logica* (1860) 40 The often quoted passage of Locke..when understood in its proper latitude.

†**b.** The range within which anything may vary.

1533 ELYOT *Cast. Helthe* (1541) 52a, Meate but a lyttel excedynge temperance..may yet kepe the body within the latitude or boundes of helthe. **1645** FULLER *Good Th. in Bad T.* (1680) 68, I find myself in the latitude of a fever: I am neither well nor ill. **1649** JER. TAYLOR *Gt. Exemp.* II. Disc. ix. 110 Our love to God consists not in any one determinate degree, but hath such a latitude, as best agrees with the condition of men. **1717** J. KEILL *Anim. Oecon.* (1738) 247 The Latitude of a natural Perspiration is from about a Pound and half to three Pound. **1796** KIRWAN *Elem. Min.* (ed. 2) I. 160 Few stones admit of a greater latitude of composition.

†**c.** Local range; wide diffusion or prevalence.

1612 DAVIES *Why Ireland*, etc. (1787) 177 The execution of all these laws had no greater latitude than the Pale. **1638** CHILLINGW. *Relig. Prot.* I. vi. §42. 363 If you should contend for latitude with any one Religion, Mahumetisme would carry the victory from you.

d. *Photogr.* The range of exposures for which an emulsion, printing paper, etc., will give acceptable contrast; *spec.* the ratio (or its logarithm) of the exposures between which the characteristic curve is straight.

1889 E. J. WALL *Dict. Photogr.* 98 The extreme latitude of exposure which most plates possess. **1907** SHEPPARD & MEES *Investigations Theory Photogr. Process* III. i. 289 The latitude may be defined as the ratio of the exposure at which over-exposure commences to that at which under-exposure commences, and these two points must be arbitrarily defined. **1939** W. CLARK *Photogr. by Infrared* iv. 60 The range or latitude of printing papers is thus always less than that of negative materials. **1962** W. G. HYZER *Engin. & Scientific High-Speed Photogr.* v. 200 Actually the toe region of the curve is usable in recording shadow detail, which somewhat increases the effective latitude of the emulsion.

3. a. Freedom from narrow restrictions; width or liberality of construction or interpretation; tolerated or permitted variety of action or opinion.

1605 BACON *Adv. Learn.* II. iii. §2 (1873) 99 Allowing.. that latitude which is agreeable and familiar unto divine prophecies; being of the nature of their author, with whom a thousand years are but as one day. **1642** CHAS. I in Rushw. *Hist. Coll.* (1692) III. I. 595 The Latitude they allow us of granting or denying of Pardons. **1647** CLARENDON *Hist. Reb.* VI. §198 A latitude of Judgement no Court can challenge to it self in any Cases. **1648** *Eikon Bas.* xiv. 115 In such latitudes of sens, I believ manie that love Mee and the Church well, may have taken the Covenant, who [etc.]. **1651** BAXTER *Inf. Bapt.* 246 A greater latitude there must be left in doctrinals then practicals. **1655** FULLER *Ch. Hist.* IX. i. §51 Christ went down to Hell (to preach to the Spirits there,) which last clause is left out in these Articles, and men left to a latitude concerning the cause, time and manner of his Descent. **1687** DRYDEN *Hind & P.* III. 160 Your sons of latitude that court your grace. [Cf. I. 187 Your sons of breadth.] **1711** ADDISON *Spect.* No. 44 ¶8 There is a much greater Latitude for comick than tragick Artifices. **1726** DE FOE *Hist. Devil* I. ii. (1840) 28 The devil has some little latitudes and advantages for mischief. **1749** FIELDING *Tom Jones* xv. ix, He gave a latitude to his friends tongue, and desired him to speak plainly what he knew. **1753** HANWAY *Trav.* (1762) I. II. xvi. 70 A latitude to kill might subject the innocent to great inconveniencies. **1779** J. MOORE *View Soc. Fr.* (1789) I. x. 68 The greatest ease and latitude allowed in behaviour and dress. **1838-9** HALLAM *Hist. Lit.* IV. iv. iv. §27. 165 Natural good has been defined by Cumberland with more latitude than has been used by Paley. **1858** LD. ST. LEONARDS *Handy-Bk. Prop. Law* ii. 7 The latitude which a court of equity allows itself in enforcing agreements against the letter. **1863** KINGLAKE *Crimea* (1877) I. xi. 150 In regard to time the Emperor grants you no latitude. **1868** STANLEY *Westm. Abb.* iv. 325 Courayer's 'Last Sentiments', which were of the extremest latitude in theology.

†**b.** Laxity of conduct or principle. *Obs.*

1670 G. H. *Hist. Cardinals* II. I. 127 They live with that latitude and licentiousness, as if there were neither God, nor Justice for them. **1679** PENN *Addr. Prot.* I. iii. (1692) 7 Which way soever this ungodly Latitude came in. **1702** *Eng. Theophrast.* 237 If statesmen..worked their heads, there would be no occasion for Latitude and insincerity.

c. *attrib.* †**latitude man** = LATITUDINARIAN.

1662 S. P. (*title*) Brief Account of the new Sect of Latitude-men. *Ibid.* 5 In opposition to that hide-bound, strait-lac'd spirit that did then prevail, they were called Latitude-men.

II. In Geography and Astronomy.

4. *Geog.* **a.** Angular distance on a meridian: only in ***degree, minute,*** etc. ***of latitude***. **b.** The angular distance on its meridian (of any place on the earth's surface) north or south from the equator; quantitatively identical with the elevation of the pole above the horizon, and with the declination of the zenith.

For *circle, parallel of latitude*, see those words.

[In their original geographical use *latitude* (L. *latitudo*, Gr. πλάτος) and *longitude* (L. *longitudo*, Gr. μῆκος) meant quite literally the 'breadth' and 'length' of the oblong map of the known world; this literal sense remained even in the expression 'degrees of latitude and longitude' (μοῖραι πλάτους καὶ μήκους). By a natural development the terms afterwards came (in late Latin, app. not yet in Greek) to denote the distance of any place, in the breadthwise and lengthwise direction respectively, from the circle assumed as the origin of measurement.]

c **1391** CHAUCER *Astrol.* Prol., A suffisaunt astralabie as for owre orizonte, compowned after the latitude of Oxenford. *Ibid.* II. §22 The latitude of any place in a regioun is the distance fro the senyth vnto the Equinoxial. **1527** R. THORNE in Hakluyt *Voy.* (1589) 253 This latitude is the measure of the world from North to South. *c* **1550** *Disc. Common Weal Eng.* (1893) 13b, How could youe knowe towarde what coste ye be sea driven withoute knowledge of the latitude of the place by the poolle and the lengthe by the starres? **1559** W. CUNNINGHAM *Cosmogr. Glasse* 123 Ther shalbe so many, as there are paralleles of latitude, whose nombre as I saide was .90. **1622** DRAYTON *Poly-olb.* xix. 316 To fortie three Degrees of North'ly Latitude. **1669** STURMY *Mariner's Mag.* IV. iv. 157 How to correct the Account, when the Dead Latitude differs from the Observed Latitude ..if the Difference of Latitude be less by Estimation than it is by Observation [etc.]. **1698** KEILL *Exam. Theory Earth* (1734) 107 The Latitude of Paris being 48°. 45'. **1706** PHILLIPS (ed. Kersey) s.v., Whenever a Ship sails to or from the Equinoctial on either side, her way thus gain'd is call'd her Difference of Latitude. **1836** MARRYAT *Midsh. Easy* xxxviii, We have made a famous run. It's twelve o'clock, and if you please I'll work the latitude. **1867** DENISON *Astron. without Math.* 9 A degree of latitude measured on any meridian is about 69 miles everywhere.

c. A locality as marked or defined by parallels of latitude; usually in *pl.* = regions, climes, parts of the world. Also *fig.*

1632 MASSINGER *City Madam* II. ii, They serve For any latitude in Christendom. **1704** *Lond. Gaz.* No. 3988/1 A French Privateer..which he took in this Latitude. **1719** DE FOE *Crusoe* I. vi. (1840) 101, I was something chilly, which I knew was not usual in that latitude. **1760-2** GOLDSMITH *Cit. of the World* cxiv. (Globe) 265/1 A lady's whole cargo of smiles, sighs, and whispers, is declared utterly contraband, till she arrives in the warm latitudes of twenty-two. **1845** FORD *Handbk. Spain* I. 59 Very little meat and wine are necessary in these hot latitudes. **1855** PRESCOTT *Phillip II* I. v. (1857) 75 The flag of Castile was seen in the remotest latitudes,—on the Atlantic, the Pacific, and the far-off Indian seas. **1871** MORLEY *Carlyle* (1878) 157 Men who have long since moved far away from these spiritual latitudes. **1882** W. R. GREG *Misc. Ess.* Ser. I. v. 103 Those latitudes and altitudes where no crops will grow. **1885** J. MARTINEAU *Types Eth. Theory* I. 115 Leaving blank vast latitudes on the map of human thought.

5. *Astron.* The angular distance of a heavenly body from the ecliptic: called spec. ***celestial latitude***. (See also ASCENDING *vbl. sb.*, GEOCENTRIC *a.* 1, HELIOCENTRIC *a.* 1, and HELIOGRAPHIC *a.* 1.)

The history of this sense appears to be as follows. Orig. the word was applied, on the analogy of the geographical use (see 4) to denote the angular distance of a point in the celestial sphere from the equator, measured along a secondary to the latter. This, however, was not accurately distinguished by name from the distance of a point from the *ecliptic*, the terms 'latitude' and 'declination' being employed indiscriminately with reference to both these ways of indicating position. (Cf. quot. 1391.) In mod. use, the terms have been differentiated, *declination* being appropriated to what was originally and with historical propriety called 'latitude', while *latitude* became the name for distance from the ecliptic.

c **1391** CHAUCER *Astrol.* II. §17 Fro the Equinoxial may the declinacion or the latitude of any body celestial be rikned, after the site north or south,..& riht so may the latitude or the declinacion of any body celestial, saue only of the sonne ..be rekned fro the Ecliptic lyne. **1551** RECORDE *Cast. Knowl.* (1556) 176 Proprelye they doo call that the Latitude of the Planetes, when they swarue from the Ecliptike line. **1594** BLUNDEVIL *Exerc.* III. I. xi. (1636) 298 The Latitude is counted from the said Ecliptique line towards any of the Poles of the Zodiaque. **1601** HOLLAND *Pliny* I. 11 Mars in his latitude leaueth the eclipticke line foure halfe degrees. **1706** PHILLIPS (ed. Kersey) s.v., Apparent Latitude, is the Distance of the apparent, or seeming Place of any Planet from the Ecliptick; and True Latitude is the Distance of its real Place from the same Ecliptick. **1868** LOCKYER *Elem. Astron.* §555. 269 The right ascension and declination are then easily converted by calculation into celestial longitude and latitude if required.

latitudinal (lætɪ'tjuːdɪnəl), *a.* and *sb.* [f. L. *lātitūdin-*, *-tūdo* LATITUDE + -AL[1].]

1. Relating to breadth or width. *rare.*

1671 GREW *Anat. Plants* I. ii §28 (1682) 17 The Latitudinal growth of the Root. **1879** J. M. DUNCAN *Lect. Dis. Women* I. (1889) 2 Bounded below by a horizontal or latitudinal line which joins the iliac crests.

2. Relating to, connected with, or depending on geographical latitude; corresponding with lines of latitude.

1778 SHUCKBURGH in *Phil. Trans.* LXVIII. 687 *note*, Between the lat. 56° and 79°..the zero of the scale moves through a space of no less than 32°; whereas, between the lat. 46° and 56° it is perfectly stationary..which great want of proportion..is of itself some argument against the existence of such a latitudinal equation. **1855** MAURY *Phys. Geog. Sea* v. §289 The latitudinal limits of the northern edge of the northeast trade-winds are variable. **1867** RAWLINSON *Anc.*

Mon. IV. i. 31 Its principal mountain ranges are latitudinal, or from west to east. **1874** Coues *Birds N.W.* 19 In respect of latitudinal distribution the Tufted Titmouse offers much the same case as the Blue-gray Gnat-catcher. **1880** Haughton *Phys. Geog.* v. 204 The latitudinal width of this part of Africa is 63°. **1897** *Allbutt's Syst. Med.* IV. 137 The latitudinal and altitudinal relations of hepatic abscess.

† **B.** *sb.* *Anat.* The name of two muscles of the epigastrium. *Obs.*

1541 R. Copland *Guydon's Quest. Chirurg.* I j b, Of what villes is the stomacke composed... Of longytudynalles to drawe in & tranuersalles to reteyne & latitudinalles to put forth. **1548-77** Vicary *Anat.* viii. (1888) 63 Two Latitiudinales comming from the backe-wards to the wombe.

Hence **lati'tudinally** *adv.*, in respect of breadth or latitude.

1853 Lytton *My Novel* ii. vii, The bones..in the skin of Jackeymo spread out latitudinally. **1884** *Manch. Exam.* 20 Aug. 6/3 This submarine swamp extends fifty miles latitudinally.

latitudi'narially, *adv.* *rare*$^{-1}$. [f. **latitudinarial* (formed as next) + -ly^2.] With latitude or laxity of distinction.

1853 De Quincey *Autobiog. Sk.*, Laxton Wks. 1863 XIV. 400 *note*, Colours were as loosely and latitudinarially distinguished by the Greeks and Romans as degrees of affinity and consanguinity are everywhere.

latitudinarian (ˌlætɪtjuːdɪˈnɛərɪən), *a.* and *sb.* [f. L. *lātitūdin-*, *lātitūdo* latitude, after *trinitarian*, etc. Cf. F. *latitudinaire.*]

A. *adj.* Allowing, favouring, or characterized by latitude in opinion or action, esp. in matters of religion; not insisting on strict adherence to or conformity with an established code, standard, formula, etc.; tolerating free thought or laxity of belief on religious questions; characteristic of the latitudinarians (see B).

1672-1702 Comber *Comp. Temple* 368 There were no such Latitudinarian Principles among the Apostles. **1697** Collier *Ess. Mor. Subj.* i. (1709) 166 When you have made the most of it, I foresee this Latitudinarian Love will be expensive. **1733** *Let. to Mr. Holden* 26 in Ellys *Plea for Sacram. Test.* (1790) 39 The prevailing opinion of England is Latitudinarian. **1794** Sullivan *View Nat.* V. 200 There was a latitudinarian harmony..among the religions of the ancient world. **1812** Shelley *Proposals* Prose Wks. 1888 I. 273 It is a very latitudinarian system of morality that permits its professor to employ bad means for any end whatever. **1822-34** *Good's Study Med.* (ed. 4) IV. 470 Herpes..being ..by others extended so widely as to include both the preceding and the ensuing genus..and in the latitudinarian sense of the term, it is employed by Mr. B. Bell. **1827** Hallam *Const. Hist.* (1876) III. xiv. 56 The men most conspicuous in the reign of Charles II..were of the class who had been denominated Latitudinarian divines. **1849** Macaulay *Hist. Eng.* vii. II. 182 His opinions respecting ecclesiastical polity and modes of worship were latitudinarian. **1858** Longf. in *Life* (1891) II. 360 The sermon..very latitudinarian in doctrine.

B. *sb.* One who practises or favours latitude in thought, action, or conduct, esp. in religious matters; *spec.* one of those divines of the English Church in the 17th century, who, while attached to episcopal government and forms of worship, regarded them as things indifferent; hence, one who, though not a sceptic, is indifferent as to particular creeds and forms of church government or worship.

1662 S. P. *New Sect Latitude-men* 7 Our Latitudinarians ..are by all means for a Liturgy. **1669** Pepys *Diary* 16 Mar., Dr. Wilkins, my friend, the Bishop of Chester..is a mighty rising man, as being a Latitudinarian. **1676** Wycherley *Pl. Dealer* i. i, Why, thou art a Latitudinarian in Friendship, that is no Friend; thou dost side with all Mankind, but wilt suffer for none. *a* **1680** Butler *Rem.* (1759) II. 177 A Latitudinarian..believes the Way to Heaven is never the better for being strait. **1684** J. Goodman *Old Relig.* (1848) 42 To be such Latitudinarians, as to think it indifferent what religion a man be of. **1696** Phillips (ed. 5), *Latitudinarians in Religion*, are those who profess a Freedom, and as it were a greater Latitude than usual in their Principles and Doctrine. It is also vulgarly applied to such as take a more than ordinary Liberty in their Lives and Conversations. *a* **1700** B. E. *Dict. Cant. Crew*, *Latitudinarian*, a Churchman at large, one that is no Slave to Rubrick..and in fine looks towards Lambeth, and rowes to Geneva. **1705** Hearne *Collect.* 22 Nov. (O.H.S.) I. 92 This Discourse is a Justification of a *Latitudinarian* (the word was first hatch'd at Cambridge) against ye Zealous Nonconformists. **1753** Wesley *Eng. Dict.*, *Latitudinarian*, one who fancies all religions are saving. **1822** Syd. Smith *Wks.* (1867) II. 6 These latitudinarians leant to Arminianism rather than to high Calvinism. **1859** *All Year Round* No. 28. 38, 'I am afraid going abroad has made you a latitudinarian', she said, anxiously. **1862** R. Vaughan *Nonconformity* 393 According to Baxter, the Latitudinarians were mostly Cambridge men.

latitudinarianism (ˌlætɪtjuːdɪˈnɛərɪənɪz(ə)m). [f. prec. + -ism.] Latitudinarian doctrine, opinions, principles, or practice; the professions or practice of a latitudinarian or the latitudinarians.

1676 R. Grove *Vind. Conforming Clergy* (1680) 25 Let us see what he understands by this fearful Bugbear of Latitudinarianism. **1771** Wesley *Wks.* (1872) V. 502 A catholic spirit is not speculative latitudinarianism. **1844** Disraeli *Coningsby* iii. ii, There must be substituted for this latitudinarianism something sound and deep. *a* **1859** Macaulay *Biog.* (1867) 12 The majority of King William's bishops were inclined to latitudinarianism. **1867** Froude *Short Stud.* (ed. 2) 57 Latitudinarianism loosens the elementary principles of theology.

lati'tudinary, *a.* [f. L. *lātitūdin-* latitude + -ary.] = latitudinarian A.

1834 Sir W. Hamilton *Discuss.* (1852) 507 The latitudinary divines of Cambridge.

† **lati'tudinism.** *Obs.* [Formed as prec. + -ism.] = latitudinarianism.

1667 Locke *Toleration* in Fox Bourne *Life* (1876) I. iv. 194 Whether toleration and latitudinism would prevent those evils. **1685** M. Barne *Authority Ch. Guides* Pref. 4 Latitudinism in Principles is evermore accompanied with Libertinism in Practice.

latitudinous (lætɪˈtjuːdɪnəs), *a.* [Formed as prec. + -ous.] **1.** Characterized by latitude of interpretation.

1838 Calhoun *Wks.* III. 223 These [impediments].. ought to be irresistible with all, except the latitudinous in construction. **1865** Greeley *Amer. Confl.* I. viii. 82 These were..accused of seeking its subversion through.. latitudinous and unwarranted construction.

2. = latitudinal *a.*

1906 *Westm. Gaz.* 5 July 4/2 The race is not straight up to the limit of the earth's atmosphere and back again, but latitudinous.

lative (ˈleɪtɪv), *a.* *Gram.* [f. L. *lāt-* ppl. stem of *ferre* to bring + -ive.] Denoting the case used in some languages, e.g. of the Finno-Ugrian group, to express motion up to or as far as. Also *absol.* Cf. allative *a.*, elative *a.*

1939 L. H. Gray *Found. Lang.* vii. 194 The termination finds further analogues in..the Uralic lative and illative, the former indicating motion up to, and the latter motion to the interior of. *Ibid.* 195 The dative occasionally has, in Indo-Iranian, Latin, Teutonic, and Slavic, a lative force denoting the place toward which, in contrast to the illative force of the accusative. **1960** B. Collinder *Compar. Gram. Uralic Lang.* 239 The lative ending denoted that something is moving to the locality (or thing) expressed by the word stem. **1964** *Language* XL. 98 The same general discussion concerning the temporal function of the assumed Finno-Ugric lative case is presented twice.

‖**latke** (ˈlʌtkə). Also **lutka**, **lutke**. [Yiddish, a. Russ. *látka* a pastry.] In Jewish cookery, a pancake, esp. one made with grated potato.

1927 *Amer. Mercury* Feb. 206 Luscious potato *latkes*—pancakes made of grated, raw potatoes, [etc.]. **1958** J. Grossinger *Art Jewish Cookery* p. ix, A Jewish cookbook can be almost considered a history book... Just one instance —the *latke* (pancake), which the wives of the soldiers of.. Judah Maccabee hurriedly cooked for their men. **1964** W. Markfield *To Early Grave* (1965) iii. 50, I make a few *latkes*, I paint the kitchen chairs. **1967** A. Bailey in L. Deighton *London Dossier* 55 If you hunger after gefillte fish or latkes when in Soho, try Grahame's Sea Fare restaurant. **1971** M. Masson *Jewish Cookery* 44 Fry the *latkes* until a golden brown on both sides. **1974** *Times* 15 Oct. 13/8 He really does need a few more of my potato lutkas.

latli, rare obs. form of loathly.

latly, -most, etc.: see lately, latemost, etc.

latoen, -one, obs. forms of latten.

latomy (ˈlætəmɪ). *Hist. rare.* [ad. Gr. λᾱτομία, f. λᾶας, λᾶς stone + -τομία cutting.] A stone quarry; *spec.* of those at Syracuse.

1656 Blount *Glossogr.*, *Latomy*, a Quarry of stones. **1798** W. Taylor in *Monthly Rev.* XXV. 504 Were these embassies mere child's play, or were there Timoleons concealed in the latomies?

laton: see latten.

Latonian (ləˈtəʊnɪən), *a.* (*sb.*) [f. L. *Lātōni-us* f. *Lātōna*, a. Gr. (Æolic) Λάτων, (Doric) Λατώ, (Attic) Λητώ: see -an.] **A.** *adj.* Pertaining to Latona (= Gr. *Leto*), the mother of Apollo and Diana. **B.** *sb.* ***the Latonian***: Apollo.

1591 Sylvester *Du Bartas* i. iv. 538 Latonian Twins.. why hide you so your shining Fronts? **1656** Blount *Glossogr.* s.v., We use Latonian lights for the Sun and Moon (Latona's children). **1819** Shelley *Lett.* Prose Wks. 1880 IV. 82 A spectacle little suited to the antique and Latonian nature of the place. **1820** —— *Hymn to Mercury* lxxi, He.. Subdued the strong Latonian, by the might Of winning music.

latony, obs. form of litany.

† **'lator.** *Sc. Obs.* In 6 **latour**. [a. L. *lātor.*] The bearer (of a letter).

1529 Earl Angus in *St. Papers Hen. VIII*, IV. 562 As forthir the said latour can mair largely mak manifest unto zour Grace.

latosol (ˈlætəsɒl). *Soil Science.* [f. lat(erite + -o + -sol.] (See quot. 1949.)

1949 C. E. Kellogg in *Technical Communications Commonwealth Bureau Soil Sci.* No. 46. 79 We should like to suggest that some new term be adopted to comprehend all the zonal soils in tropical and equatorial regions having their dominant characteristics associated with low silica-sesquioxide ratios of clay fractions, low base-exchange capacities, low activities of the clay, low content of most primary minerals, low content of soluble constituents, a high degree of aggregate stability, and (perhaps) some red colour. The word 'Latosol' has been proposed as the name for this group at the categorical level of suborder... It is a collective term for those zonal soils previously called 'lateritic soils' where the characteristics just mentioned were dominant. **1955** K. Lawton in F. E. Bear *Chem. of Soil* ii. 68 In the group of soils considered to be laterites or latosols, aluminum and iron may make up a large proportion of the soil mass... Some ferruginous latosols contain as much as 60 per cent Fe_2O_3 and thereby could be classified as low grade iron ore. **1965** B. T. Bunting *Geogr. Soil* xvii. 199 In S. America, dark latosols occur in humid areas or on base-rich rocks; red latosols on acid materials and brown latosols on ash or basaltic terrain.

latoun, obs. or arch. form of latten.

Latour (latur, ləˈtʊə(r)). [Fr., ellipt. for *Château Latour*, the vineyard where it is produced.] A red Bordeaux wine from the Haut-Médoc district of France.

1833 [see château b]. **1920** G. Saintsbury *Notes on Cellar-Bk.* iv. 48, I think the best Latour rather better. **1931** S. Jameson *Richer Dust* iv. 79 Nicholas watched his scout pouring claret into Hugh's glass... A Latour of '93. **1935** *Punch* 28 Aug. 238/2 Ah, the Old Latour and the Old Lafite, And the Old Yquem which was not too sweet. **1958** J. W. Lambert in C. Ray *Compleat Imbiber* II. 200 How, despite one's best endeavours, they echo in the mind, those great names—Lafite, Margaux, Latour, Mouton-Rothschild. **1967** A. Lichine *Encycl. Wines* 321 Full-bodied and hard when young, Latour develops into something firm, rich, and noble. **1973** [see Lafite].

† **latra'bility.** *Obs.* [f. L. *lātrābil-is* barking + -ity.] The quality or faculty of barking.

1668 H. More *Div. Dial.* iii. xxxiv. (1713) 272 These rational Creatures may..agree all in Rationality; as the sundry species of Dogs here on Earth agree in Latrability.

latrant (ˈleɪtrənt), *a.* [ad. L. *lātrant-em*, pr. pple. of *lātrāre* to bark.] Barking. Chiefly *fig.*

1702 C. Mather *Magn. Chr.* vii. App. (1852) 620 The balant and latrant noises of that sort of people. **1706** Phillips (ed. Kersey), *Latrant*, barking; as *A Latrant Writer*, an Author that does nothing but bark and snarl at others. **1714** Tickell *Fragm. on Hunting* in Steele *Poet. Misc.* 178 The Minds and Genius of the Latrant Race. **1737** M. Green *Spleen* 464 Whose latrant stomachs oft molest The deep-laid plans their dreams suggest. **1861** R. Quin *Heather Lintie* (1866) 115 Thy latrant muse aye glooms sae sour.

† **latrate**, *v.* *Obs.*$^{-0}$ [f. L. *lātrāre* to bark: see -ate.] (See quots.)

1623 Cockeram, *Latrate*, to barke like a dog. *Ibid.* ii, To Carpe, *Conlatrate*, *Latrate*.

latration (ləˈtreɪʃən). [n. of action f. L. *lātrāre* to bark.] A barking; also *fig.*

1623 Cockeram, *Latration*, a barking. **1691** E. Rawson in *Andros Tracts* I. 68 It must needs be beneath a great Mind to take notice of such Latrations, or to answer them any otherwise than with contempt. **1824** *New Monthly Mag.* XI. 424 We have no three-headed dog chained at the gate of Tartarus to startle the visitants by his tri-lingual latrations. **1828** *Blackw. Mag.* XXIII. 194 If a dog bite a pig, the narrative teems with 'virus', the 'rabid animal', and the 'latration' of the patient.

‖**latrator.** *Obs.*$^{-0}$ [L. *lātrātor*, f. *lātrāre.*]

1623 Cockeram, *Latrator*, which barketh, or rayleth, or scoffeth.

† **latrede**, *a.* *Obs. rare.* [OE. *lætrǽde*, f. *læt* late *a.* + *rǽd* counsel, rede.] Slow, tardy.

c **897** K. Ælfred *Gregory's Past.* xx. 148 Oft mon bið swiðe wandigende æt ælcum weorce & swiðe lætræde. *c* **1386** Chaucer *Pars. T.* ⁋644 Whan a man is so latrede [*v.rr.* laterede, latred, lattred] or tarying er he wil torne to god.

latreutic (ləˈtruːtɪk), *a. rare.* [ad. Gr. λατρευτικ-ός pertaining to divine worship, f. λατρεύ-ειν: see latria.] Of the nature of latria.

1845 Lingard *Anglo-Sax. Ch.* II. x. 111 *note*, He venerates, indeed, the holy images, but pays latreutic worship to the Holy Trinity alone.

la'treutical, *a. rare.* [f. prec. + -al^1.] = prec.

1627 Bp. Hall *No Peace w. Rome* §19 That in the Sacred Supper there is a sacrifice..none of vs euer doubted: but that is then either latreuticall, as Bellarmine distinguishes it not ill, or eucharisticall. **1833** Rock *Hierurg.* I. 171 Sacrifice ..is severally denominated Latreutical, or of praise and supreme adoration, Eucharistic, or of thanks-giving, Propitiatory and Impetratory.

‖**latria** (ləˈtraɪə). *Theol.* Also 7 **latreia**. [late L. *latrīa*, a. Gr. λατρεία service, service to God, divine worship, f. λατρεύ-ειν to serve, serve with prayer.] In Roman Catholic language: The supreme worship which is due to God alone (distinguished from dulia and hyperdulia).

[**1426** Lydg. *De Guil. Pilgr.* 22952 Off this place, ffolkes alle, 'Latrya' they me calle. Myne offyce is moste in wakynge, To kepe the gate aboute the kynge.] **1526** *Pilgr. Perf.* (W. de W. 1531) 44 b, This latria is holy and due reuerence to god in prayers, vowes, tythes, othes and in the seruice of god. **1635** Pagitt *Christianogr.* i. iii. (1636) 131 It is the common opinion in Spaine and Italy that Latria, or divine honor, is due to the Crosse. **1645** —— *Heresiogr.* (ed. 2) 147 The Papists make two Degrees of Religious worship; the highest they call Latreia. **1845** Lingard *Anglo-Sax. Ch.* II. x. 111 The worship of latria due to God only, and that of dulia, the respect which may justly be shewn to his creatures. **1859** I. Taylor *Logic in Theol.* 225 What now becomes of the distinction between the dulia, and the hyper-dulia, and the latria?

Hence † **latrial**, † **latrian** *adjs. rare*, of the nature of latria.

1550 Bale *Apol.* 141 They can make false Goddes, and gyve to them latryall honoure. **1635** Pagitt *Christianogr.* ii. vii. (1636) 68 The Romists say that they give to the Saints

one kinde of worship, to wit, Dulian, and to God another and a greater, Latrian.

latrine (lə'triːn). Also 7 *Sc.* **latron, lateran.** [a. Fr. (chiefly in pl. *latrines*), a. L. *lātrīna* privy, contr. f. *lavātrīna*, f. *lavāre* to wash.] **1.** A privy, esp. in a camp, barracks, hospital, or similar place.

1642 SPALDING *Troub. Chas. I* (Bannatyne Club) II. 82 He also tirred the laterans in the Colledge, whereby the studentis had not sic naturall eisment as befoir. **1673–88** FOUNTAINHALL in M. P. Brown *Suppl. Decis.* (1826) III. 293 The public river of Tweed, whose use is common, and which dimits in the sea which is the latrons and receptacle of the universe. **1808** T. CRAUFURD *Univ. Edin.* 150, 1628 and 1629, the publick latrines..were built where now they stand. **1867** *Standard* 23 Nov. 3 The longer the occupation of the camp the greater necessity for good drainage, for making new and filling up old latrines. **1869** E. A. PARKES *Pract. Hygiene* (ed. 3) 311 Cesspits are now discontinued in most barracks, and water latrines are used. **1884** *Health Exhib. Catal.* 59/1 Enamelled Earthenware Latrine. **1897** HUGHES *Mediterr. Fever* v. 181 Latrines are for want of space often in close proximity to bed-rooms.

2. *attrib.* and *Comb.* **latrine rumour** *Services' slang*, a baseless rumour believed to originate in gossip in the latrines; also *absol.*

1918 in *Amer. Speech 1972* (1975) XLVII. 73 (*title of unofficial newspaper*) La Trine Rumor. **1925** in FRASER & GIBBONS *Soldier & Sailor Words* 140. **1929** F. A. POTTLE *Stretchers* (1930) i. 15 A 'latrine', we learned, was not only a building, but also the name for any particularly exciting but quite unfounded rumour emanating therefrom. **1929** A. W. WHEEN tr. *Remarque's All Quiet on W. Front* i. 15 Not for nothing was the word 'latrine rumour' invented; these places are the regimental gossip-shops and common-rooms. **1931** S. SOUTHWOLD in *Martial Medley* 105 This short essay ..confines itself mainly to the rumours current among the fighting forces, and generally referred to as latrine-rumours and dump-rumours. **1950** PARTRIDGE *Here, There & Everywhere* 76 Late in the [First] War, tersely (*eine*) *Latrine* —the English term being *latrine-rumour*.

latrinogram (lə'triːnəʊgræm). *Services' slang.* [f. LATRIN(E + -o + -GRAM.] = *latrine rumour* (LATRINE 2).

1944 [see DINKUM B. *adj.*]. **1946** [see *bush telegraph* s.v. BUSH *sb.*¹ 11]. **1947** D. M. DAVIN *Gorse blooms Pale* 203 According to current latrino-gram we were going to be given a rest. **1966** *Sunday Times* (Colour Suppl.) 4 Dec. 73/2 GI Jargon. *Latrinogram*, latrine rumour.

latrobite ('lætrəbaɪt). *Min.* [f. the name of its discoverer, the Rev. C. J. *Latrobe* + -ITE.] A pink variety of anorthite from Labrador.

1837 DANA *Min.* 299 Latrobite has been found only on Ametik island near the coast of Labrador.

†**latrocinate,** *v. Obs.*⁻⁰ [f. L. *latrōcinārī* to rob on the highway: see -ATE.] (See quot.)

1623 COCKERAM, *Latrocinate*, to rob, to play the theefe.

†**latrocination.** *Obs.*⁻⁰ [ad. L. *latrōcinātiōn-em*, f. *latrōcinārī* (see prec.).] (See quot.)

1656 BLOUNT *Glossogr.*, *Latrocination*, theft, robbery.

†**latrociny.** *Obs.* Also 5 **-synie, -cynye,** 7 **-cinie.** [ad. L. *latrōcini-um* highway-robbery, band of robbers, f. *latro*: see next. Cf. LARCENY.]

1. Highway-robbery, brigandage, freebooting, plundering.

c **1430** *Pilgr. Lyf Manhode* III. xvii. (1869) 144 Coutte bourse it is cleped, and latrosynie the defamede. **1607** TOPSELL *Four-f. Beasts* (1658) 263 These..possessed the Mountains and Desert places of Thessaly, being given to all manner of Latrociny and Deprædation. **1619** PURCHAS *Microcosmus* xlvii. 438 Publike Latrocinies, Rapes, Murthers, Hell vpon Earth. **1657** THORNLEY tr. *Longus' Daphnis & Chloe* 40 Escaping two dangers at once, shipwreck and latrociny.

2. A band of robbers. In quots. *transf.*

1474 CAXTON *Chesse* IV. i. (1860) I viij b, A royame wyth out habundaunce of goodes..may better be callyd a latrocynye or a nest of theuys than a royame. *c* **1643** *Maximes Unfolded* 35 Because the faction sought by force to prevaile, it was aptly called a Latrocinie. **1732** STACKHOUSE *Hist. Bible* III. v. (1752) I. 389 When..Oppression rul'd, and the Government was turn'd into a mere Latrociny.

†**latron.** *Obs.* [ad. L. *latrōn-em*, *latro*, hireling, mercenary, freebooter, robber. Cf. LADRONE.] A robber, brigand, plunderer.

1613 PURCHAS *Pilgrimage* II. vii. (1614) 133, I meane those Latron-patrons and Patron-latrons, whereof these extend to the vtmost whatsoeuer might, and whatsoeuer colour of right, in Exemptions, Customes, Priuiledges and prauileges whereby euery 'John-a Stile' shall intercept the Churches due. **1634** CANNE *Necess. Separ.* (1849) 272 In their writings against the prelates..they call them all latrons. **1657** THORNLEY tr. *Longus' Daphnis & Chloe* 108 Counting such actions to suit better with a Latron than the Grand Captain of an Army. **1658** J. JONES *Ovid's Ibis* 116 What may sacrilegious latrons expect? **1879** G. MEREDITH *Egoist* III. iii. 74 The hymeneal pair are licensed freebooters levying black mail on us;..I apprehend that Mr. Whitford has a lower order of latrons in his mind.

latron, obs. Sc. variant of LATRINE, LECTERN.

†'**latronage.** *Obs. rare*⁻¹. [f. LATRON + -AGE.] Robbery, brigandage.

1619 PURCHAS *Microcosmus* lxii. 624 Abusing..the Courts and Lawyers, to Patronize his Latronage and Violence.

latrosynie, variant of LATROCINY *Obs.*

la'truncular, *a. rare*⁻¹. [f. L. *latruncul-us* robber, piece in the game of 'latrunculi' + -AR.] Pertaining to the ancient Roman game of *latrunculi*, somewhat resembling draughts or chess.

1825 FOSBROKE *Encycl. Antiq.* (1843) II. 678 Circumstantial evidence supports Montfaucon in his latruncular origin of it [chess].

-latry, *-olatry*, representing Gr. -λατρεία worship, as in εἰδωλολατρεία IDOLATRY. Other examples, legitimately formed on possible Gr. types, are *angelolatry, astrolatry, bibliolatry, cosmolatry, demonolatry, grammatolatry, Mariolatry*, q.v. Hence, in humorous nonce-use, have been formed divers hybrids, as *babyolatry* (q.v.), *crochetolatry, dutiolatry, lordolatry*. Corresponding to this is the termination -*(o)later*, representing Gr. -λατρης, as in *idolater, bibliolater*.

1848 THACKERAY *Bk. Snobs* iii. (1892) 13 How should it be otherwise in a country where Lordolatry is part of our creed? **1859** F. E. PAGET *Curate of Cumb.*, etc. 330 She was immolating health and spirits in crochetolatry. **1891** *Harper's Mag.* Oct. 770/2 The question of how far the Puritan civilization has carried the cult of the personal conscience into mere dutiolatry.

lats: see LAT³.

latschipe, -som, -sum: see LATESHIP, -SOME.

latst, obs. form of LAST *a.*

latt: see LAIT *v.*, LATE, LET.

lattee, var. LATHI.

latteen, variant of LATEEN.

latten ('lætən). Forms: 4–5 (also 9 *arch.*) **latoun, latun,** 5–6 **latyn,** 5–7, 9 **laten,** (5 **latoen, -one**), 5–8 **latin,** 6 **lattinne, -oun, -yne, -yng, latynn,** 6–7 **latine, lattyn(n,** 6–9 **lattin,** (7 **laden**), 4– **laton,** 5– **latton, latten.** [a. OF. *laton, leiton*, mod.F. *laiton* = Pr. *lato*, Sp. *laton*, Pg. *latão*, Piedmontese *loton*, It. *ottone* (the initial *l* having been dropped through being mistaken for the def. article). The relation between these forms is obscure; if the Fr. form be original, it would point to a popular L. type **lactōn-em*; if the word was originally Sp., it may be a derivative of Com. Rom. **latta* lath, tin-plate (It. *latta*, Sp., Pg. *lata*, F. *latte*; of Teut. origin: see LATH). From Fr. the word was adopted into the Teut. and Slav. langs.: cf. Du. *latoen*, ON. *látun*, Russian *latun'*.]

1. A mixed metal of yellow colour, either identical with, or closely resembling, brass; often hammered into thin sheets. Now only *arch.* and *Hist.*

The word occurs not infrequently as a translation of L. *orichalcum*.

[**1339** in Riley *Lond. Mem.* (1868) 205 Sex Instrumenta de latone, vocitata Gonnes.] **1340** HAMPOLE *Pr. Consc.* 4367 His fete er like latoun bright Als in a chymne brynnand light. **1382** WYCLIF *1 Kings* vii. 45 Alle the vessels..weren of latoun [L. *de aurichalco*]. *c* **1386** CHAUCER *Prol.* 699 He hadde a croys of laton ful of stones. —— *Frankl. T.* 517 Phebus wax old and hewed lyk laton. **14..** *Sir Beues* (MS. M) 1134 Pelouris and durris were all of brasse, With laten sett and with glasse. *c* **1425** *Voc.* in Wr.-Wülcker 653/15 *Hoc auricalcum*, latone. **1494** FABYAN *Chron.* VI. clvi. 145 An horologe or a clocke of laten. **1528** MORE *Dyaloge* I. Wks. 132/2 Whan we se dayly a great pece of siluer, brasse, laten or yron drawen at length into smale wier. **1538** *Inv.* in *Archæologia* LI. 71 Itm the laton on the larestones, *vs.* **1553** *Inv. Ch. Goods, Stafford* in *Ann. Dioc. Lichfield* (1863) 49, ij candelstyks of lattyn, one crysmatorye of latten. **1582** N. T. (Rhem.) *Rev.* i. 15 And his feete like to latten as in a burning fornace. **1600** DEKKER *Fortunatus* Wks. 1873 I. 124 Whether it were lead or lattin that haspt downe those winking casements, I knowe not. **1639** FULLER *Holy War* III. xiii. (1840) 138 It was concluded, that they should not celebrate the sacrament in glass..but in chalices of latten. **1693** EVELYN *De la Quint. Compl. Gard., Direct. Melons* 4 The Noses of the Pipes might easily be Inserted into a larger Pipe of Laton. **1715** LEONI *Palladio's Archit.* (1742) I. 5 Latten ..is another sort of Copper colour'd with *Lapis Calaminaris*. **1885** R. F. BURTON *1001 Nts.* I. 141 A dome of yellow laton from Andalusia. **1890** W. MORRIS in *Eng. Illustr. Mag.* July 755 She brought him the hand-washing water in a basin of latten.

b. ***black latten*** = latten-brass (see 3 b). ***shaven latten***, a thinner kind than black latten. ***roll latten***, latten polished on both sides ready for use (Simmonds *Dict. Trade* 1858).

1660 *Act 12 Chas. II* c. 4 Sched. Rates Inwards, Lattin vocant blacke Lattin the hundred weight..ij *li.* shaven Lattin..iij *li.* vj *s.* viij *d.* **1714** *Fr. Bk. of Rates* 413 His Majesty..does permit the Danish and Swedish Ships to come loaded with..Latten-black, or ruled. **1812** J. SMYTH *Pract. of Customs* (1821) 120 Shaven Latten is distinguished from Black Latten by its thinness and brightness on both sides of the sheets.

2. Iron tinned over, tin-plate; more explicitly ***white latten***. Also, any metal made in thin sheets. Now *dial.*

1611 COTGR., *Fer blanc*, White Lattin. **1615** *De Montfort's Surv. E. Ind.* 37 A little hollow pipe of white latten. **1669** BOYLE *Contn. New Exp.* I. (1682) 43 Pipes of..Tin or Laton as they call thin Plates of Iron Tinn'd over. **1676** WORLIDGE *Cyder* (1691) 147 Your vessel ought to be of latten..the tin yielding no bad tincture to the liquor. **1706** PHILLIPS (ed. Kersey), *Latten* or *Lattin*, Iron tinn'd over. **1728** RUTTY in *Phil. Trans.* XXXV. 630 The making of Tin-plates, or Lattin, as it is called, being not commonly practised in England. **1799** G. SMITH *Laboratory* I. 238 The art of making tin plates or latten. **1812** J. SMYTH *Pract. of Customs* (1821) 120 Iron Plates tinned over are sometimes termed Latten. *a* **1825** in FORBY *Voc. E. Anglia*, *Latten*, We do not mean any mixed metal, but give the name to common tin-plate. **1875** KNIGHT *Dict. Mech.*, *Latten*, thin metal. Metal in sheets.

3. *attrib.* often passing into *adj.* = Consisting or made of latten.

1492 *Nottingham Rec.* III. 24, j laton bason, pretii ijs. **1513** DOUGLAS *Æneis* VII. Prol. 4 Cleir schynand bemys, and goldin symmeris hew, In lattoun colour altering haill of new. **1529** *Churchw. Acc. St. Giles, Reading* 37 Laten wire for the chyme. **1608** SYLVESTER *Du Bartas* II. iv. IV. *Decay* 944 A Dry-fat, sheath'd in latton plates with-out. **1623** WEBSTER *Devil's Law-Case* IV. ii, Here's a latten spoon, and a long one, to feed with the devil. **1655** MRQ. WORCESTER *Cent. Inv.* §39 A Lattin or Plate Lanthorn. **1670–1** NARBOROUGH *Jrnl.* in *Acc. Sev. Late Voy.* I. (1711) 37 In a hole of the Pool lay a Latten or Tin Box. **1673** SHADWELL *Epsom Wells* IV. ii. Wks. (1720) 248 No people in the world can make Lattin ware, or work our tin well but they. **1714** *Fr. Bk. of Rates* 270 Latin Plates or White Iron per Barrel containing 450 double Plates. **1729** SHELVOCKE *Artillery* v. 398 Bind it upon them with Iron or Lattin Wyre. **1825** SCOTT *Betrothed* xi, A latten chain will become me as well as beaten gold. **1865** SWINBURNE *Masque Q. Bersabe* 85 Low-barred latoun shot-windows. **1877** W. JONES *Finger-ring* 89 A massive latten thumb-ring.

b. latten-brass, milled brass in thin plates or sheets, used by braziers and for drawing into wire.

1676 W. B[ROWNE] *Man. Goldsm.* 97 The Grain Weights are made of pieces of thin Brass, commonly called Latin-Brass. **1812** J. SMYTH *Pract. of Customs* (1821) 120 Black Latten, or Latten Brass, is imported in thin sheets of various sizes, sometimes scraped with a knife.

¶ Used with a pun on *Latin*.

1607 BREWER *Lingua* III. v. F 2, Congealing English Tynne, Græcian Gold, Romaine Latine all in a lumpe. **1624** BEDELL *Lett.* vi. 96 The Barbarous not *Latine* but lead of the stile,..doe conuince them of falshood. **1631** BRATHWAIT *Whimzies* 119 Of all metals, hee hates Latin: for hee hath heard how it was sometime the Roman tongue. *a* **1655** SIR N. L'ESTRANGE in *Shaks. C. Praise* 282 [Alleged saying of Shaks.], I faith Ben: I'le e'en give him a douzen good Lattin Spoones, and thou shalt translate them.

lattener ('lætənə(r)). Also 4–5, 9 **latoner,** 5 **-enere, -ennare.** [f. LATTEN + -ER¹.] A worker in or maker of latten.

1392–3 *Earl Derby's Exped.* (Camden) 157 Et ij latoners per ij dies ij *s.* **1415** *York Myst.* Introd. 26 Latoners. *c* **1440** *Promp. Parv.* 288/2 Latenere, or latennare (*S.* latonere), *erarius.* **1885** *Athenæum* 17 Oct. 513/3 'Latten' or some other word connected with the craft of the founders and latoners.

latter ('lætə(r)), *a.* (*adv.*) Forms: 1 **lator** (*adv.*), **latera, lætra** (*adj.*), 2 **leter** (*adv.*), 3 **lattre,** 3–4 **latere,** 4–5 **lattere, latir, -yr,** (*Sc.* 5 **lattire,** 5–6 **letter,** 6 **-yr,** 6–7 **-er,** 7 ? **leater**), 3–6 **later** (and 6–7 in sense 5), 3– **latter.** [OE. *lætra* (fem. and neut. *-e*) adj., *lator* adv., compar. of *læt* LATE; cf. OFris. *letora, lettera* latter, Du. *later* later, MHG. *lazzer* later, ON. *latare* more sluggish.

The mod. LATER is a new-formation on the positive; it is difficult to determine how far it goes back, as the spelling *later* may have represented the form with short vowel even as recently as the 17th c.; in sense 5 *later* is here treated as a spelling of *latter* in the more recent as well as in the earlier examples.]

A. *adj.*

†**1.** Slower. OE. and early ME.

c **1000** *Laws Eccles. Instit.* §3 in Thorpe *Anc. Laws* II. 404 Þæt he þy lætra bið to uncystum. *c* **1000** ÆLFRIC *Exod.* iv. 10 (Gr.) Siððan þu spræce to þinum þeowe, ic hæfde þe lætran tungan. *c* **1205** LAY. 5911 Weoren heo of Rome alle ridinde, þa oðre a foten..and slowen alle here hors; here hæp wes þe lættere.

2. a. Belonging to a subsequent or comparatively advanced period; later. Sometimes contextually = 'second' (cf. LATTERMATH). Now only *poet.* or *arch.* with reference to periods of the year and their productions.

c **1200** ORMIN 15409 Þin forrme win iss swiþe god, Þin lattre win iss bettre. *Ibid.* 19984 Att Cristess lattre come. *c* **1230** *Hali Meid.* 7 Hire latere were is lasse wurð & lesse haueð þen hauede ear hire earre. **1596** DALRYMPLE tr. *Leslie's Hist. Scot.* I. 4 The lattir historiographors [called us] Albians, and the Realme Albanie. *Ibid.* 86 In thir lattir dayes ..is sa brocht to passe, that in the people is gretter constancie. **1611** BIBLE *Transl. Pref.* 3 We forbeare to descend to latter Fathers. —— *Joel* ii. 23 He will cause to come downe for you the raine, the former raine, and the latter raine in the first month. **1624** QUARLES *Job* xv. 19 My kindly words were welcome as a latter Raine. **1649** MILTON *Eikon.* 136 Former with latter steps in the progress of well doing need not reconcilement. **1662** STILLINGFL. *Orig. Sacr.* III. ii. §7 The latter Platonists. **1708** SWIFT *Sentim. Ch. Eng. Man* Wks. 1755 II. I. 54 The opinion and practice of the latter Cato. **1727** BRADLEY *Fam. Dict.*, *Eddish*,..the latter Pasture or Grass that comes after Mowing or Reaping. **1801** STRUTT *Sports & Past.* I. i. 7 These pursuits are said by latter writers to have been [etc.]. **1850** TENNYSON *In Mem.* l, Be near me when my faith is dry, And men the flies of latter spring. **1863** COWDEN CLARKE *Shaks. Char.* xv. 373 Gaunt suddenly fell away from him, like the latter snow.

1864 SWINBURNE *Atalanta* 1397 Pale as grass, or latter flowers.

b. † *latter-lady (in harvest)*, the Feast of the Nativity of the Virgin Mary (cf. LADY *sb.* 3 b). † *Latter Mary day (Saint Marie day the latter*, etc.), one of the later feasts of the Virgin Mary, as the Nativity, Sept. 8, or the Assumption, Aug. 15. † *latter meat (Sc.)*, 'victuals brought from the master's to the servant's table' (Jam.). *latter Lammas*: see LAMMAS.

11.. *O.E. Chron.* an. 1052 (MS. D.) þis wæs ȝedon .vii. nihton ær þære lateran sancta Maria mæssan. **1297** R. GLOUC. (Rolls) 7843 þe morwe after seinte mari day þe later [*v.r.* latter] ded he was. **15..** *Aberd. Reg.* XV. 617 (Jam.) At the assumptioune of our Lady callit the letter Mareday. **1541** *Ibid.* XVII. (Jam.), The nativite of our Lady callit the Lettir mareday nixt to cum. **1641** BEST *Farm. Bks.* (Surtees) 11 Tuppes beinge fedde are to bee kept noe longer then Latter-lady in harvest. **1660** J. LAMONT *Diary* (Maitland Club) 124 Johne Paterson, meason in Auchtermouchtie, strake throw new doores in the leater meate roume. **1721** RAMSAY *Elegy on Patie Birnie* xv, Ane's thrawart porter wadna let Him in while latter meat was hett.

3. a. Pertaining to the end of life, of a period, a temporal sequence, the world; = LAST. *Obs.* exc. *arch.* in *latter days*.

1513 DOUGLAS *Æneis* II. v. 93 We fey peple..Quham till this was the dulefull lettir day. *Ibid.* VIII. ix. 94 At lattyr poynt [L. *digressu supremo*] quhen thai war to depart. **1530** *Proper Dyaloge* (Arb.) 129 Your fraudes, almoste at the latter cast. **1535** COVERDALE *Jer.* xxiii. 20 In the latter dayes ye shall knowe his meanynge. *a* **1547** SURREY *Æneid* II. 414 The later day and fate of Troy is come. **1588** A. KING *Canisius' Catech.* I iiij, On ye letter day of december. *Ibid.* 15 In the letter day of iudgment. **1594** MARLOWE & NASHE *Dido* II. C 1 b, At whose latter gaspe Ioues marble statue gan to bend the brow. **1597** HOOKER *Eccl. Pol.* v. lvi. §9 That life which shall make them glorious at the later day. **1609** SKENE *Reg. Maj.* 35 She may make na disposition in her letter will, anent her husbands gudes and geir. *a* **1649** DRUMM. OF HAWTH. *Hist. Jas. V*, Wks. (1711) 114 The cardinal put in his hands some blank papers, of which they composed a latter-will. **1816** JEFFERSON *Writ.* (1830) IV. 296 All the latter years of aged men are overshadowed with its gloom. **1883** R. W. DIXON *Mano* I. iv. 11 This sign moreover doth St. John transmit, That in the latter days we shall be tricked By Satan's legates.

b. *latter end*: the concluding part (of a period etc.); the end of life, (one's) death. Also *punningly*, the posteriors.

c **1290** *S. Eng. Leg.* I. 256/33 In þe latere ende of Jeneuer. *a* **1400-50** *Alexander* 3891 Him limpis all þe loose be þe lattire end. *c* **1420** *Chron. Vilod.* 2219 In þe laterhende of þe office. **1422** tr. *Secreta Secret., Priv. Priv.* 135 He that hit wil not desyre, he shall atte the latyr ende be shente. *a* **1548** HALL *Chron., Hen. VIII* 243 b, In ye latter ende of this moneth. **1568** GRAFTON *Chron.* II. 292 From the later ende of Marche untill the later ende of July. **1630** PRYNNE *Anti-Armin.* 122 What is the chiefe grounde..of most mens delaying their amendment to their latter ends. **1697** DAMPIER *Voy.* 351 About the latter end of August. **1710** PALMER *Proverbs* 247 Death..shou'd never be spoken of in jest: for a man may play with almost any thing safer than his latter-end. **1845** M. PATTISON *Ess.* (1889) I. 17 At the latter end of the spring of 577. **1852** R. COOMBES in *Aquatic Notes Cambridge* 104 Throw the body forward with a spring, as if your latter end was made of Indian-rubber. **1893** G. E. MATHESON *About Holland* 10 The latter end of the Rhine is not so romantic..as its earlier career in Germany.

† **4.** *Sc.* Hinder, hindmost. *Obs.*

1533 BELLENDEN *Livy* II. (1822) 199 The Volschis.. followit feirsly on the latter skirtis of thair armye.

5. a. That has been mentioned second of two, last of a group of more than two, or at or near the end of a preceding clause or sentence: opposed to *former*.

1555 in Strype *Eccl. Mem.* III. App. xliv. 126 This latter sort..are more hated in the sight of God than the other. **1632** SANDERSON *Serm.* 58 Of the later sort are such outward actions [etc.]. **1755** JOHNSON s.v. *Disloyal* 4 The three latter senses are now obsolete. **1780** BENTHAM *Princ. Legisl.* xvii. §6 The latter mode is not less certain than the former. **1922** JOYCE *Ulysses* 616 'Eaten alive?' a third asked the sailor. 'Ay, ay,' sighed again the latter personage. **1957** B. & C. EVANS *Dict. Contemp. Amer. Usage* 267/2 *Latter* is the older of the two comparative forms... Its chief function is as a contrast to *former*. The contrast implies that some group has been separated into two parts, but more than two elements may be involved. We may say *the three latter events*. **1971** *Guardian* 24 Dec. 17/5 The Berlin Wall stands unbreached, passes are needed to get into Bethlehem and Father Christmas has been arrested in Oxford Street. It's the latter item that fascinates me.

b. *absol.* or *ellipt.*

1608 SHAKS. *Per.* III. ii. 29 Vertue and Cunning Were endowments greater then Noblenesse & Riches; Carelesse Heyres May the two latter darken and expend; But Immortalitie attendes the former Making a man a god. **1611** BIBLE *Transl. Pref.* 8 To the later we answere; that wee doe not deny [etc.]. **1678** YOUNG *Serm. at Whitehall* 29 Dec. 7 The Civilians distinguishing a Law into parts, the Preceptive Part,..and the Distributive Part,..are pleas'd to call this later the *Sanction*..of the Law. **1841** [see FORMER *a.* 2 b]. **1853** [see FILL-UP *sb.*]. **1870** F. R. WILSON *Ch. Lindisf.* 99 A nave and chancel, with a vestry on the north side of the latter. **1903** G. B. SHAW *Man & Superman* 230 When a man teaches something he does not know to somebody else who has no aptitude for it, and gives him a certificate of proficiency, the latter has completed the education of a gentleman. **1922** JOYCE *Ulysses* 680 The former returned to the latter..a sum of money..advanced by the latter to the former. **1926** H. W. FOWLER *Mod. Eng. Usage* 316/2 *The latter* should not be used when more than a pair are in question, as in: The difficult problems involved in the early association of Thomas Girtin, Rooker, Dayes, & Turner are well illustrated..; & what was undoubtedly the best period of the latter artist is splendidly demonstrated... Neither should it be used when less than two are in question; the public and its shillings cannot be reasonably regarded as a pair of things on the same footing in: The mass of the picture-loving public, however, may be assured of good value for the shillings—whatever be the ultimate destination of the latter. **1928** [see LENATE *v.*]. **1938** *Amer. Speech* XIII. 28 Faith, hope and charity are virtues, but few possess them, particularly the latter. **1970** LOFTS & ADLEY *Saint* ii. 15 Another story..was written under the *nom de plume* of 'Leslie C. Bowyer'—the latter being his mother's maiden name. **1974** A. HUXLEY *Plant & Planet* xvi. 177 Light is also essential to the germination of many seeds such as tobacco, foxglove, many primulas and some lettuces. The dark-induced dormancy of the latter can be broken by quite low illumination.

† **B.** *adv.* **a.** More slowly. **b.** Later. *Obs.*

c **1050** *Byrhtferth's Handboc* in *Anglia* (1885) VIII. 324 Ne lator þon .ii. id. martii. *c* **1175** *Lamb. Hom.* 15 Eour eyþer sunegað bi-foran drihten and ec leter ȝe beoð sahte. *a* **1200** *Moral Ode* 131 Oðer raðer oðer later; milce he scal imeten. *c* **1200** ORMIN 13206 Þohhwheþþre comm he lattre till To lefenn uppo Criste. **1362** LANGL. *P. Pl.* A. I. 173 Þat nis no treuþe of Trinite but tricherie of helle, And a leornyng for lewed men þe latere [*v.rr.* latter(e] forte dele. *c* **1400** *Lanfranc's Cirurg.* 217 Ful seelden it comeþ of colre, & more lattere of malancoli. **1413** *Pilgr. Sowle* (Caxton 1483) v. xiv. 109 The sone dependeth of the fader nouther more ne lesse neither latter ne rather than the fader. **1422** tr. *Secreta Secret., Priv. Priv.* 220 More latre Is he [the Malencoly man] wourthe than a colerike man.

Comb. **1590** SHAKS. *Com. Err.* I. i. 79 My wife, more careful for the latter borne.

latter, variant of LAUGHTER.

'latter-day, *adj. phr.* Belonging to 'the latter days'; modern. **Latter-day Saints**, the name by which the Mormons call themselves.

1842 CASWALL *City of Mormons* 22 On the door..was an inscription to the following effect: 'Office of Joseph Smith, President of the Church of Latter Day Saints'. **1850** CARLYLE (*title*) Latter-day Pamphlets. **1851** MAYHEW *Lond. Labour* I. 22 Neither the Latter-day Saints nor any similar sect, have made converts among the costermongers. **1855** TROLLOPE *Warden* xiv. 222 The painting of some of these latter-day pictures [*sc.* of the Pre-Raffaellite School]. **1884** *Manch. Exam.* 29 Feb. 5/3 The whole circumstances were thoroughly mediæval from a latter-day English point of view. **1897** DOWDEN *Fr. Lit.* IV. iv. 329 André Chénier..a latter-day Greek or demi-Greek himself.

latterkin ('lætəkɪn). Also 7 **laperkin**, 9 ?**latherkin** (Simmonds 1858). A glazier's tool used in making lead-lights (see quot. 1825).

1688 R. HOLME *Armoury* III. 384/1 In this square are three Glasiers Tools; the first..is termed a Laperkin. It is a short piece of Wood made streight on one edge [etc]..With this, being a kind of Ruler he [the Workman] cuts Quarries of any Size. **1825** J. NICHOLSON *Operat. Mechanic* 638 The latterkin is a piece of hard wood pointed, to run in the groove of the lead, and widen it for the easier reception of the glass. **1859** GWILT *Encycl. Archit.* (ed. 4) 586.

latterly ('lætəlɪ), *adv.* [f. LATTER *a.* + -LY².]

a. At the latter end (of life or of some period). **b.** Of late, lately.

1734 J. RICHARDSON *Life Milton* 2 Latterly he [Milton] was—No; Not Short and Thick, but [etc]. **1735-6** PEGGE *Kenticisms* (E.D.S.) *Latterly*, adv., the latter part of his time. **1755** JOHNSON, *Latterly*,..a low word lately hatched. **1762-71** H. WALPOLE *Vertue's Anecd. Paint.* (1786) IV. 143 He died Sept. 23, 1766, at Hammersmith, though latterly he resided chiefly at Bath. **1821** J. FOSTER in *Life & Corr.* (1846) II. 46 A languid tone of health into which I have latterly fallen. **1883** GILMOUR *Mongols* xxix. 339 He..gave away so much that, latterly, he had little left. **1885** *Manch. Exam.* 24 Feb. 5/1 If there has been anything like an increase of ill-feeling latterly.

lattermath ('lætəmɑːθ, -mæθ). *dial.* Also 6-7 **latermath(e**, 7 **latter-meath**, **leather-math**. [f. LATTER *a.* + MATH (OE. *mǽþ*) mowing.] The 'latter' mowing; the aftermath. Also, the crops then reaped.

1530 PALSGR. 237/2 Latermathe. **1587** HARRISON *England* I. xviii. (1881) III. 133 Of such [medowes] as are twise mowed I speake not, sith their later math is not so wholsome ..as the first. **1611** COTGR., *Arriere-saison*, later math. **1660** *Charac. Italy* 84 Some Soyls..afford four Latter-meaths of Hay. **1692** TRYON *Good House-wife* vii. (ed. 2) 70 [Butter made in Summer] is much finer than that which is made of Rowings or Leather-Math (as they call it). **1736** AINSWORTH *Lat. Dict.* s.v. *Cordus*, *Fœnum cordum*, the latter math. **1813** SIR H. DAVY *Agric. Chem.* (1814) 363 Grasses..which afford..the greatest quantities of spring, summer, lattermath and winter produce. **1880** JEFFERIES *Gt. Estate* 128 The aftermath, or, as country people call it, the 'lattermath'.

'lattermint. *rare.* [f. LATTER *a.* + MINT *sb.*] ? A late kind of mint.

1818 KEATS *Endym.* IV. 579 Savory, latter-mint, and columbines.

lattermost ('lætəməʊst), *a.* [f. LATTER *a.* + -MOST.] Last.

1821 *Blackw. Mag.* X. 116 Domesticus, the foremost man, is not more of a ring-leader..than Mr. and Mrs. Crux, the lattermost. **1879** E. ARNOLD *Lt. Asia* VIII. 222 Fresh Issues upon the Universe that sum Which is the lattermost of lives.

lattern, Sc. form of LECTERN.

† **'latterness.** *Obs. rare*⁻¹. [f. LATTER *a.* + -NESS.] The condition of being later or subsequent.

1674 N. FAIRFAX *Bulk & Selv.* 14 Any other word that can ..cut off all formerness and latterness.

† **'latterward**, *a. Obs. rare*⁻¹. [f. LATTER + -WARD.] = LATEWARD.

1572 MASCALL *Plant. & Graff.* (1651) 43 Ye shall graffe them on a latterward fruit, as Pome Richard.

† **'lattew.** *Obs.* Forms: 1 **ládþéow**, **-téaw**, **-t(é)ow**, **láðððéow**, **látéau**, **-éaw**, **-éow**, **látðéow**, **-téow**, **-téuw**, **-tíow**, *Northumb.* **látua**, 2 **ladtew**, **læd-**, **lætteow**, 3 **latðæu**, **latteu**, **lattow**. [OE. *ládtéow*, *látteów*, *látðéow*, f. *lád* leading, LODE + *þéow* servant, THEW.] A leader.

c **825** *Vesp. Psalter* xxx. 4 Ladtow me ðu bist. *c* **888** K. ÆLFRED *Boeth.* xxxiii. §5 þa eart ægðer ȝe weȝ, ȝe ladþeow, ȝe sio stow ðe se weȝ to liȝð. *c* **1200** *Trin. Coll. Hom.* 161 For þat þe storres liht is hem god latðæu. *Ibid.* 197 Alse mannes heued is heȝest lime and latteu swo wisseð rihtte bi-leue þe soule. *a* **1225** *Juliana* 33 Lauerd liues lattow lead me þurh þis ..lif.

lattice ('lætɪs), *sb.* Forms: 4 **latijs**, **latis**, *pl.* **latises**, **-is**, 4-6 **latys**, 5 **lates**, **lateys(e**, 5-6 **latyse**, 6 **lateis**, **latesse**, **latise**, **lattes(e**, **-is**, **lettise**, *pl.* **lattas(s)es**, 6-7 **lattesse**, 6-8 **lattise**, **lettice**, 7 **latice**, **latteise**, *pl.* **lettases**, 6- **lattice**. [a. OF. and F. *lattis*, f. *latte* LATH.]

1. a. A structure made of laths, or of wood or metal crossed and fastened together, with open spaces left between; used as a screen, e.g. in window openings and the like; a window, gate, screen, etc. so constructed.

1382 WYCLIF *Prov.* vii. 6 Fro the windowe..of myn hous bi the latys I beheeld the ȝunge man. **14..** *Chaucer's Troylus* II. 566 (615) (Harl. MS. 3943) A! go we see, caste up the latis [*v.r.* yates] wyde, For thurgh this strete he most to palays ryde. *c* **1440** *Gesta Rom.* lxxx. 400 (Add. MS.) The pareshe preste..sate at his selle, and lokede oute at his latyse towarde the kyrke. **1452-3** in Willis & Clark *Cambridge* (1886) II. 449 Pro factura x lateys in deambulatorio. *c* **1475** *Partenay* 4747 He..The lateis unshitte. **1562** J. HEYWOOD *Prov. & Epigr.* (1867) 116 Lattise keepeth out the light and letth in the winde. **1569** *Bury Wills* (Camden) 155 The glasse lattases and bourdes belonginge to the howse. **1611** BIBLE *2 Kings* i. 2 Ahaziah fel downe thorow a lattesse in his vpper chamber. *a* **1674** MILTON *Hist. Mosc.* Wks. 1738 II. 130 Small Windows, some of Glass, some with Latices, or Iron Bars. **1693** EVELYN *De la Quint. Compl. Gard.* II. 114 A Lattice of narrow Laths nail'd a cross one another checker-wise, every square consisting of about twelve Inches. **1717** LADY M. W. MONTAGU *Let. to Lady Rich* 1 Apr., They are made a good deal in the manner of the Dutch stage coaches, having wooden lattices painted and gilded. **1741** tr. *D'Argens Chinese Lett.* xxv. 172 When they don't choose to be concealed, they open the Lettices. **1814** SCOTT *Ld. of Isles* v. i, The sunbeam, through the narrow lattice, fell Upon the snowy neck [etc.]. **1822** BYRON *Werner* v. i. 44 The flowers fell faster—Rain'd from each lattice at his feet. **1866** ROGERS *Agric. & Prices* I. xx. 488 The diamond shape of the glass of old casements was suggested by the ancient lattice.

fig. **1621** DONNE *Progr. Soul, 2nd Anniv.* Poems (1639) 243 Thou shalt not peepe through lattices of eyes, Nor heare through Labyrinths of eares. **1642** FULLER *Holy & Prof. St.* v. xiii. 409 He will..creep out at the lattice of a word. **1670** *Devout Commun.* (1688) 93 Stand not at a distance behind the walls: shew thyself through the lattice of thy ordinance. **1742** YOUNG *Nt. Th.* III. 473 Life's a debtor to the grave, Dark lattice! letting in eternal day. **1850** TENNYSON *In Mem.* lxx, Thro' a lattice on the soul Looks thy fair face and makes it still.

† **b.** A window of lattice-work (usually painted red), or a pattern on the shutter or wall imitating this (see CHEQUER *sb.*¹ 4), formerly a common mark of an alehouse or inn. *Obs.*

1575 GASCOIGNE *Glasse Govt.* IV. vi, There, at a howse with a red lattyce, you shall finde an old baude..and a yong damsell. **1589** R. HARVEY *Pl. Perc.* (1590) 15 As they which determine vpon an Ale bench whether the passenger that passeth by the lettise be a Saint or a Diuell. **1592** *Arden of Faversham* H 2, He..had beene sure to haue had his Signe puld down, & his latice borne away the next night. **1594** PLAT *Jewell-ho.* II. 15 Some Alewiues, if they had knowne this receipt..wold haue hung out holly bushes at their red lettises, and so they might haue beene mistaken for Tauerns, of many ale knights. **1597** SHAKS. *2 Hen. IV*, II. ii. 86 He call'd me euen now (my Lord) through a red Lattice. **1598** B. JONSON *Ev. Man in Hum.* III. iii, At the signe of the water-tankerd, hard by the greene lattice. **163.** WOTTON *Educ.* in *Reliq.* (1672) 97 Amongst Tradesmen..they are not poorest, whose Shop windows open over a red Lettice. **1639** MAYNE *City Match* I. ii, If he draw not A Lattice to your doore, and hang a bush out. **1689** SHADWELL *Bury F.* I. i, She by Art makes her face look like a new white wall with a red lettice. **1735** DYCHE & PARDON *Dict.*, *Lattice*..with us now is generally an ensign of an Alehouse, which to make it the more conspicuous is commonly painted of various Colours, and those who have not a real Wooden one up at their Door, cause Chequers or Squares like 'em to be painted on their Window-shutters, Walls or Side-posts of the Door, &c.

c. Work of the kind described in 1; lattices collectively; = LATTICE-WORK. Also *fig.*

1577 HARRISON *England* II. xii. (1877) I. 236 Our countrie houses, in steed of glasse, did use much lattise. **1597** SHAKS. *Lover's Compl.* 14 Some beauty peept through lettice of sear'd age. **1601** —— *All's Well* II. iii. 225 My good window of Lettice fare thee well. **1611** CORYAT *Crudities* 50 The vpper part of the window..is made of glasse or lattise. **1890** F. G. CARPENTER in *Amer. Agriculturalist* Oct. 512 (Funk) Rude frames of lattice filled with greased paper to act as windows.

2. *transf.* **a.** Something with open interlaced structure like that of a lattice.

1657 TOMLINSON *Renou's Disp.* Pref., This harmless Essay..may..induce your charity to connive at our imbecillity, by glancing through the Lattice of a diminishing Telescope. **1684** R. WALLER *Nat. Exper.* 132 Taking a sheet

of Paper, we made several little Lattices in it. **1895** C. R. B. BARRETT *Surrey* iii. 91 An oak tree with a curiously twisted lattice of roots.

b. *Her.* A charge representing lattice-work.

1828 W. BERRY *Encycl. Heraldica* I, *Lattice*, or *Lettice*, .. is formed of perpendicular and horizontal bars, .. and the lattice may be either interlaced, or not. **1889** C. N. ELVIN *Dict. Heraldry* 82/2 *Lattice*, *Tirlace*, or *Treilée*, consists of bars crossing one another at right angles, which do not interlace, but are nailed together at the crossings. **1969** FRANKLYN & TANNER *Encycl. Dict. Heraldry* 199 *Lattise*, .. alt. for 'trellis'.

c. In textile manufacture, a lattice-work apron or conveyer used to carry material into or out of a machine.

1884 W. S. B. MCLAREN *Spinning* x. 213 The wool is taken from it by a roller which combs it off, and passes it on to an endless lattice, marked 'upper lattice'. **1890** J. NASMITH *Mod. Cotton Spinning Machinery* iii. 19 In each case it is customary to attach lattices to the machine, by which the cotton is thoroughly broken up. **1967** SHAW & ECKERSLEY *Cotton* xi. 77 The machine employs a lattice and rollers to feed the thread waste to a revolving cylinder covered with steel spikes.

d. *Electr.* = *lattice network* (see 4).

1934 A. T. STARR *Electr. Circuits & Wave Filters* vi. 198 The lattice needs twice as many components as the bridged-T network. **1950** W. C. JOHNSON *Transmission Lines & Networks* xiv. 303 The filters most generally used are made up of T or π sections and L 'half sections' connected on an image basis to form a ladder network... A more general structure, called the lattice, is shown in Fig. 14.3. Not only can the performance of any T or π be duplicated at all frequencies by a lattice, but a lattice can be designed to provide characteristics unobtainable with the T or π. **1960** M. E. VAN VALKENBURG *Introd. Mod. Network Synthesis* xii. 339 If there is any symmetrical network realization for a set of specification functions at all, then there is a symmetrical lattice realization.

†3. A part of the auditorium of a theatre (see quot.). *Obs.*

1818 J. WARBURTON etc. *Dublin* II. 1113 Boxes 5*s.* 5*d.*; lattices 4*s.* 4*d.*; pit 3*s.* 3*d.*; gallery 2*s.* 2*d.* *Ibid.* 118 *note*, The interior of the house [*c* 1793] formed an ellipse, and was divided into three compartments—pit, boxes, and lattices, which were without division.

4. a. Any regular arrangement of points or point-like entities that fills a space, area, or line; *spec.* a crystal lattice or a space lattice; **Bravais lattice** ('brævei) [named after Auguste *Bravais* (1811–63), French physicist], any lattice in which every point has exactly the same environment (as regards the distances and directions of other points of the lattice); *spec.* any of the fourteen different lattices of this kind in three dimensions (cf. *space lattice*); **crystal lattice**, the space lattice underlying the arrangement of atoms or molecules in a crystal; also, the arrangement of points occupied by the atoms or molecules or of the atoms or molecules themselves.

1895 W. J. POPE tr. *Fock's Introd. Chem. Crystallogr.* ii. 12 Frankenheim .. found that fifteen different space-lattices are possible, and then, having deduced from the cleavage and general habit of the crystals that fifteen fundamental forms of crystals are possible, he showed that these latter in many respects correspond with the lattices. Frankenheim's views are not in all respects correct. **1917** *Physical Rev.* X. 441 Manganblende, MnS, is a simple cubic lattice like rock salt. **1926** [see *crystal lattice* s.v. CRYSTAL B. 2c]. **1927** T. VERSCHOYLE tr. *Haas's Atomic Theory* iii. 58 From the one-dimensional line-lattice, let us now pass to the two-dimensional plane-lattice, which will be formed by points with the coordinates $x = k_1a$, $y = k_2b$ constructed in a plane coordinate system, where *a* and *b* are two lattice constants, and k_1 and k_2 can assume every integral value. **1934** *Nature* 16 June 916/1 The electron extracted from the atom may only move through the periodic field of the lattice with certain discrete energies. **1935** *Discovery* May 132/2 The patterns in which the atoms or charged atoms are arranged are often called lattices. There are 'face-centred' lattices, and 'body-centred' lattices, hexagonal close-packed lattices, and so on. **1936** *Mineral. Abstr.* VI. 323 Recently structures have been suggested, e.g. for α-AgI, in which equivalent points are not completely filled or are occupied by different sorts of particles. These structures are said to have 'defect lattices'. **1938** W. A. WOOSTER *Text-bk. Crystal Physics* 280 A Bravais lattice is one of the fourteen possible arrangements of the points in space which have crystallographic symmetry. **1955** *Mineral. Mag.* XXX. 625 There are in all twenty types of lattices, as defined by their symmetry element[s]: one one-dimensional, five two-dimensional, and fourteen three-dimensional. *Ibid.* 626 All lattices are formed by translations, and all are characterized by inversion. **1958** W. K. MANSFIELD *Elem. Nucl. Physics* v. 39 These displacements distort solid lattices, producing effects similar to cold working, and decrease the electrical and thermal conductivity. **1966** C. R. TOTTLE *Sci. Engin. Materials* iii. 67 The crystal lattice of an ionic compound depends on the size of the ions and on their valency. **1969** A. P. CRACKNELL *Crystals* ii. 56 The mathematical condition to be satisfied in the definition of a lattice is quite stringent... In fact there are only five two-dimensional Bravais lattices. **1970** A. J. C. WILSON *Elem. X-Ray Crystallogr.* iv. 52 Thirteen of the fourteen Bravais lattices (all except the triclinic lattice) possess at least one reflexion plane passing through each point of the lattice. **1971** I. G. GASS et al. *Understanding Earth* i. 11/2 The halite lattice is built on a simple pattern in which sodium particles and chlorine particles occupy alternate corners of a continuously repeated set of cubes.

b. *Nuclear Engin.* An array of fuel and moderator in the core of a nuclear reactor.

1945 H. D. SMYTH *Gen. Acct. Devel. Atomic Energy Mil. Purposes* ii. 21 The steady production of atomic power requires a slow-neutron-induced fission chain reaction occurring in a mixture or lattice of uranium and moderator. **1959** H. JACOBOWITZ *Fund. Nucl. Energy & Power Reactors* iii. 50 The Bulk Shielding Reactor comprises little more than an assembly of enriched uranium fuel elements immersed in water. The height of the active lattice is 24 inches. **1960** S. E. LIVERHANT *Elem. Introd. Nucl. Reactor Physics* vii. 178 If the lattice or matrix arrangement (i.e., a heterogeneous system) is employed, a chain reaction becomes possible with natural uranium and graphite as moderator. **1973** *Jrnl. Nucl. Energy* XXVII. 458 For water-beryllium lattices, the band structure and Nelkin's expansion .. is [*sic*] computed for various directions.

5. *Math.* A partially ordered set in which every pair of elements has an infimum and a supremum.

1933 G. BIRKHOFF in *Proc. Cambr. Philos. Soc.* XXIX. 442 If we define a lattice to be any set of elements satisfying [axioms] I–VI, we can express our results as Theorem 3·1: The subalgebras of any algebra constitute a lattice. *Ibid.*, [F.] Klein calls a finite lattice a 'Verband'. **1951** N. JACOBSON *Lect. Abstr. Algebra* I. vii. 208 Boolean algebras were the first lattices to be studied. They were introduced by Boole in order to formalize the calculus of propositions. **1964** H. G. FLEGG *Boolean Algebra* iii. 18 The algebra of classes is frequently referred to as Boolean algebra. A rigorous treatment of the algebra has been made by Garrett Birkhoff and Saunders MacLane and of its generalizations, lattice theory, by Birkhoff alone. **1965** S. WARNER *Mod. Algebra* I. iii. 105 An ordered structure $(E, \leq)$ is a lattice and $\leq$ is a lattice ordering if for all $x, y \in E$, the subset $\{x, y\}$ of E admits a supremum and an infimum. **1966** *McGraw-Hill Encycl. Sci. & Technol.* VII. 409/2 Lattice theory deals with properties of order and inclusion, much as group theory treats symmetry. *Ibid.*, The real numbers form a lattice, if $x \leq y$ is given its usual meaning... Again, the set J of positive integers forms a lattice, if one lets $m \leq n$ mean '*m* divides *n*'.

6. *attrib.* and *Comb.*, as ***lattice-blind***, ***-bough***, ***-box***, ***-closing***, ***-edge***, ***-fence***, ***-floor***, ***-hole***, ***-maker***, ***-mast***, ***-nail***, ***-ornament***, ***-pane***, ***-pattern***, ***steel***; **lattice-bar** *Bridge-building* (see quot.); **lattice beam** = *lattice girder*; **lattice-braid**, a narrow lattice-like braid made on the lace-pillow (Caulfeild and Saward *Dict. Needlework* 1882 p. 43); **lattice-bridge** (see quot. 1857); **†lattice caltrop** (see quot.); **lattice-cell** (see quot. and cf. LATTICED 2b); **lattice conductivity** *Physics*, the contribution to the thermal conductivity of a crystalline substance arising from transfer of energy between the vibrating atomic nuclei in the crystal lattice; so ***lattice conduction***; **lattice constant** *Cryst.*, the length of a side, or the size of an angle, of the unit cell of a lattice; *spec.* the length of each of the sides of the unit cell of a cubic lattice; **lattice defect** *Cryst.*, an irregularity in a crystal lattice such as a missing atom or an interstitial one; **lattice energy** *Physics*, the energy required to separate the ions of a crystal to an infinite distance from one another; **lattice filter** *Electr.*, a filter consisting of components connected so as to form a lattice network; **lattice frame, girder**, a girder consisting of two horizontal bars connected by diagonal bars crossed so as to resemble lattice-work; **lattice leaf (plant)**, the *Ouvirandra fenestralis* or lace-leaf of Madagascar; also **lattice plant**; **lattice moss**, a moss of the genus *Cinclidotus*; **lattice network** *Electr.*, a network having four impedances and two pairs of terminals, each terminal of one pair being connected by an impedance to each of the other pair; **lattice plane** *Physics*, any plane containing lattice points; a layer of atoms or molecules in a crystal; **lattice point** *Math.* (*a*) a point on a graph or in space having integral coordinates; (*b*) any of the points of which a lattice, esp. a crystal lattice, is composed; **lattice-stitch** (see quot.); **lattice-truss**, 'one having horizontal chords and inclined intersecting braces' (Knight *Dict. Mech.* 1875); **lattice vibration** *Physics*, an oscillation of an atom or molecule about its equilibrium position in a crystal lattice; also, a lattice wave; **lattice wave** *Physics*, a displacement of atoms or molecules from their equilibrium position in a crystal which travels as a wave through the crystal; **lattice-wise** *adv.*, in the form of a lattice or lattice-work.

1885 WADDELL *Syst. Iron Railr. Bridges Japan* 246 **Lattice-bar*, a bar belonging to a system of latticing. **1850** G. D. DEMPSEY *Iron Girder Bridges* iv. 36 *Lattice beams. **1832** TENNYSON *Mariana in S.* 87 Backward the *lattice-blind she flung. **1878** SYMONDS *Many Moods* 175 The star of Love, those *lattice-boughs between. **1865** 'MARK TWAIN' *Celebr. Jumping Frog* (1867) 16 Smiley kept the beast in a little *lattice box. **1838** D. STEVENSON *Civil Engin. N. Amer.* viii. 231 Town's Patent *Lattice Bridge. **1857** HUMBER *Iron Bridges & Girders* 14 The Trellis Girder or Lattice Bridge, consisting of a top and bottom flange connected by a number of flat iron bars which are rivetted across each other at a certain angle, thus forming a lattice. **1497** *Nav. Acc. Hen. VII* (1896) 97 *Latescaltraps [*Footnote*, Perhaps coltraps united by lattice work or rods forming a kind of *cheval-de-frise*, and thus distinguished from 'casting caltrops']. **1888** *Syd. Soc. Lex.*, **Lattice-cells*, in Botany, Mohl's term for cells whose walls are irregularly thickened in such a manner as to form a kind of net-work sculptured in relief. *c* **1425** *St. Eliz. of Spalbeck* in *Anglia* VIII. 114/46 þe chapel is departyd fro þe chaumbyr wiþ a smalle *latys-closynge. **1938** *Proc. Cambr. Philos. Soc.* XXXIV. 475 The *lattice conduction is shown to be important in poor conductors. **1971** I. G. GASS et al. *Understanding Earth* v. 86/2 At moderate temperatures .. heat transfer in rocks is almost entirely by 'lattice conduction'. **1938** *Proc. Cambr. Philos. Soc.* XXXIV. 474 In good conductors the *lattice conductivity is unimportant. **1962** *Physical Rev.* CXXVII. 1888/2 The lattice conductivity was increased by high-temperature annealing. **1971** I. G. GASS et al. *Understanding Earth* v. 86/2 The lattice conductivity of the various rocks tends to converge with increasing temperatures to something like 2 to 3 W m^{-1} $°K^{-1}$. **1923** H. L. BROSE tr. *Sommerfeld's Atomic Struct. & Spectral Lines* iii. 154 The crystal of smallest known *lattice constant, namely, diamond. **1927** Lattice constant [see sense 4 above]. **1944** *Ann. Reg. 1943* 363 Siegbahn's determination of the lattice-constant of calcite at 18°C. **1969** Lattice constant [see LENGENBACHITE]. **1973** *Physical Rev.* B. VII. 674 Energy bands, Fermi surfaces, and densities of states of calcium as a function of lattice constant have been calculated. **1938** *Proc. Cambr. Philos. Soc.* XXXIV. 486 We define a free path L_i for scattering by impurities and *lattice defects on an atomic scale. **1959** *Phil. Mag.* IV. 468 When a metal is strained, the lattice defects introduced cause scattering of the phonons and electrons. **1847** TENNYSON *Princess* II. 15 Here and there on *lattice edges lay Or book or lute. **1924** *Physical Rev.* XXIII. 497 (*caption*) *Lattice energies, from compressibility data, in kg-cal/g-mol. **1942** C. E. K. MEES *Theory Photogr. Process* iv. 183 In the fifth column are given the differences between silver and sodium salts for the electrostatic lattice energy as another measure of deformation energy. **1965** *Geochem. Internat.* II. 416/1 The methods of calculations of lattice energy are based on the assumption that the crystal is ideally ionic, but such crystals do not exist, and results are always approximate. **1861** *Trans. Illinois Agric. Soc.* IV. 259 An octagon, for exhibition of fancy articles .. with a good *lattice fence to keep people from the exhibition tables. **1964** H. O. PERKINS *Espaliers & Vines* vi. 90 The lattice or Belgian fence types. **1935** E. A. GUILLEMIN *Communication Networks* II. x. 409 (*caption*) Behavior of the reactances (891 *a*) versus the frequency variable $x = \omega/\omega_1$ for the low-pass *lattice filter whose index and characteristic impedance functions are given by eqs. (889 *a*) and (890 *a*). **1970** J. EARL *Tuners & Amplifiers* ii. 43 Another arrangement employs a pair of quartz elements within a transformer, the idea then being more representative of the ordinary quartz crystal filter. Such a filter, called a crystal lattice-filter, is shown in Fig. 2.18. **1916** BLUNDEN *Harbingers* 24 When the dryer in his oast Had loaded up his *lattice-floors, He called a binman at the doors. **1838** D. STEVENSON *Civil Engin. N. Amer.* viii. 233 *Lattice-frames. **1852** *Rep. Brit. Assoc.* Notices 123 BARTON (title of art.) On the Calculation of strains in *Lattice Girders. **1897** *Daily News* 6 Sept. 5/3 A steel pillar with a lattice girder construction. **1556** J. HEYWOOD *Spider & F.* i. 32 In at a *lattes hole .. fast flew there in a flie. **1866** *Treas. Bot.* s.v. *Ouvirandra*, *O. fenestralis* .. is best known as the *Lattice-leaf plant, from its singular leaves resembling open lattice-work. **1872** OLIVER *Elem. Bot.* II. 252 Allied to the Pondweeds is the rare Lattice-leaf (*Ouvirandra fenestralis*) of Madagascar. **1562** J. HEYWOOD *Prov. & Epigr.* (1867) 116, I wishe .. *Lattise makers few, and glasiers many. **1924** *Harmsworth's Wireless Encycl.* II. 1274 **Lattice mast*, term used to describe a tall, composite structure for the support of a lofty aerial. This type of construction is carried out in both wood and metal. .. Such a mast is triangular in section, and comprises essentially three upright members held together by tie bars of metal and braced by diagonal bracing of stout timber. **1928** A. WILLIAMS *Telegr. & Telephony* xxi. 282 An aerial is carried by five 28-ton lattice masts, 287 feet high, each resting on four legs bolted to 20-ton concrete blocks. **1948** R. DE KERCHOVE *Internat. Maritime Dict.* 399/1 *Lattice mast*, steel mast constructed of riveted structural steel shapes or lattice work. **1868** TRIPP *Brit. Mosses* 108 *Cinclidotus*, .. *Lattice Moss. **1480** *Wardr. Acc. Edw. IV* (1830) 122 For dī M¹ of *latis-naille price iij*d.* **1931** H. W. BODE in *U.S. Pat. 1,828,454* 20 Oct. 1/1 An important general property of a symmetrical *lattice network is that its propagation constant and its characteristic impedance are mutually independent. **1934** A. T. STARR *Electr. Circuits & Wave Filters* vi. 196 Such a lattice network has image impedance *R* at all frequencies, no attenuation at any frequency, and a phase shift which depends upon the reactance characteristic of Z_1. **1956** AMOS & BIRKINSHAW *Television Engin.* II. ix. 126 In general a lattice network has two series and two shunt elements as shown in Fig. 68; this particular network is a symmetrical one in which both series elements are equal to Z_1 and both shunt elements are equal to Z_2... For purposes of calculation it is often more convenient to redraw the network in the form of a bridge circuit. **1923** R. G. COLLINGWOOD *Roman Brit.* 75 Coarse ware with incised *lattice-ornament. **1840** MRS. NORTON *Dream* 268 Beaming all redly thro' the *lattice-pane. **1875** FORTNUM *Majolica* viii. 71 *Lattice and diaper patterns. **1923** G. BARR tr. *Graetz's Recent Devel. Atomic Theory* iv. 96 We will call each such series of similar parallel planes a system of *lattice planes. **1937** *Amer. Mineralogist* XXII. 449 Consider any two successive lattice planes perpendicular to a screw axis. **1973** K. W. ANDREWS *Physical Metall.* II. ii. 90 If the grating is actually composed of lattice planes, i.e. layers of atoms or molecules properly located in relation to the electron beam, then an image of these layers could be formed. **1877** BENNETT *Thomé's Bot.* 457 The aquatic *Ouvirandra* or *lattice plant. **1857** in Cayley *Coll. Math. Papers* (1890) III. 40 Imagine now in a plane, a rectangular system of coordinates (*x. y*) and the whole plane divided by lines parallel to the axes at distances = 1 from each other into squares of the dimension = 1. And let the angles which do not lie on the axes of coordinates be called '*lattice points'. **1926** *Encycl. Brit.* II. 832/2 A lattice point (*Gitterpunkt*) in space of any number of dimensions is a point with integral co-ordinates. **1936** A. H. WILSON *Theory of Metals* ii. 48 We assume as zero approximation that the electron is in the neighbourhood of one particular lattice point. **1955** *Sci. News* XV. 143 The gas is usually regarded as being accommodated on the lattice of the metal by occupying positions in its interstices, rather than replacing metal atoms at some of the lattice points. **1966** OGILVY & ANDERSON *Excursions in Number Theory* x. 120 The point (20, 47), having both its coordinates integers, is called a lattice point of the plane. It is a point of intersection of a

horizontal and a vertical line of the coordinate grid, or lattice. **1967** A. H. Cottrell *Introd. Metall.* xvii. 261 This array of lattice points is the space lattice of the crystal. It is important to notice that a lattice point is not an atomic site. In certain simple crystal structures.. the pattern of atomic sites happens also to form a space lattice, but in many other structures.. there is more than one atom in the motif. **1951** *Archit. Rev.* CIX. 389/2 The *lattice-steel roof-trusses are supported on the inner leaf of the reinforced concrete walls and act as permanent shuttering for the concrete roof. **1882** Caulfeild & Saward *Dict. Needlewk.* 187 *Lattice-stitch, a stitch used in Ticking work and other ornamental Embroideries for borders and formed of straight interlaced lines. **1942** R. H. Newton *Town & Davis: Architects* ii. 42 The few sources I have consulted say nothing significant.. about Ithiel Town as the inventor of the *lattice truss. **1936** A. H. Wilson *Theory of Metals* vi. 200 The coupling between the electrons and the *lattice vibrations is due mainly to changes in the density of the solid. **1959** *Phil. Mag.* IV. 468 At low temperatures the dominant lattice vibrations are those of long wavelength which are not scattered by the impurity atoms. **1969** J. S. Blakemore *Solid State Physics* ii. 114 The particle—or phonon—aspect of lattice vibrations is particularly appropriate when we are concerned with energy transformation. **1936** A. H. Wilson *Theory of Metals* vi. 201 We should then be compelled to take into account the dispersion of the *lattice waves. **1955** H. B. G. Casimir in W. Pauli *Niels Bohr* 119 At temperatures well below the so-called Debye temperature Θ only lattice waves with a wave-length of many atomic distances are excited. **1971** Donovan & Angress *Lattice Vibrations* iv. 83 In the harmonic approximation the lattice waves travel independently, without hindrance, so that the mean free path is infinite and the thermal resistance is zero. **1538** Elyot *Dict.*, *Cancelli*, latteses, or any thynge made *lattese wyse. *a* **1548** Hall *Chron.*, *Hen. VIII* 239 Ryche cloth of golde traverced latyse wyse square. **1601** Holland *Pliny* I. 166 Some sinewes running streight out in length, others crossing ouerthwart lattise-wise. **1715** Leoni *Palladio's Archit.* (1742) II. 37 An additional Door.. made Lettice-wise; to the end that the People standing without might see what was done in the Temple.

lattice (ˈlætɪs), *v.* [f. prec.] **1.** *trans.* To furnish with a lattice or lattice-work. Also with *up*, *over*.

1428 in Heath *Grocers' Comp.* (1829) 5 The seide parlore and tresance lattizid, glazid and selyd with othir necessariis. **1538** Leland *Itin.* I. 55 A Closet in the middle of 8 Squares latisid aboute. **1565** Cooper *Thesaurus*, *Clathrare*, to close with crosse barres, or trayles: to lettise vp. **1664** Power *Exp. Philos.* I. 7 Her eye is all latticed or chequered with dimples like Common Flyes. **1726** Swift *Gulliver* II. iv. 73 Each Window was latticed with Iron Wire on the out-side. **1856** Kane *Arct. Expl.* I. xi. 117 It was a wooden structure, latticed and pierced with auger-holes. **1867** Lady Herbert *Cradle L.* i. 9 The narrow streets which are latticed over with matting.

2. *trans.* To form into a lattice, arrange as a lattice.

1950 *Amer. Speech* XXV. 24 'Homogeneous' piles and 'heterogeneous' piles, depending on whether the fissionable material is latticed with the moderating material.

lattice, obs. form of lettuce.

latticed (ˈlætɪst), *a.* Also 6 lattis(e)d, letticed, -uced, -ised, latized, 7 latised. [f. lattice *sb.* + -ed².]

1. Furnished with a lattice or lattice-work.

1565 Golding *Ovid's Met.* II. (1593) 32 Their hooves they mainely beat upon the lattisd grate. **1662** Greenhalgh in Ellis *Orig. Lett.* Ser. II. IV. 12 A low, long, and narrow latticed window. **1795** Southey *Joan of Arc* III. 2 The early sun Pour'd on the latticed cot a cheerful gleam. *a* **1845** Hood *Open Question* i, Shut the gardens! lock the latticed gate! **1863** Geo. Eliot *Romola* iii, A latticed screen.. divided the shop from a room of about equal size.

2. Shaped or arranged like a lattice. **a.** *gen.*

1577 B. Googe *Heresbach's Husb.* (1586) 25 b, You must.. harrowe it, which is don with a lettused instrument ful of teeth. **1787** Glover *Athenaid* XXVII. 108 Huge alders.. shed Disparted moonlight through the lattic'd boughs.

b. *Nat. Hist.* Having a conformation or marking resembling lattice-work. Of plant-cells: see quot. 1877 and *lattice-cell*, lattice *sb.* 6. Of leaves = cancellate.

1664 Power *Exp. Philos.* I. 25 Her eye is.. foraminulous and latticed like that of other Insects. **1816** T. Brown *Elem. Conchol.* 155 *Latticed*, having longitudinal lines or furrows, decussate by transverse ones. **1862** Cooke *Brit. Fungi* 93 The Latticed Stinkhorn (*Clathrus cancellatus*). **1862** Newman *Brit. Moths* (1869) 87 The Latticed Heath (*Strenia clathrata*). **1877** Bennett *Thomé's Bot.* 49 *Sieve-tubes*, or *bast-vessels* result from the coalescence of cells standing one over another, the partition walls of which, or *sieve-discs*, have become perforated in the manner of a sieve... Of similar construction are latticed cells, the partition-walls of which are not actually perforated, but only thickened in a sieve-like manner. **1885** A. S. Pennington *Brit. Zoophytes* 161 *Phellia Brodricii*,.. 'The Latticed Corklet'.

c. *Her.*

1847 *Gloss. Heraldry*, *Lattised*, *Treille*, or *Portcullised*, a pattern resembling fretty, but placed cross-ways. It may be interlaced or not.

lattice-window. A window furnished with a lattice; also, in mod. use, one composed of small diamond-shaped panes set in lead-work.

1515–16 in Willis & Clark *Cambridge* (1886) II. 23 Pro factura fenestrarum.. scilicet latyswyndows. *a* **1533** Ld. Berners *Huon* clviii. 609 Out of yᵉ chaumbre wheras she shal be in she shal se them all.. thrughe a lateyse wyndowe. **1560** Daus tr. *Sleidane's Comm.* 32 b, The Doctors of Divinite stande in the latesse windowes. **1611** Coryat *Crudities* 207 Brasen dores, whereof the middle.. is made of solid brasse, the other foure in the forme of latteise windowes. **1743** Pococke *Descr. East* I. 16 They [galleys] are made with lattise windows all round. **1838** Dickens *O. Twist* xxxiv, A cottage-room, with a lattice-window. **1880** Disraeli *Endym.* I. xi. 86 An old hall with gable ends and lattice windows.

lattice-work. Wood or metal work consisting of crossing strips with small openings; = lattice *sb.* 1. Also, something resembling this.

1487 *Will* in *Paston Lett.* III. 465 A nother towell of latise werk. **1600** Surflet *Country Farm* 509 The latice worke or climing and running frames made for the vine. **1664** Power *Exp. Philos.* I. 25 The like curious Lattice-work I have also observ'd in the crustaceous Cornea of the Creckets Eye. **1784** Cowper *Task* I. 42 The cane.. severed into stripes That interlaced each other, these supplied Of texture firm a lattice-work. **1838** Thirlwall *Greece* III. xx. 145 It.. was guarded on either side by a strong lattice-work of forest timber. **1853** Sir H. Douglas *Milit. Bridges* (ed. 3) 340 The bow-and-tie construction is thought to be superior in strength to lattice-work.. for a bridge.

latticing (ˈlætɪsɪŋ). [f. lattice *sb.* or *v.* + -ing¹.] The process of making a lattice or lattice-work; in *Bridge-building* (see quot.).

1885 Waddell *Syst. Iron Railr. Bridges Japan* 246, *Latticing*, a system of bars crossing each other at the middle of their lengths, used to connect the two channels of a strut in order to make them act as one member.

‖**latticinio** (lattiˈtʃinjo), **latticino** (-ˈtʃino). [It., f. L. *lacticinium* milk food.] An opaque white glass used in threads for decorative purposes in Venetian glass. Hence *attrib.*

1855 F. B. Palliser tr. *Labarte's Handbk. Arts Middle Ages & Renaissance* ix. 348 The opaque white glass, the *latticinio* most usually employed in the filagree Venetian glasses, is only a glass coloured milk-white by oxide of tin or arsenic. **1881** C. C. Harrison *Woman's Handiwork* III. 229 There are the *millefiori*,.. The *latticino*, with graceful milk-white spirals. The *avventurino*, with the lustre of pure gold. **1937** *Burlington Mag.* Nov. 218/2 Venetian *latticino* glass of the sixteenth and seventeenth centuries. **1969** *Canad. Antiques Collector* Sept. 26/2 Latticinio glass is produced by pouring clear glass around fine 'canes' or rods of white.. glass to form a thick rod with thin white rods embedded in it. **1972** *Sunday Tel.* 21 May 10/7 Collectors.. will be burying their visual senses in millefiori, butterflies, latticinio.

lattin(ne, -o(u)n, -yn(e, -yng, -ynn, latun, obs. forms of latten.

lattine, obs. variant of lateen.

lattly, obs. form of lately *adv.*

lattouce, obs. Sc. form of lettuce.

lattyn: see let *v.*

‖**latus**¹ (ˈleɪtəs). *Math.* [L. = side.] Used in the following terms in *Conic sections*: **latus rectum**, a straight line drawn through the focus of a conic at right angles to the transverse diameter, the parameter; **latus primarium** (see quot. 1706); †**latus transversum**, the transverse diameter.

1702 Ralphson *Math. Dict.* App. Conic Sections 11 In a Parabola the Rectangle of the Diameter, and Latus Rectum, is equal to the Rectangle of the Segments of the double Ordinate. **1706** Phillips (ed. Kersey), *Latus primarium*,.. a Right-line drawn thro' the *Vertex*, or Top of the Section, parallel to the Base of the Triangular Section of the Cone, and within it. *Ibid.*, *Latus Transversum*, (in an Hyperbola) is a Right-line lying between the Vertex's of the two opposite Sections. **1734** J. Ward *Introd. Math.* IV. i. (ed. 6) 367 The Diameter of a Circle being that Right-line which passes thro' its Centre or Focus.. may.. be properly call'd the Circle's Latus Rectum: And altho' it loses the Name of Diameter when the Circle degenerates into an Ellipsis, yet it retains the Name of Latus Rectum. **1859** Parkinson *Optics* (1866) 256 A luminous point is placed at one of the foci of a semi-elliptic arc bounded by the axis major: prove that the whole illumination of the arc varies inversely as the latus rectum.

‖**latus**² (ˈleɪtəs). *Antiq.* [Late L. = Gr. λάτος.] A large fish inhabiting the Nile and other regions.

1598 *Epulario* F iiij b, To dresse a Latus or shadow fish. **1706** Phillips (ed. Kersey), *Latus*,.. a huge Fish peculiar to the River Nile, which is often of Two Hundred Pounds Weight. **1753** Chambers *Cycl. Supp.*, *Latus*,.. the name of a fish of the coracinus, or umbra kind. **1857** Birch *Anc. Pottery* (1858) I. 90 Among fishes, the latus,.. and the oxyrhyncus.

Latvian (ˈlætvɪən), *a.* and *sb.* [f. *Latvia*, Lett. and Lith. *Latvija*.] **A.** *adj.* Of or belonging to Latvia, since 1940 a constituent republic of the U.S.S.R., lying on the east coast of the Baltic Sea. **B.** *sb.* **a.** A native or inhabitant of Latvia. **b.** The language of Latvia; Lettish. Cf. Lett, Lettish *a.* (*sb.*)

1920 *Contemp. Rev.* Aug. 283 Troops under German command on Latvian territory. **1924** J. M. Murry *Voyage* ii. 28 All these new languages. Lithuanian, Latvian, Esthonian, Transcaucasian. **1926** *Spectator* 31 July 176/1 Latvian is certainly not so difficult to learn as Chinese. **1941** J. H. Jackson *Estonia* ii. 38 A branch of the Estonian race, the Livs, waged endless warfare with the Letts or Latvians. **1955** *Times* 16 Aug. 9/6 The Lithuanians and Latvians, ethnologically Indo-European, are survivors of ancient peoples. **1964** G. Bennett *Cowan's War* i. 22 The defences of Riga crumbled, which prevented the workers of all three Latvian ports from declaring for Bolshevism in November. **1973** *Listener* 15 Nov. 656/3 Those who have an ethnic or religious fellow-feeling, whether they be.. Latvians or Georgians, Kurds or Nagas.

Latyn, obs. form of Latin, latten, let *v.*

latynere, -tynier: see latimer.

Latyng, -ynge, obs. forms of Latin, letting.

latynn, obs. form of latten.

‖**lau** (laʊ). [Native word.] An African water monster supposed to live in the swamps of the Nile valley.

1923 H. C. Jackson in *Sudan Notes & Rec.* VI. 187 There is also a third kind [of python] of which rumours have come to my ears... This serpent is called Lau by the Nuer and Dinka... It is reported to be of gigantic proportions. **1925** *Blackw. Mag.* Sept. 303/2 The *lau* is a composite beast; it is reputed to have a bit of the bird, snake and lizard in it, like the wyvern in coats-of-arms. **1937** *Discovery* Dec. 369/1 The *lau* and the *lukwata*, monstrous beasts whose hideous calls are heard booming through the grey night-mists of the lakes.

lau, obs. form of law, low.

lauan (læˈwɑːn). [Tagalog *lawaan*.] The Philippine name for the light hardwood timber produced by trees of the genus *Shorea* or closely related genera.

1894 H. M. Ward *Laslett's Timber & Timber Trees* (ed. 2) xxii. 226 The outside planks of the old Manilla and Acapulco galleons were of Lauan wood. **1936** *Nature* 26 Dec. 1090/2 The top and side clasps [of the tennis racket] are of Malayan lauan. **1971** N. E. Hickin *Wood Preservation* 88 Shorea. A very extensive genus of hardwood trees found chiefly in Malaysia, Indonesia, Borneo and the Philippines, the principal timbers of which are generally known as meranti, seraya and lauan, suitably qualified.

laubanite (ˈlɔːbənaɪt). *Min.* [Named by Traube, 1887, from *Lauban* in Silesia, where it was first found: see -ite.] Hydrous silicate of aluminium and calcium, resembling stilbite.

1888 *Amer. Jrnl. Sci.* Ser. III. XXXV. 418 Laubanite. A zeolite resembling stilbite.

lauber, -or, etc., Sc. forms of labour.

laubmannite (ˈlaʊbmænaɪt). *Min.* [f. the name of Heinrich *Laubmann*, 20th-century German mineralogist + -ite¹.] A basic phosphate of ferrous and ferric iron, $Fe^{II}_3Fe^{III}_6(PO_4)_4(OH)_{12}$, of yellow- to grey-green colour.

1949 C. Frondel in *Amer. Mineralogist* XXXIV. 536 The name laubmannite is proposed for the species. **1970** *Ibid.* LV. 138 A new locality was discovered, the laubmannite occurring as bright yellow-green aggregates and affording a powder pattern virtually identical with the Arkansas material. The location is Leveäniemi in the Svappavaara mining district, Norrbotten Province, Sweden.

lauch: see latch *v.*¹, laugh, law, low.

lauchful, obs. Sc. form of lawful.

laucht, obs. Sc. form of laugh *v.*, low *a.*

†ˈ**lauchtane**, *a. Sc. Obs.* [a. Gaelic *lachdunn* = Irish *lachtna*.] Dull coloured, swarthy.

1375 Barbour *Bruce* XIX. 672 A lawchtane [*MS. E* lauchtane] mantill than hym by Lyand apon the bed he saw. *a* **1568** in Pinkerton *Anc. Sc. Poems* (1786) 192 My rubie cheeks, was reid as rone, Ar leyn, and lauchtane as the leid.

lauchter, -ir, obs. Sc. forms of laughter.

lauchtfull, obs. Sc. form of lawful.

laucyouse, var. lautious *Obs.*, luxurious.

laud (lɔːd), *sb.*¹ Forms: 4–7 laude, 6–7 lawd(e, 6– laud. [a. OF. *laude*, ad. L. *laud-em*, *laus* praise.]

1. Praise, high commendation. Also † *in laud of*, *honour and laud*, *laud and glory* (*honour*, *thanks*); † *to give laud*. Now *rare* exc. in hymns.

c **1384** Chaucer *H. Fame* III. 232 Pursevantes and herauldes That crien ryche folkes laudes. *c* **1386** —— *Prioress' T.* 8 In laude.. Of thee.. To telle a storie I wol do my labour. —— *Friar's T.* 55 He was, if I shal yeven him his laude, A theef, and eek a somnour, and a baude. *a* **1470** Tiptoft *Cæsar* iv. (1530) 5 That the enterpryce myght be to the lawd and profyte of his legion. **1494** Fabyan *Chron.* v. cxviii. 94 To hym that laude & thankys shulde be geuen vnto. **1509** Hawes *Past. Pleas.* xxxvi. (Percy Soc.) 187 To the laude and glory Of wyse dame Pallas it was so edified. **1552** Lyndesay *Monarche* 4125 Onely to God be laude and glore. **1593** Q. Eliz. *Boeth.* III. pr. vi. 53 They that falsely be praised, needs must they blush at their own laude. **1622** Bacon *Hen. VII* 106 For which this Assembly and all Christians are to render laud and thankes unto God. **1640** Gent *Knave in Gr.* II. i. Eb, So well, as Æsop could discharge his scene, whereby he won most laud. **1725** Pope *Odyss.* XIV. 442 Great laud and praise were mine.. for spotless faith divine. **1819** Jefferson *Autobiog.* App., Wks. 1859 I. 117 We willingly cede to her the laud of having.. been.. 'the cradle of sound principles'. **1849** Longf. *Kavanagh* xvii. Prose Wks. 1886 II. 346 Sibylline leaves.. in laud and exaltation of her modest relative. **1858** Neale *Bernard de M.* (1865) 27 His laud and benediction Thy ransomed people raise. **1879** Dixon *Windsor* II. xxiv. 250 His chief employment being the laud of his dead lives.

b. A cause or subject for praise. *rare.*

1560 Rolland *Crt. Venus* II. 351 It was na laude, nor 3it Humanitie On sic ane wicht to schaw thame villanous. **1890**

J. H. STIRLING *Gifford Lect.* xiv. 278 That is not a fault: that is rather a laud.

†**c.** ? Praiseworthiness. *Obs.*

1576 GASCOIGNE *Compl. Philomene* (Arb.) 94 And by the lawde of his pretence His lewdnesse was acquit.

2. *pl.* The first of the day-hours of the Church, the Psalms of which always end with Pss. cxlviii–cl, sung as one psalm and technically called *laudes.*

a **1340** HAMPOLE *Psalter* lxii. 1 þis salme is ay songen in þe lauds. *a* **1400** *Prymer* (1891) 88 Here begynneth laudes. *c* **1460** *Towneley Myst.* xiii. 180 Sir, this same day at morne I thaym left in the corne, When they rang lawdys. **1526** *Pilgr. Perf.* (W. de W. 1531) 251 Meditacyons at the laudes, vnto the ende of matyns, diuided accordyng to euery psalme. *a* **1711** KEN *Hymns Festiv.* Poet. Wks. 1721 I. 20 The Evening Lamb..Was by the hallow'd Fire but half-consum'd, When Mary rose to Lauds. **1805** SCOTT *Last Minstr.* I. xxxi, Now midnight lauds were in Melrose sung. **1843** M. PATTISON *Diary* in *Mem.* (1885) 190 At 6 went to Matins, which with Lauds and Prime take about an hour and a half.

transf. **1509** HAWES *Past. Pleas.* XXXIII. (Percy Soc.) 169 The lytle byrdes swetely dyd syng Laudes to their maker early in the mornyng. **1577** VALLANS *T. Two Swannes* in *Leland's Itin.* (1759) V. p. viii, The merrie Nightingale.. Ringes out all night the never ceasing laudes Of God. **1659** HAMMOND *On Ps.* lix. 16 Paraphr. 300 To make this the matter of my daily morning lauds.

3. A hymn or ascription of praise.

1530 PALSGR. 237/2 Laude a prayse, *laude.* **1604** SHAKS. *Ham.* IV. vii. 178 (2nd Qo.) Which time she chaunted snatches of old laudes. **1657** SPARROW *Bk. Com. Prayer* 247 So was it of old ordained..that the Lauds or Praises should be said..immediately after the Gospel. **1737** WATERLAND *Eucharist* 49 The Christians offered up Spiritual Sacrifices, Prayers and Lauds. **1877** SYMONDS *Renaiss. Italy* II. 320 An author of devotional lauds [= It. *laude*] and mystery plays.

†**laud**, *sb.*² *Obs.* [ad. med.L. *laud-um*, vbl. sb. f. *laudāre* (LAUD *v.*), used in the extended sense 'to give a judgement upon'.] Decision, judgement.

c **1465** *Eng. Chron.* (Camden 1856) 77 After long trete bothe partyes submytted theym to the laude and arbytrement of the kyng. **1542** *Sc. Acts Mary* (1814) II. 416 To here and se þe decrete laude and sentence of forfaltour gevin.

‖**laud** (la'ud), *sb.*³ [Sp.: see LUTE *sb.*¹] A Spanish lute.

1876 STAINER & BARRETT *Dict. Mus. Terms* 276 The word [*sc.* lute]..is most probably from the Arabic *el'ood*, as the instruments came into Europe from the Moors through the Spaniards, who still call it *laud.* **1923** *Blackw. Mag.* July 38/1 The Spanish laud or lute Jo had bought in Murcia during the previous year. **1954** *Grove's Dict. Mus.* (ed. 5) I. 400/1 The instrument [*sc.* the bandurria] is in common use in the south of Spain, generally in conjunction with the *laud* and the *guitarra.*

laud (lɔːd), *v.* Forms: 5–7 **laude**, (5 **loud**), 6–7 **lawde**, 6– **laud**. [ad. L. *laud-āre*, f. *laud-*, *laus* praise.] *trans.* To praise, to sing or speak the praises of; to celebrate. Often ***to laud and bless*** (***praise, magnify***). Originally implying an act of worship.

1377 LANGL. *P. Pl.* B. XI. 102 Neyther for loue laude it nouȝt ne lakke it for enuye. *c* **1440** *Bone Flor.* 1883 The lady ..forthe ys gon, Loudyng the trynyte, To a noonre. **1477** EARL RIVERS (Caxton) *Dictes* 68 So ye shal be happy, & your werkes lauded. **1509** HAWES *Past. Pleas.* VIII. (Percy Soc.) 32 We ought to laude and magnify Your excellent springes of famous poetry. **1526** *Pilgr. Perf.* (W. de W. 1531) 251 We excite & moue..all creatures to laude & blesse god. *c* **1610** *Women Saints* 34 They therefore fast and pray and lawde our Lord. **1670** WALTON *Lives* IV. 317 [They] did at Night ..betake themselves to prayers, and lauding God. **1812** H. & J. SMITH *Rej. Addr., Cui Bono?* xii, To build a temple worthy of a god, To laud a monkey. **1833** HT. MARTINEAU *T. of Tyne* vii. 122 He lauded the arrangements. **1850** KINGSLEY *Alt. Locke* v, To be called..ambitious for the very same aspirations which are lauded up to the skies in the sons of the rich. **1868** HAWTHORNE *Amer. Note-Bks.* II. 1, I laud my stars, how-ever, that you will not have your first impressions of..our future home from such a day as this.

absol. **1850** NEALE *Med. Hymns* (1867) 168 Sing we lauding And applauding.

Hence **'lauded** *ppl. a.*

1824 DIBDIN *Libr. Comp.* 557 Son of the above lauded octogenarian. **1856** J. YOUNG *Demonol.* IV. vii. 437 More.. than..all the elaborate disquisitions or lauded aphorisms of ancient and modern wisdom together.

absol. **1887** *Chamb. Jrnl.* IV. 12 A rising power that would crush..the lauders and the lauded.

laud, obs. form of LEWD.

laudability (lɔːdə'bɪlɪtɪ). *rare.* [ad. L. *laudābilitās*, f. *laudābilis*: see next.] The quality of being a fit subject for praise; praise-worthiness.

1715 *Mem. Abp. Tenison* 5 Names..however instructive by the Laudability of their Characters. **1829** S. TURNER *Hist. Eng.* II. xxxi. IV. 363 This doctrine of the laudability and right of assassinating sovereigns was taught by others.. of the Jesuit fraternity.

laudable ('lɔːdəb(ə)l), *a.* Also 6 **laudabul**, **lawd(e)able**, 6–7 **laudible**. [ad. L. *laudābilis*, f. *laudāre*: see LAUD *v.* and -ABLE.]

1. Of immaterial things, actions, etc.: Praiseworthy, commendable. †Also, in early use, of the nature of praise, laudatory.

c **1420** *Chron. Vilod.* (Horstm.) 1359 And dred þus laudable wordus more in hure þouȝt. **1479** in *Eng. Gilds* (1870) 413 The..laudable custumes foresaide. **1503–4** *Act 19 Hen. VII* c. 4 After the lawdeable custome used in tyme of his moste noble progenytours. **1583** STUBBES *Anat. Abus.* II. (1882) 53 The laudable sciences of phisick and surgerie. **1605** SHAKS. *Macb.* IV. ii. 76 This earthly world: where to do harme Is often laudable. *c* **1610** *Women Saints* 178 When his precious ashes and laudable corps was caried to the martyrs seate. **1670** WALTON *Lives* IV. 278 A laudible ambition to be some-thing more than he then was. **1710** STEELE *Tatler* No. 180 ¶6 In the Sight of Reason, nothing is laudable but what is guided by Reason. **1761** HUME *Hist. Eng.* III. liv. 165 His conduct..was innocent, and even laudable. **1791** *Gentl. Mag.* 1/2 A wish that so laudable an institution may be more generally known. **1849** MACAULAY *Hist. Eng.* vi. II. 74 Using scandalous means for the purpose of obtaining a laudable end. **1879** MISS BRADDON *Clov. Foot* III. 269 He carried out this resolve with laudable firmness. **1886** RUSKIN *Præterita* I. 398 Laudable curiosity.

†**b.** Of testimony: Trustworthy. *Obs.*

1664 EVELYN *Sylva* 84 Upon laudable and unsuspected Record.

2. Of material objects and physical conditions: Of satisfactory nature, quality, or operation; healthy, sound, wholesome. Now only *Med.* of secretions, *esp.* pus (see quots.).

1514 BARCLAY *Cyt. & Uplondyshm.* (Percy Soc.) 4 The somer season men counteth now laudable. *c* **1550** LLOYD *Treas. Health* (1585) b ij, A bloudy fluxe, an hidropsy or madnesse after a frenesy, are laudable. **1607** TOPSELL *Four-f. Beasts* (1658) 464 The sheep of the Isle Chius are very small, and yet their milk maketh very laudable cheese. **1634** R. H. *Salernes Regim.* 27 Kids flesh is better and more laudable then any other flesh. **1675** EVELYN *Terra* (1676) 127 It may be a laudable Compost for moist grounds. **1669** BOYLE *Contn. New Exp.* II. (1682) 185, I found the Apple of a laudable colour. *c* **1720** GIBSON *Farrier's Guide* II. liii. (1738) 207 To promote a laudable growth of flesh. **1725** N. ROBINSON *Theory Physick* 269 If after the third Day a laudable Expectoration does not appear..then [etc.]. **1794–6** E. DARWIN *Zoon.* (1801) I. 501 Ulcers which are said to abound with laudable pus. **1829** *Health & Longevity* 229 Easier and sooner reduced to laudable chyle. **1878** T. BRYANT *Pract. Surg.* I. 19 When thick and creamy, it is known as healthy or laudable pus.

3. *sb.* in *pl.* **a.** Laudable qualities, good points. **b.** Persons of title, dignities. *Obs.* or *nonce-uses.*

1715 M. DAVIES *Athen. Brit.* I. 321 To do Justice, even to ones Enemy's Laudables. **1815** *Q. Rev.* XIV. 135 The number of these Laudables, including Dukes [etc.].

Hence **'laudableness**.

1695 J. EDWARDS *Perfect. Script.* 423 He asserts the truth of his doctrine, and the laudableness of his actions. **1730–6** in BAILEY (fol.). **1768–74** TUCKER *Lt. Nat.* (1834) I. 243 We shall..look upon the laudableness of an action as a certain evidence of its usefulness.

laudably ('lɔːdəblɪ), *adv.* [f. prec. + -LY².]

1. In a praiseworthy manner, so as to deserve praise.

1477 EARL RIVERS (Caxton) *Dictes* 87 He ansuerd to speke litil and laudably. **1533** in *Vicary's Anat.* (1888) App. xiv. 263 Occupacions lawdablye vsed and contynued withyn this Cytye. **1646** SIR T. BROWNE *Pseud. Ep.* VI. x. 322 The Chymists have attempted laudably, reducing their causes unto Sal, Sulphur, and Mercury. **1748** RICHARDSON *Clarissa* (1811) I. xxviii. 199 Would not love and pity excusably, nay laudably, make a good wife..give up her own will..to oblige a husband. **1876** BLACK *Madcap V.* vi. 52 A..young man..laudably anxious to be instructed.

†**2.** In a sound and healthy manner. *Obs. rare.*

1699 EVELYN *Acetaria* 129 Some Plants not only nourish laudably, but induce a manifest and wholsom Change.

laudanine ('lɔːdənaɪn). *Chem.* Also **-in**. [ad. G. *laudanin* (O. Hesse 1870, in *Ann. d. Chem. und Pharm.* CLIII. 49), f. LAUDAN-UM: see -INE⁶.] A colourless to pale red crystalline alkaloid contained in opium.

1871 *Jrnl. Chem. Soc.* XXIV. 1064 White crystals are thereby obtained, from which the laudanine is separated by the action of hydriodic acid, with which it forms a difficultly soluble compound. Laudanine has the composition $C_{20}H_{25}NO_4$, instead of the formula $C_{20}H_{25}NO_3$, as formerly given. **1892** MORLEY & MUIR *Watts' Dict. Chem.* III. 120 *Laudanine* $C_{20}H_{25}NO_3$. **1954** A. BURGER in Manske & Holmes *Alkaloids* IV. 57 Laudanine is optically inactive in spite of the presence of an asymmetric carbon atom in its formula.

laudanosine (lɔː'dænəʊsiːn). *Chem.* [ad. G. *laudanosin* (O. Hesse 1871, in *Ber. d. Deut. Chem. Ges.* IV. 696): see LAUDANINE and -OSE².)] Laudanine methyl ether, $C_{21}H_{27}NO_4$, the dextrorotatory form of which occurs in opium and is a strong tetanic poison.

1871 *Jrnl. Chem. Soc.* XXIV. 1065 Laudanosine.. dissolves sparingly in cold, but easily in hot benzol; it forms colourless prisms which melt at 89°. **1900** *Chemist & Druggist* LVII. 846/1 It is therefore probable that laudanosine is *d*-*N*-methyl-tetra-hydro-papaverine. **1951** [see GNOSCOPINE]. **1972** *Phytochemistry* XI. 461 The major alkaloids of the above-ground parts of *Argemone grandiflora* ..were found to be berberine, α-allocryptopine and protopine; (+)-laudanosine..and chelerythine were identified as minor alkaloids.

laudanum ('lɔːd(ə)nəm, 'lɒ-). Also 8 **lodanum**, 9 *dial.* **lodlum**, *Sc.* **lodomy**. [a. mod.L. *laudanum*, used by Paracelsus as the name of a medicament for which he gives a pretended prescription, the ingredients comprising leaf-gold, pearls not perforated, etc. (*Opera* 1658 I. 492/2). It was early suspected that opium was the real agent of the cures which Paracelsus professed to have effected by this costly means; hence the name was applied to certain opiate preparations which were sold as identical with his famous remedy.

It is doubtful whether the word as used by Paracelsus was a fanciful application of *laudanum* a med.L. variant of LADANUM, or was suggested by *laudāre* to praise or by some other word, or was formed quite arbitrarily.]

1. In early use, a name for various preparations in which opium was the main ingredient. Now only: The simple alcoholic tincture of opium.

1602–3 MANNINGHAM *Diary* (Camden) 46 There is a certaine kinde of compound called Laudanum..the virtue of it is very soueraigne to mitigate anie payne. **1643** SIR T. BROWNE *Relig. Med.* II. §12, I need no other Laudanum than this to make me sleep. **1694** SALMON *Bate's Dispens.* (1713) 267/2 It is of the Nature of other Laudanums. **1704** F. FULLER *Medic. Gymn.* (1711) 255, I was deny'd likewise the Ease which is to be obtain'd by Laudanum. **1739** 'R. BULL' tr. *Dedekindus' Grobianus* 166 Your Mischief, being fully done, Will make you sleep as well as Laudanum. *a* **1828** *Lang Johnny More* ix. in Child *Ballads* (1892) IV. 398 They ..gae him draps o lodomy That laid him fast asleep. **1852** MRS. STOWE *Uncle Tom's C.* xxxiv. 310, I gave him laudanum, and held him close to my bosom while he slept to death.

fig. *a* **1711** KEN *Dedicat.* Poet. Wks. 1721 I. 3 Pain haunting me, I court the sacred Muse, Verse is the only Laudanum I use. **1789** G. KEATE *Pelew Isl.* 293 The Laudanum of rhetoric, whose property will occasionally benumb..the power of common understandings.

†**2.** = LADANUM 1.

1616 BULLOKAR, *Laudanum*, a yellowish gumme, as some write; notwithstanding others affirm it to be made of a dew, which falleth vpon a certaine herbe in Greece. **1702** W. J. *Bruyn's Voy. Levant* lxxii. 272 Laudanum..proceeds from a Dew which falls on the leaves of a small Plant about half a foot high, which does something resemble small Sage.

3. *Comb.*, as ***laudanum-raised*** adj.

1800 WEEMS *Washington* i. (1877) 8 The fine laudanum-raised spirits of the young sparklers.

Hence **'laudanum** *v. trans.*, to dose with laudanum.

1839–40 THACKERAY *Catherine* v, You'd laudanum him.

laudation (lɔː'deɪʃən). [ad. L. *laudātiōn-em*, n. of action f. *laudāre* to LAUD.] The action of praising; an instance of this, a laudatory inscription. Also, the condition of being praised, as † ***to be*** or ***to have in laudation.***

c **1470** G. ASHBY *Dicta Philos.* 1232 Poems 99 And his figure in Recommendacion Shal be had, and in Laudacion. **1509** HAWES *Past. Pleas.* xliv. (Percy Soc.) 212 Dame Fame was in laudation. ? *a* **1550** in *Dunbar's Poems* (1893) 329 And on this day in his laudatioun Aue Redemptor Iesu! all ȝe cry. **1848** DICKENS *Dombey* vii, Notwithstanding his liberal laudation of himself, however, the Major was selfish. **1865** *Reader* 27 May 589/3 Success in this matter would stamp him as a man of talent. He would be singled out for laudation. **1868** STANLEY *Westm. Abb.* iv. 338 As we read the long laudation on the pedestal.

laudative ('lɔːdətɪv), *a.* and *sb. rare.* [ad. L. *laudātīv-us*, f. *laudāt-*, ppl. stem of *laudāre* to LAUD. Cf. F. *laudatif.*] **A.** *adj.* Expressive of praise; laudatory. Const. *of.*

1609 HOLLAND *Amm. Marcell.* XVI. i. 52 Now whatsoever in this narration shall be delivered..shall pertaine in manner to a laudative argument. **1656** BLOUNT *Glossogr.*, *Laudative*, of or belonging to commendation, wherein praise is contained. **1824** *Blackw. Mag.* XVI. 3 Strains not simply laudative of Oporto, but vituperative..of Bordeaux.

Comb. **1833** CARLYLE in Froude *Life* (1882) II. 346 A kind of lampoon, laudative-vituperative (as it ought to be).

†**B.** *sb.* A laudative expression or discourse; a eulogy, panegyric. *Obs.*

1605 BACON *Adv. Learn.* I. v. §12 (1873) 44, I have no purpose to enter into a laudative of learning. **1633** WOTTON *Let.* in *Reliq.* (1651) 456 A tempest of Panegyricks and Laudatives of their Princes. **1674** T. TURNOR *Case Bankers & Creditors* Introd. 2 Thuanus..unto other Laudatives of that Princes Reign, adds this.

laudator (lɔː'deɪtə(r)). [a. L. *laudātor*, agent-n. f. *laudāre* to LAUD.] One who praises: a eulogist.

1825 *Blackw. Mag.* XVIII. 177 Of our magazine he is a most determined reader..and frequently not a laudator. **1830** G. R. GLEIG *Country Curate* I. ix. 174 Suspecting..the design of his laudator was to pass censure upon myself. **1834** *Fraser's Mag.* X. 715 Consequences never contemplated by the laudators of the peace-loving priesthood.

‖**laudator temporis acti** (lɔː'deɪtə 'tɛmpərɪs 'æktaɪ). [See LAUDATOR.] A Latin phrase, from Horace's *laudator temporis acti se puero* 'a praiser of time past when he himself was a boy' (*Ars Poetica* 173), used of one who looks back to the past as a better time.

1736 SWIFT *Let.* 2 Dec. in Pope *Works* (1757) IX. 209 Have you got a supply of new friends to make up for those who are gone?.. I am afraid it is with friends as with times; and that the *laudator temporis acti se puero*, is equally applicable to both. **1753** CHESTERFIELD in *World* 6 Dec. 293, I am neither sour nor silly enough yet, to be a snarling *laudator temporis acti.* **1814** *Edin. Rev.* XXIII. 316 The suspected praises of any of the *laudatores temporis acti.* **1870** A. C. EWALD *Guide Indian Civil Service* 13 Some old Indians—*laudatores temporis acti*—are wont to make the most doleful prophecies regarding the results of abolishing Haileybury and introducing the Civil Service Commissioners in its place. **1923** BEERBOHM *Peep into Past* 10 Not that he [*sc.* Wilde] is a mere *laudator temporis acti.* **1931** BLUNDEN *Votive Tablets* 360 We can hardly avoid being *laudatores temporis acti* when we think even of Oxford ..as it has been, and as it now is. **1965** O. BARFIELD in J. Gibb *Light on C. S. Lewis* p. xv, He..ended his days..as a kind of..guilt-oppressed *laudator temporis acti.*

laudatory ('lɔːdətərı), *a.* and *sb.* [ad. L. *laudātōrius* adj., f. *laudāre* to LAUD.] **A.** *adj.* Expressive of praise; eulogistic. Const. *of.*

1555 ABP. PARKER *Ps.* 326 This laudatory is: and thankth God's gentlenes. *a* **1633** AUSTIN *Medit.* (1635) 190 His [Christ's] Laudatory Sermon to the People concerning John. **1821** FOSTER in *Life & Corr.* (1846) II. 44 The laudatory testimony inscribed upon it. **1824** BENTHAM *Bk. Fallacies* Wks. 1843 II. 413 The object of laudatory personalities is to effect the rejection of a measure. **1838** JAMES *Robber* viii, Wiley muttered something not very laudatory of his companion. **1858** HAWTHORNE *Fr. & It. Jrnls.* I. 291 An artist is not apt to speak in a very laudatory style of a brother artist. **1884** *Times* (weekly ed.) 10 Oct. 13/1 Monumental inscriptions, laudatory of gods and kings.

† **B.** *sb.* A laudatory discourse, a eulogy. *Obs.*

1620 E. BLOUNT *Horae Subs.* 353, I will not enter into a Laudatory thereof. **1642** MILTON *Apol. Smect.* 77 A laudatory of itselfe obtruded in the very first word.

Hence **'laudatorily** *adv.*

1847 *Blackw. Mag.* LXII. 323 A dangerous competitor recently and laudatorily noticed in the pages of Maga.

Laudean, obs. form of LAUDIAN.

laudefy, variant of LAUDIFY *Obs.*

lauder ('lɔːdə(r)). [f. LAUD *v.* + -ER¹.] = LAUDATOR.

1611 COTGR., *Louangier*, a praiser, lauder, commender. **1827** BEDDOES *Let.* in *Poems* (1851) p. lxxv, He..is a deep philosopher, a lauder of Spinosa. **1871** *Daily News* 13 Jan., We cannot sufficiently condole with the lauders of those old times.

Laudian ('lɔːdıən), *a.* (*sb.*) Also 7–8 **Laudean.** [f. name of William *Laud*, archbishop of Canterbury 1633–45 + -IAN.] Of, pertaining to, or characteristic of Laud; favouring the tenets or practices of Laud; instituted by Laud. Also as *sb.*, a follower of Laud.

1691 BAXTER *Nat. Ch.* xiv. 68 The Laudian New Church men, that are for a Forreign Jurisdiction. **1710** *Managers' Pro & Con* 47 The Modern Laudeans can scarce bear the Word Reformation. **1738** NEAL *Hist. Purit.* IV. 408 The Earl of Clarendon was a Protestant of Laudean principles in Church and State. **1853** MARSDEN *Early Purit.* 445 The tendency of the Laudian theology. **1861** W. S. PERRY *Hist. Ch. Eng.* I. xv. 555 The Laudian system of Church Government. **1874** GREEN *Short Hist.* viii. 495 The Laudian clergy..regarded it [Sunday] simply as one among the holidays of the Church.

Hence **'Laudianism**, the principles and practice of Laud and his followers.

1872 R. RAINY *Lect. Ch. Scot.* ii. (1883) 94 He will say this is Laudianism, in principle identical with the Anglican High Churchism.

laudible, obs. form of LAUDABLE.

laudifi'cation. *rare*⁻¹. [f. L. *laudific-āre* (see next) + -ATION.] The action of extolling with praise.

1890 MARQ. SALISBURY *Sp.* 6 Aug., Questions..so constructed as to conduce..in the greatest possible degree to the self-laudification of the questioner.

† **'laudify**, *v. Obs. rare.* Also **laudefy.** [ad. L. *laudificāre* (only in Gloss.) f. *laud-, laus* praise; see -FY.] *trans.* To extol with praises.

c **1470** HARDING *Chron.* XXXIX. iii, For whiche he was full greately magnified In all his realme with people laudefyed [*printed* landefyed]. *Ibid.* XLVII. iv, Ioseph [*i.e.* Josephus].. fully laudifyed [*printed* landifyed] The lawe of Christe.

lauding ('lɔːdıŋ), *vbl. sb.* [f. LAUD *v.* + -ING¹.] The action of the vb. LAUD; laudation.

1489 CAXTON *Faytes of A.* I. x. 26 Vegece thus saith to the lawdyng and praysyng of them. *c* **1500** *Melusine* xxxix. 304 Wherof they gaaf lawdyng to our lord god deuoutely. **1533** *Articles imputed to Latimer* in Foxe *A. & M.* (1563) 1310/2 Salutyng or gretyng, laudyng or praysing is not properly prayeng. *c* **1610** *Women Saints* 19 Who..talke nothing but that appertayneth to the lauding of god.

attrib. **1827** *Edin. Rev.* XLVI. 359 It is the inevitable consequence of such lauding-bouts, that the little are exalted.

lauding ('lɔːdıŋ), *ppl. a.* [f. LAUD *v.* + -ING².] That lauds or praises.

1895 H. SPENCER in *Contemp. Rev.* 229 We meet with the lauding official in his simplest form—the orator.

Laudism ('lɔːdız(ə)m). [f. *Laud* (see LAUDIAN) + -ISM.] The principles and practice of Abp. Laud.

a **1834** COLERIDGE *Lit. Rem.* (1839) IV. 154, I spoke above of 'Romanism'. But call it, if you like, Laudism, or Lambethism in temporalities and ceremonials. **1841** MIALL in *Nonconf.* I. 73 Laudism and ultra-churchism.

laudist¹ ('lɔːdıst). [f. LAUD *sb.*¹ + -IST.] One who writes 'lauds' or hymns.

1890 *Harper's Mag.* July 272/2 The thought came into [Carducci's] head..to show that..without any faith at all one might reproduce the forms of the blessed laudists of the thirteenth century.

Laudist² ('lɔːdıst). [f. *Laud* (see LAUDIAN) + -IST.] A follower of Laud or his principles.

1730 SWIFT *Vind. Ld. Carteret* 27, I do not find how his E——y can be justly censured for favouring none but High-Church, High-Flyers, Termagants, Laudists [etc.].

Laue ('laʊə). *Cryst.* The name of Max von *Laue* (1879–1960), German physicist, used *attrib.* with reference to a method of X-ray diffraction developed by him in which a narrow parallel beam of polychromatic X-radiation is directed at a thin crystal and the resulting diffraction pattern is recorded on a photographic film placed either in front of the crystal (with a hole for the passage of the incident beam) or beyond it; as ***Laue method, pattern, photograph***; also **Laue condition**, each of the three equations (one for each linear parameter of the unit cell) which must be satisfied for a diffracted beam to occur in a given direction for particular orientations of the crystal and the incident beam; **Laue spot**, a spot on a Laue photograph corresponding to a diffracted ray.

1915 W. H. & W. L. BRAGG *X Rays & Crystal Struct.* xii. 208 Each spot in a Laue photograph represents the reflection of the X-rays by a certain plane (*hkl*) of the crystal structure. **1935** *Jrnl. Chem. Physics* III. 421/1 Oscillation and Laue photographs were prepared with crystals of lepidocrocite from Eiserfeld, Westerfald, Germany. **1940** *Physical Rev.* LVII. 448/1 Crystals that are naturally in a strained condition..show 'asterism' of Laue spots. **1940** *Nature* 7 Sept. 332/2 The diffuse spot pattern changes much more slowly than the Laue pattern on successive photographs. **1955** E. S. GOULD *Inorg. Reactions & Struct.* xx. 310 The Laue method, employing polychromatic radiation, is no longer important as a tool for structure determinations. Laue photographs are used chiefly for lining up crystals preliminary to examination by filtered radiation, for partial indications of symmetry, and for indicating imperfections and deformations in crystals. **1966** D. G. BRANDON *Mod. Techniques Metallogr.* 69 (*caption*) Derivation of Laue conditions for diffraction. **1973** P. WILKES *Solid State Theory in Metall.* viii. 197 For the three-dimensional case we require that for constructive interference all three Laue conditions..be satisfied simultaneously. **1973** *Soviet Physics: Crystallogr.* XVIII. 320/1 The symmetry of the Laue pattern allowed the mineral to belong to the hexagonal system.

laue, obs. form of LAW, LOW.

Laufen ('laʊfən). The name of a place in W. Germany near Salzburg, adopted by A. Penck (in Penck & Brückner *Die Alpen im Eiszeitalter* (1909) I. ii. 157, 248) and used *attrib.* to designate a minor retreat and advance of glaciation which he believed followed the last major (Würm) glaciation in the Alps.

1927 PEAKE & FLEURE *Hunters & Artists* 4 After the maximum of the Würm glaciation came a shrinkage called the Laufen retreat, but only of relatively short duration. **1939** AUDEN & ISHERWOOD *Journey to War* 292 When we emerged from holes And blinked in the warm sunshine of the Laufen ice retreat. **1957** J. K. CHARLESWORTH *Quaternary Era* II. xlii. 1174 The Laufen oscillation is probably to be equated with the Aurignacian oscillation.

laugh (lɑːf, læf), *sb.* Also 9 *Sc.* **lauch.** [f. next vb. Cf. MHG., mod.G. *lache*, Du. *lach.*]

1. The action of laughing; laughing, or an inclination to laugh; laughter. *rare.*

1690 CROWNE *Eng. Frier* v. 45 Oh, I'me full of laugh, and must give it some vent. **1694** CONGREVE *Double Dealer* III. ix. 37 You are never pleased but when we are all upon the broad grin; all laugh and no Company. **1768** GOLDSM. *Good-n. Man* I, Do you find jest, and I'll find laugh, I promise you. **1891** S. J. DUNCAN *Amer. Girl in Lond.* 191 Mr. Pratte had very blue eyes with a great deal of laugh in them.

2. An instance of laughing; (a person's) characteristic manner of laughing.

1713 STEELE *Guardian* No. 29 ¶ 1 The laugh of men of wit is for the most part but a faint constrained kind of half-laugh. *a* **1732** GAY *Fables* II. i. 36 So monstrous like the portrait's found, All know it, and the laugh goes round. **1792** S. ROGERS *Pleas. Mem.* I. 33 The heart's light laugh pursued the circling jest. **1796** JANE AUSTEN *Sense & Sens.* (1849) 227 Elinor could have forgiven everything but her laugh. **1826** J. WILSON *Noct. Ambr.* Wks. 1855 I. 175 His licht-blue cunnin een, and that bashfu' lovin lauch. **1838** THIRLWALL *Greece* IV. 215 That the people could be expected to join in the laugh raised at the expense of the demagogues. **1848** THACKERAY *Let.* 4 Oct. in *Scribner's Mag.* I. 399/1, I laughed a sad laugh. **1857** SPURGEON *New Park St. Pulpit* II. 131 It is a figment and a fiction, a laugh and a dream.

fig. **1841** L. HUNT *Seer* (1864) 4 When she stooped..over the tinder-box on a cold morning, and rejoiced to see the first laugh of the fire. **1894** W. WATSON *To R. H. Hutton* Odes, etc. 2, I have seen the morn one laugh of gold.

3. In phr. ***to have the laugh at*** or ***of, to raise the laugh against*** (a person), ***to have*** or ***get the laugh on one's side. on the laugh***: laughing. ***to have the last laugh*** (and similar phrs.): to be successful in the end. ***to have,*** or ***get, the laugh on,*** or ***over*** (***someone***): to have (someone) at a disadvantage; so ***the laugh is on*** (someone).

c **1712** SWIFT *Hints Ess. Convers.* Wks. 1765 XIII. 257 Singling out a weak adversary, getting the laugh on his side, and then carrying all before him. **1766** GOLDSM. *Vic. W.* vii, This effectually raised the laugh against poor Moses. **1771** SMOLLETT *Humph. Cl.* 17 May, He..found no great difficulty in turning the laugh upon the aggressor. **1847** MARRYAT *Childr. N. Forest* v, You've beat us..and have the laugh on your side now. **1848** THACKERAY *Van. Fair* vi, 'Of course you did', cried Osborne, still on the laugh. **1865** KINGSLEY *Herew.* ii. 65 If I have had my laugh at them, they have had theirs at me. **1881** FREWER *Holub's 7 Years S. Afr.* II. iv. 80 Meriko had the laugh of me. **1909** J. LONDON *Let.* 1 July (1966) 280 The laugh is on me. I confess to having been fooled by Mr. Harris's canard. **1925** *Times* 21 Mar. 12/4 *The Last Laugh*, the German film which was shown at the Capitol in the Haymarket for the first time on Thursday, is another example of the new school of film production, the basis of which is the recognition of imagination in the spectator. **1937** G. & I. GERSHWIN (song) *They All Laughed* 4 They laughed at us and how! But Ho, Ho, Ho! Who's got the last laugh now? **1942** E. PAUL *Narrow St.* v. 40 Guy was hauled up, put on the carpet, and when he learned that the uncle was willing to make a rather generous cash settlement considered that he had the last laugh on his fellow workers. **1944** G. B. SHAW *Everybody's Pol. What's What?* xxx. 259 The laugh was on the mob, not on Fouquier. **1949** W. S. MAUGHAM *Writer's Notebook* 329 Sometimes we die sitting quietly in an armchair over a whisky and soda... Then, I suppose, we have the laugh over those who..never rested till the end. **1954** A. MARX *Groucho* xxiii. 200 If she happened to make an error..he would say, 'Well, who's got the last laaaaff now?' **1966** 'J. HACKSTON' *Father clears Out* 18 She's got the laugh on me this time, all right. **1968** D. GODFREY in R. Weaver *Canad. Short Stories* 2nd ser. 306 The Yankee came back about the end of August and we had to give him the last laugh. **1975** J. AIKEN *Voices in Empty House* iv. 121 The dead really have the last laugh on the living.

4. a. = LAUGHING-STOCK. *rare.*

1817 BYRON *Beppo* xcviii, He oft became the laugh of them.

b. A cause of laughter; a joke. Freq. ironic, as in phr. ***that's a laugh***, etc.

1895 G. B. SHAW *Our Theatres in Nineties* (1932) I. 51 The piece contained three or four 'laughs' which could not possibly have been explained or described at a dinner party. **1921** *Motion Picture Mag.* Oct. 21/2 There is unlimited room for the screen comedy of manners and for comedy that depends for its laughs upon the sheer power of clever situations. **1930** W. R. BURNETT *Iron Man* I. 3 Ain't that a laugh!.. That guy's been sleeping for the last half-hour, and he says we're a lot of company. **1960** J. WAIN *Nuncle* 165 'Your friends paid for it.' That was a laugh. My friends.. were a one-way valve for drinks, cigarettes and loans. **1961** A. WILSON *Old Men at Zoo* i. 51 That's a laugh. When Leacock was head of the Aquarium, he did absolutely nothing. **1966** 'H. CALVIN' *Italian Gadget* ix. 149 Embellished or not, the story would be taken as a wild laugh. **1972** D. DEVINE *Three Green Bottles* III. i. 106 She fell for Dr Kendall and he chucked her too. It's a laugh when you think of it.

5. *attrib. and Comb.*, as ***laugh-maker, -shriek***; † **laugh-dove** = LAUGHER 2; **laugh-line**, (*a*) in theatrical use, a comic line received with laughter; (*b*) = *laughter-line* (see LAUGHTER 3); **laugh track**, a recording of audience laughter added to a sound track.

1755 *Man* No. 6 ¶ 1 The cry of the laugh-dove. **1927** M. SULLIVAN *Our Times* II. 106 'Uncle Herbert's Speaker' gave text and minute directions for what modern comedians would call 'putting over the "laugh line"'. **1960** *20th Cent.* Nov. 470 The humour does not consist of laugh lines, but of moods and contrasts. **1967** 'T. WELLS' *Dead by Light of Moon* (1968) vi. 60 Bright green eyes and laugh lines around the mouth. **1969** W. GARNER *Us or Them War* i. 19 'It scared the living daylights out of me. Except it was dark,' he finished, but nobody played up to the laugh line. **1971** P. O'DONNELL *Impossible Virgin* xii. 252 The little laugh-lines at the corners of her eyes..had gone. **1834** H. CAUNTER in *Oriental Ann.* xiv. 187 The shrill laugh-shriek of the jackal. **1850** HT. MARTINEAU *Hist. Peace* II. 602 The great laugh-maker, Liston. **1962** *Variety* 22 Aug. 14 Universal is on the laugh-track for extended play. And the logic is unarguable, as witness the current 'Lover Come Back'. **1966** *N.Y. Times* 20 Nov. 19 Perhaps symptomatic of the quiet corrosion around 'The Jean Arthur Show' is the 'laugh track' or 'canned laughter' on the show. **1969** *Punch* 5 Feb. 193/3 The absence of a laugh track which would only foul up the pace. **1970** *Toronto Daily Star* 24 Sept. 30/3 (*caption*) Program's tired laugh-track..and tired non-plot.

laugh (lɑːf, læf), *v.* Forms: 1 **hlehhan, hli(e)h(h)an, hlæh(h)an,** *Northumb.* **hlæhha,** 2–4 **leiȝen,** 3 **leh-, lihȝen, lahe(n, lauhwen,** *Orm.* **lahȝhenn,** 4 **leȝe(n, leyghe, -ȝ(h)e, l(h)eȝȝe, leeȝe, leyȝe, lyhe, lyȝhe, liȝe, laȝ(h)e(n, lauȝe, lawȝhe(n, lay(g)hyn,** *Sc.* **laucht,** 4–5 **lagh(e, laȝe, lauȝw(h)e, lawȝ(e, laȝwe, loȝe,** 4–6 **laughen, lawghen, law(g)whe, lawȝh(e,** (5 **leyȝh, lawhyn**), 5–6 **lawe, laȝe, lahe,** *Sc.* **lach,** 6 **laffe, loffe,** 5–9 *Sc.* **lauch, lawch,** 5– **laugh.** *Pa. t.* 1 **hlôȝ, hlôh,** 4–5 **logh(e, lough(e, lowh(e,** 4 **loȝe, louȝ(h), louh, lou, lohu, loowȝ, lowȝ(e, looȝ, loowe,** 5 **lowgh, louȝe,** *Sc.* **lugh(e,** 5–6 *Sc.* **leughe, leuȝe,** 6 **lawgh, lewgh, low,** *Sc.* **leuche, lewch, luiche,** 6– *Sc.* **leuch, leugh.** *weak forms*, 4 **leiȝede, -ide, laȝed, laughede, loght,** *Sc.* **laucht, lucht,** 5 **leyghed, lauȝed, louched,** *Sc.* **lauchit,** 6 **lawght, lought,** 5– **laughed.** *Pa. pple.* 4 **laughen, lawhen,** 6 *Sc.* **lachin,** 5– **laughed.** [A Com. Teut. str. vb., but in the later periods of most of the langs. conjugated wholly or partially weak. OE. *hlęhhan, hliehhan*, Anglian *hlæhhan*, pa. t. *hlóȝ, hlóh*, pl. *hlóȝon*, pa. pple. **hlaȝen*, **hlæȝen*, corresponds to OFris. *hlacka*, pa. t. *hlackade*, OS. **hlahan*, pa. t. pl. *hlôgun*, pa. pple. *hlagan* (MDu. *lagchen, lachen*, pa. t. *loeg*, pa. pple. *gelaghen*, mod.Du. *lachen*, pa. t. *lachte*, pa. pple. *gelachen*), OHG. *hlahhen*, pa. t. *hlôch*, also *hlahhên*, pa. t. *hlahhêta* (MHG., mod.G. *lachen*, pa. t. *lachte*, pa. pple. *gelacht*), ON. *hlæja*, pa. t. *hló*, pl. *hlógu*, pa. pple. *hlegenn* (Sw. *le*, pa. t. *log*, Da. *le*, pa. t. *lo*), Goth. *hlahjan*, pa. t. *hlôh* (whence causative *ufhlôjan*); the Teut. root

hlah-* (:hlôh-*: **hlag-*) represents a pre-Teut. **klak-*, prob. echoic; cf. **klōk-* in Gr. *κλώσσειν* to cluck. The OTeut. type has a *-jo*-suffix in the present-stem, but not in the pa. t. or pa. pple. The mod.Eng. form descends from the Anglian *hlæhhan*.]

1. a. *intr.* To manifest the combination of bodily phenomena (spasmodic utterance of inarticulate sounds, facial distortion, shaking of the sides, etc.) which forms the instinctive expression of mirth or of sense of something ludicrous, and which can also be occasioned by certain physical sensations, esp. that produced by tickling. Also *transf.* to have the emotion (of mirth, amusement, scorn) which is expressed by laughing.

c **897** K. ÆLFRED *Gregory's Past.* xxvii. 187 Wa eow ðe nu hliehað, forðam ȝe sculon eft wepan. *c* **1000** ÆLFRIC *Gen.* xviii. 15 Þa ætsoc Sarra: Ne hloh ic na.. God cwæð þa.. ac þu hloȝe. *c* **1200** *Vices & Virtues* (1888) 127 Þat mann is swa blind ðat he farð to helle leiȝinde. *c* **1200** ORMIN 5663 He wepeþþ ec forr alle þa þatt lahȝhenn her wiþþ sinne. *a* **1225** *Ancr. R.* 230 And þeonne mid ispredde ermes leapeð lauhwinde uorð. **1297** R. GLOUC. (Rolls) 2233 Þe king bigan somdel to lyhe, þo he hurde þis. *a* **1300** *Floriz & Bl.* 477 Þis oþere loȝen and hadde gleo. **13..** *E.E. Allit. P.* B. 653 Þenne þe burde byhynde þe dor for busmar laȝed. *c* **1320** *Sir Tristr.* 1582 Sche com wiþ adrink of main and louȝ. **1340** *Ayenb.* 93 Ne þet ne is naȝt lyf of man, ac of child þet nou weþþ nou lheȝþ. *c* **1375** *Sc. Leg. Saints* i. (*Petrus*) 240 Ymagis.. of brass and stane, þat semyt to laucht all elane. *c* **1385** CHAUCER *L.G.W.* Prol. 93 Ryght so mowe ye oute of myn hert bringe Swich vois, ryght as yow lyst, to laughe or pleyn. *c* **1425** LYDG. *Assembly of Gods* 404 Pan gan to carpe of hys lewde bagpype, whyche caused the company to lawe. *c* **1460** *Towneley Myst.* xxiv. 90 So we loghe and maide good chere. *c* **1470** *Golagros & Gaw.* 1065 The lordis on the tothir side for liking thay leugh. **1481** CAXTON *Reynard* xxxii. (Arb.) 92 Ye lawhyd for ye were wel plesyd. **1555** EDEN *Decades* 26 They sawe the Lieuetenaunte laugh. **1590** SHAKS. *Mids. N.* II. i. 55 Then the whole quire hold their hips, and loffe. *a* **1657** SIR W. MURE *Misc. Poems* ii. 88 Lauching to sie my trickling teirs doune go. **1676** HOBBES *Iliad* I. 561 And then the Gods laught all at once outright. **1728** RAMSAY *Anacreontic on Love* 32 He leugh and with unsonsy jest, Cry'd, 'Nibour, I'm right blyth in mind'. **1754** CHATHAM *Lett. Nephew* v. 35 It is generally better to smile than laugh out. **1839** LANE *Arab. Nts.* I. 98 The 'Efreet laughed, and, walking on before him, said, O fisherman, follow me. **1868** G. MACDONALD *R. Falconer* I. 28 He leuch, and speirt gin I wad list, and gae me a shillin. **1890** HALL CAINE *Bondman* I. x, Then she laughed like a bell.

b. In proverbial and fig. phrases. ***to laugh in one's sleeve***: to laugh to oneself, to nurse inward feelings of amusement. ***to laugh on the other, wrong side*** (***of one's face, mouth***): to change from laughter and exultation to sadness and vexation. ***don't make me laugh***: expostulatory phr. freq. used ironically. ***to make a cat laugh***: see CAT *sb.*[1] 13j. ***laugh! I thought I'd die***: exclamatory phr. to indicate excessive laughter. ***to laugh like a drain***: see DRAIN *sb.* 1 f. ***to laugh out of court***: see COURT *sb.*[1] 12c.

1560 DAUS tr. *Sleidane's Comm.* 64 If I coveted nowe to avenge the injuries that you have done me, I myght laughe in my slyve. **1562** HEYWOOD *Prov. & Epigr.* (1867) 163 They laugh that win. **1622** MAY *Heir* III. i, Let them laugh That win the prize. **1642** ROGERS *Naaman* 228 Thou.. hast fleerd and laught in thy sleeve at the sincere. **1775** SHERIDAN *Rivals* II. i, 'Tis false, sir; I know you are laughing in your sleeve. **1779** COWPER *Love of World Reproved* 24 You laugh—'tis well—the tale applied May make you laugh on t' other side. **1809** MALKIN *Gil Blas* II. v. ¶2 We were made to laugh on the other side of our mouths by an unforeseen occurrence. **1837** CARLYLE *Diamond Necklace* iii, in *Fraser's Mag.* Jan. 7/1 By-and-by thou wilt laugh on the wrong side of thy face mainly. **1853** M. ARNOLD *Empedocles on Etna* I. ii, The Gods laugh in their sleeve To watch man doubt and fear. **1889** 'ROLF BOLDREWOOD' *Robbery Under Arms* xxxiii, I'll make some of ye laugh on the wrong side. **1894** A. CHEVALIER *Humorous Songs*, Laugh! I thought I should 'ave died, Knock'd 'em in the Old Kent Road! **1898** J. D. BRAYSHAW *Slum Silhouettes* 246 'E does a bunk dahn the street, lookin' fer all the world like a hunder-done pancake. Laugh—I thought I should ha' died. *Ibid.*, An' as fer you, my lady, wait till I've got yer, I'll make yer laugh the uvver side o' yer face. **1925** D. H. LAWRENCE *Mornings in Mexico* (1927) 21 The monkey.. mocks at you and gibes at you and imitates you... It's funny, and you laugh just a bit on the wrong side of your face. **1951** 'F. O'CONNOR' *Traveller's Samples* 43 'Who are ye laughing at?' I shouted, clenching my fists at them. 'I'll make ye laugh at the other side of yeer faces if ye don't let me pass.' **1958** *Spectator* 22 Aug. 241/3 The fact that a resolute Government (don't make me laugh) could stuff its fingers in its ears and carry on regardless makes no difference; nothing will in fact be done. **1966** *Observer* 20 Mar. 27/3 The jokes.. tended to make one laugh on the other side of one's face. **1967** J. B. PRIESTLEY *It's an Old Country* xiii. 142 'Mind you, I'll never believe there was anything between him and Mum——' 'Don't make me laugh,' Vic said, giving Tom a wink. **1975** S. JOHNSON *Urbane Guerilla* II. 70 Stanton will soon laugh on the other side of his face.

c. Attributed *poet.* and *rhetorically* to inanimate objects, chiefly with reference to movement or play of light and colour which is apprehended as the expression of joyous feeling.

c **1386** CHAUCER *Knt.'s T.* 636 Firy Phebus riseth vp so brighte That al the Orient laugheth of the lighte. **1398** TREVISA *Barth. De P.R.* XIV. I. (1495) 485 For fayrnesse and grene springynge that is therin it is sayde that meedes laughe. *c* **1420** *Anturs of Arth.* 161 (Douce MS.) My lere [was] as þe lele, louched one highte. **1535** COVERDALE *Ps.* lxv. 13 The valleys stonde so thicke with corne yt they laugh and synge. **1725** POPE *Odyss.* III 601 In the dazzling goblet laughs the wine. **1784** COWPER *Task* VI. 817 The fruitful field Laughs with abundance. **1803-6** WORDSW. *Intim. Immort.* iv, The heavens laugh with you in your jubilee. **1805** —— *Prelude* IV. Poems (1888) 261/1 The sea lay laughing at a distance. **1818** MILMAN *Samor* 9 The sparkling wine laugh'd up, As eager 'twere to touch so fair a lip. **1852** HAWTHORNE *Grandfather's Chair* II. i. (1879) 75 The wood fire.. laughs broadly through the room. **1875** LONGF. *Masque of Pandora* i, The waters of a brook.. Limpid and laughing in the summer's sun! **1894** BARING-GOULD *Deserts S. France* I. 2 This mountain plateau laughs with verdure.

†**d.** ***laugh and lay*** (or ***lie***) ***down***: an obsolete game at cards.

1522 SKELTON *Why not to Court* 928 Now nothynge but pay, pay, With, laughe and lay downe, Borowgh, cyte, and towne. **1591** FLORIO *2nd Fruites* 67 What game doo you plaie at cards? At primero, at trump, at laugh and lie downe. **1594** LYLY *Moth. Bomb.* (1632) Dd ij, At laugh and lie downe if they play, What asse against the sport can bray? **1634** S. R. *Noble Soldier* I. ii. in Bullen *O. Pl.* I. 268 Sorrow becomes me best. A suit of laugh and lye downe would wear better. *a* **1825** FORBY *Voc. E. Anglia, Laugh-and-lay-down*, a childish game at cards.

e. ***to be laughing***: to be in a fortunate or successful position (see quot. 1930). *colloq.*

1930 BROPHY & PARTRIDGE *Songs & Slang Brit. Soldier* 136 *Laughing*, comfortable, safe, fortunate, especially in contrast with others or with normal circumstances. E.g. 'He's got a job at Brigade Head Quarters, so he's laughing'; 'Once I get to the C.C.S. I'm laughing'. **1968** *Listener* 19 Dec. 812/3 Oh, Ron, he's got a job—£30 a week he can get now, you know. Skilled motor mechanic, and not put-on like it used to be. Runs his own racket as well. Old Ron's laughing. **1975** M. STANIER *Singing Time* 255 So long as you're a jump ahead you're laughing.

2. a. quasi-*trans.* with cognate object. Also, to utter laughingly or with laughter.

c **1470** *K. Estmere* 235 in *Percy's Reliq.*, The ladye lough a loud laughter, As shee sate by the king. **1606** SHAKS. *Tr. & Cr.* I. iii. 163 The large Achilles.. laughs out a loud applause. *c* **1650** *Lad of Learne* 215 in Furnivall *Percy Folio* I. 190 A loud laughter the Ladie lought. **1842** TENNYSON *Lady Clare*, He laugh'd a laugh of merry scorn. **1848** [see LAUGH *sb.* 2]. **1871** R. ELLIS tr. *Catullus* xxxi. 14 Laugh out whatever laughter at the hearth rings clear.

b. in *passive* (*nonce-use*).

1844 MRS. BROWNING *Drama Exile* Poems 1850 I. 66 For is all laughed in vain?

3. With *dat.* of person, and *to* with sb. expressing the effect, as in ***to laugh to scorn*** (now *arch.* and *literary*), †***to laugh to bismer, hething, hoker.***

The vb. in these phrases is now apprehended as transitive: cf. sense 6.

a **1225** *Ancr. R.* 270 Hwon þet ȝe habben herdi bileaue nule ȝe buten lauhwen him lude to bismare. *a* **1240** *Wohunge* in *Cott. Hom.* 283 Ha.. lahhen þe to hokere þer þu o rode hengest. *a* **1300** *Cursor M.* 15881 (Gött.) Þe feluns logh [*v.r.* lowȝe] him til hething on ilk side, allas! *c* **1340** *Ibid.* 2028 (Trin.) Cam.. was vnkynde ynouȝe To scorne he his fadir louȝe. **13..** *Minor Poems fr. Vernon MS.* xxxvii. 184 Alle wolle þei ful ȝare Lauhwhe þe to bisemare. *c* **1425** *Seven Sag.* (P.) 1995 The clerkys.. louhe to scorne the emperour. **1535** COVERDALE *Ps.* xxi[i]. 7 All they yt se me, laugh me to scorne. **1540** —— *Fruitf. Less.* i. (1593) P i b, The wisest of all is laughed to scorne. *a* **1839** PRAED *Poems* (1864) II. 395, I laughed to scorn the elements—And chiefly those of Learning. **1866** HOWELLS *Venet. Life* 306 This was too much, and we laughed him to scorn.

4. With preps. **a.** With *at*, †*of*, †*on*, *over*, indicating the cause of laughter. †Also with *on*, *upon* (rarely *up*, *to*) in the sense: To look pleasantly on, to smile on.

c **825** *Vesp. Psalter* li[i]. 8 Rehtwise.. ofer hine hlæhað. *a* **1300** *Cursor M.* 2722 (Gött.) Sare.. Herd þis word and lohu [*v.rr.* loghe, lowȝe] þar-att. *c* **1300** *Havelok* 903 The kok stod, and on him low. **1340** HAMPOLE *Pr. Consc.* 1092 Þe world laghes on man and smyles. **1377** LANGL. *P. Pl.* B. XI. 203 For thi loue we as leue bretheren shal and vche man laughe vp other. *c* **1380** WYCLIF *Serm.* Sel. Wks. I. 150 3if.. þe world leiȝe to him in killynge of his enemyes. *c* **1386** CHAUCER *Reeve's Prol.* 1 Whan folk hadde laughen at this nyce cas. *c* **1400** *Rom. Rose* 5060 She.. laugheth on him, and makith him feeste. *c* **1430** *Syr Gener.* (Roxb.) 3253 Thoo Anazaree vpon him lough. *c* **1500** *Three Kings' Sons* 37 The quene & fferaunt lough wele at the wordes of hir doughtir. **1535** COVERDALE *1 Esdras* iv. 31 Yf she laughed vpon him, he laughed also. **1622** MABBE tr. *Aleman's Guzman d'Alf.* II. 226 Whereat they laught'a good. **1654** WHITLOCK *Zootomia* 65 He had the picture of a foole at the entrance,.. laughing on an Urinall. **1669** PEPYS *Diary* 7 Jan., A bold, merry slut, who lay laughing there upon people. **1821** BYRON *Juan* IV. iv, If I laugh at any mortal thing, 'Tis that I may not weep. **1880** MRS. FORRESTER *Roy & V.* I. 7 Dreams, indeed, my dear!.. I have not forgotten them: I often laugh heartily over them.

b. ***to laugh at*** (rarely †*of*, †*upon*): to make fun of, mock at; to deride, ridicule. Also in *indirect pass.*

c **1374** CHAUCER *Anel. & Arc.* 234 He laughethe at my peyne. **1484** CAXTON *Fables of Æsop* II. xii, Of the euylle of other, men ought not to lawhe ne scorne. **1513** MORE in Grafton *Chron.* (1568) II. 781 [He] laughed upon him, as though he woulde say, you shall have neede of one sone. **15..** *Peebles to Play* ix, All that lookit them upon Leugh fast at their array. **1560** DAUS tr. *Sleidane's Comm.* 18 b, A lighte and verye weake reason.. and even laughed at of the Romanes them selves. **1604** E. G[RIMSTONE] *D'Acosta's Hist. Indies* I. i. 2 In his Commentaries vpon the Epistle to the Hebrewes, he doth laugh at those, which hold the heavens to be round. **1722** DE FOE *Plague* (1840) 12 My Brother.. laught at all I had suggested. **1724** —— *Mem. Cavalier* II. 202 Our Major was.. laughed at by the whole Army. **1786** BURNS *Ordination* iv, How graceless Ham leugh at his Dad. **1802** R. ANDERSON *Cumberld. Ball.* 25 Far maist I leugh at Grizzy Brown. **1807-8** IRVING *Salmag.* (1824) 97 Giving parties to people who laugh at them. **1866** *Reader* No. 169. 295/2 Laughed at by mere litterarians. **1880** L. STEPHEN *Pope* iv. 89 Though Pope laughed at the advice, we might fancy that he took it to heart.

†**5.** *trans.* To laugh or mock at, deride. *Obs.*

c **950** *Lindisf. Gosp.* Matt. ix. 24 ȝehloȝun hine. *c* **1000** ÆLFRIC *Hom.* II. 482 Ða apostoli hloȝon ðæra deofla leasunga. **1579** SPENSER *Sheph. Cal.* Jan. 66 She.. laughes the songes, that Colin Clout doth make.

6. With obj. and compl. or advb. phr.: To produce a specified effect upon (a person) by laughing.

1387 TREVISA *Higden* (Rolls) I. 305 Men laughe hem selve to deaþ. **1603** SHAKS. *Meas. for M.* II. ii. 123 Angels.. who with our spleenes, Would all themselves laugh mortal. **1610** —— *Temp.* II. i. 188 Will you laugh me asleepe, for I am very heauy. *Ibid.* ii. 159, I shall laugh my selfe to death at this puppi-headed Monster. **1647** TRAPP *Comm. Epist. & Rev.* 296 [2 Thess. iii. 11] Whose whole life is to eat, and drink.. and laugh themselves fat. **1668** CHAS. II in Julia Cartwright *Henrietta of Orleans* (1894) 264 James did maintaine for some time that she was not painted, but he was quickly laffed out of it. **1679** J. GOODMAN *Penitent Pardoned* II. ii. (1713) 196 The company.. laughed the cunning man out of countenance. *c* **1712** SWIFT *Hints Ess. Convers.* Wks. 1765 XIII. 262 Love, honour, friendship, generosity,.. under the name of fopperies, have been for some time laughed out of doors. **1732** BERKELEY *Alciphr.* III. §15 These authors laugh men out of their religion, as Horace did out of their vices. **1784** COWPER *Task* II. 321 Whom [has it] laughed into reform? **1827** HARE *Guesses* (1859) 248 Is there anybody living.. who has not often been laught out of what he ought to have done, and laught into what he ought not to have done. **1863** COWDEN CLARKE *Shaks. Char.* x. 268 A fellow who will joke and laugh the money out of your pocket. **1890** 'ROLF BOLDREWOOD' *Col. Reformer* (1891) 102 Sure ye'd be laughed out of any hunting-field in Britain if ye took one of them things there.

7. With adverbs. ***to laugh away***: † (*a*) to let go with a laugh; (*b*) to dismiss or get rid of with a laugh; (*c*) to while away (time) with laughter. ***to laugh down***: to subdue or silence with laughter. ***to laugh off***, ***out*** = ***to laugh away*** (*b*). ***to laugh that off***: phrase used ironically (freq. in imperative) as an invitation to dismiss or get rid of (some accomplished fact) with a laugh. ***to laugh over***: to recall or repeat with laughter or mirth. ***to laugh*** (someone) ***out of it***: to persuade (someone) out of a depressed or serious, etc., mood with laughter.

1591 SPENSER *M. Hubberd* 704 Yet would he laugh it out.. And tell them that they greatly him mistooke. **1598** SHAKS. *Merry W.* v. v. 256 Let us.. laugh this sport ore by a Countrie fire. **1604** —— *Oth.* IV. i. 113 Now he denies it faintly: and laughes it out. **1606** —— *Ant. & Cl.* II. vi. 109 Pompey doth this day laugh away his Fortune. **1715** VANBRUGH *Country Ho.* I. i, They all got drunk and lay in the Barn, and next Morning laugh'd it off for a Frolick. **1780** COWPER *Table T.* 239 And laughs the sense of misery far away. **1781** —— *Retirement* 452 He.. talks and laughs away his vacant hours. **1797** MRS. RADCLIFFE *Italian* xiii, Vivaldi tried to laugh away her apprehension. **1806** SURR *Winter in Lond.* III. 221 Though burning with envy.. her grace attempted to laugh out the scene. **1809** MALKIN *Gil Blas* XII. i. ¶8 Instead of laughing it off, I was fool enough to be angry. **1820** BYRON *Mar. Fal.* IV. i. 10, I strove To laugh the thought away. **1842** TENNYSON *Locksley Hall* 89 Baby lips will laugh me down. **1855** —— *Maud* I. xix. 60 Whenever she touch'd on me This brother had laugh'd her down. **1880** MRS. LYNN LINTON *Rebel of Fam.* ii, Clarissa.. laughed off the proposal as a joke. **1918** F. B. YOUNG *Crescent Moon* v. 96 Eva tried to laugh him out of it, to make him ashamed of being afraid. **1926** MAINES & GRANT *Wise-Crack Dict.* 11/1 *Laugh that off*, extraordinary conversational triumph. **1936** 'N. BLAKE' *Thou Shell of Death* xii. 224 Why should he want them [*sc.* footprints] preserved if it wasn't he who originally made them?.. Laugh that one off! **1944** L. MACNEICE *Christopher Columbus* I. 57 They have given me all that I asked—Let Talavera laugh that off if he can. **1974** *Times* 15 Jan. 14/6, I claim to have a complete answer to the charge, so laugh *that* off, Sir Peter.

laughable ('lɑːfəb(ə)l, 'læf-), *a.* [f. LAUGH *v.* + -ABLE.] That may be laughed at; to be laughed at.

1596 SHAKS. *Merch. V.* I. i. 56 They'll not shew their teeth in way of smile, Though Nestor sweare the iest be laughable. **1693** DRYDEN *Juvenal* Ded. (1697) 52 He [Persius] was not a laughable Writer. **1840** CARLYLE *Heroes* iv. (1858) 293 Puritanism was only despicable, laughable then; but nobody can manage to laugh at it now. **1853** READE *Chr. Johnstone* 258 [He] had fallen in love with her in a manner that was half pathetic, half laughable. **1870** OUIDA *Held in Bondage* 78 She could not see that she had said anything laughable.

¶ Similarly *laugh-at-able.* (*nonce-wd.*)

1844 J. T. HEWLETT *Parsons & W.* iv, His being deemed so laugh-at-able a character.

Hence **'laughably** *adv.*, **'laughableness**.

1815 LADY GRANVILLE *Lett.* 1 Aug. (1894) I. 68 She follows and watches him quite laughably. **1853** KANE *Grinnell Exp.* xxx. (1856) 259 All our eatables became laughably consolidated, and after different fashions. **1864** WEBSTER, *Laughableness.* **1872** 'MARK TWAIN' *Innoc. Abr.* 194 The dress of the men is laughably grotesque.

laughee (lɑː'fiː, læ'fiː). *nonce-wd.* [f. LAUGH *v.* + -EE.] The person laughed at.

1829 CARLYLE *Misc.* (1872) II. 134 Laughter seems to depend not less on the laughee than on the laughee.

laugher ('lɑːfə(r), 'læf-). [f. LAUGH *v.* + -ER[1].]

1. One who laughs; one addicted to laughing; also, a scoffer.

c **1410** LOVE *Bonavent. Mirr.* vi. (Gibbs MS.), Crystes wepynges and teers comforteth not dissolute laughers.

c **1515** *Cocke Lorell's B.* 11 Swerers, and outragyous laughers. **1597** SHAKS. *Lover's Compl.* 124 To make the weeper laugh, the laugher weepe. **1676** ETHEREDGE *Man of Mode* III. ii, Softly, these are Laughers, you do not know 'em. **1702** STEELE *Grief à la Mode* I. i. 1 You are of the Laughers [*mispr.* Laughters], the Wits that take the Liberty to deride all Things that are Magnificent and Solemn. *a* **1715** BURNET *Own Time* (1724) I. 260 For the author of the Rehearsal Transprosed had all the men of wit (or, as the French phrase it, all the *Laughers*) on his side. **1784** COWPER *Let. to W. Unwin* in *Corr.* (1824) I. 331 The laughers you mention may live to be sensible of their mistake. **1812** D'ISRAELI *Calam. Auth.* (1867) 115 The wit has gained over the laughers on his side. **1821–30** LD. COCKBURN *Mem.* ii. (1874) 92 The public sided with the best laugher. **1897** 'MARK TWAIN' *More Tramps Abr.* lxvii, Most of them are.. good-natured, and easy laughers.

2. A variety of the domestic pigeon, so called from its peculiar note.

1765 *Treat. Dom. Pigeons* 133 The laugher is about the size of a middling runt, and of much the same make. **1867** TEGETMEIER *Pigeons* xviii. 159 Under the title of the Laugher, Moore describes a variety that, like the Trumpeter, has a very peculiar voice.

laughful ('lɑːfful, 'læf-), *a.* [f. LAUGH *sb.* + -FUL.] Full of laughing, mirthful.

1825 SCOTT *Talism.* xv, The laughful look of some merry one has taken thine eye. **1883** WINGATE *Lost Laird* xvi, After one brief, laughful apology she took her whiff when she desired it.

laugh-in ('lɑːfɪn, 'læf-). [-IN[3].] A demonstration, event, or situation marked by laughter, often staged for this purpose; *spec.* as the name of an American television comedy programme.

1968 *N.Y. Times* 23 Jan. 79/2 The increasing liberality and topicality of Hollywood variety comedy was further evidenced last night in the hour of Dan Rowan and Dick Martin, whose 'Laugh In' had a preseason tryout and now has deservedly won a niche as a regular series at 8 P.M. Mondays... Their hour is an extraordinary quick succession of sight laughs and sketches, many with a deft and good-natured satirical edge to give the show a contemporary pertinency. **1968** *Manch. Guardian Weekly* 21 Mar. 6 As part of their demonstration against the Defence Minister, Mr. Healey,..students at Cambridge proposed to organise a 'laugh-in'. **1968** *Listener* 26 Dec. 854/2 There's a kind of cathartic quality about Danny la Rue that is a tremendous relief after weeks of trying to admire the Rowan and Martin Laugh-In. **1969** *Time* 6 June 56 At an airport, Fielding's baggage check-in is a laugh-in. **1969** *Guardian* 10 Feb. 8/3 'Rowan and Martin's Laugh-in' is a proudly esoteric American comedy series shown late on Sunday night on BBC-2. **1974** HAWKEY & BINGHAM *Wild Card* ii. 26 It had not been Wallcroft's scene at all, and he'd had to eat a lot of dirt to stay in the [television] business through its *Laugh-in* phase.

laughing ('lɑːfɪŋ, 'læf-), *vbl. sb.* [f. LAUGH *v.* + -ING[1].] **a.** The action of the vb. LAUGH; laughter; †an instance of this. Phrase, ***to burst out (a) laughing.***

1340 *Ayenb.* 128 He..euremo ssolle by myd god ine paise and ine leȝinge. **1382** WYCLIF *Job* viii. 21 To the time that thi mouth be fulfild with laȝhing. *c* **1440** *Jacob's Well* 171 Leyȝhyng & enioyng, in a seke body, is sygne of deth. *a* **1450** *Knt. de la Tour* (1868) 42 He saw the fende write alle the laughinges that were betwene the women atte the masse. **1563–83** FOXE *A. & M.* II. 1212/2 Whereat was good laughyng in sleeues of some. **1576** FLEMING *Panopl. Epist.* 281 At the estate of such as are to be lamented, you fall a laughing. **1650** HOBBES *Hum. Nat.* ix. 104 Laughing to ones self putteth all the rest to jealousie and examination of themselves. **1692** L'ESTRANGE *Fables, Life Æsop* (1708) 18 *bis*, They all burst out a laughing by Consent. **1737** FIELDING *Hist. Reg.* III. Wks. 1882 X. 230 He's a laughing in his sleeve at the patriots. **1801** MAR. EDGEWORTH *Angelina* iv. (1832) 69 'Nat!' exclaimed Miss Hodges, bursting out laughing. **1812** *Parl. Debate* 7 May in *Examiner* 11 May 297/2 Hear, hear, and laughing. **1848** KINGSLEY *Yeast* viii, 'Be you a laughing at a poor fellow in his trouble?'

Proverb. **13..** *Minor Poems fr. Vernon MS.* (E.E.T.S.) 534/185 Þe fol is knowen bi his lauhwhing. **1422** tr. *Secreta Secret., Priv. Priv.* 141 By ofte laghynge thow mayste know a fole.

b. *attrib.* and *Comb.*, as ***laughing-humour, -side, -thing, -time***; also **laughing death** = KURU; †**laughing-game** = LAUGHING-STOCK; **laughing-matter** (esp. in phr. ***it is no*** or ***not a laughing matter***), a subject for laughter; **laughing-muscle**, the *risorius*, or the muscle that produces the contortions attendant upon laughter; †**laughing-peal**, a peal of laughter; †**laughing-post, -stake** = LAUGHING-STOCK.

1958 *Times* 9 Jan. 10/1 The newly discovered illness in New Guinea..has become known as the '*laughing death'. .. The malady is comparable in some respects to paralysis agitans. **1967** *Acta Tropica* XXIV. 193 (*heading*) Kuru—the laughing death. **1564** tr. *Jewel's Apol. Ch. Eng.* I. (1859) 5 [They] did count them [Christians] no better than the vilest filth, the offscourings and *laughing games of the whole world. **1875** JOWETT *Plato* (ed. 2) I. 436 Though not in a *laughing humour, I swear that I cannot help laughing. **1563–83** FOXE *A. & M.* II. 1763/1 Then the audience laughed agayne: and Maister Latimer spake vnto them saying: why my maisters, this is no *laughyng matter. I aunsweare vppon lyfe and death. **1793** SHERIDAN in *Sheridaniana* 141 A joke in your mouth is no laughing matter. **1809** MALKIN *Gil Blas* VII. xiv, These little festivities were laughing matters. **1833** MARRYAT *P. Simple* ix, It was not exactly a laughing matter to me. **1593** 'FOULFACE' *Bacchus Bountie* C 3, The whole hall for ioy did ring out a loud *laffing peale. **1810** *Splendid Follies* II. 150 Nobody can't say I have stuck myself up for a *laughing post. **1864** KNIGHT *Passages Work. Life* I. i. 106 One [person] I especially remember as looking upon the *laughing side of human affairs. *a* **1625** ? FLETCHER *Faithf. Friends* I. iii, He lay in Vulcan's gyves a *laughing-stake. **1541** R. COPLAND *Galyen's Terap.* 2 F iv b, It shuld be a *laughyng thynge that so many of dyuers and often contraryes shulde be taken of a communyte. **1534** MORE *Comf. agst. Trib.* I. xiii. (1553) c v b, To proue that thys lyfe is no *laughyng tyme.

laughing ('lɑːfɪŋ, 'læf-), *ppl. a.* [f. LAUGH *v.* + -ING[2].] **a.** That laughs.

a **1300** *Cursor M.* 7366 In visage es he bright and clere, In red of heu, o laghand chere. **13..** *Gaw. & Gr. Knt.* 988 Þus wyth laȝande lotez þe lorde hit tayt makez. **1375** BARBOUR *Bruce* II. 34 [He] schawyt him, with lauchand cher, The Endentur. *c* **1532** DU WES *Introd. Fr.* in *Palsgr.* 922 A gyrle havyng laughyng eyes. **1557** *Tottel's Misc.* (Arb.) 257 Wo shall yeld thee frendes in laughing wealth to loue. *c* **1590** *Manifolde Enormities* in *Chetham Misc.* IV, The Scornefull laffinge Countenance of other som. **1709** STEELE *Tatler* No. 58 ¶ 2 A Man would be apt to think in this laughing Town, that [etc.]. **1725** POPE *Odyss.* IX. 10 O'er the foaming bowl the laughing wine. **1761** CHURCHILL *Night* Poems I. 90 Night's laughing hours unheeded slip away. **1781** E. DARWIN *Bot. Gard.* I. (1791) 5 And tunes to softer notes her laughing lyre. **1821** SHELLEY *Adonais* xlix, A light of laughing flowers along the grass is spread. **1851** CARLYLE *Sterling* III. iii. (1872) 183 A brisk laughing sea..made a pleasant outlook. **1885** J. PAYN *Talk of Town* I. 75 Maggie held up her finger reprovingly, but her laughing eyes belied the gesture.

b. In the names of animals, so called from their cry or aspect: **laughing-bird** *dial.*, the green woodpecker (*Gecinus viridis*); **laughing-crow**, a name for various Asiatic birds; by some writers used as = *laughing-thrush*; **laughing dove**, the African dove, *Stigmatopelia senegalensis*; **laughing-goose**, the white-fronted goose (*Anser albifrons*); **laughing gull**, a North American gull, *Larus atricilla*; **laughing jackass** = JACKASS *sb.* 3 (q.v. for examples), KOOKABURRA; **laughing-owl** (see quot.); **laughing-thrush**, a name given to certain Asiatic birds (see quots.). See also GULL *sb.*[1], HYENA, JACKASS.

1862 WOOD *Nat. Hist.* II. 345 The *Laughing Crow of India (*Garrulax leucolophus*). **1879** ROSSITER *Dict. Sci. Terms* s.v., Laughing Crow, *Cinclosoma erythrocephalus*, a bird belonging to *Meruliddæ*. **1881** E. E. FREWER tr. *Holub's Seven Yrs. S. Afr.* I. ii. 47 The most common birds in the Riet River valley are doves, and those almost exclusively of two sorts, the South African blue-grey turtle-dove, and the *laughing dove. **1966** E. PALMER *Plains of Camdeboo* xii. 196 The thorn trees were full of laughing dove. **1772** FORSTER in *Phil. Trans.* LXII. 415 The *laughing goose is of the size of the Canada or small grey goose. **1830** COL. HAWKER *Diary* (1893) II. 13 Bagged 3 of the white-fronted laughing geese. **1789** J. MORSE *Amer. Geogr.* 59 American Birds [include] ..*Laughing Gull, Goose, Canada Goose [etc.]. **1884** *Bull. U.S. Nat. Museum* No. 27. 169 Laughing Gull... Atlantic coast, from Maine (casually) to mouth of the Amazon. **1968** *Times* 10 Oct. 8/8 The laughing gull could be a useful animal for studying colour perception. **1873** W. L. BULLER *Birds N. Zealand* 21 *Sceloglaux albifacies* (*Laughing Owl). **1859–62** SIR J. RICHARDSON, etc. *Mus. Nat. Hist.* (1868) I. 331 The *Laughing Thrush (*Pterocyclus cachinnans*)..is especially abundant in the thick woods which clothe the Neilgherries. **1879** ROSSITER *Dict. Sci. Terms*, s.v., Laughing Thrush, *Trochaloptera phœniceum*. **1880** A. R. WALLACE *Isl. Life* iii. 44 The fine laughing-thrushes, forming the genus Garrulax.

c. ***laughing-eyed*** adj.

1851 H. MELVILLE *Moby Dick* cxxxii. 597 So have I seen little Miriam and Martha, laughing-eyed elves, heedlessly gambol around their old sire. **1896** H. BELLOC *Verses & Sonnets* 57 This is the laughing-eyed amongst them all: My lady's month. **1909** *Westm. Gaz.* 7 Aug. 9/1 Pale-faced women were hugging to their hearts their rosy-cheeked, laughing-eyed children.

Hence '**laughingly** *adv.*, in a laughing manner.

1563–83 FOXE *A. & M.* II. 1524/1 For (sayth he laughingly) his Chapleine gaue him counsel not to strike me with his Crosierstaffe, for that I would strike agayne. **1825** HONE *Every-day Bk.* I. 112 Laughingly he taunted them. **1874** GREEN *Short Hist.* ix. §3. 617 Charles laughingly bid him set all fear aside. **1894** FENN *In Alpine Valley* II. 139 To take troubles laughingly.

laughing gas. Nitrous oxide, N_2O; so called from the exhilarating effects it produces when inhaled. (See also GAS *sb.*[1] 3 d.)

1842 BRANDE *Dict. Sci.*, etc., *Nitrous oxide*... When nitrous oxide is respired, it produces effects somewhat similar to those of intoxication; hence it has been called laughing gas. **1869** *Daily News* 2 Jan., Protoxide of nitrogen, more commonly called laughing-gas.

laughing-stock. [f. LAUGHING *vbl. sb.* + STOCK.] An object of laughter; a butt for ridicule; said both of persons and things.

1533 FRITH *Bk. agst. Rastell* (1829) 219 Albeit..I be reputed a laughing-stock in this world. **1581** SIDNEY *Apol. Poetrie* (Arb.) 20 Poetry..is fallen to be the laughing stocke of children. **1667–8** PEPYS *Diary* 4 Jan, I perceive my Lord Anglesey do make a mere laughing-stock of this Act. **1775** SHERIDAN *St. Patr. Day* II. iv, You'll be a laughing stock to the whole bench, and a byword with all the pig-tailed lawyers. **1813** *Sporting Mag.* XLII. 213 He could not see any fun in being made a laughing-stock of. **1852** H. ROGERS *Ecl. Faith* (1864) 369 A numerous party to whom the old superstition was a laughing stock. **1881** *Macm. Mag.* XLIV. 118 No wonder that the parish priest becomes the laughingstock of the nobles.

laughsome ('lɑːfsəm, 'læf-), *a.* [f. LAUGH *sb.* + -SOME.] **a.** Of persons: Addicted to laughing, mirthful. **b.** Of things: Provocative of laughter; laughable.

1620 SHELTON *Quix.* III. vi, 'No more, good Sir', quoth Sancho; 'for I confess I have been somewhat too laughsome'. **1798** COLERIDGE *Anc. Mar.* I. iii, Nay, if thou'st got a laughsome tale, Mariner! come with me. **1884** G. ALLEN *Philistia* I. iv. 113 Fly away, sweet little frolicsome, laughsome creature.

laught, obs. pa. t. of LATCH.

laughter ('lɑːftə(r), 'læf-), *sb.*[1] Forms: 1 **hleahtor, hlehter,** 1, 3 **leahter,** 3 **lahter, lehter, leihter,** 4 **laghter, laȝter, laght(t)ir, lauȝtur, lauhter, leiȝter,** 5 **laghtur, laughtir, (laughtre),** 5–6 **lauchtir,** 6 **laughtur,** *Sc.* **lau-, lawchter,** 4– **laughter.** [OE. *hleahtor* str. masc. = OHG. *hlahtar* (MHG. *lahter*, whence collective *gelehter*, mod.G. *gelächter*), ON. *hlátr* (MSw. *later*, Da. *latter*):—OTeut. **hlahtro-z*, f. root **hlah-*: see LAUGH *v.*]

1. a. The action of laughing; *occas.* a manner of laughing. ***Homeric laughter*** (see *Iliad* I. 599, *Odyss.* XX. 346).

Beowulf 611 (Gr.) Ðær wæs hæleþa hleahtor. *c* **897** K. ÆLFRED *Gregory's Past.* xxxiv. 230 Hie habbað swæ micle mede oðerra monna godra weorca,..swæ we habbað ðæs hleahtres, ðonne we hlihhað gliȝmonna unnyttes cræftes. *a* **1050** *Liber Scintill.* lx. (1889) 171 Þurh leahter stunt wyrcð scylda. *c* **1205** LAY. 3045 Mid gomene & mid lehtre [*c* **1275** lihtre]. **1340** HAMPOLE *Pr. Consc.* 1451 Now es laghter and now es gretyng. **1388** WYCLIF *Job* viii. 21 Til thi mouth be fillid with leiȝter. *a* **1400–50** *Alexander* 96 A lowde laȝter he loȝe. **14..** *How Good Wife taught Dau.* 15 in *Barbour's Bruce*, Nocht lowd of lauchtir, na of langage crouss. **1535** COVERDALE *Ps.* cxxv. 3 Then shal oure mouth be fylled with laughter. **1576** FLEMING *Panopl. Epist.* 283 When I behold there undiscrete behauours,..I cannot but burst out into laughter. **1588** SHAKS. *L.L.L.* V. ii. 80 O I am stab'd with laughter. **1651** HOBBES *Leviath.* I. vi. 27 Much Laughter at the defects of others, is a signe of Pusillanimity. **1713** STEELE *Guardian* No. 29 ¶ 25 Laughter is a vent of any sudden joy. **1754** CHATHAM *Lett. Nephew* v. 35 It is rare to see in any one a graceful laughter. **1793** HOLCROFT *Lavater's Physiog.* xxx. 148 The physiognomy of laughter would be the best of elementary books for the knowledge of man. **1812** BYRON *Ch. Har.* II. xcvii, Laughter, vainly loud, False to the heart, distorts the hollow cheek. **1826** J. WILSON *Noct. Ambr.* Wks. 1855 I. 174 The..hubbub o' curses, endin' in shouts o' deevilish lauchter. **1863** GEO. ELIOT *Romola* xii, In the vain laughter of folly wisdom hears half its applause. **1866** R. CHAMBERS *Ess.* Ser. II. 180 Man..has a faculty of the ludicrous in his mental organisation, and muscles in the face ..to express the sensation in..laughter.

Personified. **1632** MILTON *L'Allegro* 32 Laughter holding both his sides.

transf. **1825** LONGF. *Spirit Poetry* 16 The silver brook.. Slips down through moss-grown stones with endless laughter.

b. An instance of this, a laugh. Now *rare*.

971 *Blickl. Hom.* 59 Hwær beoþ þonne..þa unȝemetlican hleahtras. *c* **1200** *Trin. Coll. Hom.* 149 Forlete lahtres, and idele songes. *c* **1205** LAY. 1219 His lauedi Diana hine leofliche biheolde mid wnsume leahtren. *a* **1225** *Ancr. R.* 156 To underuongen flesliche leihtren. **13..** *Gaw. & Gr. Knt.* 1217 Þus he bourded aȝayn with mony a blyþe laȝter. ? *a* **1400** *Morte Arth.* 2673 With lowde laghttirs one lofte for lykynge of byrdez. **1546** J. HEYWOOD *Prov.* (1867) 78 Better is the last smyle, than the fyrst laughter. **1560** DAUS tr. *Sleidane's Comm.* 57 b, Then with a greate laughter (he saide) they would have it so. **1651** *Life Father Sarpi* (1676) 10 Whereat the Duke breaking into a laughter, replyed. **1692** R. L'ESTRANGE *Fables, Life Æsop* (1708) 8 Whereupon Æsop brake out into a Loud Laughter. **1775** GOLDSM. *Scarron* II. 22 They broke out into a laughter for four or five several times successively. **1840** BROWNING *Sordello* III. 98 Exchanging quick low laughters.

†**c.** In various obsolete phrases.

a **1225** *Ancr. R.* 212 To bringen o leihtre hore ontfule louerd. *c* **1374** CHAUCER *Troylus* II. 1120 (1169) She for laughter wende for to dye. *a* **1375** *Lay Folks Mass Bk.* App. IV. 324 He barst on lauhtre. *c* **1400** *Destr. Troy* 5054 Diamede full depely drough out a laughter. *a* **1400–50** *Alexander* 5303 Þan has Þat hende him by Þe hand & hent vp a laȝtir. *a* **1420** HOCCLEVE *De Reg. Princ.* 3400 The Kyng tooke up a laughtir, and went his way. **1480** CAXTON *Chron. Eng.* cxxviii. (1482) 107 The kynge..a grete laughter toke vp. **1596** DALRYMPLE tr. *Leslie's Hist. Scotl.* II. VIII. 125 Al war lyk to cleiue of lauchter. **1608** ARMIN *Nest Ninn.* (1842) 32 Shee forgetting modesty, gapte out a laughter.

d. Used for: A subject or matter for laughter.

1596 SHAKS. *1 Hen. IV*, II. ii. 101 It would be argument for a Weeke, Laughter for a Moneth, and a good iest for euer. **1601** —— *Jul. C.* IV. iii. 114 Hath Cassius liu'd To be but Mirth and Laughter to his Brutus? **1864** TENNYSON *Enoch Arden* 184 All his Annie's fears, Save, as his Annie's, were a laughter to him. —— *Aylmer's F.* 498 A mockery to the yeomen over ale, And laughter to their lords.

¶**2.** An alleged name for a company of ostlers.

1486 *Bk. St. Albans* F vj b, A Laughtre of Ostelores.

3. *attrib.* and *Comb.*, as ***laughter-book, -burst, -maker; laughter-dimpled, -lighted, -lit, -loving, -stirring, -twinkling*** adjs.; †***laughter-crack*** vb.; **laughter-line**, one of the small wrinkles at the corners of the eyes or mouth supposedly formed by years of intermittent laughter.

1851 MAD. DE CHATELAIN (*title*) A *Laughter-Book for Little Folk. **1868** LD. HOUGHTON *Select. fr. Wks.* 208 Each repeated *laughter-burst. **1634** HEYWOOD *Lancash. Witches* II. Wks. 1874 IV. 188 Our sides are charm'd, or else this stuffe Would *laughter-cracke them. **1887** G. MEREDITH *Ballads & P.* 113 A *laughter-dimpled countenance. **1813** SCOTT *Trierm.* I. xviii, *Laughter-lighted eyes. **1938** M. ALLINGHAM *Fashion in Shrouds* xii. 180 His light grey eyes

were entirely without humour in spite of the *laughter-lines beside them. **1950** *Vogue Beauty Bk.* Autumn 26 You should watch for wrinkles—expression lines that run from nose to mouth, laughter lines round the eyes and frown lines on the forehead. **1971** R. FALKIRK *Chill Factor* iii. 35 Laughter-lines still cobwebbed the corners of his eyes. *a* **1847** ELIZA COOK *Rory O' More* vi, Apollo with *laughter-lit face. **1592** DANIEL *Delia, Sonn.* x, Thou..*Laughter-louing Goddesse, worldly pleasures Queen. **1807–8** W. IRVING *Salmag.* (1824) 126 One of those confounded good thoughts struck his laughter-loving brain. **1850** GROTE *Greece* II. lxvii. VIII. 456 The professional jester or *laughter-maker at the banquets of rich Athenian citizens. **1877** DOWDEN *Shaks. Prim.* vi. 66 *Laughter-stirring surprises. **1826** HOR. SMITH *Tor Hill* (1838) II. 215 The ..*laughter-twinkling eyes of the Frenchman.

Hence ˈ**laughterful**, ˈ**laughterless** *adjs.*

1825 *Blackw. Mag.* XVIII. 440 No unfit haunting place For things of..laughterless beatitude. **1897** *Ibid.* Nov. 680/1 The brute..takes himself with the most laughterless gravity. **1898** *Sat. Rev.* 9 July 39 A teacher as rich and laughterful, as mendacious and corrupting as life itself.

laughter (ˈlɑːftə(r), ˈlæf-), *sb.*² *dial.* Also 7 laiter, 8 *Sc.* lachter, 8–9 lafter, 9 *dial.* latter, lawter. [a. ON. **lahtr*, *láttr*:—OTeut. **lahtrom*, f. **lag-*, root of LAY *v.*] The whole number of eggs laid by a fowl before she is ready to sit.

1601 HOLLAND *Pliny* I. 298 Pullets lay more than old hennes, but they be lesse, especially the first and last of one laiter. **1703** THORESBY *Let. to Ray* s.v. (E.D.S.), A hen lays her laughter; that is, all the eggs she will lay that time. **1787** GROSE *Prov. Gloss.*, *Lafter* [printed *Laster*] or *Lawter*, thirteen eggs to set a hen. **1790** MORISON *Poems* 68 Her [*sc.* a goose] lachter's laid with which she's set. *a* **1825** FORBY *Voc. E. Anglia*, *Latter.* **1869** *Lonsdale Gloss.*, *Lafter*, the number of eggs laid by a hen before she begins to wish to sit.

ˈ**laughworthy**, *a.* Deserving to be laughed at.

1616 B. JONSON *Epigr.* cxxxiii, They laugh't at his laughworthy fate. **1848** THACKERAY in *Punch* 20 May 207 Because the object was laughworthy.

laughy (ˈlɑːfɪ, ˈlæfɪ), *a. rare.* [f. LAUGH *sb.* + -Y¹.] Inclined to laugh.

1837 THACKERAY *Ravenswing* i, Let us laugh when we are laughy. **1906** B. VON HUTTEN *What became of Pam* II. ix. 172, I suppose you felt teary, but now you must feel laughy. **1913** G. STRATTON-PORTER *Laddie* vii. 201 Then father, all laughy and criey, said: 'Thank God!' **1950** *Sunday Jrnl. & Star* (Lincoln, Nebraska) 29 Oct. (*headline*) Mister 880 is a charming laughy movie.

‖**lauhala** (laʊˈhɑːlə). [Hawaiian *lau* leaf + *hala* pandanus.] A Polynesian screw pine, *Pandanus tectorius*; the dried leaves of the tree, or the material plaited from them.

1826 M. GRAHAM *Voy. H.M.S. Blonde to Sandwich Is.* II. 108 A church..has lately been erected here: its walls are of reeds, lined with the woven leaves of the lauhala. **1866** 'MARK TWAIN' *Lett. from Hawaii* (1967) 99 Shady groves of forest trees..the breadfruit, the lau hala, the orange, lime. **1875** I. L. BIRD *Hawaian Archipelago* viii. 111 Then we come upon a whole cluster of grass houses under *lauhalas* and bananas. **1898** J. A. OWEN *Story Hawaii* iii. 87 Around the room are hung native mats woven from the long leaf of the 'lauhala' tree. **1933** E. H. BRYAN in *Ancient Hawaiian Civilization* 127 Much of the plaited work, such as baskets, mats, pillows, and fans, was made from *lauhala*, the leaf of the pandanus. **1954** J. SHERIDAN in J. Macdonald *Lethal Sex* (1962) 174 With *lauhala* mats and some reed furniture..it will be quite charming. **1957** P. H. BUCK *Arts & Crafts Hawaii* 250 Sandals..were quickly woven of any tough fiber at hand: *lauhala*, ti, banana leaves.

lauhter, obs. form of LAUGHTER.

‖**laulau** (ˈlaʊlaʊ). [Hawaiian, reduplicated form of *lau* leaf.] A portion of a Hawaiian dish of meat and fish wrapped in leaves and steamed or baked (see quots.). Also, this cover of leaves.

1940 K. BAZORE, *Hawaiian & Pacific Foods* i. 41 *Laulau*, an individual portion of fresh belly pork and of salted butterfish or salmon, wrapped in several taro leaves, then in ti leaves, and steamed or cooked in an imu. **1954** J. SHERIDAN in J. Macdonald *Lethal Sex* (1962) 162 We ate with the Hawaiian family..steamed *laulaus* (salt salmon, butterfish, and pork wrapped in *ti* leaves), *poi* and coconut pudding. **1957** P. H. BUCK *Arts & Crafts Hawaii* 18 Like fish, they might be wrapped in the ti-leaf cover called *laulau*. **1961** E. FODOR *Hawaii* 15 The Manoa campus is transformed..into a kind of miniature Pacific worlds fair where you can sample kim chee, laulaus, sukiyaki and other Pacific foods.

laumb(e)re, variant of LAMBER¹ *Obs.*, amber.

laumontite (ˈlɔːməntaɪt). *Min.* Earlier lomonite, laumonite. [Named (G. *lomonit*) by Werner, 1805, after Gillet de *Laumont*, its discoverer: see -ITE.] Hydrous silicate of aluminium and calcium, found in crystals which lose water when exposed to the air.

1805 JAMESON *Syst. Min.* II. 539 Lomonite. **1808** T. ALLAN *Alphab. List* 42 Laumonite. **1843** PORTLOCK *Geol.* 218 Laumonite has only been observed at Portrush, and is there very rare. **1868** DANA *Min.* (ed. 5) 400 Laumontite occurs in the cavities of trap. **1894** *Amer. Jrnl. Sci.* Ser. III. XLVIII. 190 Laumontite..Loses about ½ its water at 300°.

laumpe, obs. form of LAMP *sb.*¹

laumpron, -un, obs. forms of LAMPERN.

†**launce**¹. *Obs. rare*⁻¹. [ad. L. *lance-m* (*lanx*), It. *lance*.] A scale, balance.

1590 SPENSER *F.Q.* III. vii. 4 Need teacheth her..That fortune all in equall launce doth sway.

launce² (lɑːns, læns). *Zool.* Also 7 lawnce, lance. [? identical with LANCE *sb.*¹; the name may allude to the shape of the fish; cf. LANCELET, and G. *lanzenfisch*, a kind of chætodon.] A fish of the genus *Ammodytes*; the sand-eel; = LANT *sb.*² Also called *sand-la(u)nce*. ***sable launce***: the capelin.

1623 WHITBOURNE *Newfoundland* 89 A sufficient quantity of Herrings, Mackerel, Capeling, and Lawnce, to bait their hooks withal. *Ibid.* 114 Mackarell, Herrings, Lance, Caplin, Dogfish. **1691** RAY *Creation* (1701) 156 We found the stomach of one we dissected full of Sand-eels or Launces, which for the most part lie deep in the sand. **1769** PENNANT *Brit. Zool.* III. 123 The launce is found on most of our sandy shores during some of the summer months. **1848** C. A. JOHNS *Week at Lizard* 26 The launce or sand-eel is a small cylindrical fish from six to twelve inches long. **1883** L. Z. JONCAS *Fish. Canada* 13 (Fish. Exhib. Publ.) The cod-fish resorts..to the coast..in pursuit of the caplin or sable launce, on which it feeds.

launcelet, -ot, obs. forms of LANCELET.

launcer, launcet(te, obs. ff. LANCER², LANCET.

launch (lɔːnʃ, formerly lɑːnʃ), *sb.*¹ [f. LAUNCH *v.*]

†**1.** The action or an act of lancing; a prick. *Obs.*

1558 TRAHERON in S. R. Maitland *Ess. Reform.* (1849) 80 If I shal perceaue that it shalbe to your welth, I wil not sticke to giue you a launch or two. **1596** SPENSER *Hymn Heavenly Love* 162 What hart can feele least touch of so sore launch?

2. The action or an act of launching, shooting forth, or springing. *Obs.* exc. *dial.*

c **1440** *Promp. Parv.* 290/2 Lawnche, or skyppe, *saltus*. *a* **1825** FORBY *Voc. E. Anglia*, *Launch*, a long stride. **1897** W. C. RUSSELL *Last Entry* 241 The schooner..swept in long floating launches down upon the boat.

†**3.** *concr.* Shoots of a plant. Also *fig.* *Obs.*

a **1400** *Pistill of Susan* (Ingilby MS.) 109 þe lyly, þe louage, þe launches so lefe. *c* **1430** *Hymns Virg.* 3 Veni de libano, þou loueli in launche.

4. a. The action or process of launching a vessel. Also *fig.* and *transf.*, and with *out*. **b.** The starting off of a bird in flight.

1749 J. CLELAND *Mem. Woman Pleasure* I. 18, I soon came to a resolution of making this launch into the wide world, by repairing to London. **1814** SCOTT *Let. to Southey* 17 June in *Lockhart*, The first time I happened to see a launch. **1835–6** TODD *Cycl. Anat.* I. 298/1 The first launch of the bird into the air is produced by an ordinary leap from the ground. **1857** *Trans. Mich. Agric. Soc.* VIII. 193, I have seen the commencement of railways, and witnessed the 'launch' of the first locomotive. **1879** J. MARTINEAU *Ess.* (1891) IV. 271 Its daring launch-out on the ocean of real being. **1879** *Cassell's Techn. Educ.* IV. 223/2 Bearing surfaces should be well greased..before the launch takes place. **1969** J. ARGENTI *Managem. Techniques* v. 25 Anxiety that the launch date [of a product] will be missed. **1969** *Punch* 15 Jan. 96/2 The Ford Capri, a sort of shrunken Mustang, is being built in Britain and Germany and will be launched later this month. But, of course, 'the launch', as the trade calls it, is not as simple as that. **1971** *Sunday Express* (Johannesburg) 28 Mar. 5/1 Mr. Uys..vetoed the display of the same model's nipple when the launch advertisement was submitted.

c. The launching of a missile, spacecraft, glider, or the like. (See also sense 7 below.)

1935 C. H. LATIMER-NEEDHAM *Gliding & Soaring* x. 170 The wind velocity should be ascertained and allowed for in any method of mechanical launching or too vigorous a launch may be given unwittingly. **1952** F. GEEN *A.B.C. of Gliding* 95 The easiest launch is a full-height nose launch. **1963** *Ann. Reg. 1962* 397 The closely matched orbits of the two astronauts also required precise timing of their launches. **1966** *Economist* 18 June 1307/1 The first of three such launches which are to put a chain of 24 defence communications satellites in synchronous orbit round the earth. **1969** *Observer* 20 July 9/8 The astronauts..sleep or doze for nearly five hours before preparing for the launch.

5. *concr.* in *Ship-building*. (See quot. 1850.)

1711 W. SUTHERLAND *Shipbuild. Assist.* 23 Erecting a Ship on the Launch, and launching her from thence. **1712** *Lond. Gaz.* No. 5019/5 Wherein are two large Launches and a large dry Dock. *c* **1850** *Rudim. Navig.* (Weale) 128 *Launch*, the slip or descent whereon the ship is built, including the whole of the machinery used in launching.

6. *dial.* A trap for taking eels.

1847 in HALLIWELL.

7. *attrib.* and *Comb.* as (sense 4 c) ***launch crew***, ***date***, ***site***, ***vehicle***; **launch-block**, **launch-ways** (*Cent. Dict.*) = *launching-ways*, *launching-planks*; **launch pad** = *launching pad*; **launch window**, a period outside which the planned launch of a spacecraft cannot take place if the journey is to be completed, owing to the changing positions of the planets.

1720 DE FOE *Capt. Singleton* iii. (1840) 50 A launch-block and cradles. **1962** J. GLENN in *Into Orbit* 6 The most junior member of the launch crew. **1969** *Daily Mail* 15 Jan. 5/3 Then suddenly it was now—launch date just around the corner. **1960** *News Chron.* 29 Sept. 9/6 The 100-foot rocket sat immobile on its launch-pad. **1968** *Times* 23 Dec. 6/3 Captain Lovell and Major Anders..climbed into a van which took them to the launch pad. **1969** *Times* 3 June Suppl. p. iii/1 The world's largest tracked vehicle, 'the crawler',..carried..Saturn 5..from its lofty assembly building to launchpad 39A. **1969** *Listener* 20 Feb. 233/2 When you fly over the Soviet Union, can you see their launch sites? **1965** *New Scientist* 18 Mar. 701/1 The Gemini spacecraft, launch vehicle and target vehicle are all derived from hardware and technology already in existence. **1966** *Sci. Amer.* Jan. 54 Because of various failures in the launch-vehicle guidance system..a lunar landing was not accomplished. **1965** *Newsweek* 29 Nov. 40/3 It is thought they may even try a third shot before the launch window closes in December. **1966** *Sci. News Let.* 3 Sept. 165 The 20-day period centered around the launch date allowing travel between planets on an orbit requiring the least amount of energy. This is the so-called 'launch window' used to hurl space vehicles from earth to the moon. **1968** *Radio Times* 19 Dec. 41/4 As to timing, they must choose a launch window several days long when the Moon is in the right position relative to the Earth, when the sun is in the right position relative to the lunar landing sites, and when Apollo 8 can return to a suitable landing on Earth.

launch (lɔːnʃ, formerly lɑːnʃ), *sb.*² Also 7–8 lanch. [ad. Sp. *lancha* pinnace, perh. of Malay origin: see LANCHARA, LANTCHA.]

1. The largest boat of a man-of-war, more flat-bottomed than a long boat, for use in shallow water, usually sloop-rigged.

1697 DAMPIER *Voy.* (1729) I. 2 The Craft which carried us was a Lanch, or Long Boat. **1742** WOODROOFE in Hanway *Trav.* (1762) I. II. xvii. 76 We had..a launch of ten tuns with sixteen oars. **1833** MARRYAT *P. Simple* (1863) 248 The launch, yawl, first and second cutters, were the boats appointed for the expedition.

2. A large boat propelled by electricity, steam, etc. (***electric launch***, ***steam-launch***) used for transporting passengers, or as a pleasure-craft. *Comb.* **launchman**, a man who operates a launch.

1865 LIVINGSTONE *Zambesi* xxi. 423 Natives from all parts of the country came to see the launch. **1880** *Daily Tel.* 26 Nov., The Judge directed them that to find a verdict of guilty they must be satisfied that the defendant omitted to perform an obvious duty in navigating his launch.

Comb. **1894** C. H. COOK *Thames Rights* 21 On the Thames, some 370 launch-owners endanger the lives of many thousands of people. *Ibid.* 28 A man absolutely ignorant of steam or other vessels may be a launch-driver. **1924** J. MASEFIELD *Sard Harker* 146 Everybody was very still, except for the launchman munching his onion. **1928** *Daily Mail* 13 Aug. 13/4 The complement consists of captain, first and second mate, two cooks, two stewards, boatswain, launchman, and able seamen. **1963** M. SHADBOLT in C. K. Stead *N.Z. Short Stories* (1966) 322 So my father produced the launchman and people from the township as witnesses.

3. Special Comb.: **launch-engine** (see quot. *a* 1877).

a **1877** KNIGHT *Dict. Mech.* II. 1266/2 Launch-engines generally consist of a boiler with engines attached thereto, and are used for propelling the launches of large ocean steamers in shallow harbors, etc. **1889** P. N. HASLUCK *Model Engineer's Handybk.* vi. 69 A double cylinder launch engine fitted with reversing motion. **1909** *Westm. Gaz.* 23 Mar. 4/3 A very fine launch-engine, fitted with..reversing gear.

launch (lɔːnʃ, formerly lɑːnʃ), *v.* Forms: 4–5 launche, (5 laun-, lawnchyn, launsche), 5–6 lawnche, 5–9 lanch(e, (6 lange, launge), 6– launch. [ad. ONF. *lancher* = Central OF. *lancier*: see LANCE *v.*]

†**1. a.** *trans.* To pierce, transfix, wound; cut, slit; to make (a wound) by piercing. Also with *up*. *Obs.*

c **1400** *Destr. Troy* 6811 Toax..with a tore speire..hym launchit to dethe. **1460** *Libeaus Desc.* 293 (Kaluza) Wiþ his sper he will launche All þat aȝens him rit. **1484** CAXTON *Fables of Æsop* v. x, Two rammes within a medowe whiche with theyr hornes launched eche other. **1590** SPENSER *F.Q.* III. ii. 37 Whose love hath gryde My feeble brest of late, and launched this wound wyde. **1596** *Ibid.* VI. ii. 6 A sharpe bore-speare, With which he wont to launch the salvage hart Of many a Lyon. **1615** G. SANDYS *Trav.* 12 In the beginning of August lanch they the rine, from whence the masticke distilleth. **1622** BEAUM. & FL. *Faithf. Shepherdess* IV. iii, Hee, Directed by his fury, Bloodelye, Lanch't vpp her brest. **1670** DRYDEN *1st Pt. Conq. Granada* I. i, Nine Bulls were launch'd by his victorious arm.

†**b.** To cut with a lancet, to lance; to let out (infection) by lancing. *Obs.*

1426 LYDG. *De Guil. Pilgr.* 18357 For pouerte Is bothe medicyne and leche To launche the bocche off Properte. **1593** NASHE *Christ's T.* 82 a, So wil they giue them more.. to feede their sores then to launch them. **1598** Q. ELIZ. *Plutarch* xiv. 23 As wound that bloudies hit self while hit is Launged. **1604** DRAYTON *Owl* 310 To lanch th' infection of a poysoned state. **1612** WOODALL *Surg. Mate* Wks. (1653) 10 If you be wary, you need not launch or cut the gum at all. **1641** T. EDWARDS *Reasons agst. Independancy* 10 The foote ..is dressed, lanched and ordered, not by it selfe, but by the hands and eyes.

fig. **1625** QUARLES *Sion's Elegies* II. xiv. D 2 b, Thy Prophets..Rubb'd where they should haue launcht. **1640** FULLER *Joseph's Coat, David's Repent.* (1867) 224 Nathan, than whom was none more skilled to lanch A festered soul.

2. a. To hurl, shoot, discharge, send off (a missile) (cf. LANCE *v.* 1); *spec.* to send off (a rocket, spacecraft, or the like, or an astronaut) on its (or his) course: (cf. 4 b, from which this use may equally derive). †Also, to heave (the lead).

? *a* **1400** *Morte Arth.* 750 Schipe-mene..Launchez lede apone lufe. *c* **1489** CAXTON *Blanchardyn* xliii. 164 Launchynge and castyng to hym speres and dartes. **1697** DRYDEN *Æneid* II. 364 And launch'd against their Navy Phrygian fire. **1791** MRS. RADCLIFFE *Rom. Forest* ix, All the thunders of heaven seemed launched at this defenceless head. **1808** SCOTT *Marm.* I. Introd. 80 Nor mourn ye less his

perished worth Who..launched that thunderbolt of war On Egypt. **1837** W. IRVING *Capt. Bonneville* I. 268 Much as they thirsted for his blood, they forebore to launch a shaft. **1873** MERCIER & KING tr. *Verne's From Earth to Moon* 145 The gun destined to launch the projectile had to be fixed in a country situated between the 0 and 28th degrees of north or south latitude. *Ibid.*, Launched on the 1st of December, ..it ought to reach the moon four days after its departure. **1922** *Encycl. Brit.* XXX. 50/1 A forecastle deck large enough to enable a seaplane to be launched therefrom on a light subsidiary carriage. **1952** *Oxf. Jun. Encycl.* X. 17/2 The German guided missiles..launched against London from the French coast were driven by their own power and were automatically controlled. **1957** *Britannica Bk. of Year* 443 The first artificial earth satellite..was launched from a site in the U.S.S.R...on Oct. 4, 1957. **1960** J. N. BELL *Seven into Space* i. 15 He knows an excitement so intense that it seems he can no longer contain it. The first American has been launched into space. **1972** A. C. KERMODE *Mech. of Flight* (ed. 8) xii. 390 As with the X15 these [*sc.* lifting bodies] are launched from a mother craft. **1974** *Daily Tel.* 14 Feb. 1/3 Two more spaceships, Mars-6, and Mars-7, which were launched last August, were due to approach the planet next month.

absol. *c* **1500** *Melusine* xxi. 137 Thanne bygan the Cypryens..to shote & to launche on the paynemes.

b. with immaterial object, *e.g.* a blow, censure, threat, sentence.

1748 RICHARDSON *Clarissa* (1811) VII. 196 The best in the world to launch a guess. **1865** LECKY *Ration.* (1878) I. 251 Week after week he launched from the pulpit the most scathing invectives. **1869** FREEMAN *Norm. Conq.* (1876) III. xii. 89 The assembled Fathers at once went on to launch the censures of the church against offenders of every degree. **1875** STUBBS *Const. Hist.* II. xvi. 345 A threat launched especially at the Despensers. **1886** G. T. STOKES *Celtic Ch.* (1888) 171 Jerome, therefore, launched a treatise against him.

†**c.** To throw (a person); *refl.* to hurl oneself, dart, rush. *Obs.*

13.. *Seuyn Sag.* (W.) 1904 The louerd..in a bed he dede hire launche. **1604** E. G[RIMSTONE] *D'Acosta's Hist. Indies* IV. xxxix. 315 Then do they launch themselves foorth.

d. To dart forward (a weapon, a limb, etc.). Now only, to dart *out* (something long and flexible).

c **1386** CHAUCER *Sompn. T.* 437 Doun his hand he launcheth to the clifte. **1426** LYDG. *De Guil. Pilgr.* 461 Hyr syxthe hand she gan to launche Lowe doun vn-to hyr haunche. **1484** CAXTON *Fables of Æsop* III. ii, The booll.. smote strongly whith his feet after the man and launched his hornes at hym. **1847-9** TODD *Cycl. Anat.* IV. 293/1 The whole tongue is then launched out with a rapidity that is perfectly amazing.

3. a. *intr.* for *refl.* To be set into sudden or rapid motion; to rush, plunge, start or shoot forth; †to leap, vault; *transf.* to 'skip' in reading. *Obs.* exc. *dial.*

13.. *K. Alis.* 3746 He gan in the water launche: Up he cam in that othir side. ? *a* **1400** *Morte Arth.* 194 Of ilke a leche the lowe launschide fulle hye. *Ibid.* 2560 Who lukes to the lefte syde, whenn his horse launches. *c* **1400** *Destr. Troy* 12307 þai demet þe duke..to..launche out of towne. *c* **1440** *Promp. Parv.* 290/2 Lawnchyn, or skyppyn ouer a dyke, ..*perconto.* **1480** CAXTON *Ovid's Met.* XI. xix, The mortal floodes launchid in by the places opend. ? *a* **1500** *Chester Pl.* vii. 469 Lanch on! I will not be the last upon Mary for to marveyle. **1552** HULOET, Launche to shore, *appellere ripam.* **1570** LEVINS *Manip.* 22/34 To lanch ouer a boke, *percurrere.* **1787** BEST *Angling* (ed. 2) 45 He [a fish] will launch and plunge in such a manner, that..he will tear away his hold. **1814** W. IRVING in *Life & Lett.* (1864) I. 317 The poor animal..gazed at me..and then launching away to the left, I presently heard it plunge into the river. *a* **1825** FORBY *Voc. E. Anglia*, *Launch*, to take long strides.

†**b.** *transf.* To shoot, sprout. Also, to project.

1401 *Pol. Poems* (Rolls) II. 90 Thei ben bastard braunches that launchen from oure bileve. **1698** FRYER *Acc. E. India & P.* 49 The Cape lanches into the Sea with Three Points.

c. *fig.* (Now usually with *out.*) To enter boldly or freely into a course of action; to rush *into* expense; to burst *out* into unrestrained speech. † *to launch it out*: to flaunt, make a display.

1608 MIDDLETON *Fam. Love* v. iii. I 3, If master Gerardine..would yet be induced to take your Neece.. would you launch with a thousand pound, besides her fathers portion? **1622** FLETCHER *Sp. Curate* II. i, When you love, lanch it out in silks and velvets. **1624** BEDELL *Lett.* vii. 115 Thus Pamelius; and presently lanches forth into the Priuiledges of the See of Rome. **1685** BOYLE *Enq. Notion Nat.* vi. 196, I want time to launch into an ample discourse. **1711** STEELE *Spect.* No. 49 ¶4 He enjoys a great Fortune handsomly, without lanching into Expence. **1712-13** POPE *Guardian* No. 4 ¶6 There is no subject I could lanch into with more pleasure than your panegyrick. **1732** ARBUTHNOT *Rules of Diet* 430, I have lanch'd out of my subject in this Article. **1741** RICHARDSON *Pamela* (1824) I. 136 One launching out upon my complexion, another upon my eyes. **1745** *De Foe's Eng. Tradesman* (1841) I. vii. 49 He has perhaps launched out in trade beyond his reach. *c* **1820** S. ROGERS *Italy Descent* 38 For awhile he held his peace..But soon, the danger passed, launched forth again. **1855** MILMAN *Lat. Chr.* III. vii. (1864) II. 143 The triumphant Pontiff..launches out into a panegyric on the mercy and benignity of the usurper. **1865** CARLYLE *Fredk. Gt.* XVI. xv. (1872) VI. 316, I began to launch-out on Friedrich's actions, but he rapidly interrupted. **1887** JESSOPP *Arcady* i. 9 The small man..is..slow to launch out into expense when things are going well. **1888** BURGON *Lives 12 Gd. Men* I. iii. 358 You could not vex him more than by launching out against some common acquaintance. **1889** RUSKIN *Præterita* III. 11 She launched involuntarily into an eager and beautiful little sermon.

4. a. *trans.* To cause (a vessel) to move or slide from the land, or the stocks, into the water; to set afloat; to lower (a boat) into the water.

? *a* **1400** *Morte Arth.* 3921 He..Gers lawnche his botes appone a lawe watire. **1511** *Nottingham Rec.* III. 332 To lawnche the boote in to the water. **1523** LD. BERNERS *Froiss.* I. ccccxiii. 722 There came two other barkes..and anone they were langed into the ryuer. **1555** *Act 2 & 3 Ph. & Mary* c. 16 §7 Before the said Boate..bee lanched out of the Yarde or Grounde. *c* **1590** MARLOWE *Faust* xiii. 91 Was this the face that launch'd a thousand ships. **1653** HOLCROFT *Procopius* III. x. 92 He lancht into the Tiber also 200. Pinnaces. **1702** POPE *Sappho* 250 O launch thy bark, nor fear the wat'ry plain. **1756-7** tr. *Keysler's Trav.* (1760) IV. 45 From these sheds they are launched into the deep canals. **1821** JOANNA BAILLIE *Metr. Leg.*, *Columbus* lviii. 2 Ere from his home He launch his vent'rous bark. **1856** KANE *Arct. Expl.* II. iii. 45 Our boats must be sledged over some 60.. miles of terrible ice before launching and loading them.

b. In wider sense: To send off, start upon a course, send adrift; *spec.* to release (a balloon or its contents) into the air at the beginning of a flight. (Cf. 2.)

1627 CAPT. SMITH *Seaman's Gram.* xiii. 62 Out goes the boat, they are lanched from the ship side. *a* **1680** BUTLER *Rem.* (1759) I. 217 When Pudding-Wives were launcht in cock quean Stools. **1715-20** POPE *Iliad* VIII. 455 Haste, lanch thy chariot, thro' yon ranks to ride. **1820** SCOTT *Ivanhoe* xxxi, Fling open the door, and lanch the floating bridge. **1824** *Encycl. Brit.* Suppl. I. 83/1 It was soon found, that a balloon, launched into the atmosphere, is abandoned, without guidance or command, to the mercy of the winds. **1831** BREWSTER *Newton* (1855) I. xiii. 359 The planets, like the comets, might have been launched in different directions. **1959** *Chambers's Encycl.* I. 103/2 On 19 Sept. 1783..they launched a sheep, a cock and a duck into the air, enclosed in a basket suspended beneath the balloon.

c. *fig.* To start (a person) *in*, *into*, or *on* a business, career, etc.; to set on foot (a project); to commence (an action). Also with *out.* ***to launch into eternity***: rhetorically for 'to put to death'.

1602 MARSTON *Ant. & Mel.* IV. G b, Was neuer Prince.. With louder shouts of tryumph launched out Into the surgy maine of gouernment. **1678** BUNYAN *Pilgr.* I. 217 Being lanched again into the gulf of misery. **1711** ADDISON *Spect.* No. 108 ¶7 We find several Citizens that were lanched into the World with narrow Fortunes. **1719** DE FOE *Crusoe* II. xiii. (1840) 274, I am now launched quite beside my design. **1802** *Med. Jrnl.* VIII. 275 The mention of this term serves to launch the author into a digression. **1812** *Examiner* 30 Nov. 768/1 The platform, from whence he was to be launched into eternity. **1837** W. IRVING *Capt. Bonneville* I. 43 The worthy captain,..fairly launched on the broad prairies, with his face to the boundless west. **1839-40** —— *Wolfert's R.* (1855) 213 It was agreed that..as soon as I should be fairly launched in business we would be married. **1863** GEO. ELIOT *Romola* vi, The pretty youngster..was well launched in Bardo's favourable regard. **1872** YEATS *Growth Comm.* 275 The Mississippi scheme launched by John Law. **1884** H. B. BUCKLEY in *Law Times Rep.* 22 Mar. 115/1 The plaintiff himself has launched this action in the Chancery Division.

d. To publish (a book); to put (a product, etc.) on the market.

1870 'MARK TWAIN' *Lett. to Publishers* (1967) 45 We'll have someone standing ready to launch a book right on our big tidal wave and swim it into a success. **1919** J. QUINN *Let.* 3 Oct. in T. S. Eliot *Waste Land Drafts* (1971) p. xvii, My part in connection with launching your book is finished. **1926** H. CRANE *Let.* 5 Dec. (1965) 278 Once this first book is really launched and off my mind. **1966** *Listener* 17 Nov. 716/3 The complicated process of launching a new American car. **1969** J. ARGENTI *Managem. Techniques* v. 25 To launch a product is a complex project.

5. *intr.* Of the ship: To be launched, to pass into the water.

1665 *Lond. Gaz.* No. 5/4 The *Resolution* now in the Dock, Launches on Tuesday 28. **1677** W. HUGHES *Man of Sin* III. iii. 67 A fourth,..with some Prayers and three signings of the Cross made a Ship lanch with few men. **1769** FALCONER *Dict. Marine* (1780) H 4, Cradles, placed under the bottom, to conduct the ship..into the water whilst lanching. **1906** *Westm. Gaz.* 26 Nov. 6/2 The payment was refused on the ground that the Deal lifeboat launched to the same wreck.

6. To push *forth*, *out* from land, put to sea, advance seawards; *lit.* and *fig.* ***to launch into eternity***: rhetorically for 'to die'.

1534 TINDALE *Luke* v. 4 He sayde vnto Simon: Launche out in to the depe. **1555** EDEN *Decades* 55 He lanched from that lande and directed his course to Vraba. **1598** DRAYTON *Heroic. Ep.* xiii. 53 The Thames..That danc'd my Barge, in lanching from the stayre. **1604** E. G[RIMSTONE] *D'Acosta's Hist. Indies* I. xviii. 60, I doe not finde in ancient bookes, that they have lanched farre into the Ocean. *a* **1656** BP. HALL *Rem. Wks.* (1660) 385 What need I lanch forth into this forrain deep? **1676** DRYDEN *Aurengz.* II. i. 25 Lanching out into a Sea of strife. **1720** MRS. MANLEY *Power of Love* (1741) I. 123 He was afraid his Soul should launch into Eternity without a Guide to direct his Penitence. **1745** *De Foe's Eng. Tradesman* (1841) I. ii. 12 The time of my servitude being at length expired, I am now launched forth into the great ocean of business. **1766** HUME *Let. to H. Walpole* in *W.'s Remin.* 165, I find I am launching out insensibly into an immense ocean of common-place. **1769** BURKE *Late St. Nation* Wks. II. 160 To have launched into a new sea, I fear a boundless sea, of expence. **1773** JOHNSON *Let. to Mrs. Thrale* 21 Sept., We launched into one of the straits of the Atlantick Ocean. **1838** THIRLWALL *Greece* II. xii. 107 Before any Greek navigator ventured..to launch out beyond Sicily. **1875** LONGF. *Masque of Pandora* ii, Forth I launch On the sustaining air.

7. *trans. Naut.* †**a.** To set up, hoist (a yard). **b.** To move (casks, heavy goods, etc.) by pushing. **c.** '*Launch-ho!* The order to let go the top-rope, after the top-mast has been swayed up and fidded' (Smyth *Sailor's Word-bk.* 1867).

1627 CAPT. SMITH *Seaman's Gram.* ix. 41 Vnparrell the mizen yard and lanch it, and the saile ouer her Lee quarter. **1692** *Capt. Smith's Seaman's Gram.* (ed. 3) I. xvi. 79 When a Yard is hoisted high enough, they usually call aloud *Launch-hoe*, that is hoise no more. **1711** W. SUTHERLAND *Shipbuild. Assist.* 161 To Launch;..to leave off pulling, haling, or heaving. **1753** CHAMBERS *Cycl. Supp.*, *Launch*, a term used in several sea phrases, as *launch out the capstan bars*, that is, put them out; *launch aft*, or *foreward on*, that is, when things are stowed in the hold, to put them more aft, or foreward on. **1769** FALCONER *Dict. Marine* (1780), *Lanch*, the order to let go the *top-rope*, after any top-mast is *fided.*

8. *Public School slang.* (See quots.)

1865 G. F. BERKELEY *My Life*, etc. I. 129, I had [at Sandhurst about 1815] to undergo the usual torments of being 'launched', that is, having my bed reversed while I was asleep [etc.]. **1878** H. C. ADAMS *Wykehamica* 426 *Launch*, to drag a boy, bed-clothes, mattress, and all, off his bedstead on to the floor.

9. *intr.* To propel a boat with a pole, etc.; *spec.* in *Wild-fowl shooting* (see quot. 1824).

1824 P. HAWKER *Instr. Yng. Sportsmen* (ed. 3) 329 Off they set,..crawling on their knees, and shoving this punt before them on the mud. Thus travelling all night (by 'launching' over the mud, and rowing across the creeks). **1856** P. THOMPSON *Hist. Boston* 713 Launching—propelling a barge or small vessel in a river by means of a poy.

10. *dial.* (See quot.)

1847 HALLIWELL s.v., To launch leeks is to plant them like celery in trenches. *West.*

†**ˈlaunchant**, *a. Obs.* [a. ONF. *lanchant*, pres. pple. of *lanchier* LAUNCH *v.*] Darting, leaping.

c **1400** *Destr. Troy* 4630 With a launchant laite lightonyd the water. *Ibid.* 12006 All the cite vnsakrely þai set vppon fyre, With gret launchaund lowes into the light ayre. *c* **1450** *Merlin* 288 The toon myght not come to that other but launchant.

launched (lɔːnʃt, formerly lɑːnʃt), *ppl. a.* [f. LAUNCH *v.* + -ED[1].] In senses of the vb.

1601 WEEVER *Mirr. Mart.* F ij, With goarie sides, and deeper lanched brest. **1639** G. DANIEL *Ecclus.* xli. 54 Let thy blushes rise From a lanch't heart. **1875** BROWNING *Aristoph. Apol.* 95 The launched lie Whence heavenly fire has withered. **1896** *Daily News* 1 Apr. 6/5 A launched vessel always begins her career by [etc.].

launcher (ˈlɔːnʃə(r), formerly ˈlɑːnʃə(r)). [f. LAUNCH *v.* + -ER[1].] **1.** One who launches, in senses of the vb.

1824 P. HAWKER *Instr. Yng. Sportsmen* (ed. 3) 329 A family..who are by far the best launchers in Hampshire. **1827** —— *Diary* (1893) I. 302 The vagabond mud launchers. **1897** *Westm. Gaz.* 19 Aug. 6/3 To make the launchers of schemes responsible for their promises. **1899** *Daily News* 4 May 7/3 All hands turned out at once to launch the lifeboat, ..four of the most useful launchers..being women.

2. A device or structure that launches something or is used for launching; *spec.* (*a*) a structure that holds a rocket or missile during launching; (*b*) a rocket from which a satellite is released into orbit.

1911 T. O'B. HUBBARD et al. *Aeroplane* v. 61 There have been many..mechanical launchers invented, but none have met with any success..except the rail-and-falling-weight method originally used by the Wright biplanes. **1944** C. P. LENT *Rocket Research* 4 The photograph lower left is a German rocket launcher. **1945** *Aeroplane Spotter* 18 Oct. 250/2 Zero-type rocket-projectile launchers eliminated the drag of the earlier tube type to such an extent that the Lockheed P-38J and P-38L Lightning is able to carry seven under each wing. **1957** *Oxford Mail* 20 Aug. 1/4, I saw the 25 ft. long Bloodhound on its launcher, together with its special loading trolley, exactly as it would be on one of the coastal sites. **1958** *Times* 12 Aug. 7/3 Now that Britain can provide the launcher, she should certainly explore the field for partners in the actual launching of a satellite. **1959, 1969** [see *grenade launcher* s.v. GRENADE *sb.*[1] 3]. **1970** *Daily Tel.* 28 Apr. 1/4 America was first to use a single launcher to put eight satellites into orbit, in June, 1966. **1971** *Nature* 2 Apr. 282/2 An extensive study of the propagation of Earth surface waves, including the design of launchers for such waves, is described. **1973** *Sci. Amer.* Aug. 105/2, I devised an apparatus for launching a continuous stream of water globules indoors... The launcher consists of a small nozzle that directs a jet of water upward at an angle of approximately 45 degrees. **1974** *Daily Tel.* 14 Feb. 4/8 The ship has been fitted with four missile launchers.

launching (ˈlɔːnʃɪŋ, formerly ˈlɑːnʃɪŋ), *vbl. sb.* [f. LAUNCH *v.* + -ING[1].] **a.** The action of the vb. LAUNCH.

1592 DAVIES *Immort. Soul* xxx. lviii. (1714) 104 That Launching, and Progression of the Mind, Which all men have. **1602** *2nd Pt. Return fr. Parnass.* I. i. 95 Nought but lanching can the wound auayle. **1605** SYLVESTER *Du Bartas* II. iii. II. *Fathers* 67 Such ill-rigg'd ships would even in lanching sink. **1669** BUNYAN *Holy Citie* 259 This signifieth our launching into Eternity. **1745** *De Foe's Eng. Tradesman* (1841) I. vi. 44 Such miserable havoc has launching out into ..remote undertakings, made amongst tradesmen. **1751** LABELYE *Westm. Br.* 28 The lowering or launching of the finished Caisson. **1822** J. FLINT *Lett. Amer.* 129 The launching of a large steam-boat attracted a great assemblage of spectators. **1824** P. HAWKER *Instr. Yng. Sportsmen* (ed. 3) 332 Birds may be approached much nearer by this means than by any other kind of 'launching'. **1967** *Listener* 23 Feb. 263/3 Admittedly, the launchings will be carried out by American rockets from an American site, but the satellites themselves are purely British-built. **1971** *Nature* 6 Aug. 357/2 It is not safe to base a rocket development project on a single launching once a year.

b. *attrib.* and *Comb.*, as ***launching-cord***, ***-cradle***, ***-line***, ***platform***, ***site***, ***station***; **launching-cleat**, the block of wood fastened to a ship when in dry dock or on the slips, to catch the head of the 'shore'; **launching pad**, the area

on which a rocket stands for launching; also *fig.* and *transf.*; **launching-planks** (see quot.); **launching-punt, -sledge**, a boat used in shooting wild fowl (cf. LAUNCH *v.* 9); **launching-tube**, a tube in a war-vessel for launching torpedoes; **launching-ways**, = *launching-planks*.

1898 *Westm. Gaz.* 15 Dec. 4/1 The Princess..has only to sever the *launching cord to set the *Irresistible* free. *Ibid.*, The *launching cradle is a massive structure of wood and iron, weighing 300 tons. **1691** T. H[ALE] *Acc. New Invent.* 124 It swims at the line representing the *launching line. **1951** COOKE & CAIDIN *Jets, Rockets & Guided Missiles* 138 Under a blazing afternoon sun, at 3.14 p.m., a modified V-2 rocket carrying a WAC-Corporal in its nose rose slowly from its concrete *launching pad. **1958** *Daily Mail* 16 Aug. 1/4 The 88 ft. rocket stands poised on its concrete launching pad here tonight looking like a giant silver propelling pencil. **1959** *Encounter* Dec. 74/2 All this is by way of a launching-pad for the idea of the Non-Nuclear Club. **1963** A. HUXLEY *Let.* 17 Feb. (1969) 948 Julian tells me that your book is now definitely on the launching pad. **1973** *Guardian* 31 Jan. 13/7 The NUS sees the rent-strike movement as a launching pad for its main campaign. *c* **1850** *Rudim. Navig.* (Weale) 128 **Launching planks*, a set of planks mostly used to form the platform on each side of the ship, whereon the bilgeways slide for the purpose of launching. **1922** *Encycl. Brit.* XXX. 50/1 Ordinary aeroplanes were carried in fighting-ships with a *launching-platform. **1957** *Jane's Fighting Ships 1957–58* 413 The missile is using jet-assisted rocket bottles to launch it from its zero-length launching platform. **1824** P. HAWKER *Instr. Yng. Sportsmen* (ed. 3) 326 Hampshire *Launching-punt. **1944** *Aeronautics* Aug. 27/1 The counter attack, by bombing the *launching sites in the Pas de Calais, was intensified. **1958** *Listener* 13 Nov. 766/2 Israel had also agreed to launching-sites on her territory for United States atomic rockets and guided missiles. **1824** P. HAWKER *Instr. Yng. Sportsmen* (ed. 3) 332 The light *launching sledge is in the foreground. **1897** *Strand Mag.* June 712/1 We had better not make the *launching station a place like the bank of the river, where it can go only one way. **1944** A. HUXLEY *Let.* 9 July (1969) 507 Five thousand launching stations, firing off twenty robots [*sc.* rockets] apiece—and that would be the end of any metropolis. **1958** C. C. ADAMS et al. *Space Flight* p. xi, A space station would serve as a 'launching station' for space ships to the moon, saving fabulous amounts of precious fuel. **1846** A. YOUNG *Naut. Dict.*, **Launching-ways*, the same as *Bilge-ways*.

laund (lɔːnd). *Obs.* exc. *arch.* Forms: 4–6 launde, 5–9 lawnd(e, (5, 7 land, 7 launt), 6– laund. See also LAWN *sb.*[2] [a. OF. *launde*, F. *lande* wooded ground, a. OCeltic **landā* (Irish *lann*, Welsh *llan*, Breton *lann*): see LAND *sb.*[1]] An open space among woods, a glade (= L. *saltus*); untilled ground, pasture.

1340 *Ayenb.* 216 Þe fole wyfmen þet guoþ mid stondind.. nhicke as hert ine launde. **13..** *E.E. Allit. P.* B. 1209 Loude alarom vpon launde lulted was þenne. **1387** TREVISA *Higden* (Rolls) V. 251 Som of hem com out of hilles and laundes, þere mannes help failede. *c* **1425** WYNTOUN *Cron.* VII. i. 50 Thare thai fand A fayre brade land and a plesand. **15..** *Adam Bel* 419 in Ritson *Anc. P.P.* 21 Then went they down into a launde, These noble archares all thre. **1551** ROBINSON tr. *More's Utop.* 41 You loste no small quantity of grounde by forestes, chases, laundes, and parkes. **1593** SHAKS. *3 Hen. VI*, III. i. 2 Through this Laund anon the Deere will come. **1631** BRATHWAIT *Whimzies, Forrester* 37 The lawnd is his temple, the birds his quirresters. **1650** T. BAYLY *Herba Parietis* 3 A..bridge, between which and the palace, was a stately launt. **1700** DRYDEN *Fables, Palamon & Arc.* III. 898 That grove for evergreen, that conscious lawnd Where he with Palamon fought hand to hand. *a* **1825** FORBY *Voc. E. Anglia, Lawnd*, a lawn. **1891** ATKINSON *Last of Giant Killers* 204 Through the launds and glades, out on to the moor.

attrib. *a* **1440** *Sir Degrev.* 596 Undir a lynd or thei lente, By a launde syde. *c* **1440** *Promp. Parv.* 291/1 Lawnde kepare, *salator*. **1523** FITZHERB. *Surv.* 5 All the grounde within pale or hedge as well the launde grounde as of the wode grounde.

laund(e, obs. form of LAWN *sb.*[1] (fine linen).

launde iron, variant of LANDIRON *Obs.*

launder ('lɔːndə(r), 'lɑːndə(r)), *sb.* Forms: 4– lander, 4 *Sc.* landar, laynder, 5–7 la(u)ndre, law(e)nder(e, 5– launder. [Contraction of LAVENDER *sb.*[1]]

†**1.** A person (of either sex) who washes linen. *Obs.*

a **1350** *St. Brice* 71 in Horstm. *Altengl. Leg.* (1881) 156 A woman þat his lander was. **1375** BARBOUR *Bruce* XVI. 273 It is ane landar.. That hir childyne richt now hass tane. *c* **1440** *Promp. Parv.* 290/1 Lawndere, *lotor, lotrix*. **1477** NORTON *Ord. Alch.* v. in Ashm. (1652) 79 As Laundres witness evidently, When of Ashes thei make their Lye. *a* **1530** HEYWOOD *Play Weather* (Brandl) 894 She wolde banyshe the sonne And then were we pore launders all vndonne. **1573** TUSSER *Husb.* lxxxiii. (1878) 173 In washing by hand, haue an eie to thy boll, for launders and millers, be quick of their toll. **1584** COGAN *Haven Health* (1636) 28 Amylum is taken to be starch, the use whereof is best knowne to Launders. *a* **1603** T. CARTWRIGHT *Confut. Rhem. N.T.* (1618) 31 How small things they be, that these cunning Launders can with so small cost make white.

2. a. A trough for water, either cut in the earth, or formed of wood; *esp.* in *Mining*, a trough for washing the ore clean from dirt. **b.** A rain-water gutter. †**c.** A tube made out of a hollow tree (*obs.*).

1667 PRIMATT *City & C. Build.* 8 The water brought to the top of the wheel, in landers or troughs which cast the same into Buckets made in the wheel. **1671** *Phil. Trans.* VI. 2108 The Launder (i.e. a trench cut in the floor, 8 foot long, and 10 foot over) stopt at the other end with a turf, so that the waters run away, and the Ore sinks to the bottom. **1734** DESAGULIERS *Ibid.* XXXIX. 48 This centrifugal Wheel can in a little Time drive down Air through wooden Trunks (or Launders) of seven Inches bore. **1753** CHAMBERS *Cycl. Supp.* s.v. *Dressing*, The launder..fills up with the dressed ore. **1865** *Crt. Com. Pleas* 10 July, A lander or trough..had been constructed to carry water to his works across the defendant's land. **1884** *West. Morn. News* 9 Aug. 1/4 Lot of Launders, 14 buddles. **1891** *Blizzard of 1891* 25 Icicles hung inches long from windowsills and launders of the houses.

d. *Metallurgy.* A channel for conveying molten metal from a furnace or container to a ladle or mould.

1900 *Kynoch Jrnl.* Oct.–Nov. 20/1 The tapping hole is now cut through the bottom of the furnace, and a wrought iron channel—technically called a lander—fastened round it. **1906** W. MACFARLANE *Princ. & Pract. Iron & Steel Manuf.* x. 110 The Shoot or Launder, along which the steel and slag are conveyed from the taphole to the ladle, is a half-round gutter made of steel plates. **1929** W. LISTER *Pract. Steelmaking* x. 78 With all fixed furnaces the lander is necessarily 10 ft. to 15 ft. long, and sometimes up to 20 ft. long. **1967** P. MCGEOWN *Heat the Furnace* x. 97 We had her running down the lander as the twelve o'clock hooter sounded. **1971** W. K. V. GALE *Iron & Steel Industry: Dict. Terms* 195 The tapping spout of an open-hearth furnace is usually called a launder.

launder ('lɔːndə(r), 'lɑːndə(r)), *v.* Also 7 lander, laundre. [f. LAUNDER *sb.*]

1. a. *trans.* To wash and 'get up' (linen).

1664 BUTLER *Hud.* II. i. 171 It does your visage more adorn Than if 'twere prun'd, and starcht, and lander'd. **1818** SCOTT *Bride of Lamm.* xviii, The picture..is up in the old Baron's hall that the maids launder the clothes in. **1883** G. CABLE *Dr. Sevier* xvii, His dress was coarse but clean; his linen soft and badly laundered. **1890** *Century Mag.* Oct. 933/1 White duck, which they were permitted to send outside to be laundered.

absol. **1709** MRS. MANLEY *Secret Mem.* (ed. 2) I. 150 Some of their beggarly Soldiers Trulls does nothing but Launder for 'em, they'r always at the Wash-Tub.

transf. and *fig.* **1597** SHAKS. *Lover's Compl.* 16 Laund'ring the silken figures in the brine, That seasoned woe had pelleted in teares. **1654** [see LATHER *v.* 1]. **1878** SWINBURNE *Poems & Ball.* Ser. II. 223 (tr. Villon) The rain has washed and laundered us all five.

b. To transfer funds of dubious or illegal origin, usu. to a foreign country, and then later to recover them from what seem to be 'clean' (i.e. legitimate) sources. Also *transf.*

The use arose from the Watergate inquiry in the United States in 1973–4.

1973 *Guardian* 19 Apr. 14/2 Suitcases stuffed with 200,000 dollars of Republican campaign funds; money being 'laundered' in Mexico. **1973** *Publishers Weekly* 17 Sept. 54/2 A New York lawyer carrying $200,000 in his camera case to be 'laundered' in Switzerland. **1973** J. M. WHITE *Garden Game* 128 Phoenix is a city where the Mafia is well entrenched; its booming real-estate, building and service industries are ready-made havens for 'laundering' the extortion and gambling money from Nevada and California. **1974** *Globe & Mail* (Toronto) 3 Apr. 1 (*headline*) Kerr concedes U.S. criminals 'launder' money in Ontario.

†**2.** To 'sweat' (gold or plate). *Obs.*

1610 B. JONSON *Alch.* I. i, I'll bring..Thy necke within a nooze, for laundring gold and barbing it.

3. *intr.* Of a fabric: to admit of being laundered; to bear laundering without damage to its texture, colour, etc. Used with adverbs.

1908 *Sears, Roebuck Catal.* 916 It will launder as well as a piece of linen. **1909** *Daily Chron.* 22 July 7/5 A single initial ..done in satin stitch..is showy, quickly worked and launders well. **1923** *Daily Mail* 19 Feb. 1 (Advt.), This hard wearing fabric, which launders perfectly, can be obtained. **1951** *Good Housek. Home Encycl.* 252/1 Most silks launder well.

Hence **'laundered** *ppl. a.*

1892 *Daily News* 31 Mar. 5/5 Ravachol..is rather a dandy, and affects nicely-laundered shirts. **1893** KATE WIGGIN *Cathedral Courtship* 151 A freshly laundered cushion cover.

launderer ('lɔːndərə(r), 'lɑːndərə(r)). Also 5 lawnderer, 6–7 landerer, 7 laundrer. [f. LAUNDER *sb.*: see -ER[1] 3; now regarded as f. LAUNDER *v.*]

1. One who launders (linen). *Obs.* exc. *U.S.*

c **1475** *Cath. Angl.* (Add. MS.) 210/2 Lawnderer, *candidaria, lotrix*. **1550** J. COKE *Eng. & Fr. Heralds* §101 (1877) 89 Launderers. **1598** KITCHIN *Courts Leet* (1675) 379 The Woman which is Landerer or Nurse shall be essoined. **1631** BRATHWAIT *Whimzies, Launderer* 56 A launderer may bee as well a male as a female, by course of nature. **1666** EVELYN *Mem.* (1857) III. 185 The cook and laundrer comprehended in the number. **1876** DIXON *White Conq.* I. xvii. 171 Having their work done better and cheaper by.. Chinese launderers in Jackson Street. **1884** *Circular* [The makers of an ironing machine shown at the Health Exhibition ask the support of] launderers and laundresses. **1889** *Daily News* 8 June 5/1 A laundress, or washerwoman [in America], is now 'a lady launderer'.

fig. *a* **1680** BUTLER *Rem.* (1759) II. 386 An Anabaptist..is a Landerer of Souls, and tries them, as Men do Witches, by Water.

†**2.** One who 'launders' gold or plate; a sweater.

1632 D. LUPTON *Lond. & Country Carbonadoed* (1857) 277 Some of the men are cunning Landerers of plate, and get much by washing that plate they handle, and it hath come from some of them..a great deale the lighter.

launderette (lɔːndə'rɛt). Also laundrette. [f. LAUNDER *v.* + -ETTE.] An establishment providing automatic washing machines for the use of customers.

1949 *Vogue* Oct. 102/2 A new and interesting development in housekeeping—the advent of the self-service launderette. **1952** [see BAGWASH]. **1955** PRIESTLEY & HAWKES *Journey down Rainbow* 117 Who does not understand the sudden success of our communal laundrettes? **1967** *Which?* July 216 Launderettes are shop-like premises, usually equipped with between 8 and 20 large automatic washing machines, supplied with hot water from a central source, and with about one tumbler drier for each three washing machines. **1968** *Listener* 7 Mar. 316/1 To me the world Strindberg created is like some enclosed launderette of the spirit—the underwear goes round and round but the water has been turned off. **1970** G. GREER *Female Eunuch* 227 Perhaps the failure of such community living could be avoided by including a pub and a launderette in each block. **1973** E. BERCKMAN *Victorian Album* 113 The enemy lumbered into sight carrying two fat plastic bags: obviously bound for the launderette in the High Street.

'laundering, *vbl. sb.* [f. LAUNDER *v.*] The process or action of washing, drying, and ironing linen, etc. Also *fig.*

1894 *To-Day* 17 Mar. 182/2 French cambrics..are not to be starched in the laundering, but left soft. **1908** K. GRAHAME *Wind in Willows* x. 221 I'm in the washing and laundering line, you must know, ma'am. **1949** 'G. ORWELL' *Nineteen Eighty-Four* II. x. 221 Her life had been laundering, scrubbing, darning, cooking, sweeping, polishing, mending, scrubbing, laundering, first for children, then for grand-children. **1970** *Which?* Aug. 247/2 Many people were uninformed about certain aspects of laundering. **1974** *Globe & Mail* (Toronto) 3 Apr. 1/8 Mr. Kerr, who rose in the Legislature to answer Dr. Shulman's question last Friday about laundering of money in Ontario, began by saying, 'The washing or laundering of funds does occur in Toronto.' *Ibid.*, The laundering transaction itself is not illegal.

Launder-Ometer (lɔːndə'rɒmɪtə(r)). orig. *U.S.* Also **Launderometer, launderometer.** [f. LAUNDER *v.* + -OMETER.] The proprietary name of a machine for making standard laundry tests, consisting of a number of jars clamped to a rotating shaft in which the washing is carried out.

1928 *Amer. Dyestuff Reporter* XVII. 731/2 We will now.. introduce to you this machine, which we have baptised the 'Launder-Ometer'... It was originally invented or devised by one of our fellow members, Hugh Christison. **1929** *Official Gaz.* (U.S. Patent Office) 21 May 591/1 Launder-Ometer. For laundry washing machines. Claims use since April 27, 1928. **1938** *Year Bk. Amer. Assoc. Textile Chemists & Colorists* XV. 138 The Launder-Ometer..consists of a heavily constructed copper tank.., supported upon a rigid angle-iron frame. Within this tank there is a brass and aluminum rotor that carries the twenty standard pint jars in which the tests are made. **1958** *Observer* 30 Mar. 11/5 Cotton and other coloured materials are tested in a launderometer, a machine which reproduces as many domestic washes as are considered necessary. **1961** K. DURHAM *Surface Activity & Detergency* ix. 229 The Launderometer..is merely a tank containing a simple mechanism for holding and rotating jars, each containing steel balls, into which the fabric and solution are placed; the jars are rotated and the steel balls provide agitation. The rate of rotation and the weight of the balls are both variable.

†**laundon.** *Obs. rare*[−1]. [a. OF. *landon*, f. *lande*: see LAUND.] *o laundon*: on the field.

? *a* **1400** *Morte Arth.* 1768 The kynge of Lebe be-fore the wawurde he ledez, And alle his lele lige mene o laundone ascriez.

laundress ('lɔːndrɪs, 'lɑːndrɪs), *sb.* Forms: 6–7 landres(se, laundres(se, (7 landeress, lawndresse), 7–8 landress, 7– laundress. [f. LAUNDER *sb.* + -ESS.]

1. A woman whose occupation it is to wash and 'get up' linen.

1550 COVERD. *Spirituall Perle* vi. (1560) 75 As the dier, blecher, or the laundresse washeth..the foule, vncleanly and defiled clothes. **1555** EDEN *Decades* 319 He sent to lande certeyne of his men with the landresses of the shyppes. **1598** SHAKS. *Merry W.* III. iii. 155 Carry them to the Landresse in Datchet mead. **1623** MIDDLETON *More Dissemblers* v. i. 104 His jealous laundress, That for the love she bears him starches yellow. **1710** STEELE *Tatler* No. 189 ¶3 Write down what you give out to your Landress, and what she brings Home again. **1732** BERKELEY *Alciphr.* II. §2 She employs milliners, laundresses, tire-women. *a* **1859** MACAULAY *Hist. Eng.* xvii. V. 68 A Dutchwoman.. employed as a laundress at Whitehall.

2. A caretaker of chambers in the Inns of Court.

1592 GREENE *Groat's W. Wit* (1617) 29 His hostesse writte vp the wofull remembrance of him, his Laundresse and his boy. **1611** BARREY *Ram Alley* I. i, No punie Inne a Court But keepes a Landresse at his command To doe him seruice. **1731** *Gentl. Mag.* I. 206/2 He had been very careful to avoid the Use of the Words *Chambers, Laundress*, &c. **1836** DICKENS *Pickw.* xx, It's a curious circumstance, Sam, that they call the old women in these inns, laundresses. **1841** S. WARREN *Ten Thous. a Year* III. 357 Greatly to the surprise of his laundress, he made his appearance at his chambers between six and seven o'clock in the morning.

†**'laundress**, *v. Obs.* [f. LAUNDRESS *sb.*] **a.** *trans.* To furnish with laundresses. **b.** *intr.* To act as a laundress.

1612 WEBSTER *White Devil* G 2, Did I want Ten leash of Curtisans, it would furnish me; Nay lawndrese three Armies. **1636** SIR H. BLOUNT *Voy. Levant* 14 Their Wives are used..but to dresse their meat, to Laundresse [etc.].

c. To serve (a person) as a laundress.

1850 DICKENS *Dav. Copp.* xxvi. 281 'Sir,' said Mrs. Crupp, in a tone approaching to severity, 'I've laundressed other young gentlemen besides yourself.'

laundrette: see LAUNDERETTE.

Laundromat ('lɔːndrəʊmæt). orig. *U.S.* Also laundromat. [See -MAT.] The proprietary name of a brand of automatic washing machines; also, by extension, a launderette.

1943 *Trade Marks Jrnl.* 14 July 300/1 Laundromat. Domestic electric washing (laundering) machines. Westinghouse Electric & Manufacturing Company.. Pennsylvania. **1951** *Amer. Speech* XXVI. 166 The Westinghouse Company has a 'Laundramat', and there are also 'Laundromats'—often called 'Laundermats' and 'Laundrymats'—open for public patronage. **1955** M. MCCARTHY *Charmed Life* (1956) i. 20 The village mind was still churning up the past, tossing the old dirty linen back and forth impersonally, like one of the washing machines in the new laundromat. **1956** A. HUXLEY *Adonis & Alphabet* 148 Junior colleges, jet-plane factories, Laundromats, six-lane highways. **1957** J. KEROUAC *On Road* (1958) III. ii. 187, I..found nothing but laundromats, cleaners, soda fountains. **1963** *Punch* 2 Jan. p. vi/2 Harrods' sale..includes ..laundromats and dryers. **1964** *Economist* 30 May 1024/3 Coin operated Laundromats and dry cleaning machines. **1966** *New Scientist* 16 June 694/3 The 'local' is doomed, one day, to operate like a licensed laundromat. **1966** T. PYNCHON *Crying of Lot 49* v. 121 She found the symbol tacked to the bulletin board of a laundromat, among other scraps of paper offering cheap ironing and baby sitters. **1971** B. MALAMUD *Tenants* 219 They drag out of a laundromat, shoe store, [etc.], every Zionist they can find.

laundry ('lɔːndrɪ, 'lɑːndrɪ), *sb.* Also 6 landerie, -y, 8 landry. [Altered form of LAVENDRY after LAUNDER.]

†**1.** The action or process of washing. *Obs.*

a **1530** HEYWOOD *Play Weather* (Brandl) 896 Excepte the sonne shyne that our clothes may dry, We can do ryght nought in our laundry. *Ibid.* 1100 Then came there a nother that lyueth by laundry. *c* **1611** CHAPMAN *Iliad* XXII. 135 Where Trojan wives and their fair daughters had Laundry for their fine linen weeds. **1626** BACON *Sylva* §394 Chalkie Water is too fretting As it appeareth in Laundry of Clothes, which wear out apace, if you use such Water.

2. a. An apartment or establishment, where linen, etc. is washed and 'got up'.

1577 B. GOOGE *Heresbach's Husb.* (1586) 13 Hyther also runnes the water from the Laundry to moist it the better. **1648** MAYNE *Amorous War* II. iv, To starch, and to belong Unto their Laundries. **1715** LEONI *Palladio's Archit.* (1742) I. 51 The Wood-house, the Landry, and a pretty fine Garden. **1798** CANNING *Elegy* ii. in *Anti-Jacobin* 14 May (1852) 132 No story half so shocking By kitchen fire or laundry. **1807** CRABBE *Par. Reg.* II. 89 Fair Lucy first, the laundry's grace and pride. **1851** *Illustr. Catal. Gt. Exhib.* 194 Sample of refined Indian blue, for the laundry.

b. Articles (linen, etc.) that need to be, or that have been, laundered.

1916 W. J. LOCKE *Wonderful Year* iii. 50 The proletariat hung laundry to dry over royal salamanders and proud escutcheons. *Ibid.* v. 67 Women below at the water's edge beat their laundry with lusty arms. **1965** *Which?* Mar. 80/1 What we have done is to see how much it would cost to wash three different amounts of laundry each week, by each of these methods. **1970** *Laundry & Cleaning Internat.* June/July 1/3 The traditional attitude—that the laundry is paid for from the housewife's weekly budget.

¶ **3.** Used blunderingly for LAUNDRESS.

1598 SHAKS. *Merry W.* I. ii. 5 There dwels one Mistris Quickly, which is in the manner of his Nurse, or his dry Nurse, or his Cooke, or his Laundry.

4. *attrib.*, as ***laundry bag, -battledore, -blue, -blue-bag,*** †***-house, list*** (also *fig.*), ***-maid, -man, mark, room, soap, van, -woman, -work, -worker.***

1895 *Montgomery Ward Catal.* 23/2 *Laundry Bag; size 14 × 25 inches; made from heavy figured drapery sateen, with white cotton drawing cord and tassels. **1971** P. PURSER *Holy Father's Navy* xi. 60, I shovelled my suit into a laundry bag to send to the cleaners. *a* **1668** DAVENANT *Play-ho. to Let* Wks. (1673) 77 We'll make 'em bring Their *Laundry Battledores. **1899** *Westm. Gaz.* 8 Aug. 6/1 Large supplies of ..*laundry blue. **1880** *Plain Hints Needlework* 33 Run a tape through the holes, and it will make a '*Laundry Blue-bag'. **1585** *Wills & Inv. N.C.* (Surtees 1860) II. 108 To euerie of the maides of the *landerie house 2*s.* 6*d.* **1958** *Spectator* 4 July 24/2 Mr. Wardle makes a point of dissociating himself from the *laundry-list species of biography-making. **1968** *Time* 10 May 22 The at-large ballot is a bewildering laundry list of 75 names. **1972** *Fortune* Jan. 3/1 As the archetype of U.S. corporations, General Motors is charged by its critics with primary responsibility for a laundry list of social ills, including air pollution, congestion in the cities, ugliness in the countryside, [etc.]. **1972** *Times Lit. Suppl.* 24 Mar. 333/1 A huge panorama of names and dates, as dull as a laundry-list. **1975** *Radio Times* 16 Jan. 5/4 Everybody knows..that there are exceptions to this laundry-list of woes, and that the author can be brilliantly served. **1632** B. JONSON *Magn. Lady* IV. i, I will..cry it through..every office of the *laundry-maids. **1855** MRS. GASKELL *North & S.* ix, She was no longer Peggy the laundry-maid, but Margaret Hale, the lady. **1708** J. CHAMBERLAYNE *St. Gt. Brit.* II. III. List xlix. (1743) 162 The Matron is to take care of the Men's Linnen..& deliver it to the *Laundryman once a week. **1883** STEVENSON *Silverado Squatters* 14 There are the blacksmith's,..and Kong Sam Kee, the Chinese laundryman's. **1924** G. S. DOUGHERTY *Criminal as a Human Being* 278 An important factor in this work is a collection of *laundry marks. **1962** 'J. BELL' *Crime in our Time* II. i. 22 The..police..overlooked a conspicuous laundry mark, 599, on some of the clothing. **1972** L. LAMB *Picture Frame* xviii. 155 Laundry mark on shirt and maker's name on hand-made shoes. **1967** J. REDGATE *Killing Season* (1968) II. vi. 102 There's a new *laundry-room just behind the kitchen. **1971** *Country Life* 23 Dec. Suppl. 11/1 Unique single-story residence..kitchen, laundry room. **1937** *Discovery* Feb. 49/1 The Great Geyser had practically ceased activity, and could not be stimulated to life, even with a hundred-weight of *laundry soap—the usual stimulant. **1958** M. DICKENS *Man Overboard* xii. 190 A homely smell compounded of many things, like roasting meat and leather and dogs and laundry soap. **1952** M. ALLINGHAM *Tiger in Smoke* xv. 217 He and two other boys stole a *laundry van. **1972** *Guardian* 5 Oct. 28/2 The laundry van in which Sapper Stewart died. **1863** FR. A. KEMBLE *Resid. in Georgia* 24 The eldest son of our *laundry-woman. **1838** H. MARTINEAU *Retrospect of Western Travel* II. 185 The 10th was Sunday... There was no *laundry-work going on. **1891** *Daily News* 15 Dec. 6/2 There was possibility of a good deal of family laundry work arising. **1930** *Times Educ. Suppl.* 16 Aug. 360/2 The teacher must hold full diploma in Cookery, Laundrywork and Housewifery. **1963** F. F. LAIDLER *Gloss. Terms Home Econ. Educ.* 52 *Laundrywork*, the washing and finishing of soiled fabrics. **1894** E. BANKS *Campaigns of Curiosity* 196 She did not consider me up to the mark for a *laundry-worker. **1906** *Westm. Gaz.* 21 June 8/1 The attention of laundry-workers is drawn to this. **1975** *Times* 15 Feb. 3/3 Greater London Council..suggested that the post of..'laundry woman' should become 'laundry worker'.

laundry ('lɔːndrɪ, 'lɑːndrɪ), *v.* [f. the sb.] = LAUNDER *v.* Hence **'laundrying** *vbl. sb.*

1880 *American Mail Order Fashions* (1961) 14 The wires can be taken out..so that the entire bustle can be laundried with the greatest care. **1892** *Daily News* 15 Sept. 5/5 The great Chinese national industry is laundrying. **1901** D. SLADEN *In Sicily* I. 152 The ditch in which they did their laundrying. **1919** W. DEEPING *Second Youth* xxvi. 224 No, he can't ask you to laundry his man's clothes. **1957** B. & C. EVANS *Dict. Contemp. Amer. Usage* 268/2 The verb is *to launder*, not *to laundry*. Clothes are *laundered*, not *laundried*.

†**'laundy**, *a. Obs. rare*$^{-0}$. [f. LAUND + -Y[1].] = LAWNY *a.*[2]

1611 FLORIO, *Landoso*, laundie, full of laundes.

laune, obs. form of LAWN *sb.*

launge, obs. form of LAUNCH *v.*

launsgay, variant of LANCEGAY.

launt, variant of LAUND *Obs.*

launtern(e, obs. form of LANTERN.

‖**laura** ('lɔːrə). *Christian Antiq.* [Gr. λαύρα, lane, passage, alley.] An aggregation of detached cells, tenanted by recluse monks under a superior, in Egypt and the desert country near the Jordan.

1727–52 in CHAMBERS *Cycl.* **1819** SOUTHEY in *Q. Rev.* XXII. 66 Like one of the eastern *Lauras*—an assemblage of separate cells, each inhabited by a recluse. **1845** PETRIE *Eccl. Archit. Irel.* 425 These [separate cells] formed a Laura, like the habitations of the Egyptian ascetics. **1871** FARRAR *Witn. Hist.* v. 170 It would have perished in some lonely laura of desert cenobites.

lauraceous (lɔː'reɪʃəs), *a. Bot.* [f. mod.L. *Laurāce-æ* + -OUS.] Of or belonging to the N.O. *Lauraceæ* or laurel family.

In recent Dicts.

Laurasia (lɔː'reɪʃ(ɪ)ə). *Geol.* [mod.L. (R. Staub *Der Bewegungsmech. der Erde* (1928) ii. 121), f. *Laur(entia*, name given to the ancient forerunner of N. America (from the Laurentian strata of the Canadian Shield by which it is represented today) + *Eur)asia* (see EURASIAN *a.* 1).] A vast continental area or supercontinent thought to have once existed in the northern hemisphere and to have broken up in Mesozoic or late Palæozoic times forming North America, Greenland, Europe, and most of Asia north of the Himalayas. Also, these land masses collectively as they exist today.

1931 *Trans. Geol. Soc. Glasgow* XVIII. 578 The long history of the Tethys girdling the continental shelf of the earth between Gondwanaland and Laurasia is a clear indication of the operation of some opposing force tending to pull the continents apart. **1937** A. L. DU TOIT *Our Wandering Continents* ii. 24 Through..alternating 'polar flight' and 'polar drift' Laurasia and Gondwana have successively impinged upon or else parted from one another. **1944** A. HOLMES *Princ. Physical Geol.* xvii. 367 The [earthquake] belts form two rings..: one enclosing North America and most of Asia and Europe (known collectively as Laurasia), and the other enclosing South America, Africa and Arabia, India, Australia, and Antarctica (known collectively as Gondwanaland). **1971** I. G. GASS et al. *Understanding Earth* xv. 229 Gondwanaland..probably formed about 500 million years ago, and Laurasia, west of the Urals, about 370 million years ago. **1974** *Daily Tel.* (Colour Suppl.) 10 Apr. 20/1 Whether Laurasia and Gondwanaland were themselves joined together into a supercontinent is a question still to be resolved.

Hence **Lau'rasian** *a.*

1962 L. C. KING *Morphol. Earth* xii. 399 At the beginning of Cretaceous time virtually the whole of the vast continental interior had been reduced to a landscape of low relief—the Laurasian surface. **1973** *Nature* 1 June 278/2 The Atlantic and Indian Oceans originated from the break up of the Gondwanan and Laurasian continents.

laurate ('lɔːreɪt). *Chem.* [f. L. *laur-us* laurel + -ATE. See LAURIC.] A salt of lauric acid.

1873 *Fownes' Chem.* (ed. 11) 690 The laurates of the alkali-metals and of barium are soluble in water.

†**laure**. *Obs.* Also 1 laur, lawer. [OE. *laur*, ad. L. *laurus*. Cf. OF. *laure* (perh. the source in ME.).] The laurel or bay-tree; also, the leaves of the same woven into a chaplet. Also ***laure tree***.

971 *Blickl. Hom.* 187 Simon..mid lawere ȝebeaȝod ongan fleoȝan. *c* **1000** *Sax. Leechd.* II. 20 Wiþ healfes heafdes ece, ȝenim laures croppan dust. *c* **1384** CHAUCER *H. Fame* III. 17 Thou shalt see me go Unto the nexte laure I see And kisse hit for hit is thy tree. **1549** *Compl. Scotl.* xvii. 149 He vas crounit vitht ane croune of laure tre. **1567** *Gude & Godlie Ball.* (S.T.S.) 98 Sum tyme a Tyrane flureis haif I sene Lyke lawre tre, quhilk euer growis grene.

laureal, laurear, obs. forms of LAUREL *sb.*[1]

laureate ('lɔːrɪət), *a.* and *sb.* Also 4–5 lauriat, 5–6 lawreat, 5–7 lawriat(e, 4–9 laureat. [ad. L. *laureāt-us* crowned with laurel, f. *laurea* laurel-tree, laurel crown, fem. of *laureus* made of laurel, f. *laur-us*: see LAUREL.]

A. *adj.*

1. a. Crowned with laurel, wearing a laurel crown or wreath (as a symbol of distinction or eminence).

1616 BULLOKAR, *Laureate*, crowned with Laurell. *a* **1618** SYLVESTER *Du Bartas* (Grosart) I. 9 These laureat Temples which the Laurel grace. **1637** MILTON *Lycidas* 151 To strew the Laureat Herse where Lycid lies. **1742** COLLINS *Ode Simplicity* 33 While Rome could none esteem But Virtue's Patriot Theme, You lov'd her Hills, and led her Laureat Band. **1818** BYRON *Ch. Har.* IV. lvii, The crown Which Petrarch's laureate brow supremely wore. **1864** J. EVANS *Coins Anc. Brit.* 38 The laureate head of Apollo.

b. Of a crown, wreath: Consisting of laurel, or imitating one composed of laurel (blending with the attributive use of the sb.). Hence (*poet.*) ***laureate shade***.

1412–20 LYDG. *Chron. Troy* Prol. (1513) A ij, The palme laureat Whiche yt they wan by knygthode in theyr dayes. **1483** CAXTON *Gold Leg.* 243/1 He..sawe..saynt domynyk crowned with a crowne of gold laureate. **1597** *Pilgr. Parnass.* I. 51 There may youre templs be adornd with bays..There may you sit in softe greene lauriate shade. **1628** WITHER *Brit. Rememb.* IV. 1794 The Lawreat Wreath. **1655** H. VAUGHAN *Silex Scint.* Pref., That is the Βραβεῖον, and Laureate Crown, which idle Poems will..bring to their unrelenting Authors. **1744** AKENSIDE *Pleas. Imag.* I. 54 Unfading flowers Cull'd from the laureate vale's profound recess, Where never poet gain'd a wreath before. **1769** GRAY *Ode for Music* vii, To grace thy youthful brow The laureate wreath, that Cecil wore, she brings.

†**c.** ***laureate letters*** [tr. L. *litteræ laureatæ*], a letter or dispatch announcing a victory. *Obs.*

1508 KENNEDIE *Flyting w. Dunbar* 28 Thow fall doun att the roist, My laureat lettres at the and I lowis. **1533** BELLENDEN *Livy* v. (1822) 442 Come laureat letteris fra Posthumius, schawing all this victorie as it was fallin to Romanis. *a* **1656** USSHER *Ann.* VI. (1658) 549 Lucullus dispatched his letters laureat to the Senate.

2. With a sb. denoting an agent or the like: Worthy of special distinction or honour, pre-eminent in the (indicated) sphere or faculty.

The adj. often followed the sb., in imitation of Latin order.

a. *gen.* ? *Obs.*

1508 DUNBAR *Ballad Ld. Barnard Stewart* 4 Most valyeand, most laureat hie wictour. **1508** KENNEDIE *Flyting w. Dunbar* 524 Judas, iow, iuglour, Lollard laureate. *c* **1590** MARLOWE *Faust.* iii. 32 No, Faustus, Thou art conjuror laureat, That canst command great Mephistophilis.

b. *spec.* Distinguished for excellence as a poet, worthy of the Muses' crown. ***poet laureate***: in early use, a title given generally to eminent poets, and sometimes conferred by certain universities; in mod. use, the title given to a poet who receives a stipend as an officer of the Royal Household, his duty being to write court-odes, etc.

The first poet laureate in the modern sense was Ben Jonson, but the title seems to have been first officially given to his successor, Davenant (appointed 1638).

c **1386** CHAUCER *Clerk's Prol.* 31 Fraunceys Petrak the lauriat poete. ? *c* **1400** LYDG. *Æsop's Fab.* Prol. 8 This poyet laureate Callyd Ysopos. **1423** JAS. I. *Kingis Q.* cxcvii, Gowere and chaucere..Superlatiue as poetis laureate. **1432–50** tr. *Higden* (Rolls) I. 13 That nowble and laureate poete callede Homerus. [**1486** in Rymer *Fœdera* XII. 317 Cum Nos..concesserimus Bernardo Andreæ Poetæ Laureato quandam Annuitatem Decem Marcarum.] **1490** (*title*) The Dylectable Newesse..of the Gloryous Victorye of the Rhodyans agaynst the Turkes. Translated from the Latin of G. Caoursin by Johan Kaye (Poete Lawreate). **1508** DUNBAR *Gold. Targe* 262 O morall Gower, and Ludgate laureate. *a* **1529** SKELTON *Agst. Garnesche* iv. 84 At Oxforth, the vniversyte, Auaunsid I was to that degre; By hole consent of theyr senate, I was made poete lawreate. **1586** W. WEBBE *Eng. Poetrie* (Arb.) 19 The famous and learned Lawreat Masters of Englande. **1642** MILTON *Apol. Smect.* Wks. 1851 III. 272 The laureat fraternity of Poets. **1686** PLOT *Staffordsh.* 275 Robert Whittington..was a great Grammarian, Poet laureat of Oxford, and *Protovates Angliae*. **1691** WOOD *Ath. Oxon.* II. 255 Sir Will. D'avenant, sometimes Laureat Poet to the said King. **1697** *Verdicts Virg. & Homer* vi. 26 Our Laureat Poet tells us, that [etc.]. **1738** JOHNSON *London* 198 The laureat tribe in venal verse relate, How virtue wars with persecuting fate. **1843** DYCE *Skelton's Wks.* I. p. xv, There would..be no doubt that Skelton was..poet laureat or court poet to Henry the Eighth, if [etc.].

3. *transf.* of things: Worthy of the laurel-wreath; deserving to be honoured for eloquence, etc. In later use also: Of or pertaining to poets, or to a poet laureate.

1535 STEWART *Cron. Scot.* (1858) I. 32 With goldin toung and lippis laureat. 1560 ROLLAND *Crt. Venus* III. 13 Luifsum Ladies, of langage Laureat. *c* 1595 J. DICKENSON *Sheph. Compl.* (1878) 13 O how diuinely would the swaine haue sung In Laureate lines of beauteous Ladies praise. 1598 MARSTON *Pygmal.*, Author's Praise 136 Come, Come, Augustus, crowne my laureat quill. 1815 L. HUNT *Feast Poets* 18 The fancies that flow'd at this laureat meeting. 1821 BYRON *Juan* III. lxxx, There was no doubt he earn'd his laureate pension. 1847 GROTE *Greece* (1862) III. xliii. 556 The laureat strains of Pindar.

B. *sb.*

1. a. = *poet laureate* (see A. 2 b).

a 1529 SKELTON *Calliope* Wks. (ed. Dyce) I. 197 Calliope . . Whiche gaue to me The high degre Laureat to be Of fame royall. 1597–8 BP. HALL *Sat.* I. ix. 2 Cupid hath crowned a new laureat. *a* 1618 SYLVESTER *Epist.* Wks. (Grosart) II. 337 O thou that art the Laureat's liberall Fautor! . . Guide thou, Apollo, this first course of mine. 1687 M. CLIFFORD *Notes Dryden* ii. 7 Our Laureat has not pass'd for so Learned a man as he desires his unlearned Admirers should esteem him. 1780 COWPER *Table T.* 109 The courtly laureat pays His quit-rent ode, his pepper corn of praise. 1806 SURR *Winter in Lond.* (ed. 3) III. 134, I really think the fire of the laureat, Pye, increases with his years. 1825 KEBLE *Occas. Papers* (1877) 102 The panegyrical strains of this greatest of laureates [Spenser]. 1841 W. SPALDING *Italy & It. Isl.* II. 20 Claudian . . was the court laureate of the western empire till his patron's fall. 1884 *Chr. World* 21 Aug. 629/1 Keble may be spoken of . . as the laureate of the Church.

b. A court-panegyrist.

1863 COWDEN CLARKE *Shaks. Char.* xii. 305 He has indeed been their champion, their laureate, their brother, their friend. 1867 FREEMAN *Norm. Conq.* (1876) I. iv. 169 An author who was writing as the mere laureate of the Norman court. 1868 *Ibid.* II. vii. 3 He is very distinctly not an historian, but a biographer, sometimes a laureate.

c. *transf.*

1816 BYRON *Bards & Rev.* (ed. 5) 21 Laureat of the long-ear'd kind! *a* 1849 H. COLERIDGE *Ess. & Marginalia* (1851) II. 9 Herrick was the laureate of flowers and perfumes. 1930 R. CAMPBELL *Poems* 12 He . . demonstrates, this laureate of the pubs, That 'all good poets have belonged to clubs'. 1941 *Scrutiny* IX. 384 According to their view he [*sc.* Proust] is the laureate of a dying society. 1954 G. W. KNIGHT (*title*) Laureate of peace. On the genius of Alexander Pope.

d. ***Nobel laureate***, one who has been awarded a Nobel prize.

1947 CROWTHER & WHIDDINGTON *Science at War* 144 Professor W. N. Haworth of Birmingham, the famous organic chemist and Nobel laureate. 1965 *Listener* 2 Sept. 329/2 Three great physiologists, all Nobel laureates. 1975 *Sci. Amer.* May 53/2 (Advt.), Written by a Nobel Laureate in medicine, this is the first comprehensive treatment of DNA synthesis emphasizing its biochemical aspects and recent developments.

2. *U.S.* (See quot.) Cf. LAUREATE *v.* 2 a.

1888 BRYCE *Amer. Commw.* III. VI. cii. 445 *note*, Mr. D. C. Gilman . . mentions the following among the degree titles awarded in some institutions to women, the titles of Bachelor and Master being deemed inappropriate:— Laureate of Science, Proficient in Music, Maid of Philosophy.

3. *Numism.* = LAUREL *sb.*[1] 4.

1727–51 CHAMBERS *Cycl.* s.v. *Coin*, In England, the current species of gold are, the guinea, half-guinea, jacobus, laureat, angel, and rose-noble. *Ibid.*, The Carolus or Laureat, 23*s*.

laureate (ˈlɔːriːeɪt), *v.* *Obs.* exc. *Hist.* Pa. t. 7 (*Sc.*) laureat; pa. pple. 4–5 lauriat, 4–7 laureat(e, 5 lawriate, 6 lawreat. [f. L. *laureāt-us*: see prec. and -ATE[3].]

1. *trans.* To crown with laurel in token of honour; to crown as victor, poet, or the like; to confer honourable distinction upon.

c 1386 CHAUCER *Monk's T.* 706 To Rome agayn repaireth Iulius With his triumphe lauriat ful hye. 1430 LYDG. *St. Margaret* 497 Of martirdam thus she toke the croun . . Was laureat thurgh hir parfit suffraunce. 1430–40 —— *Bochas* III. xv. (1554) 88 b, Thus in short time this prince in his estate On land and water was twise laureate. *c* 1470 HENRYSON *Mor. Fab.* VIII. (*Preach. Swallow*) xxxix, Esope, that noble clerk, Ane poet worthie to be lawriate. 1509 BARCLAY *Shyp of Folys* (1874) II. 17 By his reygne is all Englonde lawreat. *c* 1510 —— *Mirr. Gd. Manners* (1570) D j, Before the victorie no man is laureate, At ending thou shalt haue palme, victory and mede. 1581 SIDNEY *Apol. Poetrie* (Arb.) 60 Let vs rather plant more Laurels, for to engarland our Poets heads, (which honor of beeing laureat, as besides them, onely tryumphant Captaines weare, is [etc.]).

2. *spec.* **a.** To graduate or confer a University degree upon. **b.** To appoint (a poet) to the office of 'Laureate'.

1637–50 ROW *Hist. Kirk* (Wodrow Soc.) 447 After he had past his course of philosophie, and wes laureat in St. Androes. 1662 RAY *Three Itin.* II. 157 Most of the students here . . wear no gowns, till they be laureat as they call it—that is, commence. 1695 SIBBALD *Autobiog.* (1834) 129, I was a Basler and Magistrant under Mr. William Tweedy, who laureat me July 1659. 1715 M. DAVIES *Athen. Brit.* I. 23 He [R. Whittington] supplicated the venerable Congregation of Regents . . that he might be laureated. He was very solemnly crown'd, or his Temples adorn'd with a Wreath of Lawrel; that is, doctorated in the Arts of Grammar and Rhetorick. 1729 POPE *Of Poet Laureate* Wks. 1886 X. 448 If Mr. Cibber be laureated. 1774 WARTON *Hist. Eng. Poetry* xxv. (1840) II. 332 About the year 1489, Skelton was laureated at Oxford, and in the year 1493, was permitted to wear his laurel at Cambridge. 1864 BURTON *Scot Abr.* I. v. 252 That old community of privileges which made the member of one university a citizen of all others, . . whether he were laureated in Paris or Bologna, Upsala or St. Andrews. 1884 J. HARRISON *Oure Tounis Colledge* iii. 63 In Aug[st] 1587 Rollock laureated his first class.

laureated (ˈlɔːriːeɪtɪd), *ppl. a.* [f. LAUREATE *v.* + -ED[1].] Crowned with laurel; = LAUREATE *a.*

1611 FLORIO, *Laticlanio*, a kind of long Imperiall robe, . . that . . triumphant Generals, laureated Poets . . were wont to weare in Rome. 1644 EVELYN *Diary* 14 Nov., Before this, go many crown'd and laureated figures. 1656 BLOUNT *Glossogr.*, *Laureated letters* [cf. LAUREATE A. 1 c]. 1771 *Phil. Trans.* LXI. 351 The laureated head really represents Jupiter Marnas. 1877 RUSKIN *Fors Clav.* No. 76 VII. 98 This voice, coming to you from the laureated singer of England [Tennyson]. 1879 H. PHILLIPS *Addit. Notes Coins* 8 A fine bronze medal exhibits a laureated head of Napoleon.

laureateship (ˈlɔːriːətʃɪp). [f. LAUREATE *sb.* + -SHIP.] **a.** The office of (poet) laureate.

1785 *Rolliad* I. (*title*) Probationary Odes for the Laureatship. 1813 SCOTT *Let. to Jas. Ballantyne* 24 Aug. in *Lockhart*, I have a letter by order of the Prince Regent offering me the laureateship in the most flattering terms. 1858 MASSON *Milton* I. 387 The year 1632 was (nominally) the thirteenth year of the laureateship of Ben Jonson.

b. The personality of a laureate (used jocosely, with possessive pron., as a title).

1732 *Gentl. Mag.* 563/2 Here, replied his Laureatship, are my Works, presenting a large Volume in Quarto. 1829 SOUTHEY *Epistle* in *Anniversary* 21 To personate my injured Laureateship.

laureation (lɔːriːˈeɪʃən). [f. LAUREATE *v.*: see -ATION.] The action of crowning with laurel or making laureate; in the Scottish Universities, a term for graduation or admission to a degree; also, the creation of a poet laureate.

1637–50 ROW *Hist. Kirk* (Wodrow Soc.) 422 Mr. Patrick Simson, after his laureation, went to Ingland. 1649 BP. GUTHRIE *Mem.* (1702) 21 Being a Professor of Philosophy in St. Andrews he did at the Laureation of his Class chuse Archbishop Gladstone for his Patron. 1680 G. HICKES *Spirit of Popery* 28 Yet they now complain of the King, Parliament, and Council, for obliging Expectants, and Scholars, at their Laureation to take the Oath of Allegiance. 1730 T. BOSTON *Mem.* ii. 17 Being allowed only *l*16 Scots by my father for the laureation, I borrowed 20 merks from one of my brothers. 1774 WARTON *Hist. Eng. Poetry* xxv. (1840) II. 331 These scholastic laureations, however, seem to have given rise to the appellation in question [*poeta laureatus*]. 1834 SIR W. HAMILTON *Discuss.* (1852) 483 The right of laureation conceded to the University of Vienna by Maximilian I . . constituted what may be held a distinct faculty,—a Collegium Poeticum. 1843 DYCE *Pref. to Skelton's Wks.* 11 Skelton's laureation at Oxford. 1867 MASSON *Edin. Sketches* 39 Their graduation, or, as it was called, their 'laureation', in Arts.

laurel (ˈlɒrəl, ˈlɔːrəl), *sb.*[1] Forms: α. 4 lorer(e, lorrer, 4–7 laurer(e, 5–7 lawrer(e, 5 laurear, -ier, lawrare, 6 lawryr, 7 lowrier. β. 4 laureal, 5 laurialle, -yel, lawriall, -ielle, (loryel, larel, -ielle), 5–6 lorel(l, 6–7 lau-, lawrell, 7 lawreall, 7–8 lawrel, (7 lowrell), 6– laurel. [ad. F. *laurier* for *lorier*, f. OF. *lor*:—L. *laur-us*: the β forms arise from the common substitution of *l* for a second *r* in a word. Cf. mod.Sp. *laurel*. In some of the forms there may be confusion with LAUREOLE.]

1. a. The Bay-tree or Bay-laurel, *Laurus nobilis*: see BAY *sb.*[1] 2. Now *rare* exc. as in 2.

α. *a* 1300 *Cursor M.* 8235 He . . planted tres þat war to prais, O cedre, o pine, and o lorrer. *c* 1381 CHAUCER *Parl. Foules* 182 The victor palm, the laurer [*v.rr.* lawrer, laureol] to deuyne. *a* 1400 *Med. MS.* in *Archæologia* XXX. 358 Lewys of lorere & rwe ye take. 1412–20 LYDG. *Chron. Troy.* I. viii, With ye lawrer . . They crowned ben. *c* 1500 *Lancelot* 82 To my spreit vas seen A birde, yat was as ony lawrare green. 1500–20 DUNBAR *Poems* xlvi. 6 Vpone a blisful brenche of lawryr grene. 1652 ASHMOLE *Theat. Chem.* 214 The Laurer of nature ys ever grene.

β. *c* 1350 [See *laurel-tree* in 6]. *c* 1400 *Destr. Troy* 4961 A tre . . Largior þen a lawriall & lengur withall. *c* 1420 *Anturs of Arth.* vi, By a lauryel he lay, vndur a lefe sale. 1496 *Dives & Paup.* (W. de W.) I. xxviii. 66 Some he ordeyned to be grene wynter & somer, as lorell, boxe, holme. 1561 HOLLYBUSH *Hom. Apoth.* 23 b, Take . . the leaves of Lorel or Baye. 1601 HOLLAND *Pliny* II. 173 The Lawrell, both leafe, bark, and berry, is by nature hot. 1624 CAPT. SMITH *Virginia* I. 10 *Ascopo*, a kinde of Tree like Lowrell. 1734 POPE *Ess. Man* IV. 11 'Twin'd with the wreaths Parnassian laurels yield. 1808 SCOTT in *Biog. Notices* (1880) 19 He would have twisted another branch of laurel into his garland. 1876 HARLEY *Mat. Med.* (ed. 6) 450 The Laurel or Sweet Bay, is a native of the North of Asia and the Mediterranean regions.

†**b.** The leaves of the same used medicinally.

1477 NORTON *Ord. Alch.* v. in Ashm. (1652) 67 Lawrell the Laxative. 1533 ELYOT *Cast. Helthe* (1539) 60 Lawrell.

c. Any plant of the genus *Laurus* or the N.O. *Lauraceæ*.

1846 LINDLEY *Veg. Kingd.* 535 Order ccv. Lauraceæ—Laurels. *Ibid.* 537 In some cases a volatile oil is obtained from the Laurels in large quantities.

2. The foliage of this tree as an emblem of victory or of distinction in poetry, etc.

a. *collect. sing.*

α. *c* 1386 CHAUCER *Knt.'s T.* 169 Hoom he rood anon With laurer crowned as a Conquerour. *c* 1425 LYDG. *Assembly Gods* 791 Crownyd with laurer as lord vyctoryous. 1515 BARCLAY *Egloges* I. (1570) A j b/2 Then who would ascribe, except he were a foole, The pleasant laurer vnto the mourning cowle. 1604 J. WEBSTER *Ode* in S. Harrison *Archs Tri.* B b, To euery brow They did allow The liuing Laurer which begirted round Their rusty Helmets.

β. 1387 TREVISA *Higden* (Rolls) V. 169 þere he dede meny victories, and gat a crown of laureal þat hyng bitwene tweie pilers. *c* 1460 *Play Sacram.* 882 Gyff lawrelle to that lord of myght. *a* 1631 DONNE *Epigr.* (1652) 97 It with Lawrell crown'd thy conquering Browes. 1813 SCOTT *Trierm.* III. xxxv, A crown did that fourth maiden hold, . . Of glossy laurel made.

b. A branch or wreath of this tree. *lit.* and *fig.*

α. *a* 1429 *Pol. Poems* (Rolls) II. 141 God of his grace gaf to thy kynrede The palme of conquest, the laurere of victorye. *c* 1430 LYDG. *Min. Poems* (Percy Soc.) 26 Laurear of martirs, foundid on holynes! 1607 DEKKER *Knts. Conjur.* (1842) 75 These elder fathers of the diuine furie gaue him [Spenser] a lawrer, and sung his welcome.

β. 1578 TIMME *Caluine on Gen.* 207 The Oliue . . was a sign of peace, even as the Lawrell is a token of victory. 1709 STEELE *Tatler* No. 76 ¶4 Virtue need never ask twice for her Lawrel. *c* 1718 PRIOR *Ladle* 36 Fame flies after with a laurel. 1847 EMERSON *Repr. Men, Goethe* Wks. (Bohn) I. 387 Still he is a poet—poet of a prouder laurel than any contemporary. 1850 PRESCOTT *Peru* II. 351 The laurel of the hero . . grows best on the battle-field.

c. *pl.* in the same sense, *lit.* and *fig.* Also in phr. ***to reap, win one's laurels, to repose, rest, retire on one's laurels. to look to one's laurels***: to beware of losing one's pre-eminence.

1585 JAS. I. *Ess. Poesie* (Arb.) 23 Phœbus crowns all verses . . with Laurers always grene. 1606 SHAKS. *Tr. & Cr.* I. iii. 107 Prerogatiue of Age, Crownes, Scepters, Lawrels. 1642 FULLER *Holy & Prof. St.* III. iii. 157 The Conquerours in the Olympian games did not put on the Laurells on their own heads. 1680 OTWAY *Orphan* Ded., Under the Spreading of that Shade, where two of the best [Poets] have planted their Lawrels. 1758 JOHNSON *Idler* No. 21 ¶4 They neither pant for laurels, nor delight in blood. 1805 *Med. Jrnl.* XIV. 372 Puny attempts to blast the laurels . . of Jenner. 1818 BYRON *Juan* I. cxxvi, 'Tis sweet to win, no matter how, one's laurels. 1855 MOTLEY *Dutch Rep.* v. i. (1866) 651 Here he reaped his first laurels. 1859 HELPS *Friends in C.* Ser. II. I. To Rdr. 6 They might really repose upon their laurels. 1874 DEUTSCH *Rem.* 250 Let them rest on their laurels for a while. 1882 MRS. RIDDELL *Pr. of Wales's Garden-Party* 306 The fair widow would be wise to look to her laurels. 1886 'HUGH CONWAY' *Living or Dead* xxx, Rothwell . . wrote one more book; then retired on his laurels.

†**d.** The dignity of poet laureate. *Obs.*

1700 DRYDEN *Fables* Pref. (1721) 3 My countryman and a predecessor in the Laurel [Chaucer]. 1814 *Edin. Rev.* Jan. 454 A Dramatic Poem; which we earnestly hope was written before he [Southey] came to his Laurel and Butt of Sherry.

e. As the name of a colour = *laurel-green*.

1923 *Daily Mail* 8 Oct. 5/1 (Advt.), Navy, Nigger, . . Amethyst, Laurel, Wine.

3. a. In modern use, applied to many trees and shrubs having leaves resembling those of the true laurel; esp. *Cerasus Laurocerasus*, the common laurel or cherry-laurel.

1664 EVELYN *Kal. Hort.* (1679) 33 [Plants] not perishing but in excessive Colds, . . Laurels, Cherry Laurel. 1736 BAILEY *Househ. Dict.* 378 *Laurel*, the Cherry Laurel or common Great Laurel. 1785 MARTYN *Rousseau's Bot.* vii. 79 The genus Plum, comprehending the Apricot and Cherry . . and also the Laurel. 1820 WORDSW. *To Rev. Dr. Wordsworth* i, The encircling laurels . . Gave back a rich and dazzling sheen. 1846 J. BAXTER *Libr. Pract. Agric.* (ed. 4) II. 17 The common laurel . . was brought from Constantinople to Holland in 1576. 1888 MISS BRADDON *Fatal Three* I. v, A winding walk through thickets of laurel and arbutus.

¶**b.** Some forms of this word were by certain writers of the 16th c. appropriated to the spurge laurel (see LAUREOLE).

1548 TURNER [see LAURY]. 1578 LYTE *Dodoens* III. xxxvi. 367 Lauriel groweth of the heigth of a foote and a halfe or more. 1601 HOLLAND *Pliny* I. 452 In this rank is to be reckoned the wild shrub called Lowrier or Chamædaphne.

c. With defining word: **Alexandrian laurel**, *Ruscus racemosus*; **American dwarf** or **mountain laurel** = KALMIA; **cherry laurel** (see sense 3 above); **copse laurel** = *spurge laurel*; **great laurel**, an American name for *Rhododendron maximum* (*Treas. Bot.* 1866); **Japan laurel** = AUCUBA 1; **native laurel** (Tasmania), *Anopterus glandulosus*; **Portugal laurel**, *Cerasus Lusitanica*; **seaside laurel**, *Xylophylla latifolia*; **spurge laurel**, *Daphne Laureola*; **Versailles laurel** (see quots.); **wood laurel**, spurge laurel, *Daphne laureola*. For *ground-*, *rose-*, *sheep-laurel*, see the first member.

1611 COTGR., *Laureole*, spurge Laurell, little Laurell. 1728 R. BRADLEY *Dictionarium Botanicum* II. s.v. *Laureola*, Laureola . . in English, Spurge-Laurel and Bastard-Laurel, or Wood-Laurel, is a small Evergreen, frequent enough with us, blossoming about Christmas. 1736 [see 3 a]. 1760 J. LEE *Introd. Bot.* App. 316 Laurel, Alexandrian, *Ruscus*. Laurel, Dwarf, of America, *Kalmia*. Laurel, Sea-side, *Phyllanthus*. Laurel, Spurge, *Daphne*. 1774 NICHOLLS *Let.* in *Corr. w. Gray* (1843) 174 The Portugal laurel, your favourite Portugal laurel, grows to a size here which would tempt you to poison it through envy. 1873 W. B. HEMSLEY *Handbk. Hardy Trees* 394 *Daphne Laureola*, Wood Laurel. 1882 *Garden* 4 Feb. 85/2 The Alexandrian Laurel (*Ruscus racemosus*) is one of our most precious plants for foliage with cut flowers in winter. *Ibid.* 25 Feb. 134/3 The Versailles Laurel (*latifolia*) is a large, robust, and bold foliaged form. 1889 J. H. MAIDEN *Useful Native Plants Austral.* 292 'Native Laurel'. 'Mock Orange'. 1951 *Dict. Gardening* (R. Hort. Soc.) III. 1697/2 P[*runus*] *Laurocerasus*. Common, Versailles, or Cherry Laurel. Quick-growing shrub up to 15 or 20 ft.

4. *Numism.* One of the English gold pieces (esp. those of 20*s*.), first coined in 1619, on which the monarch's head was figured with a wreath of laurel. Cf. LAUREATE *sb.* 3.

a 1623 CAMDEN *Ann. Jas. I*, an. 1619. 3 Sept., Aurea Regis moneta prodiit cum ejus capite laureato, unde Laurells nomen statim invenit apud vulgus, diversi valoris, scil. xxs. cum xx. xs. cum x. & quinque solidorum cum v. 1743 SNELLING *Gold Coin* 20 The Unite or Laurel. 1866 CRUMP

Banking x. 224 Gold laurel James I. **1884** Kenyon *Gold Coins Eng.* 137 The Laurels were also called Broad Pieces.

5. *attrib.* and *Comb.*: **a.** simple attributive, as ***laurel-band, -berry, -bough, -brake, -branch, -bush, -chaplet, -crown, -garland, -green, -leaf*** (also *attrib.*), ***-shade, -shrub, -thicket, -wreath***; **b.** parasynthetic, as ***laurel-leaved*** adj.; **c.** objective, as ***laurel-bearing, -worthy*** adjs.; **d.** instrumental, as ***laurel-browed, -crowned, -decked, -locked, -wreathed*** adjs. Also ***laurel-like*** adj.

1584 Hudson *Du Bartas' Judith* title-p. (1611), Binde your browes with *Laurer band. **1611** Florio, *Laurifero*, *laurell-bearing. **1561** Hollybush *Hom. Apoth.* 3 A penny worth of *lorel or baye berries. **1811** A. T. Thomson *Lond. Disp.* (1818) 230 Laurel berries..are imported from the Streights. **1483** Caxton *Gold. Leg.* 246/2 They that vaynquysshyd in bataylle were crowned wyth *laurier bowes. *a* **1593** Marlowe *Faustus* (1604) F 2, Cut is the branch that might haue growne ful straight, And burned is Apolloes Laurel bough. **1853** J. P. Kennedy *Blackwater Chron.* vi. 73 A man could walk about for a week,.. particularly if he got into a big *laurel-brake. **1893** *Outing* (U.S.) Oct. 61/2 Only in the wilds of the backwoods,..or in the mountains where tracts of laurel brakes give refuge against men and dogs, do the Virginia deer hold their own. **1550** Lyndesay *Test. Sqr. Meldrum* 138 Ilk Barroun beirand, in his hand, on hie, Ane *Lawrer branche, in signe of victorie. **1622** Bacon *Hen. VII* 85 Rather with an Oliue-branch..then a Laurel-branch in his Hand. **1823** Byron *Juan* xiii. xxxiii, The blaze Of sunset halos o'er the *laurel-brow'd. **1657** Trapp *Comm. Ps.* xx. 5 They presented a Palm, or *Laurel-bush, to Jupiter. **1830** Wordsw. *Russian Fugitive* iii. ii, Conquerors thanked the Gods, With *laurel chaplets crowned. **1593** Shaks. *3 Hen. VI*, iv. vi. 34 To whom the Heau'ns, in thy Natiuitie, Adiudg'd an Oliue-Branch and *Lawrell Crowne. **1882** A. Hare in *Gd. Words* May 338 The poet Empedocles, draped in purple robes, wearing a laurel crown. *c* **1374** Chaucer *Troylus* v. 1107 The *laurer crowned Phebus. *a* **1847** Eliza Cook *Song Old Year* ii. 15 Chant a roundelay over my *laurel-deck'd bier. **1577** Northbrooke *Dicing* (1843) 101 A christian man ought not to go with a *laurell garland vpon his heade. **1607** F. Mason *Author. Ch.* Ep. Ded. 3 Who..decked their victorious heads with lawreall garlands. **1938** R. Graves *Coll. Poems* 92 Grass-green and aspen-green, *Laurel-green and sea-green. **1387** Trevisa *Higden* (Rolls) IV. 295 For covetise of..*laurial leves wiþ oute eny fruyt. *c* **1450** *ME. Med. Bk.* (Heinrich) 146 Take of..percely, saueyne, lorel leues. **1747** Wesley *Prim. Physic* (1762) 56 As much as lies on a sixpence of powder'd Lawrel Leaves. **1927** Peake & Fleure *Hunters & Artists* 49 The rude Proto-Solutrean examples of the 'laurel-leaf' blades. **1973** *Times* 26 July 18/3 More than 150 unfinished and broken axes lay on the surface, with hammerstones, anvils, laurel-leaf blades, and many thousands of waste flakes. **1787** *Fam. Plants* I. 379 *Laurel-leaved Tulip-tree. **1855** A. B. Garrod *Essent. Materia Medica* 122 The bark of Canella alba or *Laurel-leaved Canella.. ; growing in the West Indies. **1833** Ht. Martineau *Cinnamon & P.* iii. 41 The *laurel-like cinnamon. **1850** Mrs. Browning *Poems* II. 223 Her [Italy] *laurel-locked..Cæsars passing uninvoked. **1894** Gladstone *Horace Odes* ii. xv. 9 Dense *laurel-shade shall stop the rays Of Summer. **1830** Tennyson *Poet's Mind* 14 Every spicy flower Of the *laurel-shrubs. **1750** T. Walker *Jrnl.* in J. S. Johnston *First Explor. Kentucky* (1898) 49 Just at the foot of the Hill is a *Laurel Thicket. **1840** Browning *Sordello* Wks. 1896 I. 132 Beneath a flowering laurel thicket lay Sordello. **1945** *Mass. Audubon Soc. Bull.* Jan. 274 It was June 25 when I sat on a log in a laurel thicket. **1616** W. Browne *Brit. Past.* ii. i, In *Laurell-worthy rymes Her loue shall Liue vntill the end of times. **1721–2** Amherst *Terræ Fil.* No. 10 (1754) 48 This..bard has..lampoon'd those, who fix'd the immortal *laurel-wreath upon his brows. **1818** Byron *Ch. Har.* iv. xvi, The true laurel-wreath which glory weaves Is of the tree no bolt of thunder cleaves. **1878** Symonds *Many Moods, Love & Death* 165 The *laurel-wreathèd choir.

6. Special comb.: **laurel-bay**, †(*a*) = *laurel-berry*; (*b*) = *bay-laurel* (sense 1); **laurel-bottle**, a bottle containing crushed laurel leaves, used by entomologists for killing insects; **laurel-cherry** = *cherry laurel*; hence ***laurel-cherry water*** = *laurel water*; **laurel magnolia** (*U.S.*), either of two species of *Magnolia*, the evergreen *M. grandiflora* or the sweet bay, *M. virginiana*; †**laurel-man**, ? a member of one of the parties disaffected to the Hanover dynasty; **laurel oak** (*U.S.*), either of two species of oak, *Quercus laurifolia* or *Q. imbricata*; **laurel-oil** = *oil of laurel*, a solid fat obtained from the berries of *Laurus nobilis* (*Syd. Soc. Lex.*); **laurel-thyme** = laurustinus; **laurel-tree** = sense 1; **laurel-water** *Med.*, the water obtained by distillation from the leaves of the cherry-laurel and containing a small proportion of prussic acid.

c **1450** *M.E. Med. Bk.* (Heinrich) 198 Tak..*lorel bayes nistad in oyle. **1813** Scott *Trierm.* iii. xxxix, Round the Champion's brows were bound The crown..Of the green laurel-bay. **1872** Wood *Insects at Home* 26 The following is the neatest way of making a *laurel-bottle. **1787** *Fam. Plants* I. 339 *Laurel-cherry. **1822–34** *Good's Study Med.* (ed. 4) I. 487 Laurel-cherry water. **1806** P. Wakefield *Excursions N. Amer.* xiv. 93 The *laurel magnolia reaches to the height of an hundred feet. **1831** J. M. Peck *Guide for Emigrants* ii. 52 From the Walnut Hills to Baton Rouge..you begin to discover the ever verdant laurel magnolia, with its beautiful foliage, of the thickness and feeling of leather. **1850** S. F. Cooper *Rural Hours* 476 The small Laurel Magnolia, or Sweet Bay, is found as far north as New York, in swampy grounds. **1893** W. Robinson *Eng. Flower Garden* (ed. 3) 520/1 *M*[*agnolia*] *grandiflora*, the great Laurel Magnolia of the southern United States, is—in England—best treated as a wall-plant. **1903** *Flora & Sylva* I. 19/1 The Laurel Magnolia or Sweet Bay..is certainly a very handsome shrub. **1911** *Encycl. Brit.* XVII. 392/1 The most beautiful species of North America is *M. grandiflora*, the 'laurel magnolia'..introduced into England in 1734. **1730** Swift *Vind. Ld. Carteret* 27 Inflamers of Quarrels between the two Nations,..Haters of True Protestants, *Lawrel-men, Annists,..and the like. **1810** F. A. Michaux *Hist. Arbres Forestiers de l' Amérique Septentrionale* I. 23 **Laurel oak*,.. dénomination secondaire dans les États à l'ouest des monts Alléghanys. **1832** D. J. Browne *Sylva Amer.* 271 East of the Alleghanies this species..is called Jack Oak, Black Oak, and sometimes from the form of the leaves, Laurel Oak. **1901** C. T. Mohr *Plant Life Alabama* 131 Between Bon Secour and Perdido Bay low, sandy hills..support a high forest..of laurel oak and Cuban and long-leaf pine. **1947** Collingwood & Brush *Knowing your Trees* 201/1 Laurel oak has been widely used, especially in the South, as an ornamental, particularly as a shade or street tree. **1838** T. Thomson *Chem. Org. Bodies* 439 *Laurel oil is expressed from the berries of the *laurus nobilis*. **1693** Evelyn *De la Quint. Compl. Gard.* II. 173 We have now..but few Flowers, except those of *Laurel-Time, or *Laurus Thymus*. *c* **1350** *Will. Palerne* 2983 Vnder a louely *lorel tre in a grene place. *c* **1415** Lydg. *Temple of Glas* 115 Daphne vnto a laurer tre Iturned was. **1549–62** Sternhold & H. *Ps.* xxxvii. 35 Flourishing..as doth the Laurell tree. **1731** Madden in *Phil. Trans.* XXXVII. 85 One Part of *Laurel-Water to four of Brandy. **1829** Carlyle *Misc.* (1857) II. 25 Counter-plottings, and laurel-water pharmacy.

Hence **'laurelship** = laureateship.

1820 *Examiner* No. 612. 1/2 Receiving the laurel which had been worn by Dryden, and Spenser, and Ben Jonson, and Daniel (a list of laurelships somewhat doubtful).

laurel ('lɒrəl, 'lɔːrəl), *sb.*² A salmon that has remained in fresh water during the summer.

1861 *Act 24 & 25 Vict.* c. 109 §4 All migratory Fish of the Genus Salmon..that is to say..Kelt, Laurel, Girling.

†**'laurel**, *a. Obs.* [f. laurel *sb.*¹] Crowned or wreathed with laurel; hence, renowned.

1579–80 North *Plutarch* (1595) 131 Lycomedes..hauing taken very rich furniture and flags, did afterwards consecrate them to Apollo laurell. [*Sic*; but perh. mispr. for *laurel-bearer*; Amyot *surnommé Portant laurier*.] **1606** Shaks. *Ant. & Cl.* i. iii. 100 Vpon your Sword Sit Laurell victory.

laurel ('lɒrəl, 'lɔːrəl), *v.* [f. laurel *sb.*¹] *trans.* To wreathe with laurel; to adorn with or as with laurel.

1631 H. Shirley *Mart. Souldier* v. in Bullen *O. Pl.* I. 242 The good, how e're trod under, Are Lawreld safe in thunder. **1663** Sir G. Mackenzie *Relig. Stoic* xvi. (1685) 143 Lawrel'd and rewarded. **1762–71** H. Walpole *Vertue's Anecd. Paint.* (1785) V. 87 Sir Edward Nicholas, secretary of state; oval frame laurelled. **1831** *Westm. Rev.* Jan. 234 Our Cæsar was bald, and we laurelled his defect. **1850** Neale *Med. Hymns* (1867) 153 Laurelled with the stole victorious. **1867** F. M. Finch *Blue & Gray* in *Atlantic Monthly* Sept. 370 They banish our anger forever When they laurel the graves of our dead!

b. To serve as a decoration for.

1821 *Sporting Mag.* VII. 192 Ever green be the garland that laurels thy fame.

laurelled ('lɒrəld, 'lɔːrəld), *ppl. a.* [f. laurel *sb.*¹ or *v.* + -ed.] **a.** Adorned, crowned, or wreathed with laurel. Hence *fig.* honoured, illustrious: cf. laureate. †***laurelled letters***: cf. laureate A. 1 c. **b.** Covered with a growth of laurel; also, made of laurel.

1682 Dryden *Dk. Guise* iii. i, The Trophies of my Lawrell'd Honesty Shou'd bar me from forsaking this bad World. **1693** —— *Persius Sat.* (1697) 496 Th' Express is come With Laurell'd Letters from the Camp to Rome. **1700** Prior *Carmen Seculare* 379 From his oozy Bed, Boyn shall raise his Laurell'd Head. **1744** Akenside *Pleas. Imag.* i. 413 The choir Of laurel'd science. **1791** E. Darwin *Bot. Gard.* i. 56 Liberty returns with laurell'd peace. **1815** W. Taylor in *Monthly Rev.* LXXVII. 471 Laurelled rather than excellent in funeral eulogy. **1822** Wordsw. *Sonn., New Churches*, Laurelled armies, not to be withstood—What serve they? **1867** M. Arnold *Heine's Grave* 57 Here no sepulchre built In the laurell'd rock. **1879** Froude *Cæsar* xxvi. 442 With laurelled fasces and laurelled wreaths. **1886** Symonds *Renaiss. It., Catholic React.* (1898) VII. viii. 32 How touching was the destiny of this laurelled exile [Tasso].

†**'laurence**¹. *Obs.* In 5–6 lowrance, -ence. [? The Christian name: see next.] A name for the fox. Cf. lowry.

c **1470** Henryson *Mor. Fab.* x. (*Fox & Wolf*) iii, The wolf was neirar nor he wend, For in ane busk he lay, and lowrence baith. **1528** Lyndesay *Dreme* 895 Lowrance..dois, but reuth, the sely scheip dounthryng.

Laurence², **Lawrence** ('lɒrəns, 'lɔː-). [ad. L. *Laurentius*.] A Christian name, used to denote a personification of indolence. ***Laurence bids wages***: a proverbial phrase meaning that the attractions of idleness are tempting. Also ***Lazy Laurence***, a reproachful designation for an idle person.

Possibly the alliteration of the last-quoted phrase may sufficiently account for the use of the name; some, however, have suggested an allusion to the heat prevalent about St. Laurence's day (Aug. 10). Another conjecture is that there was a joke to the effect that when the martyr St. Laurence told his tormentors to turn him round on his gridiron, it was because he was too lazy to turn himself. It is important to note that the equivalent G. *der faule Lenz* (Lenz = Lorenz) has been in use from the 16th c.; see Grimm s.v. *Lenz*.

1796 Pegge *Anonym.* (1809) 348 *Laurence bids wages*; a proverbial saying for *to be lazy*; because St. Laurence's day is the 10th of August, within the dog-days, and when the weather is usually very hot and faint. **1821** Clare *Vill. Minstr.* II. 23 When..the warm sun smiles And 'Lawrence wages bids' on hills and stiles. **1880** *E. Cornw. Gloss.*, He's as lazy as Larence. One wad think that Larence had got hold o'n.

Laurentian (lɒ'rɛnʃ(ɪ)ən), *a.*¹ *Geol.* [f. L. *Laurenti-us* Laurence + -an.] A designation of certain sedimentary strata found in Canada near the river St. Lawrence. Also quasi-*sb.* in collective sense.

1863 A. C. Ramsay *Phys. Geog.* v. (1878) 55 The Laurentian rocks are the oldest formations at present known in the world. **1872** W. S. Symonds *Rec. Rocks* ii. 21 The Laurentian, or Basement, sedimentary deposits are divided into two series. **1875** Dawson *Dawn of Life* vii. 176 The Lower Laurentian of Canada..is found to contain thick and widely distributed beds of limestone. **1876** Page *Adv. Text-bk. Geol.* x. 187 The Laurentian strata, till the year 1862, were regarded as metamorphic.

Laurentian (lɒ'rɛnʃ(ɪ)ən), *a.*² [f. the name of Lorenzo (Laurentius) de' Medici, who founded a library in Florence in the 15th c.] Of or pertaining to the Laurentian Library in Florence or to manuscripts preserved there. Cf. Medicean *a.*

1860 Geo. Eliot *Jrnl.* in J. W. Gross *George Eliot's Life* (1885) II. x. 216 That unique Laurentian library, designed by Michael Angelo. **1875** *Encycl. Brit.* II. 438/2 His [*sc.* Michelangelo's] principal works are..the Laurentian Library at Florence. **1879** *Ibid.* IX. 332/1 There are three large and valuable libraries in the city [*sc.* Florence]... The Laurentian, founded by Lorenzo de' Medici, and attached to the convent of San Lorenzo. **1883** R. C. Jebb in *Sophocles, Plays & Fragments* I. p. liii, The manuscripts..used..are the following: In the Biblioteca Mediceo-Lorenziana, Florence, L, cod. 32.9, commonly known as the Laurentian MS. **1936** Greenhood & Gentry *Chronol. Bks. & Printing* (rev. ed.) 14, 1437. A public library is founded at Florence on a bequest by Niccoli; becomes known later as Laurentian Library, and today is oldest existing library in Europe. **1960** G. A. Glaister *Gloss. Bk.* 214/2 *Laurentian Codex*, an 11th-century codex of the works of Sophocles, Apollonius Rhodius, and Aeschylus... It is now in the Biblioteca Mediceo-Laurenziana, Florence.

Laurentian: see Lawrentian *a.*

†**laureole**. *Obs.* Also 4, 5 **lauriol(e**, **lawryol**. [a. F. *laureole*, ad. L. *laureola*, lit. a little garland of laurel.] Spurge Laurel, *Daphne Laureola*. (In early use not clearly distinguished from laurel *sb.*¹)

c **1386** Chaucer *Nun's Pr. T.* 143 Of lawriol, Centaure, and ffumetere. *c* **1430** Lydg. *Commend. Our Lady* 73 Thou mirthe of martyrs, sweter than citole,..Unto virgynes eternal lauriole. *c* **1440** *Promp. Parv.* 291/1 La(u)ryol, herbe (lawryal *K.*, lawryol *S.*), *laureola*. **1596** P. Burrough *Meth. Phisick.* (ed. 3) 444 Laureole is more forcible in operation.

laurestinus, variant of laurustinus.

†**lauret**. *Obs.* [Corruption of laureate.] = laurel *sb.*¹ 4.

1731 in Bailey vol. II.

lauric ('lɔːrɪk), *a. Chem.* [f. L. *laur-us* laurel + -ic.] ***lauric acid***, a white crystalline compound ($C_{12}H_{24}O_2$) obtained from the berries of *Laurus nobilis*. Hence in ***lauric aldehyde, ether***: names of compounds derived from this acid.

1873 *Fownes' Chem.* (ed. 11) 689 Lauric acid is insoluble in water. **1876** Harley *Mat. Med.* (ed. 6) 680 Besides which there are small quantities of lauric aldehyd $C_{12}H_{24}O$.

†**lauricomous**, *a. Obs.*$^{-0}$ [f. L. *lauricom-us*, f. *laurus* laurel + *coma* hair + -ous.] 'Full of Bays at Top, having Hair like Bays' (Bailey vol. II, 1727).

†**lau'riferous**, *a. Obs. rare*$^{-0}$. [f. L. *laurifer*, f. *laurus* laurel + -ous.] Laurel-bearing.

1656 in Blount *Glossogr.* **1721–1800** in Bailey. Hence in mod. Dicts.

†**lau'rigerous**, *a. Obs. rare*$^{-0}$. [f. L. *lauriger*, f. *laurus* laurel + *-ger* bearing + -ous.] 'Wearing a garland of Bays' (Bailey vol. II, 1727).

laurin ('lɔːrɪn). *Chem.* [f. L. *laur-us* + -in¹.] A crystalline substance ($C_{22}H_{30}O_3$) obtained from the berries of *Laurus nobilis*.

1838 T. Thomson *Chem. Org. Bodies* 910 The laurin of Bonastre has an acrid and bitter taste, and its smell is analogous to that of laurel oil.

†**laurine**, *a. Obs.* [ad. L. (*oleum*) *laurīnum*, f. *laurus* laurel.] (Oil) of laurel.

c **1400** *Lanfranc's Cirurg.* 57 Hote oiles, as oile of coste, oile of laurine [*Add. MS.* oyle lauryne]. *c* **1420** *Pallad. on Husb.* iv. 145 Madifie hit so in oil lauryne. *c* **1450** *ME. Med. Bk.* (Heinrich) 170 Tak anoynement, þat ys y cleped agryppa, & oyle lauryne.

laurionite ('lɔːrɪənaɪt). *Min.* [Named by Köchlin, 1887, from *Laurion*, in Greece, where it was found: see -ite.] Oxy-chloride of lead, formed by the action of sea-water on ancient lead slags.

1887 *Amer. Jrnl. Sci.* XXXV. 418 Laurionite occurs in white prismatic crystals. **1900** *Brit. Mus. Return* 156.

lauristinus, variant of laurustinus.

laurite ('lɔːraɪt). *Min.* [Named by Wöhler, 1866, after Mrs. *Laura* Joy: see -ITE.] Sulphide of ruthenium, found with platinum in small brilliant crystals.
1866 *Amer. Jrnl. Sci.* XLII. 422. **1868** DANA *Min.* (ed. 5) 74 Laurite... From the platinum washings of Borneo.

†**'laurize**, *v.* *Obs. rare*⁻¹. [f. L. *laur-us* (see LAUREL *sb.*[1]) + -IZE.] *trans.* To crown with laurel.
a **1618** SYLVESTER *Sonn.* iii, Our humble notes, though little noted now,.. Lauriz'd (hereafter) 'mong the loftie-mounted; Shall sing a part that Princes shall allow.

laurustine ('lɔːrəstaɪn). Also *erron.* 7 lauri-, 9 laure-. [Anglicized form of next.] = next.
1683-4 ROBINSON in *Phil. Trans.* XXIX. 477 Myrtles,.. Bays, Laurustines. **1693** DR. T. R. in *Phil. Trans.* XVII. 686 The Lauristines or Wild Bays. **1789** G. WHITE *Selborne* lx. 290 The bays, laurustines, and laurels, were killed to the ground. **1848** THACKERAY *Bk. Snobs* xxxi, Myrtles and glistening laurustines.

‖**laurustinus** (ˌlɔːrə'staɪnəs). Also 7-8 laurus tinus, 9 *erron.* laures-, lauristinus. [a. mod.L. (orig. two words) *laurus tīnus* (L. *laurus* laurel, *tīnus* a plant, perh. the laurustinus).] An evergreen winter-flowering shrub, *Viburnum Tinus*.
1664 EVELYN *Kal. Hort.* (1679) 9, January.. Flowers in Prime.. Prim-roses, Laurus-tinus, Mezereon. **1725** BRADLEY *Fam. Dict.* s.v., There are three Sorts of the Laurus Tinus cultivated in our Country. **1765** WILKES *Corr.* (1805) II. 140 Laurels and laurustinuses were in all the hedges. **1840** BARHAM *Ingol. Leg.* Ser. I. *Spectre Tappington*, From the midst of a thickset laurustinus [he] drew forth a gardener's spade. **1861** DELAMER *Fl. Gard.* 3 Laurustinuses, .. and even Portugal laurels, are kept in tubs, that they may be housed when frost comes. **1882** J. HARDY in *Proc. Berw. Nat. Club* IX. No. 3. 435 The Laurestinuses have been sore damaged.

laurvigite, laurvikite, varr. LARVIKITE.

†**laury**. *Obs.* Also 4 lorrei, lorry, 5 lorey, 6 loury, lowrie, laurye, ? laurew, 7 lary, -ie, 8 lowry. [? f. L. *laurea*, fem. of *laureus* adj., but used as sb. for the tree itself.] = LAUREL *sb.*[1]
a **1400** *Med. MS.* in *Archæol.* XXX. 368 Whanne yis erbe is gaderid yus, In lewys of lorry it must be wounnde. **14..** *Voc.* in Wr.-Wülcker 577/26 *Dampnis*, a loreytre. *Ibid.* 592/4 *Laurus*, a loreytre. **1422** tr. *Secreta Secret.*, *Priv. Priv.* 245 Al the grene is fadid, outake the Pynes, lorreis, olyues, and few othyr tren. **1508** DUNBAR *Ballad Ld. B. Stewart* 67 Thi cristall helme with lawry suld be crownyt. **1533** BELLENDEN *Livy* II. (1822) 181 He wald not ressave the crown of laurew [*v.r.* laurer], to have the samin deformit with the public doloure. **1548** TURNER *Names of Herbes* 34 (E.D.S.) Daphnoides called of the commune sort Laureola, in englishe Lauriel, Loriel, or Loury. **1549** *Compl. Scot.* vi. 60 The laurye tree. **1598** FLORIO, *Laureola*, the herbe perwinkle. Also the shrub lowrie or lawrell. **1681** COLVIL *Whigs Supplic.* (1751) 106 Turpentine and larie berries. *Ibid.* 121 Trembling he stood, in a quandary, And purg'd, as he had eaten lary. **1706** PHILLIPS (ed. Kersey), *Lowry* or *Lowaray*, a Shrub, otherwise call'd Spurge-Laurel.

lauryl ('lɒr-, 'lɔːrɪl). *Chem.* [f. LAUR(IC *a.* + -YL.] = DODECYL; **lauryl alcohol**, $CH_3(CH_2)_{10}CH_2OH$, a crystalline, low-melting alcohol which is obtained by reduction of coconut oil and whose sulphate esters are used in detergents.
1915 P. E. SPIELMANN tr. *V. von Richter's Org. Chem.* I. iii. 227 Lauryl ketoxine, $(C_{11}H_{23})_2C{:}N.OH$, m.p. 39°. **1922** *Jrnl. Amer. Chem. Soc.* XLIV. 2649 By reducing 100 g. of ethyl laurate with 85 g. of sodium, 200 cc. of toluene and 600 cc. of absolute alcohol, there is obtained 53 to 57 g. (65–70%) of lauryl alcohol. **1960** E. L. DELMAR-MORGAN *Cruising Yacht Equipment & Navigation* xxiv. 231 Lauryl pentachlor phenol is.. very effective [for rot-proofing canvas]. **1968** J. A. MONICK *Alcohols* iii. 174 A high-quality lauryl alcohol is currently produced by the same process used for *n*-decyl alcohol, namely, the catalytic reduction of coconut oil, coconut oil fatty acids, or their esters, under high pressure. *Ibid.* 175 Lauryl alcohol is also found in oils of lime and the flowers of *Furcraea gigantea*. **1972** *Sci. Amer.* Jan. 88/2 Experiments with lauryl sulfate, a common component of commercial detergents, showed that this substance would indeed break the mucosal barrier.

laus(e, lausen, obs. ff. LOOSE *a.*, LOSE *v.*

lausenite ('laʊsənaɪt). *Min.* [f. the name of Carl *Lausen*, 20th-c. U.S. geologist + -ITE[1].] A hydrated ferrous sulphate, $Fe_2(SO_4)_3.6H_2O$, first found as aggregates of minute colourless fibres after a fire in a mine at Jerome, Arizona, U.S.A.
1928 *Amer. Mineralogist* XIII. 594 The name rogersite is already in use.. so a new name will have to be assigned to the present mineral. Dr. G. M. Butler has suggested the name lausenite, after Carl Lausen the discoverer of the new mineral. **1968** I. KOSTOV *Mineral.* II. ix. 499 Lausenite and kornelite are monoclinic, found respectively in white and pale violet globular aggregates with radial-fibrous texture.

‖**laus tibi**. *Obs.* [L. = 'praise to thee'.] A name for the White Narcissus, *Narcissus poeticus*.
1548 TURNER *Names of Herbes* (1881) 55 Narcissus.. wyth a white floure.. it is called of diuerse, whyte Laus tibi, it maye be called also whyte daffadyl. **1567** MAPLET *Gr. Forest* 48 *Laus tibi* or white Daffadill in Greeke is called *Narkissos*. **1573** TUSSER *Husb.* xliii. (1878) 96.

lauta, laute, obs. Sc. ff. LEWTY.

lautarite (laʊ'tɑːraɪt). *Min.* [ad. G. *lautarit* (A. Dietze 1891, in *Zeitschr. f. Kryst. und Min.* XIX. 447), f. Oficina *Lautar(o*, the name of the owners of the pampa where it was first found: see -ITE[1].] Calcium iodate, $Ca(IO_3)_2$, found as colourless or yellowish monoclinic crystals in Antofagasta Province, Chile.
1892 E. S. DANA *Dana's Syst. Min.* (ed. 6) 1040 (*heading*) Lautarite. **1943** R. D. GEORGE *Minerals & Rocks* vii. 198 Lautarite, calcium iodate,.. is a colorless to pale yellow, easily fusible mineral having a specific gravity of 4·6 and a hardness of 4. **1968** K. A. JONES tr. *Kirsch's Appl. Mineral.* vi. 114 Lautarite $Ca(IO_3)_2$... Monoclinic, H: 3·0–4·0, D: 4·6.

†**lautious**, *a.* *Obs. rare*⁻¹. In 6 laucyouse. [Improper formation f. L. *laut-us* (see LAUTITIOUS *a.*) + -IOUS.] Luxurious. Hence **lautiously** *adv.*
1547 BOORDE *Brev. Health* cxliii. 53 With meates and drynkes lautiously educated. *Ibid.* cclxxx. 93 This impediment [fatness] doth come of.. laucyouse fedyng.

lautite ('laʊtaɪt). *Min.* [ad. G. *lautit* (A. Frenzel 1881, in *Min. und Petr. Mittheil.* III. 516), f. *Laut-a*, the name of its original locality near Marienberg, E. Germany: see -ITE[1].] An orthorhombic, grey or black sulphide of copper and arsenic, CuAsS (possibly with silver replacing some copper), having a metallic lustre.
1883 *Encycl. Brit.* XVI. 392/1 Lautite (CuAg)As.S. **1940** *Mineral. Abstr.* VII. 489 Lautite associated with arsenic, tetrahedrite, [etc.].., is found in the Gabe Gottes mine at Sainte-Marie-aux-Mines (Haut-Rhin). It forms bunches of crystals up to 6 cm. × 6–7 mm., showing a brilliant (001) cleavage, enclosed in native arsenic. **1967** *Ibid.* XVIII. 97/1 Lautite was obtained by heating a mixture of realgar and electrolytic copper under 1000 kg/cm² to 315° C.

†**lau'titious**, *a.* *Obs. rare*⁻¹. [f. L. *lautitia* magnificence (f. *lautus* washed, sumptuous) + -OUS.] Sumptuous.
1648 HERRICK *Hesper.*, *Invitation* (1869) 281 Such lautitious meat, The like not Heliogabalus did eat.

‖**lautu** ('laʊtuː). [Quichua *ƚƚautu* (Tschudi), *llauto* (Gonçalez, 1608).] 'A band of cotton, twisted and worn on the head of the Inca of Peru, as a badge of royalty' (Webster, 1828–32, citing Barlow).
1807 J. BARLOW *Columb.* III. 136 The white lautu graced his lofty brow.

lauwhen, obs. form of LAUGH *v.*

lauwine ('lɔːwɪn, Ger. laʊ'viːnə). Also **lawine**. [ad. G. *lawine*, according to Kluge f. *lau* mild, tepid.] An avalanche.
1818 BYRON *Ch. Har.* IV. xii, Nations melt.. and downward go, Like lauwine loosen'd from the mountain's belt. **1833** *Penny Cycl.* I. 389 Generally termed Avalanches, or some-times lauwines. **1845** *Blackw. Mag.* LVIII. 34, I see.. the cliff-cradled lawine essay its first motion. **1881** J. NICHOL *Death Themistocles*, etc. 131 Down whose slope the Lauwine thunders.

lauxe, obs. form of LAX, salmon.

lauyst, obs. superl. of LOW *a.*

lav. (læv). A colloq. shortening of LAVATORY *sb.* 4.
1913 C. MACKENZIE *Sinister Street* I. vii. 99 Tell the army to line up behind the lav. at four o'clock. **1933** D. L. SAYERS *Murder must Advertise* i. 8 You've only got to warn him not to use the directors' lav., and not to tumble down the iron staircase. **1960** J. R. ACKERLEY *We think the World of You* 51, I asked instead if I could use the lav. **1961** [see ELSAN]. **1973** J. THOMSON *Death Cap* iv. 64 Gilbert Leacock went out to the lav... I heard the chain being pulled.

lava ('lɑːvə). [a. It. *lava* (f. *lavare* to wash: see LAVE *v.*[1]), orig. 'a streame or gutter suddainly caused by raine' (Florio 1611), applied in the Neapolitan dialect to a lava-stream from Vesuvius; hence adopted in literary It., where it developed the senses represented by 2 and 3 below. Hence Sp., Pg., Ger., Du., Da., Sw. *lava*, F. *lave*.]

†**1.** A stream of molten rock issuing from the crater of a volcano or from fissures in the earth.
1750 *Phil. Trans.* XLVII. x. 52 The wells.. near the places where the lava's stopped, are sometimes found full. **1767** HAMILTON *ibid.* LVIII. 6 Another lava forced its way out of the same place from whence came the lava last year.

2. The fluid or semi-fluid matter flowing from a volcano.
1760 *Ann. Reg.*, *Chron.* 86/1 On the 21st ult... all the neighbourhood of Mount Vesuvius was overflowed by a deluge of burning bitumen called lava. **1820** KEATS *Lamia* I. 157 As the lava ravishes the mead. **1832** DE LA BECHE *Geol. Man.* (ed. 2) 109 The lava burst out.. at three different points, about eight or nine miles from each other. **1885** *Times* 27 Aug. 5 The phenomenon which these people understand by 'aluvion' is really the stream of lava.
fig. **1821** SHELLEY *Lett.* Prose Wks. 1880 IV. 197 We are surrounded here in Pisa by revolutionary volcanoes.. the lava has not yet reached Tuscany. **1876** HUMPHREY *Coin Coll. Man.* xix. 247 The lava of Roman power overflowed its native crater.

3. a. The substance that results from the cooling of the molten rock.
1750 *Phil. Trans.* XLVII. xxi. 150 This lava.. is a very hard substance, like stone, of a slate colour. **1789** MRS. PIOZZI *Journ. France* II. 36 One of these towns is crushed.. under loads of heavy lava. **1806** *Gazetteer Scotl.* (ed. 2) 306 The greater part of it is composed of lava, in which the different layers or currents are very evident. **1837** W. IRVING *Capt. Bonneville* (1849) 243 Great masses of lava lay scattered about in every direction. **1882** *Rep. to Ho. Repr. Prec. Met. U.S.* 622 Volcanic breccia and volcanic conglomerates are likewise designated by the term 'lava'.

b. A kind of lava, a bed of lava.
1796 KIRWAN *Elem. Min.* (ed. 2) I. 400 Any matter that has issued out of a volcano in a liquified state.. is in general, styled a lava. **1809** BRYDONE *Sicily* vii. 71 They pierced through seven distinct lavas one under the other. **1872** DANA *Corals* ii. 154 The cavities of a lava or basalt become filled. **1882** GEIKIE *Text-bk. Geol.* III. I. i. §1. 203 Lavas differ from each other in the extent to which they are impregnated with gases and vapours.

4. *attrib.* and *Comb.*: **a.** simple attributive, as ***lava-ash, bed*** (also *fig.*), ***block, boulder, -column, -cone, -current, field*** (also *fig.*), ***-lake, -plain, -rill, -sea, -stream, -torrent***; ***lava-like*** adj.; also **lava-flag**, (see quot.); **lava flow**, a mass of flowing or solidified lava; **lava-millstone**, (see quot.); **lava-streak** *U.S.*, a basaltic dyke; **lava ware** (see quot.). **b.** instrumental, as ***lava-capped, -lit, -paved*** adjs.
1882 *Rep. to Ho. Repr. Prec. Met. U.S.* 634 The filling up .. of the old river beds by *lava-ash. **1891** *Century Mag.* Mar. 645 The general direction [of march] was towards the *lava beds of northern California. **1905** *Westm. Gaz.* 12 Aug. 13/1 She lived over a 'lava-bed of raw primeval passions'. **1937** *Discovery* Mar. 83/1 This arid lava bed. **1866** 'MARK TWAIN' *Lett. from Hawaii* (1967) 58 We climbed a hill a hundred and fifty feet high.. as full of rough *lava blocks as it could stick. *Ibid.* 223 It had *lava boulders piled around its base. **1902** *Athenæum* 30 Aug. 287/1 Where bed on bed of mountain-pinks Above the lava-boulders blow. **1882** *Rep. to Ho. Repr. Prec. Met. U.S.* 638 The bed-rock of almost every *lava-capped mountain shows the same peculiarity. **1862** G. P. SCROPE *Volcanos* 23 The *lava-column having seemingly sunk too far within the vent. **1882** GEIKIE *Text-bk. Geol.* III. I. i. §3. 246 A flat *lava-cone 13,760 feet above the sea. **1830** LYELL *Princ. Geol.* I. 327 The *lava-current.. may still be traced, by aid of the scoriæ on its surface. **1866** 'MARK TWAIN' *Lett. from Hawaii* (1967) 222 We clambered over the surrounding *lava field, through masses of weeds. **1899** *Geogr. Jrnl.* May 50 The most extensive lava-field in the island. **1906** *Daily Chron.* 21 May 7/3 The smoking lava fields of discussion. **1957** G. E. HUTCHINSON *Treat. Limnol.* I. i. 16 The lakes of the Modoc lava field are frequently regarded as lying on tilted block faults. **1811** PINKERTON *Petral.* II. 236 A.. basalt fragment .. called *lava flag. **1888** J. PRESTWICH *Geol.* II. 91 Beds of contemporaneous *lava-flows. **1866** 'MARK TWAIN' *Lett. from Hawaii* (1967) 222 Gathering up a fresh lot of specimens, having.. discarded those he dug out of the old lava flows. **1957** G. E. HUTCHINSON *Treat. Limnol.* I. i. 38 Not infrequently the surface of a newly formed lava flow may cool and produce a crust. **1974** *Country Life* 17 Jan. 66/1 The lava-flows on either side of the runway. **1895** *Lava-lake [see *blowing-cone*]. **1902** *Nature* 4 Sept. 441/1 (*heading*) The lava-lake of Kilauea. *Ibid.* 441/2, I carefully observed the then existing lava-lake during six successive days. **1802** PLAYFAIR *Illustr. Hutton. Theory* 274 Crystallized, sparry or *lava-like structure. **1876** GEO. ELIOT *Dan. Der.* IV. lxv. 294 The *lava-lit track of her troubled conscience. **1858** SIMMONDS *Dict. Trade*, **Lava-millstones*, hard and coarse basaltic millstones, obtained from quarries near Andernach on the Rhine. **1837** W. IRVING *Capt. Bonneville* III. 77 The immense *lava plain of San Gabriel. **1869** PHILLIPS *Vesuv.* iii. 83 Small *lava-rills among them. **1871** W. MORRIS in Mackail *Life* (1899) I. 268 A low mound of soft grass, rising like an island from the much-riven *lava-sea. **1872** R. B. SMYTH *Mining Statist.* 47 '*Lava streaks', or dykes, are found associated with all the main lines of reefs at Sandhurst. **1833** LYELL *Princ. Geol.* III. 184 The branches.. are formed simply of two *lava-streams. **1878** HUXLEY *Physiogr.* 192 These *lava-torrents are often of great magnitude. **1860** *Ure's Dict. Arts* (ed. 5) II. 641 **Lava-ware*, a peculiar stoneware, manufactured and coloured to assume the semi-vitreous appearance of lava.

c. similative (quasi-*adj.*).
1818 BYRON *Ch. Har.* IV. li, While thy lips are With lava kisses melting while they burn. **1878** SWINBURNE *Poems & Ballads* 2nd Ser. 182 All its lava-black Cones.

‖**lavabo** (lə'veɪbəʊ; also (senses 2 b, c) 'lævəbəʊ). [L. *lavābo*, 1st pers. sing. fut. t. of *lavāre* to wash.]

1. *Eccl.* **a.** The ritual washing of the celebrant's hands at the offertory, accompanied in the Roman rite by the saying of Ps. xxvi. 6, beginning *Lavabo inter innocentes manus meas*. **b.** The small towel used to wipe the priest's hands. **c.** The basin used for the washing.
1858 *Direct. Angl.* Gloss. 232 *Lavabo*, the *secreta oratio* of the Priest when water is poured on his fingers before the Prayer of Oblation. [An incorrect explanation.] **1870** ROCK *Text. Fabr.* I. 203 These small liturgical towels got.. the name of Lavabo cloths or Lavaboes. **1885** PATER *Marius* IV. xxiii, The.. pontiff, as he.. moved his hands.. at the *Lavabo*, or at the various benedictions.

2. a. A washing trough used in some mediæval monasteries.
1883 *Mag. of Art* Dec. 47/1 We give a reproduction of.. one aspect of the lavabo, or washing-trough, which gives its name to the lavatory.

b. A wash-stand.
a **1902** *N.E.D.*, 'In some mod. Dicts.' **1911** WEBSTER *Lavabo*, a wash basin with its necessary fittings, esp. one set in place and supplied with running water and a waste pipe.

c. = LAVATORY *sb.* 4.

1930 D. L. SAYERS *Strong Poison* xiv. 177 The little lavabo in the passage. **1934** H. MILLER *Tropic of Cancer* 83, I find a ticket in the *lavabo* for a concert. **1971** C. JOHNSTON *Mo* 58 The subject of each was unmistakeably the same—Belchamber's lavabos.

†**la'vacre.** *Obs.* Also 6 *Sc.* lavachre. [ad. L. *lavācrum* bath, f. *lavāre* to wash: see LAVE *v.*[1]] A bath or font; esp. in figurative phrases descriptive of baptism, ***e.g. lavacre of regeneration, of salvation***, after Tit. iii. 5 Vulg. *lavacrum regenerationis* (cf. LAVER *sb.*[2] 2).

1548 UDALL, etc. *Erasm. Par. Luke* iii. 47 To consecrate and halowe the lavacre or founte of eternall salvacion. *a* **1572** KNOX *Hist. Ref.* Wks. 1846 I. 304 Thei war receaved in his houshold by the lavachre of spirituall regeneratioun. **1657** TOMLINSON *Renou's Disp.* 185 They were so much taken with Lavacres that some of them.. would bathe them-selves seven times a day.

‖**lava'dero.** *Obs.* [Sp., f. *lavar* to wash: see LAVE *v.*[1]] A place for washing gold ore.

1717 tr. *Frezier's Voy. S. Sea* 110 On the Descent of the Mountain.. they shew'd me a Stream, where there is a rich *Lavadero*, or Place for washing of Gold. **1760–72** tr. *Juan & Ulloa's Voy.* (ed. 3) I. 452 The gold taken out of all these Lavaderos or mines in the province of Quito. **1799** W. TOOKE *View Russian Emp.* III. 414 To these mines belong three lavaderos.. together having 861 troughs.

lavage ('lævɪdʒ, Fr. lavaʒ). [a. F. *lavage*, f. *laver* to wash.] A washing, *spec.* in *Med.* a cleansing of the stomach by means of emetics administered in large quantities of water.

1895 MORISON *Pyloroplasty* 4 The treatment consisted of daily stomach lavage. **1898** *Daily News* 2 Aug. 5/2 This native treatment is the lavage of hot oil to stop the bleeding.

lavage, -aige, obs. forms of LAVISH *a.*

laval ('lɑːvəl), *a.* [f. LAVA + -AL.] Of or resembling lava. Also *fig.*

1891 *11th Ann. Rep. U.S. Geol. Survey* II. 199 These great springs are the outlet of a system of under-laval channels and lakes. **1931** V. WOOLF *Waves* 84 It is the speed, the hot molten effect, the laval flow of sentence into sentence that I need. **1932** W. FRANK *America Hispana* I. v. 230 Volcanic earth has made these churches and these statues. Sometimes it is stone, black and yellow as in the north; sometimes, it is adobe. And sometimes, it is tezontli, the laval rock colour of clotted blood. **1963** A. SMITH *Throw out Two Hands* (1966) xxi. 205 We were 500 feet above that exceptionally laval and unpleasant-looking region.

lava-lava ('lɑːvə'lɑːvə). [Samoan.] In Samoa and some other Pacific islands, a sort of skirt.

1891 R. L. STEVENSON *Vailima Lett.* (1895) xiii. 115 The weird figure of Faauma.. in a black lavalava (kilt). **1900** *Fortn. Rev.* Jan. 49 New Zealanders, Chinese, East and West Indians, and half-castes who are more at home in lava-lavas than bifurcated garments. **1944** *Living off Land* viii. 159 He must produce.. equipment consisting of a blanket, bowl, spoon, lava-lava. **1949** M. MEAD *Male & Female* 407 Clothes consisted of a short sarong—called a lavalava. **1957** M. B. PICKEN *Fashion Dict.* 207/2 *Lava-lava*, loincloth or waistcloth of printed calico worn by natives of Samoa and other islands in the Pacific. **1971** *Listener* 9 Sept. 334/3, I saw the famous lava-lava—the short, brightly-coloured skirt which they [*sc.* Samoans] wore below the naked torso. **1973** *Observer* (Colour Suppl.) 28 Oct. 53/1 *Lavalavas* (skirts made from a single length of cloth, originally introduced by the missionaries for reasons of modesty, often wrapped round the body from bosom to knee by Samoan women).

Lavallière (lavaljɛr). Also **Lavalière**, with lower-case initial, and without accent; **lavalier**. Name of Louise de *la Vallière*, French courtesan (1644–1710), used *absol.* or *attrib.* to designate certain styles in clothing and jewellery. Also *transf.*, a small microphone.

1873 *Young Englishwoman* July 350/1 (*heading*) White chip Lavalliere Hat. The crown is moderately high, with a rather broad brim, turned up in front and down at the back. **1916** *Daily Colonist* (Victoria, B.C.) 16 July 2/1 (Advt.), Our stock of moderately priced Necklets, Pendants and La Valieres is most attractive. **1942** *Horizon* Oct. 250 His collar and ready-made tie (a lavallière). **1951** E. PAUL *Springtime in Paris* vii. 136 Noel, with broad-brimmed felt hat, seersucker jacket and flowing *lavallière*, personified the artistic type. **1955** *Publ. Amer. Dial. Soc.* XXIV. 122 Any minor bauble such as a lavaliere.. is a *dangler*. **1959** *Times* 28 Apr. 20/6 A diamond lavalliere. **1969** D. M. DISNEY *Fatal Choice* (1970) x. 80 Marcy was wearing John's farewell gift, a lavaliere set with an aquamarine.. and seed pearls. **1970** *New Yorker* 12 Sept. 32/2 Mr. Siegel, whose clothes for public appearances are striking, running to vests and lavalieres, had a big grin on his face. **1972** R. HENDRICKSON *Human Words* 179 Today the small television microphone that hangs on a cord from the neck is also called a *lavaliere*, taking its name from the pendant necklace. **1974** *Amer. Speech 1971* XLVI. 55 A low impedance, unidirectional microphone is, I feel, better than a lavalier microphone.

lavalto, variant of LAVOLTA.

†**lavament.** *Obs.* [ad. med.L. *lavāmentum*, f. *lavāre* to wash. Cf. LAVEMENT.] A washing; *concr.*, a wash, lotion.

1597 A. M. tr. *Guillemeau's Fr. Cirurg.* 34 b/2 With cleane linnen.. and with decent and convenient lavamentes, we ought to sustayne them [fistulous guts]. *Ibid.* 49/2 We may, in this disease vse certayne exsiccating Lavamentes. **1658** A. Fox *Wurtz' Surg.* II. xii. 93 Make a Lavament of Liquorice, let it run gently into the Wound. **1823** J. BADCOCK *Dom. Amusem.* 18 Herrings.. undergo the first lavament in stale chamber-lye.

lavand, obs. Sc. form of LAVENDER *sb.*[2]

lavander, obs. form of LAVENDER.

‖**lavandera** (lavan'dera). [Sp.] In Spanish-speaking countries, a washerwoman; = LAVENDER *sb.*[1]

1841 BORROW *Zincali* I. II. vi. 316 The lavanderas engaged in purifying the linen of the capital. **1918** W. H. HUDSON *Far Away & Long Ago* vii. 97 One of the most attractive spots to me was the congregating place of the *lavanderas*, south of my street.

lavandrie, variant of LAVENDRY *Obs.*

‖**la'vange.** *rare.* [F. *lavange*, also *lavanche*, believed to be an alteration of AVALANCHE *sb.* due to association with *laver* to wash.] = AVALANCHE *sb.*

1806 J. MONTGOMERY *Wanderer Switz.* III. xxxii, Like a Winter's weight of snow, When the huge Lavanges break, Devastating all below.

lavant ('lævənt), *sb.* [? subst. use of next.] (See quot. 1774.)

1774 G. WHITE *Selborne* xix. (1789) 174 The land-springs, which we call lavants, break out much on the downs of Sussex, Hampshire, and Wiltshire. **1875** *Sussex Gloss.* s.v., How it did rain! It ran down the street in a lavant. **1900** *Academy* 28 Apr. 365/1 The waterings and 'lavants' from the hills leave her [Rye] arid.

†**lavant,** *a. Obs.* [a. F. *lavant*, pr. pple. of *laver* to wash.] That bathes; given to bathing.

1661 LOVELL *Hist. Anim. & Min.* Introd. a 5, Birds.. are .. pulveratricious lavant, as the pigeon, ring-dove [etc.].

lavatera (lævə'tɪərə, lə'vɑːtərə). [mod.L. (J. Pitton de Tournefort (1706), in *Hist. Acad. Roy. Sci. Mém.* 86), f. the name of the brothers *Lavater*, 17th- and 18th-c. Swiss physicians and naturalists.] A herb or shrub of the genus so called, belonging to the family Malvaceæ, and bearing pink, white, or purple flowers.

1731 P. MILLER *Gardeners Dict.* s.v. *Lavatera*, African Lavatera, with a most beautiful flower. **1790** *Curtis's Bot. Mag.* IV. 109 Annual Lavatera.. flowers from July to September. **1916** G. JEKYLL *Annuals & Biennials* i. 4 Where a temporary filling is desired of plants of important aspect, there are the Tobacco plants,.. Foxgloves, Solanums, and Lavatera. **1962** *Listener* 19 Apr. 708/3 Sow hollyhocks, lavatera, sweet peas.

lavatic (lɑː'vætɪk), *a.* [f. LAV-A + -ATIC.]

1830 MAUNDER *Treas. Knowl.* I, *Lavatic*, consisting of or resembling lava.

lavation (lə'veɪʃən). [ad. L. *lavātiōn-em*, n. of action f. *lavāre* to wash.] The action of washing, an instance of this; *concr.*, water for washing.

1627 HAKEWILL *Apol.* IV. i. §6. 283 Such filthy stuffe was by loose lewd varlets sung before her [Berecynthia's] charet on the solemne day of her lavation. **1652** H. C. *Looking-Glasse for Ladies* 14 If women once be cleansed by lavation. **1800** *Med. Jrnl.* IV. 27 The beneficial effects of cold lavation in febrile disorders. **1827** LYTTON *Pelham* viii, Our lavations are performed in a cracked basin. **1855** T. GUTHRIE *Gospel in Ezek.* (1856) 247 With this sacred lavation the priest sprinkles the man. **1879** SALA *Paris herself Again* (ed. 4) II. xii. 185 The lavation of their befouled linen. **1894** GOULD *Illustr. Dict. Med.*, *Lavation of the Blood*, intravenous injection of water.

Hence **la'vational** *a.*, pertaining to lavation.

1887 HALLIWELL *Life of Shaks.* II. 368 Towels.. employed for lavational purposes were called washing-towels.

†**'lavative.** *Obs.* [f. L. *lav-āre* to wash + -ATIVE.] A draught to wash down food or medicine.

1633 HART *Diet of Diseased* I. viii. 30 Now and then they will afford themselves a cup of good liquor, as a lavative, to wash downe this rubbish. *Ibid.* III. xv. 288 As for the lavative, ordinarily given after purgations.. it is hard to determine the particular houre.

lavatorial (lævə'tɔərɪəl, -'tɔː-), *a.* [f. L. **lavātōri-us*, f. *lavāre* to wash + -AL[1].] **1.** Of or pertaining to washing.

1839 LADY LYTTON *Cheveley* (ed. 2) II. iv. 117 Three pair of cotton stockings.. bearing very bilious symptoms of the lavatorial skill of Sally. **1898** *Daily News* 3 Sept. 3/1 The simplicity of the lavatorial arrangement could hardly be improved upon.

2. Of or pertaining to a style of architecture or decoration alleged to resemble that used for public lavatories.

1936 E. EATON *Summer Dust* I. vii. 42 The newer movement, which demands that every rising young lawyer should furnish an *appartement* in the neo-lavatorial style. **1957** *Sunday Times* 17 Nov. 3/3 The Examination Schools, that lavatorial building of awful omen. **1958** B. HAMILTON *Too Much of Water* ii. 42, I had to pull down an absolutely shattering piece of Victorian lavatorial Gothic. **1969** *Observer* 12 Jan. 25/3 A barber's, a lavatorial café, and nothing much else but grime and desolation. **1974** A. ROSS *Bradford Business* 63 Endless lavatorial town hall corridors.

3. Of or pertaining to lavatories; *spec.* of conversation, humour, etc.: making undue reference to lavatories and their use.

1967 *Daily Tel.* 15 Apr. 9/3 The average gent is of an aggressive disposition and a lavatorial sense of humour. **1969** *Daily Tel.* 17 Nov. 9/1 The words.. are perfectly familiar, partly lavatorial, partly sexy, ranging in length from four to seven letters. **1969** C. DERRICK *Reader's Report* vii. 120 A great many poets, when talking about their art, drop instinctively and sub-consciously into the use of obstetrical and even lavatorial imagery. **1974** *Times* 9 Nov. 10/4 The awful lavatorial embarrassment.

lavatory ('lævətərɪ), *sb.* Forms: 4–7 **lavatorie, -ye,** 6 **lavatori, lavetarye,** 4– **lavatory.** [ad. L. *lavātōrium* a place for washing, f. *lavāre* to wash: see LAVE *v.*[1]]

1. a. A vessel for washing, a laver, a bath. Also *Eccl.* †(*a*) a piscina; (*b*) (see quot. 1866).

a **1375** *Lay Folks Mass Bk.* App. IV. 606 Whon he haþ vsed he walkeþ riht To Lauatorie þer hit is diht For to wassche his hende. **1382** WYCLIF *Exod.* xxx. 18 And thow shalt make a brasun lauatory with his foot to wasshe with. **14..** LYDG. in *Lay Folks Mass Bk.* App. v. 135 Whan the preste gothe to the lauatori. **1412** *Contract for Catterick Church* (1834) 10 An awter and a lauatory acordaunt in the este end. **1435** *Contract for Fotheringhay Church* in Dugdale *Monast.* (1673) III. II. 163 Lavatoris in aither side of the wall, which shall serve for four Auters. **1519** *Test. Ebor.* (Surtees) V. 100 To be buried wtin the where, nyghte to the lavatori. **1538** *Inv.* in *Archæol.* LI. 72 Itm the lavetarye of tynne and lead. **1649** JER. TAYLOR *Gt. Exemp.* III. sect. xv. 77 They should dip in his lavatory, and be washed with his baptism. **1839** LONGF. *Hyperion* IV. iii, On a lavatory, below, sat a cherub. **1866** *Direct. Angl.* (ed. 3) 355 *Lavatory*, a water drain in the Sacristy where the Priest washes his hands before vesting.

†**b.** *fig.* and in fig. phrases. Cf. LAVACRE, LAVER *sb.*[2]

1447 BOKENHAM *Seyntys* (Roxb.) 74 The lavatorye we graunte of immortalite Here in this watir. *a* **1500** *Mankind* (Brandl 1896) 39/12 By hys gloryus passyone, þat blyssyde lauatorye. **1526** *Pilgr. Perf.* (W. de W. 1531) 60 b, As in the lauatory of grace thou mayst wasshe.. the.. by confessyon. **1631** WEEVER *Anc. Funeral Mon.* 310 The lauatorie of holy regeneration. *a* **1633** AUSTIN *Medit.* (1635) 196 Converting it [Jordan] into the Lavatory of Baptisme.

2. a. *Eccl.* The ritual washing of the celebrant's hands: (*a*) at the offertory (cf. LAVABO 1 a); †(*b*) after the cleansing of the vessels following the communion.

a **1512** FABYAN *Will* in *Chron.* Pref. 4 Wt condicion that at the tyme of the Lavatory eueryche of theym turne theym to the people, and exorte theym to pray for ye soules following. **1526** *Pilgr. Perf.* (W. de W. 1531) 261 From the latter lauatory vnto Ite missa est. **1563–87** FOXE *A. & M.* (1596) 899/2 When he had sayd Masse, he made Dukes and Earles ..to hold the bason at the Lauatories. **1896** BRIGHTMAN *Liturgies E. & W.* I. Gloss., *Lavatory*, the handwashing on the part of the minister at the offertory... While the offertory either wholly or in part has been moved back to the beginning of the [Eastern] liturgy, the lavatory has generally kept its place.

b. *gen.* The act of washing.

1620 SHELTON *Quix.* II. xxxii. 211 The Duke and Duchesse.. stood expecting what would become of this Lauatory.

†**3.** A lotion, a wash. *Obs.*

1490 CAXTON *Eneydos* xxviii. 110 They must be wasshed wyth wyne or wyth some other lauatorye. **1544** PHAER *Regim. Lyfe* (1560) H iv b, Ye may minister the lavatorie that herafter ensueth. **1665** HARVEY *Advice agst. Plague* 14 Lavatories to wash the temples, hands, wrists, and Jugulars. **1694** WESTMACOTT *Script. Herb.* 19 Barbers use them for their grateful smell to perfume their lavatories and washes.

4. An apartment furnished with apparatus for washing the hands and face, subsequently also including water-closets, etc. In the 20th c. one of the more usual words for a W.C. (and in turn giving way to more recent euphemisms: *lav.*, *loo*, *toilet*, etc.).

In some examples ellipt. for the appliance itself.

1656 BLOUNT *Glossogr.*, *Lavatory*, a place or vessel to wash in, a Font or Conduit; **1661** [*addition*] such is that at the Buttery door of the Inner Temple, where the Gentlemen wash their hands; also a *Laundry*. **1845** W. SAUNDERS *Guide Brighton* 68 By a sudden turn to the left, we attain 'The Cottage'; at the far end of its porch is the gentlemen's room, denominated by a contemporary a Lavatory. **1860** *Luck of Ladysmede* II. 78 The good Benedictine carried him off into the lavatory. **1864** *Morning Star* 2 Feb., There are separate lavatories for the men and for the women and children. **1924** F. M. FORD *Some do Not* I. ii. 37 The hotel having been a former Grand Ducal hunting-box, freshened to suit the taste of the day with varnished pitch-pine, bathrooms, verandahs, and excessively modern but noisy lavatory arrangements. **1963** J. T. STORY *Something for Nothing* iii. 106 Albert closed the door and sat down on the lavatory. **1965** *Listener* 2 Sept. 351/2 Flush Conscience down the lavatory. **1967** *Ibid.* 3 Aug. 144/3 Certain kinds of help are ..needed... Lavatories a disabled person can get in and onto. *Ibid.* 21 Dec. 802/1 'Loo' is holding its own fairly well and most of 'Toilet's' gains have been at the expense of 'Lavatory'. **1973** A. S. NEILL *Neill! Neill! Orange Peel!* (rev. ed.) II. 189 What did people use in the lavatory before the invention of paper?

5. A laundry.

1661 [see prec. sense]. **1878** STEVENSON *Inland Voy.* 180 We landed at a floating lavatory, where the washer-women were still beating the clothes.

6. = LAVADERO.

1727–52 CHAMBERS *Cycl.*, *Lavatory*, or *Lavadero*.

7. (See quot.)

185. *Archit. Dict.* (Archit. Publ. Soc.), *Lavatory*, a paved room, belonging to a dead-house, in which a corpse that is to be examined is kept under a shower of some disinfecting fluid.

8. *attrib.*: ***lavatory attendant, basin, brush, chain, cleanser, pan, paper, seat***; **lavatory humour**, unsavoury or unwholesome humour making undue reference to lavatories (cf. LAVATORIAL *a.* 3); so ***lavatory joke***; **lavatory period, style,** a period or style of architecture

with 'lavatorial' characteristics (cf. LAVATORIAL *a.* 2); † **lavatory stone**, a piscina.

1930 I. Low *His Master's Voice* xv. 217 A lavatory attendant might make a similar boast thought Nikulin. **1939** C. ISHERWOOD *Goodbye to Berlin* 29 The little old lavatory attendant in his white jacket. **1964** R. PETRIE *Murder by Precedent* i. 20 Lavatory attendants.. aren't as likely to insure their lives as professional men. **1926–7** *Army & Navy Stores Catal.* 321 'Vitrella' should be used for cleaning all porcelain baths, lavatory basins, sinks. **1931** *Times* 16 Mar. 22/1 (Advt.), Lavatory basin in best bed room. **1963** *B.S.I. News* Apr. 33 Ceramic lavatory basins. **1939–40** *Army & Navy Stores Catal.* 167/2 Lavatory brush holder. **1962** *House & Garden* Dec. 51/1 Lavatory brush and container, 12 s. **1969** A. E. LINDOP *Sight Unseen* xxix. 245 A bottle of bourbon.. stood in the stand which usually held the lavatory brush. *c* **1932** DYLAN THOMAS *Lett.* (1966) 5 Give me.. a book by Paul de Kock, and thou, thou old lavatory chain. **1964** V. S. NAIPAUL *Area of Darkness* iv. 94 At four.. we heard him rise and get ready for his walk: lavatory chain, gargling, clattering, doors. **1926–7** *Army & Navy Stores Catal.* 469/3 Harpic Lavatory Cleanser. **1963** V. NABOKOV *Gift* ii. 83 The lavatory humour and crude laughter. **1970** *Sunday Times* (Colour Suppl.) 15 Mar. 25/1 He was real blue, if you like. Some of his jokes. Lavatory humour, my Dan used to call it. **1954** N. TOMALIN in *Granta* 6 Nov. 23/2 All in all the most amazing thing about the show is the preponderance of lavatory jokes. **1966** A. E. LINDOP *I start Counting* xx. 256, I clutched my head over the lavatory pan. **1974** *Listener* 24 Jan. 100/1 After an atomic explosion, the last things to disintegrate would be articles made of vitreous porcelain—for example, wash-basins and lavatory pans. **1926–7** *Army & Navy Stores Catal.* 121/2 Lavatory Paper Holder. **1956** A. S. C. Ross in M. Black *Importance of Lang.* (1962) 103 Non-U *toilet-paper* / U *lavatory-paper*. **1974** *Times* 23 Jan. 14/4 The Americans.. had their lavatory paper panic first. **1952** A. CHRISTIE *They do it with Mirrors* iii. 24 'It's pretty ghastly, really,' said Gina cheerfully. 'A sort of Gothic monstrosity. What Steve calls Best Victorian Lavatory period.' **1939** G. HOUSEHOLD *Rogue Male* 255, I made him sit on the lavatory seat and read me the shipping news. **1973** *Country Life* 20 Sept. 784/2 Three industries of Derbyshire.. [are] the manufacture of artificial flowers, lavatory seats and mint sauce. **1487–8** *Durham Acc. Rolls* (Surtees) 651, iiij^or spultes cum j lavatory stone. **1937** H. G. WELLS *Camford Visitation* i. 5 That University affair they are building in London.. is all made, they tell me, of a sort of mineral nougat, lavatory style. **1944** J. AGATE *Red Letter Nights* 141 Liliom commits suicide, and is projected into a celestial police court, the architecture of which is copied from the Early Lavatory style of the National Liberal Club.

lavatory ('lævətərɪ), *a.* [ad. assumed L. **lavātōri-us*, f. *lavāre* to wash: see LAVE *v.*[1]] Of or pertaining to washing.

1846 in WORCESTER citing *Month. Rev.* **1865** MERIVALE *Rom. Emp.* VIII. lxvi. 217 The latter.. contrasts the lavatory resources of Rome with those of Grecian cities generally. **1890** *Cornh. Mag.* Oct. 358 His linen long-coat is a perfect marvel of the lavatory art,.. so snowy white is it.

† **lavatrine.** *Obs. rare*⁻⁰. [ad. L. *lavātrīna*, f. *lavāre* to wash; see LAVE *v.*[2]] (See quot.)

1623 COCKERAM, *Lauatrine*, a square stone in a kitchin, with a hole to auoid water, a sincker.

† **lavatrix.** *Obs. rare*⁻⁰. [assumed L. fem. (= L. *lōtrix*) of *lavātor* one who washes, f. *lavāre* to wash.] A woman who washes.

1623 in COCKERAM.

† **lavatur.** *Sc. Obs.* Also 6 lavatar. [ad. F. *lavatoire* LAVATORY.] = LAVATORY I.

1535 STEWART *Cron. Scot.* (1858) I. 101 With lauatar, lamp, with buke and mony bell Thir Drewideis thair syne did gar to dwell. **1542** *Inv. R. Wardr.* (1815) 58 Item, ane gryt clam shell gilt for the lavatur.

† **lavature.** *Obs.* [ad. L. type **lavātūra* (= cl. L. *lōtūra*), f. *lavāre* to wash.] A lotion, a wash.

1601 HOLLAND *Pliny* II. 72 A lauature [of mallows] represseth all tettars. *Ibid.* 170 The leaues boiled in rain water, together with the barke of the blacke fig-tree.. do make a lauature or water to colour the hair [blacke].

lave (leɪv), *sb.*[1] *Obs.* exc. *Sc.* Forms: 1 láf, 2 (to) lafon, 3 loave, 3–5 law(e, 4 laf(e, laffe, 4–7 laif, laiff(e, layfe, -ff, 6 le(a)ve, 7 laiv, 4– lave. [OE. *láf* = OFris. *lâva*, OLG. *lêva*, OHG. *leiba*, ON. *leif*, Goth. *laiba*:—OTeut. **laibâ* str. fem.; for the further etymology see LEAVE *v.*] What is left, is over, or remains; the remainder, the rest.

a. of persons. (In OE. the word had also the sense 'relict, widow'.)

a **1000** *O.E. Chron.* an. 867 (Parker MS.), Sio laf wiþ þone here friþ nam. *c* **1375** *Sc. Leg. Saints, Andreas* 987 Syne þe lawe ine þar degre War to met set. **1375** BARBOUR *Bruce* II. 306 The lave sone wnarmyt war. *c* **1450** HOLLAND *Howlat* 446 With lordis of Scotland, lerit, and the laif. *c* **1470** HENRY *Wallace* II. 175 All weildand God, resawe My petows spreit.. amange the law! **1513** DOUGLAS *Æneis* v. ii. 67 Quham followis all the laif in lyke maneir. **1573** *Satir. Poems Reform.* xxxix. 228 As for the leue, thair wes bot lytill leid. **1664** *Flodden F.* I. 9 Of doughty Knights the lusty lave I never could by name repeat. **1725** RAMSAY *Gentle Sheph.* I. i, My Peggy speaks sae sweetly, To a' the lave I'm cauld. **1786** *Har'st Rig* 45 Auld Rodney.. didna loiter like the lave. **1816** SCOTT *Antiq.* xlv, 'Auld Mucklebackit's gane wi' the lave.' **1881** L. B. WALFORD *Dick Netherby* v. 57 'Gif her ain fayther has his fling at my puir bairn, it's like the lave will follow.'

b. of things.

971 *Blickl. Hom.* 111 Hwæt biþ la elles seo laf buton wyrma mete. *a* **1225** *Ancr. R.* 168 Nis þis large relef? Nis þis muchel loaue? *a* **1300** *Cursor M.* 7116 His wijf fader and moder he gaue O þis hony at ete þe laue. *c* **1375** *Sc. Leg. Saints, Paulus* 351 Paulis hed, þat þar wes hyd A-mange þe lafe, a hyrd has tane. **1427** *Sc. Acts Jas. I* (1814) II. 15/1 þe quhilkis commissaris sal haf ful ande playn power of al þe laif of þe schirefdome. *c* **1450** *St. Cuthbert* (Surtees) 1306 Half his brede his horse he gaue, And kepid to him self þe laue. **1530** LYNDESAY *Test. Papyngo* 825 Androw and Ihone did leif thare possessioun, Thar schippis, & nettis, lyinnes, and all the laue. **1583** *Satir. Poems Reform.* xlv. 224 Five hundreth merkis he to him gave, And tuik in hand to pay the leave. **1721** RAMSAY *Prospect of Plenty* x, Excepting some wha a' the lave will nick. **1785** BURNS *Jolly Beggars* Air v, Your every care and fear May whistle owre the lave o't. **1816** SCOTT *Old Mort.* vi, I'll pay the lave out o' the butter siller. **1865** G. MACDONALD *A. Forbes* 44 Jist help me oot, an' lea the lave to me.

†**c.** in adj. phr. *to lave* = remaining, surviving.

971 *Blickl. Hom.* 79 þa hi ȝyt ȝenaman þæs folces þe þær to lafe wæs.. hund teontiȝ þusenda. *a* **1175** *Cott. Hom.* 221 þe niȝon werod, þe þer to lafon were. *c* **1205** LAY. 28583 þa nas þer na mare i þan fehte to laue.

lave, *sb.*[2] *rare.* [f. LAVE *v.*[1]] **a.** The sea. **b.** The action of laving, wash.

1825 'BLACKMANTLE' (Westmacott) *Engl. Spy* (1826) 177 Like the sea-mew that skims o'er the lave. **1865** *Dublin Univ. Mag.* II. 350 The crystal lymph Through sands and ivy pulsed with ceaseless lave.

† **lave,** *a. Obs.* exc. in *Comb.* Also 7 loave, 7–8 *corruptly* leaf. [See LAVE *v.*[2]] **a.** Of ears: Drooping, hanging.

a **1400–50** *Alexander* 4748 With laith leggis & lange & twa laue eres. **1606** *Wily Beguiled* 58 And I were a woman, I would lug off his laue eares. **1659** *Lady Alimony* II. vi, But take especial care You button on your night-cap—*Morisco.* After th' new fashion With his loave Ears without it. **1675** J. SMITH *Chr. Relig. Appeal* II. 9 Here the little Ear, there the lave Ear.

b. *Comb.*: **lave-ears**, drooping or hanging ears (of a horse); hence **lave-eared** (corruptly **leaf-eared**) *a.*, having 'lave-ears'.

1570 LEVINS *Manip.* 42/45 Laue eared, *plaudus.* **1597** *1st Pt. Return Parnass.* I. i. 345 Thou lave-ear'd ass, that loves dross more than arts! **1607** MARKHAM *Caval.* VII. (1617) 43 Of the disease belonging to the eares of a Horse, and first of the laue-eares, or hanging eares. **1685** *Lond. Gaz.* No. 2092/4 A large strong grey Gelding,.. somewhat leaf-ear'd. **1701** *Ibid.* No. 3750/4 Stolen or strayed.. a strong bay Cart-Horse.. very wide Lave-Ear'd. *a* **1720** GIBSON *Dict. Horses* viii. (ed. 3) 128 This Method is commonly used by the Jockeys to Leaf-eared Horses, to cause them to carry their ears more upright. **1741** *Compl. Fam.-Piece* III. 463 The hanging of the Ears is called by some the Lave-ears. **1926** *Blackw. Mag.* Sept. 431/1 If a poet.. was lave-eared; if he had the eyes of a fawn, then you might be sure that he was a poet, and fear the worst. **1932** AUDEN *Orators* II. 44 The nasty lave-eared pop-eyed bitch.

lave (leɪv), *v.*[1] Now chiefly *poet.* Forms: 1 lafian, ȝelafian, 2–3 lavin, 7 *Sc.* lawe, 4– lave. [Two distinct formations appear to have coalesced—(1) OE. had *lafian* to wash by affusion, to pour (water), corresponding formally to MDu., Du. *laven*, OHG. *labôn* (MHG., mod.G. *laben*) to refresh; cf. OHG. *laba*, mod.G. *labe* refreshment. By some scholars the OE., Du., and Ger. words are considered to represent a WGer. adoption of L. *lavāre* to wash. This view involves some difficulty, as the numerous OHG. examples refer to refreshment by food, drink, or warmth, so that the assumed primary sense 'to wash', if it ever existed, must have been quite forgotten. The L. origin, however, accounts well for the senses of the OE. word, which perh. may be only accidentally similar in form to the continental words. (2) In ME. the representative of the OE. vb. blended indistinguishably with the vb. a. F. *laver* (= Pr., Sp., Pg. *lavar*, It. *lavare*):—L. *lavāre* = Gr. λούειν, f. OAryan root **lou-* to wash (whence LATHER).]

1. *trans.* To wash, bathe.

Beowulf 2722 (Gr.) þeȝn unȝemete till winedryhten his wætere ȝelafede. *c* **1000** *Sax. Leechd.* III. 48 Lafa þin heafod mid do swa þe þearf sy. *c* **1200** *Trin. Coll. Hom.* 145 Hie his fet lauede mid hire hote teres. **1390** GOWER *Conf.* III. 337 She was anone with water laved. **1596** SHAKS. *Tam. Shr.* II. i. 350 Basons, and ewers, to laue her dainty hands. **1637** MILTON *Lycidas* 175. **1650** BULWER *Anthropomet.* 159 Who could not endure the liquid test, but were soon laved into a ridiculous aspect. **1725** POPE *Odyss.* VI. 44 The wave, Where their fair vests Phæacian virgins lave. **1735** SOMERVILLE *Chase* I. 181 Tumultuous soon they plunge into the Stream, There lave their reeking Sides. **1827–35** WILLIS *Leper* 152 He took a little water in His hand And laved the sufferer's brow. **1858** NEALE *Bernard de M.* (1865) 35 Who.. Bore with me in defilement And from defilement laved. **1871** R. ELLIS *Catullus* lxiv. 162 Now in waters clear thy feet like ivory laving.

fig. **1605** SHAKS. *Macb.* III. ii. 33 Wee must laue Our Honors in these flattering streames. **1810** SCOTT *Lady of L.* I. xv, And when the midnight moon should lave Her forehead in the silver wave. **1843** LYTTON *Last Bar.* I. ii, In those bitter tears, childhood itself was laved from her soul for ever.

b. *intr.* for *refl.* To bathe. *lit.* and *fig.*

1701 CIBBER *Love makes Man* II. ii, Happy he that.. unconfin'd may lave and wanton there. **1704** POPE *Windsor For.* 209 In her chaste current oft the goddess laves. **1801** FOSTER in *Life & Corr.* (1846) I. 129 To lave in the stream, the tide of deeper sentiments. **1811** MISS MITFORD in *Life* I. v. 129 The calm lake.. Where the young cygnets lave.

†**c.** *to lave a* (= with): to be bathed in or covered with (blood, sweat). *Obs.*

c **1205** LAY 7489 He swonc i þon fehte þat al he lauede asweote [*c* **1275** leþerede a swote]. *a* **1300** *Judas* in *Rel. Ant.* I. 144 He drou hymselve bi the cop, that al it lavede a blode.

2. *trans.* Of a river, a body of water: To wash against, to flow along or past.

1623 tr. *Favine's Theat. Hon.* II. i. 67 For this River.. commeth to laue the Towne of Namure. **1666** DRYDEN *Ann. Mirab.* cliii, Guns.. Whose low-laid mouths each mounting billow laves. **1704** ADDISON *Italy* (1733) 129 The bord'ring Ocean laves Her silent Coast. *a* **1717** PARNELL *Night-Piece on Death* 20 A place of graves, Whose wall the silent water laves. **1791** COWPER *Iliad* XXI. 318 The flood, Jove's offspring, laved his shoulders. **1814** SCOTT *Ld. of Isles* V. viii, He leant against a stranded boat,.. And counted every rippling wave, As higher yet her sides they lave. **1859** CAPERN *Ball. & Songs* 47 Where Torridge laves its banks of green. **1887** *Spectator* 30 July 1016/2 The shire is laved by a sea teeming with fish.

absol. **1808** SCOTT *Marm.* III. x, There, through the summer day, Cool streams are laving.

3. To pour out with or as with a ladle; to ladle. Also *absol.* Const. †*in, into, on, upon.*

c **1000** *Sax. Leechd.* II. 124 Hat wæter lafa on. *a* **1310** in Wright *Lyric P.* xxv. 72 Ihesu,.. The deu of grace upon me lave. **13..** *E.E. Allit. P.* A 607 He lauez hys gyftes as water of dyche. *a* **1400** *Sir Perc.* 2250 Thay wolde not lett long thone, Bot lavede in hir with a spone. *a* **1648** DIGBY *Closet Open.* (1677) 24 This being done lave and bounce it [the honey and water] very well and often. **1703** T. N. *City & C. Purchaser* 190 The Lead being melted.. is laved into the Pan. *a* **1711** KEN *Hymns Evang.* Poet. Wks. 1721 I. 81 The Saint.. on his Head the hallow'd Water lav'd. **1823** LOCKHART *Reg. Dalton* VI. i. (1842) 350 He.. laved a few cool drops upon his brow. **1862** *Macm. Mag.* Apr. 519 Lave the water.. in slight handfuls.. gently over the head and face.

†**b.** *intr.* To run, stream. *Obs.*

c **1425** *Festivals Ch.* 220 in *Leg. Rood* (1871) 217 Dropes rede as ripe cherrees, þat fro his flesshe gan lave.

†**4.** *trans.* To draw (water) out or up with a bucket, ladle, or scoop; to bale. Also with *out, up*, with complement, and *absol. Obs.*

13.. *E.E. Allit. P.* C. 154 Mony ladde þer forth-lep to laue & to kest, Scopen out the scaþel water. *c* **1374** CHAUCER *Boeth.* III. metr. xii. (E.E.T.S.) 107 [Orpheus] spak and song in wepynge alle þat euer he hadde resceyued and laued oute of þe noble welles of hys modir calliope. **1387** TREVISA *Higden* (Rolls) III. 415 þat lorde was woned to.. lave up water of pitts. **1458** in Turner *Dom. Archit.* III. 41 With xi. laborers lavyng at onys. **1508** KENNEDIE *Flyting w. Dunbar* 471 Thow fylde faster than fyftensum mycht lawe. **1601** W. PARRY *Trav. Sir A. Sherley* 6 To laue water out of this rotten boate. **1621** BURTON *Anat. Mel.* I. ii. IV. vii. (1651) 167 When I have laved the sea dry, thou shalt understand the mystery of the Trinity. **1644** EVELYN *Diary* 11 Oct., As we were weary with pumping and laving out the water. *a* **1700** DRYDEN tr. *Ovid's Met.* XI. *Cevx & Alcyone* 109 A fourth, with Labour, laves Th' intruding Seas, and Waves ejects on Waves. **1708** J. C. *Compl. Collier* (1845) 13 It were Folly and unreasonable Charge.. to Lave, or fill 20 or 30 Tubs of Water per hour.

transf. **1677** PLOT *Oxfordsh.* 5 It [a storm of wind] was yet so violent, that it laved water out of the River Cherwell, and cast it quite over the Bridge at Magdalen College.

† **lave,** *v.*[2] *Obs. rare*⁻¹. [Cf. ON. *lafa* to droop.] Of the ears: To droop, hang down.

1597–8 BP. HALL *Sat.* IV. i. 72 His eares hang laving, like a new-lug'd swine.

lave, obs. form of LAW.

laveer (lə'vɪə(r)), *v. Naut. Obs.* exc. in literary use. Forms: 6–7 lavere, (7 laver, -eir, -ier, 7–8 loft-veer), 7– laveer. [ad. Du. *laveeren*, in 17th c. also *loevéren*, MDu. *laeveren, loveren*, ad. F. (16th c.) *loveer*, now *louvoyer* (for the suffix in Du. cf. *domineren* DOMINEER *v.*), f. *lof* windward (of Du. or LG. origin: see LUFF). The Du. word has been adopted in other langs. as G. *lavieren*, Sw. *lofvera*, Da. *lavere.*] *intr.* To beat to windward; to tack.

1598 W. PHILLIPS tr. *Linschoten* I. xcvi. 179 The Indian ships.. durst not anker there; but only vsed to lauere to and fro. **1608** HIERON *2nd Pt. Def. Ministers' Reasons for Refus. Subscript.* 149 The winde being against him, he laveirs and turneth another tacke. **1648** EARL WESTMORELAND *Otia Sacra* (1879) 163 Lie on a Tack Port and Laveer, Sometimes to weather, then to Lee. **1662** DRYDEN *Astræa Redux* 65 Those that 'gainst stiff gales laveering go, Must be at once resolv'd and skilful too. **1718** J. CHAMBERLAYNE *Relig. Philos.* (1730) II. xix. §58 They can always pass through this Streight by Laveering or Tacking, even tho' the Wind be contrary. **1876** BANCROFT *Hist. U.S.* V. xxiii. 593 It went for the Chesapeake, laveering against the stiff southerly winds of the season.

fig. *a* **1667** COWLEY *Liberty* Verses & Ess. (1687) 81 To bend and turn about his own Nature, and laveer with every wind. **1800** W. TAYLOR in *Monthly Mag.* X. 319 Instead of bearing down on the point for which he is bound.. Klopstock is continually laveering. **1885** MRS. C. L. PIRKIS *Lady Lovelace* II. xxiii. 55 Neither skilful nor resolved enough to 'laveer' against them [the fates].

Hence † **la'veerer**, one who laveers.

1670 CLARENDON *Ess.* Tracts (1727) 183 They [the School-men] are the best Laveerers of the World.

† **lavel.** *Obs. rare*⁻¹. [ad. It. *lavello* 'a lauer in a Barbers shops' (Florio), ad. L. *labellum* bowl, bathing-tub.] A wide shallow pan or bowl.

1658 tr. *Porta's Nat. Magic* VI. ii. 179 Let water be often poured into the lavel [L. *in labellum*], and stirred about. *Ibid.*, Skim the lavel [L. *conca decapuletur*].

†**lavell.** *Obs.* The epiglottis.

1530 PALSGR. 237/2 Lavell that standeth in the myddes of the throte, *alovette.* 1847 HALLIWELL, *Lavell*, the flap that covers the top of the windpipe. Still used in Devon.

la'vellan. *Sc.* A kind of weasel (Jam.).

1684 SIBBALD *Scot. Illustr.* II. III. 11 Lavellan, Animal in Cathanesia frequens. 1771 PENNANT *Tour Scotl. in 1769* (1774) 175, I enquired here after the Lavellan, which, from description, I suspect to be the Water Shrew Mouse.

lavement ('leɪvmənt). [a. F. *lavement*, f. *laver* to wash; cf. LAVAMENT.]

1. The action of washing, or cleansing. *rare.*

1650 ASHMOLE *Chym. Collect.* 23 In the fourth distillation follows the Lavement. 1891 *Cornh. Mag.* Mar. 323 Those down below pause in the lavement of their hands.

2. *Med.* An injection.

1794 [J. WILLIAMS] *Crying Ep. to Col. Mack* 18 Bring a hot lavement, and infuse it Mack. 1825 W. HEBERDEN tr. *Cicero's Lett. to Atticus* x. 13 He ordered them to come again the next day, as he..was taking a lavement. 1872 *Contemp. Rev.* XXI. 149 The application of lavements to women and children. 1876 CURLING *Dis. Rectum* (ed. 4) 48 They have regularly used the cold-water lavements.

†**'lavender,** *sb.*[1] *Obs.* Forms: 4-5 **lavendere,** 4-6 **lavendre,** 5 **lavan-, -en-, -under, -dyre,** 4- **lavender.** Also in contracted form LAUNDER. [a. OF. *lavandier* masc., *lavandiere* fem. (mod.F. *lavandière* fem.) = Sp. *lavandero* masc., *-era* fem., Pg. *lavandeira* fem., It. *lavandaio* masc., *lavandaja, lavandara* fem., ad. late L. *lavandārius, -āria* (whence OHG. *laventari, ladantari* 'fullo'), f. *lavanda* (orig. neut. pl. 'things to be washed', but in Rom. used as fem. sing.: cf. It. *lavanda* washing), f. *lavāre* to wash: see LAVE *v.*

Cf. L. *lavandāria* neut. pl. (occurring once) 'things to be washed'. For the formation cf. also med.L. *referendarius.*]

A washerwoman, laundress. †Formerly also (*rarely*), a man who washes clothes, a washerman.

[*a* 1300 *Chron. Petroburg.* (Camden No. 47) 122 De catallis Johannis le Lavandere, fugitivi.] *a* 1310 in Wright *Lyric P.* xv. 49 Prude wes my plowe fere, Lecherie my lavendere. *c* 1385 CHAUCER *L.G.W.* Prol. 358 Enuye..is lauender In the grete court alway. *c* 1430 *Syr Gener.* (Roxb.) 2328 The lauenders she saw in the floode, Ful besilie washing a skert. *c* 1470 HARDING *Chron.* CXCIII. ii, Ladies faire with their gentilwomen Chamberers also and lauenders. *a* 1483 in *Househ. Ord.* (1790) 85 Of the whiche soape the seyde clerke spicers shalle take allowaunce in his dayly dockette by the recorde of the seide yeoman lavender. 1501 *Will of Wadyngton* (Somerset Ho.), My lavendre Kateryne Gybbes. *a* 1536 *Will of P'cess Catharine* in Strype *Eccl. Mem.* I. App. lxix. 170, I ordain that my lavander be paid of that which is due unto her. 1567 in Chalmers *Mary* (1818) 177 Lauandrie. Margaret Balcomie, lauander.

lavender ('lævɪndə(r)), *sb.*[2] and *a.* Forms: 3-6 **lavendre,** 5 **lavendere,** 6-7 **lavander,** 6- **lavender.** Also 6 *Sc.* **lavand.** [a. AF. *lavendre* (OF. **lavandre*, whence mod. Prov. *alebandro*) for **lavendle*:—med.L. *lavendula*, also *lavandula, livendula, livendola* (10-11th c. in Goetz *Corp. Gll. Latin.* III. 629/5), *levindula, lavindula*; cf. It. *lavendola* (Diez; not in Dicts.), Sp. *lavándula* (in Dicts. only as a botanical name); also F. *lavande* (cited from Christine de Pisan, 14-15th c.), It., Sp. *lavanda*. The med.L. *lavendula* was taken into OHG. or early MHG. as *lavendla* (in MSS. of 12th c.; see *Ahd. Glossen* III. 105), whence MHG. and early mod.G. *lavendel(e, lobendel, lobengele, laubangel, lavandel, lavander, lafander*; the standard form in Ger., Du., Sw., Da. is now *lavendel*.

The current hypothesis is that med.L. *lavendula* is a corrupt form of *lavandula*, a dim. of the shorter word which appears in It. as *lavanda* (see above). This is commonly identified with It. *lavanda* 'washing', the supposition being that the name refers to the use of the plant either for perfuming baths (so already in 16th c. writers) or as laid among freshly washed linen (see 2 below). But on the ground of sense-development this does not seem plausible; a word literally meaning 'washing' would hardly without change of form come to denote a non-essential adjunct to washing. Besides, the earliest form appears to be *livendula*; if this could be connected with L. *līvēre* to be livid or bluish, the sense would be appropriate, but the formation is obscure; M. Paul Meyer suggests, as a possibility, that the original form may have been **līvindula* for **līvidula*, f. *līvidus* LIVID. (A med.L. word of about the same date and of app. similar form is *calendula* marigold.) It is not certain that the word has not changed its application, as in early glosses *livendula, lavendula*, are given as synonymous with *samsucus* and *amaracus*, which properly mean 'marjoram'; but plant-names were applied often very loosely. The It. *lavanda*, F. *lavande*, would seem to be a back-formation from med.L. *lavandula*.]

A. *sb.*

1. a. The plant *Lavandula vera* (N.O. *Labiatæ*), a small shrub with small pale lilac-coloured flowers, and narrow oblong or lanceolate leaves; it is a native of the south of Europe and Northern Africa, but cultivated extensively in other countries for its perfume. Also applied, usually with defining word, to the two other species of *Lavandula*, *L. Spica* (distinguished as ***French lavender*** and †***lavender spike***), and *L. Stœchas* (formerly †***lavender gentle***).

oil of lavender, the essential oil obtained by distillation of the blossoms of *L. vera*, used in medicine and perfumery. An inferior kind is obtained from the two other species, and is used in making varnishes and for other industrial purposes; that from *L. Spica* is called 'oil of spike'.

c 1265 *Voc. Plants* in Wr. Wülcker 557/9 *Lauendula*, lauendre. *c* 1440 *Promp. Parv.* 290/1 Lavendere, herbe, *Lavendula.* *c* 1450 *Alphita* (Anecd. Oxon.) 92/1 *Lavendula*, gall. et angl. lauendre. 1530 PALSGR. 237/2 Lavendre an herbe, *lauende.* 1538 TURNER *Libellus*, Lavender, *pseudo-..nardus.* *c* 1550 LLOYD *Treas. Health* (1585) Lj, Take of lauender gentle ʒ. & a half. 1570 *Satir. Poems Reform.* xv. 9 Thow Lauand, lurk; thow time, be tint; Thow Margelene, swaif. 1573 BARET *Alv.*, Lauander..*lauendula.* 1577 B. GOOGE *Heresbach's Husb.* (1586) 66 Lavender is called in Latine Lavanda or Lavendula. 1578 LYTE *Dodoens* II. lxxxvi. 264 Lauender is of two sortes, male and female. 1597 GERARDE *Herbal* II. clxxix. (1633) 584 Lavender Spike is called in Latine Lavendula. 1611 SHAKS. *Wint. T.* IV. iv. 104 Here's flowres for you: Hot Lauender, Mints, Sauory, mariorum. *a* 1677 HALE *Prim. Orig. Man.* III. vi. 280 The Seeds of Lavander kept a little warm and moist, will turn into Moths. 1751 HILL *Hist. Mat. Med.* 424 Lavender has at all times been famous as a cephalic, nervous, and uterine medicine. 1796 C. MARSHALL *Garden.* xvi. (1813) 268 Lavender..is for its pleasant aromatic scent found in most gardens. 1859 GULLICK & TIMBS *Paint.* 209 The English oil of lavender, or the inferior foreign oil of spike (a larger species of lavender), is preferred in enamel painting.

b. Applied to certain other plants. **sea lavender,** *Statice Limonium*; also called † ***marsh lavender*** (*obs.*), ***lavender thrift.*** † **lavender of Spain** = LAVENDER COTTON.

1530 PALSGR. 237/2 Lavendre of Spaygne, *cipres.* 1597 GERARDE *Herbal* II. lxxxvii. §2. 333 The people neere the sea side where it groweth do call it Marsh Lauander, and Sea Lauander. 1760 J. LEE *Introd. Bot.* App. 316 Sea Lavender, *Statice.* 1837 MACGILLIVRAY *Withering's Brit. Plants* (ed. 4) 154 *S[tatice] Limonium*, Lavender Thrift.

c. Phr. ***lavender and old lace***: the title of a novel and play used to describe a gentle and 'old-fashioned' style.

The novel by Myrtle Reed was published in 1902 and the dramatized version by Rose Warner in 1938.

1966 *Guardian* 25 Nov. 14/7 Arthur Pollard..is largely concerned to dispel the notion that Mrs Gaskell is a writer of 'lavender and old lace'. 1966 M. STEEN *Looking Glass* v. 88 E. V. Lucas..never wrote twaddle: the lavender and old lace of his titles masked erudition. 1968 HOCKING & HEALEY *Murder cries Out* iv. 54 This astounded gentleman..had received a description of Miss Willoughby as all 'lavender and old lace'.

2. The flowers and stalks of *Lavandula vera*, placed among linen or other clothes in order to preserve them from moths when they are to be stored for some time. ***to lay (up) in lavender***: (*a*) to lay aside carefully for future use; (*b*) *slang*, to pawn; (*c*) to put out of the way of doing harm, as a person by imprisoning him or the like.

1584 *Stanford Churchw. Acc.* in *Antiquary* XVII. 210/1 It. lavender for the churche clothes. 1589 NASHE *Pref. Greene's Menaphon* (Arb.) 8 Bought at the deerest though they smell of the friplers lauander halfe a yeere after. 1592 GREENE *Upst. Courtier* (1871) 34 He is ready to lend the loser money upon rings..or any other good pawn, but the poor gentleman pays so dear for the lavender it is laid up in, that [etc.]. 1605 CHAPMAN, etc. *Eastw. Ho.* G2, Good faith rather then thou shouldest pawne a rag more il'e lay my ladiship in lauender, If I knew where. 1628 EARLE *Microcosm., Yng. rawe Preacher* (Arb.) 23 He..ha's a iest still in lauender for Bellarmine. *a* 1639 WOTTON *Let. to Walton* in *Reliq.* (1651) 512 Yours hath lyen so long by me (as it were in lavender) without an answer. 1648 *Petit. East. Assoc.* 9 It is the duty of a State to lay him [the king] solemnly in such kind of Lavender as grows in the 27 of Deuteronomy. *a* 1700 B. E. *Dict. Cant. Crew*, *Layd-up-in Lavender*, when any Cloaths or other Moveables are pawn'd or dipt for present Money. 1822 SCOTT *Nigel* xxiii, Lowestoffe is laid up in lavender only for having shown you the way into Alsatia. 1826 —— *Mal. Malagr.* ii, The ornaments are redeemed from the pawn-brokers, worn perhaps on the Sunday, and returned to lavender (as the phrase goes) on the next Monday. 1858 THACKERAY *Virgin.* I. xxxiii. 258 What woman..has not the bridal-favours and raiment stowed away, and packed in lavender, in the inmost cup-boards of her heart? 1888 *Academy* 18 Feb. 111/3 The old maid..with her little romance carefully preserved in the lavender of memory.

3. The colour of lavender-flowers, a very pale blue with a trace of red.

1882 *Garden* 16 Dec. 533/3 Chrysanthemums,..Fée Rageuse, a large recurved flower..colour white tinted with lavender. 1886 FENN *Master Ceremonies* i, They were of richest purple, fading into lavender and grey.

4. *Cinemat.* Positive stock, or a positive print, used for producing duplicate negatives; also (quot. 1936), a print made from such a negative.

1936 C. B. DEMILLE in *Words* Oct. 6/1 A 'lavender' is something often spoken of in the industry... It is a print made from a negative on lavender stock, which is a weak print from a weak negative, because lavender negatives are only copies of the film originally exposed in the camera and are therefore not as sharp. 1959 W. S. SHARPS *Dict. Cinematogr.* 106/1 *Lavender*, the name given to an obsolescent type of master positive stock with a lavender tinted base. The name remains in use to describe a master positive. 1973 D. A. SPENCER *Focal Dict. Photogr. Technol.* 340 *Lavender*, fine grain motion picture film used for making duplicate black and white negatives..and coated on lavender tinted base to minimise halation and prevent confusion with ordinary positive stocks. Modern duplicating stock is on a grey tinted base and differs sufficiently in appearance from ordinary positive that the lavender tint is not necessary.

5. *attrib.* and *Comb.*, as ***lavender-growing***; ***lavender-blue, -brown, -coloured, -grey, -hued, -scented*** adjs.; **lavender bag,** a bag containing dried lavender; **lavender cream,** lavender-scented cream or furniture-polish; also ***lavender furniture cream***; **lavender drawer,** a drawer containing or scented with lavender; **lavender drop,** a drop (sense 4) medicated with lavender; **lavender polish** = *lavender cream*; also ***lavender floor polish***; **lavender sachet** = ***lavender bag***; **lavender soap,** soap perfumed with lavender; also ***lavender toilet soap***; **lavender-sugar,** a sweetmeat medicated with lavender; **lavender wax** = *lavender cream.*

1865 GEO. ELIOT *Let.* 6 Feb. in J. W. Cross *George Eliot's Life* (1885) II. xii. 396, I want to send my love, lest all the old messages shall have lost their scent, like old *lavender bags. 1923 A. HUXLEY *Antic Hay* iv. 55 Give me..a lavender bag under every pillow. 1965 M. SHARP *Sun in Scorpio* III. xxv. 131 Elspet was peddling lavender-bags. 1796 KIRWAN *Elem. Min.* (ed. 2) I. 28 *Lavender blue—blue with a mixture of grey, and a shade of red. 1936 *Burlington Mag.* Jan. 9/1 Vase with lavender-blue glaze splashed or suffused with purple. 1813 *Sketches Charac.* (ed. 2) I. 218 Spangled crape petticoat, with *lavender brown train. 1901 *Westm. Gaz.* 7 Sept. 1/3 Our *lavender-coloured view of life. 1936 J. C. POWYS *Maiden Castle* (1937) 40 A vision of lavender-coloured tights. 1926-7 *Army & Navy Stores Catal.* 1128/2 Hair and toilet preparations..*Lavender cream. *c* 1938 *Fortnum & Mason Price List* 36/1 Furniture polish.. Lavender Cream..per jar 1/6. 1863 DICKENS *Mrs. Lirriper's Lodgings* i, in *All Year Round* Extra Christmas No., 3 Dec. 9/1 An advertisement..which I mean always carefully to keep in my *lavender drawer. 1811 JANE AUSTEN *Sense & Sens.* II. vii. 126 Some *lavender drops..which she was at length persuaded to take, were of use. 1969 A. E. LINDOP *Sight Unseen* xix. 158 A clean smell of *lavender floor polish. 1926-7 *Army & Navy Stores Catal.* 297/2 *Lavender furniture cream. 1834 MRS. SOMERVILLE *Connex. Phys. Sci.* xix. (1849) 181 Visible rays of a *lavender grey colour. 1936 *Burlington Mag.* Jan. 4/1 Buff ware with a crackled lavender-grey glaze. 1900 *Daily News* 28 Aug. 5/1 Some persons find *lavender-growing very profitable. 1901 *Westm. Gaz.* 7 Sept. 1/3, I speak from experience, having lately reached the *lavender-hued period. 1961 J. STROUD *Touch & Go* v. 49 The aggressive *lavender-polish aroma denoting the house-proud matriarch. 1966 L. DEIGHTON *Billion-Dollar Brain* v. 51 There was a sweet smell of lavender polish as we walked through a couple of rooms. 1938 R. FIELD *All this, & Heaven Too* (1939) iv. 65 The lavender *sachets in her bureau drawers. 1973 'S. HARVESTER' *Corner of Playground* I. 49 Who can make tea with a bloody bag like a lavender sachet? 1855 MRS. GASKELL *North & South* II. xxi. 283 Smoothing down the bed, and despatching Jenny for an armful of *lavender-scented towels. 1871 M. COLLINS *Mrq. & Merch.* I. ii. 60 Linen lavender-scented. 1938 O. SITWELL et al. *Trio* 124, I care for him [*sc.* de la Mare] less when he is in a melancholy mood, for the poems then have a tendency to become a little too lavender-scented. 1974 J. WAINWRIGHT *Evidence I shall Give* xv. 58 Lavender-scented handkerchiefs. 1875 E. SPON *Workshop Receipts* 385 **Lavender Soap.*—The basis of Windsor soap, scented with oil of lavender. 1949 D. SMITH *I capture Castle* II. ix. 133 Rose was..varnishing her nails; the varnish had been her special treat... I had lavender soap. 1961 A. WILSON *Old Men at Zoo* i. 35 The Director caught up with me, all redolent with lavender soap to greet his lady wife, as he was apt to call her. 1810 *Splendid Follies* I. 19 Hand *lavender-sugar to the old man. 1890-91 *T. Eaton & Co. Catal.* Fall & Winter 42/1 Sweet *lavender toilet soap. 1970 M. KELLY *Spinifex* vi. 97 A large bedroom scented with years of *lavender wax.

B. *adj.* **1.** Of the colour of lavender-flowers (see A. 3). Also in *Comb.*

1882 *Garden* 20 May 354/3 Clematises..with flowers of a delicate lavender shade. 1883 *Congregationalist* Nov. 900 He moved on, with springy step, wearing lavender kid gloves. 1890 'ROLF BOLDREWOOD' *Col. Reformer* (1891) 162 The lavender-kid-wearing tribe of modern youth. 1897 MARY KINGSLEY *W. Africa* 341 Obanjo evidently thought him too much of a lavender-kid-glove gentleman to deal with bush trade.

†**2.** *Photogr.* ***lavender rays,*** ultraviolet radiation. *Obs.*

1840 J. F. W. HERSCHEL in *Phil. Trans. R. Soc.* CXXX. 20 As orange, indigo, and violet, vegetable tints, are used for those of the prismatic hues, I may be allowed to express by the epithet lavender the rays which produce the tint in question, rather for the purpose of abbreviating the uncouth appellation of *ultra-violet*..than for that of laying any undue stress on the observed fact. 1842 *Ibid.* CXXXII. 191 If the action of the spectrum be prolonged, a much feebler whitening becomes sensible in the red, and a trace of it also beyond the violet into the 'lavender' rays. 1858 SUTTON & WORDEN *Dict. Photogr.* 248 The faintly luminous rays beyond the violet end of the spectrum are called 'lavender rays'. 1911 *Cassell's Cycl. Photogr.* 329/2 *Lavender rays*, a term (now practically obsolete) applied to the commencement of the ultraviolet rays just beyond the visible violet. [1922 A. E. H. TUTTON *Crystallogr.* II. li. 1139 This ultra-violet lamp is visible to the eye at close quarters owing to fluorescence of the retina of the eye itself; and the field of vision appears filled with a haze known as 'lavender fog', owing to fluorescence of the crystalline lens of the eye.]

'lavender, *v.* [f. LAVENDER *sb.*[2]] *trans.* To perfume with lavender; to put lavender among (linen).

1820 KEATS *Eve St. Agnes* xxx, In blanched linen, smooth, and lavender'd. 1839 H. ROGERS *Ess.* II. iii. 148 The word 'stench' is lavendered over into 'unpleasant effluvia', or an 'ill odour'. *a* 1845 HOOD *Two Peacocks of Bedfont* xxv, The solemn clerk goes lavender'd and shorn. 1874 M. COLLINS *Transmigr.* III. i. 3, I lay there, amid lavendered linen. 1875 TENNYSON *Q. Mary* III. v, It shall be all my study for one hour To rose and lavender my horsiness. 1893 M. GRAY

Last Sentence I. v, Snowy linen lavendered by the young bride's own hands.

¶ Used (after LAVENDER *sb.*[1]) for LAUNDER *v.* 1.

1843 WILLIS *New Mirror* (Cent.), The smell of soap, from the lavendering in the back-yard.

'lavender 'cotton. A name for Ground cypress (*Santolina Chamæcyparissus*); formerly confused with *Artemisia Abrotanon* or *maritima*.

1530 PALSGR. 237/2 Lavendre cotten, *cipres*. **1538** TURNER *Libellus*, Lavender cotton, *Absinthium*. **1577** B. GOOGE *Heresbach's Husb.* (1586) 66 b, Lavender cotten,.. some call it.. Santonia and female Sothernewood. **1579** LANGHAM *Gard. Health* (1633) 349 Lauender cotton, or garden Cypers, drunke with wine, is good against all poyson & venom: it is the female kind of Sothernwood. **1741** *Compl. Fam.-Piece* I. i. 37 Lavender-Cotton,.. Camomile, Lavender-tops.. of each of these Herbs a small Handful. **1882** *Garden* 17 June 427/1 As edging plants.. Lavender Cotton.

'lavender-,water. A perfume compounded, with alcohol and ambergris, from the distilled flowers of lavender.

1563 HYLL *Art Garden.* (1593) 99 Distil it in a limbek of glas.. into which put a little Lauender water & peper. **1758** J. S. *Le Dran's Observ. Surg.* (1771) 294 They bathed the Part with Lavender Water. *a* **1863** THACKERAY *Fitz-Boodle's Prof.* Misc. Wks. IV. 21 What a fine odour of lavender-water!

lavendery ('lævındərı), *a.* [f. LAVENDER *sb.*[2] + -Y[1].] Perfumed with lavender; fragrant. Also *fig.*

1896 G. B. SHAW *Our Theatres in Nineties* (1932) II. 10 Mr Rose has often written pleasantly about these and other more remote and lavendery antiquities. **1968** P. DICKINSON *Skin Deep* v. 107 Go now, the smile said, and I'll retain fond lavendery memories of you; stay and I'll bite. **1974** A. PRICE *Other Paths to Glory* I. v. 49 The lavendery smell of the strange room.

†**lavendry.** *Obs.* Forms: 4-5 lavendrye, 5 -drey, 6 lavandrie. [ad. OF. *lavan-*, *lavenderie*, f. *lavandier* LAVENDER *sb.*[1]] **a.** = LAUNDRY *sb.* 1; **b.** = LAUNDRY *sb.* 2; **c.** = LAUNDRESS *sb.* 1.

1377 LANGL. *P. Pl.* B. xv. 182 þanne wil he some tyme Labory in a lauendrye. **1393** *Ibid.* C. XVII. 330 And laueþ hem in þe lauandrie. *a* **1483** *Liber Niger* in *Househ. Ord.* (1790) 85 Office of Lavendrey, two yeomen;.. and if there be a Queene in housholde, then there be weomen lavendryes for the chambre, warderobe, &c. **1567** [see LAVENDER *sb.*[1]].

lavendulan (lə'vɛndjʊlən). *Min.* Also **-ane.** [Named by Breithaupt, 1837; f. mod.L. *lavendula* lavender + -AN.] Arseniate of copper with cobalt, of a lavender-blue colour.

1844 DANA *Min.* 527 Lavendulan.. Fuses easily before the blowpipe. **1872** NEVILL *Catal. Min.* 144 Erythrite.. var. Lavendulane. **1892** DANA *Min.* 814 Lavendulan.. Occurs with cobalt and other ores.

la'vendulite. *Min.* [f. as prec. + -ITE.] = prec.

1878 *Mineral. Mag.* II. 101 Lavendulite.. occurs in large blocks of cobalt ore.

lave net. [Of unknown origin; cf. LAMMET, *lamnet* (s.v. LAM *v.*).] (See quot. 1883.)

1875 BUCKLAND *Log-bk.* 346 Three fishermen were standing waist deep.. working their lave nets. **1883** *Fisheries Exhib. Catal.* (ed. 4) 125 Lave Net.. used in the estuary to take salmon on the sands in the shallow water. **1894** *Westm. Gaz.* 30 July 8/2 On Thursday Mr. Henry Cadogan, with a lave net, caught in the same water a young shark.

lavenite ('lævənaıt). *Min.* Also **laavenite, låvenite.** [Named by Brögger, 1885, from the Laven (Sw. *Låven*) islands, where it was found.] Silicate of zirconium, found in brown monoclinic crystals.

1886 *Amer. Jrnl. Sci.* Ser. III. XXXI. 230 Låvenite is a mineral of chestnut brown to yellowish color. **1887** *Mineral. Mag.* VII. 234 The laavenite occurs as small honey-yellow crystalline grains. **1927** N. H. & A. N. WINCHELL *Elem. Optical Mineral.* (ed. 2) II. x. 245 Laavenite is a monoclinic zircono-silicate of Ca, Mn, Na with some Ti, Ta, F, OH. **1967** *Mineral. Abstr.* XVIII. 48/2 A new variety of låvenite occurs in a zone of veinlet nephelinization in massive quartz syenite in the alkalic massif of Burpala in nothern Baikal [Siberia].

laventine ('lævəntın). [Corruption of LEVANTINE.] A trade name for a mixture of silk and cotton.

1893 *Funk's Stand. Dict.*, *Laventine*, a thin silk: much used for sleeve-linings. **1921** *Daily Colonist* (Victoria, B.C.) 18 Oct. 19/7 (Advt.), Umbrellas at All Prices... Strong durable covers in mercerized cotton, gloria and laventine.

laver ('leıvə(r), 'lɑːvə(r)), *sb.*[1] Also 1 laber. [a. L. *laver*.]

†**1.** A water-plant mentioned by Pliny; = Gr. σίον. *Obs.*

c **1000** *Sax. Leechd.* I. 254 Ðeos wyrt þe man sion & oðrum naman laber nemneþ byð cenned on wætum stowum. **1562** TURNER *Herbal* II. 32 Sion otherwise called lauer is found in waters with a fat bushe ryght vp with brode leues. **1601** HOLLAND *Pliny* II. 255 The roots.. are as effectual in this case as green Lauer [*margin*, Water cresses].

2. From the 17th c. applied by writers to various marine algæ, and now used as a trade or culinary name for the edible species. **laver bread** (also **lava bread**), a name in Wales for a food made from the fronds of *Porphyra umbilicalis*, which are boiled, dipped in oatmeal, and fried. **purple laver**, *Porphyra laciniata*. **green laver**, *Ulva latissima* and *Ulva lactuca*.

1611 COTGR., *Herbe marine*, Slanke, Wrake, Lauer, Seagrasse. **1701** W. KENNET *Cowell's Interpreter* (rev. ed.), *Laver-bread*, in Glamorganshire and some other parts of Wales, they make a sort of Food of a Sea plant, which seems to be the Oyster-green or Sea-Liver-wort. This they call Laver-bread. **1732** ARBUTHNOT *Rules of Diet* 257 Laver, which is the *Lactuca Marina* or Sea-Lettuce. **1766** ANSTEY *Bath Guide* v. 32 Fine potted Laver, fresh Oysters, and Pies! **1843** *Statist. Acc. Scot.* VII. 400 The *Ulva latissima* which makes a pickle called 'laver', is found on the coast. **1847** SIR J. C. ROSS *Voy. S. Seas* II. 266 The green, pink, and purple lavers of Great Britain may be readily recognized. **1873** M. COLLINS *Squire Silchester* I. xv. 191 You don't get moor mutton with hot laver sauce every day. **1894** *Daily News* 1 Dec. 5/4 Laver is now in full season, and is best imported straight from Ireland. **1949** *New Biol.* VII. 94 In the days when butter was more plentiful, laver bread was heated with butter, lemon juice and pepper, and served with roast mutton. **1953** DYLAN THOMAS *Under Milk Wood* (1954) 5 Is there rum and laverbread? **1962** *Listener* 26 July 140/2 Lava bread.. is the only truly Welsh food. It is made from seaweed. **1969** N. W. PIRIE *Food Resources* v. 127 Welsh devotion to laverbread is an important factor which restrains the managers of nuclear installations from fouling the sea more than they do now.

laver ('leıvə(r)), *sb.*[2] Forms: 4-6 lavor, lavour(e, 5 lavowre, lavre, lavyre, lawere, -owre, -orre, *Sc.* levare, 5-6 *Sc.* lavar, 6 *Sc.* lawer, lawar(e, (*dial.* leyver), 5- laver. [a. OF. *laveoir*, *lavur*:—L. *lavātōrium*: see LAVATORY.]

1. A vessel, basin, or cistern for washing; in early use, chiefly a wash-hand-basin or a water-jug, usually of metal; *occas.* a pan or bowl for water, irrespective of its purpose. Now only *poet.* or rhetorical. †Also applied to the piscina, and to the lavatory in a monastic cloister.

c **1386** CHAUCER *Wife's Prol.* 287 Assen, oxen, hors, and houndes.. been assayd at diuerse stoundes, Bacyns, lauours, er that men hem bye. *c* **1394** *P. Pl Crede* 196 þan kam I to þat cloister.. it was.. Wiþ lauoures of latun louelyche ygreithed. *a* **1400** *Octouian* 1299 Lauor and basyn they gon calle, To wassche and ayryse. **1420** *E.E. Wills* (1882) 46 Also iij. basc[i]nus,.. with ij. lauerus. *c* **1460** J. RUSSELL *Bk. Nurture* 232 þy Ewry borde with basons & lauour, watur hoot & cold, eche oþer to alay. **1483** *Act 1 Rich. III*, c. 12 §2 That no merchaunt Straungier.. brynge into this Realme.. Chafynge disshes hangynge lavers [etc.]. **1483** CAXTON *Gold. Leg.* 442 b/1 He wessheth his handes at the pyscyne or lauer for this y[t] no thynge of the Sacramente ne may abyde at his handes. **1487** *Will of Laurence* (Somerset Ho.), A water laver for the fyr. **1488** *Inv. R. Wardr.* (1815) 10 Item a levare of silver ouregilt with a cover. **1507** *Pilton Churchw. Acc.* (Somerset Rec. Soc.) 53 Item j basen and j lauer of laten. **1549** *Compl. Scot.* Ep. to Q. Mary 7 He gart delyuir to the said pure man.. ane goldin vattir lauar. **1552-3** *Inv. Ch. Goods, Staff.* in *Ann. Lichfield* (1863) IV. 31 A handbell, a crosse of wodde, a surples, and a lavor. **1557-8** *Durham Acc. Rolls* (Surtees) 715 In factura unius hostii pro le lavers, 8*d.* **1579** LANGHAM *Gard. Health* (1633) 514 Wash thy hands in a lauer, wherin is put some Sage. **1593** *Rites of Durh.* (Surtees) 70 Within the Cloyster Garth.. was a fair Laver or Conditt. **1598** FLORIO, *Vacile*, a basen to wash hands in, a lauer. **1605** TIMME *Quersit.* I. xiii. 58 Vulcan washed Phœbus in the same lauer. **1647** A. ROSS *Myst. Poet.* xvi. (1648) 388 In her temple at Cumæ.. Justin Martyr.. saw the three lavers where she used to wash her self. **1725** POPE *Odyss.* I. 182 With copious water the bright vase supplies A silver laver, of capacious size. *Ibid.* III. 558 Young Aretus.. Brought the full laver o'er their hands to pour. **1864** TYSSEN *Ch. Bells of Sussex* 11 [The Bell-founders' arms.] A chevron between three lavers.

b. Used to render Vulg. *labrum*, Heb. *kiyyōr*, applied to the large brazen vessel for the ablutions of the priests, mentioned in the descriptions of the Mosaic Tabernacle and of the Temple of Solomon.

1535 COVERDALE *Exod.* xxx. 18 Thou shalt make a brasen lauer.. to wash. —— *1 Kings* vii. 39 The lauer set he before on the righte hande towarde the south. **1647** R. BAILLIE *Anabaptism* 166 The laver.. was not of the capacity for one man to bath. **1869** W. P. MACKAY *Grace & Truth* (1875) 46 Nicodemus, as a teacher in Israel, should have been looking for the antitype of temple and laver.

c. The basin of a fountain. *Obs.* exc. *arch.*

1604 DEKKER *King's Entertainm.* E 3 b, Some prettie distaunce from them an artificiall Lauer or Fount was erected. **1645** EVELYN *Diary* 18 Jan., Many stately fountaines.. casting water into antiq lavors. **1664** PEPYS *Diary* 14 June, A mighty fine, cool place it is, with a great laver of water in the middle. **1670** BLOUNT *Glossogr.*, *Laver*, a Pond or washing place. **1825** LONGF. *Spirit Poetry* 14 Where the silver brook, From its full laver, pours the white cascade.

2. *transf.* and *fig.* The baptismal font; the spiritual 'washing' of baptism; in wider sense, any spiritually cleansing agency. After Gr. λουτρὸν παλιγγενεσίας Tit. iii. 5: cf. LAVACRE.

1340 *Ayenb.* 162 þet oþer þing is zoþe ssrifte þet is þet lauor huer he him ssel ofte wesse. **1413** *Pilgr. Sowle* (Caxton) I. xiii. (1859) 9 Eke thenne hit sheweth that he hath this lauure desalowid. **1548-9** (Mar.) *Bk. Com. Prayer, Private Baptism*, This holesome lauer of regeneracion. **1574** tr. *Marlorat's Apocalips* 29 Seeyng that Baptime is called the Lauer of newe birth. **1612** T. TAYLOR *Comm. Titus* ii. 14 This is the onely fountaine opened to the house of Dauid for Sinne and Vncleannesse, this is the onely lauer of the Church. **1631** WEEVER *Anc. Funeral Mon.* 59 At whose hands he receiued the lauer of baptisme. **1670** *Moral State Eng.* 2 Baptism is the Lavre of Regeneration. *a* **1684** LEIGHTON *Wks.* (1835) I. 115 No other laver can fetch it out but the Sprinkling of The Blood of Jesus Christ. **1846** KEBLE *Lyra Innoc.* (1873) 49 Christ's Laver hath refreshing power.

†**3.** A process or mode of ablution. *Obs.*

1671 L. ADDISON *W. Barbary* viii. 148 All the Musalmim of the Alcoran use washing in a mystic signification of internal purity, and.. the soul receives the benefit of their corporeal Lavors. **1671** MILTON *Samson* 1727 And from the stream With lavers pure and cleansing herbs wash off The clotted gore. *a* **1684** LEIGHTON *Comm. 1 Pet.* ii. 9. 303 No other Laver can do it, no water, but that fountain opened for sin.

4. *attrib.*

1660 *Act 12 Chas. II*, c. 4 Schedule s.v. *Brass*, Brass of Laver Cocks the pound j.s. iv d.

'laver, *sb.*[3] *Her.* [? For ****lever-cutter*** (alluding to the name *leversedge*): see LEVER, iris-plant.] A coulter or ploughshare when used as a bearing. Also ***laver cutter.***

1828-40 in BERRY *Encycl. Herald.* I (whence in recent Dicts.). **1894** *Parker's Gloss. Her.* s.v. *Plough*, Argent, a chevron between three laver cutters (or ploughshares, also called scythe blades) sable—Leversedge, co. Chester.

†**'laver,** *a.* *Obs. rare*[−1]. ? = BLABBER *a.*

1598 MARSTON *Pygmal.* IV. [v.] 75 Let his [the hound's] lauer lip Speake in reproch of Natures workmanship.

†**'laver,** *v.* *Obs.* [f. LAVER *sb.*[2]] *intr.* To bathe.

1607 WALKINGTON *Opt. Glass* 37 With surfets tympany he ginning swell All wan eft lavers in Saint Buxtons well.

laver, obs. form of LATHER *v.*

Laverack ('lævəræk). The name of Edward *Laverack* (d. 1877), English dog breeder, used *attrib.* in **Laverack setter** to designate the type of English setter (see SETTER *sb.*[1] 11 a) developed by him, a large hunting dog having long white fur flecked with other colours. Also *absol.*

1878 C. HALLOCK *Sportsman's Gazetteer* (ed. 4) 689/2 Belton.—the ticked or spotted Laverack setter. **1904** *Daily Chron.* 15 Aug. 3/3 In America 'Laveracks' and 'Llewellins' are household words among sportsmen. **1971** F. HAMILTON *World Encycl. Dogs* 245 These differing methods of breeding led in later years to the main division in the breed as we know it today, between show dogs and working dogs; although it must be remembered that both types originated with the Laveracks. *Ibid.*, (*caption*) An engraving of Mr. Purcell-Llewellyn's Laverack Setter, Countess.

laveracke, -cok, -oc(k, -ok(ke: see LARK *sb.*[1]

laverd, obs. form of LORD.

Laves phase ('lɑːvəs feız). *Metallurgy.* [ad. G. *Laves-phase* (G. E. R. Schulze 1939, in *Zeitschr. f. Elektrochem.* XLV. 850/1), f. the name of Fritz-Henning *Laves* (b. 1906), German crystallographer + PHASE *sb.*] Any of a group of intermetallic compounds of composition approximately AB_2 in which the relative sizes of the A and B atoms are such as to allow a stable packing arrangement with unusually high co-ordination numbers.

1940 *Chem. Abstr.* XXXIV. 1895 Laves phases are AB_2 intermetallic compds. whose structure and combination mechanism are detd. by the crystal lattice. **1956** HUME-ROTHERY & RAYNOR *Struct. Metals & Alloys* (ed. 3) v. 228 The Laves phases crystallize in one of three closely related structures, and are isomorphous with the compounds $MgCu_2$, $MgZn_2$, or $MgNi_2$. **1967** A. H. COTTRELL *Introd. Metall.* xiv. 195 In a Laves phase AB_2, each A atom has 16 neighbours (4A and 12B) and each B atom has 12 neighbours.

lavic ('lɑːvık), *a.* [f. LAVA + -IC. Cf. F. *lavique.*] Of or pertaining to lava.

1835 *For. Q. Rev.* XV. 82 The three volcanic periods termed by geologists trachytic, basaltic, and lavic.

†**la'vidnian.** *Obs. rare*[−1]. [prob. from Celtic Cornish; cf. '*Visnan, vidnan*, a sand lance or sand eel' (*West Cornw. Gloss.*).] A fish of some kind.

1606 *Act 3 Jas. I*, c. 12 For taking of Herring, Pilchards, Sprats or Lauydnyan.

laving ('leıvıŋ), *vbl. sb.* [f. LAVE *v.*[1] + -ING[1].] The action of the vb. LAVE[1] in various senses; †baling; washing. Also *attrib.*, **laving-bowl,** a baling bowl or scoop.

1458 R. FANNANDE *Inscr. St. Helen's, Abingdon* in Leland *Itin.* (1769) VII. 80 Then the strenghe of the streme astoned them stronge, In labor and lavyng moche money was lore. **1484-5** *Durham Acc. Rolls* (Surtees) 649, vij lavyng bollez. **1611** FLORIO, *Lauatura*, a washing, a lauing.

laving ('leıvıŋ), *ppl. a.* [f. LAVE *v.*[1] + -ING[2].] That laves in various senses; †flowing, washing, purifying; bathing (in quot. *intr.*).

13.. *E.E. Allit. P.* B. 366 þe mukel lauande loghe to þe lyfte rered. **13..** *S. Erkenwolde* 314 in Horstm. *Altengl. Leg.* (1881) 273 He.. to þe toumbe lokyd, To þe liche þer hit lay with lauande teres. **1671** MILTON *P.R.* I. 280 As I rose out of the laving stream. **1812** BYRON *Ch. Har.* II. xxiv, Thus bending o'er the vessel's laving side, To gaze on Dian's wave-reflected sphere.

†**lavish,** *sb.* *Obs.* Forms: 5 lavas, 6 lavess(e, lavasse, lavish. [a. OF. *lavasse*, *lavache*, deluge of rain. Cf. OF. *lavis* torrent (of words).] Profusion, excessive abundance, extravagant

outpouring or expenditure; prodigality, lavishness. Phr. *to make lavish.*

1483 CAXTON *Gold. Leg.* 364/2 Ther was no lauas in their speche ne euylle. 1534 WHITINTON *Tullyes Offices* (1540) II. 101 The other large lauesse is appropried as to flatterers of the commen people. 1548 UDALL *Erasm. Par. Luke* vii. 86 b, Dooest thou see this woman..makyng lauasse of hir precious perfumed oynctemente. 1565 T. STAPLETON *Fortr. Faith* 117 They ryot not in lauish, but liue in fasting. 1583 STUBBES *Anat. Abus.* II. (1882) 40 If euerie brooker would deale thus, their would not so many false knaues bring them such lauish of stollen goods, as they do. 1589 NASHE *Introd. Greene's Menaphon* (Arb.) 8 The sweete satietie of eloquence, which the lauish of our copious Language maie procure. *c* 1592 MARLOWE *Massacre Paris* xxiv. 102 He loves me..that makes most lavish of his blood. 1597 J. PAYNE *Royal Exch.* 11 You shall surely answere and make accowmpte for the lavess and misspendinge of your maysters goods.

lavish (ˈlævɪʃ), *a.* Forms: 5–6 **lavas, lavage,** 6 **laves, laveis, lavaige,** *Sc.* **lawage, lavash,** 6– **lavish.** [f. LAVISH *sb.*]

1. a. With reference to speech: Unrestrained, effusive; *esp.* in phrase ***lavish of (one's) tongue.*** Now only as contextual use of 2.

1485 ELIZ. C'TESS SURREY in *Paston Lett.* No. 886 III. 323 They have not ben of that disposicion to be lavas of theyr tungys, whan they had moore cause of booldnes than they have nowe. 1529 MORE *Dyaloge* IV. Wks. 245/1 [Though many confessors are] in al other thing so light and laues of theyr tong..yet finde we neuer..cause giuen of complaint, through..secretes vttred..by the confessoure. 1535 STEWART *Cron. Scot.* III. 114 'Trow ȝe', he said, 'for ȝour speiking so proude, Or lichtlie langage bayth lawage and loude,..That I dar nocht to my purpois proceid'. 1594 *1st Pt. Contention* I. i. 25 Th' excessiue loue I beare vnto your Grace, Forbids me to be lauish of my tongue. 1675 TRAHERNE *Chr. Ethics* 415 How do old men even dote into lavish discourses of the beginning of their lives. 1701 ROWE *Ambit. Step-Moth.* II. ii. 761, I bore his lavish Tongue. 1742 YOUNG *Nt. Th.* II. 284 But why on Time so lavish is my song? 1807 CRABBE *Birth of Flattery* 264 The lavish tongue shall honest truths impart.

†**b.** Of conduct or disposition: Unrestrained, impetuous; loose, wild, licentious. *Obs.*

1597 SHAKS. *2 Hen. IV*, IV. iv. 64 When Meanes and lauish Manners meete together. 1605 —— *Macb.* I. ii. 57 Curbing his lauish spirit. 1634 MILTON *Comus* 465 When lust..by leud and lavish act of sin, Lets in defilement to the inward parts. 1640 QUARLES *Enchirid.* III. 28 If he be given to lavish Company, endeavour to stave him off with lawfull Recreations.

†**c.** Extravagant or 'wild' in speculation. *Obs.*

1693 J. EDWARDS *Auth. O. & N. Test.* 252 If..I have shewed my self arbitrary and lavish in some of the derivations.

2. a. Expending or bestowing without stint or measure; unboundedly liberal or profuse; prodigal. Const. *of, in.* In early use often: Wasteful, extravagant.

c 1475 *Cath. Angl.* 210 (Add. MS.) Lavage, *prodigus.* 1546 J. HEYWOOD *Prov.* (1867) 54 He is so laueis, the stocke beginneth to droope. 1548–67 THOMAS *Ital. Dict., Discipatrici,* lauage woman, they that will spend out of reason. 1553 GRIMALDE *Cicero's Offices* I. (1558) 21 Lauisher than their goods wil beare. 1565 GOLDING *Ovid's Met.* 180 The lauas earth doth yeeld you plenteously Most gentle foode, &c. 1576 FLEMING *Panopl. Epist.* 240 Lest you be carefull in keeping..or to prodigall and lavash in wasting them. 1596 SHAKS. *1 Hen. IV*, III. ii. 39 Had I so lauish of my presence beene, So common hackney'd in the eyes of men. 1597 HOOKER *Eccl. Pol.* v. lxv. §20 The liberall harted man is..by the iudgement of the miserable lauish. 1605 *Play Stucley* in Simpson *Sch. Shaks.* (1878) I. 262, I ever fear'd that my courageous brother..would be too lavish of his person. 1643 BURROUGHES *Exp. Hosea* II. vii. (1652) 276 You often tell your lavish wasting servants, they will be glad of a crust before they dye. 1697 DRYDEN *Virg. Past.* VII. 76 Lavish Nature laughs, and strows her Stores around. 1710 HEARNE *Collect.* (O.H.S.) III. 51 When we are so lavish of our Money upon Trifles. *a* 1763 SHENSTONE *Elegies* i. 17 The mourner, lavish of his tears. 1791 BOSWELL *Johnson* (1816) IV. 482, I have not been lavish of useless letters. 1824 W. IRVING *T. Trav.* I. 113 His bounty was lavish and open-handed. 1849 RUSKIN *Sev. Lamps* iv. §3. 97 In this respect Nature is sparing of her highest, and lavish of her less, beauty. 1867 FREEMAN *Norm. Conq.* (1876) I. iv. 152 The people thus formed..were..the most lavish in gifts to holy places.

b. Expended, bestowed, or produced in unstinted profusion; profuse, abundant.

1576 FLEMING *Panopl. Epist.* 220 He writeth to Dionysius ..and alies, to leave off their lavash cheare and delicates. 1603 SHAKS. *Meas. for M.* II. ii. 24 Let her haue needfull but not lauish meanes. 1697 DRYDEN *Virg. Georg.* I. 423 The low'ring Spring, with lavish Rain, Beats down the slender Stem and bearded Grain. 1779–81 JOHNSON *L.P., Young* Wks. IV. 277 His three Plays all concluded with lavish suicide. 1832 TENNYSON *Eleanore* 12 Thou wert nursed in some delicious land Of lavish lights, and floating shades. 1848 W. H. KELLY tr. *L. Blanc's Hist. Ten Y.* II. 446 He.. received him at Neuilly with lavish marks of regard. 1883–4 O'DONOVAN *Story Merv* ii. 26 He wore a silk tunic..with lavish gold embroidery.

3. *dial.* Of grass or wheat: Rank, overgrown.

c 1730 POYNTER *Ms. Gloss.* in *N. & Q.* Ser. VI. VIII. 45 *Lavage,* rank. 1842 PULMAN *Sketches* (1871) 111 The grass is too lavidge. 1844 BARNES *Poems Rural Life* Gloss., *Lavish,* rank. 'That wheat is lavish.'

lavish (ˈlævɪʃ), *v.* Also 6 **lavesse.** [f. LAVISH *a.*]

1. *intr.* To be lavish. †**a.** To be profuse in expense; to plunge *into* (excess). Also *to lavish it. Obs.* **b.** To be lavish of words; to exaggerate. *Obs.* **c.** Of rain: To pour *along* in torrents. *rare.*

1567 MAPLET *Gr. Forest* 105 He, fearing the Female to lauish and to be no sparer of such vittailes as they haue.. stenteth the Female. 1613 R. CAWDREY *Table Alph., Lauish,* to spend extraordinarily. 1614 D. DYKE *Myst. Self-deceiving* xxii. 274 The Scripture saith not the minister may luxuriously lauish it, but onely liue of the altar. 1625 COOKE *Pope Joan* 69 You lauish when you talke of 400. yeares after. For I haue prooued vnto you alreadie, by the bookes that are yet extant, that it was knowne sooner. 1625 BP. MOUNTAGU *App. Cæsar* 217 S. Aug. in commending him did not lavish at all, where he saith, that he was..*magni nominis* [etc.]. 1642 J. BALL *Answ. Canne* I. 54 You lavish somewhat when you say without limitation [etc.]. 1698 FRYER *Acc. E. India & P.* 162 His Father dying soon,..he..lavishes into Excesses not approved of. 1830 GALT *Laurie T.* III. iii. (1849) 90 The rain came lavishing along as if the windows of heaven were opened.

2. *trans.* To bestow, deal out, distribute, or spend profusely and recklessly; also with *away, out.* Const. *in, on* or *upon,* rarely *to.*

a. with material object. Also, to shed (blood) in profusion.

1542 UDALL tr. *Erasmus' Apophth.* 135 Those persones, who of a ryottousnesse did prodigally lauesse out and waste their substaunce..vpon cookes, or reuellers [etc.]. 1592 *Nobody & Someb.* in Simpson *Sch. Shaks.* (1878) I. 288 Helpe us to lavish our abundant treasures In masks, sports, revells, riots, and strange pleasures. 1611 BIBLE *Isa.* xlvi. 6 They lauish gold out of the bagge. 1650 W. BROUGH *Sacr. Princ.* (1659) 407 Shall all be lavished away that should be so laid out? 1692 WASHINGTON tr. *Milton's Def. Pop.* xii. 229 That he might..lavish out in one House, the Riches and Wealth..of three Nations. 1713 ADDISON *Cato* II. i, We lavish'd at our deaths the blood of thousands. *a* 1715 BURNET *Own Time* (1724) I. 245 Money, which she lavished out in a most profuse vanity. 1786 BURKE *W. Hastings* Wks. 1842 II. 143 That excessive salaries and emoluments..have been lavished by the said Warren Hastings to sundry individuals. 1796 *Campaigns* 1793–4, I. I. ix. 92 'Twas a pity brave men should be lavish'd away. 1820 W. IRVING *Sketch Bk.* II. 156 The children..lavish all their holyday money in toys. 1851 D. G. MITCHELL *Fresh Glean.* 129 The savings of the week are lavished upon the indulgences of Sunday.

b. with immaterial object.

1581 SIDNEY *Apol. Poetrie* (Arb.) 67 But I haue lauished out too many wordes of this play matter. 1621 QUARLES *Esther* v. E 3 b, Each Virgin keepes her turne, and all the night They lewdly lauish in the Kings delight. 1639 FULLER *Holy War* II. xxxiv. (1840) 95 Pity it is that any pity should be lavished on them. 1653 tr. *Hales' Dissert. de pace* iv. 19 Is it credible that he will lavish out so excellent gifts..on men depraved with so many errors. 1672 DRYDEN *Conq. Granada* I. i, Ev'ry Life You lavish thus, in this intestine Strife. *a* 1704 T. BROWN *Praise Poverty* Wks. 1730 I. 100 Lavishing your favours. 1763 W. HARRIS in *Lett. Lit. Men* (Camden) 401 His good nature..was lavished away on those who had least pretence to his favour. 1766 GOLDSM. *Vic. W.* xxi, To see her lavish some kind looks upon my unfortunate son. 1845 FORD *Handbk. Spain* I. 50[Nature] lavishes..her fairest charms where most unseen. 1856 H. ROGERS *Ess.* II. viii. 368 No end of controversy has been lavished on the philosopher's precise view. 1861 J. MARTINEAU *Ess.* (1869) II. 400 The blind force of instinctive life..Plato treats with none of the admiration lavished on it by Mr. Carlyle.

Hence **ˈlavisher,** one who lavishes.

1611 COTGR., *Gaspilleur,* a spend-all,..lauisher. *a* 1619 FOTHERBY *Atheom.* II. i. §8 (1622) 189 God is not a Lauisher, but a Dispenser of his blessings. 1634 SIR M. SANDYS *Ess.* 209 Let those Lavishers then, that made the Covetous their Voyders, Live so thriftily, as to pay their debts in their life time.

lavishing (ˈlævɪʃɪŋ), *vbl. sb.* [f. LAVISH *v.* + -ING[1].] The action of the vb. LAVISH.

1573 BARET *Alv.* L 127 Lauishing or wastfull ryot. 1581 SAVILE *Tacitus, Hist.* II. lxxxii. (1591) 101 A man..firme against these lauishings to souldiers. 1812 *Examiner* 28 Sept. 620/1 These..sacrifices, and lavishings of money, are ..to be attempted for not one single good. 1850 McCOSH *Div. Govt.* III. i. (1874) 317 Love without justice is the mere lavishing of a weak affection.

lavishing (ˈlævɪʃɪŋ), *ppl. a.* [f. LAVISH *v.* + -ING[2].] That lavishes; extravagant; †given to reckless or unrestrained behaviour.

1598 GRENEWEY *Tacitus' Ann.* IV. v. (1622) 95 By reason of his owne lauishing toong. 1659 HOWELL *Lex., Prov.* Let. of Advice, Be wary of too costly and lavishing a Wife.

Hence **ˈlavishingly** *adv.*

a 1585 ABP. SANDYS *Serm.* xvi. 284 It is the wives dutie.. not lauishingly to wast or spoile their goods; but [etc.]. 1688 BUNYAN *Jerus. Sinner Saved* (1886) 71 To those that sinned not lavishingly. 1794 *Hist.* in *Ann. Reg.* 281 It was..a secret why the troops were paid for so lavishingly.

lavishly (ˈlævɪʃlɪ), *adv.* [f. LAVISH *a.* + -LY[2].] In a lavish manner.

1571 GOLDING *Calvin on Ps.* lxvi. 13 They lauishly [L. *futiliter*] force vpon God whatsoeuer comes at theire tunges ende. 1577 tr. *Bullinger's Decades* (1592) 421 They could not but bee greatly offended, to see the Gentiles so lauishly to vse the thinges prohibited. 1597 SHAKS. *2 Hen. IV*, IV. ii. 57 Some about him haue too lauishly Wrested his meaning and Authoritie. 1631 GOUGE *God's Arrows* II. vii. 142 What is violently or fraudulently gotten, will be lavishly spent. *a* 1656 USSHER *Ann.* vi. (1658) 354 So lavishly insulting over the fall of so great a person. 1769 *Junius Lett.* (1804) I. 29 Whether or no the man, who has praised him so lavishly, be himself deserving of praise. 1843 GALLENGA *Italy, Past & Pr.* (1848) I. p. xxvii, They shed blood lavishly. 1856 LEVER *Martins of Cro' M.* 207 No praise of mine—..however lavishly it was squandered—could possibly raise you in your own esteem. 1867 FREEMAN *Norm. Conq.* (1876) II. vii. 33 If they took with one hand [they] gave lavishly with the other.

lavishment (ˈlævɪʃmənt). Now *rare.* [f. LAVISH *v.* + -MENT.] The action of lavishing.

1630 LORD *Hist. Banians* 44 Yet giuen to lavishment of their gettings, if they were not admonished by their Law. 1662 J. CHANDLER *Van Helmont's Oriat.* 273 This..might.. remain safe for a long time, without a lavishment of the health. 1711 SHAFTESB. *Charac.* (1737) III. Misc. III. ii. 172 Let us suppose him..without any apparent Luxury or Lavishment in his Manners. 1814 CARY *Dante, Hell* xi. 47 Whoe'er..In reckless lavishment his talent wastes. 1839 BAILEY *Festus* (1848) 31/1 To feel..That hope, nor love, nor fear..Can check the royal lavishment of life.

lavishness (ˈlævɪʃnɪs). [f. LAVISH *a.* + -NESS.]

†**1.** Absence of restraint, recklessness. *Obs.*

c 1477 CAXTON *Jason* 141 And [Eson] shewde how he wolde punisshe his sone Iason for the lauesshenes of his body. 1553 BRENDE tr. *Q. Curtius* IV. 45 b, Ponishing with losse of lief, the lavesnes of the tounge. 1555 EDEN *Decades 72 marg.*, Hurt of lauyshenes of the tonge. 1649 JER. TAYLOR *Gt. Exemp.* II. Ad Sec. xii. 57 Lest as it happens in sudden joyes, the lavishnesse of his spirit should transport him to intemperance.

2. Unlimited bounty; extravagance, prodigality.

1590 SPENSER *F.Q.* II. vii. 12 Riches..First got with guile, ..And after spent with pride and lavishnesse. 1623 BINGHAM *Xenoph., Comp. Rom. & Mod. Wars* X 3, Lest it might be consumed by their Cabin-mates in lauishnesse and idle expences. 1663 BLAIR *Autobiog.* vii. (1848) 95 My foolish lavishness gaue to his servant two Jacobuses. 1750 JOHNSON *Rambler* No. 53 ¶13 They..scatter with a kind of wild desperation and affected lavishness. 1857 RUSKIN *Pol. Econ. Art* 12 The lavishness of pride. 1859 R. F. BURTON *Centr. Afr.* in *Jrnl. Geog. Soc.* XXIX. 213 The wondrous lavishness of Nature. 1874 GREEN *Short Hist.* vii. §5. 389 The lavishness of a new wealth united with a lavishness of life, a love of beauty, of colour, of display, to revolutionize English dress.

lavolta (ləˈvɒltə), *sb. Obs.* exc. *arch.* Also 6–7 **lavalto, -olto, levalto, -olto,** (7 **lovalto**), *anglicized* **lavolt,** 6– **lavolta.** [f. It. *la* the + *volta* turn.] 'A lively dance for two persons, consisting a good deal in high and active bounds' (Nares). Also *transf.* and *fig.*

[1584 R. SCOT *Discov. Witchcr.* III. ii. 42 These..night-dansing witches brought out of Italie into France that danse which is called *La volta*.] *c* 1590 GREENE *Fr. Bacon* viii. (1630) D 4, And draw the Dolphins to thy louely Eyes, To dance Lauoltas in the purple streames. 1599 MARSTON *Sco. Villanie* II. *Ad rithmum* 193 Come prettie pleasing symphonie of words..And daunce Leuoltoes in my poesie. 1600 S. NICHOLSON *Acolastus* (1876) 47 Behold the sunne-beames for thy Beauties sake, Dancing Lauoltoes on the liquid floare. 1603 J. DAVIES *Microcosmos* (Grosart) 94/1 In Matecheines, Lavolts, and Burgamasks. 1627 B. JONSON *Chlorida* (1630) B, Ixion..does nothing but cut capreols.. and leades Lauoltos with the Lamiæ. 1627–77 FELTHAM *Resolves* I. xiii. 21 Mortality..checks us in the frisks and levaltoes of our dancing blood. 1671 CROWNE *Juliana* v. 49 His soul shall dance Levaltoes in the aire at the Queens wedding. 1698 FRYER *Acc. E. India & P.* 128 The busy Apes..made strange Levaltoes with their hanging Brats from one Bough to another. 1879 G. MACDONALD *Sir Gibbie* III. xiv. 231 He first danced round her several times..and executed his old lavolta of delight.

†**laˈvolta,** *v. Obs.* exc. *arch.* In 6 **lavalto,** *anglicized* 6 **levalt,** 9 **lavolt.** [f. prec. sb.] *intr.* To dance a lavolta; to caper as in the lavolta.

1590 NASHE *Almond for Parrat* 19 b, The legs..they leapt, they daunced, and I leualted to the Vials of vanitie. 1599 —— *Lenten Stuffe* 36 Do but marke him on your walles.. how he sallies & laualtos. 1822 W. TENNANT *Thane of Fife* II. 65 Like spark from fire lavolting through the dance.

†**lavolteˈteer.** *Obs. rare*[−1]. [f. LAVOLTA *sb.* + -EER[1], ? after *charioteer.*] One who dances the 'lavolta'.

1625 FLETCHER *Fair Maid of Inn* III. i, A lavolteteere, a saltatory, a dancer with a Kit at his bum.

lavrock, variant of LARK.

lavrovite (ˈlævrəvaɪt). *Min.* Also **lavroffite.** [Named by von Kokscharov, 1867, in honour of N. von *Lavrov*: see -ITE.] A green variety of pyroxene, containing vanadium.

1868 DANA *Min.* (ed. 5) 216 Lavrovite..is an alumina pyroxene, colored green by vanadium. 1879 *Amer. Jrnl. Sci.* Ser. II. L. 272 Lavroffite (Lawrowite) has been..shown to be a vanadiferous diopside.

lavvy (ˈlævɪ). = LAV.

1961 PARTRIDGE *Dict. Slang* II. 1165/1 *Lavvy,* a Scottish, esp. children's, easing of lavatory. 1962 *John o' London's* 27 Dec. 588/1 An outside loo or 'lavvy'. 1971 *Guardian* 20 Jan. 8/2 A house where the lavvy is behind an arras.

lavy (ˈlævɪ). A local (St. Kildan) name for the guillemot.

1698 M. MARTIN *Voy. Kilda* (1749) 7 Eighteen of the Eggs laid by the Fowl called by them Lavy. *Ibid.* 31 The Lavy, so call'd by the Inhabitants of St. Kilda. 1766 PENNANT *Zool.* (1768) II. 410. 1802 G. MONTAGU *Ornith. Dict.* (1833) 545. 1867 in SMYTH *Sailor's Word-bk.*

law (lɔː), *sb.*[1] Forms: 1 **laᵹu** (oblique cases *laᵹe,* nom. and acc. pl. *laᵹa,* once *laᵹan*; in comb. *lah-*), 2 **laȝwe, laȝa,** 2–5 **laȝe,** 3 *Layamon* **læȝe, læwe,** 3 **laha,** 3–5 **lagh(e,** 3–7 **lau(e, lawe,** *Sc.* **lauwe,** 4 **lach(t, laght, (lake), lauh,** 4, 6 *Sc.* **la, lawch,** 5 *Sc.* **laucht, laue, laugh,** 5–9 *Sc.* **lauch,** 5– **law.** [Late OE. (*c* 1000) *laᵹu* str. fem. (pl. *laᵹa*), a. prehistoric ON. **lagu* (:—OIcel. *lǫg*), pl. of *lag* neut.; in sing. the word meant in OIcel. 'something laid or fixed' (specific senses being, e.g. 'layer, stratum', 'share in an undertaking',

'partnership', 'fixed or market price', 'set tune', etc.); the pl. had the collective sense 'law', and in ONorw. its form became (as in OE.) a fem. sing.; cf. OSw. *lagh* neut. sing. and pl., law, Sw. *lag*, pl. *lagar*, Da. *lov*. The ON. *lag* corresponds to OS. *-lag* neut. (in the compounds *aldar-lagu* pl. destined length of life, *or-lag* fate, war) :-OTeut. **lagom*, f. root **lag-*:—OAryan **logh-* (:**legh-*): see LAY, LIE *vbs.* The Lat. *lēg-*, *lēx* is not now generally believed to be cognate (being referred to the root **leg-* of *legĕre* to gather, read, λέγειν to gather, say); but in many other langs. the word for 'law' is derived from roots meaning 'to place'; cf., e.g., Eng. DOOM, Gr. θέμις, θεσμός, L. *statutum*, G. *gesetz*. The native word in OE. was *ǽ*: see Æ.

As *law* is the usual Eng. rendering of L. *lex*, and to some extent of L. *jus*, and of Gr. νόμος, its development of senses has been in some degree affected by the uses of these words.]

I. A rule of conduct imposed by authority.

* *Human law.*

1. a. The body of rules, whether proceeding from formal enactment or from custom, which a particular state or community recognizes as binding on its members or subjects. (In this sense usually *the law.*) †Also, in early use, a code or system of rules of this kind.

[As the word was in Scandinavian a plural, though adopted in OE. as a sing., this collective sense is etymologically prior to that of 'specific enactment' (sense 2).]

a **1000** *Laws of Ethelred* VI. c. 37 (Schmid) ȝif he hine laðian wille..do ðæt be ðam deopestan aðe..on Engla laȝe, and on Dena laȝe, be ðam ðe heora laȝu si. **11..** *O.E. Chron.* an. 1064 (Laud MS.) He niwade ðær Cnutes laȝe. *c* **1205** LAY. 6305 Þa makede heo ane læȝe, and læide ȝeon þat leode. *a* **1300** *Cursor M.* 19270 Þe wick þai hald þe lau for drede. *c* **1425** WYNTOUN *Cron.* IV. vii. 672 [He] governyd wytht his lauch the land. *a* **1548** HALL *Chron., Hen. VIII*, 247 All offices had by dower..to be confiscat and spent to the use and custome of the law. **1596** SHAKS. *Merch. V.* IV. i. 178 The Venetian Law Cannot impugne you as you do proceed. **1662** *Bk. Comm. Prayer* Pref., Injoyned by the Lawe of the Land. **1726** SWIFT *Gulliver* IV. v, But he was at a loss how it should come to pass, that the law, which was intended for every man's preservation, should be any man's ruin. **1764** GOLDSM. *Trav.* 386 Laws grind the poor, and rich men rule the law. **1785** PALEY *Mor. Philos.* Wks. 1825 IV. 184 The law of England constrains no man to become his own accuser. **1833** HT. MARTINEAU *Manch. Strike* i. 10 Had we not our combinations, when combination was against the law? **1896** *Law Times Rep.* LXXIII. 690/1 This court has no jurisdiction over the property in America; it is governed by the law of that country.

b. Often viewed, with more or less of personification, as an agent uttering or enforcing the rules of which it consists. Hence (*b*) *colloq.* (orig. *U.S.*), a policeman, the police; a sheriff.

1513 MORE in Grafton *Chron.* (1568) II. 774 Then the lawe maketh me his garden. **1611** SHAKS. *Wint. T.* IV. iv. 715 This being done, let the Law goe whistle. **1628** SIR J. ELIOT *Speech Parl.* in Forster *Life* II. 124 The law designs to every man his own. **1728** YOUNG *Love Fame* I. (1757) 80 When the Law shews her teeth, but dares not bite. **1794** BURKE *Corr.* (1844) IV. 228 The law is wiser than cabal or interest. **1838** DICKENS *O. Twist* li, 'If the law supposes that,' said Mr. Bumble,..'the law is a ass—a idiot'.

(*b*) **1929** M. A. GILL *Underworld Slang*, *Law*, police. **1935** A. J. POLLOCK *Underworld Speaks* 121/2 *The law*, a police officer. **1944** B. A. BOTKIN *Treas. Amer. Folklore* I. 131 There was plenty of precedent for Roy Bean in the usual Western 'Law' or sheriff. **1953** W. BURROUGHS *Junkie* (1972) x. 104 We were in the third precinct about three hours and then the laws put us in the wagon and took us to Parish Prison. *Ibid.* xii. 121 Whenever a law needs money for a quick beer, he goes over by Lupita and waits for someone to walk out on the chance he may be holding a paper [containing narcotic]. **1955** *Publ. Amer. Dial. Soc.* XXIV. 106 Some mobs have a strong prejudice against robbing any *law*, whatever he may be. **1958** F. NORMAN *Bang to Rights* 152 Two law..came up to me and grabbed hold of me. **1962** 'J. BELL' *Crime in our Time* I. 13 He had only one idea. To get rid of 'the law', clinging to his car. He drove from side to side of the road in an effort to force Meehan off. **1972** D. LEES *Zodiac* 5 Soon, car-loads of Maigret-type law would come screaming up the drive. **1972** *Times* 6 June 18/6, I inquired of the Law where I might cash a cheque, and was directed to the nearest travel agency. **1973** M. WOODHOUSE *Blue Bone* vi. 56 The Oxford law would know about this, I take it?

c. In proverbs and proverbial phrases. ***the law of the Medes and Persians***, often used (with allusion to Dan. vi. 12) as the type of something unalterable.

1382 WYCLIF *Dan.* vi. 15 The lawe of Medis and Persis. **1564** tr. *P. Martyr's Comm. Judges* xi. 189 b, It is an olde Prouerbe..Lawe and Country. For every region hath certaine customes of their owne, which cannot easelye be chaunged. **1816** SCOTT *Antiq.* xxvi, Aweel, aweel, Maggie, ilka land has its ain lauch. **1853** 'C. BEDE' *Verdant Green* I. ii, His word is no longer the law of the Medes and Persians, as it was at home. **1884** RIDER HAGGARD *Dawn* xxxv, Once given, like the law of the Medes and Persians, it altereth not.

†d. What the law awards; what is due according to law. *Obs.*

1470–85 MALORY *Arthur* VIII. ii. 275 Wel said the King Melyodas, and therfor shal ye haue the lawe. And soo she was dampned..to be brent. **1593** SHAKS. *2 Hen. VI*, I. iii. 214 This is the Law, and this Duke Humfreyes doome.

e. ***to wage one's law***, ***wager of law***: see WAGE *v.*, WAGER *sb.*

2. a. One of the individual rules which constitute the 'law' (sense 1) of a state or polity. In early use only *pl.* The plural has often a collective sense (after L. *jura*, *leges*) approaching sense 1.

a **1023** WULFSTAN *Hom.* (1883) 275 Ræde ȝe nu forð laȝan gode fyrðor. **11..** *O.E. Chron.* an. 1086 (Laud MS.) He læȝde laȝa..ðæt swa hwa swa sloȝe heort oððe hinde ðæt hine man sceolde blendian. *c* **1205** LAY. 2078 And he heom onleide þat weoren lawen gode. **1297** R. GLOUC. (Rolls) 9642 William bastard..luþer lawes made ynou. *a* **1300** *Cursor M.* 12115 Of your laues i am vttan For erthli fader haf i nan. *c* **1320** *Sir Tristr.* 904 Tvo ȝere he sett þat land His lawes made he cri. *c* **1400** *Apol. Loll.* 63 To swilk lauis & to swilk maneris schuld ilk iuge obey. *c* **1460** FORTESCUE *Abs. & Lim. Mon.* ii. (1885) 112 Therfore it is that þe lawes seyn, *quod principi placuit legis habet vigorem.* **1500–20** DUNBAR *Poems* xiv. 28 That all the lawis ar not sett by ane bene. *a* **1548** HALL *Chron., Hen. IV*, 7 b, He said that the lawes of the realme were in his head. **1560** DAUS tr. *Sleidane's Comm.* 382 b, Such thinges as were decreed in the counsel in fourmer yeares, ought not to have the force of a law. **1613** SHAKS. *Hen. VIII*, III. ii. 334 His faults lye open to the Lawes. **1637** *Decree Star Chamb.* §3 in *Milton's Areop.* (Arb.) 10 That all Bookes concerning the common Lawes of this Realme shall be printed by the especiall allowance of the Lords chiefe Justices. *c* **1670** HOBBES *Dial. Com. Laws* (1677) 32 A Law is the Command of him, or them that have the Soveraign Power. **1683** *Col. Rec. Pennsylv.* I. 21 Other duties by any law or statute due to vs. **1690** CHILD *Disc. Trade* (ed. 4) 61 The French peasantry are a slavish, cowardly people, because the laws of their country has made them slaves. *a* **1715** BURNET *Own Time* (1734) II. 189 By the Portian Law, no Citizen could be put to Death for any Crime whatsoever. **1735–8** BOLINGBROKE *On Parties* 104 The Laws of the Land are known. **1843** CARLYLE *Past & Pres.* I. iii, And other idle Laws and Unlaws. **1856** KNIGHT *Pop. Hist. Eng.* I. xxiv. 364 The Saxon King and Confessor, for whose equal laws the people had been clamouring for two centuries.

b. *Proverbs.*

c **1470** HARDING *Chron.* LXXXVI. v, Wronge lawes maketh shorte gouernaunce. *a* **1548** HALL *Chron., Hen. VI*, 169 Tholde spoken proverbs, here toke place: New Lordes, new lawes. **1578** TIMME *Caluine on Gen.* 70 According to the common Proverb 'Of evil manners spring good laws'. **1874** T. HARDY *Madding Crowd* viii, 'New lords new laws', as the saying is.

3. In generalized sense.

a. Laws regarded as obeyed or enforced; controlling influence of laws; the condition of society characterized by the observance of the laws. Often in phrase ***law and order***. Proverb: ***Necessity has*** (or ***knows***) ***no law***.

c **1175** *Lamb Hom.* 109 Ȝif þe biscop bið ȝemeles, and þet folc butan steore eft butan laȝe. *c* **1250** *Ten Abuses* in *O.E. Misc.* 184 Lond wið-ute laȝe [*v.r.* lawe]. *a* **1327** *Pol. Songs* (Camden) 150 Thus wil walketh in londe, and lawe is forlore. **1377** LANGL. *P. Pl.* B. Prol. 122 The Kyng and the comune and kynde with the thridde Shope lawe and lewte eche man to knowe his owne. *a* **1555** RIDLEY *Lament. Ch.* (1566) Div, The latter reason..includeth a necessitie which, after the common sayinge, hathe no lawe. **1598** FLORIO *Worlde of Wordes* 201/2 Legitimo..*according to law and order.* **1601** ? MARSTON *Pasquil & Kath.* I. 68 Poore and neede hath no law. **1653** H. COGAN tr. *Pinto's Trav.* xlvi. 268 Necessity, which hath no law, compelled us thereunto. **1796** *Deb. Congress U.S.* 20 Dec. (1849) 1689 A military diploma, expressive of his patriotism and attachment to law and order. **1846** *Nat. Intelligencer* (Washington) 24 Mar. 3/4 The 'Law and Order' party has clearly fulfilled..its public mission. **1847** MARRYAT *Childr. N. Forest* xvii, Her father could not do otherwise. Necessity has no law. **1881** in T. W. Reid *Life W. E. Forster* (1888) II. viii. 371 To support the Lord-Lieutenant..in maintaining law and order in this country [Ireland]. **1893** [see COMFORTABLY *adv.* 5 a]. **1932** G. F.-H. BERKELEY *Italy in Making* I. iii. 42 This repression continued until..even his allies finally began to perceive that law-and-order can be bought at too dear a price. **1952** *N.Y. Times* 11 Mar. 11/1 (*heading*) Ex-sergeant rode to power on cry of 'Law and Order', seizing reins in 1933. **1962** S. WYNTER *Hills of Hebron* ix. 118 The Commissioner..had come to use words like 'duty', 'law and order' to cover up a lack of imagination. **1967** P. HENDERSON *William Morris* II. xii. 281 The SFD and the League..started a campaign for free speech, which suddenly brought Morris into conflict with the forces of Law and Order. **1968** *Economist* 5 Oct. 41/3 Mr Nixon and..Mr Humphrey are both making concessions to this overriding concern about 'law and order'. **1970** *New Yorker* 26 Sept. 137/1 If it happens that rightists are successful in capturing most of the law-and-order vote, then, of course, the country will move to the right politically. **1972** *Daily Tel.* 24 May 15 The published motions cover a wider and more immediate political field than usual—from the economy and unemployment to the media, Ulster and law and order. **1973** *Black World* Dec. 19/1 A sense of determinism that is diametrically opposed to the ruler-class 'law-and-order' and individualism.

b. (*a*) Laws in general, regarded as a class or species of human institutions. ***court of law***: see COURT *sb.*[1] 11. (*b*) That department of knowledge or study of which laws are the subject-matter; jurisprudence.

14.. *Sir Beues* 3573 (MS. N.) Sir King, þat may not ben don bi lawe. *c* **1430** *Hymns Virg.* 61 Quod resoun, 'in age of .xx. ȝeer, Goo to oxenford, or lerne lawe'. **1611** FLORIO, *Lecito*, lawfull, good in law. **1635** SIBBES *Soul's Confl.* xvii. (1833) 136 Law being the joint reason and consent of many men for the public good hath a use for guidance of all action that fall under the same. **1644** MILTON *Educ.* 5 After this, they are to dive into the grounds of law, and legall justice. **1680** DRYDEN *Ovid's Epist.* Pref., He was design'd to the Study of the Law. **1724** SWIFT *Drapier's Lett.* vii. Wks. 1761 III. 140 In all free nations I take the proper definition of law to be, The will of the majority of those who have the property in land. **1809–10** COLERIDGE *Friend* (1865) 53 Juries do not sit in a court of conscience, but of law. **1818** CRUISE *Digest* (ed. 2) I. 114 A person having an estate..by the operation of some principle of law. **1821** J. Q. ADAMS in C. Davies *Metr. Syst.* III. (1871) 113 The pound of 15 ounces..has never been recognised in England by law. **1841–4** EMERSON *Ess., Experience* Wks. (Bohn) I. 188 The intellect..judges law as well as fact. **1842** J. H. NEWMAN *Par. Serm.* VI. xxiii. 359 He consults men learned in the law. **1882** HINSDALE *Garfield & Educ.* II. 295 If you become a lawyer, you must remember that the science of law is not fixed like geometry, but is a growth which keeps pace with the progress of society. **1891** *Law Times* XCII. 99/2 This natural sequence hardened first into custom and then into law.

c. † ***in law*** (***of wedlock***): lawfully married. Also in the combinations BROTHER-IN-LAW, FATHER-IN-LAW, etc., for which see those words; and in † ***law's father***, †***father in the law***, rarely used for 'father-in-law'; so also † ***mother of law***.

[Cf. 16th c. F. *pere en loi de mariage* (Godef.).]

c **1230** *Hali Meid.* 21 Þis is tenne hare song þat beon ilahe of wedlac. *c* **1250** *Gen. & Ex.* 2764 To wife in laȝe he hire nam. **1538** *Extracts Aberd. Reg.* (1844) I. 154 Ionat Barbour, his moder of law. **1552** LATIMER *Serm. 1st Sund. Epiph.* (1584) 301 b, The house where Jesus was, with his mother, and Joseph his Father in the lawe. **1593** Q. ELIZ. *Boeth.* I. pr. iv. 12 My holy lawes fathʳ Symmacus,..defendes vs from all suspicion of this cryme. [**1594** SHAKS. *Rich. III*, IV. i. 24 Their Aunt I am in law, in loue their Mother. **1596** —— *Tam. Shr.* IV. v. 60 And now by Law, as well as reuerent age, I may intitle thee my louing Father.]

d. In more comprehensive sense: Rules or injunctions that must be obeyed. ***to give*** (***the***) ***law*** (***to***): to exercise undisputed sway; to impose one's will †*upon* (another). † ***to have*** (***the***) ***law to do*** something: to be commanded. † ***law will I***: arbitrary rule, making one's own will law.

a **1225** *Leg. Kath.* 779 Ne lið hit nawt to þe to leggen lahe upon me. *c* **1340** *Cursor M.* 5729 (Fairf.) Moyses had þe lagh to kepe to his eldefadere shepe þat was þe prest of madian. *c* **1375** *Sc. Leg. Saints* ii. (*Paulus*) 202 To thre knychttis þane wes he tawcht, þat hym to sla son has lacht. *c* **1386** CHAUCER *Knt.'s T.* 306 Who shal yeue a louere any lawe? *a* **1564** BECON *Catech.* Wks. 1564 I. 495 To conuince them, not with fyre & fagot..or with lawe will I. **1601** R. JOHNSON *Kingd. & Commw.* (1603) 38 We have seen the Portugals, by reason of their sea forces..to have given the law to those famous princes. **1617** MORYSON *Itin.* II. 63 He hoped shortly to give law to their irregular humours. **1656** B. HARRIS *Parival's Iron Age* (1659) 142 Every body stood mute, at the expectation of a success, which was to give the Law. **1712** SWIFT *Proposal for correct. Eng. Tongue* Miscell. (1727) I. 327 A Succession of affected Phrases, and new conceited Words..borrowed..from those, who, under the Character of Men of Wit and Pleasure, pretend to give the Law. **1726–31** TINDAL *Rapin's Hist. Eng.* (1743) II. 110 The Gantois seeing their neighbours so powerful and able to give them law. **1775** JOHNSON *Tax. no Tyr.* 79 No man ever could give law to language. **1849** MACAULAY *Hist. Eng.* iii. I. 397 In literature she gave law to the world. **1852** THACKERAY *B. Lyndon* i, For a time..Mr. Barry gave he law at Castle Brady. **1866** CONINGTON *Æneid* v. 133 The wind gives law, your toil is vain.

predicatively. **1842** TENNYSON *Dora* 96 You knew my word was law, and yet you dared To slight it. **1853** 'C. BEDE' *Verdant Green* I. ii, Like a good and dutiful son, however, his father's wishes were law.

4. a. With defining word, indicating some one of the branches into which law, as an object of study or exposition, may be divided, according to the matter with which it is concerned, as ***commercial***, ***ecclesiastical***, etc. ***law***, ***the law of banking***, ***of evidence***, etc.; or according to the source from which it is derived, as ***statute law***, ***customary law***, ***case-law*** (see CASE *sb.*[1]), etc. (***the***) ***canon law***: see CANON *sb.* 1 b. See also CIVIL LAW, COMMON LAW. ***martial law***: see MARTIAL.

b. ***both laws*** [after med.L. (*doctor*, etc.) *utriusque juris*]: in mediæval use referring to the Civil and the Canon Law; in modern Scotland, the Roman Civil Law and the municipal law of the country.

1577–87 HOLINSHED *Hist. Scot.* 284/1 Peter Mallart doctor of both lawes. **1808** SCOTT *Mem.* in *Lockhart* i, We attended the regular classes of both laws in the University of Edinburgh.

c. ***international law***, ***the law of nations***, under which nations are regarded as individual members of a common polity, bound by a common rule of agreement or custom; opposed to ***municipal law***, the rules binding in local jurisdictions (see MUNICIPAL).

The term *law of nations* (L. *jus gentium*) meant in Roman use the rules common to the law of all nations (often coupled with *law of nature* in sense 9 c; so in Shaks. *Hen. V*, II. iv. 80 and *Troil.* II. ii. 184). The transition to the mod. sense was facilitated by the appeal to 'the law of nations' in relation to such matters as the treatment of ambassadors or the obligation to observe treaties.

a **1548** HALL *Chron., Edw. IV*, 229 He was an officer of armes (to whom credite, by the lawe of all nacions, ought to be geven). **1594** HOOKER *Eccl. Pol.* I. x. §12 There is a third kind of law which touches all such several bodies politic, so far forth as one of them hath public commerce with another. And this third is the Law of Nations. *c* **1651** HOBBES *Rhet.* (1681) 39 The Law or Custom of Nations. **1723** *Pres. State Russia* II. 283 Beaten, and contrary to the Law of Nations, taken into Custody. **1769** BLACKSTONE *Comm.* IV. 66 The law of nations is a system of rules..established by universal consent among the civilized inhabitants of the world. **1870** *Pall Mall G.* 24 Dec. 10 Between municipal law..and international law, there is only a qualified and even a somewhat remote analogy. **1896** LORD RUSSELL OF KILLOWEN in *Law Quart. Rev.* XII. 313 The aggregate of

the rules to which nations have agreed to conform in their conduct towards one another are properly to be designated 'International Law'. *Ibid.* 317 International Law, as such, includes only so much of the law of morals or of right reason or of natural law (whatever these phrases may cover) as nations have agreed to regard as International Law. **1899** JUSTICE GRAY in *U.S. Rep.* clxxv. 700 International law is part of our law, and must be ascertained and administered by the courts of justice of appropriate jurisdiction, as often as questions of right depending upon it are duly presented for their determination.

5. In English technical use applied in a restricted sense to the Statute and Common Law, in contradistinction to EQUITY.

1591 LAMBARDE *Archeion* (1635) 68 Besides his Court of meere Law, he must..reserve to himselfe..a certaine soveraigne and preheminent Power, by which he may both supply the want, and correct the rigour of that Positive or written Law. **1745, 1765** [see EQUITY 4]. **1818** CRUISE *Digest* (ed. 2) III. 460 He would *give* law and equity, and not *pronounce upon* law and equity. **1852** DICKENS *Bleak Ho.* lxii, Did you ever know English law, or equity either, plain and to the purpose?

6. Applied predicatively to decisions or opinions on legal questions to denote that they are correct. Also ***good*** or ***bad law***.

1593 [see 1 d]. **1765** BLACKSTONE *Comm.* I. Introd. 70 If it be found that the former decision is manifestly absurd or unjust, it is declared, not that such a sentence was bad law, but that it was not law. **179.** WOLCOT (P. Pindar) *Expost. Odes* vi, What's sound at Hippocrene, the Poet's Spa, Is not at Westminster sound law! **1891** LD. COLERIDGE in *Law Times Rep.* LXV. 580/1 We are unable to concur in these dicta, and speaking with all deference we think they are not law.

7. a. (Usually *the law.*) The profession which is concerned with the exposition of the law, with pleading in the courts, and with the transaction of business requiring skilled knowledge of law; the profession of a lawyer. Orig. in ***man of law*** (now somewhat *arch.*), a lawyer; so †(***a gentleman***) ***toward the law***.

1340 HAMPOLE *Pr. Consc.* 5942 Men of laghe [er halden] ..to travayle and to counsaile þam þat askes counsayle. *c* **1386** CHAUCER *Prol.* 309 A Sergeant of the lawe, war and wys. —— *Man of Law's Prol.* Introd. 33 'Sir man of lawe' quod he, 'so have ye blis Tel us a tale anon'. *c* **1460** *Towneley Myst.* xxx. 8 Ther may no man of lagh help with no quantyce. **1551** ROBINSON tr. *More's Utop.* II. (Arb.) 128 Euery man should tel the same tale before the iudge that he wold tel to his man of law. **1560** DAUS tr. *Sleidane's Comm.* 473 Leaving the practise of the law. **1563** B. GOOGE *Eglogs* (Arb.) 75 Lawe gyues the gayne, and Physycke fyls the Purse. **1566** *Acts & Constit. Scotl.* To Rdr. ✠iij, Our Souerane Lady seing the Lawis..to be for the maist part unknawin, bot to the Iugeis, and men of Law. **1592** GREENE *Art Conny Catch.* III. 14 They espied a Gentleman toward the lawe entring in..and a countrey Clyent going with him. *c* **1780** COWPER *Jackdaw* v, The world, with all its motley rout, Church, army, physic, law. *Mod.* Three of his brothers are in the law.

b. Legal knowledge; legal acquirements.

1630 BP. BEDELL in *Ussher's Lett.* (1686) 454 This Protestation having neither Latin, nor Law, nor common Sence, doth declare the Skill of him that drew it. **1645** MILTON *Colast.* Wks. 1851 IV. 348 These made the Champarty, hee contributed the Law, and both joynd in the Divinity. **1884** CHURCH *Bacon* iii. 63 Coke thoroughly disliked Bacon. He thought lightly of his law.

8. a. The action of the courts of law, as a means of procuring redress of grievances or enforcing claims; judicial remedy. Frequent in phrases ***to go to*** (†***the***) ***law***, ***to have*** or ***take the law of*** or ***on*** (a person), † ***to call*** (a person) ***unto the law***, † ***to draw into laws***. Hence *occas.* used = recourse to the courts, litigation. † ***the day of law***: the day of trial.

c **1450** HOLLAND *Howlat* 224 The crovss Capone..Was officiale..that the law leidis In caussis consistoriale. **1500–20** DUNBAR *Poems* xiii. 79 Sum bydand the law layis land in wed. **1523** LD. BERNERS *Froiss.* I. xii. 11 That she and her sonne shulde take ryght and lawe on them, accordyng to theyr desertis. **1526** TINDALE *1 Cor.* vi. 1 Howe dare one of you..goo to lawe vnder the wicked? **1535** COVERDALE *Prov.* xxv. 8 Be not haistie to go to the lawe. **1562** J. HEYWOOD *Prov. & Epigr.* (1867) 193 You beyng a pleader at law, Pray hir to let fall thaction at law now. **1565** T. RANDOLPH in Ellis *Orig. Lett.* Ser. I. II. 198 The Daye of Lawe agaynste the iiii Bourgois men of thys towne is lyke to holde. **1573** L. LLOID *Pilgr. Princes* (1607) 133 Being striken and spurned by the same man, Socrates was counselled to call the same vnto the law before the Judges. **1596** SPENSER *State Irel.* Wks. (Globe) 623/1 Soe as it was not..possible to drawe him into lawes..it is hard for everye tryfling dett..to be driven to lawe. *c* **1630** RISDON *Surv. Devon* §47 (1810) 54 There was a long suit in law. **1677** YARRANTON *Eng. Improv.* 24 For ten years there will be more Law than ever to clear up Titles. **1711** ADDISON *Spect.* No 122 ¶4 A Fellow famous for taking the Law of every Body. **1762–71** H. WALPOLE *Vertue's Anecd. Paint.* (1786) V. 234 Dubosc, with whom he broke and went to law. **1780** *Newgate Cal.* V. 27 Surely no man in his senses would deliberately embark in law. **1796** PAINE *Writ.* (1895) III. 239 A sharper..may find a way..to cheat some other party, without that party being able, as the phrase is, to take the law of him. **1800** MAR. EDGEWORTH *Castle Rackrent* Gloss. 24 'I'll have the law of you, so I will!'—is the saying of an Englishman who expects justice. **1809** MALKIN *Gil Blas* I. v. ¶11 The hangers-on of the law. **1848** THACKERAY *Van. F.* vi. 52 'There's a hackney-coachman down stairs..vowing he'll have the law of you'. *Ibid.* vii. 61 'She was as bad as he', said Tinker. 'She took the law of every one of her tradesmen'. **1891** E. KINGLAKE *Australian at H.* 35 The very name of 'Law' is a bogie that frightens a man out of his wits.

b. *transf.* ***to take the law into one's own hands*** (or †***fists***): to redress one's own grievance, or punish an offender, without obtaining judicial assistance. ***to have the law in one's own hands***: to possess the means of redress, to be master of the situation.

1573 G. HARVEY *Letter-bk.* (Camden) 3 The law was now in there own hands. **1847** E. BRONTË *Wuthering Heights* I. vii. 129 Next time, Master Edgar, take the law into your own fists. **1875** B. JOWETT tr. *Plato's Dialogues* (ed. 2) III. 63 Young men will take the law into their own hands. **1877** C. M. YONGE *Cameos from Eng. Hist.* 3rd ser. vii. 63 Cade took the law into his own hands. **1902** A. BENNETT *Grand Babylon Hotel* xxvii. 300, I have a few questions to put to you, and it will depend on how you answer them whether I give you up to the police or take the law into my own hands. **1942** A. BRYANT *Yrs. of Endurance* xiv. 333 The industrial workers and the starving peasants, deprived of their patrimony by enclosures, took the law into their own hands.

c. ***Halifax law***, ***Lydford law***: the summary procedure of certain local tribunals which had or assumed the power of inflicting sentence of death on thieves; the rule proverbially ascribed to them was 'hang first, try afterwards'. † ***Stafford law***: ? punningly for a thrashing. Cf. LYNCH LAW.

1565 JEWEL *Repl. Harding* (1611) 356 But heere he thought..to call vs Theeues, and wicked Judges, and to charge vs with the Law of Lydford. **1589** *Hay any Work* A iij, Non would be so groshead as to gather that I threatned him with blowes, and to deale by Stafford law. *a* **1641** WENTWORTH *Let. to Ld. Mountmorris* in *N. & Q.* 5th Ser. IV. 16 Hallifaxe lawe hath ben executed in kinde, I am already hanged, and now wee cum to examine and consider of the evidence. **1710** *Brit. Apollo* II. No. 3. 5/2 First Hang and Draw, Then hear the cause by Lidford Law.

** *Divine law.*

9. The body of commandments which express the will of God with regard to the conduct of His intelligent creatures. Also (with *a*, *the*, and *pl.*) a particular commandment.

a. *gen.* So ***God's*** (***Christ's law***), ***the law of God***.

a **1023** WULFSTAN *Hom.* (1883) 158 Godes laȝe healdan. *c* **1175** *Lamb. Hom.* 55 Halde we godes laȝe. *c* **1205** LAY. 14803 He..tahte þan folke godes læȝe. *c* **1275** *Passion our Lord* 674 in *O.E. Misc.* 56 Seoþþe in alle londes hi eoden vor to prechen, and..godes lawe techen. *a* **1300** *Cursor M.* 2690 Ful wel þis lagh sal he yeme. *c* **1330** *Spec. Gy Warw.* 38 A good man..þat liuede al in godes lawe. *c* **1380** WYCLIF *Serm.* Sel. Wks. I. 26 To þis ende shulden clerkes traveile.. for love of Goddis lawe. **1382** —— *Rom.* vii. 25, I my silf by resoun of the soule serue to the lawe of God. *c* **1440** *Promp. Parv.* 289/2 Law of Godde. *c* **1485** *Digby Myst.* (1882) III. 1857 Crystes servont and yower to be, & þe lave of hym ever to fulfyll. *a* **1548** HALL *Chron., Hen. VIII* 246 To be observed by christen men, as..consonant to the law of God. **1683** TRYON *Way to Health* xix. (1697) 419 The good and holy Fear of the Lord, and his Innocent Law.

b. as communicated by express revelation, esp. in the Bible. Hence *occas.* the Scriptures themselves.

c **1025** *Rule St. Benet* (Logeman) 88 Si ᵹeræd ætforan þam cuman seo godcunde laᵹe. *c* **1175** *Lamb. Hom.* 81 In þisse worlde [*sc.* the age before Moses] nas na laᵹe, ne na larþeu. *a* **1300** *E.E. Psalter* i. 2 Bot in lagh ofe iauerd his wille be ai, And his lagh thinke he night and dai. **1567** *Good & Godly Ball.* (S.T.S.) 190 Goddis word and lawis the peple misknawis. **1611** BIBLE *Ps.* i. 2 His delight is in the Law of the Lord. **1719** WATTS *Ps.* i. (Short Metre) 5 Who..makes the Law of God His Study and Delight.

c. as implanted by nature in the human mind, or as capable of being demonstrated by reason. Formerly often ***the law of nature*** (now *rarely*, because of the frequency of that expression in sense 17), † ***law of kind***, ***natural law***, ***the law of reason***, etc.

The expression ***law of nature*** (*lex naturæ* or *naturalis*, *jus naturale*) in Cicero, Seneca, and the Roman jurists, is ultimately derived from the *φυσικον δίκαιον* of Aristotle.

c **1225** *Leg. Kath.* 964 Hit is aȝein riht ant aȝein leaue of euch cundelich lahe. *a* **1300** *Cursor M.* 28491 (Cott.) And haf i broken wit foly, þe lagh o kynd thoru licheri. *c* **1340** *Ibid.* 1576 (Trin.) Þe lawe of soþenes ny of kynde Wolde þei no tyme fynde. **1390** GOWER *Conf.* III. 272 But he the bestes wolde binde Only to lawes of nature. *c* **1470** G. ASHBY *Active Policy Prince* 695 Poems 34 If forgoten be al lawe positife, Remembre the noble lawe of nature. **1484** CAXTON *Fables of Æsop* II. Proem, The Athenyens the whiche lyued after the lawe of Kynde. **1513** MORE in Grafton *Chron.* (1568) II. 774 The lawe of nature wylleth the mother to keepe the childe. **1531** ST. GERMAN *Doctor & Stud.* I. ii, The lawe of nature..consydered generally..is referred to all creatures as well resonable as vnresonable..the lawe of nature specially consydered, whiche is also called the lawe of reason, parteyneth onely to creatures reasonable, that is man ..As to the orderyng of the dedes of man, it is preferred before the lawe of god. And it is writen in the herte of euery man. *a* **1548** HALL *Chron., Hen. V* 73 b, I shuld not do that whiche by the lawes of nature and reason I ought to do, which is to rendre kyndnes for kyndnes. **1594** HOOKER *Eccl. Pol.* I. viii. §8 The Law of Reason or Human Nature. §9 Laws of Reason. **1597** SHAKS. *2 Hen. IV*, III. ii. 357. *a* **1614** DONNE *Βιαθανατος* (1644) 34 That part of Gods Law which bindes alwayes, bound before it was written..and that is the Law of nature. **1692** SOUTH *Serm.* (1697) I. 482 The Law of Nature,..I take to be nothing else, but the mind of God, signified to a Rational agent by the bare discourse of his Reason. **1712** BERKELEY *Passive Obed.* §33 Self-preservation is..the very first and fundamental law of nature. **1765** BLACKSTONE *Comm.* I. Introd. §2. 39 This will of his maker is called the law of nature. **1780** BENTHAM *Princ. Legisl.* Wks. 1843 I. 9 Instead of the phrase, Law of Nature, you have sometimes Law of Reason. **1878** GLADSTONE *Prim. Homer* 109 Natural law was profoundly revered, while conventional law hardly yet existed.

10. a. The system of moral and ceremonial precepts contained in the Pentateuch; also in a narrower sense applied to the ceremonial portion of the system considered separately. More explicitly, ***the law of Moses***, ***the Mosaic*** or ***Jewish law***, etc.

c **1000** ÆLFRIC *O.T.* in Grein *Ags. Prosa* I. 5 God him sette æ, þæt ys open laᵹu, þam folce to steore. *c* **1200** ORMIN 1961 Annd tatt wass ned tatt, ȝho wass þa Wiþþ Godess laȝhe weddedd. *a* **1225** *Leg. Kath.* 2500, I þe munt of Synai þer Moyses fatte þe lahe et ure lauerd. *c* **1250** *O. Kent. Serm.* in *O.E. Misc.* 26 Þo dede he somoni alle þo wyse clerekes þet kuþe þe laghe. *a* **1300** *Cursor M.* 6451 *heading*, (Gött.) Tell i sal of moyses law. *c* **1330** *Spec. Gy Warw.* 358 At þe mount of Synay..þar god him ȝaf þe firste lawe. **1398** TREVISA *Barth. De P.R.* IX. xxvi. (1495) 363 Alway in the Saterdaye preestes declaryd and expownyd the lawe to the peple. *a* **1400–50** *Alexander* 1546 Iustis of iewry & iogis of the lawe. *c* **1585** R. BROWNE *Answ. Cartwright* 54 They read in the Booke of the Lawe. **1611** BIBLE *Rom.* ii. 14 The Gentiles which haue not the Law, doe by nature the things contained in the Law.

b. In expressed or implied opposition to *the Gospel*: The Mosaic dispensation; also, the system of Divine commands and of penalties imposed for disobedience contained in the Scriptures, considered apart from the offer of salvation by faith in Christ.

1382 WYCLIF *Gal.* iii. 11 No man is iustified in the lawe anentis God. **1529** FRITH *Pistle Chr. Rdr.* (1829) 461 The law was given us, that we might know what to do and what to eschew. **1595** SHAKS. *John* II. i. 180 The Canon of the Law is laide on him. **1758** S. HAYWARD *Serm.* i. 2 To guard the Galatians against a dependence on the law. **1827** KEBLE *Chr. Y.* Easter Sunday 20 No brighter..Than Reason's or the Law's pale beams. **1842** J. H. NEWMAN *Par. Serm.* VI. i. 2 Vain were all the deeds of the Law. **1859** J. CUMMING *Ruth* vi. 109 By what he suffered I escape the law's curse.

c. The Pentateuch as distinguished from the other portions of the Old Testament Scriptures.

1382 WYCLIF *John* viii. 5 Moses in the lawe comaundide vs for to stoone siche. **1526** *Pilgr. Perf.* (W. de W. 1531) 298 b, O very messyas, promysed in the lawe for mannes redempcyon. **1611** BIBLE *2 Macc.* xv. 9 Comforting them out of the law, and the prophets.

† **11.** A 'dispensation'. ***the old law***: the Mosaic dispensation, the 'Old Covenant'; also, the books of the Old Testament. ***the new law***: the Gospel dispensation.

c **1000** *Ælfric's Past. Ep.* xl. in Thorpe *Laws* II. 380 Nu is seo ealde laᵹu ᵹeendod æfter Cristes to-cyme. *a* **1175** *Cott. Hom.* 235 Þas fif cheðen beoð fif laȝan for þan þe god is þurh þesen ȝecnowe. *c* **1200** *Vices & Virtues* (1888) 7 Aiðer ðurh ðare ealde laȝwe and iec ðurh ðare niewe. *c* **1200** *Trin. Coll. Hom.* 3 Aduent bitocneð þre time, on þe was bi-fore þe old laȝe, þe oðer was on þe holde laȝe, and þe þridde was on þe newe laȝe. *a* **1225** *Ancr. R.* 58 Uorþi was ihoten a Godes half iðen olde lawe þæt put were euer iwrien. *a* **1300** *Cursor M.* 21285 Tuin axils er tuin laghs. *Ibid.* 21644 Þe licknes o þis tre sa tru, In þe ald lagh was be-for þe neu. *a* **1340** HAMPOLE *Psalter* cxviii. 99, I vndirstode bettire þan þe docturs of þe alde laghe. *c* **1450** *Compendious olde treat.* (Arb.) 172 As kinge Antioche came in the ende wellnygh of ye olde lawe, and brent the bokes of gods lawe..So now Antichrist.. brenneth nowe nygh thende of ye new lawe theuangely of Christe. **1542** BECON *Potation for Lent* Wks. 1564 I. 50 b, Christ the true lyght of the world is com, therfore those Ceremonies of the olde law are nowe nomore necessary.

† **12.** A religious system; the Christian, Jewish, Muslim, or Pagan religion. ***by my law***: by my faith; also ***to swear one's law***. Cf. LAY *sb.*³

a **1225** *Leg. Kath.* 1349 We leaueð þi lahe..Ant turneð alle to Criste. *c* **1290** *S. Eng. Leg.* I. 17/564 Heore lawe nas riȝt nouȝt, þat ne bi-liefden nouȝt on þe rode. *a* **1300** *K. Horn* 65 Hi here laȝe asoke. **13..** *Sir Beues* (A.) 1780 Þe seue kniȝtes of heþen lawe Beues slouȝ that ilche stounde. *c* **1375** *Sc. Leg. Saints* vii. (*Jacobus Minor*) 190 Faraseis & wysmene of Iowis lach mad answere þane. *a* **1400** *Pistill of Susan* 3 He was so lele in his lawe. *c* **1400** MAUNDEV. (1839) xxiii. 252 Thei suffren, that folk of alle Lawes may peysibely duellen amonges hem. *a* **1400–50** *Alexander* 4306 In him we lely beleue & in na laȝe ellis. *c* **1450** *St. Cuthbert* (Surtees) 4824 And forsake his paynym lawe. *c* **1477** CAXTON *Jason* 86 b, By my lawe sire sayd Mopsius I see no way. *c* **1500** *Melusine* xlix. 324 He sware hys lawe that lytel or nought he shuld entrete hym. **1613** PURCHAS *Pilgrimage* (1614) 312 But the Mufti being highest Interpreter of their Law..must indeed have preeminence. **1685** STILLINGFL. *Orig. Brit.* i. 9 Here the first Disciples of the Catholick Law found an ancient Church.

*** *Combined applications.*

13. Often used as the subject of propositions equally applying to human and divine law. In juristic and philosophical works often with definitions intended to include also the senses explained in branches II and III below. (See quots.)

1594 HOOKER *Eccl. Pol.* I. ii. §1 That which doth assign unto each thing the kind, that which doth moderate the force and power, that which doth appoint the form and measure, of working, the same we term a Law. *Ibid.* xvi. §8 Of Law there can be no less acknowledged, than that her seat is the bosom of God, her voice the harmony of the world. **1611** BIBLE *Transl. Pref.* 3 The Scripture is..a Pandect of profitable lawes, against rebellious spirits. **1651** HOBBES *Leviath.* II. xxvi. 137 My designe being not to shew what is Law here, and there, but what is Law. **1690** LOCKE *Govt.* II. vi. §57 Law, in its proper Notion, is..the Direction of a free and intelligent Agent to his proper Interest. **1765** BLACKSTONE *Comm.* I. 39 This then is the general signification of law, a rule of action dictated by some superior being. **1836** J. GILBERT *Chr. Atonem.* Notes (1852) 344 Law speaks the language of indignation against crime.

1889 RUSKIN *Præterita* III. 159 Men of perfect genius are known in all centuries by their perfect respect to all law.

II. Without reference to an external commanding authority.

†**14. a.** Custom, customary rule or usage; habit, practice, 'ways'. ***law of (the) land*** : custom of the country. ***at thieves law***: after the manner of thieves. *Obs.*

c **1175** *Lamb Hom.* 25 þenne hafest þu þes hundes laȝe, þe nu speoweð and ef[t] hit fret. *c* **1200** ORMIN 2373 Ȝho wollde ben Rihht laȝhelike fesstnedd Wiþþ macche, swa summ i þatt ald wass laȝhe to ben fesstned. *c* **1220** *Bestiary* 23 Ðe ðridde laȝe haneð ðe leun. *a* **1225** *Juliana* 10 Ȝef þu wult leauen þe lahen þat tu list in. *a* **1300** *K. Horn* 1109 (Ritson) An horn hue ber an honde, For that wes lawe of londe. **13..** *Gaw & Gr. Knt.* 790 Enbaned vnder þe abataylment in þe best lawe. *c* **1330** R. BRUNNE *Chron.* (1810) 322 þe lord of Badenauh..Lyued at theues lauh. *a* **1400-50** *Alexander* 4402 A-nothire laȝe is in ȝoure lande at oure lord hatis. **1535** COVERDALE *1 Sam.* viii. 9 Yet testifye vnto them and shewe them the lawe of the kynge that shall raigne ouer them. **15..** *Adam Bel*, etc. in Hazl. *E.P.P.* II. 158 Whan they came before the kyng, As it was the lawe of the lande, They kneled downe.

†**b.** *Old Cant.* With distinctive word prefixed: A particular branch of the art of thieving.

c **1550** *Dice-Play* B iv b, Thus giue they their owne conueyance the name of cheting law, so do they other termes, as sacking law: high law, Fygging law, and such lyke. **1591** GREENE *Disc. Coosnage* (1859) 33 Hereupon doe they give their false conveyance the name of Conny-catching Lawe, as there be also other Lawes, as High-Law, Sacking Law, Figging Law, Cheting Lawe, Barnards Lawe.

†**15.** What is or is considered right or proper; justice or correctness of conduct. Also ***right and law***; ***against, in, out of, with law***. ***of a law***: with good reason. *Obs.*

c **1200** ORMIN 6256 þe birrþ himm biddenn don þe rihht & laȝhe. *c* **1250** *Gen. & Ex.* 536 Wapmen bi-gunnen quad mester..A ðefis kinde, a-ȝenes laȝe. **13..** *Guy Warw.* (A.) 410 Bi mi trewþe..Schal Y mi fader þe tiding bere, Thou worþest to hewen..Oþer wiþ wilde hors to-drawe For þi foly, & þat wer lawe. *c* **1330** R. BRUNNE *Chron.* (1810) 113 Dauid did but lawe, Mald had his seruage. *c* **1340** *Cursor M.* 13052 (Trin.) Ȝitt is she þi broþer wif whom þou shuldes not haue with lawe. **1422** tr. *Secreta Secret., Priv. Priv.* 128 To deme betwen al maner of folke..wythout goynge assyd owt of lawe. *a* **1400-50** *Alexander* 4666 Neuir-þe-les of a laȝe hald we vs driȝtins. *c* **1440** *York Myst.* viii. 10 Alle in lawe to lede þer lyffe.

16. a. A rule of action or procedure; one of the rules defining correct procedure in an art or department of action, or in a game. †Also, manner of life. *Phr.* ***a law unto*** (or ***to***) ***himself*** (or ***themselves***, etc.).

a **1225** [see 3 d]. *a* **1300** *Cursor M.* 7940 Godd mad þe king of israel, To lede þe folk wit laghes lel. **1422** tr. *Secreta Secret., Priv. Priv.* 149 Ouer al thynge the wysdome of a kyng sholde his law gouerne aftyr the law of god. *c* **1460** *Towneley Myst.* xxviii. 44 Wherfor in woman is no laghe ffor she is withoutten aghe. **1611** BIBLE *Rom.* ii. 14 These [the Gentiles] hauing not the Law, are a Law vnto themselues. **1638** BAKER tr. *Balzac's Lett.* (vol. III) 102 And the lawes of decencie are so ancient, that they seem to be a part of the ancient religion. **1671** L. ADDISON *W. Barbary* 50 Contrary to all Ingenuity and Laws of Hospitality. *Ibid.* 52 That he who aspires after..Conquest, ought not to binde himself to the Laws of a fair Gamester. **1683** TRYON *Way to Health* xix. (1697) 430 The Lord endued Man with the Spirit of Understanding, by which he might be a Guide and Law unto himself. **1736** BUTLER *Anal.* I. iv. 134 A few who shamelessly avow..their mere will and pleasure to be their law of life. **1742** HOYLE (*title*) A short treatise on the game of Whist. Containing the laws of the game. **1837** SIR W. HAMILTON *Logic* v. (1866) I. 78 For free intelligences, a law is an ideal necessity given in the form of a precept, which we ought to follow. **1856** FROUDE *Hist. Eng.* I. i. 29 Self-protection is the first law of life. **1867** (*title*) The laws of Football, as played at Rugby School. **1877** E. R. CONDER *Bas. Faith* vi. 259 A moral law states what ought to be. **1878** R. H. DAVIS (*title*) A law unto herself. **1930** J. S. HUXLEY *Bird-Watching* iv. 75 Every male [ruff] is a law unto himself. Some grow black ruffs, others ruffs that are white, sandy, brown, grey, pepper-and-salt, and half a dozen other shades. **1942** PARTRIDGE *Usage and Abusage* (1947) 129/1 Certain idiosyncratic, law-unto-themselves writers fall into vagaries when..they depart from those rules. **1962** A. NISBETT *Technique Sound Studio* xii. 221 Electronic music is a law to itself... It really can be fundamentally different from conventional music. **1965** M. SPARK *Mandelbaum Gate* ii. 23 'What was your father's Law?'..'I'm afraid he was a law unto himself.' **1968** *Listener* 27 June 850/1 Hogarth is very much a law to himself.

b. The code or body of rules recognized in a specified department of action. Also ***law of arms***: the recognized custom of professional soldiers; †also, the rules of heraldry; ***law of honour*** (see HONOUR *sb.* 9 h).

a **1300** *Cursor M.* 26276 Lagh o penance will þat [etc]. **1486** *Bk. St. Albans* E iij, By the law of venery as I dare vnder take. *c* **1500** in *Q. Eliz. Acad.* (1879) 100 Law of armys disponys ffor theme be sett and portrait with pictouris. **1530** PALSGR. 237/2 Lawe of armes, *droict darmes.* *a* **1548** HALL *Chron., Hen. VIII*, 255 He might have kepte theim in straite prison, by juste lawe of Armes. **1557** *Tottell's Misc.* (Arb.) 139 Of louers lawe he toke no cure. **1626** JACKSON *Creed* VIII. xiv. §2 Unto Satan the professed rebel against him..he did vouchsafe the benefit of the law of Armes or duel.

c. Phr. ***law of the jungle***, the code of survival in jungle life, now usu. with ref. to the superiority of brute force or self-interest in the struggle for survival.

1894 KIPLING *Jungle Bk.* 31 Baloo was teaching him the Law of the Jungle... Young wolves will only learn as much of the Law of the Jungle as applies to their own pack and tribe. *Ibid.* 34 A man's cub..must learn *all* the Law of the Jungle. **1895** —— *Second Jungle Bk.* 23 Now this is the Law of the Jungle—as old and as true as the sky;..the strength of the Pack is the Wolf, and the strength of the Wolf is the Pack. **1927** C. A. & M. R. BEARD *Rise Amer. Civilization* I. ix. 403 So the law of the jungle prevailed; and in the frightful contest that followed, the rights of neutrals were as chaff before a hurricane. **1950** A. BRYANT *Age of Elegance* x. 329 In the manufacturing districts..the old framework of society..broke down completely. Here only the law of the jungle held. **1951** M. MCLUHAN *Mech. Bride* 107/2 Mr. Queeny derives his 'law of the jungle' versus 'crusading idealist' from this later nineteenth-century phase of the older split. **1969** *New Yorker* 6 Sept. 33 (*caption*) May I remind you that here law and order means the law of the jungle. **1974** *Times* 4 Mar. 7/4 The Duke said that a purely materialistic society inevitably succumbed to the law of the jungle and political dictatorship.

III. Scientific and philosophical uses.

17. a. In the sciences of observation, a theoretical principle deduced from particular facts, applicable to a defined group or class of phenomena, and expressible by the statement that a particular phenomenon always occurs if certain conditions be present. In the physical sciences, and occasionally in others, called more explicitly ***law of nature*** or ***natural law***.

The 'laws of nature', by those who first used the term in this sense, were viewed as commands imposed by the Deity upon matter, and even writers who do not accept this view often speak of them as 'obeyed' by the phenomena, or as agents by which the phenomena are produced.

1665 *Phil. Trans.* I. 31 The changes be varied according to very odd Laws. **1665** BOYLE *Occas. Refl.* IV. vi, The Wisdome..of God does..confine the creatures to the establish'd Laws of Nature. **1690** LOCKE *Hum. Und.* I. iii. §13 A law of Nature..something that we being ignorant of may attain to the knowledge of by the use and due application of our natural Faculties. **1697** DRYDEN *Virg. Georg.* II. 698 Happy the Man, who, studying Natures Laws, Thro' known Effects can trace the secret Cause. **1755** JOHNSON, *Law*, an established and constant mode or process; a fixed correspondence of cause and effect. **1764** REID *Inquiry* vi. §13 The laws of nature are nothing else but the most general facts relating to the operations of nature. **1794** J. HUTTON *Philos. Light*, etc. 16 We..name those rules of action the laws of nature. **1827** WHATELY *Logic* (1837) 361 The conformity of individual cases to the general rule is that which constitutes a Law of Nature. **1865** *Reader* 29 Apr. 484/3 A Law expresses an invariable order of phenomena or facts. **1875** MAINE *Hist. Instit.* (ed. 4) 373 Law..has been applied derivatively to the orderly sequences of Nature. **1883** H. DRUMMOND *Nat. Law in Spir. W.* (ed. 2) 5 The Laws of Nature are simply statements of the orderly condition of things in Nature. **1898** G. MEREDITH *Odes Fr. Hist.* 62 Those firm laws Which we name Gods.

b. With reference to a particular science or field of inquiry.

law of large numbers: see LARGE *a.* 8 i. ***laws of motion***: chiefly used *spec.* for the three following propositions formulated by Newton: (1) A body must continue in its state of rest or of uniform motion in a straight line, unless acted on by some external force; (2) Change of motion takes place in the direction of the impressed force, and is proportional to it; (3) Action and reaction are equal, and in contrary directions.

1668 *Phil. Trans.* III. 864 A Summary Account given by Dr. John Wallis, Of the General Laws of Motion,..communicated to the R. Society, Novemb. 26. 1668. **1669** *Ibid.* IV. 925 A Summary Account Of the Laws of Motion, communicated by Mr. Christian Hugens in a Letter to the R. Society. **1726** tr. *Gregory's Astron.* I. 112 The Law of Attraction being the same as before. **1727-52** CHAMBERS *Cycl.* s.v. *Motion*, The general laws of motion were first brought into a system..by Dr. Wallis, Sir Christopher Wren, and M. Huygens. **1765** BLACKSTONE *Comm.* I. Introd. §2. 38 The laws of motion, of gravitation, of optics, or mechanics. **1849** MACAULAY *Hist. Eng.* i. I. 48 Whoever passes in Germany from a Roman Catholic to a Protestant principality..finds that he has passed from a lower to a higher grade of civilization. On the other side of the Atlantic the same law prevails. **1854** BREWSTER *More Worlds* xv. 221 The law of universal gravitation is established for several of these systems. **1857** S. P. HALL in *Merc. Marine Mag.* (1858) V. 11 It does seem strange that..greater attention is not given to the Law of Storms. **1860** TYNDALL *Glac.* II. xi. 289 As regards the motion of the surface of a glacier, two laws are to be borne in mind. **1864** BOWEN *Logic* ix. 308 The fact that water stands at this level is ranked among many other facts, which are comprehended under the general statement called a Law of Hydrostatics. **1877** E. R. CONDER *Bas. Faith* iii. 122 The laws of reasoning. **1884** tr. *Lotze's Metaph.* 333 Stated in its complete logical form a law is always a universal hypothetical judgment, which states that whenever *C* is or holds good, *E* is or holds good.

c. In certain sciences, particular 'laws' are known by the names of their discoverers, as in the following examples. (Most of these terms are of general European currency, their equivalents being used in Fr., Ger., It., etc.)

(*a*) *Astronomy.*

Bode's law, an empirical formula representing the distances of the orbits of the other planets from the orbit of Mercury as forming an approximate geometrical progression. **Kepler's laws**, the three propositions established by John Kepler (1571-1630) with regard to the planetary motions: (1) That the planets move in ellipses, the sun being in one of the foci; (2) That the radius vector of a planet describes equal areas in equal times; (3) That the square of the periodic time of a planet is directly proportional to the cube of its mean distance from the sun.

1781 *Chambers' Cycl., Kepler's Law*, is that law of the planetary motions discovered by Kepler. **1805** *Edin. Rev.* Jan. 443 Kepler's Laws. **1833** HERSCHEL *Astron.* Index, Bode's law of planetary distances. **1837** WHEWELL *Induct. Sci.* I. 416 One of the important rules known to us as 'Kepler's laws'.

(*b*) *Physics.*

Avogadro's law, the law that equal volumes of different gases, pressure and temperature being equal, contain the same number of molecules. **Boyle's law**, the principle, published by Robert Boyle about 1662, that the volume of a given mass of gas (the temperature being constant) varies inversely as the pressure. **Charles's law**, the law discovered by Alex. César Charles (1746-1823) that for every degree centigrade of rise in temperature, the volume of a gas increases by ·00366 of its amount at zero. **Dulong and Petit's law**, the law that all the chemical elements have approximately the same atomic heat.

1860 MAXWELL *Sci. Papers* (1890) I. 389 Boyle and Mariotte's law. **1863** ATKINSON *Ganot's Physics* 110 The laws of the compressibility of gases were studied separately by Boyle and by Mariotti... Each of these philosophers arrived at the same law, which in England bears the name of Boyle's, and on the continent of Mariotti's. *Ibid.* 288 Dulong and Petit's law may be thus expressed; the same quantity of heat is needed to heat an atom of all simple bodies to the same extent. **1880** CLEMINSHAW tr. *Wurtz' Atomic Theory* v. 95 The 'law', as it is generally called, of Avogadro and Ampère may be enunciated as follows: Equal volumes of gases or vapours contain the same number of molecules. **1884** DANIELL *Princ. Physics* 223 Then the volume varies as the 'absolute temperature' (Charles's Law, often attributed to Gay Lussac).

(*c*) *Philology.*

Grimm's law, the rule formulated by Jacob Grimm (in the 2nd ed. of his *Deutsche Grammatik*, 1822) with regard to the representation in the Germanic langs. of certain consonants of the primitive Aryan language. Grimm's statement was that original aspirates became mediæ in Gothic, Low German, English, Old Norse, etc. and tenues in High German; original mediæ became tenues in Gothic, etc., and 'aspirates' (supposed to be represented by spirants and affricates) in High German; and original tenues became 'aspirates' in Gothic, etc. and mediæ in High German. The formula is no longer accepted as correct, but the name of 'Grimm's law' is still applied to its rectified form, which is too complicated to be stated here. **Verner's law**, discovered by Karl Verner of Copenhagen in 1875, deals with a class of exceptions to Grimm's law, and is to the effect that an original Germanic voiceless spirant, when following or terminating a primitively unaccented syllable, became a voiced spirant, which in the historic Germanic langs. is under certain conditions represented by a media; the *z* which according to the 'law' results from *s* is, except in Gothic, normally represented by *r*. **Grassmann's law**, published by Hermann Grassmann in 1863, is that when primitive Aryan had two aspirates in the same or successive syllables the former of them was in Sanskrit changed into the corresponding media, and in Greek into the corresponding tenuis.

1838 W. B. WINNING *Man. Compar. Philol.* I. iii. 36 *Grimm's Law.*—I now proceed with the consideration of Grimm's important law..concerning the regular interchange of certain letters in different languages. *Ibid.* 47 On the principle of Grimm's law, we exclude the Perso-Grecians, High Germans, and Goths, from among the earliest colonists of Italy. **1841** LATHAM *Eng. Lang.* 190 An important fact relating to the change of consonants, which is currently called Grimm's Law. **1878** SWEET in *Academy* 9 Feb. 123/2 Verner's law [explained].

(*d*) *Pol. Econ.*

Gresham's law, the principle, involved in Sir Thomas Gresham's letter to Q. Elizabeth in 1558, that 'bad money drives out good', i.e. that when debased money (sc. coins reduced in weight or fineness, or both) is current in the same country with coins of full legal weight and fineness, the latter will tend to be exported, leaving the inferior money as the only circulating medium.

1858 MACLEOD *Elem. Pol. Econ.* 477 As he was the first to perceive that a bad and debased currency is the cause of the disappearance of the good money, we are only doing what is just, in calling this great fundamental law of the currency by his name. We may call it Gresham's law of the currency.

(*e*) *Meteorol.*

Buys-Ballot's law (biːzˈbælɒt) [enunciated by C. H. D. *Buys-Ballot* (1817-90), Dutch meteorologist, in 1857] (see quots.).

1875 *Encycl. Brit.* III. 29/1 Buys-Ballot's 'Law of the Winds'..may be thus expressed:—The wind neither blows round the space of lowest pressure in circles returning on themselves, nor does it blow directly towards that space; but it takes a direction intermediate, approaching, however, more nearly to the direction and course of circular curves than of radii to a centre. **1970** J. HULBERT *All about Weather* vi. 73 Buys Ballot's law..says that if a man stands with his back to the wind, the lower pressure will be to his left in the northern hemisphere, and to his right in the southern.

18. In generalized sense: Laws (of Nature) in general; the order and regularity in Nature of which laws are the expression.

a **1853** ROBERTSON *Serm.* Ser. IV. iii. (1876) 26 Such an event is invariably followed by such a consequence. This we call law. **1865** MOZLEY *Mirac.* ii. 39 In the argument against miracles the first objection is that they are against law. **1866** DK. ARGYLL *Reign Law* ii. (1867) 64 We have Law as applied simply to an observed Order of facts. **1873** H. SPENCER *Stud. Sociol.* ii. 42 The accepted conception of law is that of an established order to which the manifestations of a power or force conform. **1883** H. DRUMMOND *Nat. Law in Spir. W.* i. 1. (1884) 5 The fundamental conception of Law is an ascertained working sequence..among the Phenomena of Nature.

19. *Math.* The rule or principle on which a series, or the construction of a curve, etc., depends.

1805-17 R. JAMESON *Char. Min.* (ed. 3) 163 The law which produces an octahedron from a cube.

IV. 20. a. *Sport.* An allowance in time or distance made to an animal that is to be hunted, or to one of the competitors in a race, in order to ensure equal conditions; a start; in phrases ***to get, give, have (fair) law (of)***.

1600 R. WHYTE in Nichols *Progr. Q. Eliz.* III. 91 Hir Grace..sawe sixteen buckes (all having fayre lawe) pulled

downe with greyhoundes, in a laund. **1607** MARKHAM *Caval.* III. (1617) 82 That the formost getting his law of the hind-most, do win the wager. **1611** —— *Country Content.* I. vii. (1668) 43 That the Fewterer shall give the Hare twelve score Law, ere he loose the Greyhounds. **1666–7** DENHAM *Direct. Paint.* I. v. 7 So Huntsmen fair unto the Hares give Law. **1704** *Collect. Voy.* (Churchill) III. 40/1 If the Bird has Law of him, he will hardly overtake him. **1706** E. WARD *Hud. Rediv.* (1707) I. I. 22 The silly Hare..Having good Law, sat down to rest her. **1787** G. WHITE *Selborne* vi. (1789) 18 When the devoted deer was separated from his companions, they gave him, by their watches, law,..for twenty minutes. **1811** *Sporting Mag.* XXXIX. 142 Give her law and she'll hold it a mile. **1829** J. R. BEST *Pers. & Lit. Mem.* 77 The accident was owing to his giving his horse too much law. **1861** WHYTE MELVILLE *Mkt. Harb.* x. (ed. 12) 82 The fox..having obtained..a little law of his pursuers, takes advantage of the lull to slip away. **1883** E. PENNELL-ELMHIRST *Cream Leicestersh.* 312 The pack were now together,..the fox had gained but little law.

b. Hence, Indulgence, mercy.

1649 FULLER *Just Man's Funeral* 17 God will give them fair law. **1719** DE FOE *Crusoe* II. xi. (1840) 236 Merchant-ships show but little law to pirates, if they get them in their power. **1848** J. H. NEWMAN *Loss & Gain* 289 We shall have you back again among us by next Christmas..I can't give you greater law. **1849** E. E. NAPIER *Excurs. S. Africa* II. 101 The 'on dit' is that he has ten days more law. **1879** GEO. ELIOT *Coll. Breakf. P.* 594, I will never grant One inch of law to feeble blasphemies.

V. *attrib.* and *Comb.*

21. Simple attributive. **a.** Pertaining to the law as a body of rules to be obeyed, as in ***law-system***; pertaining to law as a department of study, as in ***law authority***, ***department***, ***dictionary***, ***-faculty***, ***firm***, ***language***, ***-learning***, ***-library***, ***-lore***, ***-pedant***, ***-point***, ***-school***, ***-student***, ***studies***, ***-tractate***, ***-vocable***, ***-word***; pertaining to the legal profession, as ***law-craft***, ***-gentleman***, ***-list***, ***-person***, †***-solicitor***; pertaining to forensic procedure and litigation, as in †***law-bar***, ***-case***, ***-charges***, ***-chicanery***, ***costs***, ***-court***, ***-fight***, ***-quirk***, ***-reports***, ***-sale***, ***-suitor***, ***-writings***; pertaining to the Mosaic dispensation or to the law in opposition to the gospel, as in ***law-covenant***, ***-curse***, ***-work***, ***-worker***.

1818 COBBETT *Pol. Reg.* XXXIII. 381 His book is the greatest of all *Law-Authorities. **1602** WARNER *Alb. Eng.* XII. lxxiii. 302 At Westminsters *Law-Barres. **1710** *Tatler* No. 190 ¶3 No one would offer to put a *Law-Case to me. **1776** FOOTE *Bankrupt* III. Wks. 1799 II. 126 The Attorney General to the paper, that answers the law cases, is not come yet. **1669** MARVELL *Corr.* cxii. Wks. 1872–5 II. 271 Your *law-charges here amount not to 5li. **1819** *Hermit in London* II. 135 Long acquainted with law-persons and law-charges. **1795** BURKE *Tracts Popery Laws* iv. Wks. IX. 394 Vexatious litigation and crooked *law-chicanery. **1618** BOLTON *Florus* IV. xii. (1636) 325 Hee durst set up a *Law-court, and sit in judgement within his Campe. **1768–74** TUCKER *Lt. Nat.* (1834) II. 258 Justification..is a term taken from the law-courts. **1878** *N. Amer. Rev.* CXXVII. 57 Condemned by the law-courts. **1803** A. SWANSTON *Serm. & Lect.* II. 168 The term of the *law-covenant might be somewhat relaxed. **1587** GOLDING *De Mornay* xx. (1617) 345 *Lawecraft hath almost as many sundry lawes as cases. **1832** SOUTHEY in *Q. Rev.* XLVII. 504 The sober follies which disgrace our law-craft. **1786** A. GIB *Sacred Contempl.* II. I. iii. 177 Through a full effect of the *law-curse to which they are naturally subjected. **1849** E. CHAMBERLAIN *Indiana Gazetteer* (ed. 3) 45 In the winter of 1838, the institution was chartered as an University, and in 1842, a *law department was established. **1594** CAREW *Huarte's Exam. Wits* xi. (1596) 154 In the *law-faculty euery law containeth a seueral particular case. **1880** MRS. OLIPHANT *He that will not*, etc. xxxi, He could not fight for his inheritance..unless indeed it were a *law-fight in the courts. *c* **1876** 'MARK TWAIN' *Lett. to Publishers* (1967) 95, I suppose *our* *law firm are [*sic*] above average. **1945** G. L. WILLIAMS *Learning the Law* xii. 130 There are law firms in the East, located in the great seaports, where young solicitors may often find good places. **1965** MRS. L. B. JOHNSON *White House Diary* 21 July (1970) 304 His greatest hope was to stabilize the law firm. **1973** *N.Y. Law Jrnl.* 31 Aug. 1/3 A New York attorney and a law firm have been found by Federal Judge Lloyd F. MacMahon of the Southern District of New York to have violated..the Code of Professional Responsibility. **1837** DICKENS *Pickw.* xlvi, If you *law-gentlemen do these things on speculation, why you must get a loss now and then you know. **1797** *Encycl. Brit.* IX. 725/1 (*heading*) *Law-Language. **1808** BENTHAM *Sc. Reform* 43 *Law-learning, with falshood for the basis of it. **1799** H. K. WHITE *Let. to bro. Neville* Rem. (1825) 179 With..a very large *law library to refer to. **1852** DICKENS *Bleak Ho.* x, Almanacs, diaries, and *law-lists. **1812** JEFFERSON *Writ.* (1830) IV. 179 The..chaos of *law-lore from which we wished to be emancipated. **1751** H. WALPOLE *Lett.* (1846) II. 382 You would easily believe this story, if you knew what a mere *law-pedant it is! **1819** *law-persons [see *law-charges* above]. **1819** SCOTT in *Biog. Notices* ii. (1880) 385 If a *lawpoint were submitted to him. **1667** *Decay Chr. Piety* vii. ¶10 Solicitous..to..leave nothing to the mercy of a *law-quirk. *c* **1840** LADY WILTON *Art of Needlework* xviii. 298 No. 50 [of *The English Mercurie*], dated July 23, 1588, is the first now in existence... In it are no advertisements—no fashions—no *law reports—no court circular. **1902** *Encycl. Brit.* XXXI. 181/2 The *Law Reports* (begun in 1884) are conducted by the large staff of *Times* law reporters, all of them barristers of at least five years' standing. **1972** *Mod. Law Rev.* XXXV. I. 22 The law reports, commonly regarded as our primary literature, tell us regularly and systematically how large claims are being determined. **1888** LIGHTHALL *Yng. Seigneur* 70 Before the parish church, just after mass on Sunday forenoon, the bailiff cries his *law-sales. **1818** *North Amer. Rev.* Mar. 428 A *Law School is established at the University. **1863** S. WARREN *Pop. & Pract. Introd. Law Stud.* (ed. 3) I. i. 89 In Ireland, there is a 'Law School' in the University of Dublin. **1893** W. K. POST *Harvard Stories* 128 'You couldn't do that if you were a biographee,' reasoned Dane Austin, the law-school man. **1966** G. WILSON in K. Boehm *University Choice* 242 It would be a rare law student who could do anything as straightforward as transfer his own house as a result of what he had learnt at law school. **1738** WARBURTON *Div. Legat.* I. 431 That known Story of two *Law Sollicitors. **1835** S. WARREN *Pop. & Pract. Introd. Law Stud.* iii. 102 Could the eye of the young *law-student be brought to..see how heavily his bodily and mental energies will be taxed..how he would husband them! **1884** *Harper's Mag.* LXVIII. 817 The next call was upon S——, a young law-student. **1945** G. L. WILLIAMS *Learning the Law* iv. 36 A teacher must consider..the amount of time actually available to a law student for his studies. **1966** Law student [see *law school* above]. **1845** C. M. KIRKLAND *Western Clearings* 42 George Burnet had just come home after finishing what he called his '*law studies'. *a* **1720** SHEFFIELD (Dk. of Buckhm.) *Wks.* (1753) I. 160 We did not, as *law-suitors for contention, Disburse more charges than the prize was worth. **1880** GLADSTONE in *Daily News* 17 June 2/4 Allowing for all the differences in the *law system of the two countries. **1649** MILTON *Eikon.* v. 45 To which and other *Law-tractats I referr the more Lawyerlie mooting of this point. **1845** CARLYLE *Cromwell* (1871) V. 60 Hundreds of *Law-vocables. *a* **1654** SELDEN *Table-T.* (Arb.) 64 *Allodium* is a *Law-word contrairy to *Feudum.* **1645** RUTHERFORD *Tryal & Tri. Faith* (1845) 198 God healeth the sinner from his guiltiness (it is a law-word). *Ibid.* 149 It is likely Judas and Cain..had some *law-work in their heart, and yet were never converted. **1818** SCOTT *Hrt. Midl.* xii, Wi' ony rag of human righteousness, or formal law-work. **1860** N. MACMICHAEL *Pilgrim Ps.* 251 Law-work keeps him struggling..for years before he finds peace in believing. **1577** VAUTROUILLIER *Luther on Ep. Gal.* 131, I haue the author and Lord of the Scripture wyth me, on whose side I will rather stand, then beleue all the rablement of *Law-workers. **1701** *Lond. Gaz.* No. 3749/6 The original Titles to Estates, and other *Law-Writings.

b. Pertaining to or commonly used for legal treatises or documents, as ***law-binding***, ***-calf***, ***-sheep***.

1727–51 CHAMBERS *Cycl.* s.v. *Book-binding*, French-binding, law-binding, marble-binding [etc.]. **1837** DICKENS *Pickw.* xxxiv, Goodly octavos, with a red label behind, and that underdone-pie-crust-coloured cover, which is technically known as 'law-calf'. **1879** *Cassell's Techn. Educ.* IV. 89/1 The uncoloured skin..is used in the peculiar style of binding called Law. **1895** J. ZAEHNSDORF *Hist. Bookbind.* 25 Law Calf.—Law books are usually bound in calf left wholly uncoloured.

c. with the sense 'as defined by law, according to the legal view', as in ***law-goodness***, ***-guilt***, ***-honesty***, ***-infant***, ***obligation***, †***power***, ***reckoning***, ***righteousness***; ***law-honest*** adj.

1850 ROBERTSON *Serm.* Ser. III. v. 65 Goodness..which is produced by rewards and punishments—*law goodness, *law-righteousness. **1645** RUTHERFORD *Tryal & Tri. Faith* (1845) 197 Not only shall justification free us..from all *law-guilt..but [etc.]. **1838** J. F. COOPER *Homeward Bound* III. xi. 333 Mr. Dodge belonged to a tolerably numerous class, that is quaintly described as being '*law honest', that is to say, he neither committed murder nor petty larceny. **1873** *Spectator* 22 Feb. 236/2 To find representatives who after a double winnowing are commonly 'law honest', will abstain from actual bribes or actual plundering of the State till. **1905** *Daily Chron.* 6 Dec. 7/7 What may be called *law-honesty, the kind of honesty necessary in order to avoid falling into the clutches of the law. **1810** *Sporting Mag.* XXXV. 62 The consent and approbation of the fair *law-infant. **1645** RUTHERFORD *Tryal & Tri. Faith* (1845) 201 Christ's pardon in like manner doth remove a *law-obligation to eternal death. **1647** *Mercurius Brit.*, *His Spectacles* 4 A King..whilest he is absent from his Parliament as a man, he is legally and in his *Law-power present. **1800** A. SWANSTON *Serm. & Lect.* I. 326 The sufferings which Christ endured are his by God's gracious imputation and in *law-reckoning.

22. **a.** Objective, as ***law-bearer***, ***-evader***, ***-framer***, ***-fulfiller***, †***-monger***, ***-preacher***, †***-racker***; ***law-catching***, ***-making***, ***-preaching*** vbl. sbs.; ***law-magnifying*** vbl. sb. and ppl. a.; also ***law-contemning***, ***-cracking***, ***-loving***, †***-monging***, ***-revering*** adjs. **b.** Instrumental, as ***law-beaten***, ***-bound***, ***-condemned***, ***-forced***, ***-governed***, ***-locked***, ***-made***, ***-ridden*** adjs. **c.** Locative, as ***law-learned*** adj.; hence ***law-learnedness***.

1483 *Cath. Angl.* 210/2 A *Law berer, *legifer.* **1645** MILTON *Tetrach.* Wks. 1851 IV. 190 Let the buyer beware, saith the old *Law-beaten terme. *a* **1613** OVERBURY *Charac.*, *Franklin* Wks. (1856) 149 To bee *law-bound among men, is like to be hide-bound among his beasts. **1625** FLETCHER & SHIRLEY *Nt. Walker* IV. i, I'll..let my Lady go a-foot a *Law-catching. **1681** FLAVEL *Meth. Grace* vi. 120, I am a *law-condemned, and a self-condemned sinner. **1805** SCOTT *Last Minstr.* IV. xxiv, Your *law contemning kinsmen. **1606** *Wily Beguiled* B 4 b, This *lawcracking cogfoyst. **1894** H. GARDENER *Unoff. Patriot* 2 Being both a law-breaker and a *law-evader. **1794** COLERIDGE *Relig. Musings* I. 102 The morsel toss'd by *law-forced charity. **1876** FOX BOURNE *Locke* III. xiii. 392–3 Expert *law-framers. **1870** SPURGEON *Treas. Dav.* Ps. xl. 8 The atoning sacrifice, the *law-fulfiller. **1938** *Burlington Mag.* Mar. 148/1 The '*law-governed' development of the language of form. **1960** H. EDWARDS *Spirit Healing* iii. 25 Every change within our comprehension is the result of law-governed forces applied to the subject. **1606** SYLVESTER *Du Bartas* II. iv. II. *Trophies* 1308 The *Law-learned Sage. **1658–9** *Burton's Diary* (1828) IV. 121 A law-learned head and an eloquent tongue. **1895** JANE MENZIES *Cynewulf's Elene* 38 The law-learned one, the ancient sage. **1826** BENTHAM in *Westm. Rev.* Oct. 492 *Law-learnedness in this and the higher grade. **1886** G. ALLEN *Maimie's Sake* xiv, We must behave ourselves like civilized people, clothed and *law-locked. **1698** SYLVESTER *Du Bartas* II. ii. III. *Colonies* 424 Th' ingenious, Towr-full, and *Law-loving Soil, Which Jove did with his Leman's name en-stile. **1622** DRAYTON *Poly-olb.* XXII. 113 His father the lord Wells, who he suppos'd might sway His so outrageous son with his lov'd *law-made brother, Sir Thomas Dymock. **1744** E. ERSKINE *Serm.* Wks. 1871 III. 185 The *law-magnifying righteousness of Christ. **1786** A. GIB *Sacred Contempl.* 337 The justice-satisfying and law-magnifying of His atonement. **1690** CHILD *Disc. Trade* (ed. 4) 33 Every nation does proceed according to peculiar methods of their own in ..*law-making. **1645** MILTON *Colast.* 18 Though this catering *Law-monger bee bold to call it wicked. *a* **1693** *Urquhart's Rabelais* III. xliv. 362 *Law-monging Attorneys. **1645** RUTHERFORD *Tryal & Tri. Faith* (1845) 144 Your *law-preachers lead men from the foundation, Christ. **1875** E. WHITE *Life in Christ* III. xxii. (1878) 322 Those ante-diluvians who had heard the *law-preaching of Enoch and of Noah. **1635** BRATHWAIT *Arcad. Pr.* 217 If I should be Judge,..*Law-rackers should be all made readers of the Anatomy Lecture in Pluto's court. **1862** S. LUCAS *Secularia* 200 Their act is memorably characteristic of our *law-revering race. **1835** MARRYAT *Olla Podr.* iii, England is no longer priest-ridden..but..she is **law*-ridden. **1874** HELPS *Soc. Press.* ii. 23 A very considerably law-ridden country.

23. Special comb.: **law-act**, (*a*) a transaction in law; (*b*) (see ACT *sb.* 8); **law-bible**, applied by Irish Roman Catholics to the Authorized Version; **law-bred** *a.*, bred or trained in legal studies; **law-church** (disparagingly), the Established Church; †**law-daughter** (see 3 c above); †**law-driver**, one who drives or works at the law; a lawyer; **law enforcement**, enforcement of the law; freq. *attrib.*; so ***law-enforcer***; †**law-father** (see 3 c above); †**law-free** *a.*, not legally convicted or condemned; **law-French**, the corrupt variety of Norman French used in English law-books; †**law-house**, a court of justice; **law-keeper**, †(*a*) a guardian of the law; = Gr. νομοφύλαξ; (*b*) an observer of the law; **law-Latin**, the barbarous Latin of early English statutes; **law-lord**, (*a*) one of the members of the House of Lords qualified to take part in its judicial business; (*b*) in Scotland *colloq.*, one of those judges who have by courtesy the style of 'Lord'; **law-lordship**, the office or dignity of a law-lord; **law-neck-cloth**, humorous for 'a pillory'; **law-office** (*U.S.*), a lawyer's office; **law-officer**, a public functionary employed in the administration of the law, or to advise the government in legal matters; *spec.* in England, ***law-officer*** (***of the Crown***), either the Attorney or Solicitor General; hence ***law-officership***; †**law-place**, (*a*) a post as law professor; (*b*) position in the eye of the law; **law-post**, ? a post marking the limit of 'law' (sense 20); †**law-prudent** *a.* [after *juris prudentia*], marked by legal learning; †**law-puddering**, pothering about the law; †**law-setter**, a lawgiver; **law station** *slang*, a police station; **law-term**, (*a*) a word or expression used in law; (*b*) one of the periods appointed for the sitting of the law-courts; **law-writer**, †(*a*) a legislator; (*b*) one who writes books on law; (*c*) one who copies or engrosses legal documents.

1645 RUTHERFORD *Tryal & Tri. Faith* (1845) 215 The renewed apprehension of the grace of God..maketh not a new forensical and *law-act. **1708** J. CHAMBERLAYNE *St. Gt. Brit.* I. III. xi. 470 After a Man has been five years Batchellor of Law, or seven years Master of Arts, he may be Doctor of Law, provided he keep two Law-Acts, and Oppose once. **1847** W. CARLETON *Traits Irish Peasantry* (1860) II. 5 The consoling reflection that he swore only on a *Law Bible. **1836** SIR H. TAYLOR *Statesman* xxxii. 251 The fault of a *law-bred mind lies commonly in seeing too much of a question, not seeing its parts in their due proportions. **1826** in Cobbett *Rur. Rides* (1885) II. 185 He wishes to support the *law-church, and the army. **1845** G. OLIVER *Biog. Jesuits* 42 A minister of the Law-church was called in for his opinion. **1583** STANYHURST *Æneis* II. (Arb.) 60 And Hecuba old Princesse dyd I see, with number, an hundred *Law daughters. **1625** FLETCHER & SHIRLEY *Nt. Walker* IV. i, She's the merriest thing among these *law-drivers, And in their studies half a day together. **1936** L. HELLMAN *Days to Come* II. iii. 70 Dowel was found knifed, dead... That gives us a little job of *law enforcement to do. **1955** D. W. MAURER in *Publ. Amer. Dialect Soc.* xxiv. 6 A problem which urgently demands the attention of the legislators, law-enforcement specialists, and the judiciary. **1956** 'E. MCBAIN' *Cop Hater* (1963) xvii. 129 If they can do away with law enforcement, the rest will be easy... First the police, then the National Guard. **1960** *Times* 3 Oct. 13/6 Their functions as law-enforcement officers. **1972** A. ROUDYBUSH *Sybaritic Death* (1974) xiii. 119 His proposal.. to help the overwhelmed police in their law-enforcement task. **1938** *Tablet* 1 Jan. 1/1 The world was pictured as consisting of the law-makers and *law-enforcers. **1975** *Listener* 16 Jan. 67/1 The law enforcers themselves were bent. **1583** STANYHURST *Æneis* II. (Arb.) 54 Next cooms thee lusty Choroebus Soon to king Priamus by law: thus he *lawfather helping. *a* **1670** SPALDING *Troub. Chas. I* (Bannatyne Club) I. 12 To quyte him who had married his sister, so long as he was *law free, he could not with his honour. **1644** MILTON *Educ.* Wks. (1847) 99/2 To smatter Latin with an English mouth, is as ill a hearing as *law French. **1876** DIGBY *Real Prop.* v. 205 *note*, The reports in the Year Books are written in the strange jargon called law-French. *a* **1610** HEALEY *Theophrastus* (1636) 91 Strouting it in the *Lawe house, saying; There is no dwelling in this Citie. **1644** MILTON *Areop.* (Arb.) 49 That no Poet should so much as read to any privat man, what he had writt'n, untill the Judges and *Law-keepers had seen it. **1894** H. GARDENER *Unoff. Patriot* 3 [A man may] be at once a law-breaker and a good man, or a law-keeper and a bad one. *a* **1613** OVERBURY *A Wife* (1638) 192 He hates all but *Law-

Latine. **1713** BERKELEY *Guardian* No. 62 ¶4 An imitation of the polite style,.. is abandoned for law-Latin. **1818** SCOTT *Hrt. Midl.* v, I ken our law-latin offends Mr. Butler's ears. **1773** BURKE *Corr.* (1844) I. 444 The measure..will not be opposed in council by any great *law-lord in the kingdom. **1883** FREEMAN in *Longm. Mag.* II. 482 There has been something like the revival of a kind of professional peerage in the persons of certain of the law-lords. **1901** *Dundee Advertiser* 12 Apr., 'Lord Newbottle'—there never was such a title in the Scottish Peerage, though it was a law-lord's title. **1958** *Times* 24 July 8/7 The sons and daughters of law lords and life peers..shall be treated for their style, rank, dignity, and precedence in the same way as the wives..of hereditary barons. **1972** *Mod. Law Rev.* XXXV. I. 63 Two Law Lords with first instance experience in the Divorce Division. **1882** *Daily News* 3 June 2/2 An Irish Judge had been nominated to fill one of the *law-lordships of the House of Lords. **1789** WOLCOT (P. Pindar) *Expost. Ode* vi. Wks. 1812 II. 228 Perchance *Law Neck-cloths, form'd of deal or oak..Shall rudely hug his harmless throat. **1873** 'MARK TWAIN' & WARNER *Gilded Age* xii. 117 In the anteroom of the *law-office where he was writing. **1896** *Chatauqua Mag.* Dec. 322/1 The daily routine and drudgery of a law-office. **1973** *N.Y. Law Jrnl.* 2 Aug. 16/6 (Advt.), Political Science undergraduate seeks 4 years law study and clerkship in law office to gain credit to take Bar. **1781** SIR W. JONES *Ess. Bailments* 85 The great *law-officer of the Othman court. **1817** *Sp. Earl Liverpool* in *Parl. Debates* 778 It might turn out, that the law officers in 1801 had acted upon their own opinion. **1896** *Daily News* 1 July 7/2 An Under-Secretaryship for India..was a poor substitute for a *Law Officership. **1587** in *Buccleuch MSS.* (Hist. MSS. Comm.) 25 A *Lawe place now voyde by the departure of Mr Doctor Day. *a* **1771** J. GILL in *Treas. Dav.* Ps. cxix. 122 Put himself in their law-place and stead, and became responsible to law and justice for them. **1741** *Compl. Fam.-Piece* II. i. 309 The first, which is next the Dog-house and Pens, is the *Law-Post, and is distant from them 160 Yards. **1645** MILTON *Tetrach.* 55 Heerin declaring his annotation to be slight & nothing *law prudent. —— *Colast.* 16 The Servitor..declaring his capacity nothing refin'd since his *Law-puddering, but still the same it was in the Pantry, and at the Dresser. **1572** L. LLOYD *Pilgr. Pr.* (1607) 65 Lycurgus that auncient *law-setter. **1958** F. NORMAN *Bang to Rights* 50 After a while we came to a *law station. **1959** ANON. *Streetwalker* x. 180, I was in the law station. They got me early. **1693** DRYDEN *Juvenal* (1697) p. lxvi, Writings, which my Author Tacitus, from the *Law-Term, calls *famosos libellos.* **1758** S. HAYWARD *Serm.* i. 11 The word Condemnation is a law-term. **1580** HOLLYBAND *Treas. Fr. Tong, Legislateur*,..a Law-maker, a *lawe-writer. **1852** DICKENS *Bleak Ho.* (1853) x. 94 Our law-writers, who live by job-work, are a queer lot.

†**law**, *sb.*[2] *Obs.* Also 5 lagh, 6 *Sc.* lacht, lauch. Cf. LAWING *sb. Sc.* [ad. ON. *lag* market-price.] Score, share of expense, legal charge.

c **1410** HOCCLEVE *Crt. Good Company* 33 Paie your lagh. **15..** *Peebles to Play* xi, Ane bad pay, ane ither said, nay, Byd quhill we rakin our lauch. **1530** *Extracts Aberd. Reg.* (1844) I. 137 The said day, Iohne Anderson was convicted in ane lacht of vj scillingis..because he [etc.].

law (lɔː), *sb.*[3] *Sc.* and *north.* Also 3–5 lau(e, 4, 7 lawe. [Northern repr. OE. *hláw* LOW *sb.*]

1. A hill, esp. one more or less round or conical. Sometimes with local designation prefixed, as *North Berwick Law, Cushat Law.*

a **1300** *Cursor M.* 4081 Wit þair fee bituix þair lauus. *Ibid.* 7393 'He es', he said, 'þar he es won, Wit our scep apon þe lau.' **13..** *E.E. Allit. P.* B. 992 Noȝt saued watz bot Segor þat sat on a lawe. *c* **1470** HENRYSON *Mor. Fab.* v. (Parl. Beasts) vii, Ane vnicorne come lansand ouer ane law. **1628** COKE *On Litt.* 5 b, Law signifieth a hill. **1807** HEADRICK *Arran* 154 Artificial hills, called laws, in various parts of the country. **1813** HOGG *Queen's Wake* 69 We raide the tod doune on the hill, The martin on the law. **1825** J. WILSON *Noct. Ambr.* Wks. I. 96 Ilk forest shaw and lofty law Frae grief and gloom arouse ye. **1892** STEVENSON *Across the Plains* 209 You might climb the Law..and be-hold the face of many counties.

attrib. *c* **1420** *Anturs of Arth.* iii, He ladde þat lady so longe by þe lawe sides.

†**2.** A monumental tumulus of stones. *Obs.*

1607 CAMDEN *Britannia* 660 In quibus quod mireris, plures sunt lapidum strues admodum magnæ Lawes vocant, quas in memoriam occisorum olim aggestas credunt vicini.

law (lɔː), *v.* [OE. *laȝian*, f. *laȝu* LAW *sb.*[1]]

†**1.** *trans.* To ordain (laws); to establish as a law; to render lawful. *Obs.*

a **1023** WULFSTAN *Hom.* li. (Napier) 274/7 Laȝiaþ gode woroldlaȝan and lecȝað þærtoeacan, þæt ure cristendom fæste stande. *a* **1225** *Leg. Kath.* 1206 As his ahne goddlec lahede hit ant lokede. **1651** N. BACON *Disc. Govt. Eng.* II. xxvii. (1739) 124 The King hath a power of Lawing and Unlawing in Christ's Kingdom.

b. To command or impose as law. *rare*$^{-1}$.

1855 BAILEY *Mystic* 82 The vast Baobab..Within whose cavernous..trunk Meet village senates, lawing peace and war To dusky tribes.

†**c.** *to law it*: to act the lawgiver. *Obs.*

1653 H. COGAN *Scarlet Gown* Ep. Ded., That pragmatique Superintendent Court, and Consistory, which Lords and Lawes it, or would willingly doe so, over the whole world.

d. *Sc.* (? *nonce-use.*) To give the law to, control.

1785 BURNS *Women's Minds* iv, But for how lang the flie may stang, Let inclination law that.

2. *intr.* To go to law, litigate. Also *to law it.* Also *colloq.* or *dial.* in indirect passive.

? *a* **1550** *Hye Way to Spyttel Ho.* 799 in Hazl. *E.P.P.* IV. 59 They that lawe for a debt vntrew. **1581** MULCASTER *Positions* xxxvi. (1887) 138 He will needes lawe it, which careth for no lawe. **1624** FLETCHER *Rule a Wife* IV. iii, Ye must law and claw before ye get it. **1712** ARBUTHNOT *John Bull* II. iii, If we law it on, till Lewis turns honest, I am afraid our credit will run low at Blackwell Hall! *a* **1734** NORTH *Lives* I. 108 There [*sc.* Ho. of Lords] the knight lawed by himself, for no person opposed him. **1866** GEO. ELIOT *F. Holt* (1868) 7 People who inherited estates that were lawed about.

quasi-trans. **1742** FIELDING *J. Andrews* II. v, Two of my neighbours have been at law about a house, till they have both lawed themselves into a gaol.

b. *trans.* To go to law with, proceed against in the courts.

1647 TRAPP *Comm. 1 Cor.* vi. 7 By your litigious lawing one another, you betray a great deal of weaknesse. **1786** NELSON in Nicolas *Disp.* (1845) I. 169 One sends me a challenge; another Laws me: but I keep them all off. **1860** READE *Cloister & H.* (1861) IV. 398 Alas, poor soul! And for what shall I law him? **1870** E. PEACOCK *Ralf Skirl.* II. 117 You can't law a man ye knaw for a job like that.

3. To mutilate (an animal) so as to render it incapable of doing mischief. Almost exclusively *spec.* to EXPEDITATE (a dog). *Obs.* exc. *Hist.*

1534 G. FERRERS tr. *Carta de Foresta* in *Gt. Charter* etc. §6 (1542) B ij b, He whose dog is not lawed [orig. *expeditatus*] & so founde shalbe amercyed [etc.]. **1610** W. FOLKINGHAM *Art of Survey* III. iv. 71 Foote-geld implies a Priuiledge to keepe Dogges within the Forrest not expeditated or lawed sans controule. **1616** *Rich Cabinet* 54 b, His own [cattle] are so ringed, and yoakt, and lawde, that they neuer trespasse on any other man. **1866** *Chamb. Jrnl.* XXVIII. 261 They were forbidden to take anything for lawing dogs. **1886** *Contemp. Rev.* XX. 505 The cur which the husbandman kept might only exist if he had been 'lawed', or so mutilated, that the idea of poaching was for ever banished from his mind.

law (lɔː), *int.* Now *vulgar.* Also 9 **laws.** [Cf. LA, LO, of which it may have been in origin an alteration prompted by an instinctive sense of expressiveness in the vowel sound; in later use it has coalesced with *lor'* = 'Lord!' as an exclamation; cf. LAWD.] An exclamation now expressing chiefly astonishment or admiration, or (often) surprise at being asked a question; in early use chiefly asseverative.

With †*law ye* cf. *la you* s.v. LA.

1588 SHAKS. *L.L.L.* v. ii. 414 To begin Wench, so God helpe me law, My love to thee is sound *sans* cracke or flaw. **1602** MARSTON *Antonio's Rev.* IV. iii. Wks. 1856 I. 125 Lawe I, I begin to swell—puffe. **1620** SHELTON *Quix.* II. xxv. 169 Law ye there (quoth Sancho) did not I tell you [etc.]. **1762** *Ann. Reg.* 134 'O law, madam', said the poor children. **1813** *Sketches Charac.* (ed. 2) I. 59 Law! I wonder at that, replied Mrs. Mansell. **1846** C. M. S. KIRKLAND *Bee-Tree* in *Amer. Short Stories* (1904) 204 Law sakes alive! **1851** MRS. STOWE *Uncle Tom's Cabin* (1852) II. xx. 49 Law, Missis, you must whip me; my old Missis allers whipped me. **1853** 'C. BEDE' *Verdant Green* I. vi, 'Law bless me, sir'. **1863–5** J. THOMSON *Sunday at Hampstead* ix, But law! Think of becoming a poor naked squaw! **1878** MRS. STOWE *Poganuc P.* iii. 26 Laws, he's an old bachelor. **1880** 'MARK TWAIN' *Lett.* (1917) I. 383 A kind-hearted, well-meaning corpse was the Boston young man, but lawsy bless me, horribly dull company. **1881** J. C. HARRIS *Nights with Uncle Remus* (1884) xii. 65 'Is dey anybody home?'.. 'Law, no, honey, folks all gone.' **1884** 'MARK TWAIN' *Huck. Finn* xvi. 142 But lawsy, how you did fool 'em, Huck. **1887** R. M. JOHNSTON in *Harper's Mag.* Apr. 729/1 Ah, law me! But it's no business of mine. *Ibid.* 729/2 Good gracious, laws o' mercy, sister! **1914** G. ATHERTON *Perch of Devil* I. 75 'Your room's pretty!' ..'mine's pink—but lawsy!' **1945** [see LAWD].

law, obs. form of LAVE, LAY *sb.*[1], LOW.

'**law-a'biding**, *a.* [f. LAW *sb.*[1] + pr. pple. of ABIDE *v.* The formation may have been due to a reminiscence of LAW-BIDING.] Abiding by, i.e., maintaining or submitting to the law.

1839 *Congress. Globe* Dec., App. 14/2 Being a law-loving and law-abiding man, he had voted to preserve the laws. **1855** *Ibid.* 26 Jan. 416/2 The people of Oregon are a law-abiding, honest and gallant people. **1867** FREEMAN *Norm. Conq.* I. vi. 558 The great Earl..who on every other occasion appears as conciliatory and law-abiding. **1878** BOSW. SMITH *Carthage* 63 If the Roman people had not been the most law-abiding people in the world all public business must have come to a standstill. **1973** C. MULLARD *Black Brit.* II. vi. 68 A racist, however intelligent, will never accept that blacks are just like other average human beings, honest, industrious, clean, law-abiding, intelligent, etc.

Hence **law-abidingness.**

1880 *Fortn. Rev.* Feb. 311 National self-respect demands a decent conformity to law-abidingness and morality. **1889** *Spectator* 28 Sept., That most useful of civic virtues, law-abidingness.

lawaier, -ayer, obs. forms of LAWYER.

lawar(e, obs. Sc. form of LAVER *sb.*[2]

†**law-biding**, *ppl. a. Sc. Obs.* [f. LAW *sb.*[1] + pres. pple. of BIDE *v.* to await.]

1. 'Waiting the regular course of law' (Jam.).

1597 SKENE *De Verb. Sign.* s.v. *Recognition*, Gif the vassall is fugitive for slauchter, and not law bidand, the superiour may [etc.].

2. a. Standing good in law. **b.** Able to answer an accusation.

1637 RUTHERFORD *Lett.* (1862) I. 268, I cannot take God's word without a caution as if Christ had lost and sold His credit and were not in my books responsal and lawbiding. **1755** *Guthrie's Trial* 112 (Jam.) The soul is pursued for guilt more or less, and is not law-biding; Christ Jesus is the city of refuge.

law-board (-brod, etc.), var. LAY-BOARD *dial.*

'**law-book.** [f. LAW *sb.*[1] + BOOK; cf. ON. *lǫg-bók.*]

1. A book containing a code of laws.

c **1200** ORMIN 16944 Þe nahht maȝȝ ec bitacnenn uss All þatt stafflike lare Off Moysæsess laȝheboc. **1860** MAX MÜLLER *Hist. Sanskrit Lit.* Introd. (ed. 2) 62 The different dates ascribed to Manu as the author of our Law-book.

2. Chiefly *pl.* A book treating of law.

1555 GARDINER *Will* in *Wills Doctors Com.* (1863) 43, I bequeath to Thomas Worliche all my humanitie and lawe bookes. **1660** *Trial Regic.* 10 Gentlemen, Let me tell you what our Law-books say. **1720–21** C. PHIPPS in *Swift's Lett.* (1766) II. 13 The oldest man alive, or any law-book, cannot give any instance of such a proceeding. **1781** GIBBON *Decl. & F.* xvii. II. 42 In the fourth century, many camels might have been laden with law-books. **1876** BANCROFT *Hist. U.S.* I. xvii. 495 Europe suffered from the multiplication of law-books.

'**law-borrow.** *Sc. Law.* Now only in *plural.* Also 5 -burgh, *pl.* -borowis, -bowrous, -boris, 7–9 -burrows. [f. LAW *sb.*[1] + BORROW *sb.*] The legal security required from a person that he will not injure the person, family, or property of another; security of the peace. Also ***action, bond of law-borrows. to swear a law-borrows against*** (a person): to make an affidavit of being in danger from him.

1457 *Sc. Acts Jas. II* (1814) II. 51/1 And gif ony man be fedyt..þe schirref sall furthwithe of bath þe parteis tak law borowis. **1474** *Extracts Aberd. Reg.* (1844) I. 406 He was nocht under law borrowis anent the said William of Cadiou. **1484** *Ibid.* 40 William Futhes is becumin law burgh that William Vmfray salbe vnscathit in tym cuming. **1597** *Sc. Acts Jas. II*, §13 *heading*, The Proclamation of generall peace: Of law-burrowes. **1609** SKENE *Reg. Maj., Crimes* 142 Gif ane complains to the Schiref, and desires lawborrows of ane other man; and the Schiref doe not his office thereanent, he sall pay fourtie poundes. **1752** J. LOUTHIAN *Form of Process* App. (ed. 2) 281 Interdictions, Inhibitions, and Law-burrows. **1864** A. LEIGHTON *Leg. Edin.* (1886) 171 Had forced the deacon to swear a lawborrows against him. **1884** *Manch. Exam.* 18 Sept. 5/5 John Fraser, sheriff officer, raised an action of lawburrows against John Norrie Anderson.

fig. **1636** RUTHERFORD *Lett.* (1862) I. 174 Men would have law-borrows against Christ's cross.

†**law-breach.** *Obs.* [OE. *lahbryce*, f. *lah-*, *laȝu* LAW *sb.*[1] + *bryce* breaking.] A breach or breaking of the law.

1014 WULFSTAN *Serm. ad Anglos* in *Hom.* xxxiii. (Napier) 166 *note*, þæt wæs ȝeworden..ðurh lædwedra lahbryce. **1382** WYCLIF *Isa.* i. 5 Lawe breche or trespassing aȝeins the lawe.

†**law-break**, *v. Obs. rare*$^{-1}$. [f. LAW *sb.*[1] + BREAK *v.*; after next sb.] *intr.* To break the law.

1382 WYCLIF *Is.* xlviii. 8, I wot forsothe, for lawe breking thou shalt lawe breke [L. *praevaricans praevaricaberis*].

'**law-breaker.** [OE. had *lahbreca* of the same meaning.] One who violates the law.

[*a* **1050** *Liber Scintill.* ii. (1889) 9 Þar healdan geþyld we na scylan ac wiðstandan þam lahbrecan.] *c* **1440** *Promp. Parv.* 289/2 Lawe brekare, *legirumpus.* *c* **1450** *Mirour Saluacioun* 3550 Lawbrekers and ydolatrers with bolde visage blamed hee. **1547** *Primer* O j, Deliuer me..out of the hande of the ..lawe breaker. **1611** SHAKS. *Cymb.* IV. ii. 75 Thou art a Robber, A Law-breaker, a Villaine; yeeld thee Theefe. **1663** KILLIGREW *Parson's Wed.* v. ii. (1664) 141 That Tongue.. which now growes hoarse with flattering the great Law-breakers. **1876** *Oxford Bible-Helps, Mountains*, It was on Mount Ebal that the cursing of the law-breakers took place.

So **law-breaking** *vbl. sb.* and *ppl. a.*

1767 *Sp. agst. Suspending & Disp. Prerogative* in Hansard *Parl. Hist.* (1813) XVI. 258 There was no such distinction in the days, when the law-making and the law-breaking prerogative walked forth at noon tide. **1881** *Times* 9 Apr. 11/5 Temporal Courts would deal more timidly with clerical law-breaking.

lawch, lawchter: see LAUGH *v.*, LAUGHTER[1].

Lawd (lɔːd). Chiefly *U.S.* Also **Lawdy.** Cf. LAW *int.* Local (esp. Black English) variants of *Lord*, *Lordy*, usually as interjections or in humorous contexts.

1881 J. C. HARRIS *Nights with Uncle Remus* (1884) xxxix. 183 Lawdy mussy, Brer Rabbit! Whar my vittles? **1898** 'J. KERR' *Cheery Bk.* 121 But, Lawdy! How dat coon can kiss! **1901** G. B. SHAW *Captain Brassbound's Conversion* I. 226 *Drinkwater.* Lawd,..wot jagginses them jurymen was! *Ibid.* II. 242 Git the plice ready for the British herristorcracy, Lawd Ellan and Lidy Wineflete? **1926** W. C. HANDY *Blues* 64 Feel so low down an' sad Lawd Lost ev'rything I ever had. *Ibid.* 91 Why did I go away? I used to be so gay There'll come a day! Oh Lawdy Lawd how happy I'll be Down home in Florida. **1928** R. BRADFORD in B. A. Botkin *Treas. S. Folklore* (1949) III. ii. 485 So about dat time de Lawd comed up on old man Noah. **1945** MENCKEN *Amer. Lang.* Suppl. I. 664 Euphemisms... For *Lord*: *land, law, lawks, lawdy, lawsy.* **1970** R. D. ABRAHAMS *Positively Black* vi. 142 Lawdy, lawdy, lawdy, lawd, I used to be your reg'lar, now I got to be your dog. **1971** *Black Scholar* Sept. 44/2 'Lawd!' he blurts out and begins to giggle. **1973** *Black World* Sept. 29 Hughes sometimes created short, vignette-type poems with the blues feeling..as he did in 'Bad Morning': Here I sit with my shoes mismated. Lawdy-mercy! I's frustrated!

lawd, obs. form of LAUD, LEWD *a.*

'**law-day.** *Obs.* exc. *Hist.* [f. LAW *sb.*[1]]

1. The day for the meeting of a court of law, esp. of the sheriff's court, once in six months, or of the court leet, once a year; hence used for the session of such a court, and the court itself.

1235–52 *Rent. Glaston.* (Som. Rec. Soc.) 189 Salvis duobus laghedaghes. **1292** *Year-bk. 20 & 21 Edw. I* (Rolls) 339 A deus lauedaues [*printed* lauedanes] par an. **1331** *Lit.*

Cantuar. 31 Oct. (Rolls) I. 403 Ad exigendum et manutenendum jura..ac etiam Curiam nostram de Godmersham, quæ dicitur Laghe daye, die Veneris proxime sequente. **1444** *Extracts Aberd. Reg.* (1844) I. 399 The law dayis eftir Michelmess. **1467** in *Eng. Gilds* (1870) 370 That the articles of the yelde aforeseid be redde and declared at the lawday. **1516** in W. H. Turner *Select. Rec. Oxford* 16 Two tymys yn yᵉ yere to kepe a lawedaye there. **1535** *Act 27 Hen. VIII*, c. 26 §23 [Lordes marchers] shall have..their Lordshippes Courtis Baron Court letes and Lawedayes. **1589** R. HARVEY *Pl. Perc.* (1860) 5, I will present you at the law day for a ryot. **1604** SHAKS. *Oth.* III. iii. 140 Who ha's that breast so pure, Wherein vncleanly Apprehensions Keepe Leetes and Law-dayes? **1613** PURCHAS *Pilgrimage* (1614) 201 Thirdly, that Thursday should be Court or law-day for deciding controversies. **1641** *Termes de la Ley* 194 Law-day signifies a Leet or Sheriffes tourne. **1710** HEARNE *Collect.* 23 Apr. (O.H.S.) II. 379 A Lawday of the Dean and Canons of Hereford. **1890** GROSS *Gild. Merch.* II. 105 The 'curia legalis' (Law-day) was held yearly the Monday next after the feast of St. Hilary.

2. A day appointed for the discharge of a bond, after which the debtor could not at common law be relieved from the forfeiture.

1492 RYMAN *Poems* xcii. 6 in *Archiv. Stud. neu. Spr.* LXXXIX. 266, I make an ende within shorte space. I sette no lawe day in the case.

lawdeable, obs. form of LAUDABLE.

lawe, obs. form of LAUGH, LAVE.

†**lawed**, *ppl. a. Obs.* [f. LAW *sb.*¹ + -ED².] Provided with laws.

1639 SALTMARSH *Policy* 109 In attempts of conquest spie out and informe your selfe first, whether they be such as are well lawed and disciplined, or carelesse and disordered.

lawed, obs. form of LEWD.

laweour, -er(e, -eyer(e, obs. ff. LAWYER.

lawer(e, obs. Sc. form of LAVER *sb.*²

lawful ('lɔːfʊl), *a.* Forms: 4 laghful, 4–6 *Sc.* lachful, (5 laffull), 5–6 *Sc.* lauch(t)ful(l, 6 laufull, law(e)foll, 6–8 lawfull, 6– lawful. [f. LAW *sb.*¹ + -FUL. Cf. ON. *lǫgfullr.*]

1. a. According or not contrary to law, permitted by law. Frequent in predicative use.

1398 TREVISA *Barth. De P.R.* XVII. xlviii. (1495) 632 It was not lawfull to defoylle the laurer tree in vnhoneste and vnlawfull vses. *c* **1440** *Promp. Parv.* 289/2 Lawfulle, *legitimus.* **1526** TINDALE *John* v. 10 It is the sabboth day, it is not laufull for the to cary thy beed. **1535** COVERDALE *Ezek.* xxxiii. 16 In so moch as he doth now the thinge that is lawfull and right, he shall lyue. **1560** DAUS tr. *Sleidane's Comm.* 250 It is lawfull for all men, to save themselves from violence. **1590** SWINBURNE *Testaments* 11 By this word lawfull is excluded..whatsoeuer is contrary to iustice, pietie, or equity. **1665** MANLEY *Grotius' Low C. Warres* 739 Upon debate of the matter in the great Council of the Kingdome, and in a lawful manner. **1718** LADY M. W. MONTAGU *Let. to C'tess Bristol* 10 Apr., He..inquired..whether it was lawful to permit it. **1796** H. HUNTER *St.-Pierre's Stud. Nat.* (1799) III. 642, I shall not examine whether that possession be lawful. **1817** W. SELWYN *Law Nisi Prius* (ed. 4) II. 922 It shall be lawful for the jury..to find a verdict for the plaintiff. **1835** I. TAYLOR *Spir. Despot.* vi. 249 Constantine's establishment of Christianity..declaring it to be a..Lawful Religion. **1849** MACAULAY *Hist. Eng.* v. I. 567 A lawful military operation.

†**b.** Permissible; allowable, justifiable. *Obs.*

1599 SHAKS. *Hen. V*, IV. viii. 122 Is it now lawfull and please your Maiestie, to tell how many is kill'd? **1717** FREZIER *Voy. S. Sea* 69 It seems lawful to believe, that, among the Children of our common Parent, God has formed three Sorts of Colours in the Flesh of Men.

†**c.** Of a disease: ? Normal. *Obs.*

1610 BARROUGH *Meth. Physick* v. xxi. (1639) 318 Foure particular orders to be kept in curing a lawfull Oedema.

2. a. Appointed, sanctioned, or recognized by law; legally qualified or entitled. Now chiefly in certain traditional collocations, as ***lawful heir, king, money, parliament, sovereign, succession, title***; also, ***lawful captive, prey, prize, (to be) lawful game.***

a **1300** *Cursor M.* 26903 Þas oþer [plightes] the quilk he bette Bot noght wit penance laghful sett. **1439** *E.E. Wills* (1882) 122, xx markes of laufull money. *c* **1440** *Jacob's Well* 98 Forȝeue þi lawefull accyoun, & seke ferst loue. **1456** *Extracts Burgh Rec. Peebles* (1872) 111 Geyf thar was ony lachful ar to that land. **1526** *Galway Arch.* in *10th Rep. Hist. MSS. Comm.* App. v. 402 No carpenter nor masson shall have no workeman but that which shallbe laufull workeman in that sience [*sic*]. **1535** STEWART *Cron. Scot.* (1858) III. 393 His eldest sone..to his place suld succeid As lauchtfull air. **1560** DAUS tr. *Sleidane's Comm.* 20 b, Lawfull succession. *Ibid.* 243 Yf they have any lawful impediment. **1562** WINȜET *Cert. Tractates* Wks. 1888 I. 2 Thre Questionis, twecheing the lauchful vocatioun of Iohne Knox. **1571** *Satir. Poems Reform.* xxvi. 118 He being Crownit in lauchfull Parliament. **1581** *Ibid.* xliv. 101 That lauchfull pastors of the Kirk sould be depryuit. **1595** SHAKS. *John* II. i. 95 Thou hast vnder-wrought his lawfull King. **1604** —— *Oth.* I. ii. 51 If it proue lawfull prize, he's made for euer. **1651** HOBBES *Leviath.* II. xxviii. 165 A Banished man, is a lawfull enemy of the Common-wealth. **1763** *Rhode Island Col. Rec.* (1861) VI. 359 All mortgages, bonds, [etc.]..wherein the payment of money is..promised, shall be taken and understood to mean lawful money. **1766** FORDYCE *Serm. Yng. Wom.* (1767) I. iii. 108 They will consider her as lawful game. **1768** BLACKSTONE *Comm.* III. 69 Prize vessels..condemned in any courts of admiralty or vice-admiralty as lawful prize. **1817** W. SELWYN *Law Nisi Prius* (ed. 4) II. 854 Having no lawful impediment. **1818** CRUISE *Digest* (ed. 2) VI. 278 So that my executrix shall pay in good time all lawful debts. **1871** FREEMAN *Norm. Conq.* (1876) IV. xvii. 54 Himself in his own reading of the law, a lawful King.

†**b.** *ellipt.* = lawful money, weight. *Obs.*

1533 *Churchw. Acc. Croscombe* (Som. Rec. Soc.) 40 For to delyver the sayd x scheppe so good as they ware or ells xiijs. iiijd. in good and lawfoll. **1778** A. ADAMS in *Fam. Lett.* (1876) 343 It takes..fifty pounds lawful for a hundred of sugar, and fifty dollars for a hundred of flour.

c. Of a marriage: Such as the law permits; and regards as valid. Of offspring: Born in lawful wedlock, legitimate.

c **1375** *Sc. Leg. Saints* xxviii. (*Margaret*) 163, I wes borne this towne within, In lauchful bed of folk mychtty. **1513** DOUGLAS *Æneis* III. v. 23 Helenus, The lachfull sone of the king Priamus. *a* **1548** HALL *Chron., Rich. III*, 49 Makyng much suite to have her joyned with him in lawfull matrimony. **1560** DAUS tr. *Sleidane's Comm.* 35 b, The same..ought nowe to be every where received for lawfull wives. *Ibid.* 424 Moste men doubted of the lawful birth of his syster. **1600** SHAKS. *A.Y.L.* III. iii. 71 Truly she must be giuen, or the marriage is not lawfull. **1606** —— *Ant. & Cl.* III. xiii. 107 Haue I..Forborne the getting of a lawfull Race. *a* **1657** SIR W. MURE *Hist. Rowallan* Wks. (S.T.S.) II. 249 The great Stewart..invited home againe Elizabeth Mure to his Lawfull bed. *a* **1699** LADY HALKETT *Autobiog.* (1875) 1 Constant to the only lawfull embraces of the Queen. **1827** JARMAN *Powell's Devises* (ed. 3) II. 247 In case M. B. should die..without leaving lawful issue of her body. **1885** *Law Rep.* 29 Ch. Div. 270 Had been the lawful wife of the testator, and Adelinda his legitimate daughter by her.

d. ***lawful age, years***: the age at which a person attains his legal majority; also, the age at which a person becomes legally competent to perform some act or to hold some office. ***lawful day***: one in which it is lawful to transact business, or some particular kind of business.

a **1548** HALL *Chron., Hen. V*, 80 b, Til my sonne come to his lawful age. **1560** DAUS tr. *Sleidane's Comm.* 424 He himselfe was of lawefull yeres. **1708** *Royal Proclam.* 11 July in *Lond. Gaz.* No. 4456/1 Upon the Tenth Day of October next to come,..if the same be a Lawful Day.

†**3.** Observant of law or duty; law-abiding, faithful, loyal. *Obs.*

c **1375** *Sc. Leg. Saints* ii. (Paulus) 218 For I am cristis lauchtful knycht. *c* **1430** *Hymns Virg.* 113 Ech man þat..loueþ a lawful lijf to lede. *c* **1475** *Rauf Coilȝear* 508 Bot as ane lauchfull man my laidis to leid. **1483** CAXTON *Cato* G iv b, It is the soueraym gyfte of god for to haue a good and lawful wyf. **1560** ROLLAND *Crt. Venus* I. 581 Lute is tressonable: Nocht lauchfull, but scho is lamentable. **1642** J. MARSH *Argum. Militia* 4 Every lawfull Subject is taken to be within the protection of the King. **1890** M. C. FRASER *Let.* Nov. in *Diplomatist's Wife Japan* (1899) II. xxviii. 143 The Japanese are a profoundly lawful people (if I may use the word in its old sense).

†**4.** Pertaining to or concerned with law. *Obs.*

1387 TREVISA *Higden* (Rolls) I. 35 Lawefulman in þe peple [L. *politici in populo*]. **1631** WEEVER *Anc. Funeral Mon.* 722 In matters lawfull to depend vpon the pleasure and direction of the Archbishop.

†**5. a.** quasi-*sb.*; **b.** quasi-*adv.*; **c.** as an exclamation. *Obs.*

1502 *Ord. Crysten Men* (W. de W. 1506) II. vi. 99 In kepynge faythe, trouth and lawfull for yᵉ loue of god pryncypally. **1656** PHILLIPS *Purch. Palt.* (1676) 2 That th' Seller be so old, That he may lawfull sell, thou lawful hold. **1787** GROSE *Prov. Gloss.*, *Lawful*, Oh lawful case, an interjection, Derb. **1790** PEGGE *Derbicisms* (E.D.S.) *s.v.*, Ah lawful, and ah lawful case! exclamations.

6. Describable or governed by laws of nature.

1939 *Nature* 14 Jan. 64/1 Newton and others have found confirmation even for their religious beliefs in the lawful character of physical phenomena. **1958** M. ARGYLE *Relig. Behaviour* i. 2 It is commonly assumed that human behaviour is lawful and that it can be predicted by means of psychological laws and explained in terms of psychological processes. **1959** M. BUNGE *Causality* i. 22 The principle of universal lawfulness..may be taken to read thus: Every single event is lawful, i.e., is determined in accordance with a set of objective laws—whether we know the laws or not. **1975** *Nature* 3 Apr. 416/2 The results show that the tendency..can be brought under lawful control in such a way as to discriminate against the above hypotheses.

lawfully ('lɔːfʊlɪ), *adv.* [f. LAWFUL + -LY².] In a lawful manner.

1. a. In accordance with law.

a **1300** *Cursor M.* 26111 Scrift es opin scheuing o breist Laufulli mad be-for þe preist. *c* **1380** WYCLIF *Wks.* (1880) 74 Þes false men seye in here doyinge þat crist was lafully don to the deþ. *c* **1400** *Destr. Troy* 3512 Qwyle ye lawfully lefe may & your lyf haue. *c* **1430** *Freemasonry* 300 Ȝet most the mayster, by good resone, Warne hem lawfully by-fore none. *c* **1470** HENRYSON *Tale of Dog* 66 This exceptioun Wes of na strenth, nor lauchfullie mycht stand. ? *a* **1500** *Chester Pl.* (Shaks. Soc.) I. 208 This woman..Was wedded lawfullye this other yeaire. **1512** *Act 4 Hen. VIII*, c. 9 Preamble, The heires males of his body laufully begoten. **1526** *Pilgr. Perf.* (W. de W. 1531) 165 b, Thus..we may perceyue what thoughtes..we may lawfully admyt..in yᵉ tyme of the seruyce of god. *a* **1548** HALL *Chron., Hen. VIII* 242 b, That the kyng might lawfully mary where he would. **1552** ABP. HAMILTON *Catech.* (1884) 5 General counsallis lauchfully gaderit in the halye spreit. *c* **1560** A. SCOTT *Poems* (S.T.S.) xxxiv. 58 Ȝit thair is lesum lufe That law fully suld lest. **1588** A. KING tr. *Canisius' Catech.*, *Confess.* 9 Adulterie lauchefullie prouen. **1609** SKENE *Reg. Maj.* Table 74 The defender being lawfullie summoned, may vse his lawfull essonzeis. **1638** R. BAKER tr. *Balzac's Lett.* III. 102 There are certain bounds..which neither you nor we can lawfully passe. **1651** HOBBES *Leviath.* I. xiv. 69 What I lawfully Covenant, I cannot lawfully break. **1765** BLACKSTONE *Comm.* I. xvi. (1793) 573 He may lawfully correct his child, being under age, in a reasonable manner. **1817** W. SELWYN *Law Nisi Prius* (ed. 4) II. 1116 The declaration ought to have stated, that the mare was lawfully on the common. **1818** CRUISE *Digest* (ed. 2) VI. 316 Without having issue on her body lawfully begotten. **1849** MACAULAY *Hist. Eng.* ii. I. 159 Each provincial assembly might lawfully have a permanent president. **1885** DUNCKLEY in *Manch. Weekly Times* 24 Feb. 5/5, I cannot pray for those who are engaged, however lawfully as men may think, in shedding blood.

b. In accordance with laws of nature.

1959 M. BUNGE *Causality* i. 22 The principle of universal lawfulness does not assert that facts are determined by laws, but in accordance with laws, or simply lawfully.

†**2.** Loyally, faithfully. *Obs.*

c **1500** *Melusine* vi. 32 And indide I lawfully [Fr. *leaulment*] promytte you that so shal I doo.

lawfulness ('lɔːfʊlnɪs). [f. LAWFUL + -NESS.]

1. The quality of being lawful; legality; respect for law.

a **1250** *Owl & Night.* 1741 Nawt for þire tale, Ah do for mire laþfulnesse. **1530** PALSGR. 237/2 Laufulnesse, *licitité, loysibleté.* **1597** HOOKER *Eccl. Pol.* v. xlviii. §7 The lawfulnesse of our prayer for deliuerance out of all [calamities]. **1631** GOUGE *God's Arrows* I. xliii. 69 This great instance of Gods being angry, gives an evident demonstration of the lawfulnesse of anger. **1635–56** COWLEY *Davideis* IV. Notes. (1669) 149 That is no more a proof of the Right, than their Practice was of the Lawfulness of Idolatry. **1741** RICHARDSON *Pamela* I. 140 Let him, who has Power to command me, look to the Lawfulness of it. **1855** MACAULAY *Hist. Eng.* xxi. IV. 566 To question the lawfulness of assassination..was to question the authority of the most illustrious Jesuits. **1924** B. WILLIAMS in *History* Jan. 273 The adventures of..the N.W. Mounted Police, in bringing half a continent to lawfulness and peace.

2. The quality of being describable by laws of nature, or of happening or behaving in accordance with certain general principles that always hold good.

1938 B. F. SKINNER *Behavior of Organisms* i. 25 The early classical examples of the reflex were those of which the lawfulness was obvious. **1956** E. H. HUTTEN *Lang. Mod. Physics* vi. 210 To say that causality is the belief in the lawfulness of nature..is therefore quite meaningless. **1959** [see LAWFUL *a.* 6]. **1972** *Science* 16 June 1208/3 Experiences..that do not show consistent patterns..will be distinguished from those phenomena which do show general lawfulness.

lawgh, obs. form of LAUGH *v.*, LOW.

lawgiver ('lɔːgɪvə(r)). [f. LAW *sb.*¹ + GIVER. Cf. Icelandic *lög-gjafari*, Da. *lovgiver.*] One who gives, i.e. makes or promulgates, a law or code of laws; a legislator.

1382 WYCLIF *Job* xxxvi. 22 Lo! heȝe God in his strengthe, and noon to hym lic in lawe ȝiueres [Vulg. *legislatoribus*]. *c* **1400** *Apol. Loll.* 74 Not only is holi writ despicid bi þat sciens, & blasfemid, but God Himsilf þat is þe law ȝeuar. **1535** COVERDALE *Isa.* xxxiii. 22 The Lorde shalbe oure lawe geuer. **1597–8** BACON *Ess.*, *Honour* (Arb.) 70 In the second place are *Legislatores*, Lawgiuers. **1611** BIBLE *Ps.* lx. 7 Iudah is my Lawgiuer. **1689–90** TEMPLE *Ess. Learning* Wks. 1731 I. 292 They are content Pythagoras should pass for a Law-giver, but by no means for a Philosopher. **1786** A. GIB *Sacred Contempl.* I. iii. 36 The Supreme Law-giver is entitled to the absolute subjection of his reasonable creature. **1835** THIRLWALL *Greece* I. 135 Minos appears in the..character..of a wise and just lawgiver. **1842** MIALL in *Nonconf.* II. 1 We bow to no law-giver in the church but Christ. **1876** BANCROFT *Hist. U.S.* VI. Index 510 [Sir Geo. Calvert] a wise and benevolent law-giver.

'**law-giving**, *vbl. sb.* Also 5 **lawes-yovyng**. [f. LAW *sb.*¹ + GIVING *vbl. sb.*] The action or process of giving laws; legislation.

1475 *Bk. Noblesse* (Roxb.) 73 They bene christen men, and lyvyng under your obeissaunce, lawes-yovyng, and yelding to youre lawes. **1645** MILTON *Tetrach.* Wks. 1851 IV. 178 This is the very end of Lawgiving, to abolish evil customs by wholsom Laws. **1876** *Oxford Bible-Helps, Mountains*, Mount Horeb was the scene of the burning-bush and of the law-giving.

'**law-giving**, *ppl. a.* [f. LAW *sb.*¹ + GIVING *ppl. a.*] That gives or makes laws. Also *occas.* that 'gives the law' to or determines.

1581 SIDNEY *Apol. Poetrie* (Arb.) 22 In Turky, besides their lawe-giuing Diuines, they haue no other Writers but Poets. **1645** MILTON *Tetrach.* Wks. 1851 IV. 196 As if the will of God were becom sinfull, or sin stronger then his direct and Law-giving will. **1827** HARE *Guesses* (1859) 310 Men would still worship the creature, under the form of abstractions and laws, instead of the living, lawgiving Creator. **1865** GROTE *Plato* I. i. 11 The nature of number was imperative and lawgiving.

law-hand. The style of hand-writing used for legal documents. Also *occas.*, matter written in this hand.

1731 *Gentl. Mag.* I. 98 It is not the Lawyers that have invented these Law-hands, to keep their clients in ignorance. **1748** HARTLEY *Observ. Man* I. iii. 302 The common Round-hand, various Law-hands, and various Short-hands. **1776** J. ADAMS *Wks.* (1854) IX. 433 You must make yourself sufficiently acquainted with law-french and with the abbreviated law-hand, to read and understand the cases reported in these books. **1852** DICKENS *Bleak Ho.* xlvii, An immense desert of law-hand and parchment.

lawhe, -hyn, obs. forms of LAUGH *v.*

lawier(e, obs. form of LAWYER.

lawine, variant of LAUWINE.

lawing ('lɔːɪŋ), *sb. Sc.* [f. LAW *sb.*² + -ING¹.] A reckoning at a tavern; a tavern-bill.

1535 STEWART *Cron. Scot.* (1858) II. 633 The Scottis countit thair lawing so deir. **1686** G. STUART *Joco-ser. Disc.*

68 Come to my house some other day I'll pay the lawing, gang your way. **1728** RAMSAY *Lure* 4 Night-drinking sots counting their lawin. *a* **1774** FERGUSSON *Leith Races* Poems (1845) 33 They rake the grunds o' ilka barrel To profit by the lawin. **1824** SCOTT *Redgauntlet* ii, No man should enter the door of a public-house without paying his lawing.

b. *Comb.*: **lawing-free** *a.*, not called upon for one's share in the bill; scot-free.

17.. *Song, Andro & his Cutty Gun* in Ramsay *Tea-t. Misc.* (1775) II. 229 She heght to keep me lawing-free. **1794** *Poems, Eng. Scot. & Lat.* 103 I'm no for letting ye, ye see, (As I ware rich) gang lawin free.

lawing ('lɔːɪŋ), *vbl. sb.* [f. LAW *v.* + -ING¹.] The action of the vb. LAW.

1. Going to law; litigation. *Obs.* exc. *arch.*

c **1485** *E.E. Misc.* (Warton Club) 51 As many as her doth here For lawing schalle they not stere. **1526** TINDALE *2 Cor.* xii. 20, I feare lest there be founde amonge you lawynge [Gr. ἔρεις, WYCL. stryuyngis, Cov. debates, 1611 variance, 1881 (R.V.) strife]. **1554–9** T. WATERTOUNE in *Songs & Ball.* (1860) 10 Behold throughe lawyng howe som be brought bar. **1586** J. HOOKER *Hist. Irel.* in *Holinshed* II. 54/2 Lawing & vexation in the towns, one dailie suing and troubling another. **1602** CAREW *Cornwall* 64a, To defray the extraordinarie charge of building, marriage, lawing, or such like. **1640** D. CAWDREY *Three Serm.* (1641) 2 Warre is but a more public kind of Lawing. **1737** OZELL *Rabelais* III. v. 33 *note*, So Lawing was his natural Element. **1891** B. HARTE *1st Fam. Tasajara* iv, It might be a matter of 'lawing' hereafter.

Proverb. **1562** J. HEYWOOD *Epigr.* (1867) 180 Great lawyng, small louyng. **1631** BP. WEBBE *Quietn.* (1657) 201 Then should we have less lawing and more love.

attrib. **1598** BARRET *Theor. Warres* 167 It is not so light a matter to skirmish among the musket bullet, as to pen out a Lawing plea.

2. The action of cutting off the claws or ball of a dog's forefeet; expeditation. *Obs.* exc. *Hist.*

1656 BLOUNT *Glossogr.*, Lawing of dogs. **1768** BLACKSTONE *Comm.* III. 72 The court of regard, or survey of dogs, is to be holden every third year for the lawing or expeditation of mastiffs. **1876** FREEMAN *Norm. Conq.* V. xxiii. 163 In his love for the chase he..kept up the cruel mutilation, the lawing, as it was called, of all dogs in the neighbourhood of the royal forests.

†'**lawing**, *ppl. a. Obs. rare*⁻¹. [f. LAW *v.* + -ING².] Given to litigation.

1640 D. CAWDREY *Three Serm.* (1641) Ep. Ded., To strangle the lawlesse contentions of this Lawing age.

†'**lawish**, *a. Obs.* [f. LAW *sb.*¹ + -ISH.] Pertaining to the law, savouring of the law. In quots. referring to the ceremonial or Mosaic law.

1560 BECON *Catech.* Wks. 1564 I. 444b, This lawysh sprinkling was a figure of the blood of Christ. **1654** VILVAIN *Theol. Treat.* iv. 118 Al Lawish Ceremonies which prefigured him [are] abolished.

lawit, obs. Sc. form of LEWD, lay.

lawk, lawks (lɔːk(s), *int.* Also 8–9 **lauk**. [vulgar form of LACK *sb.*² or deformation of LORD.]

= Lord! Also ***lawk-a-daisy (me)*** and as sb. = LACK-A-DAISY. ***lawk-a-mercy (-mussy)*** = Lord have mercy!; also as *v.* = to cry 'Lawk-a-mercy!', and as quasi-*adj.*

1768–74 TUCKER *Lt. Nat.* (1834) II. 168 Lauk! that cannot be like mistress, for she has never a blue gown. **1837** DICKENS *Pickw.* xxxix, Lauk, Mr. Weller,..how you do frighten one! *a* **1845** HOOD *Lost Heir* 25 Lawk help me, I don't know where to look. **1864** J. PAYN *Sir Massingberd* 33 Spread-eagled fruit-trees, or, as school-boys called them, 'lawk-a-daises'. **1886** *Pioneer* (N.Y.) Oct. (Cent.), 'Lawks!' exclaimed Mrs. Partington, 'what monsters these master-builders must be!' **1890** BARING-GOULD *Arminell* xlix. 464 Lawk, miss! She wouldn't stand no nonsense. **1893** —— *Cheap Jack Z.* I. 10 The servant maids..were..lawk-a-mussying and oh-mying over the bargains. **1909** J. MASEFIELD *Tragedy of Nan* I. 8 Idle lawkamercy girl. **1927** B. L. K. HENDERSON *Chats about our Mother Tongue* i. 54 Lawkamercy, lad, what's that?

lawland, Sc. form of LOWLAND.

lawle, obs. Sc. form of LOWLY.

lawless ('lɔːlɪs), *a.* [f. LAW *sb.*¹ + -LESS.]

1. a. Without law, having no laws; ignorant of, or not regulated by law. Of a law: Not based on principles of right. Now *rare*.

a **1200** *Moral Ode* 291 Þer buð þo heþenemen, þe were lawelese [*v.r.* laȝe-lease]. *a* **1327** *Pol. Songs* (Camden) 254 For miht is riht, the lond is laweles. **1340–70** *Alex. & Dind.* 906 For as bestes ȝe ben by no skile reuled,..So be ȝe, ludus, by-lad & lawe-les alse. **1470–85** MALORY *Arthur* I. xix, Ther was oomen in to their landes people that were laules. **1598** HAKLUYT *Voy.* I. 20 A barbarous and inhumane people whose law is lawlesse. *a* **1656** BP. HALL *Sp. Defence Convocation*, Shall the enemies of the Church..say we are a lawless Church? **1789** BELSHAM *Ess.* I. 4 If the determinations of the will are themselves lawless and uncertain. **1812** BYRON *Ch. Har.* II. xlvii, Albania's chief, whose dread command Is lawless law. **1836** W. IRVING *Astoria* III. 254 Commercial feuds in the lawless depths of the wilderness. **1956** E. H. HUTTEN *Lang. Mod. Physics* vi. 215 This confusion has prompted the view that chance events are lawless.

b. Exempt from law, not within the province of law, above or beyond the reach of law. †Also, in the position of an outlaw.

c **1250** BRACTON *De Legibus* III. tract. II. xi. §1 & extunc utlagabitur, sicut ille qui est extra legem, sicut Laughelesman [*v.r.* Laghelesman]. **1602** *How to choose good wife* H 4, I haue procur'd a licence, and this night We will be married in a lawlesse Church. **1632** MASSINGER *City Madam* v. ii, You shall find you are not lawless, and that your moneys Cannot justify your villanies. **1656** S. H. *Gold. Law* 49 He is not bound to it, for the Lord of the Law is Lawless. **1685** BAXTER *Paraphr. N.T.* Matt. xii. 37 Christ hath not made us lawless..in vain. **1865** MOZLEY *Mirac.* vi. 117 Such an anomalous occurrence would be lawless, and a contradiction to known law.

2. a. Of persons, their actions: Regardless of, or disobedient to law. †Occas. of an action: Illegal, unlawful (*obs.*). Of passions, etc.: Uncontrolled by law, unbridled, licentious.

a **1300** *Cursor M.* 7304 (Gött.) For nouþer er ȝe war ne wise, Bot for ȝour riches ouer lawe-lis. **13..** *E.E. Allit. P.* C. 170, I leue here be sum losynger, sum lawles wrech. *c* **1394** *P. Pl. Crede* 609 It is a laweles lijf as lordynges vsen. **14..** *Siege Jerusalem* 25/496 Lat neuer þis lawles ledis lauȝ at his harmys. **1576** FLEMING *Panopl. Epist.* 36 Great is the lawlesse laying on of the sword and warlike weapon. **1588** SHAKS. *Tit. A.* I. i. 312 A Valliant sonne in-law thou shalt enioy: One, fit to bandy with thy lawlesse Sonnes. **1591** —— *Two Gent.* IV. i. 54 That they may hold excus'd our lawlesse liues. **1594** —— *Rich. III*, I. iv. 224 He needs no indirect or lawlesse course, To cut off those that haue offended him. **1604** DEKKER *Honest Wh.* Wks. 1873 II. 133 Lawlesse desires are seas scorning all bounds. **1642** FULLER *Holy & Prof. St.* V. xiv. 411 At the Innes of Court under pretence to learn Law, he learns to be lawlesse. **1697** DRYDEN *Virg. Georg.* II. 637 Wine urg'd to lawless Lust the Centaurs Train. *a* **1704** T. BROWN *Sat. Woman* Wks. 1730 I. 56 Revenge implacable, and lawless fires. **1812** CRABBE *Tales* 3 Beneath him fix'd, our man of law, That lawless man the foe of order, saw. **1846** KEBLE *Lyra Innoc.* (1873) 40 Shaming lawless mirth. **1855** MACAULAY *Hist. Eng.* xiii. III. 326 He should be protected against lawless violence. **1888** M. MORRIS *Claverhouse* x. 183 Among these lawless spirits, he who would be obeyed must be feared.

absol. **1557** N. T. (Genev.) *1 Tim.* i. 9 The Lawe is..geuen ..vnto the lawles. **1809–10** COLERIDGE *Friend* (1865) 137, I have said that to withstand the arguments of the lawless, the Anti-jacobins proposed to suspend the law.

b. said of animals and inanimate objects.

1738 WESLEY *Psalms* LXXXIX. vi, Thou dost the lawless Sea controul. **1781** GIBBON *Decl. & F.* lxxi. III. 803 The lawless river overturned the palaces..on its banks. **1854** BADHAM *Halieut.* 154 A prison for wild lawless birds.

Hence '**lawlessly** *adv.*, in a lawless manner.

1591 SHAKS. *Two Gent.* v. iii. 14 He..will not vse a woman lawlesly. *a* **1656** BP. HALL *Imposition Hands* §14 Wks. 1808 IX. 808 How lawlessly vicious are the lives of too many. **1972** *Daily Tel.* 4 Aug. 2/8 The council is insistent that it is not behaving lawlessly.

lawlessness ('lɔːlɪsnɪs). [f. LAWLESS + -NESS.] The quality of being lawless; disregard of, or disobedience to, law or rule.

1591 SPENSER *M. Hubberd* 1310 Gluttonie, malice, pride, and covetize, And lawlesnes raigning with riotize. **1611** COTGR., *Illegalité*, .. lawlesnesse. **1855** MACAULAY *Hist. Eng.* xviii. IV. 200 A frightful instance of the lawlessness and ferocity of those marauders. **1860** J. THRUPP *Introd. to Ps.* II. 69 Unholiness and lawlessness of life. **1871** MORLEY *Carlyle* in *Crit. Misc.* Ser. I. 215 Byron, whose genius, daring, and melodramatic lawlessness, exercised what now seems such an amazing fascination over the least revolutionary of European nations.

law-like ('lɔːlaɪk), *a.* [f. LAW *sb.*¹ + LIKE.]

a. Like to law, having a resemblance to law, or to legal phraseology or proceedings. Now *rare*.

†**b.** Disposed or inclined to law or rule. *Obs.*

1553 GRIMALDE *Cicero's Offices* I. (1558) 3 Plato coulde haue spoken very grauelie and plentifully if he would haue practised ye lawlike sort of pleading. **1575** GASCOIGNE *Dulce bellum* cciii, Let not my verse your lawlike minds displease. **1638** LISLE *Ags. Monum., Lord's Prayer* &c., The ten lawlike words, that God himself taught Moyses. **1644** MILTON *Divorce* II. vii. 47 The giving of any law or law-like dispence to sin for hardnesse of heart. **1818** COBBETT *Pol. Reg.* XXXIII. 301 Provisions dressed forth with all the 'saids' and other law-like words.

c. *Philos.* Of a statement, explanation, etc.: resembling scientific laws in saying that some consequence would occur in any situation of a certain sort, though differing in containing reference to individuals; also, such as to be a law of nature if established as true.

1949 G. RYLE *Concept of Mind* iv. 89 How does the law-like general hypothetical proposition work? It says, roughly, that the glass, *if* sharply struck or twisted, etc. *would*..fly into fragments. **1961** E. NAGEL *Struct. of Sci.* ii. 21 The premises contain at least one 'lawlike' assumption. **1968** M. BLACK in R. Klibansky *Contemp. Philos.* II. 59 Scientific or 'lawlike' generalizations require, in Peirce's phrase, reference to a 'would-be'. **1973** *Nature* 27 July 241/1 Archaeological explanations should be very general, preferably of lawlike form.

†'**lawly**, *a.* and *adv. Obs.* [f. LAW *sb.*¹: see -LY¹ and ².] **A.** *adj.* Lawful. **B.** *adv.* In a lawful manner; lawfully.

c **1200** ORMIN 1965 Laȝheliȝ weddedd wiþþ aniȝ macche. *c* **1200** *Trin. Coll. Hom.* 13 Gef he ben laȝeliche bispusede, þat is unriht. *c* **1220** *Bestiary* 695 In boke is ðe turtres lif writen o rime, wu laȝelike ȝe holdeð luue al hire lif time. *a* **1250** *Prov. Alfred* 72 in *O.E. Misc.* 106 Hw he schule his lond laweliche holde. *Ibid.* 77 Þe eorl and þe eþelyng ibureþ vnder godne king, þat lond to leden myd lawelyche deden.

lawly, lawlynas, obs. ff. LOWLY, LOWLINESS.

'**law-,maker.** [f. LAW *sb.*¹ + MAKER.] One who makes laws; a lawgiver, legislator.

c **1380** *Antecrist* in Todd *3 Treat. Wyclif* 115 David seiþ Lord sett þou a lawe maker upon hem. *a* **1540** BARNES *Wks.* (1573) 207 As though I had condempned the lawemaker, lawe, and execution thereof. **1587** GOLDING *De Mornay* xxv. 381 The Scepter shall not be taken from Iuda, nor the Lawmaker from betweene her feete vntill Silo come. **1623** MASSINGER *Bondman* IV. ii, Wise lawmakers From each well governed private house derived The perfect model of a commonwealth. **1699** BENTLEY *Phal.* 335 Aristotle informs us, that the best and most of the Law-makers were Men of the middle Rank. **1833** HT. MARTINEAU *Tale Tyne* v. 94 The practice of these lawmakers agreed with their principle. **1881** *Times* 5 Feb. 9/3 No laws work uninterruptedly without the supervision of the lawmaker.

lawman ('lɔːmən). Now chiefly *Hist.* [f. LAW *sb.*¹ + MAN; the OE. *lahmann* was prob. a. ON. *laga-*, *lǫgmann-* (nom. *-maðr*), whence Anglo-Latin *lagamannus*, *lagemannus*, by some writers on legal antiquities anglicized as lageman.]

1. *OE. Law.* **a.** One whose official duty it was to declare the law. (Kingsley's use is incorrect.)

a **1000** *Ordin. Dunsætas* c. 3 in Schmid *Gesetze* 360, xii lahmen scylon riht tæcean Wealan and Ænglan, vi Englisce and vi Wylisce. ? *a* **1200** *Laws Edw. Conf.* c. 38 ibid. 518 Postea inquirat justicia per lagemannos. **1865** KINGSLEY *Herew.* xx, 'Where is the lawman of the town?' 'I was lawman last night, to see such law done as there is left', said Pery.

b. In the five Danish boroughs, one of a specified number of magistrates or aldermen (in some cases twelve). (As our knowledge of this class of officials is mainly derived from Domesday, which uses the latinized form *lagemannus*, the word often appears *Hist.* as *lageman.*)

1086 *Domesday Bk.* (1783) I. 336 In ipsa ciuitate erant .xii. Lagemen idest habentes sacam & socam. **1672** COWELL *Interpr.*, Lageman *Homo habens legem*, or as we term it, *Homo legalis*, such as we now call Good men of the Jury. **1675** OGILBY *Brit.* 156 Lincoln..in Doomsday-Book accounted..900 Burgesses, with 12 Lage-men having Sac and Soc. *c* **1818** BRITTON *Lincolnsh.* 796 In the time of the Conqueror, Stamford was governed by the lagemen or aldermen. **1864** SIR F. PALGRAVE *Norm. & Eng.* IV. 5 Lincoln's Lawmen kept their statutes. **1875** STUBBS *Const. Hist.* III. xxi. 578 York..retained..vestiges of the constitutional government by its lawmen which had existed before the Conquest. **1897** MAITLAND *Domesday & Beyond* 89 The lawmen of Stamford had sake and soke within their houses.

2. *Orkney* and *Shetland*. The president of the supreme court in the Orkney and the Shetland Islands respectively. Also ***lawman-general***. (The Scandinavian form *lagman* occurs in historical use.)

1554 tr. *Diploma Bp. Orkney* in *Bannatyne Cl. Misc.* III. (1855) 84 The seill of..Henrie Randale lawman [orig. *legiferi*]. **1576** in *Oppress. Orkney & Zetld.* (1859) 36 The electione of Nichole Ayth..to the office of Lawman-generale of all Zetland. *Ibid.* 37 Quhilk the said Lawman keipit and observit as ane just bismeyre all his dayis. **1805** BARRY *Orkney* 217 The President, or principal person in the Lawting, was named the Great Foud or Lagman. **1892** G. GOUDIE in *Proc. Soc. Ant. Scotl.* XXVI. 190 A functionary termed the 'Lawman' held the important office of legal adviser and judge of assize, and had generally the superintendence of the framing and interpretation of the law... The office of Lawman was apparently elective.

3. A man of law, lawyer. *Obs.* exc. as *nonce-wd.*

1535 STEWART *Cron. Scot.* (1858) I. 87 He hes gart seik in mony sindrie land..Leichis, lawmen, and mony vther mo. **1588** FRAUNCE *Lawiers Log.* Ded., The study of the law,..by these lawmens report, is so hard. **1694** R. L'ESTRANGE *Fables* ccxxvii. (1714) 247 Nothing Commoner in Times of Danger than for Law-Men to leave their Masters. **1830** J. HODGSON in J. Raine *Mem.* (1858) II. 177 Mr. Howard the artist, who resides..with his brother, I think, who is a lawman.

4. A law enforcement officer. *colloq.*

1959 P. COOK in *Granta* 6 June 33/1 Had he actually seen the rough law-men bundle the startled Widow into the Black Maria? **1962** R. BARKER *Clue for Murder* ix. 57 Some lawmen took a delight in seeing the criminal squirm. **1972** *Radio Times* 30 Mar. 14/4 A retired lawman, still sporting a tin star, demonstrated how he could kill with either hand. **1973** J. WAINWRIGHT *Devil you Don't* 65 He surely hated Davis... He also hated this goddam lawman.

lawmer, variant of LAMBER¹, amber.

law-merchant. *Comm.* [f. LAW *sb.*¹ + MERCHANT *a.*, in imitation of the med.L. *lex mercatoria.*] A special system of rules for the regulation of trade and commerce, differing in some respects from the Common Law.

1622 MALYNES (*title*) Consuetudo vel Lex Mercatoria, or the Ancient Law-Merchant. **1663** MARVELL *Corr.* xl. Wks. 1872–5 II. 88 Those things may better be redressed by the law merchant, or *lex mercatoria*. *a* **1687** PETTY *Pol. Arith.* i. (1691) 22 Liberty of Conscience, Registry of Conveyances, ..and Law Merchant, rise all from the same Spring, tend to the same Sea. **1777** SHERIDAN *Sch. Scand.* II. ii, Yes, madam, I would have law merchant for them too. **1856** H. BROOME *Comm. Common Law* 11 Lord Campbell remarks that the general lien of bankers is part of the law merchant.

lawmp-: see LAMP-.

lawn (lɔːn), *sb.*¹ Also 5–6 laun(e, lawnd(e, 5–7 **laund(e, lawne,** 6 **la(a)ne.** [According to Prof. Skeat, from the name of *Laon* in France.

This suggestion has since been independently made by A. Thomas (*Romania* XXIX. 182, 1900), who shows that linen manufactures were carried on extensively at Laon as late as the 18th c. A slight difficulty is presented by the fact that the earliest known form of the word is *launde*, which long remained more frequent in use than the shorter form; this, however, may be due to association with LAUND, LAWN *sb.*²]

1. A kind of fine linen, resembling cambric; *pl.* pieces or sorts of this linen.

1415 *Test. Ebor.* (Surtees) I. 382, j plice de lawnd. **1423** *Rolls of Parlt.* IV. 239 Item, 1 remenaunt de Laun, cont' viii alnz pris l'aln' iiis. iiiid. *c* **1440** *Generydes* 73 Ther was an hanged bedde, And ther vppon a shete of launde was spredde. **1483** *Acc. Coronation Rich. III*, in *Antiq. Repertory* II. 251 A coyfe made of a plyte of lawne. **1502** *Priv. Purse Exp. Eliz. of York* (1830) 50 A plyte of lawnde for a shirte for the childe of grace at Reding. *a* **1548** HALL *Chron., Hen. VIII*, 240 b, But on her head she had a cap as she ware on the saturdai before with a cornet of laune. **1594** PLAT *Jewell-ho.* III. 46 You must tie the powder hard in a rag of Laune or thin Cambrick. **1634** SIR T. HERBERT *Trav.* 38 Long haire and loose,..covered with a fine thinne vaile of Callico Lawne. **1640** in Noorthouck *Lond.* (1773) 838/2 Lawns, the whole piece 2*d.* **1692** BENTLEY *Boyle Lect.* 123 In vessels cover'd with fine lawn, so as to admit the air and keep out the insects, no living thing was ever produced. **1730–46** THOMSON *Autumn* 86 Bright in glossy silk and flowing lawn. **1764** HADLEY in *Phil. Trans.* LIV. 5 Sold in the shops for 2*s.* 4*d.* per yard, under the name of long lawn. **1793** MISS CHOWNE in *Ld. Auckland's Corr.* (1861) II. 511 If you can get fine lawns, bring them with you, for they are rare. **1813** SCOTT *Trierm.* III. xi, A summer mist arose;..It seem'd a veil of filmy lawn. **1829** *Yng. Lady's Bk.* 501 Take a common vase..and cover it entirely with widow's-lawn.

transf. and *fig.* **1555** EDEN *Decades* 186 Her bodye was..full of a laune wherof they make their webbes. **1591** SYLVESTER *Du Bartas* I. vii. 667 Then neat and nimbly her new web she [the spider] weaves, With her fine shuttle circularly drawn Through all the circuit of her open lawn. **1663** COWLEY *Hymn Light* xix, The Virgin Lillies in their White, Are clad but with the Lawn of almost naked Light.

Proverb. **1546** J. HEYWOOD *Prov.* (1867) 15 He that will sell lawne before he can folde it, He shall repent him before he haue solde it. **1598** BARNFIELD *Pecunia* xxxvi, No peece of Lawne so pure, but hath some fret.

2. *spec.* This fabric used for the sleeves of a bishop. Hence, the dignity or office of a bishop.

a **1732** GAY *Fables* II. iv, You ask me if I ever knew Court chaplains thus the lawn pursue. **1732** POPE *Ep. Cobham* 136 A Saint in Crape is twice a Saint in Lawn. **1763** CHURCHILL *Ep. to Hogarth* (ed. 2) 6 Whilst Thou In Lawn had'st whisper'd to a sleeping croud. *c* **1800** SYD. SMITH in Lady Holland *Mem.* (1855) I. ii. 28 Those who were too honest to sell them [*sc.* liberal opinions] for the ermine of the judge or the lawn of the prelate. **1894** HALL CAINE *Manxman* v. xi. 315 He took one of the two chairs under the canopy; the other was taken by the Bishop in his lawn.

†**3.** An article of dress made of lawn. *Obs.*

c **1480** HENRYSON *Test. Cres.* 422 Thy gay garmentis, with mony gudely goun, Thy plesand lawn pinnit with goldin prene. **1573–80** G. HARVEY *Letter-bk.* (Camden) 103 No laanes or the like, to bewitch delite. **1578** T. N. tr. *Conq. W. India* 204 They were covered with a lawne called Nacar. **1610** G. FLETCHER *Christ's Vict.* I. liii, Her vpper garment was a silken lawne. **1633** P. FLETCHER *Purple Isl.* II. viii, Lest eyes should surfet with too greedy sight, Transparent lawns withhold, more to increase delight. *c* **1704** PRIOR *Henry & Emma* 360 To stop the wounds, my finest lawn I'd tear. **1812** J. H. VAUX *Flash Dict.*, *Lawn*, a white cambric handkerchief.

†**b.** A piece of lawn used in torture.

For an explanation of the torture of the 'lawn', see 1569 JEWEL *Expos. 1 Thess.* Wks. 1848 VII. 42–3. (Cf. *linen-ball*, LINEN B 5.)

1590 MARLOWE *Edw. II*, v. iv. 32 (1598), I learned in Naples how..To strangle with a lawne thrust through [*later 4tos* down] the throte. **1622** S. WARD *Life of Faith in Death* i. 84 Here thou..shiuerest to hear of the strappado, the racke, or the Lawne.

4. *techn.* Short for *lawn sieve*: A fine sieve, generally of silk, through which porcelain 'slip', cement, etc., are strained, to ensure uniform fineness.

1853 URE *Dict. Arts* (ed. 4) II. 453 (s.v. *Porcelain*), The mixture [of 'slips' or fluid clays] is now passed..through fine sieves or 'lawns' woven of silk, and containing 300 threads to the square inch. **1895** *Times* 10 Jan. 3/6 [Cement-manufacture]. The use of such lawns..would..be almost impracticable.

5. *Bot.* A name for Venus' Navelwort (*Cynoglossum officinale*).

1778 MILNE *Bot. Dict.* (ed. 2) 22 *Cynoglossum*, Hound's Tongue, Venus's Navel Wort, Lawn.

6. *attrib.* and *Comb.* **a.** attributive ('made of or consisting of lawn'); **b.** objective, as †*lawn-maker*; **c.** instrumental, as *lawn-robed* adj. Also LAWN-SLEEVED *a.*

1477 NORTON *Ord. Alch.* vii. in Ashm. (1652) 103 Lawne Kercheefes fayre. *c* **1515** *Cocke Lorell's B.* 10 Golde sheres, keuerchef, launds, and reben makers. **1562** BULLEYN *Bk. Simples* 86 a, Covering the place with a Launde clothe. **1565** GOLDING *Ovid's Met.* To Rdr. (1593) 4 As Persian kings did never go abroad with open face, But with some lawne or silken scarfe. **1602** MARSTON *Antonio's Rev.* II. ii. C 4 b, Looke on those lips, Those now lawne pillowes. **1697** tr. *C'tess D'Aunoy's Trav.* (1706) 284 The Embassadors are obliged..to put on certain little Lawn Cuffs, which they wear quite flat upon their sleeves. **1710** STEELE & ADDISON *Tatler* No. 257 ¶3 The Lawn Apron that was whiter than Ermin. **1711** *Ld. Marshal's Order* 26 Apr. in *Lond. Gaz.* No. 4840/3 That the Peeresses..wear Black Silk, Laune Linnen, and White Gloves. **1719** TICKELL *To Earl Warwick, On Death Addison*, The duties by the lawn-robed prelate pay'd. **1819** KEATS *Eve of St. Mark* 53 From plaited lawn-frill, fine and thin, She lifted up her soft warm chin. **1856** MISS MULOCK *J. Halifax* ix. (1859) 101 Garnished with the snowiest of lawn frills and ruffles.

d. Special comb.: †**lawn-man** (derisively), a bishop; **lawn-sieve**, a fine sieve, made of lawn (or silk), used in cookery, porcelain-manufacture, etc.: cf. sense 4. Also LAWN-SLEEVES.

1795 WOLCOT (P. Pindar) *Liberty's last Squeak* Wks. 1812 III. 432 May those lawn-men, born to happier fate Chase not the Curate from their grand abode. **1806** A. HUNTER *Culina* (ed. 3) 32 Run it through a lawn sieve. **1807** T. THOMSON *Chem.* (ed. 3) II. 492 The clay is reduced nearly to the consistence of milk with water, and the liquid passed through lawn sieves gradually increasing in fineness.

lawn (lɔːn), *sb.*[2] Also 6 laune, 7 lawne. [Later form of LAUND.]

1. a. An open space between woods; a glade. = LAUND. Now *arch.* and *dial.*

1548 ELYOT *Dict.*, *Sallus*, a place voyde of trees, as a laune in a parke or forrest. **1591** GREENE *Farew. to Folly* (1617) D 3 b, Her stature and her shape was passing tall, Diana-like, when longst the Lawnes she goes. **1615** G. SANDYS *Trav.* 202 A goodly forrest..intermixed with fruitfull and flowry lawnes. **1637** MILTON *Lycidas* 25 Ere the high Lawns appear'd Under the opening eye-lids of the morn, We drove a field. **1730–46** THOMSON *Autumn* 405 The thistly lawn, the thick-entangled broom. **1780** A. YOUNG *Tour Irel.* I. xviii. (1892) 404 The hills..consist of a large lawn in the center of the two woods, that to the right of an immense extent. **1805** WORDSW. *Waggoner* IV. 38 Thence look thou forth o'er wood and lawn Hoar with the frost-like dews of dawn! **1876** MORRIS *Sigurd* I. 25 She came where that lawn of the woods lay wide in the flood of light. **1899** *Times* 3 Mar. 15/3 So long as the favourite feeding places—lawns, as they are called—of their cattle are not interfered with,..no possible injury can be done to the commoners [of the New Forest].

fig. **1635** BRATHWAIT *Arcad. Pr.* I. 120 Privacy was his Lawne, and discontent his Lure.

b. A stretch of untilled ground; an extent of grass-covered land. Also in generalized sense.

1674 RAY *S. & E. C. Words* 70 Lawn in a Park: Plain untilled ground. **1749** L. EVANS *Middle Brit. Col.* (1755) 11 They [Indians] fix their Towns commonly on the Edges of great Rivers for the Sake of the rich Lawns to sow their Corn in. **179.** BURNS *My Nannie's Awa* iii, Thou laverock that springs frae the dews o' the lawn. **1820** W. IRVING *Sketch Bk.* I. 124 Vast lawns that extend like sheets of vivid green. **1839** E. D. CLARKE *Trav. Russia* 47/1 The roads (if a fine turf lawn may be so denominated). **1863** W. BARNES *Dorset Gloss.*, *Lawn* or *Lawnd*, unploughed land; the unploughed part of an arable field. **1890** *Science* 12 Sept. 141 A birdseye view..would show 60 acres of beautiful lawn besprinkled with buildings.

2. A portion of a garden or pleasure-ground, covered with grass, which is kept closely mown.

(Somewhat different in early use: cf. quot. 1733 and sense 1.)

1733 MILLER *Gardeners Dict.*, *Lawn* is a great Plain in a Park, or a spacious Plain adjoining to a noble Seat... As to the Situation of a Lawn, it will be best in the Front of the House, and to lie open to the neighbouring Country and not pent up with Trees. **1761** *Descr. S. Carolina* 6 Fine Savannahs..a Kind of natural Lawns, and some of them as beautiful as those made by Art. **1829** WORDSW. *Poems Sentim.* xxx, This Lawn, a carpet all alive With shadows flung from leaves. **1856** EMERSON *Eng. Traits, Universities* Wks. (Bohn) II. 88, I had but a single day wherein to see..the beautiful lawns and gardens of the colleges. **1875** J. D. HEATH *Croquet Player* 89 Finely sifted earth must now be spread over the lawn.

3. *Bacteriology.* A layer of bacteria uniformly distributed over the surface of a culture medium.

1951 WHITBY & HYNES *Med. Bacteriol.* (ed. 5) xxiv. 433 Phage activity is readily observed on solid culture media. A plate is first thickly inoculated with susceptible bacteria to form a 'lawn' of growth. **1970** PASSMORE & ROBSON *Compan. Med. Stud.* II. xviii. 102/1 The routine test dilution (RTD) is determined by placing drops of tenfold dilutions of the phage suspension on a lawn of sensitive bacteria.

4. *attrib.* and *Comb.*, as ***lawn-shading*** adj.; ***lawn-like*** adj. and adv.; **lawn billiards** = TROCO; **lawn-cutter** = *lawn-mower*; **lawn-meet**, the meeting of a hunt in front of a gentleman's house; **lawn-mower**, a machine provided with revolving spiral or horizontal knives for cutting the grass on a lawn; **lawn-party**, a party held on a lawn, a garden-party; **lawn sand**, a top-dressing of ammonium sulphate and iron sulphate mixed with sand, used as a fertilizer and weed-killer for lawns; **lawn-sprayer**, a sprayer for diffusing a fine spray of water over a lawn; **lawn-sprinkler**, a machine with revolving tubular arms from which water is sprinkled like rain. Also LAWN-TENNIS.

1873 *Young Englishwoman* Nov. 572/2 Jean would feel obliged if the Editor would tell her..if *lawn billiards can be played on a croquet lawn?.. Is there a book of rules on lawn billiards? **1879** TROLLOPE *John Caldigate* I. xvi. 213 Hunting, shooting, fishing,..lawn-billiards. **1882** [see TROCO]. **1910** *Encycl. Brit.* III. 934/2 The game [billiards] was at one time played on a lawn, like modern croquet... A later form of 'lawn billiards' again enjoyed a brief popularity during the latter half of the 19th century. **1897** S. HALE *Let.* 24 Mar. (1919) 315 Such a delicious drive,..and the *lawn-cutters making hay smells. **1879** MISS BIRD *Rocky Mountains* 121 Flowery pastures..sloping *lawnlike to bright swift streams. **1890** *Daily News* 8 Dec. 5/5 A *lawn meet of the West Norfolk Hunt took place at Sandringham. **1875** KNIGHT *Dict. Mech.*, **Lawn-mower*. **1852** W. COLLINS *Basil* v. (1856) 17 At pic-nics, *lawn-parties, little country gatherings of all sorts. **1937** R. S. MORTON *Woman Surgeon* xxxi. 346 Many interesting people gather in our frequent outings, lawn parties and other expressions of comradeship. **1955** R. BLESH *Shining Trumpets* (ed. 3) viii. 181 Parades, picnics, funerals, Mardi Gras, lawn parties, dances—he and his band were in demand everywhere. **1973** *Lebende Sprachen* XVIII. 38/1 US lawn party—BE/US garden party—Gartenfest. **1907** *Yesterday's Shopping* (1969) p. xlii/4 *Lawn sand. **1909** T. W. SANDERS *Lawns & Greens* vii. 68 Methods of exterminating daisies are to put a pinch of salt on the crown of each plant, or to sprinkle 'Watson's Lawn Sand' over the infested parts. **1939** R. B. DAWSON *Pract. Lawn Craft* xxi. 152 It may be found more convenient for owners of quite small areas of turf to buy a ready compounded lawn sand. **1968** *Punch* 20 Aug. 304/2 Add 1 oz of iron sulphate to 15 oz of dry sludge and you have a moss killing 'lawnsand'. **1820** KEATS *Hyperion* III. 25 Poplars, and *lawn-shading palms. **1943** WYNDHAM LEWIS *Let.* 15 Aug. (1963) 362 Watching the blue jays..having a shower-bath in a *lawn-sprayer. **1884** KNIGHT *Dict. Mech.* Suppl., **Lawn Sprinkler*.

lawn (lɔːn), *v.* [f. LAWN *sb.*[2]] *trans.* To turn (arable land) into lawn or grass-land; to make (ground) lawn-like.

1766 [ANSTEY] *Bath Guide* Epil. 337 To improve an old Family Seat By Lawning a hundred good Acres of Wheat. **1781–1814** *Parliamentary Hist.* XXI. 1282 Several of the country clergy..chose to lawn their church yards and cut away the noxious yew trees. **1792** A. YOUNG *Trav. France* 99 A gently falling vale with a little stream through it, that might be made anything of for lawning and watering. **1868** DORAN *Saints & Sin.* I. 256 This led in later times to lawning cemeteries on the part of incumbents, who would not plant since they might not cut down.

lawncent, variant of LANCENT *Obs.*

lawnch(e, obs. form of LAUNCH *v.*

lawnd(e, var. LAUND *Obs.*; obs. ff. LAWN *sb.*[1]

lawndere, obs. form of LAUNDER.

lawndresse, obs. form of LAUNDRESS.

lawndyrne, variant of LANDIRON[1] *Obs.*

lawned (lɔːnd), *ppl. a.* [f. LAWN *sb.*[1] + -ED[2].] Decked with lawn, wearing lawn sleeves.

1794 MATHIAS *Purs. Lit.* (1798) 109 May the muse in lasting strains record That lawn'd Endymion of a happier age. **1848** WHITTIER *Prose Wks.* (1889) II. 358 Oxford sent up its lawned deputations.

ˈlawnly, *adv. nonce-wd.* [f. LAWN *sb.*[1] + -LY[1].] After the manner of a wearer of lawn.

18.. LANDOR *Exam. Shak.* Wks. 1846 II. 286 This is not the doctrine of the silkenly and lawnly religious.

lawn sleeves, lawn-sleeves. Sleeves of lawn, considered as forming part of the episcopal dress. Hence, the dignity or office of a bishop; also, a bishop or bishops.

c **1640** TROUTBECK in Hickeringill *Priest-Cr.* (1707) II. iii. 34 That unhappy Verdict occasion'd to me the loss of 20000*l.* of my Uncle's..Estate Dis-inheriting me..lest any of the Lawn-Sleeves..should lay their Fingers on't. **1674** *Essex Papers* (Camden) I. 177 Wee..find little assistance from those we might most justly expect it from (yᵉ Lawne Sleeves). **1710** HEARNE *Collect.* (O.H.S.) II. 355 A Man of great Note For the sake of Laun-sleeves is aturning his Coat. **1730** FIELDING *Rape upon Rape* III. v, Why, I should sooner have suspected ermine or lawn-sleeves. **1768–74** TUCKER *Lt. Nat.* (1834) II. 492 If they [parents] propose..divinity, they think of the lawn sleeves. **1859** THACKERAY *Virgin.* II. x. 73 My lords of the lawn sleeves have lost half their honours now. **1882** BESANT *Revolt of Man* viii. (1883) 188 The Bishop himself appeared, in lawn-sleeves and surplice.

Hence **lawn-sleeved** *a.*

1651 CLEVELAND *Poems* 51 A fair blew-apron'd Priest, a Lawn-sleev'd brother. **1682** O. N. tr. *Boileau's Lutrin* I. 162 [He] Tells them..what rude Affronters Of Laun-sleev'd Grandeur were these Sawcy Chanters. *a* **1743** SAVAGE *Progr. Divine* Wks. 1775 II. 125 Lawn-sleev'd, and mitred, stand he now confest.

ˈlawn-ˈtennis. [LAWN *sb.*[2]] A modification of the game of tennis (TENNIS *sb.* 1), played in the open air on a lawn, or other prepared ground.

Now usu. called simply *tennis* (TENNIS *sb.* 2).

1874 *Army & Navy Gaz.* XV. 154 A new game has just been patented by Major Wingfield..'Lawn Tennis'—for that is the name..is a clever adaptation of Tennis to the exigencies of an ordinary lawn. **1882** MISS BRADDON *Mt. Royal* I. vi. 190 And now came the brief bright season of rustic entertainments.. lawn-tennis—archery—water parties.

attrib. **1884** *Harper's Mag.* Jan 297/2 Lawn-tennis clubs.

lawnterne, -tryn, obs. forms of LANTERN.

lawny (ˈlɔːnɪ), *a.*[1] [f. LAWN *sb.*[1] + -Y.]

1. Made of lawn.

1598 BP. HALL *Sat.* IV. iv. 31 When a plum'd Fanne may shade thy chalked face, And lawny strips thy naked bosome grace. **1604** DRAYTON *Moses Map Miracles* 12 The..winde ..was..angrie with her lawnie vaile, That from his sight it enuiouslie should hide her. **1641** MILTON *Ch. Govt.* II. iii. Wks. 1851 III. 173 Not she her selfe..but a false-whited, a lawnie resemblance of her. **1657** THORNLEY tr. *Longus' Daphnis & Chloe* 2 Their vests, and lawnie-petticoats tied, and tuckt up at the waste. **1795** COLERIDGE *Lewti* v, Perhaps the breezes..Have snatched aloft the lawny shroud Of Lady fair—that died for love. **1817** KEATS *Sleep & Beauty* 374 A fold of lawny mantle dabbling swims At the bath's edge. **1825** *Blackw. Mag.* XVIII. 446 Heaven's gleam Her light loose lawny vestment silver'd. **1853** DE QUINCEY *Autobiogr. Sk.* Wks. I. 23 Visions of beds with white lawny curtains.

b. Dressed in lawn; also pertaining to a wearer of lawn, i.e. a bishop.

1647 WARD *Simp. Cobler* 71 Let Salvation come..with.. lawny embracements. **1691** C. BLOUNT *Opening of Session* in *Collect. of Poems* 21 Their Lawney Conscience, whose Designs were seen, In voting out the King to serve the Queen. **1742–8** SHENSTONE *Schoolmistr.* 134 The times when..lawny saints in smould'ring flames did burn.

2. Resembling lawn; lawn-like; †soft as lawn.

1615 CROOKE *Body of Man* v. Pref. (1631) 257 As a Spider in the center of her Lawny Canopy with admirable skil weaueth her Cipresse web. **1618** N. WARD *S. Ward's Jethro* Ep. Ded., Impatient of cure; not only of searching acrimonious waters..but shie of the most soft and lawny touches. **1880** MISS BROUGHTON *Sec. Th.* III. iii, Her eyes are absently fixed on the lawny mists that swathe the fells' fair necks.

lawny ('lɔːnɪ), *a.*[2] [f. LAWN *sb.*[2] + -Y.]

†**a.** Containing lawns or glades (*obs.*). **b.** Resembling a lawn; covered with smooth green turf.

1613–16 W. BROWNE *Brit. Past.* II. i, Through Forrests, Mountaines or the Lawny ground. **1727–46** THOMSON *Summer* 768 Stupendous rocks That..lift Cool to the middle air their lawny tops. **1809** CAMPBELL *Gertrude* III. iv, Where..pines their lawny walk encompass round. **1822** SHELLEY *Isle* 1, There was a little lawny islet. **1871** M. COLLINS *Mrq. & Merch.* III. vi. 175 The river running between lawny margins.

lawrare, -eall, -el(l, -er(e, -iall(e, -ielle, -yel, -yr, obs. ff. LAUREL.

lawrencite ('lɒrənsaɪt, -ɔː-). *Min.* [Named by Daubrée, 1877, after its discoverer J. *Lawrence* Smith: see -ITE.] Ferrous chloride found in meteoric iron.

1877 *Amer. Jrnl. Sci.* Ser. III. XIII. 318. **1892** DANA *Min.* 165 Drops of ferric chloride,..formed from lawrencite, often exude..from the surface of meteoric iron.

lawrencium (lɒ'rɛnsɪəm). *Chem.* [mod.L., f. the name of Ernest O. *Lawrence* (1901–58), U.S. physicist + -IUM.] An artificially produced transuranic element that concludes the actinide series, the longest-lived isotope of which has a half-life of a few minutes. Atomic number 103; symbol Lw.

1961 *Times* 15 Apr. 7/1 The isotope of element 103 was 'created' on February 14 by four nuclear scientists—Albert Ghiorso, Torbjorn Sikkeland, Almon Larsh, and Robert Latimer... The scientists intend to name the new element Lawrencium in honour of..the founder of the laboratory. **1972** K. M. & R. A. MACKAY *Introd. Mod. Inorg. Chem.* (ed. 2) xi. 151/1 Lawrencium behaves as expected for the $f^{14}d^1s^2$ configuration by forming only Lw(III)..and resisting oxidation or reduction. **1972** *Sunday Mail Mag.* (Brisbane) 23 Apr. 11/2 Until lawrencium was discovered, californium ..was regarded as the world's most valuable metal.

Lawrentian (lɒ'rɛnʃ(ɪ)ən), *a.* **1.** Also **Lau'rentian.** Of or pertaining to the military leader and author T. E. *Lawrence* ('Lawrence of Arabia') (1888–1935), or his deeds and writings.

1928 T. E. LAWRENCE *Let.* 20 Jan. (1938) 568 Laurentian, that sudden insult. I thought I'd sloughed off those manners with the names. **1949** KOESTLER *Promise & Fulfilment* i. 10 It would have necessitated a team of men with Byronic idealism and Lawrentian imagination. **1966** *Punch* 20 July 123/3 The great merit of Mr. Mousa's study is that while his mind is clearly weighted against the Lawrentian myth, he appears to be scrupulously fair to Lawrence.

2. Also **Laurentian, Lawrencian.** Of or pertaining to the English author D. H. *Lawrence* (1885–1930), or his work or style of writing. Hence **Lawrenci'ana, Lawrentiana** [-IANA], objects belonging to, literature about or characteristic of, D. H. Lawrence.

1930 L. P. HARTLEY in *Sat. Rev.* 15 Feb. 203/1 Morgan's description of the sisters has many Lawrentian echoes, especially in the use of the word 'dark'. **1931** R. ALDINGTON *Colonel's Daughter* v. 270 The good old Lawrentian dark abdomen. **1936** A. HUXLEY *Olive Tree* 211 A characteristically Lawrencian expression. **1938** *Times* 28 Jan. 367/3 It is..possible also to put her down as a mixture of the living and the merely Lawrentian. **1944** H. TREECE *Herbert Read* 92 Most of Read's 'Eclogues'..are filled with a dark passionate emotion, a Lawrentian impulse centred in the body. **1944** *Scrutiny* XII. 256 Levels at which the characteristic Laurentian contribution may well appear the reverse of helpful. **1948** H. T. MOORE in D. H. Lawrence *Lett. to Bertrand Russell* p. vi, Meanwhile, here is another contribution to Lawrence literature, one of the last important collections of Lawrenciana. **1959** *Listener* 16 Apr. 683/1 Dr. Leavis successfully established a Lawrentian enclave in Cambridge. **1959** *Times Lit. Suppl.* 30 Oct. 630/1 Mr. de Vries has nicely satirized..Lawrencian and Bohemian 'free livers'. **1959** *N. & Q.* Mar. 120/1 There is an immense literature of 'Lawrentiana'. **1972** *Observer* 19 Nov. 4/2 There has been a 'tremendous revival' in Lawrentiana from a purely touristic point of view. **1973** *Daily Tel.* 7 Nov. 15/2 It has a Lawrentian turn of situation, too. There is a knight, Sir Tom, whose wife Margaret is ill-served—he comes home only for weekends and is too gentle anyway for her.

lawrie, variant of LOWRIE *Sc.*, a fox.

†**lawrightman.** *Orkney* and *Shetland. Obs.* Also 6 **lawrik-, lawricht-.** [f. LAW *sb.*[1] + RIGHT *sb.* + MAN; intended as a rendering in etymological equivalents of the local *lagraetman* = ON. *lǫgréttumaðr* a member of the *lǫgrétta* (*lǫg* law + *rétta* to make right) or public court of law held during the general assembly (thing).] (See quots.)

1554 tr. *Diploma Bp. Orkney* in *Bannatyne Cl. Misc.* III. (1855) 84 The seill of..Joanne Cragy myne armyng, of Richard Fodringame lawrik-men myne, of Alexander Sinclar myne [etc.]. **1576** in *Oppress. Orkney & Zetld.* (1859) 16 Ane discreit man of ilk paroche, by the rest, callit The Lawrichtman, quha mesurit oure dewitie, callit Wadmell, and weyit our dewitie of buttir. **1708** J. CHAMBERLAYNE *State Gt. Brit.* II. I. iii. 408 Six or seven of the most honest and intelligent persons within the Parish, called Lawrightmen. These..have the Oversight of the People, in manner of Constables. **1733** GIFFORD *Description Zetld.* (1786) 48 There is also in each parish a lawright man. .. His business is to weigh and measure the rent-butter and oil, and also to judge of the quality thereof. **1805** G. BARRY *Orkney Isl.* 217 The inferior ones had their council also, composed of members denominated Lagraetmen or Lawrightmen, who were a kind of constables for the execution of justice in their respective islands. **1822** SCOTT *Pirate* xviii, To do justice betwixt man and man, like a Fowd or a Lawright-man at a lawting lang syne.

lawrok, obs. form of LARK.

lawryol, lawryr: see LAUREOLE, LAUREL *sb.*[1]

Lawson ('lɔːsən). The name of Peter *Lawson* (d. 1820) and his son Charles (1794–1873), partners in the firm of Lawson and Son, Edinburgh nurserymen, used *attrib.* or in the possessive in **Lawson('s) cypress** to designate *Chamæcyparis lawsoniana*, a conifer from Oregon first introduced to cultivation by them after seeds had been collected in 1854 by Andrew Murray (1812–78), Scottish botanist, who named the tree after the Lawsons.

1858 G. GORDON *Pinetum* 62 *Cupressus Lawsoniana*, Murray. Messrs Lawson's Cypress... A large graceful tree, growing 100 feet high, and two feet in diameter..with the branches at first curved upwards..and towards the ends hanging down like an ostrich feather. **1866** *Curtis's Bot. Mag.* XCII. 5581 The Lawson Cypress..has for the last few years been a great favourite in our gardens and shrubberies. **1914** L. H. BAILEY *Stand. Cycl. Hort.* II. 730/2 Lawson's Cypress..is one of the most beautiful conifers and very variable, about 80 garden forms being cultivated in European nurseries. **1923** DALLIMORE & JACKSON *Handbk. Coniferæ* 200 The extraordinary variability of the Lawson cypress under cultivation has resulted in a large number of forms being given varietal names. **1957** M. HADFIELD *Brit. Trees* 120 The Lawson Cypress has a very limited natural distribution..restricted to a narrow belt on the Pacific coast of the United States. **1970** C. LLOYD *Well-Tempered Garden* iii. 215 One or other form of Lawson's cypress will give you a dense hedge. **1974** *Country Life* 12 Dec. 1855/2 A golden Lawson cypress..is a narrow column of bright gold.

†**Lawson-eve, -even,** short for *Low Sunday even* = Saturday in Easter week.

1725 HEARNE *R. Brunne's Chron.* (1810) 521/1 Saturday in Easter week, or as it is also called with us Lawson even. **1841** HAMPSON *Med. Ævi Kalend.* II. 236 Lawson Even is, therefore, Low Sunday Eve.

lawsoniana (lɔsəʊnɪ'ɑːnə). [a. the specific epithet of *Chamæcyparis lawsoniana*.] = *Lawson('s) cypress* (see LAWSON).

1959 R. E. HARRISON *Handbk. Trees & Shrubs S. Hemisphere* 89/1 The well-known golden Lawsoniana with stiff erect pyramidal habit, and lemon-golden foliage. **1965** F. SARGESON *Memoirs of Peon* ix. 270 We sat in the shade of a lawsoniana hedge.

lawsonite ('lɔːsənaɪt). *Min.* [Named by Ransome, 1895, after A.C. *Lawson*: see -ITE.] Hydrous silicate of aluminium and calcium, occurring usually in light blue crystals.

1895 *Amer. Jrnl. Sci.* Ser. III. L. 75 Lawsonite..is a new rock-forming mineral.

'law-'stationer. [f. LAW *sb.*[1] + STATIONER.] A tradesman who keeps in stock stationery and other articles required by lawyers. In Great Britain and Ireland, the business includes the taking in of manuscripts and legal documents to be fairly copied or engrossed.

1836 SIR H. TAYLOR *Statesman* xxiii. 169 Paying persons in the rank of law-stationers and their hired writers at the rate of so much per folio. **1851** MAYHEW *Lond. Labour* I. 383 Some copying, that I occasionally obtain from the law-stationers.

†**lawstead.** *Obs.* In 7 lawsteed. [f. LAW *sb.*[1] + *stede* STEAD, used as equivalent of L. *jūstitium* (f. *jūs* law + *stāre* to stand) a standing still of law.] A vacation.

1600 HOLLAND *Livy* III. xxvii. 106 Then Quintius.. proclaimeth a publicke vacation or Lawsteed. **1606** —— *Sueton.* 124 The..King of Kings..dissolved the Societie of his great Peeres and Princes at his table: which among the Parthians is as much as a Law-steed.

lawsuit ('lɔːsjuːt). [f. LAW *sb.*[1] + SUIT *sb.*] A suit in law; a prosecution of a claim in a court of law.

1624 GATAKER *Transubst.* 131 As if in a Law-suite..a man taketh hold..of somewhat that falleth from his adversaries. **1685** BAXTER *Paraphr. N.T.* Matt. v. 38 etc., Patience may cost you less than a Law-suit or Revenge. **1735–6** SHERIDAN in *Swift's Lett.* (1768) IV. 153 As I do not wear a sword, I must have recourse to the weapon in my hand. It is a better method than a law-suit. **1782** PRIESTLEY *Corrupt. Chr.* II. x. 268 The bishops made themselves judges in all law suits. **1809–10** COLERIDGE *Friend* (1865) 137 As if a mere lawsuit were carrying on between John Doe and Richard Roe! **1866** GEO. ELIOT *F. Holt* (1868) 16 Ah, you've had Durfey's debts as well as the lawsuits.

lawsy, var. of *laws* (LAW *int.*).

lawta, -te, -tie, -tith, -ty: see LEWTY.

lawter, variant of LAUGHTER[2].

†**lawting,** *dial. Obs.* [a. ON. *lǫg þing*, from *lǫg* LAW *sb.*[1] + *þing* assembly.] In Orkney and Shetland, the former supreme court of judicature.

1805 BARRY *Orkney* 217 With power of holding and adjourning courts called Lawtings. **1822** SCOTT *Pirate* xix, The Lawting, with the Raddmen and Lawright men, confirmed the division.

lawty, Sc. variant of LEWTY. *Obs.*

'law-,worthy, *a.* ? *Hist.* Also **law-worth.** [f. LAW *sb.*[1] + WORTHY: a modern rendering of OE. *þæra laȝa weorðe* (*þe*, etc.), 'worthy of (i.e. entitled to) the laws (which, etc.).'] **a.** Of persons: Having a standing in the law-courts; possessed of full legal rights. **b.** Of things: Within the purview of the law; able to be dealt with by a court of law.

[**1066–75** *Charter Will. I to Lond.* in Stubbs *Select Charters* 83 Ic wylle þat ȝet beon eallra þæra laȝa weorðe þe ȝyt wæran in Eadwerdes dæȝe kynges.] **1818** HALLAM *Mid. Ages* (1872) II. 277 The strongest proof of his being, as it was called, law-worthy, and possessing a rank. **1857** TOULM. SMITH *Parish* 21 The inquiry having been made by the oath of good and law-worth men of the neighbourhood. **1884** W. O'C. MORRIS in *Contemp. Rev.* Feb. 177 This enormous and growing mass of property was not lawworthy under English law. **1896** —— *Ireland* x. 333 The claims, however, which in fact approached a joint ownership over millions of acres, continued, as before, to be not law-worthy: they had never been recognized by the State.

lawyer ('lɔːjə(r), 'lɔɪə(r)). Forms: 4 **lawyere**, 4–7 **lawer(e**, 4, 6–8 **lawier(e**, (5 **laweour, laweyer(e, laweȝer, lawyour**, 6 **lawaier, -ayer**), 6– **lawyer.** [f. LAW *sb.*[1] + -YER: see also -IER.]

1. a. One versed in the law; a member of the legal profession, one whose business it is to conduct suits in the courts, or to advise clients, in the widest sense embracing every branch of the profession, though in colloquial use often limited to attorneys and solicitors. †*high lawyer* (see HIGH *a.* 21).

1377 LANGL. *P. Pl.* B. VII. 59 Ȝe legistres and lawyeres Holdeth this for treuthe. **1387** TREVISA *Higden* (Rolls) III. 275 Anoþer Socrates was of Grees, a greet philosofer and lawiere [Higden *orator*]. **1413** *Pilgr. Sowle* (Caxton 1483) III. iv. 53 Ye aduocates ye laweours and maynteners of wrong. **1543** GRAFTON *Contn. Harding, Hen. VII* 584 He had of his counsaill..Syr Charles Booth a lawer, then byshop of Herforde. **1556** LAUDER *Tractate* 427 Sum Solistars, now thir dayis, Vincusis Laweris in thare cause. **1592** GREENE *Upst. Courtier* E, Then the lawier was a simple man, and in the highest degree was but a bare scriuener. **1611** BIBLE *Matt.* xxii. 35 Then one of them, which was a Lawyer, asked him a question. **1637** NABBES *Microcosm.* v. Gib, Bless me! who's this? one of the divells she lawyers? **1688** SHADWELL *Sqr. Alsatia* II. i. Wks. 1720 IV. 44 A modest learned Lawyer, of little Practice, for want of Impudence. **1712** STEELE *Spect.* No. 480 ¶7, I am now clerk to a lawier. **1765** BLACKSTONE *Comm.* I. 32 A lawyer thus educated to the bar. **1780** COWPER *Report Adjudged Case* 25 Then shifting his side, as a lawyer knows how. **1845** POLSON *Law* in *Encycl. Metrop.* II. 819/1 Text-books, written by eminent lawyers, have..an authority in Westminster Hall.

Proverb. **1553** T. WILSON *Rhet.* 20 b, The lawyer never dieth a begger. The lawyer can never want a livyng till the yearth want men.

b. In mod. versions of the N.T.: An expounder of the Mosaic law.

1526 TINDALE *Luke* x. 25 A Certayne Lawere [Gr. νομικός, Vulg. *legisperitus*; Wyclif 'a wise man of the lawe'] stode vp and tempted hym.

†**c.** *Sc.* 'A professor of law' (Jam.). ? *Obs.*

1567 BUCHANAN *Reform. St. Andros* (S.T.S.) 14 The College of Diuinite. Personis. Ane Principal to be Reidar in Hebrew. Ane Lawer. *Ibid.* 15 The lawar sal reid dayly an hore in law. **1579** *Sc. Acts Jas. VI* (1814) III. 180/2 That the lawer..of befoir in the new college sall [etc.].

†**2. a.** A lawgiver. **b.** A lawmaker. *Obs.*

1534 MORE *On the Passion* Wks. 1294/1 Theyr olde lawyer Moises. **1638** *New Litany* in *Bk. Sc. Pasquils* (1868) 53 From cobling acts of Parliament Against the Lawers intent.

3. *dial.* A long bramble. Also in New Zealand, etc., applied to certain creeping plants.

1857 READE *Course True Love* 52 We call these long briars lawyers. **1863** KINGSLEY *Water-Bab.* 34 The lawyers tripped him up and tore his shins as if they had sharks' teeth. **1875** *Sussex Gloss., Lawyer*, a long bramble full of thorns, so called because 'when once they gets a holt an ye, ye doant easy get shut of 'em'. **1889** H. H. ROMILLY *Verandah in N. Guinea* 56 Tearing the vines and lawyers with their teeth.

4. ***Penang lawyer***: a kind of walking-stick, made from the stem of a dwarf palm (*Licuala acutifolia*, Griffith), a native of Penang and Singapore. In England often misapplied to the Malacca cane.

App. with jocular reference to the use of the weapon in settling disputes at Penang. It has been suggested that the name may be a corruption of Malay *pinang liyar*, wild areca, or *pinang láyor* fire-dried areca. The dwarf palm has prickly stalks, so that the notion may be the same as in sense 3 and in *lawyer palm*.

1828 P. CUNNINGHAM *N. S. Wales* (ed. 3) II. 64 With a Penang lawyer hugged close under his right arm. **1894** CONAN DOYLE *S. Holmes* 10 His stick, which was a Penang lawyer, weighted with lead.

5. *Zool.* The name given locally in America to **a.** the Black-necked Stilt (*Himantopus nigricollis*); **b.** the Burbot (*Lota maculosa*), and the Bowfin or Mudfish (*Amia calva*): cf. *lake-lawyer* (LAKE *sb.*[4] 6).

*c*1850 HAMMOND *Wild Northern Scenes* 45 (Bartlett), 'What on earth is that?' said I to the fisherman. 'That', said he, 'is a species of ling; which we call in these parts a lawyer'. **1859** BARTLETT *Dict. Amer.*, *Lawyer*..the black-necked Stilt... On the New Jersey coast it is some-times called *lawyer* on account of its 'long bill'. **1884** *Riverside Nat. Hist.* (1888) III. 97 *Amia calva*, the bow-fin,..or lawyer.

6. *attrib.* and *Comb.*, as ***lawyer-craft, -life; lawyer-made, -ridden*** adjs.; ***lawyer-like*** adj. and adv.; **lawyer cane, -palm, -vine** *Austral.*, names for *Rubus australis*, *Calamus australis*, and *Flagellaria indica*, the stems of which are armed with sharp thorns.

1908 E. J. BANFIELD *Confessions of Beachcomber* I. vi. 209 The *lawyer cane or vine (*Calamus*)..is a vegetable of tortuous ambitions. **1936** *Geogr. Jrnl.* LXXXVII. 229 They wore a band..made out of lawyer cane, around their middles as a protection against arrows. **1965** *Austral. Encycl.* V. 266/2 Lawyer Cane or Lawyer Vine, a name popularly if impolitely given to species of the rattan genus *Calamus*..and to *Flagellaria indica*. **1827** BENTHAM *Ration. Evid.* Wks. 1843 VI. 351 The punishment of death..(so long as *lawyercraft reigns) will ever continue to be a favourite policy with the English lawyer. **1861** W. F. COLLIER *Hist. Eng. Lit.* 481 Pictures of middle-class *lawyer-life. **1575** *Brieff Disc. Troub. Franckford* 208 The *lawierlike hearinge off suites that appertaine to liuinges. **1637** *Documents agst. Prynne* (Camden) 83 That it was not possible Mr. Burton should drawe his aunsweare to Mr. Attornyes soe lawyerlike as it was done without the helpe of some lawyer. **1876** FOX BOURNE *Locke* I. i. 6 Most of the entries are evidently in the elder Locke's own lawyer-like handwriting. **1860** GEN. P. THOMPSON *Audi Alt.* III. cix. 27 The popular resistance in the present case is right, though the *lawyer-made law should be wrong. **1890** LUMHOLTZ *Cannibals* 103 The stem and leaves are studded with the sharpest thorns, which continually cling to you and draw blood, hence its not very polite name of *lawyer-palm. **1824** MILL in *Westm. Rev.* II. 376 Our lawyers, and *lawyer-ridden legislators. **1907** *Daily Chron.* 29 Apr. 6/6 Land reform had been too long delayed, because they had been too frightened and lawyer-ridden. **1892** G. PARKER *Round Compass Austral.* xiv. 256 Don't touch that *lawyer-vine; it will tear you properly, and then not let you go. **1908, 1965** [see *lawyer cane* above].

Hence ˈ**lawyeress**, the wife of a lawyer; a female lawyer. ˈ**lawyering** *vbl. sb. colloq.*, the following of the lawyer's profession; similarly ˈ**lawyering** *ppl. a.* ˈ**lawyerling**, a contemptuous term for a lawyer; also, a young lawyer, a law-student; also *attrib.* ˈ**lawyerly** *a.*, lawyer-like. ˈ**lawyership**, the condition or dignity of a lawyer. †ˈ**lawyery**, lawyers as a class.

1649 MILTON *Eikon.* v. 45 To which..Law-tractats I referr the more Lawyerlie mooting of this point. **1676** WYCHERLEY *Pl. Dealer* IV. I, I have taken my leave of lawyering and pettifogging. **1716** M. DAVIES *Athen. Brit.* II. To Rdr. 26 Our Magnificent Nobility,..our Munificent Lawyery, or our Wealthy Gentry. **1830** D. O'CONNELL in *Ann. Reg., Chron.* 176/2 A wretched English scribe..urged on by his paltry, pitiful lawyerlings... The English Major-general and his lawyerling staff. **1835** GREVILLE *Mem. Geo. IV* (1875) III. xxviii. 278 Dined yesterday with the Vice-Chancellor; sixteen people..almost all lawyers and lawyeresses. **1861** MRS. H. WOOD *E. Lynne* i, 'Egad! lawyering can't be such bad work, Carlyle'. 'Nor is it..But you must remember that a good fortune was left me by my uncle..'. 'I know. The proceeds of lawyering also'. **1862** MAYHEW *Prisons of London* 72 A chapel-like edifice called the 'hall'..where the lawyerlings 'qualify' for the bar. **1871** CARLYLE in *Mrs. Carlyle's Lett.* II. 374 W.H., the now lawyering, parliamenteering, &c.; loud man. **1881** MASSON *Carlyle* in *Macm. Mag.* XLV. 64 The Edinburgh..of Jeffrey in the early heyday of his lawyership and editorship of the *Edinburgh Review*. **1896** *Columbus Dispatch* (Ohio) 11 Jan. 4/4 Miss Nellie G. Robison, the Cincinnati lawyeress.

ˈ**lawyerish**, *a.* [f. LAWYER.] Befitting a lawyer; like that of a lawyer.

1918 GALSWORTHY *Five Tales* 133 His lawyerish mind habitually put two and two together.

ˈ**lawyerism.** [f. LAWYER.] The influence, or principles, of lawyers.

1915 F. S. OLIVER *Ordeal by Battle* 221 To fall back on lawyerism was perhaps inevitable in the circumstances; but to think that it was possible to substitute lawyerism for leadership was absurd.

lax (læks), *sb.*¹ *Obs.* (revived as an alien word.) In 1 leax, laex, lex, 7 lauxe, lask, (*pl.*) lack(e)s. [OE. *leax* = OHG., MHG. *lahs* (mod.G. *lachs*), Du., ON., Sw., Da. *lax*:—OTeut. **lahs-* (cons.-stem); cognate and synonymous forms are Lith. *laszisza*, Lettish *lasis*, Russian *losos'*, Polish *łosoś*.] A salmon; in later use some particular kind of salmon (see quots.).

In the 17th c. the word seems to have been obsolete exc. in the north; southern writers merely guess at the meaning; Minsheu 1617 (followed by Phillips) app. connected the word with LAX *a.* In recent examples it represents the Sw. or Norwegian word, as applied to the salmon of those countries.

*c*725 *Corpus Gloss.* E 315 *Essox*, laex. *a*1000 *Boeth. Metr.* xix. 12 Hwy ʒe nu ne settan on sume dune fiscnet eowru, þonne eow fon lysteð leax oððe cyperan? *c*1050 *Suppl. Ælfric's Voc.* in Wr.-Wülcker 180/33 *Esocius, uel salmo*, lex. *c*1300 *Havelok* 754 He tok þe sturgiun, and þe qual, And þe turbut and lax with-al. *Ibid.* 896 He bar up wel a carte lode Of segges, laxes, of playces brode. *c*1320 *Pol. Songs* (Camden) 151 Thenne mot ych habbe hennen a-rost, Feyr on fyhshe day launprey ant lax. **1488** *Acta Dom. Conc.* 89/1 Extending ʒerely to ixˣˣ of salmond laxis takin vp be him. **1589** RIDER *Eng.-Lat. Dict.* 1721 A Laxe, a fish so called, *exos, esox*. **1601** HOLLAND *Pliny* I. 242 The Lax, in the Rhene. **1617** MINSHEU *Ductor*, *Lax*, a fish so called, a fish which hath no bones. **1621** *Naworth Househ. Bks.* (Surtees) 165 One great lauxe, iiijˢ. *Ibid.* 84 Lask. **1656** W. D. tr. *Comenius' Gate Lat. Unl.* §154 The pointed Sturgeon, and gristly Lax, greatning to the length of fowr and twentie feet. **1677** JOHNSON in *Ray's Corr.* (1848) 127 In the mouth of Eden, in Cumberland, the fishers have four distinctions of yearly growth..before they come to be lackes;..the Lacks, or overgrown salmon. **1882** MRS. H. REEVE *Cookery & Housek.* xiv. 104 Norwegian Lax (Salmon). **1883** *Fisheries Exhib. Catal.* 68 Tunny, Char, Lax, Cod, Haddock, Herring, Oysters, &c.

b. *Comb.*, as ***lax-fisher***; †**lax-pink**, ? a salmon at a certain stage of growth (cf. LASPRING).

1533–4 *Act 25 Hen. VIII*, c. 7 The yonge frye spaune or broode of any kynde of Salmon called lakspynkes smowtis or salmon pele. **1543** *Extracts Aberd. Reg.* (1844) I. 187, I and Johnn Freser, laxfyschar. *a*1670 SPALDING *Troub. Chas. I* (Bannatyne Club) I. 305 The masters and lax-fishers of Dee and Don. **1875** *New Hist. Aberdeenshire.* I. 99 A very pleasant footpath for the lax fishers.

lax, *sb.*² Also 6–7 laxe. [? f. LAX *v.*]

†**1.** A laxative medicine, an aperient. *Obs.*

1526 *Pilgr. Perf.* (W. de W. 1531) 171 Pocyons, laxes,.. and other medecynes. **1544** PHAER *Regim. Lyfe* (1553) E j b, It is good to take an infusion or laxe of rubarbe.

2. Looseness of the bowels, diarrhœa (in men and cattle); = LASK *sb.*¹ *Obs.* exc. *dial.*

1540 HYRDE tr. *Vives' Instr. Chr. Wom.* (1592) Q ij, Often changing his sheets and his clouts, because he had an exceeding laxe. **1542** BOORDE *Dyetary* xxii. (1870) 286 Maces..is good for the blody flyxe and laxes. **1573** TUSSER *Husb.* xix. (1878) 53 Which so, if ye giue, with the water and chalke, thou makest the laxe fro thy cow away walke. **1607** TOPSELL *Four-f. Beasts* (1658) 298 The lax or bloudy flix. **1610** MARKHAM *Masterp.* I. lxx. 147 Of the Laxe, or too much scouring of Horses. **1737** BRACKEN *Farriery Impr.* (1756) I. 216 If the Lax or Scouring continues too long upon him. **1770** HANLY in *Phil. Trans.* LXI. 133 She was seized with a smart lax. **1876** in *Whitby Gloss.* **1877** *N.W. Linc. Gloss.*, *Lax*, a looseness of the bowels. See *Lask*.

transf. **1577** FULKE *Two Treat. agst. Papists* II. 366 Being trobled with a sore laxe of the tongue, which I take to be a like disease in yᵉ mouth that it is in yᵉ wombe.

3. ? Relief, release. *rare*⁻¹.

*a*1800 *Bonny Baby Livingston* xviii. in Child *Ballads* (1890) IV. 233/2 O wherefore should I tell my grief, Since lax I canna find?

lax (læks), *sb.*³ Colloq. abbrev. of LACROSSE.

1951 E. TAYLOR *Game of Hide-and-Seek* II. i. 128 One late afternoon after lax-practice. **1966** J. GARDNER *Amber Nine* xii. 203 A far cry from the hockey and lax sticks of Roedean or Vassar. **1968** 'P. HOBSON' *Titty's Dead* viii. 86 Thank goodness Mummy doesn't know anything about LaX.

lax (læks), *a.* [ad. L. *lax-us* loose; cogn. w. *languēre* to LANGUISH, and prob. also with Teut. **slako-* SLACK *a.*]

1. Of the bowels: Acting easily, loose. †Of a person: Having the bowels unduly relaxed.

*c*1400 MAUNDEV. (1839) xiv. 152 Men putten it [manna] in Medicynes for riche men, to make the Wombe lax, and to purge evylle Blode. **1530** PALSGR. 317/1 Laxe as one that hath the flyxe or squyrte, *foyreux*. *a*1776 R. JAMES *Dissert. Fevers* (1778) 110, I do not neglect on these occasions, proper evacuations by bleeding, and keeping the body somewhat lax. **1804** ABERNETHY *Surg. Obs.* 188 The bowels lax. **1822–34** *Good's Study Med.* (ed. 4) I. 37 A moderately lax state of the bowels lessens the risk of worse consequences from dentition.

2. a. Slack; not tense, rigid, or tight. Hence of bodily constitution or mental powers: Wanting in 'tone' or tension. Now somewhat *rare*.

1660 tr. *Amyraldus' Treat. conc. Relig.* II. i. 154 The springs are some too stiffe, and others too laxe. **1669** HOLDER *Elem. Speech* 129 Though their outward Ear be stopt by the Laxe Membrane to all Sounds that come that way. **1732** ARBUTHNOT *Rules of Diet* 409 Especially Mothers of a weak lax Constitution. **1751** JOHNSON *Rambler* No. 85 ¶7 That neither the Faculties of the one [the mind] nor of the other [the body] be suffered to grow lax or torpid for Want of Use. **1789** W. BUCHAN *Dom. Med.* (1790) 339 When it attacks the tender and delicate, or persons of weak lax fibre. **1842** ABDY *Water Cure* (1843) 64 Abdomen soft, lax, and without inequalities.

b. Of the limbs, attitude: Relaxed, without muscular tension. *rare.*

1832 L. HUNT *Hero & Leander* II. 89 His tossing hands are lax. **1887** D. C. MURRAY & HERMAN *One Trav. Returns* vi. 91 He fell back in his chair and lay lax with closed eyes.

c. Of attachment or connexion of any kind: Weak in force, easily dissolved.

1782 KIRWAN in *Phil. Trans.* LXXII. 216 Nitrous air where the union of phlogiston to the acid is of the laxest kind.

3. a. Of organic tissue, stone, soils, etc.: Loose in texture; loosely cohering or compacted; porous.

1615 CROOKE *Body of Man* 206 That it may firme, stay, and as it were knit together his soft and laxe flesh. **1653** H. MORE *Antid. Ath.* I. xi. (1712) 34 This lax pith or marrow in Man's head. **1691** RAY *Creation* II. (1692) 127 The flesh of this sort of Fish being lax and spungy, and nothing so firm, solid and weighty as that of the bony Fishes. **1695** WOODWARD *Nat. Hist. Earth* II. (1723) 77 Not only in the more lax, Chalk, Clay, and Marle, but even in the most solid, Stone. **1713** DERHAM *Phys.-Theol.* 62 Some [delight] in a lax or sandy, some a heavy or clayie Soil. **1746** SIMON in *Phil. Trans.* XLIV. 314 Wood, Vegetables, or any other lax Bodies..whose Pores, being open [etc.]. **1811** PINKERTON *Petral.* I. 295 *note*, Da Costa..mentions the whet-stone of Derbyshire as of a lax texture, easily pervaded by water. **1835–6** TODD *Cycl. Anat.* I. 11/1 The psoas muscle is covered with a lax..cellular tissue. **1873** T. H. GREEN *Introd. Pathol.* (ed. 2) 191 Those organs which possess a lax structure..as the lungs. **1875** *Lyell's Princ. Geol.* I. I. ii. 225 Their stems had also a lax tissue.

b. *Bot.* 'Said of parts which are distant from each other, with an open arrangement, such as the panicle among the kinds of inflorescence' (*Treas. Bot.* 1866).

1796 WITHERING *Brit. Plants* (ed. 3) III. 294 [*Equisetum palustre*] Sheaths larger and more lax than those of *E. arvense*. **1837** MACGILLIVRAY *Withering's Brit. Pl.* (ed. 4) 18 The Panicle..presents the following varieties: Loose or Lax, when the stalks are distant. **1845** LINDLEY *Sch. Bot.* iv. (1858) 32 Racemes lax when in fruit. **1846** DANA *Zooph.* (1848) 591 Pinnules oblique, arcuate, lax. **1877–84** F. E. HULME *Wild Fl.* p. viii, Flowers in a lax spike, purple, at times fragrant.

4. Of clothes: Loose-fitting, worn loosely. Of persons: Negligent in attire and deportment. Of handwriting: Not compact; also, careless, not precise. *nonce-uses.*

1621 BURTON *Anat. Mel.* III. ii. III. iii. (1651) 474 They.. hurt and crucifie themselves, sometimes in laxe clothes, an hundred yards I think in a gown, a sleeve. **1783** COWPER *Let.* 7 Mar., Life & Wks. (1836) II. 120 Your manuscript indeed is close, and I do not reckon mine very lax. **1812** H. & J. SMITH *Rej. Addr.*, *Theatre* 71 Lax in their gaiters, laxer in their gait. **1885** W. M. ROSSETTI in *Athenæum* 6 May 641/3 The German character for *str*..would be considerably like that for *w*..; in rapid or lax handwriting the two might be almost identical.

5. a. Of rules, discipline, conduct, observance: Loose, slack, not strict or severe. Of ideas, interpretation, etc.: Loose, vague, not precise or exact. Said also of the agent (in both uses).

*c*1450 tr. *De Imitatione* I. xxv. 37 He þat euermore sekiþ þo þinges þat are most laxe and most remisse, shal euer be in anguissh. *c*1555 HARPSFIELD *Divorce Hen. VIII* (Camden) 187 If the Queen..can be moved..to take vow of chastity, or enter in laxe religion. **1671** *True Nonconf.* 115 As for this your Laxe acceptation of a professed indifferency in externals. **1736** BUTLER *Anal.* I. vi. Wks. 1874 I. 113 In a lax way of speaking. **1755** JORTIN *Diss.* vi. 260 The word *æternus* itself is sometimes of a lax signification. **1770** BURKE *Pres. Discont.* Wks. 1842 I. 146 Under the lax and indeterminate idea of the *honour of the crown*. **1803** R. HALL *Wks.* (1833) I. 160 A lax theology is the natural parent of a lax morality. **1821** LAMB *Elia* Ser. I. *Imperfect Sympathies*, The custom of resorting to an oath..is apt..to introduce into the laxer sort of minds the notion of two kinds of truth. **1840** MACAULAY *Ess.*, *Ranke* (1851) II. 136 To this enthusiastic neophyte their discipline seemed lax and their movements sluggish. **1854** THACKERAY *Newcomes* I. 43, I was a lax and negligent attendant. **1855** MACAULAY *Hist. Eng.* xv. III. 570 The oath of allegiance, the Whigs said, was drawn in terms far too lax. **1856** FROUDE *Hist. Eng.* (1858) I. i. 86 The execution of justice was as lax in practice as it was severe in theory. **1868** E. EDWARDS *Raleigh* I. iv. 68 Writers possessing extremely lax notions of the laws of evidence. **1874** GREEN *Short Hist.* viii. §10. 581 Richard [Cromwell] was known to be lax and godless in his conduct. **1884** *Manch. Exam.* 18 June 4/7 They were lax in their attendance, losing perhaps one or two days..per week. **1884** LD. COLERIDGE in *Law Rep.* 12 Q. Bench Div. 327 Towards the close of his life the practice of the Court became somewhat easier and laxer.

b. said of versification.

1749 *Power Pros. Numbers* 47 If the antient Poetry was too lax in its Numbers, the modern is certainly too strict. **1817** MOORE *Lalla R.* (1824) 161 The lax and easy kind of metre in which it was written. **1847** L. HUNT *Men, Women, & B.* II. viii. 145 The lax metre and versification resembling those of the second order of French tales in verse.

c. *Phonetics.* Of a speech-sound, esp. a vowel: produced with the speech organs relaxed.

1909 D. JONES *Pronunc. of Eng.* I. iii. 12 The difference in quality between a tense vowel and the corresponding lax vowel..is sometimes very considerable, especially in the case of closed vowels. **1933** WESTERMANN & WARD *Pract. Phonetics for Students Afr. Lang.* vi. 36 These two sounds occur in Bari as the 'lax' forms of *i* and *u*. **1949** R.-M. S. HEFFNER *Gen. Phonetics* v. 96 Later scholars have substituted the terms tense and lax for narrow and wide. **1964** JAKOBSON & HALLE in D. Abercrombie et al. *Daniel Jones* 97 A peculiar interplay of the lax-tense and compact-diffuse features underlies the vowel harmony. **1973** *Amer. Speech 1969* XLIV. 199 The diphthongizing of lax vowels.. can be analyzed.

6. quasi-*adv.* So as to have ample room. [A Latinism: cf. LAXITY 4.]

1667 MILTON *P.L.* VII. 162 Mean while inhabit laxe, ye Powers of Heav'n. [Cf. Cicero *De domo sua* xliv. 115 *Habitare laxe et magnifice voluit*.]

7. *Comb.*, as ***lax-fibred, -flowered*** adjs.

1761 PULTENEY in *Phil. Trans.* LII. 353 Women, children, and weakly men..are lax-fibred. **1861** MISS PRATT *Flower. Pl.* V. 210 Lax-flowered Orchis. **1870** HOOKER *Stud. Flora* 356 *Aceras anthropophora*,..Spike lax-flowered.

†**lax,** *v. Obs.* [ad. L. *laxāre*, f. *lax-us* LAX *a.*] *trans.* To make lax; to loosen, relax; to purge. Also *absol.*

1398 TREVISA *Barth. De P.R.* VI. xxi. (1495) 210 Hote water clensyth and laxyth and pourgyth the wombe. *Ibid.* XVII. lv. 635 The whyte rote of Eleborus laxyth both vpwarde and dounwarde. **1528** PAYNEL tr. *Reg. Salerni* (1535) 60 a, Butter..laxethe the bealye out of measure, and prouoketh one to vomyte. **1540** RAYNOLD *Byrth Mankynde* 15 b, Yf the woman..haue ben longe sycke before her labor, yf she haue ben sore laxed [*ed.* 1552 lasked]. **1627–77** FELTHAM *Resolves* II. l. 259 That we should laxe our selves in all the corrupt..pleasures of life. **1675** EVELYN *Terra* (1676) 57 Laxing the parts, and giving easy deliverance to its off-spring. **1685** COTTON tr. *Montaigne* I. liv. (1711) 470 An extream Fear, and an extream Ardour of Courage, do equally trouble and lax the Belly.

Hence **laxed** *ppl. a.*, made loose or slack, relaxed. ˈ**laxing** *vbl. sb.*, loosening.

c **1400** *Lanfranc's Cirurg.* 268 For brekyng of þe siphac & of his laxyng. **1623** Cockeram ii, *Released*, Laxed, Relaxed. **1679** Evelyn *Sylva* xxx. (ed. 3) 176 Those laxed parts, and Vessels by which the humour did ascend, grow dry and close. **1718** Prior *Solomon* iii. 162 When the lax'd Sinews of the weaken'd Eye In wat'ry Damps or dim Suffusion lye.

† '**laxable**, *a. Obs. rare*⁻¹. [ad. L. type *laxābilis*, f. *laxāre*: see lax *v.* and -able.] Of the body: Easily purged, 'loose'.

1607 Topsell *Four-f. Beasts* (1658) 337 Drink..mingled with Mares milk, doth make the body loose and laxable.

laxaman, var. laksamana.

† **laxament**. *Obs.*⁻⁰ [ad. L. *laxāment-um* an extending, relaxation, etc., f. *laxāre* to lax.]

1623 Cockeram, *Laxament*, a release.

† '**laxate**, *v. Obs.* [f. ppl. stem of L. *laxāre* lax *v.*] *trans.* To loosen, relax. Also *absol.*

1623 Cockeram, *Laxate*, to release, to loose, to pardon. **1652** French *Yorksh. Spa* viii. 72 It corroborates, astringeth, and laxateth. *Ibid.* xi. 96 Exercise is..very necessary, as being good to laxate the passages of the body. **1661** Lovell *Hist. Anim. & Min.* 211 All fat things laxate the stomach.

Hence † '**laxated** *ppl. a.*, † '**laxating** *vbl. sb.*

1652 French *Yorksh. Spa* iv. 41 They that have very cold, weak and laxated stomacks. *Ibid.* viii. 73 If by its laxating, evacuation is promoted.

laxation (læk'seɪʃən). [ad. L. *laxātiōn-em*, n. of action f. *laxāre*: see lax *v.* and -ation.] The action of loosening or relaxing; the state of being loosened or relaxed; *occas.* an instance or means of relaxing, a laxative application.

1398 Trevisa *Barth. De P.R.* viii. xxvii. (1495) 337 Hote water is contrary to laxacion yf the heete of the ayre is not stronge for the tyme also. *c* **1550** Lloyd *Treas. Health* (1585) K iv, Beanes sodde in Veniger..do greatlye withold Laxation. **1579** Twyne *Phisicke agst. Fort.* i. xxiv. 33 a, These are the prouocations of leacherie, these are the laxations of libertie. **1640** Bp. Reynolds *Passions* v. 34 That Law, without execution whereof there cannot but follow a laxation of the whole frame [of Nature]. **1661** Lovell *Hist. Anim. & Min.* 420 The hernia,..it's cured by laxation. **1669** W. Simpson *Hydrol. Chym.* 127 By reason of the laxation and flagging of the membranes. **1699** T. Bennet *Dissenters' Pleas.* (1711) 5 By reason of..laxation of disciplin in those wars, Atheism has much increas'd. **1832** I. Taylor *Saturday Even.* 26 The movement—the *laxation* of the human mind in all countries. **1897** *Allbutt's Syst. Med.* IV. 252 An initial mercurial purge, followed by milder saline laxations..will afford some amelioration.

laxative ('læksətɪv), *a.* and *sb.* Also 4–6 laxatif, -yf(e, 6 laxitive. [a. F. *laxatif, -ive*, ad. L. *laxātīv-us*, f. *laxāre*: see lax *v.* and -ative.]

A. *adj.* Having the property of relaxing.

1. Of medicines, food, etc.: Having the property of loosening and evacuating the bowels.

1398 Trevisa *Barth. De P.R.* xvii. cxii. (1495) 675 Some oyle..is laxatyf and nesshynge. *c* **1400** *Lanfranc's Cirurg.* 184, I ne knewe no medicyn laxatif þat is so good. **1481** Caxton *Reynard* xxxii. (Arb.) 90 He knewe..alle the herbes ..whiche were viscose or laxatyf. **1547** Boorde *Brev. Health* §110 Vse laxatiue meates..if nede do require. **1598** Sylvester *Du Bartas* ii. i. iii. *Furies* 646 Our Glysters laxative. **1660** F. Brooke tr. *Le Blanc's Trav.* 185 Tortoises ..excellent meat,..but are so laxative, they cause even Disenterias. **1732** Arbuthnot *Rules of Diet* i. 244 Tamarinds, Astringent, yet laxative to the lower Belly. **1789** W. Buchan *Dom. Med.* (1790) 293 Fomentations and laxative clysters are by no means to be omitted. **1809** Pinkney *Trav. France* 222 Those countries are most healthy where, from an ordinary laxative diet, the body is always kept open. **1861** Bentley *Man. Bot.* 579 Some [of the *Compositæ*] are laxative and anthelmintic.

2. Of the bowels, or the bodily constitution: Loose, subject to 'flux' or free discharge of the fæces. Of a disease: Characterized by such discharge. Now *rare.*

1546 J. Heywood *Prov.* (1867) 34 Ye would..geue me a purgacion. But I am laxatiue inough. **1573** Baret *Alv.* L 153 Letise is good to make one laxitiue or go to yᵉ stoole. **1608** Middleton *Fam. Love* iii. iii, What a laxatiue fever shakes me. **1620** Venner *Via Recta* v. 90 A very good medicinable meate, for such as are too laxatiue, and subiect to fluxes. **1635** Brereton *Trav.* (Chetham Soc.) I. 130 My body was always..inclined to be laxative and soluble. **1708** *Brit. Apollo* No. 38. 3/2 You seem prone to Excess, Whence this Laxative Ailing arises. **1722** Quincy *Lex. Phys.-Med.* (ed. 2), *Laxative*, signifies loose in Body, so as to go frequently to stool. **1801** *Med. Jrnl.* V. 261 Bowels laxative, tongue and skin healthy. **1822–34** *Good's Study Med.* (ed. 4) I. 194 If confined in youth, in advanced life they [the bowels] are often laxative.

b. *transf.* Unable to contain one's speech or emotions. ? *Obs.*

1601 B. Jonson *Poetaster* Apol. Dial., Fellowes of practis'd and most laxatiue tongues. **1607** W. S. *Puritan* iii. F 2, I am of such a laxatiue laughter, that if the Deuill him selfe stood by, I should laugh in his face. **1622** T. Scott *Belg. Pismire* Pref. 2 My owne Countri-men haue tongues laxatiue enough, and Strangers are in their wordes.. libertines. *a* **1639** W. Whateley *Prototypes* i. vi. (1640) 85 This sinne proceedeth from a twattling laxative humour causing that a man must vent all he knows and be talking of many things.

3. Having a loosing power, affording remission or relief. *rare.*

1645 Milton *Tetrach.* Wks. 1851 IV. 216 A law giving permissions laxative to unmarry a wife and marry a lust. **1649** —— *Eikon.* xiv. 138 The simpler sort he furnishes with laxative, hee termes them general clauses, which may serve to releeve them against the Covnant tak'n.

B. *sb.* **1.** A laxative medicine; 'a slightly purgative medicine which simply unloads the bowels' (*Syd. Soc. Lex.*).

c **1386** Chaucer *Knt.'s T.* 1898 Hym gayneth neither for to gete his lif, Vomyt vpward ne dounward laxatif. —— *Nun's Pr. T.* 142 Er ye take youre laxatyues, Of lawriol, Centaure, and ffumetere. *c* **1400** *Lanfranc's Cirurg.* 333 Whanne his body is maad clene wiþ laxatiuis. **1412–20** Lydg. *Chron. Troy* i. iii, And made him [*sc.* Cerberus] voide his venym in ye strife And upwarde gaue hym suche a laxatyfe That all the worlde his brethe contagyous Infected hath. **1572** Mascall *Plant. & Graff.* (1592) 57 The iuyce of Elder,..of Turbith, or such like laxitiues. **1612** Woodall *Surg. Mate* Wks. (1653) 154 Thou maist also give the partie some laxative. **1726** Swift *Gulliver* iii. vi. 83 Lenitives, Aperitives,..Laxatives. **1822–34** *Good's Study Med.* (ed. 4) I. 37 If the bowels be confined, we must employ cooling laxatives. **1874** *R. Hooper's Physic. Vade M.* i. v. (ed. 9) 230 Brown bread often proves an effectual laxative.

† **2.** ? Relaxed condition of the bowels, 'flux'. *Obs. rare.*

c **1430** Lydg. *Reason & Sens.* 3439 The drynke..Which the mynystres of babel Maden..And gaf hyt to kyng Sedechye Wher thorgh he had a laxatyf That he shortly lost hys lyf. **1500–20** Dunbar *Poems* xxxiii. 140 He cowth gif cure for laxatyve. **1527** Andrew *Brunswyke's Distyll. Waters* A ij b, Who so drynke the same [walwort] water at eche tyme ii ounces or two ounces and a halfe causeth laxatyfe.

'**laxativeness**. [f. prec. + -ness.] Loose or relaxed condition (of the body, etc.).

1610 Markham *Masterp.* i. xii. 33 Laxatiuenesse or loosenesse of the body is a signe of a hot liuer. **1611** Cotgr., *Courance*, a flux, a laxatiuenesse in the bodie. **1615** Markham *Eng. Housew.* ii. vi. (1668) 142 It..proceedeth.. from a laxativeness or looseness of milk. **1725** Bradley *Fam. Dict.* s.v. *Scouring-long-sought*, Either by over-heating or by unwholsome Fodder, which will breed Laxativeness.

b. Looseness of tongue.

1866 *Sat. Rev.* 1 Sept. 254/2 Their silence is quite refreshing beside the rhetorical laxativeness of others.

laxator (læk'seɪtə(r)). *Anat.* [mod.L., agent-n. f. L. *laxāre* (see lax *v.*).] Name formerly given to a (supposed) muscle of the external ear.

1799 Home *Ear* in *Phil. Trans.* XC. 9 The largest of these is called the obliquus, and is the antagonist of the tensor muscle; the other is very small, and is called the laxator. **1808** *Med. Jrnl.* XIX. 393 Soemmerring again errs..in considering the muscle as entirely a laxator.

laxism ('læksɪz(ə)m). [f. lax *a.* + -ism.] The views of the 'laxists'.

1895 *Dublin Rev.* Oct. 276 Laxism and Jansenism.

laxist ('læksɪst). [f. lax *a.* + -ist.] One who favours lax views or interpretation: *spec.* the designation given by modern historians to the school of casuists in the Roman church who maintained that it was justifiable to follow any probability, however slight, in favour of liberty. Also *attrib.*

1865 F. Oakeley in *Ess. Relig. & Lit.* 144 One of two extreme attitudes; that of unpractical theorists, on the one hand, or that of practical laxists on the other. **1882** Littledale in *Encycl. Brit.* XIV. 638/2 Some of the stricter casuists say so, but Liguori sides with the laxists. **1884** *Ch. Times* 366/2 There is a disastrous recommendation of the laxist school in handling moral questions. **1890** *Guardian* 7 May 741/1 There have been 'rigorist' and 'laxist' views on points of morals and discipline.

'**laxitude**. *rare*⁻¹. [See -tude.] Laxity.

1861 Wright *Ess. Archæol.* II. xvii. 97 The laxitude of mediæval manners.

laxity ('læksɪtɪ). [a. F. *laxité*, ad. L. *laxitātem*, f. *laxus* lax *a.*] The quality of being lax.

1. Looseness, irretentiveness (of the bowels, etc.); slackness, want of tension (in the muscular or nervous fibres, etc.).

1528 Paynel tr. *Reg. Salerni* (1535) 119 b, Superfluous drynkynge of cold drynke..causeth the palsey, or laxite of the membres. **1620** Venner *Via Recta* viii. 184 The stomacke..if it be subiect to laxitie. **1672** Wisemen *Wounds* ii. v. 36 There arises a laxity and indigesture in the Wound. **1707** Floyer *Physic. Pulse-Watch* 203 The Laxity of Fibres in the Habit of the Body, or *Viscera*, is restored by Exercise, Friction, and cold Baths. **1775** Johnson *Let. to Mrs. Thrale* 13 July, In her early state of laxity and feebleness. **1789** W. Buchan *Dom. Med.* (1790) 319 This disease may..proceed from too great a laxity of the organs which secrete the urine. **1799** M. Underwood *Dis. Childr.* (ed. 4) I. 6 The great moisture and laxity of infants.

2. Looseness of texture or cohesion; openness, uncompact structure or arrangement.

1603 Holland *Plutarch's Mor.* 229 The skin..by the closenesse or laxitie thereof, as he drawes it in, or lets it out. **1660** Boyle *New Exp. Phys. Mech.* xxxvi. 300 The dif-form consistence, as to laxity and compactness of the Air at several distances from us. **1692** Bentley *Boyle Lect.* vii. (1693) 25 The former [cause] could never beget Whirl-pools in a Chaos of so great a Laxity and Thinness.

3. Looseness or slackness in the moral and intellectual spheres; want of firmness, strictness, or precision.

1623 Cockeram, *Laxitie*, pardon, chiefly cheapnesse. **1656** Blount *Glossogr.*, *Laxity*, looseness, wildness, liberty. **1775** Johnson *Tax. no Tyr.* 20 Every expedition would in those days of laxity have produced a distinct and independent state. **1795** Mason *Ch. Mus.* iii. 187, I need not observe on the laxity of that Version. **1830** Scott *Demonol.* viii. 260 Such laxity of discipline afforded scope to the wildest enthusiasm. **1838** J. H. Newman *Par. Serm.* (1839) IV. ix. 156 All these laxities of conduct impress upon our conscience a vague sense..of guilt. **1849** Macaulay *Hist. Eng.* ix. II. 422 The very faults of their colleague, the known laxity of his principles. **1858** Froude *Hist. Eng.* III. xvi. 407 Laxity of assertion in matters of number is so habitual as to have lost the character of falsehood. **1865** Tylor *Early Hist. Man.* iv. 77 Carelessness and laxity in articulation. **1870** Rogers *Hist. Gleanings* Ser. ii. 54 Laxity of belief is coupled with laxity of practice. **1875** *Protests Lords* I. Pref. 10 A laxity of language, which must have conveyed far more than the framers of the Act contemplated. **1875** Jowett *Plato* (ed. 2) III. 265 Such tales ..engender laxity of morals among the young.

† **4.** Spaciousness. [A Latinism: cf. lax *a.* 6.]

1650 Fuller *Pisgah* ii. v. 122 The hills in Palestine generally had in their sides plenty of caves, and those of such laxity and receit that ours in England are but conny-boroughs if compared to the palaces which those hollow places afforded.

laxly ('lækslɪ), *adv.* [f. lax *a.* + -ly².]

1. In physical sense: Loosely; with loose cohesion; slackly, without tension.

1756 C. Lucas *Ess. Waters* I. 24 With [it] all the other elements..are more laxly or intimately blended. **1887** D. C. Murray & Herman *One Trav. Returns* ii. 35 The queen's head fell laxly on the arm which encircled her.

b. *Bot.*, etc.: With loose or open arrangement; not closely, compactly, or densely.

1847 W. E. Steele *Field Bot.* 191 The flor. thin, laxly imbricated. **1852** Dana *Crust.* i. 586 Hand..laxly pubescent about the fingers. **1867** J. R. Jackson in *Intell. Observ.* No. 62. 129 Laxly or densely imbricate. **1870** Hooker *Stud. Flora* 101 Vicia sylvatica..Racemes laxly 6–18-flowered.

2. With moral or intellectual looseness; without strictness, precision, or exactness.

1680 *Answ. Stillingfleet's Serm.* 12 We will not speak so laxly altogether as he does there. **1773** Johnson in *Boswell* 24 Oct., Nobody, at times, talks more laxly than I do. **1779** [Burke] ibid. 12–19 Oct., I do not think that men who live laxly in the world, as you and I do, can with propriety assume such an authority. **1838–9** Hallam *Hist. Lit.* III. iii. vi. 302 The former of these corrective functions must have been rather laxly exercised. **1867** Freeman *Norm. Conq.* (ed. 3) I. iii. 102 The..Thegns would attend more laxly. **1868** *Ibid.* (1876) II. ix. 403 We must remember how laxly that word is often taken. **1889** H. D. Traill *Strafford* 74 The enforcement of the laxly administered penal statutes.

laxmannite ('læksmənaɪt). *Min.* [Named after E. *Laxmann*, a Swedish chemist: see -ite.] A synonym of vauquelinite.

1884 in *Cassell's Encycl. Dict.*

laxness ('læksnɪs). [f. lax *a.* + -ness.] The quality of being lax; laxity: **a.** in physical senses.

1634 T. Johnson tr. *Parey's Chirurg.* xxvi. xlii. (1678) 658 Cold Waters or Baths..help the laxness of the bowels. **1669** Holder *Elem. Speech* 161 It is requisite that the Tympanum be tense..; otherwise the laxness of that Membrane will.. damp the sound. **1681** Glanvill *Sadducismus* i. (1682) 155 Like some Body passing through an over-large or wide hole, where it cannot stick by reason of the laxness of the passage. **1718** Quincy *Compl. Disp.* 6 By the greater laxness of its Contexture it will not lie in so little room. **1774** Garden in *Phil. Trans.* LXV. 105 This *carina*..is very distinguishable ..by its thinness, its apparent laxness.

b. in moral or intellectual senses.

1676 W. Hubbard *Happiness of People* Pref., Too much rigidness on the one hand, or laxness on the other. **1715** *Wodrow Corr.* (1843) II. 96 The universal laxness of the age. **1841** Elphinstone *Hist. Ind.* I. 51 The laxness, confusion, and barbarism which pervade this branch of the law. **1843** Thackeray *Ravenswing* vii, Deploring..the dreadful immorality which..arose in consequence of their laxness. **1887** *Pall Mall Budget* 21 Apr. 2/2 This criminal laxness, so alarmingly on the increase, should be nipped in the bud. **1969** *Daily Tel.* 27 May 1/2 Mission Control has now been exonerated of any laxness in this respect, for it turns out that they were not required to remind the lunar module crew to operate this particular switch.

c. *Phonetics.* Of a speech-sound, esp. a vowel: the state of being lax (lax *a.* 5 c).

1909 D. Jones *Pronunc. of Eng.* i. iii. 13 The tenseness or laxness of a vowel can often be observed mechanically by placing the finger on the throat between the larynx and the chin. **1956** Jakobson & Halle *Fund. of Lang.* i. iv. 43 In the opposition of tense and lax consonants, the laxness is frequently accompanied by voicing and the tenseness by voicelessness. **1967** D. Steible *Conc. Handbk. Ling.* 71 *Laxness*, a distinctive acoustic feature of English characterized by relative relaxation of the tongue and jaw while in the act of articulation.

Laxton ('lækstən). The name of *Laxton* Brothers, a firm of English nurserymen, used in the possessive to designate several varieties of fruit bred and introduced by them, esp. the apple **Laxton's Superb**, a popular, late-ripening variety of red-skinned eating apple.

1920 *Jrnl. R. Hort. Soc.* XLV. p. xxxvii, Exhibit. Messrs. Laxton, Bedford: Apple 'Laxton's Superb'. **1926** A. J. Macself *Fruit Garden* vii. 98 Laxton's Superb.—One of the best of early Pears, ripening in August. **1933** Hall & Crane *Apple* xii. 195 Laxton's Superb.—A comparatively new seedling introduced by Messrs. Laxton in 1921, which is now beginning to be generally planted. *Ibid.* 203 Laxton's Exquisite follows closely on James Grieve. **1937** A. H. Hoare *Commercial Apple Growing* ii. 50 Laxton's Epicure.. received an Award of Merit from the Royal Horticultural Society in 1931. *Ibid.* 51 Laxton's Fortune, also a result of a Cox's Orange Pippin and Wealthy cross, is claiming attention as an early bright-coloured and attractive apple. **1966** C. R. Thompson *Pruning Apple Trees* ii. 194 Other varieties..often crop profusely and yield small apples, e.g.

.. Laxton's Fortune and Laxton's Superb. 1974 *Countryman* Summer 107/2 The Fire Blight Order of 1958 ..banished this bacterial disease of pears by prohibiting Laxton's Superb, the most susceptible variety.

† **'laxy**, *a. Obs. rare* [f. LAX *a.* + -Y¹.] = LAX *a.* 3 a.

1716-21 *Mist's Weekly Jrnl.* (1722) II. 24 Her Flesh is laxy and flabby.

lay (leɪ), *sb.*¹ *Obs.* exc. *dial.* Forms: *α.* 1 **laȝu**, 3 **laʒe**; *pl.* 3 **lawes**, 4 **lauen**. *β.* 3 **lei-e**, 3, 5 **ley**, 4 **leye**, **laie**, 4-5 **laye**, 4, 9 (*dial.*) **lay**. [OE. *laȝu* (oblique cases *laȝe*); the *β* forms may represent either an OE. **læȝe* dat., acc., or gen., or the ON. *legi* dative, *legir* plural, of the equivalent *lǫg-r*:—OTeut. **lagu-z*:—pre-Teut. **lakú-s* (= L. *lacus* LAKE *sb.*⁴). It is also probable that in some instances the *β* forms represent an adoption of OF. *lai* pool:—L. *lacum*.] A lake, pool.

α. *a* 1000 *Boeth. Metr.* ix. 40 Lyft and laȝu land ymbclyppaþ garsecg embegyrt gumena rice. *a* 1000 *Cædmon's Gen.* 211 (Gr.) Laȝo yrnende. *a* 1300 *Childh. Jesus* 314-19 in Horstm. *Altengl. Leg.* (1875) 12-13 Watur þare with inne he brouȝte, His lawes maken þare inne he þouȝte. Bote a giw of heorte wrac Alle hise lawes þare he to brac. Iesu him seide with hastiue wille..ȝwi hast þou to broke mi lay? 1340-70 *Alisaunder* 3856 Theo blod, of heom that was slawen, Ran by flodis and by lauen.

β. *c* 1330 *Arth. & Merl.* 5296 Þe blod ran in þe valaie So water out of a laie. *Ibid.* 9652 He made alle a valaye Al so it were a brod leye. 1387 TREVISA *Higden* (Rolls) III. 367 Alisaundre..hadde alle maner bestes in kepyng in hyves, in layes, in fisshe weres and pondes. 1390 GOWER *Conf.* II. 167 She was nigh the great lay Of Triton [= L. *Tritonia palus*] founde, where she lay A child for-cast. *a* 1440 *Sir Degrev.* 239 One a launde by a ley These lordus dounne lyght. 1481 CAXTON *Godfrey* cciii. 298 The cyte of tabarye, whiche stondeth on the laye of Geme. *a* 1825 FORBY *Voc. E. Anglia*, *Lay*, a very large pond. 1840 SPURDENS *Suppl. Voc. E. Anglia*, *Lays*: always, I believe, in the plural number: as 'Denham lays'. Ponds in the midst of coppice and timber.

b. *attrib.*, as ***lay-fen***, ***-mire***.

c 1205 LAY. 22835 Draȝeð hine to ane more & doð hine in an ley uen [*c* 1275 laȝe fen]. *a* 1225 *Ancr. R.* 328 So me deoppre wadeð into þe ueondes leie uenne [*MS. T.* iðe deoueles lei mure], so me kumeð later up. *a* 1225 *Marherete* 14 Ich leade ham iþe leiuen [*printed* leinen] ant iþe ladliche lake of þe suti sunne. *c* 1230 *Hali Meid.* 33 Hwase lið ileinen [*i.e.* i lei uen, *MS. B.* ileifen] deope bisunken.

† **lay**, *sb.*² *Obs.* In 3 **leȝhe**, **lai**. [a. ON. *leiga* hire, toll.] Hire. Also in comb. **leȝhemann** (= ON. *leigumaðr*), a hireling.

c 1200 ORMIN 6222 And ȝunnc birrþ ȝunnkerr leȝhemenn Rihht laȝhelike ledenn. *Ibid.* 6234 And heore leȝhe birrþ hemm beon Rædiȝ þann itt iss addledd. *a* 1300 *Cursor M.* 11814 Nu neghes tim to tak his lai [*Fairf.* mede, *Trin.* pay].

† **lay**, *sb.*³ *Obs.* Also 3 **lei**, 3-4 **lai(e**, 5 **ley**, 5-6 **laye**. [a. OF. *lei*, mod.F. *loi* law = Pr. *ley*, *lei*, Cat. *lley*, Sp. *ley*, Pg. *lei*, It. *legge*:—L. *lēgem*, *lēx* law.] Law; *esp.* religious law; hence, a religion, a faith.

a 1225 *Leg. Kath.* 166 þæt cristene weren & leaffule in godes lei. *Ibid.* 832 Sone se ich awei warp ower witlese lei. *c* 1250 *Gen. & Ex.* 1201 Ðor-of holden ðe ieuwes lay. *c* 1290 *S. Eng. Leg.* I. 457/18 Formest he wende to Orlians to prechie godes laẏ. *a* 1300 *Cursor M.* 1428 Fra abraham..Til moyses þat gaf þe lai. *Ibid.* 1474 To fight al for þe cristen lay. *Ibid.* 13593 'A prophet', said he, 'be mi lai'. 13.. *Sir Beues* (A.) 1053 þow schelt swere vpon þe lay. *c* 1375 *Sc. Leg. Saints* ii. (*Paulus*) 983 All þat euire war of Iowis lay. *c* 1385 CHAUCER *Sqr.'s T.* 10. *c* 1400 *Sowdone Bab.* 764 If he will Baptised be And lefe his fals laye. *c* 1400 tr. *Secreta Secret.*, *Gov. Lordsh.* 105 My fey, My byleue, and my ley, er þes. *c* 1440 *York Myst.* xi. 44 Now are they like to lose our layse. *Ibid.* xxxviii. 445 It is gretely against oure lay. 1513 DOUGLAS *Æneis* VI. xiv. 8 Numa Pompilius, quhilk sall.. Begyn and statut with lawis and haly layis The cheif cetie of Rome. 1534 TINDALE *Acts* xxvi. 5 After the most straytest secte of oure laye [1526 lawe], lyved I a pharisaye. 1593 PEELE *Chron. Edw. I*, B 3, 'Tis Churchmans laie and veritie To liue in loue and charitie. 1599 ? KYD *Soliman & Pers.* I. A 4 b, Welcome vnto thee renowned Turke, Not for thy lay, but for thy worth in armes.

lay (leɪ), *sb.*⁴ Also 3-4 **lai**, 4-6 **laie**, 4-7 **laye**. [a. OF. *lai* (recorded from the 12th c.) = Pr. *lais*, *lays*; of uncertain etymology.

The most likely view is that favoured by M. Gaston Paris, that the word is of Teut. origin, an adoption of some form of the word represented by OHG., MHG. *leich*, play, melody, song. The ON. *lag* (see LAW *sb.*¹), used in the sense of 'tune', would also be phonetically a possible source. Connexion with Teut. **leupo-* (OE. *léoð*, Ger. *lied*) is out of the question, as are the Celtic words commonly cited: the Irish *laoidh* is believed to represent an OCeltic type **lūdi-*; the Welsh *llais* voice, sound, is too remote in meaning, and the assumed Breton equivalent is non-existent.]

1. A short lyric or narrative poem intended to be sung.

Originally applied *spec.* to the poems, usually dealing with matter of history or romantic adventure, which were sung by minstrels. From the 16th to the 18th c. the word was a mere poetical synonym for 'song'. This use still continues, but *lay* is now often employed (partly after G. *lied*, with which it is often erroneously supposed to be etymologically connected) as the appropriate term for a popular historical ballad such as those on which the Homeric poems are by some believed to be founded. Some writers have misapplied it to long poems of epic character like the Nibelungenlied or Beowulf.

a 1240 *Ureisun* in *Cott. Hom.* 199 þet ich habbe þe i-sungen ðesne englissce lai. *c* 1320 *Sir Tristr.* 551 An harpour made alay. *c* 1320 *Orpheo* 13-16 In Brytayn this layes arne ywrytt..Of aventures that fillen by dayes, Wherof Brytons made her layes. *c* 1386 CHAUCER *Merch. T.* 637 And in a lettre wroot he al his sorwe In manere of a compleynt or a lay. —— *Frankl. Prol.* 2 Thise olde gentil Britons in hir dayes Of diuerse auentures maden layes,.. Whiche layes with hir Instrumentz they songe, Or elles redden hem for hir plesance. *a* 1400-50 *Alexander* 6 Sum has langing of lufe lays to herken. 1470-85 MALORY *Arthur* X. xxxi, Thenne came Elyas the harper..and told hym the lay that Dynadan had made by Kynge Marke. 1483 CAXTON *G. de la Tour* A j, I made songes layes Roundels balades. 1592 DAVIES *Immort. Soul* IX. iv. (1714) 60 The holy Angels Choir Doth spread his Glory forth with spiritual Lays. 1608 SHAKS. *Per.* V. Prol. 4 Shee sings like one immortall, and shee daunces As Goddesse-like to her admired layes. 1697 DRYDEN *Virg. Georg.* II. 542 To Bacchus therefore let us tune our Lays. 1714 GAY *Trivia* I. 21 My Country's Love demands the Lays. 1718 PRIOR *Solomon* II. 80 Each morn they wak'd me with a sprightly lay; Of opening Heaven they sung. *a* 1758 RAMSAY *Some of the Contents* iii, Attackis his freind Dunbar in comick layis. 1805 SCOTT (*title*) The Lay of the Last Minstrel. 1827 KEBLE *Chr. Y.*, *Catechism*, Why should we think He turns away From infants' simple lays. 1842 MACAULAY (*title*) Lays of Ancient Rome. 1849 —— *Hist. Eng.* iii. I. 418 The popular lays chaunted about the streets of Norwich and Leeds in the time of Charles the Second. 1850 TENNYSON *In Mem.* xlviii, These brief lays, of Sorrow born. 1886 F. B. JEVONS in *Jrnl. Hellenic Studies* VII. 303 The theory of the aggregationists, that the *Iliad* is an agglomeration of orginally independent lays.

b. *poet.* Applied to the song of birds.

13.. *K. Alis.* 5211 Mery time it is in May, The foules syngeth her lay. 1362 LANGL. *P. Pl.* A. IX. 57 For to leorne the layes that louely foules maden. *c* 1386 CHAUCER *Sir Thopas* 58 The thrustelcok made eek his lay. 1390 GOWER *Conf.* III. 119 Whan every bird upon his lay Among the grene leves singeth. 1593 SHAKS. *2 Hen. VI*, I. iii. 93 Madame, my selfe haue..plac't a Quier of such enticing Birds, That she will light to listen to the Layes. 1742 YOUNG *Nt. Th.* I. 443 Sweet Philomel!.. ev'ry star Is deaf to mine, enamour'd of thy lay. *a* 1788 J. LOGAN *Cuckoo* iv, The school-boy..Starts, the new voice of Spring to hear, And imitates thy lay.

† **2.** Strain, tune. *Obs.*

a 1529 SKELTON *Agst. Garnesche* IV. 6 Your chorlyshe chauntyng ys all o' lay. 1581 J. BELL *Haddon's Answ. Osor.* 118 A continuall ianglyng of this Portingall Coockoe chatteryng alwayes one maner of laye in myne eares.

† **lay**, *sb.*⁵ *Obs. rare*⁻¹. [? repr. OE. **læȝ* = ON. *lag*: see LAW *sb.*²] A bill, score, reckoning.

13.. *Metr. Hom.* (Vernon MS.) in *Archiv Stud. neu. Spr.* LVII. 267 He..bad his hostes feede hem þat day And sette heore costes in his lay.

† **lay**, *sb.*⁶ Also 5-6 **laye**, **laie**, 6-8 **ley**. [? Aphetic form of ALLAY *sb.*¹] Alloy. Chiefly *attrib.* in ***lay metal***, the name of a kind of pewter.

c 1375 *Sc. Leg. Saints* xxxiii. (*George*) 402 þi godis..Ar mad bot of handis of mene Of gold and siluir & of clay, Of stok, of stone ore of lay. 1489 *Will of Wynter* (Somerset Ho.), j C de fyne metell et j C de lay metell. 1503 *Act 19 Hen. VII*, c. 6 §3 That no manere of person..make no holowe wares of Peauter, that is to say Saltes and Pottes that is made of Peweter called Ley Metell, but that it may be after the Assise of Peauter Ley Metell wrought within the Cite of London. 1534 in Peacock *Eng. Ch. Furniture* (1866) 210 Item xxv platers of lay metall. 1538 *Inv.* in J. W. Clark *Barnwell* Introd. (1897) 23 Item j lauer of laye mettell. 1794 G. ADAMS *Nat. & Exp. Philos.* I. App. 562 Lead and tin Ley-pewter, soft sold[er].

lay (leɪ), *sb.*⁷ Also 6-7 **laye**, **laie**, **ley(e**. [f. LAY *v.*¹]

† **1.** A wager, bet, stake. Often in phr. ***even lay***, a wager in which the chances are equal on either side, an even chance. Hence (in ***fair***, ***good***, etc. ***lay***) = chance, hazard. *Obs.*

1584 R. SCOT *Discov. Witchcr.* VII. iv. (1886) 107 It is an even laie, that an idiot shall conjecture right. 1593 SHAKS. *2 Hen. VI*, V. ii. 27 *Clif.* My soule and bodie on the action both. *Yor.* A dreadfull lay. 1601 HOLLAND *Pliny* II. 495 They bound themselues by a sacred lay and oth to fight it out to the last man. 1604 DEKKER *Honest Wh.* I. i. Wks. 1873 II. 17 Done, 'tis a lay, joyne gols on it. 1610 BEAUM. & FL. *Scornf. Lady* V. i, If I had been unhandsome, old or jealous, 't had been an even lay she might have scorn'd me. 1725 *New Cant. Dict.* s.v. *Lay*, An Hazard or Chance; as, *He stands a queer Lay*; He stands an odd Chance, or is in great Danger. 1726 DE FOE *Hist. Devil* I. x. (1840) 135 By venturing my life upon an even lay with him. 1729 E. ERSKINE *Wks.* (1871) I. 453 What a fair lay sinners living under the Gospel dispensation have for the eternal Salvation of their Souls. 1769 CHESTERF. *Lett.* 296 You will stand a very good lay, for if it is a prize it shall be yours, if a blank, mine.

2. a. A place of lying or lodging; lair, couch (of animals); an oyster- or mussel-bed; = LAYING *vbl. sb.* 2 c, LAYER *sb.* 4 b.

1590 GREENE *Mourn. Garm.* (1616) 42 The Fawne doth choose his foode by the laie of the olde Bucke. *a* 1625 BEAUM. & FL. *Bonduca* I. ii, I have found ye, Your lays, and out-leaps, Junius, haunts, and lodges. 1867 F. FRANCIS *Angling* vii. (1880) 252 The boatman will probably know.. the lay of the trout. 1902 *Westm. Gaz.* 12 June 10/1 The oyster and mussel lays off the foreshore have hitherto been worked on the large scale. 1905 *Country Life* 25 Mar. 400/2 More than 200 fresh oyster 'lays' have now been staked out on the north side of the Witham.

† **b.** ? Right of pasturing cattle; ? number of cattle pastured at one time. *Obs.*

1596 in T. Harwood *Lichfield* (1806) 527 Rec. for the fyrst leye into the Churche yarde for foure and twentye beastes and a weanynge calfe—xxxvj. *s.*

† **3.** A layer, stratum; a 'course' (of masonry).

1594 PLAT *Jewell-ho.* I. 35 By making a lay of dung of a foot in thicknesse. 1599 HAKLUYT *Voy.* II. I. 214 First they layed a lay of Brickes, then a Mat made of Canes, square as the Brickes. 1626 BACON *Sylva* §280 It was devised, that a Viall should have a Lay of Wire Strings below, as close to the Belly as a Lute. 1678 MOXON *Mech. Exerc.* 65 Continue your several lays of Plaining, till the whole upside of the Stuff be plained. *c* 1682 J. COLLINS *Making Salt* 16 It was.. pressed into a Cask, with sprinklings of Salt between each Lay. 1693 EVELYN *De la Quint. Compl. Gard.*, *Refl. Agric.* 55 These..make up what we call a Bed or Lay of Roots. 1704 ADDISON *Italy* (1733) 225 Different Lays of white and black Marble. 1725 BRADLEY *Fam. Dict.* s.v. *Vertigo*, Those [Animal Spirits] that are in the Lays of the Optick Nerves. 1769 MRS. RAFFALD *Eng. Housekpr.* (1778) 221 Lay them in the same water, with a lay of leaves betwixt.

4. The act of imposing a tax; an impost, assessment, rate, tax. Now *dial.*

1558 in Picton *L'pool Munic. Rec.* (1883) I. 95 It is to be levied by force of one ley yearly to be gathered by the Bailiffs for the time being. 1597 *Churchw. Acc. Cartmel* in J. Stockdale *Ann. Cartmel*, etc. (1872) 36 A caste or laye should bee forthwith had throughout all the parish. 1601 *Acc.-Bk. W. Wray* in *Antiquary* XXXII. 79 A note of all layes and sesments..one laye of xxxs. 1624 SIR E. SANDYS 15 Apr. in Cobbett *Parl. Hist.* (1806) I. 1421 In the lay of the first Imposition,..it was promised, That [etc.]. 1647 in Picton *L'pool Munic. Rec.* (1883) I. 143 A Ley or Taxacion of xiiˡ. *c* 1860 STATON *Rays fro' th' Loomenary* 34 Its some beggar, or else its th' chap ut collects th' lays. 1861 SMILES *Engineers* I. 419 In 1750 a lay of 3*d.* in the pound produced only £6 2*s.* 1½ *d.* 1888 *Sheffield Gloss.*, *Lay*, a rate, an assessment.

5. Rate or 'terms' of purchase or remuneration. *local U.S.*

1712 *Connect. Col. Rec.* (1870) V. 333 Provided that such land..shall be sold to such possessors thereof at the same lay as the residue of said land. 1775 *N. Hampsh. Prov. Papers* (1873) VII. 425 Provided there can be more built at an easier Lay than in the country by the company. 1792 B. MARSTON in *N. Eng. Hist. & Gen. Register* (1873) XXVII. 399, I am engaged to go out with a large Company..[to Africa] as their Land Surveyor General, on a pretty good lay. 1816 PICKERING *Vocab. U.S.*, *Lay*, terms or conditions of a bargain; price. Ex. I bought the articles at a good lay; he bought his goods on the same lay that I did mine. A low word. *New England.* 1856 *Peter Gott* (Bartlett), He took in his fish at such a lay, that he made a good profit on them.

6. *slang.* A line or plan of business, occupation, adventure, etc.; a (particular) job, 'line', or 'tack': often in phr. ***on*** (a certain) ***lay***.

1707 FARQUHAR *Beaux Strat.* III. iii, Cou'd I bring her to a Bastard, I shou'd have her all to my self; but I dare not put it upon that Lay, for fear of being sent for a Soldier. 1715 *Wodrow Corr.* (1843) II. 97 To distinguish myself from the refusers upon a Jacobite lay. 1721 CIBBER *School-boy* III. Dram. Wks. 1754 I. 23 The Puppy will play, tho' he knows no more of the Lay than a Milkwoman. 1760 C. JOHNSTON *Chrysal* (1822) I. 174, I first set them on the lay. 1818 SCOTT *Hrt. Midl.* xvi, I shall be on that lay nae mair. 1852 DICKENS *Bleak Ho.* xxii, He's not to be found on his old lay. 1858 GEN. P. THOMPSON *Audi Alt* I. lii. 201 It is a sad thing for a great country..to have taken to the filibustering lay. If the word is from the vocabulary of thieves, to the conduct of thieves it is appropriate. 1876 BESANT & RICE *Gold. Butterfly* xxxiv, For a year or two he wrote poetry. But the papers in America, he found, were in a league against genius. So he gave up that lay.

7. a. The way, position, or direction in which something is laid or lies (*esp.* said of country); disposition or arrangement with respect to something. (Cf. LIE *sb.*)

1819 *Sporting Mag.* V. 50 The correctness of their [dogs'] judgment on the lay of the country. 1851 *Jrnl. R. Agric. Soc.* XII. II. 647 Where the corn has a decided lean in one direction, the machine, if worked against the lay of the straw, meets with the requisite resistance. 1864 THOREAU *Maine W.* iii. (1869) 163, I did not know the exact route myself, but steered by the lay of the land. 1867 F. FRANCIS *Angling* v. (1880) 174 If the angler pulls against the..lay of the weed. 1878 H. M. STANLEY *Dark Cont.* I. xvi. 434 Seams of white quartz travelled along the lay of the strata. 1886 WALSINGHAM & PAYNE-GALLWEY *Shooting* I. 89 The lay of a gun to the shoulder when aimed depends..upon the 'cast off' and slope of the heel-plate.

b. *Naut.* Of a rope: The direction or amount of twist given to the strands. (Cf. LAY *v.* 37.) Also in *Spinning* (see quot. 1851).

1800 CAPT. HARVEY in *Naval Chron.* XII. 195, I was inclined to attribute this defect to the soft lay of the cable. 1839 URE *Dict. Arts* 1071 In no one instance has a rope or cable thus formed, been found defective in the lay. 1851 L. D. B. GORDON in *Art Jrnl. Catal. Gt. Exhib.* v**/2 In the bobbin and fly-frames, the amount of lay, or quantity of twist given to the roving, is as little as is compatible with their being unwound without impairing their uniformity. *c* 1860 H. STUART *Seaman's Catech.* 2 By taking a half hitch round and against the lay of the rope.

c. *Printing.* The arrangement of type in the case from which a compositor takes it; in full, ***lay of the case***; also = *lay gauge*.

[1683-4 MOXON *Mech. Exerc.*, *Printing* (1962) 194 The manner how the several sorts of Letters are disposed in the several Boxes, is called, Laying of the Case.] 1871 *Amer. Encycl. Print.* (ed. Ringwalt), *Lay of the Case*, the system upon which the various letters, points, spaces, quadrats, etc., are distributed among the different boxes in a case. 1884 J. GOULD *Letter-Press Printer* (ed. 3) 29, I give the following illustration of the upper-case as it is most commonly laid. In some offices, however, the 'lay' is quite different. 1888 JACOBI *Printers' Vocab.*, *Lay*, this refers to the position of the print on a sheet of paper. 1915 *Southward's Mod. Printing* (ed. 3) I. xxvi. 150 A printed plan of the case..will also be useful to experienced compositors, for there are many variations of the lay to be found in printing offices. *Ibid.* II. iv. 45 The Feed or Laying-on Board is, in the Wharfedale machine, at the base of the cylinder... On the front of the board are the gauges, or 'lays', to which the sheet of paper is laid. 1946 A. MONKMAN in H. Whetton *Pract. Printing & Binding* ii. 20/1 There is no standardized lay in this country although the variations are

in the main only concerned with such characters as the ligatures.., figures, and lower-case k and q. **1946** V. S. GANDERTON in *Ibid.* xi. 142/1 Lays, sheet-bands, grippers, and wheels shall be in identical positions on the sheet... If ..the register is out along the grip edge, the fault may be due to the front lays lifting too early or too late. **1969** *Studies in Bibliogr.* XXII. 125 (*title*) The lay of the case. *Ibid.*, The single lay, as used for instance in Germany and Switzerland, employs one large case for a fount of type. **1970** E. A. D. HUTCHINGS *Survey of Printing Processes* 199 *Lays, machine*, the points against which a sheet is positioned on the machine prior to impression taking place. **1972** P. GASKELL *New Introd. Bibliogr.* 36 Lays for exotic founts were usually adaptations of those used for the Latin alphabet.

d. A woman who is readily available for sexual intercourse; an act of sexual intercourse. *slang* (orig. *U.S.*). Cf. LAY *v.*[1] 2 b.

1932 J. T. FARRELL in *Story* Mar.-Apr. 46 A foursome passed homeward; two of the group were girls whom Jack and George agreed were swell lays. **1934** J. O'HARA *Appointment in Samarra* (1935) vi. 159 If there was ever an easy lay she was it. **1936** J. DOS PASSOS *Big Money* 254 There never been a girl got a spoken word by givin' that fourflusher a lay. **1955** W. GADDIS *Recognitions* II. i. 317 She's the girl you used to go around with in college? She's a good lay. **1955** G. GREENE *Quiet American* II. iii. 173 You'll just keep her as a comfortable lay until you leave. **1958** E. DUNDY *Dud Avocado* III. vi. 266 Roving photographer.. blows into town on the lookout for a quick lay. **1962** *Listener* 9 Aug. 223/3 His characters are without perspective: engrossed completely in their own lives, hardly seeing.. beyond the next drink, the next lay, the next five pounds. **1971** B. MALAMUD *Tenants* 16 Tonight an unexpected party, possibly a lay with a little luck.

8. A share in a venture; *esp.* in *Whaling*, the proportion of the proceeds of a voyage which is allotted to a man.

on a lay, on shares (*Cent. Dict.*). Also, ***by the lay*** (Smyth *Sailor's Word-bk.* 1867).

1850 SCORESBY *Cheever's Whalem. Adv.* iii. (1859) 35 With eager hope to obtain the oily material wherewith to.. make good their 'lay'. **1859** *Jrnl. R. Agric. Soc.* XX. I. 113 Every one on board.. has 'a lay' in the venture. **1879** H. GEORGE *Progr. & Pov.* I. iii. (1881) 47 On American whaling ships the custom is not to pay fixed wages, but a 'lay', or proportion of the catch. **1898** F. T. BULLEN *Cruise 'Cachalot'* iv. (1900) 33 Each of us was on the two hundredth 'lay'.. which means that for every two hundred barrels taken on board, we were entitled to one.

9. ***in (good, full) lay***: laying eggs.

1885 *Bazaar* 30 Mar. 1267/3, 4 pullets, in full lay.

10. *concr.* (See quot.)

1794 W. FELTON *Carriages* (1801) II. Gloss., *Lay*, a strip of leather, which is sewed on the top of another that is broader, for the purpose of additional strength, or to confine a smaller buckle.

11. *Comb.*: **lay-edge** *Printing*, the edge of a sheet of paper which is used to determine the correct position of the sheet in a press; **lay gauge**, an attachment on a printing press that keeps the paper in the correct position; †**lay-layer**, an assessor of rates.

1892 A. POWELL *Southward's Pract. Printing* (ed. 4) I. 444 Turn over the sheet.. and place it upon the feeding or laying-on board, with the same lay-edge towards the grippers as before. **1946** V. S. GANDERTON in H. Whetton *Pract. Printing & Binding* xi. 143/2 An untrimmed lay edge is an unknown quantity, and no two sheets stand up to the lays in the same way if they have a feather edge. For exact work, paper should always be trimmed. **1892** A. POWELL *Southward's Pract. Printing* (ed. 4) xlix. 434 Now set the lay gauges on the machine, so that the paper when fed to these will.. occupy the right position on the cylinder to receive the impression where it is intended to be. **1961** T. LANDAU *Encycl. Librarianship* (ed. 2) 190/1 Lay edges. The edges of a sheet of paper which are laid against the front and side lay gauges of a printing or folding machine. **1669** in Picton *L'pool Munic. Rec.* (1883) I. 328 The common assesso[rs] or Leylayers of this towne.

lay (leɪ), *sb.*[8] *dial.* [var. LATHE *sb.*[3] and *sb.*[4]]

1. *Weaving.* The batten of a loom; = LATHE *sb.*[4]

1789 A. WILSON in *Poems & Lit. Prose* (1876) I. 16 The palefaced weaver plies the resounding lay. **1825** J. NICHOLSON *Operat. Mechanic* 412 The lay which carries the reed, is hung from a bar. **1844** G. DODD *Textile Manuf.* i. 44 The batten or lay by which the weft-thread is driven up close. **1892** J. M. BARRIE *Little Minister* iii. 20 The lay still swung at little windows like a great ghost pendulum.

b. *Comb.*: **lay-cap**, a wooden bar which lies on the top of the reed and is held by the workman in working the lay; **lay-race** (see quot. 1855).

The comb. *lay-rod, lea-rod*, in some Dicts., referred to this word, is an incorrect form of *lease-rod*: see LEASE *sb.*[4], and cf. LEA *sb.*[4].

1831 G. R. PORTER *Silk Manuf.* 217 A top piece having a longitudinal groove along its lower side which is called the *lay-cap. **1839** URE *Dict. Arts* 1287 The lay-cap.. is the part of the lay which the hand-loom weaver seizes with his hand, in order to swing it towards him. **1855** OGILVIE Suppl., **Lay-race*, that part of the lay on which the shuttle travels from one side to the other of the web.

2. Used for LATHE *sb.*[3] 2.

In parts of Scotland, the turning lathe is still called *lay.*

1797 GODWIN in C. K. Paul *Life* (1876) I. 259 The potters we saw in the morning, turning a wheel, or treading a lay.

lay (leɪ), *a.* (and *sb.*[1]) Also 5–6 laye, 6 leye, laii, 5–7 laie, 6–7 lai. [a. F. *lai* (now replaced by the learned form *laïque*):—eccl.L. *lāïcus*, a Gr. λᾱϊκός (cf. LAIC). Cf. MDu. *leec* (Du. *leek*), OHG. *leigo* (MHG. *leige, leie*, mod.G. *laie*) layman.]

A. *adj.* **1.** Of persons: Belonging to the 'people' as contradistinguished from the clergy; not in orders, non-clerical.

When prefixed to official titles, the adj. is often hyphened.

c **1330** [see B]. **1432–50** [see LAYMAN]. *c* **1440** *Jacob's Well* 34 Alle relygious men, þat to leryd or to lay-folk.. mynystren ony of þise in sacramentys. **1481** CAXTON *Godfrey* xv. 42 The maners of the Clergye and of the laye peple. **1550** CROWLEY *Inform. & Petit.* 4 The laie and priuate persons ar as well of the flocke of Christe as the other. **1577** COLET *Fruitf. Admon.* 5 If thou be lay and vnmaried. **1641** MILTON *Ch. Govt.* II. iii. 52 Neither did the first Nicene councel.. think it any robbery to require the help.. of many learned lay brethren, as they were then called. **1651** C. CARTWRIGHT *Cert. Relig.* I. 76 It is erroneous ..that a Lay-man (as your Lay-Chancellour) should excommunicate and deliver up soules to Sathan. **1654** H. L'ESTRANGE *Chas. I* (1655) 186 No Convocation having power to grant any Subsidies, or aid without confirmation from the Lay-Senate. **1717** BERKELEY *Jrnl. Tour Italy* 8 Jan., Wks. 1871 IV. 514 A good number of gentlemen, lay as well as ecclesiastic. **1766** GRAY *Corr. N. Nicholls* (1843) 65 Ansel is lately dead, a lay-fellow of your college. **1818** CRUISE *Digest* (ed. 2) III. 68 A general prescription *de non decimando* can no more be set up against a lay impropriator than against a spiritual person. **1820** SCOTT *Monast.* xiii, [A] mill, erected on the lands of a lay-baron. **1873** HAMERTON *Intell. Life* XI. i. (1875) 398 A powerful lay element is certainly separating itself from the ecclesiastical element all over Europe. **1893** *Globe* 1 July 6/4 The Lay Helpers' Association of the diocese of London.

2. Characteristic of, connected or concerned with, occupied or performed by, laymen or the laity.

1609 BIBLE (Douay) II. Index, Laiheadshippe of the Church is rejected by most Heretiques, and by al Catholiques. **1613** SHAKS. *Hen. VIII*, I. iv. 11 Had the Cardinall But halfe my Lay-thoughts in him. **1649** JER. TAYLOR *Gt. Exemp.* II. Ad Sec. xi. 25 It cannot hallow a Lay designe, and make it fitt to become a religious ministery. **1675** in *Parl. Hist.* (1808) IV. 783 This bribing men by drink is a lay simony. **1750** CARTE *Hist. Eng.* II. 129 These were levelled against lay-patronages, and the prohibitions of secular Courts. **1765** BLACKSTONE *Comm.* I. 458 Lay corporations are of two sorts, civil and eleemosynary. **1767** *Ibid.* II. 61 The four kinds of lay tenure which subsisted in England, till the middle of the last century. **1780** COWPER *Progr. Err.* 371 With reverend tutor clad in habit lay. **1816** COLERIDGE (*title*), The Statesman's Manual.. A lay Sermon, addressed to the higher classes of society. **1867** TROLLOPE *Last Chron. Barset* II. xlvii. 31 The bishop strove to get up a little lay conversation.

3. Transferred senses. †**a.** Uninstructed, unlearned. *Obs. rare.*

c **1330** R. BRUNNE *Chron.* (1810) 171 Lered men and lay, fre and bond of toune. **1535** COVERDALE *Acts* iv. 13 They sawe the boldnesse of Peter & Ihon and marueyled for they were sure yᵗ they were vnlerned and laye people.

b. Non-professional, not expert, *esp.* with reference to law and medicine.

1810 BENTHAM [see GENT *sb.*]. **1826** —— in *Westm. Rev.* Oct. 457 Lay-gents however.. will.. see a convenience in it. **1861** MAINE *Anc. Law* (1874) 31 A mine of law unrevealed to the bar and to the lay-public. **1883** W. A. JEVONS in *Law Times* 27 Oct. 431/2 Lay legislators.. jumped to the conclusion that [etc.]. **1892** *Law Times* XCIV. 171/2 There is a natural confusion in the lay mind between a trustee and an executor. **1897** J. W. CLARK *Barnwell* p. lxvii, The prevention of disease, as well as the cure of it, is too technical for lay interference.

†**c.** Unhallowed, unsanctified; unspiritual, secular, worldly, *esp.* in phr. ***lay part.*** *Obs.*

1609 BIBLE (Douay) *1 Sam.* xxi. 4, I have no lay breads [Vulg. *laicos panes*] at hand, but only holy bread. *a* **1613** OVERBURY *A Wife*, etc. (1638) 49 That goodly frame we see of flesh and blood.. it is I say But their Lay-part; but well digested food. **1615** T. ADAMS *Spir. Navig.* 40 We see but the lay-part of things with these opticke organs. **1633** G. HERBERT *Temple, Priesthood* x, Exchanging my lay-sword For that of th' holy word. *a* **1668** SIR W. WALLER *Div. Medit.* (1839) 58 Thou hast shewed mercy to my worldly part, to my lay part; O heal my spiritual part.

4. Special collocations. **lay abbot** (see quot.). **lay analysis**, psychoanalysis undertaken by an analyst who has not been medically trained; so **lay analyst, psychiatrist, psychoanalyst**, one who practises psychoanalysis without medical training. **lay baptism**, baptism administered by a layman. **lay bishop**, †(*a*) applied derisively to those who set up as teachers of morality; (*b*) a playful term for a lay-rector. **lay brother**, a man who has taken the habit and vows of a religious order, but is employed mostly in manual labour and is exempt from the studies or choir-duties required of the other members. †**lay chattels** [AF. *lai chatel*] (see quot.). **lay clerk**, (*a*) a 'singing man' in a cathedral or collegiate church; (*b*) a parish clerk: see CLERK *sb.* 2 b. **lay communion**, (*a*) the condition of being in communion with the Church as a layman; (*b*) the communicating of the laity in the Eucharist. **lay deacon**, a man in deacon's orders who devotes only part of his time to religious ministrations, while following a secular employment. **lay elder** (see ELDER *sb.*[3] 4); hence ***lay-eldership.*** **lay judge**, a judge who is not a lawyer (*Cent. Dict.*). **lay lord**, a peer who is not a lawyer; opposed to *law lord.* **lay pope**, a layman who assumes the authority of a pope. **lay preacher**, an unordained preacher, esp. among Methodists. †**lay presbyter**, ? = 'lay elder'; hence ***lay presbytery.*** **lay reader**, (*a*) a layman licensed to conduct religious services; (*b*) a reader of a book, etc., on a subject of which he has no professional or specialist knowledge. **lay rector** (see RECTOR). **lay sister**, the analogue in a female religious order of a lay brother. **lay vicar** (see VICAR). See also LAY-FEE.

1872 *Gloss. Eccl. Terms* (ed. Shipley), s.v. *Abbot*, **Lay-Abbot*, a layman in possession of abbey property. Called also Abbot Non-religious. **1927** *Internat. Jrnl. Psycho-Anal.* VIII. 174 The Central Executive of the International Psycho-Analytical Association informs us it is their intention to bring forward the question of '*Lay Analysis' at the next Congress, so that opinions may be heard and, so far as possible, decisions arrived at in the matter. **1928** A. P. MAERKER-BRANDEN tr. *Freud's Probl. Lay-Analyses* i. 25 Let me, therefore, state that the problem of Lay-Analyses expresses itself most succinctly in the question of whether medically untrained laymen should be permitted to practise psychoanalysis. *Ibid.* viii. 171 As soon as the physician has ascertained this, he may safely leave the treatment to the *lay-analyst. **1955** M. MCCARTHY *Charmed Life* (1956) ii. 36 He had been.. a lay analyst. **1726** AYLIFFE *Parerg.* 105 Such Priests as question'd the Validity of *Lay-Baptism. **1693** DRYDEN *3rd Miscell.* Ded., Those *lay-bishops, as some call them, who, under pretence of reforming the stage, would intrude themselves upon us, as our superiors. **1870** L'ESTRANGE *Miss Mitford* I. ii. 58 The Colonel [Beaumont] is the patron,.. he is what they call a lay bishop, and still receives the tributary pence from the communicants. ? **14..** in *Mirr. our Ladye* p. xxi, I N. N. broþer professyd in the order & degre of a *lay brother or ffocary. **1679** *Trials of Wakeman*, etc. 34 He is a Benedictine Monk, or at least-wise a Lay Brother. **1743** *Pope's Dunciad* IV. 576 *note*, 'A Gregorian, one a Gormogon', A sort of Lay-brothers, Slips from the Root of the Free-masons. **1865** KINGSLEY *Herew.* i. (1875) 39 He dismounted, and halloed to a lay brother to see to his horse. **1618** SELDEN *Tithes* ii. 13 After those Tenths thus disposed of the remnant of that yeers increase they called חולין מתוחנין that is, as if you should say, euery way prepared or fit for common vse, or absolutely *Lay Chattels. **1811** BUSBY *Dict. Mus.*, **Lay-Clerk*, a vocal officiate in a cathedral, who takes part in the services and anthems, but is not of the priesthood. **1877** LEE *Gloss. Liturg. & Eccl. Terms, Lay clerk*,.. a layman who in the Church of England, by the tacit consent of the bishop or ordinary, or by the direct authority of the parish priest, assists in divine service. **1892** J. C. BLOMFIELD *Hist. Heyford* 17 He was fulfilling the office of lay-clerk in that parish. **1680** ALLEN *Peace & Unity* Postscr. 149 Their concession touching the Lawfulness of *Lay-Communion with our Parish Churches. **1847** CARDL. WISEMAN *Ess., Unreality Angl. Belief* (1853) II. 406 The Host given in lay-communion. **1880** W. SMITH & CHEETHAM *Dict. Chr. Antiq.* II. 947 Offences which in a lay-man were punished by ἀφορισμός,.. were in the clergy punished by reduction to 'lay communion'. **1861** M. ARNOLD *Pop. Educ. France* 117 If the National schools of England were taught by an order of *lay deacons. **1884** *Sat. Rev.* 12 July 49/2 The proposed scheme of starting a new order of ministers in the Church of England under the strangely paradoxical designation.. of 'lay-deacons'. **1594** HOOKER *Eccl. Pol.* Pref. §4. 22 The power of your *lay elders. **1827** HALLAM *Const. Hist.* (1876) III. xvii. 314 Each parish had its minister, lay-elder, and deacon. **1641** SMECTYMNUUS *Vind. Answ.* xv. 185 Al patrons of *Layeldership. **1863** H. COX *Instit.* II. vi. 481 Certain *lay lords expressed an intention of voting, but ultimately, on the recommendation of the law lords, with-drew. **1826** W. E. ANDREWS *Rev. Foxe's A. & M.* II. 179 The mere tools of the royal *lay-pope. **1747** WESLEY *Wks.* (1872) II. 67 He expressed the most rooted prejudice against *Lay-Preachers. **1790** J. WESLEY *Works* (1872) IV. 493 Joseph Humphrys; the first Lay Preacher that assisted me in England, in the year 1738. **1823** A. CLARKE *Mem. Wesley Family* 34 From this conversation we learn.. that he was a lay-preacher. **1906** 'MARK TWAIN' *What is Man?* (1917) iii. 31 In the Adirondack woods is a wage-earner and lay preacher in the lumber camps. **1962** H. DAVIES *Worship & Theol. in England* IV. ix. 258 John Nelson.. one of Wesley's most trusted lay preachers. **1975** R. LEWIS *Double Take* ii. 58 He.. was a Methodist lay preacher and a supporter of good causes. *a* **1663** SANDERSON *Serm.* (1681) II. Pref. 7 Where are your *lay-presbyters, your classes, &c. to be found in Scripture? **1640** BP. HALL *Episc.* III. ii. 224 Wheresoever they finde mention of an Elder in the New Testament, [they] think presently of a *Lay-Presbytery. **1958** 'J. BELL' *Seeing Eye* xiv. 147 He has been more successful as a *lay psychiatrist than he has as a general practitioner. **1933** *Harper's Mag.* Jan. 186/1 A lay *psycho-analyst finds that the political philosophy of Thomas Jefferson was a product of Jefferson's infantile revolt against his father. **1883** *Official Year-bk. Ch. Eng.* 110 The importance.. of recognizing the assistance of *Lay Readers, and of assigning them their proper place in the service of the Church... The office of Lay Reader is also fully recognized in the Protestant Episcopal Church in the United States. **1885** W. JAMES *Coll. Ess. & Rev.* (1920) 282 To the lay-reader, this absolute Idealism doubtless seems insubstantial and unreal enough. **1907** —— *Pragmatism* ii. 74 Farther than that the ordinary lay-reader in philosophy.. does not venture to sharpen his conceptions. **1912** *Motor* 17 Dec. 980/1 The subject matter is.. written in a manner easily understood by the lay reader. **1947** *Mind* LVI. 156 This is done in so compressed and allusive a manner that.. the lay reader could scarcely be expected to grasp it adequately. **1709** STEELE *Tatler* No. 129 ¶4 Whether the Ladies so called are Nuns or *Lay-Sisters. **1825** SCOTT *Betrothed* xvii, Her cellaress, her precentrix, and the lay-sisters of the kitchen.

5. *Comb.*, as †***lay-conceited, -minded*** adjs.

1613 SIR H. FINCH *Law* (1636) To Rdr., The very phrase, the termes of Art, excluding all hope of accrue to Lay-conceited opinions. **1898** S. EVANS *Holy Graal* 134 We Englishmen of today, a lay-minded folk much misguided of philosophic historians.

†**B.** *absol.* and *sb.* The lay people, laity; also, a layman. *Obs.*

c **1330** R. BRUNNE *Chron.* (1810) 100 þe kyng in þe courte of þe lay þe clerkes wild justise. *c* **1511** COLET in Lupton *Life* (1887) 302 The clergies..part ones reformed..than may we with a iuste order procede to the reformation of the lays [*ed.* 1661 laities; L. *laicalis*] part. **1528** TINDALE *Obed. Chr. Man* 40 b, What other thynge causeth the laye so litle to regarde there princes, as that they se them both dispised and disobeyed of the spiritualte? *c* **1532** DU WES *Introd. Fr.* in *Palsgr.* 1020 All the men..as well clerkes & lays. **1579** SPENSER *Sheph. Cal.* May 76 Men of the laye. **1602** WARNER *Alb. Eng.* IX. l. (1612) 227 From the Laie the Scriptures light to hide. *c* **1616** JONSON *Epigr.* cxxxi. Wks. (1616) 813 The learn'd haue no more priuiledge then the lay. **1670** MILTON *Hist. Eng.* IV. Wks. 1851 V. 181 Sparing neither Preist nor Lay. **1680** G. HICKES *Spirit of Popery* 23 They were Priviledged to come to the Altar, when all other Laies were forbidden.

lay (leɪ), *v.*[1] Pa. t. and pa. pple. laid (leɪd). *Infinitive*: 1 lecgan, lecgean, 2–5 legge(n, 6–7 (sense 1 c) ledge, 3–5 leyn, 4 lein, lain, leye, lai, 4–5 leyne, leie, 4–6 laye, ley, 5 leyen, 6 *Sc.* la, 6–7 laie, 4– lay. *Indicative Present*: *sing. 1st pers.* 1 lecge, 4 legge, leye (etc.), 4– lay. *2nd pers.* 1 leȝest, 3 leist, 6 lay'st, 6– layest. *3rd pers.* *α.* 1 leȝ(e)ð, 2 leiȝð, 3 leggeð, leiȝeð, 3–4 leið, 4 layþ, leyþ, leggiþ, 4–5 leieþ, 5–6 layth, 6 laieth, 4– (now *arch.*) layeth. *β.* 4–7 layes, lais, 5 legges, 7 laies, 4– lays. *plural.* *α.* 1 lecgaþ, lecgeaþ, 3 leggeoð, leggeð, leið. *β.* 3–6 laye, 4 leyn, lein, leye, leie, 5 leyhe, 6 laie, 4– lay. *γ.* *Sc.* and *north.* 5 layez, 6 layis. *Indicative Past*: *sing. 1st and 3rd pers.* 1 leȝde, læȝde, léde, 2 leiȝde, 2–3 læide, 2–5 leide, 3 leaide, *Orm.* leȝȝde, 3–6 leyde, 4 leid, legged, lait, *Sc.* lad, 4–5 lade, 4–7 laide, 4–8 layd(e, 5 leyd, leged, leghed, layid, 5–7 layed, laied, 7–8 lay'd, 4– laid. *plural.* 1 leȝdon, læȝdon, leidon, 2–3 læiden, 2–4 leiden, 3 ledden, 4 laiden, 4–5 leyden, 5 laidon; also (in 4 and subsequently) as 1st and 3rd pers. sing. *Imperative*: *sing.* 1 leȝe, 3 *Orm.* leȝȝ, 3–5 ley, leie, 4 leye, 5 le, 6 laye, 4– lay. *plural.* 1 lecgaþ, 3–4 leggeþ, 4 leiþ, 4– lay. *β.* *north.* and *Sc.* 4 laes, lays, lais. *Gerund*: 4–6 layeng, 5 legginge, legynge, 6 (sense 1 c) ledging, 5 leying, leiyng, leyng, 5–6 layng(e, 6 laieng, laiyng, 6–7 layeing, 4– laying. *Present Participle*: *α.* 1 lecgende, 4 *north.* and *Sc.* leyond, layand. *β.* (as in the Gerund). *Past Participle*: 1 ȝeléd, ȝeleiȝd, 3 ileid, yleid, ilæid, *Orm.* leȝȝd, 3–5 leid(e, leyd, 4 ylaid(e, ylayde, leyde, 4–5 yleyd, 4–6 layde, 4–7 laide, layed, 4–8 layd, 5 ilaid, leied, leyed, led, 6 layede, (sense 1 c) ledgde, 6–7 laied, 7 lai'd, 7–8 lay'd, 4– laid. [OE. *lęcgan* = OFris. *ledsa*, *lega*, *leia*, OS. *leggian* (Du. *leggen*), OHG. *lecken*, *legen* (MHG., mod.G. *legen*), ON. *legja* (Sw. *lägga*, Da. *lægge*), Goth. (= OTeut.) *lagjan*, f. **lag-* ablaut-variant of OTeut. **leg-*: see LIE *v.*

The normal representative of the OE. inf. and of the 1st pers. sing. and the plural pres. tense, would be **ledge*; the exisitng form of the present-stem is evolved from the 2nd and 3rd pers. sing. pres. tense, in which the *g* of the OTeut. vb. was followed not by *j* but by *i*, and therefore escaped the WGer. gemination, so that OE. in these instances has *g* instead of *cg*.]

General sense: To cause to lie.

I. To prostrate.

1. a. *trans.* To bring or cast down from an erect position (in OE. often, to strike down, slay); †*fig.* to cast down, abase, humble. Now only with complement denoting prostration or extension upon a surface. *to lay low*: see the adj.

c **888** K. ÆLFRED *Boeth.* (Sedgefield) xli. §3 He..hæt fealdan þæt seȝl & eac hwilum lecgan þone mæst. *a* **1000** *Laws of Athelstan* II. c. 2 (Schmid) Hine lecge for þeof se ðe him tocume. *c* **1200** *Trin. Coll. Hom.* 165 Al riht is leid and wogh arered. **13..** *E.E. Allit. P.* B. 1650 Who-so hym lyked to lyfte, on lofte watz he sone, & quo-so hym lyked to lay, watz loȝed bylyue. **1377** LANGL. *P. Pl.* B. v. 359 [He] cauȝte hym bi the myddel, For to lifte hym alofte and leyde him on his knowes. *c* **1440** *Partonope* 7007, I leyd hym flatt than in the med. **1595** SHAKS. *John* II. i. 399 Shall we..lay this Angiers euen with the ground? **1660** F. BROOKE tr. *Le Blanc's Trav.* 6 With a mortall wound on the forehead [he] laid him dead at his feete. **1671** MILTON *P.R.* II. 332 A multitude with Spades and Axes arm'd To lay hills plain, fell woods, or valleys fill. **1785** COWPER *Poplar Field* 7 And now in the grass behold they are laid, And the tree is my seat that once lent me a shade! **1850** *Tait's Mag.* XVII. 754/1 The abbey was laid in ruins by the explosion. **1879** BROWNING *I. Ivanovitch* 95 We check the fire by laying flat Each building in its path. **1890** *Guardian* 24 Sept. 1486/1 One third of the town was laid in ashes.

†**b.** *to lay to ground, to earth* (Sc. *at eird*): to stretch upon or bring to the ground; to bring low, throw down, overthrow, destroy. *Obs.*

c **1205** LAY. 27328 We heom scullen awelden leggen heom to grunde. *c* **1330** *Arth. & Merl.* 5086 (Kölbing) Hou Wawain & his feren..Hadden..þre þousand leyd to grounde. **1375** BARBOUR *Bruce* III. 16 And weill ost..War layd at erd, but recoveryng. **1470–85** MALORY *Arthur* I. x, At the fourth passage there mette two for two, and bothe were leid vnto the erthe. **1513** DOUGLAS *Æneis* XI. xiii. 62 Mony Troianis ded to ground scho laid.

c. Of wind or rain: To beat down (crops). Chiefly in *passive*. (In 16–17th c. spelt *ledge*.)

1590 *Plain Perc.* 21 Send not a whirlwinde amongst them, least..they..be ledgde on the ground. **1613** R. C. *Table Alph.* (ed. 3), *Cadence*..properly the ledging of corne by a tempest. **1626** [see LAYING *vbl. sb.* 1]. **1727** BOYER *Fr. Dict.* s.v., The Rain has laid the Corn, *la Pluye a couché les Bleds.* **1787** WINTER *Syst. Husb.* 63 The straw grows so luxuriant, as to be beaten down and laid by high winds and heavy rains. **1799** A. YOUNG *Agric. Linc.* 162 If laid, it [*sc.* flax] will not do for seed. **1846** *Jrnl. R. Agric. Soc.* VII. II. 288 It bore wheat again,..but the weather of July laid it. **1859** TENNYSON *Geraint* 764 Yniol with that hard message went; it fell Like flaws in summer laying lusty corn. **1870** RAMSAY *Remin.* ii. (ed. 18) 26 The crops being much laid.

2. a. To 'bring to bed' *of* a child; to deliver (a mother). *Obs.* exc. *dial.* †Also *refl.* said of the mother. (Cf. 53 c.)

c **1460** *Towneley Myst.* xiii. 520 And gyll, my wyfe, rose nott here syn she lade hir. **1605** *Vestry Bks.* (Surtees) 56 Item given to the hird of Pittington for layinge a hogge, ijd. **1669** *Plymouth Col. Rec.* (1856) V. 14, I went to her father Winters house..as I was informed of her being laid; and shee haueing a young child in her lapp, I asked her whoe was the father of it. **1682** BUNYAN *Holy War* 168 The midwife that laid my mother of me. **1684** LADY R. RUSSELL *Lett.* I. xvii. 50, I hear my Lady Digby is safely laid of a girl. **1716** C'TESS COWPER *Diary* (1864) 126 The English Ladies all pressed to have the Princess laid by Sir David Hamilton. **1724** J. MAUBRAY (*title*) Female Physician Comprehending ..particular directions for laying women, in all cases of difficult and preternatural births. **1828** CARR *Craven Dial.*, *Lay, Lig*, to perform the office of an accoucheur. 'He com to lay my daam'. **1876** in *Whitby Gloss.*

b. To have sexual intercourse with (a woman). Occas. *intr.*, const. *for*: (of a woman) to have sexual intercourse with (a man). Also *intr.*: (of a woman) to be willing to have (extramarital) sexual intercourse. *slang* (orig. *U.S.*). Cf. LAY *sb.*[7] 7 d.

1934 J. O'HARA *Appointment in Samarra* ii. 38 I'm going to take Teddy out and get him laid tonight. *Ibid.* vii. 212 'You're wrong about one thing,' said Julian... 'I didn't lay that girl.' **1936** J. DOS PASSOS *Big Money* 305 'Gosh,' he was saying at the back of his head, 'maybe I could lay Elsie Finnegan.' **1938** G. GREENE *Brighton Rock* v. v. 214 I'm marrying her for your sake, but I'm laying her for my own. **1950** A. WILSON *Such Darling Dodos* 123 As soon as he laid a new wench..there was always a shift round of staff. **1955** 'H. ROBBINS' *Stone for Danny Fisher* I. vii. 55 'Does she lay, Danny?'.. His face was flushed as his eyes followed the girl on to the porch. **1956** H. GOLD *Man who was not with It* (1965) xviii. 164 Whore! Baby-whore! She been laying for you. **1960** J. UPDIKE *Rabbit, Run* (1961) 184 You've laid for Harrison, haven't you? **1966** AUDEN *About House* 15 A great-great-grandmother who got laid By a sacred beast. **1969** P. ROTH *Portnoy's Complaint* 182 All I know is I got laid, *twice.* **1973** B. BROADFOOT *Ten Lost Years* viii. 83 The guy who knew her was one of our gang and he was laying her.

3. a. To cause to subside (the sea, a tempest, a cloud of dust, etc.); †to put a stop to (an annoyance) (*obs.*); to allay (anxiety), appease (anger, appetite, etc.). Now *arch.* or *dial.* exc. in *to lay the dust.*

a **1300** *E.E. Psalter* lxxxiv. 4 þou leyed alle þi wreth þat þou was inne. *c* **1340** *Cursor M.* 5990 (Trin.) To morwe shul þo fliȝes be leide. **1398** TREVISA *Barth. De P.R.* v. vi. (1495) 112 Yf the eye lyddes..ben full of flesshe wythin..thenne he layeth the syghte [L. *visum impediunt*]. *c* **1430** *Syr Gener.* (Roxb.) 1782 If ye me doo as ye me seid, A grete part of my care is leid. **1508** DUNBAR *Flyting w. Polwart* 96 Ȝit come I hame, fals baird, to lay thy boist. **1539** TAVERNER *Erasm. Prov.* (1552) 4 Moue not an euyll that is well layed. **1579** GOSSON *Sch. Abuse* (Arb.) 25 Terpandrus with his notes layeth the tempest. **1591** SHAKS. *Two Gent.* II. iii. 35 See how I lay the dust with my teares. *a* **1645** LAUD *Serm.* (1847) 127 To show His disciples that His command could lay the sea. **1650** R. STAPYLTON *Strada's Low C. Warres* IV. 77 This report he was so farre from sleighting..that he laid it, before it could passe out of Spain. **1671** MILTON *P.R.* IV. 429 Who ..still'd the roar Of thunder, chas'd the clouds, and laid the winds. **1695** BLACKMORE *Pr. Arth.* I. 307 Th' enchanted Winds straightway their Fury laid. **1712** ADDISON *Spect.* No. 465 ¶1 The doubt which was laid revives again. *a* **1715** BURNET *Own Time* (1724) I. 60 He upon his coming over did for some time lay the heats that were among the Highlanders. **1727** BOYER *Fr. Dict.* s.v., To lay the Stomach for a while, *etourdir la grosse faim.* **1872** BLACK *Adv. Phaeton* xxii. 308 'It was merely to lay the dust', said Bell, as though she had ordered the shower. **1879** FARRAR *St. Paul* I. 181 To lay the secret misgivings which had begun to rise in his mind. **1891** *Rutland Gloss.* s.v., 'The bit of fish as you sent me laid my appetite'. **1900** *Q. Rev.* Apr. 459 These fears ought now to be laid.

b. To prevent (a spirit) from 'walking'. Often in fig. context.

1592 SHAKS. *Rom. & Jul.* II. i. 26 To raise a spirit in his Mistresse circle,..letting it stand Till she had laid it, and coniured it downe. **1678** BUTLER *Hud.* III. ii. 466 For nothing but his Interest Could lay his Devil of Contest. **1706** ESTCOURT *Fair Example* III. i, When the Devil is up in a Woman, the wisest way is to lay it. **1716** ADDISON *Drummer* II. i, He knows the secret of laying ghosts or of quieting houses that are haunted. **1850** TENNYSON *In Mem.* xcvi. 16 He faced the spectres of the mind And laid them. **1851** D. JERROLD *St. Giles* xvi. 162 With a strong will, he laid the rising ghosts of his boyish days. **1883** FROUDE *Short Stud.* IV. II. i. 170, I remember his being called upon to lay a troublesome ghost.

4. †To bring down, reduce (a swelling) (*obs.*); to smooth down, make to lie evenly.

1579 SPENSER *Sheph. Cal.* Oct. 119 When my Gates shall han their bellies layd: Cuddie shall haue a Kidde to store his farme. **1823** J. BADCOCK *Dom. Amusem.* 185 This will lay some blisters, and prevent others rising. **1892** *Leisure Hour* Nov. 72/2 Silk hats are 'renovated' by brushing them round smoothly with a wet brush to lay the nap.

5. *Naut.* To sail out to such a distance as to bring (an object) to or below the horizon. (Opposed to *raise*.)

1574 BOURNE *Regiment for Sea* xiii. (1577) 39 a, In going to the North, you doe rayse the Pole, and lay the Equinoctiall. **1711** *Milit. & Sea Dict.*, *To Lay the Land.* When they have sail'd out of Sight of Land, they say, they have Laid the Land. **1711** *Lond. Gaz.* No. 4887/3 We chased them till Ten, at which time we had laid their Hulls. **1769** FALCONER *Dict. Marine* (1780), *Laying the Land*, in navigation, the state of motion which increases the distance from the coast, so as to make it appear lower and smaller;..used in contradistinction to *raising* the land.

6. *Gardening.* = LAYER *v.* 1 b. Also *refl.* of the plant. ? *Obs.*

1565 COOPER *Thesaurus* s.v. *Sterno, Vites stratæ, quæ & constratæ.* Vines growyng close to the grounde, or layed or planted in the earth. **1664** EVELYN *Kal. Hort.* July (1679) 21 You may lay Myrtils, Laurels, and other curious Greens. **1696** PHILLIPS (ed. 5), To *Lay*, in Gardening is to bend down the Branches, and cover them that they may take Root. **1707–12** MORTIMER *Husb.* II. 185 The chief time of laying gilliflowers is in July. **1770** WARING in *Phil. Trans.* LXI. 387 Inferiour plants, that sometimes, in the phrase of gardening, lay them-selves. **1822** LOUDON *Encycl. Garden.* §1646. 978 In that case the new plants [pinks] are not so well rooted as those layed earlier. **1851** *B'ham & Midl. Gardeners' Mag.* May 68 Lay and peg your plants.

b. *dial.* '*to lay a hedge*, to trim it back, cutting the boughs half through, and then bending them down and intertwining them so as to strengthen the fence' (*Wiltsh. Gloss.*).

1765 *Museum Rust.* IV. 80 Making, plashing and laying live hedges. **1851** *Jrnl. R. Agric. Soc.* XII. II. 336 The fences ..have been plashed and laid.

II. To deposit.

7. a. To place in a position of rest *on* the ground or any other supporting surface; to deposit in some situation specified by means of an adverb or phrase. †*to lay lake*: to offer sacrifice (quot. 1225).

c **950** *Lindisf. Gosp.* Matt. xxi. 8 Hia ȝeðurscon tuiggo of treum & ȝebredon *vel* leȝdon on weȝ. *c* **1175** *Lamb. Hom.* 101 Ða ileaffullen brohton heore gersum, and leiden heo et þere apostlan fotan. *c* **1200** *Moral Ode 12* in *Trin. Coll. Hom.*, Alto muchel ic habbe ispend, to litel ileid on horde. *c* **1200** ORMIN 14666 Sniþ itt, alls itt wære an shep, & leȝȝ itt upponn allterr. *a* **1225** *Leg. Kath.* 1895 Ȝef þu leist lac to ure liuiende godes. *a* **1300** *Cursor M.* 7186 Vp [Sampson] bar þe yatis o þe tun, And laid þam on a hei dun. *c* **1350** *Will. Palerne* 3234 þat men miȝt legge him mete & wateren atte wille. *c* **1375** *Sc. Leg. Saints* i. (*Petrus*) 429 He can it ta,..and syne it lade In his slefe. **1387** TREVISA *Higden* (Rolls) VII. 369 He was wont to legge his heed uppon a forme of þe chirche. **1399** LANGL. *Rich. Redeles* II. 186 Lymed leues were leyde all aboute. *c* **1450** *Two Cookery-bks.* 109 Take brede..and make it broune, and ley hit in vynegre. **1500–20** DUNBAR *Poems* xii. 14 Thornis laid in thy way. **1535** COVERDALE *Lev.* i. 8 Yᵉ peces..shal they laye vpon the wodd. **1582** N. T. (Rhem.) *Matt.* viii. 20 The sonne of man hath not where to lay his head. [So **1611**; earlier versions 'rest'.] **1604** E. G[RIMSTONE] *D'Acosta's Hist. Indies* v. xxiv. 394 Al the people did humble themselves, laying earth vpon their heads. **1664** EVELYN *Kal. Hort.* July (1679) 21 If it prove too wet, lay your pots side-long. **1666** BOYLE *Orig. Formes & Qual.* 355, I had layd it upon a piece of white Paper by the fires side to dry. **1669** STURMY *Mariner's Mag.* I. 31 Laying a Ruler over the Intersections..draw the line GH. **1697** DRYDEN *Virg. Georg.* IV. 64 Plaister thou their chinky Hives with Clay, And leafy Branches o'er their Lodgings lay. **1701** W. WOTTON *Hist. Rome, Commodus* ii. 233 He layd the Book upon the Bed. **1838** T. THOMSON *Chem. Org. Bodies* 676 Two pieces of paper..were laid upon each other, and allowed to dry. **1849** MACAULAY *Hist. Eng.* v. I. 532 He had contrived to scatter lampoons about the terrace of Windsor, and even to lay them under the royal pillow.

b. To place documents containing information on the table (see TABLE *sb.* 5 b) in order to present the information to the members.

[**1813** *Hansard Commons* 17 Mar. 142 Mr. Whitbread then moved, that the Petition be laid upon the table; which was ordered accordingly.] **1923** *Westm. Gaz.* 3 Aug., The Premier promised to lay all the correspondence, if M. Poincaré consents. **1924** *Hansard Commons* 10 Mar. 1931 His Majesty's Government have been willing to lay the complete records, but objections have been raised. **1964** *Erskine May's Law of Parl.* (ed. 17) xiii. 274 A similar order was made..in cases where a paper was laid under an Act that prescribed a period during which objection to it could be taken.

8. With mixture of sense 1.

a. To place (a person, one's limbs, oneself) in a recumbent posture in a specified place. *to be laid*: to lie down, recline (†formerly sometimes without a specifying adv. or phrase).

c **1200** ORMIN 3401 þeȝȝ fundenn þær þe child þær itt wass leȝȝd i cribbe. *c* **1275** *Sinners Beware* 284 in *O.E. Misc.* 81 Ye me..leyden in softe bedde. *a* **1300** *Cursor M.* 8604 (Cott.) Wimmen..þat lais [*MS. Trin.* leyn] in bedd yong barn þam bi. *c* **1385** CHAUCER *L.G.W.* Prol. B. 208 Whan I was leyd, and had myn eyen hed. *c* **1475** *Partenay* 2889 But slepe myght he noght when that he was led. *a* **1548** HALL *Chron.*, *Hen. V*, 80 Kyng Henry wexed sicker and sicker, and so was layd in a horselitter. *a* **1598** PEELE *Merrie Jests* (*c* 1620) 13 With much ado her maid had her to bed, who was no sooner layd, but she fell fast asleepe. **1608** TOPSELL *Serpents* (1658) 756 When he is laid, he careth not for rising again. *a* **1701** SEDLEY *Pindaric Ode* Wks. 1778 II. 17 The bleating sheep are laid; And on the earth the nightly dew distils. **1849** MACAULAY *Hist. Eng.* iii. I. 321 The coarse jollity of the afternoon was often prolonged till the revellers were laid under the table. **1849** AYTOUN *Poems, Hermotimus* ii, Fain I'd lay me gently by thy side. **1853** M. ARNOLD *Scholar-Gipsy* iii, The bent grass where I am laid.

b. To deposit *in* the grave; to bury. Only with adv. or phrase indicating the place. ***to lay one's bones***: to be buried (in a specified place).

c **1000** *Ags. Gosp.* John xx. 15 Seȝe me hwar þu hine ledest [*c* **1160** *Hatton Gosp.* leydest]. **11..** *O.E. Chron.* an. 1075 (Laud MS.) Se cyng hi let bryngan to Westmynstre..& læȝde hi wið Eadward kyng hire hlaforde. *c* **1175** *Lamb. Hom.* 51 Efterþan þet þe mon bið dead, me leið þene licome in þere þruh. *c* **1205** LAY. 17842 Leggeð me an æst ænde inne Stan-henge. *a* **1225** *Leg. Kath.* 2251 We..þæt licome awei ledden & leiden in eorðe. *c* **1250** *Gen. & Ex.* 816 Fowre biried ðor ben; ðor was leid adam and eua, Abram siðen and sarra. *a* **1300** *Cursor M.* 17794 Lang es gan Sin þai war ded, laid vnder stan. *c* **1375** *Sc. Leg. Saints* vii. (*Katerine*) 1179 Angelis..hire body bare to mont synay, & lait It þare. **1388** WYCLIF *Acts* xiii. 36 Dauid..diede, and was leid with hise fadris. *a* **1400** *Prymer* (1891) 50 Thei leyde hym in his graue. **1578** W. HUNNIS in *Parad. Dainty Devices* 2 After they be layde in graue. **1697** DRYDEN *Æneis* XI. 310 Part, in the Places where they fell, are laid. **1698** FRYER *Acc. E. India & P.* 57 The Air so salubrious, that never any English are remembered to lay their Bones here. **1836** W. IRVING *Astoria* I. 121 My uncle was lost a few years ago on this same bar, and I am now going to lay my bones alongside of his. **1853** M. ARNOLD *Scholar-Gipsy* xiv, Thou from earth art gone Long since, and in some quiet churchyard laid. **1879** MORLEY *Burke* ix. 206 He was laid in the little church at Beaconsfield.

c. ***to lay to sleep, asleep***: to put to rest; to put in the last resting-place, to bury; also *fig.* Also ***to lay to rest***, † ***abed***, † ***to bed***.

a **1300** *Cursor M.* 14199 Lazar vr freind es laid on-slepe. **1340–70** *Alisaunder* 823 Hee sawe..How þat louelich lif laide was a bedde, And a gracious God gripte hur in armes. *c* **1400** *Destr. Troy* 10410 Thai..logget þe long nyght, layd hom to rest. **1591** SPENSER *Teares Muses* 183 O! all is gone; and all that goodly glee..Is layd abed, and no where now to see. **1606** SHAKS. *Ant. & Cl.* II. ii. 232 Royall Wench: She made great Cæsar lay his Sword to bed. **1610** —— *Temp.* II. i. 284. **1676** HOBBES *Iliad* XIV. *Table Contents*, Juno by the help of Venus layeth Jove asleep. **1692** tr. *Sallust* 33 Malice and Pride were laid asleep. **1701** W. WOTTON *Hist. Rome, Commodus* ii. 235 The Poyson soon layd him to sleep. **1814** J. HUNTER *Who wrote Cavendish's Wolsey?* 13 There is, in this, what might lay a general biographer, who was a very Argus, asleep. **1869** A. W. WARD tr. *Curtius' Hist. Greece* II. II. v. 112 He was laid to rest among his ancestors. **1881** GARDINER & MULLINGER *Study Eng. Hist.* I. x. 186 The questions springing out of the Toleration Act had long been laid asleep.

9. To produce and deposit (an egg). Also *absol.* Often in fig. contexts. Also fig. phr. ***to lay an egg***, used in various colloq. senses, *spec.*: (*a*) (of an aircraft) to drop a bomb; (*b*) orig. *U.S.* (of a performer or performance) to flop.

c **1000** *Sax. Leechd.* III. 204 Henne æȝru lecgan ȝestreon mid carfulnysse ȝe[tacnað]. *a* **1225** *Ancr. R.* 66 Þe hen hwon heo haueð ileid, ne con buten kakelen. **13..** *K. Alis.* 568 A faukon..An ay he laide. *c* **1420** *Pallad. on Husb.* I. 583 Wiltow they oftyn hacche & eyron grete They legge. **1523** FITZHERB. *Husb.* §146 Thou must take hede how thy hennes duckes & gees do ley. **1553** EDEN *Treat. Newe Ind.* (Arb.) 9, I wold be loth to lay an egge, wherof other men might hatche a serpent. **1611** BIBLE *Isa.* xxxiv. 15 There shall the great owle make her nest, and lay and hatch. **1678** BUTLER *Hud.* III. iii. 625 Like Nest-eggs, to make Clients lay. **1711** ADDISON *Spect.* No. 120 ¶14 When she has laid her Eggs in such a manner that she can cover them. **1780** COWPER *Progr. Err.* 239 Remorse, the fatal egg by Pleasure laid In every bosom where her nest is made. **1830** MARRYAT *King's Own* xli, One of the hens laid astray. **1841** *Jrnl. R. Agric. Soc.* II. I. 23 [They] lay their eggs in the bodies of other insects. **1884** *Times* (weekly ed.) 19 Sept. 6/4 [Pheasants] lay freely in the thick coverts on the hillsides. **1918** [see EGG *sb.* 3 d]. **1927** *Daily Express* 2 June 11/2 'Laying an egg' in Air Force slang means dropping a bomb. **1929** *Variety* 30 Oct. 1 (*headline*) Wall Street lays an egg... The most dramatic event in the financial history of America is the collapse of the New York Stock Market. **1940** J. O'HARA *Pal Joey* 38 You would just as well come wearing a shell if you ever took a job [singing] in a spot like this, that is how big an egg you would lay. **1947** [see EGG *sb.* 3 d]. **1949** L. FEATHER *Inside Be-Bop* iii. 30 The singer had been laying eggs at the Zanzibar..and Shaw was undecided what to do with him. **1958** *Spectator* 6 June 730/2 The second gambit, when a joke is so drearily bad..that even a studio audience can't laugh at it, is to admit, quite shamelessly, that one has, as they say, laid an egg. **1964** *People* (Austral.) 16 Dec. 45/1 A Stuka caught us in the town of Lamia. The plane duly laid an egg. I was crouched alongside a wall. The bomb landed on the other side of the wall.

† **10.** To deposit (payment). *Obs. rare.*

c **1475** *Rauf Coilȝear* 299 God forbid..That for ane nichtis harbery Pay suld be laid.

† **11. a.** With advb. phr. as complement, e.g. *to wed, to pledge, in pawn*: To deposit as a pledge or in pawn; hence, to mortgage (lands). Also, ***to lay a wed***. *Obs.*

1297 R. GLOUC. (Rolls) 8083 He..leide willam is broþer to wedde normandye. *c* **1374** CHAUCER *Compl. Mars* 205 They myghten lyghtly ley hire hede to borowe. **1377** LANGLAND *P. Pl.* B. XVIII. 31 Lyf..leyth his lif to wedde, þat [etc.]. **1389** in *Eng. Gilds* (1870) 8 Þat þey leye a suffisaunt wed. *c* **1400** MAUNDEV. (Roxb.) ii. 6 Þe emperour had layd þam [þise relyques] in wedd for a grete soume of gold. **1461** *Paston Lett.* No. 407 II. 33 A dyamaunt and a gret perle, which were leyd to plegge by oure fader. **1500–20** DUNBAR *Poems* xiii. 22 Sum bydand the law layis land in wed. **1530** PALSGR. 603/1, I lay to morgage, as one dothe his herytage. *a* **1533** LD. BERNERS *Huon* cxlvi. 552 Without..laynge to plegge any fote of londe pertenynge to my churche. **1560** DAUS tr. *Sleidane's Comm.* 246 b, That he laie to them agaiine in mortgage so mutch of hys owne landes. **1598** SHAKS. *Merry W.* II. ii. 5, I haue beene content (Sir) you should lay my countenance to pawne. **1600** HAKLUYT *Voy.* (1810) III. 365 She layd part of her owne ieuels..to gage. **1609** SKENE *Reg. Maj.* 49 Ane thing is laid in wad to ane certaine day.

1698 [R. FERGUSON] *View Eccles.* 53 (61), I do pledge and lay my Word to pawn that [etc.].

† **b.** To give up as a hostage. Also, ***to lay a hostage***. *Obs.*

13.. *Guy Warw.* (A.) 2476 My bodi þerfore in ostage I legge. **1523** LD. BERNERS *Froiss.* I. lxxxviii. 110 He layed his sonne in hostage. *a* **1533** —— *Huon* xiii. 37 Yᵉ kyng sayd that Huon muost lay hostage. *Ibid.* xviii. 51, I wyll thou layest vnto me good hostages. *a* **1557** *Diurn. Occurr.* (Bannatyne) 10 The next yeir thereafter he was redeemit and his tua sones laid for him.

12. a. To put down or deposit as a wager; to stake, bet, or wager (a sum, one's head, life, etc.). Also ***to lay a wager***.

a **1300** *Floriz & Bl.* 786 (Hausknecht) Ȝerne he wile þe bidde and preie, þat þu legge þe cupe to pleie. **1303** R. BRUNNE *Handl. Synne* 5598 A waiour dar y wyþ ȝow ley þat [etc.]. *c* **1320** *Sir Tristr.* 678 Þai ȝolden me þat y layd. *c* **1350** *Will. Palerne* 2169, I der leye mi lif hit was þe liþer treytour. **1393** LANGL. *P. Pl.* C. IX. 291 Ich dar legge myn eres. **1404** in Ellis *Orig. Lett.* Ser. II. I. 36, I durste lae my hede, that [etc.]. *c* **1449** PECOCK *Repr.* II. ii. 145 Y dare avowe and dare leie what waiour eny man wole me forto leie, that [etc.]. **1530** PALSGR. 602/1, I lay a nobyll agaynst a peny that it is nat so. **1573** *New Custom* I. ii. Bj, Harke Simplicitie hee is some preacher I wyll lay my gowne. **1597** SHAKS. *2 Hen. IV*, V. v. 111. **1632** J. PORY in Ellis *Orig. Lett.* Ser. II. III. 277 Hee would lay ten to one, the king was dead. **1711** STEELE *Spect.* No. 79 ¶5 I'll lay what Wager she pleases against her present Favourite. **1784** COWPER *Tiroc.* 863 Canst thou..Lay such a stake upon the losing side? **1802** MAR. EDGEWORTH *Moral T.* (1806) I. iv. 19 He spent his time in training horses, laying bets [etc.]. **1887** BOWEN *Virg. Eclog.* III. 29 This heifer I lay thee lest thou decline..what stake for the coming battle is thine? **1891** F. W. ROBINSON *Her Love & His Life* III. VI. iii. 135, I never lay wagers.

b. *absol.* or *intr.* To wager, bet.

In ME. poetry ***I lay, I dare lay*** is often used as little more than a riming expletive.

c **1380** *Sir Ferumb.* 2367 Of Charlemeyn ne his ferede nabbeþ þay non help, y legge. *c* **1384** CHAUCER *H. Fame* II. 166 There I seye Mo wonder thynges dar I leye. *c* **1420** *Avow. Arth.* xxxviii, Him is lefe I dar lay, To hald that he heȝte. *c* **1470** *Golagros & Gaw.* 95 Yhit ar thi latis vnlufsum and ladlike, I lay. **1535** COVERDALE *Isa.* xiv. 15 Yet darre I laye, yᵗ thou shalt be brought downe to the depe of hell. **1677** W. HUGHES *Man of Sin* III. i. 13 She offers a Wager... They lay: and 'twas for what the Friar owed. *a* **1680** BUTLER *Rem.* (1759) I. 143 Rooking Gamesters never lay Upon those Hands, that use fair Play. **1777** MAD. D'ARBLAY *Early Diary* (1889) II. 211, I ventured not to lay against her, because I thought her rather too much in the secret. **1883** STEVENSON *Treas. Isl.* IV. xx, I know a gentle-man, and you may lay to that. **1889** M. E. CARTER *Mrs. Severn* I. I. xiii. 254, I lay I'll keep drier on my own shanks.

c. To bet on (a horse).

1877 *Porcupine* 10 Mar. 790/1 Whether it is as immoral to 'bear the market' as to 'lay the favourite';..all these are irrelevant issues. **1887** W. B. GILPIN *Set of Four Hunting & Racing Stories* vi. 68 They refused to lay him except at odds on. *Ibid.* x. 97 His..plans..'to lay the horse all he could without exciting too much suspicion'. **1891** N. GOULD *Double Event* 6 The heaviest layers of odds..had laid Caloola..for considerable amounts. **1901** *Daily Chron.* 24 July 3/2 For the Derby or other important races Davis would lay a horse to the extent of £100,000 in one bet.

† **13.** *trans.* To relinquish, sacrifice (one's life); = *lay down* (51 e). *Obs.*

c **1330** *Arth. & Merl.* 7188 (Kölbing) Oȝain..bare him þurch wombe & rigge, His liif he dede him þere legge. *Ibid.* 2026, 6426. **1340** *Ayenb.* 149 We ssolle legge oure zaules uor oure broþren. *c* **1430** *Christ's Compl.* 591 in *Pol. Rel. & L. Poems* (1866) 201 For þi loue my lijf y laied. **1567** *Gude & Godlie Ball.* (S.T.S.) 142 Than suld we outher do or die, Or ellis our lyfe we suld lay for it.

† **14.** To lose the faculty of (speech). *north. Obs.*

c **1350** *Medical MS.* in *Archæologia* XXX. 354 Ȝif a man for sekenesse hat leyde speche. **1566** *Wills & Inv. N.C.* (Surtees 1835) 261 Thes things hearafter fouloing was propounded to him when he had layd spetch, and he..gau his consent by sygnes. **1637–50** ROW *Hist. Kirk* (Wodrow Soc.) 439 He hoped that he should yit speak, suppose it be said that his speech is laid, and show his awin mynde.

III. To place, set, apply.

15. a. To place close *to*; to put *to* for a purpose, to apply; sometimes const. *on, upon*. † ***to lay ear to***: to give ear to, listen or attend to. ***to lay to heart***: see HEART *sb.* 42.

a **1000** *Cædmon's Gen.* 2336 (Gr.) Abraham..leȝde hleor on eorðan. *c* **1000** ÆLFRIC *Gen.* xxi. 7 Þæt Sarra sceolde lecgan cild to hyre breoste to ȝesoce on ylde. *c* **1000** *Sax. Leechd.* III. 86 Nim winȝeardes sæt &..leȝe uppan þat sar. *c* **1200** *Trin. Coll. Hom.* 197 Þe neddre secheð a ston and leið hire on eare þer to. *c* **1220** *Bestiary* 359 Is non at nede ðat oðer lateð, Oc leiȝeð his skinbon on oðres lendbon. *a* **1300** *Cursor M.* 16340 (Cott.) Pilate..Of his clothes vn-clethes him, And oþer on him did lai. *Ibid.* 23831 (Cott.) Selden com we sarmon nere..þe ere þar-to selden we lai. *c* **1340** *Ibid.* 1241 (Trin.) Vpon his spade his brest he leide. *c* **1375** *Sc. Leg. Saints* ii. (*Paulus*) 388 Þe hevid þan to þe fete þai lad ..and..a-bowt turnyt þe ded body. **1377** LANGL. *P. Pl.* B. XVI. 44 The Fende..leith a laddre there-to, of lesynges are the ronges. *c* **1384** CHAUCER *H. Fame* I. 291 That he that fully knoweth therbe May savely ley hyt to his ye. *c* **1400** *Rom. Rose* 7611 Ley no deef ere to my speking. *c* **1450** *ME. Med. Bk.* (Heinrich) 201 Tak yarwe & le þe rotos y brused to þe teþ. **1526** TINDALE *Luke* iii. 9 Nowe also ys the axe leyd vnto the rote off the trees. **1602** SHAKS. *Ham.* III. iv. 145 Lay not a flattering Vnction to your soule, That not your trespasse, but my madnesse speakes. **1605** —— *Macb.* I. iii. 44 By each at once her choppie finger laying Vpon her skinnie lips. **1611** BIBLE *Ezek.* xxxvii. 6, I wil lay sinewis vpon you, and wil bring vp flesh vpon you. **1817** *Blackw. Mag.* II. 86/1 Instead of passing the one-horse chaise, he [a horse] laid his counter close up to it, and stopt it. **1877** MISS YONGE *Cameos* Ser. III. xiv. 124 He had laid the spark to the train.

† **b.** To attach, add, annex *to*.

a **1023** WULFSTAN *Hom.* (Napier) 274 Leofan menn, laȝiað gode woroldlaȝan and lecgað þærtoeacan, þat [etc.]. *a* **1225** *Leg. Kath.* 1434 Se rudie & se reade ilitet eauereuch leor as lilie ileid to rose. **1388** WYCLIF *Ecclus.* xviii. 5 It is not to make lesse, nether to leie to. **1560** BIBLE (Genev.) *Isa.* v. 8 Wo vnto them that ioyne house to house, and lay field to field. **1589** PUTTENHAM *Eng. Poesie* II. xi. (Arb.) 117 He conquered..Egypt, and layd it to his dominion. **1601** HOLLAND *Pliny* I. 53 The townes next to the marches..laid to Bœtica. **1647** N. BACON *Disc. Govt. Eng.* I. ii. (1739) 20 The Incumbent also of every Church had Glebe laid to the Church. *a* **1656** USSHER *Ann.* VI. (1658) 253 A multitude of townes and villages..all which he laid to Porus his Kingdom. **1819** in Picton *L'pool Munic. Rec.* (1886) II. 373 The buildings..may be removed and part of the land laid to the street in the intended line of improvement.

† **c.** ***to lay from, off***: to put away from (oneself); to take (one's fingers) off something. *Obs.*

c **1375** *Sc. Leg. Saints* iii. (*Andrew*) 684 His clathis all fra hym he lad. **1526** TINDALE *Eph.* iv. 22 Laye from you that olde man, which is corrupte thorowe the deceavable lustes. **1601** SHAKS. *Jul. C.* I. ii. 243 He was very loath to lay his fingers off it. **1611** BIBLE *Jonah* iii. 6 He laid his robe from him.

† **d.** To put *in* or commit *to* (prison). *Obs.*

c **1250** *Gen. & Ex.* 2693 Ðor ise son he leide in bonde. **1434** *Waterf. Arch.* in *10th Rep. Hist. MSS. Comm.* App. v. 297 The said citsaine..shal be commytted and layed to jayle. **1526** TINDALE *Luke* iii. 20 Then Herode..added this above all and leyd Jhon in preson. **1560** DAUS tr. *Sleidane's Comm.* 426 Hughe Latimer..whome kyng Edward delivered out of the tower, layd in there by his father for doctrine.

† **e.** To compare *with*. *Obs.*

1577 H. I. tr. *Bullinger's Decades* II. viii. 192 They conferre the one with the other & lay them with the lawe.

f. ***to lay into*** or ***in one***: to convert into one apartment or structure. ? *local.*

1849 *Jrnl. R. Agric. Soc.* X. II. 412 Two bad cottages of one room each, if laid into one, might make an extremely good one. **1861** R. WILLIS in Willis & Clark *Cambridge* (1886) III. 174 Whenever the additional structure is completed, this wall can be removed, and the whole will be laid in one.

† **g.** ***to lay a name on***: to give a name to.

a **1300** *Cursor M.* 9827 His names er þir, wit-vten les, þat þe prophet has on him laid. *Ibid.* 10577 Maria to nam on hir þai laid, Als þe angel had þam forwit said.

h. To put (dogs) *on* a scent. (Cf. 55 i.) Also, ***to lay a trail on*** (a quarry).

1781 COWPER *Expost.* 520 Thy soldiery, the Pope's well-managed pack..when he laid them on the scent of blood, Would hunt a Saracen through fire and flood. **1861** *Temple Bar* IV. 53 He gets a little 'law' before the pack are laid upon his track. **1888** *Times* 13 Oct. 7/6 A trail should be laid on a man who makes his way along both frequented and unfrequented streets and on to some railway station.

16. a. To place (affection, hope, confidence) *on* or *in* a person or thing. †Also, ***to lay praise, one's blessing***, etc. ***upon***. ***to lay*** †***prize, store upon***: to value, set store by. *arch.*

a **1300** *Cursor M.* 18341 On all his santes..His saing laid þat drightin dere. *a* **1307** *Thrush & Night.* 158 in Hazl. *E.P.P.* I. 56 Thou art ounwis, On hem to leggen so michel pris. *c* **1350** *Will. Palerne* 1448 Þe loos on hire is leide. *c* **1374** CHAUCER *Troylus* v. 1846 For he nil falsen no wight, dar I seye, That wol his herte al hoolly on him leye. *c* **1375** *Sc. Leg. Saints* i. (*Petrus*) 236 Sic loiss on hym-self he laide. **1549** *Compl. Scot.* vi. 65 My luf is laid apon ane knycht. **1580** SIDNEY *Ps.* XXI. vii, Our king In heav'n his trust hath laied. **1601** SHAKS. *All's Well* III. iii. 2 We Great in our hope, lay our best loue and credence Vpon thy promising fortune. **1719** WATTS *Ps.* CXXI. i, To heav'n I lift my waiting eyes, There all my hopes are laid. **1883** R. W. DIXON *Mano* I. xiv. 45 And though on Blanche his love was wholly laid. **1889** DOYLE *M. Clarke* xxxiii. 365 Neither now or at any time.. have I laid great store upon my life.

† **b.** ***to lay*** (one's care, concerns) ***on God***: to commit, trust to Him. *Obs.*

c **1200** ORMIN 2381 And all ȝho leȝȝde þatt o Godd & onn hiss lefe wille, þatt he þærofe shollde don All whattse hiss wille wære. **1671** MILTON *P.R.* II. 54 Let us be glad of this, and all our fears Lay on his Providence.

17. ***to lay ... before***: to place in front of, to bring to the sight of; hence, to bring to the notice of, to submit to the consideration of; †*pass.* to be in store for. (Cf. branch IV.)

c **1000** ÆLFRIC *Gen.* xxxi. 37 Leȝe hit her beforan þinum freondum. *c* **1340** *Cursor M.* 15714 (Trin.) Muchel woo if he wist is bifore him leide. *c* **1375** *Sc. Leg. Saints* vi. (*Thomas*) 102 A blak hund..gat It, & lad before þame all. *c* **1420** *Pallad. on Husb.* I. 661 When she fynt a corn, She chicketh hem and layth hit hem byfore. **1526** *Pilgr. Perf.* (W. de W. 1531) 14 They..brought the pryce therof, and layde it before the fete of the apostles. **1535** COVERDALE *Gen.* xxx. 41 He layed the staues in the drynkinge troughes before the eyes of the flockes. —— *1 Chron.* xxi[i]. 10 Thre thinges laye I before the, chose yᵉ one of them. **1712** ADDISON *Spect.* No. 457 ¶1, I shall this Day lay before my Reader a Letter. *a* **1715** BURNET *Own Time* (1734) II. 602 The Lower House ordered him to lay the Matter before the Attorney-General for his Opinion. **1729** BUTLER *Serm.* Wks. 1874 II. 90 We ought to lay these things plainly and honestly before our mind. **1766** GOLDSM. *Vic. W.* xxviii, I hope you have no objection to laying your case before the uncle. **1849** AYTOUN *Poems, Buried Flowers* 163 And I laid my heart before thee, Laid it, darling, at thy feet! **1856** FROUDE *Hist. Eng.* (1858) I. ii. 94 Cardinal Morton..laid the condition of the secular clergy before the assembled prelates.

18. a. To set (a snare, a trap, an ambush); †to set (watch). ***to lay wait***: see WAIT *sb.* (and AWAIT *sb.*).

c **1200** *Trin. Coll. Hom.* 209 Ure fo..leið grune in a wilderne to henten þe deor. *a* **1300** *Cursor M.* 16894 Ȝeming on him yee lai. *c* **1400** *Destr. Troy* 10743 The ledes with-oute

. . Laidon wacche to þe wallis, þat no wegh past. *c* **1440** *Bone Flor.* 1358 To kepe the place day and nyghtys, And wach abowte hur lay. *a* **1533** LD. BERNERS *Huon* lxxxiii. 262 We . . layde our busshement in a lytell wood. **1535** COVERDALE *Ps.* lxiv. 5 [They] commoned amonge them selues, how they maye laye snares. *a* **1548** HALL *Chron., Edw. IV,* 222 b, Watche was privilie leyd for him. **1591** SHAKS. *1 Hen. VI,* III. i. 22 Thou layd'st a Trap to take my Life. **1670** A. ROBERTS *Adv. T.S.* 111 The first time they laid an Ambuscado in their way. *a* **1859** MACAULAY *Hist. Eng.* xxiii. V. 93 Melfort was particularly active in laying traps for the young noblemen and gentlemen of the Legation.

b. intr. *to lay for*: to set an ambush or a trap for; to beset the path of; to lie in wait for, waylay.

1494 FABYAN *Chron.* VII. 300, ii. M. of his men . . were layde for, & distressyd. **1530** PALSGR. 602/1, I laye for, as hunters or fysshers layeth his nettes for his praye, *je tens.* I have layde for a pickrell, but I wene I shall catche a frogge. **1603** KNOLLES *Hist. Turks* (1621) 569 Being . . hardly laied for at sea by Cortugogli a famous pirat. **1609** HOLLAND *Amm. Marcell.* XIX. ix. 134 The inhabitants beyond Tigris, streightly layed for, were all massacred every mothers child. **1623** MASSINGER *Dk. Milan* v. i. L 3, Men in debt . . layd for by their creditors. **1648** BP. HALL *Select Th.* 84 Even our Blessed Leader . . when he found that he was laid for in Judæa, flees into Galilee. **1893** *Nat. Observer* 20 May 22/1 He was 'laid for' by a scoundrel whom, being a magistrate, he had sent up for trial. **1897** MARY KINGSLEY *W. Africa* 291 The men go and lay for a rubber-hunter.

†**c.** *trans.* To set watch or guard in (a place); to beset; to search (a place) *for. Obs.*

1560 DAUS tr. *Sleidane's Comm.* 77 Somuche as the waye is layde, that I can neyther come nor sende unto you. **1593** SHAKS. *2 Hen. VI,* IV. x. 4, I . . durst not peepe out, for all the Country is laid for me. **1607** MIDDLETON *Your Five Gallants* IV. G 4 b, Maister Primero was rob'd of a Carkanet vpon monday last; laid the Goldsmiths and found it. **1608** —— *Trick Catch Old One* I. ii, I have been laying all the town for thee. **1621** H. KING *Serm.* 3 As exquisite gluttons lay all markets for fare. *a* **1645** HEYWOOD *Fort. by Land & Sea* II. Wks. 1874 VI. 390 Continue our pursuit, all ways are layd.

19. *to lay siege to,* †*unto,* †*about,* †*against,* †*before*: to besiege; also *fig.* to attack. †Also *to lay battery, blockade to.*

c **1400** *Sowdone Bab.* 2071 The sege he did leyen a-bowte On every side of that Cite. *c* **1449** PECOCK *Repr.* 258 King Herri leieth a sege to Harflew. **1470–85** MALORY *Arthur* XX. x. 814 All his hoost made hem redy to laye syege aboute sir Launcelot. **1485** CAXTON *Chas. Gt.* 205 He layed syege before it by the space of foure monethes. **1500–20** DUNBAR *Poems* xlii. 53 Gar lay ane sege vnto ȝone fort. **1560** DAUS tr. *Sleidane's Comm.* 184 King Fernando besegeth Offen or Buda and layeth to it battery. **1598** SHAKS. *Merry W.* II. ii. 244 To lay an amiable siege to the honesty of this Fords wife. **1647** MAY *Hist. Parl.* III. v. 98 Three daies after the siege was layed. **1713** *Light to Blind* in *10th Rep. Hist. MSS. Comm.* App. v. 200 His General . . had lay'd a blocade . . to Girona with 12,000 men. **1877** MISS YONGE *Cameos* Ser. III. i. 5 He laid siege to Roxburgh Castle.

20. †**a.** To post or station (a body of soldiers, etc.); to station (post-horses) along a route. Also, to beset (a place) with soldiers. *Obs.*

1454 *Paston Lett.* I. 271 The seide Thomas . . layde dyvers folks arraied in maner of werre . . in ij busshements. **1523** LD. BERNERS *Froiss.* I. xc. 113 The lorde Loyes . . and sir Othes Dornes, were layd on the see about Gernzay. **1535** COVERDALE *2 Chron.* xxxiii. 14 He . . layed captaynes in yᵉ stronge cities of Iuda. *a* **1548** HALL *Chron., Edw. IV,* 208 Without anye army layd . . to kepe the Erle from landyng. **1577–87** HOLINSHED *Chron.* I. 87/2 They . . laie the sea coasts full of souldiers. **1596** SPENSER *State Irel.* Wks. (Globe) 664/1 There is a bande of souldiours layed in Mounster. **1689** SHADWELL *Bury F.* IV. Wks. 1720 IV. 182 He has laid horses, and will be ready to escape. **1736** LEDIARD *Life Marlborough* III. 299 Parties of Horse . . were laid on the Road between Antwerp and that Town, to Escort his Grace. **1862** *Temple Bar* VI. 566, I travelled in a manner which . . used to be . . very common in India. . . It is called 'laying horses'; that is, you 'lay' out a horse every seven or eight miles along the road you are going to take.

b. To place or locate (a scene). †Also, to assign to a specified locality. *to lay the venue*: see the sb.

1570–6 LAMBARDE *Peramb. Kent* (1826) 185 The book of Domesday (speaking of Apuldore) laieth it in the hundreth of Blackburne. **1592** SHAKS. *Rom. & Jul.* Prol. 2 (Qo. 1597) In faire Verona, where we lay our Scene. **1601** HOLLAND *Pliny* I. 145 Other Geographers . . lay it as a dependant annexed to Affrick. **1668** DRYDEN *Dram. Poesie* Ess. (ed. Ker) I. 83 The scene of it [*The Silent Woman*] is laid in London. **1784** COWPER *Task* IV. 697, I never framed a wish or formed a plan . . But there I laid the scene. **1868** GLADSTONE *Juv. Mundi* ii. (1870) 34 In the legend of the birth of Eurustheus, the scene is laid in Ἄργος Ἀχαϊκόν.

21. With object denoting a member of the body.

a. *gen.* To place (one's limbs, etc.) in a certain position.

1362 LANGL. *P. Pl.* A. VII. 115 And summe leiden the legges a-liri as suche losels cunne. **1530** PALSGR. 602/1 Laye your legges a crosse and I wyll teache you a play. **1604** SHAKS. *Oth.* II. iii. 424 (Qo.), Then layed his leg Ouer my thigh, and sigh'd, and kissed. **1842** TENNYSON *Beggar Maid* I Her arms across her breast she laid. **1859** JEPHSON *Brittany* iii. 29 The horse who was caressed in this affectionate style had scarcely the spirit even to lay back his ears.

†**b.** *to lay eyes on*: to 'set eyes on', look at.

a **1225** *Ancr. R.* 56 Heo lette him leggen eien on hire. **1676** MARVELL *Mr. Smirke* 42 The fairest thing that ever eyes were laid on. **1818** W. IRVING *Sketch-bk., Leg. Sleepy Hollow,* From the moment Ichabod laid his eyes upon these regions of delight, the peace of his mind was at an end.

c. *to lay hands* (or †*hand*) *on* or *upon* (†also *in, to*) a person or thing; (in the earliest quots. const. dat. pron. as indirect obj. with *on* adv.): (*a*) in lit. sense, to place one's hands on or apply them to, esp. for purposes of appropriation or in violence; hence (*b*) to seize, get hold of, appropriate; (*c*) to do violence to; now *to lay violent hands on* (with *oneself* = to commit suicide); (*d*) to perform the rite of imposition of hands in confirmation or ordination.

c **1000** *Riddles* lxxx. 4 (Gr.) Cwen mec hwilum hwitloccedu hond on leȝeð. *c* **1205** LAY. 8192 Ne funde he nonne swa kene mon, þat hond him durste leggen on. *c* **1250** *Gen. & Ex.* 4113 And ðine hondes ley him on, Sey him on ðin stede to gon. *c* **1300** *Havelok* 994 Neuere more he him misdede, Ne hond on him with yuele leyde. *a* **1300** *Cursor M.* 12893 (Cott.) A! Ion . . nan was worthier þan þou Hand to lai on suete iesu To giue him þat hali sacrament. *c* **1340** *Ibid.* 19393 (Fairf.) On ham þai laide þaire hali hande & a quile ware praiande. **1340** *Ayenb.* 41 Sacrilege is . . huanne me layþ hand ine kueade ine clerk. *c* **1380** WYCLIF *Sel. Wks.* III. 321 Alle þo þat leyn hond on fadir or modir in violence ben cursed of God and man. *c* **1489** CAXTON *Sonnes of Aymon* xxii. 479 It is trouth that X rybawdes cam here ryght now and layd hande vpon me. *a* **1533** LD. BERNERS *Huon* lviii. 199 Gerames . . layd handes on him, as though he toke hym prysoner. **1550** CROWLEY *Last Trump* 9 If God haue layede hys hande on the, And made the lowe. **1568** GRAFTON *Chron.* II. 362 There was no great Ship on the Sea that the French men could lay theyr handes upon. **1605** SHAKS. *Lear* IV. vi. 192 Oh heere he is: lay hand vpon him, Sir. **1606** G. W. tr. *Justine* XLIII. 135 By meanes whereof, the treason comming to light, the Ligurians were laide hand on. **1662** *Bk. Com. Prayer, Burial Dead* (Rubric), Or have laid violent hands upon themselves. **1726** *Adv. Capt. R. Boyle* 55, I loaded them with . . any thing I could lay my Hands on. **1784** COWPER *Task* II. 393 O ye mitred heads . . lay not careless hands On skulls that cannot teach, and will not learn. **1860** DICKENS *Uncomm. Trav.* xiii, Any object they think they can lay their thieving hands on. **1889** JESSOPP *Coming of Friars* ii. 99 A mob . . laid hands on a quantity of timber fit for building purposes, and took it away bodily. **1890** *Guardian* 29 Oct. 1693/3 The Government have laid hands on the last fraction of the sum reserved for the redemption of the public debt.

†**d.** *to lay* (*a*) *hand*: to assist, 'lend' a hand.

1634 SIR T. HERBERT *Trav.* 192 Happy is that man or child can lay a hand to help to draw it. **1645** PAGITT *Heresiogr.* (1662) 46 Alas our poor Church is oppressed, and who layeth hand to help?

e. *to lay a finger* or *one's finger(s upon*: see FINGER *sb.* 3 a.

1724 DE FOE *Mem. Cavalier* (1840) 157 The Parliament began to lay their fingers on the great ones. **1836** KEBLE *Serm.* viii. Postscr. (1848) 376 To select for himself a certain number of divine truths out of the great body of the Scriptures, on which he may lay his finger and say; This, and this alone, is the Gospel. **1865**, **1894** [see FINGER *sb.* 3 a].

22. *to lay hold* (*up*)*on, of*: to take into one's grasp, to grasp, seize on (with material and immaterial obj.); to avail oneself of (a pretext).

1535 COVERDALE *Prov.* iii. 18 She is a tre of life to them that laye holde vpon her. **1579** GOSSON *Sch. Abuse* (Arb.) 54 If he presume to enter our house . . we lay holde on his locks, turne him away with his backe full of stripes. **1604** E. G[RIMSTONE] *D'Acosta's Hist. Indies* IV. vi. 221 Hee was forced to lay holde vpon a braunch. **1611** BIBLE *Matt.* xiv. 3. —— *1 Tim.* vi. 12. **1613** PURCHAS *Pilgrimage* (1614) 889 Stealing closely, or openly, any thing they could lay hold on. **1710** STEELE *Tatler* No. 194 ¶12 For offering in so rude a Manner to lay hold on a Virgin. **1714** ADDISON *Spect.* No. 556 ¶5, I laid hold of all Opportunities to exert it. *a* **1715** BURNET *Own Time* (1724) I. 245 Lady Dysert laid hold on his absence in Scotland to make a breach between them. **1726** G. ROBERTS *Four Years Voy.* 26, I was willing to lay hold of the Frieght offered, for fear his Sloop should come. **1836** MARRYAT *Midsh. Easy* ii, So saying, the boatswain lays hold of the boy. **1874** HELPS *Soc. Press.* ii. 24 There is no municipality which can lay hold of this land.

23. *refl.* and *intr.* To apply oneself *to*; †to set oneself *against*.

1535 COVERDALE *1 Sam.* ii. 29 Why layest thou thy selfe then agaynst my sacrifices and meatofferinges? **1856** KANE *Arct. Expl.* II. xxix. 297 Not even after the death of the usuk did our men lay to their oars more heartily. **1865** CARLYLE *Fredk. Gt.* XVIII. xii. (1872) VIII. 21 When Friedrich laid himself to engineering, I observe, he did it well.

24. *Mil.* To set (a gun, etc.) in the correct position for hitting a mark. Also *absol.*

1480 [see LAYING *vbl. sb.* 1]. **1565** COOPER *Thesaurus* s.v. *Arcus, Tendere aliquo arcum,* to lay or leuell toward. **1859** F. A. GRIFFITHS *Artil. Man.* (1862) 103 No 1 commands and lays. **1877** CLERY *Minor Tactics* xi. 134 Not . . so much by the distance the gun can carry, as by the accuracy with which it can be laid. **1883** LD. SALTOUN *Scraps* I. 224 A young officer of the line regiment asked to be allowed to lay the gun for that shot.

25. a. To put into a condition (usually one of subjection, passivity, or exposure to view or danger: cf. the corresponding uses of LIE *v.*), which is expressed by a complementary adj., adv., or advb. phrase, as in *to lay fallow, idle*; to *lay* (land) *dry, under water*; *lay under necessity, obligation, difficulty, a command,* etc. *to lay bare*: (*a*) to denude, remove the covering from; (*b*) to expose to view, reveal. † *to lay in forbode*: to prohibit the use of. † *to lay to sight*: to reveal, disclose. *to lay under contribution*: see CONTRIBUTION 1 b. † *to lay in* (or *a*) *water*: fig. to make nugatory (see WATER). For *lay open, waste,* see the adjs.

a **1300** *Cursor M.* 765 þe midward tre is vs outtan Our lauerd in forbot has it laid. **1563** *Homilies* II. *Matrimony* (1859) 513 Let him . . never lay these matters to sight. **1703** COLLIER *Ess. Mor. Subj.* II. 42 It lays him at the mercy of chance and humour. **1736** LEDIARD *Life Marlborough* I. 156 He first laid the Country under Water. **1748** *Anson's Voy.* II. xii. 262 This laid us under a necessity of filling all our casks from the furthest part of the lake. **1748** CHESTERF. *Lett.* (1792) II. clxviii. 124 Which might . . lay him under difficulties both what to say, and how to look. **1807** SIR R. WILSON *Jrnl.* 2 July in *Life* (1862) II. viii. 291, I rowed part of the way in the queen's boat, an exercise . . of which my hands will long bear the marks, as they are laid bare over the whole of both palms. **1862** TYNDALL *Mountaineer.* vi. 44 A space of comparatively dry clay was laid bare. **1877** MISS YONGE *Cameos* Ser. III. xxxi. 311 He was laid under orders to follow the commands of the Spanish king. **1897** *Daily News* 26 Feb. 7/3 Another workmen's train was stopped . . many workmen being thus laid idle for the day.

b. *to lay fast*: to set fast, render unable to proceed or escape; †formerly, to put in fetters, imprison (also † *to lay fast by the feet*). Also *to lay by the heels*: see HEEL *sb.*[1] 19.

1560 DAUS tr. *Sleidane's Comm.* 42 b, [They] required that they might be layde faste by the feete. **1584** [see HEEL *sb.*[1] 19]. **1623** LISLE *Ælfric on O. & N. Test., Apostles Dispersed,* Then laid they his guide fast, that he might not any way escape by flight. **1677** OTWAY *Cheats Scapin* I. i, I know how to lay that rogue my son fast. **1809** HEBER in *Q. Rev.* II. 288 If we are laid fast by want of horses, or mutiny of drivers. **1889** DOYLE *M. Clarke* xxxiv. 308 He had heard that you were laid by the heels.

c. *Naut.* With advb. compl., as *alongside, by the lee,* etc. *to lay aback* (see quots. 1867, 1881).

1627 CAPT. SMITH *Seaman's Gram.* ix. 43 Lay the ship by the Lee to trie the Dipsie line. **1769** FALCONER *Dict. Marine* (1780) Eee4b, *Mettre à Scier,* . . to back the sails, or lay them aback, so as to make the vessel fall astern. **1867** SMYTH *Sailor's Word-bk.* 69 To bagpipe the mizen is to lay it aback, by bringing the sheet to the mizen-shrouds. **1869** W. LONGMAN *Hist. Edw. III,* I. xviii. 326 The King ordered his ship to be laid alongside a large Spaniard. **1881** HAMERSLY *Naval Encycl., To lay a yard aback,* is to brace it in such a way that the wind will blow against the forward side of the sail. **1891** *Cornh. Mag.* June 583 Lay her two courses to the wind.

d. Naut. *to lay . . . aboard*: to run into or alongside (a ship), usually in order to board her. So *to lay close, to lay athwart the hawse.*

1593 SHAKS. *2 Hen. VI,* IV. i. 25, I lost mine eye in laying the prize aboord. **1669** STURMY *Mariner's Mag.* I. 19 That if we should be laid aboard, we might clear our Decks. **1707** *Lond. Gaz.* No. 4369/3 The Sloop soon laid her aboard. **1731** CAPT. W. WRIGLESWORTH *MS. Log bk. of the 'Lyell'* 2 July, A Collier lay'd us athwart the Hawse, and broke our Flying Jib Boom [etc.]. **1799** NELSON *Let.* 9 Feb. in Nicolas *Disp.* (1845) III. 260 Lay a Frenchman close, and you will beat him. **1883** STEVENSON *Treas. Isl.* xi. (1886) 90 Why, how many tall ships, think ye, now, I have seen laid aboard?

†**e.** To bring *home to. Obs.*

1709 STEELE *Tatler* No. 71 ¶1 Such a Tract as shall lay Gaming home to the Bosoms of all who love . . their Families.

IV. To present, put forward (cf. *lay before,* 17).

26. a. To put forward, allege (a claim, †reason, †excuse, †example, etc.): often with clause as obj.

1387 TREVISA *Higden* (Rolls) V. 57 He leieþ [*v.r.* leiþ] for hym þe vers of þe sawter, 'God schal nouȝt be wrooþ for everemore'. **1481** CAXTON *Myrr.* III. xxiv. 193, I leye for myn excuse, that I haue to my power folowed my copye. **1481–4** E. PASTON in *P. Lett.* III. 279 My huswyffe trustythe to ley to ȝow her huswyferey for her excuse. **1491** *Act 7 Hen. VII,* c. 2 §1 Courtes where the seid proteccions shalbe pleded or leyed for any of the seid persons. **1513** MORE in Grafton *Chron.* (1568) II. 789 When he had layde for the proofe and confirmation of this sentence, examples taken out of the olde testament. **1529** —— *Dyaloge* III. Wks. 211/1 Many a witnesse was there to whom he layd none exception. *c* **1530** L. COX *Rhet.* (1899) 82 He layeth for hym that his mothers abhominable iniury constrayned him thereto. *a* **1533** LD. BERNERS *Gold. Bk. M. Aurel.* (1546) F iij, We muste not lay excuses. *a* **1540** BARNES *Wks.* (1573) 345/1 The Priests layd that they were best worthy. **1562** *Apol. Priv. Masse* 4 b, If you haue no scriptures to lay for you, then trouble our mother the holy catholike churche no longer. **1593** SHAKS. *3 Hen. VI,* I. i. 152 Plantagenet, for all the Clayme thou lay'st Thinke not, that Henry shall be so depos'd. **1601** R. JOHNSON *Kingd. & Commw.* (1603) 198 These are the reasons which I meante to lay. **1647** COWLEY *Mistr., Written in Juice of Lemon* vii, And to her Hand lay noble claim. **1847** MARRYAT *Childr. N. Forest* xxvi, I prevented it being given to any other, by laying claim to it myself.

b. To present (an information, indictment) in legal form.

1798 BAY *Amer. Law Rep.* (1809) I. 245 In an indictment for manslaughter, it is necessary to lay it to have been done voluntarily. **1838** [see INFORMATION 5 a. (*a*)]. **1870** ROGERS *Hist. Gleanings* Ser. II. 162 Information having been laid that he had forsworn himself. **1891** *Standard* 8 Apr. 5/1 Anyone, . . whether personally aggrieved or not, may lay an information.

c. † (*a*) To assign (a date). (*b*) *Law.* To state or describe *as*; to fix (damages) *at* a certain amount.

c **1440** CAPGRAVE *Life St. Kath.* v. 1699 The day of her deth eke ful fayre he leyth Of nouembre moneth. **1770** FOOTE *Lame Lover* II. Wks. 1799 II. 72 The field . . is laid in the indictment as round. **1820** GIFFORD *Compl. Eng. Lawyer* II. 248 The time of the death must be laid within a year and a day after the mortal stroke was given. *Ibid.,* The facts must be laid to be done treasonably, and against his allegiance. **1891** *Athenæum* 7 Mar. 306/1 He laid his damages at 20,000*l.*; the arbitrators gave him one farthing.

†**d.** To expound, set forth, lay open. *Obs.*

a **1586** SIDNEY *Arcadia* I. (1590) 16 b, And yet thus much I wil say for my selfe, that I haue not laid these matters, either so openly, or largely to any as your selfe.

†**e.** *intr.* To give information, tell. *Obs. rare.*

c **1470** HENRY *Wallace* VII. 31 To lord Persye off this mattir thai laid.

27. a. To bring forward as a charge, accusation, or imputation; to impute, attribute, ascribe (something objectionable). Const. *to*, †*unto*, †*against*, †*in*, *on*. ? *arch.*

c **1425** Lydg. *Assemb. Gods* 208 Thow mayst be dismayde To here so gret compleyntes ayene the layde. **1473** Warkw. *Chron.* (Camden) 5 There was leyde to him hye tresone. c **1530** *Hickscorner* (c 1550) C iv b, They sayde I was a thefe and layde felonye vppon me. a **1533** Ld. Berners *Gold. Bk. M. Aurel.* (1546) C viij b, Lette no man..lay against the goddes, that they be cruell. **1580** Sidney *Ps.* xxxv. v, Who did me wrong against me wittnesse beare, Laying such things as never in me were. **1597** Morley *Introd. Mus.* 76 These objections which you laie against me. **1611** Bible *Job* xxiv. 12 God layeth not folly to them. **1690** Wood *Life* 25 July, E. G. with child, layd on the tapster. **1749** Fielding *Tom Jones* I. iii, I'll warrant 'tis not her first [illegitimate child], by her impudence in laying it to your worship. **1795–7** Southey *Juvenile Poems* Poet. Wks. II. 236 That.. you should lay to me Unkind neglect. **1861** *Temple Bar* II. 247 This was laid to her overweening pride. **1874** Dasent *Half a Life* III. 288 He had of course to lay his sleeplessness on something, and so he laid it on the lobster salad. **1890** *Temple Bar* Oct. 296, I laid the theft on Bastonjee.

b. Phr. ***to lay to*** (a person's) ***charge***, ***at*** or ***to*** (his) ***door***, †***in*** (his) ***dish***, †***in*** (his) ***neck***: to impute to, charge upon. Also ***to lay to one's credit***, †***reproach***, etc. (See also the sbs.)

1530 Palsgr. 603/1 Wyll you laye thefte to his charge, and have no better a grounde? a **1533** Ld. Berners *Huon* xxxiii. 102 It shall neuer be layde to my reproche. **1534** Tindale *Acts* vii. 60 Lorde laye not this synne to their charge. **1551** Robinson tr. *More's Utop.* I. (Arb.) 66 The wickednesse and follye of others shalbe imputed to hym, and layde in his nekke. **1551**, **1722** [see dish *sb.* 1 d]. **1681** H. More *Exp. Dan.* 195 The Pontifician Party have no reason to lay such things in the dish of the Reformed. **1701**, **1749** [see door *sb.* 6]. **1824** Scott *St. Ronan's* xxiii, Do not force a broken-hearted sister to lay her death at your door. **1885** Mrs. C. L. Pirkis *Lady Lovelace* II. xxii. 53 You..laid his death to my charge. **1892** *Blackw. Mag.* CLI. 156/2 This..must be laid to the credit of the Tories.

V. To impose as a burden.

28. a. To impose (a penalty, command, obligation, burden, tax, etc.). Const. *on*, *upon*, (†*to*). (See also load *sb.*)

a **1000** *Guthlac* 685 (Gr.) þæt ʒe..on his wergengan wite leʒdon. **11..** *O.E. Chron.* 1064 (Laud MS.) Hi læʒdon ærende on hine to þam cynge Eadwarde. *Ibid.* an. 1137 Hi læiden gæildes on the tunes. a **1225** *Ancr. R.* 346 þe preost ne þerf..leggen oðer schrift on ou. a **1300** *Cursor M.* 18455 Sant michael for-bot on us laid. c **1380** Wyclif *Wks.* (1880) 336 It were as myche nede to leye now as myche penaunce to summe, as [etc.]. **1423** Jas. I *Kingis Q.* cxx, Thus sall on the my charge bene Ilaid. **1500–20** Dunbar *Poems* xxi. 28 On fredome is laid foirfaltour. a **1533** Ld. Berners *Huon* lxx. 240 You knowe the payne that I layde on your hedes yf Huon dyd not accomplysshe my message. **1557** N. T. (Genev.) *1 Cor.* ix. 16 For necessitie is layd vpon me [Gr. ἀνάγκη γάρ μοι ἐπίκειται], and wo is it vnto me, yf I preache not the Gospel. **1590** *Pasquil's Apol.* I. C iij b, People may not looke to lay all vppon the Parsons shoulders. **1621** Elsing *Debates Ho. Lords* (Camden) 66 Yf..the delinquent is worthy of a greate punishment; but, the question is, by whom yt is to be layed? **1662** Stillingfl. *Orig. Sacr.* II. vi. §6 We are not to think that an Oath layes any greater obligation upon God for performance, then the meer declaration of his will. **1697** Potter *Antiq. Greece* I. xxi. (1715) 121 If a pecuniary Mulct was laid upon him. **1781** D. Williams tr. *Voltaire's Dram. Wks.* II. 103 Once only do I mean to lay my commands upon you. **1790** Jefferson *Writ.* (1859) III. 153 The improbability that Congress would ever lay taxes where the States could do it separately. **1845** McCulloch *Taxation* II. x. (1852) 345 An additional duty ..was laid on windows. **1855** Macaulay *Hist. Eng.* xxi. IV. 554 Northumberland strictly obeyed the injunction which had been laid on him. **1870** Rogers *Hist. Gleanings* Ser. II. 195 The burden of proof being laid on the accused person. **1877** Miss Yonge *Cameos* Ser. III. xxiv. 230 Severe fines were laid on all the villages. **1885** E. F. Byrrne *Entangled* II. II. viii. 265 The dead mother has laid it upon you to find it.

†**b.** To quarter (soldiers) *on* or *upon*. *Obs.*

1612 Davies *Why Ireland*, etc. (1787) 43 The soldiers, for want of pay, were sessed and laid upon the subjects against their will. **1669** *Ormonde MSS.* in *10th Rep. Hist. MSS. Comm.* App. v. 102 Wee require the souldiers..to draw off from the petitioner and his tenants, and..to..shew by what authority..they are layd uppon them. *Ibid.*, It not being lawfull to lay souldiers on any persons.

†**c.** To assess, rate, tax (a person). *Obs.*

c **1330** R. Brunne *Chron.* (1810) 261 Marchaunt & burgeis to þe sext be laid. **1467** in *Eng. Gilds* (1870) 387 What persone that refuseth to paye, at that tyme as he ys assessed or leyd, shal paye to the comen cofre xl.*d.* **1707** in Picton *L'pool Munic. Rec.* (1886) II. 45 He is still lay'd and tax'd for it. **1712** Prideaux *Direct. Ch.-wardens* (ed. 4) 47 The Lands, in respect of which he is lay'd, are out of the Parish.

29. To cast (blame, †aspersions, †ridicule) *on* or *upon*; also const. †*in*, †*to*.

13.. *K. Alis.* 1553 'Byschop,' he saide, 'there is a sclaunder, Y-layd on me kyng Alisaunder'. c **1330** *Spec. Gy Warw.* 592 Many a skorn [was] on him leid [*v.r.* Ileide]. **1390** Gower *Conf.* I. 76 The blame upon the duke they laide. **1530** Palsgr. 602/2 Why lay you the blame of this faute to me? **1545** Ascham *Toxoph.* (Arb.) 30 The fault is not to be layed in the thyng whiche was worthie to be written vpon. **1560** Daus tr. *Sleidane's Comm.* 244 Yf any man shulde lay the blame in us. **1590** Spenser *F.Q.* III. i. 11 And laid the blame, not to his carriage, But to his starting steed that swarv'd asyde. **1647** May *Hist. Parl.* I. i. 14 A declaration..wherein aspertions were laid vpon some members. **1676** C. Hatton in *Hatton Corr.* (1878) 130 All ye blame wase layd on ye wine and he pardoned. **1820** W. Irving *Sketch-bk.*, *Rip van W.*, The good wives of the village..never failed..to lay all the blame on Dame van Winkle.

30. ***to lay stress, weight, emphasis on*** or ***upon***: to emphasize, bring into special prominence, attach great importance to.

1666 Pepys *Diary* 3 July, The House do not lay much weight upon him, or any thing he says. **1676** Glanvill *Ess.* vii. 33 They doated upon little, needless, foolish things, and lay'd a great stress of Religion upon them. **1686** Horneck *Crucif. Jesus* viii. 136 The Greek Church to this day lays the stress of consecration upon the prayer of the Holy Ghost. **1700** Wallis in *Collect.* (O.H.S.) I. 327 He seems to lay weight on this. **1748** J. Mason *Elocut.* 26 To see that it [the Emphasis] be always laid on the emphatical Word. **1824** L. Murray *Eng. Gram.* (ed. 5) I. 363 To lay the emphasis with exact propriety, is a constant exercise of good sense and attention. **1845** McCulloch *Taxation* II. vi. (1852) 307 The only objection..on which any stress can be fairly laid. **1890** T. F. Tout *Hist. Eng. fr. 1689.* 234 The great teachers laid all the stress on dogma.

31. To bring (a stick, etc.) down *upon*; to inflict (blows). Also ***to lay it on*** (lit. and fig.).

c **1314** *Guy Warw.* (Auchinleck MS.) 7524 And we leyd on hem dintes grete. **1399** Langl. *Rich. Redeles* III. 338 They leid on þi leigis, Richard, lasshis y-now. **1500–20** Dunbar *Poems* lxi. 14 Thane is thair laid on me ane quhip. a **1550** *Christis Kirke Gr.* xiv, The reird rais rudely with the rapps, Quhen rungs wer layd on riggis. **1601** Shaks. *Jul. C.* IV. iii. 268 Layest thou thy Leaden Mace vpon my Boy? **1833** Macaulay in *Life & Lett.* (1880) I. 337, I have laid it on Walpole..unsparingly. **1879** Froude *Cæsar* xx. 338 What if my son wishes to lay a stick on my back?

32. *absol.* and *intr.* To deal blows; to make an attack. Chiefly in phraseological expressions with preps. **a.** ***to lay on*** or ***upon***: to attack vigorously, to beat soundly. (See also *lay on*, 55 b.)

a **1225** *Ancr. R.* 292 Mid te holie rode steaue, þet him is loðest kuggel, leie on þe deouel dogge. c **1305** *Edmund Conf.* 112 in *E.E.P.* (1862) 74 And euere seide þis holi man as he leide on hire faste Maide þu schalt lurny þus awei forto caste þi fole wil of þi flesch. c **1330** *Arth. & Merl.* 4046 (Kölbing) Ich on oþer gan to legge. c **1460** *Towneley Myst.* xvi. 425 Thar was none that I spard, bot lade on and dang them. **1480** Caxton *Chron. Eng.* lxii. 46 The whyte dragon egrely assaylled the reede and layd on hym so strongly that [etc.]. **1526** *Pilgr. Perf.* (W. de W. 1531) 253 b, They layde on hym with theyr fystes and other wepens. **1590** Webbe *Trav.* (Arb.) 20 Ye Turkes woulde lay vpon them as vpon Horses, and beat them in such sort, as oft times they dyed. c **1610** *Women Saints* 146 He layeth on her with threates. **1640** tr. *Verdere's Rom. Rom.* I. x. 36 They laid upon one another with such fury, as [etc.]. **1758** Goldsm. *Mem. Prot.* (1895) II. 17 Rascal! replied the Tyrant, give me the Stick; and taking it in his Hand..with the most inhuman Barbarity he laid on the unresisting Slave. **1814** Southey *Roderick* xxv, Laying on the Moors with that good sword.

†**b.** ***to lay to, unto***: to assault, attack, press hard (*lit.* and *fig.*). Also ***to lay home, hard, hardly, to***. *Obs.*

c **1430** *Syr Tryam.* 1073 Alle the fosters to hym cun lay Wyth sterne worde and mode. **1557** N. T. (Genev.) *Mark* xiv. 68 *note*, Peter prepareth hym selfe to flee if he were farther layd vnto. **1581** B. Riche *Farew. Mil. Prof.* G iv b, The Marchaunt..with greate importunitie requested her in the waie of mariage, and so hardly he laied vnto her, that [etc.]. **1602** Shaks. *Ham.* III. iv. 1 Looke you lay home to him. **1603** Knolles *Hist. Turks* (1621) 19 The warre was again begun, and the citie more hardly laid unto than before. **1623** Bingham *Xenophon* 109 At this instant they were assaulted, and hardly laid vnto vpon the hill. **1650** Trapp *Comm., Gen.* xlii. 329 He lays it hard to them still; As who should say, the longer I hear you, the worse I like you. **1724** De Foe *Mem. Cavalier* (1840) 284, I found my major hard laid to, but fighting like a lion.

c. ***to lay at***: to aim blows or an attack at; to strike at; to attack, assail (*lit.* and *fig.*). In 15–18th c. often in *indirect passive*. Now chiefly *dial.*

? a **1400** *Arth. & Merl.* 2464 (Kölbing), A 100 Sarazens.. All att once att him layd. **1440** J. Shirley *Dethe K. James* (1818) 16 The traitours..laid at the chaumbur dors..with levours and with axes. **1548** Udall, etc. *Erasm. Par. Matt.* xii. 74, I am layed at with deadly deceytes. **1561** Hoby tr. *Castiglione's Courtier* IV. V vij, The beautiful women haue alwaies more suyters, and be more instantlye laide at in loue [It. *sono piu..sollicitate d'amor*], then the foule. **1579** Spenser *Sheph. Cal.* Feb. 214 Fiercely the good man at him did laye. **1600** Holland *Livy* v. xxiv. 196 The..Senators.. came forth to the multitude, and offered themselves to be laid at, smitten and slaine. **1611** Bible *Job* xli. 26 The sword of him that layeth at him cannot hold. **1719** De Foe *Crusoe* II. v. (1840) 102 Our men being thus hard laid at, Atkins wounded. **1728** Ramsay *General Mistake* 82 Even beauty guards in vain, he lays at a'. **1876** *Surrey Gloss.*, The rabbits have laid at that wheat unaccountably. **1899** *Expositor* Jan. 54 The lie lays at the truth and the Truth must lay at the lie.

d. ***to lay into***: to belabour; to 'pitch into'. *slang* or *colloq.*

1838 D. Jerrold *Men of Char.*, *John Applejohn* xiii, I shall be very happy..to go and hold the door, while you lay into the ruffian. **1865** Dickens *Mut. Fr.* I. iv, Laying into me with your little bonnet. **1876** 'Mark Twain' *Tramp Abr.* iii. (1880) I. 22 He [a bird] laid into his work like a nigger. **1887** G. R. Sims *Mary Jane's Mem.* 108 She would lay into Master John with her stick.

e. ***to lay about one***: to deal violent and repeated blows on all sides; occas. (trans.) ***to lay*** (a weapon) ***about one***. Hence *fig.* to act vigorously, make strenuous efforts, do one's utmost.

c **1435** *Torr. Portugal* 1036 Fast he leyd hym a-bowte All þat somyrres nyght. **1596** Spenser *F.Q.* IV. iv. 32 And with his brondiron round about him layd. a **1618** Sylvester *Sonn.* xvi. Wks. (Grosart) II. 39 When like a Lion to preserve her yong, Thou laydst about thee to redeeme the same. **1631** R. Bolton *Comf. Affl. Consc.* 49 Thou, that now laies about for the free world and wealth. **1674** *Essex Papers* (Camden) I. 279 He lays about him on all hands where there is any the least project of gaine. **1690** Locke *Hum. Und.* III. vi. (1695) 244 Those Words, with which they are so armed at all points, and with which they so confidently lay about them. **1720** Mrs. Manley *Power Love* (1741) I. 55 How they laid about them to commend your Soul to God! **1727** Boyer *Fr. Dict.* s.v., To lay about one's self..*faire tous les efforts, remuër ciel et terre.* **1837** Disraeli *Venetia* IV. xviii, They laid about them with their staves. **1889** Doyle *M. Clarke* xxxii. 353 We cut a way to his rescue, and laid our swords about us.

†**33.** *impers.* Of the wind, weather: To be violent. *Obs.*

c **1475** *Rauf Coilȝear* 139 Sa troublit with stormis was I neuer stad; Of ilk airt of the Eist sa laithly it laid. [Cf. **1825–80** Jamieson, *To Lay On.* 1. To rain, to hail, to snow heavily; as 'It's layin' o' snaw'.]

†**34.** To strike, beat (a person) *on* the face, *over* the head, etc. ***to lay on the lips***: to kiss. *Obs.*

In these uses the personal obj. is prob. to be regarded as a dative.

1530 Palsgr. 602/2, I lay hym on the face... I layde hym betweene the necke and the shoulders that I made hym grone. **1599** Massinger, etc. *Old Law* II. ii. (1656) E 1 b, Ile lay you o'th lips and leave you. **1602** Marston *Ant. & Mel.* II. Wks. 1856 I. 25 Faith, sweet, ile lay thee on the lips for that jest. **1628** Earle *Microcosm.*, *Upstart Country Knt.* (Arb.) 38 Being once laid ore the shoulder with a Knighthood. **1690** W. Walker *Idiomat. Anglo-Lat.* 228 He laid him over the face with his hands as hard as he could strike. **1712** Arbuthnot *John Bull* III. v, The cook laid them over the pate with a ladle.

VI. To dispose or arrange in proper relative position over a surface.

35. a. *trans.* To place in the proper or designed position (something that extends horizontally, e.g. a foundation (often *fig.*), a floor, stones or bricks in building, etc.).

c **1000** *Ags. Gosp.* Luke xiv. 29 Syððan he þæne grund-weall legð [c **1160** *Hatton Gosp.* leiʒð]. c **1340** *Cursor M.* 13285 (Trin.) At þe see Iame & Ion he fonde As þei were lynes leyond. **1340–70** *Alex. & Dind.* 438 To legge lym oþur ston. **1382** Wyclif *Heb.* vi. 1 Not eftsoone leggynge the foundament of penaunce fro deede werkis. c **1400** *Rom. Rose* 4149 Aboute him lefte he no masoun, That stoon coude leye, ne querrour. c **1425** Lydg. *Assemb. Gods* 596 All the baytys that ye for hym haue leyde. **1495** *Act 11 Hen. VII*, c. 23 The same heringes shuld be wele truly and justly leyed and packed. **1526** Tindale *Heb.* i. 10 Thou lorde in the begynnynge hast layde the foundacion of the erth. **1576** Fleming *Panopl. Epist.* 283 They lay traines of treason to overthrow their princes. **1644** Digby *Nat. Bodies* x. (1645) 94 Proceeding upon our grounds before layed. **1662** Gerbier *Princ.* 33 Paviors (after the Bricks are laid) throw sharp Sand over them. **1680** Moxon *Mech. Exerc.* 217 You may begin at the Verge, and so lay several Grooves close by one another till you come to the Center. **1751** Labelye *Westm. Br.* 71 The laying the Foundation of Stone-Piers. **1800** Mar. Edgeworth *Castle Rackrent* 44 She laid the corner-stone of all her future misfortunes at that very instant. **1818** Jas. Mill *Brit. India* II. v. viii. 651 The political conduct of the Governor-General lays sufficient ground for the presumption that [etc.]. **1823** P. Nicholson *Pract. Build.* 263 When you lay your floors, let the joints be fitted and tacked down. **1840** R. H. Dana *Bef. Mast* xxxiii. 125 From the time her keel was laid, she had never been so driven. **1842–59** Gwilt *Archit.* §1810 Slating is sometimes laid lozengewise. **1845** *Jrnl. R. Agric. Soc.* VI. II. 266 The ordinary mode of farming is to lay the ground in ridges. **1848** *Chambers's Inform.* I. 489/1 That manner of ploughing and laying the ridges..which will best keep the land dry. **1890** *Cornh. Mag.* Sept. 270 The first submarine cable was laid.

b. To set out (a table), to spread (the cloth), place in order (the plates, dishes, knives and forks, etc.) in preparation for a meal; hence, in later use, to set out the table for (a meal). Also *absol.* †Also, to prepare (a bed).

c **1300** *Havelok* 1722 þanne [he] were set, and bord leyd. c **1330** *Arth. & Merl.* 6508 (Kölbing) þese weschen þis gentil man & leyd tables after þan. c **1375** Barbour *Bruce* v. 388 The met all reddy grathit, Vith burdis set and clathis laid. **1530** Palsgr. 603/1 Lay the table, for we must dyne in al the haste. **1593** Shaks. *2 Hen. VI*, III. ii. 11 Haue you layd faire the Bed? **1668–9** Pepys *Diary* 8 Jan., Home to my wife's chamber, my people having laid the cloth, and got the rooms all clean. **1788** Clara Reeve *Exiles* III. 110, I made the servant lay his bed in order. **1797** Mrs. Bennett *Beggar Girl* I. viii. 257 When the cloth was laying for supper. **1836** Marryat *Japhet* lxxviii, I found that the table was laid for three. **1848** Thackeray *Van. Fair* xiv, A little dinner..was laid in the dining-room. **1861** Dickens *Gt. Expect.* iv, We found the table laid.., the dinner dressing. **1883** Black *Shandon Bells* xviii, The little maidservant..laid the cloth. **1890** Weyman *House of Wolf* iv, These gentlemen will not sup with me..Lay for them at the other end.

c. To trace (a ground-plan).

1594 Marlowe & Nashe *Dido* v, When I was laying a platform for these walls. **1601** Holland *Pliny* I. 99 Danochares the Architect laid the modell and platforme therof [*sc.* of Alexandria] by a subtil and witty deuise. **1615** G. Sandys *Trav.* 29 It is reported that when the workmen began to lay the platforme at Chalcedon, how certain Eagles conueyed their lines to the other side of the Streight.

d. †(*a*) ***to lay a buck***: to put clothes in soak for washing (*obs.*). (*b*) ***to lay leaven*** (see quot. 1891).

[Possibly confused (*a*) with some derivative of lye, and (*b*) with lay *v.*^{2}, allay *v.*; but this is uncertain.]

1573 Tusser *Husb.* (1878) 166 Maides, three a clock, knede, lay your bucks, or go brew. **1611** Cotgr. s.v. *Faire*, *Faire la buée*, to lay, or wash a bucke. **1633** D. R[ogers] *Treat. Sacraments* I. 42 Shee that cannot lay a leaven, but thinkes of the kingdome of Christ. **1891** *Sheffield Gloss.* Suppl., *Lay*, to mix; only used in the phrase 'to lay leaven', i.e. to mix the yeast with oat-meal in making oat-cake. **1893** *Northumb. Gloss.*, *Lay*, to mix dough for bread making. 'Lay the breed'—to mix the flour with the yeast, to make the dough.

e. *to lay a fire*: to place the fuel ready for lighting.

1876 JEVONS *Logic Prim.* 10 If one fire be laid and lighted exactly like another, it ought to burn like it. **1886** BESANT *Childr. Gibeon* II. i, The fire was laid..with the resinous wheels, which burn fiercely.

f. Printing. *to lay type*: 'to put new sorts in cases' (Jacobi *Printers' Voc.* 1888). Also, *to lay the case*.

1683 MOXON *Mech. Exerc., Printing* 200 The manner how the several sorts of Letters are disposed in the several Boxes, is called, Laying of the Case. **1808** C. STOWER *Printer's Gram.* vi. 151 Laying of Cases. This implies filling them with sorts of a new fount of letter.

36. To re-steel (a cutting instrument). *dial.*

1472-3 [see LAYING *vbl. sb.* 1]. **1475-6** *Durham Acc. Rolls* (Surtees) 25 Et sol. eidem pro le laynge ij axes, vj*d.* **1605** *Vestry Bks.* (Surtees) 55 For layinge the church hack with new iron, viij*d.* **1620** in Swayne *Churchw. Acc.* (1896) 172 For Layinge the pickax 1*s.* 8*d.* **1893** *Wiltsh. Gloss., To lay a tool*, to steel its edge afresh. **1893** in *Northumbld. Gloss.*

37. *Rope-making.* **a.** To twist yarn to form (a strand), or strands to form (a rope).

1486 [see LAYING *vbl. sb.* 1]. **1627** CAPT. SMITH *Seaman's Gram.* vii. 30 If the Cable bee well made, we say it is well laid. **1726** SHELVOCKE *Voy. round World* 240 Those who were ashore made twice lay'd stuff for rigging. **1793** SMEATON *Edystone L.* §281 A bridle cable was laid perfectly pliant. **1839** URE *Dict. Arts* 1070 The last part of the process of rope-making, is to lay the cordage. **1853** *Ibid.* II. 560 The manner of laying the yarns into ropes.

b. *intr.* said of the rope.

1796 *Encycl. Brit.* XVI. 485/1 Then..the top comes away from the swivel..and the line begins to lay.

38. a. *trans.* In immaterial sense: To fix the outlines of, arrange, devise (a plan, plot, scheme); †to establish (a law), settle, lay down (a principle); †to draw up the plan of (a literary composition). *to lay one's account*: see ACCOUNT *sb.* 15.

11.. *O.E. Chron.* an. 1086 (Laud MS.) He sætte mycel deorfrið & he læᵹde laᵹa þærwið. *c* **1430** *Freemasonry* 449 Suche ordynance at the semblé was layd. **1591** SHAKS. *1 Hen. VI*, II. iii. 4 The plot is laid. **1616** B. JONSON *Epigr., To weak Gamester in Poetry*, I cannot for the stage a Drama lay, Tragick or Comick. **1644** MILTON *Jdgm. Bucer* Wks. 1738 I. 87 If we retain our principles already laid. **1692** R. L'ESTRANGE *Fables, Life Æsop* (1708) 8 Several Little Tales and Jests that I take to be neither well Laid, nor well put together. **1701** W. WOTTON *Hist. Rome, Marcus* v. 83 His Design had been long laid. *a* **1715** BURNET *Own Time* (1724) I. 401 The argument for it was laid thus. **1838** THIRLWALL *Greece* II. xi. 56 His schemes also were more artfully laid. **1880** *Libr. Univ. Knowl.* (N.Y.) VIII. 381 When the conspiracy was laid to put Jesus to death.

†**b.** *gen.* To contrive, arrange. *Obs.*

1627 DONNE *Serm.* v. (1640) 51 God had laid it so, that Moses should be setled this way. *a* **1677** BARLOW *Serm.* Wks. 1716 I. 62 Is it not great imprudence so to lay our business that any other matter shall thwart or thrust out devotion? **1712** ARBUTHNOT *John Bull* III. ii, We have laid it so, that he is to be in the next room.

c. *intr.* †To make arrangements or plans *for* (*obs.*); to plan, contrive, or intend *to do* something (now *dial.* and *U.S.*). (Cf. *lay out*, 56 f.)

c **1450** *Mirour Saluacioun* 2058 Saul laide for his dethe als for hys mortale enemy. **1573** TUSSER *Husb.* lxvii. (1878) 156 Lay thou to saue,..And then thou shalt enriched be. **1587** GOLDING *De Mornay* xiv. (1617) 222 Mans mind can skill.. to lay earnestly for warre in seeking or enioying of peace. —— *Ovid's Met.* XII. 277 And what is wrought in all the world he leaies to vnderstand. **1601** HOLLAND *Pliny* I. 413 Men loue rather to haue plenty from their vines, than otherwise lay for the goodnesse thereof. **1633** BP. HALL *Hard Texts, N.T.* 11 If he lay to please the one the other will be offended. **1648** SYMMONS *Vind. Chas. I*, 113 Mahomet layed to perpetuate his religion by introducing of ignorance, [etc.]. *a* **1825** FORBY *Voc. E. Anglia, Lay*, to intend, to lay out, to lay a plan. Ex. 'I lay to plough for turnips tomorrow'. **1896** *Boston* (Mass.) *Jrnl.* 3 Dec. 4/3 Fitzsimmons evidently laying to get in right on jaw.

39. †**a.** In OE.: To direct (one's steps). **b.** Naut. *to lay one's* (or *a*) *course*: see quots. 1867, 1881.

a **1000** *Cædmon's Gen.* 2400 (Gr.) Lastas leᵹdon..oð þæt hie on Sodoman, weall stape burᵹ wlitan meahton. **1669** STURMY *Mariner's Mag.* I. 18 The Wind will be Northerly, make ready to go about; we shall lay our Course another way. **1793** RENNELL in *Phil. Trans.* LXXXIII. 190 We were driven to the north of Scilly; and were barely able to lay a course through the passage between those islands and the Land's End. **1867** SMYTH *Sailor's Word-bk., To lay her course*, to be able to sail in the direction wished for, however barely the wind permits it. **1881** HAMERSLY *Naval Encycl.* s.v., A ship *lays her course* when being close-hauled, the wind permits the desired course to be steered. **1890** W. F. RAE *Maygrove* III. ix. 307 The steamer's course was laid for Michipicoten.

†**c.** To apply or devote (one's power, affection, possessions) *to*. Also const. *into*. *Obs.*

a **1300** *Cursor M.* 26294 If..þou haf oft-sith laid might His wrangwis liuelade for to right. **1340-70** *Alisaunder* 203 He had his liking ilaide þat Ladie too wedde. *a* **1400** in *Eng. Gilds* (1870) 357 ȝif eny good man of þe town leiþ his good to þe commune nede of þe town. **1627-77** FELTHAM *Resolves* I. i. 1 He..lays his heart into pleasures, and forgets the future.

†**40.** To set down *in* writing; to put into, express or 'couch' *in* (certain language or terms). *Obs.*

c **1330** *Arth. & Merl.* 1288 (Kölbing) Merlin to Blasi þer meche seyd, þat Blasi al in writt leyd. *c* **1330** R. BRUNNE *Chron. Wace* (Rolls) 184 Als Geffrey in latyn sayd So Mayster Wace in frankis layd. *c* **1385** CHAUCER *L.G.W.* 2516 *Phillis*, Hir lettre..here & there in Ryme I haue it laide. ? *a* **1400** *Arth. & Merl.* (Douce MS.) 1792 (Kölbing) In þe Bruyt he hit layde. *a* **1631** DONNE 6 *Serm.* (1634) ii. 6 The phrase..is thus conceived and layed, *In our image* and then, *After our likenesse.* **1682** BUNYAN *Holy War* 215 [The Charter] fairly engraven upon the doors thereof, and laid in Letters of Gold. **1714** STEELE *Lover* No. 27 (1723) 160 They ..carry a secret Instruction, in that they lay the Sense of the Author still closer in Words of his own. **1775** DE LOLME *Eng. Const.* I. x. (1784) 99 In all writs, care must be taken that they be laid and formed according to their case.

41. *Art.* **a.** To put upon a surface in layers; to put or arrange (colours, †a picture) on canvas.

1570 BARET *Alv.* L 54 To laie colour on a picture. *c* **1600** SHAKS. *Sonn.* ci, Truth needs no collour, with his collour fixt; Beautie no pensell, beautie's truth to lay. **1671** MILTON *P.R.* IV. 343 Their swelling Epithetes thick laid As varnish on a Harlots cheek. **1690** LOCKE *Hum. Und.* II. x. (1695) 71 The Pictures drawn in our Minds are laid in fading Colours. **1727** BOYER *Fr. Dict.* s.v., To lay the Colours deep (in Painting), *empater.* **1781** COWPER *Retirement* 798 To teach the canvas innocent deceit, Or lay the landscape on the snowy sheet. **1859** RUSKIN *Two Paths* App. iv. (1891) 259 In every given touch [of colour] laid on canvas. *Ibid.* 261 The refinement of work consists not in laying absolutely little colour, but in always laying precisely the right quantity.

b. *to lay a ground*: to spread a coating over a surface, as a basis for colours. So in Photography, *to lay the grain*.

1762-71 H. WALPOLE *Vertue's Anecd. Paint.* (1786) V. 141 Blooteling..found out the application of the chisel for laying grounds, which much exceeded the roller. **1839** *Penny Cycl.* XIII. 94/2 Three processes are usually required in japanning; laying the ground, painting, and finishing. **1854** SCOFFERN in *Orr's Circ. Sci., Chem.* 90 The last [stage] , technically called 'laying the grain', must be effected by hand. It consists in rubbing the surface of the plate in *one direction*, by means of a buffer.

42. To cover, spread, or coat (*with* something), esp. by way of ornament (as in embroidery).

? *a* **1366** CHAUCER *Rom. Rose* 1076 A robe of purpre..it ful wel With orfrays leyd was everydel. *c* **1400** *Siege of Troy* 135 (MS. Harl. 525) in *Archiv Stud. neu. Spr.* LXXII. 15 There were sheldis gylt and leyd wyth ynde. *c* **1440** *Anc. Cookery* in *Househ. Ord.* (1790) 433 Take a faire urthen pot, and lay hit well with splentes in the bothum, that the flessh neigh hit not. **1562-3** in Willis & Clark *Cambridge* (1886) III. 296 To the Painter for leyinge the Irons of the greate Postes in oyle and red leade iijs. **1578** LYTE *Dodoens* I. xix. 29 Softe wollie leaves, as it were layde with a certayne downe or fine cotton. **1603** KNOLLES *Hist. Turks* (1621) 832 Short cloakes layed with silver lace. **1663** GERBIER *Counsel* 80 Lathed and laid with Lime and haire. **1820** SCOTT *Monast.* iii, She is convent-bred, and can lay silk broidery. **1879** E. ARNOLD *Lt. Asia* 34 Black steel, Laid with gold tendrils. **1889** FROUDE *Chiefs of Dunboy* xxvi. 399 They..dug a pit, and laid the bottom of it with thorns. **1891** *Chamb. Jrnl.* 5 Dec. 770/1 My bath-room is..a part of the veranda laid with zinc.

VII. 43. a. In intransitive uses, coinciding with or resembling those of LIE *v.*[1] *to lay low* (see LOW *a.* 18 c): an occas. use erroneously developed from *to lie low*.

In the earliest examples the verb appears to be intransitive for reflexive or passive. Now (exc. in Nautical lang., see b) it is only dialectal or an illiterate substitute for *lie*, its identity of form with the past tense of the latter no doubt accounting largely for the confusion. In the 17th and 18th centuries, it was not app. regarded as a solecism. (For *lay in wait* see WAIT *sb.*)

c **1300** *Harrow. Hell* 147 Sathanas, y bynde the, her shalt thou lay. O that come domesday. **13..** *Sir Beues* 2643 (MS. A.) þar he schel leggen ay, Til hit come domes dai. *a* **1400** in *Eng. Gilds* (1870) 363 þ[t] no man ne legge in lond ne in tenement..þe whyle þe suquestre ys þare set. *c* **1420** *Chron. Vilod.* 3340 (Horstm.) þe chest..In þe whyche þis blessud virgyn leyth y-closot inne. *c* **1489** CAXTON *Blanchardyn* li. 195 His cheff standarde ouer thrawen and layng vpon the grounde. **1498** *Will of Woodforde* (Somerset Ho.), Where my wif legges. **1530** PALSGR. 605/2 It leyeth on my herte. I tell you as it lyeth on my herte. **1625** BACON *Ess., Nature* (Arb.) 363 Nature will lay buried a great Time, and yet reuiue. **1628** EARLE *Microcosm., Pretender to Learning* (Arb.) 53 Some..Folio, which..hath laid open in the same Page this half yeere. **1662** J. STRYPE in *Lett. Lit. Men* (Camden) 179 At my first Coming, I laid alone. **1665** WOOD *Life* 25 Sept. (O.H.S.) II. 46 The lady of Castlemaine's two children began to lay at our house. *Ibid.* 56 The books layd upon the booksellours' hands. **1736** BUTLER *Anal.* II. vi. 231 The general Proof of natural Religion..does, I think, lay Level to Common Men. **1749** FIELDING *Tom Jones* I. vi, The flame which had before laid in embryo now burst forth. **1768-74** TUCKER *Lt. Nat.* (1834) II. 558 Eating when we are hungry,..laying down when sleepy. **1794** J. BIDLAKE *Poems* 4 She..on the ground, to catch each sound would lay. **1818** BYRON *Ch. Har.* IV. clxxx, Thou..dashest him again to earth:—there let him lay. **1828** J. RAINE *St. Cuthbert* 78 They found the venerable body..laying on its right side. *a* **1861** T. WINTHROP *John Brent* (1883) viii. 70 They may.. let their chances slide at cards, but my notion is they're layin' low for bigger hauls. **1890** *Daily News* 13 Oct. 7/1 A large Danish boarhound..knocked a little boy..down, laid on him, and bit him over the eye. **1894** W. T. STEAD *If Christ came to Chicago!* 225 The Democrats laid low and said nothing, for reasons of their own. **1900** F. ANSTEY *Brass Bottle* vi. 80 'They're all layin' down on the road opposite our door.' **1907** M. C. HARRIS *Tents of Wickedness* IV. iii. 359 He..laid low for the first passer-by, and slugged him.

b. *Naut.* To put oneself in the position indicated by the accompanying phrase or adv., e.g. *to lay at anchor*, *to lay by the wind*. (See also *lay along*, *lay by*, *lay in*, *lay out*, etc. in branch VIII.) *to lay on the oars*, to cease rowing.

1530 PALSGR. 605/1, I ley at anker, as a shyppe dothe, *je ancre.* **1549** EDW. VI *Jrnl.* (Roxb.) II. 227 Thei laying at anker bett the French. **1670** A. ROBERTS *Adventures of T.S.* 8 He commanded to lay by the Wind, until the Ships came within Call. **1830** MARRYAT *King's Own* xlvi, The boats laid upon their oars. **1881** HAMERSLY *Naval Encycl.* s.v., *To lay* is used (although incorrectly) in the sense of to *go* or *come*; as *lay forward, lay aft, lay down from aloft, lay out on the yards*, etc. **1894** C. N. ROBINSON *Brit. Fleet* 181 Captains are saluted by laying on the oars (in other words ceasing to row).

VIII. With adverbs in specialized uses.

44. lay about. †**a.** *trans.* To surround, beset.

14.. *Arth. & Merl.* (Percy MS.) 2452 (Kölbing), A 100 Sarazens on a rowte Att once layd him all about. **1555** J. PROCTOR *Wyat's Reb.* 33 b, The lorde Aburgaueny and the shiriffe..deuised to laye the countree aboute, that they [Wyat and others] mought not escape.

†**b.** *intr.* To contrive, plan, take measures (*to do* something); to look out or make a search *for*.

a **1618** SYLVESTER *Mayden's Blush* 66 Hee labours, and hee layes-about..that dear Issue to exterminate. **1727** BOYER *Fr. Dict.* s.v., To lay about, in order to get an Office, *briguer, rechercher un Emploi.* **1755** SHEBBEARE *Lydia* (1769) II. 176 She therefore laid about for a proper person to dispatch as an emissary to accomplish this design.

†**c.** To strike out with vigour; = *to lay about one* (32 e). *Obs.*

[*c* **1330** *Arth. & Merl.* 2874 (Kölbing) About he leyd on so hard, þat his swerd brast atvo]. **1607** ROWLANDS *Hist. Guy Warwicke* 29 He drew his sword, and laid about. **1663** BUTLER *Hud.* I. ii. 799 But when his nut-brown Sword was out Couragiously he laid about.

45. lay abroad. *trans.* To spread out; to set out for view; to spread (a net). *Obs.* exc. *arch.*

1530 PALSGR. 601/1, I laye abrode clothes in the sonne to be ayred or dried... I laye abrode, as hunters or fysshers do their nettes... I laye abrode monay, or vessell, or bookes to be vewed, *je mets au large.* **1535** [see ABROAD *adv.* 1 c]. **1570** BARET *Alv.* L 54 To laie abroade hey in the sunne to drie. **1604** E. G[RIMSTONE] *D'Acosta's Hist. Indies* v. xxiv. 395 Hauing layed abroade these bones. **1883** R. W. DIXON *Mano* I. xvi. 50 For he abroad capacious nets had laid.

†**46. lay along. a.** *trans.* To stretch at full length (also, *all along*); hence, to lay low, prostrate; to destroy, overthrow, kill.

1413, 1535, 1592, 1761 [see ALONG *adv.* 6]. **1597** A. M. tr. *Guillemeau's Fr. Chirurg.* 35 b/1 Shee is without all strength, cleane layed a-longe. **1599** *Withals' Dict.* 62 b, To ouerthrow, lay along, and destroie, *sterno.* **1697** DRYDEN *Æneid* I. 266 The Leaders first He laid along.

b. *intr.* (*Naut.*: see 43 b.) Of a ship: To lean over with a side wind. (Cf. *lie along*.)

1779 BARNARD in *Phil. Trans.* LXX. 107 That leakage, washing from side to side, will cause the ship to lay along.

†**47. lay apart.** *trans.* To put aside or away from one; to omit purposely (*to* do something.)

1526 TINDALE *Jas.* i. 21 Wherfore laye a parte all filthynes [so **1611**]. *c* **1530** L. COX *Rhet.* (1899) 52 All maters of the law layd for the tyme vtterly a part. **1563** *Homilies* II. *Rogation* 1, Wee shall..lay apart to speake of the profound and unsearchable nature of Almighty God, rather acknowledging our weakenesse, then rashly to attempt [etc.]. **1590** SPENSER *F.Q.* I. Introd. 3 Lay now thy..bow apart. **1599** SHAKS. *Hen. V*, II. iv. 78 That you divest your selve and lay apart The borrowed Glories.

48. lay aside. *trans.* **a.** To put away from one's person (as a garment, weapon, or the like); to put on one side.

c **1386** CHAUCER *Man of Law's T.* 615 They moste..leye a lyte hir holinesse asyde As for the tyme. **1540** COVERDALE *Fruitf. Less.* To Rdr. (1593) A 4 b, The old Adam ought we to lay aside. **1565** COOPER *Thesaurus* s.v. *Condo, Seponere & condere*, to lay aside and locke vp. **1595, 1611** [see ASIDE 3]. **1781** D. WILLIAMS tr. *Voltaire's Dram. Wks.* II. 140 A father cannot lay aside the father. **1824-9** LANDOR *Imag. Conv.* Wks. 1846 I. 321 On entering the apartment of the women of your country, you lay aside both slipper and turban. **1849** AYTOUN *Poems, Buried Flower* 181 Death had laid aside his terror. **1890** *Lippincott's Mag.* May 632 The editor laid aside the last proof-sheet.

b. To reject or dismiss from one's consideration or action; to abandon or postpone (a design), discontinue (an occupation).

1440 [see ASIDE 4]. **1470-85** MALORY *Arthur* IV. xx. 145, I praye to god that he send yow honour and worship. A said the Knyghte I may laye that on syde. **1530** PALSGR. 605/1, I ley away, or I laye asyde my worke to loyter. **1579** GOSSON *Sch. Abuse* (Arb.) To Gentlew. Lond. 60 When our good desires are once laide aside. **1607** [see ASIDE 4]. **1613** PURCHAS *Pilgrimage* (1614) 207 After sunne set, all this while the women lay aside their worke. *a* **1715** BURNET *Own Time* (1724) I. 66 So the design of the rising was laid aside. **1766** BROOKE *Fool of Quality* (1792) I. 152 Laying Peter aside, who think you was the greatest hero among the moderns? **1824** MACKINTOSH *Sp. Ho. Comm.* 1 June, Wks. 1846 III. 417, I think myself entitled to lay aside..the testimony of the coachman. **1877** MISS YONGE *Cameos* Ser. III. xxv. 237 The burghers laid aside their revelries.

†**c.** To put out of the way, get rid of. *Obs.*

1596 DALRYMPLE tr. *Leslie's Hist. Scot.* v. 275 Quhen he had pacifiet his cuntrey, layd asyde his alde ennimies [etc.]. **1708** SWIFT *Sent. Ch. Eng. Man* Wks. 1755 II. I. 77 When a prince was laid aside for male-administration. **1726-31** TINDAL *Rapin's Hist. Eng.* (1743) II. XVII. 110 To lay aside this troublesome Regent.

d. To set apart *for* a purpose.

1711 ADDISON *Spect.* No. 58 ¶1, I intend to lay aside a whole Week for this Undertaking.

e. *pass.* To be incapacitated for work by illness.

1879 SHAIRP *Burns* 172 At this crisis his faithful wife was laid aside, unable to attend him. **1901** *Punch* 3 Apr. 262/1 More than once laid aside by break down of health.

49. lay away. *trans.* **a.** = *lay aside* 48 a, b.

a **1400** *Ipomedon* (Kölbing) 338/7 He laid a way his horne & his hunter clothes & armed him all in white. **1526** TINDALE *Heb.* xii. 1 Lett vs..laye a waye all that preseth vs doune, and the sinne that hangeth on vs. **1563-87** FOXE *A. & M.* (1596) 70/2 They were..readie to laie awaie their

armour and weapons. 1581 SAVILE *Tacitus, Hist.* IV. (1612) 140 That passion, amongst all other, euen of wise men is last layed away. 1628 HOBBES *Thucyd.* (1822) 4 [They] laid away ..the fashion of wearing linen coats. 1641 CHAS. I in *Rushw. Hist. Coll.* III. (1692) I. 457 That laying away all disputes, you go on chearfully and speedily for the Reducing of Ireland. 1845 LONGF. *Belfry of Bruges, Curfew* ii. 4 The book is completed, And closed, like the day; And the hand that has written it Lays it away.

b. To bury. ? *U.S.*

1885 M. E. WILKINS in *Harper's Mag.* Mar. 594/1 It was hardly six months since my poor sister was laid away.

c. *Tanning.* To place (hides) flat in a vat to steep in strong tan liquor for a long period, as the final stage in the process of tanning. Also *intr.* of the hides. Cf. LAY-AWAY 1.

1885 C. T. DAVIS *Manuf. Leather* xix. 368 In tanning heavy upper leather the practice..is to first handle the sides on sticks for ten or twelve days, and then lay them away twice in bark. 1901 F. T. ADDYMAN tr. *Villon's Pract. Treat. Leather Industry* 139 Time required for Laying Away.—The hides are removed from the pit and put back three times so that the tan may be renewed. 1922 A. ROGERS *Pract. Tanning* x. 302 The hides are sometimes rocked throughout the early stages up to the time when they are laid away. 1966 G. H. W. HUMPHREYS *Manuf. Sole & Other Heavy Leathers* vii. 120 The goods may be laid away, but rarely these days with bark or other ground material as was the practice in former days when 'layers' were in general use.

50. lay by. a. *trans.* = *lay aside*, 48 a, b; †also = *lay aside*, 48 c.

1439 in Rymer *Fœdera* (1710) X. 727/2 That Matiere.. was so lightly laide by at Arras and noon Inclination shewed therto. *c* 1585 R. BROWNE *Answ. Cartwright* 6 He must.. laye by his proofe as vntrue. 1599 SHAKS. *Much Ado* v. i. 64, I am forc'd to lay my reuerence by. 1644 MILTON *Areop.* (Arb.) 38 Leaving it to each ones conscience to read or to lay by. 1674 RAY *Collect. Words, Prepar. Tin* 123 The cinder or slag..they take off with a shovel and lay it by. 1681 DRYDEN *Abs. & Achit.* 507 These were for laying honest David by On principles of pure good husbandry. 1709 STEELE *Tatler* No. 47 ¶7, I shall therefore lay by my Drama for some Time. 1736 LEDIARD *Life Marlborough* I. 118 It was Pity that so able a Man..should be laid by, as useless and forgotten. 1781 COWPER *Conversat.* 670 It views the truth with a distorted eye, And either warps or lays it useless by. 1798 LANDOR *Gebir* I. 51 His buckler and his corslet he laid by. 1867 J. B. ROSE tr. *Virgil's Æneid* 233 Lay by your wonted tasks.

b. To put away in store; to store up; to save (money). Also *absol.*

1786 BURNS *To Auld Mare* xvii, A heapit stimpart, I'll reserve ane Laid by for you. 1825 *New Monthly Mag.* XVI. 312 Of her twelve hundred a-year, she regularly lays by two-thirds. 1853 LYTTON *My Novel* IV. v, It is a great sum,..but I will lay by, as you are kind enough to trust me. 1855 MACAULAY *Hist. Eng.* XX. IV. 501 Persons who had laid by money would rather put it into the Bank. 1873 H. SPENCER *Stud. Sociol.* xv. 367 Few of them lay by in anticipation of times when work is slack.

c. To put away for future disposal or for safety.

1719 DE FOE *Crusoe* I. xiv. (1840) 239, I perceived..two miserable wretches dragged from the boats, where, it seems they were laid by, and were now brought out for the slaughter. 1821 KEATS *Isabella* lii, She wrapped it up; and for its tomb did choose A garden-pot, wherein she laid it by. 1893 *Field* 25 Feb. 297/3 She has not been put afloat yet, but is laid by till open weather sets in.

d. *pass.* To be 'laid aside' by illness (cf. 48 e).

1782 MACQUEEN in *Med. Commun.* I. 69 They are..seized with a Catarrh.., which rages so fast that in twenty-four hours, every individual..is..laid by. 1825–80 JAMIESON, *To Lay By.* 1. To overdo, to make unfit for work;..2. To be confined by ailment; as, 'He's laid by'. 1889 MRS. COMYNS CARR *Marg. Maliphant* I. xii. 237 Father is often laid by, and unable to go round the farm.

e. *intr.* (*Naut.*) = *lay to* (58 c).

1697 *Lond. Gaz.* No. 3287/3 They all laid by a considerable time, and then making Sail stood to the Westward. 1741 S. SPEED in *Buccleuch MSS.* (Hist. MSS. Comm.) I. 395 Their not hoisting their colours..and..not laying by for us.

f. To work (a crop or field) for the last time, before leaving it to grow without further husbandry. *U.S.*

1759 J. GORDON *Jrnl.* 12 July in *William & Mary College Q.* (1902) 1st Ser. XI. 106 Mowing oats & laying by corn. 1784 J. F. D. SMYTH *Tour U.S.A.* II. 127, I was also accustomed to sow a quantity of faulty wheat..in my tobacco grounds, when I gave them the last ploughing, or *laid them by*. 1835 J. H. INGRAHAM *South-West* II. 285 The ploughing generally ceases and the crop is 'laid by' about the last of July. 1868 *Rep. Iowa Agric. Soc. 1867* 158 The ground should be thoroughly rolled;..then lay by with barshear plow. 1947 *Democrat* 25 Dec. 3/4 This year when the corn was 'laid-by' the crotalaria came up voluntarily.

51. lay down. *trans.*

a. To put (something that one is holding or carrying) down upon the ground or any other surface; to put off, discard (a garment, armour). ***to lay down (one's) arms***: to surrender.

c 1205 LAY. 5070 Leie a-dun þin hære scrud & þinne rede sceld, and þi sper longe. *a* 1300 *Cursor M.* 3296 Mi hernes dun heir did i lai. *c* 1375 *Sc. Leg. Saints* i. (*Petrus*) 224, I did as myn moder saide, In þe corn myn howk doun lade, and bad it do þat do sulde I. *c* 1386 CHAUCER *Reeve's T.* 165 Lay doun thy swerd, and I wil myn alswa. 1560 DAUS tr. *Sleidane's Comm.* 423 That with al spede they laye downe theyr weapons, and devise some meanes of concorde. 1659 D. PELL *Impr. Sea* 451 *note*, They laid down their arms, and put on mourning. 1848 THACKERAY *Van. Fair* lxvii, She laid down the cup of tea. 1890 T. F. TOUT *Hist. Eng.* 142 Eighteen thousand French soldiers laid down their arms to the raw army that had defeated them at Baylen.

b. To resign, relinquish (office, power, dignity, hopes, etc.; †also *absol.* = to retire from office, etc.); †to discard, cease to bear (a name), discontinue, 'drop' (a custom, fashion); †to give up the wearing or use of.

c 1205 LAY. 2037 Þa leodene..leiden adun þene noma, & Trinouant heo nemneden. 13.. *Sir Tristr.* 1187 Tristrem he gan doun lain, And seyd tramtris he hiȝt. *a* 1450 *Knt. de la Tour* (1868) 62 Ladyes..that..hadde highe hornes, the whiche the holy man beganne to reprove, and yeue diuerse ensaumples to make hem to be layde doun. 15.. in *Dunbar's Poems* (1893) 327 In hairt be blytht and lay all dolour doun. 1577 HARRISON *England* II. xii. (1877) I. 236 Horne in windows is quite laid downe in euerie place. 1611 SPEED *Hist. Gt. Brit.* IX. xiii. (1623) 752 Those consultations of the Laitie were laide downe. 1682 LUTTRELL *Brief Rel.* (1857) I. 176 There is a discourse..that the lord chanceller will lay down, and be succeeded by the lord cheif justice Pemberton. 1697 DRYDEN *Æneis* XI. 473 What Hopes you had in Diomede, lay down. 1714 ADDISON *Spect.* No. 556 ¶1 Upon laying down the Office of Spectator. *a* 1715 BURNET *Own Time* (1724) I. 461 They [the clergy] seemed now to lay down all fears and apprehensions of Popery. 1720 DE FOE *Capt. Singleton* xiii. (1840) 226 It was a good retreat for those that were willing to leave off, and lay down. 1778 JOHNSON *Let. to Boswell* 3 July, He has laid down his coach, and talks of making more contractions of his expense. 1826 SCOTT *Woodst.* vii, Will he lay down his power?

c. To place in a recumbent or prostrate position. Often *refl.* (†in early use conjugated with *to be*). †Also, to bring to bed *of* a child (cf. 2 above).

[*a* 1225 *Ancr. R.* 288 Hwon þe heorte..leið hire salf aduneward, & buhð him ase he bit.] *c* 1250 *Old Kent. Serm.* in *O.E. Misc.* (1872) 32 Ure lord was i-leid him don to slepe. *a* 1300 *Cursor M.* 15675 Ful buxumli he laid him don apon þat erth bare. *c* 1450 *Merlin* 88 She is now leide down in hir bedde of a childe male. 1481 CAXTON *Reynard* xxxvii. (Arb.) 104 Tho wente he and leyd hym doun vnder a tre in the grasse. 1535 COVERDALE *Ps.* iv. 8 Therfore wil I laye me downe in peace, & take my rest. 1613 SHAKS. *Hen. VIII*, I. iii. 40 The slye whorsons Haue got a speeding tricke to lay downe Ladies. 1781–3 COWPER *Alex. Selkirk* 50 The sea-fowl is gone to her nest, The beast is laid down in his lair. 1791 —— *Odyss.* x. 64 Around my head Winding my mantle, [I] lay'd me down below. 1816 WOLFE *Burial Sir J. Moore* 29 Slowly and sadly we laid him down.

d. To put down (money) as a wager or a payment; †to pay (a debt).

14.. LYDG. *London Lyckpeny*, Lay down your sylver, and here you may speede. 1464–5 *Manners & Househ. Exp. Eng.* (Roxb. 1841) 487 Paid to Robart Klerke that he leid doune, xij*d*. 1560 DAUS tr. *Sleidane's Comm.* 246 b, Besydes those.. Dukates, whyche he hathe alreadye defrayde [he] shall laye downe as muche more at Venise. 1583 HOLLYBAND *Campo di Fior* 137 What shall we laye downe? What shall we stake? ? 1623 DONNE *Lett.* (1651) 230 He writ to me that 8[l] would discharge him, and that Mr Selden would lay down half. *a* 1640 MASSINGER *Very Woman* II. i, I have done nothing.. that may justly claim A title to your friendship; and much less Laid down the debt which..not I but mankind Stands bound to tender. 1692 R. L'ESTRANGE *Fables, Life of Æsop* (1708) 15 Lay down the Money upon the Nail, and the Business is done.

e. To sacrifice (one's life).

1611 BIBLE *John* x. 15, xv. 13. 1781 COWPER *Expostul.* 536 To waste thy life in arms or lay it down In causeless feuds. 1862 *Temple Bar* VI. 190 Ready..to lay down fortune, freedom, and perhaps life itself, for their sake.

f. †To put down, overthrow (*obs.*). Also *Naut.* of wind or sea: To make (a vessel) lie on her side.

c 1205 LAY. 551 A londe & a watere he heom adun leaide. *a* 1225 *Leg. Kath.* 773 Ȝef me is ileuet þurh mi leoue lauerd for to leggen ham adun. 1340 HAMPOLE *Pr. Consc.* 4415 He [Antichrist] sal drawe til hym bathe lered and lewed, And crysten law sal be doun layde. *c* 1380 WYCLIF *Wks.* (1880) 10 Lest here ypocrisie be parceyued and here wynnynge and worldly fame leid a-doun. 1387 TREVISA *Higden* (Rolls) III. 237 Foure þowsand of Spartanes fil uppon hem and leyde adoun and slouȝ of hem þre dayes to gidres. 1745 P. THOMAS *Jrnl. Anson's Voy.* 24 A raging Sea took us..with that Violence that it..laid down the Ship in a Manner quite on her Side.

g. To construct (roads, railways, ships). Also ***to lay down a keel***.

1851 *Illustr. Catal. Gt. Exhib.* 1127 Levelling instrument ..intended..for laying down railroads and highways. 1884 *Leeds Mercury* 15 Nov. 6/6 It is not..intended to lay down any new ironclads at present. 1890 T. F. TOUT *Hist. Eng.* 240 Brunel laid down the Great Western. 1897 *Daily News* 23 Jan. 3/5 Her keel will be laid down in the course of a week or two.

h. To establish, formulate definitely (a principle, rule); to prescribe (a course of action, limits, etc.).

to lay down the law: to declare what the law (with regard to something) is; hence *colloq.* to make dogmatic statements, esp. in argument.

1493 *Festiall* (W. de W. 1496) 1 b, Holy chirche leyth downe songes of melody as Te deum lau. Gloria in excelsis. 1586 A. DAY *Eng. Secretary* ii. (1625) 63, I have determined ..under this Narratory..title to lay downe my limits. 1628 EARLE *Microcosm., Medling Man* (Arb.) 89 Hee layes you downe a hundred wild plots, all impossible things. 1676 GLANVILL *Ess.* iii. 13 Laying down Rules for solving some Cubick and Biquadratick Equations. 1712 BERKELEY *Pass. Obed.* §16 If the criterion we have laid down be true. *a* 1715 BURNET *Own Time* (1724) I. 273 He assured him he would pay the debt: But did not lay down any method of doing it. 1762 FOOTE *Orators* I. i, I tell thee what, Ephraim, if thee can't but once learn to lay down the law, there's no knowing what thee may'st rise. 1765 BLACKSTONE *Comm.* I. 238 We may now be allowed to lay down the law of redress against public oppression. 1845 MCCULLOCH *Taxation* I. iv. (1852) 127 It may be safely laid down that at all times a considerable number of occupiers of land are losing by their business. 1860 TYNDALL *Glac.* II. xv. 308 He laid down the conditions of the problem with perfect clearness. 1865 TROLLOPE *Belton Est.* xviii. 205 She endeavoured to..lay down for herself a line of conduct. 1885 MRS. C. PRAED *Affinities* I. ix. 206 He was in the midst of an argument,..and was laying down the law in this fashion.

i. To set down or mark out (a plan) on paper; to delineate; †to describe (a geometrical figure).

1669 STURMY *Mariner's Mag.* I. 31 How to lay down a Triangle in a Circle. *Ibid.* v. 6 After you have taken the Angles..You must Protract or lay down the Figure. 1697 DAMPIER *Voy.* I. xvi. 448 Many shoals..that are not laid down in our Drafts. 1793 SMEATON *Edystone L.* §99, I was ..laying down the measures of the rock upon paper. 1817 SCOTT *Search after Happiness* iii, If Rennell has it not, you'll find, mayhap, The isle laid down in Captain Sindbad's map. 1853 *Jrnl. R. Agric. Soc.* XIV. I. 101 A map on which the drains of each field are laid down. 1890 T. F. TOUT *Hist. Eng.* 292 He now laid down clearly the island groups of the North Pacific.

†j. To put down in writing; to treat of. *Obs.*

1583 STUBBES *Anat. Abus.* II. (1882) 67, I will laye downe vnto you some such corruptions and abuses, as seeme to be inormous. 1634 W. WOOD *New Eng. Prosp.* To Rdr., I have laid downe the nature of the Countrey, without any partiall respect unto it. 1659 D. PELL *Impr. Sea* 131, I have laid down some of my thoughts about this word, *They that go down*. 1756 JOHNSON *Observ. St. Affairs* Wks. 1787 X. 145 It is then a proper time..to lay down with distinct particularity what rumour always huddles in general exclamations, or perplexes by undigested narratives.

†k. ***to lay down by***: to consider together with.

1614 RALEIGH *Hist. World* I. iii. §15 Lay down by those pleasures and benefits the fearful and dangerous thunders and lightnings,..with other inconveniences, and then there will be found no comparison between the one and the other.

l. To 'run and fell' (a seam); to trim, embroider. *Obs.* or *arch.*

1611 COTGR., *Rentraire*, to lay in, or lay downe, a seame. *c* 1650 *Johnnie Armstrong* vi. in Child *Ballads* (1889) III. 369 Ye shall every one have a velvet coat, Laid down with golden laces three. 1820 SCOTT *Monast.* xiv, A scarlet cloak, laid down with silver lace three inches broad.

m. *Agric.* To convert (arable land) into pasture; to put *under* grass, etc. Const. *in*, *to*, *under*, *with*.

1608 in *N. Riding Rec.* (1884) I. 122 For converting and laying down of 60 acres of arrable land in pasture. 1743 R. MAXWELL *Sel. Trans.* 52 It is a prodigious Error to overcrop Ground, before laying it down with Grass-seeds. 1789 *Trans. Soc. Arts* I. 88 Seeds for laying down arable land to grass. 1844 *Jrnl. R. Agric. Soc.* V. I. 64 The land is laid down with red or white clover. 1845 *Ibid.* II. 446 This ground was laid down with oats and grass. *Ibid.* VI. II. 528, 14 acres laid down under gorse. 1879 ESCOTT *England* I. 59 Much of this land has been newly laid down to grass.

n. To store (wine) by putting it away in cellars.

1838 DICKENS *Nich. Nick.* xxxvii, 'That was laid down, when Mr. Linkinwater first come, that wine was'. 1878 BESANT & RICE *Celia's Arb.* xv. (1887) 108 A generous flow of port, of which every respectable Briton then kept a cellar, carefully labelled and laid down years before.

†o. To cause to subside; to pacify, appease. *Obs.*

1563 W. FULKE *Meteors* (1640) 19 b, For who can affirme from whence it [wind] was raysed, or where it is laid downe? 1628 EARLE *Microcosm., High-Spirited Man* (Arb.) 92 A man quickly fired, and quickly laid downe with satisfaction.

p. *Printing.* 'To put pages on the stone for imposition' (Jacobi *Printer's Vocab.* 1888). Also (see second quot.).

1825 HANSARD *Typographia* 411 Having disposed, or 'laid down', the pages in this right order. *Ibid.* 766 To lay down a gathering, is to place the several heaps, with their signatures following each other, upon benches or forms of a proper height.

q. To deposit and fix (a coating). Also of a paving material. Hence, to cover (a surface) *with* something.

1839 *Penny Cycl.* XIII. 95/1 The composition, which is elastic and very flexible, may be immediately laid down upon the japanned surface. 1893 A. CONAN DOYLE *Mem. Sherlock Holmes* (1894) 225 The corridor..was laid down with a kind of creamy linoleum.

r. *Sporting slang.* ***to lay himself*** (or simply ***lay***) ***down to his work***: of a horse, etc., to put all his strength into a race.

1885 HOWELLS *Silas Lapham* (1891) I. 63 The mare.. understood the signal, and, as an admirer said, 'she laid down to her work'. 1893 *Illustr. Sport. & Dram. News* 20 May 375/1 He never seemed to fairly lay himself down to his work, and..Thomas won as he liked.

s. *intr.* To give up or submit; to break down or cease to act; to fail; to retire or withdraw. *U.S.*

1898 *Scribner's Mag.* XXIII. 453/2, I swear I hate to lay down to such a nincompoop. 1901 MERWIN & WEBSTER *Calumet 'K'* 64 You've never had to lay down yet, and you don't now. 1911 H. S. HARRISON *Queed* vii. 87 Your body's got to carry your mind around, and if it lays down on you [etc.]. 1923 R. D. PAINE *Comrades of Rolling Ocean* x. 193 'Any water leaking in?' 'A trickle under the floor, but the bilge pump will take care of it unless she lays down on me.' *Ibid.* xvii. 293 You stand by me and I won't lay down on you. 1927 *Cleveland Press* 4 Feb., Offered him a bribe to 'lay down' on the prosecution of George J. McKay, alleged arch-swindler.

t. To set up or establish (a certain beat). *Jazz slang.*

1950 BLESH & JANIS *They all played Ragtime* viii. 149 The backwoods pianists 'laid down the beat' and 'stacked the blues'. *Ibid.* x. 194 He laid down a terrific stomp. 1959 'F. NEWTON' *Jazz Scene* vi. 104 The 'rhythm section' laid down a rock-firm beat. 1968 *Melody Maker* 6 Apr. 8/4 The soloist can play anything he chooses to play on the time that I lay down for him. 1968 *Blues Unlimited* Sept. 23 Preston.. takes a few vocals, and lays down some swinging rhythm guitar.

52. lay forth. †a. To stretch out in a prostrate position; to bring out and display openly.

c **1420** *Chron. Vilod.* 1840 (Horstm.) For alle thyng as forthe redy þerto y-leyde. c **1430** *Hymns Virg.* 76 Now mote y leie forþ my necke, For deeþ his swerd out haþ lauȝte. **1535** COVERDALE *1 Macc.* iii. 48 They..layde forth the bokes of the lawe. **1590** SPENSER *F.Q.* I. Introd. 2 Lay forth out of thine everlasting scryne The antique rolles, where they lye hidden still. **1630** in *Descr. Thames* (1758) 65 No Fisherman ..shall at any Time hereafter ship their Draw-Nets..into their Boats, before such time as they have laid forth all their whole Net. **1667** MILTON *P.L.* IV. 259 Grots and Caves ..'ore which the mantling Vine Layes forth her purple Grape.

†**b.** To put or bring forward in argument or the like; to expound; to make patent; to expose. Also *refl.* to expatiate *upon*.

c **1386** CHAUCER *Man of Law's T.* 115 Many a subtil resoun forth they leyden. **1577** tr. *Bullinger's Decades* (1592) 1, I will..laie foorth vnto you..those things which a godly man ought to think. **1633** BP. HALL *Hard Texts, N.T.* 191 Those wonderful mercies of God wch haue been now laid forth unto you. **1665** J. SPENCER *Vulg. Proph.* Pref., The present Undertaking to lay forth the impostures wrapt up in this..instance of Enthusiasm. **1692** R. L'ESTRANGE *Fables* xiii. (1708) 16 [The Fox] lays himself forth upon the Gracefulness of the Raven's Person [etc.].

†**c.** To spend, expend, lay out. *Obs.*

1584 *Vestry Bks.* (Surtees) 16 Item laid forthe by the said churchwardens, the xxvij day of June for fower lams, vjs. ijd. **1633** BP. HALL *Hard Texts, N.T.* 318 She shall not..lay up treasure for the inriching of herselfe but shall distribute it rather and lay it forth for the benefit of Gods Saints. **1649** *Liberties & Customes of Myners* C, He shall pay 4s. for the twelve mens dinners, and the Barmaster to lay forth the mony.

d. ? To spread out with a view to ornament; to deck, array. Now *dial.* Cf. *lay out* (56 j).

1656 *Artif. Handsom.* 115 How do they exclaime..against braiding or laying forth, and powdering, or colouring their haire? **1868** ATKINSON *Cleveland Gloss., Laid out, Laid forth,* Decked out, arrayed, 'got up'.

53. lay in. a. *trans.* See simple senses and IN. †*to lay in an oar*, mentioned as an accompaniment of setting sail; also *absol.* (in quot. c 1300). *to lay in the oars*: to unship them.

c **1300** *Havelok* 718 Sone dede he leyn in an ore, And drou him to þe heye se. **13..** *E.E. Allit. P.* C. 106 þay layden in on laddeborde & þe lofe wynnes. **1485** CAXTON *Chas. Gt.* 37 At the moment whan the thorne was drawen fro the crowne he took hys syght, and whan it was layed in ageyn he recouuerd his heeryng. a **1592** GREENE *Geo. a Greene* (1599) E 4, [Shoemaker speaks in the road] Stay till I lay in my Tooles. **1769** FALCONER *Dict. Marine* (1780) C cc b, *Leve-rame!* Unship the oars! the order to the rowers to lay in their oars. **1867** SMYTH *Sailor's Word-bk., Lay in the oars*, unship them from the rowlocks, and place them fore and aft in the boat.

b. To place in store; to provide oneself with a stock of. Also said of 'taking in' food; hence *absol.* to feed vigorously (now *vulgar*). †Also *occas.* to put stores into, stock (a place).

1579 TOMSON *Calvin's Serm. Tim.* 297/2 If a man bee giuen to quaffing and laying in, he careth not..howe other be prouided for. **1625** BACON *Ess., Plantations* (Arb.) 532 And to be Laid in, and Stored vp, and then Deliuered out in Proportion. **1662** GURNALL *Chr. in Arm.* (1669) 308/2 We see in a Town besieged, though it be well laid in with Corn ..what straits they are soon put to. **1677** LADY CHAWORTH in *Hist. MSS. Comm. 12th Rep.* App. v. 37, I have laid you in some beare. **1698** FRYER *Acc. E. India & P.* 246 They observe this Maxim, Always to lay in Ballast, they eating heartily. **1709** ADDISON *Tatler* No. 131 ¶3 A great Magazine of Wines that he had laid in before the War. **1855** MACAULAY *Hist. Eng.* XV. III. 589 The rustic Jacobites were laying in arms. **1865** CARLYLE *Fredk. Gt.* XVI. xi. (1872) VI. 277 So soon as we have horses, it will not appear strange that we lay-in a little hay. **1889** 'ROLF BOLDREWOOD' *Robbery under Arms* vii, Then..the eggs and bacon—my word! how Jim did lay in.

†**c.** To put in (a claim). Also *absol.*

1603 KNOLLES *Hist. Turks* (1638) 123 The County of Tripolis layd in for himselfe, that he was discended from Raymund of Tholous. **1710** ADDISON *Whig Exam.* No. 5 ¶2 After this short preface by which..I lay in my claim to be a Politician, I shall enter on my discourse. **1734** *N. Hampsh. Prov. Papers* (1870) IV. 842 There is a new Church erected at the South end of Boston and they are laying in for Mr. Brown. **1747** *Mem. Nutreb. Crt.* I. x. 169 She applied to the then acting ministers, laying in her claim to her principality.

†**d.** *intr.* To scheme or exert oneself *to do* something. *to lay in for*: to make one's object, lay oneself out for, exert oneself to gain. *Obs.*

1599 SIR E. SANDYS *Europæ Speculum* (1629) 178 There is scant any office or estate can fall void, but they lay in by all meanes to get into it. **1642** ROGERS *Naaman* 502 If thou lay in for faith, come with an heart empty of other thoughts. **1681** DRYDEN *Abs. & Achit.* To Rdr., If I happen to please the more moderate sort, I shall be sure of..the best judges ..And I confess I have laid in for those, by rebating the satire..from carrying too sharp an edge.

e. *trans.* (*Agric.*). To enclose or reserve (a meadow) for hay. Cf. 60 b (*b*).

1600 *Sc. Acts Jas. VI* (1816) IV. 228/1 þatt all persones quha hes teillit..ony pairt..of his maiesteis..or vtheris communteis..That they within ȝeir & day..lay in the samyn communteis agane. **1727** *Cowell's Law Dict.* s.v. *Falcatura*, Meadows hay'd, or laid in for Hay. **1851** *Jrnl. R. Agric. Soc.* XII. II. 387 The proportion of hay is not great, the meadows are 'laid in' in April and May.

f. *Gardening.* (*a*) To place in position (the new wood of a trained tree). (*b*) (See quot. 1898.)

1802 W. FORSYTH *Treat. Fruit-trees* 31 It is too common a practice to lay-in the shoots at full length. **1890** BLACKMORE *Kit* III. xiv. 185, I can lay a tree in straight enough, but I am out of my line telling things. **1898** WRIGHT & DEWAR *Johnson's Gardener's Dict.* 548/2 *Laying-in* is a gardener's term for training the branches of espaliers and wall-trees. *Laying-in-by-the-heels* is his mode of describing a plant's having the roots roughly buried in the soil for some temporary purpose.

g. *Printing.* (See quot.)

1683 MOXON *Printing* 383 When the Press-man lays Sheets on the Tympan, it is stiled *Laying in Sheets*.

†**h.** ? To put (hounds) into cover. *Obs.*

1735 SOMERVILLE *Chase* II. 150 Here, Huntsman, bring.. all thy jolly Hounds, And calmly lay them in.

i. To paint (a picture or some of its parts) in the first unfinished stage.

1676 BEALE *Pocket bk.* in H. Walpole *Vertue's Anecd. Paint.* (1786) III. 135 Moneys paid my son Barth. for work, laying in the draperys of his mother's pictures. **1784** J. BARRY in *Lect. Paint.* vi. (1848) 215 Painting upon a darkish ground..will..tend to..destroy the purity..of all your lighter tints, particularly if you do not employ a great body of colour in the laying them in. **1859** SALA *Gas-light & D.* ii. 24 The whitewasher..is summoned to 'lay in' the great masses of colour. **1886** *Pall Mall G.* 8 Oct. 4/2 An artist 'laid in' a picture for an amateur, who muddled on with it for awhile and got it accepted at the Academy, but the artist who had laid the picture in was himself rejected.

†**j.** To lay (a cloth); = sense 35 b. *Obs.*

1788 G. COLMAN Jr. *Ways & Means* I. i, The cloth is laid in for breakfast.

†**k.** To 'run and fell' (a seam). *Obs.*

1611 [see 51 l].

l. To deliver, 'get in' (a blow); to shed, 'turn on' (tears).

1809 MALKIN *Gil Blas* II. ii. ¶5 Jacintha was by his bed-side, laying in her tears by wholesale. *Ibid.* VII. i. ¶9, I had no sooner laid in this home stroke [etc.]. **1865** CARLYLE *Fredk. Gt.* XV. xiii. (1872) VI. 107 A sharp brush of fighting; not great in quantity, but laid-in at the right moment.

m. To discontinue working (a colliery).

1846 M. A. RICHARDSON *Local Historians' Table-bk.* V. 78 Several collieries having been laid in this day. **1896** *Daily News* 28 Sept. 7/5 The miners at Haswell Colliery, county Durham, finished bringing their gear to bank on Saturday, and the pits are now laid in.

n. *intr.* (*Naut.*) To come in from the yards after reefing or furling. (Cf. *lie in*.)

1860 H. STUART *Seaman's Catech.* 46 The outside men will lay out and unclamp the booms,..then lay in again.

54. lay off. †**a.** *trans.* To take off, take away; to put off or remove from oneself.

c **1592** MARLOWE *Massacre Paris* (? 1600) B 4, Thou traitor Guise, lay of thy bloody hands! **1628** tr. *Tasso's Aminta* I. i. B 4 Stay for me till I haue in yon fresh fount Layd off the sweat and dust that yesterday I soyld me with. a **1631** DONNE *Serm.* lxxxviii. IV. 121 St. Gregory says that the Soul had laid off..all outward ornaments. **1727** BOYER *Fr. Dict.* s.v., To lay off a Garment, *quitter un habit*. **1919** H. L. WILSON *Ma Pettengill* ii. 46 She took me up to her little bedroom to lay my things off and then down to the parlour.

†**b.** *Naut.* To steer (a ship) away from the shore. Also *intr.*, to remain stationary outside a harbour.

1610 SHAKS. *Temp.* I. i. 52 Lay her a hold, a hold, set her two courses off to Sea againe, lay her off. **1781** JEFFERSON *Corr.* Wks. 1859 I. 291 Eight of them had got over the bar, and many others were laying off.

c. To mark or separate off (plots of ground, etc.); to plot out land in some way or for some purpose.

1748 WASHINGTON *Jrnl.* 30 Mar., This Morning began our Intended business of Laying of[f] Lots. **1765** A. DICKSON *Treat. Agric.* III. vi. (ed. 2) 400 Laying off land, after a very few crops of corn, into grass for pasture. **1795** J. PHILLIPS *Hist. Inland Navig.* 357 The partial hand of nature has laid off America upon a much larger scale than any other part of the world. **1801** A. RANKEN *Hist. France* I. 442 They ..directed that the streets should be laid off obliquely. **1847** *Jrnl. R. Agric. Soc.* VIII. II. 370 Care must be taken..to lay off the land in broad flats. **1890** *Harper's Mag.* Nov. 870/2 Laying parterres off in fanciful designs with little shells.

d. To 'set off' (distances) upon a surface.

1797 *Encycl. Brit.* (ed. 3) XVII. 393/2 Lay off the dimensions of the waste rail found in the table; and..draw a line [etc.]. **1859** RUSKIN *Perspective* xvii. 79 The dividing points..will lay off distances on the retiring inclined line. **1882** MINCHIN *Unipl. Kinemat.* 2 By laying off the different times along *Ox*.

e. *Shipbuilding.* To transfer (plans) from the paper in the full size on the floor of the mould-loft.

1863 P. BARRY *Dockyard Econ.* 139 The chief draftsman and his assistants 'lay off', or draw all the lines on the mould-loft floor, to the full size. **1893** *Field* 25 Feb. 297/2, I.. advise that the boat be 'laid off' at full size and batten-faired.

f. orig. *dial.* and *U.S.* To discontinue; to discontinue the working of; to dismiss (a workman), usually temporarily. Also *intr.*, to take a rest.

1841 *Jrnl. R. Agric. Soc.* II. II. 181 It is removed at intervals, chiefly in frost, when ploughing is laid off. **1863** W. WHITMAN *Specimen Days* (1882–3) 41 Some of the men are cleaning their sabres.., some brushing boots; some laying off, reading, writing. **1868** ATKINSON *Cleveland Gloss., Laid off*, applied to a person who from illness or other disablement is incapable of working as usual. **1886** H. JAMES *Bostonians* I. iii. 26 She would expect him to be strenuous in return; but he couldn't—in private life, he couldn't; privacy for Basil Ransom consisted entirely in what he called 'laying off'. **1888** *Daily News* 17 Sept. 2/7 One of the leading works in the district at Darlington has been laid off by a strike. **1892** *Nation* (N.Y.) 25 Aug. 135/1 To give notice of intention to 'lay off' any hands in their employ. **1897** W. D. HOWELLS *Landlord at Lion's Head* 65 When the husbands come up Saturday nights, they don't want to go on a tramp Sundays. They want to lay off and rest. **1955** *Times* 6 June 7/2 But in the course of this week stocks in some factories will begin to run out. Workers will have to be laid off. **1970** G. GREER *Female Eunuch* 242 The lowest paid employees can be and are laid off. **1972** *Daily Tel.* 1 Feb. 2/7 A pay strike by 500 clerical workers..has caused the company to lay off 2,500 car assembly workers.

g. (See quot. 1901.)

1901 J. BLACK *Illustr. Carpenter & Builder Ser.: Home Handicrafts* 43 What painters term 'laying off', that is to say, going over the work with the brush uncharged with paint and with strokes all in one direction. **1945** C. H. EATON in *Practical Painter & Decorator* iii. 90 The laying off should be vertical, that is, from ceiling to floor.. on walls, and parallel with the main source of light on ceilings. **1951** *Good Housek. Home Encycl.* 65/1 Do not attempt to 'lay off' or brush out the distemper as with paint or varnish. **1963** W. TEE *Painting & Decorating* x. 77 Finally, you lay-off, which means brushing in the direction of the grain if you are painting wood, or in the longest direction if you are painting a metal gutter or pipe.

h. To desist from (doing something); to abstain from or stop using (something); to stop bothering or pestering (a person). Also *intr.*, freq. as *imp.*: cut it out! stop it!

1908 KIPLING *Lett. to Family* ii. 17 The railways..had to find room somewhere..before Nature cried: 'Lay off!' **1919** *Amer. Mag.* May 42/2 If you guys don't lay off of me I'll bounce the two of you. **1919** *Saucy Stories* Aug. 107/2 She ..resolved to 'lay off the bright lights in the future'. **1930** D. HAMMETT *Maltese Falcon* xviii. 221 Make him lay off me then. I'm going to fog him if he keeps it up. **1931** E. LINKLATER *Juan in America* III. vii. 259 Lay off that ritzy laugh or I'll sock you. **1934** J. AGATE *More First Nights* (1937) 59 You would think, wouldn't you, that Josephine, having done enough in the way of arousing suspicion, would lay off a little. **1934** WODEHOUSE *Right Ho, Jeeves* vi. 60 Lay off the sausages. Avoid the ham. **1936** —— *Laughing Gas* iv. 49 That's all she's after—the title. For heaven's sake, Reggie, lay off while there's still time. **1946** K. TENNANT *Lost Haven* (1947) xix. 316 'For God's sake, shut up!.. Lay off, Alec, lay off.' Alec laid off. **1947** 'N. SHUTE' *Chequer Board* 62 Aw, lay off, Jim.—You're not in the South now. **1953** J. TRENCH *Docken Dead* ii. 21 How does one set about telling one's senior officer to lay off one's friend's wife? **1968** M. RICHLER in R. Weaver *Canad. Short Stories* 2nd ser. 160 'Oh, lay off,' my father said. 'Give the man air.' **1974** D. GRAY *Dead Give Away* vi. 65 I'd lay off stirring up trouble for a bit if I were you.

i. *Naut.* and *Aeronaut.* To indicate (on a chart, etc.), to work out (a course). Cf. COURSE *sb.* 12.

1942 *Tee Emm* (Air Ministry) II. 83 Always lay off Q.D.M.'s and Q.D.Y.'s as true bearings on your chart. **1943** 'T. DUDLEY-GORDON' *Coastal Command* 17 Drawing pencil lines which lay off courses of ships and aircraft, and indicate areas under patrol or to be searched. **1961** F. H. BURGESS *Dict. Sailing* 131 *Lay off a course*, work out a proposed course on a chart.

j. Of a bookmaker: to insure against a substantial loss resulting from (a large bet) by placing a similar bet with another bookmaker.

1951 E. KEFAUVER *Crime in Amer.* (1952) xvi. 184 The Nevada bookies also protect themselves by laying off their biggest bets with out-of-state operators. **1974** *New Yorker* 25 Feb. 72 An outside man..runs along the line of bookies and keeps an eye on the odds and lays off some of the money.

55. lay on. a. *trans.* To impose (an injunction, penalty, tax); †to bestow (a name) upon. (In early use with dative pronoun as in 19 b.)

11.. *O.E. Chron.* an. 1052 (Laud MS.) þe folc ȝeald heom swa mycel swa hi heom on leȝden. c **1175** *Lamb. Hom.* 31 Bluðeliche he wule herkein þet þe preost him leið on. c **1250** *Gen. & Ex.* 3994 Sal ic non wurd muȝen forð-don, Vten ðat god me leið on. c **1450** LONELICH *Merlin* 988 (Kölbing) What name they scholden leyn hym vppon. **1813** *Gentl. Mag.* May 429/2, I think laying on a tax would greatly enrich the public purse. **1833** *Act 3 & 4 Will. IV*, c. 46 §64 The meeting is for the purpose of laying on an assessment. **1881** GARDINER & MULLINGER *Study Eng. Hist.* I. x. 185 Charles I had used the special powers entrusted to him..to lay on ship-money.

b. *intr.* To deal blows with vigour; to make vigorous attack, assail. (Formerly often with dative pronoun denoting the object of attack.)

c **1205** LAY. 13708 Mid sweorde leggeð heom on. a **1225** *Juliana* 17 Leggeð on se luðerliche on hire leofliche lich. c **1330** *Arth. & Merl.* 8445 (Kölbing) He laid on wiþ schourge and bad hir go. c **1380** *Sir Ferumb.* 1533 Lokeaþ þat ȝe legge hem an & sleþ hem a-doun wyþ myȝt. a **1420** HOCCLEVE *De Reg. Princ.* 1102 He dremeth theeues comen in And on his cofres knokke, & leye on faste. **1480** CAXTON *Chron. Eng.* ccxliv. (1482) 299 Our men of armes..leyde on with stakes. **1530** PALSGR. 601/2 Laye on, lay on upon the jade. **1598** GRENEWEY *Tacitus' Ann.* I. viii. (1622) 14 They ..laide them on with stripes. **1605** SHAKS. *Macb.* v. viii. 33 Lay on Macduffe, And damn'd be him, that first cries hold, enough. **1693** DRYDEN *Juvenal* III. (1697) 68 Answer, or answer not, 'tis all the same: He lays me on, and makes me bear the blame. **1698** VANBRUGH *Prov. Wife* IV. iii, He came at us..and laid us on with a great quarter-staff. **1836** MARRYAT *Midsh. Easy* xii, The pleasure of thrashing his enemy..was quite enough—and he laid well on. **1843** MACAULAY *Lays Anc. Rome, Lake Regillus* xxvii, I will lay on for Tusculum, And lay thou on for Rome! **1882** FREEMAN in Stephens *Life & Lett.* (1895) II. 267, I fancy people will lay on more zealously for either of the extremes.

c. *trans.* To inflict (blows); to ply (the lash) vigorously. Also *to lay it on* (in quot. *fig.*).

a **1400** *Octovian* 1061 Ley on strokes with good empryse. **14..** *Libeaus Desconus* 2056 (Kaluza) Ley on strokes swifte. **1611** BEAUM. & FL. *King & No King* IV. ii. (1619) 53 You haue paid me equall, Heavens, And sent my owne rod to correct me with..Lay it on, Iustice, till my soule melt in me. **1656** BAXTER *Reformed Pastor* III. i, We disgrace them to the utmost, and lay it on as plainly as we can speak. **1732** FIELDING *Mock Doctor* viii, Those blows..which I was oblig'd to have the honour of laying on so thick upon you. **1892** *Field* 26 Nov. 799/3 A stirrup leather well laid on.

†**d.** *intr.* To set oneself vigorously (*to do* something).

1587 TURBERV. *Trag. T.* (1837) 38 The hungrie dogs,.. Layde on as fast her fleshye flankes to teare.

e. *to lay (it) on*: †(*a*) to be lavish in expense (*obs.*); (*b*) to pile on the charge for goods, etc.

1590 MARLOWE *Edw. II* (1598) E4, Thou shalt haue crownes of vs t'out bid the Barons; And, Spenser, spare them not, lay it on. **1606** SHAKS. *Tr. & Cr.* I. ii. 224 There's no iesting, laying on, tak't off, who [w]ill as they say, there be hacks. **1610** —— *Temp.* III. ii. 160, I would I could see this Taborer, He layes it on. **1611** COTGR., *Cocher sur la grosse taille*, (as wee say) to lay it on, (take it off who as will;) to spend, or borrow, exceeding much. **1612** SIR C. MOUNTAGU in *Buccleuch MSS.* (Hist. MSS. Comm.) I. 239 Here is.. much preparations at this wedding for masks.. one of eight lords and eight ladies, whereof my cousin An Dudley on[e], and two from the Inner Courts, who the[y] say will lay it on. **1727** BOYER *Fr. Dict.* s.v., I had a good Fortune, and laid on to some Tune, as long as it lasted.

f. To apply a coat of (paint, varnish, etc.) to a surface. Hence in phr. ***to lay (it) on thick, with a trowel***, to be excessive in flattery, eulogy, etc.

1600 SHAKS. *A.Y.L.* I. ii. 112 Well said, that was laid on with a trowell. **1601** —— *Twel. N.* I. v. 258 Tis beauty truly blent, whose red and white, Natures owne sweet, and cunning hand laid on. **1611** —— *Wint. T.* v. iii. 49. **1660** F. BROOKE tr. *Le Blanc's Trav.* 379 Pulverized Gold lay'd on with gumme. **1839** *Penny Cycl.* XIII. 95/1 The colours are tempered with oil and varnish, and the metallic powders laid on with gold size. **1842–59** GWILT *Archit.* §2233 All the first coats of plastering are laid on with this tool. **1875** JOWETT *Plato* (ed. 2) III. 51 Dyers first prepare the white ground and then lay on the dye of purple. **1893** *Law Times* XCIV. 452/1 It is nauseous to hear the adulation of Mr. Neville, who laid butter on with a spade.

g. *Agric.* Of cattle: To 'put on', increase in (flesh); also *absol.*

1807 SOUTHEY *Espriella's Lett.* (1808) I. 58 All the fat being laid on, as graziers speak, anew. **1813** VANCOUVER *Agric. Devon* 229 This animal would lay on from the middle of May until the middle of November, about two score per quarter. **1840** *Jrnl. R. Agric. Soc.* I. III. 333 Well-bred sheep ..lay on flesh quick.

h. *Printing.* To place the sheets of paper on the type to be printed. †Hence, to print an edition of (so many copies); *intr.* of a bookseller, ? to bespeak a number of copies from a printer (*obs.*).

1576 in *Stationers' Reg.* (Arb.) II. 137 Licenced vnto him *the praise of follie* to print not aboue xvᶜ of any impression with this condicon that any of the cumpany may laie on with him reasonablie at euery impression as they think good. **1683** MOXON *Mech. Exerc., Printing* 383 *Lay on*, a phrase used for the Number of Books to be Printed. Thus they say, There is 1000, 2000, 3000, &c. Laid on. **1849** *Chambers Inform.* II. 720/1 No alteration has been made in the manner of 'laying on' the paper.

i. To put (dogs) on the scent. Cf. 15h. Also *transf.* in jocular use.

1655 FULLER *Ch. Hist.* III. iv. §20 Such hounds are easier laid on, then either rated or hollowed off. **1861** DICKENS *Gt. Expect.* xliii, How long we might have remained in this ridiculous position it is impossible to say, but for the incursion of three thriving farmers—laid on by the waiter I think—who came into the coffee-room. **1861** THACKERAY *Four Georges* iv. (1862) 186 But now I am ashamed to mount and lay good dogs on, to summon a full field, and then to hunt the poor game. **1863** KINGSLEY *Water-Bab.* 68 Bring the dog here and lay him on. **1879** SALA *Paris Herself Again* I. xvii. 276 The oldest waiters.. had seemingly been 'laid on' to attend on the guests. **1891** *Field* 7 Nov. 696/2 No horsemen got forward with the stag before the hounds were laid on.

†**j.** To trim, embroider. Cf. *lay down* (51 l). Also, to place (thread) on a material before couching it down with a separate thread.

1563–83 FOXE *A. & M.* II. 2047/1 His Ierkin was laid on with gold lace faire and braue. **1880** L. HIGGIN *Handbk. Embroidery* i. 8 '*Japanese gold thread*'.. must.. be laid on, and stitched down with a fine yellow silk. [**1906** A. G. I. CHRISTIE *Embroidery & Tapestry Weaving* viii. 166 A bunch of threads may be laid upon the material, and an open chain, buttonhole, or feather stitch worked over in order to fix it in place.] **1959** *Chambers's Encycl.* V. 155/2 Couching or laid work is a form in which the threads are 'laid' on material and couched down with matching or contrasting colour.

k. To provide for the supply of (water, gas, etc.) through pipes from a reservoir; to provide (a telephone line). Hence, to make arrangements for, to provide (refreshments, entertainment, transport, etc.).

1845 *Punch* 1 Mar. 100/1 Announcing that the water was going to be laid on when it wasn't. **1853** *Jrnl. R. Agric. Soc.* XIV. I. 153 The water being laid on distributed itself beautifully and evenly over the surface. **1861** *Temple Bar* III. 23 Fifteen shillings an hour, to say nothing of refreshments laid on gratis and supplied at discretion. **1869** E. A. PARKES *Pract. Hygiene* (ed. 3) 319 Water in large quantities must be laid on in pipes. **1869** *St. Andrews Gaz.* 7 Aug., The special wires which the Scotch papers have 'laid on' between London and Edinburgh. **1870** DICKENS *E. Drood* xxii. 170 There is two bedrooms.. with gas laid on. **1885** *List of Subscribers, Classified* (United Telephone Co.) (ed. 6) 17 At 'The Clarendon' in Brighton.. they have a telephone laid on. **1909** *Chambers's Jrnl.* July 477/2 A large supply of hydrogen prepared by a new process is laid on for inflation. **1940** C. GARDNER *A.A.S.F.* 84 Squadron Leader Dodds.. said that he'd got my programme.. laid on. 'Laid on' was the Army term for everything—and I found myself using it. **1944** N. COWARD *Middle East Diary* 103, I was unable to give a concert as the piano.. had not been 'laid on'. **1949** *Punch* 13 May 636/2 Universities do not exist to lay on degree courses to follow the idiosyncratic requirements of a particular employer. **1959** 'J. WELCOME' *Stop at Nothing* ix. 139 As usual he had everything laid on and a car was waiting. **1964** E. O'BRIEN *Girls in Married Bliss* vi. 51 He'd have some hatchet-voiced secretary laid on to tell Kate some boring and familiar lie, like that he was in conference. **1971** B. W. ALDISS *Soldier Erect* 185 Pack your night things in a small pack and get weaving, while I lay on transport. **1973** E. PAGE *Fortnight by Sea* xvi. 177 Try and lay some coffee on. Plenty of it. Good and strong.

l. To give (something) to (a person). *U.S. slang.*

1942 *Amer. Mercury* July 86 Lay de skin on me [shake hands], pal! **1952** G. MANDEL *Flee Angry Strangers* 244 He lays some on his buddies 'n they get to like it; right, Buster? **1960** *Time & Tide* 24 Dec. 1599/3 I've fixed up a real wild basket of ribs and a bottle of juice, and I'd like you to fall by her joint and lay it on her. **1968** *New Yorker* 18 May 45/2 He .. took out a copy of his newest album. He wrote something on the back of it and picked up one of the hotel bills. 'Let me just lay this album on the man downstairs. Maybe it'll keep him quiet for two or three days.' **1970** *It* 9–24 Apr. 8/4 Of course you can't lay advice on someone.

56. lay out. a. *trans.* To extend at length; to take out and expose to view, to the air, etc.; to spread out in order; to lay so as to project outwards.

a **1400–50** *Alexander* 778 He layd owt a lang neke & hys hand likkys. **1500–20** DUNBAR *Poems* x. 45 Now spring vp flowris fra the rute.. Lay out ȝour levis lustely. **1535** in *Vicary's Anat.* (1888) I. 171 That they may have warnyng to lay owt theyre offal of theyre howses ynto the opon streates. **1580** SIDNEY *Ps.* x. vi, O, with how simple look He ofte laieth out his hook! **1619** R. HARRIS *Drunkard's Cup* 21 They bee buckt with drinke, and then laid out to bee Sunn'd and scornd. **1683** MOXON *Mech. Exerc., Printing* 383 *Lay out Sheets.* When the Press-man takes Sheets off the Tympan, and lays them on the Heap, it is stiled *Laying out Sheets.* **1748** *Anson's Voy.* III. v. 341 There is a frame laid out from her to windward. **1835** SIR J. ROSS *Narr. 2nd Voy.* xxxiii. 467 Laying out hawsers to warp her off when this should take place. **1849** THACKERAY *Pendennis* i, His letters were laid out there in expectation of his arrival. **1859** H. T. ELLIS *Hong Kong to Manilla* 239 Refreshments.. were laid out in an adjoining room. **1890** CONAN DOYLE *Firm of Girdlestone* xxxiii. 265 The deal table.. was laid out roughly as for a meal.

b. To stretch out and prepare (a body) for burial; hence (*slang*) to stretch out in death, to lay low, to 'do for'; *fig.* to put 'hors de combat'; to knock (a person) unconscious; to kill.

1595 A. COPLEY *Wits, Fits & Fancies* 195 One said to a little child whose father died that morning, and was layd out in a coffin in the Kitchin, Alas, [etc.]. **1606** SHAKS. *Tr. & Cr.* II. iii. 36 If she that laies thee out sayes thou art a fair coarse. **1848** MRS. GASKELL *M. Barton* vi. (1882) 16/1 They reverently laid out the corpse—Wilson fetching his only spare shirt to array it in. **1891** *Harper's Mag.* Oct. 777/2 Hydropathy gave him fits, and eclecticism almost lays him out. **1892** STEVENSON & L. OSBOURNE *Wrecker* xxv. 417 He gave the wretched man an opiate that laid him out within ten minutes. **1894** *Nation* (N.Y.) 22 Nov. 373/2 Never were so many demagogues laid out in one day as in the elections of a fortnight ago. **1829** [see COLD *a.* 1 c]. **1890** in Barrère & Leland *Dict. Slang* II. 9 Galletly was saying, 'I've laid one out' to the other prisoners... Witness also saw the knife, and there was blood on it. **1894** *Daily News* 26 May 8/6 If you strike me I will lay you out. **1896** *Wells Jrnl.* 3 Dec. 7/5 A disposition to 'injure, maim, and lay out an opponent, especially if he be a valuable element in the opposing team'. **1916** 'TAFFRAIL' *Pincher Martin* xviii. 337, I gits rated up ten days ago,.. death vacancy. Poor ole Byles got laid out, yer remember. **1929** J. B. PRIESTLEY *Good Companions* III. v. 589 'But do you mean to say he was laid out?' he demanded. .. 'On the jaw, I think you said?' **1973** *Scotsman* 21 Feb. 17/6 When they hit you with the word, cancer, it scares you to death. Boom! You're laid out. But I've learned a lot about cancer since then.

c. To spend, expend (money). Also *absol.*

c **1449** PECOCK *Repr.* 91 If therto thei han eny expensis bifore leid out and mynystrid. **1486–1504** *Let.* 7 Jan. in Denton *Eng. in 15th C.* (1888) 318 *note* D, Mane men wyll ley owt more to kepe vnder the porr th[en] for to helpe thaym. **1535** COVERDALE *Isa.* lv. 2 Wherfore do ye laye out youre moneye, for the thinge yᵗ fedeth not. **1596** SHAKS. *1 Hen. IV*, IV. ii. 6 *Bard.* Will you giue me Money, Captaine? *Fal.* Lay out, lay out. **1610** —— *Temp.* II. ii. 34 When they will not giue a doit to relieue a lame Begger, they will lay out ten to see a dead Indian. **1615** TOMKIS *Albumazar* III. v. F3b, Lay out some roaring oathes For me; I'le pay thee againe with interest. **1711** STEELE *Spect.* No. 54 ¶2 Most of our Professors never lay out a Farthing either in Pen, Ink, or Paper. **1843** MRS. CARLYLE *Lett.* I. 254, 2*l.* 10*s.* was more than I cared to lay out of my own money on the article. **1895** MACAULAY *Hist. Eng.* xx. IV. 471 He laid out all his gains in purchasing land.

†**d.** To employ or exercise (powers, effort). *Obs.*

1651 BAXTER *Saints' Rest* III. vi. §26 (ed. 2) 127 They.. should lay out all their strength on the work of God. **1656** *Burton's Diary* (1828) I. 24 If you do not lay out your especial endeavours in the things of God. **1665** BOYLE *Occas. Refl.* v. i. (1848) 296 A mis-expence of his Time or Talents: whether they be laid out upon Speculative Notions in Theology, or [etc.]. **1711** ADDISON *Spect.* No. 98 ¶5 Nature has laid out all her Art in beautifying the Face. *a* **1715** BURNET *Own Time* (1724) I. 190 He.. did not lay out his learning with the diligence with which he laid it in.

e. *refl.* †To exert oneself *in*, *upon* (*obs.*); to take measures, frame one's conduct with a view to effecting a purpose or gaining an object. Const. *for*, *to* with *inf.*

1659 C. NOBLE *Answ. Immod. Queries* 1 The Grandees of our Nation, who laid out themselves to the utmost in their ..contrivements for the peace.. of their Country. **1678** BUTLER *Hud.* III. i. 143 Who never fail'd.. To lay themselves out, to supplant Each other Cousin-German Saint. **1732** BERKELEY *Alciphr.* I. 194 You shall often see even the learned.. Divine lay himself out in explaining Things inexplicable. **1745** *Lett.* in *Rep. Cond. Sir J. Cope* (1746) 119, I will lay my-self out to know the Conduct and Conversation of all my Neighbours. **1757** BURKE *Abridgem. Eng. Hist.* I. iii. Wks. X. 228 If they discovered any provincial laying himself out for popularity. **1809** KENDALL *Trav.* II. xlvii. 147 A large proportion of the inhabitants lay themselves out to give entertainment. **1827** CHR. WORDSW. *K. Chas. Author Icon Basil.* (1828) 140 The running off to quite a different matter.. may fairly generate a suspicion, that the writer lays him-self out upon what is easy, and was not wanted. **1880** T. HARDY *Trumpet Major* xxii, Take it careless, my son,.. and lay yourself out to enjoy snacks and cordials.

f. *intr.* With *for*: †To make a search for, look out for (*obs.*); to take measures to win or get. Also, to scheme, plan *to* effect some purpose.

1624 T. DAVIES in *Lett. Lit. Men* (Camden) 140, I.. began to lay out for those Books you writ for. **1656** STANLEY *Hist. Philos.* v. (1701) 169/1 Dionysius laid out to take him, but could not light on him. **1712–13** SWIFT *Jrnl. Stella* 4 Feb., Lady Masham, who has been laying out for my acquaintance. *a* **1715** BURNET *Own Time* (1724) I. 397, I laid out for MSS, and searched into all offices. **1751** JOHNSON *Rambler* No. 97 ¶12 Women.. most observed when they seem themselves least to observe, or to lay out for observation. **1813** COL. HAWKER *Diary* (1893) I. 82, I had given up all idea of this buck, having laid out for him since about August 30. **1834** J. H. NEWMAN *Par. Serm.* x. I. 150 To be seen of men, to lay out for human praise. **1867** HOWELLS *Ital. Journ.* 57 He laid out to go ashore the next time he came to Venice.

g. To display, exhibit, expose; to set forth, expound, demonstrate. ? Now *rare*.

c **1440** *York Myst.* xxvi. 251 Ȝoure langage ȝe lay oute to lang, But Judas, we trewly þe trast. **1661** MARVELL *Corr.* xxxii. Wks. 1872–5 II. 76 The King's Counsell is to be heard at our barr, to lay out euidence against the King's dead and liuing judges. **1666** PEPYS *Diary* 14 July, I wrote.. to the Duke of York, laying out our want of money again. *a* **1715** BURNET *Own Time* (1724) I. 214 He.. laid out the necessity of raising some more force for securing the quiet of Scotland. **1748** RICHARDSON *Clarissa* (1811) VI. 107 Sally was laying out the law, and prating away in her usual dictatorial manner. **1789** CHARLOTTE SMITH *Ethelinde* I. 94 Sir Edward.. found it doubly delightful to lay out his whole soul in the soft and sensible society of Ethelinde. **1855** BAIN *Senses & Int.* I. i. §4 (1864) 7 The mode of laying out the subject that has occurred to an able physiologist. **1864** FROUDE *Short Stud.* (1872) I. 2 Laying out his matter as easily.. as if he had been talking to us at his own fireside.

h. To apportion (land) for a purpose; to plot or plan out (grounds, streets, etc.).

1608 [see LAYING *vbl. sb.* 1 b]. **1632** *MSS. Acc. St. John's Hosp., Canterb.*, Layd out on our selues and the land-measurer when we went to.. laye out our land. **1689** *Col. Rec. Pennsylv.* I. 298 An ordr for yᵉ laying out a Road from Philadelphia to Bucks County. **1705** ADDISON *Italy* 1 The Mountains about the Town.. laid out in beautiful Gardens. **1796** JANE AUSTEN *Pride & Prej.* xxviii, The garden.. was large and well laid-out. **1799** *Scotland Described* (ed. 2) 18 Pleasure-grounds have been in many places laid out. **1840** *Jrnl. R. Agric. Soc.* I. III. 259, I laid out the drains 30 feet apart. **1855** MACAULAY *Hist. Eng.* xii. III. 188 Those who laid out the city had never meant that it should be able to stand a regular siege. **1885** SIR J. BACON in *Law Times Rep.* LII. 509/2 The roads had been laid out, but were not completed.

i. To plan or map out; to set as a task or duty.

1742 RICHARDSON *Pamela* III. 295 Shall it be as Mrs. B. lays it out, or not? **1868** MRS. WHITNEY *P. Strong* viii. (1869) 97, I know.. what she has laid out for herself to do. **1872** BLACK *Adv. Phaeton* xxxi. 412 In laying out plans for another month's holiday. **1879** M. PATTISON *Milton* ii. 29 Lycidas is laid out on the lines of the accepted pastoral fiction.

†**j.** To put (false hair) in order. *Obs.* (Cf. 52 d.)

1580 LYLY *Euphues* (Arb.) 445 The haire they lay out groweth vpon their owne heads. **1656** *Artif. Handsom.* 59 When she laid out the combings of her own or others more youthfull haire when her own.. seemed lesse becoming her.

†**k.** *Cards.* (Piquet, Écarté, etc.) To discard, throw out (a card or cards) from one's hand.

1687 MIEGE *Gt. Fr. Dict.* II. s.v., To lay out his Cards, at Picket, *faire son écart.* **1727–52** CHAMBERS *Cycl.* s.v. *Picquet*, If one of the gamesters finds he has not a court card in his hand, he has to declare he has *carte blanche*, and tell how many cards he will lay out [etc.].

†**l.** *intr.* To incline and project outward. *Obs.*

1793 SMEATON *Edystone L.* 195 Till the stones are cleared of the boat, the shears lay out considerably.

m. *intr.* (*Naut.*) To occupy a position on a yard towards the yard arms for the purpose of manipulating the sails. (Cf. *lie out.*)

1829 MARRYAT *F. Mildmay* vii, The men laying out on the yards. **1867** SMYTH *Sailor's Word-bk.*, *Laying or Lying out on a yard*, to go out towards the yard-arms.

57. lay over. *trans.* **a.** To overlay.

1535 COVERDALE *Hab.* ii. 19 It is layed ouer with golde and syluer. **1663** GERBIER *Counsel* 84 The laying over a Wall, white in oil, twelve pence a yard. **1698** FRYER *Acc. E. India & P.* 56 Sads, laid over with Boughs. **1732** LORD TYRAWLY in *Buccleuch MSS.* (Hist. MSS. Comm.) I. 381 Crimson velvet, laid all over with gold lace.

b. *U.S. colloq.* To miss, allow to pass by; to postpone; to lay a temporary embargo on.

1885 A. GRAY *Lett.* (1893) 772 At Las Vegas, New Mexico, we laid over one train, to rest and see the Hot Springs. **1890** *St. Nicholas Mag.* Sept. 920/1, I know of tennis matches.. that have been laid over for hours because of a sprained ankle. **1890** *Standard* 20 Nov. 5/2 Great regions were 'laid over'. They were taboo to the hunter until the fur animals had time to recover themselves.

c. ? *U.S. colloq.* To excel, to 'put in the shade'.

1869 B. HARTE *Luck Roaring Camp* (1870) 15 They've a street up there in 'Roaring' that would lay over any street in Red Dog. **1876** MARK TWAIN *Tramp Abr.* (1880) I. ii. 19 In scolding.. a blue-jay can lay over anything, human or divine.

†**58. lay to. a.** *trans.* To place in juxtaposition; to apply (a medicinal remedy) to the body; also

to lay to one's ear, to listen to, obey; ***to lay to the deaf ear***, to turn a deaf ear. *Obs.*

In the Wyclif quots. merely a literalism of translation.

1382 WYCLIF *Eccl.* viii. 16, I leide to [L. *apposui*] myn herte. —— *Ecclus.* ii. 4 Alle that to thee shul ben leid to [L. *quod tibi applicitum fuerit*]. *c* **1400** *Rom. Rose* 2660 Than shalt thou stoupe, and lay to ere, If they within a-slepe be. *c* **1450** *Merlin* 261 The carll leide to the deef ere. **1513** DOUGLAS *Æneis* I. Prol. 488 To ilk cunnand wicht lay to my eir. **1551** TURNER *Herbal* I. F j b, The leues of this herbe layd to with salt. **1584** COGAN *Haven Health* (1636) 25 Being laid to outwardly, as a medecine. **1601** HOLLAND *Pliny* II. 262 The leaues..of Ephedros brought into a liniment and laid too, do discusse and dissolue them. **1620** *Frier Rush* 19 He made a great fire and set on the pot, and layed to the spit.

†**b.** To put or bring into action; to bring to bear; *esp.* in ***to lay to one's hand(s***.

c **1386** CHAUCER *Prol.* 841 Ley hond to, every man. *c* **1440** HYLTON *Scala Perf.* (W. de W. 1494) I. xxxix, Our lorde.. layeth to his honde and smyteth down the deuyll. **1530** PALSGR. 603/1, I laye to my hande to helpe that a thyng maye be doone. **1535** COVERDALE *Ps.* cxviii. [cxix.] 126 It is tyme for the (o Lorde) to laye to thine honde. **1560** DAUS tr. *Sleidane's Comm.* 233 With all hys force and power, he layeth to all hys munition. **1576** FLEMING *Panopl. Epist.* 74 Lay too all the might you can make. **1610** SHAKS. *Temp.* IV. i. 251 Monster, lay to your fingers: helpe to beare this away. *c* **1620** Z. BOYD *Zion's Flowers* (1855) 20 Lay to your armes, and help..afford.

c. *intr.* (*Naut.*) To come to a stationary position with the head towards the wind; = *lie by*.

1798 NELSON in Nicolas *Disp.* (1845) III. 20 The Terpsichore..continued to lay to under bare poles. **1866** R. M. BALLANTYNE *Shift. Winds* xiii. (1881) 131 [He] was obliged to lay-to until daylight, as the weather was thick.

59. lay together. a. *trans.* To place in juxtaposition; to add together; †to compare; †to put together, construct; †*pass.* to be composed *of*.

[*a* **1300** *Cursor M.* 29529 (Cott.) Þir pointes of cursing haf i said, and soth and scortly samen laid.] *c* **1340** *Ibid.* 550 (Fairf.) Of þer þinges þat I haue sayde was adam cors togeder layde. **1530** PALSGR. 605/1, I ley styckes or brandes togyther, to make a fyre. **1560** DAUS tr. *Sleidane's Comm.* 469 That the same fyre whiche many yeares since they had layde together, myght nowe..breake out. **1565** T. STAPLETON *Fortr. Faith* 74 All which numbres being layed together arising well toward to twenty thousand soules. *a* **1568** ASCHAM *Scholem.* II. (Arb.) 88 Whan he bringeth it translated vnto you, bring you forth the place of Tullie: lay them together: compare the one with the other. **1628** T. SPENCER *Logick* 114 *To keepe a dore, and to dwell in the tents &c.* are layd together. **1678** BUNYAN *Pilgr.* I. Author's Apol. 236 O then come hither, And lay my Book, thy Head, and Heart together. **1692** BURNET *Past. Care* ii. 15, I will..lay both the Rules and the Reproofs that are in them together. **1707** [see EYE *sb.*[1] 2 f]. **1727** BOYER *Fr. Dict.* s.v., Lay his Words and Deeds together, *comparez ses Paroles avec ses actions.* **1853** URE *Dict. Arts* II. 562 A simpler..mode of.. laying the strands together.

b. ***to lay..heads together***: to confer together.

c **1381** CHAUCER *Parl. Foules* 554 The watyr foulis han here hedis leid To gedere. **1483** *Nottingham Rec.* II. 393 [They] leyd theyr hedes to geder to vnderstand how they myght haue verrey evydence and Knolage. **1583** GOLDING *Calvin on Deut.* clxxviii. 1108 If all the greatest Doctors of yᵉ world shold lay their heads together they coulde not attaine to the vnderstanding thereof. **1650** R. STAPYLTON *Strada's Low C. Warres* VIII. 5 Then laying their heads together..[they] created them a Generall. **1760** GRAY *Corr.* (1843) 210 We shall lay our heads together, and try if we cannot hammer out as good a thing about you. **1893** *Bookman* June 83/1 [They] laid their heads together and gradually built up this picturesque mountain of lies.

†**c.** To concoct, compose (a story); also *absol.*

1603 KNOLLES *Hist. Turks* (1638) 770 At such time as the old mans fury was ouerpast, falling of purpose into talke with him about the matter, she laid together in her sons behalf, and alledged [etc.]. *a* **1715** BURNET *Own Time* (1724) I. 580 His story was so ill laid together, that the Court was ashamed to make use of it.

†**d.** *intr.* To engage (in combat). *Obs.*

c **1205** LAY. 5904 Heore wepnen weoren lihte heo leiden to-gadere & feorliche fuhten.

60. lay up. a. *trans.* See simple senses and UP; to put up and extend (one's limbs) on a couch; †to erect (a building); †to vomit, 'throw up' (*obs.*).

1570 GOOGE *Popish Kingd.* IV. 53 And miserably they reele, till as their stomacke vp they lay. **1579-80** NORTH *Plutarch* (1676) 757 Antonius being queasie stomacked with his Surfeit he had taken, was compelled to lay up all before them, and one of his friends held him his Gown instead of a Bason. **1788** J. MAY *Jrnl. & Lett.* (1873) 86 To-day finished laying up the house, and put on the roof. *c* **1830** *Houlston Tracts* No. 87. 11 Her daughter must go home, and lay up her legs till they got quite well.

b. *Agric.* (*a*) To throw up (land) in ridges as a preparation for sowing: often with compl., as *dry*, *rough*, *in ridges*. (*b*) To reserve for hay. Cf. 53 e.

1842 *Jrnl. R. Agric. Soc.* III. II. 171 Every arable field which is laid up in ridges probably requires..to be drained. **1844** *Ibid.* V. I. 167 After being fed the meadows are laid up, and in about six weeks produce an excellent crop of hay. **1852** *Ibid.* XIII. I. 62 The land..is either sown with wheat at Michaelmas or laid up dry, for barley in the spring. **1883** FROUDE *Hist. Sketches* 74 (*Norway Fjords*) There were forty or fifty acres of grass laid up for hay.

c. To deposit or put away in a place for safety; to store up (goods, provisions); to put by. Often *absol.* to save money. Also with immaterial obj. ***to lay up in lavender***: see LAVENDER *sb.*[2] 2.

? *a* **1366** CHAUCER *Rom. Rose* 184 Gret tresours up to leyn. *c* **1400** *Rom. Rose* 5680 They..ley not up for her living. **1526** TINDALE *Luke* i. 66 And all they that herde them layde them vppe in their hertes. —— *2 Cor.* xii. 14 The children ought nott to laye vppe for the fathers and mothers. [So **1611.**] **1560** DAUS tr. *Sleidane's Comm.* 229 b, That the same should be laied up into a cheste fast locked. *a* **1626** BACON *New Atl.* (1900) 9 The Strangers House is at this time Rich, and much aforehand; For it hath layd up Revenew these 37 yeares. **1651** N. BACON *Disc. Govt. Eng.* II. xxvi. (1739) 115 It encourages men to gather and lay up, when they have Law to hold by what they have. **1690** LOCKE *Ess. Hum. Und.* II. x. §10 The faculty of laying up and retaining the ideas that are brought into the mind. **1709** STEELE *Tatler* No. 91 ¶1, I have, by leading a very wary Life, laid up a little Money. **1736** LEDIARD *Life Marlborough* III. 194 The Allies design'd to lay up large Magazines at Douay. **1879** MISS YONGE *Cameos* Ser. IV. xx. 216 Lines which she had probably composed and laid up in her memory. **1879** M. PATTISON *Milton* xiii. 212 His poems he wished laid up in the Bodleian. **1885** E. F. BYRRNE *Entangled* I. I. xiii. 248 You could not bear the agony that would be laid up for you in an unhappy union.

†**d.** To place in confinement, imprison. *Obs.*

1565 COOPER *Thesaurus* s.v. *Carcer*, *Condi in carcerem*, to be layed vp in [prison]. **1569** in J. Hooker *Life Sir P. Carew* App. (1857) 233 The messenger..was layed op by the helys. **1602** *2nd Pt. Return fr. Parnass.* I. ii. 240 Sweete Constable doth take the wondring eare, And layes it vp in willing prisonment. **1632** MASSINGER *City Madam* I. iii, When laid up for debt.

e. To cause to keep indoors or in bed through illness; often in *pass.* to be (taken) ill, to keep one's bed. In recent colloquial use also *intr.*, to take to one's bed.

1554 SIR J. MASON in Tytler *Edw. VI* (1839) II. 456 The constitution of his body being so easy to be overthrowen, as a little travel taken more than it be able to bear were enough to lay him up. **1600** SHAKS. *A. Y. L.* I. iii. 7 Then there were two Cosens laid vp, when the one should be lam'd with reasons, and the other mad without any. **1676** LADY CHAWORTH in *12th Rep. Hist. MSS. Comm.* App. v. 32 This seveare weather which hath laid [me] up in the house this ten days. **1709** STEELE *Tatler* No. 82 ¶5 While he was laid up with the Gout. **1771** FOOTE *Maid of B.* III. Wks. 1799 II. 230 My gout..lays me up for four or five months in a year. **1840** R. H. DANA *Bef. Mast* xxxi. 117, I should be laid up for a long time, and perhaps have the lock jaw. **1877** MISS YONGE *Cameos* Ser. III. xxv. 241 An attack of small-pox..laid him up for a short time. **1893** A. S. ECCLES *Sciatica* 49 Busy persons who can ill afford to lay up and be absent from their affairs for some days.

†**f.** To bury. *Obs.*

1581 SAVILE *Tacitus, Agric.* (1622) 202 Yet wast thou laied vp with fewer teares. **1655** E. TERRY *Voy. E. India* 309 It [Pile] was begun by Achabar-sha..and finished by his Son, who since was laid up beside him.

g. To put away (a ship) in dock or some other place of safety. Also *intr.* for *pass.* or *refl.*

1667 PEPYS *Diary* 14 June, The counsel that brought us into this misery, by laying up all the great ships. **1701** in Picton *L'pool Munic. Rec.* (1883) I. 309 Ships that are to be layd up. **1725** DE FOE *New Voy.* 18 At length we..arrived again at the Port of St. Julian... Here we resolved to lay up for the winter. **1795** NELSON in Nicolas *Disp.* (1845) II. 69 We must both soon be laid up to repair. **1838** THIRLWALL *Greece* IV. xxvii. 25 The Peloponnesians..laid up their fleet for the rest of the winter. **1849** *Tait's Mag.* XVI. 158/1 The sands, on which a vessel is laid up, are minutely and beautifully detailed. **1885** *Times* (weekly ed.) 11 Sept. 9/3 The ice-hulks and the swift yawls..moored and laid up in ordinary. **1890** *Murray's Mag.* Oct. 469, I shall send the yacht round to Gosport to lay up.

transf. **1855** DICKENS *Dorrit* I. xxiv, Mr. F.'s Aunt was, for the time laid up in ordinary in her chamber.

h. *Ship-building.* (See quot.)

1869 SIR E. REED *Shipbuilding* x. 197 The heads of the rivets are generally laid-up, that is, are made close to the surface, against which they fit by a few heavy blows given by the workman.

i. *Rope-making.* = sense 37.

c **1860** H. STUART *Seaman's Catech.* 28 Lay up the centre strands together, take the next two strands and lay them up together..; when you have laid it up to within ten inches of the end, lay both strands up together [etc.]. **1882** NARES *Seamanship* (ed. 6) 26 Gun gear [is] laid up left handed.

j. *Naut.* (*intr.*) To direct the course.

1832 MARRYAT *N. Forster* xli, The French squadron.. tacked and laid up directly for them. **1858** *Merc. Marine Mag.* V. 71 We neither could lay up for it, nor overhaul it.

k. *Printing.* (See quot. 1841.)

1808 STOWER *Printer's Gram.* 156 A form cannot be well laid up without plenty of water. **1841** SAVAGE *Dict. Printing* s.v., Before the letter of a worked-off form is distributed,.. if the work be finished it is unlocked upon a board laid in the trough and well rinsed with water, while the compositor keeps working the pages backward and forward with his hands, and continues pouring water on them till the lye and ink are washed away..; this is termed laying-up.

†**l.** To surpass, excel. *Obs.*

1601 R. JOHNSON *Kingd. & Commw.* (1603) 40 In suffering of hunger, thirst, heat, cold, labor and extremities, they wil laie up any nation in Europe.

m. To assemble or stack (plies or layers) in the arrangement required for the manufacture of plywood or other laminated material (usu. prior to bonding into a single structure).

1927 KNIGHT & WULPI *Veneers & Plywood* xxvi. 286 Stock trucks..with suitable guides against which to jog layers of stock as the freshly glued plywood is laid up. **1942** WOOD & LINN *Plywoods* vii. 74 When working on thin 3-ply boards two panels are frequently 'laid up' between each caul. **1949** B. L. DAVIES *Technol. Plastics* xiii. 233 The dried, impregnated or coated material is cut to size..and the sheets are laid up, i.e. piled one upon the other to a predetermined number. **1962** *Newnes Conc. Encycl. Electr. Engin.* 115/2 Normally not less than three layers of tissue are laid up between the electrodes [of an industrial capacitor] for the lower voltages. **1965** *Plastics Tooling & Manuf. Handbk.* (Amer. Soc. Tool & Manuf. Engineers) vi. 114 Successive plies are laid up until the desired thickness is achieved; then the part is allowed to cure.

IX. 61. *Comb.*: **lay-down** *a.* (*a*) (also ***laid-down***), applied to a collar which is folded over instead of standing up; also as *sb.*, a 'turn-down' collar; (*b*) applied to a hand or contract at cards (esp. Bridge) which is such that success is possible against any defence, so that no harm would be done by exposing the player's cards on the table; also *ellipt.* as *sb.*, such a hand; also *fig.*; †**lay-holding** *a.*, that lays hold, tenacious; **lay-over** *a.* = *lay-down*.

a **1586** SIDNEY *Arcadia* I. (1629) 89 Vran..Laid hold on him with most lay-holding grace. **1838** DICKENS *Nich. Nick.* xxvii, A black gentleman..with a lay down collar with two tassels. **1852** R. S. SURTEES *Sponge's Sp. Tour* (1893) 339 The three Master Baskets in coats and lay-over collars. **1880** MISS BIRD *Japan* I. 47 A laid-down collar. **1889** W. S. GILBERT *Foggerty's Fairy* (1892) 151 Serious collars, substitutes for the unprofessional 'lay-downs' I usually wore. **1906** *Westm. Gaz.* 8 Sept. 16/3 Enormous cards are held and we have a lay-down great or small slam. **1934** *Amer. Speech* IX. 10/2 A *cold* game is a sure game, and a *cold* contract is a *lay-down*. **1955** I. FLEMING *Moonraker* vii. 75 It was a laydown Grand Slam for Bond against any defence. **1959** *Listener* 12 Mar. 489/1 Seven Clubs, it will be seen, is a lay-down. **1961** *Times* 6 Dec. 8/3 A lay-down slam in Clubs. **1966** 'W. HAGGARD' *Power House* ix. 92 The interview had diverted him. He'd learnt a lot about Harry Fletcher; he'd held a crushing hand and had played it as a laydown. **1974** *Country Life* 17 Oct. 1139/3 The slam is a lay down.

☞ *Phrase-key.*

To be laid (= to lie down) 8 a; it lays (*impers.* of wind and weather) 33; lay aback 25 c; *l* abed 8 c; *l* aboard 25 d; *l* about 44; *l* about one 32 e; *l* abroad 45; *l* one's account 38; *l* along 46; *l* alongside 25 c; *l* an ambush 18; *l* apart 47; *l* aside 48; *l* asleep 8 c; *l* at (= attack) 32 c; *l* at one's door 27 b; *l* athwart the hawse 25 d; *l* a-water 25; *l* away 49; *l* the axe (to) 15; *l* bare 25; *l* battery 19; *l* a bed 35 b; *l* before 17; *l* a bet 12; *l* blame (on) 29; *l* a blockade 19; *l* one's bones 8 b; *l* bread, *l* a buck 35 d; *l* a burden on 28; *l* by 50; *l* by the heels 25 b; *l* by the lee 25 c; *l* the case (*Printing*) 35 f; *l* claim 26; *l* close 25 d; *l* the cloth 35 b; *l* colours 41 a; *l* (one's) course 39 b; *l* down 51; *l* the dust 3; *l* a duty (on) 28; *l* ear to 15; *l* an egg 9; *l* emphasis 30; *l* eyes on 21 b; *l* fast 25 b; *l* a finger on 21 e; *l* a fire 35 e; *l* for (= lay wait for) 18 b; *l* for (= plan for) 38 c; *l* forth 52; *l* from one 15 c; *l* a ghost 3 b; *l* the grain, *l* a ground 41 b; *l* a gun 24; *l* a hand 21 d; *l* hands on 21 c; *l* hard(ly to 32 b; *l* (= wager) one's head 12; *l* to heart 15; *l* a hedge 6 b; *l* hold (of, on) 22; *l* home to 25 e, 32 b; *l* a horse 12 c; *l* a hostage 11 b; *l* in 53; *l* in one's dish, neck 27 b; *l* in mortgage, pawn, †wed 11; *l* in one, into one 15 f; *l* in prison 15 d; *l* in water 25; *l* in words, writing, etc. 40; *l* an information 26 b; *l* into (= belabour) 32 d; *l* it on 31, 55 e, f; *l* the land (*Naut.*) 5; *l* leaven 35 d; *l* one's life 12, 13; *l* load about one 32 e; *l* load on, see LOAD *sb.*; *l* one's love upon 16 a; *l* low 1, 43; *l* a name on 15 g; *l* off 54; *l* on 55; *l* on (= attack, belabour) 32 a; *l* on a scent or track 15 h; *l* (a person) on the face, the lips 34; *l* open 25; *l* out 56; *l* over 57; *l* (a person) over the head, etc. 34; *l* pay 10; *l* a picture 41 a; *l* the scene 20 b; *l* the sea 3; *l* siege 19; *l* a snare 18; *l* (= quarter) soldiers upon 28 b; *l* speech 14; *l* stress 30; *l* a table 35 b; *l* a tax (on) 28; *l* to 58; *l* to (= impute or attribute to) 27; *l* to (= attack) 32 b; *l* to do (= plan or intend to do) 38 c; *l* to one's charge, credit 27 b; *l* to one's door 27 b; *l* to ground, earth 1 b; *l* to heart 15; *l* to jail 15 d; *l* to pledge (gage, mortgage, pawn, †wed) 11; *l* to rest, sleep, bed 8 c; *l* to sight 25; *l* together 59; *l* a trail (on) 15 h; *l* a trap 18; *l* type (*Printing*) 35 f; *l* under contribution, obligation, etc., under water 25; *l* unto (= attack) 32 b; *l* up 60; *l* a wager 12; *l* wait 18; *l* waste 25; *l* watch 18; *l* a †wed 11; *l* weight (upon) 30; *l* the wind 3; *l* with (= compare with) 15 e; *l* with (= cover or spread with) 42.

lay, *v.*[2] *Obs.* [Aphetic f. ALLAY *v.*[2], to mix.] *trans.* To mix or ALLOY (metals).

1489 *Sc. Acts Jas. IV* (1814) II. 221/1 Tuiching the article of goldsmythis, quilkis Layis and makkis falss mixtouris of ewill metale. **1554** *Ld. Treas. Acc. Scot.* Sept., Aucht unce of siluer, to mak ane assay of siluer and layit mony. *a* **1572** KNOX *Hist. Ref.* Wks. 1846 I. 403 Sche dois sua corrupt the layit money, and hes brocht it in sick basenes, and sic quantatie of scruiff, that [etc.].

†**lay**, *int. Obs.* An exclamatory substitute for *Lord!*

1700 W. KING *Transactioneer* 33 *Gent.* Pray what's that? *Transact.* Oh lay! Why don't you know?

lay: see LEA, LEE, LEY.

lay, pa. t. of LIE *v.*[1]

†**'layable**, *a. Obs.* [f. LAY *v.*[1] + -ABLE.] Rateable, taxable.

c **1599** *Acc. Bk. W. Wray* in *Antiquary* XXXII. 279 The layable rentes of all my landes.

layabout ('leɪəbaʊt). [f. LAY *v.*[1] 43 + ABOUT *adv.* 8.] An habitual loafer, idler, or tramp. Also *attrib.* or as *adj.*

1932 G. S. MONCRIEFF *Café Bar* viii. 78 These layabouts were rotters. **1932** S. PEARSON *To Streets & Back* xxiv. 234 The 'down and outs' in Hyde Park are permanent 'layabouts'. **1959** *Punch* 19 Aug. 57/1 He simply uses any old-fashioned plot about layabout art-lecturers getting mixed up with funny spies. **1959** H. PINTER *Birthday Party* (1960) 81 Keep an eye open for low-lives [*sic*], for schnorrers and for layabouts. He didn't mention names. **1961** *John o' London's* 21 Sept. 327/1 A colourful tour of layabout London. **1968** *New Scientist* 2 May 217/2 Those of us gifted by nature with inertia but maligned by society as layabouts. **1972** D. HASTON *In High Places* ii. 35 There was another strong twosome..in the hut, otherwise only student layabouts left.

lay-away ('leɪəweɪ). Also layaway. [Lay *v.*[1] 49.]

1. *Tanning.* A vat or pit in which hides are 'laid away'; = Layer *sb.* 4 e. Freq. *attrib.*

1885 A. Watt *Art Leather Manuf.* xii. 145 The Layers.—In these pits, which are termed lay-aways by the Americans, the butts are stratified with ground oak-bark. **1885** C. T. Davis *Manuf. Leather* xix. 367 When heat is used on the head leaches the liquor sometimes enters the lay-away yard in a hot condition. **1901** F. T. Addyman tr. *Villon's Pract. Treat. Leather Industry* 137 Tan-pits or lay-away pits are large vats, sometimes round, and made of oak, bound with iron. **1922** A. Rogers *Pract. Tanning* x. 303 At this stage..the hides go to the layaways. These are vats large enough to permit the hide being spread out flat. *Ibid.* 304 All the layaway liquors are not so worked down and out, some being returned to the leach-house to be strengthened and freshened. **1957** *Encycl. Brit.* XIII. 848/1 The goods are moved from the strongest suspender vats to the layaway vats or floaters.

2. *N. Amer.* = Lay-by *sb.* 2 b.

1961 in Webster. **1967** *Boston Sunday Herald* 26 Mar. 1. 22/3 Her dress for Easter is on layaway... You can get it out. It only costs $5, but I don't own that much now. **1970** *Globe & Mail* (Toronto) 25 Sept. 32/7 (Advt.), No Dealers—All Sales Final—Christmas Lay-A-Ways... Sale at Toronto Warehouse. **1973** *Houston* (Texas) *Chron.* 21 Oct. 2/1 (Advt.), Use our layaway plan for Christmas!

'lay-back. [f. vbl. phr. *to lay back.*] **1.** The receding position of the nose of certain breeds of dog, esp. the bulldog.

1894 R. B. Lee *Hist. & Descr. Mod. Dogs Gt. Brit. & Ireland* (*Non-Sporting Division*) 233 The bones of the lower jaw in specimens [of the bulldog] which have the desired appearance, known as 'upturn' and 'lay back' are found to have the contour of a segment of a circle. **1905** H. St. J. Cooper *Bull-Dogs & Bull-Dog Breeding* 98 This well-known dog..has a grandly shaped head, with small well-carried ears, large under-jaw, turn-up and lay-back. **1909** *Ladies' Field* 28 Aug. 511/1 Bulldogs:..a brindle, good layback and under-jaw. **1968** H. Harmar *Chihuahua Guide* 239 *Layback*, the receding nose found in some of the short-faced breeds.

2. a. *Mountaineering.* A method of climbing cracks in rocks (see quot. 1968).

1925 *Jrnl. Fell & Rock Climbing Club* VII. 17 The crack ..is then climbed, utilising the lefthand edge of the crack for a 'lay back'. **1957** Clark & Pyatt *Mountaineering in Brit.* xvi. 237 A layback is almost as tiring in descent as in ascent. If the leader's arms give out he cannot retreat, and has to fall off. **1968** P. Crew *Encycl. Dict. Mountaineering* 77 *Layback*, a method of climbing cracks and flakes by gripping the edge with the hands, leaning back and placing the feet flat on the rock at the side of the crack and slightly below the hands. As the climber pulls on the edge of the crack and presses his feet against the rock, the opposing pressures exerted can be sufficient to support the body. **1971** *N.Z. Listener* 19 Apr. 56/5 Pete had a dekko up a chimney. But there was a lay-back and too much exposure at the top. **1973** C. Bonington *Next Horizon* x. 145 Only the crack in its [*sc.* the rock's] back provided a mixture of hand-jamming and lay-back holds.

b. In various sports, the movement or position of leaning backwards or lying on one's back.

1948 R. F. Herrick *Red Top: Reminisc. Harvard Rowing* 173 The chief differences between Washington and eastern rowing at that time were Washington's lack of layback, fast hands on the release and their tremendous emphasis on the catch. **1962** *Times* 6 Feb. 4/5 They [*sc.* the Cambridge crew] have a longer swing and a longer lay-back than recent crews. **1962** *Austral. Women's Weekly* Suppl. 24 Oct. 3/3 [Surfing] *Layback*, a supreme test of skill in trick riding. The rider lies flat on his back, with feet facing the way board is going. **1968** *Daily Tel.* 6 Dec. 15/6 As always, Miss Waghorn used her long legs to full advantage in the split jump, a majestic spreadeagle and well-timed lay-back and grab-parallel spins.

layband ('leɪbænd). Also (? 6 laband), 7 leyband. [f. *lay*, Lea *sb.*[4] + Band *sb.* The identity and meaning of the word in the first quot. are doubtful.] **a.** The string with which a 'lea' or skein is tied up. **b.** (See quot. 1847.)

1597 *Wills & Inv. N.C.* (Surtees 1860) 283, v els of camericke, 46*s.* 8*d.* v els of lawn 36*s.* xvj labandes 8*s.* **1598** Florio, *Bàndine*, the lay-bande of a skaine of threed. **1615** Markham *Eng. Housew.* ii. v. (1668) 137 You shall as you reel it, with a Leyband of a big twist, divide the slipping or skean into divers leyes. **1847** Halliwell, *Lay-band*, a small roller. *West.* It is explained as a towel in one MS. glossary.

lay-bed. Also 6 labed. [f. Lay *v.*[1]] The bed in which something is laid or lies: **a.** a grave (now *dial.*); †**b.** a layer, stratum.

1541 *Richmond. Wills* (Surtees 1853) 24, I gyf to the churche warks and for my labed vj*s.* viij*d.* **1728** W. Smith *Ann. Univ. College* 251 When, for ought I know, the Statue might be in its Lay-bed, and not taken out of the Quarry. **1876** *Whitby Gloss.*, *Lay-bed*, a grave.

lay-board. *Sc.* and *north. dial.* Also laboard, law-board, etc. [? f. Lay *v.*[1] Cf. G. *legebrett*, Du. *legbord*, board for laying something on.] The board on which tailors iron their seams. (Cf. *lap-board*, s.v. Lap *sb.*[1] 9.)

1804 Galloway *Luncarty* 57 (E.D.D.) His laboard gave, and gives, old bakers bread. *a* **1813** A. Wilson *Poems* (1876) II. 44 As soon's she reekt the sooty bield, Whare labrod he sat cockin'. **1829** Hogg *Sheph. Cal.* I. 180 Afore I were a landless lady, I wad rather be a tailor's lay board. **1867** Gregor *Banffs. Gloss.*, *Lay-buird.*

lay-by ('leɪbaɪ). Also lay-bye. [f. Lay *v.*[1] + By *adv.*]

A. *sb.*

1. a. A 'slack' part of a river in which barges are laid by out of use.

1826 J. Kay *Let.* 7 July in *N. & Q.* (1960) Apr. 148/1, I have given permission for a Laybye to be formed in the bank of the Canal near Thornhill Bridge. **1879** E. J. Castle *Law of Rating* 61 Pumping station, wharf, lay-by for barges. **1891** *Field* 7 Mar. 344/2 A lay-by near Windsor Bridge. **1892** *Ibid.* 17 Sept. 454/3 Screened lay-byes and deep pools. **1899** *Daily News* 9 May 3/1 There is a river frontage to the Thames of 160 ft. with private dock and lay-by for three barges.

b. A railway siding.

1906 *Westm. Gaz.* 28 Sept. 7/1 A heavy goods train had left the up-line..and run into a short lay-by. **1955** L. T. C. Rolt *Red for Danger* x. 206 He therefore signalled the L.M.S. goods out of the lay-by, but the driver stopped in Charfield station for water.

c. An area adjoining a road where vehicles may park without interfering with the traffic.

1939 [see *draw-in* (Draw *sb.* 12 a)]. **1950** *Engineering* 17 Nov. 387/2 Stopping places off the carriageway in the form of lay-bys. **1959** *Manch. Guardian* 1 July 5/4 The emergence of a new type of picnic—the lay-by high tea... On any arterial road you can see the family saloons..heave into the lay-by. **1971** *Islander* (Victoria, B.C.) 8 Aug. 4/3 We enjoyed a Sunday picnic in a forest layby and then returned to Holland. **1972** *Daily Tel.* 13 Mar. 3/2 Caravanners who park in lay-bys causing litter and hygiene problems will face prosecution. **1973** *Times* 30 Apr. 14/1 My correspondent at the front owns a weekend cottage in Norfolk and was in the habit of collecting his empty wine bottles and baked bean cans and dumping them in the lay-by bins on the way home on Sundays. **1973** *People's Jrnl.* (Inverness & Northern Counties ed.) 4 Aug. 8/2 The holidaymakers had stopped in a lay-by at Oban and Miss Coldrick thinks she left the camera on the car boot.

2. a. Something laid by or saved; savings.

1894 Baring-Gould *Kitty Alone* III. 65, I had gone with all my little lay-by to get you out of your difficulties.

b. A system of payment whereby a purchaser puts down a deposit on an article, which is then kept on one side for him until he has paid the full price. Also *transf.*, and as *vb.* Chiefly *Austral.* and *N.Z.*

1930 *Sydney Morning Herald* 16 Oct. 4 (Advt.), Avail yourself of our lay-by service. **1943** *Amer. Speech* XVIII. 95 [New Zealand] A few trade names have caught the public fancy, and become generalized..A system of hire-purchase called the 'Lay-by' has resulted in the verb 'layby', pronounced and written as one word. **1944** W. E. Harney *Taboo* (ed. 3) 154 He did not complain, for it was to him a tribal law and custom—a lay-by system to protect him when he was old. **1957** *Rhodesia Herald* 16 Mar. (Advt.), Lay-Byes Accepted Now. **1960** *Times* 25 June 9/4 When in Australia..I was bewildered to find this expression 'Lay by' used widely in large shops, until I discovered that it meant that the management would put aside articles for customers. **1969** *Sydney Morning Herald* 24 May 26/8 (Advt.), Goldfish, tropical. Full range plants, access... Lay-by or terms. Get your discount card now.

B. *attrib.* or *adj.* Intended to be 'laid by'.

1804 W. Taylor in Robberds *Mem.* I. 492 You might.. have executed..a correct and expurgated copy for a lay-by edition.

laycall, obs. form of Laical *a.*

laych(e, variant of Laigh.

laycke, obs. form of Laic.

layd, obs. pa. t. Lay *v.*[1]; obs. north. f. Load.

lay-day ('leɪdeɪ). *Comm.* [app. f. Lay *v.*[1]] One of a certain number of days allowed according to a charter-party for the loading and unloading of cargo.

1845 Stephen *Comm. Laws Eng.* (1874) II. 141 That he will..load and unload the goods within a certain number of days (usually called *lay* or *running* days). **1857** C. Gribble in *Merc. Marine Mag.* (1858) V. 5 Your consignees..do not trouble themselves until your lay days are expired.

laydman, obs. form of Loadman.

laye: see Lay *a.* (and *sb.*[1]), *v.*[1], also Leye *Obs.*, flame.

layen, obs. pa. pple. of Lie *v.*[1]

layer ('leɪə(r)), *sb.* Forms: 4 legger, leier, 4–5 leyer, 5 leyare, 5–7 lare, 6 laier, 7 lear(e, leer, layre, 8 lair, 7– layer. [f. Lay *v.*[1] + -er[1].]

I. 1. a. One who or that which lays (in various senses); one who lays siege, plots, etc. Also with sb. in comb., as †*besiege-layer*, *plate-layer*, etc.

1538 *Extracts Aberd. Reg.* (1844) I. 156 It selbe lesum to quhatsumeuer nychtbour that reprehendis the layaris of the said fulze in the place forsayd [etc.]. **1552** Huloet, Besiege laier, *obsessor.* **1674** N. Fairfax *Bulk & Selv.* 152 Layers of plots and traps. *a* **1684** Leighton *Comm. 1 Pet.* ii. 6 The Lord Himself is the layer of this corner stone. **1737** J. Chamberlayne *St. Gt. Brit.* ii. iii. 93 Layers and Takers of Paper on and from the Rolling-Presses. **1871** Proctor *Light Sci.* 311 The layer of the odds. **1884** Mrs. Houstoun *Caught in Snare* II. vi. 71 A layer of the demon of jealousy. **1891** *Pall Mall G.* 11 Nov. 6/3 At St. Ouen there was no betting, the layers refusing to do any business.

†**b.** One who lays stones; a mason. (Cf. *bricklayer*.) *Obs.*

1382 Wyclif *1 Chron.* xxii. 15 Many craftise men, masouns, and leyers [**1388** leggeris of stonys]. —— *Ezra* iii. 7 Thei ȝeve money to heweris of stonus, and to leieris [*v.r.* leggeris, **1388** liggeris]. **1425** in Dugdale *Monast.* III. ii. 164 During all the sayd werke the seid Will. Horwode shall nether set mo nor fewer Free-Masons Rogh Setters ne Leye[r]s there-upon. *c* **1440** *Promp. Parv.* 294/1 Leyare, or werkare wythe stone and mortere, *cementarius.* **1641** Sanderson *Serm.* II. 194 The workmen, and labourers (layers, fillers, servers, and the rest).

†**c.** One who lays or fixes the amount of (an impost).

1602 *Acc. Bk. W. Wray* in *Antiquary* XXXII. 80 Imp'm. one laye..of 1*d.* ob. a noble..Wm. Wray Robt. Hodgesonn and R. Atkingson beinge layers of the sayme.

d. Of a hen (with adj. *good*, etc.).

1707 Mortimer *Husb.* 191 The oldest [Hens] being always reckoned the best Sitters, and the youngest the best Layers. **1880** *Standard* 27 Dec., The hens are of a bad breed and are infrequent layers.

e. with advs. (see Lay *v.*[1] VIII): **layer-on** (*a*) *Printing*, the operator who 'feeds' a printing-machine; (*b*) *Engineering*, 'an automatic mechanism which in a coining-press, embossing-press, or other analogous machine feeds blanks to the dies of the press' (*Cent. Dict.*).

1552 Huloet, A layer out of mony, *dispensator.* **1599** Shaks. *Hen. V*, v. ii. 248 Old Age, that ill layer vp of Beautie. **1635** J. Gore *Well-doing* 25 A good layer up makes a good layer out, and a good sparer makes a good spender. **1666** Pepys *Diary* 3 July, The worst judge of matters, or layer together of what he hath read, in the world. **1708** *N. Jersey Archives* (1881) III. 280 The layers out of the High way. **1711** Shaftesb. *Charac.* (1737) II. 330 Spirit-hunters, witch-finders, and layers-out for hellish storys and diabolical transactions. **1797** Mrs. Bennett *Beggar Girl* VII. x. 384 An exceeding good dresser of hair and layer-on of rouge. **1849** Alb. Smith *Pottleton Leg.* vi, One of these [old women] was the layer-out of the village, to whom the management of the last dreary toilet for the grave was, by long usage, always conceded. **1849** *Chambers' Inform.* II. 720/2 This machine requires a layer-on and taker-off of sheets at each end. **1887** *Standard* 7 Oct. 3/2 A printer's 'layer-on'. **1895** Hardy *Jude* iv. ii. 248 In the afternoon, when everything was done, and the layers-out had finished their beer, and gone, he sat down in the silent place. **1896** W. Morris in Mackail *Life* (1899) I. 230 The layer-out of a garden. **1928** *Observer* 10 June 7/4 Poetry, it is generally known, is dead... Our critics are a generation of layers-out. **1953** R. Campbell tr. *E. de Queiroz's Cousin Bazilio* xiii. 264 The professional layer-out was a woman with a pocked face. **1958** L. Durrell *Mountolive* xvi. 318 The dead man's clothes are the perquisites of the layer-out. **1974** W. Foley *Child in Forest* i. 51 His widowed mother..acted midwife and washer-woman, or layer-out of the dead.

f. = *gun-layer* (Gun *sb.* 17).

1896 *Daily News* 6 Aug. 7/2 Two gun detachments, including layers. **1898** G. S. Robertson *Chitrál* xviii. 167 All the gunners, even the 'layers', wore bandages over their eyes. **1911** H. A. Bethell *Mod. Artillery in Field* x. 147 If any officer or layer fails to locate the target correctly, the result is likely to be considerable waste of time and ammunition. **1971** D. A. Lamb *View from Bridge* ii. 16 On the twelfth of February three of the new artillerymen became first class layers.

II. Something which is laid.

2. a. A thickness of matter spread over a surface; *esp.* one of a series of such thicknesses; a stratum, course, or bed. In early use chiefly in *Cookery.*

1615 Markham *Eng. Housew.* (1660) 83 Take Codlins.. and lay a lear thereof in the bottom of the pye. **1616** Surfl. & Markh. *Country Farme* 409 If you lay them [Damaske-plums] betweene mulberrie-leaues, or vine-leaues, one leare aboue another in a close box made for the purpose. **1641** Best *Farm. Bks.* (Surtees) 126 Just 10 boards in every chesse or layer. **1644** G. Platts in *Hartlib's Legacy* (1655) 200, I would have all the richest Farmers..to thrash up the most part of their other Corn, and to take down the foresaid Rick, and to make it up again with a leere of thrashed Corn, with chaffe and all together. *a* **1648** Digby *Closet Opened* (1677) 165 Put no more Collops into one pan at once than meerly to cover it with one Lare. **1684** T. Burnet *Theory Earth* i. 167 The inner veins and lares of the earth are also broken as well as the surface. **1703** T. N. *City & C. Purchaser* 161 Some Gutters..have a Lair of Sand for the Lead to lie upon. **1747** Mrs. Glasse *Cookery* iv. 60 Then lay in your Dish a Layer of Mince-meat, and a Layer of Yolk of Eggs,..a Layer of Anchovies [etc.]. **1774** Goldsm. *Nat. Hist.* (1776) I. 37 These layers of shells..must have been brought there by successive depositions. ?**17..** *Receipts in Cookery* 11 (Jam.) Lay in a lare of the beef, and throw on it plenty of suet with more spice, salt and fruits, do so lare after lare, till it be full. **1802** Playfair *Illustr. Hutton. Theory* 44 Rocks having their layers exactly parallel are very common. **1807** J. E. Smith *Phys. Bot.* 30 In the Fir..Each of these circular layers is externally most hard and solid. **1828** Carr *Craven Dial.*, *Layer*,..2. a slice from the breast of a fowl. **1845** Budd *Dis. Liver* 6 A layer of areolar..tissue. **1860** Tyndall *Glac.* i. xviii. 132 A deep layer of fresh snow overspread the mountain. **1880** Geikie *Phys. Geog.* iv. xxi. 187 Stripping off the layer of vegetation we see below it the layer of soil on which the plants grow.

fig. a **1658** Cleveland *Poems* (1677) 24 So mixt they are one knows not whether's thicker A Layre of Burgess, or a Layre of Vicar. **1876** Geo. Eliot *Dan. Der.* II. xxiii. 110 Gwendolen's better self..made a desperate effort to find its way above the stifling layers of egoistic disappointment and irritation.

b. A formation of aircraft flying at the same height.

1940 N. Monks *Squadrons Up!* iv. 113 One Hurricane, trying to get above the enemy aircraft, observed five layers of ten M.E. 110's each, between 10,000 and 15,000 feet. *Ibid.*, Another Hurricane spent about a quarter of an hour alternately dodging and flying in and out among the enemy layers. **1952** *Oxf. Jun. Encycl.* X. 52 The German fighters usually flew in formation well above the bomber formations. .. The R.A.F. replied by sending up layer formations, the upper layer to engage the fighters while a lower layer dealt with the bombers. **1959** R. Collier *City that wouldn't Die* v. 64 Since to-night was a 'fighter night'..the guns could

engage targets only at 12,000 feet and below—2000 feet below the bottom layer of fighters. *Ibid.* x. 167 As the youngest he had inevitably drawn the highest 'layer' on the Southend-Romford patrol line.

3. *Gardening* and *Agric.* **a.** A shoot or twig of a plant fastened down and partly covered with earth, in order that it may strike root while still attached to the parent stock, and so propagate the plant.

1664 EVELYN *Sylva* (1679) 13 Many Trees are also propagated by Cuttings, and Layers. —— *Kal. Hort.* June (1679) 19 *Cytisus lunatus* will be multiplied by slips in a moist place.. but neither by Seeds or Layers. **1712** J. JAMES tr. *Le Blond's Gardening* 141 The Dutch Lime.. is easily produced by Layers. **1772** in *Mrs. Delany's Lett.* Ser. II. I. 475 On examining the layers of my large blooming magnolia I found one remarkably vigorous. **1813** SIR H. DAVY *Agric. Chem.* (1814) 361 The grasses that propagate themselves by layers. **1846** J. BAXTER *Libr. Pract. Agric.* (ed. 4) I. 311 Many layers are lost, or prevented from striking kindly, by being covered too deep.

b. *pl.* Patches of laid or trodden corn.

1634 W. TIRWHYT tr. *Balzac's Lett.* (vol. I.) 79 When I see the Grasse trodden downe, and.. the Corne full of Layers: I am well assured it is neither Wind nor Haile, hath made this work.

c. A field of grass or clover; see also quot. 1793.

[Perh. a special development of LAIR *sb.*[1] 5 (q.v.), influenced by association with LAY *v.*]

1793 *Ann. Agric.* XXI. 611 *note*, *Layer* is the term used in Suffolk for artificial grasses, that rest longer than one year. **1895** *E. Angl. Gloss.*, *Layer*, arable land in grass and clover. **1898** RIDER HAGGARD in *Longm. Mag.* Oct. 498 Last year it and No. 39 were clover layers, but the crop they yielded was poor.

d. (See quots.)

1787 W. MARSHALL *Norfolk* (1795) II. 383 *Layer*, plants of hedgewood; quick. **1794** *Trans. Soc. Arts* XII. 106 Planted with three rows of fine white-thorn layer, intermixed with Oak and Ash. **1895** *E. Angl. Gloss.*, *Law* or *Layer*, young plants, such as whitethorn, crab, and brier.

4. Other specific and technical senses. **a.** ? Some measure of flax. ? Cf. LEA *sb.*[4] †**b.** An oyster-bed (see quots.). **c.** *Silk-manuf.* (See quot.) **d.** A pavior's flag or flag-stone. **e.** *Tanning.* = bloomer-pit (see BLOOMER[1]). **f.** (See quot.) **g.** *Cartography.* An area on a map depicted in a particular colour or tint chosen to represent all land between two specified heights. Cf. *layer system* in 5.

a. 1732 *Acc. Workhouses* 42 Every pound of six-penny flax, spun to 24 layers.

b. 1667 T. SPRAT *Hist. R. Soc.* II. 308 This Brood and other Oysters they carry to Creeks of the Sea.. and there throw them into the Channel, which they call their Beds or Layers, where they grow and fatten. **1735** DYCHE & PARDON *Dict.*, *Layer*,.. a Place in the retired Part of a River, Sea, &c. commonly called a Creek, where young Oysters are laid to grow. **1758** *Descr. Thames* 238 They [Oysters] are laid in Beds or Rills or Salt-water, in order to fat them, and these they term Layers.

c. 1825 J. NICHOLSON *Operat. Mechanic* 396 A small light rod of wood, called a layer, which has a wire eye fixed into it, is placed at a little distance from, and opposite, to each bobbin, so as to conduct the thread thereupon; and as the layer moves constantly backwards and forwards, the thread is regularly spread upon the length of the bobbin.

d. 1829 *Glover's Hist. Derby* I. 90 Paviers' flags, or layers.

e. 1797 *Encycl. Brit.* XVIII. 307/1 They [hides] are then removed into another pit, called a layer, in which they are laid smooth, with bark ground very fine strewed between each hide. **1885** *Harper's Mag.* Jan. 276/1 Hides remain in a 'first layer' for six or eight days. The same process is repeated in a 'second layer' in other vats for about two weeks, and in a third, or 'splitting layer', for about four weeks.

f. 1875 KNIGHT *Dict. Mech.*, *Layer*,.. 2. (*Leather-manufacture.*) A welt or strengthening strip.

g. 1918 BRYANT & HUGHES *Map Work* v. 84 Tints, or layers, of colour are used to denote all the land lying between any two named contours. **1932** J. W. CAMERON *Maps & Map-Work* iv. 45 Hill features are represented on the map by: 1. Contours. 2. Hachures. 3. Hill-shading. 4. Colour layers or layer-colouring. **1969** C. B. M. LOCK *Mod. Maps & Atlases* iii. 134 When the fifth (Relief) 'One inch' series was issued, relief was shown by contours in brown, hachures in orange and hill-shading in grey, with layers in buff tints.

III. 5. *attrib.* and *Comb.*: **layer-board, -boarding**, boarding for sustaining roof-gutters of lead; also *lear-board* (Ogilvie); **layer-cake**, a cake consisting of layers of sponge held together by a sweet filling, and usually iced; also *fig.*; **layer cloud** *Meteorol.*, a sheet-like cloud, having little vertical development but pronounced horizontal development; **layer colour** *Cartography*, a colour used in the layer system of showing relief on a map; so ***layer colouring, -coloured*** adj.; **layer-coral**, a fossil coral of the genus *Stromatopora*; **layer lattice** *Cryst.* [tr. G. *schichtengitter* (F. Hund 1925, in *Zeitschr. f. Physik* XXXIV. 849)], a crystal lattice in which the atoms are arranged in layers a few atoms thick that are separated by a distance greater than the interatomic distance within the layers, so that the interlayer forces are relatively weak; **layer pit** or **vat** *Tanning* = LAY-AWAY 1, LAYER *sb.* 4e; **layer-pudding**, a steamed pudding, consisting of layers of suet crust pastry with a sweet filling; **layer-reared** *a.*, reared from a 'layer'; **layer shading** *Cartography*, the use of layer tints to show relief on a map; **layer-stool**, a root from which layers are produced; **layer system** *Cartography*, on a map, the representation of land between different heights or contours by different colours or tints that are graded so as to show relief at a glance; **layer tint** *Cartography*, a layer colour, or a tint of such a colour; so ***layer tinting, -tinted*** adj.

1842–59 GWILT *Encycl. Archit.* §2350. 630 Table for guttering.. 6-inch layer-board. **1881** F. OWENS *Cook Bk.* 265 *Lemon butter*, good to eat as sauce, or for layer cakes. **1895** *Montgomery Ward Catal.* 431/2 Tins for pies and layer cakes. **1902** *Daily Chron.* 3 May 8/4 Layer cakes can be made in great varieties according to the filling used. **1905** *N.Y. Even. Post* 16 Dec., In the mixing of this literary layer cake most of the humor rose to the top. **1933** 'R. CROMPTON' *William—the Rebel* iv. 94 He.. began to eat the last piece of cream-layer cake. **1962** L. DEIGHTON *Ipcress File* xxi. 140 The sunset was a layer cake of mauve and gold. **1965** R. CARRIER *Cookbk.* xxii. 473 Mocha layer cake, a subtle blend of chocolate and coffee spiked with rum. [**1920** G. A. CLARKE *Clouds* iv. 73 The beautifully waved structure seen in nearly all of the layer-type of clouds from cirrus downward to stratocumulus is caused by the propagation upwards or downwards of the wave-motion that is produced by the flowing of air-currents of different velocities and directions over each other.] **1951** *Rep. Progress Physics* XIV. 192 Thick layer clouds often found over the oceans. **1956** *Nature* 18 Feb. 321/1 The great layer-cloud systems which are associated with cyclones and fronts. **1963** G. M. B. DOBSON *Exploring Atmosphere* iv. 78 The persistence of thick layer-clouds over a city in winter gives rise to a very dark, gloomy day. **1922** *Encycl. Brit.* XXX. 417/2 He extended and popularized the use of 'layer' colours exhibiting relief in land. **1969** C. B. M. LOCK *Mod. Maps & Atlases* iii. 135 A single-colour shadow tone in blue was printed in half-tone over the layer colours and the layer tints themselves were carefully chosen so as to reduce the 'step' effect of the layers. **1932** J. W. CAMERON *Maps & Map-Work* i. 12 There are two editions..: (*a*) In outline,.. without contours. (*b*) Contoured and layer-coloured. **1924** *Catal. Maps Ordnance Survey* 4 Relief is indicated by.. layer colouring in shades of brown and green. **1969** C. B. M. LOCK *Mod. Maps & Atlases* i. 40 For the best results of all, hill-shading is blended with layer-colouring. **1875** DAWSON *Dawn of Life* vi. 156 The Stromatoporæ, or layer-corals. **1929** *Trans. Faraday Soc.* XXV. 265 Besides cadmium iodide there are known a number of other types of layer lattices. **1966** A. CAMERON *Princ. Lubrication* xxi. 21 The low friction of graphite may not.. be directly related to its layer-lattice structure. **1901** F. T. ADDYMAN tr. *Villon's Pract. Treat. Leather Industry* 137 The object of handling is to give body to the plumped skin, so that it may be able to support the weight which will press upon it in the layer-pit. **1949** D. WOODROFFE *Stand. Handbk. Industr. Leathers* iii. 47 The butts or other leather, already completely penetrated in the previous stages of the tanning process, are placed singly in the layer pits, a layer of ground tanning material.. is sprinkled over each butt, and the process continued with more pieces of leather until the pit is full. Finally, a very strong tan liquor.. is run into the pit. **1909** *Daily Sketch* 14 Oct. 14/3 Layer pudding. **1951** *Good Housek. Home Encycl.* 489/2 Syrup is used.. as a filling for tarts and layer puddings. **1832** *Planting* (L.U.K.) 34 Grafted and layer reared species. **1952** MONKHOUSE & WILKINSON *Maps & Diagrams* ii. 61 (*heading*) Layer-shading and tinting. **1971** G. R. P. LAWRENCE *Cartogr. Methods* ii. 25 Information relating to the shapes of the floors of lakes and oceans can be presented in much the same way as relief information but in most cases only submarine contour lines are used, layer shading being found in some atlases. **1832** *Planting* (L.U.K.) 35 Transplanting trees from seed-beds, layer-stools, cutting grounds. **1903** *Man. Field Sketching & Reconnaissance* (H.M.S.O.) vi. 28 There is also the layer system of showing hills. **1953** A. H. ROBINSON *Elem. Cartogr.* x. 215/2 The larger the scale, assuming a reasonable degree of contour simplification, the more useful the layer system. **1969** C. B. M. LOCK *Mod. Maps & Atlases* iii. 135 The layer system was not used, but, instead, two printings in purple-grey tones on the shadow side of the hills and one printing in yellow on the illuminated side were added to the standard base map. **1918** BRYANT & HUGHES *Map Work* v. 84 In high country the layer tints become so dark as to obscure all detail. **1969** *Geography* LIV. 198 Relief is shown by contour and layer tint. **1934** J. BYGOTT *Introd. Mapwork & Pract. Geogr.* iv. 21 Certain layer-tinted Ordnance maps, especially the layered quarter-inch and half-inch maps. **1966** *McGraw-Hill Encycl. Sci. & Technol.* II. 534/2 On small-scale maps.. the intervals are frequently layer-tinted from green to brown. **1952** H. C. BROOKFIELD in G. H. Dury *Map Interpretation* xvi. 184 The O.S. 1/63,360 Fifth (Relief) Edition, first published in 1929, employed contours at 50-ft. intervals... There was also layer tinting in buff, the tint changing at each 500 ft. **1971** G. R. P. LAWRENCE *Cartogr. Methods* ii. 24 Colour has been used in the depiction of relief for a number of years in the method known as 'layer tinting'. **1969** T. C. THORSTENSEN *Pract. Leather Technol.* v. 70 The bends lie in the layer vats for one or two weeks in a warm vegetable tan liquor, and again the liquor may be strengthened and heated to gain better penetration and fixation of the strong tanning liquors.

layer ('leɪə(r)), *v.* [f. LAYER *sb.* 3.]

1. *Gardening.* **a.** *intr.* To bend down 'layers' to the ground and cover them partly with earth so that they may strike root and propagate the plant. **b.** *trans.* To propagate by 'layers'. **c.** To make a layer of.

1832 *Planting* (L.U.K.) 27 The root which produces the young shoots for layering is called the stool. **1841–60** T. RIVERS *Fruit Garden* (ed. 9) 4 To make this emission of roots more certain, the stem may be tongued, as usual in layering. **1845** *Florist's Jrnl.* 144 Preparation should be made for striking pinks, and layering carnations. **1858** GLENNY *Gard. Every-day Bk.* 252/1 If a healthy shoot can be layered and struck. **1891** T. E. KEBBEL *Old & New Country Life* 213 Cutting and 'layering' the stiff white-thorn hedges.

2. Of crops: To be laid flat as by wind or rain in consequence of weakness of growth.

1882 VINES *Sachs' Bot.* 851 It is on this that the upgrowth of 'layered' Wheat depends. **1890** *Carter's Seed Catal.* 1 Sept. 35 The Goldthorpe Barley is remarkable for stout long straw, rendering it less liable to layer in rainy weather than other Barleys. **1891** *Times* 10 Oct. 12/4 The layering.. of the corn rendered the use of machines impossible.

3. *trans.* To place or insert as a layer.

1906 *Times Lit. Suppl.* 12 Jan. 14/1 Mr. Lee has succeeded in neatly layering fallacies of argument. **1974** *Nature* 8 Mar. 110/2 Sample of 55 ml of a 110 ml linear density gradient.. was layered into a 110 ml jacketed isoelectric focusing column. *Ibid.* 5 Apr. 519/2 Each incubation was then layered onto a 10–30% sucrose gradient in TKM.

layer: see LAIR.

layered ('leɪəd), *a.* [f. LAYER *sb.* 2 + -ED[2].] Divided into layers; having layers (of a particular character or number); covered with layers; *spec.* in *Cartography*, having relief shown by the layer system.

1852 G. W. CURTIS *Nile Notes* in W. H. Gregory *Egypt* (1859) I. 270 Hills and regularly layered rocks. **1887** *Amer. Naturalist* XXI. 420 Certain two-layered sponge-larvæ. **1898** G. W. STEEVENS *With Kitchener to Khartum* 174 Our faces were layered with coffee colour. **1922** *Encycl. Brit.* XXXI. 842/2 These remarks apply with special force to the 'layered' maps; changes in the tones of the layers will greatly alter their character. **1969** C. B. M. LOCK *Mod. Maps & Atlases* i. 40 For reasons of economy, hachures were omitted from the fourth or 'popular' edition published after the 1914–18 war... Publication of layered or shaded maps of selected tourist areas followed.

layering ('leɪərɪŋ). *Cartography.* [f. LAYER *sb.* + -ING[1].] = *layer colouring, layer shading* (LAYER *sb.* 5).

1922 *Encycl. Brit.* XXXII. 1174 (Index), Layering of maps. **1937** *Geogr. Jrnl.* LXXXIX. 52 It is possible that the ultimate solution will be a change in the ground tint of the map over areas of rock, though experiment may show that this gives a false impression of layering.

layer-over. *dial.* Also **lare-over, lay-over, layer,** etc. (see Eng. Dial. Dict.). (See quots.)

a **1700** B. E. *Dict. Cant. Crew*, *Lare-over*, said when the true Name of the thing must (in decency) be concealed. **1725** in *New Cant. Dict.* **1785** GROSE *Dict. Vulg. Tongue*, *Lareovers for Medlers*, an answer frequently given to children, or young people, as a rebuke for their impertinent curiosity, in enquiring what is contained in a box, bundle, or any other closed conveyance. *a* **1825** FORBY *Voc. E. Anglia*, *Layer-over*, a gentle term for some instrument of chastisement. **1888** *Sheffield Gloss.*, *Layors-for-meddlers.*

layery ('leɪərɪ), *a. rare.* [f. LAYER *sb.* + -Y.] Consisting of or formed in layers.

1832 L. HUNT *Dryads* 17 From hedge to layery beech.

layery, layetie, obs. forms of LAIRY *a.*[1], LAITY.

‖**layette** (lejɛt). [Fr.]

1. A complete outfit of garments, toilet articles, and bedding for a new-born child.

1839 F. A. KEMBLE *Jrnl. Residence Georgian Plantation* (1863) 158, I have worked my fingers nearly off with making.. innumerable rolls of coarse little baby-clothes, layettes for the use of small new-born slaves. **1863** G. DU MAURIER *Let.* in *Young G. du Maurier* (1951) 212 She is now.. making the layette and things for the son and heir, whom I am beginning to look forward to with a certain amount of curious expectation. **1874** PRINCESS ALICE *Mem.* 26 Apr. (1884) 321 Let me thank you.. for the present towards the layette—a most kind assistance. **1939** [see BAJU]. **1974** *Selfridge Christmas Catal.* 47 Baby doll complete with layette.

2. (See quot.)

1885 FARROW *Mil. Encycl.*, *Layette*, A three-sided tray.. used to carry powder from one mortar to another in powder-mills.

layety, obs. form of LAITY.

layfe, obs. form of LAVE *sb.*[1]

lay-fee. *Obs.* exc. *Hist.* Forms: see LAY *a.* (and *sb.*[1]) and FEE *sb.*[2]; also 4 **laifeo**, 5 **laife, layfe**, 6 **laffye**. [a. AF. *lai fe.*]

1. A fee or estate in land held in consideration of secular services, as distinguished from an ecclesiastical fee. †Also phr. ***of lay fee*** (cf. FEE *sb.*[2] 1 b).

c **1290** *Beket* 560 in *S. Eng. Leg.* 122 ȝif ani man of holi churche halt ani-þing of lay-fe [*c* **1300** (Percy Soc.) 556 holdeth eni laifeo].. he schal done þere-fore þe seruice þat to þe kinge bi-fallez. *c* **1330** R. BRUNNE *Chron.* (1810) 285 'Sir', þe bisshop said, 'of þis we pray þe, þat.. nouht of our lay fe Be taxed with non of ȝours'. ? *a* **1400** *Plowman's Tale* 741 Therewith they purchase hem lay fee In londe there hem liketh best. **1553** BECON *Reliques of Rome* (1563) 246 b, Al yt.. maken holy churche Layfee, yt is halowed and blessed. **1651** G. W. tr. *Cowel's Inst.* 148 An Inventory of such Goods and Chattels, as they shall finde in the Lay-fee of the party deceased. **1750** CARTE *Hist. Eng.* II. 283 Arrogating to his own courts the cognisance of lay-fees in the case of persons of the first quality. **1868** FREEMAN *Norm. Conq.* (1876) II. viii. 182 Besides his archbishopric, he held the county of Evreux as a lay fee.

†2. The laity, lay people collectively. Orig. in phr. ***of the lay fee***. *Obs.*

1398 TREVISA *Barth. De P.R.* I. (1495) 6 It suffyceth to theym whyche ben of the lay fee or state. *c* **1425** *Found. St. Bartholomew's* 19 The peple of boith ordres, the Clergie And the laife. *c* **1449** PECOCK *Repr.* II. i. 136, I wote not that it is worth forto talke in resonyng with eny persoon of the laife vpon eny mater of Goddis lawe. **1481** CAXTON *Godfrey* xv. 43 For tamende clerkes & layefee. *a* **1529** SKELTON *Replyc.*

267 Why iangle you suche jestes.. To the people of lay fee. **1536** *Exhort. to North.* in Furnivall *Ballads fr. MSS.* I. 308 The intollerable exactions that longe he dyd vsse the laffye emonges, and also the spiritualtye. **1545** *Primer, Injunction,* To.. all other of the Clergie: as also al estates and degrees of the laye fee. **1568** GRAFTON *Chron.* II. 118 A great multitude, of the which the king pardoned a great number of the laye Fee. **1641** PRYNNE *Antip.* 79 More of their Tenants went to the Kings warres, then of the Tenants of them of the Lay fee.

layff, obs. form of LAVE *sb.*

lay figure (ˈleɪ ˈfɪgə(r)). [f. **lay* (abstracted from LAYMAN[2]) + FIGURE *sb.*] A jointed wooden figure of the human body, used by artists as a model for the arrangement of draperies, posing, etc.

1795 T. HURLSTONE *Crotchet Lodge* 49 The latter, in passing behind the Lay-figure, pushes it, and the Landlord down together. *Miss Crotchet.* Heav'n's! my niece's Lay-figure is destroyed. **1851** *Illustr. Catal. Gt. Exhib.* 1239 Lay figures of men and women.. for artists. **1855** MRS. GASKELL *North & S.* i, Her Aunt asked her to stand as a sort of lay figure on which to display them [shawls]. **1877** MRS. OLIPHANT *Makers Flor.* xiv. 351 Fra Bartolommeo was the inventor of the lay figure.

b. *fig.* A person of little intrinsic importance, a 'nonentity'; a character in fiction destitute of the attributes of reality.

1835 *Court Mag.* VI. 166/2 Let me.. guard myself against any possible imputation of hostility towards my proposed lay-figure. **1859** HELPS *Friends in C.* Ser. II. I. i. 20, I feel more for the mother, who is but a lay-figure, than for the daughter.

lay(g)hyn, obs. form of LAUGH *v.*

†**layheap.** *Obs.* [? f. *lay-* in LAYSTALL + HEAP *sb.*] = LAYSTALL.

1624 *Nottingham Rec.* (1889) IV. 386 To remoue cartts, and layheappes, and other annoyances.

layick(e, obs. form of LAIC.

laying (ˈleɪɪŋ), *vbl. sb.* [f. LAY *v.*[1] + -ING[1].]

1. a. The action of LAY *v.*[1] in various senses; putting, setting, placing, fixing, esp. in a designed position; †assessment, taxation; †accouchement; etc.

c **1330** R. BRUNNE *Chron.* (1810) 261 Þe lond fulle hard was sette in þat ilk laying. *c* **1440** *Promp. Parv.* 294/2 Leyynge of a thynge, *posicio.* **1472–3** *Durham Acc. Rolls* (Surtees) 644 Pro le laynge fusi et rynde molendini [cf. LAY *v.* 3 b]. **1480** CAXTON *Chron. Eng.* ccxliii. (1482) 290 Anone he leyd his ordynaunce and in the leyng of a gonne come a quarell and smote the good Erle Edmond in the hede. **1486** *Naval Acc. Hen. VII* (1896) 13 The.. openyng and newe leying of old Ropes. *a* **1548** HALL *Chron., Edw. IV,* 245 To reise the siege, at the layeng whereof he was counsayler and partener. **1611** COTGR. *Proposition d' erreur,* a Writ, or the laying, of Error. **1611** *Vestry Bks.* (Surtees) 63 Item payed for laying of thre hoggs, vj *d.* **1626** BACON *Sylva* §669 Another ill Accident is Laying of Corne with great Raines in Haruest. **1660** SHARROCK *Vegetables* 59 Circumposition is a kind of laying.. In this the mould is born up to the bough which is to be taken off. **1662** PEPYS *Diary* 25 May, They do say there are some plots in laying. **1712** PRIDEAUX *Direct. Ch.-wardens* (ed. 4) 53 The laying of the Church Rate ought to be according to the Lands and the Stock. **1796** *Encycl. Brit.* (ed. 3) XVI. 485/1 The operation of uniting them [i.e. strands of a rope] with a permanent twist is called *laying.* **1823** P. NICHOLSON *Pract. Build.* 373 Laying consists in spreading a single coat of lime and hair all over a ceiling and partition. **1859** F. A. GRIFFITHS *Artil. Man.* (1862) 112 No. 6.. attends stool bed, elevating screw and quoin in laying. **1861** HULME tr. *Moquin-Tandon* II. III. iii. 136 Godard saw a female [Meloe] deposit in two layings 2212 eggs.

b. with advs. or advb. phr. (see LAY *v.*[1] VIII).

1496 *Naval Acc. Hen. VII* (1896) 174 Mappes for layng on of piche Rosyn & talow uppon the seid ship. **1526** TINDALE *1 Tim.* iv. 14 Leyinge on of the hondes of a seniour. **1535** COVERDALE *1 Esdras* viii. 51 Because of the layenges awayte. **1576** FLEMING *Panopl. Epist.* 240 In the dispensing or laying out of your goods. **1602** SHAKS. *Ham.* v. i. 182 We haue many pocky Coarses now adaies, that will scarce hold the laying in. ? **1608** E. M. WINGFIELD *Disc. Virginia* in Capt. Smith *Wks.* (Arb.) I. p. xc, I misliked his leying out of our towne. *a* **1659** OSBORN *Misc.* (1673) 603 Her Comings-in are Mathematically adjusted to her Layings-out. **1726** LEONI *Alberti's Archit.* I. 76/1 Ware-houses or Vaults for the laying up of Goods. **1817** KEATS *Let.* Wks. 1889 III. 76 One of my chief layings-up is the pleasure I shall have in showing it to you. **1844** DICKENS *Mart. Chuz.* xix, She went to a lying-in or a laying-out with equal zest and relish. **1869** SIR E. REED *Shipbuild.* xx. 429 The laying-off of the ship is proceeded with simultaneously with the preparation of the model. **1879** ESCOTT *England* I. 60 The laying down of main roads. **1892** GARDINER *Student's Hist. Eng.* 21 The erection of fortifications, and the laying out of streets. **1900** *Daily News* 20 Sept. 6/2 The stoppage of coal traffic, and the consequent laying off of railway coal train crews. **1968** *Listener* 4 July 24/1 Nowadays in the US redundancy can mean displacement for good; then it was, at worst, a long laying-off. **1970** *Nature* 21 Nov. 709/2 Layings-off are, of course, nothing unusual in the volatile aerospace industry.

2. *concr.* **a.** What is laid, in various senses of the vb. **b.** A layer, bed, stratum. **c.** An oyster-bed. **d.** *Building.* (See quot. 1823.)

1398 TREVISA *Barth. De P.R.* XII. vii. (1495) 417 Alle byrdes that ben lyke to Culuores.. laye not the thyrde tyme but whan the seconde layenge is corrupte and dystroyed. **1683** MOXON *Mech. Exerc., Printing* xxiv. ¶9 Having laid down his Dry Laying, he takes another Quire off the Dry Heap. **1703** T. N. *City & C. Purchaser* 205 You must.. cover with Sand every Laying, or Bed of Lime. **1823** P. NICHOLSON *Pract. Build.* 391 Laying, in plastering.—The first coat on lath of two-coat plaster, or set-work. **1846** McCULLOCH *Acc. Brit. Empire* (1854) I. 637 The oysters.. are deposited for a while in beds or layings in the adjoining creeks. **1863** C. R. MARKHAM in *Intell. Observ.* IV. 624 The brood [oysters two years old] are dredged up out at sea, and placed on layings within the river Colne. **1867** SMYTH *Sailor's Word-bk., Layings,* a sort of pavement of culch, on the mud of estuaries, for forming a bed for oysters. **1960** C. M. YONGE *Oysters* ix. 154 The Colchester and other natural oyster beds and the layings along the Essex coast flourished exceedingly during the eighteenth and much of the nineteenth centuries.

3. *attrib.* and *Comb.*, as ***laying-place***; **laying-hook** (see quot.); **laying house,** (*a*) the house or building in which rope is 'laid' or made; (*b*) a building in which laying hens are kept; **laying-machine**, a machine for 'laying' strands into a rope; **laying mash, meal**, a special food for laying hens; **laying-on table** *Printing*, a table from which the machine is fed; **laying-on tool** *Bookbinding*, the tool with which gold leaf is laid on the cover or the edge of a book; **laying-press** *Bookbinding*, a press in which books are held while their edges are being cut (also called *lying-press*); **laying-tool, -trowel**, a plasterer's trowel (see quot. 1825); **laying-top**, a grooved conical piece of wood placed between the strands in 'laying' a rope, a TOP; **laying-walk**, that part of a rope-walk in which the rope is laid.

1794 *Rigging & Seamanship* 55 **Laying-Hook*, the hook on which the strands are all hung together for laying or closing. **1778** *Eng. Gazetteer* (ed. 2) s.v. *Portsmouth*, The fire was first seen to burst through the roof of the *laying-house. **1913** H. R. LEWIS *Productive Poultry Husbandry* vii. 128 (*heading*) Plans and specifications of laying houses. **1962** L. E. CARD *Lippincott's Poultry Production* (ed. 9) vii. 179 (*caption*) Interior of.. laying house, showing tiered roofs. **1839** URE *Dict. Arts* 1091 Captain Huddart constructed a *laying-machine, which has carried his inventions in rope-making to the greatest perfection. **1926** *Daily Colonist* (Victoria, B.C.) 12 Jan. 2/1 (Advt.), Feed Prices.. *Laying Mash, sack $2.75. **1972** A. A. MCARDLE *Poultry Managem. & Production* (rev. ed.) xiv. 308 (*heading*) Quantity of laying mash and grain needed. **1908** *Illustr. Poultry Rec.* Oct. p. ix (Advt.), *Laying Meal 12/6 Cwt. **1935** *Poultry Rec.* Jan. (Advt. inside cover), Alfalfa, Laying Meal, Grit, Shells etc. **1849** *Chambers' Inform.* II. 719/2 On the gallery are seen eight men at so many '*laying-on-tables', feeding the machine. **1858** SIMMONDS *Dict. Trade*, **Laying-on-tool*, a bookbinder's tool; a tip. **1865** DICKENS *Mut. Fr.* I. ix, The favourite *laying-place of several discreet hens. **1835** HANNETT *Bibliopegia* 172 The cutting or *laying press is formed of two strong cheeks of timber, connected together with two wooden screws and two square pins. **1825** J. NICHOLSON *Operat. Mechanic* 606 The *laying and smoothing tool consists of a flat piece of hardened iron, about ten inches in length, and two inches and a half wide, very thin, and ground to a semicircular shape at one end, but left square at the other. **1839** URE *Dict. Arts* 1073 In laying cables, torsion must be given both behind and before the *laying top. **1703** MOXON *Mech. Exerc.* 249 A *Laying Trowel, to lay the Lime and Hair withall upon the Laths, it being larger than a Brick Trowel, and fastned [to] its handle in a different manner. **1778** *Eng. Gazetteer* (ed. 2) s.v. *Portsmouth*, The rope-makers' *laying-walk and tarring-walk.

laying (ˈleɪɪŋ), *ppl. a.* [f. LAY *v.*[1] + -ING[2].] That lays: chiefly said of hens.

1591 PERCIVALL *Sp. Dict., Ponedera gallina*, a laying hen. **1884** ROE *Nat. Ser. Story* ii. in *Harper's Mag.* Jan. 288/2, I can keep my laying hens warm even in zero weather.

†**layit**, *a. Sc. Obs.* [Altered form of *lawit*, LEWD *a.*, influenced by LAY *a.* (and *sb.*[1]).] Lay.

1563 WINJET *Four Scoir Thre Quest.* title-p., Wks. 1888 I. 47 The Catholiks of the inferiour ordour of clergie and layt men. **1621** *Gude & Godlie Ball.* (S.T.S.) App. I. 231 The layit ȝe will not teiche.

layity, obs. form of LAITY.

layk(e, laykin, -yn, obs. ff. LAKE, LAKIN.

lay-land: see LEA-LAND.

ˈ**laylight.** [f. LAY *v.*[1] + LIGHT *sb.* 5 b.] A window or light made of glazed panels and set into a ceiling to provide natural or artificial light.

1932 H. ROBERTSON *Mod. Archit. Design* vi. 174 The architect is well advised to make a critical study.. of lighting through ceiling lay-lights, before determining his layout. **1934** *Archit. Rev.* LXXV. 31 The lay-light of the same type of glass is hung from the ceiling to provide day and artificial lighting. **1948** R. O. ACKERLEY *Introd. Sci. Artificial Lighting* III. iv. 99 Laylights designed to provide alternatively natural and artificial light through the same glazing, like most dual-purpose devices, are liable to perform both functions badly unless great care is taken in the design. **1951** W. R. STEVENS *Princ. Lighting* viii. 186 We find it difficult to provide high illumination.. in interiors without discomfort glare unless we use very large sources, such as laylights or indirectly lighted ceilings. **1966** M. M. PEGLER *Dict. Interior Design* (1967) 260 *Laylight*, a glass or translucent panel set flush into a ceiling to admit natural or artificial light.

layloc(k, obs. and dial. form of LILAC.

layman[1] (ˈleɪmən). Also 5–6 laye-, laieman, 6 leaman, leman. [Orig. two words: see LAY *a.* (and *sb.*[1]).]

1. A man who is not a cleric; one of the laity.

1432–50 tr. *Higden* (Rolls) V. 289 That noo clerke scholde receyve investiture of his benefice.. of the honde of a seculer lay man. **1520** *Caxton's Chron. Eng.* IV. 38/2 This man of a laye man was made pope. **1548** GEST *Pr. Masse* F viij, It implieth no more one christian then another, no more yͤ spiritual then the leamen. **1561** T. NORTON *Calvin's Inst.* I. 24 Let them [the papistes] no more use this shift to say that images are lay mennes bokes. *a* **1677** BARROW *Serm.* Wks. 1716 I. 210 A Lay-man should not intrude himself to administer the sacred functions. **1704** NELSON *Fest. & Fasts* iii. (1739) 473 Nor would the Primitive Church have forbidden Deacons.. to have followed secular Employments, if they had been mere Laymen. **1782** PRIESTLEY *Corrupt. Chr.* II. vii. 85 A layman.. might baptize. **1849** MACAULAY *Hist. Eng.* vi. II. 95 Of the other six commissioners three were prelates and three laymen. **1865** KINGSLEY *Herew.* iii. (1875) 82 It is as good a rule for priest as for layman.

2. *transf.* A man who is an 'outsider' or a non-expert in relation to some particular profession, art, or branch of knowledge (esp. with reference to law and medicine).

1477 NORTON *Ord. Alch.* Proem in Ashm. (1652) 6 This Boke is made, that Lay-men shulde it see, And Clerks alsoe.. Whereby all Lay-men which putteth them in prease, To seech by Alkimy great ryches to winn May finde good Counsell. **1559** MORWYNG *Evonym.* 240 Dry it lyghtly by the sun, and drawe out an oyll after the maner of the lay men. **1574** tr. *Littleton's Tenures* 69 b, To declare and expresse to the lay men that be not learned in the law. **1866** *Sat. Rev.* 7 Apr. 403/1 No prudent layman will venture to judge of the merits of a tailor's log. **1888** BRYCE *Amer. Commw.* I. 329 Sometimes this is a simple question which an intelligent layman may answer. More frequently it is a difficult one which needs.. the subtlety of the trained lawyer. **1897** *Allbutt's Syst. Med.* II. 657 The assertion so frequently made by ignorant or unscrupulous laymen that the [medical] profession has been influenced [etc.].

So ˈ**laywoman.**

1529 MORE *Dyaloge* III. Wks. 247/1 How the scripture might without great perill.. be.. taken to ley men & women both. **1553** BECON *Reliques of Rome* (1563) 95 They myght lawfully be baptised in all places.. by a Layman or by a Laywoman. **1674** HICKMAN *Quinquart. Hist.* (ed. 2) 140 Had he held that a Lay-man, or woman, may administer the Lord's Supper. **1846** MASKELL *Mon. Rit.* I. p. ccxi, Having reference to baptism in times of necessity by laymen and laywomen. **1922** *Daily Mail* 11 Nov. 8 The success of this laywoman is a.. cheerful omen of good luck for those women who.. will hold the position of practising members of the English Bar.

†**lay-man**[2]. *Obs.* [a. Du. *leeman* for **ledenman*, f. *led* 'membrum, articulus' (Kilian), now *lid* limb, joint + *man* MAN *sb.*[1] Cf. G. *gliedermann.*] = LAY-FIGURE.

1688 H. TESTLING *Sentiments Painters* 5th Table, Rather make use of Models of Wax, than a Layman of Wood. **1706** *Art of Painting* (1744) 31 The Painter ought to avoid all manner of stiffness and hardness in his folds, and be careful that they dont smell of the lay man, as we commonly say. **1762** H. WALPOLE *Catal. Engravers* (1765) 22 Crispin Pass.. describes the use of the maneken or layman for disposing draperies. **1796** CHARLOTTE SMITH *Marchmont* I. 141 She seemed as if her shape had been imagined by some joiner.. on purpose to serve as a layman for the clothes she wore.

†**layn(e.** *Obs.* [variant of LAWN *sb.*[1]] Some fine linen fabric; ? = LAWN *sb.*[1]

1561 *Inv. R. Wardr.* (1815) 150 Ane bed of layn sewit with silk. **1581** *Sc. Acts Jas. VI*, c. 113 Coastelie cleithing of silkes.. layne, cammeraige, freinzies, etc. **1612** P. LOWE *Chyrurgerie* VIII. v. 367 Couer it with a Linnen cloth, or for persons of higher dignitie take layne [*printed* layre] or camerige.

layn(e, var. LAIN; obs. Sc. f. LOAN.

laynder, obs. form of LAUNDER.

layner, obs. form of LAINER.

ˈ**lay-off.** [LAY *v.*[1] 54.] A rest, respite, spell of relaxation; a period during which a workman is temporarily dismissed or allowed to leave his work; a part or season of the year during which activity in a particular business or game is partly or completely suspended.

1889 *Gallup* (New Mexico) *Gleaner* 27 Mar. 1/3 Fred Diamond is taking a lay-off. **1904** *Minneapolis Daily Times* 8 June 8 The men who have been on for a year get a vacation of ten days. Those who have been working less than a year have to get along with only a five-day layoff. **1908** 'O. HENRY' *Gentle Grafter* vii. 285 Me and my partner.. tried to take a layoff from our professional and business duties; but.. our work followed us wherever we went. **1909** R. A. WASON *Happy Hawkins* 148 Now take a lay-off if you want to,.. then come back here. **1919** T. K. HOLMES *Man from Tall Timber* vi. 58 At the lay-off,.. he had given each man enough money on account to make their vacation.. a very wet spell indeed. **1923** *Daily Mail* 10 Sept. 8/5 As a consequence of the 'lay-off' during the summer months it often happens that the muscles of the young player are not sufficiently supple for him to face the rigours of the game. **1926** J. BLACK *You can't Win* xix. 297, I decided to take a lay-off [from burgling]. **1927** *Sunday Express* 8 May 10/3 Although his salary on the speaking stage had fluctuated between £20 and £40 a week, there were.. many lay-offs. **1928** *Sunday Dispatch* 8 July 22/2 His opponent will be a French boxer, Pierre Callior. As nothing is known of the Frenchman here we shall be.. in the dark.. as to what extent.. Teddy's long lay-off has affected his form. **1952** B. ULANOV *Hist. Jazz in Amer.* (1958) xxii. 299 The Herman band took a layoff in Detroit in June 1945. **1956** B. NANKEVILLE *Miracle of Mile* xii. 90 Chris Chataway.. had only had ten days' training following a lay-off. **1969** *Daily Tel.* 12 Apr. 1/5 Workers protested at proposed factory lay-offs. **1972** *Guardian* 17 Feb. 6/1 Jaguar is one of the British Leyland groups where extensive lay-offs occurred. **1973** *Times* 17 Oct. 25/1 (*heading*) Lay offs threaten 28,000 workers at Vauxhall as car unrest grows.

lay-out ('leɪaʊt). Chiefly *U.S.* [See *lay out*, LAY *v.*[1] 56.]

1. a. The laying out, planning, or disposition of land, streets, etc.; also, the land so laid out. Also, the plan or disposition of a house, factory, garden, etc. Also *fig.* and *transf.*

1852 *San Diego Herald* 10 Jan. 2/1 The new 'lay out', at the Wholesale Commission Warehouse and store..on California street, proves quite attractive. **1888** *Harper's Mag.* July 285/1 Although the conception of its lay-out dates back nearly half a century, the tree planting that has added so much to Washington was begun only in 1872. **1895** *Forum* (N.Y.) Sept. 80 In the lay-out and construction of a very considerable part of the railway service of this country. **1898** C. O. PARMENTER *Hist. Pelham, Mass.* 158 A portion of the town is south of the original layout. **1900** I. P. ROBERTS (*title*) The Farmstead, the Making of the Rural Home, and the Lay-out of the Farm. **1903** KIPLING *Five Nations* 212 The day's lay-out—the mornin' sun Beneath your 'at-brim as you sight; The dinner-'ush from noon till one, And the full roar that lasts till night. **1905** W. ROBINSON *Eng. Flower Garden* (ed. 9) I. ii. 15 In many books on garden design the authors misuse words... One..writes 'lay-out' for 'plan'. **1923** *Radio Times* 28 Sept. 28 (Advt.), The lay-out [of a radio set] is neat and compact; the cabinet work distinctive. **1930** *Oxford Times* 14 Mar. 13 A new 'lay-out' plan from the builders was before the meeting. **1931** H. G. WELLS *Work, Wealth & Happiness of Mankind* (1932) 2 Almost all our political and administrative boundaries, the 'layout' of the human population, have become..misfits. **1937** *Discovery* Feb. 47/2 In the planning of new factories.., the engineer and the industrial psychologist should..ensure that, both in the general lay-out and in the smallest details, due regard is paid to the view-point of the men who will actually be doing the work. **1937** D. RUNYON *More than Somewhat* i. 7, I go to see Mr. Tuesday at a Fifth Avenue hotel where he makes his home, and where he has a very swell layout of rooms. **1939** [see FERRY *sb.*[1] 3 e]. **1941** W. S. CHURCHILL *Secret Session Speeches* (1946) 37, I am satisfied that up to the present a good lay-out of our available forces has been made. **1943** J. B. PRIESTLEY *Daylight on Saturday* xxv. 195 Both of 'em are up against a pretty tough problem on floor space and general lay-out. **1946** *R.A.F. Jrnl.* May 179 A layout was begun for a new medium bomber to replace the Hampden. **1960** *Observer* 24 Jan. 5/2 How they broke in in the first place depended on the layout. It could be through a lavatory window or by tunnelling laboriously from next door. **1962** *Which? Car Suppl.* Oct. 129/1 The pedal control layouts on the *Peugeot* 403B..were generally liked. **1964** *McCall's Sewing* ii. 30/1 *Layout*, the way the pattern pieces are placed on the fabric for cutting. **1974** J. WAINWRIGHT *Hard Hit* 131 The house—this 'Diasc Farm' place—tell me about it. The layout. The approach. The grounds.

b. Typographical specifications or rough designs for a piece of printing; in extended use, the design details of a cartoon film. Also *attrib.*

1910 *Brit. Printer* Feb.–Mar. p. lxv (Advt.), The Printer will be enabled to submit to his customer both original and artistic lay-outs. **1910** E. G. GRESS *Art & Pract. Typogr.* 35/1 Every printshop should have a 'layout' man. **1913** *Technical World* XIX. 464 And the strange part of it is that from two to five good news picture layouts are made daily and enlarged in this small room. **1933** *Planning* I. VII. 2 A few years ago individualism in advertising would have rejected without hesitation the discipline of lay-out and design which has been accepted with such good effect this time. **1946** A. MONKMAN in H. Whetton *Pract. Printing & Binding* vii. 81/1 It is necessary also for the layout man to be expert in copying the numerous type faces. This is not so very important if the layout is for the compositor, because all he requires for his work is the general plan, indicating type sizes and faces and allocations of white space; but when the layout is for the client, markings showing type sizes and other particulars are not necessary. The sketch should be a clear indication of the appearance of the finished job. **1948** H. MISSINGHAM *Student's Guide Commercial Art* II. 157 To see a first-class 'visualizer' romp through one with a flat-leaded layout pencil is a sight to stir the blood. **1955** M. REIFER *Dict. New Words* 119/2 *Layout*,..2. *Cartoon Animation*... The combined elements of the animation procedure which prescribe the relationship of characters and backgrounds to define a scene and its properties. **1958** *Clarendonian* XII. 198 Throughout his service at the Press he has shown great interest in the Layout Department and has been responsible for the design of many Oxford books. **1959** HALAS & MANVELL *Technique Film Animation* III. 215 He [*sc.* the director] works closely with the lay-out artist, who in most studios is also the designer. **1967** KARCH & BUBER *Offset Processes* iii. 46 The layout man usually receives the reading matter in typewritten form, along with glossy photographs, line drawings or other artwork. **1968** J. R. BIGGS *Basic Typogr.* 122/2 The lay-out which goes to the printer with the typographic instructions 'marked up'..should be quite accurate with nothing left to chance.

2. a. Something laid or spread out; a display; a 'spread'; the tools or apparatus pertaining to some occupation, etc.; *spec.* (*U.S. slang.*) the equipment used for smoking opium.

1869 A. K. MCCLURE *Rocky Mts.* 219 His [*sc.* a miner's] necessities are appreciated by the other owners, who get up a most expensive 'lay-out' for him. **1882** H. H. KANE *Opium-Smoking* iii. 32 (*heading*) Description of the 'lay-out', pipe, etc. **1887** in *Amer. Speech* (1948) XXIII. 247 A person that had a private layout in his room. **1891** H. CAMPBELL *Darkness & Daylight* (1895) xxviii. 565 A small room at the rear of the temple contained an opium 'lay-out' for two persons. *Ibid.*, In the center of the platform was a tray which contained the smoker's 'lay-out'. **1898** MARK TWAIN in *Cosmopolitan* 12 Aug. 426 Of all the barbarous layouts that were ever contrived this was the most atrocious. **1946** MEZZROW & WOLFE *Really Blues* (1957) 376 *Layout*, set of instruments used to smoke opium.

b. A scheme, plan, or arrangement; a course of action. orig. and chiefly *U.S.*

1867 in *Amer. Speech* (1942) XVII. 71/1 A 'lay-out' is any proposed enterprise, from organizing a State to digging out a prairie-dog. **1901** S. E. WHITE *Westerners* xxxi. 292 'I'm sorry that I have this to do, Billy,' said Lafond. 'I don't want to. It's none of my lay-out.' **1904** W. H. SMITH *Promoters* ii. 53 There isn't a single move in this whole lay-out that we can't justify by history. **1928** *Sat. Even. Post* 4 Feb. 81/3 Here's the layout. The bonds bear 6 per cent. **1945** BAKER *Austral. Lang.* vii. 142 *Layout, setup*, a trickster's plan of action.

c. A number of persons associated in some way; a set, party, gang (of persons); a family. (Often in a depreciatory sense.) *U.S. colloq.* or *dial.*

1869 *Overland Monthly* III. 128 Several persons in our 'lay-out' (*i.e.*, our company) in New Mexico 'swapped' good American horses for mustangs. **1884** 'C. E. CRADDOCK' *In Tennessee Mts.* III. 143 All them Peels, the whole lay-out, war gone down to the Settlement. **1903** A. ADAMS *Log of Cowboy* vii. 47 Surround this layout, lads, and let's examine them more closely. **1904** W. N. HARBEN *Georgians* 203 I'm a-goin' to close in on that Clegg lay-out to-night, an' locate the'r still. **1927** W. ROGERS in C. M. Russell *Trails plowed Under* p. xiii, I tell you they was a pretty sad lookin outfit. They sho was a lonesome layout.

3. *Cards.* In Faro: see quot.

1889 in *Century Dict.* **1894** MASKELYNE *Sharps & Flats* 189 The layout. The designation of this adjunct to the game is derived from the fact that it forms that part of the table upon which the players 'lay out' their stakes. Usually it is a green cloth, having painted upon it a representation of the thirteen cards of one suit.

4. 'The space occupied or fished over by a haul-seine' (*Cent. Dict.*).

5. *attrib.* in **lay-out line**, 'a long line buoyed at each end, from which baited hook-lines run into deep water' (*Cent. Dict.*).

'lay-over. [LAY *v.*[1] 57.] **1.** An additional cloth laid over a table-cloth.

1777 *Monthly Rev.* LV. 108 Two servants appeared with a small table.., and laid a cloth and a lay-over upon it, in our English fashion, of the finest damask.

2. A stop or stay in a place, esp. overnight; a halt, rest, delay. *N. Amer.*

1873 J. H. BEADLE *Undevel. West* xxxv. 756 Two invalids and myself..applied for a 'lay over', unable to go further. **1903** A. ADAMS *Log of Cowboy* viii. 53 Their cattle having grown restless during their enforced lay-over. **1911** *Daily Colonist* (Victoria, B.C.) 18 Apr. (Mag.) 7/4 The object of this [*sc.* an extra train]..is to allow those going through to Alberni to reach their destination the same day. This will do away with the present lay-over en route. **1968** *Listener* 27 June 841/2 Meanwhile, some principal themes of Beat mythology are being laid down:..the pastoral theme of travelling on along the American highways with layovers for pot, mescalin. **1969** R. STARK *Blackbird* (1970) iii. 23 We have an airline ticket for this evening..with a change at New York. A four-hour lay-over there, I'm afraid. **1972** *National Observer* (U.S.) 27 May 13/5 Mrs. Bartels parks at Gateway for the three-hour layover.

layperson ('leɪpɜːs(ə)n). [f. LAYMAN[1], after *chairperson*, etc. (see PERSON *sb.* 2 f).] A member of the laity; a layman or laywoman.

One of numerous manufactured words formed to avoid alleged sexual discrimination in terminology.

1972 E. J. GOODMAN *Tenant Survival Bk.* ix. 121 Despite the prohibition against lay persons arguing at the bar, some small claims courts..are now permitting community advocates. **1975** *Publishers Weekly* 29 Dec. 63/2 He addresses himself to the layperson who has been, in his view, taken in by wrong-headed mystery-mongers. **1980** L. BOTSTEIN in Michaels & Ricks *State of Lang.* 353 The twentieth century has obliterated the skilled amateur and widened the gap between the technical professional and the layperson. **1986** *Church Times* 23 May 5/3 This [URC] Assembly was..presided over by its first layman as Moderator (not the first layperson; Mrs. Rosalind Goodfellow was that).

layr(e: see LAIR, LAYER.

layrock, obs. form of LARK.

†**lays.** *Obs.* Earlier anglicizing of Sp. *lazo* LASSO.

1726 SHELVOCKE *Voy.* 109 [Island of Chiloe on Coast of Chili] They are particularly dextrous in throwing a sliding noose at the end of a long thong of leather, wherewith they are sure of catching an ox, horse, &c. or any thing, even in its full career; this they call a *Lays*.

lays, lays-band: see LEASE *sb.*[4]

laysar, -er, -our, obs. forms of LEISURE *sb.*

layse, variant of LEESE *v.*[2] *Obs.*

layshaft ('leɪʃɑːft, -æ-). Also **lay shaft, lay-shaft.** [Prob. f. LAY *v.*[1] 43.] A short secondary or intermediate shaft driven by gearing from the main shaft of an engine; *spec.* one inside a gear-box that transmits the drive from the input shaft to the output shaft.

1888 *Lockwood's Dict. Mech. Engin.* 205 *Lay shaft*, a small secondary shaft, which is placed beside, or at the end of a horizontal engine, for the purpose of actuating the valves. It is driven from the crank shaft by means of bevel or spur-wheels. **1908** *Westm. Gaz.* 7 May 4/2 The whole of the valve mechanism being contained in a neat, hinged lay-shaft on top of the cylinder heads. **1911** G. W. HAYTER *Motor-Car Mech. for Beginners* (ed. 4) 45 For the next speed the gear wheel, B, is slid into mesh with the wheel marked C on the third or lay shaft, E. **1958** *Times Rev. Industry* Feb. 84/2 The engine, clutch, and layshaft are mounted on a light chassis and protected by a hinged bonnet which allows easy access to the power unit. **1959** *'Motor' Manual* (ed. 36) iv. 73 Spaced along the layshaft are other gears, the total number being equal to the number of ratios which the gearbox can provide.

†**'layship.** *Obs. rare*[−1]. [f. LAY *a.* (and *sb.*[1]) + -SHIP.] The condition of a layman; in quot. used (with poss. pron.) as a mock title.

1641 MILTON *Ch. Govt.* II. iii. Wks. 1851 III. 168 In respect of a woodden table and the perimeter of holy ground about it, a flagon pot, and a linnen corporal, the Priest esteems their lay-ships unhallow'd and unclean.

lay-soil. *rare*[−0]. [? corruption of LAYSTALL, after SOIL.] 'A place to lay soil or rubbish in' (Crabb *Technol. Dict.* s.v. LAY).

laystall ('leɪstɔːl). Also 6 **laye-, leystall(e**, 6–7 **lei-, leystal, laystale**, 7 **leastall, lestal(l**, ? **loystal.** [f. LAY *v.* + STALL; perh. to be regarded as an altered form of next.]

†**1.** A burial-place. *Obs.*

1527 *Lanc. Wills* (Chetham Soc.) I. 16 My bodye to be bured w[tin] the white freris of Chester..and thei to have for my laystall xiij[s]. iiij[d]. **1541** *Ludlow Churchw. Acc.* (Camden) 5 Reseyved of mastere Foxe for m[r] wardens leystalle vjs. viij*d*.

2. A place where refuse and dung is laid.

1553 *Surrey Ch. Goods* (1869) 98 A pese of grownd to make a leystall for the soyle of the hole paryshe. **1580** HOLLYBAND *Treas. Fr. Tong, Voiries d'vne ville*, the laystall of a towne. **1590** SPENSER *F.Q.* I. v. 53 Many corses, like a great lay-stall, Of murdred men. **1610** *Death Rauilliack* in *Harl. Misc.* (Malh.) III. 112 The house..to be utterly ruinated, and be converted into a common leastall. **1612** DRAYTON *Poly-olb.* Pref. A, The common Lay-stall of a Citie. **1702** *Lond. Gaz.* No. 3825/4 The Ground called the Laystal at Mile-end. **1831** CARLYLE *Sart. Res.* (1858) 26 Five-million quintals of Rags picked annually from the Laystall. **1881** *Times* 25 Aug. 7/3 It does not require a very old man to remember a universal reign of cesspools, open ditches, and public laystalls, even in our largest and best kept towns.

attrib. **1745** *De Foe's Eng. Tradesm.* iii. (1841) I. 20 The brickmakers all about London mix seacoal-ashes, or laystal-stuff, as we call it, with their clay, of which they make brick.

b. *fig.*

1629 H. BURTON *Babel no Bethel* 66 The Schoole and Laystall of all impure spirits. *a* **1637** B. JONSON *Underwoods, Little Shrub Growing by*, There he was, Proud, false, and trecherous,..the lay-stall Of putrid flesh alive! **1644** VICARS *God in Mount* 152 Stage-playes..those most dirty and stinking sinks or lestalls of all kinde of abominations. *a* **1734** NORTH *Exam.* I. iii. §99 (1740) 191 The Whole was no better than a Laystall of Lyes.

3. 'A place where milch cows are kept in London' (Simmonds *Dict. Trade* 1858).

†**laystow.** *Obs.* Also 5 **laye-**, 5–6 **ley-**, 6 **laistow(e**, 7 **laistoff** (?). [f. LAY *v.* + STOW. Cf. LAIRSTOW.]

1. = LAYSTALL 1.

1452 *Will of Vampage* (Somerset Ho.), Faciant vnum leystowe pro sepulturibus defunctorum. **1485** *Will of Rypon* (ibid.), For my leystow in the seid church.

2. = LAYSTALL 2.

1494 FABYAN *Chron.* VII. ccxxvi. 254 This place of Smythfeelde was at y[t] daye a laye stowe of all order of fylth. **1577** HARRISON *England* II. xx. (1877) I. 325 The ancient gardens were but dunghils and laistowes. *a* **1665** J. GOODWIN *Filled w. the Spirit* x. (1670) 304 The fumes and smells of Laistoffs, Dunghills, and putrified bodies.

laysure, obs. form of LEISURE *sb.*

layt(e, variant of LAIT *Obs.*; obs. f. LATE *a.*[1]

laytell, layth, obs. ff. LITTLE, LOATH, LOATHE.

laytie, -ty, obs. forms of LAITY.

laytt, variant of LATE *sb.*[1] *Obs.*

lay-up. [LAY *v.*[1] 60.] **1.** A period during which a person or thing is (temporarily) out of employment or use, as a ship in winter.

1927 *Daily Mail* 7 Apr. 3/6 During the winter lay-up of these vessels their passenger accommodation has been thoroughly overhauled. **1929** *Amer. Speech* V. 72 A compulsory stopping on the '[cattle-]drive' is a 'lay up'. **1955** *Times* 10 May 17/4 The winter demand brought tankers out of lay-up. **1959** C. OGBURN *Marauders* (1960) iii. 87 There were frequent lay-ups, and during one of these the men in a car down the train evidently spotted a couple of ducks beside the tracks. **1967** *Coast to Coast 1965–66* 160 The big hall where the Jap pearlfishers dossed during lay-up.

2. a. The operation of laying up in the manufacture of laminated material (see LAY *v.*[1] 60 m). **b.** The assembly of layers ready for bonding so produced.

1942 T. D. PERRY *Mod. Plywood* vi. 169 The lay-up..consists in assembling the layers of veneer and/or lumber with the adhesive. **1950** WEBSTER Add., *Lay-up*, an assembly of layers of veneers or cores for pressing. **1965** *Plastics Tooling & Manuf. Handbk.* (Amer. Soc. Tool & Manuf. Engineers) iii. 35 In wet layup, the workman saturates a piece of fabric in resin, and then may wring out the excess resin and drape the cloth on the laminate. **1972** *Physics Bull.* Nov. 665/2 *Layup*, a laminate that has been assembled, but not cured.

3. *Basketball.* In full, *lay-up shot.* (See quot. 1961.)

1948 A. F. RUPP *Championship Basketball* xv. 130 The drill gives the boys stamina and endurance and helps teach the lay-up shot when going in with the greatest speed. **1958** A. L. COLBECK *Mod. Basketball* iii. 59 In good-class basketball most plays are designed to get a player free for a

lay-up shot. 1959 P. ROTH *Goodbye, Columbus* ii. 35, I took my set shot and, of course, missed. With the Lord's blessing and a soft breeze, I made the lay-up. 1961 J. S. SALAK *Dict. Amer. Sports* 260 *Layup shot*,..a shot taken from underneath or very close to the basket. On this type shot, the ball usually is banked off the backboard, but on occasion the player, on a straight run toward the basket, will 'lay' the ball up to the basket without using the backboard. 1967 *Boston Herald* 1 Apr. 16/4 There wasn't anyone in the Boston contingent who could recall him ever blowing three layups in a game before. 1969 Z. HOLLANDER *Mod. Encycl. Basketball* 121 He could also score on jumpers from the corner, driving lay-ups or tip-ins of rebounds. 1974 *Greenville* (S. Carolina) *News* 22 Apr. 13/3 Havlicek sank a layup with 26 seconds left, putting Boston safely ahead.

layvel, obs. form of LEVEL.

laywoman: see under LAYMAN.

Laz (lɑːz). **a.** A group of Caucasian peoples giving its name to Lazistan in north-east Turkey. **b.** Usu. **Laze** (ˈlɑːzə) or **Lazi** (ˈlɑːzɪ). A member of any of these peoples. **c.** The south Caucasian language of the Laz people. Also (Laz) *attrib.* or as *adj.* Also ˈ**Lazic** *a.*

1836 *Jrnl. R. Geogr. Soc.* VI. 191, I embarked at Trebizond..in a galley, and kept along the shore to the Russian frontier..passing in succession the districts of Yomurah, Surmenah, O'f, Rizah, and Lázistán. All these..are known under the general name of Lázistán, and the people are called Láz. 1847 A. KERR tr. *L. von Ranke's Hist. Servia* xi. 219 The first step taken by Selim amongst the Lazes..excited open rebellion against him in his capital. 1897 *Daily News* 26 Feb. 5/4 These Lazes played an active part in the Armenian massacres. 1923 *Daily Mail* 21 Feb. 9 Travelling with Kemal is a bodyguard of 'Lazis'. Tall, robust dare-devils from the Black Sea coast..each carries an abundant supply of daggers and revolvers. 1934 *Geogr. Rev.* LXXXIV. 472 The ports and mouths of rivers have three names—Greek, Turkish, and Lazic. 1939 L. H. GRAY *Found. Lang.* 375 South Caucasian..consists of four languages: Georgian.., Mingrelian, Laz, and Svanian. 1948 D. DIRINGER *Alphabet* v. 322 According to Dr. O. N. Kazara, who is of Laz extraction, the physical type throughout Caucasia is remarkably uniform. *Ibid.*, There are various dialects, the principal of which are Kartlian, Mingrelian with Laz, and Svanian. 1950 [see ERGATIVE *a.*]. 1954 PEI & GAYNOR *Dict. Ling.* 121 *Laz*, a language spoken in the Caucasus; a member of the South Caucasian family of languages. 1963 *Times* 12 Jan. 9/7 In fact it turned out his father was a Kurd from Elazig, his mother a Laze from Trabzon.

lazar (ˈleɪzə(r)), *sb.* and *a. arch.* Forms: 4–7 lazare, lazer, laser, (4 lacer, lazre, 5 lasyar), 6 lasar, (laiser, laizer), 4– lazar. [a. med.L. *lazarus*, an application of the proper name *Lazarus*, Luke xvi. 20. Cf. F. *ladre*, It. *lazzaro*.]

A. *sb.*

1. A poor and diseased person, usually one afflicted with a loathsome disease; *esp.* a leper.

1340 *Ayenb.* 189 Ine þe uorbisne of þe riche manne, þet onworþede þane lazre. *c*1350 *St. John* 254 in Horstm. *Altengl. Leg.* (1881) 37 Þe Lacer, þat died in disese. 13.. *E.E. Allit. P.* B. 1093 Lazares ful monye, Summe lepre, summe lome, & lomerande blynde. *c*1420 *Chron. Vilod.* st. 274 Blynd lazerus and croked in chirche to lede. 1485 CAXTON *Chas. Gt.* 37 There atte laste were guarysshed & heled..viij lazars of the palesey. 1572 *Nottingham Rec.* IV. 142 A lasar of the Spyttyll' House. 1577–87 HOLINSHED *Chron.* III. 1082/2 They prouided for the lazer to keepe him out of the citie from clapping of dishes, and ringing of bels. 1610 HOLLAND *Camden's Brit.* I. 522 Lazers..so they used to tearme folke infected with the Elephantiasie or Leprosie. *a*1743 SAVAGE *Epitaph on Mrs. Jones* 15 Did piteous lazars oft attend her door? She gave—farewell the parent of the poor. ?1795 COLERIDGE *Sonn.*, *'Sweet Mercy'*, The Galilean mild, Who met the Lazar turned from rich man's doors, And called him friend, and wept upon his sores. 1884 TENNYSON *Becket* I. iv, I marked a group of lazars in the market-place—half-rag, half-sore—beggars.

†**2.** (See quot. 1710.) *Obs.*

1573 TUSSER *Husb.* xlix. (1878) 108 If Lazer so lothsome in cheese be espied, let baies amend Cisley, or shift hir aside. 1710 D. HILMAN *Tusser Rediv.* (1744) 52 What he [Tusser] calls Lazer, which is an inner Corruption, or Rottenness of divers Colours, is chiefly occasion'd from their suckling Beastings, or Milk soon after Calving.

3. *attrib.* and *Comb.*, as *lazar-like*, †*-man*, *-sore*; †**lazar's clicket, clapper, snapper** = *lazarus clapper*; **lazar-haunter**, one who frequents places where lazars are. Also LAZAR-COTE, LAZAR-HOUSE.

1611 COTGR., *Claquette*, a *Lazers Clicket, or Clapper. 1835 BROWNING *Paracelsus* III. 760 You are not a *lazar-haunter; How should you know? 1602 SHAKS. *Ham.* I. v. 72 And a most instant Tetter bak'd about, Most *Lazar-like, with vile and loathsome crust, All my smooth Body. 1552 LATIMER *Serm. 3rd Sund. Epiph.* (1584) 309 Note here also the behauiour of this *Lazer man. 1587 GOLDING *De Mornay* xxix. 463 He saw him there lapping vp his sores among the Lazermen. 1658 tr. *Bergerac's Satyr. Char.* xxvi. 98 *Lazeres snappers [orig. *cliquettes de ladres*]. 1796 BURKE *Regic. Peace* I. Wks. VIII. 123 Exposing our *lazar sores at the door of every proud servitor of the French republick.

B. *adj.* Affected with a loathsome disease, esp. leprosy; leprous. Also *fig.*

1483 CAXTON *Gold. Leg.* 108 b/1 For the cruelte of Constantyn god sente hym suche a sekenes that he becam lazare and mesell. 1530 in Weaver *Wells Wills* (1890) 157 To the lazar people beyng at St. Margarets near the towne of T[aunton] xijd. 1546 *Supplic. Poore Commons* (E.E.T.S.) 62 Blind, lame, lazar, and other the impotent creatures. 1599 SHAKS. *Hen. V*, II. i. 80 Fetch forth the Lazar Kite of Cressid's Kind, Doll Teare-sheete. 1792 D. LLOYD *Voy. Life* 148 Studious to heal a Lazar world.

Hence †ˈ**lazarly** *a.*, lazar-like, diseased.

1612–15 BP. HALL *Contempl.*, *N.T.* IV. xi, And like another Ierusalem, for those five leprous and lazarly orders, hath built five porches.

lazar, obs. Sc. form of LEISURE *sb.*

†ˈ**lazar-cote.** *Obs.* [f. LAZAR + COTE *sb.*[1]] A hut or lodge for the reception of lazars.

1470–85 MALORY *Arthur* VIII. xxxv, Syr said Gouernaile she is put in a lazar cote. 1493 *Will of Spencer* (Somerset Ho.), The iiij Lazarcottes nygh London. 1536 in *Vicary's Anat.* (1888) App. iii. 157 Thomas Barnwell..shalbe one of the visitors of the spyttelhowses, or lazar cotes, about this Citye. 1563 FOXE *A. & M.* 477 (bis) His [Bilney's] preaching at the lazar cots.

lazaret (læzəˈrɛt). Also 7 lazarett, 8–9 lazarette, lazzaret. [a. F. *lazaret*, ad. It. *lazzaretto*, now *lazzeretto*: see next.]

1. = LAZARETTO 1.

1611 COTGR., *Lazaret*, a Lazaret, or Spittle for Lazers. 1667 *Lond. Gaz.* No. 135/2 The Grand Visier..has given order for..raising a Battery near the Lazaret. 1682 WHELER *Journ. Greece* I. 16 A large Lazarett, as the Italians call a Pest-house. 1783 HAMILTON in *Phil. Trans.* LXXIII. 201 The Lazaret has some cracks in it. 1826 *Gazetteer Scot.* (ed. 2) 128 A lazaret or hospital for the reception of sick. 1888 *Daily News* 29 Nov. 4/8 The lazarets where the sick..so often find their welcome passport to the grave.

transf. and *fig.* *a*1711 KEN *Hymnotheo* Poet. Wks. 1721 III. 76 In the great Portico there Night and Day, A Lazaret of wounded Spirits lay. 1845 SIR H. TAYLOR *I. Comnenus* v. vii. Wks. 1864 II. 235 Man, for lack of manliness, is made A lazaret for the mind's maladies.

2. = LAZARETTO 2.

1721 *Act Parl.* in *Lond. Gaz.* No. 5927/5 Such Ship, House, Lazaret, or other Place. 1769 BLACKSTONE *Comm.* IV. 162 The same penalty also attends persons escaping from the lazarets, or places wherein quarentine is to be performed. 1800 *Act 39 & 40 Geo. III*, c. 80 (*title*) An Act for erecting a Lazaret on Chetney Hill, in the County of Kent, and for reducing into one Act the Laws relating to Quarantine. 1860 *Merc. Marine Mag.* VII. 147 Only one box..was left in the lazarette. 1896 *Daily News* 23 July 5/4 After purging five days' quarantine in a lazaret.

fig. 1819 BYRON *Juan* II. ccxxv, The liver is the lazaret of bile.

3. = LAZARETTO 3.

1892 STEVENSON & L. OSBORNE *Wrecker* xi. 185 From the cabin the cook was storing tins into the lazarette. 1897 R. KIPLING *Capt. Courageous* 185 He rolled to the lazarette aft the cabin.

lazaretto (læzəˈrɛtəʊ). Also 7 lazzareto, lazaretta, 8 lazeretto, lazareta, 9 lazzaretto. [ad. It. *lazareto* (Florio), now *lazzeretto*, f. *lazzaro* LAZAR.]

1. A house for the reception of the diseased poor, esp. lepers; a hospital, pest-house. (Chiefly used with reference to foreign countries.)

1549 THOMAS *Hist. Italie* 83 a, For the plague there is a house..two miles from Venice, called the *Lazaretto*. 1609 W. BIDDULPH in T. Lavender *Trav. cert. Englishmen* 6 The Lazaretta [at Zante], which is a place like vnto the pest house in More-fields. 1789 MRS. PIOZZI *Journ. France* I. 77 The Lazaretto..remains a standing monument of his piety. 1822–56 DE QUINCEY *Confess.* (1862) 31 Bare as the walls of a poor house or lazaretto. 1874 GREEN *Short Hist.* x. §1. 722 His longing..led him to examine the lazarettos of Europe and the East.

2. A building, sometimes a ship, set apart for the performance of quarantine.

1605 B. JONSON *Fox* IV. i. (1607) I. 2 b, Where they vse To lie out forty, fifty dayes, sometimes, About the *Lazaretto*, for their triall. 1615 G. SANDYS *Trav.* (1621) 6 When they haue Pratticke, they are enforced to vnlade at the *Lazaretto*. *Ibid.* 227 To be conueyed by him vnto the *Lazaretta*, there to remaine for thirtie or fortie dayes before I could be admitted into the Citie. 1785 PALEY *Mor. Philos.* (1818) II. 163 Conveyed to a lazaretto by an order of quarantine. 1853 FELTON *Fam. Lett.* xxiv. (1865) 210 We could not shake hands; for that would have sent him to the lazaretto for twenty-four hours, as a plague-stricken person.

3. *Naut.* 'A place parted off at the fore part of the 'tween decks, in some merchantmen, for stowing provisions and stores in' (Adm. Smyth 1867).

1711 in W. SUTHERLAND *Shipbuild. Assist.* 161. 1783 COLEBROOKE *Let.* in *Life* (1873) 7 The Duke of Athol, Indiaman, took fire by neglect of the steward in drawing off rum in the lazareta. 1799 in *Naval Chron.* I. 303 The fire must be in the lazaretto below. *c*1850 *Rudim. Navig.* (Weale) 129.

ˈ**lazar-house.** A house for lazars or diseased persons, esp. lepers; a leper-house, lazaretto.

1530 PALSGR. 237/2 Lasarhouse, *lasdriere*. 1543 in *Vicary's Anat.* (1888) App. iii. 149 Mr. R. H...appointed one of the gouernours and Vysytours of the lazarhouses. 1610 HOLLAND *Camden's Brit.* I. 574 A Lazarhouse of women in Wilt-shire which one of the said sisters, being herselfe infected with the Leprosie built for them that had the same disease. 1667 MILTON *P.L.* XI. 479. 1712 ADDISON *Spect.* No. 363 ¶13 A large hospital or lazar-house, fill'd with persons lying under all kinds of mortal diseases. 1794 COLERIDGE *Relig. Musings* x, The closing gates Of the full Lazar-house. 1889 JESSOPP *Coming of Friars* i. 21 Lepers..driven forth to curse and howl in the lazar-house outside the walls.

fig. 1820 BYRON *Mar. Fal.* III. i, Thou must be cleansed of the black blood which makes thee A lazar-house of tyranny. 1880 G. MEREDITH *Tragic Com.* (1881) 160 Their house would be a lazar-house, they would be condemned to seclusion.

Lazarist (ˈlæzərɪst). [ad. F. *lazariste*, f. the proper name *Lazare*, Lazarus.] 'The popular name for the "Congregation of the Priests of the Mission" founded by St. Vincent of Paul in 1624, and established a few years later in the College of St. Lazare at Paris' (*Catholic Dict.* 1885).

1747 *Gentl. Mag.* 570 Jesuits, Oratorians,..Lazarists, and other whimsical orders. 1768 BOSWELL *Corsica* i. (ed. 2) 23 There is here a convent of Lazarists or missionaries. 1900 *Ch. Times* 30 Nov. 614/2 The stupendous labours of Lazarists, of Jesuits, of Marist Fathers in China.

So †ˈ**Lazarite** in the same sense.

1727–52 CHAMBERS *Cycl.* s.v. *Lazarus, Fathers of S. Lazarus*, called also *Lazarites*.

†ˈ**lazarole.** *Obs.* [ad. It. *lazzaruolo*, now *lazzeruolo*.] The medlar-tree (*Mespilus Germanica*).

1668 WILKINS *Real Char.* II. iv. §7. 113. 1688 R. HOLME *Armoury* II. 119/1 Pomiferous Trees..Lazarole.

†ˈ**lazarous**, *a. Obs.* Also 6 lazarus. [f. LAZAR + -OUS.] Leprous. Also *fig.*

1536 in Weaver *Wells Wills* (1890) 47, v howsses of lazarus pepyll xxd. 1541 R. COPLAND *Guydon's Quest. Chirurg.*, etc. Q iij, To habyte with a lazarous woman. 1635 A. READ *Tumors & Vlcers* 225 The Germans have many lazarous persons. 1652 T. ADAMS *God's Anger & Man's Comfort* 87 When that Angel from heaven, gracious repentance hath troubled the waters, the lazarous soul doth but step into them, and is cured.

Hence †ˈ**lazarousness**, leprosy.

1648–60 HEXHAM *Dutch Dict.*, *Melaetscheyt*, Leprosie, or Lazerousnesse.

lazartus, obs. form of LACERTOSE.

Lazarus (ˈlæzərəs). *rare.* [Allusive use of the proper name: see LAZAR.] A leper; a beggar. (In the first quot. the allusion may be to the Lazarus who was raised from the dead: see John xi.)

1508 DUNBAR *Flyting w. Kennedie* 161 Thow Lazarus, thow laithly lene tramort. 1634–5 BRERETON *Trav.* (Chetham Soc.) 9 Only Lazaruses..are permitted to beg their victuals. 1850 S. G. OSBORNE *Gleanings* 15 Lazari, to whom the hated workhouse had come to be as the palace of a Dives. 1879 FARRAR *St. Paul* (1883) 491 The poor, hungry-eyed Lazaruses—half-starved slaves..sat famishing and unrelieved.

b. *attrib.*: †**lazarus-clapper**, a clapper or rattle with which a leper gave notice of his approach; †**lazarus-house** = LAZAR-HOUSE.

1560 DAUS tr. *Sleidane's Comm.* 350 By the waye they set on fyre the poore Lazarus house, cleane contrary to the lawe of armes. 1593 HOLLYBAND *Dict.*, *Le Cliquet de l'huis*, the hammer or ring of a doore, also a lazarous clapper. 1634–5 BRERETON *Trav.* (Chetham Soc.) 10 About half a mile from this town is this alms-house, this Lazarus house.

†ˈ**lazary.** *Obs.* Also 6 lazarye, lazery. [f. LAZAR + -Y.] = LEPROSY *lit.* and *fig.*

1502 ARNOLDE *Chron.* 149 Our Lord Ihesu Criste..be his gret mercy hath purged you of your gret lazarye. 1541 R. COPLAND *Guydon's Quest. Chirurg.* P j b, To..conforte the heade in palsy,..and to pale lazery. 1597 A. M. tr. *Guillemeau's Fr. Chirurg.* 41/1 In those which have the lazarye, and theire face corroded and deformed.

laze (leɪz), *sb. colloq.* [f. LAZE *v.*] The action of the vb. LAZE; an instance of this.

1862 *Temple Bar* V. 328 He will take a quiet laze. 1894 *Cycl. Tour. Club Gaz.* Sept. 262 The writer contented himself with a laze in the gardens below.

laze (leɪz), *v.* Also 7 lase. [Back-formation from LAZY *a.*]

1. *intr.* To lie, move, or act in a sleepy listless fashion; to enjoy oneself lazily. Also with advs.

*a*1592 GREENE *Alphonsus* III. Wks. (Grosart) XIII. 370 And canst thou stand still lazing in this sort? 1610 ROWLANDS *Martin Mark-all* 17 Worke is left at home vndone, and loyterers laze in the streete. 1611 COTGR., *S'endormir en sentinello*,..to laze it when he hath most need to looke about him. 1661 K. W. *Conf. Charac.*, *Lawyer* (1860) 43 He begins to lag and laze, like a tired jade. *a*1704 *Compl. Servant-Maid* (ed. 7) 7 Incline not to sloth, or laze in bed. 1802 SOUTHEY in C. C. Southey *Life* II. 195, I must sleep, and laze, and play whist till bed time. 1868 LOWELL *Lett.* (1894) I. iv. 453, I had a very pleasant time, sailing, fishing, and lazing about. 1899 *Atlantic Monthly* Aug. 199/2 We lazed along, hardly seeming to move at all.

†**b.** *to laze oneself*: to indulge in indolence.

1612 T. ADAMS *Gallant's Burden* 28 b, Hence Beggars lase themselues in the fields of idlenesse. 1620 SHELTON *Quix.* II. xxii. 146 Lazing himselfe as if he had wakened out of a..profound sleep. 1658 GURNALL *Chr. in Arm.* (1669) 119/1 In a summer's day..he lay lazing himself on the grass.

2. quasi-*trans.* To pass *away* in indolence.

1627–77 FELTHAM *Resolves* II. xxxiv. 228 So the bloodless Tortoise..lazeth his life away. 1891 E. PEACOCK *N. Brendon* II. 420 With the firm determination..of 'lazing' away the rest of the day.

Hence ˈ**lazing** *vbl. sb.*

*a*1626 W. SCLATER *2 Thess.* (1629) 283 The lazing of these loyterers is not numbred amongst mortals. 1672 PETTY *Pol. Anat.* (1691) 366 Their lazing seems to me to proceed..from want of employment. 1880 H. S. COOPER *Coral Lands* II. 309 An hour or so of downright lazing on the heath.

laze, lazer, obs. forms of LACE, LAZAR.

ˈ**laze-off.** *rare.* [f. LAZE *v.*] A rest from work.

1924 GALSWORTHY *White Monkey* I. xi. 93 Resenting regular work, enjoying a spurt, and a laze-off.

lazie, variant of LASSO.

lazily ('leɪzɪlɪ), *adv.* [f. LAZY *a.* + -LY².] In a lazy manner; without energy or spirit, sluggishly.

1587 GOLDING *De Mornay* xxxiii. 537 He that feighteth lasilie shalbe damned in hell. **1688** BUNYAN *Heavenly Footm.* (1886) 147 You run too lazily, the door is shut. **1744** ARMSTRONG *Preserv. Health* II. 527 Thro' tedious channels the congealing flood Crawls lazily, and hardly wanders on. **1865** DICKENS *Mut. Fr.* II. i, In a certain lazily arrogant air. **1887** *Spectator* 26 Mar. 415/2 The clouds that float lazily over the enchanted valley.

laziness ('leɪzɪnɪs). [f. LAZY *a.* + -NESS.] The quality of being lazy; aversion or indisposition to exert oneself; slothfulness, sluggishness.

1580 in HOLLYBAND *Treas. Fr. Tong.* **1590** SPENSER *F.Q.* III. vii. 12 Such laesinesse both lewd and poore attonce him made. **1601** SIR W. CORNWALLIS *Disc. Seneca* (1631) 38 Laysines the yonger brother of idlenes. **1631** GOUGE *God's Arrows* I. Ded. 8 Even in leisure lasinesse is to be shunned. **1796** MORSE *Amer. Geog.* II. 394 The pride, indolence, and laziness of the Spaniards. **1816** T. MOORE *Let.* 1 July in *Mem.* (1856) VIII. 216 It is not right that you and I, whatever may be our respective lazinesses, should continue so long without hearing from each other. **1869** SPURGEON *J. Ploughm. Talk* 7 Every man ought to have patience and pity for poverty; but for laziness, a long whip.

lazo, variant of LASSO.

lazre, obs. form of LAZAR.

'lazule. ? *Obs.* Also 6 lazull, 7 luzzel, 7–8 lazul. [ad. L. *lazulum* (see LAPIS LAZULI).] = LAPIS LAZULI. Chiefly attrib. *lazule-stone*.

1598 FLORIO, *Lazoli*, an azure or lazull stone. **1616** BULLOKAR, *Lazule stone*, a blewish greene stone of the kinde of marble, vsed sometime in physicke. **1639** HORN & ROB. *Gate Lang. Unl.* ix. §90 The Azure (Luzzel) stone. **1714** *Fr. Bk. of Rates* 384 Merchandizes from the Levant [etc.].. Lazule. **1757** tr. *Henckel's Pyritol.* 284 The blue resembles a beautiful sapphire and a lazul-stone. **1832** G. DOWNES *Lett. Cont. Countries* I. 320 It is handsomely wrought of marble and lazule-stone.

lazuli ('læzjʊlaɪ). Short for LAPIS LAZULI. Also *attrib.*, as **lazuli-finch**, a brilliant fringilloid bird (*Passerina amœna*) of the western U.S.

1789 E. DARWIN *Bot. Gard.* II. (1791) 157 Light piers of lazuli the dome surround. **1798** SOTHEBY tr. *Wieland's Oberon* (1826) II. 172 There gold and lazuli the walls o'erlaid. **1824** WIFFEN *Tasso* XVI. xxiii, Flowers that, like lazuli in gold, impressed A deeper charm on the beholder's mind. **1831** A. WILSON & BONAPARTE *Amer. Ornith.* IV. 132 *Fringilla amœna*, Bonaparte, Lazuli Finch.

lazuline ('læzjʊlaɪn), *a. rare*⁻¹. [f. LAZULI + -INE.] Of the colour of lapis lazuli.

1877 PATMORE *Unknown Eros* (1890) 2 Love's three-stranded ray, Red wrath, compassion golden, lazuline delight.

lazulite ('læzjʊlaɪt). *Min.* [f. med.L. *lazul-um* (see LAPIS LAZULI) + -ITE.] Hydrous phosphate of aluminium and magnesium, found in blue monoclinic crystals; also, the colour of this mineral. ¶ Sometimes used = LAPIS LAZULI.

Named by Klaproth, 1795, from its older name *lazurstein*.

1807 AIKIN *Dict. Chem. & Min.* II. 3 Lazulite..occurs disseminated in fine grains. **1818** W. PHILLIPS *Min.* 81 Lazulite..is perfectly distinct from Lapis Lazuli. **1849** MACAULAY *Hist. Eng.* viii. II. 268 In that princely house where the remains of Ignatius Loyola lie enshrined in lazulite and gold. **1861** BRISTOW *Gloss. Min.* 211 Lazulite is distinguished from Lapis Lazuli by never being accompanied by Iron Pyrites. **1883** E. ARNOLD *Pearls Faith* IV. 12 His sky is lazulite; His earth is paved with emerald-work.

attrib. **1811** PINKERTON *Petral.* II. 88 Lazulite rock. **1853** KANE *Grinnell Exp.* xlvii. (1856) 439 The rich lazulite blue that was reflected from the bergs.

Hence **lazu'litic** *a.*, of or pertaining to lazulite.

1853 KANE *Grinnell Exp.* viii. (1856) 62 It reminded me of the recent cleavage of sulphate of strontian—a resemblance more striking from the slightly lazulitic tinge of each.

† **'lazure**, *a. Obs. rare.* [See AZURE.] = AZURE *a.* 1. Also in comb., *lazure-coloured* adj.

1671 J. WEBSTER *Metallogr.* xvi. 236 Sometimes it is red and brown, mixed with a green colour: some are of a lazure colour. **1683** PETTUS *Fleta Min.* I. (1686) 230 The fair lazure colored Copper..Oars..contain likewise much and good Copper.

lazurite ('læzjʊəraɪt). *Min.* [f. med.L. *lazur* (see AZURE) + -ITE. Used first by Von Kobell in 1853, as a synonym of AZURITE.] The blue part of lapis lazuli.

1892 DANA *Min.* 433 Ordinary natural lapis lazuli is shown to contain lazurite.

lazy ('leɪzɪ), *a.* and *sb.* Forms: 6–7 laysy, -ie, lasie, -y, lazie, (6 laesie, -y, lasey, leasie), 7– lazy. [Of obscure etymology.

The earliest quoted form *laysy* would favour the derivation from LAY *v.* with suffix as in *tipsy*, *tricksy*, etc.; but the spelling is not quite early enough to have etymological significance. If the word be of early origin, and esp. if the alleged dialectal sense 'naught, bad', be genuine, there may possibly be connexion with ON. *lasenn* dilapidated, *lasmøyrr* decrepit, fragile, mod.Icel. *las-furða* ailing, *las-leiki* ailment. Prof. Skeat suspects adoption from Du. or LG., and refers to MLG. *lasich*, *losich*, mod.LG. *läösig* (Danneil), early mod.Du. *leuzig*.]

A. *adj.*

1. a. Of persons (also of animals), their disposition, etc.: Averse to labour, indisposed to action or effort; idle; inactive, slothful.

1549 BALE *Labor Journ. Leland* Pref. A vij b, Those laysy lubbers and popyshe bellygoddes. **1567** *Triall Treas.* A iv, Your lasy bones I pretende so to blisse, That you shall haue small luste to prate any more. **1578** T. N. tr. *Conq. W. Indies* 191 If they were found to be lazie and slouthfull they should be used accordingly. **1579** SPENSER *Sheph. Cal.* Feb. 9 Lewdly complainest thou laesie ladde, Of Winter's wracke, for making thee sadde. **1590** —— *F.Q.* I. iv. 36 Sathan.. forward lasht the laesy teme. **1628** PRYNNE *Cens. Cozens* 77 Who gratifie their owne lasie dispositions. *a* **1658** CLEVELAND *Wks.* (1687) 508 These lazie tender-hearted Clowns. **1697** DRYDEN *Virg. Georg.* IV. 242 All, with united Force, combine to drive The lazy Drones from the laborious Hive. *a* **1770** JORTIN *Serm.* (1771) I. i. 13 It is a lazy modesty to resign the reason God has conferred upon us. **1807** CRABBE *Par. Reg.* III. 143 The lazy vagrants in her presence shook. **1878** JEVONS *Prim. Pol. Econ.* 80 He must not be very lazy..for fear of being discharged.

b. *transf.* Applied to things, places, or conditions, favourable or appropriate to laziness.

1606 SHAKS. *Tr. & Cr.* I. iii. 147 With him Patroclus Vpon a lazie Bed the liuelong day Breakes scurrill Iests. **1669** DRYDEN *Tyrannic Love* I. i, Two tame gown'd princes, who at ease debate, In lazy chairs, the business of the state. **1670** —— *2nd Pt. Conq. Granada* III. iii, Love, like a lazy ague, I endure. **1680** OTWAY *Orphan* I. i, They cry they're weary of their lazy home. **1721** RAMSAY *Morning Interview* 87 The nymph, new-wak'd, starts from the lazy down. **1840** DICKENS *Old C. Shop* iv, The room is a cool, shady, lazy kind of place. **1851** LONGF. *Gold. Leg.* IV. *Road to Hirschau*, The great dog..Hangs his head in the lazy heat.

2. a. Of things: Sluggish, dull, slow-moving; now only *transf.* from sense 1. †Formerly of literary style, and, in physical sense, of heat or chemical agents: Languid, having little energy.

a **1568** ASCHAM *Scholem.* II. (Arb.) 100 Melancthon.. came to this low kinde of writing, by vsing ouer moch Paraphrasis in reading: For studying therbie to make euerie thing streight and easie, in smothing and playning all things to much, neuer leaueth, whiles the sence it selfe be left, both lowse and lasie. **1590** SHAKS. *Mids. N.* V. i. 41 How shall we beguile The lazie time, if not with some delight? **1592** *Arden of Faversham* E i b, The laysie minuts linger on their time. *a* **1628** F. GREVIL *Alaham* 3rd Chorus 35 A lasy calme, wherein each foole a pilot is. ? **1630** MILTON *Time* 2 Lazy leaden-stepping Hours. **1668** CULPEPPER & COLE *Barthol. Anat.* I. xx. 53 The condition of Spirituous blood, forcibly issuing forth, and of a dull and lazie urin are different. **1693** DRYDEN *Ovid's Met.* I. 362 With rain his robe and heavy mantle flow, And lazy mists are low'ring on his brow. **1734** *Phil. Trans.* XXXVIII. 298 There is a great deal more of this Substance of the Lazy or Inactive, than of the Active or Magnetick sort. **1764** GOLDSM. *Trav.* 2 Or by the lazy Scheld, or wandering Po. **1799** COLERIDGE *Lines comp. in Concert-room* 26 The lazy boat sways to and fro. **1885** R. BRIDGES *Eros & Psyche, May* 4 The sun..Sifting his gold through lazy mists.

b. Applied to an eye with poor vision which is consequently little used and tends to deteriorate further; *esp.* the unused eye in squint.

1939 R. B. SIMPKINS *Basic Mech. Human Vision* v. 62 Both exophoric and esophoric conditions are probably the most frequent causes of the development of a lazy eye. **1957** [see *heterophoria* (HETERO-)]. **1971** E. RUDINGER *Eyes Right* 42 Up to the age of 5 years there is a fair chance of success by encouraging the child to use the lazy eye.

† **3.** *dial.* Bad, worthless. *Obs.*⁻⁰

1671 SKINNER *Etymol. Ling. Angl.*, *Lazy*, in agro Linc. usurpatur pro Malus,..Pravus, Perversus. **1674** RAY *N.C. Words* 29 *Lazy*, Naught, bad. **1787** in GROSE *Prov. Gloss.*

4. *Comb.*, as *lazy-boned*, *-minded*, *-paced*, *-puffing* adjs.; **lazy arm**, a type of boom from which a microphone may be slung; **lazy-board** (*U.S.*), a short board on the left side of a waggon, used by teamsters to ride on (*Cent. Dict.*); **lazy-boots** *colloq.* = LAZY-BONES; **lazy-cock** (*U.S.*), 'a cock controlling the pipe between the feed-pump of a locomotive and the hose from the tank of the tender' (Funk); **lazy daisy (stitch)**, a petal-shaped embroidery stitch; **lazy dog** *U.S. Mil. slang*, a type of fragmentation bomb designed to explode in mid-air and scatter steel pellets at high velocity over the target area; † **lazy-gut**, a glutton; **lazy-guy** *Naut.* (see GUY *sb.*¹ 2); **lazy-jack**, 'a lifting device of compounded levers on the principle of the lazy-tongs' (Knight *Dict. Mech.* 1875); **lazy-legs** = LAZY-BONES; **lazy-painter**, 'a small temporary rope to hold a boat in fine weather' (Smyth *Sailor's Word-bk.* 1867); **lazy-pinion**, a pinion serving as a transmitter of motion between two other pinions or wheels (*Cent. Dict.*); **lazy scissors** = LAZY-TONGS; **Lazy Susan**, **lazy susan** orig. *U.S.*, a revolving (wooden) stand on a table to hold condiments, etc.; a muffin stand.

1960 O. SKILBECK *ABC of Film & TV* 76 *Lazy arm, a small, hand-held microphone Boom. **1962** A. NISBETT *Technique Sound Studio* 257 *Lazy arm*, simple form of boom consisting of an upright and a balanced cross-member from which a microphone may be slung. **1875** A. R. HOPE *My Schoolboy Fr.* 148 One or two *lazy-boned fellows worked in bed. **1831** LYTTON *Eug. Aram* I. ii, Why don't you rise, Mr. *Lazy-boots? Where are your eyes? Don't you see the young ladies? **1863** MRS. GASKELL *Sylvia's L.* xxxv, Nancy..is gone to bed this hour past, like a lazy boots as she is. **1923** *Daily Mail* 10 Mar. 14 The way the '*lazy-daisy' stitch is worked is shown at the side of the sketch. **1948** J. CANNAN *Little I Understood* x. 133 Mildred completed six lazy daisies. **1963** N. MARSH *Dead Water* (1964) viii. 221 A rumpled nightgown embroidered with lazy daisies. **1965** *Times* 23 Mar. 12/7 Asked why something more deadly was not preferred—when such things as napalm and white phosphorus incendiary bombs and '*lazy dog' fragmentation bombs are frequently in use— the spokesmen said the gas was being used in situations where the Vietcong might be holding hostages. **1967** *N.Y. Times* 13 Jan. 8 The Lazy Dog is an advanced antipersonnel weapon introduced last spring. **1968** *Punch* 21 Feb. 258 Tomorrow, we'll get three divisions in here, four, we'll get two hundred B-52s, we'll get ground-to-grounds, and whole batteries of Lazy Dogs. **1631** *Celestina* IX. 105 This same *lazy-gut was the cause..of all this stay. **1838** DICKENS *O. Twist* xxi, Don't lag behind already, *Lazy-legs! **1879** C. M. YONGE *Burnt Out* xii. 192 George..had been getting more *lazy-minded and stupid. **1929** V. WOOLF *Granite & Rainbow* (1958) 105 This lazy-minded man was quite capable..of filling a chapter or two..from a fountain of empty, journalistic phrases. **1591** SYLVESTER *Du Bartas* I. vi. 106 The *lazy-paced (yet laborious) Asse. **1592** SHAKS. *Rom. & Jul.* II. ii. 31 When he bestrides the *lazie puffing Cloudes. **1836** *Lazy scissors [see LAZY-TONGS]. **1917** *Vanity Fair* (N.Y.) Dec. 17 (Advt.), Revolving Server or *Lazy Susan. **1966** B. ASKWITH *Step out of Time* ii. 35 The home-made jam on the Lazy Susan in the middle of the table. **1971** *Sunday Australian* 8 Aug. 10/1 The best china is used. Silver pots of steaming tea and coffee spin round with wheels of gateaux on a massive lazy susan.

† **B.** *sb.* Used as a name for the SLOTH. *Obs.*

1682 SIR T. BROWNE *Chr. Mor.* I. §33 To tread a mile after ..the heavy measures of the Lazy of Brazilia, were a most tiring Pennance.

Hence **'lazyhood**, laziness. **'lazyish** *a.*, somewhat lazy.

1866 B. W. PROCTER *Mem. Lamb* 184 The imbecile, or those brought up in complete lazyhood. **1892** *Argosy* Jan. 42, I have six long, delicious weeks of lazyhood before me. **1892** *Spectator* 17 Dec. 878/2 The lazyish, slightly slatternly poor.

lazy ('leɪzɪ), *v.* [f. LAZY *a.*]

1. *intr.* = LAZE *v.* 1.

1612 SYLVESTER *Tropheis* 90 Nor waits he lazying on his bed for day. **1694** R. L'ESTRANGE *Fables* 50 They knew no reason..why the One should lye lazying and pampering itself with the fruit of the Other's labour. **1765** H. TIMBERLAKE *Mem.* 76 Hunting, and warring abroad, and lazying at home. **1876** BESANT & RICE *Gold. Butterfly* III. 81 He..lazied under the hanging willows by the shore. **1890** MRS. LAFFAN *Louis Draycott* I. II. ii. 146 A snug retreat, indeed, to read, or think, or 'lazy' in.

2. quasi-*trans.* = LAZE *v.* 2.

1885 *Century Mag.* XXXI. 197 We lazied the rest of the pleasant afternoon away. **1892** TENNYSON *St. Telemachus* 21 Wake Thou deedless dreamer, lazying out a life Of self-suppression, not of selfless love.

'lazy-back. †**a.** A sluggard. *Obs.* **b.** *Coal-mining.* (See quot. 1881.) **c.** 'A high back-bar to a carriage-seat' (Knight *Dict. Mech.* 1875). **d.** *lazy-back-chair*, a chair with a reclining back. ? *U.S.*

1611 COTGR., *Poltron*, a..sluggard lazie-backe. **1860** *Eng. & For. Mining Gloss.*, S. Staff. Terms, *Lazyback*, the place at surface where the coals are loaded and stacked for sale. **1887** *Pop. Sci. Mo.* XXX. 748 A lazy-back chair makes a capital observing-seat.

'lazy-bed. *Potato-growing.* A bed about six feet wide, on which the potatoes are laid, with a trench on each side, two or three feet wide, from which earth is taken to cover the potatoes. Also *attrib.*

1743 R. MAXWELL *Sel. Trans.* 159 In ley Ground they [Potatoes] are commonly, in Scotland, planted in Lazy-beds, as they are called. **1780** A. YOUNG *Tour Irel.* I. 300 Mr. Herbert has cultivated potatoes in the common lazy-bed method. **1813** VANCOUVER *Agric. Devon* 193 The old fresh lazy-bed mode..seems to have taken great root in Devonshire. **1846** McCULLOCH *Acc. Brit. Empire* (1854) I. 311 Potatoes..are mostly planted in the Irish fashion, or in lazy beds. **1860** DELAMER *Kitch. Gard.* 24 The lazy-bed system may be advantageously followed on stiff retentive clays.

'lazy-bones. *colloq.* A lazy person.

1592 G. HARVEY *Pierce's Super.* (1593) 185 Was..legierdemane a sloweworme, or Viuacitie a lasie-bones. **1600** BRETON *Pasquil's Madcap* (Grosart) 12/2 Go tell the Labourers, that the lazie bones That will not worke, must seeke the beggar's gaines. **1809** MALKIN *Gil Blas* II. i. ¶6 Master lazy-bones did not like sitting up! **1863** R. F. BURTON *Abeokuta* II. 168 Our lazy bones who had escorted the returner had spent four days on a two days march.

b. (See quot.) Cf. LAZY-TONGS.

1785 GROSE *Dict. Vulg. Tongue*, *Lazybones*, an instrument like a pair of tongs, for old, or very fat people, to take anything from the ground without stooping.

'lazy-tongs. A system of several pairs of levers crossing and pivoted at their centres in the manner of scissors, so connected that the movement of the first pair is communicated to the last, which is fitted with ends resembling those of a pair of tongs, for picking up objects at a distance. The name is applied also to a similar combination of levers used in machinery. Also *attrib.*

1836 *Encycl. Brit.* (ed. 7) XIV. 450/2 A combination of levers called zig-zag, or lazy tongs, or scissors. *Ibid.*, These lazy tongs are ingeniously applied by Mr. Aldous of Clapton, for conveying the motion of the beam of his steam engine to the crank which gives the circular motion. **1847** LD. LINDSAY *Hist. Chr. Art* I. 109 The other presents him

[the Saviour] the sponge of vinegar, (on the instrument commonly called a lazy-tongs). **1862** H. MARRYAT *Year in Sweden* I. 118 Our course ran zigzag, like a pair of lazy-tongs. *a* **1864** GESNER *Coal, Petrol.*, etc. (1865) 31 The Lazy Tongs..is attached by a screw-joint to the sinker bar or other suitable rod of iron, and lowered so as to catch the end of the missing tool in its jaws. **1881** G. M. HOPKINS *Let.* 14 May (1938) 100 My only resource is to ask you if you..can suggest some fetch, some boomerang or lazytongs or round-the-corner means of having at him. **1912** *Proc. Amer. Philos. Soc.* LI. 558 A series of links of the 'lazy-tongs' pattern. **1942** 'M. INNES' *Daffodil Affair* II. 70 A lazy-tongs... It used to be quite a popular toy..something rather like a pair of scissors with a piece of lattice-work pivoted to the blades. **1955** *Archit. Rev.* CXVII. 356/3 The 'lazy-tongs' effect of every door being forced to open simultaneously.

‖**lazzaro** (ˈladdzaro). Plur. lazzari (-i). [It.: see LAZAR.] = LAZZARONE.

1650 HOWELL *Revol. Naples* (1664) II. 115 The Lazzari which are the scum of the Neapolitan people. **1797** MRS. RADCLIFFE *Italian* vii, To have as swift a pair of heels to assist in carrying him off as any lazaro in Naples need desire. **1835** *Court Mag.* VI. 20/2, I do not pretend..to distinguish between the veritable lazzari, and the vagabonds.

‖**lazzarone** (læzəˈrəʊneɪ, laddzaˈrone). Chiefly *pl.* Forms: *sing.* 9 laz(z)arone; *pl.* 8 lazaroni, 9 lazzaroni. [It. *lazzarone*, augmentative form of *lazzaro* (Florio) LAZAR.] One of the lowest class at Naples, who lounge about the streets, living by odd jobs, or by begging.

1792 CHARLOTTE SMITH *Desmond* II. 121 What wretched and dangerous doctrine to disseminate among the lazzaroni of England. [*Note*] Lazzaroni, a word descriptive of people reduced to the utmost poverty and wretchedness. **1796** MORSE *Amer. Geog.* II. 439 [Naples.] About 30000 lazaroni, or black guards. **1797** MRS. RADCLIFFE *Italian* ix, A few fishermen and lazzaroni only were loitering along the strand. **1832** G. DOWNES *Lett.* I. 454 The Italian *vetturini*, a kind of peregrinating *lazzaroni*, never let slip any opportunity of paying homage to the goddess Vacuna. **1859** GEO. ELIOT *A. Bede* xvii, Neither are picturesque lazzaroni or romantic criminals half so frequent as your common labourer. **1878** H. M. STANLEY *Dark Cont.* II. iii. 74 The most ragged British beggar or Neapolitan lazzarone.

attrib. **1822** J. FLINT *Lett. Amer.* 34 Lazzaroni hucksters of fruit and sweetmeats. **1875** J. H. BENNET *Winter Medit.* I. iii. 77 Lazzarone enjoyment in midwinter of sunshine, air, and scenery.

lb., abbreviation of L. *lībra* 'pound', *pl.* **lbs.**, now only used of pounds weight, but formerly also of pounds sterling. **lbf**, the pound as a unit of force; **lbm**, the pound as a unit of mass.

1390-1 *Earl Derby's Exped.* (Camden) 11 Pro ij lb. gyngere, ijs. *xd.* **1563-7** BUCHANAN *Reform. St. Andros* Wks. (S.T.S.) 7 In silver, five hundret xlvij lbs. xs. *xd.* **1961** *B.S.I. News* Oct. 26/1 The B.S.I. committee which deals with units and symbols has accepted a form of notation in which a distinction is made between the two concepts 'mass' and 'force'. In this notation the pound has the abbreviation 'lb'; the unit called a pound-force has the abbreviation 'lbf' and is that force which, when acting on a body of mass one pound, gives it an acceleration equal to that of standard gravity. **1962** S. L. BRAGG *Rocket Engines* ix. 148 A jet velocity of 10^5 ft/s could be obtained, giving a thrust of 3 lbf for a flow of 0·0009 lbm/s. **1966** lbf [see *gravitational system*]. **1967** *Technology Week* 23 Jan. 104/1 (Advt.), Pictured from the top: 300 lbf monopropellant hydrazine rocket for orbit control. **1971** I. H. SHAMES *Introd. Statics* i. 12 (*table*) 1 slug ≡ 32·2 lbm.

l'chaim, l'chay(i)m, varr. LECHAYIM.

L-dopa (ɛlˈdəʊpə). *Chem.* and *Biochem.* Also l- (now *rare*), L-, -DOPA. [f. L 7 c + DOPA.] = LEVODOPA.

1939 *Jrnl. Physiol.* XCVI. 51 *P* Tyrosine given in the diet is partly excreted as *l*-dopa. **1942** *Ibid.* CI. 345 In tyrosinosis *l*(−)-dopa was found to be excreted in the urine after oral administration of *l*(−)-tyrosine. **1958** *Brit. Jrnl. Pharmacol.* XIII. 92/1 (*heading*) Effect of L-dopa and epinine. **1969** *3rd Symposium Parkinson's Dis.* (R. Coll. Surg. Edin.) 178 L-Dihydroxyphenylalanine (L-dopa) proved far less toxic and more effective than the racemic compound studied earlier. **1970** PASSMORE & ROBSON *Compan. Med. Stud.* II. v. 61/2 [In Parkinsonism] DOPA is given by mouth in doses up to 16 g/day of the racemic mixture or up to 8 g of L-DOPA. **1970** D. B. CALNE *Parkinsonism* x. 94 Disappointing results arise from unwanted effects of L-dopa, such as dyskinesia or psychiatric disturbances. **1970** *Times* 29 Apr. 2/3 L-Dopa, the drug used experimentally in treatment of Parkinson's Disease, has passed the clinical trial stage.

†**Le, lee.** *Obs.* [abbreviation for med.L. (*dies*) *legibilis* (day) appropriated for reading (see Du Cange).] Only in *Le day*: a day on which ordinary exercises (as distinguished from disputations) were read in the schools. Cf. DIS *sb.*

1574 M. STOKYS in G. Peacock *Observ. Stat. Univ. Camb.* App. A (1841) p. iv, The Questionists shall gyve the Bedels warnynge upon the Le Daye. *Ibid.* p. xiv, All the Determiners shall stande in the Common Schooles every Lee Daye from Ashe wensdaye untyll the last Acte.

le, obs. form of LAY, LEA, LEE, LIE.

-le, *suffix*, pronounced (-(ə)l), of various function and origin.

1. The usual mod.Eng. form of ME. *-el(e, -le*, repr. OE. *-el, -ela, -(e)le* in sbs. and *-ol, -ul, -el* in adjs. (The form -EL is retained where phonetic law or orthographical convention does not permit the change into *-le*, as after *ch, g* soft, *n, r, sh, th*, and *v*. After *m* the suffix becomes *-ble*.)

The OE. sbs. and adjs. with *l* suffixes are prob. in most cases of pre-Eng. formation. The sbs. formed on noun-stems have sometimes an originally diminutive sense, as in *bramble*; sometimes they express the notion of 'an appliance or tool', as in *thimble, handle*. In those formed on vb.-stems the function of the suffix is either agential as in *beadle*, instrumental as in *bridle, girdle*, or expressive of some less definable relation, as in *bundle*. The adjs., which are formed on vb.-stems, have the sense 'apt or liable' (to do what the vb. expresses), as in *brittle, fickle, gripple, nimble*, †*swikel*.

b. In *riddle* the suffix represents OE. -ELS, the *s* having been confused with the plural ending.

2. An occasional representative of ME. *-el(l, -elle*, in sbs. adopted from Fr. This has several different sources: in *castle, mantle*, it is OF. *-el*:—L. *-ellum* dim. suffix (see -EL); in *cattle* it is OF. *-el*:—L. *-āle*, the neut. sing., and in *battle* it is OF. *-aille* the neut. pl., of the adjective suffix *-ālis* (see -AL[1]); in *bottle* it is OF. *-eille*:—L. *-icula* dim. suffix.

3. A verbal formative, repr. ME. *-(e)len*, OE. *-lian*:—OTeut. type *-ilôjan*, with a frequentative or sometimes a diminutive sense. Among the few examples that go back to OE. are *nestle, twinkle, wrestle*. In ME. and early mod.E. the suffix was extensively used (like the equivalent forms in MHG. and mod.Ger. and in Du.) to form vbs. expressing repeated action or movement, as in *brastle, crackle, crumple, dazzle, hobble, niggle, paddle, sparkle, topple, wriggle*, etc. Many of these formations are from echoic roots, as *babble, cackle, gabble, giggle, guggle, mumble*, etc.

lea (liː), *sb.*[1] Forms: 1 léah, léa, léaȝ, léȝ, 4 leȝ, 5-6 (9) lee, 5-7 leye, 5 lie, legh, 5-6 le, 6 lighe, laie, 6-7 laye; 5-7 lay, 5-9 ley, 6- lea. [OE. *léa(h* masc. (genitive *léas, léaȝes*, nom. pl. *léas*), and *léah* fem. (genitive *léaȝe*), app. meaning a tract of cultivated or cultivable land; in spite of the difference of sense, the words appear to be etymologically identical with OHG. *lôh* neut. or masc., used to render L. *lūcus* grove (MHG. *lôh, lôch* low brushwood, clearing overgrown with small shrubs, mod.Ger. dial. *loh*), and perh. with Flem. *-loo* in place-names, as *Waterloo*; the pre-Teut. type **louqo-* occurs also in L. *lūcus* grove, and Lith. *laukas* meadow and arable land, as opposed to wood; the root is supposed by some scholars to be **leuq-* to shine (whence L. *lūcēre*, Eng. LIGHT *sb.*, etc.; for the sense cf. *clearing*); others have suggested **leu-* to loosen (Gr. λύειν, L. *so-lv-ĕre*).

The sense has been influenced by confusion with LEASE *sb.*[1] (OE. *lǽs*), which seems often to have been mistaken for a plural, and also with LEA *sb.*[2]]

A tract of open ground, either meadow, pasture, or arable land. After OE. chiefly found (exc. where it is the proper name of a particular piece of ground) in poetical or rhetorical use, ordinarily applied to grass land.

805 in Birch *Cartul. Sax.* (1885) I. 450 *Campus armentorum* id est *hriðra leah.* **944** *Ibid.* (1887) II. 540 þonne ȝeuðe ic Ælfwine & Beorhtulfe þæs leas & þæs hammes be norðan pære lytlan dic. *c* **1430** *Hymns Virg.* (1867) 95 Bi a forest as y gan walke With-out a paleys in a leye. *c* **1470** *Golagros & Gaw.* 312 Thai plantit doun ane pailyeoun, vpone ane plane lee. *c* **1470** HENRYSON *Fables* viii. 1793 in *Anglia* IX. 458 Luik to the lint that growis on yone le. **1513** DOUGLAS *Æneis* XII. Prol. 183 In lyssouris and on leys litill lammis Full tait and trig socht bletand to thar dammis. **1526** SKELTON *Magnyf.* 2093, I garde her gaspe, I garde her gle, With, daunce on the le, the le! **1535** STEWART *Cron. Scot.* (1858) I. 627 Eugenius vpoune ane lustie le Dewydit his hes his ost in battellis thre. *a* **1541** WYATT in *Tottel's Misc.* (Arb.) 90 In lusty leas at libertie I walke. **1586** *Durham Depos.* (Surtees) 320, I have bene yonder in the lighes. **1588** SPENSER *Virg. Gnat* 110 Flowres varietie With sundrie colours paints the sprinckled lay. **1610** SHAKS. *Temp.* IV. i. 60 Ceres, most bounteous Lady, thy rich Leas Of Wheate, Rye, Barley, Fetches, Oates and Pease. **1634** MILTON *Comus* 965 Other trippings..With the mincing Dryades On the Lawns, and on the Leas. **1750** GRAY *Elegy* i, The lowing herd winds slowly o'er the lea. **1790** BURNS *Elegy Capt. Henderson* v, Mourn, little hare-bells o'er the lee. **1808** COLERIDGE *Three Graves* III. xxxiv, I saw young Edward by himself Stalk fast adown the lee. **1813** HOGG *Queen's Wake* 221 Stern Tushilaw strode o'er the ley. **1849** LONGF. *Birds of Passage* v, From the land of snow and sleet they seek a southern lea. **1850** TENNYSON *In Mem.* cxv, Now dance the lights on lawn and lea. **1851** KINGSLEY *Poems, Bad Squire* 12 Where under the gloomy fir-woods One spot in the ley throve rank.

transf. **1612** DRAYTON *Poly-olb.* i. 23 Surging Neptunes leas.

¶ Used loosely for 'ground'.

c **1450** *Bk. Curtasye* III. 441 in *Babees Bk.*, On legh vnsonken hit [a pallet] shalle be made.

b. Occurring in place-names.

778 *Charter of Cynewulf* in *O.E. Texts* 427 To brad(an) leaȝe, *illo septo* bradan leaȝe. **862** *Charter of Æðelberht* ibid. 438 Bromleaȝ—an norðan fram ceddan leaȝe to langan leaȝe. *c* **1305** *St. Kenelm* 342 in *E.E.P.* (1862) 56 Heo..To-ward wynchecumbe come riȝt vnder soup leȝ. **1572** *Satir. Poems Reform.* xxxi. 75 Nor quhen thay come in feir of weir Downe to the Gallow Ley. **1620** in Willis & Clark *Cambridge* (1886) I. 126 A ground..now commonly called S. Thomas' Leyes. **1844** S. BAMFORD *Life of Radical* 39 We found ourselves traversing Hopwood ley.

lea[2], **ley, lay** (liː, leɪ). Forms: 4 leyȝe, 4-7 leye, 5 lee, 6 laie, laye; 5- ley, lay, 6- lea (now chiefly *poet.*). [Elliptical use of LEA (*ley, lay*) adj.] Land that has remained untilled for some time; arable land under grass; land 'laid down' for pasture, pasture-land, grass-land. ***clover-lay, ley***: see CLOVER *sb.* 4.

1357 *Durham Halmote Rolls* (Surtees) 19 Concelavit eos qui depast. fuerunt les leyes. **1362** LANGL. *P. Pl.* A. VIII. 5 Treuthe..bad holden hem at hom and heren heore leyȝes [B. VII. 5 leyes]. *a* **1400-50** *Alexander* 3561 Ai wald þe wise haue wale soile mare þan a wast lee. *c* **1420** *Pallad. on Husb.* VI. 30 Nowe feeldes fatte..Is good to plowe, and leyes vp to breke. *c* **1440** *Promp. Parv.* 285/1 Lay, londe not telyd. **1523** FITZHERB. *Husb.* §8 If thou haue any leys, to falowe or to sowe otes vpon, fyrste plowe them. **1573** TUSSER *Husb.* xxxv. (1878) 83 In Januiere husband that poucheth the grotes will break vp his laie, or be sowing of otes. **1610** W. FOLKINGHAM *Art of Survey* I. ii. 36 Rapes require a broken-vp lay and a rich layer. **1638** DRUMM. OF HAWTH. *Irene* Wks. (1711) 164 The husbandman..had turned his acres into leyes, his syths and ploughs into swords. **1713** *Lond. Gaz.* No. 5143/4, 12 Acres of Meadow Ground, and 4 Leys and a half in St. Ives. **1765** A. DICKSON *Treat. Agric.* xii. (ed. 2) 259 In plowing lea, where the sward is tough. **1780** A. YOUNG *Tour Irel.* I. 28 He also spreads this manure on lays he intends breaking up. **1808** CURWEN *Econ. Feeding Stock* 12 Having destroyed all old lays, I have no other hay than clover. **1886** ELWORTHY *W. Somerset Word-bk.*, *Lay, ley*, land which has been sown with annual or biennial grasses, and has come round to the time to be reploughed. **1892** *Lichfield Mercury* 20 May 5/2 Good Ley for few Horses. **1932** *Discovery* Feb. 61/1 Some progressive farmers are alternating four years of corn-growing with four years of temporary grass leys, on which bullocks and grass-land sheep are fed. **1957** *New Biol.* XXIV. 42 In many areas it was not convenient to change arable land to leys of any considerable duration. **1962** *Listener* 1 Feb. 214/1 The old permanent pastures are being replaced by temporary leys, with the plough 'going all round the farm'. **1972** *Oxford Times* 28 July 8 Don't be in a hurry to plough up and re-seed leys and permanent pastures.

b. *attrib.*

1523 FITZHERB. *Husb.* §25 Shorte hey, and leye hey is good for shepe. **1634** W. WOOD *New Eng. Prosp.* (1865) 12 Being made into Hay, the Cattle eate it as well as it were Lea-hay and like it as well with it. ? **17..** [BURNS] *There's News, Lasses* iii, I hae as gude a craft rig As made o' yird and stane; And waly fa' the ley-crap For I maun till'd again. **1799** J. ROBERTSON *Agric. Perth* 222, I learned from a nobleman.. that good ley hay is much sought after..for his Majesty's horses. **1805** R. W. DICKSON *Pract. Agric.* (1807) I. 16 This is the best object in ploughing for a ley crop. **1813** VANCOUVER *Agric. Devon* 142 Hacking is also performed where lay-wheat is sown immediately after the plough, and without a previous harrowing. **1948** L. D. STAMP *Land of Britain* iv. 65 The length of time the grass is left down is usually determined by the farmer's own judgment..a common average being seven years. This is the system of 'leys' or 'ley farming'—taking the plough round the farm.

lea (liː), *sb.*[3] *north. dial.* Also 5, 9 ley, (6 *pl.* lease), 9 lae, leigh. [a. ON. *lé* (Sw. *lia*, Da. *lee*).] A scythe.

1483 *Cath. Angl.* 211/1 A Ley, or a sythe, *falx, falcicula.* **1528** in Rogers *Agric. & Prices* (1866) III. 567/2, 3 falces called leys. **1573** *Richmond. Wills* (Surtees 1853) 242, vij lease, iij[d]. **1781** J. HUTTON *Tour to Caves* Gloss. 92 *Lea*, a sythe. **1855** MORTON *Cycl. Agric.* II. 724 *Lea* or *Leigh* (Yorks.), a scythe. **1877** *Holderness Gloss.*, *Ley.*

attrib. **1855** ROBINSON *Whitby Gloss.*, *Lea-sand*, a fine sand brought from the eastern moorlands, to lay upon the strickle or sharpening tool for the lea. **1869** *Lonsdale Gloss.*, *Lea-stone*, a scythe-sharpener.

lea (liː), *sb.*[4] Also 4-5 le(e, 7- lay, 9 ley. [The gloss in the *Promp. Parv.* suggests that the word is a derivative of F. *lier* (:—L. *ligāre*) to bind, tie. But cf. LEASE *sb.*[4]] A measure of yarn of varying quantity: see quots.

1399 *Mem. Ripon* (Surtees) III. 132 Et in xl lee luminon' [?] emp. pro præd. torchez 2s. 6d. [*Note*, A *lee* or *lea* contains 80 yards.] *c* **1440** *Promp. Parv.* 291/2 Lee of threde, *ligatura.* **1469** *Ripon Ch. Acts* 139, x les de coverlett yarn. **1615** MARKHAM *Eng. Housew.* II. v. (1668) 137 Some spinning by the pound, some by the lay, and some by the day. **1633** *N. Riding Rec.* (1885) III. 348 A Huby spinster presented for stealing 10 leas of harden yarn. **1696** PHILLIPS (ed. 5) s.v., Every Lea of Yarn at Kidderminster shall contain 200 Threds reel'd on a Reel four yards about. *a* **1704** LOCKE in Fox Bourne *Life* (1876) II. xiii. 368 Twelve lays of good sound merchandable..linen yarn or thread, each lay containing 200 yards, and the whole 12 lays not weighing above 8 oz. avoirdupois. **1776** *Act 17 Geo. III*, c. 11 §11 Every hank of..yarn shall..contain seven raps or leas, and ..every such rap or lea shall..contain eighty threads. *a* **1825** FORBY *Voc. E. Anglia*, *Lea*, forty threads of hemp-yarn. **1851** *Illustr. Catal. Gt. Exhib.* 198 Line, sliver-roving, and yarn, from 500 leas to 200 leas, from the flax... Piece of cloth, 200 leas warp and 200 leas weft. **1882** J. PATON in *Encycl. Brit.* XIV. 666/2 Throughout the United Kingdom the standard measure of flax yarn is the 'lea', called also in Scotland the 'cut' of 300 yards. **1885** F. H. BOWMAN *Struct. Wool* Gloss., *Lea*, the seventh part of a hank; in worsted 80 yards; in cotton and silk 120 yards.

b. (See quot.)

1875 KNIGHT *Dict. Mech.*, *Lay*, a quantity of wool or other fiber in a willow or carding-machine.

lea, ley, lay (liː, leɪ), *a.* Forms: 4, 6 leye, 4-7 laye, 8 lee; 5- lay, 6- ley, 7- lea. [? repr. OE. **lǽȝe* (implied in the comb. *lǽȝhrycg* LEA-RIG, where *lǽȝ-* cannot well stand for *léah* LEA *sb.*[1]), f. the root of LAY, LIE *vbs.* (cf. '*to lie* fallow'); the

formal equivalent (:—OTeut. *lǣgio-) is found with different meaning in OHG. *aba-lâgi* weary, exhausted, MHG. *lǣge*, early and dial. mod.G. *läg* low, flat, of poor quality, ON. *gras-lǣgr* lying in the grass; cf. LOW *a.*] Of land: Fallow, unploughed.

c **1330** R. BRUNNE *Chron. Wace* (Rolls) 6983 Al þe lond, leye hit lay. **1398** TREVISA *Barth. De P.R.* XIV. xlviii. (1495) 484 Euery suche felde other lyeth laye.. other beryth trees or is able to pasture. *c* **1400** *Gamelyn* 161 Thi lond that lith leie wel it shal be sowe. **1591** SYLVESTER *Du Bartas* I. vii. 392 A Field, left lay for some few years, will yeeld The richer crop when it again is till'd. **1675** EVELYN *Terra* (1676) 63 In our worn-out and exhausted lay-fields. **1788** MARSHALL *Yorks.* II. 340 *To lie ley*, to lie in grass; as lands in a common field. **1853** RAYNBIRD *Suppl. to Rham's Dict. Farm.* 466 This preparation may be made before harvest, and applied to the lea ground in October. **1883** *Contemp. Rev.* Sept. 351 Long night-watches in wet ditches and beside hedges for hares on the lea fields.

fig. *c* **1430** *Hymns Virg.* 70 To reepe myn heruest, whidir mai y winde? Mi londis of vertues liggen al lay. **1585** JAS. I *Ess. Poesie* (Arb.) 39 This subiect seame a barren ground, With quickest spreits left ley. **1612** T. TAYLOR *Comm. Titus* i. 3 Every vision is for an appointed time: let them seeme to lie lea and voide never so long. **1827** SCOTT *Jrnl.* 11 Dec., I saw.. no other receipt than lying lea for a little, while taking a fallow-break to relieve my imagination, which may be esteemed nearly cropped out.

leace, obs. form of LEASE *sb.*³

leach (liːtʃ), *sb.*¹ *Obs.* exc. *arch.* Forms: α. 4-6 leche, 5-7 leech(e, 6 leache, 6- leach. β. 5 lese, lesse, lees(s(e, leshe, lesk, 6 less. [a. OF. *lesche* (F. *lèche*).]

†**1.** A slice (of meat, etc.); a strip. *Obs.*

α. *c* **1420** *Liber Cocorum* (1862) 45 Thre leches of bacun lay þou mot In brothe. *c* **1440** *Anc. Cookery* in *Househ. Ord.* (1790) 435 Cut smal leches of two ynches of length. *c* **1500** *For to Serve Ld.* in *Babees Bk.* (1868) 370 Take of ij leches of the briste, and cowche legge and whyngge and lechis into a faire voyde plater.

β. **14..** *Noble Bk. Cookry* (Napier 1882) 30 Tak the clodde of beef and make lesks of a span longe. *c* **1460** J. RUSSELL *Bk. Nurture* 610 Put it in a dische leese by lees.

2. A dish consisting of sliced meat, eggs, fruits, and spices in jelly or some other coagulating material. Often in adoptions of AF. combinations, denoting particular varieties, e.g. *leche frye* [cf. OF. *lechefroie*, mod.F. *lèchefrite*, dripping-pan], *damask, dugard, lumbard, purple, royal*, etc. *dry leach*: a sort of cake or gingerbread, containing dates, etc. *white leach*: a gelatine of almonds.

α. ? *c* **1390** *Forme of Cury* 36 Leche Lumbard. Take rawe Pork [etc.]. *c* **1420** in *Q. Eliz. Acad.* 90 Leche ffloree... leche dalmayn. *Ibid.* 91 Leche damasque. *Ibid.* 92 Leche maskelyn... Leche rubby. *c* **1440** *Anc. Cookery* in *Househ. Ord.* (1790) 449 And therwith daryolus, and leche-fryes, made of frit and friture. *c* **1460** J. RUSSELL *Bk. Nurture* 516 Cow heelis and Calves fete ar dere y-bouȝt some tide To medille amonge leeches & Ielies. *Ibid.* 708 Quynces bake leche dugard. **1494** FABYAN *Chron.* VII. 587 Leche damask, wᵗ the kynges worde or prouerbe flourysshed. **1530** PALSGR. 238/1 Leche made of flesshe, *gelee*. **1570** in Gutch *Coll. Cur.* II. 8 For vj lb. of almones to him, for drie leche. **1573** BARET *Alv.* L 154 White Leach, *gelatina amygdalorum*. **1602** PLAT *Delightes for Ladies* (1605) §22 This is your Gingerbread vsed at the Court... It is otherwise called drie Leach. **1615** MARKHAM *Eng. Housew.* II. ii. (1668) 96 To make the best Leech take Ising-glass.. then take Almonds. **1750** E. SMITH *Compl. Housew.* (ed. 14) 195 To make white Leach. **1848** H. AINSWORTH *Lanc. Witches* I. ix, I pray you taste this pippin jelly.. or some leach of almonds.

β. *c* **1450** *Two Cookery-bks.* 75 Lese fryes. **1452** in Wood *Hist. Univ. Oxon.* (1792) I. 599 Leshe damask. *c* **1460** J. RUSSELL *Bk. Nurture* 504 Alle maner of leessez ye may forbere.

leach (liːtʃ), *sb.*² Also 7 lech, 7-9 letch, 9 leech. [app. f. LEACH *v.*² (though recorded much earlier than the vb. in the cognate sense); in senses 1-3 prob. short for attributive combs. (LETCH *sb.*¹, ditch or pool, is etymologically identical.)]

1. A perforated vessel or trough used for making lye from wood ashes by pouring water over them. *Obs.* exc. *dial.*

1673 RAY *Journ. Low C.* (1738) I. 172 This powder they mingle with a little slaked lime.. which they put into letches or troughs, and pouring water upon them make the lixivium. **1674-91** —— *S. & E.C. Words* 104 A Letch or Lech. **1840** SPURDENS *Suppl. to Forby, Leach.* **1894** *Harper's Mag.* Apr. 810 Her elbow struck the leach and knocked it into the soap-kettle.

2. *Tanning.* (See quot. 1886.)

1777 MACBRIDE in *Phil. Trans.* LXVIII. 114 The ooze is made by macerating the bark in common water, in a particular set of holes or pits, which.. are termed letches. **1852** MORFIT *Tanning & Currying* (1853) 22 The application of heat to bark in leaches. **1875** KNIGHT *Dict. Mech.* s.v., In the bark-leach, the bark is contained between two perforated horizontal partitions in the leach. **1886** W. A. HARRIS *Techn. Dict. Fire Insur.*, *Leaches*, in tanneries, are the pits in which the tan-liquors are mixed, as distinguished from the tan-pits, in which the hides are steeped.

3. *Salt-making.* (See quot.)

1886 *Cheshire Gloss.*, *Leach*, salt-making term; the brine (fully saturated) which drains from the salt, or is left in the pan when the salt is drawn out. Formerly called 'leach-brine'.

4. a. The action of 'leaching'. **b.** (See quot.)

1828-32 WEBSTER, *Leach*, a quantity of wood-ashes, through which water passes, and thus imbibes the alkali.

5. *attrib.*: †**leach-brine** = sense 3; **leach-hole** (see quot. and cf. sense 4 of the vb.); **leach-tank**, a tank for leaching metallic ores; †**leach-trough** (see quot.).

1669 *Phil. Trans.* IV. 1065 *Leach-brine, which is such Brine, as runs from their salt, when 'tis taken up before it hardens. *c* **1682** J. COLLINS *Salt & Fishery* 56 Cheshire Salt-Workers call the Liquor that drops from their Salt, being put into Wicker-baskets, Leach Brine. **1857** THOREAU *Maine W.* xvi. (1863) 313 A '*leach hole' through which the pond leaked out. **1877** RAYMOND *Statist. Mines & Mining* 403 From this line of wooden tubing the bath is to be conducted to each *leach-tank by an India-rubber tube. **1686** PLOT *Staffordsh.* 94 Through these being set in the *Leach-troughs the salt drains it self dry in 3 hours time.

leach (liːtʃ), *v.*¹ *Obs.* exc. *arch.* Forms: α. 4-5 leche, 5 lecche, leeche, leyche, 7- leach. β. 5 lese, lessh, 6 les(c)he. [f. LEACH *sb.*¹] *trans.* To cut (meat, etc.) in slices; to slice.

α. ? *a* **1400** *Morte Arth.* 188 Seyne bowes of wylde bores with þe braune lechyde, Bernakes and botures in baterde dysches. *c* **1420** *Liber Cocorum* (1862) 37 Whenne hit is sothun, thou schalt hit leche. *c* **1430** *Two Cookery-bks.* 35 Take gratyd Brede, & make it so chargeaunt þat it wol be y-lechyd. *c* **1450** *Ibid.* 71 Leche hit [brawn] faire, but not to thyn. **1486** *Bk. St. Albans* F vij b, Brawne leechyd. **1688** R. HOLME *Armoury* III. 78 Terms for Carving.. Leach that Brawn. **1864** H. AINSWORTH *Tower Lond.* 412 In the old terms of his art, he leached the brawn.

β. **14..** *Noble Bk. Cookry* (Napier 1882) 27 Then leshe it in dyshes. *c* **1440** *Douce MS.* 55 lf. 29 Mold it all to gedrys with thyn honde till it be so stiffe that it will be lesshed. **1513** *Bk. Keruynge* in *Babees Bk.* 265 Termes of a Keruer. Lesche yᵗ brawne.

Hence †**leached** *ppl. a.*, sliced, fried in slices. †'**leaching** *vbl. sb.*¹, in quot. *concr.*, a slice; also *attrib.*, as *leaching-knife*.

1416-17 *Durham Acc. Rolls* (Surtees) 613, 2 ladell de auricalco et 1 lechyngknyfe. *c* **1430** *Two Cookery-bks.* 15 Kytte hem [cakys] y lyke lechyngys. **1446** *Wills & Inv. N.C.* (Surtees 1835) I. 101, iij lesyng knyues. **1461-83** *Househ. Ord.* (1790) 38 At supper leychid beefe & mutton roste. **1488** *Will of Eliz. Brown* (Somerset Ho.), Dressing knyfys, lecchyng knyfys, choppyng knyfys.

leach (liːtʃ), *v.*² Also leech, latch, letch. [Prob. repr. OE. *leccan* to water (tr. L. *rigare*):—WGer. type *lakkjan:—*lakjan, f. *lak-: see LAKE *sb.*³ There appears to be no trace of the vb. between OE. and the examples of the technological use in the 18th c., exc. the doubtful instance in Shaks. and one other (see 1, 2 below). The form *letch* is normal; the variant *leach* is phonologically obscure.]

†**1.** *trans.* To water, wet. *Obs. rare.*

(In the Shaks. quot. the vb. may possibly belong to LATCH *v.*², in the transferred sense 'to fasten'.)

c **888** K. ÆLFRED *Boeth.* xxxix. §13 (Sedgefield) 136/17 Hæȝlas & snawas & se oftræda ren leccað þa eorðan on wintra. **1590** SHAKS. *Mids. N.* III. ii. 36 (1st Qo.) But hast thou yet latcht [*2nd Qo.* & *1st Fol.* lacht] the Athenians eyes, With the loue iuice, as I did bid thee doe?

†**2.** *intr.* To soften, melt. *Obs.*

1614 H. GREENWOOD *Jayle Deliv.* 470 Merchants wax must leach in a candle, before it can take a stampe or impression.

3. a. *trans.* To cause (a liquid) to percolate through some material.

1796 MORSE *Amer. Geog.* I. 439 Cider.. is first separated from the filth and dregs, either by leaching through sand, or straining it through flannel cloths. **1828-32** WEBSTER, *Leach*, to wash, as ashes, by percolation, or causing water to pass through them, and thus to separate from them the alkali. The water thus charged with alkali is called *lye*.

b. To subject (bark, ores, etc.) to the action of percolating water, etc., with the view of removing the soluble constituents; to lixiviate. Also used with reference to the action of water, esp. rain, on soil; also *absol.*

1839 J. BUEL *Farmer's Compan.* ix. 74 The wind and the sun dissipate its virtues, and rains leach it and waste its fertilizing powers. **1877** RAYMOND *Statist. Mines & Mining* 403 Concentrated liquid obtained by leaching the ores in this process, at Widnes, in England. **1882** PATON in *Encycl. Brit.* XIV. 382/2 The tanning materials so prepared are next leached, latched, or infused for preparing the strongest tanning solutions. **1882** *Rep. to Ho. Repr. Prec. Met. U.S.* 112 Chlorination works are needed for leaching the sulphurets. **1885** *Harper's Mag.* Jan. 276/1 Most tanners.. grind [bark] in a bark-mill, 'leaching' the bark to obtain the liquor. **1917** *Mining Mag.* XVII. 75/2 The rocks.. are altered and leached of iron. **1951** W. P. KELLEY *Alkali Soils* vii. 146 It should not be inferred that.. all the farmer needs to do in order to reclaim any alkali soil is to drain and leach with water. **1954** W. D. THORNBURY *Princ. Geomorphol.* xvi. 420 Kansan and Nebraskan tills are leached to much greater depths. **1971** D. HILLEL *Soil & Water* v. 124 They suggested that leaching soils at a water content below saturation (e.g., under sprinkling irrigation or rainfall or under intermittent irrigation) could produce more efficient leaching and thereby reduce the amount of water required.

c. *intr.* To pass through by percolation (Webster, 1864); to percolate through and pass *out*. Also *intr.* for *refl.* Of ashes: To be subject to the action of percolating water.

1883 MRS. ROLLINS *New Eng. Bygones* 68 The ashes of those ancient wood-fires.. went to leach in the spring for the making of family soap. **1931** *Forestry* V. 143 In order to avoid any possible effect of some of the preservative leaching out into the medium, some workers raise the blocks above the surface of the medium. **1961** J. N. ANDERSON *Appl. Dental Materials* (ed. 2) xxiii. 240 Dentures should be kept in water after curing in order to allow as much residual monomer as possible to leach out. **1968** *Listener* 21 Mar. 376/2 Cacodylic acid is alleged to disappear very quickly, to leech down through the soil. **1974** A. HUXLEY *Plant & Planet* xviii. 198 Many [viruses] make use of materials which leach through the [leaf] skin.

4. *trans.* To take *away*, *out*, by percolation. Also *fig.*

1860 MAURY *Phys. Geog. Sea* i. 16 The tides.. leached out of the disintegrated materials.. every soluble ingredient known in nature. **1877** N. S. SHALER *App. to J. A. Allen's Amer. Bison* 458 Whenever the rocks lie above the line of the drainage, these salts have been leached away. **1884** *Engineer* 12 Sept., After leaching out the chloride, the tails may be treated. **1900** *Nature* 19 July 277/2 A moist climate would tend to leach the calcareous matter from the rock. **1964** *Listener* 13 Aug. 225/2 It [*sc.* a modern office block] has neither virtues nor vices; it just sits there like a graceless woman, leeching away a bit more of the city's vitality. **1971** *Nature* 13 Aug. 446/3 Insecticides are leached from soil by water. **1973** *Ibid.* 20 July 165/1 Particulate material was collected on fibreglass filters from which lead was leached with hot 70% nitric acid.

Hence **leached** *ppl. a.* (*a*) that has been subjected to the action of percolating liquid; (*b*) (also *leached-out*) that has been removed by percolating liquid.

1837 *Cultivator* Aug. 93/2 (*heading*) Leached ashes as manure. *Ibid.*, Leached or drawn ashes possess a highly beneficial effect, particularly when applied to lands deficient in calcareous matters. **1862** MARSH *Eng. Lang.* 40 A melancholy heap of leached ashes, marrowless bones, and empty oyster-shells. **1895** *Offic. Mining Rep. N. Zealand* 10 Separating the cyanide solutions from the leached pulp. **1926** A. LOCKE (*title*) Leached outcrops as guides to copper ore. **1961** *Listener* 12 Oct. 559/1 So white are some leached layers [in a podsol] that they have entered archaeological literature as 'layers of ash'. **1963** D. W. & E. E. HUMPHRIES tr. *Termier's Erosion & Sedimentation* vi. 139 The lowest part is a zone of enrichment to which the leached-out soluble salts from the upper part of the soil are carried. **1972** J. G. CRUIKSHANK *Soil Geogr.* ii. 69 Part of the leached compounds are deposited in the lower zone of the soil, but some will be lost from the system through soil drainage and seepage.

leachable ('liːtʃəb(ə)l), *a.* [f. LEACH *v.*² + -ABLE.] Capable of being leached out.

1944 *Experiment Station Rec.* Apr. 450 Potassium could be changed biologically from a leachable to a nonleachable state. **1955** *Sci. News Let.* 27 Aug. 132/2 Experiments indicate that an average of only about 25% of the thorium and uranium in granite rock is 'leachable'. **1972** *Ann. Rep. Freshwater Biol. Assoc.* XL. 40 This contrasts with dead leaves from which leachable substances are said to disappear in about a week. **1972** J. G. CRUIKSHANK *Soil Geogr.* ii. 46 Maximum mobilisation of leachable substances is related to both the volume and composition of the organic leachate. **1973** *Nature* 13 Apr. 452/2 The concentrations reported include the contribution of acid leachable mercury associated with particulate material.

leachate ('liːtʃeɪt). [f. LEACH *v.*² + *-ate*, after *filtrate, precipitate*, etc.] (A quantity of) liquid that has percolated through a solid and leached out some of the constituents.

1952 *Sci. Agric.* XXXII. 606 The pH of leachates from decomposing leaves rises as decomposition progresses. **1971** *Nature* 17 Sept. 211/1 The material was then filtered, washed several times and the leachates were combined. Both the residual material and the leachate were analysed for lead. **1972** [see LEACHABLE *a.*].

leache, leacher, -y, obs. ff. LEECH, LECHER, -Y.

leaching, *vbl. sb.*¹: see LEACH *v.*¹

leaching ('liːtʃɪŋ), *vbl. sb.*² [f. LEACH *v.*² + -ING¹.] The action of the vb. LEACH². Also *leaching out*.

a **900** *Kent. Gloss.* in Wr.-Wülcker 56/16 *Et inrigatio*, and leccinc. **1877** RAYMOND *Statist. Mines & Mining* 323 The percentage of copper.. renders the ore unfit for amalgamation without previous leaching. **1906** E. W. HILGARD *Soils* ii. 24 A heavy depletion of the land by the leaching-out of this important plant food. **1938** R. W. LAWSON tr. *Hevesy & Paneth's Man. Radioactivity* (ed. 2) xxv. 265 In some minerals the ratio of lead to uranium has been altered by leaching-out processes in the course of the long periods of time involved. **1943** MILLAR & TURK *Fund. Soil Sci.* xv. 377 The leaching out of the alkali tends to leave the soil in an even worse physical condition. **1966** G. H. DURY *Ess. Geomorphol.* 56 It is the simple process of leaching out of contained salt, by groundwater, which rapidly reduces the shearing strength of the deposits.

attrib. **1850** H. CUTTS *Address Windsor Co. Agric. Soc.* (U.S.) 12 In China.. every thing is subjected to the leaching process, and in the form of liquid decoctions only, applied to the land. **1877** RAYMOND *Statist. Mines & Mining* 399 The bath may be brought in contact with the ore.. by percolation in leaching-tanks. **1884** *Harper's Mag.* Apr. 761/1 This subsoil water, after acting as a leeching agent of a surface, filled.. with.. refuse, is scarcely less foul than sewage.

leachy ('liːtʃɪ), *a.* ? *U.S.* [f. LEACH *v.*² + -Y.] Of soils: Of a nature to let water percolate through; not capable of holding water; porous.

1879 L. STOCKBRIDGE *Investig. Rainfall* 4 The whole depth was 36 inches, and it would be called a very 'leachy' soil. **1880** S. W. JOHNSON *How Crops Feed* 177 When a soil is too coarsely porous it is said to be leachy or hungry.

lead (lɛd), *sb.*¹ Forms: 1-2 léad, 3 læd, 3-4 leod(e, 4 *Kentish* lyad, 3-6 led(e, 4-6 leyde, 4-7 leed(e, *Sc.* leid(e, 5-6 ledde, (6 *dial.* lydde), 5-7 lead(e, 4- lead. [OE. *léad* str. neut. = OFris. *lâd*, Du. *lood* lead, MLG. *lôd* (whence Sw. and

Da. *lod*), MHG. *lôt* (mod.G. *lot, loth*) plummet, sounding-lead, also solder; cf. ON. *lauð* fem., doubtfully interpreted as 'draw-plate for wire' (Fritzner).

The OTeut. **laudo*ᵐ:—Pre-Teut. **loudhom* is cogn. with Irish *luaidhe* (:—**loudhiā* fem.).]

I. 1. a. The heaviest of the base metals, of a dull pale bluish-gray colour, fusible at a low temperature, and very useful from its softness and malleability. Chemical symbol Pb. Rarely *pl.* = kinds of lead. †*to lie, be wrapt in lead*: to be buried in a lead coffin. So *to lay, lap in lead*: see LAP *v.*² 3. *Obs.*

*c***900** tr. *Bæda's Hist.* I. Introd. (1890) 26 Swylce hit [*sc.* þis land] is eac berende on wecga orum ares & isernes, leades & seolfres. *c***1205** LAY. 5692 Ofte heo letten grund-hat læd [*c* **1275** leod] gliden heom an heore hæfd. *c* **1290** *S. Eng. Leg.* I. 208/272 Þe feondes welden led and bras. *c* **1300** *Seyn Julian* 171 A chetel he sette ouer þe fier, and fulde it uol of lede. *c* **1330** R. BRUNNE *Chron.* (1810) 229 Þe patriark þe legate liggis in lede. **1340** *Ayenb.* 141 Þe asse of þe melle þet ase bleþeliche berþ bere ase huite, and lyad ase þet corn. *c* **1430** LYDG. in Turner *Dom. Archit.* III. 39 Euery hous couerid was with leede. **1470–85** MALORY *Arthur* v. viii. 174 [He] leyd them in chestys of leed. **1500–20** DUNBAR *Poems* xxvi. 101 The feyndis gaif thame hait leid to laip. *c* **1540** *Pilgr. T.* 24 in *Thynne's Animadv.* (1865) App. i. 77 Houses of office on and other Where-on of leyd lay many a fowther. **1578** *Chr. Prayers* 83 We Earles and Barons were sometime: Now wrapt in lead, are turnd to slime. **1611** SHAKS. *Wint. T.* III. ii. 178 What studied torments (Tyrant) hast for me? .. What flaying? boyling? In Leads, or Oyles? **1753** CHAMBERS *Cycl. Supp.* s.v., Lead and all its products turn into glass by a strong fire. **1855** *Cornwall* 239 The Cornish and Devon leads are very rich in silver. **1871** ROSCOE *Elem. Chem.* 258 Lead does not occur free in nature.

†**b.** After L. use, lead was sometimes called ***black lead*** (= L. *plumbum nigrum*) in contradistinction to ***white lead*** (*plumbum album*), used as a name for tin. *Obs.*

1567 MAPLET *Gr. Forest* 13 There are two sortes of Lead, the one white, and the other black... That other black Lead is found most in Cantabrie. **1678** R. R[USSELL] *Geber* II. I. II. x. 59 The same Delusion they also find in Black Lead or Saturn. **1753** CHAMBERS *Cycl. Supp.* s.v. *Black-lead*, The common lead being the true black lead, so called by way of contradistinction from tin, otherwise called white lead.

c. With allusion to its qualities; e.g. its weight, colour, want of elasticity, low value, etc., in both *lit.* and *fig.* expressions.

a **1300** *Cursor M.* 16454 Þai þe fine gold for-soke, and to þam to þe lede. **1303** R. BRUNNE *Handl. Synne* 11730 Þys Ananyas fyl downe dede As blak as any lede. *c* **1425** WYNTOUN *Cron.* VII. x. 3623 Oure gold wes changyd in to lede. *c* **1440** *York Myst.* xviii. 20 Me thynke myne eyne hevye as leede. **1509** HAWES *Past. Pleas.* XVII. (Percy Soc.) 76 Dyane derlyng pale as any leade. **1551** ROBINSON tr. *More's Utop.* I. (1895) 102 They haue wrested and wriede hys [Christ's] doctryne, and lyke a rule of leade haue applyed yt to mennys maners. **1605** SHAKS. *Macb.* II. i. 6 A heauie Summons lyes like Lead vpon me. **1606** —— *Ant. & Cl.* III. xi. 72 Loue I am full of Lead. **1646** JENKYN *Remora* 9 Shall our Reformation have an heel of lead? **1656** BP. HALL *Breathings Devout Soul* (1851) 200 Pull this lead out of my bosom. **1725** YOUNG *Love Fame* II. 158 How just his grief? one carrys in his head A less proportion of the father's lead. **1798** COLERIDGE *Anc. Mar.* VII. viii, The ship went down like lead. **1861** J. EDMOND *Children's Church at Home* x. 157 He might have left everything the colour of lead. **1927** *Amer. Speech* Mar. 278/1 *Shake out the lead*, start action. **1942** BERREY & VAN DEN BARK *Amer. Thes. Slang* §578/26 Get the lead out of your pants, to play allegro. **1948** F. BROWN *Dead Ringer* i. 15 Quit asking .. questions and get the lead out. **1961** *Lebende Sprachen* VI. 101/1 He's as lazy as they come, he's got lead in his pants, shoes. **1964** WODEHOUSE *Frozen Assets* vi. 115 She knows I'm in imminent danger of dying of malnutrition unless she takes the lead out of her pants and gets a move on with that picture. **1967** —— *Company for Henry* xii. 207 Those wedding bells aren't going to ring if you don't take the lead out of your pants and get a move on.

d. With defining prefix, as *cast-, milled-, pig-, pot-, sheet-lead*, for which see the first element.

2. ***red lead***: a red oxide of lead obtained from litharge by exposing it to hot air, much used as a pigment; = MINIUM. ***white lead*** (or simply *lead*): a mixture of lead carbonate and hydrated lead oxide, much used as a pigment; = CERUSE. ***blue lead***: see BLUE 12 c.

c **1450** *ME. Med. Bk.* (Heinrich) 203 Tak .. iij quarter of whyt led Tak a quart of oile and red led. **1658** W. SANDERSON *Graphice* 54 Most excellent pure Virgin Colours are Ceruse and White leade. **1686** *Phil. Trans.* XVI. 27 Red-lead, a colour unknown to the Antients. **1716** SWIFT *Progr. Beauty* Wks. 1755 III. II. 165 White lead was sent us to repair .. A lady's face, and China ware. **1753** CHAMBERS *Cycl. Supp.* s.v., The common calx of lead, red lead. **1827** R. NESBIT in J. M. Mitchell *Mem.* iii. (1858) 80 It [the idol] was painted with red lead. **1844** FOWNES *Chem.* 294 Red oxide; red lead. *Ibid.* 295 Carbonate of lead; white lead.

3. Short for BLACK LEAD *sb.*, graphite, or plumbago. Only with reference to its use as a material for pencils. Hence, a small stick of graphite for filling an 'ever-pointed' pencil. Phr. ***lead in one's pencil***: implying (esp. sexual) vigour in a male.

1816 JANE AUSTEN *Emma* III. iv. 54 When he took out his pencil, there was so little lead that he soon cut it all away. **1840** *Penny Cycl.* XVII. 402/1 Pencils are commonly marked with certain letters to denote the quality of the lead, as H for hard, B for black [etc.].. Most [ever-pointed pencil] cases are made with a reservoir at the top, in which a supply of five or six leads may be carried. **1881** W. M. WILLIAMS in *Knowledge* No. 4. 67 A thin stick .. like vermicelli, or the 'leads' of ever-pointed pencils. **1922** S. LEWIS *Babbitt* i. 9 A silver pencil (always lacking a supply of new leads). **1941** BAKER *Dict. Austral. Slang* 43 (*This will*) *put some lead in your pencil*, this (esp. a drink of beer or spirits) will make you feel fighting fit. **1946** P. LARKIN *Jill* 190 'Well, ere's more lead in yer pencil.' He finished off his half-pint. **1969** [see CURL *v.*¹ 1 c]. **1970** *Kay's Catal.* (Worcester) Autumn–Winter 947/3 Pencil both propels and retracts, contains twelve 3 inch leads. **1970** A. DRAPER *Swansong for Rare Bird* vii. 59 She came over with two glasses. 'If that doesn't put some lead in your pencil, Auk, I don't know what will.' **1972** D. LEES *Zodiac* 107 The couscous is supposed to put lead in your pencil but with Daria I needed neither a talking point nor an aphrodisiac.

4. a. The metal regarded as fashioned into some object, e.g. †a seal, †the plummet of a plumb-line, †a pipe or conduit, a leaden coffin, a bullet, the leaden part of anything. (*cold*) *lead*, bullets.

1340 *Ayenb.* 150 He deþ al .. to þe line and to þe reule and to þe leade and to þe leuele. *Ibid.* 151 Efterward he proueþ ofte his work mid lead. *c* **1380** WYCLIF *Sel. Wks.* III. 309 Men of þis world dreden more þe popis leed. **1596** SHAKS. *1 Hen. IV*, v. iii. 35 Heauen keepe Lead out of mee. **1598** SYLVESTER *Du Bartas* II. i. I. *Eden* 58 Let not me .. be like the Lead Which to some City from some Conduit-head Brings wholsome Water. *c* **1650** *Balow* iv. in *Laneham's Let.* (1871) Pref. 172 The iudge of heavin and hell By some predestined deadlie lead, .. hath struke him dead. **1771** BURKE *Corr.* (1844) I. 330 My passions are not to be roused .. by those who lie in their cold lead. **1809** T. G. FESSENDEN *Pills Poetical* 32 Thus our sporting democrats, .. When they can't reason with a Fed, In logick substitute cold lead. **1837** W. H. WHARTON *Let.* in *Ann. Rep. Amer. Hist. Assoc. 1907* (1908) II. 190 We would give Mexico nothing but lead. **1884** *Law Times Rep.* LI. 161/2 The attachments to buildings were made .. by a bolt screwed into the lead of the ridge. **1887** *Times* (weekly ed.) 23 Dec. 6/1 If you don't stand loyal .. you will get the lead. **1891** M. E. RYAN *Told in Hills* 332 [The message] belongs to the command, and I may get a dose of cold lead before I could deliver it. **1918** C. SANDBURG *Cornhuskers* 50 Three riders emptied lead into him. **1964** F. O'ROURKE *Mule for Marquesa* 146 Get 'em up or we'll pump you full of lead!

†**b.** A plate of lead. *Obs.*

1523 FITZHERB. *Husb.* §122 Layde vpon .. a thynne sclate or leed.

5. a. A large pot, cauldron, or kettle; a large open vessel used in brewing and various other operations. (Originally, one made of lead, but early used without reference to the material.) Now only *dial.* **b.** *dial.* A leaden milk-pan.

a. *a* **1100** *Gerefa* in *Anglia* (1886) IX. 264 Hwer, lead, cytel, etc. *c* **1250** *Death* 242 in *O.E. Misc.* 182 Also beoð his eȝe-puttes ase a bruþen led. *c* **1300** *Havelok* 924 Y shal .. make the broys in the led. **13..** in *Archiv Stud. neu. Spr.* LXXIX. 449/62 A lede of bras then did he bring with pik fullfilled. **1370–80** *XI Pains Hell* 37 in *O.E. Misc.* App. iii. 224 Þer weore þei turmented in þo ledes. **1382** WYCLIF *1 Sam.* ii. 14 He putte it [the fleshhook] into the leede or into the cawdroun. *c* **1386** CHAUCER *Prol.* 202 His eyen stepe, and rollinge in his heed, That stemed as a forneys of a leed. **1428** *Surtees Misc.* (1888) 6 Yt suld hafe brynt oute his lede bothom. *c* **1430** *Two Cookery-bks.* 39 Caste hym to seþe with þin grete Fleysshe, in lede oþer in Cauderoun. **1504** *Bury Wills* (Camden) 101, I will that they shall haue all brewyng ledys. **1552** LYNDESAY *Monarche* 5103 Sum, brynt; sum, soddin in to leiddis. **1575** *Gamm. Gurton* IV. ii, Haue you not .. behind your furnace or leade, A hole where a crafty knaue may crepe in for neade? **1639** T. DE GRAY *Compl. Horsem.* 137 Put all these into a lead or chalderon. **1869** *Lonsdale Gloss.*, *Leäd*, a vat for dyeing.

b. **1750** W. ELLIS *Mod. Husbandm.* III. 129 To improve Cream. To do this, take a Pint or more of Stroakings, .. and divide it into several Pans, or Leads, or Kivers. **1813** VANCOUVER *Agric. Devon* 232 Dairy utensils, consisting of leads, kettles, pans .. &c. **1895** 'ROSEMARY' *Under the Chilterns* ii. 69 Rose always scoured the great 'leads' .. and left no half-cleaned corners to taint the milk.

6. a. A 'bob' or lump of lead suspended by a string to ascertain the depth of water; a sounding-lead. Phrases, ***to cast, heave the lead***. ***to arm the lead***: to fill the hollow in the lead with tallow in order to discover the nature of the bottom by the substances adhering (Smyth *Sailor's Word-bk.* 1867 s.v. *Arm*). †Also, the leaden sinker of a net.

c **1440** *York Myst.* ix. 199, I sall caste leede and loke þe space. *c* **1485** *Digby Myst.* (1882) III. 1440 Cast a led, & In vs gyde. **1597** MONTGOMERIE *Cherrie & Slae* 1187 Their leid ay .. Micht warn them. **1613** J. DENNYS *Secrets of Angling* I. xix, Then on that Linke hang Leads of euen waight. **1626** CAPT. SMITH *Accid. Yng. Sea-men* 29 Heaue the lead. **1628** DIGBY *Voy. Medit.* (1868) 13, I sent my shalloppes out with leades to sound the depth. **1657** TRAPP *Comm. Ps.* xxv. 1 The best heart is lumpish, and naturally beareth downward, as the poise of a clock, as the lead of a net. **1769** FALCONER *Dict. Marine* (1780) M m 4 Sounding with the hand-lead .. is called heaving the lead by seamen. **1836** MARRYAT *Midsh. Easy* xxx, A man .. lowering down the lead, sounded in seven fathoms. **1840** —— *Poor Jack* xxxv, We ran through the Swin by the lead. **1860** *Merc. Marine Mag.* VII. 248 The lead used .. was the ordinary hand-lead of 9 lbs. instead of the deep sea-lead of 28 to 32 lbs.

b. Phr. ***to swing the lead***: to idle, to shirk; to malinger. *slang.* Hence in similar phrs. and in *Comb.*, as **lead-swing** *sb.* and *v. intr.*, **-swinger**, **-swinging** *vbl. sb.* and *ppl. a.*

1917 *To-Day* 6 Jan. 243/3 It is evident that he had 'swung the lead' (using Army phrase) until he got his discharge. **1918** B. K. ADAMS *Let.* 25 Jan. in *Amer. Spirit* 71 Lead-swingers are those that stall along, doing as little as they possibly can, hoping the war will be over before they finish. **1922** C. E. MONTAGUE *Disenchantment* iv. 56 Then grey hairs should be a lot of use to you .. when you want to get swinging the lead. **1927** A. BROSNAN *At Number 15* I. 30 'If they wanted a three-man job done they had to put forty on to it to make sure it was done.' 'And so they did. That's organisation, that is. Of course, there was some lead-swingers.' **1927** *Daily Express* 2 Mar. 3/4 He said he .. had been 'swinging the lead' for the purpose of getting a permanent pension. **1930** S. BECKETT *Whoroscope* 1 The vile old Copernican lead-swinging son of a sutler! **1939** R. CAMPBELL *Flowering Rifle* II. 60 It was not we who lead-swung to the Pities, When half the loveliest of our ancient cities Were in the clouds rebuilt. **1940** J. B. PRIESTLEY *Postscripts* 70 A wary .. old soldier, a lead-swinger, a dodger of the column. **1952** M. ALLINGHAM *Tiger in Smoke* iv. 77 He went sick... It was so hopeless, so damned silly and forlorn as a lead-swing that in the end he got away with it. **1957** A. GRIMBLE *Return to Islands* ii. 32 Their number was not without its natural quota of cheerful leadswingers. **1968** *Manch. Guardian Weekly* 12 Sept. 9 Mr. Crossman .. insisted that 'lead swinging' among the unemployed was confined to a very small minority. **1969** *Daily Tel.* 8 Jan. 26/1 Overall absenteeism in the coal-fields is running slightly higher than last year... Out of this total, 4·66 per cent. is classified as voluntary absenteeism ('lead-swinging'). **1972** *Daily Colonist* (Victoria, B.C.) 12 Feb. 4/1 The mayor of Victoria accuses the four Greater Victoria members of the legislature of lead-swinging. **1973** *Daily Tel.* 29 Aug. 6/3 'It would soon put a stop to lead-swingers who take a few days off to paint the house or watch cricket,' the doctor added.

7. *pl.* **a.** The sheets or strips of lead used to cover a roof; often *collect.* for a lead flat, a lead roof, †occas. construed as sing. **b.** The lead frames of the panes in lattice or stained glass windows.

a. **1578–9** in Willis & Clark *Cambridge* (1886) I. 538 Mending the leddes over the librarie chambers. **1588** BP. ANDREWES *Serm. Spittle* (1641) 5 He looketh downe on his brethren, as if he stood on the top of a Leads. **1625** BACON *Ess., Building* (Arb.) 550 A Goodly Leads upon the Top, railed with Statua's interposed. *a* **1635** CORBET *Iter Bor.* (1647) 133 Gardens cover howses there like leades. **1726** LEONI *Alberti's Archit.* I. 78 Leads or Terrasses from whence the Soldiers may be molested with stones or darts. **1760** C. JOHNSTON *Chrysal* (1822) I. 238 A cat .. whom she used to meet in the evenings, upon the leads of the house. **1824** SCOTT *Redgauntlet* ch. xiii, Trumbull .. clambered out upon the leads. **1873** DIXON *Two Queens* II. VII. vi. 42 A blare of trumpets from the leads told every one .. that [etc.].

b. **1705** HEARNE *Collect.* 8 Nov. (O.H.S.) I. 68 After the Examination of the Books, & a slight view of the Leads. **1885** F. MILLER *Glass Painting* vii. 69 It gives the effect of weakness to see large pieces of glass leaded with narrow leads.

8. *Printing.* A thin strip of type-metal or brass, less than type-high, of varying thickness and length, used in type-composition to separate lines; before 1800 known as *space-line*.

1808 STOWER *Printer's Gram.* 515 Leads, 4 to a pica, per pound, 1*s.* 10*d.* **1824** J. JOHNSON *Typogr.* II. 125 All measures are made to pica m's, and all leads are cast to m's of the above body. **1848** CRAIG, *Leads* or *space lines.* **1889** *Harper's Mag.* Apr. 819/1 A newspaper which .. avoids double leads .. and all forms of typographical hysteria.

9. In the knitting-machine: The lead or tin socket holding the shanks of one or more needles.

1839 URE *Dict. Arts* 650 In order to fit the needles for the frame, they are now cast into the tin sockets, or leads as they are called by the workmen.

II. *attrib.* and *Comb.*

10. *simple attrib.* passing into *adj.* Made (wholly or partly) of lead, consisting of lead.

1379 *Mem. Ripon* (Surtees) III. 103 Et de j Ledepan. **1422** *Surtees Misc.* (Surtees) 16 Yat the lede pype and the shelfs be the wyfe's of Symond of Stele. **1811** SCOTT *Biog. Notices* Prose Wks. (1870) IV. 273 The copies had hung on the bookseller's hands as heavy as a pile of lead bullets. **1825** J. NICHOLSON *Operat. Mechanic* 362 Lead pipes are sometimes cast in an iron mould, made in two halves. **1868** *Rep. to Govt. U.S. Munitions of War* App. 286 These [Gatling] guns discharge half-pound solid lead-balls.

11. General comb.: **a.** attributive, as ***lead-colour, -glaze, -grain,*** †***-groove, -mine, -miner, -ore, -slag, -vein.***

1658 ROWLAND tr. *Mouffet's Theat. Ins.* 909 Poysoned Honey .. staines the honey-comb with a Kinde of *Lead-colour. **1823** P. NICHOLSON *Pract. Build.* 416 Of the Compound Colours, Lead colour is of indigo and white. **1842** PARNELL *Chem. Anal.* (1845) 276 A porcelain bason having a *lead glaze. *a* **1728** WOODWARD *Nat. Hist. Fossils* I. (1729) I. 207 *Lead-Grains so pure as nearly to approach the Fineness of Virgin Lead. *c* **1750** J. NELSON *Jrnl.* (1836) 84 A great company of men that worked in the *lead-groves. **1653** MANLOVE (*title*) The Liberties and Cvstomes of the *Lead-Mines. **1665** BOYLE *Occas. Refl.* I. iii. *heading*, Wandring .. among cover'd Lead-mines that he knew not of. **1761** WESLEY *Jrnl.* 9 June, Most of the men are *lead-miners. **1653** MANLOVE *Lead-Mines* 4 If any .. there *Lead-oar may get. **1661–9** BOYLE *Physiol. Ess.* II. i. 52 So unlike common Lead-Oar, that the workmen upon that account are pleased to call it Steel-Oar. **1854** RONALDS & RICHARDSON *Chem. Technol.* (ed. 2) I. 108 More adapted for smelting some lead-ores than the others. **1864** WATTS *Dict. Chem.* II. 523 Analyses of *Lead-slags from Blast Furnace. *a* **1728** WOODWARD *Nat. Hist. Fossils* I. (1729) I. 159 Out of a *Lead-Vein .. in Wales. **1874** RAYMOND *Statist. Mines & Mining* 313 Lead-veins, rich in silver.

b. objective, as ***lead-burner, -carving, -smelting*** (also *attrib.*); obj. genitive, as ***lead-free*** adj.

1894 *Daily News* 6 Sept. 6/7 M—— W——, *lead burner, brother of the deceased, said [etc.]. **1748** LADY LUXBOROUGH *Let. to Shenstone* Easter Sunday, The present fashion at London, is all *lead-carving. **1946** **lead-free* [see *lead glass*, sense 12]. **1960** *Farmer & Stockbreeder* 16 Feb. Suppl. 36/2 Sow Feeder .. painted [with] one coat lead-free

paint. **1970** *Guardian* 13 Apr. 13/4 Lead-free petrol. **1973** *Country Life* 29 Mar. 854/1 Modifications were also made to the engine to enable it to run on lead-free fuels. **1877** RAYMOND *Statist. Mines & Mining* p. viii, *Lead-smelting blast-furnaces. *Ibid.* 296 Lead-smelting ores can be produced.

c. instrumental, as ***lead-covered, -lapped, -lined, -ruled, -sheathed*** adjs.

1891 KIPLING *Light that Failed* xiii. 253 A hall at the foot of some *lead-covered stairs. **1908** *Westm. Gaz.* 22 Apr. 8/3 Over twenty miles of lead-covered cables have been laid in the grounds. **1830** SCOTT *Doom Devorgoil* I. i, The dry bones of *lead-lapp'd ancestors. **1828** J. M. SPEARMAN *Brit. Gunner* (ed. 2) 120 Cartridges..packed in *Lead-lined Barrels and Cases. **1895** E. A. PARKES *Health* 25 Lead-lined cisterns are, on the whole, better avoided. **1871** R. ELLIS tr. *Catullus* xxii. 8 The parchment-case *Lead-ruled. **1691** T. H[ALE] *Acc. New Invent.* 8 *Lead-sheathed Ships. **1948** G. V. GALWEY *Lift & Drop* vi. 137 The leads to the switchgear were buried. They were lead-sheathed.

d. parasynthetic, as ***lead-coloured, -lidded*** adjs. **e.** similative, esp. with adjs. of colour, as ***lead-blue, -brown, -grey; lead-like*** adj. and *adv.*

1882-4 *Yarrell's Brit. Birds* (ed. 4) III. 505 Legs and toes pale blue, becoming *lead-blue a few days after death. **1897** MARY KINGSLEY *W. Africa* 90 A slope of smooth and *lead-brown slime. **1611** COTGR., *Plombasse*,..*lead coloured. **1825** J. NEAL *Bro. Jonathan* III. 378 Spanish brown, or lead coloured roofs. **1837** GOSSE in *Life* (1890) 107 The insects were..of a *lead-grey colour. **1856** BOKER *Calaynos* III. ii, Robs the *lead-lidded god of many an hour. **1842** TENNYSON *St. Sim. Styl.* 25 Those *lead-like tons of sin. **1816** BYRON *Siege Cor.* xiii, The mail weighed lead-like on his breast.

12. a. Special combs.: **lead accumulator**, a lead-acid cell or battery; **lead-acid** *a.*, applied to a secondary cell or battery in which the anode is a plate or grid of lead (or lead alloy) coated with lead dioxide, the cathode is a similar plate coated with spongy lead, and both are immersed in dilute sulphuric acid; **lead-arming**, the tallow used for 'arming' a lead (see 6); **lead-ash, -ashes**, litharge; **lead-back** (*U.S.*), the American dunlin (*Cent. Dict.*); **lead balloon**, a failure, an unsuccessful venture; **lead-bath**, (*a*) the mass of melted lead in a lead-furnace; (*b*) the molten lead with which gold and silver ores are melted before cupellation; **lead bronze**, bronze containing lead, which is used in bearings; **lead bullion**, a mixture of lead and other heavy metals obtained as an intermediate product in the extraction of lead; **lead burning**, the welding of lead; so **lead-burn** *v. trans.*, to weld (pieces of lead); **lead cell**, a lead-acid cell; **lead chamber**, a large reaction vessel made of welded sheet lead which is used in the manufacture of sulphuric acid from sulphur dioxide, air, and steam using oxides of nitrogen as catalysts; so ***lead chamber process***; **lead-comb**, a comb made of lead, used for the purpose of darkening the hair; **lead crystal** [CRYSTAL *sb.* 5] = *lead glass* below; †**lead-dust** (see quot.); **lead-eater** *dial.* (see quot. 1855); **lead-flat** (see quots.); †**lead foam**, the oxide skimmed from the surface of molten lead; **lead-foot** *a.* = *leaden-footed*; **lead glance** [= Du. *loodglans*], galena; **lead glass**, glass containing a substantial proportion of lead oxide; **lead-glaze** *Pottery*, a glaze containing lead oxide; so ***lead-glazed*** adj., ***lead-glazier, lead-glazing*** vbl. sb.; †**lead-house**, ? a plumber's shop; †**lead-lath**, ? a batten for laying a leaden roof upon; **lead-light**, a window in which small panes are fixed in leaden cames, also *attrib.*; **lead-line**, (*a*) a sounding-lead or plumb-line; (*b*) a line loaded with leaden weights, running along the bottom of a net; (*c*) a bluish grey line along the gums at their junction with the teeth, indicating lead-poisoning; (*d*) the narrow strip of lead between two pieces of stained glass; a came; so **lead-line** *v. trans.*, to put the lead-lines in (stained glass work); †**lead-lustre**, lead oxide used as a glaze; †**lead-mall**, ? a leaden mallet or a mallet for beating lead; **lead-man**, (*a*) a dealer in lead; (*b*) a lead-miner; **lead-marcasite**, ? zinc blende (see quot.); **lead-mill**, (*a*) an establishment for producing milled or sheet lead; (*b*) (see quot. 1864); **lead-nail** (mostly *pl.*), a nail used to fasten a sheet of lead on a roof; **lead-ochre** = MASSICOT; **lead-paper**, a test-paper treated with a preparation of lead; hence **lead-papered** *a.*, covered with or containing lead-paper; †**lead-pen**, ? a metallic pencil for ruling lines; **lead-pencil**, a pencil of graphite, often enclosed in cedar or other wood; **lead-plant** (*U.S.*), a shrub (*Amorpha canescens*) found in the west of the Mississippi valley, and believed to indicate the presence of lead ore; **lead-plaster** = DIACHYLON; **lead-poisoning**, poisoning (acute or chronic) by the introduction of lead into the system; **lead-pot**, a pot or crucible for melting lead; †**lead-pound**, a measure of weight; **lead ratio**, the ratio, in a sample of rock, of the quantity of lead (or a lead isotope) to the quantity of its radioactive parents uranium and thorium (or an appropriate isotope of one of these elements), from which the age of the sample may be determined; **lead-reeve** (see quot.); **lead-sinker** (see quot. 1875); **lead-soap** (see quot.); **lead-spar** = ANGLESITE or CERUSSITE; **lead-sugar** (see quot.); **lead-tin** *a.*, containing lead and tin; also *ellipt.*, a lead-tin alloy; **lead-tree**, (*a*) *Bot.*, a West Indian name for the tropical leguminous tree, *Leucæna Glauca*; (*b*) a crystalline deposit of metallic lead or zinc that has been placed in a solution of acetate of lead; **lead-vitriol** = ANGLESITE; †**lead-walling** *Salt-making* (see quot.); **lead-wash** = *lead-water*; **lead-water** (= G. *bleiwasser*), dilute solution of acetate of lead (*Syd. Soc. Lex.* 1888); **lead wool**, lead in a fibrous state, used for caulking pipe joints; **lead-work**, plumber's work and material; work in lead *esp.* glaziers' work; **lead-works** *pl.*, an establishment for smelting lead-ore; **lead-wort**, a herbaceous plant of southern Europe (*Plumbago Europæa*); also, any plant of the genus *Plumbago* or the order *Plumbagineæ*.

1903 *Chem. News* 17 July 34/2 Dr. Lehfeldt's paper on 'The Total and Free Energy of the *Lead Accumulator' was taken as read. **1928** CRENNELL & LEA *Alkaline Accumulators* i. 5 The lead accumulator suffers from certain inherent defects of which the most important are a rather large weight for a given capacity, [etc.]. **1971** G. F. LIPTROT *Mod. Inorg. Chem.* xviii. 242 The voltage supplied by the lead accumulator is just in excess of 2 volts. **1926** W. S. IBBETSON *Accumulator Charging* iii. 26 Fig. 7 illustrates the actions and results of charging and discharging a simple *lead acid cell. **1936** *Motor Manual* (ed. 29) iv. 78 The lead-acid type [of battery] is that most general as its cost is much lower. **1972** *Dry Cells, Batteries & Accumulators* iii. 36 Lead-acid accumulators have a good life in terms of charge/discharge cycles. **1974** *Railway Mag.* Apr. 176/2 The locomotive interior is taken up by no less than 160 lead-acid battery cells, giving a 300V supply. **1882** OGILVIE, **Lead ash*, the slag of lead. **1523-4** in Swayne *Churchw. Acc. Sarum* (1896) 67 For *lede asches iij*d.* **1799** G. SMITH *Laboratory* I. 193 One of lead ashes. **1960** WENTWORTH & FLEXNER *Dict. Amer. Slang* 314/2 **Lead balloon*, a failure; a plan, joke, action or the like that elicits no favorable response; a flop; anything that lays an egg. **1962** L. DEIGHTON *Ipcress File* xxv. 158 With this boy it went over like a lead balloon. **1970** *Sunday Times* 19 Apr. 31/3 *What the Dickens?* was a lead balloon literary quiz wherein the experts showed only how little they knew. **1839** URE *Dict. Arts* 754 The smelter throws a shovelful of small coal or coke cinder upon the *lead bath. **1875** KNIGHT *Dict. Mech.*, *Lead-bath.* **1937** H. N. BASSETT *Bearing Metals & Alloys* viii. 296 Under the general title of *lead bronzes are included..the copper-tin-lead alloys..and the so-called 'tin-free' bronzes. **1951** *Engineering* 6 July 1/3 The main and big-end bearings are all fitted with steel shells, lined with lead-bronze. **1967** *Jane's Surface Skimmer Systems 1967–68* 123/2 Crankshaft... Lead-bronze bearings with steel cups. **1905** A. H. LOW *Technical Methods Ore Analysis* viii. 56 The determination of bismuth in impure lead or *lead bullion may be carried out on the same lines as described for refined lead. **1954** W. H. DENNIS *Metall. Non-Ferrous Metals* iv. 242 The crude lead bullion may contain up to 4 per cent of these reduced metallics. **1963** *Times* 22 Apr. p. iv/4 This plant is producing about 40,000 tons of good ordinary brand zinc annually together with lead bullion and by-product cadmium and sulphuric acid. **1886** D. SALOMONS *Managem. Accumulators* 14 It is frequently necessary to perform the operation of soldering or *lead burning. **1937** *Archit. Rev.* XXXI. 272/2 Leadburning is a variety of welding. As a process it has been known for centuries, but only since the invention of the gas welding flame have its possibilities been fully exploited. *Ibid.* 270 (*caption*) After casting the flat sheets [of lead] are bent round and the joint lead-burned to form the point. **1963** H. R. CLAUSER *Encycl. Engin. Materials* 368/2 Lead welding, commonly called lead burning, produces a true weld by fusing the parts together without the addition of any different material. **1897** *Physical Rev.* IV. 353 We owe the discovery of the *lead cell to Planté. **1928** CRENNELL & LEA *Alkaline Accumulators* ix. 121 The energy, or watt-hour, efficiency of alkaline cells is about 50–55 per cent., as compared with 75 per cent. for lead cells. **1867** *Chem. News* 5 July 12/1 (*heading*) *Lead-chamber process. *Ibid.*, This explains the loss of nitric acid in the manufacture of sulphuric acid, which always takes place when the sulphuric acid in the lead-chamber is below the normal strength. **1909** L. KAHLENBERG *Outl. Chem.* xiii. 198 There are commonly three lead chambers, so connected that the gases enter the top of each and pass out at the bottom. **1946** J. R. PARTINGTON *Gen. & Inorg. Chem.* xxiv. 710 The lead chamber plant..consists of (i) pyrites (or sulphur) burners, (ii) a dust separator.., (iii) a nitre oven.., (iv) a Glover tower, (v) a series of lead chambers with arrangements for supplying steam or water spray, and (vi) a Gay-Lussac tower. **1969** H. T. EVANS tr. *Hägg's Gen. & Inorg. Chem.* xxi. 529 The reaction takes place in reaction chambers, formerly lead chambers, that is, large lead-lined rooms, but now most often of other types. **1973** THOMAS & FARAGO *Industr. Chem.* viii. 133 The lead-chamber process is by no means obsolete.., and is likely to remain in operation for the production of acid not exceeding 78 per cent in concentration..and where high purity is not essential. **1715** GARTH *Claremont* 96 Nor yet *lead-comb was on the toilet plac'd. **1902** J. D. & A. EVERETT tr. *Hovestadt's Jena Glass* x. 364 Foerster recalls the fact that the resisting power of *lead crystal glass to acids is increased by long-continued exposure to acids. Were it otherwise, the use of this material for wine glasses would long ago have been given up. **1968** *Canad. Antiques Collector* Dec. 19/2 When lead crystal came into fashion about 1800, it was possible to cut the glass in glittering facets. **1969** R. F. LANG tr. *Henglein's Chem. Technol.* 835 Lead crystal contains lead (instead of Ca) and potassium and has high light refraction; it is much used in colored glasses. **1727-41** CHAMBERS *Cycl.*, **Lead Dust*, is a preparation used by the potters; made by throwing charcoal dust into melted lead, and stirring them a long time together. **1788-9** *Lead-eater [see CAOUTCHOUC 1]. **1855** ROBINSON *Whitby Gloss.*, *Lead-eater*, Indian-rubber, for removing pencil marks on paper. *a* **1877** KNIGHT *Dict. Mech.* II. 1270/1 **Lead-flat*, a level roof consisting of sheet-lead laid on boarding and joists. **1907** W. DE MORGAN *Alice-for-Short* xxv. 259 Charles remembers the lead-flat sunk in the roof. **1940** *Chambers's Techn. Dict.* 491/2 *Lead-flat*, a flat roof formed of sheet-lead laid on boarding and joists. **1552** HULOET, *Leade fome or spume, *molybditis.* **1896** K. TYNAN *Lover's Breast-Knot* 15 *Lead-foot, slow, Did the day round to evening-flame? **1810** J. T. in *Risdon's Surv. Devon* p. xv, Lead is found in the state of galena or *lead glance. **1843** PORTLOCK *Geol.* 181 Lead glance is also occasionally, but not frequently met with, in small masses. [**1830** *Phil. Trans. R. Soc.* CXX. 43 The tri-borate of *lead glass is almost as colourless as good flint glass.] **1856** W. A. MILLER *Elem. Chem.* II. xi. 764 Lead glass has..the inconvenience of being readily scratched. **1946** *Nature* 26 Oct. 582/1 Colouring oxides such as iron, copper, etc., all produce more intense colours in heavy lead glasses than in ordinary lead-free glasses. **1965** PHILLIPS & WILLIAMS *Inorg. Chem.* I. xiv. 546 Special glasses are made by adding other oxides: for example, lead glasses have a high refractive index and are used in crystal and flint glass. **1899** *Westm. Gaz.* 27 Mar. 6/2 There seems no reason..why..the operatives should still continue to be exposed to the evils which the use of *lead-glaze entails. **1969** *Canad. Antiques Collector* Jan. 28/3 Lead and lustre glazes came early from the Near East. **1901** *Daily News* 3 Dec. 3/7 He states that there is no difference now in price between the *lead glazed and leadless glazed ware. **1968** J. ARNOLD *Shell Bk. Country Crafts* 231 Medieval pottery was mainly in the form of lead-glazed earthenware..and was known as faience or majolica. **1908** *Westm. Gaz.* 23 Nov. 9/3 The deceased came under his notice twelve years ago, when he was a *lead-glazier. **1962** H. R. LOYN *Anglo-Saxon Eng.* iii. 110 The so-called Stamford ware, utilizing a type of *lead-glazing that may have originated in the Netherlands, appears to have spread from East Anglia. **1424** *Mem. Ripon* (Surtees 1888) III. 152 Item Ricardo Horner circa *ledhows a festo Annunciacionis Beatæ Mariæ usque ad Pascha per xv dies et di... 7*s* 9*d.* **1466** in Willis & Clark *Cambridge* (1886) III. 93 The said Roofe shal haue sufficient *leedlathis of herty ooke sufficiently dried. **1844** *Catholic Weekly Instructor* 103 Fixing a small copper gutter at the bottom of each *lead-light. **1895** *Jrnl. R. Inst. Brit. Archit.* 14 Mar. 350 All lead-light windows should have iron casements. **1485** *Naval Acc. Hen. VII* (1896) 51 *Leede lynes..j. **1839** BAILEY *Festus* xx. (1848) 248 Deeper than ever leadline went. **1879** *St. George's Hosp. Rep.* IX. 100 The tobacconist had a 'lead line' on the gums. **1907** W. DE MORGAN *Alice-for-Short* xxvii. 283 I'll lend you a hand over the lead-lines. *Ibid.* xii. 136 It was Pope's man, Buttivant, who lead-lines up all the windows. **1973** HARRISON & WATERS *Burne-Jones* iv. 50 All the designers had to supply were the cartoons, which were quite often bold drawings without indication of lead lines. **1485** *Naval Acc. Hen. VII* (1896) 39 *Lede malles feble.. xiiij. **1497** in *Ld. Treas. Acc. Scot.* (1877) I. 350 Item, to the *lede man, making ledin pellokkis. **1625** BACON *Ess.*, *Riches* (Arb.) 235 A Great Colliar, A Great Corne Master, a Great Lead-man. **1633** B. JONSON *Love's Welc. Welbeck*, Such a light and metall'd Dance Saw you never yet in France, And by Lead-men, for the nonce, That turne round like grindle-stones. **1889** *Times* 28 Nov. 5/6 Relaying a whole sheet of lead for a single crack is doubtless delightful to the leadmen. *a* **1728** WOODWARD *Nat. Hist. Fossils* I. (1729) I. 183 A *Lead-Marcasite..much like the Potters Lead-Ore..The Miners call this Mock-Ore, Mock-Lead, Wild-Lead, and Blinde. **1863** P. BARRY *Dockyard Econ.* 109 Chatham has a monopoly of the dockyard lead manufacture. During the year the *lead-mill turned out 21,852 cwt. 1 qr. 21 lb. **1864** CRAIG Suppl., *Lead-mill*, a circular plate of lead used by the lapidary for grinding or roughing. **1354** *Mem. Ripon* (Surtees) III. 92 In ccc *lednayle emp. 12*d.* **1476-7** *Durham Acc. Rolls* (Surtees) 95 Sol. pro iiij^{c} ledenale..12*d.* **1536-7** *Ibid.* (Surtees) 698, 100 leydnall', 5*d.* **1869** *Lonsdale Gloss.*, *Leäd-nails.* **1899** CAGNEY tr. *Jaksch's Clin. Diagn.* v. (ed. 4) 159 The brown or black stain upon the *lead-paper will again show the presence of hydrochloric acid. **1922** JOYCE *Ulysses* 659 A crinkled leadpaper bag. *Ibid.* 70 He..read the legends of leadpapered packets. **1952** M. ALLINGHAM *Tiger in Smoke* vi. 108 The final covering was a piece of lead paper off a tobacco package. **1682** WILDING in *Collect.* (O.H.S.) I. 255 For Paper, Inkhorne, and *Lead pen..00 01 05. *a* **1693** *Urquhart's Rabelais* III. xxv. 203 He with a White Lead Pen ..drew a..Number of..Points. **1688** R. HOLME *Armoury* III. iii. 144/2 Black and red *Lead Pencils. **1704** *Lond. Gaz.* No. 4044/1 A Letter..written on Horseback with a Lead-Pencil. **1863** EMERSON *Misc. Papers, Thoreau* Wks. (Bohn) III. 324 A manufacturer of lead-pencils. **1833** A. EATON *Man. Bot.* (ed. 6) 15 *Amorpha canescens*, *lead plant... Somewhat woody... Galena. **1848** W. H. EMORY *Notes Mil. Reconn.* 399 The lead plant, or tea plant..is in some places so abundant as to displace almost every other herb. **1939** *Nat. Geogr. Mag.* Aug. 220/1 Chief among the peas is a group of close relatives: lead plant,..prairie clovers, together with indigo plant. **1865** *Lead-plaster [see *lead-soap*]. **1841-2** T. D. MITCHELL in *Western & Southern Med. Recorder* (Lexington, Kentucky) I. 145 (*title*) Practical notes on *lead poisoning. **1878** BRISTOWE *Theory & Pract. Med.* 617 Chronic lead-poisoning. **1972** *National Observer* (U.S.) 27 May 10/1 The American Smelting and Refining Co. of New Jersey was accused in a civil suit of unduly polluting the air and environment with its huge smelters here and of causing lead poisoning in at least 135 children. **13..** *Measures of Weight* in *Rel. Ant.* I. 70 Sex waxpunde makiet .j. *leedpound. **1920** *Discovery* Apr. 111/2 It is of course obvious that, if a mineral is altered, it has suffered chemical changes whereby the normal *lead ratio is upset, for either introduction or elimination of lead may have taken place. *Ibid.* 112/1 In some cases the lead-ratio can be used..for determining the geological position of rocks which yield their age to no other method of investigation. **1946** F. E. ZEUNER *Dating the Past* x. 325 In practice, the analyst measures the total amount of lead present, and the expression $Pb^{total}/(U + 0{\cdot}36\ Th)$, accounting for the presence of both uranium and thorium, is the one which has

to be determined in every case. It is called the 'lead-ratio'. 1687 *Mining Laws* in Collinson *Hist. Somerset* I. 117 Any miner who finds himself aggrieved complains to an officer called the *Led reeve. 1829 *Glover's Hist. Derby* I. 242 The improvement (on the stocking-frame)..consisted in applying the *lead-sinkers, which are still in use. 1875 KNIGHT *Dict. Mech.*, *Lead-Sinker* (*Knitting-machine*), one of the devices which alternate with the jack-sinkers in the depression of the loops between the needles. 1865 WATTS *Dict. Chem.* III. 564 **Lead-soaps*, lead-salts of the fat-acids. Common lead-plaster is a preparation of this kind. 1821 R. JAMESON *Man. Min.* 85 Accompanied with galena or lead-glance, and *lead-spars. 1852 SEIDEL *Organ* 122 The oxygen contained in the atmosphere is imparted to bad brass, and produces what is called *lead-sugar..which is eagerly sought and consumed by mice. 1889 *Jrnl. Chem. Soc.* LV. 677 The first alloys experimented on were the *lead-tin alloys. 1890 *Ibid.* LVIII. 336 The two alloys always correspond with two cognate points on the solubility curves of zinc in lead-tin, and of lead in zinc-tin. 1928 H. H. COWLEY *Mod. Electr. Wiring* iv. 54 Either copper or lead-tin alloy is generally employed for ordinary wire fuses. 1931 G. O. RUSSELL *Speech & Voice* viii. 67 The author has a lead-tin, round-walled open organ pipe. 1956 *Monogr. & Rep. Ser. Inst. Metals* No. 18. 73 In the lead-tin alloys, as in many other alloy systems, precipitation is accompanied by recrystallization. 1844 FOWNES *Chem.* 199 The common.. experiment of the *lead-tree. 1864 GRISEBACH *Flora W. Indian Isl.* 785 Lead-tree, *Leucæna glauca*. 1674 RAY *Collect. Words*, *Making Salt* 142 A *Lead-walling is the Brine of twenty-four hours boiling for one house. 1876 BRISTOWE *Theory & Pract. Med.* (1878) 330 The local inflammation may be allayed to some extent by the use of *lead-wash. 1875 *Dental Cosmos* XVII. 510 Keep the gum covered with a pellet of cotton saturated with *lead-water and laudanum. 1908 *Chambers's Jrnl.* Jan. 120/1 What is called '*lead wool', consisting of pure lead cut into fine strips by machinery. 1930 *Engineering* 10 Oct. 451/1 The end bracket structure on the ends of each tube formed the lateral forms for the joint concrete. The actual face joint was made with lead wool caulked. 1641 in Willis & Clark *Cambridge* (1886) I. 95 *Leadworke in yᵉ East Range. 1825 J. NICHOLSON *Operat. Mechanic* 638 Lead-work is used in inferior offices. 1859 GWILT *Encycl. Archit.* (ed. 4) 586 Glazing..may be classed under the heads of sashwork, leadwork, and fretwork. *a*1728 WOODWARD *Nat. Hist. Foss.* I. (1729) I. 7 The Lord Derwentwater's *Lead-Works near Haden-Bridge in Northumberland. 1897 *Daily News* 25 Dec. 5/7 A lad employed at a leadworks. 1727 BAILEY vol. II, **Lead-wort*, a kind of herb. 1845 LINDLEY *Sch. Bot.* (ed. 14) 104 C, *Plumbaginaceæ*—Leadworts. 1852 MORFIT *Tanning & Currying* (1853) 82 The dentellaria, or leadwort.

b. In names of chemical compounds, as ***lead carbonate***, ***chloride***, ***iodide***, ***salts***, etc.; **lead tetraethyl** = *tetraethyl lead*.

1873 *Fownes' Chem.* (ed. 11) 450 Lead Chloride.. separates as a heavy white crystalline precipitate. *Ibid.*, Lead Iodide..dissolves in boiling water. *Ibid.* 451 Lead Carbonate..is sometimes found..crystallised in long white needles, accompanying other metallic ores. *Ibid.*, Lead Nitrate. 1887 *Jrnl. Chem. Soc.* LII. I. 572 Lead tetraethyl, Pb Ph_4. 1926 *Encycl. Brit.* II. 127/2 The tendency to knocking is suppressed by adding to the motor spirit substances such as lead tetra-ethyl which, it is assumed, act by being adsorbed by the ferriferous carbon in the cylinder. 1971 *Daily Tel.* (Colour Suppl.) 28 May 16/2 The amounts of lead in the environment have increased dramatically since the introduction of lead tetraethyl as a petrol additive in the Twenties... By controlling the rate at which fuel burns, lead tetraethyl promotes smoother ignition.

c. In the names of diseases caused by the presence of lead in the system, as ***lead-colic***, ***-distemper***, ***-encephalopathy***, ***-palsy***, ***-paralysis***, for which see also the second member in each.

1774 PENNANT *Tour Scotl. in 1772*, 114 The miners and smelters are subject here..to the lead distemper which brings on palsies. 1866 W. H. O. SANKEY *Lect. Ment. Dis.* viii. 162 Lead palsy..is accompanied with obstinate constipation or lead colic, and the gums are marked with a peculiar blue line. 1897 *Allbutt's Syst. Med.* II. 967 Many of the miners..have died from lead encephalopathy.

lead (liːd), *sb.*² Forms: 4–6 lede, (4 ledde), 5–6 *Sc.* leid, 6 leade, 7– lead. [f. LEAD *v.*¹; cf. OHG. *leitî* (MHG., mod.G. *leite*).

By Johnson, who gives one example from Herring (quot. 1745 in sense 2), it is stigmatized as 'a low, despicable word'; Todd quotes an instance of it from Burke, and says it is used somewhere by Bolingbroke.]

†**1. a.** The action of the vb. LEAD¹; leading, direction, guidance. ***to take to lead***: to take under one's direction or guidance. *Obs.*

*a*1300 *Cursor M.* 1570 þai left þe lede of þar lau. *Ibid.* 12029 þan tok ioseph iesus to ledde. *c*1400 *Destr. Troy* 10653 Hom lacked the lede of þe lorde Ector. *c*1470 HENRY *Wallace* IX. 1532 Decest scho was, God tuk hir spreit to leid. *c*1510 *Gest Robyn Hode* VII. 368 in Child *Ballads* (1888) III. 74/1 Take fyue of the best knyghtes That be in your lede.

†**b.** ***gentleman, man of lead***: one who has a recognized leading position. *Obs.*

1793 LD. WESTMORLAND in Lecky *Eng. in 18th C.* (1887) VI. 558 The men of talent and lead in his Majesty's service. 1842 WEBSTER *Wks.* (1877) II. 130 More than thirty Whigs, many of them gentlemen of lead and influence.

c. Direction given by going in front; example, precedent; esp. in phr. ***to follow the lead of***.

1863 BRIGHT *Sp. Amer.* 30 June, To accept the lead of the Emperor of the French on..one of the greatest questions. 1868 J. H. BLUNT *Ref. Ch. Eng.* I. 405 The king had set an example..and the subject was only too ready to follow the royal lead. 1875 T. W. HIGGINSON *Hist. U.S.* xxiv. 240 Under the lead of Josiah Quincy..a law was passed forbidding the importation of slaves. 1884 LADY VERNEY in *Contemp. Rev.* Oct. 546 Is the American model a success —a lead which it is desirable to follow out? 1899 CHEYNE *Chr. Use Ps.* iii. 56 The early Christians, in interpreting the Old Testament, followed the lead of the Jews.

d. *spec.* in *Hunting*, etc., chiefly in phr. ***to give a lead***, i.e., to go first in leaping a fence or the like, so as to encourage the rest; in quots. *transf.*

1859 G. A. LAWRENCE *Sword & Gown* v. 52 Two Sundays ago..a Mr. Rolleston..volunteered to give us a lead... He went off at score, and made the pace so strong, that he cut them all down in the first two verses. 1862 A. TROLLOPE *Orley Farm* I. xxxviii. 296, I lost the run, and had to see Harriet Tristram go away with the best lead any one has had to a fast thing this year. 1897 MARY KINGSLEY *W. Africa* 535 'What thing?' said I, not wishing to give him the lead.

e. A guiding indication; a clue (to the solution of something).

1851 *Jrnl. R. Agric. Soc.* XII. I. 141 As I have a small brook passing through the farm..these carriages take their lead from the stream in due succession. 1855 BAIN *Senses & Int.* II. ii. §13 (1864) 202 For the up and down direction we have a very impressive lead; this being the direction of gravity. 1910 J. LONDON *Let.* 19 Nov. (1966) 323 Again and again I have opened up leads of true life and found that it was wholly misunderstood by my reading public. 1959 *Times* 18 Feb. 8/3 The enquiry arose from a complaint.. that he had been given 'definite leads' to the questions in advance. 1971 *Daily Tel.* 17 Dec. 1/5 Three leads are being followed by detectives investigating the attempted assassination of the Jordanian Ambassador. They are a sub machine-gun.., an hotel bill..and fingerprints. 1973 *Times* 5 May 1/2 The French police have decided to shift their inquiry into the axe murder of Mr John Cartland, a Brighton schoolmaster, to Britain next week in search of new leads.

f. *Journalism.* A summary or outline of a newspaper story; a guide to a story that needs further development or exploration; the first (often the most important) item in an issue, bulletin, etc. Cf. *lead story*, etc., under sense 11 b below.

Quot. 1947 refers to a radio news broadcast.

1927 *Amer. Speech* II. 241 'Lead'..is used as a noun to refer to the initial summary of the story, or as a verb to instruct the printer what to put first. 1947 *Hansard*, *Commons* 19 Dec. 2113 There is what one calls the 'lead', which is..the first item. 1950 D. HYDE *I Believed* xvi. 189, I had several hundred accredited Worker Correspondents sending in regular reports and receiving regular 'leads' and directives from me. 1952 *Manch. Guardian Weekly* 20 Mar. 3 This discovery destroyed many a newsman's first confident 'lead'. 1961 'B. WELLS' *Day Earth caught Fire* viii. 119 Stenning's brought in a lead to something that could be big. 1973 A. BROINOWSKI *Take one Ambassador* ix. 128 He's onto some lead about a mob of fanatical rat-bags.

2. a. The front or leading place; the place in front *of* (something); freq. in phr. ***to take the*** (or ***a***) ***lead***. Also, the position or function of leading (e.g., a party, a deliberative body), leadership.

1570 *Satir. Poems Reform.* xii. 40 His Grandschir slane at Lythquo gif I leid. 1745 ABP. HERRING *Sp. at York* 24 Sept. 6 This County..takes the Lead of the inferior Ones. 1761 HUME *Hist. Eng.* II. xxvii. 127 He took the lead in every jovial conversation. 1768 STERNE *Sent. Journ.* (1775) 72 (*Rose*) They take the lead, and lose it..by turns. 1796 BURKE *Regic. Peace* iii. Wks. VIII. 137 To prevent those who compose it from having the open and avowed lead in that house. 1817 COBBETT *Taking Leave* 13 Unless they [the country gentlemen] shall cordially take the lead amongst those working classes. 1840 HOOD *Up Rhine* 5 For a mile or more the doctor took the lead and kept it. 1840 ALISON *Hist. Europe* VIII. xlix. §18. 20 Boldly assuming the lead in diplomacy. *a*1859 MACAULAY *Hist. Eng.* xxiv. (1861) V. 169 The lead of the House of Commons had, however, entirely passed away from Montague. 1860 TYNDALL *Glac.* I. xxv. 187 Each of our porters took the lead in turn. 1879 M. ARNOLD *Equality* Mixed Ess. 66 On certain lines, certain nations find their strength and take a lead. 1884 *Times* (weekly ed.) 26 Sept. 4/1 Germany has..taken the lead of other nations [in the preparation of colours from coal tar].

b. The body moving in front; the van. *U.S.*

1880 TOURGEE *Fool's Err.* xxxiii. 217 The lawyers were of course in the lead. *Ibid.* xxxviii. 281 Then we started on. I rode beside Mr. Watson in the lead.

c. *Austral.* and *N.Z.* (See quot. 1933¹.)

1933 L. G. D. ACLAND in *Press* (Christchurch, N.Z.) 4 Nov. 15/7 *Lead*, the front part of a mob of sheep. *Ibid.* 2 Dec. 15/7 An injudicious turn with a dog in an abrupt gully may stop the lead and cause some sheep to be knocked over. 1946 F. D. DAVISON *Dusty* ix. 90 Tom..sent [the sheepdog] Sapper to the flank [of the mob] and to turn the lead.

d. Finance. ***leads and lags*** (also attrib. phr. ***lead-and-lag***): see quot. 1965¹. Also *transf.*

1958 *Spectator* 31 Jan. 129/1 The 'leads and lags' are being replaced by a more natural pattern of commercial payments. 1959 *Economist* 14 Feb. 619/2 The customary 'leads and lags' are at work, postponing commercial demands for sterling and accelerating sales of sterling. 1962 S. E. FINER *Man on Horseback* xii. 220 Sometimes the demand for popular sovereignty has preceded nationalism, sometimes it has been the other way about; but the leads and lags were never very lengthy. 1964 A. BATTERSBY *Network Analysis* iii. 37 The lead-and-lag (or ladder) system has the merit of simplicity, and it draws attention to the importance of planning the sequence of individual jobs within a departmental activity. 1965 J. L. HANSON *Dict. Econ.* 253/2 *Leads and Lags*, with reference to international payments and their effect on the balance of payments this term is used on the hastening or delaying of payment, the former by residents and the latter to residents in order to take advantage of expectations of changes in the rate of exchange. 1965 *Listener* 13 May 692/2 Some foreigners, in the habit of acquiring sterling in advance of their commitments, refrained from doing so; that would be a mug's game, they thought, when sterling might be devalued before they had to pay. These are known as the 'leads and lags' in trade payments.

3. *concr.* Something that leads.

a. An artificial watercourse, esp. one leading to a mill. Also MILL-LEAT. Cf. LEAT.

1541 *Ludlow Churchw. Acc.* (Camden) 9 Item, to Roger Meysy for cuttynge downe of ellorns in the ledes..ijd. 1870 CHAMBERS *Pop. Rhymes* 17 They took..a loup in the lead and a dip in the dam.

b. A channel in an ice-field. Cf. LANE *sb.* 2.

1835 SIR J. ROSS *Narr. 2nd Voy.* Explan. Terms 15 *A lead*, a channel in a direct line through the sea. 1853 KANE *Grinnell Exp.* xi. (1856) 78 Something like 'a lead' a little to leeward. 1881 A. LESLIE *Nordenskiöld's Voy. Vega* I. x. 519 Johnsen supposed that in a couple of hours the whole lead would be completely closed.

c. A path; a garden path; an alley. ***blind lead*** = *blind alley* (see BLIND *a.* 11).

1590 *Acts Privy Council* (1899) XIX. 409 Permytt them to enjoye the libertie of the gardens and the orchards and the leades to walke in. 1885 C. F. HOLDER *Marvels Anim. Life* 51 Innumerable avenues and blind leads are built to mislead the various carnivorous beetles.

d. A leash or string for leading a dog.

1893 *Daily News* 18 July 6/3 Daykin had with him a dog, which he held by a lead. 1898 *Westm. Gaz.* 2 Sept. 5/3 Seeing defendant with a muzzle in her hand and an unmuzzled toy terrier on a lead in Holborn.

e. *N.Z.* (See quot.)

1878 E. S. ELWELL *Boy Colonists* 214 They made a 'lead' in the stockyard for branding the cattle. This was something like a 'race' for drafting sheep, with a swing gate... It had a wide entrance gradually getting narrower till it became a lane only just wide enough for one beast at a time to squeeze through.

4. *Card-playing.* The action or privilege of playing the first card in a round or trick. Also, the card so played, or proper to be played, or the suit to which it belongs. ***to return one's partner's lead***: to play from the same suit on getting the lead.

1742 HOYLE *Whist* 11 If you have a Sequence of King, Queen, and Knave, or Queen, Knave, and Ten, they are sure Leads. *Ibid.* 12 You need seldom return your Partner's Lead, if [etc.]. 1862 'CAVENDISH' *Whist* (1879) 57 If all your suits are weak, the lead is very disadvantageous. 1885 PROCTOR *Whist* i. 21 A forced lead from Queen and one other. 1896 *Daily News* 28 Jan. 6/4 The system of American leads—leads more frequently mentioned than adopted in England.

5. a. *Curling.* The first player, or the stone first played. Also, the course along which the stones are driven (Jamieson, 1825–80).

1685 *Lintoun Green* (1817) 38 Convened for a bonspeel, He..their lead, or driver leal. 1812 *Sporting Mag.* XL. 52 Whoever is last in order..is called the driver and the first the lead. 1820 *Blackw. Mag.* VI. 572 The lead, or first stone, is always, except on very drug ice, expected to lie short.

b. *Bowls.* (See quot.)

1753 CHAMBERS *Cycl. Supp.* s.v. *Bowling*, *Lead*, the advantage of throwing the block and bowling first.

c. *Boxing.* The first punch thrown (of two or more) (see also quot. 1954).

1906 [see CROSS *sb.* 22 d]. 1950 J. DEMPSEY *Championship Fighting* x. 50 The first punch thrown (by either) is a lead. 1954 F. C. AVIS *Boxing Reference Dict.*, *Lead*, a forward blow made at a fair distance from the opponent. 1970 *Times* 28 Sept. 13/5 Those sneak right leads I hit him with helped as well. 1971 *Black Scholar* Jan. 43/2 Man, this would make these fighters so mad they would forget about boxing and come out swinging wild. And that was all old Jack wanted. He'd step inside their leads and counter punch them to death!

6. *Mining.* **a.** = LODE. Also *fig.* **b.** *Gold-mining.* An alluvial deposit of gold along the bed of an ancient river. Also ***deep-lead***, ***great-blue-lead*** (see quots.).

a. 1812 BRACKENRIDGE *Views of Louisiana* (1814) 148 Leads (or loads), are the smaller fissures that connect with the larger, which are called by the miners, caves. 1869 S. BOWLES *Our New West* vii. 136 A quaint old miner of the valley, who, 'prospecting' for society that day, had struck a 'lead' in us. 1872 'MARK TWAIN' *Roughing it* xl. (1882) 218 A 'blind lead' is a lead or ledge that does not 'crop out' above the surface. 1881 RAYMOND *Mining Gloss.*, *Lead*..See *Lode*. 1893 GUNTER *Miss Dividends* 104 Capital..invested in the silver leads of the great mountains.

b. 1855 *Argus* (Melbourne) 19 Jan. 6/1 A great curiosity was discovered in a hole on this lead—a tree. 1874 RAYMOND *Statist. Mines & Mining* 16 The term 'great blue-lead' is employed by the miners to distinguish those portions of the alluvium which are found to rest in a well-defined channel. 1880 FISON & HOWITT *Kamilaroi* 272 *note*, The expression 'deep lead' refers to those ancient river-courses which are now only disclosed by deep-mining operations. 1888 F. HUME *Mad. Midas* I. i, Who knew..where the richest leads had been in the old days.

7. *Theatr.* **a.** The leading or principal part in a play. **b.** One who plays such a part.

1831 J. BOADEN *Life Mrs. Jordan* I. xi. 264 It gave him the lead in a successful play. 1865 *Punch* 7 Jan. 5/1 As a general rule an actor who plays the 'lead' ought to aim at becoming a general manager. 1874 F. C. BURNAND *My time* xxv. 229 She was a girl and playing the lead in the Northern Circuit. 1884 G. MOORE *Mummer's Wife* (1887) 126 He had been playing heavy leads in Shakesperian revivals. 1885 J. K. JEROME *On the Stage* 63 Grey-headed stars, and respectable married leads. 1937 *Daily Tel.* 14 Aug. 9/1 Many leading men and women (and some who are merely minor leads). 1939 [see *character part*]. 1953 [see *big stuff* (BIG *a.* B. 2)]. 1973 *Listener* 21 June 844/2 The lead, Martin Thurley, must surely have studied the slovenly dialect of the area.

8. a. *Change-ringing.* (See quot. 1874.) **b.** *Mus.* The giving out of a phrase or passage by one of the parts in a concerted piece, to be followed in harmony by the other parts.

1671 STEDMAN *Tintinnalogia* 55 In Ringing Half-pulls, some Peals do cut Compass, that is—the whole hunt comes to lead at the back stroke. 1834 SOUTHEY *Doctor* I. 304 A lead single was made in the middle of the peal. 1872 *Punch*

27 Apr. 170/1 You always take up that 'lead' in the anthem so dreadfully 'flat'. **1874** STAINER & BARRETT *Dict. Mus. Terms* s.v. *Bells*, A bell is said to be 'behind' when she is the last of the changing bells, and at 'lead' when she is the first. Thus the progress from 'lead' to behind is said to be 'going up', and from behind to lead is called 'going down'.

c. *Mus.* The most prominent part in a piece played by an orchestra, esp. a jazz band; the player or instrument that plays this; the leader of a section of an orchestra; also, the start of a passage played by a particular instrument. Freq. *attrib.* orig. *U.S.*

Further *attrib.* examples are given under sense 11 b below.

1934 S. R. NELSON *All about Jazz* v. 99 He evolved what he called a 'harmony chorus', the instruments all playing harmony, with a solo lead. **1937** *Amer. Speech* XII. 47 The lead melody is carried lower than the clarinet. **1952** B. ULANOV *Hist. Jazz in Amer.* (1958) xvii. 203 Hymie Schertzer's rich lead alto sounds. **1967** [see ATTACK *v.* 7]. **1968** *Blues Unlimited* Sept. 8 They played mostly Italian music and polkas, with Charlie McCoy on lead mandolin.

9. ***friendly lead*** (see FRIENDLY *a.* 2 b). Also simply *lead.*

1851–61 MAYHEW *Lond. Labour* III. 154 We went to a public-house where they were having 'a lead', that is a collection for a friend who is ill, and the company throw down what they can for a subscription, and they have in a fiddle and make it social.

10. In various technical uses.

a. *Electricity.* (*a*) The angle between the plane through the lines of contact of the brushes or collectors of a dynamo or electric motor with the commutator and the transverse plane bisecting the magnetic field. (*b*) A conductor conveying electricity from the source to the place where it is used.

1881 *Design & Work* 24 Dec. 455/2 Had properly insulated and erected 'leads'.. been employed, no serious result would have followed personal contact. **1893** SLOANE *Electr. Dict.*, *Lead of Brushes* in a dynamo electric generator, the lead or displacement in advance of or beyond the position at right angles to the line connecting the poles of the field magnet, which is given the brushes. In a motor the brushes are set back of the right angle position, or are given a negative lead. **1898** *Westm. Gaz.* 11 Nov. 9/1 The use of candles could be dispensed with by the use of a wandering lead with a hand electric light.

b. *Engineering*, etc. The distance to which ballast, coal, soil, etc. has to be carted or otherwise conveyed (see LEAD *v.*[1] 1 b) to its destination.

1852 WIGGINS *Embanking* 113 The cost of earth-work depends on the nature of the soil, and the distance it has to be conveyed, which is called 'the lead'. **1894** *Westm. Gaz.* 10 Feb. 6/1 Instead of sending the coal east and west with short 'leads', the company had to send it north and south with very long 'leads'.

c. *Horology.* The action of a tooth, as a tooth of a wheel, in impelling another tooth or pallet.

1880 TRIPPLIN & RIGG *Saunier's Mod. Horology* 40.

d. *Naut.* The direction in which running ropes lead fair, and come down to the deck (Smyth *Sailor's Word-bk.* 1867). Cf. FAIR-LEAD.

c **1860** H. STUART *Seamen's Catech.* 37 Ropes that want a lead can have one.. by using a snatch block. **1865** *Pall Mall G.* 30 Oct. 4 He knows.. the lead of the ropes, the use of a boat, and a score of other things. **1897** R. KIPLING *Captains Courageous* 73 The lead of each rope was fixed in Harvey's mind by the end of the rope itself.

e. *Sawing.* 'The overhang of a saw, to extend the cut throughout the length of the saw and to carry the saw back in the kerf during the return stroke' (Knight *Dict. Mech.* 1875).

f. *Steam-engine.* (See quots.)

1875 KNIGHT *Dict. Mech.*, *Lead of the crank*, the setting of the crank of one engine a little in advance of the right angle to the other; namely at 100° or 110° in place of 90°. This assists in rendering the motion of the piston more uniform, by moderating its velocity at the end of the stroke. **1881** *Metal World* No. 18. 274 The steam-port is open a very small amount when the crank is in this condition [on the dead centre], the amount that the steam-port is then open being termed the lead of the valve. **1895** *Mod. Steam Engine* 39 This amount of opening before the piston commences its stroke is called the lead of the slide.

11. *attrib.* and *Comb.*: **lead-bars** *Coaching*, the bars to which the traces of the leaders are attached; **lead-horse**, a horse that is guided by a lead (see 3 d); **lead-mule** (cf. *lead-horse*); **lead-net** = LEADER[1] 15 b; **lead-reins** *Coaching*, the leaders' reins; **lead-rope**, a rope used as a lead for a horse or ox; also *fig.*; **lead-screw**, 'the main screw of a lathe, which gives the feed motion to the slide-rest' (Webster 1864); **lead sheet** *U.S. slang* (see quot. 1942); also *transf.*, an overcoat; **lead-time** orig. *U.S.*, the time taken to produce some manufactured article (see also quot. 1968); also *transf.*

1840 *Congress. Globe* 5 Mar. App. 227/2 The horse broke loose from the coach, taking with him a part of what are now called '*Lead bars'. **1890** 'ROLF BOLDREWOOD' *Col. Reformer* (1891) 188 Both check-reins were carried away and the lead bars broken. **1828** J. M. SPEARMAN *Brit. Gunner* (ed. 2) 256 Total weight carried by the *lead horse. **1877** RAYMOND *Statist. Mines & Mining* 345 Give me the *lead-mule, and the rest of us will go on to camp. **1910** *Chambers's Jrnl.* Mar. 192/2 The *lead-net is about fifteen hundred feet long. The salmon strike this. **1896** *Outing* (U.S.) XXX. 111/1 The buckles on these *lead-reins should hang even over the leader's quarters... You have now both lead-reins in your left hand. **1846** R. B. SAGE *Scenes Rocky Mts.* iii. 24 Holding in one hand the *lead-rope of his horse. **1901** KIPLING *Kim* vii. 169 'We be all on one lead-rope, then,' said Kim at last, 'the Colonel, Mahbub Ali, and I.' **1958** L. VAN DER POST *Lost World of Kalahari* i. 15 Lifting the lead rope from the horns of the two guide-oxen. **1942** BERREY & VAN DEN BARK *Amer. Thes. Slang* §578/9 *Lead sheet, a sheet of music containing the melodic line and lyric only. **1945** L. SHELLY *Jive Talk Dict.* 28/2 *Lead sheet*, an overcoat. **1961** R. RUSSELL *Sound* iii. 38 You never got around to writing out a lead sheet! **1945** *Birmingham* (Alabama) *News* 19 May 8/1 The '*lead-time' normally required to bring out new models. **1957** *Manch. Guardian* 4 May, The problem is.. difficult, on account of the complex character of the equipment in question and the long lead-time involved. **1964** A. BATTERSBY *Network Analysis* iii. 36 The chain-dotted arrows.. represent *lead times* when they connect start events. **1968** J. F. MAGEE *Industr. Logistics* i. 19 'Lead time' is the response time lag of the system, the time that must be allowed at a stock point to replenish stock, including the time needed to process records, transmit information, and process and ship material. **1971** *Inside Kenya Today* Mar. 28/1 Because of the lead-time in switching the emphasis in the secondary schools, the University is under pressure to increase its Arts intake very rapidly. **1973** *Nature* 28 Sept. 179/1 The long lead time required for such a rendezvous or flyby mission makes it impossible to achieve a fruitful interception with Kohoutek.

b. Used in the sense of 'leading'.

1846 R. B. SAGE *Scenes Rocky Mts.* xxxiii. 289 Bidding them adieu, with my lead pack-animal returned to the mountains. **1857** in *Ann. Wyoming* (1939) XI. 83 The carriage sustained no injury, but one of our lead Mules became detached from the wagon. **1869** *Overland Monthly* III. 127 With the Texan driver all oxen are 'steers', and he has his 'wheel-steers', his 'swing-steers', and his 'lead-steers'. **1888** KIPLING *Barrack-Room Ballads* (1892) 117 Then the lead-cart stuck, though the coolies slaved, and the cartmen flogged. **1890** *Ibid.* 18 The rattle an' stamp o' the lead-mules. **1910** W. M. RAINE *Bucky O'Connor* 189 It was as the man in charge circled round to head the lead cows in that a faint voice carried to him. **1929** *Randolph Enterprise* (Elkins, W. Virginia) 28 Mar. 1/2 Dick Collette played the lead violin and Bryan Gainer, second. **1942** BERREY & VAN DEN BARK *Amer. Thes. Slang* §523/3 Leader, lead story, a leading news item. **1959** J. OSBORNE *World of Paul Slickey* I. vi. 55 Congratulations.. on today's lead story. **1962** *Amer. Speech* XXXVII. 87 A lead article satirizing American temperance groups. **1963** MRS. L. B. JOHNSON *White House Diary* 22 Nov. (1970) 3 In the lead car were President and Mrs. Kennedy. **1967** *Time* 25 Aug. 38 The Group Image, one of the new, first-name-only hippie groups, of which Nancy is the den mother.. and Artie the lead guitar. The tribe has about 25 musicians, artists and psychedelic experts in it. **1967** W. SOYINKA *Kongi's Harvest* 3 Superintendent. .. Seizes the lead drummer by the wrist. **1973** 'F. CLIFFORD' *Amigo, Amigo* xxi. 175 Ahead, the lead horse whinnied. **1973** *Listener* 6 Sept. 312/3 Carl Perkins.. now playing lead guitar behind Johnny Cash. **1975** *Guardian* 7 Jan. 6/7 A mob of Hell's Angels set on members of the Troggs pop group in their dressing-room and during a fight the group's lead guitarist was stabbed five times in the back.

lead (li:d), *v.*[1] Forms: 1 **lǣdan**, 2–4 **laden**, 3 **læden, læiden**, 2–5 **leden, leaden**, (3 **leoden**, *Orm.* **ledenn**), 3–5 **ledde**, 4–6 **led(e**, 4, 7 **leede**, 4–7 (chiefly *Sc.*) **leide, leyde**, 6–7 **leade**; 6– **lead.** *Pres. ind.* (*contracted forms*): *2nd sing.* 1 **lǣtst**, 3 **last**; *3rd sing.* 1 **lǣt**, 3 **lat**, 3–4 **let**, 4 **leth.** *Pa. t.* 1 **lǣdde**, 2 **leaded**, 2–6 **ledd(e**, 3 **lædde**, 3–4 **leede**, (3 **leadde, leddede**), 4–6 **ladde**, 4–8 **lad**, 5–6 **ledd**, (5 **leded**, *Sc.* **laid**), 4– **led.** *Pa. pple.* 1 **lǣded, lǣd**, 3–6 **ledde**, 4–5 **ladd(e, lede**, 4–7 **lad(e**, 7 **lead(e**, 4– **led.** Also 3–5 with prefix **i-, y-.** [A Com. Teut. wk. vb. (wanting in Goth.): OE. *lǣdan* = OFris. *lêda*, OS. *lêdjan* (MDu. *leden, leiden*, Du. *leiden*), OHG. (MHG., G.) *leiten*, ON. *leiða* (Sw. *leda*, Da. *lede*):—OTeut. **laidjan*, f. **laidâ* road, journey (see LOAD, LODE *sbs.*), related to OE. *líðan*, ON. *líða* to go, travel.

The word has always served as the usual rendering of L. *ducere*, and this has in some degree influenced the development of meaning.]

I. To conduct.

1. *trans.* To cause to go along with oneself.

†**a.** To bring or take (a person or animal) to a place. Also with *away, down*, etc. *Obs.* (Phrases like ***to lead captive*** are now understood in sense 2.)

c **825** *Vesp. Psalter* lxvii[i]. 19 Astiȝende in heanisse ȝehefte lædde heftned. *c* **1000** ÆLFRIC *Gen.* vi. 19 Of eallum nytenum.. tweȝen ȝemacan þu lætst in to þam arce mid þe. *Ibid.* xlii. 20 Læde eowerne ȝingstan broðor to me. *a* **1175** *Cott. Hom.* 221 God ȝeledde to him niatenu.. and adam ham alle namen ȝesceop. *c* **1205** LAY. 26797 [He] ladde uorð Petreiun læð þeh hit weore him. *c* **1250** *Gen. & Ex.* 858 Wifwes, and childre.. He ledden a-wei wið herte prud. *Ibid.* 2193 He dede hem binden and leden dun, And speren faste in his prisun. **1297** R. GLOUC. (Rolls) 8803 Oþer kniȝtes þer were inome,.. & ilad in to engelond. *c* **1375** *Sc. Leg. Saints* xi. (*Symon & Judas*) 408 þe forsad byschapis of þat stede al hale þe puple with þam lede. **1387** TREVISA *Higden* (Rolls) III. 97 þat þe kyng schulde be lad awey prisoner in to Babilon. *c* **1400** MAUNDEV. (1839) x. 113 The Jews ladden him upon an highe Roche. *c* **1460** *Towneley Myst.* xiv. 70 Boldly thou thaym bynde, And with the leyde. **1530** PALSGR. 604/2 Shall I leade him away with me? **1533** GAU *Richt Vay* 70 God sal leid thaime vp to the heuine with hime quhilk ar deid in christ. **1579** LYLY *Euphues* (Arb.) 168 Ieremy before the people were led awaye, apointeth their exile to continue three score and ten years. **1704** HEARNE *Duct. Hist.* (1714) I. 395 The Pannonians.. he successfully subdued, leading away the younger sort into other countries.

quasi-*passive* in *gerund. a* **1533** LD. BERNERS *Huon* cxliv. 539 The other prysoners, whom we see yonder ledyng to the dethe warde. **1757** ELIZ. GRIFFITH *Lett. Henry & Francis* (1767) II. 87 Suppose a criminal leading forth to execution.

b. To carry or convey, usually in a cart or other vehicle. Now only *north. dial.*: To cart (coal, corn, stones, turf, etc.). ***to lead in*** (grain): to house.

c **900** tr. *Bæda's Hist.* I. i. (1890) 30 Of Breotone nædran on scipum lædde wæron. *Ibid.* III. v. [vii.] 168 Hædde biscop heht his lichoman.. lædan to Wintaceastre. *c* **1205** LAY. 3548 To læden þis garisume to leuene mine fadere. *a* **1225** *Leg. Kath.* 2251 We, aȝeines þin heast, þæt licome awei ledden. *a* **1300** *Cursor M.* 5129 Siluer and gold þai wit þam ledd. **1362** LANGL. *P. Pl.* A. IV. 130 Lawe schal ben a laborer and leden [1377 lede] a-feld dounge. **1375** BARBOUR *Bruce* x. 195 Vith this Bunnok spokin had thai To leid thair hay. *c* **1386** CHAUCER *Monk's T.* 158 The vessel of the temple he with hym ladde. *c* **1400** MAUNDEV. (1839) xxiii. 248 Thei leiden hire Houses with hem upon chariottes. *c* **1420** *Liber Cocorum* (1862) 33 Whenne thou hast covered hit [venison] so, Lede hit home. *c* **1450** *St. Cuthbert* (Surtees) 5300 þare armour hame þai led. *c* **1450** *Bk. Curtasye* 813 in *Babees Bk.*, þe vssher ledes þat on hed ryȝt. *c* **1470** HENRY *Wallace* IX. 1610 A drawcht off wod to leid. *c* **1475** *Rauf Coilȝear* 597 Leidand Coillis he ȝeid To Paris the way. **1528** *Test. Ebor.* (Surtees) V. 260 To Smythson, for ledinge corne at Acclame, vjs. viijd. **1530** PALSGR. 604/2 He was ledde thorowe the towne upon a hardell and so to the galowes. **1594** *Acc. Bk. W. Wray* in *Antiquary* XXXII. 55 For leding ij lodes of haye, xij[d]. **1601** SHAKS. *All's Well* IV. iii. 298 Faith, sir, ha's led the drumme before the English Tragedians. **1603** OWEN *Pembrokeshire* (1891) 93 And being thus dried throwlie they [turfs] are led home and layed then vp. **1683** *Vestry Bks.* (Surtees) 341 For two load of lime and leading it, 5*s.* **1721** RAMSAY *Elegy Patie Birnie* v, Tho' peats and turfs and a's to lead. **1799** J. ROBERTSON *Agric. Perth* 195 In no case to reap when they ought to be leading in (housing) their grain. **1839** STONEHOUSE *Axholme* 43 One shilling a load is the price generally paid for leading a cart-load of warp. **1841** *Jrnl. R. Agric. Soc.* II. II. 191 He undertakes to convey (or lead, as the term is) all the materials for a new building. **1887** HALL CAINE *Deemster* xvi. 800 Dan was sent for the pair of oxen to where they were leading manure. **1891** ATKINSON *Moorland Par.* 64 The people of the farm in question.. had been leading, that is, carting hay in a 'catchy' time.

†**c.** Of a natural agent, e.g. the wind: To carry. *Obs.*

1297 R. GLOUC. (Rolls) 2023 He ariuede at souþ hamptone as þe wind hom adde ylad. *a* **1300** *Cursor M.* 1805 þe wind him ledd a-pon þe flodd. **1633** BP. HALL *Hard Texts* 607 Causing the Clouds to lead in store of rain.

d. To bring forward, adduce (testimony); to bring (an action). Now only in *Sc. Law.*

a **1300** *Cursor M.* 16278 Quat mister es o wijtnessing again him for to lede? *c* **1450** HOLLAND *Howlat* 224 The crovss Capone.. Was officiale but less that the law leidis. **1503** *Extracts Aberd. Reg.* (1844) I. 430 The richtis, ressonis and allegacionis of batht the said parties,.. led, herde, sene and understandin. **1564** *Warrant* in D. H. Fleming *Mary Q. of Scots* (1897) 494 Forsamekill as thair wes ane proces of forfaltoure led agains Mathew sumtyme Erle Leuenax [etc.]. **1737** RUTHERFORD *Lett.* (1862) I. 379 A process leading ags[t]. my guiltiness. **1831** SIR W. HAMILTON *Discuss.* (1852) 228 No evidence has yet been led to show. **1884** LD. WATSON in *Law Rep.* 9 App. Cases 253 In the Court below, the parties were allowed and led proof of their respective averments. **1887** *Scotsman* 19 Mar., Proof was led to-day in this action of separation and aliment.

2. a. To accompany and show the way to; to conduct, guide, *esp.* to direct or guide by going on in advance; to cause to follow in one's path. Often with advs., *astray, away, forth, in, on, out, up*, etc.

In early examples app. merely a contextual use of sense 1.

a **900** *Martyrol.* 26 in *O.E. Texts* 178 Mine englas ðec lædað in ða hiofonlican Hierusalem. **971** *Blickl. Hom.* 27 He hine lædde upon swiþe hea dune. *c* **1175** *Lamb. Hom.* 119 Monie þewas.. ledað to deþe on ende þa þe heom duseliche folȝiað. *c* **1200** ORMIN 14468 Caym ledde himm [Abæl] ut uppo þe feld. *c* **1205** LAY. 1098 Brutus nom Ignogen & into scipe lædde. *c* **1250** *Gen. & Ex.* 3607 Go, led ðis folc. *a* **1300** *Cursor M.* 24620 Vnto þe tun þan i me ledd. *c* **1350** *Will. Palerne* 2618 þe werwolf hem ladde ouer mures & muntaynes. *c* **1375** *Sc. Leg. Saints* xxxv. (*Thadee*) 47 þane till a chawmir scho hym lede mare priue. **1382** WYCLIF *Ps.* lxxvii[i]. 14 He ladde hem thennes in the cloude of the day. *c* **1475** *Rauf Coilȝear* 263 To ane preuie Chalmer beliue thay him led. **1509** HAWES *Past. Pleas.* xxxviii. (Percy Soc.) 196 The gentle porteres.. on my way then me lede. **1570** *Satir. Poems Reform.* xvi. 51 Bot he will leid him in the myre Thocht he hecht to defend him. **1603** SHAKS. *Meas. for M.* III. ii. 47 How now, noble Pompey! What, at the wheels of Cæsar? Art thou led in triumph? **1667** MILTON *P.L.* XII. 309 Therefore shall not Moses.. his people into Canaan lead. **1711** ADDISON *Spect.* No. 321 ¶9 Satan is afterwards led away to Gabriel. **1742** YOUNG *Nt. Th.* I. 45–7 O lead my Mind.. Lead it thro' various Scenes of Life. **1847** H. ROGERS *Ess.* (1860) III. 402 The criminal must be led back by the same road by which he has been led astray. **1879** MISS YONGE *Cameos* Ser. IV. xiii. 144 He was led into the chamber of presence.

b. Of motives, conditions, circumstances: To guide, direct to a place.

a **1300** *Cursor M.* 20386 Sais me quat has you hider ledde. **1821** CLARE *Vill. Minstr.* II. 44 It was a happy hour That led me up to Barnack hill. **1861** *Temple Bar* I. 467 Chance led him to Basil. **1892** *Eng. Illustr. Mag.* IX. 867 Instinct early led him into the political arena.

c. Of a clue, light, sound, etc.: To serve (a person) as an indication of the way; to mark the course for. Also absol. ***to lead in*** (Naut.): to mark the course for entering port.

1697 DRYDEN *Virg. Georg.* IV. 222 By the tinkling Sound of Timbrels led, The King of Heav'n in Cretan Caves they fed. **1824** CAMPBELL *Theodric* 185 Led by that clue, he left not England's shore Till he had known her. **1833** J. H. NEWMAN *Hymn*, Lead, Kindly Light, amid the encircling

gloom, Lead Thou me on! **1860** *Merc. Marine Mag.* VII. 316 The two latter Lights *in line* lead in.

d. *absol.*, chiefly in figurative contexts.

1580 Sidney *Ps.* i. i, He blessed is who..[never] loosely treads The straying steps as wicked councel leads. **1593** Shaks. *3 Hen. VI*, iii. i. 99 We charge you..To go with vs vnto the Officers. *King.* In Gods name lead. **1602** —— *Oth.* i. i. 311 Pray you lead on. *c* **1614** Sir W. Mure *Dido & Æneas* i. 89 Quhair ever thou dost leid We follow the. **1624** Quarles *Job* xvi. 30 My lips shall tread That ground..as Truth shall leade. **1836** I. Williams in *Lyra Apost.* (1849) 120 Into God's Word..Thou leadest on and on. **1863** Cowden Clarke *Shaks. Char.* xvi. 390 [They] who desire to lead, must at all events make a show of following.

e. *to lead the way*: †(*a*) with personal obj., to guide, show the way to (*obs.*); (*b*) in later use (influenced by sense 13), to go in advance of others, take the lead in an expedition or course of action.

c **1200** Ormin 3465 Ant teȝȝre steorrne wass wiþþ hemm To ledenn hemm þe weȝȝe. *c* **1375** *Sc. Leg. Saints* ii. (Paulus) 203 þe quhilkis ledand hym þe way praide hym [etc.]. **1590** Marlowe *Edw. II*, ii. ii. (1598) D 2, *Lan.* Lead on the way. **1599** Porter *Angry Wom. Abingt.* (Percy Soc.) 90 Lead thou the way, and let me hold by thee. **1613** Shaks. *Hen. VIII*, v. v. 73 Lead the way, lords. **1697** Dryden *Virg. Georg.* iii. 123 The first to lead the Way, to tempt the Flood. **1709** Prior *Ode to Col. Villiers*, And in their various Turns the Sons must tread Those gloomy Journeys, which their Sires have led. **1770** Goldsm. *Des. Vill.* 170 He..allured to brighter worlds, and led the way. **1832** Ht. Martineau *Ireland* ii. 22 Dora..led the way..in an opposite direction. **1847** Marryat *Childr. N. Forest* vii, I can manage it, Humphrey; so lead the way. **1874** Green *Short Hist.* ii. §6. 89 In the silent growth and elevation of the English people the boroughs led the way.

f. To aim in advance of.

1892 W. W. Greener *Breech-Loader* 267 Theoretically it is correct to lead a quartering pigeon from five to seven feet. **1968** D. Hamilton *Menacers* xxii. 176, I led him by roughly two feet and pressed the trigger of the Luger.

g. Coll. phr. *lead me to* (something previously mentioned), expressing the ability to perform or a desire to comply, or merely expressing eager assent.

1929 W. E. Miller *To you I tell It* 107 'How wood you like to urn a piece of jack?' 'Leed me to it,' says Figgars. 'What's the propozishion?' **1934** D. L. Sayers *Nine Tailors* iv. 307 'Can you ride a motor-bike?' 'Lead me to it, guv'nor!' **1938** D. Smith *Dear Octopus* ii. iii. 90 Lead me to that whiskey.

h. *to lead with one's chin* (Boxing slang), to 'stick one's neck out', to leave oneself unprotected; *fig.*, to behave or speak incautiously.

1949 E. S. Gardner in *Argosy* Apr. 110/3 Let him lead with *his* chin. We'll work undercover. **1954** F. C. Avis *Boxing Reference Dict.*, *Lead with chin*, to have a very bad stance or guard. **1968** *Listener* 18 Jan. 78/2, I thought it was a good idea to say that I was prejudiced to begin with, to lead with my chin. **1973** A. MacVicar *Painted Doll Affair* i. 19 Don't go leading with your chin, Bruce.

3. Of a commander: To march at the head of and direct the movement of. Also with *on.* †Also to conduct (warfare) = L. *ducere bellum.*

a **900** *O.E. Chron.* an. 827 (Parker MS.) Se Ecgbryht lædde fierd to Dore wiþ Norþan hymbre. *c* **1350** *Will Palerne* 1609 Wiþ þe clennest cumpanye þat euer king ladde. **1422** tr. *Secreta Secret., Priv. Priv.* 154 Where ben tho that ladd the grete hostes? *c* **1470** *Golagros & Gaw.* 655 The thrid heght schir Bantellas, the batal to leid. *c* **1470** Henry *Wallace* vii. 1171 Hew Kertyngayme the wantguard ledis he. **1513** Douglas *Æneis* xi. iii. 28 Ne na weirfair with ȝour pepill leid I. **1596** Dalrymple tr. *Leslie's Hist. Scot.* vi. 332 He leids ane armie till Northumberland. **1605** Shaks. *Macb.* v. vi. 4 You (worthy Vnkle) Shall..Leade our first Battell. **1736** Lediard *Life Marlborough* II. 267 The Prince..led them on with great Gallantry. **1821** R. Turner *Arts & Sci.* (ed. 18) 188 Many thousands of them [elephants] have at once been led to battle. **1847** Marryat *Childr. N. Forest* iv, He longed..to lead his men on to victory.

absol. *c* **1420** *Anturs of Arth.* 397 (Douce MS.) Withe a launce one loft þat louely cone lede. **1581** Savile *Tacitus' Agric.* (1622) 194 The army..cried to leade into Caledonia. **1623** Bingham *Xenophon* 10 Cyrus..told them, that his purpose was to lead against the great King. **1791** Cowper *Iliad* iv. 430 Go therefore thou, Lead on.

4. a. To go before or alongside and guide by direct or indirect contact; to conduct (a person) by holding the hand or some part of the body or clothing, (an animal) by means of a cord, halter, bridle, etc. Const. *by* (the hand, etc.). Also with advs. *away, in, off, on, out, up and down*, etc. *to lead apes* (*in hell*): see ape *sb.* 6.

971 *Blickl. Hom.* 71 His þeȝnas..læddon him to þone eosol. *c* **1000** *Ags. Gosp.* Matt. xv. 14 Se blinda ȝyf he blindne læt hiȝ feallað beȝen on ænne pytt. *c* **1175** *Lamb. Hom.* 111 þet mon..sarine frefrað oðer blindne let. *c* **1320** *Sir Tristr.* 446 Tristrem hunters seiȝe ride Les of houndes þai ledde. *c* **1375** *Sc. Leg. Saints* xxxiii. (*George*) 274 Ta þi belt & hyme [a dragon] lede, & about his hals knyt it sone. *c* **1420** *Anturs of Arth.* 447 His stede was sone stabillede, and lede to þe stalle. **1470–85** Malory *Arthur* i. xlix, The brachet was mine that the Knight lad away. **1500–20** Dunbar *Poems* xiii. 17 His fa sum by the oxstar leidis. *Ibid.* xc. 35 The ane blynde man is led forth be ane uther. **1530** Palsgr. 604/2 Lede my horse, I praye you, up and downe. **1590** Spenser *F.Q.* i. i. 4 A milke white lamb she lad. **1614** Sir A. Gorges tr. *Lucan's Pharsalia* i. 37 Then doth he take a faire large bull..And him vnto the Altar leades. **1766** Goldsm. *Vic. W.* xxiii, The captive soldier was led forth. **1813** *Sketches Charac.* (ed. 2) I. 29 [She] returned, leading in a lovely little girl. **1830** Tennyson *Ode Memory* iii. 10 In sweet dreams..Thou leddest by the hand thine infant Hope. **1862** *Temple Bar* IV. 252 The chestnut..was led off to the stable.

b. *to lead* (*a bride*) *to the altar, to church* (†also simply: ? after L. *ducere*): To marry.

1530 Palsgr. 604/2, I lede a bride to churche, *je mayne.* **1700** Dryden *Ovid's Metam.* xii. 267 He had either led Thy Mother then; or was by Promise ty'd. **1812** Landor *Ct. Julian* v. iii. 5 He leads her to the altar, to the throne. **1842** Tennyson *Ld. of Burleigh* 11 He..leads her to the village altar.

c. *fig.* (*a*) In opposition to *drive*: To guide by persuasion as contrasted with commands or threats. (*b*) *to lead by the nose* (for the allusion cf. quot. 1604): to cause to obey submissively. Also † *to lead by the sleeve.*

c **1425** Lydg. *Assemb. Gods* 1680 How false idolatry ledeth hem by the sleue. **1583** Golding *Calvin on Deut.* cxxi. 745 Men..suffer themselues to bee led by the noses like brute beasts. **1589** Puttenham *Eng. Poesie* iii. xxiv. (Arb.) 299 Princes may be lead but not driuen. **1604** Shaks. *Oth.* i. iii. 407 The Moore..will as tenderly be lead by th' Nose As Asses are. **1631** *Star Chamb. Cases* (Camden) 20 You shall meete with ignorant Juryes, your duty is to open their eyes, you may not leade them by the nose. **1749** Smollett *Gil Bl.* (1797) III. 77 They [the great] have favourite domestics who lead them by the nose. **1856** Kingsley *Plays & Purit.* 211 A mob of fools and knaves, led by the nose in each generation by a few arch-fools and arch-knaves. **1862** *Temple Bar* IV. 167 She might be led, but would not be driven.

d. *intr.* (quasi-*passive*). To be led; to submit to being led.

1607 Markham *Caval.* i. (1617) 75 Till hee be so tame..that he will leade vppe and downe quietlye. **1822** Scott *Pirate* xxiv, My mester may lead, but he winna drive. **1887** I. R. *Lady's Ranche Life Montana* 148 In the morning the pupils [colts] have learnt their lesson, and will lead anywhere.

5. To guide with reference to action or opinion; to bring by persuasion or counsel *to* or *into* a condition; to conduct by argument or representation *to* a conclusion; to induce *to* do something. Said both of persons and motives, circumstances, evidence, etc.

a **1225** *Leg. Kath.* 261 þe feont..leadeð [men] to unbileaue. *a* **1300** *Cursor M.* 26696 He said þar-till his wijf him ledde. *c* **1330** *Spec. Gy Warw.* 62 þe world þurw his foule gile Haþ me lad to longe while. *c* **1380** Wyclif *Sel. Wks.* III. 445 Herby bene man lad in to fendus temptacioun. **1422** tr. *Secreta Secret., Priv. Priv.* 217 Al accordid, that kynde lad the chylde that to done. **1538** Starkey *England* i. ii. 30 The wyl of man ever commynly folowyth that to the wych opynyon..ledyth hyt. **1586** Hunsdon in *Border Papers* (1894) I. 367 Sondrie cawses..leades me greatlie to mistrust the Kinges good meaning towards her Majesty. *a* **1605** Montgomerie *Devot. Poems* iii. 26 To lyf that leddie sall the leid. **1611** Bible *Transl. Pref.* 1 Bruit-beasts led with sensualitie. **1651** Hobbes *Leviath.* ii. xxx. 177 They ought not to be led with admiration of the vertue [etc.]. **1711** Addison *Spect.* No. 40 ⁋1 This Error they have been led into by a ridiculous Doctrine in modern Criticism. **1736** Butler *Anal.* Introd., Wks. 1874 I. 9 Our whole nature leads us to ascribe all moral perfection to God. **1859** Ruskin *Two Paths* App. i. (1891) 251 Tintoret..may lead you wrong if you don't understand him. **1861** M. Pattison *Ess.* (1889) I. 41 Edward's foreign policy led him to draw closer the ties which connected our country with Germany. **1871** B. Stewart *Heat* §239 In studying the radiation of gases we are led to some very peculiar laws. **1885** Sir H. Cotton in *Law Rep.* 29 Ch. Div. 479 There was nothing in the prospectus to lead him to such a conclusion. **1888** H. F. Lester *Hartas Maturin* II. vi. 122 She knew the colonel was easily led.

absol. **1597** Bacon *Colours Gd. & Evil* (Arb.) 138 Besides their power to alter the nature of the subiect in appearance, and so leade to error.

6. a. Of a way, road, etc.: To serve as a passage for, conduct (a person) *to* or *into* a place. Hence *absol.* or *intr.*, to have a specified goal or direction. Cf. L. *via ducit in urbem.* Often in fig. contexts.

a **1200** *Moral Ode* 337 Læte we..þe wei bene þe lat þe niȝeðe del to helle of manne. *c* **1200** Ormin 12916 Forr þiss Lamb iss þatt rihhte stih þatt ledeþþ upp till heffne. **1340** *Ayenb.* 165 þet is þe way þet let in-to þe helle of god. *c* **1375** *Sc. Leg. Saints* xviii. (*Egipciane*) 843 Gyf he..wald kene me the gat, þat mycht me led to the flume Iordane. **1382** Wyclif *Matt.* vii. 14 How streit is the ȝate and narewe the weye that ledith to lyf. **1509** *Bury Wills* (Camden) 112 Ye hygheway..ledyng toward Ipswych. **1526** *Pilgr. Perf.* (W. de W. 1531) 14 Yet bothe entendeth to go the iourney that ledeth to the hye Jerusalem. **1603** Shaks. *Meas. for M.* iv. i. 33 A little doore, Which from the Vineyard to the Garden leades. **1621** Lady M. Wroth *Urania* 452 The way of necessity leading me to follow my disdainer. **1710** Steele *Tatler* No. 194 ⁋2 There was a single Bridge that led into the Island. **1720** Ozell *Vertot's Rom. Rep.* II. ix. 48 There were but two Ways that led equally to all the Dignities of the Republick. **1780** A. Young *Tour Irel.* i. 288 The end of the lake at your feet is formed by the root of Mangerton, on whose side the road leads. **1791** Mrs. Radcliffe *Rom. Forest* ii, La Motte ascended the stairs that led to the tower. **1821** Clare *Vill. Minstr.* I. 122 My rambles led me to a gipsy's camp. **1861** *Temple Bar* II. 547 Broad steps lead down into a garden. **1884** J. Colborne *Hicks Pasha* 69 Then comes the eternal arid plain leading to the barren hills. **1889** *Repentance Paul Wentworth* I. ix. 187 Their road..led them through a little copse.

b. *intr.* To form a channel *into*, a connecting link *to* (something).

1833 *Act 3 & 4 Will. IV*, c. 46 §95 One waste or foul water pipe..to communicate with any drain..leading into a common sewer. **1851** *Illustr. Catal. Gt. Exhib.* 361 Motion is..communicated to the rudder by means of two connecting rods leading to the tiller.

c. *intr.* *to lead to*: to have as a result or consequence.

a **1770** Jortin *Serm.* (1771) IV. vi. 119 Pride seldom leads to truth in points of morality. **1845** S. Austin *Ranke's Hist. Ref.* I. 277 The general disapprobation excited by the church on such weighty points, naturally led to a discussion of its other abuses. **1861** M. Pattison *Ess.* (1889) I. 43 Several seizures of English cargoes led to reprisals on our part; reprisals led to a naval war. **1875** Bryce *Holy Rom. Emp.* iv. (ed. 5) 35 The victory of Tolbiac led to the submission of the Alemanni. **1885** *Manch. Exam.* 8 July 5/3 Mr. Beecher's former opinion that smoking leads to drinking.

7. *to lead* (a person) *a dance*: *transf.* and *fig.*, to put to the trouble of hurrying from place to place; hence, to compel to go through a course of irksome action. *to lead* (a person) *a chase*: lit. to give (a pursuer) trouble by one's speed or circuitous course; also *fig.* Also (by association with sense 12) *to lead a person a life.*

a **1529**, **1599** [see dance *sb.* 6 b]. **1601** Shaks. *All's Well* ii. iii. 49 Why he's able to leade her a Carranto. **1607** Heywood *Wom. Killed* (1617) A 3, That's the dance her Husband meanes to leade her. **1711** Addison *Spect.* No. 89 ⁋2 You know..my Passion for Mrs. Martha, and what a Dance she has led me. **1715** De Foe *Fam. Instruct.* i. iv. (1841) 77 I'll lead her such a life she shall have little comfort of me. **1850** Mrs. Jameson *Leg. Monast. Ord.* (1863) 64 They led St. Guthlac such a life, that [etc.]. **1861** *Temple Bar* IV. 53 He ..often leads them a fine chace over hill and dale. **1883** Fenn *Middy & Ensign* xvii. 107 The chaps would lead him such a life. **1892** *Cornh. Mag.* July 15 How can the captain so forget himself as to lead them a paper chase? **1892** *Sunday Mag.* Aug. 509/2 She had led him the life of a dog.

8. With an inanimate thing as object. **a.** To conduct (water, *occas.* steam) through a channel or pipe. Cf. L. *aquam ducere.* Also with *away, forth, off, out.*

c **1205** Lay. 15952 þis wæter wes al ilæde. **1382** Wyclif *Prov.* v. 16 Ben lad out thi wellis withoute forth. **1842** *Jrnl. R. Agric. Soc.* III. ii. 273 Deep beds of peat, from which the water has been led off by open drains. **1865** *Ibid.* Ser. ii. I. ii. 276 Water may be led away from a hill-side and form a perennial stream of the greatest value. **1892** *Chamb. Jrnl.* 4 June 360/1 A dam and shoot were constructed..to lead the water away faster. **1893** *Ibid.* 28 Jan. 61/1 The steam..being led by a bamboo pipe to other vessels.

b. To guide the course or direction of (something flexible); †to train (a vine), †to trace (a line, a boundary); to draw or pass (a rope, etc.) *over* a pulley, *through* a hole, etc.

c **1050** in Thorpe *Dipl. Angl.* 376 þa ilcan þe him ær landȝemære læddon. **1398** Trevisa *Barth. De P.R.* xvii. clxxvii. (1495) 719 Vynes mow be lad wyth rayllynge aboute houses and townes. **1607** Topsell *Four-f. Beasts* (1658) 441 The nose is blackish, a line being softly led through the length, and only through the top of the outside thereof. **1669** Sturmy *Mariner's Mag.* v. 3 Ten small sticks, which let him that leadeth the Chain, carry in his Hand before. **1834–47** J. S. Macaulay *Field Fortif.* (1851) 219 A charge is laid on the floor..and it is fired with a hose led outside. **1841** J. T. Hewlett *Parish Clerk* I. 79 Bleed and blister, lead a mane, dock a tail. **1869** Boutell *Arms & Arm.* viii. (1874) 142 System of pulleys, over which strong cords are led. **1876** Preece & Sivewright *Telegraphy* 37 The insulated wire..is led up through the copper sulphate. **1885** R. Bridges *Eros & Psyche, March* 25 Olive-border'd clouds o'er lilac led. **1892** *Longm. Mag.* Nov. 88 Ropes..led through blocks fixed to stakes.

c. Naut. *intr.* Of a rope: To admit of being 'led'.

c **1860** H. Stuart *Seaman's Catech.* 38 The reef tackle leads through the upper sheave of the sister block. **1867** Smyth *Sailor's Word-bk.*, *Fair-lead*, is applied to ropes as suffering the least friction in a block, when they are said to lead fair.

†**d.** To guide, steer (a boat); to guide, drive (a carriage; cf. F. *conduire*); to guide (a pen). *Obs.*

1377 Langl. *P. Pl.* B. ii. 179 Cartesadel the comissarie owre carte shal he lede. *c* **1380** Wyclif *Serm.* Sel. Wks. I. 12 Lede þe boot into þe hey see. *c* **1384** Chaucer *H. Fame* ii. 434 Pheton, wolde lede Algate his fader carte, and gye. **1430** Lydg. *Bochas* v. vii. (1554) 127 To holde the plough and lede it with his hond. **1484** Caxton *Fables of Æsop* ii. xvi, Of a carter whiche ladde a Charyot or carte whiche a Mule drewe forthe. **1552** Latimer *Serm., St. Andrew's Day* (1584) 241 Our Saviour..saith to Peter, *Duc in altum*—Lead thy boate into the deepe. **1567** *Satir. Poems Reform.* iii. 49 With Romaine hand he could weill leid ane pen.

¶**e.** In literalisms of translation; = L. *ducere* and its compounds.

1382 Wyclif *Exod.* xxvi. 37 Fyue pilers..before the whiche shal the tente be lad. —— *Ezek.* v. 1 Take to thee.. rasour, shauynge heeris;..thou shalt lede it bi thin heed, and bi thi beerd. —— *Mark* xiv. 47 Oon of men stondinge aboute, leding out a swerd, smot the seruaunt of the hiȝeste prest.

†**f.** To multiply (a number *into* another). *Obs.*

c **1430** *Arte of Nombryng* (E.E.T.S.) 15 Lede the rote of o quadrat into the roote of the oþer quadrat, and þan wolle the meene shew. *Ibid.* 17 A digit, the whiche lade in hymself cubikly [etc.].

†**9. a.** To conduct (affairs); to manage, govern.

c **1200** Ormin 17238 To ledenn a þe bodiȝ rihht All affterr Godess lare. *a* **1300** *Cursor M.* 4256 þan was ioseph bath luued and dred Wit wisdom al his werkes ledd. *c* **1320** *Cast. Love* 306 Wiþ-outen þeos foure wiþ worschipe Mai no Kyng lede gret lordschipe. ? *a* **1366** Chaucer *Rom. Rose* 400 She had no-thing hir-self to lede..More than a child of two yeer olde. **1375** Barbour *Bruce* i. 38 Alexander the King..That Scotland haid to steyr and leid. **1398** Trevisa *Barth. De P.R.* i. (1495) 2 This game rule and lede And bringe it to a good ende. *c* **1470** *Golagros & Gaw.* 48 Ask leif at the lord, yone landis suld leid. **1567** *Gude & Godlie Ball.* (S.T.S.) 41

Gif thai heir not the Law, quhilk suld thame leide Than sall thay not in ony wayis beleif.

absol. a **1300** *Cursor M.* 28277 Maister o childer i was sumquare, I ledd noght lele wit my lare. **1579** Spenser *Sheph. Cal.* July 185 For shepeheards (sayd he) there doen leade, As Lordes done other where.

†**b.** *refl.* To conduct oneself, behave, act. *Obs.*

c **1200** Ormin 1246 Ʒiff þu þe ledesst all wiþþ skill. c **1250** *Gen. & Ex.* 2301 Hu he sulden hem best leden. a **1300** *Cursor M.* 8470 Hu þat he agh him for to lede. c **1375** *Sc. Leg. Saints* xxx. (*Theodera*) 833 In vertuise..he..sa can hyme-selfe leyde þat..þai..mad hyme abbot.

†**10.** To deal with, treat (cf. guide *v.* 5). In pa. pple.: Circumstanced, situated, in such and such a condition.

c **1205** Lay. 8726 Heo weoren swiðe uuele ilæd. *Ibid.* 27713 Þer weoren Rom-leoden reouliche iledde. a **1225** *Leg. Kath.* 624 Hu me ham walde þreatin ant leaden unlaheliche. c **1340** *Cursor M.* 13787 (Trin.) For so in sekenes am I lad þat [etc.]. **1362** Langl. *P. Pl.* A. iii. 154 Heo ledeth the lawe as hire luste. c **1450** *Merlin* 331 Whan he saugh the kynge Rion so euell I-ledde, it a-noyed hym sore. c **1489** Caxton *Sonnes of Aymon* iii. 81 Thise glotons that leden our folke so cursedly.

II. To carry on.

†**11.** To engage or take part in, to perform (dances, songs), to utter (joyful or mournful) sounds. Cf. L. *ducere carmen, choros*, G. *die reihen führen*. *Obs.*

A different sense of *to lead a dance* appears under sense 13.

a **1000** *Andreas* 1477 (Gr.) He wæs eft swa ær lof lædende. c **1250** *Gen. & Ex.* 699 Of ðis kinge wil we leden songe. a **1300** *Cursor M.* 28147 Caroles, iolites, and plaies, Ic haue be-haldyn and ledde in ways. c **1325** *Coer de L.* 3739 The damyseles lede daunse. **13..** *Gaw. & Gr. Knt.* 1894 Ʒet is þe lorde on þe launde, ledande his gomnes. **1382** Wyclif *Judith* iii. 10 Ledende dauncis in trumpis and timbris. c **1489** Caxton *Sonnes of Aymon* xx. 446, I have seen Reynawd, Alard, guychard, & Rychard ledyng grete joye wyth grete company of Knyghtes. **1493** *Festivall* (W. de W. 1515) 26 b, Thou hast thyn armes spredde to lede karolles and daunces.

12. a. To go through, pass (life, †a portion of time). Cf. L. *ducere vitam*, Gr. ἄγειν βίον, etc. Rarely, †To support life *by* (bread). †Also with *forth*.

c **900** tr. *Bæda's Hist.* iv. xxviii. [xxvii.] (1890) 360 Se ær in medmyclum ealonde, þæt is Farne nemned, ancorlif lædde. a **1000** *Boeth. Metr.* vii. 40 (Gr.) Forðon orsorȝ lif ealniȝ lædað woruldmen wise buton wendinge. c **1175** *Lamb. Hom.* 89 God sette e þam israelisce folce hu heo sculden heore lif leaden. c **1200** Ormin 9359 Þatt haffdenn ledd aȝȝ þeȝȝre lif Affterr þe flæshess wille. a **1300** *Cursor M.* 4027 He ledd his liue wit-vten blam. *Ibid.* 13279 Wit þair fissing war þai fedd And pouer liuelade þai ledd. ?a **1366** Chaucer *Rom. Rose* 216 She..ladde hir lyf only by breed Kneden with eisel. **1393** Langl. *P. Pl.* C. xvii. 18 That al here lyf leden in lowenesse and in pouerte. c **1425** *Seven Sag.* (P.) 232 To have another wyf, For to ledde with thy lif. **1523** Ld. Berners *Froiss.* I. xxiii. 32 Thus this lady ledde forth her lyfe ther mekely. **1569** J. Rogers *Gl. Godly Loue* 178 Very few leade lyves..according to the lawes of Christe. **1579** Lyly *Euphues* (Arb.) 189 He may at his leasure..lead his Winter in Athens his Summer in Naples [etc.]. **1612** H. Peacham *Minerva Brit.* 46 Heere sits Repentance, solitarie, sad,..As greeuing for the life, that she hath lad. a **1661** Fuller *Worthies* (1840) I. 276 He led his old age in London. **1710** Steele *Tatler* No. 166 ¶2 The Tastless Manner of Life, which a Set of idle Fellows lead in this Town. **1819** Crabbe *T. of Hall* xii, They led in comfort a domestic life. **1821** Keats *Lamia* i. 312 In Corinth..she..had led Days as happy as [etc.]. **1856** Froude *Hist. Eng.* (1858) I. i. 13 That no human being should be at liberty to lead at his own pleasure an unaccountable existence. **1873** Browning *Red Cott. Nt.-cap* 156 Do lead your own life and let ours alone!

†**b.** To pass through (pain, suffering); to bear, endure.

a **1300** *Cursor M.* 15703 Þe strang soru þat he ledd can na man rede in run. c **1330** R. Brunne *Chron.* (1810) 15 Suffre not Sir Fretheblad long to lede þis pyne. c **1435** *Torr. Portugal* 1054 Yt ys wylle the worse to lede. c **1475** *Partenay* 3785 Non knew the sorow by thaim lade and bore.

III. To precede, be foremost. (Cf. sense 2.)

13. a. To have the first place in; to march in the front line of; *lit.* and *fig.* esp. in *to lead the dance* (see dance *sb.* 6), *to lead the van.*

c **1380**, a **1616** [see dance *sb.* 6]. **1697** Dryden *Æneid* ix. 31 Messapus leads the Van. *Ibid.* xi. 905 Asylas leads the Chase. **1736** Lediard *Life Marlborough* I. 98 The Grenadiers..led the Van. **1839** Bailey *Festus* v. (1848) 49 May our country ever lead The world, for she is worthiest. **1865** Lowell *Wks.* (1890) V. 285 A commonwealth whose greatest sin it has been to lead the van in freedom of opinion. **1869** A. W. Ward tr. *Curtius' Hist. Greece* II. iii. iii. 478 In ancient times the *choregi* themselves *led* the chorus. **1884** *Graphic* 23 Aug., Your cousin Gordon and I..had led the van all the morning. **1893** *Harper's Mag.* Feb. 385/2 Of the causes..pneumonia led the list.

b. *absol.* To go first, to have the first place. Also with *off*.

1798 Capt. Millar Aug. in Nicolas *Disp. Nelson* VII. p. cliv, The Goliath was leading, the Zealous next. **1824-9** Landor *Imag. Conv.* Wks. 1846 II. 249 The mounted slave ..led off with his master's charger. **1892** *Sat. Rev.* 2 July 10/2 The boat..was leading by two hundred yards. **1900** *Blackw. Mag.* June 789 The Admiral's frigate led.

fig. **1858** Greener *Gunnery* 300 If we take thirty or thirty-five yards' distance as an average, the latter will not 'lead' in the race. **1891** *Pall Mall G.* 20 Oct. 6/1 The small hats which are to lead for the coming season.

14. *intr.* **a.** *Mus.* (See quot. 1880.) **b.** *Change-ringing.* Of a bell: To have the 'lead' (see lead *sb.*² 8 a).

1671 Stedman *Tintinnalogia* 82 Every bell leads four times, and lies behind twice, except when [etc.] . **1880** Grove *Dict. Mus.*, *Lead, to*, in fugues or imitative music, is to go off first with a point or subject, which is afterwards taken up by the other parts successively. Thus in the Amen Chorus in the Messiah the bass 'leads'.

15. a. *trans.* To direct by one's example; to set (a fashion); to take the directing or principal part in (proceedings of any kind); to be chief of (a party, a movement); to have the official initiative in the proceedings of (a deliberative body).

1642 Fuller *Holy & Prof. St.* iii. xxv. 228 They should rather lead a fashion of thrift, than follow one of riot. **1697** Humfrey *Righteousn. God* i. 2 The Trent Doctrine (which is the perfect Papists) I must confess, is lead them by St. Austine. **1841** W. Spalding *Italy & It. Isl.* II. 266 The famous insurrection led by Masaniello. **1872** C. E. Maurice *Life S. Langton* i. 22 The Abbot..helped to lead the movement. **1880** C. R. Markham *Peruv. Bark* 335 The Government should retain the chinchona plantations, and continue to lead the cultivation. **1891** *Sat. Rev.* 31 Oct. 494/1 Disraeli still led the House of Commons. **1892** *Pall Mall G.* 15 Sept. 7/1 He was able to lead the work himself. **1892** *Eng. Illustr. Mag.* IX. 867 In conversation he seems rather to be led than to lead.

b. To take the directing part in (singing, a musical performance), to perform one's own part so as to guide the others; so *to lead a band, an orchestra.* Similarly, *to lead the prayers* (of a congregation), *to lead* (a congregation) *in prayer.* Also *absol.*

1849 *Chambers's Inform.* II. 764/2 Sometimes a tenor voice will attempt to lead the trebles. **1859** G. A. Lawrence *Sword & Gown* v. 51 He is so very anxious to get Cecil to lead the singing in church. **1866** G. Macdonald *Ann. Q. Neighb.* xiii. (1878) 245 This fine old church in which I was honoured to lead the prayers of my people. **1880** Goldw. Smith *Cowper* iii. 41 Cowper himself was made to do violence to his intense shyness by leading in prayer. **1883** Fenn *Middy & Ensign* xxvi. 159 He..led the chorus, which was lustily trolled out by all present. **1891** *Graphic* 31 Oct. 518/3 He went to lead the orchestra at the concert. **1892** *Harper's Mag.* May 821/2 A woman..led the singing.

16. Of a barrister: **a.** *trans.* To act as leading counsel in (a cause); to act as leader to (another barrister); to take precedence of. **b.** *absol.* or *intr.*

1806-7 J. Beresford *Miseries Hum. Life* (1826) i. Introd., Were I however employed to lead the cause on our side. **1862** A. Trollope *Orley Farm* I. xxxiv. 268 Of course I must lead in defending her. **1883** [see leader 3 c]. **1884** *Law Times* 11 Oct. LXXVII. 384/1 It has been the practice of English Queen's Counsel to lead colonial Queen's Counsel in appeals before the Judicial Committee.

17. *Card-playing.* **a.** *intr.* To play the first card in a round or trick. Also with *off*. Said also of the card. *to lead to* or *up to*: to play a card in order to bring out (cards held by another player). Also in *indirect pass.*

1677 Miege *Eng.-Fr. Dict.* s.v., To lead (in Cards), *jouër le premier.* **1727-52** Chambers *Cycl.* s.v. *Ombre*, Matadores ..are not obliged to attend an inferior trump when it leads. **1742** Hoyle *Whist* 11 When you lead, begin with the best Suit in your Hand. **1863** 'Cavendish' *Whist* (ed. 5) 75 You would often do better to..lead up to the weak suit of your right-hand adversary, or through the strong suit of your left-hand adversary. **1879** —— *Card Ess.*, etc. 110 Lead orginally from your strongest suit. *Ibid.* 165 He led off with his own strongest suit. **1892** *Field* 16 July 120/1 He was keeping his tenace to be led to.

b. *trans.* As first player, to play (a specified card); to play one of (a suit or a specified suit). Also with *out*.

1731 Swift *Death Dr. Swift* 239, I lead a heart. **1742** Hoyle *Whist* (1763) 5 Let us suppose the right-hand Adversary leads a Suit. **1778** C. Jones *Hoyle's Games Impr.* 90 Lead Punto. **1843** Thackeray *Ravenswing* v, You led the club. **1879** 'Cavendish' *Card Ess.*, etc. 111 It is an excellent plan to lead out first one suit and then another. *Ibid.* 171, I led knave of diamonds..The club was then led through me. *Ibid.* 198, I led the king of trumps. **1891** *Field* 28 Nov. 843/1 He ought in any case to lead trumps.

IV. In idiomatic combination with adverbs. (For the non-specialized combinations, see the several senses and the advs.)

18. lead away. a. *trans.* To induce to follow unthinkingly. Chiefly in *passive*: to yield to enthusiasm, to give credence to misrepresentation.

1736 Lediard *Life Marlborough* III. 163 Some Men are led away by the Spirit of Party. **1861** *Temple Bar* II. 395 Grace is easily led away.

b. Naut. *to lead it away*: to take one's course.

1720 De Foe *Capt. Singleton* xiii. (1840) 229 We led it away, with the wind large, to the Maldives.

19. lead off. a. *trans.* To 'open', take the first steps in (a dance, a ball); hence *gen.* to begin, make a beginning in; to open (a conversation or discussion). Const. *with.* **b.** *intr.* or *absol.* Also with *to.*

a. 1817 Jane Austen *Sanditon* vi. in *Minor Works* (1954) 389 Sir Edw: Denham & Miss Denham, whose names might be said to lead off the Season. **1847** *Punch* 27 Mar. 126/2 To lead off a list of Expiring Acts with one that is to live till the National Debt is paid off..is a delusion. **1881** Mrs. Lynn Linton *My Love* I. xiii. 229 The twins leading off the family ball. **1890** A. Gissing *Vill. Hampden* II. iv. 66 The dance.. was led off to the popular strains of the 'Keel-Row'. **1893** *Illustr. Lond. News* 28 Jan. 109/2 A well-known dramatic critic led off the congratulations.

b. 1806 R. Cumberland *Mem. of himself* 18 On some occasions, she would persist in a determined taciturnity, to the regret of the company present; and at other times would lead off in her best manner. **1809** Malkin *Gil Blas* iii. v. ¶8, I led off with five or six coxcombical bows. **1862** *Temple Bar* IV. 500 The primo tenore..leads off with 'Hard times no more'. **1882** Stevenson *Fam. Stud.* 267 A boy of fifteen to lead off with a lass of seventeen. **1893** *Harper's Mag.* Jan. 210/2 He led off with his companion in a sort of quickstep. **1911** *Chambers's Jrnl.* July 463/2 From these [wagons] rubber tubes protected by encircling wire lead off to each of the streets.

20. lead on. a. *trans.* To induce gradually to advance; to entice or beguile into going to greater lengths. **b.** *intr.* To direct conversation *to* a subject.

1598 Shaks. *Merry W.* ii. i. 98 Giue him a show of comfort in his Suit, and lead him on with a fine baited delay. **1833** Keble *Serm.* vi. (1848) 141 She will continually be led on from bad to worse. **1840** Dickens *Old C. Shop* vi, I've led her on to tell her secret. **1891** F. W. Robinson *Her Love & His Life* III. vi. ix. 195 Mike led on to the one subject which engrossed him. **1891** Mrs. Henniker *Sir George* vi. 113 Don't pretend, now, you didn't encourage and lead me on.

21. lead out. *trans.* = *lead off* 19 a. Also, to conduct (a partner) to the dance.

1818 Scott *Br. Lamm.* xxxv, The picture of Auld Sir Malise Ravenswood came down on the ha' floor, and led out the brawl before them a'. **1859** Reade *Love me little* xiv. (1868) 190 The stable-boy..leading out one of the housemaids..proceeded to country dancing.

absol. **1776** Pratt *Pupil Pleas.* (1777) I. 172 The soft things he said, while we led out.

22. lead through. *Mountaineering.* Said of two climbers: to act alternately as leaders (see quots.). Hence **leading through** *vbl. sb.*

1945 G. W. Young *Mountain Craft* (ed. 4) v. 184 Nowadays, two such experts..make a practice of 'leading through': that is..the second man on reaching his leader climbs straight on past him and leads the next section. **1955** M. E. B. Banks *Commando Climber* ix. 177 We were leading through, that is to say, one of us would climb a pitch and belay himself to the rock, whereupon the other would climb up to him and then continue beyond to lead the next pitch. **1970** A. Blackshaw *Mountaineering* (rev. ed.) v. 143 For experienced climbers two is the best number since this is quick and allows them to 'lead through'. *Ibid.* xvii. 420 Leading through may not save as much time on alpine rock as it does on British rock.

23. lead up. a. *trans.* = *lead off* 19 a. ? *Obs.*

1731 Lady M. W. Montagu *Poems, Farewell to Bath* v, I've led up many a ball. **1754** Richardson *Grandison* VI. xxvii. 166 What a frolic dance will she and her new husband, in a little while, lead up. **1766** Goldsm. *Vic. W.* ix, Mr. Thornhill and my eldest daughter led up the ball. **1799** Mar. Edgeworth *Pop. Tales, Limerick Gloves* i, She did not object to her own Jenny's leading up the ball.

b. intr. *to lead up to*: to prepare gradually for: to form a gradual preparation for.

1861 *Temple Bar* IV. 101 The circumstances which led up to the explosion of the..conspiracy. **1880** McCarthy *Own Times* III. xlv. 381 Perhaps he had deliberately led up to this very point. **1892** Westcott *Gospel of Life* Pref. 22 All earlier history leads up to the Incarnation. **1892** *Sat. Rev.* 2 Jan. 16/2 The harlequinade..is led up to by a tasteful transformation scene.

lead (lɛd), *v.*² Also 5 lede, leedyn, 6 leed. [f. lead *sb.*¹]

†**1.** *trans.* **a.** To make (something) of lead. **b.** To make dull and heavy as lead. *Obs.*

c **1420** *Pallad. on Husb.* ix. 175 Or pipis hit to condit me may lede. c **1430** *Pilgr. Lyf Manhode* ii. xc. (1869) 109 With this ax I dulle and lede [F. *j'assomme..et aplomme*] the clerkes at cherche.

2. To cover with lead. Also with *over*.

c **1440** *Promp. Parv.* 292/2 Leedyn wythe leed, *plumbo*. **1479** *Bury Wills* (Camden) 53 A new rooff to the church of Euston and ledyd. **1530** Palsgr. 604/2, I leede, I cover a thing, or a rofe of a house, with leede. **1552** *Inventories* (Surtees) 10 And the quier all leadid. a **1661** Fuller *Worthies* (1840) II. 293 She leaded and paved the Friday Market Cross in Stamford. **1691** T. H[ale] *Acc. New Invent.* 40 Sent away naked (saving in her Keel, which was Leaded). **1748** *Anson's Voy.* iii. ii. 316 The Carpenters.. caulked all the seams..and leaded them over. **1826** Scott *Woodst.* xvii, We gained the roof..which was in part leaded. **1862** [see leaded *ppl. a.*].

3. To arm, load, or weight with lead.

1481 Caxton *Reynard* viii. (Arb.) 16 A croked staf wel leded on thende for to playe at the balle. **1483** —— *Gold. Leg.* 191 b/2 They bete this holy man with..Scourges leded. **1651-7** T. Barker *Art of Angling* (1820) 25 Lead the shank of the hook. **1787** Best *Angling* (ed. 2) 12 The line should always be leaded according to the rapidity, or quietness of the river you angle in. **1842** C. J. Lever *Jack Hinton* (1843) xxv. 172, I..seated myself in the scale..and my saddle being leaded to the required weight, the operation took not a minute.

4. a. To fix (glass of a window) with leaden cames. Also with *in, up*.

1530 Palsgr. 604/2, I wyll leed no mo wyndowes, it is to costely. a **1626** Bacon *New Atl.* (1900) 26 A carved Window of Glasse, leaded with Gold and blew. **1885** F. Miller *Glass Painting* vii. 69 Where very small pieces of glass have to be leaded in the finest or 'string' lead can be used. **1886** Willis & Clark *Cambridge* I. 443 The glass [of the windows] was new leaded. **1899** Mackail *Life Morris* II. 42 The glass was burned and leaded up.

b. To set or fasten *in* firmly with molten lead.

1793 Smeaton *Edystone L.* 274 The next day..Course XXIX. was set, and its circular chain leaded in also.

†**5.** To line (pottery) with lead or lead-glaze; to glaze. Also with *over*. *Obs.*

1558 Warde tr. *Alexis' Secretes* 73 Boyle them together in an earthen panne or potte leaded. **1594** Plat *Jewell-ho.* ii. 30 Great stone pottes that bee leaded within. **1611** Bible *Ecclus.* xxxviii. 30 He [the potter] applieth himselfe to lead it ouer. **1686** Plot *Staffordsh.* 123 After the vessels are painted, they lead them, with that sort of Lead-Ore they cal Smithum, which is the smallest Ore of all, beaten into dust, finely sifted and strewed upon them.

6. *Printing.* To separate the lines of type by interposing leads (see LEAD *sb.*[1] 8).

1841 SAVAGE *Dict. Printing* 179 When a work is double leaded. **1852** W. WILKS *Half Cent.* Pref., Twenty-three sheets of bourgeois leaded. **1875** SOUTHWARD *Dict. Typogr.*, *Lead out*—a direction given in order that leads may be put between lines of matter.

7. *intr. Naut.* To use the lead; to take soundings.

1858 C. KIRTON in *Merc. Marine Mag.* V. 246 He would . . sooner haul off the land out of soundings, than run . . close in and lead.

8. *passive* and *intr.* Of a gun-barrel: To become foul with a coating of lead.

1875 'STONEHENGE' *Brit. Sports* I. I. xi. §6. 47 If either gun has its barrels leaded . . the scratch-brush must be used till the lead is removed. **1881** GREENER *Gun* 130 The barrel also leads very quickly.

9. *trans.* To smooth the inside of (a gun-barrel) with a lap of lead (see LAP *sb.*[4] b).

1881 GREENER *Gun* 146 When once rifled, the barrel cannot—as in the Henry, Ratchet, and other riflings—be leaded or otherwise regulated, except with the rifling machine.

leadable (ˈliːdəb(ə)l), *a.* [f. LEAD *v.*[1] + -ABLE.] That may be led, apt to be led.

1836 *Foreign Q. Rev.* XVII. 122 During this last most misleadable, if not most leadable, age. **1885** *Contemp. Rev.* July 131 The electorate, always . . blind and leadable.

Hence ˈ**leadableness**, docility.

1885 *Edin. Rev.* Apr. 524 Opinions which the curious docility and leadableness of her mind had made her believe.

leadage (ˈliːdɪdʒ). [f. LEAD *v.*[1] + -AGE.]

1891 *Labour Commission* Gloss., *Leadage*, distance that coal has to be conveyed from the mine to a sea-board or railway.

† ˈ**leadance.** *Obs. rare*⁻¹. [f. LEAD *v.*[1] + -ANCE.] The action of leading; guidance.

1682 G. D. *Season. Caution North to South* 7 Written Rules . . Which th' Spirits Leadance lays aside.

leadbeater[1] (ˈlɛdbiːtə(r)). The name of Benjamin *Leadbeater*, 19th-c. English naturalist, used *absol.* and in the possessive to designate a pink Australian cockatoo, *Kakatoe leadbeateri*, named after him in 1831 by N. A. Vigors (*Phil. Mag.* X. 55). In full, ***Leadbeater's cockatoo***.

1848 J. GOULD *Birds Austral.* V. 2 (*heading*) Leadbeater's Cockatoo. **1890** 'LYTH' *Golden South* xiv. 127 The birds are very beautiful—the Blue Mountain and Lowrie parrots, . . lead-beater, and snow-white cockatoos. **1900** *Daily News* 10 Feb. 7/2 The foreign birds are many, and include Amazon and grey parrots, lead-beaters, rose cockatoos, [etc.]. **1973** A. H. LENDON *Cayley's Austral. Parrots* 89 Pink Cockatoo. . . Synonyms. Major Mitchell Cockatoo, Leadbeater's Cockatoo, [etc.].

Leadbeater[2]. The name of Mr. *Leadbeater*, taxidermist at the National Museum of Victoria, Melbourne, in 1867, used in the possessive to designate **Leadbeater's possum**, *Gymnobelideus leadbeateri*, a very rare Australian opossum named after him in 1867 by F. M'Coy (*Ann. Mag. Nat. Hist.*, 3rd Ser., XX. 287).

1937 *Discovery* XVIII. 364/1 The smaller gliding 'possums . . whose ancestry is probably derived from the same stock as the extinct Leadbeater's 'Possum, feed on insects, nectar, fruit and sap. **1942** C. BARRETT *On Wallaby* iii. 36 The rarest of all Australian animals—Leadbeater's possum. **1966** G. DURRELL *Two in Bush* iv. 142 To the astonishment of incredulous naturalists, a tiny pocket of Leadbeater's Possum was discovered [in 1961] in the eucalyptus forest not far from Melbourne. **1968** *Times* 23 Jan. (Austral. Suppl.) p. xiii/3 Eric Wilkinson . . saw something that made him stare in disbelief—clinging to the trunk of a wattle tree beside the road was a small, dainty animal which much resembled the Leadbeaters possum, presumed extinct.

leaded (ˈlɛdɪd), *ppl. a.* Also 3 i-leaded. [f. LEAD *v.*[2] + -ED[1].] In senses of the vb. **a.** Covered, lined, loaded, or weighted with lead.

a **1225** *Ancr. R.* 418 Ne beate ou . . mid schurge i-leðered ne i-leaded. **1398** TREVISA *Barth. De P.R.* XVII. xxvi. (1495) 619 Smyten downe wyth leded arowes. **1538** LELAND *Itin.* V. 39 The Chirch of S. Oswalde is a very faire leddid Chirch. **1625** BACON *Ess., Building* (end), Tarrasses, Leaded aloft, and fairely garnished. **1726** CAVALLIER *Mem.* I. 108, I perceived by chance in a Dyer's House great Leaded Kettles, of above seven hundred Quintals weight. **1862** G. G. SCOTT *Rep.* in Willis & Clark *Cambridge* (1886) II. 328, I have introduced a timber leaded *flèche* as a belfry. **1887** RIDER HAGGARD *Jess* 3 He saw the ostrich's thick leg fly high into the air and then sweep down like a leaded bludgeon! **1891** T. HARDY *Tess* (1900) 124/2 The marble monuments and leaded skeletons at Kingsbere.

fig. **1889** SKRINE *Mem. E. Thring* 129 Who forgets the leaded accents with which he would say, 'that's fatal!'

b. Of panes of glass: Fitted into leaden cames.

1855 OGILVIE Suppl., *Leaded*, . . set in lead; as leaded windows. **1870** MORRIS *Earthly Par.* III. IV. 229 The drone Of the great organ shook the leaded panes. **1887** HISSEY *Holiday on Road* 27 Gothic porches, leaded latticed windows.

c. *Printing.* Having the lines separated by leads.

1864 in CRAIG *Suppl.* **1871** *Amer. Encycl. Printing* (ed. Ringwalt), *Leaded Matter*, matter with leads between the lines. **1886** *Pall Mall G.* 10 Aug. 1/1 The leaded articles penned in Fleet-street. **1893** R. KIPLING *Many Invent.* 166, I wrote three-quarters of a leaded bourgeois column.

d. Affected by lead-poisoning.

1878 J. H. BEADLE *Western Wilds* xxxv. 581 Great care must be taken by the workmen not to get 'leaded', that is, not to inhale the fumes from the melted lead, which are very poisonous. **1906** *Daily Chron.* 28 June 6/4 The children of 'leaded' mothers usually die, or if they live inherit the effects of the poison. **1914** *Dialect Notes* IV. 163 *Leaded*, among miners, ill from lead poisoning.

e. Containing added lead.

1936 *Blackw. Mag.* Mar. 359/2 It was said that Archie had obtained a special supply of leaded fuel, which would allow him to bring in the Kestrel supercharger near the ground. **1939** CARPENTER & ROBERTSON *Metals* II. xv. 1317 Alloys in the fifth group are those to which large amounts of lead are added to improve their suitability for certain types of bearings. . . These alloys are known as the 'plastic' or 'leaded' bronzes. **1963** H. R. CLAUSER *Encycl. Engin. Materials* 370/1 Sheet lead and sheets of leaded plastics are also being used to control noise. **1968** E. R. PETTY *Physical Metall. Engin. Materials* xiii. 266 Operators must be shielded from this penetrating radiation and for this purpose . . a foot of concrete or several feet of water (usually in a leaded-glass jacket) are necessary. **1972** *Lancet* 1 July 12/2 All the subjects had been simultaneously exposed to tetraethyl lead during the process of scaling a tank which had contained leaded petrol.

leaden (lɛd(ə)n), *a.* Forms: 1 léaden, 4 ledun, 4–5 leden, 5 ledyn, 6 leeden, 6– leaden. [OE. *léaden*: see LEAD *sb.*[1] and -EN[4].

The absence of umlaut shows that the word was formed in OE., not inherited from WGer. Cf. Du. *looden*.]

1. a. Consisting or made of lead.

c **1000** in Schmid *Gesetze* 414 Si þæt alfæt isen oððe æren, leaden oððe læmen. *c* **1000** ÆLFRIC *Hom.* I. 426 Mid leadenum swipum langlice swingan. **1382** WYCLIF *2 Macc.* iv. 14 Pleying with ledun dishe. **1420** *E.E. Wills* (1882) 46 Also iij[c]. of ledyn wyȝtis. **1596** SHAKS. *Merch. V.* II. vii. 15 What says this leaden casket? **1663** GERBIER *Counsel* 87 Leaden gutters. **1746–7** HERVEY *Medit.* (1818) 43 Swifter than a whirlwind flies the leaden death. **1816** J. SMITH *Panorama Sci. & Art* II. 558 Distilled in a leaden, earthen, or glass retort. **1855** MACAULAY *Hist. Eng.* xvi. III. 638 Deposited in a leaden coffin. **1875** JOWETT *Plato* (ed. 2) I. 252 She descended into the deep like a leaden plummet. **1883** R. W. DIXON *Mano* IV. xi. 177 The leaden roofs arose like terraces Behind the battlements.

b. In allegorical contexts, with allusion to qualities of the metal or to the fig. senses below, as in ***leaden key, sceptre***, attributed *poet.* to the powers of sleep or dullness; ***leaden sword***, the type of an ineffectual weapon.

1579 FULKE *Heskins' Parl.* 396 He heweth at it with his leaden sworde. **1601** SHAKS. *Jul. C.* IV. iii. 268 O Murd'rous slumber! Layest thou thy Leaden Mace vpon my Boy . . ? **1602** *2nd Pt. Return fr. Parnass.* IV. iii. 1887 Those leaden spouts, That nought downe vent but what they do receiue. **1682** O. N. tr. *Boileau's Lutrin* I. 35 When Eyes and Ears Nights leaden Key composes. **1742** YOUNG *Nt. Th.* I. 20 Night . . stretches forth Her leaden sceptre o'er a slumb'ring world. **1829** H. NEELE *Lit. Rem.* 33 The leaden sceptre of French taste was stretched over the tragic drama.

2. *transf.* and *fig.* **a.** Of base quality or composition; of little value; opposed to *golden*. **b.** Heavy as if made of lead; oppressive, burdensome; (of the limbs) hard to drag along, tardy in movement; hence said of movement, etc.; (of slumber or soporific influences) heavy, dull, benumbing. **c.** With allusion to the want of elasticity in the metal: Inert, spiritless, depressing. **d.** Of a dull, cold, pale colour; dull grey.

a. **1577** BATMAN (*title*) The Golden Booke of the Leaden Goddes. **1590** MARLOWE *Edw. II*, II. ii. (1598) D i b, Base leaden Earles, that glory in your birth. **1612** BP. HALL *Serm. Imprese of God* II. Wks. (1625) 455 The Church of Rome . . (which cares not if she haue golden vessels, though she haue leaden Prests). **1616** CAPT. SMITH *Descr. New Eng.* 33 The golden age and the leaden age.

b. **1579** LYLY *Euphues* (Arb.) 172 Though God haue leaden handes, which when they strike pay home. **1585** ABP. SANDYS *Serm.* xii. 197 It is good for a iudge commonly to haue leaden feete. **1609** *Ev. Wom. in Hum.* III. i. in Bullen *O. Pl.* IV, Lay not a leaden loade of foule reproach Upon so weake a prop. **1713** C'TESS WINCHELSEA *Misc. Poems* 13 [He] courts deforming Death, to mend his Leaden pace. **1725** POPE *Odyss.* IV. 610 Leaden slumbers press his drooping eyes. **1827–44** WILLIS *Jephthah's Dau.* 25 Onward came The leaden tramp of thousands. **1860** READE *Cloister & H.* xxxviii. (1896) 112 He has risen, and was dragging his leaden limbs along. **1878** B. TAYLOR *Deukalion* I. i. 15 That leaden weight which pressed mine eyelids to reluctant sleep. **1887** *Pall Mall G.* 9 Feb. 4/1, I have never felt the atmosphere of the House so leaden.

c. **1592** SHAKS. *Ven. & Ad.* 34 The tender boy, Who . . powted in a dull disdaine, With leaden appetite. **1641** MILTON *Ch. Govt.* vi. Wks. 1851 III. 124 To bring . . an unactive blindnesse of mind upon the people by their leaden doctrine. **1647** R. BARON *Cyprian Acad.* I. 8 Saturne, that leaden planet did cast his melancholy influence over all his intellectuals. **1865** MERIVALE *Rom. Emp.* VIII. lxiv. 90 Under its leaden rule little scope was left for the free and healthy exercise of mind. **1889** *Times* (weekly ed.) 20 Dec. 5/2 In 'the Progress of Spring' are leaden lines.

d. *c* **1386** CHAUCER *Can. Yeom. Prol. & T.* 175 Wher my colour was bothe fressh and reed Now is it wan and of leden hewe. **1576** NEWTON *Lemnie's Complex.* I. viii. 65 It declyneth to a swart and leaden colour, such as we see in men in the cold Wynter. **1840** GEN. P. THOMPSON *Exerc.* (1842) V. 131 Sleepless nights passed under the leaden eye of him he . . sent to death. **1865** GOSSE *Land & Sea* (1874) 4 The sky was leaden. **1877** BLACK *Green Past.* xxxiv. (1878) 270 The green islands lay desolate in the midst of the leaden sea. **1897** *Allbutt's Syst. Med.* II. 205 The vesicle . . has a uniform purple or leaden appearance.

3. Qualifying other adjectives.

1844 RUSKIN *Arrows Chace* (1880) I. 288 The lights being often a blaze of gold, and the shadows a dark leaden grey. **1846** BEDDOES *Let.* Poems p. cix, Prose of the leadenest drab dye has ever pursued Your humble servant. **1885** STEVENSON *Dynamiter* 126 Within, like a black and leaden-heavy kernel, he was conscious of the weight upon his soul. **1894** R. B. SHARPE *Handbk. Birds Gt. Brit.* I. 33 Bill, leaden blue.

4. *Comb.* Chiefly parasynthetic, as ***leaden-coloured, -eyed, -footed, -headed, -hearted*** (hence ***leaden-heartedness***), ***-heeled, -hued, -lidded, -locked, -natured, -pated, -skulled, -spirited, -thoughted, -weighted, -willed, -winged***; also ***leaden-stepping***, in which *leaden* is quasi-*adv.*; ***leaden-like*** adv.

1598 FLORIO, *Plombeo*, . . *leaden coloured. **1816** SHELLEY *Alastor* 557 Leaden-coloured even. **1820** KEATS *Ode Nightingale* 28 *Leaden-eyed despairs. **1596** R. L[INCHE] *Diella* (1877) 61 *Leaden-footed griefe. **1899** F. T. BULLEN *Log Sea-waif* 246 Never before . . had I felt time to be so leaden-footed. **1589** *Marprel. Epit.* E iij, Not . . so *leaden-headed as your brother Bridges. **1852** DICKENS *Bleak Ho.* i, A leaden-headed old corporation. **1596** R. L[INCHE] *Diella* (1877) 31 *Leaden-harted sleepe. **1938** C. DAY LEWIS *Overtures to Death* 14 Infirm and grey This leaden-hearted day Drags its lank hours. **1864** E. MURRAY *E. Norman* III. 28 He subsided into a sort of *leaden-heartedness. **1598** E. GUILPIN *Skial.* (1878) 35 Thys *leaden-heeled passion is to dull, To keepe pace with this Satyre-footed gull. **1877** W. BLACK *Green Past.* xxvii. (1878) 221 Water—*leaden-hued—with no trace of phosphorescent fire in it. **1946** W. DE LA MARE *Traveller* 18 His *leaden-lidded eyes. **1574** HELLOWES *Gueuara's Fam. Ep.* (1577) 169 To write so heauie or *leadenlike, your Lordship had no occasion. **1963** *Listener* 7 Mar. 429/1 A man . . Whiskered and *leaden-locked. **1889** SKRINE *Mem. E. Thring* 42 The . . *leaden-natured boy. **1603** FLORIO *Montaigne* II. viii. (1632) 220, I was the . . most *leaden-pated to learne my lesson. **1681** *Heraclitus Ridens* No. 42 (1713) II. 19 The Leaden-pated Gentleman propounded the Matter. ? *c* **1600** *Distracted Emp.* v. i. in Bullen *O. Pl.* III. 242 What a *leaden-skulld slave he makes me. **1609** J. DAVIES *Humours Heaven on Earth* (Grosart) 10/2 Let leane-fac'd *leaden-spirited Saturnists . . Prate what they list. ? **1630** MILTON *Time* 2 The lazy *leaden-stepping hours. **1596** R. L[INCHE] *Diella* (1877) 52 Now *leaden-thoughted Morpheus dyms each sight. **1888** T. W. REID *Life W. E. Forster* I. 75 *Leaden-weighted lethargy. **1596** FITZ-GEFFRAY *Sir F. Drake* (1881) 58 Summons my Muse . . Her *leaden-winged crest aloft to raise. *a* **1645** FEATLY *Reynolds* in Fuller *Abel Rediv.* (1867) II. 243 We university men were *leaden-witted, who admired so dull a man.

5. leaden fly-catcher, a small grey-green Australian bird, *Myiagra rubecula*, of the family Muscicapidæ (see FLY-CATCHER 2).

1908 E. J. BANFIELD *Confessions of Beachcomber* I. iii. 95 Leaden Fly-catcher, *Myiagra rubecula (plumbea)*. **1911** J. A. LEACH *Austral. Bird Bk.* 125 Leaden Flycatcher. . . Upper wings, tail, breast leaden-gray glossed with green. **1965** *Austral. Encycl.* IV. 121/1 The best-known [tropical flycatchers] are the leaden flycatcher (*Myiagra rubecula*) which migrates south to Tasmania, and the black-faced flycatcher.

Hence ˈ**leadenly** *adv.*, in a leaden manner; without elasticity or spring; after the manner, or with the effect of a leaden weight. ˈ**leadenness**, the quality of being leaden both in a material and an immaterial sense.

1611 COTGR., *Ternissure*, palenesse . . leadennesse of colour. **1879** G. MEREDITH *Egoist* II. vii. 141 It had sunk suddenly and leadenly under the sense of imprisonment. **1893** BEATRICE HARRADEN *Ships that pass* 99 The lovelessness and leadenness of his temperament. **1895** CROCKETT *Cleg Kelly* xxvii, She went leadenly up the steps.

leaden (lɛd(ə)n), *v.* [f. LEAD *sb.*[1] + -EN[5] or f. LEADEN *a.*] †**a.** *trans.* To fasten with molten lead. *Obs.* **b.** To make leaden or dull. **c.** *intr.* To press down like lead; only in **leadening** *ppl. a.*

1552 HULOET, Leaden or sowdre together, *plumbo*. **1835** *Fraser's Mag.* XII. 637 A leadening weight of something indescribable began to gather upon his heart. **1899** *Speaker* 29 July 107/1 The very completeness with which Mr. Mends has done his work . . leadens his narrative.

leaden, obs. dial. form of LEDEN.

Leadenhall (ˈlɛdənhɔːl). The name of an area in London, used *attrib.* in ***Leadenhall Market***, a poultry market in London; ***Leadenhall Street***, a street in London which from 1648 to 1861 contained the headquarters of the East India Company, hence designating the Company itself.

1587 J. STOW *Summarie Chron. Eng.* 407 The Northwest corner of Leaden Hall (the highest grounde of the Citie of London). **1720** STOW & STRYPE *Survey Cities London & Westminster* I. (*map facing p. 1*) Leaden Hall St. **1825** T. MOORE *Mem. Life R. B. Sheridan* I. viii. 367 The people, by the unanimous outcry with which they rose, in defence of the monopoly of Leadenhall Street . . proved how little of the '*vox Dei*' there may . . be in such clamour. **1831** J. BOADEN *Life Mrs. Jordan* II. i. 28 It showed, how the elegant mothers of Leadenhall Street, might, with the greatest gentleness, strain their young ones to bosoms equally *soft*, while they themselves were nourished by the *blood* and sweat of the unhappy peasant of Bengal. **1882** *Encycl. Brit.* XIV. 828/2 The principal markets . . are Smithfield (central meat market and poultry market), Leadenhall (poultry and game), Billingsgate (fish), Covent Garden (fruit and vegetables). **1932** P. SPEAR *Nabobs* 28 Wellesley's remark about 'the cheesemongers of Leadenhall Street' would have horrified them. **1952** M. BELLASIS *Honourable Company* p. viii, The factors and merchants, who first went out from

Leadenhall Street to 'shake the pagoda tree', were transformed in the course of two or three generations into.. self-effacing public servants. **1961** *Wonderful London* (Evening News) 56 Leadenhall market..was rebuilt in 1881.

leader[1] ('li:də(r)). Forms: 4–6 ledar(e, -er(e, (4 **ledder, leeder,** 5 **ledir, leedare),** 5–7 *Sc.* **leidar, -er,** (6 **ledair),** 6– **leader.** [OE. *lǣdere*, f. *lǣdan* LEAD *v.*[1] + -ER[1].]

I. One who leads.

1. a. *gen.* in various senses of the vb.: One who conducts, precedes as a guide, leads a person by the hand or an animal by a cord, etc. Also with adverbs, as ***leader-away, leader-on,*** for which see the corresponding verbal phrases. ***follow my leader***: see FOLLOW *v.* 1 c.

a **1300** *E.E. Psalter* liv. 14 Mi leder, and mi kowth sa gode. *c* **1374** CHAUCER *Troylus* IV. 1454 (1482) Oon thynketh þe bere But al a-nother thynketh his ledere. **1375** BARBOUR *Bruce* VII. 20 He suld ger Bath the sleuthhund and the ledar Tyne the sleuth men ger him ta. **1382** WYCLIF *Matt.* xv. 14 Thei ben blynde, and lederis of blynde men. **1398** TREVISA *Barth. De P.R.* XII. viii. (1495) 418 Curlewes haue guydes and ledars as cranes haue for they drede the goshawke. *c* **1450** *St. Cuthbert* (Surtees) 5675 Withouten ledar nedit he [a man struck blind] To abyde behynd. **1513** DOUGLAS *Æneis* I. xi. 5 Blyithlie following his ledair Achates. **1552** HULOET, Leder awaye, *abductor.* **1598** SHAKS. *Merry W.* III. ii. 3 You were wont to be a follower, but now you are a leader. **1633** FORD *Broken H.* I. ii, Without Reason, Voycing the Leader-on a Demi-god. **1667** MILTON *P.L.* VI. 451 Leader to free Enjoyment of our right as Gods. **1697** DRYDEN *Virg. Georg.* III. 526 Ample Plains, Where oft the Flocks without a Leader stray. **1838** DICKENS *Nich. Nick.* xiii, Follow your leader, boys, and take pattern by Smike if you dare. **1861** J. EDMOND *Childr. Ch. at Home* i. 17 Christ is..a leader to all that trust him.

†**b.** One who has the charge of (animals).

1495 *Act 11 Hen. VII*, c. 34 §4 The office of the Maistershippe of the leder of the Dere of the parke of Okeley.

†**c.** The driver of a vehicle (*obs.*). **d.** *dial.* A carter.

a **1300** *Cursor M.* 21283 Bath wise and war es þat leder [sc. of þe wain]. **1497** *Ld. Treas. Acc. Scot.* (1877) I. 355 Item, to the sand ledaris, xviijs. **1548** in *Burgh Rec. Edin.* (1871) II. 141 That na maner of persouns ledares of burne tak [etc.]. **1847** *Sheffield Indep.* (E.D.D.), A coal leader. **1887** DONALDSON *Suppl. to Jamieson* s.v., Until comparatively late years the occupation of water-carrier was followed by a large number of men and women, some carried by hand..; some by barrow..; and some by cart—those were the leaders. **1888** *Sheffield Gloss.*, *Leader*, a carter. 'A coal leader'.

2. One who leads a body of armed men; a commander, a captain.

a **1300** *Cursor M.* 7630 And of a thusand men o wal He made him [David] ledder and marscal. **1387** TREVISA *Higden* (Rolls) V. 217 The oost of þe Gothes was i-slawe in Thuscia, and here ledere Ragadasius was i-take. *c* **1400** tr. *Secreta Secret., Gov. Lordsh.* 108–9 Off lederes off ostes and here ordinaunce..Folwe þanne vche comandour tene vicaires, & vche vicaire tene lederes, & vche ledere tene denys. *c* **1470** HENRY *Wallace* IV. 143 Our leidar is gayne, Amang our fays he is set him allayne. **1591** SHAKS. *1 Hen. VI*, I. i. 143 A worthy Leader, wanting ayd, Vnto his dastard foe-men is betray'd. **1665** MANLEY *Grotius' Low C. Warres* 715 Sir Horace Vere..performed the duty, both of a good Leader and Souldier. **1828** SCOTT *F.M. Perth* xii, All this day..they will gather to their leader's standard. **1844** H. H. WILSON *Brit. India* III. 20 Detachments of troops were..sent..to secure the leaders.

3. a. One who guides others in action or opinion; one who takes the lead in any business, enterprise, or movement; one who is 'followed' by disciples or adherents; the chief of a sect or party. †In early use *occas.* a chieftain, governor.

Leader of the House of Commons: the member of the government who has the official initiative in the proceedings of the House; (see also quot. 1964); freq. *ellipt.* as ***Leader of the House***; so ***Leader of the House of Lords*** (or ***of the Upper House***).

1375 BARBOUR *Bruce* III. 660 Anguss..wes.. lord and ledar off kyntyr. **1495** *Act 11 Hen. VII*, c. 7 The seid.. principall or principallis leder or leders that unlaufully cause the seid people to gedre or rise. **1532** MORE *Confut. Tindale* Wks. 515/2 The leaders and maisters of the christen fayth. **1552** ABP. HAMILTON *Catech.* (1884) 47 To be ledar techar & direckar of the same kirk. **1596** DALRYMPLE tr. *Leslie's Hist. Scotl.* IX. 213 For his brotheris caus he was cheif leider of the ring. **1666** TEMPLE *Let. to Godolphin* Wks. 1713 II. 18 The Duke of Albuquerque you will find..no great Leader in Council or Business. **1719–20** SWIFT *Let. Yng. Clergyman* Misc. (1727) I. 361 Demosthenes and Cicero..each of them a Leader..in a popular State. **1771** *Junius Lett.* liv. 286, I am a partizan of the great leader of the opposition. **1828** D'ISRAELI *Chas. I*, II. xi. 269 A genius so commanding and so turbulent, was fitted to be the leader of a party. **1835** *Ann. Reg. 1834* 335/2 It was requisite to find a new chancellor of the Exchequer, and a new leader of the House of Commons. **1841–4** EMERSON *Ess., Manners* Wks. (Bohn) I. 208 If the people should destroy class after class, until two men only were left, one of these would be the leader. **1852** DISRAELI *Lord George Bentinck* xx. 397 The government abandoned this..project..scarcely with decency, for the leader of the house of lords was eulogizing its virtues..at the moment it was cast away by the chancellor of the exchequer. **1852** LD. PALMERSTON *Let.* 24 Dec. in J. Russell *Later Corr.* (1925) II. xx. 119 If the extensive duties of Leader of the House of Commons can be performed without salary why should any public officer have any? **1855** —— *Let.* 7 Feb. in Queen Victoria *Lett.* (1907) III. xxiv. 131 Proposed cabinet... Organ of the Government or Leader of the House of Lords. Marquis of Lansdowne. **1868** C. D. YONGE *Life 2nd Earl of Liverpool* I. iv. 145 According to the usage of that day, when the Prime Minister was a Commoner, the Home Secretary, if a peer, was the leader of the Upper House. **1869** A. TODD *On Parl. Govt. in Eng.* II. iv. 323 The leader of the House of Commons is at liberty to arrange the order of business appointed for government nights as he thinks fit. **1874** GREEN *Short Hist.* viii. §5. 500 The leaders in the country party..were thrown into prison. **1883** FROUDE *Short Stud.* IV. II. ii. 187 Circumstances independent of himself could alone have raised him into a leader of a party. **1908** A. E. STEINTHAL tr. *Redlich's Procedure House of Commons* I. 120 The name and function of the chief member of the Government in the House of Commons, the Leader of the House. **1964** ABRAHAM & HAWTREY *Parl. Dict.* (ed. 2) 111 The term 'Leader of the House' was originally applied to the chief spokesman for the Government in the House of Commons when the Prime Minister was a member of the House of Lords. *Ibid.*, The Leader of the House receives no salary as such... His chief responsibility is for planning and supervising the Government's legislative programme, and in particular for the arrangement..of the business of the House. *Ibid.* 112 The Leader of the House of Lords is the chief spokesman for the Government in that House. **1974** *Guardian* 30 Apr. 1/4 A statement from Mr Short, Leader of the House, on the registration of interests is promised later this week, but there are deep differences between the parties over whether the register should be compulsory or voluntary. *Ibid.*, A promised personal statement by Mr Short, Deputy Leader of the Labour Party and Leader of the House of Commons, was delayed by several hours last night.

†**b.** Phrases. ***leader of laws***: one who has power in the state, a ruler. ***leader of hail***: a guide to salvation. *Obs.*

13.. *E.E. Allit. P.* B. 1307 He..hatz..þe lederes of her lawe layd to þe grounde. *c* **1375** *Sc. Leg. Saints* i. (*Petrus*) 674 And þu [Paul] dere brothir, far wele ay lledar of heile and saweoure. *c* **1440** *York Myst.* xxx. 55 O leder of lawis. *a* **1605** MONTGOMERIE *Sonn.* xxi. 1 My lords, late lads, nou leidars of our lauis.

c. A counsel who 'leads' (see LEAD *v.*[1] 16) in the conduct of a case before the court; a barrister whose status (in England, that of a King's Counsel) entitles him to 'lead'. Also, the senior counsel of a circuit.

1856 WILKIE COLLINS *A Rogue's Life* v, He had engaged the leader of the circuit to defend me. **1878** BALL *Student's Guide to Bar* 44 At the trial itself he will generally have a 'leader' on whom the conduct of the case will wholly depend. **1883** J. H. SLATER *Guide Legal Prof.* 17 Queen's Counsel are usually termed 'Leaders', and they sit in front of the utter Barristers, whom they are said to 'lead' in any particular case in which both are engaged.

d. The foremost or most eminent member (of a profession); also, in wider sense, a person of eminent position and influence.

1858 O. W. HOLMES *Aut. Breakf.-t.* v. (1859) 115 Judges, mayors..leaders in science..were represented in that meeting. **1884** *Illustr. Lond. News* 1 Nov. 410/3 Here is Mr. F. Archer, the leader of his profession.

e. *spec.* as a rendering of G. *Führer*, It. *Duce*, or Sp. *Caudillo*: the head of an authoritarian state. Usu. with capital initial. Also *transf.* (in quot. 1934 applied to the leader of the British Fascists, Sir Oswald Mosley).

1918 [see CAUDILLO]. **1934** H. G. WELLS *Exper. Autobiogr.* II. ix. 783 Quite a quantity of pleasant boys and nice young men.. were acting as ushers, selling idiotic songs about their glorious Leader. **1937** A. HUXLEY *Ends & Means* i. 2 The twentieth [century] has already witnessed..the emergence of the sheep-like social man and the god-like Leader. **1939** S. SPENDER tr. *Toller's Pastor Hall* I. 48 I've never spoken a word against the Leader. **1952** A. BULLOCK *Hitler* iii. 123 There was persistent..grumbling at the amount of money the Leader and his friends took out of Party funds for their own expenses. **1960** H. SETON-WATSON *Neither War nor Peace* viii. 226 The head of the government was the Chancellor, Adolf Hitler, who was also Leader (*Führer*) of the party, and on the death of President Hindenburg in 1934 replaced him as Head of State with the title of Leader of the German Nation.

4. One who leads a choir or band of dancers, musicians, or singers. ***leader of praise*** (Sc.) = PRECENTOR.

1530 PALSGR. 238/1 Leeder of a daunce, *auant dancevr.* **1599** SHAKS. *Much Ado* II. i. 157 We must follow the Leaders. **1811** BUSBY *Dict. Mus.* (ed. 3), *Leader*, a performer who in a concert takes the principal violin, receives the time and style of the movements from the conductor, and communicates them to the rest of the band. **1859** JEPHSON *Brittany* xvi. 269 The leader, as in our village churches, was evidently a person of immense importance. **1892** *Glasgow Herald* 22 Apr. 2/2 Leader of Praise Wanted. **1900** *Blackw. Mag.* July 51/1 The leader trills ahead in runs and shakes up and down the scale.

5. Among Methodists, the presiding member of a 'class' (see CLASS *sb.* 7 b). Usually ***class-leader.***

1743 WESLEY *Nat. United Societies* Wks. 1872 VIII. 270 There are about twelve persons in every class; one of whom is styled the Leader. **1791** [see CLASS *sb.* 7 b].

6. a. The first man in a file, one in the front rank, one of the foremost in a moving body. In *Surveying*, the foremost carrier of the chain.

1604 EDMONDS *Observ. Cæsar's Comm.* 130 Euery one is especially to acknowledge his leader or foremost man to be the author of all his motions. **1616–1809** [see *file-leader*, FILE *sb.*[2] 11]. **1622** PEACHAM *Compl. Gent.* (1634) 240 The men in the File are to be distinguished by the names of Leaders, Bringers up and Middle-men. **1857** HUGHES *Tom Brown* I. vii, The leaders are busy making casts into the fields on the left and right. **1860** TYNDALL *Glac.* I. xxv. 188 Another person was sent forward, who drew himself up by the rope which was attached to the leader.

b. One of the front horses in a team, or the front horse in a tandem.

a **1700** B. E. *Dict. Cant. Crew*, *Leaders*..the Fore-horses in Coaches and Teams. **1784** COWPER *Tiroc.* 254 With pack-horse constancy we keep the road..True to the jingling of our leader's bells. **1825** HONE *Every-day Bk.* I. 1191 He was a capital horse, the off-leader. **1859** DICKENS *T. Two Cities* I. ii, The near leader violently shook his head. **1886** RUSKIN *Præterita* I. vi. 182 If the horses were young..there was a postillion for the leaders also.

7. a. *Cards.* The first player in a round; also, one who 'leads' from a particular suit.

1677 MIEGE *Eng.-Fr. Dict.* s.v., A leader, in Cards, *celui que joue le premier.* **1742** HOYLE *Whist* (1763) 45 If the Leader of that Suit or his Partner have the long Trump. **1876** A. CAMPBELL-WALKER *Correct Card* Gloss. (1880) 12 *Leader*, the first to play each round.

b. *Curling.* The first player: cf. LEAD *sb.*[2] 5 a.

1789 D. DAVIDSON *Seasons* 166 Next Robin o' Mains, a leader good, Close to the witter drew.

II. A thing which leads.

8. a. *gen.* **b.** *colloq.* A remark or question intended to lead conversation (cf. FEELER 4 b). **c.** *Comm.* (orig. U.S.) = LEADING ARTICLE 2; cf. *loss leader* s.v. LOSS *sb.*[1] 10.

c **1290** *S. Eng. Leg.* I. 33/124 þe steorre gan softe to glide forth, also it were þene way to teche... þe Abbot Anourede his ledare. *c* **1450** tr. *De Imitatione* III. lxi. 143 þe crosse is þe lif of a gode monke, & þe leder to paradise. **1581** MULCASTER *Positions* Ep. Ded. (1887) 4 It is an argument which craueth consideration, bycause it is the leader to a further consequence. **1851** C. CIST *Sk. Cincinnati in 1851* xv. 319 These articles [*sc.* sugar, molasses, coffee, etc.] are the leaders, as they are called, in commercial transactions, with the west. **1882** MRS. RIDDELL *Pr. Wales's Garden-Party* 34 'And what did you make of them over the dish of tea?' suggested the young man as a leader. **1888** *Chicago Tribune* 29 Apr. 4/7 Goods advertised and sold below cost are technically known as 'leaders'. **1889** *Pop. Sci. Monthly* XXXIV. 622 A new rival may inflict severe loss..through cutting the price of a staple below cost, and making it what is called a 'leader'. **1895** *Critic* 6 Apr. 263/1 In several Sixth Avenue houses, new books by popular writers have long been used as 'leaders'—the technical name, I believe, for goods sold at little or no profit, sometimes even at a loss, for the sake of drawing customers, with a view of getting them to buy other wares as well. **1963** 'R. FINDLATER' *What are Writers Worth?* 14 Most [paperback] firms produce about a dozen titles every month..at the summit the 'leader'—the smash-hit novel on which the selling machine is focused. **1967** *Times Rev. Industry* Feb. 31/1 Establishing new products is both costly and hazardous..while old leaders tend to decline over the years. **1972** *Lebende Sprachen* XVII. 34/1 US leader—BE/US loss leader, BE leading article.

9. In a tree or shrub: The shoot which grows at the apex of the stem, or of a principal branch; also, a bine.

1572 MASCALL *Plant. & Graff.* (1592) 75 Ye shall neuer leaue aboue two or three leaders at the head of any principall branch. **1822** LOUDON *Encycl. Gardening* 808 Retain a competent supply of side-shoots, with a good leader to each mother-branch. **1880** JEFFERIES *Gt. Estate* 89 The leaders of the black bryony..twist around each other. **1892** *Gardeners' Chron.* 27 Aug. 242/1 The trees are allowed to waste their energies in the formation of a plurality of leaders at the top.

10. A tendon. (Cf. *guide, guider.*)

1708 J. C. *Compl. Collier* (1845) 23 Cutting their Leaders and Nerves. **1737** BRACKEN *Farriery Impr.* (1757) II. 22 What the common People call Leaders or Sinews. **1854** OWEN *Skel. & Teeth* (1855) 3 The leaders of the leg-muscles in the turkey. **1891** *Daily News* 4 Sept. 3/7 In his second performance he severed one of the leaders of his thigh.

11. a. In agricultural drainage: A main drain. **b.** A tributary.

1844 *Jrnl. R. Agric. Soc.* V. I. 9 One of the drains that enter the leader. **1853** G. JOHNSTON *Nat. Hist. E. Bord.* I. 15 The leaders to these burns are, in some places, called sykes.

12. = LEADING ARTICLE 1.

1837 *Southern Lit. Messenger* III. 418/2 The Editor thus commenceth his leader. **1838** DICKENS *Let.* 23 Dec. (1965) I. 475, I was very much obliged indeed to you for the paper. I..was greatly amused with the 'leader'. **1844** DISRAELI *Coningsby* II. vi, Give me a man who can write a leader. **1847** R. P. MILNES in T. W. Reid *Life Ld. Houghton* (1891) I. ix. 401 You can get..a file of the *Times*, the commercial leaders of which you should get up. **1862** SHIRLEY *Nugæ Crit.* xi. 482 He thought a page of Clarendon as pleasant historical reading as a leader in the *Times*. **1892** B. MATTHEWS *Americanisms & Brit.* 22 An American..calls that an 'editorial' which the Englishman calls a 'leader'.

13. *Mining.* **a.** A drain or stream that by its colour indicates the presence of minerals. **b.** (See quot. 1846.) **c.** A small and insignificant vein, which leads to or indicates the proximity of a larger and better.

1809 A. HENRY *Trav.* 231 A green-coloured water, which tinged iron of a copper-colour, issued from the hill; and this the miners called a leader. **1846** BROCKETT *N.C. Words*, *Leader*, a small band of coal connecting the portions of a coal-seam detached by a dyke, and following which, leads the miner to the seam again. **1855** *Cornwall* 95 Frequently the prevailing mineral runs continuously through the lode for considerable lengths and depths, forming what is called the leader. **1880** C. C. ADLEY *Rep. Pioneer Mining Co.* 2 Oct. 1 Two strong veins or leaders carrying copper ore have been crossed. **1890** *Goldfields Victoria* 16 The prospects of the mine have improved, two auriferous leaders having been cut. **1900** *Daily News* 19 June 3/2 One or two tunnels had been drawn..on small leaders and..diamonds had been discovered.

14. *Fireworks* and *Gunnery.* A quick match enclosed in a paper tube for the purpose of conveying fire rapidly. Also *attrib.*, as ***leader pipe*** (see quot.).

1859 F. A. GRIFFITHS *Artil. Man.* (1862) 60 Lay a leader of quick match along the bore. *Ibid.* 282. **1878** KENTISH *Pyrotechn. Treas.* 103 Leader Pipes. These are for piping quickmatch.

15. *Fishing.* (*U.S.*) **a.** The end portion of a reel-line, consisting of gut, and having the snells of the fly-hooks attached to it; a casting-line.

1859 BARTLETT *Dict. Amer.*, *Leader*, a length of finely twisted hair, gut, or grass, for attaching an angler's hook to the line; a bottom. Called also a Snell. **1885** *Harper's Mag.* Apr. 777/1 The flies are attached to a leader, or, as our English brethren term it, a casting-line.

b. 'A net so placed as to intercept fish and lead them into a pound, weir, trap-net, etc.' (Knight *Dict. Mech.* Suppl. 1884).

16. *Machinery.* **a.** (See quots.)

1805 BREWSTER in *Ferguson's Lect.* I. 82 *note*, In a combination of wheels that which is acted upon by the power, or by some other wheel is called a leader. **1825** J. NICHOLSON *Operat. Mechanic* 21 When speaking of the action of wheel-work in general, the wheel which acts as a mover is called the *leader*, and the one upon which it acts the *follower*. **1895** *Mod. Steam Engine* 58 The wheels of a locomotive are called—1st, leaders or leading-wheels.

b. *U.S.* = *leading block.* **c.** 'A principal furrow leading from the eye to the skirt of a mill-stone' (1875 Knight *Dict. Mech.* s.v. *Millstone*). **d.** 'One of the long vertical timbers guiding the ram of a pile-driver car' (Funk's *Stand. Dict.*).

17. *Printing.* A line of dots or dashes to guide the eye in letterpress.

1824 J. JOHNSON *Typogr.* II. iii. 59 Full points are sometimes used as leaders in tables of contents. **1871** *Amer. Encycl. Printing* (ed. Ringwalt), *Leaders* (.... or ---), these consist of two or three dots, similar to full points, cast on one type, to the em body; there are also two or three em leaders, the number of dots being multiplied according to their length. Hyphen-faced leaders are also made (----).

18. *Sc.* and *U.S.* A pipe to conduct water.

1875 in Knight *Dict. Mech.* **1890** LOWSON *Guidfollow* xix. 161 The name 'Spout' was derived from a spout, stroupe, or leader, that was inserted into the bank..leading the water which ran [etc.].

19. *U.S.* A guiding ring in an animal's nose. (*Cent. Dict.*)

20. *Cinemat.* and *Tape Recording.* A short length of blank or uncoated film or tape attached at the beginning or end of a reel for purposes of threading or identification.

1917 C. N. BENNETT *Guide to Kinematogr.* xi. 185 Refrain from..cutting or punching holes in the film leaders. **1960** J. M. LLOYD *All-in-One Tape Recorder Bk.* (ed. 4) v. 63 The inside and outside leaders are usually of different colours. **1969** J. ELLIOT *Duel* III. ii. 233 She went to..learn the mysteries of..opticals and leaders and parallel and printing sync. **1969** D. N. WOOD *On Tape* vii. 82 This brings me to the other main use of the leader tape—to act as a title... It is possible to use a chinagraph pencil on the tape itself, but it is much better to use leaders for this purpose.

21. *Meteorol.* In full, ***leader stroke.*** A preliminary stroke of lightning that ionizes the path taken by the much brighter return stroke that follows.

1934 SCHONLAND & COLLENS in *Proc. R. Soc.* A. CXLIII. 657 These preliminary downward strokes will be referred to as leader strokes and the upward strokes which follow them will be called main strokes. *Ibid.*, Sometimes the leader is so faint that a portion only of the track can be seen. **1937** *Jrnl. Inst. Electr. Engin.* LXXXI. 6/2 Immediately the stepped leader stroke reaches the earth the..return stroke begins to travel..from earth to cloud. *Ibid.*, The leaders to the second and subsequent strokes of a flash usually travel from cloud to ground in a single flight. **1963** *Meteorol. Gloss.* (Meteorol. Office) (ed. 4) 154 Leader strokes directed upwards from ground to cloud may predominate in the case of very high structures. **1966** *McGraw-Hill Encycl. Sci. & Technol.* VII. 510/1 Cloud-to-cloud strokes also involve a step leader and main return stroke.

22. *attrib.* and *Comb.*, as (sense 3 e) ***leader-principle, -worship***; (sense 6 b) ***leader-mule***; (sense 12) ***leader-column, -note, -page, -writer.*** **leader board** orig. *U.S.*, a score-board, esp. at a golf-course, on which the names, etc., of the leading competitors are displayed; **leader stroke** (see sense 21); **leader tape**, uncoated tape intended for use as a leader on a reel of magnetic tape; a length of tape so used.

1970 *Golf Digest* Aug. 40/3 Last year there were not enough *leader boards and scoreboards at the PGA. **1986** *Sunday Express Mag.* 9 Nov. 79/1 The maverick of the golf course. That phrase summed up Severiano Ballesteros when he first appeared on the leader boards. **1897** *Daily News* 3 June 5/4 The problem set in our *leader columns the other day. **1890** L. C. D'OYLE *Notches* 108 Not forgetting.. to bestow an occasional cut upon the *leader-mules. **1932** J. BUCHAN *Gap in Curtain* i. 54 Each of us must concentrate on one particular part to which his special interest was pledged —Tavanger on the first City page, for example, Mayot on the *leader page, [etc.]. **1938** *Observer* 9 Jan. 5/1 (Advt.), Eugene Lyons..Assignment in Utopia..'A moving and truthful account...'—Malcolm Muggeridge (*D. Telegraph*, leader-page article). **1940** 'G. ORWELL' *Crit. Ess.* (1951) 80 The absence of the *leader-principle. There is no central dominating character. **1960** J. M. LLOYD *All-in-One Tape Recorder Bk.* (ed. 4) v. 64 *Leader tape is transparent and is shiny on both sides. **1962** A. NISBETT *Technique Sound Studio* vi. 107 A leader tape (giving summarized details of the contents) and a trailer (several feet of coloured tape to give a visual indication of the end) may be cut on to the recording. **1971** *Hi-Fi Sound* Feb. 42 (Advt.), We also carry a full range of Accessories, Leader Tape, Empty Spools, Splicing Tape etc. **1940** 'G. ORWELL' *Crit. Ess.* (1951) 83 More bloodshed, more *leader-worship. **1882** C. PEBODY *Eng. Journalism* xix. 144 It is as a *leader-writer and special correspondent that he will be best remembered. **1888** BESANT *Inner House* 3 No news came. This was especially hard on the leader-writers. **1940** *Manch. Guardian Weekly* 22 Mar. 228 But now it is stated in Berlin that Mr. Kuusinen 'has been promoted to be a leader-writer on an obscure provincial paper'.

†**'leader**[2]. *Obs. rare*$^{-0}$. [f. LEAD *v.*[2] (? or *sb.*[1]) + -ER[1].] A plumber.

c **1440** *Promp. Parv.* 292/1 Leedare or plummare.

'leadered, *pa. pple.* [f. LEADER[1] 12.] Treated in a leading article; made the subject of a leader.

1884 *Pall Mall Gaz.* 29 Nov. 3/2 If it [*sc.* an interview] had been a speech it would have been 'leadered' all round. **1897** *Westm. Gaz.* 25 Sept. 5/2 Seeing that the subject is 'leadered' in both papers.

leaderess ('liːdərɪs). Also 6 leadress(e. [f. LEADER[1] + -ESS.] A female leader.

1599 THYNNE *Animadv.* (1865) 74 They agree yt shoulde not be a 'minoresse', but a 'mooveresse' or leadresse of and to anger and yre. **1888** *Daily News* 9 Nov. 2/1 Mrs. K...a leader, or leaderess of the Ladies' Land League.

leaderette (liːdə'rɛt). [f. LEADER[1] (sense 12) + -ETTE.] A short editorial paragraph, printed in the same type as the 'leaders' in a newspaper.

1880 *Athenæum* 4 Sept. 289/2 One able to write crisp Original Leaderettes..would have preference. **1895** MAR. CORELLI *Sorrows of Satan* ix. (1897) 97 This paragraph of mine..will take the shape of a 'leaderette'.

leaderless ('liːdəlɪs), *a.* [f. LEADER[1] + -LESS.] Having no leader; without a leader.

1870 MORRIS *Earthly Par.* IV. 284 Some men must.. leaderless go forth unto the flame. **1878** LECKY *England in 18th C.* (1883) I. 326 The party..had been left leaderless by the deaths of Stanhope and Sunderland. **1894** *Times* 15 Jan. 14/4 The would-be defenders of Paris were little more than a leaderless mob.

'leaderly, *a.* [f. LEADER[1] 3 + -LY[1].] Having the character of a leader.

1918 H. G. WELLS *In Fourth Year* ii. 23 Very rarely has it [*sc.* the United States] failed to set up very leaderly and distinguished men [as Presidents]. **1922** —— *Short Hist. World* xix. 104 They distinguished certain families as leaderly and noble. **1973** *Daily Tel.* 24 Nov. 16 The engineering community..is entitled to a more leaderly and statesmanlike response.

leadership ('liːdəʃɪp). [f. LEADER[1] + -SHIP.] The dignity, office, or position of a leader, esp. of a political party; ability to lead; the position of a group of people leading or influencing others within a given context; the group itself; the action or influence necessary for the direction or organization of effort in a group undertaking. Also *attrib.*, as ***leadership behaviour, school, skill.***

1821 C. W. WYNN *Let.* 11 Mar. in *Corr.* (1920) 268 Charles writes that Tierney has regularly resigned the Leadership of the Opposition. **1834** FONBLANQUE *Eng. under 7 Administr.* (1887) III. 130 Is the leadership of the House to be conservatively settled by placing the minority in office? **1856** E. A. BOND *Russia close 16th C.* (Hakl. Soc.) Introd. 29 An invasion of the Crim Tartars..under the leadership of their khan. *a* **1859** MACAULAY *Hist. Eng.* xxiv. (1861) V. 165 That high position which has now been long called the Leadership of the House of Commons. **1870** *Pall Mall G.* 26 Aug. 1 Nothing is wanted but military leadership and military means. **1885** *Law Times* LXXIX. 351/2 The leadership of a great circuit. **1915** E. & C. PAUL tr. *Michels's Pol. Parties* IV. ii. 261 (*heading*) Analysis of the bourgeois elements in the socialist leadership. **1930** O. OESER tr. *Bühler's Mental Devel. Child* vii. 166 From the schoolgoing age onwards we find that some have the talent for leadership. **1933** M. S. VITELES *Industr. Psychol.* xxvii. 626 The substitution of morale for discipline and of integration for domination calls for a change in the quality of leadership in industry. **1939** J. D. BROWN in C. I. Barnard *Dilemmas of Leadership* 3 To treat the difficult problem of executive leadership. **1939** C. I. BARNARD *Ibid.* 24 If a system once accepted..destroys leadership or divides followers—then disorganization, schism, rebellion..ensues. **1947** SHERIF & CANTRIL *Psychol. of Ego-Involvements* vii. 182 Leadership, then, was seen to be a function of the group and its activities. **1962** K. ORVIS *Damned & Destroyed* xiv. 95 He went to a communist leadership school. **1963** J. E. GERALD *Social Responsibility of Press* v. 100 Few of the editors of mass-circulation newspapers since 1830 have risked their careers to exert strong leadership in the community. **1964** GOULD & KOLB *Dict. Social Sci.* 380/2 The manifestation of leadership behaviour can be observed only in relation to other persons who act in response to the leader and who are collectively referred to as the *following*. **1964** MRS. L. B. JOHNSON *White House Diary* 16 Jan. (1970) 51 We had an early dinner this evening..for the heads of the Senate Committees..and the Leadership on both sides and their wives. **1964** *English Studies* XLV. 50 Administrative and leadership skill. **1972** *Jrnl. Social Psychol.* LXXXVI. 29 Investigations of the relationship between personality traits and leadership behavior have failed to reveal any consistent patterns. **1973** M. TRUMAN *Harry S. Truman* xv. 306 Dad once defined leadership as the art of persuading people to do what they should have done in the first place.

leadger, obs. form of LEDGER.

'leadhillite. *Min.* [Named by Beudant, 1832, from Leadhills in Scotland, the locality where it was found: see -ITE.] A sulphato-carbonate of lead, found in whitish pearly crystals.

1835 C. U. SHEPARD *Treat. Min.* II. 6. **1852** *Phillips' Min.* 565 Haidinger..was led to suppose the crystallization of leadhillite to be oblique. **1885** ERNI *Min. Simplified* 262 Leadhillite..crystallizes in the orthorhombic system.

'lead-in. [f. vbl. phr. *to lead in* (LEAD *v.*[1] 2); cf. *leading-in* adj. (LEADING *ppl. a.* 1 c).] **1. a.** A wire that leads in from outside, *esp.* one connecting an outdoor aerial with an indoor receiver or transmitter. Freq. *attrib.*

1913 *Wireless World* Apr. p. xxxvii/2 The lead was taken from the mast in the garden down to the instruments, which were now moved to the ground floor. This gave me a lead-in wire of 65 ft. **1913** *Work* 14 June 217/3 Lead in, about 40 ft. insulated. **1924** *Wireless World* 10 Sept. 679/2 (*caption*) By fixing your lead-in in this way opening and closing the window is not interfered with. **1934** *Practical Wireless* V. 62/1 (*heading*) A weather-proof lead-in. *Ibid.*, About 6 in. from the end of the lead-in wire, bind round with a 3 in. length of..copper wire. **1950** *Jrnl. Sci. Instrum.* XXVII. 231 (*heading*) Insulated power lead-in for vacuum systems.

b. A wire in an electric lamp that carries the current between the cap and the filament or electrode. Freq. *attrib.*

1929 *Encycl. Brit.* VIII. 291/1 The lead-in wires which carry the current to the filament have to be sealed through the glass. **1962** N. H. CODLING in G. A. T. Burdett *Automatic Control Handbk.* viii. 6 Nickel-steel of 42 per cent composition, when copper-clad, is used for the lead-ins of lamps. **1970** A. BYERS *Home Lighting* ii. 45 (*heading*) Lead-in wires.

2. *transf.* and *fig.* An introduction, opening, etc.

1928 *Melody Maker* Feb. 188/2 It is electrifying to hear the solo instrumentalists rip in on some unexpected lead-in. **1952** W. R. BURNETT *Vanity Row* xiv. 118 Like a radio announcer with an embarrassingly far-fetched lead-in to the commercial. **1958** [see LEAD-OUT 1]. **1958** *Economist* 15 Nov. 579/2 The fantasy life portrayed [*i.e.*, in certain children's comics] is simply a lead-in to the more elaborate and still more depressing dreamworld of the women's magazines. **1962** W. NOWOTTNY *Lang. Poets Use* iv. 90 That opening is seen to be not an embarrassed and forced lead-in to a technically necessary comparison but rather a first and major step in the development of the whole. **1963** P. MOYES *Murder à la Mode* i. 20 Helen Pankhurst finished her lead-in blurb to the Collections feature. **1963** D. OGILVY *Confessions Advertising Man* (1964) viii. 131 Don't mess about with irrelevant lead-ins. Start selling in your first frame. **1971** *Daily Tel.* 11 Feb. 30/6 Workers who agree in writing to operate incentive bonus schemes should get a 'lead-in' payment of £1 a week. **1972** D. HASTON *In High Places* xii. 155, I heard the full story about Harsh's death and began to get some lead-in to the political infighting that had been going on. **1973** *Listener* 30 Aug. 295/1 Keep the lead-in short; some [news]papers enforce a 14-word limit on opening sentences.

leading ('liːdɪŋ), *vbl. sb.*[1] [f. LEAD *v.*[1] + -ING[1].]

1. a. The action of LEAD *v.*[1], in various senses.

a **1300** *Cursor M.* 2866 If ani fische þar-in bigane, Wit leding o þe flum iordane, þe lijf it es for-don wit stink. **1340** HAMPOLE *Pr. Consc.* 4217 Thurgh ledyng of þe fende He sal even to Ierusalem wende. *c* **1380** WYCLIF *Sel. Wks.* III. 358 No woundir ȝif men gone þikke to helle bi þe leding of suche prelatis. *c* **1440** *Three Kings Cologne* 50 þorwe þe gret mercy of god and ledyng of þis sterre, þei com..in to Ierusalem. **1555** PHILPOT in Strype *Eccl. Mem.* III. App. xlix. 157 Through his lovyng and comfortable leading and governance. **1570** DEE *Math. Pref.* dj b, Hydragogie, demonstrateth the possible leading of Water, by Natures lawe, and by artificiall helpe, from any head to any other place assigned. **1690** WOOD *Life* 15 July, So feeble that he could not goe without leading. **1805** *Trans. Soc. Arts* XXIII. 35 The filling, leading, and spreading of 2500 carts of compost. **1846** TRENCH *Mirac.* Introd. (1862) 73 Humanity is being carried forward under a mightier leading than its own. **1891** *Labour Commission* Gloss., *Leading*, conveying coals by carts from the pits to the workmen's houses.

b. with *forth*, *off*.

a **1240** *Lofsong* in *Cott. Hom.* 207 Ich bide þe..bi his ledunge forð, bi al þet me him demde, bi [etc.]. **1890** *Daily News* 6 Jan. 3/5 The leading off of the rain from the Vomero.

†**c.** A figure in dancing. *Obs.*

1694 MOTTEUX *Rabelais* v. xxiv. (1737) 105 *Coupés*, Hops, Leadings, Risings.

d. ***light or leading*** (Milton) = illumination or guidance; hence in Burke's phrase, ***men of light and leading*** (cf. quot. 1596 in 2).

1644 MILTON *Jdgm. Bucer* Wks. 1851 IV. 296, I owe no light or leading receiv'd from any man in the discovery of this truth. **1790** BURKE *Fr. Rev.* Wks. V. 191 The men of England, the men, I mean, of light and leading, in England. **1846** DISRAELI *Sp. Ho. Comm.* 15 June, The language that has been used in this House by men of great light and leading.

2. a. The action of commanding and marching at the head of armed men. † ***at one's leading***: under one's command. †Also, ability to command, generalship.

c **1400** MAUNDEV. (Roxb.) vi. 20 Ilk ane admyrall sall hafe at his ledyng foure or fyue or sex men of armes. **1411** *Rolls of Parlt.* III. 650/2 All the Knyghtes and Esquiers and Yomen that had ledynge of men on his partie. *c* **1470** HENRY *Wallace* IX. 1285 A hundreth men was at his ledyng still. **1596** SHAKS. *1 Hen. IV*, IV. iii. 17, I wonder much, being men of such great leading as you are, That you fore-see not what impediments Drag backe our expedition. *c* **1630** RISDON *Surv. Devon* §74 (1810) 75 Under the leading of the Lord Walter Manny. **1642** *Commiss.* in *Buccleuch MSS.* (Hist. MSS. Comm.) I. 529 Commanders for the governing, leading, and commanding of them. **1719** DE FOE *Crusoe* I. xvii. (1840) 293 They would be absolutely under my leading, as their..captain. **1813** SCOTT *Rokeby* III. xxiii, His gallant leading won my heart. **1828-40** TYTLER *Hist. Scot.* (1864) I. 167 The civil government in Scotland, and the leading of its armies, were in the hands of Mar and March. **1878** SIMPSON *Sch. Shaks.* I. 96 A great armada was being prepared which was said to be intended to pass the seas under the leading of Stucley. **1898** *United Service Mag.* July

406 The higher leading may go to pieces, and confusion of command may ensue.

†**b.** Government, rule. *Obs.*

c **1375** *Sc. Leg. Saints* xl. (*Ninian*) 820 A nobil knycht had þe leding of þe land. **1375** BARBOUR *Bruce* I. 579 Than thocht he to have the leding Off all Scotland. *c* **1430** *Syr Gener.* (Roxb.) 356 All that land was in hir ledyng.

†**c.** quasi-*concr.* The followers of a leader.

1375 BARBOUR *Bruce* XV. 302 Thai that war of his leding.. War all ded. **1382** WYCLIF *Gen.* l. 9 He hadde in his ledyng [Vulg. *in comitatu*] chares, and rydynge men. *c* **1400** *Rom. Rose* 5863 Al the folk of hir leding,.. never wist what was fleing.

†**3.** *Arith.* Multiplication. Const. *in, into.*

c **1430** *Art of Nombryng* (E.E.T.S.) 14 Nombre superficial is þat comethe of ledynge of oo nombre into a-nother. *Ibid.*, The solide nombre or cubike is þat þat comythe of double ledynge of nombre in nombre.

4. *Lead-mining.* (See quots.) Cf. LEADER[1] 13 c.

1653 MANLOVE *Lead-Mines* 3 If any..find a Rake, Or sign, or leading to the same. **1747** HOOSON *Miner's Dict.* s.v. *Break-off*, If it happen that it [a vein] break into several Leadings or Strings. **1802** MAWE *Min. Derbyshire* Gloss., *Leadings*, small sparry veins in the rock. **1829** *Glover's Hist. Derby* I. 65 The branches [of a vein] have a general communication by means of fine slender threads, or *leadings*, as the miners term them.

5. A directing influence or guidance; esp. a spiritual indication of the proper course of action in any case. A term used by the Quakers; also in the usage of other religious bodies, and in philosophy.

1821 *Congregational Mag.* Nov. 579 What is Christian experience, but this working in us, this leading of the spirit of God? **1859** GEO. ELIOT *Adam Bede* I. iii. 59, I thought it might be a leading of Providence for me to change my way of life. *Ibid.* 60 The strong love God has given me towards you was a leading for us both. **1889** M. C. LEE *Quaker Girl Nantucket* 8 Ann Millet..began to have 'leadings' at the age of four years. **1969** *Listener* 23 Jan. 117/3 Hence their [*sc.* Peirce and James's] characteristic teaching that all thought exists in signs or in 'leadings' from one area of experience to another.

6. *attrib.* and *Comb.*, as ***leading-cart***; **leading-block** (see quots.); **leading-business** (*Theatr.*), the parts usually taken by the leading actor; **leading-hose**, that section of the hose from which the water is discharged by a fire-engine; **leading-rein**, a rein to lead a horse or other animal; also *fig.*; **leading-staff**, † (*a*) a staff borne by a commanding officer, a truncheon; (*b*) a staff to lead a bull by means of a ring through its nose; **leading-strap** = LEAD *sb.*[2] 3 d; †**leading-weapon**, a weapon serving as a 'leading-staff'; **leading-wire** = LEAD *sb.*[2] 10 a (*b*). Also LEADING-STRING.

1859 E. A. GRIFFITHS *Artil. Man.* (1862) 317 A **leading block* is a fixed pulley, which alters the direction of the power, but does not increase it. **1867** SMYTH *Sailor's Word-bk.*, *Leading-blocks*, the several blocks used for guiding the direction of any purchase, as hook, snatch or tail blocks. **1880** *Era Almanack* 95 My First Chapter in *Leading Business. **1854** H. MILLER *Sch. & Schm.* (1858) 238 An entire sheaf that had fallen from the '*leading-cart' at the close of harvest. **1483** *Ward. Acc.* in *Antiq. Rep.* (1807) I. 32 And for *ledyng rayns, xxij yerds of broode riban silk. **1826** SCOTT *Diary* 18 Apr. in *Lockhart*, He a boy, of six or seven, was brought to visit me on a pony, a groom holding the leading-rein. **1864** J. PAYN *Sir Massingberd* 58 If you had had a leading-rein yourself..at seventeen, it would have been a great deal better for you. **1598** BARRET *Theor. Warres* II. i. 29 In musters and traynings to carie..neither Halbard, neither *leading-staffe [etc.]. **1634** FORD *P. Warbeck* III. i. *stage direct.*, Enter King Henrie, his Gorget on, his sword, plume of feathers, leading staffe. **1813** SCOTT *Trierm.* II. xix, And Gyneth then apart he drew; To her his leading-staff resign'd. **1889** T. HARDY *Mayor of Casterbridge* xxix, He ran forward towards the leading-staff, seized it, and wrenched the animal's head as if he would snap it off. **1856** 'STONEHENGE' *Brit. Sports* I. III. v. 185 If..he [dog] must be steadily dragged along by the *leading-strap. **1622** F. MARKHAM *Bk. War* V. i. 10 To conclude, the Colonell is to bee armed at all points like the Captaine, onely his *Leading-weapon, and Feather-staffe is of a much lesse proportion.

b. with advs., as *leading-in, -off, -out*; in quots. *attrib.* (and hardly distinct from *ppl. a.*).

1876 PREECE & SIVEWRIGHT *Telegraphy* 224 On to the square terminal pole a hollow facing or casing is fixed, down which the *leading-in wires are led. **1884** F. J. BRITTEN *Watch & Clockm.* 91 The large amount of power required to drive the *leading off rod. **1895** THOMPSON & THOMAS *Electr. Tab. & Mem.* 80 The *leading-out wires of electro-magnets.

leading ('lɛdɪŋ), *vbl. sb.*[2] [f. LEAD *v.*[2] + -ING[1].] The action of LEAD *v.*[2] **a.** A covering, framing, or mending with lead. **b.** *concr.* = CAME; leadwork in general. **c.** *Printing.* The action of placing 'leads' between the lines of type. **d.** quasi-*concr.* The fouling of a gun with lead from bullets; more widely, deposition of lead on a surface.

c **1440** *Promp. Parv.* 293/1 Leeding wythe leed, *plumbacio.* **1563-83** FOXE *A. & M.* II. 1799/2 Paules Church..costeth me a good deale of money by the yeare, the leading thereof. **1573** BARET *Alv.* L 157 A leading or souldring in lead, *plumbitura.* **1597** *MS. Rawl.* D. 176 fo. 275 b, The sydes of the Chauncell, the Leadding whereof being defectyve. **1611** COTGR., *Plombement*, a leading or tinning. **1691** T. H[ALE] *Acc. New Invent.* 83 The leading of the Bread room..was a preservation of the Bread;..if it had not been for the leading of it, it would not have lasted half so long. **1807** SYD. SMITH *P. Plymley's Lett.* ix. Wks. 1840 III. 440 A Protestant plumber has discovered that it [the parish church] wants new leading. **1855** OGILVIE Suppl., *Leading*, separating by leads, as in printing. **1881** GREENER *Gun* 261 This removes all 'leading' and deposit. **1884** *Harper's Mag.* Aug. 369/2 The..panes might..be whirled out of their leadings. **1894** *Athenæum* 26 May 674/1 The 'leading' of the pages of the two texts differs considerably. **1946** *Happy Landings* (Air Ministry) July 3/2 Pilots can prevent leading of plugs by clearing engines..or by using higher r.p.m. when flying in cold conditions.

leading ('li:dɪŋ), *ppl. a.* [f. LEAD *v.*[1] + -ING[2].]

1. a. That guides, directs, or leads *to* something; †also, that serves as a precedent.

a **1628** F. GREVIL *Sidney* (1652) 188 This She-David of ours..takes the truth for her Leading-Star. *a* **1633** AUSTIN *Medit.* (1635) 168 This was on..the Second Lords day that was ever kept. And now it began to be a leading custome to the Church. **1655** FULLER *Ch. Hist.* I. ii. §1 Such as make him a Britan, ground their pretence on a leading Mistake. **1681** FLAVEL *Meth. Grace* xx. 356 It is a leading introductive mercy to all other spiritual mercies that follow it. *a* **1708** BEVERIDGE *Thes. Theol.* (1710) II. 235 Have a particular care of leading sins, that seldom go alone. **1745** J. MASON *Self Knowl.* I. xvii. (1853) 125 A Man cannot live without some leading views. **1791** BURKE *Let. Member Nat. Assembly* Wks. VI. 56 One of the strongest acts of innovation and the most leading in its consequences. **1793** GOUV. MORRIS in Sparks *Life & Writ.* (1832) II. 277, I have not proof, but some very leading circumstances. **1817** COLERIDGE *Biog. Lit.* II. xxi. 126 Suppose too all this done without a single leading principle established. **1875** JOWETT *Plato* (ed. 2) IV. 277 A great principle or leading thought suggests and arranges a world of particulars.

b. Special collocations: **leading-buoy** (see quot.); **leading case** *Law*, one that serves as a precedent to decide other cases; **leading dog** *Austral.* and *N.Z.* (see quot. 1933); **leading-light** *Naut.* (cf. *leading-mark*); **leading-mark** *Naut.*, one of 'those objects which, kept in line or in transit, guide the pilot while working into port, as trees, spires, buoys, etc.' (Adm. Smyth 1867); **leading-motive** *Mus.*, occas. tr. LEITMOTIV, q.v.; **leading note** *Mus.* (see quot. 1889; cf. *sensible note*); **leading question**, one that suggests the proper or expected answer; *spec.* in *Law* (see quot. 1848); **leading seventh** *Mus.* (see quot.).

1875 KNIGHT *Dict. Mech.*, **Leading-buoy*, a buoy placed as a guide in sailing. **1655** FULLER *Ch. Hist.* II. v. §1 We cannot but gaze at the Novelty of this act (as we conceive, a *leading Case in this kind). **1855** MACAULAY *Hist. Eng.* xvii. IV. 48 The leading case was that of Athaliah. **1895** NORTH in *Law Times Rep.* LXXIII. 24/1, I will refer to *Barrow v. Barrow*, a leading case perhaps on a married woman's right and power to elect. **1897** I. SCOTT *How I stole over 10,000 Sheep in Austral. & N.Z.* ii. 9 We had no '*leading' dog. **1933** L. G. D. ACLAND in *Press* (Christchurch, N.Z.) 4 Nov. 15/7 *Leading-dog*, a dog trained to run ahead of a mob of sheep to keep them steady. **1934** *Bulletin* (Sydney) 16 May 38/3 Rock, the kelpie leading-dog..had never possessed any aspirations towards leadership. **1875** KNIGHT *Dict. Mech.*, **Leading-light.* **1804** NELSON in Nicolas *Disp.* (1845) V. 521 The *leading mark for running in, is the Light-House. **1883** F. HUEFFER *Wagner* (ed. 2) 70 The same melody forms a prominent part of the music-drama, and appears as '*leading-motive' wherever the composer wishes to suggest the idea of the love potion. **1894** *Times* 13 Apr. 10/4 A few of the 'leading-motives'..startle us by their originality. **1811** T. BUSBY *Dict. Music* (ed. 3), **Leading note.* **1889** E. PROUT *Harmony* i. §13 The seventh note of the scale, which ..has a very strong tendency to lead up or rise to the tonic is on that account called the Leading Note. **1824** STARKIE *Law Evid.* I. II. 123 Upon the examination of a witness in chief, the principal rule to be observed is that *leading questions are not to be asked. **1848** WHARTON *Law Lex.*, *Leading question*, a question which suggests to a witness the answer which he is to make. **1849** MACAULAY *Hist. Eng.* viii. II. 381 Williams put leading questions. **1889** E. PROUT *Harmony* (ed. 10) xiv. §365 The first inversion of the dominant major ninth is sometimes called the 'Chord of the seventh on the leading note', and sometimes simply the '*Leading Seventh'.

c. ***leading-in*** adj.: applied to a lead-in wire (of either kind: see LEAD-IN 1 a, b).

1876 PREECE & SIVEWRIGHT *Telegraphy* vii. 224 The leading-in wire from the terminal pole, consists of a copper conductor insulated with gutta-percha, and well protected by a coating of tarred tape. **1885** *Phil. Mag.* XX. 141 The envelope may have deposited upon it a metallic film, derived from the leading-in wires to which the carbon filament is clamped. **1891** F. C. ALLSOP *Telephones* viii. 131 The leading-in wire is joined to the line-wire close to the last shackle or insulator. **1914** S. C. BATSTONE *Electr.-Light Fitting* vii. 138 G is a long glass stem through which the leading-in wires pass for connexion to the filament F. **1924** *Wireless World* 13 Aug. 543/1 (*heading*) Doing away with the leading-in wire. **1936** ORR & FORREST *Introd. Neon Lighting* i. 2 A lighting tube consists of a length of glass tubing bent to the shape required and closed at both ends. Into each end is inserted an electrode, usually in the form of a hollow cylinder of metal, to which are attached leading-in wires, which are carried to the outside of the tube through a vacuum-tight seal.

2. That takes the lead; chief, principal, prominent. ***leading lady, man***: the chief actress or actor in a theatrical company or a film. Also LEADING-ARTICLE.

1625 B. JONSON *Staple of N.* II. i, I have read the Elements, And Accidence, and all the leading books. **1671** L. ADDISON *W. Barbary* 35 A leading Person in that part of the Countrey. **1701** SWIFT *Contests Nobles & Commons* iv. Miscell. (1711) 71, I mean Popular Orators, Tribunes, or as they are now stiled Great Speakers, Leading Men and the like. **1711** STEELE *Spect.* No. 54 ¶2 Several of the leading Men of the Sect have a great deal of the cynical Humour in them. **1734** J. WARD *Introd. Math.* II. v. (ed. 6) 176 The Solution of such Leading Questions as are in themselves very easie. **1779** BURKE *Corr.* (1844) II. 275 That profession [the bar] which is so leading in this country. **1793** SMEATON *Edystone L.* §117 The great and leading point now to be determined was, whether the house should be rebuilt with stone. **1806** A. DUNCAN *Nelson's Funeral* 27 Large sums were given for standing in a cart, in a leading street. **1817** *Parl. Debates* 565 Mr. Brougham..had admitted the leading facts of the great distresses. **1821** CRAIG *Lect. Drawing* iv. 216 The leading events of our sacred history. **1827** L. REDE *Road to Stage* 16 The salary is generally first-rate—at all events next to that of the leading man. **1849** MACAULAY *Hist. Eng.* v. I. 666 He had not been one of the leading conspirators. **1868** FREEMAN *Norm. Conq.* II. vii. 161 He had himself..played a leading part in them [commotions]. **1874** HATTON *Clytie* (ed. 10) 96, I should have put it down for a leading lady. **1885** J. K. JEROME *On the Stage* 157 Our leading man died suddenly from heart disease. **1898** *Allbutt's Syst. Med.* V. 615 Leading physicians both in Germany and America. **1900** *Daily News* 20 Jan. 6/4 'The leading hand in the teak trade', as Mr. Kipling, père, calls the elephant. **1918** Leading lady [see DOUBLE *v.* 1 e]. **1921** Leading aircraftman [see AIRCRAFTMAN]. **1939** I. BAIRD *Waste Heritage* vii. 88 He hated the way Bette's leading man looked, all slicked-up and Hollywood. **1955** T. H. PEAR *Eng. Social Differences* vi. 159 Leading-hand, charge-hand.

3. That has the front place; that goes first or in front on the line of movement. ***leading wheels***: the front pair of wheels of a locomotive (so ***leading axle, springs***; cf. LEADER[1] 16 a). ***leading card***: that which is played first; also *fig.* ***leading counsel*** = LEADER[1] 3 c. ***leading shoot*** = LEADER[1] 9.

1597 MORLEY *Introd. Mus.* 77 When we speak of a Fuge or Canon, in the vnison, fift, or eight: it is to be vnderstood from the first note of the leading part. **1683** TRYON *Way to Health* xiv. (1697) 318 Drunkenness being the leading Card to all Evils. **1690** J. MACKENZIE *Siege London-Derry* 5/2 If we come to be made a leading-Card, sit not still and see us sink. *a* **1711** KEN *Anodynes* Poet. Wks. 1721 III. 432 When I of God a Song design, Pains intercept my leading Line. **1712** J. JAMES tr. *Le Blond's Gardening* 181 Guide the leading Shoot of these young Trees higher and higher. **1727-51** CHAMBERS *Cycl.* s.v. *Fugue*, The leading parts still flying before those which follow. **1771** P. PARSONS *Newmarket* II. 32 The two leading-horses..carried about eight stone..each wheel-horse about seven stone. **1774** J. BRYANT *Mythol.* I. 80 This people..often suppressed the leading vowel. **1792** *Trans. Soc. Arts* X. 18 The vigorous leading shoots made by healthy plants from year to year. **1796** *Instr. & Reg. Cavalry* (1813) 60 Every other squadron ..and every other regiment..manœuvre from a leading flank. **1798** CAPT. MILLAR in Nicolas *Disp. Nelson* (1846) VII. p. cliv, The leading Ship to steer one point more to starboard. **1825** J. NICHOLSON *Operat. Mechanic* 129 These mortises must be square to the leading side of the whip. **1849-50** *Weale's Dict. Terms*, *Leading springs*, the springs fixed upon the leading axle-box of a locomotive engine, bearing the weight above. *Leading wheels*, the wheels of a locomotive engine, which are placed before the driving wheels. **1854** J. S. C. ABBOTT *Napoleon* (1855) II. xx. 358 Here..he encountered the leading Cossacks of Blucher's army. **1855** MACAULAY *Hist. Eng.* xv. III. 525 He had been the leading counsel for the seven Bishops. **1885** U. S. GRANT *Pers. Mem.* I. xxii. 302 The leading boat got within a very short distance of the water battery. **1889** *Pall Mall G.* 6 Aug. 3/3 A good 'leading' deer [of a sledge team] is the most valuable of a Samoyede's possessions. **1895** *Mod. Steam Engine* 67 The leading axle. **1898** *Daily News* 4 Jan. 5 The leading engine was overturned.

4. That makes to go, drives, or communicates motion; in certain technical collocations.

1762 FALCONER *Shipwr.* I. 480 The ship..waited..the leading gale. **1772-84** COOK *Voy.* (1790) VI. 2175 A shoal.. makes it necessary to warp in, unless there should happen to be a leading wind. **1841** DANA *Seaman's Man.* 113 *Leading-wind*, a fair wind. More particularly applied to a wind abeam or quartering. **1867** SMYTH *Sailor's Word-bk.*, *Leading-part*, the rope of a tackle which runs between the fall and the standing post... It is that part of the fall which is to be hauled on or overhauled, to ease the purchase. **1875** KNIGHT *Dict. Mech.*, *Leading-screw* (Lathe), the longitudinal screw between the shears of a lathe, by which the slide-rest is moved longitudinally of the lathe-bed. *Lead-screw.*

5. ***leading coach*** (sense obscure: cf. quot. 1848).

1704 *Lond. Gaz.* No. 4052/1 The Gentlemen Ushers in waiting in Her Majesty's Leading Coach. **1724** *Ibid.* 6233/2 The Morocco Ambassadour was conducted by the Master of the Ceremonies to his Audience of the young Princesses, in one of their leading Coaches and six Horses. **1736** HERVEY *Mem. Geo. II*, I. xiii. 272 He [*sc.* the Prince of Orange] came the next morning to St. James's..though the equipage the king sent to fetch him was only one miserable leading coach with only 'a pair of horses'. **1848** *Ibid.*, *footn.*, Strange to say, the peculiar meaning of 'a leading coach' has been lost in the Master of the Horse's office, though these offices are usually so conservative of etiquette.

Hence †'**leadingly** *a.* (in 3 *north. dial.* **ledand-like**), suitable for leading (a procession); '**leadingly** *adv.*, in a leading manner.

a **1300** *E.E. Psalter* xcvii. 6 In bemes ledand-like [Vulg. *in tubis ductilibus*] to se. **1801** W. TAYLOR in Robberds *Mem.* I. 368 You have no other brother so likely to be soon and leadingly settled. **1862** RUSKIN *Unto this Last* 65 Among national manufactures..a quite leadingly lucrative one.

leading article.

1. One of the longer large-type articles in a newspaper, appearing as the expression of editorial opinion on any subject; a leader.

1807 *Politics Georgium Sidus* 29 The Morning Newspapers of the metropolis..in their solemn political paragraphs, and especially in those which are called their leading articles. **1812** *Examiner* 25 May 333/2 Your leading article of last Sunday. **1868** M. PATTISON *Academ. Org.* v. 295 In the schools of Oxford is now taught in perfection the art of writing 'leading articles'.

2. *Comm.* **a.** A principal or prominent article of trade. **b.** In recent use, an article which is 'pushed' and sold at a low price in order to attract customers for other things. Cf. LEADER 8 b.

1818 JAS. MILL *Brit. India* II. IV. v. 163 A leading article in the European traffic was the salt-petre produced in Bengal. **1877** W. S. GILBERT *Sorcerer* I. 15 Sir, it is our leading article.

leading edge. [LEADING *ppl. a.*] **1.** The forward edge of a moving body; also *transf.*; *spec.* (*a*) that of a blade of a screw-propeller; (*b*) that of a wing, tailplane, or other part of an aircraft; (*c*) that of one of the plates of the earth's crust.

1877 W. H. WHITE *Man. Naval Archit.* xiv. 579 When the plane is moved obliquely, its leading edge, corresponding to the forward edge of a rudder, may be regarded as continually entering water which was comparatively little disturbed by the previous motion. **1888** *Lockwood's Dict. Mech. Engin.* 205 *Leading edge*, that edge of the blade of a screw propeller which cuts the water, as distinguished from the following edge. **1912** *Aeroplane* 12 Dec. 592/1 Looking over the leading edge of the wings from a constant position the ground disappeared regularly. **1922** GLAZEBROOK *Dict. Appl. Physics* I. 364/1 That part [of the suface]..over which the particles of fluid are being gradually retarded—i.e. the part in the neighbourhood of the leading edge of the surface such as, for example, the immersed surface of a ship. **1939** *Archit. Rev.* LXXXVI. 63/2 At the 'leading edge' of each wing-like roof, the wooden slats with which it is faced are slightly separated to allow for..ventilation. **1946** TAYLOR & ALLWARD *Spitfire* 99/2 Special wings were fitted, the leading edge portion of each being constructed as a fuel tank. **1959** H. BARNES *Oceanogr. & Marine Biol.* i. 49 On sand, where there is considerable resistance to the leading-edge of either the mud bucket or naturalist's oval dredge, only a small sample is usually brought up and deeper burrowing animals frequently avoid capture. **1967** M. CHANDLER *Ceramics in Mod. World* vi. 177 For very high-speed aircraft the sharp leading edges of engines and wings will also probably have to be made of ceramic materials. **1971** I. G. GASS et al. *Understanding Earth* xx. 289/2 A plate whose leading edge is of continental material will gradually increase in size; for new crust will be added where oceanic crust is generated at its trailing edge but little or no continental crust is being consumed at the leading edge. **1972** *Sci. Amer.* Mar. 33/3 The drifting of the continents is another theme; every continent must have a leading edge and a trailing edge.

2. *Electronics.* The part of a pulse in which the amplitude increases.

1945 *Nature* 15 Sept. 319/2 The beginning or 'leading edge' of the pulse marks a packet of energy which can be re-identified after the vicissitudes of travel, thus permitting accurate measurement of time of travel. **1962** SIMPSON & RICHARDS *Physical Princ. Junction Transistors* vii. 139 In the amplification of small pulses with sharp leading and trailing edges the frequency range may be very broad. **1972** *Radio Times* 6 Jan. 5/3 Listeners may have noticed a change in the Greenwich Time Signals broadcast since January 1... The exact time is signalled by the beginning or 'leading edge' of the long pip.

3. *fig.* The forefront or vanguard, esp. of technological development. Freq. (with hyphen) *attrib.*

1977 *Sci. Amer.* Sept. 49/2 (Advt.), We are a young, publicly held, leading-edge technology company. **1983** *Fortune* 13 June 24/3 Professors, commonly assumed to be on the leading edge of thought. **1983** *Austral. Microcomputer Mag.* Aug. 44/2 Pioneering, leading edge developments in micro applications. **1984** *Financial Rev.* 17 Jan. 8/4 Video games which are based on leading-edge technology. **1985** *Church Times* 29 Nov. 4/4 If family services were 'the leading edge' for such people, the Church needed to see that those services were available. **1986** *Daily Tel.* 26 Feb. 13/8 Three choices from the Burton Group's spring ranges. Sophisticated style from Principles... Leading-edge young fashion from Top Shop... Mainstream young fashion from Dorothy Perkins.

'leading-string. Chiefly *pl.*

1. Strings with which children used to be guided and supported when learning to walk. *to be in leading-strings*: to be still a child; *fig.* to be in a state of dependence or pupilage.

1677 WYCHERLEY *Plain Dealer* I. i. 1 But I'll have no Leading-strings, I can walk alone. *a* **1685** OTWAY *Compl. Muse* xiii. Wks. 1727 II. 366 In little time the Hell-bred Brat ..Without his Leading-strings could walk. **1779** T. A. MANN in *Lett. Lit. Men* (Camden) 417, I live in a Country where good Philosophy is still in its leading-strings. **1780** COWPER *Progr. Err.* 531 One that still needs his leading-string and bib. **1809** W. IRVING *Knickerb.* (1861) 69 He.. gallops through mud and mire..merely to show that he is a lad of spirit, and out of his leading-strings. **1851** MAYHEW *Lond. Labour* 317 Thus the 'model' lodgers are kept, as it were, in leading-strings. **1884** LOWELL *Wks.* (1890) VI. 135 His [Cervantes'] genius soon broke away from the leading-strings of a plot that denied free scope to his conceptions.

2. A cord for leading an animal. Cf. *leading rein.*

1859 *Archæol. Cant.* II. 106 At the feet of each crouches a dog with knotted leading-strings. **1886** RUSKIN *Præterita* I. v. 159 Led..by a riding master with a leading string.

Hence **leading-stringed** *pa. pple., nonce-wd.*, guided with, or kept within, leading-strings.

1859 THACKERAY *Virgin.* II. xiv. 104 A powerful mettlesome young Achilles ought not to be leading-stringed by women too much.

†'leadish, *a. Obs.* [f. LEAD *sb.*^{1} + -ISH.] Somewhat like lead. Also *Comb.*, as *leadish-coloured* adj.

1398 TREVISA *Barth. De P.R.* VII. lxiv. (1495) 280 In theym that haue the Lepra the face is ledysshe. **1530** PALSGR. 317/1 Ledysshe, *plummee, plummeux.* **1577** DEE *Relat. Spir.* I. (1659) 75 That about the center is of fuskish or leadish colour. **1597** A. M. tr. *Guillemeau's Fr. Chirurg.* 3 b/1 If the Fleshe of the wounde be leadishe-colourede. **1653** R. SANDERS *Physiogn.* 183 The Excrements, of a wan leadish colour. **1784** *Maryland Jrnl.* 27 July (Th.), There are two great-coats missing, one of which is a leadish-coloured country cloth.

leadless ('lɛdlɪs), *a.* [f. LEAD *sb.*^{1} + -LESS.] Devoid of lead.

1809 BYRON *Eng. Bards & Sc. Rev.* 466 When Little's leadless pistol met his eye. **1852** EARP *Gold Col. Australia* 127 Gentlemen, whose seconds take care that they fight with leadless pistols. **1898** *Westm. Gaz.* 25 Feb. 2/1 The itinerant vendor of plaster busts and leadless pencils. *Ibid.* 14 June 2/2 Messrs. Minton..have already taken steps..to discover a leadless glaze.

[**leadman,** 'one who leads a dance' (J.): see *lead-man* in LEAD *sb.*^{1} 12, quot. 1633.]

'lead-off. [f. vbl. phr. *to lead off* (LEAD *v.*^{1} 19).] A commencement; that which 'leads-off', the first of a series. Also *attrib.*

1886 H. BAUMANN *Londinismen* 94/2 *Lead-off*, Journalisten-Slang: erste(r) (gew. von einem bekannten Schriftsteller herrührender) Artikel. **1892** *Fun* 20 Nov. 225/2 It contains 'Seven Christmas Eves', the first or lead off being by clever Miss Graves. **1922** *Ardmore* (Okla.) *Daily Press* 6 May 3/3 His ability to judge close ones..make[s] him an ideal leadoff man. **1938** D. BAKER *Young Man with Horn* (1939) iv. 264 For 'Sam, the Old Accordian Man', it was to be a lead-off by Jeff. **1963** MRS. L. B. JOHNSON *White House Diary* 27 Dec. (1970) 22 Our foreman, Dale Malechek, took the lead-off bus... I took the second bus and Lynda..the third. **1970** *Toronto Daily Star* 24 Sept. 17/1 Morton..was greeted by a Willie Stargell leadoff single.

'lead-out. [f. vbl. phr. *to lead out.*]

1. A leading out (in various senses).

1906 *Dialect Notes* III. 158 *Stag lead-out*, a dance-number in which only men who have not brought women dance with the women present. **1958** *Spectator* 3 Jan. 13/2 In stark contrast to the Zilliacus broadcasts these received an implied disavowal in the lead-in and lead-out.

2. *attrib.* or as *adj. Electronics.* Applied to a conductor by which current may enter or leave an electronic device.

1939 *Amat. Radio Handbk.* iii. 45/2 These valves..are ordinary valve types mounted in a metal bulb, welded or brazed together, having the lead-out wires passed through eyelets..mounted in the metal bulb. **1962** F. E. DUFFIELD in G. A. T. Burdett *Automatic Control Handbk.* ix. 17 Fig. 18 illustrates a single inductance type of pressure transducer... The lead-out wires are connected to a pair of sealed terminals. **1967** F. LANGFORD-SMITH *Radio-Designer's Handbk.* (ed. 7) 1484 The lead-out groove is reduced in length due to the smaller ending diameters. **1970** J. EARL *Tuners & Amplifiers* ii. 29 There are other types [of IC] which represent a component 'block'..with leadout wires or tags. Transistors usually have three leadout wires..with a possible fourth connecting to a screen or shield.

lead-pipe. [See LEAD *sb.*^{1} 10.] Used *attrib.* with *cinch* to denote a complete certainty. *U.S. colloq.*

1898 'J. KERR' *Cheery Bk.* 71, I never had a 'lead pipe cinch'; I never had a 'pull'; I never had a 'straight' that was not beaten by a 'full'. **1911** H. QUICK *Yellowstone Nights* xi. 288 Oh its a cinch, a timelock, leadpipe cinch! **1926** *Punch* 7 July 17/1 The Office of Works does not borrow money even to back what Americans call a lead-pipe cinch. **1949** N. ALGREN *Man with Golden Arm* 23 Not early enough to move no tables, that's a lead-pipe cinch. **1973** *N.Y. Times* 25 Feb. IV. 2/6 To be sure, speculation in gold is not a lead-pipe cinch; its price can go down as well as up.

†leadsman^1. *Obs.* [f. *leads*, genitive of LEAD *sb.*^{2} + MAN.] A guide, = LODESMAN.

c **1510** *Gest R. Hode* VII. 369 in Child *Ballads* (1888) III. 74/1, I wyll be your ledës-man, And lede you the way. **1598** BARRET *Theor. Warres* 29 They find their leadsman before them in their due distance.

leadsman^2 ('lɛdzmən). [f. gen. of LEAD *sb.*^{1} + MAN.] The man who 'heaves' the lead in taking soundings.

1857 S. OSBORN *Quedah* xxii. 308 The rippling music of my gun-boat's stem..and the low call of the leadsman, were the only signs of life. **1867** SMYTH *Sailor's Word-bk.*, *Leadsman*... In Calcutta the young gentlemen learning to be pilots are called leadsmen. **1875** BEDFORD *Sailor's Pocket Bk.* v. (ed. 2) 153 The foremast awning stanchion..forms a good support for the leadsman's breast-rope. **1891** *Scribner's Mag.* Sept. 278/2 Skilful pilots; each of whom brings his own leadsman on board.

'lead-up. [f. vbl. phr. *to lead up* (cf. LEAD *v.*^{1} 23).] Something that leads up to something else.

1953 M. T. MONRO *Thinking about Genesis* I. i. 26 The lead-up is the ordinary one by which we establish, on rational grounds alone, the existence of God, His attributes, [etc.]. **1959** D. COOKE *Lang. Mus.* iii. 145 The Beethoven is the short, breathless lead-up to the final jubilant outburst of the finale of the Choral Symphony. **1959** D. D. C. P. MOULD *Peter's Boat* vi. 78, I had occasion to go into..that country's great mediaeval cathedrals now in Protestant hands... Here was a setting, a magnificent lead-up in stone..pointing to one thing and one thing only, the Mass and the Blessed Sacrament. **1972** *Lebende Sprachen* XVII. 73/1 During the vital lead-up to first flights, acceleration and deceleration tests were made during taxying trials.

leadwork ('li:dwɜ:k). Also lead work. [Origin unknown.] (See quot. 1900.)

Not connected with *lead-work* s.v. LEAD *sb.*^{1} 12.

1900 E. JACKSON *Hist. Hand-made Lace* 213 *Lead works* or *lerd works*, terms used to indicate Modes or Fillings. Fancy stitches employed to fill in enclosed spaces in needle-point and bobbin laces. **1919** T. WRIGHT *Romance of Lace Pillow* ix. 70 A Lille ground..sprinkled with *dots* (*plaits, leadworks* or *points d'esprit* as they are called). **1953** M. POWYS *Lace & Lace-Making* iv. 26 Maltese Lace. This specimen has the leaf or lead work used as an ornamental filling.

leady ('lɛdɪ), *a.* Forms: 4 leeddy, 5 ledi, 6 ledy(e, leadie, -ye, 5- leady. [f. LEAD *sb.*^{1} + -Y^1.] Resembling lead, usually in colour.

1398 TREVISA *Barth. De P.R.* VIII. xii. (1495) 319 Saturnus tokenyth sorowe..his colour is blacke leeddy and false. *c* **1400** *Lanfranc's Cirurg.* 197 þe face..is sumwhat ledi... Her nailis bicomeþ ledi. **1477** NORTON *Ord. Alch.* v. in Ashm. (1652) 65 Wann or leady Colour. **1534** ELYOT *Gov.* II. (1557) 124 His ruddy lippes wan, & his eyen ledye & holow. *a* **1536** *Beauty & Good Prop. Women* C j, And to calisto with this gyrdle celestina Shall go and his ledy hart make hole & lyght. **1638** SIR T. HERBERT *Trav.* 102 His eyes grow dim, his heart turnes leady. **1756** *Dict. Arts & Sci.* s.v. *Porcelain*, This colour has a leady cast like metal-burning mirrors. **1824** *Mech. Mag.* No. 52. 383 Every part of the iron ..will be found to be unusually soft and leady. **1892** *Harper's Mag.* LXXXIV. 570/2 Glacier water..always gray —a sort of lead-y gray.

leaf (li:f), *sb.*^{1} Pl. **leaves** (li:vz). Forms: *α. sing.* 1 léaf, 2–4 lef, 3 (6) leif, (3 lief, lieif, 4 lyeave), 3–6 lefe, (3 leve), 4–5 leyf, leff, (4 lyf), 4–6 leef, (4, 6 leof), 6 leaffe, leefe, (leave, laif), 6–7 leafe, 3– leaf. *β. pl.* 1 léaf, *Northumb.* léofo, hléofa, léofa, 3–4 levis, 3–6 leves, (4 leeves), 4 lewes, *Sc.* leivis, lewis, 5 lewys, 4–5 levys, (5 leevys), 6 *Sc.* levis, 5 le(e)fes, 6 leaffes, 7–8 leafs, 8 leafes, 6– leaves. [OE. *léaf* str. neut. (pl. *léaf*) = OFris. *lâf*, OS. *lôf*, *lôb* (Du. *loof*), OHG. *loup* masc. and neut. (MHG. *loup*, *loub-*, mod.G. *laub* neut.), ON. *lauf* neut. (Sw. *löf*, Da. *löv*), Goth. *lauf-s* (pl. *laubôs*) masc.:—OTeut. **laubo-*. By some scholars regarded as cogn. w. Lith. *lùpti*, OSl. *lupiti* to peel, strip off.]

I. The organ of the plant, etc.

1. a. An expanded organ of a plant, produced laterally from a stem or branch, or springing from its root; one of the parts of a plant which collectively constitute its foliage.

It is usually green, and in its most complete form consists of a blade, footstalk, and stipules; in popular lang. the word *leaf* denotes the blade alone. Some mod. botanists use the word in an extended sense, including all those structures which are regarded as 'modified leaves', such as stamens, carpels, floral envelopes, bracts, etc.

c **825** *Vesp. Psalter* xxxvi. 2 Forðon swe swe heȝ hreðlice adruȝiað & swe swe leaf wyrta hreðe fallað. *c* **950** *Lindisf. Gosp.* Matt. xxi. 19 And ȝesæh ðone fic-beom enne..& næniht infand in ðær..buta leofo anum. *c* **1200** *Trin. Coll. Hom.* 177 To-ȝanes wintre þenne alle leues fallen. *c* **1290** *S. Eng. Leg.* I. 7/204 A treo with bowes brode and lere, Ake þare nas opon noþur lief ne rinde. *a* **1300** *Cursor M.* 804 þai cled þam..wit leues brad bath o figer. **1375** BARBOUR *Bruce* XVI. 67 Quhen..lewis on the branchis spredis. **1422** tr. *Secreta Secret., Priv. Priv.* 239 He sholde rube his gomes with lewys of trenne. **1485** CAXTON *Chas. Gt.* 210 Eche man took his owne, and cutte of the bowes & leues. **1562** TURNER *Herbal* II. 162 They differ also in the color of the leaue. **1640** HOWELL *Dodona's Gr.* To Prince 12 They soon will cast their leafs. **1667** MILTON *P.L.* v. 480 So from the root Springs lighter the green stalk, from thence the leaves More aerie. **1722** WOLLASTON *Relig. Nat.* ix. 205 Like leaves one generation drops, and another springs up. **1830** TENNYSON *Arab. Nts.* viii, A sudden splendour from behind Flush'd all the leaves with rich gold-green. **1889** GEDDES & THOMSON *Evol. of Sex* vi. §1 In most phanerogams..male and female organs occur on different leaves (stamens and carpels) of each flower.

fig. **1377** LANGL. *P. Pl.* B. v. 138 On limitoures and listres lesynges I ymped, Tyl thei bere leues of low speche lordes to plese. *c* **1386** CHAUCER *Pars. T.* ¶41 Ne by þe braunches ne the leuys of confession. **1613** SHAKS. *Hen. VIII*, III. ii. 353 This is the state of Man; to day he puts forth The tender Leaues of hopes, to morrow Blossomes. **1860** READE *Cloister & H.* lv. (1896) 163 Yet our love hath lost no leaf, thank God. **1882** JEAN WATSON *Life R. S. Candlish* xiv. 148 How the leaves fall when the autumn of one's friendship has begun.

Phrase. **1413** *Pilgr. Sowle* (Caxton 1483) I. xv. 11, I tremble as doth a leef vpon a tree. [See also ASPEN *a.* 1.]

b. with qualifying adjs., as *compound, fleshy, lyrate*, etc. q.v.; also ***cold, hollow leaf*** (see quots.).

1831 G. DON *Gard. Dict.* I. xvii, Hollow-leaf, form of a cowl, concave above. **1897** WILLIS *Flower. Pl.* I. 192 Most of them [Alpine plants] have more or less inrolled leaves, which perhaps..act as a protection against the cold... Such leaves are termed by Jungner cold-leaves.

c. ***walking leaf***: see WALKING *ppl. a.*

2. Popularly used for: A petal; esp. in ***rose-leaf.***

1565 COOPER *Thesaurus* s.v. *Vnguis*, *Vnguis rosæ*..the thicke white parte of a rose leafe nexte the stalke. **1591** SHAKS. *1 Hen. VI*, IV. i. 92 This Fellow..Vpbraided me about the Rose I weare, Saying, the sanguine colour of the Leaues Did represent my Masters blushing cheekes. *c* **1600** *Acc. Bk. W. Wray* in *Antiquary* XXXII. 80 Take the leaues of Blew violetes. **1760** J. LEE *Introd. Bot.* (1765) 2 The Corolla, Foliation, vulgarly called the Leaves of the Flower. **1820** SHELLEY *Sensit. Plant* III. vii, The rose leaves, like flakes of crimson snow, Paved the turf. **1847** TENNYSON *Princ.* v. 189 Pure as lines of green that streak the white Of the first snowdrop's inner leaves.

3. *collect.* **a.** The foliage of a plant or tree; leafage, leaves. Chiefly in phr. ***fall of the leaf. in (full) leaf***: covered with leaves or foliage.

1537 in *Lett. Roy. & Illustr. Ladies* (1846) II. 363, I am sick at the fall of the leaf and at the spring of the year. **1545**

ASCHAM *Toxoph.* I. (Arb.) 48 Spring tyme, Somer, faule of the leafe, and winter. **1625** BACON *Ess., Gardening* (Arb.) 556 The White-Thorne in Leafe. **1660** F. BROOKE tr. *Le Blanc's Trav.* 362 The year began in March with the coming of the leaf. **1789** G. WHITE *Selborne* xvi. (1853) 68 When the leaf is out. **1863** FR. A. KEMBLE *Resid. in Georgia* 19 All in full leaf and beauty.

fig. **1605** SHAKS. *Macb.* v. iii. 23, I haue liu'd long enough, my way of life Is falne into the Seare, the yellow Leafe. **1811** W. R. SPENCER *Poems* 44 Ere yet the green leaf of her days was come.

†**b.** Used for 'season', 'year', in the description of wine. *Obs.* [Cf. F. *vin de deux feuilles.*]

1594 PLAT *Jewell-ho.* III. 71 Wine of nine or ten leaues (as they terme it) which is so many yeares olde. **1715** *Lond. Gaz.* No. 5385/9 Hermitage Claret, deep, bright, strong..and of the true Leaf. **1720** *Ibid.* No. 5832/4.

4. *spec.* The leaves of a plant cultivated for commercial purposes: **a.** of the tobacco-plant, or of other plants used for smoking; ***in the leaf***, in leaves, i.e. unstemmed and uncut.

a **1618** SYLVESTER *Tobacco Battered* 781 Impose so deep a Taxe On all these Ball, Leafe, Cane, and Pudding-packs. **1641** FRENCH *Distill.* ii. (1651) 49 Of Tobacco in the leafe three ounces. **1853** URE *Dict. Arts* (ed. 4) II. 866 Virginia leaf costs in bond 3½*d.* per lb... Ditto strips 5½*d.* **1898** *Tit-Bits* 7 May 105/3 Tobacco..in the Navy..is usually served out in the leaf. **1972** *Guardian* 29 Jan. 9/2 Mr Williams had three previous convictions for possession of cannabis... 'A man..let me have some leaf for five shillings.'

b. of the tea-plant (see quot.).

1883 *Times* 2 Apr. 4 A factory in which the 'leaf', as the green leaves gathered from the tea bushes are technically termed, is manufactured into tea.

5. A disease incident to sheep and lambs. (Cf. *leaf-sickness* in 18.) ? *Obs.*

1726 *Dict. Rust.* (ed. 3), *Leaf*, a Distemper incident to Lambs of 10 or 14 Days old. **1749** W. ELLIS *Syst. Improv. Sheep* 320 Some call it [the disease] wood evil, and others the leaf. Some suppose they get it by feeding upon wood, or some leaf upon the ground.

6. a. A representation of a leaf; an ornament in the form of a leaf; esp. in *Arch.* (see quot. 1842–59).

1459 in *Paston Lett.* I. 478, j. close bedde of palle grene and whyte, with levys of golde. **1664** EVELYN tr. *Freart's Archit.* xxix. 70 The Chapter had this in particular, that its stalks and flexures of the leaves were made in the form of Ramms horns. **1707** J. CHAMBERLAYNE *St. Gt. Brit.* I. III. iii. (ed. 22) 274 His [an Earl's] Coronet hath the Pearls raised upon Points, and Leaves low between. **1727–41** CHAMBERS *Cycl.*, *Leaves*, in architecture, are an ornament of the Corinthian capital, and thence borrowed into the Composite. **1842–59** GWILT *Archit.* Gloss., *Leaves*, ornaments imitated from natural leaves, whereof the ancients used two sorts, natural and imaginary.

†**b.** *Geom.* A leaf-shaped figure. (Cf. FOLIATE *a.* 2 b, and quot. 1796 there.) *Obs.*

1715 A. DE MOIVRE in *Phil. Trans.* XXIX. 330 Whereas the Foliate is exactly quadrable, the whole Leaf thereof being but one third of the Square of *AB*.

II. Similative uses.

7. a. One of the folds of a folded sheet of paper, parchment, etc.; *esp.* one of a number of folds (each containing two pages) which compose a book or manuscript, a folio; hence, the matter printed or written thereon.

c **900** tr. *Bæda's Hist.* I. i. (1890) 31 Man scof þara boca leaf, þe of Hibernia coman. *c* **1205** LAY. 46 Laȝamon leide þeos boc & þa leaf wende. *a* **1225** *St. Marher.* 1 Ich..habbe ired ant araht moni mislich leaf. **1340** *Ayenb.* Pref., And ine huyche half of þe lyeaue be tuaye lettres of þe abece. Þet is to wytene .A. and .b. .A. betocneþ þe uerste half of þe leave .b. þe oþerhalf. *c* **1386** CHAUCER *Miller's Prol.* 69 Who so list it nat yheere, Turne ouer the leef, and chese another tale. **1490** CAXTON *Eneydos* Prol. 2, [I] toke a penne & ynke, and wrote a leef or tweyne. **1535** JOYE *Apol. Tindale* (Arb.) 15 Read the xvj. lyne the fyrste syde of the xij. leif. **1595** SPENSER *Sonn.* i. 1 Happy, ye leaves ! when as those lilly hands..Shall handle you. **1669** STURMY *Mariner's Mag.* IV. 202 It will be fit to have a Book in Folio, that a sheet of Paper makes but two Leafs. **1726** SWIFT *Gulliver* II. vii. 131, I..began the other Page in the same manner, and so turned over the Leaf. **1849** MACAULAY *Hist. Eng.* iii. I. 389 None of these [newspapers]..exceeded in size a single small leaf.

fig. **1607** SHAKS. *Timon* IV. iii. 117 [They] Are not within the Leafe of pitty writ.

b. Phrases. ***to take a leaf out of*** (a person's) ***book***: see BOOK *sb.* 16. †***to turn down a leaf***: to cease for a time. †***to turn*** (***over***) ***the*** (***next***) ***leaf*** (obs.), ***to turn over a new leaf***, etc.: to adopt a different (now always a better) line of conduct.

1577–87 HOLINSHED *Chron.* I. 21/2 He must turne the leafe, and take out a new lesson, by changing his former trade of liuing into better. **1581** MULCASTER *Positions* xxxvii. (1887) 148 The state is now altered,..the preferment that way hath turned a new leafe. **1597** BEARD *Theatre God's Judgem.* (1631) 92 But as soone as he was exalted to honor, he turned ouer a new leafe, and began..furiously to afflict..the..faithfull seruants of Christ. **1601** *Imp. Consid. Sec. Priests* (1675) 90 Let us all turn over the leaf, and take another course. *a* **1659** OSBORN *Characters, etc.* Wks. (1673) 647 It is time to give over, at least, to turn down a Leaf. **1809** MALKIN *Gil Blas* VII. ii. (Rtldg.) 12, I took a leaf out of their book. **1861** HUGHES *Tom Brown at Oxf.* xlii. (1889) 411, I will turn over a new leaf, and write to you.

†**8.** A lobe (of the lungs). (Cf. F. *fueille de poulmon* Cotgr.) *Obs. rare*$^{-1}$.

1398 TREVISA *Barth. De P.R.* v. xxiii. (1495) 130 Thenne to shape yͤ voys thayre is receyued in yͤ leues of yͤ lounges.

9. The layer of fat round the kidneys of a pig; also applied to the inside fat of other animals.

14.. *Anc. Cookery* in *Househ. Ord.* (1790) 425 Take the lefe of porke sethen..and grynde hit smalle. **1552** HULOET, Leaffe or fat of a swyne, *vnctum.* **1563** *Wills & Inv. N.C.* (Surtees) 1835 I. 207 Leaves of ij swyne iiijd. **1630** J. TAYLOR *Gt. Eater Kent* 8 What say you to a leafe or flecke of a brawn new kild? **1697** DAMPIER *Voy.* 106, I heard of a Monstrous Green Turtle... The leaves of Fat afforded 8 Gallons of Oyl. **1753** *Scots Mag.* Jan. 48/2 The fore chine weighed 64, and the leaves 75 pounds. **1854** THOREAU *Walden* xvii. (1886) 304 A thick moist lobe, a word especially applicable to the liver and lungs and the leaves of fat. **1876** *Whitby Gloss.*, *Leeaf*, or *Leaf*, the inside layer of fat in a pig or a goose. 'Geease-leeaf.' **1886** in *S.W. Linc. Gloss.* **1886** *Harper's Mag.* July 206/2 Lard, 'made from hog round, say head, gut, leaf, and trimming', is..in demand. **1904** L. L. LAMBORN *Cottonseed Products* 166 Neutral lard is composed of the fat derived from the leaf of the slaughtered animal. **1911** *Encycl. Brit.* XVI. 214/2 The finest quality [of lard], used for making oleomargarine, is got from the leaf. **1934** F. ALLEN in *Meat Trade* II. iv. 100 The following parts [of a pig] are removed: the back bone, the blade bone,..and the flair or leaf. *Ibid.* 113 The leaf, or flair, of the pig is generally regarded as producing the best lard. **1955** W. G. R. FRANCILLON *Good Cookery* iii. 53 The leaf or caul (a lining of fat taken from the inside of the animal)..should be placed over the joint before baking.

10. a. A very thin sheet of metal, esp. gold or silver. (See also ***Dutch***, ***Florence leaf***, GOLD LEAF, SILVER LEAF.)

14.. *Voc.* in Wr.-Wülcker 580/3 *Electum*, a lefe of goolde. **1567** MAPLET *Gr. Forest* 10 Vpon a Stith with a Mallet it [gold] is brought into most thin leafe or plate. **1580** FRAMPTON *Monardes' Dial. Iron* 166 Vessels of Copper, or of the leafe of Milan... The leafe of Milan is made of Iron. **1707** *Curios. in Husb. & Gard.* 344 Put it into several Leafs of the finest Gold. *a* **1800** COWPER *Flatting Mill* vi, He must beat it as thin and as fine As the leaf that infolds what an invalid swallows. **1851** *Illustr. Catal. Gt. Exhib.* 1236 Gold and silver beaten into leaves, for gilding.

b. A thin sheet or layer of other material produced either by beating out or by splitting; a lamina (of horn, marble, wood, etc.). Also, a thin piece of soap or other detergent (larger than a 'flake'). ***lantern leaves*** (see LANTERN *sb.* 9).

1601 HOLLAND *Pliny* II. 571 The first who couered all the walls..with leaues of marble. **1640** in Entick *London* II. 175 Horns of lanthorn, the 1000 leaves. **1668** *Phil. Trans.* III. 783 Very many *vasa lacrymalia* of Glass, which by length of time were become laminated into divers leaves. **1772** NUGENT tr. *Hist. Friar Gerund* IV. ix. 199 The modern buildings at Rome..appear to be all porphyry, marble..when, in reality, they have no more of these stones than a thin superficial leaf. **1850** SCORESBY *Cheever's Whalem. Adv.* iii. (1859) 38 The bones, or rather, slabs of whalebone, radiate in leaves that lie edgewise to the mouth. **1880** *Chambers's Encycl.* (U.S. ed.) s.v. *Deals*, When a deal is sawed into twelve or more thin planks, they are called 'leaves'. **1925** G. MARTIN *Mod. Soap & Detergent Industry* II. I. ii. 35 Soap Leaves are prepared by passing continuous paper sheets over rollers through a hot solution of soap, the excess of soap attached to the surface being scraped off. The paper is then passed over drying cylinders and from thence to a cutting machine. **1959** *Which?* Nov. 152/2 There were differences between these shampoos and some of the powder or leaf varieties. *Ibid.* 154 Packet of 6 leaves.

c. One of the metal strips of a leaf spring.

1905 R. T. SLOSS *Bk. Automobile* vi. 124 The friction of the leaves decreases with the tension of the spring. **1936** F. CLUNE *Roaming round Darling* ix. 78 We left the car to have a couple of extra leaves inserted in the springs. **1971** B. SCHARF *Engin. & its Lang.* xii. 147 The individual leaves are free to slide along each other and adequate grease lubrication must be provided to minimise friction.

†**11.** The sheet of leather into which the teeth of a wool-card were inserted. *Obs.*

1688 R. HOLME *Armoury* III. 92/1 The Leaf, the Leather to set the Teeth in. Pricking the Leaf, is making holes in the Leather, into which the teeth are put.

12. a. A hinged part or one of a series of parts connected at one side or end by a hinge; a flap. Now *rare* or *obs.* exc. *spec.* as in b, c, d, e.

1420 *E.E. Wills* (1882) 46 A beme þat y weye þer-with, and ij leuys. *c* **1524** *Churchw. Acc. St. Maryhill, Lond.* (Nichols 1797) 118 A Spear with 2 leues. **1526** *Pilgr. Perf.* (W. de W. 1531) 236 He..wrote them in a payre of tables of stone, whiche tables had two leaues or two bredes. **1572** *Lanc. Wills* (Chetham Soc.) II. 205 One mucke weyne wth leaves.

b. One of two or more parts of a door, gate, or shutter turning upon hinges.

c **1380** *Sir Ferumb.* 1327 Þe wyndowes wern y-mad of iaspre..þe leues were masalyne. **1382** WYCLIF *Judg.* xvi. 3 And thens rysynge he [Sampson] took both leeues of the ȝate. **1581** LAMBARDE *Eiren.* II. vii. (1588) 265 Puttyng backe the leafe of a window with his dagger. **1611** BIBLE *Ezek.* xli. 24 And the doores had two leaues a piece, two turning leaues. **1723** CHAMBERS *Le Clerc's Treat. Archit.* I. 102 Coach-Gates..are usually made with two Leaves or Folding-doors. **1848** THACKERAY *Van. Fair* xli, Two..personages in black flung open each a leaf of the door as the carriage pulled up. **1870** MORRIS *Earthly Par.* III. IV. 106 The chanted prayer..Thrilled through the brazen leaves of the great door. **1887** *Times* 25 Aug. 4/5 One leaf of each pair of gates.

c. A hinged flap at the side of a table to be raised when required for use. Hence applied *gen.* to any movable addition to the top of a table.

1558 *Bury Wills* (Camden) 151 One plaine table wth one leafe. **1577** *Wills & Inv. N.C.* (Surtees 1835) I. 414 A table withe two leves vjs. viijd. **1665** PEPYS *Diary* 28 May, Here I saw one pretty piece of household stuff:—as the company increaseth, to put a larger leaf upon an ovall table. **1797** MAR. EDGEWORTH *Early Lessons* (1827) I. 50, I will hold up this part of the table which is called the leaf. **1830** MARRYAT *King's Own* xli, He has finished the spare-leaf of the dining-table. **1883** *Harper's Mag.* Oct. 652/2 The table was cleared off, and the leaves taken out.

d. The part of a draw-bridge or bascule-bridge which is raised upon a hinge.

1653 *Boston Rec.* (1877) II. 117 Liberty..to alter the drawe bridge, whereas it is made [to] rise in one Leafe, and..to make it to rise in two leaves. **1791** *Selby Bridge Act* 34 The leaf or leaves of the said bridge. **1894** *Westm. Gaz.* 30 June 5/2 The ponderous bascules or leaves of the [Tower] bridge were seen to rise steadily into the air.

e. A hinged sight on the barrel of a rifle.

1875 in KNIGHT *Dict. Mech.* s.v. *Leaf-sight.* **1896** *Westm. Gaz.* 16 Sept. 3/1 Half the company with the leaf of the sight raised and half with it down. **1900** *Daily News* 2 Feb. 7/1 The sighting leaf.

13. One of the teeth of a pinion. (See also quot. 1805.)

1706 in PHILLIPS (ed. Kersey). **1729** DESAGULIERS in *Phil. Trans.* XXXVI. 195 An Iron Wheel,..to be carried round by a Pinion, *u*, of a few Leaves. **1805** BREWSTER in *Ferguson's Lect.* I. 82 *note*, When the small wheel is solid and oblong, and it's teeth longer than their distance from the axis,..its teeth are named *leaves.* **1812–16** J. SMITH *Panorama Sci. & Art* I. 358 The tooth of the wheel acts upon the leaf of the pinion.

14. The brim of a hat. Chiefly *Anglo-Irish.*

1767 H. BROOKE *Fool of Qual.* IV. 210 Harry let down the leaf of his hat, and drew it over his eyes to conceal his emotions. **1841** H. AINSWORTH *Guy Fawkes* xi, His hat was..somewhat broader in the leaf than was ordinarily worn. **1842** LEVER *J. Hinton* xxi. 146 A hat..the leaf jagged and broken. **1893** P. W. JOYCE *Short Hist. Irel.* 118 The *barread* or hat was cone-shaped and without a leaf.

15. Weaving. ***leaf of heddles*** (see quot. 1839). ***twill of three, four,*** etc. ***leaves***: twill woven upon three, four, etc. leaves of heddles; hence *attrib.*, as ***eight-leaf twill.***

1831 G. R. PORTER *Silk Manuf.* 238 All varieties of twilling depend upon the..working of the different leaves of heddles. **1839** URE *Dict. Arts* 1230 The heddles being stretched between two shafts of wood, all the heddles connected by the same shafts are called a leaf. *Ibid.* 1231 The draught of the eight-leaf tweel differs in nothing..excepting in the number of leaves. **1888** J. PATON in *Encycl. Brit.* XXIV. 464/2 Regular twills of from four to eight leaves are woven in the same manner.

16. The external portion of the ear of a mammal or the nasal appendage of a leaf-nosed bat.

1851 H. MELVILLE *Moby Dick* II. xxxii. 225 The ear [of a whale] has no external leaf whatever; and into the hole itself you can hardly insert a quill. **1955** *Times* 16 July 12/1 (*caption*) A forest-living bat, with a very large nose leaf..caught by members of the expedition to British Guiana.

III. *attrib.* and *Comb.*

17. a. Simple attrib., chiefly *Bot.* and *Vegetable Phys.*, as ***leaf-axil***, ***-base***, ***-blade***, ***-cell***, ***-disease***, ***-lobe***, ***-point***, ***-rib***, ***-shadow***, ***-shape***, ***-shoot***, ***-stalk*** (= PETIOLE[1]), ***-vein***.

1870 HOOKER *Stud. Flora* 322 Flowers fascicled in the upper *leaf-axils. **1865** P. H. GOSSE *Land & Sea* 26 This plant [*sc.* a grass] grows in large stools or tussocks formed of the densely-matted *leaf-bases of successive seasons. **1894** *Pop. Sci. Monthly* XLIV. 488 The huge leaf-bases [of the banana tree]..tightly inclose each other. **1965** BELL & COOMBE tr. *Strasburger's Textbk. Bot.* 158 In many leaves..the leaf base is not specially developed. **1870** HOOKER *Stud. Flora* 367 *Leaf-blade flat. **1875** HUXLEY & MARTIN *Course Elem. Biol.* 49 The terminal *leaf-cell soon attaining its full size and not dividing. **1974** A. HUXLEY *Plant & Planet* vii. 57 In which vein the xylem and phloem fit together, so that the sugars from the leaf cells can be passed into the remainder of the plant. **1869** *Rep. Comm. U.S. Agric.* 218 Mildew and other *leaf diseases. **1870** HOOKER *Stud. Flora* 15 *Leaf-lobes longer. **1871** C. KINGSLEY *At Last* II. x. 71 The curving *leaf-points toss in the breeze. **1895** KIPLING *Second Jungle Bk.* 141 The lighting shows each littlest *leaf-rib clear. **1863** LONGF. *Wayside Inn* I. *Falcon of Ser Federigo* 50 In the *leaf-shadows of the trellises. **1909** GROOM & BALFOUR tr. *Warming's Oecol. Plants.* III. xxviii. 99 The properties of water bring forth *leaf-shapes entirely different from those of land-plants. **1946** *Nature* 13 July 64/1 When a leaf-shape is transferred from a late to an early flowering species the action of the gene is accelerated. **1946** F. E. ZEUNER *Dating Past* xii. 381 If one compares this example of an aromorph with the evolution, for instance, of a highly specialized protective character, such as the leaf-shape of a leaf-insect.., one realizes the difference between an aromorph and an ordinary adaptational character. **1865** TYLOR *Early Hist. Man.* vii. 187 A pointed flexible *leaf-shoot of wild plantain. **1776** WITHERING *Brit. Plants* Gloss. 799 *Leaf-stalk, the foot-stalk of a leaf. **1839** LINDLEY *Introd. Bot.* (ed. 3) 138 The petiole, or leafstalk. **1895** *Daily News* 27 Dec. 7/1 Both evergreens and deciduous plants are subject to this process of separation at the bottom of the leaf stalk. **1970** ROBERTSON & GOODING *Bot. for Caribbean* (ed. 2) iii. 27 The petiole or leaf-stalk varies somewhat in length and shape. **1880** C. R. MARKHAM *Peruv. Bark* xvii. 193 Distinguishable by the deep red of the *leaf-veins.

b. objective, as ***leaf-eater***, ***-shedding***; ***leaf-bearing***, ***-boring***, ***-eating***, ***-forming***, ***-shedding*** adjs. See also *leaf-miner*, *-mining* (sense 18); LEAF-CUTTER; LEAF-CUTTING *ppl. a.*

1875 BENNETT & DYER *Sachs' Bot.* 131 Leaves and *Leaf-bearing Axes. *a* **1887** R. JEFFERIES *Field & Hedgerow* (1889) 115 The coils and turns upon this leaf..are the work of a *leaf-boring larva. **1852** T. W. HARRIS *Insects Injur. Veget.* (1862) 117 *Leaf-eaters. *Ibid.* 121 The tortoise-beetles..are *leaf-eating insects. **1884** BOWER & SCOTT *De Bary's Phaner.* 63 *Leaf-forming plants. **1837** WHEELWRIGHT tr. *Aristophanes* I. 107 Smelling of bind-weed and *leaf-shedding poplar. **1876** T. HARDY *Ethelberta* (1890) 316 The leaf-shedding season being now at its height.

c. instrumental, as ***leaf-crowned***, ***-encumbered***, ***-entangled***, ***-fringed***, ***-hid***, ***-hung***, ***-laden***, ***-latticed***, ***-lined***, ***-roofed***, ***-shadowed***, ***-sheltered***, ***-strewn***, ***-strown***, ***-whelmed.***

1891 W. B. YEATS *Countess Kathleen* (1892) 125 And no one any *leaf-crowned dancer miss. **1925** V. WOOLF *Mrs. Dalloway* 21 That *leaf-encumbered forest, the soul. **1821** SHELLEY *Prometh. Unb.* IV. i. 258 The emerald light of *leaf-entangled beams. **1820** KEATS *Ode Grecian Urn* 5 What *leaf-fringed legend haunts about thy shape..? **1869** J. R. LOWELL *Under Willows* 52 Our *leaf-hid Sybaris. **1895** W. B. YEATS *Poems* 16 Down in a leaf-hid, hollow place. **1919** V. WOOLF *Night & Day* xi. 145 They swept together among the *leaf-hung trees of an unknown world. **1921** W. DE LA MARE *The Veil* 7 The listening, leaf-hung creek. **1842** FABER *Styrian Lake, etc.* 122 *Leaf-laden waters. **1863** LONGF. *Wayside Inn* I. *Birds Killingworth* 122 The dim, *leaf-latticed windows of the grove. **1895** *Outing* XXVI. 394/2, I filled one of our *leaf-lined pails with berries. **1839** BAILEY *Festus* xx. (1848) 238 Old orchards' *leaf roofed aisles. **1844** J. TOMLIN *Missionary Jrnls.* v. 120 The capital of Siam is a large, but not very magnificent city..consisting mainly of leaf-roofed wooden cottages. **1906** *Westm. Gaz.* 10 Sept. 2/3 Where the much-loved birds in their leaf-roofed halls Will herald my morning in. **1845** E. COOK *Poems* 2nd Ser. 187 The *leaf-shadow'd thicket. **1868** J. R. LOWELL *Under Willows* (1869) 22 So they in their leaf-shadowed microcosm Image the larger world. **1769** G. WHITE *Selborne* (1789) 69 To yonder bench *leaf-sheltered let us stray. **1876** T. HARDY *Ethelberta* 384 The *leaf-strewn path. **1730–46** THOMSON *Autumn* 955 These now the lonesome muse.. lead into their *leaf-strown walks. *a* **1889** G. M. HOPKINS *Poems* (1918) 89 We are *leafwhelmed somewhere with the hood Of some branchy bunchy bushybowered wood.

d. parasynthetic and similative, as ***leaf-bladed, -dark, -dry, -eyed, -legged, -light, -pointed, -shaped*** adjs.; also ***leaf-like*** adj.

1883 *Daily News* 21 Sept. 5/7 A small *leaf-bladed sheathed dagger. **1936** E. SITWELL *Victoria of Eng.* xix. 227 Their *leaf-dark hair smoothed into the Chinese style. **1946** W. DE LA MARE *Traveller* 20 He caught but *leaf-dry whisper of what they said. **1949** S. SPENDER *Edge of Being* 20 Behind the hedge of *leaf-eyed lovers. **1971** B. PATTEN *Irrelevant Song* 51 Into myth she faded, Leaf-eyed. *c* **1879** G. M. HOPKINS *Poems* (1918) 44 Low-latched in *leaf-light housel his too huge godhead. **1921** V. WOOLF *Monday or Tuesday* 37 Flaunted, leaf-light, drifting at corners, blown across the wheels. **1818** BYRON *Ch. Har.* IV. cii, Of her consuming cheek the autumnal *leaf-like red. **1845** LINDLEY *Sch. Bot.* (1862) 168 The stem..leaf-like (*foliaceus*). **1865** LUBBOCK *Preh. Times* 17 The swords of the Bronze age..are always more or less leaf-like in shape. **1870** HOOKER *Stud. Flora* 111 *Rubus fruticosus*..Sepals ascending often *leaf-pointed. **1851** D. WILSON *Preh. Ann.* (1863) II. III. i. 8 The ancient bronze *leaf-shaped sword. **1872** J. EVANS *Anc. Stone Implements Gt. Brit.* xvi. 333 Of leaf-shaped arrow-heads..there are several minor varieties. **1923** C. FOX *Archaeol. Cambr. Region* i. 4 Both the leaf-shaped and the tanged types [of arrowhead] commonly occur in the district. **1940** C. F. C. HAWKES *Prehist. Found. Europe* iii. 78 Hollow-based and leaf-shaped arrowheads.. appear in the flint industry.

18. Special comb.: **leaf-arrowhead**, an arrowhead shaped like a leaf, usu. of the Neolithic period and made of flint (cf. *leaf-shaped* adj. in sense 17 d above); **leaf-bearing** *a.*, having a leaf-like appendage; applied *spec.* to worms of the family *Phyllodocidæ*, which have gills in the form of leaves; †**leaf-beaten** *a.*, beaten to a thin plate or foil; **leaf-bed**, a layer of leaves sometimes found in the upper stratum of the earth's surface; **leaf-beetle**, a beetle of the family *Chrysomelidæ* (see quot.); **leaf-birth** [after *childbirth*], a bringing forth of leaves; **leaf blight**, one of several plant diseases causing the death of foliage; **leaf blister**, (*a*) a disease of certain fruit trees caused by a parasitic mite; (*b*) a plant disease caused by a fungus of the genus *Taphrina*; **leaf blotch**, one of several plant diseases indicated by discoloured patches on foliage, esp. = BLACK SPOT 1; **leaf-brass**, brass foil; **leaf-bridge**, a bridge constructed with a leaf or leaves (sense 12 d); **leaf brown**, the colour of (dead) leaves; **leaf-bud**, a bud from which leaves are produced (opposed to *flower-bud*); **leaf-bug** *U.S.*, a heteropterous insect of the family *Tingitidæ* (*Cent. Dict.*); **leaf-bundle**, the bundle of fibres running from the stem into the leaf of a plant; **leaf-butterfly**, one of the genus *Kallima*; **leaf-canopy** (see quot.); **leaf cast** = *larch needle cast* (LARCH 3); **leaf-climber** (see quot. 1880); so **leaf-climbing** *a.*; **leaf-crumpler** (see quot.); **leaf-cup**, †(*a*) ? a cup shaped like a leaf; (*b*) the plant *Polymnia Uvedalia* (*Treas. Bot.* 1866); (*c*) a leaf folded and used as a cup; **leaf curl**, one of several plant diseases characterized by curling leaves, esp. (*a*) = *leaf-roll*; (*b*) a disease of peach, almond, and nectarine trees caused by the fungus *Taphrina deformans*; (*c*) a virus disease of cotton; **leaf-cutting**, a leaf used as a cutting in the propagation of certain plants; **leaf-cycle** *Bot.* (see quot.); **leaf-door**, a flap- or folding-door (in quots. *transf.* and *fig.*); **leaf-drift**, a place where fallen leaves have been blown together by the wind; **leaf-eared**, a corrupt form of *lave-eared* (see LAVE *a.*); **leaf-fall**, (*a*) *poet.*, the fall of the leaf, autumn; (*b*) *Bot.*, the shedding of leaves by a plant; **leaf-fat**, the fat round a pig's kidneys; **leaf-feeder**, an insect that feeds upon plant-leaves; **leaf-finch** *U.S.*, the common bullfinch, *Pyrrhula vulgaris* (*Cent. Dict.*); **leaf-flea**, an insect of the family *Psyllidæ* which lives on plants (*Syd. Soc. Lex.* 1888); **leaf-folder**, a moth whose larvæ fold leaves together to form a protective covering; **leaf-footed** *a.*, having leaf-like feet; **leaf-frog**, a frog of the genus *Phyllomedusa* (Webster, 1897); **leaf-gap** *Veg. Phys.*, a division in the fibre of a plant, caused by the protrusion of a leaf-bud; †**leaf-gate**, a gate with folding leaves or flaps; **leaf gelatine**, gelatine manufactured in sheet form for cooking purposes; **leaf-gilding** *vbl. sb.*, gilding with leaf-gold; **leaf-green** *a.*, of the colour of green leaves; also quasi-*sb.*; *sb.* = CHLOROPHYLL; **leaf-hopper** (see quot.); **leaf-house, -hut**, a house or hut made of entwined leaves; **leaf-insect**, a name for insects of the family *Phasmidæ*, esp. the genus *Phyllium*, in which the wings and sometimes the legs resemble leaves in shape and colour; **leaf-joy** *nonce-wd.*, **leaf-lard** (see quots.); **leaf-lichen**, a lichen of the genus *Parmelia* or N.O. *Parmeliaceæ*; **leaf-louse**, one of the aphides which infest the leaves of plants; a plant-louse; **leaf-mass**, a thick growth of leaves; **leafmeal** [-MEAL] *adv.* (*nonce-wd.*), with leaves fallen one by one; **leaf-metal**, metal beaten out to a thin leaf or foil; **leaf-miner**, a small caterpillar of a tineid moth which eats its way between the cuticles of leaves; so ***leaf-mining caterpillar***; **leaf-monkey**, a monkey found in south or south-east Asia belonging to one of several species of the genus *Presbytis*; = LANGUR; **leaf-mould**, (*a*) mould having a large proportion of decayed leaves mixed with it; (*b*) a disease of tomatoes caused by the fungus *Cladosporium fulvum*; **leaf-netting** (see quot.); **leaf-nosed** *a.*, having a leaf-like appendage on the snout; *spec.* applied to the phyllostomoid and rhinolophoid bats; **leaf-opposed** *a. Bot.*, having opposite leaves; **leaf-plant**, a plant cultivated for its foliage; in quot. *attrib.*; **leaf-plate, -platter**, a leaf or leaves used as a plate or dish for food; **leaf protein**, protein, or a protein, present in leaves, esp. when extracted for use as a possible dietary supplement; **leaf-red** = ERYTHROPHYLL (*Syd. Soc. Lex.*); **leaf-roll**, a virus disease of potatoes shown by curled-up leaves; **leaf-roller**, the caterpillar of certain (tortricid) moths, which rolls up the leaves of plants which it infests; so ***leaf-rolling*** adj.; **leaf-rosette** *Veg. Phys.*, a cluster of leaves resembling a rosette; **leaf-rust**, a mould which attacks trees, producing the appearance of rusty spots on the leaves; **leaf scald**, (*a*) = *leaf scorch*; (*b*) a disease of sugar-cane caused by the bacterial pathogen *Xanthomonas albilineans*; **leaf-scale**, a scale on a plant-stem which develops into a leaf; **leaf-scar**, the cicatrix left on the bark by the separation of the leaf-stalk of a fallen leaf; **leaf scorch**, a plant disease caused by a deficiency of potassium, causing leaves to shrivel and turn brown; also, a virus disease causing similar effects; **leaf-sheath**, an expansion at the axil of a leaf in some plants, which embraces the stem and petiole; also, a covering to the leaf-bearing shoots of some grasses, e.g. the *Equisetaceæ*; **leaf-shedding**, (*a*) a disease of pine trees caused by the fungus *Hendersonia acicola*; pine needle cast; (*b*) = *leaf-fall* (*b*); **leaf shelter**, a shelter made of leaves; †**leaf-sickness** (see quot. and cf. sense 5 above); **leaf-sight** (see 12 e); **leaf-silver**, silver leaf or foil; hence **leaf-silvering** *vbl. sb.*, the process of covering with leaf-silver (*Cent. Dict.*); **leaf-skin**, (*a*) the membrane enclosing the leaf-fat; (*b*) the epidermis of a leaf; **leaf-soil** = *leaf-mould*; **leaf-spine** (see quot. 1882); **leaf-spot**, one of a large number of plant diseases caused by various fungi which mark the foliage; also *attrib.*; **leaf spring**, a spring consisting of a number of strips of metal curved slightly upwards and clamped together one above the other, each strip being longer than the one beneath; so ***leaf springing, -sprung*** adj.; **leaf-table**, a table with a leaf or flap; **leaf-tailed** *a.*, having the tail shaped like a leaf, applied to geckos of the genus *Phyllurus* (*Cent. Dict.*); **leaf-teeth** (see quot.); **leaf-tendril**, a leaf, the midrib of which grows beyond the blade in the form of a tendril; **leaf-thorn** = *leaf-spine* (*Syd. Soc. Lex.*); †**leaf-tin**, tin-foil; **leaf-tobacco** (see quot. 1851); **leaf-trace** *Veg. Phys.* (see quot. 1875); **leaf-turner**, †(*a*) *jocular*, a reader of a book; (*b*) a device for turning over the leaves of a book (Knight *Dict. Mech.* 1875); **leaf-valve**, 'a valve of a pumping-engine hinged or pivoted on one side, a flap-valve' (Knight); **leaf warbler**, a small green or yellow bird of the genus *Phylloscopus*, living in bushes or trees; **leaf-wasp**, 'a saw-fly' (Webster, 1897); **leaf-work**, ornamental work consisting of leaf-forms; †**leaf-worm**, a caterpillar that devours leaves.

1954 S. PIGGOTT *Neolithic Cultures* iii. 99 *Leaf-arrowheads are a common feature in Belgium. **1963** L. F. CHITTY in Foster & Alcock *Culture & Environment* vii. 188 Flints found range from a microlith and a leaf-arrowhead to a gun-flint. **1882** *Cassell's Nat. Hist.* VI. 232 The family of *Leaf-bearing Worms, the Phyllodocidæ, contains very beautiful Worms. **1660** HEXHAM *Dutch Dict.*, *Klater-goudt*, ..*leafe-beaten gold. **1873** *Archæologia* XLIV. 278 The upper surface of the *leaf-bed was well marked and level, as was also..the upper surface of the moss. **1894** *Nature* 26 July 295/1 If we could only meet with some fairly representative leaf-beds, such as abound in newer formations, the Wealden would yield a flora, both varied, and of enormous interest. **1954** S. PIGGOTT *Neolithic Cultures* x. 295 'Leaf bed' with no large vegetable remains, 3–4 ft. thick. **1852** T. W. HARRIS *Insects Injur. Veget.* (1862) 117 Beetles..which, as they derive their nourishment.. from leaves alone, may be called *leaf-beetles. **1887** BOWEN *Virg. Eclog.* III. 56 Now each meadow is teeming, in *leafbirth every tree. **1850** *Rep. Comm. Patents 1849* (U.S.) 440 During the last summer our seedling pears were for the first time badly affected with '*leaf-blight'. **1920** P. J. FRYER *Insect Pests & Fungus Dis. Fruit & Hops* 709 Cherry and Plum Leaf Blight..appears to be slightly on the increase. **1926** [see *frog eye*]. **1960** C. WESTCOTT *Plant Dis. Handbk.* (ed. 2) 125 *Mystrosporium adustum.* Leaf Blight, Ink Spot of bulbous iris. **1914** F. C. SEARS *Productive Orcharding* xi. 159 *Leaf Blister Mite.—Another pest which is frequently troublesome on both pears and apples is the blister mite. **1960** C. WESTCOTT *Plant Dis. Handbk.* (ed. 2) 194 A single genus, Taphrina, is responsible for most of the hyperplastic (over-growth) deformities known as leaf blister, leaf curl, or, occasionally, as pockets. **1906** M. C. COOKE *Fungoid Pests Cultivated Plants* 75 Iris *Leaf-blotch. **1925** *Gardeners' Chron.* 31 Oct. 353/3 (*heading*) A leaf blotch of the Shasta daisy. **1928** *Daily Express* 7 July 4/2 See that none of your favourites [*sc.* roses] is attacked by leaf blotch. **1971** *Country Life* 18 Feb. 389/2 The diseases of mildew, rust and leaf blotch are prevalent throughout Britain. **1708** *Phil. Trans.* XXVI. 90 The Rosin, while warm, would attract *Leaf-Brass. **1841** S. C. BREES *Gloss. Civ. Engin.*, *Leaf-Bridge, or Hoist-Bridge. **1923** *Daily Mail* 19 Feb. 1 (Advt.), French Model Jumper made of..Crepe de Chine,..Jade..*Leaf Brown, Navy and Black. **1932** W. FAULKNER *Light in August* xx. 444 Patches of Confederate grey weathered leafbrown now. **1664** EVELYN *Kal. Hort.* Jan. (1706) 4 Learn..to.. distinguish the Bearing and Fruit-buds from the *Leaf-buds. **1839** LINDLEY *Introd. Bot.* (ed. 3) 74 The usual, or normal, situation of leaf-buds is in the axil of leaves. **1906** *Westm. Gaz.* 14 Apr. 8/1 The lilac and elder-bushes..are beginning to unfold their leaf-buds. **1971** *Country Life* 10 June 1440/2 The ash..never makes the mistake of opening its leaf buds before the last night frost. **1884** BOWER & SCOTT *De Bary's Phaner.* 256 All..are, according to Wigand, 'true *leaf-bundles, since they traverse only one internode and then run into the leaf-organs. **1882** *Cassell's Nat. Hist.* VI. 232 *Leaf-butterfly of India (*Kallima inachis*). **1885** C. F. HOLDER *Marvels Anim. Life* 147 Java, the home of the beautiful leaf-butterfly. **1889** *Land Agents' Rec.* 9 Feb. 126 A forest is said to form a '*leaf-canopy' when the crowns of the trees touch each other. **1933** *Oxford Forestry Mem.* XV. 7 *Meria laricis* Vuillemin, the *leaf cast disease of larch, which was first described by Mer in 1895..is probably the most important fungal disease of European larch in nurseries in this country. **1952** E. RAMSDEN tr. *Gram & Weber's Plant Dis.* iv. 482/1 Leaf cast is the worst disease of young larch trees. **1880** GRAY *Struct. Bot.* iii. §3 (ed. 6) 52 *Leaf-Climbers are those in which support is gained by the action, not of the stem itself, but of the leaves it bears. **1880** C. & F. DARWIN *Movem. Pl.* 139 A *leaf-climbing plant. **1884–5** *Riverside Nat. Hist.* (1888) II. 444 The *leaf-crumpler, *Phycis indiginella*, of North America... The caterpillars draw together and crumple the leaves on which they feed. **1716** *Lond. Gaz.* No. 5409/3 A *Leaf Cup without a Cover. **1890** G. M. GOULD *New Med. Dict.*, *Bear's-foot*, leaf cup. A popular remedy for enlargement of the spleen, or the 'ague-cake' of malarious regions. **1901** KIPLING *Kim* x. 263 He bought sweetmeats in a leaf-cup from a Hindu trader. **1899** G. MASSEE *Text-bk. Plant Dis.* 82 The disease [of peaches], which is very widespread, is popularly known as '*leaf curl', or simply as 'curl', owing to the fact that the diseased leaves become much curled, distorted, and thickened. *Ibid.* 323 The well-known disease of the foliage of potatoes known as 'leaf curl' attacks the stem..and gradually creeps up. **1926** W. H. JOHNSON *Cotton* viii. 259 Upland cotton appeared to be less affected by a peculiar leaf-curl disease. **1951** *Dict. Gardening* (R. Hort. Soc.) III. 1654/2 The most common and probably the most serious [virus disease of potatoes] is Leaf Curl (Leaf Roll). **1965** RIPPER & GEORGE *Cotton Pests Sudan* i. 7 Leafcurl is transmitted from ratoon cotton and wild host plants to cotton by whitefly. **1967** *Punch* 18 Jan. 96/3 It [*sc.* Burgundy mixture] is a good fungicide to use on leafless trees and bushes, particularly against leafcurl in the peach family. **1882** *Garden* 4 Feb. 74/1, I have been successful with *leaf cuttings of..Bertolonias. **1877** BENNETT tr. *Thomé's Bot.* 87 If a spiral is drawn round the stem connecting the points of attachment of the [alternate or scattered] leaves... The course of the spiral from any one leaf to the next leaf which stands exactly vertically above or beneath it is therefore termed the *leaf-cycle. **1600** J. LANE *Tom Tel-troth* 113 The two *leafe-dores of quondam honestie, Which on foure vertues Cardinall were turned. **1615** CROOKE *Body of Man* 108 Nature hath ordained & scituated a certain value, leaf-doore, or floud-gate, at the beginning of this Colon. **1905** E. PHILLPOTTS *Secret Woman* I. i. 6 While death, not unlovely, appeared in *leaf-drift and touch-wood, in acorn cups..and hollow hazel-nuts. **1958** C. TOMLINSON *Seeing is Believing* (1960) 60 And it continues Falling flaking into the leaf-drift. **1840** BROWNING *Sordello* III. 95 *Leaf-fall and grass-spring for the year. **1914** M. DRUMMOND tr. *Haberlandt's Physiol. Plant Anat.* iii. 143 The arrangements [for peeling bark scales] resemble those

which occur in leaf-bases in connection with the autumnal leaf-fall. **1947** G. F. WILSON *Detection & Control Garden Pests* vi. 107 Premature leaf-fall is associated with several factors other than pest attack. **1971** *Homes & Gardens* Sept. 128/2 Most of the cornus family colour richly before leaf-fall. **1725** BRADLEY *Fam. Dict.* s.v. *Sausages*, *Leaf-Fat out of the Hogs-belly. **1845** J. J. HOOPER *Some Adventures Simon Suggs* v. 65 They've knocked the leaf fat outen him tonight, in wads as big as mattock handles. **1904** L. L. LAMBORN *Cottonseed Products* 166 In the packing plants the leaf fat is taken from the animal immediately after killing. **1853** *Zoologist* XI. 4025 The seed-feeders..not betraying themselves by the discoloured blotches as the *leaf-feeders do. **1869** *Rep. Comm. U.S. Agric.* 217 Illinois: The *leaf folder, thrips, borer, and curculio are occasionally found in vineyards. **1863** WOOD *Illustr. Nat. Hist.* III. 633 The Phyllopoda, or *Leaf-footed Entomostraca. **1884** BOWER & SCOTT *De Bary's Phaner.* 243 Narrow reticulated tracheides at the edges bordering the *leaf-gap. **1615** CROOKE *Body of Man* 236 The torne Membranes..do somtimes hang downe on either hand in the sides by the cleft like vnto values..or *leafe-gates. **1956** C. SPRY *Cookery Bk.* xxx. 957 The incorporation of gelatine with various liquids is much easier now that powdered or very fine *leaf gelatine is sold. **1957** E. CRAIG *Collins Family Cookery* 606 Ten perfect sheets of French leaf gelatine equals 1 oz. **1839** URE *Dict. Arts* 613 *Leaf gilding..is done by giving..a coat of gum water or fine size, applying the gold leaf ere the surfaces be hard dry. **1853** *Ibid.* (ed. 4) II. 867 Chlorophyle (*leaf-green). **1891** *Daily News* 19 Sept. 2/1 The hat..is in leaf green felt. **1899** *Ibid.* 27 Feb. 6/6 Laburnum-yellows, leaf-greens. **1852** T. W. HARRIS *Insects Injur. Veget.* (1862) 220 Some of the insects..are..called..frog-hoppers, and to others [*Tettigoniadæ*] may be applied the name of *leaf-hoppers, because they live mostly on the leaves of plants. **1953** A. MOOREHEAD *Rum Jungle* vii. 107 Green-ants that stitch their *leaf-houses together by holding their babies in their arms and drawing out of the babies' mouths a sticky thread. **1958** *Listener* 14 Aug. 237/1 Johnny and Silas were my two servants and lived in a leaf house near mine. **1910** W. DE LA MARE *Three Mulla-Mulgars* i. 8 He taught them..to build *leaf-huts and huddles against heat or rain. **1949** M. MEAD *Male & Female* x. 220 A leaky leaf-hut on the side of a mountain. **1861** TENNENT *Nat. Hist. Ceylon* 408 *Leaf-insects. **1863** WOOD *Illustr. Nat. Hist.* III. 486 Leaf insect, *Phyllium scythë*. **1638** RAWLEY tr. *Bacon's Life & Death* (1650) 34 Hope is as a *Leafe-Ioy [orig. *tanquam gaudium foliatum*]; Which may be beaten out, to a great Extention, like Gold. **1848** *Rep. Comm. Patents 1847* (U.S.) 538 The articles thus referred to are put up in these establishments, from the hams..*leaf lard [etc.]. **1858** SIMMONDS *Dict. Trade*, *Leaf-lard*, lard from the flaky animal fat of the hog. **1885** W. L. CARPENTER *Treat. Manuf. Soap* ii. 25 The fat immediately surrounding the kidneys yields the best and purest lard. This, and that which is obtained in flaky layers between the flesh and the skin.., is known as 'leaf' lard. **1888** W. T. BRANNT *Pract. Treat. Animal & Veg. Fats & Oils* ix. 344 The leaf lard is..kept separate from the rest. **1879** ROSSITER *Dict. Sci. Terms*, *Leaf lichens, *Parmeliaceæ*. **1774** GOLDSM. *Nat. Hist.* (1824) III. 212 The animal which some have called the *Leaf Louse, is of the size of a flea, and of a bright green, or bluish-green colour. **1908** G. JEKYLL *Colour in Flower Garden* vii. 60 We gradually return to the grey-blues, whites and pale yellows, with..the splendid *leaf-mass of a wide and high plant of *Euphorbia Wulfenii*, which..rises to a height far above my head. **1958** C. TOMLINSON *Seeing is Believing* (1960) 20 Light, swept perpendicular Into the leaf-mass Flickers out. *c* **1880** G. M. HOPKINS *Poems* (1918) 51 Though worlds of wanwood *leafmeal lie. **1812** J. SMYTH *Pract. of Customs* (1821) 155 *Leaf Metal (except of Gold) the packet to contain 250 leaves. **1830** J. RENNIE *Insect Archit.* xii. 239 Most of the solitary *leaf-miners either cannot or will not construct a new mine, if ejected by an experimenter from the old. **1883** WOOD in *Gd. Words* Dec. 763/2 Leaf-miners—tiny caterpillars which pass their lives between the inner and outer layer of leaves. **1830** J. RENNIE *Insect Archit.* xii. 233 *Leaf-mining Caterpillars. **1888** W. T. BLANFORD *Fauna Brit. India: Mammalia* I. 41 Phayre's *Leaf-Monkey is found in dense high forests. **1928** *Jrnl. Bombay Nat. Hist. Soc.* XXXII. 472 (*title*) The langurs or leaf-monkeys of British India. **1966** R. & D. MORRIS *Men & Apes* viii. 236 Various species of leaf monkeys..frequent salt licks and saline mineral springs in Borneo. **1845** *Florist's Jrnl.* 53 A compost of *leaf-mould, loam, and sand, well mixed together. **1913** M. T. COOK *Dis. Trop. Plants* vii. 217 Leaf Mould..spreads rapidly. **1931** *Times Lit. Suppl.* 24 Sept. 734/4 Leaf-mould (*Cladosporium*) is a source of much loss to growers of the tomato. **1971** T. F. PREECE in J. H. Western *Dis. Crop Plants* ii. 12 *Cladosporium fulvum.* Tomato leaf mould. **1882** CAULFEILD & SAWARD *Dict. Needle-work* 360 **Leaf Netting*, also known as Puff Netting, and worked so as to raise some of the loops of a row above the others. **1843** *List Mammalia Brit. Mus.* 21 Redman's *Leaf-nosed Bat. **1850** A. WHITE *Pop. Hist. Mammalia* 47 The bats are arranged by Mr. Gray in two great divisions—the Leaf-nosed bats and the Simple-nosed bats. **1879** WRIGHT *Anim. Life* 64 The Phyllostomidæ. This family contains the simple Leaf-nosed Bats. **1960** G. DURRELL *Zoo in Luggage* ii. 61 A handful of leaf-nosed bats with extraordinary gargoyle-like faces. **1965** R. & D. MORRIS *Men & Snakes* viii. 178 (*caption*) The leaf-nosed snake, showing an unusual form of serpentine camouflage. **1870** HOOKER *Stud. Flora* 5 Ranunculus.. Batrachium..Peduncles usually *leaf-opposed. **1896** HOWELLS *Impressions & Exp.* 214 The *leaf-plant beds before the hotel. *a* **1843** SOUTHEY *Commonplace Bk.* (1849) 2nd Ser. 422/1 **Leaf-plates.* 'Their plates and dishes are generally formed from the leaf of the plaintain tree or the nymphæa lotos... These are never used a second time.' **1962** B. HARRISSON *Orang-Utan* ii. 57 You bend slightly over and down for mouth and fingers to meet above your leaf-plate. **1901** KIPLING *Kim* xi. 281 'And we,' said Kim, turning his back and heaping a *leaf-platter for the lama, 'are beyond all castes.' **1937** *Rep. Brit. Assoc. Adv. Sci. 1937* 459 Man also eats leaves to some extent,..and these leaves are quite high in protein. In this case there has been no selection of the *leaf proteins by animal or plant, and it is probable that this leaf protein is intermediate in value to man between animal and other vegetable protein. **1953** *Jrnl. Agric. Sci.* XLIII. 136/1 Work on laboratory-extracted leaf protein suggests that such material might provide valuable protein feed as it contains many of the amino-acids essential for poultry nutrition. **1971** N. W. PIRIE *Leaf Protein* xvi. 157 People habituated to leaf protein accept its flavour so that a larger proportion can be added to a food. *Ibid.*, Freshly made slabs of leaf protein disperse in water to give a smooth paste but slabs stored in deep-freeze gradually become gritty and have to be passed through a mill. **1972** GOODWIN & MERCER *Introd. Plant Biochem.* ix. 236 The major part of the leaf protein is in the chloroplast. **1926** *Sci. Proc. R. Dublin Soc.* XVIII. 177 Twenty-nine halves or thirds of tubers..were infested with aphides from diseased sprouts. .. Only two..became infected (with *leaf-roll, the aphides being *Myzus pseudosolani*). **1946** *Nature* 14 Dec. 885/2 Bismark is resistant to leafroll. **1960** *Times* 29 July 12/6 The telltale curl..shows a potato plant has leafroll. **1830** J. RENNIE *Insect Archit.* viii. 158 The caterpillars which are familiarly termed *leaf-rollers, are perfect hermits. *Ibid.* 163 The leaf-rolling caterpillars. **1875** BENNETT & DYER *Sachs' Bot.* 169 The *leaf-rosettes of Crassulaceæ. **1865** COOKE *Rust, Smut*, etc. 111 A rare species in Britain is the oak-*leaf rust (*Uredo Quercus*). **1899** G. MASSEE *Textbk. Plant Dis.* 276 (*heading*) *Leaf scald. **1924** *Phytopathology* XIV. 587 (*title*) Java gum disease of sugar cane identical to leaf scald of Australia. **1965** G. C. STEVENSON *Genetics & Breeding Sugar Cane* v. 147 Resistance of sugar cane species and hybrids to leaf scald disease..is very much complicated by the presence, in various countries, of several different strains of the parasite. **1776–96** WITHERING *Brit. Plants* (ed. 3) II. 490 Leaves floating, long, grass-like, blunt, from *leaf-scales. **1835** LINDLEY *Introd. Bot.* (1848) I. 239 We do not ..usually find any buds in the axils of the *leaf-scars. **1897** J. C. WILLIS *Man. Flowering Plants* I. iii. 167 This [*sc.* the absciss layer] splits down the middle and leaves one half upon the stem, where it forms the *leaf scar* covering the wound. **1965** BELL & COOMBE tr. *Strasburger's Textbk. Bot.* 167 In almost all woody plants the leaves..are sooner or later shed, leaving leaf scars on the stem showing their former positions. **1921** *Ann. Rep. Agric. & Hort. Res. Station Univ. Bristol* 121 The correlation which has been noted between the amount of potash supply, root growth and the degree of *leaf scorch, points very definitely towards the liberal application of potash manures as a remedial measure. **1929** *Misc. Publ. Ministry Agric. & Fisheries* no. 70. 27 Leaf Scorch..was common on Mangolds in Devon and Cornwall in 1927, and on Sugar Beet in the East Midland and Eastern Provinces in the same year. **1933** *Jrnl. R. Hort. Soc.* LVIII. 253 Leaf scorch of apples is a deficiency disease. **1943** *Bull. Ministry Agric. & Fisheries* no. 126. 30 Leaf Scorch..was formerly attributed to *Sporidesmium putrefaciens* Fuckel but is now regarded..as a later and secondary symptom of Yellows. **1952** E. RAMSDEN tr. *Gram & Weber's Plant Dis.* iii. 342/2 Leaf Scorch (Potassium Deficiency). Potatoes that lack potassium produce a low-growing, rather dark, open haulm. **1961** *Amat. Gardening* 21 Oct. Suppl. 31/2 Leaf scorch. A common disorder of grapevines under glass, in which the leaves take on a shrivelled appearance. **1830** LINDLEY *Nat. Syst. Bot.* p. xlvii, *Leafsheaths entire..Leafsheaths slit. **1875** BENNETT & DYER *Sachs' Bot.* 370 [*Equisetum Telmateia* and *E. arvense*] After they have formed several foliar girdles and their apex is covered by a firm envelope of leaf-sheaths, they break through the base of the parent leaf-sheaths. **1891** W. SCHLICH *Man. Forestry* II. 302 In many cases a fungus (*Hysterium pinastre*) is present, and may occasion the disease, which is called '*leaf-shedding'. **1895** *Daily News* 27 Dec. 7/1 With most evergreens the process of leaf-shedding is exactly the same as in the case of deciduous trees. **1937** *Discovery* Sept. 274/2 Two dilapidated *leaf shelters. **1614** MARKHAM *Cheap. Husb.* III. xxvi. (1668) 93 The staggers, or *leaf-sickness..is ingendered in sheep by surfeiting on Oak-leaves..or such like..it is cold corrupt blood, or flegm, gathered together about the brain. **1614** CAMDEN *Rem.* 204 Eleauen ounces two pence ferling [in the lb. of coin] ought to be of so pure siluer, as is called *leafe siluer. **1712** COOKE *Voy. S. Sea* 87 Salvers, Spoons,..&c. cover'd with Leaf Silver and Gold. **1816** 'A. SINGLETON' *Lett.* (1824) 75 (Th.), Being born smokers, [the Negroes] make pouches of the inner *leafskin of a swine, peeled thin, which is soft, transparent, and tough. **1974** A. HUXLEY *Plant & Planet* xxv. 281 Alpine rhododendrons..have very thick leaf-skins reinforced with silica. **1872** *Jrnl. Horticulture* 21 Mar. 262/1 *Leaf soil decays with age, and finally becomes vegetable soil. **1894** ROBINSON *Cottage Gardening* IV. 12/2. **1877** BENNETT tr. *Thomé's Bot.* 109 *Leaf-spines as in the holly. **1882** VINES *Sachs' Bot.* 215 Leaf-spines are leaves which have developed into long, conical, pointed, woody bodies. **1901** H. M. WARD *Dis. in Plants* xii. 114 If the fungus becomes epidemic and myriads of *leaf-spots are formed, the destruction of foliar tissue..may end in rapid defoliation. **1908** *Jrnl. South-Eastern Agric. College, Wye* XVII. 316 (*title*) Leaf-spot diseases of the apple. **1933** *Jrnl. R. Hort. Soc.* LVIII. 280 Infected seed as a source of the celery leaf-spot is discussed. **1951** *New Biol.* XI. 78 The leaf-spot disease of bananas.. was not recorded in the western tropics until 1934. **1972** *Arable Farmer* Feb. 55/1 Latest list of approved products..includes: Benlate (systemic fungicide from Du Pont for control of Botrytis in green beans and leaf spot in celery). **1893** *Funk's Stand. Dict.*, *Leaf-spring. **1896** R. GRIMSHAW *Shop Kinks* 123 In finishing leaf-springs by grinding care should be taken that the grinding-marks run lengthwise. **1905** R. T. SLOSS *Bk. Automobile* vi. 123 Leaf-springs seem to give the best results in automobile construction. **1935** *Times* 22 Oct. 9/2 In applying independent front wheel suspension some designers use coil springs and others leaf springs. **1967** *Autocar* 5 Oct. 73/3 He built the car without dampers, having read somewhere that inter-leaf friction in leaf springs might be sufficient damping. It wasn't. **1958** *Times* 26 Sept. 6/4 Air suspension is confined mostly to passenger-carrying vehicles, for the normal *leaf springing is considered satisfactory for goods vehicles. **1973** *Times* 4 Oct. 43/3 All the cars have a leaf sprung back axle. **1649** *Bury Wills* (Camden) 220 A *leafe table, a forme, a great kettle. **1884** BOWER & SCOTT *De Bary's Phaner.* 374 The *leaf-teeth of Drosera... The leaf of species of Drosera..has at its edge and on its entire upper surface numerous filiform teeth with broadened ends. **1877** BENNETT tr. *Thomé's Bot.* 109 Accordingly as they belong to the stem as in the vine, or to the leaf as in the tare, they are called stem- or *leaf-tendrils. **1611** COTGR., *Orpel*,..a kind of *leafe-tinne. **1600** ROWLANDS *Lett. Humours Blood* vi. 77 Out upon Cane and *leafe Tabacco smell. **1851** *Illustr. Catal. Gt. Exhib.* 204 Tobacco..the raw material, as imported with the stalk on it, known as 'leaf', or 'unstemmed', tobacco. **1875** BENNETT & DYER *Sachs' Bot.* 431 We have here 'common' bundles [of Phanerogams], each of which has one arm that ascends and bends out into the leaf, and another which descends and runs down into the stem; the latter is called by Hanstein the 'inner *leaf-trace'. **1877** BENNETT tr. *Thomé's Bot.* 360 Leaf-traces. **1672** MARVELL *Reh. Transp.* I. 212 Where then were all your *Leaf-turners? **1926** T. A. COWARD *Birds Brit. Isles* 122 (*heading*) The *Leaf-Warblers. **1929** W. E. GLEGG *Hist. Birds Essex* 71 The Willow-Warbler is a very common summer resident, increasing, and the most numerous of the Leaf-Warblers. **1953** B. CAMPBELL *Finding Nests* vii. 96 The off-nest call [of the wood-warbler]..is easier to pick up than similar notes of the other leaf-warblers. **1974** *Lady* 2 May 622/3 Linnaeus did not distinguish all three common leaf-warblers. **1611** COTGR., *Fueillure*,..*leafe-worke, or a leauie flourishing. **1841** LONGF. *Childr. Lord's Supper* 33 Bright-curling tresses of angels Peeped..from out of the shadowy leaf-work. **1880** J. L. WARREN *Guide to Study of Book-Plates* ii. 10 Outside the inscription is some rather fine leaf-work. **1937** *Burlington Mag.* Aug. 69/1 Decorated with the famous leafwork. *c* **1000** *Ags. Ps.* lxxvii. 51 (Spelman) He sealde *leaf-wyrme [*MS. C.* treowyrme, Vulg. *ærugini*] wæstm heora. *a* **1300** *E.E. Psalter* lxxvii. 46 And to lefe-worme þar fruit gafe he. **1496** *Fysshynge w. Angle* (1883) 25 The water docke leyf worme and the hornet worme.

leaf (liːf), *sb.*[2] *Services' slang.* Also **leef.** [Var. LEAVE *sb.* 1 e.] Leave of absence, furlough; = LEAVE *sb.* 1 e.

1846 *Punch* 3 Jan. 10/2 The shabby Capting (who seames to git leaf from his ridgmint whenhever he likes). **1904** KIPLING in *Windsor Mag.* Dec. 4/1 What a lot of 'ard work one misses on leaf! **1916** 'TAFFRAIL' *Pincher Martin* viii. 124 Wot's the good o' seven days' leaf ter a bloke wot ain't got no money? **1919** *Athenæum* 8 Aug. 729/1 The soldier going on short leave speaks usually of 'going on pass'; sometimes, however, of 'going on leaf'. Why in this phrase (nowhere else) the voiceless *f* is substituted for voiced *v* in 'leave' is a mystery to me. **1929** *Papers Mich. Acad. Sci., Arts & Lett.* X. 306 *Leef*, leave, pass, furlough. **1946** J. IRVING *Royal Navalese* 107 *Leaf*, a corruption of Leave—leave of absence. .. A sailor goes 'on leaf' and *never* on furlough.

leaf (liːf), *v.* See also LEAVE *v.*[2] [f. LEAF *sb.*[1]]

1. *intr.* To put forth leaves or foliage. Also *to leaf out* (U.S.).

1611 COTGR., *Fueiller*, to leafe; or leaue; to beare, or bring forth leaues. **1695** EVELYN *Diary* 21 Apr., The Spring begins to appeare, yet the trees hardly leaf'd. **1759** B. STILLINGFL. *Cal. Flora* Pref., Misc. Tracts (1762) 233, I marked the day of the month on which certain trees leafed. **1837** LOWELL *Lett.* (1894) I. i. 19 The gooseberry bushes are beginning to leaf out. **1855** SINGLETON *Virgil* I. 19 Now leaf the woods. **1861** DELAMER *Fl. Gard.* 24 By making the bulbs leaf in a reserved ground. **1872** O. W. HOLMES *Poet Breakf.-t.* xi. (1885) 286 There it stood..leafing out hopefully in April.

2. a. *trans.* To cover with foliage. *poet. rare.*

1849 *Tait's Mag.* XVI. 670 The wood that leafs the hill-side.

b. To shade (a plant) with leafage.

1846 *Jrnl. R. Agric. Soc.* VII. II. 592 The requisites [of the pea] are early ripening, short and delicate bine, which will not leaf or house the turnips too much.

3. a. To go *through* (a book or papers) by turning the leaves, usu. in a casual manner; also *fig.* Also (now *U.S.*), to turn or turn *over* (the leaves of a book). Also used *intr.*

1663 SIR G. MACKENZIE *Relig. Stoic* xvi. (1685) 147 Children who love to leaf over talidouce pictures. **1888** *Advance* (Chicago) 9 Aug., This man in front of me who is leafing the hymn-book. **1929** *Publishers' Weekly* 19 Oct. 1928/2 There are..plenty of people who..like to leaf through a book before buying. **1936** J. G. COZZENS *Men & Brethren* II. 175 Ernest..leafed over the remaining letters. **1936** L. C. DOUGLAS *White Banners* xi. 245 He found the book, opened it on the table and leafed to the pictures he had found most amusing. **1953** *Encounter* Nov. 34/1 So it is possible to leaf through the Essays, reading a few pages and turning away at pleasure, as Montaigne himself read. **1960** 'R. EAST' *Kingston Black* x. 98 She went on leafing through the transcript. **1960** 'S. HARVESTER' *Chinese Hammer* i. 16 [He] leafed through an old issue of the *New Yorker*. **1973** W. M. DUNCAN *Big Timer* xxi. 141 He..picked up a paper and leafed through it idly.

b. To number (a leaf of a book).

1875 F. J. FURNIVALL in *Thynne's Animadv.* p. xlii, Q q iii is leaft or folio'd Fo. CC. xix.

Hence **'leafing** *vbl. sb.*, (*a*) the putting forth of leaves; (*b*) leaf-painting, leafage (*rare*); **'leafing** *ppl. a.*, that puts forth leaves.

1610 GUILLIM *Heraldry* III. vii. (1611) 104 A liuely power of growing, budding, leafing, blossoming and fructifying. **1759** B. STILLINGFL. *Cal. Flora* Pref., Misc. Tracts (1762) 233 The leafing, flowering, &c. of..plants. **1815** L. SIMOND *Tour Gt. Brit.* (1817) II. 190 Glover is a very good *paysagiste*, but his leafing is too spotty. *a* **1851** MOIR *Child's Burial in Spring* ii. Poet. Wks. 1852 I. 117 The birds sang forth from many a leafing tree. **1868** DARWIN *Anim. & Pl.* I. x. 354 The periods of leafing and flowering differ. **1870** HOOKER *Stud. Flora* 412 *Carex aquatilis*..sheaths all leafing, not filamentous.

leafage ('liːfɪdʒ). Also 6 lefage, 8 levage. [f. LEAF *sb.*[1] + -AGE.]

1. Leaves collectively; foliage.

1599 T. M[OUFET] *Silkwormes* 54 If morn and eu'n fresh lefage they may haue. **1850** BLACKIE *Æschylus* II. 374 When the leafage first comes out in spring. **1876** FARRAR *Marlb. Serm.* iv. 30 The test of their reality is not the idle leafage of profession, but the rich certainty of fruit. **1881** S. R. HOLE *Nice* iii. 36 The silvery leafage of the olive. **1883** RUSKIN *Art Eng.* i. 10 The true representation of actual Sunshine, of growing Leafage.

b. The representation of leaves or foliage, *esp.* as an ornamentation.

1703 T. N. *City & C. Purchaser* 108 The Drapery or Levage that is wrought upon the Heads of Pillars. **1762–71**

H. WALPOLE *Vertue's Anecd. Paint.* (1786) IV. 120 The leafage of his trees..is hard. **1853** RUSKIN *Stones Ven.* III. i. §2. 2 Corinthian capitals, rich in leafage. **1863** *Gentl. Mag.* Nov. 537 We have also an extreme dislike to..his adopting the modern conceit of leafage in place of the long-established..technical term of foliation. **1893** *Archæologia* LIII. 554 Their freely-carved leafage is far superior to any foliage that could have been executed.

2. Lamination. *rare.*

1833 HOLLAND *Manuf. Metal* II. 349 The leafage of the wire is produced by passing it through a numerous succession of rayed perforations.

'leaf-cutter.

1. An insect that cuts or eats out portions of the leaves of trees; *spec.* in ***leaf-cutter ant, bee.***

1815 KIRBY & SP. *Entomol.* I. 191 The leaf-cutter bee also (*Apis centuncularis*) by cutting pieces out..disfigures it [the rose] considerably. **1881** *Cassell's Nat. Hist.* V. 368 The..Bees of the genus Megachile are commonly known as Leaf-cutters. **1899** *Daily News* 26 July 8/2 Another community, Leaf-Cutter Ants, of North America.

b. A bird of similar habits.

1884 G. ALLEN in *Longm. Mag.* Jan. 291 The South American leaf-cutter has..bony bosses on its beak and palate.

2. A paper-knife. '*U.S. rare*' (*Cent. Dict.*).

So **leaf-cutting** *ppl. a.*, in ***leaf-cutting ant, bee*** = prec. (sense 1).

1802 BINGLEY *Anim. Biog.* (1813) III. 272 The Leaf-cutting Bee. **1874** LUBBOCK *Wild Flowers* i. 6 A species of acacia..is apt to be stripped of its leaves by a leaf-cutting ant.

leafdom ('li:fdəm). *nonce-wd.* [f. LEAF *sb.*¹ + -DOM.] The realm of leaves.

1856 AIRD *Poet. Wks.* 127 What life the little Creeper of the Tree To leafdom sends. **1888** MRS. M. HUNGERFORD *Under-Currents* I. i. 1 Clothed with a tender foliage, a very baby leafdom, just bursting into the fuller life.

leaf-eared: see LAVE *a.* b.

leafed (li:ft), *a.* (See also LEAVED *a.*) [f. LEAF + -ED².] Having a leaf or leaves. Chiefly in parasynthetic formations, as ***broad-, thick-, two-leafed.***

1. Having leaves or foliage; bearing (a specified kind of) foliage. *rare* except with adj. prefixed.

1552 HULOET, Braunched or leafed, *frondatus.* **1572** BOSSEWELL *Armorie* III. 236 The fielde is of the Moone, a Therebinthe tree, Saturne, floured and leafed Veneris. **1601** HOLLAND *Pliny* II. 257 Some say it is leafed after the maner of Squilla or sea-onion. **1660** BLOUNT *Boscobel* 32 The colonel made choice of a thick leafed oak. **1698** FRYER *Acc. E. India & P.* 177 Bamboos..sending from every Joint sprouts of the same form, leafed like long Five-fingered Grass. **1860** *Merc. Marine Mag.* VII. 199 A thick leafed..plant.

transf. **1659** PECKE *Parnassi Puerp.* 16 Trees regain Hair: and Fields the verdant Grass: But when will your Head Leaf'd be, as it was?

†**2.** Of a door, book, etc.: Having (a specified number of) leaves. *Obs.*

1598 YONG *Diana* 87 All the windowes were double leafed a peece. **1611** COTGR., *Valve*, a foulding, or two-leafed doore, or window. **1611** CORYAT *Crudities* 211 A two leafed brasen gate. **1626** tr. *Parallel.* A ij, A two leafed Tablet.

3. (Broad-) brimmed. Cf. LEAF *sb.*¹ 14.

1841 H. AINSWORTH *Guy Fawkes* i, With a broad-leafed steeple-crowned hat..pulled over his brows. **1861** W. F. COLLIER *Hist. Eng. Lit.* 176 A broad-leafed low-crowned hat of Flemish beaver.

'leafen, *a. rare*⁻¹. [f. LEAF *sb.*¹ + -EN⁴. (? Or misprint for *beaten.*)] In ***leafen gold*** = LEAF-GOLD.

1746 HERVEY *Refl. Flower-gard.* 57 This reddens into blood in the Veins of the Mulberry, and attenuates itself into leafen Gold to create a Covering for the Quince.

leafery ('li:fərɪ). [f. LEAF *sb.*¹ + -ERY.] Leafage.

1834 J. WILSON *Let.* in Hamilton *Mem.* V. (1859) 164 The matured and almost arid leafery of Summer. **1883** *Blackw. Mag.* July 116 The rising amphitheatre of wood behind is singularly rich in leafery.

leafe-sugger, dial. form of LOAF-SUGAR.

†**'leafful,** *a. Obs.* Forms: 1 (ȝe)léafful, 2 lefull, 3 læfful(l, lefful, leafful. [OE. (*ȝe*)*léaffull*, f. (*ȝe*)*léafa* belief, faith + -FUL.] Faithful, believing.

c **950** *Lindisf. Gosp.* Matt. xxv. 21 Forðon ofer lytla ðu were leaffull ofer moniȝo ðec ic setto. *c* **975** *Rushw. Gosp.* John xx. 27 Nelle ðu wosa unȝilefend ah leaf-full. *c* **1175** *Lamb. Hom.* 77 He nis nawiht alle monne lauerd..but lefulle monne lauerd. *c* **1200** ORMIN 19242 Wiþþ erþlic eȝhe, & ec Wiþþ læffull herrtess sihhþe. *c* **1205** LAY. 3033 Cordoille..nom hire leaf-fulne huie þat heo liȝen nolden [? *read* nolde]. *c* **1220** *Bestiary* 713 List ilk lefful man her-to. *a* **1225** *Leg. Kath.* 1038 Godd (þe leadeð euch leafful to treowe bileaue). *a* **1250** *Gen. & Ex.* 3447 If ye listen lefful to me, Ic wile min folc owen be.

leaf-gold.

1. = GOLD-LEAF.

1598 *Epulario* Cj, When the Peacocke is rosted, you may gild it with leafe gold. **1604** MIDDLETON *F. Hubburd's T.* Wks. (Bullen) VIII. 107 A quaint volume fairly bound up in principal vellum, double-filleted with leaf-gold. **1727** W. MATHER *Yng. Man's Comp.* 82 Lay a little Leaf-Gold upon a fine Earthen Plate. **1824** MISS MITFORD *Village* Ser. I. (1863) 31 Becoming thin by expansion, like leaf-gold.

fig. **1672** DRYDEN *Marr. à la Mode* IV. iv, The dull French poetry which is so thin, that it is the very leaf-gold of wit.

2. Native gold in the form of laminæ. *rare.*

1877 RAYMOND *Statist. Mines & Mining* 315 Rich nests of carbonate of lead, filled with leaf-gold, were..found.

leafiness (li:fɪnɪs). [f. LEAFY *a.* + -NESS.] The state or condition of being leafy.

1627 *Lisander & Cal.* I. 5 Solitarinesse perpetually resides there in the shadow of an impenitrable leafinesse. **1652** COTTERELL *Cassandra* I. (1676) 1/1 Trees whose thick leafiness cast a very pleasing shade. **1844** MRS. BROWNING *Vision Poets* Concl. iv, While up the leafiness profound A wind..Stood ready to blow on me when I turned that way. **1863** BATES *Nat. Amazon* xiii. (1864) 438 The margins of these streams were paradises of leafiness and verdure.

†**'leafit.** *Obs.* [f. LEAF *sb.*¹ + *-it*, ? = ET.] = LEAFLET *sb.* 1.

1787 WITHERING *Brit. Plants* Dict. Terms (1796) I. 66 *Leafit*, or little leaf (foliolum) one of the single leaves of a compound leaf. **1793** T. MARTYN *Lang. Bot.*, *Leaflets*, Foliola. Others call them *Leafits.* But I follow the analogy of the language in forming diminutives. **1816** KEITH *Phys. Bot.* II. 453 The leafits of some of the leguminous plants..are often erected into a vertical position on each side the leaf-stalk. **1819** H. BUSK *Banquet* II. 458* Smooth from the spatula, heart-shaped, or awl, The winged leafits stretch along the wall. **1820** KEATS *Isabella* liv, So that the jewel, safely casketed, Came forth, and in perfumed leafits spread. **1830** J. RENNIE *Insect Archit.* viii. 164 The leafits of the rose..expand in nearly the same manner as a fan. **1916** BLUNDEN *Harbingers* 60 The lopped tree, be it but stub or stock, Thrives, and begems its leafits in a year.

leafless ('li:flɪs), *a.* Also 6–7 LEAVELESS, q.v. [f. LEAF *sb.*¹ + -LESS.] Without a leaf; destitute of leaves or foliage. Also *fig.*

1590 T. WATSON *Eclog. Death Walsingham* 217 in Poems (Arb.) 163 Now in the woods be leafelesse eury Tree. **1697** DRYDEN *Æneid* XI. 13 Above his Arms, fix'd on the leafless Wood, Appear'd his Plumy Crest. **1776–96** WITHERING *Brit. Plants* (ed. 3) III. 390 Shoots very long, rather leafless below. **1824** W. IRVING *T. Trav.* I. 18 A cold leafless park. **1830** LINDLEY *Nat. Syst. Bot.* 330 Aphyllæ, or Leafless flowerless plants. **1839** —— *Introd. Bot.* (ed. 3) 127 The petiole may exist without the lamina, as in *leafless* Acacias. **1866** M. ARNOLD *Thyrsis* ii, Leafless, yet soft as spring, The tender purple spray on copse and briers!

b. ***leafless tree***, the gallows. *slang.*

1830 LYTTON *Paul Clifford* I. xi. 261 Oh! there never was life like the Robber's..And its end?—why a cheer from the crowd below, And a leap from a leafless tree!

Hence **'leaflessness.**

1818 MILMAN *Samor* VIII. 580 Thy o'ershadowing woods One bare, brown leaflessness. **1875** MISS BIRD *Sandwich Isl.* (1880) 89 Mist, cold, murk, slush, gales, leaflessness, and all the dismal concomitants of an English winter.

leaflet ('li:flɪt), *sb.* [f. LEAF *sb.*¹ + -LET.] A small leaf.

1. †**a.** *Bot.* A sepal. *Obs.* **b.** *Bot.* One of the divisions of a compound leaf. **c.** *popularly.* A young leaf; *rarely*, a petal.

1787 *Fam. Plants* I. 153 Perianth five-leaved: the leaflets lanced, equal, permanent. **1811** A. T. THOMSON *Lond. Disp.* (1818) 404 The leaves are..pinnate, with a terminal leaflet a little larger than the rest. **1839** URE *Dict. Arts* 344 It has a cup-shaped calyx..The leaflets are united at their base, of a heart shape and toothed; stigmas three to five. **1854** MARION HARLAND *Alone* xxviii, The willow leaflets were just putting out. **1855** LYNCH *Rivulet* XLIV. iv, When Their [blossoms'] colour fades, their leaflets dry. **1872** OLIVER *Elem. Bot.* I. vii. 76 Compound leaves..having the blade divided into leaflets. **1896** *Allbutt's Syst. Med.* I. 340 A decoction of aromatic plants, such as lavender or fresh pine leaflets.

2. *Phys.* and *Zool.* An organ or part of an organ resembling a small leaf; *spec.* the thin flap of a valve in the heart or a blood vessel.

1826 KIRBY & SP. *Entomol.* III. 392 Foliola (the Leaflets). Rigid..leaf-like anal organs. **1835–6** TODD *Cycl. Anat.* I. 695/1 Respiration is effected by means of four branchial leaflets..arranged on either side of the body. **1936** G. R. HERRMANN *Synopsis Dis. Heart & Arteries* xvii. 254 The degrees to which valvular lesions develop depend upon the extent of the allergic or inflammatory processes and the trauma to which these inflamed leaflets are subjected at the time and during the healing processes. **1961** R. D. BAKER *Essent. Path.* xiv. 333 Uncomplicated insufficiency occurs when the valve leaflets are held against the wall of the heart or of the great vessels or when the ring of the valve is dilated.

3. a. A small-sized leaf of paper or a sheet folded into two or more leaves but not stitched, and containing printed matter, chiefly for gratuitous distribution.

1867 MISS BROUGHTON *Cometh up as Flower* xv. (1878) 153 Leaflets (as Spurgeon and Co. have christened very young tracts). **1886** *Q. Rev.* Jan., 12 A generous gift of Liberation leaflets for home use and distribution among the neighbours. **1888** JACOBI *Printers' Voc.*, *Leaflets*, jobs printed on single leaves, either one or both sides.

b. *attrib.* and *Comb.*, as ***leaflet literature, party, writer;*** **leaflet raid**, a raid in which leaflets are dropped from an aircraft; also *transf.*; so ***leaflet drop.***

1903 *Westm. Gaz.* 13 Aug. 2/3 Mr. C. A. Vince, M.A., chief leaflet-writer to Mr. Chamberlain. **1904** *Ibid.* 21 Jan. 2/1 Not even the profuse distribution of Birmingham leaflet literature can alter this fact. **1940** *Flight* 11 Apr. 337/1 This same officer commanded the Whitley which made the first leaflet raid over Berlin. **1940** HARRISSON & MADGE *War begins at Home* vii. 148 The first leaflet raid—in which the R.A.F. dropped 6,000,000 leaflets over Germany. **1943** KOESTLER *Arrival & Departure* III. 94 That is why I took part in those leaflet-parties, though it was not my job. **1961** *Guardian* 11 Nov. 1 (*caption*) Leaflet raid on Lisbon. **1969** *Listener* 31 July 145/2 We would send our lecturers out into the fringes of the jungle to soften people up, we would have special leaflet drops before the troops went in. **1974** *Times* 13 Nov. 2/6 Miners from the Nottinghamshire coalfield..made leaflet raids to pits in South Yorkshire.

leaflet ('li:flɪt), *v.* [f. LEAFLET 3.] *trans.* and *intr.* To distribute leaflets to (people or places). Hence **'leafleting** *vbl. sb.*

1962 *Spectator* 24 Aug. 268/3 Thousands of campaigners will be putting this case..by leafletting and pamphleteering. **1968** *Peace News* 25 Oct. 5/3 Civilians who originally had tried to leaflet on bases were quickly kicked off. **1969** C. DAVIDSON in Cockburn & Blackburn *Student Power* 361 We should make our presence felt everywhere—in the campus news media, leafletting and poster displays. **1969** *Oxf. Univ. Gaz.* XCIX. Suppl. VII. 156 The Proctors announced the withdrawal of the regulation prohibiting indiscriminate leafleting. **1972** *Listener* 27 Jan. 119/2 Tariq Ali..refers to the question whether factories should be leafleted. **1973** *Daily Tel.* 9 June 2/8 Our friends in Germany and elsewhere will be encouraged to leaflet British soldiers stationed there. **1973** C. MULLARD *Black Brit.* I. iii. 33 The new group were people willing to leaflet, organize and demonstrate.

leafleteer (li:flɪ'tɪə(r)). [f. LEAFLET 3 + -EER.] A writer of leaflets; the author of a leaflet. (Often contemptuous.)

1892 *Sat. Rev.* 16 July 70/2 It..is written in clear, plain, simple English, the only 'leaf' we could wish our leafleteers to take from this example. **1903** *Westm. Gaz.* 6 Oct. 2/2 We do not in the least mind Professors becoming leafleteers if so they must. **1970** *Sunday Tel.* 14 June 8/2 The leafleteers have fairly polluted the streets this time.

leafull, variant of LEEFUL *a. Obs.*, permissible.

leafy (li:fɪ), *a.* (See also LEAVY.) [f. LEAF *sb.*¹ + -Y¹.]

1. Having, or abounding in, leaves; clothed with leaves or foliage; made or consisting of leaves.

1552 HULOET, Leaffy, or ful of leaues. **1697** DRYDEN *Virg. Georg.* I. 491 Soft Whispers run along the leafy Woods. —— *Virg. Past.* VII. 7 Ye Trees, whose leafy Shades those mossy Fountains keep. **1725** POPE *Odyss.* XI. 235 Autumn..The leafy honours scattering on the ground. **1798** COLERIDGE *Anc. Mar.* v. xviii, In the leafy month of June. **1817** MOORE *Lalla R.* Pref. (1850) 8 Stranger, spread Thy leafiest bed. **1864** TENNYSON *En. Arden* 97 The leafy lanes behind the down. **1893** N. GALE *Country Muse* Ser. II. 101 In leafy Warwickshire.

b. *spec.* in *Bot.* Foliate.

1776 J. LEE *Introd. Bot.* Explan. Terms 379 *Foliatus*, leafy, furnished with Leaves. **1870** HOOKER *Stud. Flora* 115 Flowering stems 3–5 in., lateral, ascending, leafy.

c. That produces broad-bladed leaves, as distinguished from other kinds of foliage.

1879 D. M. WALLACE *Australas.* xi. 222 We have many Indian genera of leafy trees, very different from the usual Australian type.

2. Of the nature of a leaf; resembling a leaf.

a. Said of the parts of a plant.

1671 GREW *Anat. Plants* I. iv. §17 (1682) 32 Every bud, besides its proper Leaves, is covered with divers Leafy Pannicles or Surfoyls. **1727** BRADLEY *Fam. Dict.* s.v *Elm*, It bears a single leav'd Flower..which turns to a membranous or leafy Fruit in the Form of a Heart. **1847** W. E. STEELE *Field Bot.* 30 Cal. of 5 leafy teeth. **1851** CARPENTER *Man. Phys.* (ed. 2) 466 They may form..fronds (expanded leafy surfaces).

b. Of other substances: Laminate.

1754 LEWIS in *Phil. Trans.* XLVIII. 668 A leafy or fibrous texture, a purplish colour..are peculiar to the mixtures with lead. **1791** PEARSON *ibid.* LXXXI. 324 A..leafy, or mica-like sediment. **1881** *Borings* II. 26 (E.D.D.) Leafy clay with scares of sand.

3. *Comb.*, as ***leafy-branched*** adj.

1837 MACGILLIVRAY *Withering's Brit. Plants* (ed. 4) 340 Leafy-branched Spurge.

leager, leagier, obs. forms of LEDGER.

league (li:g), *sb.*¹ Forms: 4–5 leghe, 4–6 lege, leuge, (4 lewge, 5 lewke, leuke, leeke), 5–6 leege, 6 legge, le(a)que, *Sc.* lig, 6–7 leag(e, 6– league. [Late ME. *leuge, lege, leghe*, etc., ad. late L. *leuga, leuca* (= late Gr. λεύγη, λεύκη), according to Hesychius and Jordanes a Gaulish word; hence OF. *liue, liwe* (mod.F. *lieue*), Pr. *lega, legua*, Cat. *llegua*, Sp. *legua*, Pg. *legoa*, It. *lega.*]

a. An itinerary measure of distance, varying in different countries, but usually estimated roughly at about 3 miles; app. never in regular use in England, but often occurring in poetical or rhetorical statements of distance. ***marine league***: a unit of distance = 3 nautical miles or 3041 fathoms.

Although the league appears never to have been an English measure, *leuca* occurs somewhat frequently in Anglo-Latin law-books (Bracton, Fleta, etc.); it is disputed whether in these works it means one mile or two.

1387 TREVISA *Higden* (Rolls) V. 245 þanne þey come to giders in þe feeldes Cathalmytes, þat conteyneþ an hondred leges [*v.rr.* leuges, leghes, **1432–50** lewkes] in lengþe and seventy in brede. **1398** —— *Barth. De P.R.* XV. xxii. (1495) 497 The walles of Babylone were acountyd for two lewges and an halfe. *c* **1400** MAUNDEV. (Roxb.) viii. 28 þis ile es cccl. leeges aboute. **1474** CAXTON *Chesse* IV. i. (1481) i vij, After the maner of lombardye they be callyd myles, and in fraunce leukes, and in englond they be callyd myles also. **1483** —— *Gold. Leg.* 223/2 Mount Joye..is but half a leeke fro seynt James. **1494** FABYAN *Chron.* v. lxxxv. 63 An Hundreth Legis..wherof euery Lege conteyneth .iii. Englysshe myles. **1502** ARNOLDE *Chron.* 66, xvi. furlong make a frensh leuge

[*printed* lenge]. **1528** LYNDESAY *Dreme* 642–4 The quantytie of the erth Circuleir Is fyftie thousand liggis.. Deuidyng, aye, ane lig in mylis two. *a* **1533** LD. BERNERS *Huon* lxxxvii. 275 A stronge castell with in a .iii. legges of Burdeux. **1555** EDEN *Decades* 1 Such as are expert sea men affyrme that euery league conteyneth foure myles. **1559** W. CUNNINGHAM *Cosmogr. Glasse* 57 The Gretians [measure] by furlonges: the Spaniardes, and French men by leques. **1594** BLUNDEVIL *Exerc.* III. II. vi. (1636) 382 The French league containeth two of our miles, the Spanish league three, and the common league of Germany foure, and the great league of Germany containeth five of our miles. **1610** SHAKS. *Temp.* I. ii. 145 They hurried vs a-boord a Barke Bore vs some Leagues to Sea. **1774** GOLDSM. *Nat. Hist.* (1776) I. 42 At Touraine, in France.. there is a plain of about nine leagues long, and as many broad. **1818** BYRON *Ch. Har.* IV. liii. *note*, I never yet saw the picture.. which came a league within my conception. **1828** J. M. SPEARMAN *Brit. Gunner* (ed. 2) 268 A league at sea.. contains 3000 geometrical paces, or 3 English miles. **1843** BORROW *Bible in Spain* 136 Before us, at the distance of about a league and a half, rose the mighty frontier chain. **1845** FORD *Handbk. Spain* I. 15 The Spanish league is somewhat less than three miles and a half English. **1855** TENNYSON *Charge Light Brigade* i, Half a league, half a league, Half a league onward. **1878** BROWNING *La Saisiaz* 25 Can I.. sharpen ear to recognize Sound o'er league and league of silence?

b. *Comb.*: ***league-wide*** adj. (*poet.*); **league-long** *a.*, that extends the length of a league.

1843 J. R. LOWELL *Prometheus* in *Poems* (1844) 83 The vast Sarmatian plain, league-wide. **1848** —— *Columbus* in *Poems* 2nd Ser. 11 Some league-wide river. **1883** TENNYSON *Charge Heavy Brigade* Prol. 27 The league-long rampart-fire. **1883** SWINBURNE *Les Casquettes* xxiv, Forth she fared.. For a league-long raid on the bounding brine. **1951** W. DE LA MARE *Winged Chariot* 56 Life's league-wide cornfields. **1957** R. CAMPBELL *Coll. Poems* II. 254 Across a league-wide valley, white with sprays.

league (liːg), *sb.*[2] Forms: 5 ligg, (? 5–) 6 leage, *Sc.* lig, 6 lege, liage, leag(ge, *Sc.* leig, lyge, lyig, 6–7 ligue, leaug(e, 6– league. [The form *ligue*, *lig*, is a. F. *ligue*, ad. It. *liga*, var. of *lega*, vbl. sb. f. *legare* to bind:—L. *ligāre*. The form *le(a)ge* is perh. ad. It. *lega*.]

1. a. A military, political, or commercial covenant or compact made between parties for their mutual protection and assistance against a common enemy, the prosecution or safeguarding of joint interests, and the like; a body of states or persons associated in such a covenant, a confederacy.

1452 in Tytler *Hist. Scot.* (1864) II. 387, I.. binds and obliss me, that I shall make na bond, na ligg.. quhilk sall be contrar till his heines. **1509** FISHER *Funeral Serm. Hen. VII*, Wks. (1876) 269 Leages and confyderyes he hadde with all crysten prynces. **1513** DOUGLAS *Æneis* III. vii. 63 And this same lyge with our posteritie Sall euir remane in faith and vnite. **1553** EDEN *Treat. Newe Ind.* (Arb.) 13 The cytiezins of Aden had.. made a leage with the Portugales. **1596** DALRYMPLE tr. *Leslie's Hist. Scot.* II. 132 This League or band being maid betweine the king and the hail natione. *Ibid.* v. 262 To make a Leagge or band wᵗ the Scotis or Peichtis against the Jnglismen. **1613** SHAKS. *Hen. VIII*, I. i. 95 France hath flaw'd the League, and hath attach'd Our Merchants goods at Burdeux. **1651** HOBBES *Leviath.* II. xxii. 121 Leagues are commonly made for mutuall defence. **1678** C. HATTON in *H. Corr.* (1878) 160 Yᵉ league offensive and defensive wᵗʰ yᵉ States Genˡˡ. **1783** WATSON *Philip III* (1839) 17 Count Hohenloe was in Germany, employed in exciting the princes of the league of Munster to take the field against the Spaniards. **1858** FROUDE *Hist. Eng.* III. xvii. 451 The danger of a Protestant league compelled the Catholic powers to bury their rivalries.

b. *spec.* in *Hist.* ***the League***, (*a*) a league formed in 1576 under the direction of the Guises, to prevent the accession of Henry IV to the French throne; (*b*) = LEAGUE OF NATIONS. ***Holy League***, a name given to several leagues in European history, as that formed by Pope Julius II against the French in 1511 and the Nuremberg League of 1538. ***Hanseatic, Latin League***: see these adjs. ***Solemn League and Covenant***: see COVENANT *sb.* 9 a.

By writers on ancient history the word is used in the designation of certain confederations of states, as the ***Ætolian league***, the ***Amphictyonic league***, etc.

1589 I. L. (*title*) The Birth, Purpose, and mortal Wound of the Romish holie League. **1684** DRYDEN (*title*) The history of the League. Written in French by M. Maimbourg. Translated into English. **1706** PHILLIPS (ed. Kersey), *Leaguer*, one concern'd in the League or Confederacy in France, in the time of King Henry III and IV. **1727–41** CHAMBERS *Cycl.* s.v., The League, by way of eminence, denotes that famous one on foot in France, from the year 1576 to 1593. **1769** ROBERTSON *Chas. V*, IV. Wks. 1813 V. 401 The king of England was declared protector of this league, which they dignified by the name of holy, because the pope was at the head of it. **1838** THIRLWALL *Greece* I. 375 The Amphictyonic league or council. *Ibid.* III. 39 The Delphians.. were.. induced.. to renounce their union with the Phocian league. **1861** DYER *Mod. Europe* II. 194 An alliance against the Sultan, called the Holy League, was.. concluded between himself [Pius V], Philip II., and the Venetians. *Ibid.* 450 The Catholic States of the Circles of Suabia and Bavaria agreed to enter into an alliance which afterwards obtained the name of the Holy League. **1917** H. N. BRAILSFORD *League of Nations* 324 Without the firm resolve to make the League itself an article, and the first article, in the settlement, our need of security will drive us inevitably to other expedients. The settlement, unless the idea of the League penetrates it and inspires it, must draw its principle from the older statecraft of anarchy and force. **1919** J. M. O'SULLIVAN in *Studies* Dec. 577 Had not the basal idea of the League been thus early formulated. **1936** A. HUXLEY *Let.* 2 Mar. (1969) 401 The.. atmosphere wd be cleared and a chance given for the reconstruction of the League on a more satisfactory basis. **1944** J. S. HUXLEY *On Living in Revolution* iii. 32 The failure of the League merely served to underline the urgent need for *some* international political organization. **1950** THEIMER & CAMPBELL *Encycl. World Politics* 260/1 The Assembly did not meet again until April 1946, when it decided to dissolve the League, already replaced by the United Nations. **1952** *Oxf. Jun. Encycl.* X. 212/2 When the United States Congress repudiated President Wilson's proposals and failed to join the League, its hope of real success was small. **1971** W. H. MCNEILL in A. Bullock *20th Cent.* 47/1 Should a government defy the League.. all the League members would be obliged to.. check aggression by imposing sanctions.

c. In recent times often adopted in the names of certain associations of individuals or of societies for some common object. ***Anti-Corn-Law League***: a political association formed in 1838 to procure the abolition of the existing Corn Laws. ***Football League***: see quot. 1899[2]. ***Land, Primrose, Reform League***: see these sbs. Similarly, ***Baseball, Cricket League***. Also ellipt. ***League***.

1846 WELLINGTON in *Croker Papers* (1884) III. xxiv. 51 There were no persons in that assembly capable of sustaining in debate the existing Corn Law against Cobden and the League. **1879** *Chicago Tribune* 17 May 7/5 A misunderstanding has arisen as to the condition of the Cleveland Club, and its inability to play, which will end in an appeal to the League. **1883** *Catholic Dict.* (1896) 554 The Catholic Total Abstinence League of the Cross was founded in 1873. **1883** *Whitaker's Almanack* 227/2 National Sunday League,.. National Temperance League. **1889** *Ibid.* 564/1 A Football League has been formed, including twelve of the leading North and Midland clubs... These clubs play a sort of American tournament for the League Championship. **1891** *Amer. Cricket Annual* 10 The organisation of the Metropolitan District Cricket League was certainly a move in the right direction. **1892** *Athletic News Cricket Ann.* 51 Lancashire Cricket League... This organisation.. has done for cricket what the League has done for football. **1892** J. A. LEIGHTON (*title*) Leighton's North-Western Rugby Football League card. Season 1892–93. **1894** *Athletic News* 5 Nov. 1/2 The position of Notts in the League is occasioning very considerable anxiety. **1899** LD. ALDENHAM *Colloq. Currency* (1900) Pref. 9 They even proposed to hear me, as president of the Bimetallic League. **1899** G. O. SMITH in *Football* (Badm. Libr.) 170 It was at this stage Mr. MacGregor.. brought forward his idea of a football union between the leading clubs of the day... The following twelve clubs were invited to form a union between themselves... Thus was the League formed. *Ibid.* 171 The League was formed chiefly for the purpose of insuring a series of first-class games [etc.]. **1910** *Encycl. Brit.* IX. 622/1 In 1888 the Football League, a combination of professional clubs of the north and midlands of England, was formed. **1921** A. HUXLEY *Crome Yellow* ii. 13 All the players in all the teams of the League. **1930** J. WILLIAMSON *Amer. Hotel* 293 The Broadway Central has been the scene of several noteworthy episodes. It was there that the National League was organized in 1876. **1935** *Encycl. Sports* 187/2 A number of [cricket] clubs form themselves into a league; each plays all the others in turn, and the championship of the league falls to the one which wins the most matches. *Ibid.* 292/2 The first league, the Football League, was then formed [in 1888]. **1951** *Football Record* (Melbourne) 8 Sept. 12 Approximately 300 visiting schoolboys were recently entertained by the League at the Melbourne ground. **1957** *Encycl. Brit.* III. 159/2 The professional [baseball] clubs usually compete as members of leagues. **1960** B. LIDDELL *My Soccer Story* vii. 48 For years the Football Association and the Football League have been trying to help players to prepare for the new life ahead when they finish with football. **1969** *Listener* 20 Mar. 384/2, I cannot believe he would still maintain that Rugby League backs 'usually run across instead of straight'. **1973** *News of the World Football Ann. 1973–74* 78 (*heading*) Football League—Division One. *Ibid.* 100 Re-elected to Division [One] when League was extended after the war. **1974** *Daily Record* (Glasgow) 15 Apr. 27/2 Yesterday Stein admitted, 'The League is almost won. We know that!' **1974** *Guardian* 1 Aug. 22/8 It is not possible to be wrapped up in all the competitions and win them as the League exists at present.

†**d.** A document in which the terms of a league are set down. *Obs.*

1642 C. VERNON *Consid. Exch.* 43 The Treasury, where the ancient Leagues of the Realme.. and divers other ancient Records doe lye. **1652** NEEDHAM tr. *Selden's Mare Cl.* 89 The Transcripts of Leagues and Treaties.

e. *transf.* and *fig.* Cf. *big league* s.v. BIG *a.* B. 2.

1935 J. T. FARRELL *Judgment Day* viii. 185 You better go back and play in a grammar-school league. **1959** N. MAILER *Advts. for Myself* (1961) 389 You want to keep a girl who was born to travel in a big league. **1961** *Listener* 12 Oct. 547/1 At the Riga brewery.. I saw a notice board with the photographs of the twelve workers who were topping the production league. **1965** *Listener* 23 Sept. 446/1 The English-speaking peoples are excellent at breakfasts, but after that they would scarcely claim to stand high in the gastronomic league. **1966** J. CHAMIER *Cannonball* xii. 115 She's out of your league, me lad, and you'll take a most almighty toss. **1970** *Washington Post* 30 Sept. B. 4/3 In such a league Paul Mellon has impeccable collections. **1971** *Austral. Seacraft* June 17/2 To join the big league [in speedboating]. **1971** *Where* Oct. 293/2 Neill has a lightness of touch, and a flair for comedy that were in the Wodehouse league. **1972** *New Society* 27 Jan. 187/1 Rory Gallagher, a minor league superstar blues guitarist. **1972** 'M. YORKE' *Silent Witness* v. 121 She was bored because he obviously wasn't in her league. **1973** *Times* 22 Feb. 5/3 The latest incident is not in the same league as the apparently endless series of espionage scandals in and around Bonn in 1968 and 1969.

2. *gen.* A covenant, compact, alliance. Now *rare.*

1509 HAWES *Conv. Swearers* 42 How that ye breke the lege of sothfastnesse. **1534** MORE *On the Passion* Wks. 1325/2 Thys is the bloud of the league, that oure Lorde hathe made with you vppon al these wordes. **1577–87** HOLINSHED *Chron.* III. 1220/1 Contrarie to the leagues and quietnesse of both the realmes of England and Scotland. **1594** SHAKS. *Rich. III*, I. iii. 281 Ile kisse thy hand, In signe of League and amity with thee. *c* **1600** —— *Sonn.* xlvii, Betwixt mine eye and heart a league is tooke. **1604** E. G[RIMSTONE] *D'Acosta's Hist. Indies* IV. x. 236 Though there be a league and simpathie betwixt golde and quicke-silver. **1611** BIBLE *1 Sam.* xxii. 8 My sonne hath made a league with the sonne of Iesse. **1621** BURTON *Anat. Mel.* I. i. II. viii. (1651) 25 The Appetite.. which by an admirable league of Nature, and by mediation of the spirit commands the organ by which it moves. **1644** MILTON *Jdgm. Bucer* Wks. 1738 I. 284 Those duties.. wherby the league of wedloc is chiefly preserved. *c* **1645** HOWELL *Lett.* I. vii. (1650) 10 Our first ligue of love, you know, was contracted among the Muses in Oxford. **1667** MILTON *P.L.* IV. 339 Linkt in happie nuptial League. **1831** BREWSTER *Newton* (1855) II. xxiv. 359 By thus uniting philosophy with religion, he dissolved the league which genius had formed with scepticism. **1833** LAMB *Elia* Ser. II. *Product. Mod. Art*, What associating league to the imagination can there be between the seers, or the seers not, of a presential miracle?

3. Phr. †**a.** ***to enter league***: to make a covenant or alliance; to INTERLEAGUE. *Obs.*

1579 LYLY *Euphues* (Arb.) 49, I studyed.. to enter league with such a one as might direct my steps. **1590** GREENE *Orl. Fur.* (1599) C 2, I maruaile Medor, what my father meanes, To enter league with Countie Sacrepant? **1618** BOLTON *Florus* (1636) 149 They did choose to enter league, when they could have made an end of him.

b. ***in league with***: having a compact with, allied with.

1565 COOPER *Thesaurus*, *Fœderati*,.. confederate: in league, or alliance with. **1611** BIBLE *Job* v. 23 For thou shalt be in league with the stones of the field. **1611** [see LEAGUE *v.*[1] 1]. **1808** SCOTT *Marm.* II. vii, Jealousy.. With sordid avarice in league. **1859** DICKENS *T. Two Cities* I. ii, For anybody on the road might be a robber or in league with robbers. **1865** KINGSLEY *Herew.* xxi, Look you, villains, this fellow is in league with you.

4. *Basket-making.* (See quots.)

1903 T. OKEY in R. M. Jacot *Useful Cane Work* I. p. ix, When a single continuous cane is used as a combined bottom stick and stake it is termed a 'League'. **1910** *Encycl. Brit.* III. 482/2 When the 'bottom-stick' and 'stake' are formed of one and the same continuous rod, it is termed a 'league'.

5. *attrib.* and *Comb.*, as ***league breaker***, ***-fellow***, †***-friend***, ***-union***; (sense 1 c) ***league championship***, ***club***, ***cricket***, ***football*** (hence ***league footballer***), ***league-game***, ***match***, ***player***, ***star***, ***system***, ***-team***; **league-hut** (see quot.); **league table**, a list of the members of a league in ranking order; also *transf.*, a systematic comparison of performance in any field of competitive activity.

1561 NORTON *Calvin's Inst.* IV. 104 Beeyng receyued by the hande of a *leaguebreaker preste. **1671** MILTON *Samson* 1184 When they took thee As a League-breaker. **1901** *Dundee Advertiser* 4 Jan. 6 That [*sc.* Guiseley] Club winning the *League championship. **1969** *Official Baseball Rules* 16 The League is a group of clubs whose teams play each other in a pre-arranged schedule under these rules for the league championship. **1972** G. GREEN *Great Moments in Sport: Soccer* iv. 58 The previous season Chelsea had won the League Championship of the First Division. **1938** C. E. SUTCLIFFE et al. *Story of Football League* 14 A meeting of the *League clubs was held on 8th February, 1909. **1973** *News of the World Football Ann. 1973–74* 163 (*heading*) Oldest League Clubs. **1961** F. C. AVIS *Sportsman's Gloss.* 125/2 **League Cricket*, that organized, outside the county championship, etc., in competitive league groups, e.g. the Central Lancashire League. **1561** DAUS tr. *Bullinger on Apoc.* (1573) 175 The Gothians, and other *league fellowes of the People of Rome. **1910** T. CHARNLEY *Let.* 13 Jan. in C. E. Sutcliffe et al. *Story of Football League* (1938) 15 Reports are continually being received that the many unfair and unscrupulous tactics indulged in by some of the players engaged in *League football are allowed to pass unpunished by the referees. **1959** I. & P. OPIE *Lore & Lang. Schoolch.* xvi. 350 The mid-century schoolchild's sporting enthusiasms are more taken up with league football, [etc.]. **1951** *Football Record* (Melbourne) 8 Sept. 18 Congratulations to Ron Clegg, who won the.. award for the best *League footballer of 1951. **1553** GRIMALDE *Cicero's Offices* II. (1558) 83 Warres were made eyther for defence of *leagfrendes or for empire. **1895** *Outing* (U.S.) XXVII. 251/2 If the American universities would send delegates to see our *league games. **1888** 'P. DARYL' *Irel. Disease* 137 These are *League-huts, a temporary shelter which the [Land] League offers to ejected tenants. **1909** A. BENNETT *Matador* (1912) 30 Knype had yet five *League matches to play. **1973** *Irish Times* 2 Mar. 3/2 Cup ties are very different to league matches. **1886** H. CHADWICK *Art of Pitching & Fielding* 132 The following are the best fielding averages of the Eastern *League players. **1938** C. E. SUTCLIFFE et al. *Story of Football League* 12 The forces outside the League were.. ready to take away League players without paying anything for them. **1967** *Australian* 26 Apr. 12 Injuries to many *League stars. **1899** G. O. SMITH in *Football* (Badm. Libr.) 171 In accordance with the *League system a certain number of clubs play home and home matches together. **1902** *Encycl. Brit.* XXVIII. 425/2 An elaboration of this competition is the 'League system' of the Association game. This.. has not been popular with Rugby players. Still it is prevalent in many districts... In the League system a certain number of clubs form a league to play one another twice each season; two points are counted for a win, and one for a draw. The club which at the end of the season comes out with most points wins the competition. **1912** *Football Chart* (G. F. Stirling, Liverpool), Note position of Club each week in *League Table and mark the ups or downs. **1930** *Daily Express* 6 Oct. 16 (*heading*) Saturday's League results and tables. **1959** *Times* 19 Mar. 12/2 He also recited with telling effect a 'league table' of unemployment percentages in western countries, ending with Great Britain as the lowest of all. **1967** COULTHARD & SMITH in Wills & Yearsley *Handbk. Managem. Technol.* 205 Large and

expensive personnel departments, which maintain extensive records, card indexes, files, annual appraisal systems, charts, league tables, and so on. **1970** F. C. AVIS *Soccer Dict.* (ed. 3) 57 *League table*, the statement of teams in relation to each other during the season, [etc.]. **1972** *Human World* May 3 In 1971 they were half way up the 'league table' of wages instead of near the top. **1972** *Times* 11 July 2/7 A league table of tar and nicotine in most brands of cigarettes seems certain to be produced. **1973** C. BONINGTON *Next Horizon* ix. 131 Already a healthy element of competition was springing up between the big league climbers of the Alpine countries... This was a little like a League Table, which we all examined with care as we decided what to do next. **1899** G. O. SMITH in *Football* (Badm. Libr.) 182 Four *League teams. **1639** GLAPTHORNE *Argalus & P.* IV. 39 Palmes (That do with amorous mixture twine their boughes Into a *league-union).

league (li:g), *v.*[1] [f. LEAGUE *sb.*[2] Cf. F. *liguer*, It. *legare*.]

1. *trans.* To form or join into a league; to band together *with*; to confederate.

1611 COTGR., *Ligué*, leagued, in league with. **1633** P. FLETCHER *Pisc. Eclogs*, etc. *Upon Picture Achmet*, Wakeful ambition leagu'd with hastie pride. **1638** DRUMM. OF HAWTH. *Irene* Wks. (1711) 166 To league a people is to make them know their strength & power. **1648** *Hamilton Papers* (Camden) 219 France, Jermin, and the Parliament of England, are leagued to obstruct his designe. **1667** MILTON *P.L.* X. 868 Out of my sight, thou Serpent, that name best Befits thee with him leagu'd. **1791** COWPER *Iliad* XII. 21 Then Neptune, with Apollo leagued, devised Its ruin. **1814** WORDSW. *White Doe* II. 32 Two Earls fast leagued in discontent. **1874** GREEN *Short Hist.* v. §6. 259 Hotspur.. leagued himself with the Scots.

†**2.** To bind, connect, join. *Obs.*

c **1645** HOWELL *Lett.* (1650) I. 51 They began to build upon those small islands.. and in tract of time they conjoined and leagued them together by bridges. **1660** tr. *Amyraldus' Treat. conc. Relig.* III. i. 304 The tyes that ligue us to God.

3. *intr.* To join in or form a league or alliance; to band together. Also *to league against* in indirect pass.

1638 DRUMM. OF HAWTH. *Irene* Wks. (1711) 166 All the world seeth, that to league is imperiously to command their king and sovereign to cut short his pinions. **1698** CROWNE *Caligula* v. Dram. Wks. 1874 IV. 416, I never knew they leagu'd or lov'd till now. **1724** DE FOE *Mem. Cavalier* (1840) 37 The king.. began to see himself leagued against.. both by protestant and papist. **1813** SHELLEY *Q. Mab* VIII. 185 Where kings first leagued against the rights of men. **1822** — *Hellas* 537 The tiger leagues not with the stag at bay Against the hunter. **1854** MILMAN *Lat. Chr.* III. iii. (1864) I. 402 Theodoric.. left.. the Bishop of Rome.. to league with the rebellious subjects of Byzantium against the Eastern Emperor.

Hence **leagued** *ppl. a.*, confederate; **'leaguing** *vbl. sb.*

1799 CAMPBELL *Pleas. Hope* I. 351 When leagu'd Oppression pour'd to Northern wars Her whisker'd pandoors and her fierce hussars. **1807** CRABBE *Library* 136 Where first the proud, the great, In leagued assembly keep their cumbrous state. **1817** SHELLEY *Rev. Islam* II. xiv, A tower whose marbled walls the leagued storms withstand! **1821** JOANNA BAILLIE *Metr. Leg.*, *Wallace* xxvii, These are the leagued for Scotland's native right. **1840** DICKENS *Barn. Rudge* xxxvi, They can sustain no harm from leaguing for this purpose. **1845** S. AUSTIN *Ranke's Hist. Ref.* III. 499 The leagued states. **1869** *Daily News* 8 Mar., His actual leaguing with the Scots against the independence of England.

†**league**, *v.*[2] *Obs. rare.* [a. F. *légue-r*, ad. L. *lēgā-re*.] *trans.* To bequeath.

1623 tr. *Favine's Theat. Hon.* V. i. 40 By his testament he leagued Normandie to Robert his eldest Sonne.

'leagueist. *rare.* In 8 leaguist. [f. LEAGUE *sb.*[2] + -IST.] A party to or member of a league.

1762 tr. *Busching's Syst. Geog.* V. 285 An agreement was made here in 1620 betwixt the United and Leaguists.

League of Nations. An association of self-governing states, dominions, and colonies created by a covenant forming part I of the Peace Treaty of 1919 'in order to promote international co-operation and to achieve international peace and security'. ***League of Nations Society*** (later ***Union***): a society formed to promote the principles of the League of Nations.

1917 H. N. BRAILSFORD (*title*) A League of Nations. *Ibid.* ii. 37 The programme of the British 'League of Nations Society' is as follows. **1917** A. HUXLEY *Let.* 30 Sept. (1969) 133, I have spent the morning in correcting.. essays on the possibility.. of a League of Nations. **1919** *League of Nations Jrnl.* Jan. 1 The Union.. Resulting.. from the amalgamation of the League of Nations Society and of the League of Free Nations Association,.. includes members of a society which has been working since May, 1915, for the establishment of a League of Nations, and of a new and vigorous association which was inaugurated in the summer of 1918. **1919** *Treaty of Peace* (H.M.S.O.) xii. art. 376 Disputes which may arise.. shall be settled as provided by the League of Nations. **1922** *Encycl. Brit.* XXII. 647/2 Perhaps the most important event which happened in Switzerland in 1920 was the first meeting of the League of Nations in Geneva. *a* **1930** D. H. LAWRENCE *Phoenix II* (1968) 442 He was the scourge of *God*: not the scourge of the League of Nations, hired and paid in cash. **1934** H. G. WELLS *Exper. Autobiogr.* II. ix. 694 The term 'League of Nations' is of English origin and it seems to have been first used by a small group of people meeting in the house of Mr. Walter Rea... (E. M. Forster in his life of Lowes Dickinson (1934) gives reasons for ascribing the term to that writer, who may have used it for the two possible 'leagues' he sketched in the first fortnight of the war.) These people founded a League of Nations Society, with Lord Shaw as president, early in 1915. **1957** *Encycl. Brit.* XIII. 832/2 The League of Nations was legally inaugurated on Jan. 10, 1920. *Ibid.*, Pres. Woodrow Wilson espoused the cause of a league of nations in May 1916. **1971** W. H. MCNEILL in A. Bullock *20th Cent.* 47/2 Most of these lands were designated League of Nations 'mandates'.

leaguer ('li:gə(r)), *sb.*[1] Also 6 legher, legar, 6–7 leagure, 7 leguer, leager, leagre, 8 leiger. [a. Du. *leger* camp, formally equivalent to OE. *leʒer* LAIR *sb.*[1]]

1. A military camp, esp. one engaged in a siege; an investing force.

1577 HOLINSHED *Chron.* I. 212/2 But when it was perceiued that theyr slender ranckes were not able to resiste the thycke leghers of the enimies. **1590** SIR J. SMYTH *Disc. Weapons* 2 They [military men] will not vouchsafe.. to use our antient termes belonging to matters of warre, but doo call a Campe by the Dutch name of Legar. *a* **1645** FEATLY in *Fuller's Abel Rediv.*, *Reynolds* (1867) II. 240 The leaguer is not yet broken up. **1647** CLARENDON *Hist. Reb.* VII. §204 It would not at first be credited at the leaguer that the earl of Essex could be in a condition to attempt such a work. **1650** T. B[AYLEY] *Worcester's Apoph.* 100 When General Fairfax came into the Leaguer before Raglan. **1724** DE FOE *Mem. Cavalier* (1840) 120, I came into the imperial leaguer at the siege of Leipsic. **1823** SCOTT *Quentin D.* i, He temporised until the enemy had broken up their leaguer. **1827** KEBLE *Chr. Y.* 2nd Sunday after Trinity, The holy house is still beset With leaguer of stern foes. **1865** PARKMAN *Huguenots* ii. (1875) 20 Villegagnon with six followers.. passed under cover of night through the infidel leaguer. **1875** STUBBS *Const. Hist.* II. xiv. 17 He had dispersed the leaguer at Lincoln.

b. *in leaguer*: in camp; engaged in a siege.

1590 MARLOWE *2nd Pt. Tamburl.* I. iii, Our men of Barbary haue.. laine in leagre fifteene moneths and more. **1600** HOLLAND *Livy* 446 Anniball now laie in leaguer, before the walls of Gerion. **1675** tr. *Machiavelli's Prince* xii. (1883) 85 They were in leaguer before a town. **1808** SCOTT *Marm.* VI. i, Where England's King in leaguer lay. **1879** BUTCHER & LANG *Odyss.* 39 Now we sat in leaguer there achieving many adventures.

2. A military investment, siege.

1598 B. JONSON *Ev. Man in Hum.* III. i, It was the first, but the best leaguer, that euer I beheld, with these eies. **1630** J. TAYLOR (Water P.) *Begger* Wks. I. 100/1 Two dangerous hurts hardly brought off from Bummill Leaguer. **1669** STURMY *Mariner's Mag.* v. 72 At the time of a Leagure he must expect often to change his Powder. **1715** tr. *Pancirollus' Rerum Mem.* I. II. vi. 81 The Waste which lay between the Houses in a Time of a Leaguer, was sown with Corn. **1855** MOTLEY *Dutch Rep.* III. ix. (1866) 533 During the infinite horrors of the Harlem siege, and in the more prosperous leaguer of Alkmaar. **1859** SMILES *Self-Help* vii. (1860) 175 The leaguer of Lucknow. **1890** *Athenæum* 13 Dec. 811/1 The long leaguer of Miletus in the Ionic revolt.

3. *attrib.* and *Comb.*, as ***leaguer-proof*** adj.; †**leaguer-basket**, a fascine; **leaguer-†lady, -lass, † -laundress**, euphemistic names for a woman attached to a camp.

1659 HOOLE *Comenius* (1672) 291 Engineres who lye behind *Leagure-baskets [L. *gerras*]. **1702** STEELE *Funeral* II. 36, I shall take care.. to keep you from Lord Hardy—From being a *Leiger Lady, From carrying a Knapsack. **1822** SCOTT *Nigel* xviii. (*motto*), This were a *leaguer-lass to love a soldier, To bind his wounds, and kiss his bloody brow. **1895** *Q. Rev.* Apr. 472 Her father had dreamed that Jeanne 'went with the soldiers', doubtless as a 'leaguer-lass'. **1629** MASSINGER *Picture* I. i, Were it not for my honesty, I could wish now I were his *leager landresse. *c* **1645** HOWELL *Lett.* II. iv, There are some beauties so strong, that they are *leager-proof; they are so barricaded that no battery.. can do good upon them.

¶**4.** This word has occasionally been substituted by confusion for *leger*, LEDGER, in attributive use and in the phrase *to lie leaguer*.

1678 H. VAUGHAN *Thalia Rediv.* Wks. (Grosart) I. 303 Angels descend, and rule the sphere; Where Heaven lies leiguer. **1727** BOYER *Fr. Dict.* II. s.v., A Leaguer Ambassador, (one that makes a continuance) *Un Ambassadeur ordinaire.* **1826** SCOTT *Woodst.* II. x. 260 He lies leaguer, as a sort of ambassador for his worthy masters.

leaguer ('li:gə(r)), *sb.*[2] [f. LEAGUE *sb.*[2] + -ER[1].]

1. a. A member of a league; in reference to *Fr. Hist.*, a member or adherent of the League formed against the Huguenots in the reign of Henry III; in modern times, a member of the Anti-Corn-Law League, the Irish Land League, etc.

1591 COLYNET (*title*) True History of the Ciuill Warres of France, between the French King Henry 4. and the Leaguers. **1683** *Apol. Prot. France* iii. 8 The Liguers.. did well to cry, To your Quarters White Scarfs, this is none of your quarrel. **1724** DE FOE *Mem. Cavalier* (1840) 168 Here was no leaguers in the field, as in the story of Nuremberg. **1729** TINDAL *Rapin's Hist. Eng.* IX. XVII. 103 *note*, After the Death of the Duke of Guise Henry III was accused by the Leaguers of having caused the Queen of Scots to be put to Death. **1844** COBDEN *Speech* 11 Dec., Speeches 1870 I. 229 One Leaguer in Manchester who has given more money.. than [etc.]. **1864** SALA in *Daily Tel.* 23 Aug., This last dirty move of the Loyal Leaguers to spite the Copperheads in view of the Chicago Convention. **1880** [see LANDLEAGUER]. **1892** 'H. LE CARON' 25 *Y. Secr. Service* (1893) 181 O'Rorke and Andrew Kettle, both Leaguers. **1943** M. WARD *G. K. Chesterton* (1944) xxvi. 435 Many leaguers.. felt.. that the spirit of criticism of others was too fully developed. **1949** M. L. DARLING *At Freedom's Door* I. ii. 52 In this year's election he stood as a Unionist, and like most Unionists was defeated by a Leaguer. **1970** *Cape Times* 28 Oct. 26/2 There are few American major leaguers earning less than $30,000 a year.

b. *attrib.*, as ***leaguer-town***.

1591 *Art. conc. Admiralty* 21 July §51 All those, that.. haue had trafficke with the Leaguers in France, or shipped .. any victuals.. for Spaine, the Islands, or any leaguer towne in Fraunce. **1647** MAY *Hist. Parl.* II. v. 93 Sir John Meldrum arrived suddenly at a Leaguer-town called Aulby.

†**2.** ? A term of reproach. ? *nonce-use.*

1615 CHAPMAN *Odyss.* XVII. 285 This same victles Leager, This bane of banquets; this most nasty begger.

leaguer ('li:gə(r)), *sb.*[3] ?*Obs.* Also 8 leagre, 8–9 leager, 9 legar. [? ad. Du. *ligger* a tun, f. *liggen* to LIE *v.*[1] Cf. G. *leger* (also *legger*, *wasserlegger*) a measure for arrack, *pl.* fresh-water casks on board ship.] **a.** A certain measure of arrack. **b.** A cask of wine or oil, ? of a particular size. **c.** *Naut.* (See quot. 1867.)

1683 in *Hacke's Collect. Voy.* (1699) I. 37 We had gotten in 36 Liggers of Water already. **1712** W. ROGERS *Voy.* 398 Half a Leaguer of Spelman's Neep, or the best sort of Arrack. **1730** CAPT. W. WRIGLESWORTH *MS. Log-bk. of the Lyell* 15 Aug., Started 3 Leagers of Arrack belonging to the Ships Crew, into 3 Butts and a small Cask. **1772–84** COOK *Voy.* (1790) I. 362 The provisions for which the French contracted this year.. one thousand two hundred leagers of wine. **1789** G. KEATE *Pelew Isl.* 83 They also discovered a cask of Arrack.. it was half a Leaguer. **1800** *Naval Chron.* III. 66 The largest casks are called leagers, and are of the following dimensions: Length.. 4 ft. 6 in., Diameter of Bouge.. 3 ft., Diameter of Chine.. 2 ft. 5 in. **1802** *Ibid.* VIII. 82 His object was to purchase 200 legars, to be filled with water.. for the use of the cattle. **1812** J. SMYTH *Pract. of Customs* (1821) 169, Butts and Leaguers. **1837** WHITTOCK *Bk. Trades* (1842) 348 [Oilmen] Both parties require roomy outskirt premises for their stores; the former for his casks and his 'leagers'. **1867** SMYTH *Sailor's Word-bk.*, *Leaguers*, the longest water-casks, stowed near the kelson, of 159 English imperial gallons each. Before the invention of water-tanks, leaguers composed the whole ground tier of casks in men-of-war. **1881** F. R. STATHAM *Blacks, Boers, & British* iv. 61 You want to see what can be done with South African wine?.. Visit a great airy shed not far from the Cape Town docks,.. the rough and ready wine has become—what? Look at it and see it as it is drawn from the huge casks —leaguers they call them here. **1959** *Cape Times* 14 Mar. 2/6 Two lorries, one carrying a 5-leaguer tank of wine (some 600 gallons) collided here yesterday. **1970** *Ibid.* 28 Oct. 20/3 (Advt.), A wine quota of 320 leaguers.

'leaguer, *v.* [f. LEAGUER *sb.*[1]]

†**1.** *refl.* and *intr.* To set one's leaguer, to encamp. *Obs.*

1629 *S'hertogenbosh* 15 Leaguering himself on the East side of the Towne. **1676** W. ROW *Contn. Blair's Autobiog.* x. (1848) 161 Where the army had leaguered the year preceding.

†**b.** To 'lie', lodge. *Obs. rare.*

1596 NASHE *Saffron Walden* 157 When I legerd by him in the Dolphin.

2. *trans.* To besiege, beleaguer. Chiefly in **'leaguered, 'leaguering** *ppl. adjs.*

1715–20 POPE *Iliad* XVIII. 593 Two mighty hosts a leaguer'd town embrace. **1794** COLERIDGE *Robespierre* II. i, That the voice of truth.. though leaguered round By envy and her hateful brood of hell, Be heard. **1816** BYRON *Siege Cor.* ii, The crescent shines Along the Moslem's leaguering lines. **1855** W. SARGENT *Braddock's Exped.* 362 His.. defence of Detroit against Pontiac and his leaguering hordes. **1860** T. MARTIN *Horace* 19 The watchfires round Troy's leaguer'd wall.

†**'leaguerer.** *Obs.* [f. LEAGUER *sb.*[1] + -ER[1].] A (Dutch) trooper.

1635 GLAPTHORNE *Hollander* II. (1640) D 1 b, My naturall Dutch too is a Clownish speech, and only fit to court a leagurer in. **1639** — *Wallenstein* III. ii. E 3 Sure, My Lord intends to write some Proclamation 'Gainst wearing holland smockes, some furious Edict 'Gainst charitable leaguerers. **1654** WEBSTER *Appius & Virg.* IV. ii. 48 Though we dine to day As Dutch men feed their soldiers, we will sup bravely, like Roman Leaguerers.

leaguite ('li:gaɪt). Also leagueite. [f. LEAGUE *sb.*[2] + -ITE[1].] = LEAGUEIST.

1841 *Times* 4 Feb. 5/4 The leagueites polled 9 dead men. **1892** E. DOWSON *Let.* 22 Nov. (1967) 253 It seeming to be very much confined to the actual Leaguites themselves.

leahter, obs. form of LAUGHTER.

leak (li:k), *sb.* Forms: 5–6 leke, 6 *Sc.* lek, 6–7 leake, 7 *Sc.* leck, 8 lake, 7– leak. [First recorded late in 15th c.; the proximate source is uncertain; perh., like many other nautical terms, adopted from LG. or Du.; cf. LG., MDu. *lek*, inflected *lēk-* (whence G. *leck*, Da. *læk*; the G. *lecke*, Sw. *läcka* are f. the vb.), Du. *lek*; equivalent forms are Ger. dial. *lech*, *leche*, ON. *leke* str. masc. It is possible that the Eng. word, notwithstanding its late appearance, may represent an adoption of the ON. form, or even an OE. cognate. The exact relation between the sb. and the adj. and vb. is undetermined.]

1. a. A hole or fissure in a vessel containing or immersed in a fluid, by which the latter enters or escapes from the vessel, so as to cause loss or injury: said orig. and esp. of ships; also in phr. † *to fall in leak, to spring a leak*.

1487 *Naval Acc. Hen. VII* (1896) 25 The stopping of lekes. **1497** *Ibid.* 131 Lost in a ship.. by occasion of a leke falling in the same. **1513** DOUGLAS *Æneis* VI. vi. 67 The jonit barge, Sa full of riftis, and with lekkis perbraik. **1531–2** *Act 23 Hen. VIII* c. 7 If.. the shippe.. happen to fall in leke. **1558** W. TOWRSON in Hakluyt *Voy.* (1589) 122 We found a

great leake in the stemme of our ship. *c* **1620** Z. BOYD *Zion's Flowers* (1855) 11 Consider well before a leck begin, It seemes I heare the water wheesing in. **1624** CAPT. SMITH *Virginia* VI. 230 The next day the lesser ship sprung a leake. **1626** —— *Accid. Yng. Sea-men* 19 Sling a man ouerboord to stop the leake. **1642** FULLER *Holy & Prof. St.* I. viii. 20 Many little leaks may sink a ship. **1727** *Philip Quarll* 56 We found our Ship had sprung a Leake. **1782** COWPER *Loss Roy. George* 19 She sprang no fatal leak. **1814** SCOTT *Ld. of Isles* I. xviii, Rent was the sail, and strain'd the mast, And many a leak was gaping fast.

b. *transf.* and *fig.*

1597 HOOKER *Eccl. Pol.* v. ix. §2 There..will be alwaies euils, which no arte of man can cure, breaches and leakes moe then mans wit hath hands to stop. **1602** MARSTON *Antonio's Rev.* IV. ii. Wks. 1856 I. 120 Fooles, That can not search the leakes of his defectes. **1622** HAKEWILL *David's Vow* vi. 229 It being the property of a foole to be full of leakes. **1806-7** J. BERESFORD *Miseries Hum. Life* (1826) xx. xxxv. 257 A leak in the waistcoat-pocket in which you carry all your money. **1873** HAMERTON *Intell. Life* x. viii. (1875) 373 An able finance minister who has found means of closing a great leak in the treasury. **1900** LD. ROSEBERY *Napoleon* xvi. 246 Russia was the fatal leak in his Continental System.

c. *Electr.* A path or component of relatively high resistance through which a small current flows.

1896 T. E. HERBERT *Electricity in Application to Telegr.* xvii. 81 B is connected to earth as is the end of our 40 ohm leak. **1919** [see *grid leak* (GRID 5 b)]. **1940** *Amat. Radio Handbk.* (ed. 2) ii. 33/2 The grid will take up a potential such that the current from grid to filament equals the current through the leak in either the positive or negative half cycle. **1966** [see *grid leak* (GRID 5 b)].

d. An improper or deliberate disclosure of information (e.g. for political purposes).

1950 H. D. LASSWELL *National Security* ii. 34 Americans are accustomed to 'government by leak'. **1957** *Economist* 28 Sept. 1004/2 The allegation of a 'leak' about last Thursday's increase in Bank rate has brought forth understandable indignation from those City dealers whose fingers were burned, and an equally understandable demand by the Labour Party for a full inquiry. **1960** L. COOPER *Accomplices* I. ii. 17 Confidential stuff about a security leak from one of our research stations. **1960** *News Chron.* 30 Apr. 4/2 No agenda, no communiqué, no inspired leaks. **1965** H. KAHN *On Escalation* iii. 56 In..1964, the United States and the Chinese engaged in a series of such semiformal leaks and announcements about the war in Vietnam. **1967** *Punch* 4 Oct. 509/3 Long among the most skilled practitioners of leak journalism. **1973** *Guardian* 10 Apr. 15/3 The EEC Commission spent an hour and a half..discussing leaks and how to plug them (or so it is reliably leaked to Miscellany).

2. a. The action of leaking; leakage.

1828-32 in WEBSTER. **1896** *Academy* 11 Apr. 399/1 In hydrogen the leak was slowest... The rate of leak in the halogens is also very rapid.

b. *Electr.* Leakage of electric charge or current (see LEAKAGE 2 b).

1863 R. S. CULLEY *Handbk. Pract. Telegr.* iv. 65 Suppose ..a fault to occur connecting the wire to the earth, and offering a resistance equal to that of 20 miles of the line. This 'leak' will lessen the total resistance of the circuit..as if a wire 20 miles long..were fixed to the line at the fault. **1893** [see LEAKANCE]. **1895** THOMPSON & THOMAS *Electr. Tab. & Mem.* 52 It will..show the position of a leak from one wire to another. **1906** *Phil. Mag.* XII. 403 With very thin paper ..no discharge could be observed, whilst in the case of aluminium leaf 0·0005 mm. in thickness a difference in the rate of leak was observed. **1939** *Post Office Electr. Engineers' Jrnl.* XXXII. 138 (*heading*) The localization of small leaks in the underground transmission line system at Cooling Radio Station.

c. *slang.* An act of urination. Freq. in phr. *to take a leak*, to urinate. Cf. LEAK *v.* 2 c.

1934 H. MILLER *Tropic of Cancer* 182, I stood there taking a leak. **1968** K. WEATHERLY *Roo Shooter* 111, I saw Sam get out of the Rover... I thought he'd got out for a leak. **1969** G. GREENE *Trav. with my Aunt* II. vi. 282 All these hours of standing without taking a leak. **1972** F. RAPHAEL *April, June & Nov.* 283 'The guest toilets at the Palace aren't really all that marvellous.' '..Thanks for the tip, I'll remember to take a leak before I go next time.'

3. *attrib.* and *Comb.*: **leak-alarm, -indicator, -signal**, devices for indicating the rising or accumulation of water in the hold of a ship (Knight *Dict. Mech.* 1875); **leak detector**, any device for detecting leaks of fluid; **leak-proof** *a.*, not subject to leaks.

1921 *Chambers's Jrnl.* July 454/2 Each bag..is inflated with air and examined all over its surface with leak-detectors. **1968** *Non-Destructive Testing* I. 215/1 Shell have developed a portable hydrocarbon leak detector to facilitate the overhaul of [gas] mains. **1926** *Kitchen Kook* (Amer. Gas Mach. Co. Inc.) 3 The fuel..is contained in an electrically welded, leakproof, steel tank. **1929** *Daily Express* 8 Jan. 8/5 Waste heat in leak-proof pipes to towns near the coalfields. **1960** *Farmer & Stockbreeder* 15 Mar. 44/2 (*caption*) It's leakproof. **1971** *Engineering* Apr. 92/2 (Advt.), Instant.. safe..leakproof joints... A pipeline which is flexible while remaining absolutely leak-proof.

†**leak**, *a.* *Obs.* Forms: 1 hlec, 6 lek(e, 6-7 leake, 7 *Sc.* leck. [In OE. *hlec*; after OE. the word does not appear until the 16th c. when it may have been adopted from LG., MDu. *lek* (inflected *lēk-*), whence mod.Du. *lek*, Sw. *läck*, Da. *læk*, G. *leck*; cogn. w. ON. *lekr*, Ger. dial. *lech* of the same meaning, and with LEAK *sb.* and *v.*

The OE. form presents difficulties; the spelling *hlec* occurs in the Hatton MS. of the *Pastoral Care* (9th c.) and in at least three glosses, so that it cannot well be a mere error; on the other hand the (apparently) cognate words in the other Teut. langs. show no trace of the *h*; in the ON. vb. *leka* the initial *l* (not *hl*) is attested by the alliteration.]

= LEAKY.

c **897** K. ÆLFRED *Gregory's Past.* lvii. 437 Swiðe lytlum siceraþ ðæt wæter & swiðe deȝellice on ðæt hlece scip. *c* **1100** in Napier *Glosses* ii. 480 *Rimosa*, hlec. *a* **1530** HEYWOOD *Play Weather* (Brandl) 800 Olde moones be leake, they can holde no water. **1544** *Extracts Aberd. Reg.* (1844) I. 205 The Inglismen..knawand that thair schip was lek, geve thaim thair leif. **1590** SPENSER *F.Q.* I. v. 35 And fifty sisters water in leke [*ed.* 1596 leake] vessels draw. **1622** R. HAWKINS *Voy. S. Sea* (1847) 131 Thus, this leake-ship went well into England. **1626** CAPT. SMITH *Accid. Yng. Sea-men* 13 A ship cranke sided, Iron sicke, spewes her okum, a leake ship. **1637-50** Row *Hist. Kirk* (Wodrow Soc.) 398 The ship not tight enough, being leck. *a* **1678** MARVELL *Poems, Char. Holland* 45 Who best could know to pump an earth so leak.

leak (liːk), *v.* Forms: 5 leke, 6 leeke, *Sc.* (also 8 *north.*) leck, 6-7 leake, *Sc.* lek(k, 6- leak. [Not found before *c* 1420, but prob. much older; a. or cogn. with ON. *leka* str. vb. (pa. t. *lak*) to drip, to leak, corresponding to OHG. **lechen* str. vb., found only in composition (pa. pple. *zelechen* leaky), MHG. and dial. mod.G. *lechen* wk., to crack from drought, become leaky, MDu. *leken* (pa. t. *lak*) to let water through, drip; f. Teut. root **lek-*, ablaut variant of **lak-*: see LACK *a.*

It is very likely that in later use the vb. was formed afresh from LEAK *sb.* or *a.* Sense 5 may be plausibly explained as a development from sense 2, but it is not wholly impossible that it may be a distinct word, a var. of LEACH *v.*, OE. *lęccan.* The LG. *lecken* (whence Sw. *läcka*, Da. *lække*, G. *lecken*) is derived from, or at least refashioned after, the equivalent of LEAK *a.* or *sb.*]

1. a. *intr.* To pass (*out, away, forth*) by a leak or leakage. Also *fig.*, to pass *away* by gradual waste.

c **1420** *Pallad. on Husb.* VI. 33 Let diche hit deep that humour out may leke, If hit be weet. **1648** WILKINS *Math. Magick* II. v. 181 It is easie to conceive how..the water, which will perhaps by degrees leak into several parts, may be emptyed out again. *a* **1728** WOODWARD *Nat. Hist. Fossils* I. (1729) I. 243 A Crack, through which a small quantity of the Liquor leak'd forth. **1791** PAINE *Rights of Man* (ed. 4) 154 The gold and silver..leak continually away by unseen means, at the average rate of about three quarters of a million a-year. **1863** R. S. CULLEY *Handbk. Pract. Telegr.* vii. 106 The dampness of the insulators enables part of the electricity to leak or escape from one wire to another, and to the earth. **1890** *Spectator* 23 Aug., A democracy that has allowed its chief political interests to leak away. **1917** G. D. SHEPARDSON *Telephone Apparatus* xiv. 224 Little talking current 'leaked' through the signaling equipment. **1959** *Which?* Winter 37/1 If there is a fault in an electrical appliance and current leaks to the exposed parts.

b. *to leak out* (fig.): to transpire or become known in spite of efforts at concealment.

1832 WEBSTER, *To leak out*,..to escape privately from confinement or secresy; as a fact or report. **1834** S. SMITH *Sel. Lett. J. Downing* 58 If it should leak out that I was going. **1840** R. H. DANA *Bef. Mast* xiv. 33 We had heard rumours of such a ship to follow us, which had leaked out from the captain. **1852** MRS. STOWE *Uncle Tom's C.* xix, I can see it leaking out in fifty different ways—just that same strong, overbearing, dominant spirit. **1884** *Manch. Exam.* 27 May 5/1 The outcry which was raised when the rumour of it leaked out. **1884** 'RITA' *Vivienne* II. v, The carefully-guarded secret had leaked out in some way or other.

2. To allow the passage of fluid through a leak: **a.** inwards.

1513 DOUGLAS *Æneis* I. iii. 50 Thai all leckit, and salt watter stremis Fast bullerand in at every ryft and boir. **1530** PALSGR. 606/1, I leeke, as a shyppe or bote dothe that taketh in water... Labour well, syrs, at the pompe, for our shyppe leaketh. **1555** EDEN *Decades* 229 One of theyr shyppes leaked and toke water very sore. *a* **1568** *Satir. Poems Reform.* xlvi. 19 Gif scho lekkis, gett men of skill To stop hir hoilis laich in þe howis. **1708** J. PHILIPS *Cyder* II. 66 Against a secret Cliff..A Ship is dash'd, and leaking drinks the Sea. **1873** BROWNING *Red Cott. Nt.-cap* 1317 Carried pick-a-back by Eldobert Big-baby-fashion, lest his leathers leak!

b. outwards.

1530 PALSGR. 606/1 This hogges heed of wyne leaketh. **1557** *N. T.* (Genev.) *Heb.* ii. 1 *note*, Lest like vessells ful of chappes we leake, and renne out on euery part. **1597** SHAKS. *2 Hen. IV*, IV. iv. 47 That the vnited Vessell of their Blood (Mingled with Venome of Suggestion..) Shall neuer leake, though it doe worke as strong As *Aconitum*, or rash Gun-powder. *a* **1605** MONTGOMERIE *Misc. Poems* xxxvii. 21 Go to —vhat rek? and gar the bealing brek; For, fra it lek, I hald the danger done. **1835** SIR J. ROSS *Narr. 2nd Voy.* vi. 86 The starboard boiler began to leak.

c. To 'make water'. (*vulgar.*)

1596 SHAKS. *1 Hen. IV*, II. i. 22 Why, you will allow vs ne're a Iourden, and then we leake in your Chimney. *a* **1661** HOLYDAY *Juvenal* 51 Some great ones drinking so hard, that they even leak'd on their supper couches. **1673** DRYDEN *Amboyna* v. i. 54 Boy, give me some Tobacco, and a Stope of Wine..And a Tub to leak in Boy; when was this Table without a leaking Vessel? **1731** SWIFT *Strephon & Chloe* 164 Twelve cups of tea (with grief I speak) Had now constrain'd the nymph to leak. **1796** in *Grose's Dict. Vulg. Tongue.* **1957** J. KEROUAC *On Road* (1958) 90 The prowl car came by and the cop got out to leak. **1971** D. E. WESTLAKE *I gave at the Office* (1972) 173, I kept thinking he'd come back from the john—how long can one man leak?

†**3.** *pass.* To have sprung a leak; to be emptied by leakage. *Obs.*

1607 SHAKS. *Timon* IV. ii. 19 Leak'd is our Barke. **1622** in Bradford *Plymouth Plantation* (1856) 138 Within 14. days after she [a ship] came againe hither, being dangerously leaked and brused with tempestious stormes. **1699** DAMPIER *Voy.* II. III. vi. 69 Some of the Rum they found,..a Cask in one place, and a Cask in another;..some staved against the Trees, and leeked out. **1748** *Anson's Voy.* III. iv. 333 We.. found many of our casks so decayed, as to be half leaked out.

4. a. *trans.* To let (water, etc.) in or out through a leak. ? Now *U.S.* only.

1687 HOOKE in *Hist. Royal Soc.* (1757) IV. 548 It would be next to impossible to make pipes to hold so perfectly as not to leak air in some parts. **1692** LOCKE *Educ.* §7 (1693) 6 To have his Shooes made so, as to leak Water. **1889** *Cent. Dict.* s.v., The pipe leaks gas; the roof leaks rain.

†**b.** *fig.* To cause to run *out* or escape.

1655 GURNALL *Chr. in Arm.* I. 94 When a Christian is flush of comfort, then Satan lies upon the catch, then to inveigle a Saint into one sin or other, which he knows will soon leak out his joy.

c. To allow the disclosure of (secret or confidential information). (Cf. sense 1 b and LEAK *sb.* 1 d.) Also *intr.* Hence **leaked** *ppl. a.*

1859 G. W. MATSELL *Vocabulum* 50 *Leak*, to impart a secret. **1916** W. OWEN *Let.* Aug. (1967) 402 Here I am beginning to 'Leak information', (when I have to read daily a solemn W.O. Letter, saying that no talk of the War is ever to be indulged in, even in private letters.) **1954** *Encounter* June 11/1 In practice [the dial number] was a secret in name only, since supervisors were instructed to 'leak' the number 'confidentially' to various employees. **1958** *Punch* 3 Nov. 10/3 It seemed pretty clear from what the F.O. had leaked to us that Bonaparte had crossed the Niemen. **1958** *Ann. Reg. 1957* 195 In a miscalculated effort to prepare the public and Congress for the new doctrine, it had been deliberately 'leaked' well beforehand. **1959** *John o' London's* 26 Nov. 265/3 A..U.S. Air Force sergeant..promptly scares off the circling sharks by leaking information about her non-existent husband. **1962** *Listener* 25 Oct. 647/2 The Council Fathers are supposed to maintain complete discretion, though almost all of them 'leak' to the press. **1971** *Daily Tel.* 14 July 3/4 It was not sufficient for the tribunal merely to establish by whose hand information..was improperly leaked. **1972** *Times* 30 Sept. 3/1 Legislation covering 'leaked' information is proposed by the Franks Committee on Official Secrets. **1973** [see LEAK *sb.* 1 d].

5. *Brewing.* To cause (liquor) to run *over, on, off*, in small quantities or by degrees. *Obs.* exc. *dial.*

Cf. Sc. 'To *lek, leck*, to pour water over bark or other substance, in order to obtain a decoction; to strain off, Clydes[dale]' (Jam.). See also LECK *v.* in Eng. Dial. Dict.

1674 RAY *N.C. Words* 29 *Leck on*, poure on more, Liquor, v.g. **1743** *Lond. & Country Brew* II. (ed. 2) 119 Put your Malt in by Degrees, and stir it..then leak on your Complement. *Ibid.* 122 Leaking over.—Is what may be called putting over the Malt, at Times, many Hand-bowls of Water, that it may run gradually off, and wash away the Flower of the Malt by a slow Degree. **1788** W. MARSHALL *E. Yorksh.* II. 339 To *Leck-on* to add more water, as in brewing. **1790** *Trans. Soc. Arts* VIII. 151 Draining the liquor through a sieve, instead of leaking it off gradually.

leakage ('liːkɪdʒ). Also 5-7 lecage, 6 lekkege, 8 leekage. [f. LEAK *v.* + -AGE. Cf. Du. *lekkage.*]

1. The action of leaking; admission or escape of water or other fluid through a hole in a vessel, etc.; loss of fluid by this means.

1490 in Arnolde *Chron.* (1811) 112 Alle maner auenturs fortunes perilles and ioperdies of alle the sayd wynes, lecage forst and egirnesse of the same oonly exepte. **1622** MALYNES *Anc. Law-Merch.* 195 Allowances made..vpon Wines in regarde of lecage of tenne or fifteene vpon the hundreth. **1633** T. JAMES *Voy.* 45, I would take no excuse of leakage or other waste. **1739** LABELYE *Short Acc. Piers Westm. Bridge* 34 By the Help of only four Pumps..we easily master'd what Leakage we had. **1748** *Anson's Voy.* II. x. 241 Jars..are liable to no leekage, unless they are broken. **1825** J. NICHOLSON *Operat. Mechanic* 198 We have seen an engine of an eight-horse power of this kind at work, with a fluid metal on the pistons: it effectually prevented the leakage. **1861** T. L. PEACOCK *Gryll Gr.* xix. 161 The sub-soil of London..converted by gas leakage into one mass of pestilent blackness. **1875** H. C. WOOD *Therap.* (1879) 509 A form of secretion, or..leakage, from mucous membranes.

2. a. *transf.* and *fig.* Diminution resulting from gradual waste or escape; improper or deliberate disclosure of information from an office, etc.; unexplained continuous disappearance of something.

1642 FULLER *Holy & Prof. St.* Pref. §7, I will stop the leakage of my soul, and what heretofore hath run out in writing, shall hereafter..be improved in constant preaching. **1673** BP. S. PARKER *Reproof Reh. Transpr.* 11 They..weaken themselves by too great a leakage of their power. **1859** 'T. TITCOMB' *Titcomb's Lett.* (ed. 12) ii. 185 It is entirely rational and right that your wife should understand the basis of all your requirements of her; and when she does this, the chances are that she will not only be economical herself, but will point out leakages in your prosperity for which you are responsible. **1863** KINGLAKE *Crimea* I. 452 The Cabinet of Lord Aberdeen was not famous for its power of preventing the leakage of state matters. **1880** E. W. HAMILTON *Diary* 30 Nov. (1972) I. 83 There have of late curiously been some leakages. My own belief is that men like Chamberlain and Forster..are most unguarded in their language outside. **1890** *Daily News* 17 Oct. 7/2 It was discovered that there was a 'leakage' in the stamp transfer forms. **1893** SIR R. BALL *Story of Sun* 270 The leakage of heat is..slow. **1894** *Westm. Gaz.* 19 Sept. 3/3 That leakage from the faith which is taking place among the poor Catholics. **1895** *Month* May 115 The 'leakage' going on in the Catholic Church in the British Isles. **1898** *Daily News* 17 Feb. 2/7 The prizes..for three best essays on the cause of the leakage in the membership of the Methodist Church,.. have been awarded. **1898** *Ibid.* 20 Oct. 6/5 Some extracts.. have found their way into the pages of the 'New York Critic'... I am unable..to account for this leakage. **1900** *Speaker* 22 Sept. 668/1 The frightful leakage from deaths, wounds and sickness. **1900** *Edin. Rev.* July 81 The tide of emigration has been stayed..the leakage is diminishing. **1904** A. B. F. YOUNG *Compl. Motorist* 347/2 Leakage of small moneys, during travel. **1908** H. G. WELLS *War in Air* i. 25 Mr. K. Butteridge..intended to keep his secret safe from any further risk of leakage. **1945** E. WAUGH *Brideshead Revisited* 10 Our new commanding officer was making an unusual display of 'security'... 'If I find any of these female camp followers waiting for us the other end, I'll know

there's been a leakage.' **1972** *Times* 30 Sept. 1/1 The [Franks] committee proposes an Official Information Act to cover leakage of information which would seriously injure the national interest. **1973** A. CHRISTIE *Postern of Fate* III. xvii. 248 There were leakages—as always there are leakages in time of war.

b. *Electr.* A gradual escape of charge or current, esp. as a result of imperfect insulation. Also, in *Magnetism*, an escape of flux from a magnetic circuit or device; flux which does not pass through the secondary of a transformer or induction coil, or through the armature of a motor or generator.

1863 R. S. CULLEY *Handbk. Pract. Telegr.* iv. 59 On a long line the leakage from wire to wire through damp air cannot be altogether without effect. **1902** *Encycl. Brit.* XXVII. 586/2 Since no substance is impermeable to the passage of magnetic flux, the only form of magnetic circuit free from leakage is one uniformly wound..over its whole length. **1922** GLAZEBROOK *Dict. Appl. Physics* II. 190/1 Allowance must be made for flux which leaks across the intervening space between the poles and does not actually enter the armature, and a magnetic circuit has to be designed so as to keep this leakage as small as possible. **1962** *Newnes Conc. Encycl. Electr. Engin.* 229/1 Danger from leakage may be prevented on metal pole lines by a continuous earth wire connected to the poles. **1962** D. F. SHAW *Introd. Electronics* i. 7 If the coil is long enough for the solenoid formula to apply there will be a considerable leakage of flux between the turns.

3. *concr.* **a.** That which leaks or oozes out. Also *fig.*

a **1661** FULLER *Worthies Hampsh.* II. (1662) 13, I behold these his Books as the Receptacle of the Leakage and Superfluities of his Study. **1793** SMEATON *Edystone* §313 A very small leakage came in. **1820** W. IRVING *Sketch Bk.*, *Stage Coach* (1865) 234 The privilege of battening on the drippings of the kitchen and the leakage of the tap-room.

†**b.** A leak. *Obs. rare.*

1776 G. SEMPLE *Building in Water* 102 Get the Water.. taken out, corking any Leakages that may happen to appear.

4. Allowance made for waste of fluid by leakage from the containing vessels.

1591 *Wills & Inv. N.C.* (Surtees 1860) II. 108, 40*s.* for freght, 40*s.* for impost, the lekkege in myne owne hand, by estimation, 26*s.* **1735** *Connect. Col. Rec.* (1873) VII. 563 The said retailer..will pay to the said commissioner the duty laid thereon by the excise act, substracting only one fifth part thereof for leakage and wastage. **1809** R. LANGFORD *Introd. Trade* 132 *Leakage*, allowance of duty for waste of liquor from the vessels leaking or other causes. **1861** SMILES *Engineers* II. 196 The lightermen claimed as their right the perquisites of 'wastage' and 'leakage'.

5. *attrib.*, as (sense 2 b) ***leakage current, flux, path***; also **leakage conductance** *Electr.* = LEAKANCE; **leakage detector**, (*a*) = *leak detector* (s.v. LEAK *sb.* 3); (*b*) = *leakage indicator*; **leakage indicator** *Electr. Engin.*, any device for indicating or measuring leakage currents flowing to earth.

1887 *Electrician* 3 June 80/2 The attenuation factor is now $\epsilon^{-R/2L\nu} \cdot \epsilon^{-K/2S\nu}$, if *K* be the leakage conductance, and *S* the permittance per unit length. **1880** *Jrnl. Soc. Telegr. Engin.* IX. 456 The additional term (*v/i*)*dx* is the leakage current of *dx*, viz., the potential of *dx* divided by its insulation resistance. **1962** J. BELL in G. A. T. Burdett *Automatic Control Handbk.* iv. 3 The insulation to earth must be maintained in the megohms region otherwise the inaccuracy due to leakage currents will be significant. **1880** *English Mechanic* Oct. 107/3 Cowan's meters, and Mr. Young's.. leakage-detector are prominent exhibits [at the Exhibition of Gas and Electrical Apparatus]. **1901** *Catal. Mech. Engin. Collection Sci. Div. V. & A. Mus.* (ed. 3) I. 220 Leakage detector... This is an instrument for rendering audible the slight sound made by water flowing in a pipe, so that if the noise continues, after certain valves are closed, the existence of a leak is indicated. **1923** MEARES & NEALE *Electr. Engin. Pract.* (ed. 4) I. xv. 499 In the Howard leakage detector a current transformer is connected in the earthing wire of, say, a switchboard frame, and the secondary of the current transformer is connected to a tripping relay. **1971** *Instruments & Exper. Techniques* XIV. 830 The leakage detector operates in stable fashion when the pickup is situated in a high vacuum. **1896** F. BEDELL *Princ. Transformer* xv. 302 The leakage flux varies inversely as the reluctance of the leakage path. **1962** CORSON & LORRAIN *Introd. Electromagn. Fields* vii. 291 Let us consider a toroid of magnetic material with a localized winding... The leakage flux, that is, the flux of **B** which leaves the core, produces poles on the surface..and these poles contribute an intensity **H** within the iron. **1920** *Whittaker's Electr. Engineer's Pocket-Bk.* (ed. 4) 276 The function of a leakage indicator is to provide information as to the insulation resistance of the whole of the electrical system..to which it is connected. **1958** J. L. WATTS *Electr. Maintenance & Repairs* iii. 43 Where the supply is obtained from a three-wire d.c. system with earthed mid-point, a suitable differential ammeter connected across shunts in the positive and negative mains will serve as a leakage indicator. **1896** Leakage path [see *leakage flux* above]. **1909** *Installation News* III. 64/1 The leakage path to the conduit or earth is now very greatly reduced. **1962** *Newnes Conc. Encycl. Electr. Engin.* 437/1 It is usual to assume that those parts of a leakage path lying in ferro-magnetic material will require a negligible proportion of the coil m.m.f.

leakance ('liːkəns). *Electr.* [f. LEAK *v.* + -ANCE as a shortening of *leakage conductance*.] Conductance attributable to leakage or imperfect insulation.

1893 O. HEAVISIDE *Electromagn. Theory* I. 453 A process ..of representing a large number of separate leaks by uniform leakance. *Ibid.*, Distribute the inductive leakance uniformly, in imagination, of course. **1928** BRADFIELD & JOHN *Telephone & Power Transmission* ii. 18 Since the insulation of the circuit..can never be perfect, there must be a certain leakance from wire to wire,..stated in 'mhos', or sometimes in 'micro-mhos' per mile of loop. *Ibid.* iv. 55 The leakance of aerial circuits varies irregularly between wide limits, owing to weather and other conditions. **1962** *Newnes Conc. Encycl. Electr. Engin.* 845/1 Leakance and capacitance effects are large [in telecommunication lines], so that the attenuation is much higher than could be tolerated in power transmission.

leake, obs. form of LATCH, LEAK, LEEK.

leakiness ('liːkɪnɪs). [f. LEAKY *a.* + -NESS.] Leaky condition.

1628 DIGBY *Voy. Medit.* (1868) 84 Because of her leakinesse and ill-sayling. **1835** SIR J. ROSS *Narr. 2nd Voy.* xxii. 324 Whence arose some of our leakiness. **1864** SALA in *Daily Tel.* 27 Sept., If a kettle..shows symptoms of leakiness.

leaking ('liːkɪŋ), *vbl. sb.* [-ING[1].] The action of the verb LEAK; leakage. Also *attrib.* in †**leaking tub, vessel** (LEAK *v.* 2 c).

1611 COTGR., *Coulement*..a leaking. **1642** ROGERS *Naaman* To Rdr. 4 As a naile fastned in a sure place from wanzing and leaking out. **1673** DRYDEN *Amboyna* v. i. 54 Never any thing of Moment was done at our Counsel Table, without a leaking Tub..great Consultations require great Drinking, and great Drinking a great leaking Vessel. **1973** *Time* 16 Apr. 53/2 The leaking and publication of classified information has always been a murky area in criminal law. **1973** *Listener* 15 Nov. 658/1 There was..some leaking to the Arabs from perhaps two EEC capitals, which had disclosed to them the line the Dutch had been taking in confidential Community discussions.

'leaking, *ppl. a.* [-ING[2].] That leaks or lets water in or out; that has a leak or leaks. †Also of weather, showery.

c **1420** *Pallad. on Husb.* I. 450 When this siment is maad, hit most insinke Vche hole & chene and euery lekyng ston. **1534** MORE *Treat. Pass.* Wks. 1386/2 Whoso lyke a foole placeth hymselfe in a leakinge shyppe. **1610** FOLKINGHAM *Art of Surv.* I. xi. 35 A loose and light Sand swords slow and thin, yet with rest and lecking sommers it yeelds good Corne. **1611** BIBLE *Heb.* ii. 1 Lest at any time we should let them slip [*marg.* run out as leaking vessels]. **1612** T. TAYLOR *Comm. Titus* iii. 1 Out of a leaking vessell good things are euer running out. *c* **1614** SIR W. MURE *Dido & Æneas* I. 290 Their leiking seames drink in the floods so fast. **1678** DRYDEN & LEE *Œdipus* II. i. (1679) 18 All dart at once their baleful influence In leaking Fire. **1863** A. B. GROSART *Small Sins* 36 Leaking timber.

'leakless, *a.* [f. LEAK *sb.* + -LESS.] Not having a leak.

1899 T. S. MOORE *Vinedresser* 4 Choose casks which thou hast seen Are leakless.

†**'leakness.** *Obs.* [f. LEAK *a.* + -NESS.] Leakiness.

1508 *Extracts Aberd. Reg.* (1844) I. 439 And cum within the hawin and port of the said burgh, be ane north eist wind and lekness of ane of thair said schippis. **1625** J. GLANVILL *Voy. Cadiz* 83 The leakness of his shipp.

leaky ('liːkɪ), *a.* [f. LEAK *sb.* + -Y[1].]

1. a. Having a leak or leaks; full of leaks; giving passage to water or other fluid through a hole or fissure.

1606 SHAKS. *Ant. & Cl.* III. xiii. 63 Sir, sir, thou art so leakie That we must leaue thee to thy sinking. **1610** —— *Temp.* I. i. 51. **1677** W. HUBBARD *Narrative* II. 67 He would not venture himself in our Leakie Canoo. **1732** BERKELEY *Alciphr.* II. §13 A leaky vessel, always filling and never full. **1791** W. JESSOPP *Rep. Riv. Witham* 15 Lining the Canal through the leaky Soil..450*l.* **1835** SIR J. ROSS *Narr. 2nd Voy.* ii. 11 The ship was so leaky as to require the constant use of two pumps. **1868** MORRIS *Earthly Par.* I. 98 We lay Leaky, dismasted, a most helpless prey To winds and waves. **1872** YEATS *Techn. Hist. Comm.* 141 Leaky casks. **1881** *Daily News* 10 Mar. 6/1 A leaky gas pipe.

b. Incontinent of urine; passing urine frequently or in large quantities.

1727 GAY *Begg. Op.* III. ii, The Dog is leaky in his Liquor. **1897** *Allbutt's Syst. Med.* III. 242 The patient..had never had an illness in his life, except that he had always been a 'leaky subject'. *Ibid.*, Such patients seem to drift imperceptibly into the 'leaky' state.

c. *fig.* Of persons, their tongues: Not reticent, blabbing. Of memory: Not retentive.

1692 R. L'ESTRANGE *Fables* ccccxxvii. 402 Women are generally so leaky, that..I have hardly met with one of the Sex that could not hold her Breath longer than she should keep a secret. **1703** QUICK *Dec. Wife's Sister* 18 Our Memories are exceeding feeble, leaky and forgetful. **1740** SOMERVILLE *Hobbinol* I. 242 But be thou, my Muse! No leaky Blab. **1805** *G. Rose's Diaries* (1860) I. 244 It is true he is leaky, but I believe would not willingly tell anything. **1845** H. ROGERS *Ess.* I. iii. 93 [It] must depend..on the doubtful authority, and leaky memory of those who report it.

d. *Electr.* Retaining electric charge only with gradual loss; connected to or having a high resistance that acts as a 'leak'; ***leaky-grid detection***, detection in which the signal is applied to the grid of a valve through a series capacitor and a resistor (the latter being connected as a grid leak or in parallel with the capacitor).

1904 A. RUSSELL *Treat. Theory Alternating Currents* I. xvii. 384 (*heading*) Inductive coil and leaky condenser. **1922** J. SCOTT-TAGGART *Wireless Vacuum Tubes* (ed. 4) iv. 89 Leaky grid condenser rectification. *Ibid.* vii. 132 If we employ a leaky grid condenser we can obtain a suitable negative grid potential without..a battery. *Ibid.* viii. 167 A leaky grid condenser may be connected in the grid circuit. **1934** *Jrnl. Inst. Electr. Engin.* LXXV. 298/2 Leaky-grid detection is used in this receiver. **1962** D. F. SHAW *Introd. Electronics* ii. 35 A leaky capacitor..in which the leakage resistance is represented by a shunt. **1968** *Radio Communication Handbk.* (ed. 4) ii. 17/1 Any d.c. voltage developed across the grid leak by the rectification of a modulated or an unmodulated signal will thus constitute a negative bias for the grid and the anode current in the triode will fall... An excessively strong signal will tend to bias the valve beyond the cut-off point, and therefore a leaky-grid detector ceases to function satisfactorily when the input voltage is too great. **1969** R. G. MIDDLETON *Transistor Television Servicing Guide* ix. 105/1 A leaky transistor, such as 22..increases in temperature.

e. Of persons: lachrymose. Also as *sb.*

1905 H. A. VACHELL *Hill* vii. 151 'I ain't the leaky sort,' she added fiercely, still gasping. **1959** I. & P. OPIE *Lore & Lang. Schoolch.* x. 187 Croydon boys have twenty names for a cry-baby:..leaky, [etc.].

2. *Genetics.* Of a mutant: producing the protein specified by the mutated gene in a form with reduced activity compared with that produced by the wild type. Of a protein so produced: having reduced activity. Cf. *hypomorphic* adj. (s.v. HYPO- II).

1955 *Proc. Nat. Acad. Sci.* XLI. 347 Under given conditions, however, the coefficient can be used as a comparative index of degree of phenotypic effect, a 'leaky' mutant having a high coefficient. **1959** *Ibid.* XLV. 204 This strain is a leaky derivative of strain 21863 [of *Neurospora crassa*]. **1961** *Nature* 30 Dec. 1227/2 Mutants produced by acridines are seldom 'leaky'; they are almost always completely lacking in the function of the gene. **1966** E. A. CARLSON *Gene* xiii. 112 The microbial geneticist today uses the term 'leaky mutant' for hypomorph. **1968** R. C. KING *Dict. Genetics* 141 *Leaky protein*, a mutant protein that has a subnormal degree of biological activity.

leaky, variant of LAKIE *Sc.*

leal (liːl), *a.* and *adv.* Forms: 3–5 lel, 3–6 lele, 4 liale, 4–5 lell(e, *Sc.* leile, leyll, 4–5 (7–8 *Sc.*) leel, 4–6 leale, 4–7 *Sc.* leill, 4–8 *Sc.* leil, 5 leell, 6 *Sc.* laill, 8– leal. [a. OF. *leel*, usually in semi-learned form *leial*, *leal* (= Pr. *leyal*, *lial*, Cat. *lleal*, Sp. *leal*, It. *leale*), mod.F. *loyal* (see LOYAL) :—L. *lēgāl-is* LEGAL.]

A. *adj.* Now *Sc.* (and *north. dial.*) and in literary use derived from Scottish.

1. Loyal, faithful, honest, true. **a.** Of persons, etc. ***land of the leal***: see LAND *sb.*[1] 3 c.

a **1300** *Cursor M.* 4891 Yon er theues we lelmen wend. *Ibid.* 27847 Lele of hert and fre of gyft. *c* **1350** *Will. Palerne* 4809 þe grettest lordes of þat land þat lellest were hold. **1375** BARBOUR *Bruce* IV. 576 He that worthy wes and leill. *a* **1400–50** *Alexander* 2877 Lede lelist to his lord leuand of lyue. *c* **1460** *Launfal* 326, I yeve the Blaunchard my stede lel. **1513** DOUGLAS *Æneis* I. Prol. 482 Thocht I be lawit, my leil hart can nocht fenȝe. *c* **1560** A. SCOTT *Poems* (S.T.S.) x. 28 Scho wat w[t]outtin faill I am hir luvar laill. **1609** SKENE *Reg. Maj.* 82 The eath of ellevin leill and vnsuspected men. **1721** RAMSAY *Prospect of Plenty* vi, Friendship makes us leal To truth and right. *a* **1776** *Cruel Mother* iii. in Child *Ballads* (1882) I. 220/2 She's counted the leelest maid o them a'. **1826** SCOTT *Jrnl.* 14 Nov., Honest Allan Cunningham..a leal and true Scotsman. *a* **1839** PRAED *Poems* (1864) I. 391 Leal subject, honest patriot, cordial friend. **1876** BLACKIE *Songs Relig. & Life* 119 Thou, Scotland's son, that wouldst be leal and true.

b. Of things, qualities, etc.

(In ME. poetry sometimes a more or less conventional laudatory epithet = 'noble', 'fair'.)

a **1300** *Cursor M.* 8294 For wit þat flur sa fress and neu, þair stode a selcut lele [*Fairf.* etc. lou(e)ly] heu. **13..** *Minor Poems fr. Vernon MS.* (E.E.T.S.) 498/204 þen maiȝt þou synge of loue lele. *c* **1350** *Parlt. thre Ages* (text A) 115 Longe legges and large and lele for to schewe. *c* **1375** *Sc. Leg. Saints* xxx. (*Theodera*) 154 Consele kane I kene þe gad & leile. **1393** LANGL. *P. Pl.* C. I. 146 With leel labour to lyue whyl lif and londe lasteth. *c* **1400** *Destr. Troy* 8800 [It] sanke..to the leell theghes, Passond by poris into þe pure legges. *c* **1475** *Rauf Coilȝear* 604 To se gif the Coilȝearis lawtie was leill. **1500–20** DUNBAR *Poems* lxvi. 13 The leill laubour lost, and leill seruice. *a* **1605** MONTGOMERIE *Sonn.* lxx. 2 Blind brutal Boy, that with thy bou abuses Leill leisome love by lechery and lust. **1721** RAMSAY *Katy's Answer* iv, There's my leal hand Win them, I'll be at your devotion. **1884** *Pall Mall G.* 25 Apr. 5/1 No man ever did more leal service than did Mackenzie during the bad days of the miserable Cabul business.

2. True, genuine; real, actual; exact, accurate; very (truth). Of a blow or shot: Well-aimed, hitting the mark. ? *Obs.*

a **1300** *Cursor M.* 6478 Ne ber þou witnes nan bot lele. *Ibid.* 7798, I come to tell þe tiþand lel. **13..** *Gaw. & Gr. Knt.* 35 þis laye..is stad and stoken, In stori stif & stronge With lel letteres loken. **13..** *E.E. Allit. P.* B. 425 Of þe lenþe of Noe lyf to lay a lel date, þe sex hundreth of his age & none odde ȝerez. *c* **1330** R. BRUNNE *Chron.* (1810) 69 þerof he mad me skrite, his hote to mak leale. **1393** LANGL. *P. Pl.* C. XI. 210 Men that buth bygetyn Out of matrimonie mowe nat haue the grace That leelle legitime by lawe may cleyme. *c* **1400** *Melayne* 8 The ryghte lele trouthe. **1560** ROLLAND *Crt. Venus* Prol. 35 The Planeitis..The quhilks are in leill number thir seuin. **1597** SKENE *De Verb. Sign.* s.v. *Bona patria*, We sall leill suith say, and na suith conceale. **1752** J. LOUTHIAN *Form of Process* (ed. 2) 83 The said Witnesses to bear leal and soothfast Witnessing. **1789** D. DAVIDSON *Seasons* 167 With that stepp'd forward Tullochfern, An'.. A leal shot ettled at the cock.

†**3.** Lawful; also, just, fair. *Obs.*

c **1350** *Will. Palerne* 1312 Whanne..alle lele lawes [were] in þat lond sette. **1352** MINOT *Poems* iii. 9 His mone that was gude and lele, Left in Braband full mekill dele. *c* **1375** *Sc. Leg. Saints* xl. (*Ninian*) 1050 Condemnyt be leile syse. *c* **1400** MAUNDEV. (Roxb.) viii. 28 Wheder þai be geten in leel spousage or noght. *c* **1425** WYNTOUN *Cron.* VII. x. 3186 Oure

Kyng Alysawndyr tuk Margret, The dowchtyr of this Kyng Henry, Into lele matrimony. *c* **1460** *Towneley Myst.* xxiv. 296 To draw cutt is the lelyst, and long cut, lo, this wede shall wyn. **1513** DOUGLAS *Æneis* III. viii. 81 Obseruyng weill ..the seremonyis lele. **1727** WALKER *Life Peden* 134 (Jam.), I have had my leal share of wrongs this way.

4. *Comb.*, as ***leal-hearted*** adj.

1721 RAMSAY *Prospect of Plenty* xi, The North Sea skippers are leal-hearted men. **1859** MASSON *Brit. Novelists* 107 The leal-hearted Scot's last visit to his native land.

B. *adv.* Now only *Sc.*

1. Loyally, faithfully.

a **1300** *Cursor M.* 6857, I..sal hald yow lel mi hight. *a* **1450** *Le Morte Arth.* 1066, I trewly many a day Haue lovid lelyest in londe. *c* **1450** HOLLAND *Howlat* 750 Luke to the leid that the so leile lufis. *a* **1605** MONTGOMERIE *Sonn.* xlv. 3 Look ony one before me loved so leill. **17..** in Herd *Sc. Songs* (1776) I. 160 Had me fast, let me not gang, If you do love me leel.

2. Honestly, lawfully. *Comb.* **leal-come** *adj.*, honestly come by.

a **1300** *Cursor M.* 4913 Of our lele bi-geten thing. **1500–20** DUNBAR *Poems* lxvi. 46 Bot beneficis ar nocht leill devydit. **1637** RUTHERFORD *Lett.* (1862) I. 443 Let us claim our leel-come and lawfully conquessed joy. **1693** *Sc. Presbyt. Eloquence* (1738) 98 Every Man hath Conversion and the New Birth, but it's not leel come by.

3. Truly, exactly, accurately; perfectly, thoroughly.

c **1400** *Destr. Troy* 3029 Nouþer lynes ne lerkes but full lell streght. *a* **1400–50** *Alexander* 5020 Sire, þou ert lele of ilk lede þe lorde and þe fadire. *c* **1460** *Towneley Myst.* iii. 446 This forty dayes has rayn beyn, It will therfor abate Fulle lele. **1513** DOUGLAS *Æneis* (*ad fin.*), Redis leill, and tak gud tent in tyme. **1637–50** ROW *Hist. Kirk* (Wodrow Soc.) 285 Therby giving Mr. Andro Melvill a faire opportunitie to light leill upon Bishop Bancroft. **1720** RAMSAY *Wealth* 51 The dawted petts of fate..By pure instinct sae leal the mark have hit. **1790** D. MORISON *Poems* 15 [She] swore she'd be ..Kiss'd leal frae lug to lug Fu' sweet that day.

†**leal**, *v. Obs. rare*$^{-1}$. In 4 lelen. [f. LEAL *a.*] *trans.* To legalize, authorize.

c **1350** *Will. Palerne* 5284 Whan..þe menskfull messangeres here message wisten & hade letteres of here lord to lelen here sawes.

leal, dial. form of LITTLE.

lea-land, lay-land (ˈliːlænd, ˈleɪlænd). Forms: 4 leylond, 5–6 leland(e, 5–9 ley-land, 7 lee-, 6– lay-land, 7– lea-land. [f. LEA *a.* + LAND *sb.*¹] Fallow land; land 'laid down' to grass.

c **1325** *Gloss. W. de Bibbesw.* in Wright *Voc.* 153/4 Le ffally lest sa tere freche [*glossed* leylond]. *c* **1460** *Towneley Myst.* xiii. 112 On a ley-land hard I hym blaw. he commys here at hand. **1553** *Short Catech. Liturgies*, etc. (1844) 525 The husbandmen, that first use to shrubbe and root out the thorns, brambles, and weeds, out of their lay-land and unlooked to. **1577–95** *Descr. Isles Scotl.* in Skene *Celtic Scotl.* III. App. 437 All teillit land, and na girs but ley land. **1671** *Shetland Document* in *Proc. Soc. Antiq. Scot.* (1892) XXVI. 194 To provyde laufull tennents for his Majesteis ley lands within the said Bailyerie. **1745** tr. *Columella's Husb.* II. ii, Smaller ploughs, which are not strong enough to rip up the fallow grounds or lay-lands. **1876** MORRIS *Sigurd* (1877) 314 They ride the lealand highways, they ride the desert plain. **1886** ELWORTHY *W. Somerset Word-bk.*, *Leylands*, arable land under a grass crop. The word is a very common name for pasture fields; to be found in the terriers of most estates. It will never be found in connection with meadow land proper, but it will usually denote land once arable but now 'laid' down.

Proverbial phrase. *c* **1500** *Payne & Sorowe Evyll Maryage* 140 in Hazl. *E.P.P.* IV. 79 Yf she than wyll be no better, Set her upon a lelande, and bydde the devyll fet her. **1599** PORTER *Angry Wom. Abingt.* (Percy Soc.) 103, I thinke she is better lost then found..and they would be ruld by me they should set her on the leland and bid the diuell split her. **1631** R. H. *Arraignm. Whole Creature* xiv. §1. 226 She..is now..abhorred..forsaken and disrespected..set on a Lea land as they say, and disrespected.

leally (ˈliːlɪ), *adv.* Forms: 4 lellik, -ich(e, -yche, leellich(e, leelly, lelli, leleli, lelyly, lelik, leeliche, leli, leyly, 4–5 lelly, lely, lele, 4–6 lelely, 5–6 lelle, -y, 6 leillellie, lelalie, lealie, leallelie, leily, 9 leally. [f. LEAL *a.* + -LY².]

1. Loyally, faithfully, truly.

a **1300** *Cursor M.* 1955 (Gött.) All þat wil leleli [*Cott.* lely; *Fairf.* lele] hald þair lede. *Ibid.* 3818 (Cott.) Of all þe god he dos me weild Lelik [*Gött.* lelely] his tend i sal him yeild. **13..** *E.E. Allit. P.* B. 1066 & lelly louy þy lorde & his leef worþe. *c* **1340** *Cursor M.* 22777 (Edin.) þai foluis lellik al his laues. *c* **1394** *P. Pl. Crede* 639 þat leeueþ fulliche on God & lellyche þenkeþ On his lore and his lawe. *c* **1400** *Destr. Troy* 3875 Was neuer kyng..lellier louyt ledys of his aune. *c* **1460** *Towneley Myst.* xviii. 182 Thise ar the commaundmentys ten, who so will lely layt. *a* **1578** LINDESAY (Pitscottie) *Chron. Scot.* (S.T.S.) I. 21 [He] sould stand his freind leillellie and trewlie. **1588** in Beveridge *Culross & Tulliallan* I. iv. 125 They suld use the offices faythfullie and lealie till all persones. **1597** SKENE *De Verb. Sign.* s.v. *Iter*, The dempster..sall leallelie and trewlie, vse and exerce his office. **1773** FERGUSSON *Poems* (1807) 304 Sae lealy I'll propone defences, As yet ye flung for my expences. **1837** R. NICOLL *Poems* (1843) 123 The men..Who by Scotland, my country, stood leally and true.

†2. Truly, really, actually. *Obs.*

c **1350** *Will. Palerne* 95 þere walked he a-boute þe walles to winne in siȝt; & at þe last lelly a litel hole he findes. *Ibid.* 117 But lelliche þat ladi in ȝouþe hadde lerned miche schame. **1377** LANGL. *P. Pl.* B. XII. 174 He that knoweth clergye can sonner aryse Out of synne..than any lewed lelly [C. xv. 113 sothliche]. *a* **1400** *Relig. Pieces fr. Thornton MS.* (1867) 30 For þat oure saule es lelly lyke vn-till þe lyknes of þe ffadyr, and þe Sone, and þe Haly Gaste. *c* **1475** *Rauf Coilȝear* 313 Tell me now lelely quhat is thy richt name.

lealness (ˈliːlnɪs). *rare*$^{-0}$. [f. LEAL *a.* + -NESS.] = LEALTY¹.

1882 in OGILVIE.

lealty¹ (ˈliːəltɪ). *Obs.* exc. *arch.* [f. LEAL *a.* + -TY. Cf. LEWTY, LOYALTY.] Faithfulness, loyalty.

[*a* **1310** in Wright *Lyric P.* xvi. 53 Heo is solsecle of suetnesse, ant ledy of lealte.] **1860** READE *Cloister & H.* (1861) I. 270 They who travel should learn to read faces; methinks you might see lealty in mine sith I have seen it in yourn. **1867** LADY G. FULLERTON *A stormy Life* III. ii. 28 As to lealty and gratitude, she showeth herself as ignorant of these sentiments as if they did not exist.

†**lealty**². *Obs. rare.* [f. *le* LAY *a.*¹ + -AL¹ + -TY (after *spiritualty*, etc.).] Laity.

1548 GEST *Pr. Masse* E iij b, So doo all Christianes & the faythfull lealtye performe yᵉ same.

leam (liːm), *sb.*¹ Now *Sc.* and *north. dial.* Forms: 1 léoma, 2 lome, 3–4 leome, lem, 3–6 (9) leme, (4 leom, lewme, lime, lym, *Sc.* leyme), 4–5 leem, (5 leeme, *Sc.* leime), 4, 6–7 leame, 6– leam. [OE. *léoma* str. masc. = OS. *liomo*, ON. *ljóme*:—OTeut. **leuhmon-*, f. **leuh-* (see LIGHT *sb.*).] Light, flame; a flash, ray, or gleam of light; brightness, gleam. Also *fig.*

Beowulf 1517 (Gr.) Fyrleoht ȝeseah, blacne leoman beorhte scinan. *c* **1175** *Lamb. Hom.* 77 He him alse þe sunne streonþ þe lome þet ho spret in to al þis wide worlde. *c* **1200** *Trin. Coll. Hom.* 107 Leomene fader we clepeð ure drihten for þan þe he sunne atend. *a* **1240** *Ureisun* in *Cott. Hom.* 183 Ihesu mi leof, mi lif, mi leome. **1297** R. GLOUC. (Rolls) 3180 Out of þe dragons mouþe tueye leomes þer stode þere. *a* **1300** *Cursor M.* 17344 Ne nankins leme [*Fairf.* lym] o dais light. **1375** BARBOUR *Bruce* XI. 191 All the felde ves in ane leyme Vith baneris richt freschly flawmand. *c* **1380** *Sir Ferumb.* 1861 Were þou he by þys leem sone þow scholdest dye. **1387** TREVISA *Higden* (Rolls) VII. 279 Of þe welle of þat place he hadde þe leme of byleve [L. *credendi flammam*]. **1388** WYCLIF *Bible, Pref. Ep.* vi, Now newe kyn cometh fre, from an hiȝ, fro heuinli lewmes. *c* **1400** *St. Alexius* (Laud 463) 439 Out of his mouþ þer stoed a leom. **1450–70** *Golagros & Gaw.* 1254 With grete lightis on loft, that gaif grete leime. *c* **1450** *Mirour Saluacioun* 1096 A sterne of fulle grete leeme. **1503** DUNBAR *Thistle & Rose* 21 All the houss illumynit of hir lemys. **1531** ELYOT *Gov.* I. i, A bright leme of a torche. **1576** FLEMING *Panopl. Epist.* 172 Glorious with the leames of learning. **1600** HOLLAND *Livy* XL. lviii. 1094 Blasted with leames of lightning that dazzeled their eie-sight. **1668** WILKINS *Real Char.* II. iii. §1. 57 Flame, Blaze, Coruscation, Flash, Leam, Lightfire. **1724** RAMSAY *Wyfe of Auchtermuchty* x, The leam up throu the lum did flow. **1813** HOGG *Queen's Wake, Kilmeny* (1814) 172 When the ingle lowed with an eiry leme. **1895** CROCKETT *Men of Moss Hags* 160 The flickering leme of pale lightning.

leam (liːm), *sb.*² *dial.* A drain or watercourse in fen districts.

1601 F. GODWIN *Bps. of Eng.* 221 Ye new leame that he [Bp. Morton] caused to be made for more conuenient cariage to his towne..many complaine that the course of the riuer Nene into the sea by Clowcrosse is very much hindred thereby. **1646** BUCK *Rich. III*, 53 Doctor Morton for his private commodity..brought certain Leames or bigger ditches to his owne grounds about Wisbitch. **1861** SMILES *Engineers* I. 67 Many droves, leams, eaus, and drains were cut. **1881** *Times* 13 Jan. 9/4 The existing 'cuts' or 'leams' cease to fulfil their functions..by a gradual alteration in their own beds.

leam, *sb.*³ *dial.* Also **limb**. The husk of a nut.

1854 MISS BAKER *Northamptonsh. Gloss.* s.v., 'Will you buy them in, or out of the limbs' is a frequent inquiry in our nut-market. *Mod.* (Northants.) The boy stained his fingers with walnut leams.

leam (liːm), *v.*¹ Now *Sc.* and *north. dial.* Forms: 3– as in LEAM *sb.*¹: also 4 lume. [f. the sb. Cf. ON. *ljóma*, also OE. *ȝeléomod* having rays (of a comet), *Saxon Leechd.* III. 272.] *intr.* To shine, gleam; to light *up*.

a **1300** *Cursor M.* 8197 On þe morn, quen dai suld lem. *c* **1310** in Wright *Lyric P.* 25 Ase jaspe the gentil that lemeth with lyht. *Ibid.* 52 Hire lure lumes liht, Ase a launterne a nyht. *c* **1330** *King of Tars* 162 Alle the feldes feor and neer Of helmes leomede lihte. *c* **1400** *Destr. Troy* 699 A triet Image..of true golde..With light that was louely lemyng þer-in. *c* **1420** *Avow. Arth.* lxv, There come fliand a gunne, And lemet as the leuyn. *c* **1475** *Rauf Coilȝear* 326 The lyft lemit vp beliue, and licht was the day. **1535** STEWART *Cron. Scot.* (1858) III. 232 With birneis bricht, Lyke ony lanterne lemit all of licht. **1575** *Mirr. Mag.*, *Elstride* xxxv, And when she spake, her eyes did leame as fire. **17..** *Dame Oliphant* xxiv. in Child *Ballads* (1886) II. 410/1 He carried the match in his pocket That kindled to her the fire..That leamd oer Lincolnshire. **1768** ROSS *Helenore* (1789) 55 Now by this time, the sun begins to leam. *a* **1878** H. AINSLIE *Pilgrim. Land of Burns*, etc. (1892) 240 There leem'd a light frae yon high tower.

leam, *v.*² *dial.* Also 8 **leem**. [Belongs to LEAM *sb.*³] **a.** *trans.* To free nuts from their husks.

1788 W. MARSHALL *Yorksh.* II. 339 *Leem.* **1824** MACTAGGART *Gallovid. Encycl.* s.v. *Benjie*, The wud sae gay, whar mony a day I leamed nits wi' thee. *Mod.* (*Northants*). He has been leaming walnuts for the gardener.

b. *intr.* Of nuts: To separate easily from the husk.

1846 BROCKETT *N.C Words*, It leams well.

leam, obs. var. LYAM; Sc. form of LOAM.

†**leamer**¹. *Obs. rare*$^{-1}$. In 5 lemer. [f. LEAM *v.*¹ + -ER¹.] One that flashes or radiates light.

c **1440** *York Myst.* xiv. 111 Hayle, my lorde, lemer of light.

ˈ**leamer**². *dial.* [f. LEAM *sb.*³ or *v.*² + -ER¹.] A nut fully ripe. Chiefly in ***brown leamer***, a nut with a brown husk.

1832 J. WILSON in *Blackw. Mag.* XXXII. 126 Clusters of ripe nuts, which you can crack when you have gathered them, brown leamers every one. **1836** GARNETT in *Q. Rev.* Feb., *Leemers*, a north-country phrase for ripe nuts. **1855** ROBINSON *Whitby Gloss.*, *Leamers*, or 'brown leamers' large filbert nuts.

leamer, variant of LIMER, a hound.

ˈ**leaming**, *vbl. sb. Obs.* exc. *dial.* [f. LEAM *v.*¹ + -ING¹.] Shining, gleaming, flashing (of light).

1387 TREVISA *Higden* (Rolls) VII. 171 Thunder lemynge brend þe cornes. **1398** —— *Barth. De P.R.* VIII. xvi. (1495) 324 The sonne hath vertue of heetynge of leemynge and of brennynge. *c* **1440** *Promp. Parv.* 198/2 Glemynge, or lemynge of lyghte, *conflagracio.*

ˈ**leaming**, *ppl. a. Obs.* exc. *dial.* [f. LEAM *v.*¹ + -ING².] Gleaming, flashing, shining.

a **1300** *Cursor M.* 5754 þan cald on him our lauerd dright, Vt of his mikel lemand light. **1387** TREVISA *Higden* (Rolls) VII. 447 A sterre wiþ a briȝt lemynge creest. *c* **1400** *Destr. Troy* 12517 The breme lowe Of the leymonde laite. **1513** DOUGLAS *Æneis* II. xii. (xi.) 90 Lemand armour and schynand scheildis brycht. **1567** DRANT *Horace's Ep.* xvi. E viij, A leminge lampe of light. **1611** COTGR., *Radieux*, radiant, shining..leaming, full of beams. **17..** *Jolly Goshawk* xxxiii. in Child *Ballads* (1886) II. 361/2 With lily-white cheeks, and lemin een. **1839** BAILEY *Festus* vi. (1848) 60 Like a shipwrecked stranger in a lighthouse, I have looked down upon the utter side Of such thoughts from the leeming room of reason.

†**lean**, *sb.*¹ *Obs.* Forms: 1 léan, 2–3 lean, lan, 3 læn, len, lyen. [OE. *léan* str. neut. = OFris. *lân*, OS., OHG., MHG. *lôn* (Du. *loon*, mod.G. *lohn* masc.), ON. *laun* neut. pl. (Sw. *lön*, Da. *løn*), Goth. *laun* neut.:—OTeut. **laun-*. The root *lau-* is referred to the same source as OSlav. *lovŭ* capture, booty, L. *lū-crum* gain, Gr. *ἀπο-λαύ-ειν* to enjoy.] Reward, recompense.

Beowulf 1021 (Gr.) Siȝores to leane. *c* **1000** *Ags. Gosp.* Matt. xix. 29 Be hundfealdon he onfehþ lean & hæfð ece lif. *a* **1200** *Moral Ode* 64 þer me scal..ȝeuen us ure swinkes lan [**12..** in *O.E. Misc.* 60 lean; *a* **1300** in *E.E.P.* 24 lyen] efter ure erninge. *c* **1200** ORMIN 1518 ȝiff þu shæwesst hemm whatt læn Iss ȝarrkedd hemm inn heoffne. *c* **1205** LAY. 16691 Nu þu scalt fon þat læn þæt þu for-ferdest Jerusalem. *a* **1250** *Prov. Ælfred* 407 in *O.E. Misc.*, þe mon þat her wel deþ he cumeþ þar he lyen foþ. *c* **1250** *Gen. & Ex.* 2838 Pharaun..Was dead and hadde is werkes len.

lean, *sb.*²: see after LEAN *a.*

lean (liːn), *sb.*³ [f. LEAN *v.*]

1. The act or condition of leaning; inclination. ***on the lean***: inclining, sloping.

1776 G. SEMPLE *Building in Water* 73 Pressure from either Side, would give them all a lean to the opposite Side. **1850** P. CUNNINGHAM *Handbk. Lond.* p. xxxvii/1 Leaden coffins piled thirty-feet high, and all on the lean from their own immense weight. **1851** *Jrnl. R. Agric. Soc.* XII. II. 647 The corn has a decided lean in one direction. **1890** CLARK RUSSELL *Ocean Trag.* I. v. 106 The rounds of her canvas whitened into marble hardness with the yearn and lean of the distended cloths.

†2. *concr.* Something to lean on; a support.

1610 HEALEY tr. *Vives' St. Aug. Citie of God* Ded. A, How holy..a man, what a light, what a leane to the christian common-wealth [L. *quale specimen columenque reip. Christianæ*], on whom onely it rested for many yeares.

lean (liːn), *a.* and *sb.*² Forms: 1 **hlǽne**, 2–6 **lene**, 3 **læne**, 3, 6–7 **leane**, 4 *Kent.* **hlene**, *Sc.* **leine**, **leyne**, 5 **leen(e**, 5–6 *Sc.* and *north.* **leyn**, 6– **lean**. [OE. *hlǽne*:—OTeut. type **hlainjo-*, perh. repr. a pre-Teut. **qloinio-*, related by ablaut to Lith. *klýnas* scrap, fragment, Lettish *kleins* feeble. (If so, the word is not related to LEAN *v.*, the pre-Teut. initial of which is *k*, not *q*.)]

A. *adj.* 1. a. Wanting in flesh; not plump or fat; thin. Also said †of the flesh, and of a person's condition, growth, appearance, etc.

c **1000** ÆLFRIC *Gen.* xli. 3 Oðre seofon oxan..þa wæron fule and swiðe hlæne. *c* **1175** *Lamb. Hom.* 37 þu scalt.. festen swa þet þin licome beo þe lenre. *c* **1205** LAY. 19445 No durste þær bilæuen na þæ uatte no þe læne. *a* **1225** *Ancr. R.* 118 Pellican is a leane fowel. *c* **1290** *S. Eng. Leg.* I. 66/435 His lene bones he wolde drawe aȝein þe harde grounde. **1340** *Ayenb.* 53þou sselt ueste al huet þou art bleche and lhene. **1377** LANGL. *P. Pl.* B. v. 83 So loked he with lene chekes lowrynge foule. *c* **1460** *Towneley Myst.* ii. 112 My wynnyngis ar bot meyn, No wonder if that I be leyn. **1513** DOUGLAS *Æneis* XII. iv. 159 Wyth chekis walxin leyn. **1601** SHAKS. *Jul. C.* I. ii. 194 Yond Cassius has a leane and hungry looke, He thinkes too much. **1774** GOLDSM. *Nat. Hist.* (1776) III. 131 Their heads are small and lean, their ears little. **1784** COWPER *Tiroc.* 656 The mere school-boy's lean and tardy growth. **1844** DICKENS *Mart. Chuz.* liv, She had a lean lank body. **1855** MACAULAY *Hist. Eng.* xii. III. 233 Nine horses were still alive..They were so lean that little meat was likely to be found upon them. **1885** *Manch. Exam.* 17 Mar. 5/2 The beet-growers find a profitable trade in fatting lean stock brought into the country.

b. with personifications.

1591 SHAKS. *1 Hen. VI*, IV. ii. 11 My three attendants, Leane Famine, quartering Steele, and climbing Fire. **1634** MILTON *Comus* 709 Praising the lean and sallow Abstinence. **1835** LYTTON *Rienzi* I. viii, Lean fears and hollow-eyed suspicions are the comrades of a hated power. **1840** DICKENS *Old C. Shop* lxv, The great manufacturing town reeking with lean misery and hungry wretchedness.

c. Proverbial phrases.

c **1386** CHAUCER *C.T.* Prol. 287 And leene was his hors as is a rake. **1588** SHAKS. *L.L.L.* I. i. 26 Fat paunches haue leane pates. **1611** COTGR., s.v. *Maigret, Maigres comme pies*, as leane as Rakes (we say). *a* **1732** GAY *New Song on New Similies* Songs, etc. 1784 II. 115 Lean as a rake with sighs and care.

d. *transf.*

1578 LYTE *Dodoens* III. lxix. 410 Trichomanes..hath the stalkes of his leaves very small and leane. **1588** SHAKS. *Tit. A.* II. iii. 94 The Trees, though Sommer, yet forlorne and leane. **1596** —— *Merch. V.* II. vi. 19 With ouer-wither'd ribs and ragged sailes, Leane, rent, and begger'd by the strumpet winde. **1606** *Sir G. Goosecappe* I. i. in Bullen *O. Pl.* III. 7 Theis two strange hungry knights [will] make the leanest trenchers that ever I waited on. **1693** C. DRYDEN in *Dryden's Juvenal* vii. (1697) 169 The lean Statue of a starv'd Renown. **1772** T. SIMPSON *Vermin-Killer* 18 The ears of the corn will be withered and lean. **1871** ROSSETTI *Poems, Even so* iii, The sea..Where the lean black craft Seem well-nigh stagnated.

e. *Shipbuilding.* = CLEAN *a.* 10 b; 'sharp': opposed to *bluff*.

1769 FALCONER *Dict. Marine* (1780) G 3, The former of these is called by seamen a *lean*, and the latter a *bluff* bow. **1874** THEARLE *Naval Archit.* 17 The lean or acute portions of the bow and stern of the ship between the extremities and the line of the inside of the timbers.

2. *fig.* Poor or meagre in quantity or quality; slight, mean. Somewhat *arch.* Of diet: Poor, innutritious. Of employment (*colloq.*): Unremunerative.

c **1325** *Poem times Edw. II* (Percy) xliii, He wild..gyf the god man to drink Lene broth that is nowȝt. *c* **1400** *Pride of Life* (Brandl 1898) 395 þing..yat þou art lenust man..& euirmor hau þout opon þi dredful ending. *a* **1420** HOCCLEVE *Let. Cupid* 407 Her heped vertu hath swich excellence That al to lene is mannes facultee To declare it. **1581** MULCASTER *Positions* xli. (1887) 250 The liuings in colledges be now to to leane. **1594** T. B. *La Primaud. Fr. Acad.* II. 561 As for that consolation [against death]..it is very leane if there be no other. **1601** SHAKS. *Twel. N.* III. iv. 378 Out of my leane and low ability Ile lend you something. **1637** MILTON *Lycidas* 123 Their lean and flashy songs Grate on their scrannel Pipes of wretched straw. **1744–50** W. ELLIS *Mod. Husbandm.* II. 5 That would..cause the Farmer a lean crop, instead of a fat one, as the usual terms are. **1784** COWPER *Task* VI. 905 With lean performance ape the work of love. **1850** PRESCOTT *Peru* II. 316 Their miserable carcases furnished a lean banquet for the famishing travellers. **1875** *Sussex Gloss.*, s.v., 'Ah sir! stone-breaking's a lean job for those that ain't used to it.' **1890** F. M. CRAWFORD *Cigarette-maker's Rom.* iv, An exceedingly lean diet.

3. Of flesh: Containing little or no fat (as distinguished from muscular tissue).

c **1430** *Two Cookery-bks.* 28 Take lene Porke, and boyle it. **1496** *Fysshynge w. angle* (1883) 33 Lene flesshe of the hepis of a cony or of a catte. **1744** ARMSTRONG *Art Pres. Health* II. (1797) 25 Chuse leaner viands. **1747** MRS. GLASSE *Cookery* iv. 59 Then cut the lean Meat off the Legs into Dice. **1837** M. DONOVAN *Dom. Econ.* II. 61 The flesh of monkeys is so lean and dry, that [etc.]. **1845** BUDD *Dis. Liver* 244 If he will ..live chiefly on lean meat..and drink water.

4. Wanting in rich elements or qualities. Said, e.g. of soils, limestone, †water, etc. Now *rare* except in various techn. senses, as: **a.** Of mortar or concrete: containing little of the binding material. **b.** Of clay: not very plastic. **c.** Of coal: of poor quality, *spec.* deficient in volatile material. **d.** Of ore: of low grade; containing little valuable mineral. **e.** Of fuel gas: of low calorific value. **f.** Of the mixture in an internal-combustion engine: containing a low proportion of fuel. **g.** Of an emulsion, painted surface, etc.: containing little oil.

c **1375** *Sc. Leg. Saints* xxvii. (*Machor*) 987 He..gert teill a mekill feild of land..It was leyne & dry. *c* **1420** *Pallad. on Husb.* v. 6 Hit dongeth londes lene, & beestes lorn ffor lene hit fedeth vp. **1523** FITZHERB. *Husb.* §20 Hawdod..groweth comonly in rye vpon leane grounde. *a* **1592** GREENE *Jas. IV*, v. i, Lands are leane where riuers do not runne. **1683** TRYON *Way to Health* vi. (1697) 104 Such Springs..are of a lean Saturnine Quality. **1684** T. BURNET *Theory Earth* I. v. 55 Seeing there are two chief kinds of Terrestrial liquors, those that are fat, oily, and light; and those that are lean and more Earthy, like common Water. **1686** PLOT *Staffordsh.* 356 Esteemed but a lean hard water. **1697** DRYDEN *Virg. Georg.* II. 293 The coarse lean Gravel, on the Mountain sides, Scarce dewy Bev'rage for the Bees provides. **1703** MOXON *Mech. Exerc.* 241 Lime..made of greasy clammy Stone, is stronger than that made of lean poor Stone. **1781** COWPER *Truth* 364 As leanest land supplies the richest wine. *a* **1817** T. DWIGHT *Trav. New Eng.* etc. (1821) II. 358 We rode through a country rough, lean, and solitary. **1899** H. SUTCLIFFE *By Moor & Fell* i. 4 Above the houses a few lean fields slope up to the heather-line.

a. 1726 J. LEONI tr. *Alberti's Archit.* I. 49/1 For small Stones, a thick lean Mortar is best; to a dry exhausted Stone, we should use a fat sort; tho' the Ancients were of the opinion that in all parts of the Walls the fattish sort is more tenacious than the lean. **1936** *Times Lit. Suppl.* 18 Apr. 325/4 Very rich concrete, one part cement with two-and-a-half sand and gravel (concrete so rich is seldom used), is hardly affected at all by sea water... But 'lean' concrete, one part cement to about ten of sand, gravel, or even pozzolani, disintegrates in a year. **1965** *Economist* 13 Nov. 745/3 Outside mining subsidence areas, one of the lower layers [in construction of 'black-top' roads] is often 'lean' (with little cement) concrete.

b. 1754 *New & Compl. Dict. Arts & Sci.* III. 2128/1 Mortar for furnaces, &c. is made with red clay wrought in water in which horse-dung and chimney-soot has been steeped..; this clay ought not to be too fat, lest it should be subject to crack; nor too lean and sandy, lest it should not bind enough. **1885** *Encycl. Brit.* XIX. 600/2 'Lean' clays —those that have a large proportion of free silica— shrink but little, and keep their form unaltered under the heat of the kiln. **1964** H. HODGES *Artifacts* i. 20 Such clays are sticky or greasy..and shrink seriously on drying... Equally a clay may be too aplastic to work, the material being crumbly, also known as short, mealy, lean, or open.

c. 1883 W. S. GRESLEY *Gloss. Terms Coal Mining* 154 *Lean*, thin, poor; of inferior quality. **1960** *Gloss. Coal Terms* (*B.S.I.*) 9 *Lean coal*, term used in several European countries for coal with a low volatile matter.

d. 1901 *Daily Colonist* (Victoria, B.C.) 20 Oct. 10/3 There are..rumors..that lean ore has been struck in the lower workings. **1965** G. J. WILLIAMS *Econ. Geol. N.Z.* v. 57/1 Yields [of gold] ranging up to 0·75 oz. were reported but most of the quartz is very lean.

e. 1924 *Jrnl. Inst. Petroleum Technologists* X. 804 In handling lean [natural] gases of this type large through-puts are necessary if the operation of extraction is to be profitable. **1960** *Economist* 15 Oct. 271/3 A national high-pressure grid supplying industry direct and local systems with lean gas for enrichment to town gas.

f. 1932 F. J. CAMM *Bk. Motors* xxxii. 253 Misfiring may be due to incorrect petrol supply, too 'lean' or weak a mixture or an occasional short circuit. **1949** FRAZEE & BEDELL *Automotive Fundamentals* iii. 174 Too low a float level results in a slightly leaner mixture as too little fuel will leave the jets. **1973** *Physics Bull.* Apr. 241/2 The cvcc engine.. was designed with pollution control in mind. It operates on extremely lean air-fuel mixture from the carburettor which is varied according to the operating conditions.

g. 1934 H. HILER *Notes Technique Painting* iii. 171 The emulsions made from yolk of egg, some gum or resin, linseed oil and sometimes a little wax, are intimate mechanical but not chemical compounds... When egg-yolk is used..a somewhat yellowish tinted 'fat emulsion' results. If gum arabic is used, the result is a whitish 'lean emulsion'. **1961** M. LEVY *Studio Dict. Art Terms* 66 *Lean Surface*, the matt surface of a layer of pigment containing a minimum of oil. It is essential that an underpainting which is to be glazed should possess a lean surface. **1967** J. N. BARRON *Lang. of Painting* 75 For obtaining better permanence in paintings.. the overlying or upper layers of paint are to be increasingly more 'fatty' and contain more oil than the layers they cover, or the 'leaner' ones.

5. a. Scantily furnished, ill provided. †Also, scant *of*, wanting *in*.

a **1340** HAMPOLE *Psalter* xxi. 32 My saule, þat is lene of couaitis & riches. **1552** T. BARNABE in Ellis *Orig. Lett.* Ser. II. II. 200 The cuntry of Kent..is veryе lene of men by the see syde. **1596** SHAKS. *1 Hen IV*, I. ii. 82 Yea, for obtaining of suites, whereof the Hangman hath no leane Wardrobe. **1623** *St. Papers Col.* 1622–4. 183 Cash is very lene. **1652** WADSWORTH tr. *Sandoval's Civil Wars Sp.* 69 Leaving the Countrie lean, poor, and dismantled of all it's fruits and wealth. **1654** tr. *Martini's Conq. China* 69 That Province which used to be most plentifull, was lean in Corn. **1677** YARRANTON *Eng. Improv.* 28 Scotland is a thin and lean Kingdom, and wanting in these things. **1784** COWPER *Task* II. 615 Dress drains our cellar dry, And keeps our larder lean. **1878** B. TAYLOR *Deukalion* I. iv. 37 My purse is lean, so rarely comes an obolus.

b. Of seasons, etc.: Characterized by scarcity.

1670 DRYDEN *1st Pt. Conq. Granada* I. i. (1672) 5 Lean times and foreign Warrs should minds unite. **1890** *Spectator* 5 Apr., Sir J. Lubbock..evidently believes that the cycle of lean years has fairly passed.

6. *Printing.* In various uses. (See quots.)

1676 MOXON *Print Lett.* 7 *Lean strokes* are the narrow strokes in a Letter, as the Left Hand stroke in Letter A, and the Right Hand stroke in V, are *Lean*. **1683** —— *Mech. Exerc., Printing* 369 *Beat Lean*, is to Take but little Inck, and often: all Small Letter must be Beaten Lean. *Ibid.* 383 *Lean Ashes*, Founders call their Ashes Lean, if they are Light; because then they have little Mettle in them. *Lean Face*, a Letter whose stems and other Stroaks have not their full width. **1841** W. SAVAGE *Dict. Printing, Lean Face*..As now understood, a letter of slender proportions compared to its height. [Cf. *lean-faced* in 7.] **1871** *Amer. Encycl. Printing* (ed. Ringwalt), *Lean work*, the opposite of fat work—that is, poor unprofitable work.

7. *Comb.* chiefly parasynthetic, as ***lean-chapt, -cheeked, -eared, -faced, -fleshed, -horned, -jawed, -looked, -looking, -minded, -necked, -ribbed, -souled, -visaged, -witted*** adjs.; †**lean-kinded** *a.*, belonging to the lean kind.

1621 QUARLES *Argalus & P.* (1678) 25 From whom, What *lean-chapt Fury did I snatch thee from? **1812** W. TENNANT *Auster F.* II. lii, *Lean-cheek'd tetchy critics. **1602** *2nd Pt. Return fr. Parnass.* v. iv. 2232 His long *leane eard lugges. **1590** SHAKS. *Com. Err.* v. i. 237 A hungry *leane fac'd Villaine. **1855** OGILVIE Suppl. *Lean-faced*.., Among printers, applied to letters which have not their full breadth. **1892** W. B. YEATS *Countess Kathleen* ii. 34 A crowd of ugly lean-faced rogues. **1953** R. S. THOMAS *Minister* 13 By a lean-faced people in black clothes. **1535** COVERDALE *Gen.* xli. 3 Other seuen kyne..which were euell fauoured and *leane fleshed. **1648** HERRICK *Hesper., Parting Verses to Wife* (1869) 188 Not many full-fac't moons shall waine, *Lean-horn'd, before [etc.]. **1678** DRYDEN & LEE *Œdipus* IV. i, *Lean-jawed famine. **1601** J. HARRINGTON *Let.* in *Nugæ Antiq.* (1779) II. 64 Many *lean kinded beastes and some not unhorned. **1593** SHAKS. *Rich. II*, II. iv. 11 And *leane-look'd Prophets whisper fearefull change. **1748** W. HAMILTON *Ode to Fancy*, In Merits lean look'd form t' appear. **1713** ROWE *Jane Shore* I. ii. 9 *Lean-looking sallow Care. **1866** CARLYLE *Remin.* I. 82 A *lean-minded controversial spirit. **1608** ARMIN *Nest Ninn.* 33 The *leane-neckt crane, who had the fat foxe to dinner. **1602** MARSTON *Antonio's Revenge* IV. i. sig. G1v, Whilst pale cheekt wisdome, and *leane ribd arte Are kept in distance at the halberts point. *a* **1845** HOOD *Lamia* vii. 82 Lean-ribbed tigers. **1925** E., O., & S. SITWELL *Poor Young People* 7 Neptune beat his lean-ribbed ass The braying sea uphill. **1638** FORD *Lady's Trial* III. i, Poor *lean-soul'd rogues. **1686** *Lond. Gaz.* No. 2159/4 He is pretty tall, black hair, *lean-visag'd. **1593** SHAKS. *Rich. II*, II. i. 115 A lunatike *leane-witted foole.

B. *sb.*

1. a. The lean part of anything; lean meat.

c **1450** *ME. Med. Bk.* (Heinrich) 121 [T]ake a peece of salt beof, þe lene, & noon of þe fat. **1598** *Epulario* C ij b, Take the leane of a legge of Veale. **16..** in *Wood's Life* (O.H.S.) II. 6 *note*, Some fat to my leane, John Haywood, I say some fat to my leane. **1670** RAY *Prov.* 211 Jack Sprat he loved no fat, and his wife she lov'd no lean: And yet betwixt them both, they lick't the platters clean. **1771** GOLDSM. *Haunch of Venison* 4 The fat was so white and the lean was so ruddy. **1774** —— *Nat. Hist.* (1776) VI. 210 The lean, which they boil, is, in his opinion not inferior to beef. **1848** *Chambers's Inform. People* I. 730/1 The lean of bacon is rendered more difficult of digestion by the same process.

b. The flesh adhering to the blubber of a whale.

1887 [see LEAN *v.*[3]]. **1888** W. T. BRANNT *Anim. & Veg. Fats & Oils* 297 Any flesh, termed lean or fat lean, that may adhere to the horse pieces is cut off.

2. *Printing.* †**a.** A thin part or stroke of a letter. **b.** 'Among printers, ill-paid work' (Ogilvie, 1882). Cf. FAT *sb.* 5 b.

1683 MOXON *Mech. Exerc., Printing* ii. 92 V. Dijcks Pearl Dutch Letters..bear such true proportion..for the Thickness, Shape, Fats and Leans, as if with Compasses he could have measur'd..every particular Member.

lean (liːn), *v.*[1] Pa. t. and pa. pple. **leaned** (liːnd), **leant** (lɛnt). Forms: 1 **hleonian, hlinian,** *Northumb.* **(h)lin-, (h)lioniȝa,** 3 **hlonen, leanen, leonien,** 2–6 **lene,** 4 **leone, leny(e, len,** 4–5 **lyne,** 5 **leene, le(y)nyn,** 5–7 *Sc.* and *north.* **lein(e, leyn(e,** 6–7 **leane,** 6– **lean.** *Pa. t.* α. 1 **hleonede, hlinode,** *Northumb.* **hlionade, -ede,** 3 **lende,** 2–4 **lened(e,** 4 **leonede, lynede,** 4–6 *Sc.* **lenyt, -it,** 6–7 *Sc.* **leynit,** 6– **leaned.** β. 5 **lente,** 5–7 **lente,** 8 *Sc.* **leint,** 8– **leant.** *Pa. pple.* 1 *Northumb.* **ȝehlionad,** 3–4 **lened;** from 14th c. onwards as in pa. t. [ME. *lēnen*:—OE. *hleonian, hlinian*, corresponding to OFris. *lena* (cf. *hlenbed* sick-bed), OS. *hlinôn* (MDu. *lēnen*, Du. *leunen*), OHG. *(h)linên* (MHG. *linen, lenen*, mod.G. *lehnen*, whence Da. *læne* refl.), f. Teut. root **hlī-* (ablaut- var. of **hlai-*: see LADDER):—OAryan **klī-* represented in Gr. κλῖμαξ ladder, L. *clīvus* declivity, etc., Skr. *çri* to lean; the formation of the Teut. vb., with *n* suffix orig. belonging to the pres.-stem, is paralleled in Gr. κλίνειν to make to slope, L. *inclīnāre* to INCLINE.

OE. had a causative *hlǣnan* to make to lean (occurring only once as simple vb. and once in each of the compounds *up-āhlǣnan* and *bihlǣnan*), corresponding to MDu. *leinen*, OHG. *hleinen* (MHG. *leinen*):—WGer. **hlainjan.* If this verb survived into ME., it would assume the form *lēnen*, thus coalescing with *hleonian*. Whether the mod. vb. actually descends from both the OE. vbs. is doubtful, but in view of the rare occurrence of *hlǣnan* in OE. it seems more probable that only *hleonian* has come down; the development of transitive senses presents no difficulty.]

1. a. *intr.* To recline, lie down, rest. *Obs.* exc. *Sc.* in reflexive construction. †Formerly conjugated with the verb *to be*.

c **950** *Lindisf. Gosp.* Mark ii. 15 Moniȝo bærsuniȝo & synnfullo ætgeadre liniȝiendo weron mið ðone hælende. *c* **1000** *Ags. Gosp.* John xiii. 23 An þæra leorning-cnihta hlinode on þæs hælendes bearme. *c* **1200** *Trin. Coll. Hom.* 39 Ðe unwreste herde hloneð and slepeð. **1362** LANGL. *P. Pl.* A. IX. 56 Vnder a lynde, vppon a launde leonede I a stounde. *c* **1375** *Sc. Leg. Saints* xix. (*Cristofore*) 228 & scantly lenyt don he was, Quhen þe woyce on hym can cry. *c* **1385** CHAUCER *L.G.W.* Prol. 179 Lenynge on myn elbowe and my syde. *c* **1450** *Merlin* 168 He..yede towarde the loges where as the thre kynges were lenynge. **1486** *Bk. St. Albans* F vij b, An haare in her forme shulderyng or leenyng. **1503** DUNBAR *Thistle & Rose* 100 This lady..leit him listly lene vpone hir kne. **1513** DOUGLAS *Æneis* VIII. Prol. 2 As I lenyt in a ley in Lent this last nycht. **1693** DRYDEN *Ovid's Met.* I. 1012 She laid her down; and leaning on her knees, Invok'd the cause of all her miseries. **1721** RAMSAY *Yng. Laird & Edinb. Katy* iii, Now and then we'll lean, And sport upo' the velvet fog. **1724** *Vision* iii, I leint me down to weip. **1871** W. ALEXANDER *Johnny Gibb* xvi. 114 She 'lean't her doon'.

†**b.** Phr. *to lean beside the* (or *one's*) *cushion*: to miss the point, be beside the mark. (Cf. CUSHION *sb.* 10 b.)

1576 FLEMING *Panopl. Epist.* 30 But this your consideration and purpose, (except I leane beside my cushing,) hath in it a certaine measure and meaning. *Ibid.* Epit. B j b, Thou leanest beside the cushing: for the epistle which thou meanest..is a president of an epistle Dehortatorie, and not an example of an epistle disuasorie.

†**c.** Of things: To lie or rest *on* a surface. *Obs.*

a **1000** *Phœnix* 25 (Gr.) Ne þær hleonað oo unsmeþes wiht. **1661** BOYLE *Examen* iv. (1682) 28 A small drop of water or Quicksilver..when it leans upon a dry or greasie plain.

2. a. To incline the body against an object for support; to support oneself *on, against* something; †formerly also const. *to, till, up* (= upon), *by.* ***to lean off something*** (colloq. in imperative): to cease to lean on. † ***to lean on the cushion*** (fig.): ? to assume the attitude or position of a preacher.

c **1250** *Gen. & Ex.* 1610 He..saȝ..A leddre stonden.. And ðe louerd ðor uppe a-buuen Lened ðoron. **1297** R. GLOUC. (Rolls) 6329 King edmond..lenede vp is sseld. **1387** TREVISA *Higden* (Rolls) III. 309 A staf for to lyne too. *c* **1450** tr. *De Imitatione* II. vii. 47 Truste not ner leene not upon a windy rede. *c* **1489** CAXTON *Blanchardyn* xli. 153 She was lenyng vpon her wyndowe. **1530** PALSGR. 606/1, I leaned with my backe against an oke to rest me. *a* **1533** LD. BERNERS *Huon* xiv. 38 There was lenynge in wyndows ladys & damesels a grete nombre. **1607** TOPSELL *Four-f. Beasts* (1658) 167 Elks..who..sleep by leaning unto trees like Elephants. *a* **1628** F. GREVIL *Five Yrs. K. James* (1643) 62 [Somerset] thought it no matter to leane on the Cushion in publique to check some of the Nobility; and amongst the

rest to make a flat Breach with my Lord of Canterbury. **1671** MILTON *Samson* 1632 To let him lean a while With both his arms on those two massie Pillars. *c* **1710** PRIOR *Cupid in Ambush* 2 Upon his arm, to let his mistress lean. **1727–46** THOMSON *Summer* 721 Mid the central depth of blackening woods.. Leans the huge elephant. **1774** GOLDSM. *Nat. Hist.* (1776) V. 248 They have hard stiff tails, to lean upon when climbing. **1829** MARRYAT *F. Mildmay* ii, Lean off that gun. **1837** DICKENS *Pickw.* vii, Let me lean on your arm. **1863** GEO. ELIOT *Romola* xx, He.. leaned against the wall. **1883** R. W. DIXON *Mano* IV. iii. 147 And ever on him leaned she lovingly, Staying on him her body's tender weight.

b. with refl. pron.

c **1220** *Bestiary* 634 A tre he sekeð.. and leneð him trostl[i]ke ðer-bi. *a* **1225** *Ancr. R.* 252 (MS. T.) ȝif þet ani weries, euchan leones him to oðer. *a* **1300** *Cursor M.* 1241 He lened him þan a-pon his hak. *Ibid.* 7805, I.. fand Saul him lenand on his sper. *c* **1470** HENRY *Wallace* VII. 67 Syne to the grece he lenyt him sobyrly. **1523** SKELTON *Garl. Laurel* 17, I lent me to a stumpe Of an oke. **1597** MONTGOMERIE *Cherrie & Slae* 7, I lay and leynit me to ane bus To heir the birdis beir.

c. *transf.* Of inanimate objects.

c **1400** *Lanfranc's Cirurg.* 161 þese .vij. boonys ben ioyned togidere in þis maner þat euery leeneþ vpon oþir. *c* **1425** *Seven Sag.* (P.) 2895 He wolde a toure rere Lenand to the mykyl toure. **1611** BIBLE *Num.* xxi. 15 At the streame of the brookes that.. lieth [*marg.* Heb. leaneth] vpon the border of Moab. **1624** WOTTON *Archit.* I. 46 That the Columnes may bee allowed somewhat aboue their ordinary length, because they leane vnto so good Supporters. **1764** GOLDSM. *Trav.* 284 Where the broad ocean leans against the land. **1887** RUSKIN *Præterita* II. 423 A burn.. with a ledge or two of sandstone to drip over, or lean against in pools.

d. *Mil.* ***to lean upon***: to be close up to something serving as a protection.

1813 *Examiner* 7 June 354/2 The right of the enemy leaned upon fortified rising points. **1838** THIRLWALL *Greece* IV. xxxiii. 303 Clearchus commanded the right wing, which leaned upon the river.

e. To press *upon*; to lay emphasis *upon*.

1736 AINSWORTH *Lat. Dict.* I. s.v. *Horse*, A horse that leaneth too hard on his bit. **1758** *Ann. Reg.* 22 The winter would lean heavier on the besiegers. **1883** *Harper's Mag.* Feb. 393 [The nickname] sounded awful enough when they leaned heavily on the first syllable.

3. *fig.* †To trust *to* for support (*obs.*); to rely or depend *on* or *upon*. Also *refl.*

a **1225** *Ancr. R.* 142 Heo owun to beon of so holi liue þet al holi chirche.. leonie & wreoðie upon ham. *a* **1340** HAMPOLE *Psalter* xxii. 5 þi stalworth help þat i len me till. *c* **1450** tr. *De Imitatione* III. li. 123 Wherfore in euery iugement recourse owiþ to be had to me, & not to leyne to propre arbitrement. **1526** *Pilgr. Perf.* (W. de W. 1531) 4 b, He sholde not lene to moche to his natural reason. **1577** HARRISON *England* Pref. (1877) I. p. cix, As one leaning altogither vnto memorie. **1592** WEST *1st Pt. Symbol.* §2 H, A simple or single Obligation is that which leaneth upon right onely. **1611** BIBLE *Prov.* iii. 5 Trust in the Lord.. and leane not vnto thine owne vnderstanding. **1621** *Gude & Godlie B.* (S.T.S.) App. 235 Confes thy synnis.. Vnto thy God.. And till him leyne for euer mair. **1697** tr. *Burgersdicius' Logic* II. viii. 31 The necessity of consecution, which we call'd the soul of syllogism, leans upon certain foundations and rules. **1736** BOLINGBROKE *Study & Use Hist.* v. (1752) I. 182 Christianity may lean on the civil and ecclesiastical power. **1849** MACAULAY *Hist. Eng.* vi. II. 148 While Clarendon was trying to lean on Rochester, Rochester was unable longer to support himself. **1869** FREEMAN *Norm. Conq.* (1876) III. xi. 55 It was on the tried friendship of that true man of God that Harold chose to lean. **1884** *Daily News* 11 Feb. 5/5 He could lean neither on the territory traversed nor on Khartoum for his supplies.

4. a. To bend or incline in a particular direction (usually indicated by an adv. or advb. phr.). Const. *from*, *over*, *towards*; also with advs. *back*, *out*, †*up*. (Also in *passive* in the same sense.)

Beowulf 1415 (Gr.) Oþ þæt he.. fyrgenbeamas ofer harne stan hleonian funde. *a* **1400–50** *Alexander* 1708 As he lenytt & lokett on hys forme. *c* **1430** *Syr Gener.* (Roxb.) 579 Oute of the bed gan she lene. *c* **1470** *Golagros & Gaw.* 1112 He lenyt vp in the place. **1530** PALSGR. 461/2, I bowe or leane out, as a clyffe of a hyll or a thynge that hangeth out-warde. *c* **1590** MARLOWE *Faust.* (1604) D i b, Over the which foure stately bridges leane. **1700** DRYDEN *Pal. & Arc.* III. 442 The gods came downward to behold the wars, Sharp'ning their sights, and leaning from their stars. **1715–20** POPE *Iliad* XI. 60 They.. leaning from the clouds, expect the war. **1818** LEIGH *N. Pict. Lond.* 303 The houses on each side [of London Bridge] overhung and leaned in a most terrific manner. **1821** KEATS *Isabella* 23 He leant into the sunrise, o'er the balustrade. *a* **1839** L. E. LANDON *Poems* (1844) II. 17 The spent stag on the grass is laid; And over him is leant a maid. **1860** TYNDALL *Glac.* I. xii. 89 A cone of ice forty feet high leaned quite over our track. **1883** F. M. CRAWFORD *Dr. Claudius* i, He leaned back in his.. chair.

fig. **1640** tr. *Verdere's Rom. of Rom.* I. xvi. 69 A Knight.. who.. so furiously bestirred himself, that he made the advantage lean to that side. **1770** GOLDSM. *Des. Vill.* 164 Ev'n his failings lean'd to virtue's side.

b. To move or be situated obliquely; to incline; to swerve (*aside*); *U.S.* to 'make tracks'.

1398 TREVISA *Barth. De P.R.* V. xxxvi. (1495) 149 The sharpe ende of the herte lenyth inwarde to the breste. *a* **1400–50** *Alexander* 5069 Qua list þis lymit ouir-lende, lene to þe left hand. **1546** J. HEYWOOD *Prov.* (1867) 47 Ye leane to the wrong shore. **1776–96** WITHERING *Brit. Plants* (ed. 3) I. 287 Filaments 4, upright, 2 leaning to the same side. **1841** CATLIN *N. Amer. Ind.* (1844) I. xiii. 98 Wraps his robe around him and 'leans' as fast as possible for home. **1883** STEVENSON *Treas. Isl.* IV. xvi, The gigs had leaned to their right. **1894** P. PINKERTON *Adriatica, Sulla Rocca, Asolo*, It [my love] may not lean Aside, nor choose between Her own and lesser beauty.

5. To incline or tend *towards*, *to* some quality or condition. Also, to have a tendency favourable *to*.

1398 TREVISA *Barth. De P.R.* IV. xi. (1495) 95 The colour of malencoly humour lynyth towarde blackenes. **1538** STARKEY *England* I. iv. 121 Hyt [the sentence] leynyth to equyte and consyence. **1734** POPE *Ess. Man* IV. 40 There's not a blessing Individuals find, But some way leans and hearkens to the kind. **1771** *Junius Lett.* lix. 306 The form of the constitution leans rather more than enough to the popular branch. **1844** LD. BROUGHAM *Brit. Const.* i. (1862) 6 The Government leans towards Democracy. **1855** MACAULAY *Hist. Eng.* xv. III. 549 His political opinions leaned towards Toryism.

6. a. To incline or tend in thought, affection, or conduct; to be somewhat partial or favourable; to be inclined or disposed *to* or *towards*. †Also, to have an inclination or desire *after*.

1530 PALSGR. 396 He leaneth to moche to the orthographye of the latyne tonge. **1557** *N. T.* (Genev.) *Matt.* vi. 24 Or els he shal leane to the one, and despise the other. **1576** FLEMING *Panopl. Epist.* 106 When you perceived the will of your.. friend leaning another way. **1596** SPENSER *State Irel.* Wks. (Globe) 613/1 They.. delight rather to leane to theyr old customes and Brehoon lawes. **1604** E. G[RIMSTONE] *D'Acosta's Hist. Indies* III. iii. 124 Aristotle leanes to the contrary opinion. **1605** VERSTEGAN *Dec. Intell.* i. (1628) 14 Such great men or commanders as some might leane vnto and follow. **1666** BUNYAN *Grace Abound.* §289, I found my spirit leaned most after awakening and converting work. **1728** NEWTON *Chronol. Amended* I. 93 Thales.. might lean a little to the opinion of former Astronomers. **1849** MACAULAY *Hist. Eng.* v. I. 585 The townsmen had long leaned towards Presbyterian divinity and Whig politics. **1868** GLADSTONE *Juv. Mundi* v. (1869) 140, I lean to another explanation of the name.

b. ***to lean against***: to be unfavourable to, not to countenance. Chiefly *legal*.

1804 CASTLEREAGH in Owen *Wellesley's Desp.* 258 The latter.. leant to Tippoo and against us. **1818** CRUISE *Digest* (ed. 2) II. 490 Which showed how strongly the Court had leaned against survivorship. **1826** SYD. SMITH *Wks.* (1859) II. 117/1 If it be true, that Judges in cases of high treason are more liable to be influenced by the Crown, and to lean against the prisoner. **1884** SIR C. S. C. BOWEN in *Law Times Rep.* I. 312/1 The courts lean against this interpretation.

†**c.** To defer *to* an opinion. *Obs.*

1538 STARKEY *England* II. iii. 199 But I wold Wee schold in our reame gyue so much to hys [i.e. the Pope's] authoryte, leynyng therto as to the Jugement of God. **1559** W. CUNINGHAM *Cosmogr. Glasse* 12, I wyll omytte it: and leane to th' authoritie of the famous king, and grave Philosopher Alphonsus. **1611** SHAKS. *Cymb.* I. i. 78 'Twere good, You lean'd vnto his Sentence, with what patience Your wisedome may informe you.

d. ***to lean on*** (someone): to put pressure on (a person) in order to extract something from him or force him to do something against his will (see also quot. 1960).

1960 WENTWORTH & FLEXNER *Dict. Amer. Slang* 315/1 *Lean against, lean on*... 2. To beat up someone; to threaten to beat up someone or a member of one's family in order to get information, to persuade someone to suppress information, or to extort money; to act or be tough with someone; to coerce. **1965** J. PORTER *Dover Three* xv. 168 If you start leaning on her and you don't make the poison-pen business stick good and proper, she'll crucify you! **1967** K. GILES *Death in Diamonds* vii. 126 I'm going to lean on him until I get to know that contact. **1967** J. MORGAN *Involved* 51 You were too much tonight.. the way you leaned on Tuttles, that was really something. **1972** J. BROWN *Chancer* vii. 101 Sandy Crump had been naughty, not telling me about Shag... I'd have to lean on him harder. **1975** *N.Y. Times* 3 Feb. 6/2 'An Attorney General would resign too if he thought he was being leaned on by the Prime Minister or senior ministers on a pending prosecution,' a former Attorney General said.

e. ***to lean over backwards***: see BACKWARDS *adv.* A.

7. Transitive (causal) uses. **a.** To cause to lean or rest, to prop (*against*, etc.). Const. as in 2.

13.. *Minor Poems fr. Vernon MS.* 614/82 Bot Godes sone ..His hed nou leoneþ on þornes tynde. *c* **1470** HENRY *Wallace* XI. 573 His bow and suerd he lenyt till a tre. **1535** COVERDALE *Amos* v. 19 He.. leeneth his honde vpon the wall. **1591** SHAKS. *1 Hen. VI*, II. v. 43 Leane thine aged Back against mine Arme. **1611** —— *Wint. T.* I. ii. 285 Is whispering nothing? Is leaning Cheeke to Cheeke? **1680** MOXON *Mech. Exerc.* 212 Clasping the Blade of it in your Left Hand, lean it steddy upon the Rest. **1697** DRYDEN *Æneid* x. 1188 His fainting Limbs against an Oak he leant. **1794** MRS. RADCLIFFE *Myst. Udolpho* vi, He leaned his head on her shoulder. **1797–1809** COLERIDGE *Three Graves* IV. xviii, She tried to smile, and on his arm Mournfully leaned her head. **1812** BYRON *Ch. Har.* II. lii, The little shepherd ..Doth lean his boyish form along the rock. **1842** TENNYSON *St. Sim. Styl.* 213 Let him.. lean a ladder on the shaft.

fig. **1603** DRAYTON *Bar. Wars* III. lxxx, Whereon their low deiected state to leane.

b. To cause to bend or incline.

1423 JAS. I *Kingis Q.* xlii, In my hede I drewe ryght hastily, And eft-sones I lent It forth ageyne. **1631** A. CRAIGE *Pilgrime & H.* 5 As I lent to my Lug, this well I heard. **1683** MOXON *Mech. Exerc., Printing* xxii. ¶4 If his Lines were Hard Justified, he cannot perhaps with the first leaning the Letters back get them clear out of the Stick. **1727** BOYER *Eng.-Fr. Dict.* s.v., To lean one's Head backward, *pencher le tête en arriere*. **1844** MRS. BROWNING *Lady Geraldine's C.* i, I would lean my spirit o'er you. **1887** BOWEN *Virg. Æneid* II. 303, I.. lean mine ear to the sounds of the air.

†**lean**, *v.*² *Obs.* In 1 hlǣnian, 3 leanen, 5 lenen, lenyn. [OE. *hlǣnian*, f. *hlǣne* LEAN *a.*] **a.** *intr.* To become lean. **b.** *trans.* To make lean.

c **897** K. ÆLFRED *Gregory's Past.* xiv. 87 Ne bið hit ðonne nohtes wan buton forhæfdnesse anre, ðæt he his lichoman suence & hlæniȝe. *Ibid.* xliii. 313 Ðonne ðonne ðæt flæsc hlænað. *c* **1230** *Hali Meid.* 35 þi rudi neb schal leanen & as gres grenen. *c* **1400** *Lanfranc's Cirurg.* Table Contents 4 Cap. viii of fastnynge a lene lyme, and to lenen a fat lyme. *c* **1440** *Promp. Parv.* 296/2 Lenyn, or make lene, *macero*. **1450–80** tr. *Secreta Secret.* 2 Of thing that leneth the body. **1616** T. ADAMS *Dis. of Soul* 23 The spirituall [dropsy].. though it leanes the carkasse, lards the conscience.

lean (liːn), *v.*³ *Whaling.* [f. LEAN *a.* and *sb.*²] *trans.* To cut away the 'lean' adhering to the blubber of a whale. Hence **ˈleaning** *vbl. sb.*, also with *up*.

1887 J. T. BROWN in *Fish. & Fish. Industr. U.S.* V. *Hist. & Meth.* II. 278 The pieces of flesh and muscles or 'lean'.. are removed.. with sharp knives... This process is called 'leaning'. *Ibid.* 281 To sever the muscles or pieces of flesh that persist in binding the fat to the body... The.. process is called.. 'leaning up'. *Ibid.* 282 The mate remains and 'leans' the blubber from the carcass.

lean(e, obs. form of LAIN *v.*, to conceal.

leaner (ˈliːnə(r)). [f. LEAN *v.*¹ + -ER¹.] One who leans, inclines, or reclines.

a **1536** TINDALE in Marbeck *Bk. of Notes* (1581) 306 To heare the law onelie & to be a professour therof and a leaner vnto it. **1631** R. H. *Arraignm. Whole Creature* i. 11 A staffe of Reedes, that deceives the leaners trust. **1646** GAULE *Cases Consc.* 3 Whereas our late leaners and lingerers after such a kinde of sect, could be content to deny all these. **1856** MRS. BROWNING *Aur. Leigh* II. 56 Strong enough to bear Such leaners on my shoulder.

leangle (ˈliːæŋg(ə)l). *Austral.* Also **langeel**, **leeangle**, **leonile**, **liangle**. [Native word, a derivation of *leang* or *liang* tooth. Other forms (see Morris) are *leeawell*, *leawill*.] A wooden club bent at the striking end. (Morris *Austral Eng.*)

1845 C. GRIFFITH *Port Phillip Distr. N.S.W.* x. 155 The liangle is.. of the shape of a pickaxe, with only one pick. **1867** G. G. MACCRAE *Māmba* 9 The long leangle's nascent form Forespoke the distant battle-storm. **1869** HOARE *Figures Fancy* 98 Beneath the dread leeangle blow Fell many a strong and swarthy foe. **1894** R. ETHERIDGE in *Jrnl. Anthrop. Instit.* XXIII. 317 On a Modification of the Australian Aboriginal Weapon, termed the Leonile, Langeel, Bendi, or Buccan, &c. **1945** BAKER *Austral. Lang.* xiii. 224 Those aboriginal words we have incorporated in our language... For example:.. wurley, leangle, mulga, [etc.]. **1966** W. S. RAMSON *Austral. Eng.* vi. 132 Leangle, 'a club', and wirri, 'a throwing stick', are Victorian, both coming from the Gippsland area.

leaning (liːnɪŋ), *vbl. sb.* [f. LEAN *v.*¹ + -ING¹.] **1.** The action of LEAN *v.*¹; inclination; reclining.

c **1000** *Ags. Gosp.* Luke xx. 46 þa forman hlininga [Vulg. *primos discubitus*]. *c* **1440** *Promp. Parv.* 295/1 Le(y)nynge, *appodiacio*. **1530** PALSGR. 238/2 Leaning to, *adhesion*. **1677** MOXON *Mech. Exerc.* 5 According to the leaning of the Chaps of your Vice. **1712** BUDGELL *Spect.* No. 277 ¶17 The various Leanings and Bendings of the Head. **1830** HERSCHEL *Stud. Nat. Phil.* 241 If the bricks.. had all a certain leaning or bias in one direction out of the perpendicular. **1883** GILMOUR *Mongols* xxvii. 321 Inexplicable leanings and movements were seen about the shoulders.

b. Something to lean upon; †*spec.* the flat horizontal surface formed by the thickness of the wall on the inner and lower side of a window.

c **1532** DU WES *Introd. Fr.* in Palsgr. 894 Lenyng *appuis*. **1663** GERBIER *Counsel* 20 Persons, who.. affect low leanings, to make use either to sit on.. or to shew themselves.. to passengers.

2. *fig.* Inclination, bias; tendency, 'penchant'.

1587 HARRISON *England* II. v. (1877) I. 130 [An 'Italianate' Englishman says:] He is a foole that.. will come in trouble for constant leaning to anie [religion]. **1795** BURKE *Th. on Scarcity* Wks. VII. 417 To these, great politicians may give a leaning, but they cannot give a law. **1838–9** HALLAM *Hist. Lit.* IV. IV. ii. 37 The latter was as little suspected of an heterodox leaning as Petavius himself. **1849** MACAULAY *Hist. Eng.* ii. I. 231 The king was suspected by many of a leaning towards Rome. **1871** SMILES *Charac.* x. (1876) 290 Frederick the Great.. manifested his strong French leanings in his choice of books.

3. *attrib.* and *Comb.* (= 'for leaning upon or against for rest or support'), as ***leaning-board***, ***-carpet***, ***-chair***, ***-cushion***, ***-place***, ***-post***, ***-staff***, ***-support***; †**leaning-height**, the height of the 'leaning' (see 1 b *spec.*) of a window from the floor; also used *adj.* = next; †**leaning-high** *a.*, of a height to lean upon; **leaning-note** *Mus.* = APPOGGIATURA; **leaning-stock**, (*a*) a support (*lit.* and *fig.*); (*b*) in an organ, the ledge on which a pipe rests.

1533 in Bayley *Tower Lond.* I. (1821) p. xx, It'm a *lenyng borde laide in yᵉ same chambre wyndow. **1656** FINETT *For. Ambass.* 53 A *leaning Carpet laid before them, and Seats to sit on. **1601** HOLLAND *Pliny* I. 485 *Leaning chairs, wherein a man or woman may gently take a nap, sitting at ease and repose most sweetly. **1586** *Wills & Inv. N.C.* (Surtees 1860) II. 129 In the greate chambre.. ij long *leaninge cushins. **1663** GERBIER *Counsel* 19 The *leaning height of the Windowes, ought to be three Foot and a half. **1664** EVELYN tr. *Freart's Archit.* 124 They served for Podia or posaries of a leaning-height for which they had a slight cornice assign'd them. **1663** GERBIER *Counsel* 49 As for the foundation of their building, it ought to be raised at first leaning hight; and then to let it rest to settle, for if only brought.. a foot high above ground, it will be pusht down again, but being *leaning high, it will be preserved. **1811** BUSBY *Dict. Mus.*, *Appogiature* or *Leaning Note. **1530** PALSGR. 238/2 *Leanyng place, *apuy*. **1533** in Bayley *Tower Lond.* I. (1821) p. xix, A great carrall wyndow.. and lenyng places made new to the same. *a* **1850** ROSSETTI *Dante & Circ.* I. (1874) 54

My face shows my heart's colour, verily, Which, fainting, seeks for any leaning-place. **1535** COVERDALE *2 Chron.* ix. 18 It had two *leanynge postes vpon both the sydes of the seate. *c* **1440** *Promp. Parv.* 295/2 *Le(y)nynge staffe, *calopodium, podium.* **1552** HULOET, Lenynge staffe, *podium.* **1530** PALSGR. 238/2 *Leanyng stoke, *apuial.* **1583** GOLDING *Calvin on Deut.* lvi. 335 They will be a sure and steadie leaning stocke to rest vppon. **1642** ROGERS *Naaman* 8 To worship Rimmon himself, and be his Masters leaning stock in that worship. **1852** SEIDEL *Organ* 56 Sometimes this ledge, or leaning-stock of the pipe, has a semi-circular cut, into which the pipe leans back. **1875** OUSELEY *Harmony* xviii. 206 *Appoggiaturas*..are supposed to be a kind of buttress or *leaning support to the note before which they are placed.

leaning ('li:nɪŋ), *ppl. a.* [f. LEAN *v.*[1] + -ING[2].] That leans or inclines; †inclining towards a person in devotion or affection.

1577-87 HOLINSHED *Chron.* III. 919/1 [Wolsey] in whome the king receiued such a leaning fantasie, for that he [etc.]. **1595** DANIEL *Civ. Wars* IV. xxix, The wel-known right of the Earle of Marche alurd A leaning loue, whose cause he did pretend. **1697** DRYDEN *Æneid* VIII. 311 The leaning head hung threatening o'er the flood, and nodded to the left. **1793** SMEATON *Edystone L.* §114 The..leaning tower of Pisa. **1835** WILLIS *Melanie* 165 Hidden by yon leaning tree. **1860** TYNDALL *Glac.* I. xii. 89 In front of us was a second leaning mass.

leanish ('li:nɪʃ), *a. rare.* [f. LEAN *a.* + -ISH.] Somewhat lean.

1647 W. BROWNE tr. *Polexander* II. 234 Her waxing leanish,..her drooping [etc.]. **1737** BRACKEN *Farriery Impr.* (1757) II. 19 The Neck..should be leanish.

leanly ('li:nlɪ), *adv.* [f. LEAN *a.* + -LY[2].] In a lean fashion; with a lean body or form; meagrely, poorly.

1580 HOLLYBAND *Treas. Fr. Tong, Maigrement,* leanely. **1669** BUNYAN *Holy Citie* 152 It was also (though but leanly) represented to us by the golden state of old Jerusalem in the days of Solomon the King. **1827** *Examiner* 67/1 Most leanly shapen. **1876** LANIER *Poems, Ps. West* 108 So leanly sails the day behind the day.

leanness ('li:nnɪs). Also 1 hlǽnnes, -nys, 4 leenes, 4-5 lenesse, 5 lennesse, leynes, 5-6 lenenes(se, 6 leanenesse, leanes, *Sc.* leinnes. [f. LEAN *a.* + -NESS.] The condition or quality of being lean; thinness; meagreness; poverty (of land); barrenness; etc.

a **1000** in Napier *Glosses* 192/33 *Macie,* mid hlænnesse. *c* **1000** ÆLFRIC *Hom.* (Thorpe) I. 522 Hwæt is þæt man besette his geðanc on nyðerlicum þingum, buton swilce modes hlænnys? **1382** WYCLIF *Ezek.* xxiv. 23 ȝe shulen.. faile for leenes in ȝoure wickidnessis. **1398** TREVISA *Barth. De P.R.* v. x. (1495) 116 Tomoche lenesse of the forheed and reuelynge of the skynne. *c* **1400** *Lanfranc's Cirurg.* 86 If þat ..þe lymes ben mene bitwene fatnes & lenenes. *c* **1400** tr. *Secreta Secret., Gov. Lordsh.* 115 He þat hauys a mene fface, in chekys and templys, bowynge to Lennesse. **1547** BORDE *Dyetary* xvii. 276 The fatnes of flesshe is not so moche nutrytyue as the leenes of flesshe. **1562** J. HEYWOOD *Prov. & Epigr.* (1867) 104 Better all be fatte..Than linger in leannesse. **1593** SHAKS. *2 Hen. VI*, I. i. 112 The poore King Reignier, whose large style Agrees not with the leannesse of his purse. **1611** SPEED *Theat. Gt. Brit.* x. (1614) 19/1 A sand ..which being spread upon the face of the earth, bettereth the leannesse thereof for grain. **1634** SIR T. HERBERT *Trav.* 147 The women..incline rather to corpulency than leannesse. **1862** STANLEY *Jew. Ch.* (1877) I. iv. 66 The sacred kine..fit symbols of the leanness or the fertility of future years. **1871** MORLEY *Carlyle* in *Crit. Misc.* Ser. I. 233 A most unlovely leanness of judgment.

lean-over ('li:nəʊvə(r)). [f. LEAN *v.*[1] + OVER *adv.*] An inclination down or forward; *concr.*, something over which one can lean.

a **1885** G. M. HOPKINS *Poems* (1918) 79 So long to this sweet spot, this leafy lean-over. **1936** E. SITWELL *Victoria of Eng.* xiii. 163 For others, again, there is the twopenny lean-over. **1969** E. H. PINTO *Treen* 334 Early pipes had a very forward tilt, or 'lean over', on the bowl.

leant, pa. t. and pa. pple. of LEAN *v.*[1]

lean-to ('li:ntu:), *sb.* (and *a.*). Also 5 lenetoo, 7-8 leantoo, -toe, lentoo, 8 lento. 9 *U.S. dial.* leanter, linter. [f. LEAN *v.*[1] + TO *adv.*]

A. *sb.* 'A building whose rafters pitch against or lean on to another building or against a wall' (Gwilt); a penthouse.

1461 in *Archæol.* XXIII. 107 Emend' unius Lenetoo juxta parlur' annex'. Magn' Aule. **1618** R. HARRIS *Samuel's Funeral* To Rdr. (1622), Me thought it handsomer to lay all my stuffe vpon the foundation, then to set vp a leane-to. **1638** in T. Lechford *Note-Bk.* (1885) 54 And also the old house and lean-toos, yard and garden thereto belonging. **1639** *Ibid.* 217 Provided that the said Brackenbury shall have ..liberty to make a leanto unto the end of the parlor. **1704** MADAM S. KNIGHT *Jrnl.* (1865) 24 Shee conducted me to a parlour in a little back Lento. **1782** *Phil. Trans.* LXXII. 358 A wall is continued eastward..having a stable built against it as a lean-to. **1854** HAWTHORNE *Eng. Note-Bks.* (1883) I. 509 On one side of the church-tower there was a little penthouse, or lean-to,—merely a stone roof, about three or four feet high, and supported by a single pillar. **1861** MRS. STOWE *Pearl Orr's Isl.* 10 A brown house of the kind that the natives call 'lean-to' or 'linter'. **1884** *Law Times Rep.* LI. 238/2 An old lean-to facing Gower-street had been raised and a room erected above it.

transf. **1871** L. STEPHEN *Playgr. Europe* iv. (1894) 101 A ledge of snow..formed a kind of lean-to against the.. precipitous rock.

B. *attrib.* (or *adj.*) Belonging to or of the nature of a building such as that described in A. Also, placed so as to lean against something.

1649 in J. Merrill *Hist. Amesbury* (1880) 42 A payer of hinges of one of yᵉ doores & yᵉ railes yᵗ lie by yᵉ leantoo side. **1666** *Dedham Rec.* (1894) IV. 122 The said bridge or foot plankes and leaneto rayles. **1833** MARRYAT *P. Simple* xxi, The buildings appropriated for the prisoners were built with lean-to roofs on one side. **1860** GEO. ELIOT *Mill on Fl.* I. iv, A lean-to pigsty. **1882** STEVENSON *New Arab. Nts.* (1884) 236 They had set fire to the lean-to outhouse.

† **'leany,** *a. Obs.* Also 5 leney. [f. LEAN *a.* + -Y[1].] Lean.

14.. *Noble Bk. Cookry* (Napier 1882) 95 Take leney beef and cut it in thyn lesks. **1579** SPENSER *Sheph. Cal.* July 199 They han fatte kernes, and leany knaues. **1602** DAVISON *Rhapsody* (1611) 39 Thou leany flocke that didst of late lament.

leap (li:p), *sb.*[1] Forms: 1 hlýp, 3 lupe (*ū*), leope, leep(e, (lip), 4-6 lepe, 6-7 leape, 6- leap. [OE. *hlýp*, Anglian **hlēp* str. masc.:—OTeut. type **hlaupi-z*, corresponds (apart from declension) to OFris. (*bec-*)*hlêp*, Du. *loop*, OHG. *hlouf* (MHG. *louf*, mod.Ger. *lauf*), ON. *hlaup* neut. (Da. *løb*, Sw. *löp-* in compounds); f. root of LEAP *v.*]

1. a. An act of leaping; a springing from the ground or other standing-place; a bound, jump, spring.

a **900** CYNEWULF *Crist* 747 (Gr.) Swa we men sculon heortan ȝehyȝdum hlypum styllan. *c* **1230** *Hali Meid.* 23 A muche lupe duneward. **1387** TREVISA *Higden* (Rolls) III. 55 And forto make þat good he lepe ouer þe wal at oo leepe. *a* **1400-50** *Alexander* 1761 þou..maa þi lepis & þi laikis & quat þe liste ellis, As ratons or ruȝe myse in a rowme chambre. *a* **1420** HOCCLEVE *De Reg. Princ.* 3436 He at a leep was at hir and hir kyste. *c* **1450** *Merlin* 142 It is grete nede a man to go bak to recouer the better his leep. **1470-85** MALORY *Arthur* III. v, The herte lepte a grete lepe. **1573** BARET *Alv.* L. 204 A leap or jump. **1660** F. BROOKE tr. *Le Blanc's Trav.* 184 They spring away with most stupendious leaps. **1700** WALLIS in *Collect.* (O.H.S.) I. 318 Mr. Bosely [was] observed..to have leaped, at six continued leaps, one and twenty yards, three quarters and some odd inches. **1711** ADDISON *Spect.* No. 223 ¶4 Those who had taken this Leap were observed never to relapse into that Passion. **1774** GOLDSM. *Nat. Hist.* (1776) VI. 322 It sometimes happens, however, that they [salmon] want strength to make the leap. **1825** *Sporting Mag.* XV. 346 Our elders took leaps, now they are all jumps. **1833** *Regul. Instr. Cavalry* I. 61 For the 'Standing Leap', bring the horse up to the bar at an animated walk... For the 'Flying Leap', the horse must not be hurried. **1867** LADY HERBERT *Cradle L.* i. 7 The spot.. from whence the Mameluke..took the famous leap on horseback.

b. *transf.* and *fig.* esp. An abrupt movement or change; a sudden transition. Also with an adv., as *leap-up*.

c **1000** *Sax. Leechd.* III. 264 *De saltu lunæ*... þæt is ðæs monan hlyp for þan þe he oferhlypð ænne dæg. *a* **1225** *Ancr. R.* 48 þe heorte is a ful wilde best, and makeð monie wilde lupes, as Seint Gregorie seið, 'nichil corde fugacius'. *c* **1400** *Ywaine & Gaw.* 72 Ful light of lepes has thou bene ay. *a* **1420** HOCCLEVE *De Reg. Princ.* 1767 And for-þi, sonē, wole I make a leepe ffrom hem [stories], and go wole I to þe empryse þat I first took. **1577-87** HOLINSHED *Chron.* (1807-8) IV. 653 Leaving the lord lieutenant for a while, we will give a little leape to actions of manhood against the enimie. **1592** BACON *Observ. Libel* Wks. 1826 V. 412 One Barrow..made a leap from a vain and libertine youth, to a preciseness in the highest degree. **1661** FELTHAM *Resolves* II. xxviii. (ed. 8) 238 'Tis justly matter of amazement, for a man in the leap of the one, or in the tumble of either of these, to retain a mind unaltered. **1701** SWIFT *Contests Nobles & Comm.* iii. Miscell. (1711) 41 Thus in a very few Years the Commons proceeded so far as to wrest the Power of chusing a King intirely out of the Hands of the Nobles; which was so great a Leap..that [etc.]. **1856** GRINDON *Life* i. (1875) 7 The leap of the stamens of the Kalmia from their niches in the corolla. **1860** TYNDALL *Glac.* II. xi. 289 The boulders and débris..came in frequent leaps and rushes down the precipice. **1875** DOWDEN *Shakspere* 86 The energy, the leap-up, the direct advance of the will of Helena. **1885** FAIRBAIRN *Catholicism* 89 Every attempt..to discover method and progress in creation, without leap or gap, violence or interference..was [etc.].

c. Phrases. ***a leap in the dark***: a hazardous action undertaken in uncertainty as to the consequences. ***by leaps, by leaps and bounds***: by sudden transitions; used *esp.* to express startling rapidity of advance or increase; ***leap forward***: an advance of a marked or notable character.

1698 VANBRUGH *Prov. Wife* v. vi, Go, now I am in for Hobbe's Voyage: a great Leap in the Dark. **1720** POPE tr. *Homer's Iliad* V. XXI. 1587 High o'er the surging Tide, by Leaps and Bounds, He wades, and mounts; the parted Wave resounds. **1721** DE FOE *Moll Flanders* (1840) 75 Make matrimony, like death, a leap in the dark. **1851** NICHOL *Archit. Heav.* 154 The telescope, in passing through it [the Milky Way], often goes by leaps from one cumulus to another. **1867** EARL DERBY in Hansard *Parl. Deb.* Ser. III. CLXXXIX. 952 No doubt we are making a great experiment, and 'taking a leap in the dark'. **1885** *Illustr. Lond. News* 8 Aug. 143/2 Electricity has been advanced 'by leaps and bounds'. **1891** GLADSTONE in *Star* 11 Dec. 2/5, I shall proceed by skips and jumps; or, as it is the fashion to say now, by leaps and bounds. **1915** MRS. BELLOC LOWNDES *Let.* 10 Mar. (1971) 57 Everything is going up, in price, by leaps and bounds. **1940** By leaps and bounds [see DOUBLE *v.* 4 c]. **1947** By leaps and bounds [see AFRIKANERIZING *vbl. sb.* and *ppl. a.*]. **1954** T. S. ELIOT *Confid. Clerk* II. 63, I make decisions on the spur of the moment, But you'd never take a leap in the dark. **1961** *Ann. Reg. 1960* 170 The convention ..would amount to a great 'leap forward' towards a virtual European federation. **1966** *Performing Right* Oct. 4 The leap forward of nearly 20 per cent in this revenue is a triumph for the skill and hard work of our administrative staff. **1973** *Times* 21 Mar. (China Trade Suppl.) p. xi/2 The back-yard steel furnaces that sprang up during the Great Leap Forward (1958-60).

2. a. A leaping-place; something to be leaped over or from. Also, the place or distance leaped.

Frequent in place-names, as *Deerleap, Hindlip, Smuggler's Leap, Lover's Leap.*

c **1205** LAY. 1928 Nu..haueð þat clif þare nome on ælche leode þat þæt weos Geomagoges lupe. *c* **1400** MAUNDEV. (Roxb.) xiii. 56 Halfe a myle fra Nazareth es þe leep þat oure Lord leped fra þe Iews. **1539** Dere leapes [see DEER 4 b]. **1613** SHAKS. *Hen. VIII*, v. i. 139 You take a Precepit for no leape of danger, And woe your owne destruction. **1692** R. L'ESTRANGE *Fables* lvii. 57 After they have carry'd their Riders safe over All Leaps. **1711** ADDISON *Spect.* No. 223 ¶4 This Place was therefore called *The Lover's Leap.* **1791** G. GAMBADO *Ann. Horsem.* vi. (1809) 90 The soil is pretty stiff, the leaps large and frequent. **1818** J. LAWRENCE *Brit. Field Sports* 410 He ran his Horse at a Leap, which every one else in the Field refused.

b. ***salmon leap***, a precipitous fall in a river (either natural or contrived artificially) over which salmon leap in ascending the river for breeding.

1387 TREVISA *Higden* (Rolls) I. 369 In Irlond beeþ þre samoun lepes. **1661** LOVELL *Hist. Anim. & Min.* 220 They [salmon] are taken at leapes. **1780** A. YOUNG *Tour in Ireland* I. 126 All the fisheries are his to the leap at Colraine.

3. Of animals: The action of leaping (the female).

1607 MARKHAM *Caval.* I. (1617) 38 [They] being desirous to get into good races, are fayne to get leapes for their Mares, either by courtesie, bribes, or stealth. **1697** DRYDEN *Æneid* VI. 36 The rushing leap, the doubtful progeny. **1708** *Lond. Gaz.* No. 4428/16 A Dapple Grey Horse..to be had for a Guinea a Leap.

transf. **1616** B. JONSON *Devil an Ass* III. iii. (1631) 124 *Meercraft*..could you ha'..Beene satisfied with a leape o' your Host's daughter. **1632** MASSINGER *City Madam* IV. ii, I well know him For a most insatiate drabber. He hath given, Before he spent his own estate..A hundred pound a leap.

4. The sudden fall of a river to a lower level.

1796 *Statist. Acc. Scotl.* XVII. 611 Where the Esk.. forms a linn or leap. **1809** A. HENRY *Trav.* 16 The Sault de Saint-Louis..is highest of the saults, falls, or leaps, in this part of the Saint-Lawrence. **1843** RUSKIN *Mod. Paint.* I. II. v. iii. §22 The quiet stream is a succession of leaps and pools. **1872** JENKINSON *Guide Eng. Lakes* (ed. 6) 286 The water makes five or six leaps in its descent.

†**5.** An alleged name for a 'company' of leopards. *Obs.*

1486 *Bk. St. Albans* F vj b, A Lepe of Lebardis.

6. *Mining.* A fault or dislocation of strata. ***a leap up*** or ***leap down***, one caused by upheaval or sinking of the strata.

1747 HOOSON *Miner's Dict., Leap*..is when the Vein is thrown of from its perpendicular Course, at once into the Side; these Leaps never happen, but at some Wayboard, or large Bed-joynt. **1855** *Cornwall* 109 Vertical Intersections. —These are commonly called leaps, or throws. **1874** J. H. COLLINS *Metal Mining* Gloss. s.v. *Fault.* If [the displacement of strata is] upwards, a leap or upthrow; if downwards, a slide or downthrow.

7. *Mus.* A passing from one note to another by an interval greater than a degree of the scale.

1674 PLAYFORD *Skill Mus.* I. xi. 45 By the taking of the greater Sixth that falls by a leap. **1811** BUSBY *Dict. Mus.* (ed. 3), *Leaps,* this word is properly applicable to any disjunct degree, but is generally used to signify a distance consisting of several intermediate intervals. **1889** E. PROUT *Harmony* (ed. 10) vi. §164 A second inversion may be approached either by leap..or by step..from the root position of another chord.

8. *Comb.*: **leap-Christian** (see quot.); †**leap-month**, February of leap year; **leap-ore**, 'the most inferior quality of tin ore' (*Cent. Dict.*); **leap pease**, ? parched-peas; **leap second** [after *leap day*], a second which on a particular occasion is inserted into (or omitted from) a scale of reckoning time in order to bring it into correspondence with another scale; †**leap-skip** *a.* (*nonce-wd.*), applied to the knight's move in chess; †**leap-staff**, a leaping-pole. Also LEAP DAY, LEAP YEAR.

1647 TRAPP *Comm. Ep. & Rev.* App. 684 *Leap-Christians are not so much to be liked, that all on the sudden, of notorious profane become extremely precise and scrupulous. **1566** PAINTER *Pal. Pleas.* IV. 36 The *leape moneth, which is February. **1648-60** HEXHAM *Dutch Dict., De Schrickelmoendt,* the Leape-month. **1620** MARKHAM *Farew. Husb.* (1625) 137 The field Pease..are onely for boyling and making of *leape Pease, or parching. **1971** *Nature* 11 June 345/1 An adjustment will be made to all GMT time signal emissions on January 1, 1972, so that a GMT time of 0 h 0 m 0 s will correspond exactly to an IAT time of 0 h 0 m 10 s; thereafter '*leap seconds' will be inserted or omitted as necessary at the end of a particular GMT month... From then on, GMT will always be exactly 10 s slow compared with IAT. A so-called positive leap second will begin at 23 h 59 m 60 s on the last day of the month selected and end at 0 h 0 m 0 s on the first day of the next month; by contrast, if the leap second is negative, 23 h 59 m 58 s will be followed one second later by 0 h 0 m 0 s. **1972** *Daily Tel.* 28 Dec. 10/2 Shortly before 11 p.m. on Sunday (4 a.m. New Year's Day in Britain) technicians at the United States National Bureau of Standards in Boulder, Colorado, will add one leap second to America's atomic clock to correct it to match the Earth's rotation. **1973** *Nature* 21/28 Dec. 444/1 Currently, the Earth loses about 3 ms a day on Atomic Time, and the leap seconds are added where

necessary..to keep UT and Atomic Time in close correspondence. *a* **1649** DRUMM. OF HAWTH. *Fam. Ep.* Wks. (1711) 146 The lady..is..inhibited from the *leap-skip bound of the knights. *c* **1626** *Dick of Devon.* IV. iii. in Bullen *O. Pl.* II. 78 One with a *leape staffe may leape over it.

leap (liːp), *sb.*² Forms: 1 léap, 3–6 lep(e, 4–5 leep(e, 6–7 leape, 7– leap; *dial.* 5 leippe, 7–8 lib, 8 lip, 9 lep(e. [OE. *léap* str. masc. = ON. *laup-r* (MSw. *löper*).]

1. A basket. Now *dial.* Cf. SEED-LIP.

c **1000** WULFSTAN *Hom.*, *De Confessione* (Napier) 293 Ða bær man up of ðan ðe hi læfdon twelf leapas fulle. *a* **1250** *Owl & Night.* 359 Thez thu nime evere oth than lepe. *a* **1300** *Cursor M.* 4486 A lepe..Wit bred þar i bar on mi heued. *Ibid.* 19719 In a lep men lete him dun Vte ouer þe walles o þe tun. **1388** WYCLIF *Exod.* ii. 3 Thanne sche took a leep of segge..and puttide the ȝong child with ynne. **1432–50** tr. *Higden* (Rolls) V. 195 Moyses thabbot..toke a lepe fulle of gravelle on his backe. **1495–6** *Durham Acc. Rolls* (Surtees) 653 Pro leippez et Scotellez pro granario. **1530** PALSGR. 238/2 Lepe or a basket, *corbeille.* **1641** BEST *Farm. Bks.* (Surtees) 23 The other leape is to putte the worst lockes of wooll into. *a* **1825** FORBY *Voc. E. Anglia*, *Lep, lepe*, a large deep basket.

†**b.** Used locally as a measure; in Sussex, according to Ray, half a bushel. ? *Obs.*

1277 *Extent Manor of Cerring, Suss.* in Du Cange s.v. *Lepa*, Et colliget de nucibus in bosco comini tertiam partem unius mensuræ, quæ vocatur Lepe, quod est tertia pars 2 bussellorum, et valet quadrantem. **1674** RAY *S. & E.C. Words* 70 A Leap or Lib; Suss. Half a bushel.

2. A basket in which to catch or keep fish.

c **1000** ÆLFRIC *Gloss.* in Wr.-Wülcker 167/14 *Nassa*, boȝenet, *uel* leap. **1297** R. GLOUC. (Rolls) 5352 In lepes & in coufles so moche viss hii ssolleþ hom bringe þat ech mon ssal wondry of so gret cacchinge. **1382** WYCLIF *Job* xl. 26 Whether thou shalt fille nettis with his skyn, and the lep [**1388** leep] of fisshis with the hed of hym? *c* **1440** *Promp. Parv.* 297/1 Leep, for fysshe kepynge, or takynge, *nassa.* **1481–90** *Howard Househ. Bks.* (Roxb.) 363 Item..for makenge of lepes and othir gere for the kechyn to kepe ynne eles ij. s. ix. d. **1530** PALSGR. 287/2 Welle or lepe for fysshe, *boutiele.* **1533–4** *Act 25 Hen. VIII*, c. 7 [No person shal take] in..any wele..lepe..or by any other engyne..the yonge frye..of any kynde of Salmon. **1603** HOLLAND *Plutarch's Mor.* 218 Weaving them close together..after the maner of a fishers leape or weele net. **1649** BLITHE *Eng. Improv. Impr.* (1653) 172 The Osier..is of especiall use for..fishermen for making Leaps & instruments to catch fish in. **1873** *Act 36 & 37 Vict.* c. 71 §15 Except wheels or leaps for taking lamperns.

3. *attrib.* and *Comb.*, as *leap maker, weel*; †**leap-head**, a weel; †**leap-hole** (see quot. 1641).

1360–1 *Durh. Acc. Rolls* 563 Johanni lepemaker pro 4 spartis pro bracina, 2 scuteles, 2 flekes [etc.], 8*s.* 4*d.* **1483** *Cath. Angl.* 213/2 A Lepe maker, *cophinarius, corbio.* **1601** HOLLAND *Pliny* I. 248 A wonderfull number of these Yeels ..insomuch as in the leapweeles and weernets..there be found somtime a thousand of them wrapped together in one ball. **1611** COTGR., *Mannequin*..also, a little basket, leape-head, or weele, made of bullrushes, and vsed by fishermen. **1641** BEST *Farm. Bks.* (Surtees) 61 When..wee feare that it will heate in the mowe, then doe wee drawe up a leape aboute the middle of each roomstead; and soe by this meanes the storme getteth a vent by the leap-holes.

leap (liːp), *v.* *Pa. t.* and *pa. pple.* leaped (liːpt), leapt (lɛpt). Forms: 1 hléapan, 3 leapen, læpen(n, leope, lupe, 4 luppe(n, lippe, lijpe, lip, leope, *Kent.* lheape, 3–4 lepen, 3–6 lepe, 5–6 *Sc.* and *north. dial.* leip, 5–7 leppe, 3, 6–7 leape, 6– leap. *Pa. t.* 1 hléop, *pl.* hlupon, (*subj.* hlíepe), 3 leope(n, leop(pe, le(o)up, lupe, 3–5 lep(pe, leep, (4, 7 leepe), 4–5 lepe, 4 lepp, lhip, lhiep, lip, loop, lup, 4–7 lope, 4, 6 *Sc.*, 9 lape, 5 lappe, laup, 6 leap, lapp, loppe, 3–9 *Sc.* and *north. dial.* lap; *weak forms* 3 leopt, 3–5 lepte, 4 leepte, lepide, lippid(e, lippte, lupten, 4–6 leped, 6 leapte, 5–7 lept, 6– leapt, leaped. *Pa. pple.* 1 hléapen, 3 ileope, 3–6 lopen, 5 lopon, 6 *Sc.* loppin, 6, 8 *Sc.* loppen, 9 *Sc.* luppen; *weak forms* 4 lippid, 6–7 lept, 6– leapt, 7– leaped. [A Com. Teut. reduplicating str. vb., which has become weak in Eng.: OE. *hléapan* (pa. t. *hléop*, pl. *hlupon*, pa. pple. *-hleapen*) corresponds to OFris. *(h)lâpa, hliapa*, pa. t. *hlêp*, pa. pple. *hlêpen*, OS. *(a-)hlôpan*, pa. t. pl. *-hliopun* (MDu. *lôpen*, Du. *loopen*, pa. t. *liep*, pa. pple. *geloopen*), OHG. *(h)lauffan, loufan* (MHG. *loufen*, mod.G. *laufen*, pa. t. *lief*, pa. pple. *gelaufen*), ON. *hlaupa*, pa. t. *hlióp*, pl. *hlióþom*, *hlupom*, pa. pple. *hlaupenn* (Sw. *löpa*, Da. *løbe*), Goth. *(us)-hlaupan*:—OTeut. **hlaupan*. The equivalent LOUP, from ON. *hlaupa*, has in Sc. and some northern dialects supplanted the native form in the present stem.

No certain affinities outside Teut. are known: some scholars have suggested connexion with Lith. *klúpoti* to remain kneeling, *klúpti* to fall on one's knees, to stumble; or with Gr. κόλυμβος diver.]

†**1. a.** *intr.* To run; to go hastily or with violence; to rush, to 'throw oneself'. Also with advs., as *forth, out.* (In OE., *út hléapan* = to escape.) *Obs.*

Beowulf (Z.) 865 Hwilum heaþo-rofe hleapan leton on ȝeflit faran fealwe mearas. **11..** *O.E. Chron.* an. 1072 (MS. D.) Her Eadwine eorl & Morkere eorl hlupon ut & mislice ferdon on wuda. *Ibid.* an. 1087 (MS. Laud), Roger het an of heom se hleop into þam castele æt Norðwic. *c* **1205** LAY. 24847 ȝif Arður ne leope to swulc hit a liun weore and þas word seide. *a* **1225** *Juliana* 38 þis eadie meiden..leop to ant lahte him. *c* **1250** *Gen. & Ex.* 2726 And to hemward swide he lep. **1297** R. GLOUC. (Rolls) 8170 Vor hor hors were al astoned..ac some stode..stille & some lepte her & þer. *a* **1300** *Cursor M.* 4541 þe boteler to þe prisun lep. *c* **1330** *Assump. Virg.* (B.M. MS.) 613 To þe beere he cam lepand. **1340** *Ayenb.* 240 þo lhip op þe mayster and him keste. **1362** LANGL. *P. Pl.* A. Prol. 94 Erchedekenes and Deknes..Beon lopen to londun. **1375** BARBOUR *Bruce* x. 242 Thai that neir enbuschit war Lap out. **1528** *St. Papers Hen. VIII*, IV. 493 The freindes of the said traiter are loppen to hym into Scotlaunde. *c* **1560** *Durham Depos.* (Surtees) 65 He hard a sturr in the streit, and therwith lap furth. **1596** DALRYMPLE tr. *Leslie's Hist. Scot.* II. 163 The Scottis couragious..leipis to straikis. **1644** R. BAILLIE *Lett.* (1841) II. 217 Coll. Macgillespick's son, who, with two thousand five hundred runagates from Ireland, are loppen over here. **1716** RAMSAY *On Wit* 15 Hameward with clever strides he lap.

b. To break *out* in an illegal or disorderly way.

a **1670** J. SCOT *Staggering State* (1754) 153 He..grieving that he had not that power in court that he thought his birth and place deserved, leapt out, and made sundry out-reds against the king.

2. a. To rise with both (or all four) feet suddenly from the ground or other standing-place, alighting in some other position; to jump, spring. Often with advs., as *aside, down, in, out.* Also with cognate object.

c **897** K. ÆLFRED *Gregory's Past.* xxxiii. 214 Ðæt hie ne hliepen unwillende on ðæt scorene clif unðeawa. *c* **1200** ORMIN 11792 þurrh þatt te laþe gast himm badd Dun læpenn off þe temmple. *c* **1386** CHAUCER *Knt.'s T.* 1829 His hors for fere gan to turne, And leepe aside, and foundred as he leepe. *c* **1450** *Merlin* 21 He hadde lepte in to the ryver and drowned hym-self. **1513** DOUGLAS *Æneis* x. x. 119 The tothir fey bruthir..Lap fra the cart. **1530** LYNDESAY *Test. Papyngo* 552 The ledder schuke, he lape, and gat one fall. **1535** STEWART *Cron. Scot.* (1858) III. 447 He suld haif gart him leip Thre lowpis in ane. **1612** DRAYTON *Poly-olb.* II. 322 Cauerns in the earth, so darke and wondrous deepe As that, into whose mouth the desperate Roman leepe. **1688** BOYLE *Final Causes Nat. Things* II. 53 He [the frog] must..shut his eyes, and so leap blindly. **1707** *Lond. Gaz.* No. 4382/4 Stolen..a bright bay Gelding,..walks, trots, gallops, and leaps. **1711** ADDISON *Spect.* No. 233 ¶2 This Account.. only mentioning the Name of the Lover who leaped, the Person he leaped for. **1725** RAMSAY *Gentle Sheph.* I. i, I..lap in o'er the dyke. **1863** GEO. ELIOT *Romola* xx. He leaped up the stone steps by two at a time. **1884** LADY VERNEY in *Contemp. Rev.* Oct. 547 To save himself by leaping from the car.

Proverb. **1546** J. HEYWOOD *Prov.* (1867) 6 Ye may learne ..to looke or ye leape. *c* **1570** *Marr. Wit & Science* IV. i. C iv, But he that leapes before he loke, good sonne, Maye leape in the myre.

b. Phrase. *(ready) to leap out of †oneself* or *one's skin* (as an expression of delight or eagerness).

1611 SHAKS. *Wint. T.* v. ii. 54 Our King being ready to leape out of himselfe, for ioy of his found Daughter. **1629** MASSINGER *Picture* III. i, Tho' a poor snake, I will leap Out of my skin for joy. **1776** FOOTE *Capuchin* I. Wks. 1799 II. 388, I should have been ready to leap out of my skin at the sight of a countryman in foreign parts.

c. To spring to one's seat *upon* a horse, *into* the saddle. Often with *up.* Also, †*to leap on*, †*to leap to horse.*

c **900** tr. *Bæda's Hist.* II. x. [xiii.] (1890) 138 [He] hleop on þæs cyninges stedan. *c* **1205** LAY. 9284 Leoup he an his stede. *c* **1290** *S. Eng. Leg.* I. 41/232 And lupe þou up bi-hynde me. *c* **1330** *Arth. & Merl.* 5278 (Kölbing) Opon her hors þai lopen swiþe. **13..** *Sir Beues* 1945 (MS. A.) Into þe sadel a lippte. **1375** BARBOUR *Bruce* II. 28 The bruss lap on, and thiddir raid. *c* **1440** *Generydes* 2262 Generydes leppe vppe vppon his stede. *c* **1450** *Merlin* 236 Thei dide his comaundement, and lepe to horse. *a* **1533** LD. BERNERS *Huon* lxii. 216 Huon & his company lept on theyr horses. **1600** *Disc. Gowrie Conspir.* in Moyses *Mem. Scot.* (1755) 265 Before his majestie..could leape on horse-back. *a* **1670** SPALDING *Troub. Chas. I* (Bannatyne Club) I. 94 Allwayes, he lap on in Aberdein, about 60 horse with swords, pistolls, [etc.]. **1841** ELPHINSTONE *Hist. Ind.* II. ii. 137 Humáyun had only time to leap on horseback.

d. Of a fish: To spring from the water.

1387 TREVISA *Higden* (Rolls) VI. 203 A greet fische leep into þe schip. **1423** JAS. I. *Kingis Q.* cliii, Lytill fischis..with bakkis blewe as lede, Lap and playit. **1536** BELLENDEN *Cron. Scot.*, *Descr. Alb.* xi. (1541) C ij b, Als sone as thir salmond cumis to ye lyn, thay leip. **1813** HOGG *Queen's Wake* 71 The troutis laup out of the Leven Louch. **1867** F. FRANCIS *Angling* ix. (1880) 334 Whenever a salmon leaps you must keep a slack line.

e. *to leap at*: to make a spring at in order to seize; *fig.* to exhibit eagerness for. Cf. *to jump at.* So †*to leap to be* or *do* something.

1606 SHAKS. *Ant. & Cl.* III. xiii. 51 If Cæsar please, our Master Will leape to be his Friend. **1632** MASSINGER *Maid of Hon.* III. i, My too curious appetite..Would leap at a mouldy crust. **1653** WALTON *Angler* 214, I could..see fishes leaping at Flies of several shapes and colours. **1665** BOYLE *Occas. Refl.* I. i, But observe this Dogg; I hold him out Meat ..: 'Tis held indeed higher than he can Leap; and yet, if he Leap not at it, I do not give it him. **1671** L. ADDISON *W. Barbary* 20 Large Incoms, the baite disloyalty still leaps at. **1824** SCOTT *Redgauntlet* Let. xiii, Saunders lap at the proposition.

3. To spring sportively up and down; to jump (with joy, mirth, etc.); to dance, skip.

c **900** tr. *Bæda's Hist.* v. iii. (1891) 390 He up astode & áa wæs gongende & hleapende & Dryhten heriȝende. *c* **1205** LAY. 24697 Summe heo gunnen lepen. **1340** *Ayenb.* 156 þe asse..beginþ to lheape and yernþ to-yens him. **1382** WYCLIF *Matt.* xi. 17 We han sungen to ȝou, and ȝe han nat lippid. **1509** HAWES *Past. Pleas.* XXXIII. (Percy Soc.) 163 My grey-houndes leped and my stede did sterte. **1583** BABINGTON *Commandm.* iv. (1637) 39 Asking us if that were to hallow the Sabbath..to swill & to bibble, to leape, to wallow & tumble in bed. **1611** BIBLE *Luke* vi. 23 Reioice yee in that day, and leape for ioy. **1792** A. WILSON *Watty & Meg*, Watty lap, and danced, and kiss'd her. **1856** MRS. BROWNING *Aur. Leigh* I. (1857) 41 And ankle-deep in English grass I leaped, And clapped my hands. **1896** A. E. HOUSMAN *Shropshire Lad* x, And brutes in field and brutes in pen Leap that the world goes round again.

4. To spring suddenly *to* or *upon* one's feet; to rise with a bound *from* a sitting or recumbent position. Often with *up.* †*to leap afoot*: to spring to the ground from horseback; to dismount.

c **1330** *Arth. & Merl.* 7135 (Kölbing) [He] gan arise of his swouȝ..Vp he lepe wiþ chaufed blod. *c* **1400** *Destr. Troy* 8646 Achilles..bound vp his wounde..Lep vp full lyuely launchit on swithe. *c* **1450** *Merlin* 195 He lepe upon hys feet vigerously. **1481** CAXTON *Godfrey* lxviii. 113 The duc leep a foote & drewe oute his swerde. **1697** DRYDEN *Virg. Georg.* IV. 498 Arethusa leaping from her Bed, First lifts above the Waves her beauteous Head. **1821** SHELLEY *Prometh. Unb.* I. 96 A pilot asleep on the howling sea Leaped up from the deck in agony. **1859** TENNYSON *Vivien* 842 Vivien..Leapt from her session on his lap and stood Stiff as a frozen viper. *fig.* **1878** BROWNING *La Saisiaz* 19 The sudden light that leapt at the first word's provocation, from the heart-deeps where it slept.

5. a. *transf.* of things: To spring, move with a leap or bound; esp. to 'fly' (by explosive or other force). Often with *advs.* Also *fig.*

c **1205** LAY. 22031 Vðen þer leppeoð ut..fleoð ut a þat lond. **1340** *Ayenb.* 27 And uor þet þe herte wes uol of uenym hit behoueþ þet hit lheape out be þe mouþe. **1398** TREVISA *Barth. De P.R.* XII. iii. (1495) 411 The goshawke..smytyth and flappyth her wynges, and in soo doynge the olde fethers lepen out and newe growe. **1420** *Liber Cocorum* (1862) 46 Fyrst sethe þy mustuls quyl shel of lepe In water. *c* **1425** *Seven Sag.* (P.) 627 Al the vertu ther schulde bee, Is lopon into the lytyl tre. **1575** GASCOIGNE *Dan Bartholomew* Posies 98 From reasons rule his fancie lightly lope. **1613** SHAKS. *Hen. VIII*, III. ii. 206 He parted Frowning from me, as if Ruine Leap'd from his Eyes. **1667** MARVELL *Corr.* xxxvi. Wks. 1872–5 II. 82 'Tis probable it [the Bill] may this very day leap beyond any man's reach for the future. **1790** BURKE *Fr. Rev.* (C.P.S.) 89, I thought ten thousand swords must have leaped from their scabbards to avenge even a look that threatened her with insult. **1814** CARY *Dante, Par.* v. 91 The arrow, ere the cord is still, Leapeth unto its mark. **1860** TYNDALL *Glac.* I. x. 65 The echos..leaped from cliff to cliff. **1879** FARRAR *St. Paul* (1883) 64 The vessel was shaken, and the name of Matthias leapt out. **1887** RUSKIN *Præterita* II. 154 Above field and wood, leaps up the Salevè Cliff, two thousand feet into the air.

†**b.** To burst, crack, 'fly'. *Obs.*

1477 NORTON *Ord. Alch.* vi. in Ashm. (1652) 95 Manie Claies woll leape in Fier. **1604** E. [GRIMSTONE] *D'Acosta's Hist. Indies* III. xxvi. 198 As a chesnut laid into the fire, leaps and breaks.

c. Of the heart: To beat vigorously, beat 'high', bound, throb. Also *rarely* of the pulse.

1526 *Pilgr. Perf.* (W. de W. 1531) 289 b, Wherfore the herte hoppeth and lepeth in the body. **1596** BP. W. BARLOW *Three Serm.* Ded. 81 Made mens hearts to leape for joy. **1688** MIEGE *Fr. Dict.* s.v. *Heart*, His Heart is ready to leap into his Mouth. **1822–34** *Good's Study Med.* III. 32 He found its [the carp's] heart leaping..four hours after a separation from the body. **1871** PALGRAVE *Lyr. Poems* 6 His heart leapt high as he look'd. **1900** *Blackw. Mag.* June 789 His pulses leaped, and his comely face Glowed with the pride of a fighting race.

d. *colloq.* Of frost: To 'give' or thaw suddenly.

1869 H. STEPHENS *Bk. Farm.* (ed. 2) I. 139/2 When frost suddenly gives way in the morning about sunrise, it is said to have 'leapt'.

e. *Mining.* (See quot.)

1747 HOOSON *Miner's Dict.* s.v., Sometimes a Vein..will Leap [as] much aside as a Yard..or more. **1802** J. MAWE *Min. Derbyshire* 206 Gloss., *Leap*, the vein is said to leap when a substance intersects it, and it is found again, a few feet from the perpendicular.

f. with reference to leap-year.

1600 [see LEAP DAY]. **1601** HOLLAND *Pliny* I. 6 Whereupon euery fifth yeere leapeth, and one odde day is set to the rest. **1604** *Bk. Com. Prayer* Rubric, When the yeeres of our Lorde may be diuided into foure euen partes, which is euery fourth yeere: then the Sunday letter leapeth. *a* **1681** WHARTON *Disc. Yrs. Months & D.* Wks. (1683) 74 By this Addition.. the Fixed Holy-days, and the like, do as it were leap one day farther into the Week.

6. *fig.* **a.** To pass abruptly or at a bound (from one condition or position to another). Also with *back, down, up.*

a **1225** *Ancr. R.* 236 Lo! hwu þe swike wolde makien hire, a last, leapen into prude. *a* **1240** *Wohunge* in *Cott. Hom.* 285 For þenne schal i lepen fra rode in to reste. *a* **1300** *Cursor M.* 8800 þat þou þarfor lepe not in ire. *c* **1380** WYCLIF *Sel. Wks.* III. 384 þus deede beggers freris, lippen up to kynges power. ? *a* **1400** *Morte Arth.* 2084 Bot some leppe fro the lyfe, that one ȝone lawnde houez. **1568** *Satir. Poems Reform.* xlvii. 101 The pairteis mett and maid a fair contrack; Bot now, allace! the men are loppin aback For oppin sklander, callit ane speikand devill. **1598** GRENEWEY *Tacitus' Ann.* VI. x. (1622) 137 He gaue him time to leape backe from their agreements. **1613** PURCHAS *Pilgrimage* (1614) 223 And (to leape back into the Talmud) a certaine Rabbi..saw [etc.]. *Ibid.* 746 Let us draw somewhat nearer the Sunne, gently marching..lest if wee should suddenly leape from one extremity to another, wee should [etc.]. *a* **1670** SPALDING *Troub. Chas. I* (Bannatyne Club) II. 319 Forgetting his oath ..he lap in to the uther syd. **1692** R. L'ESTRANGE *Josephus* IV. i. (1733) 78 Without leaping out of one Slavery into another. **1846** J. MARTINEAU *Ess.* (1891) III. 378 They leap down from Aristotle to Bentham, from Plato to Coleridge, with the fewest possible resting-places between.

b. To pass *over* at a bound; †to evade, neglect.

1596 SHAKS. *Merch. V.* I. ii. 20 A hot temper leapes ore a colde decree. **1658–9** *Burton's Diary* (1828) IV. 55, I could

leap over the rest, but this passed, I doubt it will never be recovered in any age. **1727** A. HAMILTON *New Acc. E. Ind.* I. p. xv, I can perceive several Things worth noticing, they have neglected or leapt over. **1891** CHEYNE *Orig. Psalter* viii. 408 The world's great change was expected so shortly that the brief waiting time might easily be leaped over.

c. *Mus.* To pass from one note to another by an interval greater than a degree of the scale. Also *trans.* (Cf. LEAP *sb.*¹ 7.)

1879 G. A. MACFARREN *Counterpoint* iv. 10 After several consecutive 2nds, in melody, it is bad to leap, in the same direction, upward or downward to an accented note. **1889** E. PROUT *Harmony* (ed. 3) xiii. 143 The third of the chord exceptionally leaping, instead of moving as usual by step. **1927** C. H. KITSON *Counterpoint for Beginners* 17 A part may not leap any interval greater than an octave.

7. *trans.* To spring over; to pass from one side to the other by leaping. Also in phr. ***to leap bounds*** (*lit.* and *fig.*). Also said of a bridge span.

1432–50 tr. *Higden* (Rolls) III. 57 Romulus diede afore thro lepenge the walles of Rome. **1597** MONTGOMERIE *Cherrie & Slae* 1046 Schaw skild and pithie resouns quhy That Danger lap the dyke. **1601** SHAKS. *Twel. N.* I. iv. 21 Be clamorous, and leape all ciuill bounds. **1697** DRYDEN *Virg. Georg.* III. 228 Let 'em not leap the Ditch, or swim the Flood. **1780** COWPER *Progr. Err.* 93 The Nimrod..Leaps every fence but one. **1786** BURNS *Twa Dogs* 30 He was a gash an' faithful tyke, As ever lap a sheugh or dyke. **1865** KINGSLEY *Herew.* xxviii, Come on, leap it like men! **1886** RUSKIN *Præterita* I. 293 The single arched bridge that leaps the Ain.

fig. *a* **1637** B. JONSON *Pind. Ode, Mem. Sir L. Cary & Sir H. Morison* iii, He leap'd the present age, Possest with holy rage, To see that bright eternal day.

8. To cause (an animal) to take a leap. Also *fig.*

1681–6 J. SCOTT *Chr. Life* (1747) III. 355 Those restless Furies..will never cease stimulating and spurring us on.. till they have leapt us headlong into the everlasting Burnings. **1860** RUSSELL *Diary India* II. 287 [He] had leaped his horse across a deep nullah.

9. Of certain beasts: To spring upon (the female) in copulation. Also *absol.* Also † ***to leap upon.***

1530 TINDALE *Gen.* xxxi. 10 All the rammes that leape vpon the shepe are straked, spotted and partie. **1530** PALSGR. 606/1 Kepe your horse in the stabyll, for and he leape a mare he wyll be the worse to journey a good whyle after. **1535** *Act 27 Hen. VIII*, c. 6. §4 The Lords..shall not..suffer any of the said mares to be covered or leapt with any stoned Horse. **1599** SHAKS. *Much Ado* v. iv. 49. **1656** RIDGLEY *Pract. Physick* 251 A Ram that never leaped a Sheep. **1737** BRACKEN *Farriery Impr.* (1757) II. 128 Colts got by such Horses that have leaped eight or ten Times a Day. **1772** *Ann. Reg.* 105/1 A bull..which leaps cows at 5*l.* 5*s.* a cow. **1813** *Sporting Mag.* XLII. 232 The young bull..will not leap any cows..till the first of May.

transf. *a* **1611** BEAUM. & FL. *Philaster* II. ii, I had rather be Sir Tim the schoolmaster, and leap a dairy-maid. **1639** MAYNE *City Match* II. iii. 13 Why what are you? you will not leap me, Sir, Pray know your distance.

10. *Comb.*: **leap candle** (see quot.); † **leap-land** *a.*, vagabond (cf. *land-leaper*). Also LEAP FROG.

1839 W. J. THOMS *Anecd. & Tradit.* (Camden) 96 The young girls in and about Oxford have a sport called *Leap Candle, for which they set a candle in the middle of the room in a candlestick, and then draw up their coats..and dance over the candle back and forth with these words [etc.]. **1614** D. DYKE *Myst. Self-deceiving* (ed. 8) 256 God did not allow of such rouing *lep-land-Leuites.

leapable ('liːpəb(ə)l), *a.* [f. LEAP *v.* + -ABLE.] That can be leaped.

1925 A. S. ALEXANDER *Tramps across Watersheds* 128 Some parts of the precipitous sides approach within leapable distance.

leap day. An intercalary day in the calendar, esp. that of leap-year, February 29th.

1600 HOLLAND *Livy* XLV. xliv. 1232 This yere leapt, and the leap day was the morrow after the feast *Terminalia.* **1712** SWIFT *Jrnl. Stella* 29 Feb., This is leap-year, and this is leap-day. **1833** HERSCHEL *Astron.* xiii. 412 The surplus days thus thrown into the reckoning are called intercalary or leap days. **1896** *Daily News* 22 Jan. 5/4 Rossini was born on February 29 (or 'leap-day'), 1792.

leaper ('liːpə(r)). Forms: 1 **hléapere**, 4 **lepere**, 5 **lepare**, 6– **leaper.** [OE. *hléapere*: see LEAP *v.* and -ER¹.] One who leaps.

† **1.** A runner; a dancer. Also with advs. *Obs.*

a **1000** *O.E. Chron.* an. 889 On þissum ʒeare wæs nan færeld to Rome, buton tueʒen hleaperas Ælfred cyng sende mid ʒewritum. *c* **1000** *Ags. Voc.* in Wr.-Wülcker 311 *Saltator*, hleapere. **1382** [implied in LEAPERESS]. **1393** LANGL. *P. Pl.* C. x. 107 The whiche aren lunatik lollers and leperes a-boute. *c* **1440** *Promp. Parv.* 297/1 Lepare, or rennare, *cursor.* Lepare, or rennar a-wey, *fugax.* **1580** HOLLYBAND *Treas. Fr. Tong.*, *Saulteur ou danseur*, a leaper, or daunser.

† **b.** [After Du. *looper.*] An irregular soldier.

1604 E. GRIMSTONE *Hist. Siege Ostend* 116 Generall Vere sent forth some of his Leapers or aduenturers to take some prisoner of the enemies Campe.

2. A person or an animal that leaps or jumps.

c **1325** *Names of Hare* in *Rel. Ant.* I. 133 The wilde der, the lepere. **1573** LLOID *Pilgr. Princes* (1607) 100 Wrastlers, leapers, runners and such like games were appointed. **1700** WALLIS in *Collect.* (O.H.S.) I. 318 Who did..out-leap..the next-best leaper..by seven inches. **1774** GOLDSM. *Nat. Hist.* (1776) II. 366 The Danish horses were good leapers. **1836** C. SHAW *Let.* 9 May in *Mem.* (1837) 568 The most extraordinary leaper, and perhaps most active man in Europe. **1861** WHYTE MELVILLE *Mkt. Harb.* 275 The two horses..both capital leapers.

b. An animal which uses leaping as a mode of progression.

1796 MORSE *Amer. Geog.* II. 254 They are also called springers, or leapers, from the agility with which they leap, rather than walk. **1828** STARK *Elem. Nat. Hist.* I. 332 Laurenti, in 1768, in his Synopsis of Reptiles, divides them into three orders, viz. Leapers, as the frogs; Walkers, as the lizards; and Serpents. **1881** *Cassell's Nat. Hist.* V. 121 These true Orthoptera may be readily divided into three tribes, namely, the Leapers, or *Saltatoria*, the Runners, or *Cursoria*; and the Earwigs, or *Euplexoptera.*

3. A hollow cylinder with a hook at one end, employed in untwisting old ropes. Cf. LOPER¹. (Knight *Dict. Mech.* 1875.)

† **'leaperess.** *Obs. rare*⁻¹. [f. LEAPER + -ESS.] A female dancer.

1382 WYCLIF *Ecclus.* ix. 4 With a leperesse, or tumbler [1388 daunseresse, Vulg. *saltatrice*], be thou not besy.

leaperous, obs. form of LEPROUS.

'leap-frog, *sb.* [f. LEAP *v.*]

1. A boys' game in which one player places his hands upon the bent back or shoulders of another and leaps or vaults over him. Also, a jump or leap of this description.

1599 SHAKS. *Hen. V*, v. ii. 142 If I could winne a Lady at Leape-frogge, or by vawlting into my Saddle, with my Armour on my backe. **1672** MARVELL *Reh. Transp.* I. 15 Like fair gamsters at Leap-frog. **1797** HOLCROFT *Stolberg's Trav.* (ed. 2) III. lxxxvi. 402 They..exercised themselves at leap frog. **1834** M. SCOTT *Cruise Midge* xix, Massa Twig.. clapping his hands on the old lady's shoulders cleared her and her tub cleverly by a regular leap frog. **1854** HAWTHORNE *Eng. Note-Bks.* (1883) I. 464 And ended..by jumping leap-frog over the backs of the whole company. **1888** BURGON *Lives 12 Gd. Men* I. i. 8 A double row of posts —where boys played leap-frog.

fig. **1704** SWIFT *Mech. Operat. Spirit* Misc. (1711) 299 There is a perpetual Game at Leap-Frog between both; and sometimes the Flesh is uppermost, and sometimes the Spirit. **1856** MRS. BROWNING *Aur. Leigh* I. (1857) 35 We play at leap-frog over the god Term.

2. *Croquet.* (See quot.)

1874 J. D. HEATH *Croquet Player* 33 The Leapfrog or Jump Stroke. This may be called a 'fancy' stroke..The object is, when a hoop or another ball is in the way of the striker's ball, to make the latter jump over the obstacle.

3. *Mil.* (See quot.)

1918 E. S. FARROW *Dict. Mil. Terms* 340 *Leapfrog*, a method of maintaining constant communication with a moving command by using two or more instruments with a single unit, keeping one in operation while another is moving past it to a position in front.

4. *transf.* Competing for higher wages by 'leap-frogging'. Cf. LEAP-FROG *v.* 2 a.

1958 *Spectator* 31 Jan. 123/2 Nobody has much sympathy with the wage demands of busworkers, town or country; if you use dubious methods of wage bargaining, like the leap-frog, you must expect few tears to be shed if a leap lands you into a ditch. **1961** *Daily Tel.* 14 Oct. 16/6 'Leap-frog' in pay may be checked. **1974** *Times* 25 May 13/1 The wage 'leap frog'..is the cause of a large part of our present tensions.

5. *attrib.* (in various *fig.* senses).

1904 *Daily Chron.* 13 July 6/5 Mr. Morley exposed what may be called the 'leap-frog' logic of the Protectionists. **1917** *Q. Rev.* July 190 The 'leap-frog' game of fleeting Ministries. **1952** L. ROSS *Picture* i. 41 The 'leapfrog' director..whose job it would be to arrange things so that Huston would not have to wait between scenes. **1962** *Gloss. Terms Automatic Data Processing* (*B.S.I.*) 50 *Leap-frog test*, a test program stored in locations which are progressively changed by the program itself in order to test the store. **1972** *Times* 19 Dec. 14/1 An attempt to invoke the 'leap-frog' procedure under section 12 of the Administration of Justice Act, 1969, and go direct to the House of Lords from a decision of a judge of the High Court failed.

leap-frog, *v.* [f. the *sb.*] **1. a.** *intr.* and *trans.* To leap or vault as at leap-frog.

1872 G. MACDONALD *Wilf. Cumb.* I. xiii. 215 All I had to do was to go on leap-frogging. **1891** KIPLING *Life's Handicap* 210 He..tried to leapfrog into the saddle. **1894** BLACKMORE *Perlycross* xxxii. 329 Leap-frogged it [a tombstone], hundreds of times, when I were a boy, I have.

b. *Mil.* Of detachments or units, esp. in an attack: to go in advance of each other by turns (see also quot. 1942).

1920 *National Rev.* Nov. 355 Behind them marched other divisions who, on the first momentum of the offensive slackening, were to 'leap-frog' over their comrades and continue the drive. **1922** C. E. MONTAGUE *Disenchantment* ix. 133 Leap-frogging waves of assault. **1927** *Daily Tel.* 30 Aug. 8/7 Two pairs of mobile picket groups, moving by long bounds and one pair 'leapfrogging' the other. **1942** *R.A.F. Jrnl.* 16 May 32 The Air Force followed on their heels.. leap-frogging over huge stretches of desert... As the armies retreated, they leap-frogged back again. **1966** A. J. BARKER *Eritrea* iv. 85 Due to the lack of transport it was possible only to lift two companies forward at any one time, the rest had to march. The two rear companies were picked up in turn and leap-frogged to the head of the main column.

2. *transf.* **a.** In wage negotiations: to pursue a policy of demanding higher wages every time a group or groups of comparable wage-earners have succeeded in pulling level or ahead. Chiefly as **leap-frogging** *vbl. sb.* and *ppl. a.*

1955 *Times* 6 June 7/2 And if the British Transport Commission and the Government were to give in now it could never again be fought with certainty, no matter how long the leap-frogging between the two unions went on. **1958** *Times* 30 Jan. 4/3 Sir Robert Grimston..said that there was much concern among the fare-paying public at the continual leap frogging in wages between London and the provinces. **1958** *Times Rev. Industry* June (London & Cambridge Bull.) p. x, Engineers..could not be well granted less than was granted to workers in prosperous industries. This seems to produce a threat of leap-frogging wages. **1959** *Listener* 2 July 6/1 The long-term contract relieves the strain of annual efforts to surpass the previous year's gains, or to leap-frog the advances won in another industry. **1967** *Times* 18 Jan. 16 There is leap-frogging in newspaper offices, such that when one department negotiates a rise the others follow regardless of justification. **1970** *Daily Tel.* 15 June 2/5 For the first time collective negotiations on new claims by all unions will replace individual 'leapfrogging' demands. **1973** *Times* 21 Dec. 1/7 To breach Phase Three..would lead to leap-frogging claims which would erode the miners' position in the league table.

b. Other *fig.* uses.

1935 J. C. SQUIRE *Reflections & Memories* 6 It is a time before the jolly vulgarity of Earl's Court had leap-frogged westward to the White City, and then to Wembley. **1949** I. DEUTSCHER *Stalin* xiii. 498 Only in 1943 did the newly built factories and those that had been 'leap-frogged' from the west to the Urals and beyond begin to pour out great quantities of tanks, planes, and guns. **1961** *Times* 28 Mar. 4/5 They [*sc.* Oxford] were accompanied by Imperial College, with whom they paddled in the familiar leap-frogging pattern to Chiswick Eyot. **1962** *Punch* 5 Sept. 330/2 The leap-frogged zones beyond [the Green Belts]. **1964** T. W. MCRAE *Impact of Computers on Accounting* vi. 175 In fact, they [*sc.* auditors] 'leapfrog' over the entire EDP system. **1971** P. GRESSWELL *Environment* 122 Development leap-frogs green belts. **1971** J. WAINWRIGHT *Last Buccaneer* III. 313 When a man leap-frogs me in the promotion stakes I'm human enough to feel narked. **1972** *Times* 23 Feb. 27/6 So soon as a case at first instance arose involving the ratio decidendi of *Rookes v Barnard* the parties concerned might use the 'leap-frogging' procedure now available. **1973** *Listener* 17 May 653/1 Haldeman..was put in charge of the advance men, leap-frogging ahead of the candidate and arranging for crowds.

Hence **leap-frogger**, one who plays at leap-frog.

1890 *Pall Mall G.* 4 Jan. 2/1 Sometimes a too ambitious leap-frogger ruined his party by overbalancing and falling off.

† **'leapful.** *Obs.* [f. LEAP *sb.*² + -FUL. Orig. in syntactical comb.] A basketful.

c **1000** [see LEAP *sb.*² 1]. *c* **1380** WYCLIF *Serm.* Sel. Wks. II. 14 How many leepfullis of broke mete þei token aftir. **1382** —— *Mark* viii. 8 *v. rr.* lepful, leepis ful. *c* **1440** *York Myst.* xxxi. 207 ʒa, lorde, and xij lepfull þer lefte Of releue whan all men had eten.

† **leap-gate.** *Obs.* Forms: 1 **hlýpʒeat**, 4 **lipȝet**, 5 **lypȝet(e, -zet**, 7 **leap-yeat.** [f. LEAP *sb.*¹ + GATE *sb.*¹] A low gate in a fence, which can be leaped by deer, while keeping sheep from straying.

980 in Kemble *Cod. Dipl.* III. 180/28 Ondlang ʒeardes on ðæt hlypʒeat. **13..** *Eulog. Hist.* (Rolls) III. 224 Fuit ibi una porta quæ vocatur in lingua Anglicana lipȝet [*v. rr.* **14..** lypȝete, lypzet]. **1609** in S. ROWE *Peramb. Dartmoor* (1848) 278 The corne hedges and leape yeates rounde aboute the same Common and fforest. *c* **1630** RISDON *Surv. Devon* §215 (1810) 223 The correction of the..ditches, and leap-yeats, shall be in the court.

leaping ('liːpɪŋ), *vbl. sb.* [f. LEAP *v.* + -ING¹.] The action of the vb. LEAP, in various senses.

c **1000** ÆLFRIC *Hom.* I. 480 Ða unstæððiʒan hleapunge þæs mædenes. **1398** TREVISA *Barth. De P.R.* XVIII. xxii. (1495) 781 The wylde gote is..moost lyght in lepynge and moste sharpe in sighte. *c* **1440** *Promp. Parv.* 297/1 Lepynge a-wey, *fuga.* **1529** *Supplic. to King* (E.E.T.S.) 41 Church ales in the whiche with leappynge, daunsynge, and kyssyng, they maynteyne the profett of their churche. **1611** FLORIO, *Chiarantana*, a kind of Caroll or song full of leapings like a Scotish gigge. **1622** MABBE tr. *Aleman's Guzman d' Alf.* II. 49 Which way so euer I sought to winde me, was but a leaping out of the Frying Pan into the fire. **1664** COTTON *Scarron.* 30 Our Æneas, at two leapings, Set the first foot upon the steppings. **1896** A. E. HOUSMAN *Shropshire Lad* liv, By brooks too broad for leaping The lightfoot boys are laid.

b. *attrib.* and *Comb.*, as ***leaping-bar, -pole***; **leaping-head, -horn**, the lower pommel on a side-saddle, against which the left knee presses in leaping; a hunting-horn, 'third crutch'; † **leaping house**, a brothel; **leaping-on-stone**, a stone for convenience in mounting a horse; a horse-block; **leaping time**, the time of activity, youth.

1852 WHATELY in *Life* (1866) II. 260 The Ecclesiastical Titles Bill (commonly called 'Lord John's *leaping-bar' to afford exercise in jumping over it). **1881** MRS. P. O. DONOGHUE *Ladies on Horseb.* I. iii. 35 By..pressing the left knee against the *leaping-head, you can accomplish the rise in your saddle. **1859** *Art Taming Horses* ix. 144 In case of a horse 'bucking', without the *leaping-horn there is nothing to prevent a lady from being thrown up. But the leaping-horn holds down the left knee. **1596** SHAKS. *1 Hen. IV*, I. ii. 9 What a diuell hast thou to do with the time of the day? vnlesse houres were cups of Sacke..and dialls the signes of *Leaping-houses. **1837** LOCKHART *Scott* II. ii. 63 He immediately trotted to the side of the **leaping-on-stone* of which Scott from his lameness found it convenient to make use. **1859** FARRAR *Jul. Home* xvi. 205 Trying the merits of his alpenstock as a *leaping-pole. **1893** BARING-GOULD *Cheap Jack Z.* III. 192 In the Fens, when a man requires to traverse a considerable distance, he provides himself with a leaping-pole. **1661** SHAKS. *Cymb.* IV. ii. 200 To haue turn'd my *leaping time into a Crutch.

leaping ('liːpɪŋ), *ppl. a.* [f. LEAP *v.* + -ING².] That leaps (†runs, †dances, etc.: see the vb.).

c **1000** ÆLFRIC *Hom.* I. 482 Herodes swor..ðæt he wolde ðære hleapendan dehter forʒyfan swa hwæt swa heo bæde. *c* **1380** WYCLIF *Serm.* Sel. Wks. I. 389 More sutil and sinful þan þis lepynge strumpet [*sc.* the daughter of Herodias]. ? *a* **1400** *Morte Arth.* 1460 They luyschene to-gedyres..on leppande stedes. **1607** TOPSELL *Four-f. Beasts* (1658) 12

There is a remedy to quail these wanton leaping beasts [satyrs]. 1667 DUCHESS OF NEWCASTLE in *Life Duke N.* (1886) II. 101 A grey leaping horse. 1716 *Loyal Mourner* 9 And leaping Dolphins catch a distant View. 1870 MORRIS *Earthly Par.* IV. (1871) 219 A joy as of the leaping fire Over the house-roof rising higher.

b. In the names of various animals, plants, etc., as **leaping cucumber** = *spirting* or *squirting cucumber* (see CUCUMBER 3); **leaping-fish**, the fish *Salarias tridactylus*, of Ceylon; so called because it comes on shore and leaps over the wet stones, etc.; (**Cape**) **leaping hare** = *jumping hare*: see JUMPING *ppl. a.* b; **leaping spider**, 'a jumping spider, one of the *Saltigradæ*' (W.).

1548-78 *Leaping cucumber [see CUCUMBER 3]. 1861 TENNENT *Nat. Hist. Ceylon* 495 Index, *Leaping fish. 1849 *Mammalia* IV. 44 The *leaping hare equals our common hare in size. 1859 WOOD *Nat. Hist.* I. 588 The Spring Haas, or Cape Gerboa, sometimes called, from its hare-like aspect, the Cape Leaping Hare.

c. leaping ague, †gout (see quots.).

1562 TURNER *Baths* 6 This bathe..is good for the leping goute, that runneth from one ioynte to another. 1792 *Statist. Acc. Scotl.* IV. 5 A distemper called by the country-people the leaping-ague, and by physicians, St. Vitus's dance. 1806 FORSYTH *Beauties Scotl.* IV. 375 In the mountainous part of Angus a singular disease, called there the *leaping ague*, is said to exist, bearing a resemblance to St. Vitus's dance.

Hence **'leapingly** *adv.*, by leaps.

1548 ELYOT *Dict.*, *Assultim*, leapyngly, iumpyngly.

leaprous, leapry, obs. ff. LEPROUS, LEPRY.

'leap year. [Late ME., f. LEAP *sb.*[1]; prob. of much older formation, as the ON. *hlaup-ár* is presumably, like other terms of the Roman calendar, imitated from Eng.

The name may refer to the fact that in the bissextile year any fixed festival after Feb. falls on the next week-day but one to that on which it fell in the preceding year, not on the next week-day as usual. Cf. med.L. *saltus lunæ* (OE. *mónan hlýp*), the omission of a day in the reckoning of the lunar month, made every nineteen years to bring the calendar into accord with the astronomical phenomena.]

A year having one day (now Feb. 29) more than the common year; a bissextile year. †*to make leap year of*: (fig) to pass over.

1387 TREVISA *Higden* (Rolls) IV. 199 Þat tyme Iulius amended þe kalender, and fonde þe cause of the lepe ȝere [L. *rationem bisexti invenit*]. 1481 CAXTON *Myrr.* II. xxxi. 127 Bysexte or lepe yere, whiche in iiij yere falleth ones. 1562 J. HEYWOOD *Prov. & Epigr.* (1867) 207 The next leape yere after wedding was first made. 1606 BIRNIE *Kirk-Buriall* (1833) 38 In civil entries to heritage, if it be for the better, men can make leap-yeare of their father and seeke farther uppe. 1704 HEARNE *Duct. Hist.* (1714) I. 3 That Year was called the Bissextile; and by us Leap-Year because one day of the Week is leaped over in the Observation of the Festivals. 1834 *Nat. Philos., Astron.* i. 44/1 (U.K.S.) The years 1600, 2000, 2400, would be leap years.

lear[1] (lɪə(r)). Now *Sc.* and *north. dial.* Also 5-7 lere, 6 leare, 6-7 leer(e, 9 leir. [f. LERE *v.*; but in mod.Sc. use prob. a mere graphic variant of *lair*, *lare*: see LORE.] Instruction, learning; in early use †a piece of instruction, a lesson; †also, a doctrine, religion.

*a*1400-50 *Alexander* 3759 For many leres may þe limpe slik as þou noȝt wenes! *c*1440 *Sir Gowther* 231 Y will to Rome er than y reste, To leve up another lere. *a*1450 *Le Morte Arth.* 521 The knightis þat were wise of lere. 1579 SPENSER *Sheph. Cal.* May 262 He, that had wel ycond his lere. 1586 FERNE *Blaz. Gentrie* 22 And teach our Gentiles vertuous lere. 1594 LYLY *Moth. Bomb.* II. v, He learn'd his leere of my sonne. 1647 H. MORE *Song of Soul* II. i. i. xix, Queen of Philosophie and virtuous lear! 1652 STAPYLTON tr. *Herodian* 37 So well his leere he couth. 1720 RAMSAY *Edinburgh's Salut.* vi, Classic lear and letters belle. 1837 R. NICOLL *Poems* (1842) 95 He gaed to the school, an' he took to the lear. 1882 STEVENSON *Merry Men* ii. Wks. 1895 VIII. 126 Your heid [is] dozened wi' carnal leir.

b. *Comb.* **lear-father**, a master in learning; see also quot. 1855.

1533 GAU *Richt Vay* 15 Elders techours and leirfaders. 1702 C. LESLIE *Reply to 'Anguis Flagellatus'* Theol. Wks. 1721 II. 612 The Man who was call'd G. Fox's Lear-Father. 1855 ROBINSON *Whitby Gloss.*, *Lay-father* or *Lear-father*, a person whose conduct has influenced others; an exemplar.

†lear[2]. *Obs.* Forms: 4 layour, 4-5 liour(e, lyour(e, lyre, 5 lere, 5-6 lyer(e, 6-8 leer(e, 7 leir, 8-9 lear. [a. OF. *lieure, lyeure, liure*:—L. *ligātūra-m* (see LIGATURE).]

1. Tape; binding for the edges of a fabric.

1382-3 *Durh. MS. Sacr. Roll.* In lyour empt. pro le Redill' pro magno altari, ijd. *c*1440 *Promp. Parv.* 178/1 Frenge, or lyoure, *tenia*. *Ibid.* 306/2 Lyowre, to bynde wythe precyows clothys, *ligatorium, redimiculum*. 1485 *Churchw. Acc. St. Dunstan's, Canterbury*, For lere and ryngys to the same bookeram vd. 1503 *Privy Purse Exp. Eliz. York* (Nicholas 1830) 91 Item for viij lb. of blewe lyere at xijd. the lb. viijs. 1579 LYLY *Euphues* (Arb.) 79, I meane so to mortifie my selfe, that in steede of silkes, I wil weare sackcloth: for Owches and Bracelletes, Leere and Caddys. 1736 J. LEWIS *I. of Tenet* Gloss. (E.D.S.), *Leere*, tape.

2. *Cookery.* A thickening for sauces, soups, etc.; a thickened sauce.

?*c*1390 *Form of Cury* (1780) 24 Make a layour of brede and blode and lay it þerwith. *c*1430 *Two Cookery-bks.* 33 Take Water and let boyle, and draw a lyer þer-to of Brede, of þe cromys, with wyne y-now. 1658 SIR T. MAYERNE *Archimag. Anglo-Gall.* xxviii. 29 Then make a Leer or Sawce for it. 1750 E. SMITH *Compl. Housew.* (ed. 14) 35 When 'tis baked, put in a lear of gravy with a little white wine. 1837 DISRAELI *Venetia* I. iv, One of those rich sauces of claret, anchovy, and sweet herbs,..which was technically termed a Lear.

Hence **'learing** *vbl. sb.* (in quots. *liring*, *lyring*), binding with tape.

1480 *Wardr. Acc. Edw. IV* (Nicholas 1830) 126 Liour for liring and lowping of the same arras. 1512 *Househ. Bk. Earl Northumb.* (1770) 326 For Lyring Sewing and Jouning of Stuf.

lear[3] (lɪə(r)). Also 7 leere. [Perh. a developed use of *lear*, LAIR *sb.*[1] 5; cf. quot. 1623 there.] Colour (of sheep or cattle), due to the nature of the soil.

1601 HOLLAND *Pliny* XXXI. ii. II. 403 In some places there is no other thing bred or growing but brown & duskish, insomuch as not only the cattell is all of that leere, but also the corn upon the ground. 1616 SURFL. & MARKHAM *Country Farm* I. xxv. 117 Now for the leares of sheepe, you shall vnderstand that the browne hazell leare is of all other the best, the redd leare next to it [etc.]. 1883 *Advt. Handbill*, M——'s Fly, Lear, and Vermin Powder will prevent the Sheep from being struck by the Fly, at the same time producing a good Lear, which every farmer must allow is a great advantage.

lear, obs. f. or var. of LAIR, LEER, LERE, LIAR.

'lea-rig. *dial.* [OE. *lǽȝhrycg*, f. **lǽȝe* LEA *a.* + *hrycg* back, RIDGE.] A ridge left in grass at the end of a ploughed field.

956 *Charter* in Birch *Cartul. Sax.* (1893) III. 96 To emnes þam ealdan læȝ hrycge. 1549 *Compl. Scot.* vi. 42 The end of ane leye rig. 1792 BURNS *My ain kind dearie O* i, I'd meet thee on the lea-rig, My ain kind dearie! O.

learn (lɜːn), *v.* Pa. t. and pple. learned (lɜːnd), learnt (lɜːnt). Forms: 1 leornian, *Northumb.* liorniȝa, 2 leornen, lornen, 2-3 leornie-n, 3 -in, leorny, liernin, lerni(e, 3-4 lernen, 4 leorne, lerny, l(e)urne, *Kent.* lierne, lyerne, -i, -y, 4-5 leerne, 4-6 lern(e, 4, 6, 9 *dial.* larn, 6 *Sc.* leyrne, leirne, 6-7 learne, 6- learn. *Pa. t.* 1 leornode, -ade, 3 *Orm.* lerrnde, 3-4 leornede, 4 lernid, leernde, lernd, 4-6 lerned, 5 leerned, lurned, -et, 5-6 lernyd, 6 *Sc.* lernit, leirned, -it, 7- learned, learnt. *Pa. pple.* 3 ileornet, 3-5 ilerned, 3, 6 ylerned; from 14th c. onwards as in pa. t. [OE. *leornian*, Northumb. *liorniȝa* = OFris. *lirna, lerna*, OS. *línôn* (not found in Du.), OHG. *lirnên, lernên*, (MHG., mod.G. *lernen*):—WGer. **liznējan*, **liznôjan*, f. **lis-*, wk.-grade of **lais-*, root of OTeut. **lairâ* LORE.]

I. To acquire knowledge.

1. a. *trans.* To acquire knowledge of (a subject) or skill in (an art, etc.) as a result of study, experience, or teaching. Const. *from*, *of* (arch.), †*at* (a person). Also, to commit to memory (passages of prose or verse), *esp.* in phrases *to learn by heart, by rote*, for which see the sbs.

*c*900 tr. *Bæda's Hist.* III. xvii. [xxiii.] (1890) 232 From þæm he þæt ȝemet ȝeleornade reȝollices þeodscipes. *c*975 *Rushw. Gosp.* Mark xiii. 28 From fic-beom ðonne liorniȝe bispell. *c*1050 *Byrhtferth's Handboc* in *Anglia* (1885) VIII. 308/26 þam þe lyste þisne cræft leornian. *c*1175 *Lamb. Hom.* 55 Gif we leornið godes lare! *c*1200 ORMIN 9309 Too leorenn lare att Sannt Johan Off þeȝȝre sawle nede. *c*1200 *Trin. Coll. Hom.* 17 Ate biginninge of cristendom elch man leornede pater noster and credo. *a*1225 *Leg. Kath.* 940 þes is al þe lare þat ich nu leorni. 1387 TREVISA *Higden* (Rolls) V. 167 þis Julianus in his childehode lerned nygromancie and wicchecraft. *c*1449 PECOCK *Repr.* I. xi. 58 Al that Cristen men and wommen ouȝten leerne thei mowe leerne out of the Bible. 1576 FLEMING *Panopl. Epist.* 238, I woulde have you to understand and learne this lesson. 1667 MILTON *P.L.* XI. 360 To learn True patience, and to temper joy with fear. 1715 DE FOE *Fam. Instruct.* I. i. (1841) 19 What shall I learn there of God? 1845 M. PATTERSON *Ess.* (1889) I. 16 The Frank..learned with implicit belief his faith from the mouth of the Roman priest. 1874 GREEN *Short Hist.* iv. §1. 162 It was from Earl Simon..that Edward had learned the skill in warfare which distinguished him among the princes of his time.

b. with clause as obj.

*c*1000 ÆLFRIC *Deut.* xiv. 23 Leorna þæt þu ondræde Drihten on ælc tid. *c*1200 ORMIN 4970 Lerneþþ att me þatt icc amm wiss Rihht milde and meoc wiþþ herrte. *c*1200 *Trin. Coll. Hom.* 73 Alle þo þe ne wilen listen lorspel and þeron lernen wiche ben sinnen. 1340 *Ayenb.* 233 O, þu þet art cristen, lyerne hou þou sselt louie god. *c*1400 *Cato's Morals* 62 in *Cursor M.* App. iv. 1670 Lerne..quat werk þou folow salle. 1667 MILTON *P.L.* XII. 561 Henceforth I learne that to obey is best. 1884 F. TEMPLE *Relat. Relig. & Sci.* vii. (1885) 220 Scientific men will learn that there are other kinds of knowledge besides scientific knowledge.

c. With *inf.*; also with *how* and *inf.*

*c*900 tr. *Bæda's Hist.* III. xx. [xxviii.] (1890) 246 þa ða he in wreotum leornade to donne. *c*1175 *Lamb. Hom.* 117 *Discite bene facere* þet is..leorniað god to wurchenne. 1297 R. GLOUC. (Rolls) 675 Betere him adde ibe Abbe bileued þed doune þan ilerned vor to fle. *Ibid.* 10693 So hii miȝte lerni traitour to be. *c*1340 *Cursor M.* 7496 (Trin.) þou lernedest neuer to fiȝt. *c*1500 *Merch. & Son* in Halliw. *Nugæ Poet* 23 Y wolde lerne of marchandyse to passe ovyr the see! 1547 LATIMER *2nd Serm. bef. Edw. VI* (Arb.) 70 So your grace must learne howe to do of Salomon. 1602 *2nd Pt. Return fr. Parnass.* V. i. 1999, I was a gamesome boy and learned to sing. 1729 BUTLER *Serm.* Wks. 1873 II. 47 There are times for silence: when they should learn to hear, and be attentive. 1838 LONGF. *Ps. Life* ix, Learn to labour and to wait. 1875 JOWETT *Plato* (ed. 2) IV. 32 We learn morals, as we learn to talk, instinctively.

d. Phr. ***I am (yet) to learn***: I am ignorant or unaware. Now usually ***I have (yet) to learn***.

1687 MIEGE *Gt. Fr. Dict.* II. s.v., The truth of it we are as yet to learn, *nous n'en savons pas encore la Verité*. 1726 LEONI *Alberti's Archit.* I. 82, I am not to learn [It. *Ne mi è nascoso*] that some..are of opinion that very high Walls are dangerous. 1789 CHARLOTTE SMITH *Ethelinde* I. 91 Whence he came..Sir Edward was yet to learn.

2. a. *intr.* To acquire knowledge of a subject or matter; to receive instruction. Const. as in sense 1.

971 *Blickl. Hom.* 13 Leorniað æt me, forðon þe ic eom mildheort. *c*1000 ÆLFRIC *Past Ep.* §46 in Thorpe *Laws* II. 384 Lange sceal leornian se ðe læran sceal. *c*1340 *Cursor M.* 6819 (Trin.) Lerne not of him þat is lyere. *c*1420 *Liber Cocorum* (1862) 36 Thus have I lurnet at gentil men. 1575 *Brief Disc. Troubl. Franckford* 10 God grant, we maye lerne at their ensamples. 1605 SHAKS. *Lear* II. ii. 134 Sir, I am too old to learne. 1781 COWPER *Charity* 120 'Tis thus reciprocating, each with each, Alternately the nations learn and teach. 1863 KINGSLEY *Lett.* (1878) II. 161 The great use of a public school education to you, is, not so much to teach you things as to teach you how to learn. 1884 F. M. CRAWFORD *Rom. Singer* I. 7 He was always willing to learn and to read.

†b. Const. *on* (the matter studied). *Obs.*

*c*1340 *Cursor M.* 15614 (Trin.) Folweþ him ȝoure fadir is: to lerne on his lare. *a*1400 *Pistill of Susan* 135 Wolt þou, ladi, for loue, on vre lay lerne? *a*1668 DENHAM *Old Age* 274, I have heard that Socrates the wise Learned on the lute for his last exercise.

3. a. *trans.* To acquire knowledge of (a fact); to become acquainted with or informed of (something); to hear of, ascertain. Also with *obj. clause.*

*c*1200 ORMIN 7250 He lerrnde wel þurrh hemm Whatt daȝȝ, and whære o lande, þatt ȝunge wenchell borenn wass. 1559 W. CUNNINGHAM *Cosmogr. Glasse* 151 When you will lerne the time that it shall be full sea. 1576 FLEMING *Panopl. Epist.* 278 You, whom I had learned by common voice to be a philosopher of great fame. 1599 SHAKS. *Much Ado* II. ii. 57, I will presentlie goe learne their day of marriage. 1638 BAKER tr. *Balzac's Lett.* (vol. II.) 27 This good newes I have learned by a letter of yours. 1798 JEFFERSON *Writ.* (1859) IV. 243, I..have not yet learnt his sentiments on it. 1836 W. IRVING *Astoria* I. 105 Lest the captain should learn the fate of the schooner. 1855 MACAULAY *Hist. Eng.* xxii. IV. 717 All that he knew about their treachery he had learned at second hand. 1864 BROWNING *Dram. Pers., Mr. Sludge* 221 He's dead I learn.

b. *to learn out*: to find out, discover. Now *dial.*

1629 MAXWELL *Herodian* (1635) 171 Then, secretly torturing them, he [Albinus] learnt out all their treachery. 1677 YARRANTON *Eng. Improv.* 109, I will tell you how the Trick is: And if I had not been an old Clothier and a Fulling-Boy when I was young I could not have learnt it out. 1899 RAYMOND *Two Men o' Mendip* xv. 250 But if he should find out? If any should learn it out an 'tell?

c. *intr.* To be informed, to ascertain, hear (*of*).

1756 C. LUCAS *Ess. Waters* III. 243 It has never, that I can learn, been fully observed. 1827 SIR J. BARRINGTON *Sketches* I. ii. 29 How many rogues 'ill there be at Reuben, as you larn, to-night? 1893 STEVENSON *Catriona* ii. 18 He'll have to learn of it on the deaf side of his head no later than to-morrow when I call on him.

II. To impart knowledge. Now *vulgar.*

4. *trans.* To teach. In various constructions:

a. To teach (a person).

*a*1300 *Cursor M.* 19028 In crist lai þat folk to lern. 1382 WYCLIF *Prov.* ix. 7 Who lerneth [1388 techith] a scornere, doth wrong he to hymself. *c*1440 *York Myst.* x. 20 þus lernyd he me. *a*1450 *Knt. de la Tour* (1868) 2 A man ought to lerne his doughters with good ensaumples. 1535 COVERDALE *Ps.* xxiv. 5 Lede me in thy trueth and lerne me. 1549 *Compl. Scot.* Prol. 14 Quhen ane ydiot..presumis to teche or to leyrne ane man that hes bayth speculatione ande experiens. 1650 FULLER *Pisgah* II. xii. 249 No doubt the chickens crowed as the cocks had learned them. 1763 FOOTE *Mayor of G.* II. Wks. 1799 I. 178 [An uneducated speaker] If they would but once submit to be learned by me. 1974 *Times* 16 Dec. 12/8 We asked whether he had learned the instrument at school... 'No. He learned it himself and now he's learning me.'

b. To teach (a person) *to do* or *how to do* something. (Also in *passive.*)

*c*1340 *Cursor M.* 8421 (Trin.) Set him faste to gode teching Til he be lerned him self to lede. *c*1435 *Torr. Portugal* 1897 To lerne you ffor to ride. 1480 CAXTON *Descr. Brit.* 34 Gentilmens children ben lerned and taught from their yongth to speke frenssh. *a*1540 BARNES *Wks.* (1573) 352/1 Doth hee not learne all men to come to Christ. 1590 SPENSER *F.Q.* I. vi. 25 He would learne The Lyon stoup to him. 1666 BUNYAN *Grace Ab.* ¶27 That my Father might learn me to speak without this wicked way of swearing. 1706 FARQUHAR *Recruiting Officer* III. i, The captain learned me how to take it with an air. 1792 MARY WOLLSTONECRAFT *Right Wom.* v. 181 We should learn them, above all things, to lay a due restraint on themselves. 1801 STRUTT *Sports & Past.* III. i. 115 The frequent practice of this exercise must have learned them..to become excellent horsemen. 1801 COLERIDGE *Lett.* I. 365 They learn us to associate a keen and deep feeling with all the good old phrases. 1844 DISRAELI *Coningsby* VIII. iii, Learn to know the House; learn the House to know you. 1885 G. ALLEN *Babylon* i, 'Will you learn me to draw a church?'

c. To teach (a person a thing). Also with *clause.*

*c*1200 ORMIN 19613 To lokenn watt itt lerneþ uss Off [ure] sawle nede. 1377 LANGL. *P. Pl.* B. x. 171 Logyke I lerned hir and many other lawes, And alle the musouns in musike I made hir to knowe. *c*1420 LYDG. *Assembly of Gods* 957, I shall lerne hem a new daunce. *c*1460 FORTESCUE *Abs. & Lim. Mon.* xi. (1885) 135 Wherby we bith lerned þat it schal..be goode to owre prince..that he be well indowed. 1559 W. CUNNINGHAM *Cosmogr. Glasse* 33, I pray you learne me th' use of this table. 1606 J. CARPENTER *Solomon's Solace* xiv. 58 So learneth he all children..in what honor..they

should hold those persons. **1610** SHAKS. *Temp.* I. ii. 365 The red-plague rid you For learning me your language. **1719** DE FOE *Crusoe* I. xv. (1840) 255 Having learnt him English. **1742** RICHARDSON *Pamela* III. 353 Her Ladyship asked one of the Children.. who learnt her her Catechism? **1831** J. J. STRANG *Diary* 31 Dec. in M. M. Quaife *Kingdom of St. James* (1930) 198, I have succeeded in regulating them and learning them what to do without punishing a single schollar. **1876** MORRIS *Sigurd* (1877) 86 Thou.. hast learned me all my skill. **1889** 'ROLF BOLDREWOOD' *Robbery under Arms* xliv, We made up our minds to learn him a lesson. **1914** *Sat. Even. Post* 4 Apr. 10/3, I learned him that, yuh see. **1935** WODEHOUSE *Luck of Bodkins* xv. 181 The English public school system.. isn't at all what an educational system should be... If you ask me, they don't learn the little perishers nothing. **1966** F. SHAW et al. (*title*) Lern yerself Scouse.

d. To teach (a thing) *to* a person. *rare.*

1377 LANGL. *P. Pl.* B. x. 374 Many tales ȝe tellen that Theologye lerneth. **1477** EARL RIVERS (Caxton) *Dictes* 15 b, He.. commaunded it shulde not be lerned to any Straungers. **1697** COLLIER *Ess. Mor. Subj.* I. 161 'Tis the Rod, not the Inclination, which learns the Lesson. **1893** STEVENSON *Catriona* 21 My father learned it to me.

¶**e.** Phr. ***I'll learn you***: used as a warning of impending punishment. *Non-standard.*

1822 J. GALT *Sir A. Wylie* III. xxxiii. 279 I'll learn you to fill yoursel fu'. **1873** C. D. WARNER in 'Mark Twain' & Warner *Gilded Age* xxix. 266 The conductor.. reached the bell rope, 'Damn you, I'll learn you,' stepped to the door. **1974** P. WRIGHT *Lang. Brit. Industry* iv. 41 The common *I'll learn you*.. when used ironically, has the unstandard meaning of 'I'll teach you never to do that again'.

†**5.** To inform (a person) of something; with clause or thing as second obj. *Obs.*

1425 *Rolls of Parlt.* IV. 271/1 For, as I am lerned, ther ar to consider two thinges. **1441** *Plumpton Corr.* (Camden) p. lix, The said misdoers were learned by their especialls [*sic*] .. that the said officers.. had knowledge of their said lying in waite for them. *a* **1456** LD. CROMWELL in *Paston Lett.* III. 426 There is a greet straungenesse betwix.. John Radcliff and you.. as I am lerned. *c* **1500** in *Q. Eliz. Acad.* 96 Of brutane the duk.. Richast armes is, as I lernit am. **1606** SHAKS. *Tr. & Cr.* II. i. 22 Learne me the Proclamation. **1697** tr. *C'tess D'Aunoy's Trav.* (1706) 57 You learn me Particulars I was ignorant of. *Ibid.* 69 Having learnt him all which had past.

learnability (ˌlɜːnəˈbɪlɪtɪ). [f. LEARNABLE *a.* + -ITY.] The quality or fact of being learnable.

1959 *Brno Studies in English* I. 16 The easiness or the difficulty with which it affects the person trying to acquire it (at the risk of coining another barbarous neologism one might term it 'learnability'). **1966** *Philos. Rev.* LXXV. 435 There are others of great importance: brevity, learnability, etc.

learnable (ˈlɜːnəb(ə)l), *a.* [f. LEARN *v.* + -ABLE.] That may be learnt.

1629 T. ADAMS *Medit. Creed* Wks. 1099 These bee mysteries, yet in some measure learneable. **1818** BENTHAM *Ch. Eng.* Pref. xi, I learnt for my first lesson, the matter, in so far as it was learnable, of this formulary. **1840** CARLYLE *Heroes* iii. (1858) 249 Dante,.. we need not doubt, learned better than most all that was learnable. **1857** KINGSLEY *Two Y. Ago* xviii, When the lesson comes.. I suppose it will come in some learnable shape. **1885** TENNYSON *Balin* 127 Gifts Born with the blood, not learnable, divine.

learned (ˈlɜːnɪd), *ppl. a.* [f. LEARN *v.* + ED[1].]

†**1.** In distinctly participial sense. *Obs. rare.*

c **1420** *Pallad. on Husb.* v. 121 This mone also, by rather lerned reson [L. *ea ratione qua dictum est*] To sette and graffe in places temporate Pomgarnat is. *a* **1586** SIDNEY *Arcadia* I. (1633) 25 The error committed.. becomes a sharpely learned experience. **1714** TICKELL *Fragm. Hunting* in Steele *Poet. Misc.* 179 [A hound] True to the Master's Voice, and learned Horn.

2. a. Of a person: In early use, that has been taught; instructed, educated. In later use with narrowed sense: Having profound knowledge gained by study, esp. in language or some department of literary or historical science; deeply-read, erudite. Const. *in*, †*of.* (Superseding the earlier LERED.)

learned society: a society formed for the prosecution of some branch of learning or science.

c **1340** *Cursor M.* 10416 (Laud) This lady was of muche price lovid and lernyd [*older texts* lered] ware and wyse. **1382** WYCLIF *Acts* vii. 22 And Moyses was lernd [**1388** lerned] in al the wysdom of Egipcians. *c* **1400** *Destr. Troy* 3940 Eneas.. was.. of litterure & langage lurnyt ynoghe. **1556** *Chron. Gr. Friars* (Camden) 48 The byshoppe of Wynchester, with dyvers other byshoppes & lernede men. **1639** FULLER *Holy War* III. xxix. (1840) 170 He was very learned.. especially for a prince, who only baiteth at learning. *a* **1680** BUTLER *Rem.* (1759) I. 1 A Learn'd Society of late.. Agree'd.. To search the Moon by her own light. **1698** KEILL *Exam. Theory Earth* (1734) 312 That very Learned Friend of his.. has given the World reason enough to suspect him. **1712** HEARNE *Collect.* (O.H.S.) III. 488 He was learned in the British tongue. **1772** *Junius Lett.* lxviii. 335 Learned.. you are, and quick in apprehension. **1791–1823** D'ISRAELI *Cur. Lit.* (1866) 319/2 He is a 'learned' man who has embraced most knowledge on the particular subject of his investigation. **1798** *Phil. Mag.* June 95 (*title*) Intelligence. Learned Societies. **1810** SCOTT *Biog. Notices* Prose Wks. (1870) II. 202 That dreaded phenomenon, a learned lady. **1823** —— *One Volume more*, John Pinkerton next, and I'm truly concern'd.. I can't call that worthy so candid as learn'd. **1847** TENNYSON *Princess* VII. 299 Not learned, save in gracious household ways. **1863** HAWTHORNE *Our Old Home* iv. 136 This bewildered enthusiast had recognized a depth in the man whom she decried, which scholars, critics, and learned societies, devoted to the elucidation of his unrivaled scenes, had never imagined to exist there. **1871** C. DAVIES *Metr. Syst.* II. 40 A system.. made.. by a committee of learned professors. **1897** W. JAMES *Will to Believe* 306 All our learned societies have begun in some such modest way. **1898** H. CALDERWOOD *Hume* vi. 85 The learned circles of Paris. **1958** *Observer* 13 July 3/7 The battle of the learned societies with the Inland Revenue. **1973** *LSA Bull.* Mar. 28 He defined a learned society as one which publishes a journal and holds an annual meeting; a professional society as one which is involved in matters of concern to its members.

b. *absol.* Chiefly in pl. ***the learned*** = 'men of learning', 'the literati'.

a **1568** ASCHAM *Scholem.* (Arb.) 45 This, lewde and learned, by common experience, know. **1591** SPENSER *Teares Muses* 216 Each idle wit.. doth the Learneds taske upon him take. **1610** HOLLAND *Camden's Brit.* 768 Sundry ceremonies, which I leaue to the learned in Christian antiquities. **1673** DRYDEN *Prol.* (*Silent Woman*) *to Univ. Oxford* 24 The learned in schools.. Studies with care the anatomy of man. **1736** BOLINGBROKE *Study & Use Hist.* v. (1777) 122 Let us leave the credulous learned to write history without materials. **1817** SCOTT *Search after Happiness* vi, E'en let the learn'd go search, and tell me if I'm wrong. **1879** JAS. GRANT in *Cassell's Techn. Educ.* IV. 284/2 His paper on optics speedily drew upon him the attention of all the learned in Europe.

c. Inflected in *compar.* and *superl.* Now *arch.*

1562 TURNER *Herbal* II. 43 The hop bushe is called.. of yͤ Barbarus writers humulus, of the later learneder writer lupulus. **1575–85** ABP. SANDYS *Serm.* xiv. 249 With all the learnedst of latter times. **1596** SPENSER *F.Q.* IV. ii. 35 Canacee.. was the learned ladie in her dayes. *a* **1619** FOTHERBY *Atheom.* Pref. (1622) 22 Diuers of my learnedest and best affected Friends. **1627** BP. HALL *Passion Serm.* Wks. 425, I leaue it modestly in the middest; let the learneder iudge. **1646** S. BOLTON *Arraignm. Err.* 101 The learnedst men.. may be deceivers. **1648** MILTON *Tenure Kings* (1650) 51 Among our own Divines two of the lernedest. **1661** BOYLE *Spring of Air* Pref. (1682) 6 For more learneder men than I [etc.]. **1693** W. FREKE *Sel. Ess.* xxxiv. 224, I may make myself learneder by reading. **1822** HAZLITT *Table-t.* Ser. II. x. (1869) 204 A lady had objected to my use of the word *learneder*, as bad grammar. **1824** LAMB *Let. to Coleridge* Lett. (1837) II. 164 Testimony that had been disputed by learneder clerks than I. **1870** EMERSON *Soc. & Solit., Success* Wks. (Bohn) III. 120 The gravest and learnedest courts in this country shudder to face a new question.

d. Said of one 'learned in the law'; hence applied by way of courtesy to any member of the legal profession.

c **1485** *Plumpton Corr.* (Camden) 48 Yt is thought by the forsayd lernedmen, that [etc.]. **1524** HEN. VIII in *Buccleuch MSS.* (Hist. MSS. Comm.) I. 220 Our welbiloued subgiet Edward Mountegue, lernedman. **1596** SHAKS. *Merch. V.* IV. i. 167 You heare the learn'd Bellario what he writes. **1818** CRUISE *Digest* (ed. 2) VI. 579 The learned Judges having given their opinion.. there is nothing remaining for the consideration of the House.

¶**e.** *transf.* Of an animal trained to make a show of intelligence.

1784 A. SEWARD *Let.* 29 Oct. in H. Pearson *Swan of Lichfield* (1936) 71 That amusing part of this conversation, which alluded to the learned Pig, and his demi-rational exhibitions, I shall transmit to you hereafter. **1785** W. COWPER *Let.* 22 Apr. in *Corr.* (1904) II. 314, I have a competitor for fame.. in the Learned Pig. **1833** MARRYAT *P. Simple* ix, There was also the learned pig.. and a hundred other sights. **1837** LOVER *Rory O'More* xvi. (1897) 128 Here is the wondherful larned pig that knows the five quarters o' the world, and more. **1919** CONRAD *Let.* 25 Jan. in G. Jean-Aubry *J. Conrad: Life & Lett.* (1927) II. 216 If the Alliances had been differently combined the Western Powers would have delivered Poland to the German learned pig.

3. a. Of things: Pertaining to, manifesting, or characterized by, profound knowledge gained by study.

1613 PURCHAS *Pilgrimage* (1614) 10, I will not dispute this question.. A learned ignorance shall better content me. **1625** BACON *Ess., Atheism* (Arb.) 337 Learned Times. **1632** MILTON *L'Allegro* 132 Then to the well-trod stage anon, If Jonson's learned Sock be on. **1651** FULLER *Abel Rediv., Perkins* (1867) II. 148 The scholar could hear no learneder ..sermons. **1763** DODSLEY *Pref. to Shenstone's Wks.*, The father resolved to give him a learned education. **1818** CRUISE *Digest* (ed. 2) III. 455 A treatise of tenures by a learned hand. **1823** LAMB *Elia* Ser. II. *Tombs in Abbey*, Your learned fondness for the architecture of your ancestors. **1824** *Ibid., Capt. Jackson*, The anecdote.. diffused a learned air through the apartment. **1837** WHEWELL *Hist. Induct. Sci.* (1857) I. 379 The Ancients.. were wanting in Learned Ignorance. **1874** DEUTSCH *Rem.* 264 A learned and lucid paper in the current *Edinburgh Review*.

b. In art-criticism often applied to draughtsmanship, colouring, etc., with the sense: Exhibiting thorough knowledge of method.

a **1830** HAZLITT *Fine Arts* (1873) 231 The drawing of N. Poussin.. is merely learned and anatomical.

c. Of a language, profession, or science: Pursued or studied chiefly by men of learning. Of the words in a language: Introduced by men of learning. Of plants: Known only from books (*rare*).

1581 MULCASTER *Positions* xli. (1887) 235 The three learned toungues, the latin, the greeke, the hebrew. **1623** LISLE *Ælfric on O. & N. Test.* Pref. (1638) 2 He knew moreover the learneder tongues and arts as well as they. **1696** WHISTON *Theory Earth* II. (1722) 139 The learned Sciences seem to have been anciently much better known. **1785** MARTYN *Rousseau's Bot.* Introd. 4 These learned plants however must be found in nature. **1824** L. MURRAY *Eng. Gram.* (ed. 5) I. 160 The English tongue is, in many respects, materially different from the learned languages. **1850** MRS. JAMESON *Leg. Monast. Ord.* (1863) 162 Students in the learned professions at Rome. **1869** KITCHIN *Brachet's Hist. Fr. Gram.* Introd. 32 Words of very different origin,.. the one popular, the other learned. *Ibid.* 39 This influx of learned words increases throughout the fifteenth century.

d. Of publications: devoted to (esp. some branch of) scholarship.

1883 E. B. BAX tr. *Kant's Prolegomena & Metaphysical Found. Nat. Sci.* 128 There is a good deal to be done before a learned journal.. can maintain its otherwise well-merited reputation, in the field of metaphysics as elsewhere. **1942** *Amer. Speech* XVII. 3 Since he [*sc.* the writer of detective stories] introduces characters from all walks of life, and since he usually avoids the more formal style, he is a better informant than.. the writers for the learned journals. **1951** AUDEN *Nones* (1952) 61 Lone scholars, sniping from the walls Of learned periodicals, Our fact defend. **1954** E. E. EVANS-PRITCHARD *Inst. Primitive Soc.* p. v, Monographs about primitive peoples and innumerable papers devoted to them in learned journals. **1961** A. WILSON *Old Men at Zoo* i. 50 Subscriptions to learned periodicals. **1969** M. PUGH *Last Place Left* xxii. 167 So you've just met him. And the rest you know.. from the learned journals.

Hence †**ˈlearnedish** *a.*, learned-like.

a **1680** BUTLER *Rem.* (1759) I. 250 Some write in Hebrew ..T' avoid the Critic.. And seem more learnedish, than [etc.].

learnedly (ˈlɜːnɪdlɪ), *adv.* [f. LEARNED *ppl. a.* + -LY[2].] In a learned manner.

1549 BALE *Labor. Journ. Leland* Pref. B iv b, So lernedlye, lyuelye, euydently, and groundedlye.. woulde he haue.. described.. thys oure realme. **1549** CHEKE *Hurt Sedit.* (1641) 6 Yee think it is not learnedly done. **1642** MILTON *Apol. Smect.* Wks. 1851 III. 317 They can learnedly invent a prayer of their own. **1717** LADY M. W. MONTAGU *Let. to Mrs. Thistlethwayte* 1 Apr., I can speak very learnedly on that subject. **1863** H. COX *Instit.* III. vii. 680 He most minutely and learnedly investigated the ancient course of the Exchequer.

learnedness (ˈlɜːnɪdnɪs). [f. LEARNED + -NESS.] The quality or condition of being learned.

1646 E. FISHER *Mod. Divinity* (ed. 2) 227 Are there not some who give themselves to.. learnednesse and clerklike skill in this art and that language? **1681** H. MORE *Exp. Dan.* 72 By reason of their Learnedness in the Law. **1869** *Lond. Q. Rev.* Jan. 266 He is a stumbling-block.. to all conventional learnedness. **1879** G. MEREDITH *Egoist* II. ii. 29 The doctor's learnedness would be a subject to dilate on.

learner (ˈlɜːnə(r)). Forms: 1–2 leornere, 4–5 lerner, 6– learner. [OE. *leornere*, f. *leornian*: see LEARN *v.* and -ER[1].]

1. One who learns or receives instruction; a disciple. †In early use, a scholar, man of learning.

c **900** tr. *Bæda's Hist.* IV. xxv. [xxiv.] (1890) 344 þa heht heo ȝesomnian ealle þa ȝelæredestan men & þa leorneras. *c* **1175** *Lamb. Hom.* 7 þa apostles itacned þa leorneres þet beoð þa wise witeȝa þe beoð nu ouer þe halie chirche. **1413** *Pilgr. Sowle* (Caxton 1483) v. viii. 99 No doute that Tubal ne Pyctagoras had nought be but lerners and as prentyses in theyr presence. **1526** *Pilgr. Perf.* (W. de W. 1531) 188 Nedes must the disciple or lerner byleue many thynges yͭ his mayster techeth hym. **1597** MORLEY *Introd. Mus.* 182 Thus hast thou.. my booke.. as I thought most conuenient for the learner. **1612** [see LATE *a.*[1] 2 d]. **1685** BAXTER *Paraphr. N.T., Matt.* xiii. 36 It is the part of Learners, to ask their Teachers help. **1735** BERKELEY *Free-think. in Math.* §21 Every learner hath a deference more or less to authority. **1828** J. H. MOORE *Pract. Navig.* (ed. 20) 47 To give the Learner some idea of the System of the Universe. **1867** SMILES *Huguenots Eng.* xi. (1880) 193 James II was but the too ready learner of the lessons of despotism taught him by Louis XIV.

†**2.** A teacher. *Obs.*

1382 WYCLIF *Heb.* xii. 9 We hadden fadris of oure fleisch, lerneris [*v.r.* lereris, Vulg. *eruditores*]. **1494** FABYAN *Chron.* V. cxxvii. 107 A tutoure or lerner of.. knyghtlye maners.

3. One who is learning to be competent but who does not yet have formal authorization as a driver of a motor vehicle, cycle, etc. Also *attrib.*, as **learner-driver**. (The abbrev. L is shown on the ***learner plates*** of the vehicle.)

1930 'A. ARMSTRONG' *Taxi* viii. 103 Conversational freedom between.. taximen and private 'learner drivers'. **1934** R. F. BROAD et al. *Motor Driving made Easy* (ed. 5) ix. 140 A provisional licence will be issued to enable learners to receive instruction qualifying them for the official test. **1935** *Daily Tel.* 7 Mar. 9/4 New drivers.. must start with a provisional or learner's licence. **1938** E. WAUGH *Scoop* III. ii. 276 Bonnet and back bore battered learner plates. **1961** [see BOOK *v.* 2 c]. **1970** D. MARLOWE *Echoes of Celandine* i. 15 A learner-car circling the block. **1973** *Times* 28 June 31/1 The learner driver holding up the traffic as he or she falters down the High Street is still part of the British motoring scene. *Ibid.* 21 Sept. 23/5 Although with its 1,000 cars and its 160 branches it is easy to get the impression that there are British School of Motoring learners everywhere.. it still only has something like 2½ per cent of the learner-driver population training with it.

4. *Austral.* (See quot.)

1965 J. S. GUNN *Terminol. Shearing Industry* I. 35 A learner is not a shedhand or barrower, but a budding shearer who has not yet shorn 5,000 sheep (10,000 in Queensland).

Hence **ˈlearner-like** *a.*, befitting a learner. **ˈlearnership**, the position of a learner.

1581 SIDNEY *Apol. Poetrie* (Arb.) 19 Mooued with our learner-like admiration. **1891** *Pall Mall G.* 17 Jan. 6/3 Candidates.. for male telegraph learnerships.

learning (ˈlɜːnɪŋ), *vbl. sb.* Forms: 1 leornung, 4 leorning, 4–6 lerning, -yng(h)(e, 7 *Sc.* leirning, 9 *vulg.* larnin, 6– learning. [OE. *leornung*, *-ing*, f. *leornian*: see LEARN *v.* and -ING[1]. Cf. OHG. *lirnunga*.]

1. The action of the vb. LEARN. **a.** The action of receiving instruction or acquiring knowledge; *spec.* in *Psychol.*, a process which leads to the modification of behaviour or the acquisition of

new abilities or responses, and which is additional to natural development by growth or maturation; (freq. opp. *insight*).

c **897** K. ÆLFRED *Gregory's Past.* Pref. (Sweet) 3 Hu ȝiorne hie wæron æȝðer ȝe ymb lare ȝe ymb liornunga. *c* **1340** *Cursor M.* 14811 (Trin.) To him was þe lawe bitauȝt þat he him self bi lernyng lauȝt. **1477** EARL RIVERS (Caxton) *Dictes* 67 Gladnesse whiche encresses daily in me in lernynghe. **1577–87** HOLINSHED *Chron.* III. 1165/2 He..for the pouertie of his father..not able to be mainteined here at learning. **1644** MILTON *Educ.* Wks. (1847) 98/2 The end then of learning is to repair the ruins of our first parents. **1740** J. CLARKE *Educ. Youth* (ed. 3) 18 It..renders the Learning of the *English* Rules more tedious abundantly, than they would be. **1860** RUSKIN *Mod. Paint.* V. IX. iii. 220 Vigilance..required of us, besides learning of many practical lessons. **1862** R. OWEN in *19th Cent.* Dec. (1897) 992 There's nothing so good for learning, as teaching. **1897** BRYAN & HARTER in *Psychol. Rev.* IV. 29 While there are many exceptional cases of quickness and slowness in learning, it requires from two to two and a half years to become an expert operator. **1901** E. L. THORNDIKE in *Ibid.* VIII. 442 With the monkeys, however, the association is both more rapid and more permanent, and the approach to suddenness and definiteness in their learning simulates that of human beings. **1901** —— *Human Nature Club* iii. 38 This method of learning may be called the method of trial and error..or..the animal method of learning. **1922** R. S. WOODWORTH *Psychol.* xiii. 311 To compare human and animal learning..cannot but throw light on the whole problem of the process of learning. **1924** R. M. OGDEN tr. *Koffka's Growth of Mind* ii. 41 Certain stages of development are attained only after learning has been added to growth and maturation. **1940** W. KÖHLER *Dynamics in Psychol.* (1942) iii. 114 If this is the case, retroactive inhibition..must also be a disturbance of the product of learning. **1948** E. R. HILGARD *Theories of Learning* xii. 353 It can be stated with reasonable confidence that there are changes in the nervous system accompanying learning. **1968** GELERNTER & ROCHESTER in Evans & Robertson *Cybernetics* 70 This is the learning involved when the machine uses results on one problem to improve its guesses about similar problems. **1970** M. H. MARX *Learning: Theories* p. v, It is no longer possible for one psychologist to be fully expert in all the areas of so broad and diversified a field as learning.

†**b.** Teaching; schooling. *Obs.*

c **1380** WYCLIF *Sel. Wks.* III. 393 þe gospels of Crist written in Englische to moost lernyng of oure nacioun. **1489** CAXTON *Faytes of A.* IV. x. 255 It is gode for to speke therof to the lernynge of thoos that shall moost iuge therof. **1727** *Philip Quarll* (1816) 34 The old man determined to give him his learning, if his relations would find him in board, and other necessaries. **1802** R. ANDERSON *Cumberld. Ball.* 44 O, cud I afford it, mair larnin thou'd get!

†**2.** What is learnt or taught: **a.** a lesson, instruction; **b.** information or direction; **c.** the 'teaching' of a person; a doctrine; also, a doctrine or maxim in law; **d.** a branch of learning; a science; **e.** an acquirement. *Obs.*

a. **1362** LANGL. *P. Pl.* A. I. 174 That nis no treuthe of trinite but..a leornyng for lewed men, the latere forte dele. **1483** CAXTON *G. de la Tour* cxxxvii. M vij, The thre enseygnementes or lernynges whiche Cathon gaf to his sone. **1611** SHAKS. *Cymb.* I. i. 43 The king..Puts to him all the Learnings that his time Could make him the receiuer of.

b. *c* **1386** CHAUCER *Sec. Nun's T.* 184 Right as hym was taught by his lernynge He foond this holy olde Vrban. **1606** SHAKS. *Ant. & Cl.* II. ii. 47, I did inquire it: And haue my Learning from some true reports.

c. **1526** TINDALE *Rev.* ii. 24 As many as have nott this lernynge. **1549** COVERDALE, etc. *Erasm. Par. Rom.* 34 To expounde unknowen learnynges. **1560** PILKINGTON *Aggeus* C ij (Matt. xv. 9), Teaching learninges which are the commaundementes of men. *a* **1625** BOYS *Wks.* (1629–30) 128 Christ the way, the truth and the life..The truth in his learning, the way for his liuing. *a* **1626** BACON *Max. & Uses Com. Law* Pref. (1636) 2 Particular and positive learnings of lawes doe easily decline from a good temper of justice.

d. **1570** BILLINGSLEY *Euclid* XI. xi. 315 It is no rare thing in all learninges..to haue one thing more generall then an other. **1605** BACON *Adv. Learn.* I. vi. §13 (1873) 49 He did send his divine truth into the world, waited on with other learnings. **1613** SIR H. FINCH *Law* (1636) 6 The rules of Reason are of two sorts; some taken from forreigne learnings, both diuine and humane.

e. **1602** SHAKS. *Ham.* V. ii. 35, I once did hold it..a basenesse to write faire, and laboured much How to forget that learning.

3. a. Knowledge, esp. of language or literary or historical science, acquired by systematic study; also, the possession of such knowledge, learnedness.

c **1340** *Cursor M.* 16108 (Trin.) Men han seide þat þou art wis of lernyng ȝore. **1513** BRADSHAW *St. Werburge* I. 2016 But for marchaunt men hauyng litell lernyng. **1559** W. CUNNINGHAM *Cosmogr. Glasse* 175 Oxenford..a norishe of learning, and a famous universitie. **1588** SHAKS. *L.L.L.* IV. iii. 314–15 Learning is but an adiunct to our selfe, And where we are, our Learning likewise is. **1611** BIBLE *Transl. Pref.* 2 The rare learning that he hath attained vnto. **1644** MILTON *Areop.* (Arb.) 60 The servil condition into which learning..was brought. **1676** LISTER in *Ray's Corr.* (1848) 125 [Plagiaries] being the bane and pest of learning. **1709–11** POPE *Ess. Crit.* 215 A little learning is a dang'rous thing. *a* **1732** GAY *Fables* II. xi. (1738) 100 Learning by study must be won. **1756–7** tr. *Keysler's Trav.* (1760) II. 60 That Politianus was a man of learning must be confessed. **1771** *Junius Lett.* lxi. 319 It..is not much to the credit either of their learning or integrity. **1781** GIBBON *Decl. & F.* xxx. III. 136 He had betrayed the ancient seat of freedom and learning to the Gothic invader. **1822** HAZLITT *Table-t.* I. viii. 167 Learning is the knowledge of that which none but the learned know. **1838** HALLAM *Hist. Lit.* (1847) I. I. iii. §47. 168 Ancient learning is to be divided into two great departments. **1887** LOWELL *Democr.* 122 What we want is not learning, but knowledge.

b. *the new learning*: the studies, esp. that of the Greek language, introduced into England in the 16th century; also applied to the doctrines of the Reformation.

c **1530** LATIMER in Strype *Eccl. Mem.* I. II. 119 Ye sayed that it was plaine, that this New lernyng (as ye call it) was not the trowth... Ye call the Scripture the new Lerninge; which I am sure is eldre than any lerninge, that ye wote to be the old. *c* **1550** BALE *K. Johan* (Manly) 1156, I trust ye beleve as Holy Church doth teache ye, And from the new lernyng ye are wyllyng for to fle. **1577** NORTHBROOKE *Dicing* (1843) 12 Such as impute this thing to the new learning, and preaching of the Gospell are shamefully deceiued. **1732** NEAL *Hist. Purit.* I. 28 The King's displeasure against the..Bishops of the new Learning. **1874** GREEN *Short Hist.* vi. §4. 305 On the Universities the influence of the New Learning was like a passing from death to life.

4. *attrib.* and *Comb.*, as ***learning-place***, ***process***, ***programme***, ***score***, ***-seat***, ***situation***; **learning curve**, a graph showing progress in learning; **learning machine**, a machine of the electronic computer type that can 'learn' by recording the results of attempts to solve a problem and giving preference to those which are successful; **learning resources** (also *attrib.*), collective materials for learning, e.g. microfilms, audio-visual aids, made accessible in a library, school, etc.; also ***learning-resource*** attrib. phr.; **learning theory**, theory attempting to account for the process of learning.

1922 R. S. WOODWORTH *Psychol.* xiii. 307 Learning curve for the rat in the maze. **1924** R. M. OGDEN tr. *Koffka's Growth of Mind* iv. 168 All these facts..would naturally operate to shorten the learning-curve. **1967** M. ARGYLE *Psychol. Interpersonal Behaviour* x. 183 In fact some manual operatives also learn by doing, and learning curves can be plotted which show their rate of progress. **1968** JOHANNSEN & ROBERTSON *Managem. Gloss.* 74 Learning curves indicate how the rate of learning changes with increased practice and are used to predict labour productivity. **1950** A. M. TURING in *Mind* LIX. 458 The idea of a learning machine may appear paradoxical to some readers. *Ibid.* 459 It is probably wise to include a random element in a learning machine. **1954** *Oxf. Univ. Gaz.* 15 June 1035/2 Work..on the insightful learning machine was also continued. **1963** A. M. ANDREW *Brains & Computers* 61 Future machines of this kind will certainly also be learning machines. **1967** R. WHITEHEAD in Wills & Yearsley *Handbk. Management Technol.* 57 Brains, self-organizing systems, economic systems, learning machines, computers, and automated factories are among the many subjects examined by the cybernetician. **1509** HAWES *Past. Pleas.* IV. (Percy Soc.) 20, I went to Doctryne, prayenge her good grace, For to assygne me my fyrst lernynge place. **1601** SHAKS. *All's Well* I. i. 191 The Court's a learning-place. **1922** R. S. WOODWORTH *Psychol.* xiii. 302 It makes the learning process easier to follow. **1947** A. W. MELTON in *Harvard Educ. Rev.* XXIX. 96 Educators..must know how to manage the learning process. **1949** SHURR & YOCOM *Mod. Dance* i. 13 Nothing can substitute for the physical activity which is necessary to the learning process. **1962** R. M. GAGNÉ in *Psychol. Rev.* LXIX. 355/1 Autoinstructional devices and their component learning programs. **1969** *Library Jrnl.* 1 Apr. 1536/3 (Advt.), Student body of 5000 on two campuses; 300 teachers; new learning resources center. **1970** *Ibid.* 15 Feb. 800/3 (Advt.), Curriculum adviser to work..in planning.. for new learning resource facility incorporating uses of all learning materials. **1970** *Globe & Mail* (Toronto) 25 Sept. 39/1 (Advt.), The successful applicant..will be responsible for assisting the principal in organizing, equipping and stocking a 3-level Learning Resource Centre in an innovational secondary school. **1970** *Jrnl. Gen. Psychol.* LXXXIII. 46 The analysis of variance on learning scores. **1585** JAS. I *Ess. Poesie* (Arb.) 33 That is a storehouse riche, a learning seat. **1948** E. R. HILGARD *Theories of Learning* xii. 335 Many learning situations require the selection of one or another possible mode of action. **1947** *Harvard Educ. Rev.* XXIX. 84 (*heading*) The relation of learning theory to the technology of education. **1962** *Listener* 15 Nov. 793/2 The psycho-analysts..believe that learning theory..is doomed to give only an incomplete and sometimes misleading account of personality development. **1967** M. ARGYLE *Psychol. Interpersonal Behaviour* viii. 148 Various training techniques derived from learning theory have been developed for the removal of symptoms [of mental disorders]. **1968** E. LOVEJOY *Attention in Discrimination Learning* iii. 44 This selectivity is likely to be an important part of a learning theory.

†**'learnless**, *a.* *Obs.* [f. LEARN *v.* + -LESS.] Devoid of learning.

1593 G. FLETCHER *Licia* To Rdr. A 4 b, These and such like errours..commonlie by learnelesse heades are reputed for loves kingdome. **1610–25** A. COOKE *Pope Joane* 5 That age was a learne-lesse and a witlesse age.

learwite, variant of LAIRWITE. *Obs.*

†**'leary**, *a.* *Obs.* *rare*$^{-1}$. (Origin and meaning obscure.)

1641 BEST *Farm. Bks.* (Surtees) 34 The shortest and most leary hey is allwayes accounted the best. *Ibid.* 73 Shepheards are to have an especiall eye to their hogges, and allwayes to give them the shortest, learyest, and best hey.

leary: see LEERY *a.*

leas, pa. t. of LEESE, to lose.

leasable ('liːsəb(ə)l), *a.* [f. LEASE *v.* + -ABLE.] That may be leased.

1611 COTGR., *Affermable*,..leasable, lettable, farmeable.

lease, *sb.*[1], **leaze** (liːz). Now *dial.* Forms: 1 læs, 3–6 lese, 4–5 leese, 5–9 lees, 6 leasse, 6–7 leas, 6– lease, leaze. [OE. *læs* str. fem.:—OTeut. type **læ̂swâ*; the orig. declension was nom. *læs*, acc., gen., dat. *læswe* (whence LEASOW), but in OE. there appears also an oblique form *læse*. The word has sometimes been confused with the plural of LEA *sb.*[1]

The word is prob. etymologically identical with (*blód*-)*læs*, gen. -*læswe*, (blood)-letting:—OTeut. type **læ̂swâ*:—pre-Teut. **lēd-twā* or **lēd-swā*, f. root of LET *v.*; the original meaning would thus be land 'let alone', not tilled.]

Pasture; pasturage; meadow-land; common. (Cf. *cow-*, *ewe-*, *horse-lease*.)

a **1000** ÆLFRIC *Colloq.* in Wr.-Wülcker 91/13 Ic drife sceap mine to heora læse. *a* **1100** *Voc.* ibid. 177/10 *Compascuus ager*, ȝemæne læs. *c* **1290** *St. Brendan* 134 in *S. Eng. Leg.* I. 223 An ylle fair ynouȝ, Grene & wiþ wel fair lese. **1297** R. GLOUC. (Rolls) 1005 Lese [*v.r.* leseo] last þer alle winter. *c* **1350** *Will. Palerne* 175 Hit..couþe ful craftily kepe alle here bestes & bring hem in þe best lese. **1387** TREVISA *Higden* (Rolls) I. 423 In þese hilles þere is Leese i-now for al Walis. *a* **1400** *Prymer* (1891) 17 We been his peple and scheep of his leese. **1523** FITZHERB. *Husb.* §148 Take thy horse and go tedure hym vpon thyn owne lees. **1578** LYTE *Dodoens* I. lxiii. 91 The three first Plantaynes grow almost every where..in pastures and leases. **1622** WITHER *Fair Virtue* C 6 b, And my Lambkins changed from Brome leaze, to the Mead at home. *a* **1722** LISLE *Husb.* (1757) 394 The cattle cannot go into those deep leases, they being under water. **1794** A. YOUNG in *Ann. Agric.* XXII. 231 Much.. common Down..stocked with bullock and sheep leases. **1880** JEFFERIES *Hodge & M.* II. 277 The dead, dry grass, and the innumerable tufts of the 'leaze' which the cattle have not eaten. **1887** *Kent. Gloss.*, *Lees*, a common, or open space of pasture ground. The *Leas* is the name given at Folkestone to the fine open space of common at the top of the cliffs. **1898** T. HARDY *Wessex Poems* 196 The years have gathered grayly Since I danced upon this leaze.

lease, *sb.*[2]: see LEASE *a.*

lease (liːs), *sb.*[3] Also 5 lese, leas, 6 leace. [a. AF. *les* = OF. *lais*, *leis*, *lez*, etc., a letting, leaving (mod.F., with pseudo-etymological spelling *legs*, 'legacy'), vbl. noun f. *laisser* to let, leave.]

1. A contract between parties, by which the one conveys lands or tenements to the other for life, for years, or at will, usually in consideration of rent or other periodical compensation. Also in phr. ***to put (out) to lease***; ***by lease***, ***on*** (†***in***) ***lease***. **b.** The instrument by which such a conveyance is made. **c.** The period of time for which the contract is made.

The grantor of a lease is called the *lessor*, and the grantee, the *lessee*. In popular lang. *lease* is usually confined to a conveyance by deed for a term of years.

[**1292** BRITTON III. xi. §26 Qe il ne cleime rien el tenement for qe terme des aunz de le les un tiel.] **1483** *Act 1 Rich. III*, c. 1 §1 Every astate feoffement yeft relesse graunte lesis and confirmacion of landys. **1495** *Act 11 Hen. VII*, c. 9 §2 Lessees, before..they take or occupie biforce of any suche leas any suche londes. **1573** TUSSER *Husb.*, *Ep. to Ld. T. Paget* viii. (1878) 9 Though countrie health long staid me, yet lesse expiring fraid me. **1583** STUBBES *Anat. Abus.* II. (1882) 31, I thought one might haue had a farme or a lease for a reasonable rent yeerely, without any fine or income paieng. **1616** R. C. *Times Whistle* v. 1981 A..young gentleman Put out the best part of his land to lease. **1667** PEPYS *Diary* 4 June, I cannot have a lease of the ground for my coach-house. **1690** *Lond. Gaz.* No. 2542/4 To be Lett furnished or unfurnished, by a short Lease or Yearly Rent. **1756** HUME *Hist. Eng.* II. xxviii. 134 He got possession, on easy leases, of the revenues of Bath, Worcester and Hereford. **1758** JOHNSON *Idler* No. 16 ¶7 [He] renewed his uncle's lease of a farm. **1776** ADAM SMITH *W.N.* v. ii. (1869) II. 420 All the arable lands which are given in lease to farmers. **1846** MCCULLOCH *Acc. Brit. Empire* (1854) I. 149 A tenant without a lease, and, consequently, depending on the goodwill and caprice of his landlord, may not deteriorate his farm. **1893** SIR J. W. CHITTY in *Law Times Rep.* LXVIII. 429/1 The lease..had been lent..to the plaintiff.. for perusal. *Mod.* The lease had still thirty years to run.

2. *fig.* with reference to the permanence of occupation guaranteed by a lease; esp. in phr. ***a (new) lease of life***. Also, the term during which possession or occupation is guaranteed.

c **1586** C'TESS PEMBROKE *Ps.* LXXXI. vi, Of my graunt they had enjoy'd A lease of blisse with endlesse date. *c* **1600** SHAKS. *Sonn.* cxlvi, Why so large cost, having so short a lease, Dost thou vpon thy fading mansion spend? **1605** —— *Macb.* IV. i. 99 Our high plac'd Macbeth Shall liue the Lease of Nature. **1628** RUTHERFORD *Lett.* (1862) I. 36 Remember of what age your daughter was, and that just so long was your lease of her. **1631** MILTON *Epit. Marchioness Winchester* 52 [Thou] That to give the world encrease, Shortned hast thy own lives lease. **1640** SHIRLEY *Constant Maid* IV. iii, The Statutes and the Magna Charta have taken a lease at his tongues end. **1641** —— *Cardinal* IV. i, Time has took a lease But for three lives I hope. **1647** CLEVELAND *Char. Lond. Diurn.* 4, I wonder, for how many lives my Lord Hoptons Soule took the Lease of his Body. *a* **1700** DRYDEN *Ovid's Met.* XV. *Pythag. Philos.* 603 He..the same Lease of Life on the same Terms renews. **1706** BAYNARD in Sir J. Floyer *Hot & Cold Bath.* II. 192 My Lady Loyd's Case,.. who when the vital Flame was even blinking in the Socket.. had a new Life put to Lease. **1853** MRS. CARLYLE *Lett.* II. 227 She was going to have a new lease of life with better health. **1865** DICKENS *Mut. Fr.* I. xiii, The suspense seemed to have taken a new lease. **1878** SEELEY *Stein* III. 397 Wherever Estates still existed, they seemed to have gained a new lease of life. **1897** MARY KINGSLEY *W. Africa* 685 Men and women, who looked, as the saying goes, as if you could take a lease of their lives.

3. *Austral.* 'A piece of land leased for mining purposes' (Morris).

1890 *Goldfields Victoria* 15 A nice block of stone was crushed from Johnston's lease.

4. *Comb.*, as ***lease-buyer***, ***-letter***, ***-possession***. See also LEASE-MONGER, LEASE-PAROLE.

1570 LEVINS *Manip.* 204/37 Lease letter, *locator*... Lease byer, *conductor*. **1894** A. MORRISON *Mean Streets* 286 The glories of lease-possession grew dim in his eyes.

lease (liːs). *sb.*[4] *Weaving.* Also 4 lese, leese, leys, 9 leas, lays. [app. a var. of LEASH *sb.*, perh. confused with an adoption of F. *lisse, lice* (:—L. *līcia*, pl. of *līcium*) = sense 2 below.]

†**1.** A certain quantity of thread. *Obs.*

A Fécamp document of 1235 in Du Cange has 'In eadem Ecclesia reddit Presbyter.. tres leshas cere pro candela'. Cf. LEA *sb.*[4]

1391 *Mem. Ripon* (Surtees) III. 110 Et in xxviij lb. ceræ pro ij torches ad magnum altare.. Et in xxiiij leses lintiaminis emp. pro eisdem. **1453-4** *Durham Acc. Rolls* (Surtees) 633 Pro 4*dd.* leese de lechino ad 15*d.* pro candelis inde fiendis, 5*s.* **1457** *Ibid.* 635, 1*dd.* leys de lichino.

2. The crossing of the warp-threads in a loom; the place at which the warp-threads cross. Phr. ***to keep, take the lease.*** (The corresponding Spitalfields term is *cross*.)

1839 URE *Dict. Arts* 1284 The lease being carefully tied up, affords a guide to the weaver for inserting his lease-rods. **1851** *Art Jrnl. Illustr. Catal.* p. vii**/2 Taking the 'lease' previously to the yarns being submitted to the sizing process. **1883** *Almondbury & Huddersf. Gloss.*, s.v. *Lays*,.. When the warp is made ready for the loom, the threads are separated, and passed alternately above and below a string called the *laysband*. Where the threads cross, or perhaps the whole arrangement itself, may be considered the *lays*. **1888** C. P. BROOKS *Cotton Manuf.* 30 The keeping of the lease. The latter term will be understood by all connected with weaving as being the separation of the threads alternately.

3. = LEASH 7 a.

1824 *Lond. Jrnl. Arts & Sci.* VII. 184 The improved piece of mechanism.. is to be placed immediately over the heddles or leases of the loom. **1831** G. R. PORTER *Silk Manuf.* 238 Separating the threads of the warp in forming the shed, thus according to the weaver's phrase augmenting the number of leases in the harness.

4. *Comb.*: **lease-band** (see quot. 1883 under sense 2); **lease-rod**, one of the rods placed between the warp-threads to keep the lease.

1824 *Lond. Jrnl. Arts & Sci.* 114 The warp is drawn from this roller over a small roller, and from thence is conducted to the lease-rods. **1883** A. BROWN *Power-loom* (ed. 4) 35 The lease-rods.. play a very important part in power-loom weaving... Their primary purpose is to keep the lease, so that when any of the threads are broken their proper place may be readily found in the web.

†**lease,** *a.* and *sb.*[2] *Obs.* Forms: 1 léas, 2-3 leas, 3 læs, 3-5 lese, 3-6 les, 4-5 lees, lesse, 4-6 less, 5-6 leace, *Sc.* leis(s, (5 leas(s)e, leys, 6 lase). [Com. Teut.: OE. *léas* corresponds to OFris. *lâs*, OS., OHG., MHG. *lôs* (Du., G. *los*), ON. *lauss* (Sw. *lös*, Da. *løs*), Goth. *laus*:—OTeut. **lauso-*, f. **laus-* (:**leus-*: *lus-*, whence LOSE *v.*), an extension of the OAryan root **leu-* (Gr. λύειν to loosen). The suffix -LESS is etymologically identical with the present word; LOOSE *a.* is an adoption of the ON. equivalent *lauss*.

In the Teut. langs. generally the word had the senses 'loose', 'free, unoccupied', 'destitute of', 'loose in conduct, immoral', 'vain, empty, worthless'. In OE. the only senses are 'destitute of' (see -LESS) and 'false, lying'.]

A. *adj.* Untrue, false, lying.

a **900** *Kent Gloss.* in Wr.-Wülcker 59/43 *Testem fallacem*, leasa ȝewitnesse. *a* **1200** *Moral Ode* 255 Þa þe weren swa lese [13.. in *E.E.P.* 31 lease] þet me hom ne mihte ileuen. *c* **1200** *Trin. Coll. Hom.* 71 We shule no þing seien þat les beo. *a* **1225** *Leg. Kath.* 1779 Leaueð to leuen lengre on þes lease maumez. *c* **1250** *Gen. & Ex.* 3498 Ne swer it [God's name] les to fele in gamen. *c* **1330** R. BRUNNE *Chron.* (1810) 34 Bot þe Northeren men held him no leaute.. & forsoke Edrede, þer were þei les. ? *a* **1366** CHAUCER *Rom. Rose* 8 An Authour ..That halt not dremes false ne lees. *c* **1440** *Promp. Parv.* 298/1 Lees, or false, *falsus*. *c* **1450** *Erle Tolous* 1086 So are ye lythyr and lees. *c* **1450** *Cov. Myst.* (Shaks. Soc.) 354 He droff from me the fendes lees.

B. *sb.* Untruth, falsehood, lying. Common in ME. poetry in the expletive ***without(en, but lease.***

c **888** K. ÆLFRED *Boeth.* xli. §1 Þone mon mæȝ hatan buton lease soþe sunne. *c* **1205** LAY. 28150 þat isæid ich þe habbe soð buten lease. *c* **1250** *Gen. & Ex.* 3514 False witnesse dat ðu ne bere, Ne wið ðe lese non ma[n] ne dere. *a* **1300** *Cursor M.* 5747 O moder bath and maiden clene, þat siþen lang, wit-vten less, Bar child and sco þerof wemles. *c* **1305** *St. Lucy* 155 in *E.E.P.* (1862) 105 A ioyful teþinge ic ȝou telle þat soþ is and les noȝt. *c* **1375** *Sc. Leg. Saints* xix. (*Cristofore*) 99 Sa held he furth lange but lese, til he come in a wildirnes. *c* **1385** CHAUCER *L.G.W.* 1022 (*Dido*) Thus seyt the bok withoutyn ony les. *c* **1440** HYLTON *Scala Perf.* (W. de W. 1494) I. xvi, It is soth & no lees. *c* **1460** *Towneley Myst.* i. 158 We held with hym ther he saide leasse. **1500-20** DUNBAR *Poems* I. 24 He knawis gif this be leiss. **1513** DOUGLAS *Æneis* III. ii. 115 By Olearon, and mony ilis, but les. **15..** *Adam Bel* 460 in Hazl. *E.P.P.* II. 158 Syr, we be outlawes of the forest, Certayne without any leace. **1598** HAKLUYT *Voy.* I. 188 Flanders of nede must with vs haue peace Or els shee is destroyed without lees.

lease (liːz), *v.*[1] Now *dial.* Forms: 1 lesan, 4 leese, (*pa. t.* lase, laas), 4-5 lese, 6- lease, 7- leaze. [A Com. Teut. str. vb. (in Eng. wk. since the 14th c.): OE. *lesan* (pa. t. *læs*, pl. *lǣson*) to gather, glean, corresponds to OFris. *lesa* to read, OS. *lesan* to gather (Du. *lezen* to gather, select, read), OHG. *lesan* (MHG., mod.G. *lesen* to gather, to read), ON. *lesa* to gather, pick, read (Sw. *läsa*, Da. *læse* to read), Goth. *lisan, galisan* to gather. Outside Teut. the Lith. *lesù* (inf. *lesti*), to pick up with the beak, may be cognate.]

1. *trans.* and *intr.* To glean. †Also with *up*. (In OE. used in wider sense: to gather, collect.)

c **1000** ÆLFRIC *Lev.* xxiii. 22 Ne ȝe ne gaderion þa eorþe.. ac lætað þearfan and ut acymene hiȝ lesan. **1377** LANGL. *P. Pl.* B. VI. 68 Who so helpeth me to erie.. Shal haue leue.. to lese here in heruest. **1387** TREVISA *Higden* (Rolls) I. 11 Ruth þat.. lase [*v.r.* laas] vp þe eeres after his [*sc.* Boaz'] ripe men. **1546** *Supplic. Poore Commons* (E.E.T.S.) 71 No man myght lease, rake, or gleane his grounde after he had gathered of his croppe. **1612** *Court Rolls of Taynton, co. Glouc.*, That no person shall lease or gleane vntill the corne there growing be carryed. *c* **1640** J. SMYTH *Lives Berkeleys* (1883) I. 155 How hee set with hand.. his beanes; and in the barn leazed in the eare. **1684** DRYDEN *Theocritus* Idyl iii. 72 Agreo, that in Harvest us'd to lease. *c* **1700** *Allen & Ella* in Evans *Old Ball.* (1784) II. xliv. 258 Together we'll lease o'er the field. **1825** COBBETT *Rur. Rides* (1830) I. 307 No less than eighty four men, women and boys and girls gleaning, or leasing, in a field of about ten acres. **1879** in MISS JACKSON *Shropsh. Word-bk.*

2. To pick: in various applications (see quots.).

c **1420** *Pallad. on Husb.* VIII. 48 Of wynter fruyt science Yet leseth out the smale, vnto the grete So that the tree may sende her drynke & mete. *c* **1430** *Two Cookery-bks.* 21 Take Rys, and lese hem clene. **1609** C. BUTLER *Fem. Mon.* (1634) 39 Take four or five good handfuls of wheat or Rye leazed out of the sheaf. **1703** THORESBY *Let. to Ray* (E.D.S.), *Leyse*, to pick the slain and trucks out of wheat. **1764** *Mus. Rusticum* II. 223 What we in the North call *leasing*, or *gathering out*, the blighted ears. *Ibid.* 226 The greatest care should be taken to *lease* wheat intended for seed. **1891** *Hartland Gloss.*, *Lease* (laize), to pick out weed-seeds, &c., by hand from imperfectly winnowed corn.

†**lease,** *v.*[2] *Obs.* In 4 lese, 6 leaze. [OE. *léasian*, f. *léas* LEASE *a.*; perhaps partly a back-formation from LEASING *sb.*] *intr.* To tell lies.

c **1000** *Ags. Ps.* (Spelman) lxv. 2 Leoȝað [*v.r.* leasiaþ] þe fynd þine [L. *mentientur tibi inimici tui*]. *c* **1340** *Cursor M.* 22042 (Fairf.) þer-fore he sais he lesis noȝt [*Cott.* lies, *Gött.* leies, *Trin.* lieþ]. **1594** *Knack to Know Knave* A 4, Let Honestie receiue such punishment As he deserues that leazes to the king.

lease (liːs), *v.*[3] Also 5 lese, 6 leese, lesse. [ad. AF. *lesser*, a specific use of OF. *lesser, laissier* (mod.F. *laisser*) to let, let go:—L. *laxāre* to loosen, loose, f. *lax-us* loose, LAX *a.*]

1. *trans.* To grant the possession or use of (lands, etc.) by a lease (LEASE *sb.*[3]); to let *out* on lease.

[**1292** BRITTON II. xi. §9 Si cestui.. lesse sa terre a terme de la vie le lessour.] **1570** LEVINS *Manip.* 204/43 To Lease or let leas, *locare, dimittere*. **1592** WEST *1st Pt. Symbol.* §25 B, He which letteth, lesseth or setteth any thing to be made or used, is called.. the lessor or lettor. **1593** SHAKS. *Rich. II*, II. i. 59 This land.. Is now Leas'd out.. Like to a Tenement or pelting Farme. *a* **1600** G. LONGE in Ellis *Orig. Lett.* Ser. II. III. 157 Having themselves no knowledge, [they] were driven to lease out the benefitt of their Patent to the Frenchmen. *a* **1637** B. JONSON *Pind. Ode Mem. Sir L. Cary & Sir. H. Morison* iv, Leas'd out t'advance The profits for a time. **1726** AYLIFFE *Parergon* 285 Where the Vicar leases his Glebe, the Tenant must pay the great Tithes to the Rector or Impropriator. **1776** ADAM SMITH *W.N.* V. iii. (1869) II. 536 The lands in America.. are in general not tenanted nor leased out to farmers. **1818** CRUISE *Digest* (ed. 2) I. 288 Lands were leased from the 10th October 1763, for eleven years. **1868** PEARD *Water-Farm.* ii. 21 Each proprietor leased his water to men who having no permanent interest in the river, killed every salmon they could catch.

transf. and *fig.* *c* **1665** MRS. HUTCHINSON *Mem. Col. Hutchinson* (1846) 329 He would not give up bishops, but only lease out their revenues. *a* **1845** HOOD *Plea Midsummer Fairies* xii, 'Alas', quoth she, 'ye know our fairy lives Are leased upon the fickle faith of men'.

2. To take a lease of; to hold by a lease.

1877 'H. A. PAGE' *De Quincey* I. xv. 319 In 1840.. the family was transported to Mavis Bush, a neat little cottage.. which was leased for a period of years. **1892** GRETA ARMEAR *What was it?* (ed. 2) 8 A rich Scotchman.. had leased a large property.. in order to indulge in his favourite sport with the famous Ballmore hounds. **1898** *Westm. Gaz.* 11 May 4/2 Angling on the choice streams of the South.. is hardly to be obtained unless by leasing a rod.

Hence **leased** (liːst) *ppl. a.*

1869 *Bradshaw's Railway Manual* XXI. 73 The gross earnings of the leased undertakings. **1895** A. J. WILSON *Gloss. Terms Stock Exch.*, *Leased Lines*.. those railway securities whose interest or dividends are dependent not on the earning power of the properties, but upon the rent agreed to be paid by the lessee company.

lease (liːz), *v.*[4] [f. *leas*, pl. of LEA *sb.*[4]] *trans.* To divide (yarn or thread) into leas.

1884 W. S. B. MCLAREN *Spinning* 242 The length varies from one to twelve yards, and the forms of making up, leasing, and tying are endless. **1927** T. WOODHOUSE *Artificial Silk* 67 It is quite possible that all the remaining hanks have already been leased.

lease, var. LEESE *v.*, to lose; and see LEASH.

'lease-back. [f. LEASE *sb.*[3] or *v.*[3] + BACK *adv.*] In full, ***sale and lease-back.*** The sale of a property, etc., to a purchaser on the understanding that the vendor may take out a lease on the property. Also *attrib.*

1947 J. W. KEARNS in *Amer. Bar Assoc. Proc., Section of Corporation, Banking & Mercantile Law* 46/1 The origin of the 'lease-back deal' is probably traced back to high taxes, high taxes coupled with the desire of almost any corporate manager to see a liquid balance sheet with very few fixed assets on it. The fewer the better. The lease-back deal is basically a transaction under which a corporation, which in the course of its business will use a considerable amount of real estate, sells that real estate to another entity which may be a university; it may be a charitable foundation; it may be any other type of organization which is tax free under the Internal Revenue Code. The real estate is usually sold at depreciated book value and simultaneously or concurrently a lease-back is granted to the industrial or merchandising concern that has sold the property. **1949** *Business Week* 22 Oct. 31/1 The device under attack is the sale-and-lease-back of real estate. **1964** *Financial Times* 12 Mar. 1/8 Excess cash produced by sale and lease-back arrangements. **1967** *Times Rev. Industry* July 33/2 The illusions of liquidity which can be created by.. leaseback. **1970** *Daily Tel.* 30 Dec. 16 Factory-owners who sell their premises and take a lease-back of their accommodation. **1971** *Ibid.* 27 Apr. 21 (*heading*) Leaseback raises £5m for Grand Met. *Ibid.* 17 June 19 A £6 million plus sale and lease-back agreement. **1972** *Accountant* 26 Oct. 516/1 There is an increased use of real estate sale and lease-back and the non-cancellable leasing of capital equipment for a term approximating its economic life. **1974** *Country Life* 7 Mar. 506/1 It was arranged that immediately upon the transfer of the estate, the son would lease back the property to his father. The leaseback was for a term of five years.

leasee, -er, -o(u)r, obs. ff. LESSEE, LESSOR.

leasehold ('liːshəʊld). [f. LEASE *sb.*[3], after *freehold.*] A tenure by lease; real estate so held.

1720 *Lond. Gaz.* No. 5867/3 A Leasehold of 100*l.* per Annum, for 99 Years. **1870** SPURGEON *Treas. Dav.* Ps. lxix. 17 He has but a leasehold of his acres, and death ends his tenure. **1874** HELPS *Soc. Press.* ii. 25 There is also the system of leaseholds, which must be very prejudicial to good building. **1881** GLADSTONE *Sp. on Irish Land Bill* 19 You have the leaseholds and you have the annual tenancy.

b. *attrib.* or *adj.* Held by lease.

1731 W. DERHAM (*title*) A Defence of the Churches Right in Leasehold Estates. **1817** W. SELWYN *Law Nisi Prius* (ed. 4) II. 707 In ejectment for a leasehold estate, the lessor of the plaintiff produced the original lease. **1858** BRIGHT *Sp. Reform* 27 Oct., A man.. comes into possession of leasehold houses.

Hence **'leaseholder,** one who possesses leasehold property.

1858 J. B. NORTON *Topics* 229 Which thrusts a 'long lease' upon the 'perpetual' leaseholder. **1883** T. COLBORNE in *Law Times* 27 Oct. 433/1 The leaseholder, like the agricultural tenant under the Act of 1883, is.. prevented from contracting himself out of the benefits of the Act.

lease-lend. (Level stress.) Also **lease and lend** and LEND-LEASE. [f. LEASE *v.*[3] + LEND *v.*[2]] At first (in 1941) applied to an arrangement whereby sites in British overseas possessions were leased to the United States as bases in exchange for the loan of U.S. destroyers; later in extended uses. Also *attrib.* and as *vb.*

1941 *Economist* 1 Feb. 139/2 The great reduction in American payments under the 'Lease and Lend' Bill. **1941** *Hutchinson's Pict. Hist. of War* 9 July-30 Sept. 48 Mr Harry Hopkins.. in charge of the administration of the Lease-Lend Act, arrives in England again. **1942** *Ann. Reg. 1941* 19 The signing of the Lease and Lend Bill in the United States on March 11.. caused great rejoicing in England. **1942** *R.A.F. Jrnl.* 3 Oct. 24 The Canadians argued that by lease-lend the Old Man would get one [a Jeep]. **1943** *Daily Tel.* 23 Oct. 4 Britain's new aircraft-carrier Victorious was 'Lease-lent' to the United States. **1944** G. B. SHAW *Everybody's Pol. What's What?* xv. 120 Under the American Lease and Lend arrangements England and Russia are borrowing their war stores from the United States. **1945** *Reader's Digest* July 47/1 Hatch has been particularly successful in 'breeding up' the poultry and livestock of the country by lease-lending his pure-bred bulls. **1964** *Daily Tel.* 19 May 28/6 To-night 40 Eastbourne policemen were sent to Brighton. They formed part of a 'lease-lend' arrangement entered into by Brighton, Eastbourne and Hastings police forces to help each other out in case of riots.

leaseless ('liːslɪs), *a.* [f. LEASE *sb.*[3] + -LESS.] Not having a lease.

1882 *Daily News* 4 Feb. 3/4 Leaseless tenants' rights.

†**lease-monger.** *Obs.* [LEASE *sb.*[3]] One who traffics in leases.

1549 LATIMER *7th Serm. bef. Edw. VI* (Arb.) 208 No hore mongers fayth, no lease mongers fayth, no seller of benefices fayth. **1550** CROWLEY *Epigr.* 1169 Of late a leasemongar of London laye sycke, And thyncking to dye, his conscience dyd him pricke. **1615** *Stow's Ann.* 868/1 Many houses.. were all very sudainely inhabited.. to the great.. aduantage of Landlords and Leasemongers. **1884** *Q. Rev.* Jan. 117 Either by the landlord or the 'leasemonger' farms and tenements were let to the highest bidder.

So †**lease-monging.**

1586 FERNE *Blaz. Gentrie* 99 If such a one.. through good husbandrye, cheuisauncing, leasemonging.. shall rise vp to a reuenew of hundredes.

†**lease-parole.** *Obs.* [f. LEASE *sb.*[3] + PAROLE.] (See quot. 1672.)

a **1592** LODGE & GREENE *Looking Glasse* (1598) F 2, *Clowne.* At night I wil bring home my mistresse. *Smith.* Euen when you please, good Adam. *Clowne.* When I please, marke thy words,—'tis a lease parol, to haue and to hold. *a* **1613** OVERBURY *A Wife* (1638) 131 He is tenant by custom to the Planets, of whom hee holds the 12 Houses by lease paroll: paying the yearly rent of his study and time. **1672** *Cowel's Interpr.* s.v. *Parol*, Lease-parol, that is Lease per Parol; a Lease by word of mouth, to distinguish it from a Lease in writing.

leaser[1] ('liːzə(r)). Now *dial.* Also 4 lezere, 6 lezer. [f. LEASE *v.*[1] + -ER[1].] A gleaner.

1340 *Ayenb.* 86 Hi abideþ and wylneþ þane dyaþ ase deþ .. þe lezere his haruest. **1534** *Act 25 Hen. VIII*, c. 1, *Stat.*

Irel. (1678) 46 Every such gatherer, lezer or lezers. **1586** J. HOOKER *Hist. Irel.* in *Holinshed* II. 88/1 An act against leasers of corne. **1724** SWIFT *Drapier's Lett.* Wks. 1755 V. II. 133, I knew there was no office of any kind, which a man from England might not have . . and . . I looked upon all who had the disadvantage of being born here, as only in the condition of leasers and gleaners. **1828** MISS MITFORD *Village* Ser. III. 242 You cannot proceed a quarter of a mile, without encountering some merry group of leasers.

† **ˈleaser**². *Obs. rare.* [OE. *léasere.* Agent-n. to LEASE *v.*²: see -ER¹.] A liar.

c **950** *Lindisf. Gosp.* Matt., Pref. (Skeat) 17 Leaseres *vel* leȝeras, *falsos.* **1641** 'SMECTYMNUUS' *Vind. Answ.* iii. 48 Hee . . lays on us unmercifully, calling us *Cavellers, Leasers, Slanderers.*

leaser³ (ˈliːsə(r)). [f. LEASE *v.*³ + -ER¹.] One who takes on lease; a lessee.

1877 RAYMOND *Statist. Mines & Mining* 300 The mine has been in leasers' hands.

leash (liːʃ), *sb.* Forms: *α.* 3, 5 lece, 4 leesse, 4–5 lees, 4–6 les, lese, 5–7 leace, lease, (5 leese, leys, lyes, 6 leasse). *β.* 4 *Sc.* leysche, 4–7 lesh, 5 lesshe, leeshe, 5–6 *Sc.* lische, 6 leyssche, leshe, leas(s)he, *Sc.* leish, leisch, lesch, (7 leach), 6– leash. [a. OF. *lesse, laisse* (mod.F. *laisse*) ?:—L. *laxa* fem. of *laxus* LAX *a.*]

1. The thong or line in which hounds or coursing-dogs are held. Phr. † ***with the leash***, † ***at a leash***, ***on*** or ***in*** (***the*** or ***a***) ***leash***. Proverbial phr. † ***as greyhound*** (***let out***) ***of leash***.

α. *a* **1300** *St. Gregory* 822 in *Archiv Stud. neu. Spr.* LVII. 68 Houndes þat were liȝt & lent To leten of lece, to cacche beste. **13..** *Coer de L.* 1923 As greyhounds stricken out of lese, Kyng Richard threst among the press. *c* **1330** *Arth. & Merl.* 9126 (Kölbing) Merlin smot forþ, þai after dasse On aiþer half, so grehounde of lasse. *a* **1400** *Octouian* 767 As glad as grehond y-lete of lese Florent was than. *c* **1440** *Partonope* 558 Her lees were as softe as sylk. **1475** *Bk. Noblesse* 16 Every man . . had a masty hound at a lyes. **1509** BARCLAY *Shyp of Folys* (1570) 85 In comes another his houndes at his tayle, With lynes and leases and other like baggage. **1576** FLEMING tr. *Caius' Eng. Dogs* 7 Beyng restrained and drawne backe from running at random with the leasse. **1579–80** NORTH *Plutarch* (1676) 1027 Having in his right hand a Club, and in his left hand a Leace, unto the which Thyus was tied. **1640** tr. *Verdere's Rom. of Rom.* I. xxviii. 130 Perceiving a Damsell comming in with two Lions in a lease, he went speedily down [etc.].

β. **1356–7** *Durham Acc. Rolls* (Surtees) 558 Pro catenis, chapes, et leshes, et uno Cornu pro venatore, . . 7*s.* 11*d.* **1375** BARBOUR *Bruce* VII. 414 His leysche till him drew he, And leit his houndis gang all fre. *c* **1440** *Ipomydon* 785 Furthe he went with greyhondis thre, In a lesshe he dyd hem do. **1509** BARCLAY *Shyp of Folys* (1570) 134 He that will labour a beast to hunt or chase . . His lines, colers, and leshes he must dresse. **1513** DOUGLAS *Æneis* V. ix. 104 He that the lische and lyame in schondir draue. **1688** R. HOLME *Armoury* III. 74/1 The Fewterer . . shall receive the Greyhounds matched to run together, into his Leash, as soon as he comes into the Field. **1808** WORDSW. *Force of Prayer* iii, [He] holds a greyhound in a leash, To let slip upon buck or doe. **1830** SCOTT *Demonol.* iv. 131 She led three greyhounds in a leash. **1879** OUIDA *C. Castlemaine* 5 Fretting like staghounds held in leash. **1888** *Times* 13 Oct. 7/6 The hounds, hunted on the leash. *Ibid.* 16 Oct. 10/5 The hound worked on leash from the spot where the deer had lodged.

transf. **1741** *Mem. M. Scriblerus* I. i. 10 A Paper kite which had broke its leash by the impetuosity of the wind.

† **b.** ***the leash***: (*a*) the department of the king's household concerned with the keeping of the hounds; (*b*) the art or practice of coursing.

1526 *Househ. Ord.* (1790) 194 The charge of 68 loves of bread served to the officers of the Lesh for the expences of the Kings Greyhounds. **1552** in Strype *Eccl. Mem.* II. xxxiii. 540 The office of child of the leashe to Iohn Streete for life, with the wages of 40*s.* by year. **1611** MARKHAM *Country Content.* I. vii. (1615) 104 Touching the lawes of the lease or coursing. *Ibid.* 106 Those which are chosen Iudges of the leashe, shall giue their iudgements before they depart from the field. *c* **1628** *Warrant* in *Verney Papers* (1853) 180 Lord Compton, master of his majestys leash. **1665** *Warrant* in *Sporting Mag.* XLII. 10 Like as my perdecessors masters of the Leash.

2. A set of three; originally in *Sporting* language, used of hounds, hawks, foxes, hares, deer, etc.; hence *gen.*

α. *c* **1320** *Sir Tristr.* 446 Tristrem hunters seiȝe ride, Les of houndes þai ledde. **1376–7** *Durham Acc. Rolls* (Surtees) 387 In uno lese et uno pare de turetteis. **1426** LYDG. *De Guil. Pilgr.* 21424 Swyche houndys . . God wot, I ha mo than a les. **1486** *Bk. St. Albans* F vj b, A Lece of thessame haukis, iij. **1575** TURBERV. *Bk. Faulconrie* 166 They cast off a cast or a lease of Sacres, which follow the peregrine falcon. **1624** CAPT. SMITH *Virginia* VI. 231 As we passed we see a lease of Bucks. **1690** DRYDEN *Amphitryon* IV. (1691) 42, I put in for a brace, or a lease. **1723** *True Briton* No. 15 I. 126 Giving their Suffrages for the Good of their Country . . and this too, not by Couples or Leases, but by Scores, almost, at a time.

β. *c* **1450** *Merlin* 181 Gawein . . ledde in honde a leeshe of grehoundes, and ledde also two brace folowinge hym. **1526** SKELTON *Magnyf.* 592 Here is a leysshe of ratches to renne an hare. **1582** STANYHURST *Æneis* Ep. Ded. (Arb.) 9 Thee third [posy] (for I wyl present your lordship with a leshe). **1596** SHAKS. *1 Hen. IV*, II. iv. 7 Sirra, I am sworn brother to a leash of Drawers . . Tom, Dicke, and Francis. **1609** B. JONSON *Sil. Wom.* III. ii, I . . kept my chamber a leash of daies for the anguish of it. **1663** BUTLER *Hud.* I. i. 104 Or Cerberus himself pronounce A Leash of Languages at once. **1705** *Double Welcome* xvi. 7 A Leash of Armies on thy Plains appear. **1750** JOHNSON *Rambler* No. 51 ⁋8 A leash of hares to be potted by his wife. **1792** *Munchhausen's Trav.* xxi. 88, I have acquired precisely nine hundred and ninety-nine leash of languages. **1826** SCOTT *Woodst.* xxii, A brace of wild-ducks and a leash of teal. **1838** APPERLEY *Nimrod's North. Tour* (1874) 259 We found a leash of foxes, one after another. **1859** TENNYSON *Lynette* 50 Then were I wealthier than a leash of Kings. **1882** *Gd. Words* 604, I contrived to bag a leash of trout.

3. *Hawking.* The thong or string which is passed through the varvels of the jesses to secure the hawk.

1497 *Ld. Treas. Acc. Scotl.* (1877) I. 366 Item for chessis and lischis thare vjd. **1575** TURBERV. *Bk. Faulconrie* 147 Tying . . a cryance unto your hawkes lease. **1615** LATHAM *Falconry* (1633) Gloss., *Lease* or leash is a small long thong of leather, by which the Faulconer holdeth his Hawke fast, folding it many times about their fingers. **1635** QUARLES *Embl.* v. ix. (1718) 282 But her too faithful leash doth soon retain Her broken flight, attempted oft in vain. **1686** BLOME *Gentl. Recreat.* II. 62 *Lease* or *Leach.* **1826** SIR J. S. SEBRIGHT *Hawking* (1828) 11 When he has been furnished with the necessary appendages of hood, bells, jesses, and leash, he is to be tied to the block. **1874** TENNYSON *Vivien* 123 Their talk was all of . . terms of art, Diet and seeling, jesses, leash and lure.

4. *fig.* (with allusion to senses 1 and 3); esp. in phrases, ***to hold*** or ***have in leash***, to have control over, keep in bondage.

c **1430** *Pilgr. Lyf Manhode* IV. xl. (1869) 195 She is prioresse, whiche leedeth alle þe cloystreres in les, bounden bi hondes and bi feet. **1477** EARL RIVERS (Caxton) *Dictes* 71 Wrath ledeth shame in a lese. **1560** BECON *New Catech.* IV. Wks. 1564 I. 422 For God hathe them in lease. Yea . . they are his slaues. **1611** SHAKS. *Wint. T.* IV. iv. 477 What I was, I am: More straining on, for plucking backe; not following My leash vnwillingly. **1648** BOYLE *Seraph. Love* xii. (1700) 62 The ravish'd Soul being shewn such Game as that, would hate so eagerly, that she would break those Leashes that tye her to the Body. **1821** SHELLEY *Prometh. Unb.* IV. i. 178 We lead along In leashes . . The clouds that are heavy with love's sweet rain. **1842** TENNYSON *Love & Duty* 40 Thy low voice . . would . . hold passion in a leash. **1848** KINGSLEY *Saint's Trag.* II. iv, His ministers Must lure, not drag in leash. **1856** MISS MULOCK *J. Halifax* xvii. (1859) 181 It was easy to see . . that, did he once slip the leash of his passions, it would go hard with Richard Brithwood. **1862** MERIVALE *Rom. Emp.* (1865) VI. li. 231 The soldiers, long held in the leash . . were eager to spring upon the foe.

† **5.** A snare, noose. *Obs.*

c **1374** CHAUCER *Anel. & Arc.* 233 With oon worde him list not oonys deyne To brynge ageyne my sorouful hert in pees, For he is kaught vp in a noþer lees. **1814** CARY *Dante, Par.* XXVIII. 12 Looking upon the beauteous eyes, whence love Had made the leash to take me.

† **6.** *Sc.* = LASH *sb.*¹ *Obs.* (Cf. LEASH *v.* 2.)

1508 KENNEDIE *Flyting w. Dunbar* 45 Lat him lay sax leichis on thy lendis. **1508** DUNBAR *Flyting w. Kennedie* 100 Thow art bot Gluncoch with thy giltin hippis, That for thy lounry mony a leish hes fyld.

7. *Weaving.* **a.** One of the cords (having an eye in the middle to receive the warp-thread) which extend between the parallel laths of the heddle of a loom. Also written *leish.*

1731 MORTIMER in *Phil. Trans.* XXXVII. 105 Some of these Frames are made like a Loom, with a Warp passed through the Leishes. **1878** BARLOW *Weaving* 77 The headles consist of two laths, between which are stretched the required number of 'leashes' usually made of linen thread, and having an eye formed in the middle of them.

b. = LEASE *sb.*⁴ 2.

1888 J. PATON in *Encycl. Brit.* XXIV. 463/2 At each end of the warp the threads are, by a mechanical device in the heck, made to intersect alternately, forming leashes, which are, when taken from the reel, separately tied up, and thus aid in maintaining the parallelism of the ends when they are bundled up.

8. *attrib.*, as ***leash-hound***, ***-man***; † **leash-law** (see quot.).

1679 BLOUNT *Anc. Tenures* 46 Leash-hounds or Park-hounds, such as draw after a hurt Deer in a Leash or Liam. **1721** BAILEY, *Leash-Laws*, are Laws to be observed in Hunting or Coursing. *c* **1817** HOGG *Tales & Sk.* II. 91 [He] ordered that the leashmen should exert themselves in recovering their scattered hounds.

leash (liːʃ), *v.* Also 7 lease. [f. LEASH *sb.*]

1. *trans.* To attach or connect by a leash.

1599 SHAKS. *Hen. V*, Prol. 7 And, at his heeles, (Leasht in, like Hounds), should Famine, Sword, and Fire, Crouch for employment. *a* **1658** LOVELACE *Lucasta Posth.* (1659) 33 Cerberus, from below Must leash'd t'himself with him a hunting go. **1863** W. PHILLIPS *Speeches* xvii. 374 We were then two snarling hounds leashed together.

b. *fig.* To link *together*, esp. in threes.

1854 *Jrnl. R. Agric. Soc.* XV. I. 18, I prefer leashing together these points of the discussion. **1887** SAINTSBURY *Hist. Elizab. Lit.* x. (1890) 366 He [Crashaw] was a much younger man than either of the poets with whom we have leashed him. **1898** READE in *New Century Rev.* IV. 501 Yet were these rivals leashed by sacred ties.

2. †To beat or lash with a leash (*obs.*); to whip (*dial.*).

1503 *Sc. Acts Jas. IV*, c. 103 (ed. 1566) Gif ony childer . . commit ony of thir thingis . . their fathers . . sall . . deliuer the said childe to the juge, to be leichit, scurgeit and dung. **1583** BALFOUR *Practicks* (1754) 27 Ordanis the Dean of Gilde . . to gar leisch barnis that perturbis the kirk. **1592** LYLY *Midas* IV. iii. E 4, If I catch thee in the forest, thou shalt be leasht. . . A boy leasht on the single. **1677** N. COX *Gentl. Recreat.* (ed. 2) 81 In many cases heretofore Leasing was observed; that is, one must be held, either cross a Saddle, or on a mans Back, and with a pair of Dog-couples receive ten pound and a Purse; that is, ten stripes . . and an eleventh, that used to be as bad as the other ten, called a Purse. **1893** *Northumbld. Gloss.*, *Leash, leesh*, to whip. 'Leesh yor horse up, man'.

leasie, obs. form of LAZY.

leasing (ˈliːzɪŋ), *sb. Obs.* or *arch.* exc. *dial.* (*Sc.* and *north.*) Forms: 1 léasung, -ing, 2–3 leasung, (2 lesung, 3 lesin, læs(s)inge, lasinge, leosinge), 3–4 lessinge, 3–6 lesinge, -yng(e, 3–7 lesing, (4 lesenge, -ine, leesyng, *Kent.* lye(a)singe, leazinge), 4–8 leesing, (5 -ynge, -inge, lesyn, 6 leasyng(e, *Sc.* leis-, leysing, 7 leazing), ? 2, 3– leasing. [OE. *léasung*, f. *léasian*: see LEASE *v.*² and -ING¹.] Lying, falsehood.

c **950** *Lindisf. Gosp.* John viii. 44 Miððy spreceð leasuung. *a* **1175** *Cott. Hom.* 229 Heo onscunede . . alle leasunge. *a* **1225** *Ancr. R.* 82 þe deouel . . is leas, & leasunges feder. *c* **1250** *Gen. & Ex.* 2578 He wereden hem wið lesing. *a* **1300** *Floriz & Bl.* 585 'Is þat soþ?' sede he. Heo sede, 'ȝe, sire, withute lesing'. *c* **1340** *Cursor M.* 15412 (Trin.) In to ȝoure hondes I shal him take: holde hit no lesynge. **1375** BARBOUR *Bruce* IV. 480, I wald revard the but lesing. *a* **1450** *Knt. de la Tour* (1868) 33 Ye saide ye loved us . . the which was fals lesinge. **1459** *Paston Lett.* I. 497 Walsham of Chauncery, that never made lesyng, told me that [etc.]. **1500–20** DUNBAR *Poems* ix. 106, I knaw me vicious, Lord, and richt culpable In aithis sweiring, leising, and blaspheming. **1535** COVERDALE *2 Esdras* xiv. 18 The trueth is fled farre awaye, & lesynge is hard at hande. **1595** SPENSER *Col. Clout* 102 No leasing new, nor grandams fable stale. **1601** DENT *Pathw. Heaven* 75 All your faire speeches . . are nought else but hypocrisie and leazing. **1611** BIBLE *Ps.* v. 6 Thou shalt destroy them that speake leasing. **1641** MILTON *Animadv.* Wks. 1851 III. 211 And so take againe either your manifest lesing, or manifest ignorance. **1712** PRIOR *Alma* III. 9 As folks . . prone to leasing, Say things at first because they're pleasing. **1825** SCOTT *Talism.* xiii, Satan is strong within you . . and prompts thee to leasing.

b. In particularized use: A lie, falsehood.

c **1000** *Ags. Ps.* (Th.) v. 5 þu fordest þa þe symle leasinga specað. *c* **1200** *Trin. Coll. Hom.* 163 Ðe defles sed is cheast and twispeche and curs and leasinges. *c* **1290** *S. Eng. Leg.* I. 211/400 þat we with lesingues bi-traieth men. **1303** R. BRUNNE *Handl. Synne* 633 A lesyng ys Whan þou wost þat þou seyst mys. ? *a* **1366** CHAUCER *Rom. Rose* 2 Many men seyn that in sweveninges Ther nis but fables and lesinges. *c* **1440** *Gesta Rom.* xxxvi. 145 (Harl. MS.) Vnhonest and vnleful talkinges, lesynges, & bacbitinges. **1580** LYLY *Euphues* (Arb.) 384 So that in giuing credite to thy letters, I may be deceiued with thy leasings. **1590** SPENSER *F.Q.* I. vii. 48 That false pilgrim, which that leasing told. **1599** B. JONSON *Cynthia's Rev.* I. iv, He [Lucian] doth feed you with fittons, figments, and leasings. **1614** RALEIGH *Hist. World* II. (1634) 197 The Priests . . to magnifie their antiquities, filled the Records with many leasings. **1714** GAY *Sheph. Week* Prol. 74 For Trading free shall thrive again, Nor Leasings leud affright the Swain. **1731** SWIFT *On Mr. P——y being put out of C.* Misc. (1735) V. 110 Sir R—— weary'd by Will. P——y's Teazings, Who interrupted him in all his Leasings.

c. *Comb.*, as ***leasing-bearer***; **leasing-maker**, a liar; *spec.* in *Sc. Law* (now *Hist.*), one who utters untrue and slanderous statements such as are likely to prejudice the relations between the king and his subjects; so **leasing-making**, verbal sedition; † **leasing-monger**, a liar.

c **1440** *Promp. Parv.* 298/2 *Lesynge berare, *mendifer.* **1388** WYCLIF *Prov.* xxi. 6 He that gadrith tresours by the tunge of a *leesing [maker]. **1424** *Sc. Acts Jas. I* (1814) II. 8/2 All lesingis makaris & tellaris of þaim. **1484** CAXTON *Fables of Æsop* IV. viii, The lesynge maker and flaterer. **1703** *Lond. Gaz.* No. 3953/1 Act anent Leesing-makers and Slanderers. *a* **1715** BURNET *Own Time* I. (1724) I. 25 Nor had they the nature of the paper before them, which was judged by the Court to be *leasing-making. **1863** H. COX *Instit.* I. xi. 272 *note*, By the law of Scotland . . verbal sedition or leasing-making, is inferred from [etc.]. *c* **1380** WYCLIF *Wks.* (1880) 268 þei ben . . *lesyngmongeris. **1496** *Dives & Paup.* (W. de W.) VII. ii. 277/2 Bacbyters lesyng-mongers and wycked spekers . . be the worst theues upon the erthe.

leasing (ˈliːzɪŋ), *vbl. sb.*¹ Now *dial.* Also 6 lezing. [f. LEASE *v.*¹ + -ING¹.] Gleaning. Also *concr.* = *leasing corn.*

1534 *Act 25 Hen. VIII*, c. 1 *Stat. Irel.* (1678) 46 Many . . persons . . will not labour for their living, but have their sole respect to gathering and lezing of corn in harvest time. **1772** GRAVES *Spirit. Quixote* II. 255 How much might she earn a day, then, by her leasing? *c* **1825** *Houlston Tracts* II. xlvii. 2 What was to become of the poor, now their leasing was all eaten and gone?

b. *attrib.*, **leasing-corn**, wheat got by gleaning.

1857 ELIZA ACTON *Eng. Bread-Bk.* 138 *note*, The wheat . . which her family have gleaned,—the leasing corn,—supposed to make the best bread of any.

leasing (ˈliːsɪŋ), *vbl. sb.*² [f. LEASE *v.*³ + -ING¹.] The action of LEASE *v.*³; letting out (on lease). Also *attrib.*

1521 *Bury Wills* (Camden) 124 In lesyng and lettyng yᵉ days werke. **1610** J. MORE in *Buccleuch MS.* (Hist. MSS. Comm.) 90 In case of leasing, whether you will reserve the house. **1818** CRUISE *Digest* (ed. 2) IV. 284 If actual possession were necessary, a leasing power could never be executed where land was in the hands of a tenant. **1880** *Times* 30 July 9/4 The leasing of shooting rights.

ˈleasing, *vbl. sb.*³ [f. LEASE *sb.*⁴ + -ING¹.] *Attrib.* in **leasing reed**, in weaving, a reed through which the warp threads pass as they come off the bobbins.

1927 T. WOODHOUSE *Artificial Silk* 108 The ends of the bobbins are threaded through a leasing reed. **1960** *Textile Terms & Definitions* (ed. 4) 90 (*caption*) Leasing.

leasing (ˈliːzɪŋ), *ppl. a.*¹ [f. LEASE *v.*¹ + -ING².] Gleaning.

1829 E. JESSE *Jrnl. Nat.* 361 The allowance of fourteen pence a day . . would hardly be accepted by my leasing neighbours in place of it [*viz.* gleaning].

leasing ('li:zɪŋ), *ppl. a.*² [Formed as a corresp. adj. to LEASING *sb.* Cf. LEASE *v.*²] Lying.

1873 W. S. MAYO *Never Again* xii. 166 Here, take this leasing, meeching bard, With priestly aid go bind him hard.

leasow ('li:səʊ, 'lɛzə), *sb.* Now *dial.* Forms: 1 *pl.* **læswe, léswe,** *Northumb.* **lésua,** 3 ? **lewse,** *pl.* **leswa,** 3–6 **lesewe,** 4 **leswe,** 4–6 **lesue,** 5 **leseo, liswe,** 5, 7 **lesow,** 6 **leassewe, leyssue,** *Sc.* **lesoue,** 7– **leasow.** *β.* (chiefly *Sc.*) 6 **lesur(e, lyssoure, lasor,** 7 **leissoure, leasure, lizure,** 8 **lizor,** 9 **lizzure, leissure.** [See LEASE *sb.*¹] Pasture; pasturage; meadow-land.

c **950** *Lindisf. Gosp.* John x. 9 Inn-færeð & ut-færeð & lesua [*Rushw.* leswe, *Ags. & Hatton Gosp.* læse] ȝemoetað. **10..** *Ags. Voc.* in Wr.-Wülcker 325/25 *Pascua*, læswe. *c* **1200** *Trin. Coll. Hom.* 37 Ðis oref is swiðe egerne and fecheð his leswe hwile uppen trewes, and hwile uppen cliues. *c* **1205** LAY. 2011 Bi-heold he þa leswa [*c* 1275 lesewes] & þene leofliche wode. *a* **1225** *Ancr. R.* 94 Ine heouene is large leswe. *c* **1250** *Gen. & Ex.* 1576 Ydumea, ðat fulsum lond, Of lewse god, was in hise hond. **1382** WYCLIF *Ps.* xciv. [xcv.] 7 Wee the puple of his leswe; and the shep of his hond. —— *Jer.* xxiii. 1 Wo to the shepperdis, that scateren and to-tern the floc of my leswe, seith the Lord. *c* **1440** *R. Glouc. Chron.* 1005 (MS. δ) Hor leseo lasteth euere. *Ibid.* 7701 Lesow he ȝaf þer to. **1495** *Act 11 Hen. VII*, c. 35 §4 Medowes lesues pastures. **1502** ARNOLDE *Chron.* (1811) 174 Lesurs pasturs weies pathes wetingli and uniustli.. witholden. **1513** DOUGLAS *Æneis* XII. Prol. 183 In lyssouris and on leys litill lammis Full tait and trig socht bletand to thar dammis. **1547** *Newminster Cartul.* (1878) 310 All lands medows leyssues and pastures. **1596** DALRYMPLE tr. *Leslie's Hist. Scot.* I. 27 A pasture, or as we say, a Lesoue. **1658** *Disposition* in Jamieson *Dict.* s.v. *Lesuris*, Meadows, leissoureis and pasturages. **1699** *Ibid.*, Water stanks, lizures, pasturages. **1686** PLOT *Staffordsh.* 293 Having a Lesow quite overrun with well grown broom. **1799** *Trans. Soc. Arts* XVII. 126 Coarse meadows, or what are called leasows, being rough woody pastures. **1825–80** JAMIESON, *Leissure, Lizzure.* *a* **1845** HOOD *Town & Country* xv, I hold no Leasowes in my lease, No cot set round with trees. **1852** WIGGINS *Embanking* 139 After feeding all the summer on the higher grounds, called leasows or leazes in the dairy counties. **1894** *S.E. Worcester Gloss, Lezzow*, a meadow.

'**leasow**, *v. Obs.* or *dial.* In 1 **lǽs(w)ian,** 3 **leswe, leswue,** 3–4 **lesewe,** 4 **lesuwe, lisewe,** 4–5 **lesowe,** 7 **lessow.** [OE. *lǽswian* (also *lǽsian*), f. *lǽsw-, lǽs* LEASOW *sb.*, LEASE *sb.*¹] *trans.* and *intr.* To pasture, graze.

c **950** *Lindisf. Gosp.* Luke viii. 32 Wæs ðonne ðer ede *vel* sunor berȝana moniȝo foedendra *vel* lesuuandra [*Ags. Gosp.* læsiendra]. *c* **1000** ÆLFRIC *Gen.* xli. 2 (Gr.) Hiȝ man læswode on morium lande. *c* **1200** *Trin. Coll. Hom.* 39 þe selue herdes beð þe lorþewes of holi chiriche þe leseweð here orf. *a* **1225** *Ancr. R.* 100 And leswe þine ticchenes bi heordmonne hulen, of ris & of leaues. **1382** WYCLIF *Matt.* viii. 30 A floc.. of many hoggis lesewynge was nat fer from hem. —— *1 Cor.* ix. 7 Who feedith or lesuwith a floc, and etith not of the mylk of the flok? *c* **1425** WYNTOUN *Cron.* I. v. 212 As catell lesowyde in and oute. **1604** DRAYTON *Moses* 28 Gently his faire flocks lessow'd he along. **1825–80** JAMIESON, *Lesure*, both as a *s.* and as a *v.*, is still used in the pastoral districts of Ayrs., Renfrs., and Lanarks.

Hence '**leasowed** (*lesewed*) *ppl. a.*

1382 WYCLIF *1 Kings* iv. 23 Ten fatte oxen, twenti lesewed oxen [1388 oxis of lesewe, Vulg. *pascuales*].

leasse, obs. form of LEASE.

leassee, -our, obs. forms of LESSEE, LESSOR.

leasses, variant of LESSES *Obs.*

leasshe, obs. form of LEASH.

least (li:st), *a.*, (*sb.*), and *adv.* Forms: 1 **lǽst, lǽsast, lǽsest,** *Northumb.* **léasest, léassæst, lǽssest,** 3 **læst,** 2–5 **leste,** 3–4 **last,** 3–6 **leist,** 3–7 (*rarely* 8) **lest,** 4–5 **leeste,** 4–6 **leest,** 3, 6– **least.** [OE. *lǽst, lǽsest*:—prehist. **laisisto-*, superlative f. **laisiz-* LESS; cf. OFris. *leist*. An OE. *lǽrest* = OFris. *lêrest*:—**laizisto-*, occurs in one instance.] Used as the superlative of LITTLE.

A. *adj.*

I. In concord with *sb.* expressed or understood.

1. a. Little beyond all others in size or degree; smallest; slightest; †fewest.

Not infrequently coupled with *last*: see LAST *a.* 1 c.

a **1000** *Guthlac* 741 Nis þæt huru læsast þæt seo lufu cyþeð. *c* **1000** *Sax. Leechd.* II. 268 þone læstan dæl þunges. *c* **1200** ORMIN 15277 þiss follc iss laȝhesst, & tiss lott Addleþþ þe læste mede. **1297** R. GLOUC. (Rolls) 860 And best me mai to hom truste, þat of lest wordes [*MS.* δ leste of wordys] beþ. **1377** LANGL. *P. Pl.* B. VII. 39 Men of lawe lest pardoun hadde þat pleteden for Mede. *c* **1400** *Lanfranc's Cirurg.* 294 þe veyne þat is bitwixe þe leeste too of his foot. *c* **1470** *Golagros & Gaw.* 289 Lich as leif of the lynd lest, That welteris doun with the wynd, sa wauerand it is. **1576** FLEMING *Panopl. Epist.* 35 To reckon your owne state among things of least estimation. **1697** DRYDEN *Æneid* XI. 664 Th' Italian Chiefs, and Princes, joyn their Pow'rs: Nor least in Number, nor in Name the last. **1725** LD. BOLINGBROKE 24 July in *Swift's Lett.* (1767) II. 210 Those, who had the least mind to see me in England, have made it impossible for me to live any where else. **1768** STERNE *Sent. Journ.* (1775) 128 (*Act of Charity*) A fix'd star of the least magnitude. **1778** PENNANT *Tour in Wales* I. 2 [Flint] is the lest of the twelve Welch [Counties]. **1879** DOWDEN *Southey* 8 His last and least pupil.

ellipt. *c* **1205** LAY. 28560 Fiftene he hafde feondliche wunden mon mihte i þare lasten [*c* **1275** leaste] twa glouen iþraste. *a* **1300** *Cursor M.* 16947 Ogains leist of his to drei. *Ibid.* 26252 þe ferth point es noght þe lest. **1340** *Ayenb.* 44 Huanne me.. beggeþ be þe gratteste wyȝtes.. and zelleþ by þe leste. *c* **1369** CHAUCER *Dethe Blaunche* 283 No more than coude the leste of vs. **1662** J. DAVIES tr. *Mandelslo's Trav.* 103 The effects of a deep resentment, where of the least are cudgelling or caning. **1768** STERNE *Sent. Journ.* (1775) 63 (*Gloves*) She begg'd I would try a single pair, which seemed to be the least.

b. ***the least***: often used, esp. in negative and hypothetical contexts, for 'Any, however small'. †More emphatically, ***any*** or ***one the least.*** †Formerly *occas.* with omission of the article; also in ***no least*** = 'not the least'.

c **1380** WYCLIF *Wks.* (1880) 143 þouȝ he conne not þe leste poynt of þe gospel. **1613** SHAKS. *Hen. VIII*, II. iv. 153 Whether euer I.. spake one, the least word that might Be to the preiudice of her present State. **1632** BROME *North. Lasse* I. vii. Wks. 1873 III. 19 One from whom You never had, or can expect least good. **1634** SIR T. HERBERT *Trav.* 73 Without least shew of remorse or pietie. **1659** HAMMOND *On Ps.* lxxxix. 7 There is no least comparison between all the power and operations of all those. **1664** H. POWER *Exp. Philos.* Pref. a iij, Dioptrical Glasses.. are but a Modern Invention: Antiquity gives us not the least hint thereof. **1667** MILTON *P.L.* III. 120 Without least impulse or shadow of Fate. **1687** TOWERSON *Baptism* 269 Without any the least hint of their being baptiz'd. **1697** in W. S. Perry *Hist. Coll. Amer. Col. Ch.* I. 14 Without receiving any the least assistance from those Guns. **1699** DAMPIER *Voy.* II. II. 38 Beef.. without the least sign of Fat in it. **1762** *Gentl. Mag.* 615 The least aperative [= aperient] undoes all immediately. **1763** *Mus. Rusticum* Oct. XXII. I. 109 Every the least appearance of a weed or root of grass is diligently picked off. **1824** BENTHAM *Bk. Fallacies* Wks. 1843 II. 380 Scarce in any instance will be discovered any the least danger of final deception. **1834** T. MEDWIN *Angler in Wales* I. 262 Tiger is not like pheasant-shooting.. and the least noise often scares away.. game of the forest. **1851** *Illustr. Catal. Gt. Exhib.* 330 Fire-escape.. intended to be always ready.. without the least preparation.

c. In the names of certain animal and vegetable species or varieties, distinguished by their smallness from others bearing the same name. (Cf. LESS, LESSER.)

1633 *Gerarde's Herbal* I. lxxxvi. 137 The Least Mountain White Narcissus. **1719** QUINCY *Lex. Physico-Med.* (ed. 2) 346 The least Hare's-Ear. **1766** PENNANT *Brit. Zool.* (1776) III. 171 Lest Hake. **1796** MORSE *Amer. Geog.* I. 209 Least Golden Crown Thrush. **1823** CRABB *Technol. Dict.* s.v. *Hare*, The least Hare, *Lepus minimus*, which is the size of a rat. **1831** A. WILSON & BONAPARTE *Amer. Ornith.* III. 53 The least bittern is also found in Jamaica. **1837** MACGILLIVRAY *Withering's Brit. Plants* (ed. 4) 335 Least Bog Orchis. *Ibid.* 366 Least Willow. **1870** *Amer. Naturalist* III. 234 The least Tern,.. and the Roseate Tern, still breed on our coast. **1915** A. R. HORWOOD *Story Plant Life Brit. Isles* III. i. 105 Hooker recognises three divisions [of Gamopetalæ]: Chironieæ, including Yellow Wort, Least Yellow Gentian, [etc.]. **1946** T. M. STANWELL-FLETCHER *Driftwood Valley* 42 Sometimes he and the least chipmunks .. play hide-and-seek round boxes and trees. **1955** E. B. FORD *Moths* xi. 166 This [*sc.* the Burren] is also the Irish locality for the Least Minor. **1960** M. BURTON *Wild Animals of Brit. Isles* 114 The Least weasel.. has not so far been found in this country. **1975** *Country Life* 16 Jan. 131/1 Least tern nesting area.

d. ***least common multiple, least squares, least constraint, least resistance***: see the sbs.

e. ***law*** (or ***principle***) ***of least action*** (Physics): the principle that an actual trajectory of a physical system is always such that, in comparison with any slightly different motion between the same end-points, the integral over the trajectory of the momentum with respect to distance (or more generally, of the sum of the generalized momenta with respect to generalized co-ordinates) has a minimum (or a maximum) value.

[**1748** MOREAU DE MAUPERTUIS in *Hist. de l'Acad. R. des Sci. 1744* 423 Le chemin qu'elle [*sc.* la lumière] tient est celui par lequel la quantité d'action est le moindre... La quantité d'action.. est proportionnelle à la somme des espaces multipliez chacun par la vitesse avec laquelle le corps les parcourt. **1748** —— in *Hist. de l'Acad. R. des Sci. et des Belles Lettres de Berlin 1746* 286 J'ai découvert le principe universel, sur lequel toutes ces loix sont fondées... C'est le principe de la moindre quantité d'action.] **1814** J. TOPLIS tr. *Laplace's Treat. Analytical Mech.* ii. 47 Maupertuis.. asserted, that in all the changes which take place in the situation of a body, the product of the mass of the body by its velocity and the space which it has passed over is a minimum. This he called the principle of the least action, and it was applied by him to the discovery of the laws of the refraction and the reflection of light,.. the laws of equilibrium, &c. **1834** W. R. HAMILTON in *Phil. Trans. R. Soc.* CXXIV. 252 Although Lagrange and others, in treating of the motion of a system, have shown that the variation of this definite integral vanishes when the extreme coordinates and the constant H are given, they appear to have deduced from this result only the well known law of least action. **1920** A. S. EDDINGTON *Space, Time & Gravitation* ix. 149 The law of gravitation, the laws of mechanics, and the laws of the electromagnetic field have all been summed up in a single Principle of Least Action. For the most part this unification was accomplished before the advent of the relativity theory, and it is only the addition of gravitation to the scheme which is novel. **1966** J. L. MERIAM *Dynamics* viii. 349 Hamilton's principle and the principle of least action have found important but limited applications in engineering problems. Their use will undoubtedly grow with time as the complexity and generality of design situations increase. **1973** *Nature* 28 Sept. 223/1 The mechanics section begins with Hamilton's principle (here called the principle of least action) and gives a concise and elegant account of the relation between invariance and conservation laws.

2. Lowest in power or position; meanest. (*arch.*) †With agent-noun: Having very little practice or scope. Also *ellipt.*

c **950** *Lindisf. Gosp.* Matt. v. 19 Lytel *vel* leasest [*Ags. Gosp.* læst] he bið ȝenemned in ric heafna. **1362** LANGL. *P. Pl.* A. III. 25 [She] ȝaf.. The leste man of here mayne a mutoun of gold. *c* **1400** tr. *Secreta Secret., Gov. Lordsh.* 41 Phelip þe lest of his clerks. **1567** *Gude & Godlie Ball.* (S.T.S.) 44 Bot quha is maist, sall serue the leist. **1580** SIDNEY *Ps.* XXV. x, I am poore and least of all. **1594** SHAKS. *Rich. III*, V. iii. 268 The least of you shall share his part thereof. **1611** BIBLE *Matt.* ii. 6 Thou.. art not the least among the Princes of Iuda. **1697** DRYDEN *Æneid* XI. 677, I, Turnus, not the least of all my Name. **1727** S. SWITZER *Pract. Gardiner* II. vii. 58 All which is obvious to the least practitioners in them.

†**3.** Phr. **a.** ***at the least way(s, wise***: see LEASTWAYS, LEASTWISE. **b.** ***at least hand***: at least. *Obs.*

a **1586** SIDNEY *Arcadia* III, My musicke well assures me we are (at least hand) fellow prentises to one vngratious master.

II. Absolute uses (quasi-*sb.*).

4. That which is least; the least quantity or amount; †the least part *of* something. Phrase, ***to say the least*** (***of it***).

a **1200** *Moral Ode* 112 þe ðe lest wat biseið ofte mest. *Ibid.* 353 þe þe lest haued haueð so muchel þat he bit no more. **1590** SHAKS. *Mids. N.* V. i. 105 Loue therefore, and tongue-tide simplicity, In least, speake most, to my capacity. **1591** —— *Two Gent.* II. vii. 68 That is the least (Lucetta) of my feare. **1597** BACON *Coulers Gd. & Evill* (Arb.) 150 [They] haue no other shift but to bear it out wel, and to make the least of it. **1809** *Deb. Congress U.S.* 20 Feb. (1853) 422 To say the least of it, the people will perceive.. an uncommon coincidence. **1811** *Ibid.* 17 Jan. 603 To say the least of such a measure, is to term it an experiment. **1850** MᶜCOSH *Div. Govt.* II. ii. (1874) 197 We hold the moral law to be as much, to say the least of it, the appointment of God as any natural law. *a* **1902** *Mod.* The very least I can do is to apologize for the mistake. **1928** R. CAMPBELL *Wayzgoose* i. 26 Muses Nine, Those strapping girls whose love, to say the least, Would make a rabid Mormon of a priest. **1974** D. SCANNELL *Mother knew Best* vi. 59 Mother said vanity was a besetting sin which Amy resented, to say the least of it.

Proverb. **1773** GOUV. MORRIS in Sparks *Life & Writ.* (1832) II. 289 Our Secretary of State reminds me of a maxim of his predecessor that least said is soonest mended. **1835** MARRYAT *Pirate* v, The least said the soonest mended.

5. Governed by a prep., forming an advb. phrase.

a. at least, at the least (also ME. *atte leste*, Ormin *att allre læste*). A qualifying phrase, attached to a quantitative designation to indicate that the amount is the smallest admissible. Hence, in wider use, characterizing a statement as certainly valid, even if one of a more comprehensive kind be not allowable; = 'at any rate', 'at all events'.

11.. *O.E. Chron.* an. 1049 (MS. D.) Sweȝen.. bæd Eadward cyng scypfultumes þ sceolde beon æt læstan .L. scypa. *c* **1200** ORMIN 937 þatt he ȝuw illke Sunennda33 Att allre læste lære. *a* **1225** *Ancr. R.* 164 Ihereð nu reisuns hwui me ouh for to fleon þene world; eihte reisuns et te leste. *a* **1300** *Cursor M.* 6774 And if i lent þe suilkin beist, þat ded be or spilt at leist.. þou sal it quit wit iuiement. *c* **1375** *Sc. Leg. Saints* xxvi. (*Nycholas*) 219 þane askit he þame to sel vitale A hundre medreiis at þe lest of ilke schipe. *c* **1386** CHAUCER *Man of Law's Prol.* 38 Thanne haue ye do youre deuoir atte leeste. *c* **1400** MAUNDEV. (Roxb.) xix. 86 þase ymages er ilk ane of þe stature of twa men at þe leste. **1526** TINDALE *John* xiv. 11 Att the leest beleve me for the very workes sake. **1552** *Bk. Com. Prayer, Pref. to Ordering Deacons*, .xxi. yeres of age at the least. **1563–7** BUCHANAN *Reform. St. Andros* Wks. (1892) 8 The nombre of the classis at the leist sex. **1576** FLEMING *Panopl. Epist.* 355 *note*, Man being indued with reason (or at least ought to bee), knowledge and understanding. **1605** SHAKS. *Macb.* V. v. 52 At least wee'l dye with Harnesse on our backe. **1611** BIBLE *Luke* xix. 42. **1662** J. DAVIES tr. *Olearius' Voy. Ambass.* 93 At lest I can say this, I never met with any who were glad when they were beaten. **1663** GERBIER *Counsel* 53 There are at the least in twenty thousand, five thousand unfit for work. **1667** MILTON *P.L.* I. 258 Here at least We shall be free. **1711** ADDISON *Spect.* No. 105. ¶7 The Book-Pedant is much the most supportable; he has at least an exercised Understanding. **1712** STEELE *Ibid.* No. 498 ¶3 As had disabled him from being a coachman for that day at least. **1802** MAR. EDGEWORTH *Moral T.* (1816) I. iii. 17, I hope.. you'll at least tell me, that you do not really suspect me. **1834** J. H. NEWMAN *Par. Serm.* (1837) I. iii. 44 Have you not power at least over the limbs of your body? **1847–9** HELPS *Friends in C.* Ser. I. (1857) I. 123 At least it does not contain the whole matter. **1885** *Act 48 & 49 Vict.* c. 60 §4 A session of the Council shall be held once at least in every two years.

†**b. by the least.** At least.

a **1300** *K. Horn* 616 He sloȝ þer on haste On hundred bi þe laste [*Geste Kyng Horn* 612 at the leste]. *c* **1400** *Destr. Troy* 7623 The flode was so felle, with fallyng of Rayn, Hit was like, by the lest, as oure lorde wold With water haue wastid all þe world efte. **1513** DOUGLAS *Æneis* XII. xiii. 29 Desist heirof, now at last, be the lest.

c. in the least. †(*a*) At the lowest estimate (*obs.*). (*b*) In the smallest or slightest degree.

1605 SHAKS. *Lear* I. i. 194 What in the least Will you require in present Dower with her. **1660** WOOD *Life* 29 Nov., He never suffered in the least for his cause. **1662** STILLINGFL. *Orig. Sacr.* III. iii. §4 And is it possible.. to imagine that the Scriptures do in the least ascribe the Origine of evill to God? **1702** ADDISON *Dial. Medals* ii. Wks. 1721 I. 461, I have been surprized to meet with a man in a Satire that I never in the least expected to find there. **1845** STEPHEN *Comm. Laws Eng.* (1874) II. 497 So as to restrain or diminish in the least any of his rights or interests. **1851** RUSKIN *Stones Ven.* (1874) I. xx. 218 No sculptor can in the least imitate the peculiar character of accidental fracture.

† **d.** **with the least.** (*a*) Inferior. (*b*) = At least. Also, ***to speak with the least***: to say the least. (*c*) ***with least or most***: at all, in any way. *Obs.*

c **1374** CHAUCER *Troylus* I. 281 She nas not with the leste of here stature. **1550–3** *Decaye of England* (E.E.T.S.) 100 It lesth the kings Maiesty...v. thousande markes by the yeare with the lest [*printed* left]. **1575** *Gamm. Gurton* v. ii. 247 *Bayly.* Canst thou not say any-thing to that, Diccon, with least or most? *Diccon.* Yea, mary, sir, thus much I can say: wel, the nedle is lost! *c* **1680** BEVERIDGE *Serm.* (1729) II. 586 We..who live..where the..means of grace are as.. powerfully administer'd, to speak with the least, as in any place.

† **6.** as *sb.* A most minute quantity or part; a minimum. *Obs.*

1656 STANLEY *Hist. Philos.* v. (1701) 161/2 There being in Nature no least which cannot be divided. **1682** CREECH *Lucretius* I. 23 They all affirm, that Nature never rests In breaking Bodies, and admits no Leasts. **1683** *Ibid.* Notes 17 Epicurus made all his Atoms to be leasts, and therefore insensible. **1766** AMORY *Buncle* (1770) IV. 94 By impregnating the most generous white wine, with the minims or leasts of antimony. **1813** BUSBY *Lucretius* I. 658 These particles themselves no parts contain, And hence are Nature's Leasts, or finest grain.

B. *adv.* **a.** In the least degree; in a degree less than all others, or than on all other occasions.

c **1200** *Trin. Hom.* 75 þanne þu lest wenst deað cumeþ to fecchende þe. *a* **1300** *Cursor M.* 27201 In lauerd house..þar man agh lest do dishonur. *a* **1400–50** *Alexander* 2546 He was fallen in a feuer or he lest wende. *c* **1440** *Promp. Parv.* 299/1 Leest wurthy, *eximius.* **1526** TINDALE *1 Cor.* xii. 23 Those members of the body which we thynke lest honest. *c* **1600** SHAKS. *Sonn.* xxix, With what I most inioy Contented least. **1667** MILTON *P.L.* I. 679 Mammon, the least erected Spirit that fell From Heav'n. **1732** BERKELEY *Alciph.* III. §6 Alciphron has made discoveries where I least expected it. **1833** HT. MARTINEAU *Fr. Wines & Pol.* v. 75 When the time came for giving up his watch or his rat, he thought he could least spare his live companion. **1883** R. W. DIXON *Mano* II. i. 65 And when lord Gerbert questioned privily, Of me he got but little: least of all Upon that noble knight would I be spy.

b. ***the least***: in the least degree.

1662 J. DAVIES tr. *Mandelslo's Trav.* 101 Drunkenness is a Vice they can the least of any be charged withal. **1840** MARRYAT *Poor Jack* vi, He wasn't the least groggy. **1881** FROUDE *Short Studies* (1883) IV. 351, I am not the least pretending that this has been the actual history of man in this planet.

least(e, leastall, obs. ff. LEST, LAYSTALL.

† **'leasting.** *Obs. rare.* [f. LEAST *a.* + -ING³.] N. Fairfax's word for 'atom'.

1674 N. FAIRFAX *Bulk & Selv.* 30 One atome or leasting.

† **'leastness.** *Obs. rare.* [f. LEAST *a.* + NESS.] Minimal size.

1674 N. FAIRFAX *Bulk & Selv.* 100 A least bitling is made as much for cleaving, if it had but a wherewith to be cloven; its leastness, not its bodiness forbidding it.

leastways ('li:stweɪz), *adv.* [See WAY.]

†**a.** Orig. two words (subsequently often written as one) in the phrase ***at (the) least way(s*** = 'at least' (cf. LEASTWISE). *Obs.* **b.** As one word, in the same sense. *dial.* and *vulgar.*

c **1386** CHAUCER *Clerk's T.* 910 Do thou thy devoir at the leeste weye. **1470–85** MALORY *Arthur* IV. xxi, So this same dolorous knyȝt serued hem al, that at the lest way he smote doune hors and man. **1526** TINDALE *Acts* v. 15 That at the lest waye the shadowe off Peter..myght shadowe some of them. **1548** UDALL, etc. *Erasm. Par. John* xviii. 37–40 If ye wyll not spare..hym as an innocente, at leastwaye..pardon hym his life as an offender. **1552** LATIMER *Serm. 23rd Sund. Trinity* (1584) 205 Let vs be moued at the least wayes with his promises. **1606** HOLLAND *Sueton.* 100 In expectance either of speedy succession after him, or at least waies of fellowship in the Empire with him. *a* **1825** FORBY *Voc. E. Anglia, Least-ways,* adv. at least; least-wise. **1852** DICKENS *Bleak Ho.* liv, He was own brother to a brimstone magpie—leastways Mrs. Smallweed. **1866** G. MACDONALD *Ann. Q. Neighb.* vii. (1878) 103 She lets them, leastways her sister go and see her.

leastwise ('li:stwaɪz), *adv.* [See WISE *sb.*, -WISE, and cf. LEASTWAYS.] †**a.** As two words (later often written as one) in certain phrases: ***at (the) least wise***, = 'at least'; ***in the least wise***, = 'in the least.' *Obs.* **b.** As one word = 'at least'. Somewhat *rare.*

1534 MORE *Comf. agst. Trib.* III. xi. (1553) P iij b, Though a man..abide in great authoritie til he dye, yet than at yᵉ leaste wise euery man must leaue it at yᵉ last. **1577** VAUTROUILLIER *Luther on Ep. Gal.* 243, I feele not my selfe to haue any righteousnes, or at least wise, I feele it but very litle. **1611** BIBLE *Transl. Pref.* 2 The first christened Emperour (at the leastwise that openly professed the faith). **1676** TEMPLE *Let. to M. Pomponne* Wks. 1731 II. 365, I judged it a Matter of too great Weight for me to intermeddle with in the leastwise. **1692** S. PATRICK *Answ. Touchstone* 12 Impugned..by the Authority of Holy Scripture, or at least-wise, by the Universal Councils of Catholick Priests. *a* **1825** [see LEASTWAYS]. **1861** GEO. ELIOT *Silas M.* xvi. 281 It was a sign that his money would come to light again, or leastwise that the robber would be made to answer for it. **1883** A. EDERSHEIM *Life Jesus* I. ii. 20 The old Testament, leastwise, the Law of Moses, was directly and wholly from God.

leat (li:t). Chiefly *s.w.dial.* Also 6 leate, 7 let(t, 9 leet. [OE. (*wæter*)-*ʒelǽt*(*e* water-conduit (the simple word occurs also in the sense 'junction of roads') = OHG. *gilâz* letting, letting out, junction, also in comb. *wazzer gilâz* water-conduit (MHG. *gelâz*, mod.G. *gelasz*, also MHG. *gelæze*, mod.G. *geläsze*, in many senses derived from that of the verbal root); f. *ʒe-* prefix (see Y-) + root of *lǽtan* LET *v.*¹] An open watercourse to conduct water for household purposes, mills, mining works, etc.

1590–1 in *Trans. Devon. Assoc.* (1884) XVI. 526 Item pd to 4 trumpetors that were att the leate by Mr Maiors commaundemt, vs. *a* **1642** SIR W. MONSON *Naval Tracts* iv. (1704) 432/1 Streight, River, or other Let of Water, fresh or salt. **1671** *Phil. Trans.* VI. 2098 Cut a Leat, Gurt, or Trench. **1671** F. PHILLIPS *Reg. Necess.* 235 Commissioners of Sewers to survey Streams, Gutters, Letts, and Annoyances. **1796** W. MARSHALL *W. England* II. 269 Rode to the head of Plymouth Leat. This artificial brook is taken out of the river Mew, towards its source. **1813** VANCOUVER *Agric. Devon* 319 The entrance for the leat was cut at about thirty feet above the lip of the weir. **1838** MRS. BRAY *Tradit. Devon* I. 232 *note*, Leet is used in Devonshire to signify a stream of water. **1855** KINGSLEY *Westw. Ho!* xvi, I have a project to bring down a leat of fair water from the hill-tops right into Plymouth town. **1881** *Daily News* 21 Jan. 6/4 The leats on Dartmoor are choked with snow and ice, and no water is flowing into the reservoirs.

attrib. **1882** BURTON & CAMERON *Gold Coast for G.* I. iii. 57 The water-course or leat-road of Santa Luzia.

leat, pa. t. of LOUT *Obs.*, to stoop.

leatch, obs. form of LEECH *sb.*³ *Naut.*

leath (li:θ), *sb. Obs.* exc. *dial.* Forms: 2–3 **leð, leoð, lioþ,** 3–4 **leþe,** 3–5 **leth,** (? 3–4 **lyth,** 5 **letht**), 7 **lathe,** 7– **leath.** [Early ME. *leð*, of obscure origin; not connected with LITHE *a.* Usually regarded as equivalent to the sb. from which are derived Ger. and Du. *ledig* unoccupied, also (with negative prefix) MDu. *onlede* trouble. Cf. also LETHE *a.*]

1. Cessation, intermission, rest. †***a leoð gān*** (early ME.): to make peace.

c **1175** *Lamb. Hom.* 35 Swilche pine ic habbe þet me were leofere þenne al world..most ic habben an alpi þraȝe summe lisse and summe leðe. *c* **1205** LAY. 9504 ȝif he wule a leoð gan [*c* 1275 pais makie] & halden me for lauerd. *c* **1250** *Gen. & Ex.* 3348 Wið ðis mete weren he fed, fowerti winter vten leð. *a* **1300** *Cursor M.* 23260 Of helle pines..firen bandes es þe nind, þat al þair limes ar bunden wit, witvten leth of ani lith. *a* **1400–50** *Alexander* 4593 þa þat lepros ere & lame, þat neuire of leth knewe. *c* **1460** *Towneley Myst.* xxi. 142 Oone worde myght thou speke ethe, yit myght it do the som letht. **1674** RAY *N.C. Words* 29 *Lathe*, ease or rest. *Ibid.*, *Leath*, ceasing, intermission: as no Leath of pain.

2. *Mining.* A soft part in a vein.

1747 HOOSON *Miner's Dict.*, *Blanch*, a piece of Ore grown in the hard Rock, or in hard Sparr or Tuft, or any other hard Stuff, without any Softness of Leath at all about it. *Ibid.*, *Leath.* In hard Works it is any Joynt, or softness that gives some Liberty and Advantage, for the better freeing the harder Part, in order to Cut or Blast it.

leath, *v. Obs.* exc. *dial.* Forms: 2 **leðien,** 3 **leoðien,** 4 **leþ(e,** 6, 8–9 *dial.* **lathe,** 8–9 **leath(e,** **leeth.** [ME. *leþien*, f. *leþ* LEATH *sb.*]

1. *trans.* To mitigate, soften, relax.

c **1200** *Trin. Coll. Hom.* 71 Alse wat swo þe man his sinne sore bimurneð ure drihten leðeð þe sinne bendes, and blisseð swo þe soule. *c* **1205** LAY. 21922 Leoðe [*c* 1275 slake] vre benden. *c* **1325** *Metr. Hom.* 86 Goddes graz..conforted him ..And lethed his soru and his kare. **13..** *E.E. Allit. P.* C. 13 Suffraunce may aswagend hem & þe swelme leþe. **1796** MARSHALL *Yorks.* II. 330 *Leathe*, to relax; as a cow when near calving. **1868** ATKINSON *Cleveland Gloss.* 310 *Leathe*, to soften, to render that which is rigid more or less soft and pliant.

†**2.** *intr.* To cease, abate. *Obs.*

1205 LAY. 12042þat weder leoðede. *c* **1340** *Cursor M.* 5572 (Fairf.) Of his wikkenes walde he noȝt leþ. **13..** *St. Erkenwolde* 347 in Horstm. *Altengl. Leg.* (1881) 274 þe ay-lastand life, þat lethe shalle neuer. **13..** *E.E. Allit. P.* A. 377 Now I hit se, now leþez my loþe. *Ibid.* B. 648 Er þy lyuez lyȝt leþe vpon erþe..schal Sare consayue & a sun bere.

Hence **'leathing** *vbl. sb.*

a **1300** *Cursor M.* 7438 Ai quen [saul] was trauaild mast.. And [dauid] bigan to gleu or sing, Of his vn-ro he tok lething. **1535** STEWART *Cron. Scot.* (1858) I. 219 The king of Pechtis, into siclike number, Than haistilie come ouir the watter of Humber, Without lathen, that tyme he wes not lidder; Syne in ane feild tha lichtit all togidder. *Ibid.* 401 Without lathin he maid no langar lat.

leather ('lɛðə(r)), *sb.* Forms: 1 **leðer,** 4–5 **leder, leþer,** (**leeder**), 4–6 **ledder, -yr,** 5 **ledur, -yr,** (**letheir**), 5–7, 8 *Sc.* **lether(e,** 6 *Sc.* **lathir,** 7 **lather,** 6– **leather.** [OE. *leðer* (only in compounds, as *leðer-hose, weald-leðer* bridle) = OFris. *leither, leder, lider, leer,* OSax. *leðar* (Du. *leder, leer*), OHG. *ledar* (MHG., G. *leder*), ON. *leðr* (Sw. *läder*, Da. *læder*):—OTeut. **leþrom* neut.:—pre-Teut. **létrom*, whence Irish *leathar*, Welsh *lledr*, Breton *ler* (earlier *lezr*).]

I. The simple word.

1. a. Skin prepared for use by tanning, or some similar process.

American leather, a kind of oil-cloth; 'an English name for what in the U.S. is called enameled cloth' (Funk); ***patent leather***, leather having a fine black varnished surface; ***vegetable leather***, a material consisting of a layer or layers of linen on which india-rubber is spread; ***white leather***, leather dressed so as to retain its natural colour. For *Morocco, Russia, Spanish, Turkey leather*, see the prefixed words.

a **1225** *Ancr. R.* 324 þe hund þet fret leðer..me beateð him anonriht. **13..** *E.E. Allit. P.* B. 1581 Alle þat loked on þat letter as lewed þay were As þay had loked in þe leþer of my lyft bote. *c* **1380** WYCLIF *Serm.* Sel. Wks. II. 45 So may men go on þe eyre ȝif it be closid wiþinne leþer. *c* **1420** *Liber Cocorum* (1862) 33 With leder þo mouthe þen schalt þou bynde. *c* **1440** *Jacob's Well* 256 þe preest schal clothe þe in whyȝt ledyr. *c* **1450** *Merlin* 370 Merlin made hem digge depe undir an Oke till thei fonde a vessel of lether. **1464** *Inv.* in *Turner's Dom. Archit.* III. 113 A square standarde, and covered with blaak letheir. **1513** DOUGLAS *Æneis* XI. xv. 9 Sovir weid Of curbulȝe or leddyr wyth gylt nalis. **1519** *Churchw. Acc. St. Giles, Reading* 7 For a hide of white lether viijᵈ. **1546** *Extracts Aberd. Reg.* (1844) I. 238 Ane bulget of blak ledder. *a* **1568** ASCHAM *Scholem.* (Arb.) 97 Turning of good wine, out of a faire sweete flagon of siluer, into a foule mustie bottell of ledder. **1579** LANGHAM *Gard. Health* (1633) 665 Binde the herbe to the body in Crimson lether, to stop bleeding. **1596** DALRYMPLE tr. *Leslie's Hist. Scot.* II. 140 The pennie he causet be cuinȝet of a buffill hyde, to wit of sik kynde of lathir. **1611** BIBLE *2 Kings* i. 8 Girt with a girdle of leather about his loynes. **1704** F. FULLER *Med. Gymn.* (1711) 121 We can by squeezing make Water pass through Leather. **1852** MORFIT *Tanning & Currying* (1853) 146 When placed in the tan-vats they [hides or skins] become leather. **1893** G. ALLEN *Scallywag* I. 97 That peculiar sort of deep-brown oil-cloth which is known..as American leather.

fig. **1852** MRS. STOWE *Uncle Tom's C.* v. 29 Not a cruel man exactly, but a man of leather.

b. *pl.* Kinds of leather.

1853 URE *Dict. Arts* (ed. 4) II. 65 A great variety of leathers in all conditions and states of manufacture is exhibited. **1896** *Westm. Gaz.* 5 Dec. 3/2 An elementary course on the dressing of skins and more advanced courses on the tanning of heavy and light leathers.

c. Proverbs and proverbial sayings.

1460 MARG. PASTON in *P. Lett.* III. 372 Men cut large thongs here of other men's lether. **1583** GOLDING *Calvin on Deut.* cxiii. 696 The common prouerbe which saith that wee cut large thongs of other mens lether. **1767** FENNING *Univ. Spelling Bk.* 36 A Currier, being present, said..If you have a Mind to have the Town well fortified and secure, take my Word, there is Nothing like Leather. **1837** SIR F. PALGRAVE *Merch. & Friar* (1844) 147 Depend upon it, Sir, there is nothing like leather.

d. ***leather and prunella***: an expression for something to which one is utterly indifferent.

[This is, strictly speaking, a misinterpretation of Pope's words; the context refers to the difference of rank between the 'cobbler' and the 'parson', *prunella* being mentioned as the material for the clerical gown.]

1734 POPE *Ess. Man* IV. 204 Worth makes the man, and want of it, the fellow: The rest is all but leather or prunella. **1811** BYRON *Epitaph J. Blackett*, Then who shall say so good a fellow Was only 'leather and prunella?' **1831** *Society* I. 32 A preux chevalier, to whom all others were leather and prunella. **1879** TROLLOPE *Thackeray* 192 The man to whom these delights of American humour are leather and prunello.

2. a. An article or appliance made of leather, e.g. a strap, a thong; a piece of leather for a plaster or to tighten a tap; the leathern portion of a bellows, or of a pump-sucker; a stirrup-leather. ***upper leather***: see UPPER.

c **1400** *Lanfranc's Cirurg.* 199 Herof þou schalt plane vpon a leþer, & leie it to þe lyme þat is forseid. **1486** *Bk. St. Albans* B vj, Thessame letheris that be putt in hir bellis. **1497** *Naval Acc. Hen. VII* (1896) 237 Coueryng & settyng the Newe ledders vnto the seid Bellowes. *c* **1500** *Melusine* ix. 39 At both thendes of the said thonge or leder shal spryng out of the Roche a fayre fontayne. *a* **1533** LD. BERNERS *Huon* xc. 285 He..stretched him so in his styrropes that yᵉ lethers streyned out thre fyngers. **1586** *Vestry Bks.* (Surtees) 22 Item given for the leather which it [the bell clapper] hings, iiijd. **1607** MARKHAM *Caval.* II. (1617) 75 Those.. thrustings forward with your legges, stirrops and leathers. **1702** T. SAVERY *Miner's Friend* 82 The [friction of the] others are vastly encreased by the Leathers of their Suckers. **1703** *Art & Myst. Vintners* 38 Take a course harden Cloth, and put it before the Bore..then put in your Leathers. **1731** BEIGHTON in *Phil. Trans.* XXXVII. 9 When the Leathers [of a pump] grow too soft, they are not capable of sustaining the Pillar to be raised. **1852** R. F. BURTON *Falconry Indus* iv. 47 *note*, Bewits are leathers and bells buttoned round the shank. **1853** 'C. BEDE' *Verdant Green* I. xii, They.. endeavoured to have a game of billiards..with curious cues that had no leathers. **1907** *Yesterday's Shopping* (1969) 300/2 Hunting saddle,..complete with stirrup irons and leathers. **1928** D. BYRNE *Destiny Bay* vii. §2. 314 The shorter your leathers, the less you know about your mount. **1936** J. CARY *Afr. Witch* vii. 137 'You ride too long... Take up your leathers.' Fisk obediently took up his stirrups a hole. **1952** M. ALLINGHAM *Tiger in Smoke* xiii. 197 Off you go! Shorten your leathers.

b. *pl.* Articles for wear made of leather, e.g. shoes, slippers, leggings, breeches. Hence *colloq.* 'leathers' as a name for one who wears leather breeches or leggings. Also *sing.*, a leather jacket or coat.

1837 DICKENS *Pickw.* xix, 'Out of the vay, young leathers'. **1841** LEVER *C. O'Malley* iv. 24 His own costume of black coat, leathers and tops was in perfect keeping. *a* **1845** HOOD *Agric. Distress* vi, He taps his leathers with his stick. **1849** THACKERAY *Pendennis* xx, 'Jump in, old boy—go it, leathers!' **1873** BROWNING *Red Cott. Nt.-cap* 1317 Carried pick-a-back..Big-baby-fashion, lest his leathers leak! **1883** E. PENNELL-ELMHIRST *Cream Leicestersh.* 152 They..came in the full glory of pink and leathers. **1887** I. R. *Lady's Ranche Life Montana* 64 A great big man with a beard, dressed in white leathers and jack boots. **1894** CONAN DOYLE *S. Holmes* 56, I glanced down at the new patent leathers which I was wearing. **1962** *John o' London's* 4 Jan. 20/1 A Banquo little more than an Oberon in his 'leather'. *Ibid.* 31 May 535/4 Two youths in leathers and crash-helmets. **1970** *Daily Tel.* 2 Mar. 14 Ankle-length, shiny, wet-look coats, suèdes and leathers were often trimmed with fur. **1972** ELLIS & NEWMAN in T. Kochman *Rappin' & Stylin' Out* 378 Wear 'black leathers'. **1973** P. DICKINSON *Gift* ix. 142 Ian got into his leathers, Davy put on two extra layers of clothing, the bike started first kick.

c. *Cricket* and *Football.* The ball.

1868 Box *Theory & Pract. Cricket* 22 They [the French] can see no delight in..getting in the way of 'leather'. **1882** *Daily Tel.* 17 May, Spofforth resigned the leather to Boyle. **1896** A. E. Housman *Shropshire Lad* xxvii, Is football playing.., With lads to chase the leather, Now I stand up no more?

d. As the name of a colour.

1872 *Queen* 15 June 431/3 Costume cloth in all the new colours, including pink,..leather,..and all leading colours. **1923** *Daily Mail* 16 Jan. 1 (Advt.), Coat frock..Grey, Mole, Leather,..New Brown. *Ibid.* 31 July 1/3 (Advt.), Grey, Smoke, Leather and Navy.

e. *slang.* Various articles made of, or clad in, leather, such as (*a*) a wallet or purse; (*b*) a leather-shod foot; hence a kick; (*c*) a boxing-glove; hence a punch or boxing.

(*a*) **1883** 'Mark Twain' *Life on Mississippi* lii. 511, I pulled off an old woman's leather; (*robbed her of her pocket-book*). **1899** 'J. Flynt' *Tramping with Tramps* 395 'To reef a leather' means that the pickpocket pulls out the lining of a pocket containing the 'leather'. **1914** Jackson & Hellyer *Vocab. Criminal Slang* 54 *Leather*,..Some general currency, but used chiefly by pickpockets. A pocketbook; a wallet; a billbook. **1938** F. D. Sharpe *Sharpe of Flying Squad* 331 *Leathers*, wallets. (An inveterate pickpocket is sometimes called 'A Leather Merchant'.) **1955** *Publ. Amer. Dial. Soc.* xxiv. 114 The ordinary billfold which men normally carry, folded double, in the hip pocket, is called a *leather.*

(*b*) **1931** D. Runyon *Guys & Dolls* (1932) vi. 118 Dave walks over and starts to give Waldo Winchester the leather. **1936** J. Curtis *Gilt Kid* vi. 61 Old boys never could stand the leather.

(*c*) **1936** 'R. Hyde' *Passport to Hell* v. 86 It started off as a pretty little bout, though neither knew much about the leather. **1950** J. Dempsey *Championship Fighting* ii. 12 Meehan..threw so much leather and was so rugged that he and I broke even.

3. Skin; now only *slang* exc. *spec.*, the skin on the ear-flap of a dog. *to lose leather*; to suffer abrasion of skin. Also, †a bag or pouch of skin.

1303 R. Brunne *Handl. Synne* 3451 þan wete men neuere, wheþer ys wheþer, þe ȝelughe wymple or þe leþer [*glossed* skyn]. **13..** *Gaw. & Gr. Knt.* 1360 þe lyuer & þe lyȝtez, þe leþer of þe paunchez. *c* **1400** *Lanfranc's Cirurg.* 269 Whanne a mannes bowels falliþ into his ballokis leþeris. *c* **1440** *Jacob's Well* 186 Whann she was deed, here frendys sowedyn [here] in hertys ledyr. *c* **1500** *Melusine* x. 41 As moche of grounde as the hyde or leder of a hert shall mow comprehende. **1541** R. Copland *Guydon's Quest. Chirurg.* C ij b, How many maners of skynnes or lether are there... Two, one is entrynsyke or outforth, and that is proprely called lether. **1583** Stubbs *Anat. Abus.* i. (1879) 37 Did the Lord cloth our first parents in leather? **1726** Swift *To Earl P-b-w* Misc. 1735 V. 63 Returning sound in Limb and Wind, Except some Leather lost behind. **1807** Sir R. Wilson *Jrnl.* 15 May in *Life* (1862) II. vii. 214 Others came on slowly to save their horses and their native leather. **1883** G. Stables *Our Friend the Dog* vii. 60 *Leather*—the skin, generally applied to that of the ear. **1884** J. Colborne *Hicks Pasha* 50 Most of us, to use the hunting term, were 'losing leather' rapidly. **1952** C. L. B. Hubbard *Pembrokeshire Corgi Handbk.* 112 *Leather*, the skin on the ear flap. **1960** *Times* 2 Jan. 9/2 The ear leather of the workers [*sc.* spaniels] is shorter than in show specimens. **1968** H. Harmar *Chihuahua Guide* 240 *Leather*, the skin of the earflap.

II. *attrib.* and *Comb.*

4. *simple attrib.*, passing into *adj.* **a.** Consisting or made of leather, or of a material resembling it.

c **1000** Ælfric *Gloss.* in Wr.-Wülcker 117/3 *Bulgæ*, leþer-coddas. **1497** *Naval Acc. Hen. VII* (1896) 89 Leder bagges. **1598** Barret *Theor. Warres* v. iii. 134 Lether bagges or satchels, to cary powder behind men on horsebacke. **1593** Shaks. *3 Hen. VI*, ii. v. 48 His cold thinne drinke out of his Leather Bottle. **1601** —— *Jul. C.* i. i. 7 Where is thy Leather Apron, and thy Rule? **1607** Tourneur *Rev. Trag.* ii. ii. Wks. 1878 II. 61 Lether-hindges to a dore. **1655** Moufet & Bennet *Health's Improv.* (1746) 146 Their Flesh is hardly digested of a weak Stomach, and their Leather Coat not easily of a strong. **1682** (*title of song*) The Leather Bottèl. **1862** Borrow *Wild Wales* (ed. 2) 67 Policemen..in their blue coats and leather hats. **1872** Yeats *Techn. Hist. Comm.* 159 Leather gloves, saddles and harness.

b. Some combs. of the above type occur *attrib.*

1658 Gurnall *Chr. in Arm.* (1669) 91/2 A poor Leather-coat Christian will shame and catechize a hundred of them. **1665-6** *Answ. Fr. Declar. War* in *Harl. Misc.* II. 479 A fig for France, or any that accords With those Low-country leather-apron lords. **1723** *True Briton* No. 10. I. 85 When you..consented to use your utmost Efforts for chusing Two proper Sheriffs in Opposition to a Majority of Livery Men, and to stretch your Pocket among Leather-Apron Stentors. **1769** *Dublin Merc.* 16-19 Sept. 2/2 Chairs and settee.. leather-bottom chairs. **1897** *Allbutt's Syst. Med.* III. 486 The so-called 'leather-bottle stomach'. **1900** *Everybody's Mag.* III. 497/2 Wool cards—leather back implements set with wire teeth. **1902** *Westm. Gaz.* 14 June 8/3 A fire broke out in a leather goods manufactory. **1946** J. W. Waterer *Leather* xiii. 222 An..up-to-date manual of leather goods manufacture. **1971** D. Mackenzie *Sleep is for the Rich* vi. 196 A leathergoods store downtown stayed open during the lunch hour.

5. General combs. **a.** attributive as *leather-merchant, -work*; also *leather-hard, -like* adjs.

1960 H. Powell *Beginner's Bk. Pott.* ii. 64 *Leather-hard, the condition of clay when it may be cut. Soap condition. **1967** M. Chandler *Ceramics in Mod. World* iv. 122 Each such blank, after partial drying to render it leather-hard, is turned on a semiautomatic lathe. **1971** *Islander* (Victoria, B.C.) 12 Dec. 7/1 The pot and the slip have reached a stage which is known as leather-hard. This means the pot may be handled safely without risk of damage, but is still capable of receiving the indented design. **1589** Warner *Alb. Eng.* vii. xxxvii. (1602) 182 My limber wings..were *Leather-like vnplum'de. **1776** Mendes da Costa *Conchol.* 121 A..toughish coriaceous or leather-like substance. **1851** Richardson *Geol.* (1855) 433 A soft, leather-like mouth, capable of protrusion and retraction. **1861** *Sat. Rev.* 3 Aug. 114/1 Great *leather-merchants. **1856** C. M. Yonge *Daisy Chain* i. xv. 143 Meta has been making a drawing for her papa, and is framing it in *leather work. **1870** Bryant *Iliad* I. vii. 222 Tychius, skilled beyond all other men In leather-work. **1906** Sanford & Phillips *Art Crafts for Beginners* (rev. ed.) vi. 137 The great popularity of leather-work among amateurs is due..to the fact that a small and inexpensive equipment is all that is required. **1971** H. Pluckrose *Bk. of Crafts* 53/2 In the past amateur leatherwork meant punching and thonging.

b. objective, as *leather-cutter, -dresser, -dyer, -gilder, †-parer, -sealer, -seller, -stainer, -worker*; *leather-cutting, -dressing, -stitching.* Also in the names of implements used in the manufacture or preparation of leather: as *leather-polisher, -softener, -stretcher, -stuffer.*

1804 W. Tennant *Ind. Recreat.* II. 195 *Chumars*, or *leather cutters. **1889** T. Hardy *Mayor of Casterbr.* iv, The class of objects displayed in the shop-windows, scythes..at the ironmongers..at the glover's and leather cutter's hedging-gloves [etc.]. **1875** Jowett *Plato* (ed. 2) I. 220 Do you really..know..carpentering and *leather-cutting? **1611** Cotgr., *Megissier*,..a Fellmonger, a *Leather-dresser. **1862** Mrs. H. Wood *Mrs. Hallib.* i. xxvi. 134 When the skins came in from the leather-dressers they were washed in a tub of cold water. **1850** *Rep. Comm. Patents 1849* (U.S.) 357, I claim the adjustable scraper..for the purposes and uses of *leather dressing. *c* **1515** *Cocke Lorell's B.* 11 Pardoners, kynges benche gatherers, and *lether dyers. **1692** Luttrell *Brief Rel.* (1857) II. 566 Three clippers seized..one a *leather gilder. **1725** *Lond. Gaz.* No. 6403/4 Joseph Woolley,.. *Leather-Pairer. **1662** *Public Rec. Colony of Connecticut* (1850) I. 377 The *leathr sealers..shal haue allowed vnto them for each Dicker of Leather they seale, 18d. **1798** I. Allen *Nat. & Pol. Hist. Vermont* 272 Weights and measures, leather sealers &c. are regulated according to law. *c* **1515** *Cocke Lorell's B.* 9 Bokeler makers, dyers, and *lether sellers. **1847** Grote *Greece* ii. l. (1862) IV. 356 Kleon, the leather-seller. **1825** Hone *Everyday Bk.* I. 515 Mr. Bailey,..*leather-stainer. **1891** S. C. Scrivener *Our Fields & Cities* 53 Allotments for shoemakers to dig, after ten hours of *leather-stitching per diem. **1891** E. Kinglake *Australian at H.* 81 The French *leather-workers have discovered the capabilities of their [kangaroos'] skins.

c. instrumental, as *leather-bottomed, -bound, -coated, -covered, -faced, -jacketed, -lined* (also *fig.*), *-topped, -upholstered* adjs.

1783 in E. Parkman *Diary* (1899) 298, 9 black chairs..five *leather bottomed Do. **1854** J. E. Cooke *Virginia Comedians* I. xxii. 127 A rude oaken table and some leather-bottomed chairs. **1894** H. Gardener *Unoff. Patriot* 124 He reached up and took down a *leather-bound volume. **1903** *To-Day* 4 Mar. 191/2 The implements consist of small *leather-coated balls and wooden hockey sticks about seven inches long, which are held as one would hold a pencil. **1868** *Rep. to Govt. U.S. Munitions War* 102 A *leather-covered seat. **1906** *Westm. Gaz.* 20 Nov. 4/2 Metal-to-metal clutches are ..extending in favour at the expense of the old *leather-faced bone type. **1908** *Ibid.* 29 Dec. 4/1 The three-speed gear-box..to which the power is transmitted through the medium of a leatherfaced clutch. **1916** Joyce *Portrait of Artist* ii. 81 There stood the stout *leatherjacketed vaulting horse. **1846** W. H. Emory in Frémont & Emory *Notes Trav. Calif.* (1849) 22/2 The first mouthful brought the tears trickling down my cheeks, very much to the amusement of the spectators with their *leather-lined throats. It was red pepper, stuffed with minced meat. **1903** *Work* 18 July 382/1 The clutch..pulls the band (which.., is steel, leather-lined). **1913** W. Owen *Let.* 13 Nov. (1967) 211, 2 shirts (leather-lined extra). **1911** O. Onions *Widdershins* 281 The large *leather-topped table. **1936** E. E. Evans-Pritchard in *Ess. Social Anthropol.* (1962) viii. 179 They were preceded in this romp through gardens and cultivations by a small boy beating on a leather-topped drum. **1965** G. McInnes *Road to Gundagai* vii. 119 Soft..armchairs and sofas, a big leather-topped desk. **1923** F. L. Packard *Four Stragglers* ii. v. 183 Polly Wickes rose hastily from the..big *leather-upholstered Chesterfield.

d. parasynthetic derivatives (often with similative meaning), as *leather-coated, -complexioned, -eared, -faced* (also *-face*), *-jacketed* (cf. leather-jacket 5), *-legginged, -lunged, -skinned, -winged*, adjs.

1902 W. B. Yeats *In Seven Woods* (1903) 12 And *leather-coated men, with slings. **1809** Malkin *Gil Blas* vii. xiii. (Rtldg.) 16 That little swarthy, *leather-complexioned Adonis. **1682** *Heraclitus Ridens* No. 61 (1713) II. 128 Twelve *Leather-ear'd Disciples might have been found in the Vicinage. **1884** 'Mark Twain' *Huck. Finn* xxviii. 287 You ain't one of these *leather-face people. I don't want no better book than what your face is. **1919** W. Deeping *Second Youth* xv. 128 She let this *leather-faced old rascal flirt with her quite harmlessly. **1934** T. Wilder *Heaven's my Destination* 3 Brush..chose a seat beside a tall leather-faced man. **1960** *Economist* 8 Oct. 149/1 Among the cartoonists Herblock has drawn Mr Khrushchev as a *leather-jacketed gang-leader. **1961** *Encounter* XVII. ii. 17/2 The leather-jacketed 'Teddy Boy' gangs of Western Germany. **1969** *Daily Tel.* 2 Sept. 1/3 South and East coast resorts were invaded yesterday by hundreds of leather-jacketed Rockers and teenagers in jeans and steel-tipped boots. **1973** J. Wainwright *Pride of Pigs* 114 The leather-jacketed, stocking-feeted Hell's Angel. **1837** Dickens *Pickw.* xix, Here the *leather-legginged boy laughed very heartily. **1852** R. S. Surtees *Sponge's Sp. Tour* (1893) 48 First comes a velveteen-jacketed, leather-legginged keeper. **1846** W. P. Scargill *Puritan's Grave* 20 The ruder shoutings of the *leather-lunged rabble. **1655** Moufet & Bennet *Health's Improv.* (1746) 304 The Provence Olives are..more *leather skin'd, yet better for the Stomach than the Spanish. **1896** Mrs. B. M. Croker *Village Tales* 18 An active, leather-skinned man. **1590** Spenser *F.Q.* ii. xii. 36 The *lether-winged batt, dayes enimy.

6. Special combs., **leather-back**, a large marine soft-shelled turtle, *Dermochelys coriacea*; **leather-bark**, a tree of the genus *Thymelæa*; **leather belting**, machine belting made of leather; also *attrib.*; **leather-board**, a composition of leather scraps, paper, etc., glued together and rolled into sheets, used in shoemaking (Knight *Dict. Mech.* 1875); **leather breeches (beans)** *U.S. dial.*, dried beans or dried bean-pods; beans that have been dried and then cooked in their shells; **leather-carp**, a scaleless variety of the carp; **leather-cloth** (also **leathercloth**), cloth coated on one side with a waterproof varnish; also, a synthetic product simulating leather; **leather-coat**, a name for russet apples, from the roughness of their skin; **leather-flower**, a North-American climbing-plant (*Clematis Viorna*) with thick leathery purplish sepals; **leather-head**, (*a*) *slang*, a blockhead; (*b*) *Austral.* the friar-bird; **leather-headed** *a.*, stupid, slow-witted; hence *leatherheadedness*; **leather-hungry**, †(*a*) some variety of leather; (*b*) *dial.* skim-milk cheese; **leather-hunting** *Cricket slang* (cf. sense 2 c), fielding; esp. a colloq. term for fielding when the batsman is hitting out as freely as he likes; hence *leather-hunter*; †**leather-kersner** [MHG. *kürsenære*, G. *kürschner* skinner] a pelterer; **leather-leaf**, a low evergreen shrub of the northern U.S. (*Chamædaphne calyculata*), with coriaceous leaves (*Treas. Bot.* Suppl. 1874); **leather-man**, a leather-seller; **leather medal** orig. *U.S.*, a medal made of leather instead of metal, sarcastically suggested as an award; **leather-mill** (see quot. 1727-52); **leather-mouthed** *a.*, having a leather-like mouth (see quots.); **leather-paper**, paper having a surface resembling that of leather; **leather-plant**, a composite plant of the genus *Celmisia*, a native of New Zealand (*Treas. Bot.* Suppl. 1874); **Leather-Stocking**, a North American frontiersman [from a character portrayed by J. F. Cooper]; also *attrib.*; **leather-turtle** = *leather-back*; **leather-wing**, a name for a bat; **leather-wood**, (*a*) a North American shrub of the genus *Dirca*, with a very tough bark; (*b*) a Tasmanian wood of a pale reddish mahogany colour, *Eucryphia billardieri* (Morris). Also leather-jacket.

1855 Ogilvie Suppl., **Leather-back.* **1880** *Cassell's Nat. Hist.* IV. 260 The Leather-back Turtles, whose carapace is not covered with scales of shell, but with a dense coriaceous skin. **1965** R. McKie *Company of Animals* xii. 168 On the beaches of Trengganu..the leatherback turtles lay their eggs. **1969** A. Bellairs *Life of Reptiles* I. ii. 41 The tendency nowadays is to regard the leatherback as a specialised descendant of turtles of more 'ordinary' type. **1751** J. Bartram *Observ. Trav. Pennsylv.*, etc. 28 Abundance of *leather-bark or *thymelea*, which is plentiful in all this part of the country. *a* **1877** Knight *Dict. Mech.* I. 273/1 *Leather belting is ordinarily prepared in the following manner. **1877** *Design & Work* 9 June 23 (Advt.), Charles Churchill and Co., importers of American machinery and tools,..lathes, vices, planes,..American leather belting. **1909** *Westm. Gaz.* 6 Apr. 2/1 The exposure of the graft.. behind the duty on hides was made by tanners and shoe and leather-belting manufacturers. **1946** J. W. Waterer *Leather* 304 Included in its members are all the principal manufacturers of leather belting. *Ibid.*, Persons engaged in or intending to engage in the leather belting trade. **1913** H. Kephart *Our Southern Highlanders* 292 Beans dried in the pod, then boiled 'hull and all' are called *leather-breeches (this is not slang, but the regular name). **1941** J. Smiley *Hash House Lingo* 35 *Leather breeches*, dried kidney beans. **1943** R. Chase in B. A. Botkin *Treas. S. Folklore* (1949) 470 Such communal tasks as stringing beans for canning, or threading them up to make the dried pods known as 'leather britches'. **1972** E. Wigginton *Foxfire Bk.* 15 He..dried leather Britches beans. *Ibid.* 167 *Leather breeches beans*... Take a string of dried green beans down, remove the thread, and drop them in a pot of scalding water. **1880-4** F. Day *Brit. Fishes* II. 159 The *leather-carp, *Cyprinus nudus, C. alepidotus, C. coriaceus*, or *C. nudus*, in which scales are absent, but the skin is very much thickened. **1857** *Mech. Mag.* 4 Apr. 321 A singularly close and valuable imitation [of leather] known as 'Crockett's *Leather Cloth'. **1929** *Publishers' Circular* 18 May 621/3 A revolution has taken place in the world of leather by the introduction of the synthetic product leathercloth. **1937** *Archit. Rev.* LXXXI. 291/1 The manufacturers of cheaper cars began to use leathercloth as a finish over the normal rigid type of body construction and the snob-appeal of purpose-made bodies was lost. **1961** *Times* 30 May (I.C.I. Suppl.) p. viii/1 The original amalgamation brought together..dyestuffs, leather-cloth, paints and non-ferrous metals. **1973** *Daily Tel.* 21 Nov. 14/4 This test car was upholstered in a ventilated leathercloth. **1597** Shaks. *2 Hen. IV*, v. iii. 44 There is a dish of *Lether-coats for you. **1676** Worlidge *Cyder* (1691) 203, The Leather-Coat or Golden-Russeting, as some call it, is a very good Winter-Fruit. **1866** *Treas. Bot.*, *Leather-flower, *Clematis Viorna.* *a* **1700** B. E. *Dict. Cant. Crew*, **Leather-head*, a Thick-skull'd, Heavy-headed Fellow. **1847** L. Leichhardt *Overland Exped.* xiii. 461 The Leatherhead with its constantly changing call and whistling. **1860** G. Bennett *Gatherings Nat.* x. 233 Among the Honey-suckers is that singular-looking bird, the Leatherhead, or Bald-headed Friar (*Tropidorhyncus corniculatus*). *a* **1668** Davenant *News fr. Plymouth* Wks. (1673) 20 What a *Leather-headed Dunce Am I, to ask thee. **1876** 'Mark Twain' *Tramp Abr.* (1880) I. 206 His *leather-headedness is the point I make against him. **1478-9** *Durh. Acc. Rolls* (Surtees) 646 Sol. pro corrio de *ledderhungry, iiijs. **1530** Palsgr. 238/2 Lether hungrye, *cvir bovlly.* **1804** R.

ANDERSON *Cumberld. Ball.* 103 Wi' scons, leather-hungry, and whusky. **1944** BLUNDEN *Cricket Country* i. 19 The laugh at the unfortunate '*leather-hunter' on a hot chase. **1865** J. PYCROFT *Cricketana* xiii. 224, I like science more than swiping, and enjoy 'fielding', but not *leather hunting. **1886** G. SUTHERLAND *Australia* xxvii. 178 Occasionally, in summer, there are days when..the pastime of 'leather hunting' becomes somewhat tiresome. **1896** *Westm. Gaz.* 19 June 7/1 The Westerners had a long day's leather hunting at Lord's yesterday. **1905** H. A. VACHELL *Hill* xii. 254 And then, when his 'eye' is in, he will give the Etonians such leather-hunting as they never had before. **1934** W. J. LEWIS *Lang. Cricket* 143 *Leather-hunting*, a jocular term for the exertions of the fieldsmen when the ball is hit freely to all parts of the field. **1970** *Sunday Tel.* 20 Dec. 21/7 The voracious Richards was in action once more and M.C.C. are assured of more leather-hunting today. **1226** in Gilbert *Hist. & Munic. Doc. Ireland* (Rolls) 83 Reginaldus le *letherkersnere. **1818** A. EATON *Man. Bot.* (ed. 2) 173 *Andromeda calyculata*, *leather leaf. **1870** *Amer. Naturalist* IV. 217 The Leather Leaf (*Cassandra calyculata*), and *Andromeda polifolia*, are both worthy of attention. **1831** J. MOTTE in A. H. Cole *Charleston goes to Harvard* (1940) 89 He must be a cute chap, and deserves to have a *leather medal. **1837** *Harvardiana* III. 147 (Th.), A leather medal his reward should be, A leather medal and an LL.D. **1860** *Richmond* (Virginia) *Enquirer* 20 Apr. 2/5 (Th.), The individual who conceived the leather medal idea [for identifying dogs] deserves a leather medal himself. **1889** *Kansas City* (Missouri) *Times & Star* 5 Dec., A leather medal..awaits the first misguided person this season writing it 'Xmas'. **1922** JOYCE *Ulysses* 750 He ought to get a leather medal with a putty rim for all the plans he invents. **1624** in Gross *Gild Merch.* II. 12 There have hitherto been three Companies in the town, those of the Drapers, *Leathermen, and Firemen. **1727–52** CHAMBERS *Cycl.* s.v. *Mill*, *Leather-Mills are used to scour, and prepare with oil, the skins of stags, buffaloes, elks, bullocks, &c. to make what they call buff-leather, for the use of the soldiery. **1895** *Outing* (U.S.) XXVI. 362/1 There is also a flour and leather mill. **1653** WALTON *Angler* ii. 55 By a *leather mouthed fish, I mean such as have their teeth in their throat, as the Chub or Cheven, and so the Barbel [etc.]. **1757** LISLE *Husbandry* II. 155, I told him the ewes were leather-mouthed with thick lips. **1833** J. RENNIE *Alph. Angling* 9 Such fishes as have teeth thus placed far back upon the palate and upper part of the throat while they want them in their jaws, are termed by anglers leather-mouthed. **1890** HOSIE *W. China* 153 That famous tough paper which..is wrongly called '*leather' paper. The mistake is pardonable, for the character which means 'leather' also means 'bark'. The paper is made from the fibrous inner bark of the *Broussonetia papyrifera*. [**1823** J. F. COOPER *Pioneers* I. i. 18 His limbs were guarded with long leggings of the same material as the moccasins, which gartering over the knees of his tarnished buck-skin breeches, had obtained for him, among the settlers, the nick name of *Leather-stocking.] *Ibid.* 11 The Leather-stocking has put his hounds into the hills this clear day. **1831** M. HOLLEY *Texas* (1833) v. 43 The character of Leather Stocking, is not uncommon in Texas... The dress of these hunters is usually of deerskin. Hence the appropriate name *Leather Stocking*. Their generic name..is *Frontiers-men*. **1909** *Daily Chron.* 1 July 7/3 With most birds, you must make your approach with all the art of a leatherstocking. **1965** *English Studies* XLVI. 313 In this book Cooper draws repeated parallels between the Leather-stocking hero and Moses. **1884** GOODE, etc. *Fish. Industr. U.S.* I. 147 The so-called '*Leather Turtle', or 'Luth', or 'Trunk Turtle'. **1851** GOSSE *Nat. in Jamaica* 298 The little nimble *Leather-wings pursue their giddy play in security. **1760** J. LEE *Introd. Bot.* App. 317 *Leather-wood, *Dirca*. **1882** *Garden* 8 Apr. 232/3 The Leather-wood..now in flower, though not showy, is interesting.

leather ('lɛðə(r)), *v.* [f. LEATHER *sb.*]

1. *trans.* To cover or arm with leather.

a **1225**, *c* **1400** [see LEATHERED *ppl. a.*]. **1564–5** *Acc.* in Willis & Clark *Cambridge* (1886) III. 362 For mending and newe lethering the Colledge Quisshens v^s. *a* **1774** GOLDSM. *Exper. Philos.* (1776) II. 52 The piston or sucker is leathered so tight as to fit the barrel exactly. **1794** *Rigging & Seamanship* I. 27 The round holes of all caps are leathered. **1830** ALFORD in *Life* (1873) 51 Cleaned, new-leathered, and tuned the dining-room piano. **1850** FANNY PARKES *Wander. Pilgr.* I. 135 My husband used to cut it up to leather the tips of billiard cues.

2. To beat with a leathern thong; hence *gen.* to beat, thrash.

a **1625** BEAUM. & FL. *Faithf. Friends* II. iii, I am mad,..I shall leather 'em. **1764** FOOTE *Mayor of G.* I. Wks. 1799 I. 174, I would so swinge and leather my lambkin. **1815** *Sporting Mag.* XLV. 161 Sam leather'd his man, and the mob were amazed. **1860** GEO. ELIOT *Mill on Fl.* I. v, I gave Spouncer a black eye..that's what he got by wanting to leather me. **1882** TENNYSON *Promise of May* II. Wks. (1889) 793/1 I'd like to leather 'im black and blue.

b. *fig. intr.* To work hard; with *away, on.*

1869 E. FARMER *Scrap Bk.* (ed. 6) 44 How they leather'd away at the job. **1893** CROCKETT *Stickit Minister* 239 So their minister simply kept leathering on at the fundamentals.

† **'leatherdoom.** *Obs. rare*⁻¹. [Corruption of F. *l'édredon*, = 'the eiderdown'.] Eiderdown.

1702 BAYNARD in Sir J. Floyer *Hot & Cold Bath* II. (1709) 285 Winter and Summer he was forced to wrap himself up in Flannel, and Leatherdoom.

leathered ('lɛðəd), *ppl. a.* Also 3 i-leðered. [f. LEATHER *sb.* or *v.* + -ED.] **a.** Covered, †loaded or provided with leather, or leathers. Of a servant: Wearing 'leathers'.

a **1225** *Ancr. R.* 418 Ne ne beate ou þer mide, ne mid schurge i-leðered ne i-leaded. *c* **1400** *Destr. Troy* 5500 Iche shalke hade a shild shapyn of tre, Wele leddrit o lofte. **1610** GUILLIM *Heraldry* VI. ii. (1611) 256 He beareth..a Spurre with the Rowell downwards, Leathered. **1794** W. FELTON *Carriages* (1801) II. 190 The imperial is a leathered case, placed occasionally on the roof of the Coach, for the purpose of carrying Clothes. **1837** T. HOOK *Jack Brag* xii, A strapping livery servant, jacketed, topped, and leathered for travelling. **1858** O. W. HOLMES *Aut. Breakf.-t.* vii. (1891) 168 Oars of spruce, balanced, leathered and ringed under your own special direction.

b. Made into, or like, leather.

1797 in G. B. Goode *Fisheries U.S.: Hist. & Methods* (1887) II. 435 By walking it [seal-skin] becomes leathered and soft to the foot. **1869** S. BOWLES *Our New West* 444 If you bring a liver not entirely leathered and lungs not over half consumed. **1970** L. JEFFERS *My Blackness is Beauty of this Land* 9 His face was leathered, lean, and strong, Gashed with struggle scars.

leatherette (lɛðə'rɛt). [f. LEATHER *sb.* + -ETTE.] A fabric composed of cloth and paper, in imitation of leather.

1880 *Sat. Rev.* 20 Nov. 655 Messrs. Dalziel's *Bible Gallery* is bound in vellum and leatherette. **1891** *Brit. Weekly* 10 Sept. 308 The volume can be had in leatherette for half-a-crown. **1897** G. M. HOPKINS *Exper. Sci.* (ed. 17) 329 The bags—which hold one plate each—are made of the stout black paper known in the trade as leatherette.

leathering ('lɛðərɪŋ), *vbl. sb.* [f. LEATHER *v.* + -ING[1].]

1. The action of covering, fitting, or furnishing with leather.

1517 *Acc.* in *Archæologia* XLVII. 310 For..naylyng, letheryng, bokelyng of m^l m^l xlvij complete harnes. **1794** *Rigging & Seamanship* I. 27 The..hole is..larger.., to allow for leathering. **1869** *Eng. Mech.* 26 Nov. 257/3 We next come to the very important part of the work—'leathering'.

b. *concr.* A covering or strip of leather.

1852 SEIDEL *Organ* 38 The other ends of the bellows.. called the hinges, are provided with a double or triple leathering. **1861** *Jrnl. Soc. Arts* IX. 746/1 The leathering on the oar, to prevent chafe.

2. *colloq.* A flogging, beating.

1791 A. WILSON *Poems & Lit. Prose* (1876) II. 33 Ye deserve a leathering. **1894** BARING-GOULD *Kitty Alone* II. 169 'Won't I only give that cursed beast a leathering.'

3. *Comb.* as **leathering-bed** (see quot.).

1839 MURCHISON *Silur. Syst.* I. ii. 18 '*Leathering bed*'. Name given to a bed of very hard micaceous marlstone found in the Lower Lias.

'leather-,jacket. [f. LEATHER *sb.* + JACKET.]

1. A name given to various fishes, having a thick skin; *e.g. Balistes capriscus, Oligoplites saurus*, and species of *Monacanthus*.

1770 COOK *Jrnl.* 5 May (1893) 246 They had caught a great number of small fish, which the sailors call leather jackets on account of their having a very thick skin. **1789** W. TENCH *Exped. Botany Bay* xv. 129 To this may be added bass, mullet, skait, soles, leather-jackets, and many other species. **1883** E. P. RAMSAY *Food-Fishes N.S. Wales* 31 (Fish Exhib. Publ.) The 'leather jackets', *Monacanthus*, are the only members of this family [*Sclerodermi*] used as food. **1884** GOODE etc. *Fish. & Fish. Industr. U.S.* I. 172 The Leather-jacket of Pensacola, *Balistes capriscus*, called 'Trigger Fish' in the Carolinas. *Ibid.* 332 The Leatherjacket —*Oligoplites saurus*.

2. *Austral.* A kind of pancake.

1846 G. H. HAYDON *Five Y. Australia* vi. 151 A plentiful supply of 'leather jackets' (dough fried in a pan). **1855** R. HOWITT *Two Y. Victoria* I. 117 (Morris) The leather-jacket ..is equal to any muffin you can buy in the London shops.

3. *Austral.* A name applied to various trees, on account of the toughness of their bark, e.g. *Eucalyptus punctata* (Morris).

1874 *Treas. Bot.* Suppl., *Leather-jacket* of New South Wales, *Eucalyptus resinifera*.

4. The grub of the crane-fly.

1881 ELEANOR ORMEROD *Man. Injur. Insects* 66. **1898** R. KEARTON *Wild Life at Home* 76, I watched a female [starling] collecting 'leather-jackets' on a newly-mown lawn last July.

5. A person, freq. a member of a gang or a delinquent group, dressed in a leather jacket.

1959 *New Statesman* 15 Aug. 180/1 All France has learnt about the bands of 'leather-jackets'... Why are these young rowdies called 'leather-jacket'?... Certainly leather jackets seem to be the uniform for young American delinquents. **1960** *Britannica Bk. of Year* 557/2 The characteristic dress of juvenile delinquents in several countries produced the term *leather jackets*, meaning delinquents. **1963** V. NABOKOV *Gift* v. 289 Not long before his deportation from Russia, when some revolvered leatherjackets had come to arrest him.

† **'leatherly**, *a. Obs.* [f. LEATHER *sb.* + -LY[1].] Leather-like, tough.

1573 TUSSER *Husb.* xlix. (1878) 108 Poore Cobler he tuggeth his leatherlie trash, if cheese abide tugging, tug Cisley a crash.

leathern ('lɛðən), *a.* Forms: 1 leðer(e)n, leðren, 4–5 lether(e)ne, letherin, 5 leddering, 6 leth(e)ren, lethrin, letheryn, *Sc.* ledderane, ledderyn, leddren, lethrone, leathering, 6–7 leatherne, 7 leathren, lethern, 6– leathern. [OE. *leðeren*, f. *leðer* LEATHER *sb.* + -EN; cf. Du. *lederen*, G. *ledern*. The earlier OE. form was *liðerin, liðrin* = OS. *litharin* (gloss), OHG. *lidrîn*.]

1. a. Consisting or made of leather. ***leathern convenience, -ency***: a circumlocution for a coach, originally imputed to the Quakers; hence in jocular use.

c **1000** ÆLFRIC *Gloss.* in Wr.-Wülcker 123/30 *Scortia*, leþren fæt. *c* **1050** *Suppl. Ælfric's Voc.* ibid. 179/6 *Scortius* leðern. **1362** LANGL. *P. Pl.* A. v. 110 Lyk a letherne pors lullede his chekes. **1382** WYCLIF *Lev.* xiii. 59 This is the lawe of the lepre..of all letherin purtenaunce. **1488** *Inv. R. Wardr.* (1815) 12 Item in a leddering purs...tuelf score & xvi salutis. **1521** *Churchw. Acc. Pilton* (Som. Rec. Soc.) 74 Item payde for a letheryn baag to ber ye keys—iiii^d. **1546** *Extracts Aberd. Reg.* (1844) I. 234 Ane ledderane coit worth tua crovnis of the sone. **1583** *Leg. Bp. St. Androis* 574 A cott of kelt Weill beltit in ane lethrone belt. **1634** MILTON *Comus* 626 He..Would..in requitall ope his leather'n scrip. **1683** *Brit. Spec.* 14 The poorest of them were good Leathern Shoes. **1699** E. WARD *Lond. Spy* VII. (1702) 3 Our Leathern-Conveniency being bound in the Braces to its Good-Behaviour had no more Sway than a Funeral Herse. *a* **1700** B. E. *Dict. Cant. Crew, Leathern Convenience* (by the Quakers), a Coach. **1719** D'URFEY *Pills* III. 322 Men with leathern Buckets, do quench Fire in a Town. **1796** COMBE *Boydell's Thames* II. 123 Robert Scot, the inventor of leathern artillery. **1824** SCOTT *St. Ronan's* xx, At the duly appointed hour, creaked forth the leathern convenience. **1836** W. IRVING *Astoria* I. 120 The Crow camp..was composed of leathern tents. **1861** J. Y. SIMPSON *Archæol.* 56 Human bodies..covered with the leathern and other dresses in which they died.

b. Used with reference to the skin of the living animal.

a **1325** *Names of Hare* in *Rel. Ant.* I. 134 The hert with the letherene hornes. **1600** SHAKS. *A.Y.L.* II. i. 37 Such groanes That their discharge did stretch his leatherne coat Almost to bursting. **1851** LONGF. *Gold. Leg.* IV. *Road to Hirschau*, The horses distend their leathern sides with water.

c. *nonce-use.* Skin-clad.

1596 *Edward III*, II. ii. 120 Since leathern Adam till this youngest hour.

2. Made of a substance resembling leather; leather-like. Said esp. of the bat's wings, hence of its flight, and occas. of the bat itself. Also *fig.*

1513 DOUGLAS *Æneis* XIII. Prol. 33 Vpgois the bak wyth hir pelit ledderyn flycht. **1600** FAIRFAX *Tasso* IX. xxv. 164 An hideous dragon..With iron pawes, and leathren wings displaid. **1663** BUTLER *Hud.* I. iii. 153 But..the late-corrected Leathern Ears of the circumcised Brethren. **1687** *Death's Vis.* ix. note 4 (1713) 43 It has been a Question, whether the Leathern Bat (as 'tis call'd) be to be annumber'd among Birds or Beasts. **1725** POPE *Odyss.* XII. 514 So to the beam the bat tenacious clings, And pendant round it clasps his leathern wings. **1746** COLLINS *Ode to Even.* iii, The weak-eyed bat..flits by on leathern wing. **1812** H. & J. SMITH *Rej. Addr., The Theatre* Who's that calls 'Silence'! with such leathern lungs? **1879** TODHUNTER *Alcestis* 100 Death..Thou shalt fly no more, For all thy leathern wings. **1886** ELWORTHY *W. Somerset Word-bk.*, *Leathern-bird*, the bat. **1895** MRS. B. M. CROKER *Village Tales* (1896) 100 Her wondrous loveliness stirred even the leathern hearts of these hill-men.

Comb. **1664** EVELYN *Pomona* 44 The thick skin or leathern-coat [= *leather-coat* (apple)]. **1818** W. IRVING *Sketch Bk.*, *Leg. Sleepy Hollow*, Old farmers, a spare leathern-faced race. **1875** J. G. HOLLAND *Sevenoaks* xii. 158 Blue-jays were screaming among leathern-leaved oaks.

Hence **'leathernly** *adv.*, ? clumsily.

1594 NASHE *Unfort. Trav.* 33 A Comedie..which was so filthily acted, so leathernly set forth, as would haue moued laughter in Heraclitus.

'leather-neck, 'leatherneck. *slang.* [f. LEATHER *sb.* + NECK *sb.*[1]] **1.** A sailor's name for a soldier, from the leather stock he used to wear.

1890 *Pall Mall G.* 24 Jan. 2/1 He [the sailor] despises his friend the leather-neck for a lazy and luxurious dog. **1916** 'TAFFRAIL' *Carry On!* 27 A Royal marine is a 'bullock', 'turkey', or 'Joey', while a soldier is a 'grabby' or 'leather-neck'.

b. A marine. *U.S.*

1914 *Dialect Notes* IV. 150 *Leatherneck*, a marine. **1919** *A Company, Eleventh Frapper* (U.S. Marines) 17 Apr. 1/2 We learn that between 700 and 800 warworn Leathernecks from the famous 5th and 6th Marines..arrived at Camp Covington. **1926** *Amer. Speech* I. 354/2 'Leatherneck' for a Marine..is derived from the old custom of facing the stiff neck-band of the marine uniform with leather. **1931** *Punch* 3 June 606/1 I'd just passed the remark to the leather-neck on sentry that we was 'avin' a nice peaceful forenoon when the Admiral's buzzer goes, and I 'ops in to see what 'e wanted. **1955** W. FOSTER-HARRIS *Look of Old West* i. 11 Under this collar, the troopers were supposed to wear an atrocity of a stock, of black leather. This is where the name 'leather-neck' came from, since the Marines also had to wear these dog-collar affairs. **1968** R. WEST *Sk. Vietnam* ii. 37 The U.S. Marine Corps. These legendary troops, nick-named 'leathernecks'.

2. = ROUSEABOUT 2. *Austral.*

1898 *Bulletin* (Sydney) 1 Oct. 14/3 In a shearing shed: The boss is the 'finger', the shearers the 'brutes', the rouseabouts 'leathernecks'. **1899** W. T. GOODGE *Hits! Skits! & Jingles!* 155 And he 'pinked' him like a leather-neck when squatters paid a pound! **1945** BAKER *Austral. Lang.* xvi. 286 *A leatherneck* is a marine in the U.S.; in Australia he is a station handyman.

leatheroid ('lɛðərɔɪd). [f. LEATHER *sb.* + -OID.] A fabric consisting of cotton paper, chemically treated so as to resemble raw-hide.

1882 *Knowledge* 18 Aug. 193 Leatheroid..consists of a number of thicknesses of cotton paper..The..strength and adhesion it possesses are derived from a chemical bath. **1900** *Munsey* July 517/1 Telescopes made of leatheroid.

leathery ('lɛðərɪ), *a.* [f. LEATHER *sb.* + -Y.]

a. Resembling leather in appearance or texture; frequent in botanical use = CORIACEOUS. Of the voice: As if proceeding from an organ of leather.

1552 HULOET, Letherye or of lether. **1681** GREW *Museum* 111 Wormius calls this Crust a Leathery Skin. **1787** *Families Plants* I. 256 Perianth eight-leaved, leathery. **1821** CRAIG *Lect. Drawing* ii. 127 The fleshy tints of the pictures painted in oil become brown and leathery. **1870** HOOKER *Stud. Flora* 288 *Marrubium vulgare*..Leaves..much wrinkled, leathery. **1884** BOWER & SCOTT *De Bary's Phaner.* 418 Leathery leaves of Conifers. **1888** *Century Mag.* Feb. 565/2

She thrust forward her leathery hand. **1897** *Allbutt's Syst. Med.* IV. 470 The tones of the voice were leathery. **1898** J. HUTCHINSON *Archives Surg.* IX. No. 34. 103 The valves of the heart, especially the mitral, were thickened and leathery.

Comb. **1851** MAYNE REID *Scalp Hunt.* xxi. 155 The hair was all worn off it [a cap], leaving a greasy, leathery-looking surface. **1880** C. R. MARKHAM *Peruv. Bark* 167 Several *Calisaya* trees were growing on the summit..in company with the leathery-leafed *huaturu*.

b. leathery turtle = *leather-back* (LEATHER *sb.* 6).

1875 *Encycl. Brit.* III. 112/1 The 'leathery turtle',..is herbivorous, and yields abundance of oil. **1901** [see LUTH]. **1963** J. KIRKUP *Tropic Temper* 270 The 'leathery turtles' are among the world's largest and in Malaya they haunt the beaches of Trengganu. **1966** *Festival Malaysia 1966: Calendar of Events* 8 (*caption*) A giant leathery turtle of the East Coast of the Malay peninsula. **1969** A. BELLAIRS *Life of Reptiles* I. ii. 41 Some workers have believed that the huge leathery turtle (*Dermochelys*)..is more primitive than the rest.

Leathic, Leatic: see LIATICO.

ˈleathwake, *a. Obs.* exc. *north. dial.* Forms: 1 **liðe-, leoðuwác**, 4 **leothewok**, 5 **lith-, lythewayke**, 6 **leath(i)e we(a)ke, lyeth-waike, leithweik**, 7 **leeth-, lieth-**, 9 *dial.* **leathwake**. [OE. *liðewác*, *leoðuwác*, f. *lið*, *leoðu* limb, LITH *sb.* + *wác* soft, pliant: see WEAK *a.*] Having the joints flexible; hence *gen.* pliant, soft.

c **1000** *Endowments Men* 84 in *Exeter Bk.* 298 Sum bið.. for gum-þeʒnum leoht and leoþu-wac. *c* **1330** *Rel. Ant.* II. 229 Ther oure body is leothe-wok, ȝyf strengthe vrom above. **1483** *Cath. Angl.* 218/2 Lithwayke, *flexibilis*. **1545** ASCHAM *Toxoph.* (Arb.) 129 A fedder is fit for a shafte.. bycause it is leathe weake to giue place to the bowe. *Ibid.* 139 Waxe taketh printe whan it is warme and leathie weke. **1593** *Anc. Monum. Rites Durham* (Surtees) 55 He [St. Cuthbert] was taken out of the ground..lying like to a man sleping, being found saife and uncorrupted and lyeth-waike. **1674** RAY *N.C. Words* 30 *Leethwake*, limber, pliable. **1788** W. MARSHALL *Yorksh.* II. 339 *Leathwake*, lithe, weak, flexible, limber, feeble; as a hair, a thread, an ozier twig, or an angling rod. **1828** CARR *Craven Dial.*, *Leathe-wake*, supple in the joints.

Hence † **ˈleathwakeness**.

1548 R. HUTTEN *Sum of Divinity* S i a, [Attributes of a glorified body] Leithweiknes & quicknes or redines.

leattre, obs. form of LETTER.

leavable (ˈliːvəb(ə)l), *a.* [f. LEAVE *v.*[1] + -ABLE.] Able to be left.

1923 H. G. WELLS *Men like Gods* I. i. 10 The affairs of the *Liberal* were just then in a particularly leavable state. **1946** *N.Y. Herald Tribune* 2 June (Books) 5 Her rather rubbishy mother..had finally gone off with her artist, bringing despair to her 'leavable' husband, who could not help alienating the people he loved most.

leave (liːv), *sb.*[1] Forms: 1 **léaf**, 2 **lǽf**, *dat.* **léve**, (3 **luve**), 3–6 **leve**, 4 **lef, leef, lyve**, *Sc.* **leyf(e, leife**, 4–5 **lefe, leeve**, *Sc.* **leiff**, 4–6 *Sc.* **leif**, 5 **lewe**, 6 **leffe**, *Sc.* **leive, live, lyve**, 6–7 **lieve**, 3, 6- **leave**. [OE. *léaf*, str. fem. = OHG. **louba* (MHG. *loube*, str. fem., early mod.G. *laube*):—OTeut. type **laubâ*, whence **laubjan* (see LEVE *v.*[1] to permit).

The etymological sense is prob. 'pleasure, approval'; the root is identical with that of LOVE, LIEF, BELIEVE, etc. The mod. form represents not the OE. nom. (which would have given **leaf*), but the dat. and accus. *léafe*, which was more frequent in use.]

1. a. Permission asked for or granted *to do* something: freq. in phr. ***to ask, beg, get, give, grant, have, obtain leave***; † ***beside*** (obs.), ***by, with, without*** (***the***) ***leave*** (***of***).

by your leave: used as an apology for taking a liberty; often *ironically* used when some remark is made which will be unwelcome to the person addressed.

c **900** tr. *Bæda's Hist.* IV. v. (1890) 278 Buton þæs biscopes leafe. **11..** *O.E. Chron.* an. 1048 (Laud MS.), [He] sæt on þam biscoprice þe se cyng him ær ʒeunnan hæfde be his fulre leafe. *a* **1131** *Ibid.* an. 1128 (Laud MS.), Be þes kynges leue. *c* **1200** *Trin. Coll. Hom.* 167 Ure drihten..ȝaf leue þe deuel to binimende him his oref and his ahte. *c* **1220** *Bestiary* 226 Wat if he leue haue of ure heuen louerd for to deren us. ? *a* **1300** *Shires & Hundreds Eng.* in *O.E. Misc.* 145 Myd þes kinges leaue. *a* **1300** *Fall & Passion* 75 in *E.E.P.* (1862) 14 þo pilat had igrant is luue glade y-noȝ ho was: he nem þat swet bodi adun an biriid hir in a fair plas. *a* **1300** *Cursor M.* 14744 Mi hus agh be..Hus o praier..And yee mak it, wit-vten leue, A to-draght o reuer and thefe. *c* **1325** *Deo Gracias* 33 in *E.E.P.* (1862) 125 þen seide þe prest, sone bi þi leue I most seye forþ my seruise. *c* **1374** CHAUCER *Troylus* III. 622 But execut was al bisyde hir leue At the goddes wil. **1375** BARBOUR *Bruce* XVII. 863 But leiff, he hame has tane his gat. *c* **1380** WYCLIF *Wks.* (1880) 40 Here wyues han ȝouen here housbondis lyue [*MS. W.* leeve]. *c* **1385** CHAUCER *L.G.W.* 2283 *Philomene*, At the laste leue hath she to go. *c* **1400** MAUNDEV. (Roxb.) v. 17 To haue leue for to passe mare surely thurgh þe cuntreez. **1596** SHAKS. *Merch. V.* IV. i. 395, I pray you giue me leaue to goe from hence. **1599** in *Buttes' Dyets drie Dinner* P vij b, Buttes (by thy leaue) Ile be a Guest of thine. **1608** TOPSELL *Serpents* (1658) 816 But by their leaves these reasons are very weak. **1613** PURCHAS *Pilgrimage* (1614) 293 They never goe abroad without leave, except to the Bath. **1653** A. WILSON *Jas. I*, 112 Sir Walter Rawleigh ..made Accesses to the King, whereby he got leave to visit the New World. **1705** HICKERINGILL *Priestcr.* (1721) I. 41 If the French King invade without putting off his Hat, or saying, *by your Leave*. **1713** ADDISON *Guardian* No. 140 ¶2 By my correspondent's good leave, I can by no means consent. **1815** W. H. IRELAND *Scribbleomania* 253 Upon which subject I shall beg leave to dwell a little. **1838** DICKENS *Nich. Nick.* iii, I'll speak to you a moment, ma'am, with your leave. **1840** —— *Barn. Rudge* xvi, The solitary passenger was startled by the chairmen's cry of 'By your leave there!' as two came trotting past him. **1855** BROWNING *Fra Lippo L.* 1, I am poor brother Lippo, by your leave! **1885** *Law Rep.* 29 *Chanc. Div.* 268 Pursuant to this leave, the daughter..applied to add to the decree.

b. Proverbs.

1523 FITZHERB. *Husb.* §143 Seldom doth the housbande thryve withoute the leve of his wyfe. **1546** J. HEYWOOD *Prov.* (1867) 20 Ye might haue knokt er ye came in, leaue is light. **1633** B. JONSON *Love's Welcome at Welbeck*, Leave is ever faire, being ask'd; and granted is as light, according to our English Proverbe, Leave is light.

† **c.** ***to give leave*** (*fig.*, of conditions or circumstances): to allow, permit. *Obs.*

1500–20 DUNBAR *Poems* xxix. 7 Quhen I wald blythlie ballattis breif, Langour thairto givis me no leif. **1576** FLEMING *Panopl. Epist.* 316 As the measure of my abilitie wil give me leave. **1617** MORYSON *Itin.* II. 109 He would.. keepe the field as neere Tyrone, as his meanes would give him leave. **1644** *Direct. Publ. Worship* 39 So far as the time will giue leaue. **1797** *Encycl. Brit.* IX. 14/1 One..of these.. columns will become longer..and give the lighter fluid.. leave to rise in its place.

† **d.** ***to give*** (a fish) ***leave***: to give (him) play.

1653 W. LAUSON *Comm. on Secr. Angling* C 5 When you have hookt him, give him leave, keeping your Line straight.

e. In military, naval, and official use (also sometimes in schools and gen. in offices, etc.): (*a*) ***leave of absence***, or simply ***leave***, permission to be absent from a post of duty. (See also *sick-leave*.) ***on leave***: absent from duty by permission. (*b*) Hence, the period of such absence.

1771 BURKE *Let.* 31 July, *Corr.* (1844) I. 255 He has got a leave of absence. **1802** C. JAMES *Milit. Dict.*, *Leave of absence*, a permission which is granted to officers..and soldiers, to be absent from camp or quarters for any specific period. **1829** MARRYAT *F. Mildmay* x, To-morrow my leave expires. **1831** LAMB *Ess. Elia* Ser. II. *Newspapers 35 yrs. ago* 342 On one fine summer holyday (a 'whole day's leave' we called it at Christ's Hospital). **1844** *Regul. & Ord. Army* 86 Officers, going on Leave of Absence. **1860** READE *Cloister & H.* xxxviii, He was going on leave, after some years of service, to see his kindred at Remiremont. **1864** TENNYSON *Sea-Dreams* 6 They..Came, with a month's leave given them, to the sea. **1878** *N. Amer. Rev.* CXXVI. 93 Furloughed men returned..before their 'leaves' had terminated. **1963** *Times* 28 Sept. 9/4 While not personally subscribing to the use of the term 'on leave' by office workers to describe their annual break(s), I can contribute reasons for their doing so. **1973** *Times* 17 Apr. 12/8 She will be on a six month leave-of-absence from the [National Theatre] company. **1974** P. DE VRIES *Glory of Hummingbird* xiv. 206 It'll only be a leave of absence... But..*if* there's a blowup, the firm will be able to say you were let go.

2. a. ***to take*** (***one's***) ***leave*** (const. *of*, †*at*, †*to*, †*on*): orig. †to obtain permission to depart (*obs. rare*); hence, to depart with some expression of farewell; to bid farewell. †Also rarely, ***to fang, get, have, latch leave***. (See also FRENCH LEAVE.) ***to take leave*** (const. *inf.*): used as a formula to draw attention, with a somewhat ponderous affectation of presumption, to a truth or state of affairs; cf. BEG *v.* 3.

c **1250** *Gen. & Ex.* 2697 Mai he no leue at hire taken but-if he it mai mið crafte maken. *a* **1300** *Cursor M.* 4999 þair leue þai laght [*Trin.* toke], and war ful blith. **1375** BARBOUR *Bruce* v. 253 Thar-with-all he lowtit, and his leyf has tane. *Ibid.* xx. 109 Quhen on bath halfis levis wes tane. *c* **1386** CHAUCER *Frankl. T.* 763 They take hir leue, and on hir wey they gon. *a* **1400–50** *Alexander* 899 Faire at philip þe fers þair leue þai fangen. *c* **1430** *Syr Tryam.* 52 He toke hys leve at the quene. *c* **1435** *Torr. Portugal* 946 Torrente..toke leve on kyng and knyght. **1447** BOKENHAM *Seyntys* (Roxb.) 31 Aftyr leve takyn to shyp they went. *c* **1460** J. RUSSELL *Bk. Nurture* 970 Of youre souerayne take no leue; but low to hym alowt. *c* **1500** *Melusine* lvii. 334 He toke leue to the Pope. **1523** LD. BERNERS *Froiss.* I. x. 9 This lady departed ..and all her company, with syr John of Heynaulte, who with great peyne gatte leue of his brother. **1593** SHAKS. *Rich. II*, I. iii. 50 Let vs take a ceremonious leaue And louing farwell of our seuerall friends. **1596** DALRYMPLE tr. *Leslie's Hist. Scot.* x. 458 Jlk from vther takeng thair lyue departet. **1610** B. JONSON *Alch.* v. iv, We will..take our leaues of this ore-weaning raskall. **1611** [see TAKE *v.* 21]. **1667** MILTON *P.L.* III. 739 And Satan bowing low..Took leave. **1719** DE FOE *Crusoe* II. xvi. (1840) 342 The young lord took his leave of us. **1814** T. S. RAFFLES *Substance of Minute on Java* 100, I take leave to observe, that the state of landed tenure here is very different from what it is reported to be in other parts of Java. **1820** [see TAKE *v.* 21]. **1834** M. EDGEWORTH *Helen* III. v. 93 We must take leave to pause one moment to remark..that the first little fib in which Lady Cecilia.. indulged herself..occasioned her..a good deal of..trouble. **1864** MRS. CARLYLE *Lett.* III. 236 When she took leave of me the night before starting. **1928** *Sat. Rev.* 28 July 127/1 Stephen has many excellent qualities both of heart and head, though whether her sufferings would have cradled her into a first-rate novelist we take leave to doubt. **1938** 'M. INNES' *Lament for Maker* I. viii. 53 We may take leave to think the silly body stood there in the sleet and cursed the lure of the wanderer roundly.

b. *transf.* and *fig.*

1500–20 DUNBAR *Poems* xxii. 73 Twa curis or thre hes vpolandis Michell Thocht he fra nolt had new tane leif. **1508** in *Dunbar's Poems* (1893) 321, I tak my leve at all vnstedfastnes. **1597** MORLEY *Introd. Mus.* 115, I wil then take my leaue of you for this time, till my next leisure, at which time I meane to learne of you that part of musicke which resteth. **1655** FULLER *Ch. Hist.* v. iv. §41. 225 We take our leaves of Tyndal. **1660** MILTON *Free Commw.* Wks. 1738 I. 587 They may permit us a little Shroving-time first, wherin to speak freely, and take our leaves of Liberty. **1703** MAUNDRELL *Journ. Jerus.* (1732) 108 We went to take our leaves of the holy Sepulcher. **1723** *Wodrow Corr.* (1843) III. 33 There was never a schoolboy more desirous to have the play than I am to have leave of this world. **1771** FRANKLIN *Autobiog.* Wks. 1840 I. 65, I now took leave of printing, as I thought, for ever. **1916** A. BENNETT *Lion's Share* v. 40 'Mother!' cried Audrey. 'Have you taken leave of your senses?' **1942** 'M. INNES' *Daffodil Affair* II. iv. 58, I think you've taken leave of your senses. **1968** L. GOODMAN *Sun Signs* (1970) 325 You'll think I've taken leave of my senses, if you've just met that particular Pluto person. **1972** 'M. INNES' *Open House* II. xiii. 129 Nothing of the kind... You must have taken leave of your senses.

† **3.** Leave-taking; in phr. ***audience of leave***: see AUDIENCE 6. *Obs.*

c **1400** *Destr. Troy* v. 1823 Antenor vntomly turnet his way Withoutyn lowtyng or lefe. **1711** [see AUDIENCE 6]. **1724** *Lond. Gaz.* No. 6321/1 Mr. Finch had his Audience of Leave of the King and Queen of Sweden. **1734** tr. *Rollin's Anc. Hist.* (1827) VII. VII. xvii. 226 The king having like-wise tendered them very considerable presents at their audience of leave.

4. ***to give*** (a person) ***his leave***: to give him his dismissal. ***to get one's leave***: to get one's dismissal. Now only *Sc.* (Cf. F. *congé*.)

1508 DUNBAR *Tua mariit wemen* 67 We suld..gif all larbaris thair leveis, quhan thai lak curage. *a* **1568** COVERDALE *Bk. Death* xxvi. (1579) 118 The sicke must geue all other worldely matters theyr leave. **1637** RUTHERFORD *Lett.* (1862) I. 272 He..wd. give an evil servant his leave at mid-term.

5. *attrib.* and *Comb.*, as ***leave camp, centre, -giving, list, period, permit, rota, -way***; **leave-boat**, a boat carrying troops on leave; **leave-breaker**, a sailor who breaks his leave of absence; so **leave-breaking**; **leave-day** (also *leave-out day*), at certain schools, a day on which boys are allowed to go beyond the precincts of the school; **leave draft**, a detachment of troops on leave; † **leave-niming** = LEAVE-TAKING; **leave-out**, at certain schools, permission to go beyond the school precincts; cf. *leave-day*, *leave-out day*; **leave party** *Mil.*, a group of servicemen on leave; **leave-taker**, one making his farewell; **leave-train**, a train carrying troops on leave.

1917 'CONTACT' *Airman's Outings* v. 118 Passengers on a Channel *leave-boat are quieter than might be expected. **1922** BLUNDEN *Bonadventure* iii. 21 To the Plate and back again, in a cargo ship!.. The voyage, no doubt, would be more arduous than that in the leave-boat from Boulogne to Folkestone. *c* **1860** H. STUART *Seaman's Catech.* p. v, *Leave-breakers prevent the officers from giving the indulgence. *Ibid.*, *Leave-breaking is occasioned by the indulgence of..vices. **1945** W. S. CHURCHILL *Victory* (1946) 109 Eight new *leave camps are under construction. **1961** *Reader's Digest* Feb. 24/1 Last March..the government was asked why African airmen in Her Majesty's service had been excluded from a Kenya *leave centre. **1966** *New Statesman* 14 Oct. 537/3 The lavish structure of permanent installations, family homes, schools, leave centres and the like is enormously costly. **1817** COLERIDGE *Biog. Lit.* I. 16 In my friendless wanderings on our *leave-days. [*footnote*] The Christ Hospital phrase, not for holidays altogether, but for those on which the boys are permitted to go beyond the precincts of the school. **1920** *Blackw. Mag.* May 608/2 The sallow complexions..and leanness of a *leave draft from the Palestine front. **1450–1530** *Myrr. our Ladye* 102 Wyttynge well that the blyssyng, or *leaue geuynge, longeth pryncypally to God. **1917** 'CONTACT' *Airman's Outings* v. 108 Only during the intervals of attack is the *leave-list unpigeonholed. **1340** *Ayenb.* 112 Vor he hit ous let: at his *yleave-nymynge and at his laste bequide. **1854** KEBLE in *Life* (1869) xvii. 394 When he comes here on *leave-out days. **1940** M. MARPLES *Public School Slang* 164 I've got *leave-out. **1955** *Times* 18 Aug. 10/6 When I was in College at Winchester, one of our favourite pastimes used to be hitch-hiking on leave-out days. These were free days during term when we could do as we liked. **1916** W. OWEN *Let.* 3 July (1967) 398, I had the *Leave Party to conduct to the Station the other day. **1954** W. FAULKNER *Fable* 128 During three of these two-week *leave-periods..the entire squad had vanished from France.., and reappeared one morning two weeks later. **1906** *Daily Chron.* 14 May 5/2 The report ..recommends..that traffic in *leave-permits be made illegal. **1940** 'GUN BUSTER' *Return via Dunkirk* I. x. 76 I've been looking at the *leave rota, and see you're down for January 10. **1891** KIPLING *Light that Failed* xv. 310 Bess found Dick his cabin in the wild turmoil of a ship full of *leavetakers and weeping relatives. **1922** JOYCE *Ulysses* 190 The quaker librarian came from the leavetakers. **1917** 'CONTACT' *Airman's Outings* v. 113 The train, true to the custom of *leave trains, was very late. **1918** A. BENNETT *Pretty Lady* xx. 132 Then I can't catch my train at Victoria ..the leave-train. My leave is up to-night. **1913** T. E. LAWRENCE *Let.* 29 Sept. (1938) 157 They half suggested a royalty of a pound a head a day, as *leave-way to dig.

leave (liːv), *sb.*[2] [f. LEAVE *v.*[1] 3.] In Billiards, etc., the position in which the balls are left for the next player or stroke.

1896 W. BROADFOOT et al. *Billiards* x. 319 Every leave was the result of accident rather than of design. **1903** W. MITCHELL *Cue Tips* 6 The most interesting and not the least useful way to practise billiards..is..to place the balls in certain favourable positions upon the table and attempt to make as large a break as possible from the 'leave'. **1914** LD. TOLLEMACHE *Croquet* xiv. 74 A well thought-out and finished Leave is one of the hall-marks of a first-class player. **1929** J. DAVIS *Billiards Up-to-Date* viii. 89 An exception.. is seen when, at the commencement of a break, an opponent presents you with a leave which necessitates the use of side. **1936** —— *Improve Your Snooker* xii. 69, I cannot guarantee you will bring off this shot if you are presented with a similar leave. **1968** *Croquet* July 2/2 It is when we consider how to make leaves against good shots that the fun really begins.

leave (liːv), *v.*[1] Forms: 1 **lǽfan**, 2–3 **læven, lefen, lefven, leven**, 3 **leafen, leave(n**, 4–5 **leef, leeve,**

-yn, leff(e, leif(e, lev, leyf(f, -fe, -ve, (lyve), 4–6 lef(e, leve(n, lewe, leif(f, 6 (leavy) *Sc.* laif, live, 7 leaf, leav, 8–9 *Sc.* (*colloq.*) lea', 5– leave. *Pa. t.* 1 lǽfde, 2–3 læfde, l(e)afde, læv-, lefede, 3–5 leved(e, 4–5 lefid, -it, lef(f)yt, *Sc.* lewid, -it, -yt, 4–6 lafde, laf(f)t(e, lefte, (5 leeft, lefft, levit, leyfft), *Sc.* leifit, 6 leaft, 4– left. *Pa. pple.* 1 lǽfed, 3 leaved, 4 le(v)ed, -id, -it, leift, leyved; also 4 leven, 5 leve, 4–5 laf(f)te, -yn, 4–6 lefte, *Sc.* lev-, lewyt, 6 leaft, 4– left. See also Y-LEFT. [OE. *lǽfan* trans. and intr., corresp. to OFris. *lêva* to leave, OS. *-lêƀian* in *farlêƀid* pa. pple., left over), OHG., MHG. *leiben*, ON. *leifa* to leave, Goth. *-laibjan* (in *bilaibjan* to leave behind):—OTeut. **laiƀjan*, f. **laiƀâ* remainder, relic (see LAVE *sb.*), whence also the intr. vbs. OS. *lêƀôn*, OHG. *leibên* to remain. The OTeut. **laiƀjan* is the causative of **lîƀan* str. vb., represented by the compounds OE. *belífan* (see BELIVE *v.*), OFris. *belîva*, *blîva*, MDu. *blîven* (Du. *blijven*), OHG. *belîban* (MHG. *belîben*, *blîben*, mod.G. *bleiben*), to remain.

The root (OTeut. **lĭƀ-*, **laiƀ* -:—OAryan **lip-*, **leip-*, **loip-*) has in Teut. only the sense 'to remain, continue' (so in LIFE, LIVE *v.*), which appears also in Gr. λῑπαρής persevering, importunate. This sense is usually regarded as a development from a primary sense 'to adhere, be sticky', exemplified in Lith. *lìpti*, OSl. *lĭpěti* to adhere, *lěpiti* to stick, Gr. λίπος grease, Skr. *rip-*, *lip-* to smear, adhere to.

The view of some scholars, that the Teut. words may belong to the Aryan root **leiq-* to leave (whence Gr. λείπειν, L. *linquĕre*), is plausible with regard to the sense, but the tendency of recent research is unfavourable to the admission of its formal possibility.]

I. To have a remainder; to cause or allow to remain.

1. a. *trans.* Of a deceased person: To have remaining after one (a widow, children, property, reputation, etc.).

c **1000** *Ags. Gosp.* Mark xii. 22 And ealle seofon hi hæfdon & sæd ne læfdon. **1382** WYCLIF *Ruth* i. 3 The housboond of Noemie, is deed, and she lafte with the sones. *c* **1400** *Apol. Loll.* 4 Better to die wiþ out barnes, þan to lef vnpitouse barnis aftir. **1604** E. G[RIMSTONE] *D'Acosta's Hist. Indies* VI. xii. 455 For the entertainment of the family he left. **1818** CRUISE *Digest* (ed. 2) VI. 512 In case he should..leave no lawful heir. **1838** THIRLWALL *Greece* V. 165 He left an infant son named Amyntas. **1881** GARDINER & MULLINGER *Study Eng. Hist.* I. vi. 103 The medieval saints..had left no successors. **1891** *Law Reports* Weekly Notes 201/1 He intended that whatever property he left should be divided.

b. Of things or conditions: To have remaining as a trace or consequence after removal or cessation.

1756 C. LUCAS *Ess. Waters* III. 296 Most chalybeate waters leave no common vitriol upon evaporation. **1814** WORDSW. *Excursion* VII. 27 It had left, Deposited upon the silent shore Of memory, images and precious thoughts. **1823** F. CLISSOLD *Ascent Mt. Blanc* 24 This area is so detached from the rock, as to leave a crevasse running along its base. **1885** SIR J. HANNEN in *Law Reports* 10 P.D. 87 A small blister, which subsided in a day or two leaving only a redness of the skin.

2. a. To transmit at one's death *to* heirs or successors. Hence, to direct that (something which one possesses) shall descend after one's death *to* a specified person, corporation, etc.; to bequeath or devise. Also in *indirect passive*.

Beowulf 1179 (Gr.) þinum magum læf folc ond rice. *c* **1000** *Ags. Gosp.* John xiv. 27 Ic læfe eow sibbe. *a* **1300** *Cursor M.* 24235 Sin i sal to mi fader fare, I sal þe leue a fere. **1484** CAXTON *Fables of Alfonce* iii, A good man labourer wente fro lyf to deth [and] lefte nothyng to his sone but only a hows. **1508** DUNBAR *Poems* vi. 36 Corpus meum ebriosum, I leif on to the toune of Air. **1526** *Pilgr. Perf.* (W. de W. 1531) 27 Than we made our last wyll and testament, whan we lefte to the worlde our kynne and frendes. **1559** W. CUNNINGHAM *Cosmogr. Glasse* 3 We should have left many more errours to our posteritie. **1580** SIDNEY *Ps.* XVII. xi, They in riches floorish doe, And children have to leave it to. **1651** HOBBES *Leviath.* II. xxviii. 162 It was not given, but left to him, and to him onely. **1676** LADY CHAWORTH in *12th Rep. Hist. MSS. Comm.* App. v. 29 Poore cosin Brooks hath left me 10*l.* **1713** ADDISON *Guardian* No. 97 ⁋1, I was left a thousand pounds by an uncle. **1732** BERKELEY *Alciph.* I. §1 A good collection, chiefly of old books, left him by a clergyman his uncle. **1844** DICKENS *Mart. Chuz.* xliv, If I knew how you meant to leave your money. **1849** MACAULAY *Hist. Eng.* vi. II. 127 The seventeenth century has, in that unhappy country, left to the nineteenth a fatal heritage of malignant passions. **1876** MOZLEY *Univ. Serm.* iv. (1877) 87 Suppose him suddenly to be left an enormous fortune. **1895** *Bookman* Oct. 23/1 The great engravers of the age of Louis have left us innumerable portraits.

absol. **1837** SYD. SMITH *Let. to Singleton* Wks. 1859 II, Men of Lincoln have left to Lincoln Cathedral, and men of Hereford, to Hereford.

b. In passive: ***to be*** (***well***, etc.) ***left***: to be (well, etc.) provided for by legacy or inheritance.

1606 DEKKER *Sev. Sinnes* v. (Arb.) 36 Richmens sonnes that were left well. **1875** JAS. GRANT *One of the '600'* ii. 21 Cora shall be well and handsomely left.

3. a. To allow to remain in the same place or condition; to abstain from taking, consuming, removing, or dealing with in some particular manner. ***to be left***: to remain.

c **1000** *Ags. Gosp.* Luke xix. 44 Hiȝ ne læfað on þe stan ofer stane. *c* **1205** LAY. 994 Al heora god we sculen nimen, & lutel hem læuen. *a* **1225** *Ancr. R.* 70 Muche fol he were..ȝif he grunde þe greot & lefde þene hwete. *a* **1300** *Cursor M.* 4983 Þe yongeist..þai lefte at þeir fader in. *Ibid.* 5401 Es vs noght leued bot erth bar. **1340** HAMPOLE *Pr. Consc.* 100 Wharfor that man may be halden wode, That cheses the ille and leves the gude. **1375** BARBOUR *Bruce* I. 247 Fre liking to leyve, or do That at hys hart hym drawis to. **1382** WYCLIF *Num.* ix. 12 Thei shulen not leeue of it eny thing vnto the morwe. *a* **1548** HALL *Chron., Hen. VI*, 129 It was not the poynt of a wiseman, to leave and let passe, the certain for the uncertain. **1576** FLEMING *Panopl. Epist.* 67 For, what place is left now for honestie? where lodgeth goodnes? **1693** EVELYN *De la Quint. Compl. Gard., Dict.*, To *Head* a Tree, is to cut off the Head or Top, leaving only the bare Stem without any Top Branches. **1697** DAMPIER *Voy.* I. 315 The Trunk..they leave in the Sun 2 or 3 days. **1709** STEELE *Tatler* No. 139 ⁋1 Business and Ambition take up Men's Thoughts too much to leave Room for Philosophy. **1822** LAMB *Elia* Ser. I. *Distant Correspondents*, If you do not make haste to return, there will be little left to greet you, of me, or mine. **1845** BUDD *Dis. Liver* 264 Persons who..have..very little liver left. **1898** *N. & Q.* 15 Oct. 301/2 The six [criminals]..were however 'left for death' as the phrase then went.

†**b.** *absol.*, esp. in the sense 'not to consume the whole of one's portion of food, etc.'; also with *over*.

1603 KNOLLES *Hist. Turks* 893 He..made himselfe able at his own choice and pleasure to leave or take. **1611** BIBLE *Ruth* ii. 14 She did eate, and was sufficed, and left [**1551** COVERDALE, left over]. **1642** FULLER *Holy & Prof. State* IV. xiv. 310 A worthy work (wherein the Reader may rather leave then lack).

c. To have as a remainder (in the operation of subtraction). Of a number or quantity: To yield (so much) as a remainder when deducted from some larger amount.

c **1425** *Crafte of Nombrynge* (E.E.T.S.) 18 Medie 8. þen þou schalt leue 4. **1709** J. WARD *Introd. Math.* II. ii. §2 (1734) 150, $a - b$ Taken from $a + b$ Leaves $+ 2b$ for the Remainder. **1896** A. E. HOUSMAN *Shropshire Lad* ii, And take from seventy springs a score, It only leaves me fifty more.

d. With complementary sb., adj., or phrase: To allow to remain in a specified condition; not to change from being so-and-so. Often with a negative ppl. a., ***to leave undone***, ***unsaid*** etc. = to abstain from doing, saying, etc. Also, with mixture of sense 7 b: To put into, or allow to remain in, a certain condition on one's departure.

c **1205** LAY. 1508 Nulleð heo leaue [**1275** lefuen] nenne of ous a-liue. *a* **1300** *Cursor M.* 11228 The sonne goth thorogh glas And levith yt hole as it was. **1375** BARBOUR *Bruce* IX. 453 He levit nocht about that toune Tour standand, stane no wall. **1526** TINDALE *Matt.* xxiii. 23 For ye tythe mynt annys and commen and leave the waygthtyer mattres of the lawe ondone. **1552** *Bk. Com. Prayer, Gen. Conf.*, We haue left vndone those things which we oughte to haue done. **1576** FLEMING *Panopl. Epist.* 301 Then did you leave us sticking in the myre. **1591** SPENSER *Muiopot.* 155 Ne did he leave the mountaines bare unseene, Nor the ranke grassie fennes delights untride. **1613** PURCHAS *Pilgrimage* (1614) 192 The Jewish..Wise-men, have left no part of life unprovided of their superstitious care. **1794** PALEY *Evid.* (1825) II. 101 To leave the argument without proofs, is to leave it without effect. **1803** MARY CHARLTON *Wife & Mistress* II. 62 Dolly had left the dressing-room door half open. **1809–10** COLERIDGE *Sailor's Fortune* iii, Being now on that part of his life which I am obliged to leave almost a blank. **1849** MACAULAY *Hist. Eng.* iii. I. 297 An important military resource which must not be left unnoticed. **1888** *Law Times* LXXXV. 132/2 If the timber adds beauty or shelter to the mansion-house, the tenant for life must leave it intact.

e. To allow, permit, let. *colloq.* (chiefly *U.S.*). Cf. *to leave..be* s.v. sense 13.

1840 *Southern Lit. Messenger* VI. 508/1 If you ha'nt a mind to go, you can leave it be, it's all one to me. **1863** T. D. PRICE *Diary* 14 Apr. (MS.), I left him have colt. **1910** J. HART *Vigilante Girl* iv. 55 It's all right so long as you don't leave her get loose. **1916** 'BOYD CABLE' *Action Front* 235 Prickles, me lad, it's deep enough we've dug to lave us get out to our German Gineral. **1935** Z. N. HURSTON *Mules & Men* (1970) I. vi. 127 Leave the weeds go. Somebody 'll come chop 'em some day. **1940** J. O'HARA *Pal Joey* 103 But I said to him how can I pay you if you don't leave me wear it and I lose my job.

4. †**a.** To neglect or omit to perform (some action, duty, etc.); = *to leave undone* (see 3 d); also with inf. to omit *to do* something. *Obs.*

a **1300** *Cursor M.* 3144 He left noght do his lauerd wil. *c* **1380** WYCLIF *Sel. Wks.* III. 348 Y leeve to speke of stelyng of wymmen. —— *Wks.* (1880) 328 Siþ þat crist myȝt not faile in ordynaunce to his chirche, & he left þis confessioun, it semeþ þat it is not nedeful. *Ibid.* 410 Þey leeuen þat crist biddiþ. *c* **1489** CAXTON *Blanchardyn* xxiv. 81 He sholde not leue to bringe her his two doughters. **1502** *Ord. Crysten Men* (W. de W. 1506) Prol. 6 Good werkes that a man leueth to do ayenst the mercy of god. **1538** STARKEY *England* I. i. 24 Yf wyse men..wold have bent themselfe to that purpose leuyng such fon respecte of tyme and place. **1557** NORTH *Gueuara's Diall Pr.* (1619) 69/2 They..living in flesh, did leave to use the workes..of the flesh. **1558–68** WARDE tr. *Alexis' Secr.* 24 b, Not leaving to dooe their businesse abrode notwithstanding. **1597** A. M. tr. *Guillemeau's Fr. Chirurg.* 6/1 Yet must not we leave to effecte that which this arte requireth. **1624** QUARLES *Sion's Elegies* iii. 14 Thou leav'st what thy Creator did Will thee to doe.

absol. *c* **1374** CHAUCER *Troylus* v. 1518 Weep if thou wolt, or leef. *c* **1375** *Lay Folks Mass Bk.* (MS. B.) 243 Offer or leeue, wheþer þe lyst. **1486** *Bk. St. Albans* C v, That an hauke use hir craft all the seson to flye or lefe.

b. To allow to stand over, to postpone (an action, a subject of consideration).

1559 W. CUNNINGHAM *Cosmogr. Glasse* 115, I will leave his composition untill I shewe you the making of it among other instrumentes. **1628** EARLE *Microcosm., Young-man* (Arb.) 51 Hee leaues repentance for gray hayres.

5. a. To abstain from appropriating, dealing with, or doing (something) so that another person or agent may be able to do so without interference; to suffer to be controlled, done, or decided by another instead of oneself; to commit, refer. Const. *to* or *dat.*; also *with*.

c **1300** *Harrow. Hell* 104 Heovene ant erthe tac to the— Soules in helle lef thou me. **1486** *Bk. St. Albans* E iij b, All that bere skyne and talow and Rounge leue me. **1559** W. CUNNINGHAM *Cosmogr. Glasse* 143, I..wil leave it to such as are Pilotes. **1561** DAUS tr. *Bullinger on Apoc.* (1573) 93 b, For despisyng of the simple truth, men be left vp to lying deceauers. **1590** SPENSER *F.Q.* I. vii. 9 This man forlorne And left to loss. **1638** SIR T. HERBERT *Trav.* 127, I..leave such theories to those that study Meteors. **1660** F. BROOKE tr. *Le Blanc's Trav.* 277 The flood retiring within its bounds, leaves their dwellings to their possession again. **1670** A. ROBERTS *Adventures T.S.* 180 When we had our Dispatches, we left him to his own Fortune. **1726** G. ROBERTS *Four Years Voy.* 302, I told him, I would leave all that to his management. **1771** *Junius Lett.* liv. 283, I will leave him to his suspicions. **1796** BURKE *Regic. Peace* i. (C.P.S.) 73 Nothing in the Revolution..was left to accident. **1849** MACAULAY *Hist. Eng.* ii. I. 257 The rage of the hostile factions would have been sufficiently violent, if it had been left to itself. **1890** LD. ESHER in *Law Times Rep.* LXIII. 692/1 This case ought not to have been left to the jury. **1897** *Allbutt's Syst. Med.* III. 876 The prospect of success by operation is so slight that..it is better to leave the case to nature.

b. With *obj.* and *infinitive*: To allow (a person or thing) *to* do something, *to be* done or dealt with, without interference.

1526 *Pilgr. Perf.* (W. de W. 1531) 5 b, Leauynge them and suffrynge them to be without meate and drynke a certeyn season. **1662** J. DAVIES tr. *Olearius' Voy. Ambass.* 107 The Great Duke never signs expeditions, but leaves that to be done by the Secretaries of State. **1665** HOOKE *Microgr.* 85 And what I have therein perform'd, I leave the Judicious Reader to determine. **1670** A. ROBERTS *Adventures T. S.* 152 They always left them to enjoy their own without disturbing them. **1719** WATERLAND *Vind. Christ's Div.* v. (1720) 81 In the Interim I may fairly leave you to consider it. **1818** CRUISE *Digest* (ed. 2) II. 233 To leave the title of the inheritance to go one way, and the trust of the term another way. **1818** COBBETT *Pol. Reg.* XXXIII. 116 He left him to shift for himself. **1828** SCOTT *F.M. Perth* xxxv, The Earl rode off..leaving Albany to tell his tale as he best could. **1881** GARDINER & MULLINGER *Study Eng. Hist.* I. ix. 165 The future was to be left to take care of itself. **1895** *Law Times Rep.* LXXIII. 22/1 The court..left the parties to take their own course.

c. ***to leave*** (***something, much,*** etc.) ***to be desired*** (***to wish***, etc.): to be (more or less) imperfect or unsatisfactory.

Common in journalistic use; suggested by the F. *laisser à désirer*, which is sometimes, though faultily, imitated in its ellipsis of the obj.

[**1769** F. BROOKE *Hist. Emily Montague* IV. 189 Every anxiety is removed from my Emily's dear bosom: a father's sanction leaves her nothing to desire.] **1780** F. BURNEY *Diary & Lett.* (1842) I. VIII. 335 Etty plays as if inspired, and in taste, expression, delicacy and feeling, leaves nothing to wish. **1835** *Athenæum* 16 May 371/1 Her style, too, leaves little to be desired. **1852** *Harper's Mag.* Aug. 422/2 This edition leaves nothing to be desired by the most fastidious book-fancier. **1876** F. POLLOCK *Pollock-Holmes Lett.* (1942) I. 6 Kent is a considerable advance, but leaves much to be desired. **1895** F. ESPINASSE *Life E. Renan* x. 185 Dean Stanley's French accent left much to be desired, but his volubility was indisputable. **1939** M. ALLINGHAM *Mr. Campion & Others* I. iii. 65 The staff still left much to be desired and the food..was certainly not cooked by a master. **1953** G. DURRELL *Overloaded Ark* ix. 166 Apart from his face, which left much to be desired, his feet were swollen to twice normal size with elephantiasis. **1967** A. BAILEY in L. Deighton *London Dossier* 52 The vegetables leave much to be desired, but the Stilton is worth having. **1974** *Times* 22 Jan. 2 When the clubs first applied for licences it was decided not to oppose them. 'Now that we know how they operate, we feel they leave a lot to be desired.'

6. To deposit or give in charge (some object) or station (persons) to remain after one's departure; to give (instructions, orders, information, e.g. one's name or address) for use during one's absence. Phrase, ***to leave a card on*** (a person).

c **1350** *Will. Palerne* 1858 His bag wiþ his bilfodur wiþ þe best he lafte. *c* **1380** WYCLIF *Serm.* Sel. Wks. I. 17 Leeve þi offring at þe auter. *a* **1548** HALL *Chron., Hen. VIII*, 104 b, He left another nombre and left capitaines to overse them. **1655** STANLEY *Hist. Philos.* I. (1701) 30/1 He..left order with his friends that they should carry his bones to Salamis. **1704** DE FOE in *15th Rep. Hist. MSS. Comm.* App. IV. 83 The letter has not reached your hands, though left with your porter last Friday night. *c* **1709** PRIOR *Protogenes & Apelles* 50 Will you please To leave your name? **1797** MRS. A. M. BENNETT *Beggar Girl* (1813) IV. 63 He wanted to leave his address, and she flounced away, and would not take it. **1813** COL. HAWKER *Diary* (1893) I. 65, I left word that if I won the cheese I would give it to the old man again. **1860** TYNDALL *Glac.* I. xvi. 117 Until we reached the point where we had left our wine in the morning. **1861** DICKENS *Gt. Expect.* xxxvii, He left word that he would soon be home. **1883** LD. R. GOWER *My Remin.* II. xxvi. 160 A contradictious old man..had been left in charge of a boat which he had moored to the pier.

absol. *a* **1715** BURNET *Own Time* (1724) I. 382 As she drew near a village she often ordered her coach to stay behind till she had walked about it, giving orders for the instruction of the children and leaving liberally for that end.

II. To depart from, quit, relinquish.

7. a. To go away from, quit (a place, person, or thing); to deviate from (a line of road, etc.).

a **1225** *Ancr. R.* 130 Treowe ancren beoð briddes bitocned: vor heo leaueð þe eorðe. *a* **1300** *Cursor M.* 17288 + 296 'Leues þis', he saide, '& telles fast mi brether..þat [etc.]'. *c* **1400** *Destr. Troy.* 7549 Þen fled all in fere, & the fild leuit. *Ibid.* 9498 The Troiens lighten doun lyuely, lefton

thair horses. a 1400-50 *Alexander* 330 With þat rysis vp þe renke & his rowme lefys. 1535 COVERDALE *Prov.* ii. 13 From soch as leaue the hye strete and walke in ye wayes of darcknesse. a 1557 *Diurn. Occurr.* (Bannatyne Club) 11 Quha causit the said erle leif the toun. 1584 POWEL *Lloyd's Cambria* 269 Rees leaft the castele with his wife and children. 1660 F. BROOKE tr. *Le Blanc's Trav.* 18 At two leagues from Outer we left the most part of our company. 1676 LADY CHAWORTH in *12th Rep. Hist. MSS. Comm.* App. v. 29 The Duke and his family left Whitehall for St. James's yesterday. 1724 DE FOE *Mem. Cavalier* (1840) 33, I left Italy in April. 1788 BURNS *Wks.* II. 200, I maun lea'e my bonnie Mary. 1795 *Gentl. Mag.* 543/2 Whether the antient road to the passage over the Severn left the road to Chepstow at Crick or St. Pere. 1799 *Med. Jrnl.* II. 139 A hoarseness came on the eleventh day, and did not leave him till the eighteenth. 1819 BYRON *Juan* I. clxiii, Pray, sir, leave the room. 1825 J. NICHOLSON *Operat. Mechanic* 129 If a straight line be applied to the face of the bar from the whip to the end, the face of the bar should leave the straight line about the breadth of the bar. 1837 DICKENS *Pickw.* ii, I think we shall leave here the day after to-morrow. 1865 TYLOR *Early Hist. Man.* i. 7 They think that in sleep the soul sometimes remains in the body, and sometimes leaves it, and travels far away. 1884 W. C. SMITH *Kildrostan* 50, I thought you never left your books except To trim the boat, and set the lines. 1887 M. MACKENZIE *Dis. Throat & Nose* II. 174 He could feel it [the gas] leave the stomach. 1891 E. PEACOCK *N. Brendon* I. 162 He left the table as he spoke.

absol. (*colloq.*) 1791 BENTHAM *Let.* 12 May, Wks. 1843 X. 254 So says Lord L., who himself leaves on the 1st. 1866 THIRLWALL *Lett.* II. 70, I do not leave for town until to-morrow. 1867 R. S. CANDLISH in Jean L. Watson *Life* xiii. (1882) 144 We left about eleven, with two horses.

b. With complementary adj. or phrase, indicating the place or condition of the object quitted.

a 1225 *Ancr. R.* 162 He..wende one uppon hulles, us to uorbisne, þet we schullen..climben mid him on hulles: þet is, þenchen heie, & leauen lowe under us alle eorðliche þouhtes. a 1300 *Cursor M.* 5177 Ioseph hale and sond left wee. 1377 LANGL. *P. Pl.* B. II. 67 Thus left me that lady Liggyng aslepe. a 1548 HALL *Chron., Hen. VIII*, 258 b, They..left the toune as they founde yt. 1559 SCOT in Strype *Ann. Ref.* I. App. x. 27 The inward [thinges] it dothe..so shake, that it leavithe them very..feble. 1699 DAMPIER *Voy.* II. I. 165 And when the Tide goes out, it leaves the Oaz dry a quarter of a mile from the shore. a 1708 BEVERIDGE *Thes. Theol.* (1710) I. 330 As death leaves you, judgment will find you. 1813 *Sketches Charac.* (ed. 2) I. 170, I left her very well, a few hours ago. 1883 R. W. DIXON *Mano* II. iv. 78 Him there they overwhelmed, and left him dead.

c. To pass (an object) so, that it 'bears' so and so to one's course.

1662 J. DAVIES tr. *Olearius' Voy. Ambass.* 264 As you come into the City, you leave on the right hand two very high.. Mountains. 1719 DE FOE *Crusoe* I. iii. (1840) 47 We.. steered.., leaving those isles on the east.

d. *colloq.* (orig. *U.S.*) *to get* (or *be*) *left*: to be left in the lurch.

1884 E. W. NYE *Baled Hay* 56 That is where we get left. 1891 *New York Weekly Witness* 11 Nov. 4/4 The man that does not sympathize with the Prohibition movement is afraid of being left. 1894 G. MOORE *Esther Waters* xii. 84 While our quarrel was going on Miss Peggy went after him, and that's how I got left. 1908 *Daily Chron.* 16 Nov. 5/2 'Oh, never mind those,' says the admiral; 'what has the Navy got?' 'Got left, as usual,' replies the lieutenant. 1928 D. H. LAWRENCE *Lady Chatterley* vi. 73 It was no good being really good and getting left with it.

e. *Cricket.* Of the ball, to move away from (the batsman); used of a leg break delivery which turns away from the batsman.

1952 A. BEDSER *Bowling* II. vii. 64 A type of leg-spin which, of course, makes the ball leave or go away from the batsman. 1956 R. ALSTON *Test Commentary* iii. 19 Both batsmen seemed especially fallible to the ball that left them.

8. a. To go away from permanently; to remove from, cease to reside at (a place), to cease to belong to (a society, etc.); to forsake the company, quit the service of (a person).

a 1225 *Ancr. R.* 102 Nim þerto, & lef me hwon þe so is leouere. c 1300 *Beket* 884 Meni of Seint Thomas Men Levede him for eye. c 1340 *Cursor M.* 13033 (Trin.) Herodias..drad to leue heroudes kyng. 1362 LANGL. *P. Pl.* A. I. 101 Never leue hem for loue Ne for lacchyng of syluer. c 1420 *Anturs of Arth.* 176 (Thornton MS.) Thane wille thay leue the lyghtely þat nowe wil the lowte. 1535 COVERDALE *Gen.* ii. 24 For this cause shal a man leaue father and mother. 1651 in *Fuller's Abel Rediv., Gerardus* (1867) II. 264 Leaving of the university, he travelled through most parts of France. 1700 CONGREVE *Way of World* II. i, 'Tis better to be left, than never to have been loved. 1720 OZELL *Vertot's Rom. Rep.* I. v. 297 The Soldiers..thought they cou'd not leave their Ensigns..without offending the Gods. 1845 LD. HOUGHTON in T. W. Reid *Life* (1891) I. viii. 358 My servant Frederick has just left me to set up for himself in a public-house.

absol. a 1549 *Laneham's Let.* (1871) Pref. 151 Thoch uthers luif, and leif, with all. 1882 JEAN L. WATSON *Life R. S. Candlish* vii. 87 When he left, it was with no prospect of temporal good things, but with a firm trust in God.

†b. To part with, lose (one's breath, life). *Obs.*

a 1300 *Fragm. Pop. Sci.* (Wright) 386 That other [soule deieth] whan he leveth his breth. c 1400 *Destr. Troy* 8049, I hade leuer my lyf leue in this place, Than [etc.]. c 1450 LONELICH *Grail* lvi. 14 Mordreins qwene there left hire lyf. 1570-6 LAMBARDE *Peramb. Kent* (1826) 216 Sexburga left hir life at the doore of Mylton church. 1635 PAGITT *Christianogr.* I. ii. (1636) 81 They had rather leave their lives, then their Religion.

9. To abandon, forsake (a habit, practice, etc.), to lay aside (a dress). Now *rare* or *Obs.*, exc. in *to leave off*: see 14 c (*a*).

a 1225 *Leg. Kath.* 1340 We leaueð þi lahe and al þine bileaue. c 1330 R. BRUNNE *Chron.* (1810) 98 Mald þe gode quene gaf him in conseile, To..leue alle his tirpeile. c 1380 WYCLIF *Sel. Wks.* III. 350 He shulde be holde apostata þat lefte his abite for a day. c 1380 *Sir Ferumb.* 357 'Lef', saide he, 'þy grete foleye'. c 1449 PECOCK *Repr.* I. xx. 123 But if thee wolen leue her vnwijs and proud folie. 1478 *Liber Niger* in Pegge *Cur. Misc.* (1782) 78 Their Clothing is not according for the King's Knights, therefore it was left. 1484 CAXTON *Fables of Æsop* I. v, For the loue of a vayn thynge men ought not to leue that whiche is certeyn. c 1525 *Tale Basyn* 218 in Hazl. *E.P.P.* III. 53 Then thai leuyd thair lewtnesse, and did no more soo. 1558 BP. WATSON *Sev. Sacram.* xviii. 112 The confession of a faulte is a profession to leaue the same. 1577 HARRISON *England* II. vi. (1877) I. 163 This fondnesse is not yet left with us. 1660 F. BROOKE tr. *Le Blanc's Trav.* 8 He was..resolved to leave Turkisme, and become a Christian again. 1697 DRYDEN *Virg. Georg.* IV. 647 Proteus, leave Thy fraudful Arts. 1740 JOHNSON *Lives, Barretier* Wks. IV. 471 Eighteen months, during which he ..neither neglected his studies nor left his gaiety. 1871 R. ELLIS tr. *Catullus* lxxvi. 13 What? it is hard long love so lightly to leave in a moment?

10. a. To cease, desist from, stop. With obj. a *sb.* or *gerund*; also *inf.* with *to*. Now only *arch.*; = *leave off* (see 14 c (*a*).)

c 1340 *Cursor M.* 1131 (Trin.) His blood..leueþ not wreche to crye. c 1350 *Will. Palerne* 1806 Soburli seide meliors 'sire leues youre wordes'. 1398 TREVISA *Barth. De P.R.* XVII. xxxvi. (1495) 624 Whan the leuys of Carduus dryen the pryckes leuen to prycke and stynge. c 1420 *Chron. Vilod.* 4235 Herre song þey laftone & songon nomore. 1477 EARL RIVERS (Caxton) *Dictes* 67 Leuyng to do alle thing that may cause hattered. 1490 CAXTON *Eneydos* xxxii. 121 Now shalle I leue to speke of this mater. 1513 *Life Bridget* in *Myrr. our Ladye* (1873) p. lix, But thou leue sayde he to speke of thys newe heresye..I [etc.]. a 1533 LD. BERNERS *Huon* lxxxii. 254 Lady, I desyre you to leue your sorow. 1545 ASCHAM *Toxoph.* (Arb.) 164 If a man woulde leaue to looke at his shafte..he may vse this waye. 1556 *Chron. Gr. Friars* (Camden) 20 Thys yere the mayer lefte rydynge to Westmyster, and went be watter. 1576 GASCOIGNE *Steel Gl.* (Arb.) 79 When Cutlers leaue to sel olde rustie blades. 1602 *2nd Pt. Return fr. Parnass.* III. iv. 1401 Leaue trussing your pointes, and listen. 1603 B. JONSON *Jas. I's Entertainm. Coronation*, Zeal when it rests, Leaues to be Zeal. a 1626 BACON *New Atl.* (1900) 20 And specially, farre Voyages.. were altogether left and omitted. 1686 W. DE BRITAINE *Hum. Prud.* ix. 42 Never purchase Friends by Gifts, for if you leave to give, they will leave to love. 1690 LOCKE *Toleration* ii. Wks. 1727 II. 265 It was designed only to make them leave Swearing. 1722 DE FOE *Col. Jack* (1840) 243 The English left chasing us. 1762 GOLDSM. *Cit. W.* lxxx, Whenever one crime was judged penal by the state, he left committing it. 1821 CLARE *Vill. Minstr.* I. 156 The cat at her presence left watching the mouse. 1871 R. ELLIS tr. *Catullus* xxxvi. 5 If ever I..Ceased from enmity, left to launch iambics.

†b. *intr.* To cease, desist, stop. *Obs.*

a 1300 *Cursor M.* 6036 (Cott.) He praid, þe weder it lefte þan son. c 1340 *Ibid.* 4108 (Trin.) Til he him fonde lafte he nouȝt. 1375 BARBOUR *Bruce* VI. 157 Quha vist euir men sa fouly fall As vs, gif that we thusgat leif? c 1400 *Destr. Troy* 10084 þan leuit the laike for late of þe night. 1483 CAXTON *G. de la Tour* B v b, He..bad her ones or twyes that she shold be stylle and leue. 1523 LD. BERNERS *Froiss.* I. cxcviii. 234 The companyons..hadde lerned so well to robbe and pyll the countrey..that they coude nat leaue. 1589 PUTTENHAM *Eng. Poesie* III. xxii. (Arb.) 265 If he had left at the two first verses, it had bene inough. 1594 MARLOWE & NASHE *Dido* II. i. C 2, I dye with melting ruth; Æneas leaue. 1633 BP. HALL *Hard Texts* 298 It shall devoure both your tall cedars and your low shrubs; and shall not leave till the very bryars and thornes bee consumed.

†11. a. *trans.* In the course of narration: To drop, cease speaking of. *Obs.*

c 1330 R. BRUNNE *Chron.* (1810) 235 We salle leue þat pas vnto we com ageyn. 1526 *Pilgr. Perf.* (W. de W. 1531) 1 The seconde boke leueth yᵉ lyfe of yᵉ worlde and entreateth what is the iourney of religion. a 1548 HALL *Chron., Hen. VI*, 135 b, Now leavyng Scotland, let us returne to the busines of Fraunce. 1604 E. G[RIMSTONE] *D'Acosta's Hist. Indies* III. xv. 169 But now that we have left the sea, let vs come to other kinde of waters that remaine to be spoken of.

b. *intr.* To cease, stop, break off in a narrative. Const. *of*. *Obs.*

c 1330 R. BRUNNE *Chron. Wace* (Rolls) 60 þis Mayster Wace þer leues he. c 1350 *Will. Palerne* 1836 Leef we now here. c 1435 *Torr. Portugal* 587 Leve we now of Torrent there. 1470-85 MALORY *Arthur* IX. i. *heading*, Here leue we of sire Lamorak and of sir Tristram. 1592 SHAKS. *Ven. & Ad.* 715 Where did I leaue? 1614 RALEIGH *Hist. World* II. v. §7. 180 Let us return thither where we left.

†III. 12. *intr.* To remain; to remain *behind*, *over*; to continue or stay in one place. *Obs.*

c 1000 ÆLFRIC *Hom.* II. 40 Gif ðær hwæt læfde. c 1230 *Hali Meid.* 15 Hit ne wundeð þe nawt bute hit festni oþe & leaue se longe þat [etc.]. c 1275 LAY. 22305 And wose leafde his leome he solde leose. a 1300 *Cursor M.* 7269 He left at ham for eild. 1357 *Lay Folks Mass Bk.* App. II. 120 There levyth in the auter no materyal bred. 1375 BARBOUR *Bruce* III. 282 Hym thocht he had doyne rycht nocht Ay quhill to do hym levyt ocht. 1398 TREVISA *Barth. De P.R.* IX. iv. (1495) 349 In that yere comyth vp a Lunacion a mone of thyrty dayes and thre dayes leuyth ouer. 1425 *Rolls of Parlt.* IV. 276/1 All the said Merchandises..that leven unsold.. shall be forfaited. c 1425 *Craft of Nombrynge* (E.E.T.S.) 9 Whan þou has þus ydo..sett þere þat leues of þe subtraccioun. c 1450 HOLLAND *Howlat* 948 Thar levit allane The Howlat and I. 1460-70 *Bk. Quintessence* 5 þat þat leueþ bihynde, putte it to þe fier. 1492 *Bury Wills* (Camden) 74 The torchys that shall leve after my yere day. 1535 COVERDALE *2 Kings* iv. 44 They ate, and there lefte ouer. a 1541 WYATT *Poet. Wks.* (1861) 209 Who will'th him well for right therefore shall leve; Who banish him shall be rooted away.

IV. Phraseological combinations.

13. In various idiomatic phrases. **a.** *to leave... alone* (earlier † *to leave one*): to abstain from interfering with; = 'to let alone' (see ALONE 4 and LET v.¹). In the same sense, *to leave...be* (colloq.) where *leave* has been substituted for *let* without modification of the form of the phrase. *to leave* (a person) *cold*: see COLD a. 7 e; *to leave it at that*: to proceed no further with a matter; to refrain from pressing a point; *to leave to* (*himself*, etc.): to let (a person, etc.) alone or without help or interference from another or others; *to leave* (a person) *to it*: to leave (someone) alone, esp. to allow him to proceed with a task in hand. **b.** *to leave go* (*of*), *to leave hold* (*of*), *to leave loose* (*of*) colloq.: to cease holding, to let go.

In *to leave go*, *to leave loose*, the vb. was orig. transitive, *go* being inf., and *loose* a complementary adj.; but the combinations being used *absol.* or with ellipsis of the obj. became virtually intransitive vbs., and were construed with *of*. (Cf. *let go*, under LET v.¹) The frequency in use of the three expressions *leave go*, *leave hold*, *leave loose*, varies in different parts of the country, but perhaps none of them can be regarded as merely *dial.*

The notion expressed in some Dicts. that *leave* in some of these phrases represents ME. LEVE (OE. *léfan*, *lýfan*), to permit, is quite erroneous.

c 1400 tr. *Secreta Secret., Gov. Lordsh.* (1898) 88 If þou leue þe water aloon, it shal make whit, and if þow ioynge to ffyre by þe gyft of god it shal wel fare. c 1485 in *E.E. Misc.* (Warton Club) 8 Thou woldus gladly with me fare, And leve one my talkynge. 1738 [G. SMITH] *Curious Relat.* II. 274 A few, who perhaps through Dread had left their Hold..were drowned. 1776 in *Essex Inst. Hist. Coll.* (1907) XLIII. 118 Tis said we left go pieces of heavy cannon owing to the cowardice of a body of Connecticut troops. 1798 MAD. D'ARBLAY *Diary* (1891) IV. 82 'O, leave him alone!' cried Mr. Pepys: 'take care only of his health and strength'. 1825 J. NEAL *Bro. Jonathan* I. 37 Leave me be, squeaked Miss Edith, whose foot he had caught..under the table. 1833 *Chambers's Edin. Jrnl.* II. 145/1 The individual who writes the present paper was once 'so far left to himself' as to spend several months amidst the heartless frivolities which characterise a winter of fashionable life in the Scottish.. capitals. 1841 *Jrnl. R. Agric. Soc.* II. I. 99 The operator then leaves hold of the spoke. 1851 HELPS *Comp. Solit.* vi. (1854) 99 People will not be supposed to be educated at the time of their nonage and then left sight of and hold of for evermore. 1868 F. E. PAGET *Lucretia* 205 Leave go of me..you young monkey. 1881 JEFFERIES *Wood Magic* I. v. 133 The bridge is now dry, and therefore you can pass it easily if you do not leave-go of the hand-rail. 1885 *Manch. Exam.* 5 June 5/1 We cannot but wish that Mr. Gladstone had left the matter alone. 1902 *Captain* VII. 542/1 We'll leave it at that, then. 1910 'SAKI' *Reginald in Russia* 8 Left to themselves, Egbert and Lady Anne would unfailingly have called him Fluff. 1918 C. MACKENZIE *Early Life Sylvia Scarlett* II. ii. 283 The petulant way in which she shook herself free from the embrace at last brought Sylvia up to the point of leaving Lily to herself. 1928 GALSWORTHY *Swan Song* II. ii. 114 He had looked at her, and left it at that. 1943 J. B. PRIESTLEY *Daylight on Saturday* xvi 114 'You never told her what she ought to do..,' said Freda to Jock. And then she left them to it. 1946 E. O'NEILL *Iceman Cometh* (1947) II. 102 Leave Hugo be!.. He's earned his dream! 1948 C. DAY LEWIS *Otterbury Incident* iv. 45 Ted and I left him to it. 1949 V. GROVE *Language Bar* viii. 114 If understanding and sense were not sought after, the ignorant would merely corrupt the 'meaningless' word, and leave it at that. 1958 L. A. G. STRONG *Light above Lake* xxi. 148 Toby..left him be for a while. 1966 *Oxf. Univ. Gaz.* 23 Dec. 445/2 If the House is content to leave it at that for the present,..then I would ask if we might withdraw the resolution and leave it at that for today. 1967 SINGHA & MASSEY *Indian Dances* i. 34 South India had been more or less left to itself. 1970 D. STOREY *Contractor* I. 40 I'll leave you to it before the rest of 'em arrive. 1971 M. WEST *Summer of Red Wolf* 9 Leave me be for a moment, please. 1972 R. ADAMS *Watership Down* xxxiii. 258 They'll know which way we've gone and they won't leave it at that. 1974 W. T. BURLEY *Death in Stanley St.* vii. 127 Wycliffe stood up. 'Good. I'll leave you to it.'

14. Combined with *advs.* (For unspecialized combs. see the various senses.)

a. leave behind. (Also, *to leave behind one.*) *trans.* †(*a*) To neglect, leave undone (*obs.*) (*b*) Not to take with one at one's departure, to go away without. (*c*) To have remaining after departure or removal, as a trace or consequence. (*d*) To outstrip.

a 1300 *Cursor M.* 26389 þis ypocrites..þai leue þe grettest. plight be-hind. c 1325 *Poem Times Edw. II*, 80 in *Pol. Songs* (Camden) 327 He..leveth thare behind a theef and an hore. 1390 GOWER *Conf.* II. 263 Behind was no name laft. 1509 HAWES *Past. Pleas.* xli. (Percy Soc.) 204 This worldly treasure I must leve behinde. 1660 F. BROOKE tr. *Le Blanc's Trav.* 9 Considering they might leave me behind, or sell me. 1670 A. ROBERTS *Adventures T. S.* 159 The Guards that were at the Gate obliged us to leave our Sandals behind. 1697 DRYDEN *Virg. Georg.* III. 306 He..leaves the Scythian Arrow far behind. 1711 ADDISON *Spect.* No. 50 ¶2 A little Bundle of Papers..left behind by some mistake. 1746-7 HERVEY *Medit.* (1818) 217 The rapidity of an eagle, which leaves the stormy blast behind her. 1758 *Song*, 'The girl I left behind me'. 1849 MACAULAY *Hist. Eng.* iv. I. 496 He made such rapid progress in the doctrines of toleration that he left Milton and Locke behind. 1896 A. E. HOUSMAN *Shropshire Lad* iii. 1 Leave your home behind, lad.

†b. leave down. *trans.* To discontinue, let drop. *Obs.*

1548 *Proclam.* in Strype *Eccl. Mem.* II. App. O. 46 That no maner person..do omyt, leave down,..or innovate any order, rite, or ceremony commonly used..and not commaunded to be left down..in the reign of our late sovereign lord.

c. leave off. (*a*) *trans.* To cease from, discontinue (an action), abandon (a habit); with obj. a gerund or sb., formerly also an *inf.* with *to*. Also, to cease to wear or use (something).

c **1400** *Destr. Troy* 3587 Lefe of þis langore. *c* **1440** *York Myst.* xxxii. 295 Leffe of þi talke. **1480** CAXTON *Descr. Brit.* 22 Afterward the romayns lefte of her regning in britayne. **1535** COVERDALE *Luke* v. 4 Whan he had lefte of talkinge he sayde [etc.]. **1563–83** FOXE *A. & M.* I. 259 [Francis of Assisi] left of shoes, had but one coate, and that of a course clothe. **1581** MULCASTER *Positions* v. (1887) 33 That the learning to write be not left of, vntil it be verie perfit. **1589** PUTTENHAM *Eng. Poesie* iii. xxiii. (Arb.) 279 Bid him leaue off such affected flattering termes. **1622** MABBE tr. *Aleman's Guzman d'Alf.* II. 41 His crosse fortune, which did neuer leaue off to persecute him. **1687** MIEGE *Gt. Fr. Dict.* II. s.v., Leave off this wrangling, *cessez de vous quereler.* **1704** *Lond. Gaz.* No. 4083/4 Tho. Brown..wears a Wig, but his Hair almost long enough to leave it off. **1737** WHISTON *Josephus, Antiq.* I. iii. §8 But I will leave off for the time to come to require such punishments. **1875** JOWETT *Plato* (ed. 2) III. 303 Those invalids who..will not leave off their habits of intemperance. **1885** G. ALLEN *Babylon* viii, They left off work early. **1891** *Field* 21 Nov. 774/3 We had reluctantly to leave off fishing.

†(*b*) In occasional uses, now obsolete: To give up (a possession, a business or employment); to forsake the society of (a person); to 'give up' (a patient) as incurable. *Obs.*

1534 MORE *Comf. agst. Trib.* II. Wks. 1200/2 If it so be, yt a man..perceiueth that in welth & authoritie he doth his own soule harme,..then wold I in any wise aduise him to leaue of that thing, be it spirituall benefice yt he haue,..or temporal rowm & authoritie. **1662** R. MATHEW *Unl. Alch.* xxxi. 27 Left off by a very honest and able Doctor. **1706** HEARNE *Collect.* 2 Jan. (O.H.S.) I. 154 To oblige him to leave off Pupils he made him his Curate. **1712** STEELE *Spect.* No. 264 ¶2 He left off all his old Acquaintance to a Man. **1720** DE FOE *Capt. Singleton* xx. (1840) 341 He would send her sufficient to enable her to leave off her shop.

(*c*) *absol.* and *intr.* To cease doing something implied by the context; to make an end or interruption, to stop. Of a narrative: To end, terminate. Also *Comm.* of shares, etc.: To end (*at* a certain price) on the closing of the market.

1415 HOCCLEVE *To Sir J. Oldcastle* 152 Your wit is al to feeble to despute..Stynte and leue of. *c* **1475** *Rauf Coilȝear* 174 Is nane so gude as leif of, and mak na mair stryfe. **1535** COVERDALE *Ps.* xxxvi[i]. 8 Leaue of from wrath, let go displeasure. **1563–83** FOXE *A. & M.* 1615/1 Now death draweth nye, and I [Bradford] by your leaue must now leaue of, to prepare for him. **1611** BIBLE *Ecclus.* xxxi. 17 Leaue off first for maners sake, and be not vnsatiable. **1700** DRYDEN *Pref. Fables* Wks. (Globe) 499 He knows also when to leave off, a continence which is practised by few writers. **1711** ADDISON *Spect.* No. 130 ¶4 Here the printed story leaves off. **1816** CRABB *Synonymes* (1829) 148/1 A break is made in a page of printing by leaving off in the middle of a line. **1875** JOWETT *Plato* (ed. 2) I. 206 Take up the enquiry where I left off. **1883** *Manch. Exam.* 30 Nov. 4/1 South Austrian shares left off at last night's quotations. **1895** *Bookman* Oct. 25/1 It is merely a first volume, and we leave off with an appetite.

d. leave out. To omit, not to insert or include.

a **1470** GREGORY *Chron.* (Camd.) 203 They seyng and redynge hys papyr, commaundyd to leve owte and put a way many troughtys. *c* **1484** CAXTON *Proem to Chaucer's Cant. T.*, I erryd..in settyng in somme thynges that he neuer.. made, and leuynge out many thynges that he made. **1545** ASCHAM *Toxoph.* II. (Arb.) 110 And these thynges althoughe they be trifles, yet..I woulde not leue them out. **1613** PURCHAS *Pilgrimage* To Rdr. (1614) ¶v, The most leave out their Authors, as if their owne assertion were sufficient authoritie. **1653** WALTON *Angler* ii. 46 A companion that feasts the company with wit and mirth, and leaves out the sin which is usually mixed with them. **1676** LISTER in *Ray's Corr.* (1848) 124, I shall only put you in mind that you leave not out the vinegar. **1735** LORD TYRAWLY in *Buccleuch MSS.* (Hist. MSS. Comm.) I. 387 They could not with any decency do it for him and leave me out. **1766** GOLDSM. *Vic. W.* xi, He seldom leaves anything out, as he writes only for his own amusement. **1843** H. ROGERS *Ess.* (1860) III. 79 They can leave out, if they do not put in. **1887** 'L. CARROLL' *Game of Logic* i. §1. 6 We agree to leave out the word 'Cakes' altogether.

e. leave over. *trans.* To allow to remain for future use; to let 'stand over' for subsequent consideration. Freq. in pa. pple. *left over*, remaining, not used up.

1887 *Times* (weekly ed.) 14 Oct. 3/2 He thought the matter might be left over for the present. **1892** 'MARK TWAIN' *Amer. Claimant* xii. 107 Irish stew made of the potatoes and meat left over from a procession of previous meals. **1899** G. B. BURGIN *Bread of Tears* II. i. 138 The undigested fragments which were left over after the making of the world. **1907** *Smart Set* Mar. 72/1 You can go to the boss for your time—if there's anything left over from your breakage account. **1940** J. O'HARA *Pal Joey* 114 Choice meats like steak & chops etc. that was left over from the nite before. **1955** M. PATTEN *Learning to Cook* ii. 59 (*heading*) Foods that have been left over.

†**f. leave up.** To abandon, give up, resign. *Obs.*

1430–40 LYDG. *Bochas* IX. xxxiv. (1554) 214 b, The second [sonne] left up his cleargie. **1523** LD. BERNERS *Froiss.* I. lv. 76 The kyng might be fayne..to leave up the siege at Tourney. *Ibid.* ccxv. 271 That was the cause that dyuers of them left vp their fortresses. **1530** *Compend. Treat.* (Arb.) 178 He saide that he wold leaue vp the office of Chaunceler.

leave (liːv), *v.*² [ME. *lēvi*, f. *lēf* LEAF *sb.*¹, with regular change of *f* into *v.*] *intr.* = LEAF *v.* 1. Also *to be leaved out* (U.S.): to have the leaves expanded.

c **1290** *S. Kenelm* 168 in *S. Eng. Leg.* 350 þis maister nam þe ȝeorde and sette hire on þe grounde And heo bi-gan to leui þare in well uyte stounde. **1450–80** tr. *Secreta Secret.* 27 The humydite of the erthe..makith trees and herbes to leve and flowre. **1715** PETIVER in *Phil. Trans.* XXIX. 232 It leaves like our Corn Marygold. **1789** J. MAY *Jrnl. & Lett.* (1873) 127 The apple-trees are now in blow; the oaks and chestnuts but just leaved out. **1864** WEBSTER, *Leave*, to send out leaves;—often with *out*. **1890** *Century Mag.* July 448/1 The trees had not yet leaved enough to afford..any shade. **1895** *Pop. Sci. Monthly* Mar. 578 The poplars were leaved out. **1895** KATH. HINKSON *Miracle Plays* I. 20, I..watch my lilies bud and leave.

†**leave**, *v.*³ *Obs. rare.* [ad. F. *lever*: see LEVY.] *trans.* To raise (an army).

1590 SPENSER *F.Q.* II. x. 31 An army strong she leav'd, To war on those which him had of his realm bereav'd.

leave, obs. form of LAVE *sb.*, LEAF, LIEF, LIVE.

leaved (liːvd), *a.* (See also LEAFED *a.*) [f. LEAF *sb.*¹ or LEAVE *v.* + -ED.]

1. Having leaves or foliage; bearing leaves, 'in leaf'. *lit.* and *fig.* Also *Her.*

c **1250** *Gen. & Ex.* 3839 It [Aaron's rod] was grene and leaued bi-cumen. *c* **1350** *Will. Palerne* 22 þe buschys þat were blowed grene, & leued ful louely. **1377** LANGL. *P. Pl.* B. xv. 95 There somme bowes ben leued and somme bereth none. **1470–85** MALORY *Arthur* VI. vi, They lodged hem in a lytyl leued wood. **1572** MASCALL *Plant. & Graff.* vii. (1651) 40 In the spring time before the trees be leaved. *c* **1586** C'TESS PEMBROKE *Ps.* CIV. vii, Thence, Lord, thy leaved people bud and blow. **1601** HOLLAND *Pliny* II. 216 A foursquare stem,..leaued like vnto an Oke. *a* **1711** KEN *Sion* Poet. Wks. 1721 IV. 324 The Flow'rs were blown, the Vine was leav'd. **1864** BOUTELL *Her. Hist. & Pop.* xxi. §6. 364 Three lilies, slipped and leaved.

b. Having leaves or foliage (of a specified number or kind).

1393 LANGL. *P. Pl.* C. XVIII. 48 Then grace sholde growe ȝut and grene-leued wexe. **1583** *Leg. Bp. St. Androis* 303 Sanct Jhones nutt, and the forᵉ levit claver. **1607** TOPSELL *Four-f. Beasts* (1658) 258 Three-leaved grass is also good for Horses. *a* **1729** CONGREVE tr. *Ovid's Art of Love* III, There tamarisks with thick leav'd box are found. **1787** *Fam. Plants* I. 13 Perianth one-leaved. **1847** TENNYSON *Princess* III. 159 The thick-leaved platans of the vale.

2. Resembling a (plant-)leaf.

1841 S. C. HALL *Ireland* (1842) II. 84 The base of the former [pillar in the Caves of Tipperary] is not simple, but composed of stalks cemented together, and having leaved or foliated edges. **1865** *Spectator* 14 Jan. 49 He himself describes them as more like 'willow-leaves'..These leaved forms are different in size.

†**3.** Reduced to a leaf or thin plate; laminate. *Obs.*

1559 MORWYNG *Evonym.* 240 Mixt [*sic*] the siedes of Rew pund with leued gould. **1658** SIR T. MAYERNE *Receipts Cookery* xxi. 24 Making them [minced pies] in a paste, or dough, very thin, and, as we formerly called it, a leaved paste.

4. Of a door: Having (two) leaves.

1610 GUILLIM *Heraldry* II. i. (1660) 50 The two leaved silver gates bright raies did cast. **1611** BIBLE *Is.* xlv. 1. **1611** COTGR. s.v. *Batant*, A fowlding, or two leaued, doore. **1847** C. BRONTE *J. Eyre* I. xii. 223 The great dining-room, whose two-leaved door stood open.

5. Furnished with leaves (of paper).

1629 GAULE *Pract. Theories* Rules to Rdr., 'Tis not a winged Bird, but leaued Booke. **1817** BYRON *Beppo* liv, A new Magazine With all the fashions which the last month wore, Coloured, and silver paper leav'd between That and the title-page.

†**'leaveless**, *a.* *Obs.* [variant of LEAFLESS, influenced by the pl. *leaves.*] Without leaves.

1581 T. HOWELL *Deuises* (1879) 199 When Boreas rough, had leauelesse left eche tree. *c* **1611** CHAPMAN *Iliad* II. 370 With wood, leauelesse, and kindl'd at Apposed fire, they burne the thighes. **1638** CAREW *Verses pref. to Sandys' Div. Poems* 34 Then, I no more shall court the Verdant Bay, But the dry leavelesse Trunke on Golgotha.

†**'leaveless**, *adv.* *Obs.* [f. LEAVE *sb.*¹ + -LESS.] Without permission.

c **1250** *Gen. & Ex.* 1848 Dina ðor mis-dede, ȝhe nam leueles fro ðat stede. *a* **1500** *Chaucer's Dreme* 74 Closed rounde about That levelesse none come in ne out.

leavell, obs. form of LEVEL.

leave-looker. [f. LEAVE *sb.*¹ (? in the sense of 'licence') + LOOKER *sb.*] A municipal officer in several boroughs of Lancashire, Cheshire, and North Wales, having certain duties of inspection.

1552 in Picton *L'pool Munic. Rec.* (1883) I. 59 Leavelookers John Walker Robt Mercer. **1592** in J. Hall *Hist. Nantwich* (1883) 73 The leaue lookers or one of them shall euery kinding [heating of the salt-pans] goe about wᵗʰ the stryke and measure their owne and euery Occupiers salt. **1599** *List Mayors of Chester* in *Digby Myst.* (1882) App. to Fore-words 26 This Mayor..restrayned the leaielookers [*another version* (p. 24) *has* leaulokers], for sending wine, on the feastifull dayes. **1656** D. KING *Vale Royal, Chester* II. 157 The Leave-lookers, who then were the Head and chief of the Citizens before a Maior was ordained, and still is reputed the head or chief of the fourty, or the Common-Councell of the City. **1685** in D. Sinclair *Hist. Wigan* (1882) II. 177 Your petʳ was fined in Ten shillings for the neglect of his your petʳ office of a Gatewaiter or Leave-looker. **1795** J. AIKIN *Manchester* 392 Forty common councilmen two of whom are leave-lookers, whose office it is to inform of all persons exercising trades within the city [Chester] without being freemen. **1835** *Munic. Corp. Comm. Rept.* App. IV. 2621 [Chester] The Leave lookers are..appointed annually by the mayor. *Ibid.* 2663 [Denbigh] The Leave Lookers are appointed by the common council. Their office..is quite gratuitous. *Ibid.* 2709 [Liverpool] The Leave Looker has 104*l.* a year. *Ibid.* 2850 [Ruthin] The Leave Lookers are appointed by the borough jury at the leet for a year. **1883** J. HALL *Hist. Nantwich* 68 [Town-officers formerly] Leave-lookers; or Market Inspectors.

Hence †**leave-lookerage** (see quot.).

1778 PENNANT *Tour in Wales* I. 168 Here [*sc.* at Chester] are..two annual officers, called leave-lookers... They were accustomed..to take small sums, called leave-lookerage, for leave for non-freemen to sell wares by retail.

leaven ('lɛv(ə)n), *sb.* Forms: 4–5 levayn(e, 4–8 levain(e, 4 levein, 4–6 leveyne, 5–8 leven, (5 lewan), 7 levin, 6– leaven. [a. F. *levain* (recorded from 12–13th c.) = Prov. *levam*:—L. *levāmen* means of raising (recorded only in the sense 'alleviation, relief, comfort'), f. *levāre* (F. *lever*) to raise.]

1. A substance which is added to dough to produce fermentation; *spec.* a quantity of fermenting dough reserved from a previous batch to be used for this purpose (cf. *sour-dough*). †In 16–18th c. often *plural.* Phrase, †*to lay, put leaven(s.*

1340 *Ayenb.* 205 Ase þe leuayne zoureþ þet doȝ. **1390** GOWER *Conf.* I. 294 He is the levein of the brede, Which soureth all the past about. *c* **1400** *Lanfranc's Cirurg.* 352 Take þe wombis of cantarides & grinde him wiþ leueyne. *c* **1425** *Voc.* in Wr.-Wülcker 663/21 *Hoc leuamentum*, lewan. **1471** RIPLEY *Comp. Alch.* IX. viii. in Ashm. (1652) 175 Lyke as flower of Whete made into Past, Requyreth Ferment whych Leven we call. *a* **1483** *Liber Niger* in *Househ. Ord.* (1790) 70 One yoman furnour..seasonyng the ovyn and at the making of the levayne at every bache. *c* **1532** DU WES *Introd. Fr.* in Palsgr. 946 To put the levain, *fermenter.* **1533** ELYOT *Cast. Helthe* (1539) 27 b, Breadde of fyne floure of wheate, hauynge no leuyn, is slowe of digestion. **1541** R. COPLAND *Guydon's Quest. Chirurg.* N j, And yf yᵉ veynes as yet appere nat wel, a day before he must haue a plaster of leueyne. **1573** TUSSER *Husb.* lxxxix. (1878) 179 Wash dishes, lay leauens. **1601** HOLLAND *Pliny* I. 566 The meale of Millet is singular good for Leuains. **1611** BIBLE *Exod.* xii. 15 Euen the first day yee shall put away leauen out of your houses. **1671** SALMON *Syn. Med.* III. xxii. 430 Rie, the leaven is more powerfull than that of Wheat, in breaking all Aposthumes. **1699** EVELYN *Acetaria* 53 Add a Pound of Wheat-flour, fermented with a little Levain. **1747** MRS. GLASSE *Cookery* xvii. 151 The more Leaven is put to the Flour, the lighter and spongier the Bread will be. **1809** PINKNEY *Trav. France* 33 The bread is made of wheat meal, but in some cottages consisted of thin cakes without leven. **1876** tr. *Schützenberger's Ferment.* 10 The ancients used as leaven for their bread either dough that had been kept till it was sour, or beer-yeast.

b. In wider sense: Any substance that produces fermentation; = FERMENT *sb.* 1; occasionally applied to the 'ferment' of zymotic diseases.

1658 R. WHITE tr. *Digby's Powd. Symp.* (1660) 111 Oyl of tartar fermented by the levain of roses. **1689** HARVEY *Curing Dis. by Expect.* iv. 21 [The] humours..acquire a levain so pernicious, as to deprave and subvert the animal Faculty. **1747** tr. *Astruc's Fevers* 254 Moreover such a foreign levain is so disproportioned to our nature, that its effects will be the greater; nor must we admire, that this mortal ferment should be the product of some particular countries. **1758** J. S. *Le Dran's Observ. Surg.* (1771) 137 Her Blood was loaded with a bad Leven. **1822–34** *Good's Study Med.* (ed. 4) I. 694 The activity of its [typhus'] leaven by which it assimilates all the fluids of the body to its own nature.

2. *fig.* **a.** Chiefly with allusion to certain passages of the gospels (e.g. Matt. xiii. 33, xvi. 6): An agency which produces profound change by progressive inward operation.

1390 [see sense 1]. **1555** PHILPOT *Apol.* (1599) B 8 b, What pharisaical leuen dothe they scatter abrode. **1641** MILTON *Reform.* II. Wks. 1851 III. 49 The soure levin of humane Traditions mixt in one putrifi'd Masse with the poisonous dregs of hypocrisie in the hearts of Prelates. **1647** N. BACON *Disc. Govt. Eng.* I. iii. 7 And thus the Romans levened with the Gospell..insinuated that leven by degrees, which in the conclusion prevailed over all. **1725** LD. BOLINGBROKE 24 July in *Swift's Lett.* (1767) II. 211 Lest so corrupt a member should come again into the house of lords, and his bad leaven should sour that sweet untainted mass. **1799** J. ADAMS *Wks.* (1854) IX. 8 There is a very sour leaven of malevolence in many English and in many American minds against each other. **1865** PARKMAN *Huguenots* ii. (1875) 17 To the utmost bounds of France, the leaven of the Reform was working. **1875** STUBBS *Const. Hist.* III. xxi. 542 The evil leaven of these feelings remained.

b. Used for: A tempering or modifying element; a tinge or admixture (of some quality).

1576 FLEMING *Panopl. Epist.* 410 You have your fine walkes..and therewithall communication seasoned with the leven of learning. **1699** BENTLEY *Phal.* 406 Their Style had some Leaven from the Age that each of them liv'd in. **1740** J. CLARKE *Educ. Youth* (ed. 3) 124 The latter [Seneca]..has a Mixture of the Stoick Leaven. **1793** HOLCROFT *Lavater's Physiogn.* i. 13 Virtue unsullied by the leven of vanity. **1864** SWINBURNE *Atalanta* 318 Pleasure with pain for leaven. **1883** S. C. HALL *Retrospect* II. 185 A leaven of gaiety clung to her through life. **1884** *Manch. Exam.* 23 June 6/1 We should remember their temptations and mix a large leaven of charity with our judgments.

c. Phrases. ***of the same leaven***: of the same sort or character. ***the old leaven***: after 1 Cor. v. 6, 7, the traces of the unregenerate condition; hence often applied to prejudices of education inconsistently retained by those who have changed their religious or political opinions.

1598 B. JONSON *Ev. Man in Hum.* I. ii. 73 One is a Rimer, sir, o' your owne batch, your owne levin. **1650** TRAPP *Comm. Num.* 48 A loafe of the same leaven, was that resolute Rufus. **1653** MILTON *Hirelings* Wks. 1738 I. 569 They quote Ambrose, Augustin, and some other ceremonial Doctors of the same Leven. **1722** SEWEL *Hist. Quakers* 4 The Prejudice of the old Leaven. **1727** SWIFT *To Very Yng. Lady* Wks. 1755 II. II. 42 Of the same leaven are those wives, who, when their husbands are gone a journey, must have a

letter every post. **1839** STONEHOUSE *Axholme* 191 The old leaven of dissent, in which Wesley was brought up.

3. *attrib.*

1547 BOORDE *Brev. Health* ccvii. 72 Rye breade, Levyn bread,..and all maner of crustes. **1880** KINGLAKE *Crimea* VI. vi. 134 The army of General Canrobert was often..able to provide itself with good leaven bread.

leaven ('lɛv(ə)n), *v.* Forms: see the sb. Also *pa. pple.* 5 **y-lavenyt**, 6 **levended**. [f. LEAVEN *sb.*]

1. *trans.* To produce fermentation in (dough) by means of leaven.

1422 tr. *Secreta Secret., Priv. Priv.* 241 The brede be hit made of whete and euenly y-lauenyt. **1528** PAYNEL *Salerne's Regim.* (1541) 45 b, This text declareth .v. propretes of good breadde. The fyrste is, hit must be well leuende. **1535** COVERDALE *Hos.* vii. 2 As it were an ouen y[t] the baker heateth ..till the dowe be leuended. **1611** BIBLE *1 Cor.* v. 6 Know ye not that a little leauen leaueneth the whole lumpe? **1638** RAWLEY tr. *Bacon's Life & Death* (1650) 47 Bread, a little leavened, and very little salted, is best.

absol. **1650** TRAPP *Comm. Exod.* 74 In the Meat-offering, it was not lawfull to offer leaven, or anie thing that leaveneth, as honie.

2. *fig.* (Cf. LEAVEN *sb.* 2.) To permeate with a transforming influence as leaven does; to imbue or mingle *with* some tempering or modifying element; †*rarely*, to debase or corrupt by admixture.

1550 LATIMER *Last Serm. bef. Edw. VI.* (1562) 118 b, But beware ye that are Maiestrates, theyr synne dothe leauen you all. **1576** FLEMING *Panopl. Epist.* 35 Your advise, being leavened with singular wisedome. *Ibid.* 238 When I had perceived..that your friendshippe was leavened with lightnesse and inconstancie. **1647** N. BACON *Disc. Govt. Eng.* I. iii. 7 Thus the Romans levened with the Gospell.. insinuated that leven by degrees. **1682** SIR T. BROWNE *Chr. Mor.* I. §1 Leven not good Actions nor render Virtues disputable. **1682** BURNET *Rights Princes* Pref. 29 Only they were too much leavened with a superstitious conceit of the Rights of the Church. *c***1718** PRIOR *Ladle* 166 That cruel something unpossess'd Corrodes and leavens all the rest. **1860** READE *Cloister & H.* lii, When this revelation had had time to leaven the city. **1862** GOULBURN *Pers. Relig.* IV. xii. (1873) 355 The indolent, evil thought would still insinuate itself until it leavened their entire character. **1865** MERIVALE *Rom. Emp.* VIII. lxv. 144 Bithynia..and the adjacent parts of Asia were at the time more leavened with Christian opinions than other districts of the empire. **1877** MRS. OLIPHANT *Makers Flor.* xi. 273 A mob which it was very easy to leaven with noisy men here and there.

Hence '**leavening** *vbl. sb.* and *ppl. a.*

1606 SHAKS. *Tr. & Cr.* I. i. 20, 22. *a***1626** BACON *New Atl.* (1627) 37 Breads we haue of severall Graines,.. With diuerse kindes of Leauenings, and Seasonings. **1674** N. FAIRFAX *Bulk & Selv.* 128 By..fermentation or bustle of the working or leavening particles. **1878** MACLEAR *Celts* vii. 105 It did not retain the leavening influences now introduced. **1894** *Athenæum* 10 Nov. 633/2 [The world was] seething and fermenting..under the leavening influences of Christianity.

leaven, obs. form of ELEVEN.

1549 LATIMER *Seven Sermons* A a iij b, It was a solitarye place and thyther he wente w[t] hys leauen Apostles.

leavened ('lɛv(ə)nd), *ppl. a.* [f. LEAVEN *v.* + -ED[1].] In senses of the vb.

*c***1400** MAUNDEV. (Roxb.) iii. 10 Þe Grekes also makes þe sacrement of þe autere of leuaynd breed. **1531** TINDALE *Exp. 1 John* (1537) 76 A leuended mauncher of theyr pharisaycall gloses. **1573** BARET *Alv.* L 245 Leauened bread, *panis fermentatus.* **1586** J. HOOKER *Hist. Irel.* II. 161/2 Their old leauened and wicked vsage. **1603** SHAKS. *Meas. for M.* I. i. 52 We haue with a leauen'd and prepared choice Proceeded to you. **1611** BIBLE *Exod.* xiii. 3 There shall no leauened bread be eaten. **1815** ELPHINSTONE *Acc. Caubul* (1842) II. 191 The Uzbeks breakfast on tea and leavened bread.

'**leavenish**, *a. rare.* [f. LEAVEN *sb.* + -ISH.] Resembling leaven.

1608 TOPSELL *Serpents* (1658) 695 If a perfume hereof be made & infused by a tunnel into the holes of serpents, it will drive them away, by reason of the sharp and leavenish savour thereof.

leavenless ('lɛv(ə)nlɪs), *a.* [-LESS.] Containing no leaven.

1877 J. D. CHAMBERS *Div. Worship* 240 A second meal was served, with bitter herbs and leavenless bread.

leavenous ('lɛv(ə)nəs), *a.* [f. LEAVEN *sb.* + -OUS.] Having the properties of leaven.

1649 MILTON *Eikon.* ix. Wks. 1851 III. 401 A..vitious clergy..whose unsincere and levenous Doctrine corrupting the people, first taught them loosness, then bondage. **1677** WARWICK *Mem. Chas. I* (1701) 78 When they [Dissenters] would mingle their leavenous zeal with a dissatisfied Laylump..it so fermented the blood that at last it cast the whole body into a distemper.

leaver ('liːvə(r)). [f. LEAVE *v.*[1] + -ER[1].] One who leaves (in various senses of the vb.); *spec.* a boy or girl who has just left or is about to leave school: see *school-leaver* (SCHOOL *sb.*[1] 19).

1548 UDALL, etc. *Erasm. Par. Matt.* xix. 96 This vertue is more estemed of thaffection of the leaver than of the greatnes of the thyng that is lefte. **1606** SHAKS. *Ant. & Cl.* IV. ix. 22 But let the world ranke me in Register A Master leauer, and a fugitive. **1652** J. B. *To Brome on his Joviall Crew* Brome's Wks. 1873 III. 347 The most our Leavers serve for, shews Onely that we're his friends. **1883** *Century Mag.* June 219/2 Leaders of lonely lives, and leavers of great fortunes. **1890** G. GISSING *Emancip.* III. II. xvii. 288 Hither came no payers of formal calls, no leavers of cards. **1910** *Westm. Gaz.* 17 Jan. 5/1 Of the entrants and leavers examined, approximately 3 per cent. of the children.. suffered from..eye disease. **1930** *Times Educ. Suppl.* 28 June 289/3 One teacher..wearied to despair by the listlessness and lack of interest of his class of 'leavers', persuaded his head to allow him to hire an allotment. **1969** R. LAYARD et al. *Impact of Robbins* 121 The numbers of entrants to arts faculties are expressed as a percentage of leavers with arts A levels and similarly for science. **1972** *Guardian* 3 Aug. 6/6 Employers..were most favourably impressed with leavers' basic art and design skills.

leaver, obs. form of LEVER.

Leavers: see LEVERS.

leavetail, obs. form of LEEFTAIL *a. dial.*

leave-taking ('liːv,teɪkɪŋ), *vbl. sb.* [f. LEAVE *sb.*[1]] The taking leave of a person; saying farewell; †parting speech.

1375 BARBOUR *Bruce* II. 143 [He] passyt furth but leve-taking. *c***1564** LADY MARY SIDNEY *Let. to her Son* in Symonds *Sir P. Sidney* (1889) 16 And for a final leave-taking for this time, see that you show yourself a loving obedient scholar to your good master. **1605** SHAKS. *Macb.* II. iii. 150 And let vs not be daintie of leaue-taking, But shift away. **1838** POE *A. G. Pym* xx, We had agreed..to pay a formal visit of leave-taking to the village.

attrib. **1796** CHARLOTTE SMITH *Marchmont* III. 256 Mrs. Glaston, without repeating the usual leave-taking compliments, departed. **1828** *Lights & Shades* II. 182 The Captain urged Charles to deliver a final leavetaking letter to Emily.

leaving ('liːvɪŋ), *vbl. sb.* [f. LEAVE *v.* + -ING[2].]

1. The action of the vb. LEAVE in various senses. Also in Comb. with advs., as *leaving-off*.

*c***1380** WYCLIF *Sel. Wks.* III. 350 For leevyng of dedis of charite shulde he noþing be blamed. **1450–1530** *Myrr. our Ladye* 38 And yet yf he lefte yt vnsayde he shulde synne more greuosly, what shall he then do syth he synneth bothe in the doyng & in the leueynge. **1526** *Pilgr. Perf.* (W. de W. 1531) 27 b, Not carnally vnderstandynge this rewarde, for than, for the leuyng of one wyfe thou sholdest haue an hondred wyues. **1539** TONSTALL *Serm. Palm Sund.* (1823) 97 To the Thessalonicense he writeth..Pray without any day leauynge of. **1663** GERBIER *Counsel* 27 Never..suffer them to begin their Scafflings in the morning, but before their leaving of their work. **1719** DE FOE *Crusoe* II. iv. (1840) 85 They..went in by ways of their own leaving. **1834** SIR W. NAPIER *Penins. War* XIV. iv. (Rtldg.) II. 250 His leaving of Mr. Stuart without instructions. **1861** TRENCH *7 Ch. Asia* 77 The suggestion that this leaving of the first love can refer to the abating of any other love.

2. *concr.* †**a.** *sing.* What is left; remainder, residue, remains.

*a***1340** HAMPOLE *Psalter* Cant. 496, I soght þe lefynge of my ȝeris. *c***1425** *Crafte of Nombrynge* (E.E.T.S.) 18 Medye þat þe quych leues after þe takyinge away of þat þat is odde, þe quych leuynge schalle be 3. *c***1450** LONELICH *Grail* xlviii. 468 To aleyn token they Ageyn the leveng Of that fisch In Certeyn. **1596** B. GRIFFIN *Fidessa* (1876) 35, I am no leauing of al-withering age.

b. *pl.* in the same sense (Cf. L. *reliquiæ*, which the Eng. word often translates in early examples.)

*a***1340** HAMPOLE *Psalter* xvi. 16 Þai left þaire leuyngis till þaire smale. **1432–50** tr. *Higden* (Rolls) I. 97 Off the levenges of whiche cite, after the seyenge of Seynte Ierom, ij. cities were made in Persida. **1526** TINDALE Mark viii. 20 Howe many baskettes of the leavinges of broken meate toke ye up. **1552** HULOET, Leuynges or thinges left, *reliquiæ*. **1555–8** PHAER *Æneid* III. F iv, The leauinges of Achilles wyld. **1580** HOLLYBAND *Treas. Fr. Tong, Fanfreluches*, riffe raffe, the leauings or shreds of any thing. **1611** MIDDLETON & DEKKER *Roaring Girl* III. ii, To dine on my scraps, my leavings. **1646** JENKYN *Remora* 28 Shall God have Satans leavings? **1672** DRYDEN *Conq. Granada* I. i. Dram. Wks. (1725) 34 Now you have but the Leavings of my Will. **1686** HORNECK *Crucif. Jesus* v. 72 The poorer sort..carried the leavings or fragments home. **1742** RICHARDSON *Pamela* III. 215 Truly, she'd have none of Polly's Leavings; no, not she! *c***1790** IMISON *Sch. Art* II. 74 The student should make it a rule to save the leavings of his colours. **1834** MACAULAY *Biog., Pitt* (1866) 178 He gave only the leavings of his time and the dregs of his fine intellect. **1863** KINGSLEY *Water-Bab.* 5 His master let him have a pull at the leavings of his beer. **1867** M. ARNOLD *Sonn. Immortality* Poems 1877 I. 262 And will not, then, the immortal armies scorn The world's poor routed leavings? **1884** *Graphic* 23 Aug. 207/2 Their leavings—what they did not touch—made a luxurious supper for all my waiters.

†**c. leaving out**: what has been left out, omitted matter. *Obs.*

1683 MOXON *Mech. Exerc., Printing* xxii. ¶8 He may perhaps get a small word..into the foregoing Line; and.. another..in the following Line, which if his Leaving out is not much, may Get it in.

3. *attrib.*, esp. in the sense of leaving school or college, as in ***leaving certificate***, ***examination***, ***leaving scholarship***; **leaving-age**, the age at which a pupil is legally entitled to leave school; **leaving-book**, (at Eton) a book presented by friends on the occasion of one's 'leaving'; **leaving-shop** (*slang*), an unlicensed pawnshop. Also **leaving-off time**, the time of ceasing work.

1943 J. GRAVES *Policy & Progress Secondary Educ.* xix. 125 The curriculum would vary according to the normal *leaving age and the different interests and abilities of the children. **1878** SYMONDS *Shelley* 15 Hogg says that his Oxford rooms were full of handsome *leaving books, and that he was frequently visited by old Etonian acquaintances. **1879** *Mem. Cath. & Crauford Tait* 483 His popularity at Eton was attested by the exceptionally large number of leaving-books he got from his friends. **1884** *Times* (weekly ed.) 26 Sept. 4/1 No German or Saxon can enter the mining School at Freiberg..unless he have obtained a *leaving certificate at a gymnasium or a first-class Real School. **1892** *Daily News* 30 June 5/3 The Leaving Certificate Examination. **1914** 'I. HAY' *Lighter Side School Life* i. 24 Oxford and Cambridge Locals..or, in Scotland, the Leaving Certificate. **1923** J. D. HACKETT in *Management Engineering* May, *Leaving Certificate*, a card given to laid-off employees, entitling them to consideration when work is resumed. **1963** J. FOUNTAIN in B. James *Austral. Short Stories* 275 Brilliant passes in the Intermediate and Leaving Certificate examinations. **1971** *Guardian* 2 July 7/4 With an examination reform which provides a leaving certificate.. raising the school-leaving age to 16 would be a failure. **1893** *Athenæum* 21 Oct. 555/2 For all schools a common *leaving examination. **1907** *Westm. Gaz.* 26 Aug. 10/2 It is the usual practice at *leaving-off time on Saturdays for the workmen ..to cease work at once. **1889** *Nation* (N.Y.) 7 June 464/1 This sum includes the '*leaving' scholarship given by the Clothworkers' Company. **1865** DICKENS *Mut. Fr.* II. xii, Upon the smallest of small scales, she was an unlicensed pawnbroker, keeping what was popularly called a *Leaving Shop, by lending insignificant sums on insignificant articles of property deposited with her as security. **1888** *Spectator* 7 July 942 The 'leaving-shop', or illicit pawnbroker, almost frustrates attempts at protective legislation for the poor.

†'**leavish**. *Obs. rare*$^{-0}$. [f. LEAF *sb.*[1] (pl. *leaves*) + -ISH.]

1530 PALSGR. 317/1 Leavysshe full of leaves, *fueillu*.

Leavisian ('liːvɪsɪən), *sb.* and *a.* [f. the name of the English literary critic, Frank Raymond *Leavis* (b. 1895) + -IAN.] **A.** *sb.* An admirer or follower of F. R. Leavis. **B.** *adj.* Of, pertaining to, or characteristic of F. R. Leavis or his writings.

1959 *Times Lit. Suppl.* 1 May 256/2 There are Leavisians, there are Empsonians, but, as an embattled band, preaching and practising the Master's doctrine, there are no Ricardians. **1963** *Ibid.* 17 May 357/1 The Arnoldian and Leavisian concern with 'high seriousness'. **1964** *Punch* 29 Apr. 624/2 The phrase 'quality of life'..is something of a Leavisian stock response. **1969** *Listener* 16 Oct. 508/2 Many speakers brought a Leavisian passion and concern to the study of popular culture. They kept, in other words, to a view of art as a humanising study. **1972** *Times Lit. Suppl.* 19 May 577/2 The Leavisian conceptual articulation is compact, powerful and cogent.

Leavisite ('liːvɪsaɪt), *a.* and *sb.* = LEAVISIAN *sb.* and *a.*

1958 *Times Lit. Suppl.* 17 Jan. 30/4 Mr Wain is still involved with Leavisite criticism. **1962** *Listener* 6 Sept. 364/2 The pages about which the Leavisite, or the general reader, may feel himself below G.C.E. 'O'-level on the Snow line are, happily, few. **1963** A. HARTLEY *State of England* ii. 50 Dr. Leavis seems to have been one of the rare contemporary examples of a teacher conveying a view of life to his pupils... The word 'Leavisite' is not an empty one. **1969** *Sunday Times* (Colour Suppl.) 21 Dec. 25/4 Arnoldians, Leavisites, Marxists, Fabians, Buberites were all free to get on with it. **1970** *Guardian* 16 Sept. 10/3 You can't go on writing Leavisite criticism when you've reviewed everything that relates to the great tradition.

leavy ('liːvɪ), *a.* [Earlier and more normal form of LEAFY.]

1. Having leaves; covered with leaves or foliage. *Obs.* exc. *poet.*

*c***1420** *Pallad. on Husb.* IV. 486 With leuy bowis puld ek let hem be By nyght. *c***1586** C'TESS PEMBROKE *Ps.* XCVI. vi, Leavy infants of the wood. **1608** SHAKS. *Per.* V. i. 51 The leauie shelter that abutts against the Islands side. **1634** MILTON *Comus* 278 Dim darknes, and this leavy Labyrinth. **1651–3** JER. TAYLOR *Serm. for Year* I. xxi. 266 So doth the humble vine creep at the foot of an oak..and [they] are the most remarkable of friends..of all the leavie nation. **1745** tr. *Columella's Husb.* IX. ix, A green leavy little tree. **1832** TENNYSON *Margaret* v, And faint, rainy lights are seen, Moving in the leavy beech. **1833** —— *Poems* 42, I heard.. The nightingale in leavy woods Call to its mate.

†**b.** Of a season: Abounding in foliage. *Obs.*

1599 SHAKS. *Much Ado* II. iii. 75 The fraud of men were euer so, Since summer first was leauy.

c. Consisting of or made of leaves (either natural or ornamental).

1610 G. FLETCHER *Christ's Vict.* I. xix, He fled thy sight, ..And for his shield a leavie armour weav'd. **1611** COTGR., *Fueillure*..; also, leafe-worke, or a leauie flourishing.

†**2.** Of a gate: Having leaves. *Obs.*

*c***1611** CHAPMAN *Iliad* VI. 86 Take the key, vnlocke the leauie gates.

Hence †'**leaviness**, leafiness.

1611 COTGR., *Fueillure*, Leauinesse. **1687** RYCAUT *Contn. Knolles' Hist. Turks* II. 252 The shady leaviness of two tall elms.

leaward, obs. form of LEEWARD.

leaze, variant of LEASE *sb.*[1], *v.*[1], *v.*[2]

leazing, variant of LEASING *Obs.*, lying.

‖**leban** ('lɛbæn). Also **lebban**, **leben**. [Arab. *laban*, from a root meaning 'to be white'.] A drink in use among the Arabs, consisting of coagulated sour milk.

1698 *Phil. Trans.* XIX. 158 Leben, (a thick sour Milk).. is a thing in mighty esteem in these hot Countries, being very useful to quench Thirst. **1756** *Gentl. Mag.* XXVI. 345 Their breakfast..in winter is fryed eggs, cheese, honey or leban. **1847** DISRAELI *Tancred* IV. ii, Sheikh Salem will never drink leban again. **1880** L. WALLACE *Ben-Hur* 231, I have bread and leben.

Lebanese (lɛbə'niːz), *sb.* and *a.* [f. *Leban-on* + -ESE.] **A.** *sb.* A native or inhabitant of Lebanon;

also *collect.* **B.** *adj.* Of or pertaining to Lebanon or its inhabitants.

1920 *Glasgow Herald* 5 Apr. 6 The Lebanese..have..dissociated themselves entirely from the action of the Syrian Congress. **1926** *Contemp. Rev.* Feb. 194 A distinguished Lebanese Druse. **1927** *Times* (Weekly ed.) 25 Aug. 208/3 Many..Lebanese residing in Egypt became French subjects. **1957** M. Banton *W. Afr. City* v. 77 The Lebanese and Indians are not numerous. **1972** M. J. Bosse *Incident at Naha* i. 39, I..accepted some authentic Lebanese hash. **1972** *Times* 27 June 9/1 Pressures within Lebanon to get them [*sc.* Palestine guerrilla forces] to leave Lebanese territory. **1973** *Guardian* 21 May 4/7 If the fighting had kept going, they would have been obliged to join in: Lebanese against Lebanese.

lebarde, leberde, obs. forms of LEOPARD.

lebbek ('lɛbɛk). Also labakh, lebba(c)k, lebbakh, lebbeck, lebek. [ad. Arab. *labak̲.*] A large deciduous tree, *Albizia lebbeck*, of the family Leguminosæ, native to the tropics of north Africa and Asia and bearing heads of yellowish-white flowers; = SIRIS a.

1766 tr. *Hasselquist's Voyages & Travels in Levant* 249 Acacia of Upper Egypt... The Arabs call it Lebbeck. **1803** W. Wittman *Travels in Turkey* xiv. 346 In the vicinity of Cairo..a species of the cassia fistula grows to a considerable height, and affords a very agreeable shade... By the Arabs this tree is called lebback. **1916** J. B. Cooper *Coo-oo-ee* xvii. 253 The troops went past them, down the long avenue of lebbakhs. **1920** E. H. Jones *Road to En-Dor* (ed. 2) iv. 39 Along the long, straight road near Cairo..there was an avenue of lebbak trees. **1921** *Blackw. Mag.* Feb. 155/1 They drove out through the eight-mile tunnel of lebbek-trees. **1929** Broun & Massey *Flora Sudan* 174 *A[lbizzia] Lebbek* Benth. Labakh, Lebbek. **1942** C. Barrett *On Wallaby* vi. 134 The lebek trees were in bloom and delicate foliage rippled in the cool wind. **1965** Zand & Videan tr. *'Abd al-Laṭīf al-Baghdādī's Eastern Key* 33 While the fruit of the labakh is green it has a styptic savour like a green date, but when it is ripe it becomes sweet and agreeable, and takes on a viscous quality.

‖**Lebensform** ('leːbənsfɔrm). Pl. Lebensformen. [G., 'form of life'. Used notably by L. Wittgenstein in the German text of his *Philos. Investigations.*] Any type of human activity that involves values, e.g. the artistic or political or religious life; gen., a style or aspect of life.

1937 G. W. Allport *Personality* viii. 231 These Lebensformen are at best only *categories* of value. **1959** *Times Lit. Suppl.* 11 Sept. 513/2 Mr. Stuart Hampshire in *Thought and Action* is aware of the scale of his undertaking. 'It is necessary first,' he says, 'to view the using of language as a particular form of human behaviour' (Wittgenstein called it *Lebensform*).

‖**Lebenslust** ('leːbənzlʊst). [G., = joy of living.] = JOIE DE VIVRE.

1890 W. James *Let.* 22 Aug. in R. B. Perry *Tht. & Char. W. James* (1935) I. 414 Your last two letters..breathed a spirit of youth, a sort of *Lebenslust.* **1958** P. De Vries *Mackerel Plaza* 84 Security he could give her, yes, but not, I'm afraid, something else demanded by her *Lebenslust.* **1963** *Economist* 19 Oct. 228/2 As long as the *Lebenslust* continues to drive him regularly into Bonn.

‖**lebensraum** ('leːbənzraʊm). Also **L-**. [G., f. genit. of *leben* life + *raum* space.] Territory which the Germans believed was needed for their natural development (now *Hist.*). Also *transf.*

1905 *Mind* XIV. 266 A universal activity..forms an all-comprehending *Lebensraum* in which the manifold may meet and enter into relation. **1935** [see *life-space* s.v. LIFE *sb.* 16 a]. **1939** O. Lancaster *Homes Sweet Homes* 46 These treasures were joined on..overcrowded ledges by a new wave of invaders..and..the problem of *lebensraum* had become acute. **1939** A. Salter *Dual Policy* 25 *Lebensraum*, or a place in the sun, is the historic claim and ambition of Germany, as 'encirclement' is her historic anxiety. **1939** *War Illustr.* 9 Dec. 393/1 Moravia and Bohemia had been overrun by the Nazi armies and declared German Protectorates—part of the German people's 'lebensraum'. **1940** [see APPEASEMENT 4]. **1951** S. van Valkenburg in G. Taylor *Geogr. in 20th Cent.* iv. 109 Kurt Vohwinkel (..1939)..distinguishes three kinds of German *Lebensraum.* The first kind is the real area occupied solidly by Germans; the second the area where besides Germans there are other people but the German cultural influence prevails; and the third is the one in which Germans are outnumbered by others but still because of their racial and cultural superiority have a right to dominate. **1957** *Encycl. Brit.* VIII. 881/2 Hitler was convinced that..Germany..needed Russian territory for *Lebensraum.* **1959** *Listener* 25 June 1119/1 People, both white and black, either intent on gain or simply seeking *lebensraum* and resolved not to share it. **1960** *Guardian* 14 Mar. 6/6 Music, manuscripts, and her little daughter's toys compete amiably for *lebensraum.* **1960** *Times* 30 May 13/6 Lebensraum for the Japanese. **1972** W. A. Pantin *Oxf. Life* iv. 49 The problem of *Lebensraum* for the developing natural sciences..was already beginning to appear in the early-nineteenth-century minutes of the Hebdomadal Council.

‖**lebensspur** ('leːbənsʃpuːr). Also with capital initial. Usu. as *pl.* **lebensspuren.** [a. G. *lebensspur* (O. Abel *Grundzüge der Palaeobiol. der Wirbeltiere* (1912) 65), f. *leben* life + *spur* trace, track, remains (cogn. w. SPOOR *sb.*[1]).] A small track, burrow, cast, or the like left in sediment by a living organism; *esp.* one preserved in fossil form in sedimentary rock.

1960 *Gloss. Geol.* (Amer. Geol. Inst.) Suppl. 37/2 Lebensspur. **1962** R. C. Moore *Treat. Invertebr. Paleont.* W. 178/2 Lebensspuren are very transient structures as compared with shells, skeletons, or other hard parts, and in general they have little chance of being preserved as fossils. *Ibid.* 179/2 Many fossils..which have now been identified as Lebensspuren, were considered to be remains of marine algae. **1964** Pettijohn & Potter *Atlas & Gloss. Primary Sedimentary Struct.* Plate 70A (*heading*) Lebensspuren on underside of sandstone. **1973** *Nature* 30 Mar. 323/2 In a recently completed series of laboratory studies, lebensspuren were produced by individual macrobenthic organisms on a variety of marine sand and mud substrates (freshly collected from..the Bristol Channel) from which all other macrofauna had been removed by passing it through a 1·0 mm mesh. But the resultant tracks, trails and burrows gradually disappeared when the aquarium tanks..were left undisturbed.

‖**Lebenswelt** ('leːbənzvɛlt). [Ger.] = *life-world* (see LIFE *sb.* 17).

1962 A. W. Levi *Lit., Philos. & Imagination* 138 What Husserl has called the *Lebenswelt*—the ongoing continuity of 'lived' experience. **1964** *Amer. Philos. Q.* I. 127/1 According to Wild the *Lebenswelt* is the world of direct, lived experience. **1966** *Philos. Rev.* LXXV. 394 Husserl's transcendental philosophy and..his concept of the *Lebenswelt.*

Leber ('leɪbə(r)). *Ophthalm.* The name of Theodor *Leber* (1840–1917), German ophthalmologist, used in the possessive esp. in **Leber's disease,** hereditary optic atrophy, a rare hereditary disease in which partial blindness in both eyes sets in rapidly, typically affecting young men; also called *Leber's* (*hereditary optic*) *atrophy.*

1890 Billings *Med. Dict.* II. 41/2 *Leber's disease*, hereditary optic atrophy. **1902** *Encycl. Medica* X. 358 Possibly the family cases known as Leber's atrophy may come under this heading. **1932** *Times Lit. Suppl.* 5 May 334/4 The theoretical analysis is applied to statistics of albinism, colour blindness, haemophilia and Leber's disease. **1952** C. P. Blacker *Eugenics* x. 248 Among these genes [located on the human sex chromosomes] are those believed to determine:..Leber's optic atrophy, a progressive form of blindness. **1971** Duke-Elder & Scott in S. Duke-Elder *Syst. Ophthalm.* XII. ii. 108 Leber's hereditary optic atrophy is a relatively rare condition of unknown ætiology. *Ibid.*, In the main Leber's disease is hereditary.

‖**leberwurst** ('leːbərvʊrst, 'leɪbəwɜːst). [G.] = *liver sausage.*

1855 Geo. Eliot in *Fraser's Mag.* June 706/1 Goethe..is enthusiastic about the delights of dining on blaukraut and leberwurst (blue cabbage and liver sausage). **1969** [see BLUTWURST]. **1971** R. Petrie *Thorne in Flesh* iii. 40 A packet of cane spaghetti and a jar of leberwurst.

‖**lebes** ('lɛbiːz). *Gr. Antiq.* [Gr. λέβης.] A deep round-bottomed bowl, usually set on a stand, for holding wine; often used as a wedding-gift (*lebes gamikos*).

1851 *Catal. Greek & Etruscan Vases Brit. Mus.* I. 34 Lebes..Clay ash-coloured; varnish black and maroon, [etc.]. **1885** *Encycl. Brit.* XIX. 614/1 (*caption*) On the left is a gilt pyxis with a tall lid, and an œnochoe on a low table; on the right two tall vases (lebes) on a plinth. **1935** Richter & Milne *Shapes & Names Athenian Vases* 9 *Lebes* (Greek λέβης), deep bowl with round bottom, made to be set on a stand. *Ibid.* 11 *Lebes gamikos* (Greek λέβης γαμικός), 'marriage bowl'. High foot, double handles on the shoulder, the bowl in one piece with the foot. **1937** *Antiquity* XI. 246 The large nuptial lebes. **1974** Savage & Newman *Illustr. Dict. Ceramics* 177 *Lebes* (Greek), a type of bowl of Greek pottery used for mixing wine and water. It is ovoid in form and has a high shoulder, a low neck, and two vertical handles; it usually has a rounded bottom and rests on a stand.

Leblanc[1] (ləblɑ̃). Also **LeBlanc**. The name of Nicolas *Leblanc* (1742–1806), French chemist, used *attrib.* to designate a (now obsolete) process for the manufacture of sodium carbonate in which sodium chloride is treated with hot concentrated sulphuric acid to form the sulphate ('salt-cake'), which is then heated with limestone and coal and the resulting carbonate dissolved out with water.

[**1864** *Chem. News* 5 Mar. 111/1 (*heading*) Theoretical researches on the preparation of soda by Leblanc's process.] **1880** G. Lunge *Theoret. & Pract. Treat. Manuf. Sulphuric Acid & Alkali* II. iv. 361 (*heading*) The manufacture of soda by the Leblanc process. **1930** J. A. Timm *Introd. Chem.* xxxiii. 438 During the 75 years which followed, the LeBlanc process grew to be a great industry, spreading to Germany, Austria, and England. **1965** D. Abbott *Inorg. Chem.* iv. 157 Sodium sulphate is manufactured by the first stage of the Leblanc process.

Leblanc[2] (ləblɑ̃). *Electr. Engin.* The name of Maurice *Leblanc* (1857–1923), French electrical engineer, used *attrib.* to designate apparatus invented by him, as **Leblanc connection,** a method of connecting three single-phase transformer windings to convert three-phase current to two-phase; **Leblanc exciter** or **phase advancer,** a device for advancing the phase of the rotor current of an induction motor, consisting of a direct-current armature and commutator, having three sets of brushes per pair of poles connected to the slip rings of the main motor, and driven somewhat faster than the main motor.

1924 M. Walker *Control of Speed & Power Factor of Induction Motors* vii. 117 The Leblanc exciter, consisting of an armature built like a continuous current armature and excited by the rotor currents following either the armature itself or in a field magnet surrounding the armature. **1948** M. G. Say *Performance & Design Alternating Current Machines* (ed. 2) v. 68 The Le Blanc connection has the advantage of using a standard three-phase transformer core. **1965** J. Hindmarsh *Electr. Machines* ix. 492 (*heading*) Leblanc phase advancer. **1966** Brosan & Hayden *Adv. Electr. Power & Machines* vi. 243 In the Leblanc connexion there are three magnetic cores, and the primary windings may be connected in either star or delta. *Ibid.* x. 476 Another method of power factor control utilizes the Leblanc exciter. **1968** A. R. Daniels *Performance Electr. Machines* v. 97 An alternative method of 3/2 phase conversion is the Leblanc connection.

Leboyer (ləbwaje). *Obstetr.* The name of Frédérick *Leboyer* (b. 1918), French obstetrician, used *attrib.* and *absol.* with reference to the manner of childbirth advocated by him (in *Birth without Violence* (1975)), involving gentle delivery and handling with minimum intervention and minimum stimulation of the baby.

1976 *N.Y. Times* 27 Mar. 30 One couple wanted their baby to have a Leboyer bath, but the baby didn't even want to leave his mother's arms for that long. **1977** *Sci. News* 22 Jan. 59 If additional follow-up studies continue to show beneficial effects for children born the Leboyer way, it seems likely that nonviolent delivery may become an accepted way of birth. **1979** Adams & Lee in D. Harvey *New Life* vi. 94 By keeping both light and noise at a low level, the Leboyer approach is designed to ease the trauma of birth for the baby. **1980** S. Kitzinger *Pregnancy & Childbirth* 275 An important part of the Leboyer style of birth is the warm bath in which the baby is supported shortly after delivery. **1986** M. Stoppard *Pregnancy & Birth Handbk.* ii. 34/1 Medical authorities have been slow to adopt Leboyer because research has shown that Leboyer babies appear to receive no extra benefit compared to others.

leburd(e, variant of LEE-BOARD[1] *Obs.*

lecage, obs. form of LEAKAGE.

lecam, variant of LICHAM *Obs.*, body, corpse.

lecanomancy ('lɛkənəʊmænsɪ). Also 7 lican-, lecon-. [ad. Gr. λεκανομαντεία, f. λεκάνη dish, pan, pot (f. λέκος of the same meaning) + μαντεία divination. Cf. F. *leconomantie* (Rabelais).] Divination by the inspection of water in a basin.

1610 Healey *St. Aug. Citie of God* 294 Hydromancy..done..in a basin of water, which is called Lecanomancie. **1613** Purchas *Pilgrimage* (1614) 366 They had also their Lecanomancie, which was observed in a Bason of Water, wherein certaine plates of golde and silver were put with Iewels, marked with their jugling Characters. **1656** Blount *Glossogr.*, *Licanomancy.* *a* **1693** *Urquhart's Rabelais* III. xxv. 207 By Hydromancy, by Leconomancy. **1783** T. Wilson *Archæol. Dict.*, *Lecanomancy.*

So †**lecanomancer,** †**lecanomantic** *Obs.*$^{-0}$, one who practises lecanomancy.

1623 Cockeram, *Leconomanticke.* **1670** Blount *Glossogr.*, *Lecanomancer*, a diviner by water in a bason.

lecanoric (lɛkə'nɒrɪk), *a. Chem.* [f. *Lecanora*, the name of a genus of lichens.] *lecanoric acid*: a crystalline substance obtained by Schunck from certain members of the genus *Lecanora* of lichens. Hence **lecanorate** (-'ɔərət), a salt of lecanoric acid; **lecanorin** (-'ɔərɪn) = *lecanoric acid.*

1844 Fownes *Chem.* 488 Fresh dye-lichens, exhausted by ether, yield a crystalline substance, which when purified by solution in alcohol, is perfectly white; to this the name *lecanorine* has been given. **1852** *Ibid.* (ed. 4) 577 Boiled with water for some time, erythric acid absorbs 2 eq. and yields picro-erythrin..and a new acid..which is termed by some chemists lecanoric, by others orsellinic acid. **1865** Watts *Dict. Chem.* III. 565 The lecanorates gradually decompose, especially when heated, yielding orsellinic acid, and ultimately orcin.

lecanorine (lɛkə'nɔːərɪn), *a. Bot.* [f. *Lecanora* (see prec.) + -INE.] Resembling the apothecium of the genus *Lecanora* of lichens. So **leca'noroid** *a.*

1871 Leighton *Lichen-flora* 5 Apothecia lecanorine. *Ibid.* 241 Apothecia pale, plane, lecanoroid.

leccer ('lɛkə(r)). Also **lecker, lekker.** [-ER[6].] Slang or colloquial alteration of LECTURE *sb.* (See also quot. 1900.)

1899 *Daily Tel.* 14 Aug., *Leccers*, lectures. **1900** Farmer *Public School Word-bk.* 124 *Lecker*, 1. (Oxford). A lecture. 2. (Harrow). The electric light. **1904** [see -ER *suffix*[6]]. **1907** 'B. Burke' *Barbara goes to Oxf.* (1915) 115 I'm awfully sorry that I had to cut your leccer, my mother came up quite unexpectedly. **1911** W. Elmhirst *Freshman's Diary* (1969) 10 Had 1st leccer from the Dean this morning. *Ibid.* 11 Had a caller, who..said good night saying we should meet in another sphere what one I don't know as he said he didn't row & he certainly doesn't come to P.Mods leccers. **1914** C. Mackenzie *Sinister St.* II. III. viii. 455 And you won't come out..to watch people buying copies on their way to leckers? **1928** *Daily Express* 29 June 5/3 A..dilapidated basket filled with gay-coloured 'lekker' notebooks.

lecche, obs. form of LEACH *v.*[1], LEECH *sb.*[1]

lecchour, obs. form of LECHER.

lece, obs. form of LEASH.

† **lech**, *sb.*[1] *Obs.* Also 3 læch, laich. [App. to be identified (in spite of the difficult form *laichen*, which may be corrupt) with OE. *léc* masc., cogn. w. *lócian* to LOOK.] A look, glance.

[*c* **1000** ÆLFRIC *Hom.* (Thorpe) II. 374 Wo sceolon awendan urne lec fram yfelre ȝesihþe, ure hlyst fram yfelre spræce.] *c* **1205** LAY. 1884 Laðliche læches heo leiteðeni mid eȝan. *Ibid.* 3410 He..þas worde seide mid seorhfulle laichen. *Ibid.* 13703 Mid his lechen he gon liȝen. [Often elsewhere in LAY.] *a* **1250** *Owl. & Night.* 1138 þine leches beoþ grisliche þe hwile þu art on lif-daȝe.

lech (lɛk), *sb.*[2] [ad. W. *llech* (flat) stone = Ir., Gael. *leac.* Cf. CROMLECH.] A Celtic monumental stone.

1768–9 J. CLELAND *Spec. Etym. Vocab.* 134 A Lech differs from a Cromlech, in that it means the top-stone of a Cromlech, or any sacred stone; whereas Cromlech expresses its adjunct stones and circle underneath it. **1899** BARING-GOULD *Bk. West* II. 28 [St. Patrick] did not overthrow their lechs or pillar-stones.

‖ **lech** (lɛç), *sb.*[3] [Ger.] (See quot. 1753.)

1753 CHAMBERS *Cycl. Supp.*, *Lech*, in metallurgy, a term used by the miners to express the gold ore which has been powdered, and washed, and afterwards run with the assistance of lime stone. **1756–7** tr. *Keysler's Trav.* (1760) IV. 229 The Schemnitz ore contains a greater quantity of gold..than that of Cremnitz; but the hard ore of the latter yields more lech.

lech (lɛtʃ), *sb.*[4] Also letch. [Now regarded as a back-formation from LECHER *sb.*, but cf. LETCH *sb.*[2]] **a.** A strong desire or longing, esp. sexual. **b.** = LECHER *sb.*

1796 [see LETCH *sb.*[2]]. *c* **1830** *Venus School Mistress* Pref. in 'Pisanus Fraxi' *Index Librorum Prohibitorum* (1877) 399 It [*sc.* flagellation] is, however, a *lech*, which has existed from time immemorial. **1868** *Index expurgatorius of Martial* 39 There are various rumours as to the nature of your letch. *c* **1888–94** *My Secret Life* III. 147 Did they fuck with me for fun, for letch, or for money? **1934** G. GREENE *It's a Battlefield* 204 This is when a girl gets a baby; when she's got a lech like this. **1938** S. BECKETT *Murphy* vii. 126 A man could no more work a woman out of her position on her own ground of sentimental lech than he cd outsmell a dog. **1940** S. LEWIS *Bethel Merriday* xxxiii. 387 Your letch for power over everyone around you. **1941** 'R. WEST' *Black Lamb* II. 204 Those who had a lech for violence could gratify it. **1943** H. A. SMITH *Life in Putty Knife Factory* x. 157 If anybody noticed what I was doing, they'd think I was an old letch. **1956** E. POUND tr. *Sophocles' Women of Trachis* 17 All started when he had a letch for the girl. **1958** *Spectator* 10 Oct. 482/1 A post-war working-class family..—the grey letch of a father, his jolly rolypoly wife and their prissy daughter. **1959** J. BRAINE *Vodi* xix. 220, I don't mind admitting I always had a lech for her. **1960** *Times Lit. Suppl.* 27 May 333/4 Graves is 'a lech', whose current mistress is Purling's wife, Jo. **1964** [see DROOL *v.*]. **1970** *Guardian* 13 Feb. 9/6 A rich man can have a beautiful young wife even if he is a gropy old letch! **1971** *Petticoat* 17 July 7/1 Out of ten girls who are invited back to men's flats for coffee, at least eight expect a cup of coffee and are quite shocked and horrified when they find themselves pinned to the bed, five seconds after walking into the lech's lair. **1972** *Sunday Times* 12 Nov. 40/3 Many so-called platonic friendships.. are merely one-way leches.

Lech, Lekh (lɛx), *sb.*[5] and *a.* Also Lach, L'ach (ʎax). [ad. G. *Lech*, O.Russ. *lyakh*; f. O.Pol. **lęch.*] **A.** *sb.* A member of an early Slavonic people once inhabiting the region around the upper Oder and Vistula, whose descendants are the Poles; also, the name of a legendary ancestor of this people. **B.** *adj.* Of or pertaining to the Lechs or their language. Cf. LECHISH *sb.* and *a.*, LECHITIC *sb.* and *a.*

1893 W. R. MORFILL *Poland* 23 In the sixth or seventh centuries some people settled on that river [*sc.* the Vistula] are called Lekhs, a word which has never been satisfactorily explained. The older form probably had a nasal: hence we get in the Latin chroniclers *Lenchitæ*, in Lithuanian, *Lenkas*, and in Magyar, *Lengyel.* **1911** *Encycl. Brit.* XXV. 236/2 In the north Polish is closely connected with Kašube, and this with Polab, making the group of L'ach dialects in which the nasals survived... The two Sorb dialects link the L'achs on to the Čechs and Slovaks, the whole making the N.W. group with its preference for *c, z, s* as against *č, ž, š.* **1929** *Ibid.* XVIII. 161/2 The nearest relative of Polish is Polabian, with which it forms the Lech group. **1939** G. SLOCOMBE *Hist. Poland* (new ed.) 12 The Western Slavs had become divided into three distinct sections: the Serbs..; the Czech group..; and the Lech group, in which were included the Obodrites, the Wiltzi, the Pomeranians.., and other tribes who were in the course of the succeeding centuries to form the Polish nation. **1950** A. P. GOUDY in *Cambr. Hist. Poland to 1696* i. 10 Besides the name Polanie, there existed another collective name—Lachy (Lechs). This term is used in the Chronicle of Nestor to indicate the Poles and came into frequent use by the old chroniclers.

lech (lɛtʃ), *v.* Also letch. [Back-formation from LECHER *sb.*] *intr.* To behave lustfully, to feel or to be lecherous. Occas., to have a (non-sexual) desire.

1911 J. MASEFIELD *Everlasting Mercy* 68 And drunk and leched from day till morrow. **1940** E. POUND *Let.* 18 Jan. (1971) 334, I have now the text of Erigena, and *if* I could get hold of the recent publications about him, I could write quite a chunk. Not that I am letching to. **1948** PARTRIDGE *Dict. Forces' Slang* 110 Letch, to look at women, not necessarily in a lecherous way, in spite of its derivation. **1957** C. DAY LEWIS *Pegasus* 13 Unblest, Unchecked—what a serpent flame letched at her marrow! **1963** 'M. CORRIGAN' *Why do Women—?* xiii. 89, I..letch around looking for sex thrills. **1972** M. FARHI *Pleasure of your Death* vii. 173 He was still watching the..shapely ankles when Chastity pulled him to task. 'Don't lech!' **1973** *Guardian* 27 Feb. 10/1 A fortyish factory worker..lives with..an obsessively nubile sister whom he obviously leches after.

lech, obs. form of LEECH *sb.*[1]

lechaim, var. LECHAYIM.

lechardemane, obs. form of LEGERDEMAIN.

Le Chatelier (lə ʃæ'tɛljeɪ). [The name of Henry *Le Chatelier* (1850–1936), French chemist.]

a. Used *attrib.* with reference to a test for the soundness (freedom from expansion) of cement using a small hollow brass cylinder split longitudinally and having pointers close to the split which indicate the extent of any expansion that occurs when the cylinder is filled with cement.

1904 *Specification for Portland Cement (B.S.I.)* 7 The cement shall be tested by the Le Chatelier method, and shall in no case show a greater expansion than 12 millimetres after 24 hours aeration and 6 millimetres after seven days aeration. The apparatus for conducting the Le Chatelier test..consists of a small split cylinder of brass. **1930** *Engineering* 18 July 62/1 Dry clay when adsorbing water increased in bulk and exerted..sufficient pressure to spring open the Le Chatelier gauge about 1 lb. per square inch. **1963** A. M. NEVILLE *Properties of Concrete* i. 50 The Le Chatelier test detects unsoundness due to free lime only.

b. Used *attrib.* and in the possessive († and in conjunction with the name of K. Ferdinand *Braun* (1850–1918), German physicist) to designate a principle enunciated by Le Chatelier, which states that if a constraint (such as a change in pressure or temperature) be applied to any system in equilibrium, the equilibrium will shift in such a way as to tend to counteract the effect of the constraint.

1910 *Chem. Abstr.* IV. 1600 (*heading*) New isomerization of benzopinacolins and Le Chatelier's law. **1911** *Ibid.* V. 3361 The author gives the following as the usual statement of the Le Chatelier-Braun principle. **1922** *Proc. Amer. Acad. Arts & Sci.* LVII. 25 The condition which must be satisfied in order that the Le Chatelier Principle may hold with regard to the effect of a change in the initial mass of *one* component, is that the addition of such component shall accelerate or retard the transformation (at equilibrium). **1943** *Thorpe's Dict. Appl. Chem.* (ed. 4) VI. 229/1 It would be expected from the Le Chatelier-Braun principle of mobile equilibrium that increase of pressure would exert a retarding effect upon the rate of a uni-molecular reaction. **1954** A. R. BAILEY *Text-bk. Metall.* viii. 232 A reaction involving a gaseous reactant is favoured by increase in operating pressure, and one involving a gaseous product by decrease of pressure or by sweeping it away in a gas stream; these points also follow from Le Chatelier's Principle. **1961** A. HOLDERNESS *Inorg. & Physical Chem.* xviii. 258 If the temperature of an equilibrium system..is lowered, Le Chatelier's Principle requires the equilibrium to shift so as to tend to raise the temperature again; that is, to evolve heat. **1973** *Jrnl. Chem. Education* L. 124 Since stretching a rubber band is an exothermic process, Le Chatelier's principle predicts that heat applied to a stretched rubber band will contract it.

lechatelierite (ləʃə'tɛlɪəraɪt, ləʃətɛ'lɪəraɪt). *Min.* Also † -iérite. [a. F. *lechateliérite* (A. Lacroix 1915, in *Bull. de la Soc. franç. de Min.* XXXVIII. 185), f. LE CHATELIER + -ITE[1].] Naturally occurring vitreous silica, SiO_2, formed when siliceous material is intensely heated (as by lightning).

1916 *Mineral. Mag.* XVII. 353 *Lechatelierite*, naturally occurring fused (amorphous) silica. **1928** *Amer. Mineralogist* XIII. 77 Lechateliérite is unique in that it is the only naturally occurring glass that is definite enough to be considered a mineral. **1931** *Jrnl. R. Soc. W. Austral.* XVII. 146 Digging revealed a vertical core of lechatelierite in the soil. This core was hollow and very brittle, and extended downwards for about a metre. **1963** W. A. DEER et al. *Rock-Forming Min.* IV. 180 Silica glass (vitreous silica; lechatelierite): can exist at room temperatures and up to 1000°C... It is an unstable glass at all temperatures below 1713°C. **1964** *New Scientist* 16 Jan. 160/1 The invariable signs of flow and common presence of lechatelierite (pure silica glass) indicate that tektites were formed by rapid fusion at very high temperatures.

‖ **lechayim** (lə'xaɪɪm). Also l'chaim, l'chay(i)m, lechaim, lehayim. [Heb., 'to life'.] A drinking toast: to life!

1932 L. GOLDING *Magnolia St.* III. ix. 582 'Here's mud in your eye!' says the Chicagoan. '*Lechayim!* To Life!' says Mr. Emmanuel. **1963** *Encounter* Apr. 35/1 The guests stood and raising their glasses honoured me, in Hebrew, with that most beautiful of toasts: *Lechaim!* To life! **1968** M. RICHLER in R. Weaver *Canad. Short Stories* 2nd Ser. 193 'I been here seven years ago and what we done since, it's remarkable. *L'chaym.*' '*L'chaym.*' **1968** P. DURST *Badge of Infamy* iii. 23 Chaim raised his glass. 'Good health.' '*L'chaim,*' Michael returned. **1968** L. ROSTEN *Joys of Yiddish* 205 *L'chayim*, pronounced *l-KHY-im*, with a resounding German *kh*, to rhyme with 'to fry 'em'. Hebrew: 'To life.' The toast offered, with raised glass, before sipping wine or liquor: 'To your health.' **1973** *Jewish Chron.* 2 Feb. 16/4 Miss Kitt raised her wine-glass. 'L'chayim,' she said.

leche, obs. f. LEACH, LEECH, LICH, LIKE.

leche, var. LECHWE.

lecher ('lɛtʃə(r)), *sb.*[1] *arch.* Forms: 2–5 lechur, 3 -or, 3–6 -our, 4 lichur, -o(u)re, licchour, lec(c)houre, lech-, lychure, 4–5 lichour, lecchour, 5 lecheour(e, lechowr(e, -ir, -urre, lichir, -or, lycher, lehchour, 5–6 lychour, (6 leachour, lecherd, 7 lechard), 6–8 leacher, letcher, 5– lecher. [a. OF. *lecheor, -eur, -ur, liceour, lichieor*, also *lichard*, agent-n. f. *lechier* to live in debauchery or gluttony, mod.F. *lêcher* to lick = Pr. *lecar, lechar*, It. *leccare*, ad. OHG. *leccôn* (G. *lecken*):—OTeut. **likkôjan* to LICK.] A man immoderately given to sexual indulgence; a lewd or grossly unchaste man, a debauchee.

c **1175** *Lamb. Hom.* 53 þus heo doð for to feiren heom seoluen and to draȝe lechurs to ham. *a* **1225** *Ancr. R.* 216 þe lechur iðe deofles kurt bifuleð himsulf fulliche, & alle his feolawes. **1297** R. GLOUC. (Rolls) 7208 Prustes, mid vnclene honden & mid lechors mod Al isoyled. **13..** *K. Alis.* 3916 Fy, he saide, apon the lechour: Thou schalt dye as a traytour! *c* **1340** HAMPOLE *Prose Tr.* (1866) 11 The sexte commandement es 'Thou sall be na lichoure'. *c* **1375** *Cursor M.* 31 (Laud) Of chastyte the lechour [*Bedford MS.* þe lichore] hath lyte. *c* **1386** CHAUCER *Wife's Prol.* 242 Sir olde lecchour, lat thy Iapes be. *c* **1449** PECOCK *Repr.* I. xviii. 103 Summe ben founde..to be greet lecchouris, Summe to be avoutreris. **1470–85** MALORY *Arthur* XVIII. ii, Launcelot now I wel vnderstande that thou arte a fals recreaunt knyghte and a comyn lecheoure, and louest and holdest other ladyes. **1508** DUNBAR *Tua Mariit Wemen* 174 He has bene lychour so lang quhill lost is his natur. **1598** SHAKS. *Merry W.* III. v. 147, I will now take the Leacher: hee is at my house. **1603** FLORIO *Montaigne* (1634) 477 Of Concubines they [men] may have as many as they list, and women as many lechards. **1621** QUARLES *Esther* vi, The time is come, faire Ester must Expose her beauty to the Lecher's lust. **1697** DRYDEN *Virg. Georg.* III. 148 Half-surpriz'd, and fearing to be seen, The Leacher gallop'd from his jealous Queen. **1712** STEELE *Spect.* No. 502 ¶4 You see..old letchers, with mouths open, stare at the loose gesticulations on the stage with shameful earnestness. **1728** RAMSAY *Monk & Miller's Wife* 105 The haly letcher fled, And darn'd himsell behind a bed. **1763** CHURCHILL *Gotham* III. (1764) 23 Like a Virgin to some letcher sold. **1831** TRELAWNEY *Adv. Younger Son* II. 193 If she is poor, some old lechers, their dormant passions rekindled, beset her.

Lecher ('lɛçə(r), 'lɛtʃə(r)), *sb.*[2] *Physics.* Also lecher. The name of Ernst *Lecher* (1856–1926), Austrian physicist, used *attrib.* (esp. in ***Lecher wires***) and † in the possessive to designate a pair of parallel wires in which the frequency of a high-frequency electric oscillation may be measured by means of a sliding detector or conductor placed so as to bridge the wires, positions of maximum response or absorption being separated by a distance equal to half the wavelength of the oscillation.

1897 *Phil. Mag.* XLIV. 202 In Lecher's arrangement.. the wires are of equal diameter. **1902** *Encycl. Brit.* XXVIII. 59/2 Many problems of electric waves along wires can readily be investigated by a method due to Lecher, and known as Lecher's bridge. **1929** J. A. RATCLIFFE *Physical Princ. Wireless* iii. 35 A pair of parallel wires is often used to guide the waves, instead of the single wire... This arrangement is known as the Lecher wire system. **1947** *Jrnl. Inst. Electr. Engin.* XCIV. 953/2 The tuned circuit consisted of a pair of lecher rods, the output being fed through a resonant line to a fixed end-fed half-wave vertical aerial. **1962** W. B. THOMPSON *Introd. Plasma Physics* ii. 12 In arc discharges the electron density is $10^{11}-10^{12}$ cm^{-3} and the plasma frequency ~ 100 Mc/s, so the high-frequency signals were picked up on resonant Lecher wires, rectified by a crystal and detected by a galvanometer. **1968** *Radio Communication Handbk.* (ed. 4) xix. 12/2 Lecher lines.. comprise a pair of taut parallel wires, spaced an inch or so apart to form an open wire transmission line, and a bridge to short circuit the wires which can be moved along the line as required.

† '**lecher**, *a. Obs.* [attrib. use of LECHER *sb.*[1]] Lecherous; also in wider sense, base, vile.

c **1250** *Gen. & Ex.* 776 God sente on him sekenesse & care, And lettede al his lecher-fare. *Ibid.* 1064 Al ðat burȝt folc ðat helde was on, Ðe miȝte lecher crafte don. *a* **1300** *Cursor M.* 28528 Lechur sanges haf i wroght. *c* **1400** *Destr. Troy* 13037 Thus the lady was lost for hir lechir dedis. **1603** FLORIO *Montaigne* 511 Some..disgrace alight on his lawfull wife or on his lechard mistris.

Hence † '**lecherhed** [see -HEAD], lechery; † '**lecherlike**, † '**lecherly** *advs.*, lecherously; † '**lecherness**, lechery.

c **1250** *Gen. & Ex.* 770 Ðat folc luuede lecherlike. *Ibid.* 1997 He wulde don is lechur-hed wið ioseph, for hise faire-hed. *c* **1400** *Destr. Troy* 8059 The tothur lurkes in lychernes, & laghes ouerthwert. *Ibid.* 12604 þan Vlixes the lord, licherly þai saide, Preset [etc.]. *c* **1511** *1st Eng. Bk. Amer.* (Arb.) Introd. 27 The wymen be very hoote & dyposed to lecherdnes.

† '**lecher**, *v. Obs.* [f. LECHER *sb.*[1]] *intr.* To play the lecher. Hence † '**lechering** *ppl. a.*

1382 WYCLIF *Num.* xv. 39 Thei folowen not her owne thouȝtis and eyen, by dyuerse thingis lecheryngе. **1594** NASHE *Unfort. Trav.* 11 How he must..drinke carouse, and lecher with him out of whom he hopes to wring anie matter. **1605** SHAKS. *Lear* IV. vi. 114 The small gilded Fly Do's letcher in my sight. **1611** COTGR., *Foutre*, to leacher. **1631** DONNE *Polydoron* 130 To letcher is like the spider that spinns a webb out of his owne bowells; to swill and drinke in excesse, is to turne trype-wife and wash gutts. *a* **1693**

Urquhart's Rabelais III. xlviii. 392 A Lechering Rogue. **1756** *Demi-Rep* 31 If vanity or dress allure her mind To forfeit fame and letcher with Mankind.

lechere, obs. form of LEECHER.

† **'lecherer**. *Obs.* Also 5-6 lecherour. [? f. LECHER *sb.*: see -ER[1] 3.] = LECHER *sb.*

c **1380** WYCLIF *Wks.* (1880) 102 ȝif þei meyntenen.. leccherours of here owne meynne in here housholde. **1422** tr. *Secreta Secret., Priv. Priv.* 230 Tho that haue rogh leggis bene lechureris. **1496** *Dives & Paup.* (W. de W. 1531) v. xix. 222/2 Yf a clerke saye that it is lefull to slee.. lecherors.. he is yrreguler. **1575** R. B. *Appius & Virginia* D ij b, The Gods confound such lecherers. **1591** SPARRY tr. *Cattan's Geomancie* 36 He is.. a glutton, a leacherer. **1605** *Narr. Murthers Sir J. Fitz* (1860) 11 A roysting drunkard is most commonly noted for an incontinent lecherer.

attrib. **1494** FABYAN *Chron.* VI. ccx. 225 She hath.. nempned her lecherour leman Goddes owne preest.

lecherous ('lɛtʃərəs), *a. arch.* Forms: 4 licheros, lycher(o)us, le(t)cherouse, 4-5 leccherous, 4-6 licherous, 5 lychorous, luchrus, 5-6 lichorous, 6 lecheros, -us, licharus, leicherous, 6-8 letcherous, 4- lecherous. [a. OF. *lecheros*, etc., f. *lecheur* LECHER *sb.*: see -OUS. Cf. LICKEROUS.]

1. Addicted to lechery.

1303 R. BRUNNE *Handl. Synne* 7989 Þys was a prest ryȝt amerous—And amerous men are leccherous. *c* **1386** CHAUCER *Prol.* 626 As hoot he was, and lecherous, as a sparwe. *c* **1400** MAUNDEV. (Roxb.) xv. 69 Men er so prowde, so enuyous, so grete glotouns, and so licherous. **1500-20** DUNBAR *Poems* l. 41 He said he was ane licheruss bull, That croynd bayth day and nycht. **1577** tr. *Bullinger's Decades* (1592) 315 Nero that beast and lecherous monster. **1602** SHAKS. *Ham.* II. ii. 609 Remorselesse, Treacherous, Letcherous, kindles villaine! **1613** PURCHAS *Pilgrimage* (1614) 79 Semiramis.. a lecherous and bloudie woman was worshipped by the name of the Syrian Goddesse. **1773** BRYDONE *Sicily* xx. (1809) 213 Lazy, lying, lecherous monks. **1876** BLACKIE *Songs Relig. & Life* 125 Thy murderous, and lecherous race Have sat too long i' the holy place.

b. Of action, thought, etc.: Consisting in or characterized by lechery.

c **1330** R. BRUNNE *Chron.* (1810) 65 Licheros lif þei led. **1393** LANGL. *P. Pl.* C. VII. 194 Ich had lykynge to lauhe of lecherous tales. **1398** TREVISA *Barth. De P.R.* XVI. lxxxvii. (1495) 583 It chasteth lecherous meuynges and maketh good mynde. *a* **1400-50** *Alexander* 4328 And to na licherous lustes leeue ve oure membris. **1533** GAU *Richt Vay* 16 Thay ..thinkkis lichorous thochttis. **1567** *Gude & Godlie Ball.* (S.T.S.) 216 ȝit war his factis sa lichorus. **1611** COTGR., *Saffreté*, wanton dallying, leacherous ieasting, lasciuious toying. **1884** *Chr. Treasury* Feb. 97/2 Absalom's plot to assassinate his eldest brother had no justification in the lecherous crime of that guilty brother.

c. Of drink, etc.: Inciting to lechery.

1382 WYCLIF *Prov.* xx. 1 A leccherous thing win. *c* **1386** CHAUCER *Pard. T.* 221. **1393** LANGL. *P. Pl.* C. II. 25 Loth in hus lyue thorw lecherouse drynke Wykkydlich wroghte. **1596** DALRYMPLE tr. *Leslie's Hist. Scot.* II. 152 He sett out sum leicherous lawis, that his flagitious gairt.. mycht haue occasione frilie to louse a brydle to al thair appetites. **1632** SHERWOOD, Lecherous stuffe, *poudre agrippine.* [COTGR., *Pouldre Agrippine*, any meat, that prouokes, or enables, vnto lust.]

†**2.** = LICKEROUS: **a.** fond of good living, gluttonous; **b.** (of food) rich, dainty. *Obs.*

1474 CAXTON *Chesse* 112 The sight of the noble and lichorous metis. **1483** —— *G. de la Tour* B vij, How they ought not.. to yeue flesshe ne lychorous metes to houndes. *c* **1483** —— *Dialogues* viii. 33 *Car elle est moult gloutee*, For she is moche lichorous. **1535** STEWART *Cron. Scot.* (1858) II. 228 With gluttony and lichorous appetyte.

Hence **'lecherously** *adv.*, **'lecherousness**.

1340 *Ayenb.* 128 Þe guode mannes zone þet.. leuede lecherusliche. **1382** WYCLIF *Luke* xv. 13 There he wastide his substaunce in lyuynge leccherously. *c* **1450** *Mirour Saluacioun* 1651 One leccherously lyving consumes his substaunce. **1551** BIBLE *Isa.* Iii. Notes, They were.. dryuen into yᵉ profounde and deepe sleepe of ygnoraunce, of idlenes, of lecherousnesse, and of pride. **1591** PERCIVALL *Sp. Dict., Luxuriosamente*, lecherouslie. **1895** *Min. 9th Nat. Council Congreg. Ch. U.S.A.* 138 Laws against all manner of lecherousness. **1972** *Daily Tel.* 12 May 12/8 Amorous delusions concerning.. a lecherously attentive neighbour and her kindly but pre-occupied husband.

† **'lecherwite**, a perversion (after LECHER *sb.*) of OE. *leȝerwite* (see LAIRWITE).

1228 *Mem. Ripon* (Surtees) I. 52 Lecherwyt.

lechery ('lɛtʃərɪ). Forms: 3-5 leccherie, 3-7 lecherie, (3-5 -ye), 4 lechury(e, -ure, -uri, -yry, lec(c)heri, ? lecȝery, licchery, -ie, litcheri, lychory, -ery, -eri, -ore, luchery, 4-5 lecchery(e, lechory, -i(e, lichery, -ory, 4-6 licherie, 5 lecuri ?, 6 leicherie, luchrie, li-, lychorie, lichery, 6-7 letcherie, 7-8 -ery, leachery, 5- lechery. [a. OF. *lecherie, licherie*, f. *lecheur* LECHER *sb.*] Habitual indulgence of lust; lewdness of living. †Also, an instance of this.

c **1230** *Hali Meid.* 11 Þat is te lust of leccherie þat riuleð þer wiðinne. *c* **1250** *Gen. & Ex.* 3510 Oc horedom ðat ðu ne do, Ne wend no lecherie to. *a* **1300** *Cursor M.* 10046 (Cott.) Þe chastite o þis leuidi Ouercumms al lust o lecheri [*Gött.* lichery]. *c* **1340** *Ibid.* 6476 (Trin.) Do no lecchery bi no wommon. *c* **1380** WYCLIF *Serm.* Sel. Wks. II. 79 Of þe herte comen yvel þouȝtis, in yvel wordis; mansleyingis, avoutrieris, leccheries. *c* **1386** CHAUCER *Pars. T.* ¶762 After Glotonye thanne comth leccherie. *a* **1420** HOCCLEVE *De Reg. Princ.* 3656 Leccherye.. is hogges lif. *a* **1568** ASCHAM *Scholem.* I. (Arb.) 84 To waulter, with as litle shame, in open lecherie, as Swyne do here in the common myre. *a* **1586** SIDNEY *Arcadia* (1622) 225 The Faulcons fiercenesse, Sparrowes letcherie. **1606** SHAKS. *Tr. & Cr.* v. i. 106 Nothing but Letcherie? All incontinent Varlets. **1616** R. C. *Times' Whistle* VI. 2649 And this I holde, that secret letcherie Is a lesse sinne than close hypocrisie. **1822-34** *Good's Study Med.* (ed. 4) IV. 92 The Salacity of a Debauched Life, or lechery produced and confirmed by habit. **1888** *19th Cent.* July 40 A new *motif* for art has also been discovered in death, disease, and lechery.

personified. *c* **1400** *Rom. Rose* 3914 Over-al regnith Lecchery, Whos might yit growith night and day. **1500-20** DUNBAR *Poems* xxvi. 79 Lichery, that lathly corss, Berand lyk a bagit horss. **1590** SPENSER *F.Q.* I. iv. 24 And next to him rode lustfull Lechery Upon a bearded gote. **1640** YORKE *Union Hon.* 17 You cherish three daughters, Pride, Covetousnesse and Lechery.

b. *fig.*

c **1491** *Chast. Goddes Chyld.* x. 26 Of this pryde cometh a spirituel or ghostli lechery. **1606** DEKKER *Sev. Sinnes* I. (Arb.) 17 The Vsurer liues by the lechery on mony, and is Bawd to his owne bags. **1676** MARVELL *Mr. Smirke* Wks. 1875 IV. 77 [He] will violate the ecclesiastical secret rather than lose the leachery of his tattle. **1687** SETTLE *Refl. Dryden* 38 Lash him, and mortify his Letchery of writing Nonsense. **1692** E. WALKER tr. *Epictetus' Mor.* (1737) xlvi, For Boasting is a most intemperate Vice.. 'tis the Leach'ry of the Mind.

†**c.** *transf.* Luxurious or inordinate pleasure.

1632 MASSINGER *City Madam* II. i, Didst thou know What ravishing lechery it is to enter An ordinary, cap-a-pie trimmed like a gallant!

Lechish ('lɛxɪʃ), *sb.* and *a.* [ad. G. *lechisch*; cf. LECH *sb.*[5] and *a.*] = next.

1888 J. WRIGHT tr. *Brugmann's Elem. Compar. Gram. Indo-Germanic Lang.* I. 12 The Slavonic languages fall into a South-Eastern and a Western group... To the latter [belong] Czech.., Sorabian or Wendish.. and Lechish (Polish and Polabian or Elbe-Slavonian). **1908** T. G. TUCKER *Introd. Natural Hist. Lang.* 224 The classification of the Slavonic tongues which appears to find most favour with students in that branch is as follows:—.. (ii) West Group: e. Tzech. f. Sorbian. g. Lechish [Polish, Polabish (Elbe-Slavonic)]. **1936-7** *Slavonic & East European Rev.* XV. 477 The relationship of the present and past Baltic dialects of Slavonic to the other Lechish languages.

Lechitic (lɛ'xɪtɪk), *sb.* and *a.* Also **Lechite, Lekhite, Lekhitic.** [ad. G. *lechitisch*; cf. med.L. *Le(n)chitae* and LECH *sb.*[5] and *a.*] Name given by some linguists to certain West Slavonic languages (Polish, Kashubian, Slovincian, the extinct Polabian) showing characteristic features in common and sometimes held to have once formed a single sub-dialect within the Slavonic group. Also as *adj.*, of or pertaining to the Lechs or their language. Also comb. form Lechito-, Lekhito-. Cf. prec.

1934 G. C. ENGERRAND *So-called Wends of Germany* (Univ. of Texas Bull. No. 3417) 35 Its Western subgroup.. is composed of the Polish, Kashub-Slovince, former Polab, Wendish.., Czech, and Slovak languages. If we eliminate the three latter ones from that subgroup, we have a family, to which philologists give the name of Lechitic (L'Ach, Lekhite, etc.), that is characterized by the persistency of many old Slavic nasals. **1935** *Times Lit. Suppl.* 15 Aug. 506/2 Like most of the Polish Slav philologists of the last two generations, he [*sc.* T. Lehr-Spławiński] holds the theory of a Lechitic linguistic community, that is to say, that all the Slav languages of the Baltic region from Polish in the east to Dravanian on the west bank of the Elbe constituted an unbroken chain of mutually related groups. **1939-40** *Slavonic & East European Rev.* XIX. 273 Schleicher states that Kashubian stands as a bridge between the West Lechite (Polabian) and East Lechite (Polish). **1946-7** *Ibid.* XXV. 493 Shakhmatov sees in this signs of an intermingling of certain Lechitic tribes with the Russians in North Russia. **1949-50** *Ibid.* XXVIII. 286 The Poles, as the most conservative and least mobile of the Western (Lechitic) tribes, stayed behind in the original habitat. **1950** A. P. GOUDY in *Cambr. Hist. Poland to 1696* i. 9 From the linguistic point of view Slovinzish and Kashubish belong to the Polish group and it is usual to class these languages (or dialects) along with Polish and Polabian under the title Lechitic (grupa lechicka). **1964** M. SAMILOV *The Phoneme jat' in Slavic* 144 In Lekhitic the nasals have generally preserved their nasality. **1966** H. BIRNBAUM *Ancient Indo-European Dialects* 194 The dissociation of.. the West Slavs into a Lekhito-Sorbian group.. and a Czechoslovak group. **1972** G. STONE *Smallest Slavonic Nation* 96 I. Taszycki's view that West Slavonic had first divided into two sub-groups—Lechito-Sorbian and Czecho-Slovak—was subsequently supported by Zdzisław Stieber.

† **lechne**, *v. Obs.* Forms: 1 lǽcnian, lécnian, lácnian, 2 lechnien, *pa. pple.* ilechned, 3 lacnien, lechinien, lechni(e, lecnen, 4 lechnen. [OE. *lǽcnian, lácnian* = ON. *lǽkna*, Goth. *lêkinôn*:—OTeut. **lǽkinôjan*, f. **lǽkjo-z* LEECH *sb.*[1]] *trans.* To cure, heal, *lit.* and *fig.* Also *absol.* to administer medicine.

c **900** tr. *Bæda's Hist.* IV. xviii. [xvi.] (1890) 308 Se ða in þæm ilcan dælum deaȝollice læcnod [*v. rr.* lacnad, lacnod] wæs from his wundum. *c* **950** *Lindisf. Gosp.* Luke iv. 23 La lece lecne ðec seolfne. *c* **1000** ÆLFRIC *Gram.* xxxiii. (Z.) 203 *Medeor*, ic lacniȝe. *c* **1175** *Lamb. Hom.* 83 Adam wes ilechned þurh god almihte solf. *c* **1205** LAY. 16589 To lechinien [*c* **1275** lechnie] þa wunden of leofenen his cnihten. *Ibid.* 19500 Sa me scal lacnien [*c* **1275** lechni] his leomes þat beoð sare. *a* **1225** *Ancr. R.* 330 Uorte lecnen mid þe seke, & forte healen mide hire cancre. **1393** LANGL. *P. Pl.* C. IX. 189 Lame men he lechede [*MS. M.* lechnede].

Hence † **lechning** *vbl. sb.*

c **1000** *Sax. Leechd.* I. 106 Se ærest of þyssum wyrtum læcnunge ȝesette. *a* **1225** *Juliana* 6 Wið uten lechnunge of hire libben he ne mahte. *a* **1240** *Ureisun* in *Cott. Hom.* 202 Hit beo mi lechnunge hit beo mi bote.

lechriodont ('lɛkrɪəʊdɒnt), *a.* [f. Gr. λέχριο-ς slanting + ὀδοντ-, ὀδούς tooth.] (See quot.)

1875 HUXLEY in *Encycl. Brit.* I. 760/2 The one end of the palatine.. becomes directed transversely to the axis of the skull, immediately behind the posterior nostril, its teeth continuing the transverse line of the teeth of the vomers. Salamanders with the teeth thus disposed have been termed 'lechriodont'. *Ibid.* 761/1 The 'mecodont' and 'lechriodont' *Salamandrida.*

lechwe ('liːtʃwiː). Also **lechwre, leshwe, letchwe, letshewe, lechwi, leechwe, leche.** [Sechuana: cf. Sesuto *letsa* antelope.] A South African water-buck, *Kobus leche.*

1857 LIVINGSTONE *Trav.* iii. 71 We discovered an entirely new species of antelope called leche or lechwi. It is a beautiful water-antelope of a light brownish-yellow colour. **1863** W. C. BALDWIN *Afr. Hunting* 247 My driver told me.. that he was a man who could shoot a leche ram. **1881** E. E. FREWER tr. *Holub's Seven Yrs. S. Afr.* II. vi. 128 The letshewes were larger and the pukus smaller than blessbocks, and both, like all water bucks, had shaggy, light brown hair, and horns bent forward. **1893** SELOUS *Trav. S.E. Africa* 450 The graceful water-loving leechwe antelopes. **1907** *Westm. Gaz.* 6 Sept. 3/1 The haunts of the jacana, of the waders in general, and of the Lechwe and Situtunga. **1915** *Chambers's Jrnl.* Nov. 701/2 The lechwre is remarkable for its waterloving characteristics. **1920** *United Free Ch. Miss. Rec.* Aug. 138/1 The letchwe is an antelope much addicted to knee-deep water. **1936** P. M. CLARK *Autobiogr. Old Drifter* x. 131 My first buck.. was a large lechwe with beautiful curved horns. **1946** *Cape Times* 7 Aug., Herds of elephant up to 80 strong were seen, as well as.. the rare letchwe and puku buck. **1949** *Ibid.* 30 July 5/5 An expedition.. has found many specimens in the Caprivi Strip, including.. three genets, seven leshwe, one putu, [etc.]. **1969** *Times* 24 Oct. (Zambian Suppl.) p. xi/2 One of the rarest species of game in the world, the black lechwe antelope, is faced with extinction. **1972** *Nature* 7 Apr. 265/1 He further suggested that.. the Okavango and Caprivi be set aside for species such as lechwe, puku and sitatungu.

lecideaceous (lɪsɪdɪ'eɪʃəs), *a. Bot.* [f. mod.L. *Lecidea* + -ACEOUS.] Having the characters of or resembling the genus *Lecidea* of lichens. So **leci'deiform, le'cideine** *adjs.*

1855 MAYNE *Expos. Lex.*, Lecideaceous. **1871** LEIGHTON *Lichen-flora* 154 Apothecia simply lecideine or patellaroid. *Ibid.* 392 Ardellæ.. rotundate, lecideiform. **1900** B. D. JACKSON *Bot. Terms, Lecideiform, lecideine*, like the apothecium of *Lecidea*, which has a margin of the same colour as the disk.

-lecithal ('lɛsɪθəl), *suffix* [f. Gr. λέκιθ-ος yolk + -AL], used to form adjs. describing egg cells with yolks of specified kinds, as ALECITHAL *a.*, *homolecithal* adj. (s.v. HOMO-).

lecithin ('lɛsɪθɪn). *Chem.* Also **-ine.** [F. *lécithine* (N. T. Gobley 1850, in *Jrnl. de Pharm. et de Chim.* XVII. 411), f. Gr. λέκιθος yolk of egg: see -IN[1].]

a. Any of a group of phospholipids found in plants and animals which are esters of a phosphatidic acid with choline and on hydrolysis yield choline, phosphoric acid, glycerol, and two fatty acids; also used as a generic name for these compounds. **b.** A commercial mixture of lecithin with other phosphatides and often other lipids obtained from natural products and used industrially, esp. that from soya beans.

1861 HULME tr. *Moquin-Tandon* II. III. ii. 86 Helicine.. consists.. of oleine,.. lecithine, and cerebrine. **1873** RALFE *Phys. Chem.* 75 Lecithin hydro-chlorate. **1896** *Allbutt's Syst. Med.* I. 165 A phosphoretted fat termed lecithin. **1923** [see *lysolecithin* s.v. LYSO-]. **1926** G. D. ELSDON *Chem. & Exam. Edible Oils & Fats* iii. 15 Lecithin is a complex compound.. and may be looked on as a tri-glyceride in which one of the fatty acid radicles has been replaced by a complex organic base containing phosphoric acid. *Ibid.* xii. 205 Maize oil contains 1·1 to 1·5 per cent. of lecithin. **1951** M. B. JACOBS *Chem. & Technol. Food & Food Products* (ed. 2) III. xlii. 2155 The addition of lecithin to chocolate results in a saving of cacao butter, counteracts moisture, and stabilizes the chocolate. **1951** K. S. MARKLEY *Soybeans* II. xvi. 600 It has become customary in industrial circles to call the phosphatide residue obtained in the commercial manufacture of soybean oil soybean lecithin or simply lecithin. The commercial product contains roughly two-thirds phosphatides and one-third soybean oil. *Ibid.* 601 The term commercial lecithin or lecithin is applied almost exclusively to soybean lecithin, whereas 20 years ago it would have referred to egg lecithin. **1954** *Thorpe's Dict. Appl. Chem.* (ed. 4) XI. 47/2 Lecithins and cephalins, about 2%, are present in the oil [from soya beans] and have been widely used as emulsifiers in the food, textile, cosmetic, soap, and other industries. **1961** H. F. PAYNE *Organic Coating Technol.* II. xxiii. 970 Lecithin.. is a balanced polar-non-polar compound and will concentrate at the interface between polar pigments and less polar oils and resins to reduce the interfacial tension and facilitate wetting. **1967** *Martindale's Extra Pharmacopoeia* (ed. 25) 293 Lecithins occur in all animal and vegetable cells and vary in composition according to the source from which they are obtained. The two chief commercial varieties are egg lecithin (ovolecithin).., and vegetable lecithin.. from various vegetable sources, particularly leguminous seeds. **1970** AMBROSE & EASTY *Cell Biol.* viii. 272 The main lipid constituents of plasma membranes are phospholipids (in particular phosphatidylcholine or lecithin), and cholesterol, a steroid. **1973** *Sci. Amer.* Apr. 85/1 The alveolar fluid contains trace amounts of various large molecules; among them are the two principal lipids—lecithin and

sphingomyelin—that represent the bulk of the pulmonary surfactant.

lecithinase (ˈlɛsɪθɪneɪz, -eɪs). *Biochem.* [f. LECITHIN + -ASE.] = PHOSPHOLIPASE.

1910 *Chem. Abstr.* IV. 2680 Lecithinase is itself almost or entirely free from toxicity, showing its independence from the neurotoxin of cobra venom. **1947** *Jrnl. Biol. Chem.* CLXIX. 704 Four types of lecithinases, each acting on a separate ester linkage of the lecithin molecule, were postulated by Contardi and Ercoli in 1932.., but the existence of only three of these has hitherto been demonstrated. These are (*a*) the enzyme found in cobra serum..which splits off a single unsaturated fatty acid from the lecithin molecule; (*b*) the enzyme found in rice hulls.. and *Aspergillus oryzae*.., which splits off both fatty acids; (*c*) the enzyme found in *Clostridium welchii*.., which separates the phospholipide molecule at its ester linkage between the glycerol and the phosphoric acid. **1959** *Biochem. Jrnl.* LXXI. 619/1 It may be of significance for the biological function of intestinal lecithinase that the optimum conditions for its activity are those which can be expected to prevail in the mucosal cells during absorption of fat. **1970** D. R. DILLEY in A. C. Hulme *Biochem. Fruits* I. viii. 181 Proteases and lecithinase increase lysosomal permeability.

lecithotrophic (lɛsɪθəʊˈtrɒfɪk, lɛkɪθəʊ-), *a.* [f. Gr. λέκιθος yolk of egg + -TROPHIC.] Of the larvæ of certain marine invertebrates, feeding on the yolk of the egg from which they have emerged.

1950 G. THORSON in *Biol. Rev.* XXV. 10 The lecithotrophic pelagic larvae, mainly developing from fairly large yolky eggs, are of a clumsy shape, rather unfit for locomotion. **1962** D. NICHOLS *Echinoderms* x. 119 *Heliocidaris* has a lecithotrophic larva (feeding on stored yolk). **1967** *Oceanogr. & Marine Biol.* V. 360 Experiments refer to short-lived lecithotrophic larvae.

leck (lɛk), *sb. dial.* Also 8 lack. A hard subsoil of clay or gravel. Also *attrib.*, as ***lack-clay***; **leck-stone**, a granular variety of trap rock used in some parts of Scotland for the slabs of ovens.

1780 YOUNG *Tour. Irel.* I. 199 Immediately under the moor, is a thin stratum of what they call lack-clay, which is like baked clay, the thickness of a tile. **1813** R. KERR *Agric. Surv. Berwick* 41 A half lapidified tough and compact clay, called *leck* by the quarriers. **1862** PAGE *Adv. Text-Bk. Geol.* vii. 126 Before the improved manufacture of fire-bricks, some open-textured varieties [of greenstone], known as 'leck-stones', were largely used for the linings and soles of ovens. **1899** DICKINSON & PREVOST *Cumberld. Gloss.*, *Leck*, a hard subsoil of clay and gravel.

leck (lɛk), *v. rare* exc. *dial.* [Cf. E.D.D. *leck v.*] = LEAK *v.* 2 c.

1922 JOYCE *Ulysses* 749 Shes [a cat] as bad as a woman always licking and lecking.

leck, leckar, obs. forms of LAC-, LACQUER.

lecker, var. LECCER.

Leclanché (ləˈklɑ̃ːʃeɪ). The name of Georges *Leclanché* (1839–82), French chemist, used *attrib.* and *absol.* to denote a primary cell invented by him that has a zinc cathode in contact with zinc chloride, ammonium chloride (in solution or as a paste) as the electrolyte, and a carbon anode in contact with a mixture of manganese dioxide and carbon powder.

1871 *Chem. News* 6 Oct. 166/2, I find that what I said about the Leclanché battery..has led to a false impression. .. It is used only on circuits of considerable resistance, and not much work, for which it is found very suitable. **1878** *Encycl. Brit.* VIII. 93/1 Good instances of this kind of action are furnished by the bichromate battery of Bunsen and the Léchanché [*sic*] cell, which occupy a sort of middle position between one and two fluid batteries. **1891** E. M. CAILLARD *Electr.* iv. 264 A form of Daniell's cell has been chiefly adopted in England, but the Leclanché is also excellent for telegraphic purposes. **1907** M. K. KASSABIAN *Rontgen Rays & Electro-Therapeutics* iii. 64 The Leclanché cell consists of a porous cup and a carbon plate. **1946** J. R. PARTINGTON *Gen. & Inorg. Chem.* xxix. 827 Manganese dioxide is used.. as a depolariser in the Leclanché cell. **1971** L. T. AGGER *Introd. Electr.* xi. 171 The dry form of the Leclanché cell, which was introduced towards the end of the last century, has generally replaced the wet Leclanché and is now by far the most commonly used primary cell.

lecontite (lɪˈkɒntaɪt). *Min.* [Named by W. J. Taylor, 1858, after Dr. J. L. *Le Conte*, its discoverer: see -ITE.] Hydrous sulphate of sodium and ammonium, found in colourless prismatic crystals.

1858 W. J. TAYLOR in *Amer. Jrnl. Sci.* Ser. II. XXVI. 273 Lecontite occurs in crystals varying greatly in size. **1868** DANA *Min.* (ed. 5) 635 Lecontite..crystals often have a coating of organic matter.

lecotropal (lɪˈkɒtrəpəl), *a. Bot.* [f. Gr. λέκο-ς dish + -τροπος turning.] (See quot. 1900.)

1889 in *Century Dict.* **1900** B. D. JACKSON *Bot. Terms*, *Lecotropal*, shaped like a horse-shoe, as some ovules.

-lect, terminal element, f. DIA)LECT, used to designate a regional or social variety within a language as in IDIOLECT; also used in forming a number of technical terms in linguistics, as ***acrolect***, ***basilect***, ***isolect***, ***sociolect***, etc. (see quots.). Hence (without hyphen) as *sb.*, a social variety of a language or dialect.

1965 W. A. STEWART in R. W. Shuy *Social Dial. & Lang. Learning* 15, I will refer to this topmost dialect in the local sociolinguistic hierarchy as *acrolect* (from *acro-* 'apex' plus *-lect* as in *dialect*). In most cases what is meant by 'Standard' English is either acrolect or something close to it. At the other extreme is a kind of speech which I refer to hereafter as *basilect* (from *basi-* 'bottom'). **1969** *Florida FL Reporter* VII. I. 48 Although acrolect differs also in sounds and words from basilect, grammatical differences between them create the real blocks to communication. **1971** C.-J. N. BAILEY in *Working Papers in Ling.* (Univ. of Hawaii) III. v. 39 In this case, the creole becomes a satellite (*satellect* or *acoluthOlect*) to the established language (*matrilect*). *Ibid.*, The matrilect serves as the *acrolect* in the continuum at one end, while the *basilect*..will be separated from the acrolect by a graded (systematic) series of *mesolects*. *Ibid.*, An *isolect* has been defined by me elsewhere as a form of speech different from its isolectal correlate. *Ibid.* 41, I have suggested *paralect* to denote folk creations from the related systems (e.g. middle Arabic, Punti, Slavish). **1972** J. L. DILLARD *Black English* iii. 107 Higginson recorded many clause and question forms which are much as they still are in Black English basilect today. *Ibid.* 300 Dialect refers to a set of features delimited geographically; sociolect to a socially distributed set. **1974** J. NIST *Handicapped Eng.* iii. 72 Any departure from that code ..marks the speaker as confined to either the vernacular of mesilect or to the 'folk speech' of basilect. *Ibid.*, Geographical dialects in present-day British English automatically become social-class lects. **1975** *College Composition & Communication* XXVI. I. 104/1 She is being primed to be the ideal teacher of basilect students in spite of her messy lect.

lectern (ˈlɛktən). Forms: α. 4–5 lettorne, 5 leteron(e, -vn, letteroun, letrone, -une, leyterne, letyrn, 5–7 lettron, 6 lettrone, -une, letteron, -ane, litterne, letaring, 6–8 latron(e, 6–7, 9 lettern, 7 lettren, *Sc.* lettering, 9 *Sc.* lateran, lattern. β. 5 lectrone, -un, 5–6 lectron, -yne, 5–7 lectorn(e, 6 lecteron, -erne, -urne, 9 lecturn, 6, 9 lectern. γ. 6 lecter, lector, lettour. [ME. *lettrun*, etc., a. OF. *lettrun*, *leitrun*, semi-popular form of late L. *lectrum*, 'analogium super quo legitur' (Pseudo-Isidore *Lib. Glossarum*), f. *leg-*, root of *legĕre* to read: cf. *mulctrum* milking pail, f. *mulgēre* to milk. The β. forms are influenced by the L. *lectrum*, or perh. rather by the synonymous med.L. *lectrinum*, f. the same root (cf. *textrīnum* weaver's shop, f. *tex-ĕre* to weave), which was the more usual word in eccl. Latin in the 15th c.

The mod.F. *lutrin* (15th c. *lieutrin, leutrin*) seems to represent a mixture of OF. *leitrun* (the vowel of the first syll. being influenced by that of the last) with OF. *letrin*, ad. med.L. *lectrīnum*. There seems to be no foundation for the common statement that Isidore's *lectrum* is ad. Gr. λέκτρον, for which no other sense is known in Gr. of any period than that of 'bed', 'marriage-bed'.]

1. A reading- or singing-desk in a church, esp. that from which the lessons are read; made of wood, metal, or stone, and often in the form of an eagle with outspread wings supported on a column.

α. *c* **1325** *Deo Gratias* 18 in *E.E.P.* (1862) 124 In silke þat comely clerk was clad, And ouer a lettorne leoned he. *c* **1425** *Voc.* in Wr.-Wülcker 648/27 *Hic ambo*, letrune. *c* **1440** *Promp. Parv.* 299/2 Leterone, or lectorne, deske (*K.* lectrone, *H., P.* letrone, or lectrun, *S.* leteron, or letervn), *lectrinum*. *c* **1475** *Pict. Voc.* in Wr.-Wülcker 757/1 *Hoc lectrinium, Hic ambo, Hic discus*. a leyterne. **1541** *Ld. Treas. Acc. Scot.* in Pitcairn *Crim. Trials* I. 320* To be coveringis to the Lettronis in þe Chapell, xij elnis blak Birge Sating. **1600** *Vestry Bks.* (Surtees) 278 For mending of the letaring, ivd. **1676** W. ROW *Contn. Blair's Autobiog.* ix. (1848) 159 Mr. Blair went to the lettren and took the Bible from the reader. **1845** *Ecclesiologist* IV. 147 The nave will contain both lettern and litany-stool. **1877** J. D. CHAMBERS *Div. Worship* 6 There should be Desks or Letterns in the Choir. *fig.* **1401** *Pol. Poems* (Rolls) II. 78 So longe..thou hast lerned to lyen that thi tonge is letteroun of lyes.

β. **1432–50** tr. *Higden* (Rolls) VI. 447 [He] putte his gloves on a lectryne whiles he prayede. **1483** CAXTON *Gold. Leg.* 165/1 Thenne thys felowe wente up to the lectron where as saynt James preched. **1530** PALSGR. 238/1 Lecterne to syng at, *levtrayn*. **1538** LELAND *Itin.* IV. 7 Buried yn the Paroche Chirch of S. Albane under the Place of the lectern in the Quier. **1571** GRINDAL *Injunct. at York* B ij b, So that a conuenient deske or lecterne, with a rowme to turne his face towardes the people be there prouided. **1665** in *Dean Granville's Rem.* App. in *Miscellanea* (Surtees) 263 The Lectorne and Litany Desk are meane and uncomely. **1845** *Times* 3 Feb. 5/5 The reading desk was taken away and a 'faldstool' and 'lectern' substituted. **1852** HOOK *Ch. Dict.* (1871) 437 The lectern in English cathedrals usually stands in the midst of the choir facing westwards.

γ. **1516** *Indenture* in Willis & Clark *Cambridge* (1886) II. 243 Of the Qwyer..the oon halfe thereof on every syde shall be double staulled, wyth lyke lettours, Staulls, and Seats. **1553** *Mendlesham Acc.* in *5th Rep. Hist. MSS. Comm.* 593/2 Payde to Thomas Whyghtyng for makyng of yᵉ lector that stonde on the alter iiiid. **1566** in Peacock *Eng. Ch. Furniture* (1866) 38 An old lecter wt a deske yet remayninge.

2. Chiefly *Sc.* **a.** A reading-desk in a private house. **b.** A writing desk; an escritoire. ***to be bred, sent to the lattern***: see quots. 1825–80, 1888.

1513 DOUGLAS *Æneis* VII. Prol. 145 Seand Virgill on ane lettrune stand, To writ anone I hynt ane pen in hand. **1517** WATSON *Ship of Fools* A ij, I make my lectrons and my deskes clene rygh[t] often. My mansyon is all repylnysshed with bokes. **1534** *Ld. Treas. Acc. Scot.* in Pitcairn *Crim. Trials* I. 284*, iiij½ elnis sad grene, to covir the Latronis in the Kingis Study. **1561** *MS. Acc. Treasurer Edinb.*, Ane great four-square latterane turning on ane vice. *a* **1575** *Earl Huntly's Death* in Bannatyne *Jrnl. Trans. Scot.* (1806) 486 The whole cofferis, boxis, or lettronis, that the erle him self had in handling; and had ony geir in keping in. *c* **1610** J. MELVILL *MS. Mem.* 5 (Jam.) The whole expenses of the process and pices of the lyble, lying in a several buist by themselves in my lettron. **1691** Z. HAIG in Russell *Haigs* xi. 226 At that time I desired to be put to a lettering. **1697** *Inv.* in *Sc. N. & Q.* Dec. (1900) 90/1 A writting latron and chamber box. **1719** *Wodrow Corr.* (1843) II. 442, I have forgot my book of Ministers' names... It stands behind the latron, in that shelf where my manuscript sermons stood. **1825–80** JAMIESON, 'He was bred to the Lettron'. He was bred a writer; a phrase still used by old people in Edinburgh. **1888** J. RAMSAY *Scot. & Scots. 18th C.* I. iii. 181 It was in those days [18th cent.] very common for young men intended for the bar to attend a writer's chambers... In a word, the lattern, as it was called, answered nearly the same purpose in Scotland that the Inns of Court did to the English. *Ibid.* II. 63 People of moderate estate used to send their eldest son for some time to the lattern.

†**c.** (*a*) A music-stand; (*b*) see quot. 1612. *Obs.*

1557–8 in Willis & Clark *Cambridge* (1886) II. 292 A lecturne for yᵉ orgaines in the quere. **1612** *Sc. Bk. Rates* in *Halyburton's Ledger* (1867) 297 Desks or lettrones for wemen to work on covered with veluott, the peice vil.

d. *Sc.* (in form *lateran*). The precentor's desk in a Scotch Presbyterian church.

1860 RAMSAY *Remin.* Ser. I. 208 What is commonly called the Lateran; a kind of small gallery at the top of the pulpit steps. **1871** W. ALEXANDER *Johnny Gibb* xxxv. (1873) 200 The mole-catcher..now occupied the precentor's desk, but ..on great occasions he would always have Johnny Gibb in the 'lateran' also.

lectin (ˈlɛktɪn). *Immunol.* [See quot. 1954 and -IN[1].] A substance, usu. a protein of plant origin, which has the properties of an antibody but is not produced in response to an antigen.

1954 W. C. BOYD in Neurath & Bailey *Proteins* IIB. xxii. 789 It would appear to be a matter of semantics as to whether a substance not produced in response to an antigen should be called an antibody, even though it is a protein and combines specifically with certain antigens alone. It might be better to have a different word for these substances, and the present writer would like to propose the word *lectin*, from the Latin *lectus*, the past participle of *legere*, meaning to pick, choose, or select. **1971** *New Scientist* 8 Apr. 82/2 Over a dozen different agglutinins or lectins have now been isolated from a variety of plant materials, but most work has centred on just two of them—wheat germ agglutinin and concanavalin A. Both preferentially agglutinate several sorts of transformed cells, including those transformed by polyoma virus. **1971** *Nature* 30 July 299/2 During the past eighteen months plant agglutinins, or lectins.., have become a major topic of conversation in many cancer research laboratories.

lectio difficilior (ˈlɛktɪəʊ dɪfɪˈkɪlɪɔː(r)). *Textual Criticism.* Also difficilior lectio. [L., 'harder reading', from the maxim *difficilior lectio potior*.] Of two alternative manuscript readings, the one that is less obvious, and therefore less likely to be a copyist's error; also, the practice of giving preference to such a reading.

1901 F. G. KENYON *Handbk. Textual Crit. New Testament* i. 13 One proposition is so often stated as a leading principle in textual criticism... It is..formulated by Bengel in the words, *Proclivi scriptioni praestat ardua*, or..*Difficilior lectio potior*; the harder reading is to be preferred to the easier... The 'difficilior lectio' is preferable..because a hard reading is likely to be altered into an easy one. **1901** W. EDIE tr. *Nestle's Introd. Textual Crit. Greek New Testament* iii. 157 The principle laid down in the maxim, *lectio difficilior placet* ..is perfectly sound. *a* **1955** B. FLOWER tr. *Maas's Textual Crit.* (1958) 13 It is right to prefer as a rule the '*lectio difficilior*'. **1962** E. J. DOBSON in Davis & Wrenn *Eng. & Medieval Stud.* 130 A's is the *difficilior lectio* and somewhat better in sense. **1966** *English Studies* XLVII. 284 The 'lectio difficilior' can be the better or the worse reading as the case may be. **1968** REYNOLDS & WILSON *Scribes & Scholars* v. 150 Many references to the principle of *difficilior lectio* will be found in commentaries, and there is no doubt of its value. **1969** R. RENEHAN *Greek Textual Crit.* 27 As the rarer verb, it is a *lectio difficilior* and should be received into the text here.

lection (ˈlɛkʃən), *sb.* [a. OF. *lectiun*, ad. L. *lectiōn-em*, n. of action f. *lect-*, *legĕre* to read, to choose. (Cf. LESSON.)] **I.** Reading.

†**1. a.** The act of reading. *Obs. rare.*

1669 WOODHEAD *St. Teresa* I. Pref. (1671) a, The frequent Lection of Books of Devotion. **1669** A. BROWNE *Ars Pict.* To Rdr., I am extreamly unwilling any person should..take the trouble of casting his eye here, were not I modestly of the opinion, something may not be impertinent, or unworthy curious mens Lection.

†**b.** A particular way of reading or interpreting a passage. *Obs.* Cf. F. *leçon*.

1540 COVERDALE *Confut. Standish* (1547) k viij, Now is καθολικος as much to saye as *vniuersalis*. Which worde like as ye leaue out in youre lection [etc.]. **1652** GAULE *Magastrom.* 10 What magician will account of them so, in his way of lection? Or astrologer, in his way of configuration? **1702** W. J. *Bruyn's Voy. Levant* x. 39 To know the different Lections of this Inscription.

c. *concr.* A reading of a text found in a particular copy or edition. †***various lections***, variant readings.

a **1654** SELDEN *Table-T.* (Arb.) 22 When you meet with several Readings of the Text,..be sure you keep to what is setled, and then you may flourish upon your various lections. **1659** BP. WALTON *Consid. Considered* 114 If they be critical notes they cannot be either in part or in whole Various Lections. **1699** BENTLEY *Phal.* xiv. 461 In the Vossian MS. it's πάντα for πᾶσα; which may seem the truer Lection. **1715** *Pope's Iliad* I. *note* I. 47 The grand Ambition of one sort of Scholars is to encrease the number of Various Lections. **1830** DE QUINCEY *Bentley* Wks. 1857 VII. 172, I confess that.. I myself am offended by the obtrusion of the new lections into the text. **1837–8** SIR W. HAMILTON *Logic*

xxxi. (1866) II. 149 Doctrines originating in a corrupt lection..have thus arisen and been keenly defended.

2. *Eccl.* A portion of a sacred writing appointed to be read in church; a 'lesson'. Also *attrib.*

1608 WILLET *Hexapla Exod.* 179 They write in those parchments certaine sacred lections which they call parashoth. **1695** S. HOOPER *Disc. conc. Lent* 355 To this last describ'd Iewish Order of Morning Prayers so far did the Antient Christian agree, as to begin likewise with Lections and Psalmody. **1846** MASKELL *Mon. Rit.* I. p. xxiij, On Passion Sunday, the first Lections were from Jeremiah. **1861** BERESF. HOPE *Eng. Cathedr. 19th C.* 157 The ambo or ambones..for the lections of Holy Scriptures. **1885** PATER *Marius the Epic.* II. 135 Those lections, or sacred readings, which..occurred at certain intervals amid the silence of the assembly. **1927** A. H. MCNEILE *Introd. New Testament* 383 It [*sc.* the Codex Bezae] contains certain lection marks which Brightman holds to be Byzantine.

†**3.** A professional or tutorial lecture. *Obs. rare.*

1563-7 BUCHANAN *Reform. St. Andros* Wks. (1892) 11 The portar..sal ryng..at sax to the lesson public; before viij, twys to the ordinar lection.

†**4.** A lesson to be learnt. *Obs.*

1621 *Gude & Godlie Ball.* (S.T.S.) 233, I cry in generall, on Spirituall & Temporall, This lectioun that ȝe leir.

II. = ELECTION.

a **1300** *Leg. St. Gregory* 986 (Schulz) þe cardinals.. bisouȝt God,..Her leccioun wele to do. **1462** *Burgh Rec. Peebles* (1872) 145 Ilke man be his awn vos gaf thair lectioun to the sayd Schyr John. **1525** LD. BERNERS *Froiss.* II. xlii. 129 *heading*, Howe pope Vrbane and pope Clement were at grete dyscorde togyder, and howe the crysten kynges were in varyaunce for theyr lectyons. **1535** STEWART *Cron. Scot.* (1858) II. 698 The haill lectioun that tha had gevin him till.

lection (ˈlɛkʃən), *v. rare*⁻¹. [f. the sb.] To read a lesson from.

1922 HARDY *Late Lyrics* 165, I went where my friend had lectioned The prophets in high declaim.

lectionary (ˈlɛkʃənərɪ). *Eccl.* (Also in Lat. form.) [ad. eccl. L. *lectiōnāri-um*, f. L. *lectiōn-em* LECTION *sb.*: see -ARY. Cf. F. *lectionnaire.*] A book containing 'lessons' or portions of Scripture appointed to be read at divine service; also, the list of passages appointed to be so read.

1780 T. WARTON *Life Sir T. Pope* (ed. 2) 337 *note*, [The] lectionary contained all the lessons, whether from scripture, or other books, which were directed to be read in the course of the year. **1790** R. PORSON *Lett. to Travis* 153 A Gallic Lectionary, which is reputed to be now about 1200 years old, and contains the entire epistle of John, except the three heavenly witnesses. **1802** RANKEN *Hist. France* II. ii. 197 They should be furnished with a mass-book, a lectionarium, or book of lessons. **1846** MASKELL *Mon. Rit.* I. p. xxv, Among the Lambeth MSS. there is an English Lectionary. **1865** LD. LYTTELTON in *Englishman's Mag.* Feb. 167 The question of our Lectionary generally, or of the selection of Lessons to be read in Church on Sundays and on other days. **1872** O. SHIPLEY *Gloss. Eccl. Terms* s.v. *Missal*, Before the offices were combined in a single volume, several books were necessary, the Sacramentary, Lectionary, Antiphonary, and others.

‖**lectisternium** (lɛktɪˈstɜːnɪəm). Also 7 *anglicized* lectistern(e. [L., f. *lecti-*, *lectus* couch, bed + *stern-ĕre* to spread.]

1. *Roman Antiq.* A sacrifice of the nature of a feast, in which images of the gods were placed on couches with food before them as if for them to eat.

1597 BEARD *Theatre God's Judgem.* (1631) 158 The Priests going about to pacifie the anger of their gods with Lectisterns and sacrifices. **1600** HOLLAND *Livy* v. xiii. 188 By celebrating a Lectisterne. **1702** ADDISON *Dial. Medals* I. 19 Lectisterniums and a thousand other antiquated names and ceremonies. **1857** BIRCH *Anc. Pottery* (1858) II. 290 A lectisternium to the infernal gods.

2. *Med.* (See quot.)

1722 QUINCY *Lex. Physico-Med.*, *Lectisternium* is used by some Writers for that Apparatus, which is necessary for the Care of a sick Person in Bed. [Hence in BAILEY, etc.]

lector (ˈlɛktə(r)). Also 6 lectour. [a. L. *lector* reader, agent-n. f. *legĕre*, *lect-* to read. Cf. F. *lecteur.*]

1. *Eccl.* An ecclesiastic belonging to one of the minor orders, whose duty originally consisted in reading the 'lessons'.

1483 CAXTON *Gold. Leg.* 201/2 Julyan..entrid in to relygyon..and semed to be holy and was made lector. **1588** A. KING tr. *Canisius' Catech.* 106 Four inferiours, to wit, the order of ostiars, lectors, Exorcists and Acolyts. **1637** GILLESPIE *Eng. Pop. Cerem.* IV. iv. 19 A lectors publike reading of Scripture in the Church upon the Sabbath day. **1847** LD. LINDSAY *Chr. Art* I. p. clxxix, The custom was that the lector should not begin to read till the bishop nodded to him. **1852** J. H. NEWMAN *Callista* (1890) 339 The Lector, a man of venerable age, taking the roll called *Lectionarium*, and proceeding to the pulpit, read the Prophets to the people. **1885** *Catholic Dict.* (ed. 3) 381/1 The singing of the Gospel was not always reserved to the deacon..and..the lector still recites the Gospel in the Greek Mass.

2. A reader; chiefly *spec.* a 'reader' or lecturer in a college or university (now only *Hist.* and with reference to foreign use, e.g. that of Germany).

1563-7 BUCHANAN *Reform. St. Andros* Wks. (1892) 6 Personis. The Principal. Ane Lectour Publik. Vj Regentis. *Ibid.* 7 Wagis of the Personis..The public lectour ane hundreth markis. **1658** PHILLIPS, *Lecturer*, or *Lectour*, a publick Professour, a Reader of Lectures. **1708** *Lond. Gaz.* No. 4406/1 Cardinal Carpegna, First Lector of the French College of Theatins. **1889** *Edin. Rev.* Apr. 331 Vincent de Beauvais was lector or Librarian to St. Louis. **1890** 'ROLF BOLDREWOOD' *Miner's Right* (1899) 178/1 Handing in the depositions..he desired us to read for ourselves. I was chosen lector.

Hence †ˈ**lectoress**, a female instructor.

1634 W. TIRWHYT tr. *Balzac's Lett.* 270 Now after she hath..bin threescore yeares a Lectoresse in vice [F. *a enseigné soixante ans le vice*].

lector(n, obs. forms of LECTERN.

lectorate (ˈlɛktərət). *Eccl.* [ad. eccl. L. *lectōrātus*, f. L. *lector* LECTOR.] The office of lector.

1876 T. A. DIXON tr. *Sighart's Albert Gt.* 51 The duties of his first lectorate. **1885** *Catholic Dict.* (ed. 3) 510/1 The Lectorate was the first order conferred on young clerics.

ˈ**lectorship.** [f. LECTOR + -SHIP.] The office or post of lector.

1605 H. WOTTON *Let.* 18 Aug. in L. P. Smith *Life & Lett. Sir H. Wotton* (1907) I. xii. 331 He hath since been stayed with a Lectorship in Genua. **1906** *Westm. Gaz.* 24 Mar. 3/2 It is hereby expressly stated that the Lectorship cannot be held for life. **1911** A. BRENNAN *Life St. Lawrence of Brindisi* 42 The Lectorship was but the first step in his ascent to the highest dignities of the Order.

†**lectory**¹. *Obs. rare*⁻¹. [Put for **alectory*, ad. L. *alectoria*, sc. *gemma* (Pliny), f. Gr. ἀλέκτωρ cock: cf. ALECTORIAN.] = COCK-STONE.

c **1275** *Luue ron* 172 in *O.E. Misc.* 98 Of Amatiste, of calcydone, of lectorie, and tupace.

†**lectory**². *Obs.* [ad. med.L. *lectōri-um*, f. L. *lect-*, *legĕre* to read.] A reading-place.

1387 TREVISA *Higden* (Rolls) III. 361 The seide Plato callede the howse of Aristotille the lectory or redenge place [L. *lectorium*].

lectotype (ˈlɛktəʊtaɪp). *Taxonomy.* [f. Gr. λεκτός chosen + TYPE *sb.*¹.] A specimen from the original material serving as the basis for a description of a new species, selected as the type in the absence of a holotype.

1905 SCHUCHERT & BUCKMAN in *Ann. & Mag. Nat. Hist.* 7th Ser. XVI. 103 *Lectotype*, a syntype chosen, subsequently to the original description, to take the place which in other cases a holotype occupies. **1951** G. H. M. LAWRENCE *Taxon. Vascular Plants* ix. 204 A lectotype is a specimen or other element selected from the original material to serve as the nomenclatural type, when the holotype was not designated at the time of publication, or when the holotype is missing. **1953** E. MAYR et al. *Methods & Princ. Syst. Zool.* xii. 242 A selection of lectotypes should be undertaken only when it leads to the clarification of a taxonomic problem. **1963** DAVIS & HEYWOOD *Princ. Angiosperm Taxon.* viii. 280 The lectotype should be chosen, if possible, from among the specimens actually seen by the author when he described the species. **1967** R. E. BLACKWELDER *Taxonomy* iv. 293 There can be no question that a type (at least holotype, lectotype, or neotype) belongs to the species it typifies. **1970** *Watsonia* VIII. 43 The lectotype of *E[uphrasia] rostkoviana* f. *borealis* was chosen by Mr. Sell and me [*sc.* P. F. Yeo] in 1968. **1975** *Trans. R. Entomol. Soc.* CXXVI. 615 This specimen..is here designated Lectotype and has been labelled accordingly.

lectour, obs. variant of LECTOR, LECTURE.

lectress (ˈlɛktrɪs). *nonce-wd.* [f. LECTOR + -ESS (suggested by F. *lectrice*: see next).] A female reader.

1867 MISS THACKERAY *Village on Cliff* 35 'She advanced through the countries of Devon, Somerset and Gloucester' ..says the little lectress, in a loud disgusted voice.

lectrice (ˈlɛktrɪs). [a. F. *lectrice*, ad. L. *lectrix*, fem. of LECTOR.] A woman engaged as an attendant or companion to read aloud.

1889 in *Century Dict.* **1899** G. B. SHAW *Shaw on Theatre* (1958) 73 An attempt to force the Salvation Army to have their hymns licensed by the Archbishop of Canterbury, or the daily papers to have their political leaders licensed by the Queen's Lectrice, would produce an overwhelming agitation at once.

lectron(e, obs. forms of LECTERN.

lectrure, variant of LETTRURE *Obs.*

lectual (ˈlɛktjuːəl), *a. rare*⁻⁰. [ad. late L. *lectuāl-is* (perh. a faulty reading), badly f. L. *lectu-s* bed, couch.] (See quots.)

1775 ASH, *Lectual*, confined in bed, proper to be confined in bed. **1823** CRABB *Technol. Dict.*, *Lectual*, an epithet for a distemper which requires a person to be confined to his bed.

†ˈ**lectuary.** *Obs.* Also 3-5 letuarie, 4 latuarye, letuare, 4-5 let(e)wary, -ye, 4-6 letuary, 5 lect-, lett-, lytwary, letwerye, lettorye, letuarye, 6 lectuarie. [Aphetic form of ELECTUARY. Cf. OF. *letuaire.*] An electuary.

a **1225** *Ancr. R.* 226 He haueð so monie bustes ful of his letuaries. *c* **1374** CHAUCER *Troylus* v. 741 To late cometh þe letuarye, Whan men þe cors vn-to þe graue carye. *c* **1400** *Lanfranc's Cirurg.* 183 Make herof a letuarie not to hard soden. **1422** tr. *Secreta Secret., Priv. Priv.* 240 Moche worth is the lytwary y-makyd of fuste and aloes. **1435** MISYN *Fire of Love* I. iii. (1896) 7 With þe whilk þai..has gretter comforth þen may be trowyd of gostely letwary. **1453-4** *Durh. MS. Com. Roll*, In confeccione vocat. lettorye. **1509** HAWES *Past. Pleas.* xxx. (Percy Soc.) 149, I shall provide for you a lectuary, Which after sorow into your herte shall sinke. **1528** PAYNEL *Salerne's Regim.* Y ii, Whan pepper is ministred in lectuaries it is holsome for the coughe. **1578** LYTE *Dodoens* VI. xciii. 778 Turpentine in a lectuarie with honey, clenseth the breast and the lunges.

lectuce, obs. form of LETTUCE.

lectun, variant of LEIGHTON *Obs.*, garden.

lecturable (ˈlɛktʃərəb(ə)l), *a. rare.* [f. LECTURE *v.* + -ABLE.] That can be the subject of a lecture.

1828 DISRAELI *Voy. Capt. Popanilla* v. 48 The voices of boys lecturing upon every lecturable topic.

†ˈ**lectural**, *a. Obs.* [f. LECTURE *sb.* + -AL¹.] Of the nature of a lecture.

1657 REEVE *God's Plea* Ep. Ded. to Relig. Cit. 16 Scholasticall intricacies, and lecturall disquisitions.

lecture (ˈlɛktʃə(r)), *sb.* Also 5 letture, 6 lectour, -tur, 6-7 lector. [ad. L. *lectūra*, f. *lect-*, *legĕre* to read: see -URE. Cf. F. *lecture.*]

1. The action of reading, perusal; also *fig.* Also, that which is read or perused. *arch.*

1398 TREVISA *Barth. De P.R.* VIII. x. (1495) 311 He dysposyth a man and makith him able to letture and to wrytynge. *c* **1450** LYDG. *Secrees* 379 With alle these vertues plentevous in lecture. **1490** CAXTON *Eneydos* vi. 24 By thynspection and lecture of theyr wrytyngys. *a* **1586** SIDNEY *Astr. & Stella* lxxvii, That face, whose lecture shewes what perfect beautie is. **1612** SHELTON *Quix.* I. i. 4 He plunged himselfe so deeply in his reading of these bookes, as he spent many times in the Lecture of them whole dayes and nights. **1642** BOYLE in *Lismore Papers* Ser. II. (1888) V. 115, I have receaued a great deal of contentment..by the lecture of those particularitys of my Brother's..victoryes. **1642** SIR T. BROWNE *Relig. Med.* 54 Were I a Pagan, I should not refrain the Lecture of it [the Bible]. **1741** MIDDLETON *Cicero* II. ix. 290 He addressed it [the *De Senectute*] to Atticus, as a lecture of common comfort to them both, in that gloomy scene of life on which they were entring. **1790** CATH. GRAHAM *Lett. Educ.* 130 The French poetry I would limit to Boileau [etc.]..and the Latin lectures to selected plays of Terence [etc.]. **1829** [I. R. BEST] *Pers. & Lit. Mem.* 401 No one..ought to be contented with a single lecture of a work that requires such attentive study. **1904** CONRAD *Nostromo* I. vi. 47 In about a year he had evolved from the lecture of the letters a definite conviction. **1922** JOYCE *Ulysses* 708 What fractions of phrases did the lecture of those five whole words evoke? **1929** R. BRIDGES *Testament of Beauty* I. 24 If we read but of Europe since the birth of Christ, 'tis still incompetent disorder, all a lecture of irredeemable shame.

†**2.** The way in which a text reads; the 'letter' of a text; the form in which a text is found in a particular copy, a lection. *Obs.*

c **1400** *Apol. Loll.* 32 Be þei ware þat þei knitt not falsly a wey þe witt fro þe lecture. **1538** COVERDALE *Prol. N.T.* To Rdr., Where as the Greke and the olde awncient authours reade the prayer of oure lorde in the xi. Chapter of Luke after one maner..I folowe their lecture. **1680** *Weekly Mem. Ingen.* 2 He thinks their multiplicity and various lecture prove prejudicial to many Students.

3. The action of reading aloud. Also, that which is so read, a lection or lesson. *arch.*

1526 TINDALE *Acts* xiii. 15 After the lectur of the lawe and the prophetes. **1534** SIR T. MORE *Treat. Pass.* Wks. 1301/1 And vp on thys arose thys newe counsayle..whereof oure present lecture speaketh. **1539** BIBLE (Great) *2 Cor.* iii. 14 In the lecture of the olde testament. **1597** HOOKER *Eccl. Pol.* v. lxxv. §4 With solemne recitall of..lectures, Psalmes and praiers. **1623** LISLE *Ælfric on O. & N. Test.* Pref. ¶18 He that conquered the Land could not so conquer the language, but that in memory of our fathers, it hath been preserved with common lectures. **1664** BULTEEL *Birinthea* 74 He repeated the Lecture of this Message. **1764** *Mem. G. Psalmanazar* 272, I could easily enough understand both their lectures of the Old Testament and their prayers. **1849** C. BRONTE *Shirley* xxvii. 396 She began to read. The language had become strange to her tongue: it faltered: the lecture flowed unevenly. **1849** ROCK *Ch. of Fathers* IV. xii. 126 Then came a lecture out of some pious writer. *a* **1873** LYTTON *Pausanias* II. iv. (1878) 427 She seemed listening to the lecture of the slave.

4. a. A discourse given before an audience upon a given subject, usually for the purpose of instruction. (The regular name for discourses or instruction given to a class by a professor or teacher at a college or University. Cf. sense 5.)

1536 *Act 27 Hen. VIII* c. 42 §4 To reade one opyn and publique lectour in every of the said Universities in any such Science or tonge as [etc.]. **1576** FLEMING *Panopl. Epist.* 341 In that College it was his happie lucke, to reade in the open schooles in Latine that thereby he..procured to his hearers exceeding great profite by his learned lectures. **1607** SHAKS. *Cor.* II. iii. 243 Say, we read Lectures to you, How youngly he began to serue his Countrey, How [etc.]. **1628** COKE *On Litt.* 280 b, But now Readings..haue lost..their former authorities: for now the cases are long, obscure, and intricate ..liker rather to Riddles than Lectures. **1662** GERBIER *Princ.* 5 Lectures on the Art of Architecture, which have laid before them the most necessary Rules. **1741** WATTS *Improv. Mind* I. ii. Wks. 1813 VIII. 19 Public or private lectures are such verbal instructions as are given by a teacher while the learners attend in silence. **1821** CRAIG *Lect. Drawing* viii. 420 In this, as I have shown you in a former lecture, the statues of antiquity will afford you little assistance. **1827** *Oxf. Univ. Guide* 56 The Common Law School, where the Vinerian Professor reads his Lectures. **1847** EMERSON *Poems, Monadnoc* Wks. (Bohn) I. 436, I can spare the college bell, And the learned lecture well.

b. Applied to discourses of the nature of sermons, either less formal in style than the ordinary sermon, or delivered on occasions other than those of the regular order of church

services; formerly, a sermon preached by a 'lecturer' (see LECTURER 2).

In Scottish use, the term formerly denoted a discourse in the form of a continuous commentary on a chapter or other extended passage of Scripture.

1556 *Chron. Gr. Friars* (Camden) 63 The xxv. day [of September, 1549] Cardmaker rede in Powlles, & sayd in hys lector that he cowde not rede there the xxvij. day. **1642** T. LECHFORD *Plain Dealing* (1867) 51 Upon the week dayes, there are Lectures in divers townes, and in Boston, upon Thursdays. **1675** BAXTER *Cath. Theol.* II. xii. 265 Our late Lectures against Popery. **1696** S. SEWALL *Diary* 17 Sept. (1878) I. 433 Mr. Moodey preaches the Lecture from Acts 13. 36. **1724** R. WODROW *Life J. Wodrow* (1828) 191 Those useful and necessary exercises we in this church call Lectures. **1729** in G. Sheldon *Hist. Deerfield, Mass.* (1895) I. 459 His Custom was to Preach a Lecture once a month, and a Sermon the Friday before the Sacrament. **1773** M. CUTLER in *Life, &c.* (1888) I. 41 Mr. Leslie preached the lecture, afternoon. **1895** A. R. MACEWEN *Life J. Cairns* xiii. 323 The lecture gave place to a sermon of a more or less hortatory type.

c. A course or series of lectures, given regularly according to the terms of their foundation; a foundation for a lecturer; a lectureship.

1615 SIR G. BUCK in Stow *Annals* 980 In this [Gresham] colledge are by this worthy Founder ordained seauen seuerall lectures of seauen seuerall Arts and faculties, to be read publikely. ?*c* **1650** in Wood *Ath. Oxon.* (1899) III. 149 Mr. Richard Gardner of this parish, a phisitian, gave for a catechisme lecture 200 li. **1702** C. MATHER *Magn. Chr.* III. II. v. (1852) 382 They gathered among themselves a convenient salary to support him still amongst them: though his lecture were gone. At Earl's Coln then he tarried, and prepared for the lecture to be settled the next three years in Towcester. **1730** HOADLEY *Life S. Clarke* 11 C.'s Serm. I, In the year 1704, He [Clarke] was call'd forth..to preach Mr. Boyle's Lecture, founded by that Honourable Gentleman, to assert and vindicate the Great Fundamentals of Natural and Revealed Religion. **1780** J. BANDINEL (*title*), Eight Sermons preached..in the year 1780, at the Lecture founded by the late rev. and pious John Bampton M.A.

d. The audience or class attending a lecture.

1848 J. H. NEWMAN *Loss & Gain* 7 He coloured, closed his book, and *instanter* sent the whole lecture out of the room.

5. a. The instruction given by a teacher to a pupil or class at a particular time; a lesson. Obs. exc. in University use: see 4.

1545 BRINKLOW *Compl.* xxii. (1874) 52 Let scholes be mainteyned and lectures to be had in them of the .iij. tongys, —Hebrew, Greke & Latyne. **1552** HULOET, Lectur, or readynge in scholes, called the kinges lectur, or common lectur. *a* **1568** ASCHAM *Scholem.* II. (Arb.) 87 These bookes, I would haue him read now, a good deale at euery lecture. **1596** SHAKS. *Tam. Shr.* III. i. 24 You'll leaue his Lecture when I am in tune? **1597** *1st Pt. Return fr. Parnass.* II. i. 793 Wilt please you, Sir, to sit downe and repeate youre lecture? **1644** MILTON *Educ.* Wks. (1847) 100/1 But here the main skill and groundwork will be, to temper them such lectures and explanations upon every opportunity. **1765** FOOTE *Commissary* I. Wks. 1799 II. 14 The man..attends every morning to give him a lecture upon speaking.

†**b.** *fig.* A 'lesson', an instructive counsel or example. *Obs.*

1575 GASCOIGNE *Glasse Gov.* I. v. Poems 1870 II. 23, I sawe a frosty bearded scholemaster instructing of four lusty young men erewhyle as we came in, but if my iudgement do not fayle me, I may chaunce to read some of them another lecture. **1593** SHAKS. *Lucr.* 618 And wilt thou be the schoole where Lust shall learne? Must he in thee read lectures of such shame? **1624** CAPT. SMITH *Virginia* III. xi. 89 He was againe to learne his Lecture by experience. **1633** BP. HALL *Medit.* Proem, Every thing, that we see, reads us new lectures of wisdom and piety. **1697** POTTER *Antiq. Greece* III. iv. (1715) 21 Achilles's Shield..is a Lecture of Philosophy. **1745** *Matrimony, Pro & Con* 4 Gew-gaws of Dress are Lectures of the Mind. **1755** YOUNG *Centaur* II. Wks. 1757 IV. 142 Heaven means to make one half of the species a moral lecture to the other.

6. An admonitory speech; *esp.* one delivered by way of reproof or correction; 'a magisterial reprimand' (J.). Phr. *to read* (a person) *a lecture*.

1600 SHAKS. *A.Y.L.* III. ii. 365, I haue heard him read many Lectors against it. **1602** —— *Ham.* II. i. 67 So by my former Lecture and aduice. **1622** FLETCHER *Sea Voy.* IV. ii, Ye have read me a faire Lecture, And put a spell upon my tongue for fay[n]ing. **1633–1851** [see CURTAIN-LECTURE]. **1706** *Reflex. upon Ridicule* (1707) 298 Which moral Lecture is out of its Place. **1713** ADDISON *Cato* II. i. 29 Numidia will be blest by Cato's Lectures. **1732** LEDIARD *Sethos* II. VIII. 229 Our young bridegroom receiv'd a terrible lecture. **1867** PARKMAN *Jesuits N. Amer.* xix. (1875) 283 The missionary answered with a lecture on the duty of forgiveness.

7. *attrib.* and *Comb.*, as ***lecture agency, agent, audience, -book, circuit, course, -goer, -hall, -hearing, list, note, -room, -table, -theatre, -tour*** (also as vb.); **lecture-day**, 'the appointed day for the periodical lecture of the municipality or parish; in the New England colonies it seems to have been usually Thursday' (*Cent. Dict.*); **lecture-recital**, a lecture illustrated by music; †**lecture-sermon**, a sermon of the character of a lecture, or forming part of a set course.

1925 A. HUXLEY *Let.* 25 Jan. (1969) 240 You suggest lectures for lucre in the U.S.A.:—I have had several offers from various *lecture agencies... The fatigue and the boredom of a lecture tour frighten me. **1949** DYLAN THOMAS *Let.* 1 Dec. (1966) 340 He said that the Lecture Agencies..have nowhere near his own acquaintanceship with the institutions. **1966** N. NICOLSON in H. Nicolson *Diaries & Lett.* (1966) 131 Colston Leigh Inc. was the lecture-agency. **1873** 'MARK TWAIN' & WARNER *Gilded Age* lviii. 527, I am a business man. I am a *lecture-agent. **1949** DYLAN THOMAS *Let.* 1 Dec. (1966) 341 Surely a letter from Brinnin, acting as my secretary & Lecture-Agent,..would mean something to the Treasury. **1943** WYNDHAM LEWIS *Let.* 5 Dec. (1963) 372 Seeing the gas-shortage whittles down all *lecture-audiences, I had quite a lot of people. **1974** M. FIDO *R. Kipling* 64/2 'Here's poetry at last!' he [*sc.* Professor Masson] burst out to his lecture audience on the day 'Danny Deever' appeared. **1857** PUSEY *Real Presence* i. (1869) 111 The altered confession [of Augsburg]..became the *Lecture-book in Lutheran states. **1965** *Times Lit. Suppl.* 25 Nov. 1057/3 Well-financed readings on large *lecture-circuits..are staple. **1967** O. WYND *Walk Softly, Men Praying* v. 62 He sounded like the agent for a lecture circuit telling me that I was standing on the threshold of great things. **1890** H. FREDERIC *Lawton Girl* 150 It may take the form of..a *lecture course. **1956** *Nature* 10 Mar. 455/2 The American graduate student is usually forced to complete a relatively large number of lecture-courses. **1616** HIERON *Wks.* I. 589 Let not the *lecture-day, now when the sermon is ended, be made a day of voluptuousnesse. **1677** in I. Mather *Prevalency Prayer* (1864) 264 *note*, It was agreed that Lecture-day, July 25th, 1677, should be kept as a Fast. **1753** in *Essex Inst. Hist. Coll.* (1884) XXI. 153 The meeting adjourned to the next Lecture Day. **1779** E. PARKMAN *Diary* 94 Mr. Badcock has been with me to speak about ye Singing ..on proposed Lecture day. **1897** *Lecture-goer [see *class-attender* (CLASS *sb.* 10)]. **1961** M. BEADLE *These Ruins are Inhabited* (1963) xii. 163 Oxford undergraduates aren't the inveterate lecture-goers and note-takers that American college students are. **1865** *Atlantic Monthly* XV. 369 The platform of the *lecture-hall has been common ground for.. all our social..organizations. **1870** 'FANNY FERN' *Ginger-Snaps* 179, I get a comfortable seat in church,..or lecture-hall. **1961** NEW ENG. BIBLE *Acts* xix. 9 He..continued to hold discussions daily in the lecture-hall of Tyrannus. **1967** J. HAWGOOD in Cox & Grose *Organiz. Bibliogr. Rec. by Computer* III. 70 The number of minutes that..it takes him to walk there from college or lecture-hall. **1768–74** TUCKER *Lt. Nat.* (1834) II. 207 Placing all in faith, together with *lecture-hearing, hymn-singing,..and other means of strengthening it. **1965** *Listener* 4 Nov. 700/2 It was the first time that either of these names had appeared on the Oxford *lecture list. **1892** W. WALLACE tr. *Hegel's Logic* (ed. 2) 426 Cf. *Werke*, vii. I. 314 (*lecture-note). **1920** G. SAINTSBURY *Notes on Cellar-Bk.* i. 2 An ordinary 'exercise book'.. devoted to base purposes of lecture-notes. **1944** *Mind* LIII. 269 Sometimes one gets the impression of a collection of lecture-notes. **1973** E. TAYLOR *Serpent under It* (1974) iv. 60 Could *you* continue to teach in a place where..your students knew you had cribbed your lecture notes? **1961** *Observer* 26 Nov. 28/1 (Advt.), *Lecture-Recitals..at Royal Academy of Music. **1817** COLERIDGE *Biog. Lit.* I. x. 219 Numerous and respectable audiences,..honored my *lecture-rooms with their attendance. **1829** in Willis & Clark *Cambridge* (1886) III. 104 The Lecture Rooms..to be provided with desks. **1936** *Discovery* Oct. 301/2 The various buildings which housed the sectional lecture-rooms. **1703** S. SEWALL *Diary* 5 Aug. (1879) II. 83 Mr. Thomas Bridge preaches his first *Lecture-Sermon. **1736** J. ELIOT (*title*) The Two Witnesses... Being the Substance of a Lecture-Sermon, preach'd at the North-Society in Lyme, October 29, 1735. *a* **1751** J. BAMPTON *Will*, I direct..that..a Lecturer be yearly chosen..to preach eight Divinity Lecture Sermons. **1854** in Willis & Clark *Cambridge* (1886) III. 166 A small room for the use of the Lecturer, with a separate entrance to the Lecture-Table. **1849** W. ALLINGHAM *Diary* 30 June (1907) iii. 48 We..passed into the *lecture-theatre. **1854** in Willis & Clark *Cambridge* (1886) III. 168 The Museum, and *Lecture-Theatre remain as at present. **1969** *Listener* 1 May 594/2 The ordinary university lecturer is no more exciting on film than he is in the lecture theatre. **1973** *Nature* 28 Sept. 225/1 Above the blackboards in the main physics lecture theatre of a Scottish university where I once worked there used to be written in large letters: 'Truth will in the end always flow in the direction of the greatest speculative reflection.' **1913** R. BROOKE *Let.* 24 July (1968) 486 The most unpopular person in Canada is Winston. Ever since his *lecture-tour. **1921** R. FRY *Let.* 19 Dec. (1972) II. 519, I have just got back to London after my lecture tour in the north of England. **1952** 'J. TEY' *Singing Sands* ix. 138, I hope Mr. Brown doesn't go lecture-touring in the States. **1958** *Times Lit. Suppl.* 2 May 237/2 An actress whom he meets while on a lecture-tour in South America. **1973** R. LEWIS *Of Singular Purpose* i. 5 This lecture tour in America ..is the first of many recognitions, I'm sure of it.

lecture ('lɛktʃə(r)), *v.* [f. LECTURE *sb.*]

1. *intr.* To deliver a lecture or lectures. Also †*to lecture it.*

c **1590** GREENE *Fr. Bacon* ix. 16 Men that may lecture it in Germany, To all the Doctors of your Belgicke scholes. **1637–50** J. ROW *Hist. Kirk* (Wodrow Soc.) 320 Mr. Robert Bruce,..they now haveing no minister, almost everie day, either preaching in the morning, or lectureing at even. **1774** GOLDSM. *Retal.* 86 But now he is gone, and we want a detector, Our Dodds shall be pious, our Kenricks shall lecture. **1861** *Sat. Rev.* 21 Dec. 631 No one, we should think, ever lectured at one of the common institutions without seeing the most absurd burlesque of his discourse in the next week's local paper. **1874** GREEN *Short Hist.* iii. §6. 146 The Oxford Dominicans lectured on theology in the nave of their new Church.

2. *trans.* To deliver lectures to or before (an audience); to instruct by lecture. †Also, to stir *up* by lectures or sermons.

1681 R. L'ESTRANGE *Relaps'd Apostate* (ed. 3) 48 They set to work a Preaching Ministry, and Lectur'd up the people into a Gospel-frame. **1706** *Reflex. upon Ridicule* 249 It is but a week ago that Simonet was still lectur'd in the civil law. **1735** POPE *Ep. Lady* 83 So Philomedé, lect'ring all mankind On the soft Passion. **1776** ADAM SMITH *W.N.* v. i. III. ii. (1869) II. 348 The teacher..while he is lecturing his students. **1784** COWPER *Task* VI. 182 From dearth to plenty, and from death to life, Is Nature's progress when she lectures man In heavenly truth. **1850** MRS. JAMESON *Leg. Monast. Ord.* (1863) 146 He was in the habit of lecturing his monks every morning, from some passage in Scripture.

b. To read out (tales) to (an audience). *nonce-use.*

1814 CARY *Dante, Par.* xv. 118 Another..lectured them Old tales of Troy.

3. To address with some severity, or at some length, on the subject of conduct, behaviour, or the like; to admonish, rebuke, reprimand.

1706 *Reflex. upon Ridicule* (1707) 172 The most ordinary Folly incident to old Men, is to be perpetually Lecturing Youth. **1779** MAD. D'ARBLAY *Lett.* Jan., I have been.. plentifully lectured already upon my vexation. **1818** in J. Maclean *Hist. Coll. N. Jersey* (1877) II. 175 This morning we suspended one student, and three others were lectured before the Faculty. **1855** MACAULAY *Hist. Eng.* xix. IV. 367 Those whom he had lectured withdrew full of resentment. The imputation which he had thrown on them was unjust. **1858** R. S. SURTEES *Ask Mamma* xlv. 203 Having lectured Tom well on the importance of sobriety. **1882** FROUDE *Short Stud.* (1883) IV. I. vi. 70 He [Becket] lectured the bishops for their want of understanding.

lectu'ree. *rare.* [f. LECTURE *v.* + -EE[1].] One who attends lectures.

1900 J. H. WYLIE *Council of Constance* 191 To make lectur*ees* independent of lectur*ers*. **1939** W. ALLEN *Blind Man's Ditch* 15 There were the born lecturees; like Miss Wiggin, who had been attending classes for twenty years. **1972** *Listener* 9 Mar. 316/3 Poor American lecturees.

lecturer ('lɛktʃərə(r)). Also 6 lectorer. [f. LECTURE *v.* + -ER[1]: it is possible that the earlier *lectorer* is not a misspelling, but an extension of LECTOR, and *lecturer* an interpretative alteration.]

†**1.** = LECTOR 1. *Obs.*

1570 FOXE *A. & M.* (ed. 2) 94/2 [He] was commended of Cyprian to certayne brethren to haue hym for theyr lectorer. **1647** N. BACON *Disc. Govt. Eng.* I. x. (1739) 18 Lecturers came next, who served to read and expound.

2. One of a class of preachers in the Church of England, usually chosen by the parish and supported by voluntary contributions, whose duty consists mainly in delivering afternoon or evening 'lectures'.

1583 STUBBES *Anat. Abus.* II. (1882) 87 Preachers and lecturers, that haue no peculiar flockes, nor charges appointed them. *a* **1654** SELDEN *Table-T.* (Arb.) 67 Lecturers do in a Parish Church what the Fryers did heretofore, get away not only the Affections, but the Bounty, that should be bestow'd upon the Minister. **1666** PEPYS *Diary* 15 July, To church, where our lecturer made a sorry, silly sermon. **1696** PHILLIPS (ed. 5), *Lecturer*... Used now-a-days for a Minister that preaches at a Parish Church in the Afternoon, having no settled Benefits, but only the free gift of the Parishioners. *a* **1715** BURNET *Own Time* (1724) I. 178 That the half conformity of the Puritans before the war had set up a faction in every city and town between the lecturers and the incumbents. **1732–8** NEAL *Hist. Purit.* II. 207 These Lecturers were chiefly Puritans, who..only preached in the afternoons. **1827** *Oxf. Univ. Guide* 10 Four Lecturers, appointed to preach in rotation before the Mayor and Corporation, are elected by the Mayor, Recorder, Alderman, and Assistants. **1844** *Act 7 & 8 Vict.* c. 59 §1 Whereas in divers Districts, Parishes, and Places there now are or hereafter may be certain Lecturers or Preachers in the Holy Orders of Deacon or Priest..appointed to deliver or preach Lectures or Sermons only, without the Obligation of performing other clerical or ministerial Duties.

3. One who gives lectures or formal discourses intended for instruction, esp. in a college or university. In some universities, one who assists a professor in his department or performs professorial duties without having the corresponding rank or title (equivalent to the 'Reader' of Oxford and Cambridge).

1615 SIR G. BUCK in Stow *Annals* 980 [Gresham College] To euery lecturer or reader is prouided..fiftie pounds of Annuall Fee. **1622** PEACHAM *Compl. Gent.* ix. (1634) 77 Doctour Hood, sometime Mathematicall Lecturer in London. *a* **1642** SIR W. MONSON *Naval Tracts* IV. (1704) 437/2 The Maintenance of a Lecturer of Navigation. **1705** HEARNE *Collect.* 16 July (O.H.S.) I. 8 Mr. Swinfin..was chosen Lecturer of Grammar for the University. **1845** MISS MITFORD in L'Estrange *Life* III. xi. 199 Mr. Taylor, the medical lecturer at Guy's. **1882** JEAN L. WATSON *Life R. S. Candlish* viii. 94 An institution, consisting of a professor and lecturer, should be established.

'lecturership. *rare.* [f. LECTURER + -SHIP: see next.] = next.

1891 *Athenæum* 22 Aug. 256/2 More posts, such as lecturer-ships, professorships, ordinary or extraordinary.

lectureship ('lɛktʃəʃɪp). [f. LECTURE *sb.* (sense 4c) + -SHIP. For the formation cf. *clergyship.*] The office of lecturer: **a.** in a church.

1634 CANNE *Necess. Separ.* i. §3. 51 Many of these [pastors leave their sheep] when they see a richer lectureship comming toward them. **1654** GATAKER *Disc. Apol.* 36 The Lecture-ship at the Rolls being vacant. **1720** SWIFT *Fates Clergy-men* Wks. 1755 II. II. 27 He got a lectureship in town of sixty pounds a year; where he preached constantly in person. **1827** HONE *Every-day Bk.* II. 370 He served..the curacy and lectureship of St. Botolph. **1900** *Oxf. Univ. Calendar* 35 University Patronage..Afternoon Lectureship, St. Giles, Oxford..Rhayader Lectureship.

b. in a college, university, or like place.

1707 HEARNE *Collect.* 19 Sept. (O.H.S.) II. 49 Levins.. got the Moral Philosophy Lectureship. **1863** E. HITCHCOCK *Remin. Amherst Coll.* 48 A list of the Professorships, Preceptorships, Tutorships, and Lectureships in the College to the present time. **1871** FRASER *Life Berkeley* ii. 17 Lectureships in chemistry, botany, and anatomy.

lecturess ('lɛktʃərɛs). [f. LECTURER: see -ESS.] A female lecturer.
1825 T. HOOK *Say. & Doings* Ser. II, *Man of Many Friends* I. 162 'But' continued the animated lecturess, 'you must understand that' [etc.]. **1883** BLACK *Shandon Bells* xxxi, The lecturess seemed very self-possessed.

lecturette (lɛktʃə'rɛt). Also -et. [f. LECTURE *sb.* + -ETTE.] A short lecture.
1867 J. MACFARLANE *Mem. T. Archer* iv. 89 The lecturette began. **1888** *Ch. Times* XXVI. 1109 There are twenty-three lectures in the volume, and the Preface is a lecturet in itself. **1895** *Naturalist* 114 A series of lecturettes on the lower forms of animal life.

lecturing ('lɛktʃərɪŋ), *vbl. sb.* [f. LECTURE *v.* + -ING¹.] The action of the vb. LECTURE.
a **1656** BP. HALL *Some Special. in Life* 42 Rem. Wks. (1660), Complaining of..my too much liberty of frequent Lecturings. **1694** *Acts Gen. Assembly* 10 That the ministers ..shall in their exercise of lecturing read and open up to people some large and considerable portion of the Word of God. **1841** in *Mem. G. Ewing* (1847) xvi. 610 That department of pulpit ministrations called in Scotland *lecturing*, which is so universal in the north, and so strangely rare in the south. **1861** HUGHES *Tom Brown at Oxf.* vii. (1889) 60 A little mild expostulation or lecturing. **1892** *Athenæum* 9 July 53/3 Sir Robert Ball's chapter on the observatory is..composed with that skill which has made his public lecturing so famous.
attrib. **1817** COBBETT *Pol. Reg.* XXXII. 358 There is now to be..no Lecturing place..without a Licence. **1818** MRS. SHELLEY *Frankenst*: ii, I went into the lecturing room. **1897** 'MARK TWAIN' *Following Equator* i. 25 The starting point of this lecturing-trip around the world was Paris. **1899** M. BEERBOHM *More* 140 His lecturing-tour through the States.

'lecturing, *ppl. a.* [-ING².] That lectures.
1794 MATHIAS *Purs. Lit.* (1798) 359 Hume's words are.. remarkable in this lecturing age. **1881** MISS BRADDON *Asph.* I. 163 He was always a lecturing old thing.

†**'lecturize**, *v. Obs. rare*⁻¹. [f. LECTURE *sb.* + -IZE.] *intr.* To deliver lectures, to 'hold forth'.
1643 A. BROME *Saint's Encouragemt.* vii. Poems (1661) 138 We must preserve Mecannicks now, To Lecturize and pray.

lecturn: see LECTERN.

lectuse, obs. form of LETTUCE.

lecyth ('lɛsɪθ). *Bot.* [ad. mod.L. *Lecythis* (see below).] A plant of the order *Lecythidaceæ* (typical genus *Lecythis*).
1846 LINDLEY *Veg. Kingd.* 740 Lecythidaceæ—Lecyths.

lecythid ('lɛsɪθɪd), *sb.* and *a.* [f. mod.L. family name *Lecythidaceæ*, f. the generic name *Lecythis* (P. Loefling *Iter Hispanicum* (1758) 189), f. Gr. λήκυθος a flask: see LECYTH.] **A.** *sb.* A tropical American tree of the order Lecythidaceæ. **B.** *adj.* Of or pertaining to a tree of this kind.
1871 C. KINGSLEY *At Last* II. xi. 113 The ground was strewn with large white flowers, whose peculiar shape told us at once of some other Lecythid tree high overhead. *Ibid.* 118 Some other Lecythids..go by the name of monkey-pots.

lecythus, var. LEKYTHOS.

led (lɛd), *ppl. a.* [Pa. pple. of LEAD *v.*¹]
1. In various nonce-uses (see the vb.).
1570 LEVINS *Manip.* 48/38 Ledde, *ductus.* *a* **1586** SIDNEY *Arcadia* IV. (1629) 425, I would suffer this fault..to be blotted out of my minde, by your former led life. **1754** RICHARDSON *Grandison* III. xxii. 203 Is not in his own power. He suffers himself to be a led man.
absol. **1895** *Daily News* 11 July 5/1 The fusion is adopted by the leaders and half repudiated by the led.
2. *led horse*, a spare horse, led by an attendant or groom; also a sumpter- or pack-horse. Also *transf.* in *led tub*, etc., (Mining): see quot. 1851.
1662 J. DAVIES tr. *Olearius' Voy. Ambass.* 21 Twenty led Horses, with great silver Chains instead of Bridles. **1718** *Freethinker* No. 109 ¶4 With an Hundred Led-Horses in his Train. **1806** A. DUNCAN *Nelson's Funeral* 35 The carriage was drawn by six led horses. **1842** BARHAM *Ingol. Leg.* Ser. II, *Smuggler's Leap* 19 The led-horse laden with five tubs or more. **1851** GREENWELL *Coal-trade Terms Northumb. & Durh.* 35 A led tub or corf means a spare one, for the barrowman to leave empty with the hewer, whilst the full one is being put to the flat or crane. **1887** P. M'NEILL *Blawearie* 84 Will Hood had a 'led' lamp; it soon was kindled.
3. That follows slavishly or as a sycophant. *led-captain*, a hanger-on, dependant, parasite. So also *led-†eater*, *†friend*, *poet.*
1672 WYCHERLEY *Love in Wood* I. i, Every wit has his cully, as every squire his led captain. **1679** SHADWELL *True Widow* I. Wks. 1720 III. 123 He is, in short, a Led-eater.. and Dry Jester to gaming and jockey-Lords. **1710** STEELE *Tatler* No. 208 ¶2 There is hardly a rich Man in the World, who has not such a led Friend. **1745** H. WALPOLE *Lett.* (1846) II. 68 Churchill, whose led-captain he [Sir John Cope] was. **1848** THACKERAY *Van. Fair* l, A led captain and trencher-man of my Lord Steyne. **1866** *Daily Tel.* 16 Jan. 7/4 In the last century opera singers used to keep led-captains in their pay, who..swore their employers were incomparable, and defied those who dared denial to the duello. **1881** SAINTSBURY *Dryden* 53 Elkanah Settle was one of Rochester's innumerable led-poets.
4. *led farm*: a farm held and controlled by a non-resident farmer. *Sc.*
1815 SCOTT *Guy M.* l, The Deuke's no that fond o' led farms. **1899** CROCKETT *Kit Kennedy* 58 The Back o' Beyont was a solitary place,..and was situated on a led farm.
transf. **1858** CARLYLE *Fredk. Gt.* I. II. iv. 92 He transferred the Markgrafdom to Brandenburg, probably as more central in his wide lands; Salzwedel is henceforth the led Markgrafdom or Marck.

LED (ɛliː'diː). Also l.e.d., led (lɛd). [Abbrev.] A light-emitting diode: a semiconductor diode that emits light when a voltage is suitably applied.
1968 *Electronics World* Jan. 36/1 Today, the LED is making possible vast improvements upon circuits that seem to have no obvious connection with photoelectric operations. **1971** *New Scientist* 1 Apr. 26/3 LEDs have not caught on to any great extent because they cost a great deal more. **1975** *Hi-Fi Answers* Feb. 78/2 The light pulses from the led are picked up by a photo-conductive cell and applied to the filter. **1976** *Pract. Electronics* Oct. 810 (*caption*) Block diagram of the system using two separate l.e.d. displays. **1978** PASACHOFF & KUTNER *University Astron.* ix. 271 Gallium production..is used in many solid state devices including the light-emitting diodes (LED's) that form the digits on most pocket calculators and digital watches. **1982** *What's New in Computing* Nov. 19/2 The logger can be programmed to these levels, indicating on a led display which channel is giving a fault condition signal. **1984** *What Video?* Aug. 21/2 It has an LED recording level meter.

led, ledare, obs. forms of LID, LEADER.

ledder(e, -ir(e, -yr, obs. ff. LADDER, LEATHER.

leddy, obs., Sc. and *dial.* form of LADY.

†**lede.** *Obs.* Forms: α. *sing.* 1 léod, 3–5 leode, lede, 3 ledd, 4 leude, lued, lud(e, 4–6 led, 5–6 *Sc.* leid, 5 leyde, 7 leed. β. *pl.* 1, 3 leode, 3 leoden, 3–5 ledes, 3–6 ledis, 4–6 le(e)de, 4 leodes, le(u)dez, ludes, -us, leedes, led, *Sc.* lide, 4–5 *Sc.* ledys, 5–6 *Sc.* leid, 6 *Sc.* laidis. [Repr. three different but closely related OE. words: (1) OE. *léod* fem., nation, people; not found elsewhere in Teut. as fem., but corresponding in sense with the masc. sb. OHG. *liut* (MHG. *liut*, also neut.), MDu. *liet*, ON. *lýð-r* people (whence ME. LITH followers). (2) OE. *léode*, *léoda*, Northumb. *líoda*, pl., men, people = OS. *liudi* (MDu. *liede*, Du. *lieden*), OHG. *liuti* (MHG. *liute*, mod.G. *leute*), ON. *lýðir*. (3) OE. *léod* str. masc., man (occurring only as a poetical word for 'king', and in the compounds *burhléod* (*-líod*) burgher, *landléod* inhabitant); not found in the other Teut. langs. Cognates outside Teut. are OSl. *ljudŭ* masc. sing., people, nation, pl. *ljudije* people, folks, Lettish *laudis* fem. sing., people.
The relation between the Teut. words is uncertain, but the Slavo-Lettic cognates suggest that the OTeut. type was a collective sing. **leudi-s* masc., people, the plural of which had naturally much the same sense (cf. *folk*, *folks*). The OE. masc. sing., with the sense 'man', seems to have been evolved from the plural meaning 'people'. The fem. gender of the OE. *léod* people, and the form *léoda* (*líoda*) in the pl. instead of *léode*, seem to be due to the influence of the synonymous *þéod* fem.
The Teut. word is commonly regarded as from the OAryan root **leudh-*, whence Goth. *liudan*, OS. *liodan*, OE. *léodan*, to grow, spring (from).]
1. A people, nation, race. Also, persons collectively, 'people'.
Beowulf 2732 (Gr.) Ic ðas leode heold fiftiȝ wintra. **971** *Blickl. Hom.* 201 Beneuentius & Sepontanus hatton, þa twa leode. *c* **1200** ORMIN 7166 Forr ȝiff þe riche mann iss braþ, & grimme..Hiss lede þatt iss unnderr himm Himm dredeþþ. *a* **1250** *Prov. Ælfred* 27 in *O.E. Misc.*, Þvs queþ Alured..wolde ye mi leode lusten eure louerde. *a* **1300** *Cursor M.* 4246 Men war þar o sarzin lede. *Ibid.* 8225 All naciun and lede aght vr lauerd for to drede. **1362** LANGL. *P. Pl.* A. VI. 38 Ther nis no laborer in this leod that he loueth more. *c* **1425** WYNTOUN *Cron.* v. xiii. 5800 Fra hys kyn till ane wncouth lede. *c* **1740** HENRY *Wallace* x. 227 For thai me hayt mar na Sotheroun leid.
b. *pl.* In the alliterative phrase *land and lede*, i.e. land and vassals or subjects.
a **1000** *Andreas* 1321 (Gr.) Hafast nu þe anum eall ȝetihhad land & leode. *c* **1330** *Arth. & Merl.* 86 And gaue him bothe land and lede To help his childer after his day. **1377** LANGL. *P. Pl.* B. xv. 520 When Constantyn..holykirke dowed With londes and ledes lordeshipes and rentes. *c* **1430** *Syr Tryam.* 1269 Y make the myn heyre Of londe and of lede. ?*c* **1475** *Sqr. lowe Degre* 135, I wyll forsake both land and lede, And become an hermyte. **15..** *Merch. & Son* in Hazl. *E.P.P.* I. 133 He was a grete tenement man, and ryche of londe and lede.
c. Phrases. *all lede*, all people, all the world, everybody. *in lede*, among people, in the land, on earth.
a **1275** *Prov. Ælfred* 334 in *O.E. Misc.*, Hit is said in lede cold red is quene red. *a* **1300** *Cursor M.* 5490 Quen he went al lediss wai. *Ibid.* 15480 Ha þou Iudas, traitur, thef, felunest in lede. *Ibid.* 23040 At þis dome..sal al lede in four be delt. *c* **1320** *Sir Tristr.* 1677 Þai loued al in lide. *c* **1400** *Destr. Troy* 5345 Hade he lyuyt in lede, he hade ben lorde here. *c* **1450** HOLLAND *Howlat* 288 The trewe Turtour and traist..Wrait thir letteris at lenth, lelest in leid. *c* **1460** *Emare* 702 He thowghth..That she was non erdyly wyght; He saw never non shuch yn leede.
2. *pl.* Persons collectively, 'people'; the people subject to a lord or sovereign; one's own people, countrymen.
Beowulf 260 (Gr.) We synt ȝumcynnes ȝeata leode. *c* **1000** *Ags. Gosp.* Luke xix. 14 Ða hatedon hine his leode..& cwædon; nyllað þæt þes ofer us rixie. *c* **1205** LAY. 1784 Liððen þa leoden þat heo on londe comen. *a* **1310** in Wright *Lyric P.* xii. 42 ȝef y may betere beode, To mi latere leode. **1340–70** *Alex. & Dind.* 141 As was þe langage of þe lond wiþ ludus of inde. *c* **1350** *Will. Palerne* 390 Whan þe loueli ludes seie here lord come. **1393** LANGL. *P. Pl.* C. XVI. 306 Many man hath hus Ioye here for alle here wel dedes, And lordes and ladyes ben callid for leodes that thay haue. *c* **1400** *Destr. Troy* 9056 And of his ledis ben lost mony lell hundrith.
3. *sing.* A man, person; esp. one of the 'men' or subjects of a king or chief; a subject. Also *poet.* in OE., a king.
Beowulf 341 (Gr.) Wlanc Wedera leod word æfter spræc. **13..** *Gaw. & Gr. Knt.* 1195 Þe lede lay lurked a ful longe quyle. **13..** *E.E. Allit. P.* B. 614 Lenge a lyttel with þy lede I loȝly biseche. **1362** LANGL. *P. Pl.* A. VI. 6 Thei a leod metten, Apparayled as a palmere. *c* **1400** *Destr. Troy* 6441 For all the grefe of þo Grekes, & þe grete þronge, Was no led might hym let. *c* **1430** *Hymns Virg.* 106, I warne vche leod þat liueþ in londe. *c* **1460** *Towneley Myst.* iii. 48 Euery liffyng leyde, Most party day and nyght. **1508** DUNBAR *Tua Mariit Wemen* 441 Se ȝe nought, allace! Ȝone lustlese led so lelely scho luffit hir husband. **1535** STEWART *Cron. Scot.* (1858) I. 543 Ȝouthheid..at na leid experience will leir. *a* **1650** *Earle Westmorland* 10 in Furnivall *Percy Folio* I. 318 A noble Leed of high degree.
b. As a form of address.
13.. *Gaw. & Gr. Knt.* 675 Bi Kryst, hit is scaþe, þat þou, leude, schal be lost þat art of lyf noble! **13..** *E.E. Allit. P.* A. 541 Þe lorde..Called to þe reue 'lede pay þe meyny'. **1377** LANGL. *P. Pl.* B. I. 139 To litel latyn thou lernedest Lede in thi ȝouthe. *c* **1470** HENRY *Wallace* VIII. 1639 And thus he wrait..To Wilȝam Wallace as a conquerour. 'O lowit leid, with worschip wys and wicht; Thow werray help [etc.].
4. *attrib.* and *Comb.*, as ***lede folk***, ***kemp***, ***king***, ***knight***, ***shame***, ***spel***, ***thegn***; **lede bishop**, a bishop of a district (hence **-*bishopric***); **lede-quide**, national language; **lede-rune**, ? an incantation; also, ? a mysterious doctrine.
a **1000** *O.E. Chron.* an. 971 (Cotton MS.) Se wæs ærest to Dorke ceastre to *leod bisceope ȝehalȝod. ?*a* **1300** *Shires Eng.* in *O.E. Misc.* 145 Oþe þe leod biscopryche on Rouecestre. *c* **1325** *Chron. Eng.* 322 in Ritson *Metr. Rom.* II. 283 Ant twenty-sevyn he made also Leod bischopes thereto. *c* **1205** LAY. 6627 He fræinede þis *leod-folc æfter heore kineleouerde. *Ibid.* 6025 Werren on alche legiun þus feole *leod-kempen. *Beowulf* 54 (Gr.) Beowulf Scyldinȝa leof *leodcyninȝ. *c* **1205** LAY. 867 Ich habbe þesne leod king ileid in mine benden. *Ibid.* 7459 And þene king lærde al þas *leod-cnihtes. *Ibid.* 2914 Kaer Leir..þa we an ure *leod-quide Leirchestre clepiað. *c* **1000** *Sax. Leechd.* II. 138 Wiþ ælcre yfelre *leodrunan..ȝewrit writ him þis ȝreciscum stafum. *c* **1205** LAY. 9121 Her beoð to þisse londe icumen seolcuðe leod-ronen. *Ibid.* 15488 Heo gunnen loten weorpen mid heore leod-runen. *Ibid.* 26297 Nu is hit muchel *leod-scome ȝif hit scal þus a-ligge. *Ibid.* 15757 He cuðe tellen of ælche *leod-spelle. *Ibid.* 6674 He..lette laðien him to al his *leod-þeines.

lede, obs. variant of LEAD *sb.* and *v.*

lede, variant of LEED¹, *Obs.* language.

ledeburite ('leɪdəbjʊraɪt). *Metallurgy.* [ad. G. *ledeburit* (F. Wüst 1909, in *Metallurgie* VI. 523), f. the name of Adolf *Ledebur* (1837–1906), German metallurgist + -ITE¹.] The eutectic of the iron/iron carbide system which is composed of austenite and cementite, contains about 4·3 per cent carbon, and occurs in cast iron.
1912 W. H. HATFIELD *Cast Iron* i. 16 This well-known structure, presented by the solidified eutectic, Wüst proposes to christen 'Ledeburite', after his distinguished compatriot. **1943** *Jrnl. R. Aeronaut. Soc.* XLVII. 218 A high carbon chromium steel in the cast condition..will have good sliding properties (ledeburite structure) and is widely employed in high pressure pump mechanism. **1972** G. A. CHADWICK *Metallogr. of Phase Transformations* iv. 140 The white iron eutectic, consisting of austenite and cementite, is often referred to as 'ledeburite'.

†**ledeless**, *a. Obs. rare*⁻¹. In 4 leudlez. [f. LEDE + -LESS.] Without a companion.
13.. *Gaw. & Gr. Knt.* 693 Oft, leudlez alone, he lengez on nyȝtez.

†**ledely**, *a. Obs. rare.* In 3 leodlich. Belonging to the people or nation, national.
c **1205** LAY. 14698 Al þat leodliche folc þat lueueden ure drihten.

'leden. *Obs.* exc. *dial.* Forms: 1 léden, læden, lýden, léoden, 3–4 leoden, ledene, 2–6 leden, 4–5 ledne, 4 ledone, lidene, ledyn, lyd(e)ne, ludene, 4–7 ledden, 5 lydyn, 7 leaden, 7, 9 lidden. See also LEED¹. [OE. *læden*, repr. a Celtic or early Romanic pronunciation of L. *Latīnum* LATIN, was confused with the native *léden*, *lýden*, *léoden* language, f. *léode* people, LEDE. (For the etymological sense cf. *ȝeðéod* language, f. *ðéod* people.) The confusion seems to have originated with the compound *bóc-léden* 'book-language' (see BOC-LEDEN), which was fashioned by popular etymology as a more intelligible synonym for *læden*.]
†**1.** Latin. (See also BOC-LEDEN.) Only OE.
c **897** K. ÆLFRED *Gregory's Past.* Pref. 3 Of Lædene on Englisc areccean. *c* **900** tr. *Bæda's Hist.* v. xx. (1891) 466 And Leden him wæs swa cuð & swa ȝemimor swa swa Englisc. *c* **1050** *Byrhtferth's Handboc* in *Anglia* VIII. 321 Enchiridion þæt ys manualis on lyden.

†2. The language of a nation, people or race; a 'tongue'. *Obs.*

c **1000** *Sax. Leechd.* III. 110 þæt ys on ure leodene hneccan sar. *c* **1200** *Trin. Coll. Hom.* 141 Hie is ihaten.. englene quen marie þat is on ure ledene se-steorre. *a* **1225** *Ancr. R.* 130 Vor al so muchel seið þis word Dauid, on Ebreuwische leodene, as strong toȝein þe ueond.

†**b.** The speech or utterance of a person or class of persons; form of speech; way of speaking. (Cf. LEED¹ b.) *Obs.*

c **1320** *Cast. Love* 32 No monnes mouþ ne be i-dut, Ne his ledene i-hud. *c* **1350** *Will. Palerne* 782 þan hee meeues too hur mouthe & makes his lidene. **1377** LANGL. *P. Pl.* B. xv. 253 Though he crye to Cryst.. I leue His ledne be in owre lordes ere lyke a pyes chiteryng. *c* **1400** *Destr. Troy* 13276 The songe of þo Syrens was selly to here! With a ledyn full lusty & likyng with-all. **1595** SPENSER *Col. Clout* 746 Those that do to Cynthia expound The ledden of straunge languages in charge. **1596** —— *F.Q.* IV. xi. 19 He was expert in prophecies, And could the ledden of the Gods vnfold.

†**c.** *poet.* Applied to the 'language' of birds. *Obs.*

1340-70 *Alisaunder* 601 þe ludene of þat language [*sc.* of birds] lelli þei knowe. *c* **1386** CHAUCER *Sqr.'s T.* 427 She vnderstood wel euery thyng That any fowel may in his leden seyn. **1393** LANGL. *P. Pl.* C. xv. 186 þe larke, þat is a lasse fowel is loueloker of lydene. *c* **1425** *Seven Sag.* (P.) 3238 And that wyt God hym gafe, That on fouls lydyn he couthe. **1600** FAIRFAX *Tasso* XVI. xiii. 283 A woondrous bird.. That in plaine speech sung.. Her leden was like humaine language trew. **1612** DRAYTON *Poly-olb.* xii. 503 The ledden of the birds most perfectly shee knew.

d. *dial.* Noise, chatter.

1674 RAY *N.C. Words* 29 A Leaden or Lidden; a Noise or Din. **1865** R. HUNT *Pop. Rom. W. Eng.* Ser. II. 245 Hark to his lidden. Listen to his word or talk.

leder, obs. f. LEADER, LEATHER; var. LITHER.

‖**lederhosen** ('leɪdəˌhəʊzən). [G.] Leather shorts, as worn in Alpine regions.

1937 *Night & Day* 8 July 8/2 The men, with any luck, will refuse to discard their grey flannels for lederhosen. **1953** *Time* 17 Aug. 27/2 The powerful Social Democratic Party is presided over by mild Erich Ollenhauer, a sort of chubby Clement Attlee in *Lederhosen.* **1956** WALLIS & BLAIR *Thunder Above* (1959) xv. 154 A boy in a checked sports shirt and *lederhosen.* **1973** *Listener* 25 Jan. 103/2 (*caption*) Hitler .. in lederhosen.

lederite ('lɛdəraɪt). *Min.* In the obs. sense 1 later corrected to **ledererite**. [Named after Baron Louis von *Lederer*: see -ITE.]

†**1.** A synonym of gmelinite. *Obs.*

1829 C. T. JACKSON in *Amer. Jrnl. Sci.* XVI. 207 It is the same mineral which has been.. termed Lederite. **1834** *ibid.* XXV. 80 We propose for this mineral, the name of Ledererite, in honor of the Austrian ambassador to the United States.

2. A brown variety of titanite, with splendent lustre.

1840 C. U. SHEPARD in *Amer. Jrnl. Sci.* XXXIX. 360, I shall bespeak for them the name of Lederite. **1892** DANA *Min.* 714 Lederite, brown, opaque, or subtranslucent.

ledge (lɛdʒ), *sb.* Forms: 4-6 legge, 6 lege, legg, 7 ledg, 6- ledge. [Possibly a ME. formation from *legge* (lɛdʒə) LAY *v.* The various senses of the sb. admit of being accounted for by this supposition: cf. LAY *sb.*, and MHG. *legge, lecke*, stratum, layer, edge, border.

The ON. *lǫgg* fem., rim of a cask (see LAG *sb.*) is commonly quoted as cognate, but it is doubtful whether it even belongs to the same root, as it may represent an OTeut. type **lawwâ.* One example of ONF. *lege*, app. 'ledge' of leather put on a packsaddle, is given by Godef.; the F. word may possibly be the proximate source, in which case the ultimate etym. is prob. Teut.]

1. a. A transverse bar or strip of wood or other material fixed upon a door, gate, piece of furniture, or the like. Now *dial.* and *techn.*

c **1330** *Arth. & Merlin* 5673 He toke þe gate bi þe legge & slong hem vp at his rigge. *c* **1440** *Promp. Parv.* 293/2 Legge, ouer twarte byndynge [*MS. S.* ouer wart, *MS. P.* ledge], *ligatorium.* **1453** *Mem. Ripon* (Surtees) III. 160 Legges de ligno emptis eidem stabulo, vidz. hostio ejusdem. **1504** *Nottingham Rec.* III. 322 For vj legges to þe same dore. **1530** PALSGR. 238/1 Ledge of a dore, *barre. Ibid.*, Ledge of a shelfe, *apoy, estaye.* **1566** *Churchw. Acc. St. Dunstan's, Canterbury*, Payed for bordes and palles [i.e. pales] and leges for the gatte xvjd. **1638** *MS. Acc. St. John's Hosp., Canterb.*, A dayes worke in sawinge of ledges and quarters for the steeple. **1741** RICHARDSON *Pamela* (1824) I. 86, I clambered up upon the ledges of the door, and upon the lock which was a great wooden one. *a* **1825** FORBY *Voc. E. Anglia, Ledge*, a bar of a gate or stile; of a chair, table, &c. **1825, 1881** [see *ledge-door* in sense 6].

b. *Joinery.* One of the sides of a rebate, as that against which a door closes; (see quot.). ***ledge(d) and brace(d) door*** (see quots.).

1842 GWILT *Archit.* Gloss. s.v., Ledges of doors are the narrow surfaces wrought upon jambs and sofites parallel to the wall to stop the door, so that when it is shut the ledges coincide with the surface of the door... In temporary work the ledges of doors are formed by fillets. **1901** J. BLACK *Illustr. Carpenter & Builder Ser.: Home Handicrafts* ii. 19 (*caption*) Elevation and vertical section of what is termed a ledge and brace door. **1904** GOODCHILD & TWENEY *Technol. & Sci. Dict.* 352/1 *Ledged and braced door*, the same as a ledged door, with the addition of braces or pieces of wood running diagonally across between the opposite ends of two successive ledges. **1957** *N.Z. Timber Jrnl.* Oct. 73/1 *Ledged-and-braced door*, a door similar to a batten door, but framed diagonally with braces across the back, between the battens.

c. *Naut.* pl. (See quots.)

1676 COLES, *Ledges*, small Timbers, coming thwart ships (from the wast-trees to the Roof-Trees) to bear up the Nettings. **1769** FALCONER *Dict. Marine* (1780), *Ledges*,.. small pieces of timber placed athwartships, under the decks of a ship, in the intervals between the beams. **1776** G. SEMPLE *Building in Water* 36 After it is floored, there must be Ledges nailed on to give firm Hold to the Feet of the Men. *c* **1850** *Rudim. Navig.* (Weale) 129 *Ledges*, oak or fir scantling used in framing the decks, which are let into the carlings athwartships. The ledges for gratings are similar, but arch or round-up agreeable to the head-ledges.

d. *Arch.* (See quots.)

1611 COTGR., *Cymace*, a ledge, or outward member in Architecture, fashioned somewhat like a Roman S, and tearmed a Waue, or Ogee. **1828** WEBSTER, *Ledge*.. 4. A small molding. **1875** KNIGHT *Dict. Mech.*, *Ledge*,.. a small moulding, as the Doric drop-ledge. **1889** *Century Dict.*, *Ledge*, in *arch.* a string-course.

2. †**a.** A 'lip' or raised edging running along the extremity of a board or similar object. *Obs.*

1535 COVERDALE *1 Kings* vii. 28 The seate was made so, that it had sydes betwene the ledges [Luther: *Leisten*]. —— *Ezek.* xliii. 13 This is the measure of the aulter.. his botome in the myddest was a cubite longe and wyde, and the ledge [Luther: *Rand*] that wente rounde aboute it, was a spanne brode. **1599** A. M. tr. *Gabelhouer's Bk. Physicke* 163/2 A boarde which hath round aboute ledges. **1802** MAR. EDGEWORTH *Moral T.* (1806) I. 244, I at first set this vase upon the ledge of the tray, and it was nearly falling.

b. *Printing.*

1683 MOXON *Mech. Exerc., Printing* 195 The Ledges of the Dressing-sticks. *Ibid.* 218 Placing the first Line close and upright against the lower ledge of the Galley, and the beginning of his Lines close and upright against the left hand Ledge of the Galley. **1727-41** CHAMBERS *Cycl.* s.v. *Printing*, From the right side of this plate arises a ledge about half an inch high.. serving to sustain the letters. **1808** STOWER *Printer's Gram.* 199 The page being tied up, the compositor removes it pretty far from the ledges of the galley.

3. a. A narrow horizontal surface, formed by the top of some vertical structure, or by the top of some projection in the vertical face of a wall or the like.

1558 in C. Welch *Tower Bridge* (1894) 87 For twoo powles for the water drawenge at the legg on the bridge. **1641** BP. HALL *Mischief of Faction* Rem. Wks. 77 We are like some fond spectators, that when they see the puppets acting upon the ledge, think they move alone. **1715** DESAGULIERS *Fires Impr.* 130 Make two Ledges in the Chimney,.. that the [Register] Plate may go down no further when it shuts close. **1814** SCOTT *Ld. of Isles* v. xxxi, The warder next his axe's edge Struck down upon the threshold ledge. **1833** TENNYSON *Miller's Dau.* 84 You were leaning from the ledge. **1852-61** *Archit. Publ. Soc. Dict.*, *Ledge of a window*, or *window ledge*, a name often given to a rounded window board, when the brickwork under the window is of the same thickness at the sill as the rest of the wall. **1861** M. PATTISON *Ess.* (1889) I. 45 On every projecting ledge of the heavy wainscot, was displayed.. the silver and pewter plate. **1874** MICKLETHWAITE *Mod. Par. Churches* 180, I have known clocks to be let into the ledge of the pulpit.

b. A shelf-like projection on the side of a rock or mountain.

1732 LEDIARD *Sethos* II. IX. 286 This stone shew'd.. a ledge which open'd a way to a sort of cave. **1748** *Anson's Voy.* II. viii. 218 In some parts it ran sloping with a rapid but uniform motion, while in others it tumbled over the ledges of rocks with a perpendicular descent. **1850** S. DOBELL *Roman* ii. Poet. Wks. (1875) 26 That breezy ledge of genial rock. **1860** TYNDALL *Glac.* I. xiv. 94 The face of a cliff.. afforded us about an inch of ledge to stand upon. **1871** L. STEPHEN *Playgr. Europe* iii. (1894) 78 We clung to the crannies and ledges of the rock. **1888** F. HUME *Mad. Midas* I. Prol., They were hanging on a narrow ledge of rock midway between earth and sky.

c. *Fortif.* = BERM.

1729, 1850 [see BERM 1]. **1852-61** *Archit. Publ. Soc. Dict.*, *Ledge* is applied to the 'bench' or 'berm' left on the face of a cutting.

d. *Meteorol.* A layer in the ionosphere corresponding to a point of inflexion in a graph of ionization density against height, i.e. a layer in which the ionization increases less rapidly with height than in the regions immediately above and below it.

1949 *Gloss. Terms Radio Propagation* (*B.S.I.*) 5 Distributions in which the vertical gradient [of ionization] falls to a minimum value greater than zero are sometimes referred to as 'ledges'. **1960** RATCLIFFE & WEEKES in J. A. Ratcliffe *Physics Upper Atmosphere* ix. 437 The complicated loss process.. stimulates recombination so that an *F1* ledge is produced. **1967** *Proc. IEEE* LV. 17/1 Within the F region the main features of the vertical distribution of electrons are the F1 'ledge' at about 160 to 200 km.. and the F2 'peak' which generally lies between 250 and 400 km.

4. A ridge of rocks, esp. such as are near the shore beneath the surface of the sea; †a range of mountains or hills (*obs.*); a ridge of earth.

1555 EDEN *Decades* 351 There is a ledge of rockes on the southeast parte of the rode. **1626** CAPT. SMITH *Accid. Yng. Seamen* 18 A shoule, a ledge of rockes. **1652-62** HEYLIN *Cosmogr.* III. (1673) 57/1 We must cross Mount Hermon a ledg of Hills, which.. bend directly South. **1658** EVELYN *Fr. Gard.* (1675) 13 Break away the ledge of earth. **1699** DAMPIER *Voy.* II. II. 25 To the North of these Islands lyes a long ledge of Rocks bending like a Bow. **1725** DE FOE *Voy. round World* (1840) 63 A pretty high ledge of hills. **1762** FALCONER *Shipwr.* II. 835 That buoyant lumber may sustain you o'er The rocky shelves and ledges to the shore. **1769** —— *Dict. Marine* (1780), *Ledge* is also a long ridge of rocks, near the surface of the sea. **1867** SMYTH *Sailor's Word-bk.*, *Ledge*, a compact line of rocks running parallel to the coast, and which is not unfrequent opposite sandy beaches. **1887** BOWEN *Virg. Æneid* I. 108 Three of the ships on invisible ledges the South winds drave. **1891** S. C. SCRIVENER *Our Fields & Cities* 31 We have a view of the first principal 'ledge' of land above the Fen country.

†**5. a.** A course or layer. *Obs.*

1624 WOTTON *Archit.* 25 That the lowest Ledge or Row be meerely of Stone, and the broader the better, closely layed without Morter. *Ibid.* 29 That certain courses or Ledges of more strength then the rest, be interlayed like Bones,.. to sustaine the Fabrique from totall ruine, if the vnder parts should decay.

b. *Mining.* A stratum of metal-bearing rock; also, a quartz-vein.

1847 EMERSON *Poems, House* Wks. (Bohn) I. 472 She ransacks mines and ledges, And quarries every rock. **1863** ANSTED *Gt. Stone Bk. Nat.* II. vi. 97 The half-crystalline quartz that forms reefs or ledges,—the local name for veins and bands of quartz in sandstone rock. **1872** RAYMOND *Statist. Mines & Mining* 27 The ledges are small, and mostly lie flat, but are very rich. **1883** STEVENSON *Silverado Sq.* 211 Every miner that ever worked upon it says there's bound to be a ledge somewhere.

6. *attrib.*, as ***ledge formation, matter, rock***; **ledge-door** = *ledged-door*; **ledge-handle**, a handle of distinctive shape found on Bronze Age ware.

1825 J. NICHOLSON *Operat. Mechanic* 589 A transverse piece, called a ledge nailed across, from which the door derives the name of a *ledge-door. **1881** YOUNG *Every Man his own Mechanic* §832. 384 We may look on them [doors] speaking generally as divided into ledge doors and framed doors. **1882** *Rep. to Ho. Repr. Prec. Met. U.S.* 109 An unmistakable *ledge formation carrying quartz the entire distance. **1891** W. M. F. PETRIE *Tell el Hesy* vii. 42 The *ledge-handles are very striking and quite unknown elsewhere. They belonged to large vessels with upright sides... The ledge is of various degrees... Sometimes it is very deeply and sharply waved.. or else slightly curved,.. or merely nicked,.. or lastly a plain ledge.., without ornament or hollow. **1949** W. F. ALBRIGHT *Archæol. of Palestine* iv. 78 The envelope ledge-handle. This name, given it by P. L. O. Guy, is derived from the fact that the laps of the pushed-up ledge-handle,.. are now folded over and fastened down as neatly as though each lap were the flap of an envelope. **1952** V. G. CHILDE *New Light Most Anc. East* (ed. 4) xi. 230 Four occupational layers are superimposed at Ghassul, and some rather suspicious ledge-handles are figured from the site. **1972** Y. YADIN *Hazor* III. x. 121 Large and deep bowls with ledge-handles. **1882** *Rep. to Ho. Repr. Prec. Met. U.S.* 262 At the depth it [a mine] has now attained, the *ledge matter is larger and richer than at any previous period of its history. **1894** *Outing* (U.S.) XXIV. 339/2 Up and down the mountains over *ledge rock that spread out like stair steps.

ledge, *v.*¹ *Obs.* exc. *dial.* Also 4-7 lege, legge, 5 leadge. [Aphetic form of *alegge, aledge* ALLEGE *v.*² (Perhaps sometimes confused with ME. *legge*, dial. form of *lay*: see LAY *v.*)] = ALLEGE *v.*² Also '**ledging** *vbl. sb.*

a **1300** *Cursor M.* 28646 He.. leghges [*Cotton Galba MS.* aledges] for him no for-þi þat he na scrift mai vnderly. *Ibid.* 28679 If þis man.. for-sakes penance neuer þe lese, and legges febulnes of flexse. **1387-8** T. USK *Test. Love* I. vii. (Skeat) l. 73 [They] shoulden seen the same sentence, thei legen on other, spring out of their sides, with so many branches, it wer impossible to nomber. **1401** *Pol. Poems* (Rolls) II. 41 Thou leggist oft Goddis lawe, bot to a false entente. ?*a* **1500** *Chester Pl.* (Shaks. Soc.) II. 187 Wher is the barron wher is the knighte for me to leadge the lawe? *a* **1500** *Chaucer's Dreme* 816 He said it was nothing fitting To void pity his own legging. *c* **1530** *Crt. of Love* 1065 So he hath begon To reson fast, and legge auctorite. **1556** LAUDER *Tractate* 428 For all thare ledgin of the lawis. **1596** SHAKS. *Tam. Shr.* I. ii. 28 Nay 'tis no matter sir, what he leges in Latine. **1867** GREGOR *Banffs. Gloss.*, *Ledge*, (1) to throw out suspicions; as, 'A' bodie's beginnin' t' ledge it he's nae far fae the brackan'. (2) With the preposition *upon*, to accuse; as 'They ledge upon 'im it he cheatit the minister wee the sellan o's coo'.

ledge, *v.*² *rare.* [f. LEDGE *sb.*]

1. *intr.* To form a ledge.

1598 STOW *Surv.* xvi. (1603) 139 Euery Boorde ledging ouer other. **1879** JEFFERIES *Wild Life in S. Co.* 98 It [snow] melts on the south of every furrow leaving a white line where it has ledged on the northern side.

2. *trans.* To furnish with ledges (*obs.*); to form as a ledge.

1599 NASHE *Lenten Stuffe* Wks. (Grosart) V. 231 The burdensome detrimentes of our hauen, which euery twelue-month deuoures a Justice of peace liuing, in weares and banckes to beat off the sand, and ouerthwart ledging and fencing it in. **1845** TALFOURD *Vac. Rambles* I. 239 The road .. sometimes pierced through the blasted rock, sometimes ledged along it.

ledge, obs. and dial. form of LAY *v.*¹

ledged (lɛdʒd), *ppl. a.* [f. LEDGE *sb.* + -ED².] Having or furnished with a ledge or ledges. *ledged door*: see quot. 1842-59.

1538 LELAND *Itin.* I. 55 A Desk ledgid to set Bookes on. **1727-41** CHAMBERS *Cycl.* s.v. *Printing*, The body of the galley is ledged on three sides, to contain the slice. **1842-59** GWILT *Archit.* II. iii. §5 (ed. 4) 2130 The most inferior sort of door used in building is the common ledged door, in which five or six or seven vertical boards are held together by usually three horizontal pieces called ledges to which the vertical ones are nailed. **1880** L. WALLACE *Ben-Hur* 395 Ledged and broken walls and floor. **1898** *Daily News* 15 Mar. 6/4 A vast tract of arid rock, crannied and ledged.

ledgeless ('lɛdʒlɪs), *a.* [f. LEDGE *sb.* + -LESS.] Having no ledge.

1826 *Blackw. Mag.* XX. 278 A dizzy and ledgeless bridge, over which the very goat would almost fear to clamber.

ledgement, ledgment (ˈlɛdʒmənt). *Arch.* Also 5 lege-, ligement. [app. f. LEDGE *sb.* + -MENT.]

1. ‘A string-course or horizontal suit of mouldings, such as the base-mouldings, &c., of a building’ (*Gloss. Terms Archit.* 1850). Also ***ledgement-table.***

1435 *Contract Fotheringhay Ch.* in Dugdale *Monast.* (1673) III. II. 163 When he hath..set his ground table-stones, and his ligements, and the wall thereto withyn and without. **1443** in Willis & Clark *Cambridge* (1886) I. 385 They..shal..do be made..iiijᶜ xvj fote of legement table... And they shal haue for euery ciiij fote of the same legement ..xxxiijs. iiijd. **1849–50** WEALE *Dict. Terms, Ledgment.*

2. (See quots.)

1842 GWILT *Archit.* Gloss., *Ledgement*, the development of a surface, or the surface of a body stretched out on a plane, so that the dimensions of the different sides may be easily ascertained. **1845** *Gloss. Terms Archit.* (ed. 4) 287 *note*, When an apartment, a roof, or other complex structure, is delineated by having its plan and other component surfaces laid out or developed upon the paper, each in its proper relation to the plan as if the whole had been originally constructed by folding together and was now laid flat, the structure is said to be *laid in ledgement.*

ledger (ˈlɛdʒə(r)), *sb.* and *a.* Forms: (5 legerd), 5–9 legger, 6 ledgar, leadger, lydger, -ear, ligear, -ier, legior, 6–7 lidger, liger, legier, 6–8 lieger, leager, 6–9 leger, leiger, 7 leidger, liedger, leeger, legar, lyger, leig-, lieg-, leag-, lidgier, ligyor, legyor, 6– ledger. [The senses represent Du. *ligger* and *legger*, f. *liggen, leggen*, LIE, LAY *vbs.* The Eng. forms *lidger, ledger*, cannot be direct adoptions of the Du. words, but may be formations on Eng. *liggen, leggen*, dial. forms of LIE, LAY *vbs.* + -ER¹, in imitation of these.]

A. *sb.*

1. A book that lies permanently in some place.

†**a.** *gen. Obs.*

1538 WRIOTHESLEY *Chron.* (1875) I. 85 The curates should provide a booke of the bible in Englishe, of the largest volume, to be a lidger in the same church for the parishioners to read on.

†**b.** *spec.* A large copy of the Breviary. *Obs.*

1401 in Wylie *Hen. IV*, IV. 198 [Items of expenditure] 19 portos, 3 liggers. **1444** in *Dugdale's Mon.* VI. 1427 Duo portiphoria..alias nuncupata lyggers. **1481** *Churchw. Acc. Yatton* (Som. Rec. Soc.) 112 To John Brene writer on part of payment for the legger the x day of June..£iij. vjˢ viiiᵈ. **1484** *Ibid.* 115 Payd to the Scryvener for the legerd..xxjˢ. **1496** *Will of Howneslowe* (Somerset Ho.), Portiferium alias vocat Legger. **1530** ABP. WARHAM in *Wills Doctors' Comm.* (Camden) 23 Omnes libros meos vocatos ledgers, grayles, et antiphonaria. **1691** WOOD *Ath. Oxon.* I. 572 The said Archb. [Warham] left all his..Ledgers, Grayles and Antiphonals to Wykeham Coll.

†**c.** A record-book; a register. *Obs.*

1550 *Acts Privy Council* (1891) III. 3 To..enter..all such decrees, determinacions, and other thinges..in a booke, to remaigne alwaies as a leger. **1553** S. CABOT *Ordinances* in Hakluyt *Voy.* (1589) 259 To put the same into a common leger to remain of record for the companie. **1605–47** HABINGTON *Surv. Worcs.* in *Proc. Worc. Hist. Soc.* I. 33, I was suffered by a speciall frynd to see the Legers of the Church of Worcester. **1625** GILL *Sacr. Philos.* VIII. 136 Some Liger, or booke of record, wherein such memorable things were written..as might serue for remembrance to future ages. **1666** WOOD *Life* 25 June, Perused the evidences of Queen's Coll., and afterwards a leiger, or transcript of all the evidences.

d. *Comm.* The principal book of the ‘set of books’ ordinarily employed for recording mercantile transactions.

Its distinctive feature is that its contents consist of ‘debtor-and-creditor accounts’. Usually each person (or firm) with whom the trader has business relations has an account in the ledger, headed with his name, and showing the sums charged to his debit on the left page or half-page, and on the right those credited to him. In the system of ‘double entry’ the ledger includes other accounts of similar form to these, but headed with the designations of certain branches or subdivisions of the trader's own business.

1588 J. MELLIS *Briefe Instruct.* C iv b, After you haue thus sette euery parcell orderly in your Iournal, then it behoueth you to take out the said parcelles, and compile and indite them into the third booke, called the Leager, which commonly is made of double so many leaues as is the Iournall. **1662–3** PEPYS *Diary* 7 Jan., So to my office all the morning, signing the Treasurer's ledger. **1679** R. CHAMBERLAIN *Accomptant's Guide* Pref., At the end of the Leager there is a ballance of the Leager. **1745** *De Foe's Eng. Tradesman* (1841) II. xxxii. 43 It is usual to mark the ledgers alphabetically thus—Ledger No. A. **1783** BURKE *Rep. Affairs Ind.* Wks. XI. 291 The journals and legers of the Treasury. **1838** DICKENS *Nich. Nick.* xvi, He had a thick ledger lying open before him. **1873** HAMERTON *Intell. Life* x. viii. (1875) 379 The mind is like a merchant's ledger, it requires to be continually posted up to the latest date.

fig. **1809–10** COLERIDGE *Friend* (1818) III. 315 An improved system of book-keeping for the ledgers of calculating self-love.

2. a. A horizontal timber in a scaffolding, lying parallel to the face of the building and supporting the putlogs. (Cf. *ligger.*)

1571 *Stanford Churchw. Acc.* in *Antiquary* XVII. 170/1 It. for iiijᶜ prays & a hundreth lydgers xijd. **1703** T. N. *City & C. Purchaser* 231 In Building of Scaffolds..the Ledgers.. are those pieces that lie Parallel to the side of the Building. **1703** MOXON *Mech. Exerc.* 251 Timber, or short Poles.. from the Leggers into their Brickwork. **1823** P. NICHOLSON *Pract. Build.* 303 A frame of wood, braced with strong pieces of timber, and secured by ledgers and feet. **1883** *Law Times Rep.* XLIX. 139/1 The scaffolding was constructed of five.. uprights and one ledger, this ledger being only two boards wide instead of five.

b. In Thatching, a wooden rod laid across the thatch to hold it in place. Cf. LEGGET.

1916 C. F. INNOCENT *Devel. Eng. Building Construction* xiii. 196 After the ‘yelms’ are laid, a ledger, that is, a pointed stick, is thrust into the straw, the length of it being carried across three or four ‘yelms’ and tied to the rafters at the opposite end. *Ibid.* 198 This method of securing thatch by rods laid across it is..that most generally used in England. The rods, or ‘ledgers,’ may be either tied or ‘sewn’ to the rafters, or they may be held down by ‘broaches’. **1949** H. L. EDLIN *Woodland Crafts in Brit.* xi. 67 In most parts of Britain thatching materials are secured to the roofs of thatched houses or stacks by narrow pegs of wood, usually hazel. One common name for these is *spars*, but they have many others... *Withynecks, ledgers* and *roovers* have all been recorded. **1959** G. HOGG *Country Crafts* 123 The ‘diamond’ pattern which a thatcher produces by laying strips of cleft hazel or other thin wood, which he refers to as ‘ledgers’, criss-cross along the roof a little below the ridge on each side.

3. A flat stone slab covering a grave.

c **1510** *Contr. for tomb Hen. VII*, in Britton *Arch. Antiq.* (1809) II. 21, 100 foote of blacke towchestone is sufficient for the legger and the base of the said tombe. **1852** J. L. CHESTER *Westm. Abbey Reg.* (1876) 514 *note*, Buried in the North Cloister of Westminster Abbey, under a black marble ledger, close to the North wall. **1883** KERRY *St. Lawrence, Reading* 136 The old ledger on which Barton's brass was laid. **1890** *Archæol. Jrnl.* XLVII. 100 A ledger in the chancel at Burton commemorates Sir William Goring.

4. The nether millstone. Now *dial.*

a **1530** HEYWOOD *Play Weather* (Brandl) 743 Fere not the lydger, be ware your ronner..Perchaunce your lydger doth lache good peckyng. **1686** PLOT *Staffordsh.* 170 The Mole-cop-stone being always the runner, and the Darbyshire stone, the Legier. **1825** J. NICHOLSON *Operat. Mechanic* 451 The bed of masonry which supports the legger.

5. *Angling.* Short for *ledger-bait* (see 8).

1653 WALTON *Angler* vii. 149 You may fish for a Pike, either with a ledger, or a walking-bait; and you are to note that I call that a ledger which is fix'd, or made to rest in one certaine place when you shall be absent. **1859** S. C. HALL *Bk. Thames* 278 The usual practice is to fish for barbel with the ledger. **1882** *Daily Tel.* 28 Oct. 2/4 The only chance is to fish with a leger on the submerged banks in the eddies for roach.

6. An ordinary or resident ambassador; also, a papal nuncio. *Obs.* exc. *Hist.* in form *lieger.*

1548 HALL *Chron., Hen. VIII* (1809) 724 The Viscount Rochforth retorned into England & so did the Bishop of Bathe shortly after leavyng Sir Anthony Broune behind for a Ligier. **1563–87** FOXE *A. & M.* (1596) 260/1 The realme was neuer lightlie without some of the popes ligiers with all violence exacting and extorting continuall provisions, contributions, [etc.]. **1577–87** HOLINSHED *Chron.* III. 896/2 The bishop of Bath..laie there for the king as legier. **1599** HAKLUYT *Voy.* II. 165 William Harborne was sent first Ambassadour unto Sultan Murad Can—with whom he continued as her Majesties Ligier almost sixe yeeres. **1605** BACON *Adv. Learn.* II. xxiii. §20 A Nuntio of the pope, returning from a certayne Nation, where hee serued as Lidger. **1630** M. GODWYN tr. *Bp. Hereford's Ann. Eng.* (1675) 39 Prat, Leiger here for the Emperour,..without leave withdrew himself from court. *a* **1639** SPOTTISWOOD *Hist. Ch. Scot.* VI. (1655) 351 By a letter sent from Mr. Archibald Douglas that stayed as Lieger in England, he found him not well disposed in the businesse. **1655** FULLER *Ch. Hist.* III. v. §22 A Nuncio differed from a Legate, almost as a Lieger from an extraordinary Ambassadour. **1855** COSTELLO *Stor. Screen* 3, I was then—as I am now—the lieger of the house of Nidau.

7. *transf.* and *fig.* **a.** A (permanent) representative; a commissioner; an agent; also, an ‘ambassador of the Gospel’. *Obs.* or *arch.* in form *lieger.*

1603 SHAKS. *Meas. for M.* III. i. 59 Lord Angelo hauing affaires to heauen Intends you for his swift Ambassador, Where you shall be an euerlasting Leiger. **1607** DEKKER *Knts. Conjur.* (1842) 34 The poxe lyes there as deaths legyer. **1611** BARKSTED *Hiren* (1876) 87 But sighes he sends out on this embassie, Liegers that dye ere they returne againe. **1619** HUTTON *Follie's Anat.* A 7 He..like a ledger at the Tables end Takes place for an inuited friend. **1627–77** FELTHAM *Resolves* I. xii. 19 Every good man is a Leiger here for Heaven. **1651** JER. TAYLOR *Clerus Dom.* 20 God sent at first Embassadours extraordinary and then left his Leigers in his Church for ever. **1664** BUTLER *Hud.* II. iii. 140 Has not this present Parliament A Ledger to the Devil sent, Fully empowr'd to treat about Finding revolted Witches out? **1671** FLAVEL *Fount of Life* viii. 23 The Mediator that made it, lies as a Lidger in heaven to maintain it for ever and prevent new Jars. **1791** COWPER *Iliad* xxiv. 171 Mark me, —I come, a lieger sent from Jove [Gr. Διὸς δέ τοι ἄγγελος εἰμι].

†**b.** One who is permanently or constantly in a place; a resident. *Obs.*

1599 B. JONSON *Ev. Man out of Hum.* IV. iv, Hee's a lieger at Horne's ordinarie yonder. **1611** SPEED *Hist. Gt. Brit.* VII. xiv. (1623) 416 King Ethelred thus rid of these his vnlooked for guests, sought to remoue those leigers that lay in Cumberland. **1612** BP. HALL *Serm.* v. 63 All Palestine..was but, as Jerome which was a lieger there reckons it, 160 miles long. **1650** FULLER *Pisgah* 428 Seeing it is said of Anna.. that she departed not from the Temple, it will be enquired whether any women were constantly Leigers to live therein. *a* **1661** —— *Worthies* (1662) I. 4 Of these wonders, some were transient,.. others Liegers and Permanent.

†**c.** ***Welsh ledger:*** ?‘a jocular name for the cuckoo’ (Nares). *Obs.*

1607 MIDDLETON *Five Gallants* v. i, Your deuice here is a Cuckow sitting on a tree, the Welsh Lidger; good.

8. *attrib.* and *Comb.*, as (sense 1 d) ***ledger-account, -clerk, -entry, -keeper, -man, -scroll, -work;*** also ***ledger-like*** adj.; **ledger-bait**, a fishing bait which is made to remain in one place (also *attrib.*); so ***ledger-hook, -line, -tackle;*** **ledger-blade**, in a cloth-shearing machine, the stationary straight-edged blade, placed as a tangent to and co-acting with a spiral blade on a cylinder, and used to trim the nap and reduce it to a uniform length; **ledger-millstone** = sense 4; **ledger-pole** = sense 2; **ledger-stone** = sense 3; **ledger-wall** = *foot-wall.*

1727–41 CHAMBERS *Cycl.* s.v. *Book*, The *ledger account of cash. **1902** G. H. LORIMER *Lett. Merchant* vi. 77 Some one who keeps separate ledger accounts for work and for fun. **1903** *Daily Chron.* 5 Jan. 5/5 It would be a bad day for loyalty when people considered loyalty as an item in the ledger account. **1653** WALTON *Angler* vii. 149 Your *ledger bait is best to be a living bait. **1740** R. BROOKES *Art of Angling* I. ii. 8 Ledger-Bait Angling is when the Bait always rests in one fixt and certain Place. **1839** URE *Dict. Arts*, etc. 1323 The..fixed..or..*ledger blade. **1887** *Times* 10 Oct. 3/3 The prisoner, who was employed as a *ledger clerk and accountant. **1682** SCARLETT *Exchanges* 37 A formal Journal, or *leidger Entry. **1849** FREESE *Comm. Class-bk.* 97 Forms of Ledger-Entries. **1653** WALTON *Angler* vii. 153 Having given you this direction for the baiting your *ledger hook with a live fish or frog. **1906** *Daily Chron.* 18 Sept. 3/5 A female *ledger-keeper and accountant in one office worked for 6*s.* a week. **1846** HAWTHORNE *Mosses* II. iii. (1864) 62 A folio volume of *ledger-like size and aspect. **1882** OGILVIE, **Ledger-line*,..a kind of tackle used in fishing for barbel and bream. **1883** *Fisheries Exhib. Catal.* 56 Spoon Baits, Paternosters, Ledger Lines. **1820** KEATS *Isabella* xviii, How was it these same *ledger-men could spy Fair Isabella in her downy nest? **1548** UDALL *Erasm. Par. Luke* xvii. 140 To be cast headlong into the sea with a great *lidger milstone tied about his necke. **1901** J. BLACK *Illustr. Carpenter & Builder Ser.: Scaffolding* 86 A combination of chains, clips, and screw bolts, used for securing a *ledger-pole to standard. **1949** M. L. DARLING *At Freedom's Door* I. v. 116 Till two or three years ago..Hindu Bhats from Rajputana would come every year with their long *ledger-scrolls to record in them any additions to the family. **1851** E. MOORE in *Fen & Marshland Ch.* Ser. III. (1869) 65 Two stone coffins with the *ledger stones belonging to them. **1894** JESSOPP *Random Roaming* 188 Certain rather handsome ledger stones that were lying in the chancel. **1867** F. FRANCIS *Angling* i. (1880) 51 There are many places..which..can only be fished with *ledger tackle. **1872** *Echo* 5 Aug., Heavy leger tackle. **1881** RAYMOND *Mining Gloss.*, **Ledger-wall.* **1908** *Westm. Gaz.* 24 Mar. 6/3 He came to Paris, learnt *ledger-work, and obtained a situation in a banking-house.

B. *adj.*

I. In attributive use.

†**1.** ***ledger-ambassador*** or ***ambassador ledger***: resident or ordinary ambassador. So ***ledger Jesuit.*** *Obs.*

1550 EDW. VI *Jrnl.* in *Rem.* (Roxb.) 258 That Sir John Mason shuld be embassadour ligier. **1577–87** HOLINSHED *Chron. Hist. Scot.* 344/2 Monsieur Doisell, liger ambassador for the French King. **1606** *Proc. agst. Late Traitors* 32 Baldwin the Ligier Jesuite in Flaunders. **1615** G. SANDYS *Trav.* 85 The Kings of England and of France haue here their Ledger Embassadours. *a* **1670** HACKET *Abp. Williams* I. (1692) 120 The leiger Embassador of the Catholick King. **1755** CARTE *Hist. Eng.* IV. 111 A duplicate of the order [was] sent to Sir Walter Aston, the lieger embassador. **1755** JOHNSON, *Leger*, any thing that lies in a place; as, a leger ambassador.

transf. and *fig.* *a* **1613** OVERBURY *A Wife* (1638) 286 Sleepe is Deaths Leiger-Ambassador. **1639** CADE *Serm. necess. for Times* 10 Gods Lieger Ambassadour residing in our hearts. **1649** JER. TAYLOR *Gt. Exemp.* Pref. §45 Christ having left his Ministers as Lieger Embassadours to signifie and publish the Lawes of Jesus.

†**2.** Remaining in a place; resident; permanent; stationary. Also *fig.* constantly in use; said, e.g. of a joke, ‘standing’, ‘stock’. ***ledger side***: the side on which something lies. *Obs.*

1547 *Injunct. Edw. VI* in Kitchin *Winchester Docum.* (1889) I. 184, iiij legior bybles to be hadde continually within the Churche. **1642** FULLER *Holy & Prof. St.* IV. xxi. 354 How mercifull is he to such who not out of leigier malice, but sudden passion, may chance to shed blood. **1647** CLARENDON *Hist. Reb.* v. §146 This Petition, deliver'd publickly, and read..by their Leiger Committee. **1654** GAYTON *Pleas. Notes* I. viii. 28 Like a bruised Codling Apple a little corrupted on the Leiger side. **1655** FULLER *Hist. Camb.* 156 Their habits, gestures, language, leiger-jests, and expressions. *a* **1661** —— *Worthies, Kent* (1662) II. 59 The great Soveraign, built at Dulwich, [in later edd. corrected *Woolwich*] a Lieger-ship for State, is the greatest Ship our Island ever saw. **1662** STILLINGFL. *Orig. Sacr.* II. iv. §8 God had a kind of Leiger-Prophets among his people.

3. *Mus.* **ledger line**, one of the short lines added temporarily above and below the stave to accommodate notes in a passage which cannot be contained by the usual five lines. They are numbered from the stave upward and downward, 1st, 2nd, 3rd, etc. ***ledger lines above*** or ***below***. Also ***ledger space***, a space between two ledger lines or between the stave and the 1st ledger line.

[The origin of this use is not clear; perh. the word may be the sb. used *attrib.* with allusion to sense A 2. The common statement that it represents the F. *léger* light, slight, is baseless.]

1700 PLAYFORD *Skill Mus.* i. 6 And then you add a Line or two to the five Lines, as the Song requires, those Lines so added being called Ledger-Lines. **1775** ASH, *Leg'erline*,..a line above or below the five to receive an ascending or descending note. **1793** *Trans. Soc. Arts* V. 125 The ledger or occasional lines, drawn through the heads of the notes. **1818** BUSBY *Gram. Mus.* 20 The situation of G in the first ledger space, being higher than any within the stave, that note is called *G in alt.* **1879** C. J. EVANS *Let.* in *Musical Times* 1 June, A ledger line has never been typographically either

lighter in shade or thinner in substance than its accompanying stave lines.

II. In predicative use, esp. in *to be, lie ledger*. (In many cases the word may be taken either as sb. or adj.)

4. Resident in the capacity of ambassador, commissioner or agent. *Obs.* exc. *arch.*

1560 DAUS tr. *Sleidane's Comm.* 113 His Ambassadour that was ledger at Rome. *a* **1635** CORBET *Poems* (1807) 121 He was Natures factour here, And legier lay for every sheire. **1642** W. MOUNTAGU in *Buccleuch MSS.* (Hist. MSS. Comm.) I. 300 The Committee that are to lie leiger there. **1647** CLARENDON *Hist. Reb.* II. §24 Those who..lay leiger for the Covenant, and kept up the spirits of their countrymen by their intelligence. *a* **1670** HACKET *Abp. Williams* I. (1692) 29 One that lay lieger at London for their dispatches. **1826** [see LEAGUER *sb.*¹ 4].

†**5.** Lying or resting in a place, stationary; resident. **a.** of persons.

1600 FAIRFAX *Tasso* I. lxx. 15 Returne not thou, but legier stay behinde. **1632** CHAPMAN & SHIRLEY *Ball* v. i, Two or three English spies told us they had lain leger three months to steal away the Piazza, and ship it for Covent Garden. **1638** R. WEST *To Mem. T. Randolph* 15 in *R.'s Poems*, For Humours to lye leidger they are seene. *a* **1656** USSHER *Ann.* VI. (1658) 434 Astymedes remained Lieger at Rome, that he might know what things were transacted. **1660** MILTON *Free Commw.* Wks. 1851 V. 438 They meet not from so many parts remote to sit a whole year Lieger in one place, only now and then..to convey each Man his bean or ballot into the Box.

b. of things. *Obs.*

1577 B. GOOGE *Heresbach's Husb.* 25 Wheate..yf the ground be to riche where it is sowen, it wyll growe to ranke, and lye leadge[r] vpon the grounde. **1611** MIDDLETON & DEKKER *Roaring Girl* III. i. 91 A name which Ide teare out From the hye Germaines throat, if it lay ledger there To dispatch priuy slanders against mee. **1639** FULLER *Holy War* I. xx. (1640) 32 Shiloh, where the Ark was long leiger. **1650** —— *Pisgah* II. xiv. 300 These wise men perceiving this..to be no light constantly Leiger in the skies, conclude it an extraordinary Embassadour sent upon some peculiar service. *a* **1661** —— *Worthies, Lond.* (1662) II. 223 A rusty Musket, which had lien long Leger in his Shop.

'ledger, *v. Angling.* Also leger. [f. LEDGER *sb.* (sense 5).] *intr.* To use a ledger-bait.

1688 R. HOLME *Armoury* II. 324/2 Ledger is another way of fishing for a Pike, the Angler being absent. **1859** F. FRANCIS *N. Dogvane* (1888) 19 An adept in spinning, trolling, ledgering. **1867** —— *Angling* ii. (1880) 63 The fishermen who require to cast a long line on the Thames, for ledgering or spinning. **1883** *Fisheries Exhib. Catal.* (ed. 4) 106 Jew Fish, caught by Messrs. Curtis and Senior, ledgering, Brisbane River, Queensland, Australia.

'ledger-book. Now *Hist.* (Forms: see LEDGER.) A book containing records; a register; a cartulary; a book of accounts; = LEDGER 1 b, c, d.

1553 EDW. VI *Let. to Ridley* in Strype *Eccl. Mem.* II. xxii. 421 To subscribe the same [articles] in one ledger-book to be formed for that purpose. **1599** HAKLUYT *Voy.* II. I. 96 All which particulars doe most evidently appeare out of certaine auncient Ligier bookes of the R. W. Sir William Locke Mercer of London. **1611** SPEED *Hist. Gt. Brit.* VII. xxiii. 305 The Liger booke of the Monastery of Peterborow. **1643** PRYNNE *Open. Gt. Seal* 1 Sundry ancient Charters of our English Saxon Kings, yet extant in old Leger Books of Abbeys. *c* **1645** HOWELL *Lett.* (1688) IV. 484 When I look over my leger Book of accounts, I do not find that God-Almighty is indebted to me one Penny. **1659** —— *Lex. Tetragl.*, *Proverbs* To the knowingest kind of Philologers, Touching the Method of perusing these Proverbs or Adages ..the Reder shall do well to have his Leger-Book about him when he falls upon Them, to Register therein such that Quadrat with his Conceit and Genius. **1665** WOOD *Life* 27 May, The registers leiger-books and statutes of Oryell College. **1727–41** CHAMBERS *Cycl.* s.v. *Book*, Every transaction must be entered in the ledger-book, with a balance of debt and credit. **1759** STERNE *Tr. Shandy* III. x, The ledger-book of the church of Rochester. *c* **1820** S. ROGERS *Italy* (1839) 100 Among the debtors in his leger-book Entered in full.

fig. **1599** SIR J. DAVIES *Nosce Teipsum* 47 Such formes as she doth cease to see To Memories large volume she commends. This Lidger Booke lyes in the braine behind.

ledging ('lɛdʒɪŋ). [f. LEDGE *sb.* + -ING¹.] *concr.* A ledge, or ledges collectively.

c **1817** HOGG *Tales & Sk.* (1837) I. 270 The sea in the opening was as bright as a mirror..and through it I could see the ledgins of this amazing cone [an iceberg] spreading away shelve below shelve into the channels of the ocean. **1820** A. SUTHERLAND *St. Kathleen* IV. 143 He..loupit richt ower my head, far beyont the ledgin' o' the brig. **1899** *Westm. Gaz.* 17 July 6/3 He..lay on the main deck ledging outside the saloon cabin covering board.

ledgit ('lɛdʒɪt). *Sc.* [? f. LEDGE *sb.* + *-it* = -ET¹; cf. *leafit.*] **a.** (See quot. 1867.) **b.** A label projecting from a leaf of a book.

1867 GREGOR *Banffs Gloss.*, *Ledgit*, the top of the inner half of a window. **1885** *Advt.* (from Ayr) in *Bookseller* 7 Jan. 82/2 English Catalogue of Books, 1863–74. Half-bd. With Parchment Ledgits for the Years.

ledgy ('lɛdʒɪ), *a.* [f. LEDGE *sb.* + -Y.] Abounding in or consisting of ledges or ridges of rock.

1779 LIVERMORE in *Coll. New Hampsh. Hist. Soc.* (1850) VI. 315 This swamp..has some considerable hills and ledgy mountains in it. **1878** SAWTELLE *Hist. Townsend (Mass.)* 15 It contains ledgy, waste lands, in which are wild ravines. **1882** *Harper's Mag.* LXV. 497 The small ledgy island known as 'the Nubble'.

ledi- (li:dɪ), combining form of mod.L. *Lēdum* (see LEDUM); used in chemical terms: **ledi'tannic (acid), ledi'xanthin** (see quots.).

1865 WATTS *Dict. Chem.* III. 567 *Leditannic acid*... A variety of tannic acid, obtained from the leaves of the marsh wild rosemary (*Ledum palustre*). *Ibid.*, *Ledixanthin*, a yellow or red pulverulent substance, produced by boiling leditannic acid with sulphuric or hydrochloric acid.

†**ledish,** *a. Obs.* Forms: 3 leodisc, leodiss, 4 ludych, ludisch, ledisch. [f. LEDE + -ISH.] Pertaining to the people, national.

c **1205** LAY. 2144 Cum liðen to londe þæt wes an leodisc king. *c* **1275** *Ibid.* 22684 He wolde..isen Gwenaifer þe leodisse cwene. **13..** *E.E. Allit. P.* B. 73 Þe ludych lorde. *Ibid.* 1375 Mony ludisch lordes þat ladies broȝten. *Ibid.* 1556 Ledisch lore.

‖**ledon** ('li:dən). [a. Gr. λῆδον mastic.] = LADANUM. Also *ledon-gum* (Cent. Dict.).

1884 *Cassell's Encycl. Dict.*, *Ledon.*

†**'ledor.** *Obs.*⁻⁰ [ad. Gr. λοιδορία.]

1623 COCKERAM, *Ledors*, biting taunts.

ledra ('lɛdrə). *rare.* Also **ledrah.** [Cornish *ledr, ledra.*] A cliff, steep hill.

1942 A. L. ROWSE *Cornish Childhood* vii. 197 We picnicked all day on the ledrah. **1966** —— in *Listener* 9 June 845/3 When Devon was purple Cornwall was brown, With harvesting bracken On ledra and down.

ledron, variant of LIDDERON *Obs.*

‖**ledum** ('li:dəm). [mod.L., a. Gr. λῆδον mastic.] A genus of ericaceous shrubs, commonly known as Labrador tea, used in the pharmacopœia. **oil of ledum** or **ledum-oil, ledum camphor,** products obtained from *L. palustre.*

1834 GOOD *Study Med.* (ed. 4) IV. 456 Infuse four ounces of the ledum in a quart of hot water. **1858** THOREAU *Winter* (4 Feb.) 339 The ledum bears a general resemblance to the water andromeda. **1865** WATTS *Dict. Chem.*, *Ledum, oil of*.. obtained by distilling the leaves of *Ledum palustre*, with water.

ledur, -yr, obs. forms of LEATHER, LITHER.

lee (li:), *sb.*¹ Forms: α. 1 hléo, 4 leȝ, leo, 4–6 le, 5 legh, 5–6 lie, 7 lay, ley, 7, 9 lea, 4– lee. β. 1 hléow, 3 leouwe, 5 lue, 8 *dial.* loo, 9 *dial.* lew. [OE. *hléo* (gen. *hleowes*) str. neut. or masc., cognate with OFris. *hli, hly*, OS. *hleo* neut. or masc., *hlea* fem., shelter, ON. *hlé* neut., 'lee' in the nautical sense (Sw. *lä*, Da. *læ*):—OTeut. **hlewo-*, whence **hlewjo-*, **hliujo-* in ON. *hlý* neut., shelter, warmth, *hlýja* to protect. The word is also found as a nautical term in Du. *lij*, MLG. *lê* (whence G. *lee*); the history of these forms is not clear.

The OTeut. **hlewo-* has no known cognates outside Teut. The Goth. *hlija* tent, is prob. unconnected.

It is not necessary to suppose that the nautical use in Eng. is of Scandinavian origin, though it is not recorded in OE.: the form *lee* might be either from OE. or ON., but the unequivocally native forms *lue, lew* are found in the nautical use.]

I. 1. a. Protection, shelter, rarely *pl.* Also in phrases ***in, under (the) lee (of)*** both in material and immaterial senses. †Also, a resting-place.

a **900** CYNEWULF *Crist* 605 Weder liþe under sweȝles hleo. *c* **1000** *Ags. Ps.* cviii. 10 Þonne hi to his huse hleowes wilnian. *a* **1225** *Ancr. R.* 368 Mid festen, mid wechchen..mid herd weriunge, herd leouwe. *a* **1300** *Cursor M.* 23326 Þat þai þe sorfuller sal be þat losen folili has þat le. **13..** *E.E. Allit. P.* C. 277 Þenne he lurkkes & laytes where watz le best. *a* **1375** *Lay Folks Mass Bk.* App. iv. 62 Þen most Merci.. lenge wiþ vs in leo and lede. ? *a* **1400** *Morte Arth.* 1446 We lurkede undyr lee as lowrande wreches! **1513** DOUGLAS *Æneis* VII. Prol. 79 The silly scheip and thair lytill hyrd gromis Lurkis vndir le of bankis. **1596** DALRYMPLE tr. *Leslie's Hist. Scot.* I. 55 It is a bosum of the Sey, in the ley of a hich montane conteyned. **1624** CAPT. SMITH *Virginia* II. iii. (Arb.) 446 Our quarter..was onely the open woods under the lay of a hill. **1630** *Tinker of Turvey, Sea-Mans T.* 100 To come under the lee of wedlock. *a* **1649** DRUMM. OF HAWTH. *Cypress Grove* Wks. (1711) 123 Any mariner.. arriving near the shoar, would..joyfully enter the lees of a safe harbour. **1654** H. L'ESTRANGE *Chas. I* (1655) 96 Sheltered under the Lee of Royal favour. **1821** J. W. CROKER *Diary* (1884) 3 June, He wishes to have Peel under his lee. **1847** G. MITCHELL *Fresh Gleanings* (1851) 223 Cameron was thinking of Rob Roy's cave under the Lea of Ben Lomond. **1863** WISE *New Forest* 193 The labourer still sits under the lew..of the hedge. **1873** G. C. DAVIES *Mount. & Mere* xiii. 101 There he is under the lee of the opposite bank. **1901** *Speaker* 5 Jan. 375/2 Under the lee of the Turkish guns.

b. *dial.* Something constructed as a shelter.

1791 PEGGE *Derbicisms* Ser. II, *Lee*, shelter; a Sheep-lee, a wall on the moors for the sheep to stand under in bad weather. **1794** *Annals Agric.* XXII. 273 (E.D.S.) Looes or frames..are fixed all round the kiln. **1887** *Kent Gloss. Lees*, a row of trees planted to shelter a hop-garden. *Ibid.*, *Lew*, a thatched hurdle, supported by sticks, and set up in a field to screen lambs, etc. from the wind.

2. a. Chiefly *Naut.* The sheltered side of any object; hence the side (of a ship, the land, an eminence, etc.) that is turned away from the wind. Frequent in ***beneath, under the lee (of)***.

c **1400** *Destr. Troy* 2806 Paris..Shot into ship with shene men of Armys; Lausit loupis fro the le. **1556** W. TOWRSON in Hakluyt *Voy.* (1589) 99 The 12. day we saw a saile vnder our Lee. **1583** *Leg. Bp. St. Androis* Pref. 104 He lattis his scheip tak in at luife and lie. **1590** GREENE *Never too late* (1600) 43 He that at euery gust puts to the Lee, shall neuer be good Nauigator. **1591** HARINGTON *Orl. Fur.* x. xvi, They bore To come within the lue of Scottish banke. **1595** MAYNARDE *Drake's Voy.* (Hakl. Soc.) 8 Becalmed under the lee of the land. **1627** CAPT. SMITH *Seaman's Gram.* xiii. 63 They are to come vnder the Lee of the Admirall to salute him. **1667** MILTON *P. L.* I. 207 The Pilot..Moors by his side under the Lee. **1720** DE FOE *Capt. Singleton* xvi. (1840) 274 We run in as much under the lee of the point as we could. **1762** FALCONER *Shipwr.* II. 798 For rocky shores beneath our lee appear. **1814** SCOTT *Ld. of Isles* I. xxiv, Beneath the Castle's sheltering lee, They staid their course in quiet sea. **1819** BYRON *Juan* II. xlv, A tight boat will live in a rough sea, Unless with breakers close beneath her lee. **1855** O. W. HOLMES *Poems* 164 She rends the clinging sea, That flies before the roaring wind, Beneath her hissing lee. **1860** TYNDALL *Glac.* I. xxi. 146 Against..the Matterhorn the vapour was chilled and precipitated in his lee. **1881** *Isle of Wight Gloss.*, *Lew*, the lee side. **1884** PAE *Eustace* 129 The lieutenant sails as smooth as a pinnace under his lee.

b. Nautical phrases. †***at lee***: (*a*) windbound; (*b*) under shelter. †***(to bring, fall) by the lee***: to leeward; also *fig.* †***(to bring, lay, lie) upon the lee***: with sails aback. ***on, under (the) lee***: to leeward = ALEE.

1597 J. PAYNE *Royal Exch.* 33 The ship on hull, the helme on lee. **1607** MARSTON *What You Will* II. i. Wks. 1856 I. 238 Shoot him through and through with a jest; make him lye by the lee. **1611** COTGR., *Bouter vent en penne*, to bring a ship vpon the Lee. *a* **1618** RALEIGH *Apol.* 7 The *Thunder*..by the negligence of her Master, was at Lee in the Thames. **1630** J. TAYLOR (Water P.) *Fight at Sea* Wks. III. 34/2 They.. passed from vs to lay their ships by the Lee. *a* **1642** SIR W. MONSON *Naval Tracts* v. (1704) 507/1 The Ship lay upon the Lee; and..the Master called with the Whistle to fill the Sails. **1666** *Lond. Gaz.* No. 59/2 An Hollands Man of War ..whom she fought very bravely, and at last brought by the Lee, but had not Men enough to board her. **1667** *Ibid.* No. 120/1 One of them..was so warmly received with a broadside, that he immediately fell by the Lee. **1692** *Capt. Smith's Seaman's Gram.* I. xvi. 79 *A Ship lies by the Lee*, that is, has all her sails lying flat against the Masts and Shrouds. **1769** FALCONER *Dict. Marine* (1780) Z 3, 'We saw a fleet under the lee', and 'we saw a fleet to leeward', are synonymous expressions. **1825** A. CUNNINGHAM *'A Wet Sheet and a Flowing Sea'* i, Away the good ship flies, and leaves Old England on the lee. **1887** BOWEN *Virg. Æneid* III. 478 Yonder her nearest coast fate wills thee to leave on the lee.

†**3.** A sheltered position or condition; hence, calmness, peace, tranquillity. Chiefly in ***to leng, live, rest in*** (or ***on***) ***lee***. Also, in ***lithe of*** (or ***on***) ***lee***: said of the weather. *Obs.*

The alliterative phrases, *lordings, lordship in lee*, may perh. not belong to this sense.

13.. *Minor Poems fr. Vernon MS.* (E.E.T.S.) 477/10 Þe Mon þat þenkeþ to liuen in le. **13..** *Gaw. & Gr. Knt.* 849 To lede a lortschyp in lee of leudez ful gode. *c* **1375** *Sc. Leg. Saints* xxxviii. (*Adrian*) 416 Of þe fare nowmir for to be Of haly mene & reste in le. *a* **1400–50** *Alexander* 5615 He lengis in lithis & in lee to his lyues ende. *c* **1425** WYNTOUN *Cron.* VII. x. 3620 Alysandyr..Scotland led in luwe and lé. *c* **1460** *Emare* 348 The wedur was lythe of le. *c* **1470** *Golagros & Gaw.* 341 Lordingis in le, I rede ye tent treuly to my teching. *c* **1470** HENRYSON *Mor. Fab.* XIII. (*Frog & Mouse*) xxii, Better but stryfe allane to leif in le. **1535** STEWART *Cron. Scot.* (1858) II. 128 Amang thair freindis for to leve in lie. *a* **1650** *Turke & Gowin* 47 in Furnivall *Percy Folio* I. 92, I will neuer flee from noe aduenture..whilest I may liue on lee.

II. *attrib.* and *Comb.*

4. Simple attributive, passing into adj.

a. Indicating that an object is on the lee-side of a vessel, or to leeward of some other object, e.g. ***lee-bowline, -division, -gunwale, -rail, -scupper***, etc.

1513 DOUGLAS *Æneis* v. i. 30 Himself infangis the le scheit of the saill. **1626** CAPT. SMITH *Accid. Yng. Sea-men* 28 Make ready your loufe howks and ley fagnes. **1669** STURMY *Mariner's Mag.* I. 16 Let go the Lee-Bowling of Fore-sail, and Weather-Braces. *Ibid.* 18 Set in the Lee-Braces. **1726** G. ROBERTS *Four Years Voy.* 291 They could help to stay her with a Lee Oar. **1748** *Anson's Voy.* II. iv. 163 The Commodore ordered them to bring to under his lee-quarter. **1751** SMOLLETT *Per. Pic.* (1779) II. lxiv. 209 He commanded the men to carry the vessel's lee-gunwale under water. **1805** *Log of H.M.S. Mars* 21 Oct. in Nicolas *Nelson's Disp.* VII. 165 *note*, At daylight saw the Enemy's Fleet on our lee-beam. *Ibid.* 166 *note*, At 9.5 answered Victory's signal for the Mars to lead the lee division. **1823** J. F. COOPER *Pioneer* xv. (1869) 66/2 Hauling in the slack of the lee-sheet. **1833** MARRYAT *P. Simple* xii, O'Brien..told me never to mind, but to keep in the lee-scuppers. *Ibid.* xv, She careened over so that her lee channels were under the water. **1835** —— *Pacha* v, We descried land on the lee beam. **1867** SMYTH *Sailor's Word-bk.*, *Lee-fang*, a rope rove through the cringle of a sail, for hauling in, so as to lace on a bonnet. *Ibid.*, *Lee-gunwale under*, a colloquial phrase for being sorely over-pressed, by canvas or other cause. **1893** F. M. CRAWFORD *Childr. King* I. 9 You would rather..take the lee earing too, in any gale. **1897** R. KIPLING *Captains Courageous* 188 She cuddled her lee-rail down to the crashing blue. **1913** J. LONDON *Let.* 20 Nov. (1966) 410 Sailing with lee-rail continually buried. **1961** F. H. BURGESS *Dict. Sailing* 132 *Lee rail awash, with*, heeled well over.

b. Implying motion to leeward.

1726 G. ROBERTS *Four Years Voy.* 120 The Lee-Tide being made, I fell short by half a League. **1790** BEATSON *Nav. & Mil. Mem.* I. 157 The strong lee current. **1848** CRAIG, *Lee lurch*, a sudden and violent roll of a ship to leeward in a high sea, when a large wave strikes her on the weather side. **1859** R. H. DANA *Cuba & Back* i. 7 The.. leisurely weather-roll and lee-roll.

5. Special combs.: **lee-anchor** (see quot.); **lee-bow,** the bow of a vessel that is turned away from the wind; hence *lee-bow* vb., to run under

the lee bow of; *fig.* to take advantage of; **lee-gage** (see GAUGE 5); **lee-hatch, -hitch** (see quots.); **lee-helm**, the helm when 'down' (cf. *down with the helm* s.v. HELM *sb.*² 1 c); **lee ho!, lee o!** (see quots.); **lee-latch**, 'dropping to leeward of the course' (Smyth *Sailor's Word-bk.* 1867); **lee-most** *a.*, furthest to leeward; **lee-port**, a sheltered port; **lee wheel**, 'the assistant to the helmsman' (Adm. Smyth). Also LEE-BOARD¹, LEE-SHORE, LEE-SIDE.

1867 SMYTH *Sailor's Word-bk.*, **Lee-anchor*, the leeward one, if under weigh; or that to leeward to which a ship, when moored, is riding. **1697** DAMPIER *Voy.* I. 100 Some of them appeared on our Weather-bow, some on our *Lee-bow. **1840** R. DANA *Bef. Mast* xxv. 83 The anchor on the lee bow had worked loose. **1893** *Outing* (U.S.) XXII. 96/1 Hauling her close on the wind so that she would 'lee-bow' the tide. **1867** SMYTH *Sailor's Word-bk.* s.v., *Take care of the *Lee hatch*, a word of caution to the helmsman, not to let the ship fall to leeward of her course. **1883** *Man. Seamanship for Boys' Training Ships R. Navy* (Admiralty) (1886) 78 If carrying too much weather-helm, shift the weights further aft; if *lee-helm, further forward. **1948** R. DE KERCHOVE *Internat. Maritime Dict.* 407/1 A sailing craft is said to carry lee helm when the helm has to be kept alee to counteract slackness and keep it on its course. **1962** A. G. COURSE *Dict. Naut. Terms* 120 *Lee helm*, a term used in sailing ships to indicate that the tiller is to leeward and the rudder and wheel to windward. **1867** SMYTH *Sailor's Word-bk.* s.v., **Lee-hitch*, the helmsman getting to leeward of the course. **1927** G. BRADFORD *Gloss. Sea Terms* 99/2 **Lee ho!*, a command given by English yachtsmen preparatory to bringing a boat about; same as *hard a lee*. **1961** F. H. BURGESS *Dict. Sailing* 133 *Lee-o*, the helmsman's warning to a crew before going about. **1721** BAILEY, **Lee-latch*, (Sea Phrase) have a care of the Lee-Latch, i.e. keep the Ship near the Wind. **1622** R. HAWKINS *Voy. S. Sea* (1847) 17 The vice-admirall and her consort..were *lee-most and stern-most of all. **1804** CAPT. OWEN in *Naval Chron.* XII. 132 The leemost Brigs began to get under weigh. *a* **1649** DRUMM. OF HAWTH. *Cypress Grove* Wks. (1711) 125 Lords and gods of this earth, sleeping in the *lee-port of honour.

Hence **lee** *v. rare*⁻¹, *trans.*, to put (the helm) a-lee. See A-LEE.

1659 DAVENANT *Hist. Sir F. Drake* ii. 13 The Master alowd bids, Lee the Helm, Lee!

lee (liː). *sb.*² *Obs.* exc. in *pl.* Forms: *sing.* 4 lie, 5 ley(e, lye, 7–9 lee. *pl.* 4–6 lyes, 5–6 lies, 6 leese, leeze, lyse, 6– lees. [a. F. *lie*, Gaulish L. *lia*, pl. *liæ* (10th c.); Celtic origin has been conjectured.] The sediment deposited in the containing vessel from wine and some other liquids.

†**1.** *sing.* Also *fig.* Also *upon the lee*, *to drain to the lee*. Cf. 2 d below. *Obs.*

1390 GOWER *Conf.* (M.) III. 895 (I. 309) And thus fuloften have I boght The lie, And drank noght of the wyn. *c* **1430** *Two Cookery-bks.* 32 Whan þe ley is seþin hot, caste þe Pesyn þer-to. **1481** CAXTON *Myrr.* I. i. 6 The lye whiche is thordure abideth byneth in the bottom. **1686** PLOT *Staffordsh.* 338 Which..will both stop the fermentation and precipitate the Lee. **1700** DRYDEN *Sigism. & Guisc.* 317 A man so smelling of the people's lee. **1703** *Art & Myst. Vintners* 23 The gross Lees settle quickly, and also the flying Lee in time. **1709** *Lond. Gaz.* No. 4512/14 For Sale,..70 Hogsheads of new.. Claret upon the Lee neat. **1718** PRIOR *Henry & Emma* 497 I'll mingle with the people's wretched lee. **1747** *Gentl. Mag.* 468 This cyder..should be rack'd off once at least from its gross lee. **1813** HOGG *Queen's Wake* 183 Sweet though the draught of pleasure be, Why should we drain it to the lee?

2. *pl.*

c **1384** CHAUCER *H. Fame* III. 1040 Boystes Crammed ful of lyes As euer vessel was with lyes. *c* **1460** J. RUSSELL *Bk. Nurture* 115 The reboyle to Rakke to þe lies of þe rose. **1530** PALSGR. 239/1 Lyse of wyne, *lye*. **1580** LYLY *Euphues* (Arb.) 328 Ther is..no wine made of grapes but hath leese. **1642** FULLER *Holy & Prof. St.* II. xvi. 110 Wines the stronger they be the more lees they have when they are new. **1692** BENTLEY *Boyle Lect.* iv. 11 Where all the heavier Lees may have time to subside. **1704** SWIFT *Mech. Operat. Spirit* Misc. (1711) 302 Other Spirits are produc'd from Lees, by the Force of Fire. **1763** J. BROWN *Poetry & Mus.* vi. 119 Thespis and his Company bedaubed their Faces with the Lees of Wine. **1796** MRS. GLASSE *Cookery* xxv. 377 Lay them to steep in sack lees, or any white wine lees. **1830** M. DONOVAN *Dom. Econ.* I. 257 The lees of wine, on distillation, afford the greatest quantity of oil. **1861** H. MAYHEW *Lond. Labour* II. 132 Composed of the scum and lees of all broths and soups. **1883** *Fisheries Exhib. Catal.* 352 A Bottle containing Lees of Sardine Oil.

b. *fig.* Basest part, 'dregs', 'refuse'.

1593 NASHE *Christs T.* 30 a, Twenty thousand of these dreggy lees of Libertines. **1621** S. WARD *Life of Faith* xiii. 116 In these Lees and Dregges of time. **1651** HOBBES *Leviath.* (1839) 321 Pretenders to political prudence..bred for the most part in the lees of the people. **1677** W. HUBBARD *Narrative* 119 This company of Treacherous Villains, the Dregs and Lees of the Earth. **1706** ESTCOURT *Fair Examp.* I. i. 11 A Man that will always smell of the Lees of the People. **1726–46** THOMSON *Winter* 480 He, too, with whom Athenian honour sunk, And left a mass of sordid lees behind. **1838** HALLAM *Hist. Lit.* (1841) I. ii. 216 Slowly purging off the lees of this extreme corruption. **1851** H. MELVILLE *Whale* vii. 40 My body is but the lees of my better being. **1859** KINGSLEY *Misc.* I. 166 The angler..has left for his day's work only the lees of his nervous energy. **1868** MILMAN *St. Paul's* ix. 220 It is impossible to work a revolution, especially a religious revolution, without stirring up the lees of human nature.

†**c.** construed as *sing. Obs.*

1605 SHAKS. *Macb.* II. iii. 100 The Wine of Life is drawne, and the meere Lees Is left this Vault, to brag of.

d. In various phrases, chiefly *fig.*, esp. *to drain, drink the lees*, (*to drain, drink*, etc.) *to the lees*, i.e. to the last drop, to the very end, (*to settle*) *on* or *upon the lees*.

1611 BIBLE *Isa.* xxv. 6 A feast of fat things, a feast of wines on the lees. *Ibid.*, *Jer.* xlviii. 11 Moab hath bene at ease from his youth, and hee hath setled on his lees, and hath not been emptied from vessell to vessell. **1612** T. TAYLOR *Comm. Titus* i. 7 They may not part till they have drunk..the cup of the wrath of God to the very lees. *Ibid.* ii. 6 Settle the soule vpon his lees of sinnefull lusts. *a* **1639** WOTTON *Parallel* in *Reliq.* (1651) 8 His Humours grew Tart, as being now in the Lees of favour. **1667** POOLE *Dial. betw. Protest. & Papist* (1735) 75 You are an obstinate Heretick, and settled upon the Lees. **1696** TATE & BRADY *Ps.* lxxv. 8 To drink the very Lees. **1780** COWPER *Progr. Err.* 260 Are sweet philosophy's enjoyments run Quite to the lees? **1821** KEATS *Lamia* I. 143 She felt the warmth..And, like new flowers at morning song of bees, Bloomed, and gave up her honey to the lees. **1842** TENNYSON *Ulysses* 7, I will drink Life to the lees. **1847** DISRAELI *Tancred* II. i, This Parliament will last; it will go on to the lees. **1855** MILMAN *Lat. Chr.* IV. ii. (1864) II. 206 They were doomed to drink the lees of humiliation. **1856** BOKER *Poems* (1857) II. 80 I'll drain the bitter to the very lees. **1868** J. H. BLUNT *Ref. Ch. Eng.* I. 41 The people at large were content to settle down on their lees. **1871** PUSEY *Lenten Serm.* vii. (1883) 141 We reverse the Apostle's rule, rest on our lees, remember 'the things which are behind', and forget 'those which are before'.

e. *attrib.*

1706 *Art of Painting* (1744) 107 Leonardo's carnations have too much of the lees-colour in them.

†**lee**, *a. Obs.* Also 5–6 le, 6–8 lee. Cf. LEW *a.* [f. LEE *sb.*¹] Sheltered from the wind.

c **1400** *Destr. Troy* 4675 Þai..logget hom to lenge in þat le hauyn. *c* **1450** HOLLAND *Howlat* 18 The land lowne was and le, with lyking and luf. *c* **1470** HENRYSON *Mor. Fab.* VII. (*Lion & Mouse*) xxxviii, The fair forest with leuis lowne and le. **1513** DOUGLAS *Æneis* X. iv. 121 The famy stour of stremis le Vp weltis from the braid palmis of tre. **1674** RAY *S. & E. C. Words* 70 *Lee* or *Lew*, Calm, under the wind. *Suss.*

¶ The ballad phrase in quot. below may possibly contain this word, used vaguely for 'pleasant'.

a **1800** *Sweet Willie & Faire Annie* xxxv. in Child *Ballads* (1885) II. 189 He is on to Annie's bower By the lei light o the moon. [**1875** J. VEITCH *Tweed* 81 Exploits by lee light of the moon.]

lee: see LE, LIE, LYE.

leeangle, var. LEANGLE.

'lee-board¹. *Obs.* Forms: 4 leburde, 6 leburd, lea boord, leebord. [a. ON. *hlé-borð*, f. *hlé* LEE *sb.*¹ + *borð* BOARD.] The lee-side (of a vessel).

? *a* **1400** *Morte Arth.* 3625 Ledys one leburde, lordys and oþer. **1570** *Henry's Wallace* IX. 56 Leidis on leburd [*MS.* luff burd]. **1582** N. LICHEFIELD *Castanheda's Conq. E. Ind.* lxxix. 161 The other Captayns being a Lea boord, and hearing the sound of the ordinance, did returne. **1585** JAS. I *Ess. Poesie* (Arb.) 16 Graunt syne, o Neptune, god of seas profound, That readars think on leebord.

lee-board² ('liːbɔəd). [f. LEE *sb.*¹ + BOARD.] A strong frame of plank, fixed to the side of a flat-bottomed vessel, which, being let down into the water diminishes her drift to leeward.

1691 T. H[ALE] *Acc. New Invent.* 126 Of the Lee-boards, their use, dimension and place. **1732** LORD TYRAWLY in *Buccleuch MSS.* (Hist. MSS. Comm.) I. 381 The Molettas ..steer almost altogether by their lee-board. **1813** *Gentl. Mag.* June 522/1 With respect to keeping to windward, lee-boards and sliding keels will effect this. **1829** MARRYAT *F. Mildmay* ii, The lee-board of a Dutch schuyt.

'lee-boarded, *a.* [f. LEE-BOARD².] Fitted with a lee-board.

1897 KIPLING *Five Nations* (1903) 40 Do you know the shallow Baltic..Where the bluff, lee-boarded fishing-luggers ride?

leech (liːtʃ), *sb.*¹ Forms: 1 lǽce, *Northumb.* léce, 2–6 leche, 3 lache, læche, liache, 3, 6 leache, 4 leyche, 4–5 leeche, 4–6 lech, 5 leeche, lieche, 6 *Sc.* leiche, leitche, 6–9 leach, 6– leech. [OE. *lǽce* str. masc. (once *lǽca* wk.), corresponds to OFris. (dative) *letza*, *leischa*, OHG. *lâhhi*, MSw. *läkir* (Da. *læge*; ON. has the cognate *lǽknir*, and mod.Sw. *läkare*, from the vb. *läka* to heal), Goth. *lêkeis*:—OTeut. **lǣkjo-z*:—pre-Teut. **lēgio-s*; the synonymous Irish *liaigh* (OIr. *liaig*, dat. pl. *legib*) is app. related in some way.]

1. A physician; one who practises the healing art.

Now *arch.* (chiefly *poet.*) or *jocular*; often apprehended as a transferred use of LEECH *sb.*² In the 17th c. it was applied in ordinary prose use only to veterinary practitioners, and this sense survives in some dialects. (See also the combs. *bullock-leech*, *cow-leech*, HORSE-LEECH, etc.)

c **900** tr. *Bæda's Hist.* IV. xxi. [xix.] (1890) 320 Cyneferð læce, se æt hire wæs, þa heo forðferde. *c* **950** *Lindisf. Gosp.* Luke iv. 23 La lece lecna ðec seoline. *c* **1175** *Lamb. Hom.* 83 Nu bihoueð þe forwunded wreche þet he habbe leche. *c* **1290** *S. Eng. Leg.* I. 101/7 On leches heo hadde i-spendet Muche del of hire guod. *a* **1300** *Cursor M.* 26322 Als lech þou suld seke man hale. *a* **1340** HAMPOLE *Psalter* vi. 1 þe hand of þe leche brennand or sherend. *c* **1386** CHAUCER *Sompn. T.* 248 What nedeth hym þat hath a parfit leche To sechen othere leches in the toun? *c* **1450** *Merlin* 574 The kynge delyuered hem leches to couer theire woundes. **1513** DOUGLAS *Æneis* XIII. Prol. 80 Als stern of spech As he had bene ane medycyner or lech. **1590** SPENSER *F.Q.* I. v. 17 Many skilfull leaches him abide To salve his hurts. *a* **1656** HALES *Serm. at Eton* (1673) 40 They that come and tell you what you are to believe,..and tell you not why, they are not *Medici*, but *Veterinarii*, they are not Physicians, but Leaches. **1715** ROWE *Lady Jane Grey* I. i. 2 The hoary wrinkled Leach has ..Try'd ev'ry health-restoring Herb and Gum. **1776** *Phil. Trans.* LXVI. 498 A farrier and bullock-leach. **1807** CRABBE *Par. Reg.* III. (1810) 43 Can this proud leech, with all his boasted skill, Amend the soul or body, wit or will? **1820** SCOTT *Abbot* vi, A learned leech with some new drug. *a* **1839** PRAED *Poems* (1864) II. 85 Grudging the leech his growing bill. **1870** MORRIS *Earthly Par.* I. I. 121 As one who lays all hope aside, Because the leech has said his life must end.

b. *transf.* and *fig.* Applied often to God and Christ, and spiritual persons.

a **1200** *Moral Ode* 303 Ich kan beo ȝif i scal lichame and soule liache. *c* **1200** *Trin. Coll. Hom.* 41 Ure louerd ihesu crist is alre herdene herde and alre lechene leche. *a* **1225** *Ancr. R.* 182 Þus is sicnesse soule leche, & salue of hire wunden. **1340** *Ayenb.* 129 Þe holi gost is þe guode leche þet amaystreþ his ziknesse. *c* **1386** CHAUCER *Sompn. T.* 184 God that is oure lyues leche. *c* **1420** *Pallad. on Husb.* XII. 129 The best Of benes boyled water may be leche To sle the frost. *a* **1547** SURREY in *Tottel's Misc.* (Arb.) 221 My hartes delight my sorowes leche mine earthly goddesse here.

†**2.** = *leechman*, LEECH-FINGER. *Obs.*

c **1290** *S. Eng. Leg.* 308/311 Þe nexte finguer hatte 'leche'. *c* **1475** *Pict. Voc.* in Wr.-Wülcker 753/2 *Hic medius*, the longman. *Hic medi[c]us*, the leche. *Hic auricularis*, the lythylman.

3. *attrib.* and *Comb.*, as **leech-fee**, 'a physician's fee' (*Cent. Dict.*); †**leech-house**, a hospital; **leechman**, †a physician; also (now *dial.*) = LEECH-FINGER.

14.. *Camb. MS. Ff.* v. 48 lf. 82 (Halliw., s.v. *Fingers*) The lest fyngir hat lityl man, for hit is lest of alle; The next fynger hat leche man, for quen a leche dos oȝt, With that fynger he tastes all thyng, howe that hit is wroȝt. **1483** *Cath. Angl.* 211/1 A Leche house, *laniena*, *quia infirmi ibi laniantur*. **1591** SYLVESTER *Du Bartas* I. iv. 401 Light-bringer, Laureat, Leach-man, all-Reviver. **1600** F. L. *Ovid's Remedy of Love* B 2, The Leachmans skill. **1888** *Syd. Soc. Lex.*, *Leechman*, a practitioner of medicine.

leech (liːtʃ), *sb.*² Forms: 1 lǽce, (lýce), 3 liche, 4–6 leche, 5 *Sc.* leiche, 6–9 leach, 6– leech. [OE. *lǽce*, Kentish *lýce* str. masc. = MDu. *lake* (Kilian *laecke*, *lijck-laecke*, mod.Flemish *lijklake*), *lieke*, *leke* fem.

Commonly regarded as a transf. use of LEECH *sb.*¹; this is plausible, but the forms OE. *lyce*, early ME. *liche*, MDu. *lieke*, suggest that the word was originally distinct, but assimilated to *lǽce* LEECH *sb.*¹ through popular etymology.]

1. a. One of the aquatic blood-sucking worms belonging to the order *Hirudinea*: the ordinary leech used medicinally for drawing blood belongs to the genus *Hirudo* or *Sanguisuga*. (See also HORSELEECH, *land-leech* (LAND *sb.*¹ 11 b), *sea-leech*, *water-leech*, etc.)

a **900** *Kentish Glosses* in Wr.-Wülcker 85/11 *Sanguissuge*, lyces. *c* **1000** ÆLFRIC *Gloss.* ibid. 121/36 *Sanguisuga*, *uel hirudo*, læce. *a* **1275** *Prov. Ælfred* 472 in *O.E. Misc.* 131 Suket þuru is liche, so dot liche blod. *c* **1440** *Promp. Parv.* 291/2 Leche, wy(r)m of þe watur, *sanguissuga*. **1508** KENNEDIE *Flyting w. Dunbar* 45 Lat him lay sax leichis on thy lendis. **1533** ELYOT *Cast. Helthe* (1541) 61 Evacuation by wormes, founde in waters called bloudde suckers or leaches. **1656** RIDGLEY *Pract. Physick* 154 Leeches set behind the Ears. **1794** BURKE *Sp. Impeachm. W. Hastings* Wks. XV. 351 He was driven out of it finally by the rebellion, and, as you may imagine, departed like a leech full of blood. **1803** *Med. Jrnl.* X. 430 The application of four leeches to each ankle. **1822–34** *Good's Study Med.* (ed. 4) IV. 2 The *hirudo viridis* or green leech [is well known to multiply] by longitudinal sections. **1861** HULME tr. *Moquin-Tandon* II. III. iv. 140 There are three principal varieties of Leeches employed in France. These are—1st, the Grey Leech; 2nd, the Green Leech; 3rd, the Dragon Leech ..(true English or Speckled Leech).

transf. **1833** ALISON *Hist. Europe* (1849–50) II. viii. §34. 261 Those female furies, aptly termed the 'leeches of the guillotine'.

Proverbial phrase. *c* **1839** W. E. FORSTER in Reid *Life* (1888) I. iv. 115 He [Cobden] is..likely to mistake a crotchet for a principle and stick to it like a leech.

b. Surg. ***artificial leech***: see quot. 1875.

1858 in SIMMONDS *Dict. Trade*. **1875** KNIGHT *Dict. Mech.* s.v., *Artificial Leech*, a light glass tube from which the air is expelled by the vapor of ether, and whose mouth is then applied to a previously scarified portion of the body. **1879** *St. George's Hosp. Rep.* IX. 497 The artificial leech was applied to the temple on three occasions.

c. *fig.* One who 'sticks to' another for the purpose of getting gain out of him.

1784 COWPER *Task* III. 817 The spendthrift, and the leech That sucks him. **1794** PIGOTT *Female Jockey Club* (ed. 4) Pref. 20 Are the hearts of these leeches softened by the possession of such scandalous monopoly? **1842** TENNYSON *Will. Waterproof* xxv, Ere days, that deal in ana, swarm'd His literary leeches. **1883** J. PARKER *Tyne Ch.* 86 It's a sticking leech you have laid on me this time, and a famous biter.

2. *attrib.* and *Comb.*, as ***leech-bite***, ***-bleeder***, ***-breeder***, ***-dealer***, ***-family***, ***-gatherer***, ***-tribe***; ***leech-like*** *adj.* and *adv.*; **leech-eater**, a name for the Spur-winged Plover (*Holopterus spinosus*) and the Crocodile-bird (*Pluvianus ægyptius*); **leech-extract**, an extract prepared from leeches, used in physiological experiments for intravenous or intraperitoneal injections; **leech-gaiter**, a kind of gaiter worn in Ceylon as a protection against land-leeches; **leech-glass** *Surg.*, a glass tube to hold a leech which it is

required to apply to a particular spot; †**leech-worm** = 1.

1882 DE WINDT *Equator* 57 We..reached the bungalow.. none the worse, with the exception of *leech-bites and cut feet. **1851** in *Illustr Lond. News* 5 Aug. (1854) 119 *Leech-bleeder, *leech-breeder. **1839** *Penny Cycl.* XIII. 383/2 The *leech-dealers of Bretagne. **1885** *Riverside Nat. Hist.* (1888) IV. 100 The so-called spur-winged plover (*Hoplopterus spinosus*)..claims the distinction of being the '*leech-eater' or 'trochilos' of Herodotus. **1898** *Allbutt's Syst. Med.* V. 420 Organic substances such as fibrin ferment, hemi-albumose, peptones, nuclein, and *leech extract..have the effect on injection, of bringing about a marked and rapid diminution in the number of leucocytes. **1839** *Penny Cycl.* XIII. 383/1 Cuvier thinks it doubtful whether the species of this genus [*Clepsina*] should be arranged with the *leech family. **1859** TENNENT *Ceylon* I. 303 The coffee planters, who live among these pests, are obliged..to envelope their legs in '*leech gaiters' made of closely woven cloth. **1802** WORDSW. *Resolut. & Indep.* xx, I'll think of the *leech-gatherer on the lonely moor. **1839** *Penny Cycl.* XIII. 384/1 It is difficult to make them fix themselves on the particular spot wished; but a *leech-glass will generally effect this. **1682** DRYDEN *Medal* 149 The Witnesses, that, *Leech-like, liv'd on bloud. **1819** SHELLEY *Eng. in 1819*, 5 Rulers who neither see nor feel nor know, But leech-like to their fainting country cling, Till they drop, blind in blood, without a blow. **1905** *Westm. Gaz.* 8 Jan. 3/2 He is prepared to stick to it with almost leech-like tenacity. **1908** *Ibid.* 6 Oct. 10/2 Parasitical and leech-like characteristics. **1963** R. P. DALES *Annelids* ix. 176 The parasitic leech-like branchiobdellids also belong to the Prosopora. **1835-6** TODD *Cycl. Anat.* I. 170/2 There is observed in the *leech-tribe something analogous to the lesser circulation. **1794** *Sporting Mag.* IV. 271 Observations on the *Leech worm, by a Gentleman who kept one several Years for the purpose of a Weather-glass.

leech (liːtʃ), *sb.*³ *Naut.* Forms: 5 lek, leche, lyche, 7 leatch, 7, 9 leach, 7- leech. [Of obscure origin; app. related in some way to ON. *lík* (a nautical term of obscure meaning; the Sw. *lik*, Da. *lig* mean 'bolt-rope'), Du. *lijk*, G. *liek*, leech-line.] **a.** Either vertical edge of a square sail; the aft edge of a fore-and-aft sail. Also with qualifications, as ***after-leech, mast-leech, roach-leech, weather-leech.***

1485 [see b]. **1496** *Ld. Treas. Acc. Scotl.* (1877) I. 300 Item, to Dauid Gourlay, for making of a bonat and the lek to it. **1611** COTGR., *Penne d'un voile*,..the Leech of a sayle. **1627** CAPT. SMITH *Seaman's Gram.* vii. 32 The Leech of a saile is the outward side or skirt of the saile from the earing to the clew, the middle betwixt which wee account the Leech. **1762** FALCONER *Shipwr.* II. 62 The leeches taught, the hallyards are made fast. **1835** MARRYAT *Jac. Faithf.* xvii, They were handing in the leech of the sail, when snap went one bunt-line. **1881** CLARK RUSSELL *Sailor's Sweetheart* I. v. 123 The leech of the top-gallant sail. **1948** R. DE KERCHOVE *Internat. Maritime Dict.* 407/1 *Leech*, the side of a square sail, or the afteredge of a fore-and-aft sail. Also called skirt when referring to square sails.

b. *attrib.* in †**leech-hook**, a hook for attaching the leech-line to the sail; **leech-line**, a rope attached to the leech, serving to truss the sail close up to the yard; **leech-lining** (see quot. 1883); **leech-rope** (see quot. 1769).

1485 *Naval Acc. Hen. VII* (1896) 38 Shanke hokes.., Pakke hokes.., *Leche hokes. **1495** *Ibid.* 158 Lyche hokes of Yron,..loff hokes of yron. **1626** CAPT. SMITH *Accid. Yng. Sea-men* 30 Cleare your *leach-lines. **1627** —— *Seaman's Gram.* v. 23 Leech lines are small ropes made fast to the Leech of the top-sailes. **1860** *Merc. Marine Mag.* VII. 113 A leach-line is bent on each yard-arm. **1883** *Man. Seamanship for Boys' Training Ships R. Navy* (Admiralty) (1886) 53 *Q.* What is a goring cloth? *A.* A side cloth of a topsail,..or lining of a topsail, called by sailmakers the *leech lining. **1769** FALCONER *Dict. Marine* (1780), **Leech-rope*, a name given to that part of the bolt-rope, to which the border, or skirt of a sail is sewed. **1800** *Asiat. Ann. Reg., Chron.* 23/2 The leech ropes of the fore-sail, main-sail, fore-top sail, and mizen-top-sail. **1885** LADY BRASSEY *The Trades* 465 Repaired leech rope of mizen and set the sail.

leech (liːtʃ), *sb.*⁴ (See quots.)

1805 LUCCOCK *Nat. Wool* 15 The part of the staple through which the shears passed to separate it from the sheep (and which is commonly called the leech of the fleece). *Ibid.* 310 In some instances a quantity of dirt is concealed by the custom of winding fleeces with the leech outwards. **1892** SIMMONDS *Dict. Trade* Suppl., *Leech*, the technical name for a bundle or small parcel of human hair.

leech (liːtʃ), *v.*¹ Now *rare* and *arch.* Forms: 3 liache, *Orm.* læchenn; 3-6 leche, 4-5 liche, 5-6 lech, 5, 7 leach, 6 leeche, 9 leech. [Early ME., f. LEECH *sb.*¹; cf. Sw. *läka*, Da. *læge*. The sense was expressed in OE. by *lácnian, lǽcnian*: see LECHNE *v.*] *trans.* To cure, heal.

c **1200** ORMIN 4274 He comm her to læchenn uss Off all þatt dæþess wunde. *Ibid.* 17227 Hiss gast Iss clennsedd & rihht læchedd. *a* **1300** *Cursor M.* 176 Iesu crist..openlik bigan..alle þat sek ware to leche. *Ibid.* 11841 þai moght not leche his wa. **1382** WYCLIF *Job* v. 18 [The Lord] woundeth and lecheth; smyteth, and his hondis shuln helen. *c* **1440** *York Myst.* xvii. 156 A barne is borne þat shall..leche þam þat ar lorne. *c* **1450** *St. Cuthbert* (Surtees) 1832 He taght goddis wordes..And synfull' men lyues lechyd. **1564** *Louth Corporat. Acc.* (1891) 78 Paid for leching my horses verie sicke, vs. **1618** FLETCHER *Loyal Subj.* III. v, Have ye any crack maidenhead to new leach or mend? **1820** SCOTT *Ivanh.* xviii, Let those leech his wounds for whose sake he encountered them. **1850** BLACKIE *Æschylus* I. 63 A disease that none may leech.

leech, *v.*² [f. LEECH *sb.*²] *trans.* To apply leeches to medicinally. Also *absol.*

1828 G. EWING in *Mem.* (1847) xiv. 5, I was leeched and bled in the arm and am almost quite well. **1834** FORBES *Laennec's Dis. Chest* (ed. 4) 427 The patient was bled and leeched with relief. **1861** GEO. ELIOT *Silas M.* xvi, When I'm leeching or poulticing. **1897** *Allbutt's Syst. Med.* III. 346 The protruding tongue must be leeched.

leech, obs. form of, or variant of LEACH.

leecha, variant of LITCHI.

leechcraft ('liːtʃkrɑːft, -æ-). *arch.* Forms: see LEECH *sb.*¹ [OE. *lǽcecræft*, f. *lǽce* LEECH *sb.*¹ + *cræft* CRAFT.] The art of healing; medical science, †medical attendance. †*at leechcraft* under treatment. †Also *concr.* Remedy, medicine.

c **888** K. ÆLFRED *Boeth.* xvi. §3 Swa mæȝ eac se dreamcræft ðæt se mon bið dreamere, & se læcecræft þæt he bið læce. *c* **1000** *Sax. Leechd.* II. 8 Læcecræftas & dolȝsealfa & drencas wiþ eallum wundum. *c* **1200** ORMIN 1869 þurrh Crisstenndomess læchecrafft. *c* **1205** LAY. 7616 Ne þurh nenne læche-cræfte ne mihte he lif habben. *a* **1225** *Ancr. R.* 370 God & his deciples speken of soule lechekreft. *c* **1315** SHOREHAM 2 For siknesse lechecreft, And for the goute sealve Me makethe. **1393** LANGL. *P. Pl.* C. VII. 81 Til þat ich dispice Leche-craft of oure lorde and leyue on a wicche. **1471** J. PASTON in *P. Lett.* No. 670 III. 7 My horse that was at lechecraft at the Holt. *Ibid.*, My leche crafte and fesyk, and rewardys to them that have kept me..hathe cost me sythe Estern Day more then *vli.* **1500-20** DUNBAR *Poems* xxxiii. 33 In leichecraft he was homecyd. **1577** STANYHURST *Descr. Irel.* in *Holinshed* (1807-8) VI. 68 Their common schooles of leachcraft and law. **1592** DAVIES *Immort. Soul* Introd. xxvi. (1714) 7 We Leech-craft learn, but others cure with it. **1626** *Vicary's Anat.* 111 Letchcraft is in two manners, that is both Physicke and Chirurgerie. **1814** SCOTT *Chivalry* (1874) 19 The quality of leech-craft..was essential to the character of an accomplished princess. **1843** LYTTON *Last Bar.* I. v, Nature, to say nothing of Madge's leechcraft ultimately triumphed. **1870** MORRIS *Earthly Par.* III. IV. 196 The black folk E'en saved my life from that ill stroke, By leech-craft.

leechdom ('liːtʃdəm). *arch.* [OE. *lǽcedóm*, f. *lǽce* LEECH *sb.*¹ + *-dóm* -DOM.] A medicine, remedy.

a **900** *Kentish Glosses* in Wr.-Wülcker 59/38 *Medicinam*, lecedom. *c* **900** tr. *Bæda's Hist.* IV. xxvi. [xxv.] (1890) 350 Micel wund behofað micles læcedomes. *c* **1175** *Lamb. Hom.* 111 Mon..unhalne lechnað ȝif he lechedom con. *c* **1200** ORMIN 1851 Drihhtiness hallȝhe læchedom & sawless eȝhesallfe. **1864** COCKAYNE (*title*) Leechdoms, Wortcunning, and Starcraft of Early England. **1894** CREIGHTON in *Daily News* 3 Sept. 6/2 A collection of receipts, prescriptions, or leechdoms, for the various injuries.

leechee, variant of LITCHI.

'leecher. *rare.* Also 4 lechere. [f. LEECH *v.*¹ + -ER¹.] One who 'leeches'; a physician.

c **1374** CHAUCER *Boeth.* IV. pr. vi. 108 (Camb. MS.) Who is ellis kepere of good or dryuere a-wey of yuel but god gouernour and lechere [*Add. MS.* leecher] of thowthes [orig. *rector ac medicator mentium*]. **1887** *Athenæum* 31 Dec. 890/1 There were also [in Aberdeen]..the Leechers or barber-surgeons, each with their deacon and constitution.

leechery ('liːtʃəri). *rare*⁻¹. [f. LEECH *sb.*¹ + -ERY.] The art or practice of healing; leechcraft.

[**1600** SURFLET *Country Farm* I. xxviii. 196 *marg.*, The horseleacherie of P. Vegetius. **1688** see HORSE-LEECHERY.] **1892** C. M. ANDREWS *Old Eng. Manor* v. 256 The Anglo-Saxon 'wyrt'..included not only herbs..but flowers and vegetables, shrubs and trees, and their importance in Saxon leechery is well attested.

†**leech-finger.** *Obs.* [OE. *lǽcefinger*, a transl. of L. *digitus medicus*, Gr. δάκτυλος ἰατρικός. Cf. ON. *lǽknisfingr*; also the Eng. synonyms †*medical finger*, †*physic finger*.] The finger next to the little finger.

c **1000** *Sax. Leechd.* I. 394 Sing on ðine læcefinger in pater noster. *a* **1100** *Voc.* in Wr.-Wülcker 307/2 *Medicus*, læcefinger. **1387** TREVISA *Higden* (Rolls) II. 313 þe fourþe fynger þat is y-cleped þe leche by cause of þe more hiȝtynge and fairenesse, for in þat fynger is a veyne þat streecheþ to þe herte. *c* **1400** *Lanfranc's Cirurg.* 158 Bitwene þe litil fyngir & þe leche fyngir. **1506** *Kalender of Sheph.* A vj (Sommer) III. 15 The lytell seconde fynger..the medyll fyngers..the leche fyngere. **1681** W. ROBERTSON *Phraseol. Gen.* (1693) 607 The leach-finger, or ring-finger.

'leeching, *vbl. sb.*¹ [f. LEECH *v.*¹ + -ING¹.] The action of LEECH *v.*¹; healing, medical treatment. † *a* or *in leeching*: under medical treatment.

c **1000** ÆLFRIC *Gloss.* in Wr.-Wülcker 114/16 *Pharmacia*, sealflæcung. *a* **1240** *Ureisun* in *Cott. Hom.* 187 Min heouenliche leche þet makedest us of þi seolf se mihti medicine..hit beo mi lechunge. *a* **1300** *Cursor M.* 15064 Welcum lauerd þat leches all And leching giues to lame. **1393** LANGL. *P. Pl.* C. xx. 73 He..lefte hym þere a lechinge to lyuen if he myghte. *c* **1400** *Ywaine & Gaw.* 2823 Stil in lecheing thar sho lay. **1533** GAU *Richt Vay* 8 Quhair thay sal..find help and lechine of thair spiritual seiknes. **1540** *Extracts Aberd. Reg.* (1844) I. 168 The saids Egiptianis to pay the barbour for the leyching of the said Barrowne. *c* **1650** *Sir Cawline* vii. in Child *Ballads* (1885) II. 58/1 Sir Cawline's sicke, and like to be dead Without and a good leedginge.

'leeching, *vbl. sb.*² [f. LEECH *v.*² + -ING¹.] The medicinal application or use of leeches.

1802 *Med. Jrnl.* VIII. 6 The leeching and bleeding had succeeded well. **1869** CLARIDGE *Cold Water-cure* 188 By steam-baths and leeching the inflammation was in some degree subdued.

leechwe: see LECHWE.

leed¹ (liːd). *Sc.* and *north. dial.* Forms: 3-6 lede, 4 leyd, 6-7 leid, (6 lead), 8-9 leed, 8 leet, 9 lied. [app. a shortened form of LEDEN.] †Language, 'tongue' = LEDEN 2. *Obs.*

1513 DOUGLAS *Æneis* III. iv. 1 Strophades in Grew leid ar nemmit so. **1567** *Satir. Poems Reform.* iii. 140 Than sall I wryte in prettie poetrie, In Latine leid. *a* **1578** LINDESAY (Pitscottie) *Chron. Scot.* (S.T.S.) I. 158 Alexander..was send to France to leairne the leid witht wther lettres.

Proverb. **1808** JAMIESON, Ilk land has its ain leid.

b. The speech of a person or class of persons, talk, utterance; manner of speaking or writing; phraseology, 'patter'. *Obs.* exc. *Sc.*

a **1300** *Body & Soul* 21 in *Map's Poems* (Camden) 334 Ȝwere is al thi michele pride, And thi lede that was so loud? **13..** *Sir Tristr.* 1004 Tristrem..schortliche seyd in lede: We no owe þe noþing. *c* **1375** *Sc. Leg. Saints* ix. (*Bertholomeus*) 68 Al langage spek he cane, & vndirstand al leyd of mane. *a* **1400-50** *Alexander* 5007 In quatkyn manir of lede sall me þir treis sware? **1560** ROLLAND *Crt. Venus* Prol. 284 The other that ȝe it reid, Ȝe sall the better tak baith the sence, and leid. **1599** JAS. I Βασιλ. Δωρον (1603) 115 Not using any rusticall corrupt leid, as booke language. **1746** E. ERSKINE *Serm.* Wks. 1871 III. 305 Let faith get up its head and it will speak its own particular leed. **1790** D. MORISON *Poems* 77 Let Matrons round the ingle meet..An' in a droll auld farran' leet, 'Bout fairys crack. **1826** G. BEATTIE *John o' Arnha* 22 To hersel' this leed she mutter'd, 'Frae the east —fra the wast' [etc.]. *a* **1828** '*Hynd Horn*' xviii. in Child *Ballads* (1882) I. 207/1 Auld man, come tell to me your leed; What news ye gie when ye beg your bread. **1850** W. JAMIE *Stray Effusions* 146 Nae jockeyship kent he Nor ploughman leed. **1867** GREGOR *Banffs. Gloss.*, *Leed*..One line of conversation or argument; as, 'He got intil a leed, an oot o' that he cudna get'.

c. *poet.* applied to the 'language' of birds.

a **1310** in Wright *Lyric P.* 27 The lutel foul hath hire wyl on hyre lud to sing. **184.** LAING in *Whistle-Binkie* (Scot. Songs) (1890) I. 374 That wonderfu calf Has Scripture by heart, as the gowk has its lied.

leed² (liːd). *local.* The grass *Glyceria aquatica.*

1607 CAMDEN *Brit.* 360 Cum aquæ se in suos alueos receperint, lætissimo gramine & fœno crassiori (*Lid* vocant) ita luxuriat. **1878** MILLER & SKERTCHLY *Fenland* x. 298 [After quoting Camden on *Lid*] This grass is most likely the *Glyceria*, formerly *Poa aquatica*..and is still usually known by the name of 'White Leed'. It was once the principal grass of the Wash lands.

leed, obs. pa. pple. LAY *v.*¹; obs. f. LIDE, March.

leeder, obs. form of LEATHER.

Leeds (liːdz). [Name of a city in West Yorkshire.] Used *attrib.* or *absol.* as the designation of a cream-ware type of pottery made at Leeds.

[**1783** *Hartley, Greens Trade Catal.* in *Art Jrnl.* (1911) Jan. 25/1 Designs of sundry Articles of Queen's or Cream colour'd Earthen-Ware, manufactured by Hartley Greens & Co., at Leeds Pottery: with A Great Variety of other Articles. The same Enamel'd, Printed or Ornamented with Gold to any Pattern; also with Coats of Arms, Cyphers, Landscapes, etc., etc. Leeds 1783.] **1863** W. CHAFFERS *Marks Pott. & Porc.* 133 *Leeds pottery*, earthen-ware, manufactured by Hartley, Greens, and Co. Leeds, 1786. This ware has much perforated or basket work. **1872** C. SCHREIBER *Jrnl.* (1911) I. 139 A very pretty Leeds sucrier and cover. **1876** *Ibid.* 485 We..arranged to come and look at his Leeds ware next week. **1903** MRS. H. WARD *Lady Rose's Daughter* xi. 169 The Leeds and Wedgwood dessert dishes that Cousin Mary Leicester had used for half a century. **1968** *Canad. Antiques Collector* June 17/2 What is Mocha Ware? Sometimes referred to as 'Leeds Ware' or 'banded creamware' it is a creamware decorated with seaweed or tree silhouettes. This was made from 1787 up to 1903.

leedsite ('liːdzaɪt). *Min.* [Named by J. D. Dana in 1850 from *Leeds*, its locality: see -ITE¹.] A mixture of barium and calcium sulphates.

1850 DANA *Min.* 704.

Lee-Enfield (liː'ɛnfiːld). The names of J. P. *Lee* (1831-1904), Amer. designer of the bolt action, and *Enfield*, a town in Greater London, site of the British Royal Small Arms Factory, designers of the rifling form, used to designate a type of rifle used by the British Army in the S. African War and, modified, in the wars of 1914-18 and 1939-45. Also ***Lee-Enfield bullet.***

1902 *Encycl. Brit.* XXXII. 241/1 The Lee-Metford Mark II. rifle has been further improved in its rifling to resist the wear of smokeless powder,..and is now known as the Lee-Enfield rifle. **1910** *Ibid.* I. 874/1 A cone-shaped sharp-pointed bullet, named the Spitzer bullet, has been tried in the United States..in a Springfield rifle, which is practically identical with the British..Lee-Enfield. This bullet is lighter than the Lee-Enfield bullet. **1917** A. G. EMPEY *Over Top* 297 *Lee Enfield*, name of the rifle used by the British Army. Its caliber is ·303 and the magazine holds ten rounds. When dirty it has a nasty habit of getting Tommy's name on the crime sheet. **1959** [see ENFIELD]. **1966** *Guardian* 8 July 1/2 The Royal Navy laid the No. 4 short magazine Lee-Enfield ·303 service rifle to rest... The Army and the Royal Marines said goodbye to the rifle a few years ago. **1970** F. WILKINSON *Guns* 135 In 1895 the Lee-Enfield rifle was introduced and was to remain the standard arm until 1902 when a shorter version was approved. This, the Short Magazine Lee-Enfield, was to continue in service..through two world wars.

leef, obs. f. LEAF, LIEF; var. LEVE *v.*[1] *Obs.*

leefekie, variant of LYFKIE *Obs.*, bodice.

† ˈ**leefkyn.** *Obs. rare*$^{-1}$. [a. obs. Du. *liefkyn*: see LIEF *a.* and -KIN.] = 'Darling'.

1540 PALSGR. *Acolastus* III. v. R j b, I must nedes enbrace the my lyfe, i. O my leefekyn.

leefsel, variant of LEVESEL, bower.

leeftail, *a. dial.* Forms: 7 leftal, 8 lieftel, leave-, 9 leef-, leevetail. [? repr. OE. *léoftǽle* high in favour, desirable, f. *léof* LIEF, dear + *-tǽle*, f. root of *tellan* to count, TELL.] Much in demand; having a quick sale.

1674 RAY *N.C. Words* Collect. 30 *Lestal* [*read* leftal]; saleable, that weighs well in the hand, that is heavy in lifting, from the Verb Lift, as I suppose. 1781 HUTTON *Tour to Caves* 92 *Leavetail*, being a great want of, or demand for. 1790 ANN WHEELER *Dial.* 58 En wur a varra lieftel Market. 1847 HALLIWELL, *Leeftail*, quick sale. *Cumb.* 1869 *Lonsdale Gloss.*, *Leef-tail*, *Leevetail*, much in demand.

leef tenaunte, obs. form of LIEUTENANT.

† ˈ**leeful**, *a. Obs.* Forms: α. 3 læfful, leafful, 4–5 leveful, 5 lieveful, 5–6 levefull(e. β. 4 leffel, -ol, li(e)fful, leyffull, leoful, leefful(l, lefulle, 5 laifull, lefful, 4–6 leful(l, leifull, 4–7 leeful(l, 5–6 leafull, 6 lieful(l, leiffull, leyfull, lyefull. [ME. *leveful*, f. *leve*, LEAVE *sb.*[1] + -FUL. Some of the forms may be due to association with LAY *sb.*[3]] Permissible, right, lawful; just.

c 1205 LAY. 3033 [Heo] nom hire leaf-fulne hure [c 1275 laþfolne oþ]. *Ibid.* 10854 For he wes swiðe læfful, alle Brut luueden. c 1374 CHAUCER *Boeth.* I. pr. iv. 10 (Camb. MS.) Ne I trowe nat by the Iugement of socrates þat it weere Leueful to me to hide the sothe. c 1380 WYCLIF *Sel. Wks.* III. 84 Wiþ þre condiciouns it is leefful to swere. 1387 TREVISA *Higden* (Rolls) IV. 431 Wherto wilt þou lyve while it is not covenable, noþer leoful [*v.rr.* leefful, leffol, leeful], noþer semeliche? c 1400 *Destr. Troy* 2948 Þof it be laifull to ladys and oþer les wemen. 1445 *Extracts Aberd. Reg.* (1844) I. 14 It sal be lieveful to the alderman and balyheis for to tak [etc.]. a 1450 *Cov. Myst.* (Shaks. Soc.) 301 It is not lefful to us, ȝe seyn, No maner man for to slen. 1485 *Act 1 Hen. VII*, c. 10 §10 That it be leeful to youre Highnesse to graunt to youre seid besechers youre lettres of sauf-conduyt. 1508 DUNBAR *Gold. Targe* 166 Leuefull Company, and Honest Besynes. 1526 TINDALE *Matt.* xii. 12 It is lefull to do a good dede on the saboth daye. 1530 LYNDESAY *Test. Papyngo* 274 Halkyng, hountyng, armes, and leiffull amour. c 1575 BALFOUR *Practicks* (1754) 13 It sall be leifful to us to put our handis thairto quhen we pleis. 1600 HOLLAND *Livy* VIII. x. 288 It is not leefull the enemie to seise thereon. 1614 J. DAVIES *Eclogue* in Browne's *Sheph. Pipe* G 6 b, Hence forward then I must..con My leere in leefull lore. 1802 SCOTT *Minstr. Scot. Bord.* (1803) III. 77 Tell your sister Sarah To come and lift her leafu' lord! 1814 —— *For a' that an' a' that*, The true and leilfu' cause.

¶ **b.** ***leeful lane***: substituted for *lee-lane* (see LEE-LONE). (Cf. LEESOME *a.*[1] b.)

a 1758 RAMSAY *Address Thanks* xviii, Whilk gart some aft their leeful lane, Bring to the warld the luckless wean. 1832–52 LAING in *Whistle-Binkie* (Scot. Songs) Ser. III. 9 The auld gudewife gade out at e'en, An' owre the craft her leefu' lane.

Hence † ˈ**leefully** *adv.*, permissibly, lawfully; † ˈ**leefulness**, lawfulness.

c 1340 HAMPOLE *Prose Tr.* (1866) 20 Worldely men or women the which hauntene leuefully worldely goodes. c 1380 WYCLIF *Wks.* (1880) 132 In many cases sugetis may leffly wiþholde tiþis. c 1449 PECOCK *Repr.* II. i. 136 Leefulnes and vnleefulnes. 1483 *Cath. Angl.* 212/1 To do Leffullness (*A.* to do Vnlefulnesse), *illicebrare*. 1490 CAXTON *Eneydos* ii. 14 His sone yolus..beynge..soo fayr..it maye leefully be sayd that nature hadde doon her deuoyr. 1534 MORE *On the Passion* Wks. 1336/1 The liefulnesse thereof, was knowen and taught by the tradicion of thapostles theymselfe. 1540 in W. H. Turner *Select. Rec. Oxford* 159 Leffally chossen and elected Bayllyffs. 1548 GEST *Pr. Masse* B vj b, Then could not Irenee leyfully call y[e] one part of the sacrament a substaunce but an earthlye accidente.

leeger, obs. form of LEDGER.

leegte, var. LAAGTE.

leek (liːk). Forms: 1 léac, 3 lec, 3–5 lek, 4 lik, 4–6 leke, *Sc.* leik(e, (5 *pl.* lecus), 5–7 leeke, 6 like, 7 lieke, leake, 8 leak, 4– leek. [OE. *léac* str. neut. = MDu. *looc* (Du. *look*) neut., OHG. *louh* (MHG. *louch*, mod.G. *lauch*) masc., ON. *lauk-r* (Sw. *lök*, Da. *løg*):—OTeut. **lauko-*, whence Finnish *laukka*, OSl. *lukŭ*; no affinities outside Teut. are known.]

1. A culinary herb, *Allium Porrum* (N.O. *Liliaceæ*), allied to the onion, but differing from it in having the bulbous part cylindrical and the leaves flat and broad.

c 1000 *Sax. Leechd.* II. 234 Gebeat þæt leac & þa rudan ȝegnid togædere. c 1265 *Voc. Plants* in Wr.-Wülcker 555/7 *Porius*, poret, lek. c 1375 *Sc. Leg. Saints* xl. (*Ninian*) 404 In þe ȝard [he] sone has sene caile & leikis faire & grene. c 1400 *Lanfranc's Cirurg.* 291 Wiþ þe iuys of a strong oynoun, or wiþ ius of lekis. c 1420 *Liber Cocorum* (1862) 47 Grynd þy lecus in morter fre. 14.. *Nom.* in Wr.-Wülcker 710/23 *Hic bilbus*, a lekes hed. 1528 PAYNEL *Salerne's Regim.* (1535) 31 a, Garlike, oynions, and also likes are nat holsome for temperate bodyes. 1597 GERARDE *Herbal* I. lxxxvi. 138 The Leeke is hot and dry, and doth attenuate. 1656 COWLEY *Pindar. Odes*, *Plagues Egypt* i, But we, alas, the Flesh-pots love, We love the very Leeks and sordid roots below. 1722 *Lond. Gaz.* No. 6043/2 All the Company wore Leeks in Honour to the Princess [of Wales]. 1807 CRABBE *Par. Reg.* I. Wks. 1834 II. 148 The leek with crown globose and reedy stem. 1845 DARWIN *Voy. Nat.* xviii (1852) 428 A leek has over-run whole districts [in New Zealand]..; it was imported as a favour by a French vessel.

2. Applied with qualifications to: **a.** Other species of *Allium*, as **stone leek**, the Welsh onion, *A. fistulosum* (Treas. Bot. 1866), formerly called HOLLEKE, q.v.; **vine leek** († **leek of the vine**), *A. Ampeloprasum* (Treas. Bot.); **wild leek**, *A. ursinum*; **French leek** (see FRENCH *a.* 5). **b.** Bulbous plants of other genera, as † **corn-leek** (see quot. 1551); **dog('s) leek**, (see DOG *sb.* 20 d). Also CROW-LEEK, HOUSE-LEEK.

1551 TURNER *Herbal* I. G v b, Bulbine..may be called in English Corne leeke or wyldeleeke. 1577 B. GOOGE *Heresbach's Husb.* (1586) 60 The headed or sette Leeke..in Latine Capitatum. 1611 COTGR., *Oignon sauvage*..the wild field Onyon, Bulbine,..Corne Leeke. *Ibid.*, *Porreau de chien*, Dogs Leeke, wild Leeke, French Leek, Leeke of the Vine. *Porreau sectil, ou tondu*, the cut Leeke, maidens Leeke, blade Leeke, vnset Leeke. *Porreau testu*, the headed or knobbed Leeke, set Leeke, vncut Leeke. 1853 G. JOHNSTON *Nat. Hist. E. Bord.* 198 *Allium ursinum*. Ramps: Wild Leeks. Moist woods and deans, abundant and gregarious. 1874 C. GEIKIE *Life in Woods* xiii. 205 The wild leeks in the bushes.

† **3.** Taken as a type of something of little value. Also ***a leek's blade, a leek's clove*** (CLOVE *sb.*[1] 1).

13.. *Guy Warw.* (A.) 3644 Bodi & soule no nouȝt þer-of No is nouȝt worþ a lekes clof. c 1386 CHAUCER *Merch. T.* 106 Every man that holt him worth a leek. —— *Can. Yeom. Prol. & T.* 242. a 1400–50 *Alexander* 4228 Ȝour lare of a leke suld neuire þe les worth. c 1460 *Towneley Myst.* i. 129 Now, therof a leke what rekes vs? a 1483 *Pol. Poems* (Rolls) II. 278 Thay were not of thayre entent the nere of a leke. 14.. *Childe of Bristowe* 8 in Hazl. *E.P.P.* I. 111 The beste song that ever was made ys not worth a lekys blade, but men wol tende ther-tille. a 1529 SKELTON *Col. Cloute* 183 They make her wynche and keke, But it is not worth a leke. 1591 SYLVESTER *Du Bartas* I. iii. 515 And breaking Laws for Bribes, profane your Place, To leave a Leek to your unthankfull Race. c 1600 MONTGOMERIE *Cherrie & Slae* 1374, I knaw na liquor worth a leik To quench his deidlie drouth. ? a 1800 *Willie's drowned in Gamery* iii. in Child *Ballads* (1890) IV. 181/1, I dinna value their love a leek.

4. Proverbial and allusive phrases, referring to the colour of the leek, to its being the national emblem of the Welsh, etc. ***as clean as a leek*** (Sc.): perfectly, completely, entirely.

1362 LANGL. *P. Pl.* A. v. 65 As a leek that hedde i-leiȝen longe in the sonne, So loked he, with lene chekes lourede he foule. ? a 1366 CHAUCER *Rom. Rose* 212 Ful sad and caytif was she eek, And al-so grene as any leek. c 1386 —— *Reeve's Prol.* 25 To have an hoor heed and a grene tayl, As hath a leek. 1401 *Pol. Poems* (Rolls) II. 43 A lewid frere that men callen frere Daw Topias, as lewid as a leke. c 1430 *Syr Gener.* (Roxb.) 7684 To his face she leid hir cheke She felt it cold as yse or leke. 1546, 1589 [see LARK *sb.*[1] 1 c]. 1575 GASCOIGNE *Dan Bartholmew* Poems 1869 I. 137 His flecked cheekes, Nowe cherrye redde, nowe pale and greene as leekes. 1604 DEKKER *Honest Wh.* Wks. 1873 II. 103 Tho my head be like a Leeke, white: may not my heart be like the blade, greene? 1714 GAY *Sheph. Week*, *Monday* 83 Leek to the Welch, to Dutchmen Butter's dear. 1719 D'URFEY *Pills* (1872) III. 118 St. David, you know, loves Leeks and toasted Cheese. 1725 RAMSAY *Gentle Sheph.* I. i, For now, as clean's a leek, Ye've cherish'd me since ye began to speak.

b. ***to eat the*** (or ***one's***) ***leek***: to submit to humiliation under compulsion (in allusion to the Shaks. passage below).

1599 SHAKS. *Hen. V*, v. i. 10 Hee is come to me, and prings me pread and sault yesterday, looke you, and bid me eate my Leeke. 1835 DISRAELI *Let.* 20 Aug. in *Corr. Sister* (1886) 43 It was whispered the Whigs meant to swallow the Corporation leek. 1859 *All Year Round* No. 29. 61 The Welshmen very humbly ate their leek. 1882 STEVENSON *New Arab. Nts.* (1884) 303 There was nothing for it but to obey. .. But it was a leek to eat, and there was no denying it.

† **5.** A cant term for a Welshman. *Obs.*

c 1700 *Street Robberies Consider'd*, Leake, Welshman. 1725 *New Cant. Dict.*, *Leaks*, Welshmen.

† **6.** (See quot.) *Obs.*

1688 R. HOLME *Armoury* II. 172/2 The Porrum, or Leek of the Eye [in Cows] is a swelling tumor in the eye.

7. ***green-leek*** (***parrot***): see GREEN *a.* 13 b.

8. *attrib.* and *Comb.*, as ***leek-bed***, ***-blade***, ***-colour***, ***-garth***, ***-green*** sb. and adj., ***-porridge***, ***-pottage***, ***-seed***, ***-wort***; † **leek-head** (see quot.).

14.. *Voc.* in Wr.-Wülcker 604/12 *Porretarium*, a *lekbed. 1573–80 BARET *Alv.* L 285 A leeke bed, or a place set with lekes. 1886 ELWORTHY *W. Somerset Word-bk.*, *Leek-bed*, it is usual in talking to children, when of an inquiring turn, to tell boys that they were dug up in the leek-bed. 1538 ELYOT *Dict.*, *Porraceus*, of the coloure of *leeke blades. 1658 ROWLAND *Moufet's Theat. Ins.* 990 Three feet and shanks on each side of a *leek colour. 1570 LEVINS *Manip.* 34/12 Ye *Leekegarth, *porretum*. 1662 MERRETT tr. *Neri's Art of Glass* xxxii, A very fair Sea-green, called *Leek green. 1864 R. F. BURTON *Dahome* 58 A broad leek-green swamp. 1865 GROTE *Plato* I. i. 81 Blue, violet, leek-green, nut-brown. 1726 *Dict. Rust.* (ed. 3), **Leek-Heads*, a kind of Warts that come about a Horse's Pasterns and Pastern-joints. 1795 WOLCOT (P. Pindar) *Lousiad* IV. Wks. 1812 I. 281 *Leek-porridge, stir-about, we'll sooner want. c 1440 *Promp. Parv.* 295/2 *Leek pottage *porrata*. 1781 [C. JOHNSTON] *John Juniper* II. II. vii. 176 It will agree with the stomach of a Welshman as well as leek-pottage. 1393 LANGL. *P. Pl.* C. XIII. 190 Lynneseed and *lik-seed and lente-seedes alle Aren nouht so worthy as whete. 1528 PAYNEL *Salerne's Regim.* (1535) 91 b, The.. ieuse of henbane with the leke sede muste be bourned to gether. 1297 R. GLOUC. (Rolls) 6999 It wolde finde hom lec & worten [*v.rr.* *lek worten, like worten, lekwort] inowe bi þe ȝere.

leek(e, obs. form of LEAK, LIKE.

† ˈ**leekish**, *a. Obs.* [f. LEEK + -ISH.] Resembling a leek in colour.

1576 NEWTON *Lemnie's Complex.* II. v. 133 b, There is also an other kinde of Choler, called Leekish, so named because it is as grene as a Leeke.

† ˈ**leeky**, *a. Obs.* [f. LEEK + -Y[1].] = prec.

1552 HULOET, Leeky or of leekes, *porraceus*. 1607 WALKINGTON *Opt. Glass* 108 The second is..of a leeky nature or greene coulour. 1662 J. CHANDLER *Van Helmont's Oriat.* 227 It had confected or made a Leeky liquor above the greater Flint.

leel, obs. Sc. form of LEAL.

lee-lang, Sc. form of LIVELONG.

leeliche, obs. form of LEALLY.

leelite (ˈliːlaɪt). *Min.* [Named by Clarke, 1818, after J. F. *Lee*, from whom it was received; see -LITE.] A waxy-looking variety of orthoclase.

1818 *Ann. Philos.* IX. 367 Specimens of Leelite are at present more common than those of petalite. 1868 DANA *Min.* (ed. 5) 356 Leelite..is a deep, flesh-red variety.

leell, -ich(e, -y, obs. forms of LEAL, LEALLY.

lee-lone. *dial.* Also *Sc.* **lee-lane.** [An emphasized form of LONE *a.* The first element is of doubtful origin; Ramsay has *liefu' lane* in the same sense: see LEEFUL.] Chiefly in phrase ***by*** (***one's***) ***lee-lone***: quite alone, by (one)self.

1878 STEVENSON *Merry Men* ii, Praying..that God would 'remember..fower puir, feckless, fiddling, sinful creatures here by their lee-lane beside the great and dowie waters'. 1893 —— *Catriona* II. xxii. 265 What would become of you here, and you your lee-lone in a strange place? 1920 N. MUNRO in *Northern Numbers* 35, I heard a maiden sing, All in the lee-lone Sabbath morn. 1928 D. BYRNE *Destiny Bay* i. §19. 128 Will you..leave your cousin Jenico and Miss Ann-Dolly by their lee lone? 1966 T. H. RADDALL *Hangman's Beach* IV. xxvi. 399, I thought 'twas only love letters a gel went off tae read by her lee-lone.

leem, obs. f. LEAM; Sc. form of LOAM, LOOM.

Lee-Metford (liːˈmɛtfəd). The names of J. P. *Lee* (see LEE-ENFIELD) and W. E. *Metford*, used *attrib.* to designate a type of rifle in use before the Lee-Enfield rifle. Also ***Lee-Metford bullet***.

1897 G. B. SHAW *Our Theatres in Nineties* (1932) III. 257 If he does not actually regard it [*sc.* the Bible] as an amulet, and believe that if a soldier carries it into battle it will magically attract and stop the Lee-Metford bullet. 1898 [see DUM-DUM]. 1902 [see LEE-ENFIELD]. 1967 *Everyman's Encycl.* VI. 202/2 The British War Office adopted..the Lee-Metford Mark I in 1888. In 1891 the Lee-Metford Mark II was adopted... This rifle was subsequently.. improved, and became known as the Lee-Enfield rifle.

leeming, variant of LEAMING, LEMMING.

leen, obs. f. LEAN, LEND *v.*[2], LIN *v.*, to cease.

leend, leenes, obs. ff. LEND, LEANNESS.

leenge, leeper, obs. ff. LING, LEPER.

leep (liːp), *v. Anglo-Indian.* [ad. Urdu (Hindi) *līpna.*] *trans.* To wash with cow-dung and water.

1895 KIPLING *Second Jungle Bk.* 80 The big wicker-chest, leeped with cow-dung. 1920 *Blackw. Mag.* Oct. 464/1 As you smell the fresh leeped earth of the picquet floor.

leepwynke, obs. form of LAPWING.

† **leer**, *sb.*[1] *Obs.* Forms: 1 hléor, hlíor, 2–4 leor, 3–5 ler, lire, 3–6 lere, 4 lure, lewre, 4–6 lyre, 5 lyr, leyre, 5–6 lyer(e, 6–7 leer(e. [OE. *hléor*, *hlíor* neut. = OS. *hleor*, *hlear*, *hlier* (MDu. *liere*, MLG. *ler*), ON. *hlýr* (only pl.).

Some scholars have regarded the word as cogn. w. Gr. πλευρόν side; but the *z*-umlaut in the ON. form indicates an OTeut. type **hleuzo*[m]:—pre-Teut. **kleusóm*; E. Zupitza suggests that this is the neuter of an adj. with the sense 'adjacent to the ear', f. **kleusó-* ear (root **kleu-* to hear: see LISTEN).]

1. The cheek.

c 1000 *Sax. Leechd.* I. 86 Gif hwylcum wearȝbræde weaxe on þam nosum oððe on þam hleore. c 1000 ÆLFRIC *Gloss.* in Wr.-Wülcker 157/8 *Malae*, hleor. c 1205 LAY. 30266 Urnen þa teres uppen þes kinges leores. a 1300 *Floriz & Bl.* 501 Þe tieres glide of hire lere. c 1300 *Havelok* 2918 The heu is swilk in hire ler, So the rose in roser. 13.. *Metr. Hom.* (Vernon MS.) in *Archiv Stud. neu. Spr.* LVII. 273 As he eode wiþ leores weete. c 1330 *Spec. Gy Warw.* 842 Of þin eiȝen þe hote teres þat goþ adoun bi þine leres. 1398 TREVISA *Barth. De P.R.* v. xiv. (Tollem. MS.), 'Mala' is þe lower, and in þe face ben twey lewres þat schetteþ in ayþer side of þe nose. c 1410 *Sir Cleges* 153 Hys teris..That ran dovn be his lyre. 1470–85 MALORY *Arthur* IX. xxii. 371 This lytel brachet.. lyched his learys and his erys. 1582 STANYHURST *Æneis* I. (Arb.) 33 With tears his lyers ful he blubbred. 1586 J. HOOKER *Hist. Irel.* in *Holinshed* II. 106/1 The tears trilling downe his leeres.

2. The face, countenance; hence, look or appearance (of the face and skin), 'hue', complexion. Often in alliterative phrases, as ***lovely*** or ***lovesome of leer***, ***lily leer***.

a 700 *Epinal Gloss.* 438 *Frons*, hleor. a 1000 *Guthlac* 305 Þonne he to eorðan on þam anade hleor onhylde. a 1225 *Leg. Kath.* 316 Þi leor is, meiden, lufsum, & ti muð murie. a 1310

in Wright *Lyric P.* 52 Hire lure lumes liht, Ase a launterne a nyht. *c* **1350** *Will. Palerne* 227 Of lere ne of lykame lik him nas none. **1377** LANGL. *P. Pl.* B. x. 2 A wyf.. That lene was of lere and of liche bothe. *c* **1400** *Ywaine & Gaw.* 2510 The mayden with lely lire. *c* **1460** *Towneley Myst.* xxxi. 145 Youre rud that was so red, youre lyre the lylly lyke. *a* **1529** SKELTON *E. Rummyng* 12 Her lothely lere Is nothynge clere. —— *P. Sparowe* 1031 The whytnesse of her lere. **1588** SHAKS. *Tit. A.* IV. ii. 119 Fie trecherous hue, that will betray with blushing The close enacts and counsels of the hart: Heer's a young Lad fram'd of another leere, Looke how the blacke slaue smiles vpon the father. **1806** JAMIESON *Sir Oluf* in Whitelaw *Sc. Ballads* (1875) 466/1 Whareto is your lire sae blae and wan?

3. ? Temper, disposition.

(The identity of the word in this example is very doubtful.)

a **1575** *Wyfe Lapped in Morrelles Skin* 1109 in Hazl. *E.P.P.* IV. 226 Thus endeth the iest of Morels skin, Where the curst wife was lapped in; Because she was of a shrewde leere, Thus was she serued in this maner.

leer (lɪə(r)), *sb.*² [f. LEER *v.*] A side glance; a look or roll of the eye expressive of slyness, malignity, immodest desire, etc.

1598 SHAKS. *Merry W.* I. iii. 50 Shee discourses: shee carues: she giues the leere of inuitation. **1667** MILTON *P.L.* IV. 503 Aside the Devil turnd For envie, yet with jealous leer maligne Ey'd them askance. **1681** OTWAY *Soldier's Fort.* III. i. Wks. 1728 I. 372 What a Hang-dog Leer was that. **1712** ARBUTHNOT *John Bull* III. ii, The fellow has a roguish leer with him, which I don't like by any means. **1735** POPE *Prol. Sat.* 201 Damn with faint praise, assent with civil leer. **1743** FIELDING *J. Wild* III. vii, She accompanied these words with ..so wanton a leer, that [etc.]. **1851** LAYARD *Pop. Acc. Discov. Nineveh* xiii. 353 Old Gouriel, the Kiayah, still rejoicing in his drunken leer, was there to receive us. **1863** WHYTE MELVILLE *Gladiators* I. 143 A short, square, beetle-browed man, with a villanous leer.

leer (lɪə(r), lɛə(r)), *sb.*³ *Glass-making.* Also **lehr**. Also 8–9 **lear**, 9 **lier**. **a.** An annealing-furnace. Also *attrib.*, as ***lear-annealing***; **leer-pan** = FRACHE.

1662 MERRETT tr. *Neri's Art of Glass* 243 The Leer (made by Agricola, the third furnace, to anneal and cool the vessels ..) comprehends two parts, the tower and leer. **1727–51** CHAMBERS *Cycl.* s.v. *Furnace*, The leer is an avenue five or six yards long, continued to the tower. **1797** P. WAKEFIELD *Mental Improv.* (1801) I. 143 The lear or third furnace. **1797** *Encycl. Brit.* (ed. 3) VII. 768/2 The third oven or leer. **1832** G. R. PORTER *Porcelain & Gl.* 158 The annealing oven, or lier, is a long low rectangular chamber..furnished with numerous shallow iron trays... These trays are called lier pans, or fraiches. **1839** URE *Dict. Arts* 579 The cooling or annealing arch, or leer, is often built independent of the glass-house furnace... The leer pans or trays of sheet iron. **1890** GORDON *Foundry* 140 The tunnel is the 'lear', and the process is known as lear-annealing. **1908** W. ROSENHAIN *Glass Manuf.* x. 165 The split cylinders are taken to a special kiln, generally known as a 'lear', or 'lehr', where they are.. raised to a dull red-heat. **1918** P. MARSON *Glass* x. 72 These tunnels, or lehrs, are about 40 ft. long. **1937** *Nature* 18 Dec. 1072/1 There has been a corresponding improvement..in lehrs for annealing the finished product. **1943** *Amer. Speech* XVIII. 309/1 Among the latter were boys who carried hot glassware from the molds to the leer and toward the end of a shift they began a chant, 'Ten more trips to the layer O,' 'Nine more trips to the layer O,' and so on... They said 'layer' distinctly in two syllables. **1949** *Jrnl. Soc. Glass Technol.* XXXIII. 287 The term 'lehr' to denote an apparatus or plant for the continuous annealing of glass first appeared in factory usage in the U.S.A. between 1890 and 1900. The word arose most probably by corruption of the original form 'leer', but whether by accident or design is obscure. **1958** *Times* 22 Dec. 1/4 (Advt.), Practical experience of design and construction of glass furnace lehrs also essential. **1965** E. TUNIS *Colonial Craftsmen* vi. 139/1 A boy carried the new bottle to the leer where he snapped the punty off its bottom. **1971** *Atom* May 118/1 A ribbon of glass up to 11 feet wide leaves the float tank and enters the annealing lehr at temperatures in the region of 600°C.

b. **leer man**, **lehr man**, one who works at a leer.

1849 A. PELLATT *Curiosities of Glass Making* 67 The instruction to the lear-man, or fireman, rather to run the risk of melting goods by excess of heat than subject them to fly by insufficient. **1912** G. SOWERBY *Rutherford & Son* 27 The new lear man's shaping all right then. **1965** E. TUNIS *Colonial Craftsmen* vi. 139/1 A leer man stood the bottle on a hot iron tray in the leer.

Hence **'leering**, treatment in the 'leer'.

1889 *Standard* 5 Jan. 2/1 The English glass is brighter and better from lead being used, instead of lime, for 'learing', the lead 'learing' being more expensive.

†**leer**, *sb.*⁴ *Obs.* exc. *dial.* [? repr. OE. *lira* the fleshy part of the body.] The flank or loin; the hollow under the ribs.

c **1386** CHAUCER *Sir Thopas* 146 He dide next his white leere Of clooth of lake fyn and cleere A breech and eek a sherte. **1725** *Lond. Gaz.* No. 6397/2 Stolen,..a..Mare,.. several white Spots on her Body, one larger than the rest on the further Leer. **1746** *Exmoor Courtship* 355 (E.D.S.) A geed ma a Vulch in tha Leer. **1777** *Horæ Subsecivæ* 249 (E.D.D.) Under the leer. **1886** ELWORTHY *W. Somerset Word-bk.*, *Leer*, the flank—applied to man and beast.

leer (lɪə(r)), *a.*¹ Forms: 3–7 (9) **lere**, 5 **ler**, 6 **leare**, 6–7 **leere**, 7 **leir**, 7, 9 *dial.* **lear**, 9 *dial.* **lair**, 4– **leer**. [OE. **lǽre* (implied in *lǽrnes* emptiness) = OS., OHG. *lâri* (MHG. *lǽre*, mod.G. *leer*, MDu. *laer*, Du. *laar*):—WGer. **lâri*, of uncertain origin; according to some repr. an OTeut. **lǽzjo-*, cogn. w. Goth. *lasiws* weak.]

†**1.** Empty. Also, clear *of*. Of a burden: Useless. *Obs.*

a **1250** *Owl & Night.* 1527 [He] haveth attom his riȝte spuse, Wowes weste [an] lere huse. **1297** R. GLOUC. (Rolls) 1800 þo was bruteine þis lond of romeins al mest lere. **1387** TREVISA *Higden* (Rolls) II. 283 ȝif þey fyndeþ it [Fortune's horn] empty [*v.r.* leer], þanne þey makeþ sorwe. *Ibid.* III. 311 How longe schal a fool bere lere fardelles? **1398** —— *Barth. De P.R.* XVII. cxxxv. (1495) 691 The pyth wythin is wasted and therfore the hole is voyde and lere. *c* **1430** *Two Cookery-bks.* 50 Take þin cofyns, & put in þe ovynne lere. *c* **1440** *Gesta Rom.* lxi. 252 (Harl. MS.) 'Do gete me', quod she, 'a ler tonne, withe oute onye delaye'. **1519** HORMAN *Vulg.* 158 b, Let all your leere pottis [L. *vasa inania*] stande the mouthe downwarde. **1567** TURBERV. *Ovid's Ep.* 16 b, Some lustfull lasse will not permit Achylles couch be leare. [**1864** SIR J. K. JAMES *Tasso* XIX. xxx, Carnage had choked the town, no spot was leer.]

b. Proposed as a *Pathological* term.

1893 S. GEE *Auscult. & Percuss.* iii. (ed. 4) 58 Skoda.. distinguishes percussion sounds according as they are full or leer. *Ibid.*, *note*, Skoda's word 'leer' is translated by Markham 'empty'. I formerly suggested 'scanty'. But indeed the word 'leer' needs no translation, for it is English as well as German, and bears the same meaning in both tongues.

2. Having no burden or load; said also of a horse without a rider. *Obs.* exc. *dial.*

1387 TREVISA *Higden* (Rolls) I. 413 þe foot man lere [*printed* lereþ] synge to fore þe þeef. **1542** UDALL *Erasm. Apoph.* 8 Went he leere (quoth Socrates) or els charged with the charge of any burden? **1591** HARINGTON *Orl. Fur.* XXXV. lxiv, The horse runs leere away without the man. **1609** HOLLAND *Amm. Marcell.* XVII. xi. 94 Leading also after them in hand one lere horse. **1609** C. BUTLER *Fem. Mon.* i. (1623) B iv, Bees..that are loaded seeme greater and longer then those that are leere. **1654** 'PALAEMON' *Friendship* 32 An Asse,..over burthen'd with his Masters Carriage desired a Horse..led leer by him, to ease him by bearing a Part. **1688** WOOD *Life* 7 Nov., 60 horsmen went thro Oxford,—with leir and sumpter horses. **1787** GROSE *Prov. Gloss.*, *Leer*, empty. Wilts. A leer waggon, an empty waggon. **1886** *Tip Cat* xv. 199 They were on the top of a load..on their way to the rick-yard, promising to come back in what they call in those parts the 'leer' waggon. **1891** *Athenæum* 22 Aug. 255 In the country between Plymouth and Exeter between forty and fifty years ago any 'unladen' cart was familiarly spoken of as a lair or a lairy-cart.

3. *dial.* **a.** Of the stomach: Empty of food. **b.** Of persons and animals: Having an empty stomach; hungry, faint for want of food.

1848 KINGSLEY *Saint's Trag.* I. ii. 83 Then what's the friar to the starving peasant? Just what the abbot is to the greedy noble—A scarecrow to lear wolves. **1853** AKERMAN *Wilts. Tales* 97 His bill was zharp, his stomach lear, Zo up a snapped the caddlin pair. **1862** HUGHES in *Macm. Mag.* V. 243/2 'Em be aggravatin' birds, plaguey cunnin' let 'em be never zo lear. **1870** LADY VERNEY *Lettice Lisle* 308 Do ye tell Madam to send me a sup o' broth, or summat, I feel so leer. **1878** JEFFERIES *Gamekeeper at H.* 15 I'm rather lear at supper.

Proverb. **1860** READE *Cloister & H.* I. 312 Better a lean purse than a lere stomach.

†**leer**, *a.*² *Obs.* In 7 **leare**, **lere**. [app. f. LEER *v.*] Looking askance; oblique, indirect; sly, underhand.

1629 B. JONSON *New Inn* IV. i, Ile to bed and sleepe, And dreame away the vapour of Loue, if th' house And your leere drunkards let me. **1633** EARLE *Microcosm.* (Arb.) 103 A Suspitious, or Iealous Man Is one that watches himselfe a mischiefe, and keepes a leare eye still, for feare it should escape him. *a* **1680** BUTLER *Rem.* (1759) II. 207 He had rather have them bear two Senses in vain and impertinently, than one to the Purpose, and never speaks without a Lere-Sense. *Ibid.* 459 He has a lere Trick,..to cry down all those Paces which he wants. *a* **1830** *Yng. Musgrave* viii. in Child *Ballads* (1885) II. 249/1 The laddie gae a blythe leer look, A blythe leer look gave he.

leer (lɪə(r)), *v.* Also 6 **lere**, 6–7 **leare**, **leere**. [Perh. f. LEER *sb.*¹ in the sense 'cheek'; the early examples of the vb. suit well the explanation 'to glance over one's cheek'.]

1. *intr.* To look obliquely or askance; to cast side glances. Now only, to look or gaze with a sly, immodest, or malign expression in one's eye. Also with adverbs, as *aside*, *up*, *back*; occas. with clause.

1530 PALSGR. 606/2, I leare or lere, as a dogge dothe underneth a doore. *Je regarde de longue veue.* **1575** *Gamm. Gurton* I. iii. 32 By chaunce a-syde she leares, And Gyb, our cat, in the milke pan she spied ouer head and eares. **1576** GASCOIGNE *Philomene* (Arb.) 106 And now on hir, and then on him, Full lowringly did leare. **1591** SYLVESTER *Du Bartas* I. v. 1012 Even as a wolf,..Flyes with down-hanging head, and leareth back Whether the Mastife doo pursue his track. **1597** SHAKS. *2 Hen. IV*, v. v. 7, I will leere vpon him, as he comes by: and do but marke the countenance that hee will giue me. **1647** H. MORE *Song of Soul* I. II. xcv, Here Graculo learing up with one eye View'd the broad Heavens. **1663** BUTLER *Hud.* I. iii. 6 Though Dame Fortune seem to smile And leer upon him for a while. **1720** GAY *Tales, Mad-dog* 35 They leer, they simper at her shame. **1735** POPE *Ep. Lady* 9 Here Fannia leering on her own good man. **1821** LAMB *Elia* Ser. I. *Grace bef. Meat*, C.V.L. when importuned for a grace used to inquire, first slily leering down the table, 'Is there no clergyman here?' **1851** THACKERAY *Eng. Hum.* vi. (1858) 310 The foul Satyr's eyes leer out of the leaves constantly. **1853** KINGSLEY *Hypatia* xix. 218 He passed out through the ante-chamber, leering at the slave-girls.

fig. *a* **1745** SWIFT (J.), I wonder whether you taste the pleasure of independency, or whether you do not sometimes leer upon the court.

†**2.** To walk stealthily or with averted looks; to slink *away*. *Obs.*

1586 FERNE *Blaz. Gentrie* 260 He came learing softlye on the other side the hedge. *a* **1634** RANDOLPH *Muses Looking-gl.* II. ii, Who knows but they come learing after us To steale away the substance? **1666** BUNYAN *Grace Ab.* ¶144 Methought I saw as if the Tempter did lear and steal away from me, as being ashamed of what he had done. **1678** —— *Pilgr.* I. (1862) 71, I met him once in the Streets, but he leered away on the other side, as one ashamed of what he had done. **1847–78** HALLIWELL, *Leer*, to go or sneak away. *North.*

3. *trans.* **a.** To give a leer with (the eye).

1835 MARRYAT *Jac. Faithf.* xi, Leering his eye at his father. **1838** D. JERROLD *Men of Char.*, *Matthew Clear* ii. (1851) 141 [A parrot] cocking his head, leering his eye, and working his black tongue.

b. To beguile or reduce *to* by leering.

1681 DRYDEN *Sp. Friar* I. 6 But Bertran has been taught the Arts of Court, To guild a Face with Smiles; and leer a man to ruin.

Hence **'leering** *vbl. sb.*

1619 FLETCHER *M. Thomas* IV. ii, Footra for leers, and learings. *c* **1685** in *Roxb. Ballads* VII. 426 She knew him a Knave by his learing.

leer(e, obs. form of LEAR *sb.*²

leere, var. LERE *v. Obs.*, to teach, learn.

leereboord, obs. form of LARBOARD.

leerfish ('lɛəfɪʃ). *S. Afr.* [Partial tr. of Afrikaans LEERVIS.] A large game fish, *Hypacanthus amia*, of the family Carangidæ, found off the Atlantic coast of southern Africa.

1843 J. C. CHASE *Cape Good Hope* II. 169 Leer Fish—A species of Pike, affording considerable sport to the angler. **1902** *Trans. S. Afr. Philos. Soc.* XI. 217 Probably the Cape Leer-fish was so named by the early Dutch sailors, who brought the name from the East Indies. **1930** C. L. BIDEN *Sea-Angling Fishes of Cape* ii. 54 For the past two or three generations the word has been commonly written and accepted by the English-speaking people as leerfish. **1957** S. SCHOEMAN *Strike!* iii. 106 The average weight of leerfish is 20–35 lbs. **1973** *Eastern Province Herald* 28 Nov. 37 Out in the darkness came the unmistakeable sound of a leerfish hurling itself in frenzy after its prey.

leering ('lɪərɪŋ), *ppl. a.* [f. LEER *v.*] That leers, or looks with side glances.

1546 J. HEYWOOD *Prov.* (1867) 57 My cats leeryng looke. **1598** FLORIO *Ital. Dict.* To Rdr. A v b, There is another sort of leering curs, that rather snarle then bite. **1602** ROWLANDS *Greenes Ghost* 18 All the while he is telling his tale, he cast a leering eye about the shop, to see if there were euer a cloake ..or anie other bootie. **1697** DRYDEN *Virg. Past.* III. 13 We know..what the Goats observ'd with leering Eyes. **1746** SMOLLETT *Reproof* 139 Behold the leering belle, caress'd by all. **1859** W. COLLINS *Q. of Hearts* (1875) 49, I..managed to get between his leering eyes and the book-case.

Hence **'leeringly** *adv.*

1702 BP. NICOLSON *Let. to Dr. Kennet* 9 He leeringly produces a Passage, wherein I maintain that [etc.]. **1839** THACKERAY *Major Gahagan* i, 'How do you do?' said the old hag leeringly.

leerne, obs. form of LEARN.

leerness ('lɪənɪs). [f. LEER *a.*¹ + -NESS.] Emptiness.

c **1000** *Sax. Leechd.* II. 60 Se micla ȝeoxa..cymð..of to micelre fylle, oððe of to micelre lærnesse. **1398** TREVISA *Barth. De P.R.* XIV. ii. (Tollem. MS.), Mounteynes ben sumtyme withinne ful of holownesse, and of dennes; and so by cause of voydenesse and of lerenesse it draweþ and soukeþ in water. *Ibid.* VII. xliv. (1495) 257 Appetite of the stomak comyth by cause of lerenes and voydnes. **1656** RIDGLEY *Pract. Physick* 25 Arthrite..often causeth learness with weaknesse of the joynts. **1893** S. GEE *Auscult. & Percuss.* iii. (ed. 4) 62 The prime property assigned by Skoda to a percussion-sound, its fulness or its leerness..is in fact a compound perception.

‖**leervis** ('leːrfəs). *S. Afr.* Also **leervisch**. [Afrikaans, f. *leer* leather + *vis* fish.] = LEERFISH.

1853 L. PAPPE *Synopsis Edible Fishes Cape Good Hope* 24 *Lichia Amia*, Cuv. & Val. (Leervisch.)..Taken occasionally in Table Bay, but not in great repute, its flesh being deemed dry and rather insipid. **1913** W. W. THOMPSON *Sea Fisheries Cape Colony* 156 *Lichia amia* L... Leer-visch; Leather-fish; Garrick (Natal). **1945** *Cape Argus* 27 Jan., Many leervis, kob and yellowtail have fallen for spoons, spinners and wobblers of many kinds. **1951** *Cape Times* 13 Nov. 2/3 Anglers know Swartvlei as a place where the sporting *leervis* abounds. **1953** J. L. B. SMITH *Sea Fishes S. Afr.* (rev. ed.) 222 The Leervis always seizes a fish across the middle and then works it about in the jaws until head-on for easy swallowing. **1956** *Cape Times* 2 Mar. 2/5 He caught a 32-lb. *leervis* near the lighthouse at Cape Agulhas. **1974** *Eastern Province Herald* 1 Aug. 21 In mid-December..leervis were caught in large numbers off the breakwater.

leery ('lɪərɪ), *a.*¹ *Obs.* exc. *dial.* Forms: 7 **leirey**, 8–9 **leary**, **leery**, 9 **lairy**. [f. LEER *a.*¹ + -Y¹.] = LEER *a.*¹ in various senses. (In quot. 1676 = containing empty spaces or hollows.)

1676 J. BEAUMONT in *Phil. Trans.* XI. 734 These Stones are generally found in Leirey places (as they call it) that is, Cavernous. **1787** GROSE *Prov. Gloss.*, *Leary*, empty. Dorsetsh. **1796** W. MARSHALL *W. Eng.* I. 328 *Lear* or *Leary*, empty, as an unloaded cart or waggon. **1874** W. CORY *Lett. & Jrnls.* (1897) 372 My cart goes 'leery' (= empty) to fetch coals. **1889** T. HARDY *Mayor Casterbr.* xx, I've been strolling in the Walks and churchyard, father, till I feel quite leery. **1891** —— *Tess* (1900) 44/1 And he so leery and tired that 'a didn't know what to do.

leery ('lɪərɪ), *a.*² *slang.* Also 9 **leary**. [? f. LEER *a.*² + -Y¹.] **1. a.** Wide-awake, knowing, 'fly'. **b.**

orig. *U.S.* Doubtful, suspicious (*about*, *of*). Cf. LAIRY *a.*[2]

1718 C. HITCHING *Regulator* 20 The Cull is leery, *alias* the Man is shy. **1796** *Grose's Dict. Vulg. Tongue*, *Leery*, on one's guard. **1812** J. H. VAUX *Flash Dict.*, *Leary*, synonymous with *fly*. **1817** *Sporting Mag.* I. 118 Frequently dropping their hands when at leary distance. **1820** *Ibid.* VI. 80 It was evident to the leary ones that his condition was bad. **1846** *Swell's Night Guide* 46 The president..who is generally the most cheeky, *leary*, downy cove they can tumble to. **1882** *Five Y. Penal Servit.* iii. 71 A 'leary look', in which fear, defiance and cunning are mixed up together. **1885** *Bazaar* 2 Jan. 1/2 The deep earth bank from a hole in which a leary water rat peeps upward at the terrier. **1893** *Oxford Mag.* 24 May 382/2 The leery lawyer simply stepped inside. **1896** ADE *Artie* iii. 29 The old lady's a little leary of me, but I can win her all right. *Ibid.* xii. 105 I'm leary of it. **1905** *Dialect Notes* III. 63 He is *leery* of book agents. **1909** R. A. WASON *Happy Hawkins* 122, I was rather leery about Jabez. **1923** L. J. VANCE *Baroque* vi. 56 If you hadn't..made me leary that maybe you'd tip your friends off. **1942** E. PAUL *Narrow St.* xx. 165 The Surrealists discovered that they were not, in fact, Communists and that Moscow was leery of their antics. **1956** B. HOLIDAY *Lady sings Blues* (1973) xii. 108, I was leery of any man who could throw those things back at me in a quarrel. **1960** B. CRUMP *Good Keen Man* 113 Harry didn't entirely agree with my suggestion that [my dog] Flynn was probably a bit leery of boars since the one that 'killed' him at Maran. **1965** *Listener* 9 Sept. 391/3, I am..leary of theatrical revivalism. **1966** *Economist* 5 Feb. 489/1 At first, centre voters may be fed up with the government in power, but they are leery of voting for the other side, so they stop halfway and vote Liberal. **1969** *Southerly* XXIX. 9 Leery though I am of Greeks, Sophocles sums up my preoccupations effectively. **1970** *New Yorker* 10 Oct. 174/2 Many tennis authorities have been a little leery about placing her on a level with Lenglen. **1971** [see GEHEIMRAT]. **1973** *Tucson* (Arizona) *Daily Citizen* 22 Aug. 28/1 The Braunlichs will also tell you that, sad as it is, middle America is leery of things it gets for free.

2. *U.S. slang.* Careful.

1911 H. QUICK *Yellowstone Nights* xii. 300 But be leery that we don't get stuck for non-performance.

Hence **'leerily** *adv.*, in a leery manner.

1859 FARRAR *J. Home* 242 No, you very leerily managed to make the other fellow shoot him.

lees, obs. f. LEACH *sb.*[1], LEASE, LEASH, LESS.

lees, *pl.* (dregs): see LEE *sb.*[2]

† **leese**, *v.*[1] *Obs.* Forms: (1 -léosan), 2–4 leosen, (3 -ien), (3 *2nd pers. sing.* lust), 2–5 lesen, 3–4 leose, (*Kent.* 3 liese, 3–4 lyese, *3rd sing. pres.* lyest, liest), 3–6 lese, 3, 5–6 lease, 4 *Sc.* leiss, 4–5 les, 4–7 leese, (5 lesyn, ? lyse), 5–6 lesse, leze, lees, *Sc.* leis, 6 leeze. *Pa. t.* α. *strong.* (1 -léas), 3 læs, las, leos, 3–4 leas, (*pl.* and *subj.* 3 lure, 3–4 lore, 4 *pl.* lorn), 4 lese, lees, *Kent.* lyeas, (5 ? lyse), 6 *Sc.* leis. β. *weak.* 3 leosede, *Kent.* liesed, 4 leste, leest, 4–5 lest, *Sc.* lessit, -yt. *Pa. pple.* α. *strong.* (1 -loren), 3 i-loren, 3–5 ilore, 4 yloren, lorin, losen, -in, 4–5 ylore, ylorn(e, lore(n, 5 yloore, 4–7 lorne, 4– lorn (see LORN *ppl. a.*). β. *weak.* 3 ileosed, 4–5 lest(e, 6 *Sc.* lesit. [A Com. Teut. str. vb.: OE. *-léosan*, only in compounds, *beléosan*, *forléosan* (*-léas*, *-luron*, *-loren*) corresponds to OFris. *ur-liasa*, OS. *far-liosan* (Du. *ver-liezen*), OHG. *vir-liosan* (MHG. *verliesen*, mod.G. *verlieren*, influenced by the pa. t. and pa. pple.), Goth. *fra-liusan*; other derivatives of the root (**leus-*: *laus-*: *los-*) are LEASING *sb.*, -LESS, LOOSE *a.* and *v.*, LOSE *v.*, LOSS.

The root **leus-* is usually regarded as an extension of the **leu-*, **lu-* in Gr. λύ-ειν, L. *so-lv-ĕre* to loosen.]

1. *trans.* = LOSE, in its various senses; to part with or be parted from by misadventure, through change in conditions, etc.; to be deprived of; to cease to possess; to fail to preserve, or maintain; to fail to gain or secure; to fail to profit by, to spend (time) unprofitably; to use (labour) to no advantage. Also *refl.*

a. In present stem.

c **1205** LAY. 20112 Þat he scal þat lif leosen & leosien his freonden. *Ibid.* 24914 Idelnesse makeð mon his monscipe leose [*c* **1275** lease]. *a* **1225** *Ancr. R.* 102 Þe cat of helle.. makede hire to leosen boðe God & mon, mid brod schome & sunne. *c* **1250** *Kent. Serm.* in *O.E. Misc.* 26 He was ofdred for to liese his king riche of ierusalem. *a* **1300** *Cursor M.* 6 Þere many thosand lesis þer lijf. *a* **1300** *Beket* (Percy Soc.) 859 Thu must do so. Other thu lust thi bischop-riche: other peraventure thi lyf. **1340** *Ayenb.* 52 Þos he lyest al his time, and þe ni3t and þane day. **1362** LANGL. *P. Pl.* A. III. 131 Heo doth men leosen heore lond and heore lyues after. ? *a* **1366** CHAUCER *Rom. Rose* 448 For a litel glorie veine, They lesen god and eek his reine. **1387** TREVISA *Higden* (Rolls) VII. 49 He is worþy to lese [*MS.* γ luse] his heed. **1398** —— *Barth. De P.R.* XII. xxxii. (1495) 432 The pecok lesyth his fetheres whan the fyrste tree lesyth his leues. *Ibid.* XIV. xliv. 483 This mount is perylous to stranges that knowe not the wayes therin, for they may lightly lese themself. ? *a* **1400** *Arthur* 231 As þu wold nat leze þy lyf, Fulfylle þys wythoute stryff. *c* **1430** *Hymns Virg.* 46, I leese on him so myche trauaile. **1485** *Galway Arch.* in *10th Rep. Hist. MSS. Comm.* App. v. 384 To lesse and forfayte one hundred shillinges. **1523** LD. BERNERS *Froiss.* I. cclix. 384 He that all coueteth al leseth. *a* **1547** EARL SURREY in *Tottel's Misc.* (Arb.) 7 Farre of I burne, in both I wast, and so my life I leze. **1553** *Douglas' Æneis* XI. viii. 75 Thou sall neuer leis [*ed. Small* los]..Sic ane peuische and catiue saule as thine. *a* **1568** ASCHAM *Scholem.* I. (Arb.) 63, I do not meene..that yong Ientlemen ..by vsing good studies, shold lease honest pleasure. *c* **1600** SHAKS. *Sonn.* v, Flowers distil'd,..Leese but their show, their substance still liues sweet. **1601** HOLLAND *Pliny* I. 168 Mans memorie..oftentimes it assaieth and goeth about to leese it selfe, euen whiles a mans body is otherwise quiet and in health. **1605** BACON *Adv. Learn.* II. Ded. to King §3 Water..doth scatter and leese itselfe in the ground, except it be collected into some Receptacle. **1611** BIBLE *1 Kings* xviii. 5 Peraduenture we may finde grasse to saue the horses and mules aliue, that we leese not all the beasts. **1625** BACON *Ess.*, *Empire* (Arb.) 307 For that that he winnes in the Hundred, he leeseth in the Shire. **1626** —— *Sylva* §390 Flowers Pressed or Beaten, do leese the Freshness and Sweetness of their Odour. **1675** HOBBES *Odyssey* (1677) 119 Your life, quoth he, amongst the rest you'll leese.

b. In pa. t. and pa. pple.

α. *strong.*

c **1205** LAY. 15519 Þe King his swinc læs. *Ibid.* 18202 Ne les [*c* **1275** leos] he næuere leouere mon. *Ibid.* 20463 Þenne [wes] heore wurðscipe iloren a þissere worlde-richen. *a* **1225** *Ancr. R.* 54 Heo leas hire meidenhod, & was imaked hore. *c* **1275** *XI Pains Hell* 139 in *O.E. Misc.* 151 Heo heore mayden-hod lure. **1297** R. GLOUC. (Rolls) 6287 He dradde wanne he lore þat lif, & were ybro3t to deþe. *a* **1300** *Body & Soul* in *Map's Poems* (Camden) 337 Al mi love on the I las. *a* **1300** *Cursor M.* 714 (Gött.) To win þat bliss þat he ha lorin [*Fairf.* lorne]. **1307** *Elegy Edw. I*, ix, Jerusalem, thou hast ilore The flour of all chivalerie. **13..** *Sir Tristr.* 1116 Þai lorn all her swink. **1340** *Ayenb.* 85 Ac þis lhordssip he leas be zenne. *Ibid.* 203 Be huam he wes ouercome, and be huam he lyeas his mi3te. **1375** BARBOUR *Bruce* VII. 44 [He] Persauit the hund the sleuth had lorn. *c* **1385** CHAUCER *L.G.W.* Prol. 26 If that olde bokis weryn aweye I-loryn were of remembrance the keye. *Ibid.* 945 *Dido*, By the weye his wif Crusa he les [*v.r.* lees]. **1393** LANGL. *P. Pl.* C. VIII. 132 The sonne for sorwe ther-of lees lyght for a tyme. *c* **1400** *Beryn* 3731 Fond this blynd seching..Grasping al aboute to fynd that he had lore. **1406** HOCCLEVE *Misrule* 349 My purs his stuf hath lore. *c* **1425** *Seven Sag.* (P.) 892 As dyde the knyght ..That slew his hounde and lyse hys lyfe, For a worde of hyse wyfe. **1447** BOKENHAM *Seyntys* (Roxb.) 39 Here shal I hope no labour be lorn. **1513** DOUGLAS *Æneis* III. x. 104 The port of Drepanoun, and the raid quhar..I leis my fadir.

β. *weak.*

c **1205** LAY. 10629 Þa Pohtes weoren uuele, he leoseden heore aðele. *Ibid.* 26360 While þine aldren France ieoden.. and seoðen heo hit leoseden [*c* **1275** losede]. *Ibid.* 28337 Nu ich ileosed habbe mine sweines leofe. *c* **1250** *Kent. Serm.* in *O.E. Misc.* 30 Alle þo..þet..þurch yemer i-wil liesed þo blisce of heuene. *a* **1300** *Cursor M.* 2084 Nine hundreth 3ere and tensith fiue Was noe wen he lest his liue. **13..** *E.E. Allit. P.* A. 9 Allas! I leste hyr in on erbere. **1393** LANGL. *P. Pl.* C. x. 269 Ich leyue, for thy lacchesse thow leest meny wederes. **1430–40** LYDG. *Bochas* I. i. (1544) 2 b, They lost the dominacion Of Paradise..Their fredome lest, and became mortal. *c* **1470** HENRY *Wallace* IX. 477 Feyll lessyt thar..lyff apon the Sotheroun sid. *a* **1555** LYNDESAY *Tragedie* 120 Efter that boith strenth and speche wes lesit.

2. *absol.* and *intr.* To lose, be a loser.

c **1275** LAY. 12492 We habbeþ for oure loue ilore of [*c* **1205** ilosed] vre leode. **1375** BARBOUR *Bruce* XII. 347 Thai haf tald ..how thai lessit off thair men. **1481** CAXTON *Myrr.* I. iii. 10 He may wynne by doyng well and also lese by doyng euyll. **1484** —— *Fables of Auian* xviii, Suche supposen to wynne somtyme whiche lesen. *a* **1592** GREENE *Geo. a Greene* (1599) D 2 b, To know whether we shall win or leese. **1599** HAKLUYT *Voy.* II. I. 68 Whereby the Empire of Constantinople leeseth, and is like to leese. **1605** BACON *Adv. Learn.* I. viii. §6 (1873) 72 Copies cannot but leese of the life and truth. **1610** HOLLAND *Camden's Brit.* (1637) 59 All things [are] to follow in an easie and expedite course if you win, but all against you, if you leese.

3. *trans.* To destroy; to bring to ruin or perdition; to spoil. = L. *perdere*.

a **1325** *Prose Psalter* v. 6 Þou shalt lesin [L. *perdes*] alle þat speken lesyng. *c* **1330** *Spec. Gy Warw.* 130 Þurw þat sinne he was lorn. *c* **1350** *Will. Palerne* 988 Þerfor, come-liche creature..les nou3t is liif 3ut for a litel wille. *c* **1375** *Sc. Leg. Saints* Prol. 52 Hou þat crist ves of hire borne, to ransone mankynd þat ves lorne. *c* **1420** *Pallad. on Husb.* III. 462 Oyl pausia, whil hit is grene is best, But sone in age hit is corrupt & lest. *c* **1460** FORTESCUE *Abs. & Lim. Mon.* xix. (1885) 155 It is no prerogatyff or power to mowe lese any good, or to mowe wast, or put it awey. *c* **1485** in *E.E. Misc.* (Warton Club) 30 Sone after the sperit with a dredly speche Begane to crye and sayd,—I am lorne! **1496** *Dives & Paup.* (W. de W.) I. viii. 39/2 The fendes that ben besy nyght & daye to lese us. **1553** *Douglas' Æneis* x. vi. 64 Syne smate he Lycas, and him has al to lorne [*ed. Small* torn], That of his dede moderis wame furth was schorne.

b. With dative: To cause (a person) the loss of.

1550–3 *Decaye of Engl.* (E.E.T.S.) 100 It leseth the kings Maiesty in prouision for his noble housholdes,..v. thousande markes by the yeare.

4. *intr.* To come to ruin, to be 'lost'. *rare.*

c **1175** *Lamb. Hom.* 109 Vniseli bið þe 3itsere þe þurh his iselhðe leosað. *c* **1470** HENRY *Wallace* XI. 646 To succour thaim that was in poynt to leis.

5. To fail *to do* something. *rare.*

13.. *E.E. Allit. P.* B. 887 Þay lest of Lotez logging any lysoun to fynde.

¶ **6.** Spenser uses the vb. in the str. pa. t. and pa. pple. (*lore*, *lorn*) incorrectly with the sense 'to forsake, desert, leave'. Cf. the corresponding sense of LORN *a.*, which first appears in the 16th c.

1590 SPENSER *F.Q.* I. iv. 2 After that he had faire Una lorne, Through light misdeeming of her loialtie. *Ibid.* III. i. 44 Neither of them she found where she them lore.

† **leese**, *v.*[2] Forms: 1 líesan, lýsan, lésan, 2–4 lese(n, 4 les, lais(e, layse, 5 lesse, 6 *Sc.* leis, 7 leese. *Pa. t.* 1 lýsde, 3 lesede, 4 lais(e)d. [OE. *líesan* wk. vb. = OS. *lôsian* (MDu. *lôsen*, *lôzen*, Du. *loozen*), OHG. *lôsen* (MHG. *lœsen*, mod.G. *lösen*), ON. *løysa* (Sw. *lösa*, Da. *löse*), Goth. (and OTeut.) *lausjan*, f. OTeut. **lauso-*: see LOOSE *a.* The forms *laise*, *layse*, are from ON. Cf. ALESE.]

1. *trans.* To set free, deliver, release (in material and immaterial senses).

a **900** CYNEWULF *Crist* 1209 Hu se sylfa cyning mid sine lic-homan lysde of firenum þurh milde mod. *c* **975** *Rushw. Gosp.* Luke xii. 58 Sel 3eornlice ðætte ðu se 3ilesed from him [L. *da operam liberari ab illo*]. *c* **1175** *Lamb. Hom.* 71 Lif and saule beon..ilesed ut of sor3en. *c* **1200** *Trin. Coll. Hom.* 69 Ure helendes wille þe lesde us of deaðe. *a* **1300** *Cursor M.* 16442 He barabas, es laisd o prisun. *Ibid.* 18327 For us artu hider soght Fra ded of hell all to lais us. *a* **1310** in Wright *Lyric P.* vii. 29 Levedy, of alle londe Les me out of bonde. *a* **1340** HAMPOLE *Psalter* cxxv. 5 We ere lesyd of syn. *c* **1430** *Syr Gener.* (Roxb.) 7342 Generides was lessed of his thoght. **1560** ROLLAND *Crt. of Venus* II. 558 Perauenture thay wold 3ow leis of cair. **1607** MIDDLETON *Five Gallants* IV. viii, Keep thou thine owne heart, thou liu'st vnsuspected, I leese thee agaiine now.

2. To loosen, unloose; to unfasten, open; to relax (the body).

c **1250** *Gen. & Ex.* 3152 Heued and fet..lesen fro ðe bones and eten. *a* **1300** *Cursor M.* 18640 Leon o rightwisnes has raised Him-self, and his prisun laisd [*Fairf.* laused, *Gött.* laised]. **13..** *E.E. Allit. P.* A. 836 Lesande þe boke with leuez sware [= square]. *c* **1400** *Lanfranc's Cirurg.* 16 To myche slepinge..coldiþ & lesiþ al his bodi. ? **1507** *Communyc.* (W. de W.) A iij, Lorde, let these werkes lesse my bandes.

leese, obs. form of LEACH *sb.*[1], LEASE, LEASH.

leese, obs. pl. of LEE *sb.*[2]

† **'leeser**[1]. *Obs.* Also 4 lesar, -er. [f. LEESE *v.*[1] + -ER[1].]

1. A destroyer. (Cf. LEESE *v.*[1] 3.)

c **1380** WYCLIF *Sel. Wks.* III. 31 Þe fals world þat is leser of alle þat it loven. *Ibid.* 470 Lesars of mennys soulis.

2. A loser.

1546 *St. Papers Hen. VIII*, XI. 366 The Protestantes ar leesers by the withdrawinge of theyr armye. *a* **1575** R. CHENEY *Let.* in *Abp. Parker's Corr.* (Parker Soc.) 139 If your pleasure be that I only shall be a leeser..I will hold me content with 40*l.* loss. **1591** HARINGTON *Orl. Fur.* XXIII. xxvii, Then winners bost, when leesers speake their fill.

'leeser[2]. In 4 leser. [f. LEESE *v.*[2] + -ER[1].] A deliverer.

a **1300** *E.E. Psalter* cxliii. 2 Mi helper and leser mine.

leeshance, dial. form of LICENCE.

leeshe, obs. form of LEASH.

lee shore. [LEE *sb.*[1]]

1. A shore that the wind blows upon.

1579–80 NORTH *Plutarch* (1595) 127 Themistocles..knew the enemies must of necessitie fall vpon the lee shore for harborow. **1697** DAMPIER *Voy.* (1729) I. 498 Never did poor Mariners on a Lee-shore more earnestly long for the dawning Light. **1748** *Anson's Voy.* I. x. 104 To keep clear of this lee-shore. **1817** JAS. MILL *Brit. India* II. v. v. 525 The English were so alarmingly close upon a lee shore, that one of the ships actually touched the ground.

attrib. **1871** WHITTIER *Sisters* 26 If in peril from swamping sea Or lee shore rocks.

† **2.** A shore that affords shelter from the wind.

1653 H. COGAN tr. *Pinto's Trav.* xliii. (1663) 171 We weighed Anchor, and..put ourselves under the lee-shore of a Creek. **1711** SHAFTESB. *Charac.* (1737) III. 96 To retire under the lee-shore, and ply our oars in a smooth water.

lee side. Also *dial.* lew side. [LEE *sb.*[1]]

a. That side of any object which is turned away from the wind. Opposed to *weather-side*.

1577–87 HOLINSHED *Chron.* III. 815/2 The Carrike was on the weather side, and the Regent on the lie side. **1609** C. BUTLER *Fem. Mon.* i. (1623) C iv, They fly alow by the ground..in the..lee-sides of the hedges. **1748** *Anson's Voy.* III. v. 340 The proa..has..her two sides very different; the side, intended to be always the lee-side, being flat. **1833** MARRYAT *P. Simple* xii, I waited under the bulwark on the lee side. **1855** MAURY *Phys. Geog. Sea* 96 The weather side of all such mountains as the Andes is the wet side, and the lee side the dry. **1894** *Q. Rev.* Apr. 418 The valleys that lie on the 'lew' side of the prevailing winds.

fig. **1812** SCOTT *Fam. Lett.* (1894) I. viii. 240 You see I keep on the leeside of prudence.

b. *Geol.* The 'down-stream' side of a mound of rock which has undergone erosion by a glacier.

1886 [see *drag-line* s.v. DRAG *sb.* 9]. **1920** A. W. GRABAU *Textbk. Geol.* I. xiv. 374 The eroded bottom of such a valley often shows hummocky surfaces, sloping and smooth on the side from which the glacier moved (stoss-side) and with striated surfaces, but rough and cliffed on the side away from the movement (lee side). **1969** J. L. DAVIES *Landforms Cold Climates* ix. 171 The characteristic roche moutonnée presents a streamlined appearance with smoothed, more gently sloping, upstream end and sides and a steeper lee side sometimes smooth but characteristically plucked.

† **'leesing**, *vbl. sb.*[1] *Obs.* [f. LEESE *v.*[1] + -ING[1].] Losing, loss. Also *occas.* destruction, perdition.

1362 LANGL. *P. Pl.* A. v. 93 Of his leosinge I lauhwe..Ac for his wynnynge I wepe. *c* **1380** WYCLIF *Wks.* (1880) 369 It is..mooste lykynge to þe fende and lesynge of soulis. *c* **1400** *Lanfranc's Cirurg.* 37, I suppose þat a wounde be compound wiþ holownes & lesynge of fleisch & of skyn. *c* **1440** *Promp. Parv.* 298/2 Lesynge, or thyngys loste,..*perdicio.* **1483** CAXTON *Gold. Leg.* 133/2 She..conceyued the sonne of God and was delyueryd without leesyng of her virgynyte. **1523** LD. BERNERS *Froiss.* I. xcviii. 119 They of Vannes were in moost ieopardy, and in peryll of lesyng. **1585** PARSONS *Chr. Exerc.* I. vi. 49 The offence of God, that is, the leesing of his friendship by that sin if we do it.

† **'leesing**, *vbl. sb.*[2] *Obs.* [f. LEESE *v.*[2] + -ING[1].] **a.** Deliverance; redemption. **b.** Loosening.

c **950** *Lindisf. Gosp.* Luke i. 68 Gesohte & dyde lesing folces his. *c* **1440** *Promp. Parv.* 298/2 Lesynge, or losynge of a thynge bowndyn,.. *solucio*.

† **'leesing**, *vbl. sb.*[3] [? f. *lees* pl. of LEE *sb.*[2] + -ING[1].] ? Impregnation with lees (of better wine).

c **1460** J. RUSSELL *Bk. Nurture* 116 ȝiff swete wyne be seeke or pallid put in a Rompney for lesynge.

leesome ('liːsəm), *a.*[1] *Obs.* exc. *Sc.* Also 3 lefsum, leofsum, 6 lesum, 8 leisum, [Early ME. *leofsum*, f. *leof* LIEF *a.* + *-sum* -SOME.] Lovable; pleasing; pleasant.

c **1200** *Trin. Coll. Hom.* 181 Wowe beð wunsum þeih hit ne bie naht lefsum. *a* **1225** *Juliana* 17 Towart te liuiende godd mi leofsume leofmon. **1535** STEWART *Cron. Scot.* (1858) I. 195 He culd nocht find that he had far misgane, Sen lesum wes to haif ma wyffis nor ane. **1792** BURNS *'In simmer when the hay was mawn'* v, The tender heart o' leesome luve, The gowd and siller canna buy. ? *a* **1800** *Thomas o Yonderdale* x. in Child *Ballads* (1892) IV. 410/1 Fair and leesome blew the wind. **1819** W. TENNANT *Papistry Storm'd* (1827) 62 Some gentle cushie-dows, That saw The leesome la'rick's wae.

¶ **b.** *leesome lane*: a variation of *lee-lane* (see LEE-LONE). (Cf. LEEFUL b.)

1824 SCOTT *Redgauntlet* let. xi, There sat the Laird his leesome lane.

† **'leesome**, *a.*[2] Chiefly *Sc. Obs.* Forms: 4-5 lefsum, *Sc.* 5-6 lesum, (6 lesume, 7 lesome), 6 leifsum (?), le(i)uesom, 6-7 leasum, leasom(e, leisoum, leisome(e, 7 leisum, 8 leesome. [ME. *lēfsum*, f. *lēf* LEAVE *sb.*[1] + *-sum* -SOME.] Lawful, permissible, right.

? *a* **1400** *Langland's P. Pl.* B. xi. 92 *MS. B.* [*reads* lefsum *for* licitum *of other texts*; *MS. O has* leueful]. **14..** HENRYSON in *Bannatyne Poems* (1873) 611 Hir kirtill suld be of clene constance, Lasit with lesum lufe. **1513** DOUGLAS *Æneis* IV. iii. 25 So that it lesum be Dido ramane In spousage bund. **1552** LYNDESAY *Monarche* 6079 The Secretis quhilk he saw Thay wer nocht leifsum [? leissum] for to schaw To no man. **1560** ROLLAND *Crt. Venus* I. 776 To set ane Court in leissum time and place. **1560-78** *Bk. Discipl. Ch. Scot.* (1621) 75 Without this lawfull calling it was never leasome to any person to meddle with any function Ecclesiasticall. *a* **1578** LINDESAY (Pitscottie) *Chron. Scot.* (S.T.S.) I. 15 Puir men labouraris hauntand to thair lesum bussenes. *a* **1600** MONTGOMERIE *Sonn.* lxx. 2 Blind brutal Boy, that with thy bou abuses Leill leesome love by lechery and lust. **1681** *Act Secur. Peace Kingd. Scot.* in *Lond. Gaz.* No. 1648/4 His Majesty.. Declares, that in this Case, it shall be leisum to Heritors to put their Tennants off their Lands. *a* **1758** RAMSAY *Jenny Nettles* iii, The leel and leesome gate o't.

Hence **'leesomely** *adv.*, lawfully.

1552 ABP. HAMILTON *Catech.* (1884) 21 We may lesumlie desyre o' God our necessarie sustentatioun. **1609** SKENE *Reg. Maj.* 46 He may lesomelie distrenzie them, for the releiue and service aucht to him for his lands.

leesse, obs. form of LEACH *sb.*[1], LEASH.

leest(e, leester, obs. ff. LEAST, LEST, LEISTER.

leet (liːt), *sb.*[1] *Obs.* exc. *Hist.* Forms: 5-6 lete, 6-7 leete, 5- leet. [ad. AF. *lete* or AL. *leta*, of obscure origin; perh. ad. OE. *lǣþ*: see LATHE *sb.*[1] Prof. Skeat conjectures that it represents an OE. **lǣte* connected with *lǣtan* LET *v.*[1] (cf. LEET *sb.*[3]), but no evidence of this has been found.]

1. A special kind of court of record which the lords of certain manors were empowered by charter or prescription to hold annually or semi-annually; = COURT-LEET.

1292 *Year Bks. 20 Edw. I.* (Rolls) 297 E par la reson ke yl ad une lete en tel luy, a la quele presente fut ke Jon deynz la purceynte de sele lete fut resident. **1294** *Abbr. Placit. 22 Edw. I*, Norf. rot. 2. 291 (Du Cange) Et quia predicta transgressio.. magis sonat injuria senescalli quam injuria eorum qui fuerunt præsentatores, nec præsentacio in Leta alicujus facta, est fundamentum judicii [etc.]. **1303** *Year Bks. 31 Edw. I* (Rolls) 399 Par la resoun qe presente fut a lour lete de tiel lieu par deceyners qe [etc.]. *c* **1440** *Promp. Parv.* 11 Amercyn in a corte or lete, *amercio*. **1486** *Nottingham Rec.* III. 243 Expenses at ij. Letes at Snaynton. **1523** FITZHERB. *Surv.* 36 b, Suite of court from thre wekes to thre wekes and to the two great letes. **1538** —— *Just. Peas* 80 b, The lorde in his Lete, and the Shyriffe in his Tourne to enquere and to have for every defaute xxd. *a* **1577** SIR T. SMITH *Commw. Eng.* (1633) 164 The Leet and Law day is all one [in a manor]. This Leet is ordinarily kept but twice in the year. **1583** STUBBES *Anat. Abus.* II. (1882) 9 In euerie which shire or countie, be courts, lawe daies, and leets, as they call them, euery moneth. **1603** OWEN *Pembrokeshire* vi. (1891) 52 And in those sheeres there were no manours or Lordships neyther anye Courtes Baron or leetes kept or holden. **1643** SIR J. SPELMAN *Case of Affairs* 2 Every single man of twelve yeares of age ought by Law in some or other of His Majesties Leetes to swear Alleageance to His Majestie. **1778** *Eng. Gazetteer* (ed. 2) s.v. *Rumney Marsh*, Priveleges of leet, lawday, and tourn. **1846** MCCULLOCH *Acc. Brit. Empire* (1854) II. 153 Inferior courts of known jurisdiction.. such as a leet or a civil court within a borough. **1854** TOULM. SMITH *Parish* (1857) 107 Every Leet shall enquire of all offences against the Statute. **1877** R. W. DIXON *Hist. Ch. Eng.* I. iii. 197 In their renewal of this system the Commons seem to make sheriffs in their leets answer for the provincial synod.

† **b.** *transf.* Used in pl. as transl. of L. *comitia*.

1600 HOLLAND *Livy* I. xliii. 31 In the grand-leetes and solemne elections of Magistrates.

† **c.** A commission or committee. *Obs. rare*[−1].

1665 J. BUCK in Peacock *Stat. Cambridge* (1841) App. B. 59 There be certain priviledged Persons and Townsmen appointed for the Paving Leet.

2. The jurisdiction of a court-leet; the district over which this jurisdiction extended, in some cases including only the manor, in other cases a wider area, often that of the hundred.

1477 *Paston Lett.* No. 807 III. 211, I trow it to the lord of the soylle and not to the lete; for the maner holdyth nothyng of hyr. **1503-4** *Act 19 Hen. VII*, c. 30 §16 Whiche landis tenementes services and a lete with the appurtenaunces the seid John Vynter purchased. *c* **1630** RISDON *Surv. Devon* §308 (1810) 316 All this circuit, now the leet of Womberley, was timbered with tall trees. **1671** F. PHILLIPS *Reg. Necess.* 291 Where a Leet being a more large or greater Jurisdiction hath been granted to a man and his heirs. **1710** *Act 8 Anne* in *Lond. Gaz.* No. 4681/3 This Act shall not prejudice the Right of the City of London, or the Lords of any Leet. **1818** HALLAM *Mid. Ages* (1872) II. 293 The courts of the tourn and leet were erected.

† **b.** *transf.* A district generally. *Obs.*

1565 GOLDING *Ovid's Met.* VIII. (1593) 206 For fate forbiddeth famine to abide within the leete where plentie is.

3. *attrib.*, as ***leet-court***, ***-day***, ***-jury***, ***-juryman***; ***leet-ale***, a drinking of ale at the time of the leet.

1781 WARTON *Hist. Eng. Poetry* III. 129 *note*, *Leet-ale, in some parts of England, signifies the Dinner at a court-leet of a manor for the jury and customary tenants. **1651** W. G. *Cowel's Inst.* 96 To goe twice a year to the Sheriffs Courts, or *Leet Courts. **1690** W. WALKER *Idiomat. Anglo-Lat.* 517 Whole court or *leet-days. **1868** BROWNING *Ring & Bk.* IX. 1167 So, all's one lawsuit, all one long leet-day! **1720** STRYPE *Stow's Surv. Lond.* I. II. ii. 25 The *Leet Jury of the Manour of East Smithfield. **1766** ENTICK *London* IV. 398, 20 inquest or *leet jurymen.

leet (liːt), *sb.*[2] Now chiefly *Sc.* Also 5, 7, 9 lite, 6 liet, lyet, lytt, 7 lyte, leit. [app. an aphetic form of ELITE *sb.*[2] (a. OF. *eslite*, *eslete*), election. (With the phrase *to be in leet* cf. OF. *estre en eslite* 'to be at the choice or disposal' of a person.) Sense 2 may be a development of sense 1; but cf. LITE *sb.* = ELITE *sb.*[1], (bishop) elect.]

1. A list of persons designated as eligible for some office. Phrases, ***to be in leet***, ***to be on the leets***, ***to put in leet***, ***to put on the leet***, etc. ***short leet***: a select list of a prescribed number of candidates, which is to be submitted to the elective body or the appointing authority.

1441 *Extracts Aberd. Reg.* (1844) I. 7 Quhasaeuer that happynnis to be put furth at lites to be chosin alderman. *a* **1550** *Ordinances* in Boyle *Hedon* (1895) App. 66 The maior and crowner, with the other of his cowncell, shall nayme two men to be that daye in liet of the mayre, and iiij[or] men to be in liet as baylyffis. And when suche lyetts are writtyne, the said mayre or crowner shall fyrst tell to the towne clerke, and cawsse hym writte, whiche of them as is in lyet shalbe chosyne the mayre by hyme, and so the baylyffis. **1612** *Sc. Acts Jas. VI* (1816) IV. 518/1 To present ane Leit to my Lord [of] aucht persones. **1614** BP. COWPER *Dikaiologie* 180 You will not finde any Bishop of Scotland whom the general Assemblie hath not first nominated and giuen vp in lytes to that effect. *c* **1635** W. SCOT *Apol. Narr.* (Wodrow Soc.) 15 The Assemblie put in leits the said Mr. Alexander and Mr. Robert Pont.. [and] ordained edicts.. for the admission of one of them to the superintendentship. **1637-50** ROW *Hist. Kirk* (Wodrow Soc.) 152 That they would put on the leet five or six of the discreetest of the ministrie, that his Majestie may make choise of two of them to be ministers in his houss. **1639** in *Baillie's Lett.* (Bannatyne Club) I. 124 The Moderator for the time offered to my Lord Commissioner a lite, whereupon voices might passe for the election of a new Moderator. **1718** *Wodrow Corr.* (1843) II. 375 Mr. Chambers, Mr. Clark, and Mr. Rodgers, were on the leet. **1822** GALT *Provost* vii. 51 The policy of gentlemen putting themselves on the leet to be members of Parliament. **1865** *Reader* 21 Oct. 450/2 The chair of Scots Law.. is vacant. The patrons are the Faculty of Advocates and the Curators, the former having the right of presenting to the latter a leet of two, from which the appointment must be made. **1884** SIR A. GRANT *University Edinb.* II. 279 The Town Council .. placed him on a leet of persons eligible for the Principalship.

2. *pl.* The candidates forming a 'leet'.

The only use which is known to us outside Scotland is with reference to the annual election of Wardens of the Trinity House, Hull. Four 'lites' are nominated, from whom the two wardens are chosen.

1533 BELLENDENE tr. *Livy* III. (1822) 298 The candidatis and new litis [tr. L. *candidati*]. **1552** in *Rec. Convent. Roy. Burghs* (1870) I. 3 Quhilk new counsale and auld counsale to convene on Fryday.. and cheis the litis to the offices.. It is of.. auld vse, that the provest than present, the dene of gild, and thesaurare ar litis to that samin office for the zeir to cum. **1583** in Maitland *Edin.* (1753) 232 To proceid to the cheising of the Lytts to the Magistratts and Officemen.

† **leet**, *sb.*[3] *Obs.* [repr. OE. (*weʒa*) *ʒelǣte* = OHG. *kalâz* (*dero wego*) junction (of roads):—OTeut. type **galǣtjo*[m], f. **ga-* together + **lǣt-*: see LET *v.*[1]

A form *releet* given in the East Anglian glossaries is due to a wrong division of *threer eleet*, *four-eleet*, repr. OE. **préora ʒelǣte*, *féower-ʒelǣte*. (See Skeat in *Academy* 2 Mar. 1878.)]

A meeting of the ways, a cross-way; only in ***two-***, ***three-***, ***four-way leet***.

[*c* **1000** *Ags. Gosp.* Matt. xxii. 9 Gað nu witodlice to weʒa ʒelætum.] **1603** HARSNET *Popish Imposture* 134 Our children, old women, and maides afraid to crosse a Churchyeard, or a three-way leet. **1608** GOLDING *Epit. Frossard* II. 95 Arriuing at a three-way leete, and consulting among themselues which way was to be taken. **1618** BOLTON *Florus* I. ix. (1636) 24 Situated in the middest, betweene Latium and Tuscanie, as it were in a two-way-leet. **1656** W. D. tr. *Comenius' Gate Lat. Unl.* §923. 289 There are four principal ones—the Heathenish, Jewish, Christian, Mahometan—of which scrupulous four-way-leet, to take an Historical short delineation. **1674-91** RAY *S. & E.C. Words* 105 A Three or four-way Leet,.. where three or four ways meet.

leet (liːt), *sb.*[4] *dial.* [Of uncertain origin: by some referred to OE. (**hlíete*) *hléte* ON. *hløyti* share, portion; the OE. word, however, is recorded only in the sense 'casting of lots'.] A stack of peat, etc. (see quots.).

1744-50 W. ELLIS *Mod. Husbandm.* IV. x. 98 In Hertfordshire.. the same Morning the Grass is mown.. we ted.. it.. the same day.. it may be.. raked into Windrows, and then put into Grass-cocks. The second [day] we shake it into square Leets.. then put it into Bastard-cocks. **1793** *Statist. Acc. Scot.* V. 101 Peats are estimated by the leet, which is a solid body piled up like bricks, 24 feet long, and 12 ft. broad at bottom and 12 feet high. **1892** *Blackw. Mag.* Oct. 475 *Carage*, carting and leading a leet or stack of peats.

leet (liːt), *v. Sc.* Also 7 leit, 8 lytt. [f. LEET *sb.*[2]] *trans.* To place in a list of selected candidates; to nominate. Hence **'leeted** *ppl. a.*; **'leeting** *vbl. sb.*

1583 in Maitland *Edin.* (1753) 231 Theirefter the said Provest, Baillies, and Counsell, sall nominate, and lytt three Persones.. of the saids fourten Crafts. **1612** *Sc. Acts Jas. VI* (1816) IV. 518/1 To leit and present twa persounes with the auld thesaurar to the Thesaurie of the said cietie. *Ibid.*, To haue the fre leitting and electioun of thair said prouest deane of gild baillies and thesaurar. **1637-50** ROW *Hist. Kirk* (Wodrow Soc.) p. xxi, Thair wer six persones leitit to be sent to the King that he myght chuse ane of them for that kirk. *Ibid.* 290 Sitting doune as moderator without any leeting or voycing. **1647** in *Baillie's Lett.* (Bannatyne Club) III. 20 Mr. David Calderwood.. hes pressed soe a new way of leetting the moderator for time to come, that [etc.]. *a* **1670** SPALDING *Troub. Chas. I* (1792) I. 314 They referred their leeted [*Bannatyne Club ed.* listed] men with eiking paring or changing to the next provincial assembly.

leet, obs. form of LET *v.*; dial. var. LIGHT.

leethwake, obs. form of LEATHWAKE.

leetle ('liːt(ə)l), a jocular imitation of a hesitating or deliberately emphatic pronunciation of LITTLE.

1687 PHILLIPS *Don Quixote* 496 The Taylour.. held up five leetle Cloaks. **1755** JOHNSON *Grammar* in *Dict.* cj, There is another form of diminution among the English, by lessening the sound itself, especially of vowels; as there is a form of augmenting them [*sic*] by enlarging, or even lengthening it;.. as.. *little* pronounced long, *lee-tle*. **1835** B. HOFLAND in L'Estrange *Friendships Miss Mitford* (1882) I. xi. 280 A gentleman, somewhat a leetle too much dressed. **1838** DICKENS *O. Twist* ii, Just a leetle drop, with a little cold water, and a lump of sugar. **1894** G. W. APPLETON *Co-respondent* I. 45, I am sure he went just a leetle wrong.

† **'leetor.** *Obs. rare*[−1]. [f. LEET *sb.*[1] + -OR.] A member of a leet; one bound to appear at a leet.

1714 SCROGGS *Courts-Leet* (ed. 3) 4 Then call over the leetors, and mark every one that appears.

leeve, variant of LEVE *Obs.*

leevetail, variant of LEEFTAIL *dial.*

leeward ('liːwəd, 'ljuːəd), *a.* (*sb.*) and *adv.* Forms: 6 leaward, *Sc.* leuart, 7 le(y)ward, 7- leeward; also (repr. Naut. pronunc.) 9- looard. Also see LEEWARDS. [f. LEE *sb.*[1] + -WARD.]

A. *adj.*

† **1.** Of a ship: That makes much leeway. *Obs.*

a **1618** RALEIGH *R. Navy* 13 The high charging of ships it is that.. makes them extreame Leeward. **1691** T. H[ALE] *Acc. New Invent.* 127 What makes her Leeward or keep a good Wind. **1769** FALCONER *Dict. Marine* (1780), *Leeward ship*, a vessel that falls much to leeward of her course, when sailing *close-hauled*, and consequently loses much ground.

2. *gen.* Situated on the side turned away from the wind; having a direction away from the wind. Opposed to WINDWARD. Const. *of*. Hence *occas.* Sheltered. ***leeward shore*** = LEE-SHORE. ***leeward-tide***, ***-trade***, (see quots. 1721, 1735). ***leeward-way*** = LEE-WAY.

1666 DK. ALBEMARLE in Quaritch *Rough List* Oct. (1900) 102 Being Leeward of them standing to ye eastward. *a* **1687** PETTY *Pol. Arith.* iii. (1691) 53 The Windward Ship has a fairer Mark at a Leeward Ship, than *vice versa*. **1696** PHILLIPS, *Leeward Tide*, is when the Tide and Wind go both one way. **1705** *Lond. Gaz.* No. 4113/2 The Wind slackened upon a Leeward Tide. **1727** ARBUTHNOT *Tables Anc. Coins, Navig. Ancients* 230 Because of the great quantity of leeward way. **1735** BAILEY, *Leeward Trade*, is when the Tide and Wind go both one Way. **1762** FALCONER *Shipwr.* Introd. 38 Wanderers shipwreck'd on a leeward shore. **1804** *Naval Chron.* XI. 340 There was a small island leeward of the launch. **1814** SCOTT *Ld. of Isles* I. xxv, For our storm-toss'd skiff we seek Short shelter in this leeward creek. **1853** PHILLIPS *Rivers Yorksh.* v. 157 The annual fall of rain is not the same in amount.. on the windward side as on the leeward side of a mountain. **1893** *Academy* 25 Nov. 467/2 The dirty Ainus can be leeward of deer and not be scented by them. **1886** H. BAUMANN *Londinismen* 100/1, *Looard*. **1963** NANCE & POOL *Gloss. Cornish Sea-Words* 109 *Looard*, leeward, is common sea-language.

3. *absol.* or quasi-*sb.* = LEE *sb.*[1] 2, 2 b. In phrases ***on***, ***upon***, ***to*** (***the***) ***leeward*** (***of***).

1549 *Compl. Scot.* vi. 41 Heise the myszen, and change it ouer to leuart. **1595** MAYNARDE *Drake's Voy.* (Hakl. Soc.) 22 We saw a shippe on the leaward of us. **1612** DRAYTON *Poly-olb.* i. 422 They sun-burnt Africk keepe Upon the leeward still. **1695** *Lond. Gaz.* No. 3135/3 It blowing a fresh Gale, Captain Dowglass.. was necessitated to Fight to Leeward.

1748 *Anson's Voy.* III. v. 341 The proa..as she appears when viewed from the leeward. **1800** WEEMS *Washington* xiv. (1877) 209 Finding he was going fast to leeward. **1859** JEPHSON *Brittany* vi. 77 The priest..exhorted the lazar..not to speak to any, or to answer unless to leeward of the person spoken to. **1872** BAKER *Nile Tribut.* viii. 135 Forked sticks, driven into the ground to leeward of the fire. **1910** 'O. HENRY' *Whirligigs* ii. 33 Morgan lived in a bamboo shack to 'loo'ard'.

fig. **1826** SCOTT *Woodst.* xxii, His friend..ought not..to be suffered to drop to leeward in the conversation.

B. *adv.* Toward the lee (see LEE *sb.*[1] 2).

1785 BURNS *Death & Dr. Hornbook* v, Tho' leeward whyles, against my will, I took a bicker.

leewardly ('liːwədlɪ, 'ljuːədlɪ), *a.* [f. LEEWARD + -LY[1].] Of a ship: Apt to fall to leeward. Opposed to WEATHERLY.

1683 HACKE *Collect. Voy.* I. (1699) 31 So leewardly a Ship, that she would not make her way better than N. by W. with this Sea. **1801** NELSON in Nicolas *Disp.* (1843) IV. 274 She was such a leewardly ship..that I should often be forced to anchor on a lee shore. **1865** *Examiner* 18 Mar. 163 They are far too leewardly to work to windward.

fig. **1890** CLARK RUSSELL *My Shipm. Louise* II. xxiv. 216 There's the Whole Dooty o' Man—a bit leewardly; I couldn't fetch to windward of it myself.

leewardmost ('liːwədməʊst), *a.* [f. LEEWARD + -MOST.] Situated furthest to leeward.

1693 *Lond. Gaz.* No. 2887/3 He was the Leewardmost Ship of the whole Fleet. **1726** G. ROBERTS *4 Years Voy.* 291 By the Time that it was high Water, under the Leewardmost of the little Islands. **1797** NELSON in Nicolas *Disp.* (1845) II. 341 The leewardmost and sternmost Ships in their Fleet. **1840** R. H. DANA *Bef. Mast* xxvi. 86 We..were glad to reach the leewardmost point of the island.

†'**leewardness.** *Obs.* [f. as prec. + -NESS.] The quality of being leeward, tendency to fall to leeward.

1624 CAPT. SMITH *Virginia* III. iii. 50 Such was the lewardnesse of his Ship..by stormy contrary winds was he forced so farre to Sea. *a* **1642** SIR W. MONSON *Naval Tracts* IV. (1704) 452/1 The others cannot beat it up, because of their Leewardness.

†'**leewards.** *Obs.* [f. LEEWARD + advb. *-es, -s.*] = LEEWARD A. 3.

1574 BOURNE *Regiment for Sea* xv. (1577) 43 b, Whether the shippe goeth to leewardes, or maketh hir way good.

'**lee-way, 'leeway.** [f. LEE *sb.*[1] + WAY.] The lateral drift of a ship to leeward of her course; the amount of deviation thus produced. Also *to make, fetch up, make up lee-way.* ***angle of lee-way***: the angle made by the direction of a ship's keel, with that of its actual course.

1669 STURMY *Mariner's Mag.* II. 145 To give allowance to your Course according to the Lee-way you have made. **1743** *Phil. Trans.* XLII. 414 The same Theory is applied to the Motion of Ships, abstracting from the Lee-way, but having regard to the Velocity of the Ship. **1762** FALCONER *Shipwr.* II. 576 The angle of lee-way, seven points, remain'd. **1771** SMOLLETT *Humph. Cl.* 8 Aug., To fear that the tide would fail before we should fetch up our lee-way. **1840** R. H. DANA *Bef. Mast* Gloss., When sailing close-hauled with all sail set, a vessel should make no leeway. **1883** STEVENSON *Treas. Isl.* v. xxiii, Do as you pleased, she [the boat] always made more leeway than anything else.

fig. **1827** SCOTT *Jrnl.* 2 Dec., Laboured to make [? *read* make up] lee-way, and finished nearly seven pages to eke on to the end of the missing sheets when returned. **1835** W. IRVING in *Crayon Misc.* (1849) 196 He..made great leeway toward a corn-crib, filled with golden ears of maize. **1871** L. STEPHEN *Playgr. Europe* iv. 221 Both in time and space it is rapidly making up its leeway. **1884** *Daily News* 16 Feb. 5/1 We have a great deal of leeway to make up with the Australians.

leeze, obs. pl. of LEE *sb.*[2]

leeze me. *Sc.* Also 6 leis(s, 8 leez. [Short for *lief is me* dear is to me.] An expression of lively satisfaction; 'pleased am I with'. Const. *for, on.*

15.. *Wowing of Jok & Jynny* 15 in *Bannatyne Poems* (1873) 388, I schro the, lyar, full leis me yow. *a* **1568** CLERK *Ibid.* 297 Fow leiss me that graceles gane. **1724** RAMSAY *Tea-t. Misc.* (1733) I. 25 Leez me on thy snawy pow, Lucky Nansy. **1792** BURNS *Bessy & Spinning Wheel* i, Oh leeze me on my spinning-wheel, Oh leeze me on my rock and reel. **1861** RAMSAY *Remin.* Ser. II. 29 Leeze me abune them a'..for yon auld clearheaded man.

lef(e, obs. form of LEAF, LEAVE, LIEF, LIVE *v.*

leffel, -ol, -ul, variant forms of LEEFUL *a. Obs.*

leffly, lefally, variant forms of LEEFULLY *Obs.*

lefsilver, *Obs.*: see LESSILVER.

lefsum, obs. form of LEESOME.

left (lɛft), *a., adv.,* and *sb.* Forms: 2-4 luft, 3 leoft, 3-5 lift(e, 4-5 lyft(e, 4-6 lefte, 4- left. [ME. *left, lift*:—OE. *left* (Kentish), *lyft*, occurring only in the gloss 'inanis, *left*' (Mone *Q. & F.* I. 443), and in the comb. *lyft-ádl* paralysis; the primary sense 'weak, worthless' is represented also in East Fris. *luf*, Du. dial. *loof*, and the derived sense 'left' (hand) in MDu., LG. *luchter, lucht, luft*, North Fris. *leeft, leefter.*

Cf. further (though connexion is very doubtful) OE. *léf* weak, *léfung* paralysis, *ʒeléfed* weak, old, OFris., OS. *léf* weak, OS. *gilêbod* lamed.]

A. *adj.*

1. a. The distinctive epithet of the hand which is normally the weaker of the two (for examples see LEFT HAND), and of the other parts on the same side of the human body (occas. of their clothing, as in *left boot, glove, sleeve*); hence also of what pertains to the corresponding side of any other body or object. Opposed to *right.* Phr. ***two left feet***: signifying a clumsy person.

c **1205** LAY. 27693 [He] smat Leir þene eorl sære a þa lift side þurh ut þa heorte. **13..** *E.E. Allit. P.* B. 981 Hit watz lusty lothes wyf þat [looked] ouer her lyfte schulder. **1340** HAMPOLE *Pr. Consc.* 818 Þe lefte eghe of hym þan semes les And narower þan þe right eghe es. **1393** LANGL. *P. Pl.* C. IV. 75 Let nat þy lyft half, oure lord techeþ, Ywite what þow delest with þy ryht syde. *c* **1449** PECOCK *Repr.* 530 Thei baren scrowis in her forehedis and in her lift arme. **1559** W. CUNNINGHAM *Cosmogr. Glasse* 27 Orions left foote. **1667** MILTON *P.L.* VIII. 465 Who stooping op'nd my left side, and took From thence a Rib. **1709** STEELE *Tatler* No. 127 ¶ 1 With his Hat under his Left Arm. **1833** *Regul. Instr. Cavalry* I. 13 Place the right heel against the hollow of the left foot. **1895** *Punch* CVIII. 49/1 The peculiar striping of his [a tiger's] left shoulder. **1915** WODEHOUSE *Psmith Journalist* xviii. 132 Mr. Dawson..gave it as his opinion that one of the lady dancers had two left feet. **1959** E. L. MASCALL *Pi in the High* 7 Or dance with two left feet the *valse triste.* **1975** D. RAMSAY *Descent into Dark* iii. 92 Clumsy..you've got two left feet.

b. *left side,* † *half* (also LEFT HAND), used (with a preceding prep.) for: The position or direction (relative to a person) to which the left hand points.

a **1175** *Lamb. Hom.* 141 Þer stod a richt halue and a luft alse an castel wal. *c* **1200** *Trin. Coll. Hom.* 67 He setteð þe synfulle on his lifthalf. **13..** *Gaw. & Gr. Knt.* 698 Alle þe iles of Anglesay on lyft half he haldez. **1362** LANGL. *P. Pl.* A. II. 7 'Loke on þe lufthond', quod heo..I lokede on þe luft half as þe ladi me tauhte. *c* **1400** MAUNDEV. (1839) iv. 31 On the lift syde of the hille Carmelyn is a towne. **1474** CAXTON *Chesse* 16 She shold sitte on the lift side of the kyng.

c. ***left jabber***, a boxer whose characteristic punch is the left jab.

1950 [see CROSS *sb.* 22 d].

2. †**a.** In various obsolete proverbial expressions, e.g. ***to see with the left eye, to work with the left hand***, implying inefficiency in performance; ***to take a thing by the left ear*** (cf. quot. *a* 1684). †**b.** ***to go over the left shoulder***: to be squandered. **c.** ***over the left shoulder***, now ***over the left*** simply, a slang phrase implying that the words to which it is appended express the reverse of what is really meant.

c **1450** tr. *De Imitatione* III. xliii. 114 Þat beholden þinges transitory wiþ þe lifte eye ande hevenly þinges wiþ þe riȝt eye. **1650** B. *Discolliminium* 14 Some of our new Architectors, have read some Authors about alterations of States with their left eyes, which makes them work with their left hands, so sinisterly. *a* **1684** LEIGHTON *Comm. 1 Pet.* ii. I. (1693) 225 Taking all things by the left Ear; for (as Epictetus says) Every thing hath two handles. **1705** *Rec. Hartford County Court* (*U.S.*) 4 Sept. in *Newcastle Daily Jrnl.* 28 July 1891, The said Waters, as he departed from the table, he said, 'God bless you over the left shoulder'. **1748** RICHARDSON *Clarissa* I. 218 With t'other, perhaps, you'll have an account to keep, too; But an account of what will go over the left shoulder; only of what he squanders, what he borrows, and what he owes, and never will pay. **1837** DICKENS *Pickw.* xlii, Each gentleman pointed with his right thumb over his left shoulder. This action, imperfectly described in words by the very feeble expression of 'over the left'..its expression is one of light and playful sarcasm. **1843** W. T. MONCRIEFF *Scamps Lond.* I. i, I think she will come. *Ned.* Yes, over the left—ha, ha, ha! **1852** R. S. SURTEES *Sponge's Sp. Tour* (1893) 137 'All over the left', said Frosty..'He's come gammonin' down here that he's a great man..but it's all my eye'.

3. a. That has the relative position of the left hand with respect to the right. (Sometimes said with reference to the appearance to a spectator, and sometimes with reference to the direction in which the object is considered to face.) In predicative use with const. *of*; in attributive use now chiefly replaced by LEFT-HAND, exc. in certain special collocations, as LEFT WING (of an army), ***left branch*** (of a stream). ***left bank*** (of a river): that to the left of a person looking down the stream; applied *spec.* to a part of Paris lying south of the Seine noted for its 'advanced' intellectual views; = *Latin Quarter* (LATIN *sb.* 5); also *attrib.*; hence ***left-bankish*** adj.

c **1400** MAUNDEV. (1839) xi. 128 Uppon the lyfte way, men goon fyrst un to Damas, by Flome Iordane. **1838** THIRLWALL *Greece* IV. xxxiii. 319 They then proceeded along the left bank of the Tigris. **1845** M. PATTISON *Ess.* (1889) I. 28 A prison..the ruins of which long after, remained on the left bank of the Seine. **1882** CUSSANS *Her.* (ed. 3) 45 That part of the shield which appears on the left side is called the dexter. *Mod.* The greater part of the town is left of the railway.

1893 H. S. EDWARDS *Old & New Paris* I. iii. 10/1 On the 'left bank', ..stand the Institute, the Pantheon, [etc.]. **1911** W. J. LOCKE *Glory of Clementina Wing* ix. 129 Paris of the Left Bank, of the studios, of struggle and toil. **1929** E. WILSON *I thought of Daisy* iv. 243 She was staying..in a little Left Bank hotel. **1932** 'F. ILES' *Before the Fact* ii. 42 Some unpretentious little restaurant on the left bank. **1943** D. GASCOYNE *Poems 1937-42* 45 In a Left-bank café. **1949** *Oxf. Jun. Encycl.* III. 335/1 The streets..on the left bank are noted for the numerous book-stalls. **1952** A. WILSON *Hemlock & After* II. iii. 168 She had carefully preserved her Left Bank student get-up for this bourgeois gathering. **1958** *Times Lit. Suppl.* 14 Feb. 85/1 The intense form of *Angst* that one associates..with French intellectualism is not confined to the Left Bank. **1958** *Manch. Guardian* 27 Feb. 7/6 The highly complicated 'left-bankish' and somehow heartless fairy story which it tells in its three acts grows no more likeable with renewed acquaintance. **1964** *Economist* 2 May 478/1 Mr Gomulka strongly criticised their 'left-bank' attitudes. **1974** 'S. HARVESTER' *Forgotten Road* vi. 72 Their meal took on a sort of Chelsea or Greenwich Village or Left Bank atmosphere.

b. In politics: cf. LEFT *sb.* 2 c and LEFT WING; **left-leaning** *a.*, sympathetic towards the left in politics.. For *left centre* see CENTRE *sb.* 15.

1837 CARLYLE *Fr. Rev.* I. VI. ii. 308 The Left side [of the Assembly] is also called the d'Orleans side. **1919** T. E. LAWRENCE *Let.* 27 Sept. (1938) 293 So long as we are the more liberal ('left' in the Parliamentary sense) we call the tune... Our remedy and safeguard will be to trend continually 'left'. **1953** M. LOWRY *Sel. Lett.* (1967) 330, I am even 'left' of de Voto on the subject. **1957** J. OSBORNE *Entertainer* VIII. 62 A chap at my school..managed to get himself in to the Labour Government, and they always said he was left of centre. **1961** *Times* 23 Jan. 13/6 The left-leaning Captain Kong Lae was, moreover, partly educated in Siam. **1962** J. BRAINE *Life at Top* x. 135, I asked the Warden who Graffham was. 'He's very Left,' the Warden said. **1962** *Listener* 19 July 87/1 A left-of-centre party not unlike the British Labour Party. **1964** GOULD & KOLB *Dict. Social Sci.* 383/2 The word *left* was used in England from the 1920s onwards,..sometimes covering Communists and Socialists and sometimes Liberals as well. **1966** T. PYNCHON *Crying of Lot 49* iii. 50 Peter Pinguid was really our first casualty. Not the fanatic our more left-leaning friends..chose to martyrize. **1972** *Times* 4 Aug. 13/4 The constitution of..the Donovan Commission, was on any showing a fair way left of centre.

c. Further special collocations: (in sport) ***left arm, -armer, back, half (-back)***. Also ***left field*** (Baseball): the part of the outfield to the left of the batter as he faces the pitcher; also, a fielder in this position; also *fig.*, a position away from the centre of activity or interest; ***left fielder***: a fielder in the left field; also *fig.*

1955 *Times* 9 May 15/1 Goddard opened the bowling with him, left arm over the wicket at a gentle medium pace. *Ibid.* 10 June 4/2 Splendid bowling by Hampshire's young, left-arm bowler Sainsbury, whose seven wickets for 25 runs was the best performance of his career. **1974** *Times* 11 Nov. 8/2 Titmus chopped Bright's orthodox left-arm spin into his stumps. **1960** E. W. SWANTON *W. Indies Revisited* 277 New bowling talent will have to be unearthed, for instance..a slow left-armer. **1897** *Encycl. Sport* I. 419/2 [Assoc. Football] The left back and half-back deal with the opposing right wing. **1955** *Times* 9 May 14/3 Eckersley, the Blackburn Rovers left-back, who has not played for England since November, 1953, has been selected to accompany the Football Association party. **1960** B. LIDDELL *My Soccer Story* xvi. 98 The tragedy of Munich robbed England of one of her finest post-war left-backs in Roger Byrne. **1974** *Guardian* 18 May 19/2 Willie Ormond, the Scotland manager, has..kept Danny McGrain..at left-back. **1857** *Spirit of Times* 29 Aug. 404/3 Enterprise Club. Maxfield, catcher;..Webber, left field. **1867** H. CHADWICK *Base Ball Player's Bk. Reference* 51 A ball similarly hit to the right or left fields. **1896** KNOWLES & MORTON *Baseball* 77 Harry Athol..played left field for the Thespians in all their games. **1949** *Minot* (N. Dakota) *Daily News* 22 July 8/8 Marinari spoiled Lettau's chance for a no-hitter, lining a solid single to left field in the fifth frame. **1961** *Amer. Speech* XXXVI. 147 *Out in left field*, disoriented, out of contact with reality. **1970** *Time* 9 Mar. 19 An increasing number of candidates are emerging from leftfield to give voters surprising options. **1974** *Publishers Weekly* 11 Mar. 48/3 Novak's use of religious metaphor may put him in left field (Reinhold Niebuhr was there before him). **1867** H. CHADWICK *Base Ball Player's Bk. Reference* 70 Suppose the left-fielder should be the third striker on the list. **1957** *Encycl. Brit.* III. 160/2 The outfielders are called right fielder, centre fielder and left fielder with relation to a man standing on home plate and facing out across the diamond. **1973** *Publishers Weekly* 29 Jan. 259/1 Sober, necktie-wearing citizens will get a bang out of the book, left-fielders not at all. **1897** *Encycl. Sport* I. 418/2 [Assoc. Football] Three half-backs are played nowadays... They are called..the right, centre and left half-back. **1914** *London Opinion* 19 Sept. 445/1 A 'rising young left-half' for Sludberry Rangers. **1960** B. LIDDELL *My Soccer Story* vi. 40 Bobby Paisley was at left-half.

4. *Comb.*: parasynthetic, chiefly in sense 'having the left limb more efficient than the right'; as ***left-eyed*** (hence ***left-eyedness***), ***-footed*** (hence ***left-footedness***), ***-legged*** (hence ***left-leggedness***); also ***left-sided, -witted*** (see quots.). **left-brained**, having the left-hand side of the brain as the dominant half; **left-footer** *slang*, a Roman Catholic. Also LEFT-HANDED.

1890 W. JAMES *Princ. Psychol.* I. ii. 39 Most people..are *left-brained, that is, all their delicate and specialized movements are handed over to the charge of the left hemisphere. **1902** *Daily Chron.* 22 May 3/4 Each half [of the cerebrum] governs the opposite side of the body, and..as we are right-handed, so we may be called left-brained. **1622** MASSINGER *Virg. Mart.* IV. ii, I wud not giue vp the cloake of your seruice to meet the splay-foot estate of any *leftey'd kingdom aboue the Antipodes, because they are vnlucky to meete. **1900** *Westm. Gaz.* 20 Jan. 5/2 [In rifle-shooting] a left-eyed man can easily fire from his left shoulder. **1937** S. T. ORTON *Reading, Writing & Speech Probl. in Children* i. 52 A boy found..difficulty in using the rifle because of his right-handedness and *left-eyedness. **1891** SIR D. WILSON *Right Hand* 169, I am myself *left-footed. *Ibid.*, Right and *left-footedness prevailed about equally. **1944** J. H. FULLARTON *Troop Target* 26 'What about the R.C.s?' 'Oh, yes. Leave the *left-footers behind as gun-picquets.' **1959** I. & P. OPIE *Lore & Lang. Schoolch.* xvi. 344 In Lancashire Roman Catholics are known as 'Micks', and in Dundee as 'Left-footers'. **1964** M. CRITCHLEY *Developmental Dyslexia*

viii. 51 Others attached less importance to the role of *left-handedness than to left-eyedness. **1728** POPE *Dunc.* II. 68 Bernard..*left-legg'd Jacob seems to emulate. **1829** MARRYAT *F. Mildmay* xvi, He was left-legged as well as left-handed. **1890** W. K. SIBLEY in *19th Cent.* May 773 (art.), *Left-leggedness. **1880** BARWELL *Aneurism* 84 The *left-sided destination of fibrinous concreta. **1616** B. JONSON *Horace's Art of Poetry* 389 O I *left-witted [*A. P.* 301 *o ego lævus*], that purge every spring For choller!

B. *adv.* On or towards the left side.

a **1300** *Cursor M.* 21639 Ouer and vnder, right and left, In þis compas godd all has left. **1796-7** *Instr. & Reg. Cavalry* (1813) 228 Squadrons—left wheel! **1832** *Prop. Regul. Instr. Cavalry* II. 35 Rear Divisions left incline. **1833** *Regul. Instr. Cavalry* I. 125 Draw back the body and 'Left Parry'. **1884** *Times* 3 Mar. 5/3 'Troops, left about', was sounded immediately. **1885** R. BRIDGES *Eros & Psyche, March* 23 She.. Lookt left and right to rise and set of day. **1886** *Manch. Exam.* 14 Jan. 5/6 Mr. Gladstone was supported right and left by Lord H. and Sir W. H. **1918** *Daily Chron.* 2 Dec., In Kiel, where the revolution started, matters appear to be going 'left' with a vengeance.

C. *sb.*

†**1.** A mean, worthless person. *Obs.*

1377 LANGL. *P. Pl.* B. IV. 62 Conscience hym tolde þat wronge was a wikked luft. *c* **1425** *Seven Sag.* (P.) 1284 His wyf, that cursyd lyfte, Brewed the childys deth that nyght.

2. a. = LEFT HAND. Often in advb. phrases referring to relative position or direction (cf. A. 1 b), where it is now apprehended as merely *absol.* of the adj. Also, a blow dealt with the left hand.

a **1240** *Sawles Warde* in *Cott. Hom.* 257 þe middel sti bituhhe riht and luft. *a* **1300** *Cursor M.* 2463 Queder þou ches, on right or left, I sal ta me þat þou haues left. **1667** MILTON *P.L.* VI. 558 Vangard to Right and Left the Front unfould. **1669** STURMY *Mariner's Mag.* V. 73 If the Shot graze to the right or left. **1697** DRYDEN *Æneid* IX. 864 Jove ..thunder'd on the left. **1842** TENNYSON *Vision Sin* 138 In her right a civic wreath, In her left a human head. **1855** —— *Charge Light Brig.* iii, Cannon to right of them, Cannon to left of them,.. Volley'd and thunder'd. **1859** *Field Exerc. Infantry* 35 A squad will be formed to the front, left, or left about, on the same principle. **1897** *Encycl. Sport* I. 136 (*heading*) Stop for lead-off at body with the left. **1898** *Daily News* 24 Nov. 7/3 Corbett kept trying to push his left in Sharkey's face. **1912** *Chambers's Jrnl.* 394/2 Out went Reid's murderous 'left' to our unutterable surprise, and down went the man on the platform. **1914** J. H. & A. LAMBERT *Boxing* (ed. 2) 41 If possible send in a straight left to the head. **1930** *Daily Express* 8 Sept. 1/6 Siki fell to a left on the body and was counted out. **1948** 'P. WOODRUFF' *Whatever Dies* 126 An odious person who could be neatly floored by one skilful left to the chin. **1967** G. F. FIENNES *I tried to run a Railway* i. 5 Out shot a telescopic left, and I had the shiner of all time for weeks.

b. *Mil.* The left wing (of an army). Also in *pl.*, the men whose place is on the left.

1707 *Lond. Gaz.* No. 4334/4 Our Right was then at Louvignies, and our Left at Naast. **1780** A. HAMILTON *Wks.* (1886) VIII. 14 We see the consequences. His left ran away, and left his right uncovered. **1796-7** *Instr. & Reg. Cavalry* (1813) 191 The left's go about by three's. **1832** *Prop. Regul. Instr. Cavalry* II. 33 Their Centres and Lefts move up. **1881** HENTY *Cornet of Horse* xvi. (1888) 165 He formed..a heavy column of attack opposite the French left.

c. In continental legislatures, the section of the members who occupy seats on the left side of the chamber (as viewed from the president's chair), a situation which is by custom assigned to those holding relatively liberal or democratic opinions. Hence applied *transf.* to the more advanced or innovating section of a philosophical school, a religious sect, or the like, and esp. to a political group holding radical or socialist views.

For the origin of the party significance of the term, see CENTRE *sb.* 15.

1837 CARLYLE *Fr. Rev.* II. v. ii. 285 Still less is a *Coté Gauche* wanting: extreme Left. **1898** BODLEY *France* II. 327 The combats between the Moderates and the Extreme Left. **1939** *John o'London's Weekly* 2 June 321/1 A defiant glare at the Left..with an equally defiant glare at the Right. **1940** W. TEMPLE *Thoughts in War-Time* iii. 24 The Right tends to have a fuller sense of historical continuity than the Left. **1950** THEIMER & CAMPBELL *Encycl. World Politics* 260/2 The communists are referred to as the 'extreme' or 'far' left. **1971** W. LAQUEUR *Dict. Politics* 310 Popularly the Left has favoured rapid social change... During the thirties, Left was associated with opposition to fascism. **1974** 'W. HAGGARD' *Kinsman* ix. 93 The tiresomely modern bishop.. was..very far to the Left.

3. A glove, boot, etc. for the left hand or foot.

1864 F. LOCKER *My Mistress's Boots* vii, Cinderella's lefts and rights To Geraldine's were frights.

4. A shot fired at game with the left barrel of a double-barrelled shotgun; a bird or beast hit by such a shot.

1893 H. A. MACPHERSON et al. *Partridge* II. iii. 131 Now thoroughly awake, you kill three neatly, quickly followed by a smart right and left— one in front and one behind—at a brace that come straight at you. **1908** R. H. BENSON *Conventionalists* I. iii. 82 On Saturday he had killed three rights and lefts, and had not missed more than one single bird flying alone. **1910** *Blackw. Mag.* Jan. 140/1, I got a right and left with the big gun. **1958** M. BRANDER *Rough-shooter's Sport* XX. 217 When..a covey of grouse was flushed.., I only managed to drop one bird. The others, however, performed more than adequately, each bringing down a right and left. **1974** *Field* 5 Dec. 1311/1 Congratulate anyone on a good piece of dog work..as one would if he achieved a right and left.

5. *Surfing.* The (use of the) left foot. Cf. GOOFY *a.* 2.

1968 W. WARWICK *Surfriding in N.Z.* 17/3 Calculate where the waves are shaping up the best for your style of riding. Obviously..goofy footers will favour lefts. **1970** *Surf '70* (N.Z.) 17/2 Wayne Charlton was one of the best goofy footers to ever surf the left at Fitzroy.

Hence '**leftness**, the condition of being on the left.

1530 PALSGR. 238/1 Leftnesse, *gavcheté*. **1884** [see BILATERALITY]. **1887** W. JAMES in *Mind* Jan. 14 Rightness and leftness, upness and downness, are again pure sensations differing specifically from each other. **1890** [see DOWNNESS].

left (lɛft), *ppl. a.* [pa. pple. of LEAVE *v.*]

1. In senses of the vb. Now rare exc. in ***left-luggage*** (***office***, etc.).

c **1586** C'TESS PEMBROKE *Ps.* LIX. vi, They babling prate, How my left life extinguish may Their deadly hate. **1627-77** FELTHAM *Resolves* II. lviii. (1709) 432 How often does the lavish Gamester squander away a large left Patrimony. **1724** RAMSAY *Wyfe of Auchtermuchty* xii, The twa left gaislings gat a clank. **1816** A. C. HUTCHISON *Pract. Obs. Surg.* (1826) 173 He uniformly every night made a hearty repast from the left provisions. **1861** H. RHYS *Theatr. Trip Canada & U.S.* xi. 96 Arrived at the depôt, I discovered in the doubtful light the 'left luggage' room. **1888** LD. HERSCHELL in *Law Reports, Ho. Lords* XIII. 53 Left-luggage offices for luggage brought to the station. **1945** G. B. GRUNDY *55 Yrs. at Oxf.* 167 He left it in the left-luggage office. **1963** [see *baggage-room*]. **1971** 'E. CANDY' *Words for Murder Perhaps* xiii. 158 He..came straight back, leaving his case and holdall in the left luggage.

2. a. With advs. or advb. phrase; see LEAVE *v.*¹ 14.

1783 COWPER *Let. to Newton* 17 Nov., He came to thank me for some left-off clothes. **1841** J. T. HEWLETT *Parish Clerk* I. 23 The squire's left-off chintz dressing-gown. **1852** R. S. SURTEES *Sponge's Sp. Tour* (1893) 166 Our left-in-the-lurch friends. **1861** SALA *Dutch Pict.* xxi. 324 The subject of left-off garments has always been an interesting one to me. **1873** 'S. COOLIDGE' *What Katy Did* i. 7 In almost every large family, there is one of those..left-out children. **1888** W. MORRIS in Mackail *Life* (1899) II. 211 The town is the queerest left-behind sort of a place. **1909** *Daily Chron.* 14 Jan. 1/5, I believe the left-out millions are more miserable. **1941** E. BOWEN *Look at Roses* 242 Emma's left-behind silver things. **1965** B. SWEET-ESCOTT *Baker St. Irreg.* i. 38 The section was for a few weeks engaged in organising 'left behind' parties all over the British Isles.

b. *absol.* passing into *sb.* Chiefly *colloq.*

1890 *Standard* 14 Apr. 2/6 Witness had given her some of his family's left-offs. **1908** *Westm. Gaz.* 18 Apr. 3/1 (*title*) The little brothers. Or, the land of the left-behind. **1965** *Economist* 21 Aug. 674/2 They [*sc.* Negroes who rioted, esp. in Los Angeles] believe—some of them rightly—that they could have risen out of the ghetto of the left-behind but for their colour. **1974** W. FOLEY *Child in Forest* II. 220 Getting my swollen inflamed feet back into Leah's left-offs.

leftal, obs. variant of LEEFTAIL *a. dial.*

left-branching, *a. Linguistics.* [LEFT *adv.*] (Of grammatical constructions) having the majority of its constituents on the left of its tree diagram. Also **left-branching** *vbl. sb.*

1961 N. CHOMSKY in *Proc. Symposia Appl. Math.* XII. 14 Left-branching should offer no problem... A hearer will tend to group left-branching units of a complex sentence (as, e.g., in 'many more than half of the rather obviously much too easily solved problems') as units quite readily. **1965** —— *Aspects of Theory of Syntax* i. 13 A left-branching structure is of the form [[[···]···]···]—for example, in English, such indefinitely iterable structures as [[[[*John*]'*s brother*]'*s father*]'*s uncle*]... There are no clear examples of unacceptability involving only left-branching or only right-branching.

leftenaunt, obs. form of LIEUTENANT.

left hand. Forms: (See LEFT *a.* and HAND.)

1. (See LEFT *a.* 1.)

c **1205** LAY. 28047 Ich igrap mi sweord..mid mire leoft honde. *a* **1300** *Cursor M.* 28968 þat þi left hand wijt noght for roos, þe almus þat þi right hand doos. **1340** *Ayenb.* 196 Huanne þou dest elmesse ne wyte naȝt þi left hand huet deþ þi riȝt hand. **1387** TREVISA *Higden* (Rolls) I. 229 [He] halt his bridel in his lift hand. *c* **1450** *Mirour Saluacioun* 3847 Vndere myne heved softly mot he lay his left hande. **1480** CAXTON *Chron. Eng.* ccxxx. (1482) 245 Charlys leyde..his lift hond on the missale. **1581** MULCASTER *Positions* xxxviii. (1887) 169 To vse the left hand, as well as the right. **1611** BIBLE *Matt.* vi. 3. **1727-41** CHAMBERS *Cycl.* s.v. *Marriage*, In Germany, they have a kind of marriage called morganatic, wherein a man of quality contracting with a woman of inferior rank, he gives her the left hand in lieu of the right. **1856** EMERSON *Eng. Traits, Race* Wks. (Bohn) II. 29 The French say that the English women have two left hands. **1879** BROWNING *Halbert & Hob* 42 Right-hand with left-hand linked,—He faced his son submissive.

2. In phrases. ***on, to the left hand*** (***of***): on the left side (of), in the direction of the left side; also *fig.* ***to take the left hand*** (***of***): to place oneself on the left side (of). † ***to give*** (***a person or thing***) ***the left hand of friendship***: to deal unfriendly with. ***to marry with the left hand***, to contract a morganatic marriage with; hence ***a wife of the left hand*** (see quot. 1727-41 in 1); (***a daughter***) ***by the left hand***, one born of such a marriage (in quot. used for 'illegitimate').

c **1200** *Trin. Coll. Hom.* 37 þe get..an ure louerd ihesu cristes lift hond. *a* **1300** *Cursor M.* 6323 On his left hand loked he. *c* **1300** *Ibid.* 23042 (Edin.) þe wik in tuin on his lef hand. *c* **1450** tr. *De Imitatione* III. xl. 110 þou art impugned on þe riȝt honde & on þe lifte honde. *c* **1483** CAXTON *Dialogues* ix. 49 *A le main senestre*, on the lyfte honde. **1502** *Ord. Crysten Men* (W. de W. 1506) III. iii. 145 Unto theym the whiche shall be on the lyfte hande. **1526** *Pilgr. Perf.* (W. de W. 1531) 21 And neyther declyneth on the ryght hande, ..ne on yᵉ lefte hande. *c* **1585** R. BROWNE *Answ. Cartwright* 1 Some being enemies will giue it their left hande of friendshippe. **1613** PURCHAS *Pilgrimage* (1614) 820 On the right and left hand of Dariene are found twenty Rivers, which yeelde Gold. **1669** STURMY *Mariner's Mag.* IV. 203 The Figures to the left hand signifie Leagues in this Journal, or Miles. *c* **1720** *Mist's Weekly Jrnl.* (1722) I. 252 When once a Man has been any Time on the left Hand of Gain, it must be [etc.]. **1756-7** tr. *Keysler's Trav.* (1760) I. 237 On the left-hand..is the mountain of Rochemelon. **1762** GOLDSM. *Cit. W.* lxxii, He would take the left hand at feasts. **1778** C. JONES *Hoyle's Games Impr.* 75 Place of every Suit in your Hand the worst of it to the Left-hand. **1788** CLARA REEVE *Exiles* II. 196 She is only my wife of the left hand. **1818** J. W. CROKER *Jrnl.* 7 Dec. in *C. Papers* (1884) I. iv. 122 The Prince certainly married Mrs. Fitzherbert with the left hand. **1883** LD. R. GOWER *My Remin.* II. xxx. 337 One of the Grand Monarque's daughters by the left hand married a Duc de Chevreuse.

3. *attrib.* (usually hyphened *left-hand*) passing into *adj.*, chiefly signifying 'placed or situated on the left side', or 'taking the direction towards the left side', occas. also 'ill-omened', 'sinister', 'underhand', 'inferior'. Also in special collocations: **left-hand blow**, one delivered with the left hand; **left-hand drive**, a (motor vehicle) steering system with the steering wheel and other controls fitted on the left side; also, such a vehicle; hence ***left-hand driving***; **left-hand man**, †(*a*) a left-handed man; (*b*) one who has his place at one's left; **left-hand marriage** = *marriage with the left hand* (see 2); so ***left-hand wife***, ***queen***; **left-hand rope**, rope laid up and twisted 'against the sun'; †**left-hand tongue**, a language written from right to left, as Hebrew or Arabic.

c **1440** *Promp. Parv.* 293/2 Left hande man [*MSS. K and S* (*a* 1485) left handid man], *mancinus*. *c* **1450** *Mirour Saluacioun* 2771 Like to the lefthande thefe. **1586** W. WEBBE *Eng. Poetrie* (Arb.) 74 Oft did a left hand crow foretell these thinges in her hull tree [tr. Virg. *Ecl.* i. 18 *sinistra..cornix*]. **1598** ROWLANDS in Farr *S.P. Eliz.* (1845) II. 352 A little from that place Vpon the left-hand side. *a* **1632** SIR J. WHITELOCKE *Liber Famelicus* (Camden) 13 An obscure.. man..but expert in all the lefthand tongs, as hebrew [etc.]. **1635** QUARLES *Embl.* IV. iv. 197 If left-hand Fortune give thee left-hand chances, Be wisely patient. **1650** BAXTER *Saints' R.* III. vi. §26 (1651) 127 God..hath given them the very cream and quintessence of his blessing, when the rest of the world are..put off with common, and temporal, and left-hand-Mercies. **1664** *Flodden F.* v. 46 Then next the Left-hand wing did wield Sir M. C. old. **1669** STURMY *Mariner's Mag.* IV. 202 Put down the Title of the Voyage, over the left-hand Page. **1683** TRYON *Way to Health* xix. (1697) 429 Most Men inclining to the left-hand way, are thereby precipitated into all Vncleanness. **1687** DRYDEN *Hind & P.* I. 353 Then by a left-hand marriage [he] weds the dame. **1711** S. SEWALL *Dairy* 9 Feb. (1879) II. 300 His place at the Council Board..will hardly be filled up. I have lost a good Left-hand man. **17..** BURNS *Epitaph Holy Willie* i, His saul has taen some other way, I fear the left-hand road. **1818** J. W. CROKER *Jrnl.* 7 Dec. in *C. Papers* (1884) I. iv. 123 The lady..affected..scruples, which the left-hand marriage.. silenced. **1828** J. H. MOORE *Pract. Navig.* (ed. 20) 173 Find ..the given latitude in the left-hand column. **1860** TYNDALL *Glac.* I. xvi. 117 For a long time we kept at the left-hand side of the glacier. **1871** R. ELLIS tr. *Catullus* xii. 2 Left-hand practices o'er the merry wine-cup. **1872** LEVER *Ld. Kilgobbin* lxvii, Regrets that beset us for not having taken the left-hand road in life instead of the right. **1894** FRANCES ELLIOT *Rom. Gossip* iv. 127 The beautiful villa..where lived his left-hand queen. **1913** A. L. CLOUGH *Dict. Automobile Terms* 187 Left-hand Drive. **1931** *N.Y. Times* 19 July IX. 8/8 It was not..until 1909 that left-hand drive and centre control were introduced, reputedly by Henry Ford. **1933** P. MACDONALD *Mystery of Dead Police* vii. 51 Its a left-hand drive. **1956** *Collier's Year-Bk.* 670/1 Sweden is the only Scandinavian country with left-hand driving, and the desirability of changing to right-hand driving has been discussed off and on for many years. **1966** J. WEATHERHEAD *Force of Innocence* iv. 28, I was finding my left-hand drive difficult in London. **1975** *Guardian* 20 Jan. 7/3 All this year's production will be left-hand drive.

left-handed, *a.* (Stress variable.) [-ED².]

1. Having the left hand more serviceable than the right; using the left hand by preference.

a **1485** [see LEFT HAND 3]. *c* **1530** L. COX *Rhet.* (1899) 62 The yonge man after warde was named Sceuola, whiche is as muche to say in Englyssh as lefte handed. *a* **1627** MIDDLETON & ROWLEY *Changeling* III. iii. 121 I'll go up and play left-handed Orlando amongst the madmen. **1709** STEELE *Tatler* No. 59 ¶5 They are all Left-handed, and have always been very expert at Single Rapier. **1892** *Pall Mall G.* 4 July 6/1 Perhaps some physiologist can explain..why a left-handed bowler is nearly always a right-handed bat.

2. *fig.* †**a.** Crippled, defective. *Obs.* **b.** Awkward; clumsy, inapt. (Cf. L. *lævus*, F. *gauche*.) †**c.** Characterized by underhand dealings. *Obs.*

a. 1629 *Leather* 10 How many..Manuall Trades must be left-handed and go lame, if Leather..bee taken from them. **1636** J. TAYLOR (Water P.) *Catal. Tavernes* (1877) 52 Chertsey..there is a decayed left-handed bridge over the river: I wish it mended.

b. 1613 BEAUM. & FL. *Captain* III. v, That thou mayst know him perfectly, hee's one Of a left-handed making, a lanck thing. **1655** FULLER *Hist. Camb.* (1840) 110 A good artist is left-handed to no profession. **1806-7** J. BERESFORD *Miseries Hum. Life* (1826) xviii. 197 A minor critic.. puzzling himself to death with twenty left-handed conjectures about nothing. **1863** A. BLOMFIELD *Mem. Bp.*

Blomfield I. vii. 203 Disproving the assertion of Fuller.. that spiritual men are generally left-handed in secular affairs. c. **1694** MOTTEUX *Rabelais* v. v. (1737) 19 Ill-natur'd Left-handed Godlings and *Vejoves*. **1707** J. STEVENS tr. *Quevedo's Com. Wks.* (1709) 328 'Tis not safe trusting a Left Handed Man with Money.

3. Ambiguous, doubtful, questionable. †In medical language: Spurious.

1612 SIR G. PAULE *Life Abp. Whitgift* 44 [They] are close hypocrites and walke in a left-handed policie. **1625** GILL *Sacr. Philos.* I. 39 For the avoyding of some left-handed opinions concerning Him. **1650** B. *Discolliminium* 17 They are dextrously pragmatick in all Left-handed worke. **1735–8** BOLINGBROKE *On Parties* 2 There is need of that left-handed Wisdom. **1775** ADAIR *Amer. Ind.* 452 Lest necessity should compel her.. to pay.. dear for her left-handed wisdom. **1804** *Med. & Phys. Jrnl.* XII. 63 The spurious left-handed inflammation of erysipelas. **1807–8** W. IRVING *Salmag.* xiii. (1860) 307 We are indebted to the world for little else than left-handed favors. **1809** MALKIN *Gil Blas* IV. vii. §18, I gave a left-handed blessing to Euphrasia. **1824–9** LANDOR *Imag. Conv.* Wks. 1846 II. 228 Thou hast some left-handed business in the neighbourhood, no doubt. **1881** SAINTSBURY *Dryden* i 6 To diminish the force of this very left-handed compliment. **1892** *Nation* (N.Y.) 22 Dec. 481/3 Dr. White .. had to put up with a left-handed Scotch ordination to his bishopric. **1899** *Law Jrnl.* 11 Nov. 577/2 If this exemption .. was designed as a concession to farmers, it is a curiously left-handed one. **1914** 'HIGH JINKS, JR.' *Choice Slang* 14 *Left handed compliment*, one that may be taken either as a compliment or in the opposite way. **1953** *Time* 3 Aug. 36/1 An enthusiastic patter of applause came from the British press, including a left-handed compliment from the *Manchester Guardian* that he was not at all like the movie-type American. **1972** *Ulster Folklife* XVIII. 94 In the dialect of Donegal.. *left-handed* betokens 'malicious, underhand'; a *left-handed blessing* is a euphemism for a malediction or curse, and *a left-handed friend* is 'an enemy'. **1974** A. DOUGLAS *Noah's Ark Murders* vi. 54 'I'm not trying to date you.' 'Well, that's a left-handed compliment,' she complained.

4. Ill-omened, inauspicious, sinister. Of a deity: Unpropitious. (Cf. L. *lævus*.) ? *Obs.*

1609 B. JONSON *Sil. Wom.* III. ii, That would not be put off with left-handed cries. **1650** T. B[AYLEY] *Worcester's Apoph.* Ep. Ded. 2 The (Left-handed) stroaks of fortune, which have lately fallen so heavily upon your Illustrious Family. **1678** DRYDEN & LEE *Œdipus* I. i. D.'s Wks. 1883 VI. 151 And while Jove holds us out the bowl of joy.. 'tis dashed with gall By some left-handed god. **1809** MALKIN *Gil Blas* VI. i. ¶9 Was not that a left-handed dream for him, master secretary?

5. Of a marriage: *Literally*, one in which the bridegroom gives the bride his left hand instead of his right (as was the custom at morganatic weddings in Germany); hence, morganatic. Said also of the parties so married, and of the issue of the marriage.

Occasionally applied to fictitious or illegal marriages, or to unions formed without marriage, and to their offspring.

a **1642** KILLIGREW *Parson's Wed.* I. i, Do you not know he's married according to the Rogue's Liturgy? a Left-handed Bridegroom. **1653–4** WHITELOCKE *Jrnl. Swed. Emb.* (1772) I. 280 He marryed the king of Denmarke's daughter by a left-handed wife (as they are there called). **1760** FOOTE *Minor* I. Wks. 1799 I. 235 A left-handed marriage, in the language of the newspapers. **1788** H. WALPOLE *Remin.* i. 19 The children of a left-handed alliance are not entitled to inherit. **1835** SOUTHEY *Cowper's Life & Wks.* I. 102 His mistress, whom he [Churchill] considered now as his left-handed wife, united to him by moral ties. **1839** *Lett. fr. Madras* xxv. (1843) 274 The half-caste young left-handed ladies look down upon the poor little honestly-born Europeans. **1861** THACKERAY *Four Georges* i, [They] contracted left-handed marriages after the princely fashion of those days. **1885** *Manch. Exam.* 21 Jan. 5/2 Caroline Bauer.. represents herself.. as having.. become the left-handed wife of the late King of Belgium. **1925** T. DREISER *Amer. Trag.* (1926) II. xxii. 308 The pleasures of this left-handed honeymoon were at full tide. **1935** A. J. POLLOCK *Underworld Speaks* 70/2 *Left handed wife*, a kept woman. *fig.* **1865** LOWELL *Scotch the Snake* Prose Wks. 1890 V. 260 Shall we succeed better in trying a second left-handed marriage between democracy and another form of aristocracy?

6. In various uses. **a.** Of an implement: Adapted to the left hand or arm, or for use by a left-handed person. **b.** Placed on the left hand. **c.** Of a blow: Delivered with the left hand.

a **1653** G. DANIEL *Idyll* v. 42 Rather then want a Target, Perkins Tents Are Search't vp, for Left-handed Implements. **1752** HUME *Ess. & Treat.* (1817) II. 450 It is drawn only.. from the left-handed vessel. **1814** *Sporting Mag.* XLIV. 240 Hall met him with a left-handed facer. **1825** KNAPP & BALDW. *Newgate Cal.* IV. 335/1 A left-handed gun, as the lock was at this side.

7. In scientific and technical use: Characterized by a direction or rotation to the left; producing such a rotation in the plane of a polarized ray. (Cf. LÆVO-.)

1812–16 J. SMITH *Panorama Sci. & Art* I. 74 As the tool meets the wood, so it cuts a left-handed screw. **1825** J. NICHOLSON *Operat. Mechanic* 143 If the stone revolves the other way.. the mill is termed a left-handed one. **1831** BREWSTER *Optics* xxvi. 218 Hence, in reference to this quality, quartz may be divided into right-handed and left-handed quartz. **1851–6** WOODWARD *Mollusca* 46 Left-handed, or reversed varieties of spiral shells have been met with. *c* **1865** J. WYLDE in *Orr's Circ. Sci.* I. 84/2 If.. these colours succeed each other in any body when the analyser is turned towards the left hand, then such is said to have a left-handed polarisation. **1884** F. J. BRITTEN *Watch & Clockm.* 141 [A] left-handed movement. *Ibid.* 227 [A] Left Handed Fusee.

Hence **left'handedly** *adv.*, **left'handedness**.

a **1631** DONNE *Poems* (1633) 77 Although a squint left-handednesse Be ungracious; yet we cannot want that hand. **1854** SCOFFERN in *Orr's Circ. Sci., Chem.* 82 The amount of right-handedness or left-handedness displayed by the solution. **1872** O. W. HOLMES *Poet. Breakf.-t.* viii. (1885) 203 The subject of what we may call moral left-handedness. **1882** *Athenæum* 30 Dec. 904/3 A representation of the Apollo Belvedere.. holding out.. left-handedly enough, a problematical scaring ægis.

left-handed, *adv.* [f. LEFT HAND.] Towards the left; with the left hand.

1848 *Sporting Life* 1 Jan. 241/2 He also bats left-handed. **1851** *Illustr. London News* XVIII. 133/2 This nut is cut.. left-handed. **1909** *Chambers's Jrnl.* Oct. 651/2 The great stag.. swinging left-handed.. passed Culworth. **1909** E. H. MILES *Lessons Lawn Tennis* (ed. 3) xv. 79, I do not know why ladies should not beat right-handed men players if the latter were compelled to play left-handed. **1928** *Observer* 19 Feb. 24/4 You leave the Oundle road and turn left-handed for Uppingham. **1929** *Morning Post* 30 Dec. 13/1 Hounds.. swinging left-handed past Edgecote House. **1974** *Country Life* 7 Mar. 477/1 We rode left-handed beyond the Letham woods as our fox set his mask for Canty hall.

,left-'hander. [f. LEFT HAND + -ER[1].] **a.** One who uses the left hand instead of the right; *spec.* in *Cricket* and other games, one who bats, bowls, etc., left-handed. **b.** In mediæval fencing, a dagger carried in the left hand to parry a stroke or thrust. **c.** A blow delivered with the left hand. **d.** A left-handed compliment.

a. **1881** *Standard* 28 June 3/2 The left-hander was immediately hit to leg for four. **1900** *Daily News* 12 June 8/4 For two hours and forty minutes the young left-hander had withstood the Middlesex bowling. **1937** [see CHINAMAN 4]. **1937** S. T. ORTON *Reading, Writing & Speech Probl. in Children* i. 49 Prejudice.. is so strong as to amount to the belief that the left-hander is abnormal. *Ibid.* 52 Parson.. went so far as to hold that all left-eyed and right-handed individuals were native left-handers who had been shifted by training. **1940** G. MARX *Let.* 5 Sept. (1967) 25 A tennis player with the weirdest assortment of strokes... He's a left-hander. **1961** RUSSELL & ESPIR *Traumatic Aphasia* iv. 29 The left hemisphere is usually dominant.. for left-handers. **1970** *Daily Tel.* 29 Dec. 10 Not all the evidence.. supports his inference that left-handers have exceptional ability, even if they do range from Leonardo da Vinci to Sir Compton Mackenzie. *Ibid.*, A nice assortment of.. 40 offensive slang words for left-handers, from kack to cuddy-wifter. **1974** *Times* 6 Nov. 13 He continues to make runs for Western Australia.. and has the advantage of being a left-hander.

b. **1869** BOUTELL *Arms & Armour* ix. 180 The weapon that in the 16th century was called a *main gauche* (a *left-hander*) was a dagger especially used in duels.

c. **1861** *Macm. Mag.* Feb. 273 He let fly a tremendous left-hander at the doctor. **1884** *Graphic* 13 Dec. 625/1 He received a straight left-hander in the chest that sent him back reeling.

d. **1959** *Times* 28 Apr. 11/4 'Not bad' might appear a good enough specimen of the simplest type of left-hander.

left-handiness. *nonce-wd.* [f. **left-handy* adj. (f. LEFT HAND) + -NESS.] Awkward manner. Cf. F. *gaucherie*.

1749 CHESTERF. *Lett.* cx. (1892) I. 249 An awkward address, ungraceful attitudes and actions, and a certain left-handiness (if I may use that word) loudly proclaim low education.

leftie, var. LEFTY.

leftish ('lɛftɪʃ), *a.* [LEFT *sb.* 2c + -ISH[1].] Inclined to the political views of 'the left'. Hence **'leftishness**.

1934 H. G. WELLS *Exper. Autobiogr.* II. ix. 809 The violent persecution of Jewish and leftish writers in Germany. **1934** WYNDHAM LEWIS *Let.* 29 Nov. (1963) 226 The strong *Leftish* political colouration of so much of the newest poetry. **1959** *Listener* 6 Aug. 195/1 There were leftish magazines on the tables. **1966** *Economist* 15 Oct. 254/2 This probably has little to do with the [Syrian] regime's 'leftishness'. **1972** *Observer* 6 Aug. 19/3 The leftish Left, the revolutionary Left.

Leftism ('lɛftɪz(ə)m). Also leftism. [f. LEFT *sb.* 2c + -ISM.] The political views or principles of 'the left'.

1920 *Oxf. Mag.* 19 Nov. 94/1 Mr. Clutton-Brock has consented to read a paper on 'Left-ism'. **1921** N. ANGELL *Fruits of Victory* v. 165 No sooner does the Left of some party break off and found a new party than it is immediately confronted by its own Leftism. **1945** 'G. ORWELL' in *Contemp. Jewish Record* VIII. 169 During the past few years there has been what amounts to a counter-attack against the rather shallow Leftism which was fashionable in the previous decade. **1960** *Guardian* 13 June 9/3 The 40th anniversary of the publication of Lenin's book on Leftism. **1967** C. SETON-WATSON *Italy from Liberalism to Fascism* iv. 160 Labriola was the first Italian to present socialism not as the natural offspring of the leftism of the Risorgimento but as a philosophical system. **1971** *Guardian* 4 Aug. 10/4 There is still a lot of old fashioned and sentimental Leftism (hanging over from much bad verse written in the late 1930s). **1973** *Listener* 19 July 91/2 The infantile Leftism of the fellow-traveller.

'Leftist. Also leftist. [f. as prec.] An adherent of 'the left' in politics. Also *attrib.* or as *adj.*

1924 *Contemp. Rev.* July 20, I would support either a violent reactionary, or extreme Leftist. **1937** E. SNOW *Red Star over China* II. iii. 67 The Leftist Kuomintang general. **1951** E. PAUL *Springtime in Paris* xi. 206 The anti-Communist Leftists, Existentialists, Trotskyists, Titoists and Anarchists published plans for a rival meeting. **1960** *Guardian* 12 Apr. 8/3 Most of the leaders of the Labour party were probably Leftist rebels at the age of twenty. **1960** *Economist* 8 Oct. 134/2 Many of the speeches were vaguely leftist. **1962** *Listener* 4 Jan. 36/2 It refutes the leftist legend that Dollfuss was simply a Fascist. **1964** L. NKOSI *Rhythm of Violence* 29 She's a bit of a Leftist, but I thought you wouldn't mind. **1967** H. V. DICKS *Marital Tensions* 61 This vivacious, carefree girl with her disdain for tradition was matched by this progressive, leftist scholar. **1974** *Times* 12 Oct. 5/4 It is difficult to find Spanish politicians who do not say they are leftists.

'leftmost, *a.* Also leftermost. [f. LEFT *a.* + -MOST.] Situated furthest to the left.

1863 KINGLAKE *Crimea* II. 443 The Grenadiers.. were making good use of that delicate bend in the formation of their leftmost company. **1875** *Ibid.* (1877) V. i. 269 The leftermost portion of them, under the direction of Serjeant O'Hara. **1894** O. O. HOWARD in *Voice* (N.Y.) Sept., Mansfield.. pushed out toward Lee's leftmost troops.

left-over, *a.* and *sb.* [LEFT *ppl. a.* 2. Cf. LEAVE *v.*[1] 14e.] **A.** *adj.* Remaining over; not used up or disposed of.

1897 R. M. STUART *In Simpkinsville* 65 A bundle of left-over flowers. **1905** *Westm. Gaz.* 28 Dec. 2/1 If.. they find themselves with a left-over stock of life-force. **1907** *Smart Set* Feb. 13/1 She tacitly avoided him, and his left-over moments had.. been spent philandering. **1967** N. FREELING *Strike Out* 103 The rice had left-over ham and chicken in it. **1968** *Listener* 4 Apr. 438 (*caption*) Is that leftover macaroni cheese.. still in the fridge? **1972** *Guardian* 30 Dec. 13/3 Many senior EEC officials.. make regular bookings out of Brussels, and the casual visitor has to battle for the left-over seats.

B. *sb.* Something remaining over; *esp.* a portion of some article of food left over from a meal. Freq. *pl.* Also *transf.*

1891 *Cassell's Family Mag.* May 374/1 They all like change of diet, so I provide all sorts of things, with the result that the 'left-overs', as I call them, are appalling. **1897** R. M. STUART *In Simpkinsville* 64, I try to keep the Potter's field a-bloomin' with my left-overs. **1906** *Daily Chron.* 19 Sept. 4/4 We are almost yawning at the 'left-overs' of the scandal banquet. **1950** H. J. MASSINGHAM *Curious Traveller* iv. 71 Now only the shoddy left-overs from the export trade can be bought at inflated prices. **1964** *Punch* 8 Jan. 73/2 Adlibbing madly on Mrs. Hannah Glasse's 'Domestic Cookery Made Easy' (1747) he will combine assorted garden leftovers, crab-apples, damsons, blackberries, radish-pods. **1974** *Sunday Express* 21 Apr. 23/1 (Advt.), As for the babies' left-overs—well, I really scoffed those.

b. A survival.

1902 KIPLING *Traffics & Discov.* (1904) 169 'E's a left-over from Majuba—one of the worst kind. **1911** L. ABBOTT *Amer. in Making* 94 The dread of this Executive power is a curious left-over from Colonial days. **1927** H. E. FOSDICK *Pilgrimage to Palestine* 252 In this ancient monastery these left-overs of a bygone age guard their relics. **1971** I. G. GASS et al. *Understanding Earth* vii. 102/1 Meteoritic debris (probably representing left-overs from the time of formation of the solar system).

†**'leftsomes,** *adv. Obs. rare*$^{-1}$. In 4 liftsoms. [f. LEFT *a.* + SOME, with advb. *-s*.] In a leftward direction, leftwards.

1398 TREVISA *Barth. De P.R.* IX. i. (1495) 345 Streyghte and forthryghte menynge is ryghtsoms other liftsoms.

leftward ('lɛftwəd), *adv.* and *a.* [f. LEFT *a.* + -WARD.]

A. *adv.*

1. On the left hand. Also *to (the) leftward (of)*.

1483 *Cath. Angl.* 212/1 Leftwarde, *leuorsum*. **1509** BARCLAY *Shyp of Folys* (1570) 89 Many a thousande Fast runneth leftwarde, but fewe on the right hande. **1848** CLOUGH *Bothie* ix. 42 Is it well that the soldier whose post is far to the left-ward Say, I will go to the right? **1864** LD DERBY *Iliad* XII. 218 A sign from heav'n Appear'd, to leftward of the astonish'd crowd. **1895** *Blackw. Mag.* Nov. 643/2 We soon caught the sound of the sea leftward. **1898** G. W. STEEVENS *Egypt in 1898*, xix. 220 Leftward and behind us is the desert.

2. In the direction of the left hand. Freq. in political contexts: towards 'the left'. Also *to (the) leftward*.

1579 DIGGES *Stratiot.* 2 Reckning all the characters afore that point leftward. **1791** COWPER *Iliad* XII. 150 Leftward he drove furious. **1814** CARY *Dante, Purg.* XXX. 43, I Turn'd me to leftward. **1829** SCOTT *Anne of G.* ix (end), We have yet, keeping leftward.. nearly a mile to make. **1883** *Century Mag.* XXVII. 33 A trail strikes up the main hill to the leftward. **1885** MISS MCCONKEY *Hero of Cowpens* xiii. 118 He [Burgoyne] extended his intrenchments leftward to the river-bank.

1957 *Economist* 28 Dec. 1119/1 The Singapore city council elections last Saturday may be taken as an accurate indication of the political trend in the island colony. That trend is clearly leftward. **1973** *Listener* 15 Nov. 668/1, I was rather Conservative as a young man. I've moved gently leftward.

B. *adj.* Situated on the left; directed or tending towards the left, esp. politically.

1813 SCOTT *Trierm.* III. xxiii, Against the leftward foe he flung The ready banner. **1825** *Blackw. Mag.* XVIII. 452 'Twas the leftward corridor She glided down. **1886** W. R. EVANS *Rustic Walking Routes* 20 In five-eighths of a mile, just beyond a leftward bend.

1936 M. SCHACHTMAN in J. G. Wright tr. *Trotsky's Third International after Lenin* p. xxii, In the message to the Sixth Congress entitled 'What Now?' Trotsky touches upon this Leftward evolution in the European working class. **1939** H. G. WELLS *Holy Terror* III. i. 220 The Group turned its attention to the existing leftward papers. **1949** I. DEUTSCHER *Stalin* 403 Stalin's leftward switch in Russia was not only an earnest affair; it had the grandeur of national drama. **1957** *Times* 11 May 7/2 It is no surprise that in the borough elections the leftward movement seen in national by-elections has been repeated—though not, it seems, carried any further. **1973** *Guardian* 10 Mar. 1/5 Mr Roy Jenkins.. is calling on those who share his views.. to dig in their feet against what is seen as a dangerous Leftward drift.

ˈleftwardly, *adv.* = LEFTWARDS *adv.*

1908 HARDY *Dynasts* III. I. iii. 335 With that in eye he has bundled leftwardly Thomière's division.

ˈleftwardness. *rare.* [f. LEFTWARD *a.* + -NESS.] The quality of being leftward in politics.

1944 *Politics* Sept. 247/2 What does *Politics* offer them? A center for leftwardness? **1966** *New Statesman* 5 Aug. 203/2 His leftwardness is smilingly excused, but we are not reminded that Eluard was a communist.

ˈleftwards, *adv.* [f. as LEFTWARD *adv.* and *a.* with advb. *-s.*] = LEFTWARD *adv.*

1863 KINGLAKE *Crimea* II. 433 Going thence leftwards to the Coldstream..brigade. **1893** *Horse & Hound* 18 Nov. 734 The pack made a sudden turn leftwards. **1899** *Allbutt's Syst. Med.* VI. 389 If the aneurysm..extends backwards.. or to any considerable extent leftwards from the above position, it will [etc.]. **1971** *Guardian* 3 July 11/8 When the Chinese civil war began in 1946 Liu wobbled to the Right. .. Then he lurched Leftwards.

left wing. [f. LEFT *a.* + WING *sb.*]

1. a. The division on the left side of an army or fleet in battle array.

1535 COVERDALE *1 Macc.* ix. 16 When they which were of the lefte wynge, sawe that the right side was discomfited. **1670** EACHARD *Cont. Clergy* 47 He falls a fighting with his text, and makes a pitch'd battel of it, dividing it into the right-wing and left-wing. **1844** H. H. WILSON *Brit. India* III. 149 The European divisions were directed severally against the left and right wings.

b. In football and similar games: the position of a player on the left side of the centre(s); a player occupying this position; the part of the field in which a left wing normally plays. Cf. WING *sb.* 7 b.

1882 in Charles-Edwards & Richardson *They saw it Happen* (1958) 300 He was instantly robbed by Strachan, who passed it [*sc.* the football] to the left wing. **1889** *Field* 5 Jan. 29/3 [Hockey] The left wings played to each other well, and the backs..were seen at their best. **1921** in B. James *England v Scotland* (1969) vi. 125 Remember he was against probably the finest left wing in the three countries; certainly the cleverest outside-left, Alan Morton. **1974** *Liverpool Echo* (Football ed.) 4 May 1/3 He raced down the left wing..to cross the ball into the goalmouth.

2. In Politics. (See LEFT *a.* 3 b.) Freq. *attrib.* Also *transf.*

1884 W. JAMES *Will to Believe* (1897) 171 In theology, subjectivism develops as its 'left wing' antinomianism. *Ibid.*, If the Hegelian gnosticism, which has begun to show itself here and in Great Britain, were to become popular philosophy, as it once was in Germany, it would certainly develop its left wing here as there, and produce a reaction of disgust. **1898** BODLEY *France* II. 427 Significant also is the attitude of the Socialists, who now compose the Radical left wing. **1905** W. JAMES *Meaning of Truth* (1909) v. 124 If the formula ever became canonical, it would certainly develop both right-wing and left-wing interpreters. **1921** H. CRANE *Let.* 25 Dec. (1965) 74 You have met about all the personalities in the younger left-wing at all worth while. **1923** G. D. H. COLE *Trade Unionism & Munitions* p. i, One of the principal contentions of the 'left-wing' elements in the Trade Union and Socialist movements. **1940** W. TEMPLE *Thoughts in War-Time* iii. 23 The Left Wing tends to identify the Government and the community. **1957** *Times Lit. Suppl.* 1 Nov. 653/1 Mr Humphreys has been very ambitious here, in an attempt to analyse the relationships between a rich magazine publisher with Left-wing political ambitions and his family. **1972** *Times* 5 Sept. 2/3 The left-wing challenge over Europe is expected to unseat at least one member of the Labour Party National Executive Committee.

Also **left-ˈwinger, -ˈwingery, -ˈwingism; left-ˈwingish** *a.*

Quots. 1891, 1896, 1967 are sense 1 b, the remainder sense 2.

1891 *Peel City Guardian* IX. 7/3 A beautiful bit of passing by the Peel left wingers. **1896** Left winger [see WINGER 2]. **1923** G. D. H. COLE *Workshop Organiz.* 17 The rise of 'left-wingism' inside the Trade Union movement. **1924** *Glasgow Herald* 5 Apr. 9 The unscrupulous, untiring representative of the leftest of left-wingers. **1951** R. CAMPBELL *Light on Dark Horse* 249, I have never been Left-Wingish. **1955** *Times* 2 May 8/5 Mr. Zilliacus is a left winger who has often been a thorn in the side of the party leadership. **1963** *Guardian* 10 May 22/7 Vague Left-Wingism. **1967** J. POTTER *Foul Play* (1968) viii. 90 Good left wingers are in short supply. **1968** *Economist* 7 Sept. 25 Voted on to the general council were Mr Cousins's new ally from the engineers, Mr Hugh Scanlon, and the draughtsmen's militant leader, Mr George Doughty. This gives the sensation of more imminent left-wingery. **1972** *Listener* 2 Nov. 615/3 A period atmosphere of Thirties left-wingery. **1975** *Daily Tel.* 22 Feb. 10/4 Perry Worsthorne was allowed about 30 seconds to question how far Jenkins' left-wingery was an opportunist gimmick, to 'shock and provoke' his opponents.

leftwise (ˈlɛftwaɪz), *adv.* *rare*$^{-1}$. [f. LEFT *a.* + -WISE.] Toward the left.

1860 T. MARTIN *Horace*, Epode ix, Steering leftwise [L. *sinistrorsum*] o'er the sea.

lefty (ˈlɛftɪ). Also **leftie.** [-Y^{6}.] **1.** A left-handed person. Also *attrib.* or as *adj.*

1886 *Sporting Life* 7 Apr. 2/4 In last Wednesday's [baseball] game Nashville presented her left-handed battery,..to offset our 'lefty' battery. **1927** *Glasgow Herald* 7 Apr. 12 He was a patriotic Roman youth who allowed his right hand to be burned off..and was henceforward designated by a term which..would be rendered by his comrades of to-day as 'Leftie'. **1969** *New Scientist* 6 Nov. 277/2 Such illustrious lefties as Leonardo da Vinci, Michelangelo..and Paul McCartney.

2. A left-winger in politics. Also *attrib.* or as *adj.*

1935 C. ODETS (*title*) Waiting for Lefty. **1937** in Partridge *Dict. Slang* (1951) 1097/2 (*caption*) Counter-blast to lefties. **1939** R. CAMPBELL *Flowering Rifle* II. 40 As I who've lived beneath the two regimes And have not dreamed the Leftie Teacher's dreams. **1967** *Listener* 10 Aug. 164/1 The lefties are almost completely in control of the nation's communication. **1970** K. AMIS *What became of Jane Austen?* 204, I mean the kind of person who..buys unexamined the abortion-divorce-homosexuality-censorship-racialism-marijuana package; in a word, the Lefty. **1972** *Times* 6 Oct. 14/7 A leader of the left who is no fair-weather Lefty but the genuine article. **1972** *Observer* 22 Oct. 29/1 These groups pump out quantities of magazines and news-sheets, frequently repetitive, full of Lefty names and too-ready inferences. **1974** *Oxford Times* 8 Mar. 11/3 This word, victimisation, has become a substitute, in leftie jargon, for just punishment.

leful, lefulle, variants of LEEFUL *a. Obs.*

lefve, variant of LEVE *v. Obs.*

leg (lɛg), *sb.* Also 3–7 *pl.* legges, (4–7 leggis, leggys), 4–5 lege, 6–7 legge. [a. ON. *legg-r* leg, (in compounds) leg or arm, limb (Sw. *lägg*, Da. *læg*, calf of the leg):—OTeut. type **lagjo-z*.

Cf. Lombard *lagi* 'coxa super genuculum' (*Ed. Roth.* 384). By some scholars the word is referred to the West Aryan root **laq-* of Gr. λακτίζειν to kick, L. *lacertus* arm.]

I. The limb.

1. a. One of the organs of support and locomotion in an animal body; *esp.* one of the two lower limbs of the human body; in narrower sense, the part of the limb between the knee and foot.

abdominal or ***false leg***, one of the fleshy legs which support the abdomen of some insects and which disappear in the perfect insect. ***Barbados leg***: see BARBADOS. See also BLACK-LEG(S *sb.*

c **1275** LAY. 1876 Hii soten hire legges [*c* 1205 sconken]. **13..** *K. Alis.* 1808 He drawith leg over othir. *c* **1340** *Cursor M.* 7449 (Fairf.) Goly..of body grete of leggis lange. *a* **1400–50** *Alexander* 5473 Wormes As large as a mans lege. **14..** LYDG. & BURGH *Secrees* 2681 Smale leggys be tokne of symple konnyng. **1530** PALSGR. 238/2 Legge fro the kne to the fote. **1588** SHAKS. *Tit. A.* IV. ii. 102 All the water in the Ocean, Can neuer turne the Swans blacke legs to white. **1667** MILTON *P.L.* x. 512 His Leggs entwining Each other ..down he fell, A monstrous Serpent. **1837** DICKENS *Pickw.* xix, 'What's the matter with the dogs' legs?' whispered Mr. Winkle. **1864** TENNYSON *Grandmother* iii, 'Here's a leg for a babe of a week!' says doctor. **1896** NEWTON *Dict. Birds* s.v. *Stork*, Its contrasted plumage..with its bright red bill and legs, makes it a conspicuous and beautiful object.

Proverb. Phrase (*vulgar*). **1662** WILSON *Cheats* II. iv. (1664) 26 All's well, and as right as my Leg. **1719** D'URFEY *Pills* IV. 141 This Lady is as right as my Leg.

b. *esp.* with reference to the use of the legs in standing, walking, running, etc.

1382 WYCLIF *Ps.* cxlvii. 10 He shal not han wil in the strengthe of hors; ne in the leggis of a man shall be wel plesid to hym. **1555** J. PROCTOR *Wyat's Rebell.* 14 b, He..ranne away no faster than his legges could carye hym. **1596** SHAKS. *Merch. V.* II. ii. 6 Vse your legs, take the start, run awaie. **1638** BROME *Antipodes* I. vi. Wks. 1873 III. 248 Mandevile went farre. Beyond all English legges that I can read of. **1749** FIELDING *Tom Jones* VII. vii, I thank Heaven my legs are very able to carry me. **1839** SIR C. NAPIER in Bruce *Life* iv. (1885) 132 Gashes that would frighten a thousand of their companions into the vigorous use of their legs. **1867** BAKER *Nile Tribut.* xi. 287 He would rather trust to his legs.

transf. and *fig.* **1590** *Pasquil's Apol.* I. C iv b, He perceiueth not.., that I haue his leg in a string still. **1597** J. PAYNE *Royal Exch.* 15 Buyenge and sellinge is one of the leggs whervpon euery common welthe dothe stand. **1635** QUARLES *Embl.* IV. iii. 193 The sprightly voice of sinew-strengthning Pleasure Can lend my bedrid soule both legs and leisure. **1652** COLLINGES *Caveat for Prof.* xviii. (1653) 77 Mr. Fisher..saves himselfe upon the legs of his old distinction. *a* **1700** DRYDEN *Ovid's Met.* VIII. *Baucis & Philemon* 148 They haste, and what their tardy Feet deny'd, The trusty Staff (their better Leg) supply'd. **1780** COWPER *Progr. Err.* 561 One leg by truth supported, one by lies, They sidle to the goal.

2. Phrases. **a.** General references. ***all legs and wings***, said of an overgrown awkward young person; also Naut., of an overmasted vessel. ***on the leg***, (of a dog or horse) long in the leg, leggy. ***the boot is on the other leg*** (see BOOT *sb.*^{3} 1 b). ***to pull*** (or ***draw*** Sc.) ***a person's leg***, to impose upon, 'get at', befool him (colloq.). †***to fight at the leg*** (see quot. 1785). ***to give a person a leg up***, to help him to climb up or get over an obstacle, mount (a horse, etc.); *fig.*, to help over a difficulty; hence ***leg-up*** sb., a help, support, boost. ***to hang a leg*** (see HANG *v.* 4 c). ***to have a bone in one's leg*** (see BONE *sb.* 9). ***to have a leg***: to be physically attractive, to have a fine appearance (*Obs.*). ***to have one's leg over the harrows***, to be out of control. ***to lift, lift up*** (or ***heave up***) ***the leg***: said of a dog voiding urine. ***to show a leg***: to get out of bed; to make one's appearance. ***to be tied by the leg***: to be prevented from doing something by some circumstance.

1591 SHAKS. *Two Gent.* IV. iv. 41 When did'st thou see me heaue vp my leg, and make water against a Gentlewomans farthingale. **1602** *2nd Pt. Return fr. Parnass.* IV. ii. 1659 Nor any bold presumptuous curr shall dare To lifte his legge against his sacred dust. **1785** GROSE *Dict. Vulgar T.* s.v. *Leg*, *To fight at the leg*, to take unfair advantages, it being held unfair by back sword players to strike at the leg. **1816** SCOTT *Old Mort.* viii, 'She has her leg ower the harrows now', said Cuddie, 'stop her wha can'. *a* **1817** JANE AUSTEN *Persuasion* (1818) II. vi. 116 She, poor soul, is tied by the leg. She has a blister on one of her heels. **1831** B. HALL *Fragments Voy. & Trav.* I. 247, I say, Master Doughy, do you mean to relieve the deck tonight? Here it's almost two bells, and you have hardly shewn a leg yet. **1832** F. TROLLOPE *Dom. Manners Amer.* I. xviii. 281 We should be obliged to pass the whole of Monday there, as the coach..would not arrive.. till Tuesday morning. Thus..we were to be tied by the leg for four-and-twenty hours. **1837** DICKENS *Pickw.* xvi, The wall is very low, sir, and your servant will give you a leg up. **1837** MARRYAT *Dog-fiend* x, [He] came shambling, all legs and wings, up the hatchway. **1854** 'C. BEDE' *Further Adventures Verdant Green* vii. 61 He used to sing out, 'You must show a leg, sir!' and..kept on hammering at the door till I *did*. **1865** MILTON & CHEADLE *N.W. Passage by Land* i. 13 The dogs kept tumbling off..until hauled back again with the help of a 'leg up' from the people inside [a stage coach]. **1867** ANDERSON *Rhymes* 17 (E.D.D.) He preached, an' at last drew the auld body's leg, Sae the kirk got the gatherins o' our Aunty Meg. **1867** SMYTH *Sailor's Word-bk.*, Legs and wings: see *Overmasted*. **1879** G. MEREDITH *Egoist* I. ii. 16 And, says Mrs Mountstuart, while grand phrases were mouthing round about him '*You see he had a leg*'. **1888** CHURCHWARD *Blackbirding* 216 Then I shall be able to pull the leg of that chap Mike. He is always trying to do me. **1890** W. E. NORRIS *Misadventure* iv, She was now devoting all her energies to giving them a leg up. **1893** *Kennel Gaz.* Aug. 213/3 A little dog..with..good carriage of stern, but a trifle 'on the leg' and out of coat. *Ibid.* 215/2. **1899** *Pall Mall Mag.* Apr 474 'She wouldn't marry you?' 'My dear fellow, the boot was on the other leg. I wouldn't marry her.' **1901** *Chambers's Jrnl.* 27 July 554/2 He had.. strong introductions to a great financier in Park Lane, who seemed to have good reasons for obliging him in such matters as club nominations and social 'legs-up' generally. **1901** J. N. MCILWRAITH *Curious Career R. Campbell* iv. 45 He might not have managed to mount had not Gib been at hand to give him 'a leg up'. **1908** *Westm. Gaz.* 28 Mar. 2/2 He first wore breeches at the Coronation of Queen Victoria, and there was a curious anticipation of a phrase immortal in literature in his statement that his first Court suit revealed to him 'that he had a leg'. **1916** 'TAFFRAIL' *Pincher Martin* ii. 19 All hands! turn out, turn out, turn out! show a leg, show a leg, show a leg! **1936** C. S. LEWIS *Allegory of Love* ii. 72 We can all but hear the voices shouting 'Show a leg—show a leg'. **1937** B. DE HOLTHOIR tr. *Duhamel's Pasquier Chron.* I. 73 Never mind, if you think it will give him a leg up. **1946** J. IRVING *Royal Navalese* 156 *Show a leg!*.. The boatswain's mates' early morning shout..is a direct link with pre-Nelsonic days when certain women were permitted to live on war-ships in harbour. **1950** A. L. ROWSE *England of Elizabeth* vi. 233 The family owed its leg-up in the world to Robert's grandfather. **1957** *New Yorker* 12 Jan. 25/1 For Nora, who came from a poor and an ugly lower-middle-class home, political action was a leg up. **1965** *Observer* (Colour Suppl.) 30 May 34 *On the leg.* A horse whose legs look too long for his body—he has a lot of daylight underneath him. **1969** 'P. ALDING' *Murder among Thieves* xii. 12 Kerr awoke to find someone was rocking his shoulders... 'Come on, me sleeping beauty, rise and shine, show a leg,' said P. C. Mottram, with indecent cheerfulness. **1969** *Listener* 9 Jan. 43/2 The boys are here..because local parents think it will give them a social leg-up. **1973** *Weekly News* (Glasgow) 11 Aug. 26/2 Then he got the leg-up on a horse called Native Copper. **1974** *Times* 5 Feb. 24/5 (Advt.), Want a leg up? There's more than one way with N.O.P. Secretary.

b. With reference to walking or running. ***to change leg***, (of a horse) to change step. ***to have the legs of***, to travel faster than, to outrun. ***to put*** (or ***set***) ***one's best leg foremost***, to go at one's best pace; to exert oneself to the utmost. ***to shake a leg***, to dance. ***to shake a loose*** (or ***free***) ***leg***, to lead an irregular life, live freely. ***to stretch one's legs***, †(*a*) to increase one's stride, walk fast (*obs.*); (*b*) to exercise the legs by walking. ***to take to*** (or ***betake oneself to***) ***one's legs***, to run, run away; so ***to take leg*** (lit. and fig.), ***give legs.***

1530 PALSGR. 749/1, I take me to my legges, I flye a waye, *je me mets en fuyte.* **1579** TOMSON *Calvin's Serm. Tim.* 17/2 They..set the better legge before. **1592** SHAKS. *Rom. & Jul.* I. iv. 34 Come knocke and enter, and no sooner in, But euery man betake him to his legs. **1653** WALTON *Angler* i. 1, I have stretch'd my legs up Tottenham Hil to overtake you. **1790** J. FISHER *Poems* 83 When ance her chastity took leg. **1834** AINSWORTH *Rookwood* III. ix. 1878) 233 While luck lasts, the highwayman shakes a loose leg! **1844** W. H. MAXWELL *Sports & Adv. Scotl.* xii. (1855) 116 We have landed to ..'stretch our legs'. **1856** MAYHEW *Gt. World Lond.* 87 Those who love to 'shake a free leg', and lead a roving life, as they term it. **1857** G. A. LAWRENCE *Guy Liv.* ix, He [the horse] is in a white lather of foam, and changes his leg twice as he approaches. **1861** HUGHES *Tom Brown at Oxf.* xli, The beggar had the legs of me. **1881** BESANT & RICE *Ten Yrs.' Tenant* v, It would be positively indecent for a man at a hundred to shake a leg as merrily as a man at thirty. **1882** BESANT *All Sorts & Cond.* xviii, I explain that the stage is ready for them, if they like to act;..or the dancing-room, should they wish to shake a leg. **1883** *Daily News* 15 May 7/2 The best way is to make a snatch and give legs for it, it's better than loitering. **1886** HOBART *Sk. Life* 135, I knew we had the legs of her [a gunboat].

c. ***on one's legs***: (*a*) in a standing attitude; said *esp.* of a parliamentary or other public speaker; so jocularly ***on one's hind legs***; (*b*) well enough to go about; 'on one's feet'; (*c*) *fig.* in a prosperous condition, established, *esp.* in ***to set*** (a person) ***upon his legs***; also *transf.* of things. ***to fall on one's legs***: to be lucky or successful. ***to get on one's hind legs***: *lit.* of a horse, hence jocularly of a person, to go into a rage. ***to stand*** (or †***come***) ***upon one's own legs***: to be self-reliant. ***not a leg to stand on***: no support whatever.

1594 NASHE *Unfort. Trav.* sig. B4 Faine he would have patcht out a polt-foot tale, but (God knowes) it had not one true leg to stand on. **1624** SANDERSON *Serm.* I. 251 A pound, that would.. put him into fresh trading, set him upon his legs, and make him a man for ever. *a* **1628** PRESTON *Effectual Faith* (1631) 54 Then a man cometh upon his own legs. **1666** PEPYS *Diary* 7 Jan., I do fear those two families.. are quite broken, and I must now stand upon my own legs. **1697** COLLIER *Immor. Stage* (1730) Pref., Throwing in a Word or two; to.. keep the English upon its Legs. **1760–72** H. BROOKE *Fool of Qual.* (1809) III. 117, I engage in a few weeks to set you once more upon your legs. **1771** SMOLLETT *Humph. Cl.* 17 Apr., I.. might have been upon my legs by this time, had the weather permitted me to use my saddle-horse. **1792** *Anecd. W. Pitt.* (1797) I. xii. 249 Mr. Pitt, upon his legs, in the House of Commons, charged [etc.]. **1799** *Med. Jrnl.* I. 22 He was obliged to be on his legs the whole day. **1801** G. ROSE *Diaries* (1860) I. 321 We found Mr. Sheridan on his legs, moving the adjournment. **1818** COBBETT *Pol. Reg.* XXXIII. 9 A thing totally destitute of talent could never expect long to stand upon its own legs. **1825** J. NEAL *Bro. Jonathan* I. 8 As if the Yankee man were determined to leave the.. brigadier without a leg to stand upon, as a lawyer would say. **1841** LYTTON *Nt. & Morn.* II. iii. II. 121 A man who has plenty of brains generally falls on his legs. **1856** DICKENS *Dorrit* (1857) II. viii. 393 He had better confess, for he had not a leg to stand on. **1884** *Sat. Rev.* 7 June 731/1 That English credit is not good enough to set Egypt.. on her legs again. **1889** MIVART *Truth* 131 The latter hypothesis.. has not a leg to stand on. **1897** *Daily News* 15 Oct. 7/4 Mr. S. was on his hind legs arguing with.. force. **1897** W. E. NORRIS *Marietta's Marr.* xxx. 217 'Don't get on your hind legs', returned Betty composedly. **1910** H. BELLOC *Pongo* xix. 289 The Pongo was to get on to his very short hind legs and talk of the gravity of the situation and all his party was to listen in awed silence. **1925** V. WOOLF *Mrs. Dalloway* 114 Solemnly Richard Dalloway got on his hind legs and said that no decent man ought to read Shakespeare's sonnets. **1944** E. S. GARDNER *Case of Black-Eyed Blond* (1948) xvi. 158 Mildred had gone to a lawyer, and the lawyer had advised her that she didn't have a legal leg to stand on. **1960** M. SPARK *Bachelors* ii. 21 She hasn't a leg to stand on in the case. He's divorcing her, she's not divorcing him. **1964** J. MASTERS *Trial at Monomoy* i. 26 That's why I'm on my hind legs now, asking you folks to keep calm. **1973** J. WAINWRIGHT *Pride of Pigs* 179 You haven't a leg to stand on... You don't even out-rank me.

d. ***one's last legs***, the end of one's life; *fig.* the end of one's resources; said also of things; chiefly ***on*** or ***upon one's last legs***.

1599 MASSINGER, etc. *Old Law* v. i, *Eugenia*. My Husband goes upon his last hour now. *1st Courtier*. On his last legs, I am sure. **1668** DRYDEN *Evening's Love* II. i. Wks. 1883 III. 287 He had brought me to my last legs. **1764** FOOTE *Mayor of G.* II. Wks. 1799 I. 184 You was pretty near your last legs. **1846** DE QUINCEY *Syst. Heavens* Wks. (1854) III. 174 If the Earth were on her last legs. **1857** A. TROLLOPE *Barchester T.* i, The bishop was quite on his last legs; but the ministry also were tottering.

e. ***to dance*** (***run walk***, etc.) a person ***off his legs***: to cause (him) to dance, etc. to exhaustion.

1663 BUTLER *Hud.* I. iii. 326 Purging Comfits and Ants Eggs, Had almost brought him off his legs. **1668** PEPYS *Diary* 25 Nov., These people.. will run themselves off of their legs. **1736** AINSWORTH *Lat. Dict.* II s.v. *Hag*, I am hagged off my legs. **1890** 'ROLF BOLDREWOOD' *Col. Reformer* (1891) 159 Girls, who will dance him off his legs, unless he's very fit indeed. **1894** FENN *In Alpine Valley* I. 205 Soon walk him off his legs.

f. Put for 'the power of using the legs', as in ***to feel one's legs*** (FEEL *v.* 6 d), ***find one's legs***. ***to keep one's legs***, to remain standing or walking. ***sea-legs***: see SEA.

1593 SHAKS. *2 Hen. VI*, II. i. 147 We must haue you finde your Legges. Sirrha Beadle, whippe him till he leape ouer that same Stoole. **1706** [E. WARD] *Wooden World Dissected* (1708) 5 They.. walk firm, where all other Creatures tumble; and seldom can keep their Legs long, when they get upon *Terra firma*. **1855** MACAULAY *Hist. Eng.* xii. III. 233 The fighting men.. were so much exhausted that they could scarcely keep their legs. **1858** MRS. CARLYLE *Lett.* II. 345 Carried most of the way, not able to keep his legs.

g. ***in high leg***: in high spirits, exalted.

1808 SYD. SMITH *Let. to Lady Holland* 8 Oct. *Mem.* (1855) II. 38 The Mufti in high leg about the Spaniards.

3. a. The leg cut from the carcass of an animal or bird for use as food.

1533 ELYOT *Cast. Helthe* II. i. (1541) 16 b, Biefe is better digested than a chykens legge. **1599** H. BUTTES *Dyets drie Dinner* A a, A breast or legge of Mutton. *a* **1625** BEAUM. & FL. *Bonduca* II. iii, What say you to a leg of Beef now, sirha? **1722** DE FOE *Col. Jack* (1840) 118 Then came up a leg of mutton. **1875** A. WOOD *Havard's Dead Cities Zuyder Zee* 75 The butcheress.. still had a leg of veal.

b. leg-of-mutton *adj. phr.*, resembling a leg of mutton, *esp.* in shape. **leg-of-mutton sail**, a kind of triangular sail (also called shoulder-of-mutton sail); so ***leg-of-mutton rig***. **leg-of-mutton sleeve**, one very full and loose on the arm but close-fitting at the wrist; a gigot-sleeve.

1840 *P. Parley's Ann.* I. 218 Mrs. Button had dressed herself in leg-of-mutton sleeves [etc.]. **1883** *Harper's Mag.* Dec. 146/1, I had rigged her with a leg-of-mutton sail. **1884** *Girl's Own Mag.* 29 Mar. 410/1 The old-fashioned 'gigot', or leg-of-mutton sleeve. **1885** F. GORDON *Pyotshaw* 26 He brandished his leg-of-mutton fist. **1894** *Outing* (U.S.) May 148/1 The leg-of-mutton rig.. is the simplest.

4. An obeisance made by drawing back one leg and bending the other; a bow, scrape. Also in phrase ***to make*** (rarely ***cast away, scrape***) ***a leg***. Now *arch.* or *jocular*.

1589 *Tri. Love & Fortune* v. (Roxb. Club) 141 Hang rascall, make a leg to me. **1596** NASHE *Saffron Walden* (Grosart) III. 146 Whither.. haue you brought mee? To Newgate, good Master Doctour, with a lowe leg they made answer. **1599** HAKLUYT *Voy.* II. I. 152, I turned me to the Basha, and made a long legge, saying, Grand mercie Signior. **1602** *2nd Pt. Return fr. Parnass.* III. ii. 1212 His hungry sire will scrape you twenty legges, For one good Christmas meale. **1606** *Sir G. Goosecappe* IV. i. in Bullen *O. Pl.* III. 64 To shew my Courtship In the three quarter legge, and setled looke. **1609** DEKKER *Gvlls Horne-bk.* 64 A Jew never bends in the hams with casting away a leg. **1629** P. SMART *Holy Commun. Durham Cath.* 14 To teach the Coristers going up to the Altar to make legs to God. *a* **1654** SELDEN *Table-T.* (Arb.) 85 'Tis good to learn to dance, a man may learn his Leg, learn to go handsomly. **1725** DE FOE *Voy. round World* (1840) 97 The governor.. gave them the compliment of his hat and leg. **1839** LONGF. *Hyperion* I. vii, He is one that cannot make a good leg. **1857** TROLLOPE *Barchester T.* xxiii, Each made a leg in the approved rural fashion.

fig. **1858** *Sat. Rev.* 31 July 98 The India Bill came simpering on.. and made its little leg to an applauding public.

5. *slang.* Short for BLACKLEG 2.

1815 *Sporting Mag.* XLV. 39 The Goose that laid the Golden Egg should be a lesson to the legs on the turf. **1837** DICKENS *Pickw.* xlii, He *was* a horse chaunter: he's a leg now. **1884** H. SMART *From Post to Finish* xxiii. 172 The world regards me as a compound of leg and money-lender.

6. *Cricket.* **a.** ***leg before wicket***: the act of stopping with the leg, or other part of the person, a straight-pitched ball, which would otherwise have hit the wicket (a fault in play for which the batsman may be given 'out'). Also, simply, ***leg before***. Abbreviated *l.b.w.*

[**1774** *Laws Cricket* in Lillywhite *Cricket Scores* (1862) I. 17 Or if a striker puts his leg before the wicket with a design to stop the ball, and actually prevent the ball from hitting his wicket by it [he is out].] [**1795**: cf. *l.b.w.* under L (*the letter*) 7.] **1850** 'BAT' *Cricket Man.* 47 The hitter is given out as.. 'leg before wicket'. **1862** LILLYWHITE *Cricket Scores* I. 191 In this match [in 1795], 'leg before wicket' is found *scored* for the first time. **1882** *Daily Tel.* 20 May, Blackham was out leg before to Lillywhite.

b. (Also ***the leg***.) (*a*) That part of the 'on' side of the field which lies behind, or about in a line with, the batsman. Chiefly in (a hit) *to* (*the*) *leg*. (*b*) The side of the pitch on which the batsman stands.

(*a*) **1843** 'A WYKHAMIST' *Pract. Hints Cricket* Frontisp., The 'long on'.. is for the most part done away with, and placed either.. between the slip and cover-point, or to the 'leg'. *Ibid.* 17 The hitting to the leg is by far the most effective. **1857** HUGHES *Tom Brown* II. viii, A beautifully pitched ball for the outer stump, which the.. unfeeling Jack.. hits right round to leg for five. **1866** LE FANU *All in Dark* I. viii. 66 William, whose hit to leg was famous.

attrib. **1882** *Daily Tel.* 24 June, The South Australian got his first ball to the leg boundary.

(*b*) **1843** 'A WYKHAMIST' *Pract. Hints Cricket* 17 As soon as ever the ball is pitched to the leg. **1851** PYCROFT *Cricket Field* ix. 181 So a cricket ball, with lateral spin, will work from Leg to Off, or Off to Leg, according to the spin. **1859** *All Year Round* No. 13. 306 The first ball they bowled me was slow, overpitched, and to leg. **1888** *Cricket* (Badm Libr.) vii. 282 Farmer Miles.. bowled under-arm.. his balls curling in from the leg.

c. Hence, the position of a fieldsman placed to stop balls hit 'to leg' (see above); also, the fieldsman so placed. ***long, short, square leg***, the fieldsman, or his position, at a long or short distance from the wicket or about square with it.

1816 in Box *Eng. Game Cricket* (1877) 34 *Leg*, the person who takes this place should stand a little back from the straight line of the popping crease. **1850** 'BAT' *Cricket Man.* 44 Long Leg must be occupied by a good thrower. **1857** *Chambers' Inform.* II. 688/2 Leg should stand rather behind the striker, in a diagonal line, about twelve or sixteen yards from the wicket. **1877** Box *Eng. Game Cricket* Gloss., *Short Leg*, the fielder stationed within a few yards of the wicket behind the batsman. *Square Leg*, this fielder stands nearly square with the batsman. **1880** *Times* 28 Sept. 11/5 The men were placed thus:—Mr. Jarvis, wicket-keeper;.. Bannerman, leg [etc.]. **1894** *Ibid.* 23 May 7/3 He was taken at short-leg.

II. Something more or less resembling a leg, or performing its function as a support for a 'body'.

7. a. A representation or figure of a leg; *esp.* in *Her.*

c **1500** *Sc. Poem Heraldry* in *Q. Eliz. Acad.* 100 Thire be also raschit, as lege or heid. **1725** COATS *New Dict. Her.*, *Legs* are born in Coat-Armour, either naked, or shod, or booted. **1797** *Encycl. Brit.* (ed. 3) VIII. 457/2 'Gules, three Legs armed proper, conjoined in the Fess-point'... This is the coat of arms of the Isle of Man... 'Or, three Legs couped above the knee Sable'; borne by the name of *Hosy*.

†**b.** *Sc.* Short for *leg-dollar*. *Obs.*

1687 [see *leg-dollar* in 17].

8. An artificial leg. Also ***cork leg, wooden leg***: see the adjs.

1426 LYDG. *De Guil. Pilgr.* 23199, I made me a leg of tre.

9. (See quot.)

1727 BOYER *Eng.-Fr. Dict.* s.v. *Leg*, A Leg of Wood to put in a Stocking, *forme, pour enformer les Bas*.

10. That part of a garment which covers the leg.

1580 *Stanford Churchw. Acc.* in *Antiquary* XVII. 171/2 It. for a payre of boote Leggs to mende bawdrycks, viij*d*. **1861** DICKENS *Gt. Expect.* ii, To put my hunk of bread-and-butter down the leg of my trousers.

11. a. A bar, pole, or the like used as a support or prop; *esp.* in *Shipbuilding* and *Mining*.

1497 *Naval Acc. Hen. VII* (1896) 324 Carpenters whuch made the seid ledders and legges of tymbre. **1699** DAMPIER *Voy.* II. I. 73 One end of the Carriage is supported with two Legs, or a Fork of three Foot high. **1712** J. JAMES tr. *Le Blond's Gardening* 81 'Tis set upon the Ground by means of three Legs or Staves.. put into as many Sockets below the Ball... The lesser sort.. require but one Leg. **1883** GRESLEY *Gloss. Coal-mining*, *Leg*. 1. S[cotland]. A wooden prop supporting one end of a bar. 2. Y[orkshire]. A stone which has to be wedged out from beneath a larger one. **1886** R. C. LESLIE *Sea-painter's Log* iv 68 The yacht is likely to fall over, and, breaking her leg under her, receive serious damage.

b. One of the poles or masts of a sheers.

1896 *Law Times Rep.* LXXIII. 634/2 The engine then brought the other waggon under the shear legs to have it unloaded. **1898** *Daily News* 30 June 4/5 A pair of steel legs eighty-seven feet in height, which had a lifting power of 75 tons.

12. One of the comparatively long and slender supports of a piece of furniture or the like.

1680 MOXON *Mech. Exerc.* 177 The Legs and Cheeks are to be fastned with Braces to the Floor.. of the Room the Lathe stands in. **1784** COWPER *Task* I. 19 Joint-stools were then created; on three legs Upborne they stood. **1837** DICKENS *Pickw.* xliv, I was always used to a four-poster afore I came here, and I find the legs of the table answer just as well. *Ibid.* xlvii, Mr. Pickwick grated the legs of his chair against the ground. **1852** MRS. CARLYLE *Lett.* II. 175 Tables with their legs in the air.

13. A beam upon which tanners dress skins.

1727–41 CHAMBERS *Cycl.* s.v. *Shammy*, They [skins] are.. laid on a wooden leg or horse.

14. a. One of the branches of a forked, jointed, or curved object.

1683 MOXON *Mech. Exerc.*, *Printing* xiii. ¶4 The Legs of a Carpenter's Joynt-Rule. **1726** tr. *Gregory's Astron.* I. 490 Imagine a Canal fill'd with a Fluid, and bent,.. the Fluid in the Leg of the Canal *AC* is in equilibrio with the Fluid in the Leg *PC*. **1727–41** CHAMBERS *Cycl.*, Compasses of three legs. **1801** JEFFERSON *Writ.* (ed. Ford) VII. 482 A rainbow, therefore,.. plunges one of it's legs down to the river. **1828** J. H. MOORE *Pract. Navig.* (ed. 20) 18 The Sector. This instrument consists of two legs or rulers, representing the radii of a circle. **1866** *Croquet* 10 A ball is Wired when it cannot effect the stroke desired on account of the leg of a hoop (wire) intervening. **1893** SLOANE *Electr. Dict.*, *Leg of circuit*, one lead or side of a complete metallic circuit.

b. One of the sides of a triangle, viewed as standing upon a base (so Gr. σκέλος); one of the two parts on each side of the vertex of a curve. ***hyperbolic, parabolic leg*** (see quot. 1727–41).

1659 MOXON *Globes* VI. i. (1674) 184 The Legs of a Right Angled Spherical Triangle. **1702** RALPHSON *Math. Dict.*, *Isosceles* Triangle is a Triangle that has two equal Legs. **1727–41** CHAMBERS *Cycl.* s.v. *Curve*, Lastly, the legs of curves.. are either of the parabolic or hyperbolic kind: an hyperbolic leg, being that which approaches infinitely towards some asymptote; a parabolic, that which has no asymptote.

c. *Gold-mining.* One of the two nearly vertical lateral prolongations of the saddle of a quartz-reef.

1890 *Melbourne Argus* 16 June 6/1 In payable saddle formations a slide intersects the reef above the saddle coming from the west, and turning east with a wall of the east leg, where the leg of reef is observed to go down deeper.

d. *Lace-making.* A strand of the net-work which connects the patterns in lace. Usu. *pl.*

1865 F. B. PALLISER *Hist. Lace* xxii. 263 Early guipure of Venice or darned network, in which the raised flowers were strung together by legs or brides. **1900** E. JACKSON *Hist. Handmade Lace* 214 *Legs*,.. the connecting threads thrown across spaces in needlepoint and bobbin laces. **1922** MRS. R. E. HEAD *Lace & Embroidery Collector* 232 *Brides*. Fr. Syns.: bars, legs (Eng.).

e. *U.S. Broadcasting.* A branch or supplementary network attached to the main network and providing coverage for a particular region (see also quot. 1937).

1937 *Printers' Ink Monthly* May 39/1 *Leg*, a regional chain, i.e., one link of stations in a network. **1951** E. E. WILLIS *Foundations in Broadcasting* iii. 47 Supplementary stations are added to the basic network in order to expand the coverage of a particular program. Often these supplementary stations are organised into groups or legs, which provide coverage of an entire section. The networks all have West Coast legs, for example. **1966** *McGraw-Hill Encycl. Sci. & Technol.* XI. 252/2 An appended supplementary network circuit, feeding more than one station from an intermediate point along a reversible or a round-robin system, is called the leg of a network. Network legs are usually.. one-way circuits from the AT&T office to the leg office and the stations they feed.

15. *Naut.* **a.** A name applied to various short ropes (see quot. 1794). ***leg along*** (see quot. 1867).

1627 CAPT. SMITH *Seaman's Gram.* v. 24 Legs are small ropes put thorow the bolt ropes of the maine and fore saile, neere to a foot in length, spliced each end into the other in the leech of the saile, hauing a little eye whereunto the martnets are fastened by two hitches. **1711** W. SUTHERLAND *Shipbuild. Assist.* 143 Cat-harping Legs. **1794** *Rigging & Seamanship* I. 169 *Legs*, short ropes which branch out into two or more parts, as the bowline-legs or bridles, buntline-legs, crowfoot-legs, &c. **1860** *Merc. Marine Mag.* VII. 113 The two meet and fall to deck in one leg. **1867** SMYTH *Sailor's Word-bk.*, *Leg along*, ropes laid on end, ready for manning.

b. A run made on a single tack. Chiefly in ***long, short leg, a good leg***, 'a course sailed on a tack which is near the desired course' (Webster, 1897).

1867 in SMYTH *Sailor's Word-bk.* **1892** H. HUTCHINSON *Fairway Island* 20 I'll fetch down on a long leg, and catch the 'Pengelley' on a single tack. **1895** *Daily News* 8 July 8/6 Valkyrie.. preferred a series of short legs off Wemyss Bay to weather the Skelmorlie.

c. A part of, or stage in, a journey, race, competition, etc.

1920 *Blackw. Mag.* Feb. 166/1 On each new 'leg' of our zigzags, our eyes were straining over ever-new horizons.

1927 *Nat. Geogr. Mag.* Aug. 185/2 (*heading*) First non-stop leg of the journey was 1,400 miles. **1938** W. L. Hughes *Bk. Major Sports* xxx. 345 Each man on a relay team is said to run one leg of the race. **1953** R. Chisholm *Cover of Darkness* xiv. 151 We began a square search, flying five-minute legs. **1955** *N.Y. Times* 23 Jan. 3/6 Wiggins swam his leg of the relay in 56 seconds flat. **1958** *Times* 8 Sept. 6/3 Where an alien's visit to Britain was split into two parts by a trip to another country, each 'leg' of the United Kingdom visit had, by law, to be dealt with separately by the immigration authorities. **1972** *Nature* 31 Mar. 196/2 The first leg of this route traverses Arctic tundra regions of Alaska and Canada's Northwest Territories. **1973** C. Bonington *Next Horizon* xiii. 196 We squeezed out of the snow cave for the last leg down to Scheidegg.

III. 16. *attrib.* and *Comb.* Simple attrib., as ***leg bath***; objective and obj. gen., as ***leg-maker***, ***-tripping***; locative, as ***leg tired***, ***-weary*** adjs. (so ***leg-weariness***); also ***leg-like*** adj.

1869 Claridge *Cold Water-cure* 56 *Leg Bath. The thighs and legs..ought to be put into a bath. **1897** *19th Cent.* Aug. 297 Others unmistakably *leglike. **14..** *Nom.* in Wr.-Wülcker 686/29 *Hic tibiarius*, *legmaker. **1737** Bracken *Farriery Impr.* (1757) II. 149 If he..change his Feet, it denotes he is *Leg-tired. **1871** B. Taylor *Faust* (1875) II. iii. 211 He overcame In *leg-tripping. **1880** W. Day *Racehorse* xix. 183 Horses often pull up lame from *leg-weariness. **1755** Shebbeare *Lydia* (1769) I. 243 The exciseman began to be *leg-weary. **1890** 'Rolf Boldrewood' *Col. Reformer* (1891) 319 The slow, hopeless, leg-weary jog.

17. a. Special combinations: **leg art** *slang* (orig. *U.S.*) = cheese-cake 2; **leg-bird**, a dial. name for the Sedge Warbler; **leg-bone**, the shin-bone, tibia; **leg-boot**, a boot for a horse, covering the leg between the knee and hoof; **leg-business** *slang*, ballet-dancing; **leg-dollar** (see quot. 1687); **leg drive**, in rowing, drive imparted by movement of the rower's legs; **leg-foot**, the foot of a post or the like; **leg-guard**, a protection for the leg; in *Cricket*, a covering for the knee, shin and ankle, worn by the batsmen and wicket-keeper as a protection against injury from the ball; **leg-ill**, a disease of sheep, causing lameness; **leg-iron**, a shackle or fetter for the leg (whence ***leg-ironed*** adj.); **leg-lock** = prec.; **leg man**, **woman** orig. *U.S.*, an assistant who does leg work, *spec.* a journalist who goes from place to place gathering information; †**leg money** (see quot.); **leg-muff**, 'one of the fleecy or downy puffs or tufts about the feet of many humming-birds' (*Cent. Dict.*); **leg-pad** *Cricket* = *leg-guard*; †**leg payment** (see quot. and cf. leg-bail); **leg piece**, †(*a*) in *pl.*, greaves; (*b*) *Theatrical slang* (= F. *pièce aux jambes*), a play in which 'leg-business' is prominent; **leg-pull** [f. the phr. *to pull one's leg*: see leg *sb.* 2 a], the act of deceiving a person in a playful way, a humorous deception (so ***leg-puller***, ***-pulling*** sbs.); **leg-rest**, a contrivance for supporting the leg of an invalid when seated; **leg-ring**, an aluminium strip wrapped round a bird's leg to mark it; hence **leg-ringing** *vbl. sb.*; **leg-room**, space for the legs, *spec.* in a car; **leg-rope** *v.* (*Austral.* and *N.Z.*), to catch an animal by the leg with a noosed rope; *sb.* (*Austral.* and *N.Z.*), a noosed rope for securing an animal by one hind leg; also **leg-roping** *vbl. sb.*; †**leg-saw** (meaning obscure); **legs eleven**, a jocular catch-phrase in the game of bingo (or housey-housey), etc., for 'eleven'; also *ellipt.* as *legs*; **leg-shield**, a shield to protect the leg from being crushed against the barrier in justing; **leg shop** *colloq.*, a theatre in which 'leg-shows' are produced (*Obs.*); **leg-show** *colloq.* (orig. *U.S.*), a theatrical production in which dancing girls display their legs; **leg-splint**, a plate of armour to protect the leg; **leg-stretcher**, (*a*) a walker; (*b*) a walk (see *to stretch one's legs* s.v. stretch *v.* 3 c); **leg warmer**, either of a pair of tubular (usu. knitted) garments covering the leg from ankle to thigh, orig. worn by ballet dancers at rehearsal, and subsequently by (young) women, often as a fashion accessory; usu. in *pl.*; **leg woman** (see *leg man* above); **leg-wood** *dial.*, large branches cut from trees (also *attrib.*); **leg work**, work which involves running errands, going from place to place in search of information, etc.; **leg-worm**, the Guinea worm (q.v.) which attacks the legs. Also leg-harness.

1940 *Amer. Speech* XV. 359/1 *Leg art, exploitation of sex appeal in pictures. **1958** *Spectator* 10 Oct. 481/1 The Cameo Royal, the leg-art cinema by London's Leicester Square. **1848** *Zoologist* VI. 2290 The sedge warbler, a '*leg bird'. **1885** in Swainson *Prov. Names Birds*. **1615** Crooke *Body of Man* 1003 The whirle and the *Leg-bone are ioyned by adarticulation. **1871** Mrs. Ann. Edwardes *Ought we to visit her?* III. i. 11 She was..in the '*Leg Business', your Grace. **1670** *Proclam.* in Cochran-Patrick *Coinage Scot.* (1876) II. 158 These dollors commonly called *leg dollors. **1687** A. Haig in J. Russell *Haigs* xi. (1881) 331 To Daick,..a rex-dollar and halfe a legg, which is £04 . 06 . 0. [*Note*, A rix-dollar was worth £2 18*s.* Scots, or 4*s.* 10*d.* sterling; a leg-dollar £2 16*s.*, or 4*s.* 8*d.* sterling. The latter coin was so-called from having on it the impression of a man in armour with one leg, the other being covered by a shield containing a coat of arms.] *Ibid.* 332 A legg-dollar for parchment and drink-money. **1928** *Observer* 1 July 30/3 They are lacking in *leg-drive, and their boat does not run evenly between the strokes. **1968** *Encycl. Brit.* XIX. 668/2 Fairbairn.. emphasized leg drive and arm pull and considered smooth bladework more important than what he called the 'showy style' of body work. **1893** Stevenson *Catriona* iii. 29 Old daft limmers sit at a *leg-foot [of a gibbet] and spae their fortunes. **1844** *Bell's Life* 12 May 1/3 (Advt.), Robert Dark, the Inventor and sole Manufacturer of..the improved *leg guards, begs respectfully to inform the lovers of the Game of Cricket that they can be supplied at the shortest notice. **1849** 'Bat' *Cricket Man.* Advt., Gauntlets, Leg Guards [etc.]. **1890** [see *face-screen* (face *sb.* 26)]. **1952** C. Day Lewis tr. *Virgil's Aeneid* vii. 160 Working polished leg-guards from malleable silver. **1807** *Ess. Highl. Soc.* III. 431 *Leg ill. **1861** Dickens *Gt. Expect.* xvi, A convict's *leg-iron which had been filed asunder. **1884** E. Yates *Recoll.* I. iii. 115 Convicts ..handcuffed and *leg-ironed. **1860** [Mrs. W. P. Byrne] *Undercurrents Overlooked* II. 218 Manacles and chains, whips and *leg-locks. **1923** *Nation* (N.Y.) 24 Oct. 454/2 Newsboys and '*legmen' and a foreign news service keep the streets of Mecca aware of all that goes on. **1951** E. Paul *Springtime in Paris* xi. 195 The Paris police, leg men and cameramen from the Paris newspapers began tailing Nordmann and Tixier-Vignancour day and night. **1960** *Woman's Own* 5 Mar. 9/1 Jeannie supposed he'd have to get another secretary. He had two already, one more or less a leg-man, another who came in by the day. **1967** *Economist* 1 July 26/1 He was Mr Macmillan's leg man during the break-up of the Central African Federation. **1812** *Examiner* 7 Sept. 575/1 If not able to pay *leg money, or a fee for knocking off the irons [at Newgate]. **1850** 'Bat' *Cricket Man.* 51 *Leg-pads. **1611** Cotgr., *Payer en gambades*, to make *leg-paiments, to runne away in debt. **1676** Hobbes *Iliad* (1677) 151 His *leg-pieces he down to th' anckles ti'd, With silver buckles leg-pieces of brass. **1918** G. B. Shaw *Let.* Sept. in W. Loraine *Robert Loraine* (1938) xiii. 247 So long as you have a mouth left and one lung to keep it going, you will still be better than the next best: my pieces are not leg pieces. **1923** J. Manchon *Le Slang* 179 *Leg-piece*,..ballet. **1915** *Truth* Nov. 848/1 What you describe as a swindle was only a brain-wave of mine ending in a *leg-pull. **1938** *Times Lit. Suppl.* 12 Feb. 112/3 In point of fact they appear to have been no more than a not very subtle leg-pull. **1950** T. S. Eliot *Cocktail Party* iii. 148 You always did enjoy a leg-pull, Julia. **1965** M. Spark *Mandelbaum Gate* iv. 106 Sometimes, Abdul, I wonder if you're just treating me to a big leg-pull. **1970** J. Ardagh *New France* xi. 549 His whole operation might be partly a leg-pull at the expense of serious literature. **1923** *Motor Cycling* 7 Nov. 2/1 You are a confirmed *leg-puller. Just fancy kidding me about the speed of the bus I bought from you. **1969** *Mind* LXXVIII. 31 Most samples are fair samples (God is not a leg-puller). **1908** *Westm. Gaz.* 30 June 2/1, I, too, have lived in Australia, where *leg-pulling is one of the chief joys of life. **1926** T. E. Lawrence *Seven Pillars* ix. civ. 553, I could hardly tell my own self where the leg-pulling began or ended. **1946** *R.A.F. Jrnl.* May 178 'Liz' and 'Sally'..will take any amount of leg pulling—and give it. **1963** *Times* 30 May 17/2 Mr. Rovere is patently civilized, thoughtful and well-informed in his leg-pulling. **1833** J. C. Loudon *Encycl. Archit.* iii. vi. 1050 A *Leg Rest..is sometimes used in dining-rooms by old gentlemen after the ladies are gone. **1854** Mrs. Gaskell *North & South* (1855) II. v. 68 He was busy..contriving a leg-rest for Dixon, who was beginning to feel the fatigues of watching. **1860** Geo. Eliot *Mill on Fl.* III. 8 Tom advanced before him, carrying the leg-rest. **1970** *Stoke Mandeville Dict. Managem. Paraplegic Patients* 23 *Leg-Rest*, attachment to wheelchairs used to keep a paralysed leg elevated. **1973** *Green Shield Stamps Catal.* No. 12. 133 (*caption*) Garden Chair with Leg Rest. Adjustable to 8 positions. [**1909** A. L. Thomson in *Brit. Birds* II. 362 Various investigators..are endeavouring to obtain fuller and more accurate data with regard to migration, by liberating birds marked with metal foot-rings.] **1938** *Brit. Birds* XXXI. 242 Each bird was marked with a light, numbered, metal *leg-ring of the British Birds Marking Scheme. **1959** *New Biol.* XXIX. 111 Leg-rings in different colours have been distributed to a large number of I.G.Y. bases in the hope that some of the mysteries associated with this bird's [*sc.* the Antarctic skua's] activities can be solved. **1963** *Times* 5 June 14/4 During the time he has been in Cyprus, Mr. Nicholson has helped in many major ornithological achievements, notably in the hazardous but successful *leg-ringing of young Eleanora's falcons. **1928** *Punch* 18 Apr. p. xxii (Advt.), Carries four full-sized people. Ample *leg-room... A wonderful performer for such a small horse-powered car. **1958** *Times* 19 Aug. 11/6 They [*sc.* Ford designers] succeeded in giving the passengers sufficient legroom. **1972** *Drive* Spring 147/3 The height, legroom and squab level of the driver's seat can be adjusted. **1878** E. S. Elwell *Boy Colonists* 235 She kicked out at Ernest, who was trying to get the *leg-rope on. **1889** 'Rolf Boldrewood' *Robbery under Arms* (1890) 7 We could milk, leg-rope, and bail up for ourselves. **1911** H. Foston *In Bell Bird's Lair* 36 Each cow was to be carefully 'leg-roped'. *Ibid.*, Ted was shown how to 'leg-rope' a cow and bail up. **1950** *N.Z. Jrnl. Agric.* Feb. 169/2 Milk stools, door handles, leg ropes, posts and walls must be kept clean. *Ibid.* Nov. 465/3 The tail of the cow should be prevented from waving about and, if necessary, the animal comfortably leg-roped. **1963** *Landfall* Mar. 13, I..let the cow out into the race where, taking the leg-rope with her, she squittered off wild in the eyes. **1912** B. E. Baughan in D. M. Davin *N.Z. Short Stories* (1953) 189 Much to my surprise, there was no *leg-roping, and hardly any bailing-up [of the cows being milked]. **1662** *Stat. Irel.* (1765) II. 464 *Leg-saws the piece 6*s.* 8*d.* **1919** W. H. Downing *Digger Dial.* 32 *Legs eleven, ..the number eleven in the game of 'house'. **1933** L. A. G. Strong *Sea Wall* 256 A game of 'house' was in progress and a voice monotonously droned the numbers: '..legs... Kelly's eye.' **1945** E. Waugh *Brideshead Revisited* ii. i. 230 Kelly's eye—number one; legs, eleven; and we'll Shake the Bag. **1965** Brophy & Partridge *Long Trail* 144 *Legs eleven*, ..in the game of House, eleven. **1860** Hewitt *Anc. Arm.* III. 390 The *leg-shield of the saddle is found in woodcut No. 49. **1871** 'Mark Twain' *Screamers* xxviii. 144 They're playing 'Undine' at the Opery House, and some folks call it the *leg shop. **1882** J. J. Jennings *Theatr. & Circus Life* 238 Burlesque with its blonde attributes kept the country in a rage..and the minor musical attractions of the *quasi* legitimate stage have usurped its principal feature—the *leg show. **1900** *Amer. Jrnl. Sociol.* VI. 447 Next follows a cinematograph reproduction of a prize-fight, and then, in striking contrast with the first, a 'leg show' of the most shameless character. **1930** Brophy & Partridge *Songs & Slang 1914–18* 137 At a leg-show of these days you saw far less of the female form than is now exhibited in the streets. **1930** J. Dos Passos *42nd Parallel* v. 420 Doc wanted to go to see a legshow. **1952** 'J. Guthrie' *Paradise Bay* vi. 57 He took me to exciting spectacles which I now know were leg shows. **1969** *Listener* 20 Mar. 399/1 We often use the cliché of the tired business-man to define the low response..that sustains leg-shows. **1828–40** Tytler *Hist. Scot.* (1864) II. 78 Breastplate, greaves, and *leg-splints. **1616** T. Coryat *Traveller for English Wits* 42 Your..most obliged Countreyman..the..*Legge-stretcher of Odcomb in Somerset, Thomas Coryate. **1942** 'M. Home' *House of Shade* iii. 57 Marigny was suggesting a leg-stretcher... The two made their way out to the glare of the sun. **1970** *Daily Tel.* 23 May 9 Now lonely, neglected, and often overgrown, they provide delightful leg-stretchers, on the springy turf, for the motorist with an hour or so to spare. **1974** *Dance Mag.* June 80/1 (Advt.), At last a fashion-wise..line of garments that can be worn for dance, sports..or street wear. ..*Leg Warmers..Midriff Top..Swing Skirt. **1975** *New Yorker* 26 May 30/3 Mr. Grigorovich was sitting on a bench at the front of the room watching fifty-odd perspiring dancers, in leotards and leg warmers, moving through the complicated patterns of a lilting Tchaikovsky waltz. **1976** *Times* 30 Mar. 10 Leg-warmers, accessory of every freezing dance rehearsal room, emerged as a stylish cover-up for girls. **1984** S. Townsend *Growing Pains A. Mole* 146 No Selina this morning, so I had to make do with going into town with Pandora, who wanted to buy a pair of neon pink legwarmers. **1960** M. G. Eberhart *Jury of One* (1961) i. 9 An old school friend, a fashion writer, had needed an assistant, a *leg woman. **1872** T. Hardy *Greenw. T.* I. iii. (1876) 22 We shall have a rare *leg-wood fire directly. **1898** *Oxford Chron.* 22 Jan. 1 A large number of Faggots and Legwood. **1891** *Dialect Notes* I. 207 Reporters characterize a task in which there is more running than writing by the expression **leg-work*. **1942** E. Paul *Narrow St.* xxxi. 285 The Greek madonna did the leg work faithfully while La Absalom cackled orders through a rift in the portières. **1959** G. Cobden *Murder for his Money* iv. 51 He wouldn't come himself for Patey was no man of action, but he might send ..a man we used a great deal for leg work. **1972** *Daily Tel.* 21 June 13/8, 1,700 men..do the surveying leg-work needed for keeping local maps up to date. **1973** L. Heren *Growing up Poor in London* vii. 179, I would earn a few bob working on the edge of big stories... The reporters who came down from Fleet Street were nearly always willing to pay for leg work. **1699** Dampier *Voy.* II. ii. 79 Two hairy Worms growing in the Authors Leg. Dangerous *Leg-worms in the West Indies. **1857** tr. *Küchenmeister's Man. Parasites Hum. Body* I. 398 Amongst the Germans it is known as..the skin-worm,..leg-worm,..and Pharaoh's worm.

b. in *Cricket*: **leg bail**, **stump**, that nearest the batsman; **leg ball**, **break**, a ball which pitches on or breaks from the leg side; hence ***leg-breaker***, a leg-break bowler; **leg-bye** (see bye *sb.* 1); **leg-cutter** (see quot. 1966); **leg glance**, **glide**, a shot in which the ball is glanced fine on the leg side; **leg hit**, **stroke**, a hit to leg (hence ***leg-hitter***, ***-hitting*** sbs.); **leg play** (see quot. 1934); **leg side** = leg *sb.* 6 b; **leg slip**, (a fielder in) a position corresponding to that of the slips (see slip *sb.*[3] 14 a), but on the leg side; **leg spin**, a type of spin which causes the ball to turn from leg side to off (so ***leg-spinner***); **leg sweep**, a sweeping stroke which sends the ball to leg; **leg theory**, the technique of bowling to leg with a concentration of fielders on the leg side; **leg trap**, fielders stationed for catches close to the wicket on the leg side.

1882 *Daily Tel.* 27 May, The new-comer..immediately afterwards had his *leg-bail removed. **1830** Miss Mitford *Village* Ser. iv. 29 He missed a *leg ball of Ned Smith's. **1888** A. G. Steel in Steel & Lyttelton *Cricket* iii. 114 The '*leg break' ball is usually bowled from round the wicket. **1927** W. E. Collinson *Contemp. English* 19 Only gradually did the mysteries of yorkers, full tosses and leg-breaks penetrate to us. **1955** *Times* 9 May 15/1 Mansell..bowled 17 steady overs of leg-breaks. **1969** M. Parkinson *Cricket Mad* x. 57 We had our suspicions confirmed in the Indian's first over which contained five leg breaks. **1905** *Strand Mag.* June 703/2 Armstrong is a *leg-breaker. **1956** R. Alston *Test Commentary* i. 13 Benaud, potentially a most dangerous leg-breaker. **1956** N. Cardus *Close of Play* 37 What is action break? In what way is it a term with a meaning more demonstrable..than 'seamer' and '*leg-cutter'? **1963** *Times* 25 Apr. 4/5 He went to Lord's last year to play his first match for Warwickshire and within a couple of overs had bowled everything from a leg-cutter to an inswinger. **1966** B. Johnston *Armchair Cricket* 102 *Leg-cutter*, is really a fast leg-break which is bowled by 'cutting' across the seam of the ball. **1883** *Cricket* 19 Apr. 39/1 Horan came in after lunch, and soon commenced to score in his own peculiar style, *leg glances being his favourite stroke. **1966** B. Close *Close on Cricket* iii. 35 *Leg glance*, this is a refined stroke played against a ball pitched on or outside the leg stump but not far enough up to drive efficiently. **1920** D. J. Knight in P. F. Warner *Cricket* 33 The first of the leg strokes, the *leg glide, is a glorious one to watch, and is exceedingly paying. **1955** *Times* 12 July 12/4 Just before luncheon he had lost Brookes, who, after a beautiful leg glide, missed one from Smith to be out leg before. **1836** in 'Bat' *Cricket Man.* (1850) 100 Pilch ..wrote down three with a *leg hit. **1843** 'A Wykhamist' *Pract. Hints Cricket* 17 He will soon become an effective *leg-hitter. *Ibid.*, On *leg-hitting. **1888** R. H. Lyttelton in Steel & Lyttelton *Cricket* xvi. 411 It is the bowlers who have most cause to grumble at the modern *leg play. **1898** K. S. Ranjitsinhji *With Stoddart's Team* (ed. 4) v. 96 His [*sc.* S. P. Jones's] cutting and his leg play being particularly well-timed. **1928** *Daily Express* 28 June 3/4 If leg-play were more severely penalised and wickets less like polished concrete,

the balance between bat and ball would be more redressed and the game restored to its former attractiveness. 1934 W. J. Lewis *Lang. Cricket* 147 *Leg play*, 1. Stopping a breaking or curling ball with the leg instead of with the bat... 2. The playing of balls on the leg side. 1816 W. Lambert *Cricketer's Guide* (ed. 6) ii. 32 If the Ball should come 4 or 5 inches on the *leg side, the Striker should move his right foot back at the moment of hitting, playing the Ball between his left leg and the wicket. 1956 N. Cardus *Close of Play* 26 No opposing captain dreamed of setting a close leg-side field for him. 1969 P. Pocock *Bowling* i. 19 The majority of seam bowlers swung the ball away from the batsman, using six fielders on the offside and three on the leg side. 1956 R. Alston *Test Commentary* xvi. 143 Miller swept him through the hastily retreating *leg-slips. 1963 A. Ross *Australia 63* vii. 134 Benaud gave Davidson his most aggressive field for some time; neither long leg nor third man, three slips, gully, leg slip and backward short leg. 1888 A. G. Steel in Steel & Lyttelton *Cricket* iii. 116 The ball, coming from a great distance round the wicket and with a considerable amount of *leg spin, would be gradually working away to the batsman's off side. 1966 B. Close *Close on Cricket* v. 55 We have a quantity of good finger-spin bowlers but few leg-spin bowlers in first-class cricket. 1927 *Observer* 29 May 28/4 It was a clear case for old Brown's *leg-spinners. 1965 P. Walker *Winning Cricket* iv. 57 Nowadays you have to bowl leg spinners with the accuracy of an orthodox right hander to achieve even moderate success. 1906 *Westm. Gaz.* 12 July 4/1 This *leg-stroke off a straight ball has two great merits—it scores runs and it puts the bowler off. 1955 *Cricket—How to Play* (M.C.C.) 47 (*heading*) Practising leg-strokes. 1833 C. C. Clarke *Nyren's Cricketer's Guide* (1888) 23 A ball.. pitched on the inside of the *leg stump. 1937, 1956 Leg stump [see *Chinese cut*]. 1846 W. Denison *Cricket Sk. Players* 17 His [*sc.* G. Brockwell's] '*leg sweeps' are very powerful, and generally speaking they are along the ground—not lifted. 1955 A. Ross *Australia* 55 xii. 168 His leg-sweep was comfortably finished before the ball had got anywhere near him. 1898 G. Giffen *With Bat & Ball* x. 153 Cooper bowled the *leg-theory almost as remarkably as the off-theory is practised nowadays. 1923 *Daily Mail* 11 Aug. 7/4 Newman, following the fashion of the match, bowled the leg theory with a crescent of fieldsmen close in on the leg side. 1956 N. Cardus *Close of Play* 26 He would have discovered a way of retaliation against leg-traps and leg-theories. 1923 *Wisden's Cricketers' Almanack* 329 His stock ball is the inswinger and here again he often hits the wicket and has not got to rely on his *leg-traps. 1924 N. Cardus *Days in Sun* 50 The good balls were pushed for singles through the leg-trap—when they did not get wickets. 1953 R. Warner *Escapade* ii. iii. 93 It's a leg-trap... You see, my dear, the batsman is absolutely forced to play every ball to the leg. 1963 *Times* 5 June 4/2 He took a pace to Titmus only to turn him gently into the leg trap.

leg (lɛg), *v.* [f. Leg *sb.*]

1. *intr.* ***to leg it***: To use the legs, to walk fast or run; also simply *to leg* (Sc. and dial.).

1601 Deacon & Walker *Spirits & Divels* 3 Let vs legge it a little. 1790 D. Morison *Poems* 7 The wives leg hame an' trim their fires. 1837 Haliburton *Clockm.* Ser. i. xxiv, He was a leggin it off hot foot. 1899 R. Kipling *Stalky & Co.* i. 4 We're goin' along the cliffs after butterflies.. We're goin' to leg it, too. You'd better leave your book behind.

†**2.** ***to leg it***, to 'make a leg'. ***to leg unto***, to bow to (*indirect passive* in quot.). *Obs. rare.*

1628 Sir F. Hobart *Edw. II*, cclii, [They] Are legg'd and crouch'd unto for feare they sting. 1633 Shirley *Bird in a Cage* v. i, He'l kisse his hand and leg it.

3. *trans.* To propel or work (a boat) through a canal-tunnel by means of the legs (see quot. 1861); to navigate (a tunnel) in this way; also ***to leg through***.

1836 Sir G. Head *Home Tour* 144 Two hours is the time occupied in 'legging' a boat through. 1861 Smiles *Engineers* I. 441 *note*, The men who 'leg' the boat.. lie on their backs .. and propel it along by means of their feet pressing against the top or sides of the tunnel. *Ibid.* II. 421 After legging Harecastle Tunnel.. the men were usually completely exhausted. 1885 *Harper's Mag.* May 863/1 To 'leg through' this 'ere tunnel. 1891 V. C. Cotes *2 Girls on Barge* 86 A little .. boy was lying on his back, legging the boat along.

4. ***to leg up*** (a yacht): to shore up or support with legs or props when in dry harbour.

1886 R. C. Leslie *Sea-painter's Log* iv. 68 To lay ashore and leg-up a yacht.

5. a. To hit on the leg. (Cf. Wing *v.*)

1852 *Blackw. Mag.* LXXII. 303 Those [pebbles] aimed at his head and body he turned aside, and jumped over those that threatened to leg him.

b. To seize or hold by the leg.

1876 *Coursing Calendar* 149 Birkdale.. came round on the outside and legged the hare, which Stolen Moments killed. 1951 L. G. D. Acland *Early Canterbury Runs* 385 To *leg* a sheep is to haul him from the pen to the board by his hind leg, a practice much objected to, especially by owners of heavy sheep.

6. *dial.* and *slang.* To trip up (a person) by seizing his leg.

1882 *Sat. Rev.* 22 Apr. 488/1 The policeman ordered them to move on... Presently they 'legged the copper', and he fell to the ground.

7. *Cricket.* To send to leg.

1902 *Westm. Gaz.* 11 July 5/2 The newcomer at once started scoring... Nicholl followed him by legging Hopley to the covered stands. 1903 *Star* 8 July 3/4 His first ball was legged by Ranji for what would really have been 3 with a couple of smart sprinters.

legable, *a.* *rare*⁻⁰. [ad. mod.L. *lēgābilis*, f. L. *lēgāre* to bequeath.] (See quot.)

1721 Bailey, *Legable*, that is not intail'd as Hereditary, but may be bequeathed by Legacy.

legacy ('lɛgəsɪ), *sb.* Forms: 4 legasy, 4–7 -cie, 6 -cye, -sey, (*pl.* legaces), 7 leagacie, 5– legacy. [a. OF. *legacie* a legateship (see 1 b), = Sp. *legacía*, ad. med.L. *lēgātia* (see -acy) the district of a legate, f. *lēgātus* Legate *sb.*]

I. Legateship, legation.

†**1.** The function or office of a delegate or deputy. (Cf. Embassy 1.) *Obs.*

1382 Wyclif *2 Cor.* v. 20 Therfore we ben sett in legacie [L. *legatione fungimur*].. for Crist. 1555 Eden *Decades* 133 As I passed by in my legacie to the Soldane of Alcayr. 1563–83 Foxe *A. & M.* II. 1178/1 Who.. conferred.. with Tho. Cromwell to associat him in that legacie.

†**b.** *spec.* The function or office of a papal legate; a legateship. ***to send in legacy***: to send as legate. ***legacy of the cross***: see Legate *sb.*[1] 1.

1387 Trevisa *Higden* (Rolls) VIII. 260 Þis Baldewyn had þe office of legacie of the cros [L. *crucis legatione fungens*]. 1537 Throgmorton *Let. to Cromwell* in Froude *Hist. Eng.* (1858) III. 228, I suppose you have a great desire for a true knowledge of his mind and acts in this legacy. *a* 1548 Hall *Chron.* (1809) 448 Innocent Bishop of Rome had sent in legacye Adryan of Castella. *a* 1562 G. Cavendish *Wolsey* (1893) 174 A strawe, quoth my lord of Norfolk, for your legacye. 1577–87 Holinshed *Chron.* III. 920/1 Two great crosses of siluer, the one of his archbishoprike, the other of his legacie. 1726 Fiddes *Wolsey* ii. 189 There were no fires in Smithfield during his [Wolsey's] Legacy.

†**2.** The message or business committed to a delegate or deputy. *Obs.*

1550 Bale *Eng. Votaries* ii. 75 b, His legacye there performed, and all his bagges wele stuffed, he returned agayne to London. 1555 Eden *Decades* 75 Quicedus and Colmenaris were brought before the king and declared theyr legacie in his presence. 1573 *Satir. Poems Reform.* xlii. 602 God gave to þame giftis mair large Thair legacie for till discharge. 1599 Minsheu *Sp. Dict.*, *Legacia*, a legacy, an embassage, a message from a Prince. *c* 1611 Chapman *Iliad* vii. 349 He came, and told his Legacie. 1654 tr. *Martini's Conq. China* 113 This Legacy comming to nothing,.. both parties prepare to take the Field.

†**3.** A body of persons sent on a mission, or as a deputation, to a sovereign, etc.; also, the act of sending such a body. (Cf. Embassy 3.) *Obs.*

c 1375 *Sc. Leg. Saints* vii. (*Jacobus Minor*) 555 In þis sammyne tyme com legasy to vaspaciane reuerently. 1582 N.T. (Rheims) *Luke* xiv. 32 Otherwise whiles he is yet farre of, sending a legacie, he asketh those things that belong to peace. 1598 Hakluyt *Voy.* I. 125 Offa by often legacies solicited Charles le Maigne the king of France, to be his friend.

II. †**4.** The action or an act of bequeathing = Bequest 1. Also ***legacy parole***, nuncupative bequest. *Obs.*

1494 Fabyan *Chron.* vi. cciii. 213 Henry, than duke of Burgoyne.. bequethed his dukedome vnto Kyng Robert; but the Burgonyons withstode that legacy. 1606 Holland *Sueton.* 86 Sundry parcels gave hee besides by legacie parole.

5. A sum of money, or a specified article, given to another by will; = Bequest 2. †Formerly also in generalized sense, what one bequeaths.

c 1460 Henryson *Test. Creseid* 597 Quhen he had hard hir greit infirmite Hir legacy and lamentatioun. 1514 Pace *Let. to Wolsey* in Ellis *Orig. Lett.* Ser. iii. I. 176 To thin-tent they be not deprividde off suche legaces as my late lorde didde bequest unto them. 1577 H. I. tr. *Bullinger's Decades* ii. v. 162 Thou art left wealthie enough by thy fathers legacie, if yᵗ thou art godly, painful, heedful and honest. 1590 Swinburne *Treat. Testaments* 14 A Legacie.. is a gifte lefte by the deceased, to bee paide or performed by the Executor, or administrator. 1601 Shaks. *Jul. C.* iii. ii. 141 Bequeathing it as a rich Legacie Vnto their issue. *a* 1660 C. Maund in *Wood's Life* (O.H.S.) I. 350 *note*, I have given Mr. Powell 5*li.* for a legacie. 1770 *Junius Lett.* xl. 204 You have paid.. his legacy, at the hazard of ruining the estate. 1818 Cruise *Digest* (ed. 2) I. 528 It has been stated that a purchaser is bound to see to the payment of legacies. 1858 Ld. St. Leonards *Handy Bk. Prop. Law* xx. 155 The residue greatly exceeded in value the aggregate amount of all the legacies.

b. *transf.* and *fig.*; esp. = anything handed down by an ancestor or predecessor.

c 1586 C'tess Pembroke *Ps.* lxxxix. x, His sonnes.. Shall find like blisse for legacie bequeathed. 1697 Dryden *Æneid* x. 1263 Forbear thy Threats, my Bus'ness is to dye; But first receive this parting Legacy, He said; And straight a whirling Dart he sent. 1711 Addison *Spect.* No. 166 ⁋3 Books are the legacies that a great Genius leaves to mankind. 1845 Ford *Handbk. Spain* i. 9 One of the many fatal legacies left to Spain by the French, was [etc.]. 1850 Tennyson *In Mem.* lxxxiv, Leaving great legacies of thought, Thy spirit should fail from off the globe. 1863 W. G. Blaikie *Better Days Working People* v. (1864) 117 The difficulty has left sundry legacies behind it.

6. *attrib.* and *Comb.*, as ***legacy-duty***; **legacy-hunter, -monger**, one who pays court to old and rich persons in hope of obtaining a legacy; so ***legacy-hunting***.

1810 W. Campbell (*title*) The Value of Annuities.. with the amount of the several Rates of *Legacy Duty, payable on the value of Annuities. 1894 Lely *Stat. Pract. Utility* 1263 *note*, Foreign or colonial personalty is liable to legacy duty if [etc.]. 1693 T. Power in *Dryden's Juvenal* (1697) 304 He exercises his Satyrical Vein upon the Hæredipetæ, or *Legacy-Hunters. 1828 Miss Mitford *Village* Ser. iii. 286 Her decline was rapid, and her latter days much tormented by legacy-hunters. 1794 Charlotte Smith *Wand. Warwick* 105 To stoop to the pitiful expedient of *legacy-hunting. 1647 Stapylton *Juvenal* 287 Which made Coranus, like a common captator or *legacy-monger, court his owne sonne.

†'**legacy**, *v.* *Obs.* Also 6 legace, -asy. [f. prec.]

1. *trans.* To send as a legate.

1563 Foxe *A. & M.* 1373/2 You are legasyd by thautoritie of the Pope.

2. a. To give or leave as a legacy. **b.** To bequeath a legacy to.

1546 *Wills & Inv. N.C.* (Surtees 1835) 126 The reste of all my goodes not beinge legaced noʳ gyuen. 1594 Nashe *Unfort. Trav.* Wks. (Grosart) V. 185 Where yet liuing, hee might behold his flesh legacied amongst the foules of the aire. 1623 tr. *Favine's Theat. Hon.* ix. vi. 392 Inheritances might be legacied to them. 1643 Sir T. Browne *Relig. Med.* ii. §3 My acquired parts must perish with my self, nor can be Legacied among my honoured Friends. 1798 Jane Austen *Northang. Abb.* (1833) II. xv. 206 Her intimacy there had made him seriously determined on her being handsomely legacied hereafter. 1886 A. G. Murdoch *Readings* Ser. i. (ed. 2) 29 The ten pounds legacied to.. Kate Dalrymple.

legal ('liːgəl), *a.* [ad. L. *lēgālis* (perh. through F. *légal*, recorded from 14th c.), f. *lēg-*, *lēx* law. The popular OF. representative of the L. adj. was *leial*, *loial*: see Leal, Loyal.]

1. a. Of or pertaining to law; falling within the province of law.

1529 More *Dyaloge* i. Wks. 161/2 Albeit the matter of the precepte is morall and the daie legall, so that it maie be chaunged, yet wil.. no man thinke [etc.]. 1665 Boyle *Occas. Refl.* Introd. Pref. (1848) 29 To make use of a Legal Artifice to hinder.. the Publication. 1671 Milton *Samson* 313 [God] hath full right to exempt Whomso it pleases him.. From National obstriction, without taint Of sin, or legal debt. 1728 Veneer *Sincere Penitent* Pref. 7 Sharp rebukes and legal severities. 1765 Blackstone *Comm.* I. i. 18 The rudiments of legal knowledge. 1818 Cruise *Digest* (ed. 2) VI. 238 A system of legal construction had been established in former cases. 1838 Thirlwall *Greece* IV. 135 One Menecles having raised some legal objection to the decree. 1844 H. H. Wilson *Brit. India* I. 241 Debarred from the aid of the legal advisers of the state. 1849 Macaulay *Hist. Eng.* iv. I. 452 His legal knowledge.. was merely such as he had picked up. 1861 Graham *Eng. Word Bk.* Introd. 8 Words of Latin origin relating to legal and military affairs. 1898 *Eclectic Mag.* LXVII. 603 Protected.. by skillful legal advice.

¶**b.** ***legal man***: = Law Latin *legalis homo*, a man who has full legal rights, being neither outlawed, excommunicated, nor in any way disqualified from appearing in courts of law. So ***legal person***.

1660 R. Coke *Power & Subj.* 183 Let the Minister of the Bishop and his Clerks come thither.. with legal men of that province. 1689 S. Johnson *Rem. Sherlock's Bk.* 40 The next thing requisite to a Person being Commissionated is that he be a Legal Person.

c. Belonging to or characteristic of the profession of the law.

1819 Byron *Juan* i. clxiv, As he [the attorney] revolv'd the case, The door was fasten'd in his legal face. 1837 Dickens *Pickw.* lv, As all this here property is a wery great temptation to a legal gen'l'm'n. *Mod.* Whether he is a lawyer or not, he seems to have a legal mind.

d. *nonce-uses.* Observant of law; devoted to law.

1872 Bagehot *Physics & Pol.* (1876) 218 Each generation must be born better tamed, more calm, more capable of civilisation—in a word, more legal than the one before it. 1873 Stubbs *Const. Hist. Eng.* (1896) II. xiv. 111 Edward was by instinct a lawgiver, and he lived in a legal age.

e. ***legal cap***: ruled writing paper used chiefly for legal documents. *U.S.*

a 1877 Knight *Dict. Mech.* I. 455/2 Foolscap and legal cap are of various sizes, from 7½ × 12 to the size of a flat cap-sheet folded 8½ × 14. 1902 W. N. Harben *Abner Daniel* i. 3 Old man Bishop.. was carefully reading a long document written on legal-cap paper. 1937 E. J. Labarre *Dict. Paper* 142 *Legal cap*, a size of paper 14″ × 8½″.

f. ***legal beagle, eagle***, rhyming collocations designating a lawyer, *spec.* one who is keen and astute.

1949 *Law Library Jrnl.* XLII. 187/1 Legal Eagles and Stuffed Owls in Detroit. 1953 B. Glemser *Dove on his Shoulder* xii. 230 Since these letters are evidence they ought to be handed over to our legal beagles. 1961 I. T. Ross *Requiem for Schoolgirl* vii. 118 He's got some sort of legal beagle who protects him. 1963 N. Freeling *Because of Cats* vii. 116 According to the legal eagles you'll never get away with prosecuting them. 1967 Wodehouse *Company for Henry* vii. 117 You allowed your mind to wander when the legal eagle was doing his stuff. 1968 M. Allingham *Cargo of Eagles* iv. 57 That's the only good thing I've ever heard about your infernal legal eagle. 1974 *Economist* 30 Nov. 75 Legal eagles agree... The meeting, only the second of the justice council in EEC history.., was civilised.

g. ***legal positivism***: see Positivism.

2. a. Such as is required or appointed by law; founded upon law; deriving authority from law. ***legal aid***: official assistance allowed under certain conditions towards the expense of litigation (cf. Aid *sb.* 2 and 2 b); ***legal capacity***: the authority under law of a person to engage in a particular undertaking, or maintain a particular status; ***legal charity***: relief dispensed under the Poor Laws; ***legal fiction***: see Fiction 5 a; ***legal memory*** (see quots.).

1610 Healey *St. Aug. Citie of God* xxi. viii. (1620) 793 What more legall and fixed order doth any part of nature keepe? 1651 Baxter *Inf. Bapt.* 14 It [a marriage] is not compleat till the legall conjunction or solemnizing. *a* 1680 Butler *Rem.* (1759) I. 202 Assume the legal Right to disengage From all it had contracted under Age. 168. in Somers *Tracts* I. 273 It is not enough to say that it is a legal House without them; for a House of Commons of forty Persons is a legal House. 1751 Johnson *Rambler* No. 153 ⁋11 Preparing to take a legal possession of his fortune. 1766 Blackstone *Comm.* II. ii. iii. 31 It seems unaccountable,

that the date of legal prescription or memory should still continue to be reckoned from an aera so very antiquated. **1771** *Junius Lett.* xliv. 239 There is no..legal power without a legal course to carry it into effect. **1834** HT. MARTINEAU *Moral* II. 67 There are many who believe that an immediate abolition of our legal charity would cause less misery than its long continuance. **1844** H. H. WILSON *Brit. India* I. 447 All disputes were referable to legal tribunals. **1861** Legal fiction [see FICTION 5 a]. **1875** JEVONS *Money* (1878) 207 A bill of lading entitles the legal holder of it to certain..packages of goods. **1876** Legal fiction [see FICTION 5 a]. **1882** *Encycl. Brit.* XIV. 650/1 By the Statute of Westminster the First,..the beginning of the reign of Richard I. was fixed as the date of limitation for such actions. This is the well known 'period of legal memory'. **1882** C. SWEET *Dict. Eng. Law* 525 When a person alleges in legal proceedings, that a custom or prescription has existed from time whereof the memory of man runneth not to the contrary..this is..called time of living memory, as opposed to time of legal memory, which runs from the commencement of the reign of Richard I. **1890** (*title*) Constitution and bye-laws of the Deutsche Rechts-Schutz Verein (German Legal Aid Society). **1890** LELY & GEARY *Chitty's Pract. Treat. Law of Contracts* (ed. 12) vii. 194 The age of twenty-one years..has been fixed, as the period when an absolute and unlimited legal capacity to contract shall commence. **1903** *Act 3 Edw. VII* c. xxxviii. §1 Where it appears..desirable in the interests of justice that [any poor prisoner] should have legal aid in the preparation and conduct of his defence, and that his means are insufficient to enable him to obtain such aid..the committing justices..may certify that the prisoner ought to have such legal aid. **1928** Legal aid [see INTERSTATE *a.*]. **1937** R. H. LOWIE *Hist. Ethnol. Theory* v. 51 The same holds for the principle of legal fiction, which Maine also treated at length. **1959** *Daily Tel.* 18 Mar. 19/6 In eight years legal aid has been given to more than 238,000 litigants. **1966** BLACK & BROWN *Outl. Eng. Law* v. 43 Sometimes such a presumption takes the form of a *Legal Fiction*. For instance if two persons die in such a way that it is uncertain which of them died first the law presumes..that the younger outlived the older. **1967** E. RUDINGER *Wills & Probate* 91 The other [leaflet] explained how to get legal advice under the legal aid scheme. **1968** *Lebende Sprachen* XIII. 82/2 The customer will bear any loss incurred by the bank resulting from the fact that the bank..does not obtain knowledge of any restrictions of the customer's..legal capacity. **1969** J. B. SAUNDERS *Words & Phrases legally Defined* (ed. 2) IV. 171/1 By the ancient rule of the common law, enjoyment of an easement has to be proved from time 'whereof the memory of man runneth not to the contrary', that is to say, during legal memory or since the commencement of the reign of Richard I. **1971** 'M. UNDERWOOD' *Trout in Milk* ii. 27 Thanks to 'legal aid' it was much easier to get started at the criminal than the civil Bar. **1972** *Times* 28 Jan. 16/4 All concerned—the parties' advisers, the legal aid committees, ..—should put children's cases at the top of the list.

b. ***legal tender***: coin or other money, which a creditor is bound by law to accept, when tendered in payment of a debt. Also *attrib.*

1740 W. DOUGLASS *Disc. Curr. Brit. Plant. Amer.* 6 The Court of France were obliged to ordain, that there should be no other legal Tender but Silver-Coin. **1816** *Act 56 Geo. III*, c. 68 §12 Whereas it is expedient that the Silver Coin of the Realm should be a legal Tender by Tale,..to any Amount not exceeding the Sum of Forty Shillings. **1833** *Act 3 & 4 Will. IV*, c. 98 §6 A Tender of a Note or Notes of the ..Bank of England..shall be a legal Tender, to the Amount expressed in such Note or Notes. **1865** H. PHILLIPS *Amer. Paper Curr.* II. 49 The Virginia convention had made the continental bills a legal tender. **1870** *Act. 33 Vict.* c. 10 §4 A tender of payment of money..shall be a legal tender—In the case of gold coins for the payment of any amount: In the case of silver coins for a payment of an amount not exceeding forty shillings... In the case of bronze coins for a payment of an amount not exceeding one shilling. **1870** *N. Amer. Rev.* Jan. 8 The objectionable features of legal-tender laws.

c. That is such in the eye of the law.

1840 DICKENS *Old C. Shop* xxxvi, Miss Brass..had passed her life in a kind of legal childhood.

d. Such as is recognized by 'law' as distinguished from 'equity'.

1818 CRUISE *Digest* (ed. 2) I. 386 Having treated of legal and customary estates, we now come to discuss the nature and properties of what are called equitable estates. **1827** JARMAN *Powell's Devises* II. 153 A general devise of real estate..passed the legal estate in lands of which the devisor was mortgagee in fee. **1875** DIGBY *Real Prop.* vii. §4. 293 The legal estate is vested in the trustee, in trust for the *cestui que* trust, who has the equitable estate.

3. Permitted, or not forbidden, by law; lawful.

1647 CLARENDON *Hist. Reb.* I. §11 It is as legal..for the king to pardon, as for the party to accuse. **1671** L. ADDISON *W. Barbary* 35 His fourth was a Virgin Daughter of.., which made up the legal number of four, so many being allowed by their Prophet. **1691** LOCKE *Lower. Interest* (1692) 9 The Lender..will rather lend it to the Banker at the legal Interest, than [etc.]. **1817** W. SELWYN *Law Nisi Prius* (ed. 4) II. 970 If it were a legal capture, they were entitled [to a return of premium]. **1844** H. H. WILSON *Brit. India* III. 260 The periods fixed for the regular gaol-deliveries had been protracted beyond the legal limits. **1849** RUSKIN *Sev. Lamps* iv. §14. 106 Those false forms of decoration which are most dangerous in our modern architecture as being legal and accepted.

4. *Theol.* **a.** Of or pertaining to the Mosaic law; existing under or founded upon that law. **b.** Of, pertaining to, concerned with, or based upon the law of works, i.e. salvation by works, as opposed to salvation by faith. †Of persons: Upholding the law of works.

?*a* **1500** *Chester Pl.* viii. 290 Rites Ceremoniall of the old Testament, with legall obseruacon shall vtterly cease. **1640** J. DYKE *Worthy Commun.* 195 Paul..for legall righteousnesse, a man before men unblameable. *a* **1652** J. SMITH *Sel. Disc.* vii. 349 Under the gospel there are many that do judaize, are of as legal and servile spirits as the Jews. **1659** PEARSON *Creed* (1839) 184 Neither could he be opposed to the legal priest, as not dying himself, but giving another. **1666** BUNYAN *Grace Ab.* ¶45 These [Ranters] would..condemn me as legal and dark. **1756** LAW *Lett. Import. Subj.* 154 What folly to tell you, that you are only in a legal state, unless he could prove to you that [etc.]. **1786** A. GIB *Sacr. Contempl.* I. III. ii. 124 A legal bias toward a doing for life, in opposition to a believing on Christ for life. **1884** FAIRBAIRN *Catholicism* (1899) 26 Christ without any of the notes distinctive of sacerdotal and legal piety.

5. a. quasi-*sb.* Something connected with law; a legal formality; a legal notice. Also in *Sc. Law*, short for *legal reversion*: see REVERSION.

1526 *Pilgr. Perf.* (W. de W. 1531) 5 Our lorde wolde not that we sholde take the drosse of the lawe of Moyses, neyther the cerymonyes, nor legalles and customes. **1822** SCOTT *Fort. Nigel* x, If it [the money] is not raised, there will be an expiry of the legal, as our lawyers call it. **1896** *Daily News* 30 Dec. 10/2 A Gentleman who has influence with advertisers and is successful in obtaining Prospectuses, Legals, and Auctions.

b. The exact fare without any tip; a passenger who pays such a fare. Chiefly *taxi-drivers' slang*.

1923 J. MANCHON *Le Slang* 179 The legal = the legal fare. **1939** H. HODGE *Cab, Sir?* vii. 84 The last, and probably most common, cause of the inadvertent 'legal' is the super-sensitive meter. *Ibid.* 85 Some 'legals' are simply mean, and give excuses instead of a tip. **1963** M. LEVINSON *Taxi!* vii. 88 If his next passenger gives him another 'legal' (the exact fare) he will naturally take a very dim view.

legalese (liːgəˈliːz). *colloq.* [f. LEGAL *a.* + -ESE.] The complicated technical language of legal documents.

1914 C. J. C. HYNE *Firemen Hot* 189 He signed his name at the foot of a bald formal agreement, written in the most incomprehensible legalese. **1966** A. SACHS *Jail Diary* xvii. 155 After all these weeks I am not used to reading legalese any more. **1967** 'J. H. ROBERTS' *February Plan* I. iii. 81, I won't go into the legalese, Mr. Corman, but he claims he had a contract with you. **1973** *Black Panther* 5 May 13/3 Is it any measure of excellence to assemble glossy paragraphs of smart untried legalese? **1973** *N.Y. Times* 11 Aug., Gordon Strachan spoke openly of his resort to legalese.

legalism (ˈliːgəlɪz(ə)m). [f. LEGAL + -ISM.]

1. *Theol.* Applied reproachfully to the principles of those who are accused of adhering to the Law as opposed to the Gospel; the doctrine of justification by works, or teaching which savours of that doctrine.

1838 *Fraser's Mag.* XVII. 748 The theory of Dissenters is national legalism; the theory of Churchmen is national gospel. **1856** R. S. VAUGHAN *Mystics* (1860) II. x. i, The frigid legalism of the creed of Islam. **1861** TRENCH 7 *Ch. Asia* 83 The first great battle which the Church had to fight was with Jewish legalism. **1876** *Macm. Mag.* XXXIV. 533 A new system of Christian legalism arose which reigned for centuries. **1901** *Expositor* Jan. 12 It is by its relation to legalism that Paul has to define Christianity.

2. A disposition to exalt the importance of law or formulated rule in any department of action.

1878 R. H. HUTTON *Scott* i. 3 That disposition towards..legalism of mind. **1885** DICEY *Lect. Stud. Law Const.* 160 Federalism, lastly means legalism..the prevalence of a spirit of legality among the people. **1898** *Atlantic Monthly* LXXXII. 444/2 Englishmen and Americans..are profoundly influenced by the spirit of legalism.

legalist (ˈliːgəlɪst). [f. LEGAL + -IST.]

1. *Theol.* An adherent or advocate of legalism; one who believes in or inclines to the doctrine of justification by works.

1646 E. F[ISHER] *Mod. Divinity* Title-p., Wherein every one may cleerly see how far he..deserveth the name of Legalist. **1651** BAXTER *Saints' R.* I. i. §6 (ed. 2) 8 To make Salvation the end of Duty, is to be a Legalist. **1678** R. BARCLAY *Apol. Quakers* viii. §8. 252 There were no difference..betwixt those who are under the Gospel, and meer Legalists. **1826** J. JAY *Chr. Contemplated* III. 78 They were not Antinomians: they were not Legalists. **1860** TRENCH *Serm. Westm. Abb.* xxxii. 370 He is not afraid of being called a legalist, a preacher of good works, instead of a preacher of faith. **1879** FARRAR *St. Paul* II. 73 Becoming a Jew to the Jews, a legalist to legalists.

2. A stickler for legality.

1865 *Pall Mall G.* 19 Dec. 1 They are so far from being disorderly that they are the most prudish of legalists.

3. a. One versed in the law; one who views things from a legal standpoint.

1829 SOUTHEY *All for Love* IX. xxii, A sorry legalist were he Who could not in thy boasted plea Detect its fatal flaw. **1838** D. JERROLD *Men Charac., J. Runnymede* ii. Wks. 1864 III. 174 John, however, could not silently assent to the position of the legalist. **1861** GEN. P. THOMPSON *Audi Alt.* III. clxvi. 187 No legalist dares maintain that [etc.]. **1897** FAIRBAIRN *Catholicism* (1899) 473 The whole attitude was..that of the legalist rather than the moralist.

b. An officer of the law; a bailiff. *jocular.*

1835 *Blackw. Mag.* XXXVII. 867 The prostrate legalist ..lay motionless.

Hence ˌ**legaˈlistic** *a.*, of or pertaining to a legalist; characterized by legalism.

1882-3 SCHAFF *Encycl. Relig. Knowl.* III. 1770 Legalistic Jewish Christians. **1894** *Thinker* V. 439 Malachi was compelled to raise his voice against the extreme legalistic standpoint.

legality (lɪˈgælɪtɪ). Also 5 **legalite**, 6 **legalitee**. [ad. (directly or through) F. *légalité*, med.L. *lēgālis*, f. L. *lēgālis* LEGAL.]

1. Attachment to or observance of law or rule.

c **1460** G. ASHBY *Dicta Philos.* 1126 Poems 94 A[nd] for trouthe a[nd] noble legalite [L. *et propter veritatem et legalitatem*]. **1656** BLOUNT *Glossogr.*, *Legality*, the keeping the Law. **1849** RUSKIN *Sev. Lamps* iii. §3. 65 Much contest between two schools, one affecting originality, and the other legality. **1859** MILL *Liberty* ii. (1865) 29/1 It made an idol of asceticism, which has been gradually compromised away into one of legality.

b. *Theol.* Insistence on the letter of the law; reliance on works for salvation, rather than on free grace. Also *personified*.

1678 BUNYAN *Pilgr.* I. 29 He to whom thou wast sent for ease, being by name Legality. **1771** FLETCHER *Checks* Wks. 1795 II. 200, I have heard them cry out against the Legality of their wicked hearts.

c. The spirit or way of thinking characteristic of the legal profession; *pl.* points of manner or speech indicative of this.

1880 W. CORY *Mod. Eng. Hist.* I. 225 Legality delights in the ingenious contrivance of delays. **1893** D. C. MURRAY *Time's Revenges* III. xlvii. 268 Their militarisms and legalities made the more..sentimental-minded folk altogether ill at ease.

2. The quality of being legal or in conformity with the law; lawfulness. In early use, Legitimacy.

1533-4 *Act 25 Hen. VIII*, c. 22 §1 The right legalitee of the succession. **1637** C. DOW *Innov. Charged upon Ch. & State* Pref., The legality of the bishops exercising their jurisdictions. **1642** FULLER *Holy & Prof. St.* III. xiii. 183 In these, as in all doubtful recreations, be well assured first of the legality of them. *a* **1677** BARROW *Pope's Suprem.* (1680) 340 By signifying their approbation..concerning..the legality of their Ordination. **1792** SIR W. H. ASHURST in *Term Rep.* IV. 595 The expences of litigating the legality of the fine. **1838** THIRLWALL *Greece* III. 339 The legality of their conduct had been virtually recognised by the Eleans. **1863** H. COX *Instit.* I. ix. 213 To try the legality of the proceedings..against him. **1871** FREEMAN *Norm. Conq.* (1876) IV. xvii. 54 It was the master-piece of William's policy of outward legality.

3. *pl.* Obligations imposed by law.

1855 *Cornwall* 243 Mines not so conducted are established under the provision of the joint-stock act, and shareholders in them become liable to its legalities.

4. *slang.* The name of a gambling game.

1888 *Pall Mall G.* 30 May 2/2 Betting on the tape is quite a tame affair in comparison to 'legality'..At the 'legality' table I saw a person, whom I [etc.].

legalize (ˈliːgəlaɪz), *v.* [f. LEGAL + -IZE.]

1. *trans.* To make legal or conformable to law; to invest with the authority of law; to authorize, justify, sanction.

a **1716** SOUTH *Serm.* (1723) VII. 75 The conditions required to legalize such a defence of ourselves and fortunes. **1791** MACKINTOSH *Vind. Gallic.* Wks. 1846 III. 143 It..could not..legalise the acts of the body which created it. **1824**—— *Sp. Ho. Com.* 1 June ibid. 410 We may now be said annually to legalise military law. **1860** HOOK *Lives Abps.* I. i. 2 There was a period in our history..when oppression was legalised. **1884** SIR H. HAWKINS in *Law Times Rep.* L. 816/1 The intention of the Legislature to legalise..mere games of skill.

2. To imbue with the spirit of the (Mosaic) law; to pervert in the spirit of legalism. *rare.*

1774 FLETCHER *Grace & Justice* Wks. 1795 IV. 181 What, will you still persist to legalize the gospel?

¶**3.** *intr.* To practise as a lawyer. *nonce-use.*

1855 *Cornwall* 244 Jobson still legalizes in Gray's Inn.

Hence ˈ**legaliˌzation**, the action of legalizing.

1805 W. TAYLOR in *Ann. Rev.* III. 286 As soon as he has completed the form of legalization. **1848** MILL *Pol. Econ.* III. xxxiii. §3 (1876) 389 The legalization of joint stock associations with limited liability. **1862** M. HOPKINS *Hawaii* 373 The open encouragement and legalisation of vice.

legalized (ˈliːgəlaɪzd), *ppl. a.* [f. LEGALIZE + -ED[1].]

1. Made legal, sanctioned by law. Of a wife: Legally married.

1788 H. WALPOLE *Remin.* ii. 20 The extreme outward devotion of the duchess..seems to announce a legalized wife. **1806** *Weekly Polit. Rev.* 27 Dec. 947 The recruiting service, this legalized crimping. **1828** SEWELL *Oxford Prize Ess.* 2 Legalized facilities for divulging the property and resources of individuals. **1878** DOWDEN *Stud. Lit.* 332 The Church remained in the legalised servitude to which Napoleon had reduced it.

2. Imbued with the legal spirit.

1818 SCOTT *Hrt. Midl.* ix, The doctrines of a legalised formalist, such as Saddletree.

legally (ˈliːgəlɪ), *adv.* [f. LEGAL + -LY[2].] In a legal manner; according to law, lawfully. Also, in a legal sense; from the point of view of law.

1561 T. NORTON *Calvin's Inst.* III. xxii. (1634) 460 Hee..bindeth not himselfe with a certaine law to call all men legallie. **1622** T. SCOTT *Belg. Pismire* 1 That man might..performe actions.. legally according to a rule. **1647** CLARENDON *Hist. Reb.* II. §68 The King was as Legally possessed of that Right, as of any thing else he had. **1713** BERKELEY *Hylas & Ph.* iii. Wks. 1871 I. 332 Putting a criminal legally to death, is not thought sinful. **1766** GOLDSM. *Vic. W.* xxxi, I never was legally married to any woman. **1818** CRUISE *Digest* (ed. 2) VI. 24 His trustees would be legally seised according to the uses of his will. **1834** PRINGLE *Afr. Sk.* v. 190 The laws of Holland had..prohibited the aborigines from being legally sold. **1845** S. AUSTIN *Ranke's Hist. Ref.* II. 213 They determined to pursue the matter legally before the judges.

ˈ**legalness.** *rare.* [f. LEGAL + -NESS.] = LEGALITY (in quot. sense 1 b).

a **1665** J. GOODWIN *Filled w. the Spirit* (1867) 387 They impute legalness, as they call it..to the ministry, under which they have no mind to continue. **1727** in BAILEY (vol. II).

legantine (ˈlɛgəntɪn), *a.* [as if ad. Lat. type **lēgantīnus*, f. *lēgant-*, pr. pple. of *lēgāre*: see

LEGATE and -INE.] Incorrect synonym of LEGATINE.

1533–4 *Act 25 Hen. VIII*, c. 21 §1 Jurisdictions legantine. *a* **1562** G. CAVENDISH *Wolsey* (1893) 65 There was made a solempne procession, and my lord Cardynall went presently in the same, apparelled in his legantyn ornaments. **1641** MILTON *Animadv.* Wks. 1851 III. 229 Sending..Bishops and Archbishops..with a kind of Legantine power. **1759** HUME *Hist. Eng.* (1778) IV. 16 Wolsey..erected an office, which he called the legantine court. **1769** ROBERTSON *Chas. V*, III. XI. 304 To exercise his legantine functions with the most ample power. **1847** YEOWELL *Anc. Brit. Ch.* xi. 118 The summons..to attend a legantine Council. **1868** STANLEY *Westm. Abb.* vi. (ed. 2) 517 They met..under his [Wolsey's] Legantine authority.

legar, obs. form of LEDGER.

†**lega'tarian**, *a. Obs. rare*$^{-1}$. [f. med.L. *lēgātāri-us* (f. *lēgātus* LEGATE) + -AN.] Of or pertaining to a legate or deputy.

1766 AMORY *J. Buncle* (1770) IV. 83 Jesus Christ came with a legatarian power from God, the Supreme Being, to declare his will to mankind.

legatary ('lɛgətərɪ), *a.* and *sb.* Also 6–7 **legatarie**, 6, 8 **legatory**, (7 **ligatory**, 8 **legotary**). [ad. L. *lēgātārius*, f. *lēgāt-um* a bequest, f. *lēgāre* to bequeath.]

A. *adj.* Of or pertaining to a bequest; of the nature of a bequest.

1676 R. DIXON *Two Testaments* 30 The Promissory and Legatary part thereof [Gods Testament] was the second time confirmed by a solemn Oath. **1818** CRUISE *Digest* (ed. 2) VI. 201 The testator intended to use his subsequent words of recommendation in a legatary sense.

B. *sb.* One to whom a bequest is left; a legatee.

1542 RECORDE *Gr. Artes* (1575) 411 The mind of the Testatour is to be taken fauorably, for the ayde of the legataries [**1646** ligatories] when there ryseth suche doubts. **1570** DEE *Math. Pref.* 11 Contributed by the legataries to the heire. **1615** DONNE *Serm.* cxlii. V. 538 But if those goods be liable to other debts, the legataries shall have no profit. **1700** *Rhode Isl. Col. Rec.* (1858) III. 424 If any executor shall refuse or neglect to appear..upon the complaint of a legatory. **1726** AYLIFFE *Parergon* 21 As when a Man makes his Debtor his universal Heir or Legatary. **1795** WYTHE *Decis. Virginia* 26 The Law supposes the benevolence of the testator toward the legatary to have continued. **1802** *Levity & Sorrow* II. 148 (F.H.) Legatary.

legate ('lɛgət), *sb.*¹ Also 2–7 **legat**, (6 **lyget**). [a. OF. *legat*, ad. L. *lēgātus*, pa. pple. of *lēgāre* to send as a deputy (also, to bequeath).]

1. An ecclesiastic deputed to represent the Pope and armed with his authority. † ***legate of the cross***: one entitled to have a cross borne before him, as an emblem of dignity.

1154 *O.E. Chron.* an. 1123 (Laud MS.) On þa ilca tyma com an Legat of Rome Henri wæs ȝehaten. *c* **1205** LAY. 24501 Of Rome he wes legat and of þan hirede prelat. *a* **1300** *Cursor M.* 29358 Alle þaa lais hand on clerk behouis ga to þe pape or his legate, to soilled be. **1387** TREVISA *Higden* (Rolls) II. 115 Bonefas, archebisshop of Canterbury, þat was legat of þe croys. **1516** *Plumpton Corr.* (Camden) 217 Ther comes a lyget from Rome to my lord Cartdenall. **1595** SHAKS. *John* v. ii. 65 Looke where the holy Legate comes apace. **1638** *Penit. Conf.* xii. (1657) 323 In his dayes there entred this Kingdom a Legat from Rome. *a* **1745** SWIFT *Hist. Stephen* in *Lett.* (1768) IV. 291 Henry the youngest was bishop of Winchester, and the pope's legate in England. **1754** HUME *Hist. Eng.* (1762) I. 244 The Pope..made the archbishop of Canterbury his legate. **1875** TENNYSON *Q. Mary* III. i, I hear this Legate's coming To bring us absolution from the Pope.

b. The ruler of a legation, i.e. one of the provinces of the Papal States.

1653 H. COGAN *Scarlet Gown* 85 Urban..sent him Legate to the City of Ferrara. **1670** G. H. tr. *Hist. Cardinals* II. III. 188 At present he is Legat of Ferrara, a considerable Legation. **1756–7** tr. *Keysler's Trav.* (1760) III. 243 The most illustrious Domenico Maria Cursi being legate..of Ravenna.

c. ***legate a*** (or †***de***) ***latere*** (†also in semi-English or English form, ***of latere***, ***of the side***): the designation of a legate of the highest class, one whose acts are regarded as virtually those of the Pope himself.

1521 ABP. WARHAM in Ellis *Orig. Lett.* Ser. III. I. 239 Which wer forboden by your Graces auctoritie as Legate de latere of the See apostolique. **1528** ROY *Rede me* (Arb.) 50 He hath a tytle of S. Cecile, And is a Legate of latere. *a* **1550** *Image Ipocr.* IV. 28 in *Skelton's Wks.* (1843) II. 439 And then the Cardinall With tytles all of pride, As legates of the side. **1554** *Act 1 & 2 Ph. & Mary* c. 8 §1 The Pope's Holiness..sent hither..the Lord Cardinal Pool, Legate *de latere*. **1670** G. H. tr. *Hist. Cardinals* I. III. 77 Any Cardinal that goes *Legat a latere* to any Foreign State. **1708** *Lond. Gaz.* No. 4444/2 The Pope chang'd his design of sending a Legate Latere to her Majesty. **1839** KEIGHTLEY *Hist. Eng.* I. 133 A further hardship was the sending of special ministers, legates 'a latere'.

transf. **1618** T. ADAMS *Heaven made sure* Wks. (1629) 904 These [God's ministers] are *Legatia latere*—Dispencers of the Mysteries of Heauen.

2. *gen.* An ambassador, delegate, messenger.

1382 WYCLIF *Isa.* lvii. 9 Thou..sentist thi legates aferr. *c* **1400** *Destr. Troy* 5038 The dishonour ye did to my dere legat. *c* **1450** *St. Cuthbert* (Surtees) 2732 Legates with letters aftir him went. **1579** LYLY *Euphues* (Arb.) 146 A certaine Gentleman heere in Athens invited the kings Legats to a costly and sumptuous feast. **1671** L. ADDISON *W. Barbary* 119 We gave also to your Legates two special horses. **1692** S. PATRICK *Answ. Touchstone* 18 The Apostles were the Legats and Interpreters of Christ. **1784** COWPER *Task* ii. 338 There stands The legate of the skies. **1855** MOTLEY *Dutch Rep.* III. v. II. 291 He suffered the legates from Utrecht to return..with their heads upon their shoulders.

3. *Rom. Hist.* The deputy or lieutenant of a general, or of the governor of a province; under the empire, the governor himself. Also *transf.*

1474 CAXTON *Chesse* 45 The rookes ben vycayrs and legates of the kynge. **1577–87** HARRISON *Descr. Brit.* x. in Holinshed *Chron.* I. 31 It [Wight] was..wonne from the Britons by Vespasian the legat. **1601** R. JOHNSON *Kingd. & Commw.* (1603) 120 With the armie they sende divers of their gentlemen as Legats or providitors, who never stirre from the side of the captaine Generall. **1869** RAWLINSON *Anc. Hist.* 483 The legates who commanded legions upon the frontiers.

† **'legate**, *sb.*² *Obs.* Also **legatte**. [a. OF. *legat* = It. *legato*, ad. L. *lēgātum*, neut. pa. pple. of *lēgāre* to bequeath.] A legacy or bequest.

1447 *Rolls of Parl.* V. 129/2 John Brokley..by his Testament..made other diversez Legatez to diversez persones, grete and notable. **1479** J. PASTON in *P. Lett.* No. 849 III. 267 The funeral costes, dettes, and legattes. **1501** *Bury Wills* (Camden) 91 These my legattes herin conteynyth truly fulfyllyd. *c* **1530** *Pol. Rel. & L. Poems* 32 In dysposyng thy legatys, pay firste thy servanntis.

legate (liː'geɪt), *v.* Also 6 **leggett**. [f. L. *lēgāt-*, ppl. stem of *lēgāre*.] *trans.* To give by will, to bequeath. Often, ***to give and legate***.

1546 *Will* in *Trans. Cumbld. & Westmld. Arch. Soc.* X. 26, I gif and leggett vnto Richerd my sonn all my housholde stuf. **1582** *Will of R. Milles* (Consistory Crt. Canterbury), The towe hundred poundes to them legated shall..come wholy vnto my sonne Thomas. **1671** *True Nonconf.* 497 Legating peace as his proper blessing to all his followers. **1880** MUIRHEAD *Gaius* Digest 528 There were four forms of legating,—vindication, damnation, permission, and preception. **1888** *Law Rep., Ho. Lords* XIII. 376 The oval inlaid table I legate to——.

† **'legate**, *pa. pple. north. Obs.* [ad. L. *lēgātus*, pa. pple. of *lēgā-re* to bequeath.] Legated, disposed of by will.

1533 *Wills & Inv. N.C.* (Surtees 1835) 111 The resydue of my goodes not legate nor bequest.

legatee (ˌlɛgə'tiː), *sb.* [f. LEGATE *v.* + -EE¹.] A person to whom a legacy has been bequeathed.

1679–88 *Secr. Serv. Money Chas. & Jas.* (Camden) 99 Thomas Hayter, a legatee to John Moorhouse. **1693** T. POWER in *Dryden's Juvenal* xii. (1697) 313 The former Legatees are blotted out. **1781** COWPER *Charity* 45 Mammon makes the world his legatee Through fear, not love. **1822** HAZLITT *Table-t.* I. xii. 281 Legacies and fortunes left, on condition that the legatee shall take the name and style of the testator. **1880** MUIRHEAD *Ulpian* xxiv. §20 A legacy cannot be charged on a legatee.

Hence †ˌ**lega'tee** *v. rare*$^{-1}$, *trans.*, to hand over to a legatee, to transfer by will.

1797 *Stat. Acc. Scotl.* XIX. 189 A mortification, legateed by Mr. John Kemp.

legateship ('lɛgət-ʃɪp). [f. LEGATE *sb.*¹ + -SHIP.] The dignity and office of a legate.

1556 *Chron. Gr. Friars* (Camden) 96 Thomas Creme some tyme archebyshoppe of Cantorbery..was desgraded of hys leggatsheppe. **1653** H. COGAN *Scarlet Gown* 86 In his Legateship of Ferrara he carried himself very wisely. **1774** J. COLLYER *Hist. Eng.* II. 203 The cardinal Anagni..had succeeded Albano in the legateship. **1876** TENNYSON *Q. Mary* v. v, The Holy Father Has ta'en the legateship from our cousin Pole.

'legatess, *nonce-wd.* A female legate.

1827 CARLYLE *Germ. Rom.* III. 212 She was..his Castle-Stewardess, and Legatess *a Latere* for his domestics.

legatine ('lɛgətɪn), *a.* [f. LEGATE *sb.*¹ + -INE¹. Substituted for the earlier LEGANTINE and LEGATIVE.] Of or pertaining to a legate; having the authority of a legate. ***legatine constitution*** (see quot. 1765). ***legatine synod***: one held under the presidency of a (papal) legate.

1611 SPEED *Hist. Gt. Brit.* IX. viii. 487/2 [The Papal Legate] studied to make vpp that by his Legatine Glory which hee wanted by his Princes countenance. **1630** tr. *Camden's Hist. Eliz.* Introd. 3 The Bishops..had acknowledged his Legatine authority, in preiudice of the Kings pre-eminence. **1647** N. BACON *Disc. Govt. Eng.* I. viii. 26 This was allowed of by Offa the great in a legatine Synod. **1754** HUME *Hist. Eng.* (1761) I. viii. 178 Becket had obtained from the pope a legatine commission over England. **1765** BLACKSTONE *Comm.* I. 82 The legatine constitutions were ecclesiastical laws, enacted in national synods, held under the cardinals Otho and Othobon, legates from pope Gregory IX and pope Clement IV. **1879** MISS YONGE *Cameos* IV. iii. 36 Having accepted the legatine commission without the King's consent. **1883** C. BEARD *Reform.* ix. 308 The acceptance by the clergy of Wolsey's legatine authority.

legation (lɪ'geɪʃən). Also 5–6 **legacion**, **-yon**. [ad. L. *lēgātiōn-em*, n. of action f. *lēgāre*: see LEGATE *sb.*¹ Cf. F. *legation*, Sp. *legacion*, Pg. *legação*, It. *legazione*.]

1. The action of sending a deputy or representative, esp. a (papal) legate; the fact of his being so sent. Also, † ***to send in legation***.

1460 CAPGRAVE *Chron.* (Rolls) 260 To whech Parlement cam the duke of Gloucetir fro Yrlond expressing the Kyngis costis in Yrlond; and his legacion was so acceptabil, that the clergy graunted him a dyme, and the lay fe a fiftene. **1649** JER. TAYLOR *Gt. Exemp.* II. x. 1 To the Priests and Levites sent in legation from the Sanhedrim, he professed that himself was not the Christ. **1738** WARBURTON (*title*) The Divine Legation of Moses. **1794** SULLIVAN *View Nat.* II. 214 The object of Moses was to support his divine legation. **1875** STUBBS *Const. Hist.* III. xviii. 108 The legation of a cardinal was..bound up in the popular mind with heavy fees.

2. The object for which an ambassador or legate is sent, his mission or commission.

1470–85 MALORY *Arthur* v. viii, [They] wente toward Rome and shewed theyr legacyon & message to the potestate and Senate. **1490** CAXTON *Eneydos* xxii. 77 Anne her [Dido's] suster went incontynent towarde eneas, to make unto him her feble legacion. **1494** FABYAN *Chron.* VI. clix. 148 The sayde Lewys..gaue answers concernynge theyr legacions and messagys. **1530** PALSGR. 238/1 Legation, a message, *legation*. **1660** R. COKE *Power & Subj.* 144 Alfred ..could not give any assent to their legation. **1855** MILMAN *Lat. Chr.* IX. ii. (1864) V. 208 Innocent had chosen a German by birth, perhaps from his knowledge of the language, for this important Legation.

3. *concr.* The body of deputies sent on a mission; a diplomatic minister and his suite. Now chiefly (exc. in ***secretary of legation***) used when the minister has not the titular rank of 'ambassador'.

1603 *North's Plutarch* (1612) 1161 (*Cæsar Augustus*) Cornelius the Centiner chief of this legation or ambassade. **1619** VISCT. DONCASTER *Let.* in *Eng. & Germ.* (Camden) 148 To give him thankes for honoring this legation thus. **1756–7** tr. *Keysler's Trav.* (1760) IV. 420 A secretary of legation.. supplying their place. *a* **1859** MACAULAY *Hist. Eng.* xxiii. V. 74 The report which the English legations made of what they had seen and suffered in Russia.

b. The official residence of a diplomatic minister.

1832–3 *Reg. Deb. Congress U.S.* 22nd Congress 2 Sess. App. 90/2 The proceedings..are not recorded in the legation. *Ibid.*, The instructions are not in the legation [in London]. **1863** FORTUNE *Yedo & Peking* iv. 72 His Excellency..gave me quarters in the Legation. **1886** MISS GORDON CUMMING *Wand. China* II. 257 Really good robes ..are..offered for sale at all the Legations and other European dwellings. **1901** ALLEN *Siege Peking Legations* v. 113 Next morning we heard that the Belgian Legation had been burnt.

c. *attrib.*

1886 MISS GORDON CUMMING *Wand. China* II. 337 The recently restored Legation buildings. **1900** MARTIN *Siege in Peking* v. 84 The marines..were occupying commanding points on the legation walls, or making sorties from the legation gates. **1901** ALLEN *Siege Peking Legations* vi. 211 Answer was returned that the Legation guard were simply acting on the defensive.

4. The dignity and office of a legate (see LEGATE *sb.*¹ 1, 3); a legateship.

1603 KNOLLES *Hist. Turks* (1638) 93 By vertue of his Legation it belonged vnto him to dispose of all things taken in that sacred war. *a* **1639** SPOTTISWOOD *Hist. Ch. Scot.* II. (1677) 58 He had accepted a Legation from the Pope. **1701** W. WOTTON *Hist. Rome* 270 He was appointed to go as Legate to the Proconsul of Afric. That Legation being performed, Marcus [etc.]. **1855** MILMAN *Lat. Chr.* VII. iv. (1864) IV. 149 The Archbishop had..received from him the legation to France. **1864** W. FORSYTH *Cicero* (1867) 438 He wrote..to Anthony to request that he might have a legation given him.

5. Formerly, one of the provinces of the Papal States, governed by a legate.

1841 W. SPALDING *Italy & It. Isl.* III. 30 Deputies.. assembled in the end of 1796, and erected the two papal legations with the Modenese duchy into a commonwealth. **1848** W. H. KELLY tr. *L. Blanc's Hist. Ten Y.* I. 583 Cardinal Bernetti notified..his holiness's determination to send his troops into the legations.

†**6.** A gift by will, a legacy. *Obs. rare*$^{-1}$.

1586 FERNE *Blaz. Gentrie* 301 He..is bounde to beare the name,..by cause this is a condicionall legation or gift.

Hence **le'gation** *v. intr.*, to go on a legation. **le'gationary** *a.*, of or pertaining to a legation, qualified or ready to go on a legation.

1864 CARLYLE *Fredk. Gt.* IV. 460 Now Legationing in foreign parts. *Ibid.* 506 Plenty of legationary Sieurs. **1865** *Ibid.* V. 623 The Marischal's legationary function.

legative ('lɛgətɪv), *a.* (*sb.*) [ad. late L. *lēgātīvus*, f. *lēgāre*: see LEGATE *v.* and -ATIVE.]

A. *adj.* **a.** In ***legative bull***, ***commission***: Empowering as a representative, deputing; conferring the authority of a legate. **b.** Of or pertaining to a legate. **c.** *rarely.* Of or pertaining to an ambassador.

1537 *Irish Act 28 Hen. VIII*, c. 19 §1 Appeales, jurisdictions legative,..and instruments of sundry natures. *a* **1548** HALL *Chron.*, *Hen. VI*, 100 b, By a Bull legatyve, whiche he purchased at Rome, he gathered so muche treasure, that [etc.]. **1613** SHAKS. *Hen. VIII*, III. ii. 339 All those things you haue done of late By your power Legatiue [*mod. edd.* legatine] within this kingdom. **1631** J. BURGES *Answ. Rejoined* 86 If the Church haue a ministery to appoint ..then must shee needs haue a commission legatiue. **1638** SIR R. COTTON *Abstr. Rec. Tower* 27 Thus did Cardinall Wolsey with Wareham the Arch-Bishop of Canterbury and all other the Bishops of the Kingdome after hee had got his Legative power. **1886** *Law Times* LXXX. 146/2 An *attaché*, not being a domestic servant of an ambassador, was not entitled to the legative privilege of exemption from process in the courts.

†**B.** *sb.* ? Something entrusted with a message.

1657 J. PETTUS in *Loveday's Lett.* (1659) A iv, The latter Age hath even robb'd the poor of their raggs, torturing them with Mills and other Engines, till in paper they are made Legatives to most of our humane affairs.

†**legatnait.** *Sc. Obs. rare*$^{-1}$. [ad. med.L. *lēgāt-us nāt-us* lit. 'legate born', i.e. having an inherent right to the dignity of a legate. Cf. F. *légat-né.*]

An archbishop (e.g. of Canterbury) who in virtue of his office exercised the rights of a papal legate.

1552 ABP. HAMILTON *Catech.* (1884) 1 Johne Archbischop of sanct Androus Legatnait and primat of the kirk of Scotland.

‖**legato** (le'gato, lə'gɑːtəʊ), *a.* (*adv.*, *sb.*) [It.: lit. 'bound', pa. pple. of *legare* to bind:—L. *ligāre.*] Smooth and connected, with no breaks between the successive notes: used as *adj.* or *adv.*, esp. as a direction to a performer to render a passage or piece in this style; also as *sb.* (Opposed to *staccato.*)

1811 in BUSBY *Dict. Mus.* (ed. 3). **1815** *European Mag.* LXVIII. 154 Var. 11 is another instance of good legato style. **1848** RIMBAULT *1st Bk. Piano* 91 *Legato*, in a smooth and connected manner. **1885** W. GLOVER *Mem. Cambr. Chorister* I. xxiv. 275 All the niceties and varieties of legato, staccato [etc.].

legator (lɪ'geɪtə(r)). [a. L. *lēgātor*, agent-n. f. *lēgāre* to bequeath.] One who gives something by will; a testator.

1651 G. W. tr. *Cowel's Inst.* 132 A Legator may make a Substitution Pupillary. **1687** DRYDEN *Hind & P.* II. 375 A fair estate, Bequeath'd by some Legator's last intent. **1845** MᶜCULLOCH *Taxation* II. vi. §3 (1852) 298 The greater number of legators might have defeated the tax. **1878** J. STARK *Scot. Claims* 18 The residue of the legator's estate.

Hence **lega'torial** *a.*, of or pertaining to a legator or testator.

1883 J. PAYN *Thicker than Water* III. xli. 115 Knowing that his codicil was secure, the legatorial anxieties which were obviously consuming those about him were not without their charms for him.

legatory, obs. form of LEGATARY.

†'**legature.** *Obs. rare*⁻¹. [f. LEGATE *sb.*¹ + -URE.] The dignity and office of a legate; legateship.

a **1674** CLARENDON *Relig. & Policy* vi. (1811) I. 278 The Parliament..forbade him to usurp the privileges of his Legature.

legaunce, legauns, obs. forms of LIGEANCE.

leg-bail. Used in the jocular phrase *to give* (Sc. *take*) *leg-bail*, to run away, decamp: see BAIL *sb.*¹ 5 c. Hence sometimes used (in allusion to this phrase) = unauthorized absence or departure, 'French leave', etc.

1774 FERGUSSON *Poems* (1807) 234 They took leg-bail and ran awa Wi' pith and speed. **1785** GROSE *Dict. Vulg. Tongue* s.v. *Leg*, To give leg bail and land security, to run away. **1808** *Sporting Mag.* XXXII. 122 We have more occasion.. for leg-bail than they have. **1861** HUGHES *Tom Brown at Oxf.* xi. (1889) 107 [He] was giving them leg-bail as hard as he could foot it. **1889** *Century Mag.* Feb. 632/1 Judgment was enforced by the scalping-knife, with leg-bail or a tribal warfare as a court of last resort.

lege, obs. form of LEAGUE, LEDGE, LIEGE.

†**legeance**¹. *Obs.* Aphetic f. ALLEGEANCE¹.

13.. *Minor Poems fr. Vernon MS.* xxix, He felede no leggaunce of his peyne.

†**legeance**². *Obs.* Aphetic f. ALLEGEANCE².

c **1425** *Saints' Lives* Prol. in *Anglia* VIII. 107 Legeauns and auctorites of holy writte. *c* **1425** *St. Mary of Oignies* Prol. ibid. 134 Amonge his writynge..hee puttiþ legeauns and figuratif spekynges.

legea(u)nce, obs. form of LIGEANCE.

lege-bell = *lich-bell*: see LICH, body, corpse.

leged, obs. pa. t. LAY *v.*; obs. f. LEGGED.

†**lege de moy.** *Obs.* ? Also **lege moy**. App. the name of some dance.

a **1529** SKELTON *Col. Clout* 953 And howe Parys of Troy Daunced a lege de moy [*MS.* a lege moy]. —— *E. Rummyng* 587 She made it as koy As a lege de moy [*v.r.* lege moy].

‖**legem pone.** *Obs.* The first two words (forming the heading) of the fifth division of Psalm cxix, which begins the psalms at Matins on the 25th day of the month; they were consequently associated with March 25th (quarter day), and hence used as an allusive expression for: Payment of money; cash down.

1573 TUSSER *Husb.* x. (1878) 22 Use (*legem pone*) to paie at thy daie, but vse not (*Oremus*) for often delaie. **1592** HARVEY *New Letter* 18 Without *Legem pone*, wordes are winde and without actuall performance, all nothing. **1594** BARNFIELD *Sheph. Content* xxxix, If *legem pone* comes, he is receau'd, When *Vix haud habeo* is of hope bereau'd. **1611** G. RUGGLE *Ignoramus* II. vii. (1630) 64 Hic est *legem pone*; hic sunt sexcentæ coronæ. **1618** MYNSHUL *Ess. Prison* 26 All their speech is *legem pone*, or else with their ill custome they will detaine thee. **1694** MOTTEUX *Rabelais* IV. xii. 48 They were all at our service for the *Legem pone*.

legen, obs. form of LAGGIN.

†**legence.** *Obs.* Also 5 **legeans**. App. = LICENCE.

14.. *MS. Cantab.* Ff. v. 48, lf. 44 (Halliw.), If he myȝt have legeans For his synnes to do penans, Schrifte he thouȝte to take. **1518** *Extracts Aberd. Reg.* (1844) I. 94 The legence gevin to vnfremen to saill with merchandeise.

legend ('lɛdʒənd), *sb.* Forms: 4-5 **legand(e**, 4, 6 **legeand**, 4-7 **legende**, 5-6 **-ent(e**, 6 **-eant**, 5- **legend.** [a. F. *légende* (recorded from 12th c.) = Sp. *leyenda*, Pg. *legenda*, *lenda*, It. *leggenda*, ad. med.L. *legenda* 'what is read', f. *legĕre* to read.

For the formation of fem. verbals from the gerundive stem, cf. med.L. *præbenda* 'prebend', It. *lavanda* washing, etc.]

1. The story of the life of a Saint.

c **1375** *Sc. Leg. Saints* xiii. (*Marcus*) 108 To sancte march turnand myn hand, as I in his legand fand. *c* **1386** CHAUCER *Nun's Pr. T.* 301 In the lyf of seint kenelm, I rede.. how.. I hadde leuere than my sherte That ye hadde rad his legende, as haue I. *c* **1430** *Life St. Kath.* (1884) 65 Thys glorious virgyn seynt Kateryne had alle these ȝeftes as hir legende sheweth tofore. **1500–20** DUNBAR *Poems* xxx. 21 In haly legendis haif I hard allevin, Ma sanctis of bischoppis, nor freiris, be sic sevin. **1597** HOOKER *Eccl. Pol.* v. xx. §9 Legends being growne in a manner to be nothing els but heapes of friuolous and scandalous vanities.

2. A collection of saints' lives or of stories of a similar character. ***the Legend***, spec. a mediæval collection of saints' lives written by Jacobus de Voragine, Archbishop of Genoa, in the 13th century; now usually called ***the Golden Legend*** (*Legenda Aurea*), the name popularly given to it in the Middle Ages.

c **1340** *Cursor M.* 20900 (Fairf.) Qua wille haue mare of þis matere rede þe legende & ȝe mai here. *c* **1380** WYCLIF *Sel. Wks.* III. 344 Aftir bileve of hooli writt, þat tellip of Petre and oþir apostlis..taken we biside bileve of many oþir þat þei ben seintis, as of Clement and Laurence and oþir þat þe Legende spekiþ of. **1483** CAXTON (*colophon*) Thus endeth the legende named in latyn *legenda aurea*, that is to saye in englysshe the golden legende. **1611** COTGR., *Legendier*, the golden Legend; a booke of the liues of the Saints. **1612** BACON *Ess.*, *Atheisme* (Arb.) 330, I had rather beleeue all the fables in the Legend, and the Alcaron, then that this vniuersall frame is without a minde. **1649** *Alcoran* p. ix, They [Mohammedans] invoke their Saints, of whom they have a large Legend. **1662** STILLINGFL. *Orig. Sacr.* I. v. §5 The next Legend the world hath should be called *Legenda Orientalis*. **1740** LADY M. W. MONTAGU *Let. to Lady Pomfret* 29 June, A belief in all the miracles in the Legend.

†**3.** A story, history, account. *Obs.*

c **1385** CHAUCER *L.G.W.* Prol. 473 The moste partye of thyn lyf spende In makynge of a gloryous legende Of goode wemen. *c* **1386** —— *Shipman's T.* 145 Thanne wolde I telle a legende of my lyf, What I haue suffred sith I wasa wyf. **1508** DUNBAR *Tua mariit wemen* 504 This is the legeand of my lif. **1560** ROLLAND *Crt. Venus* III. 653 Allegeand baith the ald and new Testamentis Historyis, Scriptouris, & vtheris lang legentis. **1601** CHESTER in *Shaks. C. Praise* 43 The true legend of famous King Arthur. **1613** JACKSON *Creed* II. xxxi. §11 Christ Jesus, who hath left us these his sacred laws, and legend of his most blessed life. **1616** BULLOKAR, *Legend*, a story of olde matters. *c* **1645** HOWELL *Lett.* (1650) 98 Those rambling letters..are nought else than a legend of the cumbersom life and various fortunes of a cadet. **1671** MILTON *Samson* 1737 Acts enroll'd In copious Legend, or sweet Lyric Song.

†**4.** A roll, list, record. *Obs.*

1377 LANGL. *P. Pl.* B. x. 376 Þat I man made was and my name yentred In þe legende of lyf longe er I were. **1536** BELLENDEN *Cron. Scot.* (1821) II. 100 Thocht he be nocht nowmerit amang the legend of papis. **1601** MARSTON *Pasquil & Kath.* I. 356 Sir, I enrowle you in the Legend of my intimates.

5. *Eccl.* A book of readings or 'lessons' for use at divine service, containing passages from Scripture and the lives of saints. *Obs.* exc. *Hist.*

c **1440** *Promp. Parv.* 293/2 Legende (*S.* boke), *legenda*. **1459** *Paston Lett.* I. 489 Inprimis, ij. antyfeners. Item, j. legande of hoole servyce. **1482** *Will of M. Paston* ibid. III. 283 A compleet legende in oon book, and an antiphoner in an other book. **1549** *Act 3 & 4 Edw. VI*, c. 10 §1 All Bookes called..Processionalles, Manuelles, Legends, Pyes, Portuyses, Prymars..shalbe..abolished. **1556** in Warton *Life Sir T. Pope* (1772) App. xvi. 319 A fair legeant of parchmente lymned with gold. **1605–6** *Act 3 Jas. I*, c. 5 §15 Missals, Breviaries, Portals, Legendes, and Lives of Sainctes. *a* **1746** LEWIS in Gutch *Coll. Cur.* II. 165 A Legend; in which were written the Lessons to be read at Mattins. **1849** ROCK *Ch. of Fathers* IV. xii. 212 The Legend contained all the lessons out of Holy Writ, and the works of the fathers, read at matins.

6. a. An unauthentic or non-historical story, esp. one handed down by tradition from early times and popularly regarded as historical.

1613 PURCHAS *Pilgrimage* (1614) 506 That yee may know the Indians want not their Metamorphoses and Legends, that tell that a man..had a daughter, with whom the sunne was in love. **1685** STILLINGFL. *Orig. Brit.* i. 11 Having their minds naturally framed to believe Legends. **1687** T. BROWN *Saints in Uproar* Wks. 1730 I. 77 The kingdom..is ten times as populous as when the legend supposes you and your sister-trollops to have lived there. **1768** H. WALPOLE *Hist. Doubts* 84 *note*, It would have required half the court of Edward the Fourth to frame a consistent legend. **1838** THIRLWALL *Greece* I. 89 To Æolus himself no conquests and no achievements are attributed by the legends of his race. **1860** HOOK *Lives Abps.* I. vi. 323 The legend which would attribute to Alfred the foundation of the University of Oxford. **1900** G. C. BRODRICK *Mem. & Impressions* 156 It was deliberately and skilfully employed to break down what has been called the Gladstonian legend. **1901** *Spectator* 23 Feb. 277/2 The voracity of the pike is the subject of innumerable legends.

b. in generalized sense.

1847 EMERSON *Repr. Men, Swedenborg* Wks. (Bohn) I. 334, I think of him as of some transmigrating votary of Indian legend. **1855** MILMAN *Lat. Chr.* IV. x. (1864) II. 434 Legend dwells with fond pertinacity on the holiness of the saint.

7. a. A writing, inscription, or motto; chiefly *spec.* in *Numismatics*, the words or letters impressed upon a coin or medal.

For attempts to distinguish *legend* and *inscription*, not now recognized by numismatists, see quots. 1611, 1727-41.

1611 COTGR., *Legende*, a Legende, a Writing; also, the words that be about the edge of a peece of coyne. **1702** ADDISON *Dial. Medals* iii. 153 We are now come to the Legend or Inscription of our Medals. **1727–41** CHAMBERS *Cycl.* s.v., In strictness, the *legend* differs from the *inscription*; this last properly signifying words placed on the reverse of a medal, in lieu of figures... Every medal has properly two legends; that on the front, and that on the reverse. **1855** MACAULAY *Hist. Eng.* xxi, As..their edges were inscribed with a legend, clipping was not to be apprehended. **1863** *Reader* 4 July 5 'Who is Griffiths?' is now a legend marked in paint on many of the walls about London. **1869** FREEMAN *Norm. Conq.* (1876) III. xi. 38 No legend or effigy marks the graves of these royal Ladies.

b. *gen.* Written character; writing. *rare.*

1822 SHELLEY *Fragm. Unfin. Drama* 152 Like a child's legend on the tideless sand, Which the first foam erases half, and half Leaves legible. **1836** CARDL. WISEMAN *Sci. & Relig.* II. viii. 67 The learned..applied themselves to the study of the enchorial, or as it has since been called, the demotic legend.

c. The written explanatory matter accompanying an illustration, map, etc. Also *attrib.*, as ***legend-line***.

1903 *Westm. Gaz.* 8 Jan. 2/1 The sort [of satire] I should employ if—if I were writing legend-lines for a halfpenny comic paper. **1951** D. BLAND *Illustration of Bks.* ix. 142 After the blocks have been made and the proofs approved, a paste-up should be prepared for the printer, to include legends or captions. **1963** *Which?* July 200/1 The symbols used on a map should be..explained clearly in the legend (or key). **1970** *Watsonia* VIII. 31 Figure 4. For legend see above. **1974** *Times Lit. Suppl.* 23 Aug. 910/5 The information provided in caption and legend is clear and exactly what is needed.

¶ Misused for LEGION.

1598 SHAKS. *Merry W.* I. iii. 59 She has all the rule of her husbands Purse: he hath a legend of Angels. **1682** MRS. BEHN *Roundheads* v. i, A Legend of his Divels take him for't.

8. *attrib.* and *Comb.*, as ***legend*** †***book***, ***-king***, ***lay***, ***-lust***, ***-maker***, ***-monger***, ***tale***; ***legend-circled***, ***-haunted***, ***-like***, ***-stored*** adjs.

1495 DUCHESS OF YORK in *Wills Doctor's Comm.* (Camden) 4, I geve to Sir John More, a *legend boke and a colett boke. **1842** FABER *Styrian Lake* etc. 316 Thou *legend-circled thing, dread Euxine Sea! **1905** *Westm. Gaz.* 25 Mar. 5/3 Its famous, *legend-haunted Jews' quarter. **1908** *Daily Chron.* 5 Oct. 7/1 As a poor and lonely boy he wove his day-dreams by the legend-haunted cliffs of Tintagel. **1930** BLUNDEN *Poems* 319 And thence, before to-morrow's dawn, it springs That they are one with elves and *legend-kings. **1821** JOANNA BAILLIE *Metr. Leg.*, *Wallace* ii, My *legend lay receive. **1563–87** FOXE *A. & M.* (1596) 80/1 They seeme more *legendlike than truthlike. **1674** *Essex Papers* (Camden) I. 282 Legend-like storys. **1911** E. POUND *Canzoni* 42 Nay, on my breast thou must Forget and rest and dream there For thine old *legend-lust. **1621** FLETCHER *Wildgoose Chase* II. i, A glorious talker, and a *Legend maker Of idle tales. **1820** W. TOOKE tr. *Lucian* I. 519 *note*, The Christian legend-makers. **1871** FREEMAN *Norm. Conq.* (1876) IV. xvii. 61 Norman panegyrists and legend-makers. **1680** H. MORE *Apocal. Apoc.* 233 No *Legend-mongers, nor intruders of absurd and impossible doctrines. **1893** W. C. BORLASE *Age Saints* 13 Gilbert de Stone, a legend-monger of the fourteenth century. **1840** T. A. TROLLOPE *Summer Brittany* I. 2 The traditions of its gloomy and *legend-stored history. **1605** BACON *Adv. Learn.* I. vii. §5. 34 That *legend tale of Gregorius Magnus.

b. Applied to the estimated or planned displacement, speed, etc., of a ship before construction or testing. Also *absol.*

1908 *Westm. Gaz.* 31 July 1/3 A ship..in the Bay would exceed her legend speed by a knot or two. **1921** *Glasgow Herald* 17 Dec. 12 The British Government may construct two new ships, not to exceed 35,000 legend tons each. **1936** W. S. CHURCHILL in *Second World War* (1949) I. I. ix. 144 If you ask your people [the Admiralty] to give you a legend for a 16-inch-gun ship, I am persuaded they would show you decidedly better proportions than could be achieved at 14-inch.

†'**legend,** *v. Obs.* [f. LEGEND *sb.*] *trans.* **a.** with *out*: to tell stories of; to tell of in legend. **b.** To tell as a legend.

1597–8 BP. HALL *Sat.* I. i. 2 Nor ladies wanton love, nor wandring knight Legend I out in rimes all richly dight. **1647** TRAPP *Comm. Rom.* xi. 2 Some have legended of him [*sc.* Elias], that when he drew his mothers brests, he was seen to suck in fire. **1670** MILTON *Hist. Eng.* III. Wks. 1851 V. 131 Some of these perhaps by others are legended for great Saints.

legendarian (lɛdʒən'dɛərɪən). [f. LEGENDARY + -AN.]

†**1.** The writer of a legendary. *Obs.*

1677 W. HUGHES *Man of Sin* Pref. B iv a, Which is the Case of all their Legendarians, brought as Witnesses here.

2. One who regards something (in quot. the gospel history) as of legendary character.

1882–3 in Schaff *Encycl. Relig. Knowl.* I. 748 The Broad-Church type of thought..also includes the rationalist and the legendarian.

legendary ('lɛdʒəndərɪ), *a.* and *sb.* [ad. med.L. *legendārius* adj. and sb. (F. *légendaire*, OF. also as sb. *legendier*), f. *legenda*: see LEGEND *sb.* and -ARY.]

A. *adj.*

1. Pertaining to or of the nature of a legend; connected or concerned with legends;

celebrated or related in legend. ***legendary period, age***: one of which the accounts are mostly of the nature of legends.

1563-87 FOXE *A. & M.* (1596) 66/2 All which legendarie miracles I leave to the reader to judge of them as shall seeme good unto him. **1641** MILTON *Prel. Episc.* Wks. 1851 III. 78 That other legendarie piece found among the lives of the Saints..does bear the name of Polycrates. **1679** J. GOODMAN *Penitent Pardoned* III. iv. (1713) 332 These things are no Romances, nor have I dressed up any legendary Hero. **1748** *Anson's Voy.* III. ix. 393 The character given of them in the legendary accounts of the Roman Missionaries. **1762-71** H. WALPOLE *Vertue's Anecd. Paint.* (1786) V. 6 Confining his labours almost wholly to religious and legendary histories. **1796** BP. WATSON *Apol. Bible* 237 Had they agreed in nothing, their testimony ought to have been rejected as a legendary tale. *a* **1854** H. REED *Lect. Eng. Hist.* ii. (1855) 47 The legendary period of British history. **1856** STANLEY *Sinai & Pal.* ii. (1858) 132 The view, whether historical or legendary, of Mahomet over Damascus. **1875** JOWETT *Plato* (ed. 2) I. 261 The legendary Pythagoras is said to have sacrificed a hecatomb. **1900** J. G. FRAZER *Pausanias*, etc. 45 Relics of a mythical or legendary past.

absol. **1871** EARLE *Philol. Eng. Tongue* 25 Something of the legendary hangs over his personal history.

b. Of writers: Relating legends.

1646 SIR T. BROWNE *Pseud. Ep.* I. viii. 33 Not to meddle at all with miraculous Authours, or any Legendary relators. **1685** STILLINGFL. *Orig. Brit.* i. 45 These Proofs..depend chiefly on the authority of Simeon Metaphrastes or other Legendary Writers. **1748** *Anson's Voy.* II. vii. 212 These legendary writers, of whose misrepresentations and falsities we had almost daily experience.

2. Containing the 'legend' on a coin.

1830 [E. HAWKINS] *Anglo-Fr. Coinage* 9 Between the outer angles and the inner legendary circle.

B. *sb.*

1. A collection of legends, esp. of lives of saints; *occas.* = the Golden Legend.

1513 BRADSHAW *St. Werburge* I. 2586 Amonge her systers all She caused to be redde..The swete legendary, for a memoryall. **1571** GRINDAL *Injunc. at York* B iv, Antiphoners, Masse bookes..Processionals, Manualles, Legendaries. **1577** DE L'ISLE (*title*) A Legendarie conteining an Ample Discourse of the life and behaviour of Charles Cardinal of Lorraine, and the house of Guise.

2. A writer of legends.

1625 JACKSON *Creed* v. xxxii. §3 The Legendaries, the latter Iewish Rabbines, and the Poeticall Encomiasts of heathen Gods or Heroikes. **1630** W. T. *Justific. Relig. Professed* x. 80 Their shamelesse Legendaries report indeed, that we haue put men into Beares skinnes, and set dogges to worry them. **1663** J. SPENCER *Prodigies* (1665) 398 The ancient Grecian Historians and more Modern Legendaries studied onely to make their Relations miraculous enough. **1749** BP. LAVINGTON *Enthus. Methodists & Papists* (1752) 57 The Legendaries own that St. Catharine was slandered as a fond and light woman. **1849** JAS. GRANT *Kirkaldy of Gr.* vii. 67 A..monastery, built..by special desire (say the legendaries) of St. Michel the archangel.

†**3.** A legendary or unhistorical personage. *Obs.*

a **1662** HEYLYN *Laud* (1668) 474 The expunging of some Saints (which they falsly call Legendaries) out of the Kalendar.

'legended, *a. rare.* [f. LEGEND *sb.* + -ED².]

1. Bearing a legend or inscription.

a **1849** POE *Ulalume* viii, The door of a legended tomb. **1886** *Century Mag.* XXXII. 595 The land of the legended fan and the lacquered box.

2. Celebrated in legends.

1893 *Illustr. Lond. News* Christm. No. 9/1 The legended pursuit of Daphne by Apollo.

†**'legender.** *Obs. rare*⁻¹. [f. LEGEND *sb.* + -ER¹.] A writer of a legend.

1611 SPEED *Hist. Gt. Brit.* IX. vi. §11. 487 Which to be true, a Legender of his Miracles can best relate.

legendist ('lɛdʒəndɪst). [f. LEGEND *sb.* + -IST.] A writer of legends.

1664 H. MORE *Myst. Iniq.* 472 Lying Legendists. **1832** SOUTHEY *Lett.* (1856) IV. 312 This was decidedly an invention of the legendist. **1859** RILEY *Liber Albus* Pref. 10 The Legendist..the Romancer, and the Poet.

legendize ('lɛdʒəndaɪz), *v. rare*⁻⁰. [f. LEGEND *sb.* + -IZE.] *trans.* To affix a legend to; to inscribe with a legend.

1889 in *Century Dict.*

'legendless, *a. rare*⁻¹. [f. LEGEND *sb.* + -LESS.] Of a coin: Bearing no legend.

1884 TRAILL *New Lucian* 130 That coin of language which, once so glittering and clean-cut, has been worn down to an unmeaning counter, deviceless and legendless.

†**'legendous**, *a. Obs. rare*⁻¹. [f. LEGEND *sb.* + -OUS.] Legendary.

1686 *Spec. Beatæ Virginis* 29, I have also passed over the many Legendous stories that are told of her.

Legendre (ləʒɑ̃dr). *Math.* The name of A. M. *Legendre* (see LEGENDRIAN *a.*), used *attrib.* and in the possessive to designate certain expressions investigated by him, esp. (*a*) the differential equation $(1 - x^2)d^2y/dx^2 - 2xdy/dx + n(n + 1)y = 0$, (*b*) its solutions $y = P_n(x)$, where $P_n(x)$ is a polynomial that is the coefficient of h^n in the expansion of $(1 - 2xh + h^2)^{-1/2}$, and (*c*) the associated functions $P_n{}^m(x)$, equal to $(1 - x^2)^{m/2}\frac{d^m}{dx^m}P_n(x)$.

1875 I. TODHUNTER *Elem. Treat. Laplace's Functions* i. 1 The coefficient of a^n will be a function of x which we shall denote by $P_n(x)$, and shall call Legendre's Coefficient of the nth order. **1880** *Encycl. Brit.* XIII. 21/2 Legendre's function. **1885** A. R. FORSYTH *Treat. Differential Equations* v. 152 We have now obtained the complete integral of Legendre's equation in all cases when n is a real constant, by deducing two integrals which are linearly independent..of one another. **1902** *Encycl. Brit.* XXXII. 798/1 (*heading*) Legendre associated functions. **1930** *Engineering* 26 Dec. 812/3 There are also tables of Legendre functions. **1938** S. DUSHMAN *Elem. Quantum Mech.* vi. 153 The Legendre polynomials form an orthogonal system, since $\int_{-1}^{1}P_k(x)P_n(x)dx = 0$ (for $k \neq n$) [or] $= 2/(2k + 1)$ (for $k = n$). *Ibid.* 158 Since the value of any function $P_k(\cos\theta)$ exhibits $k - 1$ loops, there are $2(k - 1)$ circles parallel to the nodal circles at which the function has the same absolute value. It is for this reason that the Legendre coefficients of zero order are known as zonal harmonics. **1953** A. D. & K. H. V. BOOTH *Automatic Digital Calculators* xvi. 189 The Legendre polynomials..are such that, if any function is expanded in a series of the polynomials, the first n terms of this series will give the best nth degree polynomial approximation to the given function, in the least squares sense. **1962** CORSON & LORRAIN *Introd. Electromagn. Fields* iv. 172 The solutions of Legendre's equation are called Legendre polynomials, which we denote by $P_n(\cos\theta)$, there being a different polynomial for each value of the index n. **1970** G. K. WOODGATE *Elem. Atomic Struct.* ii. 17 The solutions are proportional to the associated Legendre functions.

Legendrian (lɪ'dʒɛndrɪən), *a. Math.* [f. name of Adrien Marie *Legendre* (1752–1833), an eminent French mathematician.] Pertaining to or invented by the mathematician Legendre, as ***Legendrian coefficient, function, symbol.***

1882 *Encycl. Brit.* XIV. 414/1 The theory of the Legendrian Coefficients.

legendry ('lɛdʒəndrɪ). [f. LEGEND *sb.* + -RY.] Legends collectively.

1849 RUSKIN *Sev. Lamps* iv. §8. 100 In places where its legendry may be plainly read, as in painted windows. **1880** T. SINCLAIR in *Academy* 3 Apr. 247 Mr. Gilbert's fairy legendry. **1882** BERESF. HOPE *Brandreths* II. xxix. 226 The broidure bright of homespun legendry On Homer's and on Virgil's awful robe.

†**'leger**, *sb.*¹ *Obs.* Also legier, lieger. 'A cant term for a Londoner who formerly bought coals of the country colliers at so much a sack, and made his chief profit by using smaller sacks, making pretence he was a country collier' (Nares). Hence †**'legering** *vbl. sb.*

1591 GREENE *Disc. Coosnage* (1592) D 2 b, The Law of Legering which is a deceit that Colliars abuse the Commonwealth withall, in hauing vnlawfull sacks. *Ibid.*, The Leger, the craftie Collier I mean. *Ibid.*, He carryeth the countrey colliar home to his legering place, and there at the back gate causeth him to vnloade, and, as they say, shoot the coles down. **1592** —— *Uspt. Courtier* E iij b, I am..a Collier of Croyden, and one sir that haue solde many a manne a false sacke of coales... Indeede I haue beene a Lieger in my tyme in London, and haue played many madde pranckes, for which cause..the Pillory hath eaten off both my eares.

Leger ('lɛdʒə(r)), *sb.*² Shortened f. *St. Leger* (see SAINT *a.* 4 c).

1871 [see EGG *sb.* 4 b]. **1880** TROLLOPE *Duke's Children* I. xvii. 206 Who would like to bet me fifteen to one in hundreds against the two events,—the Derby and the Leger? **1924** GALSWORTHY *Forest* II. i. 41 I'd give all mine [*sc.* my ancestors] to know what's won the Leger. **1961** F. C. AVIS *Sportsman's Gloss.* 230/2 *Leger Day*, the day upon which the St. Leger is actually run.

†**'leger**, *a. Obs.* Also 6 lieger, lyger, 7 leagar. [a. F. *léger* (= Sp. *ligero*, Pg. *ligeiro*, It. *leggiero*):—popular L. type **leviārius*, f. *levis* light.] Light, not heavy; slight, trifling. Also, nimble. Hence **'legerly** *adv.*

1481-90 *Howard Househ. Bks.* (Roxb.) 425 Item, my Lord payde to the armerer of Flaunderes apon his leger harnes vjs. viijd. *a* **1533** LD. BERNERS *Huon* cxi. 382 Huon, who was lyger and light, lept by the syde of the serpent and gaue hym a great stroke. **1565** COOPER *Thesaurus*, *Agilis*, nimble, light, lieger, quicke, quiuer. *Ibid.*, *Agiliter*, nymbly, lightly, liegerly, quiuerly. **1598** DALLINGTON *Meth. Trav.* G iv b, By his Physiognomy ye would iudge him leger and inconstant.

leger, obs. form of LEDGER.

†**legerdeheel.** *Obs. nonce-wd.* [An alteration of *legerdemain* by the substitution of *heel* for the last syllable.] 'Light-heeled' pranks.

1605 CHAPMAN *All Fools* Plays 1873 I. 151 If your wiues play legerdeheele, though you bee a hundred miles off, yet you shall be sure instantly to find it in your forheads.

legerdemain (ˌlɛdʒədɪ'meɪn). Forms: 5 lygarde de mayne, lechardemane, legerdemayn, 6 legerdemane, -dymeyne, -du-maine, -dimeane, ledgerdemaine, -mayne, ligier de meyne, -demayne, du mayne, legier du mane, ligerdemayne, lieger-du-mayne, liger, legyier, lygier demaine, 6–7 legerdemaine, -mayne, -mane, legierdemain(e, -dumain(e, leigerdumain, -demaine, 7 leger du main, mein, leiger du mayn, legger-, legeirdemaine, 8 leidger demain, 6– legerdemain (in 6–8 written as two or three words, and with hyphens). [a. F. *léger de main*, lit. 'light of hand': cf. LEGER *a.*]

1. Sleight of hand; the performance of tricks which by nimble action deceive the eye; jugglery; conjuring tricks.

14.. LYDG. *Daunce of Macabre*, Lygarde-de-mayne now helpith me right noughte. *c* **1475** *Cath. Angl.* 212/2 (Add. MS.) To play lechardemane, *pancraciari.* **1528** ROY *Rede me* (Arb.) 114 O churche men are wyly foxes More crafty then iuggelers boxes To play ligier du mayne teached. **1562** BULLEYN *Bk. Simples* 30 a, Many Inkepers with their hostlers through a cast of legerdemain: can make a pecke of draffe and Beanes, buye three bushelles of cleane Pease or Beanes. **1584** R. SCOT *Discov. Witchcr.* XIII. xxii. (1886) 263 The true art..of juggling consisteth in legierdemaine; to wit, the nimble conveiance of the hand. **1596** SPENSER *F.Q.* v. ix. 13 For he in slights and jugling feates did flow, And of legierdemayne the mysteries did know. **1613** R. C. *Table Alph.* (ed. 3), *Legeirdemaine*, light-handednesse, craftie slights, and conueiance. **1622** BEAUM. & FL. *Beggar's Bush* III. i, Will ye see any feates of activity, Some sleight of hand, leigerdemaine? **1707** FARQUHAR *Beaux Strat.* v. v, What's here? Legerdemain! By this light, my lord, our money again! **1756** C. LUCAS *Ess. Waters* III. 220 The name of a magician..has..been assumed and abused by masters of leger de main. **1817** COLERIDGE *Biog. Lit.* 116 The professors of legerdemain at our village fairs, pull out ribbon after ribbon from their mouth. **1856** DOVE *Logic Chr. Faith* II. ii. 115 The legerdemain of the skilful trickster who deceives our very senses.

2. *transf.* and *fig.* Trickery, deception, hocus-pocus.

1532 MORE *Confut. Tindale* Wks. 639/2 Hys lygier demaine in stealing. **1565** JEWEL *Def. Apol.* (1611) 529 Wel may we iest at your vnhandsome and open legierdumaine, that so vainly seeke to blinde vs with a painted shadow of the Spirit of God. **1679** *Hist. Jetzer* 13 This whole business was nothing but pure Legerdemain and Knavery. **1711** SHAFTESB. *Charac.* (1737) I. *Advice to Author* I. i. 155 There is a certain Knack or Legerdemain in argument. **1796** MRS. GLASSE *Cookery* vii. 134 By this sort of legerdemain, some fine estates are juggled into France. **1823** LINGARD *Hist. Eng.* VI. 282 The theological legerdemain, by which Cranmer pretended to nullify the oath of obedience..to the pontiff. **1875** JOWETT *Plato* (ed. 2) IV. 134 We are inclined to regard the treatment of them [paradoxes]..as a mere legerdemain of words.

†**b.** An instance of this; a trick, a juggle. *Obs.*

1550 BALE *Eng. Votaries* II. I iv, Theyr preuy leger-demaines wer not muche to be trusted. **1579** LYLY *Euphues* (Arb.) 119, I would not that all Women should take Pepper in the nose, in that I haue disclosed the legerdemaines of a few. **1625** *Gonsalvio's Sp. Inquis.* Contents, The treacheries and legerdemaines of the Inquisition in practice and exercise. **1663** GERBIER *Counsel* 48 He must with his Eyes follow..the line wherewith the Joyners work is measured, that it be not let slide through the Measurers fingers, since ..a Leger de Mayne may be prejudicial to the paymasters purse.

†**3.** A sleight-of-hand performer, a conjurer. *Obs. rare*⁻¹.

1695 CIBBER *Love's Last Shift* II. (1696) 25 The Fool diverted me and I gave him my hand, as I wou'd lend my Mony, Fan, or Hankerchief to a Legerdemain, that I might see him play all his Tricks over.

4. *attrib.* or as *adj.* Pertaining to or of the nature of legerdemain or jugglery; juggling; tricky.

1576 NEWTON *Lemnie's Complex.* II. ii. 101 Some Iuglers, & Legier du maine players. **1683** DRYDEN *Life Plutarch* Ded. 25 These legerdemain authors are for telling stories to keep their tricks undiscover'd. **1707** *Curios. in Husb. & Gard.* 91 Jugglers, who show Legerdemain Tricks. **1742** *Lond. & Country Brew.* I. (ed. 4) 39 In such a Legerdemain Manner, as gulled and infatuated the ignorant Drinker. **1760** J. RUTTY *Spirit. Diary* (ed. 2) 171 A legerdemain-man getting four guineas a day. **1812** SOUTHEY in *Q. Rev.* VIII. 96 Phantasmagoric and legerdemain miracles. **1836** J. GILBERT *Chr. Atonem.* ii. (1852) 47 The legerdemain kind of criticism resorted to by our adversaries.

Hence, †**legerde'main** *v. intr.* (also with *it*), to perform tricks, to use deceit; **legerde'mainish** *a.*, resembling that of legerdemain; **legerde'mainist**, a performer of legerdemain, a conjurer.

1483 *Cath. Angl.* 212/2 To Legerdemayn..*pancraciari.* *a* **1678** MARVELL *Hist. Poem* in *Poems Affairs State* (1697) 99 Baal's wretched Curates Legerdemain'd it so, And never durst their Tricks above-board shew. **18..** WORCESTER 1860 (citing *Observer*) Legerdemainist. **1877** F. C. BURNAND *Ride to Khiva* 10 You know what a good Legerdemainist I am. **1888** *Sat. Rev.* 21 Jan. 71 No one ever performed that operation in a more legerdemainish fashion. **1891** *Critic* (U.S.) 31 Jan. 57/2 The handkerchief tricks of the legerdemainist.

†**le'gerity.** *Obs.* Also 6 liger-, leiger-, legieritie. [ad. F. *légèreté*: see LEGER *a.* and -ITY.] Lightness (*lit.* and *fig.*); nimbleness.

1561 THROCKMORTON *Let. to Eliz.* 29 Apr. in Tytler *Hist. Scot.* (1864) III. 146 Some others of her nation that be inclined to greater legerity, inconstancy, and corruption. **1598** BARRET *Theor. Warres* I. ii. 12 A signe of great ligeritie and lightnesse. **1599** SHAKS. *Hen. V*, IV. i. 23 The Organs.. newly moue With casted slough and fresh legeritie. **1599** B. JONSON *Ev. Man out of Hum.* II. i, I have..the Leigeritie, for [certain feats of legerdemain]. **1600** *Dr. Dodypoll* III. iv. in Bullen *O. Pl.* III. 133 The legieritie of her sweet feete. **1640** tr. *Verdere's Rom. of Rom.* II. 164 Considering that his legerity would more advantage him then his force, he concluded to combat him with judgement. **1822** W. TENNANT *Thane of Fife* vi. 37 Worming his way with strange legerity. **1830** GALT *Lawrie T.* III. xvi. (1849) 138 Had I not cause for thankfulness on this occasion that I had been formed with such legerity.

† **legge**, *v.* *Obs. rare.* [Aphetic form of ALLEGE *v.*[1]] *trans.* To alleviate.
c **1400** *Rom. Rose* 5016 Som socour, To leggen hir of hir dolour.

legge, obs. form of LEDGE *v.*[1]

legge(n, obs. form of LAY *v.*

legg(e)aunce, obs. forms of LIGEANCE.

legged (lɛgd), *a.* [f. LEG *sb.* + -ED[2].] Having legs (of a particular kind, shape, or colour); freq. in parasynthetic combination with adjs., as BAKER-*legged*, *bare-legged*, *black-legged*, BOW-LEGGED, *crook(ed)-legged*, *long-legged*, *two-legged*, etc. In *Heraldry*, having legs of a specified tincture.
1470 SIR J. PASTON in *P. Lett.* No. 637 II. 394 He is legged right i now, and it is reportyd that hys pyntell is as long as hys legge. *a* **1529** SKELTON *E. Rummyng* 50 Legged lyke a crane. **1552** HULOET, Legged crokedly and ill fauored. *c* **1570** *Pride & Lowl.* (1841) 64 But he were legged as was Actæon. **1572** BOSSEWELL *Armorie* III. 26 An Owsell d'Argente, beaked golde, legged gules. **1610** SHAKS. *Temp.* II. ii. 35 Leg'd like a man. **1652** GAULE *Magastrom.* 186 The spindle legd are fearful; hairy legg'd, lustful; stump legg'd servile; bow-legg'd, various. **1697** tr. *Le Comte's Mem. China* ii. (1737) 39 A row of eunuchs.. stood on each hand close legged. **1765** *Treat. Dom. Pigeons* 134 The Trumpeter is a Bird.. very feather-footed and leg'd. **1822** SCOTT *Pirate* vii, Triptolemus was a short, clumsy, duck-legged disciple of Ceres. **1864** BOUTELL *Her. Hist. & Pop.* xv. §15 (ed. 3) 204 Three popinjays or, collared and legged gu. **1898** *Daily News* 24 Nov. 2/2 Stiffbacked, legged chairs, legged sofas.. are out of place in an Eastern house.
b. *legged dollar* = *leg-dollar* (see LEG *sb.* 17).
1672 *Corshill Baron-Crt. Bk.* in *Archæol. & Hist. Coll. Ayr & Wigton* (1884) IV. 104 Withholding from him ane leged dolour, at 5*s*., anent the niffer of ane horse. *c* **1689** *Depred. Clan Campbell* (1816) 100 Ane leggit dollor.
Hence **ˈleggedly** *adv.*
1659 TORRIANO, *Gambescaménte*, leggedly, according to the fashion of shanks.

legger[1] (ˈlɛgə(r)). [f. LEG *v.* + -ER[1].] A man who propels a canal barge through a tunnel by thrusting his legs against the walls.
1836 SIR G. HEAD *Home Tour* 143 These men.. are called 'leggers' for they literally work the boat with their legs, or kick it from one end of the tunnel to the other. **1841** BREES *Gloss. Terms Civ. Engin.*, *Leggers*, the name given to the men employed in conveying a barge through a canal tunnel, by means of pushing with their legs against the side walls.

legger[2] (ˈlɛgə(r)). [f. LEG *sb.* + -ER[1].] **1.** In a slaughter-house, a butcher or packer who works on the legs of the carcasses.
1905 F. W. WILDER *Mod. Packing House* v. 116 The number of men necessary in [different sized] beef killing groups.. are given in the following table... 2 front leggers.. 3 hind leggers. **1923** R. A. CLEMEN *Amer. Livestock & Meat Industry* xv. 332 A string of butchers now follow each other in rapid succession. The 'leggers' remove the hind legs at the hoof and the forelegs at the knee. **1949** K. STRONACH in A. E. Woodhouse *N.Z. Farm & Station Verse* (1950) 188 The legger slits as a surgeon does And the puncher strips the pelt. **1966** *Mate* (Auckland) Aug. 42 Legger, the man who cuts out the legs from the newly killed lamb in the freezing works.
2. (See quot.)
1927 T. WOODHOUSE *Artificial Silk* 95 In the manufacture of stockings on such frames two machines are used... One of these machines, termed the 'legger', knits the upper and longer part of the stocking, whereas the other machine, termed the 'footer', knits the remainder of the stocking.

legger[3] (ˈlɛgə(r)). *U.S. colloq.* Shortened f. BOOT-LEGGER. Also (with preceding hyphen) as the second element of *Combs.*, an illegal seller (of something indicated in the first element).
1926 [see HIP *a.*]. **1929** *Variety* 5 June 58/2 Leggers claim the tonic is as potent as a fifth of gin selling for three times the price. **1934** *Time* 29 Jan. 49/1 Hundreds of U.S. citizens have smuggled copies through the customs or bought them from book-leggers. **1937** *Time* 4 Jan. 11/2 Unlike Prohibition's liquor 'leggers', they are not growing rich. **1945** *Chicago Daily News* 12 July 12/2 Most of the counterfeits have been used by steakleggers down East. **1945** MENCKEN *Amer. Lang.* Suppl. I. 366 But of more interest.. are the words showing recent vogue affixes, *e.g.* ..*-legger*, as in *bootlegger* and *meatlegger*. **1973** *Times Lit. Suppl.* 20 Apr. 451/5 A sinister group of organ-leggers who go beyond the resurrectionists and try to keep the hospitals supplied with adequate numbers of fresh organs for transplants.

legger, variant of LEDGER.

leggery (ˈlɛgərɪ). *nonce-wd.* [f. LEG *sb.* + -ERY.] A manufactory or storehouse of legs.
1830 COLERIDGE *Const. Ch. & State* 212 That mundus immundus on which we, and other less scantily furnished from nature's *Leggery*, crawl, delve, and nestle.

legget (ˈlɛgət). Also leg(g)at(t), leg(g)et(t). [Etym. unknown.] In Thatching, a tool made from a flat board attached to a handle and studded with nails, used for dressing and driving the reeds into place. Cf. LEDGER *sb.* 2 b.
c **1555** in *Norfolk Antiquarian Misc.* (1883) II. 9 A Cardynall legat & a trowell wt suche other tooles. **1787** W. MARSHALL *Rural Econ. Norfolk* II. xxxii. 61 The eaves being thus completely set, they are adjusted and formed;.. nor are they formed by cutting; but by 'driving' them with a 'legget'. **1927** *Observer* 24 July 5/3 The tools and appliances used in Devon are more or less similar to those used in Norfolk. The 'leggett', however, is called a 'driff'. **1941** [see BIDDLE]. **1949** K. S. WOODS *Rural Crafts Eng.* IV. xiii. 204 The beating tool is called a 'legatt'; it is a square of thick wood studded with horseshoe nails set alternately, nail and space, in the rows. **1961** *Guardian* 21 Sept. 5/2 Ramming home one corner with a Chaucerian tool known as a leggett. **1969** E. H. PINTO *Treen* xxv. 406 The leggat, legget or reed bat.. is used for patting or beating reeds into position. **1971** *Country Life* 18 Nov. 1403/3 The Norfolk thatching reed is then beaten up tight under the hazel rods using an instrument called a leggett. **1972** *Daily Tel.* 28 Oct. 15/2 Each 'yelm' is pegged into place and beaten with a flat piece of wood or 'spud' (reed thatchers use a corrugated surface, called a 'leggat').

leggett, obs. form of LEGATE *v.*

† **leggiadrous**, *a.* *Obs. rare.* [f. It. *leggiadro* light, sprightly + -OUS.] Graceful, elegant.
1648 JOS. BEAUMONT *Psyche* XVIII. xl, Those beams of leggiadrous Courtesy Which smil'd in her Deportment. *Ibid.* XIX. xvii, The queen of soft leggiadrous Love.

‖ **leggiero** (ledˈdʒɛro), *a.* *Mus.* [It.] Of musical movement: light and nimble. Also used as *adv.*
1880 GROVE *Dict. Mus.* II. 113/2 Leggiero passages are usually, though not invariably, *piano*, and they may be either legato or staccato. **1939** *Internat. Cycl. Mus.* 988/2 *Leggiero* (Italian), lightly, usually applied to a rapid passage for the pianoforte. **1960** *Times* 4 June 9/5 Katchen's *leggiero* playing is predictably delightful.

legginess (ˈlɛgɪnɪs). Leggy condition.
1893 *Kennel Gaz.* Aug. 213/3 She [a bitch].. was much out of coat, which increased her legginess.

legging (ˈlɛgɪŋ), *sb.* Chiefly *pl.* Also 8–9 *pl.* **leggins.** [f. LEG *sb.* + -ING[1] (but cf. -ING[3]).] **a.** In *pl.* A pair of extra outer coverings (usually of leather or cloth), used as a protection for the legs in bad weather, and commonly reaching from the ankle to the knee, but sometimes higher.
1763 in F. B. Hough *Siege Detroit* (1860) 200 The Men to be clothed, but in a light Manner; a cloth Jacket, flannel Waistcoat, Leggins, &c. will be sufficient. **1809** A. HENRY *Trav.* 156 A pair of leggings, or pantaloons, of scarlet cloth, which.. cost me fifteen pounds of beaver. **1821** CLARE *Vill. Minstr.* II. 26 With leather leggings on, that stopt the snow. **1839–40** W. IRVING *Wolfert's R.* (1855) 203 A hunting-shirt of dressed deer-skin.. and leggins of the same, fringed from hip to heel. **1869** E. A. PARKES *Pract. Hygiene* (ed. 3) 415 Long leggings reaching over the knees, and made of half-tanned leather.
b. *Cricket* = PAD *sb.*[3] 3 c. Now *rare* or *Obs.*
1858 in *Cricket Q.* (1963) I. 21. **1875** *Baily's Monthly Mag.* May 11 Beldham also, without either leggings or gloves, scored 72 against Brown.. when fifty-two years old. **1934** W. J. LEWIS *Lang. Cricket* 146 *Leggings*, leg-guards of a primitive type.
Hence **ˈlegginged** *a.*, having leggings.
1837, 1852 [see *leather-legginged* in LEATHER *sb.* 5 d]. **1891** MISS DOWIE *Girl in Karp.* 39 My yellow legginged feet.

legging (ˈlɛgɪŋ), *vbl. sb.* [f. LEG. *v.* + -ING[1].]
1. Making a 'leg' or obeisance.
1872 BLACKMORE *Maid of Sk.* (1881) 160 All the bowing and legging I had seen in the Royal Navy.
2. Propelling a boat through a canal-tunnel by human labour (see quot. 1949). Cf. LEG *v.* 3. Also *attrib.*
1861 S. SMILES *Lives Engineers* II. VIII. x. 421 It [*sc.* the tunnel] was little larger than a sewer, and admitted the passage of only one narrow boat, seven feet wide, at a time, involving very heavy labour on the part of the men who worked it through. This was performed by what was called *legging*. **1949** *Archit. Rev.* CVI. 13/2 In the early tunnels towpaths were never constructed and boats were propelled through them either by shafting or legging... Legging was carried out by two men, one on each side of the boat lying on their backs and pushing against the tunnel sides with their feet. **1963** *Times* 4 May 6/4 They will stare in amazement at the legging boards used in the navigation of tunnels in the days when horse power meant what it said. **1975** *Times* 13 Mar. 4/7 The police have concentrated on the eighteenth-century 'legging' tunnel, built by Grindley, so called because boatmen had to propel their craft through by thrusting their legs against the roof.
3. *Austral.* and *N.Z.* Of dogs, the biting of an animal on the leg. Cf. LEG *v.* 5 b.
1933 L. G. D. ACLAND in *Press* (Christchurch, N.Z.) 4 Nov. 15/7 Some dogs get a bad habit of biting sheep on the leg in yards; others of laming other dogs while fighting. Both these vices are called *legging*. **1960** [see FORCE *sb.*[1] 7 e].

ˈlegging, *ppl. a.* [f. LEG *v.* + -ING[2].] That makes a 'leg' or obeisance.
1602 W. BAS *Sword & Buckler* B, A legging foote, a well-embracing hand.

leggism (ˈlɛgɪz(ə)m). *colloq.* [f. LEG *sb.* 5 + -ISM.] The practice, or an act, of 'black-legging' (Cf. BLACK-LEG, -LEGS 2).
1847 *Sporting Life* 28 Aug. 16/2 The system of adopting leggism as a legitimate part and parcel of horse-racing is one that must soon explode. **1896** FARMER & HENLEY *Slang* IV. 178/2 *Leggism*,.. the character, practices, or manners of a leg. **1937** PARTRIDGE *Dict. Slang* 477/1 *Leggism*, the art or the character of a 'leg'.

leggo (lɛˈgəʊ), a representation of a colloq. or vulgar pronunciation of *let go!*
1884 'MARK TWAIN' *Huck. Finn* xxx. 310 Leggo the boy, you old idiot! **1889** J. K. JEROME *Three Men in Boat* ii. 24 What are *you* up to?.. leggo, can't you? **1906** KIPLING *Actions & Reactions* (1909) 207 Leggo my collar! **1932** L. GOLDING *Magnolia St.* II. xiii. 450 Leggo of my 'ead! **1961** 'F. RICHARDS' *Bunter the Ventriloquist* xxv. 145 'Ow! Leggo!' Bunter, wriggling, blinked round in alarm at the captain of the Remove. **1973** 'D. SHANNON' *Spring of Violence* (1974) x. 168 You're crazy, man. Leggo of me.

leggy (ˈlɛgɪ), *a.* [f. LEG *sb.* + -Y.]
a. Conspicuous for legs; having disproportionately long legs; lanky-legged. Also *transf.*, long-stemmed.
1787 'G. GAMBADO' *Acad. Horsemen* (1809) 32 If you are a short man, you spur the saddle cloth; if you are leggy you never touch him [the horse] at all. **1827** *Sporting Mag.* XX. 170 Great numbers of our racers.. have always been too leggy. **1860** O. W. HOLMES *Prof. at Breakfast-Table* x. 310 The white meeting-house, and the row of youthful and leggy trees before it. **1883** STEVENSON *Silverado Sq.* (1886) 67 He looked neither heavy nor yet adroit, only leggy, coltish, and in the road. **1932** *Times Educ. Suppl.* 9 July 267/4 If plants are crowded under glass they will grow 'leggy'. **1965** H. G. W. FOGG *Small Greenhouse* v. 39 Put the boxes, etc., on a shelf close up under the glass of the greenhouse, to prevent the seedlings from becoming drawn and 'leggy'.
b. *slang.* Characterized by a display of legs.
1866 *Daily Tel.* 10 Jan. 7/3 This festival.. has been pitiably vulgarised.. by Christmas numbers of periodicals, Christmas concerts, leggy burlesques. **1887** *Pall Mall G.* 17 Oct. 1/2 'Leggy' burlesques.

legh (liː). Also leigh. [Etym. unknown.] = *Irish deer, elk* (IRISH *a.* 2 b).
1774 T. WEST *Antiquities Furness* p. xlvi, That the legh was a native of Furness, is evident from the heads of those animals frequently found in Furness. **1795** A. RADCLIFFE *Journey* 483 A remarkably large breed of deer, called Leghs, the heads of which have frequently been found buried at a considerable depth in the soil. **1835** WORDSWORTH *Guide through District of Lakes* (ed. 5) ii. 38 The leigh, a gigantic species of deer which has long been extinct. **1974** J. W. SMYSER in Wordsworth *Prose Works* III. 403 Wordsworth drew on West for his information about the 'leigh'.

legh, obs. form of LEE *sb.*[1], LIE *sb.*[1], LYE.

† **leg-harness.** *Obs.* Forms: see LEG *sb.* and HARNESS *sb.* Armour for the leg.
1388 WYCLIF *1 Sam.* xvii. 6 And stelyn legharneis [1388 bootis of bras] he [Goliath] hadde in the hipis. **1426** LYDG. *De Guil. Pilgr.* 8178 Legharneys ys lefft be-hynde, That thow mayst, at lyberte, Hyr dartys and hyr brondys fle. **1513** DOUGLAS *Æneis* XII. vi. 114 Hys lymmis in leg-harnes gold begane, Claspyt full clos. **1601** HOLLAND *Pliny* II. 514 Nailes, studs and tackes imploied about greeues and leg-harneis. *a* **1653** GOUGE *Comm. Heb.* x. 36 Shooes, or leg-harnesse, whereby men are enabled to hold out in their way. **1828–40** TYTLER *Hist. Scot.* (1864) II. 67 Armed with.. leg-harness, sword, spear, and dagger.
fig. **1509** HAWES *Past. Pleas.* xxvii. (Percy Soc.) 130 Good hope his legge harneys sholde be.

leghe, obs. form of LEAGUE *sb.*[1], LIE.

leghed, obs. pa. t. LAY *v.*, LIE *v.*[2]

leghere, obs. form of LIAR.

Leghorn (lɛˈgɔːn, ˈlɛghɔːn). [Use of the place-name *Leghorn*, ad. It. *Legorno* (16–17th c.), now replaced by *Livorno*, repr. the classical L. name *Liburnus*.]
1. The name of a straw plaiting for hats and bonnets, made from a particular kind of wheat, cut green and bleached, and so called because imported from Leghorn in Tuscany; a hat or bonnet made of this plaiting or some imitation of it. (Used both *simply* and in *attrib.* use, as ***Leghorn bonnet, chip, hat, plait.***)
1740 *Pennsylvania Gaz.* 22 May 7/2 Leghorn hats. **1742** *Boston News-Let.* 24 June 2/2 Just imported.. from London .. Leghorn Hats for women. **1804** *European Mag.* XLV. 412/2 Hats of a foreign manufacture, imported from Italy, and therefore denominated Leghorn Chip. **1805** *Trans. Soc. Arts* XXIII. 223 The Gold Medal of the Society was this session voted to Mr. William Corston, of Ludgate-Hill, for a substitute, of his invention, for Leghorn Plait, for Hats, &c. *Ibid.* 231 A specimen of plaited straw, manufactured.. in this country, similar to that imported from various parts of Europe, under the denomination of Leghorn. **1818** LADY MORGAN *Autobiog.* (1859) 64, I bought myself a *chapeau de soleil*, with corn flowers stuck in the side of it—a regular Leghorn. **1823** *Spirit Publ. Jrnls.* (1825) I. 6 She.. split the young lady's Leghorn by one thump of her fist. **1893** PEEL *Spen Valley* 271 The great leghorn bonnets which they prized so highly. **1969** GISH & PINCHOT *L. Gish* iii. 33 Dorothy and I were cool in our full-skirted summer frocks and wide-brimmed leghorn hats. **1975** R. PLAYER *Let's talk of Graves* ii. 46 Her big grey saucer eyes, shaded by the big Leghorn hat.
2. The name of a breed of the domestic fowl.
1869 *Rep. U.S. Commissioner Agric.* 485, 15 hens, mostly Leghorns and Black Hamburgs. *Ibid.*, Mixture of Leghorn and native breed. **1874** L. WRIGHT *Illustr. Bk. Poultry* 423 While most Spanish breeds are delicate, the Leghorns are extraordinarily hardy, besides being much superior as layers. *Ibid.* 425 The white Leghorn cock.

legia(u)nce, obs. form of LIGEANCE.

legibility (lɛdʒɪˈbɪlɪtɪ). [f. LEGIBLE: see -ITY.] The quality or condition of being legible.
1679 J. GOODMAN *Penitent Pard.* I. iv. (1713) 105 The divine goodness did supply that defect, as to the greater lines of vertue and vice, by the plain legibility of his providence. **1812** W. TAYLOR in *Monthly Rev.* LXXIX. 181 Perhaps they.. should have been accompanied with an expurgatory index, pointing out the papers which it would be fatiguing to peruse, and thus decimating the contents into legibility.

1838 DICKENS *Nich. Nick.* iv, The words emblazoned in all the legibility of gilt letters and dark shading. **1862** LADY LLANOVER in *Mrs. Delany's Corr.* Ser. II. III. 289 *note*, A hand which for clearness, compactness, and legibility exceeded any writing the Editor ever saw. **1880** EARLE *Philol. Eng. Tongue* 143 A few slight variations, often repeated, will make a great difference in the legibility of a page, to the eye that is unaccustomed to such variations.

legible ('lɛdʒɪb(ə)l), *a.* (*sb.*) Also 4 **legeable**, 5 **legibylle**. [ad. late L. *legibilis* (6th c.), f. *legĕre* to read: see -BLE.] That can be read.

a. Of writing: Plain enough to be read; easily made out or deciphered.

c **1375** *Sc. Leg. Saints* xlii. (*Agatha*) 283 And wrytine ves in þat tabil rycht fare lettire & legeable. **1483** *Cath. Angl.* 212/2 Legibylle, *legibilis*. **1560** WARDE tr. *Alexis' Secr.* II. 8 b, Dresse the letters after thys maner.. and they shalbe legible. **1620** MIDDLETON *Chaste Maid* v. i, A fair, fast, legible hand. **1662** J. DAVIES tr. *Olearius' Voy. Ambass.* 403 Strange Characters.. so eaten out by time, that they were not legible. **1719** SWIFT *To Yng. Clergym.* Wks. 1755 II. II. 11 Their heads held down.. within an inch of the cushion, to read what is hardly legible. **1874** MICKLETHWAITE *Mod. Par. Churches* 218 Over each box should be a legible inscription.

b. Of compositions: Accessible to readers (*nonce-use*); also, easy to read, readable. *rare*.

1676 W. HUBBARD *Happiness of People* Pref., For their sakes who.. were denied the opportunity to be of the Auditory, I have condescended to make it Legible. **1820** SHELLEY *Lett.* Prose Wks. 1880 IV. 178, I am translating in *ottava rima* the Hymn to Mercury... My next effort will be, that it should be legible, a quality much to be desired in translations. **1840** MILL *Diss. & Disc.* (1859) II. 121 French books are supposed to be sufficiently legible in England without translation.

c. *transf.* and *fig.*

1605 BACON *Adv. Learn.* II. iii. §2. 16 That excellent correspondence, which is betweene Gods revealed will and his secret will.. is not legible to the Naturall Man. **1649** BLITHE *Eng. Improv. Impr.* (1653) To Rdr., I have.. endeavoured to make my thoughts as legible as I can. **1691** WOOD *Ath. Oxon.* (O.H.S.) III. 112 His epitaph is legible in the larg volumes of his workes. **1703** COLLIER *Ess.* II. 102 People's opinions of themselves are commonly legible in their countenances. **1774** JEFFERSON *Autobiog.* App., Wks. 1859 I. 141 The great principles of right and wrong are legible to every reader. **1825** LAMB *Elia* Ser. II. *Superannuated Man*, My fellows in the office would sometimes rally me upon the trouble legible in my countenance.

d. as *sb. pl.* Matter for reading. *rare*$^{-1}$.

1864 *Realm* 10 Feb. 1 Natonal education too much resembles the powerful winch of a literary air-pump, screwing up the demand for legibles, and lightening the atmospheric pressure of criticism on the supply.

Hence **'legibleness**, legibility.

1727 in BAILEY vol. II.

legibly ('lɛdʒɪblɪ), *adv.* [f. LEGIBLE + -LY^2.] In a legible manner; in legible characters; so as to be easily read. Also *fig.*

1586 WARNER *Alb. Eng.* II. lxi. (1612) 269 His banner had the picture, and in gold King Edwards Cozen Elenor was legibly inrould. **1664** H. MORE *Myst. Iniq.* 97 Whether written in the outward Word, or legibly engraven upon the Table of his Heart. **1699** BENTLEY *Phal.* 240 It's yet legibly and plainly *ΠΡΩΤΟΣ ΟΣ*. **1709** STEELE & ADDISON *Tatler* No. 101 ⁋7 A shaking Hand does not always write legibly. **1833** *Act 3 & 4 Will. IV*, c. 46 §84 The rules.. shall be legibly painted upon boards. **1859** KINGSLEY *Misc.* (1860) I. 364 Whether his books treat of love or political economy, theology or geology, it is there, the history of man legibly printed. **1869** FREEMAN *Norm. Conq.* (1876) III. xiv. 356 The great tale of which it became the theatre is legibly written on its natural features.

legicide ('lɛdʒɪsaɪd). *rare*$^{-1}$. [f. L. *lēgi-*, *lēx* law + -CIDE I.] A destroyer of laws.

1689 TUTCHIN *Heroick Poem* 7 A Tyrant Troop of Legicides.. Such as Free Rome of old, Destroy'd and Fought.

legier, obs. form of LEDGER; var. LEGER *sb. Obs.*

legierdemain, etc., obs. ff. LEGERDEMAIN.

†**'legifer.** *Obs.* [a. L. *lēgifer*, f. *lēgi-*, *lēx* law + *-fer* bearing, bringing.] A legislator.

1602 W. WATSON *Decacordon* 53 Thus haue all lawes and legifers with great maiesty, ordained a distinction of place, regard, and esteeme to be had of euery person. **1604** T. WRIGHT *Passions* v. iv. 213 That the Legifers should have no lesse regard to Love, then to Lawes. **1612** T. JAMES *Jesuits' Downf.* 57 Such Lords, lawlesse Sirs, and Legifers they take themselues to be.

†**le'giferous**, *a. Obs.*$^{-0}$ [f. prec. + -OUS: cf. -FEROUS.] 'That maketh or giveth laws' (Blount *Glossogr.* 1656).

legific (liː'dʒɪfɪk), *a.* [ad. L. type **lēgificus*, f. *lēgi-*, *lēx* law + *-ficus*: see -FIC.] Pertaining to the making of laws.

1865 J. GROTE *Treat. Mor. Ideas* x. App. (1876) 224 Practically, in many cases, authority or legific competence has begun in bare power.

†**legiformal**, *a. Obs. rare*$^{-1}$. [f. assumed L. **lēgiform-is* (f. *lēgi-*, *lēx* law + *forma* FORM *sb.*) + -AL^1.] ? Of a legal form or character.

a **1693** *Urquhart's Rabelais* III. xlii. 344 There are Heaps of these Legiformal Papers.

†**'legify**, *a. Obs. rare*$^{-1}$. [f. L. *lēgi-*, *lēx* law + -FY.] *intr.* To make laws.

1658–9 *Burton's Diary* (1828) IV. 95 Is it fit that those that have no right nor foundation should legify amongst us?

legion ('liːdʒən). Also 3–5 **legiun**, 4 **legioun**, **lygioun**, 4–5 **legyoun**, 5–6 **legyon**. [a. OF. *legiun*, *legion* (mod.F. *légion*), a. L. *legiōn-em*, *legio*, f. *legĕre* to choose, levy (an army): cf. -ION^1.]

1. a. *Rom. Antiq.* A body of infantry in the Roman army, composed of different numbers at different periods, ranging from 3,000 in early times to 6,000 under Marius, and combined usually with a considerable complement of cavalry.

c **1205** LAY. 6024 Werren on alche legiun þus feole leodkempen, six þusend & six hundred & sixti iferen. *c* **1330** R. BRUNNE *Chron.* (1810) 30 Fro Charles kyng sanz faile thei brought a gonfaynoun þat Saynt Morice in bataile [bare] befor þe legioun. **1387** TREVISA *Higden* (Rolls) II. 75 When at the prayer of Genuis þe queene.. legiouns of Rome were i-sende in to Irlond, þo was Caerleon a noble citee. **1494** FABYAN *Chron.* III. lv. 36 Claudius sent certayne Legions of his Knyghtes into Irlande to rule that Countre, and retourned hym selfe to Rome. **1598** BARRET *Theor. Warres* Gloss. 251 Legion, amongst the auncient Romaines, was certaine companies of their people of warre: consisting of 5 or 6000 footemen, and 300 horsemen. **1606** SHAKS. *Ant. & Cl.* III. vii. 72 You keepe by Land the Legions and the Horse whole, do you not? **1611** —— *Cymb.* IV. iii. 24 The Romaine Legions, all from Gallia drawne, Are landed on your Coast. **1697** DRYDEN *Virg. Georg.* II. 378 As Legions in the Field their Front display, To try the Fortune of some doubtful Day. **1838** ARNOLD *Hist. Rome* I. i. 25 The thirty centuries which made up the legion. **1856** EMERSON *Eng. Traits, Ability* Wks. (Bohn) II. 33 [The Roman] disembarked his legions, erected his camps and towers. **1869** RAWLINSON *Anc. Hist.* 398 The legion was light, elastic, adapted to every variety of circumstance.

b. Applied to certain military bodies of modern times. ***foreign legion*** [= F. *légion étrangère*]: a body of foreign volunteers in a modern army, esp. that formed in the French army during the 19th c., and employed in colonial territories or on distant expeditions; also *transf.*

1598 [see LEGIONARY B.] **1802** JAMES *Milit. Dict.* s.v., The British legion which served in America. *Ibid.*, The Polish and Belgic legions, that form part of the French army. **1809** WELLINGTON in Gurw. *Desp.* V. 219 A legion is I understand a corps consisting of one, two or more battalions of infantry and a proportion of cavalry and artillery. **1815** *Ibid.* XII. 313 It appears impossible for the Hanoverian Government to bear the expence of the Legion as now constituted. **1838** *Murray's Hand-bk. N. Germ.* 154 The Farm of La Haye Sainte.. was at first occupied by the soldiers of the German Legion. *a* **1877** MRS. NORTON *Bingen on the Rhine*, A soldier of the legion lay dying in Algiers. **1897** E. A. BARTLETT *Battlefields Thessaly* vii. 144 There was a small foreign legion of about five hundred men, made up chiefly of Italians and English. **1924** M. MAGNUS (*title*) Memoirs of the foreign legion. **1957** P. KEMP *Mine were of Trouble* ii. 19 The Foreign Legion, or Tercio, was founded in the early 1920s by General Millán Astray. **1968** *Encycl. Brit.* XIII. 905/2 The term 'foreign legion' is often used for irregular volunteer corps of foreign sympathizers raised by states at war.

2. Vaguely used for: A host of armed men.

c **1325** *Chron. Eng.* 633 (Ritson) The spere That Charlemayne wes wonet to bere Tofore the holy legioun. ?*a* **1400** *Morte Arth.* 605 The lege-mene of Lettow with legyons ynewe. *c* **1440** *Partonope* 2691 Wyth hym a legyoun Of his knyghtis. **1595** SHAKS. *John* II. i. 59 The aduerse windes.. haue giuen him time To land his Legions all as soone as I. **1715–20** POPE *Iliad* XIII. 845 Nor knew great Hector how his legions yield. **1738** GLOVER *Leonidas* II. 318 With legitimering blast their legions.

3. a. A vast host or multitude (of persons or things): freq. of angels or spirits, with reminiscence of Matt. xxvi. 53.

a **1300** *Cursor M.* 15809 If i mi fader wald be-seke, I moght wit-vten lett Haf tuelue thusand legions. **1362** LANGL. *P. Pl.* A. I. 109 Lucifer with legiouns lered it in heuene. *c* **1380** WYCLIF *Sel. Wks.* III. 264 Many lygiouns of aungels. **1413** *Pilgr. Sowle* (Caxton) v. xiv. (1859) 79 No doute but many a legyon wenten to the foote of Olyuet, ordeynyng theyr procession to brynge hym therupon. **1500–20** DUNBAR *Poems* viii. 9 With angellis licht, in legionis, Thow art illumynit all about. **1605** SHAKS. *Macb.* IV. iii. 55 Not in the Legions Of horrid Hell, can come a Diuell more damn'd In euils, to top Macbeth. **1634** CANNE *Necess. Separ.* (1849) 234 To sustain even a legion of reproaches. **1667** MILTON *P.L.* I. 301 He.. called His Legions, Angel Forms, who lay intrans'd. **1751** JOHNSON *Rambler* No. 96 ⁋10 Innumerable legions of appetites and passions. **1824** W. IRVING *T. Trav.* II. 19 As I approached the house, a legion of whelps sallied out. **1865** J. H. NEWMAN *Gerontius* §4 So now his [Satan's] legions throng the vestibule. **1865** LECKY *Ration.* I. i. 25 The air was filled with unholy legions.

b. In Mark v. 9 and echoes of this passage; *esp.* in the (somewhat inaccurate) allusive phrase ***their name is Legion*** = 'they are innumerable'.

1382 WYCLIF *Mark* v. 9 A legioun is name to me; for we ben manye. **1526** TINDALE *ibid.*, My name is Legion, for we are many. **1601** SHAKS. *Twel. N.* III. iv. 95 If all the diuels of hell be drawne in little, and Legion himselfe possest him. **1665** GLANVILL *Scepsis Sci.* xviii. 116 The same undivided essence.. is here multiplyed into Legion. **1848** DICKENS *Dombey* xlv, 'Their name is Legion', she replied. **1873** HELPS *Anim. & Mast.* vi. (1875) 143 The number of such sayings anticipated by this original maxim is legion.

4. a. ***Legion of Honour*** [= F. *légion d'honneur*]: an order of distinction, founded by Napoleon Bonaparte in 1802, conferred as a reward for civil or military services, etc.

1827 SCOTT *Napoleon* V. 63. **1837** MARRYAT *Olla Podr.* xxix, The innkeeper was a Chevalier of the Legion of Honour. **1841–4** EMERSON *Ess.*, *Nom. & Real* Wks. (Bohn) I. 250 The world is full of masonic ties, of guilds, of secret and public legions of honour.

b. ***Legion of the lost*** (***ones***): people who are destitute or abandoned; *spec.* (see quot. 1961).

1870 D. J. KIRWAN *Palace & Hovel* xlii. 587 Those fair and frail members of the Legion of the Lost. **1892** KIPLING *Barrack-Room Ballads* 63 To the legion of the lost ones, to the cohort of the damned. **1899** —— *From Sea to Sea* I. ix. 299 Raising a Legion of the Lost for colonial service—of men who would do their work in one place for ever and look for nothing beyond it. **1961** PARTRIDGE *Dict. Slang* Suppl. 1167/1 *Legion of the lost, the*, those elderly or mentally infirm persons in homes or institutions who have been abandoned by relations and friends and who receive neither visits nor letters.

c. ***American Legion***, a national association of ex-servicemen instituted in 1919 in the U.S.A.; ***British Legion***, a similar association founded in 1921 and incorporated by Royal Charter in 1925 (since 1971 called the Royal British Legion); also *ellipt.*, as *Legion*.

1919 G. S. WHEAT *Story Amer. Legion* 8 At that dinner [in Paris, 16 Feb. 1919] the American Legion was born. *Ibid.* 32 That was the crux of the initial success of the Legion. **1921** *Times* 16 May 6/4 The arrangements for uniting various ex-Service men's societies into one big organization were completed.. yesterday. The new organization will be known as the British Legion. **1953** *New Statesman* 13 June 696/2 A thousand business dinners, Legion reunions and family gatherings. **1968** *Encycl. Brit.* I. 764/1 Nonpolitical and nonsectarian, the American Legion's membership requirement is honourable service and an honourable discharge. **1970** *British Legion Jrnl.* Jan. 11/3 'Don' as he was affectionately known by all was a true member of the Legion, always to the fore in all branch and club activities. *Ibid.* 21 Are you going to Jersey for your holiday this year? The Appeals Department of the British Legion will send you.. an interesting brochure. **1974** A. PRICE *Other Paths to Glory* vi. 72 Secretary of the Elthingham branch of the British Legion. *Ibid.* 73 He invariably sought information first from the local Legion secretary. **1974** T. KENRICK *Two for Price of One* xii. 101, I love my country... Been in the [American] Legion twenty years.

5. *Nat. Hist.* (See quot.)

1859 PAGE *Handbk. Geol. Terms*, *Legion*.. A term occasionally used in Natural History classification to express an assemblage of objects intermediate in extent between a *class* and *order*. A class may thus embrace several legions, and a legion contain many orders.

6. *attrib.* or *adj.* **a.** = Innumerable, multitudinous.

1678 NORRIS *Coll. Misc.* (1699) 282 By this it [Pride] becomes a Multiplied, a Legion evil. **1795** SOUTHEY *Joan of Arc* x. 443 When pouring o'er his legion slaves on Greece, The eastern despot bridged the Hellespont. **1891** C. JAMES *Rom. Rigmarole* 148 The poor curate's wife.. with the legion family clothed from the odds and ends of her rich sister's cast-offs.

b. Legion disease, fever, etc., *slang* (esp. *Journalists'*) = *legionnaires' disease* s.v. LEGIONNAIRE 2; also *ellipt.*

1976 *Time* 16 Aug. 64/2 Several Legionnaires had entered Williamsport hospital with symptoms of something that soon came to be known as 'Legion Disease'. **1976** *Birmingham* (Alabama) *News* 13 Oct. 44/1 The mysterious 'Legion fever' that killed more than a score of Americans last summer. **1978** *Dædalus* Spring 151 Nobel laureate George Wald.. likened an imaginary outbreak of recombinant DNA organisms to Legion fever. **1985** *Times* 16 May 2/1 (*heading*) New Legion disease alert. **1985** *Sunday Times* 19 May 2/1 (*heading*) Legion checked.

legionary ('liːdʒənərɪ), *a.* and *sb.* [ad. L. *legiōnārius*, f. *legiōn-em* LEGION *sb.*: see -ARY.]

A. *adj.*

1. Of or belonging to a legion.

1577–87 HOLINSHED *Chron.* I. 37/2 Ostorius.. had no legionarie souldiers, but certeine bands of aids. **1581** SAVILE *Tacitus Hist.* Annot. (1591) 52 In former times.. the Legionary Cohorts were equall, of fiue hundreth a piece. **1646** SIR T. BROWNE *Pseud. Ep.* v. x. 249 Of the foure principle or Legionary standards, that is of Judah, Ruben, Ephraim, and Dan. **1796** MORSE *Amer. Geog.* II. 112 Altars and monumental inscriptions, which instruct us as to the legionary stations of the Romans in Britain. **1838** ARNOLD *Hist. Rome* (1846) I. xiii. 223 The whole multitude of legionary soldiers. **1893** *Archæologia* LIII. 550 The bronze eagle, probably rightly supposed by Mr. Joyce to have been a legionary one.

b. Of an inscription, mark, etc.: Designating a particular Roman legion.

legionary ring (Rom. Antiq.): a finger-ring bearing a number, formerly thought to have been worn by Roman soldiers, the number being supposed to be that of the legion. This view is now abandoned, as the numbers go up to 100, while the highest legionary number was 28.

1851 D. WILSON *Preh. Ann.* (1863) II. III. ii. 38 Its legionary inscriptions indicate the several portions—erected by the different legions and cohorts. *Ibid.* 67 The legionary tablets of the Scottish wall are its most interesting relics. **1863** *Q. Rev.* CXIV. 382 The legionary mark of the tile. **1869** FORTNUM in *Archæol. Jrnl.* XXVI. 146 Bronze 'Legionary ring'.. on which is engraved the so-called legionary number.

2. Constituting or consisting of a legion or legions.

1670 MILTON *Hist. Eng.* II. Wks. 1851 V. 55 The Silures .. besett the Prefect of his Camp, left there with Legionarie Bands to appoint Garrisons. **1776** GIBBON *Decl. & F.* (1869) I. i. 25 The whole body of legionary infantry amounted to six thousand one hundred men. **1827** DE QUINCEY *Murder*

Wks. 1862 IV. 52 The Roman legionary force. **1871** FARRAR *Witn. Hist.* iii. 100 Without one earthly weapon she faced the legionary masses.

fig. **1646** SIR T. BROWNE *Pseud. Ep.* I. iii. 12 Too many.. betwixt jest and earnest, betray the cause of truth, and incensibly make up, the legionarie body of errour.

B. *sb.* A soldier of a legion, ancient or modern; a legionary soldier. Also, a member of the Legion of Honour.

1598 DALLINGTON *Meth. Trav.* Lb, As touching the [French] Infantry, Francis the first was the first that instituted the Legionaries.. 8 Legions, and every Legion to containe sixe thousand. **1608** E. GRIMSTONE *Hist. France* (1611) 675 Twelue thousand Legionaries, Picards, Normands and Champanois. **1781** GIBBON *Decl. & F.* xxx. III. 173 If any of the legionaries were permitted to return from the Italian expedition. **1827** SCOTT *Napoleon* xxvi. Wks. 1870 XI. 276 Three hundred and fifty legionaries [of the Legion of Honour]. **1832–4** DE QUINCEY *Cæsars* Wks. 1859 X. 154 The cowering legionary, with whom to hear was to obey. **1892** *Pall Mall G.* 26 Oct. 4/3 Day was just dawning when the Marine Infantry and the Legionaries advanced.

legioned (ˈliːdʒənd), *a. poet.* [f. LEGION + -ED¹.] Arrayed in legions.

1818 SHELLEY *Rev. Islam* x. xxxii, An Iberian Priest.. who led the legioned West. **1818** KEATS *Endym.* II. 43 So once more days and nights aid me along, Like legioned soldiers. **1820** —— *Eve St. Agnes* xix, While legion'd fairies paced the coverlet. **1822** SHELLEY *Hellas* 515 We met the vultures, legioned in the air. **1851** J. B. HUME *Poems* 150 The clarions of all the legion'd winds!

legionella (liːdʒəˈnɛlə). *Bacteriol.* Pl. **-ellæ**. [mod.L., f. LEGION + L. *-ella* -EL².] Any bacterium of the genus *Legionella*, that includes the cause of legionnaires' disease and comprises aerobic Gram-negative rods mostly pathogenic for man.

1979 *Lancet* 3 Feb. 270/2 We have succeeded in staining legionellæ in these materials using only the first dye in Gram's procedure. **1981** *Brit. Med. Jrnl.* 16 May 1585/1 (*heading*) Postoperative legionella pneumonia diagnosed by percutaneous lung aspiration. **1983** *Oxf. Textbk. Med.* I. v. 331/2 More recently other legionella species besides *L. pneumophila* have been associated with sporadic respiratory infections in man. **1985** *Times* 8 May 2/5 The treatment they were carrying out was not aimed at the legionella bacteria. **1985** *New Scientist* 19–26 Dec. 28/1 Amoebae live by ingesting and digesting bacteria, but legionellae turn the tables on their predators by breaking down the amoeba's destructive enzymes into amino acids, upon which the bacteria feed.

Hence ˌ**legioneˈllosis**, infection with or a disease caused by legionellæ.

1979 *Lancet* 7 Apr. 786/1 The ætiological agent of legionellosis.. has been tentatively named *Legionella pneumophila*. **1984** HOLT & KRIEG *Bergey's Man. Systematic Bacteriol.* (ed. 9) I. 281/1 The two main types of legionellosis caused by *L. pneumophila* are Legionnaires' disease (LD) and Pontiac fever (PF).

† ˈ**legioner**. *Obs. rare*⁻¹. [f. LEGION + -ER¹.] A legionary soldier.

1579–80 NORTH *Plutarch* (1595) 992 The legioners did couer themselues as they had done before with their shields.

† **legionet**. *Obs. rare*⁻¹. [f. LEGION + -ET¹.] A small legion.

1600 HOLLAND *Livy* xxxv. xlix. 917 You should see in this kings camp hardly two pretie legionets [L. *legiuncula*], and those but lame ones neither.

† ˈ**legionize**, *v. Obs. rare*⁻¹. [f. LEGION + -IZE.] *trans.* To form into legions.

1609 J. DAVIES *Holy Rood* I 4, Descend sweet Angels (Legioniz'd in Rankes).

legionnaire (liːdʒəˈnɛə(r)). Also **legionaire**, or with capital initial. [ad. F. *légionnaire*, f. *légion* LEGION 1 b.] **1.** A member of the American, British, Foreign, or other Legion.

1818 SHELLEY *Let.* 20 Nov. (1964) II. 55 The marks of the chisels of the legionaires of the Roman Consul are yet evident. **1927** *Daily Express* 26 Apr. 1/5 Each legionnaire automatically becomes a member of the branch of the Canadian Legion nearest to the settlement on which he lives. **1927** *Daily Tel.* 14 June 7/2 The American Legion.. assembles in Paris in September... The legionnaires will be over two weeks on the Atlantic. **1932** KIPLING *Limits & Renewals* 322 His speech.. ran From pure Parisian to gross peasant, With interludes North African If any Legionnaire were present. **1965** C. D. EBY *Siege of Alcázar* (1966) xi. 222 Captain Tiede and his Legionnaires filed into the Alcázar through the swimming pool door. **1974** *Northern Times* (Golspie, Sutherland) 23 Aug. 3/2 The Legion piper, Mr. Donnie McKenzie, played Mr. Bain's favourite pipe tune, while Legionaires paid their last respects.

2. *legionnaires' disease*: a severe form of bacterial pneumonia (often accompanied by mental confusion) which is caused by *Legionella pneumophila* and is associated esp. with infected water systems. [So called from the outbreak in July 1976 that affected people attending a Legionnaires' Convention in Philadelphia.]

1976 *Kingston Whig-Standard* (Ontario) 5 Aug. 1/4 Further clues to the flu-like 'legionnaires [*sic*] disease' may come today when first results are available from tests being conducted at the state health laboratories in Philadelphia. **1977** *Lancet* 17 Dec. 1266/1 It is already important for clinicians to think of legionnaires' disease when severe pneumonia proves resistant to standard therapy. **1978** G. VIDAL *Kalki* vii. 173 Every bright-faced child on earth is scheduled to die sooner or later, of cancer, legionnaire's disease, swine flu, whatever. **1983** *Oxf. Textbk. Med.* I. v. 332/2 Two cases of Legionnaires' disease in an Oxford transplant unit were associated with infected shower water. *Ibid.*, It has been suggested that Legionella pneumonia be the term used to describe pneumonia due to *Legionella* species and reserve Legionnaires' disease for outbreaks similar to that in Philadelphia. **1985** *Sci. Amer.* Oct. 70/3 It is a DNA probe designed to recognize the presence in a patient of any one of the 22 species of the bacterial genus *Legionella*, the agents of various pneumonias of which the best-known is Legionnaires' disease.

legionry (ˈliːdʒənrɪ). [f. LEGION + -RY.] Legions collectively.

1827 POLLOK *Course T.* VII, To drive away From earth the dark infernal legionry Of superstition, ignorance and hell.

legior, obs. form of LEDGER.

legislate (ˈlɛdʒɪsleɪt), *v.* [Back-formation from LEGISLATOR, LEGISLATION.]

1. *trans.* To make laws for. *rare*⁻¹.

1719 D'URFEY *Pills* (1872) II. 66 The Parliament sate.. Legislating the Nation.

2. *intr.* To perform the function of legislation; to make or enact laws.

1805 BP. WATSON *Charge* (1808) 16 Solon, in legislating for the Athenians, had an idea of a more perfect Constitution than he gave them. **1841** W. SPALDING *Italy & It. Isl.* II. 119 The emperor had a right to legislate for the whole country. **1846** MᶜCULLOCH *Acc. Brit. Empire* (1854) II. 247 The renunciation by the British Parliament of the right to legislate for that kingdom [Ireland]. **1875** JOWETT *Plato* (ed. 2) V. 135 All states legislate under the idea that there are two classes of actions, the voluntary and the involuntary.

3. quasi-*trans.* To bring or drive by legislation *into* or *out of*. Also rarely *trans.* to bring about or control by legislation.

1845 [see LEGISLATED *ppl. a.* below]. **1847** R. W. HAMILTON *Disq. Sabbath* ii. (1848) 39 The same power which legislated the very circumstances, alone can release them. **1849** *Tait's Mag.* XVI. 401/2 Trades' unions.. should be educated, and not legislated into usefulness. **1854** *Act U.S.A. Congress* in *Encycl. Brit.* (1860) XXI. 442/2 Not to legislate Slavery into any Territory or State. **1859** W. CHADWICK *Life De Foe* iv. 237, I do not want to see a people legislated into poverty. **1887** RIDER HAGGARD *Jess* i. (1899) 78 It [this sentiment] is beginning to die down and to be legislated out of our national character.

Hence ˈ**legislated** *ppl. a.*, ˈ**legislating** *vbl. sb.* and *ppl. a.*

1845 R. W. HAMILTON *Pop. Educ.* viii. (ed. 2) 178 Schemes of legislated instruction. **1890–1** J. ORR *Christian View God* (1893) 131 The.. presence of a morally legislating and commanding Reason within us. **1898** *Westm. Gaz.* 16 May 2/1 The legislated depreciation of this one estate.. had cost him.. not less than £120,000. **1899** A. E. GARVIE *Ritschlian Theol.* 33 He analyses the conceptions of the condemning and of the legislating conscience.

legislation (lɛdʒɪsˈleɪʃən). [a. late L. *lēgislātiōn-em*, properly two words = 'bringing of a law' (*lēgis*, genitive of *lēx* law + *lātiōn-em* bringing: see LATION). Cf. F. *législation*.]

1. The action of making or giving laws; the enactment of laws, lawgiving; an instance of this.

a **1655** J. GOODMAN *Winter Even. Conf.* III. (1705) 116 Let me to intreat you to explain what you mean by this way of Divine Legislation. **1675** BAXTER *Cath. Theol.* II. I. 213 Gods Legislation was a real Action; but the Law made doth not act at all. **1747** LD. LYTTLETON *Observ. Convers. Paul* 18 Pythagoras, who join'd Legislation to his Philosophy, and.. pretended to Miracles.. to give a more venerable Sanction to the Laws he prescribed. **1828** CAROLINE FRY *Script. Rdr.'s Guide* ix. 124 When the inspired historian tells his story of.. the wars and legislations of other ages. **1876** FREEMAN *Norm. Conq.* V. xxiv. 395 Legislation, as we understand it, did not, in the ideas of those times, fill any prominent place among the duties of a king.

†**2.** A legislative body, a legislature. *Obs.*

1693 *Humours Town* 96 The Common-Council-Man is a Man of Authority, a Member of the City-Legislation.

3. The enactments of a legislator or legislature; the whole body of enacted laws.

1838 THIRLWALL *Greece* viii. I. 297 A legislation in which, as in that of Moses, religion is.. the main element. **1872** YEATS *Growth Comm.* 137 The acts.. are largely taken up with legislation affecting the national commerce.

Hence **legiˈslational** *a.*, pertaining to legislation.

1829 BENTHAM *Justice & Cod. Petit., Abr. Petit. Justice* 22 A legislational proceeding.

legislative (ˈlɛdʒɪslətɪv), *a.* and *sb.* [Formed after LEGISLATION, LEGISLATOR, by substitution of suffix: see -ATIVE. Cf. F. *législatif* (recorded from the 14th c.), Sp., Pg., It. *legislativo*; a med.L. **lēgislātīvus* probably existed.]

A. *adj.*

1. That legislates or makes laws; having the function of legislating.

legislative assembly (Fr. Hist.), the body of legislators which succeeded the National or Constituent assembly in 1791; also, the legislature which succeeded the Constituent assembly of 1849.

1651 BAXTER *Inf. Bapt.* 269, I have learned to distinguish between.. the Decretive and Legislative will of God. **1654** CROMWELL *Sp.* 12 Sept. in *Carlyle*, It is the conversion of a parliament.. to a legislative power always sitting. **1674** *Baker's Chron.* 584/1 The peoples Legislative Deputies in Parliament. **1765** BLACKSTONE *Comm.* I. ii. 146 If half of the members met, and half absented themselves, who shall determine which is really the legislative body, the part assembled, or that which stays away? **1797** *Encycl. Brit.* (ed. 3) XVI. 173/1 On the 30th of September [1791], this National Assembly.. dissolved itself, and gave place to the succeeding Legislative National Assembly. **1858** J. B. NORTON *Topics* 154 The Legislative Council [of India].

2. Of or pertaining to legislation or the making of laws.

c **1641** DENHAM *On Strafford's Trial & D.* 25 Their Legislative Frenzy they repent, Enacting it should make no President. **1651** HOBBES *Leviath.* II. xx. 106 It belongeth therefore to the Soveraigne.. to præscribe the Rules of discerning Good and Evill.. and therefore in him is the Legislative Power. **1763** J. BROWN *Poetry & Mus.* v. 79 During the early Periods of Civilization, the legislative Art is always of an imperfect Form. **1795** BURKE *Scarcity* Wks. VII. 383 Legislative acts require the exactest detail of circumstances.. in order.. to elicit principles.. to direct a practical legislative proceeding. **1870** D. MACRAE *Amer. at Home* II. x. 151 All the Legislative Halls throughout the country.

b. Enacted or appointed by legislation.

1855 MACAULAY *Hist. Eng.* xiii. III. 290 Nor did the Estates mention the use of torture among the grievances which required a legislative remedy. **1872** YEATS *Growth Comm.* 308 Legislative penalties were imposed. **1878** LECKY *Eng. in 18th C.* II. v. 50 The remedy for the evil was found in the legislative emancipation of Scotch industry.

B. *sb.*

1. The power of legislating or making laws; the body in which this power is vested, the legislature. Opposed to 'executive'. Now *rare*.

1642 JER. TAYLOR *Episc.* (1647) 292 What authority is equall to this Legislative of the Bishops? **1689** W. A. *Ld. Chief Just. Herbert's Acc. Examined* 5 The King has not the Legislative exclusive of others. **1689** LOCKE *Govt.* II. §141 xi. (1694) 276 The Legislative cannot transfer the Power of making Laws to any other hands. **1712** BERKELEY *Pass. Obedience* §22 To pay an absolute submission to the decrees of some certain legislative. **1836** ALISON *Hist. Europe* (1847) V. 26 It [the Polish constitution] fell when the legislative became more corrupt then the executive.

†**2.** ? Something appointed by legislative enactment. *Obs.*

1650 ELDERFIELD *Civ. Right Tythes* xvi. 94 He this Edgar, had them questionless from Alfred,.. from Ina, Offa, Ethelbert, &c. to whose tendries he added what seemed fit of the Legislatives of West-Saxony.

legislatively (ˈlɛdʒɪsleɪtɪvlɪ), *adv.* [f. prec. + -LY².] In a legislative manner; by legislation.

1643 SIR J. SPELMAN *Case of Affairs in Law* 6 Whatsoever passed before, it [the absolute supreme Court] *pro re natâ* legislatively judgeth, maketh, and declareth Law. **1650** R. HOLLINGWORTH *Exerc. Usurped Powers* 27 Those who.. assume a power not legally in them, and act legislatively. **1820** *Ann. Reg.* I. 154 It was only legislatively that the Lords could have to deal with this matter. **1869** *Pall Mall G.* 8 July 3/2 Our national characteristic is.. a tendency to deal legislatively in a permissive or tentative style.

legislator (ˈlɛdʒɪsleɪtə(r)). [a. L. *lēgis-lātor*, properly two words, = 'proposer of a law' (*lēgis*, genitive of *lēx* law + *lātor*, used as agent-n. to *ferre* to bear, carry, bring).] One who makes laws (for a people or nation); a lawgiver; a member of a legislative body.

1605 SYLVESTER *Du Bartas* II. iii. III. *Law* 168 This Boat ..saves from wrack the future Legislator [Moses]. **1607** *Schol. Disc. agst. Antichr.* II. v. 10 He draweth the absolute authoritie of Man, not from God as he is God, but as he is *Legis-lator* only. **1651** HOBBES *Leviath.* II. XXVI. 139 For the Legislator is he, not by whose authority the Lawes were first made, but by whose authority they now continue to be Lawes. **1711** POPE *Temp. Fame* 74 Heroes in animated marble frown, And Legislators seem to think in stone. **1809–10** COLERIDGE *Friend* (1865) 44 Laws in doubtful points are to be interpreted according to the design of the legislator. **1878** JEVONS *Prim. Pol. Econ.* 77 Legislators have long since discovered the absurdity of attempting to fix prices by law.

transf. **1821** BYRON *Two Foscari* IV. i, I will be a legislator in this business. **1831** BREWSTER *Newton* (1855) II. xxvii. 403 The alleged legislator of science. **1873** SYMONDS *Grk. Poets* i. 29 Aristotle is the legislator for the human intellect through eighteen centuries after his death.

Hence ˈ**legislatorship**, the position of legislator.

1654 J. SPITTLEHOUSE *Vind. Fifth Monarchy Men* 19 Do they not.. dethrone and degrade the Lord Jesus of his Legislatorship and Judicature? *a* **1695** LD. HALIFAX *Cautions Choice Members in Parlt.* (1699) 16 There ought to be a difference made between coming out of Pupilage, and leaping into Legislatorship. **1890** J. HATTON *By Order of Czar* I. II. i. 223 The principle of hereditary legislatorship.

legislatorial (lɛdʒɪsləˈtɔərɪəl), *a.* [f. as next + -AL¹.]

1. Having the power to legislate, acting as a legislator or legislature.

1819 *Gen. Hist.* in *Ann. Reg.* 104/2 At a public meeting holden on July 12.. the managers.. proposed that the same Sir Charles [Wolseley] should be sent up to parliament as 'legislatorial attorney and representative of Birmingham'. **1841** DE QUINCEY *Homer* Wks. 1857 VI. 349 Solon, the legislatorial founder of Athens. **1882** *Encycl. Brit.* XIV. 357 One may imagine a community governed by a dependent legislatorial body or person.

2. Of or pertaining to a legislator or legislation.

1774–5 BENTHAM *Commonplace Bk.* Wks. 1843 X. 76 A System of Rules for the Conversion of Long Sentences into Short Ones, for the Legislatorial Style. **1829** *Examiner* 306/2 A capital legislatorial *jeu d'esprit*. **1833** *Fraser's Mag.* VIII. 246 He would have done better to stick to his legislatorial duties.

Hence **legislaˈtorially** *adv.*

1827 *Westm. Rev.* VII. 30 The judges legislatorially refuse to acknowledge certain rights of the landlords.

† **legislatory**, *a.* *Obs.* [ad. mod.L. type **lēgislātōrius*, f. *lēgislātor* LEGISLATOR.] = prec.

a **1639** SPOTTISWOOD *Hist. Ch. Scot.* II. (1677) 26 The judgment of Matrimonial causes,.. Legislatory actions [etc.].. should be committed to the Bishops.

legislatress (ˈlɛdʒɪsleɪtrɪs). [f. LEGISLATOR + -ESS.] A female legislator.

1711 SHAFTESB. *Charac.* (1737) II. II. ii. 252 See what that Country of the Mind will produce, when by the wholesom Laws of this Legislatress it has obtain d its Liberty! **1771** H. WALPOLE *Lett. to C'tess Ossory* (1848) I. 24 That lamb and legislatress the Czarina would suffer no patriot orations. **1846** MRS. GORE *Eng. Char.* (1852) 83 Queen Bess, that shrewdest of legislatresses. **1885** MAINE *Pop. Govt.* 155 Nature, a beneficent legislatress.

legislatrix (ˌlɛdʒɪsˈleɪtrɪks). [L. fem. of *lēgislātor.*] A female legislator.

1677 GALE *Crt. Gentiles* IV. 53 This right Reason is the great Legislatrix and Judge of al human affaires. **1797** W. TOOKE *Cath. II* (1798) II. v. 45 No woman had yet been a legislatrix. **1832** AUSTIN *Jurispr.* (1879) II. xxx. 565 Laws supposed to emanate from.. the fancied legislatrix nature.

legislature (ˈlɛdʒɪslətjʊə(r)). [Formed after LEGISLATOR by substitution of suffix: cf. -URE. Cf. F. *législature*, cited by Hatz.-Darm. from 1789.]

1. 'The power that makes laws' (J.); a body of persons invested with the power of making the laws of a country or state; *spec.* (*U.S.*) the legislative body of a State or Territory, as distinguished from Congress.

a **1676** HALE *Hist. Common Law* (1713) 2 Without the concurrent Consent of all Three Parts of the Legislature, no such Law is, or can be made. **1708** SWIFT *Sentim. Ch. Eng. Man* Miscell. (1711) 131 By the Supreme Magistrate is properly understood the Legislative Power... But the Word Magistrate seeming to denote a single Person, and to express the Executive Power, it came to pass, that the Obedience due to the Legislature was, for want of knowing or considering this easy Distinction, misapplyed to the Administration. **1716** ADDISON *Freeholder* No. 16 ¶6 In the very Notion of a Legislature is implied a Power to change, repeal, and suspend what Laws are in being, as well as to make.. new Laws. **1781** COWPER *Fable* 9 Twas April, as the bumpkins say, The legislature called it May. **1783** *Gentl. Mag.* LIII. I. 166 The Congress shall earnestly recommend it to the Legislatures of the respective States. **1821** J. Q. ADAMS in C. Davies *Metr. Syst.* III. (1871) 85 The Statute books are filled with ineffectual attempts of the legislature to establish uniformity. **1839** KEIGHTLEY *Hist. Eng.* II. 57 The legislature gave to the King's proclamations the force of statutes of parliament. **1863** H. COX *Instit.* III. v. 656 Bills of the colonial legislatures relating to trade.

attrib. and *Comb.* **1829** BENTHAM *Justice & Cod. Petit.* 124 Here and there a patch of real law—of legislature-made law—stuck in. **1843** MARRYAT *M. Violet* xx, He once said to them in the legislature room of Matagorda [etc.].

† **2.** The exercise of the function or power of legislation. *Obs.*

a **1715** BURNET *Own Time* (1724) I. 319 It was very inconvenient to have both the legislature and the execution in the same hands. **1724** SWIFT *Drapiers' Lett.* Wks. 1755 V. II. 30 Mr. Wood takes upon him the entire legislature, and an absolute dominion over the properties of the whole nation. *a* **1734** NORTH *Lives* II. 395, I think them very considerable in the science of legislature. **1765** BLACKSTONE *Comm.* I. 46 For legislature.. is the greatest act of superiority that can be exercised by one being over another.

legist (ˈliːdʒɪst). [ad. F. *légiste* (recorded from 13th c.), ad. med.L. *lēgista*, f. *lēg-*, *lēx* LAW: see -IST.] One versed in the law (cf. JURIST); *spec.* one of a group of legal philosophers in the early Han dynasty in China. Also *attrib.* or as *adj.*

1484 CAXTON *Fables of Æsop* v. x, My fader was no legist ne neuer knewe the lawes. **1536** BELLENDEN *Cron. Scot.* (1821) I. 195 Ulpianus, the floure of legistis in his dayis. **1586** FERNE *Blaz. Gentrie* To Gentl. Inner Temple, The honorable assembly of the Inner Temple with all the gentlemen, students and professed Legists in the same. **1616** BACON *Let. to King* 12 Feb. *Lett. & Life* (1869) V. 242 As legists, they will agree in magnifying that wherein they are best. **1691** WOOD *Ath. Oxon.* II. 474 He had a Legists place and took the degrees in the Civil Law. **1821** *Edin. Rev.* XXXV. 169 We shall.. bring together the names of some of the great legists of Britain. **1858** M. PATTISON *Ess.* (1889) II. 327 An able legist.. he brings into literature the habits and prepossessions of his position. **1895** RASHDALL *Universities* II. 568 Ten were to be Legists, and seven Canonists. **1956** A. TOYNBEE *Historian's Approach to Relig.* ii. 22 In China the uncompromisingly rationalistic Legist school of philosophy was eventually driven off the field by a Confucian school which tempered its Rationalism with a conservative respect for a pre-rationalist tradition. **1957** *Chinese Culture* (Taipei) I. I. 77 As we know, School of the Legists prevailed during the earlier Han dynasty. **1965** *New Statesman* 24 Dec. 1004/1 Eventually the Romans did adopt that model but not, unfortunately, 'deliberately planned and executed in advance by an act of far-sighted and well-calculated statesmanship' (as Princes Hien and Hiao had done in China with the help of a 'sophist of the Legist school, Shang Yang').

† **ˈlegister**[1]. *Obs.* Forms: 4–5 legistre, -ystre, 5 legistery, 6 legistere, 5, 7 legister. [a. OF. *legistre* variant (influenced by *ministre*, etc.) of *legiste* LEGIST.] = LEGIST.

1303 R. BRUNNE *Handl. Synne* 5410 Lordynges cunseylours Wykkede legystrys [F. *legistre*] or fals acountours. **1362** LANGL. *P. Pl.* A. VIII. 62 ȝe legistres and lawyers ȝe witen where I lyȝe. **1387–8** T. USK *Test. Love* II. ii. (Skeat) I. 69 Amonge legystres there dare I not come. **14..** *Nom.* in Wr.-Wülcker 680/43 *Hic legista*, a legistery. **1430–40** LYDG. *Bochas* III. xviii. (1554) 90a, Legistres folowyng their ententes Greatly reioyce in lucre. **1440** J. SHIRLEY *Dethe K. James* (1818) 26 He was.. a grete legister of lawe positive, and canone, and civille bothe. **1555** ABP. PARKER *Ps.* lx. 170 Juda legistere. **1616** BULLOKAR, *Legisters*, Lawyers. **1656** in BLOUNT *Glossogr.*

† **ˈlegister**[2]. *Obs.* [App. f. L. *legĕre* to read + -STER fem. agent-suffix.] In a nunnery: A woman charged with the duty of reading aloud.

14.. in Aungier *Hist. Syon Monast.* (1840) 374 Whan al be sette, anone the legister schal begyn to rede.. And sche muste rede suche mater as the abbes or chauntres assignethe.

‖ **ˈlegit** *sb.*[1] *Obs.* [L. *lĕgit* he reads, or *lēgit* he has read, pres. or pa. t. 3rd pers. of *legĕre* to read.] Claim to 'Benefit of Clergy' based upon the fact of being able to read a verse of the Bible.

1653 BAXTER *Chr. Concord* 76 They took the drunken Readers (that could scarce yet have a *Legit* to save their necks, if they needed it) to be fitter men then we to edefie the Flocks.

legit., **legit** (lɪˈdʒɪt), *a.* and *sb.*[2] Colloq. abbrev. of LEGITIMATE *a.*, *sb.*, esp. of sense 2 b of the adj. Also in phr. ***on the legit***, within the law.

1897 *National Police Gaz.* (U.S.) 26 May 6/1 Bob is envious of Corbett's success as a 'legit'. It pained him to see Jim strutting through four acts of a real play. *Ibid.*, Bob now wants to go into the 'legit'. **1904** *Daily Chron.* 22 Oct. 7/4 At the Hippodrome, four more 'legits' make their first appearance in 'variety'. **1908** 'ONE OF THE OLD BRIGADE' *London in Sixties* xiv. 177 Scene shifters, stage carpenters, actors, everything and everybody strictly 'legit' should have the preference of guzzling and swilling to the memory of the immortal poet. **1923** H. RUBY *Let.* 16 Aug. in G. Marx *Groucho Lett.* (1967) 184 He clicked as a legit actor on Broadway. **1931** G. IRWIN *Amer. Tramp & Underworld Slang* 138 *On the legit*, honest. **1936** N. COWARD *Tonight at 8.30* I. 93 When she stabs herself—she takes such a time about it—that's legits all over. **1946** MEZZROW & WOLFE *Really Blues* ii. 21 Once Sid got.. a hundred cases of booze on the legit.. but.. would sooner have his throat cut than push them at legit prices at the drugstores. **1952** W. R. BURNETT *Vanity Row* (1953) v. 41 In the early 'twenties he'd served time.. for bootlegging. .. Since then.., he'd been.. on the legit. **1955** E. BOWEN *World of Love* xi. 206 Left no children—anyway, no legits. **1957** J. OSBORNE *Entertainer* v. 38 I'd gone legit. for a while.. and I'd been in 'The Tale of Two Cities'. **1961** *Times* 29 Nov. 11/5 It provided funds for penetration into 'legit' business for the gang lords. **1965** J. B. PRIESTLEY *Lost Empires* I. ii. 16 She used to be legit and pretends to be very haigh-clarss,.. though she's only playing feed to a comedian. **1967** J. HORTON in T. Kochman *Rappin' & Stylin' Out* (1972) 22 Identified as white, a lame, and square, I had to build up an image of being at least 'legit' (not working for the police). **1969** B. MALCOLM in A. Chapman *New Black Voices* (1972) 384 First time I was sweet sixteen Marriage license, zircon ring—all legit. **1970** C. WOOD *Terrible Hard* viii. 112 I've never been 'legit' as you might say.., just an old-fashioned song and dance girl. **1972** R. HILL *Fairly Dangerous Thing* II. vii. 185 A business acquaintance. Runs an escort service. Legit. High class. **1972** *New Society* 7 Dec. 559/1 The age of legit drinking will come down from 18 to 17. **1973** 'H. HOWARD' *Highway to Murder* x. 127 This dough isn't strictly legit.

legitim: see LEGITIME.

legitimacy (lɪˈdʒɪtɪməsɪ). [f. LEGITIMATE: see -ACY.] The fact of being legitimate.

1. a. The fact of being a legitimate child.

1691 LUTTRELL *Brief Rel.* (1857) II. 207 A virulent libell ..endeavouring to prove the legitimacy of the prince of Wales, is printed. **1754–62** HUME *Hist. Eng., Hen. III*, II. 54 It had been formerly usual for the civil courts to issue writs to the spiritual, directing them to inquire into the legitimacy of the person. **1856** FROUDE *Hist. Eng.* (1858) I. ii. 107 The innumerable refinements of the Romish canon law, which affected the legitimacy of children.

† **b.** *transf.* Genuineness. *Obs.*

1695 WOODWARD *Nat. Hist. Earth* I. (1723) 36 The Legitimacy and Reality of these Marine bodies vindicated.. I now re-assume my original design.

2. Of a government or the title of a sovereign: The condition of being in accordance with law or principle. Now often, with respect to a sovereign's title, in a narrower sense: The fact of being derived by regular descent; *occas.* the principle of lineal succession to the throne, as a political doctrine.

1812 *Niles' Reg.* I. 404/1, I never hear an American citizen speak of the '*legitimacy*' of princes without indignation or pity. **1817** J. SCOTT *Paris Revisit.* (ed. 4) 233 No one.. will be found in this country to maintain that mere birth alone constitutes royal legitimacy. **1818** LADY MORGAN *Autobiog.* (1859) 215 We were seated near the princesses.. in the very *foyer* of ultra legitimacy. **1825** MACAULAY *Milton* Ess. (1880) 16 The doctrine of Divine Right, which has now come back to us, like a thief from transportation, under the *alias* of Legitimacy. **1872** J. L. SANFORD *Estim. Eng. Kings* 368 His [Oliver's] rule only wanted the stamp of legitimacy to entitle it to nearly unmixed praise. **1884** A. R. PENNINGTON *Wiclif* vi. 180 We may differ in opinion as to the legitimacy of Urban or Clement.

3. *gen.* Conformity to rule or principle; lawfulness. In *Logic*, conformity to sound reasoning.

1836 J. GILBERT *Chr. Atonem.* vi. (1852) 158 It has, however, been objected, that the difference in circumstances forbids the legitimacy of our assumption. **1864** BOWEN *Logic* vii. 175 It seems better to test the legitimacy of each step. **1874** RAYMOND *Statist. Mines & Mining* 28 It is easy to see the causes which have led to this large advance, and impossible not to recognize their legitimacy. **1885** J. RAE in *Contemp. Rev.* June 904 An argument.. in favour of the legitimacy of such philanthropic labours.

† **4.** *Austral. slang.* (See quot.) *Obs.*

1827 P. CUNNINGHAM *2 Yrs. N.S. Wales* I. i. 16 The suspicion each entertains of legitimacy being the cause of the other's appearance. *Note*, Legitimacy, a colonial term for designating the cause of the emigration of a certain portion of our population; i.e. having legal reasons for making the voyage.

legitimate (lɪˈdʒɪtɪmət), *a.* Also 5–6 **legyttymat(e**, 6 **-ytymat**, **-ittimat**. [ad. med.L. *lēgitimāt-us*, pa. pple. of *lēgitimāre* to declare to be lawful, to cause to be regarded as lawful offspring, f. L. *lēgitimus* lawful, f. *lēg-*, *lēx* law.

Etymologically, the word expresses a status which has been conferred or ratified by some authority; = LEGITIMATED. In English, however, it has taken the place of the older LEGITIME, and even in the earliest examples shows no trace of the original participial sense.]

A. *adj.* **1. a.** Of a child: Having the status of one lawfully begotten; entitled to full filial rights. Said also of a parent, and of lineal descent. (The only sense in Johnson.)

According to English common law, all children are legitimate who are born in lawful wedlock, and no others. According to the civil and canon law, a child born of unmarried parents who might at the time lawfully contract marriage becomes legitimate if his parents afterwards are lawfully married. By the Legitimacy Acts of 1926 and 1959 a child born of unmarried parents becomes legitimate if they subsequently marry.

1494 FABYAN *Chron.* VII. ccxxv. 253 This Kynge Wyllyam vsed alwey lemmans, wherfore he dyed without issu legyttymat. **1555** EDEN *Decades* 137 The children of their owne wyues they counte to bee not legitimate. **1602** MARSTON *Antonio's Rev.* v. v. Wks. 1856 I. 141 Thy true begotten, most legitimate And loved issue. **1683** *Brit. Spec.* 173 By Lineal and Legitimate Descent the true and unquestionable Heir. **1754–62** HUME *Hist. Eng., Hen. III*, II. 54 The common law had deemed all those bastards who were born before wedlock: By the canon law they were legitimate. **1827** JARMAN *Powell's Devises* (ed. 3) II. 347 A person who at the date of the will was dead, leaving.. no legitimate children. **1841** LANE *Arab. Nts.* I. 62 The offspring of his female slave.. if begotten by him.. he may recognise as his own legitimate child. **1882** A. MACFARLANE *Consanguin.* 4 Legitimate co-parent of a child.

† **b.** *transf.* Genuine, real: opposed to 'spurious'. *Obs.*

1551 BIBLE *Apocrypha* To Rdr., They are not receaued nor taken as legyttymate and leafull, as wel of the Hebrues as of the whole Churche. **1634** T. JOHNSON *Parey's Chirurg.* XXVI. vii. (1678) 633 By the Taste.. we.. distinguish the true legitimate [Medicins] from the adulterate. **1699** BENTLEY *Phal.* 327 Mr. B. maintains *Astypala* to be a legitimate word, because we read it Ἀστυπάλη in the present copy of Scylax. **1804** *Europ. Mag.* XLV. 347/2 The above remarks do not apply to what I shall call collections of legitimate remains. **1818** TODD, *Legitimate*.. 2. Genuine; not spurious: as, a legitimate work, the legitimate production of such an author.

2. a. Conformable to law or rule; sanctioned or authorized by law or right; lawful; proper.

1638 BAKER tr. *Balzac's Lett.* (vol. II.) 13 An evill that should last so long, might in some sort seeme to be made legitimate. **1645** MILTON *Tetrach.* Wks. 1738 I. 226 The Text therfore uses this phrase, that they shall be one flesh, to justify and make legitimate the rites of Marriage-bed. **1664** H. MORE *Myst. Iniq.* 257 A Legitimate Husband. **1832** W. IRVING *Alhambra* I. 79 They [Moors] are a nation.. without a legitimate country or a name. **1849** MACAULAY *Hist. Eng.* vii. II. 238 What would, under ordinary circumstances, be justly condemned as persecution, may fall within the bounds of legitimate selfdefence. **1852** H. ROGERS *Ecl. Faith* (1853) 436 There is.. a legitimate way of influencing the will. **1859** J. CUMMING *Ruth* ix. 152 Its ancient and legitimate owner.

b. Normal, regular; conformable to a recognized standard type; †*spec.* of a gun (cf. BASTARD *a.* 6 a); †of a disease (= EXQUISITE). In *Sporting*, applied to flat-racing as opposed to hurdleracing or steeplechasing. ***the legitimate drama***: the body of plays, Shakespearian or other, that have a recognized theatrical and literary merit; also ellipt. (*Theatr. slang*) ***the legitimate***. Also in other collocations. So as *sb.*, an actor of legitimate drama.

1669 STURMY *Mariner's Mag.* v. 64 Gunners call them Legitimate Pieces, as have due length of their Chase, according to the height of their bores; Bastard Pieces are such as have shorter Chases, than the Proportion of their Bore doth require. **1684** tr. *Bonet's Merc. Compit.* v. 161 The Physician must not use astringents, in a legitimate Burning fever. **1727–51** CHAMBERS *Cycl.* s.v. *Delivery*, A legitimate delivery is that which happens at the just term, i.e. in the tenth lunar month. **1799** *Sporting Mag.* XV. 135/2 A lady to whom the public are so much indebted for the support which the legitimate drama has received from her exertions, and who.. has disdained the pantomime and spectacle to which the German muse so often stoops. **1812** *Theatrical Inquisitor* Oct. I. 72 Mr. E treads closely upon the heels of the legitimate stage. **1821** BYRON *M. Faliero* Pref. 18 *note*, While I was in the sub-committee of Drury Lane Theatre.. we did our best to bring back the legitimate drama. **1838** DICKENS *Let.* 16 Jan. (1965) I. 355 Let the Legitimate Drama put this, and Joan of Arc.. into her pipe. **1855** MACAULAY *Hist. Eng.* xiv. III. 468 Tillotson still keeps his place as a legitimate English classic. **1877** *Era Almanack* 97 Always willing to patronise the legitimate. **1884** YATES *Recoll.* I. v. 211 My youthful admiration of Shakespeare and the legitimate drama. **1888** *Sportsman* 28 Nov. (Farmer), The winding up of the legitimate season. **1909** P. G. WILLIAMS in *Sat. Even. Post* 5 June 17/2 The vaudeville actor is much more thrifty than his colleague in the legitimate. **1933** P. GODFREY *Back-Stage* xvi. 207 The

principal comedian of *Have a Nibble*..scandalizes the 'legitimates' by discarding the jacket of his sprightly plus-four suit. **1947** N. MARSH *Final Curtain* v. 84, I haven't got the wind for dancing..and the 'legitimate' gives me a pain in the neck. **1952** *N.Y. Herald Tribune* 28 Aug. 16/7 A revision of New York City's building code to spur the construction of new legitimate theaters. **1968** *Globe & Mail* (Toronto) 17 Feb. 24 Nor is it [*sc.* the city] avoiding the inevitable responsibility of building a smaller legitimate house. **1972** *N.Y. Times* 3 Nov. 1/1 The new hotel would include..a legitimate theater. **1975** *Scottish Field* Jan. 9/1 With his feet now firmly planted in both acting spheres—the so-called legitimate theatre and the pantomime lark—this young-looking veteran [*sc.* Rikki Fulton]..feels fit to accept any professional challenge.

c. Of a sovereign's title: Resting on the strict principle of hereditary right. Hence, said of a sovereign, a kingdom, etc.

1812 *Niles' Reg.* I. 404/2 The 'legitimate' sovereigns of Russia, Austria and Prussia. **1821** H. COLERIDGE *Ess.* (1851) I. 8 We like the style of the Legitimate poets, as we respect the court and Legitimate monarchs. **1847** DISRAELI *Tancred* III. vi, But in these days a great capitalist has deeper roots than a sovereign prince, unless he is very legitimate. **1860** *Sat. Rev.* 14 Apr. 457/1 It is not in irony, but in sober earnest, that we express our belief, that any throne is, in practice, called legitimate which has not had the consent of the nation to its..existence. **1885** FAIRBAIRN *Catholicism* iii. (1899) 96 In literature it [the Catholic Revival] appeared as Romanticism, in politics as legitimate and theocratic theory.

d. Sanctioned by the laws of reasoning; logically admissible or inferrible.

1797 *Encycl. Brit.* (ed. 3) x. 221/2 If the first principles be clear and evident, and every syllogism in some legitimate mode or figure, the conclusion of the whole must infallibly be admitted. **1814** D. STEWART *Hum. Mind* II. iii. §1. 247 Every such process of reasoning..may be resolved into a series of legitimate syllogisms. **1840** MILL *Diss. & Disc.* (1875) I. 397 Both [methods] were legitimate logical processes. **1850** MCCOSH *Div. Govt.* III. ii. (1874) 409 We have followed them [principles] to their legitimate consequences. **1855** PRESCOTT *Philip II*, I. II. ix. 249 This bloody catastrophe was a legitimate result of the policy which he advised.

e. In *Jazz colloq.*, designating 'serious' music as distinct from jazz or popular music.

1927 *Melody Maker* Apr. 359/2 The number lends itself exceptionally well to the symphonic treatment it has been given, the orchestration is very fine and the modulated passages and general arrangement make it, although a little too 'legitimate' for dancing, perfect from a concert point of view. **1933** *Fortune* Aug. 94 Other jazz heroes such as the Dorseys..have become more or less legitimate musicians for radio purposes. **1946** MEZZROW & WOLFE *Really Blues* (1957) xvii. 341 The New Orleans drum patterns..were closest to 'legitimate' music. **1969** *New Yorker* 20 Dec. 52/3 It would have been interesting if he had made similar measurements during a performance by a 'commercial'—that is, a jazz or dance-band—player..to compare with those of a 'legitimate', or symphonic, player.

†**3.** quasi-*adv.* *Obs.*

1578 *Galway Arch.* in *10th Rep. Hist. MSS. Comm.* App. v. 427 Both he and his chyldren of his body legytymat begotten.

B. *sb.* **1. a.** A legitimate child.

1583 STUBBES *Anat. Abus.* I. (1879) 97, I had rather we had many legittimats than many illegittimates. **1842** C. WHITEHEAD *R. Savage* (1845) III. vi. 381 Their legitimates do them small honour, sometimes. **1865** *Dublin Univ. Mag.* I. 8 Legitimates and natural children were brought up..or shaken up together.

b. A legitimate sovereign. Also, one who supports or advocates the title of such sovereigns. Cf. A. 2 c.

1821 H. COLERIDGE *Ess., On Parties in Poetry* (1851) I. 6 Waller, a true Legitimate in politics. **1830** GEN. P. THOMPSON *Exerc.* (1842) I. 268 The experiment of what has been termed constitutional government, has been tried and failed. The legitimates refused this, while they might have had it. **1847** EMERSON *Repr. Men, Napoleon* Wks. (Bohn) I. 374 No longer the throne was occupied..by a small class of legitimates.

†**c.** *Austral. slang.* (See quot. and cf. LEGITIMACY 4.) *Obs.*

1827 P. CUNNINGHAM *2 Yrs. N.S. Wales* II. xxiv. 116 Our society is divided into circles as in England... Next, we have the legitimates, or cross-breds,—namely, such as have legal reasons for visiting this colony; and the illegitimates, or such as are free from that stigma.

†**2.** Something to which one has a legitimate title. *Obs. rare*$^{-1}$.

1649 MILTON *Eikon.* (1770) 31 Many princes have been rigorous in laying taxes on their subjects by the head, but of any King heretofore that made a levy upon their wit, and seized it as his own legitimate, I have not whom beside to instance.

legitimate (lɪˈdʒɪtɪmeɪt), *v.* [f. med.L. *lēgitimāt-*, ppl. stem of *lēgitimāre* (see prec.). Cf. F. *légitimer*, Sp., Pg. *legitimar*, It. *legitimare.*]

1. *trans.* To render (a bastard) legitimate; to establish the legitimacy of (a person) by an authoritative declaration or decree.

1597 BEARD *Theatre God's Judgem.* (1631) 280 With the Popes auouch, who legitimated him. **1663** PEPYS *Diary* 9 Nov., It is much talked of that the king intends to legitimate the Duke of Monmouth. **1701** DE FOE *Power Coll. Body People* Misc. (1703) 149 Another Parliament Legitimated Queen Elizabeth. **1809** J. ADAMS *Wks.* (1854) IX. 317 What is impressment of seamen?.. No parliament ever dared to legitimate or sanction it. **1818** HALLAM *Mid. Ages* (1872) III. 75 One object of which was to legitimate the duke of Lancaster's ante-nuptial children. **1868** FREEMAN *Norm. Conq.* (1876) II. viii. 176 The children were according to the law..legitimated by the subsequent marriage of their parents.

fig. **1612** T. TAYLOR *Comm. Titus* ii. 15 Straining their wittes to legitimate bastardly broods of opinions. *a* **1640** JACKSON *Creed* XI. xviii. §5 The seeds of this accursed sin are more than legitimated, ranked amongst the essential parts of honour.

2. To render lawful or legal, to give a lawful or legal character to; to authorize by legal enactment. In early use, To give (a person) a legal claim *to* (something).

1531 *Dial. on Laws Eng.* II. xlv. (1532) 115 Whether the Pope may legittimate one to temporall thynges. **1586** WARNER *Albion's Eng.* II. lxvii. 285 With Marriage, that legitimates our Propagation. **1658** T. WALL *Charac. Enemies Ch.* 65 These men can do more then God, they can legitimate any wickedness. **1715** BENTLEY *Serm.* x. 348 Nay, a particular edition shall be legitimated and consecrated. **1798** W. TAYLOR in *Monthly Rev.* XXV. 566 Their feudal laws, by legitimating orderly gradations of oppression, completed the misfortune of the times. **1869** *Pall Mall G.* 1 Sept. 10 He not only supplies himself with a magazine of arms, but with a portfolio of judges' orders legitimating their use.

3. To affirm or show to be legitimate; to authorize or justify by word or example; to serve as justification for.

1611 W. SCLATER *Key* (1629) 164 [An hypocrite] countenanceth, yea, legitimateth, wilfull rebellion against the law of God. **1651** JER. TAYLOR *Holy Dying* iii. §8 (1727) 108 Our Blessed Lord was pleased to legitimate fear to us, by his agony and prayers in the garden. **1681** FLAVEL *Meth. Grace* xxvii. 466 The Gospel legitimates no hopes of salvation, but such as are accompanied with serious efforts of mortification. **1713** NELSON *Life Bp. Bull* 292 All such terms and Phrases as are not expressly legitimated by the sacred writers. **1719** DE FOE *Crusoe* I. xvii. (1840) 306 Necessity legitimates my advice; for it is the only way to save our lives. *c* **1750** SHENSTONE *Economy* I. 179 Unless Economy's consent Legitimate expense. *c* **1820** FUSELI in *Lect. Paint.* xii. (1848) 557 Sculpture lent her hand to legitimate the sacrilege. **1824–9** LANDOR *Imag. Conv.* Wks. 1846 I. 215 National safety legitimates all means employed upon it. **1846** TRENCH *Mirac.* Introd. (1862) 4 He warns him that Pharaoh will require him to legitimate his mission.

Hence **leˈgitimated** *ppl. a.*

1670 COTTON *Espernon* II. VIII. 415 Gabrielle a legitimated Daughter of France, one of his own natural Sisters. **1723** *Lond. Gaz.* No. 6161/1 *Paris*... The King has settled the Ranks and Honours of the legitimated Princes. **1799** W. TOOKE *View Russian Emp.* II. 130 According to a legitimated statement already mentioned. **1874** GREEN *Short Hist.* vi. §1. 267 Henry Beaufort, Bishop of Winchester, a legitimated son of John of Gaunt.

legitimately (lɪˈdʒɪtɪmətlɪ), *adv.* [f. LEGITIMATE *a.* + -LY².] In a legitimate or lawful manner; in accordance with rule or propriety; legally, properly.

1593 NASHE *Christ's T.* (1613) 97 But sure legitimately (or as they shold) they are not brought vp. **1651** HOBBES *Govt. & Soc.* vii. §3. 112 A King legitimately constituted in his Government. **1794** SULLIVAN *View Nat.* I. 320 Whatever the result may be, it shall at least legitimately grow out of the premises. **1841** MYERS *Cath. Th.* IV. v. 193 Biblical Theology can legitimately extend no farther than Revelation does.

legitimateness (lɪˈdʒɪtɪmətnɪs). [f. as prec. + -NESS.] The quality or condition of being legitimate, in various senses.

1618 *Barnevelt's Apol.* D, If *New-kerke*..will giue you a Testimonie of your legitimatenesse, I will easily beleeue it. **1664** H. MORE *Myst. Iniq.* Apol. 536 They cannot make the least scruple concerning the legitimateness of the Instrument. *a* **1677** BARROW *Pope's Suprem.* (1680) 352 The Fathers of Constantinople..highly asserting the legitimateness of his Ordination. **1831** SOUTHEY in *Q. Rev.* XLV. 181 Babeuf..maintained the merit and the legitimateness of the Constitution of 1793.

legitimation (lɪdʒɪtɪˈmeɪʃən). [ad. med.L. *lēgitimātiōn-em*, n. of action f. *lēgitimāre* to LEGITIMATE. Cf. F. *légitimation.*]

1. The action or process of rendering or authoritatively declaring (a person) legitimate.

1460 CAPGRAVE *Chron.* 263 The duke of Lancastir purchased a legittimacion for the childyrn that he had begoten of dame Katerine Swynforth. **1543** *Extracts Aberd. Reg.* (1844) I. 188 The lettres of legittimatioun maid to the said Robert. **1577–87** HOLINSHED *Chron.* III. 1093/1 Cranmer..alledging manie reasons..for the legitimation of both the kings sisters. **1611** GUILLIM *Heraldry* II. v. (1660) 63 By such legitimation they are discharged of all those dishonours which in former time they were subject unto. *a* **1683** SIDNEY *Disc. Govt.* III. xxvi. (1704) 342 The intricacys of his Marriages, and the legitimation of his Children were settled by the same Power. **1726** AYLIFFE *Parergon* 110 Legitimation or the Tryal of Bastardy. **1791** BOSWELL *Johnson* 22 Mar. an. 1776, I talked of legitimation by subsequent marriage, which obtained in the Roman law, and still obtains in the law of Scotland. **1845** POLSON *Eng. Law* in *Encycl. Metrop.* II. 843/1 Nor can his agnates succeed to him [a bastard], unless he has obtained letters of legitimation from the king.

†**2.** The condition of being legitimate; legitimacy. *Obs.*

1535 STEWART *Cron. Scot.* (1858) III. 392 The quhilk wedding wes lauchfull probatioun Of his barnis legitimatioun. **1595** SHAKS. *John* I. i. 248, I haue disclaim'd Sir Robert and my land, Legitimation, name, and all is gone. **1634** SIR T. HERBERT *Trav.* 77 His infancie and doubt of legitimation, secluding him awhile from enjoying any Soveraigntie. **1660** BOND *Scut. Reg.* 50 That Son giveth cause of suspition of his Legitimation who will not mourn at his Mothers death. **1689** LOCKE *Govt.* §123 (1694) 120 From whence also will arise many Questions of Legitimation, and what in Nature is the difference betwixt a Wife and a Concubine.

fig. **1672** MARVELL *Reh. Transp.* I. 137 Mr. Bayes having gone so many months, more than the Civil Law allows for the utmost term of legitimation.

b. *transf.* Of a literary work: The fact that it is the work of its reputed author; authenticity, genuineness. Now *rare.*

1635 E. BAGSHAWE *To Rdr.* in R. Bolton *Two Serm.* (1635) A ij b, These Sermons are truely his owne..There are hundreds of people..who..can with me..attestate their legitimation. **1640** BP. HALL *Episc.* II. xi, We are yet beholding to him for asserting the truth, and legitimation of these seven Epistles of our Martyr. **1670** WALTON *Lives* III. 238 In this relation concerning these three doubtful Books of Mr. Hookers..I leave my Reader to give sentence, for their legitimation. **1884** D. HUNTER tr. *Reuss's Hist. Canon* x. 167 The legitimation refused to this book [the Apocalypse] is therefore not the authenticity in the literary sense of the word.

†**3.** The action of naturalizing (an alien). *Obs.*

1579 J. STUBBES *Gaping Gulf* C j b, The most large and most benificiall Legitimation made to any alien.

†**4.** The action of giving a lawful character to something forbidden by law; a dispensation. *Obs.*

a **1550** *Image Ipocr.* II. 376 in *Skelton's Wks.* (1843) II. 427 He robbeth all nations With his fulminations.. Legittimations. **1726** AYLIFFE *Parergon* 219 A Dispensation is..in our Books sometimes stiled a Legitimation.

5. *gen.* The action of making lawful; authorization; rarely *concr.* a document of authorization.

1660 JER. TAYLOR *Duct. Dubit.* I. v, A direct uncharitableness..which can receive no warrant or legitimation by the intention of the propounder. *a* **1680** BUTLER *Rem.* (1759) II. 193 The judicious and mature Legitimation of tipling Houses. **1799** *Carlton Ho. Mag.* 293 The legitimation of Money, and the giving it its denominated value, is one especial part of a King's prerogative. **1841–4** EMERSON *Ess., Poet* Wks. (Bohn) I. 164 Herein is the legitimation of criticism, in the mind's faith, that the poems are a corrupt version of some text in nature. **1870** *Daily News* 1 Dec., Persons going about their lawful business, and fortified by adequate legitimations.

leˈgitimatist. *rare.* [f. as next + -IST.] = LEGITIMIST.

a **1860** WORCESTER cites *Month. Rev.*

legitimatize (lɪˈdʒɪtɪmətaɪz), *v.* [f. LEGITIMATE *a.* + -IZE.] *trans.* To render legitimate or lawful, in various senses, *esp.* to render (a child) legitimate by legal enactment or otherwise.

1791 MACKINTOSH *Vind. Gall.* Wks. 1846 III. 32 The approbation of the men legitimatizes the government. **1853** J. H. NEWMAN *Hist. Sk.* (1876) I. [II.] I. iii. 115 The Turk does not deign to legitimatize his possession of the soil he has violently seized. **1856** FROUDE *Hist. Eng.* (1858) II. vii. 158 She might have been legitimatized by act of parliament. **1868** FFOULKES *Ch. Creed or Crown's C.* 60 The wily forger ..sought to legitimatise them by the high authority which he claimed. **1883** *Daily Tel.* 20 June 7/4 The alteration.. will have the effect of legitimatizing the offspring of past marriages.

Hence **leˈgitimatized** *ppl. a.*

1856 DORAN *Knts. & their Days* xvii. 285 The legitimatised son of himself [Louis XIV] and Madame de Montespan. **1885** *Athenæum* 29 Aug. 271/2 Joan Beaufort, the legitimatized daughter of John of Gaunt.

leˈgitimature. *nonce-wd.* [f. LEGITIMATE *a.* + -URE.] An office to which one has a legitimate claim.

1865 CARLYLE *Fredk. Gt.* XVI. ii. (1872) VI. 144 Regent having stripped her Husband of his high legitimatures and dignities.

legitime (ˈlɛdʒɪtɪm), *a.* and *sb.* Also 6 **legytym**, 6–7 **legittime**, 8–9 **legitim.** [a. F. *légitime* adj. and sb., ad. L. *lēgitimus*, f. *lēg-*, *lex* LAW.]

†**A.** *adj.* *Obs.*

1. = LEGITIMATE *a.* 1. In early use *absol.* or quasi-*sb.*

1393 LANGL. *P. Pl.* C. XI. 210 þe grace That leelle legitime by lawe may cleyme. **1536** in Strype *Eccl. Mem.* I. App. lxxvi. 182 The Kings highnes should make and declare the said Lady Mary to bee legitime. **1568** MARY *Let.* Jan. in H. Campbell *Love Lett. Mary Q. Scots* App. (1824) 30 To.. cause him [the Erle of Murray] to be declarit legitime to succeid unto the crowne of Scotland.

b. *transf.* Genuine: = LEGITIMATE 1 b.

1614 W. BARCLAY *Nepenthes* in Arb. *App. to Jas. I Counterbl.* 116 To apparell some European plants with Indian coats, and to enstall them in shops as righteous and legittime Tabacco.

2. = LEGITIMATE 2.

c **1430** *Pilgr. Lyf Manhode* III. cxlii. (1869) 131 Engendred in legitime mariage. **1502** *Ord. Crysten Men* (W. de W. 1506) IV. xxi. 258 If after the legittime appellacyon he hath proceded in cause. *c* **1530** L. COX *Rhet.* (1899) 46 Aristotle deuideth Justice in .ii. kyndes, one, legitime or legall, and an other, equyte. **1660** J. LLOYD *Prim. Episc.* 37 He calls it [the Lord's Prayer] the legitime and ordinary prayer. **1669** *Treaty betw. Chas. II & Dk. Savoy* in Magens *Insurances* (1755) II. 639 To constitute Sir John Finch Knt..his true and legitime Plenipotentiary. **1676** MARVELL *Mr. Smirke* I ij, The Elders and Brethren..were assembled in a legitime Council at Ierusalem. **1795** WYTHE *Decis. Virginia* 50 A species of right never adopted for legitime before 1779.

b. Of persons: Obedient to law.

1677 GALE *Crt. Gentiles* IV. 47 Those things wherein the order and ornament or goodness of the mind consistes, we cal legal and Law: whence men become legitime and orderly.

c. = LEGITIMATE 2 b.

1651 E. PRESTWICH *Hippolitus* Ep. Ded., A Legitime Poem often falls a sacrifice to the many-headed and no brained Multitude.

d. = LEGITIMATE 2 d.

c **1530** L. COX *Rhet.* (1899) 82 State legitime is whan the controuersy standeth in definicyon.

B. *sb. Civil* and *Sc. Law.* (See quot. 1845.) = L. *lēgitima* (*pars*).

a **1768** ERSKINE *Inst. Law Scot.* (1773) 606 That which falls to the children, is sometimes, from the Roman law, styled the legitim, or the portion given them by the law. **1845** POLSON *Eng. Law* in *Encycl. Metrop.* II. 851/1 Children are entitled..after their father's death, to a share of his moveable property, which is called their legitime, or portion natural, or bairns' part of gear. **1881** *Times* 9 Feb. 10 The Yorke Prize for 1880..was offered for the best essay on 'The History of the Law of Legitim'.

legitimism (lɪ'dʒɪtɪmɪz(ə)m). [ad. F. *légitimisme*, f. *légitime*: see next and -ISM.] In French or Spanish politics: Adherence to the claim of the so-called 'legitimate pretender to the throne'.

1877 *Chr. World* 12 Oct. 1/4 The patrons of Napoleonism and Legitimism. **1883** MAINE *Early Law & Custom* v. 143 The theory of sovereignty and government called Legitimism..is still a factor in French and Spanish politics.

legitimist (lɪ'dʒɪtɪmɪst). [ad. F. *légitimiste*, f. *légitime*: see LEGITIME and -IST.] A supporter of legitimate authority, esp. of a monarchical title claimed on the ground of direct descent; *spec.* in France, a supporter of the elder Bourbon line, driven from the throne in 1830.

1841 W. SPALDING *Italy & It. Isl.* III. 66 The papal secretary of state was denounced as a secret adherent of the legitimists. **1865** MAFFEI *Brigand Life* I. 231 Naples became the rallying point of the legitimists. **1865** *Examiner* 11 Mar. 145/1 The legitimists and clericals soon tied a stone to it and sent it to the bottom. **1870** *Sat. Rev.* 2 Apr. 430 Isabella II. was, in the eyes of Legitimists and extreme Catholics, a revolutionary usurper.

b. *attrib.* or *adj.* Of or pertaining to the legitimists; brought about by legitimists; expressing their sentiments.

1867 FREEMAN *Norm. Conq.* (1876) I. App. 627 He is not likely to have made the strong legitimist harangue which is put into his mouth. **1875** STUBBS *Const. Hist.* III. xviii. 190 The accession of the house of York was strictly a legitimist restoration.

Hence **legiti'mistic** *a.*, inclined to the opinions of the legitimists.

1877 *Tinsley's Mag.* XX. 381 He is too Legitimistic for me.

legi'timity. *rare*⁻¹. [ad. F. *légitimité*, f. *légitime*: see LEGITIME *a.* and -ITY.] Legitimacy.

1828 LANDOR *Imag. Conv.* III. 457 Ferocious..man, enemy to legitimity and religion!

legitimize (lɪ'dʒɪtɪmaɪz), *v.* [f. L. *lēgitimus* (see LEGITIME *a.*) + -IZE.] = LEGITIMATIZE.

1848 W. H. KELLY tr. *L. Blanc's Hist. Ten Y.* II. 148 The French laws oblige me to do so in order to legitimise my child. **1859** G. MEREDITH *R. Feverel* xl, He seemed to be legitimizing his presence. **1892** A. B. BRUCE *Apologetics* III. x. 495 Such a comparison..is not indispensable to legitimise the Christian's exclusive homage to Jesus.

Hence **le,gitimi'zation**, the action of legitimizing.

1860 FROUDE *Hist. Eng.* VI. 113 Had Elizabeth's prospects been liable to be affected by the legitimization of her sister, the queen would [etc.]. **1886** in *Antiquary* Feb. 70/2 In consideration of..25,000 crowns..his Holiness is willing to grant the act of legitimization.

†**le'gitimously,** *adv. Obs. rare*⁻¹. [f. **legitimous* adj. (f. L. *lēgitim-us* + -OUS) + -LY².] In a lawful or proper manner.

1657 W. MORICE *Coena quasi Κοινὴ* xxiv. 244 The Sacraments legitimously administred for matter and form.

leglen ('lɛglən). *Sc.* Also 8-9 leglin, 9 leglan. [? variant of LAGGIN.] A milk pail. Also *attrib.* **leglen-girth**, the lowest hoop upon a leglen. ***to cast a leglen-girth***: to have an illegitimate child (cf. LAGGIN 3).

1725 RAMSAY *Gentle Sheph.* II. iv, [When] I to milk the ewes first tried my skill, To bear a leglen was nae toil to me. *c* **1750** MISS ELLIOT *Song, 'Flowers of the Forest'* ii, Ilk ane lifts her leglin, and hies her away. **1822** SCOTT *Let. to Joanna Baillie* 10 Feb. in *Lockhart*, Miss Edgeworth..carries her literary reputation as..easily as the milk maid in my country does the leglan. **1822** —— *Nigel* xxxii, Ganging a wee bit gleed in her walk through the world; I mean in the way of..casting a leglin-girth, or the like. **1881** SANDS *Sketches of Tranent* 20 A leglen or milking pail of excellent small beer.

legless ('lɛglɪs), *a.* [f. LEG *sb.* + -LESS.]

a. Having no legs; deprived of legs.

1597 MIDDLETON *Wisdom Solomon* ix. 4 A legless body is my kingdom's map. **1848** C. LANMAN *Angler in Canada* 207 His [a seal's] clumsy and legless body. **1879** LUBBOCK *Sci. Lect.* iii. 69 The larvæ of ants..are small, white, legless grubs.

b. *slang.* Drunk, esp. too drunk to stand.

1976 A. FAIRWEATHER Low (*song-title*) Wide eyed and legless. **1977** *O.D.* No. 3. 4/2 Gigs were a cheap way of getting pissed. We were usually legless by half 8. **1978** *Times* 7 Apr. 4/8 The only thing that annoyed us with the *Sailor* programme was that they showed too much of the lads getting legless in pubs. **1982** B. BEAUMONT *Thanks to Rugby* xiii. 176 Jeff Squire was doctoring each drink with..vodka. By the end Noel was plastered and legless. **1986** *Daily Tel.* 1 Sept. 5/3, I must have had well over half a bottle... In the end I was legless and couldn't talk.

'leglessness. [f. LEGLESS *a.* + -NESS.] The condition of being legless.

1902 *19th Cent.* Feb. 254 Sir Richard Calmady's leglessness is never for an instant forgotten. **1911** G. B. SHAW *Doctor's Dilemma* Pref. p. xiv, The leg may mortify—it is always safer to operate—..evolution is towards motors and leglessness.

leglet ('lɛglɪt). [f. LEG *sb.* + -LET.]

1. A little leg.

1821 *Blackw. Mag.* Jan. 424 High raised in air to..wap his [a jointed toy soldier's] supple leglets in their view. **1855** *Fraser's Mag.* LI. 263 [A nurse tells a child] to put down her frock, and cover two very pretty white leglets.

2. An ornament for the leg. (After *armlet*, etc.)

1836 CAROLINE FOX *Jrnl.* (1882) 9 Numbers of anklets and leglets. **1866** LIVINGSTONE *Last Jrnls.* (1873) I. viii. 198 It [wire] is used chiefly as leglets. **1887** RIDER HAGGARD *K. Solomon's Mines* 200 A pair of sandals, [and] a leglet of goats' hair..made up his equipment.

‖**legong** (lɛ'gɒŋ). [Indonesian.] A stylized Balinese dance performed by young girls. Also *attrib.* Also, one of the performers of such a dance.

1926 E. MORDAUNT *Further Venture Bk.* xxiii. 291 For three days preparations have been going on for a..Legong..given by a man who has won a law-suit. **1930** H. POWELL *Last Paradise* xii. 109 Runis and Madé Réi were nine years old... They danced the sacred traditional measures of the *legong*. **1937** M. COVARRUBIAS *Island of Bali* (1972) viii. 224 As the archetype of the delicate and feminine, the *legong* is the finest of Balinese dances... The *legong* is performed at feasts, generally in the late afternoon when the heat of the day has subsided. *Ibid.* 228 A very popular dance that seems related to the *legong* is the *djogéd*, performed by a girl in a variation of the *legong* costume and in the traditional *legong* steps. **1971** *Walkabout* (Austral.) Nov. 73/1, I was sitting at this beautiful bar, listening to the distant flurry of the Legong dance.

legouane, var. LEGUAN.

legrandite (lə'grɒndaɪt). *Min.* [f. *Legrand*, the name of a 20th-c. Belgian mine manager who collected the first specimen + -ITE¹.] A basic hydrated zinc arsenate, $Zn_2AsO_4OH.H_2O$ occurring as colourless to yellow transparent monoclinic crystals at Lampazos, Mexico.

1932 DRUGMAN & HEY in *Mineral. Mag.* XXIII. 175 A chemical analysis..showed it to be indeed a new mineral, a basic zinc arsenate, and the name 'legrandite' is proposed for it in recognition of the collector. **1971** *Soviet Physics: Doklady* XVI. 421/2 Analyses of legrandite from various deposits reveal up to 2% Mn isomorphously replacing Zn.

leguan ('lɛgjʊən). Also **legouane**. [? a. F. *l'iguane* (*iguane* iguana, with def. art.).] = IGUANA, GUANA.

1790 E. HELME tr. *Le Vaillant's Trav. Afr.* I. 391 The Hottentot who fired at the Hippopotamus came home late..and was obliged to meet the sarcasms of my Hottentot wits, who tried to persuade him he had fired at a *Legouane* (a kind of large lizard, common in the rivers of Africa). **1834** PRINGLE *Afr. Sk.* vi. 210 Frequented by numbers of the large amphibious lizard called the leguan or guana. **1877** J. A. CHALMERS *Tiyo Soga* xviii. 347 The second [doctor] removes the cause of disease, which is either a lizard, a serpent, or a leguan.

leguleian (lɛgjuː'liːən), *a.* and *sb.* [f. L. *lēgulēi-us* a pettifogger (f. *lēg-*, *lex* law) + -AN.]

A. *adj.* Of or pertaining to petty questions of law or to law language; pettifogging. *rare.*

1677 NEEDHAM *2nd Pacquet Adv.* 21 It is a small matter with our Factious Leguleian Scriblers to form up Opinions upon forged Interpretations of Law. **1847** DE QUINCEY *Protestantism* Wks. 1858 VIII. 90 It seems impossible to determine whether he uses it in the classical English sense, or in the sense of leguleian barbarism.

B. *sb.* A pettifogger; a contemptuous term for a lawyer.

1631 BP. WEBBE *Quietn.* (1653) 254 Our spruce aturnies, and upstart Leguleians. **1692** WASHINGTON tr. *Milton's Def. Pop.* ix. M.'s Wks. 1851 VIII. 209 You do but that over again..which some silly Leguleians now and then do, to argue unawares against their own Clients. **1864** *Macm. Mag.* Dec. 124 To distinguish a jolly young medical from a prematurely sharp leguleian.

So **legu'leious** *a.* = LEGULEIAN *a.*

1660 H. MORE *Myst. Godl.* IV. xiii. 131 The leguleious Cavils of some Pragmatical Pettifoggers.

legume ('lɛgjuːm, lɪ'gjuːm). Also 7 **legum**. [a. F. *légume*, ad. L. *legūmen*, f. *leg-ĕre* to gather, in allusion to the fact that the fruit may be gathered by hand.]

1. **a.** The fruit, or the edible portion of a leguminous plant, e.g. beans, peas, pulse. **b.** By extension: A vegetable used for food; chiefly in *pl.*

a. **1676** *Phil. Trans.* XI. 621 The boyling of Legums. **1704** *Collect. Voy.* (Churchill) III. 7/2 There is a great Plenty of Legumes, and Garden-product. **1732** ARBUTHNOT *Rules of Diet* 263 Farinaceous Legumes, as Pease, Beans, &c. **1792** A. YOUNG *Trav. France* 443 Chesnuts, maiz, harricots, and other legumes, form principal objects of consumption.

b. **1693** EVELYN *De la Quint. Compl. Gard.* Pref., In those early times 'tis probable they knew no other Gardens than those of Fruits and Legumes. **1725** BRADLEY *Fam. Dict.* s.v. *Turnips*, Turneps are a legume used in several sauces. **1824-9** LANDOR *Imag. Conv.* Wks. 1846 I. 131 The tyrant of Sicily demanded a tenth of the corn, but not a tenth of..hay or legumes. **1875** JOWETT *Plato* (ed. 2) III. 696 The dry edible fruit and other species of food, which we call by the general name of legumes.

2. A leguminous plant.

1693 ROBINSON in *Phil. Trans.* XVII. 826 The Arachydna's, and some other Legumes, which flower above, but seed under ground. **1725** BRADLEY *Fam. Dict.*, *Legumes*, ..in Botany it is that Species of Plants, which we call Pulse. **1870** J. YEATS *Nat. Hist. Commerce* II. 137 The legumes of temperate climates are familiar plants. **1969** *Oxf. Bk. Food Plants* 34/2 There are a number of other tropical legumes which are only of very minor or local importance as sources of food. *Ibid.* 44/1 Cowpea..is an annual legume, originating in Africa. **1974** A. HUXLEY *Plant & Planet* xxx. 365 Various legume seeds have proved the best sources [of vegetable protein] so far.

3. The pod or seed-vessel of a leguminous plant.

1785 MARTYN *Rousseau's Bot.* iii. (1794) 36 The legume or pod. **1787** *Fam. Plants* I. 29 Legume long, compress'd, cloath'd with a double bark. **1811** A. T. THOMSON *Lond. Disp.* (1818) 376 The legume compressed, brown, ciliated. **1863** BATES *Nat. Amazon* viii. (1864) 230 The fruit..although a legume, is of a rounded shape.

legumen (lɪ'gjuːmən). Pl. **legumens**, ‖**legumina**. [a. L. *legūmen*: see prec.] **a.** = LEGUME 1 a. **b.** = LEGUME 2. Also *collect. sing.* **c.** = LEGUME 3.

a. **1398** TREVISA *Barth. De P.R.* XVII. xcv. (1495) 662 Greynes that ben..gretter..thanne greynes of whete other of barly be properly callyd legumina. **1680** BOYLE *Produc. Chem. Princ.* II. iv, Some legumens, as peas, or beans; which if they be newly gathered and distilled in a retort..will..afford..an acid spirit. **1721** CHAMBERLAYNE in *Phil. Trans.* XXXI. 200 These Vessels..are more easy to be discover'd in Beans and Pease, than in any sort of Legumens or Grains.

b. **1675** EVELYN *Terra* (1676) 71 The haulm of beans, pease, and other *legumina*. *a* **1722** LISLE *Husb.* (1757) 354 Grass-butter rises in price by reason of its consumption of those legumens. **1727** A. HAMILTON *New Acc. E. Ind.* I. vi. 54 The Country adjacent produces Barley, Wheat, and Legumen. **1789** G. WHITE *Selborne* xxxiv. (1853) 123 They are to be met with in gardens on kidney-beans or any legumens.

c. **1760** J. LEE *Introd. Bot.* I. vi. (1765) 13 *Legumen*, a Pod..is a Pericarpium of two Valves, wherein the seeds are fastened along one suture only. **1776-96** WITHERING *Brit. Plants* (ed. 3) III. 619 Lotus. Legumen cylindrical; filled with cylindrical seeds. **1832** *Veg. Subst. Food Man* 211 The seeds are contained in an oblong legumen, or pod..of two valves.

legumin (lɪ'gjuːmɪn). *Chem.* Also **legumine**. [f. LEGUME + -IN.] A proteid substance resembling casein, found in leguminous and other seeds.

1838 T. THOMSON *Chem. Org. Bodies* 690 A peculiar principle, to which he [Braconnot] has given the name of legumin. *c* **1865** *Circ. Sci.* I. 329/2 The largest proportion of phosphorus exists in legumine. **1886** A. H. CHURCH *Food Grains Ind.* 119 Legumin occurs in largest proportion and in the larger number of kinds of pulse.

le'guminar, *a. Bot.* [f. L. *legūmin-*, *legūmen* + -AR.] Resembling or characteristic of a legume: said of dehiscence by a marginal suture.

In some mod. Dicts.

,legu'miniform, *a.* [f. as prec. + -(I)FORM.] Having the form of a legume.

In some mod. Dicts.

leguminose (lɪ'gjuːmɪnəʊs), *a.* [f. as next + -OSE.] = next.

1693 in *Phil. Trans.* XVII. 764 Herbaceous and arborescent Plants, the greatest part of them pomiferous or leguminose. **1713** PETIVER ibid. XXVIII. 207 Leguminose or Pea-bloom Plants. **1837** WHEWELL *Hist. Induct. Sci.* (1857) III. 252 We have the leguminose plants.

leguminous (lɪ'gjuːmɪnəs), *a.* [f. L. *legūmin-*, *legūmen* + -OUS.]

1. Of or pertaining to pulse; of the nature of pulse.

1656 in BLOUNT *Glossogr.* **1767** A. YOUNG *Farmer's Lett. to People* 45 Raising leguminous crops like field pease. **1827** STEUART *Planter's G.* (1828) 498 This practice will by no means preclude the cultivation of leguminous crops. **1898** *Allbutt's Syst. Med.* V. 591 Meat, leguminous vegetables and bread contain the same alkali.

2. *Bot.* Of or pertaining to the N.O. *Leguminosæ*, which includes peas, beans, and other plants which bear legumes or pods.

1677 GREW *Anat. Plants* IV. III. v. (1682) 187 The Cod of the Garden Bean (and so of the rest of the Leguminous kind) opens on one side. **1785** MARTYN *Rousseau's Bot.* iii. (1794) 39 The greater part of the leguminous or pulse tribe. **1807** J. E. SMITH *Phys. Bot.* 446 Linnæus..asserts..that 'among all the leguminous or papilionaceous tribe there is no deleterious plant to be found'. **1830** LINDLEY *Nat. Syst. Bot.* 88 Myrospermum, a spurious Leguminous genus. **1854** HOOKER *Himal. Jrnls.* I. ii. 50 A most elegant leguminous tree. **1890** A. R. WALLACE *Darwinism* 24 Climbing leguminous plants escape both floods and cattle.

b. Resembling what pertains to a leguminous plant.

1688 R. HOLME *Armoury* II. 97/1 The top [of Goats Rue] is branched, upon each stands many leguminous, or pulse-like flowers. **1725** BRADLEY *Fam. Dict.* s.v. *Sainfoin*, They are leguminous Flowers, White and sometimes Red. **1830** LINDLEY *Nat. Syst. Bot.* 87 Another and a more invariable character [of the Pea tribe] is to have a leguminous fruit.

legyor, obs. form of LEDGER.

lehȝen, obs. form of LAUGH *v.*

lehiite (ˈliːhaɪaɪt). *Min.* [f. *Lehi*, the name of the city in Utah near which it occurs + -ITE[1].] A basic hydrated phosphate of calcium, potassium, sodium, and aluminium, of a white to grey colour.

1930 LARSEN & SHANNON in *Amer. Mineralogist* XV. 329 (*heading*) Lehiite, a new mineral. **1942** *Ibid.* XXVII. 294 Material identified by this writer as lehiite differs somewhat from that described by Larsen and Shannon. It forms dense, light gray layers on the outer shells of the nodules, and is made up of fine to moderately coarse fibers generally in subparallel bands. **1955** M. H. HEY *Index Min. Species* (ed. 2) 236 *Lehiite*, $(K,Na)_2Ca_5Al_8(PO_4)_8(OH)_{12}.6H_2O$ (?).

‖**lehm** (leːm). *Geol.* [Ger. = LOAM.] = LOESS.

1833 LYELL *Princ. Geol.* III. 151 There is a remarkable alluvium filled with land-shells of recent species, which overspreads a great part of the valley of the Rhine, between Basle and Cologne... This deposit is provincially termed 'Loess', or, in Alsace, 'Lehm'. **1876** PAGE *Adv. Text-Bk. Geol.* xx. 405 The 'loess' or 'lehm' of the Rhine—a pulverulent yellowish, sandy loam.

lehmanite (ˈleːmənaɪt). *Min.* Also lem-. [Named by J. C. Delamétherie, 1797, after Lake *Lehman* (*Leman*), its locality: see -ITE.] An obsolete synonym of saussurite.

1811 PINKERTON *Petral.* I. 207 Lehmanite of felspar and quartz, from Cornwall. **1837** DANA *Min.* 293 Lemanite.

ˈlehmannite. *Min.* [Named by H. J. Brooke and W. H. Miller, 1852, after Prof. J. G. *Lehmann*, of St. Petersburg, its discoverer: see -ITE.] An obsolete synonym of crocoite.

1852 BROOKE & MILLER *Phillips' Min.* 557 Lehmannite.

lehr, var. LEER *sb.*[3]

lehrbachite (ˈlɛərbaxaɪt). *Min.* [Named by H. J. Brooke and W. H. Miller, 1852, after *Lehrbach* in the Harz Mountains, its locality: see -ITE.] Selenide of lead, found in blackish grey masses.

1852 BROOKE & MILLER *Phillips' Min.* 153 Lehrbachite.. decrepitates when heated. **1885** ERNI *Min.* 236 Lehrbachite gives with soda on coal, globules of lead.

‖**Lehrjahre** (ˈleːrjɑːrə), *sb. pl.* [G. *lehr(en* to teach + *jahre* years; cf. G. *lehrling* apprentice.] Apprenticeship, usu. *fig.*

1865 J. A. SYMONDS *Let.* 15 May (1967) I. 539 The retrospective view you take there of your last two years is the just one. They have been Lehrjahre in a high sense. **1891** E. B. BAX tr. *Schopenhauer's Sel. Ess.* p. x, They settled at Hamburg... It was here that Arthur Schopenhauer spent his *lehrjahre*. *a* **1892** G. C. ROBERTSON *Elem. Gen. Philos.* (1896) xx. 201 The Socratic stage (407–399)—his *Lehrjahre* as they have been called—when he was the pupil of Socrates. **1973** *Times* 14 June 16/2 Julian Fane has written an updated, nineteenth-century *Lehrjahre* book.

lehter, var. LAHTER *Obs.*; obs. f. LAUGHTER.

†**lehtrie**, *v. Obs.* [OE. *leahtrian*, f. *leahtor* LAHTER, vice.] *trans.* To reproach.

c **1000** ÆLFRIC *Gram.* xxv. (Z.) 144 *Criminor* ic leahtrje. *c* **1200** *Trin. Coll. Hom.* 215 þat he.. lehtrie þo þe on sinne lið.

lehua (leɪˈhuːə). [Hawaiian.] An evergreen tree, *Metrosideros collina*, of the family Myrtaceæ, native to the Polynesian and Melanesian islands of the Pacific Ocean and bearing panicles of scarlet flowers; also called *ohia* or *ohia lehua*.

1888 W. HILLEBRAND *Flora Hawaiian Islands* 125 *M[etrosideros] polymorpha*... The most generally prevailing tree on all Islands between 1500 and 6000 ft., usually gregarious. Nat[ive] name: 'Ohia lehua', or simply 'lehua'. .. The wood is very hard, furnishes the best fuel, and is also used for building houses. **1917** *Nature* 20 Sept. 57/2 Lehua, resembles, in the appearance of the trunk, our white oak, but bears beautiful clusters of scarlet flowers with long, protruding stamens. **1937** D. & H. TEILHET *Feather Cloak Murders* ix. 152 From the lehua trees the fragrance hung. **1965** M. C. NEAL *In Gardens of Hawaii* 637 The lehua, a favorite native Hawaiian tree, is the commonest kind.. in some forests.

leˈhuntite. *Min.* [Named after Captain *Lehunt*: see -ITE.] An obsolete synonym of natrolite.

1831 BRYCE *Tables Min.* etc. (Chester). **1843** PORTLOCK *Geol.* 221 The Lehuntite of Thomson is met not uncommonly at Glenarm.

lei (leɪ). [Hawaiian.] A Polynesian garland made of flowers, feathers, shells, etc., often given as a symbol of affection.

1843 J. JARVES *Hist. Hawaiian or Sandwich Islands* iii. 65 Garlands of flowers, necklaces of shells, and *leis*, beautiful wreaths fabricated from red or yellow feathers, encircled the limbs of the females. **1883** W. H. D. ADAMS *Mountains & Mountain-Climbing* 300 These crimson tassels, deftly strung on thread or fibres, are much used by the natives for their *leis*, or garlands. **1905** A. R. H. MONCRIEFF *World of To-Day* IV. 208 Bedecked by *leis*, garlands of bright flowers or feathers. **1956** J. MASTERS *Bugles & Tiger* xxii. 292 The garlands round my neck [at Honolulu] were called leis but they smelled much the same as the ones in India. **1966** MRS. L. B. JOHNSON *White House Diary* 25 Oct. (1970) 434 There were more 'Blue Ladies'—Mrs. Marcos' hostess committee—with fragrant leis of sampaguita for each of the First Ladies. **1970** N. ARMSTRONG et al. *First on Moon* xiv. 364 Jan Armstrong was wearing a carnation lei sent by friends in Hawaii. **1975** *Times* 2 May 7 (*caption*) Governor George Ariyoshi welcoming the Queen to Hawaii with a lei of orchids.

lei, obs. form of LAY, LIE.

lei: see LEU.

Leibni(t)z (ˈlaɪbnɪts). *Philos.* [Name of the German philosopher and mathematician: see LEIBNITZIAN *a.* and *sb.*] ***Leibniz'(s) law***: the principle of the identity of indiscernibles (see INDISCERNIBLE *sb.* 2).

Leibniz is now the more usual spelling.

1941 O. HELMER tr. *Tarski's Introd. Logic* §17. 55, *x* = *y* if, and only if, *x* has every property which *y* has, and *y* has every property which *x* has... [This] was first stated by Leibniz.. and hence may be called Leibniz's law. **1965** *Philos. Rev.* LXXIV. 341 Physicalism violates Leibniz' law, which requires that if two things are identical they have all their non-intensional and nonmodal properties in common. **1968** *Aristotelian Soc. Suppl. Vol.* XLII. 99 Let us consider Leibniz's law firstly as a principle about the identity of individuals.

Leibnitzian (laɪbˈnɪtsɪən), *a.* and *sb.* Also **Leibnitian, -izian.** [f. the name of Gottfried Wilhelm *Leibnitz* (1646–1716) + -IAN.]

A. *adj.* Pertaining to Leibnitz or his philosophical doctrines or mathematical methods.

1765 MACLAINE tr. *Mosheim's Eccl. Hist.* (1768) V. 23 *note*, The Leibnitian and Wolfian philosophy. **1778** MILNER in *Phil. Trans.* LXVIII. 362 The Leibnitzian doctrine. *a* **1818** COLERIDGE *Lit. Rem.* (1838) III. 73 The Leibnitzian distinction of the Eternal Reason, or nature of God.. from the will or personal attributes of God. **1877** E. CAIRD *Philos. Kant* II. xiii. 504 The Leibnitzian Monadism. **1884** MERZ *Leibniz* 211 The great body of Leibnizian and Kantian thought.

B. *sb.* A follower of Leibnitz.

1754 *Dict. Arts & Sci.* II. 1293 Some Leibnitians do not assume.. that action or force is proportional to the pressure and space. **1882** W. WALLACE *Kant* 101 Still the Leibnitians have almost all the experiences on their side.

Hence **Leibˈnitzianism**, the doctrines of Leibnitz or his followers.

1874 MORRIS tr. *Überweg's Hist. Philos.* II. 120.

Leica (ˈlaɪkə). [f. *Leitz* (see below) + CA(MERA.] The proprietary name of cameras made by the German firm of Ernst Leitz Wetzlar Gesellschaft.

1925 *Brit. Jrnl. Photogr.* 26 June 387/2 New apparatus... Leica cine film camera... Quite an innovation in pocket cameras is one just issued by the well-known firm of Leitz, designed to take about 5 feet of ordinary standard perforated cinematograph film. **1930** *Trade Marks Jrnl.* 23 July 1135/1 Leica... Photographic cameras. Ernst & Leitz Gesellschaft mit beschränkter Haftung, (a Company organised under the laws of Germany),.. London,.. and Wetzlar, Germany; Manufacturers. **1933** W. ALEXANDER *Mod. Photogr. with Mod. Miniature Cameras* ii. 29 *Leica* and *Contax* have now become words.. familiar in the mouths of men throughout .. the earth. **1934** H. NICOLSON *Let.* 9 Oct. (1966) 184 Lindbergh.. helped me to unload my Leica camera. **1936** P. FLEMING *News from Tartary* v. 36 The Leicas turned out very satisfactorily. **1948** 'N. SHUTE' *No Highway* v. 136 The print was an enlargement from a Leica frame. **1953** C. DAY LEWIS *Italian Visit* v. 53 Armed with good taste, a Leica and a guide. **1958** G. GREENE *Our Man in Havana* I. iii. 25 The victim's Leica had been smashed as well. **1959** P. H. JOHNSON *Unspeakable Skipton* vii. 57 An American.. was photographing the swans with his Leica. **1973** R. THOMAS *If you can't be Good* (1974) iii. 28 Using.. an old Leica with some fast film, Sarah turned out striking, informal portraits.

Leicester (ˈlɛstə(r)). [The name of an English county town.] **a.** Used *attrib.* or *adj.*, and hence ellipt. as sb., to designate a valuable long-woolled variety of sheep and a long-horned variety of cattle originally bred in Leicestershire. In *Austral.* and *N.Z.* freq. as *English Leicester*. Cf. *Border Leicester*. Also **Leicestershire.**

1798 J. MIDDLETON *View Agric. Middlesex* xiii. 348 The Lincoln and Leicester sheep come to Smithfield in perfection. **1798** JANE AUSTEN *Let.* 17 Nov. (1952) 29 One of his Leicestershire sheep, sold to the butcher last week, weighed 27 lb. and ¼ per quarter. **1804** A. YOUNG *Gen. View Agric. Hertfordshire* 189 The cross is with the new Leicester: he sells no lambs. **1809** [see KENT *sb.*[3]]. **1834** YOUATT *Cattle* vi. 208 Where a few of the long-horns do linger, the improved Leicesters are gone. **1839** *Penny Cycl.* XIII. 291/2 The improved Leicester has gained a footing, and will not soon lose it. **1874** A. BATHGATE *Colonial Experiences* xv. 210 In cultivated lands the Leicester is the favorite. **1923** W. PERRY et al. *Sheep Farming in N.Z.* iv. 32 Thus Romney Marsh, English Leicesters, and Lincolns, have been improved or adapted to suit New Zealand conditions. **1950** H. G. BELSCHNER *Sheep Managem. & Dis.* ii. 21 The Leicester crosses well with the big-framed Merino, but it is not so much in favour for this purpose in Australia... The following description of the English Leicester is taken from the flock book of the Australian Society of Breeders of British Sheep. **1956** G. BOWEN *Wool Away!* (ed. 2) xii. 142 The English Leicester is another of the British breeds which has played a notable part in developing New Zealand's sheep farming, but is now more or less on the way out.

b. Leicester (occas. **Leicestershire**) **cheese**, a firm-textured full milk cheese originally made in Leicestershire.

1880 J. P. SHELDON *Dairy Farming* 241/1 The finest qualities of.. Leicester cheese are generally admitted to be, with the single exception of genuine Stilton, the best cheese produced in these islands. **1902** *Encycl. Brit.* XXVII. 355/2 Derby cheese in its best forms is much like Leicester, being 'clean' in flavour and mellow. **1950** J. G. DAVIS *Dict. Dairying* 124 Leicester cheese is made from evening's and morning's milk. **1965** T. FITZGIBBON *Art Brit. Cooking* 133 Leicestershire cheese is a hard-pressed, flaky textured cheese.. usually coloured a pale orange with annatto. **1970** *Guardian* 6 June 13/2 Leicester, an excellent dessert cheese with a mild flavour.

leiche, leicht, obs. forms of LEECH, LIGHT.

Leichhardt (ˈlaɪkɑːt). The name of the German explorer of Australia, Friedrich Wilhelm Ludwig *Leichhardt* (1813–48), used *attrib.* in **Leichhardt-tree, -pine** to designate a tree native to Australia and India, *Nauclea orientalis*, of the family Rubiaceæ, which bears heads of yellow flowers; also *absol.*; **Leichhardt's bean** (see BEAN *sb.* 4).

1860 F. VON MUELLER *Essay on Plants collected by Mr. Eugene Fitzalan* 12 The opportunity is an apt one for offering here some remarks on the 'Leichhardt-tree' of the settlers of Rockhampton. **1874** M. K. BEVERIDGE *Lost Life* 40 Groaning beneath the friendly shade That by a Leichhardt-tree was made. **1885** H. FINCH-HATTON *Advance Australia!* 258 The Leichhardt is a very symmetrical tree that grows to a height of about sixty feet, and has leaves rather like a big laurel. **1888** F. M. BAILEY *Queensland Woods* 76 *S[arcocephalus] cordatus*... Leichhardt-tree or Canary-wood... A large tree with a thick, soft, corky bark of a more or less yellowish colour. **1907** MRS. A. GUNN *We of Never-Never* 64 The camp had been fixed up in the silent depths of a dark Leichhardt-pine forest. **1908** E. J. BANFIELD *Confessions of Beachcomber* II. i. 252 'Koo-badg-aroo' (Leichhardt-tree, *Sarcocephalus cordatus*), resembling a strawberry in shape, but brown, spicy and hot. **1944** W. E. HARNEY *Taboo* (ed. 3) 27 Those huge Leichhardt trees.. would then be fashioned into canoes.

leid(e, obs. pa. t. and pple. of LAY *v.*

leide, obs. form of LEAD.

leidger, obs. form of LEDGER.

leidyite (ˈlaɪdɪaɪt). *Min.* [Named by G. A. Koenig, 1878, in honour of Dr. Joseph *Leidy*: see -ITE.] A complicated hydrous silicate found in fine yellowish-green scales.

1878 in *Proc. Acad. Nat. Sci. Philad.* 84. **1882** DANA *Min.* App. 68 Leidyite.. consisting of fine scales with silky lustre.

leie, obs. form of LAY, LIE.

leif, obs. f. LEAF, LIEF, LIVE; Sc. f. LEVE *v.*[2]

leifite (ˈliː-, ˈleɪfaɪt). *Min.* [ad. Da. *leifit* (O. B. Bøggild 1915, in *Meddelelser om Grønland* LI. 427), f. the name of *Leif* Ericson (fl. 1000), Norse voyager: see -ITE[1].] An acidic aluminosilicate and fluoride of sodium occurring as colourless hexagonal prisms.

1917 *Jrnl. Chem. Soc.* CXII. II. 147 (*heading*) Leifite, a new mineral from Narsarsuk, Greenland. **1968** I. KOSTOV *Mineral.* II. v. 406 Leifite, $Na_2AlSi_4O_{10}F.H_2O < 1$, found as acicular hexagonal crystals in pegmatites is similar to cancrinite.

leifull, leiffull, variants of LEEFUL.

leige, obs. form of LIEGE.

leigeance, obs. form of LIGEANCE.

leiger, obs. form of LEAGUER, LEDGER.

leigeritie, variant of LEGERITY *Obs.*, lightness.

leigh, obs. pa. t. of LIE *v.*[1] and *v.*[2]

leigh, var. LEGH.

†**leighster.** *Obs. rare*[−1]. [repr. OE. type **líeȝestre*, fem. agent-n. to *léoȝan*, f. LIE *v.*[2]: see -STER.] A female liar.

c **1325** *Lai le Freine* 106 Yif ich say ich hadde a bi-leman .. Than ich worth Be hold leighster and fals of tong.

†**leighton.** *Obs.* Forms: 1 léc-, léah-, léhtun, 3 ley(h)tun, leiȝhton, 4 lahtoun, leiȝ-, leyȝton, lectun, 7 liten, 8 laghton, laighton. [OE. *léahtún*, earlier **léactún*, f. *léac* LEEK + *tún* enclosure: see TOWN.] A garden.

c **950** *Lindisf. Gosp.* Luke xiii. 19 Onȝelic is corne senepes þætte ȝenumen wæs monn sende in lehtune his. *c* **1050** *Voc.* in Wr.-Wülcker 460/30 *Ortus olerum*, leahtun. *c* **1275** *Passion Our Lord* 291 in *O.E. Misc.* 45 Iwis þu were myd ihesu crist in þe leyhtune. **13..** *Childh. Jesu* 1618 in Horstm. *Altengl. Leg.* (1875) 54 Jacob.. bad him go.. A non riȝht doun into þe leiȝhtone, For to bringuen heom wuyrtone. *a* **1327** *Treat. Dreams* in *Rel. Ant.* I. 264 Lahtoun make ant to-delve. **1398** TREVISA *Barth. De P.R.* XIII. xvi. (Tollem. MS.), Some of pondes beþ stremes to water and moyste gardines and leiȝtons [*ed.* 1535 orcheyardes]. *Ibid.* XVII. I, Some tren and herbes groweþ in leyȝtons [*ed.* 1535 croftes]. **1674** RAY *N.C. Words* 30 *Liten*, a Garden. **17..** R. RICHARDSON in *Leland's Itin.* (ed. Hearne 1745) I. 140, I have met with several British Words that are still in use, such as Laghton for a Garden. **1775** WATSON *Hist. Halifax* 542 Laighton, a Garden.

Hence †**leightonward**, a gardener.

c **1000** ÆLFRIC *Gloss.* in Wr.-Wülcker 127/14 *Olitor*, lectunward. *c* **1275** *Passion Our Lord* 576 in *O.E. Misc.* 53 Heo wende hit were þe leyhtunward þat to hire spek.

leightonite ('leɪtənaɪt). *Min.* [f. the name of Tomas *Leighton* (b. 1894), Chilean mineralogist + -ITE[1].] A hydrated sulphate of potassium, calcium, and copper found as transparent, pale blue to greenish blue, triclinic crystals at Chuquicamata, Chile.

1938 C. PALACHE in *Amer. Mineralogist* XXIII. 34 Leightonite, as the new species will be named, is triclinic, as shown by optical examination. **1962** *Canad. Mineralogist* VII. 276 It is interesting to note that leightonite has a chemical homologue—polyhalite, $K_2Ca_2Mg(SO_4)_4.2H_2O$. **1963** *Acta Crystallogr.* XVI. A10/1 Leightonite, $K_2Ca_2Cu(SO_4)_4.2H_2O$, is triclinic, but it is pseudo-orthorhombic (face-centred) to the extent that no departure from 90° has been found in the angles of the unit cell as determined by the usual X-ray diffraction techniques.

leigier, obs. form of LEAGUER, LEDGER.

leihe, obs. form of LYE, lixivium.

leihter, obs. f. LAUGHTER; var. LAHTER *Obs.*

leik, obs. form of LICH, LIKE.

leil(e, leill, obs. forms of LEAL.

leime, obs. Sc. form of LEAM *sb.*[1]

lein, lein(e, obs. forms of LAY *v.*, LEAN.

†**leind**, *sb. Obs.* Also **lend**. [a. ON. *løynd*, f. *løyna*: see LAIN *v.*] A hiding-place, refuge.

a **1300** *Cursor M.* 9652 Aha! þat wreche wit-vten freind, þat on na side mai gett him leind [*Gött.* lend]. *Ibid.* 24728 We prai þat liuedi be vr leind [*Edinb.* lend].

leind, variant of LEND *v.*[1] *Obs.*

leing, obs. form of LYING.

leint, obs. Sc. pa. t. and pple. of LEAN *v.*[1]

leio- ('laɪəʊ), also lio-, comb. form of Gr. λεῖος smooth, appearing as the first element of certain scientific words, as: **leiodere** ('laɪəʊdɪə(r)) *Zool.* [Gr. δέρος skin], one of the genus *Leiodera* of American iguanoid lizards (*Cent. Dict.*). **leioglossate** (-'glɒsət) *a.* [Gr. γλῶσσα tongue], having the characteristics of the group *Leioglossa* of octopod cephalopods, which have no radula. ‖**leiomyoma** (-maɪ'əʊmə) *Path.* [see MYOMA], 'the form of myoma which is composed of unstriated muscular fibre' (*Syd. Soc. Lex.* 1888). **leiophyllous** (-'fɪləs) *a. Bot.* [Gr. φύλλον], having smooth leaves. **leiotrichous** (laɪ'ɒtrɪkəs) *a.* [Gr. τριχ-, θρίξ hair], smooth-haired, belonging to the group ‖**lei'otrichi**, one of the two primary divisions into which mankind is considered by some to be divisible; hence **lei'otrichy**, the condition of having straight lank hair.

1855 R. G. MAYNE *Expos. Lex. Med. Sci.* (1860) 581/2 *Leiotrichus*, having smooth hair: leiotrichous. **1866** HUXLEY *Preh. Rem. Caithn.* 132 Bory de St. Vincent's two primary divisions of the genus *Homo*, the *Leiotrichi*, or smooth-haired, and the *Ulotrichi*, or crisp-haired. **1881** WEST in *Jrnl. Bot.* X. 115 This species belongs to the orthocarpous leiophyllous Hypnaceae. **1909** Leiotrichous [see CYMOTRICHOUS *a.*]. **1924** A. C. HADDON *Races of Man* (ed. 2) 5 For practical purposes these varieties of hair-form may be grouped as follows: (1) Leio-trichy.., or straight hair, [etc.]. **1935** HUXLEY & HADDON *We Europeans* iv. 114 Leiotrichy: the condition of straight lank hair, hanging straight down, as among the Chinese and certain other yellow-skinned peoples of Asia, and among the Eskimo. **1936** Leiotrichy [see CYMOTRICHOUS *a.*].

leiotropic, erron. form of LÆOTROPIC.

leip(o)-: see LIP(O)-.

leir, obs. form of LAIR, LERE *v.*, LIEFER.

leir, var. LEAR[1], learning; LEAR[2] *Obs.*

leirne, obs. Sc. form of LEARN.

leis, Sc. var. LEASE *a.* and *sb.*[2], LEESE *v.*[1], LEEZE (*me*), LESE(-MAJESTY).

leisar, leisour, obs. forms of LEISURE *sb.*

leisch, leiser(e, obs. ff. LEASH, LEISURE *sb.*

leish, obs. f. LEASH; var. LISSE, fine thread.

Leishman ('liːʃmən, 'laɪʃ-). *Med.* The name of W. B. *Leishman* (1865–1926), British pathologist, used *attrib.* and in the possessive with reference to his work in pathology, as **Leishman('s) body** = LEISHMAN-DONOVAN BODY; **Leishman('s) stain**, a mixture of eosin and methylene blue used to stain blood smears.

1903 *Brit. Med. Jrnl.* 28 Nov. 1401/1 (*heading*) Further notes on Leishman's bodies. *Ibid.*, There is never any contour line suggestive of a cell-wall, as with the Leishman bodies themselves. **1904** *Ibid.* 28 May 1250/1 A film prepared from the peripheral blood was examined.., Romanowsky and Leishman's stains being used. *Ibid.* 1252/1 These bodies stain purple or violet with the Leishman stain. **1961** *Lancet* 5 Aug. 315/2 In staining blood-films we obtained just as good results as with Leishman's stain prepared by the standard method. **1972** W. C. JOHNSON in J. H. Graham et al. *Dermal Path.* xix. 455/2 A definite diagnosis [of leishmaniasis] depends upon the demonstration of the Leishman bodies.

Leishman-Donovan body (-'dɒnəvən-). *Med.* [f. prec. + the name of C. *Donovan* (1863–1951), Irish physician.] One of the numerous ovoid structures consisting of a single non-flagellated leishmania found in the macrophages of sufferers from leishmaniasis.

1904 *Brit. Med. Jrnl.* 28 May 1249/2 (*heading*) Note on the occurrence of Leishman-Donovan bodies in 'cachexial fevers' including kala-azar. **1966** WRIGHT & SYMMERS *Systemic Path.* II. xxxix. 1601/2 (*caption*) Large numbers of Leishman-Donovan bodies are seen in the cytoplasm of many of the macrophages in this field.

leishmania (liːʃ'mænɪə, laɪʃ-). *Zool.* and *Med.* Pl. **-ia, -iæ, -ias**. [mod.L., f. LEISHMAN + -IA[1].]

a. Any protozoon of the genus *Leishmania* (family Trypanosomidæ), comprising three species which are parasitic in man (and occas. other mammals), occurring as non-flagellated Leishman-Donovan bodies, and which are transmitted by sandflies of the genus *Phlebotomus*, wherein they occur as flagellated individuals in the alimentary canal. **b.** Any flagellate of the family Trypanosomidæ when existing in a leishmanial form.

[**1903** R. ROSS in *Brit. Med. Jrnl.* 28 Nov. 1401/2 Laveran has given the name *Piroplasma donovani* to these organisms; and the specific name must therefore be permanently adopted. But if, as I suppose, they are found to belong to a new genus, it would be only fair to give the name *Leishmania* to that genus. In that event the full name would be *Leishmania donovani*, Laveran.] **1914** *Trop. Dis. Bull.* III. 141 Large numbers of leishmania were found in the lesions. **1926**, etc. [see LEPTOMONAS]. **1952** M. E. FLOREY *Clin. Applic. Antibiotics* I. viii. 247 The lesion had again broken down and leishmania were found in smears. **1961** [see LEPTOMONAD]. **1962** J. D. SMYTH *Introd. Animal Parasitol.* v. 63 Leishmanias are unusual in living entirely within the cells of the reticulo-endothelial system. **1968** E. J. L. SOULSBY *Helminths, Arthropods & Protozoa Domesticated Animals* 567 Endothelial and macrophage cells contain masses of leishmaniae.

Hence **leish'manial, leish'manian** *adjs.*, caused by leishmaniæ; typical of a leishmania as it occurs in man and other mammals (i.e. as a non-flagellated Leishman-Donovan body). Also **leishma'niasis** (pl. **-ases**) [-ASIS], **-mani'osis** (pl. **-oses**) [-OSIS], any of several diseases, principally kala-azar (visceral leishmaniasis), oriental sore (cutaneous leishmaniasis) and espundia (muco-cutaneous or American cutaneous leishmaniasis), which are caused by species of *Leishmania*; **(dermal) 'leishmanoid** [-OID, after VARIOLOID *a.* and *sb.*], a condition occurring as a sequel to kala-azar and characterized by an eruption of whitish patches on the skin.

1911 STEDMAN *Med. Dict.* 470/1 *Leishmaniosis*, infection with a species of *Leishmania*. **1912** *Trop. Dis. Bull.* I. 363 (*heading*) Fourth series of haematological researches on leishmanial anaemia. **1912** *Brit. Med. Jrnl.* 2 Nov. 1194/2 (*heading*) Papers dealing with leishmaniasis. **1914** *Chem. Abstr.* VIII. 1466 (*heading*) Possibility of the excitation of leucopoiesis in Leishmanian infection in childhood. **1916** *Jrnl. Amer. Med. Assoc.* 22 Nov. 1635/2 (*heading*) Tartrate of antimony and potassium in treatment of superficial leishmaniosis. **1920** W. E. MASTERS *Essent. Trop. Med.* i. 55 (*heading*) The leishmaniases. **1922** U. N. BRAHMACHARI in *Indian Med. Gaz.* LVII. 127/1 In view of the fact that the eruptions are due to leishmania infection whose virus has been modified by antimonial treatment, I propose to call this form of cutaneous leishmaniasis *dermal leishmanoid* just as small-pox modified by vaccination is called varioloid. **1942** [see LEPTOMONAD]. **1966** WRIGHT & SYMMERS *Systemic Path.* II. xxxix. 1596/2 Cutaneous leishmaniosis (oriental or tropical sore) is caused by the protozoon, *Leishmania tropica*. **1967** A. C. ALLEN *Skin* (ed. 2) xiv. 541/1 The so-called post-kala-azar dermal leishmanoid is a familiar sequel of visceral leishmaniasis... The leishmanoid begins as patches of erythematous macules on the face and body. **1967** *New Scientist* 17 Aug. 349/2 Small rodents which are carriers of the disease leishmaniasis which causes suppurating sores in humans. **1968** E. J. L. SOULSBY *Helminths, Arthropods & Protozoa Domesticated Animals* 565 Developmental stages of the genus [sc. *Leishmania*] occur in the leishmanial form in vertebrates and in the leptomonad form in the insect vector and in culture. **1968** WEINMAN & RISTIC *Infectious Blood Dis. Man & Animals* I. viii. 160 These lack the physiological character possessed by the leishmanial parasites of mammals of being able to grow at temperatures of 34°–38°C.

leisk, Sc. form of LISK, flank.

Leisler ('laɪzlə(r)). The name of the early 19th-c. German zoologist, T. P. *Leisler*, used in the possessive to designate **Leisler's bat**, a small black bat, *Nyctalus leisleri*, named after him in 1817 by H. Kuhl (*Deutsch. Fledermäuse* 38), and formerly called the hairy-armed bat.

1904 J. G. MILLAIS *Mammals Great Brit. & Ireland* I. 76 Leisler's Bat is considerably smaller than the noctule. **1910** G. E. H. BARRETT-HAMILTON *Hist. Brit. Mammals* I. 83 Leisler's Bat, or species closely resembling it, is found in the wooded districts of boreal and transitional Europe and Asia. **1941** H. CORY *Mammals Brit. Isles* 255 Leisler's Bat.. is rare in England, but occurs in greater numbers in eastern Ireland. **1960** *Times* 14 June 14/7 Of the Leisler's bat.. I recall no obvious distinguishing character.

leisom(e, leisoum, variants of LEESOME.

leispound, variant of LISPOUND.

leiss, Sc. var. LEASE, LEESE *v.*[1], LEEZE (*me*).

leist, obs. form of LEAST, LEST, LIST.

leist, obs. 2nd sing. ind. pres. of LAY *v.*[1]

leister ('liːstə(r)). Also 6 leyster, 6, 9 lister, 7–8 leester, 9 liester. [a. ON. *ljóstr* (Norw. dial. *lioster*, Sw. *ljuster*, Da. *lyster*), f. *ljósta* str. vb., to strike.] A pronged spear for striking and taking fish, chiefly salmon.

1533-4 *Act 25 Hen. VIII*, c. 7 No.. person.. shal.. take.. in.. any.. crele, raw web, lister, fier, or any other engine.. the yonge frie.. of any kinde of salmon. **1551** TURNER *Herbal* I. F vj, Their leysters or sammon speres. **1638** *N. Riding Rec.* IV. 101 A yeoman presented for that he did kill .. with a certain engine called a leister much salmon. **1785** BURNS *Death Dr. Hornbook* vi, A three-taed leister. **1834** M. SCOTT *Cruise Midge* xi, [He] came running up the stairs with a salmon lister in one hand. **1843** W. SCROPE *Salmon Fish. Tweed* xi. 239 The men.. wielding their long leisters. **1895** *Chamb. Jrnl.* XII. 753/2 Celebrated.. as a poacher and as a great hand at the leister in autumn.

b. *Comb.*, as ***leister grain***; ***leister-shaped*** adj.

1634 *Acts Durham High Comm. Crt.* (Surtees) 102 Did see Mr. Haslehead take upp the leester graines and throw them awaie. **1863** ATKINSON *Stanton Grange* (1864) 23 Rather leister-shaped in construction, with five barbed prongs.

'leister, *v.* [f. LEISTER *sb.*] *trans.* To spear with a leister.

1834 HOGG *Dom. Mann. Scott* (1882) 11 He [Scott] and Skene of Rubislaw, and I were out one night about mid-night, leistering kippers in Tweed. **1861** J. BROWN *Horæ Subs.* II. 243 The poaching weaver who had the night before leistered a prime kipper. **1881** *Blackw. Mag.* Apr. 530 They burned the water and leistered the salmon.

Hence **'leistering** *vbl. sb.* Also **'leisterer**.

1843 W. SCROPE *Salmon Fish. Tweed* xi. 237 The side on which the leisterers strike the fish. **1867** *Times* 30 Dec. 9/6 Conviction of Salmon Leisterers. *Ibid.*, The process of salmon leistering by night with the aid of torch and spear.

leisum, variant of LEESOME *a.*

leisurable ('lɛʒ(jʊ)ərəb(ə)l), *a.* [f. LEISURE *sb.* + -ABLE; perh. on the supposed analogy of *comfortable, honourable*: cf. *pleasurable*.]

1. Proceeding or acting without haste; leisurely, deliberate.

[*a* **1540** implied in LEISURABLY.] **1581** J. BELL *Haddon's Answ. Osor.* 479 Chosing rather to broyle him with leasurable tormentes.. then to kill him at once. **1618** BOLTON *Florus* IV. ii. (1636) 264 His [Pompey's] over-great power.. moved envy among the leisurable [L. *otiosos*] Citizens. *a* **1691** BOYLE *Hist. Air* xiii. (1692) 81, I shall humbly reserve [this] to a more leasurable inquiry.

2. Not requiring haste; leisure (time). *rare.*

1607 MARKHAM *Caval.* v. (1617) 40 You must doe it by such leasurable times, that nature hauing no more then she is able to digest, may.. come to be orderly satisfied. **1643** SIR T. BROWNE *Relig. Med.* Pref., This I confesse.. I had at leisurable hours composed. **1848** *Jrnl. R. Agric. Soc.* IX. II. 261 A leisurable period of the year. **1885** PATER *Marius the Epic.* II. ix. (ed. 2) I. 149 Such a theory, at more leisurable moments, would, of course, have its precepts to propound.

leisurably ('lɛʒ(jʊ)ərəblɪ), *adv.* Now *rare.* [f. prec. + -LY[2].] In a 'leisurable' manner; leisurely, without haste, deliberately.

a **1540** BARNES *Wks.* (1573) 358/2 If thou wilt leasurably lysten and beholde to the ende of the tragedye. **1658** SIR T. MAYERNE *Receipts Cookery* cxl. 90 Let it boyl leasurably. **1695** BP. ROCHESTER *Disc. Clergy* 13 Setting forth the public Prayers to all their due Advantage, by pronouncing them leasurably, fitly, warmly, decently. **1806** *Med. Jrnl.* XV. 172 Let him speak leisurably. **1889** *Longm. Mag.* June 164 He.. pricked leisurably down the slope.

leisure ('lɛʒ(jʊ)ə(r), 'liːʒ(jʊ)ə(r)), *sb.* Forms: 4 leisere, leysir, *Sc.* lasere, 4–5 leiser, leysere, *Sc.* lasair, 4–6 laiser, layser, leyser, *Sc.* laser, -are, 5 laisir, -our, -ure, laysar, -ir, leyzer, -soure, lesure, 5–6 leysar, *Sc.* lasar, 6 laisere, -ure, layso(u)r, -ure, leisar, -our, leaser, -our, leesar, leser, leysour(e, leys(s)or, *Sc.* laseir, lasar, lazar, laisar, 5–7 leysure, 6–8 leasure, 7 liesure, leizure, 6– leisure. [a. OF. *leisir* (mod.F. *loisir*), subst. use of the infinitive *leisir*, repr. L. *licēre* to be permitted.

In Fr. the word has undergone much the same development of sense as in Eng.]

†**1. a.** Freedom or opportunity to do something specified or implied. *Obs.*

1303 R. BRUNNE *Handl. Synne* 28 Þe seruyng man þat serueþ yn þe 3ere Oweþ to come when he haþ leysere. *c* **1330** —— *Chron.* (1810) 229 Whan þou sees leysere, þat he ne perceyue þi witte.. with þe knyfe him to smite. ?*a* **1366** CHAUCER *Rom. Rose* 462 No more was there.. To clothe her with.. Gret leyser hadde she to quake. *c* **1386** —— *Miller's T.* 107 She wol been at his comandement, Whan that she may hir leyser wel espie. *c* **1400** *Destr. Troy* 3119 Þai hade laisure at lust þere likyng to say. *c* **1440** *Promp. Parv.* 295/2 Leysere, *oportunitas*. *c* **1489** CAXTON *Blanchardyn* xliii. 169 Sadoyne folowed hym of so nyghe.. that with grete peyne gaf them leyser to saue hem self. **1500-20** DUNBAR *Poems* ix. 8, I cry the mercy, and lasar to repent. **1513** DOUGLAS *Æneis* IV. x. 83 Quhy will thow nocht fle spedely be nycht, Quhen

for to haist thow hes laisar and mycht? *a* **1533** LD. BERNERS *Huon* xci. 291 Huon mette with hym so hastly that he had no layser to stryke hym. **1640** BP. HALL *Chr. Moder.* I. viii. 75 The Jewes..hold, that after twenty yeares of age, who so finds (the lezer) in himselfe, is bound under paine of sin to marry.

b. An opportunity. *Obs.*

c **1386** CHAUCER *Sqr.'s T.* 485 Whil þat I haue a leyser and a space Myn harm I wol confessen. **1390** GOWER *Conf.* II. 95 If so is, that I may hent Somtime amonge a good leiser. *Ibid.* II. 242 That she with him had [= might have] a leiser To speke and telle of her desir. **14..** *Epiph.* in *Tundale's Vis.* (1843) 116 They haue a leysar found To take hor leyve. **1412-20** LYDG. *Chron. Troy* I. v, Euer eft on him she cast an eye Whan that she founde a leyser opportune. **1430-40** —— *Bochas* IX. xxxiii. (1554) 212 b, To their entent a leysure they did spie.

2. a. In narrower sense: Opportunity afforded by freedom from occupations.

c **1375** *Sc. Leg. Saints* iii. (*St. Andrew*) 999 Waitand bot lasare quhen he mycht purchess oportunitie. **1375** BARBOUR *Bruce* xx. 234 Gif God will me gif Laser and space so lange till liff. *c* **1400** MAUNDEV. (Roxb.) xxx. 137, I..saw all þis.. and mykill mare þan I hafe layser for to tell. **1489** CAXTON *Faytes of A.* I. xxii. 70 Noo layser they had to putte hem self in ordynaunce. **1526** TINDALE *Mark* iii. 20 They had nott leesar so moche as to eate breed. **1553** T. WILSON *Rhet.* Ep. A ij, I traveyled so muche as my leasure myghte serve therunto. **1599** SHAKS. *Much Ado* III. ii. 84 If your leisure seru'd, I would speake with you. **1667** MILTON *P.L.* x. 510 He wonderd, but not long Had leasure, wondring at himself now more. **1712** ADDISON *Spect.* No. 418 ¶5 It does not give us Time or Leisure to reflect on ourselves. **1791** MRS. RADCLIFFE *Rom. Forest* ii, They had leisure to laugh at their late terrors. **1857** BUCKLE *Civiliz.* I. ii. 38 As long as every man is engaged in collecting the materials necessary for his own subsistence, there will be neither leisure nor taste for higher pursuits.

b. Duration of opportunity; time allowed before it is too late. Now *rare.*

1553 BALE *Vocacyon* 41 More than .xxvj. dayes of layser for the payment therof [of the ransom] might not be graunted. **1555** EDEN *Decades* 100 That Tumanama.. myght haue no leasure to assemble an armye. **1603** KNOLLES *Hist. Turks* (1621) 1331 The Turkes had scarce leasure to leape to land, and to flie into the country. **1781** GIBBON *Decl. & F.* xxxi. III. 259 The unfortunate youth had scarcely leisure to deplore the elevation of his family. **1818** JAS. MILL *Brit. India* II. v. v. 547 The authority of the government of Batavia, for whose sanction there was no leisure to wait. **1828** SCOTT *F.M. Perth* xxix, He found himself unexpectedly in Eachin's close neighbourhood, with scarce leisure to avoid him. **1846** J. BAXTER *Libr. Pract. Agric.* (ed. 4) I. 383 The young blades in the field have leisure to expand and grow again before the scythe returns to cut them down a second time.

3. a. The state of having time at one's own disposal; time which one can spend as one pleases; free or unoccupied time.

13.. *K. Alis.* 234 Heo thougte heo wolde him y-here, Whan heo was of more leisere. **1479** in *Eng. Gilds* (1870) 413, I..praye [them]..at theire ceasons of leysoure to rede ..this present boke. *c* **1540** GARDINER in Strype *Cranmer* II. (1694) 75 To spend some of my laysor to wryte..to your G[race] who hath lesse laysor. **1576** FLEMING *Panopl. Epist.* 255 To the perfourmance of such an enterprise, much leasure and labour is required. *c* **1600** SHAKS. *Sonn.* xxxix, Oh absence what a torment wouldst thou proue Were it not thy soure leisure gaue sweet leaue To entertaine the time with thoughts of loue. **1672** TEMPLE *Ess. Govt.* Wks. 1731 I. 97 Where Ambition and Avarice have made no Entrance, the Desire of Leisure is much more Natural, than of Business and Care. **1780** JOHNSON *Let. to Mrs. Thrale* 25 Aug., I am not grown, I am afraid, less idle; and of idleness I am now paying the fine by having no leisure. **1830** D'ISRAELI *Chas. I,* III. vi. 91 Charles commanded his Lordship to employ some of his leisure in a dramatic composition. **1887** RUSKIN *Præterita* II. 143 The first volume of 'Modern Painters' took the best of the winter's leisure.

personified. **1632** MILTON *Penseroso* 49 And adde to these retired Leasure, That in trim Gardens takes his pleasure.

b. In particularized sense: A period or spell of unoccupied time. Now *rare.*

c **1449** PECOCK *Repr.* II. xv. 236 That thei go in pilgrimage thanne or in sum other leiser which thei hem silf point. *a* **1535** FISHER *Wks.* (E.E.T.S.) 432 To spare a leysoure for hym to here the bottom of his mynde. **1597** MORLEY *Introd. Mus.* 115, I will then take my leaue of you for this time, till my next leisure. **1654** R. CODRINGTON tr. *Iustine* I. 2 In the leisures which in this City I enjoyed. **1856** EMERSON *Eng. Traits, Lit.* Wks. (Bohn) II. 110 It is because he [Bacon] had imagination, [and] the leisures of the spirit.. that he is impressive to the imaginations of men. **1873** LOWELL *Among my Bks.* Ser. II. 181 In keeping with that sense of endless leisures which it is one chief merit of the poem to suggest.

c. *to tarry, attend or stay (upon) a person's leisure*: to wait until he is unoccupied; to wait his time. Also *fig. arch.*

1517 in Ellis *Orig. Lett.* Ser. I. II. 4 *note*, If ye be not contente to tary my Leysure, departe when ye wille. **1535** COVERDALE *Ps.* xxvi[i]. 14 [16] O tary thou yᵉ Lordes leysure. **1595** SHAKS. *John* II. i. 58 The aduerse windes Whose leisure I haue staid, haue giuen him time To land his Legions all as soone as I. **1596** —— *Merch. V.* I. i. 68 Wee'll make our leysures to attend on yours. **1605** —— *Macb.* I. iii. 148 Worthy Macbeth, wee stay vpon your leysure. **1656** JEANES *Fuln. Christ* 91 Not contented to wait the Lords Leisure.

†**4.** Leisureliness, deliberation. *Obs.*

a **1300** *Cursor M.* 29370 þe toþer [case] es of dorward or porter..þat clerk wit laiser smites oght. **1450-80** *Secreta Secret.* 25 Ete with leyser and good masticacioun. **1486** *Surtees Misc.* (1888) 55 Sex kinges..with certaine convenient laisour, avisedly shall commyt a ceptour unto Salamon. **1563-7** BUCHANAN *Reform. St. Andros* Wks. (1892) 8 Tellyng..to thayme the lettres..in sik lasar that the barnis may easely writ eftyr his pronunciation. **1664** POWER *Exp. Philos.* II. 123 Much leisure and accurateness were used in filling the Tube. **1677** MARVELL *Corr.* cccvi. Wks. 1872-5 II. 563, I having presented him your letter, he read it with great leisure.

5. Phrases. **a.** *at leisure*: with free or unoccupied time at one's disposal; without haste, with deliberation. Also with qualifying adjs., as *all, best, convenient, full, less, more.*

c **1340** *Cursor M.* 7239 (Trin.) Hir tyme she toke a leiser þere And whil he slepte kut his here. **1375** BARBOUR *Bruce* v. 390 He.. sat and ete at all lasare. *c* **1386** CHAUCER *Pars. T.* ¶761 Som folk stonden of hir owene wyl to eten at the lasse leyser. **1444** *Pol. Poems* (Rolls) II. 219 Whoo hath no dyneer, at leyser must abyde, To staunche his hungir abyde upon his ffood. *c* **1450** *Merlin* 7 Go youre wey, and anothir tyme, we shall speke more at leyser. **1522** SKELTON *Why nat to Courte?* 622 My lorde is nat at layser. **1590** SHAKS. *Com. Err.* IV. i. 100, I will debate this matter at more leisure. **1598** *Epulario* H iv, And so let it bake at leisure, strawing Sugar.. vpon it. **1613** HEYWOOD *Silver Age* I. i. Wks. 1874 III. 92 The full circumstance I shall relate at leasure. **1655** FULLER *Ch. Hist.* I. v. §17 We for the present are well at Leisure, we will present the Reader with the Description of their severall Principalities. **1687** CONGREVE *Old Bach.* v. i. (1693) 50 Marry'd in Haste, we may repent at leisure. **1823** BYRON *Juan* XIII. vi, Men love in haste, but they detest at leisure.

Const. *for*; also *inf.* or a clause introduced by *that.*

1603 KNOLLES *Hist. Turks* (1621) 1250 They were not at liesure now to send such great forces as they had before used, into Hungarie. **1669** CLARENDON *Ess.* Tracts (1727) 95 We complain..of those who are in place and authority.. that they are never at leisure that we may speak to them. **1732** BERKELEY *Alciphr.* VI. §20, I am not at leisure to peruse the learned writings of divines. **1852** MRS. STOWE *Uncle Tom's C.* vii, The dinner being now fairly sent in, the whole kitchen was at leisure to gossip with her. **1875** JOWETT *Plato* (ed. 2) V. 334 The wardens..shall be men of ability, and at leisure to take care of the public interest.

b. *at one's leisure*: when one has unoccupied time at one's disposal; at one's ease or convenience. Also with adjs. as in a.

1481 CAXTON *Godfrey* Prol. 5 To whom I humbly beseche, at theyr leyzer and playsyr, to see & here redde this symple book. **1483** —— *G. de la Tour* D iv, Wherfore atte his beste leyser he shewed her his deceyuable purpos. *c* **1592** SHAKS. *Ven. & Ad.* 518 A thousand kisses buyes my heart from me, And pay them at thy leisure, one by one. **1601** —— *Jul. C.* III. i. 5 Trebonius doth desire you to ore-read (At your best leysure) this his humble suite. **1605** —— *Macb.* II. i. 24 At your kind'st leysure. **1605** —— *Lear* II. iv. 232 Mend when thou can'st, be better at thy leisure. **1636** SANDERSON *Serm.* (1681) II. 48 [They] think they can continue in their sins..and then repent of them and forsake them at their leasure, whensoever they list. **1901** KIPLING *Kim* in *Cassell's Mag.* Jan. 176/2 He would go to Umballa at his leisure.

†**c.** *by leisure* (also *by good leisure*): with deliberation, in a leisurely manner; at one's leisure; in course of time, by degrees; slowly. Also (= Gr. σχολῇ), barely, not at all. *Obs.*

c **1386** CHAUCER *Melib.* ¶65 Thilke Iuge is wys that soone vnderstondeth a matiere and Iuggeth by leyser. **1430-40** LYDG. *Bochas* (1544) Prol. 34 From the trueth shall I not remoue But on the substance, by good leysar abyde. *c* **1483** CAXTON *Dialogues* viii. 46 William the brusshemaker Selleth the brusshes by leyzer. **1522** MORE *De quat. Noviss.* Wks. 99/1 By the stuffing of his paunch so ful, it bringeth in by leysour, the dropsy [etc.]. **1555** in Strype *Eccl. Mem.* III. App. xxxiii. 87 Let him tary, and..work by leysure. **1588** SHAKS. *Tit. A.* I. i. 301 Ile trust by Leisure him that mocks me once. **1589** R. HARVEY *Pl. Perc.* (1590) 20 Though it take fire quickly, yet it takes light by leisure. **1607** COLLINS *Serm.* (1608) 41 He gaue order to Salomon to see to the execution of them by leasure. **1633** BP. HALL *Hard Texts* I Not all together and at once, nor in this perfect form, at first..but by leisure and degrees. *c* **1700** *To Celia* in *Coll. Poems* 54, I must to lengthen on the Pleasure, Dwell on thy Lips, and Kiss by leisure.

†**d.** *in (good) leisure*: at leisure. *Obs.*

c **1315** SHOREHAM 61 Ine leyser other in haste. *c* **1375** *Sc. Leg. Saints* iii. (*St. Andrew*) 904 þe bischope..made hym chifte In gud lasere to here hyr schrift. *Ibid.* xxix. (*Placidas*) 34 He þat..penance to do here wil begyne & in gud lasare mend his syne.

e. *lady* (or *woman*) *of leisure*, a woman who has no regular employment or whose time is free from obligations to others.

1948 R. M. AYRES *Missing the Tide* v. 164 She was no longer a lady of leisure in her own house but a paid companion with irksome duties to perform. **1951** M. McLUHAN *Mech. Bride* (1967) 40/1 The woman of leisure might wear long skirts, but the working woman was put into adolescent short skirts. **1955** L. P. HARTLEY *Perfect Woman* xxii. 190 Or as the lady of leisure, reading a book? **1975** D. RAMSAY *Descent into Dark* i. 26 She had a whole afternoon to play lady of leisure.

6. *attrib.* often passing into *adj.* **a.** Of periods of time: = Free, unoccupied; *occas.* compared with *more* and *most.* †**b.** Leisurely (*obs.*). **c.** Leisured.

1669 STURMY *Mariner's Mag.* IV. 161 Some will expect.. other sort of Questions..For them, and their leisure-time, I have inserted these.. following. **1673** O. WALKER *Educ.* (1677) 112 The product of his leasure hours. **1681** DRYDEN *Abs. & Achit.* 612 If any Leisure time he had from Pow'r. **1694** ATTERBURY *Serm.* (1723) I. 90 It did not establish it self like other kingdoms in a slow and leisure manner. **1712** ARBUTHNOT *John Bull* III. vii, In his leisure minutes, he was posting his books. **1742** *Lond. & Country Brew.* I. (ed. 4) 34 By the leisure Putting over the Bowls of Water, the Goodness of the Malt is the more extracted and washed out ..than if the Wort was drawn out hastily. **1772** *Ann. Reg.* 198 This was the most leisure time of the year. **1785** BURNS *To Jas. Smith* iv, Hae ye a leisure-moment's time To hear what's comin? **1809** CAMPBELL *Gertr. Wyom.* II. xiii, His leisure pace. **1816** JANE AUSTEN *Emma* I. ii. 25 He had still a small house in Highbury, where most of his leisure days were spent. **1841** CATLIN *N. Amer. Ind.* (1844) I. xxiv. 194 A more leisure occasion. **1845** *Athenæum* 1 Feb. 110 That the leisure classes are not more misled and perverted than they are. **1850** H. MILLER *Footpr. Creat.* (1874) 325 They are in part the fruits of a leisure fortnight spent this autumn. **1859** SMILES *Self-Help* x. (1860) 258 This is an advantage which the working classes..certainly possess over the leisure classes. **1875** JOWETT *Plato* (ed. 2) III. 249 Let us pass a leisure hour in story telling. **1899** T. VEBLEN (*title*) The theory of the leisure class. **1907** F. H. BURNETT *Shuttle* xxxiv. 347 In another generation there will be a male leisure class [in America]. **1907** BELLOC *Cautionary Tales* 31 Learn To pass your Leisure Time In Cleanly Merriment. **1912** J. H. MOORE *Ethics & Educ.* vi. 22 The school in its origin was a leisure-class institution. **1941** E. WILSON *Wound & Bow* i. 61 They [*sc.* Estella and Pip] are left with their leisure-class habits and no incomes to keep them up. **1947** O. BARFIELD in *Essays presented to Charles Williams* 121 It has no particular significance if poetry is to be regarded *only* as..a pleasurable way of diverting our leisure hours. **1951** M. McLUHAN *Mech. Bride* (1967) 40/1 Competitive drives and ambitious impulses will be transferred increasingly to leisure and home occupations. **1954** *Encounter* Mar. 78/2 A master-race recruited solely from the leisure-class and endemic to English shores: 'Of such was The Breed.' **1961** D. JENKINS *Equality & Excellence* vii. 143 Problems of adjustment..connected with housing and leisure-time activities. **1963** *Punch* 15 May 710/3 Fashion shows of men's outerwear, underwear, leisure-wear, rainwear. **1964** A. WYKES *Gambling* iv. 80 Watching other people play games has been one of man's favorite leisure-time occupations for a long while. **1965** *New Society* 26 Aug. 5/3 Buxton is trying to..latch on to the leisure revolution, without becoming a coach tours nightmare. **1966** *Guardian* 16 Feb. 6/3 A case for subregional leisure centres—which would help people in small towns to feel less dependent on cities—was made out yesterday by Professor Arthur Ling. **1968** *Economist* 4 May 38/2 One should not conclude that Frenchmen have reached the stage of the fabled leisure civilisation. **1968** *Daily Tel.* 28 Dec. 21/1 The ever-increasing attraction of boating as a leisure-activity and a sport. **1969** *Times* 7 Nov. 14/2 With the increasing demand for leisure wear, formal wear people have softened their lines. **1972** *Accountant* 17 Aug. (Suppl.) 11/3 Expanding construction company specialising in growth market of the leisure industry. **1974** *Times* 12 Feb. 11/7 Silhouette's swimwear and leisurewear sales manager.

leisure ('lɛʒ(jʊ)ə(r), U.S. 'liːʒ(jʊ)ə(r)), *v. rare.* [f. the sb.] **a.** *intr.* To have or enjoy leisure. **b.** *trans.* To make leisurely.

1928 BLUNDEN *Undertones of War* 304 There to tarry in careless ways,.. Leisuring after fiery days. **1929** BRIDGES *Testament of Beauty* i. 32 Science comforting man's animal poverty and leisuring his toil. **1970** G. F. NEWMAN *Sir, You Bastard* vi. 173 Sneed rose late..and leisured with the papers in the coffee-house opposite his flat.

leisured ('lɛʒ(jʊ)əd), *a.* [f. LEISURE *sb.* + -ED².]

1. Of time, action: Characterized or accompanied by leisure.

1631 HEYWOOD *2nd Pt. Faire Maid of W.* Ded., Wks. 1874 II. 2 Please you at any of your more leisured hours to vouchsafe the perusal of these slight papers. **1647** BOYLE *Let. to Hartlib* 8 Apr., Wks. 1772 I. Life 39 The particulars ..do not only ask a profound knowledge..but likewise a leisured and a great multiplicity of reading. **1899** *Allbutt's Syst. Med.* VI. 56 A leisured and level life, free from excitement, hurry and physical exertion or fatigue.

2. Of persons: Having ample leisure, esp. in *the leisured class(es.*

1794 *Gentl. Mag.* II. 1132 Foliage op'ning to the day Courts the leisur'd mortal's stray. **1848** MILL *Pol. Econ.* II. ii. §4 (1876) 140 The services which a nation having leisured classes is entitled to expect from them. **1877** MORLEY *Crit. Misc.* Ser. II. 347 The leisured student. **1891** A. CALDECOTT *Eng. Coloniz.* 101 The absorption of energy in the making of fortunes has prevented the formation of any such leisured class. **1923** W. S. MAUGHAM *Our Betters* II. 85 American wealth has reached a pitch where it was bound to give rise to a leisured class. **1926** B. WEBB *My Apprenticeship* i. 9 The rulers of the country..ought in the main to be drawn from a leisured class. **1929** D. H. LAWRENCE *Pansies* 43 Obviously he's not one of the leisured classes. **1949** A. WILSON *Wrong Set* 111 The many leisured-class hypotheses by which Mr. Cockshott obviously lived. **1960** M. BRADBURY *Phogey!* III. 105 The leisured classes demonstrated their leisure by indulgence in useless pursuits (personal relationships, scholarship, etc.).

leisureful ('lɛʒ(jʊ)əfʊl), *a.* [f. LEISURE *sb.* + -FUL.] **a.** Having abundant leisure. **b.** Leisurely.

c **1449** PECOCK *Repr.* v. xi. 541 If this present argument be take..into depe leiserful consideracioun. **1553** GRIMALDE *Cicero's Offices* III. (1558) 114 He was neuer more leasurelesse than when he was leasurefull and neuer less alone than when he was all alone. **1883** MRS. MACQUOID *About Yorksh.* 63 A large, leisureful handwriting. **1885** —— *Louisa* I. xii. 226 It always cost his easy, leisureful nature an effort.

'leisureless, *a.* [-LESS.] Having no leisure.

1536 LD. BUTLER in *St. Papers Hen. VIII*, II. 358 Being as nowe leyserles, I omytt moche other mater. **1553** [see LEISUREFUL]. **1877** RUSKIN *Fors Clav.* VII. 337 Making all Time leisureless. [Plato *Legg.* 831 C πάντα χρόνον ἄσχολον ποιεῖν.] **1901** H. ROBERTS *Chron. Cornish Gard.* Ded., To the gardenless, the leisureless toilers of the world.

'leisureliness. [f. LEISURELY *a.* + -NESS.] The quality or condition of being leisurely.

1829 *Blackw. Mag.* XXVI. 147, I thought you might have a leisureliness at tea-time. **1863** J. BROWN *Horæ Subs.* (ed. 3) 144 There was a fine leisureliness and vague stare. **1879** FARRAR *St. Paul* (1883) 133 The habitual leisureliness of Eastern travelling.

leisurely ('lɛʒ(jʊ)əlɪ), *a.* [f. LEISURE *sb.* + -LY¹.]

1. Of persons: Having leisure or unoccupied time; proceeding without haste.

1613 PURCHAS *Pilgrimage* (1614) 515 With these and manifold other antiquities, Gillius can best acquaint the more leasurely Reader. **1816** COLERIDGE *Lay Serm.* 318 The men of leisurely minds. **1824–9** LANDOR *Imag. Conv.* Wks. 1846 II. 236 The leisurely and rich agriculturist, who goeth out a-field after dinner.

2. Of actions or agents: Performed or operating at leisure or without haste; deliberate.

1604 E. G[RIMSTONE] *D'Acosta's Hist. Indies* VII. ii. 500 They spent fourescore yeares in this manner of leisurely travell, the which they might have done in a moneth. **1711** ADDISON *Spect.* No. 159 ¶4 Upon a more leisurely Survey of it. **1746** BERKELEY *Sec. Let. Tar-water* §10 Wks. 1871 III. 475 The same medicine..is a leisurely alterative in chronical disorders. **1875** J. H. BENNET *Winter Medit.* IV. xix. 614 A leisurely journey across the south of France.

ˈleisurely, *adv.* [f. as prec. + -LY[2].] At leisure, without haste; with deliberate or leisurely motion or action.

1486 *Bk. St. Albans* B iv b, Than softe and layserly fall oppon yowre kneys. **1526** *Pilgr. Perf.* (W. de W. 1531) 161 b, That he synge or saye his duty distinctly and leyserly. **1598** *Epulario* G j, Let it broile very wel and leisurely. **1670** MILTON *Hist. Brit.* Wks. 1738 II. 2 After the Flood, and the dispersing of Nations, as they journey'd leisurely from the East. **1796** MRS. GLASSE *Cookery* v. 53 Let it do leisurely, keep it basting. **1807** WORDSW. *Misc. Sonn.* I. xiv, A flock of sheep that leisurely pass by One after one. **1860** TYNDALL *Glac.* I. xvi. 105 In the afternoon we..proceeded leisurely with our two guides up the slope.

ˈleisureness. *rare.* [f. LEISURE *sb.* (taken as adj.) + -NESS.] Leisureliness.

1742 *Lond. & Country Brew.* I. (ed. 4) 18 The Leisureness of their Drying endows them with a Softness. **1867** C. PRITCHARD *Anal. Progr. Nat. & Grace* i. (1868) 6 The majestic leisureness of unbounded power.

leit, variant of LAIT *Obs.*; obs. form of LET.

leitacamp, variant of LETACAMP *Sc. Obs.*

leitche, obs. form of LEECH.

leith, obs. f. 3rd sing. pres. ind. of LAY *v.*[1]

leith, obs. form of LITH, LOATH.

‖**leitmotiv** (ˌlaɪtməʊˈtiːf). *Mus.* Also **-motif, -motive.** [Ger., f. *leit-* leading- + *motiv* MOTIVE.] In the musical drama of Wagner and his imitators, a theme associated throughout the work with a particular person, situation, or sentiment. Also in extended use.

1876 STAINER & BARRETT *Dict. Mus. Terms, Leitmotif.* **1880** PARRY in Grove *Dict. Mus.* II. 115/2 When these situations recur, or the personages come forward in the course of the action, or even when the personage or idea is implied or referred to, the figure which constitutes the leitmotif is heard. **1881** F. HUEFFER *Wagner* (1883) 120 Another feature of the score of Parsifal is the variety and number of its representative themes, or 'leit-motives'. **1896** H. ELLIS in *Savoy* I. 70 Zola..introduced this sort of *leit-motiv* into literature. **1898** G. MEREDITH *Let.* 6 July (1970) III. 1303, I long to hear from him of [the] Leit-motif—though indeed he has taken the world more or less into his confidence. **1899** KIPLING *Stalky & Co.* 84 A tune whose *leit-motif* was the word 'stinker'. **1912** WODEHOUSE *Prince & Betty* iv. 61 The name Scobell had been recurring like a *leit motif* in Mr Crump's conversation. **1937** KOESTLER *Spanish Testament* iv. 94 It provides the *leitmotif* of German foreign policy in Spain. **1955** *Times* 28 May 8/4 But the method remains, the orchestral tapestry of leitmotifs is more resplendent than ever, the drama is even more closely knit into the texture of sound. **1970** G. GREER *Female Eunuch* 151 Self-sacrifice is the leit-motif of most of the marital games played by women. **1972** *Composer & Conductor* Aug. 1/1 Ninety-nine music graduates out of a hundred..will say that the Leitmotiv (or Leitmotif, or leading motive)..was invented by Wagner. Wrong... The correct answer is: Friedrich Wilhelm Jähns, and even he applied it not to Wagner but to Weber. **1974** *Times Lit. Suppl.* 15 Feb. 162/4 There are plenty of *leitmotivs* which recur time and time again.

leiv, leivin, obs. ff. LEAVE, LEVEN (lightning).

lek (lɛk), *v.* [? a. Sw. *leka* to play: see LAKE *v.*[1] (cf. quot. 1884 s.v. LAKING *vbl. sb.*[1]).] *intr.* of certain birds: To take part in a pattern of behaviour centred upon a lek; hence **ˈlekking** *vbl. sb.* Also **lek** *sb.*[1], a patch of ground used by groups of birds of certain species, esp. blackcock, during the breeding season, as a setting for the males' display and their meeting with the females; the display itself or the season during which it takes place.

1871 DARWIN *Desc. Man* xiv. (1883) 405 As many as forty or fifty, or even more birds congregate at the leks. The lek of the capercailzie lasts from the end of March to the..end of May. **1884** DIXON in H. Seebohm *Hist. Birds* II. 436 Some particular spot is chosen in their haunts, where they [black grouse] congregate, or *lek*, as it is sometimes called. **1942** E. A. ARMSTRONG *Bird Display* xv. 215 The lek [of blackcock] is larger than the ruffs' assembly ground and the individual territories are not so clearly defined. **1964** A. L. THOMSON *New Dict. Birds* 432/1 The lek is usually maintained at the arena for considerable periods of time and many species revive the performance at the same display-ground year after year. *Ibid.* 432/2 During lek displays the birds tend to stimulate one another. **1970** *Country Life* 26 Feb. 490 (*caption*) A pair of blackcocks lekking. **1971** *Ibid.* 16 Sept. 693/2 Then came January, when instinct bade her [*sc.* a partridge] to that lekking field that had served as a partridge lekking area since time immemorial. **1972** C. WILLOCK *Death in Covert* (new ed.) i. 6 A randy old blackcock displaying triumphantly on a Highland lek. **1974** *Country Life* 26 Sept. 865/3 The strongest birds are nearest the centre of the [black grouse] lek because it is there that the females first land.

‖**lek** (lɛk), *sb.*[2] Pl. **lekë, leks.** [Albanian.] A unit of currency in Albania.

1927 *Times* 18 Nov. 24/4 The monetary unit chosen is the gold franc (5 lek).., with a parity of approximately 25 to the £. **1937** M. COMENCINI *Coins Mod. World* 2 Albania Currency unit: the Franka Ari or Gold Franc of 5 Lek or 200 Qindar. One Lek corresponds to 8 5-Qindar Leku..bronze coins. **1962** R. A. G. CARSON *Coins* 408 The republic of Albania, established in 1925, issued a coinage with the franka as the unit, divided into 5 lek, divided in turn into 40 qindar. **1966** *New Statesman* 8 Apr. 500/3 The plans are already drawn, 120 million lekë (nearly £500,000) promised by the state. **1967** *Spectator* 22 Dec. 775/3 Whitaker's [Almanack]..is no sure guide to the rate at which the British traveller can hope to exchange his pittance for Albanian *leks.* **1974** *Albania Today* (Tirana) Jan.–Feb. 16/3 The rate was fixed at 83.72 leks per ruble, as against 100 leks per ruble previously.

lek, obs. form of LATCH, LEAK.

‖**lekach** (ˈlɛkax). [Yiddish.] A traditional Jewish cake made with honey.

1932 L. GOLDING *Magnolia St.* III. viii. 573, I will fill large bags for them with *ingber* and *strudel* and *lekkach.* **1955** L. W. LEONARD *Jewish Holiday Cook Bk.* 20 A good standby for holiday entertaining is the traditional Lekach, or Honey Cake. **1960** S. BECKER tr. *Schwarz-Bart's Last of Just* (1961) v. 239 That's a *lekach!* A honey cake. **1973** CARR & OBERMAN *Gourmet's Guide to Jewish Cooking* 124 Foods associated with Rosh Hashanah are honey and honey cake (Lekach).

lekame, variant of LICHAM.

‖**lekane** (lɛˈkaːneɪ). *Gr. Antiq.* [ad. Gr. λεκάνη a bowl or dish.] A small shallow bowl, usually with handles and a cover. Also dim. **lekanis** (pl. **-ides**).

[**1905** H. B. WALTERS *Hist. Anc. Pott.* I. iv. 164 The word λεκάνη, however, seems to indicate a large bowl rather than a covered jar, and no satisfactory name has yet been found.] *Ibid.* 177 A method of divination sometimes practised.. consisted in placing waxen images in a lekane full of water. *Ibid.* xi. 469 A new form is that known as the *lekane*, a jar for holding sweetmeats; it has vertical handles and a cover of elaborate form, often surmounted by a small vase. **1918** J. D. BEAZLEY *Attic Red-Figured Vases* xix. 188 Milchhöfer mentions four lekanides in the style of the Meidias painter. *Ibid.*, The toilet-vase called lekanis is rarely decorated with pictures before the free period. **1935** RICHTER & MILNE *Shapes & Names Athenian Vases* 23 The word λεκάνη..was widely used to signify flattish bowls employed for different purposes... The word lekanis, on the other hand, apparently signifies a bowl used for a special purpose. **1946** G. M. A. RICHTER *Attic Red-Figured Vases* 13 The lekanis [was] a covered dish often used as a wedding present. **1950** H. L. LORIMER *Homer & Monuments* vii. 448 The well-known Boeotian lekane in the British Museum. **1967** R. S. FOLSOM *Handbk. Gk. Pottery* 132 Shapes of pots: Kantharos, tripod pyxis, lekane, skyphos, and cup.

leke, obs. form of LAKE *sb.*[3], LEAK, LEEK.

lekerous, variant of LICKEROUS.

Lekhite, Lekhitic: see LECHITIC *sb.* and *a.*

lekk, lekkege, obs. ff. LEAK, LEAKAGE.

‖**lekker** (ˈlɛkə(r)), *a.* *S. Afr. colloq.* [Afrikaans, f. Du. *lekker* (cf. G. *lecker*), rel. to Du. *likken* LICK *v.*] Pleasant, sweet, nice.

1900 A. CARTER *Let.* 8 Feb. (MS.), On Monday these left and in moving round the mountain was 'verneuked' as Hannes said 'lekker'. **1926** E. LEWIS *Mantis* II. viii. 123 To Mr Dan Hugo nothing tasted so *lekker* as a good cup of coffee at that hour. **1953** F. ROBB *Sea Hunters* viii. 137 'Fish soup and baked fish to follow. Lekker!' Olley drooled. **1961** *Personality* 16 May 27 It's a lekker language. **1963** A. SMITH *Throw out Two Hands* vii. 82 Charl Pauw..had the thickest of South African accents... 'But the place is lekker, I tell you, its lekker.' **1970** *Rand Daily Mail* 28 Feb. 7/4 Some South African English colloquialisms, again mainly of Afrikaans origin, he regards as downright 'barbarisms', such as..lekker.

lekker, var. LECCER.

lekyn, obs. form of LIKEN.

‖**lekythos** (ˈliːkɪθɒs, ˈlɛ-). *Gr. Antiq.* Also **lecythus** (ˈlɛsɪθəs). Pl. **lecythi, lekythoi** (-ɔɪ). [a. Gr. λήκυθος (whence late L. *lēcythus*).] A vase or flask with a narrow neck.

1851 *Catal. Greek & Etruscan Vases Brit. Mus.* I. 27 Lékythos... Clay ash-coloured; round the body brown and crimson bands. **1857** BIRCH *Anc. Pottery* (1858) I. 40 A small vase in the Museum..exactly resembles a lecythus, or oil cruse. **1889** *Athenæum* 4 May 575/3 Two white and black lecythi. **1899** R. GLAZIER *Man. Hist. Ornament* 77 A vase produced specially for funeral purposes was the Athenian Lekythos, the body of which was covered with white slip, then painted in polychrome with subjects of singular appropriateness. **1931** *Times Lit. Suppl.* 31 Dec. 1054/1 Athenian white lekythoi. **1948** A. LANE *Greek Pott.* iv. 54 The white slip was easily chipped or abraded, and the technique was mainly reserved for..lekythoi that were buried with the dead. **1960** R. G. HAGGAR *Conc. Encycl. Cont. Pott. & Porc.* 246/2 *Lekythos*,..a narrow-necked flask or vase well adapted (from its long narrow neck) for the slow pouring of oil, chiefly used in funeral rites. **1972** *Oxf. Univ. Gaz.* CII. Suppl. No. 3. 20 White ground lekythos by the Inscription Painter, Attic, mid-5th century B.C.

Hence **ˈlecythoid** *a.*, resembling a lekythos.

1889 *Athenæum* 4 May 575/3 From the same tomb came.. a black-figured lecythoid vase.

lel, lelalie, obs. forms of LEAL, LEALLY.

leland(e, obs. form of LEA-LAND.

lele, leleli, -ly, leli(k, obs. ff. LEAL, LEALLY.

lelile, -y, obs. forms of LEALLY.

lell, obs. form of LEAL; variant of LILL *v. Obs.*

lelli, -ich(e, -ik, -yche, lelly, obs. ff. LEALLY.

lely, obs. form of LILY.

lely, lelyly, obs. forms of LEALLY.

Lem (lɛm). [f. the initials.] A lunar excursion module (LUNAR *a.* 1 c). See also *L.E.M.* s.v. L 7.

1962 *Listener* 26 July 150/2 We had a discussion of Project Apollo, the American scheme for getting a man on the Moon. The secondary space-craft for this formidable task has been dubbed a 'lunar excursion module', or Lem for short. **1967** *Economist* 11 Nov. 627/1 The lunar excursion module—the Lem or bug—..will make the actual touch-down on the moon when the great day comes.

lem, obs. form of LEAM *sb.*[1]

lemaille, obs. variant of LIMAIL, filings.

leman (ˈlɛmən, ˈliːmən). *arch.* Forms: 3 **lef-, leof-, leove-, levemon,** 3–7 **lemman, -on,** 3–4 **lefman** (*pl.* **-men**), 4–5 **lemmone,** 4–8 **lemmane,** 5 **lemanne, lemone, lemmande, limman,** 5–6 **lemane,** 5–7 **lemon,** 6 **leymon, lemonde, lefe man** (*pl.* **-men**), *Sc.* **lamen,** 7 **leyman, leiman, leaman, lemain,** 3– **leman.** [Early ME. *leofmon*, f. *leof* LIEF, dear + MAN.]

1. A person beloved by one of the opposite sex; a lover or sweetheart; †*occas.* a husband or wife.

c **1205** LAY. 18611 To Tintaieol he sende his leofmon [*c* **1275** wif] þa wes hende. *c* **1250** *Gen. & Ex.* 782 Ðo sente he after abram, And bi-taȝte he him is leman. *a* **1300** *Floriz & Bl.* 53 Þo floriz iherde his lemman nempne. *a* **1300** *Cursor M.* 4345 'Ioseph,' sco said, 'to þe lemman, Hendest of all i mak mi man.' *c* **1375** *Sc. Leg. Saints* xxiv. (*Alexis*) 494 My blyse, my beld, my lef-man dere. *c* **1386** CHAUCER *Reeve's T.* 320 Now deere lemman quod she go fareweel. **1480** CAXTON *Chron. Eng.* clxxxviii. 166 Maydens of englond sare may ye morne for ty3t haue ye lost your lemmans at bannokesborne. **1513** DOUGLAS *Æneis* XII. Prol. 198 Ane sang, The schip salis ouer the salt fame, Wil bring thir merchandis and my lemane hame. **1535** STEWART *Cron. Scot.* (1858) I. 106 And ilk ȝoung man in courtlie caroling With his lamen thairfoir to dance and sing. **1590** SPENSER *F.Q.* III. viii. 40 He..offred kingdoms unto her in vew, To be his Leman and his Lady trew. **1601** SHAKS. *Twel. N.* II. iii. 26, I sent thee sixe pence for thy Lemon, hadst it? **1725** *Song, 'The Cock-laird'* i, Thou'-se be my ain lemmane Jo, Jennie, quo' he. **1739** MELMOTH *Fitzosb. Lett.* (1763) 291 The tender parley which these lemans held.

†**b.** Often used, in religious or devotional language, of Christ, the Virgin, etc. *Obs.*

a **1225** *Juliana* 17 Mi luue..towart te liuiende godd mi leofsume leofmon. *c* **1230** *Hali Meid.* 5 Godes spuse, Jeshu cristes brude, þe lauerdes leofmon. *a* **1300** *Cursor M.* 10664 To godd þan haue i giuen me..O þair husband mai i haf nan, Of him haf i made mi leman. *Ibid.* 20517 Cums wit me to mi lemman, Mi moder es scho, hir sun i am. *a* **1310** in Wright *Lyric P.* 69 Ihesu, mi lemman. **13..** *E.E. Allit. P.* A. 805 In Iherusalem was my lemman slayn. *c* **1460** *Towneley Myst.* x. 65 Hayls that madyn, my lemman, As heyndly as thou can. *Ibid.* xxviii. 337 Mercy, ihesu, rew thi leman, mans saull, thou bought full soure.

2. In bad sense (cf. *paramour*): One who is loved unlawfully; an unlawful lover or mistress. In later archaistic use chiefly applied to the female sex.

c **1275** LAY. 6356 Þeos Damus..hadde a lemman hende [*c* 1205 ane chiuese]. **1297** R. GLOUC. (Rolls) 7069 He..huld ire as is lefmon, as wo seiþ in hordum. *Ibid.* 10206 Alle clerkene lefmen in prisoun the king brouȝte. *c* **1340** *Cursor M.* 8887 (Trin.) Quenes had he hundrides seuen, Þre hundride lemmons [*Cotton* concubins]. *c* **1386** CHAUCER *Manciple's T.* 100 His wyf anon hath for hir lemman sent Hir lemman? certes this is a knauyssh speche. **1393** LANGL. *P. Pl.* C. IV. 188 And prestes hue menteyneþ To holde lemmanes and lotebyes al here lif-dayes. *a* **1450** *Knt. de la Tour* (1868) 10 On a derke night, as she yede towardes her lemman to foly. *c* **1470** HENRY *Wallace* v. 693 With my gud will I wyll no lemman be To no man born. **1515** *Nottingham Rec.* III. 343 We present Wyllyam Perkynsun and hys leymon for bawdre. **1553** T. WILSON *Rhet.* 28 b, They founde greater gaines by priestes lemmans then they were like to haue by priestes wives. **1598** GRENEWEY *Tacitus' Ann.* IV. i. (1622) 90 He [Sejanus] putteth away Apicata his wife..lest his lemmon should haue her in iealousie. **1650** BULWER *Anthropomet.* 237 It is a bravery much used to their Wives and Lemons. **1671** H. M. tr. *Erasm. Colloq.* 22 It may be his wife ith' mean time had got her self another Lemon and therefore she acknowledged not her husband. **1794** MATTHIAS *Purs. Lit.* 187 And Rochester's address to lemans loose. **1812** BYRON *Ch. Har.* I. ix, Yea! none did love him—not his lemans dear. **1833** H. COLERIDGE *Poems* I. 50 Hope Love's leman is, Despair his wife. **1871** DIXON *Tower* IV. v. 45 A lover whom his lemans dupe and cheat.

Hence **ˈlemanless** *a.*, without a leman. **ˈlemanry** (in 6 *Sc.* **lamenry, -ie**), illicit love.

1483 *Cath. Angl.* 213 A Lemanry, *concubitus, concubinatus.* **1560** ROLLAND *Crt. Venus* III. 481 Gif siclik lufe cummis of ȝour Lamenrie. **15..** *Priests of Peblis* (1603) C 4 b, He beddit nocht richt oft, nor lay hir by, Bot throw lichtnes did lig in Lamenry. *a* **1755** *Edom of Gordon* xxviii. in Child *Ballads* III. 434 And mony were the fair ladys Lay

lemanles at heme. *a* **1828** *Twa Knights* iv. ibid. V. 25 Lay never your love on lemanry. *a* **1830** *Lady Margery* xxiii. ibid. III. 119/2 I'll make many lady lemanless.

leman, obs. form of LEMON *sb.*[1]

lemanite, var. LEHMANITE, *Min.*

lembeck, -bike, etc., obs. ff. LIMBECK.

‖**lembing** (ləm'bɪŋ). Also 9 limbing, lambing. [Mal. *lembing.*] A Malay spear characterized by a ridged blade.

1839 T. J. NEWBOLD *Pol. & Statistical Acct. Straits of Malacca* II. xii. 211 The arms of the Orang Laut..are the limbing, or lance; the tampuling, a large hook, [etc.]. **1894** N. B. DENNYS *Descr. Dict. Brit. Malaya* 370 For the javelin, or half-pike, the Malays have the name *lambing.* **1936** G. B. GARDNER *Keris & Other Malay Weapons* iv. 85 Plate 80 shows an iron *lĕmbing.* **1947** R. O. WINSTEDT *Malays* ix. 165 The origin of the lance (*tombak*) and spear (*lembing*)..await study.

leme, obs. f. LEAM *sb.*[1] and *v.*[1], LIMB *sb.*[2]

†**lemeke, lem(o)ke, lempke, leomeke.** *Obs.* (See BROOKLIME.)

c **1265** *Voc. Plants* in Wr.-Wülcker 556/13 Fauida, fauede, leomeke. *c* **1450** *ME. Med. Bk.* (Heinrich) 85 Take groundeswele, lemke, chiken mete. *c* **1450** *Alphita* (Anecd. Oxon.) 61/2 *Fabaria aquatica*, angl...lempke. *Ibid.* 86/2 *Iposmia*..lemeke uel lemoke.

lemel, mod. technical form of LIMAIL, filings.

lemma[1] ('lɛmə). Pl. lemmas, ‖lemmata ('lɛmətə). [a. (either directly or through Lat.) Gr. λῆμμα, pl. λήμματα (f. root of λαμβάνειν to take, *pf. pass.* εἴλημμαι) something received or taken; something taken for granted; an argument, title. Cf. F. *lemme.*]

1. *Math.*, etc. A proposition assumed or demonstrated which is subsidiary to some other. See also quot. 1837-8.

1570 BILLINGSLEY *Euclid* II. xxxiii. 347 The Mathematicall occasion, whereby..Hippocrates..was led to the former Lemma. **1656** HOBBES *Six Less.* Wks. 1845 VII. 209 The sixth definition is but a lemma. **1678** CUDWORTH *Intell. Syst.* I. iv. §3. 194 We must first lay down this lemma or preparatory proposition. **1748** *Phil. Trans.* XLV. 367 From these Lemmata..are deduced the following Propositions. **1822** WHATELY *Commpl. Bk.* (1864) 73, I lay down, then, these Lemmas: 1st [etc.]. **1837-8** SIR W. HAMILTON *Logic* xiv. (1866) I. 267 Lemmata, that is, propositions borrowed from another science in order to serve as subsidiary propositions in the science of which we treat. **1845** DE QUINCEY *Hazlitt* Wks. 1862 XI. 299 Whatever is—so much I conceive to have been a fundamental lemma for Hazlitt—is wrong. **1885** LEUDESDORF *Cremona's Proj. Geom.* 189 The foregoing lemma.

2. a. The argument or subject of a literary composition, prefixed as a heading or title; also, a motto appended to a picture, etc. **b.** The heading or theme of a scholium, annotation, or gloss.

1616 B. JONSON *Poetaster* To Rdr., I will onely speake An Epigramme I here haue made: It is *Vnto true Souldiers.* That's the lemma. Marke it. **1623** COCKERAM, *Lemma*, an argument. **1660** tr. *Amyraldus' Treat. conc. Relig.* Pref. 9 The Discourses seem to divert a little from the subject which the Lemma's of the Chapters promise. **1679** T. BARLOW *Popery* 25 The lemma or title to that impious extravagant of Pope Boniface the eighth. **1722** SWIFT *Let. to Earl Oxford* 11 Oct., Wks. 1765 XVI. 185, I have hitherto taken up with a scurvy print of you, under which I have placed this lemma: *Veteres actus primamque* [etc.]. **1778** WARTON *Hist. Eng. Poetry* II. 201 *note*, In the year 1445, several pageaunts were exhibited..with verses written by Lydgate, on the following lemmata. *Ingredimini et replete terram* [etc.]. **1896** W. G. RUTHERFORD *Schol. Aristoph.* I. p. vii, Adequate information about..the lemmas, the spelling, the accentuation [of scholia]. *Ibid.* p. xxvii, He marks off the lemma from the body of the note in cases in which a lemma is given.

lemma[2] ('lɛmə). Pl. lemmata ('lɛmətə). [ad. Gr. λέμμα, f. λέπ-ειν to peel.] **1.** †**a.** The husk or shell of a fruit. **b.** *Embryol.* (See quot.)

a. 1753 CHAMBERS *Cycl. Supp.*, *Lemma*, in pharmacy, a term used to express the husk or shell of certain fruits, as the almond..; and in general, whatever is taken off in decortication. Thus the husks of oats, barley, &c. are the lemmata of those seeds.

b. 1880 PASCOE *Zool. Classif.* (ed. 2) Gloss. 280 *Lemma*, the primary or outer layer of the germinal vesicle.

2. *Bot.* In grasses, the lower bract of a floret.

1906 C. V. PIPER in *Contrib. U.S. Nat. Herbarium* X. 8 We have taken the liberty to introduce the word lemma to apply to the..'flowering glume' of authors. **1934** A. ARBER *Gramineae* vii. 110 The idea that the grass flower is unique, and requires a special vocabulary..has led to..a series of names [for bracts], such as *gluma florifera, palea inferior, flowering glume* and *lemma*, of which the two latter are the more generally familiar in England and America. *Ibid.* viii. 141 In Ichnanthus the lemma may show remarkable winglike appendages at the base. **1968** F. W. GOULD *Grass Systematics* ii. 51 Glumes, lemmas, and paleas are floral bracts. *Ibid.* 53 Lemma characters of taxonomic importance are shape, texture, size in respect to the glumes, nervation, awn development, and surface features.

lemma, erroneous variant of LEMNA.

lemman, obs. form of LEMON *sb.*[1]

†**le'mmatical,** *a. Obs.* [f. Gr. λημματ-, λῆμμα LEMMA + -IC + -AL[1].] Of or pertaining to a lemma; of the nature of a lemma.

1665 BARROW in Rigaud *Corr. Sci. Men* (1841) II. 45 Some short scholiums, that might be conveniently interserted, as lemmatical and preparatory to their demonstrations. **1671** *Phil. Trans.* VI. 2260 Of those five Lectures the two first are Lemmatical. **1704** *Ibid.* XXV. 1608 Lemmatical Propositions.

lemmatization (ˌlɛmətaɪ'zeɪʃən). [f. next + -ATION.] The action or process of lemmatizing; an instance of this.

1967 *Computers & Humanities* II. 75 Method:... 3. Alphabetic sorting into word forms with context. 4. Lemmatisation. **1971** A. J. AITKEN in R. A. Wisbey *Computer in Lit. & Ling. Res.* 14 The methods of lemmatization..so far mentioned necessitate informing the computer explicitly of the destination in terms of head-word of every single instance of each word which it has to treat. **1972** *Computers & Humanities* VI. 212 Not all lemmas could, of course, be made to come out correctly from the computer... In fact, the accomplished wrong lemmatizations are more notable than the missing correct ones.

lemmatize ('lɛmətaɪz), *v.* [f. Gr. λημματ-, λῆμμα LEMMA[1] + -IZE.] *trans.* To sort (words as they occur in a text) so as to group together those that are inflected or variant forms of the same word.

1967 *Computers & Humanities* II. 78 We have..tested programs for concordances, for lemmatizing with computer dictionary, and for transcribing from historical to phonologic alphabet. **1971** J. B. CARROLL et al. *Word Frequency Bk.* p. xiii, The AHI Corpus is coded for capitalization. It is not parsed or lemmatized. **1971** A. J. AITKEN in R. A. Wisbey *Computer in Lit. & Ling. Res.* 13 From a text prepared in this way the computer could deliver an output resembling a fully sorted collection for a traditional dictionary (already ordered and lemmatized) without further human attention. **1973** *Computers & Humanities* VII. 132 The vocabulary lists were next lemmatized by hand. *Ibid.*, The computer program made no attempt to lemmatize words or to distinguish homographs, but simply counted the number of occurrences of each distinct word-type.

Hence '**lemmatized** *ppl. a.*

1969 *Computers & Humanities* IV. 134 Method: Punching frequency lists and lemmatized texts; transferring to tapes; [etc.].

lemme ('lɛmiː). Colloq. contraction of *let me* (see LET *v.* 12, 14). Cf. GIMME.

1876 'MARK TWAIN' *Tom Sawyer* ii. 19 Come now; lemme just try... Now lemme try. **1894** KIPLING *Day's Work* (1898) 64 Lemme hide back o' you peoples, so's they won't see what I'm at. **1905** H. G. WELLS *Kipps* I. i. 27 Ann—lemme kiss you. **1910** C. E. MONTAGUE *Hind let Loose* iv. 58 Lemme alone. I'm an old man. Gimme a drink. Lemme alone. **1923** 'R. CROMPTON' *William Again* iv. 64 'Lemme help!' he pleaded. **1930** E. POUND *XXX Cantos* xix. 86 And in came the street 'Lemme-at-'em' Like a bull-dog in a mackintosh. **1946** K. TENNANT *Lost Haven* (1947) ii. 34 Lemme go... Oo-h, you're breaking my arm! Auntie, make 'im lemme go. **1972** C. WESTON *Poor, Poor Ophelia* (1973) xxii. 138 Okay, man, lemme think.

lemming ('lɛmɪŋ). Also 8 leming, 9 leeming. [a. Norw. *lemming*; other forms are Sw. *lemmel*, 16th c. *lemb* (pl. *lemmar*), Norw. *lemende, limende*; cf. Lapp. *luomek* (Ihre).]

1. a. A small arctic rodent, *Myodes lemmus*, of the family *Muridæ*, resembling a field-mouse, about 6 in. long, with a short tail, remarkable for its prolific character and its annual migrations to the sea. Also *lemming-mouse, -rat.*

[**1555** OLAUS MAGNUS *Hist. de Gentibus Septentr.* XVIII. xx. 617 Quod..in Noruegia..euenit, scilicet vt bestiolæ quadrupedes, Lemmar, vel Lemmus dictæ, magnitudine soricis, pelle varia, per tempestates & repentinos imbres è cœlo decidant.] **1607** TOPSELL *Four-f. Beasts* 727 There are certaine little Foure-footed beastes called *Lemmar*, or *Lemmus*, which in tempestuous and rainy weather, do seeme to fall downe from the cloudes. **1713** DERHAM *Phys.-Theol.* 56 *note*, A kind of Mice, (they call Leming..) in Norway, which eat up every green thing. They come in such prodigious Numbers, that they fancy them to fall from the Clouds. **1774** GOLDSM. *Nat. Hist.* II. 283 The leming..is often seen to pour down in myriads from the Northern Mountains. **1802** BINGLEY *Anim. Biog.* (1813) I. 376 The Lemming Rat. These animals feed entirely on vegetables. **1822-56** DE QUINCEY *Confess.* (1862) 69 Under such a compulsion does the leeming traverse its mysterious path. **1862** H. MARRYAT *Year in Sweden* II. 225 In Elfdal, says the chronicler, on the 2nd of August 1635 there rained from the sky a fall of lemmings. **1884** GURNEY & MYERS in *19th Cent.* May 807 The migratory instinct that carries the lemming into the deep sea.

b. Used *fig.* to denote a person bent on a headlong rush, often towards disaster. Also *attrib.* or quasi-*adj.*; *lemming-like* adj.

[**1959** M. GILBERT *Blood & Judgement* iii. 35 Home-going office workers..potent in mass as a lemming migration.] **1968** M. BRAGG *Without City Wall* I. x. 116 To opt out..in a way, you could say that was just as lemming-like as what *you're* doing. **1969** D. F. HORROBIN *Sci. is God* i. 9 This lemming unconcern may have dangerous consequences. **1969** *New Yorker* 12 Apr. 61/2 In Dr. Langseth's view, going to the moon is an impulse in-grained in the national character, as though Americans were astronautical lemmings. **1970** *Islander* (Victoria, B.C.) 15 Feb. 12/1 No one had the slightest idea of what was happening, yet all had joined in the mad lemming-like scramble for the waterfront. **1970** P. MOYES *Who saw her Die?* xx. 256 It was Saturday, the lemming rush was in full spate, the suburbs pouring their millions in bus, tube, train and car into the central sea. **1972** 'J. BELL' *Death of Poison-Tongue* viii. 80 Lemmings..was only the present vogue word..to describe a collection of mindless people moved by a common purpose. **1972** *Guardian* 11 Dec. 12/6 The only way to stop multiple motorway crashes is by educating us all in roadcraft so that our individual intelligence becomes more powerful than our lemming instincts. **1975** *Sunday Times* 16 Feb. 51/1 Last week there were ample signs that the lemming-like rush to pile in at any price was wearing itself out.

2. Applied to other rodents of the same or allied genera. **banded lemming** (Lydekker, *Nat. Hist.* 1894 III. 136); **collared** or **Snowy lemming** (*Riverside Nat. Hist.* 1885 V. 105), *Cuniculus torquatus.*

lemmon, obs. form of LEMON.

lemna ('lɛmnə). Also 8-9 *erron.* lemma. [a. mod.L. (Linnæus *Genera Plantarum* (1737) 417) *lemna*, Gr. λέμνα.] A genus of aquatic plants; = DUCKWEED.

[**1753** CHAMBERS *Cycl. Supp.*, *Lemma*..is..the name of a small water plant well known to the antients..confounded by late writers among the duck weed kinds.] **1789** G. WHITE *Selborne* II. liv. 269 Gold and silver fishes..will also feed on the water-plant called *lemna* (ducks' meat). **1801** M. EDGEWORTH *Belinda* II. xxi. 298 'This,' replied Belinda, 'is what "Th'unlearned, duck-weed; learned, lemma [*sic.*], call," and it is to be found in any ditch or standing pool.' **1802** BINGLEY *Anim. Biog.* (1813) III. 490 The Convallarian Vorticella is frequently found on the stalks of the lemma or duckweed. **1967** C. D. SCULTHORPE *Biol. Aquatic Vasc. Plants* vii. 204 As a result of its small size and the ease with which it may be cultured..*Lemna* is eminently suitable for laboratory experiments.

attrib. **1882** G. F. ARMSTRONG *Garland fr. Greece* 80 Not hid..under..thick Lethe's lemna-scum.

'**lemnad.** *Bot.* [f. LEMNA + -AD.] Lindley's term for a plant of the N.O. *Lemnaceæ* (Duckweeds).

1846 LINDLEY *Veg. Kingd.* 123, 124 [*in text* Lemnod; corrected in Index].

Lemnian ('lɛmnɪən), *a.* [f. L. *Lēmni-us*, Gr. Λήμνι-ος (f. Λῆμνος the island Lemnos) + -AN.] Of or pertaining to Lemnos. ***Lemnian earth*** (see quot. 1797) = SPHRAGIDE. ***Lemnian reddle*** (see quot. 1865). ***Lemnian smith***: Hephæstus or Vulcan.

1611 COTGR., *Spargitide. Terre spar.* Lemnian earth. **1622** MASSINGER *Virg. Mart.* III. i, The Lemnian Smith Sweats at the forge for hire. **1625** HART *Anat. Ur.* II. iv. 73 After the taking of a little Lemnian earth [he] did recouer. **1665** BRATHWAIT *Com. Chaucer* (1901) 63 It seems our Venus had been at her Lemnian Forge. **1797** *Encycl. Brit.* (ed. 3) IX. 784/2 Lemnian Earth, *Terra Lemnia*, a medicinal, astringent sort of earth, of a fatty consistence and reddish colour... It derives its name from the island of Lemnos, whence it is chiefly brought. **1816** W. PHILLIPS *Min.* (1823) 54 Lemnian earth is yellowish grey, or white, frequently with ochreous spots on the surface. **1865** PAGE *Handbk. Geol. Terms* (ed. 2), *Lemnian reddle*, an ochre of a deep-red colour and firm consistence, occurring in conjunction with the Lemnian Earth, and used as a pigment.

†'**lemnisc.** *Obs.* Also 8 lemnisk. [ad. L. *lēmniscus*, Gr. λημνίσκος in sense 1.]

1. A ribbon.

a **1706** EVELYN *Sylva* (1776) 397 The ends and stalks of the tender branch were tied together with a lemnisc or ribbon.

2. = LEMNISCUS 1.

1718 PRIDEAUX *Connect. O. & N. Test.* II. I. 55 The Lemnisk was a strait line drawn between two points (as thus ÷).

lemniscate (lɛm'nɪskət). *Math.* [ad. mod.L. *lēmniscāta*, fem. of L. *lēmniscātus* adj., adorned with ribbons, f. *lēmniscus*: see LEMNISC.]

a. *Geom.* The designation of certain closed curves, having a general resemblance to the figure 8. **b.** *Alg.* Used *attrib.* in ***lemniscate function***, one of a class of elliptic functions first investigated by Gauss (*Werke* III. 404), in connexion with formulæ relating to the properties of this class of curves.

1781 *Chambers' Cycl.* (ed. Rees), *Lemnisicate* [sic]. **1801** *Encycl. Brit.* (ed. 3) Suppl. II. 74/2 *Lemniscate.* **1837** WHEWELL *Hist. Induct. Sci.* XV. v. 218 The rings and lemniscates produced by dipolarizing crystals. **1873** G. SALMON *Higher Plane Curves* ii. (1879) 44 The curve being then known as the lemniscate of Bernouilli. **1879** CAYLEY in *Coll. Papers* (1896) XI. 65 The formulæ given by Gauss..for the lemniscate functions sin lemn ($a \pm b$) and cos lemn ($a \pm b$). **1891** —— *ibid.* (1897) XIII. 191 The elliptic function *snl* of the lemniscate form.

‖**lemniscus** (lɛm'nɪskəs). Pl. lemnisci (-'nɪsaɪ). [L.; see LEMNISC.]

1. The character ÷ used by ancient textual critics in their annotations.

1849 W. FITZGERALD *Whitaker's Disput.* 125 Origen marked these texts with various asterisks and obeli, lemnisci and hypolemnisci.

2. One of the minute ribbon-like appendages of the generative pores of some entozoans.

1855 in OGILVIE, Suppl. **1877** HUXLEY *Anat. Inv. Anim.* xi. 652 The development of the Echinorhyncus now approaches completion. The lemnisci appear.

lemon ('lɛmən), *sb.*[1] Forms: 5-7 lymon, 6 leman, lemonde, limone, *pl.* lemmanz, 6-7 lemmon,

limmon, 6–8 limon, 7 leamon(d, leimon, lemond, 7– lemon. [ad. F. *limon* (now restricted to the lime; formerly of wider application) = Sp. *limon*, Pg. *limão*, It. *limone*, med.L. *limōn-em*, related to F. *lime*: see LIME *sb.*² The words are prob. of Oriental origin: cf. Arab. *laimūn*, Pers. *līmūn*, Arab. *līmah*, collective *līm*, fruits of the citron kind, Skr. *nimbū* the lime.]

1. a. An ovate fruit with a pale yellow rind, and an acid juice. Largely used for making a beverage and for flavouring. The juice yields citric acid; the rind yields *oil* or *essence of lemons*, used in cookery and perfumery.

c **1400** MAUNDEV. (Roxb.) xxi. 98 þai enoynt þam..with þe ius of þe fruyt þat es called lymons. *c* **1430** LYDG. *Min. Poems* (Percy Soc.) 15 Orengis, almondis, and the pomegarnade, Lymons, datez. **1533** ELYOT *Cast. Helthe* (1539) 45 b, The iuyce of orenges or lymons may be taken after meales in a lyttell quantitie. **1575** LANEHAM *Let.* (1871) 8 Poungarnets, Lemmanz, and Pipinz. **1594** LADY RUSSELL in Ellis *Orig. Lett.* Ser. I. III. 46, I..drank..water and limmons, by Phisitions advise. **1645** WALLER *Summer Islands* I. 6 That happy Island where huge Lemmons grow. **1660** BOYLE *New Exp. Phys. Mech.* ii. (1682) 79, I cut a Limon asunder and put both halfs into two Recievers. **1695** CONGREVE *Love for L.* IV. xvi, Safer..than Letters writ in Juice of Limon, for no Fire can fetch it out. **1727–46** THOMSON *Summer* 664 The lemon and the piercing lime.. Their lighter glories blend. **1773** GOLDSM. *Stoops to Conq.* I. ii, I'll be with you in the squeezing of a lemon. **1838** T. THOMSON *Chem. Org. Bodies* 459 Oil of lemons is extracted from the rind of the lemon. **1870** YEATS *Nat. Hist. Comm.* 180 The scurvy has hardly been known in our navy since limes and lemons were ordered by law to be carried by all vessels sailing to foreign parts.

b. A person with a tart or snappy disposition (quot. 1863). More usually (*slang*), a simpleton, a loser; a person easily deluded or taken advantage of (see also quot. 1950).

1863 P. S. DAVIS *Young Parson* xxvii. 222 Mrs. Trimble.. had a great deal to say, and no little acrimony in her way of saying it. Indeed, she was what the knowing ones denominated 'a lemon'. **1908** J. M. SULLIVAN *Criminal Slang* 21 *Sucker* or *lemon*, a victim of criminals and tramps. **1916** J. B. COOPER *Coo-oo-ee* xiv. 208 There was always a danger of offending a man who has been runner-up in a boxing championship if you make him appear 'like a lemon'. **1931** WODEHOUSE *Big Money* i. 27, I don't know why it is, rich men's sons are always the worst lemons in creation. **1950** PARTRIDGE *Slang To-day & Yesterday* (ed. 3) iii. 313 If she is unpopular, she is *a pill, a pickle, a lemon*. **1966** J. PORTER *Sour Cream* x. 137 Criminal carelessness, that's what it was! Leaving me standing here like a lemon. **1973** 'A. HALL' *Tango Briefing* i. 17 They'd sent me down to show me something and they knew I couldn't see it and I felt a bit of a lemon.

c. *slang* (orig. *U.S.*). Something which is bad or undesirable or which fails to meet one's expectations.

Phr. ***the answer is a lemon***: used to denote that a reply is unsatisfactory or non-existent.

1909 *Sat. Even. Post* 20 Feb. 38/2 The wheel goes around; wherever the little indicator at the point of the pin stops, there is your prize—or your lemon. **1912** C. MATHEWSON *Pitching in a Pinch* x. 220 The papers were mentioning him as the '$11,000 lemon'. **1914** 'HIGH JINKS, JR.' *Choice Slang* 14 *Lemon*, a disappointment. **1922** M. ARLEN *Piracy* I. v. 59 'What would happen if *we* went on strike?'.. No one among them..dreamed of answering. The answer was a lemon. **1927** *Daily Express* 13 Dec. 17/1 Middlesbrough seem to have 'picked a lemon', for the draw gives them South Shields as opponents. **1930** P. MACDONALD *Link* iv. 75 The answer at first seems to be a lemon, but they're at least the sort of questions that make one think. **1931** *Morning Post* 19 June 6 'I sold five lemons for £210,' said a witness... 'Lemon' was a term used in the trade for second-hand cars of little value. **1959** M. T. WILLIAMS *Art of Jazz* (1960) ix. 85 This great record would have been a lemon commercially in 1925. **1961** C. MABEE *Seaway Story* vii. 70 He first politely wished success to New York's lemon, the new twelve-foot Erie Barge Canal. **1963** *Guardian* 21 Jan. 16/6 The French nuclear deterrent..is a military lemon of the first order. **1969** N. FREELING *Tsing-Boum* x. 68 One makes requests through official channels and the answer is a lemon. **1972** *Sat. Rev.* (U.S.) 17 June 7/3 Mechanics are less than delighted to see lines of lemons converging on their service department. **1972** *Sydney Morning Herald* 26 Aug. 1/2 The effect of this on consumers is too many lemons or part lemons coupled with near impossibility of obtaining redress from the manufacturer.

d. Phr. ***to hand*** (someone) ***a lemon***: to pass off a sub-standard article as good; to swindle (a person), to do (someone) down.

1906 H. GREEN *At Actors' Boarding House* 36 Him gettin' handed a lemon in that English act, puts us up. [**1922** WODEHOUSE *Clicking of Cuthbert* x. 233 'It did indeed begin to appear as though our beloved monarch..had been handed the bitter fruit of the citron.' The quaint old idiom is almost untranslateable, but one sees what he means.] **1939** E. S. GARDNER *D.A. draws Circle* (1940) vi. 87 The way things are now, I co-operate with them. If they hand me a lemon, I can walk up and down the streets cussing them out for letting politics interfere with the administration of justice. **1970** *New Yorker* 12 Dec. 131/1 These senators felt that the President had handed them two lemons, had gone to the mat for his choices when he didn't have to.

e. *slang*. The head.

1923 WODEHOUSE *Inimitable Jeeves* i. 13 'What might you have missed?' I asked, the old lemon being slightly clouded. **1952** *Coast to Coast* 195 If you had any brains in that big lemon you'd wipe me. You'd get away.

f. *U.S. slang*. An informer, one who turns State's evidence (see also quot. 1931).

1931 *Amer. Speech* VI. 439 *Lemon*, one who testifies for the prosecution. **1935** G. INGRAM *'Stir' Train* ii. 30 'You think you got the low-down on me: well, see me put it on you!' 'You talk like a "lemon"!' **1935** A. J. POLLOCK *Underworld Speaks* 70/2 *Lemon*, one who turns state's evidence.

2. The tree (*Citrus Limonum*) which bears this fruit, largely cultivated in the South of Europe and elsewhere. Cf. *lemon-tree* in 7.

1615 G. SANDYS *Trav.* (1621) 3 Groues of Oranges, Lemonds, Pomegranates, Fig-trees [etc.].

3. With modifying word prefixed. Applied to plants of different families bearing a yellow fruit. ***sweet lemon***: the *Citrus Lumia*, cultivated in the South of Europe (*Treas. Bot.*). ***water lemon***: *Passiflora laurifolia* of the W. Indies. ***wild lemon***: (*a*) *Podophyllum peltatum*; (*b*) an Australian timber tree (*Canthium latifolium*).

1756 P. BROWNE *Jamaica* 328 The Water Lemon. It grows frequent in the woods. **1760** J. LEE *Introd. Bot.* App. 317 Water Lemon, *Passiflora*. **1882** *Garden* 25 Feb. 127/1 The flowers..are succeeded in May by oval yellowish fruits called wild Lemons.

4. The colour of the lemon; pale yellow. More fully *lemon-colour*.

1796 KIRWAN *Elem. Min.* (ed. 2) I. 28 [Colours] Lemon or gold yellow—the purest. **1901** *Speaker* 12 Jan. 396/2 The reds and lemons and greens of its [Upsala's] houses..form a charming bouquet of colour.

5. *attrib.* and *Comb.* **a.** simple attributive, as ***lemon-bloom, -bush, -colour, -decoction, -flower, -garden, -grove, -hue, -juice, -kernel, -orchard, -peel, -pickle, -pip, -tea, -water***; also of things flavoured with oil of lemons or lemon-juice, as ***lemon-cake, -cheesecake, cordial, -cream, -ice, pie, -pudding, -puff, sauce***; **b.** instrumental, parasynthetic, and similative, as ***lemon-coloured, -faced, -flavoured, -scented, -tinted, -yellow*** adjs.

1820 SHELLEY *Fiordispina* 47 Rods of myrtle-buds and *lemon-blooms. **1884** *Leisure Hour* Feb. 82/2 Entangled its long fleece in a thorny *lemon-bush. **1769** MRS. RAFFALD *Eng. Housekpr.* (1778) 269 To make *Lemon Cake. **1728** E. SMITH *Compleat Housewife* (ed. 2) 120 To make *Lemon Cheese-cakes. **1747** MRS. GLASSE *Cookery* xvi. 142 To make Lemon Cheesecakes. **1598** FLORIO, *Lemonino*, a kinde of *lymond colour. **1707** MORTIMER *Husb.* v. xvii. (1708) 128 The Dyers use it [Weld] for dying of bright Yellows and Limon-colours. **1758** REID tr. *Macquer's Chem.* I. 218 As soon as the Sulphur is melted it will sublime in *lemon-coloured flowers. **1836** *Mag. Domestic Econ.* I. 182 *Lemon cordial. **1747** MRS. GLASSE *Cookery* xvi. 143 *Lemon Cream. **1898** P. MANSON *Trop. Dis.* vi. 126 Crudeli speaks highly of *lemon decoction..as a prophylactic [for malaria]. **1865** M. ARNOLD *Ess. Crit.* v. 178 The unfortunate husband of that *lemon-faced woman with the white ruff. **1819** SHELLEY *Rosal. & Hel.* 1250 Bowers, Of blooming myrtle and faint *lemon-flowers. **1864** M. J. HIGGINS *Ess.* (1875) 188 The celebrated *lemon-gardens of the old principality. **1830** TENNYSON *Recoll. Arab. Nts.* 67 Far off, and where the *lemon grove In closest coverture upsprung. **1845** BUDD *Dis. Liver* 125 A jaundice, bearing the lighter tints, from a sallow suffusion to a fainter or more decided *lemon hue. **1617** F. MORYSON *Itin.* I. 255 A little Greeke Barke loaded ..with tunnes of *Lemons Juyce (which the Turks drinke like Nectar). **1709** *Lond. Gaz.* No. 4584/4 Also 11 pieces of Lemon Juice, neat, an entire Parcel. **1897** *Allbutt's Syst. Med.* III. 19 We now can ascribe little or no therapeutic value to the lemon juice treatment first introduced by Owen Rees. **1731** *Gentl. Mag.* I. 40 Sow Orange and *Lemon-kernels in Pots. **1611** FLORIO, *Limonáro*, a *Lemmon hort-yard. **1875** J. H. BENNET *Winter Medit.* I. i. 13 Even at Palermo..the lemon orchards are protected by walls. **1672** WYCHERLEY *Love in a Wood* III. ii. 43 Warrant her breath with some *Lemmon Peil. **1694** R. L'ESTRANGE *Fables* cxxxvi. (1714) 152 Never without Limon-Pill in her Mouth, to correct an unsavoury Vapour of her Own. **1900** *Blackw. Mag.* June 815/2 His round face the colour of lemon-peel. **1769** MRS. RAFFALD *Eng. Housekpr.* (1778) 73 A tea spoonful of *lemon pickle. **1909** A. ARNOLD *Century Cook Bk.* Suppl. 584 *Lemon pie. 2 lemons..sugar..butter..4 eggs..corn-starch. **1911** C. HARRIS *Eve's Second Husband* 154 Then you ate lemon pie, pound-cake and boiled custard. **1972** J. POTTS *Trouble-Maker* (1973) ii. 10 Their first square meal in three days. Corn and chicken. Homemade relishes. Lemon pie. **1889** T. HARDY *Mayor of Casterbr.* i, Grains of wheat, swollen as large as *lemon-pips. **1769** MRS. RAFFALD *Eng. Housekpr.* (1778) 309 To make a *Lemon Posset. **1852** READE *Peg Woff.* (1853) 194 He never failed to eat of a certain *lemon-pudding. **1769** MRS. RAFFALD *Eng. Housekpr.* (1778) 277 To make *Lemon Puffs. **1747** H. GLASSE *Art of Cookery* ii. 36 To make *Lemon-Sauce for boiled Fowls. **1861** MRS. BEETON *Bk. Househ. Managem.* 220 (*heading*) Lemon sauce for boiled fowls. **1948** *Good Housek. Cookery Bk.* i. 15 Something piquant should be served with a dish that is very bland, as..lemon sauce with steamed sponge pudding. **1868** HOLME LEE *B. Godfrey* xliii. 234 A bushy *lemon-scented geranium. **1725** WATTS *Logic* I. iv. §4 (1822) 64 Tea..is now-a-days become a common name for many infusions of herbs, or plants, in water, as ..*limon-tea &c. **1932** L. GOLDING *Magnolia St.* II. xi. 425 Reb Feivel sat sucking lemon-tea through a cube of sugar. *a* **1963** S. PLATH *Crossing Water* (1971) 62 It'll be *lemon*-tea for me. **1975** *Times* 8 Feb. 7/4 There is no licence, but the lemon tea is fresh and good. **1897** *Allbutt's Syst. Med.* IV. 288 It is this pigment [urobilin] that causes..the *lemon-tinted skin. *a* **1625** FLETCHER *Woman's Prize* IV. v, If you want *limon-waters, Or anything to take the edge o' th' sea off, Pray speak. **1807** T. THOMSON *Chem.* (ed. 3) II. 417 An extraordinary portion of carbon gives..a *lemon-yellow colour. **1900** J. HUTCHINSON *Archives Surg.* XI. 40 With his pallor was mixed a certain degree of lemon-yellow tint.

6. quasi-*adj.*, short for *lemon-coloured*. So in names of pigments, ***lemon cadmium, lemon chrome***.

1875 J. D. HEATH *Croquet Player* 89 The finest vermilion, 'drop black', and 'lemon chrome', for red, black, and yellow respectively. **1882** *Garden* 22 July 64/3 The Evening Primrose covers the ground with large pale lemon flowers. **1886** *York Herald* 7 Aug. 8/2 A Lemon and White Setter Dog.

7. a. Special combs.: **lemon-balm**, the *Melissa officinalis* (*Syd. Soc. Lex.* 1888); **lemon-bird** (see quot.); **lemon cheese (curd)**, **lemon curd**, a confection made with lemons, butter, eggs, and sugar, and used as a spread or filling; **lemon cling** *U.S.*, a variety of clingstone peach; **lemon-cutting**, the feat of cutting in two a suspended lemon with a sword when riding at full speed; **lemon-drop**, a sugar-plum flavoured with lemon; **lemon-game** *U.S. slang*, a type of confidence trick (see quots.); also *ellipt. lemon*; **lemon-grass**, a fragrant East Indian grass (*Andropogon schœnanthus*) yielding the grass oil used in perfumery; also *attrib.*; **lemon-house**, a building where lemons are stored; **lemon-kali**, a mixture of tartaric acid and soda bicarbonate, which when dissolved form an effervescing drink; **lemon meringue (pie)**, an open pie consisting of a pastry case with a lemon filling and a topping of meringue; **lemon oil**, an essential oil obtained from lemons; **lemon-plant** (*Aloysia citriodora*), the so-called lemon-scented verbena; **lemon platt**, a flat sugar-stick, flavoured with lemon; **lemon-rob** (see quot.); **lemon scurvy grass**, the *Cochlearia officinalis* (Mayne *Expos. Lex.* 1855); **lemon-squash**, a drink made from the juice of a lemon, with soda-water, ice, and sometimes sugar; also a liquid preparation sold under this name for mixing with water; **lemon-squeezer**, (*a*) an instrument for expressing the juice from a lemon; also *fig.*; (*b*) *Austral.* and *N.Z. colloq.*, a hat with a peaked crown and broad flat brim worn by New Zealand troops; **lemon-thyme**, a lemon-scented variety of thyme; **lemon-tree**, (*a*) = sense 2; (*b*) = *lemon-plant*; **lemon-verbena** = *lemon-plant*; also **lemon-scented verbena**; **lemon-walnut**, 'the butter-nut (*Juglans cinerea*), so called on account of its fragrance' (*Cent. Dict.*); **lemon-weed** = SEA-MAT; **lemon-wood**, (*a*) a New Zealand tree, the Tarata; (*b*) a name for several tropical American trees or their light-coloured wood, esp. the Cuban *Calycophyllum candidissimum*.

1885 SWAINSON *Prov. Names Birds* 65 Linnet (*Linota cannabina*)..*Lemon bird (West Riding). A name given to those male linnets in the breeding season which have a yellowish hue on the breast. **1853** G. W. FRANCIS *Dict. Pract. Receipts* (ed. 3) 211/2 *Lemon cheese curd. **1891** R. WELLS *Mod. Flour Confectioner* 101 Lemon cheese. **1909** *Daily Chron.* 17 Aug. 6/4 Boiling lemon cheese over a gas cooking apparatus. **1848** *Rep. Comm. Patents 1847* (U.S.) 196 Fifteen specimens..of the *lemon cling..measured over a foot in circumference. **1895** *Army & Navy Co-op. Soc. Price List* 17/2 *Lemon curd, for making Cheesecakes. **1948** J. BETJEMAN *Sel. Poems* 35 Lemon curd and Christmas cake. **1968** V. S. PRITCHETT *Cab at Door* iii. 36 On Thursday, she made her second baking, concentrating..on ..her Eccles cakes, her puffs, her lemon-curd. **1889** *Daily News* 21 June 6/1 In *lemon-cutting the most dexterous performers were [etc.]. **1807** M. E. RUNDELL *New Syst. Domestic Cookery* 203 (*caption*) *Lemon drop. **1854** C. M. YONGE *Heartsease* II. xiv. 316 Here were some lemon-drops for papa. **1938** D. RUNYON *Furthermore* x. 187 A young guy by the name of The Lemon Drop Kid, who is called The Lemon Drop Kid because he always has a little sack of lemon drops in the side pocket of his coat, and is always munching at same. **1908** J. M. SULLIVAN *Criminal Slang* 15 **Lemon game*, defrauding a sucker at a pool game. **1914** JACKSON & HELLYER *Vocab. Criminal Slang* 5 *Lemon*,..a confidence game in which skill at pool is the bait, though its successful negotiation is based upon the dishonesty or avarice of the victim. **1937** E. H. SUTHERLAND *Professional Thief* iii. 68 The lemon is an agreement between the inside man, an expert pool player, and a prospect, by which the prospect will win bets on the pool games played by the expert. Through a supposed fluke the expert wins the game which the prospect had bet he would lose, and the prospect thereby loses his money. **1837** ROYLE *Ess. Antiq. Hindu Med.* 82 *Andropogon Schœnanthus* or *Lemon-grass. **1859** TENNENT *Ceylon* (1860) I. 25 These sunny expanses..are covered with tall lemon-grass. **1887** MOLONEY *Forestry W. Afr.* 423 An odour somewhat analogous to that of lemon-grass oil. **1901** *Chambers's Jrnl.* Nov. 719/2 On the very day of the picking they must be carried to the *lemon-house, and great care must be taken that the fruit is not exposed to the sun or bruised in any way. **1916** D. H. LAWRENCE *Twilight in Italy* 85 We passed through, and stood at the foot of the lemon-house. **1858** SIMMONDS *Dict. Trade*, **Lemon-kali*, a drink made from citric and tartaric acid. **1914** S. LEWIS *Our Mr. Wrenn* i. 13 Hey, Drübel, got any *lemon merang? Bring me a hunk, will yuh? **1922** *Hotel World* 15 Apr. 15/1 Lemon meringue pie. **1959** N. MAILER *Advts. for Myself* (1961) II. 126 There was roast chicken with stuffing, lemon meringue pie and chocolate cake. **1973** J. WILSON *Truth or Dare* vi. 75 It was lemon meringue pie for dinner. **1896** J. T. LAW *Grocer's Manual* 408/2 The essence of lemon coming into commerce..is greatly made up of..the ethereal oil which is present in *lemon oil. **1957** *Encycl. Brit.* XIII. 908/1 Among the important by-products resulting from the processing of lemons, after removal of the juice, are citric acid..lemon oil and pectin. **1862** ANSTED *Channel Isl.* IV. xxi. (ed. 2) 499 The *Aloysia citriodora* of botanists, the common *lemon plant, formerly called a verbena. **1867** SMYTH *Sailor's Word-bk.*, *Lemon-rob*, the inspissated juice of limes or lemons, a powerful anti-scorbutic. **1916** JOYCE

Portrait of Artist (1969) i. 7 The moocow came down the road where Betty Byrne lived: she sold *lemon platt. **1965** *Amer. N. & Q.* III. 117/2 'Lemon Platt', commonly sold as 'Yellow Man' at fairs in the North of Ireland,.. derives its name.. from its flavor. **1900** M. THORN in W. D. Drury *Bk. Gardening* xi. 469 *Lemon-scented Verbena should be represented in gardens where shrubs with fragrant leaves are cherished. **1969** D. GOOLD-ADAMS *Cool Greenhouse Today* xvii. 198 Lippia (Lemon-scented Verbena). Half-hardy deciduous shrub from Chile with insignificant flowers but grown in the greenhouse for the glorious scent of its crushed leaves. **1876** *World* V. No. 115. 14 The orator sipped his accustomed glass of *lemon-squash. **1781** *Salem Gaz.* 3 July, Isaac Greenwood.. makes Flutes.. Back-Gammon Boxes Men and Dies, Chess-Men, Billiard-Balls, Maces, *Lemon Squeezers. **1856** 'OCKSIDE' & 'DOESTICKS' *Hist. & Rec. Elephant Club* 118 One.. had been hit over the head with the lemon-squeezer. **1875** KNIGHT *Dict. Mech.*, *Lemon-squeezer.* **1884** *Health Exhib. Catal.* 110 Lemon Squeezers. **1887** *Century Mag.* Aug. 489/1 The 'Chunkers' were frequently of the 'lemon-squeezer' pattern. **1949** *Nat. Geogr. Mag.* Aug. 235 Knap-sack's a Nuisance in the 'Lemon Squeezer' [*sc.* a narrow defile]. **1953** BAKER *Australia Speaks* vii. 177 A few other words of wartime vintage.. *lemon squeezer*, the peaked hat worn by New Zealand troops (apparently originated by the troops themselves). **1957** T. S. ELIOT *On Poetry & Poets* 113 It might be called the lemon-squeezer school of criticism. **1959** B. KOPS *Hamlet of Stepney Green* I. 10 Julius Caesar, such a silly geezer, caught his head in a lemon squeezer. **1964** *N.Z. News* 24 Nov. 2/1 The 'lemon squeezer' was no longer suitable headgear for ceremonial rifle exercises and would never be worn by the New Zealand Army again, said the Chief of General Staff. **1629** J. PARKINSON *Parad.* cxxxi. 454 *Lemon Tyme. The wilde Tyme that smelleth like unto a Pomecitron or lemon, hath many weake branches trayling on the ground. **1657** R. VERNEY in M. M. Verney *Mem.* (1894) III. xi. 409 Sweet Marjoram & Lemon Time. **1713** J. PETIVER in *Phil. Trans.* XXVIII. 193 Its Leaves plain and small as Lemon Tyme. **1861** MRS. BEETON *Bk. Househ. Managem.* 220 *Lemon thyme.* Two or three tufts of this species of thyme, *Thymus citriodorus*, usually find a place in the herb compartment of the kitchen garden. **1971** *Country Life* 20 May 1252/2 Lemon-thyme has a lovely little golden cultivar which should be in all gardens. **1974** PAGE & STEARN *Culinary Herbs* 44 Those who find the flavour of garden thyme too dominating may prefer the milder and fruity flavour of lemon thyme. **1573** BARET *Alv.* L. 445 A *Limon tree, *citrea.* **1621** LADY M. WROTH *Urania* 302 They went into an Orchard beyond.. the trees being Orange and Lemond trees. **1879** BRITTEN & HOLLAND *Plant-n.*, *Lemon Tree*, a frequent name for *Lippia* (*Aloysia*) *citriodora* Kth., in allusion to the scent of the leaves. The verbena. **1869** C. L. BRACE *New West* iii. 37 *Lemonverbenas.. are small trees. **1952** J. & L. BUSH-BROWN *America's Garden Bk.* (ed. 2) xxi. 723 Plants suitable for pot culture... Lemon Verbena. **1971** *Country Life* 20 May 1207/1 A huge lemon verbena (*Lippia citriodora*) is said to be pre-1903. **1883** WOOD in *Good Words* Sept. 603/1 Very few persons, if they were shown a gigantic octopus, an oyster, and a piece of 'sea-mat', or '*lemon-weed', could believe that they belonged to the same class. **1879** J. B. ARMSTRONG in *Trans. N. Zealand Instit.* XII. 329 The tarata or *lemonwood, *Pittosporum eugenioides*, a most beautiful tree also used for hedges. **1924** RECORD & MELL *Timbers Trop. Amer.* 513 *Aspidosperma tomentosum* Mart... Lemon wood... Color mostly bright, clear canary-yellow. **1934** A. L. HOWARD *Man. Timbers of World* (rev. ed.) 148 Degame wood. *Calycophyllum candidissimum...* Lemon-wood. **1947** J. C. RICH *Materials & Methods Sculpture* x. 290 Lemonwood, also referred to as Degame, is a yellowish or creamy-white hardwood that is sometimes used for carving. Cuba is the major source of this wood. **1969** T. H. EVERETT *Living Trees of World* 162/2 The lemonwood of New Zealand.. has masses of honey-scented yellowish green flowers and leaves that emit a lemon-like odor when bruised. **1972** *Handbk. Hardwoods* (Building Res. Establishment) (ed. 2) 66 Degame. *Calycophyllum candidissimum.* Other name: lemonwood (United States).

b. Abbrev. of LEMONADE, *lemon-juice*; also ***bitter lemon***, a mineral drink.

1885 *List of Subscribers* (United Telephone Co.) p. xv. Kindly send us.. one gross of seltzer, one gross of soda, one gross of lemon, and half that quantity of splits. **1898** J. D. BRAYSHAW *Slum Silhouettes* 228 'Oh! a lemon an' dash'll do me,' she says... So I calls fer two lemons, wiv a dash o' bitter. **1956** R. POSTGATE in C. Ray *Complete Imbiber* I. 182 'Port 'n lemon', which was an evidence of feminine folly some years ago, was I suppose a sort of proletarian equivalent of pink champagne. **1962** *Guardian* 27 Aug. 3/1 His sister.. drinks nothing but orange juice or bitter lemon. **1965** I. FLEMING *Man with Golden Gun* viii. 110 Mr Hendriks.. nursed a Schweppes Bitter Lemon.

lemon ('lɛmən), *sb.*² [app. a. F. *limande.*] Used *attrib.* in **lemon-dab**, **lemon-sole**, names given in various parts of England to certain species of plaice or flounder.

In London *lemon-sole* is the fishmonger's name for a kind of plaice somewhat resembling the true sole. In Australia this name has been transferred, through association with LEMON *sb.*¹, to a flat-fish of a pale yellow colour, and in New Zealand it is applied to the Turbot.

1835 JENYNS *Man. Brit. Vertebr. Anim.* 457 *Platessa microcephala*, Flem. (*Lemon Dab.) **1884** *St. James's Gaz.* 18 Jan. 6/1 The.. lemon-dab or queen.. belong to that strange family of fish. **1876** *Trans. N. Zealand Instit.* VIII. 215 *Ammotretis rostratus*,.. a fish not uncommon in the Dunedin market, where it goes by the name of '*Lemon Sole'. **1880** E. P. RAMSAY *Food-Fishes N.S. Wales* 26 (Fish. Exhib. Publ.) *Plagusia unicolor*.. is known under the name of the lemon sole; it is of a pale olive-yellow when alive. **1890** *Daily News* 8 Jan. 2/6 Prices... Soles, 1s to 1s 4d per lb.. lemon soles, 6d per lb.

lemon ('lɛmən), *v.* [f. LEMON *sb.*¹] *trans.* To flavour with lemon. Hence '**lemoned** *ppl. a.*

1767 MRS. GLASSE *Cookery* 352 To make a lemoned honey-comb. **1869** *Pall Mall G.* 21 Aug. 10 The Spaniards take strong cups of chocolate, followed by glasses of water, sugared and lemoned. **1883** P. ROBINSON *Sinners & Saints* xxi. 264 [It] throws into an over-sweet landscape just that dash of sin and suffering that lemons it pleasantly to the taste.

lemonade (lɛmə'neɪd). Also 7-8 **limonade.** [ad. F. *limonade*, f. *limon* lemon.] **a.** A drink made of lemon-juice and water, sweetened with sugar.

In England now very commonly applied to 'aerated lemonade', which consists of water impregnated with carbonic acid with the addition of lemon-juice and sugar.

1663 KILLIGREW *Parson's Wed.* IV. v, Captain, make some Lemonade. **1697** *C'tess D'Aunoy's Trav.* (1706) 2 We wanted not for Limonade, and other refreshing waters. **1712** ARBUTHNOT *John Bull* IV. vi, Thou and thy wife and children should walk in my gardens,.. drink lemonade. **1791** GIFFORD *Baviad* 51 With lemonade he gargles first his throat. **1812** T. MOORE *Intercepted Lett.* vi. 33 A Persian's Heav'n is eas'ly made, 'Tis but—black eyes and lemonade. **1817** BYRON *Beppo* lxv, Her lover brings the lemonade. **1831** J. DAVIES *Manual Mat. Med.* 63 It [sulphuric acid] is administered with great success in the form of lemonade in bilious and typhoid fevers. **1867** LADY HERBERT *Cradle L.* vi. 159 Deliciously cool lemonade and Turkish coffee preceded the more substantial evening meal.

b. *attrib.* and *Comb.*, as ***lemonade bottle***, ***crystal***, ***powder***, ***syrup***.

1972 *Country Life* 30 Nov. 1481/3 The screw-topped or marble-stoppered lemonade bottles of long ago. **1902** J. T. LAW *Grocer's Manual* (ed. 2) 528/2 *Lemonade powders* or *crystals*, these usually consist of a compound of.. bicarbonate of soda,.. tartaric acid,.. icing sugar,.. essence of lemon with.. essence of pineapple. *c* **1938** *Fortnum & Mason Price List* 43/1 Lemonade crystals.. per bot. 9½d. **1896** J. T. LAW *Grocer's Manual* 413/1 *Lemonade powders*,.. usually consist of a compound of.. bicarbonate of soda,.. tartaric acid,.. icing sugar. **1938** L. MACNEICE *I Crossed Minch* II. x. 140 A plump school-girl.. had a tin.. containing lemonade powder. **1822** M. EDGEWORTH *Let.* 20 Feb. (1971) 355 You are welcome to the lemonade-Syrop. I have sent my aunt another bottle.

†**lemo'nado.** *Obs.* [ad. Sp. *limonada*, f. *limon* LEMON: see -ADO.] Lemonade.

c **1640** SHIRLEY *Capt. Underwit* IV. i. in Bullen *O. Pl.* II. 375 The Lemonados cleere sparkling wine The grosser witts too, doth much refine. **1668** T. ST. SERFE *Tarugo's Wiles* 18 Cooling those fiery Blisters upon the Liver that's procur'd by extraordinary drinking of Lemonado. **1676** SHADWELL *Libertine* I. 9, I saw at a Villa not far off, a grave mighty bearded Fool, drinking Lemonado with his Mistris.

lemonish ('lɛmənɪʃ), *a.* Also 8 **limonish.** [f. LEMON *sb.*¹ + -ISH.] Somewhat resembling the colour or taste of the lemon.

1719 LONDON & WISE *Compl. Gard.* 57 Full of Juice, but of a little Limonish Tartness. **1897** *Allbutt's Syst. Med.* IV. 70 The skin may have a lemonish yellow hue.

lemony ('lɛmənɪ), *a.* [f. LEMON *sb.*¹ + -Y.]

a. Resembling the smell of the lemon, tasting of lemon.

1859 W. H. GREGORY *Egypt* II. 293 [They] ordered our *sherba*, or soup, to be made more lemony and peppery than ever. **1894** FENN *In Alpine Valley* I. 23 The sweet lemony scent of the pines floated in.

b. *Austral.* and *N.Z. slang.* Irritated, angry, esp. in phr. ***to go lemony at***: to become angry with (someone).

1941 in BAKER *Dict. Austral. Slang* 31. **1945** BAKER *Austral. Lang.* vi. 121 A man in a temper is said.. *to go lemony*.. at a person. **1946** D. STIVENS *Courtship of Uncle Henry* 75 He's as lemony as hell when he opens the door and doesn't say a word to me. **1952** *Coast to Coast* 97 Ironbark got lemony. He bellowed like a thousand bulls.

lempeck, lempet, Sc. forms of LIMPET.

lemur ('li:mə(r)). Pl. **lemurs,** ‖**lemures** ('lɛmjʊəri:z). [a. L. **lemur*, pl. *lemures.*]

1. In Roman mythology: *pl.* The spirits of the departed.

[**1555** EDEN *Decades* 26 In these they graue the lyuely Images of such phantasies as they suppose they see walke by night which the Antiquitie cauled Lemures.] *c* **1580** JEFFERIE *Bugbears* III. iii. in *Archiv Stud. neu. Spr.* (1897) 68 Harpyes, Gogmagogs, lemures. **1629** MILTON *Nativity* 191 The Lars and Lemures moan with midnight plaint. **1657** H. PINNELL *Philos. Ref.* 26 To the Earth doe belong Gnoms, Lemurs, Sylphs [etc.] **1834** LYTTON *Pompeii* IV. vi, Lest he beheld one of those grim *lemures*, who.. haunted the threshold of the homes they formerly possessed.

2. *Zool.* A genus of nocturnal mammals of the family *Lemuridæ*, found chiefly in Madagascar, allied to the monkeys, but having a pointed muzzle like that of a fox; an animal of this genus.

1795 tr. *Thunberg's Cape Gd. Hope* (ed. 2) II. 206 This species of Lemur somewhat resembles a cat, with its long tail, diversified with black and white ringlets. **1863** LYELL *Antiq. Man* xxiv. 474 His order Primates.. embraced not only the apes and lemurs, but the bats also. **1865** LIVINGSTONE *Zambesi* x. 213 A little lemur was once seen to leap about from branch to branch.

Lemuria (lɪ'mjʊərɪə). [f. LEMUR + -IA¹.] A hypothetical continent stretching from Africa to south-east Asia, formerly supposed to have existed in the Jurassic period.

1864 P. L. SCLATER in *Q. Jrnl. Sci.* I. 219 In Madagascar and the Mascarene Islands we have existing relics of this great continent, for which as the original focus of the '*Stirps Lemurum*', I should propose the name Lemuria! **1876** A. R. WALLACE *Geogr. Distribution Animals* I. iv. 76 Lemuria.. is undoubtedly a legitimate and highly probable supposition, and it is an example of the way in which a study of the geographical distribution of animals may enable us to reconstruct the geography of a bygone age. **1880** —— *Island Life* II. xix. 398 Atlantis is now rarely introduced seriously.. But 'Lemuria' still keeps its place—a good example of the survival of a provisional hypothesis which offers what seems an easy solution of a difficult problem.. long after it has been proved to be untenable. **1944** 'PALINURUS' *Unquiet Grave* iii. 85 To have set foot in Lemuria is to have been close to the mysterious sources of existence... Wild ghost faces from a lost continent who will soon be extinct. **1957** P. J. DARLINGTON *Zoogeogr.* x. 590 Some persons have claimed a broad connection or union of Africa, Madagascar, and India even in the Tertiary and have named it Lemuria, but there is decisive evidence against it.

lemurian (lɪ'mjʊərɪən), *a.* [f. LEMUR + -IAN; but sense 1 is derived from LEMURIA.] **1.** (With capital initial.) Of or pertaining to LEMURIA.

1871 *Nature* 30 Mar. 429/1 The Máldive and the Láccadive coral-islands belong strictly to the Lemurian region.. and I am not sure that the latter does not reach the main-land of India. **1893** A. NEWTON *Dict. Birds* 354 The hypothesis of a Lemurian continent was.. unnecessary.

2. Of or pertaining to lemurs; characteristic of lemurs.

1891 *Ann. Rep. Board of Regents Smithsonian Inst. 1889–90* 621 An unsymmetrical face, the nasal overture of a pheleiform type, and lemurian attachment of the under jaw. **1893** A. NEWTON *Dict. Birds* 355 Lemurian remains have been found fossil in France.

lemurid ('li:mjuːrɪd, 'lɛm-). [f. mod.L. family name *Lemuridæ*, f. *Lemur* (Linnæus *Systema Naturæ* (ed. 10, 1758) I. 29), ad. L. *lemures* ghosts.] A member of the family Lemuridæ.

1884 *American* VIII. 218 True monkeys are scarce, but galagos and certain other lemurids are common. **1972** T. A. VAUGHAN *Mammalogy* vii. 115/2 The fossil record of lemurids is from Pleistocene and sub-Recent deposits in Madagascar.

lemuridous (lɪ'mjʊərɪdəs), *a.* [f. mod.L. *Lemuridæ* (see LEMUR 2) + -OUS.] Belonging to the family Lemuridæ.

1830–1 *Proc. Zool. Soc.* 109 The other [was stated by Mr. Bennett to be] a Lemuridous species. **1855** in MAYNE *Expos. Lex.* **1879** in WEBSTER, Suppl.

le'muriform, *a.* [f. LEMUR + *i* + -FORM.] Resembling the lemurs. Also as *sb.*

1887 A. HEILPRIN *Geogr. & Geol. Distribution Animals* 174 Lemurs or lemuriform insectivores (Adapis, Necrolemur). **1972** *Nature* 24 Mar. 180/1 *Archaeolemur* and *Hadropithecus* are cited as the few lemuriforms with symphysal fusion. **1973** *Ibid.* 30 Mar. 353/1 The author has his first sub-order Prosimii embrace Tupaiidae and Tarsiidae as families of equal rank to five lorisiform and lemuriform families.

'lemurine, *a.* and *sb.* [f. LEMUR + -INE¹.] = LEMUROID.

1864 *Spectator* No. 1875. 650 Here the Professor [Owen] incontestably proves the lemurine.. affinities of Chiromys. **1877** LE CONTE *Elem. Geol.* iii. (1879) 495 In the Fort Bridger beds of the Green River basin Marsh finds.. some Lemurine Monkeys.

lemuroid ('lɛmjʊərɔɪd), *a.* and *sb.* [f. LEMUR + -OID.] **A.** *adj.* Resembling the lemurs; pertaining to the sub-order *Lemuroidea*, of which the genus *Lemur* is the type.

1873 MIVART *Man & Apes* 70 They are the largest animals of the Lemuroid sub-order. **1880** HAUGHTON *Phys. Geog.* vi. 296 The extreme antiquity of the Lemuroid fauna. **1883** G. ALLEN in *Knowledge* 368/1 The fruit-bats seem to be.. specialised lemuroid animals.

B. *sb.* A lemuroid animal.

1873 MIVART *Man & Apes* 69 All the Lemuroids eat vegetable food or insects. **1885** *Riverside Nat. Hist.* V. 481 America can so far lay as good a claim to having been the original home of the lemuroids.

lemyet, obs. form of LIMIT.

†**lemyre,** *v. Obs. rare*⁻¹. [f. *leme* LEAM, after *glimmer.*] *intr.* To glimmer.

c **1435** *Torr. Portugal* 291 In to the hale sche hym lad, That lemyred ase gold bryght.

len, obs. variant of LEND *sb.*² and *v.*²

Lenape (lə'nɑ:peɪ). Also **Lenne-** or **Lenni-Lenape.** [See quot. 1819.] **a.** An Algonquian Indian people, also called Delaware Indians, formerly inhabiting the north-eastern United States; a member of this people. **b.** The language of this people.

1728 P. GORDON *Let.* 2 Sept. in S. Hazard *Pennsylvania Arch.* (1852) I. 230 Our Lenappys or Delaware Indians know nothing of it. **1785** T. JEFFERSON *Notes State Virginia* (1801) 198 Delawares, or Linnelinopies. **1819** J. HECKEWELDER *Hist. Indian Nations* (1876) p. xl, *Lenni Lenape* being the national and proper name of the people we call 'Delawares', I have retained this name, or for brevity's sake, called them simply *Lenape*, as they do themselves in most instances. Their name signifies 'original people', a race of human beings who are the same that they were in the beginning, unchanged and unmixed. *Ibid.* iii. 76 'It was we,' say the Lenape, Mohicans, and their kindred tribes, 'who so kindly received them on their first arrival into our country.' **1826** J. F. COOPER *Last of Mohicans* II. vii. 191 The Delaware, or Lenape, claimed to be the progenitors of that numerous people, who once were masters of most of the eastern and northern states of America. **1849** E. G. SQUIER in W. W. Beach *Indian Misc.* (1877) 9 (*heading*) A translation of the Walum-Olum, or bark record of the Lenni Lenape. **1885** D. G. BRINTON *Lenâpé & their Legends* iii. 35 *Lenape*, therefore, does not mean 'a common adult male', but rather 'a male of our kind', or 'our men'. **1888** BRINTON &

ANTHONY (*title*) A Lenâpé-English dictionary. **1913** *Handbk. Indians of Canada* (Geogr. Board of Canada) 125/1 The early history of the Lenàpe is contained in their national legend, the Walum Olum. **1934** F. W. HODGE *McKenny & Hall's Indian Tribes of N. Amer.* III. 32 The Delawares were situated principally upon tide-water in New Jersey, Pennsylvania, and Delaware. Their own appellation of *Lenne Lenape*, or original people, has been almost forgotten by themselves, and is never used by the other tribes. **1959** E. TUNIS *Indians* 21/1 It was taken from the Lenape, an Algonquian language.

lenard (ˈlɛnəd). *Obs.* exc. *dial.* Forms: 6 lenarde, 7 lenaret, 9 *dial.* len(n)ard, lennert, linnard, etc. (see *Eng. Dial. Dict.*). [Of obscure origin; perh. adopted from some unrecorded OF. derivative of *lin* flax: cf. the OF. *linereul* and *linot*, linnet.] = LINNET.

1530 PALSGR. 238/2 Lenarde a byrde, *linette*. **1615** BRATHWAIT *Strappado* (1878) 87 When the cheerful Robin, Larke, and Lenaret, Tun'de vp their voices.

lenate (liːˈneɪt), *v. Phonology.* [f. L. *lēn(is* soft + -ATE³.] = LENITE *v.* Hence **le'nated** *ppl. a.* Also **le'nation** *sb.* = LENITION.

1909 J. STRACHAN *Introd. Early Welsh* 12 When an adjective in the positive degree precedes, the noun is lenated. *Ibid.*, After proper nouns there is lenation of a following noun or adjective. *Ibid.* 13 In poetry, when the genitive precedes the noun, it may lenate. **1928** E. EKWALL *Eng. River-Names* p. lxxii, Quite different is the state of things in regard to lenated *t* (*d*). *Ibid.* p. lxxiii, British **b, d, g** were lenated to *v, ð, ȝ*, which latter often disappears.

†**lench**, *sb.*¹ *Sc. Obs.* [Sc. variant of LAUNCH, *sb.*¹] A leap, spring.

1606 BIRNIE *Kirk-Buriall* (1833) 37 That being prevented by death (as he was by the lyons lench) he should neuer see home.

lench, *sb.*² *dial. Mining.* (See quots.)

1747 HOOSON *Miner's Dict.* L iij b, *Lench*. These happen in Shafts or Sumps, and may happen by the Vein taking some small leap, or by [etc.]..in which Cases the best or softest part of the Vein flyes more to one Hand, and there stands jutting out a part of the Side within the Shaft, Sump or Gate..this we call a Lench. **1886** *Cheshire Gloss.*, *Lench*, salt-mining term; the middle portion of a seam of rock salt, lying under the Roof Rock; usually from four to six feet thick. **1888** *Sheffield Gloss.*, *Lench* or *Lencheon*, a shelf of rock. A Derbyshire word.

†**lench**, *v. Obs. intr.*

c **1325** *Old Age* in *Rel. Ant.* II. 211, I lench, I len, on lyme I lasse. **1847** HALLIWELL, *Lench*, to stoop in walking. *Linc.* [**1900** 'Not known to our correspondents' (*Eng. Dial. Dict.*).]

†**lend**, *sb.*¹ *Obs.* Forms: *pl.* 1 lendenu, lændenu, lendu, 3 lendin, *Orm.* lendess, 3–4 lenden, 4–5 lendes, -is, -ys, leendes, lyndes, 6 leyndis, 7– lends. *sing.* 3–5 lend(e, 4–5 leend(e, 5–6 lind. [OE. **lęnden* (only in pl. *lęndenu*) = OFris. *lenden* fem., OS. *lendi-* (in *lendibrêda* kidney), MDu. *lendene* fem. (Du. *lende* fem.), OHG. *lentin* fem. (MHG. *lende*, OHG. *lende*), ON. *lend*, pl. *lendir* (Sw. *länd*, Da. *lend*, *lænd*); the OTeut. form is perh. **landwinjâ*:—Pre-Teut. **londhw-* whence L. *lumbus* (whence ultimately LOIN), OSl. *lędvija*. An ablaut var. is ON. *lundir* loins.] Chiefly *pl.* The loins; also, the buttocks.

c **975** *Rushw. Gosp.* Matt. iii. 4 [Iohannes] hæfde hræᵹl of olbendena herum & fellen gyrdels ymb his lendu [*Ags. Gosp.* lendenu, *Hatton* lændene]. *a* **1100** *Voc.* in Wr.-Wülcker 292/13 *Lumbos*, lændenu. *c* **1200** ORMIN 4772 And cnes, & fet, & shannkess, & lende, & lesske. *a* **1300** *Christ on Cross* 9 in *E.E.P.* (1862) 20 His lendin so hangiþ as cold as marbre stone. *a* **1300** *Cursor M.* 22074 Right sua þe deuil sal descend, In anticrist moder lend. **13..** *Gaw. & Gr. Knt.* 139 His lyndes & his lymes so longe & so grete. *c* **1386** CHAUCER *Miller's T.* 51 A barm-cloth Vp on hir lendes, ful of many a goore. *c* **1440** *Gesta Rom.* xxxii. 126 (Harl. MS.) Gurdiþe youre lendys in chastite. **1508** KENNEDIE *Flyting w. Dunbar* 45 Lat him lay sax leichis on thy lendis. **1513** DOUGLAS *Æneis* XII. ii. 90 And with thar holl luyffis gan thame cheir, Did clap and straik thare leyndis to mak thame stere. *a* **1550** *Christis Kirke Gr.* vi, He lap quhill he lay on his lendis.

b. *attrib.*, as *lend-bone*.

c **1000** ÆLFRIC *Gloss.* in Wr.-Wülcker 159/23 *Sacra spina*, lendenban neoþeweard. *c* **1220** *Bestiary* 360 Oc leiȝeð his skinbon on oðres lendbon.

lend (lɛnd), *sb.*² *Sc.* and *north. dial.* Also *Austral.* and *N.Z. colloq.* Also *Sc.* lenne, len. [f. LEND *v.*² (Not repr. OE. *lǣn*: see LOAN *sb.*)] A loan.

c **1575** *Balfour's Practicks* (1754) 197 *margin*, Quhat is ane lenne, and of the restitutioun thairof. **1594** *Sc. Acts Jas. VI* (1816) IV. 70/2 Quha euir committis vsurie..(That is to say) takis mair proffite for the len [1597 leane] of money. ? *a* **1598** FERGUSSON *Sc. Prov.* xxix. (1785) 3 A borrowed len should come laughing hame. **1609** SKENE *Reg. Maj.* 47 Debt may be aweand, be borrowing and lenning, or be buying and selling; or be reason of ane lenne. **1749** J. STEUART *Let.* 29 Dec. in *Publ. Scottish Hist. Soc.* (1915) 2nd Ser. IX. 464, I ..sent him inclosed a letter..in which I desire the lend of 20£ sterlin for 18 months. **1826** J. WILSON *Noct. Ambr.* Wks. 1855 I. 246 Do ye think Mr. Awmrose could gie me the lend of a nichtcap? **1876** *Whitby Gloss.*, *Len*, the loan. 'I thank you for t' len on 't'. **1946** F. SARGESON *That Summer* 77 Could you give me the lend of a bob? **1965** *Listener* 2 Sept. 339/1 Thanks for the lend of your earhole, mate.

†**lend**, *v.*¹ *Obs.* Forms: 1 lendan, 3 lænde, *Orm.* lendenn, 3–6 lende, 4 lenden, 4–5 leende, 4–6 leind, lend, leynd(e, 5 leend, (lynd). *Pa. t.* 3 lænde, lende, 4 lend, lended, -id, -it, -yd, -yt, 4–5 lente, 4–6 lent, 5 leende. *Pa. pple.* 4 lende, lente, 4–6 lent. [OE. *lęndan* = OHG. *lenten* (MHG. *lenden*), ON. *lenda*:—OTeut. **landjan*, f. **lando*ᵐ LAND *sb.*¹ Cf. LAND *v.*]

1. *intr.* To arrive, come. Also *refl.*

Sometimes conjugated with the verb *to be.*

11.. *O.E. Chron.* an. 1036 Man hine lædde to Eliᵹ byriᵹ swa ᵹebundenne, sona swa he lende, on scype man hine blende. *c* **1200** ORMIN 2141 Swa þatt he [þe steoressmann] muȝhe lendenn rihht To lande wiþþ hiss wille. *a* **1300** *Cursor M.* 1868 þe schipp on land bigan to lend. *Ibid.* 22053 An angel..i sagh lendand Wit a mikel cheigne in hand. **13..** *Sir Beues* 4277 (MS. A.) þai lende ouer þe se beliue, At Souþhamtoun þai gonne vp riue. **13..** *E.E. Allit. P.* C. 201 Of what londe art þou lent. *a* **1400** *Octouian* 615 The seuende day har schyp lente At Japhet. *a* **1400–50** *Alexander* 573 Than lendis him vp þe leue kyng his lady to vysite. *c* **1450** *St. Cuthbert* (Surtees) 4488 To morne or none to þe leendys Fyue hundreth' of þi best frendys. **15..** *Geste Rob. Hode* VII. xlii, Now shalte thou se what lyfe we lede, Or thou hens wende, Than thou may enfourme our kynge, When ye togyder lende.

b. To go, depart.

[*a* **1310**: see 2.] *a* **1375** *Joseph Arim.* 207 A child cominge þorw, his come was nout seene, Siþen lenges a while and a-ȝein lendes. *Ibid.* 709 þei lenden of þe toun and leuen hit þere. *c* **1430** *Hymns Virg.* 105 Lete fleischeli knowynge from þee be lent.

2. To light (*up*)on. *lit.* and *fig.*

This would seem to be the original meaning and in the common ME. alliterative phrase *love is lent*, but the verb may have been subsequently otherwise interpreted as = *lean*, to incline; in some contexts it was perh. associated with next vb.: cf. LEND *v.*² 2 *a* (quot. 1430).

a **1300** *Cursor M.* 4214 Al mi luue on him was lend. *Ibid.* 10776 A duu þat was fra heuen send þare lighted dun, and þar-on lend. *a* **1310** in Wright *Lyric P.* vi. 28 From alle wymmen mi love is lent ant lyht on Alysoun. *Ibid.*, Levedi, al for thine sake longinge is y-lent me on. *c* **1340** *Cursor M.* (Cotton Galba) 29322 þe elleuynd poynt [of cursing] opon þam lendes þat witandly with-haldes tendes. *c* **1400** *Melayne* 1044 Thynk appon Marie brighte, To whayme oure lufe es lentt. *c* **1430** *Hymns Virg.* 28 Longinge is in me so lent. *c* **1460** *Emare* 404 The kynges love on her was lent. *c* **1460** *Towneley Myst.* xxv. 35 Sich light can on vs leynd In paradyse full playn. **1508** DUNBAR *Tua Mariit Wemen* 498 Gif his lust so be lent, into my lyre quhit.

3. To tarry, remain, stay; to dwell, abide.

a **1300** *Cursor M.* 2966 He dred þe folk was ful o pride, Quils he war lendand þam biside. *c* **1320** R. BRUNNE *Medit.* 1039 A! sone, here may y no longer lende. **1352** MINOT *Poems* vii. 36 Thai lended thare bot litill while, Til Franchemen to grante thaire grace. **1375** BARBOUR *Bruce* III. 747 And, quhill him likit thar to leynd, Euirilk day thai suld him seynd Wictalis for three hundred men. *c* **1450** *St. Cuthbert* (Surtees) 729 On englisch marche sall' þou lende. *c* **1460** *Towneley Myst.* xi. 352 Thus long where haue ye lent? **1513** DOUGLAS *Æneis* IV. x. 9 Quhatsumevir in the braid lochis weir, Or amang buskis harsk leyndis ondir the spray. **1535** STEWART *Cron. Scot.* 26140 That we ressaue him alway for oure freind, At oure plesour in oure landis to leind.

b. Conjugated with the vb. *to be*. ***to be lent*** = sense 3. ***lent*** (pa. pple.) = remaining, abiding, dwelling.

13.. *E.E. Allit. P.* B. 1084 Aungelles..Aboutte my lady was lent, quen ho delyuer were. **13..** *Gaw. & Gr. Knt.* 1319 þe lorde of þe londe is lent on his gamnez. *c* **1375** *Sc. Leg. Saints* xxi. (*Clement*) 229 With me is lent a ȝung man, callit to nam clement. *c* **1400** *Destr. Troy* 13857 He fraynit..In what lond he was lent. *a* **1440** *Sir Eglam.* 87 Evyr syth thou were a chylde Thou haste byn lente wyth me. *c* **1475** *Rauf Coilȝear* 591 Thair was na leid on lyfe lent in this land. **1513** BRADSHAW *St. Werburge* I. 3207 Theyr company and mynysters that were there lent. **1513** DOUGLAS *Æneis* VIII. Prol. 14 Langour lent is in land, all lychtnes is lost.

c. *refl.* To make one's abode, settle. *rare.*

a **1300** *Cursor M.* 2479 Abram lendid him o-nan Biside þe folk of chanaan.

4. *causal.* To cause to come; to bring, place.

a **1200** *Moral Ode* 122 God ȝeue þet vre ende bo god and wite þet he vs lende [*Egerton MS.* lende, *later copy* lenne]. *c* **1205** LAY. 1989 Neh him he heom lænde [*c* **1275** lende].

lend (lɛnd), *v.*² *Pa. t.* and *pa. pple.* lent. Forms: *Infin.* α. 1 lǣnan, (*3rd sing. pres. ind.* lǣn(e)þ, lénþ), 2–3 leanen, 3 læne(n, (*2nd sing. pres. ind.* lenst), 3–4 lenen, 3–6 lene, 3, 7 leane, 4 lyne, 4–5 leen(e, leyn(e. Also *Sc.* and *north.* (with short vowel) 4–6 len, lenne, 6 lenn, 8–9 len', len. β. 3–6 lende, (4 *3rd sing. pres. ind.* lent), 5 leendyn, 6 lind, 4– lend. *Pa. t.* α. 2–6 lende, 4 lened(e, 5 land. β. 4, 6 lante, 6 leant, 6–7 lended, 3– lent. *Pa. pple.* α. 2–3 ilænd, ilend, 3 lenedd, ile(a)net, 3–5 lend, 5 iland, lande, lende. β. 3–5 lant(e, lente, 5 lendid, 5–6 lentt(e, 7 lended, 3– lent. [OE. *lǣnan*, f. *lǣn* (see LOAN *sb.*). The other Teut. langs. have vbs. derived from the sb., but they differ in conjugation from the OE. vb.; cf. OFris. *lêna*, *lênia*, Du. *leenen*, OHG. *lêhanôn* (MHG. *lêhenen*, mod.G. *lehnen* to enfeoff).

The substitution of *lend-* for *lēn-* in the present-stem, which began early in ME., is explained by the fact that the pa. t. *lende* would regularly correspond either to *lēnen* or *lenden* in the infinitive, and the preponderance of analogy (cf. LEND *v.*¹, also *bend, rend, send, wend*) was on the side of the latter form. The Sc. and northern form *len, lenn(e*, owes its shortened vowel to the influence of the pa. t. and pa. pple.]

1. a. *trans.* To grant the temporary possession of (a thing) on condition or in expectation of the return of the same or its equivalent. Also with second (datival) obj. of the person; hence *rarely* in *indirect passive*.

α. *c* **1000** ÆLFRIC *Gram.* xxiv. (Z.) 135 Læne me ða boc to rædenne. *c* **1200** [see 1 d α]. *a* **1225** *Ancr. R.* 248 þeo ancre þet wernde an oðer a cwaer uorto lenen. *c* **1275** LAY. 25178 For to bi-ȝeten þin rihtes ich leane þe ten þousend cnihtes. *a* **1300** *Sarmun* in *E.E.P.* (1862) 3 þoȝ man hit [*i.e.* wealth] hab, hit nis noȝt his: hit nis ilend him bot alone fort to libbe is lif. *a* **1300** *Cursor M.* 15197 þat he yow wald len sum place, To mak vr mangeri. *c* **1380** WYCLIF *Serm.* Sel. Wks. II. 153 Lene þou me þre loves. *c* **1386** CHAUCER *Can. Yeom. Prol. & T.* 473 Leene me a marc quod he, but dayes three And at my day I wol it quiten thee. *c* **1400** *Ywaine & Gaw.* 737, I sal lene the her mi ring, Bot yelde it me at myne askyng. **1470–85** MALORY *Arthur* XVIII. ix, I wold praye yow to lene me a shelde that were not openly knowen, for myn is wel knowen. **1523** LD. BERNERS *Froiss.* I. cccxiv. 481 So the kynge lende or gaue him, I cannat tell wheder, a lx. thousande frankes. **1595** DUNCAN *App. Etymol.* (E.D.S.), *Praesto*, to len. **1608** *Vestry Bks.* (Surtees) 213 That neyther the Clarke nor Sacriston shall lenn or carrie forthe of the churche any ledders. *c* **1630** P. YOUNG in *Lett. Lit. Men* (Camden) 144 Desire his Worship to leane me Marianus his Chronicon..for the tyme he is in the countrie.

β. *c* **1330** R. BRUNNE *Chron.* (1810) 135 Fifty þousand marcs had he lent abbeis þat wer in pouerte. **1467** *Waterford Arch.* in *10th Rep. Hist. MSS. Comm.* App. v. 304 Women that borowid or lendid any manere of goodes. *c* **1491** CAXTON *Chast. Goddes Chyld.* 69 Riches and worshippes ben but lente to man for a tyme to yelde rekeninge of hem how they ben spended. **1573** BARET *Alv.* L 275 To lende one his house to solemnise a mariage in. **1593** SHAKS. *2 Hen. VI*, III. i. 77 Is he a Lambe? his Skinne is surely lent him, For hee's enclin'd as is the Rauenous Wolues. **1653** WALTON *Angler* iv. 95 This minnow I will..if you like it, lend it you, to have two or three made by it. **1718** POPE *Let. to Lady M. W. Montagu* 1 Sept., I have..passed part of this summer at an old romantic seat of my Lord Harcourt's, which he lent me. **1785** H. WALPOLE *Let. H. Mann* 3 Feb., I have very lately been lent a volume of poems. **1840** DICKENS *Barn. Rudge* ii, Lend it me for a moment. **1893** SIR J. W. CHITTY in *Law Times Rep.* LXVIII. 429/1 The lease..had been lent ..to the plaintiff..for perusal.

b. *spec.* To grant the possession and use of (money) for a fixed charge; to let out at interest.

α. *a* **900** *Kent. Gloss.* in Wr.-Wülcker 74/34 *Fenerator*, lenð. *a* **1300** *Cursor M.* 14033 It was a man quilum was wont Penis for to lene vm-stunt. *c* **1440** *York Myst.* xxxii. 354 If it ware youre lekyng, my lorde, for to lene it, xxx pens I wolde ȝe lente on-to me. *a* **1450** MYRC 1293 Hast þou I-land any thynge To haue the more wynnynge? *c* **1483** CAXTON *Dialogues* viii. 39 Neuertheles leneth he The pound for thre halfpens. **1502** *Ord. Crysten Men* (W. de W. 1506) IV. xxi. 227, I lenne the an hondred crownes.

β. *a* **1300** *Cursor M.* 28404 Agains will i lent my thing, And quilum tok þar-for okeryng. *c* **1440** *Promp. Parv.* 296/1 Leendyn, *presto, fenero*. **1596** SHAKS. *Merch. V.* I. iii. 123 You call me dog: and for these curtesies Ile lend you thus much moneyes. **1607** MIDDLETON *Five Gallants* I. i, Lent the fift day of September to mistresse Onset vpon her gowne ..three pound fifteene shillings. **1611** BIBLE *Lev.* xxv. 37 Thou shalt not..lend him thy victuals for increase. *c* **1648–50** BRATHWAIT *Barnabees Jrnl.* II. (1818) 61 What I spent the miser lended. **1776** ADAM SMITH *W.N.* II. iv. (1869) I. 353 The stock which is lent at interest is always considered as a capital by the lender. **1818** CRUISE *Digest* (ed. 2) IV. 498 All bonds, contracts, and assurances whatsoever, for payment of any principal money to be lent.

†**c.** With cogn. obj. (*loan*). *Obs.*

a **1240** *Sawles Warde* in *Cott. Hom.* 257 Se riche lane..þat he haueð ileanet him. *a* **1300** *Cursor M.* 7506, I had na help bot me allan, And drightin þat me lent his lan.

d. *absol.* or *intr.* To make a loan or loans.

α. *c* **1000** *Ags. Gosp.* Luke vi. 34 Gyf ᵹe lænaþ þam þe ᵹe eft æt onfoð hwylc þanc is eow? *c* **1200** *Vices & Virtues* 11 Ðat we sculen bliðeliche ȝiuen and leanen..alle ðe..us for his luue besecheð of ðan ilche gode ðe he us hafð ilænd. *a* **1340** HAMPOLE *Psalter* xxxvi. 27 All day he has mercy & lennys. ? *a* **1366** CHAUCER *Rom. Rose* 186 That is she that for usure Leneth to many a creature. *c* **1491** CAXTON *Chast. Goddes Chyld.* 22 They ben soo harde that neyther thei wyll yeue ne lene. **1500–20** DUNBAR *Poems* xxiii. 4 And with thy nychtbouris glaidly len and borrow. **1572** *Satir. Poems Reform.* xxxiii. 24 To borrow and len glaidlie.

β. **1388** WYCLIF *Exod.* xii. 36 The Lord ȝaf grace to the puple bifor Egipcians, that the Egipcians lenten to hem. **1535** COVERDALE *Ps.* cxi. 5 Wel is him that is mercifull, & lendeth gladly. **1573** BARET *Alv.* L 276 To lend vpon a bill or an obligacion. *c* **1600** SHAKS. *Sonn.* iv. 3 Natures bequest giues nothing but doth lend, And being franck she lends to those are free. **1611** BIBLE *Prov.* xix. 17 Hee that hath pity vpon the poore, lendeth vnto the Lord. **1625** BACON *Ess.*, *Of Usury* (Arb.) 545 Let there be Certaine Persons licensed to Lend, to knowne Merchants, vpon Vsury at a Higher Rate.

e. ***to lend out*** (or †*forth*): = 1, 1 b; now esp. used of lending libraries.

1550 CROWLEY *Last Trump.* 1118 To lende thy goodes out for vnlawful gayne. **1580** *Extracts Burgh. Rec. Edinb.* (1882) IV. 183 Nane of the saidis buikis sall be nawayis lentt furth ..bot vpon the conditioun [etc.]. **1596** SHAKS. *Merch. V.* I. iii. 45 He lends out money gratis. **1637–8** in Willis & Clark *Cambridge* (1886) I. 120 If he should lend out his Lodgings himselfe. **1681** R. KNOX *Hist. Relat. Ceylon* IV. vii. 149, I perceived a Trade in use among them which was to lend out Corn. **1734** BERKELEY *Let. to Johnson* 4 Apr., Wks. 1871 IV. 221 As to lending out the books of your library. **1855** BROWNING *Fra Lippo* 307 God uses us to help each other so, Lending our minds out. **1890** *Spectator* 14 June, 20,000 books of reference (which are not, of course, to be lent out).

2. a. To give, grant, bestow; to impart, afford. (The obj. usually denotes something which though capable of being bestowed by the subject is not in his possession, or which is viewed as an adventitious or temporary possession or attribute.)

α. *a* **1000** *Cædmon's Gen.* 2059 (Gr.) Ece drihten eað mihte æt þam sperenîðe spede lænan. *c* **1175** *Lamb. Hom.* 5 We ahte..þonkien hit ure drihten þe hit us lende. *Ibid.* 105 þet

mon wisliche spene þa þing þe him god lene on þisse liue to brukene. *c* **1200** ORMIN 5159 Afftерr þatt little witt tatt me Min Drihhtin hafeþþ lenedd. *c* **1205** LAY. 228 þis lond he hire lende. *Ibid.* 11494 Læn [*c* **1275** lean] me Mauric þinne sune þe is a swiðe wis gume. *a* **1225** *Leg. Kath.* 1084 ȝef he nere soð godd..hu mahte he lenen lif to þe deade? *c* **1340** *Cursor M.* 4882 (Fairf.) Lorde lene grace atte hit so be. *a* **1400–50** *Alexander* 3108 With all þe Iolyte & Ioy þat Iubiter vs lenes. *c* **1430** *Hymns Virg.* 23 Ihesu, þat me loue hast lende. *c* **1450** *St. Cuthbert* (Surtees) 2532 Yit grete God slik grace him len. *a* **1510** DOUGLAS *K. Hart* 351 Sythen scho ask, no licence to her len. **1538** STARKEY *England* I. iii. 84 The partys in proportyon not agreyng, but havyng of some to many, and of some to few, lene much enormyte. **1598** SYLVESTER *Du Bartas* II. ii. II. *Babylon* 532 A zeal to len A gainfull pleasure to my Countrymen. *a* **1600** MONTGOMERIE *Sonn.* xliv. 9 Let Mercure language to me len, With Pindar pennis, for to outspring the spheirs.

β. *a* **1300** *Cursor M.* 649 þe mikel ioy þat þam es lent. *c* **1375** *Lay Folks Mass Bk.* (MS. B) 342 My lyue, my lymmes þou has me lent. *c* **1430** *Hymns Virg.* 106 He [God] haþ lant þe lyf and liht. **1500–20** DUNBAR *Poems* lxxxiii. 26 Welcum, my benefice, and my rent, And all the lyflett to me lent. **1589** GREENE *Menaphon* (Arb.) 40 He rested satisfied with her answere, and therupon lent her a kisse. **1592** SHAKS. *Ven. & Ad.* 539 Her armes do lend his necke a sweet imbrace. **1613** —— *Hen. VIII*, III. ii. 151 And euer may your Highnesse yoake together, (As I will lend you cause) my doing well, With my well saying. **1623** MIDDLETON *Tri. Integrity* Wks. (Bullen) VII. 386 A speaker lends a voice to these following words. **1634** MILTON *Comus* 938 Com Lady while Heaven lends us grace, Let us fly this cursed place. **1760** FOOTE *Minor* II. Wks. 1799 I. 269 Your father talks of lending me a lift. **1790** BURNS *Tam Glen* i, Some counsel unto me come len'. **1799** CAMPBELL *Pleas. Hope* I. 7 'Tis distance lends enchantment to the view. **1805** SCOTT *Last Minstr.* I. ix, And many a flower and many a tear Old Teviot's maids and matrons lent. **1832** TENNYSON *Lady of Shalott* iv, God in his mercy lend her grace. **1849** MACAULAY *Hist. Eng.* v. I. 536 Grey, who..was ready for any undertaking, however desperate, lent his aid. **1871** R. ELLIS tr. *Catullus* xli. 8 A mirror Sure would lend her a soberer reflexion. **1883** GILMOUR *Mongols* xxxi. 362 The Mongols of lower rank lending dignity to their superiors by attending them to and from the palace.

absol. or *intr.* *a* **1310** in Wright *Lyric P.* xv. 51 God us lene of ys lyht. **1362** LANGL. *P. Pl.* A. VII. 210 Loue hem, and lene hem so the lawe of kynde wole. **1387–8** T. USK *Test. Love* III. ix. (Skeat) I. 78, I pray to the holy gost, he lene of his oyntmentes, mennes wittes to clere. *a* **1529** SKELTON *E. Rummyng* 131 Wyth all theyr myght runnynge To Elynour Rummynge, To haue of her tunnynge: She leneth them on the same.

†**b.** with *acc.* and *inf.* or *clause*: To grant. *Obs.*

The sense closely resembles that of LEVE *v.*; in MSS. it is often uncertain whether the word is *lene* or *leue* (*leve*).

c **1250** *Gen. & Ex.* 4159 In swilc ðewes lene us to cumen. *c* **1340** *Cursor M.* 27820 (Cotton Galba) God len vs to forgif man kyn. *c* **1374** CHAUCER *Troylus* v. 1750 (Harl. MS.) God lene vs for to take it for the beste. *c* **1385** —— *L.G.W.* 2083 *Ariadne*, God..lene [*v.rr.* leen, leue] me neuere swich a cas be-falle..And leue [*v.rr.* leve, leen, lyve, lene] here aftyr that I may ȝow fynde..so kynde. ?*a* **1500** *How Merchande dyd Wyfe betray* 215 in Hazl. *E.P.P.* I. 206 Were sche dedd (god lene hyt wolde!).

†**c.** To hold out (a hand) to be taken. *Obs.*

c **1386** CHAUCER *Knt.'s T.* 2224 Lene me youre hond, for this is oure accord. **1588** SHAKS. *Tit. A.* III. i. 188 Lend me thy hand, and I will giue thee mine. **1601** —— *All's Well* v. iii. 340 Your gentle hands lend vs, and take our hearts. **1611** —— *Wint. T.* IV. iii. 71 Lend me thy hand, Ile helpe thee.

d. *to lend an ear* or *one's ears*: to listen, pay attention; often with qualifying adj. †*to lend a deaf ear*: to refuse to listen. †Also *to lend audience, hearing*.

c **1375** *Sc. Leg. Saints* xxx. (*Theodora*) 92 þane wald scho ..til hym len a def ere ay. **1580** SIDNEY *Ps.* XXII. ii, O God ..to my plaint thou hast not audience lent. **1583** STUBBES *Anat. Abus.* II. (1882) 6 The sweeter the Syren singeth, the dangerouser is it to lend hir our eares. **1597** SHAKS. *Lover's Compl.* 278 Lending soft audience to my sweet designe. **1601** —— *Jul. C.* III. ii. 78. **1602** —— *Ham.* I. v. 5 Lend thy serious hearing To what I shall vnfold. **1671** MILTON *P.R.* IV. 272 To sage Philosophy next lend thine ear. **1777** WATSON *Philip II* (1793) I. IX. 351 The King..lent a deaf ear to all the representations that were made to him. **1843** MRS. CARLYLE *Lett.* I. 266 A song about Adam that John should lend all his ears to. **1848** W. H. KELLY tr. *L. Blanc's Hist. Ten Y.* I. 136 Charles X..lent a cold ear to the.. reports brought him by the general. **1863** GEO. ELIOT *Romola* xxi, The young king seemed to lend a willing ear.

e. To afford the use or support of (a part of the body); esp. in *to lend a hand* (or *a helping hand*), to render assistance, assist, help.

1598 FLORIO Ep. Ded. 4 The retainer doth some seruice, that now and then..lendes a hande ouer a stile. **1602** MARSTON *Antonio's Rev.* II. i. Wks. 1856 I. 91 Too squemish to..lend a hand to an ignoble act. **1603** SHAKS. *Meas. for M.* v. i. 447 Sweet Isabel, doe yet but kneele by me..Oh Isabel; will you not lend a knee? **1608** —— *Per.* v. i. 264 Sir, lend me your arme. **1632** MASSINGER *City Madam* I. ii, I'll lend a helping hand To raise your fortunes. **1694** MOTTEUX *Rabelais* IV. xx. (1737) 85 Lend's a Hand here. **1763** FOOTE *Mayor of G.* I. Wks. 1799 I. 168 Thinking that this would prove a busy day..I am come..to lend you a hand. **1809** MALKIN *Gil Blas* I. xiii. ¶2 Lend a helping hand. **1813** SHELLEY *Q. Mab* v. 206 Without a shudder, the slave-soldier lends His arm to murderous deeds. **1816** J. WILSON *City of Plague* II. iii, I could not sleep If I had lent a hand to rob a church. **1894** BARING-GOULD *Kitty Alone* II. 175 Lend me your arm, said Pepperill. **1940** *Times* 11 Dec. 5/4 In war-time a good many people take to what is vaguely called 'lending a hand' in the domestic circle. **1951** E. PAUL *Springtime in Paris* iv. 69 The local heroes all were known, except two passing strangers who had lent a hand at the barricade and died anonymously. **1961** NEW ENG. BIBLE *Luke* x. 40 Tell her to come and lend a hand.

f. To give or deal (a blow). Now *dial.*

c **1460** *Towneley Myst.* xxii. 136 A swap fayn, if I durst, wold I lene the this tyde. *a* **1550** *Christis Kirke Gr.* xiv, With forks and flails thay lent grit flappis. **1591** GREENE *Art Conny Catch.* II. (1592) 25 The women..among whom he leant some lustie buffets. **1598** GRENEWEY *Tacitus' Ann.* II. ii. (1622) 154 A blow which the Tribune lent her. **1612** DRAYTON *Poly-olb.* II. 281 Vpon the head hee lent so violent a stroke That the poor emptie skull like some thin potsheard broke. **1783** FIELDING *Quix. Eng.* III. xiv, If thou dost any more, I shall lend thee a knock. **1790** MRS. WHEELER *Westmld. Dial.* (1821) 67 Tom gat up and lent a girt drive at Sam. **1833** L. RITCHIE *Wand. by Loire* 140 [She] lent him such a slap upon the face as made the wood ring again!

g. To spend (one's energies), devote (one's strength) *to*. *rare.*

1697 DRYDEN *Æneid* VII. 534 [They] lend their little Souls at ev'ry Stroke [L. *dant animos plagae*]. **1809–12** MAR. EDGEWORTH *Absentee* xiii. (1893) 221 Plying the whip, and lending his very soul at every lash. **1878** H. M. STANLEY *Dark Cont.* II. xiii. 367 A man who could thus lend every fibre of his body to mere work.

h. *to lend colour* (*to*): see COLOUR *sb.*[1] 12 e.

3. *refl.* To accommodate or adapt oneself *to*. Of things: To admit of being applied *to* a purpose or subjected *to* a certain treatment.

1854 S. BROOKS *Aspen Crt.* I. ix. 122 She wore a plain blue cloth dress, which lent itself to her exquisite figure. **1874** MICKLETHWAITE *Mod. Par. Churches* 227 None lends itself better to architectural purposes. **1874** CARPENTER *Ment. Phys.* I. vi. §3 (1879) 308 Playing on the credulity of such as lent themselves to his clever deceptions. **1879** FROUDE *Cæsar* xii. 150 Cæsar neither then nor ever lent himself to popular excesses. **1885** *Manch. Exam.* 3 Nov. 5/1 He loves Ireland too well to lend himself to such a policy.

lendable ('lɛndəb(ə)l), *a.* [f. LEND *v.*[2] + -ABLE.] That may be lent.

1611 COTGR., *Prestable*,..lendable, which may be lent. **1807** SOUTHEY *Lett.* (1856) II. 13, I shall direct Artaxerxes to send you a copy, for it will be more lendable than the quarto. **1813** JEFFERSON *Writ.* (1830) IV. 196 A government may always command, on a reasonable interest, all the lendable money of their citizens. **1887** *Standard* 12 May, Money was lendable yesterday at ¾ per cent.

†**'lended,** *ppl. a. Obs.* [f. LEND *v.*[2] + -ED[1].] = LENT *ppl. a.*

1592 WYRLEY *Armorie* 145 Let no man then shee [*viz.* Fortune] seemes to fauor most To highlie of her lended faunings bost. **1650** FULLER *Pisgah* III. xii. 346 As he [*viz.* Jesus] lived in lended houses, so he was buried in a borrowed sepulchre.

lender ('lɛndə(r)). Forms: *α.* 1 lǽnere, 4 leenere, lenere, 4–5 lener, 5 leyner, 5–7 lenner. *β.* 5 lendare, 6– lender. [OE. *lǽnere*, agent n. f. *lǽnan* LEND *v.*[2] The mod. word is a new formation on LEND *v.*[2] + -ER[1].] One who lends; *esp.* one who makes a business of lending money at interest.

α. *c* **1050** *Suppl. Ælfric's Gloss.* in Wr.-Wülcker 189/21 *Creditor*, lænere. **1340** *Ayenb.* 35 þer is anoþer lenere corteys þet leneþ wyþ-oute chapfare makiinde. **1483** *Cath. Angl.* 213/2 A Leyner (*MS. A.* Lenner), *accomadator*. **1487** *Act 3 Hen. VII*, c. 6 §3 The same forfeyture to renne upon the Seller or lener therof. **1502** *Ord. Crysten Men* (W. de W. 1506) IV. xxi. 227 As yf..the lenner were in domage. **1633** *Sc. Acts Chas. I* (1817) V. 40/1 Ordaines the lenners to pay the same yeirlie and termlie.

β. *c* **1440** *Promp. Parv.* 296/1 Lendare, or he þat [lendythe] a thynge, *fenerator*. **1526** TINDALE *Luke* vii. 41 There was a certayne lender which had two detters. **1602** SHAKS. *Ham.* I. iii. 75 Neither a borrower, nor a lender be. **1625** BACON *Ess.*, *Of Usury* (Arb.) 546 Let these Licensed Lenders be in Number Indefinite. **1781** GIBBON *Decl. & F.* xliv. (1869) II. 658 The merit of generosity is on the side of the lender only. **1875** JOWETT *Plato* (ed. 2) III. 103 To insist that the lender shall lend at his own risk.

†**'lending,** *vbl. sb.*[1] [f. LEND *v.*[1] + -ING[1].] The action of LEND *v.*[1]; in quot. *concr.* dwelling-place, abode.

c **1375** *Sc. Leg. Saints* xxvii. (*Machor*) 1170 One a bere brocht till a kirk þat befor to þaim lendyng was.

lending ('lɛndɪŋ), *vbl. sb.*[2] Forms: *α.* 4 lennynge, lynynge, 4–5 lening, -yng(e. *β.* 5– lending, (5–6 -ynge, -inge, etc.). [f. LEND *v.*[2] + -ING[1].]

1. The action of LEND *v.*[2]; *esp.* the letting out of money at interest.

α. *a* **1340** HAMPOLE *Psalter* xxxvi. 27 [The rightwis] lennys, lerand and gifand almusdede till pore..and that is bot lennynge til god. **1340** *Ayenb.* 35 þis is þe uerste manere of gauelynge þet is þe leninge kueadliche. *c* **1380** WYCLIF *Wks.* (1880) 277 þat..borwyng & lynynge be frely don to pore men for goddis sake. *c* **1440** *Jacob's Well* 204 þe encres þat þou takyst for þe lenyng. **1474** CAXTON *Chesse* III. iv. G iij, Hit is sayd in reproche whan I lene I am thy frende, and whan I axe I am thyn enemye; as who saith, god at the lenyng, and the deuyll atte rendryng. **1496** *Dives & Paup.* (W. de W.) VII. xxiv. 312 Yf wynnynge come frely to the lener for his lenynge without couenaunt.

β. *c* **1440** *Promp. Parv.* 296/1 Lendynge, *mut(u)acio*. **1516** *Galway Arch.* in *10th Rep. Hist. MSS. Comm.* App. v. 397 The lendinge or sellinge of anny the said vessells. **1651** HOBBES *Leviath.* II. xxii. 117 It is left to mens own inclinations to limit lending. **1785** PALEY *Mor. Philos.* III. I. x. (1786) 133 There exists no reason, in the law of nature, why a man should not be paid for the lending of his money.

2. *concr.* Something lent; **a.** *gen.* (*fig.* in *plural*).

1602 MARSTON *Ant. & Mel.* IV. v, Thou lost a good wife, thou lost a trew friend, ha? Two of the rarest lendings of the heauens. **1605** SHAKS. *Lear* III. iv. 113 Vnaccommodated man, is no more but such a poore, bare, forked Animall as thou art. Off, off you Lendings: Come, vnbutton heere. **1884** H. D. TRAILL in *Macm. Mag.* Oct. 439/1 If we except the lendings of recognised slang, the total number of such additions..is itself not considerable.

†**b.** *spec. pl.*, money advanced to soldiers when the regular pay cannot be given. *Obs.*

1593 SHAKS. *Rich. II*, I. i. 89 Mowbray hath receiu'd eight thousand Nobles, In name of lendings for your Highnesse Soldiers. **1599** MINSHEU *Span. Dialog.* 59/2 The other [ducate] was taken out for lendings. [*Note*, Succors or lendings which they giue souldiers when there is no paie, and when the paie comes they take it off.] **1611** COTGR., *Capesoulde*, a Gentleman of a Companie; or one that hath extraordinarie Lendings; also extraordinarie Lendings, or entertainment. **1633** T. STAFFORD *Pac. Hib.* I. xviii. (1810) 193 The ready money which was payed to the Companie yearly for their Lendings. **1637** R. MONRO *Exped.* II. 131 To satisfie our hunger a little, we did get of by-past lendings three paid us in hand, and Bills of Exchange given us for one and twentie lendings more.

3. *attrib.*, as *lending-department*; **lending-house** *Hist.*, applied spec. to certain institutions for lending money without interest or at a low rate to the poor.

1797 W. JOHNSTON tr. *Beckmann's Invent.* III. 21 Those who have as yet determined the origin of lending-houses.. place it..from 1464 to 1471. **1890** *Spectator* 14 June, 34,000 [books] for the general lending department [of the Edinburgh Public Library]. **1897** *Tablet* 9 Oct. 567 It was Fra Barnaba who, in the 15th century..recommended the establishment of charitable lending-houses.

'lending, *ppl. a.* [f. LEND *v.*[2] + -ING[2].] That lends. **lending library**, a library from which books are lent out.

c **1586** C'TESS PEMBROKE *Ps.* CXII. v, He is..Most liberall and lending. **1708** J. CHAMBERLAYNE *St. Gt. Brit.* III. xii. 475 [The Libraries] of Cambridge are Lending-libraries; that is, he that is qualified may borrow out of it any book he wants. **1886** WILLIS & CLARK *Cambridge* III. 401 The.. collection was..divided into what we should now term a Lending Library, and a Library of Reference.

lend-lease. (Level stress.) = LEASE-LEND. Also *attrib.* and in extended uses. Also as *vb.* So **lend-leased** *ppl. a.*

1941 *Economist* 15 Feb. 214/1 Future disposition of the armaments now being produced is before Congress in the 'Lend-Lease' Bill. **1942** *Times* (Weekly ed.) 9 Sept. 9/2 Thousands of barrage balloons were lend-leased to the United States soon after Pearl Harbour. *Ibid.*, Lend-leased British anti-aircraft guns help to defend American cities. **1942** *R.A.F. Jrnl.* 3 Oct. (recto rear cover), The contribution of experienced pilots and planes in the fight to clear our side of the Atlantic is an element of the Lend-Lease programme in reverse. **1945** W. S. CHURCHILL *Victory* (1946) 178 Your friendship and great help as Lend-Lease Administrator and Secretary of State will always be remembered with gratitude. **1949** I. DEUTSCHER *Stalin* 512 More than 400,000 lorries were supplied to Russia under Lend-Lease. **1951** KOESTLER *Age of Longing* i. 18 Your hand, my child, is on lend-lease to a vicious old man. **1957** *Times Lit. Suppl.* 18 Oct. 625/1 Great Britain has undertaken to lend-lease to the United States nothing less than the Victorian Age in its entirety. **1962** *Listener* 15 Feb. 307/3 The abrupt ending of Lend-Lease. **1972** *National Observer* (U.S.) 27 May 3/1 Talks in the State Department are aimed at ending a U.S.-Soviet dispute over lend-lease that goes back to World War II. From 1942 to 1945, the United States supplied Russia with some $10.8 billion in military and civilian equipment under the lend-lease program.

†**lene,** *a.* and *sb. Phonetics. Obs.* [ad. L. *lēnis* smooth.] A designation formerly applied to a voiceless stopped consonant; by some later writers, to a stopped consonant generally.

In Worcester and later U.S. Dicts. the word is marked as disyllabic, and regarded as a. L. *lēne*, neut. sing. of *lēnis*: but there is no analogy for such a use of the neuter.

1751 WESLEY *Wks.* (1872) XIV. 79 The rest are mutes; of which *π, κ, τ*, are termed lenes. *Ibid.*, A lene consonant, when its vowel is cut off, before an aspirate, is changed into an aspirate. **1841** LATHAM *Eng. Lang.* ii. 107 *P, b, t, d, k, g, s, z*, are Lene; *f, v, þ, ð, κ, γ, σ, ζ*, are Aspirate. *Ibid.* 108 All the so-called Aspirates are Continuous: and with the exception of *s* and *z*, all the Lenes are Explosive. **18..** D. R. GOODWIN (Worcester), By lene we mean a determinate consonant sound defined by a simple contact or particular position of the organs; and by aspirate we mean [etc.].

lene, obs. f. LAIN *v.*, to conceal; obs. f. LEAN.

lenefie, obs. form of LENIFY.

†**'lenend.** *Obs.* In 1 lǽnend, 4 *Kent.* lynend. [Substantival use of OE. pres. pple. of *lǽnan* (see LEND *v.*[2]).] A lender, usurer.

a **1000** *Ags. Voc.* in Wr.-Wülcker 237/40 *Fenerator*,.. lænend, *uel* strude. **1340** *Ayenb.* 35 by þeyþ zeue manere gaueleres: lynende þat leneþ zeluer uor oþren [etc.].

leneret (Cockeram 1623), obs. f. LANNERET.

lenesse, obs. form of LEANNESS.

†**leng,** *adv. Obs.* Also 1 lencg, 4 lenge. [OE. *lęng* = OS. *leng*:—OTeut. **laŋgiz*, adverbial comparative of **laŋgo-* LONG *a.*] Longer.

c **1000** *Ags. Gosp.* Luke xvi. 2 Aȝyf þine scire, ne miht þu lencg tun-scire bewitan. *c* **1000** ÆLFRIC *Exod.* xix. 19 And þære byman sweȝ weox swa leng swa swiðor. *c* **1205** LAY. 11015 Hit heold hine bi þan ribben, þat ne mihte he na leng libben. **13..** *Sir Beues* 3808 (MS. A) Out of þe renge he com ride, & Beues nolde no leng [*MS. O.* lenger] abide. *c* **1386** CHAUCER *Reeve's Prol.* 18 That ilke fruyt is euer leng the wers, Til it be roten in mullok or in stree.

†**leng,** *v. Obs.* Forms: 1 lengan, 3–4 lengen, 4 lengin, ling, 4 lengh, 4–5 lenge, 4–6 lenge, lynge, 6 ling. [OE. *lęngan* wk. vb. = OS. **lengian*

(MLG., Du. *lengen*), OHG. *lengian* (MHG. *lengen*, mod.G. *längen*), ON. *lengja*:—OTeut. **laŋgjan*, f. **laŋgo-* LONG *a.* The normal mod. form, if the OE. word had survived, would be *linge*.]

1. *trans.* To lengthen, prolong; to delay.

a **1000** *Cædmon's Daniel* 646 Ne lengde þa leoda aldor witeȝena wordcwyde, ac he wide bead metodes mihte. *c* **1175** *Lamb. Hom.* 13 Þenne beoð þine daȝes ilenged. *a* **1275** *Prov. Ælfred* 391 in *O.E. Misc.* 127 Ne miȝt þu þi lif lengen none wile. *a* **1300** *Cursor M.* 12408 We sal it lengh [*Gött.* lenth, *Fairf.* lenght, *Trin.* lengþe] a quantite. *a* **1340** HAMPOLE *Psalter* cxix. 5 Wa til me for my wonynge is lenghid [Vulg. *prolongatus est*]. **1340** *Ayenb.* 198 Hi habbeþ ylengd þet lyf of þe poure be hare elmesse.

2. *intr.* To linger, tarry, remain, abide, dwell; to continue in some condition. Also const. *inf.*

Sometimes conjugated with the verb *to be*.

a **1300** *Cursor M.* 1890 On messager þat lengs lang to bring answare. *Ibid.* 12127 Þat wat i wel..hu lang þi life sal last, For to be lengand in þis werld. *c* **1340** *Ibid.* 14138 (Trin.) In his sekenes he lenged so þat he had no fote to go. *c* **1350** *Will. Palerne* 1457 Þe grete lordes of ȝour land beþ lenged now here. **1393** LANGL. *P. Pl.* C. VII. 158 Ich haue no lust..to lenge a-mong monkes. *a* **1400-50** *Alexander* 461 Now hafe I ..all to lange lengid fra hame. *Ibid.* 2162 If any life lenge in oure brestis. *c* **1420** *Anturs of Arth.* 415 (Douce MS.) If þou be curteys kniȝte, Late lenge [*Thornton MS.* Lyghte, and lende] al nyȝte, And tel me þi nome. *c* **1440** *Ipomydon* 1014 At this tyme I will not lynge. **1522** *World & Child* (Roxb. Club) Bj, With hym I loue to lynge. *a* **1586** in *Maitland Poems* (1786) 183 Mony gay gelding Befoir did in our mercat ling.

b. To lean or rely *on*. *rare*⁻¹.

c **1400** *Destr. Troy* 11769 Who graidly may trist Any lede on to leng, as for lele true?

Hence †**'lenging** *vbl. sb.*, dwelling; †**'lenging** *pres. pple.* used as *prep.* = DURING.

c **1400** *Dest. Troy* 12329 All þat left were on lyue, lengand þat tyme. *c* **1420** *Sir Amadace* (Camden) lxix, Fere!..my lenging is no lengur her.

lenge, obs. form of LING, the fish.

lengenbachite (lɛŋən'bɑːxaɪt). *Min.* [f. *Lengenbach*, the name of the quarry in Valais, Switzerland, where it was found + -ITE¹.] A sulphide of silver, copper, lead, and arsenic, $(Ag,Cu)_2Pb_6As_4S_{13}$, occurring as steel-grey blade-shaped crystals.

1904 *Nature* 1 Dec. 118/2 Mr. R. H. Solly exhibited and described various minerals from the Lengenbach quarry, Binnenthal. Three of these were new, viz. marrite and bowmanite..and lengenbachite. **1944** *Trans. R. Soc. Canada* XXXVIII. IV. 59 An *x*-ray study of lengenbachite shows that this mineral is monoclinic. **1969** *Mineral. Abstr.* XX. 227/2 Lengenbachite gave space group $P1$ or $P\bar{1}$, lattice constants of a subcell a' 35·10 ± 0·03, b' 5·75 ± 0·01, c' 36·92 ± 0·03Å, $\alpha' \sim 90°$, β' 92°35′, $\gamma' \sim 90°$.

†**lenger**, *a.* and *adv.* *Obs.* [OE. *lęngra*, neut. and fem. *lęngre*:—OTeut. **laŋgizon-*, compar. of LONG *a.*]

A. *adj.* Longer.

c **900** tr. *Bæda's Hist.* I. i. (1890) 26 Þis ealond hafað mycele lengran daȝas on sumera..þonne ða suðdælas middanȝeardes. *c* **1340** *Cursor M.* 490 (Trin.) He fel wiþouten lenger abade [*Cott.* langer bade]. *c* **1386** CHAUCER *Prol.* 330 Of his array telle I no lenger tale. *a* **1450** *Knt. de la Tour* (1868) 42 The parchemyn that he wrote in was shorte, and he plucked harde to have made it lengger with his tethe. *c* **1450** *Merlin* 110 The barouns hadde sente for hym that he sholde come with-oute lenger a-bidinge. **1526** *Pilgr. Perf.* (W. de W. 1531) 100b, We haue made this chapyter somwhat lenger than we entended. **1558** *Bury Wills* (Camden) 152 My saide iiij children or the lenger lyver of them. **1561** NORTON & SACKV. *Gorboduc* IV. ii. (Shaks. Soc.) 136 Our present hande coulde staie no lenger tyme.

B. *adv.* Longer.

c **1200** *Trin. Coll. Hom.* 139 Ðo ne mihte his holinesse ben no lengere for-hole. *c* **1290** *Beket* 219 in *S. Eng. Leg.* I. 113 Þis child wolde lengore gon to scole, ake is fader him nolde finde. *c* **1340** *Cursor M.* 3948 (Trin.) Iacob..So shal þi name no lenger be [*Cott.* Sal þou na langer hetten sua]. *c* **1385** CHAUCER *Anel. & Arc.* 129 And euer the lenger she loued him tendirly. *c* **1450** *St. Cuthbert* (Surtees) 5296 Þe scottys þare na lenger duell. **1521** FISHER *Serm. agst. Luther* Wks. (1876) 340 This persecucyon lenger continued than the other twayne. **1533** MORE *Answ. Poysoned Bk.* Wks. 1047/1 These folke do not long to eate and drincke, to lyue the lenger, but long to liue, to eate and drincke the lenger. **1590** SPENSER *F.Q.* I. vii. 22 Why do ye lenger feed on loathed light?

b. Farther. *rare*⁻¹.

c **1425** *Found. St. Bartholomew's* 10 An hospitall howse a litill lenger of from the chirche by hymself.

†**lengest**, *a.* and *adv.* *Obs.* Also 3 **lenguest**, 4 **lynguste**. [OE. *lęngest*:—OTeut. **laŋgisto-*, f. **laŋgo-* LONG *a.*; cf. prec.]

A. *adj.* Longest, very long.

c **1000** *Ags. Gosp.* Mark xii. 40 Þa onfoð lengestne [*Lindisf.* lengra] dom. *c* **1290** *Michael* 313 in *S. Eng. Leg.* 308 'Longueman' hatte þe middleste [*sc.* finguer] for he lenguest is. **13..** *E.E. Allit. P.* B. 256 And lengest lyf in hem lent of ledez alle oþer. **1387** TREVISA *Higden* (Rolls) VIII. 65 Arthures scheen boon..was lenger by þre ynches þan þe leg and þe kne of þe lengest man þat was þoo i-founde. *c* **1400** *Destr. Troy* 3776 A large man of lyms, lengest of stature. *c* **1449** PECOCK *Repr.* 133 Bi eeldist and lengist vce of bileeuyng in the Chirche. **1530** R. WHYTFORD *Werke for Househ.* A, The longest lyfe of this worlde is very short.

B. *adv.* Longest.

a **1000** *O.E. Chron.* an. 755 (Parker MS.) He hæfde þa oþ he ofslog þone aldormon þe him lengest wunode. *a* **1250** *Prov. Ælfred* 351 in *O.E. Misc.* 124 So me may þane loþe lengust lede. *a* **1300** *Cursor M.* 26652 Qua lenges [*Fairf.* langest] lijs in sin Vnnethes he mai þar-vte win. *c* **1380** WYCLIF *Wks.* (1880) 18 Rancour and euyl wille dwelliþ lengest amonges hem of alle oþere men. **1387** TREVISA *Higden* (Rolls) VII. 427 And wheþer of hem lyvede lengest [*MS. γ* lynguste] schulde be oþere heyre. **1470-85** MALORY *Arthur* XVIII. xviii, They began fyrst and lengest endured.

†**lengh.** *Obs.* Forms: 1 **leng(o, lengu, 1-2 læng,** 5 **leyngh,** 4-5, 7 **lengh(e.** [OE. *lęng(u, lęngo* wk. fem. = OHG. *langî* (MHG. *lenge*, mod.G. *länge*), Goth. *laggei*:—OTeut. **laŋgîn-*, n. of quality f. **laŋgo-* LONG *a.*] Length (of time or space); in OE. also height, stature. ***at the lengh***: in the long run.

c **888** K. ÆLFRED *Boeth.* (Sedgefield) xviii. §3 Tele nu þa lengu [*MS. B.* lenge] þære hwile. *c* **900** tr. *Bæda's Hist.* IV. xiv. [xi.] (1890) 296 Heo..toætecton lengeo þære þryh tweȝra fingra ȝemet. *a* **1000** *Salomon & Sat.* (Kemble) 180 Hu lang wæs Adam on lenge ȝesceapen? *c* **1200** *Vices & Virtues* (1888) 39 Ne wraðde mid ðe ne wuneð ones daiȝes længe. *a* **1300** *Cursor M.* 12393 A treen bedd, þat suld o lengh [*Fairf.* lenght, *Gött.* lenth] thre eln haf. **13..** *E.E. Allit. P.* A. 416 In lenghe of dayez þat euer schal wage. *a* **1340** HAMPOLE *Psalter* xx. 2 Þou gaf til him lenghe of dayes. *a* **1400-50** *Alexander* 5086 Lamprays sloȝis, þat sex cubettis clere was of clene lenghe. *c* **1400** tr. *Secreta Secret.*, *Gov. Lordsh.* 72 In þis tyme þe day and þe nyght ys of oon lengh. *c* **1450** *Lyarde* in *Rel. Ant.* II. 281 Elevyne myle on lenghe the parke es mett. **1483** *Act 1 Rich. III*, c. 8 Preamb., Clothes..drawen out in leyngh and brede. **1612** in *2nd Rep. Rec. Irel.* 265 They knew that they must be emprisoned at the length, and therefore (said they) as good now as hereafter. *a* **1699** LADY HALKETT *Autobiog.* (1875) 67 The third was a man that had a horne on the left side of the hinder part of his head..and his wife told mee shee had cutt the lengh of her finger off..because the weight of itt was troublesome.

length (lɛŋθ), *sb.* Forms: 1 **lengþ, lengþo,** 3-7 **lengthe, 4 leinth, lenkith, leynthe, lingþe, lyngþe, lynt(h,** 4-5 **lenkþe,** 4, 6 **linth,** 4-6 **lenght, lenthe,** 4-8 **lenth,** 5 **laynth, lennthe,** 5-6 **lenketh,** 4- **length.** [OE. *lęngðu* fem. = Du. *lengte*, ON. *lengd* (Da. *længde*, Sw. *längd*):—OTeut. **laŋgiþâ*, noun of quality f. **laŋgo-* LONG *a.* Cf. LENGH.]

I. Quality of being long.

1. a. The linear magnitude of any thing as measured from end to end; the greatest of the three dimensions of a body or figure; longitudinal extent.

1154 *O.E. Chron.* an. 1122 (Laud MS.) Hi sæȝon on norð east fir micel & brad wið þone eorðe & weax on lengþe. *c* **1275** LAY. 21993 Hit his on lengþe four and twenti mundes. *a* **1300** *Cursor M.* 8244 A-boute þat tre, A siluer cercle son naild he..to..knau þe wax o gret and length [*other MSS.* lenght, lenthe]. **13..** *Gaw. & Gr. Knt.* 210 Þe hede of an elnȝerde þe large lenkþe hade. *a* **1400** *Octouian* 407 The Frensch seyd he was of heghth Ten foot of length. *c* **1400** MAUNDEV. (Roxb.) ii. 6 Þe crosse..was of lenth viii. cubits. **1434** *E.E. Wills* (1882) 101 Another bordcloth..in lenkethe ij ȝerdes, & on halfe large. **1526** TINDALE *Rev.* xxi. 16 The lenght and the breth, and the heyght off hit, were equall. **1559** W. CUNNINGHAM *Cosmogr. Glasse* 25, I gather the lengthe of a degree to be the .360. parte of the heaven. **1570** BILLINGSLEY *Euclid* I. Def. ii. 2 A line..is conceaued to be drawne in length onely. **1653** WALTON *Angler* viii. 162 The Carp..will grow to a very great bigness and length. **1667** MILTON *P.L.* II. 893 A dark Illimitable Ocean..With-out dimension, where length, breadth, and highth, And time and place are lost. **1774** M. MACKENZIE *Maritime Surv.* 11 Taking the Length of *X Y* from a Scale of equal Parts, set it off from *X* to *Y*. **1777** PRIESTLEY *Philos. Necess.* 177 The most exalted piece of matter possible must have length, breadth, and thickness. **1860** TYNDALL *Glac.* I. xvi. 117 The full length of the rope between us.

†**b.** ***in length and*** (***in***) ***breadth*** (or ***brede***), ***length and breadth***, etc.: throughout the whole area (of a country), in all parts or directions.

a **1250** *Owl & Night.* 174 Ich habbe on brede and ek on lengþe Castel god on mine rise. *c* **1290** *S. Eng. Leg.* I. 38/138 Ne scholde no man so euene a þrovȝ in lengþe and in brede. **1297** R. GLOUC. (Rolls) 7911 Þat folc..robbede Wircestressire In lengþe & in brede. *a* **1300** *Cursor M.* 2130 Þe folk..fild þe werld o lenth and brede. *Ibid.* 5027 Lauerd ..þat..taght adam on lenth and wide. **13..** *Sir Beues* 537 (MS. A) A fairer child neuer i ne siȝ, Neiþer a lingþe ne on brade. *c* **1350** *Will. Palerne* 3055 Deliver þi londes aȝen in lengþe & in brede. **1362** LANGL. *P. Pl.* A. III. 196 He hedde beo lord of that lond in lenkthe and in brede. [**1377** —— B. III. 202 A lengthe and a brede]. *c* **1375** *Sc. Leg. Saints* xiii. (*Marcus*) 50 Of al þis world, lynth & bred. *a* **1400** *Octouian* 548 Ten schypmen to londe yede To se the yle yn lengthe and brede. *c* **1470** HENRY *Wallace* v. 20 About the park thai set on breid and lenth..All likly men. **1500-20** DUNBAR *Poems* lxxii. 65 Unto the crose of breid and lenth, To gar his lymmis langar wax. **1535** COVERDALE *Gen.* xiii. 17 Arise, and go thorow the londe, in the length and bredth [**1611** in the length of it, and in the breadth of it].

c. Phrases. ***to find, get, know the length of*** (a person's) ***foot***: see FOOT *sb.* 26 c. ***the length of one's nose, tether***: see NOSE, TETHER.

d. with *a* and *pl.* An instance of this.

1709 BERKELEY *Th. Vision* §61 Inches, feet, &c. are settled, stated lengths. **1838** *Penny Cycl.* XI. 153/1 Given, the area of a parallelogram, and the ratio of its sides; required, the lengths of those sides. **1853** SIR H. DOUGLAS *Milit. Bridges* (ed. 3) 229 Three lengths are given in the above table, for each mean girth.

2. a. Extent from beginning to end, e.g. of a period of time, a series or enumeration, a word, a speech or composition. † ***in length of time***: in course of time.

a **1240** *Sawles Warde* in *Cott. Hom.* 261 Þe imeane blisse is seouenfald lengðe of lif. **13..** *E.E. Allit. P.* B. 425 Þe lenþe of Noe lyf. **1340-70** *Alex. & Dind.* 444 To..leden þerinne our lif þe lengþe of our daies. *c* **1375** *Sc. Leg. Saints* xxvi. (*Nycholas*) 882 God hym lent lynt & space hyme to repent. **1523** LD. BERNERS *Froiss.* I. cccxxxii. 519 The lenght of the siege. **1577** tr. *Bullinger's Decades* (1592) 363 The equinoctiall is, when the daie and night is both of one length. **1697** DRYDEN *Virg. Georg.* III. 273 In length of Time produce the lab'ring Yoke. **1726** LEONI *Alberti's Archit.* I. 31/1 The Stone has in length of time closed up the Mouth of the Valley. **1860** MRS. CARLYLE *Lett.* III. 34 A stay of any length there would not suit me at all. *Mod.* The chapters of the book are very unequal in length.

b. An instance of this; a period or duration of time, *esp.* a long period.

1697 DRYDEN *Virg. Georg.* III. 717 After such a length of rowling Years. —— *Æneid* XII. 1280 She drew a length of sighs [L. *multa gemens*]. **1786** A. GIB *Sacr. Contempl.* I. iv. 52 There are consistent delays of it for various lengths of time. **1824-8** LANDOR *Imag. Conv.* Ser. I. Wks. 1846 I. 4 How delightful it is to see a friend after a length of absence. **1838** J. H. NEWMAN *Par. Serm.* (1839) IV. xx. 348 He had to bear a length of years in loneliness. **1877** L. MORRIS *Epic Hades* I. 8 The weary lengths of Time.

c. *Bridge.* Four or more cards of the same suit held in a Bridge hand.

1927 M. C. WORK *Contract Bridge* iii. 43 The game-goer may be bid with a blank suit or a worthless singleton if the trump length be satisfactory. **1930** E. CULBERTSON *Contract Bridge Blue Bk.* xxii. 285 To build up, if possible, a great minor suit length in the strong hand. **1948** —— *Contract Bridge for Everyone* (1949) 77 When your principal length or strength is in the suit your opponent has bid, do not overcall. **1958** *Listener* 2 Oct. 541/1 West, from the bidding, is probably aware of his [*sc.* North's] great Club length. **1973** *Sunday Times* (Colour Suppl.) 20 May 90/2 It is easy to enter for East holding length in diamonds by playing the Ace and the Queen.

3. a. The quality or fact of being long; opposed to shortness. † ***of length***: long.

1388 WYCLIF *Ps.* xci. 16, I schal fille hym with the lengthe of daies [COVERDALE & **1611** long(e life]. **1593** SHAKS. *Rich. II*, IV. i. 11 Is not my arme of length, That reacheth from the restfull English Court As farre as Callis. **1606** —— *Tr. & Cr.* I. iii. 136 To end a tale of length. **1611** BIBLE *Job* xii. 12 With the ancient is wisedome, and in length of dayes, vnderstanding. **1651** HOBBES *Leviath.* II. xxvi. 139 Such Customes have their force, onely from Length of Time. **1667** MILTON *P.L.* XI. 778 Peace would have crownd With length of happy days the race of man. **1762** LD. KAMES *Elem. Crit.* (1774) II. 164 Secondly, the length of an Hexameter line hath a majestic air. **1805** WORDSW. *Waggoner* II. 146 'A bowl, a bowl of double measure', Cries Benjamin, 'a draught of length!' *Mod.* The length of the journey was the chief objection to it.

b. Prolixity, lengthiness. Now *rare.*

1593 SHAKS. *Rich. II*, V. i. 94 Come, come, in wooing Sorrow let's be briefe, Since wedding it, there is such length in Griefe. **1606** —— *Ant. & Cl.* IV. xiv. 46, I will o're-take thee Cleopatra, and Weepe for my pardon. So it must be, for now All length is Torture. **1781** COWPER *Conversat.* 87 The clash of arguments and jar of words..Decide no question with their tedious length. **1791** BURKE *Let. Member Nat. Assembly* Wks. VI. 67 Excuse my length. **1875** JOWETT *Plato* (ed. 2) V. 456 There is no reason why brevity should be preferred to length.

4. a. A distance equal to the length of something specified or implied. ***at arm's length***: see ARM *sb.*¹ 2 b. ***cable('s) length***: see CABLE *sb.* 2 c.

1413 *Pilgr. Sowle* (Caxton 1483) IV. xxvi. 71 A litel hows whiche hath in euery side skars a mannes lengthe. **1474** *Waterford Arch.* in *10th Rep. Hist. MSS. Comm.* App. v. 311 Within the laynth of a myle unto the citie. *a* **1572** KNOX *Hist. Ref.* Wks. 1846 I. 223 Nott two payre of boot lenthis distant frome the toune. **1602** SHAKS. *Ham.* II. i. 88 He tooke me by the wrist, and held me hard; Then goes he to the length of all his arme. *a* **1674** CLARENDON *Hist. Reb.* XII. §89 When they come within little more than a horse-length. **1686** J. DUNTON *Lett. fr. New-Eng.* (1867) 31 We could scarce see the Ship's length before us. **1717** tr. *Frezier's Voy.* 261 Adorn'd with Porticos of Timber Work, the Length of the Building. **1722** DE FOE *Plague* (1840) 19, I might..have gone the Length of a..Street. **1843** MACAULAY *Lays Anc. Rome, Horatius* xli, Six spears lengths from the entrance Halted that deep array. **1851** MAYNE REID *Scalp Hunt.* xxxi. 241 They had got the mustang some fifty lengths of himself out on the prairie. **1885** SIR C. P. BUTT in *Law Times Rep.* LIII. 61/1 The look-out..saw..at a distance of two ship's lengths, a red light on board the smack.

b. ***one's length***: the extent of one's body or form from head to foot or end to end.

a **1586** SIDNEY *Arcadia* II. (1590) 118b, Laying all her faire length vnder one of the trees. **1590** SHAKS. *Mids. N.* III. ii. 429 Faintnesse constraineth me, To measure out my length on this cold bed. **1709** POPE *Ess. Crit.* 357 A needless Alexandrine ends the song That, like a wounded snake, drags its slow length along. **1784** COWPER *Task* VI. 74 The roof, though moveable through all its length As the wind sways it, has yet well sufficed. **1821** SHELLEY *Prometh. Unb.* IV. 567 The serpent that would clasp her with his length. **1847** TENNYSON *Princess* V. 56 All her fair length upon the ground she lay. **1870** RAMSAY *Remin.* iv. (ed. 18) 81, I fell all my length.

c. *Sport.* The measure of a boat, a horse, etc., engaged in a race, taken as a unit in measuring the amount by which the race is won.

1664 BUTLER *Hud.* II. III. 1190 Left danger, fears, and foes, behind, And beat, at least three lengths, the wind. **1700** DRYDEN *Cinyras & Myr.* 381 Time glides along with undiscover'd haste, The Future but a Length behind the past. **1812** *Sporting Mag.* XXXIX. 186 This was a most excellent race, and only won by a length. **1834** MEDWIN *Angler in Wales* II. 116 Owen..was some lengths behind in the last hundred yards. **1887** O. W. HOLMES *100 Days Europe* i. 52 One [horse] slides by the other, half a length, a

length, a length and a half. **1894** *Times* 19 Mar. 12/2 The Oxford crew won by three and a half lengths.

d. *Swimming.* The length of the swimming-bath taken as a measure of distance swum. Also *attrib.*

1912 F. SACHS *Compl. Swimmer* 237 They.. arrange their races to suit the baths, and their handicaps.. are measured by its length, *i.e.* '3 lengths (90 yards) handicap'. **1931** G. H. CORSAN *Diving & Swimming Bk.* viii. 74 Have the fastest swimmers swim a three lengths race. *Ibid.*, Finish with relay races of two lengths. **1972** B. TURNER *Solden's Women* xvii. 154 I'm not such a good swimmer as Patricia was. Three lengths at the baths is about my limit.

5. a. With a demonstrative or other defining word: Distance. ***the length of***: as far as. Now *Sc.*

c **1450** *Merlin* 161 Ye myght here the strokes half a myle of length. ? *a* **1550** *Mery Jest Mylner of Abyngton* 77 in Hazl. *E.P.P.* III. 103 The mylners house is nere, Not the length of a lande. **1578** HUNNIS in *Par. Dainty Devices* 2 They be the lines that lead the length, How farre my race is for to runne. *a* **1674** CLARENDON *Hist. Reb.* VIII. §90 He [Essex] had marched to the length of Exciter. **1687** *Lond. Gaz.* No. 2251/4 Which we had scarce done when the other three Ships had got our length. **1726** SHELVOCKE *Voy. round World* (1757) 73 We had found it very cold, before we came this length, but now we began to feel the extreme of it. **1772–84** COOK *Voy.* (1790) IV. 1198 When you get that length, you are very carefully.. to explore, such rivers.. as may appear to be of considerable extent. **1870** RAMSAY *Remin.* v. (ed. 18) 111 The loan of a horse 'the length' of Highgate. **1886** K. OLIPHANT *New English* I. 295 In Scotland they say, 'I will come your length'.

fig. **1753** *Scots Mag.* Jan. 8/2 That [treaty] never came any great length. **1837** CARLYLE *Let.* 28 Aug. in *Atlantic Monthly* (1898) LXXXII. 305/1 You do not say that the disorder has got that length with you.

b. *fig.* in advb. phrases: The distance or extent to which one 'goes' (in a line of action, opinion, etc.); the degree of extremity to which something is 'carried'. Chiefly, ***to go (to) the length of, to go a (great,*** etc.) ***length, to go (all,*** etc.) ***lengths.***

1697 COLLIER *Immor. Stage* i. (1730) 6 The Royal Leonora.. runs a Strange Length in the History of Love. **1718** HICKES & NELSON *J. Kettlewell* III. lxvi. 351 Others who could not.. go their lengths. **1719** DE FOE *Crusoe* II. x. (1840) 224 They had not come to that length. **1749** FIELDING *Tom Jones* XVIII. viii, I think you went lengths indeed. **1779** HUME in H. Calderwood *Hume* (1898) iii. 30 Your spirit of Controversy.. carries you strange lengths. **1792** WASHINGTON *Let.* Writ. 1891 XII. 177 When matters get to such lengths, the natural inference is, that both sides have strained the cords beyond their bearing. **1844** DISRAELI *Coningsby* VII. iv, He would go.. any lengths for his party. **1865** CARLYLE *Fredk. Gt.* v. vi. (1872) II. 104 The cunningest of men, able to lie to all lengths. **1875** JOWETT *Plato* (ed. 2) I. 404 They do not go the length of denying the pre-existence of ideas.

†6. The extent of space within which it is possible to touch or act upon something; reach. *Obs.*

c **1400** *Destr. Troy* 6573 Er he be led out of lenght, & lost of your sight. **1608** SHAKS. *Per.* I. i. 168 If I can get him within my Pistol's length. **1628** DIGBY *Voy. Medit.* (1868) 60 They could not open my shippes till they were within halfe the length of our ordinaunce.

7. *Archery.* The distance to which an arrow must be shot in order to hit the mark.

1545 ASCHAM *Toxoph.* II. (Arb.) 106 *Phi.* Howe manye thynges are required to make a man euer more hyt the marke? *Tox.* Twoo. *Phi.* Whiche twoo? *Tox.* Shotinge streyght and kepynge of a lengthe. *Ibid.* 150 The greatest enemy of shootyng is the wynde and the wether, wherby true kepyng a lengthe is chefely hindred. **1801** T. ROBERTS *Eng. Bowman* 290 *Length*, the distance shot.

8. *Pros.* Quantity (of a sound or syllable). Also, long quantity (opposed to *shortness*).

1762 LD. KAMES *Elem. Crit.* (1774) II. 10 The emotion raised by the length or shortness, the roughness or smoothness, of the sound. *Ibid.* 103 The different lengths of syllables, i.e. the difference of time taken in pronouncing. **1884** A. GOSSET *Fr. Prosody* i. 1 Some theorists forbid rhymes between syllables, whose difference of length is marked by a circumflex accent.

b. length-mark, a phonetic symbol used to indicate the relative length of a vowel sound.

1926 ARMSTRONG & WARD *Handbk. Eng. Intonation* p. vii, Length marks (: long and half-long) are used to indicate length only and not difference in vowel quality. **1932** D. JONES *Outl. Eng. Phonetics* (ed. 3) 65 The letter *i* without the length-mark stands for the members of the English *i*-phoneme used when the sound is relatively short. **1965** *English Studies* XLVI. 359 No allophonic length-marks are used.

†9. = LONGITUDE. *Obs.*

1581 W. STAFFORD *Exam. Compl.* i. (1876) 24 Without knowledge of the latitude of the place by the Poale, and the length, by other starres.

10. a. *Cricket.* The proper distance for pitching a ball in bowling; that distance which constitutes a good pitch. Also = *length ball.* Hence ***length bowler.***

1776 in C. C. Clarke *Nyren's Cricketer's Guide* (1888) 14 Ye bowlers.. measure each step, and be sure pitch a length. **1833** C. C. CLARKE *ibid.* 4 How to stop a ball dropped rather short of a length. **1850** 'BAT' *Cricketer's Man.* 41 Good lengths depend entirely on the pace. **1897** *Daily News* 18 June 2/6 Such a good length did the bowlers keep that during the first half-hour only 20 runs were made. **1910** *Blackw. Mag.* Jan. 91/1 Only at the last gasp was any serious effort made to knock him off his length. **1937** *Daily Herald* 5 Jan. 14/1 [Verity] The best length bowler in England. **1956** N. CARDUS *Close of Play* 176 The old-fashioned 'length' bowlers, ball after ball on the same spot. **1958** D. BRADMAN *Art of Cricket* 97/1, I prefer to think in terms of a 'good length ball' and to define it thus—'The type of delivery which has the striker in two minds as to whether he should play forward or back.' **1969** *Listener* 1 May 622/3 At first Powell hit the ball all around the field and, just as it looked as if Miller might be finding his length, the item ended.

b. In racket games: the quality of making shots which pitch well back in the court and deny the opponent an easy return; the placing of a shot in this way; the 'form' required to make such shots consistently.

1924 G. W. HILLYARD *40 Yrs. Lawn Tennis* viii. 136 He.. went on hitting.. until he did get his 'length', and then it was.. a case of woe betide the other man. **1930** *Morning Post* 19 July 14/6 The Italian's fine mixture of pace and length was pitted against Lott's youth, power, and cunning. **1948** S. NOEL *More about Squash Rackets* i. 24 Angles, drop-shots.. and reverse angles are all the stock-in-trade of the professional, in addition to a sound length game. **1961** J. H. GILES *Squash Rackets* viii. 41 It [*sc.* the lob shot] can also be used as an attacking shot, providing as it does a complete change of pace and flight from the orthodox drive and length shots. **1964** R. LAVER *How to play Winning Tennis* vii. 57 You can get good length with the topspin I use. **1966** *Observer* 8 May 19/5 She was quick to switch from her steady baseline game into a counter attack whenever Miss Niessen lost her length.

II. Concrete senses.

11. a. A long stretch or extent.

1595 SHAKS. *John* I. i. 105 Large lengths of seas and shores Betweene my father, and my mother lay. *c* **1600** —— *Sonn.* xliv, To leape large lengths of miles. **1697** DRYDEN *Virg. Georg.* IV. 415 That length of Region, and large Tract of Ground. **1709** POPE *Ess. Crit.* 222 From the bounded level of our mind Short views we take, nor see the lengths behind. **1715–20** —— *Iliad* II. 649 Down their broad shoulders falls a length of hair. **1784** COWPER *Task* I. 252 Not distant far, a length of colonnade Invites us. *Ibid.* IV. 355 He brandishes his pliant length of whip. **1847** TENNYSON *Princess* I. 3 With lengths of yellow ringlet, like a girl.

b. A piece of a certain or distinct length, esp. one cut off or separable from a larger piece.

1645 *Rec. Dedham, Mass.* (1892) III. 112 Samll Milles hath libertie to cut 400 lengthes of hoopes poles on the common. **1683** MOXON *Mech. Exerc., Printing* ii. ¶2 The Compositer may cut them into such Lengths as his Work requires. **1703** —— *Mech. Exerc.* 247 Line Pins of Iron, with a length of Line on them about sixty feet in length. **1832** HT. MARTINEAU *Hill & Valley* iii. 37 Cut into lengths like twigs. **1851** *Illustr. Catal. Gt. Exhib.* 328 The structure is in separate lengths, each having an independent spring.

c. *slang.* A penis; sexual intercourse; so ***to slip*** (someone) ***a length***: (of a man) to have sexual intercourse with.

1949 PARTRIDGE *Dict. Slang* Add. 1173/2 *Slip* (her) *a length*, to coït with (a woman). **1952** C. MACINNES *June in Spring* vi. 156 'Is it hard to get a job on board a ship without experience?' 'Not if you work for nix and don't mind the stokers slipping you a length.' **1968** H. C. RAE *Few Small Bones* III. viii. 216 Beefy, randy-arsed wives crying out for a length. **1970** C. WOOD *Terrible Hard* v. 58 Come on, Suggy, you're 'is batman, 'e's never slipped you a crafty length 'as 'e?

12. *Theatr. slang.* A portion of an actor's part, consisting of forty-two lines.

1736 FIELDING *Pasquin* I. Wks. 1882 X. 129, I have a part in both too; I wish any one else had them, for they are not seven lengths put together. **1838** DICKENS *Nich. Nick.* xxiii, I've got a part of twelve lengths here, which I must be up in tomorrow night. **1865** LD. BROUGHTON in *Edin. Rev.* CXXXIII. 293 Kean said [*c* 1815] that 'Iago was three lengths longer than Othello'. A length is forty-two lines.

13. *Brewing.* (See quot. 1830.)

1742 *Lond. & Country Brew.* I. (ed. 4) 71 It is the common Length I made for that Purpose. **1743** *Ibid.* II. (ed. 2) 129 In making your Length short, and then making it longer with Small-Beer. **1830** M. DONOVAN *Dom. Econ.* I. 159 A.. copper boiler,.. sufficiently large to.. boil each of the lengths drawn from the different mashings... By the word *lengths* the brewer means the quantity of wort drawn off from a certain quantity of malt.

III. Phrases.

14. at length. a. To or in the full extent; fully, in full; without curtailment. Also ***at full, great, some,*** etc. ***length.*** †Rarely, ***at the length.***

c **1500** *Sc. Poem Heraldry* 30 in *Q. Eliz. Acad.* 94 The.. most populus, mortal were, wes at thebes, quhiche at linth I did write. *c* **1530** LD. BERNERS *Arth. Lyt. Bryt.* 157 Whan Arthur had red wel at length these letters. **1530** BAYNTON in *Palsgr.* Introd. 12 Whiche thyng for substantives, he declareth some thyng at the length in his thyrde boke. **1567** *Gude & Godlie Ball.* (S.T.S.) 16 The Catechismus buke Declairis it at lenth. **1713** STEELE *Englishman* No. 4. 28 The Fellow talks of Rogue and Rascal at full Length. **1727** SWIFT *Let. Eng. Tongue* Wks. 1755 II. I. 188 The words pronounced at length sounded faint and languid. **1827** JARMAN *Powell's Devises* (ed. 3) II. 91 Lord Eldon, though he spoke at some length on the other question, did not advert to this. **1838** TREVELYAN in *Life Macaulay* (1876) II. vii. 33 Macaulay gives his impressions at greater length. **1882** J. H. BLUNT *Ref. Ch. Eng.* II. 138 Gardiner spoke at some length respecting the Holy Sacrament. **1886** *Athenæum* 30 Oct. 559/3 While Australia is described at length, the development of Canada since the Peace is hardly mentioned.

b. After a long time; at or in the end; in the long run. †Also ***at the length.***

1525 LD. BERNERS *Froiss.* (1812) II. xxiv. 64 They were all withdrawen into the castell, for they knewe well at length the towne wolde nat holde. **1526** SKELTON *Magnyf.* 1275 Euer at the length I make hym lese moche of theyr strength. **1548** UDALL, etc. *Erasm. Par. Mark* i. 117 To come at the length to highest perfeccion. **1590** SPENSER *F.Q.* I. i. 11 At length it brought them to a hollowe cave. **1611** BIBLE *Prov.* xxix. 21 He that delicately bringeth vp his seruant from a child, shall haue him become his sonne at the length. **1631** MASSINGER *Emperor East* III. iv, This was the mark I aimed at; and I glory, At the length, you so conceive it. **1671** MILTON *P.R.* IV. 506 Of thy birth at length, Announc't by Gabriel, with the first I knew. **1753** WASHINGTON *Jrnl.* Writ. 1889 I. 31 They.. pressed for Admittance.. which at Length was granted them. **1768** FOOTE *Devil on 2 Sticks* III. Wks. 1799 II. 271 Thou wilt find, at the length,.. that the first will do us best service. **1864** TENNYSON *En. Ard.* 210 At length she spoke, 'O Enoch! you are wise'.

†c. (*a*) At a distance; (*b*) in an extended line; tandem-fashion; (*c*) of a portrait = FULL LENGTH I.

c **1611** CHAPMAN *Iliad* XV. 503 Now no more Our fight must stand at length [Gr. ἀποσταδόν], but close. **1628** DIGBY *Voy. Medit.* (1868) 60, I had so fitted my selfe that gallies could not hurt mee att length. **1642** FULLER *Holy & Prof. St.* I. viii. 20 As he is good at hand, so is he good at length. **1715** *Lond. Gaz.* No. 5384/10 Drawing any Carriage with more than five Horses at Length. **1786** W. HERBERT *Ames' Typogr. Antiq.* II. 1287 A copper-plate portrait of Chaucer, at length, with his pedigree and arms.

d. With the body fully extended, to the full extent of the body or the limbs. Now usually ***at (one's) full length.***

1607 TOPSELL *Four-f. Beasts* (1658) 19 When they sleep they lie at length. **1613** PURCHAS *Pilgrimage, Descr. India* (1864) 7 [They] pray vpon the earth, with their armes and legs at length out. **1667** FLAVEL *Saint Indeed* (1754) 120 The.. serpent.. is never seen at his full length till dying. **1809** MALKIN *Gil Blas* IV. vi. ¶4 We.. discovered two men stretched at their length in the street. **1818** BYRON *Juan* I. xc, He threw Himself at length. **1887** BOWEN *Virg. Eclog.* VI. 14 Laid at his length in a cavern, Silenus slumbering sound.

†15. in length. a. Lengthwise. **b.** To the full length or extent. **c.** To a long distance; for a long time. *Obs.*

c **1400** *Lanfranc's Cirurg.* 45 If þat a senewe were woundid in lenkþe [*Add. MS.* in lengþe, L. *per longum*]. **1580** BLUNDEVIL *Curing Horses Dis.* lxxxvii. 37 b, The Horse will forsake his meat, and will stand stretching himselfe in length, and neuer couet to lie downe. **1581** SAVILE *Tacitus' Agric.* (1612) 198 Agricola.. fearing, lest he should be assailed on the front and flanckes both at one instant, displaied his army in length [L. *diductis ordinibus*]. **1607** TOPSELL *Four-f. Beasts* 757 Their position runneth all in length. **1609** BIBLE (Douay) *Num.* ix. [x.] 5 But if the trumpeting sound in length and with a broken tune [Vulg. *si autem prolixior atque concisus clangor increpuerit*].

†16. on length. a. At length, finally. **b.** To a distance, away. **c.** To the full extent of the body. *Obs.*

c **893** K. ÆLFRED *Oros.* III. xi. §3 On lengðe mid him he beȝeat ealle þa eastlond. *c* **1220** *Bestiary* 552 Wo so listneð deueles lore, on lengðe it sal him rewen sore. **13..** *Gaw. & Gr. Knt.* 1231 My lorde & his ledez ar on lenþe faren. **1340** HAMPOLE *Pr. Consc.* 7946 Þe lyght of þe son.. May fleghe fra þe est tylle þe west on lenthe. **1387–8** T. USK *Test. Love* II. xiv. (Skeat) l. 99 She streight her on length and rested a while. *c* **1400** *Destr. Troy* 8179 Tristly may Troiell tote ouer the walle, And loke vpon lenght, er his loue come. *Ibid.* 13561 Fowle folowet the hert, Thurgh the londes on lenght. *c* **1440** *York Myst.* xxxvi. 379 Laie hym on lenthe on þis lande. *c* **1450** *Bk. Curtasye* 188 in *Babees Bk.*, Fro stryf and bate draw þe on lengþe.

17. † ***to draw (out) in, into, at,*** or ***on length***: to prolong, protract; *rarely* with personal obj. = to delay, prolong the stay of (*obs.*). Now only ***to draw out to a great,*** etc. ***length.***

a **1300** *Cursor M.* 5806 He sal me drau wit lite and lenth [*Gött.* lith and lenkith, *Trin.* drawe forþ on lengþe]. *c* **1375** *Sc. Leg. Saints* xxix. (*Placidas*) 9 Men cesis.. to spedful pennance to begyne, bot drawis It erare in to lynth, til of his body falȝeis strinth. **1483** *Cath. Angl.* 107/1 To Drawe on longe or on lenght, *crastinare, prolongare, differre.* **1565** COOPER *Thesaurus, Ambages*,—a circuite of woordes, a tale drawen in length. **1589** PUTTENHAM *Eng. Poesie* II. xii. (Arb.) 134 A sound is drawen at length either by the infirmitie of the toung [etc.]. **1596** SHAKS. *Merch. V.* III. ii. 23, I speak too long, but 'tis to peize the time.. and to draw it out in length, To stay you from election. **1611** BIBLE *Ps.* xxxvi. 10 O continue [*marg.* draw out at length] thy louing kindnesse vnto them. **1611** COTGR., *Alonger*, to.. draw out in length. *a* **1713** ELLWOOD *Autobiog.* (1714) 30, I Prayed often, and drew out my Prayers to a great length. **1787** JEFFERSON *Writ.* (1859) II. 191 They will draw their negotiations into length. **1893** *Temple Bar* XCIX. 68 Breakfast was drawn out to a most unusual length.

IV. 18. *attrib.* and *Comb.*: **length ball** *Cricket*, a ball pitched a 'length' (see sense 10); **†length compass,** ? a ship's 'log' (see quot.); **†length keeping** *Archery* (see sense 7); **lengthman,** a man appointed to maintain a certain stretch of road or railway; (the form *lengthsman* in quot. 1902 is an isolated use.)

1833 C. C. CLARKE *Nyren's Cricketer's Guide* (1888) 19 The reaching in to stop a *length-ball will prevent it from rising or twisting. **1851** PYCROFT *Cricket Field* vii. 99 All balls that can be bowled are reducible to 'length balls' and 'not lengths'. **1627** DRUMM. OF HAWTH. *Lit. de Fabr. Machin. Militar.* Wks. (1711) 235 [*List of D.'s inventions*] Instrumentum quoddam, quo itineris marini quantitas exacte supputatur, & longitudinis locorum differentiæ.. Μηκοδείκτης, vulgo le *Length Compass appellatur. **1545** ASCHAM *Toxoph.* II. (Arb.) 151 Howe muche it [the wynde] wyll alter his shoote, eyther in *lengthe kepynge, or els in streyght shotynge. **1902** *Times* 22 Sept. 2/5 Every *lengthsman or fettler on the Government railway gets 8s. a day for eight hours' work. **1921** *Dict. Occup. Terms* (1927) §577 *Lengthman*,.. an underman in a gang engaged on maintenance of a specific section.. of permanent way. **1959** *New Scientist* 16 Apr. 852/1 The mixed plant community was largely maintained by.. the regular cutting with scythe and sickle by.. the County Council 'lengthmen'. **1968** *Telegraph* (Brisbane) 3 June 18/1 Our legislators should modernise transport for railway lengthmen. **1970** *E. Anglian Daily Times* 31 Aug. 4/5 In days of cheaper labour many county council roadmen known as 'lengthmen' were each

responsible for the maintenance of a limited number of miles of road in which they took great pride and knew all the peculiarities. **1971** *Times* 8 Apr. 15/3 An old man who lived at Spelbrook... His home was..the lengthman's cottage. **1972** L. LAMB *Picture Frame* xviii. 157 A road (or 'length') man, with broom and shovel strapped to his bicycle cross-bar.

†**length**, *v. Obs.* [f. LENGTH *sb.*]
1. *trans.* To lengthen, prolong.
a **1300** *Cursor M.* 5400 Now haue we noght ware-wit we mai Lenght our liue wit fra þis dai. *Ibid.* 21099 Thomas soght þat estrin thede..And tar he lenthid his sermon, Bituix-and til his passion. *Ibid.* 28850 Almus..it lenkithes man in life to lende. *c* **1350** *Will. Palerne* 4353 Lengþeþ now my lif for loue of heuene king. **1393** LANGL. *P. Pl.* C. XXI. 53 And beden hym drynke Hus deþ to lette and hus dayes lengthen. *c* **1440** *Jacob's Well* 196 Lengthe þou þe handyl of þi penauns wyth þis iiij. spanne of lengthe, þat is, of restitucyoun. *a* **1450** *Story Alexander* in *Alexander* (1886) 281 Howe might a man make other mennes liues euerlastyng whan he may not lennthe hys awne life one houre? **1513** DOUGLAS *Æneis* II. xi. [x.] 139 Gif goddis likit lynth my life langer space. **1530** PALSGR. 606/1, I length a thyng, I make it longer, *je alongis*. **1610** DANIEL *Tethys Festiv.* F 3 b, When your eyes haue done their part, Thought must length it in the hart. *c* **1614** SIR W. MURE *Dido & Æneas* II. 472 A rod he bears, by which he..Lenthes and abridges life, as he desires. **1622** J. TAYLOR (Water P.) *Water-Cormorant* Wks. (1630) III. 5/2 Drinke was ordain'd to length mans fainting breath.
2. *intr.* To become longer.
c **1400** tr. *Secreta Secret., Gov. Lordsh.* 74 In þat tyme þe nyght lenghthys, þe days shorten. **1574** BOURNE *Regiment for Sea* Introd. (1577) C ij b, The day dooth..length and short according unto the swiftnesse and slownesse of the Sunnes declination.

lengthed (lɛŋθt), *a. rare.* [f. LENGTH *sb.* + -ED².] Having length; only in *Comb.*, as ***equal-lengthed***, †***well-lengthed***.
1494 FABYAN *Chron.* VI. clvi. 144 His body was .viii. foote long, and his arms and leggys well lengthed and strenghted after the proporcion of yᵉ body. **1870** *Contemp. Rev.* XIV. 622 To the version there given we prefer, as more equal-lengthed and compact, Mr. Garnett's version.

lengthen (ˈlɛŋθ(ə)n), *v.* Also 6 *Sc.* **lenthin**, 7 **lenthen**. [f. LENGTH *sb.*; cf. LENGTH *v.* and -EN⁵.]
1. *trans.* To make longer, increase the length of, whether in material or immaterial sense; to elongate, prolong, protract. Also with *out* (†rarely *on*).
1500–20 DUNBAR *Poems* lxix. 6 Quhen that the nycht dois lenthin houris. **1555** EDEN *Decades* 215 All suche as sayled towarde the West dyd greatly lengthen the day. **1593** SHAKS. *2 Hen. VI*, I. ii. 12 Put forth thy hand, reach at the glorious Gold. What, is't too short? Ile lengthen it with mine. **1602** MARSTON *Ant. & Mel.* III. Wks. 1856 I. 43 This vengeance ..will lengthen out My daies unmeasuredly. **1611** BIBLE *1 Kings* iii. 14 Then I will lengthen thy dayes. **1614–15** *Acc.* in Willis & Clark *Cambridge* (1886) II. 487 For lenthning a wymble. *c* **1700** *To Celia* in *Coll. Poems* 54, I must to lengthen on the Pleasure Dwell on thy Lips, and Kiss by leisure. **1711** ADDISON *Spect.* No. 112 ¶3 Sometimes he will be lengthening out a Verse in the Singing-Psalms, half a Minute after the rest of the congregation have done with it. **1712** W. ROGERS *Voy.* 5 We lengthen'd our Mizen-Mast four Foot and a half. **1797** MRS. RADCLIFFE *Italian* i. (1826) 6 He lengthened his visit till there was no longer an excuse for doing so. **1805** WORDSW. *Prelude* xiii. 317 The bare white roads Lengthening in solitude their dreary line. **1858** HAWTHORNE *Fr. & It. Jrnls.* (1872) I. 35 The corridor was of immense length, and seemed to lengthen itself before us. **1875** JOWETT *Plato* (ed. 2) V. 101 The life of peace is that which men should chiefly desire to lengthen out and improve. **1885** *Spectator* 18 July 945/2 Twenty-nine such works are enumerated, and the list might be lengthened.
b. with reference to phonetic quantity.
1666 [see LENGTHENING *vbl. sb.*]. **1755** JOHNSON *Gram.*, *Of Vowels*, It [E] does not always lengthen the foregoing vowel, as glŏve, live, give. **1891** H. BRADLEY *Stratmann's ME. Dict.* Pref. p. viii, A short vowel which has been lengthened by position.
†**c.** Used for: To eke out, cause to last longer. Also with *out. Obs.*
1670 NARBOROUGH in *Acc. Sev. Late Voy.* I. (1711) 56, I do intend to salt up a quantity of each, to carry to Sea with me to lengthen out my Provisions. **1712** W. ROGERS *Voy.* 255 We agreed for the Gallapagos to get Turtle to lengthen our Provisions. **1748** *Anson's Voy.* II. viii. 220 We took a number of them [green turtle] with us to sea, which proved of great service..in lengthning out our store of provision.
2. *intr.* To become longer.
1695 LOCKE *Further Consid. Value Money* 21 One may as well make a Yard, whose parts lengthen and shrink, as [etc.]. **1707** *Curios. in Husb. & Gard.* 257 The stems will soon show themselves, and lengthen. **1725** POPE *Odyss.* XXIV. 408 His breath lengthens, and his pulses beat. **1798** LANDOR *Gebir* I. 205 And eyes that languished, lengthening, just like love. **1813** SHELLEY *Q. Mab* v. 52 The chain That lengthens as it goes. **1877** MARCH *Gram. Anglo-Saxon* 26 Under the accent the simple vowels *a, i, u*, lengthen by prefixing *a* and *â*. **1878** M. A. BROWN *Nadeschda* 82 Daylight fades, the shadows slowly lengthen.
b. *Mil.* (See quot.)
1802 JAMES *Milit. Dict.*, To *lengthen out*, in a military sense, means to stride out.
Hence †ˈ**lengthener**.
c **1560** *Misogonus* IV. i. 158 (Brandl *Quellen* 482) Thou art the lengthner of my lif, the curar of my care.

lengthened (ˈlɛŋθ(ə)nd), *ppl. a.* [f. LENGTHEN *v.* + -ED¹.] Made longer. Also, extended in duration, prolonged, long; (of compositions, etc.) extending to great length, lengthy.
1594 SHAKS. *Rich. III*, I. iii. 208 After many length'ned howres of griefe. **1611** —— *Cymb.* v. iii. 13 Cowards liuing To dye with length'ned shame. **1705** BOSMAN *Guinea* 260 Is not this Letter fairly lengthened?..Wherefore 'tis high time to end the same. **1728–46** THOMSON *Spring* 431 At once he darts along, Deep-struck, and runs out all the lengthened line. **1776–96** WITHERING *Brit. Plants* (ed. 3) II. 498 Seeds crowned with the hairy lengthened styles. **1788** J. MAY *Jrnl. & Lett.* (1873) 67, I am too busy to make lengthened remarks. **1854** SCOFFERN in *Orr's Circ. Sci., Chem.* 251 Professor Faraday undertook a lengthened investigation of the theory. **1861** GLADSTONE *Sp.* 15 Apr. *Financ. Statem.* (1863) 218 Before absolutely closing this lengthened retrospect, I must say [etc.]. **1871** SMILES *Charac.* ii. (1876) 49 After a lengthened interview.

lengthening (ˈlɛŋθ(ə)nɪŋ), *vbl. sb.* [f. LENGTHEN *v.* + -ING¹.] The action of the vb. LENGTHEN.
1573 BARET *Alv.* L 280 The lengthning of the dayes. **1611** BIBLE *Dan.* iv. 27. **1663** GERBIER *Counsel* F v a, You might.. have been invited for the lengthening of her dayes in this world. **1666** DRYDEN *Ann. Mirab.* Pref., Besides so many other helps of grammatical figures, for the lengthening or abbreviation of them [syllables]. **1748** *Anson's Voy.* II. iii. 148 The lengthning of the long-boat. **1853** MARKHAM *Skoda's Auscult.* 169 A rapid contraction of the organ is not absolutely indispensible to the lengthening of the aorta. **1869** A. J. ELLIS *E.E. Pronunc.* I. 13 The use..of the long mark (-) for the lengthening of vowels generally short.
b. *attrib.*
c **1860** H. STUART *Seaman's Catech.* 66 They are distinguished as..futtocks, top timbers, and lengthening timbers. **1879** *Cassell's Techn. Educ.* I. 12/2 A 'lengthening-bar'..is an extra brass rod, which fits into the socket in the leg of the compass.

lengthening (ˈlɛŋθ(ə)nɪŋ), *ppl. a.* [f. LENGTHEN *v.* + -ING².] That lengthens, in senses of the vb.
1764 GOLDSM. *Trav.* 10 My heart..drags at each remove a lengthening chain. **1797** MRS. RADCLIFFE *Italian* vii, He heard only the lengthening echoes of his own voice. **1865** J. H. NEWMAN *Gerontius* §2 Is this peremptory severance Wrought out in lengthening measurements of space? *a* **1872** B. HARTE *Lost Galleon* 141 To cut a lengthening story short.

ˈ**lengthenment.** *rare.* [f. LENGTHEN *v.* + -MENT.] The fact of being lengthened.
1814 *Ann. Reg., Chron.* 300 Mr. Park, for the defence, admitted the lengthenment of the risk by [etc.].

lengthful (ˈlɛŋθfʊl), *a. Poet.* (Now *rare.*) [f. LENGTH *sb.* + -FUL.] Of great length, long.
c **1611** CHAPMAN *Iliad* XI. 182 He..shooke his lengthfull dart. **1621** G. SANDYS *Ovid's Met.* XIV. (1626) 295 The lengthfull keele. **1715–20** POPE *Iliad* XI. 359 The driver whirls his lengthful thong. **1855** SINGLETON *Virgil* I. 30 The latest stage Of such a lengthful life!

lengthily (ˈlɛŋθɪlɪ), *adv.* [f. LENGTHY *a.* + -LY².] In a lengthy manner; at length.
1787 JEFFERSON *Writ.* (1859) II. 334, I have written somewhat lengthily to Mr. Madison. **1827** *Blackw. Mag.* XXI. 729 Informing her very lengthily,—to borrow an Americanism..that her father has promised her hand. **1866** GEO. ELIOT *F. Holt* II. xvi. 33 The reasons against it need not be urged lengthily. **1886** *Manch. Exam.* 21 May 5/4 The case was lengthily and learnedly argued on both sides.

lengthiness (ˈlɛŋθɪnɪs). [f. LENGTHY *a.* + -NESS.] The quality of being lengthy; prolixity.
[**1812** I. POLLEXFEN in *Examiner* 28 Dec. 828/2 (*In pseudo-archaic spelling*) If the pledyng bee of ordynarie longthynesse.] **1829** BENTHAM *Justice & Cod. Petit.*, *Abr. Petit. Justice* 31 In lengthiness of delay..vying with..the equity courts. **1863** LYTTON *Caxtoniana* I. ix. 144 Oratory, like the Drama, abhors lengthiness. **1871** EARLE *Philol. Eng. Tongue* §658 If we want to see lengthiness of language carried out to an extreme and exaggerated development. **1875** MASKELL *Ivories* v. 44 Characterised by sharpness and meagreness of form, and lengthiness of proportion.

†ˈ**lengthing**, *vbl. sb. Obs.* [f. LENGTH *v.* + -ING¹.] = LENGTHENING *vbl. sb.*
c **1375** *Sc. Leg. Saints* xxxvi. (*Baptista*) 223 þat tyme of þe ȝere..quhene þat þe dais takis linthynge. *c* **1450** HOLLAND *Howlat* 34 Bot all thar names to nevyn as now it nocht neid is, It war prolixt and lang, and lenthing of space. **1493** *Bury Wills* (Camden) 85 All the resydew of mony..I wyll jt be bestowyd vpon the lenghtyng of the north yle. **1543** *Privy Purse Exp. P'cess Mary* (1831) 114 Payed to Mabell the goldesmyth for the lenghtyng of a girdle of goldesmyth worke, and a pomandur lxixs. **1595** in *Norf. Antiq. Miscell.* (1883) II. 330 Pᵈ for the Lengthing of owle bares ijˢ.

ˈ**lengthsome**, *a. rare.* [f. LENGTH *sb.* + -SOME.] Lengthy. Hence ˈ**lengthsomeness**.
1836 in *Fraser's Mag.* (1837) XV. 611 We have here the fanatic Newton's lengthsome letters. **1849** ROCK *Ch. of Fathers* IV. iv. 21 This music of the Alleluia at the gradual, in losing its lengthsomeness, also lost its name.

†ˈ**lengthway.** *Obs.* [f. LENGTH *sb.* + WAY.] The direction of the length of something. Only used in advb. phrase (***the lengthway of***...), and *attrib.* (quasi-*adj.*) = LENGTHWISE *a.*
1691 T. H[ALE] *Acc. New Invent.* 121 The three perpendicular lenth-way sections following. **1763** *Museum Rusticum* I. 3 A notch, in which..lies the end of a pole, the length way of the frame.

lengthways (ˈlɛŋθweɪz), *adv.* [f. as prec. with advb. *-s*.] In the direction of the length.
1599 H. BUTTES *Dyets drie Dinner* M 4 b, Cut lengthwayes in halfes, and applied to the soles of the feete. **1634–5** BRERETON *Trav.* (Chetham Soc.) 45 A long table..placed length-ways in an aisle which stands over across the church. **1753** HOGARTH *Anal. Beauty* x. 53 Imagine the horn..to be cut lengthways by a very fine saw. **1822** COLERIDGE *Lett.*, *Convers.* etc. xxvi. II. 68 A hollow tube split lengthways. **1865** LUBBOCK *Preh. Times* xv. (1878) 561 The ornaments of the chiefs are actually pierced lengthways.
†**b.** quasi-*sb. Obs.*
1702 *Providence Rec.* (1894) V. 168 The lengthwayes of the said land lieing Eastward and westward. **1703** *Ibid.* 150 The lengthwayes of this sd Piece of land last mentioned Also lieth Northward and southward.

lengthwise (ˈlɛŋθwaɪz), *adv.* and *a.* [See -WISE.]
A. *adv.* = LENGTHWAYS.
c **1580** JEFFERIE *Bugbears* III. iii. in *Archiv Stud. neu. Spr.* (1897) 90 Slend thys square sticke length-wyse in-to two. **1774** GOLDSM. *Nat. Hist.* I. 362 Beginning about two degrees north of the line and so downward length-wise for about a thousand miles. **1842** *Act 5 & 6 Vict.* c. 79 §13 Allowing for every passenger..a space..of sixteen inches, measuring in a straight line lengthwise on the front of each seat. **1894** HALL CAINE *Manxman* IV. viii. 228 The child slept, and Grannie put it on the pillow turned lengthwise at Kate's side.
B. *adj.* Following the direction of the length; longitudinal.
1871 TYLOR *Prim. Cult.* I. 112 Lengthwise splits mean going on well. **1878** W. K. CLIFFORD *Dynamics* 132 The component velocity of any point on the [moving] line may be called the lengthwise velocity of the line. **1891** C. JAMES *Rom. Rigmarole* 133 That wretched driver..was reposing in a sort of doubled-up, lengthwise position.

lengthy (ˈlɛŋθɪ), *a.* Also 9 **lengthey**. [f. LENGTH *sb.* + -Y. Before the 19th c. found only in American writers; in many of the early British instances it is referred to as an Americanism.
'We have 10 examples from Jefferson between 1782 and 1786; Washington and A. Hamilton also use the word very frequently. T. Paine (quot. 1796), though of English birth, resided much in America.'—N.E.D.]
Characterized by length; having unusually great length. **a.** Of compositions, speeches, discussions, etc.: Extending to a great length; often with reproachful implication, prolix, tedious. Hence *occas.* of a writer or speaker.
1759 J. ADAMS *Diary* 3 Jan., I grow too minute and lengthy. **1773** FRANKLIN *Lett.* Wks. 1887 V. 190 An unwillingness to read any thing about them [such remote countries as America] if it appears a little lengthy. **1793** *Brit. Critic* Nov. 286 We shall, at all times, with pleasure, receive from our transatlantic brethren real improvements of our common mother-tongue: but we shall hardly be induced to admit such phrases as that at p. 93—'more lengthy', for longer, or more diffuse. **1796** PAINE *Writ.* (1895) III. 251 In the mean time the lengthy and drowsy writer of the pieces signed Camillus held himself in reserve to vindicate every thing. **1812** SOUTHEY in *Q. Rev.* VIII. 320 That, to borrow a trans-atlantic term, may truly be called a lengthy work. **1816** BENTHAM *Chrestomathia* App., Wks. 1843 VIII. 178 One most lengthy and perplext proposition. **1823** *New Monthly Mag.* VIII. 476. I must not be lengthy, though I have hardly skimmed the poems. **1827** SCOTT *Chron. Canongate* Introd. ii, The style of my grandsire..was rather lengthy, as our American friends say. **1834–43** SOUTHEY *Doctor* clx. (1862) 494 When he publishes what in America would be called a lengthy poem, with lengthy annotations. **1837** DICKENS *Pickw.* xxxviii, This address..was unusually lengthy for him. **1844** H. H. WILSON *Brit. India* I. 379 After much lengthy correspondence. **1871** FREEMAN *Hist. Ess.* Ser. I. iii. 67 The lengthy pleadings in the great suit. **1879** GEO. ELIOT *Coll. Breakf. P.* 200 But I grow lengthy.
b. said with reference to physical length. *rare.* exc. U.S. and *techn.* of animals.
1760 P. COFFIN in *N.E. Hist. & Gen. Register* (1855) IX. 341 There is an Hill..the most steep and lengthy to ascend which I have ever seen. **1795** in *W. Guthrie's Syst. Mod. Geog.* II. 330 The lengthy moss, depending on almost every branch. **1803** J. DAVIS *Trav. U.S.* 126 And is Jack Douglas there? said the horseman. He is a great, lengthy fellow. [*Author's note*: Lengthy is the American for long.] **1806** M. LEWIS in *Lewis & Clark's Exped.* (1893) 994 *note*, Down a steep and lengthey hill. **1808** PIKE *Sources Mississ.* II. App. (1810) 4 Which would still leave the Arkansaw near 800 miles more lengthy than the White river. **1849** THOREAU *Week Concord Riv.* (1894) 248 Many a lengthy reach we've rowed. **1850** SCORESBY *Cheever's Whalem. Adv.* vii. (1859) 101 Dealing his blows unsparingly..with all the force of his lengthy frame. **1878** H. M. STANLEY *Dark Cont.* II. xii. 347 On our left..rose a lengthy and stupendous cliff line. **1890** 'ROLF BOLDREWOOD' *Col. Reformer* (1891) 312 He sees the steers grow glossy of hide, thicker, lengthier, ripen into marketable bullocks. **1893** *Kennel Gaz.* Aug. 213/3 A nice lengthy bitch.

Lengua (ˈlɛŋgwə). [f. Sp. *lengua* tongue (see quot. 1904¹).] **a.** A member of a tribe of South American Indians inhabiting the Paraguayan Gran Chaco area; also *attrib.* or as *adj.* **b.** The language of this tribe.
1822 S. COLERIDGE tr. *Dobrizhoffer's Acct. Abipones* I. 125 The equestrian nations remaining in Chaco, and still formidable to the Spaniards, are the Abipones,..and Oekakalots, Guaycurus, or Lenguas. **1904** W. B. GRUBB *Among Indians Paraguayan Chaco* vii. 57 The *labret* is an extension of the lower lip, which has the appearance of a protruding tongue. Hence the Spanish term *Lengua* was applied indiscriminately by the early colonists to any tribe who adopted this custom. *Ibid.* x. 94 Unless the circumstances are known, some expressions in Lengua are quite meaningless. **1908** *Westm. Gaz.* 11 Sept. 8/2 During the past year sections [of the Bible] have been printed in Lengua, a language spoken by the Indians of the Paraguayan Chaco. **1911** J. G. FRAZER *Golden Bough*: *Taboo* (ed. 3) ii. 38 The Lengua Indians of the Gran Chaco hold that the vagrant spirits of the dead may come to life again. **1950** J. G. KERR *Naturalist in Gran Chaco* ix. 175 The main work of the Mission was..among a set of Lengua (i.e. Mushcui) Indians

known as the Paisiapto or black-food people. **1973** B. J. SUSNIK in J. R. Gorham *Paraguay: Ecological Ess.* 121 (*table*) Lengua... Since 1850, contacts (bartering) with Spanish Americans.

† **'leniate**, *v. Obs.* [f. L. *lēni-s* mild + -ATE.] *trans.* To render mild or soft; to soften, soothe.

1622 *Strangling Gt. Turk* 2 Yet, in these cases, as the Emperor's fury is leniated, they many times escape. **1624** T. SCOTT *Belg. Souldier* 26 Those hearts..were leniated with a more iustifiable triable [triacle?]. **1657** TOMLINSON *Renou's Disp.* 15 Others [catharticks] which onely by leniating and solving the belly, educe humours.

† **'lenic**, *a.* (*sb.*) *Mining. Obs. rare*⁻¹. [? f. Gr. ληv-ός wine-press + -IC.] (See quot.)

1612 S. STURTEVANT *Metallica* 37 Lenicks are peculiar Metallical instruments which worke their opperation and effect by pressing, impressioning, or moulding... There is great vse of these Lenick instruments, for the tempering and commixing of Sea-coale and Stone-coale.

lenience ('liːnɪəns). [f. LENIENT: see -ENCE.] Lenient action or behaviour, indulgence.

1796 ANNA SEWARD *Lett.* (1811) IV. 163, I am indebted rather to this skiey-lenience, than to any great decrease in the complaint itself. **1815** HOBHOUSE *Substance Lett.* (1816) II. 211 It will be necessary that this acceptance should be followed up by measures of the utmost lenience. **1826** R. H. FROUDE *Rem.* (1838) I. 84 To look with lenience on the faults. **1876** GEO. ELIOT *Dan. Der.* IV. 185 An ignorant unkindness, the most remote from Deronda's large imaginative lenience towards others.

leniency ('liːnɪənsɪ). [f. LENIENT: see -ENCY.] The quality of being lenient.

1780 MAD. D'ARBLAY *Let.* 9 June, After all the leniency and forbearance of the ministry. **1794** COLERIDGE *Lett.* (1895) I. 71 All the fellows tried to persuade the Master to greater leniency, but in vain. **1844** H. H. WILSON *Brit. India* II. 392 No leniency towards him could appease his resentment. **1868** E. EDWARDS *Ralegh* I. iii. 38 Leniency to malefactors..was cruelty to the good and peaceable subjects.

lenient ('liːnɪənt), *a.* and *sb.* [ad. L. *lēnient-em*, *lēniens*, pr. pple. of *lēnīre* to soothe, f. *lēnis* soft, mild.]

A. *adj.*

1. Softening, soothing, relaxing, both in a material and immaterial sense; emollient. †Const. *of*. Somewhat *arch.*

1652 FRENCH *Yorksh. Spa* viii. 74 Taking..a little Cassia, or some such lenient medicament. **1671** MILTON *Samson* 659 Lenient of grief and anxious thought. **1732** ARBUTHNOT *Rules of Diet* 271 One should begin with the gentlest [Remedies] at first, as the lenient, relaxing, diluent, demulcent. **1760** DODD *Hymn to Good-Nature* Poems (1767) 4 Touch with the lenient balm of thy soft love..the heart morose. **1781** E. DARWIN *Bot. Gard.* I. (1791) 84 The rapturous God..With lenient words her virgin fears disarms. **1805** FOSTER *Ess.* IV. viii. 251 Softened by the lenient hand of time. **1810** CRABBE *Borough* viii. Wks. 1834 III. 147 Nor these alone possess the lenient power Of soothing life in the desponding hour. **1832** BRYANT *Poems, Hymn to Death* 103 When thy reason..taught Thy hand to practise best the lenient art.

2. Of persons, their actions and dispositions, also of an enactment: Indisposed to severity; gentle, mild, tolerant. Const. *to*, *towards*.

1787 WINTER *Syst. Husb.* 170 The lenient laws of this happy isle do not compel men to get or save. **1828** D'ISRAELI *Chas. I*, I. vi. 153 This venerable Protestant was..disgusted at the lenient measures pursued by the Queen. **1832** HT. MARTINEAU *Ella of Gar.* vii. 86 Archie's family thought him much too lenient towards Mr. Callum. **1857** BUCKLE *Civiliz.* I. iv. 201 The greatest observer and the most profound thinker is invariably the most lenient judge. **1870** DICKENS *E. Drood* xiii, We have so much reason to be very lenient to each other. **1879** FROUDE *Cæsar* xii. 155 Cicero, who was inclined at first to be severe, took on reflection a more lenient view.

† **B.** *sb.* A soothing appliance; an emollient.

1672 WISEMAN *Wounds* I. ix. 99, I..cleansed the wound, and drest him up with lenients. **1684** tr. *Bonet's Merc. Compit.* III. 50 In the Stone in the Kidneys..I think it safer to use Lenients. **1767** GOOCH *Treat. Wounds* I. 205 How necessary it may sometimes be found..to use lenients and anodynes.

leniently ('liːnɪəntlɪ), *adv.* [f. prec. + -LY².] In a lenient manner; gently, indulgently.

1845 S. AUSTIN *Ranke's Hist. Ref.* II. 247 He..exhorted his brother to act prudently and leniently. **1855** MACAULAY *Hist. Eng.* xvii. IV. 33 The tribunal..had dealt with him more leniently than his former friends. **1884** *Spectator* 4 Oct. 1325/1 It is easy to look leniently upon his tortuous diplomacy at the Congress of Westphalia.

lenify ('liːnɪfaɪ), *v.* Also 6-7 lenefie, -ifie. [f. L. *lēni-s* soft, mild + -FY.]

† **1.** *trans.* with material object: To relax, make soft or supple (some part of the body); to render (cider) mellow. Also, to mitigate (a physical condition). *Obs.*

1574 NEWTON *Health Mag.* 29 Egges..poched..do aswage and lenifie it [the lower part of the belly]. **1612** WOODALL *Surg. Mate* Wks. (1653) 49 Oyle of Elder-flowers doth lenifie and purge the skin. *a* **1640** JACKSON *Creed* x. xxi. §7 He must..enforce himself..to lenify the rotten sores of their ulcerous consciences. **1657** W. COLES *Adam in Eden* lx, The Mucilage [of Fleawort]..helps to lenifie the drynesse of the mouth and throat. **1664** EVELYN *Pomona* Gen. Advt. (1729) 95 Two or three Eggs whole put into an Hogshead of Cider..sometimes rarely lenifies and gentilizes it. **1694** SALMON *Bate's Dispens.* I. (1713) 250 It is an excellent Pectoral,..lenifies Roughness, takes away Hoarsness.

absol. **1710** T. FULLER *Pharm. Extemp.* 145 The uses of this [Emulsion] are great..summarily to Lenify, Supple. **1712** tr. *Pomet's Hist. Drugs* I. 57 Unrefined [Sugar] to levigate and lenify.

2. With immaterial object: To assuage, mitigate, soften, soothe (pain, suffering, etc.). Also, to mitigate (a sentence). Now *rare*.

1568 tr. *P. Martyr's Comm. Rom.* 355 The feare is eyther lenified, or els sometymes vtterly layd away. **1569** PAINTER *Pal. Pleas.* (1575) II. Ep. Ded., Musike..lenifyeth sorrowe. **1594** NASHE *Unfort. Trav.* 76 She hung about his knees, and ..desired him the sentence might be lenefied. **1622** FLETCHER *Sp. Curate* IV. v, This Cataplasme of a well cozen'd Lawyer, Laid to my stomach, lenifies my Fever. **1656** BAXTER *Reformed Pastor* 447 Lenifie their minds by a deprecation of offence in a word. **1681** EVELYN *Mem.* (1857) III. 260 Lord Treasurer Clifford..could not endure I should lenify my style. **1697** DRYDEN *Æneid* XII. 594 These first infused, to Lenifie the pain. **1707** *Reflex. upon Ridicule* 184 To lenifie the ill Humour of our Slanderers. **1882** *Gd. Words* 786 She was able to look on the whole blunder with calmness, lenified in the humility it brought.

Hence **'lenifying** *vbl. sb.* and *ppl. a.*

1612 WOODALL *Surg. Mate* Wks. (1653) 36 It hath a lenifying and anodine quality. **1626** BACON *Sylva* §51 Cow milke..is..proper for..all manner of Lenifyings. **1650** BAXTER *Saint's R.* II. (1654) 259 The lenifying of exasperated and exulcerated minds. **1662** H. STUBBE *Ind. Nectar* iii. 37 This he reputes to be hot and moist, and of a lenifying nature. **1758** *Descr. Thames* 177 The Fat of a Trout is of a lenifying and dissolving Nature.

† **'leniment.** *Obs. rare*⁻⁰. [ad. L. *lēnīment-um*, f. *lēnīre* (see LENITIVE).]

1623 COCKERAM, *Leniment*, an asswaging, an appeasing.

Leninism ('lɛnɪnɪz(ə)m). [f. *Lenin*, the assumed name of Vladímir Il'ích Ulyánov (1870–1924), the founder and leader of the Bolsheviks and of the Soviet State + -ISM.] The political and economic doctrines of Marx as interpreted and applied by Lenin to the governing of the Soviet Union, to the theory of the international proletarian revolution, and to the dictatorship of the working class. So **Leninism-Stalinism**, Lenin's doctrines as interpreted and applied by Stalin.

1918 *Times* 19 Jan. 5/1 (*caption*) From Tsardom to Leninism. **1928** E. & C. PAUL tr. *Stalin's Leninism* I. vi. 53 This second formulation was directed against some critics of Leninism, against the Trotskyists. *Ibid.* II. iii. 94 The endeavour of 'practical' persons to have no truck with 'theories' runs counter to the whole spirit of Leninism and is a great danger to our cause. **1935** *Economist* 12 Jan. 73/2 'Leninism' is a series of brilliant footnotes to the Marxist philosophy made by an experimenter. **1948** J. TOWSTER *Political Power in U.S.S.R.* 3 The teachings of this theory are called Marxism, Leninism,..Marxism-Leninism, or Leninism-Stalinism. **1959** *Times Lit. Suppl.* 21 Aug. 479/3 The remainder of the book follows more familiar lines, Leninism being opposed to Stalinism. **1964** E. H. CARR *Socialism in One Country* III. I. xxxv. 500 In Bolshevik doctrine Leninism meant the adaptation of Marxism to the conditions not of a particular country, but of a particular historical period. **1966** P. HEATH tr. *Wetter's Soviet Ideology Today* 328 If history has declined to develop in the manner prescribed by Marx, the endeavour must be made to adapt her to this plan. Hence the explicitly voluntaristic element in Leninism. **1966** L. LEMPERT tr. *Vinogradov's Socialist Nationalisation of Industry* 19 Leninism maintains, and historical experience confirms, that the ruling classes do not yield power of their own free will. **1971** *Times Lit. Suppl.* 21 May 589/1 Scholastic disputes about orthodoxy are no longer a feature of studies of Marxism and Leninism.

Leninist ('lɛnɪnɪst), *a.* and *sb.* [f. *Lenin* (see prec.) + -IST.] **A.** *adj.* Of, pertaining to, or characteristic of Lenin, his followers or his doctrine. Hence ***Leninist-Marxist*** (cf. *Marxist-Leninist* adj. s.v. MARXIST *sb.*¹ and *a.*¹), ***Leninist-Stalinist***. **B.** *sb.* A follower or supporter of Lenin or his doctrine.

1917 *Times* 10 Nov. 6/4 General Korniloff has been placed under the same ban as M. Kerensky, and renewed instructions for the arrest of both have been issued by the Leninist committee. *Ibid.* 23 Nov. 7/2 Trotsky, one of the Leninist chiefs, has just declared that violence done by his supporters is a right, but violence in resisting them is immoral. **1920** *Q. Rev.* Apr. 474 The Socialists and the Leninists. **1928** E. W. DICKES tr. *Marcu's Lenin* 187 The Leninists, as the closer adherents of Ulianov now called themselves. **1934** H. G. WELLS *Exper. Autobiogr.* II. ix. 806 His [*sc.* Stalin's] was not a free impulsive brain nor a scientifically organized brain; it was a trained Leninist-Marxist brain. **1949** H. READ *Existentialism, Marxism & Anarchism* 16 Humanism is a term which..even an intransigent Marxist like Lukacs does not disdain—he calls the Leninist theory of knowledge a militant humanism. **1950** tr. *M. Djilas's On New Roads of Socialism* 29 The Soviet Government and the subordinate governments have ..organized against her [*sc.* Yugoslavia] an economic blockade and violent pressure..by which all Leninist principles on relations amongst Socialist countries have been trampled underfoot. **1953** *Mind* LXII. 68 The Leninist..is able to demonstrate the inexorable nature of the 'withering away of the state'..because his definition of the state requires that it disappears when classes have been abolished. **1964** D. CAUTE *Communism & French Intellectuals* I. iii. 54 A demand that henceforth the intellectuals cultivate the spirit of the Party in the Leninist-Stalinist sense of the term. **1966** P. HEATH tr. *Wetter's Soviet Ideology Today* ii. 32 If the Leninist concept of matter seeks to constitute a definition, it ought to explain what the nature of matter is. **1971** *Times Lit. Suppl.* 21 May 589/1 A critique of specific points of Leninist doctrine. **1973** E. HYAMS *Final Agenda* ii. 20 He was a literal, not a nominal Leninist, and he believed..that wisdom..lay in Lenin's profound distrust of the bureaucracy.

Leninite ('lɛnɪnaɪt), *a.* and *sb.* [f. *Lenin* (see above) + -ITE¹.] = LENINIST *a.* and *sb.*

1917 *Times* 7 Dec. 7/3 Trotsky, on behalf of the Leninite 'Government', has telegraphed to all the representatives of Russia abroad. **1918** *Times* 1 Jan. 5/1 The Leninites.. earmarked for their own disposal both the food and the credits that had been set aside for the soldiers' sustenance. **1920** E. E. CUMMINGS *Let.* 22 June (1969) 72, I do *not* need money..being a good (if innocuous) Leninnite [*sic*] or Trotskyite. **1920** *Glasgow Herald* 3 July 6 The Constitution of 1919 which recognised the existence of soviets, though not in the Leninite sense.

lenis ('liːnɪs), *a.* and *sb. Phonology.* [a. L. *lēnis* soft.] **A.** *adj.* Of one of two or more homorganic consonants: articulated with less energy. Opp. FORTIS B. *adj.*

1929 G. K. ZIPF in *Harvard Stud. Classical Philol.* XL. 63 Then, if our theory be true, the German *p* must be *fortis*, the German *b lenis*. *Ibid.* 64, I hazard the guess..that the same condition of *lenis-fortis* obtains there also. **1962, 1964** [see FORTIS B. *adj.*]. **1969** *Word* XXV. 20, l is sometimes realized as a very lenis unreleased t and ŋ as a nasalized vowel. **1971** F. W. HOUSEHOLDER *Ling. Speculations* xi. 206 In Iranian Azerbaijani..the back velar stop is normally lenis only, unopposed by any fortis aspirated [*k*].

B. *sb.* (pl. -es). A lenis consonant.

1932 W. L. GRAFF *Lang.* vii. 274 In Alsace people..of French tongue often pronounce voiceless sounds or lenes as in Southern German. **1933** L. BLOOMFIELD *Lang.* 99 Pressure and action are gentle in lenes, vigorous in fortes... In English the unvoiced stops are aspirated fortes, but other types occur as non-distinctive variants, notably the unaspirated lenis type after [s]. **1935** G. K. ZIPF *Psycho-Biol. of Lang.* iii. 63 In the *voiceless fortes* and the *voiceless lenes* we have stops which differ appreciably in magnitude. **1965** *Amer. Speech* XL. 7 Four groupings within the lenes.

lenite ('liːnaɪt), *v. Phonology.* [Back-formation from LENITION.] **a.** *trans.* To make lenis in articulation. **b.** *intr.* (Of consonants), to become lenis. Hence **'lenitable** *a.*; **'lenited** *ppl. a.*

1912 F. W. O'CONNELL *Gram. Old Irish* 5 A true lenited *f* occurs in Modern Irish and is pronounced *h*. *Ibid.* 61 The absolute forms of the copula lenite the following anlaut. **1953** K. JACKSON *Lang. & Hist. Early Brit.* 550 The Bretons lenited the consonants. *Ibid.* 556 British *c*, lenited to *g*. *Ibid.* 474 The consonants ordinarily regarded in Breton as lenitable. **1967** —— *Hist. Phonol. Breton* 309 The geminates, which were not lenitable, constitute a special case. **1971** *Canad. Jrnl. Ling.* Fall 20 Affrication of the yod element would create a consonant cluster which would not lenite. **1972** H. KURATH *Stud. Area Ling.* ix. 153 It should be further noted that 'lenited' /t, k/ appear as the voiced plosives /d, g/ only in the British branch of Insular Celtic.

lenitic (lɛ'nɪtɪk), *a. Ecol.* [f. L. *lenitas* mildness + -IC.] Of fresh-water organisms or habitats: situated in still water. Cf. LOTIC *a.*

1916 NEEDHAM & LLOYD *Life Inland Waters* vi. 315 Organisms..may be roughly divided into two primary groups for which are suggested the following names: I. *Lenitic* or still-water societies. II. *Lotic* or rapid-water societies. **1931** R. N. CHAPMAN *Animal Ecol.* xiv. 285 Quantitative methods for the study of benthonic organisms have made important contributions to our knowledge of the quantity of life in lenitic environments.

le'nition (liː'nɪʃən). [f. L. *lēnis* soft + -ITION.]

† **1.** An assuaging, a mitigation. *Obs. rare*.⁻¹

1541 R. COPLAND *Galyen's Terap.* F iij b, But of the cure of phlegmon by barly meale is sooner lenition than curacyon.

2. *Phonology.* [After G. *lenierung*.] In Celtic languages, the process or result of making or becoming lenis; softening of articulation; (see quots.). Also *attrib.*

1912 F. W. O'CONNELL *Gram. Old Irish* 5 In Old Irish a single consonant between two vowels was more loosely articulated than in absolute anlaut, and this phonetic change has been termed both *aspiration* and *lenition*. **1913** J. MORRIS-JONES *Welsh Gram.* §103. 162 Continental scholars use 'Lenition' as a term embracing the Welsh 'soft mutation' and the corresponding Irish 'aspiration'. **1935** *Mod. Lang. Notes* L. 518 The term *lenition* might to advantage have been recorded; in recent Celtic grammars this term has taken the place of the older *aspiration*. **1953** K. JACKSON *Lang. & Hist. Early Brit.* 424 IE. and Latin *d*..in lenition position initially and internally they became Late Brit. *d*. **1954** PEI & GAYNOR *Dict. Ling.* 121 *Lenition*, in Celtic languages, the phonetic change which consonants undergo when occurring between vowels, as well as the change of the initial consonant of a word under the influence of the final sound of the immediately preceding word. **1963** J. P. HUGHES *Sci. of Lang.* xiv. 251 A tendency arises..to shift the single medial consonant to a spirant... This process is prominent in the Celtic languages, and is known as *lenition*. **1971** *Canad. Jrnl. Ling.* Fall 17 There is some advantage to (1 a), which treats lenition in terms of point of articulation classes.

lenitive ('lɛnɪtɪv), *a.* and *sb.* Also 7 lenative, lenetive; also *corruptly* lenety, lenity. [ad. med.L. *lēnītīv-us* (cf. F. *lénitif*), f. L. *lēnīre* to soften, assuage, soothe. In sense 2, taken as if f. LENITY + -IVE.] **A.** *adj.*

1. Of medicines and medical appliances: Tending to allay or soften; mitigating, soothing; gently laxative; esp. in ***lenitive electuary***.

1543 TRAHERON *Vigo's Chirurg.* 100 b/2 Lenitiue clysters & suppositories. **1562** W. TURNER *Bathes* 10 Cassia fistula or suche lykewise lenitiue or gentell purger. **1610** MARKHAM *Masterp.* I. xcii. 179 This [glister] is lenitiue and a great easer of paine. **1621** BURTON *Anat. Mel.* II. ii. II. (1651) 237 Where

nature is defective, art must supply, by those lenitive electuaries [etc.]. *c*1623 LODGE *Poore Mans Talentt* (1881) 43 A Clister lenety made of the decoction of malloweis [etc.]. **1642** FULLER *Holy & Prof. St.* v. xix. 436 As if she meant to cure a gangren'd arm with a lenitive plaister. **1684** tr. *Bonet's Merc. Compit.* III. 52 Lenitive Purgers should be made use of. **1732** ARBUTHNOT *Rules of Diet* I. 246 Apples are likewise pectoral, cooling, and lenitive. **1822–34** *Good's Study Med.* (ed. 4) I. 192 The pulp of Cassia, alone or in the compound of lenitive electuary.

†**2.** Of persons, their dispositions, etc.: Displaying leniency, gentle. *Obs.*

1620 *Swetnam Arraign'd* (1880) 78 Old Iago is a froward Lord, Honest but lenatiue. **1625** PURCHAS *Pilgrims* II. 1848 Taking some advantage of the lenative and tractable disposition of the Emperour. *a* **1652** BROME *Love-sick Crt.* I. i, He has been Too long too lenetive. **1655** FULLER *Ch. Hist.* x. Ded., Such Writers..use the most lenitive language in expressing distastfull matter.

B. *sb.*

1. A lenitive medicine or appliance. Also *fig.*

1563 T. GALE *Enchirid.* 14 (Stanf.) Suppositorie, clyster or ientle lenytiue. **1593** Q. ELIZ. *Boeth.* I. pr. vi. 18, I will assay a while therfore with lenitiues, & meane fomentations. **1641** EARL MONM. tr. *Biondi's Civil Warres* IV. 87 The gangren'd sores of their soules were not to be cured by Lenities. **1681** DRYDEN *Abs. & Achit.* 926 But Lenitives fomented the Disease. *c* **1720** W. GIBSON *Farrier's Dispens.* v. iii. (1734) 137 It is so gentle a Lenitive, that three times the Quantity they usually give, will hardly move any Horse. **1751** EARL ORRERY *Remarks Swift* (1752) 74 The gentle lenitives of virtue..: might have proved healing ingredients to so deep..a wound. **1788** *New Lond. Mag.* 429 He demanded a lenitive which would put fire into the wound. **1822** LAMB *Elia* Ser. I. *Praise Chimneysw.*, Nature..caused to grow out of the earth her sassafras for a sweet lenitive. **1860** MOTLEY *Netherl.* (1868) II. xv. 240 Festering wounds had more need of corrosives than lenitives.

2. Anything that softens or soothes; a palliative.

1614 A. JACKSON (*title*) Sorrow's Lenitive. **1640** HOWELL *Dodona's G.* (1645) 72 Soul-solacing Lenitives of the Gospel. **1677** HALE *Contempl.* II. 179 He hath under his greatest Misery the Lenitive of Hope. **1715** tr. *C'tess D'Aunoy's Wks.* 161 If such an enormous Crime can admit of any Lenitive. **1743** FIELDING *Journey* I. xxi, It wants the lenitive which palliates and softens every other calamity. **1781** MAD. D'ARBLAY *Let. to Mrs. Thrale* 12 Nov., This consanguineous fondness..I consider..one of the lenitives of life. **1825** R. HALL *Wks.* (1833) I. 376 Friendship..the lenitive of our Sorrows and the multiplier of our joys. **1878** DOWDEN *Stud. Lit.* 412 Against the artificial he used the artificial as a lenitive. **1891** SHORTHOUSE *Blanche Lady F.* 205 Mundane prosperity, which is a wonderful lenitive to some natures.

Hence **'lenitively** *adv.*, **'lenitiveness.**

a **1627** MIDDLETON *Anything for Quiet L.* I. i, Yet should these waste you but lenatively. **1726** PENN *Life* Wks. I. 37 All Laws are to be considered Strictly and Literally, or more Explanatorily and Lenitively. **1727** BAILEY vol. II, *Lenitiveness*, softening or assuaging Quality.

lenitude ('lɛnɪtjuːd). *rare.* [ad. L. *lēnitūdo*, f. *lēnis* soft, mild.] †**a.** In a material sense: Smoothness. *Obs.* **b.** = LENITY (in the first quot. perh. misused for *lentitude*).

1627 W. SCLATER *Exp. 2 Thess.* (1629) 269 Lenitude, rather than lenity of Magistrates. **1656** BLOUNT *Glossogr.*, *Lenitude*, the same [as *Lenity*]. **1657** TOMLINSON *Renou's Disp.* 34 Some [purge] by lenitude as viscid..medicaments.

lenity ('lɛnɪtɪ). Also 6–7 lenitie. [ad. OF. *lenité* or L. *lēnitāt-em*, *lēnitās*, f. *lēnis* soft, mild.] Mildness, gentleness, mercifulness (in disposition or behaviour). Also, an instance of this.

1548 UDALL, etc. *Erasm. Par. Mark* xii. 1–8 But they now made worse through his lenitie and gentlenes, cast stones at him. **1592** *Nobody & Someb.* in Simpson *Sch. Shaks.* (1878) I. 300 Hee is the verie soule of lenitie. **1603** SHAKS. *Meas. for M.* III. ii. 103 A little more lenitie to Lecherie. **1612** T. TAYLOR *Comm. Titus* ii. 6 That he do not there exercise lenitie, where the case requireth seueritie. **1649** BP. REYNOLDS *Hosea* v. 38 Such stiffenesse and sowrnesse as is inconsistent with the lenity of holiness. **1692** E. WALKER *Epictetus' Mor.* (1737) xvi, If I indulge, and not chastise my Boy, My Lenity his Morals may destroy. *a* **1711** KEN *Lett.* Wks. (1838) 93 To apply such ghostly lenities to her sorrow, as may set her at ease. **1748** BUTLER *Serm.* Wks. 1874 II. 308 It is said, that our common fault towards the poor is..too great lenity and indulgence. **1779** JEFFERSON *Corr.* Wks. 1859 I. 234 If it produces a proper lenity to our citizens in captivity, it will have the effect we meant. **1833** I. TAYLOR *Fanat.* i. 13 Shall we, as Christians, wish to creep under the shelter of a corrupt lenity? **1863** GEO. ELIOT *Romola* lviii, Lenity to the prisoners would be the signal of attack for all its enemies.

lenity, obs. incorrect form of LENITIVE.

lenn, lenner, obs. ff. LEND *sb.*², *v.*², LENDER.

lennesse, lennet, obs. ff. LEANNESS, LINNET.

lennilite ('lɛnɪlaɪt). *Min.* [f. *Lenni* in Pennsylvania, the locality where it was found + -LITE.] A greenish variety of orthoclase.

1866 *Proc. Philad. Acad.* 110 'Lennilite'. **1868** DANA *Min.* 356 Lea has named..a greenish orthoclase..Lennilite.

'lennow, *a. Obs.* exc. *dial.* Also 7 lenow, 9 *dial.* lennaow. [Of obscure origin; the Lancashire dialect has *lennock* in the same sense (see *Eng. Dial. Dict.*).] Flabby, limp.

1589 R. ROBINSON *Gold. Mirr.* (Chetham Soc.) 61 My lennow limnes grow dry and stiffe. **1611** COTGR., *Gavache*, lennow, flaggie, limber. **1616** SURFL. & MARKH. *Country Farme* 607 The branch falleth broad, lenow, and soft. **1882** *W. Worcester Gloss.* s.v., When I were young an' lennaow I'd a gambolled over that stile like one o'clock.

lennthe, obs. form of LENGTH.

leno ('liːnəʊ). [Possibly a corruption of F. *linon* (pronounced linɔ̃).] A kind of cotton gauze, used for caps, veils, curtains, etc. Also *attrib.* Hence, the type of weave used for this fabric. Also *attrib.* and *Comb.*, as ***leno brocade, weave***; **leno loom**, a loom which produces leno weave.

1821 M. BROWNE *Diary* 11 Aug. (1905) 173 We at last got a leno cap and an under cap to wear with it. *c* **1828** J. R. PLANCHÉ *Green-Eyed Monster* 8 Leno slip, over white satin, ornamented with leno puffs of white and pink. **1851** MAYHEW *Lond. Labour* I. 388 Twenty year ago..I bought a lot of 'leno' cheap—it was just about going out of fashion for caps then. **1866** MRS. H. WOOD *St. Martin's Eve* ix. (1874) 83 The broad leno lappets of her cap thrown off from her face. **1881** G. MACDONALD *Mary Marston* I. ii. 38 He looked up from a piece of leno he was smoothing out. **1894** *Daily News* 2 June 5/3 A large space cut away..and filled in with fine net or leno. **1940** *Chambers's Techn. Dict.* 494/2 *Leno*, a fabric with an openwork or an embroidered effect, produced by cross-weaving; fabrics of this character that are of regular texture are usually termed *gauze*. *Ibid.*, *Leno brocade*, a brocade cotton, or cotton and rayon cloth, produced by a combination of ordinary and cross-weaving. **1964** H. HODGES *Artifacts* x. 141 Gauze or leno..is produced by crossing adjacent warps before passing the weft, and re-crossing the warps again before passing the next weft. **1964** *McCall's Sewing* iv. 52/2 (*caption*) Leno weave; gauze weave. *Ibid.*, Some major fabrics woven on leno looms are marquisette, netting, mesh shirting. **1968** J. IRONSIDE *Fashion Alphabet* 239 *Leno*,..a type of weave—an open-work fabric with warp yarns twisted before weaving.

†**le'nocinant**, *a. Obs.* [ad. L. *lēnōcinant-em*, pr. pple. of *lēnōcinārī* to pander, wheedle, f. *lēno* pander.] Enticing to evil.

1664 H. MORE *Myst. Iniq.* xv. 52 Animated and emboldened by the counsel or example of their lenocinant Leaders. **1848** in CRAIG; hence in later Dicts.

†**le'nocinate**, *v. Obs. rare.* [f. L. *lēnōcināt-*, ppl. stem of *lēnōcinārī*: see prec.] *intr.* To wheedle. Hence † **le'nocinating** *ppl. a.*

1609 BP. W. BARLOW *Answ. Nameless Cath.* 305 Bellarmine (the lenocinating Pander to the Whore of Babilon).

†**le'nociny.** *Obs. rare.* [ad. L. *lēnōcinium* allurement, f. *lēno* pander.] An enticing medicine.

1657 TOMLINSON *Renou's Disp.* 140 We mix benevolent lenocinyes with purgatives.

†**le'nonian**, *a. Obs. rare*⁻⁰. [f. L. *lēnōni-us* (f. *lēno* a bawd) + -AN.] 'Belonging to a bawd'.

1656 in BLOUNT *Glossogr.*

lenow, variant of LENNOW *Obs.*

lens (lɛnz), *sb.* Pl. **lenses**; also 8 **lens, lens's**, and in Latin form **lentes**. [a. L. *lens* lentil, from the similarity in form.]

1. a. A piece of glass, or other transparent substance, with two curved surfaces, or one plane and one curved surface, serving to cause regular convergence or divergence of the rays of light passing through it.

Now sometimes applied to analogous contrivances for producing similar effects on radiations other than those of light, as in ***acoustic lens, electric lens***.

1693 E. HALLEY in *Phil. Trans.* No. 205. 960 Finding the focus of any sort of lens. **1704** NEWTON *Opticks* I. (1721) 8 A Glass spherically Convex on both sides (usually called a Lens). *Ibid.* 57 According to the difference of the Lenses, I used various distances. **1719** DESAGULIERS in *Phil. Trans.* XXX. 1017 Telescopes made up of Convex *Lentes*. **1726** tr. *Gregory's Astron.* I. 347 By the help of Speculums or Lens. **1781** COWPER *Charity* 385 He claps his lens, if haply they may see, Close to the part where vision ought to be. **1831** BREWSTER *Optics* v. §51. 45 Images are formed by lenses in the very same manner as they are formed by mirrors. *c* **1865** J. WYLDE in *Circ. Sci.* I. 65/1 The Coddington lens is an equally valuable little microscope. **1881** ROUTLEDGE *Science* xii. 279 The property of a lens to form an image depends upon its power of refracting the rays of light. **1931** [see *electron lens* s.v. ELECTRON² 2 b]. **1945** *Jrnl. Sci. Instrum.* XXII. 239/1 Another material useful for ultrasonic lenses, especially when the liquid is incompatible with plastics, is lithium. **1951** V. E. COSSLETT *Pract. Electron Microsc.* ii. 35 Use is made of a surrounding shield of iron to concentrate the field into a small region near the middle of the lens. **1972** *Science* 16 June 1236/1 The spherical concave lens focused the sound at a nominal 3 cm from the transducer and provided a field 1 mm wide, extending from 2 to 4 cm in range.

b. *spec.* A lens or combination of lenses used in photography.

1841 FOX TALBOT in *Proc. Roy. Soc.* IV. 313 The object lens. **1889** *Harper's Mag.* Jan. 258/1 So thoroughly has this region been set forth by the pen and the pencil and the lens.

2. *Anat.* **a.** = *crystalline lens* (see CRYSTALLINE *a.* 6). **b.** One of the facets of a compound eye.

a. 1719 QUINCY *Lex. Physico-Med.* (1722) s.v. **1806** *Med. Jrnl.* XV. 106 Indistinct vision..can only be remedied by the depression of the lens. **1840** G. ELLIS *Anat.* 96 It is this artery..that is to be avoided when the needle is used to depress the lens. **1870** ROLLESTON *Anim. Life* Introd. 54 Except in Owls and aquatic Birds, the lens is flat.

b. 1868 DUNCAN *Insect World* Introd. 2 Eyes [of insects] composed of many lenses.

3. *Geol.* A body of ore or rock similar in shape to a biconvex lens.

1903 *Bull. U.S. Geol. Survey* No. 213. 113 The principal mines..have revealed valuable ore bodies of two great types, those which occur as lenses, roughly parallel to the bedding, and those which occur in fracture or fissure zones. **1935** *Economist* 21 Dec. 1283/3 Further lenses of valuable ore would be discovered in that section. **1939** *Proc. Prehist. Soc.* V. 40 Towards the top of the ferruginous gravels appears a lens of non-ferruginous, grey, clayey sand. **1969** BENNISON & WRIGHT *Geol. Hist. Brit. Isles* vi. 128 These Lower Palaeozoic rocks occur as discontinuous outcrops or lenses in what has been termed the Meneage Crush Zone... Included lenses may be up to 1 mile in length.

4. *attrib.* and *Comb.*, as (sense 1, 1 b) ***lens aperture, barrel, -board, -holder, mount, -shutter, -tube, -work; lens-like, -shaped*** adjs.; (sense 2) ***lens-capsule, -matter, -sector***; **lens cap**, a cap that fits over the end of a lens tube, used to protect the lens and, in early cameras without shutters, for regulating exposures; **lens coating**, a thin transparent coating applied to a lens to reduce reflection of light at its surface; **lens-eye** = 2 b; **lens-form** = LENTIFORM; **lens hood**, a tube, usually circular in cross-section and with outwardly sloping sides, fitted in front of a lens to shield it from light coming from outside the field of view; **lens louse** *slang* (see quots.); **lensman** = *camera-man* (CAMERA 3 d); **lens paper**, a kind of soft, thin, absorbent paper suitable for wiping lenses; **lens tissue** = *lens paper*; **lens turret**, a mounting fitted to the front of a camera and carrying several lenses, any of which can be brought into use by rotating the mounting.

1916 *Brit. Jrnl. Photogr.* LXIII. 166/2 (*heading*) Some matters concerning *lens apertures. **1958** *Oxford Mail* 19 May 7/4 The length of exposure and the size of the lens aperture are linked to ensure that the right amount of light reaches the film at every shutter speed. **1971** L. B. HAPPÉ *Basic Motion Pict. Technol.* ii. 62 The brightness of the image formed by the lens is determined not only by the diameter of the lens aperture but also the size of the image. **1940** *Chambers's Techn. Dict.* 495/1 **Lens barrel*, the metal tube in which one or more lenses are mounted. **1958** *Newnes Compl. Amat. Photogr.* iv. 60 Camera body—the choice is between folding bellows or extending lens-barrel. **1967** KARCH & BUBER *Offset Processes* v. 143 The lens barrel contains a slot..used to insert filters for color work. **1892** *Photogr. Ann.* II. 289 The most important feature is the novel and convenient mode of attaching the front *lens board to the baseboard. **1941** R. M. ALLEN *Photomicrogr.* ii. 67 Most manufacturers provide some type of fixture, preferably with focusing means incorporated in it, for carrying the lenses on the lens board. **1967** KARCH & BUBER *Offset Processes* v. 143 The lensboard, located directly in front of the copyboard, houses the lens. **1882** *Photogr. at Home: its Appliances & Apparatus for Amateurs* 11 A little shield covered with black velvet..occupies the place of the ordinary *lens cap. **1897** *Sears, Roebuck Catal.* 474/2 The front of the camera can be removed if desired and exposure made with a lens cap. **1965** MRS. L. B. JOHNSON *White House Diary* 17 June (1970) 290, I wanted to be darned sure I didn't lose the lens cap on the camera. **1966** LACOUR & LATHROP *Photo Technol.* iv. 48/2 It should seldom be necessary to clean a lens which has been protected from dust and fingerprints with a lens cap. **1874** G. LAWSON *Dis. Eye* 128 The *lens-capsule may be so tough that the point of the needle will puncture but not lacerate it. **1952** C. B. NEBLETTE *Photogr.* (ed. 5) ii. 48/1 *Lens coatings are a remedial measure and do not entirely remove reflections. **1966** LACOUR & LATHROP *Photo Technol.* iv. 48/2 Finger prints on the lens..are detrimental to the lens coating. **1839–47** TODD *Cycl. Anat.* III. 769/1 The *lens-eyes of insecta. **1787** *Fam. Plants* I. 16 Seeds solitary, *lens-form. **1876** tr. *G. Tissandier's Hist. & Handbk. Photogr.* 223 The ordinary *lens-holder being removed from the front of the camera. **1894** S. H. GAGE *Microscope* (ed. 5) i. 4 (*heading*) Adjustable lens holder with universal joint. **1891** W. E. WOODBURY *Encycl. Photogr.* 405 (*heading*) *Lens screen or hood. **1908** *Brit. Jrnl. Photogr.* LV. 245/1 The lens-hood..has recently revived, owing to the necessity of shading the lens from direct light in the case of anastigmats which possess large aperture. **1955** E. HILLARY *High Adventure* xii. 210, I clipped on [to my camera] the lenshood and ultra-violet filter. **1968** L. A. MANNHEIM tr. *Brandt's Photogr. Lens* xv. 166 Lens hoods not only have to shield the lens against stray light, but also protect it against accidental finger marks and rain or snow. **1836–9** TODD *Cycl. Anat.* II. 960/1 It [i.e. the facet] is convex on its external and internal surface, or *lens-like. **1928** *Amer. Speech* III. 368 Actors who strive for the most advantageous positions are also called '*lens lice'. **1950** J. HALL in *Daily Mail* 24 May, Bane of the news-reel cameraman is what he calls a 'lens louse'. They.. never miss a chance of getting in front of a news-reel camera. **1951** *N.Y. Herald Tribune* 26 Aug. IV. 4/4 It was common to see a Leatherneck *lensman wield a 45-automatic pistol in one hand and a 16-mm. camera in the other, firing both simultaneously at the enemy only a few hundred yards away. **1964** *Punch* 5 Aug. 183/1 He's one of the best lensmen in the business. **1972** I. HAMILTON *Thrill Machine* vi. 27, I held back with the pen and ink men while the lensmen pushed forward to the press barricades. **1874** G. LAWSON *Dis. Eye* 157 In cases where there is some *lens matter enclosed between the anterior and posterior layers of the capsule. **1892** *Photogr. Ann.* II. 43 Unscrew the back combination and use the front alone *in situ*, thus gaining the length of the *lens mount. **1938** H. WINDISCH *New Photo-School* vi. 166 A focusing screen is applied to the lens mount. **1972** HORNE & MARKHAM in A. M. Glauert *Pract. Methods Electron Microsc.* I. II. iii. 354 Optical bench manufacturers make a large number of lens mounts and carriers. **1925** A. F. COLLINS *Amat. Photographer's Handbk.* iv. 61 Dirt that forms on the surfaces [of a lens] in an almost imperceptible film can usually be wiped off with a dry *lens paper, which is a very soft Japanese tissue paper especially made for this

purpose. **1973** *Nature* 27 July 233/1 Each portion [of ovary] was placed on defatted lens paper on a stainless steel mesh grid in a vitreosil dish. **1879** *Rep. St. George's Hosp.* IX. 484 A zone of central opacity in each lens, with the normal *lens-sectors strongly marked therein. **1839** LINDLEY *Introd. Bot.* (ed. 3) 447 *Lens-shaped..; resembling a double convex lens; as the seeds of Amaranthus. **1887** W. PHILLIPS *Brit. Discomycetes* 365 The conical points expand into lens-shaped..discs. **1891** *Anthony's Photogr. Bull.* IV. 158 Your *lens shutter, note book and other trifles are bestowed in your pockets. **1941** A. SUSSMAN *Collins's Amat. Photographer's Handbk.* (rev. ed.) iii. 75 Use some dry *lens tissue, or an old linen handkerchief that has been freshly laundered. **1955** S. C. GILMOUR *Paper* 305 *Lens tissue*, British-made paper of very thin substance and transparent texture, resembling Japanese tissue. Long fibres, great strength for the substance, and extreme absorbency are characteristics. Used for cleaning optical and microscope lenses. **1858** SUTTON & WORDEN *Dict. Photogr.* 260 The diaphragms within the *lens-tube entirely prevent the reflection of light from the inside of the tube. **1890** *Anthony's Photogr. Bull.* III. 198 The hood is..arranged to slide out and in on the *lens tube. **1918** Lens-tube [see HOOD *sb.* 5 m]. **1971** L. B. HAPPÉ *Basic Motion Pict. Technol.* iv. 142 On 8 mm amateur cameras..the lens hood is usually limited to a deep flange extension to the lens tube itself. **1951** R. SPOTTISWOODE *Film & its Techniques* iii. 64 Camera noise readily seeps through a *lens turret and tends to interfere with dialogue recording. **1963** *Movie* July/Aug. 26/3 Brault's insistence on leaving in blank frames as he shifts the lens turret in mid-reel occasionally gets in the way. **1971** L. B. HAPPÉ *Basic Motion Pict. Technol.* x. 311 A lens turret mounting is often preferred for unit lenses and is more convenient for automated operations. **1888** G. M. HOPKINS *Let.* 1 May (1938) 144 Photography proper now is mere scaffolding..a poor bastard art succeeds the *lens-work and disguises what that gives.

Hence **lensed** *a.*, provided with a lens or lenses. **'lensless** *a.*, having no lens or lenses.

1859 SALA *Tw. round Clock* (1861) 274 If you eye him narrowly through the many-lensed lorgnette. **1892** *Illustr. Lond. News* 1 Oct. 431/3 An eye lensed like a microscope, though also lensed like yours and mine. **1899** CAGNEY tr. *Jaksch's Clin. Diagn.* i. (ed. 4) 80 The lensless spectroscope consists of two tubes.

lens (lɛnz), *v.* *Geol.* [f. the sb.] ***to lens out*** (intr.): of a body of rock: to become gradually thinner (along a particular direction) to the point of extinction.

1921 G. H. COX et al. *Field Methods Petroleum Geol.* 11 The effects of irregularities in sands may be considered to be of three types; those in which the sand lenses out entirely, those in which it loses its porosity, and those in which the porous sand continues but is of changing thickness. **1965** G. J. WILLIAMS *Econ. Geol. N.Z.* viii. 108/2 Mining went down to the 500-ft level below which the calcite bodies themselves lens out—as proved by angled diamond-drill-holes.

†**lense**, *v.* *Obs.* [OE. *hlǣnsian*, f. *hlǣne* lean; cf. *clǣnsian* to cleanse.] **a.** *trans.* To make lean; to macerate. **b.** *intr.* To become lean.

a **1000** in Napier *OE. Glosses* 32/1156 *Macero*..ic hlænsiȝe. *c* **1175** *Lamb. Hom.* 147 Mon lenseð his fleis hwenne he him ȝefeð lutel to etene and lesse to drinke. *c* **1200** *Trin. Coll. Hom.* 207 Mannes lichame ihalsneð [*Lamb. MS.* lenseð] iwis, þenne me hine pined mid hunger and mid þurste.

Hence †**'lensing** *vbl. sb.*, macerating.

c **1175** *Lamb. Hom.* 147 Ac he munegeð us an oðer rode to berene þet is inemned *Carnis maceratio* fleises lensing. *c* **1200** *Trin. Coll. Hom.* 207 An oðer [rode]..þat is cleped *Carnis maceracio* þat is lichames hlensing.

†**lensher.** *Obs.* App. early Sc. f. LANDSHARD.

1672 *Sc. Acts Chas. II* (1820) VIII. 139/2 Lenshers, aqueducts..water workes, and others vsefull and necessar for winning and vpholding of the saids coalls & coallhewghs.

lensoid ('lɛnzɔɪd), *a.* [f. LENS + -OID.] = LENTOID *a.*

1930 *Jrnl. Geol.* XXXVIII. 450 There are in effect..two main outcrops: a large lensoid northern one,..and a much thinner southern one. **1965** G. J. WILLIAMS *Econ. Geol. N.Z.* iv. 35/2 The quartz bodies are lensoid, seldom more than 5 ft in thickness, discontinuous longitudinally and overlapping in places. **1973** *Nature* 27 July 215/1 The cherts occur chiefly as intercalations, sometimes of wide lateral extent and sometimes lensoid, between the extrusives.

Lent (lɛnt), *sb.*[1] Forms: 3–5 **leinte, leynte,** 4–6 **lente,** 6– **lent.** [Shortened from LENTEN.]

1. The season of spring. *Obs.* exc. in *Comb.* (see 4).

c **1275** LAY. 30626 þar after com leinte [*c* **1205** leinten] and daȝes gonne longy. **1387** TREVISA *Higden* (Rolls) VI. 107 þe evenes of þe day and of þe nyȝt is ones in þe Lente, and efte in hervest.

2. *Eccl.* The period including 40 weekdays extending from Ash-Wednesday to Easter-eve, observed as a time of fasting and penitance, in commemoration of Our Lord's fasting in the wilderness. †Also ***Clean Lent.***

c **1290** *S. Eng. Leg.* I. 229/352 Fram þulke tyme forto in leinte no lond huy ne i-seiȝe. **1377** LANGL. *P. Pl.* B. XIII. 350 As wel in lente as oute of lente. *c* **1400** A. DAVY *Dreams* 117 On Wedenysday in clene leinte. *c* **1430** *Two Cookery-bks.* 12 An ȝif if it be in lente, lef þe ȝolkys of Eyroun. **1527** *Warden's Acc. Morebath, Devon*, The 2 Sonday in clene Lente. *a* **1548** HALL *Chron., Hen. VIII*, 241 The first Sondaie in Lent, Stephyn Gardiner Bishop of Winchester, preached at Paules crosse. **1592** SHAKS. *Rom. & Jul.* II. iv. 143 An old Hare hoare is very good meat in Lent. **1616** R. C. *Times' Whistle* IV. 1434 Cocus..hath an intent, To curry favour, to dresse meat in Lent. **1769** GRAY in *Corr. with Nicholls* (1843) 87 Palgrave keeps Lent at home, and wants to be asked to break it. **1797–1809** COLERIDGE *Three Graves* xix, Ellen always kept her church All church-days during Lent. **1861** M. PATTISON *Ess.* (1889) I. 46 Many a cargo of salt cod for Lent..was there.

b. An instance of this; the Lent of some specified year.

1387 TREVISA *Higden* (Rolls) VII. 251 But þe nexte Lente [MSS. α and β leynte] þerafter he wente into Normandie. **1538** COVERDALE *N.T., Ded. to Cromwell*, This last lent I dyd with all humblenesse directe an Epistle vnto the kynges most noble grace. **1597** SHAKS. *2 Hen. IV*, II. iv. 376 What is a Ioynt of Mutton, or two, in a whole Lent? **1740** GRAY *Let.* Poems (1775) 78 The diversions of a Florentine Lent. **1842** TENNYSON *St. Sim. Styl.* 179 If it may be, fast Whole Lents, and pray.

c. *transf.* (cf. 3 b) and *fig.*

1598 TOFTE *Alba* (1880) 102 The Carnouale of my sweet Love is past, Now comes the Lent of my long Hate at last. **1599** H. BUTTES *Dyets drie Dinner* A a iij, Spice sweetens White-meats Lent. **1613** PURCHAS *Pilgrimage, Descr. India* (1864) 157 After that weeke of cleane Lent without eating or drinking. **1634** BP. HALL *Charac. Man* (1635) 6 If, in the former, there be a sad Lent of mortification; there is in the latter, a chearfull Easter of our raising and exaltation. **1642** FULLER *Holy & Prof. St.* v. xiii. 408 He is half starv'd in the lent of a long vacation. **1660** MILTON *Free Commw.* Wks. 1851 V. 421 Before so long a Lent of Servitude, they may permit us a little Shroving-time first wherin to speak freely. **1713** SWIFT *Cadenus & Van.* 90 There live with daggled mermaids pent, And keep on fish perpetual lent.

d. *pl.* At Cambridge: The Lent-term boat-races.

1893 *Westm. Gaz.* 27 Feb. 11/2 In the Lents' on Saturday both Jesus and Trinity Hall pursued their victorious career.

†**3.** In extended senses. **a.** A period of forty days, esp. in ***lent of pardon***, an indulgence of forty days.

1483 CAXTON *Gold Leg.* 158b/2 There is seuen yere and seuen lentys of pardon. **1502** ARNOLDE *Chron.* 146 And aboue this is grauntyd xxviij. C. yere of pardon, and the merytis of as many lentis or karyns. **1535** *Godly Primer* Admon. to Rdr., Promising moche grace, and many yeres, dayes, and lentes of pardon.

†**b.** A period of fasting prescribed by any religious system. *Obs.*

c **1380** WYCLIF *Eng. Wks.* (1880) 41 þo holy lenten þat bygynneþ fro þe twelþe day of cristemasse to þe fulle fourti daies. **1555** EDEN *Decades* 99 They haue obserued a longer and sharper lent then euer yowre holinesse inioyned. **1613** PURCHAS *Pilgrimage* (1614) 541 They observe their houres, and two Fasts or Lents. **1653** GREAVES *Seraglio* 143 The Ramazan being ended, which is their day lent. **1718** LADY M. W. MONTAGU *Let. to C'tess [Bristol]* Lett. 1887 I. 241 Their lents..are at least seven months in every year. **1727–41** CHAMBERS *Cycl.* s.v., The antient Latin monks had three Lents; the grand Lent before Easter; another before Christmas, called the Lent of S. Martin; and a third after Whit-sunday, called the Lent of S. John Baptist: each of which consisted of forty days. **1757** HUME *Ess., Nat. Hist. Relig.* (1817) II. 446 The four lents of the Muscovites. **1781** GIBBON *Decl. & F.* xlvii. (1788) IV. 604 Five annual lents, during which both the clergy and laity abstain..even from the taste of wine [etc.].

4. *attrib.* and *Comb.*, as (sense 1) ***lent-corn, -crop, -grain(s; lent-sown*** adj.; (sense 2) ***Lent-diet, -fast, -meat, -provisions, -season, -seed, -sermon, stuff, -time***; †**Lent-cloth**, a cloth hung before images in Lent; **lent-lily**, (*a*) the yellow daffodil, *Narcissus Pseudo-narcissus*; (*b*) *adj.* of the colour of this flower; **lent-rose** = *lent-lily* (*a*); also, in S. Devon, *N. biflorus* (Britten & Holland); **Lent-term** (at the Universities), the term in which Lent falls.

1495–6 in Swayne *Churchw. Acc. Sarum* (1896) 45 Pro anulis pro le *lentecloth coram S. Nich. Ep. iijd., et pro factura eiusdem iiijd. **1552** *Inv. Ch. Goods* (Surtees) 44 One great clothe of canves cauled Lente clothe. **1523** FITZHERB. *Husb.* §148 Vnto the tyme that thou haue sowen agayne thy wynter-corne & thy *lente-corne. **1889** *N.W. Linc. Gloss.*, *Lent-corn*, barley and oats; also beans, if sown in the spring. **1744–50** W. ELLIS *Mod. Husbandm.* II. I. 113 Whether it be a Wheat, or **Lent-Crop*, that is set on the Soils, Rolling is one main Preservative of such a Crop. **1855** MORTON *Cycl. Agric.* II. 721/2 *Breach* or *Lent Crops* (*East Eng.* &c.), all spring crops. **1732** ARBUTHNOT *Rules of Diet* 286 In a *Lent Diet People commonly fall away. **1651** C. CARTWRIGHT *Cert. Relig.* II. 58 And the like also for the different manner of observing the *Lent-fast in respect of the time. **1744–50** W. ELLIS *Mod. Husbandm.* II. I. 55 The two first [sc. Barley and Pease] as well as Oats, etc. are called **Lent-Grains*, as being to be sown about *Lent* time. **1869** *Lonsdale Gloss.*, *Lent-grain*, the spring crops. **1826–7** K. DIGBY *Broadst. Hon.* (1846) II. 364 The early daffodil was *Lent-lily. **1872** TENNYSON *Gareth & Lyn.* 911 A silk pavilion..all Lent-lily in hue. *c* **1200** *Trin. Coll. Hom.* 67 Ete nu *leinte mete and enes o dai. **1483** CAXTON *Gold. Leg.* 375b/1 In aduent he ete neuer but lente mete. **1663–4** PEPYS *Diary* 10 Feb., My wife ..being with my aunt Wight to day to buy *Lent provisions. **1796** W. MARSHALL *W. Eng.* I. 328 *Lent rose..the Narcissus or Daffodil. **1573** BARET *Alv.* L 284 *Lent season, *quadragesima*. **1393** LANGL. *P. Pl.* C. XIII. 190 Lynne-seed and lik-seed and *lente-seedes alle. *a* **1695** WOOD *Ath. Oxon.* (1899) III. 178 And therin doth the Vicechancellour sit, to heare the *Lent-sermons preached. **1795** *Gentl. Mag.* 539/2 The dryness of April and May was against the vegetation of the *Lent-sown seed. **1573** TUSSER *Husb.* lvi. (1878) 37 Take shipping or ride *Lent stuffe to prouide. **1861** T. HUGHES *Tom Brown at Oxf.* I. iv. 68 We're only half through *Lent term. **1950** *Cambridge 1950* (Varsity) 8 The Cardinal's Ball ..seems to have taken over the position of chief social event of the Lent term from the now banned Granta Ball. **1974** *Univ. Exeter Calendar 1974–5* 4 Wed. 8 [January] Lent term begins. **1721** AMHERST *Terræ Fil.* No. 42 (1754) 223 These disputations..are so order'd, that they last all *Lent-time.

†**lent**, *sb.*[2] *Obs.* Also **lente.** [ad. L. *lent-em*, *lens*.] *collect. sing.* Lentils.

1382 WYCLIF *Ezek.* iv. 9 Take thou to thee whete, and barli, and bene, and lent. **1388** —— *2 Kings* xxiii. 11 Forsothe there was a feeld ful of lente.

lent, *sb.*[3] *Obs.* exc. *dial.* Also 5 **lente,** 7 **lenth,** 9 **length.** [f. *lent*, pa. pple. of LEND.] The action of lending; loan.

14.. in Arnolde *Chron.* 281 That for yᵉ most part the conuenable seson of themployinge of the good lente was passed. **1646** *Mass. Col. Rec.* (1853) II. 163 Maior Nehemiah Bourne..is granted ye lent of one drake from Dorchestr. **1682–3** *Hartland Ch. Acc.* (Hartland Gloss.), Pd for the lenth of two sarges 1*s.* 6*d.* *a* **1704** DE LA PRYME *Diary* (Surtees) 163 Thanking him exceedingly for the lent therof. **1740** TWELLS *Life Pocock* (1816) I. 207 Upon the lent of Mr. Pocock's copy. **1797–1805** S. & HT. LEE *Canterb. T.* III. 456 Owens offered him the lent of his scythe. **1883** *Hampsh. Gloss.*, *Lent, length*, the loan of a thing.

lent (lɛnt), *a.* Also **lente.** [a. F. *lent*, ad. L. *lentus*.]

†**1.** Slow, sluggish; said esp. of a fever, a fire. *Obs.*

14.. in *Lanfranc's Cirurg.* (1893) 297 *note*, Boile hit with a lente fyre. **1590** BARROUGH *Meth. Phisick* 392 Make a distillation with a lente and soft fire. **1610** B. JOHNSON *Alch.* III. ii, We must now encrease Our fire to *Ignis ardens*, we are past *Fimus equinus*, *Balnei*, *Cineris*, And all those lenter heates. **1658** BAILLIE in Z. Boyd *Zion's Flowers* (1855) App. 36/2 A lent feaver and defluxion. **1662** —— *Lett. & Jrnls.* (Bannatyne Club) III. 433 The last trick they have fallen on, to usurp the Magistracie, is..to get the deacons..created on their side;..but this lent-way does no satisfie. **1732** ARBUTHNOT *Rules of Diet* (1736) 342 A continual Lent-Fever, with Rigors invading with uncertain Periods.

†**b.** quasi-*sb.* Slowness, delay. *Obs.*

c **1435** *Torr. Portugal* 2561 Withoute lent, They wesh and to mete went.

2. *Mus.* = LENTO. Now *rare.*

1724 [see LENTO]. **1726** BAILEY, *Lent* [in *Musick Books*] denotes a slow Movement, and signifies much the same as Largo. **1876** STAINER & BARRETT *Dict. Mus. Terms*, *Lent* (F.), Slow, *lento.* **1882** JAS. WALKER *Janet to Auld Reekie*, etc. 31 Wha played like thee a lente solo, Reel or Strathspey.

lent (lɛnt), *ppl. a.* Also 4–5 **lant(e.** [pa. pple. of LEND *v.*[2]] In senses of the vb. LEND. (Formerly often used where we should now say 'borrowed'.)

13.. *S. Erkenwolde* 192 in Horstm. *Altengl. Leg.* (1881) 270 He [the dead man] dryues owte wordes þurghe sum lant goste, lyfe of hyme þat al redes. *c* **1420** *Sir Amadace* (Camd.) xxxviii, For gud his butte a lante lone, Sum tyme men haue hit, sum tyme none. **1560** BECON *New Catech.* Wks. 1564 I. 402 Examples..which may assertain vs of this liberality and lent good wil of God toward us. **1619** C. BROOKE *Ghost Rich. III*, H 3, In happy howre, I pai'd th' arrerages of his lent Good. **1631** A. CRAIGE *Pilgr. & Heremite* 5 When pale Ladie Luna, with her lent light, Through the dawning of the Day was driven to depart.

†**lent**, *v.* *Obs.* [f. *lent*, obs. pa. pple. of LEAN *v.*[1]] *intr.* To lean.

1658 A. FOX *Wurtz' Surg.* v. 363 A Child overturning himself or lenting backward..may soon get hurt.

lent, obs. pa. t. and pple. of LEAN *v.*[1]

-lent, *suffix*, occurring in adjs. from Latin. The L. ending *-lentus* (which in some words has an alternative form *-lens*) has approximately the sense of the Eng. -FUL. It is believed to have been orig. a compound, formed by the addition of the suffix *-ento-*, *-ent-* (cf. *cruentus* gory) to derivative stems in *-lo-* or *-li-*; these stems, however, have not been preserved (exc. in the case of *gracilis* slender, whence *gracilentus* †gracilent), and in classical times *-lentus* was a productive suffix. Normally it is preceded by *u*, as in *turbulentus* turbulent, *pulverulentus* pulverulent (see -ULENT); but there are a few cases in which the stem-vowel of the primary sb. appears, as *pestilentus* (*-lens*) pestilent, f. *pestis* plague, and some which have an unexplained *o*, as *violentus* (*-lens*) violent, f. *vi-s* force (cf. *violāre* to violate), *sanguinolentus* bloody, f. *sanguin-*, *sanguis* blood.

†**'lentally.** *Her.* *Obs.* [Origin and meaning obscure.] (See quots.)

1486 *Bk. St. Albans, Her.* b iij b, Lentalli is calde in armys whan yᵉ cootarmure is Endentid with .ij. dyuerse colowris in the berde of the cootarmure. **1562** LEIGH *Armorie* (1597) 79 He beareth Ermine and Ermines parted per Fesse dented. This is called Lentally. **1586** FERNE *Blaz. Gentrie* 208 The second manner of Endentelies, was called Lentally, and that was, an indenting of the coate with two diuers cullors in the bend of the coate-armor.

‖**lentamente** (lenta'mente), *adv.* *Mus.* [It., f. *lento* slow.] Slowly, in slow time.

1762 STERNE *Tr. Shandy* VI. xi, What Yorick could mean by the words *lentamente*,—*tenutè* [sic],—*grave*,—and sometimes *adagio*,—as applied to theological compositions ..I dare not venture to guess. **1876** in STAINER & BARRETT *Dict. Mus. Terms*, *Lentamente.*

‖**lentando** (len'tando). *Mus.* [It. pr. pple. of *lentare* to become slow.] A direction to the performer to play more and more slowly.

1854 J. W. MOORE *Encycl. Mus.*, *Lentando*, a word indicating that the notes over which it is written are to be played, from the first to the last, with increasing slowness.

†**'Lented**, *ppl. a. Obs. rare*⁻¹. [f. LENT *sb.*¹ + -ED.] That shows traces of Lent or fasting; emaciated.

1594 WILLOBIE *Avisa* (1880) 94 Well met friend Harry, what's the cause You looke so pale with Lented cheeks?

Lenten ('lɛnt(ə)n), *sb.* and *a.* Forms: α. 1 lencten, leng(c)ten, lenten, -on, 2 læng-, lengten, 2–3 leinten, 3 læncten, *Orm.* lenntenn, 4 lentene, -in, -oun, 4–5 lentone, 5 lentyn(ne, 5–7 lenton, 4– lenten. β. *Sc.* and *north.* 4 lenteryne, lentrine, 4–5 lentryn(e, 4–6, 9 lentrin, lentrone, 5 lenterne, lentyren, 6 lantern, lentern, lenterane, lentran, lentren(e, lentroun, 6–7 lentron. [OE. *lęncten* str. masc. corresponds to MDu. *lentin*, OHG. *lengizin* (*mânôth*), shortened *lenzin*: app. a derivative or a compound of the shorter synonym which appears as MLG., MDu., Du. *lente* fem., OHG. *langiz*, *langaz* str. masc. (MHG. *langez*, mod. Ger. dialects *langis*, etc.), also OHG. *lenzo* wk. masc. (MHG. *lenze*, mod.G. *lenz*). The shorter form (? OTeut. type **laŋgito-*, **laŋgiton-*) seems to be a derivative of **laŋgo-* LONG *a.*, and may possibly have reference to the lengthening of the days as characterizing the season of spring. It is doubtful whether the ending of the longer form is a mere derivative suffix, or whether it represents an OTeut. **tino-* day, cognate with *-*tîno-* in Goth. *sinteins* daily, and with Skr. *dina*, OSl. *dĭnĭ*, Lith. *dënà* day.

The ecclesiastical sense of the word is peculiar to Eng.; in the other Teut. langs. the only sense is 'spring'. As an ordinary sb. *lenten* has been superseded by the shortened form LENT *sb.*¹; but the longer form has survived in attributive use, and is now apprehended as an adj., as if f. *lent* + -EN⁴.

With the β. forms cf. the ONorthumbrian *éfern* = WS. *æfen*, *fæstern* = *fæsten*, *wéstern* = *wésten*.]

†**A.** As a separate *sb. Obs.*; superseded by LENT *sb.*¹

1. Spring; = LENT *sb.*¹ 1.

c **1000** *Sax. Leechd.* II. 148 Nis nan blodlæstid swa god swa on foreweardne lencten. *a* **1100** *Gerefa* in *Anglia* (1886) IX. 262 On længtene erȝian and impian. *c* **1200** ORMIN 8891 Illke Lenntenn forenn þeȝȝ Till Ȝerrsalæmess chesstre Aȝȝ atte te Passkemessedaȝȝ. *c* **1205** [see LENT *sb.*¹ 1]. *a* **1310** in Wright *Lyric P.* 43 Lenten ys come with love to toune.

2. = LENT *sb.*¹ 2. Also ***Clean Lenten***. ***Lenten's day***: ? Easter-day.

α. *a* **1023** WULFSTAN *Hom.* lviii. (Napier) 305 þe ma, þe man mot on lenctene.. flæsces brucan. *a* **1225** *Ancr. R.* 70 Holdeð silence.. iðe leinten þreo dawes. **1340** *Ayenb.* 175 Efterward ine one time þanne in an-oþre ase in lenten oþer in ane heȝe messedaye. **1389** in *Eng. Gilds* (1870) 106 Ye secounde [morwespeche] shal bene ye first sunday of lentone. **1393** LANGL. *P. Pl.* C. XIV. 81 To lene ne to lere ne lentenes to faste. **14..** *Customs Malton* in *Surtees Misc.* (1888) 60 Exceppyd Burgese þᵗ sellys heryng in Lentyn. *a* **1450** MYRC 75 Leste he forȝet by lentenes day [*v.r.* ester day]. **1492** *Bury Wills* (Camden) 74, I wole that the seyd prest abyde in Rome alle Lenton. **1513** BRADSHAW *St. Werburge* I. 2083 Truly for to fast the holy tyme of Lenton. **1553** BECON *Reliques of Rome* (1563) 244 The fyrst Sonday in cleane lenton.

β. **1375** BARBOUR *Bruce* x. 815 Fra the lenteryne, that is to say, Quhill forrouth the Saint Iohnnis mes. *c* **1375** *Sc. Leg. Saints* xviii. (*Egipciane*) 1135 þe next lentryn, quhen begonnyn was þe fastine. *c* **1425** WYNTOUN *Cron.* VIII. xvii. 2698 At Sayntandrewys than bad he, And held hys Lentryen in reawté. *c* **1470** HENRYSON *Mor. Fab.* IX. (*Wolf & Fox*) viii, ' Schir', said the fox, 'it is lenterne, ye see; I can not fische'. **1500–20** DUNBAR *Poems* xii. 1 Off Lentren in the first mornyng. **1536** BELLENDEN *Cron. Scot.* (1821) I. xxiv, Passand, in the time of Lentroun, throw the seis Mediterrane, ay selland thair fische. **1562** WINȜET *Cert. Tractates* iii. Wks. 1888 I. 27 The ȝeirlie abstinence of fourty dayis afore Pasche, callit Lentren. **1637–50** ROW *Hist. Kirk* (Wodrow Soc.) 7 On a Sabbath day in the tyme of Lentron.

B. *attrib.* and as *adj.*

1. Of or pertaining to Lent, observed or taking place in Lent, as in ***Lenten day***, ***discipline***, ***fast***, ***indult***, ***lecture***, ***pastoral***, ***penance***, ***sermon***, ***tide***, ***time***.

c **1020** *Rule St. Benet* xli. (Logeman) 73 On længtene fæsten oð eastran. *c* **1050** *Byrhtferth's Handboc* in *Anglia* (1885) VIII. 312 Uer ys lengten tima. *c* **1175** *Lamb. Hom.* 25 In leinten time uwilc mon gað to scrifte. *a* **1300** *Cursor M.* 12921 Til he had fasten his lententide. **1532** MORE *Confut. Tindale* Wks. 514/1 By these tradicions haue we the holy Lenton faste. **1563** WINȜET *Four Score Thre Quest.* Wks. 1888 I. 127 Quhy obeyt ȝe nocht ȝour selfis the last lentrene tyme ȝour magistratis. *a* **1572** KNOX *Hist. Ref.* Wks. 1846 I. 46 Sermones hie had tawght befoir the haill Lentrantyde preceding. **1610** WILLET *Hexapla Dan.* 39 Pintus vpon this example groundeth the lenten-fast of 40. daies. **1628** W. PEMBLE *Worthy Receiv. Lord's Supper* 16 As Popish Postillers and Preachers doe in their Lenton Sermons. **1638** SHIRLEY *Duke's Mistress* II. C 4, To read morall virtue, And lenton Lectures to you. **1644** MILTON *Areop.* (Arb.) 42 And perhaps it was the same politick drift that the Divell whipt St. Jerom in a lenten dream, for reading Cicero. **1703** MAUNDRELL *Journ. Jerus.* (1732) 75 This being the day in which their Lenten disciplines expir'd. **1812** BYRON *Ch. Har.* II. lxxviii, Yet mark their mirth—ere lenten days begin. **1876** SPURGEON *Commenting* 94 To listen to these sermons must have afforded a suitable Lenten penance to those who went to church to hear them. **1901** *Edin. Rev.* Apr. 440 The Lenten Pastoral Letters of the Catholic Bishops have appeared.

2. Such as is appropriate to Lent; hence of provisions, diet, etc., such as may be used in Lent, meagre; of clothing, expression of countenance, etc., mournful-looking, dismal.

1577–87 HOLINSHED *Chron.* II. *Descr. Scot.* 7/2 For the Lenten prouision of such nations as lie vpon the Levant seas. **1601** SHAKS. *Twel. N.* I. v. 9 A good lenton answer. **1602** —— *Ham.* II. ii. 329 To thinke, my Lord, if you delight not in Man, what Lenton entertainment the Players shall receiue from you. **1613** BEAUM. & FL. *Honest Man's Fort.* IV. i, Who can reade In thy pale face, dead eye, or lenten shute, The liberty thy ever giving hand Hath bought for others. **1660–61** PEPYS *Diary* 10 Mar., Dined at home on a poor Lenten dinner of colewurts and bacon. **1687** DRYDEN *Hind & P.* III. 27 Meanwhile she.. with a lenten salad cooled her blood. **1722** *Prol. to Steele's Conscious Lovers*, Believe me 'tis a Lean, a Lenten Dish. **1745** WESLEY *Wks.* (1872) I. 489 He was welcome.. if he could live on our lenten fare. **1750** CARTE *Hist. Eng.* II. 702 There were large quantities of Lenten food, particularly herrings. **1840** BARHAM *Ingol. Leg.* Ser. I. *St. Nicholas* xiv, His lenten fare now let me share. **1855** BROWNING *Twins* v, For Dabitur's lenten face No wonder if Date rue.

3. Special combs. and collocations: †**Lenten-chaps**, contemptuously applied to a person with a lean visage; †**Lenten-cloth** = *Lent-cloth* (LENT *sb.*¹ 4); **Lenten-corn**, corn sown about Lent; **Lenten-faced** *a.*, lean and dismal of countenance; **Lenten fig**, †(*a*) a dried fig; (*b*) *dial.* a raisin; **Lenten-grain** = *Lenten-corn*; **Lenten-kail** *Sc.*, broth made without meat; **Lenten lily** *rare* = *lent-lily* (LENT *sb.*¹ 4); **Lenten man** *nonce-wd.*, an observer of Lent; **Lenten pie**, a pie containing no meat; **Lenten rose**, a variety of *Helleborus orientalis*, blooming in late winter and early spring; †**Lenten stuff**, provisions suitable for Lent; †**Lenten top**, some kind of toy, ? used at Shrovetide; **Lenten-veil** = *lenten-cloth* (*Cent. Dict.* 1889).

1622 FLETCHER *Sp. Curate* v. ii, I'll have my swindge upon thee; Sirha! Rascall! You *lenten Chaps, you that lay sick, and mockt me. **1485** *Inv.* in J. M. Cowper *Churchw. Acc. St. Dunstan's, Canterbury* xii, j *Lentyncloth called a vayle. **1546–7** in Swayne *Churchw. Acc. Sarum* (1896) 274, vij yardes of Oscon brigges for to make Seynt Thomas a lenton' clothe at iiijd the yarde. **14..** *Tretyce* in *W. of Henley's Husb.* (1890) 44 *Lenten corne as.. otys pecys barly & soyche oþer graynes. **1901** *Times* 11 Feb. 3/1 Warm seed-beds for Lenten corn are likely to be the exception. **1604** T. M. *Black Bk.* C 1 b, Hee.. was conducted through two or three hungry roomes.. by a *Lenten faced Fellow. **1611** COTGR., *Figue de Caresme*, a drie fig, a *Lenten fig. **1669** WORLIDGE *Syst. Agric.* (1681) 266 This is a principal Seed-month for such they usually call *Lenten-Grain. **1805** A. SCOTT *Lentrin Kail* Poems 39 (Jam.) O *lentrin kail, meed of my younger days. **1820** SCOTT *Abbot* xiv, Monks.. are merriest .. when they sup beef-brewis for lenten-kail. **1896** A. E. HOUSMAN *Shropshire Lad* xxix, And there's the *Lenten lily That.. dies on Easter day. **1698** M. LISTER *Journ. Paris* (1699) 21 And the Flesh Eaters will ever defend themselves, if not beat the *Lenten Men. **1592** SHAKS. *Rom. & Jul.* II. iv. 139 No Hare sir; vnlesse a Hare sir in a *Lenten pie. **1884** J. WOOD *Hardy Perennials* 137 (*heading*) Helleborus Orientalis... Sometimes also called the *Lenten Rose, as it may often be seen in flower during Lent. [**1897** S. HIBBERD *Familiar Garden Flowers* I. 35 As the trumpet daffodils are called 'Lent lilies', so the spring flowering hellebores are called 'Lent roses'.] **1900** W. D. DRURY *Bk. Gardening* x. 330 Equally deserving of praise are the Lenten Roses (*H. orientalis*), whose flowers embrace all the shades of rose and purple, as well as white and cream. **1948** P. M. SYNGE *Flowers in Winter* 57 Lenten Roses.. always look well in a mixed winter bowl of flowers. **1970** C. LLOYD *Well-Tempered Garden* v. 378 The main flush of blossom from Lenten roses is borne from February till April. **1494** FABYAN *Chron.* VII. 638 *Lentyn stuffe for yᵉ vytaylynge of hyr hoost. *a* **1548** HALL *Chron.*, *Hen. VI* (1809) 147 The most part of the carriage was heryng & Lenten stuffe. **1630** J. TAYLOR (Water P.) *Praise Cleane Linen* Wks. II. 169/1 Round like a whirligigge or *lenten Top.

Lenterane, -eryne, Lenterne: see LENTEN.

lenth(e, obs. form of LENGTH.

lentic ('lɛntɪk), *a. Ecol.* [f. L. *lentus* slow, calm + -IC.] = LENITIC *a.*

1935 P. S. WELCH *Limnology* ii. 13 The lentic environments, sometimes known as the standing-water series, include all forms of inland water (lakes, ponds, swamps, and their various intergrades) in which the water motion is not that of a continuous flow in a definite direction. **1940** L. H. HYMAN *Invertebrates* I. iii. 80 Fresh-water habitats classify as lentic or standing-water bodies: lake-pond-swamp series, and lotic, or running-water formations. .. Among the smaller lentic environments, such as pools, ditches, ponds, and swamps, the animals are practically all littoral and benthonic. **1960** N. POLUNIN *Introd. Plant Geogr.* xv. 498 The stalks of inhabitants of swift currents tend to be much shorter than those of their lentic relatives.

lenticel ('lɛntɪsɛl). [ad. mod.L. *lenticella* (De Candolle, F. *lenticelle*), dim. f. *lent-em*, *lens* lentil: see LENS *sb.*]

1. *Bot.* A lenticular corky spot on young bark, corresponding to one of the epidermal stomata.

1870 BENTLEY *Bot.* 61. **1875** BENNETT & DYER *Sachs' Bot.* 91 Lenticels are a peculiarity of cork-forming Dicotyledons.

2. *Anat.* A lenticular gland.

1888 in *Syd. Soc. Lex.*

Hence **lenti'cellate** *a.*, producing lenticels; having corky spots on the bark.

1855 MAYNE *Expos. Lex.*, *Lenticellatus*,.. lenticellate. **1870** HOOKER *Stud. Flora* 174 *Viburnum Opulus*... Guelder-rose.. branches slender, lenticellate.

lentick(e, obs. form of LENTISK.

lenticle ('lɛntɪk(ə)l). *Geol.* [ad. L. *lenticula* (see LENTICULAR *a.* and *sb.*).] A lentil (sense 5) or a lenticular piece of rock.

1898 J. E. MARR *Princ. Stratigr. Geol.* iv. 35 The lenticles will be wider in a direction at right angles to that of the strike. **1902** *Encycl. Brit.* XXVIII. 654/2 Lenticles or eyes of uncrushed diorite may be traced. **1930** [see HORNBLENDITE]. **1931** CISSARZ & JONES *German-Eng. Geol. Terminol.* 179 Gash veins.. are usually of small lateral and vertical extent, in the form of small lenticles.

lenticular (lɛn'tɪkjʊlə(r)), *a.* and *sb.* [ad. late L. *lenticulāris*, f. *lenticula*, dim. of *lent-*, *lens* lentil: see LENS *sb.*. Cf. F. *lenticulaire*.]

A. *adj.*

1. a. Having the form of a lens or of a lentil; resembling a lens or lentil in form; double convex.

1658 ROWLAND *Moufet's Theat. Ins.* Ep. Ded., Lenticular optick Glasses of crystal. **1691** RAY *Creation* II. (1692) 24 The Crystalline Humour, which is of a lenticular Figure. **1777** LIGHTFOOT *Flora Scot.* II. 1049 The lenticular seed-vessels white. **1811** PINKERTON *Petral.* I. 521 They have all a lenticular form very much flattened. **1830** R. KNOX *Béclard's Anat.* 46 Hewson.. found the red particles of the human blood to be lenticular. **1845** LINDLEY *Sch. Bot.* viii. (1858) 151 It [duckweed] consists of lenticular floating fronds. **1867–77** G. F. CHAMBERS *Astron.* I. vii. 93 The Zodiacal Light is a peculiar nebulous light of a conical or lenticular form. **1875** BENNETT & DYER *Sachs' Bot.* 58 Lenticular grains (*e.g.* in the endosperm of wheat) have a lenticular nucleus.

b. Special collocations: **lenticular bed** *Geol.*, 'a bed which thins away in all directions' (Green *Phys. Geol.* 1877); **lenticular bone** = the orbicular bone (*Syd. Soc. Lex.* 1888); †**lenticular fever**, a fever attended with an eruption of small red pimples (Worc. 1860 citing Dunglison); **lenticular ganglion** = *ciliary ganglion* (see CILIARY); **lenticular gland**, (*a*) = LENTICEL 1; (*b*) one of the lentiform mucous follicles at the base of the tongue; **lenticular instrument**, **knife**, a scraper used in osteotomy; **lenticular loop**, a set of fibres that pass outward beneath the optic thalamus through the internal capsule; **lenticular nucleus**, the lower of the two grey nuclei of the *corpus striatum*; **lenticular ore** (see quot. 1862); **lenticular process**, a process on the incus of a mammal; **lenticular stereoscope** (see quot. 1869).

1849 MURCHISON *Siluria* viii. 176 Including some *lenticular beds of conglomerates. **1793** YOUNG in *Phil. Trans.* LXXXIII. 174 The *lenticular ganglion. **1840** G. V. ELLIS *Anat.* 94 The ophthalmic or lenticular ganglion, a small roundish-shaped body, is redder in colour in one subject than in another. **1835** LINDLEY *Introd. Bot.* (1839) 67 *Lenticular glands are brown oval spots found upon the bark of many plants. **1672** WISEMAN *Wounds* I. ix. 95 This is to be done by the *Lenticular instrument made for that purpose. **1846** BRITTAN tr. *Malgaigne's Man. Oper. Surg.* 167 The disc of bone having been removed, and the edges levelled with a *lenticular knife. **1899** *Allbutt's Sys. Med.* VI. 501 That degeneration of the central link of the bulbar nuclei associated with symmetrical lesions of the cortex.. and in particular of the outer segment of the *lenticular nucleus. **1862** DANA *Man. Geol.* 234 Beds of red argillaceous iron-ore, called *lenticular ore, from the small flattened grains which compose it. **1852** *Phil. Mag.* III. 17 (*heading*) The *lenticular stereoscope. **1869** TYNDALL *Notes Lect. Light* 31 The instrument most used by the public is the Lenticular Stereoscope of Sir David Brewster. In it the two projections are combined by means of two half lenses with their edges turned inwards.

2. a. Of or pertaining to a lens; employing a lens or lenses.

1875 BEDFORD *Sailor's Pocket Bk.* v. (ed. 2) 132 Its consumption of oil and stores.. is not more than that of the lenticular light. **1903** *Sci. Amer.* 7 Feb. 98/2 The lenses revolve at a given speed.. proportioned to the diameter of the illuminant and the lenticular apparatus. **1961** *Listener* 26 Oct. 670/1 The first lenticular light-house.

b. Of or pertaining to the (crystalline) lens of the eye.

1822–44 *Good's Study Med.* (ed. 4) III. 166 The most frequent species of lenticular cataract is that called hard or firm. **1879** *St. George's Hosp. Rep.* IX. 493 Tension of the left eye, in which there was commencing lenticular opacity.

3. *Photogr.* **a.** Embossed with minute lenses, as ***lenticular film***, a film having the non-emulsion surface formed into minute lenses (usually cylindrical lenses, giving a corrugated pattern), so that two or more images (as of different primary colours to make up a colour photograph) can be interspersed on the same area of film.

1934 *Photogr. Jrnl.* LXXIV. 206/1 The list of patents relating to the duplicating of lenticular films grows. **1950** A. W. JUDGE *Stereoscopic Photogr.* (ed. 3) xvii. 297 A more recent method of making Lenticular stereograms.. employs

a lenticular screen, made up of contiguous cylindrical-type lenses, of very small width, placed in front of the sensitive emulsion. **1962** W. G. HYZER *Engin. & Scientific High-Speed Photogr.* i. 42 A lenticular plate, comprised of an array of spherical lenslets, is employed to produce a corresponding array of spots on the photo-sensitive film. A primary lens having an aperture of $f/6\cdot3$ is used to project the image of the event onto the front surface of the lenticular plate, whereupon each individual lenslet converges the image rays intercepted by its surface onto a tiny spot at the focal plane. Sequential images may be obtained by producing relative motion between the lenticular plate and the photographic emulsion. **1966** R. J. Ross *Television Film Engin.* xi. 445 A method of recording on 35 mm lenticular film was at one time employed by the National Broadcasting Company. **1967** *Electronics* 6 Mar. 79/1 (Advt.), The tube's light output is 30,000 foot lamberts, which results in a light level of 15-foot lamberts on a 3′ × 4′ lenticular screen.

　b. Applied to a method of colour photography using a film with cylindrical lenticulations and filters with bands of the primary colours parallel to the lenticulations during exposure and projection.

　1936 R. M. FANSTONE *Colour Photogr.* xvii. 157 (*heading*) Lenticular colour photography. **1942** C. B. NEBLETTE *Photogr.* (ed. 4) xxxii. 797 The Lenticular process is essentially a screen method in which the screen is formed optically on the emulsion during exposure. **1964** E. S. BOMBACK *Man. Colour Photogr.* iii. 56 The first commercial film based on the lenticular process was marketed by Kodak in 1928 as 16 mm. cine film . . called Kodacolor.

　4. *Comb.*, as *lenticular-shaped*.

　1835 POE *Adv. Hans Pfaall* Wks. 1864 I. 17 The lenticular-shaped phenomenon . . called the zodiacal light. **1879** *Cassell's Techn. Educ.* IV. 63/2 Filled up with lenticular shaped blocks. **1884** F. J. BRITTEN *Watch & Clockm.* 191 These pendulums have generally lenticular shaped bobs.

　† B. *sb. Obs.*

　a. A lenticular glass or lens. **b.** = A lenticular knife (see A. 1 b).

　1658 tr. *Porta's Nat. Magic* XVII. 368 A Convex Lenticular kindleth fire most violently. **1758** J. S. tr. *Le Dran's Observ. Surg.* (1771) 68 We . . contented ourselves with removing some Asperities at the Circumference of the Fracture with the Lenticular. **1802** *Med. Jrnl.* VIII. 484 The Lenticular is an instrument, apparently better adapted to its intent, than experience can allow to be the case.

lenticularity (lɛntɪkjuˈlærɪtɪ). [f. LENTICULAR *a.* + -ITY.] Lenticular form or quality.

　1912 E. H. C. CRAIG *Oil-Finding* viii. 141 Many of the discrepancies between prediction and results nowadays are attributed to lenticularity of the oil-bearing strata. **1925** A. BEEBY-THOMPSON *Oil-Field Explor. & Devel.* I. iv. 111 No cautious operators fail to appreciate the importance of lenticularity and lateral variation of sands. **1928** *Bull. Amer. Assoc. Petroleum Geologists* XII. 248 Lenticularity is a characteristic feature of the Lower Pico beds. **1965** G. J. WILLIAMS *Econ. Geol. N.Z.* xix. 345/1 Lenticularity of the sands may have prevented up-dip migration of the oil, although a slight arching of a 4° south-westerly dip may have assisted.

lenˈticularly, *adv.* [f. LENTICULAR *a.* and *sb.* + -LY[1].] In a lenticular manner; after the fashion of a lens.

　1833 HERSCHEL *Astron.* xii. 407 It is manifestly in the nature of a thin lenticularly-formed atmosphere, surrounding the sun.

lenticulated (lɛnˈtɪkjuleɪtɪd), *a. Photogr.* [f. LENTICUL(E + -AT(E[3] + -ED[1].] = LENTICULAR *a.* 3 a.

　1925 *Brit. Jrnl. Photogr.* LXXII. 65/2 (*heading*) Lenticulated films for colour cinematography. **1950** A. W. JUDGE *Stereoscopic Photogr.* (ed. 3) xvii. 296 The positive (print or transparency) is viewed through a similar lenticulated screen to that used for the negative. **1970** R. J. ROSS *Color Film for Color Television* xv. 147 (*heading*) Lenticulated film systems using black-and-white emulsions on a specially processed base material.

lenticulation (lɛntɪkjuˈleɪʃən). *Photogr.* [f. LENTICUL(E + -ATION.] **a.** The condition of being lenticulated. **b.** Each of the minute lenses of a lenticular film.

　1916 *Brit. Jrnl. Photogr.* LXIII. 117/2 It is known to obtain the lenticulation of such films by rolling them at a suitable temperature between a smooth cylinder and a cylinder carrying in intaglio the engraving of the embossing to be formed on the film. **1932** *Discovery* Dec. 383/1 If the embossed lenticular film is copied on another embossed film, the lenticulations, being so minute, give rise to interference or 'watering', which causes grave defects in the quality of the copy. **1975** *Movie Maker* Feb. 87/2 Many of these materials have a very bright surface with a whiter-than-white look . . , and have some type of surface texture in the form of diamond shaped lenticulations or similar. *Ibid.* 90 (Advt.), 'Hi-Flect' Blankana-White with the unique hexagonal lenticulation.

lenticule (ˈlɛntɪkjuːl). [ad. L. *lenticula* lentil.] **a.** A lentil-shaped body.

　1884 in OGILVIE.

　b. *Photogr.* A minute lens of a lenticular film; = LENTICULATION b.

　1942 H. C. COLTON in C. B. Neblette *Photogr.* (ed. 4) xxxii. 799 Kodacolor film contained about 600 lenticules per inch. **1966** R. J. Ross *Television Film Engin.* xi. 445 A banded color filter acted on the light passing through the camera lens, with the bands parallel to the lenticules, producing three color separation records on a single frame of film.

lenticulite (lɛnˈtɪkjulaɪt). [f. L. *lenticul-a* (see LENTICULAR) + -ITE.] A fossil shell of a lenticular form.

　1848 in CRAIG. Hence in later Dicts.

lentiform (ˈlɛntɪfɔːm), *a.* [f. L. *lent-*, *lens* lentil + -(I)FORM.] Having the form of a lentil or of a lens.

　1706 PHILLIPS (ed. Kersey), *Lentiform Prominences.* **1830** LINDLEY *Nat. Syst. Bot.* 165 Seeds lentiform, pendulous. **1850** H. MILLER *Footpr. Creat.* (1874) 337 The form of the eye-orbit . . was lentiform in the Coccosteus.

lentigerous (lɛnˈtɪdʒərəs), *a.* [f. L. *lenti-*, *lens* + -ger- carry + -OUS.] Having a crystalline lens; said of the eyes of some molluscs.

　1883 E. R. LANKESTER in *Encycl. Brit.* XVI. 680/2 The two lines of development of the Molluscan eye . . the punctigerous and the lentigerous. **1889** in *Century Dict.*

lentiginose (lɛnˈtɪdʒɪnəus), *a.* [f. as next + -OSE.] (See quot.)

　1866 *Treas. Bot., Lentiginose*, covered with minute dots, as if dusted. [Also in mod. Dicts.]

lentiginous (lɛnˈtɪdʒɪnəs), *a.* Also 9 lentigenous. [f. L. *lentigin-*, *lentigo* + -OUS.] Full of freckles; affected with lentigo. Also *absol.*

　1597 A. M. *Guillemeau's Fr. Chirurg.* 52/1 Of the lentiginouse, theire bloode is to sharpe or tarte. **1681** in BLOUNT *Glossogr.* **1755** in JOHNSON. **1880** GRAY *Struct. Bot.* 418/2. **1888** in *Syd. Soc. Lex.*

‖lentigo (lɛnˈtaɪgəu). Pl. **lentigines** (lɛnˈtɪdʒɪniːz). [L. f. *lent-em*, *lens* lentil.] A freckle or pimple; now usually *collect.* for an affection of the skin (see quot. 1876).

　*c*1400 *Lanfranc's Cirurg.* 190 Lentigines ben purgid wiþ a strong purgacioun. **1706** PHILLIPS (ed. Kersey), *Lentigo*, a Pimple, or Freckle; a small red Spot in the Face, or other Part, resembling a Lentil. **1842** BURGESS *Man. Dis. Skin* 244 Lentigo generally occurs in persons with a fine, white skin. **1876** DUHRING *Dis. Skin* 336 Lentigo consists in a pigment deposit, characterized by small, pin-head or pea-sized, yellowish or yellowish-brown spots, occurring for the most part about the face and the backs of the hands.

lentil (ˈlɛntɪl). Forms: 4-6, 8 lentille, 5 lentylle, 6 lintell, lyntell(e, 6-8 lintel, 6-9 lentile, 7 lentill, lintile, ? lintle, 3- lentil. [a. F. *lentille:*—popular L. **lenticula* (= class.L. *lenticula*), dim. of *lent-*: see LENS *sb.*

The other Rom. forms represent the class. L. word with unchanged quantity: Sp. *lenteja*, Pg. *lentilha*, It. *lenticchia*.]

　1. a. Chiefly *pl.*, in early use occas. *collective sing.* The seed of a leguminous plant (*Ervum lens, Lens esculenta*); also the plant itself, cultivated for food in European countries.

　*c*1250 *Gen. & Ex.* 1488 Iacob An time him seð a mete ðat man callen lentil ȝete. *c*1425 *Voc.* in Wr.-Wülcker 664/25 *Hec lens*, lentylle. **1548** TURNER *Names of Herbes* 47 Lentilles are sowen in corne fieldes and growe as Tares do. **1577** HARRISON *England* II. vi. (1877) I. 153 Horssecorne, I meane, beanes, otes, tares and lintels [etc.]. **1611** BIBLE 2 *Sam.* xxiii. 11 A piece of ground full of lentiles. **1688** R. HOLME *Armoury* III. 331/1 The dreggs of Chaff, and the small Seeds of Tares & Lintels which are in it. **1747** tr. *Astruc's Fevers* 260 Spots, which are here sometimes as big as a lentile. **1795** J. PHILLIPS *Hist. Inland Navig.* Add. 47 Beans, pease, vetches, lintels. **1840** HOOD *Up Rhine* 174 Our black bread, and black puddings, and lentils! **1853** SOYER *Pantroph.* 58 His corn was exhausted, and his men were obliged to have recourse to lentils! **1877** C. GEIKIE *Christ* I. xv. 222 [In the bazaar] there were booths for Egyptian lentiles.

　† b. A name for DUCKWEED (*Lemna*). More fully, *water lentil* [= F. *lentilles d'eau*]. *Obs.*

　1548 TURNER *Names of Herbes* 47 Lens palustris . . is called in englishe Duckes meate or water Lentilles, in duch wasser linse. **1579** LANGHAM *Gard. Health* (1633) 355 Kanker to kill, apply water Lentils with Barrows grease. **1579-80** NORTH *Plutarch* (1895) IV. 69 Water lintels which the Romanes take for a token of death and mourning. **1597** GERARDE *Herbal* II. ccci. (1633) 829 Ducks Meat . . some term it . . Lentils.

　† 2. *pl.* Freckles or spots on the skin. (Cf. LENTIGO.) *Obs.*

　1558-68 WARDE tr. *Alexis' Secr.* 30 There is neither spotte nor lyntell or any kynde of redde burgeons in the face of a man, the whiche being washed with this water . . will not go out. **1578** LYTE *Dodoens* III. xxxiv. 365 The iuyce of the roote [of Thapsia] with honie, taketh away all lentils and other spots of the face. **1612** WOODALL *Surg. Mate* Wks. (1653) 80 Wheat flower . . cleanseth the face from lentils and spots. **1694** SALMON *Bate's Dispens.* (1713) 689/1 The Face, or other Parts of the Skin troubled with Lentils.

　† 3. A lentil-shaped metal disc. *Obs. rare*[-1].

　1770 *Phil. Trans.* LX. 365 This pendulum, which is no other than a simple steel rod fixed to a lentile, made at Para 98740 oscillations in 24 hours of mean time.

　4. A lens-shaped bulb in an apparatus for rectifying alcohol.

　In mod. Dicts.

　5. *Geol.* A mass of rock distinct in character and having the shape of a bi-convex lens; *spec.* one regarded as a subdivision of a formation.

　1895 J. W. POWELL in A. Keith *Descr. Knoxville Sheet* (U.S. Geol. Survey Atlas), The kinds of rocks are indicated . . by appropriate symbols. . . The following are generally used . . Limestones . . Lentils in strata. **1910** *Ann. N.Y. Acad. Sci.* XIX. 177 The gray sandstone of the Grès Noirs more than 20 feet thick, containing a thin irregular lentil of coal. **1953** *Bull. Amer. Assoc. Petroleum Geologists* XXXVII.

2410 Formations may be subdivided into members, lentils, 'tongues', beds, *et cetera.* **1970** *Earth-Sci. Rev.* VI. 275 Examples of informal rock units are: . . (*b*) beds (e.g., quarry layer, coal beds, oil sands, tongues, lentils, etc.).

　6. *attrib.* and *Comb.*, as *lentil-broth, -form, -porridge, -pottage, -seed, -soup*: *lentil-grey, -shaped* adjs.; † *lentil-dew* [a. F. *lentille d'eau*] = sense 1 b; **lentil-ore, -powder** (see quots.); † **lentil-pulse** = 1; **lentil-shell** (*Zool.*), the genus *Ervillia*.

　1820 W. TOOKE tr. *Lucian* I. 553 note, The *lentil-broth was boiled and served up with fowls and vegetables in it. **1800** W. TAYLOR in Robberds *Mem.* (1843) I. 345 *Lentil-dew, a name given to the duckweed . . in old herbals. **1900** *Daily News* 9 Apr. 5/6 Lady A. . . was dressed in *lentil-grey cloth. **1896** CHESTER *Dict. Names Min.*, *Lentil-ore, an early name for liroconite, because its crystals are lentil-shaped. **1622** MABBE tr. *Aleman's Guzman d'Alf.* II. 275 Vpon fish-dayes we had a messe of *lentill porrige. **1649** JER. TAYLOR *Gt. Exemp.* III. Disc. xiv. 27 He prefers a dish of red *lentill pottage before a venison. **1885** *Cassell's Encycl. Dict.*, *Lentil-powder, Pharm., a powder made of the pulverized seeds of the lentil. **1660** HOWELL *Lex. Tetragl.*, A *Lentil pulse, or lentle; *lentille*. **1555** EDEN *Decades* 102 Certayne smaule graynes of golde no bygger then *lintell seedes. **1607** TOPSELL *Hist. Four-f. Beasts* (1658) 65 Take thereof the quantity of a Lintel seed. **1796** WITHERING *Brit. Plants* (ed. 3) IV. 11 Tubercles *lentil-shaped. **1851** WOODWARD *Mollusca* 313 Ervilia, Turton. *Lentil-shell. **1820** W. TOOKE tr. *Lucian* I. 553 That the cook may . . from inadvertence pour the fish-brine into their *lentil-soup.

† ˈlentile, *a. Obs. rare*[-1]. [f. L. *lent-*, *lens* lentil + -ILE.] Of or pertaining to a lens or lentil.

　1763 *Brit. Mag.* IV. 103 A gentleman . . produced a circular piece of ice . . which he reduced to a lentile form.

† ˈLentiner. *Obs.* Also **Lentner.** [? f. LENTEN + -ER[1].] A hawk taken in Lent; a March hawk.

　1575 TURBERV. *Faulconrie* 204 And of the same condition are Lentiners for the most part, the which are called with us March Hawkes, or Lentiners, bycause they are taken in Lent with lime, or such like meanes. **1655** WALTON *Angler* i. (1661) 14 The Ramish-Hawk, the Haggard, and the two sorts of Lentners. **1677** *Lond. Gaz.* No. 1219/4 A Lentiner Faulcon of the Kings lost from Chelsey the 24 of this instant July, with the Kings Vervells on. **1727** in BRADLEY *Fam. Dict.* s.v. *Hawk.*

lentiscine, *a. rare.* Also 5 lentescyne. [ad. L. *lentiscin-us*, f. *lentiscus*: see next.] Of or belonging to the mastic-tree.

　*c*1420 *Pallad. on Husb.* II. 428 Oyl lentescyne. *Ibid.* 433 As oyl lauryne is lentiscyne of take. **1656** in BLOUNT *Glossogr.*

‖lentiscus (lɛnˈtɪskəs). Pl. **lentisci, lentiscus's.** [L.: see LENTISK.] = LENTISK.

　1398 TREVISA *Barth. De P.R.* XVII. xxv. (1495) 619 Cypres is a medycynall tree and hyght Lentiscus by a nother name. **1587** MASCALL *Govt. Cattle, Oxen* (1627) 85 The buds or branches of Lentiscus and wild oliue trees. **1664** EVELYN *Kal. Hort.* Mar. (1679) 13 Such Plants . . as . . Lentiscus, Myrtle-berries [etc.]. **1698** M. LISTER *Journ. Paris* (1699) 204 Lentiscus's and most other Greens, had suffered miserably. **1717** BERKELEY *Let. to Pope* 22 Oct., Thickets of myrtle and lentiscus. **1884** MRS. C. PRAED *Zero* xiii, Foam dashed over the low undergrowth of lentiscus and myrtle. *Comb.* **1882** *Garden* 23 Sept. 273/1 The Lentiscus-leaved Ash . . is a medium-sized tree of somewhat upright habit.

lentisk (ˈlɛntɪsk). Forms: 5-7 lentiske, 7 lentick(e, 7, 9 lentisc, 8 lentisck, 7- lentisk. Also 7 in It. or Sp. form lentisco. [ad. L. *lentisc-us.* Cf. F. *lentisque.*] The mastic tree (*Pistacia lentiscus*). Also *attrib.*

　*c*1420 *Pallad. on Husb.* II. 429 Lentiskis greynes fele and ripe a slepe Thou brynge a day and nyght to hete yfere. **1562** TURNER *Herbal* II. 29 The rosine of yᵉ lentiske tree called mastick deserueth . . prayse. **1616** B. JONSON *Devil an Ass* IV. i, Oyles of Lentisco. **1624** CAPT. SMITH *Virginia* I. 2 The Lentisk that beareth Mastick. **1625-6** PURCHAS *Pilgrims* II. 1277 The Lenticke tree . . is well nigh onely proper to Sio. **1644** EVELYN *Diary* 30 Sept., Rosemary, lavender, lentiscs, and the like sweet shrubes. **1694** MOTTEUX *Rabelais* IV. lxiii. (1737) 257 Gymnast was making Tooth-pickers with Lentisk. **1751** SIR J. HILL *Mat. Med.* 694 The Lentisc Wood, distill'd by the Retort, yields an acrid Phlegm in considerable Quantity. **1766** FAWKES tr. *Theocritus' Idyl* vii. 154 Who courteous bad us on soft beds recline Of lentisk, and young branches of the vine. **1840** BROWNING *Sordello* IV. 390, Where I set her Moorish lentisk, by the stair, To overawe the aloes. **1866** *Cornh. Mag.* Nov. 540 Lentisk and beach-loving myrtle, both exceeding green and bushy. **1894** P. PINKERTON *Adriatica, Dream*, By the lentisks of Taȯrmina.

lentitude (ˈlɛntɪtjuːd). [ad. L. *lentitūdo*, f. *lentus* slow. Cf. F. *lentitude* (Cotgr.).] Slowness, sluggishness.

　1623 COCKERAM, *Lentitude*, slownesse. **1668** WILKINS *Real Char.* II. viii. §3. 207 *Lentitude*, Stupor. **1832** I. TAYLOR *Saturday Even.* (1833) 210 There is a serenity—might we say a lentitude of the physical temperament. **1862** MRS. SPEID *Our Last Y. Ind.* 41 The struggle between English punctuality and oriental lentitude.

lentiˈtudinous, *a. rare.* [f. L. *lentitūdin-, lentitūdo* (see prec.) + -OUS.] Slow, sluggish.

　1801 W. TAYLOR in *Monthly Mag.* XI. 646 The . . rehearsal of the lentitudinous representations of Rastadt.

† ˈlently, *adv. Obs. rare*[-1]. [f. LENT *a.* + -LY[2].] Slowly.

　1654-66 EARL ORRERY *Parthen.* (1676) 154 He therefore past lently the River Vulturnus.

Lentner, variant of LENTINER. *Obs.*

‖**lento** ('lɛnto). *Mus.* [It.] **a.** A direction indicating a movement slower than *Adagio*.
1724 *Explic. For. Words Mus.*, Lent, or Lento, or *Lentement*, do all denote a Slow Movement. **1736** in BAILEY (fol.). **1876** in STAINER & BARRETT *Dict. Mus. Terms*.
b. *Philol.* Applied to a word or phrase pronounced more slowly than in normal speech. Cf. ALLEGRO B. 2.
1939 [see ALLEGRO B. 2]. **1964** J. VACHEK in D. Abercrombie et al. *Daniel Jones* 205 Yet the pronunciation with [əl], characteristic of a *lento* style of speech,.. can hardly be credited with exercising a decisive influence on the much more frequent *allegro* form with the syllabic [l]. **1968** *Language* XLIV. 87 Another main type of downdrift is in steps, with deliberate lento articulation. **1973** *Word 1970* XXVI. 39 The last two words in lento speech.

lentoid ('lɛntɔɪd), *a.* [f. L. *lent-* LENS *sb.* + -OID.] Having the form of a lens or lentil; lens-shaped.
1879 in WEBSTER, Suppl. **1880** *Athenæum* 21 Aug. 245/2 The other lentoid gems take their places in series with those which have been collected from the Greek islands. **1884** SAYCE *Anc. Emp. East* 230 The lentoid gems.. are all closely allied in artistic style to the Hittite carved stones. **1900** A. S. MURRAY in *Brit. Mus. Return* 64 Haematite lentoid seal, engraved with the figure of a man with horse's head.

lento(o), **Lenton(e**, obs. ff. LEAN-TO, LENTEN.

lentor ('lɛntə(r), 'lɛntɔː(r)). Also 7 lentour. [ad. F. *lenteur* or L. *lentor* (sense 1), f. *lentus* slow.]
1. Of the blood, etc.: Clamminess, tenacity, viscidity. Now *rare*.
1626 BACON *Sylva* §900 All Matter whereof Creatures are produced by Putrefaction haue euermore a Closenesse, Lentour, and Sequacity. **1684** tr. *Bonet's Merc. Compit.* xiv. 486 In this Disease the whole Blood does not presently acquire that lentor or sliminess. **1699** EVELYN *Acetaria* 36 Arborescent Holi-hocks.. by reason of their clamminess and Lentor, banished from our Sallet. **1744** BERKELEY *Siris* §52 There is lentor and smoothness in the blood of healthy strong people. **1797** J. DOWNING *Disord. Horned Cattle* 3 This medicine.. extinguishes the inflammatory lentor. **1822-34** *Good's Study Med.* (ed. 4) I. 560 That [hypothesis] of Boerhaave founded on the doctrine of a peculiar viscosity, or lentor of the blood.
†**b.** *concr.* A viscid component of the blood.
c **1720** W. GIBSON *Farrier's Guide* II. viii. (1738) 38 A great deal of Lenter may undoubtedly be squeezed through the smallest vessels. **1722** QUINCEY *Lex. Phys.-Med.* (ed. 2), *Lentor* hath been used.. to express that sizy, viscid, coagulated Part of the Blood, which in malignant Fevers obstructs the capillary Vessels.
2. Slowness; want of vital activity.
a **1763** SHENSTONE *Wks. & Lett.* (1768) II. 228 Persons of a phlegmatic constitution have.. a lentor which wine may naturally remove. **1779** J. LOVELL in *J. Adams' Wks.* (1854) IX. 487 Nor can I omit to call to your mind.. that the lentor of proceedings here should account for the appearances of injustice done you. **1847-9** TODD *Cycl. Anat.* IV. 297/1 The extreme lentor of all their [serpents'] digestive functions.

Lentoun, obs. form of LENTEN.

†'**lentous**, *a. nonce-wd.* [f. L. *lent-us* slow + -OUS.] Clammy, viscid.
1646 SIR T. BROWNE *Pseud. Ep.* II. i. 54 Chrystall.. is a minerall body.. made of a lentous colament of earth, drawne from the most pure and limpid juyce thereof. **1656** BLOUNT *Glossogr.*, *Lentous*, soft, tender.

Lentran(e, **-tren(e**, **-trin(e**, obs. ff. LENTEN.

†'**lentrinware**. *Sc. Obs.* Also 5 lentrynvar, lentrinva(i)r, lenterwar(e, 6 lentrenvare, lentreneveyr. [f. *lentrin*, Sc. form of LENTEN + WARE.] Skins of lambs that have died soon after being dropped; 'still called *lentrins*' (Jam.).
1435 *Exch. Rolls Scotl.* IV. 604 De custuma 760 pellium que dicuntur *lentrinware. **1492** *Extracts Aberd. Reg.* (1844) I. 47 A lettre, vnder the sam seil, of the freing of the custum of lenterwar, futevel, and other sic. **1493** *Ibid.* 49 ij dusane lentrinvair.. j dusan of lentrinware. **1496** HALYBURTON *Ledger* (1867) 115, 2 sekis skynis contenand 986 skyns, and 350 lentrynvar, and 300 futfell. **1535** *Aberd. Reg.* (Jam.), vj dossane of Lentrene veyr skynnis. **1592** *Sc. Acts Jas. VI* (1814) III. 580/2 Skynnis vndirwrittin callit in the vulgar toung Scorlingis, scaldingis, futefaillis, lentrenvare.

Lentron(e, **Lentroun**, obs. ff. LENTEN.

lent-stock, variant of LINSTOCK.

†'**lentular**, *a. Obs. rare*$^{-1}$. [as if L. *lentul-us, dim. of *lent-em* LENS *sb.* + -AR.] Lens-shaped.
1761-9 tr. *Voltaire's Wks.* XXVI. 196 (Jod.) A lentular spectacle glass.

Lentz (lɛnts). The name of Hugo *Lentz*, 20th-c. German engineer, used *attrib.* to denote a type of poppet valve invented by him for use in steam engines, and a locomotive valve gear employing such valves operated by a camshaft.
1925 *Marine Engineer* XLVIII. 19/2 In developing the Lentz poppet valve for marine engines, those first fitted were applied to engines of the triple and.. quadruple-expansion types. **1930** *Engineer* 31 Jan. 132/1 L.N.E.R. locomotive with Lentz valve gear. **1949** C. J. ALLEN *Locomotive Pract. & Performance 20th Cent.* iv. 40 The most extensive application of poppet-valves to locomotives in Great Britain has been that of Lentz valves to the 'Hunt' class 4-4-0s of the late L.N.E.R. **1966** O. S. NOCK *Brit. Steam Railway Locomotive 1925-65* viii. 99 (*caption*) L.M.S.R. Horwich 2-6-0 with Lentz R.C. poppet valve gear.

l'envoy, **lenvoy**, *sb.* See ENVOY *sb.*[1] 1.
1430-40 LYDG. *Bochas* VIII. xxv. (1494) E iij b/1 Make a Lenuoy that men all may it rede. [The 'Lenuoye' follows.] **1570** *Barclay's Ship of Fooles* 2 b, The Lenuoy of Alexander Barclay Translatour. [Also in other passages; but ed. 1509 has always *The Enuoy* or *Thenuoy*.] **1588** SHAKS. *L.L.L.* III. i. 81 *Pag.* Is not *lenuoy* a *salue?* *Ar.* No, Page, it is an epilogue. *a* **1625** BEAUM. & FL. *Wit without M.* II. iv, After these, a Lenvoy to the Citty for their sinnes? **1636** MASSINGER *Bashf. Lover* IV. i, Do I know my self? I kept that for the Lenvoy. *a* **1656** USSHER *Annals* VI. (1658) 276 Of 10 thousand talents brought forth, there were 130 left all paid, with this lenuoy over and above of Curtius [Latin: *a Curtio etiam hoc adjecto epiphonemate*], So that, saith he, that army .. brought yet more honour and glory, then spoil and riches out of Asia.
Hence †**lenvoy** *v. trans.*, to give (a person) his lenvoy; to say farewell to him.
1596 NASHE *Saffron Walden* 134 Wee shall lenuoy him, and trumpe and poope him well enough if.. he will needes fall a Comedizing it.

leny(e, obs. form of LEAN *v.*[1]

†'**lenye**, *a. Sc. Obs.* Also 6 lenȝe, linȝe, 7 lenyie. [a. OF. *ligne*, *linge*, thin, slender (said both of textile fabrics and of a person's figure: see Godef.):—L. *līneus* made of linen, f. *līnum* flax.] Fine, thin, slender.
1513 DOUGLAS *Æneis* VII. i. 30 Rych lenȝe [L. *tenues*] wobbis natly weiffis sche. *Ibid.* VIII. i. 73 A linȝe wattry garmond dyd hym vaill [L. *eum tenuis glauco velabat amictu Carbasus*]. ? **16..** *Barbour's Bruce* (1616) I. 387 His body wes weyll maid and lenye [*MS. has a blank*; *ed.* 1670 lenyie].

lenyn, obs. form of LINEN.

lenzinite ('lɛnzɪnaɪt). *Min.* [Named by J. F. John, 1816, after Dr. J. G. *Lenz*: see -IN and -ITE.] An opal-like variety of halloysite.
1823 W. PHILLIPS *Min.* (ed. 3) 87 Lenzinite.. has been divided into two varieties. **1837** DANA *Min.* 250 The Lenzinite of John, from Kall,.. in Prussia.

Lenz's law ('lɛntsɪz, 'lɛnzɪz). *Electr.* [Named after H. F. E. *Lenz* (1804-65), German physicist, who first enunciated it (in *Ann. d. Physik u. Chem.* (1834) XXXI. 483).] The law that the direction of an induced current is always such as to oppose the change in the circuit or the magnetic field that produces it.
1866 E. ATKINSON tr. *Ganot's Elem. Treat. Physics* (ed. 2) x. vi. 696 On the induction produced between a closed circuit and a current in activity when their relative distance varies, Lenz has based the following law, which is known as Lenz's law. **1931** L. B. LOEB *Fund. Electr. & Magn.* i. 35 Unless Lenz's law holds we could by induction effects get energy out of nothing. **1962** CORSON & LORRAIN *Introd. Electromagn. Fields* vi. 222 Lenz's law is a particular case of Le Chatelier's principle. **1973** *Physics Bull.* Dec. 715/2 Any change in the external field induces an appropriate supercurrent which (by Lenz's law) is just sufficient to counter the effect of the field variation.

‖**Leo** ('liːəʊ). *Astron.* [L.: see LION.] **1.** The Lion, the Zodiacal constellation lying between Cancer and Virgo. Also, the fifth sign of the Zodiac (named from this constellation), entered by the sun about the 21st of July. ***Leo Minor***, a modern constellation containing stars of minor magnitude, lying between the Great Bear and Leo.
a **1000** *Ags. Man. Astron.* in *Pop. Treat. Sci.* (1841) 7 An þæra tacna ys ȝe-haten *aries*,.. fifta *leo*; syxta *virgo*. *c* **1391** CHAUCER *Astrol.* II. §6 As thus euery degree of aries bi ordre is nadir to euery degree of libra by ordre &.. leo to aquarie [etc.]. **1611** COTGR., *Lion*, a Lyon; also, the (Zodiacall) Signe Leo. **1667** MILTON *P.L.* x. 676 Thence down amaine By Leo and the Virgin and the Scales. **1797** *Encycl. Brit.* (ed. 3) II. 548/1 Hevelius's Constellations made out of the unformed stars. Lynx, The Lynx.. Leo minor, The Little Lion. *Ibid.* 568/1 When the sun is in Aries, Taurus, Gemini, Cancer, Leo, and Virgo, the north pole of the earth is enlightened by the sun. **1868** LOCKYER *Elem. Astron.* 135 The pole of the globe being represented by a point in the constellation Leo.
2. *Astrol.* A person born under the sign of Leo. Also *attrib.* and as *adj.*
1894 E. KIRK *Influence of Zodiac upon Human Life* ix. 51 Leo people are fine conversationalists, excelling in repartee. **1936** 'J. TEY' *Shilling for Candles* vi. 63 Aries people are often talkative... Now you, Mr. Grant, are a Leo person. *c* **1960** S. PLATH *Crossing Water* (1971) 55 The astrologer at her elbow (a Leo) Picked his trip-date by the stars. *a* **1963** L. MACNEICE *Astrol.* (1964) i. 16 The delight most people take in *Classification*.. 'Are you Virgo?' 'Oh no, I'm Leo.' **1973** L. MEYNELL *Fatal Flaw* ii. 20 'Now, I would guess you to be a Leo, sir.' Vyvyan's birthday was August the ninth.

leo, OE. and early ME.: see LION.

leo, obs. form of LEE *sb.*[1], LO *int.*[1]

leof, **leofsum**, obs. ff. LEAF, LIEF, LEESOME.

leoful, variant of LEEFUL.

leom(e, obs. form of LEAM *sb.*[1]

leon, obs. f. LION; rare obs. var. LYAM, leash.

leonard(e, var. LANNARD *Obs.*, a kind of falcon.
1550 J. COKE *Eng. & Fr. Heralds* viii. (1877) 60 We have hawkes of the towre, as leonardes, leonerettes, fawcons [etc.]. **1623** COCKERAM *Eng. Dict.* III. *Hawks*, A *Leonard*, the male is called a *Leneret*. **1706** PHILLIPS (ed. Kersey), *Leonard Hawk*, a kind of Hawk, so call'd by Fowlers.

Leonardesque (ˌliːənɑː'dɛsk), *a.* [f. the name of *Leonardo* da Vinci (1452-1519) + -ESQUE.] Resembling in subject or style, or in the manner of, the works of Leonardo da Vinci.
1864 CROWE & CAVALCASELLE *New Hist. Painting Italy* II. xxii. 547 Nothing can exceed the Leonardesque precision of the drawing or the softness and fusion of the impasto. **1904** E. MCCURDY *Leonardo da Vinci* 100 How eminently Leonardesque it was to make the angel point at S. John. **1939** *English* II. 276, I had early waited for a Leonardesque sweetness and subtlety which visited his features. **1960** *Times* 24 Feb. 15/1 Sir Kenneth [Clark].. had for some time discerned a Leonardesque presence in the painting. **1971** A. SMART *Renaissance & Mannerism in Italy* xvi. 135 There is nothing here of Leonardo's mystery, but rather a calm objectivity and a cold grace that are the reverse of Leonardesque 'romanticism'.

Leonberg ('liːənbɜːg). The name of a town in south-western Germany used *attrib.* or *absol.* to designate a large dog, a cross between a St. Bernard and a Newfoundland, often golden in colour, of a breed first developed there about 1855. Also '**Leonberger**.
1907 K. LEIGHTON *New Bk. Dog* XVII. 518/1 The Leonberg dog.. is supposed also to be a worker among flocks and herds. **1945** C. L. B. HUBBARD *Observer's Bk. Dogs* 179 The Leonberg is now regarded on the Continent as a distinct race. **1954** M. K. WILSON tr. *Lorenz's Man meets Dog* vii. 75 A great, strong Leonberger,.. a member of one of the largest breeds of dog, adopted as mistress the youngest sister. **1962** J. M. BERNSTEIN tr. *Levi's Two-Fold Night* x. 86 Two enormous dogs.. of the rare Leonberg breed. **1971** F. HAMILTON *World Encycl. Dogs* 158 The popularity of the Leonberger increased and by 1872 other breeders were competing with similar crosses to obtain large, handsome, utility dogs.

leone (liː'əʊn). [f. the name of Sierra *Leone*.] The principal unit of currency in Sierra Leone; a banknote of the value of one leone.
1964 *Times* 4 Aug. 6/5 The new basic unit is the leone with a value equal to 10s. **1972** *Whitaker's Almanack 1973* 987 Sierra Leone.. Leone of 100 Cents.

leone, obs. form of LEAN *v.*[1]

†**leonell**, *a. Obs. rare*$^{-1}$. [app. a derivative of L. *leōn-* LION.] Of or resembling that of a lion.
1625-6 PURCHAS *Pilgrims* II. 1495 They themselues are of darke yellow colour, commonly called Leonell colour.

leonerett, obs. f. LANNERET, a kind of falcon.
1550 [see LEONARD].

Leonese (liːə'niːz), *a.* and *sb.* [f. Sp. *León*, the name of a town and region in Spain + -ESE.]
A. *adj.* Of or belonging to León, an ancient kingdom of Spain and now a province, or to the town of León in this region. **B.** *sb.* **a.** A native or inhabitant of León; also *collect.* **b.** The language of León, a dialect of Spanish with Portuguese affinities.
1845 R. FORD *Hand-bk. for Travellers Spain* II. viii. 558 The minor traits of Leonese character are influenced by local differences. *Ibid.* 559 The houses of the humble Leonese, like their hearts, are always open to an Englishman. **1865** H. O'SHEA *Guide to Spain* 236/2 The present Jesuits.. with their usual refinement, tact, and educational talents, will soon.. ungothicise the good Leonese. *Ibid.* 245/2 The Leoneses differ considerably in character, according to the nature of the different regions which they inhabit. **1887** *Encycl. Brit.* XXII. 351/2 *Leonese*. Proceeding on inadequate indications, the existence of a Leonese dialect has been imprudently admitted in some quarters. **1893** H. E. WATTS *Spain* ii. 52 Almanzor marched into the Christian kingdom,.. scattering Castilians and Leonese as the Goths had been scattered three hundreds years before. **1932** W. L. GRAFF *Lang.* x. 377 Spanish group, with the Castilian, Andalusian, Aragonese, and Leonese dialects. **1936** W. J. ENTWISTLE *Spanish Lang.* v. 39 Mozarabic co-operation in many important settlements brought the use of Arabic terminology to a maximum in Leonese. **1964** *Archivum Linguisticum* 2 At that stage he [*sc.* Diez] did not yet identify the dialect at issue as Leonese.

leonhardite (liːən'hɑːdaɪt). *Min.* [Named by Blum (1843) in honour of C. C. von *Leonhard*: see -ITE.] A variety of LAUMONTITE, containing less than the usual amount of water.
1848 in CRAIG. **1868** DANA *Min.* (ed. 5) 401 *Leonhardite*.. Lustre of cleavage-face pearly, elsewhere vitreous... Usually whitens on exposure like laumontite.

†**Le'onic**, *a. Obs. rare*$^{-1}$. [f. L. *leōn-* LION + -IC.] Pertaining to the constellation Leo.
a **1658** CLEVELAND *Engag. Stated* 14 The Sign's in Cancer and the Zodiack turns Leonick.

Leonid ('liːənɪd). *Astron.* Also *pl.* in L. form Leonides (liː'ɒnɪdiːz). [f. L. *leōn-* LION (LEO) + -ID.] One of a group of meteors which appear to radiate from the constellation Leo.
1876 G. F. CHAMBERS *Astron.* 799 The *Leonids* and the *Andromedes* of November 14 and 27. **1878** *Times* 25 Nov., Knowing thus.. the true velocity of the Leonides as they rush into our air. **1880** PROCTOR *Rough Ways* 116 If the path tends from that particular part of the constellation Leo.. the probability of the meteor being a Leonid is increased.
attrib. **1899** *Edin. Rev.* Oct. 319 A practised observer can thus distinguish an Andromede from a Leonid meteor.

†**Leonine**, *sb.*[1] *Obs.* Also 8 lionine. [ad. med.L. *leōnīna*, app. fem. of *leōnīnus* (see next), but the reason of the name is not clear; cf. quot. 1749.] A counterfeit coin, of the reign of Edward I, brought into England from abroad.

[*c* **1350** W. HEMINGBURGH *Chronicon* (1849) II. 187 Monetas plurimas et pessimi metalli, pollardorum.. leoninarum dormientium, et aliorum diversorum nominum.] **1577–87** HOLINSHED *Chron.* III. 309/1 There were diuerse monies in those daies [1300] currant within this realme, as pollards, crocards, staldings, eagles, leonines,.. and all these were white monies, artificiallie made of siluer, copper, and sulphur. **1749** J. SIMON *Ess. Irish Coins* 15 *note*, These..foreign coins, called Mitres, Lionines, Rosaries, ..&c. from the stamp or figures impressed on them, were privately brought from..beyond the seas, and uttered here for pennies.

leonine, *sb.*[2]: see LEONINE *a.*[2]

leonine (ˈliːənaɪn, -nɪn), *a.*[1] [a. L. *leōnīn-us*, f. *leōn-* LION. Cf. F. *léonin*.]

1. a. Resembling a lion or that of a lion; lion-like.

c **1386** CHAUCER *Monk's T.* 656 So was he ful of leonyn corage. *c* **1430** LYDG. *Reas. & Sens.* (E.E.T.S.) 168/6422 They ben of wisdam Serpentyne And of force leonyne. **1631** BRATHWAIT *Eng. Gentlew.* (1641) 338 Neere resemblance had Leëna's name with her Leonine nature. **1660** GAUDEN *Serm. Funeral Dr. Brounrig* Q vj b, And bring them from that which in their Physiognomy is..leonine (for so we read some men had lionly looks). **1822** WORDSW. *Eccl. Sonn.*, I. *Rich. I*, Redoubted King, of courage leonine, I mark thee, Richard! **1851** CARLYLE *Sterling* III. v. (1872) 208 Great sensibility..which he had an over-tendency to express even by tears,—a singular sight in so leonine a man. **1869** DIXON *Tower* I. iii. 30 In her youth she had none of that leonine beauty of her later years. **1887–9** T. A. TROLLOPE *What I remember* II. xiv. 245 Landor..was a man of somewhat leonine aspect.

b. *leonine monkey*: the *Macacus leoninus* (Cent. Dict.). *leonine seal*: ? the SEA-LION.

1802 BINGLEY *Anim. Biog.* I. 185 Leonine Seals are found in great numbers on the eastern shores of Kamtschatka... The Leonine Seal has the head and eyes large..and along the neck of the male there is a mane of stiff curled hair.

c. Designating that form of leprosy called leontiasis, and the lion-like facies characteristic of it.

The allusion to the resemblance to the lion's face can be traced back to the ancient Arab physicians.

[**1749** J. BARROW *Dictionarium Medicum Universale, Leontiasis, Leontion*, or *Leonina lepra*, a name for Elephantiasis, or leprosy.] **1813** T. BATEMAN *Pract. Synopsis Cutaneous Dis.* 295 Haly Abbas says the countenance was called leonine, because the white of the eyes becomes livid, and the eyes of a round figure; and Avicenna observes that the epithet was applied to the disease, because it renders the countenance terrible to look at, and somewhat of the form of the lion's visage. **1867** *Rep. Leprosy* (R. Coll. Physicians) 242 The prominent blotches on the forehead gave a sombre character to his countenance; not as yet approaching the leonine expression of tubercular elephantiasis. **1899** T. L. STEDMAN *20th Cent. Pract.* XVIII. 623 The lower part of the frontal skin is drawn downwards and conceals the eyes, as in mad persons and lions. This is why the affection is also called leonine. **1959** R. G. COCHRANE *Leprosy in Theory & Pract.* 367 The 'leonine' appearance in Hansen's disease is ..attributable to the nodular leprosy. **1970** G. J. HILL *Leprosy in Five Young Men* 65 Patient 5 was a large dark-skinned man with moderately severe leonine facies.

2. Of or relating to a lion.

1500–20 DUNBAR *Poems* xlviii. 91 And first the Lyone.. With visage bawld, and curage leonyne. **1755** JOHNSON, *Leonine*, belonging to a lion; having the nature of a lion. *Ibid.*, *Tiger*, a fierce beast of the leonine kind. **1794** G. ADAMS *Nat. & Exp. Philos.* III. xxv. 59 As is the piper's art to the pipe..so is the soul of the lion to the body leonine. **1861** GEIKIE & WILSON *E. Forbes* ix. 248 They styled themselves 'Red Lions', and, in proof of their leonine relationship, made it a point of always signifying their approval or dissent by growls and roars.

3. Roman Law. ***leonine convention*** or ***partnership*** [L. *leonina societas*] (see quot.).

Cf. Sp. *contrato leonino*, in S. America a contract in which the advantage is, in the judgement of the Court, manifestly and unfairly one-sided; such a contract may be held void.

1875 POSTE *Gaius* III. Comm. (ed. 2) 426 Aristo records the decision of Cassius that a partnership on the terms that one should take all the profits and another bear all the loss, which he calls a leonine partnership, is not binding.

4. Comb.: *leonine-coloured* adj.

a **1697** AUBREY *Lives, S. Butler* (1898) I. 138 He was of a leonine-coloured haire, middle-sized, strong.

Hence ˈ**leoninely** *adv.*, in the manner of a lion.

1751 J. HARRIS *Hermes* I. xi. (1765) 209 Adverbs may be derived..from Substantives, as from λέων, a Lion, λεοντωδῶς, Leoninely.

leonine (ˈliːənaɪn, -nɪn), *a.*[2] and *sb.*[2] [ad. L. *leōnīn-us*, f. *Leōn-*, *Leo* proper name: see -INE.]

A. *adj.*

1. Pertaining to one of the popes named Leo. ***Leonine City*** [mod.L. *Civitas Leonina*], that part of Rome in which the Vatican stands, which was walled and fortified by Leo IV (*c* 850).

1870 *N. & Q.* Ser. IV. VI. 294/1 In describing the present course of events in Italy, constant mention is made by the papers of the 'Leonine City'. **1892** *Daily News* 16 Dec. 5/2 The Pope's plea for jurisdiction over the Leonine City.

2. ***leonine verse***: a kind of Latin verse much used in the Middle Ages, consisting of hexameters or alternate hexameters and pentameters, in which the final word rimes with that immediately preceding the cæsural pause. So ***leonine poet, rime.***

[Prob. named from some mediæval poet called Leo (or Leonius) who made use of this kind of versification: for conjectures as to his identity see Du Cange.]

1658 W. BURTON *Itin. Anton.* 61 These rimedoggrill verses, not Leonine, as I think they are usually called. *a* **1771** GRAY *Corr.* (1843) 276 If the date of this poem be true, the general opinion, that the Leonine verse owes its name to Leonius, seems to be false. **1837–9** HALLAM *Hist. Lit.* (1847) I. i. §87. 77 Those who attempted to write verse have lost all prosody and relapse into Leonine rhymes. **1845** *Encycl. Metrop.* XXI. 385/1 Sir A. Croke has given examples from more than fifty Leonine poets from the IIId to the XVth centuries. **1862** H. B. WHEATLEY *Anagrams* 15 Leonine verses were invented, according to Camden, in the reign of Charlemagne.

B. *sb. pl.* Leonine verse.

1846 WRIGHT *Ess. Mid. Ages* I. v. 186 Its author has mixed leonines with his elegiacs. **1861** *Sat. Rev.* 21 Sept. 306 The *Speculum* is not..written either in classical metre or in leonines.

leonite (ˈleɪ-, ˈliːənaɪt). *Min.* [ad. G. *leonit* (C. A. Tenne 1896, in *Zeitschr. d. deut. geol. Ges.* XLVIII. 637), f. the name of *Leo* Strippelmann, 19th-c. German salt-works director: see -ITE[1].] A hydrated sulphate of potassium and magnesium, $K_2Mg(SO_4)_2.4H_2O$, found as transparent, colourless, or yellowish prismatic crystals.

1897 *Jrnl. Chem. Soc.* LXXII. II. 269 There is no crystallographic relation between this mineral and blödite .., so that the older but unpublished name, leonite, is used in preference to kaliblödite. **1932** *Bull. U.S. Geol. Survey* No. 833. 44 In the Joe Mitchell well at a depth of 1,368 feet pale-yellow leonite with a waxy luster is intimately mixed with kainite... In places leonite occurs in larger blebs. **1970** *Mineral. & Petrogr. Acta* XVI. 14/2 This appears to be the first occurrence of leonite for Vesuvian fumaroles. Leonite is known to be associated in salt deposits of oceanic origin, at Stassfurt with halite, at Leopoldshall with kainite, and at Ascherleben.

leonnceaux: see LIONCEAU.

‖**leontiasis** (ˌliːɒnˈtaɪəsɪs). *Med.* [mod.L., a. Gr. λεοντίασις, f. λεοντ-, λέων LION: see -ASIS.] A form of leprosy in which the face assumes a dusky, wrinkled, and somewhat lion-like appearance.

1753 in CHAMBERS *Cycl. Supp.* **1884** *Contemp. Rev.* Aug. 211 Elephantiasis, Satyriasis, Leontiasis. **1898** P. MANSON *Trop. Diseases* xxvi. 396 The bloated, dusky, wrinkled, greasy, passive countenance [of the leper] acquires the repulsive appearance very appropriately designated 'leontiasis'.

‖**leontodon** (liːˈɒntədən). [mod.L., f. Gr. λεοντ-, λέων LION + ὀδοντ-, ὀδούς tooth: a transl. of DANDELION.] A plant of the genus *Leontodon*, of which the Dandelion was the original type.

1807 CRABBE *Par. Reg.* I. Wks. 1823 I. 64 There Arums, there Leontodons we view.

leonys, obs. form of LIONESS.

leopard (ˈlɛpəd). Forms: α. 4 **labarde, lubard,** 4–6 **lebarde, libarde, lybard,** 4–8 **libard,** 5 **leberde, labbarde,** 5–6 **lybarde, lybbard(e, lyberd(e, liberd(e,** 4–7 (and 8–9 *arch.*) **libbard.** β. 3 **leupar,** 3–5 **lepard,** 4–5 **lupard(e,** 4–6 **leparde,** 4 **lepart, lip(p)ard,** (5 **lupart, lupaerd, lyepart(e, lyppart,** 6 **lyparde**). γ. 4 **leoperd(e,** 4–5 **leopart,** 4, 6 **leoparde,** 4, 6– **leopard.** [ME. *leopard*, also *lebard, lubard, leupard*, etc., a. OF. *leopard, lebard, leupard*, etc. (mod.F. *léopard*), ad. late L. *leopardus* (*Hist. Aug.*), ad. late Gr. λεόπαρδος (S. Ignat., Galen), also λεοντόπαρδος (and λεοντοπάρδαλος, ? 4th c.), f. λεοντ-, λέων LION + πάρδος PARD.

The animal orig. so named was supposed to be a hybrid between lion and 'pard': cf. Plin. *N.H.* VIII. xvii, '[Leones] quos pardi generavere'.]

1. a. A large carnivorous quadruped, *Felis pardus*, otherwise called the Panther, a native of Africa and southern Asia. Its coat is yellowish fawn shading to white under the body, with dark brown or black rosette-like spots. (In popular language, the name is often restricted to the smaller varieties of the species, the larger being called panthers.)

black leopard, a black-coated variety of the leopard, formerly regarded as a distinct species, found in Southern India and the Malay peninsula, Java, etc.

α. **13..** *Coer de L.* 2182 Then answered Kyng Richard, In deed lyon, in thought libbard. *c* **1330** R. BRUNNE *Chron. Wace* (Rolls) 13795 Was neuere lubard ne lyoun..þat was so wod. *c* **1386** CHAUCER *Monk's T.* 271 Leons, leopardes [*v.r.* lebardis, luperdes] and Beres. *a* **1400** *Isumbras* 189 A labarde ther com and tuk that othir. *c* **1440** *Promp. Parv.* 291/2 Labbarde (*K., S., P.* lebbard), *leopardus*. *c* **1440** *Gesta Rom.* I. lx. 246 (Harl. MS.) A litle Ile, fulle of liounes, leberdes, berys, and oþere wylde bestes. **1531** ELYOT *Gov.* I. xviii, In the vacation season from warres they hunted lions, liberdes, and suche other bestis. *a* **1599** SPENSER *F.Q.* VII. vii. 29 He in forrest greene had hunted late the Libbard or the Bore. **1613** PURCHAS *Pilgrimage* VI. i. 466 The Libard is not hurtfull to men except they annoy him: but killeth and eateth Dogges. **1635** SWAN *Spec. M.* (1670) 396 There is no Leopard or Libbard but such as is begotten between the Lion and the Panther, or the Panther and the Lioness. **1784** COWPER *Task* VI. 773 The lion, and the libbard, and the bear, Graze with the fearless flocks. **1820** KEATS *Lamia* II. 185 Twelve sphered tables..rear'd On libbard's paws.

β. *a* **1290** *S. Eustace* 410 in Horstm. *Altengl. Leg.* (1881) 219 Liouns and leuparz..And bestes suiþe fel[l]e. *a* **1300** *Cursor M.* 11638 Moder, he said, haf þou na ward, Noþer o leon ne o lepard [*Gött.* lippard]. **1340** *Ayenb.* 14 Vor þet bodi of þe bestes wes ase lipard. *c* **1386** CHAUCER *Knt.'s T.* 1328 Aboute this kyng ther ran on euery part ful many a tame leon and leopard. **1387** TREVISA *Higden* (Rolls) I. 159 Camelion is..in colour liche to a lupard. *c* **1430** LYDG. *Reas. & Sens.* (E.E.T.S.) 3249, I wot..thou woldest twynne And fle from hir..As doth an hare the lyppart. *c* **1450** *Merlin* 304 In that londe is the wolf that the lupart shall bynde. **1481** CAXTON *Reynard* (Arb.) 52 Tho spak sir firapeel the lupaerd whiche was sybbe somwhat to the kynge. **1483** —— *Gold Leg.* 416/1 There was a lyeparte there aboutes whiche destroyed the people of the contre. **1535** COVERDALE *Ecclus.* xxviii. 23 It shal..deuoure them as a leparde. **1635** SWAN *Spec. M.* ix. § 1 (1643) 435 The Panther is a beast little differing from a Leopard or Lippard.

γ. **13..** *K. Alis.* 5228 Vnces grete, and leopardes. **1377** LANGL. *P. Pl.* B. XV. 93 Ac þere ne was lyoun ne leopart þat on laundes wenten..þat ne fel to her feet. **1398** TREVISA *Barth. De P.R.* XVIII. xxii. (1495) 781 The Leoperde drynkith mylke of the wylde gote. *c* **1450** *Merlin* 304 Is not the leopart more of strength than is the wolf. **1535** COVERDALE *Prov.* xxvi. 13 The slouthfull sayeth: there is a leoparde in yᵉ waye. **1607** SHAKS. *Timon* IV. iii. 343 Wert thou a Leopard, thou wert Germane to the Lion, and the spottes of thy Kindred, were Iurors on thy life. **1727–46** THOMSON *Summer* 918 The lively shining leopard speckled o'er With many a spot, the beauty of the waste. **1834** PRINGLE *Afr. Sk.* viii. 246 The South-African leopard differs from the panther..in the form of its spots.

b. Applied to other animals of the genus *Felis*, as **American leopard**, the jaguar, *F. onca*; **hunting leopard**, the cheetah (see HUNTING *vbl. sb.* 3 b); **snow leopard**, the ounce, *F. irbis*.

2. With reference to its spotted coat, as a type of unchangeableness, after Jer. xiii. 23.

1382 WYCLIF *Pref. Ep. St. Jerome* vii. 71/1 [*Mentions Jeremiah's allusion to*] the leparde spuylide his colours. **1560** BIBLE (Genev.) *Jer.* xiii. 23 Can the blacke More change his skin? or the leopard his spottes? **1593** SHAKS. *Rich. II*, I. i. 174. **1624** F. WHITE *Repl. Fisher* 573 They haue washed off their Libbards spots. **1631** BRATHWAIT *Eng. Gentlew.* (1641) 308 The Blackmoore may sooner change his skin, the Leopard his spots. **1920** *New Statesman* Apr. 20/1 For the moment the public is not likely to get a thorough grounding in economics, nor does the Press leopard show any signs of changing his spots. **1930** D. JERROLD *Lie about War* 35 As for the leopard who failed to change his spots, why blame the war? **1955** W. GADDIS *Recognitions* II. v. 487 You wanted to marry a Christian, you wanted to marry a good Catholic. Well leopards can't change their spots. **1972** G. OAKLEY *Church Mouse* 20/2 The schoolmouse..said that..Sampson was a leopard in sheep's clothing and that a wolf couldn't change its spots. **1973** *Times* 21 Nov. 19/8 There is no evidence to show that the Communist Party leopard has changed its spots.

3. a. A figure of a leopard in painting, heraldry, etc.

13.. *Coer de L.* 5121 Many wer the fayre geste Theron were wryten, and wylde beste, Tygrys, dragons, leons, lupard. ? *a* **1366** CHAUCER *Rom. Rose* 894 With briddes, lybardes, & lyouns, And othir beastis wrought ful welle. *c* **1400** *Destr. Troy* 1573 And all of marbill was made with meruellus bestes, Of lions & Libardes & other laithe wormes. **1523** SKELTON *Garl. Laurel* 590 Wheron stood a lybbard crownyd with golde and stones. **1588** SHAKS. *L.L.L.* v. ii. 551 With Libbards head on knee.

b. *Anc. Her.* A lion passant guardant [F. *lion léopardé*], as in the Arms of England.

[*c* **1300** *Siege of Carlaverock* (Nicolas 1828) 22 En sa baniere trois luparte.] *c* **1330** R. BRUNNE *Chron.* (1810) 305 þei sauh kynge's banere, raumpand þre lebardes. **1475** *Bk. Noblesse* 24 The said King Henry the seconde bare in armes frome that day forthe the saide libarde of gold withe the other two libardis of the same that is borne for Duke of Normandie. **1525** LD. BERNERS *Froiss.* II. ccii. [cxcviii.] 623 He lefte the beryng of the Armes of Englande, or the lybardes, and flour delyces quarterly. **1614** SELDEN *Titles Hon.*, In royal blazonry leopards and lions were synonymous terms, and used indifferently. **1814** SCOTT *Ld. of Isles* VI. xxxv, Though ne'er the leopards on thy shield Retreated from so sad a field, Since Norman William came.

c. A gold coin, having on the obverse a lion passant guardant, struck by Edward III, *c* 1344, and by the Black Prince, for circulation in France.

In the proclamation authorizing its issue 18 Edw. III, it is called 'a gold coin with one leopard', and is stated to be of the value of a florin of Florence. A coin called *leopardus auri* is mentioned in a monastic document of Bordeaux dated by Du Cange *a* 1305; but the date may be an error.

†**d.** The ***leopard's*** (i.e. lion's) ***head*** seems to have been used as an assay-mark for silver. *Obs.*

1423 *Rolls of Parlt.* IV. 257/1 That no Goldsmyth..nor other Man that worketh Selver Hernois, put noon therof to the sale..or that it be touched wyth the touche of the Liberdisheed.

4. a. The fur of the leopard. Also, the skin of the leopard; a coat made from this.

1490 *Will of Peyton* (Somerset Ho.), Gown..furred wᵗ lybbards. **1506** *Ld. Treas. Acc. Scotl.* (1901) III. 249 It [ane cote] was lynyt with leopardis. **1924** *Vogue* early Sept. 42 (*caption*) Even smarter..is a suède coat lined and trimmed with leopard. **1930** M. BACHRACH *Fur* xv. 197 All Leopards are open-handled and..there is very little natural grease on the skin. **1938** —— *Selling Furs Successfully* ix. 91 It is preferable when manufacturing Leopards into garments that as few seams as possible show after the garments are finished. **1951** R. T. WILCOX *Mode in Furs* vii. 157 Such peltries as bear, lynx, fox, wolf and goat were popular though lamb, civet cat and leopard are noted too [in the early 20th century]. *Ibid.* 208 (*caption*) Hooded circular cape of Somali leopard. **1973** E. MCBAIN *Let's hear It* iii. 44 'My

good jewelry..[has] gone.' 'Anything else?' 'Two furs. A leopard and an otter.'

b. *attrib.* or quasi-*adj.* Made of leopard skin or material resembling leopard skin.

1772 *Town & County Mag.* 71 To consult about the cut of his next coat, or the trimming of his next leopard sourtout. **1938** M. BACHRACH *Selling Furs Successfully* ix. 100 'This Leopard coat is rather heavy' is sometimes remarked by customers. **1951** R. T. WILCOX *Mode in Furs* vii. 199 (*caption*) Leopard jacket belted with dark blue antelope—leopard gloves with antelope palms. **1958** *Listener* 28 Aug. 316/3 Scowling Continental 'helps' in leopard slacks. **1974** *Times* 11 Nov. 28/7, 1 sable, skins worked down; 1 absolutely beautiful dark leopard coat. Both made by top furriers.

5. sea leopard = *leopard-seal*: see SEA.

6. *attrib.* and *Comb.*, as ***leopard skin, spot, whelp***; ***leopard-coloured, -like -spotted*** adjs.; **leopard-man**, one who has charge of a leopard; a member of a leopard society (see below); **leopard-skin** *attrib.*, made of leopard skin; resembling a leopard skin in appearance; mottled; **leopard-skin chief, priest**, among the Nuer people of East Africa, a mediator or arbitrator who settles disputes (so called from the leopard skin which by custom he wears); **leopard society**, in West Africa, a native secret society whose members dress as leopards and attack their victims in the manner of leopards.

1847 EMERSON *Poems* 73 Gayest pictures rose to win me, *Leopard-coloured rills. **1889** W. B. YEATS *Wanderings of Oisin* 78 Or in autumnal solitudes Arise the leopard-coloured trees. **1611** COTGR., *Leopardé*, *libbard-like. **1647** WARD *Simp. Cobler* 5 The Religion of that place was but motly and meagre, their affections Leopard-like. **1390-1** *Earl Derby's Exped.* (Camden) 257 Item pro lecto, vino, candelis et pro aliis expensis, per le *libardman ibidem, j scut. **1929** F. W. BUTT-THOMPSON *W. Afr. Secret Soc.* xiv. 283 *Tongo-players*, the Sierra Leonean society..said to have been started about the Eighties..as an organisation of leopard-men hunters. **1936** G. GRIFFIN tr. *Schebesta's My Pygmy & Negro Hosts* iv. 67, I think that I have been the first to obtain any detailed information about these 'Anyoto'—the dreadful 'leopard-men'. **1973** G. GALE in Johnson & Gale *Highland Jaunt* II. iv. 143 He now was happy..telling the bar about the Leopard Men in West Africa. **1599** HAKLUYT *Voy.* II. I. 113 Coates of the Turkes fashion, of *Libard skinnes. **1739** *Will* in Payne *Eng. Cath.* (1889) 55 My leopard-skin saddle trimmed with gold fringe. **1895** F. B. & W. H. WORKMAN *Algerian Memories* x. 93 Besides the oasis of Biskra..a number of others were visible, the dark colour of which, contrasting with the lighter hues of the plain, gave the leopard-skin appearance. **1929** E. SITWELL *Gold Coast Customs* 8 Courie shells..outline The leopardskin musty Leaves. **1975** *Times* 25 Feb. 6/7 Bagpipers of the Royal [Nepalese] Army in leopard-skin gaiters. **1940** E. E. EVANS-PRITCHARD *Nuer* iv. 190 There is no central administration, the *leopard-skin Chief being a ritual agent whose functions are to be interpreted in terms of the structural mechanism of the feud. **1956** —— *Nuer Relig.* iv. 110 In this particular ceremony several groups were opposed to each other, and the leopard-skin priest was acting in his priestly capacity as mediator between them. **1959** G. D. MITCHELL *Sociol.* v. 89 If one man kills another he will go immediately to a person known as a leopard-skin chief... He is in no sense a chief but rather a person who performs certain ritual acts. **1915** K. J. BEATTY *Human Leopards* i. 6 To deal with this extraordinary class of crime the Government of the Colony of Sierra Leone decided that drastic and exceptional legislation was necessary, and a Bill entitled the Human *Leopard Society Ordinance, 1895, was introduced and passed. **1929** F. W. BUTT-THOMPSON *W. Afr. Secret Soc.* i. 20 Most of the criminal associations are 'animal' societies... They include Alligator, Baboon, Boa, Leopard, Panther societies. **1968** *Encycl. Brit.* XIII. 975/2 There were many leopard societies, of which the most renowned was the *anyota* society of the Bali tribe, eastern Congo. **1939** T. S. ELIOT *Old Possum's Pract. Cats* 13 Her coat is of the tabby kind, with tiger stripes and *leopard spots. **1972** *Times* 23 Nov. 8/2 The presence of communist cadres within Government-held areas could produce more 'leopard spots', to use the accepted phrase, than the map [of S. Vietnam] suggests. **1931** V. WOOLF *Waves* 239 Different lights fall, making the ordinary *leopard-spotted and strange. **1884** SYMONDS *Shaks. Predecessors* vii. §3. 262 She ..led lyric poetry, like a tamed *leopard-whelp.

b. in the names of animals, etc. spotted or marked like the leopard, as **leopard cat**, (*a*) the African wild cat, *Felis Serval*; (*b*) the wild cat of India and the Malay Archipelago, *F. bengalensis*; (*c*) the American ocelot, *F. pardalis*; **leopard frog** *U.S.*, a green frog with black markings, *Rana pipiens*; **leopard lily** orig. *U.S.*, a name used for several spotted lilies, esp. *Lilium pardalinum* (cf. *panther-lily* (PANTHER 5)); **leopard-mackerel**, a scombrid fish, *Scomber leopardus* Shaw, *Cybium interruptum* Cuv., common in India; **leopard moth**, a collector's name for a large white black-spotted moth, *Zeuzera æsculi* or *Z. pyrina*; **leopard-seal, -shell** (see quots.); **leopard-spotted goby**, a small brown goby with orange spots, *Gobius forsteri*, found close to the shore in parts of the western coast of Britain and France; **leopard-tortoise**, *Testudo pardalis*; **leopard-tree** *Austral.*, a name for either of two species of *Flindersia*, *F. maculosa* or *F. collina*; also used for the South American tree *Cæsalpinia ferrea*; **leopard-wood**, (*a*) the wood of a S. American tree, *Brosimum Aubletii*; (*b*) *Austral.* = *leopard-tree*.

1773 *Gentl. Mag.* XLIII. 219 The *Leopard Cat. **1863** SPEKE *Discov. Nile* 273 A..young man, who had the skin of a leopard-cat..tied round his neck. **1884** *Riverside Nat. Hist.* (1888) V. 459 The Leopard Cat (*Felis bengalensis*) is either very variable in color and markings, or there are, as enumerated by Dr. Gray, four or five distinct species. **1839** D. H. STORER in Storer & Peabody *Rep. Fishes, Reptiles & Birds Mass.* 237 *Rana halecina*..[is] better known in this state as the *leopard frog from its ocellated appearance. **1840** THOREAU *Jrnl.* 16 June in *Writings* (1906) VII. 141 Twelve hours of genial and familiar converse with the leopard frog. **1948** *Sierra Club Bull.* (San Franciso) Mar. 140 Migration is a part of the story of the American merganser, hibernation of the leopard frog. **1973** *Sci. Amer.* Oct. 26/3 The leopard frog (*Rana pipiens*) is particularly susceptible to a kidney carcinoma. **1902** *Out West* Sept. 349 The *leopard-lily lights the heather dun. **1938** J. H. McFARLAND et al. *Garden Bulbs* 136 Lilium pardalinum. Sometimes called the Western Tiger Lily, this highly esteemed California native also has the common names of Leopard Lily and Panther Lily. **1949** H. MOLDENKE *Amer. Wild Flowers* 323 A great favorite of the Southeast is the leopard lily or pine lily, *L. catesbaei*, found in pinelands and acid swamps on the coastal plain from North Carolina to Florida and Louisiana. **1969** HAY & SYNGE *Dict. Garden Plants* 318/2 [*Lilium*] *pardalinum* Leopard Lily. Summer. Fl[ower] turkscap, orange flushed and spotted with red or maroon, pendulous. **1862** BEVERIDGE *Hist. India* I. Introd. 12 The *leopard-mackerel and the mango fish. **1819** G. SAMOUELLE *Entomol. Compend.* 246 *Zeuzera Æsculi* (wood *leopard-moth). **1870** J. R. S. CLIFFORD in *Eng. Mech.* 21 Jan. 449/3 A memorable wood-boring..caterpillar is that of the Leopard Moth (*Zeuzera Æsculi*). **1894** *Royal Nat. Hist.* (ed. Lydekker) II. 142 The *leopard-seal (*Ogmorhinus leptonyx*) may be taken as the best known representative of four genera confined to the Southern and Antarctic Seas... The leopard-seal or, as it is often called, the sea-leopard. **1711** *Phil. Trans.* XXVII. 350 A neat Rhombus, spotted with black and white, call'd therefore by some the *Leopard Shell. **1959** A. HARDY *Fish & Fisheries* x. 212 Mr. P. G. Corbin..is naming it after its discoverer, *Gobius forsteri*; it will also be known by the English name of *leopard-spotted goby. **1971** *Nature* 30 Apr. 581/1 Closer examination should reveal the presence of the leopard-spotted goby along the Scottish west coast. **1880** *Cassell's Nat. Hist.* IV. 252 The Ethiopian region of natural history has the greatest number of species of Tortoises, and the *Leopard Tortoise (*Testudo pardalis*),..and the little Geometric Tortoise are familiar examples. **1927** *Austral. Encycl.* I. 474/2 *F*[*lindersia*] *maculosa* (*Leopard Tree, so called from its spotted trunk) is a small tree (20-30 feet), found in the dry interior. **1933** *Bulletin* (Sydney) 20 Sept. 20/2 The leopard tree starts as a straggly, spiny bush, from the centre of which the stem shoots up. **1965** *Austral. Encycl.* V. 288/2 Leopard-tree, a name used for two species of *Flindersia*—the graceful inland *F. maculosa*, which has spotted bark, and the tall rain-forest species *F. collina* (broad-leaved leopard tree or leopard ash). The South American tree *Caesalpinia ferrea*, much grown as an ornamental flowering and shade tree in coastal Queensland, is also called leopard-tree and leopard-wood. **1859** *Handbk. Turning* 41 Partridge and *leopard woods. **1888** F. M. BAILEY *Queensland Woods* 76 *F*[*lindersia*] *maculosa*... Spotted tree or leopard-wood... Wood bright yellow, nicely marked. **1911** C. E. W. BEAN '*Dreadnought' of Darling* xv. 140 It seems a wonder that Australians on the coast do not make a much bigger use of these delicate Western trees for their gardens, especially the leopard-wood. **1936** F. CLUNE *Roaming round Darling* xviii. 177 Spotted a splendid leopard-wood, reputed to attract lightning more than any other tree.

leopardess ('lɛpədɪs). Also 6 libardesse. [f. LEOPARD + -ESS.] The female of the leopard.

1567 MAPLET *Gr. Forest* 92 The Lion and Libardesse [having conjunction] bring forth a third kind. **1883** MRS. LYNN LINTON *Ione* I. xi. 263 She had the supple grace of movement of..a leopardess.

attrib. **1873** LOWELL *Among my Bks.* Ser. II. 317 This glimpse of her, with her leopardess beauty..is all we have.

Leopardian (liːə'pɑːdɪən), *a.* [f. the name of Count Giacomo *Leopardi* (1798–1837) + -IAN.] Of, pertaining to, or characteristic of the Italian poet and scholar Leopardi, or his works.

1881 *Fraser's Mag.* XXIV. 571 In England we have had as yet no notice of the flood of Leopardian recollections, memoirs, and posthumous correspondence that has recently appeared in Italy. **1934** *Times Lit. Suppl.* 21 June p. xi/1 This return to the Leopardian tradition in the more recent poets has been one of the most striking developments. **1947** *Horizon* Apr. 195 Articles and books have been written on 'Leopardian optimism'. **1970** I. ORIGO *Images & Shadows* viii. 181, I remember telling the distinguished Leopardian scholar and critic, Giuseppe de Robertis..that..I was just beginning a second life of the poet. He began to laugh. 'I see that you have caught it, too,' he said, '*il vizio leopardiano*.'

†'**leopardine**, *a. Obs. rare*⁻¹. [f. LEOPARD + -INE.] Characteristic of a leopard.

1641 J. JACKSON *True Evang. T.* I. 26 There was a transmigration of the same Wolvish, Leopardine, Leonine spirit into Domitian the Emperour.

†'**leopardized**, *ppl. a.* ? *nonce-wd.* [f. LEOPARD + -IZE + -ED¹; after F. *léopardé*.] A lion represented as passant guardant.

1762 tr. *Busching's Syst. Geog.* I. 77 A lion leopardized azure, with nine hearts gules.

leopardling ('lɛpədlɪŋ). *rare*⁻¹. [f. LEOPARD + -LING.] A young leopard.

1861 DU CHAILLU *Explor. Equat. Afr.* xii. 167, I beheld an immense leopard,..with a tiny little leopardling near her side.

leopard's bane. Forms: 6 lyberdes, libardis, leopardes bayn(e, libardbain(e, -bayne, 7 lib(b)ard, libbard's bane, libbardsbane, 6– leopard's bane. [See BANE *sb.*¹ 2 b.] A plant of the genus *Doronicum*, esp. *D. Pardalianches*. Also applied to *Arnica montana*, *Paris quadrifolia* (Herb Paris), etc.

1548 TURNER *Names of Herbes* (E.D.S.) 8 The one kynde [of Aconitum] is called Pardalianches, which we may call in englishe Libardbayne or one bery. **1551** —— *Herbal* I. B ij, Leopardes bayne layd to a scorpione maketh hyr vtterly amased and Num. **1579-80** NORTH *Plutarch* (1676) 739 Libardbain or Wolf-bain. **1609** B. JONSON *Masque Queens*, Night-shade, moon-wort, libbard's bane. **1658** ROWLAND *Moufet's Theat. Ins.* 909 The venomous herb called Libbardsbane, or Wolf-wort. **1682** WHELER *Journ. Greece* VI. 478 Leopard's-bane whose root is like a scorpion. **1785** MARTYN *Rousseau's Bot.* xxvi. (1794) 394 Leopard's-bane, a wild plant of the Alps, and now common among the perennials of the garden. **1822-34** *Good's Study Med.* (ed. 4) I. 137 When a more active stimulant is necessary, that of leopard's bane (*arnica montana*) may be found useful. **1882** *Garden* 15 Apr. 247/1 The Leopard's-bane..grows in great patches in the woods.

leopoldite ('liːəpəʊldaɪt). *Min.* [Named from *Leopoldshall* in Prussia, its locality.] = SYLVITE.

1882 DANA *Man. Min.* Gen. Index, Leopoldite *v.* Sylvite.

leorne, obs. form of LEARN.

leos, str. pa. t. LEESE *v.*¹

leose(n, variant of LEESE *v.*¹

leotard ('liːətɑːd). [The name of Jules *Léotard* (1830–70), French trapeze artist.] A close-fitting one-piece garment worn by acrobats and dancers; a similar fashion garment. So '**leotarded** *a.*

1920 J. W. MANSFIELD *Let.* Jan. (MS. in G. & C. Merriam Co. files), Leotards..are used by acrobats and aerial performers. **1930** *Theatre Arts Monthly* Jan. p. viii/3 (Advt.), The improved Nat Lewis leotards. Lovely, yet sturdily constructed for hard usage. **1939** ADELER & WEST *Remember Fred Karno* ii. 39 The gymnasts' costume worn by Westcott consisted of the classic leotard, a sort of vest specially designed to leave the arms free, spangled neckpiece and trunks. **1953** *Ballet Ann.* VII. 66/1 The simplest of costumes—white *tutus* for the girls, black *leotards* for boys. **1957** *N.Y. Times Mag.* 3 Mar. 42/1 (Advt.), Low and behold, the *leotard*..the shape they said could never be built into a corselette. **1957** *Life* 12 Aug. 91/2 (*caption*) Short skirt worn over striped leotards. **1957** *Vogue* 15 Aug. 42/1 (Advt.), Worsted knit leotard pants. **1958** *Daily Express* 8 Aug. 2/7 Leotards will be the rage with teenage girls this autumn—ballet tights made of stretch nylon. **1966** T. PYNCHON *Crying of Lot 49* iii. 63 One of the girls, a long-waisted, brown-haired lovely in a black knit leotard. **1969** *Sears Catal.* Spring/Summer 21 Swimsuit. Knit of stretch nylon. Popular one-piece styling takes added fashion interest with its smart leotard look. Suit can also be worn as a leotard. **1972** *Listener* 20 Jan. 93/3 Leotarded, limbs akimbo. **1972** *Village Voice* (N.Y.) 1 June 40/4 Her dance, more leotarded than veiled, was attitude rather than movement.

†**leoth.** *Obs.* [OE. *léoð* str. neut. = Du. *lied*, OHG. *liod* (MHG. *liet*, inflected *lied-*, mod.G. *lied*), ON. *lióð*, Goth. **liuþ* (in *awiliuþ* thanksgiving):—OTeut. **leuþo*ᵐ.] A song.

Beowulf 1159 (Gr.) Leoð wæs asungen. *c* **1050** *Suppl. Ælfric's Gloss.* in Wr.-Wülcker 188/29 *Poema*, leoð. *c* **1200** *Trin. Coll. Hom.* 163 Ðe defles sed is..hoker and scorn, spel and leoð. *c* **1205** LAY. 22078 Þer suggen beornes seol-cuðe leoðes of Ardure þan kinge. **1230** *Hali Meid.* 21 Ah schulen weimeres leod ai mare in helle [singen].

b. *Comb.*, as **leoth-scop**, a poet.

c **1205** LAY. 22976 Ne al soh [*read* nis al soð] ne al les þat leod-scopes singeð.

leou, obs. form of LO *int.*¹

leoun, leounesse, obs. ff. LION, LIONESS.

leouwe, obs. form of LEE *sb.*¹

leove, variant of LEVE *v.*² *Obs.*; obs. f. LIEF.

Léoville (leɪəʊviːl). [Fr.] A red wine from any of three vineyards in the commune of Saint-Julien, district of Haut-Médoc, department of Gironde, France.

[**1833** C. REDDING *Hist. Mod. Wines* v. 149 St. Julien de Reignac..is the eighteenth commune of the Medoc vine country... The inferior growths of La Rose and Léoville are the produce of this commune.] **1875** TROLLOPE *Prime Minister* (1876) I. x. 155 'Oh yes, I remember the wine. You call it '57, don't you?' 'And it is '57;—'57, Léoville.' **1903** H. JAMES *Ambassadors* III. 73 Another degustation of the Léoville, another wipe of his mustache. **1966** H. YOXALL *Fashion of Life* xxv. 238 The Léovilles, it seems to me, are the characteristic wines of St Julien.

leowse, obs. form of LOOSE.

lep, obs. or Sc. form of LAP, LEAP.

lepadoid ('lɛpədɔɪd), *a.* and *sb.* [f. Gr. λεπαδ-, λέπας limpet + -OID.] **a.** *adj.* Resembling a barnacle or goose-mussel. **b.** *sb.* A lepadoid animal.

1843 OWEN *Invertebr. An.* I. xiii. 155 The Cirripedes are divided..into two primary groups,—viz. the pedunculated, or Lepadoids, and the sessile, or Balanoids.

'**lepal.** *Bot.* [f. Gr. λεπίς scale, after *petal*, *sepal*.] A barren stamen transformed into a scale.

1835 LINDLEY *Introd. Bot.* (1839) 181 Dunal calls these sterile stamens *lepals* (*lepala*); a term which has not yet been adopted. **1880** in GRAY *Struct. Bot.* 418/2.

lepamine ('lɛpəmaɪn). *Chem.* [f. LEP(IDINE + AMINE.] (See quot.)

1865 WATTS *Dict. Chem.* III. 571 *Lepamine*, a volatile base containing the elements of 1 at. diamylamine and 1 at. lepidine; $C_{10}H_{23}N.C_{10}H_9N = C_{20}H_{32}N_2$, produced by the action of iodide of amyl on lepidine. *Ibid.* 573 Diamyline-lepidine or Lepamine.

lepard(e, -art, obs. forms of LEOPARD.

Lepcha ('lɛptʃə), *sb.* and *a.* Also **Lapcha**. [Native name.] **A.** *sb.* A member of a Mongoloid people, native to Sikkim; the Tibeto-Burman language of this people. **B.** *adj.* Of or pertaining to this people or its language.

1819 F. HAMILTON *Acct. Kingdom Nepal* II. i. 118 The most eastern principality, in the present dominions of Gorkha, is that of the Lapchas, called Sikim. *Ibid.* 125 At this custom-house or mart is a Lapcha collector. **1839** *Jrnl. Asiatic Soc. of Bengal* VIII. 624 These neighbours of the hills are the Limboos, Kerantis, Lepchas, Murmis, and Bhotias. **1840** *Ibid.* IX. I. 393 Hill tribes,..whose language, exhibiting a mere dialectic difference from the Lepcha, may be expressed in symbols not dissimilar. **1848** J. D. HOOKER in L. Huxley *Life J. D. Hooker* (1918) I. xiii. 256 The Lepchas or mountaineers of Sikkim I like extremely. **1862** H. DE SCHLAGINTWEIT et al. *Results Sci. Mission India & High Asia* II. 268, I had with me natives from a great variety of tribes, Górkhas, Kerántis, and Nevâris from Nepál, and Límbus, Lépchas, and Bhútias from Sikkim. **1877** E. L. BRANDRETH in *Jrnl. R. Asiatic Soc.* X. I. 10 These determinatives are generally affixed in the languages of Nepál and in the Dhimal language; prefixed in the Lepcha language, [etc.]. *Ibid.* 15 In Lepcha, also, not only the adjective, but the demonstrative pronoun, as in Tibetan, follows the substantive. **1912** A. GORDON *Life A. H. Charteris* xiv. 339 The aboriginal Lepchas, a gentle race, are devil worshippers. **1940** F. S. CHAPMAN *Helvellyn to Himalaya* iv. 70 We wandered downhill to Dikchu... Most of the people here were sallow-faced Lepchas. **1948** D. DIRINGER *Alphabet* vi. 356 The Lepcha character seems to have been invented or revised by the Sikkim raja. **1965** *Evening Standard* 17 Sept. 6/2 The Sikkimese are Buddhists, and ethnically consist of Bhutias from neighbouring Bhutan; of Tibetans and of the neighbouring Lepchas. **1973** *Times* 12 Apr. 8/6 The Bhutias asserted themselves over the Lepchas, the aboriginal inhabitants, with whom they are now more or less integrated.

lepe, obs. or Sc. variant of LAP, LEAP.

† **'leper,** *sb.*[1] *Obs.* Forms: 3-6 lepre, 4-6 leper, 5 lepyr, -ur, leepre, 5-6 lepir, 6 lypper, lipper, lypre, lippre, leaper. [a. OF. *lepre, liepre* (mod.F. *lèpre*), ad. L. *lepra*, a Gr. λέπρα, properly fem. of λεπρός adj., scaly, f. λέπος scale.] Leprosy.

c **1250** *Gen. & Ex.* 3690 Ðor wurð ȝhe ðanne wið lepre smiten. *c* **1250** *Kent. Serm.* in *O.E. Misc.* 31 Si lepre be-tokned þo grete sennen þet biedh diadliche. *c* **1380** WYCLIF *Wks.* (1880) 67 þe leper of naaman cleuyd to hym..euere aftir. *c* **1400** tr. *Secreta Secret., Gov. Lordsh.* 81 Wyn þat ys takyn abundanly.. norsshes gretnes of body, and..brynges yn lepre. **1482** *Monk of Evesham* (Arb.) 92, ii. yonge vyrgyns ..ful sore infecte with the grete plage of lepur. **1525** LD. BERNERS *Froiss.* II. xlii. 132 He was syke of the lypper, so yt his flesshe fell in peces. **1562** TURNER *Baths* 9 The disease now called Lepre, but Elephantiasis of olde writers. **1565** JEWELL *Def. Apol.* (1611) 152 He pronounced not, who was cleane of Leaper, who was not, before that hee had viewed the colour.

fig. *c* **1440** *Gesta Rom.* lxii. 267 (Harl. MS.) Receyve medicyn of satisfaccion; and thenne þou shalt be clansyd fro all synfull lepr. **1588** A. KING tr. *Canisius' Catech.* 90 Nocht to iudge of ye lepre of ye body bot of ye saull.

leper ('lɛpə(r)), *sb.*[2] and *a.* Forms: 4 lepyre, 4-6 lepre, 5 leepre, lepere, lypre, 5-6 lipper, 6 lippir, lepar, liper, 6-8 leaper, 7 leeper, 4- leper. [Related to prec.; perh. originating as adj. from the attributive use of LEPER *sb.*[1]; the ending *-er* would naturally confirm the tendency to regard the word as a personal designation.]

A. *sb.* **a.** One affected with leprosy; a leprous person.

The term is often avoided in medical use because of its connotations.

1387 TREVISA *Higden* (Rolls) VI. 387 A leper þat was i-heled. *c* **1440** *Gesta Rom.* lxix. 317 (Harl. MS.) þe brothir of hure husbond..was a foul lypre. **1514** BARCLAY *Cyt. & Uplondyshm.* (Percy Soc.) p. li, Sometime a leper is 'signed to thy bed. **1545** BRINKLOW *Compl.* xxiv. (1874) 65 Pore blind peple, which thynck themseluys to be healed, whan thei remayne lepers stylle. **1593** SHAKS. *2 Hen. VI*, III. ii. 75, I am no loathsome Leaper, looke on me. **1603** OWEN *Pembrokeshire* (1891) 21 Gave certaine landes to the Mawdlens of Tenbye towardes the relieffe of the Leepers. **1611** BIBLE *2 Kings* v. 27 A leper as white as snow. **1722** DE FOE *Plague* (1884) 313 Ten Leapers were healed. **1846** TRENCH *Mirac.* x. (1862) 217 *note*, When through the Crusades leprosy had been introduced into Western Europe, it was usual to clothe the leper in a shroud, and to say for him the masses for the dead. **1871** J. MILLER *Songs Italy* (1878) 75 Lonely..as a leper cast out. **1948** R. G. COCHRANE in *Leprosy Rev.* XIX. 39, I feel that it is necessary for me to launch a protest at the constant use of the word 'leper' in medical literature. *Ibid.*, The Conference of the Leonard Wood Memorial held in Manila in 1931 recommended that the word 'leper' should not be used, but I fear this recommendation is completely ignored even by those leprologists who attended the conference. **1964** *Observer* 8 Nov. 33/5 To use the word 'leper' as a synonym for 'untouchable' is to perpetuate the ignorance and prejudice of former days. **1970** *Daily Tel.* 11 May 12/7, I regret to see that your columns have again been defaced twice by the word 'leper'... Its use has been banned by such ..bodies as the World Health Organisation and the International Leprosy Association. **1970** *Ibid.* 21 May 18 Those most entitled to say whether they suffer more from the disease or from the stigma attached to the word 'leper' are the patients themselves. The campaign against the word was started by patients in the famous American leprosarium in Carville. **1974** *Ibid.* 30 Jan. 16 Like some friendly leper, Mr Mick McGahey, the Communist vice-president of the National Union of Mineworkers, moves among Labour politicians spreading terrified unease with every jovial slap on the back. **1974** *Times Lit. Suppl.* 15 Mar. 263/4 In 1941 the reappearance of leprosy led to the prohibition of the movement of Aborigines below the 20th parallel—the 'leper line'. **1975** *Daily Tel.* 11 Apr. 3/1 He decided to dedicate his life to the Indian people, and for many years was in charge of 13 hospitals, two for lepers.

fig. **1552** LATIMER *Serm. 3rd Sund. Epiph.* (1584) 310 Euen as he was a leper of his body, so are we lepers of our soules. **1825** R. NESBIT in *Mem.* i. (1858) 23, I have..been afraid to join the society of the pious... I looked upon myself as a leper. **1847** TENNYSON *Princess* IV. 203 A moral leper, I, To whom none spake.

b. *attrib.* and *Comb.*, as *leper asylum, centre, lodge, spital*; **leper-house** = LAZAR-HOUSE; **leper-juice**, the liquid matter of a leproma; † **leper's herb**, a name for St. Paul's Betony, *Veronica serpyllifolia*; **leper('s) window**, name given to a supposed hagioscope for lepers.

1898 P. MANSON *Trop. Diseases* xxvi. 384 The rulers and clergy..took measures by instituting *leper asylums..to restrict the spread of [leprosy]. **1898** J. HUTCHINSON in *Arch. Surg.* IX. 381 As the country was..a *leper centre, some individuals were contaminated. **1616** SURFL. & MARKH. *Country Farme* 204 The distilled water of Paules Betonie, doth perfectly cure the Leprosie..this is the cause why this hearbe is called the *Leapers hearbe. **1855** STANLEY *Mem. Canterb.* ii. (1857) 104 This hospital, or *leper-house,..was then fresh from the hands of its founder. **1898** P. MANSON *Trop. Diseases* xxvi. 407 Pricking the now pallid leproma, and then collecting on a cover-glass the droplet of '*leper juice' which exudes from the puncture. *c* **1480** HENRYSON *Test. Cres.* 438 This *lipper ludge [ed. *Thynne* leper loge] tak for thy burelie bour. **1891** C. CREIGHTON *Hist. Epidemics* 99 The *leper-spitals of Scotland. **1850** *N. & Q.* 1st Ser. II. 111/1 'The *Leper's window' through which, it is concluded, the lepers who knelt outside the building witnessed the elevation of the host at the altar. **1882** HARDY in *Proc. Berw. Nat. Club* IX. No. 3. 470 There was a leper window at Elsdon church.

B. *adj.* Leprous.

1388 WYCLIF *Lev.* xiii. 46 In al tyme in which he is lepre [1382 leprows, Vulg. *leprosus*] and vnclene. **1427** *Sc. Acts Jas. I* (1814) II. 16/1 þat na lippir folk nothir man nor woman fra thyn furth enter na cum in to na burghe. **1429** *Wills & Inv. N.C.* (Surtees 1835) 78 It' to ye lepremen of Newcastell xls. *c* **1480** HENRYSON *Test. Cres.* 372 He luikit on hir ugly lipper face. **1483** CAXTON *G. de la Tour* F vij b, God was wrothe with her and made her to become lepre. **1508** DUNBAR *Flyting w. Kennedie* 154 Ane laithly luge that wes the lipper mennis. **1562** WINȜET *Cert. Tracates* Wks. 1888 I. 7 Playand..the part of lippir Giezi in this mater, sayand, Quhat wyll ye geve me? *a* **1600** MONTGOMERIE *Sonn.* xxxiv, Cative Cresside, vhair she lipper lay.

absol. **1533** GAU *Richt Vay* 63 Ye crippil gangis, ye liper ar maid cleyne.

Hence **'leperdom**, the realm of lepers; † **leperize** *v. trans.*, to smite with leprosy; † **leperness**, leprosy.

c **1550** CHEKE *Matt.* viii. 3 And bi and bi his lepernes was clensed. **1592** SYLVESTER *Tri. Faith* IV. vii, Moses by Faith doth Myriam leperize. **1889** *Cornh. Mag.* Aug. 141 Curiosities of Leperdom.

'leper, *v.* [f. LEPER *sb.*[2]] *trans.* To affect with leprosy; *fig.* to infect, taint.

1850 CLOUGH *Dipsychus* I. iii. 57 Some vagrant miscreant meets, and with a look Transmutes me his, and for a whole sick day Lepers me.

leper, obs. form of LOPPER *v.*, to curdle.

† **lepered,** *a. Obs.* [f. LEPER *sb.*[1] or *v.* + -ED.] Affected with leprosy; *fig.* foully infected.

1598 E. GUILPIN *Skial.* (1878) 34 This sinne leapered age. **1602** MARSTON *Antonio's Rev.* I. v. Wks. 1856 I. 87 If he is leapred with so foule a guilt.

† **'leperhead, -hood.** *Obs.* Also 6 lepored, lypored. [f. LEPER *a.* + -HEAD, -HOOD.] Leprosy.

1398 TREVISA *Barth. De P.R.* VII. lxiv. (1495) 279 The fourth manere leprehede cometh of redde Colera corrupte in the membres with Melancoly. **1493** *Festivall* (W. de W. 1515) 101 b, He was heled of a leperhode that he had. **1542** BOORDE *Dyetary* xxxi. (1870) 293 The .xxxi. Chapytre treatyth of a dyete for them the whiche haue any of the kyndes of lypored. He that is infectyd wyth any of the .iiii. kyndes of the lepored [etc.].

leperous, obs. form of LEPROUS.

† **'lepery,** *a. Obs. rare*⁻¹. In 6 leparie. [f. LEPER *sb.*[1] + -Y[1].] Leprous.

1558-68 WARDE tr. *Alexis' Secr.* 8 b, By this same secret haue bene healed certaine persons; which had their faces as it were Leparie [It. *il viso come leproso*].

† **lepi,** *a. Obs.* [See ANLEPI, ONLEPY.] Single.

a **1300** *E.E. Psalter* xiii. 2 [xiv. 3] Whilke þat gode dos es þare nane, Es þare nane to lepi ane. **1303** R. BRUNNE *Handl. Synne* 9147 Ne slepte onely a lepy wynke.

lepid ('lɛpɪd), *a.* Now *rare.* [ad. L. *lepid-us.*] Pleasant, jocose, facetious, amusing. Sometimes, Charming, elegant.

1619 SIR S. D'EWES *College Life* (1891) 73 In guessing at the lepid derivation [of English words]. **1649** BULWER *Pathomyot.* II. i. 84 From this Tonique motion Taurellus took his Lepid Paradox. **1658** PHILLIPS, *Terræ filius*, one that is allowed to make lepid or jesting speeches at an Act at Oxford. **1660** F. BROOKE tr. *Le Blanc's Trav.* I. xxxiii. 149 Apes, the greater part black as jet, some small ones black and white, very lepid. *a* **1677** BARROW *Serm.* Wks. 1716 I. 142 Some..figures..of rhetorick..are not easily differenced from those sallies of wit wherein the lepid way doth consist. **1691** WOOD *Ath. Oxon.* I. 22 He was..esteemed..for his lepid and jocular discourse. **1708** *Brit. Apollo* No. 49. 3/2 Solve the Above, ye Lepid Gods. **1804** *Edin. Rev.* III. 339 These histories..are probably not many degrees elevated above the lepid fables of Mrs. Goose. **1807-8** SYD. SMITH *Plymley's Lett.* Wks. 1859 II. 163/1 As for the joyous and lepid consul, he jokes upon neutral flags and frauds [etc.].

Hence **'lepidly** *adv.*

1650 BULWER *Anthropomet.* (1653) 66 Lucian very lepidly derides an old Woman, who..would have her Haire of a yellow tincture.

lepidine ('lɛpɪdaɪn), *sb. Chem.* [f. mod.L. *Lepidium*, a botanical genus, ad. Gr. λεπίδιον, dim. of λεπίς scale; see -INE.] A volatile oily base obtained by distilling quinine, cinchonine, and other alkaloids.

1856 FOWNES *Chem.* (ed. 6) 580 Lepidine contains $C_{20}H_9N$, cryptidine $C_{22}H_{11}N$. **1862** MILLER *Elem. Chem.* VI. 456.

lepidine ('lɛpɪdaɪn), *a.* [f. Gr. λεπιδ-, λεπίς scale + -INE.] Composed of scales.

1859 TODD *Cycl. Anat.* V. 481/2 In C the scale widening ..the edges of its 'Lepidine' layer do not remain in contact with the ganoin layer.

† **le'pidity.** *Obs.* [ad. L. type **lepiditās*, f. *lepid-us*: see LEPID *a.* and -ITY.] Facetiousness, wit; an instance of this.

1647 WARD *Simp. Cobler* 84 For Levity, read Lepidity. **1656** BLOUNT *Glossogr.*, *Lepidity*, delectableness, or good grace in speech. **1694** HOWE *Wks.* (1834) 144/2 In a discourse upon so grave a subject some lepidities had been left out.

lepido- ('lɛpɪdəʊ), repr. Gr. λεπιδο-, combining form of λεπίς scale, used in certain scientific terms (the more important are given as main words): **'lepidochlore** (-klɔə(r)) *Min.* [Gr. χλωρός green], an impure chlorite containing mica. **,lepidocrocite** (-'krəʊsaɪt) *Min.* [Gr. κροκίς fibre], a red to reddish-brown hydroxide of iron, FeO(OH), which is found as scaly or fibrous orthorhombic dipyramidal crystals, often in association with goethite, $HFeO_2$ (with which it was formerly identified). **,lepido'dendroid** (-'dɛndrɔɪd) *a.*, pertaining to or resembling plants of the genus *Lepidodendron*; *sb.*, a plant of this genus or of the group of which it is the type; also **,lepido'dendrid** *sb.* ‖ **,lepido'dendron** (-'dɛndrɒn) [Gr. δένδρον tree], a genus of fossil plants common in coal-measures, characterized by the presence on the trunk of leaf-scars; a plant of this genus; also *attrib.* **,lepido'ganoid** (-'gænɔɪd) *a. Ichthyol.* [see GANOID], pertaining to the *Lepidoganoidei*, a group of ganoid fishes having regular scales instead of plates; *sb.*, a fish of this group. **,lepidoga'noidean** *a.*, = prec. adj. **,lepidomelane** (-mɛ'leɪn) *Min.* [Gr. μέλας, μέλαν-ος black], a highly ferruginous mica, usually found in aggregations of small black scales. **,lepido'morphite** (-'mɔːfaɪt) *Min.* [Gr. μορφή form], a fine scaly mica, the result of the alteration of oligoclase (Chester *Dict. Min.* 1896). **,lepido'phæite** (-'fiːaɪt) *Min.* [Gr. φαιός dun], a fibrous and scaly variety of lampadite (Cassell 1884). **,lepido'saurian** (-'sɔːrɪən) [see SAURIAN] *a.*, pertaining to the sub-class *Lepidosauria* of Reptiles, characterized by a scaly integument; *sb.*, one of the *Lepidosauria*. ‖ **,lepido'siren** *Ichthyol.* [see SIREN], a genus of dipnoan fishes; a fish of this genus. **,lepi'dosteid** (-'dɒstiːɪd), **lepi'dosteoid** (-'dɒstiːɔɪd) *a.*, pertaining to the family *Lepidosteidæ* of rhomboganoid fishes; *sb.*, a fish of this family. **lepido'trichium** [Gk. θρίξ, τριχ- hair], (usu. in pl. **lepido'trichia**) in most teleost fishes, the bony rays supporting the outer part of the fins.

1859 C. V. SHEPARD *Rep. Mt. Pisgah* 6 (Chester) *Lepidochlore. **1823** H. J. BROOKE *Crystallogr.* 476 *Lepidokrokite. **1868** DANA *Min.* (ed. 5) 170 Scaly-fibrous, or feathery columnar..the Lepidocrocite. **1919** *Amer. Jrnl. Sci.* XLVII. 322 Optical studies of the reddish, scaly crystals called rubinglimmer and lepidocrocite, led Lacroix to propose that they be classed together as lepidocrocite and separated from goethite, with which they had formerly been identified. **1944** C. PALACHE et al. *Dana's Syst. Min.* (ed. 7) I. 644 The name goethite properly belongs to the species here described, since the name was originally given by Lenz to the material from Eiserfeld now known to be lepidocrocite. Goethite, however, is in general use to designate the compound $HFeO_2$. **1951** *Amer. Mineralogist* XXXVI. 31 Lepidocrocite has the hydrogen atom in a discrete OH group... Hence the decomposition of lepidocrocite occurs at a lower temperature than goethite. **1967** *New Scientist* 13 July 92/3 Professor Lowenstam has discovered that some chitons have a second iron mineral in their teeth—lepidocrocite. **1971** R. J. GETTENS *Two Early Chinese Bronze Weapons* iv. 23 The iron blade which served as the cutting edge has been drastically altered by corrosion. .. X-ray powder diffraction analysis of samples of rust showed that it consists of two hydrated iron oxides, goethite ..and lepidocrocite. **1863** DANA *Geol.* 395 The large

*Lepidodendrids of the Coal era. **1877** Le Conte *Elem. Geol.* (1879) 316 Gigantic Lepidodendrids and Sigillarids. **1876** Page *Adv. Text-bk. Geol.* xiii. 223 Year after year these *lepidodendroid stems are becoming better known. **1872** Nicholson *Palæont.* xliii. 475 The Lepidodendroids and Sigillaroids have now [in the Trias] completely disappeared. **1875** W. C. Williamson in Bennett & Dyer *Sachs' Bot.* 421 The Lepidodendroid plants. **1836** Buckland *Geol. & Min. Consid.* I. 468 The internal structure of the *Lepidodendron. **1867** H. Macmillan *Bible Teach.* iv. (1870) 82 Lepidodendrons and Sigillarias were intermediate between pines and club-mosses, though approaching more nearly the former. **1861** Henry *Gloss. Sci. Terms*, **Lepidoganoid*, a sub-order of fossil fishes. **1863** Dana *Geol.* 279 Scale-covered Ganoids, or *Lepidoganoids. **1844** —— *Min.* (ed. 2) 322 *Lepidomelane..was named in allusion to its structure and color. **1879** Rutley *Stud. Rocks* x. 136 Lepidomelane occurs in small disc-sided tabular crystals, or in aggregations of minute scales. **1854** Owen *Skel. & Teeth* in *Circ. Sci., Organ. Nat.* I. 172 The *lepidosiren, and many fossil fishes. **1848** Carpenter *Anim. Phys.* ii. (1872) 99 The Lepidosiren or mud fish. **1904** E. S. Goodrich in *Q. Jrnl. Microsc. Sci.* XLVII. 472 In the majority of Teleostean fish the median and paired fins are covered with a smooth scaleless skin, below which lie the dermal fin-rays. For reasons which will appear later, I propose to call these rays the *lepidotrichia. **1963** P. H. Greenwood *Norman's Hist. Fishes* (ed. 2) iii. 29 The outer part of the fin [of sturgeons] is supported not by horny rays but by bony fin rays, actually modified scales, called lepidotrichia.

lepidoid (ˈlɛpɪdɔɪd), *a.* and *sb. Ichthyol.* [f. Gr. λεπιδ-, λεπίς scale + -oid; cf. λεπιδοειδής scale-like (Galen).] **A.** *adj.* Scaly; pertaining to the *Lepidoidei*, a family of fossil fishes having large rhomboidal scales. **B.** *sb.* A fish belonging to this family.

1836 Buckland *Geol. & Min. Consid.* I. 282 (*heading*) Lepidoid Fishes. *Ibid. note*, The Pycnodonts, as well as the fossil Sauroids, have enamelled scales, but it is in the Lepidoids that scales of this kind are most highly developed. **1854** A. Adams etc. *Man. Nat. Hist.* 562 All the lepidoid and sauroid fishes which [etc.].

lepidolite (ˈlɛpɪdəlaɪt). *Min.* [f. Gr. λεπιδο-, λεπίς scale + -lite.] A variety of mica containing lithia.

1796 Kirwan *Elem. Min.* (ed. 2) I. 208 *Lepidolite*, Lilalite of some. **1837** Dana *Min.* 264 A violet variety [of common mica] occurring in small scales, has been distinguished by the name lepidolite. **1863** *Fownes' Chem.* 298 The best material for the preparation of rubidium, is lepidolite, which has been found to contain..0·2 per cent. of that metal. **1879** Rutley *Stud. Rocks* x. 134 Before the blowpipe lepidolite colours the flame purple-red.

lepidopter (lɛpɪˈdɒptə(r)). *Ent.* [ad. mod.L. *Lepidoptera* (see next).] One of the Lepidoptera.

1828 in Webster. **1863** Dana *Geol.* 420 *note*, Lepidopters have large wings covered with minute scales; as the Butterfly and Moth. **1881** Elwes tr. *De S. Pinto's How I crossed Afr.* I. v. 120 This gigantic lepidopter, when young, feeds upon the grasses.

‖**Lepidoptera** (lɛpɪˈdɒptərə), *sb. pl. Ent.* [mod.L., f. Gr. λεπιδο-, lepido- + πτέρον wing.] A large order of insects, characterized by having four membranous wings covered with scales; it comprises the butterflies and moths.

[**1735** Linnæus *Syst. Nat.* (1758) I. 458.] **1773** T. P. Yeats *Inst. Entomol.* 18 *Lepidoptera*, which have four wings, all membranaceous, and imbricated. **1866** Dk. Argyll *Reign of Law* i. (ed. 4) 38 Baits to tempt the nectar-loving Lepidoptera.

Hence **lepiˈdopteral** *a.*, lepidopterous; **lepiˈdopteran** *a.*, lepidopterous; also as *sb.*

1828 Webster, *Lepidopteral*, belonging to the order of Lepidopters. **1855** Hyde Clarke *Dict.*, *Lepidopteral*, *-terous*, *-teran*. **1865** Wood *Homes without H.* xix. 409 The tiny cylindrical cases that are made by certain lepidopteran larvæ. **1923** J. S. Huxley *Ess. Biologist* ii. 96 It is not only the burnt child who dreads the fire (although a study of moths and candles will convince us that 'Lepidopteran' cannot be substituted as subject of the proverb). **1971** *Nature* 13 Aug. 484/1 Similar responses of hymenopteran parasites to the mandibular gland secretions of their lepidopteran hosts may occur in other species. **1973** *Ibid.* 3 Aug. 253/1 One abundant lepidopteran is the southern armyworm, *Prodenia eridania*, a polyphagous species. **1973** Proctor & Yeo *Pollination of Flowers* iv. 96 The lepidopteran proboscis is very differently constructed from that of the Diptera.

lepidopterist (lɛpɪˈdɒptərɪst). [f. Lepidopter-a + -ist.] One who studies the natural history of Lepidoptera.

1826 Kirby & Sp. *Entomol.* xliii. IV. 192 If a Lepidopterist goes into the wood to capture moths in the day-time. **1872** O. W. Holmes *Poet Breakf.-t.* ii. (1885) 48 Great competition..between the dipterists and the lepidopterists. **1971** *Daily Tel.* (Colour Suppl.) 8 Jan. 21/2 If she is an amateur lepidopterist..the candids should obviously show her chasing butterflies. **1975** *Sci. Amer.* Jan. 92/3 The first person in the area who is known to have captured a dark-colored peppered moth was an active lepidopterist, R. S. Edleston, who obtained a specimen in 1849.

lepidopterology (ˌlɛpɪdɒptəˈrɒlədʒɪ). [f. Lepidoptera *sb. pl.* + -ology.] The branch of entomology which deals with the study of Lepidoptera. Hence **ˌlepidopteˈrologist**; **ˌlepidopteroˈlogical** *a.*

1899 *Proc. 4th Internat. Congress Zool. 1898* 232 An important phenomenon that my studies in Lepidopterology have revealed. *Ibid.*, England and English-speaking America possess the greatest number of Lepidopterologists. *Ibid.* 337 Matters other than Lepidopterological must be settled by a general committee of Zoologists. **1921** (*title*) Bulletin of the Hill Museum: a magazine of lepidopterology. **1967** V. Nabokov *Speak, Memory* (ed. 2) vi. 123 Since the middle of the century, Continental lepidopterology had been..a simple and stable affair. *Ibid.* 129 Among the very few lepidopterological images in English poetry, my favorite is Browning's.

lepidopterous (lɛpɪˈdɒptərəs), *a.* [f. Lepidoptera + -ous.] Of or pertaining to the Lepidoptera.

1797 J. Abbott (*title*) The Natural History of the rarer Lepidopterous Insects of Georgia. **1826** Kirby & Sp. *Entomol.* IV. 533 With regard to setting Lepidopterous insects. **1835** *Trans. Zool. Soc. Lond.* I. 188 *note*, A detailed generalization of the Lepidopterous wing. **1861** W. Barnes in *Macm. Mag.* June 131 The lepidopterous insect 'colias edusa', is bright with orange and green.

lepidote (ˈlɛpɪdəʊt), *a. Bot.* [ad. mod.L. *lepidōt-us*, a. Gr. λεπιδωτός, f. λεπιδ-, λεπίς scale.] Covered with scurfy scales; leprose, leprous. Also **ˈlepidoted** *a.*, in the same sense.

1836 *Penny Cycl.* V. 253/1 *Lepidote*, covered with a sort of scurfiness. **1845** Lindley *Sch. Bot.* i. (1858) 19 Scurfs (*lepides*) are roundish minute scales, attached to plants by their middle..; a part covered by them is said to be *lepidote*. **1860** Worcester, *Lepidote*, *Lepidoted*. **1870** Hooker *Stud. Flora* xvi, Elæagneæ... Shrubs with lepidote scales.

lepocyte (ˈlɛpəsaɪt). [ad. mod.L. *lepocyta*, f. Gr. λέπος scale + κύτος cell.] 'A nucleated cell provided with walls' (*Syd. Soc. Lex.* 1888).

lepolite (ˈlɛpəlaɪt). *Min.* [Named, 1847 (*lepolit*), by A. A. Jossa, f. Gr. λέπο-ς husk + -lite.] A variety of anorthite from Finland.

1885 in *Cassell's Encycl. Dict.* **1896** Chester *Dict. Min.*

lepored: see leperhead.

leporicide. *rare.* [f. L. *lepor(i)-*, *lepus* hare + -cide 1, 2.] **1.** A killer of hares.

1788 Burke *Corr.* (1844) III. 77 If he could pay the duty ..he would cut off every soul of all the hares in the country ..He will depute a gamekeeper; and then, lo you! he executes all his threats by deputy, and by deputy becomes a leporicide and a gentleman.

2. The killing of hares.

1914 W. de Morgan *When Ghost meets Ghost* I. xviii. 200, I..went..dreading that I should find Achilles [a dog] awaiting applause for an achievement in—in leporicide, I suppose.

leporide (ˈlɛpəraɪd). [ad. F. *léporide*, f. L. *lepor-*, *lepus* hare: see -ide.] An alleged 'cross' between a hare and a rabbit.

1880 *Libr. Univ. Knowl.* VIII. 817 Leporide, the name given by the French to a remarkably prolific hybrid between the common European hare and the rabbit. **1886** *Encycl. Brit.* XX. 193/1 Some few years since many of these animals were sold as leporides or hybrids, produced by the union of the hare and rabbit; but the most careful experimenters have failed to produce any such hybrid.

leporiform (ˈlɛpərɪfɔːm), *a.* [f. L. *lepor(i)-*, *lepus* hare + -form.] Having the form of a hare; lagomorphic.

1889 in *Century Dict.*

leporine (ˈlɛpəraɪn), *a.* and *sb.* [ad. L. *leporīnus*, f. *lepor-*, *lepus* hare: see -ine[1].]

A. *adj.* Pertaining to a hare or hares; of the nature or form of a hare; lagomorphic.

† *leporine seal*: perh. *Phoca barbata* (Fabr.).

1656 Blount *Glossogr.*, *Leporine*, of or pertaining to an Hare. **1781** Pennant *Hist. Quadrupeds* II. 523 Leporine Seal, *Phoca Leporina*..S[eal] with fur, soft as that of a hare, upright and interwoven. **1855** Mayne *Expos. Lex.*, *Leporinus*, hare-like; leporine; but chiefly applied to denote resemblance to the mouth of the hare. **1877** Coues & Allen *N. Amer. Rod.* 44 The large, leporine, grooved-incisor species of South America.

B. *sb.* = leporide.

1862 *Melbourne Leader* 13 Sept. 13 The bill of fare included..leporine, which is betwixt hare and rabbit.

lepospondyl (lɛpəʊˈspɒndɪl), *sb.* and *a.* [f. mod.L. name of suborder *Lepospondyli* (K. A. Zittel *Handbuch der Palæontologie* (1887–90) I Abth. III. 348), f. Gr. λέπος husk + σπονδύλος vertebra.] An extinct amphibian belonging to the suborder Lepospondyli, distinguished by vertebrae shaped like hour-glasses; of or pertaining to an amphibian of this type. Also **lepoˈspondylous** *a.*

1901 H. Gadow in *Cambr. Nat. Hist.* VIII. iv. 79 The vertebræ [of Stegocephali] exhibit three types... 1. Lepospondylous and pseudocentrous.—The vertebra consists of a thin shell of bone surrounding the chorda dorsalis. **1902** C. R. Eastman tr. *Zittel's Text-bk. Palaeontol.* II. 118 (*caption*) Lepospondylous vertebrae of *Hylonomus*. **1933** A. S. Romer *Vertebr. Paleontol.* v. 112 In the lepospondyls the vertebral centrum was a single hollow spool-shaped ossification. *Ibid.*, The divergence of the various lepospondyl groups must have taken place at an extremely early date. **1958** C. K. Weichert *Anat. Chordates* (ed. 2) xix. 850 Stegocephalia... Fossil forms: labyrinthodonts, lepospondyls, and phyllospondyls, varying primarily in structure of vertebral column. **1971** E. C. Olson *Vertebr. Paleozool.* vii. 296 (*caption*) A lepospondyl (microsaur) skull. *Ibid.* 297 Like the other lepospondyls they [*sc. Lysorophus* and its relatives] are highly specialized.

lepper (ˈlɛpə(r)). A local variant of leaper, freq. of horses in hunting parlance.

1907 J. M. Synge *Playboy of Western World* III. 66 There you are! Good jumper! Grand lepper. **1920** *Baily's Mag.* Jan. 37/2 There are plenty of 'leppers' at Newmarket this season. **1931** A. J. Cronin *Hatter's Castle* I. ii. 41 We'll kick off on the leppers. All aboard for the Donegal Hunt. **1937** R. Westerby *Wide Boys Never Work* 173 'I put a couple of nicker on Tenderloin. He's a good lepper at that.'..'Got all the jargon, haven't you? "Good lepper"!—strewth!' **1948** Mencken *Amer. Lang.* Suppl. II. 362 Among American horse fanciers a jumping horse is called a *lepper*.

leppey, *a. Mining.* ? *Obs.* Soft.

1747 Hooson *Miner's Dict.*, *Leppey*. 'Tis when Work is Soft, Kind and Winable enough, without any Hardship, as Boreing, Cuting, Blasting, or such like. *Ibid.* U ij b, We drive at the Vein Head in the first Place, because there it is likely that the Vein may be the most Kind or Leppey.

‖**lepra** (ˈlɛprə). *Path.* [Late L., a. Gr. λέπρα: see leper *sb.*[1]] A skin disease characterized by desquamation: (*a*) formerly used as a synonym for psoriasis; (*b*) now commonly applied to leprosy (*Lepra cutanea* or *Elephantiasis Græcorum*).

1398 Trevisa *Barth. De P.R.* VII. lxiv. (1495) 279 In foure manere wyse Lepra meselry is dyuerse as the foure humours ben passyngly and dyuersly medlyd. *c* **1400** *Lanfranc's Cirurg.* 196 Lepra is a foul sijknes þat comeþ of malancolie corrupt. **1671** Salmon *Syn. Med.* I. xlviii. 114 *Lepra* the Leprosie is that which affecteth the whole Body or a part thereof with Scurff like Scales. **1811** A. T. Thomson *Lond. Disp.* (1818) 152 Scrofulous swellings, lepra, and some other cutaneous diseases. **1864** W. T. Fox *Skin Dis.* 43 Lepra and psoriasis are identical, though the two names are retained. **1876** tr. *Wagner's Gen. Pathol.* (ed. 6) 439 The common form of Lepra is characterized by a nodular formation. **1881** *Med. Temp. Jrnl.* XLVI. 76 Attended with lepra or psoriasis.

attrib. **1897** *Allbutt's Syst. Med.* II. 56 A large collection, or several clusters, of characteristic lepra-cells. **1898** P. Manson *Trop. Diseases* xxvi. 391 A direct and early implication of the nervous system by the lepra bacillus. *Ibid.* 412 A Sandwich Islander..was inoculated from a lepra tubercle.

b. *Bot.* 'A white mealy matter, which exudes or protrudes from the surface of some plants; leprosy' (*Treas. Bot.* 1866).

lepre: see leper and lepry.

leprechaun (lɛprəˈxɔːn, ˈlɛprəkɔːn). *Irish.* Forms: 7 **lubrican**, 9 **leprehaun**, **lepreehawn**, **leprechaun**. [Written *lupracán*, *lugharcán*, *lugracán*, in O'Reilly *Irish. Dict.* Suppl.; in the body of the Dict. it is spelt *leithbrágan*, doubtless by etymologizing perversion, the sprite being 'supposed to be always employed in making or mending a single shoe' (*leith* half, *bróg* brogue); O'Reilly also gives *luacharman* as a synonym. In some mod. Irish books the spelling *lioprachán* occurs. All these forms may be corrupted from one original; cf. Middle Irish *luchrupán* (Windisch *Gloss.*), altered form of Old Irish *luchorpán* (Stokes in *Revue Celtique* I. 256), f. *lu* small + *corp* body.] In Irish folk-lore, A pigmy sprite 'who always carries a purse containing a shilling' (O'Donovan in O'Reilly *Irish Dict.* Suppl. 1817).

1604 Middleton *2nd Pt. Honest Wh.* III. i. Wks. III. 175 As for your Irish lubrican, that spirit Whom by preposterous charms thy lust hath rais'd In a wrong circle. **1620** Dekker *Dreame* (1860) 28 Mounted on a spirits back, which ran With mandrake-shrikes, and like a lubrican. **1627** Drayton *Agincourt*, etc. 127 By the Mandrakes dreadfull groanes, By the Lubricans sad moanes. **1818** Lady Morgan *Fl. Macarthy* (1819) I. v. 289 There, your honor, them's my cordaries, the little Leprehauns, with their cathah heads, and their burned skins. **1860** *All Year Round* No. 38. 282 A little, lisping, attenuated falsetto voice, such as you would fancy would have proceeded from an Irish leprechaun. **1895** Jane Barlow *Strangers at Lisconnel* 231 A little ould lepreehawn.

Comb. **1883** W. Black *Shandon Bells* xvii, This little red-haired leprechaun-looking Andy.

†**ˈlepress.** *Obs.* [f. leper *sb.*[2] + -ess.] A female leper. Also quasi-*adj.*

1541 R. Copland *Guydon's Quest. Chirurg.*, *Exam. Lazares* Q ij b, Yf the mother be a lepresse. *Ibid.* Q iij, Than ought ye to enquyre yf he hath had y[e] company of any lepresse woman.. A woman is nat so daungerous to be a lepresse to habyte with a lazare, as it shulde be a man to habyte with a lazarous woman.

lepric (ˈlɛprɪk), *a. rare*[−0]. [ad. mod.L. *lepric-us*, a. Gr. λεπρικός, f. λέπρα lepra: see leper *sb.*[1]] Pertaining to lepra.

1855 in Mayne *Expos. Lex.* **1864** J. Thomas *Med. Dict.*, *Lepricus*, belonging to lepra; lepric.

leprolin (ˈlɛprəʊlɪn). *Med.* [f. lepro(sy + *-lin*, after tuberculin.] = lepromin.

1904 E. R. Rost in *Indian Med. Gaz.* XXXIX. 168/2 The next thing that was attempted was the manufacture of a leprolin on the lines of the manufacture of tuberculin. **1934** *Brit. Med. Jrnl.* 21 Apr. 703/2 The typical reaction to leprolin..when applied to healthy persons in an area free from endemic leprosy, differs from the intracutaneous tuberculin reaction in remaining for some days negative or

doubtful. **1947** R. G. COCHRANE *Pract. Textbk. Leprosy* vii. 64 Neural (N) Type [of Leprosy]... These cases..are of relatively good prognosis as regards life..and usually react positively to leprolin. [*Note*] Now termed lepromin. **1971** *Internat. Jrnl. Leprosy* XXXIX. 719/2 We deemed it worthwhile to determine the capacity of lymphocytes from leprosy patients to produce lymphotoxin in the presence of PHA and leprolin.

leprologist (lɛˈprɒlədʒɪst). [f. LEPRA + -(O)LOGIST.] A medical expert in leprous diseases.

1900 *Brit. Med. Jrnl.* 12 May 1164 With the assistance of a number of well-known leprologists. **1948** [see LEPER *sb.*²]. **1950** G. W. McCOY in R. L. Pullen *Communicable Dis.* xlii. 631 Promin..has been used in recent years by a group of leprologists working..at Carville, Louisiana. **1961** G. GREENE *Burnt-Out Case* v. i. 156 There is an old Danish doctor..who became a leprologist. **1970** *Daily Tel.* 21 May 18 Dr Browne is one of the leading leprologists in the world.

‖**leproma** (lɛˈprəʊmə). *Path.* Pl. **lepromas, lepromata.** [f. LEPRA, on the analogy of words like *sarcoma*.] A leprous tubercle.

1895 N. WALKER tr. *Hansen & Looft's Leprosy* ii. 5 The leprous nodes [of nodular Leprosy] or nodular Lepromata are of different size and colour; their consistence is at first firm and hard... Their form is usually semi-spherical, but they are often oblong. **1898** P. MANSON *Trop. Diseases* xxvi. 385 The leproma, the nerve lesions, and the lepra cell. **1947** R. G. COCHRANE *Pract. Textbk. Leprosy* viii. 81 We are convinced..that the majority of lepromas commence from pre-lepromatous macules..; some, however, develop from the simple macular lesions. **1970** G. J. HILL *Leprosy in Five Young Men* iv. 103 The mixture [*sc.* lepromin] is essentially a sterile emulsion of lepromas—that is, nodules excised from patients with lepromatous leprosy.

Hence **leˈpromatous** *a.*, of the nature of a leproma; characterized by or exhibiting lepromas: used *spec.* to designate one of the two principal forms of leprosy (see quot. 1938).

1898 P. MANSON *Trop. Diseases* xxvi. 397 The eyes also [in a leper] are sooner or later attacked, lepromatous growth spreading from the conjunctiva on to the cornea. **1938** *Internat. Jrnl. Leprosy* VI. 390 [Report of the Sub-committee on Classification of the First International Congress on Leprosy.] Objections have repeatedly been raised to both of the current names of the two types [of leprosy] (i.e., 'neural' and 'cutaneous')... It is the opinion of the committee... (*b*) That because 'cutaneous' has proved particularly confusing its use should be discontinued, and replaced by the term 'lepromatous'. *Ibid.*, Lepromatous (L) type.—All cases of the 'malignant' form of leprosy, relatively nonresistant and of poor prognosis, usually negative to leprolin, exhibiting lepromatous lesions of the skin and of other organs, especially the nerve trunks. **1947** [see above]. **1962** *Lancet* 26 May 1116/2 If the altered tissue response could be maintained by repeated B.C.G. vaccination, this might prove a beneficial adjunct to chemotherapy in lepromatous leprosy. **1970** [see above]. **1971** *Nature* 7 May 48/1 Leprosy, caused by *Mycobacterium leprae*, has two clinico-pathological forms: lepromatous, associated with impaired delayed hypersensitivity, and tuberculoid, with intact cutaneous reactivity.

lepromin (ˈlɛprəʊmɪn). *Med.* Also **-ine.** [a. G. *lepromin* (P. Bargehr 1927, in *Zeitschr. f. Immunitätsf. und exper. Ther.* XLIX. 347): see LEPROMA and -IN¹.] A boiled saline extract of lepromatous tissue. So **lepromin test**, a test involving intradermal injection of lepromin and examination for a nodule at the site (see quot. 1951).

1932 *Monthly Bull. Philippine Health Service* XII. 300 The leprolin (lepromin) used by Mitsuda, Bargehr, de Langen, de Vogel, Mariani, Muir and Hayashi were prepared in different ways. **1940** ROGERS & MUIR *Leprosy* (ed. 2) 248 The lepromin test is thus of use in measuring the natural resistance of the patient to leprous infection. **1951** WHITBY & HYNES *Med. Bacteriol.* (ed. 5) xiv. 267 The lepromin test consists of the intradermal injection of a small quantity of the extract. The test is positive in milder types of leprosy and in many healthy contacts; it is negative in the more severe types of the disease which have a bad outlook. **1959** G. GREENE *Congo Jrnl.* in *In Search of a Character* (1961) 89 Lepromine used to determine the resistance of an undetermined patient. **1973** BRYCESON & PFALTZGRAFF *Leprosy for Students Med.* vi. 62 Infection with *M*[*ycobacterium*] *tuberculosis*, immunization with BCG or previous skin testing with lepromin may, but does not necessarily, induce lepromin positivity in a normal person.

lepron, var. LAPRON *Sc. Obs.*, young rabbit.

1501 *Ld. Treas. Acc. Scotl.* (1900) II. 112 Ane man that brocht lepronis..to the King.

leprophil (ˈlɛprəʊfɪl). [f. LEPRO(SY + -PHIL.] One who is attracted to sufferers from leprosy. So **leproˈphilia** [Gr. φιλία affection], such an attraction.

1959 G. GREENE *Congo Jrnl.* in *In Search of a Character* (1961) 24 Should one class Father Damien among the leprophils? **1961** —— *Burnt-Out Case* I. ii. 19 You know very well that leprophils exist... Schweitzer seems to attract them. They would rather wash the feet with their hair like the woman in the gospel than clean them with something more antiseptic. **1963** P. WEST *Mod. Novel* II. i. 97 Leprophilia is the extremist answer. **1964** P. FEENY *Fight against Leprosy* ix. 90 The most serious charge..is that he was a 'leprophil', that is, that he fell in love with leprosy... This disease does hold an inverted glamour for a handful of people. *Ibid.* 91 He [*sc.* Damien] rushed into his work on Molokai like a back-row forward rushing into a scrum. He saw suffering and ran to alleviate it... Leprophilia does not enter into it.

leprophobia (lɛprəʊˈfəʊbɪə). Also **lepraphobia** (lɛprəˈfəʊbɪə). [f. LEPRO(SY + -PHOBIA; cf. LEPRA (*b*).] A morbid or insane fear of leprosy; *spec.* such a fear showing itself in the conviction of a person actually healthy that he is suffering from leprosy.

1894 GOULD *Dict. Med.* 670/1 *Leprophobia*, morbid or insane dread of leprosy. **1911** STEDMAN *Med. Dict.*, Lepraphobia. **1948** *Leprosy Rev.* XIX. 40 Euphemisms will not eradicate leprophobia. **1948** E. MUIR *Man. Leprosy* xiv. 98 Leprophobia may centre round any well-known symptom of leprosy. **1973** BRYCESON & PFALTZGRAFF *Leprosy for Students Med.* iv. 40 Do not treat for leprosy unless the diagnosis is established. Nothing is harder to cure than leprophobia.

leprosarium (lɛprəʊˈsɛərɪəm). Pl. **leprosaria.** [f. L. *lepros*(*us* leprous + ARIUM.] A hospital for sufferers from leprosy.

1846 DUNGLISON *Dict. Med. Sci.* (ed. 6) 430/1 An hospital for the reception of the leprous, *Leprosarium*. **1927** *Lancet* 23 July 212/2 (*heading*) The leprosarium at Makogai. **1935** *Nature* 4 May 757/2 A leprosarium being provided at Darwin. **1938** *Internat. Jrnl. Leprosy* VI. 399 The services of an ophthalmologist, a rhino-laryngologist and a dentist should..be made available in all leprosaria. **1966** *New Statesman* 15 Apr. 525/3 (Advt.), We will channel your gifts... *Against disease*. To hospitals, clinics, leprosaria. **1970** [see LEPER *sb.*² and *a.*].

leprose (ˈlɛprəʊs), *a. Bot.* [ad. L. *leprōsus*, f. LEPRA.] Having a scaly or scurfy appearance; lepidote; *esp.* said of crustaceous lichens in which the thallus adheres to trees or stones like a scurf.

1856 W. L. LINDSAY *Pop. Hist. Lichens* 34 Leprose species are also exceedingly common from our sea-coasts to our mountain summits. **1871** LEIGHTON *Lichen-flora* 46 Thallus leprose or powdery, effuse or evanescent.

¶ In pseudo-L. combining form *leproso-*, with the meaning 'leprose and...'

1871 LEIGHTON *Lichen-flora* 228 *L*[*ecanora*] *erysibe*.. leproso-granulose, thin, diffract. *Ibid.* 258 Thin, effuse, leproso-pulverulent.

†**ˈleprosed, ˈleproused,** *a. Obs.* [f. L. *leprōs-us* or Eng. LEPROUS *a.* + -ED¹.] Made leprous.

1550 BALE *Votaries* II. (1551) 96 So many sycke..leprosed ..hanged, and deade. **1656** S. H. *Golden Law* 61 Miriam was leprous'd as white as snow. *a* **1839** J. GALT *Demon of Destiny* VII. (1840) 49 And you, ye lepros'd ills..Make your abiding with the shunn'd and fear'd.

leprosery, leproserie (lɛˈprɒsərɪ). [ad. F. *léproserie* (also used) or Sp. *leprosería*.] A leper-house or -colony.

1884 *N.Y. Med. Jrnl.* 6 Sept. 275/2 In many parts of the country [*sc.* Brazil] *léproseries* have been established outside the city walls, to which are consigned all lepers excepting those of the very wealthiest families. **1891** J. L. ALLEN in *Century Mag.* Feb. 592 Mother Marianne would herself have written, but she was called away to the leprosery. **1897** *Dict. Nat. Biogr.* XLIX. 218/1 He founded the leprosery of St. Thomas the Martyr. **1961** G. GREENE *Burnt-Out Case* I. ii. 13 There was a rule that the leproserie should take contagious cases only.

leprosied (ˈlɛprəsɪd), *a. rare.* [f. LEPROSY + -ED².] Tainted with leprosy. (In quot. *fig.*)

1709 *Brit. Apollo* II. No. 51. 3/2 They're Leprosy'd with Scandal.

†**leˈprosity.** *Obs.* [ad. med.L. *leprōsitātem*, f. *leprōsus* LEPROUS. Cf. OF. *leprosité*.] Leprous quality or condition. In *Alchemy*, metallic impurity.

1555 EDEN *Decades* 28 With the..tortoyses of this Ilande, many leprous men are healed and clensed of theyr leprositie. **1626** BACON *Nat. Hist.* §326 If the Crudities, Impurities and Leprosities of Metals were cured, they would become Gold. **1635** A. READ *Tumors & Vlcers* 222 The Grecian leprosity may be thus described.

leprosy (ˈlɛprəsɪ). Also 6 **lepresie**, 6–7 **leprosie**, 7 **leaprosie, leprousie.** [? ad. med.L. **leprōsia* (Du Cange has *leprosia* leper-house), f. *leprōsus* LEPROUS. Cf. It. *lebbrosia*.]

1. An infectious bacterial disease (*Elephantiasis Græcorum*), which slowly eats away the body, and forms shining white scales on the skin; common in mediaeval Europe.

In the Eng. Bible it renders the Heb. *çārá*ʕ*ath*, Gr. λέπρα, which seem to have been used as comprehensive terms for various skin diseases.

1535 COVERDALE *Lev.* xiii. 3 Then is it surely a leprosy [1382 WYCLIF a plaage of lepre]. **1563** *Mirr. Mag.*, *Buckingham* ci, Thy deare doughter stroken with leprosye. **1597** MORLEY *Introd. Mus.* 163 Like vnto a hereditarie lepresie in a mans bodie is vncurable without the dissolution of the whole. **1613** PURCHAS *Pilgrimage* (1614) 216 They say it procureth the Leprosie in the children which are then gotten. **1673** RAY *Journ. Low C.* 71 These Waters dry up and heal..Leprosie and other Affections of the Skin. **1798** COLERIDGE *Anc. Mar.* III. xi, Her skin was white as leprosy. **1801** COLEBROOKE *Jrnl.* in *Life* (1873) 176 Last month, a young man..was going to be buried alive, on account of the leprosy. *Ibid.* 177 When one of the family dies of a leprosy. **1863** BARING-GOULD *Iceland* 176 The people suffer severely from scorbutic attacks and leprosy.

b. *fig.*

1598 ROWLANDS *Betray. Christ* 14 My leprosie is a defiled soule. *a* **1623** W. PEMBLE *Wks.* (1635) 9 The tongues, the pens, the practises of not a few discover unto us this leprosie of Atheisticall contempt of God's wisdome arising in their foreheads. **1651** HOBBES *Leviath.* III. xli. 265 Such men as are cleansed of the Leprousie of Sin by Faith. **1751** J. BROWN *Shaftesb. Charac.* 237 What this leprosy of false knowledge may end in, I am unwilling to say. **1781** COWPER *Expost.* 96 When nations are to perish in their sins, 'Tis in the church the leprosy begins. **1836** HOR. SMITH *Tin Trump.* (1876) 202 Idleness is a moral leprosy, which soon eats its way into the heart.

†**c.** A similar disease in horses. *Obs.*

1580 BLUNDEVIL *Order Curing Horses Dis.* iii. 2 The cankred mangenesse, most commonlie called of the old writers the Leprosie. *Ibid.* cliv. 65 b, The Leprosie or vniuersall manginesse, called of the old writers Elephantia.

d. *attrib.* and *Comb.*

1648–60 HEXHAM *Dutch Dict.*, *de Kleppe van een Lazarus*, the Clicket which a Leprosie man beggs with. **1705** *Lond. Gaz.* No. 4106/4 His Cordial Antidote for eradicating all.. Leprosie Humours out of the Blood. **1897** *Allbutt's Syst. Med.* II. 62 The leprosy bacillus is by no means evenly distributed throughout the body. *Ibid.* 69 Instances of transmission in leprosy-free countries.

2. A leper-house. *rare*⁻¹.

1834 L. RITCHIE *Wand. by Seine* 89 A malady for which a few centuries ago there were more than twenty thousand lazarettos in Europe. In the fourteenth century, in the domains of the Seigneur de Courcy alone, there were ten of these leprosies.

leprous (ˈlɛprəs), *a.* Forms: 3–5 **leprus**, 3, 6–7 **leperous**, 4–5 **leprows, -ros, -rys**, 5 **-rose, leperus**, (? **luprus**), 5–6 **leprouse**, 6 **leporous(e, lyporous(e**, 7 **leap(e)rous**, 3– **leprous.** [a. OF. *lepros, leprous* (mod.F. *lépreux*), ad. late L. *leprōs-us*, f. *lepra* leprosy.]

1. Afflicted or tainted with leprosy.

'Simon leprous' is a common ME. translation of *Simon leprosus* of the Vulgate (Matt. xxvi. 6, Mark xiv. 1) = 'Simon the leper' of the A.V.

a **1225** *Ancr. R.* 148 Moiseses hond..bisemede oðe spitel-vuel, & þuhte leprus. *c* **1290** *S. Eng. Leg.* 464/79 A man of þat contreye þat heiȝte symond leperous. **1382** WYCLIF *Lev.* xiii. 46 Al tyme that he is leprows and vncleene. *a* **1400–50** *Alexander* 4593 As þa þat lepros ere & lame. **1483** CAXTON *Gold. Leg.* 216 b/1 The hous of Symon leprous where as our lord dyned. **1535** COVERDALE *2 Kings* v. Contents, Gehasi Eliseus seruaunt is made leporous. **1535** *Act 27 Hen. VIII*, c. 25 All leprouse and pore beddred creatures. **1611** BIBLE *Exod.* iv. 6 And when hee tooke it out, behold, his hand was leprous as snowe. **1732** BERKELEY *Alciphr.* VI. §24 Leprous Egyptians, driven from their country on account of that loathsome distemper. **1876** BRISTOWE *Theory Pract. Med.* (1878) 275 The children of leprous parents are more likely to become affected [with leprosy] than are the children of healthy parents.

†**b.** Causing or inducing leprosy. *Obs.*

1542 BOORDE *Dyetary* xvi. (1870) 271 Olde beefe..doth ingender melancolye and leporouse humoures. **1602** SHAKS. *Ham.* I. v. 64 And in the Porches of mine eares [he] did poure The leaperous Distilment.

c. Pertaining to, resembling, or accompanying, leprosy.

1635–56 COWLEY *Davideis* II. 619 Leprous scurf o're his whole body cast. **1774** GOLDSM. *Nat. Hist.* (1776) II. 241 That the whiteness of the Negroe skin..might be called rather a leprous crust than a natural complexion. **1827–35** WILLIS *Leper* 125 The dull pulses..beat beneath the hot And leprous scales. **1875** JOWETT *Plato* (ed. 2) III. 669 Generating leprous eruptions and similar diseases. **1898** P. MANSON *Trop. Diseases* xxvi. 421 Nerve stretching..has been strongly advocated..for the cure of leprous neuralgia.

d. *fig.*

1598 DALLINGTON *Meth. Trav.* B j b, Who so bringeth home a leprous soule and a tainted body. **1629** MILTON *Nativity* 138 And leprous sin will melt from earthly mould. **1632** SANDERSON *Serm.* 493 The leaprous humour of Popery. **1697** JOS. WOODWARD *Rel. Soc. Lond.* x. (1704) 176 Heal my leperous soul. **1796** COLERIDGE *Sonn.*, 'Thyself redeeming from that leprous stain Nobility. **1868** FARRAR *Silence & V.* iii. (1875) 65 Her literature..a leprous fiction which poisoned every virtue.

2. *transf.* Having a surface resembling the skin of a leper; covered with white scales. In *Bot.* = LEPROSE.

1620 MARKHAM *Farew. Husb.* xiii. 100 Myst and fog, which being naughty vapours, drawn from the infected parts of the earth, and falling vpon the corne, doe..make the graine leprous. **1820** SHELLEY *Sensit. Plant* III. 70 Spawn, weeds, and filth, a leprous scum. **1830** LINDLEY *Nat. Syst. Bot.* 68 Its leprous leaves, superior fruit, and apetalous flowers, will at all times distinguish the Oleaster tribe. **1839** —— *Introd. Bot.* (ed. 3) 470 Leprous..; covered with minute peltate scales. **1840** DICKENS *Barn. Rudge* xxxi, One old leprous screen of faded Indian leather. **1842** G. TURNBULL in *Proc. Berw. Nat. Club* II. No 10. 8 Where lichens make the trunks all leprous.

†**b.** *Alchemy.* Cf. LEPROSITY. *Obs.*

1605 TIMME *Quersit.* I. xiii. 58 The phylosophers haue the same [*sc.* lead] in great esteeme,..they cal it their sunne or leperous gold. **1660** tr. *Paracelsus' Archidoxis* I. IV. 38 The Quintessence of Gold is as to its Quantity, exceeding small; and the residue of it is a leprous body.

†**3.** *absol.* (quasi-*sb.*) A leper. *Obs.*

c **1250** *Kent. Serm.* in *O.E. Misc.* 31 Swo kam a leprus, a sik man. *c* **1325** *Metr. Hom.* 129 This forsaid leprous was made hale. *c* **1380** WYCLIF *Wks.* (1880) 205 þei ben.. lemmans of foule sathanas þat is foulere þan ony mesel or leprous in þis world. **1464** *Rolls of Parlt.* V. 521/1 Certeyn Leprus of oure menialx Servauntez.

Hence **ˈleprously** *adv.*, **ˈleprousness.**

1471 RIPLEY *Comp. Alch.* VII. in Ashm. (1652) 170 Clensyng theyer Leprosenes. **1527** ANDREW *Brunswyke's Distyll. Waters* B ij, The same water..preserveth the body from leprousnes. **1547** BOORDE *Brev. Health* Pref. 6 b, Leprousnes and many other infectious sicknesses. **1607** TOURNEUR *Rev. Trag.* IV. iv, How leprously That Office would haue cling'd vnto your forehead. **1611** COTGR.,

Lepreserie, leaprousnesse. **1883** *Harper's Mag.* Aug. 464/2 It shone leprously white and blue.

leproused, variant of LEPROSED *a. Obs.*

†**lepry.** *Obs.* Forms: 5–7 lepry, -rie; 5 leperiȝ, 6 leprye, -raye, leaperie, 6–7 leprey, leaprie, -ry. (For the form *lepre*, which may possibly in some instances belong to this word, see LEPER¹.) [f. LEPER *sb.*² + -Y.] = LEPROSY.

1430–40 LYDG. *Bochas* II. xviii. (1554), God..smote him with leprie [*ed.* 1494 lepre]. *a* **1483** *Liber Niger* in *Househ. Ord.* (1790) 43 If any of this courte be infected with leperiȝ or pestylence. **1545** BRINKLOW *Lament.* 24 b, No parson, ones hauing the leperye, shuld come amonge the congregacion of the whole. **1563** HYLL *Profit. Art Garden.* (1593) 82 To heale a red leapry... Lay vpon the blisters and leaprie. **1587** HARRISON *England* II. xxiii. (1878) I. 350 This [spring] is good for scabs and leaperie. **1607** TOPSELL *Hist. Four-f. Beasts* 503 The dust of a mole being brent, mingled with the white of an Egge, and anointed vpon a sheepe, is an excellent and medicinable remedy against the Leprie which commeth oftentimes vpon them. **1621** AINSWORTH *Annot. Pentat.* (1639) 66 These sundry sorts of Leprie in the body. **1660** tr. *Paracelsus' Archidoxis* I. IV. 42 The Leapry is a more grievous infirmity then the Cholick is.

fig. **1526** *Pilgr. Perf.* (W. de W. 1531) 35 Where is worse lepry than property in religyon. *c* **1586** C'TESS PEMBROKE *Ps.* LI. iv, Thy hisop..shall clense the leaprie of my minde. **1647** WARD *Simp. Cobler* 17 Their breath is contagious, their leprey spreading. **1654** VILVAIN *Theol. Treat.* i. 29 A spiritual Lepry which hereditarily infects the whol Man.

Comb. **1608** TOPSELL *Hist. Serpents* (1658) 663 Rough, hard, mangy, or leprie-like nails.

leptandrin (lɛp'tændrɪn). *Chem.* [f. mod.L. *Leptandra* + -IN.] A bitter glucoside obtained from *Veronica* (or *Leptandra*) *virginica*.

1880 *Libr. Univ. Knowl.* VIII. 818 The resinoid extracted from it [*leptandra* or *veronica virginica*] has the name of leptandrin in the books and at the drug-stores.

leptazol ('lɛptəzɒl). *Pharm.* [f. ANA)LEPT(IC *a.* and *sb.* + AZ(O- + -OL.] A white, crystalline, bicyclic compound, $C_6H_{10}N_4$, which stimulates the respiratory and motor centres, is used as an analeptic, especially after poisoning by narcotics, and was formerly employed in convulsive psychotherapy.

1946 *Analyst* LXXI. 308 Leptazol (pentamethylenetetrazole) is commonly encountered in the form of a 10% w/v solution containing 0·25% of sodium phosphate. **1953** *Brit. Jrnl. Psychol.* XLIV. 58 After an intravenous injection of Leptazol, given during the course of electro-encephalographic studies, he had a generalized convulsion. **1968** W. C. BOWMAN et al. *Textbk. Pharmacol.* xxii. 603 In animals it [*sc.* meprobamate] protects against convulsions which occur after strychnine, leptazol and electric-shock.

lepto-, combining form of Gr. λεπτός fine, small, thin, delicate, used in many terms of Zoology and Botany: **leptocardian** (-'kɑːdɪən) *a. Zool.* [Gr. καρδία heart], belonging to the *Leptocardii*, the lowest group of true vertebrates, having contractile pulsating sinuses instead of a heart; *sb.*, a vertebrate belonging to this group (*Cent. Dict.* 1889). **leptocephalan** (-'sɛfələn), **-cephalid** (-'sɛfəlɪd) *Ichthyol.* [Gr. κεφαλ-ή head], a fish of the family *Leptocephalidæ*. **leptocephalic** (-sɪ'fælɪk) *a.*, having a narrow skull; exhibiting leptocephaly; *Ichthyol.*, as the designation of certain flat-fish (cf. *leptocephalid*). **leptocephaly** (-'sɛfəlɪ), narrowness of skull. **leptodactyl** (-'dæktɪl) *Ornith.* [Gr. δάκτυλος toe] *a.*, having thin or slender toes; *sb.*, a bird with slender toes. **lepto'dactylous**, *a.* [-OUS], = prec. *a.* **leptodermous** (-'dɜːməs) *a. Bot.* [Gr. δέρμα skin], having thin skin, said of moss-capsules when pliable (*Syd. Soc. Lex.* 1888). **leptoglossal** (-'glɒsəl) *a. Zool.* [Gr. γλῶσσα tongue], of or pertaining to the division *Leptoglossa* of lizards, having slender tongues (*Cent. Dict.*). **leptoglossate** (-'glɒsət) *a.*, leptoglossal; *sb.*, a lizard of this group (*ibid.*). ‖**leptomeningitis** (-mɛnɪn'dʒaɪtɪs) *Path.*, inflammation of the pia mater and the arachnoid (the *leptomeninges*). ‖**leptophloem** (-'fləʊɛm) *Bot.* [see PHLOEM], in certain mosses (see quot.). **leptophyllous** (-'fɪləs) *a. Bot.* [Gr. φύλλον leaf], slender-leaved (Mayne *Expos. Lex.* 1855). **leptoprosope** (-'prɒsəʊp) [Gr. πρόσωπον face], narrowness of face; the condition of having a long narrow-faced skull (*Cent. Dict.*). Hence **leptopro'sopic** *a.*, having a long narrow face. **leptorrhine** ('lɛptəʊrɪn) *a.* [Gr. ῥῖν-, ῥίς nose], having a long narrow nose; having a nasal index of 47 or under; also **lepto'rrhinian, -'rrhinic** *adjs.* **'leptosperm** (-spɜːm) [Gr. σπέρμα seed], a plant of the genus *Leptospermum* of myrtaceous shrubs (*Cent. Dict.*). ˌ**leptospo'rangiate** (-spəʊ'rændʒɪət) *a. Bot.* [see SPORANGIUM], having sporangia which are developed from a single epidermic cell. ‖**leptothrix** ('lɛptəʊθrɪks) [Gr. θρίξ hair], 'a fungus belonging to the Order *Schizomycetes*, consisting of very thin and long, indistinctly segmented, straight threads' (*Syd. Soc. Lex.*); also *attrib.* **lepto'xylem** *Bot.* [XYLEM], a structure in certain mosses (see quot.).

1842 BRANDE *Dict. Sci.* etc., **Leptocephalans, Leptocephalidæ*, the name of a family of fishes characterized by the smallness of the head, of which the genus *Leptocephalus* is the type. **1886** *Pop. Sci. Monthly* XXIX. 114 Many young flat-fish..assume that peculiarly elongated and strange form known as *leptocephalic. **1882** *Q. Rev.* Jan. 251 These *Leptocephalids are small, narrow, elongate. **1864** *Vogt's Lect. Man* ii. 30 Platycephaly stands opposed to *leptocephaly, though connected with it by gradual transitions. *a* **1864** HITCHCOCK (cited in Worcester), **Leptodactyl*..*Leptodactylous*. **1855** MAYNE *Expos. Lex.*, *Leptodactylus*, *leptodactylous. **1866** A. FLINT *Princ. Med.* (1880) 693 Sometimes inflammation of the pia mater is denominated *leptomeningitis, in distinction from pachymeningitis which is inflammation of the dura mater. **1889** BENNETT & MURRAY *Cryptog. Bot.* 146 A *leptophloem or rudimentary phloem, in which the storing up and conduction of the food-material takes place. **1889** GARSON in *Jrnl. Anthrop. Inst.* XVIII. 23 The midfacial index..in the three Yasinese skulls..is very constant and averages 54·2, making them dolichofacial, or *leptoprosopic. **1880** DAWKINS *Early Man* vii. 192 The *leptorhine rhinocerous. **1884** J. E. LEE *Romer's Bone Caves Ojcow* 31 In both the Wierzchow skulls the nose is leptorrhine. **1878** BARTLEY tr. *Topinard's Anthrop.* II. ii. 257 The *leptorrhinians, with the nasal skeleton elongated. **1891** *Athenæum* 25 July 132/3 Dr. Topinard communicates documents on the nasal index of the living... 49½ per cent... were leptorhinian..and 43 per cent. mesorhinian. **1887** GARNSEY *Goebel's Classif. Plants* 193 Two divisions of the Filicineae, the *Leptosporangiate and the Eusporangiate. **1877** BENNETT tr. *Thomé's Bot.* 259 The forms known as Termo, Bacterium, Vibrio, Spirillum, *Leptothrix, &c. **1882** *Pop. Sci. Monthly* XX. 718 Bacteria attached end to end in a string form filaments of leptothrix. **1885** KLEIN *Micro-Organisms* 89 Long leptothrix filaments composed of short joints. **1897** *Allbutt's Syst. Med.* IV. 743 The leptothrix fungus and spores are almost invariably present in the concretions of tartar that gather round the teeth. **1889** BENNETT & MURRAY *Cryptog. Bot.* 146 A *leptoxylem or rudimentary xylem which serves for the conduction of the transpiration-current to the lower portion of the sporange furnished with stomates.

leptocaul ('lɛptəʊkɔːl), *sb.* and *a. Bot.* [f. LEPTO- + Gr. καυλός stem, stalk.] A tree having a relatively thin primary stem and branches; also *attrib.* or as *adj.* Hence **lepto'caulous** *a.*; **'leptocauly** *sb.*, development of this type. Cf. PACHYCAUL.

1949 E. J. H. CORNER in *Ann. Bot.* XIII. 392 Leptocauly. I use this name to indicate the modern tree with relative[ly] slender primary axis and branches in contrast with the pachycaulous cycad. *Ibid.* 393 The leptocaul, or modern tree, thus comes to dominate in height and spread and distribution.., forming the modern forests. **1964** E. J. H. CORNER *Life of Plants* ix. 154 'Leptocaul' (with thin primary stem) denotes the slender willow construction. *Ibid.* 155 Leptocaul plants predominate in temperate and subtropical climates. *Ibid.* (*caption*) Difference between pachycauly and leptocauly as shown by sections of the young twigs of figs. *Ibid.* xv. 275 Some of the herbaceous forms relate, like the banana, directly to the pachycaulous, others to the leptocaulous. **1973** F. EHRENDORFER in V. H. Heywood *Taxonomy & Ecology* xvi. 319 There is evidence for repeated changes from little-branched monopodial and pachycaulous types..to strongly branched, sympodial, leptocaulous, growth-forms. **1974** *New Phytologist* LXXIII. 977 Leptocauls do not become pachycaul on islands.

leptocentric *a.*: see LEPTOME.

leptocephalus (lɛptəʊ'sɛfələs). [mod.L. (L. T. Gronovius *Zoophylacium Gronovianum* (1763) I. 135), f. LEPTO- + Gr. κεφαλή head.] The transparent leaf-shaped larva of a fish of the order Anguilliformes, or eels, or one belonging to the genus *Elops* or *Albula*. The larva was first described as a distinct genus; see *leptocephalan, leptocephalid* (LEPTO-), MORRIS *sb.*³

1769 T. PENNANT *Brit. Zool.* III. 125 We communicated it [*sc.* the fish] to that accurate Ichthyologist Doctor Laurence Theodore Gronovius, of Leyden, who has described it in his *Zoophylacium*, under the title of *Leptocephalus*, or small head. **1880** A. C. L. G. GÜNTHER *Introd. Study Fishes* xiii. 179 No instance is more remarkable than that of the so-called *Leptocephali*, which for a long time have been regarded either as a distinct group of Fishes, or as the larval stages of various genera of fishes. **1931** J. R. NORMAN *Hist. Fishes* xvi. 336 The first British *Leptocephalus* was discovered in 1763 by one William Morris near Holyhead. **1971** *Nature* 2 Apr. 278/3 In January 1930, the Danish Dana Expedition captured a leptocephalus on the Agulhas Bank, south of Africa, which was 184 cm long.

leptokurtic (lɛptəʊ'kɜːtɪk), *a. Statistics.* [f. LEPTO- + Gr. κυρτ-ός bulging + -IC.] Of a frequency distribution or its graphical representation: having greater kurtosis than the normal distribution.

1905 K. PEARSON in *Biometrika* IV. 173 Given two frequency distributions which have the same variability as measured by the standard deviation, they may be relatively more or less flat-topped than the normal curve. If more flat-topped I term them platykurtic, if less flat-topped leptokurtic, and if equally flat-topped mesokurtic. **1954** *Brit. Jrnl. Psychol.* XLV. 96 These curves were clearly leptokurtic as well as skewed. **1966** *New Scientist* 28 July 213/1 The leptokurtic or 'peaked' distributions that geodesists often meet with.

Hence ˌ**leptokur'tosis** [KURTOSIS], the property of being leptokurtic.

1907 *Phil. Mag.* XIII. 372 There is..sensible skewness and sensible leptokurtosis. **1937** YULE & KENDALL *Introd. Theory Statistics* (ed. 11) ix. 165 By a slip leptokurtosis is there [*sc.* in *Biometrika* (1905) IV. 169 ff.] inadvertently applied to distributions for which $\beta_2 < 3$ [instead of $\beta_2 > 3$]. **1949** DARLINGTON & MATHER *Elem. Genetics* 401 *Kurtosis*, the departure of a symmetrical frequency distribution from the normal by excess (platykurtosis) or deficiency (leptokurtosis) in its shoulders as opposed to tails and centre.

†**lep'tology.** *Obs.* [ad. Gr. λεπτολογία subtle discourse, quibbling, f. λεπτό-ς small, fine, subtle + -λογία: see -LOGY. Cf. F. *leptologie*.]

1. (See quot.) *rare*⁻⁰.

1681 BLOUNT *Glossogr.*, *Leptology*, a description of mean and sordid things. **1823** in CRABB; and in later Dicts.

2. Used for LEPTONOLOGY. *rare*⁻¹.

1928 *Amer. Naturalist* LXII. 208 The underlying basis of crystal form is now known... In fact, a complete science of the fine structure of matter—leptology—is being built up as a result of modern physical research.

leptome ('lɛptəʊm). *Bot.* Also **leptom.** [ad. G. *leptom* (G. Haberlandt *Physiologische Pflanzenanatomie* (1884) vii. 229), f. Gr. λεπτ-ός thin + -OME.] (See quot. 1965.) So **lepto'centric** *a.*, having the leptome surrounded by hadrome.

1898 H. C. PORTER tr. *Strasburger's Text-bk. Bot.* 102 The vascular portion is also termed the xylem or hadrome, and the sieve-tube portion the phloem or leptome. **1902** *Encycl. Brit.* XXV. 409/1 The tissue developed to meet the demands for conduction..is known as leptom. **1914** M. DRUMMOND tr. *Haberlandt's Physiol. Plant Anat.* vii. 347 The protein-conducting elements..form..the delicate leptome portion..of the strand... If the leptome has no fibrous sheath, it of course becomes synonymous with phloem. *Ibid.* 349 If the hadrome is central and the leptome peripheral, the bundle may be termed hadrocentric... The opposite or leptocentric..condition is exemplified by the leaf-trace bundles in many monocotyledonous rhizomes. **1940** *Chambers's Techn. Dict.* 495/2 *Leptocentric vascular bundle*, a concentric vascular bundle, in which a central strand of phloem is surrounded by xylem. **1965** K. ESAU *Plant Anat.* (ed. 2) xii. 272 The term *leptom* deserves special mention. It refers..to the soft-walled conducting part of the phloem.

leptomonad (lɛp'tɒmənæd). *Zool.* [f. LEPTO- + MONAD.] **a.** = LEPTOMONAS **a. b.** Any flagellate of the family Trypanosomidæ when existing in an elongated form with a flagellum emerging from the anterior end and arising near a kinetoplast at this end, which form is assumed only in the invertebrate host (and in culture); freq. *attrib.* or as *adj.*

1909 *Jrnl. R. Microsc. Soc.* 362 (*heading*) New leptomonad in muscids. **1931** R. R. KUDO *Handbk. Protozool.* xi. 145 Genus *Leishmania* Ross... In culture the organism develops into leptomonad forms. **1942** D. L. BELDING *Textbk. Clin. Parasitol.* xi. 143 The species of the genus *Crithidia* occur in the leishmanian, leptomonad and crithidial forms. *Ibid.*, The species of the *Phytomonas* pass through both leishmanian and leptomonad stages. **1961** M. HYNES *Med. Bacteriol.* (ed. 7) xxviii. 433 In man leishmaniæ appear as ovoid organisms with no flagella, but in insects and in culture they turn into flagellated leptomonads. **1962** J. D. SMYTH *Introd. Animal Parasitol.* v. 52 Genus *Leptomonas*. The leptomonads are exclusively parasites of invertebrates. *Ibid.* 64 The morphological changes [of leishmanias] within the sandfly gut are simple. In the mid gut they become leptomonad flagellates which multiply rapidly, spreading forwards to enter the oesophagus and pharynx by the fourth or fifth day. When introduced into the mammalian skin by a bite, the flagellates become rounded and assume the leishmanial form.

leptomonas (lɛp'tɒmənæs). *Zool.* Pl. **leptomonas.** [mod.L., f. LEPTO- + -MONAS.]

a. Any flagellate of the genus *Leptomonas* (family Trypanosomidæ), which comprises species parasitic in invertebrates (esp. in the alimentary tract of insects) and existing in both leptomonad and leishmanial forms. **b.** = LEPTOMONAD **b**; freq. *attrib.* or as *adj.*

[**1880–1** W. SAVILLE-KENT *Man. Infusoria* I. 243 Genus IV. *Leptomonas*, S.K... Animalcules free-swimming, persistent in shape, elongate fusiform or aciculate, bearing a single long undulating flagellum at the anterior extremity, no distinct oral aperture yet detected. The above generic title combined with the following specific one is here introduced for the reception of the monoflagellate animalcule figured and briefly described..by O. Bütschli.] **1926** C. M. WENYON *Protozool.* I. 312 They are the true trypanosomes typically seen in the blood of vertebrates or their invertebrate hosts: the leptomonas, crithidia, and herpetomonas, which have only an invertebrate host..; the leishmania, which..have both a vertebrate and an invertebrate host..; and the phytomonas, which have both an invertebrate and plant host. *Ibid.* 319 Flagellates of the genus *Leishmania* resemble those of the genus *Leptomonas* in having only the leishmania and leptomonas forms. **1931** BLACKLOCK & SOUTHWELL *Guide Human Parasitol.* ix. 71 In *Phlebotomus argentipes* which has been fed experimentally on infected persons, the leishmania develop in the gut into leptomonas. **1942** J. T. CULBERTSON *Med. Parasitol.* ix. 86 The organisms of the genus *Leishmania*..have in their development only two stages: a leishmania and a leptomonas. **1971** BECK & BARRETT-CONNOR *Med. Parasitol.* iv. 38/2 *Phlebotomus* flies, while feeding, regurgitate leptomonas forms..into the wound.

‖**lepton**¹ ('lɛptɒn). Pl. **lepta** (-ə), *erron.* **leptas.** [Gr. λεπτόν (sc. νόμισμα coin), neut. of λεπτός

small.] **a.** An ancient Greek coin of the value of about one-fourth of a farthing; the 'mite' of the Eng. versions of the N.T. **b.** The smallest coin ('centime') of modern Greece, being the one-hundredth part of a drachma.

1727-41 CHAMBERS *Cycl.* s.v. *Coin*, Lepton..os.od. $\frac{31}{336}$ *qrs.* Sterl. **1858** *Merc. Marine Mag.* V. 86 Vessels of 20 tons, 50 leptas per ton. **1877** C. GEIKIE *Christ* lvii. (1879) 687 Among others, came a poor widow, with her two lepta.

lepton² ('lɛptɒn). *Nuclear Physics.* [f. Gr. λεπτ-ός small, slight, slender + -ON¹.] Any of the sub-atomic particles that do not participate in the strong interaction and have a mass less than that of a nucleon and a half-integral spin (viz. the electron, the muon, and the neutrinos, and their anti-particles); in recent use extended to include any other (hypothetical) particle, of whatever mass, which does not participate in the strong interaction. (Orig. introduced in a wider sense: see quot. 1948.)

1948 L. ROSENFELD *Nucl. Forces* p. xvii, This can be achieved..by postulating a special kind of interaction between a nucleon and a pair of light particles, or leptons, consisting of an electron and a neutrino. [*Note*] Following a suggestion of Prof. C. Møller, I adopt—as a pendant to 'nucleon'—the denomination 'lepton' (from λεπτός, small, thin, delicate) to denote a particle of small mass, irrespective of its charge. **1959** *Sci. News.* LII. 101 A similar conservation law holds for leptons, a group of particles including neutrinos, electrons, and muons. **1964** *Cambr. Rev.* 24 Oct. 53/1 The..equality of the Fermi coupling constant for many different particles, baryons, mesons and leptons. **1967** *New Scientist* 8 June 578/1 These, the leptons, consist of the electron, the muon, two types of the massless, chargeless neutrino..and the anti-particles of these four. **1969** R. E. MARSHAK et al. *Theory Weak Interactions Particle Physics* i. 2 The fact that the weak interaction takes place at approximately the same level of strength between leptons.., between leptons and hadrons.., and between hadrons is a major distinguishing feature of the weak interaction. *Ibid.* 7 The names lepton, meson, and baryon were originally invented to denote light, intermediate mass, and heavy particles respectively, but we now know that the particles in each of the three classes share certain important properties in common; both the leptons and baryons are fermions.. whereas the mesons are bosons. However, of greatest importance is the presence of the strong interaction for the meson and baryon classes but not for the lepton class. **1971** *New Scientist* 17 June 669/3 If heavy leptons..exist, Pontecorvo argues that they must have neutrinos also. **1973** *Sci. Amer.* Oct. 111/2 There may well exist a spectrum of leptons of increasing mass. The heavy leptons, if they exist, could be produced, like muons, in pairs in electron-positron annihilation reactions. *Ibid.* Nov. 36/2 The few particles that feel only weak or electromagnetic forces are classed as leptons. Electrons, muons and neutrinos are the only known leptons.

b. lepton number, a quantum number assigned to sub-atomic particles that is ± 1 for leptons and 0 for other particles and is conserved in all known interactions.

1958 *Physical Rev.* CX. 1483/2 Such selection rules.. consist of giving opposite lepton numbers to μ^- and e^-. **1967** L. M. LEDERMAN in E. H. S. Burhop *High Energy Physics* II. 342 Conservation of lepton number now is a matter of N_μ and N_e being separately conserved. **1973** *Sci. Amer.* Aug. 33/2 The preference of the neutrino for the electron and of the antineutrino for the positron has been included in the theory of weak interactions by assigning a.. lepton number to the various weakly interacting particles. The convention is that the electron and the neutrino have a lepton number of + 1, whereas their anti-particles, the positron and the antineutrino, have a lepton number of − 1.

Hence **lep'tonic** *a.*, of, pertaining to, or involving leptons; ***leptonic number*** = *lepton number.*

1957 *Ann. Physics.* II. 422 Particles labelled by leptonic charge and electrical charge permit a complete identification with the known leptons. **1958** *Proc. 2nd Internat. Conf. Peaceful Uses Atomic Energy* (United Nations) 53 The law of conservation of leptons..states that if a leptonic number is assigned to each particle then the sum of leptonic numbers must be conserved in all reactions. **1969** *Nature* 23 Aug. 780/2 The Λ hyperon has leptonic decays of a very similar kind to those of the Σ.

†**lepto'nology.** *Obs. rare.* [ad. G. *leptonologie* (F. Rinne 1916, in *Neues Jahrb. f. Min., Geol. u. Paläont.* II. 48), f. Gr. λεπτός (neut. λεπτόν) small, slight, slender: see -OLOGY.] (See quot.)

1917 *Jrnl. Chem. Soc.* CXII. II. 166 Alongside the science of stereochemistry is developing a stereophysics, and these, together with the study of crystal structure, form a new branch of science, which the author terms 'Feinbaulehre der Materie' (the study of the ultimate structure of matter), or Leptonology.

leptosomic (lɛptəʊ'səʊmɪk), *a.* [f. Gr. λεπτό-ς fine, small, thin + σῶμ-α body: see -IC.] In Kretschmer's system, designating a type of physique characterized by leanness and tallness. Also **leptoso'matic** *a.*, in same sense.

Orig. used by Kretschmer as a synonym of asthenic (ASTHENIC *a.* b) in his tripartite classification of human physique into pyknic, athletic (ATHLETIC *a.* 3), and asthenic types. Later he employed a bipartite classification in which only pyknic and leptosomic types were recognized.

1936 E. MILLER in W. J. H. Sprott tr. *Kretschmer's Physique & Character* (ed. 2) 272 Kolle..[discovered] the existence of many cases with leptosomic physique who suffered from cyclothymia in one form or another. **1937** Leptosomatic [see ATHLETIC *a.* 3]. **1959** *Chambers's Encycl.* XI. 335/1 The two characteristic types of physique were termed the asthenic, or leptosomatic, and the pyknic respectively. **1960** J. COMAS *Man. Physical Anthropol.* vi. 341 E. Schreider believes that Kretschmer's classification can be reduced to two bipolar types, pyknic and leptosomic, with the inclusion in the latter group of the following varieties: the asthenic, the true leptosomic and the athletic. It should be mentioned that in later editions of his book, Kretschmer abandoned the third (athletic) type, and fell back upon a dichotomy consisting of the pyknic and asthenic (leptosomic).

Hence **'leptosome** *sb.*, (a person with) a leptosomic physique; also as *adj.*, = LEPTOSOMIC *a.*

1931 *Times Lit. Suppl.* 10 Dec. 1004/2 The two main classes of white man, which he calls 'linear' and 'lateral' (corresponding to the 'pyknic' and 'leptosome'..of other anthropologists). **1935** *Nature* 9 Feb. 236/1 Of Kretschmer's three types, the leptosome corresponds to the Nordic, the athletic to the Dinaric and the pycnic to the Mediterranean and the Alpine. **1960** J. COMAS *Man. Physical Anthropol.* vi. 341 According to the Italian biotypologists, the average or normal type is located between the leptosomes (slender type) and the pyknics (broad type). **1971** J. Z. YOUNG *Introd. Study Man* xxxix. 573 Kretschmer tried to force everyone into one of three classes, pyknic (round and fat), leptosome (long and thin), and athletic (broad and strong). *Ibid.* 576 Leptosomes were introverted.

leptospira (lɛptəʊ'spaɪərə). *Bacteriology.* Pl. **-spiræ.** [mod.L., f. Gr. λεπτό-ς fine, small + σπεῖρα coil.] Any bacterium of the genus *Leptospira* (family Treponemataceæ), structurally similar to the genus *Spirochæta* and consisting of a few species either free-living or parasitic, of which *L. icterohæmorrhagiæ* is parasitic in rats and the cause of Weil's disease in man.

[**1917** H. NOGUCHI in *Jrnl. Exper. Med.* XXV. 759 It calls for a new genus, and on account of its fine and minute windings, the name *Leptospira* is suggested.] **1918** *Ibid.* XXVII. 588 Figs. 1 to 4 are intended to show the appearance of the leptospiræ in an air-dried specimen. **1922** *Lancet* 18 Nov. 1058/1 Uhlenhuth and Zuelzer record a leptospira (*L. pseudoicterogenes*) in salt springs. **1966** WRIGHT & SYMMERS *Systemic Path.* I. xxi. 629 Leptospirae are demonstrable in the blood or urine in only half the fatal cases [of Weil's disease].

Hence **lepto'spiral** *a.*, of, characteristic of, or caused by leptospiræ; ***leptospiral jaundice***, infectious or spirochætal jaundice, Weil's disease.

1924 *Brit. Med. Jrnl.* 23 Feb. 314/1 In sections of the liver ..leptospiral forms were abundant. **1935** *Ibid.* 24 Aug. 339/1 Men who have been exposed to risk of leptospiral infection. **1937** *Proc. R. Soc. Med.* XXX. 746 Dr. J. Smith has informed us in a letter that he investigated an outbreak of leptospiral jaundice in a fox farm near Aberdeen, and that three foxes died of the disease. **1960** *Guardian* 10 Nov. 9/4 Leptospiral jaundice (Weil's Disease)..is contracted from the urine of rats. **1973** *Times* 31 Oct. 14/2 Some leptospiral serotypes cause serious disease in Man.

leptospire ('lɛptəʊspaɪə(r)). *Bacteriology.* [Anglicized form of LEPTOSPIRA.] = LEPTOSPIRA.

1957 R. S. BREED et al. *Bergey's Man. Determinative Bacteriol.* (ed. 7) 907 Pathogenic leptospires were first isolated from human cases of Weil's disease... Since that time [*sc.* 1915] other leptospires..have been recognized as causing disease in man and other animals. **1969** *New Scientist* 20 Feb. 414/2 The leptospiral structures, too, bud out from the surface of the leptospire itself.

leptospirosis (ˌlɛptəʊspaɪə'rəʊsɪs). *Med.* and *Vet. Sci.* [f. LEPTOSPIR(A + -OSIS.] Infection with, or a disease caused by, leptospiræ.

1926 STEDMAN *Med. Dict.* (ed. 9) 558/2 *Leptospirosis*, infection with some species of *Leptospira*. **1934** *Brit. Med. Jrnl.* 7 July 10/1 Weil's disease (spirochaetal jaundice, infective jaundice, leptospirosis) has been recognized in many different countries. **1961** *Times* 6 Dec. 14/6 The bulls ..have been tested for tuberculosis, brucellosis, and leptospirosis. **1970** *Daily Tel.* 11 May 12/7 In one area the Medical Officer of Health has made notifiable seven tropical diseases—plague, cholera, malaria, yellow fever, leprosy, typhus, and also leptospirosis. **1973** *Massey Ferguson Rev.* (N.Z.) Mar.-Apr. 8/1 Leptospirosis in man and cattle is recognised as a serious rural problem in parts of New Zealand.

leptotene ('lɛptəʊtiːn). *Cytology.* [ad. F. *leptotène* (H. von Winiwarter 1900, in *Arch. de Biol.* XVII. 55): see LEPTO- and -TENE.] The first stage of the prophase of the first meiotic division, in which the chromosomes are apparent as fine slender threads. Also *attrib.* or as *adj.*

[**1900** *Jrnl. R. Microsc. Soc.* 654 The reticulum gives rise to a chromatic thread.., which at first fills the nuclear cavity (leptotænic stage).] **1912** *Jrnl. Exper. Zool.* XIII. 360 The pre-synaptic leptotene. *Ibid.* 362 Are the leptotene-threads of this period chromosomes? *Ibid.* 368 Figs. 73 *a* and 73 *b* show two early leptotene-nuclei of this species. **1925** E. B. WILSON *Cell* (ed. 3) vi. 541 In the case of animals..the leptotene-spireme is not continuous but consists of separate segments. **1964** G. H. HAGGIS et al. *Introd. Molecular Biol.* vii. 197 The chromosomes at leptotene must each consist of two chromatids so closely apposed as to give the appearance of a single structure. **1970** AMBROSE & EASTY *Cell Biol.* x. 325 The cell nuclei at this stage contain chromosomes in the form of very fine single threads, hence the name leptotene, meaning 'slender ribbon'.

leptynite ('lɛptɪnaɪt). *Min.* Also leptinite. [app. f. Gr. λεπτύν-ειν (see next) + -ITE.] The same as granulite.

18.. DANA (Worc.), Leptynite. **1879** RUTLEY *Stud. Rocks* xii. 211 Granulite (Weiss-stein or leptinite) is also composed of felspar and quartz, the felspar being orthoclase.

†**leptyntic** (lɛp'tɪntɪk). *Med. Obs.* Also leptuntic. [ad. late L. *leptyntic-us*, a. Gr. λεπτυντικ-ός, f. λεπτύνειν to make thin, f. λεπτός thin.] An attenuant.

1721 BAILEY, *Leptunticks*, attenuating cutting Medicines which Part the Crass and viscous Humours, with their acute Particles.

ler: see LEER, LERE.

lerbord, lerch, obs. ff. LARBOARD, LURCH.

†**lere,** *v. Obs.* Forms: 1 lǣran, *Kentish* léran, 2-4 leren, 2-3 learen, 3 læren, *Orm.* lærenn, 3-4 lare(n, 3-6 lere, 3-5 ler, (4 lerin), 4-5 leere, 5 leryn, *Sc.* leyr, 5-9 *Sc.* leir, 5-8 lear(e. Also *pa. pple.* 3 i-læred, -learet, -lered, 4-5 y-lered. [OE. *lǣran* = OFris. *léra*, OS. *lērian* (Du. *leeren*), OHG. *lêran* (Ger. *lehren*), ON. *lǽra*:—OTeut. **laizjan* (for which Goth. has *laisjan*), f. **laizâ* LORE *sb.*]

1. *trans.* To teach; = LEARN *v.* 4. In various constructions: To give instruction to (a person); to teach (a person something, or *to do* something); to give instruction in (a science, art, etc.).

c **900** tr. *Bæda's Hist.* IV. iv. (1890) 272 He wæs sended Ongolþeode Godes word to bodienne & to læranne. *a* **1100** *Gerefa* in *Anglia* (1886) IX. 260 Ac ic lære þæt he do swa ic ær cwæð. *c* **1175** *Lamb. Hom.* 95 ʒif þe halia gast ne learð þes monnes heorte. *c* **1200** ORMIN 18147 Sannt Johan Bapptisste comm to lærenn þe follc to rihhtenn here lif. *c* **1205** LAY. 4312 þeo alche dæie hine larden luðere craftes. *a* **1250** *Owl & Night.* 1053 þu..lerdest hi to don schome And unriht of hire lichome. **1297** R. GLOUC. (Rolls) 1934 Constantin let also In ierusalem cherchen rere & wide aboute elles ware cristendom to lere. *c* **1320** R. BRUNNE *Medit.* 13 Y wyl þe lere a medytacyon. *c* **1375** *Sc. Leg. Saints* xxx. (*Theodora*) 700 He..þe barne in with hyr tuke to lere. **1393** LANGL. *P. Pl.* C. IV. 162 Hue..lereþ hem to lecherie þat louyeþ here ȝyftes. *a* **1400** *Prymer* 97 The wey of thi riȝtwesnesses lere thou me. *c* **1400** *Apol. Loll.* 33 Prestes schal be dampned for wickidnes of þe peple, if þei lere hem not wan þei are vnkunnand. *c* **1400** tr. *Secreta Secret., Gov. Lordsh.* 100 þe kyng thoht to do lere him vpon sciences. *a* **1420** HOCCLEVE *De Reg. Princ.* 1856 Of alle thre þou oghtist be wele leerid. *c* **1449** PECOCK *Repr.* 426 He is..tauȝt and leerid of an holi man. **1486** *Bk. St. Albans* E j, Lystyn to yowre dame and she shall yow lere. **1513** DOUGLAS *Æneis* VIII. Prol. 145, I sall leir the ane lessoun to leys all thi pane. **1556** LAUDER *Tractate* (1864) 151 And, now, geue that ȝe wald be leird To bruke and to Inioye the eird. **1596** DALRYMPLE tr. *Leslie's Hist. Scot.* VII. 37 Able to..leir thame to knawe thair dutie. **1600** FAIRFAX *Tasso* XII. xl. 221, I did thee leare A lore, repugnant to thy parents faith. **1832-52** MOTHERWELL in *Whistle-Binkie* (Sc. Songs) Ser. I. 42 'Twas then we sat on ae laigh bink, To leir ilk ither lear.

b. To show the way to, lead, guide; to lead (the way).

c **1320** *Sir Tristr.* 400 To wite þe riȝt way þe styes for to lere. *c* **1394** *P. Pl. Crede* 343 Lere me to som man my Crede for to lerne. *c* **1420** *Chron. Vilod.* 25 For Hengestes was þe first duke of hem, And into þis lond he dede hem lere. *c* **1470** HENRY *Wallace* IX. 1753 Graith gydys can thaim leyr.

2. To inform; = LEARN *v.* 5. Const. rarely *of*; chiefly with sb. or clause as second obj.

1300 *Cursor M.* 21494 Me war leuer yow for to lere Quar lijs your lauerd rode-tre. **1430-40** LYDG. *Bochas* Prol. (1554) 7 In which processe, like as I am leared, He [etc.]. *c* **1435** *Torr. Portugal* 1110, I wott welle ye are leryd, My lordys dowghter shalle be wed To a man off myght. *c* **1470** HARDING *Chron.* LXXIII. xxii, [Arthure] also gate, as Chronycles haue vs lered, Denmarke [etc.]. ? *a* **1500** *Chester Pl.* viii. 122 It is good that we enquyre if any the way can vs leere. **1513** DOUGLAS *Æneis* III. ii. 156 Apollois ansueir speir, Beseiking him of succouris ws to leir. *a* **1643** W. CARTWRIGHT *Ordinary* IV. i. (1651) 60 Lere me whylk way he wended.

3. To learn, acquire knowledge of (something); to study, read (a book); to learn *to* do something. Also with clause as obj.

c **1220** *Bestiary* 328 And ȝingið him ðus ðis wilde der So ȝe hauen nu lered her. *c* **1250** *Gen. & Ex.* 354 Nu wot adam sum-del o wo, Her-after sal he leren mo. *c* **1300** *Havelok* 796 Y wile with þe gange, For to leren sum god to gete. **1362** LANGL. *P. Pl.* A. XI. 270 Thanne wrouȝte I unwisly with alle the wyt that I lere! *c* **1375** *Sc. Leg. Saints* vi. (*Thomas*) 398 Wyt is þat gerris þe fynd Ite, þat þu lerit [nocht], & memore syne Is þat þu laris, þu nocht tyne, & vndirstandynge is [etc.]. *c* **1400** *Beryn* 790 Yf yee lust to lere Howe they were I-clepid. *c* **1400** MAUNDEV. (Roxb.) xxix. 132 All þe Iews.. lerez for to speke Hebrew. *c* **1450** *St. Cuthbert* (Surtees) 1548 He bade him lere John evangelist. **1466** *Burgh Rec. Peebles* (1872) 155 Master Jhon Doby swld haiff all the skwll, owttakand thai that leyryt to syng. **1500-20** DUNBAR *Poems* lxiii. 54 Thay.. will at na man nurtir leyr. **1552** ABP. HAMILTON *Catech.* (1884) 5 Ane scholar quhilk is to leir ony special science. **1567** *Gude & Godlie B.* (S.T.S.) 87 Leir him to dreid, and traist in till him syne. **1585** JAS. I *Ess. Poesie* (Arb.) 37 Then ye your self, in teaching men shall leir The rule of liuing well. **1596** DALRYMPLE tr. *Leslie's Hist. Scot.* I. 8 They haue leiret nocht to defend thair townes wᵗ wallis. **1600** FAIRFAX *Tasso* X. xxv. 184 On that sad booke his shame and losse he leared. **1719** RAMSAY *Prol. to Orphan* 8 And lear —O mighty crimes!—to speak and act! **1724** —— *Some of Contents Evergr.* v, The sons may leir, How their forbeirs were unacquaint with feir. *a* **1818** MACNEILL *Poems* (1844) 124 'Twas then my native strains ye leared.

4. *absol.* and *intr.* To acquire knowledge; to be informed; = LEARN 2, 3 c. Const. *of*, *on*, *at*.
a **1300** *Cursor M.* 1832 þai wald noght lere on noe lare. *Ibid.* 19538 þat he moght of his craftes lere. *c* **1375** *Sc. Leg. Saints* xxxvi. (*Baptista*) 958 Of þir barnis herrod send twa to rome, to lere. *c* **1384** CHAUCER *H. Fame* II. 3 And listeneth of my dreme to lere. **14..** *Parlt. Love 3* in *Pol. Rel. & L. Poems* 48 Now ȝee that wull of loue lere, I counsell yow þat ȝe cum nere. *c* **1425** LYDG. *Assembly of Gods* 887 Lothe to Offende, and Louyng ay to Lere. *c* **1460** *Urbanitatis* 1 in *Babees Bk.*, Who-so wylle of nurtur lere, Herken to me & ȝe shalle here. *c* **1470** HENRY *Wallace* VII. 671 Lerand at scule in to thair tendyr age. **1500–20** DUNBAR *Poems* xli. 21 Be ȝe so wyiss that vderis at ȝow leir. **1552** LYNDESAY *Monarche* 6326 Wald God, said I, ȝe did remane all ȝeir, That I mycht of ȝour heuinlye Lessonis leir. **1562** WINȜET *Cert. Tractates* Wks. 1888 I. 24 Childer of happy ingynis, mair able to leir than I wes to teche. **1721** KELLY *Scot. Prov.* 13 As the old Cock crows, the young Cock lears.

lere: see LEAR, LEER, LURE *sb.*[1]

'lered, *ppl. a. Obs.* exc. *dial.* Also 2 læred, 3–6 lerd, 4–5 *Sc.* leyryt, 5–6 lerid, -it, 9 leared. [pple. of LERE *v.*] = LEARNED. Also *absol.*, esp. in ***lered and lewd***.
c **1154** *O.E. Chron.* an. 1137 þe biscopes & lered men heom cursede æure. *c* **1200** *Trin. Coll. Hom.* 129 þe bisshupes, and þe oðre lerede þe wuneden in þe lond. *a* **1300** *Cursor M.* 24806 þis abbot.. Was chosin.. A lerd man o mikel lare. *c* **1375** *Sc. Leg. Saints* xxii. (*Laurentius*) 782 Quhethyre þai leyryt ore lawit ware. *c* **1386** CHAUCER *Doctor's T.* 283 For be he lewed man or ellis lered. *c* **1450** HOLLAND *Howlat* 122 Patriarkis and prophetis, of lerit the laif. *c* **1450** *Abce Aristotill* 21 in *Q. Eliz. Acad.* 65 Bothe lewid And lerid, Magnifie his mageste þat most is of myght. **1500–20** DUNBAR *Poems* lx. 41 The lerit sone of erll or lord. **1556** *Chron. Gr. Friars of Lond.* (Camden) 89 The lerdemen of both the universytes. **1855** ROBINSON *Whitby Gloss.* s.v. *Lare*, He was, after all, a mensefully leared man.

†**lerer**. *Obs.* [f. LERE *v.* + -ER[1]; cf. OHG. *lêrari* (mod.G. *lehrer*), Sw. *lärare*, Da. *lærer*, Goth. *laisareis*.]
1. A teacher.
a **1300** *Cursor M.* 21179 Spellers o trouth, lerers o lede. *a* **1340** HAMPOLE *Psalter* cxxxiv. 7 Cloudis are lerers of goddis worde. *c* **1375** *Lay Folks Mass Bk.* (MS. B) 164 Bothe þo reders & þo herers has mykil nede, me þenk of lerers. *c* **1440** *Promp. Parv.* 297/2 Lerare,.. *doctor*.
2. A learner, disciple. *rare.*
c **1440** *Promp. Parv.* 297/2 Lerare, or lernare, or he þat receyvythe lore,.. *discipulus*.

lerge, lergeness, obs. Sc. ff. LARGE, -NESS.

†**'lering**. *Obs.* [f. LERE *v.* + -ING[1]. Cf. ON. *læring*.] **a.** Learning. **b.** Instruction, teaching; doctrine.
a **1300** *Cursor M.* 14811 For til him was þe lai bi-taght, þat he him thoru lering laght. **1340** HAMPOLE *Pr. Consc.* 170 For a man excuses noght his unkunnyng That his wittes uses noght in leryng. **1357** *Lay Folks Catech.* 28 And all the knawing þat we have in þis world of him, Is of heryng, and leryng and techyng of othir. **1377** LANGL. *P. Pl.* B. x. 16 Anima that lady is ladde bi his lerynge. *c* **1460** J. RUSSELL *Bk. Nurture* 831 Yowre sawces to make y shalle geue yow lerynge.

†**lerion**. *Obs.* [? corruptly a. F. *liron*.] ? The grey dormouse.
c **1470** HENRYSON *Mor. Fab.* v. (*Parlt. Beasts*) xvii, The mertrik.. The bowranbane and eik the lerion.

leripoop(e, -pup, variants of LIRIPOOP.

lerk: see LIRK *sb.* and *v.*, *dial.*

lerkere, obs. form of LURKER.

lerky ('lɜːkɪ). [dial., of unknown origin.] In the Nottinghamshire area, the local name of a children's game (see quot. 1902).
1902 *Eng. Dial. Dict.* III. 576/1 *Lerky*, a noisy game, played with any old tin; this being placed in a ring, while all except one hide themselves, then rush out if unobserved and kick the tin out of the ring. Somewhat similar to hide-and-seek. **1913** D. H. LAWRENCE *Sons & Lovers* I. iv. 75 Paul was towed round at the heels of Annie, sharing her game. She raced wildly at lerky with the other young wild-cats of the Bottoms. **1969** I. & P. OPIE *Children's Games* iv. 167 The game seems to have been well known in city streets before the First World War... Other names: 'Ecky'.. 'Kick the Bucket'.. 'Lerky' (Nottinghamshire).

†**lerm**, *v. Obs. rare*[−1]. [ad. OF. *lermer*, *larmer* to weep, f. *larme* a tear.] *intr.* To weep.
c **1530** LD. BERNERS *Arth. Lyt. Bryt.* (1814) 268 Whan Arthur sawe.. the bysshop mytred and all barefoted, hys herte lermed and wepte for pyte.

lern, obs. form of LEARN.

Lernæan (lɜː'niːən), *a.* and *sb.* Also lernean. [f. L. *Lernæ-us*, Gr. Λερναῖος (f. L. *Lerna*, Gr. Λέρνη, the name of a marsh in Argolis) + -AN. The mod. use is prob. an allusion to the Lernæan Hydra, a monster inhabiting this marsh.]
A. *adj.* Pertaining to the *Lernæa*, a Linnæan genus of parasitic entomostracans, now limited to certain species infesting the gills of the cod.
1835 KIRBY *Hab. & Inst. Anim.* II. xiv. 25 A very remarkable Lernean parasite. **1852** DANA *Crust.* I. 4 The most degraded Lernæan forms have the sluggishness.. of the lowest worms.
B. *sb.* One of the genus *Lernæa*.
1835 KIRBY *Hab. & Inst. Anim.* II. xiv. 22 The Lerneans ..he [Cuvier] has placed.. in his first order of Intestinal Worms. **1876** *Beneden's Anim. Parasites* 97 The Lernæans also have females excessively various in size and appearance.

Lernæoid (lɜː'niːɔɪd), *a.* [f. mod.L. *Lernæa* (see LERNÆAN) + -OID.] Having the appearance of a Lernæan; resembling the Lernæans.
1846 DANA *Zooph.* vii. (1848) 107 The Lernæoid division appears to reach the Polygastrics in the Acephalocist.

lernilite, erroneous form of LENNILITE.

lerot ('lɛrət). *Zool.* [a. F. *lérot*, f. *loir*, repr. pop. L. *glīr-em* (L. *glīr-em*, *glīs*) dormouse.] The garden dormouse (*Myoxus nitela*).
1774 GOLDSM. *Nat. Hist.* VI. i. (1862) I. 453 The middle [Dormouse], which he [Buffon] calls the Lerot. **1849** *Sk. Nat. Hist.*, *Mammalia* IV. 29 The Garden Dormouse, or Lerot... The greater Dormouse of Shaw.

lerp (lɜːrp). Also laap, leurp. [Native Australian.] A sweet secretion, or the scales formed from it, produced by larvæ of jumping plant-lice of the family Psyllidæ on the leaves of eucalypts and other plants. Also *attrib.*
1848 W. WESTGARTH *Australia Felix* vi. 73 The natives of the Wimmera prepare a luscious drink from the laap. **1878** R. B. SMYTH *Aborig. Victoria* I. 211 Lerp. **1907** W. W. FROGGATT *Austral. Insects* 363 Their popular name of 'Lerp Insects' [comes] from the habit of the larvae of many species of forming 'lerp scales', shell-like protective coverings formed from exudations from the insects. **1945** K. C. MCKEOWN *Austral. Insects* 104 The Psyllidae, or Lerp-insects, form an important group in Australia. *Ibid.* 106 In its immature stages the insect lives as a squat little larva or nymph beneath the lerp-scale. **1962** *Proc. Linn. Soc. New South Wales* LXXXVII. 283 The encyrtid parasites described in this paper form one of the lesser groups of parasites of lerp-forming psyllids on eucalypts. **1965** *Austral. Encycl.* V. 290/2 Lerp-insects, a large and common group of jumping plant-lice.. which suggest miniature cicadas... Some of them give themselves, through sugary exudations, protective and often picturesque coverings known as lerp scales. *Ibid.* IV. 479/2 The lerp scales secreted by the larvae are often of beautiful design and characteristic of the species. **1970** T. E. WOODWARD et al. in *Insects of Australia* (Commonwealth Sci. & Industr. Res. Organization) xxvi. 418/2 Lerp formation has probably evolved because of the need to protect the nymphs from desiccation. *Ibid.* 419/1 Most species of *Glycaspis* and *Lasiopsylla* are lerp-builders, but some form large bubble-shaped galls with an orifice at the base plugged with the same waxy or sugary material as is used by other species to build lerps.

lerre(i)poop, variant of LIRIPOOP.

lerret ('lɛrɪt). *dial.* Also lerrett, -it. [Etymology unknown.] A boat suitable for heavy seas, used on the coast about the Isle of Portland.
1828 *New Sailor's Mag.* 155 The 'Portland Lerret', or boat adapted for approaching this extraordinary isthmus, 'Chesel Beach'... A lerret of large size, about five tons burden. **1869** *Daily News* 14 Sept., Pilot George Brown, with a crew of four men, went in a 'lerrit' to her assistance. **1877** *Times* 13 Sept. 4/3 In the face of such a sea.. none other than the well known Portland 'lerretts' could have been launched or beached. **1880** T. HARDY *Trumpet-Major* III. xxxiv. 120 The trip in the stern of the lerret had quite refreshed her.

lerrie, lerry: see LURRY.

lerroch, variant of LARACH *Sc.*

lerrup, dial. variant of LARRUP.

Les (lɛz). Also Les., Les(s)ie, Lessy, Lez(z), Lezzy, and with lower-case initial. Colloq. abbrev. of LESBIAN *a.* 2 and *sb.* Cf. LIZZIE 1.
1929 M. LIEF *Hangover* 235 'Certainly,' responded the Les, 'where is she?' **1956** B. HOLIDAY *Lady sings Blues* (1973) ix. 90 I've known black chicks in show business who were as feminine as me, but before long they got acting like lezzies because it's so easy. **1958** F. NORMAN *Bang to Rights* III. 146, I didn't see why there should be a law against queers and lezes. **1959** C. MACINNES *Absolute Beginners* 52 Jill is a Les. and, what is more, you may not believe this, but a Les. ponce. **1965** L. MEYNELL *Double Fault* I. viii. 71 These Lessies are touchy; they just can't stand it when the girl friend leaves them. **1966** I. JEFFERIES *House-Surgeon* iii. 37 'Is she like that with all the house-men?' 'Not the girls; she's lezzy as hell.' **1966** 'L. LANE' *ABZ of Scouse* 62 *Lezzy*, a lesbian woman. **1968** L. BERG *Risinghill* 122 What is a 'Lesie'..? **1970** E. BERCKMAN *She asked for It* xi. 135 So you're a couple of Lezzes, you and little Monica? **1972** L. P. DAVIES *What did I do Tomorrow?* vi. 74 There's so much homo and lessie stuff knocking about these days. **1972** *New Society* 11 May 301/1, I reckon she's a les you know. **1973** J. JONES *Touch of Danger* xxxii. 188 They're all leses, those extra-girl types.

les, obs. form of LEASH, LESS; var. LEESE.

lesar, variant of LEESER[1] *Obs.*

lesarde, obs. form of LIZARD.

Lesbian ('lɛzbɪən), *a.* and *sb.* [f. L. *Lesbi-us*, Gr. Λέσβιος + -AN.] **A.** *adj.* **1. a.** Of or pertaining to the island of Lesbos, in the northern part of the Grecian archipelago. ***Lesbian rule***: a mason's rule made of lead, which could be bent to fit the curves of a moulding (Aristotle *Eth. Nic.* v. x. 7); hence *fig.*, a principle of judgement that is pliant and accommodating. (Very common in 17th c., but app. not always correctly understood.)
1601 S. DANIEL *To Sir T. Egerton* 131 That Lesbian square, that building fit, Plies to the worke, not forc'th the worke to it. **1605** TIMME *Quersit* II. ii. 111 The composition and wonderful nature thereof is, as it were, a certaine example and Lesbian rule of our worke. **1606** SYLVESTER *Du Bartas* II. iv. II. *Magnif.* 1117 Another, leveld by the Lesbian Squire Deep under ground (for the Foundation) joyns Well-polisht Marble. *a* **1628** PRESTON *New. Covt.* (1630) 233 Thou goest not by a straight rule, but by a leaden Lesbian rule. **1703** ROWE *Ulysses* II. i. 945 The Chian and the Lesbian Grape. **1711** W. KING tr. *Naude's Rej. Politics* v. 188 It [artificial, politic Justice] is soft and pliant enough to accommodate itself as the Lesbian rule to human and popular weakness. **1724–41** CHAMBERS *Cycl.* s.v. *Cymatium*, Lesbian cymatium, according to Vitruvius, is what we otherwise call talon.
b. *absol.* Short for 'Lesbian wine'.
1775 E. BARRY *Observations Wines of Ancients* vi. 99 The best Greek Wines, the Chian, Lesbian, Coan, &c. were equally prepared in the same manner. **1824** A. HENDERSON *Hist. Anc. & Mod. Wines* I. viii. 123 The dessert-wines most commonly mentioned as in use among the Greeks are the Thasian and Lesbian. **1846** R. FORD *Gatherings from Spain* xiv. 163 Manzanilla.. may be compared to the ancient Lesbian, which Horace quaffed so plentifully in the cool shade, and then described as never doing harm.
2. (Freq. with lower-case initial.) [After the alleged practice of Sappho, the poetess of Lesbos; cf. SAPPHIC *a.* and *sb.*, SAPPHISM.] Of a woman: homosexual, characterized by a sexual interest in other women. Also, of or pertaining to homosexual relations between women.
1890 BILLINGS *Med. Dict.* II. 47/1 *Lesbian love*, tribadism. **1892** C. G. CHADDOCK tr. *Krafft-Ebing's Psychopathia Sexualis* v. 429 We are indebted to Parent-Duchatelet.. for interesting communications concerning Lesbian love. **1931** R. CAMPBELL *Georgiad* i. 13 No Lesbian governess had got the start of him. **1933** H. S. WALPOLE *Vanessa* IV. 781 She disliked people to take it for granted that unless she was Lesbian she was uninteresting. **1972** *Jrnl. Social Psychol.* LXXXVII. 52, 50 adult female respondents who would define themselves.. as being Lesbian or homosexual or both. **1974** *Ms* July 118/1 Testimony from a group of bright articulate lesbians covering: lesbian sexuality, problems of lesbian mothers.. and the lesbian lifestyle.
B. *sb.* A female homosexual.
1925 A. HUXLEY *Let.* 21 Apr. (1969) 246 After a third-rate provincial town, colonized by English sodomites and middle-aged Lesbians, which is, after all, what Florence is, a genuine metropolis will be lively. **1936** C. DAY LEWIS *Friendly Tree* i. 23, I shall never write real poetry. Women never do, unless they're invalids or Lesbians or something. **1940** 'G. ORWELL' *Inside Whale* 132 Gruff-voiced Lesbians in corduroy breeches.. could walk along the streets without attracting a glance. **1947** E. TAYLOR *View of Harbour* x. 170 'I think I look like a Lesbian,' Beth said doubtfully. **1973** [see HOMOSEXUAL *a.*].
Hence '**Lesbianism**, female homosexuality.
1870 A. J. MUNBY *Diary* 2 May in D. Hudson *Munby* (1972) 283 Swinburne.. expressed a horror of sodomy.. and an actual admiration of Lesbianism, being unable.. to see that that is equally loathsome. **1895** A. DOUGLAS *Let.* in H. M. Hyde *Trials Oscar Wilde* (1948) 360 Thus in England there are no laws against 'Lesbianism' or intercourse of an erotic character between women, and yet there are several women in London whose friendship with other women does carry a taint and a suspicion, simply because these women are obviously 'sapphic' in their loves. **1897** H. ELLIS *Stud. Psychol. Sex* I. iv. 82 Casanova remarked that the women of Provence are especially inclined to Lesbianism. **1965** [see HOMOSEXUAL *a.*]. **1971** C. WOLFF *Love between Women* iii. 40 No theory has so far been evolved which deals exclusively with lesbianism.

lesbic ('lɛzbɪk), *a.* = LESBIAN *a.* 2.
1892 D. H. TUKE *Dict. Psychol. Med.* II. 865/2 For many years a whole literature of romance and plays has been occupied in the description of Lesbic love, to the great damage of girls and neuropathic women. **1922** JOYCE *Ulysses* 205 Sons with mothers,.. lesbic sisters, loves that dare not speak their name.

lesbo ('lɛzbəʊ). Also Lesbo. Colloq. abbrev. of LESBIAN *sb.* Similarly **Lesbie**.
1940 J. O'HARA *Pal Joey* 175, I am all set to be m.c. in a crib where the Lesbos even come and watch the dress rehearsals. **1969** C. HIMES *Blind Man with Pistol* xiii. 145 'One was a man; a good-looking man at that.' 'Man my ass, they were lesbos.' **1970** S. ELLIN *Man from Nowhere* liv. 271, I don't dig Lesbies.

leschenaultia (lɛʃə'nəʊtɪə). Also lechenaultia. [mod.L. (R. Brown *Floræ Novæ Hollandiæ* (1810) 581), f. the name of L.T. *Leschenault* de la Tour (1773–1826), French botanist and traveller + -IA[1].] A herb or evergreen shrub of the Australian genus so called, belonging to the family Goodeniaceæ and bearing red, blue, white, or yellow flowers.
1825 *Curtis's Bot. Mag.* LII. 2600 (*heading*) Handsome Lechenaultia. **1916** L. H. BAILEY *Stand. Cycl. Hort.* IV. 1844/2 The leschenaultias require special care in watering. **1955** A. ROSS *Australia 55* 44 Thick clusters of blue and red leschenaultia. **1966** *Times* 11 Nov. (W. Austral. Suppl.) p. iv/2 The exquisite sky-blue leschenaultia, fragile as gossamer, shows its versatility by appearing, in different regions, in scarlet, crimson, blood-red, yellow, orange and green-blue. **1967** A. M. BLOMBERY *Guide Native Austral. Plants* 279 It [*sc.* the genus] is probably best known by the Blue Lechenaultia of W[estern] A[ustralia]. **1972** *Southerly* XXXII. 18 The coffin draped in scarlet with a single bunch of blue leschenaultia, gathered by her friends in the hills.

Lesch-Nyhan (lɛʃ'naɪhən). *Med.* The names of Michael *Lesch* and William L. *Nyhan* (b. 1926),

U.S. physicians, used with reference to a rare hereditary syndrome they described in 1964 which affects young boys (usu. causing early death) and is marked by compulsive self-mutilation of the head and hands, esp. the lips, together with mental retardation and muscular movements of choreiform and athetoid character.

1966 Reed & Fish in *Arch. Dermatol.* XCIV. 195/2 Indications are that this syndrome is probably sex-linked... Since Lesch and Nyhan first described the signs and symptoms as an entity, the condition should be called the Lesch-Nyhan syndrome. **1969** *Sci. News Let.* 11 Oct. 327 Skin cells from patients with a genetic defect known as the Lesch-Nyhan syndrome lack an enzyme essential for incorporation of purine bases into new nucleic acids. **1975** *Amer. Jrnl. Human Genetics* XXVII. 219 The mothers of Lesch-Nyhan cases will be either heterozygous (+/−) or homozygous normal (+/+). In the latter case the Lesch-Nyhan patient would have received a complete mutation from his mother.

lescun, lesczoun, obs. forms of LESSON.

lese, obs. f. LEACH *sb.*[1] and *v.*[1], LEASE, LEASH.

lese, variant of LEESE *v.*[1] and [2].

lesed, *pa. pple.* and *ppl. a. Sc.* Also 8 læsed. [f. L. *læs-us*, pa. pple. of *lædĕre* to hurt + -ED[1].] That has suffered LESION, q.v.; damaged, injured.

16.. in Hector *Judicial Rec.* (1876) 100 (E.D.D.) To assythe the sd John Barr as the pairty lesed. **1708** Chamberlayne *St. Gt. Brit.* II. II. vi. (1743) 385 If the ordinary be clear to pronounce an Interloquitor to the dissatisfaction of either party, he who thinks himself lesed, may get Redress. **1724** Dr. Houstoun in *Phil. Trans.* XXXIII. 12 The Elasticity of these læsed Parts was.. impair'd. **1741** A. Monro *Anat. of Nerves* (ed. 3) 34 The lesed Part of the Body.

lese-majesty ('liːz'mædʒəstɪ). *Civil Law.* Also 6 lease-, leis-, 7 læse-, 8-9 leze-. [ad. F. *lèse-majesté*, ad. L. *læsa mājestās* hurt or violated majesty, i.e. of the sovereign people.] Any offence against the sovereign authority; treason.

[**1430-40** Lydg. *Bochas* IV. xii. (1494) sig. p iij, Lyst he were accused to thestates Of cryme called *lese magestatis.*] **1536** Bellenden *Cron. Scot.* (1821) I. 12 Nochtwithstanding quhatsumever offence of *lese majeste* committit be thaim. *a* **1578** Lindesay (Pitscottie) *Chron. Scot.* (S.T.S.) I. 397 G. D... was banischit in Ingland ffor certane crymes of leismaiestie. **1609** Skene *Reg. Maj.* 6 The crime, quhilk in the Civill law, is called the crime of lese Majestie. *a* **1651** Calderwood *Hist. Kirk* (1843) II. 356 The conspirators ashamed to expresse the king's murther, committed this fained rapt, a crime of lese-majestie. **1726** Cavallier *Mem.* IV. 332, I confess I am loaded with the Crime of Leze Majesty. **1818** Scott *Hrt. Midl.* xi, Perduellion is.. muckle warse than lese-majesty, or the concealment of a treasonable purpose. **1830** Bentham *Const. Code* Wks. 1843 IX. 38 Under a representative democracy.. there can be no lese majesty. **1873** Longf. *Wayside Inn, Rhyme Sir Christopher* 20 Not having been at court Seemed something very little short Of treason or lese-majesty.

transf. *a* **1649** Drumm. of Hawth. *Hist. Jas. I*, Wks. (1711) 9 King Henry [8th] was.. a rebel guilty of lese-majesty divine. **1841** Emerson *Addr., Meth. Nature* Wks. (Bohn) II. 227 Why then goest thou as some.. listening worshipper to this saint or to that? That is the only lese-majesty.

¶ Both in Fr. and Eng., the first member of this word has been treated as a verb-stem, to which a sb. may be attached in an objective relation, forming compounds with the general sense of 'outrage upon the rights or dignity of' (what is expressed by the sb.). So in Fr. *lèse-catholicité, lèse-faculté, lèse-société*, etc. (see Littré); the Eng. examples below are mere nonce-wds.

1790 Burke *Fr. Rev.* 104 Persons whom the leze nation might bring under the administration of his executive powers. **1814** Southey *Lett.* (1856) II. 361 All flogging in schools is prohibited, as a crime of leze-liberty in a free country. **1831** Gen. P. Thompson *Exerc.* (1842) I. 424 There is scarcely an honest or independent man among them, who has not in some way or other been guilty of Lèse-Toryism. **1833** Sir W. Hamilton *Discuss.* (1852) 570 To enfeeble them [classical studies] would.. be.. in a certain sort, the crime of lese-humanity. **1870** Lowell *Poems, Cathedral*, I was a poacher on their self-preserve Intent constructively on lese-anglicism.

lesenge, obs. form of LOZENGE.

leser(e, var. LEESER[1] *Obs.*; obs. f. LIZARD.

lesewe, variant of LEASOW *dial.*

Lesghian ('lɛzgɪən), *sb.* and *a.* Also Lesghi(e), Lesghien, Lesgian, Lezg(h)ian, Lezgin. [ad. Russ. *Lezgin.*] **A.** *sb.* A member of a tribe of the north-eastern Caucasus; also (in earlier quots.), one of a mountain people of Daghestan. Also, the language of these people. **B.** *adj.* Of or pertaining to these people. Also 'Lesĝ(h)ic *a.*

1854 Max Müller *Suggestions in Learning Lang. Seat of War in East* 116 *Lesghic Branch.* Leshistan, or the country of the Lesghi, also called Daghestan.. lies between the rivers Koisu, Alazani, and the Caspian Sea. The Lesghi or Leski.. may.. be the same as the 'Legae' mentioned by Strabo. *Ibid.* 117 The Lesghians are Mahometans. **1875** C. Heneage tr. *M. von Thielmann's Journey Caucasus* I. iv. 280 The name Lesghie, used by the Russians in a general sense, and especially applicable to the inhabitants of Southern Daghestan, does not convey to the latter either the idea of a population or even of a single tribe. **1878** [see Finnic *a.*]. **1879** *Trans. Philol. Soc. 1877-79* 602 Here.. *Lesghian* must be struck out, since it denotes no particular tribe or people. **1921** *19th Cent.* May 871 The bon-bons of the new faith were cast indiscriminately among Circassians,.. Lesghiens.. and Negroes. **1939** L. H. Gray *Foundations of Lang.* xii. 376 This alleged family has four sub-groups, characterised respectively by a sibilant.., a spirant plus a sibilant.., a spirant (e.g. in.. Chechen, Avar, Lesghian..) and a spirant plus a sonant. **1959** B. Geiger et al. *Peoples & Lang. Caucasus* 38 Lezgian.. has the status of a literary language in the Dagestan ASSR. **1968** *Encycl. Brit.* XIII. 1012/2 The Lezgian group of languages includes.. the Agul, Tabasaran, Rutul, Tsakhur, Budukh and Dzhek languages.

lesh(e, obs. form of LEACH *sb.*[1] and *v.*[1], LEASH.

leshpund, variant of LISPOUND.

Lesie, var. LES.

lesion ('liːʒən). Also 6 *Sc.* lessioun, 9 læsion. [ad. F. *lésion*, ad. L. *læsiōn-em*, n. of action f. *lædĕre* to hurt.]

1. Damage, injury; a hurt or flaw, whether material or immaterial.

1452 Dk. York in Ellis *Orig. Lett.* Ser. I. I. 11 What.. lesion of honour, & villany is said & reported generally unto the English nation. *c* **1460** G. Ashby *Dicta Philos.* 659 Yf ye finde any spotte, fylth, or lesion In any personne or in creature, Dishonnour hym not with derision. **1858** *Times* 5 Oct., Looking for faults, for lesions, for bubbles in the gutta-percha. **1859** R. F. Burton *Centr. Afr.* in *Jrnl. Geog. Soc.* XXIX. 89 If the hand after being dipped [in boiling water] shew any sign of lesion, the offence is proven. **1875** Blackmore *A. Lorraine* I. xxvi. 292 Nay, nay, Struan, be not thus hurt by imaginary lesions.

2. Damage or detriment to one's property or rights. Now only in legal use; chiefly in *Civil* and *Scots Law*, applied to such injury involved in a contract as may be pleaded as a ground for setting it aside.

1582-8 *Hist. Jas. VI* (1804) 161 Sum men of his.. distroyed all his coirnes and housses, to his great enorme lessioun. **1839** W. O. Manning *Law Nations* v. vii. (1875) 352 The contingency of lesion to the rights of those who are not parties to the contest. **1875** Poste *Gaius* I. (ed. 2) 152 The first condition is a Laesion by the operation of civil law, i.e. a disadvantageous change in civil rights or obligations brought about by some omission or disposition of the person who claims relief.

3. *Path.* Any morbid change in the exercise of functions or the texture of organs.

1747 tr. *Astruc's Fevers* 301 The physician should.. examine the lesions of the different functions of these organs. **1808** *Med. Jrnl.* XIX. 441 Affected with tetanic symptoms, from the læsion of a nerve. **1866** A. Flint *Princ. Med.* (1880) 185 A lesion called anthracosis of the lungs. *fig.* **1835** Sir W. Hamilton *Discuss.* (1852) 532 The lesion of moral and religious principle in the delinquent himself. **1873** H. Rogers *Orig. Bible* ii. 98 That great moral lesion of man's nature with which the Bible deals.

lesk, obs. form of LEACH *sb.*[1], slice.

leske, obs. form of LASK *v.*; var. of LISK.

†**lesness.** *Obs.* Forms: 1 lésnis(s, 3, 4 lesnes(se. [OE. *lésnis*, f. *lésan, lísan* to loose.] Absolution, redemption, forgiveness (of sins).

c **950** *Lindisf. Gosp.* Luke i. 68 Forðon gesohte & dyde lesnise [**975** *Rushw.* lesnisse] folces his. *c* **1290** *S. Eng. Leg.* I. 273/73 Þou most in lesnesse of þine sunnes: habbe þine woneȝingue þere. **1297** R. Glouc. (Rolls) 3604, & wo so her is aslawe is deþ him sal be In lesnesse of al is sinne. **1340** *Ayenb.* 14 Þe enlefte [article of the Creed] is to leue þe lesnesse of zenne.

lespedeza (lɛspɛ'diːzə). [mod.L. (A. Michaux *Flora Boreali-Americana* (1803) II. 70), blunderingly (by a misreading of the surname) f. the name of V. M. de *Céspedez* (fl. 1785), Spanish governor of East Florida.] A herb or shrub of the genus so called, belonging to the family Leguminosæ, native to North America, Asia, or Australia, and bearing clusters of white, pink, or purple flowers; esp. a plant of this kind used in the southern United States as a hay or fodder crop; also called *bush clover*.

1891 *Garden & Forest* 25 Feb. 88/2 A tall, bushy Lespedeza (*L. Prainii*) is a highly ornamental shrub some ten feet high, bearing large panicles of fine purple-blue flowers. **1900** L. H. Bailey *Cycl. Amer. Hort.* II. 903/1 There are a number of native Lespedezas. **1929** W. Faulkner *Sartoris* (1932) 5, I expect every spring to find corn or lespedeza coming up in the hyacinth beds. **1943** J. S. Huxley *TVA* vi. 45 Lespedeza and other legumes.. bind soil and provide nitrates. **1965** Ripper & George *Cotton Pests Sudan* i. 6 Lespedezas, which come from China and Korea, are now widely used in the South East of the U.S.A. to renew worn out soil. **1975** *Country Life* 13 Feb. 373/1 In the crops of shot birds we found.. the seeds of beggar weed, wild peas and lespedeza.

lespund, variant of LISPOUND.

less (lɛs), *a.* (*sb.*), *adv.*, and *conj.* Forms: 1 *inflected adj.* lǽssa (lǽsse *fem.* and *neut.*), *Northumb.* léassa, *uninflected* lǽs, 2-5 lasse, 2-7 les, 3-7 lesse, (4 lass, 4, 6 *Sc.* lese), 4-5 las, 4- less. [(1) The OE. *lǽs* adv. (occas. used quasi-sb. and as uninflected adj.) corresponds to OFris. *lês*:—OTeut. type **laisiz*, f. **laiso-* (not elsewhere found with the sense 'small') + *-iz* comparative suffix (see -ER[3]), which in OE. disappears by phonetic law, as in BET, LENG *advs.* (2) The OE. *lǽssa* adj. corresponds to OFris. *lêssa*:—OTeut. type **laisizon-*, f. **laisiz*: see above, and cf. -ER[3] A. The disappearance of the middle vowel was presumably prior to the WGer. change of *z* into *r*; the OFris. *lêssera* is doubtless, like Eng. LESSER, a new formation.

The OTeut. type **laiso-*, pre-Teut. **loiso-*, appears to be cogn. w. Lith. *lësa-s*:—**leiso-*, small. Whether there is any connexion with **leid-*, **līd-* in Goth. *leitils* little is very doubtful. Cf. the alleged Crim-Gothic *lista* 'parum'.]

A. *adj.* Used as the comparative of LITTLE.

I. In concord with sb. expressed or understood.

1. a. Of not so great size, extent, or degree (as something mentioned or implied); of inferior dimensions, bulk, duration, etc.; smaller. Opposed (in mod. Eng.) to *greater*. *Obs.* with reference to material dimensions (superseded by *smaller*); still current with reference to number, degree, etc.

c **1000** Ælfric *Gen.* i. 16 Þæt mare leoht to þæs dæȝes lihtinge and þæt læsse leoht to þære nihte lihtinge. *c* **1200** *Trin. Coll. Hom.* 179 Þe more fishes in þe se eten þe lasse. **1297** R. Glouc. (Rolls) 11689 Þe bissop.. prechede hom þat hii adde of deþ þe lasse fere. ? *a* **1300** *Shires, etc. Eng.* in *O.E. Misc.* 145 On engle londe syndon two and þrytti schire, summe more and summe lasse. *a* **1300** *Cursor M.* 436 (Gött.) Summe of less [*v. rr.* lesse, lasse] and sum of more prise. **1398** Trevisa *Barth. De P.R.* III. iv. (1495) 51 The soule is noughte more in a more body, nother lasse in a lasse body. *c* **1400** *Destr. Troy* 5961 The light wax las. *c* **1440** *Gesta Rom.* I. iv. 10 (Harl. MS.) Hit is wreten that of too Evelis þe lasse Evill is to be chosyn. *c* **1449** Pecock *Repr.* I. xiv. 74 Herfore it is the lasse merveil. **1567** Maplet *Gr. Forest* 49 Akoniton.. hath leaves like the Cucumber, but somewhat more lesse and rough. **1598** Yong *Diana* III. 70 Other kindes of lesse trees.. twyning about the greater. **1610** Shaks. *Temp.* I. ii. 335 Teach me how To name the bigger Light, and how the lesse That burne by day, and night. **1673** Ray *Journey Low C.* 38 Shags.. are very like to Cormorants, only less. **1692** R. L'Estrange *Fables* xix. (1708) 26 Rather than bear a Less Misfortune to Hazzard a Greater. **1718** Prior *Henry & Emma* 430 Fine by degrees and beautifully less. **1757** Jos. Harris *Coins* 41 Every one will see and understand that 19 is less than 20. **1794** S. Williams *Vermont* 83 The female is less than the male. **1816** Byron *Prisoner Chillon* viii, And then the sighs he would suppress.. grew less and less. **1871** Morley *Voltaire* (1886) 1 The peculiarities of his individual genius changed the mind and spiritual conformation of France, and in a less degree, of the whole of the West.

b. Of smaller quantity or amount; not so much. Opposed to *more*.

c **1314** *Guy Warw.* (A.) 1697 In lasse while þan þat was Might falle mani wonder cas. **1375** *Sc. Leg. Saints* xl. (*Ninian*) 443 Þan to þe catel þai tuk les kepe. **1484** Caxton *Fables of Auian* xxv, Somtyme the children whiche ben preysed and loued done lesse good than they whiche ben despreysed and hated. **1591** Shaks. *1 Hen. VI*, IV. iv. 34, I owe him little Dutie, and lesse Loue. **1596** —— *2 Hen. IV*, IV. v. 7 Lesse noyse, lesse noyse. **1655** Fuller *Ch. Hist.* IX. i. §44 The Queen knowing it less difficulty and danger to keep him, then to cast him out of her Dominions. **1664** J. Webb *Stone-Heng* (1725) 19 We cannot yet give Credit, and less shall, to one Word he saith. **1667** Milton *P.L.* IV. 854 More glorie will be wonn, Or less be lost. **1669** Sturmy *Mariner's Mag.* v. 72 With less Trouble and Charge. **1853** Brimley *Ess., Bleak House* 285 We should then have less crowd and no story. **1853** Gladstone *Sp.* 18 Apr. *Financ. Statem.* (1863) 5 The estimate for the present year cannot, I fear, be expected to be much less, if at all less, than 530,000*l.*

c. A smaller number of; fewer. This originates from the OE. construction of *lǽs* adv. (quasi-*sb.*) with a partitive genitive. Freq. found but generally regarded as incorrect.

c **888** K. Ælfred *Boeth.* xxxv. §5 [6] Swa mid læs worda swa mid ma, swæðer we hit ȝereccan maȝon. **1481** Caxton *Godfrey* cl. 222 By cause he had so grete plente of men of hys owne countre, he called the fewer and lasse to counseyll of the noble men of the Cyte. **1579** Lyly *Euphues* To Gentl. Oxf. (Arb.) 208, I thinke there are few Vniuersities that haue lesse faultes than Oxford, many that haue more. **1862** M. D. Colt *Went to Kansas* 84, I may see them all doing with still less comforts. **1873** *Nature* 1 May 15/2 The determination of position in the given manifoldness is reduced to a determination of quantity and to a determination of position in a manifoldness of less dimensions. **1874** *Rep. Brit. Assoc. Adv. Sci. 1873* 53 To return to the history of logarithmic tables to a less number of figures. **1904** *Amer. Jrnl. Philol.* XXV. 234 There might have been less barbed wire, less flaring flowers. **1971** *Guardian* 16 Dec. 16/1 The 47-page prospectus.. shows that there are less restrictions.. than is generally supposed. **1972** 'E. Lathen' *Murder without Icing* (1973) ii. 21 You've seen less hockey games than my wife.

2. a. Of lower station, condition, or rank; inferior. *Obs.* exc. in phrases like ***no less a person than.***

c **950** *Lindisf. Gosp.* Matt. xi. 11 Seðe uutedlice læssa [*Rushw.* lessa] is in ric heofna mara is of ðæm. *a* **1200** *Moral Ode* 390 Al þat is & al þat wes is wurse þenne he [God] and lesse. *a* **1300** *Cursor M.* 12166 Noght yee ne vnderstod for-þi Less i wat er yee þan i. *c* **1380** Wyclif *Serm.* Sel. Wks. I. 19 Þis secounde feste was algatis lasse. *c* **1400** *Destr. Troy* 2948 Ladys and oþer les wemen. **1444** *Rolls of Parlt.* V. 113/1 By colour of tenure of lasse Tenentz. *a* **1450** *Knt. de la Tour* (1868) 14 To poure gentilmen, or to other of lasse degre. *c* **1450** tr. *De Imitatione* I. xx. 24 'As ofte tymes as I was amonge men, I come a lasse man', þat is to say lesse holy. **1609** Bible (Douay) *Hos.* Comm., Foure are called the greater prophetes, and twelve the lesse. **1652** Needham tr.

Selden's Mare Cl. 40 Cotzensis and Moses Maimonides besides others of a less account. **1869** TENNYSON *Coming of Arthur* 12 And so there grew great tracts of wilderness, Wherein the beast was ever more and more, But man was less and less, till Arthur came.

†**b.** Of action: Not so great, worthy, or excellent. *Obs. rare*$^{-1}$.

1685 EARL HALIFAX *On Death Chas. II*, 104 'Tis less to conquer, than to make Wars cease.

†**c.** *less of, in*: inferior in point of. *Obs.*

1307 *Elegy Edw. I*, x, God lete him ner be worse man Then is fader, ne lasse of myht. **13..** *E.E. Allit. P.* A. 598 Þe lasse in werke to take more [is] able. **1375** *Sc. Leg. Saints* ii. (*Paulus*) 49 Paule wes lese of dingnite. **1535** COVERDALE *2 Esdras* v. 55 Ye are lesse of stature, then those that were before you. **1593** SHAKS. *Rich. II*, II. iii. 15 And hope to ioy, is little lesse in ioy, Then hope enioy'd. **1594** —— *Rich. III*, IV. iv. 299 A Grandams name is little lesse in loue, Then is the doting Title of a Mother. **1654** EARL MONM. tr. *Bentivoglio's Warrs Flanders* 32 By how much the Regent went every day less in her authority.

3. a. Used *spec.* to characterize the smaller, inferior, or (after Latin use) younger, of two persons or things of the same name; = L. *minor*. (Cf. *lesser*.) †*Less Britain*, †*Britain the less*: Brittany. *Obs.* exc. in the designation *James the Less*, and occasional imitations of this.

c **950** *Lindisf. Gosp.* Mark xv. 40 Ðæs iacobes leasse [*Jacobi minoris*]. **1297** R. GLOUC. (Rolls) 2120 To þe lasse brutaine þer ne come aliue none. *a* **1300** *Cursor M.* 13299 Þe less jam and sant Thomas. *c* **1400** MAUNDEV. (1839) xxv. 259 Ynde the lesse. **1432–50** tr. *Higden* (Rolls) I. 145 Asia the lesse towcheth in the este parte Capadocy. *c* **1550** LLOYD *Treas. Health* (1585) S ij, With .ix graines of leasse spurge or of Pioni. **1597** MORLEY *Introd. Mus.* Annot., Betwixt *mi* and *fa* is not a full halfe note, but is lesse then halfe a note by a comma: and therefore called the lesse halfe note. **1598** SYLVESTER *Du Bartas* II. ii. IV. *Columnes* 490 The Tyrant of lesse-Asia. **1613** ZOUCH *Dove* 39 Allan, the Earle of lesse Brittain. **1614** SELDEN *Titles Hon.* 344 Barons with the rest vpward we call the Greater Nobilitie, the others beneath them the Lesse Nobilitie. **1843** MACAULAY *Mme. D'Arblay* Ess. 1865 III. 310 Dr. Franklin, not, as some have dreamed, the great Pennsylvanian Dr. Franklin,..but Dr. Franklin the less.

†**b.** *the less world* = MICROCOSM.

a **1300** *Cursor M.* 552 Man es clepid þe lesse werld. **1398** TREVISA *Barth. De P.R.* VIII. i. (1495) 293 Man is callyd the lasse worlde, for he shewyth in hymselfe lyknesse of all the worlde. *c* **1400** tr. *Secreta Secret., Gov. Lordsh.* 88 It holdys yn him alle þe elymentz, and it is callyd þe lesse world..þe Eye [*i.e.* egg] of Philosophers. **1526** *Pilgr. Perf.* (W. de W. 1531) 1 Lyke as the great worlde was made perfecte in vij dayes, so yᵉ lesse worlde, that is man, is made..perfecte by grace in these vij spirituall dayes.

†**c.** *less age* (*Sc.*): minority.

1524 ARRAN in *St. Papers Hen. VIII*, IV. 158 Not as ane pupile in juvente and lese aige, bot as ane maist noble excellent Prince of perfit mature aige. **1531** HEN. VIII ibid. 590 Laying apart thexcuses of mynorite and les age. *a* **1572** KNOX *Hist. Ref.* Wks. (1846) I. 403 Money, cunȝeit in our Soveraneis less age. **1609** SKENE *Reg. Majest.* II. lxx. §2 Gif she being of les age, falles in the warde of her over-lord.

4. Preceding (†formerly also, following) a numeral or other quantitative expression, used to denote that the number or quantity indicated is to be subtracted from a larger one mentioned or implied; = MINUS. Also *transf.*, used (like *minus*) for 'not including', 'except'.

O.E. Chron. an. 641 (Laud MS.) He rixode twa læs .xxx. ȝeara. *c* **1000** ÆLFRIC *Gram.* xlix. (Z.) 287 Man cweð eac *undeuiginti* an læs twentiȝ, *duodeuiginti* twam læs twentiȝ, *duodetriginta* twam læs þrittiȝ. *a* **1300** *Cursor M.* 2168 Tuelue scor o yeires bot an lesse [*Trin.* saue oon las]. *c* **1320** *Sir Tristr.* 2508 Tvelmoneth þre woukes las. **1523** LD. BERNERS *Froiss.* I. lxiii. 84 This siege endured a long season, the space of a xi. wekes, thre dayes lesse. **1695** ALINGHAM *Geom. Epit.* 1, $a - b$ is thus read *a* less *b*, or the remainder after *b* is taken from *a*. **1869** *Bradshaw's Railway Manual* XXI. 304 Dividends were declared at the rate of 5 per cent. per annum in the preference shares, amounting, less income tax, to 1,218 *l.* **1880** GOLDW. SMITH in *Atlantic Monthly* 213 The foundations of natural theology, less the mere name of Deity. **1910** *Chambers's Jrnl.* Oct. 661/1 If I borrow £100.. I pay my interest, less tax. **1911** *Rep. Labour & Social Conditions Germany* (Tariff Reform League) III. VI–VII. 20 All meat is sold less the bone. **1930** *Times* 25 Mar. 24/2 A full year's dividend on the Preference Shares, less tax, absorbing £16,800. **1972** *Times* 2 Sept. 18/8 Cost of paint.. Less VAT input tax..£500.

¶**5.** Used peculiarly by Shaks. with words expressing or implying a negative, where the sense requires 'more'. Cf. LESS *adv.*

1611 SHAKS. *Wint. T.* III. ii. 57, I ne're heard yet, That any of these bolder Vices wanted Lesse Impudence to gaine-say what they did, Then to performe it first. —— *Cymb.* I. iv. 23 To fortifie her iudgement, which else an easie battery might lay flat, for taking a Begger without lesse quality.

II. *absol.* (quasi-*sb.*)

From the point of view of the modern language, these substantival uses may be referred to the adj., though in OE. some of them originated from the adv., and the indeclinable form is therefore used.

6. *the less*: that which is smaller (of two things compared). Also of persons: He who is or they who are less.

1413 *Pilgr. Sowle* (Caxton) v. i. (1859) 70 Nedes must the lesse be conteyned within the more. **1591** SHAKS. *Two Gent.* III. i. 372 The haire that couers the wit, is more then the wit; for the greater hides the lesse. **1594** DANIEL *Cleopatra* III. Wks. (Grosart) III. 59 Nemesis..Who..Doth raze the great, and raise the lesse. **1611** BIBLE *Heb.* vii. 7 The lesse is blessed of the better. **1865** J. H. NEWMAN *Gerontius* §3 For spirits and men by different standards mete The less and greater in the flow of time.

7. a. A less amount, quantity, or number (*than* one that is specified or implied). *less than no time*: a jocular hyperbole for an exceedingly short time.

c **1000** ÆLFRIC *Exod.* xvi. 17 And Israhela bearn dydon swa and gaderodon sum mare sum læsse. *c* **1050** *Byrhtferth's Handboc* in *Anglia* (1885) VIII. 304 ȝif þær beo læs þon seofon. *a* **1225** *Ancr. R.* 6 Sum..mei..paie god mid lesse. **1387** TREVISA *Higden* (Rolls) VII. 403 Ȝif þey wil þey mowe have lasse in þe somer tyme. *a* **1500** *Chaucer's Dreme* 1869 Which herbe in lesse than halfe an houre Gan over all knit. **1500–20** DUNBAR *Poems* xv. 12 Sum askis far less than he servis. **1591** SHAKS. *Two Gent.* I. i. 111 Lesse then a pound shall serue me for carrying your Letter. **1700** DRYDEN *Pal. & Arc.* III. 841 Though less and less of Emily he saw. **1809** MALKIN *Gil Blas* IV. vii. ¶11 Trust me for sinking, burning, and destroying him in less than no time. **1844** STANLEY *Arnold* (1858) I. v. 208 Our little may be more inexcusable than their less was in them. **1850** TENNYSON *In Mem.* cxi, Not being less but more than all The gentleness he seem'd to be. **1853** J. H. NEWMAN *Hist. Sk.* (1876) 192 The Turks of this day are still in the less than infancy of art. **1877** SPURGEON *Serm.* XXIII. 588 The less said about her the better. **1879** WHITNEY *Sanskrit Gram.* 236 Less than thirty roots form their present-system. **1885** O. W. HOLMES *Emerson* i. 38 Even so late as less than half a century ago.

b. Qualified adverbially by *far*, *little*, *much*, *nothing*, *something*, or phrase denoting quantity. Also *no less* = 'nothing less'; for examples see NO.

It is often impossible to say whether in the combinations *nothing less*, *something less*, the former word is used advb. or whether it is an indefinite pronoun in apposition with *less* used absol. The combination *nothing less than* has two quite contrary senses; in the use here treated it means 'quite equal to, the same thing as'; for the opposite meaning see B. 3.

c **1200** *Vices & Virtues* (1888) 45 Ȝif he arrer dede litel te gode, ðar after he doð michele lasse. *c* **1330** R. BRUNNE *Chron.* (1810) 174 For ten mark men solde a litille bulchyn, Litille lesse men told a bouke of a moutoun. **1387** TREVISA tr. *Higden* (Rolls) IV. 251 Iohn hadde tweie dayes lasse in his moder wombe. **1593** SHAKS. *1 Hen. VI*, II. v. 100 But yet methinkes, my Fathers execution Was nothing lesse then bloody Tyranny. **1652** T. GATAKER *Antinomianism* 5 In those words of mine nothing les was intended, then this Autor would..enforce them to speak. **1836** C. FOX *Jrnl.* 23 Sept. (1972) 32 'A gentleman' was announced, who proved to be nothing less than Professor Sedgwick! **1856** DICKENS *Dorrit* (1857) II. I. xxiii. 79 You couldn't do it when your Uncle George was living; much less when he's dead. **1863** J. A. FROUDE *Hist. Eng.* (ed. 3) II. xi. 298 But Elizabeth meant nothing less than to recall Sidney. **1865** *Daily Tel.* 2 Dec. 7/1 We may rest satisfied that the dispute will end in nothing less than a battle royal. *c* **1874** D. BOUCICAULT in M. R. Booth *Eng. Plays of 19th Cent.* (1969) II. 174 You are not mistress in your own house, much less lady of the manor. **1895** *Bookman* Oct. 22/2 His policy became nothing less than a series of gigantic blunders.

†**c.** *o* or *of less than, in less than*: unless. *Obs.* (For the fuller treatment of these phrases see UNLESS.)

c **1400** MAUNDEV. (Roxb.) xxv. 118 Na man schall come nere him but lordes, o less þan he call any man till him. **1414** *Rolls of Parlt.* IV. 22/2 [That] no Lawe be made of lasse than they yaf therto their assent. **1461** *Paston Lett.* II. 46 Beware that ye aventure not your person..by the See, till ye haue oder word from us, in less than your person cannot be sure there as ye ar.

B. *adv.*

1. a. To a less or smaller extent; in a lower degree; to an inferior extent, amount, etc. Often in neg. phr., as *none the less*, *no less*, *not the less*: see NO, NOT, etc.; also NATHELESS, NEVERTHELESS, etc.

c **900** tr. *Bæda's Hist.* v. xii[i]. (1890) 424 Oðer [dæl] wes nohte þon læs unaarefndlice cele hæȝles & snawes. *c* **1290** *S. Eng. Leg.* I. 205/176 Þe lasse he was of heom a-drad. *a* **1300** *Cursor M.* 11207 Ihesu crist hir barn sco bar, Hir child, and maiden neuer less [*Gött.* neuer þe lesse]. *c* **1386** CHAUCER *Pard. Prol.* & *T.* 274 If that a prince use hasardrie.. He is ..Holde the lasse in reputacioun. **1422** tr. *Secreta Secret., Priv. Priv.* 242 The natural hette atte myde-day is lasse stronge. *a* **1450** *Knt. de la Tour* (1868) 102 No goode woman shulde..sette the lasse bi hym for ani sikenesse that God sendithe. **1508** DUNBAR *Tua mariit wemen* 322 The mair he loutit for my luf, the les of him I rakit. **1541** BECON *News out of Heaven* Prol. (1542) A v b, His worde is, that they shoulde sanctify the Sabbothday... But what do they lesse? **1596** DALRYMPLE tr. *Leslie's Hist. Scot.* I. 5 He fand heit and calde lesse vehement in Scotlande than in france. **1667** MILTON *P.L.* IV. 478 Less faire, Less winning soft, less amiablie milde, Then that smooth watry image. **1701** DE FOE *True-born Eng.* 147 None talk on't more, or understand it less. **1798** COLERIDGE *Anc. Mar.* VI. xvii, The rock shone bright, the kirk no less. **1808** SCOTT *Marm.* I. ii, As the fading ray Less bright and less was flung.

b. Qualifying an adj. or ppl. adj. used attrib.: often hyphened.

1593 SHAKS. *Rich. II*, II. i. 49 The enuy of lesse happier Lands. **1664** H. MORE *Myst. Iniq., Apol.* 538 He is to serve God though in that less-seemly or less-perfect Habit. *a* **1674** MILTON (*title*) A Brief History of Moscovia: and of other less-known Countries. London..1682. **1689** BURNET *Tracts* I. 54 If I were writing to a less knowing Man than yourself. **1711** SHAFTESB. *Charac.* (1737) II. 255 There are other over-officious and less-suspected hands. **1818** COBBETT *Pol. Reg.* XXXIII. 108 In the less-enslaved cities and towns. **1866** M. ARNOLD *Thyrsis* xv, The less practised eye of sanguine youth. **1875** JOWETT *Plato* (ed. 2) I. 399 Some other less-known members of the Socratic circle. **1886** W. J. TUCKER *E. Europe* 231 Less costly benefits and emoluments, and less extended patronage.

2. *much less*, *still less* (†formerly also simply *less*): used to characterize a statement or suggestion as still more unacceptable than one that has been already denied.

1632 B. JONSON *Magn. Lady* III. iii, You never fought with any, lesse, slew any. **1663** GERBIER *Counsel* G iv b, Dimensions and Formes, which are not to be mended, lesse contradicted. **1671** MILTON *P.R.* III. 236 The world thou hast not seen, much less her glory. **1718** HICKES & NELSON *J. Kettlewell* App. 55 It is not easily to be expected that any should contradict those Inclinations, less that the Generality should do so. **1719** DE FOE *Crusoe* II. xv, It had no power to help itself,..much less help them. **1721** RAMSAY *Content* 250 Mere empty spectres..Which merit not your notice, less your care. *Mod.* I do not even suggest that he is negligent, still less [*or* much less] that he is dishonest.

3. †*nothing less*: least of all things, anything rather (than the thing in question) (*obs.*). *nothing less than*: far from being, anything rather than; = F. *rien moins que*. (Now *rare*.)

1548 GEST *Pr. Masse* I viij b, Therfore the before mencioned boke is nothinge lesse then canonical. **1551** ROBINSON tr. *More's Utop.* I. (1895) 29 He retorned again into hys countreye, nothynge lesse then lokyd for. **1567** HARMAN *Caveat* (1869) 31 Hee..saythe that he woulde be glad to take payne for his lyuinge, althoughe he meaneth nothinge lesse. **1593** SHAKS. *Rich. II*, II. ii. 34 *Bush.* 'Tis nothing but conceit (my gracious Lady). *Qu.* 'Tis nothing lesse. **1598** GRENEWEY *Tacitus' Ann.* XII. x. (1622) 169 The Barbarous people know nothing lesse then engines and subtile deuises in besieging and assayling of fortresses. **1656** R. ROBINSON *Christ all* 158 Pretending themselves to be the companions of Christ, when indeed they are nothing less. **1827** SCOTT *Napoleon* xxvii, Who, trusting to the laws.., expected nothing less than an attack.

4. For OE. *þý lǽs þe*, early ME. *þi les þe*, see LEST *conj.*

C. *conj.* Unless. In early use *less than*, *less that*, Sc. *less nor*. *Obs.* exc. *U.S. dial.* and *colloq.*

When written *'less* it represents a contracted form of *unless*.

1422 tr. *Secreta Secret., Priv. Priv.* 137 Lasse than a kynge ..dred god..he shall..fall..in a shorte tyme. **1442** *Rolls of Parlt.* V. 60/2 Lesse þan..[þei] leve a sufficiaunt man..in their stede. *c* **1470** HENRY *Wallace* III. 304 That thai sall do him nocht..less it be on thaim socht. **1513** DOUGLAS *Æneis* I. Prol. 233 Les than wyse autouris lene [*i.e.* lie]. **1553** KENNEDY *Compend. Tractive* in *Wodrow Soc. Misc.* (1844) 128 Les nor this medicyne be applyit dewlie, it is not proffitable. **1567** *Satir. Poems Reform.* vii. 28 Les schamefullie thair office thay abuse. **1601** B. JONSON *Poetaster* Dial. Hor. & Trebatius, Less learn'd Trebatius censure disagree. **1632** MILTON *Penseroso* 56 And the mute Silence hist along, 'Less Philomel will daign a Song. **1640** GLAPTHORNE *Wit in Constable* III. Wks. 1874 I. 206 For Musicke, lesse the Virginalls, I never car'd for any. **1760–72** H. BROOKE *Fool of Qual.* (1809) II. 7, I am sorry..my nothings should be talked of, less it should intimate that other people are less ostentatious. **1892** KIPLING *Many Inventions* (1893) 41 'Less you want your toes trod off, you'd better get back. **1900** 'FLYNT' & WALTON *Powers that Prey* 62 If any of 'em knows us they'll beef dead sure, 'less we square 'em. **1929** W. FAULKNER *Sound & Fury* 22 They wont know you got wet... Less me and Jason tells. **1973** *Black World* Apr. 61 Don't no broad be puttin' me down, less I go upside her head. **1973** J. DRUMMOND *Bang! Bang! you're Dead!* xxxvii. 129 You gonna be like Jinx Janeiro soon, less you listen to me.

†**less**, *v. Obs.* Also 3–6 **lasse**, 4 **lessi.** [ME. *lasse*, *lessi*, f. *lasse*, *lesse* LESS *a.*]

1. *intr.* To become less, decrease.

a **1225** *Leg. Kath.* 1718 Þe neauer ne linneð nowðer ne lesseð, ah leasteð aa mare. ?*c* **1325** *Old Age* vii. in *E.E.P.* (1862) 149, I lench, i len on lyme, i lasse. *c* **1330** *Arth. & Merl.* 414 His men lassed alway tho. *c* **1450** *Cov. Myst.* xxiv. (Shaks. Soc.) 223 My grett desesse I hope xall lesse. **1480** CAXTON *Chron. Eng.* cxcvii. 174 Syr Thomas men lancastre lassed and slaked. **1483** —— *G. de la Tour* E vij, And thenne shalle lasse the pestylence and pees shalle be. **1496** *Dives & Paup.* (W. de W.) I. xlvii. 88/1 Our synnes alwaye encreaseth & lesseth not. **1502** *Ord. Crysten Men* (W. de W. 1506) v. ii. 357 That [the fire] of hell is eternall, & neuer lesseth. **1523** LD. BERNERS *Froiss.* I. ccxlix. 369 The englishmen were sore displeased, for their strength dayly lassed. **1602** T. FITZHERBERT *Apol.* 36 The samin lessed when seuen of Sauls offspring were deliuered to the Gabaonits.

2. *trans.* To make less, lessen, diminish. *occas.* const. *of* = by (a certain amount).

a **1300** *E.E. Psalter* xi. 2 Lessed ere sothenes fra mennes sones. *c* **1315** SHOREHAM 127 Hyre poer nys nouȝt y-lessed. *c* **1400** tr. *Secreta Secret., Gov. Lordsh.* 55 His dedys shall be defamyd, and his empir lessyd. **1429** in Rymer *Foedera* (1710) X. 420/2 Nowe that the Poeple of this Land is Lessed and Decressed of late tyme, by Mortalite. *c* **1450** *Merlin* 401 Holy cherche was lessed full sore of xxᵗⁱ thousande peple that ther was slain of oon. **1481** CAXTON *Godfrey* 164 They had ben mynysshed moche and lassed in the batayle. **1500–20** DUNBAR *Poems* lxiii. 76 It wald me sumthing satisfie, And less of my malancolie. **1534** MORE *Comf. agst. Trib.* I. Wks. 1168/2 Wee..shall..fynd our heartes lighted, and thereby the grief of our tribulacion lessed. **1562** TURNER *Herbal* II. 4 Polypody drieth and lesseth or thinneth the body. **1633** P. FLETCHER *Poet. Misc.* 77 But silence thou mayst add but never lesse it.

b. To lower in position or station; to humble, degrade.

c **1375** *Sc. Leg. Saints* xxxvi. (*Baptista*) 233 In-to man lessit are we, to god þat we ma grewande be. *a* **1400** *Prymer* (1891) 18 Thou hast lassed hym a litel fro angeles. **1483** CAXTON *G. de la Tour* L vij, Yf she tooke hym her parentes and frendes shold hold her lassed and hyndered.

c. *pass.* To decrease (in respect *of*).

?**1520** BARCLAY *Jugurth* 19 But for all this suffrance of Adherball: the mynde of Jugurth was nat more pacified, nor lessed of his cruelte.

-less (lɪs), *suffix*, forming adjs. The OE. *léas*, like its equivalents in the other Teut. langs. (see LEASE *a.*, LOOSE *a.*), was used in the sense 'devoid (of)', 'free (from)', both as a separate adj., governing the genitive, as in *firena léas* free from crimes, and (more frequently) as the second element of compounds, the first element being a sb., as in *fácnléas* guileless, *wifléas* without a wife. The adj., as a separate word in the relevant sense, did not survive in ME., and the ending *-léas* became a mere suffix, which was, and still is, very freely attached to sbs. to form adjs. with privative sense.

In many instances the sb. to which the suffix was attached was a noun of action, coincident in form with the stem of a related vb., and some of the adjs. so formed had the sense 'not to be ——ed', 'un——able', as in *countless*, *numberless*. On the supposed analogy of these words, the suffix has been appended to many verbs, as in *abashless*, *dauntless*, *describeless*, *expressless*, *quenchless*, *resistless*, *tireless*, † *topless* (= not overtopped), *weariless*.

Of the very common recent use of the suffix in the formation of nonce-wds. a few examples are subjoined.

1840 THACKERAY *Catherine* iv, Moneyless, wifeless, horse-less, corporal-less. **1870** FURNIVALL *Boorde's Introd.* etc. Pref. 14 The possibility that the undated dedicationless Wyer was issued before 1542. **1885** *Athenæum* 12 Dec. 764 Butcherless, bakerless, tailorless, coblerless, doctorless, bookless, milkless, postless..jungle. **1892** W. H. HUDSON *Nat. La Plata* 136 These peaceful gnatless days. **1897** MARY KINGSLEY *W. Africa* 341, 'I have not brought my card-case with me.'.. I said I was similarly card-caseless.

lesse, obs. form of LEACH *sb.*[1]

lesse, var. LEASE *a.* and *sb.*[2], *v.*[3], LEESE *v.*[1]

†**lessed**, *ppl. a. Her. Obs.* In 5 lassed. [f. LESS *v.* + -ED[1].] (See quot.)

1486 *Bk. St. Alban's, Her.* b ij b, A lassed cotarmure is on the moderis parte. A lassed cootarmure is calde the coote of a gentylwoman hauyng lyuelode weddyd to a man hauyng noo cootarmure.

lessee (lɛˈsiː). Also 6–7 leas(s)ee, 7 lesse. [a. AF. *lessee*, OF. *lessé*, pa. pple. of *lesser*, *lessier*, mod.F. *laisser* to leave: see LEASE *v.*[3] and -EE.] A person to whom a lease is granted; a tenant under a lease.

[*a* **1481** LITTLETON *Inst.* §57 Il y ad le Feoffor, & le Feoffee, le Donor & le Donee, le Lessor & le Lessee.] **1495** *Act 11 Hen. VII*, c. 9 §2 Lessees..[shall] fynde goode and suffycient suertie. **1533–4** *Act 25 Hen. VIII*, c. 8 The lessees ..shall defalke, abate, and reteine..as muche of the rentes dewe to the lessours, as thei can proue, to haue expended on the same pauinge. **1587** HARRISON *England* II. xii. (1877) I. 242 If the leassee be thought to be worth an hundred pounds. **1614** W. B. *Philospher's Banquet* (ed. 2) 260 The Lesse most leaudly the rent did retaine. **1683** PETTUS *Fleta Min.* II. 17 The Leasees of our Society did work the Mines of Consumlock and Talibont. **1817** W. SELWYN *Law Nisi Prius* (ed. 4) II. 1209 If executrix of lessee for years of a rectory take husband, the husband and wife may [etc.]. **1884** YATES *Recoll.* I. v. 187 The lessee..placed my name on his free list, and for years I went to his theatre once or twice a week.

Hence **le'sseeship**, the condition or position of a lessee.

1812 HOLT in *Examiner* 28 Dec. 831/2 That lesseeship was worth nothing. **1884** YATES *Recoll.* I. v. 186 Mr. E. T. Smith ..in his time entered on theatrical lesseeship on a large and varied scale.

lessen (ˈlɛs(ə)n), *v.* Also 4 lasnen, 5 lessyn, 7 leasen. [f. LESS *a.* + -EN[5] I.]

1. *intr.* To become less in size, quantity, amount, scope, etc.; to decrease.

13.. *E.E. Allit. P.* B. 438 Þenne lasned þe llak þat large watz are. *Ibid.* 441 Þenne lasned þe loȝ lowkande togeder. **1423** JAS. I *Kingis Q.* 187 Quhen lessen gan my sore. **1480** CAXTON *Chron. Eng.* iv, For kyng Goffarus peple might every day encrease mo & mo & Brute's lessen. **1633** P. FLETCHER *Purple Isl.* I. xli, The world might die to live, and lessen to increase. **1725** DE FOE *Voy. round World* (1840) 262 The river..lessened every step we went. *a* **1728** WOODWARD *Nat. Hist. Foss.* I. (1729) I. 51 A Flint of Cylindric Figure, only lessening a little toward each end. **1745** WESLEY *Answ. Ch.* 10 My Regard for them lessen'd. **1798** LANDOR *Gebir* I. 182, I..seemed to lessen and shrink up with cold. **1821** LAMB *Elia* Ser. I. *New Year's Eve*, In proportion as the years both lessen and shorten.

2. To decrease in apparent size by the effect of distance: orig. said with reference to a bird's flight (also *refl.*).

1611 SHAKS. *Cymb.* v. v. 472 The Romaine Eagle From South to West, on wing soaring aloft Lessen'd her selfe, and in the Beames o' th' Sun So vanish'd. **1660** FULLER *Mixt Contempl.* v. 9 The wealth of the Land doth begin (to use the Faulconer's phrase) to flie to lessen. *a* **1720** SHEFFIELD (Dk. Buckhm.) *Wks.* (1753) I. 93 Away she flies,..She lessens to us, and is lost at last. *a* **1771** GRAY *Ode Pleas. fr. Viciss.* ii, The sky-lark..lessening from the dazzled sight Melts into air and liquid light. **1795–7** SOUTHEY *Juvenile & Minor P.* Poet. Wks. II. 56 As the white sail is lessening from thy view. **1807** J. BARLOW *Columb.* I. 195 Spain, lessening to a chart, beneath it swims. **1859** KINGSLEY *Misc.* (1860) I. 145 The warm dark roof lessening away into endless gloom.

3. *trans.* To make less in size, quantity, amount, scope, etc.; to diminish.

a **1400–50** *Alexander* 5368 Ser, if þou lessen my life, na lowere þou wynnes. *c* **1440** *Jacob's Well* 196 To lessyn his blood in blood-letyng. **1530** PALSGR. 607/1 His treasure is lessened sythe I knewe hym first. **1632** HEYWOOD *1st Pt. Iron Age* I. Wks. 1874 III. 283 It could not..Leasen my zeale to you. **1651** HOBBES *Leviath.* IV. xlvi. 373 Other things that serve to lessen the dependance of Subjects. **1713** STEELE *Englishm.* No 34. 220 The late Tax upon Books and Pamphlets will lessen the Number of Scriblers. **1748** *Anson's Voy.* I. vi. 60 We once or twice lessened our water to forty fathom. **1793** *Blackstone's Comm.* I. 277 *note*, The increase of our paper has only a tendency to lessen the value of money at home. **1850** HAWTHORNE *Scarlet L.* xv. (1879) 199 She upbraided herself for the sentiment, but could not overcome or lessen it. **1878** JEVONS *Prim. Pol. Econ.* 64 It is one thing to lessen the hours of work; it is another thing to increase the rate of wages per hour.

absol. **1611** SHAKS. *Cymb.* III. iii. 13 Consider, When you aboue perceiue me like a Crow, That it is Place, which lessen's, and sets off.

†**b.** *Math.* ? To reduce (an equation). *Obs.*

1676 GLANVILL *Ess.* iii. 15 How to convert the false Roots into true, to avoid Fractions, and to lessen Æquations.

†**c.** *pass.* To suffer loss or curtailment *of*; to be reduced *in* (some quality). *Obs.*

c **1400** tr. *Secreta Secret., Gov. Lordsh.* 114 Kepe þe fro vche mysauentrous man, þat ys lesnyd of any membre. **1647** N. BACON *Disc. Govt. Eng.* I. xvii. (1739) 34 The Lords thus lessened in their judiciary power. **1691** T. H[ALE] *Acc. New Invent.* 38 Lessened..in that only quality upon which our Friggats most value themselves. **1793** NELSON 21 Feb. in Nicolas *Disp.* (1845) I. 301, I will not suffer any poor fellow to be lessened of his due.

4. To make less in estimation, represent as less; to extenuate, palliate (faults); to disparage, cast a slur upon. *Obs.* or *arch.*

1585 FETHERSTONE tr. *Calvin on Acts* xxvi. 12. 564 They goe about to lessen or paint [L. *extenuare aut fucare*] these thinges, for which they ought humbly.. to craue pardon. **1612** T. TAYLOR *Comm. Titus* ii. 14 They obscure the brightnesse of this our sunne of righteousnesse, and lessen the merits of his sufferings. **1677** WYCHERLEY *Pl. Dealer* I. i. 2, I never attempted to abuse, or lessen any person, in my life. **1714** STEELE *Lover* No. 24 (1723) 143 Whenever..you have the evil Spirit upon you to lessen any Body you hear commended. **1769** *Junius Lett.* xxviii. 129, I am far from wishing to lessen the merit of this single benevolent action. **1799** NELSON 9 Nov. in Nicolas *Disp.* (1845) IV. 96 Your Royal Highness will not believe that I mean to lessen the conduct of the Army; I have the highest respect for them all. **1877** MRS. OLIPHANT *Makers Flor.* xii. 290 The meaner pleasure with which the ordinary observer often exerts himself to lessen a heroic figure.

†**5.** To lower the dignity, position, or character of; to humble; to degrade, demean. *Obs.*

a **1654** SELDEN *Table-t.* (Arb.) 69 The making of new Lords lessens all the rest. **1667** MILTON *P.L.* III. 304 Nor shalt thou, by descending to assume Mans Nature, less'n or degrade thine owne. **1706** PRIOR *Ode to Queen* 192 When swift-wing'd rumour told..How lessen'd from the field Bavar was fled. **1706** DE FOE *Jure Div.* XII. 243 King Charles the First..when ever he invaded their Priviledges, had the Misfortune to see his Mistake, and lessen himself, by undoing all he had done before. *a* **1715** BURNET *Own Time* (1724) I. 245 It lessened him much in esteem of all the world. **1788** *Disinterested Love* I. 102 (F.H.).

lessen (ˈlɛs(ə)n), *conj. U.S. dial.* Also less'n. Unless. Cf. LESS *conj.*

1881 J. C. HARRIS *Nights with Uncle Remus* (1884) xix. 94 But less'n we gits dat Moon out er de pon', dey aint no fish kin be ketch. **1912** MULFORD & CLAY *Buck Peters* (1921) xxiii. 207 'Ain't that yore pinto?' queried Slick. 'Less'n I'm blind,' agreed the cow-punch. **1929** W. FAULKNER *Sound & Fury* 35 And they aint going to be no luck in saying that name, lessen you going to set up with him while he cries. **1938** M. K. RAWLINGS *Yearling* iii. 23 None o' the dogs bayed him, Pa. Lessen I didn't hear, for sleepin'. **1970** H. WAUGH *Finish me Off* (1971) 133 He's not bothering with girls less'n they're going to do him some good.

lessened (ˈlɛs(ə)nd), *ppl. a.* [f. LESSEN *v.* + -ED[1].] Diminished.

1676 DRYDEN *Aureng-z.* I. 12 You hold the Glass, but turn the Perspective; And farther off the lessen'd Object drive. **1811** W. R. SPENCER *Poems* Ded., My eyes Upon its lessen'd garland casting. **1817** DAWSON in *Parl. Deb.* 6 The prospect of a lessened expenditure. **1880** BRIDGES *London Snow*, *Shorter P.* III. ii, With lessened load a few carts creak and blunder.

lessening (ˈlɛs(ə)nɪŋ), *vbl. sb.* [f. as prec. + -ING[1].] The action of LESSEN *v.*, in various senses. Diminution; †a degradation, disparagement.

1428 *Surtees Misc.* (1888) 8 Lessenyng of yᵉ sumes of yᵉ paymentes. **1631** MASSINGER *Beleeve as you list* v. ii, I take it as A lessening of my torments. **1661** PEPYS *Diary* 12 Nov., Though I love the play as much as ever I did, yet I do not like the puppets at all, but think it to be a lessening to it. **1692** LOCKE *Educ.* §214 Their Thoughts run after Play and Pleasure, wherein they take it as a Lessening to be controll'd. **1714** MANDEVILLE *Fab. Bees* (1725) I. 292 We contribute to the relief of him we have compassion with, and are instrumental to the lessening of his sorrows. **1732** SIR C. WOGAN in *Swift's Wks.* (1841) II. 669/1 The very distinction [of English and Irish] carries in the face of it a lessening, and strikes the fancy with the ungrateful idea of misery. **1891** *Athenæum* 18 Apr. 503/3 There is no lessening of this defect, but rather increase.

†**b.** See LESSEN *v.* 2. *Obs.*

1697 COLLIER *Immor. Stage* ii. (1730) 47 A Flight of Madness, like a Faulcon's Lessening, makes them the more gaz'd at!

'lessening, *ppl. a.* [f. as prec. + -ING[2].]

†**1.** In transitive senses: Disparaging; degrading, lowering. *Obs.*

1674 N. FAIRFAX *Bulk & Selv.* 138 This kind of leaping not being successive, but all together, 'tis but even a lessening and underly way of speaking to call it Motion. **1704** J. TRAPP *Abra-Mulé* IV. i. 1965 I'll strip off this vile less'ning Habit And deck myself with all the Pomp of War. *a* **1705** BERKELEY *Comm.-pl. Bk.* Wks. 1871 IV. 426 The most lessening, vilifying appellations. **1711** ADDISON *Spect.* No. 255 ¶8 Such Indecencies as are lessening to his Reputation.

2. In intr. senses: Growing less, diminishing.

1730 SWIFT *Power of Time*, If Mountains sink to Vales, if Cities die, And less'ning Rivers mourn their Fountains dry. **1792** S. ROGERS *Pleas. Mem.* II. 45 From Guinea's coast pursue the lessening sail. **1810** SCOTT *Lady of L.* I. iv, And of the trackers of the deer Scarce half the lessening pack was near. **1895** P. WHITE *King's Diary* 8 Amongst the lessening throng of dancers.

lesser (ˈlɛsə(r)), *a.* and *adv.* [A double comparative, f. LESS *a.* + -ER[3].]

A. *adj.*

1. a. = LESS *a.* Chiefly, and now only, used *attrib.*

1459 *Inv.* in *Paston Lett.* I. 478 Item, ij. pillowes of lynen clothe of a lasser assyse. *Ibid.* 487 Item, ij. aundyrys, grete, of one sorte. Item, ij., lasse, of anothyr sorte. Item, iij. lesser aundiris. **1552** HULOET, Beate..a thynge, wherby to make it lesser or thynner. **1561** T. NORTON *Calvin's Inst.* I. 29 To offer Sacrifices to spirites, lesser Gods or dead men of honor. **1611** BIBLE *Gen.* i. 16 The greater light to rule the day, and the lesser light to rule the night. **1698** FRYER *Acc. E. India & P.* 171 Setting the lesser Lords at variance with their Prince. **1756** BURKE *Subl. & B.* IV. xxiv, These lesser and if I may say more domestick virtues. **1787** WINTER *Syst. Husb.* 83 The less the height of their descent, the lesser is the resistance they meet with in the air. **1842** TENNYSON *Locksley Hall* 151 Woman is the lesser man. **1863** KINGLAKE *Crimea* (1876) I. x. 145 The lesser minds gave way to the greater. **1896** HOWELLS *Impressions & Exp.* 259 The lights of lesser craft dipped by, and came and went in the distance.

ellipt. **1489** CAXTON *Faytes of A.* II. xx. 135 Thre other gonnes wherof one grete and two lesser. **1594** BARNFIELD *Aff. Sheph.* II. lv, For lesser cease, when greater griefes begin. **1660** BARROW *Euclid* I. iii, To take away the right line *BE* equal to the lesser *A*. **1665** BOYLE *Occas. Refl.* IV. xiv, The parting with a great Fortune, as freely as with a lesser. **1710** PRIDEAUX *Orig. Tithes* ii. 61 It must be either for a larger portion, or for a lesser. **1842** JAMES *M. Ernstein* I. x. 185 When the lesser of the two scoundrels comes to me.

†**b.** Followed by *than*. *Obs.*

1579 FULKE *Heskins' Parl.* 115 This is in nothing lesser then that. **1673** RAY *Journ. Low C.* 40 We judged it [Amsterdam] to be..lesser than one half of London. **1692** S. PATRICK *Answ. Touchstone* 71 In these, none was greater or lesser than another. **1710** PRIDEAUX *Orig. Tithes* ii. 62 The work and duty of the Christian Priesthood is lesser than was that of the Levitical.

2. In special or technical use, opposed to *greater*. **a.** *Astron.* in the names of certain constellations, as ***the Lesser Bear***. †Also ***lesser circle***, a 'small circle' of a sphere (*obs.*). Also *Geog.* in ***Lesser Asia*** (now *arch.*), Asia Minor. **b.** *Mus.* Applied to intervals which are now usually called MINOR. **c.** in the names of plants and animals. **d.** *Anat.* **e.** For ***lesser excommunication, line, litany***, see the sbs.

a. 1551, 1727–51 [see GREATER *a.* 4 a]. **1559** W. CUNNINGHAM *Cosmogr. Glasse* 39 The iiij. lesser Circles, which are the tropicke of Cancer, the tropick of Capricorne, the circle Articke, and the circle Antarticke. **1594** [see CIRCLE *sb.* 2 a]. **1613** J. DENNYS *Secr. Angling* III. xxi, When cold Boreas..Lookes out from vnderneath the lesser beare. **1676** MOXON *Tutor Astron.* (ed. 3) 221 Canis Minor, the Lesser Dog. **1768** HUME *National Char., Essays* xx, Throughout..Greece, the Lesser Asia, Sicily [etc.].

b. 1674, 1727–51 [see GREATER *a.* 4 b]. **1818** BUSBY *Gram. Mus.* 323 Lesser Sixth, with Lesser Third. **1855** BROWNING *Toccata Galuppi's* vii, Those lesser thirds so plaintive, sixths diminished, sigh on sigh. **1873** BRIDGES *Shorter P.* I. xiv, But let the viol lead the melody, With lesser intervals, and plaintive moan Of sinking semitone. **1876** STAINER & BARRETT *Dict. Mus. Terms*, *Lesser*, minor, as: *with the lesser third*, in the minor key; *lesser sixth*, a minor sixth.

c. 1678 RAY *Willughby's Ornith.* 144 The lesser Reed-Sparrow. **1822** COUCH in *Linnæan Trans.* XIV. 75 Lesser forked Hake. **1837** MACGILLIVRAY *Withering's Brit. Plants* (ed. 4) 341 Lesser Cat's-tail or Reed-mace. **1861** MISS PRATT *Flower. Pl.* V. 190 Common Frog-bit... This plant was called by the old writers Lesser Water Lily.

d. 1842 E. WILSON *Anat. Vade M.* (ed. 2) 419 The lesser internal cutaneous nerve or nerve of Wrisberg. **1872** MIVART *Elem. Anat.* 180 The lesser ischiatic notch.

3. *attrib.* and *Comb.*, as ***lesser-angled***, ***-sized*** adjs.; ***lesser breed***, applied allusively after Kipling (*Recessional*: see quot. 1897) to persons of inferior status; ***lesser light***, applied allusively (after Gen. i. 16 'the greater light to rule the day, and the lesser light to rule the night') to a person of less eminence or importance.

1889 *Anthony's Photogr. Bull.* II. 4 A longer-focussed and lesser-angled lens. **1897** KIPLING *Recessional* in *Times* 17 July 13/6 Such boasting as the Gentiles use Or lesser breeds without the Law. **1955** C. PEARL *Girl with Swansdown Seat* iv. 135 Wilfrid Scawen Blunt..was an English gentleman who shamed his class by championing the lesser breeds in Egypt and India. **1963** BROWN & FOOTE *Early Eng. & Norse Studies* 39 The next stanza, which begins with the hope that the text will not be miswritten nor mismetred by scribes and lesser breeds without the law of final *-e*. **1971** A. PRICE *Alamut Ambush* ix. 113 The authentic supercilious voice of England—the lesser breeds shall not show unfitting qualities of sportsmanship towards each other! **1973** 'H. HOWARD'

Highway to Murder vii. 82 You and your kind think you can order the lesser breeds around. **1608** SHAKES. *Pericles* II. iii. 41 None that beheld him, but like lesser lights, Did vaile their Crownes to his supremacie. **1873** R. BROWNING *Red Cott. Nt.-Cap* i. 34 Pilgrimage, Concourse, procession with, to head the host, Cardinal Mirecourt, quenching lesser lights. **1893** G. MOORE *Mod. Painting* 45 In the seventeenth century were Poussin and Claude; in the eighteenth Watteau, Boucher, Chardin, and many lesser lights. **1906** GALSWORTHY *Man of Property* III. v. 328 His interest was soon diverted from these lesser lights of justice by the entrance of Waterbuck, Q.C. **1943** K. TENNANT *Ride on Stranger* xiii. 152 One of the lesser lights of the announcers' staff had his face slapped by a young lady. **1964** *Ann. Reg. 1963* 22 At all events the most senior Ministers..turned up on Saturday 27 April, and the lesser lights on the Sunday morning. **1974** *Times* 21 Jan. 14/7 His deepest affection was reserved for the Romantics—Coleridge, Shelley, Keats, and the lesser lights. **1713** G. C. *Pref. H. More's Div. Dial.* vi, The lesser-sized Bodies.

†**B.** *adv.* Less. In quot. 1625 = to less purpose. *Obs.*

1594 SHAKS. *Rich. III*, III. iv. 54, I thinke there's neuer a man in Christendome Can lesser hide his loue, or hate, then hee. **1611** —— *Cymb.* V. v. 187 He (true Knight) No lesser of her Honour confident Then I did truly finde her. *a* **1625** FLETCHER *Laws Candy* II. i, I was an eare-witness When this young man spoke lesser then he acted, And had the souldiers voice to helpe him out.

†**'lesserness.** *Obs. rare*⁻¹. [f. LESSER + -NESS.] The quality or condition of being lesser.

1540 SIR T. WYAT in *St. Papers Hen. VIII*, VIII. 241 In the originall it hathe no such relation to lessernes or gretternes of parsones.

†**lesses,** *sb. pl. Hunting. Obs.* Also 7 leasses. [a. obs. F. *laisses* (also *laiz* in Godefroy; cf. mod.F. *laissées*), *quasi* 'leavings', ? f. *laisser* to leave.] The dung of a 'ravenous' animal, as a wild boar, wolf, or bear.

14.. *Master of the Game* (MS. Bodl. 546) lf. 75 He shal clepe fumes of an hert croteynge, of a bukke and of þe roo bukke, of þe wilde boor, & of blake beestys, & of wolfes, he shal clepe it lesses. **1576** TURBERV. *Venerie* 97 In beasts of ravyne or pray, as the bore, the beare and such like, they shall be called the Lesses. **1611** COTGR., *Laisses*, the lesses (or dung) of a wild Boare, Wolfe, or Beare. **1616** BULLOKAR, *Lesses*, dongue of a rauenous beast, as of a Beare, Bore, etc. **1630** [see FIANTS]. **1711** PUCKLE *Club* (1817) 90 At last falling upon the fumets of a deer, the lesses of a badger. **1807** *Sportsman's Dict.* s.v. *Bear*, [Bears] cast their lesses sometimes in round croteys.

'lessest, *a. Obs.* or *dial.* [f. LESS *a.* + -EST, after *lesser*.] Least. (Also *absol.*)

1553 BECON *Reliques of Rome* (1563) 200* Betwene two euils the lessest is to be chosen. *a* **1564** —— *Humble Supplic.* Wks. III. 25 If these spiteful spiritual Sorcerers can not do the lessest, we can neuer beleue, that they are able to doe the greatest. **1823** MOOR *Suffolk Words* 513 *Lessest*, least. Sometimes leasest—lessest—leasest—little, and littlest.

lesshe, obs. form of LEASE *sb.*¹, LEASH.

†**'Lessian,** *a. Obs.* [f. name of Leonard *Lessi-us* (died 1623) + -AN.] Of or pertaining to Lessius, esp. in *Lessian diet* (see quot. 1656).

1655 BAYLY *Life Fisher* i. 3 Austerely curbing his wanton appetite with the most spare and Lessian dyet. **1656** BLOUNT *Glossogr.*, *Lessian*, pertaining to Lessius, a modern Writer, who wrote a Rule of severe temperance, wherein he prescribed Fourteen Ounces every day, whence that is called a Lessian Diet. **1677** TEMPLE *Ess.*, *Gout* Wks. 1731 I. 144 Nor can this be determined by Measures and Weights, or any general Lessian Rules. *a* **1694** TILLOTSON *Serm. Evil Covetousness* Wks. 1717 I. 264 All the Religion he values himself upon, is a strict observance of the Lessian diet, which he recommends to those few that can deny themselves to Dine with him.

Lessie, var. LES.

†**lessilver.** *Obs.* [Etym., sense, and form doubtful. The form *lef-silver* in 1706, possibly the original, would point to LEAVE *sb.*¹ Cf. LADY-SILVER (*ladesilver*), *lathe silver* (s.v. LATHE *sb.*¹ b).]

1287 *Placit. Essexi* Rot. 6 in *Placit. Abbr.* (1811) 212 De.. aliis pascentibus..pro quolibet equo ii den. pullano.. quinque bidentibus i den. que præstacio vocatur Lessylver. *c* **1300** *Battle Abbey Custumals* (Camden) 60 Debet etiam quilibet eorum pro quolibet animali ætate duorum annorum vel amplius, dare domino ad festum Sancti Johannis Baptistæ unum denarium quod vocatur Lesselver. **1706** PHILLIPS (ed. Kersey), *Danger*.. In the Forest-Law, a Duty paid by the Tenants to the Lord, for leave to plough and sow in the time of Pannage, or Mast-feeding. In some Places, it is call'd *Lef-silver*, or *Lyef-silver*.

†**'lessing,** *vbl. sb.* [f. LESS *v.* + -ING¹.] The action of the verb LESS; lessening, diminution; abatement.

c **1340** HAMPOLE *Prose Tr.* (1866) 4 This es full joye..and if we vse it we sall be fyllyde euer withowttyne lessynge. **1357** *Lay Folks Catech.* 335 In lessyne [*Lamb. MS.* lessyng] of payne. *c* **1375** *Sc. Leg. Saints* xli. (*Agnes*) 5 As of habundance is na lessing na of his riches ne mynissing. **1438** *Buke Alex. Great* 107 To get lessing of my torment. *c* **1440** *Jacob's Well* 196 A lessyng of blood doth awey þe maladye. **1500–20** DUNBAR *Poems* lxvi. 100 Quhilk is ane lessing of my pane.

lessioun, obs. Sc. form of LESION.

lessit, -yt, wk. pa. t. LEESE *v.*¹

lessive ('lɛsɪv). *rare.* [ad. F. *lessive*:—L. *lixīva* neut. pl. adj. used as sb.] A lye of wood-ashes, soap-suds, etc., used in washing.

a **1790** B. FRANKLIN *Works* (1836) II. 104 One [way] is, to soak it [*sc.* the grain] all night in a *lessive* or lye. **1826** [J. R. BEST] *4 Yrs. France* 303 The lessive, so the washing is called from the wood ashes employed in it. **1875** FORTNUM *Majolica* vi. 59 Take out the wares and allow them to soak in a lessive of soap-suds.

lessness ('lɛsnɪs). *rare.* [f. LESS *a.* + -NESS.] The quality or condition of being less; inferiority.

1635 GILL *Sacr. Philos.* 59 Otherwise there should bee a greaternesse in being, and a lessenesse in working. **1868** A. SANDEMAN *Pelicotetics* 188 The Multiple Test of the greaterness and lessness of the ratio. **1889** MOULE *Secr. Prayer* v. (1890) 84 Unspeakable lessness, dependence and obligation. **1961** R. B. LONG *Sentence & its Parts* iv. 99 Sometimes negation is semantically specialized to convey meanings of 'lessness', as in *I don't have a dime.* **1970** S. BECKETT (*title*) Lessness.

lesson ('lɛs(ə)n), *sb.* Forms: 3 lescun, 3–5 lessoun, lessun, (4 les(c)zoun, 5 lession, lessown), 4–5 lessone, 5, 7 lessen, 4– lesson. [ad. OF. *leçon*, F. *leçon*:—L. *lectiōn-em*, n. of action f. *legĕre* to read. Cf. LECTION *sb.*]

†**1. a.** The action of reading. *Obs.*

1382 WYCLIF *Ecclus.* Prol., Aftir that hymself he ȝaf more to besynesse of lessoun [L. *ad diligentiam lectionis*] of lawe, and of profetes.

b. A public reading; a lecture; also, a course of lectures. *Obs.*

c **1340** *Cursor M.* 10123 *heading* (Laud), Lystyn now to my lesson That wille here of the concepcion. *c* **1375** *Sc. Leg. Saints* ii. (*Paulus*) 61 Ierome ws sais in his lessone þat [etc.]. *a* **1470** GREGORY *Chron.* (Camd.) 230 Doctor Ive kepte the scolys at Poulys..and there he radde fulle nobylle lessonnys to preve that Cryste was lorde of alle. *c* **1500** in Peacock *Stat. Cambr.* (1841) App. A. p. xxx, The Bedell shall fett every Inceptour in Arte to Scolys to rede his solemn Lesson. **1546** R. SMITH *Def. Sacram. Altar* title-p., Reader of the Kynges Majesties Lesson in His Grace's Universitie of Oxforde. **1599** *Life More* in Wordsw. *Eccl. Biog.* (1853) II. 52 He red openly in Sᵗ Laurence churche London, Sᵗ Austin's booke De Civitate Dei... His lesson was much frequented. **1724** R. WODROW *Life Jas. Wodrow* (1828) 27 He waited on the divinity lessons of that great man Mr. Robert Baillie.

transf. *c* **1645** HOWELL *Lett.* (1650) I. 187 His wife falling to read him a loud lesson.

2. *Eccl.* A portion of Scripture or other sacred writing read at divine service.

Now chiefly applied to the portion of the O.T. ('first lesson') and to that of the N.T. ('second lesson') appointed in the Church of England to be read at Morning and Evening Prayer. (For *proper lesson*, see PROPER *a.*) In the technical language of ritual, the word *lesson* is not applied to the Gospel of the mass, but sometimes to the Epistle.

a **1225** *Ancr. R.* 22 Siggeð Dirige, mit þreo psalmes, & mit þreo lescuns eueriche niht sunderliche. *c* **1330** *Spec. Gy Warw.* 500 þu most ben ofte in orisoun And in reding of lesczoun. *c* **1386** CHAUCER *Prol.* 709 Wel koude he rede a lesson or a storie. *c* **1400** *Table* in *Wyclif's Bible* IV. 683 Here bigynneth a rule, that tellith in whiche chapitris of the bible ȝe mai fynde the lessouns, pistlis, and gospels, that ben rad in the chirche al the ȝeer, after the vss of Salisbire. *c* **1422** HOCCLEVE *Learn to Die* 925 The .ixᵉ. lesson which is rad In holy chirche vp-on all halwen day. **1548–9** (Mar.) *Bk. Com. Prayer* Ord. Holy Script., The olde Testament is appoynted for the first Lessons..the newe..for the second Lessons. **1691** WOOD *Ath. Oxon.* II. 525 May it please your Maj. it is the proper lesson for the day, as appears by the Kalendar. **1802, 1865** [see LECTIONARY]. **1883** *Cath. Dict.* (1897) 554/2 Our Breviary lessons for the first nocturn. *Ibid.* 555/1 Their [the Greeks'] daily offices contain no lessons from Scripture. **1895** H. LITTLEHALES *Prymer* Pref. x, Dirige (Matins). Consisting of 3 Nocturns; each composed of:—3 Psalms..3 Lessons.

3. a. A portion of a book or dictated matter, to be studied by the pupil for repetition to the teacher. Hence, something that is or is to be learnt.

a **1225** *Ancr. R.* 66 Eue..told hire [the serpent] al þet lescun þet God hire hefde ilered. *a* **1300** *Cursor M.* 6859 Suilk was þi lessun and þi lare. **1303** R. BRUNNE *Handl. Synne* 422 Catun..techyþ chyldryn þys lessun, ' Ȝeue no charge to dremys [etc.].' **1362** LANGL. *P. Pl.* A. v. 118 Furst I leornede to lyȝe a lessun or tweyne, And wikkedliche or to weie was myn oþer lessun. *c* **1374** CHAUCER *Troylus* III. 34 (83) His lesson, þat he wende konne, To preyen hire is þurgh his wit y-ronne. **1486** *Bk. St. Albans* E ij b, Forrgeet not this lession for thyng that may fall. **1526** *Pilgr. Perf.* (W. de W. 1531) 180, I beshrewe his herte yᵗ taught the that lesson. **1599** SHAKS. *Much Ado* I. i. 295 To learne Any hard Lesson that may do thee good. **1613** PURCHAS *Pilgrimage* (1614) 605 This Psaphon..had let them flie into the Woods, where chanting their lesson, they inchanted the rude people. **1716** BOLINGBROKE *Refl. Exile* (1777) 352, I learned this important lesson long ago. **1727–41** CHAMBERS *Cycl.* s.v. *Helps*, Helps in the manage.—To teach a horse his lessons, there are seven helps, or aids, to be known. These are the voice, rod [etc.]. **1818** BYRON *Ch. Har.* IV. lxxv, The drill'd dull lesson, forced down word by word. **1838** JAMES *Robber* iv, The mind moralised upon it, and the heart took the lesson home. **1861** J. EDMOND *Childr. Ch. at Home* iii. 47 They should be industrious at their lessons.

†**b.** *transf.* Subject of discourse. *Obs.*

c **1330** R. BRUNNE *Chron.* (1810) 318 Now salle we turne ageyn tille our owen lessoun. *c* **1350** *Will. Palerne* 1944 But for to telle þe atiryng of þat child..It wold lengeþ þis lessoun a ful long while.

4. a. A continuous portion of teaching given to a pupil or class at one time; one of the portions into which a course of instruction in any subject is divided. ***to give, take lessons***: to give, receive systematic instruction *in* a specified subject. Hence occas. in text-books, a section of such length as to be suitable to be studied continuously.

c **1290** *S. Eng. Leg.* I. 437/216 Euereche dai bi custome he seide þis oresun, he nolde bi-leue for no scole, ne for no lessoun. **1398** TREVISA *Barth. De P.R.* I. (1495) 2 In the fyrste lesson that i toke thenne i lerned a. and b. And other letters by her names. **1660** PEPYS *Diary* 21 June, Mr. Blagrave..did give me a lesson upon the flageolette. **1732** LEDIARD *Sethos* II. IX. 305 The conversation..was..not less profitable..than their lessons. **1854** THACKERAY *Newcomes* I. ii. 22 A distinguished officer..engaged in London in giving private lessons on the fiddle. *Ibid.* Tom Newcome took no French lessons on a Sunday.

b. *transf.* An occurrence from which instruction may be gained; an instructive example; a rebuke or punishment calculated to prevent a repetition of the offence. ***to read*** (one) ***a lesson***: see READ *v.* 11 b.

a **1586** SIDNEY *Arcadia* II. (1590) 119 b, She woulde giue her a lesson for walking so late, that should [etc.]. **1822** LAMB *Elia* Ser. I. *Dist. Corresp.*, The kangaroos..with those little short fore puds, looking like a lesson framed by nature to the pickpocket. **1850** L. HUNT *Autobiog.* I. iii. 94 He [a monitor] showed me a knot in a long handkerchief, and told me I should receive a lesson from that handkerchief every day, with the addition of a fresh knot every time. **1882** J. L. WATSON *Life R. S. Candlish* xiii. 140 His self-denial in the little things of daily life was a constant lesson. **1900** R. T. DRUMMOND *Apost. Teach. & Teach. of Christ* ii. 77 Christ is their Teacher. He is also their Lesson: not His words only, but His Life.

†**5.** *Mus.* **a.** An exercise; a composition serving an educational purpose. **b.** A piece to be performed, a performance. *Obs.*

1593 (*title*) A New Booke of Citterne Lessons. **1596** SHAKS. *Tam. Shr.* III. i. 60 My Lessons make no musicke in three parts. **1622** DEKKER & MASSINGER *Virg. Mart.* I. B 3, *stage direct.*, A lessen of Cornets. **1626** BACON *Sylva* §161 Let there be a Recorder made, with two Fipples, at each end one..and let two play the same Lesson upon it, at an Unison. **1640** BROME *Antipodes* V. ix. *stage direct.*, A solemne lesson upon the Recorders. **1665** CHAS. II in Julia Cartwright *Henrietta of Orleans* (1894) 214, I have heere sent you some lessons for the guittar. **1674** PLAYFORD *Skill Mus.* II. 112 Lessons for the Violin by Letters are prick't on four lines..but Lessons by Notes are prick'd upon five Lines. **1754** RICHARDSON *Grandison* (1781) VI. xviii. 76 She made Lucy give us a lesson on the harpsichord. **1811** BUSBY *Dict. Mus.* (ed. 3), *Lesson*, a word formerly used by most composers to signify those exercises for the harpsichord or piano-forte which are now more generally called sonatas. The length, variety, and style of *Lessons*..entirely depend on the fancy and abilities of the composer, and the class of practitioners for whose use the pieces are designed.

6. *attrib.* and *Comb.*, as ***lesson-book, -hour, -money***; **lesson-piece**, a piece of material on which to practise needlework.

1863 W. G. BLACKIE *Better Days Wrkng. People* i. (1864) 25 Superior *lesson-books. **1890** 'L. FALCONER' *M'lle. Ixe* i. 24 Her *lesson-hour was not till the afternoon. **1847** MEDWIN *Life Shelley* II. 59 Receiving..part of the *lesson money. **1880** *Plain Hints Needlework* 36 Let each child work a..button-hole on her *lesson-piece in blue cotton.

lesson ('lɛsən), *v.* [f. LESSON *sb.*]

1. *trans.* To give a lesson or lessons to, to instruct, teach; to admonish, rebuke. Const. *in*, *on*, and with *inf.* or dependent clause. Also, To bring *into* or *to* (a certain state) by lessoning.

1555 W. WATREMAN *Fardle Facions* II. x. 223 He yet bothe harkened the complainte of his felowes, and lessoned them agaime. **1586** J. HOOKER *Hist. Irel.* in *Holinshed* II. 87/1 Willing to lesson you with sound and sage aduise. **1632** J. HAYWARD tr. *Biondi's Eromena* 110 Metaneone..had before hand lessoned him what he should say. *a* **1661** FULLER *Worthies, Kent* (1662) II. 58 To lesson the Clergy to content themselves with Decency without sumptuousness. **1682** tr. *Erastus' Treat. Excommun.* 20 The Disciples..had been severely lesson'd by the Synagogue. **1763** CHURCHILL *Duellist* I 1, Each Stripling, lesson'd by his Sire, Knew when to close, when to retire. *a* **1774** GOLDSM. *Surv. Exp. Philos.* (1776) II. 361 When the eye has been for a short time lessoned to ocular succession, there will arise [etc.]. **1795** BURKE *Lett., to R. Burke* Wks. 1842 II. 459 It ought to lesson us into an abhorrence of the abuse of our own power in our own day. **1812** BYRON *Ch. Har.* II. lxviii, To rest the weary and to soothe the sad, Doth lesson happier men. **1856** MISS WARNER *Hills of Shatemuc* xxviii. 312 If you will lesson me to find trouble is no trouble..I will thank you much for that. **1873** SYMONDS *Grk. Poets* vii. 196 Oedipus has been purged and lessoned to humility before the throne of Zeus. **1887** RUSKIN *Præterita* II. 230 There was yet another young draughtsman in Florence, who lessoned me to purpose.

absol. **1807** D. GILSON *Serm. Pract. Subj.* x. 211 The apostle lessons well when he says that the man who provideth not for his own hath denied the faith.

2. To teach (a thing) as a lesson, to inculcate.

1821 [see the *ppl. a.*].

Hence **'lessoned** *ppl. a.*

1821 JOANNA BAILLIE *Metr. Leg.*, *Columbus* xlii, Better than lesson'd saw.

lessoning ('lɛsənɪŋ). [f. LESSON *v.* + -ING¹.] The action of the vb. LESSON; the action of giving a lesson or lessons; instruction, admonition.

1583 GOLDING *Calvin on Deut.* cxxxii. 811 No longer any lessoning or warnings to be hearkened vnto. *a* **1619** FOTHERBY *Atheom.* II. i. §1 (1622) 171 As being conscious vnto himselfe, euen by Natures inward lessoning, that his seruice is due vnto him [God]. **1791** MAD. D'ARBLAY *Diary* V. v. 220 My last day..was filled with..packing, leave-taking, bills-paying, and lessoning to Mdlle. Jacobi. **1812** W. TAYLOR in *Monthly Mag.* XXXIII. 239 Our national usages and lessonings. **1887** RUSKIN *Præterita* II. 206, I

never needed lessoning more in the principles of the three great arts.

lessor ('lɛ-, lɛ'sɔː(r)). Also 6 leas(s)or, -our, 6–7 lessour(e, 7 leaser. [a. AF. *lessor, lessour*, f. *lesser*: see LEASE *v.* and -OR.] One who grants a lease; one who lets (property) on lease.

[**1278** *Act 6 Ed. I, Stat. Glouc.* c. 4 Establi est qe apres les deus annz passez eit le lessour acciour a demander la terre en demeine. *a* **1481** LITTLETON *Inst.* §57 Le Lessor est properment lou un home lessa a vn auter certaine terres ou tenements purterme de vie ou pur terme des ans, ou a tener a volunt.] **1487** *Act 4 Hen. VII*, c. 16 The Occupier and termer of theym from thense be discharged ayenst his lessour of the rente reserued vpon the same leeses. **1533–4** [see LESSEE]. **1592** WEST *1st Pt. Symbol.* §43 Where the leassor graunteth his lands or other things to the leassee. *a* **1626** BACON *Max. & Uses Com. Law* xii. (1636) 52 If tenant for life and his lessor joyne in a lease for yeares. **1715** *Act 1 Geo. I*, Stat. II. c. 55 §1 A Verdict shall be given for the Lessor of the Plaintiff in such Ejectment. **1813** VANCOUVER *Agric. Devon* 442 Tenants for lives are now most commonly obliged, on the death of certain persons named in their leases, to surrender to their lessors their best beast. **1880** BLACKMORE *Mary Anerley* II. ii. 27 The lessee being bound to a multitude of things, and the lessor to little more than acceptance of the rent.

lessow, obs. form of LEASOW.

Lessy, var. LES.

lest (lɛst), *conj.* Forms: 1 **þý lǽs þe, þe lǽs þe, þe lǽste**, 2 **þi les ðe**, 3–5 **last(e, leste, les**, 5 **lesse**, 4–8 **leest**, 4–5 **lyst(e**, 6–8 *Sc.* **leist**, 6–9 **least(e**, 4– **lest**. [OE. phrase *þý lǽs þe*, lit. 'whereby less' = L. *quōminus* (*þý* instrumental of the dem. and rel. pron. + *lǽs* LESS *a.* + *þe* relative particle). In ME. the first word of the phrase was dropped, and *les þe* became *les te* in accordance with the general rule that *þ* after *s* changed into *t*.]

1. Used as a negative particle of intention or purpose, introducing a clause expressive of something to be prevented or guarded against; = L. *nē*, Eng. *that..not, for fear that.*

c **1000** *Ags. Gosp.* John v. 14 Ne synga þu þe-læs þe þe on sumon þingon wyrs ȝetide. *a* **1100** in Napier *O.E. Glosses* i. 3675 *Ne..offenderit*, þe læste ȝehremde. *c* **1175** *Lamb. Hom.* 117 Vnderfoð steore þi les ðe god iwurðe wrað wið eou. *a* **1240** *Lofsong* in *Cott. Hom.* 209 Ne bi-hold þu ham [mine sunnen] nout leste þu wreoke ham on me. *c* **1330** *Spec. Gy Warw.* 856 Go, man, while þat þu hast liht, Lest þe of-take þe derke niht. *c* **1385** CHAUCER *L.G.W.* 723 *Thisbe*, I-kept.. ffful streyte lyst they dedyn sum folye. **1393** LANGL. *P. Pl.* C. XXI. 337 Ich sotelide how ich myghte Lette hem þat louede hym nat lest þei wolde hym martyre. *a* **1400–50** *Alexander* 732 (Ashm.) Haue a gud eȝe, Les [*Dublin MS.* lest] on þine ane here-efterward þine ossyngis liȝt. *Ibid.* 1372 (Dubl.) And band hir..Lest sho flechett or faylett with fyfe score ankers. **1526** TINDALE *Mark* xiii. 5 Take hede lest eny man deceave you. **1567** *Gude & Godlie B.* (S.T.S.) 41 That he my fyve brether aduerteis may, Leist thay in to this cairfull place discend. **1599** H. BUTTES *Dyets drie Dinner* A iv b, The which least I should seeme only idlely to wish, I have [etc.]. **1677** MOXON *Mech. Exerc.* 41 Forge your work as true as you can, least it cost you great pains at the Vice. **1741** RICHARDSON *Pamela* (1824) I. 175 But, least you should be alarmed, if I don't come home by ten, don't expect me. **1795** BURNS *'Last May a braw wooer'* vi, But owre my left shouther I gae him a blink Leest neebours might say I was saucy. **1797** JEFFERSON *Writ.* (1859) IV. 174 Nobody scarcely will venture to buy or draw bills, lest they should be paid there in depreciated currency. **1815** W. TAYLOR in Robberds *Mem.* II. 454, I did not like to write to you without the book at my elbow, least I should misremember. **1855** *Cornwall* 262 Look to the Purser well, lest he look to himself too well. **1897** R. KIPLING *Recessional*, Lord God of Hosts, be with us yet, Lest we forget, lest we forget.

†**b.** *lest that*: in the same sense. *Obs.*

c **1400** *Lanfranc's Cirurg.* 43 Nouȝt to hot a medycine, leste þat he make þe lyme toswellyn. **1426** LYDG. *De Guil. Pilgr.* 8204 Lyst that she were wroth with me, I suffrede. *c* **1491** *Chast. Goddes Chyld.* 9 Leest that ye lese him in your owne defawte. **1559** W. CUNNINGHAM *Cosmogr. Glasse* 115 Least that the difficultie of the thing mighte somwhat discouragie you, I will [etc.].

†**c.** *lest when* = L. *nequando*: lest at any time.

a **1300** *E.E. Psalter* ii. 12 Gripes lare, leswhen [Vulg. *nequando*] lauerd wrethide be. *a* **1340** HAMPOLE *Psalter* cxxxix. 9 Forsake me noght leswhen [L. *ne forte*] þai be heghid.

2. Used after verbs of fearing, or phrases indicating apprehension or danger, to introduce a clause expressing the event that is feared; equivalent to the L. *nē*, and in Eng. often admitting of being replaced by *that* (without accompanying negative).

c **1000** ÆLFRIC *Gen.* xxxii. 11 For þam þe ic hine [Esau] swiðe ondræde, þe læs þe he cume and ofslea þas modra mid hiora cildum. **1297** R. GLOUC. (Rolls) 10415 Þe king was nei for drede wod..Laste þe king of fraunce & mansing him ssolde ssende. *c* **1350** *Will. Palerne* 953 He was a-drad to þe deþ last sche him dere wold. ? *a* **1400** *Arthur* 289 We dowteþ last he wel do soo, For he ys Myghty know þer-too. *a* **1533** LD. BERNERS *Huon* lxii. 214 My hert trymbleth for fere leest he be deed. **1560** DAUS tr. *Sleidane's Comm.* 270 There is daunger, lest or euer they be ready, the enemy wyl haue inuaded his countrey. **1596** DALRYMPLE tr. *Leslie's Hist. Scot.* I. 95 A reuerend feir..leist thay offend in things of honestie. **1657** AUSTEN *Fruit Trees* I. 42 All the danger is least we take too much liberty herein. **1750** H. WALPOLE *Lett.* (1846) II. 316 Lady Catherine grew frightened, lest her infanta should vex herself sick. **1823** F. CLISSOLD *Ascent Mt. Blanc* 20, I felt a strong inclination to sleep, and feared lest I should drop down. **1881** *Punch* 29 Oct. 198 Fearing lest they should succumb.

lest, obs. form of LAST, LEAST, LIST *sb.* and *v.*

lest(e, wk. pa. t. and pple. of LEESE *v.*[1]

lestage, leste, obs. ff. LASTAGE, LEAST.

leste ('lɛsteɪ). [a. Pg. *leste* east wind.] (See quot. 1967.)

1864 *Chambers's Encycl.* VI. 248/2 Sometimes a waft of the *lesté*, or east wind, raises it [*sc.* the temperature in Madeira] to 90°. **1911** *Encycl. Brit.* XVI. 499/2 The Leste is commonly accompanied by clouds of fine red sand. **1967** R. W. FAIRBRIDGE *Encycl. Atmospheric Sci.* 1155 *Leste.* This is a hot, dry, easterly wind occasionally encountered in Madeira and the Canary Islands at any season except in summer. Essentially it is an extension of the harmattan that blows across the Sahara and is accordingly hot and dry... It is similar to the sirocco of the Mediterranean and the leveche of Spain.

leste(n, obs. form of LAST *v.*[1], LISTEN.

lestercock ('lɛstəkɒk). *dial.* [f. OCornish *lester* a ship, Breton *lestr*, Irish *leastar* small boat + COCK *sb.*[3]] (See quots.)

1602 CAREW *Cornwall* 34 Upon the North coast where want of good harbours denieth safe roade to the fisher boats, they have a device of two sticks filled with corks and crossed flatlong, out of whose midst there riseth a thred, and at the same hangeth a saile; to this engine termed a Lestercock, they tie one end of their Boulter. **1880** *W. Cornw. Gloss.*, *Lestercock*, a toy-boat sent out before the wind by fishermen in rough weather with a string of hooks.

†'**Lestrigon.** *Obs.* [ad. L. *Læstrȳgon-es* pl., Gr. Λαιστρῡγόν-ες a cannibal people of Italy (Hom. *Odyss.* x. 116).] An inhuman monster, a cannibal. So **Lestri'gonian**, in the same sense.

1591 SYLVESTER *Du Bartas* I. vi. 388 Inhumane Monster, hatefull Lestrigon. **1656** BLOUNT *Glossogr.*, *Lestrigons*, a kind of giants or fierce people of Italy, often mentioned in the Odysses of Homer. **1693** *Dryden's Juvenal* xiv. (1697) 342 Lest..their Sons should..become..Tyrants, Lestrigons, and Cannibals to their Servants. *a* **1887** JEFFERIES *Field & Hedgerow* (1889) 70 They were perfect cannibals with the tongue, perfect Lestrigonians.

†'**lesty**, *a. Sc. Obs. rare*[−1]. [? repr. OE. **listiȝ*, f. *list* skill.] Skilful, sagacious.

1423 JAS. I *Kingis Q.* clvii, There sawe I..The lesty beuer, and the ravin bare.

lesue, obs. form of LEASOW.

lesum, Sc. form of LEESOME.

lesur(e, -uwe, leswa, -w(u)e, obs. ff. LEASOW.

†'**lesure.** *Obs.* [ad. late L. *læsūra*, f. L. *lædĕre, læsum* to hurt.] Hurt, injury, wound. Cf. LESION.

c **1420** *Pallad. on Husb.* III. 733 And xxx foot asonder for lesure Is hem to sette. **1447** BOKENHAM *Seyntys* (Roxb.) 46 He venquyshd þat causyd þe lesure. *c* **1460** G. ASHBY *Dicta Philos.* 648 Of whom ye shal haue no shame ne lesure.

let (lɛt), *sb.*[1] Forms: 2–6 **lette**, *pl.* **letten**, 4 **leet, leit**, 4–5 **late, lete**, 4–6 **lat**, 4–9 **lett**, 5 **lytt**, 6 **leatte**, 4– **let**. [f. LET *v.*[2]] Hindrance, stoppage, obstruction; also, something that hinders, an impediment. Now *arch.*: most common in phrase ***let or hindrance***. (Cf. ME. LITE.)

In ME. verse the phr. ***without(en let*** (Sc. ***but let***) is frequent, often as a mere expletive.

a **1175** *Cott. Hom.* 239 Oðer hit wrð ȝewasse iþer pine of þe deaðe þe he her þaleð oðer efter mid eðelice lette. *c* **1275** LAY. 4572 He þohte habbe Delgan cwene of Denemarche ac him com mochel lette [*c* 1205 lætting] ase him was alre loþest. *a* **1300** *Cursor M.* 7395 (Gött.) Þai did him fett widuten lett. *Ibid.* 8123 (Cott.) On nan-kyn lim ne had þai lett, For in þair sted ilkan war sette. **1375** BARBOUR *Bruce* II. 179 Syne to Scone in hy raid he, And wes maid king but langir let. **1387** TREVISA *Higden* (Rolls) II. 321 Moyses..hadde a lette of his tonge. **1390** GOWER *Conf.* II. 92 Ther ben othre vices slowe, Whiche unto love don gret lette, If thou thin herte upon hem sette. **1432** *Paston Lett.* I. 31 For the..eschuyng of eny thing that mighte yeve empeschement or let therto. **1513** DOUGLAS *Æneis* v. xii. 142 Quhat is the let I may the nocht embrace? **1545** RAYNOLD *Byrth Mankynde* I. ii. (1634) 21 By which meanes for foresayd muscles..haue the lesse impediment or let in their motion. **1549** *Act 3 & 4 Edw. VI*, c. 1 §2 The said Offices have remained void for a long Time, to the great Let of Justice. **1562** BULLEYN *Bk. Simples* 55 b, The herbe wil growe in Englande also, if idlenes wer not the let. **1603** KNOLLES *Hist. Turks* (1621) 118 After which so great a victorie..the Turks without let or stay overran all the countrey. **1607** MIDDLETON *Michaelmas Term* IV. i, He may undoubtedly enter upon it without the let or molestation of any man. **1635** BARRIFFE *Mil. Discipl.* xcv. (1643) 306 Vneven, rough, bushie, and hilly grounds, are all lets and impediments to the horse. **1640** BROME *Sparagus Gard.* I. ii. Wks. 1873 III. 123 Love..through a thousand lets will find a way To his desired end. **1649** ARNWAY *Tablet* (ed. 2) 67 As singularity of Gifts recompenced His natural let in speech. **1704** F. FULLER *Med. Gymn.* (1711) 200 There is a great Lett of insensible Perspiration. **1710** BERKELEY *Princ. Hum. Knowl.* Introd. §4 Those lets and difficulties, which stay and embarrass the mind in its search after truth. **1842** S. LOVER *Handy Andy* viii. 79 At last all let and hindrance to the merry lady ceased by the sudden death of her husband. **1857** RUSKIN *Pol. Econ. Art* ii. 159 Each man would have a portion of time to himself in which he was allowed to do what he chose without let or inquiry. **1867** FREEMAN *Norm. Conq.* (1876) I. v. 370 The enemy wrought his will without let or hindrance. **1875** STUBBS *Const. Hist.* III. xxi. 532 To maintain quarrels..to the let and disturbance of the common law.

2. In *Fives, Rackets*, and *Lawn-tennis*. Obstruction of the ball in certain ways specified in the rules, on account of which the ball must be served again.

1871 'STONEHENGE' *Rural Sports* (ed. 9) 635/1 [Rackets.] After the service..a ball hitting the gallery-netting, posts, or cushions, in returning from the front wall, is a let. **1885** *Laws Lawn Tennis*, It is a let if the ball served touch the net, provided the service be otherwise good... In case of a let, the service or stroke counts for nothing, and the Server shall serve again. **1890** A. C. AINGER *Fives* in *Tennis*, etc. (Badm. Libr.) 465 *Rules.* A 'let' may be claimed when a player is in any way prevented from returning or impeded in his attempt to return the ball by one of the opposite side.

attrib. **1819** *Examiner* 7 Feb. in *Hazlitt's Table Talk* (1870) 118 His [Cavanagh the five-player's] blows were not ..let balls like the Edinburgh Review. **1890** PLEYDELL-BOUVERIE *Rackets* in *Tennis*, etc. (Badm. Libr.) 403 Do not be absurdly modest about claiming a 'let' ball.

let (lɛt), *sb.*[2] [f. LET *v.*[1]] A letting for hire or rent. (The sense in the first quot. is doubtful.)

1684 in A. Nora Royds *Reg. Par. Felkirk* (1896) 3 By ye Ancyant Lett it amounts to 35 Pounds Yearly. **1838** DICKENS *Nich. Nick.* xxiv, 'We've had a pretty good Let,' said Mr. Crummles. 'Four front places in the centre, and the whole of the stage-box.' **1868** *Perth. Jrnl.* 18 June, John Dewar, at the Farm, will show the Boundaries; and the Conditions of Let may be learned on application. **1878** *Daily News* 24 Oct. 6/6 The reason the stair was not included in the lease was that the executors wanted to utilise it for the empty rooms, and make a separate let of it.

let (lɛt), *v.*[1] Pa. t. and pa. pple. let. Forms: 1 **lǽtan**, *Northumb.* **léta**, (*3rd sing. pres. ind.* **léttes**), 2–3 **læten**, (*Orm.* **-enn**), 3 **leaten, leoten**, (*3rd sing.* **lat, let**), 2–4 **leten**, 3–4 **laten**, 3–6 **late, lete, latt(e, lette**, 3–8 **lett**, 3–9 (now *dial.*) **lat**, 4 **leet(e**, 4–5 **latyn**, 4–6 *Sc.* **leit**, 5 **lait, laatyn, leett**, 3– **let**. *Pa. t.* 1 **lét(t, léot**, *Northumb.* **leort**, (*2nd pl.* **letten**), 3 **liet**, 3–5 **lett, leet**, (*3rd pl.* **lætten**), 3–6 **lete, lette**, 4 **leite, lat**, 4–5 *Sc.* **leyt**, 4–6 *Sc.* **leit**, 5 **late**, 6 *Sc.* **lait, luit, lut(e**, 8–9 *Sc.* **loot**, 2– **let**. *β. weak*: 5–6 **letid**, 5 **lettid**, 7 **-ed**. *Pa. pple.* 1 (**ȝe**) **lǽten**, 3 **ilete(n, ilet, (i)late**, 3–5 **leten, -in**, 5 **leeten**, 3–5 **latin**, 3–6 **laten**, 4 **ylat, ylet(e, ilaten**, 4–5 (**y**)**lete, lattyn**, 4–6 **lattin**, 5–7 **lett**, 5–9 (now *dial.*) **letten**, 6 **letton, lat(t)ne, lette, leate**, 7, 9 *Sc.* **latten**, 9 *Sc.* **lotten, looten**, 7–9 **lett**, 4– **let**. [A Com. Teut. reduplicating str. vb.: OE. *lǽtan* (Northumb. *léta*), pa. t. *lét, leort* (chiefly Anglian and *poet.*), pa. pple. *ȝelǽten*, corresponds to OFris. *lêta*, pa. t. *lît, lêt*, pa. pple. *lêten*, OS. *lâtan*, pa. t. *liet, lét*, pa. pple. *gilâtan* (Du. *latan*, pa. t. *liet*, pa. pple. *gelaten*), OHG. *lâȝan*, pa. t. *liaz*, pa. pple. *gilâȝan* (MHG. *lâzen*, pa. t. *liez*, also shortened *lân*, pa. t. *lie*, pa. pple. *gilân*; mod.G. *lassen*, pa. t. *liesz*, pa. pple. *gelassen*), ON. *láta*, pa. t. *lét*, pa. pple. *látenn* (Sw. *låta*, Da. *lade*), Goth. *lêtan*, pa. t. *lailôt*. The root, Teut. **lǣt-*:—pre-Teut. **lēd-*, is related by ablaut to Teut. **lat-* (whence LATE *a.*):—pre-Teut. **lad-* (whence L. *lassus* weary); Brugmann compares Gr. ληδεῖν (Hesychius) 'to be weary'. The primary sense of the vb. would thus seem to be 'to let go through weariness, to neglect'; cf. the development of the Romanic synonym (F. *laisser*:—L. *laxāre*, f. *laxus* loose). In all the Teut. langs., however, the word has the same senses as in OE.

The shortening of the root vowel (which is curiously parallel to the change of MHG. *lâzen* into mod.G. *lassen*) has not been satisfactorily explained, and no precisely analogous instance has been found, though in the vbs. *fret* and *get* the normal lengthening of OE. *e* in open syllables has not taken place before *t*, and the OE. *ǽ, éa* are very generally shortened before *d* and *þ*, as in *dread, bread, breath*.]

I. To leave; to allow to pass.

†**1. a.** *trans.* To allow to remain; to leave behind; to abstain from taking away, using, consuming, occupying, etc. *Obs.*

971 *Blickl. Hom.* 125 Hwilce hwile hine wille Drihten her on worlde lætan. *c* **1205** LAY. 14778 Saxes..letten i þissen londe wiues & heore children. *c* **1220** *Bestiary* 777 Amonges men a swete smel he let her of his holi spel. *c* **1300** *Havelok* 1924 Summe in gripes bi þe her Drawen ware, and laten þer. **13..** *Coer de L.* 4136 Stondyng hous wyl he non lete. **13..** *Guy Warw.* (A.) 1620 Herhaudes bodi wiþ him he bar, For he nold it nouȝt lete þar. *c* **1330** *Spec. Gy Warw.* 218 And ȝaf to man fre power..þe euel to late and god to take. *c* **1374** CHAUCER *Boeth.* IV. pr. iv. 101 (Camb. MS.) As to the wyse folk ther nis no place Ileten to hate þat is to seyn that ne hate hath no place amonges wyse men. *c* **1400** *Rom. Rose* 6556 If men wolde ther-geyn appose The naked text, and lete the glose. **1561** HOLLYBUSH *Hom. Apoth.* 32 In that pouder growe little wormes, let the same therin. **1611** SHAKS. *Wint. T.* I. ii. 41 Ile giue him my Commission, To let him there a Moneth, behind the Gest Prefix'd for's parting. **1651** tr. *De-las-Coveras' Don Fenise* 76 He asked me where I let my traine.

b. To loose one's hold of, let go. *Obs.*

c **1250** *Gen. & Ex.* 1811 Quad iacob, ðe ne leate ic noȝt, Til ðin bliscing on me beð wroȝt.

†**2. a.** To leave undone, omit to do; to leave out, omit (in reading, recitation, etc.). Also with negative complement, to leave *undone*, etc. See also *let alone* (18 b). *Obs.*

c **900** tr. *Bæda's Hist.* Pref. (1890) 4 þæt ic sylf onȝeat, ne let ic þæt unwriten. *a* **1225** *Ancr. R.* 8 Þeos..beoð alle ine

freo wille to donne oþer to leten hwon me euer wule. *Ibid.* 38 Hwo se þuncheð to longe lete þe psalmes. c1230 *Hali Meid.* 17 þu wult lete lehtliche & abeore bliðeliche þe derf þat tu drehest. 1340 *Ayenb.* 74 Hit ne is naȝt ynoȝ to lete þe kueades: bote me lyerny þet guod to done.

b. with *inf.* as *obj.*: To omit or forbear *to* do something. Cf. LET *v.*² 2, to which some of the instances given here may belong. *Obs.*

c1330 R. Brunne *Chron.* (1810) 80 Clefe justise he satte, þe sothe to atrie, For lefe no loth to lette þe right lawe to guye. c1350 *Will. Palerne* 1186 Lettes nouȝt for ȝoure liues ȝour lord forto socoure. c1400 Maundev. iv. (1839) 27 ȝif thou lette to go, thou schalt have a gret harm. c1450 *St. Cuthbert* (Surtees) 4918 It was nyght, þarfore he lett to fyght, bot bade day lyght. 1535 Coverdale *Ecclus.* xviii. 22 Let not to praye allwaye. 1558–68 Warde tr. *Alexis' Secr.* 41 b, Let not in the meane tyme to use other remedies. 1593 Shaks. *Lucr.* 10 Colatine..did not let To praise the cleare vnmatched red and white. 1604 Edmonds *Observ. Cæsar's Comm.* 78 Thereupon he did not let to put them in mind of his opinion. 1620 Bradford *Plymouth Plant.* ix. (1856) 75 Ther was a proud and very profane yonge man [who] did not let to tell them [the sick], that he hoped to help to cast halfe of them over board before they came to their jurneys end. 1653 H. Cogan tr. *Pinto's Trav.* ii. 4 How violent soever the Tempest was..we letted not to discover the isles of Curia [etc.].

c. *absol.* and *intr.* To desist, forbear. Const. *of*, *from*. Cf. LET *v.*² 2. *Obs.*

c1200 *Trin. Coll. Hom.* 75 þe haueð michel sineged and nele lete ne bete. a1310 in Wright *Lyric P.* xxxvii. 103 Thus hit geth bituene hem tuo, That on saith, let, that other seyth, do. c1374 Chaucer *Troylus* ii. 1451 (1500) Now spek, now prey, now pitously compleyne, Lat not for nyce shame, or drede, or slouthe. c1380 *Sir Ferumb.* 224 'Let of þy speche' þe Erl hym saide. c1400 *Destr. Troy* 712 He sware..All tho couenaundes to kepe, & for no cause let. *Ibid.* 6458 He light doune full lyuely, lettid he noght. c1450 *Lay Folks Mass Bk.* (MS. F.) 85 Offere or lete, whethere thu list. c1450 *St. Cuthbert* (Surtees) 1062 Of his foly scho bad him lete. 1526 *Pilgr. Perf.* (W. de W. 1531) 49 The other houndes that seeth yᵉ game, foloweth yᵉ same..& letteth for nothynge. 1547 *Homilies* i. (1859) 79 When they..do swear..not to let from saying the truth. c1554 *Interl. Youth* B iij b, We wil let for none expence.

3. *trans.* To omit or cease to speak of. Also *intr.* (const. *of*).

c1205 Lay. 25069 Lete we nu of Costantin..and speken of Maximiæn. c1300 *Havelok* 328 Of Goldeboru shul we nou laten. c1350 *Will. Palerne* 382 But trewely of hem at þis time þe tale y lete. a1400 *Octouian* 1459 Now schull we lete here of Clement And telle how [etc.]. ? a1400 *Arthur* 636 On þe frensch boke..he schalle fynde..þynges þat y leete here.

†4. a. To leave *to* some one else. *Obs.*

a1000 in Earle *Land Charters* 203 Ic hæbbe ealle ða spæce to Ælfheȝe læten. 1297 R. Glouc. (Rolls) 7659 Hii..lete þe king þe maistrie & flowe to scotlonde. a1325 *Prose Psalter* xlviii[i]. 10 Hij shal laten her riches vn-to stranges. c1386 Chaucer *Pars. T.* ¶883 So heigh a doctrine I lete to diuines. c1400 *Rom. Rose* 6998 Alle desertes, and holtes hore..I lete hem to the Baptist Iohan. 1422 tr. *Secreta Secret., Priv. Priv.* 174 Smale thynges thay lettyn to Smale men. 1590 Spenser *F.Q.* ii. vi. 16 She [the lily]..neither spinnes nor cards..But to her mother Nature all her care she letts. 1612 Davies *Why Ireland*, etc. 64 King Henrie the seuenth had sent neither horse nor foote hither, but let the Pale to the Guard and defence of the fraternitie of Saint George.

b. To bequeath. *Obs.*

1340 *Ayenb.* 191 Hi hedde y-write ine hare testament þet hi let a þousend and vyf hondred pond.

c. *to let to borgh* (*Sc.*): to hand over upon security. *Obs.*

1482 *Acta Audit.* (1839) 100/2 For þe wrangwis takin..of i scheip & a kow, quhilkis war ordanit of before be the lordis of consale to haue bene lattin to borgh to þe saide alexʳ.

†5. To quit, abandon, forsake. To abandon *to* (the flames). *Obs.*

c1175 *Lamb. Hom.* 39 Leteð eower stale and eower reaflac. a1200 *Moral Ode* 337 Læte we þe brode strete, and þe wei bene. c1250 *Gen. & Ex.* 725 Thare let hur, and ðeðen he nam, And wulde to lond canahan. 13.. *K. Alis.* 5812 The kyng lete the waye of the est, And by a ryuer tourned west. c1330 *Spec. Gy Warw.* 902 It is noht euel so to biginne, For drede of pine to late þi sinne. 1362 Langl. *P. Pl.* A. xi. 22 Til thow be a lorde and haue londe leten the I nelle. c1385 Chaucer *L.G.W.* Prol. 411 Leteth youre ire, and beth sumwhat tretable! c1386 —— *Pars. T.* ¶768 A man shal lete fader and mooder, and taken hym to his wif. c1430 *Hymns Virg.* 30 If þat þou wolt þi synnes leett. 1430–40 Lydg. *Bochas* i. i. (1544) 3 b, God bad us not our countreyes for to lete To underfong thinges impossible. 1599 Massinger etc. *Old Law* v. i, Eneas..Who letting all his Jewels to the flames ..tooke his bedrid father on his back.

†6. a. To lose (one's life, virtue, honour, etc.). *Obs.*

c1200 *Trin. Coll. Hom.* 181 Hie goð welneih to hire liues ende, and fele here lif fulliche lated. a1225 *Juliana* 75 þis lif ȝe schulen leoten & nuten ȝe neauer hwenne. a1240 *Wohunge* in *Cott. Hom.* 273 Ofte moni wummon letes hire mensket þurh þe luue of wepmon þat is of heh burðe. 1297 R. Glouc. (Rolls) 10883 Isabel is wif..let at bercamstude þat lif. c1430 *Syr Gener.* (Roxb.) 9244 Many a knight his lyve lete. 1530 Palsgr. 607/2, I lette my lyfe, I departe out of the worlde. 1577–87 Holinshed *Chron.* III. 1165/1 His ..testament, which he made not long before he let his life.

b. *intr.* To abate, allow a deduction of. *Obs.*

c1200 *Trin. Coll. Hom.* 213 þe sullere lat sumdel of his lofe and þe beggere ecneð his bode.

7. a. To allow the escape of (confined fluid); to shed (tears, blood); to emit (breath, sounds, etc.). Also, to discharge (a gun). *to let blood* (*Surg.*): see BLOOD *sb.* 1 d. *Obs.* or *dial.*

c1000 *Sax. Leechd.* II. 46 Læt þu him blod on ædre. c1205 Lay. 18980 þa cnihtes scullen suggen..þat þu ært ilete blod. 1297 R. Glouc. (Rolls) 8507 þe teres þat hii lete so riue. c1374 Chaucer *Boeth.* iii. metr. i. 50 (Camb. MS.) The wynd nothus leteth hise plowngy blastes. c1390 Gower *Conf.* I. 268 Tho was ther manye teres lete. 14.. *A.B.C. on Pass. Christ* 202 in *Pol., Rel. & L. Poems* 249 þe blod þat cryst let for mankende. 1553 Bale *Vocacyon* 40 Than caused the Captaine a pece of ordinaunce to be fiered, and a gunne to be lete, to call backe the purser. 1559 Morwyng *Evonym.*, Take the bloud of sanguin yong men using a good diet whyles it is newly letten. 1600 Holland *Livy* xxvi. xiv. 594 Before they let their last breath. 1662 J. Davies tr. *Mandelslo's Trav.* 190 Over-reaching her self to take a flaggon that stood a little too far from her, she chanced to let a wind backwards. 1712 Arbuthnot *John Bull* iii. v, The oak, that let many a heavy groan, when he was cleft with a wedge of his own timber. 1715 Ramsay *Christ's Kirk Gr.* ii. i, The bauld good-wife..loot an aith. 1785 Burns *Halloween* xxiii, He..loot a winze. 1820 Shelley *Œdipus* i. 266 I'll slyly seize and Let blood from her weasand. 1832 Lytton *Eugene A.* i. v. Mr. Walter..wants to consult you about letting the water from the great pond.

†b. *intr.* Of blood: To issue. *Obs. rare.*

c1330 R. Brunne *Chron.* (1810) 36 þe blode was boþe warme and fresh, þat of þe schankes lete [AF. *le saunk pur veirs issist*].

c. *to let at* (now *Sc.*): to discharge missiles at; to assail; to aim at. Also *to let into* (*slang*): to attack.

1598 Grenewey *Tacitus, Ann.* ii. v. (1622) 39 The Captaine..commaunded the sling-casters..to let freely at them and drive them from their fence. c1800 *Christmas Ba'ing* in Skinner *Poet. Pieces* (1809) 42 He first leit at the ba'. 1851–61 Mayhew *Lond. Labour* III. 138 They got from six to nine months' imprisonment; and they would let into the police, eighteen months. 1871 W. Alexander *Johnny Gibb* xxii. (1873) 131, I see brawly fat ye're lattin at. 1872 *Punch* 2 Mar. 89/1 The Premier 'let into' the other gentleman with a fire and fury delightful to all but himself.

8. a. To grant the temporary possession and use of (land, buildings, rooms, movable property) to another in consideration of rent or hire. †Formerly also, to lend (money) at interest. (For *to let to hire*, *to farm*, see the sbs.)

909 in Birch *Cart. Sax.* (1887) II. 289 Eadward cyning & þa hiwan in Wintan ceastre lætað to Dænewulfe bisceope twentiȝ hida landes be Ticceburnan. a1100 *O.E. Chron.* an. 852 (Laud MS.) On þis tima leot Ceolred..Wulfrede to hande þet land of Sempiȝaham. 1340 *Ayenb.* 42 þe vifte [boȝ of auarice] is ine ham þet be markat makinde leteþ hare benefices. 1485 *Naval Acc. Hen. VII* (1896) 57 The said ship was letten on marchaundise..to Sʳ William Capell of London marchaunt. 1558 *Galway Arch.* in *10th Rep. Hist. MSS. Comm.* App. v. 388 We..have gyvin, grauntid, and for ever more leate unto John Lynch..a parcell of our ground. 1593 Shaks. *Rich. II*, ii. i. 110 It were a shame to let his Land by lease. 1616 W. Haughton *Englishmen for My Money* i. i, By the sweete loude trade of Usurie, Letting for Interest, and on Morgages, Doe I waxe rich. 1686 *Lond. Gaz.* No. 2109/4 The Blackamoor's Head in West-Smithfield is to be Lett. 1690 Child *Disc. Trade* (1694) 242 If Money were let as it is in other Countries. 1709 *Tatler* No. 88 ¶12 She had..let her Second Floor to a very genteel youngish Man. 1780 A. Young *Tour Irel.* I. xvi. (1892) 368 The farmer who lets the cows must [etc.]. 1815 Shelley in Dowden *Life* (1887) I. 522 Whether there is in any remote and solitary situation a house to let for a time. 1833 Ht. Martineau *Brooke Farm* xi. 128 He went..to let his labour where it would obtain a better reward. 1838 Dickens *Nich. Nick.* ii, A quarter of the town that has gone down in the world, and taken to letting lodgings. 1844 L. Hunt *Blue-Stocking Revels* i. 50 A 'House to Let', facing Hyde Park.

b. *intr.* in passive sense = *to be let*.

1855 *Jrnl. R. Agric. Soc.* XVI. i. 156 Lands let at from 10d. to 4s. 6d. per acre. 1884 *Law Rep.* 27 Ch. Div. 51 A large number of chambers now letting at many thousands a year. 1885 Sir J. Bacon in *Law Times Rep.* LII. 570/2 There was some reason to suppose that all the mortgaged houses would speedily let.

†9. To set free, liberate; also with complement, *to let free*, *at large*. *Obs.* (but cf. *let loose*, 19).

c1000 Ælfric *Exod.* xxi. 26 Læte hiȝ friȝe. a1400 *Octouian* 767 As glad as grehond y-lete of lese. 1525 Ld. Berners *Froiss.* II. clvii. [cliii.] 433 To let the ladyes and damoselles at large. 1582–8 *Hist. Jas. VI* (1804) 74 Being taken prisoner [he] was condemnit to the death, bot thairefter was lattin free. 1609 Skene *Reg. Maj.* 4 In other pleyes of felonie..he quha is accused vses to be lettin frie. 1670 Narborough *Jrnl.* in *Acc. Sev. Late Voy.* i. (1711) 33, I let the Greyhound at them.

10. a. To allow to pass or go; to admit *to*, *into* a place. Also *occas.* (with notion of *let down*, 32) to lower gradually *over*, *through* something.

c1400 Maundev. (Roxb.) xi. 49 Scho lete þam ouer þe wall ..by a rape. 1697 Potter *Antiq. of Greece* II. iv. (1715) 223 Such Persons were purified by being let thro' the lap of a Woman's Gown. 1854 Ld. Lonsdale in *Ld. Malmesbury's Mem. Ex-Minister* (1884) I. 419 They would not let a single Englishman on board of her. 1856 Mrs. Browning *Aur. Leigh* ii. 501 The creaking of the door, years past, Which let upon you such disabling news. 1894 Baring-Gould *Deserts S. France* I. 140 The proprietor absolutely refused to let me over it [a factory].

†b. *to let to bail* (*Sc. borgh*): to admit to bail.

1454–5 *Chart. Edinburgh* 12 Jan. (1871) 81 Nocht be ill pittit na prisonyt bot lattyn to borgh gif he has ony borowis. 1533–4 *Act 25 Hen. VIII*, c. 14 Suche person..may be letten to baile by the ordinaries. 1581 Lambarde *Eiren.* iii. ii. (1588) 339 Iustices of the Peace might..have letten to baile such persons as were indited of Felonie. 1609 Skene *Reg. Maj.* 4 He may be latten to borgh, be the Kings letter.

11. When construed with certain prepositions the verb assumes senses which it has with the cognate adverbs.

a. *to let into*: (*a*) to admit to, give entrance to, allow to enter (*lit.* and *fig.*); †also *absol.* and in *indirect pass.*; (*b*) to insert in the surface or substance of; †(*c*) to introduce, bring to; (*d*) to introduce to the knowledge of, make acquainted with, inform about; also, †*to let into one's knowledge*. (Cf. *let in*, 34.)

(*a*) 1596 Dalrymple tr. *Leslie's Hist. Scot.* ix. 201 Sum latne in to the castel haldeng the forme and schaw of a parleament. a1599 Spenser *F.Q.* vii. vi. 11 She bid the Goddesse downe descend, And let her selfe into that Ivory throne. 1615 G. Sandys *Trav.* 111 A spacious Court, let into by a number of streets. 1646 Boyle *Let. to Marcombes* 22 Oct. Wks. 1772 I. Life 33 To let new light into the understanding. 1671 L. Addison *West Barbary* 56 The Avenue that let into Gaylaus Country. 1680 *Let. to Person of Honour* 20 It is not possible he should be further let into the Government. 1712 Addison *Spect.* No. 411 ¶5 A Man of a polite Imagination is let into a great many Pleasures, that the Vulgar are not capable of receiving. 1860 Tyndall *Glac.* i. xvii. 119 The mass turned over and let me into the lake. 1860 Dickens *Uncomm. Trav.* xvi, He lets us into the waiting-room. 1873 Black *Pr. Thule* xix, He let himself into the house by his latch-key. 1885 *Daily News* 16 July 4/7 If we let the Conservatives into office again. 1885 *Law Rep.* 14 Q. Bench Div. 956 B.W.M...was let into possession under this agreement.

(*b*) 1623 Gouge *Serm. Extent God's Provid.* §15 Two girders were by tenents and mortaises let into the midst of it [the maine Summier]. 1694 *Acc. Sev. Late Voy.* ii. (1711) 215 Which colour they let into the Skin, by pricking it with a sharp Bone. 1858 Hawthorne *Fr. & It. Jrnls.* I. 277 A pointed arch of stone let into the plastered wall. 1859 Jephson *Brittany* xviii. 291 A slab let into the wall. 1874 Micklethwaite *Mod. Par. Churches* 180, I have known clocks to be let into the ledge of the pulpit.

(*c*) 1654 Cromwell *Sp.* 12 Sept. in *Carlyle*, That which I have now to say to you will need no preamble to let me into my discourse.

(*d*) c1665 Mrs. Hutchinson *Mem. Col. Hutchinson* 21 It is time that I let into your knowledge that splendour which [etc.]. 1703 Dk. Queensberry in Ellis *Orig. Lett.* Ser. ii. IV. 238 He says he was let into all the secrets of the correspondence of Scotsmen with St. Germains. 1708 Partridge *Bickerstaff detected*, I have let the learned world fairly into the controversy depending. 1712 Arbuthnot *John Bull* ii. iv, Gentlemen, I beg you will let me into my affairs a little. 1714 *Fr. Bk. of Rates* 3 Such..Explications.. as may serve to let the Reader into the Reason and Nature of what is before him. 1742 Richardson *Pamela* III. 39, I am glad thy honest Man has let thee into the Affair of Sally Godfrey. 1773 Goldsm. *Stoops to Conq.* ii. i, In the meantime my friend Marlow must not be let into his mistake. 1791 'G. Gambado' *Ann. Horsem.* Pref. (1809) 57 By the putting forth of this work the public must be let into much useful knowledge. 1809 Malkin *Gil Blas* vii. i. ¶5 He had no objection to letting me into the fun, on condition that I would not blab. 1841 Catlin *N. Amer. Ind.* (1844) I. iii. 17 Before I let you into the amusements and customs of this delightful country. 1887 L. Carroll *Game of Logic* iv. 93 That lets me into a little fact about you!

b. *to let* (a person) *off* a penalty, etc. (Cf. *let off* 35 c.)

1885 Sir H. Cotton in *Law Time Rep.* LII. 336/2 The judge..only lets the man off imprisonment on the terms of his paying the costs.

II. Uses requiring a following infinitive (normally without *to*).

12. a. *trans.* Not to prevent; to suffer, permit, allow.

971 *Blickl. Hom.* 51 Hwæt dest þu þe ȝif Drihten..þe læteþ þone teoþan dæl anne habban. a1100 *Gerefa* in *Anglia* (1886) IX. 260 Ne læte he næfre his hyrmen hyne ofer wealdan. 12.. in *Trin. Coll. Hom.* 258 Let vs, louerd, comen among þin holi kineriche. a1225 *Leg. Kath.* 2123 Ich schal ..leoten toluken þi flesch þe fuheles of þe lufte. a1300 *Cursor M.* 20198 Haf þis palme..Kepe it wel i prai it te, Lat tu neuer it be fra þe. c1330 R. Brunne *Chron. Wace* (Rolls) 4821 Hys pleyn londes he let hym haue. c1440 *Promp. Parv.* 289/1 Latyn, or sufferyn a thynge to been. c1500 in Denton *Eng. in 15th C.* Note D (1888) 318, I thynke for dyuers consyderacions it were better to lett the tenantes haue it. a1548 Hall *Chron., Hen. IV*, 23 Yᵉ kyng gave hym faire wordes, and let hym depart home. 1590 Spenser *F.Q.* i. i. 53 Love of your selfe..and deare constraint, Lets me not sleepe. 1602 *Life T. Cromwell* i. ii, Your son Thomas will Not let us work at all. 1611 Bible *Acts* xxvii. 15 When the ship was caught, and could not beare vp into the winde, we let her driue. 1634 Milton *Comus* 378 She plumes her feathers, and lets grow her wings. 1675 E. W[ilson] *Spadacr. Dunelm.* 64 If it be let stand and settle any long time. 1734 Pope *Ess. Man* iv. 356 Let thy enemies have part. 1816 Scott *Old Mort.* xl, I loot naebody sort it but my ain hands. 1834 J. H. Newman *Lett.* (1891) II. 24, I was not let see him. 1849 Thackeray *Pendennis* vi, Bows had taken her in hand and taught her part after part... She knew that he made her: and let herself be made. 1885 *Law Rep.* 29 Ch. Div. 539 Lomer..was right in letting Newman have the funds.

¶ b. A few examples of the use of *to* before the infinitive in this construction occur in all periods; now chiefly when *let* is used in the passive.

1523 Ld. Berners *Froiss.* I. vii. 6 That he shuld let the quene his suster to purchas for her selfe frendis. 1560 Whitehorne *Machiavel's Art of Warre* 90 Some haue vsed to deuide the enemies force, by lettyng him to enter into their countrie. 1671 H. M. tr. *Erasm. Colloq.* 43, I pray him not to let his pretious bloud to be shed for me in vain. a1677 Barrow *Serm. Wisdom* Wks. 1687 I. 4 It will not let external mischances..to produce an inward sense which is beyond their natural efficacy. 1678 Cudworth *Intell. Syst.* i. iv. §26. 437 Why does he let so many other Gods to do nothing at all? 1713 Steele *Englishm.* No. 17. 186 He was one of those mad Folks who are let to go abroad. 1812 Moore in *Mem.* (1853) I. 266, I never am let to write half so much as I wish. a1866 Keble *Lett. Spir. Counsel* (1870) 201 If they be indulged and let to run wild.

c. with ellipsis of the infinitive.

a1550 *Christis Kirke Gr.* iv, He wald haif lufit, scho wald not lat him. 1681 Dryden *Sp. Fryar* v. 77 My dear, dear Lord Remember me; speak, Raymond, will you let him? 1700 Penn in *Pa. Hist. Soc. Mem.* IX. 8 We are as well as the heat will let us. 1853 Lytton *My Novel* i. xiii, I am very

much obliged to my father for letting me. **1892** M. Morris *Montrose* ix. 172 A..declivity, by which they might march directly down upon Montrose's left flank—if Montrose would let them.

†**d.** *absol.* To allow, give permission. *Obs.*

1567 *Satir. Poems Reform.* vii. 95 Sum douts..of quhilk rycht faine, Gif laser lat, I wald resoluit be. **1725** Ramsay *Gent. Sheph.* I. ii, The maist thrifty man could never get A well-stor'd room, unless his wife wad let.

e. ***let 'em all come***: a catch-phr. denoting cheerful defiance.

1903 *To-Day* 19 Aug. 99/1 'Let 'em all come,' said Billy Frew, cheerfully. **1909** J. R. Ware *Passing Eng.* 167/2 *Let 'em all come*.., cheery defiance. Outcome of the plucky way in which the British, in the first days of the new year, accepted the message of congratulation by the Emperor of Germany to President Kruger on the repulse of the Jameson raid.

13. To cause. Now only in *to let* (a person) ***know*** = to inform (of something).

In early use, often with ellipsis of an indefinite personal object, so that the active infinitive has virtually assumed a passive sense; cf. G. *lassen*.

c **900** tr. *Bæda's Hist.* III. xiv. [xviii.] (MS. Ca.), He sette scole, & on þære he let cnihtas læran. *a* **1123** *O.E. Chron.* an. 1102 He let þær toforan castelas ȝemakian. *c* **1175** *Cott. Hom.* 221 Se almihti sceappende..hi alle..let befallen on þat ece fer þe ham ȝearcod was. *c* **1200** Ormin 6362 To letenn swingenn himm. *c* **1205** Lay. 586 He hine leatte wel witen. *a* **1225** *Ancr. R.* 54 Al þus þe holi Gost lette writen one boc uor to warnie wummen of hore fol eien. *c* **1290** *S. Eng. Leg.* I. 14/457 He liet..maken him king of al is fader lond. **1297** R. Glouc. (Rolls) 541 Ibured he was in londone þat he let verst rere. *c* **1350** *Will. Palerne* 2171 Lete wite swiþe at þe kichen weþer þei misse any skinnes. *c* **1440** *Gesta Rom.* I. vi. 15 (Harl. MS.) He lete make a proclamacion þorȝ all his Empire. **1490** Caxton *Eneydos* vi. 24 Ye thynges that they desireden to late to knowen to theyr frendis. **1530** Palsgr. 607/2, I lette one to wyte, *je sinue.* **1589** Cooper *Admon.* 125 They were let to vnderstande, what plots and meanes were made. **1602** Shaks. *Ham.* IV. vi. 11 If your name be Horatio, as I am let to know it is. **1630** Ld. Dorchester in Ellis *Orig. Lett.* Ser. II. III. 260 To let the Ambassador know this Doctor may returne as hee is come. **1706** Pope *Let. to Wycherley* 10 Apr., Pray let me know your mind in this, for I am utterly at a loss. **1781** [C. Johnston] *Juniper Jack* II. IV. v. 230 On my arrival at her house, I was not let to wait long. **1794** Burns '*O saw ye my dear*', She lets thee to wit that she has thee forgot. **1829** Scott *Tales Grandfather* Ser. III. lxxxiv. (1841) 446/2, I will let them know that they are the King's subjects, and must likewise submit to me. **1883** *Manch. Exam.* 7 Nov. 5/1 There was always some body of Church-men which disliked them, and took every opportunity of letting them know it.

14. a. The imperative with sb. or pronoun as obj. often serves as an auxiliary, forming the equivalent of a first or third person of the vb. which follows in the infinitive. Also (*U.S. colloq.*) in irregular phr. ***let's you and me*** (or ***you and I,*** or *us*): let us (do something).

The transition to this use from senses 12 and 13 may be seen in instances such as quot. 1423 below, in which *let* may be taken either in its ordinary sense, expressing a request addressed to a person, or in its function as an auxiliary.

1375 Barbour *Bruce* I. 498 Lat me ta the state on me, And bring this land out off thyrllage. *c* **1386** Chaucer *Man of Law's T.* 855 Lat vs stynte of Custance but a throwe, And speke we of the Romayn Emperour. **1423** Jas. I *Kingis Q.* xcix, Vnto ȝoure grace lat now ben acceptable My pure request. **1470–85** Malory *Arthur* IV. ii, Lete vs set vpon hym or day. **1500–20** Dunbar *Poems* xix. 49 Latt every man say quhat he will. *a* **1533** Ld. Berners *Gold. Bk. M. Aurel.* (1546) D iij, Leat vs call to memorie, the princes of times past. **1535** Coverdale *Song 3 Child.* 52 O let the earth speake good of the Lorde: yee lett it prayse him. **1583** Stubbes *Anat. Abus.* II. (1882) 102 Let it be granted that they are most necessarie. **1588** Shaks. *L.L.L.* v. ii. 228 If you denie to dance, let's hold more chat. **1669** Sturmy *Mariner's Mag.* v. 84 Let there be an hole about an Inch deep, which shall serve to Prime it with Powder-dust. **1707** Addison *Pres. St. War* Misc. Wks. 1830 III. 222 Let her wealth be what it will. **1742** Richardson *Pamela* II. 300 But come, I must love him! Let's find him out. **1840** Dickens *Old C. Shop* xii, Let us begone from this place. **1875** Jevons *Money* (1878) 254 Let us suppose that there is a town which is able to support two banks. **1929** W. Faulkner *Sartoris* III. 186 Let's you and I take 'em on for a set. **1950** J. D. MacDonald *Brass Cupcake* vi. 55 Let's you and me duck out of here. **1953** M. Dickens *No More Meadows* ii. 123 Let's you and me have a drink together first. **1961** R. B. Long *Sentence & its Parts* i. 23 In informal *let's us go too* strongly stressed *us* is an appositive which actually repeats its principal, the *us* of *let's*. **1964** Mrs. L. B. Johnson *White House Diary* 24 Mar. (1970) I. 101 Lady Bird, after this is over, let's you and me go out and have a drink.

¶**b.** Occasionally the nominative has been incorrectly used for the objective before the infinitive.

1634 *Malory's Arthur* IV. iii, Let we [1485 lete vs] hold us together till it be day. **1647** T. Hill *Paul* (1648) A Letter a ij, Finally, let you and I counsell, encourage, watch over, and pray much one for another. *c* **1650** *Chevy Chase* (Percy MS.) xxiii, Let thou and I the battell trye. **1795** Southey *Joan of Arc* VII. 424 Awhile Let thou and I withdraw. **1875** Dasent *Vikings* III. 131 Let thou and all Bui's men do their best.

c. with ellipsis of *go.* (Very common in Shaks.; now *arch.*)

1590 Shaks. *Com. Err.* III. i. 95 Let vs to the Tyger all to dinner. **1611** —— *Cymb.* IV. ii. 152 Ile throw't into the Creeke Behinde our Rocke, and let it to the Sea. **1634** Milton *Comus* 599 But com let's on. **1638** Sir T. Herbert *Trav.* (ed. 2) 219 Let us now into the Towne. **1791** Cowper *Iliad* VI. 505 Then let me to the tomb, my best retreat, When thou art slain. **1820** Scott *Ivanhoe* i, Let us home ere the storm begins to rage. **1822** Shelley *Faust* II. 326 When one dance ends another is begun; Come, let us to it.

III. To behave, appear, think.

†**15.** *intr.* To behave, comport oneself; to have (a particular) behaviour or appearance; to make *as though*, to pretend. Also with cognate obj. ***to let lates*** (cf. ON. *láta látum*). *Obs.*

c **1000** *Ags. Gosp.* Luke xx. 20 Ða sendun hiȝ mid searwun þa ðe riht-wise leton [*Hatton Gosp.* lætenn; Vulg. *qui se justos simularent*]. *a* **1023** Wulfstan *Hom.* lvii. (1883) 298 He..læt him eaðelice ymbe þæt. *c* **1200** Ormin 1296 Bule lateþþ modiliȝ, & bereþþ upp hiss hæfedd. *c* **1220** *Bestiary* 429 He lat he ne wile us noȝt biswike. *c* **1250** *Gen. & Ex.* 2168 He let he knew hem noȝt. *a* **1300** *Cursor M.* 12496 (Cott.) Þe late þai thoru þe cite let. *Ibid.* 14608 (Gött.) Als wittles men sli late þai lete. *a* **1310** in Wright *Lyric P.* xv. 49 Lord, that hast me lyf to-lene, such lotes lef me leten! *a* **1340** Hampole *Psalter* lxxvii. 12 Þai let as þai armyd þaim to stand wiþ god. *a* **1350** *St. Laurence* 137 in Horstm. *Altengl. Leg.* (1881) 114 He saw þam al lat sarili. ?*a* **1400** *Morte Arth.* 3832 Letande alles a lyone, he lawnches theme thorowe. *c* **1400** *Ywaine & Gaw.* 1809 Sho lete als sho him noght had sene. **1461** *Paston Lett.* II. 9 Sche letteth as thow sche wyst not where he were. *c* **1470** Henry *Wallace* XI. 502 Wallace assayed at all placis about, Leit as he wald at ony place brek out. **1508** Dunbar *Tua mariit wemen* 228, I cast on him a crabbit E..And lettis it is a luf-blenk. **1529** Rastell *Pastyme, Hist. Brit.* (1811) 103 Vortyger..letid as thoughe he had been wroth with that deede. **1787** Grose *Prov. Gloss.* Suppl., *Leeten*, you Pretend to be. *Chesh.* You are not so mad as you leeten you.

†**16.** To think (highly, lightly, much, etc.) *of* (occas. *by*, *to*, OE. *embe*). ***to let well of***: to be glad of, welcome. *Obs.*

c **1000** *Inst. Polity* c. 6 in Thorpe *Laws* II. 310 Eala fela is ..þæra þe..embe bletsunga oððe unbletsunga leohtlice lætað. *a* **1200** *Moral Ode* 260 Þet lutel let of godes borde, and godes worde. *c* **1200** Ormin 3750 Þatt te birrþ..lætenn swiþe unnornliȝ & litell off þe sellfenn. *c* **1230** *Hali Meid.* 33 Ȝif þu him muche luuest & he let lutel to þe. *c* **1325** *Metr. Hom.* 43 He..lates of pouer men hetheli. *c* **1330** R. Brunne *Chron.* (1810) 195 So wele it was of leten. **1362** Langl. *P. Pl.* A. XI. 29 Luytel is he loued or leten bi. **1375** Barbour *Bruce* XII. 250 Thai leit of ws lichtly. *a* **1400** *Relig. Pieces fr. Thornton MS.* 88 Þare was na lyueande lede he lete mare by. *c* **1400** *Ywaine & Gaw.* 2007 So wele the lyon of him lete. *c* **1430** *Syr Gener.* (Roxb.) 6764 He saw comyng Nathanael, He lete therof right wel. **1496** *Dives & Paup.* (W. de W.) VI. x. 247/2 Adam and Eue..well lete of themselfe byfore they ete of the tree. *c* **1600** Montgomerie *Cherrie & Slae* 1436 Quod Danger, 'Let not licht'.

†**17. a.** *trans.* with *complement.* To regard as. Also with obj. and inf., or clause: To consider *to be*, *that* (a person or thing) *is.* *Obs.*

c **893** K. Ælfred *Oros.* III. i. § 5 Þæt hi hi selfe leton æȝþer ȝe for heane ȝe for unwræste. *a* **1100** *O.E. Chron.* an. 1097 Maniȝe men leton þ hit cometa wære. *c* **1200** *Trin. Coll. Hom.* 125 He let hit unleflich and ne lefde hit noht. *a* **1225** *Ancr. R.* 130 [Heo] leteð al nouht wurð þet heo wel doð. *a* **1300** *Cursor M.* 19524 Godds virtu or gret prophet, Or angel elles þai him let. *c* **1374** Chaucer *Boeth.* II. pr. iii. 25 (Camb. MS.) Thow shalt nat wylne to leten thi self a wrecche. **1377** Langl. *P. Pl.* B. xv. 5 Somme..leten me for a lorel. *c* **1420** Wyntoun *Chron.* VIII. xxx. 4556 Inglis man ..gert his folk wyth mekil mayne Ryot halyly the cwntré; And lete, that all hys awyne suld be. *c* **1450** Holland *Howlat* 907 Thus leit he no man his peir.

†**b.** *absol.* To think. *Obs.*

c **1200** *Trin. Coll. Hom.* 105 Ech god giue..cumeð of heuene dunward..þeh þe unbileffulle swo ne lete. *c* **1440** *Promp. Parv.* 288/2 Laatyn, wenyn, or demyn. *Ibid.* 289/1 Latyn, or demyn in word, or hert. *c* **1470** Harding *Chron.* LIV. ii, Nothyng is more redy for to mete Then couetous and falshode as man lete.

IV. Phraseological combinations.

* *with adj. as complement.*

18. let alone. (In OE. also *lǽtan án*, ME. †*let one.*)

†**a.** To leave (a person) in solitude. *Obs.*

13.. *Guy Warw.* (A.) 525 Þe leches gon, & lete Gij one, Þat makeþ wel michel mone. *a* **1400–50** *Alexander* 1828 Þen lete þe lord þam allane & went till his fest.

b. To abstain from interfering with or paying attention to (a person or thing), abstain from doing (an action). ***to let well alone***: see WELL.

c **897** K. Ælfred *Gregory's Past.* xxxiii. 226 Læt ðonne an ðæt ȝefeoht swæ openlice sume hwile. ?*a* **1400** *Cursor M.* 2898 (Fairf.) Sibbe and spoused ȝe lete an [*Cott.* tak yee nan]. *a* **1483** Earl Rivers *Let.* in Gairdner *Life Rich. III* (1878) App. B. 395 Take hede to the vice that Maundy makes, and loke yef the foundacion and the wallis be sufficiaunt..than lete hym alone with his worke. **1530** Palsgr. 607/1 Let that alone, *laissés cela.* **1576** Fleming *Panopl. Epist.* 269 The corrupt natures of women, if they be let alone to live at libertie. **1596** Shaks. *1 Hen. IV*, II. iv. 95 Let them alone awhile, and then open the doore. **1601** —— *Twel. N.* II. iii. 145 For Monsieur Maluolio, let me alone with him. **1611** Bible *2 Kings* xxiii. 18 Let him alone; let no man move his bones. So they let his bones alone. **1667** Pepys *Diary* 30 Apr., So home..to my accounts, and finished them ..they being grown very intricate, being let alone for two months. **1711** Addison *Spect.* No. 57 ⁋5, I would..advise all my Female Readers..to let alone all Disputes of this Nature. **1830** Gen. P. Thompson *Exerc.* (1842) I. 293 Why not avoid all this, as Napoleon might have done, by letting well alone? **1838** Dickens *O. Twist* v, Why don't you let the boy alone? **1884** Rider Haggard *Dawn* xix, He is gentle as a lamb, if only he is let alone. **1886** *Manch. Exam.* 4 Nov. 5/6 It was best to let them alone to think quietly over their own position.

c. *absol.*

a **1400–50** *Alexander* 2688 Nay, leue, lat ane [*Dubl. MS.* lett be]. *a* **1592** Greene *Geo. a Greene* (1599) E i b, For his other qualities, I let alone. **1891** H. Jones *Browning as Philos. Teacher* ii. 45 There is given to men the largest choice to do or to let alone, at every step in life.

d. *colloq.* in imper.: ***let me*** (***him,*** etc.) ***alone to*** (do so and so) = I (he, etc.) may be trusted to do, etc. Also const. *for*, †and in early use *ellipt.*

c **1350** *Will. Palerne* 4372 Lete me allone, mi lef swete frende, anoie þe na more. [**1413** *Pilgr. Sowle* (Caxton) I. i. (1859) 2 Lete me alone therfore, to do that my ryght is; for nothing skilfully may lette me therof.] **1601** Shaks. *Twel. N.* III. iv. 201 Let me alone for swearing. **1681** Dryden *Sp. Fryar* IV. 48 Let me alone to accuse him afterwards. **1843** Dickens *Chr. Carol* iv, Let the char-woman alone to be the first.

e. The imperative ***let alone***, or the pres. pple. used *absol.*, is used colloq. with the sense 'not to mention'. (The obj., whether sb., adj., or clause, in this use follows *alone.*)

1812 M. Edgeworth *Absentee* in *Tales Fashionable Life* VI. xiii. 269, I didn't hide, nor wouldn't from any man living, *let alone* any woman. **1816** Jane Austen *Lett.* (1884) II. 263 We shall have no bed in the house..for Charles himself—let alone Henry. **1843** Fr. A. Kemble *Rec. Later Life* III. 33 Going out of town is very agreeable to me on my own account, letting alone my rejoicing for my children. **1853** Trench *Proverbs* 98 It..declares that honesty, let alone that it is the right thing, is also..the wisest. **1892** *Guardian* 20 Jan. 86/1 It is hard to get a gardener who can prune a gooseberry-bush, let alone raise a cucumber. **1961** R. B. Long *Sentence & its Parts* xi. 264 The use of adjectives as complements of transitive verbs is quite limited... She isn't even pretty, let alone beautiful. **1966** *Listener* 20 Oct. 569/3, I cannot say that I ever felt anything like twice as old (let alone twice as wise) as my Polish friends. **1974** L. Deighton *Spy Story* ix. 100 He'd never be considered for a high security clearance, let alone a job in the Service.

f. as *sb.*; now only *attrib.* in the sense of 'laisser-aller'.

1605 Shaks. *Lear* v. iii. 79 *Gon.* Meane you to enioy him? *Alb.* The let alone lies not in your good will. **1826** Miss Mitford *Village* Ser. II. (1863) 298 By dint of practising the let-alone system. **1859** Smiles *Self-Help* xii. (1860) 325 The old let-alone proprietors. **1873** H. Spencer *Stud. Sociol.* (1882) 351 Such a let-alone policy is eventually beneficial.

19. let loose. To liberate, set free; now chiefly, a fierce animal or some destructive agency. Also, †to relax, loose (one's hold, control), slacken (a bridle); †to abandon (an opinion). †Rarely *intr.* to give way *to.*

1530 Palsgr. 607/2, I let lose, *je mets au large...* Lette lose your houndes, we shall go hunte the foxe. **1576** Fleming *Panopl. Epist.* 286 Not letting loose the bridle of libertie to his concupiscence. **1582–8** *Hist. James VI* (1804) 286 It hes not bein the custome of England to let louse onie grip that they haue hade of Scotland at ony tyme. **1597** T. Beard *Theatre God's Judgem.* (1612) 430 Their tongues are let loosse to opprobrious speeches. **1610** Shaks. *Temp.* II. ii. 36, I doe now let loose my opinion. **1611** Bible *Gen.* xlix. 21 Naphtali is a hinde let loose. **1646** Sir T. Browne *Pseud. Ep.* I. x. 38 God intendeth only the care of the species or common natures, but letteth loose the guard of individualls. **1667** Milton *P.L.* II. 155 Will he, so wise, let loose at once his ire? **1667** *Causes Decay Chr. Piety* i. ⁋1 If we should so far let loose to speculation, as to forget our experience. **1683** Burnet tr. *More's Utopia* 136 When their Enemies..have let themselves loose into an irregular Pursuit. **1711** Addison *Spect.* No. 123 ⁋1 He was let loose among the Woods as soon as he was able to ride on Horse-back. **1821** Lamb *Elia* Ser. I. *Old & New Schoolmaster*, He can no more let his intellect loose in Society, than the other can his inclinations. **1836** W. Irving *Astoria* II. 43 Like so many bedlamites or demoniacs let loose. **1877** C. Geikie *Christ* lvii. (1879) 696 Fierce wrath will he let loose on this nation.

** *with a verb in the infinitive.*

20. let be (dial. *let-a-be*; †also contracted *labee*, *labbe*).

a. To leave undisturbed, not to meddle with; to abstain from doing (an action); to leave off, cease from; = *let alone*, 18 b. †Also const. *inf.*

c **1175** *Lamb. Hom.* 57 Let þu þet uuele beon. *c* **1250** *Gen. & Ex.* 3726 Leteð ben swilc wurdes ref. *a* **1300** *Cursor M.* 20271 Lat be weping, it helps noght. **13..** *Gaw. & Gr. Knt.* 1840 Lettez be your bisinesse. *c* **1385** Chaucer *L.G.W.* Prol. 475 Lat be thyn arguynge Ffor loue ne wele nat Countyrpletyd be. *c* **1425** Lydg. *Assembly of Gods* 2070 Take therof the best & let the worst be. **1470–85** Malory *Arthur* XXI. iv, Syr late hym be..for he is vnhappy. **1513** Douglas *Æneis* IV. vi. 159 With thi complayntis..Lat be to vex me. *c* **1560** A. Scott *Poems* (S.T.S.) iii. 1 Luvaris, lat be the frennessy of luve. **1599** Shaks. *Much Ado* v. i. 207 Soft you, let me be, plucke vp my heart, and be sad. **1641** Milton *Animadv.* Wks. 1738 I. 10 Let be your prayer, ask not Impossibilities. **1700** Dryden *Theod. & Hon.* 287 'Back on your lives! let be', said he, 'my prey'. **1822** Shelley *Faust* II. 383 Let it be..pass on. **1884** W. C. Smith *Kildrostan* 75, I do not understand Why you should harp on Ina. Let her be. **1896** A. E. Housman *Shropsh. Lad* xxxiv, Oh, sick I am to see you, will you never let me be?

†**b.** To cease to speak of; also *intr.* Const. *of.*

c **1205** Lay. 30455 Lette we nu beon Cadwaðlan and ga we to Edwine aȝan. *c* **1430** *Syr Tryam.* 127 Of the quene let we bee.

c. *absol.*

c **1000** *Sax. Leechd.* II. 206 Læt beon ealne dæȝ. *a* **1250** *Owl & Night.* 1735 Lateþ beo and beoþ isome. *c* **1320** *Seuyn Sag.* (W.) 1757 Lat ben, moder, for hit is nede. *c* **1386** Chaucer *Pard. T.* 619 Lat be quod he, it shal nat be. **1450–80** tr. *Secreta Secret.* 18 God saith him silf..'lete be, lete be, for in me is the vengeaunce, and y shalle quyte it'. *c* **1475** *Rauf Coilȝear* 293 'Lat be, God forbid', the Coilȝear said. **1526** Tindale *Matt.* xxvii. 49 Other sayde let be: let vs se whyther Helias wyll come and delyver hym. **1606** Shaks. *Ant. & Cl.* IV. iv. 6 Ah let be, let be, thou art The Armourer of my heart. **1651** Cleveland *Poems, Sq.-Cap* ii, She replies, good Sir, La-bee, If ever I have a man, Square-cap for mee. **1746** *Exmoor Scolding* 306 (E.D.S.) Labbe, labbe, Soze, labbe... Gi' o'er, gi o'er. **1847** Tennyson *Princess* VII. 338, I waste my heart in signs: let be. **1884** Child *Ballads* I. 322/2 When Thomas is about to pull fruit..the elf bids him let be. **1891** *Athenæum* 21 Feb. 242/2 The good old doctrine of Let Be.

d. = *let alone*, 18 e. Chiefly *Sc.*

1600 J. Melvill *Diary* (Wodrow Soc.) 246 He could skarse sitt, to let be stand on his feet. *a* **1653** Binning *Serm.* (1743) 619 These baser things are not worthy of an immortal spirit, let be a spirit who is a partaker of a divine nature. **1683** Dk. Hamilton 9 June in Napier *Dundee* (1859) I. ii. 333 They would scarce give me civil answers, let be to confess a word. **1816** Scott *Antiq.* xxxix, She .. speaks as if she were a prent book,—let a-be an auld fisher's wife. **1828** Moir *Mansie Wauch* Prelim. p. vii, Let-a-be this plain truth, another point of argument is [etc.].

21. let drive (see drive *v.* 11).

22. let fall.

†**a.** To put (clothing) *on* a person. *Obs.*

a **1300** *Cursor M.* 4655 þe kyng .. did on ioseph hand þe ring; And clahtyng on him lette he fall.

b. To lower (a bridge, a portcullis, a veil); *Naut.* to 'drop' an anchor; also (see quot. 1867).

c **1500** *Melusine* xxvi. 252 Clerevauld .. lete fall the bridge. **1508** Dunbar *Gold. Targe* 139 Than ladyes fair lete fall thair mantillis grene. **1535** Stewart *Cron. Scot.* (1858) II. 13 Tha .. Drew draw briggis, and lute portcul3eis fall. **1594** [see fall *v.* 4]. **1627** Capt. Smith *Seaman's Gram.* ix. 38 Let fall your fore-saile. **1638** Sir T. Herbert *Trav.* (ed. 2) 12 We let fall our Anchor. **1784** Cowper *Task* iv. 248 In letting fall the curtain of repose On bird and beast. **1867** Smyth *Sailor's Word-bk.*, *Let fall!* The order to drop a sail loosed from its gaskets, in order to set it.

c. †To allow (one's anger) to abate (*obs.*); to allow to lapse, proceed no further with, 'drop' (a business). ? *Obs.*

c **1430** *Syr Gener.* (Roxb.) 3238 His angre somdele lete he fall. **1594** O. B. *Questions Profit. Concernings* 31 b, It seemed better vnto him to let fall his reuenge. **1621** Elsing *Debates Ho. Lords* (Camden) 70 They lett the buissiness of Flood be lett fallen, and they to proceed no further in yt. **1677** Yarranton *Eng. Improv.* 66 Some progress was made in the work, but within a small while after the Act passed it was let fall again. **1692** R. L'Estrange *Josephus* v. i. (1733) 102 Having lost their Labour with-out making any Discovery, they let the Business fall. *a* **1715** Burnet *Own Time* (1724) I. 453 Seimour's election was let fall: But the point was settled, that the right of electing was in the House, and that the confirmation [by the King] was a thing of course.

†**d.** To lower (a price). *Obs. rare*$^{-1}$.

c **1475** *Rauf Coil3ear* 833 Sa laith thay war .. to lat thair price fall.

e. To 'drop', utter (a word, a hint), esp. carelessly or inadvertently.

1586 A. Day *Eng. Secretary* ii. (1625) 51 The least word .. that you let fall out of your overflowing venemous mouthes. **1676** Dryden *Aureng-z.* ii. i. 27 My grief let unbecoming speeches fall. **1710** Steele & Addison *Tatler* No. 256 ¶4 Some Expressions which the Welshman let fall in asserting the Antiquity of his Family. **1849** Macaulay *Hist. Eng.* x. II. 627 H.F. let fall some expressions which [etc.]. **1890** *Lippincott's Mag.* Mar. 412 Vague hints .. let fall by the dying officer.

f. To shed (tears).

1816 Scott *Jock of Hazeldean*, But aye she loot the tears down fa' For Jock of Hazeldean. **1822** Hazlitt *Table-t.* II. ii. 20 He .. lets fall some drops of natural pity over hapless infirmity.

g. Of a solution, etc: To deposit.

1838 T. Thomson *Chem. Org. Bodies* 688 On cooling it lets fall a yellow matter similar to wax.

h. *Geom.* To draw (a perpendicular) to a line from a point outside it. Const. *on, upon.*

1667 [see fall *v.* 4]. **1774** M. Mackenzie *Maritime Surv.* 14 Find its Latitude, by letting fall the Perpendicular *S b* on the true Meridian drawn through *X*. **1825** J. Nicholson *Operat. Mechanic* 9 The length of perpendiculars let fall upon the lines of direction.

23. let fly: see fly *v.*¹ 10.

24. let go.

a. *trans.* To allow to escape; to set at liberty; to lose one's hold of; to relax (one's hold); to drop (an anchor).

a **1300** *Cursor M.* 16330 þe pouste es min to spill or latte ga? *c* **1375** *Sc. Leg. Saints* ii. (*Paulus*) 173 Nero .. þane leit paule a quhill ga. *c* **1384** Chaucer *H. Fame* ii. 443 He .. lat the reynes gon Of his hors. *c* **1440** *York Myst.* xxxii. 254 What, wolde þou þat we lete hym ga? **1530** Palsgr. 607/2 Let go your capestan, and some be lyke to have a knocke. **1581** *Act 23 Eliz.* c. 10 §4 So as they .. do presentlye loose and let goe everye Fesaunte and Partridge so taken. **1591** Shaks. *Two Gent.* v. iv. 60 Ruffian: let goe that rude vnciuill touch. **1629** Earle *Microcosm.* lxvi. (Arb.) 90 He .. will not let the least hold goe, for feare of losing you. **1665** Sir T. Herbert *Trav.* (1677) 150 Letting go their hold they were killed by the fall. **1704** Newton *Optics* iii. (1721) 356 A Solution of Mercury in *Aqua fortis* being poured upon Iron, Copper, Tin or Lead, dissolves the Metal, and lets go the Mercury. **1727** Boyer *Fr. Dict.* s.v. *Go*, To let go the Anchor. **1807** T. Thomson *Chem.* (ed. 3) II. 214 The oxygen of the acid combines with the carbon .. and at the same time lets go a quantity of caloric. **1849** *Tait's Mag.* XVI. 308/1 The Dauphin let go his father's hand. **1850** *Ibid.* XVII. 26/1 He requested the pipe-seller to let go his hold. **1894** Clark Russell in *My First Bk.* 34 A big ship .. let go her anchor in the Downs.

b. *intr.* = to let go one's hold. Const. *of.*

c **1420** *Anturs of Arth.* 470 (Douce MS.) 'Let go', quod sir Gawayne, 'god stond with þe ri3te!' **1605** Shaks. *Lear* iv. vi. 241 Let go Slaue, or thou dy'st. **1712** J. James tr. *Le Blond's Gardening* 174 A Spring that lets go immediately, and shuts the Mouth of the Trap. **1851** Thackeray *Eng. Humourists, Steele* (1853) 112 Hill let go of his prey sulkily. **1889** *Spectator* 9 Mar., If once the heart lets go of the faith to which it used to cling.

c. To dismiss from one's thoughts; to abandon, give up; to cease to attend to or control. Phr. *let it go at that* (see go *v.* B. 21 e).

1535 Coverdale *1 Sam.* ii. 3 Let go youre greate boostinge of hye thynges. **1550** Crowley *Epigr.* 110 Such .. do turne into the alehouse, and let the church go. **1594** Marlowe & Nashe *Dido* v. ii. G 2, Iarbus, talke not of Æneas, Let him goe. *a* **1600** Hooker *Eccl. Pol.* vii. ii. §3 To let go the name, and come to the very nature of that thing which is thereby signified. **1666** Pepys *Diary* 22 July, I finding that accounts but a little let go can never be put in order by strangers. **1868** Tennyson *Lucretius* 113 Letting his own life go. **1878** *Scribner's Mag.* XV. 859/1 Do only what is imperative and let the rest go. **1886** Sir F. Pollock *Oxford Lect. etc.* iv. (1890) 107 Let go nothing that becomes a man of bodily or of mental excellence.

†**d.** To fire off (ordnance), discharge (missiles).

c **1500** *Three Kings' Sons* 45 All suche ordenaunce as they had they lete go at ones. **1580** Sidney *Ps.* vii. xii, Thou .. ready art to lett thyne arrowes go. *a* **1670** Spalding *Troub. Chas. I* (Bannatyne Club) I. 109 Ane sudden fray .. throw occasion of ane shot rakelesslie lettin go.

e. To cease to restrain; to allow to take its course unchecked. *to let oneself* (or *it*) *go*: (*a*) to give free vent to one's enthusiasm; (*b*) to neglect one's appearance, personal habits, etc.

1526 Tindale *Acts* xxvii. 15 When the shippe was caught, and coulde not resist the wynde, we let her goo and drave with the wedder. **1535** Coverdale *Job* vi. 9 That he wolde let his honde go, and hew me downe. **1890** *Spectator* 1 Nov., Once, and once only, does he let himself 'go', and then not till he has threatened to throw down his pen. **1893** *National Observer* 1 Apr. 488/2 The multitude is taking its pleasure, is letting itself go. **1923** A. Bennett *Riceyman Steps* v. i. 239 Her sole concern .. was the condition of the shop. Ought she to clean it, or ought she to 'let it go'? **1960** *Woman* 23 Apr. 17/3 The first step towards 'letting yourself go'. **1963** N. Streatfeild *Vicarage Family* ii. 20 There is a flower garden. It's been let go rather but I saw some nice rose trees. **1970** G. Greer *Female Eunuch* 186 She tries not 'to let herself go', keeps young-looking. **1971** R. Rendell *One Across* v. 48 She's made a nice job of my hair, hasn't she? I wouldn't want Ethel to think I'd let myself go.

f. as *sb.* An act of letting go.

1631 T. Powell *Tom All Trades* 31 Shipping is subject ever, at the let goe, to bee stayed. **1702** in *12th Rep. Hist. MSS. Comm.* App. iii. 7 [A dog match] for a Guinea each Dog, five let-goes out of hand, .. which goes fairest and furthest in wins all. **1885** Cholmondeley-Pennell *Fishing* 84 Catastrophes .. averted only by an ignominious let-go of the gaff.

†**25. let pass.** *Obs.* as a combination; for *to let* (a person or thing) *pass*, see pass *v. trans.* To let slip, miss (an opportunity); to pass by, neglect; to discontinue (a practice).

1530 Palsgr. 608/1, I lette passe a thyng, I let it go, or passe on. **1537** tr. *Latimer's Serm. bef. Convocation* A viij b, I lette passe to speake of moche other suche lyke countrefayte doctrine. **1577** Hanmer *Anc. Eccl. Hist.* (1619) 303 Although he let passe the vnsatiable tyrannie practised in the time of Diocletian, yet ceassed he not altogether from persecuting. **1598** Grenewey *Tacitus' Ann.* ii. xviii. (1622) 59 Letting passe the Ilands [to] take wide and open sea. **1648** *Hamilton Papers* (Camden) 164 That a people so wise .. can let passe ane opertunitie of so much credit and interest. **1667** Milton *P.L.* ix. 479 Let me not let pass Occasion which now smiles. **1671** —— *P.R.* ii. 233, I shall let pass No advantage.

26. let run. *Naut.* (See quot. 1867.)

1748 *Anson's Voy.* ii. iv. 163 Having let run their sheets and halyards. **1769** Falconer *Dict. Marine* (1780), *Faire courir*, .. to let run, or over-haul any rope. **1867** Smyth *Sailor's Work-bk.*, *Let run*, or *let go by the run*, cast off at once.

27. let slide (see slide *v.* 5 b).

28. let slip. (See also slip *v.*)

a. *trans.* To unfasten what is tied; to loose (a knot). ? *Obs.*

1526 Tindale *Luke* v. 4 Cary vs in to the depe and lett slippe thy nett to make a draught. **1530** Palsgr. 608/1, I lette slyppe a thyng that is tyed fast.

b. To liberate, loose (a hound) from the leash in order to begin the chase. Also *absol.*

1530 Palsgr. 608/1, I let slyppe, as a hunter dothe his grayhoundes out of his leashe. **1596** Shaks. *1 Hen. IV*, i. i. 278 Before the game's afoot, thou still let'st slip. **1601** —— *Jul. C.* iii. ii. 273 Cry hauocke, and let slip the Dogges of Warre. **1688** R. Holme *Armoury* ii. 186/2 Let slip the Grey-hound. [**1855** Macaulay *Hist. Eng.* xx. IV. 517 The cry .. was that Nottingham had kept his bloodhounds in the leash, but that Trenchard had let them slip.]

c. To allow to escape through carelessness; to miss (an opportunity).

1550 Crowley *Last Trump.* 882 Take hede by time, let not slyppe this occasion. **1611** Bible *Heb.* ii. 1 We ought to giue the more earnest heede to the things which we haue heard, lest at any time we should let them slip. **1634** Milton *Comus* 743 If you let slip time. **1730** Berkeley *Let.* Wks. 1871 IV. 176, I would not let slip the opportunity of returning you an answer. **1776** Paine *Com. Sense* (1791) 61 Most nations have let slip the opportunity.

*** *With adverbs.*

†**29. let abroad.** To allow to go abroad; to permit or cause to 'get about'. *Obs.*

1633 P. Fletcher *Purple Isl.* Ep. Ded., In letting them abroad I desire onely to testifie [etc.]. **1727** Pope, etc., *Art of Sinking* 76 Small beer .. is .. vapid and insipid, if left at large and let abroad.

†**30. let away.** *Obs.*

a. To allow to go away, permit to depart.

11.. *O.E. Chron.* an. 1011 (Laud MS.) Ælmær abbot hi lætan aweȝ. *a* **1300** *Cursor M.* 5858 Ne i ne wil lat þe folk a-wai. *Ibid.* 6217 Quat ha we don, þat we let þus þis folk awai? **1826** Moore in *Mem.* (1854) V. 37 [I] consented on condition of being let away early to my mother.

b. (*a*) To omit; to drop (a letter in a word). (*b*) To put away or aside; to have done with.

a **1000** in Thorpe *Dipl. Ævi Sax.* 289 Ða let he þone aþ aweȝ. *c* **1000** Ælfric *Gram.* xxviii. (Z.) 174 Ðas oðre lætaþ ðone n aweȝ on sopinum. *a* **1250** *Owl & Night.* 177 Lete we a wei þeos cheste. *c* **1275** *Moral Ode* 344 (Jesus MS.) þeos leteþ awei al heore wil, for godes hestes to fulle.

†**31. let by.** *Sc.* = *let alone* 18 e.

1577 Lochleven *to Morton* in Robertson *Hist. Scot.* App. 72 Your own particulars [= personal friends] are not contented lat by the rest.

32. let down.

a. To lower (a drawbridge, portcullis, steps of a carriage, etc.); in restricted sense, to cause or allow to descend by gradual motion or short stages. Also occas. *intr.* for *passive.*

1154 *O.E. Chron.* an. 1140 (Laud MS.) Me læt hire dun on niht of þe tur mid rapes. *a* **1300** *Cursor M.* 19844 A mikel linnen clath four squar Laten dun. *c* **1450** Lonelich *Grail* xxxvi. 367 So wenten they Into the towr .. and leten hym down ful Softelye. *c* **1470** Henry *Wallace* i. 90 Leit breggis doun, and portcules thai drew. **1530** Palsgr. 607/1 Come let me downe from my horse. **1539** Tonstall *Serm. Palm Sund.* (1823) 55 A vysion of a shete latten downe from heauen. **1662** J. Davies tr. *Olearius' Voy. Ambass.* 35 They would have let down the Anchor. **1664** Evelyn *Kal. Hort.* in *Sylva*, etc. (1729) 207 Letting the Tree down into a Pit of four or five Foot Depth. **1737** tr. *Le Comte's Mem. & Rem. China* i. 12 We were let down into the hold. **1819** Shelley *Cenci* iv. iii. 59 The draw-bridge is let down. **1840** Dickens *Barn. Rudge* liii, A passing carriage stopped, and a lady's hand let down the glass. **1844** —— *Mart. Chuz.* liii, Draymen letting down big butts of beer into a cellar. **1853** Lytton *My Novel* i. xii, Lights were brought in, the curtains let down. **1864** Mrs. H. Wood *Trevlyn Hold* I. 313 A large board or table which would put up or let down at will. **1881** Besant & Rice *Chapl. of Fleet* I. 89 Throwing the door wide open with a fling, and letting down the steps. *fig.* **1659** *Gentl. Calling* i. (1679) 6 We can let down our thoughts but one step lower, and that is into the bottomless pit.

b. To lower in position, intensity, strength, or †value; to depress; to abase, humble. Also, to disappoint; to fail in supporting, aiding, or justifying (a person, etc.); freq. in phr. *to let the side down.* Also (chiefly *U.S.*) *intr.*, to diminish, deteriorate; to relax.

1486–1504 *Let.* in Denton *Eng. in 15th c.* (1888) 318 *note D*, Yff ye suld support a synglere man to dryue yowr tenants owt and lett downe yowre tenandres [*i.e.* tenantries] as they doo. **1681** Dryden *Sp. Fryar* v. ii. 74 Every slackn'd fiber drops its hold, Like Nature letting down the Springs of Life. **1747** Chesterf. *Lett.* (1792) I. cxxviii. 343 Nothing in the world lets down a character more than that wrong turn. *a* **1791** Wesley *Serm.* lxii. 15 Wks. 1811 IX. 161 He lets himself down to our capacity. **1795** Burke *Let. to W. Elliot* Wks. VII. 348 When I found that the great advocate, Mr. Erskine, condescended to resort to these bumper toasts .. I was rather let down a little. **1798** Mad. D'Arblay *Diary* (1846) VI. 162 Poor M. de Narbonne! how will he be shocked and let down! **1800** Mrs. Hervey *Mourtray Fam.* I. 149 This cold laconic note, that, at once, let down all Emma's hopes of surprising her friend agreeably. **1832** *Examiner* 790/1 Nothing lets down a smart hit so lamentably as a hitching verse or hobbling rhyme. **1855** Macaulay *Hist. Eng.* xviii. IV. 187 He was .. gently let down from his high position. **1913** E. C. Bentley *Trent's Last Case* xv. 307 That's good. I judged you would not let me down. **1925** W. Deeping *Sorrell & Son* xii. 110, I leave it to you, Stephen. I know you'll not let me down. **1927** *Daily Express* 12 Dec. 2/4 A boy who lets his group down .. is made to feel ashamed of himself. **1952** M. Steen *Phoenix Rising* i. 22 Why .. should she present herself to him against this sordid background .. letting down her own side? **1958** 'A. Gilbert' *Death against Clock* x. 137 He couldn't guess his Frau was going to let down the side like that. **1969** *Guardian* 8 Sept. 7/2 'House and Garden' let the side down .. by advancing very confident pro-reproduction arguments. **1971** J. Tyndall *Death in Lebanon* xii. 223 George .. let the side down by his boat running out of juice. **1973** D. Robinson *Rotten with Honour* 20 You have a way of looking at people as if they're about to let the side down. **1974** N. Freeling *Dressing of Diamond* 99 He's my partner... He doesn't let me down, I won't let him down.

1866 'Mark Twain' *Lett. from Hawaii* (1967) 250 This Injun don't seem to know anything but 'Owry ikky', and the interest of that that begins to let down after it's been said sixteen or seventeen times. **1870** —— *Lett. to Publishers* (1967) 33, I shall watch this Galaxy business pretty closely, and whenever I seem to be 'letting down', I shall withdraw from literature and recuperate. **1926** *Publishers' Weekly* 20 Feb. 563 Sales are increasing instead of letting down. **1964** Mrs. L. B. Johnson *White House Diary* 14 Jan. (1970) 45 The meeting had broken up a little after midnight, and after a little letting down .. Lyndon had arrived at 2 a.m. for—shall we call it dinner.

†**c.** To reduce (overfed beef or mutton) by bleeding the animal before it is killed. *Sc. Obs.*

1555 *Burgh Rec. Peebles* (1872) 215 That all flescheouris bring thair flesche to the mercat croce .. and that thai blaw nane thairof, nor yit let it doune. **1574** *Burgh Rec. Glasgow* (1876) I. 26 That thair be na muttoun scoirit on the bak .. nor yit lattin doun before [*i.e.* bled at the breast].

d. *techn.* (*a*) To lower the temper of (metal). (*b*) See quot. 1886.

1677 Moxon *Mech. Exerc.* 57 If your Steel be too hard .. you must let it down (as Smiths say) that is, make it softer, by Tempering it. **1875** Knight *Dict. Mech.*, *Letting-down*, the process of lowering the temper of a steel tool or spring which [etc.]. **1886** W. A. Harris *Techn. Dict. Fire Insur.*, s.v., Shellac and other resins, and similar substances, are said to be 'let-down' when they are, by means of spirit-solvents, reduced or dissolved ready for use. The solvent itself is also known as 'let-down'.

(*c*) *intr.* Of an aircraft or its pilot: to descend prior to making a landing. Cf. let-down *sb.* 2.

1946 *Shell Aviation News* No. 100. 8/3 Another frequently used system was 'Lorenz' blind approach, which assisted aircraft to let-down in adverse visibility. **1947** *Jrnl. R. Aeronaut. Soc.* LI. 391/2 There remain the periods when so many accidents occur, just after taking off, or when the aircraft is letting down to land. **1958** 'N. Shute' *Rainbow &*

Rose ii. 42 Over Macquarie Harbour I started to let down. **1971** K. WHEELER *Epitaph for Mr. Wynn* (1972) xxxii. 399 I'll be letting down now... On the ground in ten minutes.

e. *to be let down*: (of the claws of a hound) to be in contact with the ground. Also, the sinew of a horse, = 'to be broken down' (see BREAK *v.* 51 d).

1684 *Lond. Gaz.* No. 1987/4 She is a pretty large Hound, very handsome, all her Claws are let down of one of her fore feet. **1737** BRACKEN *Farriery Impr.* (1749) I. 338 If the Horse be, what the Jockies call, let down in the Sinew..such a Horse can never be made so strong in the Part, but a hard Course, or Running a Race upon hard Ground, will let him down again. *Ibid.* (1757) II. 271 When a Horse..is quite let down (as the Jockeys call it) the Tendon is quite broken.

f. *to be well let down in the girth*: (of a horse, also of a hound) to be 'deep' in the girth.

1737 BRACKEN *Farriery Impr.* (1757) II. 122 When a Horse is well let down in the Girth, he is a good-winded Nag... He was a Round barrell'd Horse, and did not look much let down in the Girth.

g. *to let* (a person) *down gently, softly* or *eas(il)y*: to treat considerately so as to spare (his) self-respect. *colloq.*

1754 RICHARDSON *Grandison* VI. xxii. 120 It will give him consequence in the eye of the world, and be a gentle method of letting his pride down easy. **1834** M. SCOTT *Cruise Midge* xvi. (1842) 313 By way of letting him down gently, I said nothing. **1843** H. GAVIN *Feigned & Fictit. Dis.* 32 It is always a prudent measure to afford a malingerer an opportunity of giving in..or in the language of the hospital, to let him softly down. **1863** *Country Gentleman* 2 Apr. 227/3 The object of these ambiguous expressions is to 'let the applicant down easy'. **1866** *Harper's Mag.* Sept. 537/1 How to have the Colonel transferred, or 'let down easy',.. was the question. **1883** F. M. CRAWFORD *Dr. Claudius* vi, She would let him down easily, so to speak, that there might be no over-tender recollections on his part. **1907** [see COTTON *v.*[1] 8]. **1928** G. B. SHAW *Intelligent Woman's Guide Socialism* lvii. 274 The State..must let the loser down easily; and there is no other way of doing this except the way of purchase and compensation.

h. Of cows: To yield (milk). *dial.*

1863 MRS. GASKELL *Sylvia's L.* xv, She's a bonny lass, she is; let down her milk, there's a pretty! **1881** J. P. SHELDON *Diary Farming* 56/1 All cows will not let down their milk to strangers.

†**i.** *intr.* To deliver a blow *at*. *Obs.*

1640 tr. *Verdere's Rom. of Rom.* III. 219 Taking his curtelas in both his hands, he let down at Rozalmond with such force that [etc.].

j. To lengthen (a garment); to lower (a hem) in order to lengthen a garment.

1890 *Monthly Packet* Christmas 182 Mrs. Thorpe was thinking that Babie's pink frock wanted 'letting down' an inch. **1952** E. COXHEAD *Play Toward* v. 125 They both wore cotton [dresses], Sophia's showing where it had been let down, and Madeleine's dating back to the war years. **1953** K. TENNANT *Joyful Condemned* xxxiii. 316 Philippa was.. letting down the hem of Margot's green organdie. **1974** N. FREELING *Dressing of Diamond* 121 She liked to sit and sew; a frock whose hem needed letting down.

k. *to let one's hair down*: see HAIR *sb.* 8 l.

l. To deflate (a tyre).

1968 M. WOODHOUSE *Rock Baby* ix. 91, I..hoped she hadn't had any bright ideas like letting down my tyres or removing the distributor cap. **1973** 'M. YORKE' *Grave Matters* v. i. 81 There was no trace of a hole in it [*sc.* a tyre] when the wheel was brought in for repair. It must have been let down. Deliberately.

†**33. let forth. a.** To allow to pass forth or out; to give passage to. **b.** (See quot. 1573). *Obs.*

1535 STEWART *Cron. Scot.* (1858) II. 598 Neuir ane of thame he wald lat furth by. **1573** BARET *Alv.* L 292 To Let forth, or make a leasse of a piece of land, *foras locitare agellum* Ter. *a* **1578** LINDESAY (Pitscottie) *Chron. Scot.* (S.T.S.) I. 26 Schir James and his brother wer lattin furth at the request of the chancellar. **1590** SHAKS. *Mids. N.* v. i. 388 The graues, all gaping wide, Euery one lets forth his spright. **1593** —— *Lucr.* 1029 To let forth my fowle defiled blood. **1626** BACON *Sylva* §464 Pricking vines, or other trees ..and thereby letting forth gum or tears. **1667** MILTON *P.L.* VII. 207 Heav'n op'nd wide Her ever during Gates..to let forth The King of Glorie.

34. let in.

a. To admit, give admittance to (a person), *esp.* into a dwelling-house; to open the door of a house to; hence *refl.* to enter the house where one lives, usually by means of a latch-key. Also *fig.*, to include; to allow (someone) to share (confidential information, privileges, etc.); freq. const. *on*.

c **1000** ÆLFRIC *Hom.* II. 382 Petrus cnucode oþ ðæt hi hine inne leton. *a* **1240** *Sawles Warde* in *Cott. Hom.* 257 Let him in seið wit ȝef godd wule he bringeð us gleade tidinges. *a* **1300** *Cursor M.* 18096 Hell..open up þin yates wide, Lete in þe king, wit-vten bide. ? *a* **1366** CHAUCER *Rom. Rose* 700 She the dore of that gardyn Hadde opened, and me leten in. *c* **1400** MAUNDEV. (Roxb.) ii. 6 Seth went forth to Paradys; bot the aungel wald noȝt late him in. **1423** JAS. I *Kingis Q.* cxxv, The maister portare..frely lete vs in, vnquestionate. **1509** HAWES *Past. Pleas.* IV. (Percy Soc.) 21 At the chambre in ryght ryche araye We were let in. *a* **1550** *Freiris of Berwik* 154 in *Dunbar's Poems* (1893) 290 His knok scho kend, and did so him in lett. **1603** SHAKS. *Meas. for M.* IV. ii. 94 There he must stay vntil the Officer Arise to let him in. **1667** MILTON *P.L.* VII. 566 Open, ye everlasting Gates..let in The great Creator from his work returnd Magnificent. **1709** STEELE *Tatler* No. 45 ⁋1, I was let in at the Back-Gate of a lovely House. **1724** RAMSAY *Tea-t. Misc.* (1733) II. 134 And now she thanks the happy time That e'er she loot me in. *c* **1815** JANE AUSTEN *Persuas.* (1833) II. ix. 389 Nurse Rooke ..was delighted to be in the way to let you in. **1889** J. K. JEROME *Three Men in Boat* 167 George went home again, musing as he walked along, and let himself in. **1891** NAT. GOULD *Double Event* 74, I have a latch-key, and I let myself in. **1904** G. S. PORTER *Freckles* xiv. 307, I guess you'll have to let me in on that, too. You mustn't be selfish, you know. **1910** E. A. WALCOTT *Open Door* xiii. 162 Let me in on the game, Tommy. **1923** L. J. VANCE *Baroque* vii. 39 I'll let you in on a secret. **1928** E. WALLACE *Double* xv. 239 He had been 'let in' by acquaintances on the Stock Exchange to several good things. **1942** BERREY & VAN DEN BARK *Amer. Thes. Slang* §197/5 *Inform; give inside information*,..let *or* leave in on.

b. To give entrance or admittance to (light, water, air, etc.). Also *transf.* and *fig.*

1558 BP. WATSON *Seven Sacram.* xviii. 112 So wee maye lette in shame into oure soule. **1577** B. GOOGE *Heresbach's Husb.* (1586) 44 The water may be let in by Trenches when you lyst. **1650** JER. TAYLOR *Holy Living* ii. §6 (1686) 134 The more tender our spirits are made by Religion, the more easie we are to let in grief if the cause be innocent. **1685** WALLER *Divine Poems, Last Verses*, The Soul's dark Cottage, batter'd and decay'd, Lets in new Light thro' chinks that time has made. **1697** VANBRUGH *Æsop* v. 62 A Womans Heart's to be enter'd forty ways... An Essenc'd Peruke, and a Sweet Handkerchief; let's you in at her Nose. **1705** STANHOPE *Paraphr.* I. 221 Though God do not let in Heaven upon us. **1710** STEELE *Tatler* No. 203 ⁋8 A sashed Roof, which lets in the Sun at all Times. **1748** *Anson's Voy.* I. viii. 78 She let in the water at every seam. **1819** CRABBE *T. of Hall* XVI, And fears of sinning let in thoughts of sin. **1848** CLOUGH *Bothie* IX. 96 Half-awake servant-maids..letting-in the air by the door-way. **1871** R. H. HUTTON *Ess.* (1877) I. 11 Skylights opened to let in upon human nature an infinite dawn from above.

c. To insert into the surface or substance of a thing; see also quot. 1867. (Cf. *let into*, 11 a (*b*))

1575–6 in Swayne *Churchw. Acc. Sarum* (1896) 289 White the mason lettinge in the boltes above the quier dore 6*d.* **1663** H. POWER *Exper. Philos.* 97 A Lead-Pipe..into which at the top was let in a short neck'd weather-glass, or bolt-head. **1711** W. SUTHERLAND *Shipbuild. Assist.* 26 Let in all the Half-timbers, and then get in your Kelson. **1867** SMYTH *Sailor's Word-bk.*, *To let in*, to fix or fit a diminished part of one plank or piece of timber into a score formed in another to receive it, as the ends of the carlings into the beams. **1932** D. C. MINTER *Mod. Needlecraft* 214/1 Joins can be made decorative by letting in a piping cord down the centre. **1968** J. ARNOLD *Shell Bk. Country Crafts* 257 Handles are constructed by letting in a cane as a foundation.

d. To make a way for something to happen; to give rise to. *Obs.* or *arch.*

1655 FULLER *Ch. Hist.* III. v. §19 They pleaded also that the Churlishnesse of the Porter let in this sad Accident, increased by the Indiscretion of those in his own Family. **1818** CRUISE *Digest* (ed. 2) V. 502 The bar or extinguishment of both, by the recovery..lets in the reversion in fee after both. **1893** SIR J. W. CHITTY in *Law Times Rep.* LXVIII. 430/1 It would..let in all the mischief against which the statute was intended to guard.

e. Of ice, etc.: To give way and allow (a person) to fall through into the water. Hence *fig.* (*colloq.*) to involve in loss or difficulty by fraud, financial failure, etc. *to let in for* (cf. *in for*, IN *adv.* 8): to involve in the performance, payment, etc. of.

1832 *Examiner* 826/2 The Major..had become security for several friends, who..taxed his friendship too much, by 'letting him in' to the amount of the security. **1837** HALIBURTON *Clockm.* Ser. I. vi, An old sea captain, who was once let in for it pretty deep by a man with a broader brim than common. **1849** ALB. SMITH *Pottleton Leg.* 124, I was so confoundedly let in by the Patent Artificial Flour Company. **1873** *Punch* 12 Apr. 149/1 If we interfere to promote the object, Turkey will infallibly let us in for the cost. **1886** LUCY *Diary Two Parl.* II. 348 A young man to whom nothing is sacred would probably find peculiar pleasure in 'letting-in' his own father. **1913** GALSWORTHY *Fugitive* II. 48 Mr Malise, I know what I ought to be to you, if I let you in for all this. **1925** D. H. LAWRENCE *Let.* 29 Dec. (1962) II. 873 We sort of let ourselves in for these things. **1938** E. WAUGH *Scoop* I. v. 86 We've been having a row with you lately. Something about a libel action one of our boys let you in for. **1955** *Times* 29 June 12/6 But never once has she let-in her passengers for a major breakdown in foreign parts, or otherwise far from home. **1971** E. LEMARCHAND *Death on Doomsday* i. 16 You're..spelling out the horrors we've let ourselves in for with appalling clarity. **1973** *Listener* 15 Nov. 661/1 Princess Anne, did you explain to Captain Phillips.. what he was letting himself in for?

f. *intr.* To become connected or implicated with. ? *University slang.*

1861 HUGHES *Tom Brown at Oxf.* I. i. 14 He has also been good enough to recommend to me many tradesmen..but.. I shall make some inquiries before 'letting in' with any of them.

g. *Motoring.* To engage (the clutch) by releasing one's pressure on the clutch pedal.

1933 D. L. SAYERS *Hangman's Holiday* 173 Mr. Egg acknowledged the courtesy with a wave of his smart trilby, and let his clutch in with quiet determination. **1960** I. JEFFERIES *Dignity & Purity* iv. 61, I let in the clutch and zoomed off. **1968** *Listener* 19 Dec. 811/2 The Fiddler chuckled as he let in the clutch. **1973** C. EGLETON *Seven Days to Killing* xx. 213 He slipped the handbrake, raced the engine and then let the clutch in fast.

h. As *ppl. adj.* (See quots.)

1882 J. SOUTHWARD *Pract. Printing* xxvii. 257 Let-in notes are, as the name indicates, let into the text. **1894** *Amer. Dict. Printing & Bookmaking* 336/1 *Let-in notes*, another term for cut-in notes, or those let into the text, as distinct from side notes. **1973** *Collins's Authors & Printers Dict.* (ed. 11) 247/2 *Let-in notes*,..those let into the text, as distinct from side-notes.

35. let off.

†**a.** *intr.* To cease, 'let be'. *Obs.*

c **1392** CHAUCER *Compl. Venus* 52, I so long haue been in youre seruyce, þat for to leet of wol I neuer assente. **1422** tr. *Secreta Secret., Priv. Priv.* 182 'Lete of', he sayde, 'no man be So hardy to do hym any harme'.

b. To discharge with an explosion. Hence *fig.* To fire off (a joke, speech, etc.). *to let off steam*: see STEAM *sb.*

1714 *Lond. Gaz.* No. 5271/2 The Firework..will be let off. **1726** SWIFT *Gulliver, Lilliput* ii, Charging it [my pistol] only with Powder..I let it off in the Air. **1741** CHESTERF. *Lett.* (1792) I. lxxiv. 206 Instead of saying that tastes are different..you should let off a proverb, and say [etc.]. **1817** BROUGHAM in *Parl. Debates* 1873 An occasion for letting off his long meditated speech on that question. **1821** *Examiner* 509/2 He let off his puns with great dexterity. **1871** L. STEPHEN *Playgr. Europe* vi. (1894) 139 It reminds too much of letting off crackers in a cathedral. **1876** GEO. ELIOT *Dan. Der.* v. xxxix, I cannot bear people to keep their minds bottled up for the sake of letting them off with a pop.

c. To allow to go or escape; to excuse from punishment, service, etc. (Cf. 11 b.)

1814 J. CONSTABLE *Let.* 25 Oct. in *Corr.* (1964) II. 135 Mr. Roberson our curate was so polite as to ask me to dine with him as he had a party the other day, but I begged to be 'let off'. **1816** JANE AUSTEN *Emma* II. xiii. 244 It will be a good thing over..and I shall have been let off easily. **1828** J. W. CROKER *Diary* 4 Mar. in *C. Papers* (1884) I. xiii. 409 The poor devil had no shirt, and was so humble and penitent that he let him off. **1849** THACKERAY *Pendennis* lxx, I will let Clavering off from that bargain. **1866** MRS. OLIPHANT *Madonna Mary* I. ii. 25, I am not able for any more. Let me off for today. **1875** JOWETT *Plato* (ed. 2) I. 322 Did you ever hear any one arguing that a murderer or any sort of evil-doer ought to be let off? **1890** *Times* 21 Mar. 3/6 He was let off with an admonition and four strokes with the birch rod.

d. To allow or cause to pass away.

1823 J. BADCOCK *Dom. Amusem.* 21 Cocks..for letting off the sediment.

e. To lease in portions.

1852 DICKENS *Bleak Ho.* x, The house is let off in sets of chambers. **1853** *Jrnl. R. Agric. Soc.* XIV. I. 157 He mowed some worth 3*l.* and let off the grass of other land at 2*l.*

f. as *sb.* (*a*) A display of festivity, a festive gathering. (*b*) A part of a property which is 'let off'. (*c*) An outlet (*fig.*). (*d*) A failure to utilize some manifest advantage in a game; e.g. in *Cricket*, the failure on the part of a fielder to get a batsman out when he gives a chance. (*e*) *Weaving.* The 'paying off' of the yarn from the beam; *concr.* a contrivance for regulating this; also attrib. as *let-off mechanism* (Posselt *Techn. Textile Design*, 1889). (*f*) A release or exemption from punishment or obligation. (*g*) *Rifle-shooting.* The pulling of the trigger.

1827 SCOTT *Diary* 1 Oct. in *Lockhart*, I am to set off tomorrow for Ravensworth Castle, to meet the Duke of Wellington; a great let-off, I suppose. **1836** D. CROCKETT *Exploits & Adventures Texas* 52, I was for backing out and fighting shy; but there was no let-off, for the cock of the village..determined not to stay whipped. **1837–40** HALIBURTON *Clockm.* Ser. II. viii, My old lady..is agoin' for to give our Arabella..a let off to-night. **1854** *Punch* 23 Sept. 114/2 A light let-off that will be for the murderer of more than half-a-million! **1864** in *Cricket Q.* (1963) I. 21 He had a couple of let offs. **1876** *Baily's Monthly Mag.* July 45 After this let off, Lord Harris hit in his usual free and dashing style. **1887** *Religious Herald* 2 June (Cent.), Ah, the poor horses! how many a brutal kick and stripe they got..just as a let-off for the angry passions of their masters. **1893** *Daily News* 19 May 3/5 At the time of this let-off M...had scored 102. **1894** P. H. HUNTER *James Inwick* i. 10 He was ahint wi' his rent, and no' like to get muckle o' a let-aff frae the laird. *a* **1902** *Mod. Newspaper Advt.*, Wine and Spirit Vaults... Let-offs could pay all rent. **1913** A. G. FULTON *Notes on Rifle Shooting* 7 Position, holding, aim and let-off can be learned to perfection, and these things are the basis of successful Service rifle shooting. **1932** J. A. BARLOW *Elem. Rifle Shooting* ii. 9 Of the three essentials, holding should be placed foremost in order of importance, aiming next, and trigger pressing, trigger pulling, let-off, or whatever you like to call it, last. As far as possible I have purposely refrained from referring to let-off as trigger pressing. **1960** *Pistol Shooting* (Nat. Small-Bore Rifle Assoc.) (ed. 2) 21 The most difficult thing in shooting is to acquire an invariably good trigger let-off.

36. let on. a. *intr.* To reveal, divulge, disclose, or betray a fact by word or look. Const. *to* (a person); often with dependent clause. orig. *dial.* and *U.S.*

App. an absolute use of the phrase in quot. 1637.

[**1637** RUTHERFORD *Lett.* (1664) xxviii. 67 He..lets a poor soul stand still & knock, & never let it on him that He heareth.] **1725** RAMSAY *Gentle Sheph.* II. iii, Let nae on what's past 'Tween you and me. **1795** BURNS *'Last May a Braw Wooer'* iii, I never loot on that I kenn'd it, or car'd. **1825** SCOTT in *Lockhart* lxiv, I was more taken aback with Wright's epistle than I cared to let on. **1848** LOWELL *Biglow P.* Poems (1890) II. 109, I don't make no insinovations, I jest let on I smell a rat. **1889** 'ROLF BOLDREWOOD' *Robbery under Arms* xiv, Don't go planting in the gully, or some one'll think you're wanted and let on to the police. **1893** STEVENSON *Catriona* 225, I..was more wise than to let on. **1914** C. MACKENZIE *Sinister St.* II. IV. ii. 862 You'd better not let on you know he used to have a shop of his own. **1923** T. E. LAWRENCE *Let.* 5 Feb. (1938) 399 My private opinion is that she's read it, and he hasn't: and can't: but is much afraid to shock her by letting on. **1946** K. TENNANT *Lost Haven* (1947) xi. 173 Maybe Orry didn't like to let on he'd made a mistake in the first place. **1974** M. INGATE *Sound of Weir* viii. 62 'Would you say that he is very feeble?' 'Stronger than he lets on if you ask me. He don't need t' walk like that.'

b. To pretend. orig. *dial.* and *U.S.*

1822 J. GALT *Provost* xlvii. 354 The Provost maun ken nothing about it, or let on that he does na ken. **1828** *Yankee* (Portland, Maine) 23 Apr. 132/3 [In the South] to let on signifies to make believe. **1846** W. CROSS *Disruption* v. 48 She..had the sense to..let on to be just as ill pleased as her mistress. **1876** 'MARK TWAIN' *Old Times Mississippi* 137 If I wanted to..'let on' to prove what had occurred in the

remote past..what an opportunity is here! **1929** *Randolph Enterprise* (Elkins, W. Virginia) 28 Mar. 1/1 We..found out that Mr. Van let on to take the proposal seriously. **1961** *John o' London's* 12 Jan. 41/4 In the positive it [*sc.* let on] means 'pretend' or 'simulate' as in 'He let on to be angry'.

37. let out.

a. To give egress to; to cause or allow to go out or escape by an opening, esp. through a doorway (also *absol.*); to set free, liberate; to release from prison or confinement. †Also *intr.* (for *refl.*), to get out into the open. Also *fig.*, to excuse, to release (from some obligation). Also, to release (the clutch of a motor vehicle). ***to let the cat out of the bag***: see BAG *sb.* 19.

1154 *O.E. Chron.* an. 1140 (Laud MS.) Sua ð me sculde leten ut þe king of prisun. *a* **1240** *Sawles Warde* in *Cott. Hom.* 247 Wit..cleopeð warschipe forð ant makið hire durewart þe warliche loki hwam ha leote in ant ut. **1297** R. GLOUC. (Rolls) 263 Þat he ssolde þe noble folc..Oout of seruage lete. *a* **1300** *Cursor M.* 16814 + 28 Þer-with he thirled his hert, Bothe blode & water oute lett. **1382** WYCLIF *Gen.* viii. 10 He lete out of the arke a culuer. *c* **1386** CHAUCER *Knt.'s T.* 348 Duc Theseus hym leet out of prison. *c* **1450** *Merlin* 206 Merlin..seide than to the porter, 'Lete oute, for it is tyme'. **1535** COVERDALE *Isa.* xlii. 7 That thou..let out the prysoners, & them that syt in darknesse. **1588** SHAKS. *L.L.L.* IV. iii. 98 A Feuer in your bloud why then incision Would let her out in Sawcers. **1611** BIBLE *Prov.* xvii. 14 The beginning of strife is as when one letteth out water. **1633** P. FLETCHER *Purple Isl.* XI. i, The early Morn lets out the peeping day. **1684** T. HOCKIN *God's Decrees* 215 The ripening of an impostumation to be let out and evacuated by the lance. **1692** BEVERLEY *Disc. Dr. Crisp* 8 Why should we keep our selves and hearers so close muffled up in this thick Atmosphere of time, and not let out more into the open Air of Eternals? *c* **1710** C. FIENNES *Diary* (1888) 140 A demy Circle of open pallasadoe, yt lets you out to ye prospect of ye grounds beyond. **1715–20** POPE *Iliad* XII. 168 Till some wide wound lets out their mighty soul. **1824–9** LANDOR *Imag. Conv.* Wks. 1846 II. 48 A slight puncture will let out all the wind in the bladders. **1853** LYTTON *My Novel* III. x, Letting themselves out from their large pew under the gallery. **1869** B. HARTE *Luck of Roaring Camp* 41, I ran the whole way, knowing nobody was home but Jim,—and—and—I'm out of breath—and—that lets me out. **1884** 'MARK TWAIN' *Huck. Finn* vi. 43 They said he [*sc.* the Negro] could *vote* when he was at home. Well, that lets me out! **1889** *Times* (weekly ed.) 20 Dec. 5/4 They might be let out on ticket-of-leave. **1889** *Century Mag.* Aug. 590/2 Wide windows that let out between fluted Corinthian pilasters upon the broad open balcony. **1922** WODEHOUSE *Girl on Boat* v. 101 But this is splendid! This lets you out. **1945** E. WAUGH *Brideshead Revisited* II. i. 222 Oh, that's quite different. It lets you out completely. **1958** C. WATSON *Coffin scarcely Used* vi. 63 The driver..glanced swiftly behind him before letting out the clutch. **1973** J. LEASOR *Host of Extras* viii. 152, I..let out the clutch and we were off. **1974** 'E. LATHEN' *Sweet & Low* xiii. 129 'They've started casting around for motives.' 'That lets all of us out.'

b. ***to let out of***: to permit to be absent from.

a **1300** *Cursor M.* 22656 Es na man in erth wroght þat agh to lat it vte o thoght [*Trin.* to lete hit out of his þouȝt]. **1840** THACKERAY *Catherine* xi, He could not let the money out of his sight.

c. †To 'let loose' (one's tongue) (*obs.*); to give vent to (anger, etc.).

a **1250** *Owl & Night.* 8 Eiþer aȝen oþer swal And let þat uvele mod ut al. **1582** GOSSON *Playes Confuted*, To the Univ. A7b, These they very impudently affirme to be written by me since I had let out my inuectiue against them. *a* **1677** BARROW *Serm.* Wks. 1716 I. 340 Letting out their virulent and wanton tongues against him. **1685** BAXTER *Paraphr. N.T., Matt.* v. 21 Whoever lets out this passion of hurtful and uncharitable anger against any man. **1853** LYTTON *My Novel* II. x, 'He is Mr. Egerton's nephew, and', added Randal, ingenuously letting out his thoughts, 'I am no relation to Mr. Egerton at all'. **1873** OUIDA *Pascarel* I. 39 [She] could not forbear letting out her wrath to me.

†**d.** To set free *to* (some action), to let loose *upon*; to allow to go forth freely *to* (an object). *Obs.*

1613–18 DANIEL *Coll. Hist. Eng.* (1621) 11 The wildness of war by reason of these perpetual conflicts with strangers had so let out the people of the land to unlawful riots and rapine that [etc.]. **1646** P. BULKELEY *Gospel Covt.* I. 131 God being good, he will let out himself unto his people. **1659** BOYLE *Motives Love God* 35 The letting out our love to mutable Objects doth but inlarge our hearts and make them ..capable of being wounded in more places. **1809** SYD. SMITH *Wks.* (1867) I. 173 A timid and absurd apprehension ..of letting out the minds of youth upon difficult and important subjects.

e. To spread out; to slacken, *spec.* to increase the width of (a garment) by allowing extra material at the seams; to alter (the seams) in order to increase the width of a garment. Also *Naut.* (see quot. 1867).

c **1380** WYCLIF *Serm.* Sel. Wks. I. 12 Lede þe boot into þe hey see, and late out your nettis to takyng of fishe. **1712** W. ROGERS *Voy.* 104 We immediately let our Reefs out, chas'd and got ground of her apace. **1791** F. BURNEY *Jrnl.* Dec. (1972) I. 97 Miss Cambridge said she thought I was grown fat... I assured her I had been obliged to have a Gown let out, that had been made last year. **1863** QUEEN VICTORIA *Let.* 22 Sept. in R. Fulford *Dearest Mama* (1968) 271 She has increased very much in size—her waist being quite broad and her clothes having all to be let out. **1867** SMYTH *Sailor's Word-bk.*, *To let out*, or *shake out*, *a Reef*, to increase the dimensions of a sail, by untying the points confining a reef in it. **1877** A. SEWELL *Black Beauty* (*c* 1878, ed. 5) xxxiii. 158 When the crupper was let out a hole or two, it all fitted well. **1888** KIPLING *Under Deodars* (1889) 69, I shall say that I am going to Phelps's to get it [*sc.* a frock] let out. **1926** S. T. WARNER *Lolly Willowes* I. 17 Nannie would let out another tuck in Laura's ginghams and merinos. **1953** K. TENNANT *Joyful Condemned* xxxvi. 358 You've grown quite plump... I looked out a dress of mine... I'll let out the seams. **1974** R. HARRIS *Double Snare* viii. 54 'The dress is too tight...' 'Perhaps it could be let out.'

f. To lend (money) at interest (? *obs.*); to put out to hire; to distribute among several tenants or hirers.

1526 TINDALE *Matt.* xxi. 33 There was a certayne housholder whych set a vyneyarde..and lett it out to husbandmen. **1550** CROWLEY *Epigr.* 1372 A manne that had landes ..Surueyed the same, and lette it out deare. **1607** SHAKS. *Timon* III. v. 107 They haue..let out Their Coine vpon large interest. **1671** H. M. tr. *Erasm. Colloq.* 267 He..calls upon him that let out the Horses. **1690** CHILD *Disc. Trade* (ed. 4) 13 In Italy money will not yield above three per cent. to be let out upon real security. **1734** J. WARD *Introd. Math.* II. xii. (ed. 6) 254 What Principal or Sum of Money must be put (or Let) out to Raise a Stock of 385*l.* 13*s.* 7½*d.*? **1795** J. SULLIVAN *Hist. Maine* 168 The proprietors..letted out the lands for settlement. **1859** JEPHSON *Brittany* v. 59 A girl who let out chairs for hire. **1875** JOWETT *Plato* (ed. 2) IV. 508 The hireling who lets himself out for service. **1886** J. R. REES *Pleas. Bk.-Worm* i. 23 The easily accessible rooms.. are let out as offices.

g. To disclose, divulge; freq. with clause as obj.

1833 HT. MARTINEAU *Brooke Farm* x. 114 That would be letting out my secret. **1857** READE *Course True Love* 60 That dear old man's fault for letting out that he loves me still. **1880** MRS. LYNN LINTON *Rebel of Family* iii, She might as well let the murder out! **1892** MRS. H. WARD *David Grieve* II. vii, You'll be letting out my private affairs, and I can't stand that.

h. To strike out with (the fist, the heels, etc.). Chiefly *absol.* or *intr.* To strike or lash out. Hence, to give way to invective, use strong language.

1840 H. COCKTON *Val. Vox* xxxix. 330 A month after marriage she begins to let out in a style of which he cannot approve by any means. **1869** H. J. BYRON *Not such a fool as he looks* I. 8 *Mur.* What did he do? *Mou.* Well, he let out. *Mur.* What! his language? *Mou.* No, his left. **1882** *Daily Tel.* 24 June, At length Grace let out at Garrett, again driving him to the on amongst the spectators for 4. **1883** C. J. WILLS *Land Lion & Sun* 102 The horses..playfully biting and letting out at each other.

i. To give (a horse) his head; to drive (a motor vehicle) very fast. Also *absol.*, to ride with increased speed. *colloq.*

1849 F. PARKMAN *Calif. & Oregon Trail* 427 Let out your horse, man; lay on your whip! **1885** HOWELLS *Silas Lapham* (1891) I. 63 'I'm going to let her out, Pert', and he lifted and then dropped the reins lightly on the mare's back. **1889** 'ROLF BOLDREWOOD' *Robbery under Arms* ix, Jim's horse was far and away the fastest, and he let out to head the mare off from a creek. **1938** H. G. WELLS *Apropos of Dolores* vi. 321, I don't like these minor tracks. I can't let her [*sc.* his car] *out*. **1968** A. MARIN *Clash of Distant Thunder* (1969) xii. 91 There is a nineteen-kilometer stretch of road..that is almost straight, and I let the Alfa out all the way. **1970** 'D. HALLIDAY' *Dolly & Cookie Bird* iv. 50, I..overtook..the lorry..and then let her right out. I did a ton up that road, and probably more.

j. *intr.* Of a meeting: To end, break up. *U.S.*

1888 E. EGGLESTON *Graysons* x. 114 He..would meet her at the door of the Mount Zion tent when meeting should 'let out'. **1895** *San Francisco Weekly Exam.* 19 Sept. 4/2 *Q.* What did the cooking class let out? *A.* About five minutes to 3.

38. let up.

a. *trans.* †In OE., to put ashore (*obs.*); to raise (*lit.* and *fig.*).

11.. *O.E. Chron.* an. 1014 (Laud MS.) He com to Sandwic & let þær up þa ȝislas. **1400** *Gamelyn* 311 Gamelyn ȝede to þe ȝate & lete it up wide. **1822–34** *Good's Study Med.* (ed. 4) II. 442 The system can only be let up or let down by slow degrees.

b. *intr.* To cease, stop. Also, to relax. ***to let up on***: to cease to have to do with, talk of, interfere with, trouble, etc. *orig. U.S.*

1787 G. WASHINGTON *Diaries* (1925) III. 185 The Plows, after the rain let up, proceeded to finish this part of field No. 5. **1841** J. F. COOPER *Deerslayer* I. vi. 172 Let up, you painted riptyles—let up! **1882** B. HARTE *Flip* iv, I promised you I'd let up on him. *Ibid.*, Don't go back on your promise about lettin' up on the tramps and being a little more hightoned. **1888** *Century Mag.* Aug. 610 This caused me to let up on the creature, when it lumbered away till it tumbled down a precipice. **1891** C. ROBERTS *Adrift Amer.* 45 When the storm let up. **1897** HOWELLS *Landl. Lion's Head* 420 What do you suppose was the reason Jeff let up on the feller? *Ibid.* 452 What Jeff would natch'ly done would b'en to shake the life out of him; but he didn't;..he let him go. **1933** D. L. SAYERS *Murder must Advertise* v. 94 Never let up! Never go to sleep! **1936** H. HAGEDORN *Brookings* xv. 254 He was resourceful, steady, determined, he never let up on a man; and just wore people out. **1943** J. B. PRIESTLEY *Daylight on Saturday* xxx. 243 Bob's a chap that needs to let up, and now he can't let up... So he's angry inside all the time. **1970** C. MAJOR *Dict. Afro-Amer. Slang* 76 *Let up*, command to restrain from verbally abusing someone. **1974** E. LEMARCHAND *Buried in Past* viii. 138 The girl was..on the brink of tears... 'Why not let up a bit?' he suggested.

c. as *sb.* Cessation, pause; release from strain or stress, relaxation. orig. *U.S.*

1837 *Congress. Globe* 25th Congress 2 Sess. App. 47/3 There was no let up in the matter: the people had so ordered it, and the gentleman ought to be satisfied. **1841** J. F. COOPER *Deerslayer* I. viii. 240 There's no let-up in an Indian's watchfulness when he's on a war-path. **1856** MISS WARNER *Hills of Shatemuc* xxiii. 245 'It is the habitual command over oneself that I value'. 'No let-up to it?' said Rufus. 'No'. **1883** ANNA GREEN *Hand & Ring* ii, Blows like that haven't much let-up about them. **1884** *Century Mag.* XXVIII. 588 Our little let-up on Wednesday afternoons. **1891** E. ROPER *By Track & Trail* ix. 125 The snow was falling fast, and there was no appearance of a 'let-up'. **1892** *Eng. Illustr. Mag.* Sept. 884 (E.D.D.), There is no let-up, no change of undergarments, no camp. **1895** *Educat. Rev.* Sept. 168 Fine arts and music as a let-up with any of the severer studies. **1912** BELLOC *Green Overcoat* vii. 141 There was a gap in their conversation... A let up. An interval of repose. **1956** D. D. C. P. MOULD *Celtic Saints* xii. 126 The basis of Celtic prayer..is very simple... The background is ascetic, penitential, and without let-up. **1968** *Globe & Mail* (Toronto) 17 Feb. 23/5 The only let-up in policy is that non-profit groups get it [*sc.* a theatre] cheaper than shows booked by impresarios. **1973** *Nature* 21 Sept. 117/2 There is little prospect of a letup in fuel shortages for the next few years.

let (lɛt), *v.*[2] *arch.* Forms: 1 lettan, 2–5 letten, 3 lætten, laten, 3–5 lat(te, 3–6 lette, 4 leitt, 4–5 lete, 4–7 lett, 5 late, (leit), lettyn, 7 *Sc.* lat, 3– let. *Pa. t.* 3 lettede, 4 let, lettide, *Sc.* lettit, -yt, letyt, 4–7 letted, 5 lettid, -yd. *Pa. pple.* 3 ilet, ilette, 4 lated, y-lat, *Sc.* lettit, 4–5 lettid, 4–5, 7 y-let, 4–6 lett(e, 4–9 letted, 5 y-lettyd, 5–6 lettyd, (8 letten), 4– let. [OE. *lęttan* = OFris. *letta*, OS. *lettian* (Du. *letten*), OHG. *lezzan*, *lezzen* (MHG. *lezzen*, *letzen*), ON. *letja* to hinder, Goth. *latjan* intr. to delay, f. OTeut. **lato-* LATE *a.*]

1. *trans.* To hinder, prevent, obstruct, stand in the way of (a person, thing, action, etc.).

c **888** K. ÆLFRED *Boeth.* xxxvi. §4 Ac ic þe halsiȝe ðæt ðu me no leng ne lette, ac ȝetæc me þone weȝ. *c* **1000** ÆLFRIC *Hom.* II. 336 Hwi wille ȝe lettan ure siþfæt? *c* **1200** ORMIN 14117 Swa summ þe waterr erneþþ forþ, 3iff þatt itt nohht ne letteþþ. *c* **1200** *Trin. Coll. Hom.* 139 Seint Iohan hit wið seide and lettede hit bi his mihte. *a* **1340** HAMPOLE *Psalter* cxviii. 60, I am redy and i am noght lettid. **1375** BARBOUR *Bruce* III. 241 The rayne thus lettyt the fechtyn. *c* **1400** MAUNDEV. (Roxb.) xix. 87 Þai schuld see na thing þat schuld lette þaire deuocioun. *c* **1450** *St. Cuthbert* (Surtees) 1141 Bot þai war lett be wynd and flode. **1526** TINDALE *1 Pet.* iii. 7 That youre prayers be not lett. **1552** *Bk. Com. Prayer* Pref., Beyng at home, and not being otherwyse reasonably letted. **1584** COGAN *Haven Health* ccxii. (1636) 216 Much meat eaten at night, grieveth the stomack, and letteth naturall rest. **1647** H. MORE *Song of Soul* II. i. III. xii, And her bright flowing hair was not ylet By Arts device. **1650** TRAPP *Comm. Exod.* 26 There was som man there..which disturbed and letted all his doings. **1658** BROMHALL *Treat. Specters* II. 201 [An] open plain place, and letted with no brambles or shades. **1725** BRADLEY *Fam. Dict.* s.v. *Tea*, Those who have a mind to..study by Night, will find themselves no ways letten or embarrassed. **1799** S. FREEMAN *Town Off.* 262 Persons who wilfully let or hinder any sheriff or constable. **1814** SCOTT *Ld. of Isles* VI. xxiii, No spears were there the shock to let. **1856** RUSKIN *Mod. Paint.* IV. v. vii. §6 None letting them in their pilgrimage. **1867** INGELOW *Story Doom* IV. 21 Pray you let us not; We fain would greet our mother. **1885–94** R. BRIDGES *Eros & Psyche* July ii, If 'tis so, her child Will be a god, and she a goddess styled, Which, though I die to let it, shall not be.

†**b.** with infinitive or clause, indicating the action from which one is hindered. *Obs.*

a **1023** WULFSTAN *Hom.* lv. (Napier) 285 Gyf þonne þissa þreora þinga æniȝ hwylcne man lette, þæt hine to ðam fæstene ne onhaȝie. *c* **1205** LAY. 22009 What letteð þene fisc to uleoten to þan oðere. **1375** BARBOUR *Bruce* x. 320, I trow thai sall lettit be To purchas mair in the cuntre. *c* **1386** CHAUCER *Knt.'s T.* 1034 Whan a man was set on o degree He lette nat his felawe for to see. **1393** LANGL. *P. Pl.* C. IV. 239 Conscience hym lette, þat he ne felde nat hus foes. **1419** *Surtees Misc.* (1888) 14 Rutes, wedys and erthe..the whilk lettys the water to hafe the ryght issue. **1529** *Supplic. to King* (E.E.T.S.) 56 Whereby they be letted to execute their offyce. **1532** HERVET *Xenophon's Househ.* (1768) 9 What letteth you, that ye may not haue the same science? **1570–6** LAMBARDE *Peramb. Kent* (1826) 160 Al the Popish ceremonies of espousing the Sea..cannot let, but that the Sea continually by little and little with-draweth it selfe from their Citie. **1591** SHAKS. *Two Gent.* III. i. 113 What letts but one may enter at her window? **1601** —— *Twel. N.* v. i. 256 If nothing lets to make vs happie both. **1603** KNOLLES *Hist. Turks* (1621) 528 But the consideration of this war letted that he did not at first comming oppresse him. **1612** DRAYTON *Poly-olb.* xv. 17 They suddainly reply, what lets you should not see [etc.]. **1622** BACON *Hen. VII*, 129 Hee could not let her to dispose of her owne. **1670** LENNARD tr. *Charron's Wisd.* I. xiv. §2. 51, I let no man to sing.

c. const. *from*, †*of* (OE. *genitive*).

a **1000** *Prose Life Guthlac* v. (1848) 30 We þe þæs nu nellað lettan þæs þu ær ȝeþoht hæfdest. *a* **1225** *Ancr. R.* 352 Monie þinges muwen letten him of his jurneie. *c* **1300** *Havelok* 2253 Mouthe noþing him þer-fro lette. ? **13..** *Cursor M.* 27691 (Cott. Galba) And þus þai let gude men of gude lose. **1377** LANGL. *P. Pl.* B. v. 303 What he lent ȝow of owre lordes good to lette ȝow fro synne. **1430–40** LYDG. *Bochas* I. xviii. (1554) 33 b, Thou hast (quod he) no lordship of ye sunne; Thy shadowe letteth his bemes fro my tunne. **1470–85** MALORY *Arthur* VII. xxix. 260 Whan a good knyghte doth soo wel vpon somme day, it is no good knyghtes parte to lette hym of his worship. *a* **1533** LD. BERNERS *Huon* lxxxviii. 280 She coulde not let him of his enterpryse. **1588** J. UDALL *Diotrephes* (Arb.) 32 These men..are letted and stopped from dooing those notable dueties of their calling. **1611** BIBLE *Exod.* v. 4 Wherfore doe ye let the people from their workes? **1666** DRYDEN *Ann. Mirab.* ccxxii, And now, no longer letted of his prey, He leaps up at it with enraged desire. **1859** TENNYSON *Elaine* 96 'Sir King, mine ancient wound is hardly whole, And lets me from the saddle'. **1866** J. H. NEWMAN *Gerontius* iii. 22 *Soul.* What lets me now from going to my Lord? *Angel.* Thou art not let. **1870** MORRIS *Earthly Par.* I. I. 228 And let none think that any brazen wall Can let the Gods from doing what shall be.

†**d.** with double object. *Obs.*

a **1300** *Cursor M.* 12418 Ioseph þam it letted noght. *Ibid.* 28253 And haue i thoru mi frauwardnes letted oþer men þaire mes. **1390** GOWER *Conf.* II. 72 Ther was no ston.. Which mihte letten hem the weie. *a* **1440** *Sir Degrev.* 1583 A gret buschement hadde he (sette)..And thouȝth syre Degrivaunt lette The wayes ful grene. **1523** LD. BERNERS *Froiss.* I. 742 We shall fynde none that wyll let us the way.

†**e.** *absol.* To hinder, to be a hindrance. *Obs.*

1362 LANGL. *P. Pl.* A. III. 152 Heo lihth aȝeyn the lawe and letteth so faste, That feith may not han his forth hir florins gon so thikke. **1382** WYCLIF *Heb.* xii. 15 That no roote of bitternesse vpward burionynge lette [Vulg. *impediat*]. **1535** COVERDALE 2 *Thess.* ii. 7 Tyll he which now onely letteth, be taken out of the waye. **1572** J. JONES *Bathes of Bath* III. 22 b, Not without aduisement, and censure to speak it, what letteth? **1597** MORLEY *Introd. Mus.* Annot., You may..fall to the fourth, in the due order of the six notes, if the property let not. **1642** ROGERS *Naaman* 16 If sin had not letted.

†**2.** *intr.* To check or withhold oneself, to desist, refrain; to omit *to do* (something). *Obs.*

Coincident with LET *v.*¹ 2 b, 2 c, to which some of these examples may belong; but the instances in Chaucer with weak conjugation and double *t* seem not to admit of such an explanation. Prob. in the intransitive use the two verbs were confused.

[*c* **1330** etc.: see LET *v.*¹ 2 b.] *c* **1374** CHAUCER *Troylus* II. 1040 (1089) Ther-with a þousand tymes er he lette, He cussed þo þe lettre þat he shette. **1375** BARBOUR *Bruce* XIX. 210 Hym worthit neyd to pay the det That na man for till pay may let. *c* **1380** WYCLIF *Wks.* (1880) 313 Here may we see openliche hou crist lettede not for loue of petre to reproue hym sharpliche. *c* **1386** CHAUCER *Melib.* ¶435 The cause final was for to sle thy doghter; it letted nat in as muche as in hem was. **1390** GOWER *Conf.* II. 51 A gret mervaile it is forthi, How that a Maiden wolde lette, That sche hir time ne besette To haste unto that ilke feste, Wherof the love is al honeste. *c* **1400** *Destr. Troy* 934 He laid on þat loodly, lettyd he noght, With dynttes full dregh, till he to dethe paste. *c* **1460** *Play Sacram.* 848 To tell yow the trowth I wylle nott lett. **1535-1653** [see LET *v.*¹ 2 b].

†**b.** To delay, tarry, wait. *Obs.*

c **1385** CHAUCER *L.G.W.* 2167 *Ariadne*, And in that yle half a day he lette. *c* **1386** —— *Shipman's T.* 250 And doun he gooth, no lenger wolde he lette. —— *Clerk's T.* 333 And to his paleys, er he lenger lette,..Conveyed hir. *c* **1435** *Torr. Portugal* 2058 He bare it to the cite grett, There the kyng his fader lett, As a lord of jentille blood.

let, *ppl. a. rare.* [pa. pple. of LET *v.*¹ Cf. LETTEN.] In senses of the verb, chiefly with advs.

1594 MARLOWE & NASHE *Dido* III. ii, And feed infection with his let-out [*printed* left out] life. **187.** *Dict. Archit.* (Archit. Publ. Soc.), *Let work.* When a master builder agrees with a tradesman, or a workman for the execution of a portion of his contract, it is said to be 'let work'. **1892** MARQ. CLANRICARDE in *Daily News* 5/8 The attack of this Commission upon my low-let property.

let, obs. f. LATE *a.*¹, LEAT, watercourse.

let, obs. 3rd sing. pres. ind. of LEAD *v.*¹

-let, *suffix*, appended to sbs. The oldest words in Eng. with this ending are adoptions of OF. words formed by adding the dim. suffix *-et*, *-ete* (see -ET¹) to sbs. with the ending *-el*, in some cases repr. the L. dim. suffix *-ellum*, *-ellam*, and in others the L. ending *-āle* of neuter adjs. (see -AL¹). Examples are *bracelet*, *chaplet*, *crosslet*, *forcelet*, *frontlet*, *gauntlet*, *hamlet*, *mantelet*. It is somewhat difficult to see how these words gave rise to the Eng. use of *-let* as a diminutive suffix, as none of them, exc. the heraldic *crosslet*, have the appearance of being diminutives of Eng. words; possibly Fr. diminutives like *enfantelet*, *femmelette*, *osselet*, *tartelette*, were directly imitated by some Eng. writers.

An early diminutive in *-let* is *armlet* (sense 2, 'little arm of the sea', recorded 1538); others are *ringlet* (Shaks.), *kinglet* (Florio 1603, after F. *roitelet*). The formation did not become common until the 18th c.; from the first half of the century we have *streamlet* (Thomson), from near the end of it, *cloudlet*, *leaflet*. In the 19th c. the number of derivatives formed with the suffix is very great; among those recorded in this Dictionary are *booklet*, *brooklet*, *courtlet*, *crownlet*, *dukelet*, *hooklet*, *jokelet*, *keylet*; and in the formation of nonce-wds. *-let* is now perh. the most frequent of dim. endings.

In addition to its diminutive force, the suffix is in a few words (*anklet*, *armlet*, *leglet*, *necklet*, *wristlet*) appended to sbs. denoting parts of the body, forming names for articles of ornament or attire. The oldest word of this type, *armlet*, was perh. suggested by a false analysis of *frontlet* (cf., however, OF. *armillet*); in the formation, or at least the use, of the later words the analogy of *bracelet* has prob. been chiefly operative.

†**'letabund**, *a. Sc. Obs. rare*⁻¹. [a. L. *lætābundus*, f. *lætāri* to be joyful.] Full of joy.

1535 STEWART *Cron. Scot.* II. 505 Of quhois come this nobill king Edmound, As bird on breir wes blyth and letabund.

†**letacamp**. *Sc. Obs.* Also 6 leit-, let(t)-de-camp, leittacampt, lettgant. [a. F. *lit de camp* (*lit* = bed). Cf. Du. *ledekant*.] A camp-bed. Also *attrib.* in *letacamp-bed*.

1494 *Ld. Treas. Acc. Scotl.* (1877) I. 239 Ane harnes to turss the Kingis letacampbed. **1502** *Ibid.* (1900) II. 36 Ane pane to the Kingis let-de-camp. **1501-2** *Ibid.* 134 The leit de camp. **1505-6** *Ibid.* (1901) III. 46 For ane lett de camp to the King. **1530** —— in Pitcairn *Crim. Trials* I. 273* To cary the Kingis Leittacampt and Stule to the Oist. **1574** *Glasgow Burgh Recs.* (1876) I. 32 Item, ane lettgant bed furneist witht Flandreis werdour, blancattis [etc.].

let-alone, *sb.* and *attrib.*: see LET *v.*¹ 18.

letanie, var. LETTANIE; obs. form of LATTEN.

letany(e, obs. form of LITANY.

†**letating**, *ppl. a. Obs. rare*⁻¹. [f. **letate* vb. (f. L. *lætāre* to make glad) + -ING².] That makes joyful; gladdening.

1694 MOTTEUX *Rabelais* v. (1737) 230 Their plaisant Notes..wake your Soul with their letating Sound.

letation, var. LÆTATION *Obs.*, a manuring.

letch (lɛtʃ), *sb.*¹ *Sc.* and *north. dial.* Forms: 6, 9 lache, 6-7 letch, 8-9 lach, 9 latch, leach. [? f. OE. *lęccan* vb.; see LEACH *v.*², and cf. LEACH *sb.*²] A stream flowing through boggy land; a muddy ditch or hole; a bog. Also, see quot. 1781.

1138 *Newminster Cartul.* (Surtees) 9 De cruce ad crucem in Appeltreleche. **1570** LEVINS *Manip.* 5/43 A Lache, *lacus.* **1598** *Mem. St. Giles' Durh.* (Surtees) 26 Paid for scowringe of the bridge letch, ijᵈ. **1607** MARKHAM *Caval.* VI. (1617) 10 A rotten ground full of letches. *c* **1630** *Scot. Pasquil* 8 At euery river, spring, or letch, I drinke. **1781** HUTTON *Tour to Caves* Gloss., *Lyring* and *lach*, a gutter washed by the tide on the sea shore. **1815** SCOTT *Guy M.* xxiii, Wither-shins' latch ..a narrow channel, through which soaked, rather than flowed, a small stagnant stream.

b. *transf.* A pool (of blood).

1868 B. BRIERLEY *Irkdale* viii. 163 He found that instrument to be broken in several fragments, one of which lay in a 'leach' of blood.

letch (lɛtʃ), *sb.*² [Of obscure origin; possibly f. LATCH *v.*¹, but cf. LECH *sb.*⁴] A craving, longing.

1796 *Grose's Dict. Vulg. Tongue*, *Letch*, a whim of the amorous kind, out of the common way. **1814** *Monthly Mag.* XXXVIII. 126/2 [Somerset wds.] *Latch*, fancy, wish. **1830** DE QUINCEY *Bentley* Wks. 1857 VII. 40 Some people have a 'letch' for unmasking impostors, or for avenging the wrongs of others. **1834** SIR H. TAYLOR *1st Pt. Artevelde* II. vi. 134 Then will the Earl..pardon us our letch for liberty. **1862** *Sat. Rev.* 4 Jan. 5 The letch for blood which characterizes the savage. **1870** SWINBURNE *Ess. & Stud.* (1875) 81 No trace..of the fretful and fruitless prurience of soul which would fain grasp..a creed beyond its power of possession,—no letch after Gods dead or unborn. **1893** *National Observer* 23 Dec. 141/2 The unconquerable letch he had upon sombre sorceries.

letch, variant of LEACH *sb.*²

letch: see LECH *sb.*⁴ and *v.*

letcher, -ous, -y: see LECHER, etc.

letchi, variant of LITCHI.

letchwe, var. LECHWE.

let-down ('lɛtdaʊn), *sb.* [f. vbl. phr. *to let down* (LET *v.*¹ 32).] **1.** An act or instance of 'letting down': (*a*) a drawback, incident, disadvantage; (*b*) a come-down, a 'drop' in circumstances; (*c*) a disappointment. *slang.*

1768 *Woman of Honor* I. 235, I met with such a let-down. **1840** GEN. P. THOMPSON *Exerc.* (1842) V. 14 The let-down to what is known as the 'cottage and cow system', has always been, that [etc.]. **1861** *Times* 17 Sept., Here comes another 'let-down', really worse than any before. **1866** *Lond. Misc.* 3 Mar. 57 (Farmer), I don't think that's no little let-down for a cove as has been tip-topper in his time. **1894** 'J. S. WINTER' *Red-Coats, Amyatt's Child Fr.* i, It would be hard to say positively that any trace of a disappointment—what Arlington called a 'let-down'—marked his pleasant fresh face. **1933** N. COWARD *Design for Living* II. iii. 68 The human race is a let-down, Ernest; a bad, bad let-down! **1934** J. T. FARRELL *Young Manhood* ii. 41 He was lassitudinous in a mood of let-down, already lonesome for yesterday. **1938** J. STEINBECK *Long Valley* 135 Mike knew it was all over. He could feel the let-down in himself. **1946** W. STEVENS *Let.* 19 Feb. (1967) 523 There is not the..let-down between the two that one finds so often. **1960** M. SPARK *Bachelors* x. 182 And now *she's* in for a let-down, though she won't admit it. **1971** *Daily Tel.* 4 Nov. 8/4 What intrigues Mr Barstow is the inevitable let-down which is the result of getting older, of getting bored, of finding that passion can flicker out.

2. The descent of an aircraft or spacecraft prior to landing. Cf. LET *v.*¹ 32 d (*c*).

1945 *Jrnl. R. Aeronaut. Soc.* XLIX. 74/1 Extra fuel to allow for errors in navigation, errors in weather forecasts and technical inabilities to make let-downs and landings through conditions of ice, clouds, or bad ground visibility. **1949** *Flight* 30 June 754/2 From its pilot, Col. Gray, we learned that, on the let-down from 35,000 ft, while the B-29 was still in formation, its port inner engine had over-speeded to 4,500 r.p.m. **1960** 'N. SHUTE' *Trustee from Toolroom* v. 97 The note of the engines changed as the let-down began. **1969** *Guardian* 13 Oct. 18/2 The precision of landing depends predominantly on the accuracy with which the spacecraft's orbital position is known at the moment let-down begins.

3. The action of a cow yielding milk. Cf. LET *v.*¹ 32 h.

1960 *Farmer & Stockbreeder* 5 Jan. 69/3 A time-lag between the end of let-down and stripping is too prevalent. **1965** LEE & KNOWLES *Animal Hormones* ii. 32 Thus the ejection of milk at suckling, or the 'let-down' of milk as it is referred to by agricultural workers, is a neurohormonal reflex.

4. *attrib.* or as *adj.*, in the senses of the vbl. phr. *to let down* or of the sb. (see above).

1907 M. C. HARRIS *Tents of Wickedness* II. vii. 193 The next was one of these 'let-down' mornings which everybody must remember having awakened to. **1945** E. BOWEN *Demon Lover* 72 The car was a two-seater, with a let-down hood. **1948** [see *fan marker* (FAN *sb.*¹ 11)]. **1956** *Nature* 24 Mar. 582/1 In studying the function of the milk gland, with the view of increasing milk production, particular attention has been devoted in recent years to the milk-ejection mechanism (the let-down reflex). **1957** R. H. SMYTHE *Conformation of Dog* vi. 88 The exhibition Greyhound has always been noted for length of tibia, low set-on hocks, well let-down stifles. **1964** *Yearbk. Astron. 1965* 135 At a fixed height the lunar let-down engine will fire to reduce the descent rate and, landing legs having been extended, the vehicle will complete a vertical descent on to the lunar surface, hovering for short periods before making the final touchdown. **1973** M. MACKINTOSH *King & Two Queens* ii. 24, I had talked myself out of the let-down feeling and was determined to make the most of the trip. **1974** P. FLOWER *Odd Job* i. 6 Somebody had called it an escritoire... It had a letdown flap you could write on.

†**lete.** *Cookery. Obs.* Also 5 led(e, let(te, lethe. In Combs. ***lete lardes***, ***lete lory***, of obscure origin and meaning. Cf. LEACH *sb.*¹

? *c* **1390** *Form of Cury* lxviii. (1780) 38 Lete Lardes. **14..** *Noble Bk. Cookry* (Napier 1882) 87 To mak ledlardes of iij coloures. *c* **1420** in *Q. Eliz. Acad.* 91 Lete lardes y-fryed. *c* **1420** *Liber Cocorum* (1862) 13 Lede lardes. *c* **1430** *Two Cookery-bks.* 17 Let lory. *Ibid.* 36 And ȝif þow wolt haue it Motley, take þre pottys, & make letlardys in eche. *c* **1450** *Ibid.* 85 Lethe lory.

lete, variant of LATE *sb.*¹ *Obs.*, look.

letew(e)s, obs. form of LETTUCE.

†**let-game.** *Obs.* [f. LET *v.*² + GAME *sb.*] One who hinders the game; a spoil-sport.

c **1374** CHAUCER *Troylus* III. 478 (527) Dredeles it cler was in þe wynde Of euery pye and euery lette game. **1387-8** T. USK *Test. Love* I. iii. (Skeat) l. 124 Let games, and purpose breakers. *c* **1440** *Promp. Parv.* 299/2 Lette game, or lettare of play.

†**leth.** *Obs.* Also 3 **leððe.** [OE. *lǽððu*, *lǽðu*:—OTeut. **laiþiþâ*, f. **laiþo-* LOATH.] Hatred, ill-will.

971 *Blickl. Hom.* 63 Ac us is to witenne þæt þreora cynna syndon morþras, þæt is þonne þæt ærest, þæt man to oþrum læþþe hæbbe, & hine hatiȝe. *c* **1200** *Trin. Coll. Hom.* 141 Ure drihten..forgiaf hire hire sinnen for two þinge an is muchel leððe to hire sunne oðer muchel luue to him. *c* **1425** WYNTOUN *Cron.* III. ii. 229 Tyll his wyff he kest sik leth. *Ibid.* IV. xviii. 1750 Gendyre leth mare than delyte.

leth, variant of LEATH, LITH, LITHE.

lethal ('liːθəl), *a.* and *sb.* Also 6-7 **lethall**, **læthall**. [ad. L. *lēt(h)āl-is* deadly, f. *lēt(h)um* death.]

A. *adj.* **1. a.** That may or will cause death; deadly, mortal. Said, e.g. of weapons, drugs, wounds. Now *esp.* of a dose of poison: Sufficient to cause death.

1613 R. CAWDREY *Table Alph.* (ed. 3), Lethall, mortall, deadly. **1659** T. PECKE *Parnassi Puerp.* 127 There's no more need to throw the lethal Spear. **1671** E. PANTON *Spec. Juvent.* 96 Among beasts some live by what is lethal to others. **1706** MAULE *Hist. Picts* in *Misc. Scot.* I. 39 Lethal wounds. **1816** SOUTHEY *Lay Laureate* liv, There needs no outward wound! Through her whole frame benumb'd, a lethal sleep, Like the cold poison of the asp will creep. **1855** GARROD *Mat. Med.* (ed. 6) 123 Small doses raise the blood pressure..lethal ones cause immediate paralysis of the heart. **1860** GOSSE *Rom. Nat. Hist.* 240 Implements so terribly lethal, that the slightest puncture of the skin..is inevitably..followed by..death. **1885** HUXLEY *Addr. Roy. Soc.* 30 Nov., Those lethal agencies which are commonly known as the pleasures of society.

b. Resulting in death.

1850 BLACKIE *Æschylus* I. 104 The occasion..out of which the lethal quarrel arose.

c. ***lethal chamber***: a chamber containing gases, in which to destroy animals or human beings painlessly; also *fig.*

1884 *Punch* 27 Dec. 309/1 A sort of Lethal Chamber and Cat Trap combined. **1888** in *Syd. Soc. Lex.* **1901** *Blackw. Mag.* Jan. 50/1 They were quietly disposed of by euthanasia in a lethal chamber. **1928** 'M. HOFFE' *Many Waters* III. ix. 106 It [*sc.* the Bankruptcy Court] lacks of all the glitter of splendid sin; it is simply the paltry lethal chamber of the vanquished. **1933** *Punch* 4 Oct. 366/2 To a modern it is clear that age must be abhorrent. The best modern thought advocates a lethal chamber for all over fifty years of age.

d. *Genetics.* Of an allele or chromosomal abnormality (such as a deletion): resulting in the death of an individual possessing it before the normal span or before sexual maturity, or (if recessive) capable of causing such premature death when homozygous.

1917 *Proc. Nat. Acad. Sci.* III. 620 The difficulty which was experienced in getting pure stock was due to the fact that the chief factor for beaded—B_d'—is lethal, killing all flies homozygous for it. *Ibid.* 620 This remarkable genetic situation, wherein both types of homozygotes are prevented from appearing by the action of lethal factors lying in opposite chromosomes, may be termed a condition of 'balanced lethal factors'. **1939** STURTEVANT & BEADLE *Introd. Genetics* (1940) x. 160 It may be noted at once that the lethal genes ordinarily studied are recessive; a gene with a dominant lethal effect is necessarily lost before it can be studied. **1962** I. H. HERSKOWITZ *Genetics* xxviii. 239 Autosomes II, III, and IV of wild-type flies were individually made homozygous to detect the presence of recessive mutants..that are lethal (causing death of all individuals before adulthood), or semilethal (causing more than 90 and less than 100 per cent mortality before

adulthood), or subvital (causing significantly less than normal but greater than 10 per cent survival to adulthood). .. About 25% of all autosomes tested this way carried a recessive lethal or semilethal mutant. **1973** K. Mather *Genetical Struct. Populations* ii. 21 Not all genes that affect viability are, however, completely lethal. Of some 3000 chromosomes tested in *Drosophila willistoni*..over 35% carried genes that were lethal or semi-lethal. About half of the remainder carried other genes affecting the viability of flies homozygous for them.

2. Causing or resulting in spiritual death; deadly; †esp. of sin = *mortal*.

1583 Stubbes *Anat. Abus.* I. (1879) 27 Two kindes of sinne, the one veniall, the other lethall. **1603** Florio *Montaigne* II. xv. 358 To rouze, and awaken..the godly and religious soules, and raise them from out a lethall security. **1647** Ward *Simp. Cobler* 41 Such Epidemicall and lethall formality in other disciplinated Churches. **1860** Reade *Cloister & H.* lv. (1896) 157 Discoursing of sinners and their lethal end.

3. Of or pertaining to death.

1607 E. Sharpham *Cupid's Whirligig* IV. G 4, Vengeance wings brings on thy lethall day. **1794** Coleridge *Monody death Chatterton* 57 On thy wan forehead starts the lethal dew.

B. *sb. Genetics.* A lethal allele or chromosomal abnormality (see A. 1 d).

1917 *Proc. Nat. Acad. Sci.* III. 621 We must therefore believe that lethals are very frequent among recessive factors also. **1926** J. S. Huxley *Ess. Pop. Sci.* 59 Sometimes the impairment of vitality is so great that the organism pure for these factors cannot exist at all: such factors are styled lethals. **1934** *Mycologia* XXVI. 360 (*heading*) A lethal for ascus abortion in Neurospora. **1956** [see deficiency 1 e].

Hence **'lethally** *adv.*, in a deadly manner.

1661 Lovell *Hist. Anim. & Min.* 328 A..contagious matter, hurting all the actions of the heart suddainly and lethaly. **1971** *Nature* 10 Dec. 328/3 Lethally irradiated F_1 hybrid mice.

lethal ('liːθəl), *v. rare.* [f. lethal *a.*] *trans.* To kill (animals) painlessly; = lethalize *v.* So **'lethalling** *vbl. sb.*

1922 *Daily Mail* 7 Dec. 6 (Advt.), Cat. Dying from internal injuries..: Lethalled. **1925** *Observer* 27 Sept. 13/6 Proper lethalling establishments where cats can be put to sleep free of charge.

lethality (liːˈθælɪtɪ). [f. lethal *a.* + -ity. Cf. F. *léthalité*.] The condition or quality of being lethal; ability to cause death; deadliness; *pl.* (? nonce-use) lethal agencies. Also *fig.*

1656 Blount *Glossogr.*, *Lethality*, mortality, frailty. **1735** J. Atkins *Voy. Guinea* (1737) 104 The certain Punishment being preferable to the doubtful Lethality of the Fetish. **1890** *Sat. Rev.* 22 Nov. 595/1 Why a person surnamed 'Deathless'..should have succumbed to such commonplace lethalities as a horse's hoof and Prince Ivan's club we know not. **1912** *Phil. Trans. R. Soc.* B. CCII. 2 The lethality of the venom was determined for frogs, rabbits,..and pigeons. **1930** G. Blake *Press & Public* 20 Mr. Baldwin..has lately discovered for himself the dread lethality of the powers I have described. **1953** *Sci. News* XXVIII. 18 Myxomatosis in the European rabbits is unique in its very high lethality. **1957** *Times* 26 Apr., Our early missiles will carry high-explosive warheads. Their lethality will be high. **1958** 'P. Bryant' *Two Hours to Doom* 81 The radioactive cloud.. would retain its lethality for hundreds of years. **1973** D. Jordan *Nile Green* xxviii. 125 Significant strides have been made in the past two decades on the lethality of conventional and nuclear warheads.

lethalize ('liːθəlaɪz), *v. rare.* [f. lethal *a.* + -ize.] *trans.* To destroy in a lethal chamber.

1897 *Daily Tel.* 5 Feb. 7/4 If the proprietress consented to have the animal lethalised, as it was unfit for work.

†**letharge.** *Obs. rare*$^{-1}$. [ad. L. *lētharg-us*: see lethargy.] A lethargic patient.

1615 Brathwait *Strappado*, etc. (1878) 255 He cannot sleepe nor wake, but twixt them both, sleeping and waking as a letharge doth.

letharge, obs. form of litharge.

†**lethargean**, *a. Obs. rare*$^{-1}$. [? f. lethargy + -an.] Lethargic.

1659 J. Tatham *London's Tryumph* 6 Idleness, the Nurse of Ignorance; Which lulls mens braines, in a Lethergean Trance.

lethargic (lɪˈθɑːdʒɪk), *a.* and *sb.* Forms: 4 litargik, -yk, 7-8 lethargick(e, (6-7 lethargique), 7- lethargic. [ad. L. *lēthargic-us*, ad. Gr. ληθαργικ-ός, f. λήθαργ-ος: see lethargy. Cf. F. *léthargique*.] **A.** *adj.*

1. Affected with lethargy or morbid drowsiness.

1398 Trevisa *Barth. De P.R.* xviii. xxix. (1495) 791 The litargik man that hath the slepynge euyll. **1720** *Wodrow Corr.* (1843) II. 528 He was very lethargic, and was cupped.

b. *transf.* Affected with inertness or inactivity; dull, sleepy, sluggish, apathetic.

1612 Donne *Progr. Soul* 2nd Anniv. 64 To be thus stupid is Alacritie; Men thus Lethargique have best Memory. *a* **1649** Drumm. of Hawth. *Poems* Wks. (1711) 31 Blind and Lethargick of thy heavenly Grace. **1752** Hume *Ess. & Treat.* (1777) I. 153 [Nature] allows not such noble faculties to lie lethargic. **1817** J. Scott *Paris Revisit.* (ed. 4) 58 The numerous, populous, bustling, and neat towns of that country, are likely to present..striking contrasts to the lethargic Flemish cities. **1835** Lytton *Rienzi* x. vi, Those he employed were lukewarm and lethargic. **1876** Bancroft *Hist. U.S.* I. iii. 83 The exiles of a year had grown familiar with the favorite amusement of the lethargic Indians; and they introduced into England the general use of tobacco.

2. Of or belonging to a state of lethargy.

1595 Jas. VI *to Q. Eliz.* in *Lett.* (Camd.) lviii. 111 That ye quho uas so uachfull..as..to foruairne me of my perrell,.. should nou, in the uerrie heicht..thairof, be fallen in so lethargique a sleip, as [etc.]. *a* **1649** Drumm. of Hawth. *Poems* Wks. (1711) 25 Sin's lethargick Sleep. *a* **1674** Clarendon *Hist. Reb.* x. §81 His constitution and temper might very well incline him to the Lethargick indisposition of which he dyed. **1692** Luttrell *Brief Rel.* (1857) II. 501 The lord Trevors is said to be recovered of a lethargick fitt. **1734** tr. *Rollin's Anc. Hist.* (1827) I. 132 They sank into a lethargic sloth and effeminacy. **1844** Lever *T. Burke* xxxv. (1857) 340 My lethargic apathy increased upon me. **1853** Kane *Grinnell Exp.* xxx. (1856) 262, I felt that lethargic numbness mentioned in the story books. **1860** Motley *Netherl.* (1868) II. xviii. 422 The lethargic condition of Germany rendered such threats superfluous. **1875** H. C. Wood *Therap.* (1879) 228 In three to six hours he comes out of his lethargic condition.

3. Causing lethargy.

1715-20 Pope *Iliad* xv. 876 Too long Jove lull'd us with lethargic charms. *c* **1765** Flloyd *Tartarian T.* (1785) 127/1 A lethargick vapour deprived me of my senses. **1865** Dickens *Mut. Fr.* v, Found to possess lethargic properties.

B. *sb.* A lethargic person; one who is affected with lethargy. ? *Obs.*

c **1470** Harding *Chron.* ccxl. xxvii, The frowarde heretykes That..strayen oute as they were litargykes. **1694** Salmon *Bate's Dispens.* (1713) 58/2 It..revives Apoplecticks and Lethargicks. **1750** tr. *Leonardus' Mirr. Stones* 136 (216) The white, we think, restores health to the lunatic and lethargic.

Hence † **le'thargicness**.

1633 G. Herbert *Temple, Ch.-Porch* lvi, A grain of glorie mixt with humblenesse Cures both a fever and lethargicknesse. **1727** in Bailey vol. II.

lethargical (lɪˈθɑːdʒɪkəl), *a.* [f. as prec. + -al[1].]

1. Affected with lethargy.

1651 Jer. Taylor *Holy Dying* v. § 4 (1686) 216 Distracted persons, lethargical, apoplectical, or any ways senseless and uncapable of humane and reasonable acts. **1818** in Todd; and in later Dicts.

b. *fig.* of things.

1661 Cowley *Disc. Cromwell* in *Verses & Ess.* (1669) 76 If the desire of rule and superiority be a Virtue (as sure I am it is more imprinted in humane Nature than any of your Lethargical Morals). **1668** H. More *Div. Dial.* ii. xxii. (1713) 159 Terrestrial Goodness would even grow sluggish and lethargical, if it were not..quickened by [etc.].

2. Of or pertaining to lethargy.

1617 J. Taylor (Water P.) *Taylor's Trav.* Ded. to Coriat, Tongue-tide taciturnity should haue imprisoned this worke in the Lethargicall Dungeon or bottomlesse Abisse of euer-sleeping obliuion. **1840** Hood *Up Rhine* 179 The Constrictor After dinner, while deep In lethargical sleep.

Hence **le'thargically** *adv.*, **le'thargicalness**.

1633 T. Adams *Exp. 2 Peter* ii. 6. 619 They are lethargically secure, no ruine but their owne can stirre them. **1651** N. Biggs *New Disp.* Pref. 4 Lethargically content to snore. **1664** H. More *Seven Ch.* ix. (1669) 160 That thou mayst be the more effectually rowzed up out of this Tepidity and Lethargicalnesse. **1695** *Whether Parlt. be not dissolved*, etc. 13 The old Loyalty of the Church of England Party will rouse it self out of that Lethargicalness. *a* **1777** Fawkes *Voy. Planets* 111 In dismal gloom here drones inactive lull The lazy hours, lethargically dull. **1836** E. Howard *R. Reefer* l, I became..lethargically drowsy. **1882** Miss Woolson *Anne* 7 The cold kept them lethargically honest.

†**lethargine**, *a. Obs. rare*$^{-1}$. [f. letharg-y + -ine.] Lethargic.

1656 W. Montague *Accomplish'd Woman* 4 It is a Lethargine feeling..they seem rather resuscitated than waked.

†**le'thargious**, *a. Obs. rare.* Also 6 lytargious. [f. lethargy + -ous.] Affected with or causing lethargy; lethargic.

a **1548** Hall *Chron., Ed. IV* (1809) 339 Daily obfuscate and seduced, with that lethargious and deceiable serpent, called hope of long life. *Ibid.*, *Hen. VII*, 12 Duke Fraunces was an impotent man, lytargious,..all well stryken in age. **1570** Levins *Manip.* 226/14 Lethargiouse, *lethargicus*.

lethargize ('lɛθədʒaɪz), *v.* [f. lethargy *sb.* + -ize. Gr. had ληθαργίζεσθαι *pass.*, to be forgotten.] *trans.* To affect with lethargy. Hence **'lethargized**, **'lethargizing** *ppl. adjs.*

1614 T. Adams *Devil's Banq.* v. 254 The Lethargiz'd is not lesse sicke, because hee complaines not so loud as the aguish. **1633** —— *Exp. 2 Peter* iii. 10. 1307 Others are lethargiz'd with a drousie dulnesse. **1805** Southey *Madoc* i. i, Some philtre..to lethargize The British blood that came from Owen's veins. **1817** Lady Morgan *France* (1818) I. 53 A..sergeant was giving a sort of lethargized attention..to the details which the elder dame was communicating. **1830** Coleridge *Table-t.* 23 May, All bitters are poisons, and operate by stilling, and depressing, and lethargizing the irritability. *a* **1834** —— in *Lit. Rem.* (1836) III. 8 The surest preventive or antidote against the freezing poison, the lethargizing hemlock, of the doctrine of the Sacramentaries.

lethargy ('lɛθədʒɪ), *sb.* Forms: 4 litergi, litargi, -y, lytargye, 4-6 litargie, li-, lytarge, (7 lytargie), 5-6 letargie, -ye, 6 letarge, letharge, 6-7 lethargie, (6 lithargie, lethergie), 6- lethargy. [a. L. *lēthargia* (med.L. *litargia*, after med.Gr. pronunciation), a. Gr. ληθαργία, f. λήθαργος forgetful, a derivative or compound of ληθ-, λανθάνειν to escape notice, λανθάνεσθαι to forget. Cf. F. *léthargie* (OF. *litargie*), Pr. *litargia*, Sp. *letargia*, Pg. *lethargia*, It. *letargia*.

The ME. forms in *-arge* may represent L. *lēthargus*, Gr. λήθαργος; the adj. was used subst. as a name for the disease.]

1. *Path.* A disorder characterized by morbid drowsiness or prolonged and unnatural sleep.

Negro lethargy, a disorder peculiar to the Negroes of the west coast of Africa, characterized by attacks of somnolence, and ending fatally in most instances in three to twelve months (*Syd. Soc. Lex.* 1888).

c **1374** Chaucer *Troylus* i. 674 (730) What slomberyst þou as in lytargye. **1398** Trevisa *Barth. De P.R.* xvii. iii. (Tollem. MS.), Floures þerof [of almonds] sode in oyle awakeþ hem þat haueþ þe litargy, the slepynge euel. *c* **1400** *Lanfranc's Cirurg.* 310 And þis cauterie is good for sijknes þat ben in þe partie bihinde of a mannes brayn as for þe litarge. **1501** Douglas *Pal. Hon.* i. xxvi, My daisit heid fordullit disselie, I raisit vp half in ane litargie. **1534** More *Comf. agst. Trib.* i. Wks. 1144/1 Regarding nothing, thinking almost of nothing, no more then if they laye in a letarge. **1579** Langham *Gard. Health* (1633) 227 Stroake it on the temples for the Lytargie. **1593** R. Harvey *Philad.* 26 At last a lethargy made an end of him. **1604** Shaks. *Oth.* iv. i. 54 The Lethargie must haue his quyet course: If not, he foames at mouth. **1732** Arbuthnot *Rules of Diet* 367 A Lethargy is a lighter sort of Apoplexy. **1833** *Cycl. Pract. Med.* I. 445/1 By lethargy is meant a torpor both mental and corporeal, with deep quiet sleep... This is the slightest form of coma. **1840** Dickens *Barn. Rudge* lxvi, He soon fell into a lethargy.

2. A condition of torpor, inertness, or apathy.

c **1380** Wyclif *Wks.* (1880) 372 Well myȝte we seuer þat slepe of litergi þat is fallen upon vs. **1593** Nashe *Christ's T.* 87 We (surprised with a lethargy of sinne) do nothing but laugh and iest in the midst of our sleepie security. **1601** Shaks. *Twel. N.* i. v. 132 Cosin, Cosin, how haue you come so earely by this Lethargie? **1606** Warner *Alb. Eng.* xiv. xcii, Had not hate in scottish hearts bread Lethargie of feare. **1642** in Clarendon *Hist. Reb.* vi. §196 It was a strange fatal Lethargy which had seized Our good People, and kept them from discerning, that [etc.]. **1672** Dryden *2nd Pt. Conq. Granada* Def. Epil. 174 Falling..into a carelessness, and (as I may call it) a Lethargy of thought. **1702** Pope *Sappho* 128 No tear had pow'r to flow, Fix'd in a stupid lethargy of woe. **1761** Hume *Hist. Eng.* II. xxix. 148 Men, roused from that lethargy in which they had so long slept. **1837** Dickens *Pickw.* ii, That gentleman had gradually passed through the various stages which precede the lethargy produced by dinner. **1842** Tennyson *St. Sim. Styl.* 101 Oft I fall, Maybe for months, in such blind lethargies, That Heaven, and Earth, and Time are choked. **1879** Froude *Cæsar* xxi. 356 Desperate at the lethargy of their commander, the aristocracy tried to force him into movement.

transf. **1869** Phillips *Vesuv.* v. 152 The expiring stages or intermittent lethargy of a volcano.

†**3.** A lethargic or sleepy person. *Obs.*

1634 Shirley *Example* i. i, Dormant, why Dormant, thou eternall sleeper! Who would be troubled with these lethargies about him? Dormant, are you come Dreamer.

†**'lethargy**, *v. Obs. rare.* [f. lethargy *sb.*] *trans.* To affect with lethargy.

1605 Shaks. *Lear* i. iv. 249 His Discernings Are Lethargied. **1769** Colman *Prose Sev. Occas.* (1787) III. 182 If lethargied by dulness here you sit. **1893** F. Thompson *Poems* 75 It grew lethargied with fierce bliss.

lethargy, obs. form of litharge.

‖**Lethe** ('liːθiː). Also 6 Læthe, 7 Lethee. [L. *Lēthē*, a use of Gr. λήθη forgetfulness, f. ληθ-, ablaut-var. of λαθ-, root of λανθάνεσθαι to forget.

In Gr. Λήθη is not the name of the river, though it occurs as a personification; the river is Λήθης ὕδωρ 'water of Lethe'.]

1. *Gr. Myth.* A river in Hades, the water of which produced, in those who drank it, forgetfulness of the past. Hence, the 'waters of oblivion' or forgetfulness of the past.

1567 *Gismond of Salern* ii. Chorus (Brandl *Quellen* 560), The flood of Lethe can not wash out thy fame. **1593** Peele *Hon. Garter* C 3 b, The Carle Obliuion stolne from Læthes lake. **1594** Shaks. *Rich. III*, iv. iv. 250. **1667** Milton *P.L.* ii. 583 Farr off from these a slow and silent stream, Lethe the River of Oblivion roules Her watrie Labyrinth. **1709** *Tatler* No. 63 ¶5 Who had long since been drowned in the Whirlpools of Lethe. **1872** W. R. Greg *Enigmas Life* 191 Severances of Soul for which there is neither balm nor lethe. **1883** R. W. Dixon *Mano* i. viii. 20 Thou poppy, that of Lethe art the flower.

¶**2.** [? Influenced by L. *lēt(h)um*.] Death. *rare*$^{-1}$.

1601 Shaks. *Jul. C.* iii. i. 206 Heere was't thou bay'd, braue Hart, Heere did'st thou fall, and heere thy Hunters stand Sign'd in thy Spoyle, and Crimson'd in thy Lethee.

3. *attrib.* and *Comb.*, as ***Lethe-flood***, ***lake***, ***wharf***; ***Lethe-wards*** adv.

1579 Spenser *Sheph. Cal.* Mar. 23 Tho will we little Love awake, That nowe sleepeth in Lethe lake. **1602** Shaks. *Ham.* i. v. 33 And duller should'st thou be then the fat weede That rots it selfe in ease, on Lethe Wharfe. **1613** J. Dennys *Secr. Angling* iii. xxiii, As if that Lethe-floud ran euery where. **1820** Keats *Ode to Nightingale* 4 As though of hemlock I had drunk,..One minute past, and Lethe-wards had sunk.

lethe, *a. Obs. rare.* Also 5 leyth. [Of obscure origin: perh. shortened from *lethy*, lithy, or from leathwake.] Flexible, supple.

c **1440** *Promp. Parv.* 302/1 Lethy, or weyke (*S.* leyth), *flexibilis*. **1530** Palsgr. 317/1 Lethe delyver of ones lymmes, *souple*.

lethe, obs. form of leath.

Lethean (liːˈθiːən), *a.* Also 7-8 Lethæan. [f. L. *Lēthæ-us* (a. Gr. ληθαῖος, f. λήθη Lethe) + -an.] Pertaining to the river Lethe; hence, pertaining to or causing oblivion or forgetfulness of the past.

c **1645** Howell *Lett.* III. vi. 10, I did not think Suffolk waters had such a lethæan quality in them. **1667** Milton

P.L. II. 604 They ferry over this Lethean Sound. **1697** DRYDEN *Virg. Georg.* IV. 786 Nine Mornings thence, Lethean Poppy bring. **1784** COWPER *Task* IV. 475 The craftsman there [at the tavern] Takes a Lethean leave of all his toil. *a* **1849** POE *Poems, Ulalume* v, The Lethean peace of the skies. **1850** TENNYSON *In Mem.* xliv, If Death so taste Lethean springs. **1888** A. S. WILSON *Lyric of Hopeless Love* LV. 178 No murmured Lethean lullaby.

¶ **b.** (See quot.; as if from L. *lēt(h)um* death.)

1670 BLOUNT *Glossogr.*, *Lethean*,..deadly, mortal, pestiferous.

lethed, *a. rare.* [? f. L. *lēt(h)um* death + -ED.] (See quot.)

1632 COCKERAM II, *Dead*, Defunct, Lethed, Amort. **1895** F. THOMPSON *Sister Songs* 2 On the dull earth's lethèd ear.

letheon ('liːθiːɒn). [In some way from Gr. λήθη (see LETHE); perh. meant for Gr. ληθαῖον, neut. of ληθαῖος LETHEAN *a.*] Sulphuric ether when used as an anæsthetic (see quot. 1880).

1847 *N. Brit. Rev.* VII. 173 The discoverer of what has been termed 'the Letheon'—or, at least, of the system of 'Letheonizing'. *Ibid.* 205 A convict lately..has begged to be executed while under the Letheon's influence. **1880** *Libr. Univ. Knowl.* (N.Y.) X. 241 Dr. [W. T. G.] Morton [of Boston] obtained a patent for the use of ether [as an anæsthetic], under the name of 'letheon', in 1846.

Hence **'letheonize** *v.*, *trans.* to subject to the action of letheon.

1847 *N. Brit. Rev.* VII. 178 A Mr. H. Wells..dentist, is announced as having practised letheonizing since October 1844.

lether, obs. form of LADDER *sb.*

1741 *Churchw. Acc.* in *Rutland Gloss.*, For two Rounds for yᵉ uper lether, *2d.*

lether, variant of LITHER *Obs.*, evil, bad.

† **'Lethied,** *a. Obs. rare*⁻¹. [app. for *Lethe'd* (as printed in mod. edd.) f. LETHE + -ED.] ? = LETHEAN.

1606 SHAKS. *Ant. & Cl.* II. i. 27 Epicurean Cookes, Sharpen with cloylesse sawce his Appetite, That sleepe and feeding may prorogue his Honour, Euen till a Lethied dulnesse——.

lethiferal (liː'θɪfərəl), *a. rare*⁻¹. [formed as next + -AL¹.] Causing death, fatal. In quot. *fig.*

1848 LOWELL *Biglow P.* Ser. I. Introd., I have noted two hundred and three several interpretations, each lethiferal to all the rest.

lethiferous (liː'θɪfərəs), *a.* Also **letiferous.** [f. L. *lēt(h)ifer*, f. *lēt(h)um* death: see -FEROUS.] That causes or results in death, deadly.

1651 BIGGS *New Disp.* ⁋85 Lethiferous poisons. **1653** H. MORE *Conject. Cabbal.* (1713) 29 There is none..that bears so lethiferous and poisonous fruit, as the Tree of the knowledge of the good and evil. **1684** tr. *Bonet's Merc. Compit.* XIX. 794 Convulsion and other lethiferous accidents. **1830** LYTTON *P. Clifford* iii, As we murder bishops, so is there another class of persons whom we only afflict with letiferous diseases. **1866** ROSE *Ovid's Met.* VII. 561 Pending lethiferous blasts by Auster shed.

Hence † **le'thiferousness.** *rare*⁻⁰.

1727 BAILEY vol. II, *Lethiferousness*, Death bringing Quality.

lethir, obs. Sc. f. LEATHER; var. LITHER *Obs.*

† **lethy,** *a. Obs. rare*⁻¹. In 7 **leathy.** [f. LETHE + -Y.] = LETHEAN.

1613 MARSTON *Insatiate Countess* IV. G 2 A diuell..That ha's..drown'd thy soule in leathy faculties.

lethy, obs. var. LITHY *a.*, supple, pliant.

letificant, -ate, etc.: see LÆTIFICANT, etc.

1547 BOORDE *Brev. Health* lxxxvi. 35 Wyne moderately taken doth letyfycate and dothe comforte the herte. **1599** R. LINCHE *Fount. Anc. Fict.* X iv b, Discreet taking of wine.. dooth letificate the spirits of men. **1657** TOMLINSON *Renou's Disp.* 219 It letificates man's heart.

letil, obs. form of LITTLE.

let-in, *ppl. a.*: see LET *v.*¹ 34 h.

† **'letless,** *a. Sc. Obs. rare*⁻¹. In 4 **letles.** [f. LET *sb.*¹ + -LESS.] Without let or hindrance.

1375 BARBOUR *Bruce* XVI. 568 Thai all sammyn raid thame fra, And the land letles leit thame ta.

† **'letment.** *Obs.* [f. LET *v.*¹ + -MENT.] Letting.

1574 tr. *Littleton's Tenures* 52 If the particion so made betwene them were such, yᵗ at tyme of lettement were egall of yerely value.

let-off, *sb.*: see LET *v.*¹ 35 f.

letony, obs. form of LITANY.

let-out ('lɛtaʊt), *sb.* [f. vbl. phr. *to let out* (LET *v.*¹ 37).] **1.** An entertainment on a large or lavish scale. *Anglo-Irish.*

1836 F. MAHONEY *Rel. Father Prout* (1859) 70 As if resolving the mighty project of a 'let out'.

2. An excuse, a justification, a method of avoiding (a difficulty), a release from (an embarrassing situation). Also *attrib.*

1935 M. HODGE *Grief goes Over* in *Famous Plays* 331 That's not the trouble. I am glad she is. It's a let-out. **1942** H. C. BAILEY *Dead Man's Shoes* xx. 81 The open verdict let him out, old boy... He may want a good let out over Clavell. **1955** J. L. AUSTIN *How to do Things with Words* (1962) I. 10 Yet he provides Hippolytus with a let-out, the bigamist with an excuse for his 'I do' and the welsher with a defence for his 'I bet'. **1957** *Economist* 5 Oct. 17/1 And there is no easy let-out for the complacent in the notion that landladies are by definition a narrow-minded lot. **1961** *John o' London's* 17 Aug. 195/2 When we have made all possible allowance for apotropaic amulets..and any other let-out you can think up, we are left with a solid residue of crude, unimaginative.. obscene paintings. **1971** C. BONINGTON *Annapurna South Face* xi. 138 'It would be best if you could stay at camp tomorrow and dig a platform for the second box before we arrive.' I was so tired that this sounded an easy let-out, and I agreed. **1971** 'D. HALLIDAY' *Dolly & Doctor Bird* xi. 153 Thanks for the let-out. I was just too bloody nosy. **1973** *Fremdsprachen* XVII. 57/1 It is understood that the proposed agreement would provide for a let-out clause. **1973** *Listener* 13 Sept. 346/3 The really essential problem is the increase of population..of the poor world. This is a very nice let-out for the rich countries.

3. *attrib.* or as *adj.* (See quot. 1954.)

1949 *Amer. Speech* XXIV. 92 A peltry is said to be let in if it is cut and resewed in such a manner as to fashion it broader and shorter than the original. Similarly, it is said to be let out if it is rendered longer and narrower than its first shape. **1954** WEBSTER Add., *Let-out*, of furs, subjected to a method of preparation involving cutting the pelt in strips and reassembling them to form a longer, narrower piece in which good features of color and texture are emphasized. **1967** *Boston Sunday Herald* 7 May III. 3/3 (Advt.), The recent weakness in prices in the fur market enabled us to hand pick choice lush let out natural Mink Jackets.

letovicite (lɛtəʊ'vɪtsaɪt, -'vɪsaɪt). *Min.* [ad. G. *letovicit* (J. Sekanina 1932, in *Zeitschr. f. Krist.* LXXXIII. 117), f. *Letovic-e*, the name of its original locality in Moravia, Czechoslovakia + *-it* -ITE¹.] An acid ammonium sulphate, $(NH_4)_3H(SO_4)_2$, found as colourless prismatic crystals in coal-mine waste-heaps.

1932 *Mineral. Abstr.* V. 145 Associated with this are gypsum and a new mineral (letovicite) as minute colourless pseudo-hexagonal plates. **1968** I. KOSTOV *Mineral.* II. ix. 503 Letovicite, lecontite, and mirabilite..are optically negative.

let-pass (lɛt'pɑːs, -'pæs). [f. vbl. phrase *let pass*: see LET *v.*¹] A permission to pass; a permit.

1635 COKE in *Strafford's Lett.* (1739) I. 423 The Abuse of Let-Passes. **1647** SPRIGGE *Anglia Rediv.* (1854) 65 Having seen the petitions upon which a Let-pass is desired. **1657** W. MORICE *Coena quasi κοινὴ* Def. xxiv. 243 Suffering none to come to the Sacrament without their Let-passe. **1767** T. HUTCHINSON *Hist. Mass.* (1768) II. 357 All vessels took from the governor a let pass. **1776** ADAM SMITH *W.N.* v. ii. II. (1869) II. 498 Without requiring any permit or let-pass. **1792** *Act 32 Geo. III*, c. 50 §2 Nothing..shall..require any ..letpass..where the ship..does not go to open sea. **1867** SMYTH *Sailor's Word-bk.*, *Let-pass*, permission given by superior authority to a vessel, to be shown to ships of war, to allow it to proceed on its voyage.

Letraset ('lɛtrəsɛt). The proprietary name of a system of alphabet transfers used for lettering.

1957 *Trade Marks Jrnl.* 27 Feb. 200/1 Letraset... Transfers. Art & Technics Ltd.,..London,..publishers. **1962** HANSELL & OLLERENSHAW *Longmore's Med. Photogr.* (ed. 7) xliv. 519 For both prints and slides it is a simple matter to produce a positive transparency at the same scale as the intermediate, with the lettering correctly disposed... Instant Letraset is well suited to all these requirements. **1964** *Trade Marks Jrnl.* 11 Mar. 397/1 Letraset Instant Lettering... Transfers (decalcomanias) of letters, numerals and punctuation symbols, in sheet form. Letraset Limited, ..London,..manufacturers and merchants. **1966** R. ROBERTS *Typogr. Design* iii. 51 The invention of such hand transfer lettering systems as Letraset. **1971** *Physics Bull.* Sept. 527/2 His diagrams are beautifully drawn..with lettering carried out with stencils or even Letraset.

letrure, variant of LETTRURE *Obs.*

letshewe, var. LECHWE.

letsome, -ness, var. ff. LATESOME, -NESS *Obs.*

1647 TRAPP *Comm. Matt.* xiii. 54 Be it but..the letsomness of his delivery,..it is enough. **1650** —— *Comm. Exod.* 13 Slow of speech. Of a letsome deliverie, word-bound.

let's pretend (ˌlɛts prɪ'tɛnd), *sb. phr.* [PRETEND *v.* 15 b.] A game of pretence or make-believe. Also *attrib.*, *transf.*, and *fig.*

1904 *Daily Chron.* 12 July 8/5 She entered into the spirit of the thing as heartily as if we were at games of 'Let's pretend'. **1907** *Ibid.* 16 May 5/5 It is just a song, a jig, and 'let's pretend'. **1948** *United Nations World* Dec. 92/1 The New Look..was a 'Let's Pretend' fashion. **1963** *Ingenue* Dec. 45 A Short..wrap of let's-pretend beaver (called Norba). **1964** W. GOLDING *Spire* iv. 85 But there comes a point when vision's no more than a child's playing let's pretend. **1967** *Listener* 21 Sept. 371/1 The dividing line between reality and 'let's pretend'. **1969** N. FREELING *Tsing-Boum* xii. 85 Then—everything was queer then. Double-think and let's-pretend. **1970** *Guardian* 23 Dec. 9/6, I told all the children..that Santa Claus wasn't real but a let's pretend person.

Lett (lɛt). [a. G. *Lette*, ad. the native name *Latvi.*] **a.** A member of a people living near the Baltic, mainly in Latvia; a Latvian. **b.** The language of this people; = LETTISH, LATVIAN.

1831 *For. Q. Rev.* VIII. 61 The Letts, a simple-mannered and now-existing people. *Ibid.* 70 Henry the Lett, who wrote in the 13th century. **1862** *Lond. Rev.* 16 Aug. 150 The Lithuanian proper... The Lett, one of its branches, is spoken in Esthonia, Livonia, and Courland. **1884** *Sat. Rev.* 7 June 761/1 Any Lett could make himself understood in India.

lett, obs. form of LATE *a.*¹, LEAT, LET.

lettable ('lɛtəb(ə)l), *a.* Also **letable.** [f. LET *v.*¹ + -ABLE.] That may be let.

1611 COTGR., *Affermable*,..leasable, lettable. **1796** MAD. D'ARBLAY *Lett.* Oct., We mean to make this a property saleable or letable. **1860** TROLLOPE *Framley P.* xviii, Whether the house is letable or not..I do not know. **1893** DK. ARGYLL *Unseen Found. Soc.* x. 308 This absence of hireable land in a new country is 'the cause and origin' of lettable value 'arising'. **1894** MRS. FR. ELLIOT *Roman Gossip* x. 244 A favourable position on account of..the limited number of letable quarters elsewhere.

† **'lettage.** *Obs. rare*⁻¹. In 6 **letage.** [f. LET *v.*¹ + -AGE.] The action or process of letting.

1530 *Bury Wills* (Camden) 249 Too melche nete to be leten by yᵉ churchwardens for the tyme beyng, and halfe part of the mony comyng yeerly of the letage of the sayd nete to go to [etc.].

lettanie, letanie, obs. forms of LATTEN.

1648-60 HEXHAM s.v. *Bleck*, Lettanie, that is as thinne as a leafe of gold. *Ibid.*, *Eere*, Brasse, Copper, or Letanie.

lettar(e, obs. form of LETTER *sb.*³

lett-de-camp, variant of LETACAMP.

† **'letted,** *ppl. a. Obs. rare*⁻¹. [f. LET *v.*² + -ED¹.] Hindered, impeded.

1388 WYCLIF *Exod.* iv. 10, Y am of more lettid [Vulg. *impeditioris*] and slowere tunge.

† **'letten,** *ppl. a. Obs. rare.* [obs. pa. pple. of LET *v.*¹] Let; demised, leased.

1767 *Conn. Col. Rec.* (1881) XII. 616 The rents of the said letten premises. **1798** in Root *Amer. Law Rep.* I. 463 All his right in said letten premises.

letter ('lɛtə(r)), *sb.*¹ Forms: 3 **leattre, letere,** 3-5 **let(t)re,** 5 **lettere,** 4-6 **lettur,** (4 **litter,** 5 **lettyr**), 3- **letter.** [a. or ad. OF. and F. *lettre*:—L. *littera* a letter of the alphabet (pl. *litteræ* an epistle, written documents, records), also *lītera* (in inscriptions *leitera*), of obscure origin; the hypothesis that it is connected with *linĕre* 'to smear' is now generally rejected.]

I. An alphabetic character.

1. a. A character or mark designed to represent one of the elementary sounds used in speech; one of the symbols that compose the alphabet. † *these letters* = this inscription. For ***capital, double, Roman,*** etc. ***letter,*** see the adjs.

a **1225** *Ancr. R.* 42 Þe uif lettres of vre lefdi nome. *a* **1240** *Sawles Warde* in *Cott. Hom.* 249 A gret boc..iwriten wið swarte smeale leattres. *c* **1250** *Gen. & Ex.* 993 His name ðo wurð a lettre mor..For ðo wurd abram abraham. *c* **1300** *Havelok* 2481 And þare be writen þise leteres: 'þis is þe swike' [etc.]. *c* **1375** *Sc. Leg. Saints* xliii. (*Cecile*) 111 Vith goldine lettris wrytine brad. *c* **1391** CHAUCER *Astrol.* II. §3 A capital lettre that is cleped an X. *c* **1400** MAUNDEV. (Roxb.) iii. 9 Þai wrate letters with þaire fingers. **1430-40** LYDG. *Bochas* II. xiii. (1554) 51 b, Cadmus found first letters for to wryte. *a* **1548** HALL *Chron.*, *Hen. VIII*, 73 Over whose hedde was written in letters of Romayn in gold, *faicte bonne chere quy voudra.* **1598** GRENEWEY *Tacitus, Ann.* XI. iv. (1622) 145 He added and published new letters and characters. *c* **1620** A. HUME *Brit. Tongue* (1865) 16 Thus have I breeflie handled the letteres and their soundes. **1651** HOBBES *Leviath.* II. xxvi. 141 In antient time, before letters were in common use. **1709** BERKELEY *Theory Vision* §140 The monosyllable consisting of six letters. **1809** MALKIN *Gil Blas* I. i. ⁋2 By teaching me my letters he brushed up his own learning. **1840** LARDNER *Geom.* 116 The letters *a*, *b*, *c* express respectively the sides of the triangle.

b. *sing. collective* for *pl.* Now only in ***before the letter*** (= the more usual *before letters*): a proof taken from an engraved plate before the lettering is inserted.

c **1400** *Lanfranc's Cirurg.* 93 Þe cankre haþ a propre sauour, þe which mai not be write wiþ lettre. **1642** C. VERNON *Consid. Excheq.* 43 His Clerk..writeth upon every Tally the whole letter of the Tellers Bill, that when the Tally is cloven both the foile and the stocke thereof, may have like letter upon them. **1849** THACKERAY *Pendennis* xviii, Your Stranges, and Rembrandt etchings, and Wilkies before the letter.

c. Phrases. † ***to affect, hunt, lick the letter***: to practise, or study alliteration. ***letter-by-letter***: taking each letter in its turn; also *attrib.*

1579 E. K. *Ep. Ded. to Spenser's Sheph. Cal.*, I scorne and spue out the rakehellye route of our ragged rymers (for so themselues vse to hunt the letter). **1588** SHAKS. *L.L.L.* IV. ii. 56, I will something affect the letter, for it argues facilitie. **1605** [see LICK *v.* 3]. **1624** BP. MOUNTAGU *Gagg* Pref. 18, I could have played the fool in alliteration and hunted the letter as you have done. **1836** SOUTHEY *Cowper's Wks.* III. 226 'In a firm and delicate hand'..(no doubt the same letter-by-letter writing that has before been noticed). **1951** [see COMPARATIST]. **1961** T. LANDAU *Encycl. Librarianship* (ed. 2) 194/2 *Letter by letter filing*, a method of filing..entries in a list,..the basic principle being that each heading, whether consisting of one word or more, is regarded as one unit. **1964** F. BOWERS *Bibliogr. & Textual Crit.* III. vii. 92 Palaeographical 'explanations' have a marked tendency to take it for granted that every letter must be confused with another, as if the scribe were puzzling out the word in detail, letter by letter... In reprints,..the letter-by-letter misreading posited by palaeographers is impossible. **1967** COX & GROSE *Organiz. Bibliogr. Rec. by Computer* II. 13 The ability to sort word-by-word or letter-by-letter.

d. *pl.* A round game in which the players have to form words out of letters inscribed on separate pieces of card or ivory.

1856 WHYTE MELVILLE *Kate Cov.* xxi, We sat round a large table and played at 'letters', sedulously 'shuffling' the handsome capitals as we gave each other long jaw-breaking words.

e. *colloq.* (freq. in *pl.*). A university degree or other honour (denoted by its initial letters following the name of the holder). Also (esp. *U.S.*), some other mark of distinction, usu. for achievement in sport, e.g. an abbreviation or monogram representing the name of a college or other institution.

1888 KIPLING *Plain Tales from Hills* 54 It was pleasant to be singled out by a Commissioner with letters after his name. **1915** *Chicago Daily Maroon* 10 June 1/4 The Board of Athletic Control will meet today to award letters to this year's members of the track, baseball, tennis and gymnastic teams. **1951** PARTRIDGE *Dict. Slang* (ed. 4) 1098/2 *Letters*, degree-letters after one's name: coll.: mid-C. 19–20. **1964** MRS. L. B. JOHNSON *White House Diary* 10 June (1970) 163 An Illinois boy, totally deaf, who had won awards in science and in English, and a school letter in wrestling, was scheduled.. to become a scientist. **1970** *New Yorker* 23 May 54/1 He had earned his high-school letter in four sports. **1974** L. LAMB *Man in Mist* x. 66 The heads of departments knew me... Letters arter their names as long as Dick's hatband.

2. *Printing.* **a.** *pl.* Types. ? *Obs.*

1563 *Edin. City Rec.* in *Ann. Scott. Print.* xv. (1890) 157 [He] desyrit thair lordschippes to deliuer him the saidis irnis and letteris. **1588** *Marprel. Epist.* (Arb.) 22 Waldegraves printing presse and Letters were takken away. **1613** PURCHAS *Pilgrimage* (1614) 14 Wee can no more ascribe these things to chance, than a Printers Case of letters could by chance fall into the right composition of the Bible which he printeth. **1683** S. SEWALL *Diary* I. 50 The last half-sheet was printed with my letters at Boston. **1854**, **1884**, **1892** [see LIFT *v.* 3 g].

b. *sing.* Types collectively. Also, a fount of type; a particular style of printed characters.

1588 *Marprel. Epist.* (Arb.) 23 Another printer, that had presse and letter in a place called Charterhouse. **1599** THYNNE *Animadv.* (1875) 71 Caxtone..first printed Chaucers tales in one colume in a ragged letter, and after in one colume in a better order. **1618** BOLTON *Florus* To Rdr., The words..inserted in a different letter through the text of Florus. **1683** MOXON *Mech. Exerc., Printing* 370 By broken Letter is not meant the breaking of the Shanks of any of the Letters, but the breaking the orderly Succession the Letters stood in in a Line, Page, or Form, &c. and mingling the Letters together, which mingled Letters is called Py. **1699** BENTLEY *Phal.* Introd. 3, I have distinguish'd the Former Dissertation by printing it in a Greater Letter. **1706** HEARNE *Collect.* 14 Mar. (O.H.S.) I. 204 He..is resolv'd to print in a Less Letter & in columns. **1709** *Lond. Gaz.* No. 4617/4 Printed upon Extraordinary Paper, and with a New Brevier Letter. **1719** SWIFT *Baucis & Philemon*, The ballads pasted on the wall..Now seem'd to look abundance better, Improv'd in picture, size, and letter. **1816** J. SCOTT *Vis. Paris* (ed. 5) 221 Lying pretensions..in all the varieties of a large and small letter. **1823** J. BADCOCK *Dom. Amusem.* 144 When the usual page of letter (fusil type) has been made ready for press, it is..surrounded with a moveable square of wood, which rises nearly as high as the beard of the letter. **1842** BRANDE *Dict. Sci.*, etc. s.v., There is plenty of letter.

II. Something written.

†**3. a.** *sing.* Anything written; an inscription, document, text; a written warrant or authority. **b.** *pl.* Writings, written records. *Obs.*

a. *c* **1325** *Metr. Hom.* 10 Malachye, And..Ysaie..Thai scheu bathe an wit sere letter. **13..** *E.E. Allit. P.* B. 1580 Alle loked on þat letter as lewed þay were. **1375** BARBOUR *Bruce* x. 353 The gud erll Thomas Assegit, as the lettir sais, Edinburgh. **1377** LANGL. *P. Pl.* B. XI. 198 In the olde lawe, as holy lettre telleth, Mennes sons men called vs vchone. *c* **1380** *Antecrist* in Todd 3 *Treat. Wyclif* 136 þei wole þat men preche fables & lesyngis & þerto graunte lettre. *c* **1386** CHAUCER *Monk's T.* 218 In al that lond Magicien was noon That koude expounde what this lettre mente. *c* **1475** *Songs & Carols 15th C.* (Percy Soc.) 56 To a lettere alone I me ledde, That wel was wretyn upon a wal. **1534** MORE *Treat. Passion* Wks. 1316/1 Then foloweth it in the letter. 'Hee came then vnto Simon Peter' [etc.].

b. *c* **1250** *Gen. & Ex.* 2527 And he ðat ðise lettres wrot, God him helpe weli mot. *a* **1533** LD. BERNERS *Gold. Bk. M. Aurel.* (1546) B v, For except the diuyne letters, there is nothyng so well written, but that there maie bee founde necessitie of correction. **1557** F. S[EAGER] *Sch. Vertue* 185 in *Babees Bk.* 340 If letters had not then brought them to lyght The truth of suche thynges who could nowe resyght? **1789** BRAND *Hist. Newcastle* II. 380 By letters alone the accounts of past actions can be handed down to us with accuracy.

4. a. A missive communication in writing, addressed to a person or body of persons; an epistle. Also, in extended use, applied to certain formal documents issued by persons in authority.

a **1225** *Ancr. R.* 422 Ȝe ne schulen senden lettres, ne under uon lettres, ne writen buten leaue. *c* **1275** LAY. 4496 þo sende Delgan..one deorne lettre. **13..** *Coer de L.* 1173 Kyng Rychard dede a lettre wryte (A noble clerk it gan adyte). **1362** LANGL. *P. Pl.* A. VIII. 25 Vndur his secre seal Treuþe sende a lettre. **1390** GOWER *Conf.* I. 288, I wole a lettre unto mi brother..With al my wofull herte endite. **1509** HAWES *Past. Pleas.* xxx. (Percy Soc.) 149, I shall a letter make Unto your lady, and send it by my sonne. **1535** COVERDALE *Isa.* xxxvii. 14 When Ezechias had receaued ye lettre of the messaungers, & red it. **1630** MILTON *2nd Poem Univ. Carrier* 33 His Letters are deliver'd all and gon. **1676** RAY *Corr.* (1848) 123, I have been lately solicited..by an unknown person who sent me a letter. *c* **1700** PRIOR *Epist. to F. Shepherd* 12 By penny-post to send a letter. **1777** COWPER *Let.* 20 Apr., I once thought Swift's Letters the best that could be written; but I like Gray's better. **1848** in *Gilbart's Treat. Banking* I. 150 Government were obliged to interpose by a letter, in order to protect the public from the restrictive effects of the Act. **1852** MRS. STOWE *Uncle Tom's C.* xxii, I'd teach them to..write their own letters, and read letters that are written to them. **1885** *Law Times Rep.* LIII. 479/2 Her trustees..applied by letter to Messrs. Thompson for delivery of their bills of costs.

b. *pl.* with sing. meaning, after L. *litteræ.* Chiefly in the formal or legal sense, as in ***letters dimissory***, ***letters patent***, ***letters rogatory***, etc., for which see the adjs. Also ***letters of administration***, ***caption***, ***ejection***, ***fraternity***, ***horning***, etc., for which see those words.

c **1290** *Becket* 1219 in *S. Eng. Leg.* I. 141 To þe kinge of Fraunce heo comen and lettres with heom bere fram þe king of engelond. *c* **1350** *Will. Palerne* 4842 Loo here hire owne letteres to leue it þe beter. *c* **1400** MAUNDEV. (Roxb.) xi. 41, I had lettres of þe sowdan with his grete seele. **1429** *Rolls Parlt.* IV. 345/2 Sende your Letters of Prive Seal. **1501** *Ld. Treas. Acc. Scotl.* (1900) II. 126 Ormund pursewant, to pas to summond the lard of Fivee and his folkis with lettrez in the secund forme. **1604** SHAKS. *Oth.* IV. i. 286 Did the Letters worke vpon his blood. **1629** LAUD in *Ussher's Lett.* (1686) 410, I..prevailed with his Majesty that I might write these Letters to you, which are to let your Grace understand that [etc.]. **1651** EVELYN *Mem.* (1857) I. 274, I had letters of the death of Mrs. Newton, my grandmother-in-law. **1883** R. W. DIXON *Mano* I. xvi. 53 And I shall give thee letters unto those Who there abide.

c. In phrases and special collocations. **letter of advice** (*Comm.*), a letter notifying, e.g. the drawing of a bill on, or the consignment of goods to, the correspondent. **letter of attorney**, a formal document empowering another person to perform certain acts on one's behalf (now more usually 'power of attorney'). **letter of brotherhood**, = *letter of fraternity* (see FRATERNITY 4). **letter of credit**: see CREDIT *sb.* 2 c and 10 b. **letter of intent**, a letter or similar document containing a declaration of the intentions of the writer. **St. Agatha's letters**, letters written on her day (Feb. 5) as a charm against fire (see quot. 1563). **King's Letters** (see quot. 1770). **Queen's Letter**, a circular letter to the clergy first issued by Queen Anne (see quot. 1715). **letters of slains** (*Scots law*): see SLAIN. ***to run one's letters*** (*Scots law*): see quot. 1861.

1401 *Pol. Poems* (Rolls) II. 21 Why aske ye no letters of bretherheads of other mens praiers? **1467** in *Bury Wills* (1850) 50, I will..that myn executours..make hym a letter of attorney if need be. **1563** *Homilies* II. *Idolatry* III. (1859) 225 Instead of Vulcan and Vesta..our men have placed St. Agatha and make letters on her day for to quench fire with. **1683** W. LLOYD in *Lett. Lit. Men* (Camd.) 187, I desire that whensoever you send any thing for me you would be pleased to send your letter of advice by the Post. **1715** NELSON *Addr. Pers. Qual.* 120 The Queen's Letter for making a Collection in several Parishes, in and about London and in several Cities. **1770** HAILES *Henryson's Tale of Dog, Bannatyne Poems* 280 Charges to pay or to perform, issued in the name of the Sovereign, are still termed the King's letters. **1770** COWPER *Let.* 21 Apr., To receive it [a dividend] by letter of attorney. **1825** KNAPP & BALDW. *Newgate Cal.* IV. 286/2 Having run his letters against His Majesty's advocate. **1849** FREESE *Comm. Class-bk.* 31 The letter wherein the drawing of the bill is advised, commonly called the 'letter of advice'. **1861** W. BELL *Dict. Law Scot.* s.v. *Liberation*, The prisoner may run his letters, that is, he may apply in writing to any of the Lords of Justiciary..and within twenty-four hours the judge must issue precepts to intimate to the public prosecutor and party concerned..to fix a diet for trial. **1961** WEBSTER, *Letter of intent*, a written authorization enabling officers of the federal government in time of imperative need for war materials and supplies to order the making or furnishing of such materials and supplies before the issuance of a formal contract and providing reimbursement for the contractor's expenses if no contract is subsequently issued. **1970** R. JOHNSON *Black Camels* v. 75 The news of his oil strike reached New York with a copy of the letter of intent he had exchanged with Sheikh Rasul.

d. (See quot. 1825.) *dial.* and *U.S.*

1825 JAMIESON *Suppl.* s.v. *Letter*, a spark on the side of the wick of a candle; so denominated by the superstitious, who believe that the person to whom the spark is opposite will soon receive some intelligence by letter. **1854** B. F. TAYLOR *Jan. & June* 220 Two 'letters' are snuffed from the candles. **1902** in *Eng. Dial. Dict.*

e. An article, report, or the like, setting out the social, political, or cultural, etc., tendencies in a specified place.

1782 M. G. J. DE CRÈVECOEUR (*title*) Letters from an American Farmer; describing certain provincial situations, manners, and customs, not generally known; and conveying some idea of the late and present interior circumstances of the British colonies in North America. **1848** *Manch. Guardian* 22 Nov. 5/1 (*heading*) Letters from London. (From a Private Correspondent.) **1874** GEO. ELIOT *Let.* 7 Jan. (1955) VI. 4 The Parisian letter is nicely done... The single paragraph on the pressure of radiation is worth more than the price of the paper. **1913** W. J. LOCKE *Stella Maris* v. 52 He was..the contributor..of a weekly London Letter to an American syndicate. **1955** *Radio Times* 25 Apr. 16/3 Letter from America, by Alistair Cooke. **1966** K. MARTIN *Father Figures* ix. 173 Dore was an excellent lobby correspondent, who for many years had written paragraphs about Parliament, mainly for the London Letter. **1974** *Spectator* 21 Dec. 787/3 American letter—The President gets smart—[by] Al Capp.

5. The precise terms of a statement; the signification that lies on the surface. ***the letter***: often used (after St. Paul's τὸ γράμμα) for the literal tenor of a law or statement, opposed to ***the spirit***. †***after the letter***: literally. †***in letter***: in the more literal meaning (opposed to ***in spirit***). ***to the letter***: implicitly, to the fullest extent.

1340 HAMPOLE *Pr. Consc.* 6759 þir wordes, aftir þe lettre, er hard to here. **1382** WYCLIF *2 Cor.* iii. 6 The lettre sleith, forsoth the spirit quykeneth. *c* **1400** MAUNDEV. (Roxb.) xv. 68 þai vnderstand noȝt haly writte spiritually, bot after þe letter. **1526** *Pilgr. Perf.* (W. de W. 1531) 3 God hath no suche bodyly membres, as this texte to the lettre dothe pretende. **1613** PURCHAS *Pilgrimage* (1614) 6 Cleauing as fast as we can to the letter..let vs draw as neare as we may to the sense of Moses work. **1636** MASSINGER *Bashf. Lover* v. i, To tread on My sovereign's territories with forbidden feet The severe letter of the law calls death. **1642** J. EATON *Honey-c. Free Justif.* 219 That truth which they seemed before to hold, at leastwise in letter. **1678** BUTLER *Hud.* III. ii. 609 To ..Disdain the Pedantry o' th' Letter. **1700** ASTRY tr. *Saavedra-Faxardo* I. 160 A Prince is not oblig'd by the strict Letter of the Law. **1724** A. COLLINS *Gr. Chr. Relig.* 107 And to look on reasoning from the letter to be mean and low. **1776** BENTHAM *Fragm. Govt.* Wks. 1843 I. 270 A King may ..impair the happiness of his people without violating the letter of any single Law. **1809–10** COLERIDGE *Friend* (1865) 27 He who most faithfully adheres to the letter of the law of conscience. **1821** BYRON *Sardan.* v. i. 354, I shall obey you to the letter. **1844** LD. BROUGHAM *Brit. Const.* xix. §2 (1862) 311 Applying the strict letter of the law to the circumstances. **1858** FROUDE *Hist. Eng.* III. xvi. 406 The English criminal law was in its letter one of the most severe in Europe. **1886** 'HUGH CONWAY' *Living or Dead* iv, You had better follow your father's commands to the letter. **1888** BRYCE *Amer. Commw.* II. liii. 326 Jefferson..without venturing to propose alterations in the text of the Constitution, protested against all extensions of its letter.

6. Literature in general; hence, acquaintance with it, learning, study, erudition.

†**a.** *sing. Obs.*

a **1400–50** *Alexander* 624 Arystotill.. one of the coronest clerkis þat euer knew letter. **1494** FABYAN *Chron.* VI. clxxix. 176 Lower than his fader in letter and connynge.

b. *pl.* †Also ***good letters*** (*obs.*). Occasionally, the profession of literature, authorship. ***man of letters*** [= F. *homme de lettres*]: a man of learning, a scholar; now usually, a man of the literary profession, an author. ***Commonwealth***, ***republic of letters***: see those words.

a **1250** *Prov. Ælfred* in *O.E. Misc.* 106 Ne may non ryhtwis king..Bute if..he cunne lettres lokie him seolf one, hw he schule his lond laweliche holde. **1483** CAXTON *Cato* B j b, By letters and by scyence is the man made semblable or lyke to god. *c* **1532** DU WES *Introd. Fr.* in Palsgr. 894 Well lerned in good lettres. **1577** NORTHBROOKE *Dicing* (1843) 54 Learning and good letters to yong men bringeth sobrietie. **1611** BIBLE *John* vii. 15 How knoweth this man letters, hauing neuer learned? **1645** EVELYN *Mem.* (1857) I. 146 There were likewise the effigies of the most illustrious men of letters. **1693** WOOD *Life* (O.H.S.) IV. 50, I..have from my youth laboured in good letters. **1708** PARTRIDGE *Bickerstaff detected*, He was bred to letters, and is master of a pen. **1720** WATERLAND *Eight Serm.* 330 Such an Abuse of the Readers, as one shall seldom meet with among Men of Letters. **1751** HARRIS *Hermes* (1841) 111 He has always been a lover of letters. **1766** GOLDSM. *Vic. W.* xiv, It was sufficient to show me that he was a man of letters. **1811** SCOTT *Prose Wks.* IV. *Biographies* II. (1870) 191 Lord Minto, himself a man of letters, a poet and a native of Teviotdale. **1827** HALLAM *Const. Hist.* (1876) II. x. 188 That life of exile and privacy which religion and letters would have rendered tolerable to the King. **1855** PRESCOTT *Philip II*, I. vi. (1857) 95 Letters kept pace with art. **1880** *Athenæum* 10 Jan. 56 Several guests well known in letters were present. **1891** *Speaker* 2 May 532/1 Metaphysics have again condescended to speak the language of polite letters.

7. = *French letter* s.v. FRENCH *a.* 3.

c **1888–94** *My Secret Life* II. 318 My cock and the letter would not agree. **1916** [see CAP *sb.*[1] 13 d].

8. *attrib.* and *Comb.* **a.** simple attributive, chiefly in sense 4, as ***letter-bag***, ***-boy***, ***-change***, ***-clip***, ***-envelope***, ***-file***, ***-form***, ***-name***, ***-post***, ***-sequence***, ***-shape***, ***-slit***, ***-string***, ***-tray***. **b.** objective and obj. gen., as ***letter-bearer***, †***-kerner***, ***-opener***, ***-sorter***; ***letter-copying***, ***-writing***.

1809 T. BROWN in *Naval Chron.* XXII. 294 The *letter-bag was saved. **1838** DICKENS *O. Twist* xlviii, The guard was standing at the door, waiting for the letter-bag. *c* **1340** *Cursor M.* 7907 (Fairf.) Al *letter-berers for-þi ta ensaumple be vrry. **1816** JANE AUSTEN *Emma* II. ix. 176 A stray *letter-boy on an obstinate mule. **1846** R. GARNETT in *Proc. Philol. Soc.* II. 233 On certain Initial *Letter-changes in the Indo-European Languages. **1859** SALA *Gas-light & D.* xviii. 204 *Letter-clips, portfolios, music-cases. **1858** in *Abr. Specif. Patents Printing* II. (1864) 3 Stands for *letter-copying presses. **1798** W. HUTTON *Autobiog.* 24 Pencils, Cards, ..*Letter-files, Maps and Pictures. **1895** *Montgomery Ward Catal.* 40/1 The 'Boss' File is the very best letter file ever sold at the price. **1911** O. ONIONS *Widdershins* 294 The shelf on which I kept my letter-files... My files contained..my agent's letters. **1955** E. POUND *Section: Rock-Drill* lxxxvii. 33 Windeler's vision: his letter file the size of 2 lumps of sugar, But the sheet legible. **1908** *Westm. Gaz.* 22 Aug. 14/1 He looks forward to the invention of *letter-forms that will be much simpler and much more legible than the traditional symbols. **1937** *Discovery* Dec. 362/2 The letter-form of the calligrapher. **1963** *Times Lit. Suppl.* 4 Jan. 16/3 The changing use of type and letterforms in English. **1683** MOXON *Mech. Exerc., Printing* xiii. ¶4 They..left the *Letter-Kerner, after the Letter was Cast, to Kern away the Sholdering. **1889** *Cent. Dict.*, *Letter-name. **1934** PRIEBSCH & COLLINSON *German Lang.* v. iii. 261 Rhyme-forms and spelling out names by means of new letter-names applied to the alphabet. **1961** R. B. LONG *Sentence & its Parts* xvii. 388 Examples are *IQ* and *TV*, in which the component letters are given their individual letter-name pronunciations. **1898** *Westm. Gaz.* 8 Dec. 3/1 New ideas in pencil-cases and *letter-openers. **1823** BENTHAM *Not Paul* 286 Between Thessalonica and Athens..there was not..any established *letter-post. **1929** D. H. LAWRENCE *Let.* 9 July (1962) II.

1163 If I seal them letter-post they may hold them and make more fuss. **1953** *Language* XXIX. 72 The *letter-sequences QL, TSR, SSS.. never occur in English spelling. **1964** W. R. LEE in D. Abercrombie et al. *Daniel Jones* 288 There are various *letter-shapes to grasp. **1845** *Punch* VIII. 53 The Clerk.. hearing a knocking at the outer door, looks through the *letter-slit. **1851** H. MELVILLE *Whale* xxxi. 147 No ordinary *letter-sorter in the Post-office is equal to it. **1964** *Language* XL. 168 The omission of a given *letter-string from a dictionary is no assurance that the combination is not an English word. **1907** *Yesterday's Shopping* (1969) 356/2 *Letter Trays. Fitted with spring clip, 4to..0/9. **1788** COWPER *Let. to Mrs. King* 6 Dec., My *letter-writing time is spent, and I must now to Homer. **1791** BOSWELL *Johnson* 8 May an. 1781 We talked of letter-writing. **1837** LOCKHART *Scott* xlix. (1839) VI. 235 He varied his style of letter writing according to the character.. of his.. correspondents.

9. Special Combs.: **letter-balance**, a contrivance for ascertaining the weight of a letter; **letter-ballot**, a ballot in which the papers are sent by post; **letter-board** (*Printing*), a board on which matter in type is placed for convenience in handling; **letter-bomb**, an explosive device sent through the post as a weapon of terror; **letter-book**, a book in which letters are (†written or) filed, or in which copies of letters are kept for reference; **letter-bound** *a.*, characterized by close adherence to the letter of a law; **letter-box**, (*a*) a box in which letters are kept; (*b*) one in which they are deposited for transmission by post or on delivery; (*c*) *Mountaineering* (see quot. 1968); (*d*) in espionage (see quot. 1961); hence **letter-box** *v. nonce-wd.*, to put (a letter) into a letter-box; **letter-carrier**, one who carries letters either as a private messenger or as a public official; **letter-case**, (*a*) a case to hold letters; †(*b*) an envelope; **letter-corporal**, one entrusted with the duty of fetching and delivering letters; †**letter-cover**, an envelope; **letter-cutter**, one who makes punches for type-founding; so **letter-cutting**; **letter-drop** (*U.S.*), a slot into which letters may be dropped, as into a post-office or postal car (*Cent. Dict.*); **letter-dropper** *nonce-wd.* (see quot.); **letter-founder, -founding, -foundry** = *type-founder*, etc.; **letter-head**, (*a*) a sheet of letter-paper with a printed or engraved heading giving address, date, or the like; (*b*) *dial.*, a postage stamp; **letter-heading** (see quot.); **letter-high** *a.* (*Printing*), of the same height as the ordinary printing-type; **letter-house** *dial.* = POST-OFFICE; **letter-leaf**, an epiphytic orchid of the genus *Grammatophyllum*, so named from the markings on the leaves; **letter-learned**, †(*a*) learnt from letters or books; (*b*) = BOOK-LEARNED; **letter-learning** = BOOK-LEARNING; **letter-lichen**, a lichen of the genus *Opegrapha* or order *Graphidei* (see quot.); **letter-lock**, a lock which can be opened only by arranging letters attached externally so as to form the word on which the lock is set; **letter-man**, (*a*) one of the Chelsea pensioners who was entitled to extra pay on the ground of a letter from the sovereign; (*b*) *U.S.*, a sportsman who has received a letter of distinction (see sense 1 e above); **letter-mark**, a letter used as a contraction or symbol; †**letter-money**, in the Civil War, the money contributed to the support of the royal army in response to Charles I's letters; †**letter-monger** *nonce-wd.*, a forger of letters; **letter-office** = POST-OFFICE; **letter-ornament**, a decoration made up of the forms of letters; **letter-paper**, paper for writing letters; as a trade term, restricted to the quarto size, the smaller sizes being called *note-paper*; **letter-perfect** *a.*, (*a*) *Theatr.*, knowing one's part to the letter; (*b*) literally correct, verbally exact; *fig.* flawless, unexceptionable; **letter-plant** = *letter-leaf*; **letter plate**, a plate for fixing to the outside of a door or wall and having a rectangular aperture, covered by a flap, through which letters may be put; **letter-punch**, a steel punch used in making matrices for type; **letter-quality** *a.*, that produces print of a quality suitable for business letters (esp. of a printer attached to a computer); of correspondence, etc.: printed to this standard; **letter-rack**, (*a*) a tray with divisions to hold an assortment of types; (*b*) a small frame in which letters or papers are kept; **letter-racket** *slang* (see quot.); †**letter-receiver**, one who receives letters for transmission by post; **letter-scale**, a scale for weighing letters; **letter-space** *Printing*, a space inserted between the letters of a word; so **letter-spaced** *a.*, **letter-spacing** *vbl. sb.*; **letter-stamp**, a stamp used at a post-office for cancelling postage-stamps or for impressing notifications on letters or parcels; **letter-struck** *a. nonce-wd.*, smitten with the love of learning; **letter-weigher**, a device for weighing letters; **letter-weight** = *paper-weight*; †**letter-will** *Sc.*, one's testament; **letter-winged** *a.*, of a kite, having the wings marked as if with letters (*Cent. Dict.*); **letter-wood**, the wood of the South American tree *Brosimum Aubletii*, which is marked with black spots resembling letters or hieroglyphics; **letter-word**, a runic symbol or ideogram signifying both the name for something and a specific single letter; a word wholly or partly consisting of a letter or letters which are abbreviations in themselves; **letter-worship**, an undue attention to the letter of a law or commandment; **letter-writer**, (*a*) one who writes letters (hence used in the titles of manuals of letter-writing); (*b*) a machine for taking copies of letters. Also LETTER-CARD, LETTER-PRESS.

1880 G. N. LAMPHERE *U.S. Govt.* 240/1 Supplying the post-offices entitled thereto with blanks,..twine, *letter-balances, and cancelling-stamps. **1901** *Chambers's Jrnl.* Sept. 577/1 A German firm brought out a folding letter-balance, on the pan of which were engraved the British postal rates and the legend, 'Made in Germany'. **1961** *Lebende Sprachen* VI. 70/1 Letter scale (or: balance), die Briefwaage. **1898** *Engineering Mag.* XVI. 126/1 This resolution.. submitted to the Society at large in the form of a *letter-ballot. **1683** MOXON *Mech. Exerc., Printing* vii, *Letter-Boards are Oblong Squares..of clean and well-season'd Stuff. **1948** *Times* 4 Aug. 4/5 Each of the *letter bombs which he has examined contained sufficient explosive to cause fatal injuries if detonated at close quarters. **1949** KOESTLER *Promise & Fulfilment* xiii. 149 His brother was killed by a letter-bomb sent by the Stern Group. **1972** *Times* 20 Sept. 1/3 One of the unexploded letter bombs. **1973** *Guardian* 28 June 26/5 A letter bomb exploded yesterday in the hands of a Londonderry solicitor ..the first casualty of the letter-bomb campaign in Northern Ireland. **1974** *Ibid.* 26 Jan. 26/5 A letter bomb exploded at the head office of Pilkington Brothers, the glass manufacturers. **1776** J. ADAMS in *Fam. Lett.* (1876) 224 It would fill this *letter-book to give you all the arguments for and against this measure. **1892** SIR R. V. WILLIAMS in *Law Times Rep.* LXVII. 234/1 The letter-book satisfies me that Mr. Norton was right. **1643** MILTON *Divorce* II. xx, That *letter-bound servility of the canon doctors. **1812** *Examiner* 30 Nov. 766/1 The libel was found in the *letter-box of the Newspaper. **1849** THACKERAY 4 Sept. in *Scribner's Mag.* I. 683/1, I put the letter into the unpaid-letter box. **1951** E. COXHEAD *One Green Bottle* iii. 78 The rib bore them upward, perpetually varied,.. now parallel cracks, now a groove, now a letter box... The climb above the crux was even more delightful. **1955** J. THOMAS *No Banners* xvi. 144 A circuit had to be organized into leak-proof compartments with letter-boxes or couriers as the only links between them. **1961** R. SETH *Anat. Spying* iii. 44 The 'letter-box' is a long-standing method of channelling information to the chief. It may be an accommodation address..or it may be a loose brick in a wall. Sometimes one member of a group acts as a 'letter-box' under his own name and at his home address. **1968** P. CREW *Encycl. Dict. Mountaineering* 79/1 *Letter-box*, a rectangular hole in a narrow rock ridge; a hole formed by jammed blocks or flakes of rock anywhere on a rock face. **1969** HURD & OSMOND *Smile on Face of Tiger* vii. 241 The silly girl popped out of the Home Office and they [*sc.* minutes] were in her usual letter-box within the hour. **1971** R. PETRIE *Thorne in Flesh* xv. 187 Aury, apparently, had been a live letterbox for a French security organisation. **1807** W. TAYLOR in Robberds *Mem.* II. 187 It is better.. that I should *letter-box it here. **1552** HULOET, *Letter carier, *ambulus, libellio, tabellarius.* **1697** LUTTRELL *Brief Rel.* (1857) IV. 304 A warrant is come from his majestie, appointing Mr. Vanhulse, the Dutch secretary, to be court letter carrier. **1828** MISS MITFORD *Village* Ser. III. 20 Such another Dick and such another donkey, who acted as letter-carriers to that side of the village. **1967** *Boston Sunday Globe* 23 Apr. 13/1 Letter carriers in the 25 cities and towns in the Boston Postal District are delivering notices to 565,000 families and business firms, advising them of their own Zip code for use in return addresses. **1973** WODEHOUSE *Bachelors Anonymous* ix. 123 'You're American, aren't you?' said Amelia Bingham. 'I thought so. It was your saying "letter-carrier" instead of postman.' **1973** *Black Panther* 15 Sept. 5/2 Attrition is also used to get rid of workers, especially letter carriers. **1672** T. JORDAN *Lond. Triumph.* 16 By Ladies *Letter-case, [He] Shall have a better place. **1790** MAD. D'ARBLAY *Diary* Nov., My memorial was always in my mind; my courage never rose to bringing it from my letter-case. **1823** J. BADCOCK *Dom. Amusem.* 44 Let a person choose any one of them [cards], and inclose it in a letter-case. **1896** MRS. CROKER *Village Tales* I Tips to the mess-servants, the *letter-corporal, and colour-sergeant. **1742** RICHARDSON *Pamela* IV. 233 Her Handkerchief, and *Letter-cover. **1683** MOXON *Mech. Exerc., Printing* xii. ¶1 A *Letter-Cutter should have a Forge set up. *Ibid.* p. 81 *Letter-Cutting is a Handy-Work hitherto kept so conceal'd among the Artificers of it. **1711** ADDISON *Spect.* No. 59 ¶2 The Lipogrammatists or *Letter-droppers of Antiquity. **1683** MOXON *Mech. Exerc., Printing* xi. ¶23 To let you know how the *Letter-Founder Cuts the Punches. **1887** T. B. REED (*title*) History of the Old English Letter Founders. **1769** *Connect. Col. Rec.* (1885) XIII. 273 Resolved..that the Treasurer.. pay out of the public treasury to said Buel one hundred pounds.. conditioned that he set up and pursue the art of *letter-founding in this Colony. *a* **1887** JEFFERIES *Field & Hedgerow* (1889) 88 At the village post-office they ask for '*Letterhead, please Sir', instead of a stamp. **1887** *Harper's Mag.* Mar. 649/2 He drew up a note upon the 'tavern' letter-head. **1871** *Amer. Encycl. Printing* (ed. Ringwalt), *Letter-Headings*, lines printed at the head of sheets of letter-paper, containing the residence, and generally the name and place of business, of the party for whom such work is done. **1683** MOXON *Mech. Exerc., Printing* ii. ¶2 In the choice of his Brass Rules, he examines that they be exactly *Letter high. **1832** MISS MITFORD *Village* Ser. v. 47 The *letter-house had lately acquired another occupant. **1866** *Treas. Bot.*, *Letter-leaf* or *Letter-plant*. **1649** *Warn. Jac. Beem* xxviii. 18 That selfe-reason which without Gods spirit is onely *letter-learned. **1770** WHITEFIELD *Wks.* (1772) VI. 30 The letter-learned Scribes and Pharisees in our Saviour's time. **1678** R. BARCLAY *Apol. Quakers* (1841) 283 As for *letter learning, we judge it not so much necessary to the well being of one. *a* **1845** HOOD *To Tom Woodgate* ix, All letter-learning was a line you, somehow, never crossed. **1856** W. L. LINDSAY *Brit. Lichens* 245 *Graphideaceæ*..in allusion to the resemblance of the apothecia..to ancient hieroglyphics or written characters. For the same reason the *Graphideæ* are popularly designated '*Letter Lichens' or 'Scripture-worts'. **1850** CHUBB *Locks & Keys* 6 Another description of lock is that well known by the name of the '*Letter Lock'. **1724** *Lond. Gaz.* No. 6230/2 All the Out-Pensioners (as well *Letter-men as others) belonging to the said Hospital [Chelsea]. **180.** in A. H. Craufurd *Gen. Craufurd & Light Div.* (1891) 34 An increase in the pay and in the number of letter men. **1926** *Chicago Tribune* 19 Sept. II. 5/4 The letter men in the line are Wolf and Neff, guards, and Rouse, center. **1974** *Spartanburg* (S. Carolina) *Herald-Jrnl.* 21 Apr. B1/1 Now he is well on the way to becoming Spartanburg High School's first four-sport letterman in at least seven years. **1907** *Congregational Year Bk.* p. xxix, The following *letter-marks and signs are adopted:—B. (Baptist); C.H. (Countess of Huntingdon's Connexion). *a* **1674** CLARENDON *Hist. Reb.* IX. §27 The *Letter Money and Subscription Money being almost exhausted. **1699** BENTLEY *Phal.* 171 Our *Letter-monger has Herodotus's very words. **1689** *Lond. Gaz.* No. 2486/4 Whoever gives notice of the said Robbers to the General *Letter-Office at London, shall be very well rewarded. **1711** *Royal Proclam.* 23 June, ibid. No. 4866/1 That..there be one General Letter-Office and Post-Office established in the City of London. **1837** DICKENS *Pickw.* xxxiii, Sam..stepped into the stationer's shop, and requested to be served with a sheet of the best gilt-edged *letter-paper. **1888** JACOBI *Printer's Vocab.*, *Letter-paper.* This term is applied to quarto paper—note paper being octavo. **1845** *Ainsworth's Mag.* VII. 83 'I am *letter-perfect,' said another [actor]. **1867** *Harper's Mag.* Aug. 405/1 Where [legal] papers are to be served, and copies must be letter-perfect. **1885** J. K. JEROME *On the Stage* 133 He would be letter perfect in all by the following Thursday. **1894** 'MARK TWAIN' in *Century Mag.* Apr. 822 Tom's conduct had remained letter-perfect during two whole months. **1929** F. M. FORD *Let.* 10 July (1965) 186 If you will send me the better copy to look through I will certainly make it as letter-perfect as I can. **1969** *Time* 31 Jan. 1 The performances by such Bergman regulars as Max von Sydow and Gunnar Björnstrand are letter-perfect. **1898** F. W. MACEY *Specifications in Detail* 247 Knockers and *letter plates are..made in iron and gun-metal, and vary in price from 3s. to £1 10s. **1923** *Work* 17 Nov. 161/2 A section through the door, showing the relative positions of the letter-plate and the box, is given by Fig. 3. **1971** *Country Life* 1 Apr. 752/3 Letter plates are easily bought. **1977** *Forbes* (N.Y.) 1 Aug. 27/2 At one end of the low-to-medium priced *letter-quality printing equipment spectrum is the typewriter. **1981** *Computer Design* June 192/1 (*heading*) Character printers provide letter quality hard copy at 55 chars/s. **1985** *Personal Computer World* Feb. 71/1 (Advt.), Qume's Sprint 11 Plus is the smartest choice in a letter-quality printer for your IBM PC. **1871** *Amer. Encycl. Printing* (ed. Ringwalt), **Letter-rack*, a rack for containing wood and metal letters of such a size that it would be inconvenient to keep them in cases. **1812** J. H. VAUX *Flash Dict.*, **Letter-racket*, going about to respectable houses with a letter or statement, detailing some case of extreme distress, as shipwreck, sufferings by fire, &c. **1683** *Lond. Gaz.* No. 1812/4 Many of the *Letter-Receivers are Tradesmen. **1895** *Montgomery Ward Catal.* Index, *Letter scale. **1900** A. UPWARD *Wonderful Career E. Lobb* 307 Be it enough To move the index of a letter-scale But in the estimation of a hair. **1961** Letter scale [see *letter-balance*]. **1934** WEBSTER, *Letter-space. **1967** KARCH & BUBER *Offset Processes* iv. 125 Modification is possible to condense, expand,..letter-space and drop-out shadows in Benday screens. **1959** R. HOSTETTLER et al. *Technical Terms Printing Industry* (ed. 3) 120/2 One point *letter-spaced, espacé un point. **1954** *Southward's Mod. Printing* (ed. 8) I. xxix. 178 *Letterspacing. Spaces are also used for rendering uniform the thick perpendicular lines of capitals and fancy letters. **1961** T. LANDAU *Encycl. Librarianship* (ed. 2) 195/1 *Letter-spacing*, extra spacing between the letters of a word, especially in a running title or title-page. **1973** *Collins's Authors & Printers Dict.* (ed. 11) 247/2 *Letterspacing*,.. shown in MS. by a stroke between letters, and # above (one word). **1667** EVELYN *Pub. Employm.* 77 There is nothing more stupid than some of these μουσοπάτακτοι, *letter-struck men. **1862** *Illustr. Catal. Internat. Exhib., Industr. Dept., Brit. Div.* II. No. 5825, Inkstand, pen-tray, blotting-book, book-slide, *letter-weigher. **1907** *Yesterday's Shopping* (1969) 366/2 Folding Portable Letter Weigher.. to weigh up to 16 oz...each 1/8. **1880** GEO. ELIOT *Let.* 7 Feb. (1956) VII. 249 He left me the beautiful *letter-weight. **1923** P. SELVER tr. *Čapek's R.U.R.* I. 5 A large 'knee-hole' writing-table on which stand an electric lamp,.. letter-weight, [etc.]. **1596** in Dickson & Edmond *Ann. Scot. Printing* 478 Followis the Deidis Legacie and *Lettrewill. **1598** *Ibid.* 365 Made his Testament and Lettre-Will. **1698** FROGER *Voy.* 129 *Letter-wood (as they call it). **1892** *Manufacturer's Circular*, Letterwood, £12 10s. to £50 per ton. **1927** JOYCE *Let.* 2 Mar. (1957) I. 250 A Chinese student sent me some *letterwords I had asked for. The last one is ɯ. It means 'mountain' and is called 'Chin'. **1934** PRIEBSCH & COLLINSON *Germ. Lang.* v. 253 The emergence of 'letter-words' like *D-zug..L-zug..P.S...G.m.b.H.* **1948** D. DIRINGER *Alphabet* 519 A manuscript containing the poem ..of King Alfred's time..which describes in verse each runic letter-word. **1879** FARRAR *St. Paul* (1883) 117 The subtler..idolatry of formalism and *letter-worship. **1710** ADDISON *Whig Exam.* No. 2 ¶4 Our *Letter-writer here alludes to that known verse in Lucan. **1759** (*title*) The Complete Letter-Writer. **1855** OGILVIE, Suppl., *Letter-writer*..an instrument for copying letters. **1888** *Athenæum* 14 Jan. 43/2 The same desire impels thousands of persons to write letters to the newspapers; but these letter-writers are not usually journalists.

Hence **'letterlet, 'letterling** *nonce-wds.*, a little letter. †**'letterly** *adv.*, to the letter; literally.

c **1440** HYLTON *Scala Perf.* (W. de W. 1494) II. xxvi, Yf they may fulfill letterly [*corrected* letterally 1499] the commaundementes of god. **1781** TWINING in *T. Papers* (1887) 5 Your reproaches about stretch-work, short lines,

and letterlings. **1836** *Coleridge's Lett., Convers.*, etc. II. 109, I judge..from the numberless Letter-lets in my possession.

letter ('lɛtə(r)), *sb.*^{2} Also 5 letere, 8 *Sc.* latter. [f. LET *v.*^{1} + -ER^{1}.] One who lets, in senses of the vb.; *esp.* one who allows another the use of (apartments, a horse, house, etc.) for hire.

1552 HULOET, Letter of house or lande, *cœnacularius.* **1671** CROWNE *Juliana* I. Dram. Wks. 1873 I. 28 By his tone a kind of letter of lodgings. **1723** *Lond. Gaz.* No. 6175/6 Thomas Jenkins,..Letter of Horses. **1851** MAYHEW *Lond. Labour* (1861) II. 230 The letters of rooms are the most exacting in places crowded with the poor. **1885** *Law Reports* 14 Q. Bench Div. 892 The relation..between hirers and letters of private carriages. **1893** *Field* 10 June 832/1 Builders and letters of boats might object.

b. In *Comb.*, as agent-noun corresponding to various phrasal combinations of the vb., as † *letter-blood, letter-loose, letter-out*; **letter-go**, one who 'lets go'; in Sc. use (*letter-gae*) a jocular synonym for 'precentor', after A. Ramsay (quot. 1715).

c **1400** *Lanfranc's Cirurg.* 299 A man þat schal be letere blood schal be ȝong. **1611** MARKHAM *Country Content.* I. vii. (1615) 104 He which was chosen Fewterer or letter loose of the Grey-hounds. **1616** B. JONSON *Horace's Art Poetry* 234 A careless letter-go Of money. **1671** H. M. tr. *Erasm. Colloq.* 267 The letter out of the Horses at first was silent. **1715** RAMSAY *Christ's Kirk Gr.* II. xvi, The latter gae of haly rhime, Sat up at the boord-head. *c* **1750** ASTON *Suppl. to Cibber* 8 She [Mrs. Bracegirdle] was the Daughter of a..Letter-out of Coaches. **1815** SCOTT *Guy M.* xi, There was no sae money hairs on the warlock's face as there's on Letter-Gae's ain at this moment. **1847** *Whistle-Binkie* (Scot. Songs) Ser. v. (1890) II. 169 The lettergae trying new tunes.

† **'letter**, *sb.*^{3} *Obs.* Also 4 lettere, -our, 4–6 lettar(e. [f. LET *v.*^{2} + -ER^{1}.] One who lets or hinders.

a **1300** *Cursor M.* 16888 Yond traitur, yond letter of vr lai. **1362** LANGL. *P. Pl.* A. I. 67 He is a lettere of loue. **1387–8** T. USK *Test. Love* I. iii. (Skeat) l. 126 For soche lettours, it is harde any soche iewell to winne. **1434** MISYN *Mending Life* 107 Violence he doys to all his lettars. **1494** FABYAN *Chron.* VII. ccxlii. 283 The letter of this iourney..was Rycharde duke of Guyon. **1523** *Act 14 & 15 Hen. VIII*, c. 1 If any clothmaker..be letted..than the letter..to..forfait..xiid. **1563** ABP. PARKER *Articles*, Whether your Persons, Vicars and Curates be..letters of good religion. **1616** J. DAVIES *Complim. Verses* in *Capt. Smith's Descr. New Eng.*, Thy Letters are as Letters in thy praise.

letter ('lɛtə(r)), *v.* [f. LETTER *sb.*^{1}]

† **1.** *trans.* To instruct in letters or learning. *Obs.*

c **1460** G. ASHBY *Policy Prince* 648 Poems (E.E.T.S.) 33 Yf god sende you children..Do theim to be lettred right famously.

2. To exhibit or set forth by means of letters; also, to distinguish by means of letters.

1668 WILKINS *Real Char.* IV. iv. 440 It would be convenient, that every one of these Instances should be Philosophically Lettered. **1869** TYNDALL *Notes Lect. Light* 46 Fraunhofer..lettered them and made accurate maps of them. **1877** FARRAR *In Days of Youth* i. 3 He [God] letters it [his name] in fire amid the stars of heaven.

3. To affix a name or title in letters upon (a book, a shop, etc.); to inscribe (a name) in letters. Also, to inscribe *with* (something).

1712 ADDISON *Spect.* No. 463 ¶7, I observed one particular Weight lettered on both sides. **1714** *Lond. Gaz.* No. 5225/3 The binding each Book will be..4*s.* Letter'd on the Back. **1755** JOHNSON *Let. to Warton* 20 Mar. in *Boswell*, I hope to see my Dictionary bound and lettered next week. **1844** E. WARBURTON *Crescent & Cross* (1845) II. 420 The greater number of the shops are lettered in the same tongue [Italian]. **1876** GEO. ELIOT *Dan. Der.* IV. xxxiii, There might be a hundred Ezra Cohens lettered above shop-windows. **1877** *Act 40 & 41 Vict.* c. 60 §3 Every canal boat..shall be lettered, marked, and numbered in some conspicuous manner.

4. *intr.* In occasional uses. **a.** To carry letters. **b.** To write letters.

c **1645**, **1681**, **1813** [see LETTERING]. **1840** DICKENS *Barn. Rudge* xxiv, Our people go backwards and forwards.. lettering, and messaging. **1861** BP. WILBERFORCE *Diary* 22 Feb. in *Life* (1882) III. i. 15 Did not go out at night, but lettered.

letterane, obs. form of LECTERN.

‖**lette'rato.** *Obs.* [It.:—L. *litterātus*; cf. LITERATUS.] A man of letters; a learned man.

1656 EARL MONM. *Advt. fr. Parnass.* 14 That unluckie Laconick Letterato.

letterature, obs. form of LITERATURE.

letter-card. [Cf. F. *carte-lettre*, G. *kartenbrief*.] The official designation of a folded card, having a gummed and perforated edging, so as to be closed and sent through the post (with an impressed or an affixed stamp) as an ordinary letter.

Introduced in Belgium in 1882, in Great Britain in 1892, and now used in many countries of the world.

1892 (Feb.) *Instructions on Letter Card*, To open the letter card, tear off the edge at the perforation. **1892** *Daily News* 12 Feb., Letter-cards impressed with a penny postage stamp.. are now on sale at every post-office... The letter-cards will be subject to all the regulations affecting letters. **1898** G. B. SHAW *Philanderer* II. 107, I wish you'd ask her not to write on letter-cards. **1939** E. AMBLER *Mask of Dimitrios* x. 194 He bought a *pneumatique* letter-card. **1954** I. MURDOCH *Under Net* viii. 116 We..bought two letter cards. **1971** D. POTTER *Brit. Eliz. Stamps* ix. 94 A popular item in the suite of stationery is the familiar letter-card. They combine the convenience of envelope and paper with the secrecy of an ordinary letter.

lettered ('lɛtəd), *ppl. a.* Forms: 4–5 lett(e)rid(d, -yd, 4–6 lett(e)red, *Sc.* letterit, -yt, 5–6 letterd(e, 6 *Sc.* lettiret, 4– lettered. Also 4 y-lettrede. [f. LETTER *sb.*^{1} or *v.* + -ED.]

1. Acquainted with or instructed in letters; learned, literate, educated.

1303 R. BRUNNE *Handl. Synne* 7894 Prest wel y-lettrede ys to blame, þat [etc.]. *c* **1350** *Will. Palerne* 4088 A ful loueli lady lettered at þe best. *c* **1375** *Sc. Leg. Saints* xxvii. (*Machor*) 957 Twa of Irland þat..sum dele letteryt ware. *a* **1400–50** *Alexander* 2241 Lettrid berne Quare-to feynys þou þis fare? **1481** CAXTON *Godfrey* clxi. 238 Peter bertilmewe, clerk and but litil lettred. **1535** STEWART *Cron. Scot.* (1858) II. 684 Ane letterit man profound in all science. **1561** DAUS tr. *Bullinger on Apoc.* (1573) 12 Agaynst those lettered heretickes Iohn speaketh playnly. **1571** HANMER *Chron. Irel.* (1633) 125 They inquired not whether..their Ministers were lettered. **1588** SHAKS. *L.L.L.* v. i. 48 Mounsier, are you not lettred? **1605** CAMDEN *Rem., Epigr.* 14 A man well borne and better lettered. **1689** EVELYN *Mem.* (1857) III. 305 London, abounding with so many wits and lettered persons. **1713** STEELE *Guardian* No. 94 ¶5 The lettered coxcombs without good-breeding give..just occasion to rallery. **1750** JOHNSON *Rambler* No. 2 ¶14 It may not be unfit for him who makes a new entrance into the lettered world..to suspect his own powers. *a* **1822** SHELLEY *Def. Poetry* Pr. Wks. 1888 II. 17 The bucolic writers, who found patronage under the lettered tyrants of Sicily and Egypt. **1855** MILMAN *Lat. Chr.* (1864) II. 3 The unlettered barbarians willingly accepted the aid of the lettered clergy.

absol. **1362** LANGL. *P. Pl.* A. I. 125 Lereþ hit þis lewed men for lettrede hit knoweþ. *c* **1425** *Eng. Conq. Irel.* lvii. 134 He ..toke, both of letred & of lewed, þe cursed tallages of gold & of siluer. **1433** LYDG. *S. Edmund* App. 374 Symple and lettryd ther heedys did enclyne.

2. Of or pertaining to learning or learned men; characterized by learning or literary culture.

1709 PRIOR *To Dr. Sherlock on Death* 31 Wit may admire, and letter'd Pride be taught. **1775** JOHNSON *West. Isl.* Wks. X. 317 And entertained with all the elegance of lettered hospitality. **1798** S. ROGERS *Ep. to Friend* 137 This sheltered scene of lettered talk. **1826** DISRAELI *Viv. Grey* I. i, He was a man of lettered tastes. **1850** HAWTHORNE *Scarlet L.* Introd. (1883) 45 This was my all of lettered intercourse. **1875** TENNYSON *Q. Mary* II. i, He loved the more His own ..letter'd peace.

3. Composed of a (specified) number of letters.

1608 WILLET *Hexapla Exod.* 346 That foure lettered name of God.

4. Inscribed with letters; *spec.* of a book: Having the title, etc. on the back in gilt or coloured letters.

1665 J. WEBB *Stone-Heng* (1725) 163 A letter'd and straight and long Order denotes..the Conflicts of Combatants. **1707** *Lond. Gaz.* No. 4293/3 Gilt-back, and Letter'd. **1712** ADDISON *Spect.* No. 463 ¶6, I observed one particular Weight lettered on both Sides. **1740** DYER *Ruins Rome* 324 Phoebus' letter'd dome. **1746–7** HERVEY *Medit.* (1818) 12 The next thing which engaged my attention was the lettered floor. **1809** R. LANGFORD *Introd. Trade* 80 Hervey's Meditations, calf lettered. *a* **1813** A. WILSON *Th. Churchyard* Poet. Wks. (1846) 13, I woo thee, thoughtful, from this letter'd stone. **1868** BROWNING *Ring & Bk.* I. 82 One glance at the lettered back. **1872** W. S. SYMONDS *Rec. Rocks* vi. 169 Camden, who speaks of a lettered stone he saw.

letteree (lɛtə'riː). [f. LETTER *sb.*^{1} + -EE.] (See quot.)

1672 PETTY *Pol. Anat.* (1691) Advt., By Letterees are meant persons restored to Land by virtue of the Letters of King Charles the Second. *Ibid.* 2 There was restored to Letterees and Nominees..60 [acres].

letteret ('lɛtərɪt). [f. LETTER *sb.*^{1} + -ET^{1}.] A little or short letter.

1817 BYRON *To Moore* 25 Mar., I have written to you..six letters, or letterets. **1822** LAMB *Lett.* xii. *To B. Barton* 114 Begging you to accept this letteret for a letter. **1835** HOOD in *Mem.* (1860) I. 107 A little letteret that cannot do anybody any harm.

lettergram ('lɛtəgræm). [f. LETTER *sb.*^{1} + TELE)GRAM.] A telegram delivered by the postman with the ordinary mail. (Disused.)

1911 *World's Work* XVII. 447/2 'Lettergrams' of fifty words..for an inclusive fee of about two shillings over any distance. **1915** J. WEBSTER *Dear Enemy* 19 When you feel so bursting with talk that only a hundred word telegram will relieve an explosion, at least turn it into a night lettergram. **1921** *Chambers's Jrnl.* Dec. 834/1 An attendant handed him a night lettergram. **1966** *Commonwealth of Australia Post Office Guide* 294 Lettergrams are reduced rate messages which may be lodged only at capital cities and certain other offices having extended hours of service. They are transmitted by telegraph and delivered to addressees by the earliest post on the following working day.

lettering ('lɛtərɪŋ), *vbl. sb.* [f. LETTER *v.* or *sb.*^{1} + -ING^{1}.]

1. The action of writing letters; letter-writing.

c **1645** HOWELL *Lett.* (1650) II. 118 You may give the law of lettering to all the world. **1681** *Disc. Tanger* 3 If I exceed the Laws of Lettering, your command is my Apology. **1813** BYRON in Moore *Lett. & Jrnls.* (1830) I. 464, I hate lettering.

2. The action or process of putting letters upon (anything) by inscribing, marking, painting, gilding, printing, stamping, etc. Also *concr.*, the letters inscribed.

1811 L. M. HAWKINS *C'tess & Gertr.* I. 261 The letterings of his books had..afforded her a high hope of pleasure. **1832** G. R. PORTER *Porcelain & Gl.* 241 The dial-plate is complete, with the exception of the figures or lettering. **1869** J. RAVEN *Ch. Bells Cambr.* (1881) 12 The rudeness of the lettering seems to suggest an early date. **1877** *Act 40 & 41 Vict.* c. 60. §3 Such lettering, marking, and numbering shall include the word 'registered'..and the registered number. **1879** MISS BRADDON *Vixen* III. 146 The book was to have.. a smooth grey linen binding with silver lettering.

3. *attrib.* and *Comb.*: **lettering block, -box** (see quots.); **lettering piece**, the piece of leather on which the title of a book is stamped; **lettering-tool**, 'a bookbinder's tool for stamping the gilt titles on the backs of books' (Knight *Dict. Mech.* 1875).

1871 *Amer. Encycl. Printing* (ed. Ringwalt) 74 **Lettering-block*, a piece of wood, the upper surface being rounded, upon which side-labels are lettered. **Lettering-box*, the box in which the type are screwed up preparatory to lettering. **1818** *Art Bookbinding* 30 Working the letters firm and straight on the *lettering-piece. **1880** *Print. Trades Jrnl.* No. 31. 11 Some account-book lettering-pieces produced..for the trade are certainly wonderful specimens of lettering.

lettering, obs. Sc. form of LECTERN.

letterize ('lɛtəraɪz), *v.* [f. LETTER *sb.*^{1} + -IZE.] *intr.* To write letters.

1824 LAMB *Lett.* xiv. *To B. Barton* 134 The idea of letterising has been oppressive to me of late. **1837** B. BARTON *Select.* (1849) 11, I have felt unequal to any letterizing.

letterless ('lɛtəlɪs), *a.* [f. LETTER *sb.*^{1} + -LESS.] Devoid of letters.

1. Unacquainted with letters or literature; illiterate. Also *absol.*

a **1618** SYLVESTER *Quadrains of Pibrac* xcvii, 'Tis to be more than Sylla Letter-lesse. **1653** WATERHOUSE *Apol. Learning* 125 A meer daring letterless Commander can.. promise himself no more successe in his Enterprise then [etc.]. **1756** LAW *Lett. Import. Subj.* 24 They help the ignorant and letterless to..a knowledge of God. **1860** *Q. Rev.* CVIII. 225 Silbury Hill..the attempt of a letterless race to perpetuate the memory of some event. **1880** P. GREG *Errant* II. v. 59 Bookless captain and letterless subaltern. **1884** *Century Mag.* XXVIII. 157 There was an illiterate generation, and a letterless race to be educated.

2. Having no letters or correspondence.

1837 *Lett. fr. Madras* (1843) 62 Unfortunate beings so letterless as to be able to pay them [*sc.* visits]. **1884** BP. THOROLD *Yoke Christ* 105 A London Sunday..is absolutely letterless. **1886** MRS. A. HUNT *That other Person* II. 49 She wrote to him each day, and bemoaned her letterless condition.

3. Having no letters inscribed or appended.

1881 *Education* Feb., The title..was only retained by those who would have been absolutely letterless but for this domestic honour. **1886** MACLEOD *Clyde District Dumbartonsh.* i. 6 This ancient letterless slab.

letterlet, -ling, letterly: see LETTER *sb.*^{1}

lettern, letteroun, obs. forms of LECTERN.

'letter-press. [f. LETTER *sb.*^{1}]

1. (Now commonly written *letterpress.*) **a.** The text of a piece of printing, distinguished from illustrations, etc. **b.** Material printed from a relief surface, distinguished from lithographic or intaglio printing. Also *attrib.*, as in ***letterpress printing*** (for which the use of the word in this sense may be elliptical).

1758–65 GOLDSM. *Ess.* ii, Four extraordinary pages of letter-press. *a* **1764** LLOYD *Puff* Poet. Wks. 1774 I. 176 Plain letter-press shall do the feat. **1772** *Hartford Merc.* 18 Sept. Suppl. 4/3 Letter-press Printing is neatly perform'd. **1802–12** BENTHAM *Ration. Judic. Evid.* (1827) III. 473 *note*, In the case of letter press, any such alterations are as yet, perhaps, without example. **1825** J. NICHOLSON *Operat. Mechanic* 711 Plaster of Paris..is poured over the letter-press page. **1828** MISS MITFORD *Village* Ser. III. Introd. 1 They who condescend to read the letter-press will have the advantage of my fair correspondent. **1840** LARDNER *Geom.* 137 In letter-press printing, the types..are put together.. with their faces upwards. **1860–1** FLO. NIGHTINGALE *Nursing* ii. 11 The places where..letter-press printers.. have to work for their living. **1861** *Sat. Rev.* 7 Dec. 591 William and Mary Howitt have contributed the letterpress. **1889** *Spectator* 14 Dec. 830 In this cartoon, and the letterpress concerning it, are commemorated [etc.]. **1892** A. POWELL *Southward's Pract. Printing* (ed. 4) i. 2 *Letterpress printing.* In this the subject is printed from a relief *above* the surface. *Ibid.* 3 Letterpress printing is done with types, blocks of wood, casts in metal, india-rubber, celluloid; electrotypes, &c. **1925** *Southward's Mod. Printing* (ed. 5) II. xxxiii. 274 These methods [of illustration] may be tabulated thus:—For printing by the letterpress method—Wood engravings; Engravings on type metal; Process blocks in line; Process blocks in half-tones... All the above blocks are in relief. **1939** *Guide Exhib. in King's Library* (Brit. Mus.) 9 The Old Testament types are explained in two paragraphs of woodcut letterpress in the upper corners of the design. **1946** W. L. HAYES in H. Whetton *Pract. Printing & Binding* xxv. 287/1 Relief printing, as its name implies, is that in which the printing surface stands in relief, that is, above the surrounding non-printing area; identified in this category is letterpress from type, plate, half-tone and line blocks, wood and lino cuts. **1959** *Penrose Annual* LII. 113 It was.. decided to use a plate etched as shallow as was practicable and to print by 'letterpress-offset'. **1966** *Print* (Wynkyn de Worde Soc.) iv. 39 The basic characteristic of the lithographic process is that the printing image is flat: not raised as in letterpress or recessed as in gravure. **1970** K. LINDLEY *Woodblock Engravers* ii. 29 They [*sc.* Bewick's woodcuts]..enabled the letterpress printer once more to think in terms of books equal to those with copperplate illustrations. **1971** M. MOORMAN in D. Wordsworth *Jrnls.*

107 In 1809–10 W[ordsworth] wrote the letter-press for Wilkinson's drawings of the Lake District.

2. A weight to keep one or more letters in place.

1848 C. A. JOHNS *Week at Lizard* 78 They [pieces of rock] are often worked into.. letter-presses, &c.

3. A press for taking copies of letters.

1901 *Westm. Gaz.* 13 June 9/2 Van Helden.. slipped a handcuff upon his wrist, and fastened the other to the letter-press.

letter(r)ure, variant of LETTRURE *Obs.*

letterset ('lɛtəsɛt). [f. LETTER(-PRESS + OFF)SET *sb.*] (See quot. 1963.) Cf. DRIOGRAPHY.

1963 *Publishers' Weekly* 5 Aug. 87/1 A new name, 'Letterset', for what was formerly called 'dry litho' has been coined. Letterset refers to printing through the use of relief wrap-around plates and an intermediate blanket cylinder to transfer the image to the surface being printed. **1967** V. STRAUSS *Printing Industry* vi. 288/1. In 1962 Miehle and du Pont coined the term 'letterset'.. for indirect relief printing. Dry offset of the past and contemporary letterset are based on the same principle but differ widely in actual performance. **1973** S. JENNETT *Making of Bks.* (ed. 5) x. 166 Indirect letterpress or letterset are terms used for letterpress printing on to a blanket cylinder and then on to paper, after the manner of litho offset; the printing surface is a shallow etched metal or plastic plate curved round the plate cylinder.

lettes(se, lettewys, obs. ff. LETTUCE, LETTICE.

Lettic ('lɛtɪk), *a.* (*sb.*) [f. LETT + -IC.] Of, pertaining to, or related to the Letts; = LETTISH. Also, in wider sense, applied to the group of languages (by some philologists called *Baltic*) comprising Lettish, Lithuanian, and Old Prussian, and to the group of peoples speaking these languages. Also *absol.* as *sb.*, the Lettic or Lettish language.

1872 R. MORRIS *Eng. Accidence* i. 8 The Lettic Languages. (1) Old Prussian.. (2) Lettish or Livonian.. (3) Lithuanian. **1880** *Libr. Univ. Knowl.* (N.Y.) VIII. 835 The Lettic race proper still in Courland, in Livonia. **1881** FREEMAN *Hist. Geog. Eur.* I. xi. 466 *note*, A common name for these closely allied nations is sometimes needed. *Lettic* is the most convenient.

†**'lettice.** *Obs.* Also 5 letuse, -uce, letvis, 6 letewis, letuis, lettewys, lettis(e, -yce, -ys, -ushe, 6–7 letwis. See also LITUIT. [a. OF. *letice*, *-is(s)e*, etc., app. a. OHG. *illitiso*, mod.G. *iltiss* polecat; but the application of the name has varied at different times.] A kind of whitish grey fur (Cotgr.).

[**1363** *Act 37 Edw. III*, c. 12 Qels ne usent revers dermynes ne de letuses esclaire. **1373** in *Exch. Rolls Scot.* II. 440 In empcione trium timbrarum de letysses cum dimidio, et septem letisses varii precii.] *a* **1450** *Knt. de la Tour* (1868) 65 Her good and gay clothing, and furres of gray meniuere and letuse. **1457** *Sc. Acts Jas. II* (1814) II. 49/2 As to þeir gownys þt na woman weir mertrikes nor letviss. **1502** *Will of Wrattesley* (Somerset Ho.), My secunde cap of letewis. **1542** *Inv. R. Wardrobe* (1815) 100 Ane gown.. quhairof the slevis hes bein liynit with letuis. *a* **1548** HALL *Chron.*, *25 Hen. VIII* (1809) 803 The lorde Chauncellor in a robe of Scarlet open before bordered with Lettice. **1662** *Stat. Irel.* (1765) II. 406 Letwis tawed, the timber, containing forty skins 8s. 4d.

b. *attrib.* and *Comb.*, as ***lettice-bonnet***, ***-fur***; **lettice-cap**, a cap of this fur, apparently worn as a means of inducing sleep; **lettice-ruff**, a person wearing a ruff or collar of this fur.

1599 MINSHEU *Sp. Dict.*, A *Lettice bonnet or cap for gentlewomen, v. *Albanéga*. [*Ibid.*, *Albanega*, a kind of networke coife that women weare on their heads.] **1544** *Will of R. Cressey* (Somerset Ho.), *Lettys cappes. **1583** STUBBES *Anat. Abus.* I. (1879) 69 Some weare Lattice cappes with three hornes, three corners I should saie, like the forked cappes of Popishe Priestes. **1619** FLETCHER *M. Thomas* III. i, Bring in the Lettice cap. You must be shaved sir, And then how suddenly wee'l make you sleep. **1621** —— *Thierry & Theod.* v. ii. K 2 Phisitians, some with glisters, Some with lettice caps, some posset drinkes, some pills. **1533** WRIOTHESLEY *Chron.* (1875) I. 20 Gownes of scarlett edged with white *lettushe furre. **1624** FLETCHER *Wife for month* II. iv, Is this *Lettice Ruffe your husband?

lettice, obs. form of LATTICE, LETTUCE.

‖**lettiga** (let'tiga). Also lettica, latiga. [It. *lettica*, *lettiga*:—L. *lectica* a litter.] (See quots.)

1805 W. IRVING in *Life & Lett.* (1864) I. 114 Wynn and Wadsworth were seated in a Lettiga, a kind of sedan chair that accommodates two persons who sit facing each other. **1811** J. BOWDLER *Select Pieces* (1817) I. 54 Mr. Burgman had been so good to provide me with proper mules and a latiga for travelling. **1821** EARL ABERDEEN in Sir H. Gordon *Life* iii. (1893) 68, I must positively have you carried to the spot in a lettica. **1838** H. G. KNIGHT *Normans in Sicily* 148 The lettiga is a small vis-à-vis, carried on long poles by two mules.

letting ('lɛtɪŋ), *vbl. sb.*¹ [f. LET *v.*¹ + -ING¹.] The action of LET *v.*¹ in various senses.

1. The action of allowing the movement or passage of, giving loose or vent to; chiefly with adverbs, as *down*, *in*, *off*. Also *letting blood*, *letting go*.

1423 JAS. I *Kingis Q.* xli, Onely throu latting of myn eyen fall. **1482** *Monk of Evesham* (Arb.) 107 The lyftyngys vppe of the crosse and the lettyngys done ageyne. **1530** PALSGR. 239/1 Lettyng of blode, *seignee*. **1662** STILLINGFL. *Orig. Sacr.* III. i. §16 Man is formed with a mouth.. for receiving and letting forth of air. **1665** MANLEY *Grotius' Low C. Warres* 149 The letting in of the Waters, and other things.. were hindred. **1668** WILKINS *Real Char.* II. i. §5. 38 Letting go. **1839** BAILEY *Festus* (1854) 219 The good we do is of His own good will,—The ill, of His own letting. *a* **1849** H. COLERIDGE *Ess.* (1851) I. 97 Some wise-acres.. would think it a woful letting-down. **1852** MRS. STOWE *Uncle Tom's C.* ix, She couldn't wear one of your gowns, could she, by any letting down? *a* **1861** CLOUGH *Mari Magno* 692, I.. knew the letting-off of steam, and rose. **1861** TRENCH *Sev. Ch. Asia* 78 Such a letting go of first love. **1864** MRS. GATTY *Parables fr. Nat.* Ser. IV. 109 He thought his father's argument a letting down of principle. **1917** J. AGATE *Buzz, Buzz!* 9, I hold such statement of the actual and practical scope of current criticism not to be a letting-down of the art we hold dear. **1940** *Chambers's Techn. Dict.* 496/1 *Letting-down*, the process of tempering hardened steel by heating it until the desired colour is reached and then quenching. **1958** *Ibid.* 990/1 *Letting down*, the reduction of altitude from cruising height to that required for the approach to landing. **1966** J. & R. GODDEN *Two under Indian Sun* iii. 68 The letting down of hems or takings in, as dresses were handed down.

2. The action of allowing the use of (houses, lands, etc.) on payment of rent, etc.; leasing. Also with *out*.

1538 *Lichfield Gild Ord.* (E.E.T.S.) 8 All men which haue or hold ony tenement of the lettyng of the master and the wardens. **1656** H. PHILLIPS *Purch. Patt.* (1676) 1 The letting and taking of Leases. **1669** WOODHEAD *St. Teresa* II. xxii. 139 Not the Season for letting of houses. **1790** BURKE *Fr. Rev.* Wks. V. 252 Where the letting of their land was by rent [etc.]. **1833** HT. MARTINEAU *Cinnamon & Pearls* ii. 20 The letting of the Pearl banks had been accomplished. **1883** R. RITCHIE *Bk. Sibyls* ii. 83 He.. reorganized the letting out of the estate. **1885** *Act 48 & 49 Vict.* c. 77 §7 If any land is comprised in a lease for.. lives, or in a letting for a term of years. **1894** *Times* 5 Feb. 4/3 The Irish grass lettings are making high prices.

letting ('lɛtɪŋ), *vbl. sb.*² *arch.* [f. LET *v.*² + -ING¹.] The action of LET *v.*²; delaying, hindering, an instance of this; also quasi-*concr.*, a hindrance, an obstacle; frequent in † ***but, without letting***, without hindrance, without delay.

c **1020** *Rule St. Benet* (Logeman) 87 Oðer lettincge þæt he na þoliȝe. *a* **1122** *O.E. Chron.* an. 1101 (Laud MS.) Se cyng syððan scipa ut on sæ sende his broðer.. to lættinge. *a* **1240** *Ureisun* in *Cott. Hom.* 187 þe bitternesse of mine sunnen attri is þe lettunge. *c* **1250** *Gen. & Ex.* 3204 Non man on hem letting dede. *c* **1290** *S. Eng. Leg.* I. 263/76 With-oute lettingue In heo ȝeode. *a* **1300** *Cursor M.* 3199 O þis letting was he ful glad. *Ibid.* 4914 For drightin dos vs na letting. **1375** BARBOUR *Bruce* II. 12 The lord the bruce, but mar letting, Gert priuely bryng Stedys twa. *c* **1375** *Sc. Leg. Saints* iii. (*St. Andrew*) 974 þat mycht be hendringe to myn fame, and lattinge als to ȝore gud name. *c* **1380** WYCLIF *Sel. Wks.* III. 425 Seynt Poule biddes men preye wiþouten lettynge. *c* **1400** *Melayne* 1503 Go we to your company.. Late ther be no Lettynge. *c* **1470** HENRY *Wallace* IX. 1183 And our he swam; for lattyng fand he nocht. **1486** MARG. C'TESS OXFORD in *Four C. Eng. Lett.* 7 To the letting of his seid purpose. **1502** *Ord. Crysten Men* (W. de W. 1506) I. i. 8 He maye be in the waye of saluacyon if he haue none other lettynge. **1657** *Divine Lover* 299 The waye is.. full of.. theiues, and many other greate lettings.

†**b.** Wasting (of time). *Obs.*

1398 TREVISA *Barth. De P.R.* XVII. xx. (1495) 616 Whiche were ouer noyouse and gretly lettynge of tyme to reherse theym here al arowe. **1494** FABYAN *Chron.* v. cxvii. 92 To shewe here the vayne and dissymulyd sorowe that Fredegunde made for the Kynge, it were but lettynge of tyme.

†**'letting,** *ppl. a. Obs. rare.* [f. LET *v.*² + -ING².] That lets or hinders; hindering.

c **1450** tr. *De Imitatione* I. xxi. 26 Blisfull is he þat may putte awey euery letting distraccion.

lettirmareday: see LATTER.

lettis(e, obs. f. LATTICE, LETTICE, LETTUCE.

Lettish ('lɛtɪʃ), *a.* (*sb.*) [f. LETT + -ISH.] Pertaining to the Letts or their language. Also *absol.* as *sb.*, the language of the Letts.

1831 *For. Q. Rev.* VIII. 63 One of the most important personages of the ancient Lettish mythology. **1841** LATHAM *Eng. Lang.* 3 The Livonian (or Lettish) of Livonia and of Courland. **1842** PRICHARD *Nat. Hist. Man* 183 These dialects are the Lettish, Lithuanian, and the Proper Pruthenian. **1881** FREEMAN *Hist. Geog. Eur.* I. xi. 466 *note*, *Lett*, with the adjective *Lettish*, is the special name of one of the obscurer members of the family. **1888** KING & COOKSON *Sound & Inflex.* ii. 34 The Baltic family contains the three divisions of Old Prussian, Lithuanian, and Lettish.

Letto- ('lɛtəʊ), combining form repr. mod.L. *Lettŏn-*, *Letto*, used with adjs. or sbs. denoting other languages or peoples, signifying 'Lettish and..', as ***Letto-Lithuanian***, ***-Slavonic***, etc.

1880 A. H. SAYCE *Introd. Sci. of Lang.* II. vii. 107 The old middle or intransitive voice.. has been lost in Keltic and Letto-Slavonic. **1913** L. W. LYDE *Continent of Europe* 419 These are the Letto-Lithuanians and Finnic (Esht) peoples of the Baltic Provinces. **1920** *Glasgow Herald* 21 July 8 A Polono-Lithuanian, a Polono-Lettish, and a Letto-Lithuanian question still unsettled. **1935** HUXLEY & HADDON *We Europeans* vii. 221 The Letto-Lithuanians tend to be of medium height, but taller where remote from Slav influence.

Lettonian (lɛ'təʊnɪən), *a.* and *sb.* [f. mod.L. *Lettōn-*, *Letto* LETT + -IAN. Cf. LAPPONIAN, and F. *Letton* = LETT.] = LETTISH.

1880 *Libr. Univ. Knowl.* (N.Y.) VIII. 835 The Lettonian differs from the other Lithuanian dialects in having an admixture of Finnish words.

lettorne, obs. form of LECTERN.

lettorye, obs. form of LECTUARY.

lettour, obs. form of LECTERN, LETTER *sb.*³

‖**lettre** (lɛtr). The French word for 'letter' in:

a. lettre de cachet (lɛtr də kaʃɛ), lit. 'letter of seal', a warrant issued in the France of the *ancien régime* for the imprisonment of a person without trial at the pleasure of the monarch. Also *transf.* Cf. CACHET 1.

1718 VANBRUGH *Let.* 30 Aug. in *Athenæum* (1890) 30 Aug. 290/2, I am far from having the least doubt of his intentions to me; I fear only those same letters [*sic*] de cachet, that surprise folks every now and then. **1745** H. WALPOLE *Let.* 1 Aug. in *Corr.* (1941) IX. 23 Before the play itself is suppressed by a *lettre de cachet* to the booksellers. **1799** MALTHUS *Diary* 16 July (1966) 159 [Norway] These men seemed to have been placed by lettres de cachet exactly similar to those in France. **1824** SCOTT *Redgauntlet* III. vi. 163 There are sharp laws in France against refractory pupils—*lettres de cachet* are easily come by. **1849** THACKERAY *Pendennis* I. vii. 70 Why are there no such things as *lettres-de-cachet*—and a Bastille for young fellows of family? **1895** S. WEYMAN *From Mem. Minister of France* 138 M. de Clan.. is for shutting him up. Getting a *lettre de cachet*.. and away with him. **1916** A. HUXLEY *Let.* 31 Mar. (1969) 96 A lettre de cachet from a Lord Lieutenant.. can put one snugly away in the Jail or Jug without any prospect of a trial for periods quite indefinitely coextensive with the war or even eternity. **1957** C. BROOKFIELD tr. *Durkheim's Professional Ethics & Civic Morals* vii. 87 Louis XIV, clearly, was able to issue his *lettres de cachet* against anyone he wished.

b. Used as the first element in **lettre bâtarde, lettre de forme, lettre de somme**, to designate groups of early type-faces based on manuscript forms then current, now more often described as BASTARDA, TEXTURA, and ROTUNDA or fere-humanistica types.

1887 T. B. REED *Hist. Old Eng. Letter Foundries* i. 53 The Gothic letter employed by the inventors of printing for the *Bible*, *Psalter*, and other sacred works, was an imitation of the formal hand of the German scribes... This letter, as a typographical character, took the name of Lettre de Forme. *Ibid.*, The term [sc. *lettre de forme*].. was used by both Tory and Ycair to denote a class of letter which the former denominated *Canon*, or cut according to rule, as opposed to the more fanciful *lettres bâtardes*. *Ibid.* 54 The Lettre de Somme of the Germans.. became in the hands of the fifteenth century printers a rival to the Gothic. **1922** D. B. UPDIKE *Printing Types* I. iv. 60 Fifteenth century Gothic type-forms may be roughly sub-divided into Pointed, sometimes called *lettre de forme*, Round, sometimes called *lettre de somme*, and a vernacular Cursive black-letter, like the French *lettre batarde*... These three type-forms were the black-letter equivalents of the formal, less formal, and cursive manuscript-hands of the Roman period. *Ibid.* 63 The *lettre de somme* is said (without much authority) to derive its name from the *Summa* of St. Thomas Aquinas, for which.. it was early employed. **1927** R. B. MCKERROW *Introd. Bibliogr.* 289 The *lettre de forme*,.. derived from the most formal script,.. is in general of a rather narrow and pointed character, tending everywhere to angularity. *Ibid.*, Certain of the smaller sizes used by Wynkyn de Worde and Grafton.. seem very definitely to have that feeling of breadth and openness which is characteristic of the *lettre de somme*. *Ibid.*, The *lettre bâtarde* represents the cursive hand of its time. **1962** N. E. BINNS *Introd. Historical Bibliogr.* (ed. 2) xiv. 182 The rigid and formal types of this group are known as *Textura* types, or.. *Lettre de Forme*. *Ibid.*, A broader, rounder, and less formal kind of type known as *Fere-Humanistica*, or *Lettre de Somme*. *Ibid.* 185 The early German and French printers also used various cursive types.. known as *Bastarda*, or *Lettre Bâtarde*.

lettren, -on(e, -une, obs. forms of LECTERN.

lettrine (lɛ'triːn). [a. Fr.] An initial letter, often decorated, and larger than the size of the text it accompanies.

1932 JOYCE *Let.* 11 Nov. (1957) II. 326 He liked her alphabet and has written to the manager of Burns and Oates about using these *lettrines* for a reprint of Chaucer's A.B.C. poem. **1934** *Ibid.* 25 Apr. (1966) III. 302, I enclose.. two *lettrines* of hers. **1970** *Private Library* III. 174 Wood engravings such as the 'lettrine' (initial letter) that figures at the beginning of this article.

lettrism ('lɛtrɪz(ə)m). Also in Fr. form **lettrisme**. [ad. F. *lettrisme*, f. LETTER *sb.*¹ + -ISM.] Applied to a movement in French art and literature, characterized by a repudiation of meaning, and the use of letters (sometimes invented) as isolated units. So **'lettrist, lettriste** *sb.* and *a.*

1946 *Time* 2 Dec. 31/2 Lettrism, founded by Isidore Isou.. is a theory of poetry as 'rhythmic architecture'. The rapidly growing hordes of Lettrists.. prefer meaningless combinations of letters to dictionary words. **1948** *Spectator* 9 Apr. 432/2, I have been reading this week some poems written in the new mode of '*lettrisme*'. **1949** *Commentary* VIII. 183/2 'The new art,' declared Isou (his real name is Isidore Goldstein), 'accepts as its subject matter the letters reduced to, and become simply, themselves, replacing completely all poetic and musical elements which go beyond the letters in order to shape them into coherent works.' Thus was born Lettrisme, which may be regarded as a resurrection of some old avant-garde theories, or as a postwar symptom comparable to the explosions of Surrealism and Dada after World War I. **1951** *Amer. Mercury* LXXII. 659 In no time at all he [*sc.* Isidore Isou] was writing 'lettrist' poetry and he and his followers were assaulting the ears of everybody in the cafés of the Latin Quarter. **1962** *Times Lit. Suppl.* 13 Apr. 246/4 Hausmann's lettrist interview with some hypothetical French *lettristes*.

1964 *Ibid.* 3 Sept. 796/3 Lettrism is a creative movement.. which claims to be able first to revolutionize every aesthetic discipline.. from poetry to the theatre, by way of painting, and then to renovate the other cultural domains, whether philosophical or scientific. **1971** J. WILLETT in A. Bullock *20th Cent.* 244/2 The Lettrists in Paris and the Brazilian concrete poets of the 1950s, who were alike in their concentration on the appearance and sound of words or individual letters.

†**lettrure.** *Obs.* Also 4–5 letterure, (4 letrure, letterrure, lettyreure, 5 lectrure, litterure). [ad. OF. *letrëure, lettrëure*:—L. *litterātūra*, f. *littera* letter.]

1. A writing, a written book, a story. ***holy lettrure*** = Holy Scripture.

13.. *K. Alis.* 3516 Ac, for that lettrure seith ther ageyn, Nul Y schewe hit to no mon. **1377** LANGL. *P. Pl.* B. x. 27 'Lo!' seith holy letterrure 'whiche lordes beth this shrewes'. *a* **1400–50** *Alexander* 2170 Luctus it hiȝt, þe letterure & þe line þus it callis. *c* **1450** LONELICH *Grail* lv. 240 In Caldev was this scripture, whiche Is to vndirstonde As be lettrure.

2. Knowledge of letters or books; learning.

13.. *E.E. Allit. Poems* A. 750 Ne arystotel nawþer by hys lettrure Of carpe þe kynde þese propertez. *a* **1340** HAMPOLE *Psalter* lxx. 9 For .i. not knew lettyreure. **1393** LANGL. *P. Pl.* C. I. 137 For in loue and in letterure lith þe grete eleccion. *c* **1400** *Lanfranc's Cirurg.* 138 He cowde not no lettrure. *a* **1420** HOCCLEVE *De Reg. Princ.* 2073 Simple is my goost, and scars my letterure. **1447** BOKENHAM *Seyntys* (Roxb.) 275 She of lettrure no Kunnyng had. **1483** CAXTON *Gold. Leg.* 276/2 Seynt Augustyn was quycke in engyne Swete in speche wyse in lettrure.

3. Science of or skill in (arms).

13.. *Gaw. & Gr. Knt.* 1513 Þe lel layk of luf, þe lettrure of armes.

lettsomite (ˈlɛtsəmaɪt). *Min.* [Named by Percy, 1850, after Dr. W. G. *Lettsom*: see -ITE.] A synonym of cyanotrichite (see CYANO-).

1850 DANA *Min.* 523 Lettsomite.. occurs in spherical globules. **1883** *Encycl. Brit.* XVI. 402 Lettsomite.. [occurs] in tufts of capillary crystals.

lettuce (ˈlɛtɪs). Forms: 3–6 letus(e, 4–6 lettuse, 5 latewes, 5–6 letews, letuce, 6 let(t)yse, lettes(se, -is, -us, -uze, -yce, lectuse, lacteux, -use, laictuce, *Sc.* lattouce, 6–7 lactuce, lettise, 6–8 lettice, 7 lectuce, 8 lattice, 6– lettuce. [ME. *letuse*, connected with OF. *laituë* (Cotgr. *laictuë*, mod.F. *laitue*):—*lactūca*, f. *lact-*, *lac* milk, the name having reference to the milky juice of the plant.

The exact origin of the Eng. word is uncertain. Prof. Skeat conjectures that it may be a. OF. **letuse*, **laituse*:—L. **lactūcea*, an adjectival derivative of *lactūca*. Palsgrave in 1530 gives *lectus* as a Fr. form, and a vocabulary of *c* 1475 (Wright-Wülcker 787) gives *letusa* as the Latin equivalent of Eng. *letuse*; but the genuineness of these is doubtful.]

1. a. Any plant of the genus *Lactuca*; esp. *Lactuca sativa* or Garden Lettuce, the leaves of which are much used as a salad; often *collect.* in *sing.* for the plants or their leaves. ***wild lettuce***: some plant of this genus growing wild; *spec.* in England = *L. Scariola* and *L. virosa*; in America = *L. Canadensis*. Also applied to various plants resembling this genus. For ***cabbage, cos, hare, Indian, Lamb's lettuce*** etc., see the first member.

c **1290** *S. Eng. Leg.* I. 18/598 A fair herbe, þat men cleopez letuse. *a* **1300** *Cursor M.* 6079 Wit therf bred and letus wild. **1382** WYCLIF *Exod.* xii. 8 Therf looves with wylde letuse. *c* **1400** tr. *Secreta Secret., Gov. Lordsh.* 73 Wylde letus þat feldmen clepin skarioles. *c* **1420** *Pallad. on Husb.* II. 176 Letuce is to be sette in Ianyueer. *c* **1483** CAXTON *Dialogues* iv. 13 Yet ben in the gardynes.. Letews, porselane. **1533** ELYOT *Cast. Helthe* (1539) 39 Breade steped in white brothe, with sodden lettyse, or cykorie, are good to be vsed. **1562** TURNER *Herbal* II. 26 Muche vse of lettes hurteth the eysight. **1566** PAINTER *Pal. Pleas.* I. 39 When the yong lactuse begin to growe, I cutte of the bitter and sower stalkes from them. **1614** J. COOKE *Greene's Tu Quoque* L 3 b, Did I eate any Lettice to supper last night, that I am so sleepie. **1633** JOHNSON *Gerarde's Herbal* II. xxxviii. 309 The greater wilde Lettuce smelling of Opium. **1651–3** JER. TAYLOR *Serm. for Year* (1678) 108 A dish of Lettice and a clear Fountain can cool all my Heat. **1671** H. M. tr. *Erasm. Colloq.* 100 It is very fine Broth which he is served up in; the Lettice are very choyce ones. **1733** POPE *Hor. Sat.* II. i. 18 If your point be rest, [take] Lettuce and cowslip-wine. **1760** J. LEE *Introd. Bot.* App. 317 Lettuce, Wild, *Prenanthes*. **1876** HARLEY *Mat. Med.* (ed. 6) 540 Lettuce has glaucous vertical leaves.

b. *slang* (orig. *U.S.*). Money.

1929 *Amer. Speech* June 357 If you wish to boast of having a great deal of money, you may speak of having.. wads of it, or a wad of lettuce, meaning a big roll of bills. **1932** J. Dos PASSOS *1919* 57 He still had more'n fifty iron men, quite a roll of lettuce for a guy like him. **1967** WODEHOUSE *Company for Henry* v. 84 How are you fixed for lettuce, Hank?.. Dough. Cash. Glue... Money. **1974** J. WAINWRIGHT *Cause for Killing* 216 'They spend money, in Beirut...' 'Phoenicia Street,' murmured Gantley. 'Anything... Any out-of-this-world luxury. Any service. Anything! You have the lettuce... Phoenicia Street can oblige.'

c. = *lettuce green*.

1963 *New Yorker* 1 June 115 *These* shirts.. in.. cedar, lettuce, navy or red.

†**2.** Proverb. ***like lips, like lettuce*** = 'like has met its like'; an echo of L. *similem habent labra lactucam*, an alleged saying of M. Crassus, when he saw an ass eating thistles.

a **1540** BARNES *Wks.* (1573) 189/1 No doubt the prouerbe is true, such lippes such lectuse, such saintes such miracles. **1583** *Leg. Bp. St. Androis* 433 Sic lipps, sic lattouce; lordis and lownes. **1587** FLEMING *Contn. Holinshed* III. 1017/2 Like lips, like lettice, as is their cause so are the rulers. **1589** GREENE *Menaphon* (Arb.) 92 He left such lettice as were too fine for his lips. **1599** H. BUTTES *Dyets Drie Dinner* To Rdrs., Here are Lettuses for euery mans lips. **1619** *Pasquil's Palin.* (1877) 130 If he like not these Lettice, let him pull backe his lips. **1677** W. HUGHES *Man of Sin* III. iv. 140 Well, but the Lettice and the Lips do well together.

3. *attrib.* and *Comb.*, as ***lettuce-bed, -juice, -leaf, -seed***; †**lettuce-cabbage** = *cabbage-lettuce*; **lettuce green**, a medium shade of green; also *attrib.*; **lettuce-opium** = LACTUCARIUM; **lettuce-water**, a decoction of lettuce.

1897 MARY KINGSLEY *W. Africa* 380 The fierce currents of the wet season.. play great havoc with these *lettuce beds. **1731** *Gentl. Mag.* I. 408 Make Plantations of *Lettuce Cabbage for Winter use. **1897** *Sears, Roebuck Catal.* 222/2 Delicate tintings of.. lemon, *lettuce green, scarlet. **1929** E. WILSON *I thought of Daisy* i. 3, I saw lettuce-green cocktail glasses. **1970** *Guardian* 2 June 7/8 Mimosa, Lettuce Green, Lavender Blue. **1971** D. BEATY *Temple Tree* 157 A lettuce-green shirt. **1832** *Veg. Subst. Food* 299 The narcotic property of *lettuce-juice has been long familiarly known. *c* **1540** *Vicary's Anat.* (1888) App. 227 Nightshade leaves, *lactuce leaves, henbayne leaves. **1816** A. DUNCAN in *Mem. Caled. Hortic. Soc.* (1819) II. 312 A substance.. which I have denominated Lactucarium or *Lettuce Opium. **1577** MOUNTAINE *Gardener's Labyrinth* II. 43 *Lettice seedes. **1683** SALMON *Doron Med.* III. 660 Oyl of Lettice Seeds. **1713** DERHAM *Phys.-Theol.* 9 *note*, Some Lettice-Seed being sown.. in the open Air. **1836** J. M. GULLY *Magendie's Formul.* (ed. 2) 104 *Lettuce water 4 ounces.

†ˈ**lettucer.** *Obs. rare*⁻¹. In 6 letticer. [f. LETTUCE + -ER.] (See quot.)

1562 TURNER *Herbal* II. 45 The female (Mandrag) is called the letticer with lesse leues and narrower then lettice.

lettus(e, -uze, obs. forms of LETTUCE.

lettushe, obs. form of LETTICE.

lettwary, var. LECTUARY *Obs.*, electuary.

letty (ˈlɛtɪ), *a. dial.* Also 7 lette. [f. LET *v.*² + -Y.] That lets or hinders.

1642 BEST *Farm. Bks.* (Surtees) 110 When there is any lette Weather in Harvest time. **1886** ELWORTHY *W. Somerset Word-bk.*, *Letty-weather*, showery; rainy; lit. hindering weather—i.e. hindering harvesting or out-door work.

letty (ˈlɛtɪ), *sb. slang.* [ad. It. *letto* bed.] A bed, a lodging.

1846 *Swell's Night Guide* 71 While the old rum cull.. cannot wag from his Letty,.. the accumulation of dirt thrives monstrously. **1875** T. FROST *Circus Life* xvi. 279 'Letty' is used both as a noun and a verb, signifying 'lodging' and 'to lodge'. **1933** E. SEAGO *Circus Company* v. 80 All the people of the smaller show dwell in wagons of their own, and do not seek for 'letties' in the town. **1957** J. OSBORNE *Entertainer* III. 77 *Jean*: We can't all spend our time nailing our suitcases to the floor, and shin out of the window. *Archie*: Scarper the letty.

lettyce, -ys(e, obs. forms of LETTICE, LETTUCE.

lettyreure, variant of LETTRURE. *Obs.*

letuare, -ie, -y(e: see LECTUARY.

letuce, -uis, -us(e, obs. ff. LETTICE, LETTUCE.

let-up, *sb.*: see LET *v.*¹ 38 c.

letvis, letwis, obs. forms of LETTICE.

letwary(e, -werye: see LECTUARY.

letyrn, letys, obs. ff. LECTERN, LETTUCE.

Letzeburgesch (lɛtsəˈbʊrgɛʃ). Also Letzeburg, Letzeburgisch, Lezebuurjesh, etc. [Local name.] The name of the West Moselle Franconian dialect of German spoken by the natives of Luxembourg. Cf. LUXEMBURGISCH.

1921 R. J. CASEY *Land of Haunted Castles* 152, I asked a young woman of Gosseldange.. who.. the 'Letzeburgers' were. She replied, proud of her ability to tell me in English: 'They are people who live in the Stadt Luxemburg... They speak a language that is very *difficile* to understand. It is not French. It is not German. It is not Luxemburg. It is Letzeburg.' **1944** *Luxembourg* (Geogr. Handbk. Ser. B.R. 528, Admiralty, Naval Intelligence Div.) 43 The native dialect, *Letzeburgesch*, is a Moselle Franconian dialect belonging to the West Middle German group. **1956** B. MILES *Attic in Luxembourg* xxviii. 215 Letzeburgesch, the Luxembourg dialect.. although based upon old Teutonic origins,.. borrowed extensively from Celtic, Roman and French. **1961** R. E. KELLER *German Dial.* 10 *Letzeburgisch* might be considered with some hesitation as a *Halbsprache* but *Schwyzertütsch* is for Kloss beyond the pale and he merely concedes that certain circumstances make it difficult to decide whether it might not after all qualify for the status of a *Halbsprache*. **1964** S. H. MULLER *World's Living Lang.* i. 16 The speech of 300,000 citizens of Luxemburg has diverged from standard German so much that it must be considered a distinct language, Luxemburgian (self-designation *lezebuurjesh*). **1965** W. B. LOCKWOOD *Informal Hist. German Lang.* 146 Some 300,000 persons.. speak as their native idiom a now fairly uniform German dialect *Luxemburgisch* or, as they call it themselves, *Letzebursch*. **1972** *Guardian* 19 Sept. 14/3 The vast majority of Luxembourgers speak Letzeburgesch at home. **1973** *Times* 26 May (Benelux Suppl.) p. v/4 Luxembourg.. is a case apart. Its 320,000 inhabitants speak a regional language called *Letzeburgisch* on which the official language, French, is superimposed.

leu (ˈleɪuː). Pl. lei (ˈleɪ). [Rumanian, = lion.] The basic monetary unit of Rumania.

1879 *Coin Chart Manual* (N.Y.) 2 Value of U.S. Dollar... Roomania... 5 Lei 18½ Ben Paras. **1896** *Hist. Banking* III. VII. 333 Up to 1877 Roumania had no paper money. In that year, however, the Government issued non-compulsory notes of 5, 10, 20, 50, 100, and 500 lei. **1902** *Encycl. Brit.* XXXI. 291/1 In Rumania the unit of account is the *leu* of 100 *bani*. **1921** S. GRAHAM *Europe* viii. 107 The twenty, the hundred, the thousand-crown notes are almost identical... Roumanian lei are also much the same in appearance. **1940** G. CROWTHER *Outl. Money* viii. 305 Germany pushes up the value of the Reichsmark relatively to, say, the Roumanian leu; that enables her to quote a very attractive price, in lei, for wheat, without it costing her too much in Reichsmarks. **1967** *Economist* 19 Aug. (Suppl.) p. xlii/3 All families with a joint income of 2,000 lei.. are now obliged to buy their flat.

Leucadian (l(j)uːˈkeɪdɪən), *sb.* and *a.* [f. *Leucadia* (see below) + -IAN.] **A.** *sb.* A native or inhabitant of Leucadia or Leucas, an island in the Ionian Sea. **B.** *adj.* Of or pertaining to Leucadia.

1615 G. SANDYS *Rel. Journey* I. 4 It was a custome amongst the Leucadians in their yearely solemnities, as a propitiatory sacrifice to Apollo, to throw some one from the top, condemned before for his offences. **1890** J. G. FRAZER *Golden Bough* II. iii. 213 From the Lover's Leap, a white bluff at the southern end of their island, the Leucadians used annually to hurl a criminal into the sea as a scapegoat. **1952** R. CAMPBELL tr. *Baudelaire's Poems* 181 Since then I watch on the Leucadian height. **1968** *Encycl. Brit.* XIII. 998/2 It was from the extremity.. of this cape that in ancient times the 'Leucadian leap' was made, an ordeal whereby at the feast of Apollo accused persons were tried, those who survived the leap being picked up by boat.

leucæthiop (l(j)uːˈsiːθɪəp). Also leucoethiop. [f. Gr. λευκ-ός white (see LEUCO-) + Αἰθίοπ-, Αἰθίοψ an Ethiopian.

Some have written *leucœthiop*, perh. influenced by the transliteration *leucæ Æthiopes* (for λευκοί Αἰθίοπες) in the ordinary text of Pliny *N.H.* v. viii.]

An albino of a negro race. So ˌ**leucæthiˈopia**, the constitution of a leucæthiop. ˌ**leucæthiˈopic** *a.*, characterized by leucæthiopia.

1819 W. LAWRENCE *Physiol.* 287 Their peculiar constitution.. may be conveniently termed, after some modern authors, leucæthiopia. *Ibid.* 510 The same parents at different times have leucæthiopic children, and others with the ordinary formation, and characters. **1860** R. F. BURTON *Centr. Afr.* I. 109 The people.. call these leucœthiops [*sic*; *but* leucæthiops *in Index*] Wazungu, 'white men'. [Mod. Dicts. have chiefly *leucoethiop, leucœthiop.*]

leucate (ˈl(j)uːkət). *Chem.* [f. LEUC-IC + -ATE.] A salt of leucic acid.

1865 WATTS *Dict. Chem.* III. 576 Leucate of barium.

leuchæmia, obs. var. of LEUKÆMIA.

leuchtenbergite (lɔɪxtənˈbɜːgaɪt). *Min.* [named by A. Komonen, 1842, in honour of Maximilian, duke of *Leuchtenberg*: see -ITE.] A variety of clinochlore, often resembling talc.

1844 DANA *Min.* 317. **1887** *Min. Mag.* VII. 222.

leucic (ˈl(j)uːsɪk), *a. Chem.* [f. LEUC-IN + -IC.] ***leucic acid***, a diatomic fatty acid, also called *oxyhexoic acid*, obtained by treating leucin with nitrous acid. ***leucic ether***, an oily liquid obtained by the action of zinc-ethyl on oxalic ether.

1865 WATTS *Dict. Chem.* III. 576 Leucic ether. *Ibid.*, Leucic acid. **1873** RALFE *Phys. Chem.* 54 Leucic Acid... This acid only exists in the body in its ammoniated form, leucin.

leucine (ˈl(j)uːsiːn). *Chem.* Also † leucin. [a. F. *leucine* (H. Braconnot 1820, in *Ann. de Chim. et de Physique* XIII. 119), f. Gr. λευκ-ός white + -INE⁵.] A white crystalline substance, known also as *amido-caproic acid* ($C_6H_{13}NO_2$), one of the principal products of the decomposition of nitrogenous matter: an amino-acid that is one of the principal constituents of proteins.

1826 HENRY *Elem. Chem.* II. 395 A peculiar white matter, called by Braconnot leucine. **1847–9** TODD *Cycl. Anat.* IV. 164/2 Leucin.. is a crystalline substance closely resembling cholesterine in appearance. **1885** REMSEN *Org. Chem.* (1888) 194 Leucine is found very widely distributed in the animal kingdom, as in the spleen, pancreas, and brain.

attrib. **1896** *Allbutt's Syst. Med.* I. 177 Microscopic examination.. might shew.. leucin balls.

leucite (ˈl(j)uːsaɪt). *Min.* Also 8 leucit. [a. G. *leucit* (A. G. Werner, 1791), f. Gr. λευκός white: see -ITE.] Silicate of aluminium and potassium, usually found in glassy trapezohedrons, occurring in volcanic rocks, esp. in lavas from Vesuvius.

1799 *Med. Jrnl.* I. 300 In the decomposition of the fossil, called leucit, he [Klaproth] found from 20 to 22 parts of potass in the hundred. **1800** HENRY *Epit. Chem.* (1808) 363 The volcanic leucite contained less potash than other kinds. **1876** PAGE *Adv. Text-Bk. Geol.* vii. 146 Many of the older lavas yield agates.. leucite.. and other precious minerals.

attrib. **1878** LAWRENCE tr. *Cotta's Rocks Class.* 135 Leucite rock may be regarded as a dolerite, in which the labradorite is replaced by leucite.

Hence **leu'citic** *a.*, containing or of the nature of leucite. **'leucitoid** (*Crystallogr.*), the trapezohedron or tetragonal trisoctahedron; so called as being the form of the mineral leucite. **leu'citophyr(e** [G. (*por*)*phyr* porphyry; cf. GRANOPHYRE], 'a dark-grayish fine-grained cellular volcanic rock consisting of augite and leucite together with some disseminated magnetic iron' (Dana *Man. Geol.* 1868).

1830 LYELL *Princ. Geol.* I. 352 The foundations of the town [Pompeii] stand upon the old leucitic lava of Somma. **1879** RUTLEY *Study Rocks* x. 109 As in the little leucite crystals of the sperone or leucitophyr which occurs near Rome. **1880** G. F. RODWELL in *Nature* XXI. 352 The lava is very leucitic.

leuco- ('l(j)uːkəʊ), before a vowel **leuc-**, a. Gr. λευκο-, combining form of λευκός white; (*b*) In *Med.* used to represent 'leucocyte' (as in *leucopenia*, *-poiesis*); (*c*) In *Chem.* [after its use in *Dyeing*: see b], used to form the names of some colourless compounds that are chemically transformed to coloured ones (as in *leucoanthocyanin*). **leu'caniline** *Chem.*, a white crystalline coal-tar base ($C_{20}H_{21}N_3$) obtained from rosaniline by reduction and from other substances; **leu'canthous** *a. Bot.* [Gr. ἄνθ-ος flower + -OUS], white-flowered (Mayne *Expos. Lex.* 1855); **leu'caugite** *Min.* [AUGITE], a white or greyish variety of augite (Dana, 1868); **,leucoanthocy'anidin** *Chem.*, any colourless substance which yields an anthocyanidin on heating with mineral acid; **,leucoantho'cyanin** *Chem.*, a leucoanthocyanidin; *spec.* any that is a glycoside; **'leucoblast** *Biol.* [-BLAST], one of the spheroidal cells from which leucocytes develop; **leu'cocholy** *nonce-wd.* [after MELANCHOLY] (see quot.); **leuco-, leuko'cidin** († **-ine**) *Bacteriology* [a. F. *leucocidine* (H. van de Velde 1894, in *La Cellule* X. 434): see -CIDE 1], any leucotoxin produced by a microorganism; **leuco'cratic** *a. Petrol.* [ad. G. *leukokrat* (W. C. Brögger *Eruptivgesteine des Kristianiagebietes* (1898) III. 264), f. Gr. κρατ-εῖν to rule, prevail], (of a rock) light-coloured; rich in light-coloured minerals; **,leuco'cyclite** *Min.* [Gr. κύκλ-ος + -ITE], a synonym of apophyllite; **'leucoderm** (also *leuco-*) *sb.* and *a.* [Gr. δέρμ-α skin], (of, pertaining to, or being) a person of a white-skinned race; **leuco'derma** *Path.* [Gr. δέρμα skin], deficiency of colouring matter or unnatural whiteness in the skin; **leuco'dermia** *Path.* = *leucoderma*; **'leuco,dermic** *a.*, (*a*) pertaining to, or exhibiting leucoderma (*Cent. Dict.*); (*b*) (naturally) white-skinned; **,leuco'melanous** *a.* [Gr. μελαν-, μέλας + -OUS], having a fair complexion with dark hair; **,leuco'penia** *Path.* [Gr. πενία poverty] (see quot.); hence **,leuco'penic** *a.*, characterized by leucopenia; **leucophore** [a. G. *leukophore* (R. Keller 1895, in *Pflügers Archiv Ges. Physiol.* LXI. 147)] = IRIDOCYTE; **,leuco'phosphite** *Min.*, a hydrated basic phosphate of potassium and ferric iron found as white or greenish fine-grained masses; **'leucophyll** *Bot.* [Gr. φύλλ-ον leaf], a colourless substance found in the corpuscles of an etiolated plant, capable of being transformed into chlorophyll; **,leuco'plakia**, † **-placia** *Path.* [Gr. πλακ-, πλάξ a flat surface], white patches appearing on the tongue or on the mucous membrane within the mouth; hence **leuko'plakial** (now *rare*), **-'plakic** *adjs.*; **'leucoplast** *Biol.* [Gr. πλαστ-ός moulded] = next; **,leuco'plastid** *Biol.* [PLASTID], one of the colourless corpuscles found in the protoplasm of vegetable cells around which starch accumulates; **leuco-, leukopoiesis** (-pɔɪ'iːsɪs) *Physiol.* [-POIESIS], the production of leucocytes; so **leuco-, leukopoi'etic** *a.*; **leu'copterin** *Chem.* [PTERIN], a white pigment found esp. in certain butterflies; 2-amino-4, 6, 7-trihydroxypteridine, $H_2NC_6N_4(OH)_3$; **'leucoscope** [-SCOPE], an instrument contrived by Helmholtz for comparing the relative whiteness of lights or colours, or for testing the power of the eye to distinguish colours; **,leuco'spermous** *a. Bot.* [Gr. σπέρμα seed + -OUS], having white seeds; **'leucosphere** *Astron.* [SPHERE], the inner corona; **leuco-, leuko-'taxin(e** *Physiol.* [Gr. τάξις arrangement, order], a nitrogenous material found in injured tissue and inflammatory exudates which on injection causes inflammation, increase in the permeability of capillaries, and the attraction of leucocytes to the site; **leuco-, leuko'toxin** *Med.*, any substance which destroys leucocytes; **leu'coxene** *Min.* [Gr. ξένος guest], a white decomposition product of titanic iron; probably titanite (*Cent. Dict.*).

Many medical words with first element *leuco-* are also spelt *leuko-*.

1863 *Fownes' Chem.* 673 The action of sulphide of ammonium upon rosaniline gives rise to a base *leucaniline which contains two additional equivalents of hydrogen. **1935** G. M. & R. ROBINSON in *Jrnl. Chem. Soc.* 745 Probably class (b) [of leuco-anthocyanins] consists of relatively simple glycosides or diglycosides, whereas members of class (c) are sugar-free and should be regarded as *leuco-anthocyanidins. **1962** J. CLARK-LEWIS in T. A. Geissman *Chem. Flavonoid Compounds* viii. 218 Choice between the terms leucoanthocyanin and leucoanthocyanidin seems so far to have rested on the preference of individual authors, but there are sound reasons for using leucoanthocyanidin for the sugar-free molecules, and as the general term, and for reserving the term leucoanthocyanin for leuco-anthocyanidin glycosides. The terminations thus have the same significance as in anthocyanin and anthocyanidin. All the compounds of this class and known constitution so far discovered in nature are leucoanthocyanidins, i.e. do not contain sugar residues. **1967** J. B. HARBORNE *Compar. Biochem. Flavonoids* ix. 302 Leuco-anthocyanidins (or condensed tannins) can be classified into three groups: (1) low molecular weight substances, which are probably dimers formed by linkage of a flavan-3,4-diol with a catechin .., (2) soluble oligomers, containing 4 to 8 flavan units, and (3) insoluble polymers (flavolans) of 10 or more units. **1967** *New Scientist* 4 May 270/3 The culprits that cause colour change in African mahogany are katechin and leucoanthocyanidin. **1920** O. ROSENHEIM in *Biochem. Jrnl.* XIV. 185 In the young leaf, however, the pseudo-base does not occur in the free state, but in combination with either a carbohydrate or possibly another complex. For this combination the general name *leuco-anthocyanin is proposed. **1960** L. H. MEYER *Food Chem.* vii. 251 Catechins and leucoanthocyanins are present in the tissues of those woody plants studied such as apples, peaches, grapes, almonds, and some pears, while they are absent in herbaceous plants. **1962** T. SWAIN in T. A. Geissman *Chem. Flavonoid Compounds* xvi. 536 It has been presumed by many workers that the term leucoanthocyanin, like the term catechin, refers to the monomeric C_{15} molecule. **1971** *Ann. de Technol. Agricole* XX. 32 Different methods for the dosage of leucoanthocyanins of white wines have been compared. **1901** *Brit. Med. Jrnl.* 29 June 1606 A partial exhaustion of the *leucoblastic function of the bone marrow. **1742** T. GRAY *Let.* 27 May *Wks.* 1884 II. 113 Mine..is a white Melancholy, or rather *Leucocholy, for the most part; which, though it seldom laughs or dances, nor ever amounts to what one calls Joy or Pleasure, yet is a good easy sort of a state. **1894** *Jrnl. R. Microsc. Soc.* 732 The virulent cocci [of *Staphylococcus*]..secrete a special substance. This, which causes the death of the leucocytes, is termed 'substance leucocide' or *leucocidine. **1909** J. G. ADAMI *Princ. Path.* I. III. viii. 489 The leukotoxins are also known as leukocidins. **1970** AMBROSE & EASTY *Cell Biol.* xiv. 470 Some bacteria not only resist phagocytosis but produce substances, known as leucocidins, which kill phagocytes. **1909** A. HARKER *Nat. Hist. Igneous Rocks* v. 112 The former [*sc.* camptonite, is] a melanocratic type..and the latter [*sc.* mænaite] *leucocratic. **1954** H. WILLIAMS et al. *Petrogr.* ii. 33 In Johannsen's classification four rock classes are distinguished according to the volume-content of dark minerals, the limits being placed at 5, 50, and 95 percent. Shand also distinguishes four classes, but with different limits, as follows: leucocratic rocks, with less than 30 percent mafic minerals; mesocratic rocks, with 30–60 percent; melanocratic rocks, with 60–90 percent; and hypermelanic rocks, with more than 90 percent mafic minerals. **1965** G. J. WILLIAMS *Econ. Geol. N.Z.* xiv. 216/1 The Separation Point granite..is a massive white leucocratic soda-granite. **1829** *Nat. Philos., Polaris. Light* ix. 34 (U.K.S.) In other specimens of apophyllite, which Mr. Herschel calls *leucocyclite, from the rings being white and black. **1924** A. C. HADDON *Races of Man* (ed. 2) 13 Occasionally in *leucoderms, sometimes in Negroes, and as a rule in Mongoloid peoples, a fold of skin..covers the inner angle of the eye. *Ibid.* 84 The western steppe lands seem to have been the original home of fair (leucoderm) dolichocephals. **1935** HUXLEY & HADDON *We Europeans* iv. 115 A broad and convenient classification of skin-colour is as follows: (1) Leucoderms, or white-skinned (Caucasian) peoples; (2) Xanthoderms, or yellow-skinned peoples; (3) Melanoderms, or black-skinned peoples. **1884** MAX MÜLLER in *19th Cent.* June 1017 A semi-human progenitor, suffering, it may be, from leprosy or *leucoderma. **1888** *Syd. Soc. Lex.*, *Leucodermia, see Leukoderma. **1908** *Practitioner* Aug. 349 They [*sc.* freckles] are an example of excess of pigment in the skin, a condition known as hyperchromasia, in contradistinction to achromasia, or leucodermia, in which there is a deficiency of pigment in the skin. **1926** H. H. WILDER *Pedigree of Human Race* vi. 348 Members of the *Leucodermic race in Europe or America. **1898** *Allbutt's Syst. Med.* V. 418 Any number of leucocytes below the arbitrary limit of 6000 [per cubic millimetre of blood] will constitute a hypoleucocytosis, or *leucopenia as the condition is also named. **1961** R. D. BAKER *Essent. Path.* ii. 18 In some inflammations the total white blood cell count is decreased (leukopenia). **1964** W. G. SMITH *Allergy & Tissue Metabolism* ii. 16 Marked reductions in the number of leucocytes (leukopenia) and platelets (thrombocytopenia) circulating in the blood were described. **1898** *Allbutt's Syst. Med.* 420 He was able to distinguish..a *leucopenic phase, or hypoleucytosis, during which the number of hæmic leucocytes falls [etc.]. **1924** L. HOGBEN *Pigmentary Effector Syst.* ii. 24 In the skin of the Chameleon there are present, immediately below the epidermis, cells charged with yellow pigment variously described as guanophores (Schmidt), *leukophores or ochrophores (Keller), iridocytes (Pouchet), or interference cells (Brucke). **1963** M. FINGERMAN *Control of Chromatophores* i. 4 When the guanine consists of fine granules that can migrate the term leucophore is usually employed. **1932** E. S. SIMPSON in *Jrnl. R. Soc. W. Austral.* XVIII. 71 No previously described mineral approaches this in composition except minervite, a potassium aluminium phosphate, from which it differs in possessing a much greater basicity... It appears therefore to be a new species for which the name *Leucophosphite is suggested. **1963** *Prof. Papers U.S. Geol. Survey* No. 475-C. 103/2 Leucophosphite and gypsum represent in large part only a recombination of the elements already present in the phosphatized wood when uplift of the enclosing Moreno Formation exposed it to weathering. **1972** *Amer. Mineralogist* LVII. 397 Leucophosphite, $K_2[Fe^{3+}{}_4\text{-}(OH)_2(H_2O)_2(PO_4)_4].2H_2O$, possesses an atomic arrangement based on a discrete octahedral tetramer. **1865** WATTS *Dict. Chem.* III. 584 *Leucophyll. **1885–8** FAGGE & PYE-SMITH *Princ. Med.* (ed. 2) I. 124 A similar affection of the tongue often follows *leucoplacia, or white syphilitic patches, at the end of several years. **1920** W. E. MASTERS *Essent. Trop. Med.* vi. 477 Leucoplakia may also affect the penis, vulva and vagina. **1962** *Lancet* 1 Dec. 1170/2 Leucoplakia (or lichen sclerosus) diagnosed by the clinician on naked-eye appearances shows variable and non-specific histological features. **1962** *Ibid.* 8 Dec. 1228/2 Here operating is undesirable, except in those few patients in whom leukoplakia develops as well. **1973** *Daily Colonist* (Victoria, B.C.) 7 Sept. 2/1 Leukoplakia is a thickening of the membrane of a mucous surface, commonly on the lip or in the mouth. **1908** *Practitioner* Sept. 354, I believe that if sufficient examinations were made in syphilitic patients ..*leucoplakial patches would be found in the mucous membrane from time to time. **1923** *Surg. Gynecol. & Obstetr.* XXXVI. 189/1 The leukoplakial conditions of the urinary tract have received relatively little attention. **1907** *Arch. Middlesex Hosp.* IX. (6th Rep. Cancer Res. Lab.) 65 Those *leucoplakic conditions of vulva, tongue, and lips which..often precede the development of squamous cell carcinoma. **1917** J. BLAND-SUTTON *Tumours, Innocent & Malignant* (ed. 6) xxx. 331 In some patients an ulcer appears in a leucoplakic patch. **1962** *Lancet* 1 Dec. 1170/2 If all vulvas described as leucoplakic on clinical grounds are subjected to biopsy, approximately 5% are found to be cancerous at the outset. *Ibid.* 8 Dec. 1228/2 Changes in vulval skin..are very common... Among other features, they are often white, but this does not mean that they are precancerous or leukoplakic. **1886** *Jrnl. R. Microsc. Soc.* 640 In the lower plants..the formation of *leucoplasts is a subsequent process, a transformation of the coloured into a colourless chromatophore. **1887**, **1902** Leucoplast [see CHLOROPLAST]. **1964** *Oceanogr. & Marine Biol.* II. 199 All species [of the genus *Caulerpa* of green algae] possess amyliferous leucoplasts as well as the ordinary green plastids. **1885** GOODALL *Physiol. Bot.* (1892) 43 *Leucoplastids..are found in parts which are normally devoid of chlorophyll, such as tubers, rhizomes, etc. **1913** DORLAND *Med. Dict.* (ed. 7) 512/2 *Leukopoiesis, production of leukocytes. **1942** M. M. WINTROBE *Clin. Hematol.* i. 26 Erythropoiesis in the spleen is at first more pronounced than leukopoiesis but it is short-lived. **1973** WOODLIFF & HERRMANN *Conc. Haematol.* viii. 113 Disorders of leucopoiesis are usually reflected by changes in the peripheral blood. **1913** DORLAND *Med. Dict.* (ed. 7) 512/2 *Leukopoietic, forming or producing leukocytes. **1927** A. PINEY *Recent Adv. Hæmatol.* iii. 35 Hyperplasias of a character similar to those occuring in the leucopoietic tissue may affect the erythropoietic one. **1973** WOODLIFF & HERRMANN *Conc. Haematol.* viii. 113 A progressive malignant proliferation of the leucopoietic tissues. **1927** *Chem. Abstr.* XXI. 224 (*heading*) *Leucopterin, the white wing pigment of cabbage butterflies (*Pieris brassicae* and *P. napi*). **1954** *Sci. News* XXXIV. 91 The purines and pterines contribute a major source of colour to the wings of butterflies... These compounds are only present in small amounts representing in the case of white leucopterin of Pierid butterflies about 0·18 milligramme per specimen. **1883** *Nature* XXVII. 277 Professor Helmholtz's new instrument, called the *leukoscope. **1871** tr. *Schellen's Spectr. Anal.* lvi. 272 For this envelope the name '*leucosphere' has been proposed. **1937** V. MENKIN in *Proc. Soc. Exper. Biol. & Med.* XXXVI. 167 For the sake of convenience the name *leukotaxine is tentatively proposed for this active crystalline nitrogenous substance which is evidently released by injured tissue and is readily recovered in inflammatory exudates. **1947** *New Biol.* II. 135 The most reasonable hypothesis is..that leucotaxine is released from the killed and damaged cells of the injured skin we are considering, and is mainly responsible for the escape of fluid from nearby undamaged capillaries. **1957** *Amer. Jrnl. Physiol.* CLXXXIX. 99 (*caption*) A preliminary intravenous injection of 25 mg of cortisone acetate was performed in the tested rabbit to inactivate the masking effect of any leukotaxine possibly present in the acid exudate to be injected. **1964** W. G. SMITH *Allergy & Tissue Metabolism* iii. 39 This material, which Menkin called leucotaxin, can upon injection into the skin induce increased capillary permeability and chemotactic attraction of polymorphs to the injection site. **1908** *Practitioner* Mar. 392 Roentgen-rays appear to lead to the production of veritable '*leucotoxins'. Normal leucocytes, exposed in vitro and in vivo to the action of such leucotoxins present in the serum of animals, which have been exposed to Roentgen-rays, undergo a specific disintegration. **1931** *Biol. Abstr.* V. 488/2 The virulent streptococci do not possess in the same degree the power of leukotoxin production. **1956** *Proc. Soc. Exper. Biol. & Med.* XCIII. 493/2 A leucotoxin develops in the blood of the rabbit in hemorrhagic shock, and..this leucotoxin severely impairs the antibacterial potential of the animal.

b. In Combs. in which *leuco* may be used *attrib.* (without a hyphen) as quasi-*adj.*, or be joined by a hyphen to the second element: chiefly in *Dyeing*, where *leuco* is used to denote the reduced, water-soluble colourless form of a dye which is fixed on the fibre and subsequently oxidized to the dye proper by the air; as ***leuco-base*** (so ***leuco-basic*** adj.), ***-compound***, ***-cyanide***, ***-dye***, ***-form***, ***-fuchsin***.

1886 E. KNECHT tr. *Benedikt's Chem. Coal-Tar Colours* 79 These compounds, called 'leuco-bases', are colourless and yield colourless salts with acids. By oxidation they are transformed..into the colour-bases, which differ from the 'leuco-bases' by containing one atom of oxygen. **1947** L. S. PRATT *Chem. & Physics Org. Pigments* viii. 140 The dyestuff is prepared by condensing *o*-chlorobenzaldehyde with dimethylaniline and then oxidizing the leuco base to the color base. **1958** J. R. BAKER *Princ. Biol. Microtechnique* xvii. 309 Schiff's reagent..is often regarded as a leucobase, but this is an error; for a leucobase becomes coloured on oxidation and could not possibly serve in Feulgen's reaction. **1971** E. GURR *Synthetic Dyes* 108 The leuco bases of

triphenylmethane dyes (e.g. crystal violet and malachite green) are extremely light sensitive. **1956** *Nature* 14 Jan. 92/2 Leuco-basic fuchsin is specific for deoxyribonucleic acid. **1970** *Watsonia* VIII. 23 Root tips..were..stained in leucobasic fuchsin. **1888** *Jrnl. Chem. Soc.* LIV. 493 The anthraquinone-dyes yield leuco-compounds on reduction. **1906** *Notices Proc. R. Inst. Gt. Brit.* XVII. 107 What we are pleased to call leucocompounds, are in the majority of cases by no means colourless. Indigo-white itself is not white but yellow in its alkaline solution which we call a vat. Other vat-dyes have leucocompounds which are even more strongly coloured. **1961** COCKETT & HILTON *Dyeing Cellulosic Fibres* viii. 280 All methods used in practice to apply vat dyes to cellulosic fibres involve, at some stage, the conversion of the insoluble vat dye to the soluble sodium salt of the so-called leuco compound of the dye. **1931** *Trans. Faraday Soc.* XXVII. 571 The pure alcoholic leuco cyanide solution is very suitable for a laboratory method [of measuring ultra-violet light]. **1965** J. KOSAR *Light-Sensitive Syst.* viii. 370 Aside from the photographic applications, light-sensitive leucocyanides are useful for detecting, measuring, and recording short wave ultraviolet light. **1954** *Textile Terms & Definitions* (Textile Inst.) 24 *Leuco dye*, a reduced form of dye from which the original dye may be regenerated by an oxidation process. **1973** J. F. WILLEMS in R. J. COX *Proc. Symposium Photogr. Processing Univ. Sussex* 95 These leuco dyes are strong reducing agents, which in the adsorbed state on the silver halide grain start the development. **1959** *Nature* 15 Aug. 545/1 The production of a coloured dye by transformation of the leuco form. **1945** *Chem. Abstr.* XXXIX. 6288/1 (Index), Leuco-fuchsin. **1965** E. GURR *Rational Use Dyes Biol.* 94 Solutions of reduced dyes, such as Schiff's reagent (leuco fuchsin), leuco acid fuchsin and leuco patent blue in distilled water, are oxidized on heating and consequently restored in colour. **1967** *Jrnl. Med. Lab. Technol.* XXIV. 48 (*heading*) Nitric acid leucofuchsin technique for myelinated nerves.

leucochalcite (ˌl(j)uːkəʊˈkælsaɪt). *Min.* [Named by Sandberger, 1881, f. LEUCO- + Gr. χαλκ-ός brass: see -ITE.] Arsenate of copper, often found in silky white needles.

1883 DANA *Min.* App. iii. 69. **1892** *Ibid.* 837 Leucochalcite ..occurs as a delicate coating with malachite.

leucocyte (ˈl(j)uːkəsaɪt). *Phys.* Also **leukocyte.** [f. LEUCO- + -CYTE.] A colourless corpuscle, e.g. one of the white blood-corpuscles, or one of those found in lymph, connective tissue, etc.

1870 ROLLESTON *Anim. Life* Introd. 18 *note*, In the absence..of certain animal 'cytoids' or 'leucocytes' the vaccine poison is inoperative. **1898** *Allbutt's Syst. Med.* V. 415 At the present day, the name 'leucocyte' has a somewhat wider significance than that of a mere synonym for the different forms of the white corpuscles. **1911** *Jrnl. Amer. Med. Assoc.* 25 Feb. 581/1 Alexin increases in the serum under conditions which favor disintegrating of leukocytes. *Ibid.*, The 'alexin' is synonymous with Metchnikoff's leukocytic ferment. *Ibid.*, Leukocytic extract is essentially the same in its action as alexin. *Ibid.*, The alexin varies with the degree of leukocytosis. **1947** Leukocytosis [see GRANULOCYTOSIS]. **1951** A. GROLLMAN *Pharmacol. & Therapeutics* xxxi. 732 Mercurial poisoning is sometimes accompanied by a leukocytosis. **1971** J. SONG *Path. Sickle Cell Dis.* xviii. 355 Fever, vomiting, nausea, and leukocytosis. **1973** *Nature* 1 June 290/1 We cultured peripheral blood leukocytes for 24 or 48 h with phytohaemagglutinin.

Comb. **1879** J. R. REYNOLDS *Syst. Med.* V. 237 A scraping of the cut surface presents under the microscope a large number of..leucocyte-like corpuscles.

Hence ˌ**leucoˈcytal** *a.*, of or pertaining to leucocytes. ˌ**leucoˈcytary** = prec. ˌ**leucoˈcytic** *a.*, of or pertaining to leucocytes; characterized by the presence of leucocytes. ˌ**leucocyˈtosis** [after Gr. words in -ωσις] (see quot. 1866).

1879 J. R. REYNOLDS *Syst. Med.* V. 217 An overgrowth of this tissue..may be associated with..*leucocytal excess. **1900** *Pop. Sci. Monthly* Jan. 382 We can see the coloring matter penetrating the *leucocytary protoplasmic mass. **1879** J. R. REYNOLDS *Syst. Med.* V. 232 The albumen in *leucocytic blood is said to be diminished. **1898** *Allbutt's Syst. Med.* V. 637 Other organs [than the spleen] are not infrequently the seat of diffuse leucocytic infiltrations. **1866** A. FLINT *Princ. Med.* (1880) 68 According to the nomenclature proposed by Virchow, a temporary increase in the number of white corpuscles in the blood is called *leucocytosis. **1897** *Allbutt's Syst. Med.* II. 563 The leucocytosis diminishes rapidly with the fall of temperature.

‖**leucocythæmia** (ˈl(j)uːkəʊsɪˈθiːmɪə). *Path.* Also **leucocythemia.** [f. LEUCO- + Gr. κύτος -CYTE + αἷμα blood.] J. H. Bennett's name for LEUKÆMIA.

1852 J. H. BENNETT (*title*) Leucocythæmia or White Cell-blood in Relation to the Physiology and Pathology of the Lymphatic Glandular System. **1885** WOODHEAD *Pract. Pathol.* (ed. 2) 128 Leucocythemia of the Liver.

Hence **leucocyˈthæmic** (also *-emic*) *a.*, affected with or characterized by leucocythæmia.

1873 RALFE *Phys. Chem.* 41 Gelatin..is sometimes found in the blood of leucocythæmic patients. **1876** [see LEUKÆMIA].

leucoethiop, leucœthiop: see LEUCÆTHIOP.

leucol (ˈl(j)uːkɒl). *Chem.* Also **leukol.** [f. LEUCO- + -OL.] = next.

1844 FOWNES *Chem.* 537 Leukol has somewhat the odour of bitter almonds. *c* **1865** LETHEBY in *Circ. Sci.* I. 116/1 There are evolved..aniline, leukol, picoline.

leucoline (ˈl(j)uːkəlaɪn). *Chem.* [f. as prec. + -INE.] An organic base derived from coal-tar, identical with quinoline. Hence **leucoˈlinic (acid)**: see quot. 1892.

1852 FOWNES *Chem.* 562 Chinoleine (Leucoline). **1892** MORLEY & MUIR *Watts' Dict. Chem.*, *Leucoline* C_9H_7N. This base, occurring in coal tar, has been shown..to be identical with quinoline. *Leucolinic acid* $C_9H_9NO_3$. Obtained from coal-tar quinoline (leucoline).

‖**leucoma** (ljuːˈkəʊmə). *Path.* [mod.L., a. Gr. λεύκωμα, f. λευκοῦν to make white, f. λευκός white.] A white opacity in the cornea of the eye, the result of inflammation or of a wound; = ALBUGO.

1706 PHILLIPS (ed. Kersey), *Leucoma*, a white Scar in the Horney Coat of the Eye. **1802** *Med. Jrnl.* VIII. 399 The disease Leucoma, or Albugo. **1853** H. WALTON *Operat. Ophth. Surg.* 605 The lower edge of the pupil adhered to the leucoma.

Hence **leuˈcomaine** (-meɪn) *Chem.*, an alkaloid found in the living body as distinguished from one found in a dead or putrefying body (*ptomaine*). **leuˈcomatous** *a.*, affected with leucoma.

1887 *Athenæum* 20 Aug. 247/3 It treats of the ptomaines and leucomaines..in relation to scientific medicine. **1898** P. MANSON *Trop. Diseases* xxvi. 404 The cornea ulcerates or turns leucomatous, and in the end sight is entirely lost. **1899** *Allbutt's Syst. Med.* VI. 321 At present we know very little about the injurious effects of leucomaines and ptomaines.

leucopathy (l(j)uːˈkɒpəθɪ). Also in L. form **leucopathia.** [f. LEUCO- + Gr. -πάθεια, πάθος suffering.] = ALBINISM. Also *transf.*

1841 *Blackw. Mag.* L. 587 The arts are infected with a 'leucopathy', architecture and painting rejoicing in universal glare. **1868** *Nat. Encycl.* I. 383 The name [Albino] is now used to designate any individual who exhibits peculiarities, which are very generally styled leucopathy. **1875** *Encycl. Brit.* I. 445/1 Albinism, or Leucopathia.

leucophane (ˈl(j)uːkəfeɪn). *Min.* [Named by Esmark, 1840, f. late Gr. λευκοφάνης, f. λευκό-ς white + φαν-, φαίνεσθαι to appear, from its often showing whitish reflections.] Silicate of glucium, calcium, and sodium. Also **leuˈcophanite.**

1844 DANA *Min.* 235 Leucophane occurs in syenite with albite. **1868** *Ibid.* (ed. 5) 260 Leucophanite.., crystals tabular and nearly rectangular. **1891** T. S. HUNT *Min. Phys.* 327 With these is also placed leucophanite.

†**leucoˈphlegmacy.** *Path. Obs.* Also in mod.L. form **leucophlegmatia.** [ad. Gr. λευκοφλεγματία, f. λευκό-ς white + φλεγματ- PHLEGM.] 'A dropsical tendency, denoted by a pale, tumid and flabby condition of body' (*Syd. Soc. Lex.*).

1657 *Physical Dict.*, *Leucophlegmatia*, a kind of dropsie. **1681** tr. *Willis' Rem. Med. Wks.* Vocab., *Leucophlegmacy*, the kind of dropsy that riseth of white phlegm throughout all the body, and makes the flesh spongy. **1732** ARBUTHNOT *Rules of Diet* 381 It [Cachexy] sometimes disposeth to Consumptions, sometimes to Leucophlegmacy. **1747** tr. *Astruc's Fevers* 139 The urine thus retained in the blood, soon joins with the other humours of the body; whence the lymphatic ducts are over-loaded, and a *leucophlegmatia* induced.

leucophlegmatic (ˌl(j)uːkəʊflɛgˈmætɪk), *a.* [f. as prec. + -IC.] Affected with or characterized by leucophlegmacy.

1668 CULPEPPER & COLE *Barthol. Anat.* II. vii. 110 Leuco-phlegmatick persons. **1732** ARBUTHNOT *Rules of Diet* 363 Old Age attended with a..leucophlegmatic Constitution. **1771** SMOLLETT *Humph. Cl.* 20 Apr. (1815), He told me.. my case was dropsical, or, as he called it, leuco-phlegmatic. **1839** *Blackw. Mag.* XLV. 356 The vast expanse of his leuco-phlegmatic countenance. **1861** T. J. GRAHAM *Pract. Med.* 185 A leucophlegmatic temperament.

Hence ˌ**leucophlegˈmatical** *a.* = prec.

1658 ROWLAND *Moufet's Theat. Ins.* 988 They hurt not dropsie persons, nor such as are leucophlegmatical.

leucopyrite (l(j)uːkəʊˈpaɪəraɪt). *Min.* [f. LEUCO- + PYRITE.] A variety of löllingite.

1837 DANA *Min.* 400 Leucopyrite..occurs associated with copper nickel at Schladming, in Styria; with serpentine at Richenstein, in Silesia [etc.].

‖**leucorrhœa** (ˌl(j)uːkəˈriːə). *Path.* [f. Gr. λευκό-ς white + ῥοία a flow.] A mucous or mucopurulent discharge from the lining membrane of the female genital organs; the whites.

1797 *Encycl. Brit.* (ed. 3) XI. 231/1 The Leucorrhœa, Fluor Albus, or Whites. **1875** H. WALTON *Dis. Eye* 870 Some mothers with leucorrhœa infect all their children.

Hence ˌ**leucoˈrrhœal, leucorrhœic** (also **-rrhoic**, on Gr. type -ρροϊκός; cf. F. *leucorrhoïque, -rrhéique*) *adjs.*, of or pertaining to leucorrhœa.

1804 *Med. Jrnl.* XII. 521 The suppression of a leucorrhoic running. **1806** J. ROBERTON *Treat. Cantharides* II. vi. 41 The leucorrhœal discharge. **1885** G. H. TAYLOR *Pelvic Therap.* 129 A local leucorrhœal outflow. **1888** *Syd. Soc. Lex.*, *Leucorrhœic.*

‖**leucosis** (l(j)uːˈkəʊsɪs). Pl. leucoses. [a. Gr. λεύκωσις, f. λευκοῦν to make white, f. λευκός white.] **a.** Pallor, whiteness (*Syd. Soc. Lex.* 1888). **b.** The process of becoming an albino; the condition of an albino. **c.** The formation of leucoma (*Syd. Soc. Lex.*).

1706 PHILLIPS (ed. Kersey), *Leucosis*, a whitening of the Face, Teeth, or other Parts of the Body. **1842** PRICHARD *Nat. Hist. Man* 79 Symptoms of leucosis in their eyes, hair, and skin.

d. Also **leukosis.** [a. G. *leukosis* (Ellermann & Bang 1908, in *Centralbl. f. Bakteriol. Parasitenkunde u. Infectionskrankh.* (*Erste Abteil., Originale*) XLVI. 609).] = LEUKÆMIA; *esp.* any of various leukæmic diseases of animals. Also ***bovine leucosis***, a leukæmic disease of cattle; (***avian*** or ***fowl***) ***leucosis complex***, a group of poorly-differentiated leukæmic diseases of poultry which are typically transmissible.

1922 V. ELLERMANN *Leucosis of Fowls & Leucemia Probl.* i. 9 Finally, it must be mentioned that Ellermann & Bang have proposed the word 'leucosis' as a common designation for leucemic and aleucemic cases, myeloses as well as lymphadenoses. **1927** A. PINEY *Recent Adv. Hæmatol.* iii. 35 The name 'leucosis' is suitable for all forms, either lymphatic or myeloid, and is much to be preferred to leukæmia. **1935** WHITBY & BRITTON *Disorders of Blood* xviii. 357 (*heading*) The leukæmias (leucoses). **1936** *Jrnl. Amer. Vet. Med. Assoc.* LXXXIX. 681 (*heading*) A study of transmissible fowl leukosis. **1941** *Ibid.* XCIX. 214/1 (*heading*) Studies on production of specific antibodies against the agent of the fowl-leucosis complex. **1943** BARGER & CARD *Dis. & Parasites Poultry* (ed. 3) vii. 177 The cause of the avian leukosis complex or fowl paralysis is a filter-passing agent. **1946** *Physiol. Rev.* XXVI. 48 The term leukemia or leukosis implies neoplasia of a blood cell (hemoblastosis) including both the aleukemic and leukemic types of the disease. **1960** *Proc. 7th Congr. European Soc. Haematol.* II. 291 (*heading*) The haematology of bovine leucosis. **1961** *Brit. Vet. Jrnl.* CXVII. 326 The separation of fowl paralysis granuloma from the leucoses has been suggested by Campbell. **1970** *Times* 13 Apr. 11/4 Only non-vaccinated maiden heifers and young bulls will be allowed in, and the stock will have to be cleared..of foot-and-mouth disease, tuberculosis, brucellosis, leucosis, leptospirosis, and Johnes disease.

leucosoid (ˈl(j)uːkəsɔɪd). *Zool.* [f. mod.L. *Leucos-ia* (f. Gr. λευκός white) the name of the typical genus + -OID.] One of a family belonging to the tribe *Oxystomata* or pointed-mouth crabs.

1852 DANA *Crust.* I. 48 But in the Leucosoids, there is a higher perfecting of the branchial system.

leucotic (l(j)uːˈkɒtɪk), *a.* Also **leukotic.** [f. LEUC(OSIS + -OTIC.] Of, pertaining to, or affected with leucosis (in any sense).

1888 *Syd. Soc. Lex.*, *Leucotic*, of, or belonging to, Leucoma. **1935** BARGER & CARD *Dis. & Parasites Poultry* vii. 162 The leukotic type of the disease. **1960** *Proc. 7th Congr. European Soc. Haematol.* II. 291 In 'leucotic' herds.. 17 animals died. **1961** *Brit. Vet. Jrnl.* CXVII. 316 It has been calculated by Blaxland (1956) that seven to eight million pounds sterling are lost annually in Britain because of the leucotic complex, which in this particular context is taken to include the various types of fowl paralysis.

leucotomy (l(j)uːˈkɒtəmɪ). *Surg.* [ad. F. *leucotomie* (E. Moniz *Tentatives Opératoires dans le Traitement de certaines Psychoses* (1936) viii. 195): see LEUCO- (here signifying the white matter of the brain) and -TOMY.] = LOBOTOMY (in *spec.* sense).

1937 E. MONIZ in *Amer. Jrnl. Psychiatry* XCIII. 1379 (*heading*) Prefrontal leucotomy in the treatment of mental disorders. **1947** *Times* 13 Feb. 6/4 At intervals in the past 10 years details of the brain operation of leucotomy performed on patients with certain types of mental illness have appeared in the Press. **1950** M. GREENBLATT et al. *Stud. in Lobotomy* ii. 10 The English, however, use rather uniformly the more correct term 'leucotomy', in their description of the psychosurgical technic, whereas, in this country [*sc.* the U.S.A.], many still prefer the term 'lobotomy'. **1951** *Lancet* 21 July 91/2 (*heading*) Rostral leucotomy. **1958** *Listener* 5 June 931/2 People make moral objections to pre-frontal leucotomy even as a remedial measure. **1964** M. ARGYLE *Psychol. & Social Probl.* vi. 87 Other kinds of physical treatment, like insulin treatment and leucotomy, have declined in importance since the new methods have been discovered. **1967** [see GYRECTOMY]. **1969** *Times* 22 Mar. 3/2 The symptoms of pre-frontal leucotomy..include lack of inhibitions and inability to concentrate.

So **leucotome** [a. F. *leucotome* (E. Moniz 1936, in *Bull. de l'Acad. de Méd.* CXV. 390): see -TOME[1]], an instrument used to perform leucotomy; **leuˈcotomize** *v. trans.*, to perform leucotomy on; **leuˈcotomized** *ppl. a.*

1937 E. MONIZ in *Amer. Jrnl. Psychiatry* XCIII. 1380 Sections were made in the subcortical white matter by a leucotome with a steel loop, tending to crush the white matter... At the present time we are using a leucotome with a steel band that cuts rather than compresses. **1951** *Lancet* 21 July 92/1 From the number of patients so leucotomised who have come to me for more extensive operations, the results do not appear very satisfactory. **1959** *Times* 24 July 4/4 Where not so long ago some of these patients might have been leucotomized we now no longer do so. **1964** M. ARGYLE *Psychol. & Social Probl.* xii. 149 Authoritarians, psychotics and leucotomized patients are all poor at person perception. **1969** *New Scientist* 30 Jan. 229/2 The destruction of localized areas in the brain has also been achieved by..the excision of a segment of tissue with an instrument (a leucotome).

leucoturic (l(j)uːkəʊˈtjuːrɪk), *a. Chem.* [f. Gr. λευκός white + URIC, with inserted *t*, after *allanturic*.] Only in ***leucoturic acid*** (see quot. 1866).

1847 *Turner's Elem. Chem.* (ed. 8) 787 Leucoturic acid. **1866** ODLING *Anim. Chem.* 135 Leucoturic acid is a diamerone of lantanuric acid and oxaluric or parabanic acid.

leucous ('l(j)u:kəs), *a.* [f. Gr. λευκ-ός white + -OUS.] Having a white skin; light-complexioned, blonde. Said esp. of albinos. Also *ellipt.*

1842 PRICHARD *Nat. Hist. Man* 78 To these two varieties we must add a third, the leucous or the albino. **1849–52** TODD *Cycl. Anat.* IV. 936/2 The leucous races of man.. afford the most numerous examples of the sanguine temperament. **1859** R. F. BURTON *Centr. Afr.* in *Jrnl. Geogr. Soc.* XXIX. 85 They [albinos] much resemble Europeans of the leucous complexion.

leucovirus, var. LEUKOVIRUS.

leucovorin (l(j)u:'kɒvərɪn). *Biochem.* [f. mod.L. *Leuco(nostoc* (f. Gr. λευκο- LEUCO- + NOSTOC), the generic name + *citro)vor(um* (f. CITR-, CITRO- + L. *vor-āre* to devour + *-um*) the specific epithet, of the bacterium whose growth it was originally found to promote: see -IN[1].] = *folinic acid*.

1951 H. P. BROQUIST et al. in *Federation Proc.* X. 167/1 A crystalline substance with the properties of the 'citrovorum factor' (CF) was prepared from pteroylglutamic acid... The amounts of this crystalline substance, 'leucovorin', required for half-maximum growth per ml. of PGA-deficient medium were 0·00015 μg. for *Leuconostoc citrovorum* 8081. **1954** *Poultry Sci.* XXXIII. 111/1 Leucovorin (synthetic citrovorum factor) appeared to be inferior to folacin in the nutrition of the chick. **1966** [see FOLINIC *a.*]. **1971** *Cancer* XXVIII. 899/1 The combination of methotrexate with Leucovorin rescue is a well-tolerated therapeutic maneuver.

†**leucrocutanized**, *ppl. a. Obs. rare*[−1]. [f. L. *leucrocuta* (Pliny) a fabulous beast + -AN + -IZE + -ED[1].] Uttered as by a 'leucrocuta'.

1600 TOURNEUR *Transf. Metamorph.* xxvii, She soothes with Leucrocutanized sound.

leud (l(j)u:d). *Hist.* Also in Latin pl. form leudes ('l(j)u:di:z). [repr. med.L. *leudēs*, a. OHG. *liudi*, *liuti*: see LEDE.] In the Frankish kingdoms: A vassal or feudatory.

c **1756–67** BURKE *Eng. Hist.* Wks. X. 338 This chief [of the ancient Germans] was styled Senior, Lord [etc.]..the followers were called Ambacti, Comites, Leuds, Vassals [etc.]. **1845** M. PATTISON *Ess.* i. (1889) 17 The king, attended by some of his leudes, armed only with their swords, entered. **1863** J. WHITE *Eighteen Chr. Cent.* vii. 137 The Leud, as he was called—or feudatory, as he would have been named at a later time. **1872** ROBERTSON *Hist. Ess.*, *Introd.* p. xxxv, They had exchanged the position of Leudes ..for that of Antrustions.

leud, leude, obs. forms of LEDE, LEWD.

leuge, obs. form of LEAGUE *sb.*[1]

leugh, obs. Sc. pa. t. of LAUGH.

leuid, obs. form of LEWD.

leuk, Sc. form of LOOK.

‖**leukæmia** (l(j)u:'ki:mɪə). *Path.* Also leukemia, †leuch-. [ad. G. *leukämie* (R. Virchow 1848, in *Arch. f. path. Anat.* I. III. 563), f. λευκ-ός white + αἷμα blood.] A progressive disease of man and other warm-blooded animals characterized by the hyperplastic trans-formation and greatly increased activity of leucopoietic tissue, leading to abnormal accumulations of leucocytes (freq. of immature or abnormal form) first at the site of leucopoiesis and then (usually) in the blood and elsewhere.

1855 in MAYNE *Expos. Lex.* **1873** T. H. GREEN *Introd. Pathol.* (ed. 2) 148 Leukæmia. **1876** DUHRING *Dis. Skin* 503 Leucocythemic lymphadenoma, or leucæmia. **1885–8** FAGGE & PYE-SMITH *Princ. Med.* (ed. 2) I. 114 Leuchæmia. **1898** *Allbutt's Syst. Med.* V. 635 Bennett gave the name leucocythæmia to the disease, whilst Virchow called it leukæmia. **1938** M. N. RICHTER in H. Downey *Handbk. Hematol.* IV. xlii. 2889 The type of cell and tissue primarily involved, the extent and distribution of infiltrations, and the presence or absence of immature cells in the peripheral blood make the lesions observed in different cases and different types of leucemia quite diverse, the only feature common to all being the increase in number of white corpuscles and their relative immaturity. **1942** C. L. HEEL tr. *Engelbreth-Holm's Spontaneous & Exper. Leukæmia in Animals* i. 3 While leukæmia has not been observed in the lower vertebrates, the condition is known in many kinds of birds. *Ibid.* ii. 29 Detailed information is available about leukæmia in dogs, pigs, cattle, and..rodents. **1951** *New Biol.* XI. 97 In the treatment of leukaemia, a cancer-like disease of the white blood cells, several different classes of chemicals show some value. **1955** *Sci. News Let.* 19 Mar. 182/3 Leukemia, always fatal cancer of the blood, is showing up in survivors of the world's first military atom bombing. **1960** F. G. J. HAYHOE *Leukaemia* ii. 10 Patients with chronic leukaemias nearly always survive more than a year from the time of first symptoms, commonly for 3 to 5 years, and occasionally for very much longer. *Ibid.* 11 Subleukaemic and aleukaemic forms are more often encountered in the acute than in the chronic leukaemias, and they usually become fully leukaemic at a later stage in the progress of the disease. **1964** *Daily Tel.* 3 Jan. 13/3 A second British child suffering from leukemia..arrived with his mother in Ajaccio, Corsica, to-day for treatment with a new serum which is claimed to cure the disease. **1966** WRIGHT & SYMMERS *Systemic Path.* I. iv. 181/2 Post-mortem findings in acute leukaemia... Gross enlargement of the liver and spleen, such as is common in the chronic forms of leukaemia, is unusual.

leu'kæmic, *a.* and *sb.* [f. LEUKÆM(IA + -IC.]

A. *adj.* Affected with or characterized by leukæmia; characteristic of or resembling leukæmia; *spec.* marked by an increased number of leucocytes in the blood.

1876 *Clinical Soc. Trans.* IX. 83 On finding the leuchæmic state of the blood I gave him phosphorus. **1897** *Allbutt's Syst. Med.* IV. 445 Leukæmic tumours are small, scattered, roundish patches of lymph-cells. **1922**, **1946** [see LEUCOSIS]. **1942** M. M. WINTROBE *Clin. Hematol.* xvi. 616 In many cases peculiarities can be observed in leukemic cells which are like those of neoplastic cells. **1949** [see ALEUKÆMIC *a.*].

B. *sb.* An individual with leukæmia.

1964 *New Scientist* 13 Feb. 402/3 Nineteen of the 24 leukaemics were positive, one was doubtful and four were negative. **1973** *Nature* 12 Jan. 99/1 We have found that the response of lymphocytes from normals or leukaemics to low ..doses of PHA [*sc.* phytohaemagglutinin] is often greatly reduced in the presence of serum obtained from patients with untreated AML [*sc.* acute myeloid leukaemia] and ALL [*sc.* acute lymphoblastic leukaemia].

leukæmogenic (l(j)u:ˌki:məʊ'dʒɛnɪk), *a. Med.* Also leukemogenic. [f. LEUKÆM(IA + -O + -GENIC.] Capable of producing leukæmia; pertaining to the production of leukæmia.

1942 *Jrnl. Nat. Cancer Inst.* (U.S.) III. 231/2 Previous experiments indicated that X-rays are leukemogenic. **1953** *Cancer Res.* XIII. 267/2 Exposure to leukemogenic doses of x-rays. **1971** *New Scientist* 8 July 64/2 If these tumours were then removed.., these could then be shown to have leukaemogenic activity characteristic of leukaemia viruses. **1971** H. J. WOODLIFF *Leukaemia Cytogenetics* v. 47 Chromosomal abnormalities may be produced by many of the agents discussed above and many of these are also thought to be leukaemogenic, such as viruses, ionising radiation, chemicals and drugs. **1973** *Nature* 9 Feb. 397/1 Thymus dependent lymphatic leukaemia was induced [in mice] by irradiation or by a leukaemogenic virus.

So **leu'kæmogen**, a substance or agent capable of producing leukæmia; **leukæmo'genesis**, the production or development of leukæmia.

1942 *Jrnl. Nat. Cancer Inst.* (U.S.) III. 239/1 A systematic study of changes in the blood pictures during the early phases of leukemogenesis was beyond the scope of this work. **1944** DORLAND & MILLER *Med. Dict.* (ed. 20) 804/1 Leukemogen. **1946** *Physiol. Rev.* XXVI. 48 Organisms are subject to accidental exposure to chemical, physical and other agents which may be powerful leukemogens. **1953** *Cancer Res.* 268/1 Genetic factors determine susceptibility to specific leukemogens. **1961** *Lancet* 30 Sept. 748/1 We have been interested in the role of the thymus in leukæmogenesis. **1971** *Brit. Med. Bull.* XXVII. 67/1 The back-lash effects could in fact be mistaken for the advent of a new leukaemogen. **1973** *Nature* 12 Jan. 95/1 Viruses are associated with leukaemogenesis in both laboratory and outbred animals.

leukæmoid (l(j)u:'ki:mɔɪd), *a. Med.* Also leuc-, -emoid. [f. LEUKÆM(IA + -OID.] Resembling (that found in) leukæmia but due to some other cause.

1926 *Amer. Jrnl. Med. Sci.* CLXXII. 529 Was it leukemia, simulating Banti's in an aleukemic early stage, or was it Banti's with a terminal leukemoid picture? **1940** *Acta Med. Scand.* CIII. 568 In another case of sepsis with marked hyperglobulinemia there was a leucemoid reaction with crowds of plasma cells. **1946** *Physiol. Rev.* XXVI. 62 The aerobic glycolysis values of preleukemic, leukemic and leukemoid lymph nodes, spleens and livers were 50 per cent to 100 per cent above normal. **1960** F. G. J. HAYHOE *Leukaemia* xvi. 318 The haematological findings in the myeloproliferative and lymphoproliferative syndromes provide a wide borderline between leukaemic and leukaemoid pictures,..but we shall now be concerned with the unquestionably leukaemoid reactions occasionally observed in association with certain infections, metastasizing tumours, and some non-leukaemic blood diseases.

leuke, leun, obs. ff. LEAGUE, LUKE, LION.

leuko-, var. LEUCO-.

leukocyte, -cytic, etc.: see LEUCOCYTE.

leukovirus ('l(j)u:kəʊvaɪrəs). *Virology.* Also leuco-. [f. LEUKO- (in LEUKÆMIA and *leukosis*, LEUCOSIS) + VIRUS.] Any of a group of pleomorphic viruses consisting of enveloped single-stranded RNA, different members of which cause leucosis or tumours in mammals and birds.

1968 F. FENNER *Biol. Animal Viruses* I. i. 26 The viruses which are associated with leukosis of chickens and murine leukemia have as their genetic material a molecule of single-stranded RNA of about 12 million daltons atomic weight. The pathogenic potential of both groups of agents is similar, as are the virions. These viruses can therefore be grouped together into a new group, for which we propose the name 'leukovirus'. *Ibid.* 28 Most infections with leukoviruses are latent for prolonged periods, but they may eventually cause fatal disease, usually apparent as a disturbance of the lymphoid or hemopoietic systems. **1970** *Nature* 14 Nov. 622/1 The RNA tumour viruses (leucoviruses) seem to have a different mode of replication from other RNA-containing viruses. **1971** MARAMOROSCH & KURSTAK *Compar. Virol.* xvi. 514 The more euphonious term *leukovirus* suggested by Fenner (1968) has recently been approved by the International Commission for the Nomenclature of Viruses and will be used here. **1972** *Sci. Amer.* Jan. 25/3 A group of viruses, variously called the RNA tumor viruses, the leukoviruses or the rousviruses.., replicate by another mode of information transfer.

leungyie, obs. Sc. form of LOIN.

leurne, leuse, obs. ff. LEARN, LOOSE *v.*

leuterer, -ing: see LOITERER, -ING.

lev (lɛv). Also (erron.) leva. Pl. leva, levas, levs. [Bulg. *lev* (pl. *leva*), lion.] The basic monetary unit of Bulgaria.

1902 *Encycl. Brit.* XXVI. 451/2 Bulgaria..has adopted the metric system... The monetary unit is the *lev*,.. nominally equal to the franc. **1908** *Daily Chron.* 31 Oct. 1/6 The East Roumelian tribute amounts to 2,951,000 leva. **1921** S. GRAHAM *Europe* ii. 33 Bulgarian francs or levas are ..worth a bare three-farthings each today. **1928** *Daily Tel.* 16 Oct. 18 The Budget 1927–28 showed a surplus of sixty-five million levs. **1928** *Morning Post* 20 Oct. 11/5 The booty is estimated at many hundreds of thousands of levas (the leva is valued at about 600 to the £). **1959** *Chambers's Encycl.* II. 674/2 In May 1952 a drastic monetary reform was carried out whereby the lev was linked to the Russian rouble at the rate of 1·70 leva = 1 rouble. **1972** D. DAKIN *Unification of Greece* xiii. 188 Bulgaria had borrowed from France 245 million *leva* in 1904 and 1907.

†**levable**, *a. Obs.* [a. OF. *levable*, f. *lever* to raise, LEVY.] That may be levied; = LEVIABLE.

1432 *Rolls of Parlt.* IV. 403/2 If any oder..somme, be apon any Decenne..putt, that hit be for noght, voide, and noght levable. **1450** *Petit. City Winchester* in *Archæologia* (1770) I. 91 The xv penny or taxe is graunted to your highnesse..the whiche whenne it is levable [etc.]. **1496–7** *Act 12 Hen. VII*, c. 12 §5 Then the levyeng and payment of the seid xvme..[shall be] put in suspence and not levable nor paied.

‖**levada** (lɛ'vɑ:də). [Pg.] In Madeira, a canal for irrigation.

1885 J. Y. JOHNSON *Madeira* vi. 68 Besides the great levadas there are minor ones in every parish. **1920** *National Rev.* Nov. 408 Levadas are narrow canals cut out of the solid rock of volcanic basalt of which the island consists: watercourses of masonry, which intersect Madeira like a network, for the purposes of irrigation. *Ibid.* 409 One of the more hazardous levada walks. **1963** *Times* 28 Mar. 14/6 We ..set off from the rest-house on the *levada* at Queimadas. **1975** *Country Life* 13 Feb. 400/1 Every farm is irrigated by *levadas*—a network of channels which carry rainwater down from the mountains.

‖**levade** (lə'vɑ:d). [Fr., f. *lever* to raise.] (See quot. 1954.)

1944 E. BYNG *World of Arabs* 246 The three widely celebrated specialties of Vienna's 'Spanish' Riding School.. are known as the levade, the piaffe, and the capriole. **1953** G. BROOKE *Introd. Riding* vii. 69 A system that he believed would enable him to demonstrate the 'levade' and 'croupade' and similar gymnastics. **1954** A. PODHAJSKY *Spanish Riding School* (ed. 2) 22/1 Training above the ground is usually started either with the Levade or Pesade. In both these exercises which are constructed from the Piaffe, the hind quarters, deeply bent in the haunch, support the entire weight of the body, whilst the fore quarters with the fore feet drawn up under the body, rise more or less high above the ground; the duration of this position depends upon the dexterity and strength of the stallion. If the horse raises the fore quarters so high that his body reaches an angle of 45° with the earth, this is called 'Pesade'; on the other hand, if it raises the fore quarters less high, one speaks of a Levade.

levain(e, levalto, obs. ff. LEAVEN, LAVOLTA.

Levallois (lə'vælwɑ:). *Archæol.* [f. the Fr. place-name *Levallois* in north central France, NW. of Paris.] Used *attrib.* as a term for one of the main palæolithic cultures, post-Acheulian and pre-Mousterian. Hence **Levalloisean** (-'wɑ:zɪən), **-ian** *adjs.* Also **Levalloisoid** (-'wɑ:zɔɪd) *a.*, related to, or similar to, this culture. Also in *Comb.*, as **Levalloiso-Mou'sterian** *a.*

1921 R. A. S. MACALISTER *Text-bk. European Archæol.* I. 239 The transition from Lower to Middle Palaeolithic is marked by the introduction of two important types of implement; the miniature coup-de-poing..and the Levallois scraper. **1932** [see CLACTONIAN *a.*]. **1934** *Jrnl. R. Anthrop. Inst.* LXIV. 342 Partly Chellean, partly local Acheulean with a hint of Levalloisean. **1937** *Ann. Reg. 1936* 52 Associated with Levalloisian culture. **1937** GARROD & BATE *Stone Age Mt. Carmel* I. I. ii. 8 The majority of these [*sc.* flints] were of Levalloiso-Mousterian type, but a fair number could be referred to the Lower Aurignacian. **1938** *Encycl. Brit. Bk. of Year* 49/1 A Mousterian using the Levallois technique. **1938** *Proc. Prehist. Soc.* IV. 19 A Levalloisian flake industry forms part of the latest Acheulian. **1952** *Ibid.* XVIII. 10 They include Acheulean hand-axes and Levalloisoid flakes. **1959** J. D. CLARK *Prehist. S. Afr.* ii. 40 The Middle Stone Age is essentially the time of the specially prepared core and the flake tool derived from it. This is the technique known in Europe as 'Levallois' technique' and in Africa as 'prepared platform technique'. **1961** L. D. STAMP *Gloss. Geogr. Terms* 532 In East Anglia Clactonian is contemporaneous with Acheulian; Levalloisian with Mousterian.

†**levament.** *Obs. rare*[−0]. [ad. L. *levāment-um*, f. *levāre* to lighten.] (See quot.)

1623 COCKERAM, *Leuament*, the comfort which one hath of his wife.

levan ('li:væn). *Chem.* [f. LÆVO-, LEV(O- + *-an*, after *dextran*.] A lævulosan (fructan); *esp.* any fructan of the kind produced by certain bacteria, in which the linking of adjacent fructose units is between the second carbon atom of one unit and the sixth of the next.

1902 R. G. SMITH in *Proc. Linn. Soc. New South Wales* XXVI. 603 From a review of the lævo-rotatory gummy

substances that are hydrolysed to levulose, it appears that this bacterial gum has not hitherto been described. I therefore propose for it the name levan, which was suggested by the polariscopic nature of the gum and derived glucose, and also from the fact that another bacterial gum, which is derived from dextrose, and which yields dextrose on hydrolysis, is known as dextran. **1948** W. PIGMAN *Chem. Carbohydrates* xv. 604 Fructosans or levans are found widely distributed throughout the plant kingdom..and generally serve as reserve polysaccharides in place of, or in addition to, starch. **1953** WHISTLER & SMART *Polysaccharide Chem.* xi. 276 D-Fructose polymers occurring in plants..are designated as fructans while those elaborated by microorganisms are called levans... Actually the levans are structurally similar to some of the plant polyfructoses. **1965** T. AKAZAWA in Bonner & Varner *Plant Biochem.* xii. 287 Although the size of these substances is small, 3–30 hexose residues per molecule, their structure is basically the same as that of the high molecular bacterial levan produced by several microorganisms... The name grass levan has therefore been given to this group of plant compounds. A further interesting point is..that fructosans of inulin type, β-(2→1), and of levan type, β-(2→6), are the main constituents of stem and ear tissues, respectively, of cereal plants.

'levance. [See next and -ANCE.] = next.

1886 BLACKMORE in *Harper's Mag.* May 874 If.. prescription for levance and couchance conferred any right undefeasible.

levancy ('lɛvənsɪ). *Law.* [f. LEVANT *a.*: see -ANCY.] In phrase ***levancy and couchancy***: the fact of being levant and couchant.

1695, **1818** [see COUCHANCY]. **1866** *Law Rep. 1* Ex. 172 The condition of levancy and couchancy is only to be taken as the measure of the capacity of the land to maintain the cattle. **1872** *Law Rep.* 7 Com. Pl. 593 Levancy and couchancy is a mere measure of the number of cattle or other animals that may be put upon the common.

levand, obs. form of LEVANT, LIVING.

Levant (lɪ'vænt), *sb.*[1] (and quasi-*adj.*) Also (in sense 4b) 6 **levand**, 7 **leven**. [a. F. *levant*, pres. pple. of *lever* to rise, used subst. for the point where the sun rises; hence as in senses 1 and 2. (In Milton stressed '*levant*.)]

1. *Geog.* †**a.** The countries of the East. ***the High Levant*** = the far East (cf. HIGH *a.* 3). ***cloth of Levant*** = BEZETTA (see quot. 1558). *Obs.* **b.** *spec.* The eastern part of the Mediterranean, with its islands and the countries adjoining.

1497 *Naval Acc. Hen. VII* (1896) 218 A viage to be made into the levaunt. **1558** WARDE tr. *Alexis' Secr.* IV. 80 To make a kinde of cloth, called cloth of Leuant wherwith women vse to colour their faces. **1561** EDEN *Arte Nauig.* III. i. 54b, The Hydrographers..haue chaunged the names, Callyng the Leuant or Orient, East. The Ponent or Occident, West. **1599** HAKLUYT *Voy.* II. I. 99 My voiage to the Ilands of Candia and Chio in the Leuant. **1605** BACON *Adv. Learn.* II. xvi. §2 It is the use of China, and the Kingdoms of the High Levant. **1688** *Lond. Gaz.* No. 2320/3 Not to allow Pratique to any Ships coming from the Levant. **1727–41** CHAMBERS *Cycl.*, *Levant*, in geography, signifies any country situate to the east of us. **1839** *Penny Cycl.* XIII. 453/1 Levant..is also commonly used..to designate the eastern or Asiatic shores of that sea [the Mediterranean]. **1844** KINGLAKE *Eothen* v. (1864) 66 That Grecian race against which you will be cautioned so carefully as soon as you touch the Levant.

2. An easterly wind blowing up the Mediterranean; a levanter. ? *Obs.*

1628 DIGBY *Voy. Medit.* (1868) 81 The 29. there came a fresh gale att S.E.; which..blowed constantely a strong Leuante. **1693** *Dryden's Juvenal* xiv. (1697) 367 Carpathian Gale... We term it at Sea, a strong Levant. **1762** MORE in *Phil. Trans.* LII. 450 Setting sail with a light Levant, to pass the strait to the westward. **1867** SMYTH *Sailor's Word-bk.*, *Levant*, a wind coming from the east, which freshens as the sun rises.

3. A kind of leather = *levant morocco* (see 4b).

1880 *Times* 25 Sept. 4/5 The leathers known..as Levants, Memels and Cordovans.

4. *attrib.* and *Comb.*: **a.** passing into adj. with sense 'east-, eastern', as ***levant sea, wind***.

1601 HOLLAND *Pliny* I. 129 It begins at the Levant sea of Oriental Indians. **1657** HOWELL *Londinop.* 386 She is built upon the utmost levant point of Europe. **1667** MILTON *P.L.* x. 704 Forth rush the Levant and the Ponent Windes. **1691** *Lond. Gaz.* No. 2655/2 She was driven by a strong Levant Wind from her Anchor in that Bay. **1798** LADY HUNTER 16 Nov. in *Jrnl. Sir M. & Lady Hunter* (1894) 131 Some days before the rain came we had what they call a levant wind. **1819** H. BUSK *Vestriad* III. 656 Breathless, the ponent wind in vain he plies, Nor can the levant lift him.

b. (sense 1 b, 'pertaining to or coming from the Levant'), as ***Levant feathers, morocco, sea, skin, taffeta, thrift*** (a plant).

1503–4 *Ld. Treas. Acc. Scotl.* (1900) II. 239 Tua gret beddis of levand fedderis. **1597** GERARDE *Herbal* II. clxxvii. §2. 482 *Caryophyllus Mediterraneus* Leuant Thrift, or Lea Gilloflower. *a* **1625** BEAUM. & FL. *Wit without M.* II. iv, A sharpe Prognostication that shal scowre them..like leven taffaties. **1701** *Lond. Gaz.* No. 3719/4 The Hon. Company of Merchants Trading to the Levant Seas. **1818** HALLAM *Mid. Ages* ix. II. (1819) III. 391 Sanuto..has left us a curious account of the Levant trade. **1879** *Cassell's Techn. Educ.* IV. 88 The French have the pre-eminence in the species of Levant skins marked with a handsome full-grain. *Mod. Bookseller's Catal.*, Choicely bound in half crimson levant morocco.

levant (lɪ'vænt), *sb.*[2] [f. LEVANT *v.*[1]] The action of LEVANT *v.*[1]; a bet made with the intention of absconding if it is lost. Only in phrases ***to come the levant, run*** or ***throw a levant***.

1714 T. LUCAS *Mem. Gamesters* (ed. 2) 111 He hath ventur'd to come the Levant over Gintlemen. **1728** VANBR. & CIB. *Prov. Husb.* I. i. 17 Throw a familiar Levant upon some sharp lurching Man of Quality. **1731** FIELDING *Lottery* III. Wks. 1882 VIII. 483 Matter! Why, I had a Levant thrown upon me. **1749** —— *Tom Jones* VIII. xii, Never mind that, man; e'en boldly run a levant. **1812** J. H. VAUX *Flash Dict.*, *Levanting* or *Running a Levant*.

levant ('lɛvənt), *a. Law.* [a. F. *levant*, pr. pple. of *lever* to raise, *refl.* to rise.] Only in phrase ***levant and couchant*** (= med.L. *levans et cubans*, in continental as well as Eng. use): lit. 'rising up and lying down'; said of cattle. (For the specific interpretation see quot. 1768.)

1594 WEST *2nd Pt. Symbol.* Chancerie §100 To have common of pasture for their beasts and cattel upon the said lands levant and cowchant at all times of the yeare. **1768** BLACKSTONE *Comm.* III. 9 If the lands were not sufficiently fenced so as to keep out cattle, the landlord cannot distrein them, till they have been levant and couchant (*levantes et cubantes*) on the land; that is, have been long enough there to have laid down and rose up to feed; which in general is held to be one night at least. **1864** *Brumby Enclosure Application* 38 Right of common which may be exercised in all times of the year for cattle levant and couchant. **1872** *Law Rep.* 7 Com. Pl. 592 All cattle, sheep, and other commonable animals levant and couchant within the borough.

levant (lɪ'vænt), *v.*[1] Also **livant**. [? ad. Sp. *levant-ar* to lift (*levantar la casa* to break up housekeeping, *levantar el campo* to break up the camp), f. *levar*:—L. *levāre* to lift.]

1. *intr.* To steal away, 'bolt'. Now *esp.* of a betting man or gamester: To abscond.

1797 MARY ROBINSON *Walsingham* (1805) IV. xc. 261 She found that the sharps would dish me, and levanted without even bidding me farewell. **1809** *Sporting Mag.* XXXIV. 57 [He] must produce a certificate that he has never levanted at any race-course. **1848** THACKERAY *Bk. Snobs* xxxix, One day we shall hear of one or other levanting. **1863** MISS BRADDON *Eleanor's Vict.* III. xix. 289 The clerk had levanted before his employer returned from America. **1880** V. L. CAMERON *Our Future Highway* I. iii. 46 He took the opportunity of his host falling asleep to levant. **1912** D. H. LAWRENCE *Let. c* 5 Nov. (1962) I. 154 F. had carefully studied *Anna Karenina*, in a sort of 'How to be happy though livanted' spirit. *Ibid.*, I am the fellow she livanted with.

†**2.** *trans.* Only in ***levant me!***, a mild form of imprecation. *Obs.*

1760 FOOTE *Minor* I. Wks. 1799 I. 241 Levant me, but he got enough last night to purchase a principality.

Hence **le'vanting** *vbl. sb.* and *ppl. a.*

1788 G. A. STEVENS *Adv. Speculist* I. 96 This [*sc.* gaming when one will not be able to pay in the event of losing] at Hazard-table is called Levanting. **1847** THACKERAY *Brighton* ii, Guttlebury House was shut up by the lamented levanting of the noble Earl. **1855** —— *Newcomes* II. 314 The levanting auctioneer's wife. **1866** MISS BRADDON *Lady's Mile* i. 1 Distracted by vague fears of levanting tenants and bad debts.

levant (lɪ'vænt), *v.*[2] [f. LEVANT *sb.*[1]] *trans.* To make (leather) look like levant morocco.

1869 *Eng. Mech.* 17 Dec. 336/3 Can [he] give me any information about the plan of memelling or levanting leather?

Levanter[1] (lɪ'væntə(r)). [f. as prec. + -ER[1].]

1. a. An inhabitant of the Levant; = LEVANTINE *sb.* 1. *rare.* **b.** A ship trading to the Levant. *rare.*

1667 EVELYN *Mem.* (1857) III. 211, I herewith enclosed send you the relation of Signor Pietro, as unpolished as the usual styles of the Levanters are. **1812** W. TENNANT *Anster F.* II. xlviii, Then brought him home in hold of stout Levanter. **1893** F. F. MOORE *I Forbid Banns* (1899) 146 The Levant and the Levanters..are usually in need of cash.

2. A strong and raw easterly wind in the Mediterranean (Smyth *Sailor's Word-bk.* 1867).

1790 BURKE *Fr. Rev.* 86 Let them not break prison to burst like a Levanter. **1799** NELSON 28 Nov. in Nicolas *Disp.* (1845) IV. 115, I shall not keep the Perseus by detaining her a moment with this fine Levanter. **1829** MARRYAT *F. Mildmay* v, We..tumbled down the Mediterranean before a strong Levanter. **1891** HALL CAINE *Scapegoat* I. 155 The rippling of the levanter in her hair.

fig. **1831** *Blackw. Mag.* XXIX. 906 The angry philosopher himself, by a fierce levanter of indignation, [was] driven westwards to America. **1873** F. HALL *Mod. Engl.* 334 Such is the procedure, which..has provoked a very levanter of ire and vilification.

levanter[2] (lɪ'væntə(r)). [f. LEVANT *v.*[1] + -ER[1].] One who absconds; esp. one who does so after losing bets.

1781 G. PARKER *View Society* II. 168 Levanters, these are of the order and number of Black-Legs. *Ibid.* 170 If the horse which the Levanter betted upon has lost. **1811** *Sporting Mag.* XXXVII. 303 Newmarket Levanter! **1833** *New Sporting Mag.* V. 35 Boulogne whose inhabitants are partly composed of broken-down sportsmen and Levanters. **1888** TRAILL *Will. III*, iv. (1892) 36 A royal martyr is a much more impressive object than a royal levanter.

†**Le'vantian.** *Obs.* [f. LEVANT *sb.*[1] + -IAN.] = LEVANTINE *sb.* 1.

1660 F. BROOKE tr. *Le Blanc's Trav.* 380, I saw an Indian truck pearls with a Levantian (so they term us).

Levantine (lɪ'væntɪn, 'lɛvəntɪn), *a.* and *sb.* [f. as prec. + -INE. Cf. F. *levantin* (masc.), *-ine* (fem.).]

A. *adj.* Of or pertaining to the Levant; †in early use, pertaining to the east, eastern. Also, recalling or resembling the manners of the Levantines. Of a vessel: Trading to the Levant.

1649 JER. TAYLOR *Gt. Exemp.* I. §4. 43 This star did not trouble Herod till the Levantine princes expounded the mysteriousnesse of it. **1664** EVELYN *Sylva* xxii. 58 [The seeds of the Platanus] should be gather'd late in Autumn, and brought us from some more Levantine parts then Italy. **1784** COWPER *Task* III. 583 Those Ausonia claims, Levantine regions these. *a* **1844** CAMPBELL *Spectre Boat* iii, Where Mount Ætna lights the deep Levantine sea. **1897** *Daily News* 23 Sept. 8/3, I must say that his [Bourbaki's] manner was very Levantine. **1900** *Speaker* 3 Mar. 599/1 Even in the days of Thomas Cromwell a Duke of Norfolk would own Levantine merchantmen.

B. *sb.*

1. An inhabitant or native of the Levant.

1706 PHILLIPS (ed. Kersey), *Levantines*, the Natives or Inhabitants of the Levant, the Eastern People; also those that are employed on the Mediterranean. **1821** BYRON *Don Juan* III. xxix, The Pyrrhic dance so martial, To which the Levantines are very partial. **1844** KINGLAKE *Eöthen* xviii. (1864) 221 Europeans settled in the East, and commonly called Levantines. **1897** *Daily News* 23 Sept. 8/3 A Levantine in blood, he [Bourbaki] instinctively understood how to appeal to the imagination of the Arabs.

2. [F. *levantine.*] (See quot. 1882.)

1831 PORTER *Silk Manuf.* 298 Levantine is a stout, close-made, and twilled silk. **1835** *Court Mag.* VI. 1/2 Tigrine is a levantine of the very richest kind, spotted like a tiger's skin. **1882** CAULFEILD & SAWARD *Dict. Needlework*, *Levantine*, a very rich-faced stout twilled black silk material, exceedingly soft, and of excellent wear. Its face and back show different shades; if the former be a blue-black, the latter will be a jet and *vice versâ*.

Levantinism (lɪ'væntɪnɪz(ə)m). [f. LEVANTIN(E *a.* and *sb.* + -ISM.] The spirit or culture of the Levant.

1949 KOESTLER *Promise & Fulfilment* III. iv. 330 What kind of a civilization will Israel's be? Will it be..the superficial veneer of Levantinism? **1961** *Guardian* 6 Feb. 8/2 Mr Ben-Gurion warned his countrymen against letting 'Levantinism' creep into their national life. **1973** *Observer* 6 May 6/6 Israel's leaders worry about 'levantinism'.

le'vantinize, *v.* [f. as prec. + -IZE.] *trans.* To make Levantine in form or character.

1929 *Times* 5 Nov. 17/4 The Government's policy of 'Europeanizing' a somewhat levantinized Administration. **1930** *Times Lit. Suppl.* 4 Sept. 691/1 The rest of the Turks remained farmers..and thereby escaped the contamination of the Levantinized Ottomanism. **1946** KOESTLER *Thieves in Night* 112 Our small community will..become levantinised, submerged in the Arab sea.

†**Levantisco.** *Obs. rare*[−1]. [Sp. (properly adj. = Levantine), f. *Levante* LEVANT *sb.*[1] + *-isco*: see -ISH.] A Levantine ship.

1597 in *St. Papers, Dom.* 360 There remain 70 ships of all sorts: six Levantiscoes.

†**Levantisk.** *Obs. rare*[−1]. [ad. F. *levantisque*, ad. Sp. *levantisco*: see prec.] = LEVANTINE *sb.* 1.

1660 F. BROOKE tr. *Le Blanc's Trav.* 354 A Frenchman, who under the stile of a Levantisk..had before made a voyage that way.

levar, Sc. f. *liever* comp. of LIEF.

levare, obs. Sc. form of LAVER *sb.*[2]

‖**levari facias** (liː'vɑːrɪ 'feɪʃɪæs). *Law.* [L., = cause to be levied, f. *levari*, to be levied, f. *levāre* to raise + *facias* cause, 2nd pers. sing. pres. subj. of *facĕre* to do, make.] (See quot. 1768.)

a **1625** H. FINCH *Law* (1627) IV. xlvi. 471 A *Leuari facias*. .. *Leuari facias* to leuie execution of the profits of his land and Chattels. **1768** BLACKSTONE *Comm.* III. xxvi. 417 A third species of execution is by writ of *levari facias*; which affects a man's goods and the *profits* of his lands, commanding the sheriff to levy the plaintiff's debt on the lands and goods of the defendant;..little use is now made of this writ. **1818** [see FIERI-FACIAS]. **1888** *Encycl. Brit.* XXIV. 696/2 *Levari facias* is the means of levying execution for forfeited recognizances. **1959** JOWITT *Dict. Eng. Law* II, *Levari facias*..had been practically superseded before 1883 by the writ of *elegit*; and the Bankruptcy Act, 1883, s. 146 (2), enacted that it should no longer be issued in any civil proceeding.

†**levation.** *Obs.* Also 4–6 **levacion**. [ad. L. *levātiōn-em*, n. of action f. *levāre* to lighten, raise, levy. Cf. OF. *levacion* (in sense 1).]

1. *Eccl.* The lifting up of the Host for the adoration of the people; = ELEVATION 1 c.

c **1375** *Lay Folks Mass Bk.* (MS. B.) 406 And so þo leuacioun þou behalde. **1434** *E.E. Wills* (1882) 101 At the leuacion at the hie masse. **1494** FABYAN *Chron.* VI. ccx. 225 In the tyme of the leuacion of yᵉ sacrement, he laught. **1532** in Pocock *Rec. Ref.* (1870) II. 230 After the levation the deacon turneth to the people. **1559** BECON *Display. Popish Mass* Wks. 1563 III. 43b, The author of your Leuation and liftyng vp yᵉ bred aboue your head was Pope Honorius the third.

†**2.** (See quot.) *Obs.*

1656 BLOUNT *Glossogr.*, *Levation*, an easing, or diminishing of grief or pain.

†**3.** *concr.* Something levied; a duty, tax. *Obs.*

1690 CHILD *Disc. Trade* (1694) 118 Without paying the same Duties or Levations towards the Company's charge.

†**levative**, *a.* and *sb.* *Obs.* [ad. L. type **levātīvus*, f. L. *levāre* to lighten.]

A. *adj.* Tending to alleviate or soothe; soothing. **B.** *sb.* A soothing medicine.

1657 TOMLINSON *Renou's Disp.* 160* Gargarismes.. whose faculty is either levative or repressive or evocative. **1657** *Physical Dict.*, *Levative*, medicines easing pain.

levator (lɪˈveɪtə(r)). Also 7 *erron.* **levitor.** [a. late L. *levātor*, agent-n. f. L. *levāre* to raise.]

1. *Anat.* A muscle whose function is to raise the part to which it is attached = ELEVATOR 1 a; also *attrib.*, as ***levator-muscle***.

1615 CROOKE *Body of Man* 741 Euery leuator or lifting muscle hath a depressor or sinking muscle. **1826** KIRBY & SP. *Entomol.* IV. xliii. 171 Levator muscles that raise an organ. **1874** ROOSA *Dis. Ear* (ed. 2) 56 The levator is the largest of the three muscles. **1877** HUXLEY *Anat. Inv. Anim.* vi. 262 The large levator muscle of the appendage.

†**2.** *Surg.* An instrument used to raise a depressed portion of bone; = ELEVATOR 2. *Obs.*

1672 WISEMAN *Wounds* I. x. 118, I put in a Levator, and raised up the deprest bone even with the rest. **1688** R. HOLME *Armoury* III. 398/2 If [acheing teeth] chance to break in the pulling, the Levitor helpeth to prise out the roots. **1698** FRYER *Acc. E. India & P.* 176 Two Bones of the Bigness and Figure of a Levator. **1789** T. WHATELY in *Med. Commun.* II. 388 With levators and nippers I separated it piecemeal.

†**levatory.** *Obs. rare*⁻¹. In quot. *erron.* lavatory. [as if ad. L. **levātōrium*, f. *levāre* to raise. So OF. *levatoire*.] = ELEVATOR 2.

1612 WOODALL *Surg. Mate* Wks. (1653) 4 The Lavatory is a necessary instrument to elevate the depressed Cranium. **1706** PHILLIPS (ed. Kersey), *Levatory.*

levayn(e, obs. form of LEAVEN.

†**leve**, *sb.* *Obs.* Forms: 1 (ȝe)léafa, 2 i-leafe, leave, 3 leaf, lefve, *Orm.* læfe, 3–4 leve. [OE. *ȝeléafa*, *léafa* str. masc. = OFris. *láva*, OS. *gilôbo* (MDu. *gelôve*, Du. *geloof*), OHG. *giloubo* (MHG. *geloube*, G. *glaube*); Goth. has *galaubeins*, with different suffix; related to Goth. *galaubjan*: see Y-LEVE, BELIEVE *vbs.*] Belief, faith; *occas.* trust.

c **950** *Lindisf. Gosp.* Matt. viii. 10 Ne fand ic suæ miclo leafa [*c* **1000** *Ags. Gosp.* ȝeleafan] in israhel. *c* **1000** ÆLFRIC *Gram.* Pref. (Z.) 3 Forðan ðe ðurh lare byð se ȝeleafa ȝehealden. *c* **1175** *Lamb. Hom.* 5 We sulen habben ure heorte and habben godne ileafe to ure drihten. *Ibid.* 57 Mid al þis haue þu charite and soðfeste leaue. *c* **1200** ORMIN 2776 Godess þeoww birrþ habbenn her Aȝȝ soþfasst læfe o Criste. *c* **1205** LAY. 16840 ȝif heo wulleð cristindom mid gode lefue vnder-fon. *a* **1225** *Leg. Kath.* 384 Ich iseo wel..þat tu were iset ȝung to leaf & to lare. *a* **1275** *Prov. Ælfred* 548 in *O.E. Misc.*, Haue þu none leue to þe þad after þe bileued. *c* **1330** R. BRUNNE *Chron.* (1810) 247 Noþeles he wild haf briggid, þe fals leue & erroure.

†**leve**, *v.*¹ *Obs.* Forms: 1 léfan, lýfan, 2–5 leve(n, 3 le(a)fen, 4 leeve, *Sc.* lewe, 5 leef. [OE. (Anglian) *léfan*, (WS.) *lýfan* = OHG. (*ar*)*louban* (MHG., mod.G. (*er*)*louben*), ON. *løyfa*, Goth. (*us*)*laubjan*, f. OTeut. **laubâ* LEAVE *sb.*¹] *trans.* To grant permission to; allow, permit. Also (esp. of God or Christ), to grant. With personal obj. (? orig. *dat.*) and *inf.* or clause; also *absol.*

c **897** K. ÆLFRED *Gregory's Past.* Pref. 4 We hit nohwæðer ne selfe ne lufedon ne eac oðrum monnum ne lifdon. *c* **1000** *Ags. Gosp.* Matt. xix. 8 Moyses..lyfde eow eower wif to forlætenne. *c* **1175** *Lamb. Hom.* 11 Þet he us leue swa libben on þisse scorte liue þet [etc.]. *c* **1200** ORMIN 8873 Godd Allmahhtiȝ lefe uss swa To forþenn Cristess wille. *c* **1220** *Bestiary* 303 Vre louerd crist it leue us ðat his laȝe us fede. *a* **1225** *Juliana* 28 Lef me þat ich mote þe treowliche luuien. *a* **1225** *St. Marher.* 12 Leaf me gan. *a* **1225** *Ancr. R.* 88 Vre Louerd..ne leue ou neuer stinken þene fule put. *c* **1250** *Gen. & Ex.* 2532 God leue hem in his blisse spilen among engeles & seli men. *c* **1375** *Sc. Leg. Saints* xxvi. (*Nycholas*) 632 þat he wald lewe þam to say þe story of sancte nicholas. *c* **1375** BARBOUR *Bruce* XIX. 126 Of the kyngis curtasye, That levit him debonarly Till do of his land his liking. *c* **1385** CHAUCER *L.G.W.* 2083 *Ariadne*, And leue me nevere swich a cas be-falle. **1393** LANGL. *P. Pl.* C. I. 149 Crist..leue þe lede so þy londe þat leaute þe louye. *c* **1400** *Destr. Troy* 8048 And þes wordes ho warpit, as hir wo leuit. *c* **1400** *Apol. Loll.* 28 þat onely a man vse his power in to ilk þing, as God..lefiþ him to vse it. *c* **1450** HOLLAND *Howlat* 534 As our Roy levit, The Dowglass in armes the bludy hart beris. *c* **1470** HENRY *Wallace* IV. 38 Thocht a subiet in deid wald pass his lord, It is nocht lewyt be na rychtwis racord. *Ibid.* VI. 262 Wemen thai lewit and preistis, on the morn, To pass thar way. *c* **1510** *Gest Rob. Hode* I. in Arb. *Garner* VI. 430 God leve that he be true. **1513** DOUGLAS *Æneis* III. vi. 203, I am levit with my wordis the to charge.

†**leve**, *v.*² *Obs.* Forms: 1 léfan, líefan, lýfan, 2–3 luven, 2–5 leve(n, 3, 5 lefen, (3 leaven, leove), 3–4 live(n, (4 lieve, lyff, lyve), 5–6 leev(e, *Sc.* leif. [OE. (Anglian) *léfan*, (WS.) *líefan*, a shortened form of *ȝeléfan*, *ȝelíefan*: see Y-LEVE, BELIEVE *vbs.*]

1. *intr.* To believe *in*, *on*, *up*, *upon*; also to trust, give credence *to* a person or thing; = BELIEVE 1.

c **1175** *Lamb. Hom.* 75 To luuene ine god mote fif þing. *c* **1200** *Trin. Coll. Hom.* 11 Cursed be þe man þe leueð upen hwate. *c* **1200** ORMIN 939 Hu ȝuw birrþ leden ȝuw And lefenn uppo Criste. *a* **1225** *Leg. Kath.* 328 Me hwet is mare medschipe þen for to leuen on him. **1377** LANGL. *P. Pl.* B. XVII. 20 Lo here in my lappe þat leued on þat charme, Iosue and Iudith. **1382** WYCLIF *Ecclus.* xxxii. 27 Who leeueth to God, taketh heed to the hestes. *a* **1400** *Pistill Susan* 358 Who so leviþ [*MS. A.* leeueþ] on our lord dar hym not lese. *c* **1430** *Hymns Virg.* 73 ȝhe, Conscience, now to þi wordis y leeue. *c* **1430** *How Good Wife taught Dau.* 159 in *Babees Bk.*, Nocht leif to vantoune giglotriss. *c* **1450** *Erle Tolous* 555 My wele, my wytt, ys all away, But ye leue on my lore. *c* **1470** *Golagros & Gaw.* 1107 To leif in thi laute. *c* **1475** *Rauf Coilȝear* 944 My treuth I the plicht, That I sall lelely leef on thy Lord ay. **1535** STEWART *Cron. Scot.* (1858) II. 168 That all quhilk leuit vpone Christis lair, In his defence sould follow.

b. Without construction: To exercise faith.

a **900** *O.E. Martyrol.* 8 Nov. 202 Ða lyfde se gode ond fulwihte onfeng. *c* **1200** *Trin. Coll. Hom.* 81 We wolden sen sum fortocne of þe Warbi we mihten..leuen. **13..** *E.E. Allit. P.* B. 1703 Þenne he laued þat lorde & leued in trawþe. *a* **1352** MINOT *Poems* iii. 16 Leves wele it es no lye. **1382** WYCLIF *Ecclus.* xix. 4 Who leeueth sone, is liȝt in herte. **14..** *How Wise Man taught Son* in Ritson *Anc. Pop. Poetry* 36 Common women, as j leve Make ȝong men evyle to spede. *c* **1440** *Partonope* 83 Levyth [*printed* lenyth] well this ys no fable. ? *a* **1500** *Chester Pl.* (E.E.T.S.) 396 Ther he lyves in flesh and blood, as fully leeven we.

2. *trans.* **a.** To believe, give credence to (a person); occas. to believe in, to trust. **b.** To believe, give credence to (a thing, also with obj. clause either with or without *that*); to accept (an alleged fact, a statement); = BELIEVE 5–8.

971 *Blickl. Hom.* 11 Swa is to lyfenne þæt englas hie ȝeorne beheoldan. *c* **1175** *Lamb. Hom.* 75 Þet ne leueð nan bute þe gode cristene Mon. *a* **1225** *Leg. Kath.* 430 ȝef ha nalde leauen þat ha ȝet lefde. *c* **1250** *Gen. & Ex.* 935 Abram leuede ðis hot in sped. **1297** R. GLOUC. (Rolls) 6858 Þe kyng leuede him wel ynou. **13..** *E.E. Allit. P.* A. 69 Þe lyȝt of hem myȝt no mon leuen. **13..** *Guy Warw.* (A.) 1584 Allas! Allas!..That y no hadde leued thi word! *a* **1330** *Roland & V.* 302 Who þat wil nouȝt leue me, In spaine men may þe soþe y-se. *c* **1330** *Arth. & Merl.* 925 (Kölbing) Þine tale ich no leue. **1362** LANGL. *P. Pl.* A. I. 36 Leef not þi licam, for lyȝere him techeþ. **1377** —— *P. Pl.* B. XVIII. 187 Leuestow that ȝond liȝte unlouke myȝte helle. *c* **1385** CHAUCER *L.G.W.* Prol. 10 But goddis forbode but men schulde leue Wel more thyng than men han seyn with eye. *c* **1400** *Lanfranc's Cirurg.* 333 It wole liȝtly be leeued of lewid men. *c* **1400** MAUNDEV. (1839) xx. 221 We wolde never han leved it, had wee not seen it. **1414** BRAMPTON *Penit. Ps.* (Percy Soc.) 31 Now may no man othir levyn. **1426** AUDELAY *Poems* 12 Leve he is a lyere. *a* **1450** *Knt. de la Tour* (1868) 82 That ye take no yeftes, nor leuithe none euelle counsaile. *c* **1450** *Merlin* 11 The lecherye that thow hast told, wher-of I can not leve the. *c* **1470** *Golagros & Gaw.* 71 Leif ye the lele. **1513** BRADSHAW *St. Werburge* I. 852 A mountayne or hyll soner, leue ye me, Myght be remoeued. *Ibid.* 2266 They toke hym tenderly, ye may me leue full sure. *a* **1547** SURREY *Æneid* II. 314 Cassandra then..Her prophetes lippes, yet neuer of vs leeued, Disclosed eft. *c* **1570** *Pride & Lowl.* (1841) 67 And choose him how this matter he wyl leeven.

Hence †ˈ**leving** *vbl. sb.*, believing.

1533 MORE *Confut. Tindale* VIII. Wks. 799/2 Because it is a presumpteous hope, loking to be saued with damnable deuelyshe lieuing.

†**leve**, *v.*³ *Obs. rare*⁻¹. [ad. F. *lever* to raise.] *trans.* To lift *up*.

c **1489** CAXTON *Blanchardyn* xlix. 191 Sadoyne..leued vp his guysarme vpon him.

leve, obs. form of LAVE, LEAF, LIEF, LIVE *v.*

†ˈ**leveable**, *a.* *Obs. rare.* Also 4 leevable. [f. LEVE *v.*² + -ABLE.] That may be believed or trusted; credible, trustworthy.

1382 WYCLIF *2 Chron.* vi. 18 Thanne whethir leeuable [Vulg. *credibile*] it be, that [etc.]. *a* **1483** *Liber Niger* in *Househ. Ord.* (1790) 74 Fower yomen leveable and discrete.

levecel, variant of LEVESEL *Obs.*

‖**leveche** (leˈbetʃe). [Sp.] A hot, dry, more or less southerly wind of south-eastern Spain, the local counterpart of the sirocco.

1887 *Encycl. Brit.* XXII. 296/2 The eastern part of this [southern] zone is the part of Spain which is liable to be visited from time to time by the scorching and blasting *leveche*, the name given in Spain to the sirocco. **1927** [see GIBLI]. **1962** J. E. VAN RIPER *Man's Physical World* vii. 222/2 The Mediterranean area also is the home of a hot, searing, dust-laden wind off the Sahara, known in various localities as *sirocco*, *khamsin*, *leveche*, or *samiel*.

leved, levedi, obs. forms of LEAVED, LADY.

levee (lɪˈviː, ˈlɛviː), *sb.*¹ *U.S.* Also 9 levy. [ad. F. *levée*, fem. of *levé*, pa. pple. of *lever* to raise.]

1. a. An embankment to prevent the overflow of a river.

1718–20 DUMONT *Plan N. Orleans* in J. Winsor *Mississ. Basin* (1895) 151. **1770** P. PITTMAN *Europ. Settlem. Mississ.* 10 The town [New Orleans] is secured from the inundations of the river by a raised bank, generally called the Levée. **1812** J. CUTLER *Topogr. Descr. Ohio* 90 Here commences the embankment or Levee, on the western side of the river. **1850** B. TAYLOR *Eldorado* i. (1862) 6 Broad fields of sugar cane.. came down to the narrow levee which protects them from the floods. **1883** *Encycl. Amer.* I. 197/1 The levee—or levy, as it is often written—is the name of the embankment itself. **1895** J. WINSOR *Mississ. Basin* 158 Perier had completed his levee along the river.

attrib. **1877** BURROUGHS *Taxation* 29 A levee tax was laid.

b. *Geol.* A low broad ridge of water-laid sediment running along the side of a stream channel; also, any of various similar natural embankments, as those formed by mud flows or lava flows, or along a submarine channel.

1870 in L. C. Cramton *Early Hist. Yellowstone Nat. Park* (1932) 129 Passing over a sand levee, grown up with sagebrush, we found ourselves on the open beach of the great Yellowstone Lake. *Ibid.* 137 The shoreline is bordered by a levee of obsidian, lava pebbles, and calcareous fragments, cutting off and inclosing ponds of water behind it. **1910** *Proc. Indiana Acad. Sci.* 1909 260 Deltas occasionally take the form of long, narrow ridges upon one or both sides of a stream, resembling the natural levees in the 'goosefoot' of the Mississippi. **1942** *Jrnl. Geomorphol.* V. 222 (*heading*) Mudflow levees. **1957** G. E. HUTCHINSON *Treat. Limnol.* I. i. 99 Levees may form along the water courses. **1962** E. A. VINCENT tr. *Rittmann's Volcanoes* i. 33 When the supply of lava diminishes and finally comes to an end, the still-fluid lava inside the stream continues to flow out and the mantle of scoriae collapses, leaving a more or less even flow of scoriaceous block lava (clinker lava), flanked on both sides by upstanding block walls, called lava moraines (scoria moraines, lava levées). **1964** *Bull. Amer. Assoc. Petroleum Geol.* XLVIII. 1141/2 Trawl No. 23 was taken from a natural levee [of the Congo Submarine Canyon] and although the water depth was more than 500 fathoms greater than that of trawl No. 22, there was no marked decrease in diversity and abundance of animal life. **1968** R. W. FAIRBRIDGE *Encycl. Geomorphol.* 651/2 Alluvial streams flowing on flood plains commonly develop natural levees. Each levee is a low, wide ridge located immediately adjacent to the channel. **1972** G. A. MACDONALD *Volcanoes* v. 84 Overflows spread lava a few feet on either side of the river. .. Repeated overflows gradually build up natural levees.

2. A landing-place, pier, quay.

1842 H. CASWALL *City of Mormons* 3 The landing-place (or levée, as it is denominated).

attrib. **1858** SIMMONDS *Dict. Trade*, *Levee-dues*, shipping or landing dues paid at a levee.

levee (ˈlɛviː), *sb.*² Also 8 levy, 9 levée. [ad. F. *levé*, variant of *lever* (Littré *lever* sb. 3) rising (subst. use of *lever* inf. to rise): cf. COUCHEE.

All our verse quotations place the stress on the first syllable. In England this is the court pronunciation, and prevails in educated use. The pronunciation (lɪˈviː) or (lɛˈviː), which is given by Walker, is occasionally heard in Great Britain, and appears to be generally preferred in the U.S.]

†**1.** The action of rising, *spec.* from one's bed. *Obs.*

1700 CONGREVE *Way of World* IV. i, O, nothing is more alluring than a Levee from a Couch, in some Confusion. **1727** *Philip Quarll* (1816) 75 An old monkey..quietly waiting his levee, to entice him to come. **1784** R. BAGE *Barham Downs* I. 129 Their levee was honoured with the presence of the constable. **1796** STEDMAN *Surinam* II. xviii. 55 He [the planter] is next accosted by his overseer, who regularly every morning attends at his levee. **1827** R. POLLOK *Course T.* VII, Birds, In levee of the morn, dawn's advent hailed.

2. A reception of visitors on rising from bed; a morning assembly held by a prince or person of distinction.

1672 DRYDEN *Marr. à la Mode* II. i, You shall be every day at the king's levee and I at the queen's. **1697** VANBRUGH *Relapse* I. iii, Sure my Gentleman's grown a Favourite at Court, he has got so many People at his Levee. **1719** D'URFEY *Pills* (1872) I. 110 At his Levy no Crowds you see. **1732** POPE *Ep. Bathurst* 58 Sir, Spain has sent a thousand jars of oil; Huge bales of British cloth blockade the door; A hundred oxen at your levee roar. **1765** GOLDSM. *Double Transform.* 54 Fond to be seen, she kept a bevy Of powder'd coxcombs at her levy. **1819** BYRON *Juan* I. cxxxix, Without a word of previous admonition, To hold a levee round a lady's bed. **1820** LAMB *Elia* Ser. I. *Christ's Hosp.*, The Lions in the Tower—to whose levee..we had a prescriptive title to admission. **1874** GREEN *Short Hist.* x. §1. 716 The levees of the Ministers were crowded with lawn sleeves. **1887** E. DOWDEN *Life Shelley* I. i. 7 Louis XVI's last levée.

b. In Great Britain and Ireland, an assembly held (in the early afternoon) by the sovereign or his representative, at which men only are received.

1760–72 H. BROOKE *Fool of Qual.* (1792) I. 110 The minister had afterwards introduced him to his majesty in full levee. **1770** *Publ. Advertiser* 10 Mar., His Majesty's Levee began at a quarter past two. **1797** MAD. D'ARBLAY *Let. to Dr. Burney* 13 Sept., A levee is announced for Wednesday..and a drawing-room on Thursday. **1809** G. ROSE *Diaries* (1860) II. 411 At the Levée..Mr. Wellesley Pole kissed hands. **1825** JEFFERSON *Autobiog.* Wks. 1859 I. 63 My presentation, as usual, to the King and Queen, at their levées. **1834** MACAULAY *Ess.*, *Pitt* (1851) 301 The King would be civil to him at the levee. **1837** THACKERAY *Ravenswing* vii, He goes to the Levée once a year. **1896** *Law Times* C. 408/1 On the occasion..of Lord Cadogan's first Viceregal levée in Dublin Castle.

c. A miscellaneous assemblage of visitors, irrespective of the time of day; applied (*U.S.*) to the President's receptions.

1766 M. CUTLER in *Life*, etc. (1888) I. 12 A second grand levee at Ellis' Inn. **1831** SIR J. SINCLAIR *Corr.* II. 100 Several ladies attended the evening levee of the Minister of the Home Department. **1837** HT. MARTINEAU *Soc. Amer.* III. 96 The President's levee presents many facilities for ridicule. **1842** DICKENS *Amer. Notes* viii, It was on the occasion of one of those general assemblies which are held on certain nights, between the hours of nine and twelve o'clock, and are called, rather oddly, Levees.

transf. **1825** HONE *Every-day Bk.* I. 993 The dogs..held a levee.

†**3.** The company assembled at a levee; attendance of visitors. *Obs.*

1701 FARQUHAR *Sir H. Wildair* II. i, They were fisted about among his dirty Levee of Disbanded Officers. **1717** L. HOWEL *Desiderius* (ed. 3) 180 Sanctify my heart, that I may be worthy to be one of thy divine Levy. **1753** HANWAY *Trav.* (1762) I. III. xxix. 127, I was again honored with a numerous levee. **1756** C. LUCAS *Ess. Waters* I. 171 Charlemagne received his levee in a great bath. **1771** SMOLLETT *Humph. Cl.* 5 June, Going round the levee, [he] spoke to every individual.

4. *attrib.* and *Comb.*, as ***levee-day***, ***-dress***, ***-haunting***, ***-hunting***, ***-man***, ***-morn***, ***-room***, ***vow***.

1726 SWIFT *Gulliver* III. vi, At every *levee-day repeat the same operation. **1789** HAMILTON *Wks.* (1886) VII. 44 The President to have a levee day once a week for receiving visits. **1833** MARRYAT *P. Simple* xl, The day after his arrival.. was a levee day. **1897** *Geneal. Mag.* Oct. 325 All gentlemen present wore *levée dress. **1712** ADDISON *Spect.* No. 547 ¶5 Such as are troubled with the Disease of *Levee-haunting. **1744** WARBURTON *Rem. Occas. Refl.* 143 *Levy-hunting. **1721-2** AMHERST *Terræ Fil.* xiii. (1726) 67 To domineer over their masters' clients, and *levee-men. **1812** MOORE *Intercepted Lett.* ii. 20 Last *Levee-morn he look'd it through. **1760-72** H. BROOKE *Fool of Qual.* (1809) III. 133 The earl left his young friend a while in the *levee-room. **1836** in *Byron's Wks.* (1846) 533/2 On entering the levee-room at Holyrood. **1763** CHURCHILL *Duellist* III. 48 The private squeeze, the *Levee vow.

levee (lɪ'viː), *v.*¹ *U.S.* [f. LEVEE *sb.*¹] *trans.* To raise a levee or embankment along (a river); to raise levees or embankments in (a district). Also, to shut or keep *off* by means of a levee.

1832 R. BAIRD *View of Valley of Mississippi* xxii. 269 Much has been done to levee or embank the Mississippi River. **1837** J. L. WILLIAMS *Territory of Florida* 45 Where there is clay enough in the soil, to form good embankments, the waters might be leveed off. **1847** J. PALMER *Jrnl. Trav. Rocky Mts.* 121 Several islands in the river might be *leveed* and successfully cultivated. **1877** BURROUGHS *Taxation* 75 An act incorporated certain persons for the purpose of leveeing and draining a district.

So **le'veeing** *vbl. sb.*

1845 *Indiana Senate Jrnl.* 364 An act to authorize the leveeing of Blue river, in Shelby county. **1858** *De Bow's Review* Oct. (Bartlett), How are we to be protected [from overflow]? By leveeing.

† **'levee**, *v.*² *Obs.* [f. LEVEE *sb.*²] *trans.* To attend the levees of; to pursue at levees.

1725 YOUNG *Love Fame* IV. 129 Warm in pursuit, he Levées all the great. **1757** MRS. GRIFFITH *Lett. Henry & Frances* (1767) IV. 158 You may levee him fifty Times, without being admitted by his Swiss porter. **1770** FOOTE *Lame Lover* I. 7 The paltry ambition of levying and following titles.

‖**levée en masse** (ləve ɑ̃ mas). [Fr.] Mass mobilization, orig. in Revolutionary France, in response to invasion; = LEVY *sb.*¹ 3. Also *fig.*

1813 F. BURNEY *Let.* 12 Oct. (1905) VI. 95 Were he not essentially necessary in some department of civil labour and use, he would surely be included in some *levée en masse.* **1832** *Edin. Rev.* Apr. 254 A *levèe* [sic] *en masse* was decreed. The zeal of the Polish patriots was unbounded. **1895** T. A. WALKER *Man. Public Internat. Law* 135 It is, in fact, clear law that a combatant to be lawful must be formally authorised by a recognised Government, or be a member of a *levée en masse* rising on the approach of an invader. **1940** *Economist* 22 June 1067/1 There has been an outcry.. for an immediate *levée en masse*, for the calling up now of every able-bodied man not busy on war work. **1943** J. M. THOMPSON *French Revolution* xxii. 424 A decree of February 24th, '93, ordered the levying of three hundred thousand men—..less than half the necessary number was procured. It became clear that the Convention must fall back on..a *levée en masse*, or wholesale compulsory enlistment. This plan..finally took shape in Carnot's decree, as it is generally called, of August 23rd. **1949** I. DEUTSCHER *Stalin* v. 143 They were the 'activists'..behind which there moved into battle a genuine political *levée en masse.* **1972** *Times* 29 Dec. 11/7 A levée en masse is one thing, assassination is quite another.

leveful(le, variant of LEEFUL.

levein, obs. form of LEAVEN.

level ('lɛvəl), *sb.* Also 4 livel, 5 lewel, 5–7 levell, 6 leavell, 6–7 levill. [a. OF. *livel* (13th c.), later *nivel*, mod.F. *niveau* = Pr. *livell, nivel*, It. *livello*, Sp. *nivel*, Pg. *livel, nivel*:—popular L. **libellum* = classical L. *lībella*, dim. of *libra* balance.]

I. 1. a. An instrument which indicates a line parallel to the plane of the horizon, used in determining the position as to horizontality of a surface to which it is applied.

There are various forms of this instrument according to the materials used and the art in which it is employed, as *carpenter's, dumpy, foot, mercurial, plummet, spirit, surveying, water level*, etc.: see these words.

1340 *Ayenb.* 150 He deþ al to wylle and to þe line, and to þe reule, and to þe leade, and to þe leuele. **1362** LANGL. *P. Pl.* A. XI. 135, I..lered hem liuel [*v.r.* leuel] and lyne, þauȝ I loke dimme. *c* **1391** CHAUCER *Astrol.* II. §38 Ley this ronde plate vp-on an euene grond..& ley it euen bi a leuel. **1412-20** LYDG. *Chron. Troy* II. xi, To make them ioyne by leuell and by lyne. **1573** BARET *Alv.* L 243 A Leauell, lyne, or carpenters rule. **1594** BLUNDEVIL *Exerc.* IV. i. (1636) 443, I..do thinke it better for you to have such a little levell made of purpose. **1616** *Inv. of P. Oldfeild* in Earwaker *Sandbach* (1890) 136 A Levill and a staffe vjᵈ. **1703** MOXON *Mech. Exerc.* 123 If the Plumb-line hang just upon the Perpendicular *dd*, when the Level is set flat down upon the Work, the Work is Level. *a* **1763** SHENSTONE *Elegy* x. 35 The poor mechanic wanders home Collects the square, the level, and the line. **1823** P. NICHOLSON *Pract. Build.* 385 The Level, used by bricklayers, is similar to that of the carpenter. **1866** R. M. FERGUSON *Electr.* (1870) 20 A level is..hung on the axis of the telescope.

fig. **1578** TIMME *Calvin on Gen.* 281 The deeds of Men.. are..to be examined by Gods level and line. **1583** STUBBES *Anat. Abus.* II. (1882) 11 The lawe in it selfe, is the square, the leuell, and rule of equitie and iustice. **1610** SHAKS. *Temp.* IV. i. 239 We steal by lyne and leuell, and 't like your grace. **1641** MILTON *Ch. Govt.* I. ii. Wks. 1851 III. 103 Should not he..by his owne prescribed discipline have cast his line and levell upon the soule of man? **1647** WARD *Simp. Cobler* 34 Statesmen frame and build by the levell and plummet of his wisdome.

¶ **b.** Erroneously glossed as = plumb-line.

c **1440** *Promp. Parv.* 301/1 Level, rewle, *perpendiculum.* **1483** *Cath. Angl.* 215/1 A Levelle, *perpendiculum* (*MS. A.* plemmett). **1552** HULOET, Leuel or lyne called a plomblyne, *perpendiculum.*

† **c.** *fig. to give level to*: ? to take as one's rule or standard. *Obs.*

1569 J. SANFORD tr. *Agrippa's Van. Artes* xcvi. 166 Neither doo they alowe the Traditions of auncient Doctoures & Fathers, sayinge, that they maie be deceaued and deceaue, but they doo geue leauell to the Churche of Rome alone, which, as they saie, cannot erre.

† **2. a.** Level condition or position: horizontality. Chiefly in phrases: ***on, upon a level***, in a horizontal line or plane; ***the level***, the horizontal; ***in level***, on the ground (cf. L. *in plano*). *Obs.*

a **1400-50** *Alexander* 3261 Now in leuell, now on-loft, now on lawe vndire. **14..** *Voc.* in Wr.-Wülcker 580/30 *Equilibrium*, a lewel. **1594** PLAT *Jewell-ho.* II. 15 Hee commeth to spread it [dung] all ouer the ground, and layeth the same in equall leuill. **1683** MOXON *Mech. Exerc., Printing* xiii. ¶3 File off the rising side of the Punch, which brings the Face to an exact Level. **1719** DE FOE *Crusoe* I. iv, The rising of the water brought me a little more upon a level; and a little after, the water still rising, my raft floated again. **1726** SWIFT *Gulliver* III. iv, The current of a river whose course is more upon a level.

b. ***on the level***, (in a) fair, honest, or straightforward (way); reliable, true. Freq. as *adv. phr.* = honestly; truthfully. *colloq.* (orig. *U.S.*).

1872 G. P. BURNHAM *Mem. U.S. Secret Service* p. vii, *On the level*, meeting a man with honorable intentions. **1896** ADE *Artie* vi. 50, I see barrel-house boys goin' around for hand-outs that was more on the level than you are. **1901** 'J. FLYNT' *World of Graft* iii. 89 When a man who has been a known thief makes up his mind to quit stealing and live 'on the level', they say in the Under World that he has 'squared it'. **1932** A. J. WORRALL *Eng. Idioms* 50 You may be quite sure that the business is quite on the level. **1936** N. MARSH *Death in Ecstasy* xvii. 209 I've had no more'n my fair share. Same goes for Raveenje. He's on the level all right. **1958** R. GRAVES in *Times Lit. Suppl.* 15 Aug. p. x/3 He also prefers pools to premium-bond gambling—in which a bloke can't choose his own combination of numbers, so how does one know that it's on the level? **1970** G. F. NEWMAN *Sir, You Bastard* ii. 47 If you're on the level, we won't object.

1896 ADE *Artie* v. 42 On the level, I'm surprised you ain't on to that. **1914** WODEHOUSE *Man Upstairs* 63 'You look good to muh,' he said gallantly. 'The idea!' said Maud, tossing her head. 'On the level,' Mr. Shute assured her. **1923** R. D. PAINE *Comrades of Rolling Ocean* iii. 44 This was no fault of mine, on the level. **1931** E. LINKLATER *Juan in Amer.* III. iii. 231 'You're kidding,' said Buddy. 'On the level!' replied Olympia. **1942** T. RATTIGAN *Flare Path* II. ii. 137 On the level. I couldn't really.

3. a. Position as marked by a horizontal line; an imaginary line or plane perpendicular to the plumb-line, considered as determining the position of one or more points or surfaces. ***on a*** (or †***the***) ***level with***: in the same horizontal plane as.

1535 *Act. 27 Hen. VIII*, c. 18 Suche groundes as lye within the leuell of the said water marke. *a* **1682** SIR T. BROWNE *Tracts* 152 At least twenty foot in direct height from the level whereon they stand. **1712** W. ROGERS *Voy.* 367 A Stage is made above the Water, on a Level with the Side of the Boat. **1717** tr. *Frezier's Voy. S. Sea* 93 Two natural Ditches..sunk down almost to the Level of the Sea. *Ibid.* 313 The Rampart behind it is generally upon the Level with Earth-work. **1774** GOLDSM. *Nat. Hist.* (1776) I. 190 It has been said, that all fluids endeavour to preserve their level; and..that a body pressing on the surface, tended to destroy that level. **1820** KEATS *Hyperion* I. 46 To the level of his ear Leaning with parted lips, some words she spake. **1860** TYNDALL *Glac.* I. xv. 99 The line which marks the level of the ancient ice. **1879** HARLAN *Eyesight* viii. 116 Light coming from below the level of the head is worse than useless. **1880** HAUGHTON *Phys. Geog.* iv. 170 The level of the lake will continue to fall.

b. ***to find one's*** or ***its level***: said of persons or things arriving at their proper place with respect to those around or connected with them.

The primary use seems to be that referring to the tendency of two bodies of liquid to 'find their level', i.e. to equalize the vertical elevation of their upper surfaces, when free communication is established between them.

1799 J. ROBERTSON *Agric. Perth* 413 We have adopted a cant-phrase, That things will find their level..It is true with regard to prices, and was at first introduced under this acceptation; But with regard to population it is most incorrect. **1809** MALKIN *Gil Blas* V. i. ¶64 It was in vain to fret about it; and I soon found my level. **1817** COLERIDGE *Lay Serm.* 101 Instead of the position that all things *find*, it would be less equivocal..to say that Things are always *finding* their level. **1822** HAZLITT *Table-t.* Ser. II. i. (1869) 30 A member of parliament soon finds his level as a commoner.

† **c.** ***to hold its level with***: to be on an equality with. *Obs.*

1596 SHAKS. *1 Hen. IV*, III. ii. 17 Could such inordinate and low desires..hold their leuell with thy Princely heart?

d. A position (on a real or imaginary scale) in respect of amount, intensity, extent, or the like; the relative amount or intensity of any property, attribute, or activity. Freq. preceded by a sb. denoting the property, etc., referred to, as ***danger, energy, noise level.***

1897 *Lancet* 5 June 1541/1 The pulse had been rising, and by 8.30 P.M. had reached its normal level (72 in the sitting posture). **1926** *Encycl. Brit.* III. 281/1 Nothing is to be gained by amplifying a signal below the 'noise level' at the location of the receiver. **1931** A. W. NYE in L. Cowan *Recording Sound for Motion Pict.* ii. 31 The sensation level of any sound reaching the ear is the number of decibels it is above the threshold level of audition. *Ibid.*, A change of the level of a sound by 1 db is approximately the smallest that the ear can detect. **1934** G. B. SHAW *On Rocks* I. 208 By the last returns the export of Spanish onions has again reached the 1913 level. **1935** [see *danger level* s.v. DANGER *sb.* C]. **1942** W. B. BOAST *Illumination Engin.* x. 166 Recommended levels of illumination must provide an adequate safety factor ..to maintain visibility well above threshold values for critical tasks. **1948** W. E. STYLER in M. Beloff *Hist.* xv. 320/1 Unemployment reached previously unknown levels, and overseas markets collapsed. **1958** H. G. M. SPRATT *Magn. Tape Recording* vii. 207 When recording it is essential to provide some means of indicating the level of the signal applied to the tape to ensure that it is neither too high nor too low. *Ibid.* 208 Low signal levels. **1967** [see *danger level* s.v. DANGER *sb.* C]. **1968** MILLER & SAWERS *Technical Devel. Mod. Aviation* vii. 223 The level of general passenger comfort aboard the four-engined jets. **1971** *Times* 17 Mar. 21 (Advt.), I am encouraged by the current general level of orders and I am sure that because of the action which has been taken since the merger, [etc.]. **1973** HARRISON & WATERS *Burne-Jones* iii. 25 Possessing a high level of natural skill Edward Jones made rapid progress. **1973** *Nature* 23 Nov. 183/1 That could result in dangerous levels of sulphuric acid and sulphates in city air. **1974** *Daily Tel.* 11 Mar. 16 New house starts over the last three months are down to 40 per cent. of their level at this time last year.

e. *Physics.* More fully, ***energy level.*** An amount of energy associated with an atom or other quantized system and capable of being possessed by one of its constituents, being usu. measured relative to the minimum possible energy of that constituent; also, a discrete state of a quantized system characterized by such energy; *spec.* a state or group of states of an atom characterized by the quantum numbers ***n, L, S***, and ***J***, as distinguished from a 'term' (a group of levels: see TERM *sb.*) and a 'state' so called (a constituent of a level: see STATE *sb.*).

1922 A. D. UDDEN tr. *Bohr's Theory of Spectra* III. iv. 116 The values of the atomic energy corresponding to these [stationary] states are frequently referred to as the 'energy levels' of X-ray spectra. **1925** RUSSELL & SAUNDERS in *Astrophysical Jrnl.* LXI. 69 When the series limit—or ionization level—can only be found inaccurately..the common convention of measuring terms from this level becomes inconvenient... A desirable alternative might be to set the zero-level at the *lowest* term and measure the others upward from this... In such cases, the numerical values referred to the lowest level might be called 'levels' to distinguish them from 'terms', referred to ionization as zero-point. **1926** R. W. LAWSON tr. *Hevesy & Paneth's Man. Radioactivity* vii. 75 This suggests that even in the nucleus of an atom there are different energy levels. **1934** H. E. WHITE *Introd. Atomic Spectra* v. 78 [In sodium] just as in hydrogen these energy levels represent certain possible energy states of an electron, and transitions between them represent spectrum lines. **1935** CONDON & SHORTLEY *Theory Atomic Spectra* iv. 122 All except *s* configurations split into two levels, corresponding to $j = l + \frac{1}{2}$ and $j = l - \frac{1}{2}$... The (one or) two levels into which each configuration is split are together said to constitute a doublet term. **1955** R. D. EVANS *Atomic Nucleus* iv. 122 After the emission of the *β* ray, each residual nucleus of Si^{28} is left in an excited level at about 1·78 Mev above its ground level. **1962** D. F. SHAW *Introd. Electronics* ix. 170 There are important modifications to the arrangement of energy levels when, as in a crystalline solid, the atoms are separated by distances of the same order of magnitude (10^{-8} cm) as the atomic diameters themselves. .. The valence electrons may no longer be associated with a particular atom. They become a group of 'free electrons' in energy levels which belong to the lattice as a whole. **1962** R. E. DODD *Chem. Spectroscopy* ii. 78 Transitions between rotational levels [of a molecule] without change in vibrational or electronic energy, give lines in the far infrared and microwave region. **1970** G. K. WOODGATE *Elem. Atomic Struct.* i. 5 The spin-orbit interaction is the largest relativistic effect and is responsible for fine structure. Each term splits into levels whose separations are of the order of 1–1,000 cm^{-1}. *Ibid.* 6 The levels are split further into states by the application of a laboratory magnetic field... This is called the Zeeman effect.

f. *Statistics.* In full, ***level of confidence*** or ***significance.*** A number chosen as the maximum (or minimum) value of the probability with which any statistical result must be false (or true) for that result to be accepted as having been demonstrated.

1925 R. A. FISHER *Statistical Methods for Research Workers* vi. 157 Taking the four definite levels of significance, represented by P = ·10, ·05, ·02, and ·01, the table shows for each value of *n*, from 1 to 20, and thence by larger intervals to 100, the corresponding values of *r*. **1931** L. H. C. TIPPETT *Methods of Statistics* iii. 48 Adopting the 0·05 level of significance, a deviation in the mean greater than twice its standard error is statistically significant. **1937** YULE & KENDALL *Introd. Theory Statistics* (ed. 11) xxii. 425 There are..two values of *P* [*sc.* a probability] which are widely used to provide a rough line of demarcation between acceptance and rejection of the significance of observed deviations. These values are $P = 0·05$ and $P = 0·01$, and are said to define 5 per cent. and 1 per cent. levels of significance. **1950** W. FELLER *Introd. Probability Theory* I. vii. 142 However, no sample size can give absolute assurance that $|p' - p| < 0·005$... Since absolute certainty is unattainable, we settle for an arbitrary confidence level *α*, say $α = 0·95$, and require that $|p' - p| < 0·005$ with probability 0·95 or better. **1972** *Jrnl. Social Psychol.* LXXXVII. 39 The situations variable was significant at the ·01 level for all four dependent variables. *Ibid.* 48 A *t* value of 2·33 or greater indicates that differences between the high and low criterion group means are significant at the ·01 level of confidence.

g. Contextually in *Broadcasting*, etc.: the sound level or signal level as it shows up in the

different pieces of equipment. Also *attrib.* in **level test**, a test of signal levels to determine whether changes in control settings, microphone positions, etc., are required.

1940 E. McGILL *Radio Directing* ix. 184 If many sound effects are devised it will be found that a great amount of rehearsal time will be consumed in trying to bring to perfection the levels and balances of sounds against orchestra.. under unfavorable acoustic circumstances. **1941** *B.B.C. Broadcasting Terms* 17 Level test. **1962** A. NISBETT *Technique Sound Studio* iv. 79 The purpose of control of levels and lining-up of equipment.. is to make the best use of the region between which noise and distortion overtake the recording. **1966** *Listener* 4 Aug. 181/3 Delius's *Requiem* ..seemed harassed by eccentric studio management, with levels all over the place. **1966** B. GLEMSER *Dear Hungarian Friend* xiii. 223 We must do a level test... Just talk naturally ..and we will see what we pick up. **1969** J. ELLIOT *Duel* III. iii. 251 He wants you to say a few words..just for the level.

4. a. Position, plane, standard, in social, moral, or intellectual matters. ***on*** or ***upon a level***: on the same 'plane', on an equality (*with*).

1609 DANIEL *Civ. Wars* IV. xviii, Aboue the leuell of subiection. **1665** BOYLE *Occas. Refl.* IV. xvii. (1848) 269 All these shall sink themselves to his Level. **1666** DRYDEN *Ann. Mirab.* Pref., They inspired me with thoughts above my ordinary level. **1693** SOUTH *Serm.* 331 Men whose aspiring intellectuals had raised them above the common level. **1710** SWIFT *Let. to Abp. King* 10 Oct., Lett. 1767 I. 56 Their two lordships might have succeeded easier than men of my level are likely to do. **1712** BERKELEY *Pass. Obedience* §20 Wks. 1871 III. 119 The precept against rebellion is one on a level with other moral rules. **1712** ADDISON *Spect.* No. 295 ⁋4 Where the Age and Circumstances of both Parties are pretty much upon a level. **1732** BERKELEY *Alciphr.* I. §13 To degrade human-kind to a level with brute beasts. **1809** MALKIN *Gil Blas* I. xii. ⁋5 It was only reducing feasts and fasts to the level of bread and water. **1828** CARLYLE *Misc.* (1857) I. 189 The popular man stands on our own level. **1832** HT. MARTINEAU *Life in Wilds* vii. 94 The calamity.. had reduced all to one level. **1856** FROUDE *Hist. Eng.* (1858) II. vii. 182 A present madness which has brought down wisdom to a common level with folly. **1869** FREEMAN *Norm. Conq.* (1876) III. xi. 3 We must place English and Norman writers on a level. **1874** SWEET *Engl. Sounds* 40 Middle English is practically on a level with Dutch. **1882** J. H. BLUNT *Ref. Ch. Eng.* II. 348 A much higher level of doctrine and ritual.

b. A plane or status in respect of rank or authority; position in a hierarchy. Freq. with a qualifying adj.

1933 L. BLOOMFIELD *Language* iii. 49 Provincial colorings of standard English are tied up with differences of social level. **1937** A. HUXLEY *Ends & Means* x. 148 Examples of non-violence on the governmental level are seldom of a very heroic kind. **1944** *Amer. Speech* XIX. 234/1, I have often been amused at the constant recurrence of certain catchwords and phrases in [Government] memoranda... *level* ('This matter will be handled at the regional *level*'). **1945** *N.Y. Times* 24 June IV. 6/4 One of the reporters asks if he knows of any obstacle to our perfect cooperation with the Russians. Quick as a flash General Eisenhower replied, 'On my level, none.' **1948** MASTERSON & PHILLIPS *Federal Prose* vi. 30 Until a program for personnel induction at the infant level can be coordinated with the Federal Prose tutorship objectives, this situation will continue to create embarrassments at the administrative and higher levels. **1952** *Economist* 20 Sept., How long it takes to get even a simple low-level decision. **1955** *Times* 10 May 10/1 The western Foreign Ministers have agreed in Paris to invite Russia to a four-Power conference, though the level at which the meeting should be held is not yet decided. **1960** *B.S.I. News* Jan. 9/2 This sort of progress can only be achieved through full consultation from and with users at the national level. **1962** *Sci. Survey* III. 263 There exist equally interesting relationships between odours and animal behaviours on a different and more profound level. **1971** *Guardian* 24 Sept. 22/7 On instructions from director-level, the estimates..had been prepared. **1974** *Daily Tel.* 1 Apr. 6/7 At the next level of responsibility are the 14 regional health authorities. **1974** *Nature* 17 May 210/2 In talking about the recognition of [alien] life at the microscopic level the decision is largely an aesthetic one. **1974** GREEN & HOOPER *C. S. Lewis* x. 253 The stories can be read and enjoyed on at least two levels: by the child who perhaps knows nothing..of any of the authors whose works Lewis knew; and by the reader who knows many.

c. *Linguistics.* (See quots.)

1935 *Trans. Philol. Soc.* 61 Now to illustrate this empirical analysis of meaning at the phonetic, morphological, syntactical, and semantic levels. **1942** C. F. HOCKETT in *Language* Jan.-Mar. 3 Linguistics is a classificatory science. The starting-point in such a science is to define (1) the universe of discourse and (2) the criteria which are used in making the classification. Selection and preliminary ordering of data determine the *range* of analysis; the choice of criteria fixes the *level* of analysis. In linguistics there are various ranges,..and two basic levels, *phonological* and *grammatical*. **1958** C. RABIN in *Aspects of Translation* 130 Items which are the same at all levels (e.g. numbers) do not function as level-markers. **1959** M. HALLE *Sound Pattern Russ.* i. 25 The rules of translation which make up the grammar can all be subsumed under the formula 'replace x by y under condition z'... A set of rules yielding representations of a particular type is called a *linguistic level*. **1964** E. BACH *Introd. Transformational Gram.* iv. 59 The word 'level' is also used occasionally in another sense to refer to the ordering of rules within a single level and also to the ordering of the PS, transformational, and phonological rules with respect to each other. **1964** M. A. K. HALLIDAY et al. *Ling. Sci.* i. 10 From these three types of patterning are derived the three principal levels: substance, form and context. **1964** R. H. ROBINS *Gen. Ling.* 12 By extension the term level of language is used to designate those aspects of a language on which at any time the linguist is focusing his attention. **1969** *Pocket Oxf. Dict.* (ed. 5) (Suppl. Austral. & N.Z. Words) 1017 There are 'levels of usage' in Australia and New Zealand as there are elsewhere and the cautionary labels colloq., sl. (= slang), etc., are therefore employed here in the customary manner as a guide to currency. **1973** *Archivum Linguisticum* IV. 17 In the field of English intonation studies, bones of contention..spring readily to mind: levels versus configurations.

5. a. A (more or less) horizontal superficies; a level or flat surface. Also *fig.*

1634 W. TIRWHYT tr. *Balzac's Lett.* 80 To affoord vs meanes to catch Trouts and Pykes, leauing them vpon the leuill [F. *sur la terre*]. **1725** POPE *Odyss.* xii. 187 The vessel light along the level glides. **1798** in Picton *L'pool Munic. Rec.* (1886) II. 274 The levels of many of the new streets improperly and irregularly laid out. **1820** SHELLEY *Œdipus* I. 99 There's something rotten in us—for the level Of the State slopes, its very bases topple. **1840** MILMAN *Lat. Chr.* III. 367 The level of ecclesiastical or episcopal dignity gradually broke up. **1842** TENNYSON *Morte d'Arth.* 51 He, stepping down By zig-zag paths..Came on the shining levels of the lake. **1874** MICKLETHWAITE *Mod. Par. Churches* 86 Of the Chancel levels and steps.

b. ***the level***, the earth's surface. *rare*⁻¹.

1848 DICKENS *Dombey* ii, 'Where have you worked all your life?' 'Mostly underground, Sir, 'till I got married. I come to the level then.'

c. ***on the level***: moderate in ambition or aim.

1790 SIR J. REYNOLDS *Disc.* xv. (1842) 269 The Caracci.. formed..a most respectable school, a style more on the level, and calculated to please a greater number.

6. A level tract of land; a stretch of country approximately horizontal and unbroken by elevations: applied *spec.* (as a proper name) to certain large expanses of level country, e.g. *Bedford Level* or *the Great Level* in the fen district of England; ***The Levels*** (formerly ***The Level***), the tract including Hatfield Chase in Yorkshire.

1623 E. WYNNE in Whitbourne *Newfoundland* 109 Our high leuels of land are adorned with Woods. **1642** SIR C. VERMUIDEN *Disc. Drain. Fens* 4 The Levell lyeth in sixe Counties. **1661** N. N. (*title*) A Narrative of all the Proceedings in the Draining of the Great Level of the Fens, Extending into the Counties of Northampton, Lincoln, Norfolk, Suffolk, Cambridge, and Huntingdon; and the Isle of Ely. **1698** FRYER *Acc. E. India & P.* 253 Such Tombs as we met with at Bonaru Level. **1751** J. BARTRAM *Observ. Trav. Pennsylv.*, etc. 64 We..crossed a run and rode along a rich level for several miles. **1774** GOLDSM. *Nat. Hist.* (1776) I. 284 The levels of Hatfield-Chace, in Yorkshire. **1835** *Penny Cycl.* IV. 138/1 Bedford Level..is divided into three parts, which are distinguished as the North, the Middle, and the South Levels. **1841** J. C. BOOTH *Mem. Geol. Surv. Maryland* 89 The beautiful tract of land.. appropriately called the Levels. **1859** *All Year Round* No. 33. 162 In one level alone, fifteen thousand sheep were drowned. **1890** 'ROLF BOLDREWOOD' *Col. Reformer* (1891) 222 The great saltbush levels of the interior.

7. *Mining.* **a.** A nearly horizontal 'drift', passage, or gallery in a mine. **b.** A 'drift'; often (more fully ***water-level***) one serving for drainage purposes; also see quot. 1860. For *blind*, ***diphead***, ***drowned***, etc. ***level*** see the first member.

1721 *Connect. Col. Rec.* (1872) VI. 253 Any disagreement that may happen..amongst..lessees..concern'd in the mines aforesaid, about making any levels (or clearing and cleansing the said levels or shafts). **1805** R. FORSYTH *Beauties Scotl.* I. 270 This gentleman opened a level or mine from the sea,..it drained the upper coal-works. **1827** JARMAN *Powell's Devises* II. 137 The leaseholds had mostly been demised as 'coal-mines and levels at rents'. **1851** GREENWELL *Coal-trade Terms Northumb. & Durh.* 35 *Level*, a drain cut in the bottom stone, to set away or convey water. A pair of levels are a pair of drifts, driven in the water-level direction of the coal, for the purpose of winning coal. **1860** *Mining Gloss. Newcastle Terms*, *Levels*, gutters for the water to run in. **1867** W. W. SMYTH *Coal & Coal-mining* 129 When the coal to be cut away is a short block, as in the driving of levels.

†8. The equinox. *Obs.* (? *nonce-use*).

1548 ELYOT *Dict.*, *Æquidiale*, the tyme whan the dayes and the nyghtes bee of one lengthe, the leuell of the yere.

II. Senses derived from the verb.

†9. a. The action of aiming a missile weapon, aim. ***to give level to***: to aim (a gun). ***to lay, bend, take level***: to take aim, to aim. Also, the line of fire, the range of the missile. Often in fig. context. *Obs.*

a **1548** HALL *Chron.*, *Hen. VIII*, 36 b, They shotte out of their towers peces of ordinaunce and hurt such as came within there levell. **1576** FLEMING *Panopl. Epist.* 388 The thing whereat you lay the levell of your thoughtes and purposes. **1576** —— tr. *Caius' Dogs* in Arb. *Garner* III. 245 Missing our mark whereat we directed our level. *c* **1586** C'TESS PEMBROKE *Ps.* CVI. i, O blessed they whose well advised sight Of all their life the levell straight doe bend, With endlesse ayming at the mark of right. **1587** FLEMING *Contn. Holinshed* III. 1321/2 Hir statelie seat is set so high, as that no leuell can be laid against hir walles. **1592** SHAKS. *Rom. & Jul.* III. iii. 103 As if that name shot from the dead leuell of a Gun, Did murder her. **1601** —— *All's Well* II. i. 159, I am not an Impostrue [*sic*], that proclaime My selfe against the leuill of mine aime. **1602** MARSTON *Ant. & Mel.* III. Wks. 1856 I. 38 If you discharge but one glance from the levell of that set face, O, you will strike a wench. **1611** SHAKS. *Wint. T.* III. ii. 82 My Life stands in the leuell of your Dreames. **1622** F. MARKHAM *Bk. War* Ded. 2 All his leuels are at true Pietie. **1669** STURMY *Mariner's Mag.* v. 78 How by the Table to give Level to a Piece of Ordnance, without the Gunner's Rule. **1700** DRYDEN *Sigism. & Guisc.* 142 But in what quarter of the cops it lay His eye by certain level could survey. **1718** PRIOR *Solomon* III. 43 Be the fair level of thy actions laid, As temperance wills, and prudence may persuade.

b. That which is aimed at; a mark. *Obs.*

1525 LD. BERNERS *Froiss.* II. xxxviii. 115 The genoways crosbowes shotte so surely, that lightly they myst nat of their leuell. **1591** SPENSER *Bellay's Vis.* iii. 4 So far as Archer might his level see. **1600** HEYWOOD *2nd Pt. Edw. IV* Wks. 1874 I. 101 My breast the leuell was, though you the marke.

c. *fig.* Aim, purpose, design. *Obs.*

a **1592** H. SMITH *Yng. Man's Task* Serm. (1594) 239 This then is the leuel of our message. —— *Humil. Paul* ibid. 465 That this should be the leuell of all our thoughts that [etc.]. **1605** *Play Stucley* in Simpson *Sch. Shaks.* (1878) I. 187 That is the end or levels of my thought.

†10. The 'sight' of a gun. *Obs.*

1611 COTGR., *Mire*, the leuell, or little button at th' end of a Peece.

11. *Surveying.* † ***to make a level of***: to ascertain the differences of elevation in (a piece of land). *Obs.* Also, ***to take a level*** = LEVEL *v.* 5 (*absol.*).

[OF. *liveau* occurs in this sense.]

1693 [see LEVELLER 1]. **1798** I. ALLEN *Hist. Vermont* 4 In 1785 Captain Twist made a survey and level to ascertain the expence of a canal from the River St. Lawrence to Lake Champlain. **1839** *Penny Cycl.* XIII. 454/2 Among the operations of levelling, which, within a few years, have been performed on an extensive scale, may be mentioned the series of levels taken across the lands between the Black and the Caspian seas.

12. *Comb.*: **level-error** (see quot.); **level-point** (see quot. 1839); **level-range** (see quot.); **level-staff** = *levelling staff*; **level test** (see 3 g); **level tube** = *bubble-tube* s.v. BUBBLE *sb.* 6.

1867 SMYTH *Sailor's Word-bk.*, **Level-error*, the microscopic deviation of the axis of a transit instrument from the horizontal position. **1797** *Encycl. Brit.* (ed. 3) X. 10/2 The height of the *level-point determined on the staff at this place. **1839** *Penny Cycl.* XIII. 453/2 The relative heights of a series of points on the ground are obtained by means of their vertical distances from others which, on the supposition of the earth being a sphere, are equally distant from its centre; and these..are called level-points. **1706** PHILLIPS (ed. Kersey), **Level-Range*, (in Gunnery) the same as Point-blank Shot, or the Distance that a piece of Ordinance carries a Ball in a direct Line. **187.** *Dict. Archit.* (Archit. Publ. Soc.), **Level staff*, an upright staff five feet long, graduated to feet and decimals of a foot... The staff contains two thinner leaves called vanes. **1890** *Level tube [see *bubble-tube* s.v. BUBBLE *sb.* 6]. **1950** J. CLENDINNING *Princ. & Use of Surveying Instruments* v. 121 The level tube consists of a glass tube, partially filled with liquid, the inner surface of which is carefully ground.

level ('lɛvəl), *a.* and *adv.* [f. LEVEL *sb.*]

A. *adj.*

1. a. Having an even surface; 'not having one part higher than another' (J.).

1538 ELYOT *Dict.*, *Planities*, a playne or leuell grounde. **1559** W. CUNNINGHAM *Cosmogr. Glasse* 83 In any levell and plaine place, with your compasse make a circle. **1597** SHAKS. *2 Hen. IV*, III. i. 47 That one might..see the reuolution of the Times Make Mountaines leuell. **1637** MILTON *Lycidas* 98 On the level brine. **1663** GERBIER *Counsel* 21 The Hearth of a Chimney ought to lie levell, without a border, raised hearths being dangerous. **1715-20** POPE *Iliad* xx. 272 Along the level Seas they flew. **1725** DE FOE *Voy. round World* (1840) 261 We found the vale fruitful, level, and inhabited. **1835** ALISON *Hist. Europe* (1849-50) IV. xxv. §17. 429 Switzerland..comprises the undulating level surface between the Alps and the Jura. **1840** LARDNER *Geom.* 186 A cylindrical roller passing in one direction only will not produce a level surface. **1871** PALGRAVE *Lyr. Poems* 92 The level waves of broad Garonne.

b. *fig.* Of quantities: Expressed in whole numbers. Of a race: Showing no difference between the competitors. (Cf. EVEN *a.* 16.)

1826 *Sporting Mag.* XVIII. 316 At the close it was considered a level thing. **1883** GRESLEY *Gloss. Coal Mining*, *Level Tons*, weight of mineral wrought in tons, any odd cwts. not being taken into account.

2. Lying in a plane coinciding with or parallel to the plane of the horizon; horizontal; perpendicular to the plumb-line. ***level lines*** (*Shipbuilding*): see quot. 1850.

1559 W. CUNNINGHAM *Cosmogr. Glasse* 137 Placing your Instrument (which I name a Geographicall plaine Sphere) Flat, and levell. **1669** STURMY *Mariner's Mag.* v. 70 The first ..graze of the Bullet on the Level-Line, or on the Ground called the Horizontal Plain. **1679** MOXON *Mech. Exerc.* 126 The Work is Level. **1727-41** CHAMBERS *Cycl.* s.v., When the instrument is level. *c* **1850** *Rudim. Navig.* (Weale) 129 *Level lines.* Lines determining the shape of a ship's body horizontally, or square from the middle line of the ship. **187.** *Dict. Archit.* (Archit. Publ. Soc.) s.v., As applied to a line, this word means any which lies at right angles to one drawn to the centre of the earth, or to a plumb line; or any line which is parallel to the horizon. As applied to a plane, the term 'level' signifies any in which all lines drawn in any direction are level lines as before defined.

3. a. Lying in the same horizontal plane as something else; on a level *with*. Also *fig.*, on an equality *with*; readily accessible or intelligible *to*.

1559 W. CUNNINGHAM *Cosmogr. Glasse* 16 So that a man inhabiting under..th' equinoctial, do perceive both..the North pole, and..the South, level with th' earth. **1597** SHAKS. *2 Hen. IV*, IV. iv. 7 Euery thing lyes leuell to our wish. **1606** —— *Ant. & Cl.* IV. xv. 66 Young Boyes and Gyrles Are leuell now with men. **1642** FULLER *Holy & Prof. St.* I. iii. 8 He overshoots such low matter as lie levell to a womans eye. **1643** CARYL *Sacr. Covt.* 14 All our actions ought to be levell with reason. **1703** DAMPIER *Voy.* III. 32 Just by the Landing-place there is a small Fort, almost level with the Sea. **1729** BUTLER *Serm. Ignor. Man* Wks. 1874 II. 207 We should..apply ourselves to that which is level to our capacities. **1813** SHELLEY *Q. Mab* v. 11 When the tall trees ..Lie level with the earth to moulder there. **1864** LOWELL *Biglow P.* Poet. Wks. (1879) 228 Lincoln was master..of a truly masculine English,..level at once to the highest and lowest of his countrymen. **1888** SWEET *Hist. Eng. Sounds*

Pref. p. vii, I have done my best to keep level with the latest results of foreign investigation.

b. ***level crossing***: a place at which a road and a railway, or two railways, cross each other at the same level. Also *attrib.*

1841 Brees *Gloss. Civil Engin.*, *Level or Paved Crossing* (on a railway). **1851** *Illustr. Catal. Gt. Exhib.* 117 Simultaneously-acting level-crossing gates for railways. **1879** Sala in *Daily Tel.* 26 Dec., The perils of level-crossings. **1895** *Law Times* C. 133/2 A man who had been killed at a level crossing by a railway train.

4. a. Of two or more things with respect to one another: Situated in the same level or plane. Also *fig.*

1601 Shaks. *All's Well* I. iii. 118 Where qualities were leuell. **1795** J. Phillips *Hist. Inland Navig.* 8 To raise or fall Vessels out of one Canal into another, where they are not level. **1820** Keats *Eve St. Agnes* iv, The level chambers.. Were glowing to receive a thousand guests.

b. Equal in quality or position. *slang.*

1894 Astley *50 Years Life* II. 328 I'll toss yer who pays for level drinks.

5. Lying, moving, or directed in an (approximately) horizontal plane: esp. *poet.*, e.g. of the rays of the sun when it is low down on the horizon.

1667 Milton *P.L.* II. 634 He.. Now shaves with level wing the Deep, now soares [etc.]. **1760** Beattie *Virg. Past* II. 108 The setting sun now beams more mildly bright, The shadows lengthening with the level light. **1801** Campbell *Hohenlinden* 21 Scarce yon level sun Can pierce the war-clouds, rolling dun. **1832** Ht. Martineau *Life in Wilds* viii. 103 The last level rays were glittering on the stream. **1840** Browning *Sordello* III. 205 The level wind carried above the firs Clouds. **1851** *Illustr. Catal. Gt. Exhib.* 375 The shafts, being bent, bring the body level when at work. **1885–94** R. Bridges *Eros & Psyche* Aug. ii, The level sunbeams search'd the grassy ground For diamond dewdrops.

6. a. Of even, equable, or uniform quality, tone, or style; of even tenor.

1655 Fuller *Ch. Hist.* I. v. §21 In which Relation we much commend the even tenour thereof, consisting of so level Lies, that no one swelling Improbability is above the rest. **1764** Goldsm. *Trav.* 221 Their level life is but a mould'ring fire. **1802** *Sketch of Paris* II. lv. 214 Her voice was formerly very full in the medium or level-speaking. **1841** L. Hunt *Seer* II. 62 A passage.. delivered.. all in a level tone. **1861** *Illustr. Lond. News* 7 Dec. 569/3 The best of the pair.. a nice level animal. **1873** M. Arnold *Lit. & Dogma* (1876) 212 A very plain and level account. **1894** *Field* 1 Dec. 828/1 The owner of a beautifully level pack of hounds. **1899** *Allbutt's Syst. Med.* VI. 56 A leisured and level life.

b. ***level-dyeing***: a method of dyeing devised to prevent unequal absorption of the colouring matter.

In recent Dicts.

7. †**a.** 'Equipoised, steady' (Schmidt). *Obs.*

1597 Shaks. *2 Hen. IV*, II. i. 123 It is not a confident brow, nor the throng of wordes.. can thrust me from a leuell consideration. **1601** —— *Twel. N.* II. iv. 32 Let still the woman take An elder then her selfe, so weares she to him, So swayes she leuell in her husbands heart.

b. Said of the 'head' or mental 'make up': Well balanced. So ***level head***, a well-balanced person. orig. *U.S.*

1869 'Mark Twain' *Innoc. Abr.* xl. 426 The wanderers were right, and the heads of the same were level. **1870** *Orchestra* 12 Aug. 331/1 To tell a woman her head is level is apparently a compliment in America. **1876** Bret Harte *Gabriel Conroy* VI. vii, There is a strong feeling among men whose heads are level that this Minstrel Variety performance is a bluff. **1891** —— *1st Fam. Tasajara* II. 71 Mrs. Ashwood's head was about as level as it was pretty. **1906** 'O. Henry' *Four Million* 204 James Williams belonged among the level heads.

8. Plain, point-blank. *rare.*

1820 Keats *Lamia* 701 He look'd and look'd again a level —No!

9. ***one's level best***: one's very best; the utmost one can possibly do. Also ***levelest*** in the same sense, and similarly ***level worst***, etc. *colloq.* or *slang* (orig. *U.S.*).

Of these only *level best* is standard in the U.K.

1851 *An Arkansaw Doctor* 87 (Th.), We put our horses out at their level best. **1873** E. E. Hale (*title*) His Level Best. **1882** *Illustr. Sport. News* 29 July 467/2 His was an honest old hairy-heeled hunter, no doubt, and did her level best. **1884** 'Mark Twain' *Huck. Finn* xxviii. 270 The old man.. was on hand and looking his level pisonest. **1885** Rider Haggard *K. Solomon's Mines* (1887) 102 Then came a pause, each man aiming his level best. **1891** *Harper's Mag.* July 208/2 The pony will not do his level worst again. **1898** H. S. Canfield *Maid of Frontier* 97 She told me.. that she was goin' to do her levelest to make our little home comfortable. **1920** Galsworthy *In Chancery* II. vii. 186 Val walked out behind his mother, chin squared, eyelids drooped, doing his level best to despise everybody. **1933** M. Lowry *Ultramarine* 205 You've been doing your level best to make life a misery to me since we left home. **1937** V. Bartlett *This is my Life* xi. 179 Everyone was doing his level best to make me feel nervous. **1953** R. Lehmann *Echoing Grove* II. 89 When the pain nagged he thought about the relation between worry and his acid juices, and did his level best to stop worrying. **1969** *Listener* 24 Apr. 556/1 He did his level best to suppress the views of other members of the embassy.

10. *Comb.* (chiefly parasynthetic), as ***level-backed***, ***-balanced***, ***-bellied***, ***-browed***, ***-grown***, ***-lidded***, ***-mouthed***, ***-ranked***, ***-tempered***, ***-topped*** adjs.; **level-compounded** *a. Electr. Engin.*, applied to a compounded generator in which the windings are such as to produce the same voltage on full load as on no load (and usually on intermediate loads also); = *flat-compounded* adj. s.v. Flat *a.* 15; **level-handed** *a.*, having the same amount in hand; **level-lander** *nonce-wd.*, a dweller on level land; **level luffing**, luffing in which the load is maintained at constant height; freq. *attrib.*, as ***level luffing crane***.

1926 Kipling *Debits & Credits* 232 *Level-backed and level-bellied watch 'em move. **1917** D. H. Lawrence *Look! we have come Through!* 66 She Put back her fine, *level-balanced head. **1926** *Level-bellied [see *level-backed* above]. **1938** Belloc *Sonnets & Verse* 199 *Level-browed divine Touraine. **1915** W. T. Maccall *Continuous Current Electr. Engin.* viii. 204 The point, B, at which the generator is *level-compounded, *i.e.* has the same P.D. as at no load, can be made to occur at any one load. **1957** A. T. Starr *Appl. Electr.* vii. 182 An over-compounded generator really acts as a level-compounded generator plus a booster. **1971** L. T. Agger *Introd. Electr.* xvi. 298 In the level-compounded generator L the p.d. on full load is the same as on no load, and it varies only slightly in between. This is useful where the load changes rapidly, as in traction systems. **1866** G. M. Hopkins *Jrnl.* (1959) 136 Beech branches.. with *level-grown pieces of pale window-like green. **1835** *Ann. Reg.* 49 Now we are *level-handed, you've got £5, and I've got £5. **1864** Miss Yonge *Trial* I. 65 'Much you know of hills, you *level landers!' **1926** E. Bowen *Ann Lee's* 146 Miss Phelps' blue, calm, *level-lidded eyes. **1922** H. H. Broughton *Electr. Handling of Materials* III. 33 Few *level-luffing arrangements have been devised by crane makers on the Continent. **1963** R. Hammond *Mobile & Movable Cranes* iv. 110 Level luffing is achieved by the Babcock 'swan neck' supported by a fixed guy rope. **1971** *Engineering* Apr. 65 (Advt.), Level luffing cranes. **1948** C. L. B. Hubbard *Dogs in Brit.* 301 The muzzle is long, powerful and *level-mouthed. **1867** G. M. Hopkins *Jrnls. & Papers* (1959) 153 Very *level-ranked sunset. **1939** D. Cecil *Young Melbourne* i. 23 *Level-tempered and rational, she found scenes and caprices as tiresome as they did. **1796** Withering *Brit. Plants* (ed. 3) IV. 16 Crust forming cylindrical *level-topped bundles. **1847** W. E. Steele *Field Bot.* 172 Umbel level-topped.

†**B.** *adv.* With direct aim; on a level *with*. *Obs.*

1601 Marston *Pasquil & Kath.* Wks. 1878 III. 27 Welcome, Basilisco, thou wilt carrie leuell, and knock ones braines out with thy pricking wit. **1602** Shaks. *Ham.* IV. i. 42 Whose whisper o'er the world's diameter, As level as the cannon to his blank, Transports his poison'd shot. *Ibid.* v. 151 It shall as leuell to your Iudgement pierce As day do's to your eye. **1649** Bp. Reynolds *Serm. Hosea* vi. 92 If he mount a canon, and point that levell against the enemie. **1659** *Gentl. Calling* I. (1697) 4 If he chuse either to look level on the same nature with himself, or direct his eyes upward.

level ('lɛvəl), *v.*[1] Inflected levelled, levelling (*U.S.* leveled, leveling). Also 5–7 levell, (6 levelle, leavell, -ill, leyvel). [f. Level *sb.*]

I. 1. a. *trans.* To make (a surface) level or even; to remove or reduce inequalities in the surface of. †Also, to spread or distribute in a flat layer.

c **1440** *Jacob's Well* 3 Levell þi ground of þi welle be-nethe wyth þe leuell of equyte. **1509** in *Bury Wills* (Camden) 112 That ye hygheway.. be made and levelde at my cost and charge w^{t} grawell and stonys. **1530** Palsgr. 609/2, I levell, as a carpenter or mason dothe his grounde, or their tymber, or stones or they square them, with a lyne.. This florthe is well leavelled: *cest astre est bien aplanyée.* **1641–2** in Swayne *Sarum Churchw. Acc.* (1896) 213 Leveling ye ground in ye body of ye Ch. **1703** Moxon *Mech. Exerc.* 257 The Foundation being all made firm, and levelled. **1795** J. Phillips *Hist. Inland Navig.* Add. 40 The rubbish, &c. dug in making the canal, is to be leveled on the adjoining ground in a proper manner. **1856** Emerson *Eng. Traits, Aristocr.* Wks. (Bohn) II. 87 The road that grandeur levels for his coach. **1874** Green *Short Hist.* ii. §6. 92 Street and lane were being levelled to make space for the famous Churchyard of S. Paul's.

fig. **1812** *Gen. Hist.* in *Ann. Rev.* 132 Inflammatory writings inculcating levelling notions.

b. ***to level out***: to extend on a level; †*fig.* to contrive, procure (an opportunity).

1606 G. W[oodcocke] *Hist. Iustine* XVI. 65 b [Demetrius hoped] to leauell out fit opportunity himselfe to inuade the kingdome. **1644** Milton *Divorce* II. xiv. 59 To limit and level out the direct way from vice to vertu, with straitest and exactest lines on either side. *c* **1850** *Rudim. Navig.* (Weale) 129 *Levelled-out*, a line continued out in a horizontal direction from the intersection of an angle; or where the cant-timbers may intersect the diagonal or riband lines.

†**c.** To balance, settle (accounts). *Obs.*

1660 in *1st Cent. Hist. Springfield, Mass.* (1898) I. 270 Theire last Rate did not Levell all aco^{ts}, But.. there is still £2 17*s.* 4*d.* for ye Towne to allow, for ye clearing of all aco^{ts}.

d. *Dyeing.* To make (colour) uniform or even.

1874 Crookes *Dyeing*, etc. 549 This liquid [tartar] is employed by some dyers for 'levelling' certain colours.. upon woollen and worsted goods.

e. *Phonology.* To alter (a sound) so that it falls together with a similar sound. Usu. const. *under.*

1884 H. Sweet *First Middle Eng. Primer* 5 The old diphthongs *ea*, *ēa*, *eo*, *ēo* became monophthongic, *ea* being levelled under O.E. *æ*, written *e* in M.E., and *ēa* under O.E. *ǣ*, so that such a pair as the O.E. *heard* and *pæt* were both pronounced with the same vowel. **1888** —— *Hist. Eng. Sounds* 178 In North. *ā* has been preserved unrounded up to the present day in the Scotch dialects, where it has been levelled under new long *ā*. **1972** *English Studies* LIII. 503 There is, however, another type of development by which ME *ǭr* and ME *ōr* were levelled under the same sound as early as the fifteenth century.

2. To place (two or more things) on the same level or (horizontal) plane. Also *fig.*

1563 Hyll *Art Garden.* (1593) 14 You shall leuell your beds and borders of a height and breadth by a line laide out, whereby to weede the hearbes. **1599** *Broughton's Let.* xiii. 44 The two passages were leuelled vpon one floore, the one leading into Elysium, the other into Tartarus. **1863** W. Phillips *Speeches* iii. 44 Gunpowder leveled peasant and prince. **1867** Ouida *C. Castlemaine* I Cecil Castlemaine was the beauty of her country and her line.. her face levelled politics, and was cited as admiringly by the Whigs.. as by the Tories.

3. a. *fig.* ***to level*** (a person or thing) ***with*** (now rare), ***to***, †***unto***: to bring or reduce to the level or standard of; to put on a level, equality, or par with. Also occas. *intr.* for *pass.*, to be on a par with (? *obs.*). Also *refl.*

1603 Jas. I in Ellis *Orig. Lett.* Ser. I. III. 79 Sa mon ye levell everie mannis opinions.. unto you as ye finde thaime agree or discorde with the reulis thaire sett doun. **1604** Shaks. *Oth.* I. iii. 240 With such Accomodation and besort As leuels with her breeding. *a* **1626** Middleton & Rowley *Changeling* I. ii, To levell him with a Headborough, Beadle, or watchman, were but little better then he is. **1667** *Causes Decay Chr. Piety* v. 85 Those brutish appetites which would ..level its superior with its inferior faculties [etc.]. **1671** Flavel *Fount. Life* v. 13 The Arians denied his Deity levelling him with other men. **1769** *De Foe's Tour Gt. Brit.* (ed. 7) I. 86 To see a Person of Distinction.. level himself with a Groom.. is a Thing scarce credible. **1800** Mrq. Wellesley in Owen *Desp.* (1877) 739 In the nature of their duty, they are levelled with the native and Portuguese clerks. **1824** B. Travers *Dis. Eye* (ed. 3) 327 It levels with the proposal to extract through the sclerotica. **1828** Sewell *Oxf. Prize Ess.* 31 His arrogance levelled the slave with the brute creation. **1849** Prescott *Peru* (1850) II. 204 Its heaven-descended aristocracy was levelled almost to the condition of the peasant. **1879** Dixon *Windsor* II. xiii. 137 The recently created dukes were levelled to their ancient rank. **1907** *Daily Chron.* 25 May 1/7 Another halfpenny may possibly be put on the loaf before prices level themselves again.

b. ***to level up, down***: to bring up, down to the level of something (expressed or implied). Also *absol.*, and *intr.* for *refl.*

1763 Johnson in Boswell 21 July, Sir, your levellers wish to level *down* as far as themselves; but they cannot bear levelling *up* to themselves. **1809** Sir J. Anstruther *Sp. Ho. Commons* 11 May in Cobbett *Pol. Reg.* 20 May 754 Another party.. whose object was to level down all public men to their own very humble state. **1873** Hamerton *Intell. Life* III. viii. (1876) 111 To which he may level up. **1897** Morley *Speech* 16 Jan., To level up the beer and spirit duties.

c. *simply.* To lower the position of, bring down.

1712 Steele *Spect.* No. 485 ¶1 'Tis infinite pleasure to the majority of mankind to level a person superior to his neighbours.

4. a. To bring to the level of the ground; to lay low, lay 'even with the ground', to raze. Also ***to level to*** or ***with the ground, in the dust.***

1614 Raleigh *Hist. World* I. iii. §5. 41 All downe-right raines doe.. beate down and leuell the swelling and mountainous billow of the Sea. **1618** Bolton *Florus* III. x. (1636) 205 He.. levelled Alexia to the ground with fire. **1684** Otway *Windsor Castle* (1685) 13 The Hero levell'd in his humble Grave. **1713** Warder *True Amazons* (ed. 2) 33 Here twice ten thousand Houses levell'd are. **1794** Mrs. Radcliffe *Myst. Udolpho* xxxiii, Many noble trees were levelled with the ground. **1807** G. Chalmers *Caledonia* I. III. vii. 395 Many of those tumuli have been levelled of late. **1870** Bryant *Iliad* I. IV. 106 Should I design to level in the dust Some city. **1878** Browning *Poets Croisic* 12 May-dawn dews Saw the old stucture levelled.

b. To knock (a person) down. Cf. Leveller.

1760–72 H. Brooke *Fool of Qual.* (1809) IV. 94, I ran one of the assassins through the body, Tirlah levelled two more with his oaken staff. **1816** *Sporting Mag.* XLVIII. 187 The unfortunate Mordecai, who had been levelled very often by the rough son of Neptune.

c. *transf.* and *fig.* To reduce or remove (inequalities). Also with *out.*

1642 Rogers *Naaman* 3 Preparing and levelling their rough and high spirits for the Lord Jesus. **1812–16** J. Smith *Panorama Sci. & Art* I. 82 These inequalities are soon levelled by a file. **1821** Lamb *Elia* Ser. I. *Imperfect Sympathies*, The mercantile spirit levels all distinctions. **1856** Sir B. Brodie *Psychol. Inq.* I. vi. 220 Circumstances of trial, which, more than anything else, level all artificial distinctions. **1938** *Times* 24 Jan. 21/4 Later he took up with the heads of the motor industry.. the question of their co-operating with the Government to level out the production and sales of cars. **1971** *Fremdsprachen* xv. 227/1 Much can be done to level out these differences by proper use of incentive and social purpose funds derived from the profits of enterprises.

d. To get rid of, put *away*, by levelling. Also *intr.*, with *away*: to become level.

1910 Galsworthy *Sheaf* (1916) 132 All the natural weaknesses and limitations of the dwellers shall be.. levelled away and minimized. **1921** —— *To Let* II. ii. 140 Those two crumpled rose leaves, Fleur's caprice and Monsieur Profond's snout, would level away if he lay on them industriously.

5. *Surveying.* To ascertain the differences of level in (a piece of land); to ascertain the vertical contour of, 'run' a section of; hence, to lay out. Also *absol.* or *intr.*, to take levels.

1598, etc. [see Levelling *vbl. sb.* 2]. **1712** J. James tr. *Le Blond's Gardening* 118 Taking the Profil of a Mountain, is, to level the Slope of it exactly. *Ibid.* 189 You may level the Hill according to the following Practice. **1727–41** Chambers *Cycl.* s.v. *Levelling*, We are now able to level distances of one or two miles, at a single operation.

6. ***to level off*** (or ***out***): **a.** to bring an aircraft into horizontal flight (*intr.* and *trans.*); (of an aircraft) to assume horizontal flight, to flatten out.

1928 *Lit. Digest* 12 May 74/2 A 'pancake landing' occurs when the ship is leveled off several feet above the ground.

1928 *New Republic* 15 Aug. 331/2 In a straight dive down, coming out of a 'stall'..which stopped only when I levelled off and began to fly straight. *Ibid.*, When it gets into the diving position, it responds to all the controls and can be gradually levelled out. **1937** D. & H. TEILHET *Feather Cloak Murders* viii. 135 Climbing in the still blue atmosphere to five thousand feet, the ten-passenger Sikorsky amphibian levelled off above Honolulu. **1952** A. Y. BRAMBLE *Air-Plane Flight* xviii. 306 Some air-planes take a considerable time to reach cruising air speed, with cruising power setting, after levelling off. **1963** Level off [see AUTO-[1] b].

b. *fig.* To cease increasing or decreasing.

1958 *Listener* 10 July 40/1 If the recent signs of improvement in American business are not followed up, if production levels off again and unemployment rises..then [etc.]. **1968** *Guardian* 24 Apr. 11/5 The American war effort can begin to level off and eventually to be reduced. **1968** *Times* 16 Dec. 7/1 Yields have been tending to level off, or even to fall. **1972** *Guardian* 21 July 21/5 There are a few signs..that the property market is beginning to level off and prices are steadying somewhat.

II. 7. a. To aim (a missile weapon); to 'lay' (a gun); also *rarely*, to bring (a spear) to the proper level for striking. Also *to level one's aim*. (Freq. in fig. contexts.) Const. *at*, *against*, †*toward*, †*to*, †*unto*.

1530 PALSGR. 609/2 He leavelleth his crosse bowe to shote at some dere. **1586** HOOKER *Hist. Irel.* in *Holinshed* II. 130/1 He charged his peece, and leueled the same vnto the said Peter Carew. **1599** SHAKS. *Much Ado* IV. i. 239 If all ayme but this be leuelld false. **1655** MRQ. WORCESTER *Cent. Inv.* viii, A way how to level and shoot Cannon by night as well as by day. **1667** MILTON *P.L.* II. 712 Each at the Head Level'd his deadly aime. **1695** WOODWARD *Nat. Hist. Earth* I. (1723) 48 They [the Means] were both levell'd wide, and fell all short of the Mark. **1757** BURKE *Abridgm. Eng. Hist.* Wks. 1842 II. 586 The papal thunders, from the wounds of which he was still sore, were levelled full at his head. **1810** SCOTT *Lady of L.* II. xxxii, Against his sovereign, Douglas ne'er Will level a rebellious spear. **1845** DARWIN *Voy. Nat.* x. (1879) 219 In the very act of levelling his musket. **1879** J. BURROUGHS *Locusts & W. Honey* (1884) 57 Levelling his bill as carefully as a marksman levels his rifle. **1883** R. W. DIXON *Mano* I. xv. 48 Forth from Ravenna's fort he levelled aim Against the popedom.

†**b.** To shoot (a missile) *out* (*of* a weapon). *Obs.*

1592 STOW *Ann.* 235 [He] leuelled a quarrel out of a cros bowe. **1610** HOLLAND *Camden's Brit.* (1637) 250 A bullet levelled out of a great piece of ordnance. **1664** *Floddan F.* viii. 72 Roaring Guns..levell'd out great leaden lumps.

c. To direct (one's looks); to dart (rays).

1594 J. DICKENSON *Arisbas* (1878) 40 To..leuell the eye..at a gainefull, though inglorious obiect. **1667** MILTON *P.L.* IV. 543 The setting Sun..Against the eastern Gate of Paradise Leveld his eevning Rayes. **1725** POPE *Odyss.* XXI. 459 The chord he drew, Thro' ev'ry ringlet levelling his view. **1749** FIELDING *Tom Jones* IX. v, The fair one..hastily withdrew her eyes and levelled them downwards. **1817** BYRON *Beppo* lxvii, Others were levelling their looks at her.

d. *fig.* To aim, direct, point.

1576 FLEMING *Panopl. Epist.* 273 All our actions are leveled..unto two ends. **1591** SPENSER *M. Hubberd* 772 All his minde on honour fixed is, To which he levels all his purposis. **1690** LOCKE *Toleration* ii. Wks. 1727 II. 279 You proportion your Punishments..contrary to the Common Discretion,..which levels the Punishments against refractory Offenders. **1704** HEARNE *Duct. Hist.* (1714) I. 383 Pompey..made two Laws particularly levelled against him [Cæsar]. **1742** FIELDING *J. Andrews* I. xvii, This fellow's writings..are levelled at the clergy. **1856** FROUDE *Hist. Eng.* (1858) II. ix. 325 Considerable sarcasm has been levelled at the assumption by Henry of this title. **1894** *Solicitor's Jrnl.* XXXIX. 2/2 It is not necessary for the official receiver to level an accusation of fraud against any individual.

†**e.** Const. *inf.* To aim at doing something; to intend *to*. *Obs.*

1708 SWIFT *Sentim. Ch. Eng. Man* Wks. 1755 II. I. 65 A few men, whose designs..were levelled to destroy the constitution both of religion and government. **1752** BEAWES *Lex. Mercat. Rediv.* 257 My endeavours have been levelled ..to obtain this satisfaction. **1809** MALKIN *Gil Blas* V. i. ¶ 12 This exclamation produced all the astonishment it was levelled to excite in the old citizen.

8. *absol.* or *intr.* **a.** To aim with a weapon; † *occas.* said of the weapon. Also freq. *transf.* and *fig.* as in 7 (with the same const.). Somewhat *arch.*

c **1500** *Three Kings' Sons* 75 That..they shold leuelle & shote alle at ones. **1579** SPENSER *Sheph. Cal.* Mar. 85, I leuelde againe, And shott at him with might and maine. **1579** GOSSON *Sch. Abuse* (Arb.) 59 A wanton eye is the darte of Cephalus, where it leueleth, there it lighteth. **1590** GREENE *Orl. Fur.* (1599) B 3 b, I, so they gesse but leuell farre awry. **1597** SHAKS. *2 Hen. IV*, III. ii. 286 The foe-man may with as great ayme leuell at the edge of a Pen-knife. **1604** T. WRIGHT *Passions* I. i. 1 There can be no man, who works by right reason but..he aymeth at some end, he levels at some good. **1626** T. H. *Caussin's Holy Crt.* 6 Euery Christian is obliged to leuell at perfection. **1664** BUTLER *Hud.* II. iii. 449 He to his engine flew..And rais'd it till it levell'd right. **1699** POMFRET *Poems* (1724) 31 He levels blindly, yet the mark does hit. **1699** DAMPIER *Voy.* II. I. 72 When they shoot at a mark, they level, and fire at first sight. **1704** POPE *Windsor For.* I. 129 He lifts the tube and levels with his eye. **1728** T. SHERIDAN *Persius* iv. (1739) 54 The Author in this Satyr levels at Nero. **1879** BROWNING *M. Relph* 103 They level: a volley, a smoke and the clearing of smoke.

†**b.** To guess *at*. *Obs.*

1580 LYLY *Euphues* (Arb.) 227 If thou couldest as well conceiue the cure of a father as I can leuel at the nature of a child. *Ibid.* 289 Since your eyes are..so cunning that you can leuell at the dispositions of women whom you neuer knew. **1596** SHAKS. *Merch. V.* I. ii. 41 As thou namest them [my suitors], I will describe them, and according to my description leuell at my affection.

9. To be honest or truthful; to tell the truth, speak frankly, behave honestly or deal straightforwardly (*with*). *slang* (orig. *U.S.*).

1920 H. C. WITWER *Leather Pushers* (1921) 174 'Are you levelin' with the Kid in this one?' 'We level in all of 'em!' **1931** *Amer. Mercury* Dec. 416/2 Hymie, the mug, falls in love with her right off, Don't laugh, I'm levellin', honest to God. **1936** R. CHANDLER in *Black Mask* Mar. 28/1 'I was on the cops, but they bounced me.' I liked his telling me that. 'You must have been levelling,' I said. **1951** I. SHAW *Troubled Air* vii. 107 You're not levelling with me. **1962** K. ORVIS *Damned & Destroyed* ix. 64 But see that you level with me about the new pusher. **1966** E. MCGIRR *Funeral was in Spain* 100 'Think Songbird was levelling?' 'Oh yes... Mr. Songbird wouldn't mislead you.' **1972** 'R. CRAWFORD' *Whip Hand* I. viii. 49 I'll level with you. I've been paid to find your brother. **1973** *Tucson* (Arizona) *Daily Citizen* 22 Aug. 55/8 Not often enough will a company truly level with its employes. It won't say, 'These are hard times and here's why.' **1974** L. DEIGHTON *Spy Story* iv. 97 I'd better level with you, son... From now on, control is through me.

'level, *v.*[2] *Obs.* exc. *dial.* [? Corruption of LEVY, by association with prec.; but cf. OF. *levaille* tax; also It. *livellare* to levy (Florio, 1611).] = LEVY *v.*

1552 T. BARNABE in Ellis *Orig. Lett.* Ser. II. II. 202 The chefe of the Frenche kinges revenewe is levelled uppon salte. *a* **1825** FORBY *Voc. E. Anglia*, *Level*, to assess. Ex. 'I will pay whatever you level upon me'. **1886** ELWORTHY *W. Som. Word-bk.* s.v., Mr. Jones to shop 've a level'd a distress 'pon 'em vor the quarter's rent.

levelage ('lɛvəlɪdʒ). [f. LEVEL *v.* + -AGE.] Levelling.

1882 *Rep. to Ho. Repr. Prec. Met. U.S.* 389 The Rara Avis Mining Company..give the best showing of any mine..for ..development made through levelage.

†**level-coil.** *Obs.* Forms: 6-7 level(l coyl(e, coile, 7 levell acoile, leve le cull, leve-le-queue. [Corruptly ad. Fr. phrase (*faire*) *lever le cul* (*à quelqu'un*), to make a person rise from his seat (*lever* to raise, *cul* buttock): see Cotgr., and cf. COIL *sb.*[4] The Fr. name of the game is *lève-cul* (Littré s.v. *lever*): cf. the Eng. equivalent in quot. 1656. Florio has an It. *levaculo*.] A rough, noisy game, formerly played at Christmas, in which each player is in turn driven from his seat and supplanted by another; cf. LEVEL-SICE. Hence = riotous sport, noisy riot; phr. *to keep level-coil*. Also used *advb.* = turn and turn about, alternately.

1594 NASHE *Unfort. Trav.* 33 The next daie they had solempne disputations, where Luther and Carolostadius scolded leuell coyle. **1605** ARMIN *Fool upon Fool* (ed. Grosart) 21 They..entred the Parler, found all this leuell coyle, and his pate broken, his face scratcht [etc.]. **1611** FLORIO, *Leuaculo*, itch-buttocke, leue le cull. **1616** BEAUM. & FL. *Faithf. Friends* I. ii, What coil is here? Level-coil, you see, every man's pot. **1621** QUARLES *Argalus & P.* I. (1629) 18 The mothers smile Brought forth the daughters blush; and leuell coyle They smil'd and blusht; one smile begate another. **1633** B. JONSON *Tale Tub* III. ii, Young Justice Bramble has kept level-coyl Here in our quarters, stole away our daughter. **1647** HERRICK *Noble Numbers*, *To God, his gift* 72 As my little Pot doth boyle We will keep this Levell Coyle. **1654** H. L'ESTRANGE *Chas. I* (1655) 157 Thus did Episcopacy and Presbytery play Leve-le-queve, and take their turns of Government for about 30 years. **1656** BLOUNT *Glossogr.*, *Level-Coile* is when three play at Tables, or other Game, where onely two can play at a time, and the loser removes his Buttocks, and sits out, and therefore called also Hitch-Buttock. **1684** *Observator* No. 129 An Ecclesiastical way of (Leve-Cul, or) Level-Coyle.

'level-free, *a.* Of a mine: Admitting of being worked or drained by means of a level or levels.

1805 R. FORSYTH *Beauties Scotl.* III. 411 The mine..is nearly 700 feet above the level of the valley, and must therefore always be level-free. **1883** GRESLEY *Gloss. Coal-Mining*, *Level-free*, old coal or ironstone workings at the outcrop, worked by means of a day level driven into the hillside.

ˌlevel-'headed, *a.* [f. LEVEL *a.* 7 b.] Having a 'level' head; mentally well-balanced or cool. Hence **ˌlevel-'headedness**.

1876 *Rep. Vermont Board Agric.* III. 156 That same steadiness, or, in horse parlance, level-headedness,..is quite as essential on the race track..as any where else. **1879** TOURGEE *Fool's Err.* i. 8 Clear-headed, or, as they would now be called, level-headed, were these children of the Berkshire hills. **1886** *New Englander* (New Haven, Connecticut) Feb. 179 This unexampled success is due..to the levelheadedness of its clerical guardians. **1896** *Alma Mater* 11 Nov. 43/2 A man whose great characteristic is level-headedness. **1898** S. LEE *Life Shaks.* xiv. 245 The terse and caustic comments which Anthony's level-headed friend Enobarbus..passes on the action. **1916** *Daily Chron.* 13 Oct. 4/5 The British Air Service is now a great army,..all endowed with two sterling qualities required by the pilot of the air, courage and levelheadedness. **1927** *Daily Express* 9 Aug. 8/2 A tribute to the level-headedness of the country which in his puny way he tries to wreck. **1937** KOESTLER *Spanish Testament* iv. 84 English journalists..with their traditional feeling for level-headedness and decency, have often had to complain of this difficulty.

levelish ('lɛvəlɪʃ), *a.* Somewhat level.

1894 CROCKETT *Raiders* (ed. 3) 166 Over levelish, boggy country.

levelism ('lɛvəlɪz(ə)m). Also 7 levellism, 8 levillism. [f. LEVEL *a.* or *v.* + -ISM.] The principle of levelling distinctions in society. In early use *spec.* the principles advocated by the 'Levellers'.

1659 *Democritus turned Statesm.* in *Harl. Misc.* (1810) VI. 194 This day a Republican, to-morrow what you please; a favourer of Levellism [etc.]. **1708** S. SEWALL *Diary* 15 Jan. (1879) II. 210 He speaks against Levillism, Buying and Selling Men. **1831** *Fraser's Mag.* III. 480 We had given sufficient evidence of our ability to grapple with the leviathan of levelism in matters ecclesiastical.

levelization (ˌlɛvəlaɪ'zeɪʃən). [f. LEVEL *a.* + -IZATION.] 'The act of levelling or reducing to equality'.

a **1860** *Gentl. Mag.* cited in Worcester.

levelled ('lɛvəld), *ppl. a.* Also 6 levyled, 7 leveld. [f. LEVEL *v.* + -ED[1].] Made level; placed in a level position; aimed, directed.

1567 DRANT *Horace Epist.* To Rdr. *vj, A smothe, and plat leuyled poesye. **1607** SHAKS. *Timon* I. i. 47 No leuell'd malice Infects one comma in the course I hold. **1616** R. C. *Times' Whistle* III. 1098 The infection Of thy high leveld thoughts. **1667** MILTON *P.L.* VII. 376 Opposite in leveld West was set His mirror. **1769** SIR W. JONES *Pal. Fort.* Poems (1777) 23, I..fix'd my level'd telescope on man. **1800** *Asiat. Ann. Reg.*, *Misc. Tr.* 11/2 They poured in one well-levelled fire, and then a second. **1823** BYRON *Juan* VIII. xxxiv, Who kept their..levell'd weapons still against the glacis. **1869** BOUTELL *Arms & Arm.* iii. (1874) 43 The points of six levelled pikes. **1892** WOODBURY *Encycl. Photogr.* 228 [It] is placed upon the..levelled glass plate.

leveller ('lɛvələ(r)). Also 8-9 (now *U.S.*) leveler. [f. LEVEL *v.* + -ER[1].] One who or that which levels.

1. In material senses:

†**a.** One who takes soundings. †**b.** One who aims, an aimer. †**c.** A level (the instrument). **d.** One who levels ground. Also, 'an earth-scraper for levelling a site' (Knight *Dict. Mech.* 1875). **e.** *Pugilism.* A knock-down blow. **f.** One who uses a level or levelling-instrument. **g.** 'A billiard-table foot having a screw adjustment for height, in order to level the table' (Knight). **h.** (See quot. 1891.)

1598 FLORIO, *Scandagliatore*, a sounder, a leueller, or fadomer of the sea. **1611** COTGR. s.v. *Coup*, The farre-off leueller shall neuer hit the white. **1693** EVELYN *De la Quint. Compl. Gard.* I. 41 Every Level..must be taken with the Rule and Leveller, which every body knows is a Triangular Instrument with a Lead..hung to a small Cord, and that fix'd to the obtuse Angle. **1712** J. JAMES tr. *Le Blond's Gardening* 115 Customs that are ordinarily follow'd by Levelers. **1814** *Sporting Mag.* XLIII. 68 B. put in some good body hits, but C. returned them by a leveller. **1834** *Blackw. Mag.* XXXV. 548 The leveller and the shoveller.. have taken the crown off his [a hill's] head. **1860** J. MULLAN *Rep. Constr. Road to Ft. Benton* (1863) 85 The level was used by myself until..sickness forced me to leave the party, Mr. Johnson taking my place as leveller. **1891** *Labour Commission* Gloss. s.v. *Cokemen*, In making coke, the coal is deposited in the oven by a tub which runs to the top eye, and is there tipped up, the coal naturally forming a conical heap at the bottom of the oven. The leveller rakes this coal level.

2. (Often with capital initial.) One who would level all differences of position or rank among men. The term first arose as the designation of a political party of Charles I's reign, which professed principles of this character; in later use, it has been applied more widely.

1644 NEEDHAM *Case Commw.* 77 Our Levellers now exclaim against the Parliament. **1647** *Newsletter* 1 Nov. (Clarendon MSS. 2638), They have given themselves a new name viz. Levellers, for they intend to sett all things straight, and rayse a parity and community in the kingdom. **1658** J. HARRINGTON *Prerog. Pop. Govt.* I. viii. 44 The People..are not Levellers, nor know they why, and yet it is, because to be levellers, were to destroy themselves. **1697** COLLIER *Ess. Mor. Subj.* I. (1709) 44, I see, you are an everlasting Leveller; you won't allow any Encouragement to extraordinary Industry and Merit. **1790** BURKE *Fr. Rev.* Wks. 1808 V. 104 The levellers..only change and pervert the natural order of things. **1827** HALLAM *Const. Hist.* (1876) II. x. 223 The commonwealth's men and the levellers ..grew clamorous for the king's death. **1876** BANCROFT *Hist. U.S.* I. xi. 386 The republicans, the levellers, the fanatics,—all ranged themselves on the side of the new ideas.

3. *pl.* The name of a rebel secret society in Ireland in the 18th c. (see quots.); identical with or similar to the 'Whiteboys'.

1762 *Gentl. Mag.* 183 What you, in Dublin, think of the White Boys, or Levellers, I cannot say. **1763** *Brit. Mag.* IV. 162 The mischiefs committed by those people called Levellers, in the county of Tipperary; by levelling park walls, breaking down fences, &c.

4. A thing which reduces all men to an equality.

1659 *Gentl. Calling* (1679) 77 Such a Leveller is Debauchery, that it takes off all distinctions. **1755** YOUNG *Centaur* ii. Wks. (1757) IV. 146 Is diversion grown a leveller, like death? **1758** JOHNSON *Idler* No. 32 ¶ 5 Sleep is equally a leveller with death. **1829** LYTTON *Devereux* II. i, Emotion, whether of ridicule, anger or sorrow, is your grandest of levellers. **1874** HELPS *Soc. Press.* xiii. 179 Familiarity is the great leveller, and a most unjust leveller.

levelling ('lɛvəlɪŋ), *vbl. sb.* Also 8-9 (now *U.S.*) leveling. [f. LEVEL *v.* + -ING[1].]

1. Aiming, aim.

1580 HOLLYBAND *Treas. Fr. Tong*, *Visée*, leuelling. **1607** HIERON *Wks.* I. 429 A smooth stone, by which I may, if the Lord shall please so to blesse my leuelling, smite this Goliah in the forehead. **1627** tr. *Bacon's Life & Death* (1651) 50 Our Aiming and Levelling at the End. **1796-7** *Instr. & Reg. Cavalry* (1813) 263 In the firings, the loading is quick, the levelling is just.

2. a. The action of bringing to a uniform horizontal surface; the action of placing in an accurately horizontal position by means of a level.

1598 [see 4 below]. **1712** J. JAMES tr. *Le Blond's Gardening* 105 The Words Dressing, Leveling..signify the Action of harrowing or raking the Ground, to lay it every where smooth and eaven. **1786** in Picton *L'pool Munic. Rec.* (1886) II. 260 The levelling of the streets. **1861** MUSGRAVE *By-roads* 289 The levelling of two or three hills, and the filling in of a few ravines.

b. *fig.* (See LEVEL *v.* 3.) Also with *up*, *down*, *off*, *out*.

1618 J. SMITH *Lives Berkeleys* (1883) II. 417, I have, for 550 years, traced the waies wherein they severally walked, for the better levelling of the life of the present lord George. **1658** J. HARRINGTON *Prerog. Pop. Govt.* I. xi. 84 By Levelling, they who use the word, seem to understand, when a People rising invades the Lands and Estates of the richer sort, and divides them equally among themselves. **1705** STANHOPE *Paraphr.* III. 476 The Jews..disdained such a Levelling with People held by them in the utmost Contempt. **1831** LAMB *Elia* Ser. II. *To Shade of Elliston*, O ignoble levelling of Death! **1837** CARLYLE *Fr. Rev.* II. v. iv, Levelling is comfortable but only down to oneself. **1869** DOWDEN *Stud. Lit.* (1890) 353 Thus, by a process of levelling-up, Lamennais made the supernatural, in the ordinary sense of the word, disappear. **1871** H. SWEET *King Alfred's West-Saxon Version of Gregory's Pastoral Care* p. xxxvii, The change is not phonetic,..but is due to inflectional levelling, the nom. terminations being made uniform, regardless of gender. **1888** SWEET *Hist. Eng. Sounds* Pref. p. vi, To justify Rapp's and Ellis's levelling of Chaucer's long *es* under one sound. **1888** J. WRIGHT *Old High-German Primer* 16 The regular operation of this law was often disturbed by new formations made by levelling. **1903** G. B. SHAW *Revolutionist's Handbk.* vii, in *Man & Superman* 201 To them the limit of progress is, at worst, the completion of all the suggested reforms and the levelling up of all men to the point attained already by the most highly nourished and cultivated in mind and body. **1932** F. R. LEAVIS in *Scrutiny* I. 137 Mass-production, standardization, levelling-down—these three terms convey succinctly, what has happened. **1953** *Manch. Guardian Weekly* 13 Aug. 7/2 Housewives..cheered the heavy drop in the price of beef and thankfully attributed it to..the 'levelling-off' of inflation. **1955** *Times* 17 Aug. 5/5 Efforts by the employers to make them [*sc.* piece rates] realistic have foundered on the insistence of the men that they shall be changed only by levelling up. **1962** SIMPSON & RICHARDS *Physical Princ. Junction Transistors* vi. 112 The beginning of this levelling-off process can be seen in the figure. **1964** F. BOWERS *Bibliogr. & Textual Crit.* I. ii. 13 This evidence also suggests that authors' papers and not a levelling-out scribal transcript formed the printer's copy. **1971** *Cabinet Maker & Retail Furnisher* 24 Sept. 518/1 Important social changes and a levelling-off of income groups are playing a strong part in the expanding consumer market. **1972** *Guardian* 30 Mar. 14/3 Labour came to office with a strategy of levelling-up, of faster growth to finance greater equality.

3. *Surveying.* (See quot. 1887.)

1812-16 PLAYFAIR *Nat. Phil.* (1819) I. 169 Levelling is the art of drawing a line at the surface of the earth, to cut the directions of gravity every where at right angles. **1830** LYELL *Princ. Geol.* I. 293 The levellings recently carried across that isthmus..to ascertain the relative height of the Pacific Ocean at Panama. **1831** LARDNER *Hydrost.* iv. 72 Instruments for levelling or determining the direction or position of horizontal lines. **1887** GEN. WALKER in *Encycl. Brit.* XXII. 707 Levelling is the art of determining the relative heights of points on the surface of the ground as referred to a hypothetical surface which cuts the direction of gravity everywhere at right angles... The trigonometrical determination of the relative heights of points at known distances apart by the measurements of their mutual angles ..is a method of levelling. But the method to which the term 'levelling' is always applied is that of the direct determination of the differences of height from the readings of the lines at which graduated staves, held vertically over the points, are cut by the horizontal plane which passes through the eye of the observer.

4. *attrib.*: **levelling-instrument**, an instrument used in surveying and consisting essentially of a telescope fitted with a spirit-level; **levelling pole, rod, staff**, an instrument, consisting essentially of a graduated pole with a vane sliding upon it, used in levelling; †**levelling-rule** = LEVEL *sb.*^{1}; **levelling-screw**, a screw used to adjust parts of a contrivance to an exact level; **levelling-stand** (*Photography*), an instrument used to support a glass plate in a horizontal position.

1690 LEYBOURN *Curs. Math.* 456b, The *Levelling Instrument to be used in this Work. **1851** *Illustr. Catal. Gt. Exhib.* 1087 Theodolites,..sextants, levelling instruments. **1598** FLORIO, *Scandaglio*, a plummet, or line to sounde with, a *leuelling rule. **1849** R. V. DIXON *Heat* I. 51 A strong T-shaped bar of iron, furnished with two levels, and placed on a board provided with *levelling screws. **1866** R. M. FERGUSON *Electr.* (1870) 19 Upon a tripod provided with levelling screws stands the pillar. **1727-41** CHAMBERS *Cycl.*, **Levelling Staves*, are instruments used in levelling; serving to carry marks to be observed, and at the same time to measure the heights of those marks from the ground. **1875** KNIGHT *Dict. Mech.*, **Leveling-stand.* **1890** *Anthony's Photogr. Bull.* III. 220 The solution may be flowed on and off the plate or the plate placed on a levelling stand.

'levelling, *ppl. a.* Also leveling. [f. LEVEL *v.* + -ING^2.] That levels; *esp.* bringing all to the same social, moral, or intellectual level; also, of or pertaining to levellers and their principles.

a **1635** SIBBES *Confer. Christ & Mary* (1656) 63 If God be a Father, and we be brethren, it is a levelling word, it bringeth mountains down, and filleth up vallies. **1648** BOYLE *Seraph. Love* xi. (1700) 56 So familiar and levelling an affection as Love. *a* **1674** CLARENDON *Hist. Reb.* x. §136 The barbarity of the Agitators and the levelling party. **1763** JOHNSON in *Boswell* 21 July, I..showed her the absurdity of the levelling doctrine. **1796** BURKE *Let. Noble Lord* Wks. VIII. 39 A levelling tyrant, who oppressed all descriptions of his people. **1841-4** EMERSON *Ess.*, *Compensation* Wks. (Bohn) I. 42 There is always some levelling circumstance that puts down the overbearing, the strong, the rich, the fortunate. **1847** DISRAELI *Tancred* I. vi, If anything can save the aristocracy in this levelling age, it is an appreciation of men of genius.

levelly ('lɛvəlɪ), *adv.* [f. LEVEL *a.* + -LY^2.] In a level or horizontal position or direction; on a level; †uniformly; with a level surface.

1610 GUILLIM *Heraldry* II. iii. (1611) 43 [The line] is carried leuelly or equally thorowout the Escocheon without either rising or falling. **1628** HOBBES *Thucyd.* (1822) 96 Neither would praises and actions appear so levelly concurrent in many other of the Grecians. **1669** STURMY *Mariner's Mag.* v. 75 Every Shot..equally Oblique or Levelly directed. **1837** *New Monthly Mag.* L. 470 A dense, slow-moving stream,..flowing levelly on for a few yards. **1851** *Jrnl. R. Agric. Soc.* XII. II. 639 See the standing corn shorn levelly low. **1881** MRS. C. PRAED *Policy & P.* I. viii. 175 Looking at him levelly with her own large eyes.

levelness ('lɛvəlnɪs). [f. LEVEL *a.* + -NESS.] The quality or condition of being level.

1634 PEACHAM *Gentl. Exerc.* II. ii. 109 So you must remember to draw them to expresse their levelness with the earth. **1787** ROY in *Phil. Trans.* LXXVII. 190 *Romney-Marsh*, from its levelness..seeming..to afford the best base. **1824** SOUTHEY *Sir T. More* (1831) II. 107 The very levelness of the political platform. **1891** J. WINSOR *Columbus* 543 Levelness of head. **1897** *Outing* (U.S.) XXX. 126/1 Her rich black and tan markings are American, but her clean physical levelness comes from her English ancestry.

levelode, obs. form of LIVELIHOOD.

leve longe, obs. form of LIVELONG.

level-pegging, *vbl. sb.* (passing into *adv.*). (Level stress.) [Cf. PEGGING *vbl. sb.*] On equal terms (competitively), neck-and-neck, neither falling behind nor getting ahead (used of two individuals, groups, etc.). Also (as a back-formation) **level-peg** *v.*

1927 W. E. COLLINSON *Contemp. Eng.* 30 Cribbage is scored with pegs on a triangular board with two rows of holes on each side and supplied us with the technical expressions: level pegging or neck and neck (*from the racecourse*), [etc.]. **1959** *Motor* 16 Dec. 704/1 Two competitors..[one of which] lost one less mark than [the other] on the fourth section which was the first section on which they were not level pegging. **1962** *Listener* 13 Dec. 1027/2 The sociologist is level-pegging with the psychologist to replace the priest in the cure-of-souls business. **1965** *Observer* (Colour Suppl.) 28 Mar. 16 While air and sea were roughly level-pegging at a million passengers each in 1958, last year's split was 3·5 million to the airlines and 714,000 to the sea. **1973** J. WAINWRIGHT *Touch of Malice* 155 They were level-pegging—in rank, in age and in service. **1974** *Listener* 21 Feb. 244/2 ITV first made the running in the coverage of election news... Initiative reverting to the BBC? Let's call it level pegging.

†**'Levelry.** *Obs. nonce-wd.* [f. LEVEL *a.* or *v.* + -RY, with reference to *leveller*: cf. *revelry*.] The principles of the Levellers.

1661 *Sir H. Vane's Politics* 5 There is no State nor Seat more suitable for a Levelry then a Court-Livery. *Ibid.* 5 From this Levellry I should never have dissented, had not the fulnesse of my Fortunes made me their Enemy.

†**level-sice.** *Obs.* Also 6 leuell suse. [app. from an altered form of the Fr. phr. *lever le cul* (see LEVEL-COIL), in which *assise* (seat) was substituted, as more decent, for *cul*. Skelton's form may be due to association with F. *sus* up.] = LEVEL-COIL.

1522 SKELTON *Why not to Court?* 139 We haue cast vp our war, And made a worthy trewse, With, gup, leuell suse! **1608** SYLVESTER *Du Bartas* II. iv. IV. *Decay* 41 Ambitious hearts do play at Level sice [orig. F. *Ces cœurs ambitieux iouent au boute hors*].

†**levely,** *a. Obs. rare.* In 3 *north.* **levelike.** [f. LEVE *v.* + -LY^1.] Credible.

a **1300** *E.E. Psalter* xcii. 7 Þine wittenesses leuelike [*MS. H.* Mikel leuandlic: Lat. *credibilia*] are þai.

levelyheede, obs. form of LIVELIHEAD.

leven (in 4 *Sc.* lewine, lewyne, 6-7 leaven), clipped f. ELEVEN and ELEVENTH. **leventh** (in 4 *Sc.* lewint. 6 *Sc.* levint), clipped f. ELEVENTH.

c **1375** *Sc. Leg. Saints* vi. (*Thomas*) 429 Þe lewine is: þat cheryte To frend & fa euire haf we. *Ibid.* vii. (*Jacobus Minor*) 477 And þare-for he llewyne Iowis of his consent tuk with hym. *Ibid.* xxxii. (*Justin*) 30 Als þare-[of] is mad mencione in þe lewint distinccion. **1570** LEVINS *Manip.* 69 Y^e^ Leuenthe, *vndecimus*. **1578** in *Maitl. Cl. Misc.* I. (1840) 8 The levint buik of the Amades de Gaule. **1611** SHAKS. *Wint. T.* IV. iii. 33 Euery Leauen-weather toddes. **1883** JESSOP in *19th Cent.* Oct. 591 In Arcady we have an institution called 'levens, when the labourers knock off work for awhile..and make pretence of enjoying a social meal [see ELEVENS].

leven, var. LEVIN *sb.* and *v.*; obs. f. LEAVEN.

†**'leveness.** *Obs.* Also 5 lefnesse. [app. f. LEVE *v.* + -NESS.] Faith, confidence.

c **1400** *St. Alexius* (Laud 622) 627 And lered hem her lefnesse. *c* **1440** *Promp. Parv.* 301/1 Levenesse, or belevenesse, *fides*. *Levenesse*, or grete troste.

lever ('li:və(r), *U.S.* 'lɛ-), *sb.*^{1} Forms: 3 levere, 4 levor, 4-5 levour, 6-8 leaver, 5-lever. [ME. *levere*, *levour*, a. OF. **levere*, *leveour* (F. *leveur*), agent-n. f. *lever* to raise; in the sense 'lever' recorded only once (1487) as *leveur*; the usual Fr. word is *levier* (recorded from 12th c.) formed on the same vb. with different suffix; *leviere* fem. occurs in the 14th c.]

1. a. A bar of iron or wood serving to 'prize up' or dislodge from its position some heavy or firmly fixed object; a crowbar, handspike, or the like.

In mod. use, this sense is more or less coloured by the scientific sense 2, which is alone formally recognized by Johnson.

1297 R. GLOUC. (Rolls) 3103 Hii..cables vette ynowe & laddren, & leuours & uaste ssoue & drowe. **13..** *Coer de L.* 1935 Ever men bare them up with levours. **1382** WYCLIF *Isa.* xxvii. 1 In that dai visiten shal the Lord..vp on leuyathan, an eddere, a leuour [Vulg. *serpentem vectem*]. **1433** LYDG. *St. Edmund* III. 1202 Oon with a leuour to leffte the doore on barre. **1481** CAXTON *Godfrey* clxxx. 265 Other had grete leuers and plente of ropes and Cordes. **1553** T. WILSON *Rhet.* (1580) 223 An other speakes, as though his woordes had neede to bee heaved out with leavers. **1642** FULLER *Holy & Prof. St.* II. xxiii. 147 Surely so heavy a log needed more levers than one. **1697** POTTER *Antiq. Greece* III. xx. (1715) 148 The heavy Ship into the Sea they thrust With Leavers. **1736** BUTLER *Anal.* I. i. 36 As carriages and leavers and scaffolds are in architecture. **1813** SCOTT *Rokeby* I. vi, Then clanking chains and levers tell, That o'er the moat the draw-bridge fell. *a* **1825** FORBY *Voc. E. Anglia*, *Lewer*, *lower*, a lever. **1881** S. H. HODGSON *Outcast Ess.* 402 (Hor. *Od.* III. xxvi) The lever, the bright torch, the bow, For laying doors and warders low.

fig. **1831** *Society* I. 230 Jealousy is a potent lever for quickening love. **1855** MOTLEY *Dutch Rep.* (1861) II. 433 The new religion was only a lever by which a few artful demagogues had attempted to overthrow the King's authority.

†**b.** *gen.* A bar, pole, or rod. *Obs.*

1297 R. GLOUC. (Rolls) 2680 Eldol erl of gloucestre.. Hente an stronge leuour. *c* **1320** *Sir Beues* 1861 (MS. A) He tok a leuour in is hond, And forth to the gate he wond. *c* **1400** *Ywaine & Gaw.* 2386 The geant..bar a levor of yren ful strang. *c* **1530** LD. BERNERS *Arth. Lyt. Bryt.* (1814) 366 Gonemar helde in bothe hys handes a gret leuer, wherwith he layd on amonge those knyghtes. **1609** BIBLE (Douay) *Numb.* xiii. 24 They cutte of a branch with the grapes therof, which two men carried upon a leaver. **1613** PURCHAS *Pilgrimage* (1614) 504 Fish-shells..so great that two strong men with a leaver can scarse draw one of them after them.

2. *Mechanics.* Adopted as the name for that type of 'simple machine' which is exemplified in the 'lever' (sense 1). It consists of a rigid structure of any shape (a straight bar being the normal form), fixed at one point called the fulcrum, and acted on at two other points by two forces, tending to cause it to rotate in opposite directions round the fulcrum.

The force which is regarded as intended to be resisted by the use of the lever is called the *weight*, and the force which is applied for this purpose is called the *power*. Levers are said to be of the *first*, *second*, or *third kind* or *order* according as the fulcrum, the weight, or the power is in the midmost position of the three.

1648 WILKINS *Math. Mag.* I. iv. 20 The second Mechanical faculty is the Lever. **1710** J. CLARKE *Rohault's Nat. Phil.* (1729) I. 43 Two Bodies hung at the Ends of a Balance or Leaver. **1803** J. WOOD *Princ. Mech.* iv. 50 The Lever is an inflexible rod, moveable upon a point which is called the fulcrum. **1812-16** PLAYFAIR *Nat. Phil.* (1819) I. 117 Let A and B be two given weights, applied to the ends of the arms of a lever. **1829** *Nat. Philos.*, *Mechanics* II. iii. §13. 6 (U.K.S.) If the power be in the middle, it is a lever of the third kind. **1837** WHEWELL *Hist. Induct. Sci.* (1857) I. 186 Archimedes had established the doctrine of the lever. **1841** T. R. JONES *Anim. Kingd.* 168 The levers attached to the jaws are five long and slender processes. **1851** CARPENTER *Man. Phys.* (ed. 2) 172 The hard envelopes.. serve, like the bones of the Vertebrata, as levers by which the motor powers of the muscles are more advantageously employed.

3. Special applications. **a.** A roof-beam of naturally curved timber, forming one of the couples or principals supporting the roof (*obs.* exc. *dial.*). **b.** *Steam-engine.* †(*a*) = BEAM *sb.*^{1} 11 (*obs.*); (*b*) a starting-bar. **c.** The piece by which the barrel of a breech-loader is opened. **d.** In *Dentistry* and *Surgery* = ELEVATOR 2. In *Midwifery* = VECTIS (*Syd. Soc. Lex.*). **e.** The first row of a fishing-net. **f.** Short for *lever-watch*.

a. 1481-2 in *Charters Finchale* (Surtees) p. ccclv, Pro.. meremio empto pro j lever in tenemento Roberti Jakson.

b. 1758 FITZGERALD in *Phil. Trans.* L. 727 The lever of the fire-engine [*i.e.* steam-engine] works up and down alternately. **1836** HEBERT *Engin. & Mech. Encycl.* II. 702 The attendant pushes the handle or lever which he holds.

c. 1881 [see *lever-pin*].

d. 1846 BRITTAN tr. *Malgaigne's Man. Oper. Surg.* 74 *With the Lever.*—Its extremity is passed between two teeth, a sound and the decayed one, or a sound one and a stump.

e. 1884 J. PATON in *Encycl. Brit.* XVII. 359/1.

f. 1865 *N. & Q.* 27 Jan. 27/2 (Advt.), The prettiest gift for a lady is one of Jones's gold levers at 11*l* 11*s*. **1895** in *N. & Q.* (1941) 20 Sept. 160/1 It couldn't have been a stop watch. It was a lever.

4. *attrib.* and *Comb.* **a.** with sense 'belonging to a lever', as ***lever-actuation***, ***-edge***, ***-pin***; also ***lever-like*** adj. **b.** with sense 'acting as a lever, worked by a lever', as ***lever-brace***, ***-corkscrew***,

-drill, -hoist, -jack, -knife, -pallet, -pendulum, -press, -punch, -shears, -spar, -valve.

1889 G. FINDLAY *Eng. Railway* 79 The frame.. known as *lever actuation. **1860** *All Year Round* No. 57. 162 The *lever corkscrew gave a zest to his wine. **1884** F. J. BRITTEN *Watch & Clockm.* 207 *Lever Edges.. are polished in a swing tool. **1867** J. MACGREGOR *Voy. Alone* 41 The pantry is beside them with.. pepper.. mustard, corkscrew, and *lever-knife for preserved meat tins. **1891** ATKINSON *Last of Giant Killers* 190 The steel point of Sir Jack's Staff was inserted beneath it, and *lever-like pressure applied. **1825** J. NICHOLSON *Operat. Mechanic* 524 The centre of the *lever-pallet.. is in a right line between the centre of the scape-wheel and the centre of the verge. *Ibid.* 526 In Ellicott's pendulum the ball was adjustable by levers, thence called the *lever pendulum. **1881** GREENER *Gun* 263 Next turn out the *lever pin on top of lever. **1873** W. CORY *Lett. & Jrnls.* (1897) 316 The *lever-spar of a water-lift.

5. Special combs.: **lever-beam** *Steam-engine* (see BEAM *sb.*[1] 11); **lever-board, -bridge** (see quots.); **lever-engine**, †(*a*) = *beam-engine* (*obs.*); (*b*) = *side-lever engine* (1876 in Knight *Dict. Mech.* and in later Dicts.); **lever escapement** (*Watchmaking*), an escapement in which the connexion between the pallet and the balance is made by means of two levers, one attached to the pallets and the other to the balance staff (Britten); **lever-fly**, a punching machine worked by a fly-wheel and a lever; **lever frame**, (*a*) (see quot. 1950); (*b*) 'in a railroad hand-car, a wooden frame shaped somewhat like a letter A, which supports the lever-shaft and lever on the platform' (*Cent. Dict.*); **lever-man** *U.S.*, one employed to work the levers in a railway signal-box; **lever watch**, a watch with a lever escapement; **lever-wood**, the Virginian hop-hornbeam or ironwood, *Ostrya Virginica* (*Treas. Bot.* 1866).

1824 R. STUART *Hist. Steam Engine* 159 As the *lever-beam was dismissed, he communicated the motion to the paddle-wheels by a rod and crank attached to the piston. **1823** P. NICHOLSON *Pract. Build.* 587 **Lever-boards*, a set of boards, parallel to each other, so connected together that they may be turned to any angle, for the admission of more or less air or light; or so as to lap upon each other and exclude both. **1853** SIR H. DOUGLAS *Milit. Bridges* 312 That which is called a *Lever Bridge is made by cutting down trees, and sinking the buts of them in the bank on each side sufficiently deep that the parts which are buried may exceed in weight those which are out of the ground. **1744** DESAGULIERS *Experim. Philos.* II. 489 The *Leaver Engine, often call'd Newcomen's. **1838** *Penny Cycl.* XII. 303/2 *Lever-escapement. **1884** F. J. BRITTEN *Watch & Clockm.* 141 The Lever Escapement.. is generally preferred for pocket watches. **1831** J. HOLLAND *Manuf. Metal* I. 131 The holes .. are punched in the metal by the assistance of what the boiler makers call a *lever fly. **1869** *Bradshaw's Railway Manual* XXI. App. 116 (Advt.), Patent locking *lever frames. **1950** *Times Rev. Industry* 21/1 All points and signals are worked from a mechanical or manual lever frame. **1955** *Railway Mag.* May 307/2 At Stockport No. 2 signalbox, the existing mechanical lever frame has been retained. **1963** KICHENSIDE & WILLIAMS *Brit. Railway Signalling* vi. 74 (*caption*) The interior of London Bridge signal box.. showing the miniature lever frame. **1901** *Daily News* 12 Jan. 6/2 A saving.. has been effected in the wages of *lever men. **1848** *Chambers's Inform.* I. 285/2 The *lever watch is so named from the lever escapement of Mudge.

† **'lever**, *sb.*[2] *Obs. rare*[−1]. [f. LEVE *v.*[2] + -ER[1].] = BELIEVER.

c **1340** *Cursor M.* (Trin.) 18719 þe leuer [*Cott. and Gött.* truand] & þe baptized boþe Shulde be saued from alle loþe.

‖ **'lever**, *sb.*[3] *Obs. rare*[−1]. [Fr.: see LEVEE *sb.*[2]] = LEVEE *sb.*[2] 2.

1742 MISS ROBINSON in *Mrs. Delany's Lett.* (1861) II. 191 We do not appear at Phœbus's Levér.

lever ('liːvə(r)), *v.* [f. LEVER *sb.*[1]]

1. a. *intr.* To apply a lever; to work with a lever.

1856 KANE *Arct. Expl.* II. ii. 31 It was all in vain that Hans and I.. lifted, levered, twisted and pulled. **1897** *Daily News* 16 Mar. 6/5 They delved, and levered, and sweated.

b. To make way by leverage.

1883 S. BARING-GOULD *John Herring* I. i. 9 When he took his weight off,.. the plough levered out of the ground.

2. *trans.* a. To lift, push, or otherwise move with or as with a lever; also with *along, away, out, over, up.* Also *refl.* with *into.* b. To bring into a specified condition by applying a lever.

1876 PREECE & SIVEWRIGHT *Telegraphy* 209 The bottom of the pole being 'levered' out of the ground. **1882** JEFFERIES *Bevis* I. i. 11 He began to lever the raft along. **1887** BARING-GOULD *Gaverocks* I. vi. 89, I flung with such force that I levered the boat away. **1891** MISS DOWIE *Girl in Karp.* vi. 75, I levered up an eyelid with difficulty. **1896** *Daily Chron.* 15 Aug. 9/3 On no account should the canoe be levered with one end of the pole on the ground. **1898** *Daily News* 19 May 5/3 The concrete fell.. and levered the pier over. **1898** *Cycling* 77 By passing a bar through the frame.. and levering it straight.

fig. **1890** *Graphic* 11 Oct. 406/1 He seeks this by levering out of his place his best friend. **1910** *Westm. Gaz.* 24 Mar. 2/3 The Moderates have levered themselves into a position they have no claim to occupy on the Council.

Hence **'levering** *vbl. sb.* Also *attrib.*

1869 MRS. WHITNEY *We Girls* x. (1878) 174 A few more vigorous strokes, and a little smart levering, and the nails loosened. **1897** *Daily News* 3 Nov. 6/6 Snapped off by means of some powerful levering tool.

lever, obs. f. LIVER *sb.*, LIVER *v.*, to deliver.

lever, obs. var. *liever*, comparative of LIEF *a.*

leverage ('liːvərɪdʒ), *sb.* [f. LEVER *sb.*[1] + -AGE.]

1. The action of a lever; the arrangement by which lever-power is applied; also *concr.* a system of levers.

1724 *Lond. Gaz.* No. 6273/8 An Engine.., which.. by means of a Leveridge and an Horizontal Fly,.. can Raise.. Water. **1839** R. S. ROBINSON *Naut. Steam Eng.* 99 It resolves itself into a system of leverage. **1884** tr. *Lotze's Logic* 258 The length of leverage must vary inversely as the strength of the force.

2. The power of a lever; the mechanical advantage gained by the use of a lever. ***leverage of a force*** (see quot. 1830).

1830 KATER & LARDNER *Mech.* x. 135 The distance of the direction of a force from the axis is sometimes called the leverage of the force. **1845** TODD & BOWMAN *Phys. Anat.* I. 146 The extension of the os calcis.. affords a considerable leverage to the muscles of the calf of the leg. **1860** O. W. HOLMES *Elsie V.* xvi. (1891) 221 Leverage is everything. **1879** G. MACDONALD *Sir Gibbie* II. xiii. 224 The stream worked at the roots, and the wind laid hold of him with fierce leverage. **1882** *Knowledge* No. 19. 403/2 The actual leverage increases as A W is increased, supposing the oar's length to remain unchanged.

b. *fig.* Advantage for accomplishing a purpose; increased power of action.

1858 GLADSTONE *Homer* III. 113 The leverage of this straightforward speech.. produces an initial movement towards concession on the part of the great hero. **1868** HELPS *Realmah.* v. (1876) 86 And it will be putting additional leverage into his hands. **1883** *Contemp. Rev.* Dec. 790 With regard to such men the moralist has no leverage whatever.

3. *attrib.*

1838 POE *A. G. Pym* Wks. 1864 IV. 162 A vast leverage power was obtained. **1851** H. STEPHENS *Bk. of Farm* (ed. 2) I. 258/1 This bend gives a leverage power to the handle, when the graip is used to lift rank wet litter.

'leverage, *v. U.S.* [f. the sb.] *trans.* and *intr.* To lever; *spec.* to speculate or cause to speculate financially on borrowed capital expecting profits made to be greater than the interest payable. Hence **'leveraging** *vbl. sb.*; also **leveraged** *ppl. a.*, freq. as ***leveraged buy-out*** (chiefly *U.S.*), the buy-out of a company by its management with the help of outside capital.

1937 *Harper's Mag.* June 63 Acey leveraged the arm upward. **1957** *Robert R. Young & Alleghany Corp.* 2 Founded in 1929.., Alleghany was a classic example of the highly leveraged holding companies of that period. **1968** *N.Y. Times* 20 Feb. 64 Short-term trading,.. selling short and leveraging through borrowing are all speculative techniques which carry with them greater risk of loss. **1971** *Atlantic Monthly* July 49 He gave her the benefit of his experience, leveraging her up to the ears in convertible bonds. **1972** 'A. SMITH' *Supermoney* IV. i. 209 The corporation discovered that the more it borrowed, the higher the earnings and the higher the stock, so it began to leverage. **1973** *N.Y. Law Jrnl.* 26 July 3/3 Tight credit tends to put some of the marginal builders (that are very highly leveraged and have tiny working capital positions) under additional pressures. **1976** *Forbes* (N.Y.) 15 July 83/1 We have eased into the safer waters of secondary financings and leveraged buyouts. **1980** *Financial Rev.* (Melbourne) 8 July 19/3 John Polmear had engineered what the Americans call the 'leveraged buy-out'. **1984** *USA Today* 6 Apr. 4B/5 Many.. clients want to buy companies in leveraged buy-outs. **1985** *Times* 2 May 21/5 Leveraged buyouts are commonly used in the United States to defeat hostile takeover bids, but have yet to be successfully tested in Britain.

leveray, -ey, levere, obs. forms of LIVERY.

‖ **lever de rideau** (ləve də rido). [Fr.] = *curtain-raiser.* Also *fig.*

1860 *Players* I. 107 As a lever de rideau it was favourably received. **1891** G. B. SHAW *How to become Mus. Critic* (1960) 193 Signor Lago has produced a few miserably-mounted fragments of worn-out Italian operas by way of *levers de rideau* for Cavalleria. **1906** W. DE MORGAN *Joseph Vance* v. 38 The Man went up into 'the Nursery' to look at the bricks in the chimney.. This was a mere *lever-de-rideau*—the principal stage business of the day being an examination of the Drains. **1970** *Brewer's Dict. Phr. & Fable* (ed. 12) 638/2 *Lever de rideau*, a short sketch, etc., performed on the stage before the main play begins.

Leveresque (liːvə'rɛsk), *a.* [f. the name of Charles *Lever* (1806–72), Irish novelist.] Characteristic of the novels of Charles Lever in matter or style. Also **'Leverish** *a.*

1903 *Westm. Gaz.* 18 Mar. 4/2 There are some good stories, old or new, told in a racy and Leverish style. **1905** *Daily Chron.* 15 June 3/1 Of Anglo-Irish lords, of Leveresque landowners, of eighteenth-century spendthrifts. **1922** *Glasgow Herald* 6 June 3 The Leveresque pictures of Irish life.

leveret ('lɛvərɪt). Forms: 6 leverette, leav-, lyveret, 7 leverit, levoret, levart, -et, -it, 5– leveret. [ad. OF. *levrete, levrette*, dim. of *levre* (F. *lièvre*) hare.]

1. A young hare, strictly one in its first year.

14.. *Voc.* in Wr.-Wülcker 592/22 *Lepusculus*, a leveret. **1544** PHAER *Regim. Lyfe* (1553) H vj b, The mawe of a yong leuerette with the iuice of plantaine, is excedinge profitable. **1607** TOPSELL *Four-f. Beasts* (1658) 211 In ancient time, if the Hunters had taken a young Leverit, they let her go again in the honour of Diana. **1688** J. CLAYTON in *Phil. Trans.* XVIII. 123, I have seen Leverets there with the white spot in the Head, which the Old ones have not. **1759** JOHNSON *Idler* No. 81 ¶6 [It] is the claim.. of the vulture to the leveret. **1814** CARY *Dante's Inf.* XXIII. 16 More fell They shall pursue us, than the savage hound Snatches the leveret. **1835** GRIMSHAWE *Life Cowper* (1865) 35/2 On his expressing a wish to divert himself by rearing a single leveret,.. his neighbours supplied him with three.

†2. *transf.* and *fig.* a. A pet, a mistress. b. A spiritless person. *Obs.*

1617 S. COLLINS *Def. Bp. Ely* (1628) 54 Theres a Leuite of the Iesuits, or a prettie leuorite rather, to sucke a Kings heart-blood in time. **1630** LENNARD tr. *Charron's Wisd.* III. iii. §28 (1670) 371 Arrogant Boasters,.. leverets in dangers. **1637** SHIRLEY *Gamester* I. i, Some wife will bid her husband's leverets welcome. **1640** DK. NEWCASTLE *Country Capt.* II. i. (1649) 23 You meane, one wenche betweene us too is nothing: I know a hundred Leveretts.

3. *attrib.*: **leveret-skin**, a Japanese glaze applied to ceramic ware, supposed to resemble leveret's fur.

(In recent Dicts.)

levero(c)k, -ucke, obs. forms of LARK *sb.*[1]

'levers[1]. *Obs.* exc. *dial.* Also 1 læfer, leb(e)r, 5 levre. [OE. *læfer.*] (See quot. 1879.)

c **725** *Corpus Gloss.* 1823 *Scirpea*, eorisc, leber. *c* **1000** *Voc.* in Wr.-Wülcker 278/29 *Scirpia* [read *Scirpea*], læfer. *c* **1000** ÆLFRIC *Voc.* ibid. 138/30 *Pirus, gladiolus*, læfer. *c* **1000** *Sax. Leechd.* I. 382 Genim læfre neoðowearde. *c* **1450** *Alphita* (Anecd. Oxon.) 72 *Gladiolus*,.. gallice glaiol, anglice leure. **1578** LYTE *Dodoens* II. xli. 199 The wilde yellow Iris is now called.. in English Lauers or Leuers. **1879** BRITTEN & HOLLAND *Plant-n.* 304 *Levers*,.. a name applied by Lyte.. to *Iris Pseudacorus*, L.; but bestowed on 'any sword-bladed plant'.

Levers[2] ('liːvəz). Also *erron.* **Leavers.** The name of John *Levers* (1786–1848), who effected improvements in lace-making machines in the early 19th c., used *attrib.*, *absol.*, or in the possessive in the names of the lace-making machinery he developed, and of the lace thus produced.

1828 J. LEVERS *Brit. Pat.* 5741 18 Dec., My improvements in machinery for making lace consist in a certain combination and arrangement of mechanism to be adapted to lace machines constructed upon the principle commonly called or known by the name of Levers' principle. *Ibid.*, The movements of all the working parts of an ordinary Levers' machine are well understood by practical mechanics. **1865** F. B. PALLISER *Hist. Lace* xxxvi. 425 The machines now in use are the Circular, Leaver, Transverse Warp and Pusher. **1867** W. FELKIN *Hist. Machine-Wrought Hosiery* xviii. 281 In February, 1835, T. Allcock.. took out a patent.. for a new kind of Levers'. *Ibid.* xix. 294 Goods made upon Levers' Jacquard machines. *Ibid.* xxii. 329 Velvet patterns on circular Levers' bobbin net. **1890** *Chambers's Encycl.* VI. 474/2 The lace-making machine now principally used is known as the Levers machine. **1911** *Encycl. Brit.* XVI. 44/2 The Leavers lace machine does not make either a buttonhole stitch or a plait. **1959** D. E. VARLEY *Hist. Midland Counties Lace Manufacturers' Assoc.* i. 4 John Brown, John Leavers, and Clark and Mart, inventors of the traverse warp, the leavers and the pusher bobbin-net machines respectively, were all Nottingham artisans. **1968** J. IRONSIDE *Fashion Alphabet* 235 *Leavers lace*, any lace made on the machine invented by John Leavers, an Englishman, in 1813. This was the first really satisfactory lace-making machine.

leves, obs. Sc. pl. of LEAF.

† **'levesel.** *Obs.* Forms: 4 le(e)fsel, levesselle, levecel, 4–5 levesel, 5 leef-sele, levesell, lef-sale, lefe sal(e. [? repr. OE. **léafsele*, f. *léaf* LEAF + *sęle* hall; cf. Sw. *löfsal*, Da. *løvsal.*] A bower of leaves; a canopy or lattice.

13.. *E.E. Allit. P.* C. 448 Such a lefsel of lof neuer lede hade. *c* **1386** CHAUCER *Reeve's T.* 141 The clerkes hors ther as it stood ybounde Behynde the Mille, vnder a lefsel. —— *Pars. T.* ¶337 As the gaye leefsel atte Tauerne is signe of the wyn that is in the Celer. *c* **1400** *Destr. Troy* 337 A playne, Full of floures.. With lef-sales vppon lofte lustie and faire, Folke to refresshe for faintyng of hete. *a* **1420** HOCCLEVE *De Reg. Princ.* 600 To Bachus signe & to þe leuesel His youþe him haliþ. *c* **1440** *Promp. Parv.* 300/2 Levecel be-forne a wyndowe, or other place, *umbraculum.* **1480** CAXTON *Chron. Eng.* ccxxii. 215 She hath the keyes and leith hem vnder the leuesell of the bed vnto the morow.

† **levet**[1]. *Obs. rare.* [f. *leve* (LEAVE *v.*[1]) + -ET[1].] Only *pl.* Leavings, fragments.

1528 ROY *Rede me* (Arb.) 80 When they have eaten ynowe. .. Then gadder they vp their levettis. *Ibid.* 98 The best meate awaye they carve... Then proll the servynge officers .. so that their levettis are but thynne.

† **levet**[2]. *Obs.* Also 7 levett, 7–8 levit(t. [? ad. It. *levata* 'the name of a march vpon a Drumme and Trumpet in time of warre' (Florio), f. *levare* to raise.] A trumpet call or musical strain to rouse soldiers and others in the morning.

a **1625** FLETCHER *Doub. Marriage* II. i, Come sirs, a queint Levet. [Trump. a levet.] To waken our brave Generall. **1656** W. MEREDITH *Narr. Passages Irel.* in *8th Rep. Hist. MSS. Comm.* App. 600/1 The enemy.. were some distance from vs sounding levitts for joy of there supposed victory. *a* **1687** COTTON *Winter* xxxii. Poems (1689) 649 The Æolian Trumpetters By their Hoarse Levets, do declare That the bold General Rides there. **1705** S. SEWALL *Diary* 1 Jan. (1879) II. 121 Col. Hobbey's Negro.. sends in.. to have leave to give me a Levit and wish me a merry new year.

levetenaunt, obs. form of LIEUTENANT.

levey, leveyne, obs. forms of LEVEE, LEAVEN.

leviable ('lɛvɪəb(ə)l), *a.* Also 6–9 **levyable**. [f. LEVY *v.* + -ABLE.]

1. Of a duty, tax, etc.: That may be levied.

1484 J. PASTON in *Paston Lett.* III. 313 All syche money as is not levyable of dyvers of the seyd fermors and tenauntes. **1512** *Act 4 Hen. VIII*, c. 19 §8 The same some ..[shall be] due & levyable immediatly uppon demaunde hade and denyed. **1540** *Act 32 Hen. VIII*, c. 46 The sayd yerely tenth, that was..due and leuiable to the kinges vse. **1622** BACON *Hen. VII* Mor. & Hist. Wks. (1860) 409 To make the sums which any person had agreed to pay,..to be leviable by course of law. **1752** CARTE *Hist. Eng.* III. 815 An aid..due to the crown for the marriage of a king's eldest daughter and levyable from the time she attained the age of seven years. **1861** *All Year Round* 27 July 417 The amount of rates leviable under the Sewers Act..is now unlimited. **1881** *Standard* 16 June 3/4 The import duties now leviable in France upon live stock and agricultural produce. **1899** *Daily News* 16 May 3/1 The levyable expenses of a borough.

2. a. Of a person: That may be called upon for payment of a contribution.

1897 *Daily News* 15 Sept. 5/1 The number of leviable members is over 60,000.

b. *U.S.* Of a thing: That may be levied upon, capable of being seized in execution.

(In recent U.S. Dicts.)

†'**leviate**, *v. Obs. rare*⁻¹. [f. late L. *leviāt-*, ppl. stem of *leviāre*, f. *levis* light.] *trans.* To relieve; = ALLEVIATE 2.

1545 RAYNOLD *Byrth Mankynde* IV. vi. (1552) 146 b, This oft wasshing shal..leuyate and lyghten the head with al the senses therin contayned.

leviathan (lɪ'vaɪəθən). Forms: 4–6 **levyathan**, (4 **-ethan**), 5 **lyvyatan, -on**, 5– **leviathan**. [a. L. (Vulg.) *leviathan*, a. Heb. *livyāthān*.

Some scholars refer the word to a root *lāwāʰ* = Arab. *lawaʸ* to twist (cf. *livyāʰ*, conjecturally rendered 'wreath'); others think it adopted from some foreign lang.]

1. The name of some aquatic animal (real or imaginary) of enormous size, frequently mentioned in Hebrew poetry.

1382 WYCLIF *Job* xl[i.] 20 [21] Whether maist thou drawen out leuyethan with an hoc? **1535** COVERDALE *Ps.* ciii[i.] 26 There is that Leuiathan, whom thou hast made, to take his pastyme therin. **1555** EDEN *Decades* To Rdr. (Arb.) 51 The greate serpente of the sea Leuiathan, to haue suche dominion in the Ocean. **1591** SPENSER *Vis. World's Van.* 62 The huge Leuiathan, dame Natures wonder. **1667** MILTON *P.L.* VII. 412 Leviathan, Hugest of living Creatures, on the Deep Stretcht like a Promontorie. **1713** YOUNG *Last Day* I. 35 Leviathans but heave their cumb'rous mail, It makes a tide. **1725** POPE *Odyss.* XII. 119 She [Scylla] makes the huge leviathan her prey.

b. *transf.*; esp. = a ship of huge size.

[? **1801** CAMPBELL *Battle of the Baltic* ii, Like leviathans afloat.] **1816** J. SCOTT *Vis. Paris* (ed. 5) 91 They [floating baths]..stretch their long sprawling forms on the water, like so many painted Leviathans. **1818** BYRON *Ch. Har.* IV. clxxxi, The oak leviathans. **1858** BRIGHT *Sp., Reform* 21 Dec. (1876) 312 Your splendid river, bearing the leviathans of noble architecture, constructed on its banks. **1892** SUFFLING *Land of the Broads* (ed. 2) 13 These immense winged leviathans [wherries].

c. *fig.* A man of vast and formidable power or enormous wealth.

1607 DEKKER *Knts. Conjur.* (1842) 60 The lacquy of this great leuiathan promisde he should be maister. *c* **1630** SANDERSON *Serm.* II. 310 So can the Lord deal..with the great..leviathans of the world. **1782** PENNANT *Journ. Chester to Lond.* 96 The leviathan who swallowed these manors, was Sir William Paget. **1796** BURKE *Let. Noble Lord* Wks. VIII. 35 The duke of Bedford is the leviathan among all the creatures of the crown. **1839** DE QUINCEY *Recoll. Lakes* Wks. 1862 II. 155 A legal contest with so potent a defendant as this leviathan of two counties. **1884** *Punch* 1 Mar. 97/1 Punters, plungers, leviathans, little men.

†**2.** (After Isa. xxvii. 1.) The great enemy of God, Satan. *Obs.*

[**1382** WYCLIF *Isa.* xxvii. 1 In that dai viseten shal the Lord in his harde swerd,..vp on leuyathan,..a crookid wounde serpent.] *c* **1400** *Destr. Troy* 4423 This fende was the first þat felle for his pride..þat lyuyaton is cald. **1412–20** LYDG. *Chron. Troy* II. xvii, The vile serpent the Leuiathan. **1447** BOKENHAM *Seyntys* (Roxb.) 150 By the envye deceyvyd of hys enmy Clepyd serpent behemot or levyathan. **1595** B. BARNES *Spir. Sonn.* li, Breake thou the jawes of olde Levyathan, Victorious Conqueror!

3. Used by Hobbes for: The organism of political society, the commonwealth. (See quot. 1651.)

1651 HOBBES *Leviath.* (1839) 158 The multitude so united in one person, is called a Commonwealth... This is the generation of that great Leviathan, or rather, to speak more reverently, of that mortal god, to which we owe under the immortal God, our peace and defence. **1657** R. LIGON *Barbadoes* 20 What it is that makes up..harmony in that Leviathan, a well governed Commonwealth. **1690** LOCKE *Hum. Und.* I. iii. (1695) 17 An Hobbist..will answer; Because..the Leviathan will punish you, if you do not. **1714** MANDEVILLE *Fab. Bees* (1725) I. 195 The gods have.. design'd that millions of you, when well joyn'd together, should compose the strong Leviathan.

4. *attrib.* passing into *adj.* when sense: Huge, monstrous.

1624 MIDDLETON *Game at Chess* II. ii, This leviathan-scandal that lies rolling Upon the crystal waters of devotion. **1751** H. WALPOLE *Lett.* (1846) II. 398, I had suspected that this leviathan hall must have devoured half the other chambers. **1861** A. SMITH *Med. Stud.* 12 He has duly chronicled every word..in his leviathan note-book. **1892** W. BEATTY-KINGSTON *Intemper.* v. 32 The leviathan liquor interests.

Hence **leˌvia'thanic** *a.*, huge as a leviathan.

1848 *Tait's Mag.* XV. 789 The leviathanic railway that stretches out its fins amongst its contemporaries like Captain McQuhae's sea-serpent.

†**levi'ation**. *Obs.* [f. LEVY *v.*: see -ATION.] The levying of a tax; quasi-*concr.* a tax.

1538 *St. Papers Hen. VIII*, II. 544 We desire and pray youe to be now..diligent in the leviation thereof. **1681** *Treat. E. India Trade* 30 They..settle a Tax, which they call Leviations, upon the Trade. *Ibid.* 37 How shall they maintain..them? By Leviations upon Goods.

levi'cellular, *a.* [f. L. *lēvi-s* smooth + CELLULAR.] Consisting of smooth muscular fibre.

(In recent Dicts.)

levie, obs. form of LEAVY.

levier ('lɛvɪə(r)). Also 5, 8–9 **levyer**, 6 **leavier**. [f. LEVY *v.* + -ER¹.] One who levies (in senses of the vb.).

1494 FABYAN *Chron.* VII. 436 Of this taxe to be leuyers or gaderers was assygned yᵉ pryncypall men of the sayd townes. **1611** FLORIO, *Liuellatore*, a leauier or raiser of taxes or fines. **1656** PRYNNE *Rights Eng. Freemen* 30 Any Levier of them [*sc.* taxes], or imprisoner of refusers of them. **1701** DE FOE *Power People* Misc. (1703) 136 You are..the Levyers of our Taxes. **1831** GEN. P. THOMPSON *Exerc.* (1842) I. 482 Here is a distinct levying of war against the King's people; officers pointed out on whom the leviers think dependence can be placed. **1885** STEVENSON *Dynamiter* 203 The levyers of a..war. **1888** R. DOWLING *Miracle Gold* II. xiv. 7, I am not a levier of blackmail.

levigable ('lɛvɪgəb(ə)l), *a.* [ad. med.L. *lēvigābilis*, f. *lēvigāre* (see LEVIGATE *v.*).]

†**a.** That can be polished. *Obs.* **b.** That can be reduced to powder. *rare*⁻¹.

1670 EVELYN *Pomona* viii. 24 Useful is the Pear-Tree..for its excellent colour'd Timber, hard and levigable.. especially for Stools, Tables [etc.]. **1850** BROWNING *Christm. Eve* xviii, Dust and ashes levigable.

†'**levigate**, *pple. Obs.* [ad. late L. *levigāt-us*, pa. pple. of *levigāre*, f. *levis* light.] Lightened.

1531 ELYOT *Gov.* I. iii, His labours beinge leuigate and made more tollerable.

levigate ('lɛvɪgeɪt), *ppl. a. Bot.* and *Ent.* Also **lævigate**. [ad. L. *lēvigāt-us*, pa. pple. of *lēvigāre* (see next).] Smooth as if polished.

1826 KIRBY & SP. *Entomol.* IV. 269 *Levigate* (*Lævigata*), without any partial elevations or depressions. **1880** in GRAY *Struct. Bot.* 418/1.

levigate ('lɛvɪgeɪt), *v.* Also *erron.* **læv-**. [f. L. *lēvigāt-*, ppl. stem of *lēvigāre* to make smooth, f. *lēvis* (sometimes erron. *lævis*) smooth.]

†**1.** *trans.* To make smooth; to polish. *Obs.*

1612 WOODALL *Surg. Mate* Wks. (1653) 70 White starch ..levigateth the parts exasperated. **1620** VENNER *Via Recta* vii. 121 By reason of their lenifying and detersiue faculty, [they]..leuigate the roughnesse of the winde-pipe. **1650** FULLER *Pisgah* 410 A stone turned, rolled, and tossed about, to smooth, and levigate every side thereof. **1676** BOYLE *New Exper.* II. in *Phil. Trans.* XI. 805 To enable them, by the help of Gravity,..to levigate..or polish each others surfaces. **1791** COWPER *Odyss.* XII. 95 No mortal man might climb it or descend..For it is levigated as by art. **1811** *Self Instructor* 536 Bran..levigates its surface. **1826, 1835** [see LEVIGATED *ppl. a.*].

†**b.** in immaterial sense. *Obs.*

1650 FULLER *Pisgah* III. i. 314 The turning of a tender melting B. into a surly rigid R. is not to levigate or mollifie but to make the name harder in pronunciation. **1794** MRS. PIOZZI *Synon.* I. 374 Such a soul levigated by prosperity soon mounts into airiness of temper.

2. To reduce to a fine smooth powder; to rub down; to make a smooth paste of (*with* some liquid).

1694 SALMON *Bate's Dispens.* (1713) 334/1 Levigate it upon a Marble, till it becomes an impalpable Powder. **1718** QUINCY *Compl. Disp.* 181 Some have got the Art of levigating the testaceous Powders. **1782–3** W. F. MARTYN *Geog. Mag.* I. 9 Levigating it with the oil of sweet almonds. **1802** A. ELLICOTT *Jrnl.* (1803) 245 Shells, and other calcareous matter, levigated by the friction of the particles. **1807** T. THOMSON *Chem.* (ed. 3) II. 345 It is sufficient to levigate them with water to obtain them very white. **1824** *Mech. Mag.* No. 30. 32 Machinery for Levigating or Grinding Colours. **1894** SMILES *J. Wedgwood* ii. 15 This clay, carefully levigated,..yielded a red ware.

fig. **1868** BROWNING *Ring & Bk.* I. 1153 He..makes logic levigate the big crime small.

Hence '**levigating** *vbl. sb.* (*attrib.*) and *ppl. a.*

1710 T. FULLER *Pharm. Extemp.* 272 A Levigating Lohoch. *c* **1790** IMISON *Sch. Art* II. 67 Mix it with a levigating knife with spirits of wine. **1812–16** J. SMITH *Panorama Sci. & Art* II. 787 The glue is then to be put warm on a levigating stone, and kneaded with quicklime.

'**levigated**, *ppl. a.* [f. LEVIGATE *v.* + -ED¹.]

†**1.** Made smooth; polished. *Obs.*

1578 BANISTER *Hist. Man* I. 29 The outer syde of Radius is rounde, and leuigated. **1801** FUSELI in *Lect. Paint.* i. (1848) 350 A board, or a levigated plane of wood, metal, stone, or some prepared compound. **1826** KIRBY & SP. *Entomol.* III. xxx. 250 The eye-cases..surrounded on their inner side by a crescent-shaped lævigated piece. **1835** KIRBY *Hab. & Inst. Anim.* I. vi. 208 The base is concave so as to play upon the levigated centre of the above protuberance.

2. Finely powdered; reduced to a smooth consistency.

1641 FRENCH *Distill.* iii. (1651) 81 Take of this levigated Lime 10 ounces. **1732** ARBUTHNOT *Aliments* (1735) 67 The Chyle is white, as consisting of Salt, Oil and Water of our Food, much levigated or smooth. **1766** SMOLLETT *Trav.* 70 Our porcelain seems to be a partial vitrification of levigated flint and fine pipe clay. **1823** J. BADCOCK *Dom. Amusem.* 65 Finely levigated chlorate..of potash. **1881** J. GEIKIE *Preh. Europe* 161 The finely-levigated material derived from the grinding of glaciers.

levigation (lɛvɪ'geɪʃən). *Pharmacy.* [ad. L. *lēvigātiōn-em*, n. of action f. *lēvigāre*.] The action of LEVIGATE *v.*; 'the trituration or rubbing down of a substance in a mortar or on a slab, with sufficient moisture to make it soft' (*Syd. Soc. Lex.*).

1471 RIPLEY *Comp. Alch.* I. in Ashm. (1652) 133 Then of thy Water make Ayre by Levygacyon. **1612** WOODALL *Surg. Mate* Wks. (1653) 272 Levigation is the reduction of any hard and ponderous matter by comminution, and diligent contusion into fine powder, like Alcool. **1718** QUINCY *Compl. Disp.* 11 Either by the Mortar, or by Levigation upon a Marble. **1833** J. HOLLAND *Manuf. Metal* II. x. 246 The most ancient mills were undoubtedly those in which the method of levigation was rudely employed. **1879** RUTLEY *Stud. Rocks* viii. 73 In such crude examinations levigation may occasionally be advantageous. **1885** W. ROBERTS *Urin. Dis.* II. iii. (ed. 4) 325 They were easily separated from the urine by levigation and decantation.

levigator ('lɛvɪgeɪtə(r)). [f. LEVIGAT(E *v.* + -OR 2 c.] An iron or steel disc, several inches thick and about a foot in diameter, which is rubbed over the surface of a lithographic stone to smooth it.

1914 H. J. RHODES *Art of Lithogr.* ii. 11 The operator.. guides the revolving levigator (disc) over the surface, applying sand and water as required. **1965** ZIGROSSER & GAEHDE *Guide to Collecting Orig. Prints* iv. 39 The metal [for a carbograph] is scratched with carborundum crystals and a levigator, producing a fair approximation of a mezzotint ground with much less labor and time. **1967** E. CHAMBERS *Photolitho-Offset* i. 7 The method of preparing the stone for printing is..a mechanical operation in which a smaller stone, or a flat metallic jigger or levigator..is rubbed..over the surface.

levill, obs. form of LEVEL.

levin ('lɛvɪn), *sb. arch.* Forms: 3–5 **levene**, 4 **leyven, leivin**, 5 **levyn**, 5–6 **lewyn(e**, 6 **leav'n**, 3–7, 9 **leven, levin**. [ME. *leven(e*, of obscure origin.

By some conjectured to represent an unrecorded ON. or OE. cognate of ON. *leiptr* fem., lightning; but this is very doubtful. Phonetic laws as known at present do not allow of connecting ME. *levene* with MSw. *ljung-elder* (mod.Sw. *ljung-*), *lyghna*, Da. *lyn-ild*, lightning, Da. *lyne*, to lighten; these words are cogn. w. OE. *līȝ* LEYE, and ultimately with LIGHT *sb.*]

Lightning; a flash of lightning; also, any bright light or flame.

c **1250** *Gen. & Ex.* 3265 Ðhunder, and leuene..God sente on ðat hird. *a* **1300** *Cursor M.* 22477 þe sterns wit þair leman [*Gött.* lemand] leuen. *c* **1300** *Havelok* 2690 And forth rith al so leuin fares. *c* **1386** CHAUCER *Wife's Prol.* 277 With wilde thonder dynt and firy leuene Moote thy welked nekke be to-broke. **1390** GOWER *Conf.* III. 77 The thonder with his fyri levene So cruel was upon the hevene. **1412–20** LYDG. *Chron. Troy* I. ii, Out of whose mouthe, leuen and wylde fyre, Lyke a flawme euer blased out. *c* **1460** *Towneley Myst.* xiii. 650 All the wod on a leuyn me thoght that he gard Appere. **1494** FABYAN *Chron.* VII. ccxxvii. 255 Out of the east parte appered a great leuyn or beam of bryghtnes. **1513** DOUGLAS *Æneis* VII. Prol. 10 All thocht he be the hart and lamp of hevin, Forfeblit wolx his lemand giltly lewyne, Throw the declyning of his large round speir. **1594** CAREW *Tasso* (1881) 109 Mars he resembles thee, when from fift heau'n Thou comst down guirt with ire and ghastly leau'n. **1596** SPENSER *F.Q.* V. vi. 40 As when the flashing Levin haps to light Vppon two stubborne oakes. **1647** H. MORE *Song of Soul* II. i. I. xxii, Swift as the levin from the sneezing skie. **1808** SCOTT *Marm.* I. xxiii, The Mount, where Israel heard the law, 'Mid thunder-dint, and flashing levin, And shadows, mists, and darkness, given. **1851** LONGF. *Gold. Leg.* v. *At Sea*, See! from its summit the lurid levin Flashes downward. **1855** SINGLETON *Virgil* I. 348, I would that..the almighty sire Would hurl me with his leven to the shades. **1880** SWINBURNE *Songs Springtides, Gard. Cymodoce* 90 The leaping of the lamping levin afar.

b. *attrib.* and *Comb.*, as *levin-bolt, -brand* († *brond*), *-fire, -flame*; *levin-darting* adj.

1820 SCOTT *Monast.* ii, 'God-a-mercy, my little *levin-bolt,' said Stawarth. **1864** CONINGTON *Æneid* VI. (1873) 200 The levin-bolt's authentic fire. *a* **1599** SPENSER *F.Q.* VII. vi. 30 And eft his burning *levin-brond in hand he tooke. **1805** SCOTT *Last Minstr.* VI. xxv, Resistless flash'd the levin-brand. **1847** C. BRONTE *J. Eyre* Pref. (2nd ed.), Some of those..over whom he flashes the levin-brand of his denunciation. **1805** SCOTT *Last Minstr.* IV. xviii, They were not arm'd like England's sons, But bore the *levin-darting guns. **1820** —— *Ivanhoe* xxxii, Crash after crash, as with wild thunder-dints and *levin-fire. **1813** —— *Rokeby* v. xxxiii, Like wolves before the *levin flame. **1866** J. B. ROSE tr. *Ovid's Met.* 229 The leven flame Forth from his eyes, forth from his nostrils came.

†'**levin**, *v. Obs.* [f. LEVIN *sb.*] *intr.* To lighten, emit flashes of light or lightning. Also *trans.* with cognate object.

13.. *E.E. Psalter* cxliii. 7 Leuen brightnesses [Vulg. *fulgura coruscationem*]. *c* **1400** *Destr. Troy* 7723 His Ene leuenaund with light as a low fyn. **14..** *Voc.* in Wr.-Wülcker 665/7 Fulgurat, lewnes. *c* **1440** *Promp. Parv.* 304/1 Lyghtenyn, or leuenyn, *coruscat, fulmino.* **1483** [see

LEVINING *vbl. sb.*]. **1530** PALSGR. 609/2 It leveneth, as the lygtenyng dothe... Dyd you nat se it leven right nowe?

Hence †'**levining** *ppl. a.*

a **1340** HAMPOLE *Psalter* Cant. 510 In shynynge of þi leuenand spere. *c* **1400** *Destr. Troy* 1988 With a leuenyng light as a low fyre.

leviner, corrupt form of LIMER, kind of hound.

leving, obs. form of LIVING.

†**levining**, *vbl. sb. Obs.* Forms: 2–4 **levening**, 4 **levynynge, levennyng,** 5 **leyfnyng, lewenynge.** [f. LEVIN *v.* + -ING¹.] Lightning. Also, the bright flashing of any light.

a **1300** *Cursor M.* 533 Wynd þat blaws o loft, O quilk es thoner and leuening ledd. *a* **1340** HAMPOLE *Psalter* lxxvi. 18 þi leuynyngis shane til þe erth. *c* **1400** MAUNDEV. (Roxb.) xxxi. 139 With grete thunders and leuennynges and hidous tempestez. *c* **1400** *Ywaine & Gaw.* 377 In my face the levening smate. *c* **1400** *Melayne* 815 The levenynge of [þair] baners clere Lyghtenes all þat lande. **1483** *Cath. Angl.* 215/1 To Levyn or to smytte with yᵉ lewenynge.

attrib. *a* **1547** SURREY *Æneid* II. 853 Sins that the sire of Gods and king of men Strake me with thonder, and with leuening blast.

levir ('liːvə(r)). *Anthropology.* [a. L. *lēvir* brother-in-law; a common Aryan word = Skr. *dēvar*, Gr. δαήρ, Lith. *dëverì-s*, OSl. *deverĭ*, OHG. *zeihhur*, OE. *tácor*.] A brother-in-law, or one acting as such under the custom of the LEVIRATE.

1865 MCLENNAN *Prim. Marr.* viii. 203 In the earliest age the Levir had no alternative but to take the widow. **1898** *Folk-Lore* June 105 She is taken over by some other clansman, usually a widower, But in this case.. the new husband is compelled to repay to the Levir the bride-price.

levir, obs. form of LIVER; obs. compar. LIEF.

levirate ('liːvɪrət). [f. L. *lēvir* brother-in-law + -ATE¹.] The custom among the Jews and some other nations, by which the brother or next of kin to a deceased man was bound under certain circumstances to marry the widow.

1725 T. LEWIS *Antiq. Hebr. Republ.* III. 268 The Law of Levirate. **1783** T. WILSON *Archæol. Dict., Levirate.* **1855** W. H. MILL *Applic. Panth. Princ.* (1861) 202 Reasoning from the spirit of the law of levirate, as concerning only succession to property. **1870** LUBBOCK *Orig. Civiliz.* iii. (1875) 94 The next stage was.. that form of polyandry in which brothers had their wives in common, afterwards came that of the levirate. **1883** MAINE *Early Law & Cust.* iv. 100 An institution.. known commonly as the Levirate, but called by the Hindus, in its more general form, the Niyoga.

b. *attrib.* passing into *adj.*

1865 tr. *Renan's Life Jesus* xvii. 203 The Mosaic code had consecrated this partriarchal theory by a strange institution, the levirate law. **1879** FARRAR *St. Paul* I. 264 The law of levirate marriage might be set aside if [etc.].

Hence **levi'ratic, levi'ratical** *adjs.*, pertaining to or in accordance with the levirate; **levi'ration,** leviratical marriage.

1815 in J. ALLEN *Mod. Judaism* (1816) 415 *note*, The design of the precept of leviration was [etc.]. **1849** ALFORD *Grk. Test.* I. 159 (Matt. xxii. 24), The firstborn son of a leviratical marriage was reckoned.. as the son of the deceased brother.

levis, obs. pl. of LEAF.

Levi's, Levis ('liːvaɪz). orig. *U.S.* Also (in *attrib.* use) **Levi, Levies,** and with small initial. [f. name of the original Amer. manufacturer, *Levi* Strauss.] A type of (orig. blue) denim jeans or bibless overalls, with rivets to reinforce stress-points, patented and produced as working clothes in the 1860s, and adopted as a fashion garment in the 20th century.

The form *Levi's* is a proprietary term in the U.S.

1926 R. SANTEE *Men & Horses* 125 My Levis was brand-new. **1928** *Official Gaz.* (U.S. Patent Office) 18 Sept. 519/1 Levi's ..for Overalls. **1934** *Street & Smith's Western Story Mag.* 10 Mar. 132/1 The cowboy's.. overalls are called 'Levi's' from the name of Levi Straus, of San Francisco, the pioneer overalls manufacturer of the West. **1935** *N.Y. Herald-Tribune* 28 Apr. XI. 13/2 Old timers advise the prospective dude rancher to.. buy in the West a pair of Levi overalls. *Ibid.* 13/3 Levi's, or copper riveted, blue denim riding pants, have been found to be excellent. **1941** *Yankee* Dec. 39/1 Red-flannel underwear, Peavey axes, copper-riveted Levi's, etc. **1944** *Life* 15 May 66/2 Blue jeans ('levis') or corduroys, rolled at the bottom, are worn by almost all boys. **1950** *Time* 27 Feb. 88 When dude ranches became popular in the '30s, Haas introduced 'Levis for Ladies'. **1957** M. B. PICKEN *Fashion Dict.* 212/2 Levies, work pants of extra heavy denim, having pockets attached with rivets. Originally worn by ranchers, lumbermen, and industrial workers... Also overalls, especially the bibless type. **1957** J. KEROUAC *On Road* (1958) III. vi. 217 Dean was wearing washed-out tight levis and a T-shirt. *Ibid.* IV. iii. 266 Stan was wearing a levi outfit, jacket and all. **1961** *Sunday Express* 2 Apr. 14/6 The big rush this summer will be:—*for* parchment-coloured American Levi jeans. **1970** *Guardian* 15 Oct. 11 Whatever social stigma might have been attached to wearing a pair of blue jeans could hardly have been held to apply to 'white Levi's'. **1973** C. BONINGTON *Next Horizon* vii. 100, I can always see her in my mind's eye—bare footed, clad in a pair of old Levis and a simple sweater worn outside her trousers. **1973** E. BULLINS *Theme is Blackness* 59 Her sandy hair is tied by a bandanna and the blue Levis are faded dull.

levish, obs. variant of LOVAGE.

†**levi'somnous**, *a. Obs. rare*⁻⁰. [f. L. *levisomnus* (f. *levi-s* light + *somnus* sleep) + -OUS.] 'Watchful, soon waked' (Blount *Glossogr.* 1656).

levit, variant of LEVET² *Obs.*

levitant ('lɛvɪtænt). [ad. L. *levitant-em*, pres. pple. of *levitāre* to LEVITATE.] One who practises ('spiritualistic') levitation.

1875 *Q. Jrnl. Sci.* XII. 42 About three centuries after this ..we find the pair of levitants, Abaris and Pythagoras.

levitate ('lɛvɪteɪt), *v.* [f. L. *levi-s* light, after GRAVITATE *v.*]

1. *intr.* To rise by virtue of lightness; opposed to GRAVITATE 2 b. Now only with reference to 'spiritualism'.

1673 MARVELL *Reh. Transp.* II. 186 A Lecture.. upon the Centers of Knowledge and Ignorance, and how and when they Gravitate and Levitate. **1685** BOYLE *Enq. Notion Nature* vi. 183 When 'tis there, it ceases either to gravitate, or, as some schoolmen speak, to levitate. **1879** *Whitehall Rev.* 13 Sept. 412/2, I have a stepson who levitates. **1887** HUXLEY in *19th Cent.* Feb. 201 It is asserted that a man or a woman 'levitated' to the ceiling, floated about there, and finally sailed out by the window. **1971** *Daily Tel.* 19 Nov. 14/4 The demonstrators linked arms in a great circle.. and repeated the invocation in the hope that the entire building would levitate.

2. *trans.* †**a.** To make lighter or of less weight. *Obs.* **b.** Chiefly in the language of 'spiritualists': To cause to rise in the air in consequence of lightness, or by reversing the action of gravity. Also in scientific use: To cause (something heavier than the surrounding fluid) to rise or remain suspended without visible means (e.g. using magnetic forces).

1686 GOAD *Celest. Bodies* II. v. 221 The Air being of a sudden levitated to such a measure. **1875** *Q. Jrnl. Sci.* XII. 54 Many were levitated only in these unconscious states. **1884** *Longm. Mag.* V. 167 Tables turn, furniture dances, men are 'levitated'. **1892** W. S. LILLY *Gt. Enigma* 114 No reasonable man would receive Mrs. Guppy as an ambassadress from the Infinite and Eternal, merely because she was levitated. **1894** *Century Mag.* Apr. 834/1 The extra amount of gas required to levitate my person to the clouds. **1952** *Jrnl. Electrochem. Soc.* XCIX. 206/2 Slugs of any shape of various conductive metals could be levitated in the space between the coils. **1961** *Ann. Reg. 1960* 398 Sceptre 4.. was to be rebuilt with an aluminium ring 'levitated' inside its ring-shaped chamber. **1971** *Daily Tel.* 5 Apr. 7/2 Superconducting magnets are now being investigated to levitate fast-moving trains into the air above the rails. **1973** *Nature* 9 Feb. 359/2 It is now feasible both to levitate and to propel a hovertrain using only a linear induction motor.

fig. **1954** C. P. SNOW *New Men* xxxiv. 240 The touch of the metal.. levitated me to the forgotten happiness of a joyous summer night.

Hence '**levitated,** '**levitating** *ppl. adjs.* Also '**levitative** *a.*, adapted for or capable of levitation. '**levitator,** one who believes in levitation or professes ability to practise it.

1859 HERSCHEL *Fam. Lect. Sci. Subj.* iii. §45 (1866) 131 The *levitating* portion of it being hurried off—the *gravitating* remaining behind. **1875** *Q. Jrnl. Sci.* XII. 52 At least one Christian and one heathen case of levitated persons are recorded. **1887** HUXLEY in *19th Cent.* Feb. 202 Our reply to the levitators is just the same. Why should not your friend 'levitate'? **1890** *Edinb. Rev.* July 109 It had not indeed altogether escaped notice that bodies gain in weight through combustion; but the difficulty.. was evaded by attributing to phlogiston a 'levitative' power. **1892** A. M. CLERKE *Fam. Stud. Homer* x. 263 The dream of a levitative art lurked nowhere within the Homeric field of view. **1893** A. LANG in *Contemp. Rev.* Sept. 380 The levitated boy.. flew over a garden.

levitation (lɛvɪ'teɪʃən). [f. LEVITATE *v.* (see -ATION).]

1. a. The action or process or levitating or rising in virtue of lightness. Opposed to GRAVITATION 1. (Later examples: in mod. use chiefly *transf.* from 1 b.)

1668 H. MORE *Div. Dial.* I. ix. (1713) 18 There being no such hard Pressure, no Levitation or Gravitation. **1802** PALEY *Nat. Theol.* xii. §6 (1819) 206 The lungs also of birds contain in them a provision distinguishingly calculated for ..levitation. **1902** *Q. Rev.* July 125 Many such victims of levitation [*sc.* deep-sea fishes] have been picked up at sea. **1909** H. G. WELLS *Tono-Bungay* III. iii. 364, I lay in my customary glider position, horizontal and face downward, and the invisibility of all the machinery gave an extraordinary effect of independent levitation. **1966** *New Statesman* 18 Feb. 242/3 (Advt.), Atmospheric levitation. Learn to glide.

b. The action or process of rising, or raising (a body), from the ground by 'spiritualistic' means.

1874 GEO. ELIOT *Legend of Jubal* 191 On all points he adopts the latest views; Takes for the key of universal Mind The 'levitation' of stout gentlemen. **1875** *Fam. Herald* 13 Nov. 29/2 Levitation is an old claim of the marvellous, as old as Pythagoras. **1881** *Times* 30 Mar. 11/6 Levitation.. or moving at will,.. wholly independent of the laws of gravitation, is a universal dream. **1888** BESANT *Herr Paulus* 89 The séances, manifestations, levitations [etc.].

c. The process of raising or supporting by invisible means something heavier than the surrounding fluid. Cf. LEVITATE *v.* 2 b.

1939 *Gen. Electric Rev.* XLII. 231 (*caption*) As if by magic the shallow metallic dish rises into the air and appears to obey the gestures of the demonstrator's hand. Actually, the levitation results from a special application of electromagnetic principles. **1952** *Jrnl. Electrochem. Soc.* XCIX. 205 Stable levitation.. of various metals in the solid state was obtained between the coils.. both in air and in vacuum. **1952** *Jrnl. Appl. Physics* XXIII. 552/1 If electromagnetic levitation can be expanded to a larger scale, the following advantages can be anticipated: 1. The specimen touches no crucible or container during the heating, melting and drainage stages. 2. The heated or molten specimen can be protected by a suitable atmosphere or a vacuum. [Etc.] **1956** *Philips Res. Rep.* XI. 45 The possibilities.. of levitation by auxiliary gravitational forces, by reaction forces and by forces in electromagnetic fields are investigated. **1961** *Lancet* 25 Nov. 1181/1 Levitation. It occurred to me that supporting a patient on air might solve some of the problems of nursing patients whose illness necessitates the avoidance of contact with their beds. **1971** *Observer* 28 Nov. 9/4 'Magnetic levitation'.. could turn out to be the most important advance in transport technology since the internal combustion engine.

†**2.** The action or process of becoming lighter; also, the quality of being comparatively light; = BUOYANCY. *Obs.*

1686 GOAD *Celest. Bodies* II. v. 221 The Currents in the Sea, as all Tides, are made by Levitation of the Humid Body. **1739** LABELYE *Short Acc. Piers Westm. Bridge* 25 The Sides must rise by their own Levitation or Buoyancy.

3. *fig.*

1909 *Q. Rev.* Jan. 78 In other words, it [*sc.* Labour] obeys its own law of economic levitation, if we may be permitted to coin a phrase. **1962** W. NOWOTTNY *Lang. Poets Use* vi. 123 The poet.. has not yet figured as one who soars into a sphere where diction takes forms so conspicuously unprosaic.. that [etc.]... It is my purpose now to begin to enquire at what point levitation into such a sphere may be said to have taken place. **1966** *New Statesman* 28 Jan. 138/3 In his third phase.. Tippett concentrates on the spiritual 'levitation' effected by his winging lines and springing rhythms.

So **levi'tational** *a.*, of or pertaining to levitation.

1903 *Edin Rev.* Apr. 329 These people sought.. for a levitational quality akin to the dormitive quality of opium, but never found it. **1912** J. STEPHENS *Crock of Gold* v. xiv. 206 Birds have atmospheric and levitational information which millions of years will not render accessible to us. **1969** *New Scientist* 17 Apr. 117/1 If the curve is anti-spatial (particle extinction) the field is anti-gravitational or levitational.

Levite ('liːvaɪt). Also 4–5 **levyte.** [ad. L. *levīta*, also *levītēs*, ad. Gr. λευίτης, f. Λευί Levi (Heb. *Lēvī*, which also means 'Levite').]

1. *Israelitish Hist.* **a.** A descendant of Levi; one of the tribe of Levi. **b.** One of that portion of the tribe who acted as assistants to the priests in the temple-worship.

a **1300** *Cursor M.* 21241 Marc.. efter his kind.. was leuite. **1377** LANGL. *P. Pl.* B. XII. 115 *Archa dei* in þe olde lawe leuites it kepten. *a* **1420** HOCCLEVE *De Reg. Princ.* 1755 In þe abhomynable oppressioun Of þe leuytes wyfe. **1567** *Gude & Godlie B.* (S.T.S.) 180 The Leuites at thair awin hand Thay reft thair teind. **1726** AYLIFFE *Parergon* 197 In the Christian Church, the Office of Deacons succeeded in the Place of the Levites among the Jews. **1891** CHEYNE *Orig. Psalter* II. i. 59 *note*, The singers were Levites.

†**2.** *transf.* (from 1 b). A deacon. *Obs.*

A frequent rhetorical use of the word in med. Latin.

1393 LANGL. *P. Pl.* C. III. 130 Laurens þe leuite lyggynge on þe gredire, Loked vp to oure lorde. **1570** LEVINS *Manip.* 151/26 A Leuite,.. *diaconus.* **1604** E. G[RIMSTONE] *D'Acosta's Hist. Indies* v. xiv. 365 The divell.. hath placed in the order of his priests, some greater or superiors, and some lesse, the one as Acolites, the other as Levites.

†**3.** Used somewhat contemptuously for: A clergyman. Also, in allusion to Judges xvii. 12, a domestic chaplain. *Obs.*

1640 GLAPTHORNE *Wit in Constable* IV. G b, There shall a little Levite Meet you, and give you to the lawfull bed. **1655** SIR G. SONDES *Narr.* in *Harl. Misc.* (1813) X. 51 If I had not a Levite in my house, I performed the office myself. **1687** CONGREVE *Old Bach.* IV. i, I say he is a wanton young Levite. *a* **1704** T. BROWN *Sat. Marriage* Wks. 1730 i. 58 The Levite it keeps from parocial duty. **1849** MACAULAY *Hist. Eng.* iii. I. 327 A young Levite—such was the phrase then in use—might be had for his board, a small garret, and ten pounds a year.

†**4.** A loose dress, so called from its supposed resemblance to the dress of the Levites. *Obs.* [After F. *lévite.*]

1779 H. WALPOLE *Let. to C'tess Ossory* 15 Nov. (1848) I. 379 A habit-maker.. is gone stark in love with Lady Ossory, on fitting her with the new dress. I think they call it a Levite, and says he never saw so glorious a figure.. but where the deuce is the grace in a man's nightgown bound round with a belt?

Levitic (lɪ'vɪtɪk), *a.* [ad. late L. *levīticus*, ad. Gr. λευιτικός, f. λευίτης LEVITE.] = next.

1632 B. JONSON *Magn. Lady* I. (1640) 11 For of the Wardmote Quest, he better can, The mysterie, then the Levitick Law. **1669** GALE *Crt. Gentiles* I. II. ix. 139 This sacred Institution received a new stamp.. under the Levitic Constitution. **1879** FARRAR *St. Paul* II. 3 The vow which St. Paul undertook is highly significant as a proof of his personal allegiance to the Levitic institutions.

Levitical (lɪ'vɪtɪkəl), *a.* [f. as prec. + -AL¹.]

1. Pertaining to the Levites or the tribe of Levi.

1535 COVERDALE *Mal.* iii. *heading*, Off the abrogation of the olde leuiticall priestheade. **1650** TRAPP *Comm. Exod.* 74 The Sacrifice of Consecration shewed the difference between the Levitical Priests and Christ. **1776** G. HORNE *Ps.* II. 297 We read, 1 Chron. ix. 33 that the Levitical singers were 'employed in their work day and night'. **1867** LADY HERBERT *Cradle L.* vii. 168 Later, it became a Levitical city.

1898 *Expositor* Oct. 255 Deuteronomy 18. 6–8 does not invest a Levite with priestly but Levitical functions.

2. Of or pertaining to the ancient Jewish system of ritual administered by the Levites; also, pertaining to the book of Leviticus. ***Levitical degrees***: the degrees of consanguinity within which marriage is forbidden in Lev. xviii. 6–18.

1540 *Act 32 Hen. VIII*, c. 32 §2 Any mariage without the leuiticall degrees. *a* **1665** GOODWIN *Filled w. the Spirit* (1867) 140 Framers of the whole Mosaical economy and Levitical dispensation. **1726** AYLIFFE *Parergon* 52 By the Levitical Law, both the Man and the Woman were stoned to death. **1892** E. P. BARROW *Regni Evangel.* i. 56 The proselyte's bath of Levitical purification. **1895** J. A. BEET *New Life in Christ* III. xiii. 103 We have here under levitical forms important Gospel truth.

†**b.** *nonce-use.* Pertaining to ritual. *Obs.*

1670 MILTON *Hist. Eng.* IV. Wks. (1847) 515/2 Austin.. sent to Rome..to acquaint the pope of his good success in England, and to be resolved of certain theological, or rather levitical, questions.

Hence **Le'viticalism** = LEVITICISM. **Leviti'cality** *nonce-wd.*, Levitical character or obligation. **Le'vitically** *adv.*, in a Levitical manner, according to Levitical law. †**Le'viticalness**, Levitical character or quality.

1892 A. B. BRUCE *Apologetics* II. vii. 204 *Leviticalism.. may be conceived of as a husk to protect the kernel of ethical monotheism. **1900** *Speaker* 8 Sept. 624/1 We do not find in St. Paul any conception of Leviticalism as possessing a religious significance. **1621** BP. MOUNTAGU *Diatribæ* 387 The *Leuiticality..of Tithing, being confined vnto place, the Land of Promise. **1641** MILTON *Ch. Govt.* I. v, What right of jurisdiction soever can be from this place *Levitically bequeath'd, must descend upon the Ministers of the Gospell equally. **1892** *Times* 4 Feb. 6/2 An example of any Levitically clean animal. **1639** F. ROBERTS *God's Holy Ho.* vii. 48 The *Leviticalnesse of things of the Tabernacle, or Temple, consisted not in their materials..but in their typical relation to Christ.

Leviticism (lɪ'vɪtɪsɪz(ə)m). [f. LEVITIC + -ISM.] Levitical tenets and practice; an instance of this.

1888 A. CAVE *Inspir. O.T.* v. 257 Are we not also 'in full Leviticism' at the environment of Jericho? *Ibid.* 268 This long list of Leviticisms may be brought to a close.

Leviticus (lɪ'vɪtɪkəs). [a. late L. *Lēvīticus* adj. (sc. *liber* book): see LEVITIC.] The name of the third book of the Pentateuch, which contains details of the Levitical law and ritual.

c **1400** WYCLIF *Lev.* Prol., Here begynneth the bok of Leuiticus. **1579** FULKE *Heskins' Parl.* 8 In Exodus and Leuiticus..are many thinges..very easie and plaine. **1649** ROBERTS *Clavis Bibl.* (ed. 2) 45 Leviticus, so denominated by the Greek, from the chief subject or matter of the Book. **1891** CHEYNE *Psalter* VII. 357 The ceremonialism of Leviticus.

Levitism ('liːvaɪtɪz(ə)m). [f. LEVITE + -ISM.] = LEVITICISM.

1879 FARRAR *St. Paul* II. xxxvi. §2. 192 *note*, By 'works' Paul meant Levitism. *Ibid.* xxxix. 264 They went far beyond the requirements of Levitism.

levitor, erron. form of LEVATOR.

levitron ('lɛvɪtrɒn). *Physics.* [f. LEVI(TATE *v.* + -TRON.] A type of fusion reactor in which stability of the plasma inside a toroidal container is achieved by the combination of a magnetic field parallel to the sides of the torus, produced by an external winding, with a second field everywhere at right angles to the first, produced by a toroidal current-carrying core magnetically levitated inside the tube.

1960 COLGATE & FURTH in *Physics of Fluids* III. 999/2 The toroidal analog of the linear hard-core tube is the 'levitron', a toroidal pinch tube with a central ring core, levitated by magnetic field or held in place transiently by inertia. **1966** *McGraw-Hill Encycl. Sci. & Technol.* X. 234/2 Several Levitrons are built or under construction.

levitt, variant of LEVET² *Obs.*

levity¹ ('lɛvɪtɪ). Forms: 6 levitye, 7 -tie, 7- levity. [ad. OF. *levité* = It. *levità*, ad. L. *levitātem*, *levitās*, f. *levis* light: see -ITY.]

1. a. As a physical quality: The quality or fact of having comparatively little weight; lightness. Also †*specific levity*: cf. *specific gravity* (GRAVITY 4 c).

1597 A. M. tr. *Guillemeau's Fr. Chirurg.* 40/2 Consideringe theire ponderousnes or levitye. **1645** EVELYN *Mem.* (1857) I. 221 He abounded in things petrified,..a morsel of cork yet retaining its levity, sponges, etc. **1684** BOYLE *Porousn. Anim. & Solid Bod.* iii. 85 Marble itself abounds with internal Pores..as may be rationally conjectured from the Specifick Levity of it, in comparison of Gold and Lead. **1756** C. LUCAS *Ess. Waters* I. 26 Rain-water ..comes nearest to dew in levity, subtility and purity. **1787** WINTER *Syst. Husb.* 82 When they [vapours] ascend into that region of the atmosphere of the same specifick levity, there they float. **1802** PALEY *Nat. Theol.* xii. (1824) 482/1 A covering which shall unite the qualities of warmth, levity, and least resistance to the air. **1818** FARADAY *Exp. Res.* xxx. (1825) 166 The re-absorption..being..retarded in consequence of the superior levity of the fluid. **1869** MRS. SOMERVILLE *Molec. Sci.* I. i. 12 Hydrogen..rises in the air on account of its levity.

b. In pre-scientific physics, regarded as a positive property inherent in bodies in different degrees, or varying proportions, in virtue of which they tend to rise, as bodies possessing gravity tend to sink. Cf. GRAVITY 4 a. *Obs.* exc. *Hist.* or *allusively*.

1601 HOLLAND *Pliny* II. 406 That leuitie whereof they spake, can hardly and vnneath bee found and knowne by any other meanes than [etc.]. **1614** RALEIGH *Hist. World* I. (1634) 10 Hee..gave to every nature his proper forme; the forme of levitie to that which ascended. **1644** DIGBY *Nat. Bodies* x. (1658) 100 There is no such thing among bodies, as positive gravity or levity. **1672** PETTY *Pol. Anat.* (1691) 334 What alterations are made in the gravity or levity of the air from hour to hour. **1775** PRIESTLEY *Exper. Air* I. 267 That phlogiston should communicate absolute levity to the bodies with which it is combined, is a supposition that I am not willing to have recourse to. **1794** G. ADAMS *Nat. & Exp. Philos.* III. xxxiv. 381 As paradoxical as the weighing of levity. **1830** HERSCHEL *Stud. Nat. Phil.* 142 We know of no natural body in which the opposite of gravity, or positive levity, subsists. **1854** H. MILLER *Sch. & Schm.* (1858) 249, I had not levity enough in my framework to float across the lever.

c. *fig.* applied to immaterial things.

1704 SWIFT *T. Tub* Introd., Little starued conceits are gently wafted up by their extreme leuity to the middle region. **1779–81** JOHNSON *L.P.*, *Prior* Wks. 1787 III. 147 The burlesque of Boileau's Ode on Namur has, in some parts, such airiness and levity as will [etc.].

†**2.** Lightness in movement; agility. *Obs.*

1607 TOPSELL *Four-f. Beasts* (1658) 257 The natural constitution of a Horse is hot..because of his Levity, and Velocity. **1610** HOLLAND *Camden's Brit.* I. 122 The Levitie of men made shift to enter thorow places scant passable.

3. As a moral or mental quality, in various senses.

a. Want of serious thought or reflexion; frivolity. Also (now chiefly), 'Trifling gaiety' (J.); unbecoming or unseasonable jocularity. (The prevalent sense.)

1564 *Brief Exam.* A iij, As though they were ledde with a certayne irreligious leuitie, to ouerthrowe and abolyshe all thynges vsed before in religion. **1606** SHAKS. *Ant. & Cl.* II. vii. 128 Our grauer businesse Frownes at this leuitie. **1647** CLARENDON *Hist. Reb.* I. §4 The levity of one, and the morosity of another. **1671** MILTON *Samson* 880, I.. unbosom'd all my secrets to thee, Not out of levity, but overpowr'd By thy request. *a* **1686** B. CALAMY *Serm.* (1687) 6 He never employed his omnipotence out of levity or ostentation; but onely as the necessities and wants of Men required it. **1806** *Med. Jrnl.* XV. 108 The subject has been treated with indecent and disgusting levity. **1830** D'ISRAELI *Chas. I*, III. vi. 116 It is mortifying to disclose the levity of feeling of men of genius. **1841–4** EMERSON *Ess.*, *Politics* Wks. (Bohn) I. 237 But politics rest on necessary foundations, and cannot be treated with levity. **1882** JEAN WATSON *Life A. Thomson* iii. 44 He could be gay without levity.

b. Incapacity for lasting affection, resolution, or conviction; heedlessness in making and breaking promises; instability, fickleness, inconstancy.

1613 R. C. *Table Alph.* (ed. 3), Leuitie, lightnesse, inconstancie. **1633** P. FLETCHER *Poet. Misc.* 76 The Cause that with my verse she was offended, For womens levitie I discommended. **1685** BAXTER *Paraphr. N.T.*, *Acts* xiv. 19 This is the levity of the vulgar, that one day will sacrifice as to Gods, to those, whom after they would kill as malefactors. **1781** GIBBON *Decl. & F.* xvii. II. 94 The Sarmatians soon forgot, with the levity of Barbarians, the services which they had so lately received. **1832** tr. *Sismondi's Ital. Rep.* xiv. 296 Maximilian forgot, with extreme levity, his promises and alliances. **1834** MACAULAY *Ess.*, *Pitt* (1851) 303 Sick of the perfidy and levity of the First Lord of the Treasury.

c. 'Light' or undignified behaviour; unbecoming freedom of conduct (said esp. of women); an instance of this.

1601 MARSTON *Pasquil & Kath.* II. 11, I know that women of leuitie and lightnesse are soone downe. **1699** BURNET *39 Art.* xx. (1700) 195 Vain Pomp and indecent Levity ought to be guarded against. **1702** PENN in *Pennsylv. Hist. Soc. Mem.* IX. 171 Give him the true state of things, and weigh down his levities. **1710** STEELE *Tatler* No. 76 ¶6 An un-becoming Levity in their Behaviour out of the Pulpit. **1727** SWIFT *What passed in Lond.* Wks. 1755 III. I. 184 Those innocent freedoms and little levities so commonly incident to young ladies of their profession. **1766** FORDYCE *Serm. Yng. Wom.* (1767) II. xiii. 239 Their natural graces..are lost in levity. **1791** MRS. RADCLIFFE *Rom. Forest* viii, Distinguishing between a levity of this kind and a more serious address. **1828** SCOTT *F.M. Perth* xxiii, So many charges of impropriety and levity. **1849** MACAULAY *Hist. Eng.* vii. II. 256 Her elder sister..had been distinguished by beauty and levity.

†**d.** *nonce-use.* Lightness (of spirit), freedom from care. *Obs.*

1630 DONNE *Serm.* xxvi. (1640) 264 To what a blessed levity (if without levity we may so speake) to what a cheerefull lightnesse of spirit is he come, that comes newly from confession.

4. A saying or expression marked by levity.

1930 BLUNDEN in *Nation* 6 Dec. 327/1 *Coleridge*, wonderfully well edited by his grandson.., lacks his epigrams and levities.

†**'levity**². *Obs. rare*⁻¹. [ad. L. *lēvitāt-em*, *lēvitās*, f. *lēvis* smooth.] Smoothness; an instance of this, a smooth surface.

1613 M. RIDLEY *Magn. Bodies* 20 Unlesse they be drawne aside by excrescenses and levities.

levo-, variant of LÆVO-.

levodopa (ˌliːvəʊ'dəʊpə). *Chem.* and *Biochem.* Also lævo- (*rare*). [f. LÆVO-, LEVO- + DOPA.] The lævorotatory L form of dopa (see L 7 c and DOPA).

1970 *Brit. Med. Jrnl.* 7 Feb. 331 (*heading*) Treatment of Parkinsonism with laevo-dopa. **1970** *Jrnl. Amer. Med. Assoc.* 16 Mar. 1857/3 Levodopa increased the severity of depression. **1971** *Lancet* 19 June 1272/2 It seems unlikely that levodopa will have a favourable therapeutic effect on acne vulgaris. **1972** *Approved Names 1970* (Brit. Pharmacopœia Comm.) Suppl. 1, *Levodopa*, (−)-3-(3, 4-Dihydroxyphenyl)-L-alanine. **1974** *Times* 8 Jan. 14/6 The weakness and tremor of Parkinson's disease are thought to be caused by a lack of the chemical dopamine. Treatment with levodopa corrects that deficiency, as the drug is converted to dopamine within the body.

levolto, obs. form of LAVOLTA.

levor, levoret, obs. ff. LEVER, LEVERET.

levour, levrat, -it, obs. ff. LEVER, LEVERET.

levulin, variant of LÆVULIN.

levy ('lɛvɪ), *sb.*¹ Forms: 5 leve(e, levye, 5, 7 levie, 6 levey, 7 leavy, 5- levy. [a. F. *levée*, f. *lever* to raise, levy:—L. *levāre* to raise.]

1. The action of levying: **a.** The action of collecting an assessment, duty, tax, etc.

1427 *Rolls of Parlt.* IV. 318/2 Labour and coustes hade for þe levee of þe same [revenue]. **1434** *Waterf. Arch.* in *10th Rep. Hist. MSS. Comm.* App. v. 297 The said Maire and Baliffs have leve of the said citsaine or dynsyn twies as much. **1496–7** *Act 12 Hen. VII*, c. 12 §4 The Collectours deputed for the levy of the seid xv^mes and x^mes nowe graunted. **1512** *Act 4 Hen. VIII*, c. 19 §7 Suche direccion and order for the levey and payment therof as..shall theyr seme requysyte. **1635** *Mass. Col. Rec.* (1853) I. 134 The constable of Dorchestr is ffined xx^s for not retorneing his warrant for the last levy into the Court. **1714** STEELE *Lover* No. 16 (1723) 94 Sir Anthony stole the manner of this Levy from Lord Peters Invention. **1828** D'ISRAELI *Chas. I*, II. x. 252 The sole object of the Government was to settle the legal levy of the duties. **1862** MERIVALE *Rom. Emp.* (1865) IV. xxxviii. 312 He decreed the levy of one-twentieth upon the succession to property. **1874** GREEN *Sort Hist.* v. §4. 244 In the eastern counties its levy [poll-tax] gathered crowds of peasants together.

transf. **1872** YEATS *Growth Comm.* 51 A levy was made upon nature for every delicacy of food and wines with which to spread the table.

b. The action of enrolling or collecting men for war or other purposes.

1607 SHAKS. *Cor.* v. v. 67 To..giue away The benefit of our Leuies. *a* **1653** BINNING *Serm.* (1845) 490 What meant the Levy appointed immediately after Dunbar. **1843** JAMES *Forest Days* x, Arrange with bold Robin for a levy of as many yeomen as possible. **1859** JEPHSON *Brittany* viii. 107 The Government endeavoured to carry out the celebrated levy of three hundred thousand men. **1879** FROUDE *Cæsar* xxi. 354 As to the levies, the men enlist unwillingly.

†**c.** The action of collecting debts or enforcing the payment of fines. *Obs.*

1463 *Bury Wills* (Camden) 43 That my executours..make levy of my dettys. **1702** J. LOGAN in *Pennsylv. Hist. Soc. Mem.* IX. 150 As to fines—I have promoted and pressed their levy in this county to my utmost.

2. The amount or number levied: **a.** †A duty, impost, tax. *Obs.* In a trade or benefit society: A call or contribution of so much per head.

1640 in *Virginia Mag. Hist. & Biog.* V. 364 Francis Moryson..being appointed to collect and receive the levy belonging to Mr. George Sandys. **1647** N. BACON *Disc. Govt. Eng.* I. xi. 33 Offa charged this Leavy upon the Inhabitants dwelling in Nine several Diocesses. **1662** PETTY *Taxes* Pref., Great and heavy Leavies upon a poor people. *a* **1680** BUTLER *Rem.* (1759) I. 171 None but Kings have Pow'r to raise A Levy, which the Subject pays. **1765** BLACKSTONE *Comm.* I. I. viii. 280 The other ancient levies were in the nature of a modern land-tax. **1901** *Scotsman* 8 Mar. 5/4 It was decided to call up a special levy from next week to cover the amount necessary.

transf. **1873** TRISTRAM *Moab* x. 192 The only levy on our stores had been four bottles of raki.

b. A body of men enrolled; also *pl.* the individual men.

1611 BIBLE *1 Kings* v. 13 The leuie was thirtie thousand men. **1642** CHAS. I *Message Parlt.* 8 Apr. 4 With the Addition of these Leavies. **1775** J. TRUMBULL in Sparks *Corr. Amer. Rev.* (1853) I. 37 Our new levies will be at your camp with all convenient expedition. **1810** WELLINGTON in Gurw. *Desp.* (1838) VI. 475 It has brought the Portuguese levies into action. **1826** J. F. COOPER *Mohicans* (1829) I. vi. 79, I teach singing to the youths of the Connecticut levy. **1845** S. AUSTIN *Ranke's Hist. Ref.* I. 181 The levy was to consist of 1058 horse, and 3038 foot. **1865** CARLYLE *Fredk. Gt.* (1872) VIII. XVIII. xii. 18 Daun..is..perfecting his new levies. **1867** FREEMAN *Norm. Conq.* (1876) I. v. 312 The Danes put the irregular English levies to flight. **1887** M. MORRIS *Claverhouse* x. (1888) 177 Some new levies of horse.

3. ***levy in mass*** [F. *levée en masse*]: a levy of all the able-bodied men in a country or district for military service.

1807 SOUTHEY *Espriella's Lett.* (1808) I. 179 The levy in mass, the telegraph, and the income-tax are all from France. **1830** W. TAYLOR *Hist. Surv. Germ. Poetry* III. 425 Körner ..stimulated the levy-in-mass of the nation.

4. In some public schools: A meeting called for discussion of any matter relating to the school.

1857 HUGHES *Tom Brown* I. viii, A levy of the School had been held, at which the captain of the School had got up, and after premising that [etc.]. *Ibid.*, A levy of the sixth had been held on the subject. *Ibid.* I. ix, Holmes called a levy of his house.

5. *Comb.*: **levy-money**, †(*a*) bounty-money paid to recruits; (*b*) contributions called for from the members of a trade or benefit society.

1671 R. MONTAGU in *Buccleuch MSS.* (Hist. MSS. Comm.) I. 503 To learn at what rate they may have men, both as to the levy-money and the constant pay. **1702** LUTTRELL *Brief Rel.* (1857) V. 134 That there be allowed for levy money for the dragoons, £12 for man and horse. **1777** *Hist. Eur.* in *Ann. Reg.* 70/1 An unexpected demand made by the Landgrave of Hesse for levy money. **1894** *Westm. Gaz.* 16 July 2/3 The..refusal of the Federationists to share with them the English levy money.

levy ('lɛvɪ), *sb.*² [Short for *eleven pence* or *eleven-penny bit.*] †**a.** (See quot. 1859.) **b.** *local U.S.* 'The sum of twelve and a half cents; a "bit"' (*Cent. Dict.*). Also *local U.K.*, a shilling (*obs.*).

1829 C. SEALSFIELD *Tokeah* II. ii. 22 'But them fips and levies,' throwing a dirty leather bag with a dozen small silver coins upon the table, 'must first go.' **1832** F. TROLLOPE *Dom. Manners Amer.* I. 171 He drew from thence [*sc.* from his pocket] rather more dollars, half-dollars, levies, and fips, than his dirty little hand could well hold. **1837-47** NEAL *Charcoal Sk.*, *Crooked Disciple* (1872) 204 (Funk), Give us a fip's worth of sheet and levy's worth of blanket. **1859** BARLETT *Dict. Amer.*, *Levy*,..In..Pennsylvania, Maryland, and Virginia, the Spanish real..twelve and a half cents. Sometimes called an elevenpenny bit. **1864** HOTTEN *Slang Dict.* 170 *Levy*, a shilling.—*Liverpool.*

levy ('lɛvɪ), *v.* Forms: 4, 6 leve, (6 lewe), 5 levee, 5-6 levie, 6-7 leavie, -y(e, levey, 5- levy. [f. LEVY *sb.*¹ The early form *leve* may possibly be monosyllabic, and in that case would be a different word (cf. LEAVE *v.*³), a. F. *lever* to raise, levy, from which the Eng. vb. *levy* derives most of its senses.]

1. a. *trans.* To raise (contributions, taxes); to impose (an assessment, rate, toll, etc.). Const. †*of, on, upon.*

1388 *Waterf. Arch.* in *10th Rep. Hist. MSS. Comm.* App. v. 292 If the Maire..wil not leve and areyse the said xls. **1494** FABYAN *Chron.* VI. cxcviii. 204, xl. M. li...was leuyed of his subiectes, and named..Dane Gelt. **1509-10** *Act 1 Hen. VIII*, c. 19 *Preamble*, Your said Oratour..levyed severall Fynes of all the foresaid Manours. **1550** CROWLEY *Epigr.* 1205 To leauye greate fines, or to ouer the rent. **1608** *Vestry Bks.* (Surtees) 60 A sesment of ijs. the pounde shalbe leveyed presently through this parish. **1647** CLARENDON *Hist. Reb.* II. 104 Ship-money was levied with the same severity, and the same rigour used in ecclesiastical courts. *a* **1674** —— *Surv. Leviath.* (1676) 170 That he hath power to leavy mony. *a* **1687** PETTY *Pol. Arith.* (1690) 30 Bank keepers..must have power to levy upon the general, what they happen to loose unto particular men. **1726** SWIFT *Gulliver* I. vi, The pension..is levied by the emperor's officers. **1786** BURKE *W. Hastings* Wks. 1842 II. 135 Levying the tribute of the whole on the little that remained. **1828** D'ISRAELI *Chas. I*, II. v. 129 [They] declared, that these rates could no longer be levied without a grant of Parliament. **1832** BABBAGE *Econ. Manuf.* xxx. (ed. 3) 294 A fine should be levied on the delinquent. **1853** BRONTE *Villette* xiv, A subscription was annually levied on the whole school for the purchase of a handsome present. **1874** GREEN *Short Hist.* ii. §6. 90 No toll might be levied from tenants of the Abbey farms.

†**b.** To raise (a sum of money) as a profit or rent; to collect (the amount of) a debt; also, to take the revenues of (land). *Obs.*

1469 *Bury Wills* (Camden) 48 That the ferme of the seid londys..go to myne doughter Margerye tyll the summe of x marke be levyed for the seid Margerye. **1496** W. PASTON in *P. Lett.* III. 469 For as moche as..my dettis cannot be redely levied. **1523** LD. BERNERS *Froiss.* I. xxix. 43 He..wolde leuey the moyte of their landes to his owne vse. **1613** *Bury Wills* (Camden) 162 My..mynde is yt he enter into the said tenemente and hould the same vntill owte of the revenewes therof he shall have levyed the same. **1768** BLACKSTONE *Comm.* III. 419 To hold, till out of the rents and profits thereof the debt be levied.

c. To raise (a sum of money) by legal execution or process. Const. *on* (*the goods of*). Also, *to levy execution for* (a specified sum).

c **1506** *Plumpton Corr.* (Camden) 198 The berer shall goe to the Shereff with this exigent, & have from him a warrant to leve the sayd money, or els to take your body. **1669-70** MARVELL *Corr.* Wks. 1872-5 II. 308 [The fine] shall be levyd on the goods of any one or more persons that were there. **1795** WYTHE *Decis. Virginia* 13 By directing the execution to be levied for £1,000.

absol. **1885** *Law Times* LXXVIII. 389/2 An execution creditor..levied on their goods for the purpose of realising his debt.

d. To impose (service) *upon*; to require (a person's) attendance.

[**1611** BIBLE *1 Kings* ix. 21 Vpon those did Solomon leuie a tribute of bond-seruice vnto this day.] **1862** STANLEY *Jew. Ch.* (1877) I. x. 203 They willingly undertook the tributary service which was levied upon them. **1871** B. TAYLOR *Faust* (1875) I. xxi. 179 Ho, there! my friend! I'll levy thine attendance.

e. *U.S.* = CHARGE *v.* 18.

1837 CALHOUN *Wks.* III. 36 Mr. Madison, under the impression that these papers would be favorably received by the Public..had levied several legacies upon them.

f. To impose a levy on (a person). Also *refl.*

1902 *Westm. Gaz.* 17 June 9/1 The members will be levied 1s. yearly to support their candidate. **1921** *Ibid.* 24 May 2/4 When the stoppage ceases the miners will levy themselves in order to meet these promissory notes.

2. a. *Law. to levy a fine*: see FINE *sb.* 6 b. (The expression also occurs with different sense: see 1.)

1483 *Act 1 Rich. III*, c. 7 §1 Notes and Fines levied in the King's Courts..should be openly and solemnly read. **1642** *Perkins' Profit. Bk.* iv. §256. 114 If..either of them levie a fyne unto other of the same land. **1818** CRUISE *Digest* (ed. 2) I. 420 When a fine was levied..the estate was in the cognizee or feoffee..by the common law. *Ibid.* V. 67 If the fine was proved to have been duly levied, then the party who refused to adhere to it was attached. **1844** WILLIAMS *Real Prop.* (1877) 55 She was also prohibited from levying a fine.

b. To draw up (an objection, protest) in due form.

1660 STILLINGFL. *Iren.* I. i. (1662) 7 This objection will be soon leavied, that it is [etc.]. **1868** SEYD *Bullion* 82 He must send the Bill to a Notary..who then levies Protest in due form.

†**3.** In various obsolete senses: **a.** To set up (a fence, weir, etc.); to erect (a house); = AF. *lever*, Law Latin *levare*. **b.** To plan out (ground). **c.** To weigh (an anchor).

a. 1495 *Act 11 Hen. VII*, c. v, Weares and other Engynes for fisshing ther made levyed fixed. **1513** in Fowler *Hist. C.C.C.* (O.H.S.) 60 The sayd Master and Prior of St. Frideswith hath begunne to build and levie one house for a College. **1549** *Act 3 & 4 Edw. VI*, c. 3 §2 It hapneth sometime, that some Man..hath made or levied a Ditch or Hedge. **1619** DALTON *Country Just.* I. (1630) 135 The new levying or inhancing of Weares Mills [etc.]. **1741** VINER *Abridgm.* XVI. 23 Levying of a Goss to intercept the Course of Fish.

b. 1500-18 *Acc. Louth Steeple* in *Archæologia* X. 74 Paid to William Thomas and William Palmer, levying the ground for to sett the broach upon.

c. 1648 GAGE *West. Ind.* xxi. (1655) 195 We levying our anchor went on to Panama.

4. To enlist (armed men), enrol, bring into the field (soldiers, an army); to muster the available force of (a district). Also, *to levy up.*

c **1500** *Melusine* 135 The men of armes, that he leuyed fro the garnysons. **1557** *Act 4 & 5 Phil. & Mary* c. 3 §1 To muster their Maties People..and to levie a nomber of them for the Service of their Maties. *a* **1586** SIDNEY *Arcadia* v. (1629) 447 With sufficient authoritie to leauie forces. **1614** RALEIGH *Hist. World* III. (1634) 63 This was the last Fight of that huge Army leavied against Greece. **1649** H. GUTHRY *Mem.* (1702) 45 The General and his Council appointed the Earl of Montross..to levy Fife, Strathern, Angus, and Merne. **1671** L. ADDISON *W. Barbary* 40 A small Cavila, not able to levy above 500 in all. **1761-2** HUME *Hist. Eng.* (1806) IV. lxiv. 745 An army of twelve thousand men was suddenly levied. **1797** WELLINGTON in Gurw. *Desp.* (1837) I. 17 Tippoo Sultaun suffered the military force which they had levied..to land in his country. **1843** H. GAVIN *Feigned Dis.* 11 Men apprehensive of being levied, or actually levied, or forced into the military or naval services.

fig. **1599** MIDDLETON & ROWLEY *Old Law* IV. ii, Why should nature have that power in me To leavy up a thousand bleeding sorrowes. **1705** J. PHILIPS *Blenheim* 176 As when two adverse winds,..Engage with horrid shock,..Levying their equal force with utmost rage.

5. To undertake, commence, make (war). Const. *against, on, upon.*

Johnson says: 'This sense, though Milton's, seems improper', presumably because there is no similar use of F. *lever*; but it is a natural development from sense 4.

1471 in *Warkworth's Chron.* (Camd.) 57 To levee werre ayenst him. **1543-4** *Act 35 Hen. VIII*, c. 12 The kynge..is forced..to leuy warre, and to prosecute his saide ennemies. ? **1659** *Priv. Devotions* in *Gentl. Calling* (1679) 160 So levying War against Thee with thine own Treasure. **1667** MILTON *P.L.* XI. 219 The Syrian King..Assassin-like had levied Warr, Warr unproclam'd. *a* **1720** SHEFFIELD (Dk. Buckhm.) *Wks.* (1753) II. 111 A meer design of deposition, imprisonment, or levying war, are not within the bare words of this law. **1761** HUME *Hist. Eng.* I. xi. 238 They..then proceeded without further ceremony to levy war upon the king. **1789** *Constitution U.S.* iii. §3 Treason against the United States shall consist only in levying war against them. **1814** CARY *Dante, Par.* xxvii. 47 [Those] that do levy war On the baptized. **1855** MILMAN *Lat. Chr.* VII. vi. (1864) IV. 202 Crusades will hereafter be levied against those who dared impiously to [etc.].

†**6.** To raise, discontinue (a siege); to break up (a camp). *Obs.*

1542 SEYMOUR in *St. Papers Hen. VIII*, IX. 201 The segge beynge lewed from beforre the towne of Pest the 7th day of October. ? **1548** EDW. VI *Jrnl.* in *Lit. Rem.* (Roxb.) II. 223 The sieg being levied th'erle of Shrewsbery entred it. **1579** FENTON *Guicciard.* (1618) 256 There was made no more doubt to leuie the Campe. **1588** *Exhort. to Faithf. Subj.* in *Harl. Misc.* (Malh.) II. 102 Porcenna..forthwith levied the siege. **1600** HOLLAND *Livy* XXXVI. x. 925 Albeit hee saw that the siege was levied..yet [etc.]. **1628** HOBBES *Thucyd.* (1629) 74 They sent Ambassadours againe to Athens commanding them to leuy the Siege from before Potidæa.

¶**7.** Wrongly used for LEVEL *v.*

1618 BRETON *Court & Country* (Grosart) 6/1 Winking with one eye, as though hee were leuying at a Woodcocke. *a* **1634** RANDOLPH *De Histrice* 2 Poems (1638) 26 Fam'd Stymphall, I have heard, thy birds in flight Shoot showers of arrowes forth all levied right.

Hence '**levied** *ppl. a.*

1768 HUME *Ess.* xxxiii. 243 How distinguish the new from the old levied soldiers? **1819** R. CHAPMAN *Life Jas. V*, 160 They are only new levied men, and undisciplined. **1837** W. IRVING *Capt. Bonneville* III. 105 A new levied band of hunters and trappers.

levy, obs. form of LEAVY *a.*, LEVEE¹ and ².

levying ('lɛvɪɪŋ), *vbl. sb.* [f. LEVY *v.* + -ING¹.] The action of the vb. LEVY in its various senses.

1496-7 *Act 12 Hen. VII*, c. 12 §5 Then the levyeng and payment of the seid xvme..[shall be] put in suspence. ? **1548** EDW. VI *Jrnl.* in *Lit. Rem.* (Roxb.) II. 223 [Thei] levied their siege, in the month of September; in the levieng of wich ther cam [etc.]. **1587** Q. ELIZ. in *Buccleuch MSS.* (Hist. MSS. Comm.) I. 225 That ye do assist the said Captains in the levying of their bands. **1712** PRIDEAUX *Direc. Ch.-wardens* (ed. 4) 51 The levying and disposing of them [the Rates]. **1769** BLACKSTONE *Comm.* IV. 82 To resist the king's forces by defending a castle against them, is a levying of war. **1815** ELPHINSTONE *Acc. Caubul* (1842) I. 229 The levying fixed proportions of troops or money, or both, from each tribe. **1818** CRUISE *Digest* (ed. 2) IV. 160 The levying or suffering any such fines or recoveries. **1828-40** TYTLER *Hist. Scot.* (1864) I. 222 Opponents to the regular levying of the tithes.

†**b.** *gerundially* with omission of prep.

1642 *Roy. Comm.* in *Buccleuch MSS.* (Hist. MSS. Comm.) I. 527 There are now at or near..London great forces levying and moneys raising.

levyist ('lɛvɪɪst). [f. LEVY *sb.*¹ + -IST.] One who imposes, or advocates imposing, a levy.

1923 *Glasgow Herald* 5 Mar. 4 Without the investment of money in any form which the levyist could reach.

levyled, obs. form of LEVELLED.

levyne ('lɛvɪn). *Min.* [named by Brewster, 1825, after Prof. Armand Levy.] A silicate of aluminum and calcium, found in colourless or slightly tinted tabular crystals.

1825 *Edin. Jrnl. Sci.* II. 334, I propose to distinguish this species by the name of Levyne. **1831** BREWSTER *Optics* xvii. 148 Levyne. **1843** J. E. PORTLOCK *Geol.* 219 Levyne of the ordinary form of crystals, at Magilligan Carnowry.

levyne, variant of LEWYN *Obs.*, a kind of linen.

levynge, obs. form of LIVING.

levynite ('lɛvɪnaɪt). *Min.* [f. LEVYNE + -ITE.] = LEVYNE.

1868 DANA *Min.* 431 Levynite occurs in crystals, usually tabular. **1894** *Amer. Jrnl. Sci.* XLVIII. 188 For the first group..we have thomsonite..levynite, gmelinite.

levys, obs. pl. of LEAF.

†**lew**, *sb.*¹ *Sc. Obs.* Also (*pl.*) leois. [perh. a sing. inferred from *lewis* (a. F. *louis*) treated as a plural.] The name of a French gold coin formerly current in Scotland; ?the *louis d'or* (Jam.).

1467 *Sc. Acts Jas. III* (1814) II. 88/2 That..þe Ingliss noble, henry, ande Eduarde wt þe ross, þe franche crowne, þe salute þe lewe and þe Ridar sall haif courss in þis realme [etc.]. **1488** in *Inv. R. Wardr.* (1815) 13 Four hundreth tuenti & viii Lewis of gold. **1497** in *Ld. Treas. Acc. Scotl.* I. 314 Thre Harj nobles, and tua leois.

lew (lju:, lu:), *a.*¹ and *sb.*² Now *dial.* Forms: 1 (ʒe)hléow, 2-7 lewe, 5, (9) lue, 8- loo(e, 4- lew. [OE. **hléow* (implied in *hléowe* adv.), *ʒehléow* (cf. *unhléow*; all three occur only once) = ON. *hlýr* warm, mild.

The relation of this word to the synonymous OHG. *lâo* (MHG. *lâ*, *lâw-*, G. *lau*) is obscure; no cognates outside Teut. are known.]

A. *adj.* **1.** †**a.** Warm; sunny (in OE.). **b.** Lukewarm, tepid.

[*c* **1000** *Sax. Leechd.* II. 280 þonne..ʒereste him swiðe wel hleowe þær & wearme gleda bere man ʒelome inn.] *c* **1000** in Cockayne *Narr. Angl. Conscript.* (1861) 23 Ond ða on ʒehliwran dene and on wearmran we ʒewicodon. *c* **1300** *Havelok* 498 [He] Withdrou the knif, that was lewe Of the seli children blod. *Ibid.* 2921 þe sunne, brith and lewe. **1382** WYCLIF *Rev.* iii. 16 For thou art lew [Vulg. *tepidus*], and nether coold, nether hoot. ? *c* **1390** *Form of Cury* in Warner *Antiq. Culin.* 19 Take calwar samon, and seeth it in lewe water. *c* **1420** *Liber Cocorum* (1862) 33 Boyle hit..And kele hit, that he be bot lue. **1688** R. HOLME *Armoury* III. 333/1 A Scimming Dish..is to scum the Cream of the Lew Milk to Churn for Butter. **1881** *Leicester Gloss.*, *Lew* and *Lew-warm*, luke-warm. *Mod. Sc.* (*West*) The water is quite loo. (In eastern Sc. the current word is LEW-WARM.)

2. Sheltered from the wind.

1674 [see LEE *a.*]. **1735-6** PEGGE *Kenticisms* (E.D.S.), *Lew*, sheltered; an house is said 'to lye lew', i.e. the house lies snug under the wind. **1825** J. JENNINGS *Observations Dial. W. Eng.* 52 *Lew*, shelter; defence from storms or wind. **1844** W. BARNES *Poems Rur. Life* 225 Milch cows in carners dry an' lew. **1863** [see LEE *sb.*¹ 1]. **1871** W. CORY *Lett. & Jrnls.* (1897) 278 The bit of brick wall gives me a very lew corner facing the east. **1887** [see LEE *sb.*¹ 1 b]. **1889** 'M. GRAY' *Reproach of Annesley* (ed. 5) VI. iii. 276 'Tis fine and loo here, ..and you med set down and hrest. **1892** H. C. O'NEILL *Devonshire Idyls* 7 His house..was 'loo' from the cold north winds. **1899** W. RAYMOND *Two Men o' Mendip* i. 7 The primroses an' cowslips too be out beautiful in the lew between Black-rocks. **1906** *Daily Chron.* 16 Aug. 3/6 It is cool and pleasant to find a 'loo' corner on the Esplanade [in Penzance]. **1909** S. REYNOLDS *Poor Man's House* VII. vi. 209 We crouched, all humped up, in the lew of a drifter's bows, whilst the rain water washed around our boots and coat-tails. **1963** NANCE & POOL *Gloss. Cornish Sea-Words* 109 *Loo*,..(2) lee, sheltered out of a wind.

B. *sb.*

1. Warmth, heat. *Obs.* exc. *Sc.*

1591 SYLVESTER *Du Bartas* I. iv. 656 To th' end a fruitfull lew [orig. *chaleur*] May every Climat in his time renew. **1633** GERARD *Part. Descr. Somerset* (1900) 11 Lockombe. So called I should rather deeme from the lowe situation or Lucombe from the warmnes, which wee yett call Lewe. **1824** MACTAGGART *Gallovid. Encycl.* s.v., Stacks of corn are said to take a 'lew', when they heat.

2. Shelter. See *house-lew*, OE. *húshléow* (HOUSE *sb.*¹ 24), and LEE *sb.*¹ 1, 1 b.

lew, *a.*² *dial.* [Of obscure origin; cf. OE. *ʒeléwed* 'debilitatum' (Ælfric *Exod.* xxii. 10 *Laud MS.*; Grein conjectured *ʒeléfed*), also *-lǽwe* in

limlǽweo lame in a limb, *léwsa* 'inopia.'] Weak. Also, of a leaden or pale colour; pale, wan.

c **1325** *Old Age* in *Rel. Ant.* II. 211 Mi bodi wexit lewe [gloss *debile*]. **1611** COTGR., *Decoulouré*, .. pale, bleake, wan, lew. *Ibid.*, *Livide*, wan, lew, bleake, pale, of a leaden, earthie, or dead colour. **1882** *Lancash. Gloss.*, *Liew*, thin, poor, diluted.

lew, *v. Obs.* exc. *dial.* Also 7 lue, 9 loo(e. [OE. *hlíewan*, f. *hléow* LEW *a.* Cf. ON. *hlýja* to cover, shelter, make warm.]

1. a. *trans.* To make warm or tepid. †**b.** *intr.* To become warm. *Obs.*

971 *Blickl. Hom.* 51 þære sunnan hæto þe þas eorþan hlyweþ [*MS.* hlypeþ]. *a* **1400-50** *Alexander* 4374 All þe land with his leme lewis & cleres. **1808** JAMIESON, *To Lew*, to warm any thing moderately; usually applied to liquids; *lewed*, warmed, made tepid.

2. To shelter.

1664 EVELYN *Sylva* 101 This done, provide a Screene .. to keep off the wind; .. so as to be easily remov'd as need shall require for the luing of your pit. **1887** *Kentish Gloss.* s.v., Those trees will lew the house when they're up-grown.

†**lew**, *int. Obs.* Lo! behold!

c **1460** *Towneley Myst.* iii. 507 Hence bot a litill, she commys, lew, lew!

lew, dial. form of LEE *sb.*^{1}; variant of LUE *v.*

lewan(e, variant of LEWYN *Obs.*

lewce, obs. form of LOOSE.

lewd (ljuːd), *a.* Forms: α. 1-2 lǽwede, lǽwde, (2 ilewede, ileawede), 2-3 leawede, leawde, 2-6 lewed(e, 3 læwed, (*Orm.* læwedd), leouwede, loȝede, 3-5 leuid, 3-7 leude, 3-8 leud, 4 lewet, (? lowed), 4-5 lewid(e, lewyd, leewid, (louwed(e), ? lood, 5-7 leaud(e, 6 leawde, *Sc.* lewit, 6-7 lude, 4-7 lewde, 4- lewd. β. (chiefly *north.* and *Sc.*) 2-5 lawed, 3-4 laued, laud, 3-6 lawid(e, 4 lawyt, 4-6 lawd(e, 4-6 (9 *arch.*) lawit. [OE. *lǽwede*, of difficult etymology.

The sense suggests formation on Rom. *laigo:—eccl. L. *lāicus* (see LAY *a.* with suffix *-ede* -ED^{2}; but it is not easy to see the phonological possibility of this. The attempt to trace the word to a late L. type **lāicātus* (*u* stem) is still more open to objection. It has been proposed to obviate the phonetic difficulties by assuming influence from the vb. *lǽwan* to betray; but the sense is too remote, and *lǽwede* is not participial in form.]

†**1.** Lay, not in holy orders, not clerical. Also *absol. Obs.*

c **890** tr. *Bæda's Hist.* v. xii[i]. (1890) 428 Þara manna sum wæs .. bescoren preost, sum wes læwde [*v.r.* læwede], sum wæs wifmon. *Ibid.* xiii[i]. 436 Sum wær inn læwdum hade [L. *vir in laico habitu*]. *c* **1175** *Lamb. Hom.* 131 Ihadede men he muneȝeð wel to lerene ilewede men. Ihadede and lewede feier lif and clene to leden. *c* **1290** *Beket* 574 in *S. Eng. Leg.* I. 123 ȝif bi-twene tweie lewede men were ani striuingue, Oþur bi-tuene a lewed man and a clerk. *a* **1300** *Cursor M.* 26143 If þou mai no preist to wine, þus scau a leud [*Fairf.* lawed] man þi sine. **13..** *Minor Poems fr. Vernon MS.* 269 Hit wol a-vayle boþe lewed and clerk. **1382** WYCLIF *1 Sam.* xxi. 4, I haue not leeuyd loouys [Vulg. *laicos panes*] at hoond, but oonli hooli breed. *c* **1386** CHAUCER *Prol.* 502 For if a preest be foul, on whom we truste No wonder is a lewed man to ruste. *c* **1400** MAUNDEV. (Roxb.) xiii, 60 Þai hafe þaire crownes schauen, þe clerkes rownde and þe lawed men foure cornerd. **1530** LYNDESAY *Test. Papyngo* 1002 Lawit men hes, now, religious men in curis. **1553** BECON *Reliques of Rome* (1563) 246* Al thoe bene accused that purchasen writtes or letters of any leude courte. **1819** W. TENNANT *Papistry Storm'd* (1827) 212 The hail o' them, by lawit fists, Were haurl'd and howkit frae their kists.

†**b.** ***lewd frere***, a lay-brother. *Obs.*

c **1380** WYCLIF *Wks.* (1880) 41 Late lewid freris seie four & twenti pater nostris for matynes. *c* **1425** *St. Eliz. of Spalbech* in *Anglia* VIII. 116/30 Wee .. made hym a conuers, þat is to seye, a lewde frere. *c* **1483** CAXTON *Dialogues* vii. 24 Bogars, lewd freris. **1530** PALSGR. 239/1 Leude frere, *bovrdican.*

†**2.** Unlearned, unlettered, untaught. *Obs.*

a **1225** *Juliana* 2 Alle lewede [*v.r.* leawede] men þat understonden ne mahen latines ledene. *a* **1300** *Cursor M.* 249 To laud and Inglis man i spell þat understandes þat i tell. *c* **1325** *Poem temp. Edw. II* (Percy) xix, Then is a lewed priest No better than a jay. **1362** LANGL. *P. Pl.* A. I. 125 Lereþ hit þis lewed men for lettrede hit knoweþ. *c* **1430** *Art of Nombryng* (E.E.T.S.) 3 This boke is called þe boke of algorym, or Augrym after lewder vse. *c* **1460** *Towneley Myst.* vii. 143 Both to lawd man and to clark. **1513** DOUGLAS *Æneis* Pref. 412, I say nocht this of Chaucer for offence Bot till excuse my lawit insuffitience. **1536** BELLENDEN *Cron. Scot.* (1821) I. 224, I have maid this translation mair for pleseir of lawit men, than any vane curius clerkis. **1589** PUTTENHAM *Eng. Poesie* I. i. (Arb.) 21 Making .. the poore man rich, the lewd well learned, the coward couragious. **1601** HOLLAND *Pliny* I. 31 Much adoe there is here, and great debate betweene learned men; and contrariwise those of the leaud and ignorant multitude.

†**b.** *absol.*, esp. in the phrases ***learned*** (or ***lered***) ***and lewed***, ***lewed and clerks***. *Obs.*

c **1200** ORMIN 967 And mikell hellpe to þe follc, to læredd & to læwedd. *c* **1205** LAY. 31830 Quelen þa lareden, quelen þa leouweden. *c* **1320** *Sir Beues* 4020 (MS. A.) ȝong and elde, lewed and lered. *c* **1400** *Destr. Troy* 4424 And for the case is vnknowen be course to þe lewd, Here sumwhat I say. *c* **1470** HARDING *Chron.* CCXLI. vi, Thei bee as manly, learned and lewed, As any folke. **1529** MORE *Dyaloge* III. Wks. 224/2 The Jewes bee not letted to reade theyr law bothe learned & lewde. *a* **1568** ASCHAM *Scholem.* I. (Arb.) 45 This, lewde and learned, by common experience, know to be most trewe.

†**c.** Of speech and the like: Rude, artless.

c **1425** LYDG. *Assembly of Gods* 403 Othyr mynstrall had they none, safe Pan gan to carpe Of hys lewde bagpype. **1513** DOUGLAS *Æneis* I. Prol. 21 With bad harsk speche and lewit barbour tong. **1560** ROLLAND *Crt. Venus* Prol. 326 For commoun folk will call the [this book] lawit and lidder.

†**3.** Belonging to the lower orders; common, low, vulgar, 'base'. *Obs.* (In the latest quot. used *arch.* with allusion to sense 7.)

c **1380** WYCLIF *Serm.* Sel. Wks. I. 40 Sum tyme weren mounkes lewede men, as seintis in Jerusalem. *c* **1386** CHAUCER *Pars. T.* ¶408 (Harl. MS.) Þe secounde is to chese þe lewedest [*other MSS.* lowest, loweste] place ouer al. *c* **1394** *P. Pl. Crede* 568 He loueþ .. lowynge of lewed men in Lentenes tyme. *c* **1470** HENRY *Wallace* XI. 266 Rewid in his mynd at it was hapnyt sa, Sa lewd a deid to lat him wndyrta. **1548** W. PATTEN *Exped. Scot.* Hij b, Howbeit hereby I cannot count ony lost whear but a fewe leude souldiers ran rashely out of array without standard or Captayn. **1552** LYNDESAY *Monarche* 5339 Rychtso the sterris thay do compare To the lawd common populare. **1598** BARRET *Theor. Warres* II. i. 25 Many men .. shall you see in a lewd Ale house. **1612** DAVIES *Why Ireland*, etc. (1787) 173 The march-law, which in the statutes of Kilkenny, is said to be no law, but a lewd custom. **1640** YORKE *Union Hon.* 252 Robert Riddesdale, Captaine of the lewd people in Northamptonshire. [**1796** BURKE *Regic. Peace* i. Wks. VIII. 179 A lewd tavern for the revels and debauches of banditti, assassins, bravos, smugglers, and their more desperate paramours.]

†**4.** Ignorant (implying a reproach); foolish, unskilful, bungling; ill-bred, ill-mannered. *Obs.*

c **1380** WYCLIF *Wks.* (1880) 409 Þis is þe lewiderste fendis skile þat euere cam out of his leesingis. *c* **1386** CHAUCER *Merch. T.* 1031 Ye men shul been as lewed as gees. *a* **1420** HOCCLEVE *De Reg. Princ.* 3864, I am as lewed and dulle as is an asse. *c* **1440** *Gesta Rom.* viii. 21 (Harl. MS.) Þes too knyȝtis .. þe wise knyȝt and þe lewde. *c* **1449** PECOCK *Repr.* v. ii. 488 A lewder and febler skile or argument can noman make. **1509** BARCLAY *Shyp of Folys* (1874) I. 60 Alas the Shepherd is lewder than the shepe. **1522** *World & Child* (Roxb. Club) Cij b, Ye, I praye the, leue thy lewde claterynge. *a* **1568** ASCHAM *Scholem.* I. (Arb.) 18 The small discretion of many leude Scholemasters. **1570** *Homilies* II. *Agst. Wilful Rebell.* IV. (1859) 581 Not those wounds which are printed in a clout by some lewd painter. **1603** KNOLLES *Hist. Turks* (1621) 961 Amurath .. rated them all exceedingly, reproving their lewd counsell. **1620** J. WILKINSON *Coroners & Sherifes* 75 A lewd or an ignorant undersheriff may both undoe his high Sherife and himselfe. *a* **1639** MARMION *Antiquary* II. i. (1641) D 1 b, I might have .. gone on In the lewd way of loving you. **1710** PHILIPS *Pastorals* ii. 73 A lewd Desire strange Lands and Swains to know.

†**5.** Of persons, their actions, etc.: Bad, vile, evil, wicked, base; unprincipled, ill-conditioned; good-for-nothing, worthless, 'naughty'. *Obs.*

c **1386** CHAUCER *Manciple's T.* 80 The lewedeste wolf þat she may fynde Or leest of reputacion. **1413** *Pilgr. Sowle* (Caxton 1483) III. viii. 55 Al be hit that for somtyme theyr lewd lyf displesid to them seluen. *c* **1481** E. PASTON in *P. Lett.* III. 279 Plese zow .. to forgeve me, and also my wyffe of owr leude offence that we have not don ower dute. **1538** STARKEY *England* I. iv. 139 Every lude felow, now-a-days, and idul lubbur, that can other rede or syng, makyth hymselfe prest. **1569** GOLDING *Heminges Post.* Ded. 2 The Scripture accounted him a leude seruant, that hidde his Talent in the ground. **1581** SAVILE *Tacitus, Hist.* I. lxxxiii. (1591) 46 A state gotten by lewde meanes [L. *scelere quæsitum*] cannot be retayned. *a* **1607** MARKHAM in *Topsell's Four-f. Beasts* 415 If the Smith that driueth such a naile be so lewd, as he wil not looke vnto it before the horse depart. **1611** BIBLE *Acts* xvii. 5 Certaine lewd fellowes [Gr. ἄνδρας πονηρούς] of the baser sort. **1633** T. STAFFORD *Pac. Hib.* I. viii. 58 Dermond O'Conner hath played a lewd part amongst us heere. **1667** MILTON *P.L.* IV. 193 So since into his Church lewd Hirelings climbe. **1698** FRYER *Acc. E. India & P.* 169 To desist from his lewd Courses of Robbing and Stealing. **1709** J. JOHNSON *Clergym. Vade M.* II. p. c, So the lewd boy when he had set his mother's house on fire because she had corrected him .. cried out [etc.]. [**1829** SOUTHEY *Sir T. More* (1831) I. 97 If not ashamed to beg, too lewd to work, and ready for any kind of mischief.]

†**6.** Of things: Bad, worthless, poor, sorry.

1362 LANGL. *P. Pl.* A. I. 163 Chastite withouten Charite .. Is as lewed as a Laumpe þat no liht is Inne. *c* **1430** LYDG. *Min. Poems* (Percy Soc.) 115 Hys merthys wer but lewed, He was so sore dred of dethe. **1462** *Paston Lett.* II. 107 He hathe here of Avereyes xxiiij. tune wyn, whereof at the long wey he shal make the seyd Averey a lewd rekenyng. **1575** CHURCHYARD *Chippes* (1817) 107 For this assault, lewd ladders, vile and nought The souldiours had, which were to shorte God wot. **1581** T. HOWELL *Deuises* (1879) 245 Ne lewde is he on whom lewde luck doth light. **1596** SHAKS. *Tam. Shr.* IV. iii. 65 A Veluet dish: Fie, fie, 'tis lewd and filthy. **1618** FLETCHER *Loyal Subj.* III. iii, I love thy face .. Tis a lewd one, So truely ill Art cannot mend it. **1678** MRS. BEHN *Sir Patient Fancy* I. i, Then, Madam, I write the lewdest hand. **1692** R. L'ESTRANGE *Josephus, Antiq.* I. xvi. (1733) 21 His way lay through Macedonia .. which .. is a lewd and incommodious Passage for Travellers.

7. [Developed from 5.] Lascivious, unchaste. (The surviving sense.)

c **1386** CHAUCER *Miller's Prol.* 37 Lat be thy lewed dronken harlotrye. *c* **1430** *Freemasonry* 620 In holy churche lef nyse wordes Of lewed speche, and fowle wordes. **1551** ROBINSON tr. *More's Utop.* II. vi. (1895) 195 The peruerse and malicious flickeringe inticementes of lewde and vnhoneste desyres. **1594** SHAKS. *Rich. III*, III. vii. 72 He is not lulling on a lewd Loue-Bed. **1602** WARNER *Alb. Eng.* X. lix. (1612) 259 Lewde Ammon, thou didst lust in deede, and then thy Rape reiect. **1634** MILTON *Comus* 465 When lust .. by leud and lavish act of sin Lets in defilement to the inward parts. **1682** BURNET *Rights Princes* v. 176 Being a lewd and vicious Prince, who had delivered himself up to his pleasures. **1712** ARBUTHNOT *John Bull* IV. i, He had been seen in the company of lewd women. **1759** JOHNSON *Idler* No. 38 ¶12 The lewd inflame the lewd. **1838** LYTTON *Leila* I. iv, Their harlot songs. and their dances of lewd delight. **1871** R. ELLIS tr. *Catullus* lxiv. 147 If once lewd pleasure attain unruly possession. **1883** OUIDA *Wanda* I. 296 A singer of lewd songs.

†**lewdhede.** *Obs. rare*$^{-1}$. In 5 lewidheed. [See -HEAD, HEDE 2.] Ignorance; = LEWDNESS 1.

1401 *Pol. Poems* (Rolls) II. 75 A, Iak, mafey, me merveilith moche of thin lewidheed.

lewdly ('ljuːdlɪ), *adv.* [f. LEWD *a.* + -LY^{2}.]

†**1.** In unlearned fashion; ignorantly; foolishly.

c **1380** WYCLIF *Wks.* (1880) 289 Her-to þei leggen but lewydly goddis lawe. *c* **1386** CHAUCER *Sec. Nun's T.* 430 Ye han bigonne your question folily .. ; ye axed lewedly. *c* **1449** PECOCK *Repr.* III. xix. 415 And so thilk opinioun .. was take childeli and lewidli. **1477** NORTON *Ord. Alch.* ii. in Ashm. (1652) 28 Theie lewdly beleeve every Conclusion.

†**2.** Wickedly, evilly, vilely, mischievously.

1382 WYCLIF *2 Macc.* ix. 2 Antiochus after the fliȝt loodly [1388 viliche; Vulg. *turpiter*] turnyde aȝein. **1501** DOUGLAS *Pal. Hon.* I. 149 Our wit aboundit and vsit was lewdlie. **1561** T. NORTON *Calvin's Inst.* IV. 27 In this they most lewdly corrupte the olde institution. **1593** SHAKS. *2 Hen. VI*, II. i. 167 A sort of naughtie persons, lewdly bent. **1596** SPENSER *State Irel.* Wks. (Globe) 675/2, I thinke they are most lewdly abused. **1600** HOLLAND *Livy* I. xlix. 34 Fearing .. that he had given an ill precedent for others, to take vantage against himselfe, attaining to the crown so leaudly. **1653** H. COGAN tr. *Pinto's Trav.* iv. 9 The goods you have so lewdly gotten by your wicked and cunning devices. **1667** MILTON *P.L.* VI. 182 Thy self not free, but to thy self enthrall'd; Yet leudly dar'st our ministring upbraid.

†**3.** Badly, poorly, ill. ***to think lewdly of***, to have a poor opinion of. *Obs.*

c **1386** CHAUCER *Manciple's Prol.* 59 Bycause drynke hath dominacion Vpon this man, .. I trowe he lewedly wolde telle his tale. **1596** SPENSER *State Irel.* Wks. (Globe) 621/1 Those sayd gentellmens children, being thus in the ward of those Lordes, are .. therby brought up lewdly, and Irish-like. **1673** DRYDEN *Assignation* I. i, For his Violin, it squeaks so lewdly, that Sir Tibert in the gutter mistakes him for his Mistriss. **1678** MRS. BEHN *Sir Patient Fancy* II. i, I'll make such aukward love as shall persuade her .. to think most lewdly of my parts.

4. Lasciviously.

1608 SHAKS. *Per.* IV. ii. 156 As my giuing out her beautie stirs vp the lewdly enclined. **1621** QUARLES *Esther* v. E 3 b, Each Virgin keepes her turne, and all the night They lewdly lauish in the Kings delight. **1624** HEYWOOD *Gunaik.* IV. 169 This Macareus and Canace having most leaudly and incestuously loved one another. **1871** R. ELLIS tr. *Catullus* xv. 5 Touch not lewdly the mistress of my passion.

lewdness ('ljuːdnɪs). [See -NESS.]

†**1.** Ignorance; want of skill, knowledge, or good-breeding; foolishness. *Obs.*

1362 LANGL. *P. Pl.* A. III. 33 Schal no lewednesse hem lette, þe lewedeste þat I loue, þat he ne worþ avaunset. *c* **1386** CHAUCER *Melib. Prol.* 3 Thou makest me So wery of thy verray lewednesse. **1387** TREVISA *Higden* (Rolls) VII. 299 Among his oþer lewednes and folie. *c* **1440** *Promp. Parv.* 301/2 Lewdenesse of clergy, *illitteratura*. *c* **1440** *Gesta Rom.* viii. 21 (Harl. MS.), I am a foole, And he is a wise man, And þerfore he shold not so liȝtely haue levid my lewdenesse. **1540** HYRDE *Vives' Instr. Chr. Wom.* (1592) R vj, What a lewdnesse is it, not to consider how vaine a thing that money is. **1563** *Homilies* II. *Agst. Images* III. (1859) 265 There is like foolishness and lewdness in decking of our images. **1576** FLEMING *Panopl. Ep.* 80 That is supposed a loose kinde of writing, to talke of any man unreverently, for therein is leudnesse discovered.

†**2.** Wickedness; evil behaviour. *Obs.*

1387 TREVISA *Higden* (Rolls) VI. 239 So it is greet lewednesse and wrecchednesse to forgendre what is detty and riȝtful. *c* **1460** SIR R. ROS *La Belle Dame sanz Mercy* 607 (655) That to þe werste turneth by his leudenesse a yifte of grace. **1563** *Homilies* II. *Repentance* II. (1859) 541 When any thing ordained of God is by the lewdness of men abused. **1579** FULKE *Refut. Rastell* 736 It is great leudenesse and deceiptfulnes to vrge the termes vsed by the doctors. **1613** PURCHAS *Pilgrimage* (1614) 321 The leaudnesse of the Cappadocians grew into a Proverbe; if any were enormously wicked, he was therefore called a Cappadocian. **1623** BINGHAM *Xenophon* 99 What Citie, as friend, will receiue vs, when they see such lewdnesse in our conuersation?

3. Lasciviousness, lascivious behaviour.

1579 LYLY *Euphues* (Arb.) 44 A perfect wit is never bewitched with leaudenesse neither entised with lasciviousnesse. *a* **1592** H. SMITH *Serm* (1614) 568 If harlots intice thee to leaudnesse, .. flie from them. **1661** PEPYS *Diary* 17 Aug., The lewdnesse and beggary of the Court. **1685** H. MORE *Illustrat.* 155 Their gross idolatries and sensual Ludenesses. **1754** SHERLOCK *Disc.* (1759) I. iv. 145 The Lewdness of their History renders it unfit to be narrated. **1769** BLACKSTONE *Comm.* IV. iv. 64 The last offence which I shall mention .. is that of open and notorious lewdness; either by frequenting houses of ill-fame .. or by some grossly scandalous and public indecency.

†**lewdsby.** *Obs.* [f. LEWD *a.*: cf. *rudesby*, etc.] A lewd person.

1594 O. B. *Quest. Profit. Concernings* 31 b, Such mechanicall lewdsbies are said to get more sleeping, then others can do waking.

'**lewdster.** *rare.* [See -STER.] = prec.

1598 SHAKS. *Merry W.* V. iii. 23 Against such Lewdsters, and their lechery, Those that betray them do no treachery. **1839** J. ROGERS *Antipopopr.* XIV. ii. 307 To play the lewdster with their female confitents.

†**lewe**, *a.* [Adjectival use of OE. *lǽwa* traitor, betrayer.] Treacherous.

c **1000** *Ags. Gosp.* Luke vi. 16 Iudam scarioð se wæs læwa [*Lindisf.* hleȝa]. *c* **1175** *Lamb. Hom.* 7 Þeos world is whilende and ontful and swiðe lewe an swincful.

lewe, obs. f. or var. LEAVE, LEVE, LIVE.

-lewe, ME. *suffix*, OE. *-lǽwe*, forming a few adjectives: OE. *hungorlǽwe*, ME. *chekelewe, chokelewe, costlewe, drunk(e)lewe, gastlewe, siklewe, thurstlewe*. The general sense is 'affected by, liable to, or characterized by' (something undesirable); in some of the instances above there are parallel and synonymous formations in -LY[1]. The etymology is obscure, no corresponding suffix being known in any other Teut. lang.; connexion with Goth. *lêw*, occasion, may be suspected; cf. also LEW *a.*[2]

1433 LYDG. *St. Edmund* II. 223 His wounde bloody, his face ded and pale, His eyen gastlewh reuersid bothe tweyne.

lewer: see LEVER, LOUVER, LURE.

lewes, obs. pl. of LEAF.

lewge, obs. form of LEAGUE *sb.*[1]

lewgh, obs. pa. t. of LAUGH.

lewidore, obs. form of LOUIS D'OR.

lewine, -ing, obs. forms of LIVING.

lewine, lewint: see LEVEN, -TH[1] (eleven, -th).

lewis ('luːɪs), *sb.*[1] Also **lewiss, louis, luis.** [Of obscure origin; possibly f. *Lewis* or *Louis* as a surname or Christian name. A dial. form *levis* (*Whitby Gloss.* 1876) suggests connexion with F. *lever* to raise; but the formation and the phonology are not easily explained on this hypothesis.] An iron contrivance for raising heavy blocks of stone. Also called LEWISSON.

It consists of three pieces arranged so as to form a dovetail, the outside pieces being fixed in a dovetail mortise by the insertion of the middle piece. The three pieces are then connected together by the pin of the clevis passing through them.

1743 W. STUKELEY in *Bibl. Topogr. Brit.* (1790) III. 387 At each extremity a stone of Arthur's Oon to be suspended by the lewis in the hole of them. **1793** SMEATON *Edystone L.* §39 The instrument we now call the Lewis, is of an old date. **1816** *Chron.* in *Ann. Reg.* 93/2 [They] succeeded in boring the stone securing a lewiss and making fast a purchase for heaving it up. **1851** *Illustr. Catal. Gt. Exhib.* 317 Speedy louis, invented to expedite the hoisting of light stones in the erection of buildings. **1883** *Stonemason* Jan., A chain attached to a pair of lewises fixed in the face of the rock, and worked by a crane.

b. *attrib.*: **lewis-bolt**, 'a wedge-shaped bolt secured in its socket by lead, and used as a lewis in lifting' (Knight *Dict. Mech.* 1875); **lewis-hole**, the hole into which a lewis is fitted.

1740 PINEDA *Sp. Dict.*, *Impleóla*..by us call'd a Luis hole. **1742** *De Foe's Tour Gt. Brit.* (ed. 3) II. 254 The Lewis-holes are still left in many of the Stones. **1893** *Reliquary* Jan. 13 The..walls are almost, if not entirely, of Roman worked stone. Cramp holes and grooves, lewis holes, and broached tooling are everywhere visible.

lewis ('luːɪs), *sb.*[2] [f. the name of the inventor.] 'The name of one kind of shears used in cropping woollen cloth' (Ure *Dict. Arts* 1839).

In mod. Dicts.

Lewis ('luːɪs), *sb.*[3] [f. the name of the inventor, Col. Isaac Newton *Lewis* (1858–1931) of the U.S. Army.] In full, ***Lewis (machine) gun.*** A light, magazine-fed, gas-operated, and air-cooled machine gun. So **Lewis-gunner** and other *attrib.* and *Comb.* uses.

1913 *Aeroplane* 4 Dec. 606 The Lewis Machine-Gun. **1914** E. A. POWELL *Fighting in Flanders* iii. 72 The Lewis gun..is air-cooled. **1916** *War Illustr.* V. 11/2 Lewis gun-team. **1917** *Ibid.* VI. 466 A 'Lewis' gunner. **1919** *King's Royal Rifle Corps Chron. 1916* 81 Stokes mortars and Lewis gun fire subdued the enemy's resistance. **1923** KIPLING *Irish Guards in Gt. War* I. 134 Strong training at bombing and Lewis-gunnery. **1926** T. E. LAWRENCE *Seven Pillars* (1935) xv. 104 If we strengthened them by light automatic guns of the Lewis type..they might be capable of holding their hills. **1937** *Granta* 3 Feb. 219/1 Memories of John taking command of two Lewis gun crews in a dispersal under barrage fire. **1946** [see BREN]. **1964** H. L. PETERSON *Encycl. Firearms* 190/1 The Lewis machine gun..was the first machine gun ever fired from an airplane (1912), and it was adapted for ground and naval use as well. **1974** M. BUTTERWORTH *Man in Sopwith Camel* vi. 58 Flip the cocking handles of the twin Lewises.

Lewis ('luːɪs), *sb.*[4] *Chem.* [The name of Gilbert Newton *Lewis* (1875–1946), U.S. chemist, who introduced the concepts.] ***Lewis acid***, any compound or ionic species which can accept an electron pair from a donor compound; similarly ***Lewis base***, one which can donate an electron pair to an acceptor compound.

1944 I. M. KOLTHOFF in *Jrnl. Physical Chem.* XLVIII. 54 The following terminology is suggested. Acids which satisfy the Lewis definition are called Lewis acids or proto-acids. **1961** G. R. CHOPPIN *Exper. Nuclear Chem.* ix. 148 Ketones, ethers and many other oxygen containing organic solvents may act as Lewis bases. **1962** COTTON & WILKINSON *Adv. Inorg. Chem.* x. 179 Various Lewis bases, such as amines, phosphines, ethers, and sulfides, form 1:1 complexes with BX_3 compounds. *Ibid.* 180 There is good evidence that the relative strengths of the boron halides as Lewis acids are in the order $BBr_3 \geqq BCl_3 > BF_3$. **1969** LOWRIE & CAMPBELL-FERGUSON *Inorg. & Physical Chem.* xix. 219/2 All Brønsted acids and bases are also Lewis acids and bases respectively. However, the term Lewis acid can be applied to substances which do not contain protons and are not therefore Brønsted acids. **1973** J. J. LAGOWSKI *Mod. Inorg. Chem.* xiv. 522 Cationic halogen species can be stabilized by Lewis bases.

lewis ('luːɪs), *v.* [f. LEWIS *sb.*[1]] *trans.* To fasten by means of, or after the manner of, a lewis.

1837 *Civil Engin. & Arch. Jrnl.* I. 72/1 When the stone is broken..it is separated on the bed by a very large iron crowbar or gavelock, and this is either lewised or chained, and raised by the large crane or 'gin'. **1883** *Proc. Assoc. Municipal Engin.* IX. 88 The only ties are wrought-iron 'lewis' bolts, 'lewised' into the old arch stones and turned down and cemented into the new ones.

lewis, obs. pl. of LEAF; obs. f. LOUIS.

lewisia (luːˈɪzɪə, -ˈɪsɪə). [mod.L. (F. Pursh *Flora Americæ Septentrionalis* (1814) II. 368), f. the name of Meriwether *Lewis* (1774–1809), American explorer + -IA[1].] A small perennial herb of the genus so called, belonging to the family Portulacaceæ, native to western North America, and bearing solitary or clustered pink or white flowers and leaves arranged in a rosette at ground level.

1863 *Curtis's Bot. Mag.* LXXXIX. 5395 (*heading*) Spatlum, or Reviving Lewisia. **1917** C. F. SAUNDERS *Western Flower Guide* 52 The large root of *Lewisia* is a conspicuous feature. **1961** *Amat. Gardening* 23 Dec. 2 The alpine gardener could feast on the roots of his lewisias. **1963** *Times* 11 May 11/5 Lewisias have come through with flying colours. **1974** J. BERRISFORD *Window Box & Container Gardening* vii. 60 In peaty composts..one might try.. beautiful lewisias.

Lewisian (luːˈɪsɪən), *a. Geol.* [f. *Lewis*, name of the northern section of the largest island of the Outer Hebrides + -IAN.] Of, pertaining to, or characteristic of Lewis: applied to the earlier of the two main groups of Pre-Cambrian rocks in NW. Scotland. Also *absol.*, the Lewisian rocks or strata.

1859 R. I. MURCHISON in *Q. Jrnl. Geol. Soc.* XVI. 240 If this most ancient gneiss required a British name, it might indeed with propriety be termed the 'Lewisian System', seeing that the large island of the Lewis is essentially composed of it..; but the term 'Laurentian' having been already applied to rocks of this age in North America by our distinguished associate Sir W. Logan, I adhere to that name. **1887**, **1911** [see HEBRIDEAN *a.* and *sb.*]. **1938** A. K. WELLS *Outl. Hist. Geol.* vi. 49 The dykes can be followed right up to the junction of the Lewisian with the Torridonian. **1943** *Jrnl. R. Anthrop. Inst.* LXXIII. 75/1 The inconceivably old Lewisian rocks of the north-west Highlands. **1957** G. E. HUTCHINSON *Treat. Limnol.* I. i. 57 Peach and Horne (1910) record many irregular basins formed in this way on the Lewisian gneiss of the western seaboard of Sutherland and Ross, and also in the Outer Hebrides.

lewisite[1] ('luːɪsaɪt). *Min.* [f. the name of W. J. *Lewis* (1847–1926), British mineralogist + -ITE[1].] An antimonate and titanate of calcium, iron, and sodium, $(Ca,Fe,Na)_2(Sb,Ti)_2O_7$, which is found as small yellow to yellowish brown octahedral crystals and may be regarded as a titanian romeite.

1895 HUSSAK & PRIOR in *Mineral. Mag.* XI. 83 We have given the name of Lewisite to this new titano-antimonate from Brazil in honour of Prof. W. J. Lewis, during whose tenure of office the study of Mineralogy in the University of Cambridge has been so much encouraged. **1932** *Mineral. Abstr.* V. 185 Lewisite is a cubic mineral, whose composition is probably $(Ca,Fe,Na)_2(Sb,Ti)_2(O,OH)_7$. **1951** C. PALACHE et al. *Dana's Syst. Min.* (ed. 7) II. 1022 Romeite... In Minas Geraes, Brazil, with cinnabar in eluvial sands at Tripuhy near Ouro Preto (lewisite).

Lewisite[2] ('luːɪsaɪt). Also **lewisite.** [f. the name of Winford Lee *Lewis* (1878–1943), U.S. chemist + -ITE[1].] A dark oily liquid (colourless when pure) which is a powerful respiratory irritant and causes painful blisters on contact with the skin; 2-chlorovinyldichloroarsine, $ClCH{:}CHAsCl_2$.

1921 FRIES & WEST *Chem. Warfare* ii. 23 One of the most interesting and valuable of the compounds which would have found extensive use had the War continued, is an arsenic compound called Lewisite. **1923** R. F. HORTON *Mystical Quest of Christ* xxi. 223 A new poison gas, called by the barbarous name Lewisite, is of such potency that, released over London by twenty or thirty aeroplanes, it would asphyxiate the whole population in three or four hours. **1937** A. HUXLEY *Ends & Means* xii. 216 In 1937 the 'instrument of God for the protection of the people' was all the armaments existing in 1914..plus arsenic smokes, plus Lewisite. **1938** *Times* 12 Jan. 11/6 There are probably millions of people..who do not realize..that the much discussed lewisite can be dealt with by a scrubbing brush and soap, if treated quickly. **1943** [see *B.A.L.* s.v. B III]. **1970** *Amer. Rev. Respiratory Dis.* CII. 173 Almost one half of the men who had been exposed repeatedly to mustard gas or lewisite before 1945 had a persistent productive cough.

Lewisman ('luːɪsmən). [f. *Lewis* + MAN *sb.*[1]] A native or inhabitant of Lewis, the northern section of the island of Lewis with Harris in the Outer Hebrides.

1927 [see FIFER[2]]. **1938** L. MACNEICE *I crossed Minch* i. 4 Drinking beer with some Lewismen while one of them sang a love-song in Gaelic. **1971** *Stornoway Gaz.* 10 July 4/1 The initiative for advancing the prosperity of Lewis must come from the Lewisman himself.

lewisson. Also (? *erron.*) **lewising.** = LEWIS *sb.*[1]

1842–59 GWILT *Archit.* Gloss. (ed. 4), Lewis or Lewisson. **1851** *Illustr. Catal. Gt. Exhib.* 328 This breakwater is moored by lewising bolts [etc.]. **1864** in WEBSTER.

lewistonite ('luːɪstənaɪt). *Min.* [f. *Lewiston*, the name of the city in Utah, U.S.A., near which it was found + -ITE[1].] A basic phosphate of calcium, potassium, and sodium, $(Ca,K,Na)_5(PO_4)_3(OH)$, found as colourless to pale green hexagonal crystals; potassian hydroxyapatite.

1930 LARSEN & SHANNON in *Amer. Mineralogist* XV. 326 Some of the hexagonal prisms which are very much like the dehrnite have less alkali and much more water. Chemically they are so different from dehrnite as to give them species rank and the name lewistonite is proposed after Lewiston, Utah. **1942** *Ibid.* XXVII. 297 Lewistonite..shows wide variation in its properties. Stout hexagonal crystals associated with oolites of pseudowavellite are divided into six biaxial negative segments. **1968** I. KOSTOV *Mineral.* II. ix. 458 Dehrnite and lewistonite for alkali-bearing apatites.

lewit, obs. Sc. form of LEWD.

lewke, obs. form of LEAGUE, LUKE.

†**Lewkes.** *Obs.* [ad. Flem. *Luiksch* adj., f. *Luik* Liège.] Epithet of wares made at Liège.

1547 BOORDE *Introd. Knowl.* xii. (1870) 155 The cheefe towne is the cytie of Lewke; there is Lewkes veluet made, and cloth of Arys. **1550–1600** *Customs Duties* (B.M. Add. MS. 25097), Iron, voc. Lewkes or Spruse iron.

lewme, obs. form of LEAM *sb.*[1]

lewn. *dial.* Also 7 **leaune**, 9 **leun, lune.** [Of obscure origin.] A tax or rate, *esp.* a church-rate.

1582 in MISS JACKSON *Shropsh. Word-bk.* **1642** *Bridgnorth Rec.* in *10th Rep. Hist. MSS. Comm.* App. IV. 429 [Order] concerning a lewn lately laid by the Bayliffes towardes the charge of coales and candles for his Majesties army. **1690** (leaune), **1776**, **1840** in MISS JACKSON *Shropsh. Word-bk.* **1886** in *Cheshire Gloss.* (lewne, leun, lune, leur).

lewne, variant of LUNE, falcon's leash.

†**'lewness**[1]. *Obs. rare*$^{-1}$. [f. LEWE *a.* + -NESS.] Treacherousness.

c **1175** *Lamb. Hom.* 21 Summe of us for þisse weorlde lewnesse..ne maȝen alre coste halden crist bibode.

†**'lewness**[2]. *Obs. rare*$^{-0}$. [f. LEW *a.*[2] + -NESS.] Paleness, lividity.

1611 COTGR., *Lividité*, liuiditie, lewnesse, wannesse, bleakenesse, palenesse, blewishnesse.

lewre, var. LEER *sb.*[1] *Obs.*; obs. f. LURE.

lewse, obs. form of LOOSE, LUCE.

lewte, obs. f. LUTE; var. LEWTY, LOUT *v.*

lewtennand, obs. Sc. form of LIEUTENANT.

lewter, obs. form of LOITER.

lewth (luːθ). Now *dial.* Also 6 **lothe.** [OE. *hléowþ, hlýwð*, f. *hléow* LEW *a.*[1]: see -TH[1].]

a. Warmth. **b.** Shelter (cf. *house-lewth*, HOUSE 24).

c **1000** *Hexam. St. Basil* xx. (1849) 28 Ðonne him cælð he cepð him hlywðe. *c* **1000** ÆLFRIC *Hom.* II. 144 To neste bæron, heora briddum to hleowþe. *a* **1100** *Ags. Voc.* in Wr.-Wülcker 336/31 *Apricitas*, hleowð. **1554** *Survey Malling Church* in *Sussex Arch. Coll.* XXI. 180 Cattell & swyne come daylye in to the churche, in the somer for hette, and now for lothe. **1825** BRITTON *Beauties Wilts* III. 375 Lewth, warmth. **1887** T. HARDY *Woodlanders* III. xv. 311 With the sun or against the sun, uphill or downhill, in wind or in lewth. **1898** —— *Wessex Poems* 204 In the lewth of a codlin-tree.

†**'lewtifull**, *a. Sc. Obs.* In 6 **laute-, lawti-.** [f. LEWTY + -FUL.] Loyal.

1563 WINȜET *Four Score Thre Quest.* Wks. 1888 I. 61 The lautefull and faithful peple. **1584** *Sc. Acts Jas. VI* (1814) III. 327/1 Maist loving and lawtifull subiectis to their souerane lord.

†**'lewty, 'lawty.** Chiefly *Sc. Obs.* Forms: α. 4 **leute(e, lewete, leautee,** 4–5 **leaute,** 4–6 **lewte(e,** 5 **lewted, leutye.** β. *Sc.* (4 **leawte**), 4–6 **lawte, lawty, laute,** 5 **lauta, lawta,** 5–6 **lawtie,** 6 **lautie, lawtay,** 7–8 **lata,** 8 **lawtith, lateth.** [a. AF. *leuté, lewté*, F. *leaute, lealte, lealted*, mod.F. *loyauté* (= Pr. *leyaltat, leiautat, lealtat*, Sp. *lealted*, It. *lealtà*):—med.L. *lēgālitāt-em*: see LEGALITY; cf. LOYALTY, LEALTY.] Fidelity, loyalty. Often in phr. ***by*** or ***for my, thy*** (etc.) ***lewty.***

a **1300** *Cursor M.* 1655 (Gött.) Ȝe eyth, for ȝour treu leute Alone i haue granted mi gre. *Ibid.* 12252 (Gött.) Queþen he come..I ne wate, be mi laute. **13..** *Guy Warw.* (A.) 1743 Gode man..for thi leute, What is thi name, telle thou me. **1375** BARBOUR *Bruce* I. 364 Larg and luffand als wes he, And our all thing luffyt lawte. **1422** tr. *Secreta Secret., Priv. Priv.* 144 Thay brake the lewted that Stablid was to Profite of mann and hele. **1460** *Lybeaus Disc.* 1940, I woll yelde me, In trewthe and lewte, At thyn owene wylle. *c* **1470** HENRY *Wallace* VIII. 11 Fra this tyme furth kepe lawta till our croune. *c* **1510** *Gest R. Hode* III. in Arb. *Garner* VI. 438 'Now God so me help!' said Little John, 'And be my true lewte!' **1535** STEWART *Cron. Scot.* II. 116 Ȝone on the leid that lawtie hes forlorne. *a* **1572** KNOX *Hist. Ref.* Wks. 1846

I. 354 Upoun our lautie, fidelitie, and honour. **1670** RAY *Prov.* 286 Lata is lang and tedious. **1721** KELLY *Sc. Prov.* 230 Lata is long and dwigh [*read* dreigh]. **1728** RAMSAY *Step-daughter* ii, She neither has lawtith [*ed.* 9 lateth] nor shame.

lew-warm, *a.* Now *dial.* Forms: see LEW *a.*[1]; also 6 **leau-, leuwarm.** [f. LEW *a.* (used advb.) + WARM *a.*] Lukewarm.

c **1450** *M.E. Med. Bk.* (Heinrich) 207 Hete hyt lew warm. **1486** *Bk. St. Albans* C vij b, Let it stonde and wax lew warme. **1513** DOUGLAS *Æneis* IV. xii. 81 Feche hiddir sone the well wattir lew warm. **1588** A. KING tr. *Canisius' Catech.* 134 Thay..quhilk ar idil, sleuthfull, and quhome the scripture callis leuwarme. **1596** DALRYMPLE tr. *Leslie's Hist. Scot.* x. 462 Now thair conschiences ar compellit..in thair muk to clag and fyle thame selfe, that is for the baptisme of thair saluatioune to receiue water I wat not how lue warme. **1863** READE *Hard Cash* xxiv. II. 93 Scalded dog fears lue-warm water. **1878** STEVENSON *Inland Voy.* 16 The..egg was little more than loo-warm. **1879** MISS JACKSON *Shropsh. Word-bk.*, *Lew-warm*, tepid, lukewarm.

So †**lew-warmed** *a.*, lukewarm.

1588 A. KING tr. *Canisius' Catech.* Cert. Deuot. Pray. 33 Lat thy maist mightie gudenes fulfil that quhilk my maist leauwarmed vaikenes desyres to doe.

lewxern, lewzern, obs. forms of LUCERN.

†**lewyn.** *Obs.* Also 4 **leuwyn, levyne,** 5 **lewan(e.** [f. Flemish *Leuven*, Louvain.] A kind of linen cloth.

1360 *Finchale Acc.* (Surtees) p. iii, Et xij ulnæ de leuwyn pro mappis. **1373** in *Exch. Rolls Scot.* II. 444 In empcione 35 vlnarum de levyne, varii precii, xxs. xd. **1390–1** *Earl Derby's Exp.* (Camden) 80 Et pro lewyn pro dictis torches et torticiis. **1485** *Inv.* in *Ripon Ch. Acts* (Surtees) 366 De panno lineo vocato lewan j par linthiaminum de lewane.

lewyn(e: see LEVIN.

lewyn(g, obs. Sc. form of LIVING.

lewys, obs. pl. of LEAF.

‖**lex domicilii** (lɛks dɒmɪˈsɪlɪaɪ). *Law.* [L.] The law of the country in which a person is domiciled; the determination of the rights of a person by establishing where, in law, he is domiciled.

1832 BARNEWALL & CRESSWELL *Rep. Cases King's Bench* X. 909 The lex domicilii is to be regarded, yet it is not adverted to where the domicile was when the contract was entered into. **1961** *Times* 26 Oct. 19/2 Capacity and consent were matters that fell to be decided by the *lex domicilii*. **1965** *Mod. Law Rev.* XXVIII. v. 540 Unilateral acts of divorce, for example, the *talak* under Moslem law or the Jewish *gett*, have raised important questions whether an English court would recognise these acts as divorces obtained according to the *lex domicilii* of the parties.

lexeme (ˈlɛksiːm). *Linguistics.* [f. LEX(ICON + -EME. Cf. MORPHEME.] A word-like grammatical form intermediate between morpheme and utterance, often identical with a word occurrence; a word in the most abstract sense, as a meaningful form without an assigned grammatical role; an item of vocabulary.

1940 B. L. WHORF *Lang., Thought, & Reality* (1956) 160 C. F. Voegelin has accomplished the difficult and signal work of analyzing an immense number of baffling stem compounds of Shawnee into their component lexemes (stems) and other morphemes (formatives). **1946** M. SWADESH in C. Osgood *Ling. Struct. Native Amer.* 319 Lexeme building is accomplished mainly by readaptation of lexemes, paradigmatic forms, or syntactic constructions to new uses without change of form. **1950** *Archivum Linguisticum* II. 10 Discriminating between 'word' and 'lexeme'. **1954** S. NEWMAN in H. Hoijer *Lang. in Culture* 87 It is taken for granted..that no English lexeme is a perfect semantic equivalent of a Zuni lexeme. **1958** C. F. HOCKETT *Course in Mod. Ling.* xix. 171 The lexemes in the two-word sequence *twenty-eighth* are *twenty*, *eight*, and *-th...* *Red-haired* is two words; but it is a single minimum free form, since the ICs are *red hair* (free) and *-ed* (bound); and it is three lexemes, *red*, *hair* and *-ed*. *Ibid.* 174 The definition of lexeme follows unpublished work of Bernard Bloch. **1963** *Amer. Speech* XXXVIII. 50 The meaning of *actor*, a minimum free form, is predictable from its structure, as is the meaning of *wants*, a lexeme. **1963** J. LYONS *Structural Semantics* iii. 40 Certain lexemes and expressions are quickly learnt. **1964** E. PALMER tr. *Martinet's Elem. Gen. Ling.* i. 25 A lexeme like *travaill-* is normally listed in the lexicon in the form *travailler*. **1968** J. LYONS *Introd. Theoret. Ling.* 197 The orthographic word *cut* represents three different inflexional 'forms' (i.e. three different grammatical words) of the lexeme *cut*. **1971** G. ANSRE in J. Spencer *Eng. Lang. W. Afr.* 156 If the phoneme is the minimal phonological unit and the morpheme is the minimal grammatical unit, then [the] lexeme will be the minimal lexical unit. **1971** *Archivum Linguisticum* II. 48 The view has already been expressed that words are names (of lexical items) derived from the combination of roots (or lexemes) and affixes (or morphemes). *Ibid.* 50 The concept and term of 'collocation' has to be seen partly in relation to that of 'root' or 'lexeme'.

lexemic (lɛkˈsiːmɪk), *a.* and *sb.* *Linguistics.* [f. LEXEM(E + -IC.] **A.** *adj.* Of or relating to lexemes. **B.** *sb. pl.* The branch of linguistics concerned with the study of lexemes.

1954 S. NEWMAN in H. Hoijer *Lang. in Culture* 89 The most difficult problem in this lexemic study is that of establishing valid methods. **1957** *Language* XXXIII. 588, I believe that..*all borrowing is lexemic*, i.e. a transfer of lexemes by imitation from one language into another, using 'lexeme' here to mean a free construction of one or more morphemes. **1962** E. F. HADEN et al. *Resonance-Theory for Ling.* iii. 37 The zero-resonance formula expresses the fact that in morphology *easily* and *gladly* are equivalent. Of course they can be dealt with separately in lexemics. **1963** J. LYONS *Structural Semantics* vi. 122 A definite level of analysis—phonological, .. lexemic. **1973** *Archivum Linguisticum* IV. 119 These sememic graphs..must then be converted into syntactic or 'lexemic' representations.

lexer, obs. aphetic form of ELIXIR.

a **1500** in Ashm. *Treat. Chem.* (1652) 347 After that thy Lexer ys, Be hit White or Rede I wys.

‖**lex fori** (lɛks ˈfɔəraɪ). *Law.* [L.] The law of the country in which an action is brought, as determining the nature and modes of the proceedings.

1836 H. WHEATON *Elem. Internat. Law* I. II. ii. 188 The extrinsic evidence by which the existence and terms of the contract are to be proved in a foreign tribunal is regulated by the *lex fori*. **1841** CLARK & FINNELLY *Rep. Cases Lords Appeals & Writs of Error* V. 13 The law on this point is well settled in this country, where this distinction is properly taken, that whatever relates to the remedy to be enforced, must be determined by the *lex fori*, the law of the country to the tribunals of which the appeal is made. **1960** *Times* 5 Mar. 10/2 Further the *lex fori*—English law—did not provide a cause of action and relief appropriate to the enforcement of the foreign right. **1970** *Internat. & Compar. Law Q.* XIX. 173 The Soviet system contains an extremely large number of imperative rules which impose the application of the *lex fori*.

lexic (ˈlɛksɪk), *a.* *rare.* [f. Gr. λεξικ-ός: see LEXICON.] = LEXICAL *a.*

1900 *19th Ann. Rep. U.S. Bureau Amer. Ethnol. 1897–8* 832 Primitive languages are essentially structural or morphologic; only incidentally lexic.

lexical (ˈlɛksɪkəl), *a.* [f. Gr. λεξικ-ός pertaining to words, λεξικ-όν LEXICON + -AL[1].]

1. Pertaining or relating to the words or vocabulary of a language. Often contrasted with *grammatical*. ***lexical meaning***, the meaning of a base in a paradigm, e.g. of *love* in *loves*, *loved*, *loving*, etc.; ***lexical change, class, form, item, morpheme, rule, set, unit, word*** (see quots.).

1836 CARDL. WISEMAN *Sci. & Relig.* I. ii. 71 These methods may be respectively called, lexical and grammatical comparison. **1864** PUSEY *Lect. Daniel* viii. 512 The grammatical and lexical peculiarities..which establish its late date. **1873** WHITNEY *Orient. Stud.* 7 The language of the Vedas is an older dialect varying both in its grammatical and lexical character from the classical Sanskrit. **1933** L. BLOOMFIELD *Lang.* x. 166 To contrast the purely lexical character of a linguistic form with the habits of arrangement to which it is subject, we shall speak of it as a lexical form. *Ibid.* xvi. 271 Languages with an elaborate part-of-speech system..have parallel forms with the same lexical meaning for use in different syntactic positions. *Ibid.* 277 The relative frequency of the various lexical and grammatical units (morphemes and tagmemes) in a language can be studied. **1942** BLOCH & TRAGER *Outl. Ling. Analysis* iv. 68 The meaning of the base itself..is called lexical meaning. **1951** G. A. MILLER *Lang. & Communication* iv. 89 In the Oxford English Dictionary there are nearly half a million lexical units. **1958** C. F. HOCKETT *Course in Mod. Ling.* 429 Back-formation can..lead to lexical change, in the form of new morphemes. **1962** H. C. CONKLIN in Householder & Saporta *Probl. Lexicogr.* 124 Minimally, a *lexical set* consists of all semantically contrastive lexemes which in a given, culturally relevant context share exclusively at least one defining feature. **1963** BLOOMFIELD & NEWMARK *Ling. Introd. Hist. Eng.* iv. 145 Lexical morphemes are those whose grammatical characteristics can be accounted for by identifying them as members of morphological classes. *Ibid.* vi. 257 All lexical units generated from the same grammatical unit by the same lexical rule are said to belong to a single lexical class. *Ibid.* 282 The lexical word *debtors* has the root *debt* and the affixes *-or* and *-s*. **1964** R. A. HALL *Introd. Ling.* liii. 254 Archaic features may be preserved in different lexical items in different places. **1965** N. CHOMSKY *Aspects of Theory of Syntax* ii. 85 The lexical rule..now allows us to insert *sincerity* for the first complex symbol. **1966** G. N. LEECH *Eng. in Advertising* ii. 21 There are thousands of examples of lexical items composed of a sequence of words: *put out* (= 'extinguish'). **1967** R. A. WALDRON *Sense & Sense Devel.* v. 102 A system of this kind, a limited group of words forming some kind of range or scale of mutually excluding terms is often called a *lexical set*. **1967** *Lingua* XVII. 34 Lexical words imply absence of grammatical meaning and vice versa. *Ibid.* 113 All members of the same paradigm are labeled as the same 'word' (lexical unit, lexeme). **1971** J. B. CARROLL et al. *Word Frequency Bk.* p. l, The basic color terms have often been studied as a lexical set, or semantic field. **1972** P. H. MATTHEWS *Inflectional Morphol.* ii. 11, I shall use orthographic forms in small capitals..to refer to Latin verbs *qua* lexical items.

2. Pertaining to, of the nature of, or connected, with a lexicon.

1873 *Brit. Q. Rev.* LVII. 602 All the most important grammatical, exegetical, and lexical works have been laid under tribute. **1885** *Academy* 3 Oct. 217/2 Lexical defining affords a wide scope for the application of the critical apparatus. *Ibid.* 432/2 The lexical index is, we think, too long. **1892** F. S. ELLIS (*title*) A Lexical Concordance to the Poetical Works of P. B. Shelley.

So **lexiˈcalic** *a.* *rare* = prec. 1.

1860 MARSH *Lect. Eng. Lang.* 141 The new element does not much affect the lexicalic character, but exhibits itself in the structure, the inflections and the syntax.

Hence **ˈlexicalist** and **ˈlexicalness** (see quots.).

1967 *Lingua* XVII. 35 There seem to be degrees of both 'lexicalness' and 'grammaticalness' in English. **1970** N. CHOMSKY in Jacobs & Rosenbaum *Readings Eng. Transformational Gram.* 188 We might extend the base rules to accommodate the derived nominal directly (I will refer to this as the 'lexicalist position').

lexicalize (ˈlɛksɪkəlaɪz), *v.* *Linguistics.* [f. LEXICAL *a.* + -IZE.] Usu. in *pass.* **1.** To accept into the lexicon, or vocabulary, of a language.

1937 C. E. BAZELL in *Jrnl. Eng. & Germ. Philol.* Jan. 3 But in a form early lexicalized a shortening previous to the considerable dialectal differentiation of the dialects would be in harmony with Indo-European tendencies. **1954** PEI & GAYNOR *Dict. Ling.* 122 *Lexicalize*, to incorporate a word, etc., into the lexicon of a language. **1972** A. MAKKAI *Idiom Struct. Eng.* 81 Should the morpheme *flation* become widely accepted.., it would be lexicalized, and Webster's new edition would list it. **1972** *Times Lit. Suppl.* 13 Oct. 1229/3 The uncharted waters of contemporary slang, where what appears ephemeral today may become lexicalized tomorrow, and conversely.

2. To express (a difference that is already expressed in the grammatical structure, or could be) by means of a different lexical item.

1968 J. LYONS *Introd. Theoret. Ling.* viii. 352 Consider the ..two sentences:..*Bill died*..*John killed Bill*. In such instances, we may say that the relationship of the transitive to the intransitive is 'lexicalized'.

Hence **ˈlexicalized** *ppl. a.*; also **ˌlexicaliˈzation,** the action or process of lexicalizing.

1949 *Archivum Linguisticum* I. 10 The adverb differs from a combination of noun and case by a strong tendency to lexicalisation. *Ibid.* 181 'Immotive'..or 'lexicalised' words. **1961** *Brno Studies in English* III. 28 All this richness was gradually done away with (except for a very small number of adverbial or lexicalized survivals). **1968** J. LYONS *Introd. Theoret. Ling.* viii. 369 The difference between obligatory and optional 'lexicalization' in three-place constructions. *Ibid.*, *Kill* is the 'lexicalized' two-place causative form of *die*. **1971** F. W. HOUSEHOLDER *Ling. Speculations* vii. 103 Lexicalization is here assumed to follow at least some transformations.

lexically (ˈlɛksɪkəlɪ), *adv.* [f. LEXICAL + -LY[2].] **a.** In respect of vocabulary. **b.** According to the lexicons of a language; in the manner of a lexicon.

1858 ELLICOTT *2 Thess.* iii. 5 A meaning..not lexically defensible. **1862** MARSH *Orig. Eng. Lang.* 48 The Anglo-Saxon is not grammatically or lexically identifiable with the extant remains of any continental dialect. **1866** *Contemp. Rev.* II. 148 The Psalms are lexically easier, but syntactically more difficult than Job. **1880** GINSBURG *Massorah* I. title-p., The Massorah, compiled from manuscripts alphabetically and lexically arranged.

lexico- (ˈlɛksɪkəʊ). [f. Gr. λεξικό-ς.] In some mod. linguistic terms denoting 'lexical and..', as in ***lexico-dynamics*** (see quot.); ***lexico-behavioural, -grammatical*** adjs. See also LEXICOSTATISTIC *a.*

1964 E. A. NIDA *Toward Sci. Transl.* iii. 36 Bloomfield.. sought to define the semantic value of symbols in terms of lexico-behavioral distinctiveness. **1970** LANCASTER & GILLESPIE in *Ann. Rev. Information Sci. & Technol.* V. 38 The structure and uses of a large, dynamic controlled vocabulary for one-line implementation have been discussed by Harley and Lancaster... The authors have coined the term 'lexicodynamics' to express the concept of construction, maintenance, use and change of controlled vocabularies for IR purposes. **1953** Y. R. CHAO in *Language* XXIX. 379 (*title*) Popular Chinese plant words, a descriptive lexico-grammatical study. **1964** E. A. NIDA *Toward Sci. Transl.* xi. 243 In treating such lexico-grammatical features, both form and content must be dealt with, since special forms, e.g. poetry, liturgy, parables, proverbs, epigrams and epistolary formulae, are all important factors in determining meaning. **1971** *Archivum Linguisticum* II. 42 Valéry and also Eliot spoke, I believe, of their experience of composing first the formal rhythmic frame of a poem and letting the lexical and grammatical structures follow, but there are also discernible abstract arrangements of a lexico-grammatical order.

†**lexicographal,** *a.* *Obs.* *rare.* [f. Gr. λεξικογράφος (see next) + -AL[1].] Lexicographical.

1685 *Reflect. on Baxter* 5 [It] is as fond, as to pretend to give the..Meaning,..of a Greek or Latin Author, while one is very raw and ignorant in the Lexicographal Part.

lexicographer (lɛksɪˈkɒgrəfə(r)). [f. late Gr. λεξικογράφ-ος, f. λεξικό-ν LEXICON + -γράφος writer: see -ER[1].] A writer or compiler of a dictionary.

1658 ROWLAND *Moufet's Theat. Ins.* 935 Calepine and other Lexicographers of his gang. **1665** BOYLE *Occas. Refl.* v. vii. (1675) 322 Suidas, Stephanus, Hesychius, and I know not how many Lexicographers and Scholiasts. **1755** JOHNSON, *Lexicographer*, a writer of dictionaries; a harmless drudge, that busies himself in tracing the original, and detailing the signification of words. **1811** BYRON *Hints fr. Horace* 76 Pitt has furnish'd us a word or two Which lexicographers declined to do. **1860** MACAULAY *Biog.* (1867) 104 The best lexicographer may well be content if his productions are received by the world with cold esteem. **1875** WHITNEY *Life Lang.* v. 88 We use each word as we have learned it, leaving to the lexicographer to follow up the ramifications to their source.

lexicoˈgraphian, *a.* *rare.* [f. as prec. + -IAN.] Lexicographical.

1815 W. H. IRELAND *Scribbleomania* 238 He would have produced a labour unparalleled in the annals of lexicographian literature.

lexicoˈgraphic, *a.* and *sb.* *rare.* [f. Gr. λεξικογράφος (see prec.) + -IC.] **A.** *adj.* = next. †**B.** *sb. pl.* Lexicographical writings.

1716 M. DAVIES *Athen. Brit.* III. *Crit. Hist.* 2 Pomey's Onomasticks and Tachard's Lex[ic]ographicks..are far surpass'd by our Oxford Grammar. **1816** J. GILCHRIST *Philos. Etym.* p. vii, Whether that gentleman shall choose a

lexicographic department in the field of philology. **1843** J. F. DAVIS in *Proc. Philol. Soc.* (1845) I. 59 In addition to their uses in lexicographic arrangement, these roots [etc.].

lexicographical (ˌlɛksɪkəʊˈɡræfɪkəl), *a.* [f. as prec. + -AL¹.] Pertaining to lexicography.

1791 BOSWELL *Johnson* 15 Apr. an. 1755 When they find him displaying a perfect theory of lexicographical excellence. **1882–3** SCHAFF *Encycl. Relig. Knowl.* II. 870/1 These grammatical labors [of Gesenius] did not meet with the same general favor as the lexicographical.

Hence **lexicoˈgraphically** *adv.*, with regard to lexicography.

1879 FURNIVALL *Prospectus Philol. Soc. Engl. Dict.*, To place English lexicographically in a position abreast of any modern language.

lexiˈcographist. *rare.* [f. as LEXICOGRAPHER: see -IST.] A lexicographer.

1834–43 SOUTHEY *Doctor* clxxxiv. VI. 150 The good old lexicographist, Adam Littleton. **1880** MORRIS in J. A. H. Murray *Addr. Philol. Soc.* 48 A new dictionary will no doubt follow the plan adopted by Sanskrit lexicographists.

lexicography (lɛksɪˈkɒɡrəfɪ). [f. Gr. λεξικο- LEXICON + -γραφία -GRAPHY.] The writing or compilation of a lexicon or dictionary; 'the art or practice of writing dictionaries' (J.).

1680 DALGARNO *Deaf & Dumb Man's Tutor* vii. 59, I shall therefore only make some few reflexions upon Etymology and Syntax, supposing Orthography to belong to Lexicography. **1755** JOHNSON *Dict.* Pref. B ij, Such is the fate of hapless lexicography, that not only darkness, but light, impedes and distresses it; things may be not only too little, but too much known, to be happily illustrated. **1791** BOSWELL *Johnson* (1848) 58/2 He..exerted his talents in occasional composition very different from Lexicography. **1878** *N. Amer. Rev.* CXXVII. 157 A master-work of lexicography. **1900** *Expositor* Oct. 270 Hebrew grammar and lexicography flourish a little later than Arabic grammar and lexicography.

lexicology (lɛksɪˈkɒlədʒɪ), *sb.* [f. Gr. λεξικο- LEXICON + -λογία -LOGY.] That branch of knowledge which treats of words, their form, history, and meaning. Hence **lexicoˈlogical** *a.*, pertaining to lexicology; **lexiˈcologist**, one skilled in lexicology (Ogilvie 1882); **lexicoˈlogically** *adv.*

1828–32 WEBSTER, *Lexicology* [citing *Med. Repos.*]. **1867** LANE *Arab. Lex.* Pref. 8 The vast collection of lexicons and lexicological works composed by Arabs. **1937** J. ORR tr. *Iordan's Introd. Romance Ling.* iv. 287 In some, the arbitrary character of the linguistic signs is more apparent..and these Saussure calls lexicological languages. **1949** *Jrnl. Theol. Stud.* L. 104 The fifth is devoted to doctrine; the sixth and seventh to remarks on syntax and lexicology respectively. **1952** *Archivum Linguisticum* IV. 71 Units which the application of formal and semantic criteria enables the grammarian to detach from lexicologically analysable groupings.

lexicon (ˈlɛksɪkən). [? mod.L., a. Gr. λεξικόν (sc. βιβλίον), neut. sing. of λεξικός of or for words, f. λέξι-ς diction, word, phrase, f. λεγ- to speak.]

1. a. A word-book or dictionary; chiefly applied to a dictionary of Greek, Hebrew, Syriac, or Arabic.

The restricted use is due to the fact that until recently dictionaries of these particular languages were usually in Latin, and in mod.L. *lexicon*, not *dictionarius*, has been the word generally used.

1603 SIR C. HEYDON *Jud. Astrol.* ii. 44 Any other translation or Lexicon. **1607** TOPSELL *Four-f. Beasts* ¶¶ 1 b, He doth not neglect the profit of Lexicons (wherein all sayings and speeches are numbred). **1616** BULLOKAR, *Lexicon*, a Greek Dictionarie for words. **1641** MILTON *Prel. Episc.* 6 [They] must make a new Lexicon to name themselves by. **1645** —— *Tetrach.* Wks. 1851 IV. 238 They who are so exact for the letter, shall be dealt with by the Lexicon, and the Etymologicon too if they please. *a* **1682** SIR T. BROWNE *Tracts* 85 Lexicons and Dictionaries by Zizania do almost generally understand Lolium. **1702** S. SEWALL *Diary* 30 Jan. (1879) II. 52 Upon enquiry about a Hebrew word, I found he had no Lexicon. **1791** BOSWELL *Johnson* (1848) 69/1 He thought it right in a lexicon of our language to collect many words which had fallen into disuse. **1807** *Med. Jrnl.* XVII. 49 Let Mr. D. go to his Lexicon for the word urethra. **1817** BYRON *Beppo* lii, And take for rhyme, to hook my rambling verse on, The first that Walker's Lexicon unravels. **1847** LIDDELL & SCOTT (*title*) A Greek-English Lexicon.

b. *fig.* (*a*) The vocabulary proper to some department of knowledge or sphere of activity; the vocabulary or word-stock of a region, a particular speaker, etc. (*b*) A list of words or names.

1647 COWLEY *Mistress, Discretion* 66 This barbarous Term you will not meet In all Love's Lexicon. **1656** —— *Pindar. Odes, to Dr. Scarborough* iii, The vast and barbarous Lexicon Of Mans Infirmitie. **1654** WHITLOCK *Zootomia* 419 Fate, or Fortune, (in the Profane Lexicon, and in the Christians undiscovered Providence). **1724** SWIFT *Use Irish Manuf.* Wks. 1755 V. II. 3 All silks, velvets, callicoes, and the whole lexicon of female fopperies. **1751** EARL ORRERY *Remarks Swift* (1752) 25 Such, who, in the Lexicon of Party, may be found ranged under that title [Whig]. **1823** BYRON *Juan* VIII. xvii, Fifty thousand heroes, name by name.. Would form a lengthy lexicon of glory. **1839** LYTTON *Richelieu* II. ii. 362 In the lexicon of youth..there is no such word As—fail! **1954** [see EUROPEAN *sb.* 2]. **1963** *Amer. Speech* XXXVIII. 143 French-speaking Canadians..are developing a 'standard' form of Canadian French..with the same categories of variation (phonetics and lexicon) from the speech of the mother country as are found in American and Canadian English. **1972** *Archivum Linguisticum* III. 1 They constitute a regular part of his stylistic lexicon. **1973** K. JOHNSON in T. Kochman *Rappin' & Stylin' Out* 142 These racial-identity labels are part of what can be called 'the black lexicon' (words that are used exclusively by black people) formulated to designate concepts derived from the unique experience of black people within their culture. **1973** *Times* 31 July 6/7 He [*sc.* Mr. Ehrlichman] said the term 'deep six'—meaning throw in the river—had not been 'part of my lexicon'.

c. *attrib.* and *Comb.*

1826 SYD. SMITH *Wks.* 1859 II. 100/1 The boy who is lexicon-struck in early youth looks upon all books afterwards with horror. **1848** CLOUGH *Bothie* IX. 120 Leaving vocabular ghosts undisturbed in their lexicon limbo.

2. *Linguistics.* The complete set of meaningful units in a language; the words, etc., as in a dictionary, but without the definitions. (Opp. GRAMMAR *sb.*)

1933 L. BLOOMFIELD *Lang.* x. 162 The total stock of morphemes in a language is its lexicon. **1964** R. H. ROBINS *Gen. Ling.* 63 The categories of phonetics, phonology, and grammar are general; the components of the lexicon of a language are particular. **1968** J. LYONS *Introd. Theoret. Ling.* iv. 159 He can afford to make a less exhaustive classification of the lexicon.

3. (With capital initial.) The proprietary name of a game played with cards marked with the letters of the alphabet.

1932 *Trade Marks Jrnl.* 22 June 798 Lexicon... Card games. John Waddington Limited,..Leeds; manufacturers. **1945** D. WHITELAW *Lexicon Murders* i. 15 This card..was one from a pack of Lexicon cards, one bearing the letter V. *Ibid.* iii. 59 A Wop, eh...ever play Lexicon? **1960** *Guardian* 9 Dec. 9/7 Didn't we all learn to spell by playing Lexicon? **1965** R. PETRIE *Running Deep* ii. 28 One of them produced a packet of Lexicon from her bag and spread the letters over the table. **1974** 'J. LE CARRÉ' *Tinker, Tailor* xxii. 187 Smiley appeared to examine the lexicon cards, reading off the words longways and sideways.

Hence **ˈlexiconist**, a compiler of a lexicon.

1828–32 WEBSTER cites *Orient. Col.*

lexiconize (ˈlɛksɪkənaɪz), *v.* [f. LEXICON + -IZE.] **a.** *intr.* To compile a lexicon. **b.** *trans.* To reduce or make into (the form of) a lexicon.

1892 G. MEREDITH *Let.* 3 Jan. (1970) II. 1056 Your Lexiconizing is clever and I cannot go beyond it. **1908** F. GALTON *Mem. my Life* 254 They admit of being so classified or 'lexiconised', that it would be possible for him to tell.. whether a similar set had been already registered. **1952** C. P. BLACKER *Eugenics: Galton & After* 49 Galton spent about eight years on this work... It was only in the last of these, the *Finger-Print Directory*, published in 1895, that the process of 'lexiconizing' or indexing the material was completed.

lexicostatistic (ˌlɛksɪkəʊstəˈtɪstɪk), *a. Linguistics.* [f. LEXICO- + STATISTIC *a.*] Of or relating to the statistics of vocabulary. Also **ˌlexicostaˈtistics** *sb. pl.* const. as *sing.*, a branch of linguistics closely allied to GLOTTOCHRONOLOGY.

1952 M. SWADESH in *Proc. Amer. Philos. Soc.* XCVI. iv. 452 (*title*) Lexico-statistic dating of prehistoric ethnic contacts. **1956** S. C. GUDSCHINSKY in *Word* XII. 175 Lexicostatistics is a technique which attempts to provide dates for the earlier stages of languages much as carbon 14 dating provides dates for archaeological finds. **1961** [see GLOTTOCHRONOLOGY]. **1964** R. H. ROBINS *Gen. Ling.* viii. 318 The attempt to quantify linguistic divergence from a common source [etc.]..is known as lexicostatistics or glottochronology. **1965** *Canad. Jrnl. Ling.* Spring 94 Certain special methods, such as lexicostatistic list comparison, rest on comparative method. **1969** R. A. HALL in *Neuphilol. Mitt.* LXX. 199 Despite the failure of glottochronology, due to basic theoretical faults, a certain amount of interest has been maintained in other, less aprioristic aspects of lexicostatistics.

Also **ˌlexicostaˈtistical** *a.*, **ˌlexicostaˈtistically** *adv.*

1955 *Internat. Jrnl. Amer. Ling.* XXI. 138 (*heading*) Lexico-statistical skewing from dialect borrowing. **1963** *Language* XXXIX. 60 (*heading*) Lexicostatistically determined borrowing and taboo.

lexigraphy (lɛkˈsɪɡrəfɪ). [f. Gr. λέξι-ς word, expression + -γραφία writing, -GRAPHY.] A system of writing in which each character represents a word. Hence **lexiˈgraphic**, **-ˈgraphical** *adjs.*, pertaining to or characterized by lexigraphy. (In quot. 1895, *lexigraphical* is used for 'lexical': cf. note below.) Also **lexiˈgraphically** *adv.*

In Dicts. from Webster 1828 onwards, *lexigraphy* has been defined as 'the art or practice of defining words', with corresp. definitions for *lexigraphic*, *-graphical*. Cf. late Gr. λεξιγράφος 'lexici scriptor, vocabularius' (Stephanus).

1828–32 WEBSTER, *Lexigraphy*, the art or practice of defining words (citing *Med. Repos.*). **1836** DU PONCEAU *Chinese Syst. Writing* (1838) 36 The Chinese system of writing is improperly called ideographic; it is a syllabic and lexigraphic alphabet... It is lexigraphic because every syllable is a significant word. **1838** *Ibid.* Introd. 14 Instead of ideas, it only represents words, by means of the combination of other words, and therefore I have called it lexigraphic. [In a quotation from this in *For. Q. Rev.* XXI. 323, *lexigraphy* is substituted for *lexigraphic*.] **1838** *Ibid.* 32 Those nations..who use the Chinese characters lexigraphically. **1855** OGILVIE, Suppl., *Lexigraphic, Lexigraphical*, expressing words by distinct characters; representing words by the combination of other words. *Lexigraphy*, a representation of words by the combination of other words. **1895** W. BOSCAWEN *Bible & Monuments* vi. 165 The lexigraphical tablet in which this important word is found throws considerable light on the meaning. In the list of words from which the name is taken [etc.].

‖**Lexiphanes** (lɛkˈsɪfəniːz). [Gr. λεξιφάνης phrase-monger (the title of one of Lucian's dialogues), f. λέξι-ς word, phrase + φαν-, φαίνειν to show.] One who uses bombastic phraseology. Hence **Lexiˈphanic** (-ˈfænɪk) *a.*, **Lexiˈphanicism**.

1767 A. CAMPBELL *Lexiph.* Ded. 7, I generally found them [modern writings] more or less Lexiphanick in proportion to the share of fame and reputation their several authors enjoyed. *Ibid.* Ded. 17 Those Lexiphaneses, those Shiners, those dealers in hard words. *Ibid.* 131 Come, Doctor, let us have no more of your medical terms and solemnity... 'Tis no better than downright Lexiphanicism. **1841** D'ISRAELI *Amen. Lit.* (1867) 140 The encumbering Lexiphanicisms of the ponderous numerosity of Johnson. **1887** *Sat. Rev.* 5 Nov. 624 Its Lexiphanic contortions of the tongue.

lexis (ˈlɛksɪs). [ad. Gr. λέξις diction, word, f. λεγ- to speak.] **1.** The diction or wording, in contrast to other elements, of a piece of writing (see also quot. 1950).

1950 *Mod. Philology* XLVII. IV. 243/1, I have already distinguished, in the first part of this essay, between speech as action (*praxis*) and speech as meaningful (*lexis*). **1957** N. FRYE *Sound & Poetry* p. xxiii, Singing and chanting are, in modern times, radically different methods of associating melos and lexis.

2. *Linguistics.* **a.** = LEXICON 2; items of lexical, as opp. esp. to grammatical, meaning; the total word-stock of a language. **b.** The study of words as lexical items.

1960 E. DELAVENAY *Introd. Machine Transl.* v. 67 During the early days of research the priority of lexis over morphology in preparing the way for machine translation was taken for granted. *Ibid.* 131 *Lexis*, used here, and by M.T. linguists, to designate the words of a language, contained in its dictionary or lexicon, as opposed to the morphology and syntax of that language. **1961** *Language* XXXVII. 325 A distinction..between grammar and lexis seems to be necessary if the patternings are to be economically stated or defined. **1962** R. QUIRK *Use of English* v. 72 The word-stock—also known as the *vocabulary* or *lexis*. **1963** R. M. W. DIXON *Ling. Sci. & Logic* ii. 45 Theories of grammar and lexis are both needed. **1964** *English Studies* XLV. 24 Patterns of vocabulary, or *lexis*, which describe the company words keep. **1966** *Listener* 14 Apr. 534/2 Dr. Steiner's problems with the gaucho's lexis and the Amerindian's grammar..are linguistic and not literary problems. **1971** *E. Afr. Jrnl.* Mar. 35/2 Presentation of lexis is balanced by the introduction of grammatical structures.

‖**lex loci** (lɛks ˈləʊsaɪ). *Law.* [L.] The law of the country in which a legal transaction is performed, a tort is committed, or a property is situated; freq. followed by a defining word or phrase.

1832 BARNEWALL & CRESSWELL *Rep. Cases King's Bench* X. 905 The decisions of both English and Scotch courts shew that the construction of personal contracts depends on the lex loci contractus. **1836** H. WHEATON *Elem. Internat. Law* I. II. ii. 173 A necessary consequence of the rule relating to the application of the *lex loci rei sitæ*. **1848** WHARTON *Law Lexicon* 375/1 All the formalities, proofs, or authentications of them [*sc.* contracts], which are required by the *lex loci*, are indispensable to their validity everywhere else. **1858** J. WESTLAKE *Treat. Private Internat. Law* iv. 64 The fact of status must be referred to the domicile, but the incapacities attendant on the given status to the *lex situs* for immovable property, and to the *lex loci actus aut contractus* for other matters. *Ibid.* xi. 318 Both the form and the legality, the extrinsic and intrinsic validity, depended on the *lex loci celebrationis*. *Ibid.* 335 The *lex loci*..by which the conduct of married persons is to be regulated,..must always be referred, not to the place where the contract was entered into, but where it subsists for the time. **1896** A. V. DICEY *Digest Law Eng.* i. 66 '*Lex loci solutionis*' means the law of the country where a contract is to be performed. *Ibid.* xxvii. 669 It is not necessary that the *lex fori* and the *lex loci delicti* should be identical; it is sufficient if they are similar. **1970** *Internat. & Compar. Law Q.* XIX. 26 This at once gives rise to the problem whether it is the *lex fori* or *lex loci* which gives the plaintiff this cause of action.

lext, obs. 2nd sing. pres. ind. of LIE *v.*²

‖**lex talionis** (lɛks tælɪˈəʊnɪs). [L.] The law of retaliation, 'an eye for an eye, a tooth for a tooth'. (The accus. and abl. forms no longer occur in Eng. contexts.)

1597 MORLEY *Introd. Mus.* III. 146 Wherefore I may *Lege talionis* laugh at incongruity as well as you might at vnformality. **1600** J. PORY tr. *Leo's Africa* II. 56 He is presently without any iudgement to haue *Legem talionis*, that is, like for like, inflicted vpon him. **1646** EVANCE *Noble Ord.* 23 Gods *Lex talionis* is as firme as the lawes of the Meads and Persians. **1731** MEDLEY tr. *Kolben's Cape G. Hope* (1738) I. 287 They take the Field with their best Force, not only to recover their Wives, but, *Lege Talionis*, to plunder the Robbers of theirs. **1821** JEFFERSON *Autobiog.* Writ. (1892) I. 60 For other felonies should be substituted hard labor..and in some cases, the *Lex Talionis*. **1857** J. W. CROKER *Ess. Fr. Rev.* iv. 171 The *lex talionis* with which the revolutionary Nemesis requited her votaries.

ley (liː, leɪ). [Var. LEA *sb.*¹] The supposed line of a prehistoric track in a straight line usually from hilltop to hilltop with identifying points such as ponds, mounds, etc., marking its route (see also quot. 1932).

1922 A. WATKINS *Early Brit. Trackways* 12 The sighting line was called the ley or lay. *Ibid.* 13 Previous writers, treating, say, of Roman or of mediæval roads, not knowing

of the existence of the ley, assume that they are speaking of original primary structures, when they are only describing a route evolved from a number of the leys I describe. **1925** —— *Old Straight Track* 220 When you get a good ley on the map, go over it in the field, and fragments and traces of the trackways may be found, always in straight lines. **1932** D. MAXWELL *Detective in Surrey* v. 86 A ley..is an invisible and imaginary line, drawn from one point in the landscape to another, mathematically straight... The key positions..are points where two or more leys cross... The crossing places ..would be places of meeting. **1971** *It* 2–16 June 24/4 The leys..interlaced over the whole country. **1974** *Bookseller* 26 Jan. 192 (Advt.), Alfred Watkins' theory about leys which connect ancient sites.

ley, obs. form of LAY, LEE *sb.*, LYE; var. LEA².

leyar, variant of LAIR *sb.*³ *Obs.*

leycesteria (lɛ'stɪərɪə). [mod.L. (N. Wallich in W. Carey *Roxburgh's Flora Indica* (1824) II. 181), f. the name of William *Leycester* (fl. 1820), Chief Justice of Bengal + -IA¹.] A shrub of the genus so called, belonging to the family Caprifoliaceæ, native to India, and bearing yellow or purple flowers; also called Himalayan honeysuckle or pheasant-berry.

1838 J. C. LOUDON *Arboretum et Fruticetum Britannicum* II. 1060 The beautiful Leycesteria..is a rambling shrub, with the general appearance of a honeysuckle. **1899** G. JEKYLL *Wood & Garden* ix. 101 We come back to Leycesteria, put rather in a place of honour. **1961** *Amat. Gardening* 23 Dec. 9 Quick growing shrubs which make long wands of growth annually..are..buddleia, leycesteria.

leyche, obs. form of LEECH.

Leyden ('laɪdən). The name of a city in Holland, used in the names of certain electrical apparatus, invented there in 1745–6: ***Leyden jar*** (formerly ***phial*** or ***bottle***), an electrical condenser consisting of a glass bottle coated inside and outside with tinfoil to within a certain distance of its mouth, and having a brass rod surmounted by a knob passing through the cork, and communicating with the internal armature. Also ***Leyden battery***, a battery consisting of a number of Leyden jars.

1755 FRANKLIN *Lett.* etc. Wks. 1840 V. 348, I taught him ..to charge the Leyden phial, and some other experiments. **1762** *Ibid.* 380 A Leyden bottle, charged and then sealed hermetically. **1812** SIR H. DAVY *Chem. Philos.* 133 A stratum of air is charged in the same manner as a glass bottle ..is charged in the Leyden experiment. **1825** J. NEAL *Bro. Jonathan* I. 29 She was..like a Leyden jar always ready to be let off. **1840** CARLYLE *Heroes* (1858) 191 As if it were a poor dead thing, to be bottled up in Leyden jars, and sold over counters. **1855** MAYNE *Expos. Lex.*, *Leyden Battery*, term for a number of Leyden jars, connected externally by being placed on tinfoil, or other good conductor.

Leydig ('laɪdɪg). *Anat.* The name of Franz von *Leydig* (1821–1908), German anatomist, used *attrib.*, in the possessive, and with *of-* adjunct to designate various anatomical structures described by or associated with him, *esp.* the interstitial cell of the testis, a large, polyhedral cell occurring in large numbers in the connective tissue around the seminiferous tubules and believed to be the site of androgen production in the testis.

1904 *Amer. Jrnl. Anat.* III. 167 (*heading*) The embryonic development of the interstitial cells of Leydig. *Ibid.*, Boll.. believed that Leydig's cells composed the walls of capillaries. **1936** NEAL & RAND *Compar. Anat.* xii. 448 The interstitial Leydig cells of the testis. **1956** *Nature* 21 Jan. 144/1 In all cases the Leydig cell cytoplasm of the interstitium had become sprinkled with lipid droplets. **1962** *Gray's Anat.* (ed. 33) 1522 The interstitial cells of the testis (cells of Leydig) are large polyhedral cells lying in the connective tissue between the seminiferous tubules.

†**leye**. *Obs.* Forms: α. 1 lé3, 2–4 lei, 3 lai, le3e, ley3e, 3–4 lei3e, ley, 3–6 leye, 4 leyhe, 4, 7–8 (*dial.*) laye. β. 1 líe3 li3, lý3, 4 lie, ly3e, lyghe, 4–5 lye, 5 ly. [OE. *líeʒ* (Anglian *léʒ*) str. masc. corresponds to OHG. *louc*, *lauc* (MHG. *louc*, gen. *louges*), ON. *løyg-r*:—OTeut. **laugi-z*:— pre-Teut. **louk-* abl.-var. of **leuk-*: see LIGHT *sb.*] Flame, blaze, fire. (*on*) *a leye*: on fire.

α. *Beowulf* 3115 (Gr.) Wonna le3. **971** *Blickl. Hom.* xii. 133 Hie onfengon þæm Hal3an Gaste to heora heortan on fyrenra le3a onlic-nesse. *c* **1175** *Lamb. Hom.* 41 He him sceaude an ouen on berninde fure he warp ut of him seofe leies. *c* **1200** *Trin. Coll. Hom.* 49 Ech cristene oh to habben on honden to-dai in chirche le3e bernende. *a* **1225** *Leg. Kath.* 1369, I þe reade leie, & i þe leitinde fur. *a* **1240** *Lofsong* in *Cott. Hom.* 215 Wið þe lai louerd of þe holigost..tend mine heorte. *c* **1330** *Arth. & Merl.* 6796 (Kölbing) Þo sei3e þai al þe cuntray Stonden brenand on rede lei3e. **1377** LANGL. *P. Pl.* B. XVII. 207 As wex and weyke and hote fyre togyderes Fostren forth a flaumbe and a feyre leye [C. xx. 172 lye]. **1398** TREVISA *Barth. De P.R.* XVI. xxviii. (1495) 562 This stone..Crisalitus..yf it be set by the fyre anone it wexyth on a laye [*Helmingham MS.* it wexeþ a lie, *ed.* 1535 on a flame]. **1447** BOKENHAM *Seyntys* (Roxb.) 78 The leye off the flaumyd furnes. **1573** *Art of Limming* 11 You may.. blacke over your paper with the leye of a Kandle or of a lynke. **1674–91** RAY *S. & E.C. Words* 104 *Laye*, as *Lowe* in the North, the Flame of Fire; tho it be peculiarly used for the steam of Charcoal or any other burnt Coal. [Hence **1787** in GROSE *Prov. Gloss.* Suppl.]

β. *Beowulf* 727 (Gr.) Him of ea3um stod li3e 3elicost leoht unfæ3er. *a* **1000** *Cædmon's Gen.* 325 (Gr.) Brand & brade li3as. *c* **1300** *St. Brandan* 496 The Lie of the fur stod on he3 as hit a was were. **13..** *K. Alis.* 3458 The fuyr was on so gret lyghe, That Darie hit sone syghe. **1340–70** *Alex. & Dind.* 555 He was..lechourus of kinde þat in his licamus lust as a lie brente. **1398** [see α] **1422** *Secreta Secret., Priv. Priv.* 229 Tho that haue a brandynge colure like the lye of fyre. **14..** *Tundale's Vis.* 716 Owt of the mowthe the fure brast And fowle stynkyng lye com owt fast.

leye, obs. form of LAY, LEA, LEE.

leye(n, obs. f. LAY *v.*¹; obs. pa. pple. of LIE *v.*

leyerwit(e, variant of LAIRWITE *Obs.*
1696, 1706 in PHILLIPS.

leyf, obs. form of LEAF, LIEF.

leyff, leyffand, -ing, obs. ff. LIVE, LIVING.

leyf(f)ull, variant of LEEFUL *a. Obs.*

†**ley-gager**. *Law. Obs.* [cf. AF. *gager sa ley* to WAGE one's law: see LAY *sb.*³] Wager of law.

1625 *Act 1 Chas. I*, c. 3 §2 No Priviledge, proteccion, Inhibicion, or Injunccion, Ley Gager, or Essoine shalbe allowed to the Defendant. [Hence in BLOUNT, PHILLIPS, etc.]

leygh(e, obs. or var. f. LAUGH *v.*, LEYE *Obs.*, LYE.

leyhe, obs. or var. f. LAY *v.*¹, LEYE *Obs.*

leyk(e, leyland, obs. ff. LAKE, LEA-LAND.

Leyland ('leɪlənd). The name of Christopher John *Leyland* (1849–1926), of Haggerston Castle, used *attrib.* or in the possessive in **Leyland('s) cypress** to designate a hybrid conifer, × *Cupressocyparis leylandii* (*Chamæcyparis nootkatensis* × *Cupressus macrocarpa*), first raised by him from seedlings collected at Leighton Hall, Welshpool, in 1888.

[**1926** A. B. JACKSON in *Kew Bull.* 114 As this new cypress has already been named *Cupressus Leylandii* by Mr. Leyland, we propose to describe it under that name.] **1933** W. J. BEAN *Trees & Shrubs Hardy in Brit. Is.* III. 124 Leyland's Cypress..is a tree of dense pyramidal habit. **1960** N. J. PROCKTER *Garden Hedges* vi. 107 Leyland's Cypress.. is still looked upon as something new, and I regret to say is at present little known. **1970** C. LLOYD *Well-Tempered Garden* iii. 215 The great favourite now (although it is by no means new) is Leyland's cypress. **1974** A. MITCHELL *Field Guide to Trees of Britain* 68 At least three [hybrid cypresses] exist, but only one, the Leyland Cypress, is commonly grown.

leyll, leyly, obs. Sc. forms of LEAL, LEALLY.

leyme, obs. Sc. form of LEAM *sb.*¹

leyn(e, obs. f. LAIN *v.*, LAY *v.*¹, LEAN.

leyn(e, obs. pa. pple. of LIE *v.*¹

†**leyne**. *Obs.* [Cf. LAIN *sb.*²] A layer or 'bed'.
(The word in quot. 1530 is of doubtful identity.)

?*c* **1390** *Forme of Cury* (1780) 43 Take brede itosted in wyne, lay þerof a leyne. *c* **1440** *Jacob's Well* 37 Tythe owyth to be payed of all manere wode, of leynys of oystrys, of leynys of fysch, of pondys [etc.]. **1530** PALSGR. 238/2 Leyne [*no French*].

leynes, obs. form of LEANNESS.

leyngh, variant of LENGH *Obs.*, length.

leyond, obs. pres. pple. of LAY *v.*¹

ley-pewter: see LAY *sb.*⁶

leyr(e, obs. form or variant of LAIR, LERE.

leyrewite, variant of LAIRWITE *Obs.*

leyrn, leyrne, obs. ff. LIERNE, LEARN.

leys, leysche, leysshe, obs. ff. LEASH.

leystall(e, obs. form of LAYSTALL.

leyt(e, variant of LAIT *Obs.*, lightning.

leyth(e, obs. form of LOATH, LOATHE.

leyve, leyven, obs. ff. LEAVE *v.*¹, LEVIN.

leyward, obs. form of LEEWARD.

Lez, Lezz(y), varr. LES.

leze-majesty: see LESE-MAJESTY.

L-form: see L 7 c.

lhapwynche, obs. form of LAPWING.

Lhasa ('lɑːsə). Also **lhasa, Lhassa**. The name of the capital of Tibet, used *attrib.* in **Lhasa apso** to designate a small long-coated dog, often gold or grey and white, belonging to a breed originally developed there, and formerly called the **Lhasa terrier**, a name also once used for the *Tibetan terrier* (TIBETAN). Also *ellipt.*

1904 *C. B. Fry's Mag.* June 364/1 The little toy dog of Tibet, which Kennel Club edicts have declared shall properly be known as the 'Lhassa Terrier', is no novelty in our midst, although his numbers in an unkind climate possibly do not reach a round dozen. **1905** P. LANDON *Lhasa* I. 403 The Lhasa terrier is an entirely distinct breed. **1935** W. HUTCHINSON *Dog Encycl.* II. 1142/2 [The] Lhasa Apso ..has only become known in England in very recent years. **1948** C. L. B. HUBBARD *Dogs in Brit.* 303 The Lhasa Apso has had many names given it in the course of its comparatively short British history. **1955** W. GADDIS *Recognitions* I. vi. 206 The lhasa turned to stare at the Coca-Cola machine. **1974** *Radio Times* 14 Feb. 3/2 Polluche is a Lhasa apso—literally translated, it means a Lhasa terrier.

lherzolite ('lɜːzəlaɪt). *Min.* [Named from Lake *Lherz* in the Pyrenees: see -LITE.] A variety of pyroxene of a deep green or olive green colour.

1823 W. PHILLIPS *Introd. Min.* (ed. 3) 63 When mixed with serpentine it [Coccolite] has been termed Lherzolite. **1879** RUTLEY *Study Rocks* x. 120 Enstatite occurs in lherzolite.

lheuc, variant of LUKE *a.*

‖**lhiamba, liamba**. [Native African name.] Hemp, *Cannabis sativa*. (Cf. *bhang*, *hemp*.)

1861 DU CHAILLU *Equat. Afr.* xxiv. 419 The leaf is used to smoke..and has..narcotic effects..: this liamba is nothing else than the..*Cannabis Indica*. **1897** MARY KINGSLEY *W. Africa* 667 The imported gin keeps the African..from his worst intoxicant lhiamba (*Cannabis sativa*).

lhiep, lhip, obs. pa. t. of LEAP *v.*

Lhooshai, var. LUSHAI *a.* and *sb.*

‖**li**¹ (liː). Also 6 lii, 9 le(e. [Chinese.] The ordinary Chinese itinerary measure (see quot. 1886).

1588 PARKE tr. *Mendoza's Hist. China* I. vi. 12 The Chino's haue amongst them, but only three kind of measures: the which in their language are called Lii, Pu, and Icham, which is as much as to say, or in effect, as a forlong, league, or iorney. **1827** H. E. LLOYD tr. *Timkowski's Trav.* I. 65 The Chinese li contains two hundred and eighty-five Russian fathoms. **1884** G. WILLIAMSON *Old Highw. China* 209 At a small town forty li from Peking we spent the night. **1886** YULE & BURNELL s.v. *Lee*, According to Mr. Giles, 27⅘ *li* = 10 miles... From several concurrent statements we may conclude that often the *li* is generalised so that a certain number of *li*, generally 100, stand for a day's march.

‖**li**² (liː). Also 8 lai, 9 le. [Chinese.] A Chinese weight, one-thousandth part of a liang.
(A li of silver is equivalent to the copper coin called by Europeans a CASH.)

1771 J. R. FORSTER tr. *Osbeck's Voy.* I. 262 Kas, which the Chinese call Lai, is the only current coin which is struck in China. **1858** SIMMONDS *Dict. Trade*, *Li*, another name for the Chinese copper cash.

‖**li**³ (liː). [Chinese.] (See quots.)

1912 J. J. M. DE GROOT *Relig. of Chinese* iv. 95 The original *li* and *teh*, the only classical rules and ethics which keep man..in perfect harmony with the order of the universe. **1937** D. BODDE tr. *Fung Yu-Lan's Hist. Chinese Philos.* iv. 46 The 'Rites' (*Li*) were used in diplomatic relations. **1942** D. D. RUNES *Dict. Philos.* 168/1 *Li*, reason; law; the rational principle. This is the basic concept of modern Chinese philosophy. To the Neo-Confucians.., Reason is the rational principle of existence whereas the vital force (ch'i) is the material principle. **1953** *Oxf. Jun. Encycl.* V. 101/1 The word *li* used by Confucius, which is often translated by the English word 'religion', really means something more like ceremonial or ritual, the correct observance of which is needed for maintaining friendly relations with the Power or Powers of the unseen world. **1955** A. FANG in E. Pound *Classic Anthol.* p. xvi, Read in that context, Confucius must be understood as trying to integrate music with rites (*li*), just as he tried to integrate poetry with music. **1962** A. F. WRIGHT in Wright & Twitchett *Confucian Personalities* 7 The *li*, spread by fathers, village elders, and government officials, and supplemented by the discipline of ordered family life, would in turn foster social virtues: filial submission, brotherliness, righteousness, good faith, and loyalty.

li., obs. abbrev. L. *libra* pound, *libræ* pounds.

c **1450** *ME. Med. Bk.* (Heinrich) 82 Take iij lī [*sic*] of rosyn, and .i. lī of wax. *c* **1489** CAXTON *Sonnes of Aymon* xiv. 322 Here is xx. li of money. **1521** *Pilton Churchw. Acc.* (Som. Rec. Soc.) 74 For a li and a q. wexe. **1634** R. VERNEY *Let. J. Dillon* in Forster *Gr. Remonstr.* (1860) 256 He was fined in foure thousand pounds by some, by others in 5,000ˡⁱ, in 6,000ˡⁱ, in 10,000ˡⁱ.

liability (laɪə'bɪlɪtɪ). [f. LIABLE + -ITY.]

1. *Law.* The condition of being liable or answerable by law or equity.

1794–1809 E. CHRISTIAN *Note* in *Blackstone's Comm.* III. 165 It exempts them from all liability to answer for a loss occasioned by fire. **1817** W. SELWYN *Law Nisi Prius* (ed. 4) II. 1031 Of the Liability of the Master in respect of a tortious Act done by the Servant. **1875** MAINE *Hist. Inst.* ix. 259 The Pignoris Capio could be generally resorted to in the absence of the person under liability.

b. *Comm.* ***limited liability***: the position or state of being legally responsible only to a limited extent (usually the amount of one's stock or shares) for the debts of a trading company of which one is a member. Also *attrib.* in ***limited liability company***. (For the shortened form ***limited company***, see LIMITED.) Also *transf.*

1855 in *Hansard's Parl. Deb.* Ser. III. CXXXIX. 358 Bill read 2°, as was also the Limited Liabilities Bill. **1858** LD. ST. LEONARDS *Handy-Bk. Prop. Law* xxi. 162 A private company..has been formed for the purpose of executing trusts and executorships, but limited. Such associations are

not only open to all the objections which I have pointed out, but their limited liability would deter a prudent man from intrusting them with his fortune. **1890** *Review of Rev.* II. 541/1 Barings were as good as the Bank once. Now they are only a limited liability firm. **1894** SALA *Lond. up to Date* 147 Those were the days of Joint Stock Companies, and the Act authorizing the formation of companies with Limited Liability had not yet been passed. **1897** *Times* 15 Feb. 9/3 This does not give her [Greece] a right to assume that she can make war with limited liability.

2. The condition of being liable or subject *to* something, apt or likely *to do* something.

1809 A. HENRY *Trav.* 118 Their mode of life..accounts for their liability to these diseases. **1815** L. HUNT *Feast of Poets &c.* Notes 120 A genius for poetry is nothing but a finer liability to impressions. **1874** GREEN *Short Hist.* ix. §1. 596 His [Bacon's] noble confession of the liability of every inquirer to error. **1883** FROUDE *Short Stud.* IV. iii. 294 Liability to military service is a universal condition of citizenship.

3. That for which one is liable; esp. *pl.* the debts or pecuniary obligations of a person or company.

1842 MISS MITFORD in L'Estrange *Life* (1870) III. ix. 169 At the suggestion of friends a subscription was raised to meet these liabilities. **1844** H. H. WILSON *Brit. India* III. 561 Although it was relieved of a part of its liabilities, it was burthened with a heavy annual payment. **1861** GOSCHEN *For. Exch.* 18 The effect of profits and commissions on the mutual liabilities of nations.

liable (ˈlaɪəb(ə)l), *a.* Also 6–7 lyable, (7 layable). [Plausibly explained as a. AF. **liable* = med.L. **ligābilis* that can be bound, f. *ligāre*, F. *lier* to bind; but if this be the origin, it is strange that the word is not known in AF. or Law Latin.]

1. *Law.* **a.** Bound or obliged by law or equity, or in accordance with a rule or convention; answerable (*for*, also const. †*to* with the same sense); legally subject or amenable *to*.

1542–3 *Act 34 & 35 Hen. VIII*, c. 4 §4 His landes..and cattalles, shall be charged and lyable to the execucion of the sayde recouery. **1627** *Crt. & Times Chas. I* (1848) I. 208 None were liable to martial law but martial men. **1636** FEATLY *Clavis Myst.* x. 131 Those that are lyable to your authority and jurisdiction. **1649** LANGBAINE *Answ. Univ. Oxford* 40 Their having the Custody..of the Gaole,..and their being liable to Escapes. **1651** HOBBES *Leviath.* II. xxii. 120 Every Member is lyable by himself for the whole [debt]. **1761** *Descr. S. Carolina* 34 The Species of Goods liable to Duties, are Sugar, Rum, Madeira Wine. **1765** BLACKSTONE *Comm.* I. 107 The territory of England is liable to two divisions; the one ecclesiastical, the other civil. *Ibid.* 470 The freehold was vested in the parson; and,..on his death.. would be liable to his debts and incumbrances. **1818** CRUISE *Digest* (ed. 2) I. 493 It is some-what doubtful whether trusts were originally liable to Crown debts. **1832** LEWIS *Use & Ab. Pol. Terms* iii. 26 A sovereign..can never be liable to any legal duties. **1866** CRUMP *Banking* v. 126 A premature release of a party liable on the bill. **1867** C. S. PARKER in *Quest. for Ref. Parl.* 158 Persons liable to income-tax. **1886** SIR J. PEARSON in *Law Rep.* 32 Ch. Div. 46 Every one of the partners is liable to the full extent of his fortune for all the debts incurred by the partnership. **1891** *Law Times Rep.* LXIII. 765/1 The defendants were liable as principals, as they had contracted in their own names without any qualification.

b. const. *inf.*

1637 *Crt. & Times Chas. I* (1848) II. 268 There is a little demur whether an executor is liable to answer damages. **1683** *Boston Rec.* (1881) VII. 160 Candles made up for sale shall..be liable to be weighed and forfeited for want of being full weight. **1688** *Col. Rec. Pennsylv.* I. 219 Wherein Land were made Layable to pay debts. **1765** BLACKSTONE *Comm.* I. 254 It is reasonable that, wherever they transgress it, there they shall be liable to make atonement. **1808** PIKE *Sources Mississ.* (1810) III. App. 45 The property of any officer or soldier, who is killed on the field of battle..is not liable to be taken for debt. **1818** CRUISE *Digest* (ed. 2) II. 460 The estate descended is the creditor's, and liable to pay his debts. **1825** *Act 6 Geo. IV*, c. 50 §1 Every man..who shall occupy a house containing not less than fifteen windows, shall be..liable to serve on juries. **1832** HT. MARTINEAU *Ella of Gar.* ii. 27 Will our growing rich make us liable to pay what your honour calls real rent?

2. Of land: ? Subject to taxation. †Also said of the tax. ? *Obs.*

a **1626** BACON *Max. & Uses Com. Law* (1636) 46 The land was not lyable longer than his owne life time. **1647** in W. S. Pattee *Hist. Old Braintree* (Mass.) (1878) 33 His tax shall be still liable as heretofore. **1817** J. BRADBURY *Trav. Amer.* 292 No land tax is expected until five years after the purchase, when land becomes liable.

3. a. Exposed or subject to, or likely to suffer from (something prejudicial); in older use with wider sense, †subject to the operation of (any agency), likely to undergo (a change of any kind). Normally const. *to*; rarely †*of*, also † *for* with acc. and inf.

1593 NASHE *Christ's T.* 8 You should not be lyable to so much blame. **1609** HOLLAND *Amm. Marcell.* 157 To shew himself lyable to no fault [*L. nulli obnoxium culpæ*]. **1627** PERROT *Tithes* 62 He..is lyable to all those curses. **1643** BURROUGHES *Exp. Hosea* ch. 2. iii. 263 She shall be laid open, lyable for all wilde beasts to come in and to devoure her. **1646** SIR T. BROWNE *Pseud. Ep.* II. i. 52 [Crystall] by the art of Chymistry is separable unto the operations whereof it is lyable, with other concretions, as calcination, reverberation, sublimation, distillation. **1662** *Bk. Com. Prayer* Pref., Either of doubtful signification, or otherwise liable to misconstruction. **1667** MILTON *P.L.* VI. 397 Not liable to fear or flight or paine. **1668** HOWE *Bless. Righteous* (1825) 55 Those [perfections] which are less liable to our apprehension. **1692** BENTLEY *Boyle Lect.* i. 23 Some.. Wretches or..Hypocrites are mostly justly..liable to these horrors of mind. **1711** ADDISON *Spect.* No. 56 ¶4 He.. found that though they were Objects of his Sight, they were not liable to his Touch. **1712** *Ibid.* No. 421 ¶5 The Imagination is as liable to Pain as Pleasure. **1752** HUME *Ess. & Treat.* (1777) I. 171 There is one mistake to which they seem liable. **1769** *Junius Lett.* v. 27 Your declaration..is liable to two objections. **1801** A. HAMILTON *Wks.* (1886) VII. 213 Reasons..which..are omitted as being more liable to dispute. **1848** DICKENS *Dombey* i, Her eyes were liable to a similar affection. **1860** RUSKIN *Mod. Paint.* V. VI. ix. 83 At edges of loose cliffs..and in other places liable to disturbance. **1880** GEIKIE *Phys. Geog.* v. §31. 352 Sea breezes are not liable to the same extremes of temperature as those from the land.

b. Const. *inf.* Subject to the possibility of (doing or undergoing something undesirable).

1682 CREECH *Lucretius* I. 27 All would be liable to die, Subject to powerful Mortality. **1683** PENN *Wks.* (1782) IV. 302 The multitude of trees..being liable to retain mists and vapours. **1736** BUTLER *Anal.* I. iv. Wks. 1874 I. 79 Human creatures are..continually liable to go wrong voluntarily. [**1749** CHESTERF. *Let.* 24 Nov., He thought that gentleman was more liable to be thanked and rewarded than censured. You know, I presume, that liable can never be used in a good sense.] **1786** BURKE *W. Hastings* Wks. 1842 II. 178 They were..liable to suffer the greatest extremities of penury. **1800** BENTHAM *Wks.* (1843) X. 352 Difficulties, I am sensible, may be liable to occur. **1858** RUSKIN *Arrows Chace* (1880) I. 130 Some colours are..liable to darken in perpetual shade. **1893** LIDDON, etc. *Life Pusey* I. xvi. 376 The method, however equitable the intention, is liable to be inequitable in effect. **1896** *Portfolio* June 80 Ground so liable to be overflowed must surely at one time have been a swamp.

c. *dial.* and *U.S.* Likely.

1886 F. T. ELWORTHY *West Somerset Word-Bk.* 433 Speaking of a wounded hen pheasant a farmer said, 'Tis very liable he's a-croped into one o' these here hovers. **1890** R. D. BLACKMORE *Kit & Kitty* I. ix. 95 Ould dog be put out at zix o'clock riglar, and 'tis liable he'll hurn straight to 'e. **1901** MERWIN & WEBSTER *Calumet 'K'* xi. 198 He's liable to call our men out to-night, ain't he? **1903** *N.Y. Even. Post* 22 Aug., Norman Hunter's new record..is liable to stand unmolested for many years. **1935** H. W. HORWILL *Dict. Mod. Amer. Usage* 189/1 'Boston is liable to be the ultimate place for holding the convention.' 'If the lawmakers get back before the frosts kill the vegetation, many of them are liable to think it a reproach to the nation that grass should be growing in the streets of the national capital.' **1957** B. & C. EVANS *Dict. Contemp. Amer. Usage* 273/1 An American might say *we are liable to be in Chicago next week* without meaning that that would be a calamity.

¶ **4.** Inaccurately used for: Incident *to*. *Obs.*

1631 DENISON *Heav. Banq.* 246 The curse of God is liable to euery one. **1746** ELIZA HEYWOOD *Female Spect.* No. 24 (1748) IV. 285 The faults of inadvertency are liable to us all.

† **5.** Subject or subservient *to*; attached or belonging *to*. *Obs.*

1571 CAMPION *Hist. Irel.* 26 Other lawyers they haue, liable to certaine families. **1595** SHAKS. *John* II. i. 490 Angiers, and..all that we vpon this side the Sea..Finde liable to our Crowne and Dignitie. *Ibid.* v. ii. 101. **1596** *Edw. III*, I. ii. 8 Those are her own, still liable to her. **1602** WARNER *Alb. Eng.* II. lxi. (1612) 268 If sad were she, then sad was he, if merrie, merrie too. His senses liable to all, she did, or did not doe. **1616** BULLOKAR, *Liable*, subject to, belonging to.

† **6.** Suitable, apt. Also const. *inf.* *Obs.*

1570 *Q. Councell's Let.* 7 Feb. in *N. & Q.* (1857) 1 Aug., To chewse persons lyable to give good informacion. **1588** SHAKS. *L.L.L.* v. i. 97 *Pedant.* The *posterior* of the day..is liable, congruent, and measurable for the after-noone. **1595** —— *John* IV. ii. 226 Finding thee..Apt, liable to be employ'd in danger.

'**liableness.** Now *rare.* [f. LIABLE + -NESS.] The condition or quality of being liable; liability.

1645 W. JENKYN *Stil-Destroyer* 40 Our liableness and readiness to be overtaken by it. **1665–6** PEPYS *Diary* 31 Jan., By which I am..eased of a liablenesse to pay the sum. **1736** BUTLER *Anal.* I. vi. 117 Our Liableness..to Prejudice and Pervertion. **1869** WARDLAW *Lect. Jas.* iv. 65 Mutability and liableness to change.

liache, liage, obs. ff. LEECH, LEAGUE *sb.*[2]

liaise (lɪˈeɪz), *v.* orig. *Services' slang.* Also (erron.) liase. [Back-formation from LIAISON.] *intr.* To make liaison *with* or *between.* Hence **liˈaising** *vbl. sb.* and *ppl. a.*

1928 C. F. S. GAMBLE *Story N. Sea Air Station* xiii. 221 [Lord Fisher said in 1916] 'I want a soldier..to keep in touch with the Navy and so "liaise" or exchange inventions which may be suitable.' **1941** *Amer. N. & Q.* Dec. 141/1 The kind of grammatical economy found in a recent (British) Home Guard instruction sheet—in the event of certain circumstances, it stated, two groups were ordered to 'liase' with two others. **1942** *New Statesman* 1 Aug. 75/1 'To liaise'..was at first frowned on by the pundits: its usefulness ..soon came to outweigh its objectionableness. **1942** *Tee Emm* (Air Ministry) II. 128 He then hurriedly climbed into a Spit and shot off to 'liaise' with his old Squadron. **1946** A. LEE *German Air Force* 25 Göring never acquired the happy knack of liaising satisfactorily with Germany's senior army generals. **1948** L. MACNEICE *Holes in Sky* 71 The liaising aircraft mounts. **1952** *World Rev.* Sept. 20 The manufacturer, too, has advertizing people on his own staff who liaise with the advertizing agency. **1958** L. DURRELL *Mountolive* vi. 139 For convenience it can work to us and liaise with our Service Departments. **1959** *Guardian* 15 Oct. 10/7 He would expect absolute obedience from his subordinates... It remains to be seen whether he could also 'liaise' successfully. **1962** *Times* 28 Mar. 3/1 He will liaise between the dressing room and the press. **1965** *New Statesman* 10 Dec. 919/3 Paris..was..in a state of great confusion... There seemed little liaising to be done. **1970** *Country Life* 1 Oct. 846/3 It would seem advisable for the host to detach well briefed members of the shoot staff to liase with the field trial stewards. **1974** *Times* 18 Feb. 20/8 It would seem that the Government statisticians do not: (a) Liaise with other departments, [etc.].

‖**liaison** (lɪˈeɪzən, -zɒn, Fr. ljɛzɔ̃). Also 8 liason. [F.:—L. *ligātiōn-em*, n. of action f. *ligāre* to bind.]

1. *Cookery.* A thickening for sauces, consisting chiefly of the yolks of eggs; †also, the process of thickening. (Cf. LEAR[2] 2.)

a **1648** DIGBY *Closet Open.* (1671) 146 The last things [Butter, Bread, Flower] cause the liaison and thickening of the liquor. **1759** W. VERRAL *Cookery* xv. 92 Prepare a liaison, or four or five yolks of eggs and some cream. **1797** *Lond. Art Cookery* 142 Make ready a liason of two or three eggs and cream, with a little minced parsley and nutmeg. *Ibid.* 146 Skim and sift the sauce, add a little cullis to make it a liason. **1877** in *Cassell's Dict. Cookery*.

2. a. *gen.* An intimate relation or connexion.

1809 *Edin. Rev.* XIV. 226 The *liaisons* of Merlin with this man and Bazire gave rise to the following *jeu d'esprit*. **1870** *Putnam's Mag.* May 545/2 The knowledge gained from these new sources..has..given new zest to the alleged *liaisons* of the Republic. **1974** *Country Life* 5 Dec. 1814/2 Florence..remained..a home from home for the British... It is a liaison that seems to have lasted happily down the years.

b. *spec.* An illicit intimacy between a man and a woman.

1816 BYRON *Let.* 24 Dec. in *Works* (1900) IV. 29 She is by far the prettiest woman I have seen here... I believe I told you the rise and progress of our *liaison* in my former letter. **1821** BYRON *Juan* III. xxv, Some chaste *liaison* of the kind —I mean An honest friendship with a married lady. **1821** SHELLEY *Lett.* Prose Wks. 1888 II. 333 He [Byron] has a permanent sort of liaison with Contessa Guiccioli. **1849** THACKERAY *Pendennis* ix, 'If it were but a temporary liaison,' the excellent man said, 'one could bear it... But a virtuous attachment is the deuce'. **1853** GREVILLE *Mem. Geo. IV*, Ser. III. I. ii. 35 He was always much addicted to Gallantry, and had endless liaisons with women.

3. *Phonetics.* The joining of a final consonant (which would in pause or before a consonant be silent) to a following word beginning with a vowel or 'mute' *h*. Also in *Music*, in wider sense.

1884 GOSSET *French Prosody* 43 There is one letter in English, *r*, which admits in some cases of a sort of *liaison* in correct modern pronunciation. **1905** *Daily Chron.* 7 Feb. 4/7 The nightly false 'liaison' made by a clever actress... 'Take Lady Agatha-r-out,' she says with terrible distinctness. **1917** G. B. SHAW *How to become Mus. Critic* (1960) 292, I will not blame the singer for putting in a little *liaison* of her own at the reprise. **1929** *Amer. Speech* V. 87, I noticed recently a curious instance of consonant *liaison* (if that is the term for a carrying-over that is commoner in French than in English). **1962** *Listener* 6 Sept. 369/3 To our singers the style, the flavour, the true placing of the sounds, the liaisons—every aspect is elusive and deceptive.

4. *Mil.* Close connection and co-operation between two units, branches, allies, etc., esp. during a battle or campaign. Also *transf.*

1816 H. CLARKE *Hist. War* I. xliii. 702/1 Other advantages of a great and important nature arise from the combinations of the various corps of their invading armies maintaining their *liaison* or correspondence, by means of the..staff-establishments attached to every division. **1915** *Oxf. Mag.* 29 Oct. 18/2 The 'overseer' of the Press..an unrivalled artist in the liaison of departments. **1920** G. H. PERRIS *Battle of Marne* xi. 225 With the I Army pulling north-west, the II Army pulling south-east,..how could anything more than a pretence of liaison be kept up? **1920** *Q. Rev.* July 138 It acted rather as a liaison between the Admiralty and the Press Bureau than as a branch of the latter. **1922** *Encycl. Brit.* XXXII. 967/2 The welfare supervisor..is thus able to refer all matters calling for attention direct to the general manager and may be regarded by him as a *liaison* between him and the various departments dealing with the women employees. **1930** A. W. MYERS *Lawn Tennis* ix. 113 Mind and body must be working in liaison. **1964** B. B. SCHOFIELD *Russ. Convoys* ii. 27 The main trouble during the first years of the war was the shortage of aircraft—otherwise the liaison between the two services was as good as it could be.

5. *attrib.* and *Comb.*, esp. **liaison officer**, an officer in the Services who is concerned with the liaison of units, etc.; also *transf.*

1915 'I. HAY' *First Hundred Thousand* xix. 285 He is one of that most efficient body, the French *liaison* officers, who act as connecting-link between the Allied Forces. **1916** *War Illustr.* 9 Dec. 405 (*caption*) Army liaison dog leaving with a message attached to his collar. **1917** *Times* 5 June 7/1 Members of Parliament have tended less and less in recent times to fulfil their primary duty as *liaison* officers between Parliament and the constituencies. **1918** *Daily Chron.* 19 June 2/2 This position as 'liaison Minister' between the House and the War Cabinet. **1930** *N. & Q.* 5 Apr. 250/2 This [book] is a *liaison* treatise of which ethics is the warp, and economics the very much less important woof, while the whole is coloured with a tinge of metaphysics. **1942** *R.A.F. Jrnl.* 3 Oct. 23 'L' [stands] for 'Liaison pilot'. **1946** *Sun* (Baltimore) 18 Feb. 11/5 The Navy has tabbed entertainment with the high-sounding name liaison unit. **1954** A. HUXLEY *Let.* Apr. (1969) 704 You unquestionably *are* the man to act as liaison officer between pure science and the rest of the world in this matter of the nature of the Mind. **1964** *Amer. Speech* XXXIX. 233 Compares duration of liaison consonants, as in *des airs*, with that of medial consonants, as in *désert*. **1966** *B.B.C. Handbk.* 75 The main duty of the department is to act in a liaison capacity. **1973** *Times* 14 Nov. 8/1 The Israeli liaison officer said he had still not received permission for the journalists to go on to Suez.

liale, liam, obs. ff. LEAL, LYAM, leash.

liamba: see LHIAMBA.

liana, liane (lɪˈɑːnə, lɪˈɑːn). Also 8 lianne. [The form *liane* is a. F. *liane* (1658 *liene* in Rochefort), supposed to be a deriv. of *lier* to bind. The form

liana is either a latinization of *liane*, or has arisen from the notion that the word was of Sp. origin.] The name given to the various climbing and twining plants which abound in tropical forests.

[1796 STEDMAN *Surinam* I. 231 The *nebees*, called by the French *liannes*, by the Spaniards *bejucos*, and in Surinam *tay-tay*.] **1796** H. HUNTER tr. *St. Pierre's Stud. Nat.* (1799) III. 748 Liannes interwoven from trunk to trunk. **1833** CARLYLE *Misc.* (1857) IV. 267 Spite of all its brambles and lianas. **1845** DARWIN *Voy. Nat.* ii. 25 Many of the older trees presented a very curious appearance from the tresses of a liana hanging from their boughs, and resembling bundles of hay. **1885** LADY BRASSEY *The Trades* 136 Palms of every variety, all covered with gigantic lianes. **1890** 'ROLF BOLDREWOOD' *Miner's Right* xxxvi. 321 A stone bridge.. clasped with close lianas.

‖**liang** (ljæŋ). Also leang. [Chinese.] A Chinese weight, about $1\frac{1}{3}$ oz. avoirdupois; this weight in silver as a money of account. Also called *tael*.

1827 H. E. LLOYD tr. *Timkowski's Trav.* I. 17 *note*, A lan (liang) is a Chinese weight containing about $8\frac{3}{4}$ zolotnicks; the value of two roubles in silver. *Ibid.* II. 316 A good camel was sold for twenty or thirty liang.

liar ('laɪə(r)). Forms: 1 léoȝere, *Northumb.* léȝere, 2 li(h)ȝere, 3 lieȝer, liare, 3–4 leier, 3–5 lyere, 3–6 lier, (4 ly(e)ȝere, lyȝer, liȝer, leeȝer, leigher, liere, liyher), 4–5 legher(e, ligher, lygher, lyare, 4–6 *Sc.* lear, 4–7 lyer, 5–8 lyar, (7 lyarr), 7– liar. [OE. *léoȝere* (= OHG. *liugari*, Icel. *ljúgari*), agent-n. f. *léoȝan* LIE *v.*[2] See -AR[3], -ER[1] 2.] **a.** One who lies or tells a falsehood; an untruthful person. *I'm a liar*, (in trivial use) I am mistaken.

c **950** *Lindisf. Gosp.* Matt. vi. 5 Mið ðy ȝie ȝebiddas ne wosas ȝe suæ leȝeras [*other versions* liceteras; L. *hypocritæ*]. *a* **1023** WULFSTAN *Hom.* (Napier) 79 Up arisað lease leoȝeras. *c* **1175** *Lamb. Hom.* 13 Ne beo þu lihȝere ne for eye ne for luue. *c* **1290** *S. Eng. Leg.* I. 333/362 A strong liare and man of false lawe. **1340** *Ayenb.* 62 Þe lyeȝere is ylich þe dyeule þet is his uader. *c* **1374** CHAUCER *Troylus* III. 260 (309) Auauntoure and a lyere al is on. *c* **1375** *Sc. Leg. Saints* i. (*Petrus*) 422 Quhedir he a lele man or a lear be. *c* **1400** *Destr. Troy* 12590 Thus lytherly þo lyghers lappit þere tales. **1413** *Pilgr. Sowle* (Caxton) I. xvii. (1859) 18 He.. hath ben found an open lyer. **1470–85** MALORY *Arthur* XX. xiv, They that told yow the tales were lyers. **1552** ABP. HAMILTON *Catech.* (1884) 25 He is ane lear and in him thair is na verite. **1581** SIDNEY *Apol. Poetrie* (Arb.) 51 Of all Writers vnder the sunne, the Poet is the least lier. **1614** RALEIGH *Hist. World* II. (1634) 466 Poets are lyars, and for verses sake Will make the gods of humane crimes partake. *a* **1764** LLOYD *Ep. to J.B. Esq.* Poet. Wks. 1774 I. 96 Who are known lyars by profession. **1782** V. KNOX *Ess.* (1819) I. ii. 12 An habitual liar.. must possess a poor and pusillanimous heart. **1865** DICKENS *Mut. Fr.* I. xiv, 'Now tell me I'm a liar', said the honest man. **1875** JOWETT *Plato* (ed. 2) I. 359 You are a liar, Meletus, not believed even by yourself. **1940** *Sunday Express* 31 Mar. 3/5 'That's not my brother Sid you met in here last Thursday. Or was it Friday?' We said we didn't remember... 'I'm a liar. It was Wednesday.' **1972** W. GARNER *Ditto, Brother Rat!* xv. 105 Last winter, was it? No, I'm a liar. The spring. That's right.

Proverbs. *c* **1250** *Ten Abuses* in *O.E. Misc.* 184 Old mon lechur, ȝunch mon lieȝer [*2nd text* lyere]. **1539** TAVERNER *Erasm. Prov.* (1552) 35 A lyer ought not to be forgetfull. *a* **1555** LATIMER in *Godly Confer. w. Ridley* (1556) b2b, Lyers had nede to haue good memories. **1631** CHETTLE *Hoffmann* I 2b, Lyer, lyer, licke dish.

b. **liar's bench** (see quot.).

1859 NARES, *Liars'-bench*, a place in St. Paul's Cathedral in the sixteenth century, so called because it was stated that the disaffected made appointments there.

c. *attrib.* or *adj.* Lying, deceitful. **liar dice**, a gambling game resembling poker dice, in which the thrower conceals the dice thrown and sometimes declares a false score; also *ellipt.* (in *pl.*).

a **1300** *Cursor M.* 6819 Tak þou noght wit tunge leier. **1946** J. SCARNE *On Dice* (ed. 2) xvii. 386 Liar or Doubting Dice. A popular game on transpacific liners and in the Far East, it is now gaining rapidly in popularity in the United States. **1956** M. MCMINNIES *Flying Fox* I. iv. 55 Everybody was round the bar playing liar dice. **1959** R. KIRKBRIDE *Tamiko* v. 37 'Which do you play, Balin?' 'Which?' 'Liars, Horses, Cameroon—.' 'I don't play dice.' **1966** O. NORTON *School of Liars* i. 2, I spent two months in graduating from the empty lounge to the bar, two more in.. reaching the inner group, the liar-dice school. *Ibid.* ii. 23 We sat there playing liars until twenty past two. **1971** C. BONINGTON *Annapurna South Face* ix. 107 After the meal we played liar dice or Scrabble, with our tape-recorder blasting out music in the background.

d. *the liar* (Logic): the name of the paradox involved in a speaker's statement that he is lying or is a (habitual) liar; so *liar paradox*, *paradox of the liar*.

1871 T. M. LINDSAY tr. *Ueberweg's Syst. Logic* v. §77. 245 This case happens when, and only when, the *truth of the judgment* is itself *the object of the judgment*, or belongs to the object of the judgment. The ancients have empirically discovered this case, without.. giving an account of its logical nature. What is called *'The Liar'* represents it. Epimenides, the Cretan, says, all the Cretans are liars. **1906** J. N. KEYNES *Stud. & Exerc. Formal Logic* (ed. 4) App. B. 457 The sophism known as *Ψευδόμενος* or *The Liar*. **1908** B. RUSSELL in *Amer. Jrnl. Math.* XXX. 240 Hence his statement is false, and yet its falsehood does not imply, as that of 'I am lying' appeared to do, that he is making a true statement. This solves the liar. **1940** —— *Inquiry into Meaning & Truth* iv. 62 The inference from the paradox of the liar is.. as follows. **1959** E. W. BETH *Found. Math.* VI. xvii. 485 The natural first reaction to the liar paradox is to ascribe the contradiction to the fact that the statement involved refers to itself. **1967** *Encycl. Philos.* V. 46/1 But one, the Liar,.. is still of great interest to us. **1970** R. L. MARTIN (*title*) The paradox of the liar. **1971** *Philos.* XLVI. 133 (*heading*) Tarski, Frege, and the liar paradox.

liar, variant of LYAR *Sc. Obs.*

‖**liard**[1] (ljar). Also 6 lier(de, lyard (*quasi-It.* liardo), *Sc.* lyart. [F.; prob. subst. use of *liard* adj. grey (see LYARD *a.*). Cf. *grey groat*.] A small coin formerly current in France, of the value of the fourth part of a sou. Hence, typically, a coin of small value.

1542 BOORDE *Introd. Knowl.* xxvii. (1870) 191 In bras they [French] haue mietes, halfe pens, pens, dobles, lierdes.. a lier is worth three brasse pens. **1572** *Satir. Poems Reform.* xxxii. 15 Haue we ane lyart, na baid bot all is thairis. **1583** STOCKER *Civ. Warres Lowe C.* IV. 53 b, A pounde of course Cheese, one Sous and one Lyard. **1600** PORY tr. *Leo's Hist. Africa* III. 134 For the selling of euery duckats-woorth they haue two Liardos allowed them. **1657** DAVENANT *Entertainm. Rutland Ho.* Dram. Wks. 1873 III. 224 His fare being two brass liards. **1751** SMOLLETT *Per. Pic.* (1779) II. xxxix. 29 He knew to a liard what was given to each. **1820** SCOTT *Ivanhoe* xxxii, Neither I nor any of mine will touch the value of a liard. **1847** DISRAELI *Tancred* IV. xi, He would push about in the throng like a Hercules, whenever any one called out to him to fetch a liard.

liard[2] (lɪ'ɑːd). *Canadian.* [a. F. *liard*, subst. use of OF. *liard* grey: see LYARD. (Continental Fr. has *liardier* black poplar.)] The balsam poplar, *Populus balsamifera*, of North America.

1809 A. HENRY *Trav.* 128 *note*, *Populus nigra*, called, by the Canadians, liard.

liard, variant of LYARD, grey.

lias ('laɪəs). Also 5, 7–8 lyas. [Introduced into mod. geology from dialects; a. OF. *liois* (mod.F. *liais*) a compact kind of limestone.]

1. A blue limestone rock occurring in certain south-western counties of England. Also *attrib.*

1404 *Durham Acc. Rolls* (Surtees) 397 In custodia vitrarii ij par petrarum ex officio et j par vocat. lyas. **1649** GLANVILL in *Phil. Trans.* IV. 978 A sort of hard stone, commonly call'd a Lyas, blue and white, polishable. **1778** *Eng. Gazetteer* (ed. 2) s.v. *Launsdon, Som.*, On the N.W. side of this plain are dug a sort of head-stones, called lyas, which are blue and white, and polishable. **1793** SMEATON *Edystone L.* §202 *note*, Lyas is the general term for strata of stone of the species of Aberthaw, in several counties. **1813** VANCOUVER *Agric. Devon* 27 A stratum of blue lais [*sic*] lime-stone. **1832** DE LA BECHE *Geol. Man.* (ed. 2) 155 On the coast of the S.W. part of Somersetshire.. a high shingle beach, principally composed of lias (the rock of the vicinity). **1881** YOUNG *Every Man his own Mechanic* §1154 Blue lias lime is charged 24/- per yard.

2. *Geol.* A series of strata forming the lower division of the Jurassic series, consisting of thin layers of blue argillaceous limestone, and containing a great wealth of fossils.

1833 LYELL *Princ. Geol.* III. Gloss. 72 *Lias*, a provincial name adopted in scientific language for a particular kind of limestone. **1833** —— *Elem. Geol.* (1865) 415 The name of Gryphite limestone has sometimes been applied to the lias. **1873** BURTON *Hist. Scot.* I. iii. 82 The lias, oolite, and other recent formations.

liason, obs. form of LIAISON.

liassic (laɪ'æsɪk), *a.* *Geol.* Also liasic. [f. LIAS + -IC.] Pertaining to the lias formation.

1833 LYELL *Princ. Geol.* III. 378 Metamorphic rocks of the Eocene or Liassic eras. **1854** A. ADAMS, etc. *Man. Nat. Hist.* 561 In the Liasic period of the secondary formations. **1854** H. MILLER *Sch. & Schm.* ii. 37 The first ammonite I ever saw was a specimen.. from one of the liasic deposits of England. *Ibid.* xxi. 451 Both shale and nodules bore, instead of the deep liasic gray, an olivaceous tint.

†**Liatico.** *Obs.* Forms: 7 leathick, leaticke, liatica. [a. It. *liatico* = *Aleatico* (Florio).] A red wine made in Tuscany.

1622 J. TAYLOR (Water P.) *Farew. Tower Bottles* A4, With Malmesie, Muskadell, and Corcica, With White, Red, Clarret, and Liatica. **1625** PURCHAS *Pilgrims* II. 1837 Maluosey, Muscadine, and Leaticke. **1657** REEVE *God's Plea* 25 Thou wouldest.. drink nothing but Frontiniack, white Muscadines, Leathick-wine, and Vine de pary.

liatris (laɪ'ætrɪs, 'laɪətrɪs). [mod.L. (J. C. D. von Schreber in *Linnæus's Genera Plantarum* (ed. 8, 1791) II. 542), of unknown derivation.] A North American perennial herb of the genus so called, belonging to the family Compositæ and bearing spikes or clusters of purple or white flowers.

1811 *Curtis's Bot. Mag.* XXXIV. 1411 (*heading*) Spiked Liatris. **1870** W. ROBINSON *Wild Garden* xv. 139/2 Plants for very moist rich soils... Liatris, in var. **1931** M. GRIEVE *Mod. Herbal* II. 746/2 Several varieties of *Liatris* are largely used in Southern United States to flavour tobacco. **1961** *Amat. Gardening* 14 Oct. 3/4 Cimicifugas, golden rods, liatris and lobelias.

†**lib**, *sb.*[1] *Obs.* [OE. *lyb*(*b*, *libb* medicine, drug, potion. Cf. CHEESELIP.] A charm.

a **700** *Epinal Gloss.* 711 *Obligamentum*, lybb [*Erfurt* libb, *Corpus* lyb, lybsn]. **1577** in Pitcairn *Crim. Trials* I. 77 [In Perthshire] ane commoune usare of sorcerie, libbis, and charmes.

†**lib**, *sb.*[2] *Cant. Obs.* [f. LIB *v.*[3]] Sleep.

1665 HEAD *Eng. Rogue* I. iv. (1666) 29 Bien Darkmans then, Bouse Mort and Ken The bien Coves bings awast, On Chates to trine by Rome-Coves dine, For his long lib at last.

lib, *sb.*[3], colloq. abbrev. LIBERATION, freq. preceded by *adj.* (as *gay lib*) or a *sb.* in the possessive (as *men's lib*, *women's lib*). See the defining words.

1970 *Atlantic Monthly* Mar. 116 The Lib Movement was rich in documentation of the conditioning processes. **1971** *Daily Tel.* 2 Dec. 7/2 Children's lib. notwithstanding, it would be hard to write a children's book without setting up some sort of standard for the child reader to admire. **1973** *Guardian* 3 Feb. 13/1 Lillian Thomas is a member of the Suffrage Fellowship Movement.. and is delighted with the Libs. **1973** *Black World* Dec. 12/1 The various 'lib' movements, therefore, are white derivatives of the Black movement. **1974** *Listener* 25 Apr. 520/3 With Scots Lib, as with Women's Lib, it's no good the oppressors expecting the past to be forgotten when convenient.

lib (lɪb), *v.*[1] Also 7–8 libb. Now *dial.* [? repr. an OE. *lybban = MDu. *lubben* to maim, geld, f. Teut. root *lub-: see LEFT *a.*] *trans.* To castrate, geld, 'cut'.

1396 [see *libbing*, below]. **1500–20** DUNBAR *Poems* lv. 5 Thair wyffis.. baid tham betteis soun abyd At hame, and lib tham of the pockis. **1536** BELLENDEN *Cron. Scot.* (1821) I. p. lv, The steirkis.. ar.. libbit to be oxin. **1597–8** BP. HALL *Sat.* II. vii. 19 Who pares his nailes, or libs his swine. **1607** TOPSELL *Four-f. Beasts* 324 They have used to lib their Horsses and take away their stones. **1618** CHAPMAN *Hesiod* 37 The bellowing Bullock lib, and Gote. **1624** MASSINGER *Renegado* II. i, I am libbed in the breech already. **1649** DAVENANT *Love & Honour* IV. Dram. Wks. 1873 III. 164 Sure he is lib'd; he hath certainly No masculine business about him. *a* **1733** *Shetland Acc.* 28 in *Proc. Soc. Ant. Scot.* (1892) XXVI. 200 That none libb any beast upon Sunday. **1788** MARSHALL *Yorksh.* II. 340 To *Lib*, to geld male lambs and calves (horses and pigs are 'gelded'). **1855** ROBINSON *Whitby Gloss.*, *Scribb'd* and *Libb'd*, farmers' terms, or rather they are used as one word,—castrated.

b. *fig.* (Cf. CASTRATE *v.* 4.)

1577 FULKE *Two Treat. agst. Papists* II. 250 In the latter end where he libbeth of the conclusion of Origens wordes, he translateth [etc.].. when he hath clipped, shauen, pared, gelded and falsified all that he can [etc.]. **1621** BP. MOUNTAGU *Diatribæ* 419 Aristotle.. wrote cxxvi. Bookes, or thereabout, *περὶ πολιτειῶν*.. and yet none of these were libbed by Abbreuiators.

Hence **libbed** *ppl. a.*, **'libbing** *vbl. sb.*

1396 *Whitby Abbey Rolls* (Whitby Gloss.) Pro libbyng porcorum 10d. **1500–20** DUNBAR *Poems* lv. 20 Sum.. hes forsaekin all sic gammiss, That men callis libbing of the pockis. *a* **1600** *Hist. Fryer Bacon* in Thoms *E.E. Prose Rom.* (1858) I. 192 When the best libbing is. **1616** *N. Riding Rec.* II. 123 A libbed gilt. **1638** FORD *Fancies* I. ii, What a terrible sight to a libb'd breech is a sow-gelder! *a* **1693** *Urquhart's Rabelais* III. xxxi. 256 Like a libbed Eunuch. **1790** BURNS *'Kind Sir, I've read your Paper'*, How libbet Italy was singin'.

lib, *v.*[2] *dial.* (Suffolk.) 'Of a child or young animal: To suck persistently' (*Eng. Dial. Dict.*).

1662 GURNALL *Chr. in Arm.* III. xii. §1 (1669) 274/1 The growing child that lies libbing oftenest at the Breast.

†**lib**, *v.*[3] *Cant. Obs.* Also 6 lyp. [Origin unknown.] *intr.* To sleep.

1567 HARMAN *Caveat* (1869) 84 In what lipken has thou lypped in this darkemans, whether in a lybbege or in the strummel? **1611** MIDDLETON & DEKKER *Roaring Girl* v. i, Oh I wud lib all the lightmans, Oh I woud lib all the darkemans. *a* **1700** B. E. *Dict. Cant. Crew*, *Lib*, to Tumble or Lye together. **1859** MATSELL *Vocab.* s.v. (F.), The coves lib together, the fellows sleep together.

lib, dial. form of LEAP *sb.*[2]

†**lib.**, abbrev. of L. *libræ* pounds.

1442 *Extracts Aberd. Reg.* (1844) I. 8 The sowm of iiij[xx] of lib. **1528** *Ibid.* 121 Tuenty lib. Scottis. **1596** DALRYMPLE tr. *Leslie's Hist. Scot.* VI. 333 Ane hunder libs stirling. **1655** in A. Laing *Lindores Abb.* xx. (1876) 238, 8 lib. of pledge in money. **1705** HEARNE in *Rel. Hearn.* (1869) *passim*.

'libament. *Obs.* exc. *arch.* [ad. L. *lībāment-um*, f. *lībā-re* to LIBATE + -MENT.] = LIBATION.

1582 N. T. (Rhem.) *Luke* xxii. 17 *note*, That solemne cuppe of wine, which belonged as a libament to the offering and eating to the Paschal lambe. **1603** HOLLAND *Plutarch's Mor.* 1289 Before his time they dranke it [wine] not at all, neither made they libaments thereof unto their gods. **1855** SINGLETON *Virgil* I. 324 Andromache was pouring libaments To th' ashes.

libaniferous (lɪbə'nɪfərəs), *a.* [f. L. *libanus*, Gr. *λίβανος* incense + -(I)FEROUS.] Yielding incense.

1895 *19th Cent.* Oct. 595 The.. libaniferous country.

†**libanomancy.** *Obs.* [ad. F. *libanomantie* (Rabelais), f. Gr. *λίβανος* incense + *μαντεία* (see -MANCY).] Divination by the burning of incense.

1652 GAULE *Magastrom.* 165 Livanomancy [*sic*]. **1656** in BLOUNT *Glossogr.* *a* **1693** *Urquhart's Rabelais* III. xxv. 208.

libanophorous (lɪbə'nɒfərəs), *a.* [f. Gr. *λιβανοφόρος*, f. *λίβανος* incense + *-φόρος* bearing, *φέρειν* to bear: see -OUS.] Producing incense.

1847 *Jrnl. R. Asiat. Soc., Bombay br.* II. 387 Ptolemy's Libanophorous region is misplaced.

libanotophorous (lɪbənəʊˈtɒfərəs), *a.* [f. Gr. λιβανωτοφόρος, f. λιβανωτός incense (f. λίβανος: see prec.) + -φόρος bearing.] Producing incense.
1879 *Encycl. Brit.* IX. 710/1 The libanotophorous region of the ancients.

libant (ˈlaɪbænt), *a.* [f. L. *lībant-em*, pr. pple. of *lībā-re* LIBATE *v.*] Tasting; touching lightly.
1798 LANDOR *Gebir* VI. 131 She touched his eyelashes with libant lips.

libard(e, libardesse, obs. ff. LEOPARD, -ESS.

†**libardine.** *Obs.* Also 6 libardaine. [f. *libard* LEOPARD; the formation is obscure.] ? A plant of the genus *Aconitum*, ? = LEOPARD'S BANE.
1567 MAPLET *Gr. Forest* 49 Libardaine of the Greeks is called Akoniton, it hath leaves like the Cucumber, but somewhat more lesse and rough. **1607** TOPSELL *Four-f. Beasts* (1658) 32 The herb Wolfeban or Libardine is poison to..all beasts that are littered blinde.

libate (laɪˈbeɪt), *v.* [f. L. *lībāt-*, ppl. stem of *lībāre* to taste, pour out as an offering, etc.]
a. *trans.* To pour out (wine, etc.) in honour of a god. Also, to make a libation to (a god). **b.** *intr.* To pour out libations.
1866 J. B. ROSE tr. *Ovid's Fasti* VI. 762 She libated the wine In sacrifice. **1867** —— tr. *Virgil's Æneid* 227 Around the tables all libating stand, Invoking heaven. **1880** L. WALLACE *Ben-Hur* VII. xi. 441 A son of Israel has no gods whom he can libate.
Hence **liˈbated** *ppl. a.*
1866 J. B. ROSE tr. *Virg. Georg.* I. 360 Pay unto Ceres, rustics rites divine, With milk and honey and libated wine.

libation (laɪˈbeɪʃən). Also 4 libacioun, 5 lybacion. [ad. L. *lībātiōn-em*, n. of action f. *lībā-re* to LIBATE.] The pouring out of wine or other liquid in honour of a god; *concr.* the liquid so poured out; a drink-offering.
1382 WYCLIF *Ezek.* xx. 28 Thei..sacrifieden her libaciouns. **1490** CAXTON *Eneydos* xxii. 81 The good wynes of swete odour ordeyned for the lybacions or washynges of the sacryfices. **1603** HOLLAND *Plutarch's Mor.* 1196 They used this water for the solemne libations at sacrifices. **1697** DRYDEN *Æneid* I. 1030 Sprinkling the first Libations on the Ground. **1743** J. DAVIDSON *Æneid* VII. 184 Pour forth bowls in Libation to Jove. **1834** LYTTON *Pompeii* I. iii, The guests followed the prayer, and then, sprinkling the wine on the table, they performed the wonted libation. **1877** C. GEIKIE *Christ* xlix. (1879) 584 Water to be poured out at the time of the morning offering as a libation.
b. *transf.* (somewhat *jocular*). Liquid poured out to be drunk; hence a potation.
1751 EARL ORRERY *Remarks Swift* (1752) 47 Libations to his health, or, in plain english, bumpers were poured forth to the Drapier. *a* **1797** H. WALPOLE *Mem. Geo. III* (1845) I. xxii. 313 Some jovial dinners and libations of champagne cemented their friendship. *c* **1850** *Arab. Nts.* (Rtldg.) 412 In consequence of their repeated libations, they began both of them to be considerably heated. **1856** SIR B. BRODIE *Psychol. Inq.* I. App. 254 They prepared themselves for the task by a plentiful libation of gin.
c. *fig.*
1781 COWPER *Retirement* 226 He..weeps a sad libation in despair. **1817** MOORE *Lalla R.* (1824) 273 Never yet..hath the sword More terrible libations poured! **1879** FARRAR *St. Paul* I. 344 Willing, nay glad, to pour out his whole life as a libation.
d. *attrib.*
1776 BURNEY *Hist Mus.* I. ii. 40 The spondean melody, that is the libation tune of Olympus. **1865** J. H. INGRAHAM *Pillar of Fire* (1872) 256 Bearers of libation-vases. **1877** A. B. EDWARDS *Up Nile* iv. 80 A libation-table on which was engraved a hieroglyphic inscription to Apis-Osiris.

liˈbationary, *a.* [f. LIBATION + -ARY[1].] = LIBATORY *a.*
1896 W. J. LOCKE *Study in Shadows* vi. 93 Mme. Popea scattered scraps of stuff about her room, in a kind of libationary joy. **1909** *Westm. Gaz.* 16 Feb. 5/2 The new Empress-Dowager had finished performing the libationary sacrifices to the memory of the late Empress-Dowager.

liˈbationer. [f. LIBATION + -ER[1].] One who pours out libations (to a god).
1920 *Brit. Mus. Return* 47 in *Parl. Papers* XXXVI. 673 Black stone squatting figure of Ser, a divine father and libationer of Amen.

libatory (ˈlaɪbətərɪ), *a.* and *sb.* [ad. L. *lībātōri-us*, f. *lībāre*: see LIBATE *v.* and -ORY.]
A. *adj.* Pertaining to or consisting of libations.
1834 MEDWIN in *Fraser's Mag.* IX. 559 Phoebus has..received my libatory offerings. **1846** ELLIS *Elgin Marb.* I. 163 Bearers of libatory vessels.
†**B.** *sb.* A libatory vessel. *Obs.*
1609 BIBLE (Douay) *1 Macc.* i. 23 The libatories [L. *libatoria*] and the phials.

†**libature.** *Obs.* In 7 libatour. [As if ad. L. type **lībātūra*, f. *lībāre* to LIBATE.]
1632 HOLLAND *Cyrupædia* 71 Hee there procured the gracious favour of Dame Tellus, with Libatours and liquid offerings.

libbard, arch. variant of LEOPARD.

libbe, obs. form of LIVE.

libbege. *Old Cant.* [f. LIB *v.*[3]] A bed.
1567 [see LIB *v.*[3]]. **1665** R. HEAD *Eng. Rogue* I. iv. (1666) 33 *Libbege*, a Bed. *a* **1700** B. E. *Dict. Cant. Crew*, *Libbege*, a Bed.

libber[1] (ˈlɪbə(r)). Now *dial.* [f. LIB *v.*[1] + -ER[1].] A gelder.
14.. *Nom.* in Wr.-Wülcker 693/32 *Hic castrator*, lybbere. **1641** BEST *Farm. Bks.* (Surtees) 141 Libbers have for libbinge of pigges, pennies a peece for the giltes, and half pence a peece for the gowtes or bore pigges. **1674-91** RAY *N.C. Words* 44 *A Libber*, a Sow-gelder. **1683** G. MERITON *Yorks. Dialogue* 4 The Libber comes to Morn; weese Libb th' awd Piggs.

ˈlibber[2]. colloq. abbrev. LIBERATIONIST. Cf. LIB, WOMAN *sb.* 10.
1971 *Tel.* (Brisbane) 19 May 17/1 Women's libbers are preparing to do battle with the police in Baltimore. **1972** *Village Voice* (N.Y.) 1 June 26/4 Now the star-maker has decided to calm the libbers with another token. **1973** *Times* 1 Nov. 12/6 *The Female Woman* sorts out..the contemporary confusion of ideas about the sexes which the Libbers have..worse confounded. **1973** *Daily Tel.* 24 Nov. 11/8 The..debate set things off by producing a truly appalling female whose anti-male views were so extreme and so crudely expressed that orthodox Libbers in the audience showed dismay.

†**libberla.** *Sc. Obs.* A staff, cudgel.
c **1500** *Rowlls Cursing* 112 in Laing *Anc. Poet. Scotl.*, Thair sall thay [devils] cary in thair clukis Sum libberlais, and sum hell crukis. ? *a* **1550** *Freiris Berwik* 505 in *Dunbar's Poems* (1893) 302 Vp he start, and gat a libberla In-to his hand.

libbet[1] (ˈlɪbɪt). Now *dial.* Also 6 lyb(b)et, (also 9) libbat, 7 libbit, 20 livett. [Cf. OF. *libe*, *libbe* block of stone.] A billet of wood; a stick to beat or throw at anything with.
1562 J. HEYWOOD *Prov. & Epigr.* (1867) 210 Leaue that woorde or Ile baste ye with a libet. **1567** HARMAN *Caveat* 26 A longe lastinge lybbet. **1586** WARNER *Alb. Eng.* IV. xxi. (1602) 99 With that he tooke a Libbat vp, and beateth out his braines. **1589** *Ibid.* Pr. Add. (1602) 345 Libbats newly snatched from burning. **1736** LEWIS *Isle of Tenet* 37, I took up a Libbit that lay by the Sole, and hove it at the Hagister. **1847** HALLIWELL, *Libbet*, a billet of wood; a staff, stick, or club. *South.* **1908** G. SANGER *70 Yrs. a Showman* xiv. 48 We could see the big sticks—'livetts' they were termed—hurtling towards..the prizes.

libbet[2] (ˈlɪbɪt). Now *dial.* [Of obscure origin; cf. LAPPET.] **a.** A flap or lobe. **b.** A fragment, rag, jag.
1627 HAKEWILL *Apol.* (1630) Pref. 3 One who lookes onely upon some libbet, or end of a peece of Arras. *Ibid.* 418 The tender libbets of their eares. **1844** W. BARNES *Poems Rur. Life* Gloss., *Libbets*, rags in strips. **1893** *Wiltsh. Gloss.*, *Libbet*, a fragment. 'All in a libbet', or 'all in libbets and jibbets', torn to rags. Also *Lippet*.

‖**libeccio** (lɪˈbɛtʃəʊ, It. liˈbettʃo). Also *erron.* -ecchio. [It., f. L. *Lib-s*: see LIBS.] The Italian name for the south-west wind.
1667 MILTON *P.L.* x. 706 Eurus and Zephir with thir lateral noise, Sirocco and Libecchio. **1820** SHELLEY *Lett.* Prose Wks. 1880 IV. 178 The Libecchio here howls like a chorus of fiends all day. **1821** MRS. SHELLEY in Dowden *Life Shelley* (1887) II. 395 After a whole week of libeccio rain and wind. **1873** OUIDA *Pascarel* II. 314 The libeccio was blowing keenly as we crossed the square of Fiesole.

libel (ˈlaɪbəl), *sb.* Forms: 4-8 libell, 5 libelle, 5-7 lybell(e, 6-7 lybel, (6 *Sc.* libal), 3- libel. [a. OF. *libel* masc., *libelle* fem. (mod.F. *libelle*), ad. L. *libellus*, dim. of *liber* book. Cf. Sp. *libelo*, Pg., It. *libello*, used in legal senses.]
†**1.** A little book; a short treatise or writing.
1382 WYCLIF *Num.* v. 23 And the preest shal wryte in a libel [1388 litil book] thes cursid thingis. **1436** *Pol. Poems* (Rolls) II. 157 Here beginneth the prologe of the processe of the Libelle of Englyshe Polycye. **1494** FABYAN *Chron.* v. cxxiii. 102 As before is shewyd in the .C. and .xiii. Chapitre of this libell. **1529** MORE *Dyaloge* III. Wks. 234/1 Y[e] no man should..translate..by way of boke, lybel, or tretice. **1530** LYNDESAY *Test. Papyngo* 20 Quintyng, Mersar, Rowle, Henderson, hay, & holland, Thocht thay be ded, yar libells bene leuand. **1576** A. FLEMING *Pref. to Caius' Dogs* in Arb. *Garner* III. 228 Caius spared no study..which seemed..requisite to the performance of this little libel. *a* **1709** ATKYNS *Parl. & Pol. Tracts* (1734) 86 Certain Books, which he termed Codicello's; which in our Dialect, is the same with Libels or Little Books. **1715** M. DAVIES *Athen. Brit.* I. 69 His English Libels were these, viz. *A Merry Jest* [etc.].
†**b.** A written paper. Sometimes = LABEL *sb.*[1], for which it may have been substituted as etymologically more intelligible. *Obs.*
1603 *North's Plutarch* (1612) 1183 With his testament there were three litle libels or codicils. **1642** tr. *Perkins' Prof. Bk.* ii. §136. 60 That [the seal] was so fixed againe to the libell [*ed.* 1657 label, *orig. AF.* (*ed.* 1601) label] of the deed. **1682** KEIGWIN *Mt. Calvary* (1826) clxxxix, This lybell was fastened on y[e] cross fast..And over the head of Christ put. **1689** MOYLE *Sea Chyrurg.* I. 16 With every Medicament its Lybel upon it.
2. A formal document, a written declaration or statement. *Obs.* exc. *Hist.* (as occasional rendering of L. *libellus*), and *Law* (see 3).
1297 R. GLOUC. (Rolls) 10234 Hii sende him libel, & esste ek articles, þat nere noȝt to graunti wel. **1382** WYCLIF *Matt.* v. 31 Who euere shal leeue his wyf, ȝeue he to hir a libel, that is, a litil boke of forsakyng [**1388** a libel of forsakyng]. **1432-50** tr. *Higden* (Rolls) V. 161 A cownsayle was kepede ..where a libelle porrecte to Constancius. **1525** LD. BERNERS *Froiss.* II. ccxlv. [ccxlii.] 754 The knyght toke the kyng a lybell, the whiche was red; therin was conteyned that if there was nother knight..that wolde say that kyng Henry was not rightfull kyng, he was there redy to fyght with him. **1563-87** FOXE *A. & M.* (1596) 16/2 The Arrians returning from their Arrianisme, offered vp and exhibited vnto the bishops of Rome their libels of repentance. **1565** HARDING *Confut. Jewel's Apol.* IV. 161 b, Moses permitted a libell of diuorce. **1596** DALRYMPLE tr. *Leslie's Hist. Scot.* x. 366 Quha tuik al priuat libalis and accusatiounis, and causet exeme thame. **1607** TOPSELL *Four-f. Beasts* (1658) 15 With their image did Augustus sign all his Grants, Libels, and Epistles. **1608** WILLET *Hexapla Exod.* 750 The libels or billes of dowrie. **1652** NEEDHAM *Selden's Mare Cl.* 294 A Libel, or Bill of Complaint. **1781** GIBBON *Decl. & F.* xxviii. III. 75 A formal reply to the petition or *libel* of Symmachus.
3. a. *Civil Law.* The writing or document of the plaintiff containing his allegations and instituting a suit. **b.** *Eccl. Law.* The first plea, or the plaintiff's written declaration or charges, in a cause. **c.** *Sc. Law.* The form of complaint or ground of the charge on which either a civil or criminal prosecution takes place.
1340 *Ayenb.* 40 Þe ualse notaryes..ualseþ þe celes makeþ þe kueade libelles and to uele oþre ualshedes. *c* **1386** CHAUCER *Friar's T.* 297 May I nat axe a libel, sir Somnour, And answere there, by my procutour, To swich thing as men wol opposen me? *c* **1410** LOVE *Bonavent. Mirr.* xviii. (1510) F v b, He that was domysman made the lybelle in theyre cause. *c* **1440** *Jacob's Well* 131 A fals notarye, þat makyth false letterys, libellys, or false actys. **1535** COVERDALE *Job* xxxi. 35 Let him that is my contrary party, sue me with a lybell. **1548** *Act 2 & 3 Edw. VI*, c. 13 §14 The same partie ..shall bringe and deliver..the verie true copie of the libell dependinge in the ecclesiasticall Courte. **1592** *Sc. Acts Jas. VI* §73 All criminall libellis sall contene that the personis complenit on ar airt and pairt of þe cryme libellit. **1601-2** FULBECKE *1st Pt. Parall.* 68 You lay and alleage in your libell as the ground of your action things farre distant in nature. **1681** *Act* in *Lond. Gaz.* No. 1648/4 Providing always that the Libel, whereupon the foresaid Sentence proceeded be special. **1708** J. CHAMBERLAYNE *St. Gt. Brit.* I. II. viii. (1737) 76 First [in Eccl. causes] goes forth a Citation, then a Libel, and Answer. **1721** WODROW *Hist. Ch. Scot.* I. 51 Upwards of thirty different Libels were formed against him, for alledged Injuries, Oppressions, and the like. **1800** A. CARLYLE *Autobiog.* 319 Cuming, Webster, and Hyndman.. were the committee who drew up the libel. **1818** SCOTT *Hrt. Midl.* xii, Surely the pursuer is bound to understand his own libel. **1863** H. COX *Instit.* II. xi. 568 In Causes not criminal and not summary, the first plea is the complainants libel which corresponds to the declaration at common law. **1876** GRANT *Burgh Sch. Scotl.* II. i. 89 The libel having been served on the accused, he compeared.
†**d.** Used jocularly for: The collective body (of lawyers). *Obs. rare*[−1].
1515-20 *Vox Populi* 722 in Hazl. *E.P.P.* III. 293 With iij or iiij greate clothiars, And the hole lybell of lawyars.
†**4.** A leaflet, bill, or pamphlet posted up or publicly circulated; *spec.* one assailing or defaming the character of some person (in early use more fully, ***famous libel*** = Law Latin *libellus famosus*).
1521 BP. LONGLAND in Ellis *Orig. Lett.* Ser. III. I. 253 Suche famous lybells and bills as be sett uppe in night tymes upon Chirche doores. **1577-87** HOLINSHED *Chron.* III. 1240/1 The bishops..durst not openlie publish the excommunication of the king, but secretlie cast libels about the high waies, which gaue notice thereof. **1594** SHAKS. *Rich. III*, I. i. 33 Plots haue I laide..By drunken Prophesies, Libels, and Dreames, To set my Brother Clarence and the King In deadly hate. **1622** BACON *Hen. VII* 94 Who when he turned his backe (more like a Pedant then an Ambassadour) dispersed a bitter Libell, in Latine Verse, against the King. **1647** CLARENDON *Hist. Reb.* II. §86 Cheap senseless libels were scattered about the city,..traducing some, and proscribing others. **1689-90** WOOD *Life* 12 Mar., Two malitious fellowes were found sticking up a libell reflecting on the fast. **1727** SWIFT *Further Acc. E. Curll* Wks. 1755 III. I. 155 Singeing a pig with a new purchased libel. **1776** GIBBON *Decl. & F.* xi. (1869) I. 218 He scattered libels through their camp.
5. *Law.* Any published statement damaging to the reputation of a person. In wider sense, any writing of a treasonable, seditious, or immoral kind. Also, the act or crime of publishing such a statement or writing.
a **1631** DONNE *Serm.* ix. 87 And by the way, that which it may sometimes concerne us to know, yet it may be a Libell to publish it [surplusage]. **1768** BLACKSTONE *Comm.* III. 125 With regard to libels in general, there are..two remedies; one by indictment and another by action. **1810** BENTHAM *Packing* (1821) 2 In point of actual law, a libel is any paper in which he, who to the will adds the power of punishing for it, sees any thing that he does not like. **1840** B'NESS BUNSEN in Hare *Life* (1879) II. i. 12 Condemned to imprisonment for publishing seditious libels. **1862** TROLLOPE *Orley F.* xix. (ed. 4) 134 It may be very difficult to obtain evidence of a libel. **1888** *Pall Mall G.* 24 Nov. 4/1 The judge answered.. that it was clearly possible to publish a libel for the public good.
b. In popular use: Any false and defamatory statement in conversation or otherwise. *transf.*, applied to a portrait that does the sitter injustice, or to a thing or circumstance that tends to bring undeserved ill repute on a person, a country, etc.
1618 WITHER *Motto* Introd. Wks. (1633) 504 If any should confesse Those sinnes in publike, which his soul oppresse; Some guilty fellow (moov'd thereat) would take it Unto himselfe; and so, a Libell make it. **1650** FULLER *Pisgah* I. vii. 18 The false report of the spies was in some respect but a libell of this land. **1667** *Causes Decay Chr. Piety* i. 10 Are we reproacht for the name of Christ, that Ignominy serves but to advance our future Glory; every such Libel here, becomes Panegyrick there. **1673-4** DK. LAUDERDALE in *L. Papers* (1885) III. xix. 27 Thos addresses..have proved rether leik libells than treuth. **1693** *Humours Town* 132 They [Men] are living Libels [as to Women's virtue]. **1694** DRYDEN *To Sir G. Kneller* 163 Good heav'n! that sots and knaves should be so vain, To wish their vile resemblance may remain! And stand recorded, at their own request, To future days, a libel or a jest! **1725** YOUNG *Love Fame* I. 160

A rich knave's a libel on our laws. **1777** SHERIDAN *Sch. Scand.* I. i, His whole conversation is a perpetual libel on all his acquaintance. **1781** COWPER *Conv.* 450 Or make the parrot's mimicry his choice, That odious libel on a human voice. **1850** LYELL *2nd Visit U.S.* II. 163 The tale of suffering.. was not authentic... Such libels are hailed with pleasure by the Perpetualists as irritating the feeling of that class of slave-owners who [etc.].

6. *attrib.* and *Comb.*, as (sense 5) ***libel-spawning*** adj., (sense 3) ***libel summons***.

Libel Act, the title of the Act 32 *Geo.* 3. c. 60, as shortened by Act of Parliament in 1896 (59 & 60 *Vict.* c. xiv).

1682 TATE *Abs. & Achit.* II. 520 Parasites and libel-spawning imps. **1870** J. K. HUNTER *Life Stud.* xlvii. 289, I saw the auld chap go direct to the Fiscal's office, and next day I had a libel summons chargin' me wi' every conceivable way of killing game on my neighbour's grun'.

libel ('laɪbəl), *v.* [f. LIBEL *sb.*; OF. *libeller*, med.L. *libellāre* existed in certain senses.]

†**1.** *intr.* To make libellous accusations or statements; to spread defamation. Const. *against*, *on*; *by*, *of* (Sc.). *Obs.*

1570 *Satir. Poems Reform.* xii. 157 Suppois ȝe crak, ȝe ly abak, And lybellis be the Law. **1583** *Leg. Bp. St. Androis* 1008 What suld I lyble of this lowne? Not all the paper of this towne.. May had the half that he hes done. **1588** SHAKS. *Tit. A.* IV. iv. 17 What's this but Libelling against the Senate? **1596** NASHE *Saffron Walden* 80 He is verie seditious and mutinous in conuersation.. libelling most execrably and inhumanely on Iacke of the Falcon. **1610** B. JONSON *Alch.* III. ii, Nor shall you need to libell 'gainst the Prelates. **1637** LAUD *Sp. Star-Chamber* 14 June 9 Hee Libels against the King and the State.

2. *trans.* To defame or discredit by the circulation of libellous statements; to accuse falsely and maliciously; *spec.* in *Law*, to publish a libel against.

1601 B. JONSON *Poetaster* IV. vii, Thou shalt libell, and I'le cudgell the Rascall. **1654** H. L'ESTRANGE *Chas. I* (1655) 4 With a spirit which equally disdaines to libel or to flatter him. **1709** POPE *Jan. & May* 44 But what so pure, which envious tongues will spare? Some wicked wits have libell'd all the fair. **1732** SWIFT *Beasts' Confess. to Priest* 202, I would accuse him [fabling Æsop] to his face For libeling the four-foot race. **1803** WELLINGTON in Gurw. *Desp.* (1837) II. 492 Those who have deserted this service have been allowed to libel and defame his character. **1884** *Manch. Exam.* 7 Oct. 5/1 The Grub-street hacks, who in former times lived by libelling political personages.

fig. a **1716** SOUTH *Serm.* (1744) II. 158 It.. misrepresents and libels God to the Conscience. *a* **1862** BUCKLE *Civiliz.* (1869) III. v. 480 Beware of libelling what you profess to defend.

3. *Eccl.* and *Sc. Law.* To institute a suit against (a person) by means of a libel; also, to specify in a libel.

1582-8 *Hist. Jas. VI* (1804) 220 Thai shall haue alswa the King's licence.. to reduce thair foirfaultors, upoun sick causes and considerations as they may libell. **1711** *Countrey-Man's Let. to Curat* 48 When he was Lybell'd, the Missal and Breviary had not receiv'd the Rasures before spoken of. **1752** J. LOUTHIAN *Form of Process* (ed. 2) 35 In all capital Crimes, the Facts are to be libelled, with the Hour, Day, Month.. and Place in which the Fact happened. **1753** S. FRASER in *Scots Mag.* Apr. 179/1 The facts.. are not sufficient to infer the crime libelled. **1754** ERSKINE *Princ. Sc. Law* (1809) 457 If these adminicles afford sufficient conviction, that the deed libelled did once exist. **1868** *Act 31 & 32 Vict.* c. 101 §59 It shall be lawful to libel and conclude and decern for General Adjudication without such Alternative.

b. To bring suit in admiralty against (a vessel, cargo, or its owner).

1805 *East's Reports* V. 317 The vessel and her cargo have been libelled in the Court of Admiralty for condemnation. **1811** J. ADAMS *Wks.* (1854) IX. 628 Nickerson was libelled in the Special Court of Vice-Admiralty by Jonathan Sewall. **1829** MARRYAT *F. Mildmay* xxi, The *True-blooded Yankee* was libelled in the Vice-Admiralty Court at Cape Town. **1894** *Daily News* 20 Sept. 6/5 The owners of the steamer instructed a firm of solicitors at Halifax to 'libel' the vessel for 10,000 dollars.

Hence '**libelled** *ppl. a.*, '**libelling** *vbl. sb.* and *ppl. a.*

1574 *Burgh Rec. Glasgow* (1832) 33 Anent þe libellit precept rasit at þe instance of maister Robert Herbertsoun. **1587** FLEMING *Contn. Holinshed* III. 368/2 False and infamous railings and libellings. **1641** MILTON *Animadv.* Wks. 1738 I. 80 The practices.. of libelling Separatists. **1668** CLARENDON *Contempl. Ps.* Tracts (1727) 668 A libelling look hath begotten very tragical mischiefs. **1697** DRYDEN *Virgil* (1721) I. Life 29 Marc Antony.. vex'd him with a great many Libelling Letters, in which he reproaches him with the Baseness of his Parentage. **1727** SWIFT *Further Acc. E. Curll* Wks. 1755 III. I. 159 That towards the libelling of the said Pope there be a sum employed not exceeding six pounds sixteen shillings and ninepence. **1794** MATHIAS *Purs. Lit.* (1798) 385 His pictur'd person and his libel'd shape. **1830** D'ISRAELI *Chas. I*, III. xi. 245 The art of libelling is no inefficient prelude to revolutionary measures.

†**li'bella.** *Ent. Obs.* [mod.L. (Moufet 1634); perh. an application of L. *lībella* (see LEVEL *sb.*), with reference to the horizontal extension of the wings.] An early scientific name for the dragon-fly. (Cf. LIBELLULA.)

1694 *Libellæ* [see DRAGON-FLY]. **1774** GOLDSM. *Nat. Hist.*, *Insects* II. ii, Of the Libella, or Dragon-fly.

libellant ('laɪbələnt). Also libelant. [f. LIBEL *v.* + -ANT; after *appellant*, *defendant*, etc.]

1. *Law.* One who institutes a suit in an ecclesiastical or admiralty court. Also as *adj.*

1726 AYLIFFE *Parergon* 352 The party Libellant seems to confess whatever is contain'd within the compass and Words of his Libel. *Ibid.*, If the Libellant propounds any thing in his Libel which makes against himself, he must abide by it. **1804-17** W. CRANCH *Rep.* (Webster 1828), The counsel for the libelant contended [etc.]. **1874** DEADY in *Law Times Rep.* XXXI. 201/1 The libellants shipped on the Hermine.. as ordinary seamen. **1890** *Law Times* LXXXIX. 164/1 Successful libellants in a collision suit.

2. One who publishes a libel; a libeller.

In some recent Dicts.

libellary ('laɪbələrɪ), *a. Roman Law.* [ad. late L. *libellārius* (Du Cange), f. *libellus* LIBEL *sb.*] Characterized by the issuing of a libel, or written statement of his cause of action, by the plaintiff as the commencement of a suit.

1875 POSTE *Gaius* IV. Comm. (ed. 2) 532 The Libellary system which prevailed in the time of Justinian. *Ibid.* 657 The Libellary procedure.. having superseded the Formulary procedure.

†'**libellate**, *pple.*, *a.*, or *sb. Obs. rare.* [ad. med.L. *libellātus*, pa. pple. of *libellāre*: see LIBEL *v.*] = *libelled* pa. pple., or LIBELLEE.

1565 *Child Marriages* 45 Christofer Hartley.. vncle to the said James libellate. **1604** *Chichester Registry Dep.*, Nov. (*MS.*), The said Julian Legate, libellate,.. is accompted among her neighbours to be an honest woman.

libellatic (laɪbə'lætɪk), *sb. Eccl. Hist.* [ad. L. *libellāticus*, f. *libellus*: see LIBEL *sb.* Cf. F. *libellatiques* sb. pl.] A Christian who, under persecution, obtained from a magistrate a false certificate that he had sacrificed to the heathen gods.

1873 J. C. ROBERTSON *Hist. Chr. Ch.* (1874) I. 164.

†**libe'llatic**, *a. Obs. rare*$^{-1}$. In 8 -atick. [ad. L. *libellāticus* (cf. prec.): see LIBEL *sb.* and -ATIC.] That writes libellous matter.

1715 M. DAVIES *Athen. Brit.* I. Pref. 81 Those Libellatick Pamphleteers.

libellee (laɪbə'liː). *Law.* [f. LIBEL *v.* + -EE.] One against whom a libel has been filed.

1856 BOUVIER *Amer. Law Dict.*, *Libellee*, a party against whom a libel has been filed in chancery proceedings, or in admiralty, corresponding to the defendant in a common law suit. **1860** in WHARTON *Law Lex.* **1886** *Homilet. Review* (N.Y.) Jan. 91 Vermont first put restrictions on the re-marriage of the libellee.

libeller ('laɪbələ(r)). Also 7 libellour. [f. LIBEL *v.* + -ER^{1}.] One who libels another; one who publishes a libel or libels.

1589 COOPER *(title)* An Admonition to the People of England: wherein are answered.. the slaunderous vntruethes vttered by Martin [Marprelate] the Libeller. **1626** MASSINGER *Rom. Actor* I. iii, In thee, as being the chiefe of thy profession, I doe accuse the qualitie of treason, As libellers against the state and Cæsar. **1634** PEACHAM *Gentl. Exerc.* I. iii. 9 To buy it [pleasure].. with losse.. of his eares for a libeller. **1642** MILTON *Apol. Smect.* Wks. 1851 III. 285 If he hop't the Prelats had no intelligence with the libellours. **1709** *Tatler* No. 88 ⁋7 The Squibs are those who in the common Phrase of the World are call'd Libellers, Lampooners and Pamphleteers. **1742** LD. HARDWICKE in *Atkyns' Rep.* (1794) III. 479 All the libellers of the kingdom know now, that printing initial letters will not serve their turn. **1820** BYRON *Mar. Fal.* II. i. 240 Oh! had this false and flippant libeller Shed his young blood for his absurd lampoon. *a* **1862** BUCKLE *Civiliz.* (1869) III. v. 298 The Scotch divines.. were the libellers of their species; they calumniated the whole human race.

Comb. **1600** W. WATSON *Decacordon* (1602) 106 Became an officious Agent, libeller-like to Rome, by writing against his brethren the seculars.

libellist ('laɪbəlɪst). [f. LIBEL *sb.* + -IST. Cf. F. *libelliste.*] = LIBELLER.

1794 C. PIGOTT *Female Jockey Club* (ed. 4) 200 In continuing to prosecute petty, insignificant cavillers, while they allow such a Gigantic Libellist.. to go unmolested. **1801** HEL. M. WILLIAMS *Sk. Fr. Rep.* I. v. 37 Every friend of liberty.. was branded as a libellist. **1852** *Fraser's Mag.* XLV. 615 The law could not give more latitude to a libellist. **1899** *Academy* 28 Oct. 479/2 From Butler downwards they [satirists] are all inveterate libellists.

†'**libellize**, *v. Obs. rare.* [f. LIBEL *sb.* + -IZE.] *intr.* To deal in libels, to practice slander.

c **1620** T. ROBINSON *M. Magd.* 4/27 To reprehend In sharpe-fang'd Satyres, is to libellize, To raise vile slaunders, and false infamies. **1628** WITHER *Brit. Rememb.* 285 Such a president will hearten them To libellize.

libellous ('laɪbələs), *a.* [f. LIBEL *sb.* + -OUS.] Containing or constituting a libel, of the nature of a libel: also, engaged upon libels.

1619 VISCOUNT DONCASTER *Let.* in *Eng. & Germ.* (Camden) 138 A libellous booke. *a* **1631** DONNE in *Select.* (1840) 238 An itching ear, delighting in the libellous defamation of other men. **1693** in *Wood's Life* (1848) 374 The clauses and sentences.. pretending to be reflecting and libellous upon Edward late earl of Clarendon. **1769-72** *Junius Lett.* Pref. 11 The paper.. contained no treasonable or libellous matter. **1809-10** COLERIDGE *Friend* (1865) 53 The publication of actual facts may be.. criminal and libellous, when directed against private characters. **1827** HALLAM *Const. Hist.* (1876) I. iv. 207 The libellous pen of Martin Mar-prelate. **1848** DICKENS *Dombey* xv, It seemed hardly less libellous in him to imagine her grown a woman.

Hence '**libellously** *adv.*

1832 L. HUNT *Sir R. Esher* (1850) 96 The phrase.. was first given him libellously by Lord Rochester. **1865** *Sat. Rev.* 5 Aug. 168/2 Certain naturalists.. libellously represented Aristotle as saying that goats breathed through their ears.

‖**Libellula** (lɪ'bɛljuːlə). *Ent.* [Mod.L. (Linnæus); dim. of the earlier name LIBELLA.] A genus of neuropterous insects, originally corresponding in extent to the modern family *Libellulidæ* (Dragon-flies); now one of three genera composing that order.

1752 HILL *Hist. Anim.* 73 The mouth of the Libellula is furnished with jaws: the antennæ are short [etc.]. **1774** GOLDSM. *Nat. Hist.* VII. 330 A large and beautiful fly of the libellula kind. **1854** H. MILLER *Sch. & Schm.* x. (1866) 100 Different species of libellula that used to come and deposit their eggs.

Hence **li'bellulid** *sb.*, one of the family *Libellulidæ*. **li'belluline** *a.* pertaining to the *Libellulidæ*; *sb.* an insect of this family. **li'belluloid** *a.*, resembling the *Libellulidæ*.

1848 CRAIG, *Libellulines*, the Dragon-flies. **1855** MAYNE *Expos. Lex.*, *Libelluloides* adj.,.. libelluloid.

†'**libence.** *Obs. rare*$^{-1}$. [ad. L. *libentia*, f. *libent-em*, *libens* willing.] Willingness.

1654 VILVAIN *Theol. Treat.* ii. 47 This volence is a meer libence, free from coactiv violence.

†**li'bentiously**, *adv. Obs. rare*$^{-1}$. [As if f. **libentious* (f. as prec. + -OUS) + -LY^{2}.] Willingly.

1606 WARNER *Alb. Eng.* XV. xcvi. 383 That for them libentiously Fooles-Catholike should erre.

‖**liber** ('laɪbə(r)). *Bot.* [L. *liber* bark.] The inner bark of exogens; bast. Also *attrib.*

1753 CHAMBERS *Cycl. Supp.* s.v. *Bark*, The inner bark or liber. **1797** *Encycl. Brit.* IX. 603/2 It is the liber, or inner bark, that constitutes the cinnamon. **1857** HENFREY *Elem. Bot.* §765 The bast.. consists of the separate liber-layers of the Lime-tree. **1861** BENTLEY *Man. Bot.* 31 The liber-cells are among the longest that occur in any of the tissues. **1881** *Philad. Rec.* No. 3438. 4 Care is necessary to bring the liber of both stock and graft [of the vine] into contact.

[**liber**, a spurious word in recent Dicts., is evolved from a misprint in *Ure's Dict. Arts* (ed. 7, 1875) III. 333 (*libers* for *limbers*; in edd. 1-4 the word is given correctly).]

liberal ('lɪbərəl), *a.* and *sb.* Forms: 4-5 **liberale**, (5 **libral**), 4-7 **liberall(e**, 5-6 **lyberal(l**, 4- **liberal**. [a. OF. *liberal* (F. *libéral*) = Sp., Pg. *liberal*, It. *liberale*, ad. L. *līberālis* pertaining to a free man, f. *liber* free.]

A. *adj.*

1. Originally, the distinctive epithet of those 'arts' or 'sciences' (see ART 7) that were considered 'worthy of a free man'; opposed to *servile* or *mechanical*. In later use, of condition, pursuits, occupations: Pertaining to or suitable to persons of superior social station; 'becoming a gentleman' (J.). Now *rare*, exc. of education, culture, etc., with mixture of senses 3 and 4: Directed to general intellectual enlargement and refinement; not narrowly restricted to the requirements of technical or professional training. Freq. in ***liberal arts***.

c **1375** *Sc. Leg. Saints* xxiv. (*Alexis*) 111 þai set hyme ayrly to þe schule, artis liberalis for-thy þat he suld cone. **1422** tr. *Secreta Secret.*, *Priv. Priv.* 144 Libral Sciencis, that is to Say fre scyencis, as gramer, arte, fisike, astronomye, and otheris. **1509** HAWES *Past. Pleas.* XVI. (Percy Soc.) 62 Physyke can not be lyberall As the vii. science by good auctorite. **1557**, **1579** [see ART 7]. **1589** GREENE *Menaphon* (Arb.) 61 It behooued her to further his Destinies with some good and liberall education. **1638** F. JUNIUS *Paint. Ancients* 232 None among all other liberall arts do require.. so great helps. *a* **1661** FULLER *Worthies* (1840) III. 209 He made any liberal employment beseem him; reading, writing [etc.]. **1680** EVELYN *Diary* 18 Apr., A painting by Verrio, of Apollo and the Liberal Arts. **1741** MIDDLETON *Cicero* I. i. 7 Agriculture was held the most liberal employment in old Rome. **1749** CHESTERF. *Lett.* (1792) II. cciii. 272 If you have not.. liberal and engaging manners.. you will be nobody. **1753** W. SHIPLEY in D. G. C. Allan *William Shipley* (1968) 229 (*title*) Proposals for raising by subscription a fund to be distributed in premiums for the promoting of improvements in the Liberal Arts and Sciences, Manufactures, etc. **1757** BURKE *Abridgm. Eng. Hist.* II. i. Wks. (1812) 256 They are permitted.. to emerge out of that low rank into a more liberal condition. **1776** ADAM SMITH *W.N.* v. ii. II. 478 The ingenious arts and the liberal professions. **1801** STRUTT *Sports & Past.* I. iii. 40 Two centuries back horse-racing was considered as a liberal pastime, practised for pleasure rather than profit. **1818** HALLAM *Mid. Ages* (1872) I. 342 Rarely met with except in persons of good birth and liberal habits. **1845** STEPHEN *Comm. Laws Eng.* (1874) I. 1 Men of liberal education and respectable rank. **1849** MACAULAY *Hist. Eng.* vi. II. 55 They wandered to countries which neither mercantile avidity nor liberal curiosity had ever impelled any stranger to explore. **1868** M. PATTISON *Academ. Org.* v. 192 The distinction.. will always remain as fundamental between the liberal and professional. **1875** JOWETT *Plato* (ed. 2) IV. 335 The free use of words and phrases.. is generally characteristic of a liberal education. **1906** P. ABELSON (*title*) The seven liberal arts, a study in mediæval culture. **1950** E. H. GOMBRICH *Story of Art* xv. 215 The so-called Liberal Arts such as rhetorics, grammar, philosophy and dialectic. **1951** [see CLINIC *sb.*^{2} 3]. **1961** *New Scientist* 16 Mar. 662/1 The better public schools.. should be converted to liberal-arts colleges on the American pattern. **1965** *Listener* 11 Mar. 387/2 (Advt.), The major part of the work will be teaching

Sociology,..but appropriately qualified candidates will be expected to teach Liberal studies. **1973** *Jrnl. Genetic Psychol.* CXXII. 183 The educational problems of the troubled liberal arts college student.

2. a. Free in bestowing; bountiful, generous, open-hearted. Const. *of*.

1387 TREVISA *Higden* (Rolls) VII. 119 In fiȝtinge he was strong, in giffynge liberal. **1426** LYDG. *De Guil. Pilgr.* 22438 They seyne eke they be lyberal, Though they be streyte and ravynous. *c* **1430** *ABC of Aristotle* in *Babees Bk.* 12, L to looth for to leene, ne to liberal of goodis. **1513** MORE in Hall *Chron., Edw. V* (1548) j b, Somwhat aboue his power liberall. **1520** *Caxton's Chron. Eng.* IV. 31 b/2 He was full lyberall to all men. **1535** COVERDALE *Ecclus.* xxxi. 23 Who so is liberall in dealynge out his meate, many men shall blesse him. **1596** SHAKS. *Merch. V.* IV. i. 438, I see sir you are liberall in offers. *a* **1625** FLETCHER *Love's Pilgr.* III. iii, As you are a gentleman, be liberal. **1659** HAMMOND *On Ps.* lxvi. 15 Paraphr. 324 This I will now doe in the liberallest and most magnificent manner. **1785** COWPER *Task* IV. 413 Knaves in office..liberal of their aid To clamorous importunity in rags. **1860** DICKENS *Uncomm. Trav.* xi, The bearers..are persons to whom you cannot be too liberal. **1863** COWDEN CLARKE *Shaks. Char.* v. 124 With Cassio he is patronising, and liberal of his advice. **1886** RUSKIN *Præterita* I. vi. 184 Wisely liberal of his money for comfort and pleasure.

absol. **1611** BIBLE *Isa.* xxxii. 8 The liberall deuiseth liberall things. **1692** LOCKE *Educ.* §105 Let them find by experience, that the most liberal has always most plenty.

b. Of a gift, offer, etc.: Made without stint. Of a meal, an entertainment, etc., also of a fortune: Abundant, ample.

1433 *Rolls of Parlt.* IV. 425/1 Of the whiche his liberall offre ye said Lords þankid hym. **1513** MORE in Hall *Chron., Edw. V* (1548) iij b, Wyth ouer liberall and wanton diet, he waxed somewhat corpulent & bourly. **1535** COVERDALE *Ps.* xx[i]. 3 Thou hast preuented him with liberall blessinges. **1602** *Life T. Cromwell* III. i. 97 Therefore, kind sir, thanks for your liberal gift. **1607** TOPSELL *Four-f. Beasts* (1658) 360 The lion, having been lately filled with some liberal prey, did not presently fall to eat him. **1672–5** COMBER *Comp. Temple* (1702) 332 Some of our liberalest foundations..are of their Erection. **1689** BURNET *Tracts* I. 19 To correct the moisture of the Air with liberal entertainments. **1828** SCOTT *F.M. Perth* xxxiv, 'A liberal offer'..said the Host of the Griffin. **1843** R. S. CANDLISH in Jean L. Watson *Life* viii. (1882) 88 My cordial thanks for the liberal provision you have made for me. **1853** KANE *Grinnell Exp.* xxxvi. (1856) 327 The men drank it [beer] in most liberal quantities.

c. Hence *occas.* of outline, parts of the body, etc.: Ample, large.

1616 B. JONSON *Devil an Ass* I. iii. (1631) 109 Against this husband; Who, if we chance to change his liberall eares To other ensignes, and with labour make A new beast of him. **1798** LANDOR *Gebir* I. 204 More of pleasure than disdain Was in her dimpled chin and liberal lip. **1897** *Allbutt's Syst. Med.* IV. 381, I think I have observed that women of slender frame more often contract renal disease under pregnancy than those of more liberal outline.

3. †a. Free from restraint; free in speech or action. In 16–17th c. often in a bad sense: Unrestrained by prudence or decorum, licentious. ***liberal arbitre*** (= F. *libéral arbitre*, L. *liberum arbitrium*): free will. *Obs.*

1490 CAXTON *Eneydos* xii. 44 Wyll thou commytte & vndresitte thy lyberal arbytre to thynges Impossyble. **1526** *Pilgr. Perf.* (W. de W. 1531) 131 And where there is a quicke wytte & a liberall tong, there is moche speche. *c* **1594** KYD *Sp. Trag.* (1620) I 4, It lyes not in Lorenzos power To stop the vulgar liberall of their tongues. **1599** SHAKS. *Much Ado* IV. i. 93 A ruffian Who hath indeed most like a liberall villaine, Confest the vile encounters they have had. **1604** —— *Oth.* II. i. 165 Is he not a most prophane, and liberall Counsailor? **1608** MIDDLETON *Fam. Love* v. ii, I stand The theme and comment to each liberal tongue. **1613** BEAUM. & FL. *Captain* II. ii, And give allowance to your liberall jests Upon his person. **1670** COTTON *Espernon* III. IX. 469, I shall not..attempt to pass so liberal a judgment upon a person I am, for so many respects, oblig'd to honour. **1689** WOOD *Life* 31 Aug., Mr. Henry Dodwell..liberal in his discourse at London, so much that a gent. threatened to bring him into danger. **1709** STEELE *Tatler* No. 79 ¶4 The Old Devil at Temple-Bar,..where Ben. Johnson and his Sons used to make their liberal Meetings.

b. Of passage, etc.: Freely permitted, not interfered with. *Obs.* exc. *arch.*

1530–1 *Act 22 Hen. VIII*, c. 14 His lyberall and free habytations resortes and passages to and fro the vniuersall places of this realme. **1532** *Act 23 Hen. VIII*, c. 18 Ships should haue their liberall and direct passage in the mids of the streames of the said riuer of Ouse and water of Humber. **1871** R. ELLIS tr. *Catullus* lxviii. 69 He in a closed field gave scope of liberal entry.

c. Of construction or interpretation: Inclining to laxity or indulgence; not rigorous. †Also of a translation: Free, not literal.

1778 JEFFERSON *Autobiog.* Wks. 1859 I. 146, I have added Latin, or liberal English translations. **1792** A. HAMILTON *Let. to E. Carrington* Wks. (ed. Lodge) VIII. 264 A disposition on my part towards a liberal construction of the powers of the national government. **1818** CRUISE *Digest* (ed. 2) III. 407 The learned Commentator..put a much more liberal construction on the *dictum* in the Year Book.

†d. With agent-noun: That does something freely or copiously. *Obs.*

1668 CULPEPPER & COLE *Barthol. Anat.* II. i. 87 So much ..as may suffice a Child that is a liberal Sucker.

4. a. Free from narrow prejudice; open-minded, candid.

1781 GIBBON *Decl. & F.* xxx. III. 142 A Grecian philosopher, who visited Constantinople soon after the death of Theodosius, published his liberal opinions concerning the duties of kings. **1803** *Med. Jrnl.* IX. 444 A liberal investigation of the curative power of topical cold to arthritic inflammation. **1817** J. EVANS *Excurs. Windsor* etc. 20 The late Dr. Watson..published a liberal reply to the Historian in his Apology for Christianity. **1818** JAS. MILL *Brit. India* II. v. viii. 684 Liberal enquiries into the literature and institutions of the Hindus. **1849** MACAULAY *Hist. Eng.* iv. I. 467 The resentment which Innocent felt towards France, disposed him to take a mild and liberal view of the affairs of England.

b. *esp.* Free from bigotry or unreasonable prejudice in favour of traditional opinions or established institutions; open to the reception of new ideas or proposals of reform.

Hence often applied as a party designation to those members of a church or religious sect who hold opinions 'broader' or more 'advanced' than those in accordance with its commonly accepted standard of orthodoxy, e.g. in *Liberal Catholic*. *Liberal Christian*: in the U.S. chiefly applied to the Unitarians and Universalists; in England somewhat more vaguely to those who reject or consider unessential any considerable part of the traditional system of belief; so ***liberal Christianity, liberal theology***. Also in application to *Judaism*.

1823 (*title*) The liberal Christian. **1828** (*title*) Which society shall you join, liberal or orthodox? **1846** O. W. HOLMES *A Rhymed Lesson* 308 Thine eyes behold A cheerful Christian from the liberal fold. **1862** *Dublin Rev.* Nov. 48 Our friends the 'liberal' Catholics may be interested in a note to F. Faber's treatise. **1876** O. B. FROTHINGHAM *Transcendentalism New Eng.* vi. 128 It may be inferred that Transcendentalism in New England was a movement within the limits of 'liberal' Christianity or Unitarianism as it was called. **1886** W. P. ROBERTS *Liberalism in Religion* 56, I maintain that Liberal Protestantism, Liberal Christianity, is not anti-dogmatic, is not anti-theological. *Ibid.* 59 Now I am positively for dogma, and so I am sure is every Liberal Christian. **1886** W. BARRY in *Fortn. Rev.* Feb. 185 It would still appear to me..that the Liberal Protestantism of the day is a makeshift. **1900** *Jewish Q. Rev.* July 618 (*heading*) Liberal Judaism in England. *Ibid.*, These liberal Jews have no organization. **1920** R. MACAULAY *Potterism* VI. v. 253 Modernist liberal-catholic vicars asked him to preach. **1957** *Oxf. Dict. Chr. Ch.* 807/1 The 'Liberal Catholics' who formed a distinguished group in the RC Church in the 19th cent. were for the most part theologically orthodox, but they favoured political democracy and ecclesiastical reform... 'Liberal Protestantism'..developed into an anti-dogmatic and humanitarian reconstruction of the Christian faith. **1965** *Sunday Times* 5 Feb. 5/3 A plan for a national conference of non-orthodox synagogues, Reform (progressive) and Liberal. **1968** B. M. G. REARDON (*title*) Liberal Protestantism. **1974** *Times Lit. Suppl.* 19 Apr. 424/4 Judaism is divided into Orthodox, Conservative and Reform varieties following the American terminology, and not into the British Orthodox, Reform and Liberal camps.

5. Of political opinions: Favourable to constitutional changes and legal or administrative reforms tending in the direction of freedom or democracy. Hence used as the designation of the party holding such opinions, in England or other states; opposed to *Conservative*. ***Liberal-Labour***, of or pertaining to (persons associated with or sympathetic to) both the Liberal and the Labour parties. So ***Liberal Labourism***. Cf. LIB-LAB *a.*

In *Liberal Conservative*, the adj. has rather sense 4 than this sense; the combination, however, is often hyphened, which perhaps indicates that it is interpreted as = 'partly Liberal, partly Conservative.' *Liberal Unionist*: a member of the party formed by those Liberals who refused to support Mr. Gladstone's measure of Irish Home Rule in 1886.

1801 HEL. M. WILLIAMS *Sk. Fr. Rep.* I. xi. 113 The extinction of every vestige of freedom, and of every liberal idea with which they are associated. **1842** COBDEN *Speech* in Morley *Life* x. (1882) 34/2, I believe the right hon. Baronet [Peel] to be as liberal as the noble Lord [J. Russell]. **1847** LD. COCKBURN *Jrnl.* II. 191, I have scarcely been able to detect any Candidate's address which, if professing Conservatism, does not explain that this means 'Liberal Conservatism'. **1866** GEO. ELIOT *F. Holt* (1868) 29 Harold meant to stand on the Liberal side. **1879** G. B. SMITH *Life Gladstone* I. i. 9 Principles..which we usually associate with the name of Liberal-Conservative. **1881** LADY HERBERT *Edith* 190 The Liberal Government had outlived its popularity. **1899** LD. ROSEBERY in *Westm. Gaz.* 31 Oct. 2/2 There is no such party known..to the Speaker or the Whips, as the party of the Liberal Imperialists. **1901** *Scotsman* 12 Mar. 6/2 Liberal Unionism is still a vital force in British politics. **1909** *Daily Chron.* 14 July 1/7 Mr. Hancock, the Liberal-Labour candidate for Mid-Derbyshire. **1929** M. BEER *Hist. Brit. Socialism* (new ed.) II. IV. xvi. 315 In 1898 Gladstone died, and with him one of the main pillars of Liberal Labourism disappeared from British politics.

6. *Comb.* as ***liberal-anarchic, -bourgeois, -cultural, -democratic, -empiricist, -hearted, -humanist, -minded, -scientific, †-talking*** adjs.; ***liberal-anarchism, -mindedness***.

1964 *New Society* 13 Feb. 17/2 The progressive schools have been liberal-anarchic, the product of free enterprise in unorthodox educational ideas. *Ibid.*, Liberal-anarchism will no longer do. **1951** KOESTLER *Age of Longing* vi. 103 Where did you pick up this idea out of the liberal-bourgeois philosophy of law? **1953** A. K. C. OTTAWAY *Educ. & Soc.* v. 88 The supporter of the pure liberal-cultural tradition. **1940** Liberal-democratic [see CULTURE *sb.* 5 a]. **1949** *Mind* LVIII. 254 More than anyone, except perhaps Bertrand Russell, he [*sc.* L. T. Hobhouse] may be regarded as the inheritor of the liberal-empiricist mantle of John Stuart Mill. **1597** HOOKER *Eccl. Pol.* v. lxv. §20 The liberall harted man is by the opinion of the prodigall miserable. **1957** N. FRYE *Anat. Crit.* 6 It would be easy to compile a long list of such determinisms in criticism, all of them, whether Marxist.. liberal-humanist..or existentialist, substituting a critical attitude for criticism. **1756** JOHNSON in Boswell *Johnson*, The booksellers are generous Liberal-minded men. **1818** SHELLEY *Rev. Islam* Pref., Can he who the day before was a trampled slave suddenly become liberal-minded? **1850** TENNYSON *In Mem.* Concl. 38 Thou art..liberal-minded, great, Consistent. **1925** BEERBOHM *Observations* 16 Too proud to fight?..or too liberal-minded?—or what? **1961** NEW ENG. BIBLE *Acts* xvii. 11 The Jews here were more liberal-minded than those at Thessalonika. **1971** 'D. HALLIDAY' *Dolly & Doctor Bird* v. 71 Mini Adult Show for the Liberal Minded. **1783** *Gentl. Mag.* LIII. II. 938 What the liberal-mindedness of the present age amounts to [etc.]. **1874** SPURGEON *Treas. Dav.* Ps. lxxxix. 43 Indifference to all truth, under the name of liberal-mindedness, is the crowning virtue of the age. **1958** *Times Lit. Suppl.* 17 Jan. 26/4 The obvious charge which can be brought against this picture of a suppressed liberal-scientific element is the undeniable fact that it never showed any signs of formulating a practical alternative to current political or ethical machinery. **1612** N. FIELD *Woman a Weathercock* III. i. F 1 b, Next to that, the fame, Of your neglect, and liberall talking tongue, Which bred my honour an eternall wrong.

B. *sb.*

1. A member of the Liberal party (see A. 5).

a. in continental politics.

1820 *Edin. Rev.* XXXIV. 3 Our travellers..continue to resort to Paris..and occasionally take part with *Ultras* or with *Liberals*. **1823** SOUTHEY in *Q. Rev.* XXVIII. 496 The Liberals of that day [end of 18th c.].. flew at high game... There was a scheme for establishing a society of Liberals at Cleves, where..they were to employ themselves in the task of destroying Christianity by means of the press. **1848** W. H. KELLY tr. *L. Blanc's Hist. Ten Y.* I. 52 The part played by the liberals during this time was as follows. **1885** LOWE *Prince Bismarck* I. 469 This was evidently the calculation of the Liberals in the Reichstag, when..they began a series of attempts to cobble at the Constitution.

b. in British politics.

Early in the 19th c. the sb. occurs chiefly as applied by opponents to the advanced section of the Whig party: sometimes in Sp. or Fr. form, app. with the intention of suggesting that the principles of those politicians were un-English, or akin to those of the revolutionaries of the Continent. As, however, the adj. was already English in a laudatory sense, the advocates of reform were not reluctant to adopt the foreign term as descriptive of themselves; and when the significance of the old party distinctions was obliterated by the coalition of the moderate Whigs with the Tories and of the advanced Whigs with the Radicals, the new names 'Liberal' and 'Conservative' took the place of 'Whig' and 'Tory' as the usual appellations of the two great parties in the state.

[**1816** SOUTHEY in *Q. Rev.* XV. 69 These are the personages for whose sake the continuance of the Alien Bill has been opposed by the British *Liberales*. **1826** SCOTT *Jrnl.* 19 Nov., Canning, Huskisson, and a mitigated party of Liberaux. **1834** MAR. EDGEWORTH *Helen* xxxv. III. 66 That one born and bred such an ultra exclusive..should be obliged after her marriage..to open her doors and turn ultra liberale, or an universal suffragist.] **1822** (*title*) The Liberal. Verse and Prose from the South. **1828** *Blackw. Mag.* XXIII. 174 What lurking conspirator against the quiet of his native government..has failed to ask and receive the protection of our Liberals? **1850** L. HUNT *Autobiog.* II. xi. 77 Newer and more thorough-going Whigs..were known by the name of Radicals, and have since been called.. Liberals. **1865** J. S. MILL in *Morn. Star* 6 July, A Liberal is he who looks forward for his principles of government; a Tory looks backward. **1879** MCCARTHY *Own Times* II. xix. 51 A large number of Liberals were no doubt influenced by this view of the situation.

c. In extra-European politics, and in wider application.

1832 *Liberal* (St. Thomas, Ontario) 20 Sept. 3/4 We shall first notice the slanderous imputations cast upon the Liberals, that they are a discontented set of men, ever on the watch to find occasion for complaint and clamour. **1854** *N.Y. Tribune* 22 Apr. 5/5 The 'Liberals' of Maine have called a 'State Democratic Mass Convention' at Portland. **1918** H. V. EVATT *Liberalism Austral.* x. 66 The Sydney press claimed that its own free traders were the Liberals. **1940** *N.Y. Times* 23 Jan. 20/4 Since then [*sc.* the Russian Revolution] Liberal has been a word of confusion. Everybody who was not a Conservative became a Liberal or Radical or Red, whichever came first to the mind. **1955** D. VIKLUND tr. Tingsten's *Probl. S. Afr.* x. 116 A Communist in South Africa is often, according to the general usage of the word, a liberal. **1957** *New Yorker* 12 Jan. 25/1 Both she and Robbie were campus liberals; they had met at a gathering that had something to do with the Spanish war. *a* **1964** H. HOOVER in W. Safire *New Lang. Politics* (1968) 232/2 Fuzzy minded totalitarian liberals who believe that their creeping collectivism can be adopted without destroying personal liberty and representative government. **1969** *New Yorker* 14 June 44/2, I don't think he is a liberal. He's tight with his money, and he wants to see the poor work for their money.

2. One who holds 'liberal' views in theology. Chiefly *U.S.*

1887 *Beacon* (Boston U.S.) 8 Jan., In Boston a minister is called a liberal when he rejects the Andover creed, and, perhaps, the Apostles' Creed.

liberalism (ˈlɪbərəlɪz(ə)m). [f. LIBERAL *a.* + -ISM. Cf. F. *libéralisme*.] The holding of liberal opinions in politics or theology; the political tenets characteristic of a Liberal.

1819 LADY MORGAN *Autobiog.* (1859) 17 He is worthy of a conversion to liberalism. **1826** E. IRVING *Babylon* I. III. 246 Religion is the very name of obligation, and liberalism is the very name for the want of obligation. **1837** T. HOOK *Jack Brag* xii, The liberalism of the King of the French. **1841** J. H. NEWMAN in *Apol.* 313 The more serious thinkers among us are used..to regard the spirit of Liberalism as the characteristic of the destined Antichrist. **1859** MILL *Liberty* i. 11 This mode of thought..was common among the last generation of European liberalism. **1881** *Sat. Rev.* 23 July 101/1 The ecclesiastical Liberalism which shaped the Dean's peculiar view.

liberalist ('lɪbərəlɪst). [f. LIBERAL *a.* + -IST.] An advocate of liberalism in politics or religion; a liberal.

1802-12 BENTHAM *Ration. Judic. Evid.* (1827) IV. 410 We are forced to draw up: we are forced, little by little, to turn liberalists. **1817** W. TAYLOR in *Monthly Rev.* LXXXIII. 490 He had insensibly acquired the confidence of the entire party of continental liberalists. **1823** KEBLE *Lett. Spir. Counsel* viii. (1870) 18 Of course, if this be true of dissenters, it is more so of those who are mere liberalists.

attrib. or *adj.* **1846** BROWNSON *Wks.* V. 522 Faith is not, as our liberalist divines hold, something in addition to the Christian life. **1889** *Times* 19 June, The opposition of the Liberalist party has a basis in principle. **1958** A. PATON *Hope for S. Afr.* ii. 7 Further, the word 'liberal' has for the white enemies of South African Liberalism another meaning; it shares this further meaning with the words 'liberalist' and 'liberalistic'. This meaning is derogatory and carries the stigma of 'loose', 'careless', 'promiscuous'. **1972** *Times Lit. Suppl.* 27 Oct. 1272/2 Liberal or (in the pejorative corruption of her Afrikaner opponents) liberalist.

liberalistic (lɪbərə'lɪstɪk), *a.* [f. prec. + -IC.] Pertaining to liberalism; inclined or tending to liberalism.

1836 J. H. NEWMAN *Let.* 17 Feb., Whoever succeeds [to the Professorship of Divinity] will be virtually curbed in any liberalistic propensities by our present proceedings. **1888** *Dublin Rev.* July 206 The attempts made by the Liberalistic party to make capital of the Holy Father's action respecting Poland. **1898** *Catholic News* 13 Aug. 1/2 Cardinal Antonelli ..could not suffer his Liberalistic tendencies. **1958** [see prec.]. **1958** G. M. CARTER *Politics of Inequality* iii. 104 W. A. Maree..brought out well the Nationalist view of the difference between what he called 'the liberalistic approach and the approach of nationalism' to education.

liberality (lɪbə'rælɪtɪ). Also 4 **liberalte**, 4-6 **-ite**, 5-6 **lyberalite**, **-yte**, **-ytie**, 5-7 **liberalytie**, 6 **-itee**, **-ytye**, 6-7 **-itie**, **-itye**. [a. OF. *liberalité* (1262 in Hatz.-Darm.), ad. L. *līberālitāt-em*, n. of quality f. *līberāl-is* LIBERAL.]

1. The quality of being liberal or free in giving; bountiful bestowal of gifts; generosity, munificence.

13.. *St. Ambrose* 641 in *Altengl. Leg.* (1878) 18 In mony þinges he was comendable, Furst in liberalite. **1387** TREVISA *Higden* (Rolls) VII. 159 He was of so moche liberalte þat he made þe kynges and messes [? *read* kynges messes; L. *fercula regalia*] be diȝt redy foure tymes in a day. **1390** GOWER *Conf.* II. 390 Liberalite, Which is the vertu of Largesse. *c* **1460** FORTESCUE *Abs. & Lim. Mon.* vii. (1885) 124 At thair departynge thai most nedis haue grete giftes and rewardes; ffor þat besitith þe kynges magnificence and liberalite. **1494** FABYAN *Chron.* II. xlviii. 32 A..feest was holden by the Kynge to all that wolde come, with most lyberalytie and plentie in all that was necessary to suche a feest. **1530-1** *Act 22 Hen. VIII*, c. 15 The Kynge..of his mere mocion benygnitee and lyberalitee..hath gyuen and granted.. pardon. **1553** EDEN *Treat. Newe Ind.* (Arb.) 30 The Canibales beyng allured by the lyberalitie & gyftes of our men. **1566** *Prayers* in *Liturg. Serv. Q. Eliz.* (1859) 261 Good Lord, bless us and all thy gifts which we receive of thy large liberality. **1651** HOBBES *Leviath.* I. x. 41 Riches joyned with liberality, is Power; because it procureth friends, and servants. *a* **1661** FULLER *Worthies* (1840) III. 436 His liberality knew no bottom but an empty purse, so bountiful he was to all in want. **1741** BUTLER *Serm.* Wks. 1874 II. 263 Liberality..is apt to degenerate into extravagance. **1769** *Junius Lett.* ii. 13 He was formed to excel in war, by nature's liberality to his mind as well as person. **1839** THIRLWALL *Greece* VII. 229 The extraordinary liberality with which Antipater weakened his own army to strengthen that of Antigonus. **1881** BESANT & RICE *Chapl. of Fleet* I. 150 Thanks to the Doctor's liberality in the matter of my weekly board [etc.].

b. An instance of this; a liberal gift or bounty; a largess. Now *rare.*

1526 TINDALE *1 Cor.* xvi. 3 Them will I sende to brynge youre liberalite vnto Jerusalem. **1552** *Bk. Com. Prayer, Litany*, Wee receyuinge thy bountiefull lyberalytye. **1598** GRENEWEY *Tacitus' Ann.* XII. x. (1622) 167 There was.. giuen..a donatiue to the souldiers, and a liberalitie to the people. **1658** *Whole Duty Man* xiii. §31 This was to be paid, not as a charity, or liberality, but as a debt. **1751** JOHNSON *Rambler* No. 169 ¶5 Enriched by uncommon liberalities of nature. *a* **1774** GOLDSM. *Hist. Greece* I. 374 He..found himself in a position to bestow great liberalities amongst the soldiers. **1859** J. CUMMING *Ruth* ii. 15 An attempt to escape responsibilities, duties, liberalities at home. **1865** GROTE *Plato* I. iv. 154 The name of Ptolemy was popular from his liberalities.

2. Breadth of mind; freedom from bias or prejudice; liberal-mindedness.

1808 JEFFERSON *Writ.* (1830) IV. 109 Our opponents, who had not the liberality to distinguish between political and social opposition. **1849** MACAULAY *Hist. Eng.* iv. I. 491 With a liberality rare in his time, he considered questions of ecclesiastical polity as of small account when compared with the great principles of Christianity. **1853** LYTTON *My Novel* v. xiii, Where look for liberality, if men of science are illiberal to their brethren?

¶ **3.** Liberalism in politics; liberals collectively. Only in allusive nonce-uses.

1841 *Fraser's Mag.* XXIII. 204 Liberality proving..quite as careful of its pounds, shillings, and pence, as Toryism. **1843** *Tait's Mag.* X. 637 A strange jumble of all the systems, and philosophies, bigotries, and liberalities that have each had its day and its party in France. **1874** RUSKIN *Fors Clav.* IV. xxxviii. 39 With all the liberality of republican Europe rejoicing in his dignities as a man and a brother.

liberalization (,lɪbərəlaɪ'zeɪʃən). [f. next + -ATION.] The action or process of liberalizing; the fact of being liberalized or becoming liberal; *spec.*, the removal by a government of restrictions placed upon the import of goods, the movement of capital, etc.

1835 DE QUINCEY in *Tait's Mag.* II. 372 Students seeking only the liberalization and not the profits of academic life. **1854** —— *Autobiog. Sk.* Wks. II. 24 In all that concerned the liberalization of his views. **1862** R. H. PATTERSON *Ess. Hist. & Art* 144 The extensive reforms and liberalisation of the government recently undertaken by the Ottoman rulers. **1897** *Atlantic Monthly* LXXIX. 53 The growing liberalization of ideas. **1940** *Economist* 5 Oct. 431/2 The liberalisation of bank loans to farmers still left unresolved the problem of the bad..credit proposition. **1961** *Ann. Reg. 1960* 496 During the year the liberalization of imports, especially from the dollar area, continued.

liberalize ('lɪbərəlaɪz), *v.* [f. LIBERAL + -IZE. Cf. F. *libéraliser.*]

1. a. *trans.* To render liberal; to imbue with liberal ideas or principles; to make liberal-minded; to free from narrowness; to enlarge the intellectual range of. Also (*nonce-use*) *to* ***liberalize away***, to do away with by such means.

1774 BURKE *Amer. Taxation* Sel. Wks. I. 123 He was bred to the law..; a science which does more to quicken and invigorate the understanding, than all the other kinds of learning put together; but it is not apt..to open and to liberalize the mind exactly in the same proportion. **1790** —— *Fr. Rev.* 148 We liberalize the church by an intercourse with the leading characters of the country. **1796** MORSE *Amer. Geog.* I. 341 If they do not break the proper bound, and liberalize away all true religion. **1830** DE QUINCEY *R. Bentley* Wks. 1857 VII. 103 Classical education..liberalizes the mind. **1878** *N. Amer. Rev.* CXXVI. 521 The readiness with which he enlarged his needs and liberalized his habits to the standard he found here. **1898** J. E. C. BODLEY *France* II. IV. i. 325 The Empire, for which, when liberalised, he predicted a glorious and popular career.

b. To make Liberal in politics.

1853 LEWIS *Lett.* 262 He is Liberalizing them, instead of their Torifying him. **1884** *Manch. Exam.* 2 Dec. 5/1 The small boroughs will go to liberalise the counties. **1887** *Spectator* 30 July 1014/2 The Conservative Party has been liberalised..by the Household Suffrage Act.

c. To incline to liberality. *nonce-use.*

1890 'ROLF BOLDREWOOD' *Col. Reformer* (1891) 310 Liberalise the ideas of Messrs. Oldstile and Crampton.

d. To remove restrictions on (the import of goods, outflow of capital, etc.).

1940 *Economist* 5 Oct. 431/2 All the joint-stock banks decided..to liberalise their policy of agricultural loans. **1955** [see LIBERALIZED *ppl. a.*].

2. *intr.* To favour liberal opinions; be or become liberal in one's ideas or principles.

1791-1823 D'ISRAELI *Cur. Lit.* (1858) III. 248 In the Memoirs of James the Second..the catholic reasons and liberalises like a modern philosopher. *a* **1836** FROUDE *Mem.* (1849) 152 We were all liberalizing as we were going on, making too much of this world, and losing our hold upon the next. [**1839** LADY LYTTON *Cheveley* (ed. 2) I. viii. 184 Demosthenes said of the Pythian oracle, that it philipized; and from the moment the Reform Bill began to thrive, Herbert Grimstone liberalized.] **1848** *Tait's Mag.* XV. 828 Russia must liberalize, or be convulsed.

Hence **'liberalized**, **'liberalizing** *ppl. adjs.* Also **'liberalizer**, one who or something which liberalizes.

1820 FOSTER *Ess. Evils Pop. Ignor.* 158 Liberalized feeling and deportment. **1824** *Ann. Reg.* 40 The Irish clergy,..an educated, liberalized, well-conducted order of men. **1833** J. H. NEWMAN *Lett.* (1871) I. 490 The liberalisers in and out of Parliament. **1850** GROTE *Greece* II. lxviii. VIII. 634 Intolerance is the natural weed of the human bosom, though its growth or development may be counteracted by liberalizing causes. **1860** EMERSON *Cond. Life, Culture* Wks. (Bohn) II. 368 Archery, cricket, gun and fishing-rod..are all educators, liberalizers. **1868** M. PATTISON *Academ. Org.* v. 259 The course was not truly, what it claimed to be, liberalising. **1884** *Chr. Commw.* 24 Jan. 347/2 Notions that it [Sunday] is but a relaxed or liberalised Jewish Sabbath. **1955** *Times* 6 Aug. 6/3 The French Government has agreed to the German request that the 'liberalized' sector of French trade with the O.E.E.C. countries shall be restored.

liberally ('lɪbərəlɪ), *adv.* [f. LIBERAL *a.* + -LY².] In a liberal manner.

1. As befits a gentleman or man of culture. (Cf. LIBERAL *a.* 1.)

1711 STEELE *Spect.* No. 157 ¶4 A certain Hardness and Ferocity which some Men, tho' liberally educated, carry about them in all their Behaviour. **1900** *Longm. Mag.* Oct. 591 Not to know Queen Anne's wits and their works is not to be liberally educated.

2. Bountifully, freely, generously.

1387 TREVISA *Higden* (Rolls) VII. 181 William.. liberally rewarded..went aȝen to Normandye. *c* **1489** CAXTON *Blanchardyn* xliii. 168 Blanchardyn..right lyberaly graunted to hym his requeste. **1526** *Pilgr. Perf.* (W. de W. 1531) 147 b, Whiche..mynistreth to theyr neyghbours liberally suche goodes..as they haue receyued of god. *c* **1620** Z. BOYD *Zion's Flowers* (1855) 49 For such a one they lib'rally will give. **1682** NORRIS *Hierocles* 119 How can God, though of his own nature never so liberally disposed, give to him who has liberty of asking, and yet does not? **1811** SCOTT *Prose Wks.* IV. Biographies (1870) II. 165 His..poetic talents were..liberally exerted for the support of this undertaking. **1843** PRESCOTT *Mexico* (1850) I. 284 Promises, and even gold,..were liberally lavished. **1848** C. BRONTË *J. Eyre* vi. (1873) 53 And, if I do anything worthy of praise, she gives me my meed liberally. **1885** SIR H. COTTON in *Law Times Rep.* LIII. 481/2 The bill..is one which the clients are not bound to pay unless they are minded to deal liberally with the solicitors.

b. Without stint; abundantly, amply, plentifully.

1509 HAWES *Past. Pleas.* XXVII. (Percy Soc.) 131 With golden droppes so lyberally indewed. **1585** FETHERSTONE tr. *Calvin on Acts* vi. 2 Their windowes were not so liberallie relieued. **1612** DRAYTON *Poly-olb.* i. 123 That vertue which she could not liberallie impart Shee striveth to amend by her owne proper Art. **1709** STRYPE *Ann. Ref.* (1824) I. II. lv. 345 As they were both riding home from a treat, at which they had drunk liberally. *a* **1713** ELLWOOD *Autobiog.* (1714) 63 He spared not to blame him liberally for it. **1809** *Med. Jrnl.* XXI. 23 Acid fruits should be liberally offered. **1860** DICKENS *Uncomm. Trav.* iv, It was not by any means a savage pantomime..; was often very droll; was always liberally got up, and cleverly presented. **1884** *Mil. Engineering* I. II. 111 After allowing liberally for casualties during the advance.

†**3.** Chiefly with reference to speech: Without reserve or restraint; freely; often, with unbecoming freedom, insolently, licentiously. Also, without constraint; voluntarily. *Obs.*

a **1533** LD. BERNERS *Gold. Bk. M. Aurel.* (1546) Q vj, Your daughter may speke lyberally with hir cousyns. **1535** *Act 27 Hen. VIII*, c. 3 The Mayre..shall..suffre all thinhabitauntes..lyberally and freely without interrupcion ..to..bringe their saide hearinges. **1568** MARY, Q. SCOTS *Let.* in H. Campbell *Love Lett.* (1824) App. 301 Thay would have persuadit me be craft to have liberallie dimittit my crown. **1614** J. COOKE *Tu Quoque* C 1 b, Had mine owne brother spoke thus liberally, My fury should haue taught him better manners. **1646** BP. MAXWELL *Burd. Issach.* 32 Some may thinke, I speake liberally; God forbid I should doe it.

†**b.** In a lax or loose manner. *Obs.*

1596 DALRYMPLE tr. *Leslie's Hist. Scot.* I. 109 Vthiris in the meine tyme leiuet sa liberallie.

'liberalness. *rare.* [-NESS.] Liberality.

1387 TREVISA *Higden* (Rolls) VII. 155 þe covetise..stered þe robbour þerto, and nouȝt my liberalnes. **1595** DANIEL *Civ. Wars* III. xci, Though this bountie, and this liberalness, a glorious vertue be.

liberaloid ('lɪbərəlɔɪd), *a.* [f. LIBERAL *a.* + -OID.] Resembling liberal (attitudes, etc.); in a bad sense, exhibiting liberal characteristics, pseudo-liberal.

1951 R. CAMPBELL *Light on Dark Horse* xxiii. 346 The imbeciles of the King's Party in the French Revolution.. tamely handed over the keys of all the forts to the Reds because of the liberaloid mentality that they had acquired from reading the masturbations of that *pisse-froid* Rousseau. **1963** *Spectator* 29 Mar. 400 The mixture of French puritan bourgeois and liberaloid ideologist that emerges.

liberary, obs. form of LIBRARY.

‖**liberate** (lɪbə'reɪtiː), *sb. Law. Obs.* exc. *Hist.* Also 6 **-at.** [subst. use of med.L. *līberāte* 'deliver ye' (imperative pl. of *līberāre* to deliver), the word with which the writ commenced.]

1. a. A writ issued out of Chancery for the payment of a pension or other royal allowance. **b.** A writ to the sheriff of a county for the delivery of land and goods taken upon the forfeiture of a recognizance. **c.** A writ issued out of Chancery to a jailer for the delivery of a prisoner who has put in bail for his appearance.

[**1535** FITZHERB. *Nat. Brev.* (1567) 132 Vn briefe al vicount hors de chancery a deliuer a luy ceux terres et biens al value de dette &c. le quel briefe est appell'vn liberate.] **1581** LAMBARDE *Eiren.* III. ii. (1588) 349, I will shew you one forme of a Baile, and another of the Liberate. **1590** *Acts Privy Council* (1899) XIX. 297 A writ of extent with a liberat therin unto the Shreef of the said towne hath bene sued out of that Court of the Common Pleas. *a* **1625** SIR H. FINCH *Law* (1636) 181 If a Liberate be deliuered to the Clarke of the Hamper, who hath assets in his hands. **1674** T. TURNOR *Case Bankers & Creditors* ii. 7 The King hath charged himself to the Subject by Talley and liberate to pay a summe of money out of his Customes.

2. *transf.*

1639 FULLER *Holy War* IV. v. (1640) 174 Denying the Infallibility of the Church..the overplus of Merits, Service understood, Indulgences, Liberties out of Purgatorie, and the like.

3. *attrib.*: **liberate day**, a day on which liberates were issued; **liberate roll**, the account formerly kept of pensions and other allowances made under the great seal.

1642 C. VERNON *Consid. Exchequer* 18 The said Treasurers Remembrancer is..at the next Liberate or Sealing day, to make forth the strongest proces to the Sheriffes. **1874** STUBBS *Const. Hist.* I. xiii. 598 The Pipe Rolls of Henry II are supplemented under John by Oblate, Liberate, and Mise Rolls.

†**liberate**, *a.* (and *pa. pple.*) *Obs.* [ad. L. *līberāt-us*, pa. pple. of *līberāre* to LIBERATE.] Liberated, free. Const. *from.*

1597 A. M. tr. *Guillemeau's Fr. Chirurg.* 46 b/2 That the matter might have the liberater a passage to enter forth at. **1637** GILLESPIE *Eng. Pop. Cerem.* I. viii. 25 The Christian Church..is liberate from the Pedagogicall instruction of the Ceremoniall Law. **1671** *True Nonconf.* 125 The old dispensation from which we are liberate. **1752** J. LOUTHIAN *Form of Process* (ed. 2) 63 The Prisoner [shall be] immediately liberate from his Imprisonment.

liberate ('lɪbəreɪt), *v.* Also 7 **-at.** [f. L. *līberāt-*, ppl. stem of *līberāre*, f. *līber* free.] *trans.* **a.** To set free, set at liberty; to free, release *from* (something). *Chem.* To set free from combination.

1623 COCKERAM, *Liberate*, to free one. *c* **1650** *Don Bellianis* 206 Four thousand Knights that came to liberate their King. **1671** *True Nonconf.* 131 Jesus Christ..liberats the Worship of God from the shadows. **1776** ADAM SMITH *W.N.* v. iii.

(1869) I. 533 By liberating the public revenue, they might restore vigour to that government of which they themselves had the principal direction. **1784** COWPER *Task* IV. 97 Advanced to some..more than mortal height, That lib'rates and exempts me from them all. **1805** W. SAUNDERS *Min. Waters* 377 The portion of acid thus liberated. **1841** LANE *Arab. Nts.* I. 112, I will liberate him from his present sufferings. **1867** SMILES *Huguenots Eng.* x. (1880) 172 The six slaves..were eventually liberated by the crew of an English vessel. **1878** BROWNING *La Saisiaz* 52 Walking slow ..Liberates the brain o'erloaded.

b. To free (an occupied territory) of the enemy; also *ironically*, to subject to a new tyranny.

1944 G. B. SHAW *Let.* 4 Dec. in *To a Young Actress* (1960) 181 All your Italian friends must be starving now that we have 'liberated' them. **1955** *Ann. Reg. 1954* 303 Chu Teh.. expressed China's intention of 'liberating' Formosa. **1961** *Listener* 28 Dec. 1100/2 President Sukarno's warning to Indonesian troops to be ready to 'liberate' West New Guinea. **1964** A. MCKEE *Caen* xix. 314 'This place sure has been liberated,' said an American M.P. to an H.C.R. crew, when eventually they reached the waste of brick and stone which had been Vire. **1971** A. BULLOCK *20th Cent.* III. 76/2 The West had the great advantage of being liberated by the Americans and British, neither of whom wanted to stay. **1975** *Times* 1 May 1/2 At 11.30 am local time (03.30 GMT), according to Hanoi Radio, Saigon was 'liberated'.

c. To loot (property), to misappropriate. *slang.*

1944 *Daily Express* 7 Oct. 4/3 (*caption*) Excuse me, Canon, but I rather think you've liberated my matches. **1946** E. LINKLATER *Private Angelo* viii. 86 Those soldiers, who said they had liberated the turkeys and the geese, had taken a most drastic way of giving them their freedom. **1957** [see CAREEN *v.* 5]. **1965** G. MELLY *Owning-Up* vi. 59 He..wore a sombrero liberated, I suspect, from the wardrobe of some Latin American group he had worked with in the past. **1970** *Daily Tel.* (Colour Suppl.) 1 May 9 Shoplifting—'liberating' to hippies—costs the English retail trade the staggering sum of £75 million a year. **1974** S. E. MORISON *European Discovery of America: Southern Voyages* viii. 164 Drake's flagship *Golden Hind* carried no bell, but his men 'liberated' one from the church of Guatulco, Mexico, in 1579.

d. To free from social or male-dominated, etc., conventions.

1970 *New Yorker* 5 Dec. 49/1 It is not only men liberated. It is *women* liberated. **1971** *E. Afr. Jrnl.* Mar. 9/1 Aunt Bimp ..goes into the construction business..She knows nothing about cement and sand but the corruption of the system has served to liberate her. **1975** D. RAMSAY *Descent into Dark* i. 25 Put '*Ms* Joyce Chandler'. Let them get the idea you're liberating yourself from the Kitchen on principle.

Hence **'liberating** *ppl. a.*

1868 BROWNING *Ring & Book* III. 1296 Thanks to His liberating angel Death. **1883** R. ZIMMERMANN in *Athenæum* 29 Dec. 844/3 The prophet of a liberating..movement.

liberated ('lɪbəreɪtɪd), *ppl. a.* [f. LIBERATE *v.* + -ED[1].] Set free, set at liberty.

1794 BURKE *Pref. to Brissot's Addr.* Wks. VII. 305 This liberated galley-slave. **1860** TYNDALL *Glac.* I. xxi. 147 The partially liberated streams flowed..over their own ice.

b. *spec.* in *Bot.* (see quot. 1888).

1855 MAYNE *Expos. Lex.*, *Liberatus* (Bot.),..liberated. **1888** *Syd. Soc. Lex.*, *Liberated*, in Botany, applied to a structure which is in part adherent to another and in part free.

c. In sense d. of LIBERATE *v.* Cf. EMANCIPATED *ppl. a.* 2.

1970 R. LOWELL *Notebk.* 191 The liberated girl with a build. **1970** *Globe & Mail* (Toronto) 25 Sept. 12/7 Liberated school. The co-eds from women's colleges in Virginia are going to attend formerly all-male Davidson College. **1973** D. JORDAN *Nile Green* ix. 41 He resents me because I'm a liberated woman who can support herself.

liberation (lɪbə'reɪʃən). [ad. L. *līberātiōn-em*, n. of action f. *līberāre* to LIBERATE. Cf. F. *libération* (14th c. in Hatz.-Darm.).] The action of liberating or condition of being liberated; setting free; release.

Liberation Society: the designation of the 'Society for the Liberation of Religion from State Patronage and Control', the object of which is to advocate the disestablishment and disendowment of all established churches in the British dominions. Cf. LIBERATIONIST.

c **1440** *Gesta Rom.* xcv. 426 (Add. MS.) The contricion that he had in his Ende was the signe and token of his liberacion. **1532** BP. CLARK in Ellis *Orig. Lett.* Ser. II. I. 306 For the liberation off Italye. **1623** COCKERAM, *Liberation*, a deliuerance. **1776** ADAM SMITH *W.N.* v. iii. (1869) I. 515 The future liberation of the public revenue they leave to the care of posterity. **1782** POWNALL *Study of Antiq.* 155 This mode of analysing requires perfect liberation from all prejudged system. **1800** HENRY *Epit. Chem.* (1808) 55 Those gases that require, for their liberation, a red heat. **1875** LIGHTFOOT *Comm. Col.* ii. 15 A liberation from the dominion of the flesh. **1879** R. T. SMITH *Basil Gt.* x. 127 The separation of soul and body is liberation from all evil. **1886** *Q. Rev.* CLXII. 8 The Liberation Society had a balance on its Legacy Account of 10,334*l.* 15*s.* **1945** *Sun* (Baltimore) 28 Sept. 11/2 Liberation is only four months old. **1952** *Ann. Reg. 1951* 'Liberation' of the island [*sc.* Formosa] remained one of the primary stated objectives of the régime. **1956** *Ann. Reg. 1955* 314 On 15 August, the tenth anniversary of the 'Liberation' of Korea by the Soviet Russian army. **1966** *Punch* 5 Jan. 14/2 Each member of the crew would apply for his equipment to be 'written off', and for replacements to be issued. And each member of the crew would become the proud owner of the liberation loot. **1966** G. JACKSON *Let.* 23 Feb. in *Soledad Brother* (1971) 94 Some ..commit unpardonable crimes..that must in the end bar them from partaking in the benefits of the liberation that is planned for tomorrow. **1967** *Daily Tel.* 14 Mar. 21/1 Negro and Puerto Rican parents who are organising a boycott of a school in Harlem began establishing 'liberation schools' today... They are demanding a say in running the school and in choosing a headmaster. **1970** [see *game-playing* sb. and adj. s.v. GAME *sb.* 16 b]. **1971** *Black Scholar* Jan. 58/1 Those in the struggle have to deal with black separatists because they stand today as a potent obstacle to full black liberation. **1973** *Black Panther* 3 Mar. 8/1 The Black Panther Party is..an organization dedicated to the liberation of oppressed peoples in different communities. **1973** *Black World* Oct. 5 Development for us is liberation. It's liberating this person who, until now, has been suffering under colonialism..and under all kinds of superstitious beliefs. **1973** *Listener* 20 Dec. 841/1 The Arabs..are to give financial and diplomatic support to the African liberation movements.

liberationist (lɪbə'reɪʃənɪst). [f. LIBERATION + -IST.] **a.** One who sympathizes with the aims of the 'Liberation Society' (see LIBERATION); an advocate of disestablishment. **b.** An advocate of women's liberation. Also *attrib.*

1869 *Echo* 12 Oct., He served Mr. Gladstone against the Church on the political platform with Cardinal Cullen and the Liberationists. **1885** *Ch. Q. Rev.* Apr. 75 A conclusive reply to Dissenting Liberationists. **1886** *Q. Rev.* CLXII. 8 According to the wonted Liberationist style of reasoning. **1888** C. A. LANE *Notes Eng. Ch. Hist.* II. xxviii. §8. 242 Liberationist agitators. **1970** G. GREER *Female Eunuch* 13 The organized liberationists are a well-publicized minority. **1971** *Guardian* 18 Jan. 9/2 The whole point..of bra-burning seems to have vanished from some English liberationist minds.

So **libe'rationism**, the principles or practice of liberationists.

1881 *Ch. Times* 1 July 437 The evil spirit of Liberationism will be for ever cast out. **1886** *Q. Rev.* CLXII. 8 Democracy ..acting in obedience to Liberationism.

liberation theology. [tr. Sp. *teología de la liberación* (G. Gutiérrez 1968).] A theory, originating amongst Roman Catholic theologians in Latin America, which interprets liberation from social, political, and economic oppression as anticipating the historical process of eschatological salvation. Also called ***theology of liberation.***

1969 G. GUTIÉRREZ in *In Search of Theol. of Devel.* 116 The question of a theology of liberation must be placed in its proper perspective. **1970** —— in *Theol. Stud.* XXXI. 243 (*heading*) Notes for a theology of liberation. **1972** R. R. RUETHER (*title*) Liberation theology. **1973** P. E. BERRYMAN in *Theol. Stud.* XXXIV. 364 Latin American liberation theology arises out of an experience: the discovery of institutionalized violence and the dimensions of oppression. **1973** *Time* 23 Apr. 42 Jesuits are at loggerheads in Latin America over a Christian-Marxist synthesis known as the 'theology of liberation'. **1979** J. B. NELSON *Embodiment* i. 15 'Political theology' and the 'liberation theology' stimulated by Third World Christians..take seriously the human political struggle for liberation as an arena for God's continuing self-disclosure. **1982** P. B. HINCHLIFF *Holiness & Politics* ix. 197 Liberation theology appears to be saying that what matters is that the just cause must be made to succeed. **1984** *Times* 30 Aug. 12/2 The Vatican is expected to produce a document clarifying its objections to 'liberation theology' to coincide with the hearings next month against Father Leonardo Boff, the Brazilian theologian who is one of its leading exponents. **1986** A. M. KABAL *Bad Money* II. ix. 193 Why would the Vatican finance arms for right-wing guerrillas? Did they hate Liberation Theology as much as that?

Hence **liberation theologian**, a theologian who teaches liberation theology.

1976 *Christian Socialist* Mar. 2/2 The radical Catholics of South America (who include Archbishop Helder Camara of Brazil and the 'liberation theologians'). **1979** E. NORMAN *Christianity & World Order* iv. 53 The biblical exegesis of Liberation theologians is in fact very conservative. **1982** P. B. HINCHLIFF *Holiness & Politics* ix. 196 Liberation theologians do not appear to be much concerned to examine the moral issues raised by political action. **1986** *Sunday Tel.* 6 Apr. 40/1 His chosen method is to approve the concern of the liberation theologians but insist that their teaching should in future reflect the full Christian message.

liberative ('lɪbərətɪv), *a.* [f. L. *līberāt-* (see LIBERATE *v.*) + -IVE.] That liberates or favours liberation.

1843 CARLYLE *Francia* Misc. Ess. (1872) VII. 2 A liberative cavalier. **1863** J. F. MAGUIRE *Father Mathew* 300 The writer..resolves to be free, whether Father Mathew should give him permission or not; still a liberative line from his reverence would be a triumph [etc.].

liberator ('lɪbəreɪtə(r)). [Agent-n. in L. form, f. LIBERATE *v.*] One who liberates; a deliverer.

'The Liberator (of Ireland)' was a designation applied by his followers to Daniel O'Connell, the advocate of 'Repeal of the Union' between Great Britain and Ireland.

1650 HOWELL *Giraffi's Rev. Naples* 138, I have reverenced him as much as possibly I could, as Liberator of his Country. **1658** HEWYT *Last Serm.* 155 The exploits of the Judges and Kings given to the people of God for Liberators. **1659** B. HARRIS *Parival's Iron Age* 127 The King of Sweden ..was expected by all, as a true Liberatour, or Deliverer. **1835** LYTTON *Rienzi* I. i, The future liberator of Rome. **1843** CARLYLE *Francia* Misc. Ess. (1899) IV. 262 Bolivar, 'the Washington of Columbia,' Liberator Bolivar. **1848** W. J. O'N. DAUNT *Recoll. O'Connell* I. 16 In..1834, I was in Dublin, and met the Liberator at a Repeal meeting. **1881** *Academy* 16 Apr. 272 The invading army of liberators was closely blockaded.

liberatory ('lɪbərətərɪ), *a. rare.* [f. L. *līberāt-* (see LIBERATE *v.*) + -ORY.] = LIBERATIVE.

1592 WEST *1st Pt. Symbol.* §46 Instruments..of their effects be either Constitutiue and making, or remissorie and liberatorie. **1843** CARLYLE *Past & Pr.* IV. vii, Strong men and liberatory Samsons.

liberatress ('lɪbəreɪtrɪs). [f. LIBERATOR + -ESS.] A female liberator.

1798 W. TAYLOR in *Monthly Mag.* VI. 4 Joan..was received with the honours due to the liberatress of the town. **1849** THACKERAY *Pendennis* xxvii, He had run over to Laura, his liberatress, to thank her for his recovered freedom. **1894** *Catholic News* 12 May 4/6 The memory of the great 'liberatress' belongs to all the French.

Also **liberatrice** [with Fr. suffix], **liberatrix** [with L. suffix], in the same sense. *rare.*

1820 SCOTT *Monast.* xxix, Beneficent liberatrice. **1893** *Leisure Hour* Mar. 343/2 The liberatrix of France.

liberd(e, obs. form of LEOPARD.

Liberian (laɪ'bɪərɪən), *a.*[1] [f. *Liber(ius* (see below) + -IAN.] Of or pertaining to Liberius (Pope, 352–66). So ***Liberian basilica***, one of the early churches of Rome, formerly believed to have stood on the site of S. Maria Maggiore; ***Liberian calendar***, a calendar attributed to the pontificate of Liberius; ***Liberian catalogue***, a list of the Popes until and including Liberius.

a **1773** A. BUTLER *Lives Saints* (1779) X. 316 The Liberian calendar places him [*sc.* St. Callistus] in the list of martyrs. **1840** E. COX tr. *J. J. I. von Döllinger's Hist. Church* I. i. 36 The Liberian catalogue would make him to have been bishop during the lifetime of the apostle. **1858** N. WISEMAN *Recoll. Last Four Popes* II. iv. 295 The recollection..will come back..in images..of solemn entrance into..an open basilica... The Liberian speaks to you of Bethlehem..the Sessorian of Calvary. **1913** E. R. BARKER *Rome of Pilgrims & Martyrs* I. iv. 50 Philocalian (Liberian) Calendar of 354.—This Calendar is named *Liberian*, since it was compiled in 354 under Pope Liberius. It is called *Philocalian*, after its author Philocalus. *Ibid.* vi. 85 Sixtus III. (432–440) embellished the Liberian basilica. **1957** *Encycl. Brit.* VII. 4/2 Damasus was nominated.., but the intransigents of the Liberian party..set up against him another deacon, Ursinus.

Liberian (laɪ'bɪərɪən), *a.*[2] and *sb.* [f. *Liber(ia* (see below) + -IAN.] **A.** *adj.* Of or pertaining to Liberia, a West African state founded in 1822, or its people. **B.** *sb.* A native or inhabitant of Liberia; also, a Liberian ship.

1854 A. H. FOOTE *Afr. & Amer. Flag* xxxiv. 386 The Liberians are freemen. *Ibid.* 388 Captain Cooper will not take exception at the remark, that it is 'the day of small things' with the Liberian navy. **1855** *Wesleyan-Methodist Mag.* I. 307 The Liberians..have acquired lands which no European power could peaceably gain from the natives. **1868** J. A. HORTON *W. Afr. Countries* xvii. 270 The entrance to Monrovia, the capital of the Liberian Republic, reminds one of the entrance to a purely native town. **1882** *Encycl. Brit.* XIV. 508/1 The Liberian variety of coffee held in such high esteem. **1906** H. H. JOHNSTON *Liberia* I. i. 7 The governing class..consists of approximately twelve thousand Negroes and Mulattos of American origin, to whom may be added..about thirty thousand 'civilised' Liberians of local origin. **1914** W. H. PAGE *Let.* 5 July in B. J. Hendrick *Life & Lett. W. H. Page* (1925) III. ix. 120 About half the Liberian Cabinet..have asked for an audience with me this week. **1944** *Amer. Speech* XIX. 164 In Liberia the descendants of returned American slaves who constitute the ruling caste of the country used to call themselves Americo-Liberians... But I am informed by Mr. Ben Hamilton, Jr., formerly of the Liberian consulate in Los Angeles, that ..'Liberians consider the term Americo-Liberian opprobrious... Hence they prefer to be called civilized or Monrovian Liberians to distinguish themselves from the natives of the hinterland.' **1952** A. G. L. HELLYER *Sanders' Encycl. Gardening* (ed. 22) 121 *Coffea..liberica*, 'Liberian Coffee', white, fragrant, 15 to 20 ft., Trop. Africa. **1971** B. CALLISON *Plague of Sailors* iii. 98 Now, when you get aboard the Liberian... **1973** R. THOMAS *If you can't be Good* (1974) ii. 13 A Dutch freighter, flying a Liberian flag of convenience. **1973** *Times* 17 Apr. (Liberia Suppl.) p. ii/6 By 1970..this group employed 1,500 Liberians and was the largest of Liberian concerns.

libero-motor ('lɪbərəʊ,məʊtə(r)), *a.* [irreg. f. L. *līberāre* to LIBERATE + MOTOR.] Disengaging or liberating motor energy.

1855 H. SPENCER *Princ. Psychol.* I. iii. (1872) I. 47 Each ganglion is a libero-motor agent. **1880** BASTIAN *Brain* 38 Libero-motor elements.

libertarian (lɪbə'tɛərɪən), *sb.* (*a.*). [f. LIBERTY + *-arian*, as in *unitarian*, etc.]

1. One who holds the doctrine of the freedom of the will, as opposed to that of necessity. Opposed to *necessitarian.* Also *attrib.* or *adj.*

1789 BELSHAM *Ess.* I. i. 11 Where is the difference between the Libertarian..and the Necessarian? **1838** SIR W. HAMILTON *Logic* xxx. (1866) II. 113 When the Libertarian descends to arguments drawn from the fact of the Moral Law. **1882–3** F. L. PATTON in Schaff *Encycl. Relig. Knowl.* III. 2524/1 The libertarian doctrine is now taught by appealing to consciousness. **1886** H. SIDGWICK in *Mind* XI. 144 His psychology inevitably precludes him [Plato] from being really Libertarian. **1895** G. J. ROMANES *Th. Relig.* 129 If libertarians grant causality as appertaining to the will.

2. One who approves of or advocates liberty. Also as *adj.*

1878 SEELEY *Stein* III. 355. **1901** F. W. MAITLAND in *Eng. Hist. Rev.* July 419 A supply of competent editors was wanted [for the Rolls Series]... In such matters Englishmen are individualists and libertarians. The picture of an editor defending his proof sheets..before an official board of critics is not to our liking. **1906** *Westm. Gaz.* 2 Oct. 2/1 No wonder the libertarian woman rebels. **1966** *New Statesman* 22 Apr. 602/2 She is a libertarian and was not happy under the dictatorship of Hassan II. **1969** *Listener* 15 May 666/1 The political activists..belong to what is known as the libertarian Left. **1972** *Science* 12 May 615/3 It gives fair play

to the objections of civil libertarians. **1973** *Observer* (Colour Suppl.) 11 Nov. 44/4 Now he's suddenly the darling of the civil libertarians.

Hence **liber'tarianism**, the principles or doctrines of libertarians.

1830 W. TAYLOR *Hist. Surv. Germ. Poetry* III. 10 *note*, The general drift of his [Kant's] system..is not libertarianism. **1886** H. SIDGWICK in *Mind* XI. 144 [This] is to make him [Plato] talk modern Libertarianism in a quite unwarrantable way.

liberticidal (lɪˈbɜːtɪˌsaɪdəl), *a.* [f. LIBERTICIDE *sb.*[1] + -AL[1].] = LIBERTICIDE *a.*

1794 *State Papers* in *Ann. Reg.* 193 Their liberticidal measures. **1822** *Examiner* 381/2 The liberticidal system of Divine Right. **1887** R. GARNETT *Carlyle* vii. 119 He is a noble patriot in the first half of his career, and a liberticidal usurper in the second.

liberticide (lɪˈbɜːtɪsaɪd), *sb.*[1] and *a.* [a. F. *liberticide* (recorded only as adj.; used by Babœuf, *a* 1797), f. *liberté* LIBERTY + *-cide*, -CIDE 1.] **A.** *sb.* A 'killer' or destroyer of liberty.

1795 SOUTHEY *Maid of Orleans* II. 328 Cæsar..the great liberticide. **1837** CARLYLE *Fr. Rev.* III. II. ii, What if he should prove too prosperous, and become Liberticide, Murderer of Freedom! **1863** *Scotsman* 28 Mar. (Kinglake's Crimea), He abhors Louis Napoleon..because he sees in him a liberticide. **1895** OUIDA in *Contemp. Rev.* Aug. 241 He was, in his prime, a regicide; he is, in his old age, a liberticide.

B. *adj.* Destructive of liberty.

1793 A. YOUNG *Example France* (ed. 3) 60 *note*, Spare not the liberticide members, who vote in favour of Louis. **1817** BENTHAM *Parl. Ref. Catech.* (1818) 122 As to the tongue, under one of the late liberticide Acts, two London Aldermen ..have sufficed to put an end to all public use of that instrument. **1819** SHELLEY in Dowden *Shelley* (1886) II. vii. 294 Two liberticide wars undertaken by the privileged classes of the country. **1842** *Blackw. Mag.* LII. 431 The most violent, haughty, and liberticide of all despotisms.

liberticide (lɪˈbɜːtɪsaɪd), *sb.*[2] *rare.* [f. as prec.: see -CIDE 2.] The 'killing' of liberty.

1819 SHELLEY *Eng. in 1819*, 8 An army which liberticide and prey Make as a two-edged sword to all who wield. **1898** OUIDA in *Review Rev.* Sept. 251 All that has been done by the State since the revolt of May is liberticide of the most violent character.

libertinage (ˈlɪbətɪnɪdʒ). [f. next + -AGE.]

1. The conduct or practice of a libertine; habitual licentiousness with regard to the relation of the sexes; = LIBERTINISM 2.

1611 COTGR., *Libertinage*, Libertinage, Epicurisme, sensualitie, licentiousnesse, dissolutenesse. **1639** MARCOMBES in *Lismore Papers* Ser. II. (1888) IV. 98 Hauing tasted allready a litle drope of y^e Libertinage of y^e Court. **1798** MALTHUS *Popul.* (1878) 20 The libertinage which.. prevails must..render them..unfit for bearing children. **1819** *Metropolis* (ed. 2) II. 181 The General..was..famous for libertinage and debauchery. **1844** *For. Q. Rev.* XXXIII. 189 The suppers of the Duke of Orleans became a school of libertinage. **1873** SMILES *Huguenots Fr.* I. xiii. (1881) 259 The upper classes..were given up for the most part to frivolity and libertinage.

2. Free-thinking in religious matters; = LIBERTINISM 1.

1660 BLOME *Fanat. Hist.* i. 5 Anabaptism, being a doctrine of licentiousness and libertinage. **1767** WARBURTON *Serm. Linc. Inn* xiii. Wks. 1788 V. 194 *note*, Erasmus.. thought he saw, under all their fondness for the Language of old Rome, a growing libertinage, which disposed them to think slightly of the Christian Faith.

libertine (ˈlɪbətɪn), *sb.* and *a.* Also 6 lyb-, 7-8 -in. [ad. L. *lībertīn-us* (in sense 2 perh. through F. *libertin*, recorded from 1542), f. *lībertus* made free, cogn. w. *līber* free.]

A. *sb.*

1. *Rom. Antiq.* A freedman; one manumitted from slavery; also, the son of a freedman.

1382 WYCLIF *Acts* vi. 9 Summe risen of the synagoge, that was clepid of Libertyns. **1533** BELLENDEN *Livy* IV. (1822) 315 Quhidder ane servand or ane libertine war maid consull. **1540-1** ELYOT *Image Gov.* 34 Libertine, that is to saie, any man of a bonde ancestour. **1601** HOLLAND *Pliny* I. 411 A mean commoner of Rome, descended from the race of Libertines or Slaues newly infranchised. **1631** SELDEN *Titles Hon.* (ed. 2) Ep. Ded., As if one could be put into the state of a Libertine, without a former seruitude! **1644** *Jus Pop.* 52 Who could more powerfully sway in the Palace than Eunuchs, Grooms and Libertines? **1726** AYLIFFE *Parergon* 24 There are some Persons forbidden to be Accusers..as Libertines against their Patrons. **1727** LARDNER *Credib. Gosp. Hist.* I. iii. §4.

¶**b.** Misused for: A freeman (of a city). *rare*$^{-1}$.

c **1611** CHAPMAN *Iliad* XVI. 50 He..vsde me like a fugitiue; an Inmate in a towne, That is no citie libertine, nor capable of their gowne.

2. a. *pl.* The name given to certain antinomian sects of the early sixteenth century, which arose in France and elsewhere on the continent. **b.** Later, in wider sense: One who holds free or loose opinions about religion; a free-thinker.

1563-83 FOXE *A. & M.* II. 1613/1 Euen the infidels, Turkes, Iewes, Anabaptistes, and Libertines, desire felicitie as well as the Christians. **1589** *Acts Privy Council* (1898) XVII. 424 In those Lowe Countryes there are Sectaryes, as Annabaptystes, Lybertines, and soche lyke. **1604** R. CAWDREY *Table Alph.*, *Libertine*, loose in religion, one that thinks he may doe what he listeth. **1612** T. TAYLOR *Comm. Titus* ii. 14 Neither wanted their Libertins in those daies, that..thought They might doe what they listed. **1646** P. BULKELEY *Gospel Covt.* IV. 297 The old plea of loose Libertines in the Apostles time; I have faith, saith one, and though I have no works, yet my faith will save me. **1698** NORRIS *Pract. Disc.* IV. 254 The Libertins, and Profane Spirits of the Age are apt to Reason, or rather Mutiny against the Ways of God. **1762** GOLDSM. *Nash* 48 People of all ways of thinking, even from the libertine to the methodist. **1831** BREWSTER *Newton* (1855) II. xviii. 163 Flamsteed never scrupled to denounce Halley as a libertine and an infidel. **1876** J. PARKER *Paracl.* II. xvii. 283 The intellectual libertine who denies everything that cannot be certified by the senses.

c. *transf.* One who follows his own inclinations or goes his own way; one who is not restricted or confined.

1599 SHAKS. *Hen. V*, I. i. 48 When he speakes, The Ayre, a Charter'd Libertine, is still. **1612** T. TAYLOR *Comm. Titus* iii. 1 Romish policie, that they might become the absolute libertines of the world..hath withdrawn the neckes of the clergie from vnder Ciuill Power. **1628** BP. HALL *Serm. Chr. Liberty* Rem. Wks. (1660) 27 What is this, but..to professe our selves, not Libertines, but licentiate of disorder? **1642** ROGERS *Naaman* 116 Those Pharisees in the Gospel.. Christ himselfe was a libertine to them and their strictnesse. **1698** LISTER *Journey Paris* (1699) 39 Though Rubens in his History is too much a Libertine in this respect, yet there is in this very place, which we now describe, much truth in the habit of his principal Figures. **1870** DICKENS *E. Drood* iv, He is the chartered libertine of the place.

3. A man who is not restrained by moral law, esp. in his relations with the female sex; one who leads a dissolute, licentious life. †Rarely applied to a woman.

1593 G. HARVEY *Pierce's Supererog.* 45 The whole brood of venereous Libertines, that knowe no reason but appetite, no Lawe but Luste. **1593** NASHE *Christ's T.* 29 b, Twenty thousand of these dreggy lees of Libertines hiu'd vnto him in a moment. **1602** SHAKS. *Ham.* I. iii. 49. **1633** MASSINGER *Guardian* II. v, The plump Dutch Frow, the stately dame of Spain, The Roman libertine, and sprightful Tuscan. **1713** ROWE *J. Shore* i, That man the lawless libertine may rove, Free and unquestion'd through the wilds of love. **1750** JOHNSON *Rambler* No. 77 ¶14 The giddy libertine, or drunken ravisher. **1828** SCOTT *F.M. Perth* xiv, Since when is it that the principal libertine has altered his morals so much? **1855** PRESCOTT *Philip II* (1857) 80 His life..was that of a libertine.

4. At Aberdeen University: A student who has no bursary.

1782 OREM *Chanonry Aberd.* 175 The janitor..hath twenty shillings Scots from every bursar, and two shillings and six pence sterling from libertines. **1818** KENNEDY *Ann. Aberd.* II. 392 Since the original foundation of the college, the students have been distinguished by the titles of *bursars*, and *libertines*, or free scholars.

B. *adj.*

1. Manumitted from slavery (see A. 1). *rare.*

1600 HOLLAND *Livy* XXII. i. 432 The verie Libertine or enfranchised women. **1795** MACKNIGHT *Apost. Epistles* (1820) IV. 547, 4000 of the Libertine race were transported.

2. Acknowledging no law in religion or morals; free-thinking; antinomian. Also *occas.* Pertaining to the sects known as 'Libertines'.

1577 NORTHBROOKE *Dicing* (1843) 36 The doctrine of the gospell is not a libertine docrtine. **1640** BP. HALL *Chr. Moder.* II. x. 82 Even among the Christians themselves, what foule charges of libertine doctrine are layd upon them by false teachers! **1693** TILLOTSON *Pref. to Wilkins' Nat. Relig.*, The pernicious doctrines of the Antinomians, and of all other libertine-enthusiasts. **1702** C. MATHER *Magn. Chr.* II. ii. (1852) 115 Religion..had like to have died..through a libertine and Brownistick spirit. **1708** SWIFT *Sentim. Ch. Eng. Man* Wks. 1755 II. I. 55 Persons of libertine and atheistical tenets. **1858** M. PATTISON *Ess.* (1889) II. 18 The Libertine party instantly saw the opportunity afforded of turning opinion against the pastors. **1861** TRENCH *7 Ch. Asia* 84 In the Apocalypse of St. John we find these libertine errors already full blown. **1901** *Expositor* June 412 The libertine tendencies of Gentile Christians in Asia Minor.

3. Free or unrestrained in constitution, habit, conduct or language. Now *rare* or *Obs.*

1589 G. HARVEY *Pierce's Supererog.* (1593) 139 Although that same French Mirrour be..stuffed with geere homely enough, fit for a Libertine & frantique Theame; yet doth it [etc.]. **1631** T. POWELL *Tom All Trades* (1876) 167 A more libertine disposition. **1668** EVELYN *Mem.* (1857) II. 36 Amongst other libertine libels, there was..a bold petition of the poor w——s to Lady Castlemaine. **1689-90** TEMPLE *Ess. Poetry* Wks. 1731 I. 238 There is something in the Genius of Poetry, too libertine to be confined to so many Rules. **1768-74** TUCKER *Lt. Nat.* (1834) II. 79 The libertine ant will choose her own settlement. **1847** EMERSON *Wood Notes* II. Poems 70 He is free and libertine, Pouring of his power the wine To every age, to every race.

†**b.** Of literary composition, translation: Extremely free. *Obs.*

1656 COWLEY *Pindar. Odes* Pref., The Grammarians perhaps will not suffer this libertine way of rendring foreign Authors to be called Translation. *a* **1683** OLDHAM *Poet. Wks.* Pref. (1686) 3 The Satyr and Odes of the Author..I have translated in the same libertine way. **1710** STEELE *Tatler* No. 172 ¶2, I have rambled in this Libertine Manner of Writing by way of Essay. **1760** H. WALPOLE *Let. to Sir D. Dalrymple* 3 Feb., The transitions are as sudden as those in Pindar, but not so libertine.

4. Characterized by habitual disregard of moral law, esp. with regard to the relation of the sexes; licentious, dissolute; characteristic of or resembling a libertine.

1605 BACON *Adv. Learn.* II. xxv. §3. 121 The heathen Poets, when they fall upon a libertine passion, doe still expostulate with lawes and moralities, as if they were opposite and malignant to nature. **1699** BURNET *39 Art.* Pref. (1700) 4 A tendency not only to Antinomianism, but to a Libertine course of life. **1762** GIBBON *Misc. Wks.* (1814) IV. 132 The frank libertine wit of their old stage. **1804** ANNA SEWARD *Mem. E. Darwin* 375 A band of libertine lovers.. plight their promiscuous hymeneals. *a* **1831** MACKINTOSH *Rev. of 1688* Wks. 1846 II. 11 The attractions of his lively and some-what libertine conversation were among the means by which he maintained his ground with Charles II. **1886** F. HARRISON *Choice of Bks.* iii. 51 The Decameron.. is redolent of that libertine humanism which stamps the Renascence.

libertinism (ˈlɪbətɪnɪz(ə)m). [f. LIBERTINE + -ISM.]

1. The views or practice of a libertine in religious matters; freedom of opinion or non-recognition of authority as to religion; free-thinking.

1641-51 *Lanc. Tracts* (Chetham Soc.) 10 A zealous Defender of the established Doctrine..of our Church, from Heresie, Libertinisme, and Prophanenesse. **1664** H. MORE *Myst. Iniq.* Apol. 566 Fed with the sweet sugar sops of Libertinism and Antinomianism. **1699** BURNET *39 Art.* xxxii. (1700) 356 The Marriage of most of the Reformers was urged..as a Doctrine of Libertinism, that made the clergy look too like the rest of the World. **1704** HEARNE *Duct. Hist.* (1714) I. 110 His Design was to abolish all Religion.. and establish Atheism and Libertinism, leaving every Body to their Liberty of believing what they pleased. **1748** HARTLEY *Observ. Man* II. iv. Concl. 446 If Men reject Revealed Religion, great Libertinism must ensue. **1861** TRENCH *7 Ch. Asia* 84 Heathen false freedom and libertinism.

2. Disregard of moral restraint, esp. in relations between the sexes; licentious or dissolute practices or habits of life.

1611 COTGR., *Sensualité*, Sensuality, libertinisme, or epicurisme. **1650** BAXTER *Saints' R.* III. (1651) 283 Troden under foot by Libertinism, and sensuality, as meat for Swine. **1754** RICHARDSON *Grandison* (1781) II. xvii. 186 Thus are wickedness and libertinism, called a knowledge of the world, a knowledge of human nature. **1761-2** HUME *Hist. Eng.* (1806) V. lxxi. 339 Wicherley was ambitious of the reputation of wit and libertinism, and he attained it. **1852** THACKERAY *Esmond* I. xiii, The lord made a boast of his libertinism.

3. Freedom of life or conduct; unrestrained liberty. *rare.*

1647 HAMMOND *Chr. Oblig. to Peace* iii. 71 Dignified with the title of Freeman, and denied the libertinisme that belongs to it. **1753** HANWAY *Trav.* (1762) II. II. i. 71 If libertinism is carried to a certain degree, the coercive power must become arbitrary. **1875** JOWETT *Plato* (ed. 2) III. 451 The freedom and libertinism of useless and unnecessary pleasures.

†**liber'tinity.** *Obs. rare*$^{-1}$. [ad. med.L. *lībertīnitās*, f. *lībertīnus* LIBERTINE: see -ITY.] The condition of a freedman. Also = LIBERTINAGE.

a **1577** SIR T. SMITH *Commw. Eng.* III. x. (1609) 128 To bring the owners..thereof into a certaine seruitude, or rather libertinity. **1656** BLOUNT *Glossogr.*, *Libertinism*, *Libertinage*, or *Libertinity*. **1721** in BAILEY.

libertinous (lɪˈbɜːtɪnəs). *a.* [f. L. *lībertīn-us* + -OUS.] = LIBERTINE *a.*

1632 LITHGOW *Trav.* x. 432 The other abuse is, their Libertinous Masses. **1906** *Daily Chron.* 14 Aug. 3/2 The tale of a bold bad knight, who made libertinous love to a virtuous young woman. **1966** *Punch* 30 Nov. 800/1 We red-eyed supporters of riotous and libertinous Sundays have no other lord before Ted.

†**'libertism.** *Obs. rare.* [app. f. LIBERTY + -ISM.] = LIBERTINISM 1.

1644 MILTON *Judgm. Bucer* Wks. 1851 IV. 304 A Writ of Error, not of Libertism. **1681** *Ess. Peace & Truth Ch.* 33 To avoid both the confusion of Libertism, and the Tyranny of pretended Ecclesiastical Infallibility.

'libertist. *rare.* [f. LIBERT(Y *sb.* + -IST.] An advocate of liberty.

1887 *Voice* (N.Y.) Aug. 11 But not for a moment can the radical personal libertist accept such a heresy.

liberty (ˈlɪbətɪ), *sb.*[1] Also 4-6 lib-, lyberte(e, 5-7 -tie, -tye, 6 libartye. [a. F. *liberté* (14th c. in Littré) = Pr. *libertat*, It. *libertà*, Sp. *libertad*, Pg. *liberdade*, ad. L. *lībertāt-em*, f. *līber* free.]

1. a. Exemption or release from captivity, bondage, or slavery.

c **1386** CHAUCER *Manciple's T.* 70 His libertee this brid desireth ay. *c* **1425** LYDG. *Assembly of Gods* 1272 By duresse & constreynt to put thys creature Cleerly from hys liberte. **1514** BARCLAY *Cyt. & Uplondyshm.* (Percy Soc.) p. xlix, The caytif beggar hath meate & libertie. **1535** COVERDALE *Ps.* xvii[i]. 19 He brought me forth..in to lyberte. **1611** BIBLE *Isa.* lxi. 1 To proclaime libertie to the captiues. **1727** DE FOE *Syst. Magic* I. iii. (1840) 71 Moses and Aaron were to assure Pharaoh that God sent them, and they were in his Name to demand liberty for the Children of Israel. **1852** MRS. STOWE *Uncle Tom's C.* vii. 42 She gazed..on the sullen, surging waters that lay between her and liberty.

b. In religious use: Freedom from the bondage of sin, or of the law.

1382 WYCLIF *2 Cor.* iii. 17 Forsoth where is the spirit of God, there is liberte. *c* **1410** HOCCLEVE *Mother of God* 76 Þat vn-to libertee Fro thraidam han vs qwit. **1526** TINDALE *Jas.* i. 25 Whosoever loketh in the parfait lawe off libertie, and continueth there in. **1543** BECON *Nosegay* K vj b, This spirituall liberte maketh vs not free from our obedience & dutye towarde the temporal power. **1604** HIERON *Wks.* I. 482 This libertie, which Christians haue, is a spirituall libertie, a heauenly liberty, a liberty of the soule..which setteth the soule at liberty from destruction. **1823** SIMEON in *Memoirs* (1847) 587 The boundaries of Christian liberty and Christian duty.

2. a. Exemption or freedom from arbitrary, despotic, or autocratic rule or control. ***cap of liberty***: see CAP *sb.*[1] 4 f.

1484 CAXTON *Fables of Æsop* II. i, Fredome and lyberte is better than ony gold or syluer. 1565 COOPER *Thesaurus*, s.v. *Libertas*, To defende the libertie of the common weale. 1649 CULPEPPER *Phys. Direct.* A, The Prize which We now.. play for is The Liberty of the Subject. 1654 BRAMHALL *Just. Vind.* i. (1661) 4 They.. vindicate that liberty left them as an inheritance by their Ancestours, from the incroachments.. of the Court of Rome. 1690 LOCKE *Govt.* II. iv. §22 Wks. 1727 II. 165 The Liberty of Man, in Society, is to be under no other Legislative Power, but that established by Consent in the Commonwealth. 1759 FRANKLIN *Ess.* Wks. 1840 III. 429 Those who would give up essential liberty, to purchase a little temporary safety, deserve neither liberty nor safety. 1789 BURKE *Corr.* (1844) III. 105 You hope, sir, that I think the French deserving of liberty. I certainly do. 1816 J. SCOTT *Vis. Paris* (ed. 5) p. xxxiv, Liberty is the chief distinction of England from other European countries. 1845 MILL *Ess.* II. 244 The modern spirit of liberty is the love of individual independence. 1854 J. S. C. ABBOTT *Napoleon* (1855) II. xxvii. 493 Be careful not to suffer liberty to degenerate into license, or anarchy to take the place of order. 1874 GREEN *Short Hist.* viii. §5. 500 Eliot died, the first martyr of English liberty, in the Tower.

b. ***natural liberty***: the state in which every one is free to act as he thinks fit, subject only to the laws of nature. ***civil liberty***: natural liberty so far restricted by established law as is expedient or necessary for the good of the community. ***liberty of conscience***: the system of things in which a member of a state is permitted to follow without interference the dictates of his conscience in the profession of any religious creed or the exercise of any mode of worship. ***liberty of the press***: the recognition by the state of the right of any one to print and publish whatever he pleases without previous governmental permission.

The *liberty of the press* is not understood to imply absence of liability to judicial punishment for the publication of libellous or criminal matter, nor to be inconsistent with the right of the courts to prohibit a particular publication as involving a wrong to some person.

*a*1572 KNOX *Hist. Ref.* Wks. 1846 I. 364 To suffer euerie man to leaf at libertie of conscience. 1580 J. HAY in *Cath. Tract.* (1901) 61 Quhy in the beginning of your new Euangell preached ye libertie of conscience. 1601 R. JOHNSON *Kingd. & Commw.* (1603) 250 That he woulde suffer them to enjoy the libertie of their conscience. 1644 MILTON *Areop.* (Arb.) 31 When complaints are freely heard, deeply consider'd, and speedily reform'd, then is the utmost bound of civill liberty attain'd, that wise men looke for. 1651 HOBBES *Leviath.* II. xxi. 108 Naturall liberty, which only is properly called liberty. 1678 WANLEY *Wond. Lit. World* v. i. §98. 4687 In the treaty of Passaw was granted Liberty of Conscience to the Professors of the Augustane Confession. 1769 BLACKSTONE *Comm.* IV. 151 The liberty of the press is ..essential to the nature of a free state. 1771 SMOLLETT *Humph. Cl.* 2 June, Let. ii, As for the liberty of the press,.. it must be restrained. 1832 AUSTIN *Jurispr.* (1879) I. vi. 281 Political or civil liberty is the liberty from legal obligation which is left or granted by a sovereign government to any of its subjects. 1858 [see CONSCIENCE 4].

3. a. The condition of being able to act in any desired way without hindrance or restraint; faculty or power to do as one likes.

*c*1374 CHAUCER *Troylus* v. 285 It lay not in his libertee No-wher to gon. *c*1386 —— *Clerk's T.* 89, I me reioysed of my libertee, That selde tyme is founde in mariage. 1390 GOWER *Conf.* III. 180 He kepte his liberte To do justice and equite. 1530 PALSGR. 298 Suche as writeth in ryme use in this thyng their lyberte. 1590 SHAKS. *Com. Err.* II. i. 7 A man is Master of his libertie. 1690 LOCKE *Hum. Und.* II. xxi. §8. 118 The Idea of Liberty is the Idea of a Power in any Agent to do or forbear any particular Action. 1781 COWPER *Truth* 195 Thought, word, and deed, his liberty evince, His freedom is the freedom of a prince. 1831 TRELAWNY *Adv. Younger Son* I. 45 I've liberty now—not under the pennant —do as I like. 1849 RUSKIN *Sev. Lamps* vii. §1. 184 If there be any one principle.. more sternly than another imprinted on every atom of the visible creation, that principle is not Liberty but Law. 1872 DE MORGAN *Budget Paradoxes* 464 We have a glorious liberty in England of owning neither dictionary, grammar nor spelling-book. 1873 HAMERTON *Intell. Life* x. vii. (1876) 372 The liberty of the wild bee.

b. *Philos.* The condition of being free from the control of fate or necessity; = FREEDOM 5.

(Now chiefly in expressed antithesis to *necessity*; the phrase ***liberty of the will*** occurs, but *freedom* is more common in this connexion.)

1538 STARKEY *England* I. ii. 30 Many men vtturly take away the lyberty of wyl. 1654 HOBBES (*title*) Of Libertie and Necessitie. 1687 MIEGE *Gt. Fr. Dict.* II, Liberty of Will, *franc Arbitre.* 1814 CARY *Dante, Par.* v. 21 Supreme of gifts which God.. gave Of his free bounty.. Was liberty of will. 1868 BAIN *Ment. & Mor. Sci.* IV. xi. (*chapter-heading*), Liberty and Necessity. *Ibid.* 400 These terms are supposed to involve.. the Liberty of the Will.

4. a. Free opportunity, range, or scope *to* do or †*of* doing something; hence, leave, permission.

14.. *Epyphanye* in *Tundale's Vis.* (1843) 112 For they in hart rejoysed not a lyte On hym to loke that they have lybarte. *c*1430 LYDG. *Reason & Sens.* (E.E.T.S.) 131 A lady callyd Curtesy, whiche graunted him lyberte to goo wher him lyst. 1463 *Bury Wills* (Camden) 22, I will she haue hire liberte at alle leffull tymes to go in to the chapell. 1526 TINDALE *Acts* xxvii. 3 Iulius.. gave him liberte to goo vnto his frendes. 1530 PALSGR. 239/1 Lybertie leave, *faculté, liberté.* 1590 SHAKS. *Com. Err.* v. i. 53 Youthfull men, Who giue their eies the liberty of gazing. 1604 —— *Oth.* II. ii. 10 There is full libertie of Feasting from this present houre. 1642 SIR T. BROWNE *Relig. Med.* I. (1896) 26 There is no liberty for causes to operate in a loose and stragling way. 1671 MILTON *P.R.* I. 365, I enjoy Large liberty to round this Globe of Earth. 1749 FIELDING *Tom Jones* XVI. viii, You have my full liberty to publish them. 1796 BP. WATSON *Apol. Bible* (ed. 2) 190 You have the liberty of doing so. 1833 HT. MARTINEAU *Briery Creek* i. 4 Bid him come in and wait for liberty to talk. 1840 DICKENS *Barn. Rudge* iii, Have they no liberty, no will, no right to speak?

b. Unrestricted use of, or access to, permission to go anywhere within the limits of: chiefly in phr. ***to have the liberty of.*** (Cf. FREEDOM 13 b.) ? *Obs.*

1603 SHAKS. *Meas. for M.* IV. ii. 156 He hath euermore had the liberty of the prison. 1621 ELSING *Debates Ho. Lords* (Camden) 22 He desyres not to be at libertye, but to have the libertye of the house. 1630 WADSWORTH *Pilgr.* viii. 90, I was freed from the Cage.. and had the liberty of the dungeon. 1719 DE FOE *Crusoe* I. viii. (1840) 133, I might be more happy in this Solitary Condition, than I should have been in a Liberty of Society. 1724 —— *Mem. Cavalier* (1840) 270 They allowed him the liberty of the town. 1796 JANE AUSTEN *Pride & Prej.* iv. (1813) 12 He was now provided with a good house and the liberty of a manor.

c. *Naut.* Leave of absence. (Cf. *liberty man* in 10.)

1758 J. BLAKE *Plan Mar. Syst.* 12 They shall be allowed to complete the remainder of the aforesaid time of liberty. *Ibid.* 13 The seaman ashore on liberty. 1867 SMYTH *Sailor's Word-bk., Breaking liberty*, not returning at the appointed time.

5. a. Unrestrained action, conduct, or expression; freedom of behaviour or speech, beyond what is granted or recognized as proper; licence. (*Occas.* personified.) Now only in particularized sense: An instance of freedom, an overstepping or setting aside of rules; a licence.

1558 KNOX *First Blast* (Arb.) 7 John the Baptist, whom Herode.. had beheaded for the libertie of his tonge. 1562 FILLS *Stat. Geneva* Ep. Ded. *iv b, They charge vs.. with libertie and licenciousnesse. 1590 SHAKS. *Com. Err.* I. ii. 102 Nimble Iuglers.. Disguised Cheaters, prating Mountebankes; And manie such like liberties of sinne. 1603 —— *Meas. for M.* I. iii. 29 Libertie plucks Iustice by the nose. 1638 BAKER tr. *Balzac's Lett.* (vol. III) 124 These liberties are not sufferable in the freest conversations, they draw on other more dangerous liberties. 1670 COTTON *Espernon* I. IV. 146 A Captain that very well understood.. the pest of great Bodies to be sloath and liberty, which debauch Souldiers from their Duty. 1704 SWIFT *T. Tub* Postscr., Wks. 1760 I. p. xvii, Using no other liberties, besides that of expunging certain passages. 1709 FELTON *Classics* (1718) 18 The Poem [Æneid] is still more Wonderful, since without the Liberty of the Grecian Poets, the Diction is so Great and Noble, so Clear.. that [etc.]. 1727 GAY *Begg. Op.* I. vii, If I allow captain Macheath some trifling liberties. 1868 FREEMAN *Norm. Conq.* (1876) II. vii. 119 Those who may venture on liberties with the men of fargone times which to the historian are forbidden. 1881 JOWETT *Thucyd.* I. Introd. 11 Thucydides has rarely.. allowed himself liberties not to be found somewhere in other writers.

b. Phr. ***to take the liberty to*** do or ***of*** doing something: to go so far beyond the bounds of civility or propriety, be so presumptuous as to (etc.). ***to take liberties*** (or ***a liberty***): to be unduly or improperly familiar (*with* a person; sometimes *euphemistic*); to use freedom in dealing *with* (rules, facts, etc.).

1625 BACON *Ess., Friendship* (Arb.) 169 Mæcenas took the liberty to tell him that [etc.]. 1704 N. N. tr. *Boccalini's Advts. fr. Parnassus* II. 127 Catullus.. took the Liberty to call the Nobleman Bastard. 1719 DE FOE *Crusoe* II. x. (1840) 220 The poor man had taken liberty with a wench. 1739 *Wks. of Learned* I. 83 *note*, Mr. Dryden.. takes great Liberties with the Authors he translates. 1749 *Power Pros. Numbers* 71 The first Foot of the first Line.. is defective by two short Syllables; which is a Liberty seldom taken. 1749 J. CLELAND *Mem. Woman Pleasure* I. 219, I had seen him taking the last liberties with my servant-wench. 1818 COBBETT *Pol. Reg.* XXXIII. 101, I will.. take the liberty to give them.. my opinion. 1824 MRS. SHERWOOD *Waste Not* II. 9 Mayhap you have made a stolen march, and taken what they call thieves' liberty. 1862 BORROW *Wild Wales* I. xii. 124 The creature [*sc.* a cat] soon began to take liberties, and in less than a week after my arrival at the cottage, generally mounted on my back, when it saw me reading or writing. 1883 GILMOUR *Mongols* xxiii. 286 He thought I was taking some undue liberty with his dignity. 1924 A. A. MILNE *When we were very Young* 57 Excuse me, Your Majesty, For taking of The liberty, But marmalade is tasty, if It's very Thickly Spread. 1967 *Listener* 23 Feb. 271/1 A scene in which he is wrongfully accused of 'taking a liberty' with one of the female guests.

6. As a feminine personification; with reference to the preceding senses, esp. sense 2.

1508 DUNBAR *Gold. Targe* 175 Will, Wantonness, Renoun, and Libertee. 1632 MILTON *L'Allegro* 36 The Mountain Nymph, sweet Liberty. 1768 STERNE *Sent. Journ.* (1775) 87 (*Hotel at Paris*) Liberty.. no tint of words can spot thy snowy mantle. 1798 COLERIDGE *France: An Ode* 89 O Liberty! with profitless endeavour Have I pursued thee. 1818 HALLAM *Mid. Ages* (1872) I. 92 Liberty never wore a more unamiable countenance than among these burghers, who abused the strength she gave them.

7. *Law.* **a.** A privilege or exceptional right granted to a subject by the sovereign power; = FRANCHISE *sb.* 2 b.

[1166-7 *Pipe Roll 13 Hen. II* (1889) 107 Burgenses de Bedeford' reddunt Computum de. xl. *marcis* pro Carta Regis *habenda*, ut sint in libertate Burgensium de Oxineforde.] 1404 *Rolls of Parlt.* III. 549 Als ferre as he may by the lawe of his land, or by his prerogatif, or libertee. 1414 *Ibid.* IV. 22 So as hit hath ever be thair liberte & fredom, that thar sholde no Statut no Lawe be made oflasse than they yaf therto their assent. 1557 [see FRANCHISE *sb.* 2 b]. 1612 DAVIES *Why Ireland*, etc. (1787) 106 Then had the Lord of Meath the same royal liberty in that territory. *a*1626 BACON *Uses Com. Law* (1635) 8 Many men of good quality have attained by charter.. within mannors of their owne liberty of keeping law-dayes. 1647 FULLER *Good Th. in Worse T.* 13 A grant of liberty from Queene Mary to Henry Ratcliffe. 1710 PRIDEAUX *Orig. Tithes* iv. 195 Grant to be held by inheritance and with perpetual liberty. 1767 BLACKSTONE *Comm.* II. iii. 31. 1848 WHARTON *Law Lex.* s.v., A liberty to hold pleas in a court of one's own.

b. *pl.* (†rarely *collect. sing.*) Privileges, immunities, or rights enjoyed by prescription or by grant.

[1180 *Mag. Rot. 26 Hen. II*, Rot. 56 in Madox *Hist. Exchequer* (1711) 273 Homines de Preston reddunt computum de C marcis, Pro habenda Carta Regis, ut habeant Libertates quas Homines de Novo Castro habent.] *c*1380 WYCLIF *Wks.* (1880) 162 þe lawis & þe libertes of holy chirche. 1467 in *Eng. Gilds* (1870) 392 That he be disfraunchised of his libertees. 1587 FLEMING *Contn. Holinshed* III. 1491/2, I thought meet to passe ouer the antiquitie of.. Douer, with the liberties thereof. 1602 FULBECKE *Pandectes* 55 The Heluetians did bestow the liberties of their citie vpon Lewis the eleuenth. 1607 SHAKS. *Cor.* II. iii. 223 They haue chose a Consull, that will from them take Their Liberties. 1669 MARVELL *Corr.* cxxix. Wks. 1872-5 II. 294 After long debate what to do with the Lords in point of our Libertys now. 1855 PRESCOTT *Philip II*, I. v. (1857) 76 The liberties of the commons were crushed at the fatal battle of Villalar.

c. †Hence *occas.* a person's domain or property. The district over which a person's or corporation's privilege extends. Also (in England before 1850), a district within the limits of a county, but exempt from the jurisdiction of the sheriff, and having a separate commission of the peace. (See also quot. 1876.)

liberty or ***liberties of a city***: the district, extending beyond the bounds of the city, which is subject to the control of the municipal authority. ***liberties of a prison*** (esp. the Fleet and the Marshalsea in London): the limits outside the prison, within which prisoners were sometimes permitted to reside.

1455 *Rolls of Parlt.* V. 325/2 Within ye said Citee, and Libertee of the same. 1510 in *Vicary's Anat.* (1888) 210 Commaundement gyven to the Surgeons of this Citie, that they.. dwell within the libertie of this Citie. 1535 COVERDALE *1 Macc.* x. 43 Who so euer they be that fle vnto the temple at Ierusalem or within the liberties thereof [Vulg. *in omnibus finibus ejus*]. 1596 SPENSER *State Irel.* Wks. (Globe) 623/1 To distrayne the goodes of any Irish, being found within theyr libertye, or but passing through theyr townes. 1659 RUSHW. *Hist. Coll.* I. 199 Within and without the Walls of the City of London, and in the Liberties and Nine out Parishes. 1724 SWIFT *Drapier's Lett.* Wks. 1755 V. II. 128, I will begin the experiment in the liberty of St. Patrick's. 1778 *Eng. Gazetteer* (ed. 2) s.v. *Warwicksh.*, This county.. is divided into four hundreds and one liberty. 1787 *Generous Attachment* I. 144 The worthy knight demanded.. what she meant by strolling into his liberty at that hour of the night. 1792 CHIPMAN *Rep.* (1871) 11 Bond conditioned that J. a prisoner should not depart the liberties of said prison. 1848 DICKENS *Dombey* iv, The offices of Dombey and Son were within the liberties of the City of London, and within hearing of Bow-Bells. 1876 DIGBY *Real Prop.* I. ii. §3. 52 When a large district comprising several manors was held by a single lord in whom was vested by grant or long usage the complete jurisdiction of the hundred, the district was called a liberty or honour.

8. ***liberty of the tongue*** (see quot.). So F. *liberté.*

1753 CHAMBERS *Cycl. Supp.* s.v., *Liberty of the tongue*, in the manege, is a void space left in the middle of a bit, to give place to the tongue of a horse, made by the bit's arching in the middle, and rising towards the roof of the mouth... In forging the bit, care must be taken not to make the liberty too high, or at least tickle the palate.

9. Governed by *at*, forming advb. or predicative phrase. **†a.** ***at one's liberty*** (later ***at liberty***): at one's own choice, as one pleases, 'ad libitum'.

1426 BP. BEAUFORT in Ellis *Orig. Lett.* Ser. II. I. 102 Att his owen fredam and libertee.. for to mowe passe the See in parfourmyng of the said avowe. 1426 LYDG. *De Guil. Pilgr.* 8386 Thow shalt no thyng do.. But at thyn owne lyberte. 1480 *Bury Wills* (Camden) 63 Wherof my seyd chauntry priest to be one of them at his liberte. 1524 HEN. VIII in *Buccleuch MSS.* (Hist. MSS. Comm.) I. 220 To.. were his bonet on his hed.. aswel in our presence as elleswhere, at his libertie. 1627 C. LEVER *Q. Eliz. Teares* xlv. (Grosart) 80 Painefull to get, but lost at libertie.

†b. ***at*** (a person's) ***liberty***: in his power or at his disposal. *Obs.*

*c*1477 CAXTON *Jason* 111 b, Yf I nowe had her at my liberte I sholde make her to deye a cruell deth. 1542-3 *Act 34 & 35 Hen. VIII*, c. 27 §77 The shireffe.. maie awarde a Capias ad satisfaciendum.. or elles a Fieri fac. at libertie of the partie pursuant. 1547 *Homilies* I. *Falling fr. God* II. (1859) 86 They take this for a great benefit of God, to have all at their own liberty. 1642 tr. *Perkins' Prof. Bk.* v. §319. 141 It is at the Libertie of the wife to have dower. 1698 NORRIS *Pract. Disc.* IV. 303 'Tis at their Liberty whether they will do any Works of Mercy.. or not.

c. ***at liberty*** (in early use † ***at one's*** or ***one's own liberty, at all, good, liberty***): not in captivity or confinement; esp. in phr. ***to set at liberty***, to liberate, free. Also, free to act, move, think, etc.; const. *to* with *inf.*, occas. with *clause.*

*c*1430 LYDG. *Compl. Bl. Knt.* 661 Ye may togider speke What so ye liste, at good libertee. 1470-85 MALORY *Arthur* VI. iii, Were I at my lyberte as I was. 1485 CAXTON *Pref. to Malory's Arthur* 3 But for to.. byleue that al is trewe that is conteyned herin, ye be at your lyberte. 1489 —— *Faytes of A.* III. viii. 184 A man is not atte hys owne lyberte that byndeth hym self to another. 1526 TINDALE *Luke* iv. 18 Frely to sett att liberte them that are brused. 1585 FETHERSTONE *Calvin on Acts* i. 5 The Lord openeth the prison for them that they may be at libertie to fulfil their function. 1594 SHAKS. *Rich. III*, I. i. 133 More pitty, that the Eagles should be mew'd, Whiles Kites and Buzzards

play at liberty. **1611** BIBLE *Transl. Pref.* 11 They..had rather haue their iudgements at libertie in differences of readings, then to be captiuated to one. **1692** R. L'ESTRANGE *Fables, Life Æsop* (1708) 2 The Reader is at Liberty what to Believe and what Not. **1709** STEELE *Tatler* No. 109 ¶1 Some particular Matters, which I am not at Liberty to report. **1758** REID tr. *Macquer's Chem.* I. 253 Its Acid being set at liberty. **1857** TROLLOPE *Three Clerks* xlv, 'If you knew it was coming..why didn't you tell a chap?' 'I was not at liberty', said Mr. Snape, looking very wise. **1866** J. MARTINEAU *Ess.* I. 26 He is quite at liberty to think so. **1882** ALEXANDER in Watson *Life Candlish* xv. 174 His right arm was at liberty. **1886** 'HUGH CONWAY' *Living or Dead* viii, You are at perfect liberty to repeat my words to him.

d. *at liberty*: (of persons or things) unoccupied, disengaged.

1847 C. BRONTË *J. Eyre* v. I. 75, I dressed as well as I could for shivering, and washed when there was a basin at liberty. **1853** MRS. GASKELL *Cranford* i. 4, I have no doubt they will call: so be at liberty after twelve. **1931** *Amer. Mercury* Nov. 351/1 *At liberty*, out of work. **1933** P. GODFREY *Back-Stage* v. 70 It takes many years before the superseded actors and actresses will admit to themselves that the professional terms 'at liberty' and 'disengaged' are no longer applicable to them in a temporary sense.

10. *attrib.* and *Comb.*, as ***liberty-monger***; ***liberty-loving***, ***-taking*** adjs.; **liberty act**, a circus act performed by liberty horses; **liberty boat** *Naut.*, a boat carrying liberty men; **liberty bodice**, a close-fitting under-bodice; **liberty bond**, one of the interest-bearing bonds of the 'Liberty' loans issued by the U.S. government in 1917–18; **liberty boy**, (*a*) *Anglo-Irish* (see quot. 1765 and cf. *liberty-corps*); (*b*) *transf.* or *allusive*, a noisy zealot for liberty; (*c*) *U.S.* a supporter of a freedom movement; (*d*) (see quot. 1826); (*e*) (see quot. 1842); **liberty cabbage** *U.S.*, sauerkraut; **liberty cap** = *cap of liberty* (see CAP *sb.*[1] 4 f); **liberty corps** (see quot.); **liberty-day** *Naut.*, a day on which part of a ship's crew are allowed to go ashore; **liberty hall** (see HALL *sb.*[1] 11); **liberty horse** (see quot. 1946); **liberty-liquor**, 'spirits formerly allowed to be purchased when seamen had visitors; now forbidden' (Smyth *Sailor's Word-bk.* 1867); **Liberty-loan**, one of the four issues of liberty bonds; **liberty man** *Naut.*, a sailor having leave to go ashore; **liberty-party** *U.S. Hist.*, a political party which made the abolition of slavery its leading principle; **liberty-pole**, a tall mast or staff with a Phrygian cap or other symbol of liberty on the top; †**liberty post**, a post marking the boundary of the Liberties of the City of London; **liberty** (or **Liberty**) **ship**, a type of merchant vessel built in the United States by rapid mass-production methods during the 1939–45 war; also *ellipt.* ***Liberty***; **liberty-ticket** *Naut.*, 'a document specifying the date and extent of the leave granted to a seaman or marine proceeding on his private affairs' (Smyth); **liberty tree** = *tree of liberty*; †**liberty-wife**, a mistress.

1933 P. GODFREY *Back-Stage* xvii. 214 The training of a team of spirited thoroughbreds for the '*Liberty' or 'Haute École' acts. **1837** *United Service Jrnl.* Aug. 474 They knew ..that the *liberty-boat would be on shore for them at that hour. **1901** *Daily Chron.* 16 Nov. 4/3 The destroyer..ran down a liberty boat..with the loss of three lives. **1956** A. THORNE *Baby & Battleship* I. 33 They..had no intention of coming back until it was nearly time to catch the Liberty Boat. **1916** *Child* May 433/1 The 'Liberty Bodice' Factory, of Market Harborough, have made a speciality of the '*Liberty Bodice'... The bodice is made of durable but soft and elastic material, and is porous and pliable and arranged with well-placed straps carried over the shoulders to take the weight of underclothes and stand the pull of suspenders. **1932** S. GIBBONS *Cold Comfort Farm* xiv. 193 Give me my liberty bodice. **1968** J. IRONSIDE *Fashion Alphabet* 70 *Liberty bodice*, bodice to the waist,..worn by girls. The bodice has built-up shoulders and buttons at front or back. It..has gone out of fashion for all but very young children. **1973** *Radio Times* 18 Jan. 18/1 (Advt.), The wiser you are, the more you appreciate the comfort of a liberty bodice. **1918** in WEBSTER Add., *Liberty bond. **1919** E. E. CUMMINGS *Let.* 25 Nov. (1969) 64 Very nice of you all to include me in the liberty bond donation. **1922** *Encycl. Brit.* XXXI. 760/2 The Liberty Bonds and Victory Notes were issued under authority of the Acts of Congress approved April 24 1917, Sept. 24 1917, [etc.]. **1928** Liberty bond [see DRIVE *sb.* 1 g]. **1760** FOOTE *Minor* Introd., Wks. 1799 I. 229 A Dublin mechanic..heading the *liberty-boys in a skirmish on Ormond Quay. **1765** *Ann. Reg.* 120 Several soldiers and the liberty boys (that is, journeymen weavers living in the earl of Meath's liberties adjoining to the city) broke open Newgate. **1774** in C. F. Aspinall-Oglander *Admiral's Widow* (1942) 51 They are distinguished here by the name of Tories, as the Liberty Boys—the tarring feathery gentry—are by the title of Whigs. **1781** S. PETERS *Gen. Hist. Connecticut* 393 The liberty boys were..honoured with the presence of ministers, deacons [etc.]. **1788** V. KNOX *Winter Even.* I. II. xvii. 223 A Greek political ballad, which used to be sung by the Athenian liberty-boys. **1826** *New Monthly Mag.* II. 79 While the paying spectator..applauded, when his feelings prompted, the *liberty boy* [*sc.* free-ticket holder].., if he clapped at all, would clap with gloved hands. **1827** *Blackw. Mag.* XXII. 593 Enacting the part of liberty-boys. **1842** *N.Z. Gaz.* II. 112 People from ships called 'liberty boys' are only allowed to come on shore on Sundays for recreation. **1858** *Texas Almanac 1859* 33 The Liberty boys..joined Austin's Company. **1927** *Haldeman-Julius Q.* July–Sept. 7/2 Here we were..calling sauerkraut '*Liberty Cabbage'. **1967** *Listener* 18 May 642/1 In America it was more than a restaurant owner's life was worth to keep sauerkraut on the menu: it was changed to liberty cabbage. **1803** *Lit. Mag.* (Philadelphia) Dec. 172 A liberty pole..decorated with party coloured flags and *liberty caps. **1835** *Mechanics' Mag.* 10 Jan. 256/2 It is wholly at variance with classic authority to place the Pileus or Liberty Cap on the head of the figure representing Liberty. **1843** L. M. CHILD *Lett. from N.Y.* xl. 274 This age and country, in which liberty-caps abound. **1887** LECKY *Eng. in 18th C.* VI. 360 The '*Liberty' corps of the volunteers—so called because it was recruited in the Earl of Meath's liberties. **1840** R. H. DANA *Bef. Mast* xii. 27 Sunday..is the *liberty-day among merchantmen. **1930** E. SMITH *Red Wagon* xxvii. 225 The time came to exhibit his beloved *liberty horses, four dapple-grey cobs exactly resembling painted rocking-horses. **1946** M. C. SELF *Horseman's Encycl.* 264 Liberty horses are those which perform in the circus without a rider. **1952** N. STREATFEILD *Aunt Clara* 103 The comedy horse turn was coming to an end, the liberty horses would follow. **1972** *New Statesman* 7 Jan. 14/2 Yasmin Smart is the only lady ring-master in the world... Since the age of 10 she has been learning to train Liberty horses. **1917** ADE *Let.* 12 June (1973) 64 We find it hard work to induce the farmers and other small investors to take the *Liberty Loan bonds. **1921** E. L. BOGART *War Costs* 208 The First Liberty Loan Act of April 24, 1917, authorized a bond issue of $2,000,000,000 and advances to allies of $3,000,000,000. **1922** B. J. HENDRICK *Life & Lett. W. H. Page* II. xxii. 273 The American Government finally paid this over-draft out of the proceeds of the first Liberty Loan. **1897** *Daily News* 23 Jan. 7/2 The *liberty-loving elements of our town. **1758** J. BLAKE *Plan Mar. Syst.* 18 Such *liberty-men..shall..forfeit all benefit from their liberty ticket. *c* **1860** H. STUART *Seaman's Catech.* 9 Pinnaces are the boats usually selected for.. carrying working parties, liberty men, &c. **1909** *Daily Chron.* 25 Feb. 1/6 The packet boats which convey the 'liberty' men to Chatham after the day's routine. **1964** R. BRADDON *Year Angry Rabbit* xii. 110 A few hundred liberty men on each side.., their flights delayed by bad weather, returned to the firing line too late. **1702** DE FOE *Test. Ch. Eng. Loyalty* in *Somers Tracts* 4th Collect. (1751) III. 14 Stubborn, refractory, *Liberty-Mongers. **1828** SYD. SMITH *Mem.* (1855) II. 290 Without making ourselves the liberty-mongers of all Europe. **1843** WHITTIER *What is Slavery?* Prose Wks. 1889 III. 105 It is against this system..that the *Liberty Party is, for the present, directing all its efforts. **1775–83** THACHER *Mil. Jrnl.* (1823) 22 *Liberty poles were erected in almost every town and villge..under which the tory is compelled to sign a recantation. **1789** GOUV. MORRIS in Sparks *Life & Writ.* (1832) II. 70 The soldiers were then paraded in triumph to the Palais Royal, which is now the liberty pole of this city. **1644** NYE *Gunnery* (1670) 50 The *liberty post standing amongst the desolate ruines of Fore-gate street. **1941** *Marine Digest* 28 June 8/2 The emergency cargo ships, known as the EC-2 type, *Liberty ships, will have an overall length of about 425 feet, width 57 feet, approximately 10,000 deadweight tons, and will be oil-burning. **1942** W. S. CHURCHILL *End of Beginning* (1943) 183 The launching of the *Patrick Henry*, the first Liberty ship. **1945** *Seafarers Log* 3/2 The first of the Liberties to be scrapped, the Banvard was delivered into service on April 8, 1943. **1961** W. VAUGHAN-THOMAS *Anzio* iv. 47 DUKWs were already chugging in from the big Liberty ships lying out to sea. **1966** C. R. TOTTLE *Sci. Engin. Materials* vii. 170 Some of the wartime 'liberty' ships fractured when lying in port, without operational loads. **1836** *Going to Service* xiii. 161 *Liberty-taking men-servants. **1758** *Liberty ticket [see quot. for *liberty man*]. **1776** A. ADAMS in *J. Adams' Fam. Lett.* (1876) 180, I..ventured just as far as the stump of *Liberty Tree. **1825** *Sweet William & Yng. Colonel* ii. in Child *Ballads* II. 291/1 I'll keep her for my *liberty-wife.

Hence †ˈ**libertyless** *a.*, deprived of liberty.

1643 T. CASE *Serm.* in Kerr *Covt. & Covenanters* (1895) 248 Thy sword..has made many a faithful minister libertyless.

Liberty (ˈlɪbətɪ), *sb.*[2] [The name of a London drapery firm, Messrs. *Liberty* and Co.] Used *attrib.* to designate materials, styles, colours, etc., characteristic of textile fabrics or articles sold by Messrs. Liberty.

1888 MRS. H. WARD *R. Elsmere* I. II. vii. 173 Bits of Liberty stuffs with the edges still ragged, or cheap morsels of Syrian embroidery. **1888** *Daily News* 23 Apr. 6/4 Her dress was of two kindred shades of almost indescribable colour, belonging to the class now commonly known..as Liberty tints. **1891** *Ibid.* 19 Jan. 3/1 'Liberty styles' are to be had in every large drapery establishment. **1892** 'F. ANSTEY' *Voces Populi* 2nd Ser. 112 Putting on a turban and a Liberty sash. **1892** G. & W. GROSSMITH *Diary of Nobody* ix. 126 Carrie has arranged some Liberty silk bows on the four corners. **1894** W. J. LOCKE *At Gate of Samaria* (1895) ix. 103 It had long been dismantled of the Liberty curtains, Persian rugs, and cheap Japaneseries. **1900** *Munsey's Mag.* July 517/2 Tying a brown liberty silk veil over my hair. **1901** *Daily News* 7 Mar. 8/4 Dresses and costumes (familiarly known as 'Liberty' gowns and frocks). **1903** A. BENNETT *Leonora* viii. 238 She had changed her Liberty dress for the dark severe frock of her studious hours. **1913** R. BROOKE *Let.* 22 Nov. (1968) 535 Hindus..in Liberty-coloured garments. **1923** R. MACAULAY *Told by Idiot* I. vi. 31 She looked round the Liberty room. **1957** M. B. PICKEN *Fashion Dict.* 283/1 *Liberty s[atin]*, trade name for soft, closely woven, piece-dyed satin fabric with raw-silk warp and single spun-silk filling. **1972** *Daily Tel.* 6 May 21/3 In spite of its French name, the 'new art' [*sc. art nouveau*] started in England and was originally known as the 'Liberty Style' deriving its name from the famous store which was started by Arthur Lazenby Liberty in 1875. Libertys sold many articles in this new style. **1973** *Country Life* 8 Feb. 365/2 Coat and skirt in a natural-coloured Swiss cloth with a lining and blouse in Liberty lawn.

b. Used *absol.*

1898 *Daily News* 19 Nov. 6/2 Another instance of the vogue enjoyed by English materials on the Continent is the universality of the word 'Liberty'. **1903** *Daily Chron.* 19 Sept. 8/4 Soft satin, called in Paris Liberty, is again being employed as a blouse fabric. **1909** *Westm. Gaz.* 1 Oct. 8/4 With pannier draperies over an under-skirt of Liberty.

ˈ**liberty**, *v.* *Obs.* exc. *dial.* [f. prec. sb.] *trans.* **a.** To endow with liberties or privileges. **b.** To give liberty to; *dial.* to allow to run loose.

c **1425** *Found. St. Bartholomew's* 16 The kynge..made this Chirche with all his pertynencys with the sam fredommys that his Crowne ys liberttid with or ony othir chirch yn all Inglonde that is most y-freid. **1494** FABYAN *Chron.* VII. 360 He was lybertied to be at large in the Kynges courte. **1893** *Wiltsh. Gloss., Liberty*, to allow anything to run loose. 'It don't matter how much it's libertied', the more freedom you give it the better.

‖**liberum arbitrium** (ˈlɪbərəm ɑːˈbɪtrɪəm), Lat. phr. (occurring in Livy 4. 43. 5): full power to decide, freedom of action.

1652 N. CULVERWEL *Act of Oblivion* in *Lt. Nature* [II.] 38 The great Creator of Heaven and Earth, must wait upon mans *liberum arbitrium*. **1880** W. JAMES *Coll. Ess. & Rev.* (1920) 194 Shall I move my index finger or my little finger to show my '*liberum arbitrium indifferentiae*'?

libethenite (lɪˈbɛθənaɪt). *Min.* [Named (*Libethenit*) by Breithaupt, 1823, from *Libethen* in Hungary: see -ITE.] An olive-green phosphate of copper found in crystals and reniform masses.

1832 SHEPARD *Min.* 174. **1868** DANA *Min.* (ed. 5) 563 Libethenite..occurs in quartz.

libidinal (lɪˈbɪdɪnəl), *a.* *Psychoanalysis.* [f. L. *libīdin-*, *libīdo* lust + -AL[1].] Pertaining to or connected with libido.

1922 J. RIVIERE tr. *Freud's Introd. Lect. Psycho-Anal.* 283 For a son, the task consists in releasing his libidinal desires from his mother, in order to employ them in the quest of an external love-object in reality. **1949** M. MEAD *Male & Female* xiii. 278 The pleasure of irresponsibility, untidiness, undirected libidinal behaviour. **1957** *Essays in Crit.* VII. 333 There remains the charge of brutality and its libidinal content. **1970** E. FROMM *Crisis of Psychoanal.* (1971) p. ix, One can speak of a non-neurotic character trait when libidinal impulses are transformed into relatively stable and socially adapted traits.

†**liˈbidinist.** *Obs. rare.* [f. L. *libīdin-*, *libīdo* lust + -IST.] A lustful person; a lecher.

1628 FELTHAM *Resolves* II. [= I. in later edd.] lxxviii. 224 Nero would not beleeue, but all men were most foule Libidinists. **1634** SIR T. HERBERT *Trav.* 198 This Ceremony..to Libidinists may seeme mirthful.

†**libidiˈnosity.** *Obs.* Also 6 lybidinosite. [a. F. *libidinosité*.] Lustfulness.

a **1529** SKELTON *Bk. 3 Foles* Wks. (1568) X vij b, Sardanapalus, that for his lecherye and lybidinosite fell into hell. **1656** BLOUNT *Glossogr., Libidinosity*, lustfulness, lasciviousness, luxury, incontinency.

libidinous (lɪˈbɪdɪnəs), *a.* Also 5 **lybidynous, lybydynous.** [ad. L. *libīdinōs-us*, f. *libīdin-*, *libīdo* lust: see -OUS. Cf. F. *libidineux*.]

1. Of persons, their lives, actions, desires: Given to, full of, or characterized by lust or lewdness; lustful, lecherous, lewd.

1447 BOKENHAM *Seyntys* (Roxb.) 241 He was lybydynous Thorgh fleshly lust. **1490** CAXTON *Eneydos* ix. 36 The grete kyng barbaryn by whom he is repressed fro his lybidynous desire. **1548** HOOPER *Decl. 10 Command.* x. 157 A dissolute, commune, and libidinous liefe. **1641** MILTON *Ch. Govt.* II. Pref. Wks. 1738 I. 61 Libidinous and ignorant Poetasters, who..do..lay up vicious Principles in sweet Pills. **1711** ADDISON *Spect.* No. 90 ¶1 A lewd Youth..advances by Degrees into a libidinous old Man. **1784** COWPER *Task* v. 660 Libidinous discourse Exhausted, he resorts to solemn themes Of theological and grave import. **1835** J. B. ROBERTSON tr. *Von Schlegel's Philos. Hist.* (1846) 40 Polygamy is indulged in to the most libidinous excess. **1837** CARLYLE *Misc.* (1857) IV. 15 A debauched, merely libidinous mortal.

†**2.** Provocative of lust. *Obs. rare*[−1].

1601 HOLLAND *Pliny* I. 426 Thus is wine drunke out of libidinous cups.

Hence **liˈbidinously** *adv.*, lustfully; **liˈbidinousness**, lustfulness.

1602 FULBECKE *Pandectes* 25 Boldlie and libidinously. **1611** SPEED *Hist. Gt. Brit.* VI. vii. §3. 65 For bloud and libidinousnesse hee was held a most vnsatiate fury. **1797** W. TAYLOR in *Monthly Rev.* XXIV. 195 The unbridled libidinousness of Giovanni Gaston. **1818** *Chron.* in *Ann. Reg.* 302 Witness was not prepared to say that laudanum would produce libidinousness. **1882** BERESF. HOPE *Brandreths* II. xxix. 224 Tigress women, Libidinously baleful.

libido (lɪˈbiːdəʊ, -ˈaɪdəʊ). *Psychoanalysis.* [f. L. *libīdo* desire, lust.] Psychic drive or energy, particularly that associated with the sexual instinct, but also that inherent in other instinctive mental desires and drives. Also *transf.* and *attrib.*, as ***libido theory***.

1909 A. A. BRILL tr. *Freud's Sel. Papers on Hysteria* vi. 147 The anxiety neurosis goes along with the most distinct diminution of the sexual libido or the psychic desire. **1913** C. G. JUNG in *17th Internat. Congr. Med.* XII. I. 66 This infantile fixation, which is understood as an unconscious attachment of the sexual libido to certain infantile phantasies and habits. **1922** J. STRACHEY tr. *Freud's Group Psychol.* 37 Libido is an expression taken from the theory of the emotions. We call by that name the energy..of those instincts which have to do with all that may be comprised under the word 'love'. **1929** *Encycl. Brit.* VIII. 399/2 The tenets of leading psycho-analysts assume a libido, with either one or two fundamental departments, sex, or sex and ego... The physiological basis of the libido and its emotions is hazy, to say the least. **1932** *Brit. Jrnl. Psychol.* Jan. 249

The attempt to find the foundation of group behaviour in instinctive tendencies fails, as does the psycho-analytic 'libido' theory. **1944** J. S. Huxley *On Living in Revolution* xv. 192 *Libido* is the nearest to such a term [*sc.* energy], but its use implies complete acceptance of orthodox psychoanalytic theory and has certain unsatisfactory connotations. **1953** *Encounter* Nov. 25/2 We accept the fact that our sexual libido is thwarted. It is time for us to recognise that our political libido is just as complex-ridden, repressed, and twisted, if not even more. *Ibid.* 26/2 The political libido can be defined as the individual's need to feel himself as part of a community, his urge to belong. **1971** *Sci. Amer.* Sept. 529/3 He shares the libido for new military systems that his entire guild displays. **1972** *Ibid.* Aug. 46/2 It has also been observed that removal of the ovaries does not reduce the libido of human females.

libinioid (lɪˈbɪnɪɔɪd), *a. Zool.* [f. mod.L. *Libinia* + -OID.] Having the characteristics of the genus *Libinia* of brachyurous crustaceans.

1852 Dana *Crust.* I. 50 The genus Trichia..is Libinioid in aspect.

†**libitinarian**, *Obs.*$^{-0}$ [f. L. *libitīnāri-us* (f. *Libitīna* goddess of corpses) + -AN.] (See quot.)

1661 Blount *Glossogr.* s.v. *Libitina*, They also who were employed to carry forth and bury Corps, were called Libitinarians, as well as Vespilons.

†**libitude**. *Obs.*$^{-0}$ [irreg. f. L. *libit-*, ppl. stem of *libet* it is pleasing: see -TUDE.] 'Will, pleasure' (Blount *Glossogr.* 1656).

libken. *Old Cant.* Also 6 lipken, 7 libkin. [f. LIB *v.*[3] + KEN *sb.*[2]] A place to sleep in.

1567 [see LIB *v.*[3]]. **1611** Middleton & Dekker *Roaring G.* v. i. K 4, If you come to our lib ken. **1621** B. Jonson *Gipsies Metamorph.* (1640) 50 To their libkins at the Crackmans. *a* **1700** B. E. *Dict. Cant. Crew*, *Libkin*, a House to Lye in; also a Lodging. **1816** Scott *Guy M.* xliv, These are the fees I always charge a swell that must have his lib-ken to himself.

Lib-Lab (ˌlɪbˈlæb), *a.* Abbrev. of *Liberal-Labour* (see LIBERAL *a.* 5); also as *sb.* Hence ˌ**Lib-ˈLabbery**.

1903 *Review of Reviews* Aug. 113/1 The Progress of the Lib-Labs. The Lib-Lab party is carrying all before it. **1944** G. B. Shaw *Everybody's Pol. What's What?* xxx. 263 Despotic dictators came into fashion as fast as Lib-Lab prime ministers lost face. **1952** H. Nicolson *King George V* vii. 94 Of the 53 Labour members elected in 1906, twenty-nine belonged to the Independent Labour Party and twenty-four were affiliated to the Liberal Party and known as 'Lib-Labs'. **1960** T. I. J. Jones in A. J. Roderick *Wales through Ages* II. 203 There were a few working class members of parliament before that date [*sc.* 1900]..but they counted themselves Liberals or at the most 'Lib-Lab'. *Ibid.* 205 The early years of the twentieth century saw the appearance of a new more militant type of leader..and his appearance was to bring about the decline of the 'Lib-Lab' ideal. **1960** *Guardian* 18 Feb. 3/6 A famous 'Lib-Lab.' family. **1963** *Ann. Reg. 1962* 14 Mr Gaitskell stiffly shot down the idea of a formal Lib-Lab alliance. **1965** *Economist* 26 June 1496/1 This is the hoary dilemma of Lib-Labbery. **1970** *Guardian* 6 Aug. 10/3 North Cornish Liberals are to urge the Liberal Assembly to fight every parliamentary seat and to have no truck with Lib-Labbery. **1972** *Times* 30 Sept. 15/3 A Lib-Lab party would be well placed in terms of the central argument which is concerned with inflation. **1973** *Daily Tel.* 19 Oct. 16 Mr Wilson shudders at the very thought of a return to the old 'Lib-Lab.' combination.

liblong, obs. form of LIVELONG.

[**liboya**, blunder for JIBOYA, boa-constrictor.

1718 In *W. Rogers' Voy.* (ed. 2); ed. 1 (1712) has correctly *Jiboya*. Hence **1774** in Goldsm. *Nat. Hist.* VII. 195 (but p. 225 *jiboya*), and **1796** in *Encycl. Brit.* (ed. 3) III. 517/2.]

‖**libra** (ˈlaɪbrə, ˈliːbrə). [L. *lībra* pound (12 ounces), balance, constellation so called. (In med.L. used for 'pound'; hence the mod.Eng. abbreviations. £ = pound(s) sterling, lb. = pound weight.)]

1. *Antiq.* A (Roman) pound.

1398 Trevisa *Barth. De P.R.* xix. cxxx. (1495) 939 Twelue vnces makith Libra and is therfore acountyd a perfyghte weyghte. **1797** *Encycl. Brit.* (ed. 3) X. 25/1 The Roman libra was used in France for the proportions of their coin till the time of Charlemagne. **1875** Jevons *Money* ix. 89 Units of weight, such as the shekel, the talent, the as, the stater, the libra, the mark, the franc, the lira.

†**2.** An arm of a balance. *Obs.*

1797 *Encycl. Brit.* (ed. 3) IX. 19/1 At the other end of the libræ, or levers.

3. (With initial capital.) *Astron.* One of the zodiacal constellations, lying between Scorpio and Virgo. **b.** The seventh sign of the zodiac (♎), which the sun enters on the 23rd of September. **c.** *Astrol.* A person born under the sign of Libra. Also *attrib.* or as *adj.*

1398 Trevisa *Barth. De P.R.* iii. x. (1495) 312 The signe that hight Libra in mannes body rulyth the nether guttes of the wombe. *c* **1491** *Chast. Goddes Chyld.* 19 In certen tyme of the yere the sonne begynneth in a planete that men call libra. **1559** Cunningham *Cosmogr. Glasse* 35 Aries and Lybra. **1591** Nashe *Prognostication* Wks. (Grosart) II. 167 This autumnall reuolution..beginneth in Libra. **1616** T. Adams *Plain-dealing* 22 We liue under Libra, Iustice and Equitie...we feare not Taurus the Bull. **1667** Milton *P.L.* iii. 558 From Eastern Point Of Libra to the fleecie Starr that bears Andromeda farr off Atlantick Seas. **1708** Swift *Predict. for 1708*, Wks. 1755 II. i. 150 The time that he enters Libra,..which is the busy period of the year. **1868** Lockyer *Elem. Astron.* §74. 29 The magnificent star-clusters, in the constellations..Libra and Aquarius. **1894** E. Kirk *Influence of Zodiac upon Human Life* xii. 88 Libra people are psychic collectors of thought. **1947** A. Leo *Astrol. for All* 31 This causes Libra persons to love harmony. **1969** 'V. Packer' *Don't rely on Gemini* (1970) xix. 164 Mrs. Muckermann's a Libra. **1976** *Billings* (Montana) *Gaz.* 7 July 9A/2 Miss Jillison, a libra, is married to a slim libra, Joseph Gallagher, film-production executive at 20th Century Fox—a marriage that took place after three dates and her reading his chart.

libral (ˈlaɪbrəl), *a.* [ad. L. *lībrālis*, f. *lībra* (see prec.).] (See quot. 1656.) ***libral as***: the Roman 'as' weighing a pound.

1656 Blount *Glossogr.*, *Libral*, that is or pertains to a pound weight, or measure, also belonging to the sign Libra. **1872** E. W. Robertson *Hist. Ess.* 245 The heavy libral Asses of the early Monetary system.

†**librament**. *Obs. rare*$^{-1}$. [ad. L. *lībrāment-um*, f. *lībrāre* to balance, level, set in motion.] Fall or escape (of liquid).

c **1420** *Pallad. on Husb.* ix. 131 On either side a pitte most ha descent Vntil thi sought licouris librament.

Libran (ˈliːbrən). *Astrol.* [f. LIBRA + -AN.] = LIBRA 3 c.

1911 I. M. Pagan *From Pioneer to Poet* vii. 94 The Libran is a capital hand at jotting down the annals of the present day. **1947** A. Leo *Astrol. for All* 32 To sum up the individuality of the Librans we may consider them as inspirational and perceptive characters. **1972** D. Lees *Zodiac* 98 Gordon Langford is a Libran. He was born on the fourth of October which means he is ruled by Venus. **1979** *Radio Times* 5 May 19/4 She is a Libran and claims that sense of balance supposed to belong to the zodiacal sign.

‖**liˈbranza**. *Obs.* [Sp., 'warrant, order', f. *librar* = F. *livrer* to deliver.] A ticket authorizing delivery of military stores.

1598 Barret *Theor. Warres* v. iii. 132 The Clarke of the Artillerie..who keepeth account of the payes..by Libranzas or tickets. *Ibid.* iv. 137 Which [articles] they are to distribute and deliuer out by Librazas, or Tickets.

†**librar**. *Sc. Obs. rare.* [a. F. *libraire*, ad. L. *librārius*: see LIBRARIAN.] A bookseller.

1596 in Dickson & Edmond *Ann. Scot. Printing* xxxiv. (1890) 478 Katherne Norwell, spous to Robert Smyth, Librar, Burges of Edinburgh.

librar, obs. Sc. form of LIBRARY.

librarian (laɪˈbrɛərɪən). [f. L. *librāri-us* concerned with books (hence as *sb.* a bookseller or scribe) + -AN.]

†**1.** A scribe, copyist. *Obs.*

1670 Gale *Crt. Gentiles* ii. iv. i. 370 The Booksellers got these books transcribed..by unmeet Librarians. **1725** W. Broome *Notes on Pope's Odyss.* xii. 131 This is the error of the Librarians, who put τρὶς for δὶς.

2. The keeper or custodian of a library. (This word has supplanted the older *library-keeper*.)

1713 Steele *Englishman* No. 1. 8 Why mayn't I be witty, as a Man that keeps a Librarian is Learned? **1791** Boswell *Johnson* an. 1754, Mr. Wise, Radclivian librarian, with whom Johnson was much pleased. **1829** *University Instr.* in Willis & Clark *Cambridge* (1886) III. 104 A projecting Room ..for the use of the Librarian.

†**3.** A dealer in books. *Obs. rare*$^{-1}$.

a **1734** North *Lives* (1826) III. 290 This Mr. Scot was in his time the greatest librarian in Europe: for, besides his Stock in England he had warehouses at Frankfort [etc.].

Hence **liˈbrarianess**, a female librarian; **liˈbrarianship**, the office or work of a librarian.

1818 Todd, *Librarianship*. **1862** Trollope *N. Amer.* I. 360 The librarianesses looked very pretty and learned..; the head librarian was enthusiastic. **1871** *Daily News* 12 Apr. 5 In depriving the learned book-fancier of his librarianship. **1886** *Academy* 19 June 432/3 An essay on some subject in librarianship or bibliography.

†**liˈbrarier**. *Obs. rare.* [f. L. *librārius* (see LIBRARIAN) + -ER[1].] **a.** A bookseller. **b.** A librarian.

c **1483** Caxton *Dialogues* 2/23 *Des chaudeliers & libraries*, Of ketelmakers and librariers. **1667** Waterhouse *Fire Lond.* 70 Mr. Spencer, the..Aboriginal Librarier, yet living, and yet faithfully attending the remains of the Books.

librarious (laɪˈbrɛərɪəs), *a. rare.* [f. L. *librāri-us* (see LIBRARIAN) + -OUS.] Pertaining to, or having to do with, books.

1656 Blount *Glossogr.*, *Librarious*, pertaining to books. **1884** *Macm. Mag.* July 182 The acted Shakespearian drama now attracts crowds of studious people, or librarious people at any rate.

library[1] (ˈlaɪbrərɪ). Also 4–7 librarie, 5 lyberary, 6 liberary, librarye. *β.* 4–5 librair(e, *Sc.* **librar**. [a. F. *librairie* (1380 in Godefroy), now only in sense 'bookseller's shop' = It. Sp. *libreria*, Pg. *livraria*, repr. Com. Rom. **libraria* (with suffix *-īa*, -Y), f. L. *librāri-um* (F. *libraire* bookseller), subst. use of *librārius* adj., concerned with or employed about books, f. *libr-*, *liber* book, believed to be a use of *liber* bark (see LIBER), the bark of trees having, according to Roman tradition, been used in early times as a writing material. Late L. *librāria* (sc. *taberna*) occurs with the sense 'bookseller's shop'.

The Rom. word admits of being viewed as f. *libro* book + *-aria*, but this leaves the ultimate analysis unaltered.]

1. A place set apart to contain books for reading, study, or reference. (Not applied, e.g. to the shop or warehouse of a bookseller.) In various applications more or less specific.

a. Applied to a room in a house, etc.; also, †a bookcase. In mod. use, the designation of one of the set of rooms ordinarily belonging to an English house above a certain level of size and pretension.

c **1374** Chaucer *Boeth.* i. pr. v. 15 (Camb. MS.) The walles of thi lybrarye aparayled and wrowht with yuory and with glas. **1430–40** Lydg. *Bochas* vi. i. (1554) 142 Bochas pensief stode in his library. **1488** *Inventory* in *Archæologia* XLV. 120 On the south side of the Vestrarie standeth a grete library. **1779** M. Tyson in *Lett. Lit. Men* (Camden) 195, I there saw his library, i.e. the Room which once contained his Books. **1794** Mrs. Radcliffe *Myst. Udolpho* i, The library occupied the west side of the chateau. **1854** W. Collins *Hide & Seek* ii. ii. (1861) 161 Zack descended cautiously to the back parlour, which was called a 'library'.

b. A building, room, or set of rooms, containing a collection of books for the use of the public or of some particular portion of it, or of the members of some society or the like; a public institution or establishment, charged with the care of a collection of books, and the duty of rendering the books accessible to those who require to use them.

For *lending*, *reference library*, see those words. ***free library***, a library which the public are permitted to use without payment, esp. one maintained by a municipality out of the rates.

c **1449** Pecock *Repr.* i. vi. 30 In caas a greet clerk wolde go into a librarie and ouer studie there a long proces of feith writun in the Bible. **1530** Palsgr. 35 A boke in the library of Gyldehall in London. **1637** *Decree Star Chamb.* in *Milton's Areop.* (Arb.) 23 To be Sent to the Librarie at Oxford. **1708** *Act 7 Anne* c. 14 §1 Whereas of late Years several Charitable..Persons have..erected Libraries within several Parishes and Districts. **1847** *Howitt's Jrnl.* I. 119/1 A scheme of free libraries. By Dr. Smiles. *Ibid.* 119/2 Samuel Brown, the author of the system of Free Libraries, (or, as he styled them, 'Itinerating Libraries',) was a merchant of the small town of Haddington. **1850** *Act 13 & 14 Vict.* c. 65 §7 That Admission to such Libraries and Museums [established by Town Councils] shall be free of all Charge. **1850** *Manch. Guardian* 28 Dec., A Free Library and Museum for Manchester. **1855** *Act 18 & 19 Vict.* c. 70, An Act for further promoting the Establishment of Free Public Libraries and Museums in Municipal Towns. **1900** G. C. Brodrick *Mem.* 210 The Merton library is..the oldest specimen of mediæval libraries in England. **1902** *Daily Chron.* 4 Mar. 3/2 These things are surely axioms to the free-library reader. **1960** M. Sharp *Something Light* vi. 49 The meeting-place for intellectuals was the Free Library.

c. (More fully, ***circulating library***.) A private commercial establishment for the lending of books, the borrower paying either a fixed sum for each book lent or a periodical subscription.

'These are of two kinds: the establishments on a large scale that issue books to subscribers all over the country, and the smaller establishment, usually in the hands of a bookseller, which circulate among local subscribers books either kept in stock or borrowed from one of the larger 'libraries'. In watering-places, the 'libraries' sometimes have reading-rooms attached, and were formerly places of social resort (cf. quots. 1835). In the West end of London some of the 'libraries' act as agencies for the sale of tickets for places of amusement.' (N.E.D.)

1835 Dickens *Sk. Boz, Tales* i. (1892) 261 The 'dear girls' ..had been at different watering-places for four seasons; they had gambled at libraries,..sold at fancy fairs [etc.]. *Ibid.* iv. 325 The library [at Ramsgate] was crowded. There were the same ladies and the same gentlemen who had been on the sands in the morning. *Mod. Advt.*, Now ready at all the libraries, Mr. ——'s great novel, ——.

d. A theatre-ticket agency.

1827 W. Clarke *Every Night Bk.* 108 It is..necessary.. to procure tickets of admission prior to the opening of the doors: they may be had at the libraries of Ebers, or Andrews, in old Bond Street. **1902** W. H. Chantrey *Theatre Accounts* i. 7 The next source of income is derived from Library Bookings. It is usual for the management of a Theatre to allow a discount of from 5 to 10 per cent. upon seats booked by Libraries. **1959** *Financial Times* 23 June, The word 'library' is used in the trade to designate a central source of tickets—a 'ticket wholesaler' might be a better term. **1973** *Sunday Times* (Colour Suppl.) 28 Oct. 101/1 Ticket agencies..are..organised in the Combined Libraries Association ('library' is theatrical term for ticket agency).

2. a. The books contained in a 'library' (sense 1); 'a large collection of books, public or private' (J.).

13.. *S. Erkenwolde* 155 in Horstm. *Altengl. Leg.* (1881) 269 We haue oure librarie laitid þes longe seuene dayes. *a* **1540** Barnes *Wks.* (1573) 195/1 Let all the Liberaries bee sought in England. **1613** R. C. *Table Alph.* (ed. 3), *Librarie* ..a great number of books. **1760** tr. *Keysler's Trav.* III. 52 Cardinal Brancaccio has bequeathed a good library to this church. **1838** Thirlwall *Greece* II. 64 Pisistratus..is said to have been the first person in Greece who collected a library. **1872** Yeats *Techn. Hist. Comm.* 373 In universities, as well as in cloisters, libraries were very small.

β. **1390** Gower *Conf.* I. 14 And slouthe kepeth the libraire Which longeth to the Saintuaire. *c* **1420** *Pallad. on Husb.* Prol. 96 In deskis xij hymselue, as half a strete, Hath boked thair librair vniuersal. **1513** Douglas *Æneis* i. Prol. 100 (*Comment*) Ptolome..gadderit togidder in ane librar xxxvj thousand volummys. **1580** *Extracts Burgh Rec. Edinb.* (1882) IV. 183 *marg.*, New librare.

b. Often used in the titles given by publishers to a series or set of books uniform or similar in external appearance, and ostensibly suited for some particular class of readers or for students of a particular subject, as in 'The Library of Useful Knowledge' (1826–1856), 'The Parlour

Library' (consisting of novels, 1847–1863), 'Bohn's Standard Library', etc. Formerly also in the titles of bibliographical works, and of periodicals.

1692 (*title*) The Compleat Library: or News for the Ingenious. Containing Several Original Pieces. An Historical Account of the Choicest Books Printed... Notes on the Memorable Passages happening in May. As also the State of Learning in the World. To be Published Monthly. **1713** The Student's Library: a choice Collection of Books, In all Faculties and Parts of Learning. [A catalogue of books.] **1714** (*title*) The Ladies Library. Vol. I. Written by a Lady. Published by Mr. Steele. **1844** A. W. Kinglake *Eothen* xviii. 282 The books were thorough-bred Scotch... He prided himself upon the 'Edinburgh Cabinet Library'. **1974** *British Bks. in Print* I. p. ccxxvi/1 Home University Library. Oxf. U.P.

c. *transf.* and *fig.*; esp. used to denote (*a*) a great mass of learning or knowledge; (*b*) the objects of a person's study, the sources on which he depends for instruction. In quot. 1523 = a catalogue, list.

a **1450** *Cov. Myst.* (Shaks. Soc.) 88 We xal lerne ȝow the lyberary of oure Lordys law lyght. *c* **1485** *Digby Myst.* (1882) v. 227 The lybrary of reason must be vnclosed. **1523** Skelton *Garl. Laurel* 780 Of all ladyes he hath the library Ther names recountyng in the court of Fame. **1549** *Compl. Scot.* Ep. Ded. 7, I began to reuolue the librarye of my vndirstanding. **1570** Dee *Math. Pref.* 27 One Drop of Truth ..more worth then whole Libraries of Opinions. **1654** Trapp *Comm. Ezra* vii. 6 Ye may be as learned as Tostatus ..who was a living library. **1665** Boyle *Occas. Refl.* (1848) 74 Able to make the world both his Library and his Oratory. **1686** J. Dunton *Lett. fr. New Eng.* (1867) 75, I darken his Merits if I call him less than a Walking Library. *a* **1703** Burkitt *On N.T.* Matt. xxiii. 7 These Pharisees were for carrying a library of God's law on their clothes, scarce a letter of it in their hearts. **1883** J. Hawthorne *Dust* I. 104 Cards and men formed the library of the Duchess of Marlborough.

(*c*) A collection of films, gramophone records, music, etc.

1926–7 *Army & Navy Stores Catal.* 1095 Circulating library for music rolls. Arrangements can be made..for Members to subscribe to a Player Roll Library. **1937** *Amer. Speech* XII. 47/1 *Library*, collection of sheet music. **1957** *B.B.C. Handbk.* 101 Some types of material are recorded specially for the library, as for example, folk-music, dialect, natural history, and sound effects. **1962** H. Orton *Survey Eng. Dial. Introd.* 20 The British Broadcasting Corporation's Permanent Sound-Record Library. **1969** *Listener* 12 June 836/3 Proms are no longer..regarded as the poor man's record library. **1974** *Guardian* 26 Mar. 32/3 The transcription service..provides a library of BBC programmes on slow-speed recordings. **1974** *Times* 7 Oct. 13/4 Borrowers frequently make tape-recordings..from the material borrowed and can thus acquire..an extensive library of recorded music without paying the composer a penny.

3. *Computers.* An organized collection of routines, esp. of tested routines suitable for a particular model of computer.

1950 *Proc. R. Soc.* A. CCII. 576 It is convenient to have a 'library' containing sub-routines for performing such standard operations as the evaluation of a sine, or a scalar product. **1951** *Ibid.* CCVI. 539 There are..some eighty sub-routines in the EDSAC library. **1951** *Math. Tables & Other Aids to Computation* V. 46 Routines for solving standard problems will be established on tape and stored in a 'library'. **1958** *Oxf. Mag.* 29 May 469/1 Their 'library' consists of 'routines', 'sub-routines', and even 'quickies', programmes already existing and tested. *Ibid.*, As the library grows in extent, programming for new problems becomes easier. **1964** F. L. Westwater *Electronic Computers* ix. 143 Soon, 'libraries' of standard subroutines were available for each particular computer. **1966** A. Battersby *Math. in Managem.* viii. 195 Standard computing routines are always available for widely-used techniques such as network analyses or linear programming, and the range over which they extend is constantly widening. They are often referred to as 'library programs' or under the general term 'software'. **1967** *Technology Week* 23 Jan. 11/2 (Advt.), Software for Sigma 5 includes..a library of mathematical, business and utility routines.

4. *attrib.*, as ***library apartments, book, card, centre, chair, committee, company, desk, door, house, material, room, stairs, stamp, style, table, ticket***; **library binding**, a special strong binding of books for lending libraries; **library edition**, an edition of good size and print and strongly bound, *spec.* a uniform edition of a writer's works; also (quot. 1917) an edition of a newspaper for depositing in certain libraries; **library frame, glasses, spectacles**, spectacles with heavy frames suitable for use when reading; †**library-keeper**, a librarian; **library shot** (see quot.); **library steps**, a step-ladder for use in libraries; **library tax**, the obligation imposed by law on publishers to supply gratis a copy or copies of the books published by them to certain public libraries.

1832 G. Downes *Lett. Cont. Countries* I. 486 One of the *library apartments is handsomely adorned with statues. **1903** J. D. Brown *Man. Libr. Econ.* xxvi. 333 The principal leathers for public *library bindings are pig-skin, Persian and Levant moroccos, and roan. **1952** W. McGill in *Library World* Dec. LIV. 90 (*heading*) A note on how some publishers produced reinforced or special library bindings for public libraries nearly 50 years ago. **1863** 'G. Hamilton' *Gala-Days* 146 There was the long service, Sunday school and *library books. **1916** A. Bennett *Lion's Share* xxiv. 180 The women play golf all day on that appalling golf course, and then after tea they go into the town to change their library books. **1973** K. Giles *File on Death* iii. 66 My old girl retires to bed around eight, with her library book. **1966** A. Sachs *Jail Diary* xviii. 164 The station commander..has spoken to his wife and she doesn't mind if I use one of the family's *library cards. **1960** *Library Assoc. Rec.* Aug. 261/2 A *library centre is a static service-point, whether or not under the control of paid staff, which does not comply with the definitions for full-time or part-time branches. **1883** *Heal & Son Catal.* 181 Dining room and *library chairs. **1970** *Country Life* 31 Dec. 16/2 (Advt.), William IV mahogany library chair upholstered in antiqued Havana brown leather. **1831** *Congress. Rec.* 7 Feb. 618 It was referred to the *Library Committee. **1965** D. Davinson *Academic & Legal Deposit Libr.* ii. 24 All British universities have a library committee formed from the Senate or similar body. **1745** B. Franklin *Let.* 11 Dec. in *Writings* (1905) II. 296 Our *Library Company sends for about twenty pounds sterling worth of books yearly. **1837** W. Jenkins *Ohio Gazetteer* 99 The public institutions are a bank, a library company and a mechanics society. **1895** M. A. Jackson *Mem. Stonewall Jackson* (ed. 2) xi. 197 Between them is a *library desk. **1861** J. Edmond *Children's Ch. at Home* iii. 49 A gentle tap at the *library door. **1869** Geo. Eliot *Let.* 19 Feb. (1956) V. 16 Ticknor and Field have intimated some intention to bring out a *library edition of all my books. **1917** *Times* 2 July 1 (*top right-hand corner*) Library Edition. **1939** A. Huxley *Let.* 19 Feb. (1969) 440 The idea of a library edition makes me feel most horribly posthumous. **1960** S. Unwin *Truth about a Publisher* x. 150 They were..available only in the huge 38-volume Library Edition. **1948** *Optical Practitioner* II. vi. p. vi (Advt.), Frames of unusual design specially made... The '*London*' **Library* frame. **1962** L. S. Sasieni *Princ. & Pract. Optical Dispensing* i. 10 The heavy frame..is often called a 'library' frame. **1971** W. Garner *Andra Fiasco* ix. 56 She stared at him, reaching for a pair of library-frame glasses. **1959** *A.O.P. News* 31 Dec. 9/1 Modern spectacles for men, such as *library glasses..can give the wearer a distinguished appearance. **1837** W. Jenkins *Ohio Gazetteer* 281 The *library house is a handsome brick edifice. **1647** Trapp *Comm. Rom.* iii. 2 This was their prime privilege, that they [the Jews] were God's *library-keepers. **1743** Birch *Life Boyle* Wks. 1772 I. p. lvi, Dr. Thomas Barlow, then chief library-keeper of the Bodleian Library. **1962** *Listener* 16 Aug. 259/2 John Elliot's production adroitly wove the tropical *library material among the studio scenes. **1785** Boswell *Tour Hebrides* 61 At the college there is a good *library-room. **1953** K. Reisz *Technique Film Editing* 280 **Library shot*, shot used in a film but not recorded specially for it; shot taken from a library or store of shots kept for future use. **1962** *Listener* 22 Feb. 346/1 The other, the one with the *library spectacles, also lowered his paper. **1962** *Gloss. Ophthalmic Lenses & Spectacle Frames* (*B.S.I.*) 58 *Library spectacles*, spectacles of heavy weight with broad sides and usually of tortoiseshell or plastics. **1598–9** in Willis & Clark *Cambridge* (1886) II. 482 The seelinge of the *Library staires. **1861** *Catal. Cathedral Libr. Calcutta* App. 120 To stamp the title page and other parts of each volume with the *Library-stamp. *c* **1762** Ince & Mayhew *Universal Syst. Houshold Furnit.* 3/1 (*heading*) Plate XXII. Two Designs of *Library Steps; the First intended for a large Room. **1793** T. Sheraton *Cabinet-Maker & Upholsterer's Drawing-Bk.* App. 9 There are other kinds of library steps which I have seen, made by other persons, but..these must have the decided preference. **1848** Thackeray *Pendennis* (1849) I. iii. 24 He would sit.. perched upon the topmost bar of Doctor Portman's library steps with a folio on his knees. **1970** B. Cartland *Secret Fear* i. 5 He would notice the rosewood library steps below the place in the cabinet from which the book had been extracted. **1952** *Vision* VI. iii. 15/2 (*caption*) Heavy semi-rimless *library style in dark mottled material. **1741** in *Publ. Colonial Soc. Mass.* (1925) XVI. 712 [The cross table was] compos'd of three *Library Tables. **1853** Geo. Eliot *Let.* 29 Oct. (1954) II. 121, I wish to exchange my present one [*sc.* bookcase] for a Library Table, of which I am sorely in need. **1969** *Canad. Antiques Collector* Dec. 9/1 One of the most remarkable series of library tables (bureaux plats) to be found anywhere. **1971** *Country Life* 10 June Suppl. 52 (Advt.), A rare small George III library table with pull-out steps, reading top and two slides, constructed with fine quality solid mahogany. Height 32″. Circa 1790. **1877** M. W. Chapman in H. Martineau *Autobiogr.* III. 63 Heaps of concert tickets, museum tickets, *library tickets. **1950** O. Blakeston *Pink Ribbon* vi. 72 Amelia lent me her library tickets. **1965** C. Fremlin *Jealous One* xiv. 110 The usual contents of a hand-bag—comb, purse, powder compact, cheque book, library ticket.

Hence **ˈlibraryize** *v.* (*nonce-wd.*) *trans.*, to place in a library; **ˈlibraryless** *a.*, without a library.

1642 Fuller *Holy & Prof. St.* iii. xviii. 199 Once a dunce, void of learning but full of Books, flouted a library-lesse Scholar with these words. **1796** Coleridge *Biog. Lit.* (1847) II. 361 If you see nothing in it [Beddoes's Essay] to library-ize it, send it me back next Thursday.

†**library**². *Obs.* In 4 *pl.* librarijs. [ad. L. *librāri-us*: see librarian.] A scribe.

1382 Wyclif *Esther* viii. 9 The scribis and the librarijs [**1388** writeris, Vulg. *librariis*] of the king.

librate (ˈlaɪbreɪt), *sb. Hist.* Also 7 **librat**. [ad. med.L. *lībrāta* (sc. *terra*), f. *lībra* pound: see -ate¹.] A piece of land worth a pound a year.

1610 W. Folkingham *Art Survey* ii. vii. 59 Then must the Obolat be ½ Acre, the Denariat an Acre, the Solidat 12. acres, & the Librat 240. **1778** Pennant *Tour Wales* I. 26 Henry III..grants..ten librates [Dugdale *decem libratas terræ*] in Longenedale in Derbyshire. **1865** Nichols *Britton* II. 143 Twenty librates of land with the appurtenances. **1875** Stubbs *Const. Hist.* (1896) II. xiv. 119 The sheriffs were ordered to send all persons who possessed more than twenty librates of land.

librate (ˈlaɪbreɪt), *v.* [f. L. *lībrāt-*, ppl. stem of *lībrā-re*, f. *lībra* balance.]

†**1.** *trans.* **a.** To place in the scales, to weigh. **b.** To poise, balance. **c.** To produce or cause libration in: see quot. 1806 s.v. *librating* below. *Obs.*

1623 Cockeram, *Librate*, to weigh. **1657** Tomlinson *Renou's Disp.* 144 All seeds..are librated by weight [orig. *pondere semper librantur*]. **1667** *Phil. Trans.* II. 423 The Needles be touched by good Load-stones, and well librated. **1674** *Ibid.* IX. 219 The manner of Librating the Apogéum.

2. *intr.* To oscillate like the beam of a balance; to move from side to side or up and down.

1694 W. Holder *Harmony* (1731) 28 Librating after the Nature of a Pendulum. **1730** Savery in *Phil. Trans.* XXXVI. 298, I was obliged to keep it in a Motion..librating up and down like the Beam of a Pair of Scales. **1770** *Ibid.* LX. 70 The whole limb of Venus would sometimes librate towards the limb of the sun. **1867** G. Macdonald *Disciple*, etc. 109 To drop, and spin away, Librating.

b. To oscillate or waver *between* one thing and another.

1822 *Examiner* 250/2 He..is librating between vice and virtue. **1856** Kane *Arctic Expl.* II. 34 The barometer slowly librating between 29.20 and the old 30.40.

3. Of a bird, etc.: To be poised, balance itself.

1786 tr. *Beckford's Vathek* 198 The birds of the air, librating over me, served as a canopy from the rays of the sun. **1791** E. Darwin *Bot. Gard.* i. 138 Her playful sea-horse..librates on unmoving fins. **1829** *Jrnl. Naturalist* 263 Made to flutter and librate like a kestrel over the place.

Hence **ˈlibrated** *ppl. a.*, balanced (*fig.*); **ˈlibrating** *vbl. sb.* and *ppl. a.*

1665–6 *Phil. Trans.* I. 241 Some kind of Librating motion. **1801** Fuseli in *Lect. Paint.* ii. (1848) 404 The academic vigour, the librated style, of Annibale Carracci. **1806** Robertson in *Phil. Trans.* XCVII. 73 The librating force or pressure, or the force causing libration. **1839** Bailey *Festus* (1854) 332 These strange librating bonds of birth and death. **1862** T. Z. Lawrence in R. H. Patterson *Ess. Hist. & Art* 15 A librating circular smoky spectrum will be perceived at the end of the tube.

libration (laɪˈbreɪʃən). [ad. L. *lībrātiōn-em*, n. of action f. *lībrā-re* to librate. Cf. F. *libration*.]

1. a. The action of librating; motion like that of the beam of a balance oscillating upon its pivot; swaying to and fro. **b.** The state of being balanced or in equipoise; equipoise, balance.

1603 Sir C. Heydon *Jud. Astrol.* xviii. 381 This Thebit.. perceiuing the quantitie of the tropike yeare to varie, first inuented the libration of the 8. sphere. **1625** N. Carpenter *Geog. Del.* i. iv. 73 Some others..imagine the Center..of the Earth to be moued vp and down by a certaine motion of Libration. *Ibid.* ii. vi. 85 This libration or motion of the Water cannot bee caused by the winde or Aire. **1653** Jer. Taylor *Serm. Gold. Grove, Winter* v. 60 The poor bird was beaten back..descending more at every breath of the tempest then it could recover by the libration and frequent weighing of his wings. **1684** T. Burnet *Th. Earth* ii. 51 This must needs make it lose its former poise and libration. **1694** W. Holder *Harmony* (1731) 29 The Librations of the Pendulum. **1728–46** Thomson *Spring* 742 Their pinions still, In loose libration stretched. **1791** E. Darwin *Bot. Gard.* ii. 26 So turns the needle to the pole it loves, With fine librations quivering, as it moves. **1853** Kane *Grinnell Exp.* xlviii. (1856) 446 Others [*viz.* icebergs] a congeries of rubbish, and illustrating every possible condition of libration. **1874** H. R. Reynolds *John Bapt.* v. iii. 341 A dazzling brightness above the Splendour of the Sun was drawing nearer with gentle librations of its wings.

c. *transf.* and *fig.*

1650 *Anthroposophia Theomagica* 92 Such chiming and clinching of words, Antithetall Librations, and Symphonicall rappings. **1659** H. More *Immort. Soul* ii. x. 218 The Libration or Reciprocation of the Spirits in the Tensility of the Muscles. **1659** J. Harrington *Lawgiving* Wks. (1700) 431 Such a libration or poize of Orders. **1659** Walker *Oratory* 97 The short [period] is adverse to Metaphors &c. the long to exact correspondence and libration of its parts. **1670** Dryden *2nd Pt. Conq. Granada* iii. i. Wks. 1808 IV. 151 The bounds of thy libration here are set. **1840** *Blackw. Mag.* XLVII. 719 The tremulous libration of the equipoise. **1882** J. H. Blunt *Ref. Ch. Eng.* ii. 480 Oxford has its regular periods of theological libration.

2. *Astron.* A real or apparent motion of an oscillating kind. ***libration of the moon***: an apparent irregularity of the moon's motion which makes it appear to oscillate in such a manner that the parts near the edge of the disk are alternately visible and invisible. (There are three kinds, called ***libration in latitude, libration in longitude***, and ***diurnal*** or ***parallactic libration***.)

1669 J. Flamstead in *Phil. Trans.* IV. 1109 If the Libration of the Moon be known, the protraction of the Star's way in this Appearance will be facile. **1670** *Ibid.* V. 2061 Doubtless, as there is a certain Libration in the Moon, so 'tis not absurd to me, to hold a kind of Libration in the Earth, from the Annual and Diurnal motion of the same. **1678** Norris *Coll. Misc.* (1699) 181 We are nonplus'd at a thousand Phenomenas in Nature, which if they were not done, we should have thought them absolutely impossible, as for instance the central Libration of the Earth. **1690** Leybourn *Curs. Math.* 754 Now this Libration of the Eccentrick they commonly call the Deviation. **1728** tr. *Newton's Treat. Syst. World* 61 The Moon's libration in longitude. **1804** Herschel in *Phil. Trans.* XCIV. 374 Some small annual variation, or libration of position, which might lead to a discovery of the parallax of the fixed stars. **1812–16** J. Smith *Panorama Sci. & Art* I. 547 Her libration in latitude, is when either of her poles appears to dip a little towards the earth. **1831** Brewster *Newton* (1855) I. vi. 128 Galileo had discovered and explained the diurnal libration, arising from the spectator not viewing the moon from the centre of the earth. **1834** Mrs. Somerville *Connex. Phys. Sci.* ix. (1849) 78 The moon..is liable to librations depending upon the position of the spectator. **1867–77** G. F. Chambers *Astron.* i. vii. 79 When the North Pole [of the Moon] leans towards the earth we see somewhat more of the

region surrounding it;..this is known as libration in latitude. **1874** FARRAR *Christ* 51 There is one hemisphere of the lunar surface on which in its entirety, no human eye has ever gazed, while at the same time the moon's librations enable us to conjecture of its general character.

†3. Weighing (*lit.* and *fig.*). *Obs.*

1657 W. MORICE *Coena quasi Κοινὴ* xiii. 185 We..have made libration, what weight the judgment and practice of the ancient Church doth bear. **1667** WATERHOUSE *Fire Lond.* 48 Prudent libration of what weight they will and will not beare. **1770** EMERSON (*title*) Calculation, libration and mensuration, or the arts of reckoning, weighing and measuring.

Hence **li'brational** *a.*, pertaining to (the moon's) libration.

1880 PROCTOR *Rough Ways made Smooth* 110 Photographs of the moon should be taken in every aspect..of her librational swayings.

libratory ('laɪbrətərɪ), *a.* [f. L. *lībrāt-*, ppl. stem of *lībrā-re* to LIBRATE.] Having a motion like that of the beam of a balance; oscillatory.

1668 *Phil. Trans.* III. 809 That there is a Libratory motion in Comets as well as in the Moon. **1801** *Trans. Soc. Arts* XIX. 257 The beam..acquired a libratory motion. **1804** C. B. BROWN tr. *Volney's View Soil U.S.* 203 Just as the sea experiences a libratory motion, while its interior currents remain undisturbed. **1874** *Edin. Rev.* No. 285. 87 The libratory swaying to and fro of the moon.

†**libre**, *a. Obs.* [a. F. *libre*, L. *līber* free.] Of the will: Free.

1590 A. HUME *Hymns* etc. (1832) 10 He Adam lent a libre will to follow what he list. **1600** F. WALKER *Sp. Mandeville* 107a, Such thinges as are within the vse of free will and Lybre arbitrement.

librettist (lɪ'brɛtɪst). [f. LIBRETTO + -IST.] The writer of a libretto; a writer of librettos.

1862 *Sunday Times* 3 Aug., Of all themes, we imagine the captivity of Judah the most likely to make a librettist rhapsodical, and a musician uninteresting. **1891** *Times* 8 Oct. 7/4 The oratorio..set, not to the compilation of the ordinary librettist, but to a real poem.

libretto (‖li'bretto, lɪ'brɛtəʊ). Pl. libretti (-'etti). [It. = 'little book', f. *libro* book.] The text or 'words' to which an opera or other extended musical composition is set; = BOOK *sb.* 9.

1742 RICHARDSON *Pamela* IV. 113 If the Libretto, as they call it, is not approved, the Opera..will be condemned. **1845** *Athenæum* 22 Feb. 204 The libretto, on the subject of Blue Beard, by Tieck. **1880** RUSKIN *Arrows Chace* II. 281 The libretto of *Jean de Nivelle* is very beautiful, and ought to have new music written to it.

'**libricide.** *rare*⁻¹. [f. L. *libr-*, *liber* book + -CIDE 2.] The 'killing' of a book.

1856 W. BLAIR *Chron. Aberbrothock* iv. 11 Milton ranks libricide or book-slaughter with homicide or man-slaughter.

libriform ('laɪbrɪfɔːm), *a. Bot.* [f. L. *libr-*, *liber* bark: see -FORM.] Of the nature or character of liber.

1877 BENNETT tr. *Thomé's Bot.* 364 Simple bast-like wood-fibres, or libriform fibres. **1885** GOODALE *Physiol. Bot.* (1892) 81 Libriform cells are variable in length in different plants.

Librium ('lɪbrɪəm). *Pharm.* Also librium. The proprietary name of a white crystalline compound, $C_{16}H_{14}N_3OCl.HCl$, used as a tranquillizer.

1960 *Official Gaz.* (U.S. Patent Office) 15 Mar. TM 90/1 Hoffman-La Roche Inc...*Librium* for psychotherapeutic agent. **1968** *New Scientist* 21 Mar. 623/2 Hostile tendencies can often be remarkably controlled by drugs, like Librium and diazepam, which are *not* sedatives, and which do not depress the general level of cerebral activity. **1970** *Times* 22 Sept. 10 In the first cafe he went into someone sold him six librium pills. 'It was my sort of cafe, my sort of people—of course they had gear.' **1972** T. P. MCMAHON *Issue of Bishop's Blood* (1973) xvi. 228, I decided the pills Dolly had left with Julio were Librium. I use them when the shakes get bad. **1975** N. MITCHISON *All change Here* ix. 92, I took a tablet of librium, but had the father and mother of a nightmare.

‖**Libs** (lɪbz). *poet. rare.* [L. *Libs* (also *Lips*), a. Gr. *Λίψ*, *Λιβ-*.] The south-west wind.

1742 SHENSTONE *School-mistr.* 57 The childish faces of old Æol's train, Libs, Notus, Auster.

†'**libstick.** *Obs.* [Anglicization of med.L. *libisticum*, corrupt f. *levisticum* (see LOVAGE). Cf. F. *levestic* (Cotgr.).] Lovage.

1688 R. HOLME *Armoury* II. 98/2 Libstick, or Sermountain, hath at the joints a long slender leaf [etc.]. [Cf. **1802** A. RANKEN *Hist. France* II. IV. ii. 292 He (*sc.* Walafrid Strabo, in his poem *Hortulus*) treats of..libisticum, chervil, the lily, etc.]

Libyan ('lɪbɪən), *a.* and *sb.* [f. *Libya* + -AN.]

A. *adj.* Of or pertaining to Libya, the ancient name of a large country in North Africa, or to the modern state of Libya. By some philologists used as a designation for the Berber language, or for the group of mod. Hamitic langs. to which Berber belongs.

1592 NASHE *Pierce Penilesse* 34 And such a spirit it was that possest the Libian Sapho, and the Emperorer Dioclesian. **1607** TOPSELL *Four-footed Beasts* 115 The Lybian Roes..are..inferiour to the Lybian horses. **1882** [see KABYLE]. **1921** *Handbk. Libya* viii. 147 Head-quarters of the Libyan Battalion. **1956** H. S. VILLARD *Libya* xii. 154 In the suppression of native rebellions most of the educated Libyan leaders were exterminated. **1971** *Encycl. Judaica* XI. 205 During the Six Day War (1967)..widespread strikes of Libyan oil workers..brought the flow of oil to a temporary stop.

B. *sb.* **a.** An inhabitant of ancient or modern Libya. **b.** The Libyan language.

1607 TOPSELL *Four-footed Beasts* 41 Beares are tamed.. for sports among the Roxolani and Libians. *c* **1620** T. ROBINSON *M. Magd.* 12 The Thyme of Hybla, and the Libyan flore. **1667** MILTON *P.L.* IV. 277 Whom Gentiles Ammon call and Libyan Jove. *Ibid.* XII. 634 A Comet..with torrid heat, And vapour as the Libyan Air adust. **1725** E. COMBE tr. *Huet's Weakness of Hum. Und.* 117 He might be call'd a Libyan, because he stay'd a long while at Cyrene, a City in Libya. **1832** TENNYSON *Dream Fair Women* 145 We drank the Libyan sun to sleep. **1838** THIRLWALL *Greece* III. 61 The Libyan prince, Psammetichus. **1886** SHELDON tr. *Flaubert's Salammbô* 11 A Libyan of colossal stature. **1937** H. POPE *St. Augustine of Hippo* i. 18 In the purple-producing island of Girba..Libyan was spoken, as Berber indeed is to this day. **1939** L. H. GRAY *Found. Lang.* xii. 366 *Graffiti*..of uncertain date and in a script which marks them off from ancient Libyan and from modern Tuareg alike. **1956** H. S. VILLARD *Libya* xii. 155 The Libyans..continue to place restrictions on the entry of Italian citizens into Cyrenaica. **1975** *Times* 11 Jan. 12/6 The Libyans, still the most active of the governmental supporters of Arab extremists.

So †**Libyc** (*occas.* **Lybic**) [ad. Gr. *Λιβυκός*], †**Libycan** *adjs.*

a **1541** WYATT *Song of Iopas* in *Tottel's Misc.* (Arb.) 93 The wanderyng Troian knight, whom Iunos wrath with stormes did force in Libyk sands to light. **1590** SPENSER *F.Q.* II. ii. 22 On lybicke Ocean wide. **1607** TOPSELL *Four-f. Beasts* (1658) 28 Æmonian bears,..night-ranging, Lybican, menacing. **1618** BOLTON *Florus* III. vi. (1636) 192 Gellius was set to waft upon the Tuscan Sea;..Lentulus upon the Libyc. **1654** VILVAIN *Epit. Ess.* 175b, Which dwelt in utmost Lybic coasts.

Libyo-, comb. form of LIBYAN, = Libyan and (something else), as **Libyo-Phœnician**, **Libyphœnician** *Archæol.*, a Phœnician living in Libya, a person of mixed Libyan and Phœnician ancestry, or a Libyan vassal or ally of the Phœnicians.

1876 *Encycl. Brit.* V. 160/2 In Africa her [*sc.* Carthage's] subjects consisted of three classes—(1) Libyo-Phœnicians, [etc.]. **1890** BRINTON *Races & Peoples* iv. 106 This is the typical appearance..of the ancient Libyans, and is still preserved..in Morocco and Algiers; hence I shall call it the Libyo-Teutonic type. **1948** *Antiquity* XXII. 142 Hanno tells us that he set sail..under orders..to proceed outside the Pillars of Heracles and found cities of Libyphoenicians. *Ibid.*, Libyphoenicians can mean either Phoenicians from Africa or African allies or vassals of the Carthaginians. **1962** D. HARDEN *Phoenicians* 223 Some think that it is the Berber inhabitants of the *territorium* who are the Libyphoenicians so frequently mentioned in ancient texts.

licaym, Sc. variant of LICHAM *Obs.*

licca. [Origin unknown.] (Usually *licca tree.*) A West Indian tree (*Tobinia emarginata*, *Sapindus spinosus*, or *Xanthoxylum emarginatum*).

1756 P. BROWNE *Jamaica* 207 Licca-tree. This shrub..is very remarkable for the prickliness of its trunk. **1864** GRISEBACH *Flora W. Ind.* 785 Licca tree, *Tobinia emarginata.*

liccam(e, variant of LICHAM *Obs.*

liccorish, obs. form of LICKERISH.

lice, pl. of LOUSE.

‖'**liceat.** *Obs.* [L. *liceat* 'let it be allowed', pres. subj. of *licet* 'it is lawful'.] In University use: Some kind of licence or permit.

1686 WILDING in *Collect.* (O.H.S.) I. 265 For a Liceat.. 00 01 00.

†**lice-bane.** *Obs.* [f. *lice* pl. of LOUSE + BANE.] Some plant. (Cf. FLEA-BANE.)

1706 in PHILLIPS (ed. Kersey). **1755** in JOHNSON.

'**liceling.** *nonce-wd.* [irreg. f. *lice*, pl. of LOUSE + -LING.] A little louse.

1791 *2nd Ep. to J. Priestley* in *Poet. Reg.* (1808) 404 He.. could tell On one small louse how many licelings dwell!

licence ('laɪsəns), *sb.* Forms: 4-6 li-, **lycens**, 4-7 **lycence**, 5-6 **lysence**, **-ens**, (6 **laysance**, **lysans**, **-aunce**, *Sc.* **lecens**, 7 **licience**), 5-9 **license**, 4- **licence**. [a. F. *licence*, ad. L. *licentia*, f. *licēre* to be lawful. Cf. Sp. *licencia*, Pg. *licença*, It. *licenza*.

The spelling *license*, though still often met with, has no justification in the case of the sb. In the case of the vb., on the other hand, although the spelling *licence* is etymologically unobjectionable, *license* is supported by the analogy of the rule universally adopted in the similar pairs of related words, *practice* sb., *practise* vb., *prophecy* sb., *prophesy* vb. (The rule seems to have arisen from imitation of the spelling of pairs like *advice* sb., *advise* vb., which expresses a phonetic distinction of historical origin.) A slight argument for preferring the *s* form in the vb. may be found in the existence of the derivatives *licensable* and *licensure* (U.S.) which could not conveniently be spelt otherwise.

Johnson and Todd give only the form *license* both for the sb. and the vb., but the spelling of their quots. conforms, with one exception, to the rule above referred to, which is recognized by Smart (1836), and seems to represent the now prevailing usage. Late 19th-c. Dicts., however, almost universally have *license* both for sb. and vb., either without alternative or in the first place.]

1. a. Liberty (to do something), leave, permission. Now somewhat *rare.* †Also *occas.* exemption *from* (something). †Formerly often in phr. ***licence and leave***; ***by, with, without*** (a person's) ***licence***; ***to get, give, have, obtain, take (a) licence.*** (Cf. LEAVE *sb.*¹ 1.)

1362 LANGL. *P. Pl.* A. Prol. 82 And askeþ leue and lycence at londun to dwelle. *c* **1386** CHAUCER *Wife's Prol.* 855 If I have licence of this worthy frere. **1422** HOCCLEVE *Min. Poems* (1892) 223 Now, sire, yit a word, by your licence. *c* **1450** *Merlin* 17 She ansuerde prayinge she myght speke with hir confessour; and they yaf hir lycence. **1493** *Charter* in A. Laing *Lindores Abbey* xvii. (1876) 179 Anentis the making of out men burges but licens of the said abbot. **1513** BRADSHAW *St. Werburge* I. 146 Whose names we purpose to shewe with lycens. **1526** TINDALE *John* xix. 38 And Pilate gave him licence. **1532** *Fortescue's Abs. & Lim. Mon.* (1714) 119 Hou long any of them may be absent, hou he schal have his leve and licence..may be conceyvyd by leysure. **1548** HALL *Chron., Hen. IV*, 10 The duke was banished..and yet without license of Kyng Richarde he is returned again into the realme. **1549** *Compl. Scot.* xvii. 146 He gat neuyr lecens to marye quhil on to the tyme that [etc.]. **1551** ROBINSON tr. *More's Utopia* II. (1895) 148 The people..haue geuen a perpetual licence from labour to learnyng. **1640** *Order Ho. Commons* in Rushw. *Hist. Coll.* III. (1692) I. 143 Mr. R. H. has License to go and speak with Sir G. R. **1675** BAXTER *Cath. Theol.* II. I. 122 Doth God forbid it? No; he commandeth it, which is more than leave or licence. **1719** DE FOE *Crusoe* II. x. (1840) 225 It would be difficult to go from hence without their license. **1761** HUME *Hist. Eng.* I. App. ii. 256 If he sold his estate without licence from his lord. **1765** BLACKSTONE *Comm.* I. I. i. 133 The king..may ..prohibit any of his subjects from going into foreign parts without licence. **1807** CRABBE *Village* II. 61 Who take a licence round their fields to stray. **1838** THIRLWALL *Greece* V. 81 The declaration..was now interpreted..as a license to restore their political unity. **1861** MILL *Utilit.* v. 66 Others would confine the license of disobedience to unjust laws. **1888** M. MORRIS *Claverhouse* vi. 110 The same license was granted to him for dealing with all future criminals of the same class.

†**b.** *spec.* Leave or permission to depart; chiefly in phrase, ***to take one's licence***, to take one's leave; also ***licence and congee***. *Obs.* (Cf. CONGEE *sb.* 2 b and LEAVE *sb.*¹ 2.)

[*c* **1450** LONELICH *Grail* xvi. 67 The king hem ȝaf license Forto gon from his precense.] **1475** *Bk. Noblesse* 30 Good men of armes..discoragethe them as sone as paiment failethe, and takethe theire congie and licence of theire prince. **1509** HAWES *Past. Pleas.* v. (Percy Soc.) 24 Of her than I dyd take my lycence. **1556-8** PHAER *Æneid* IV. Kjb, Fayne wold he flee, and of that contrey sweete his licence take.

2. a. A formal, usually a printed or written permission from a constituted authority to do something, *e.g.* to marry, to print or publish a book, to preach, to carry on some trade, etc.; a permit. Also in phrases †***book of licence*** (see BOOK *sb.* 1), ***letter of licence and composition*** (see quot. 1809), ***licence of mortmain*** (see MORTMAIN); ***(to marry) by licence*** in opposition to *by banns*.

1433 *Rolls of Parlt.* IV. 467/1 To praye..the kynge to graunte licence of Exchaunge, under his grete Seal. **1463** *Mann. & Househ. Exp.* (Roxb.) 187 We..charge you to suffyr hym..to enjoye our sayd lycence wyth outyn any let. **1526** *Pilgr. Perf.* (W. de W. 1531) 81 This is she that in maner hath destroyed all religyons by the reason of dispensacyons or lycences. **1549** in *Vicary's Anat.* (1888) App. III. i. 136 [To] requyre yow..to drawe a booke of Lysaunce from his Maiestie, to the Maior and Auldremen [etc.]. **1552-3** *Inv. Ch. Goods, Staffs.* in *Ann. Lichfield* IV. 46, xl s. peyd to the byshope for his laysance to byrrey. **1611** BIBLE *Transl. Pref.* 6 They must first get a Licence in writing before they may vse them [the Scriptures]. **1617** in *Grosart's Spenser* (1882) III. p. ci, John ffforio, esquier, and Rose Spicer marrᵈ by licence from Mr. Weston's Office. **1641** *Declar. Both Houses* in Rushw. *Hist. Coll.* III. (1692) I. 515 Captain S. did by vertue and authority of Your Majesties License, embark at White-Haven. **1649** THORPE *Charge at York Assizes* 20 For a Badgers or Drovers License two shillings. **1683** *Robin Consc.* 15 If I [a publican] my Licence should observe,..Both I and mine alas would starve. **1724** R. WODROW *Life J. Wodrow* (1828) 53 The form of his licence [to preach] I insert from the original. **1748** *Anson's Voy.* III. x. 410 A licence for the shipping of his stores and provisions. **1763** *Brit. Mag.* IV. 495 Would you keep your pearls from tramplers, Weigh the licence, weigh the bans. **1767** BLACKSTONE *Comm.* II. 269 It..is.. necessary, for corporations to have a licence of mortmain from the crown. **1776** ADAM SMITH *W.N.* I. vi. (1869) I. 52 He must pay for the licence to gather these fruits. **1797** BURKE *Regic. Peace* iii. Wks. VIII. 406 Licences to dealers in spirits and wine. **1809** R. LANGFORD *Introd. Trade* 108 A Letter of License is an instrument or writing granted to a debtor by his creditors, giving him respite and time for payment of his debts... When..they not only grant respite and time for payment, but agree to allow an abatement on their respective accounts, then this instrument is called a *Letter of License and Composition.* **1833** HT. MARTINEAU *Berkeley the Banker* I. iv. 92 A fine of £100 for every act of issue after the term of license has expired. **1840** MACAULAY *Ess., Ranke* (1843) III. 240 A congregation is formed. A license is obtained. A plain brick building,..is run up, and named Ebenezer or Bethel. **1841** LYTTON *Nt. & Morn.* I. i, Do you marry by license? No; my intended is not of age. **1851** DIXON *W. Penn* vii. (1872) 61 'The Sandy Foundation Shaken' was printed without a license from the Bishop of London. **1851** R. NESBIT in *Mem.* xii. (1858) 305 After receiving 'licence', he preached in the Mission Lecture Room.

b. The document embodying such a permission.

1598 YONG *Diana* 393 The Kings licence being now come. **1625** MASSINGER *New Way* IV. i, Pray ride to Nottingham, get a license. **1683** in *Songs Lond. Prentices* (Percy Soc.) 81, I bade her [an alewife] on her licence look. **1888** *Daily News* 28 Sept. 3/3 There was a custom among cab proprietors of 'chair-marking' their drivers' licences. **1899** RAYMOND *Two Men o' Mendip* xv. 249 He'd have no choice but to marry us, when I did come, licence in han'.

c. In some Universities, a certificate of competency in some faculty.

1727–41 CHAMBERS *Cycl.*, Licence is also applied to the letters, or certificates, taken out in universities, whether in law, physic, or divinity. **1900–1901** *Durh. Univ. Cal.* 141 Final Examination for the Licence in Theology. *Ibid.* 487 Licence in Sanitary Science.

3. a. Liberty of action conceded or acknowledged; an instance of this.

?*a* **1400** *Morte Arth.* 457 Thy lycence es lemete in presence of lordys. *a* **1605** MONTGOMERIE *Misc. Poems* xxxvi. 48 That nou sik licience haif we none. **1606** SHAKS. *Ant. & Cl.* I. ii. 112 Taunt my faults With such full License, as both Truth and Malice Haue power to vtter. **1656** STANLEY *Hist. Philos.* v. (1701) 157/1 The true Licence of Disputations. **1748** RICHARDSON *Clarissa* (1811) I. vi. 39 Do you so understand the license you have, Miss? **1818** JAS. MILL *Brit. India* II. IV. ix. 299 English law..has neither definition nor words to..circumscribe the license of the Judge. **1834** MAR. EDGEWORTH *Helen* xxxvii. (1883) 312 The first little fib in which Lady Cecilia, as a customary licence of speech, indulged herself the moment she awoke this morning. **1850** KINGSLEY *Alt. Locke* xi. (1876) 127, I thanked him again for what license he had given me. **1868** E. EDWARDS *Ralegh* I. xiii. 249 He..allowed great and public licence to his tongue. **1875** BROWNING *Aristoph. Apol.* 5225 The rooted plant aspired to range With the snake's license. **1884** *Manch. Exam.* 20 Feb. 4/7 Ordinary license of speech has seldom been more shamefully exceeded.

b. Excessive liberty; abuse of freedom; disregard of law or propriety; an instance of this.

c **1450** tr. *De Imitatione* I. xvi. 18 Oper mennes large licence displesiþ us, but we to ourself wol have no þinge denyed þat we aske. **1601** SHAKS. *Twel. N.* III. ii. 48 Taunt him with the license of Inke. **1644** MILTON *Areop.* (Arb.) 35, I should be condemn'd of introducing licence, while I oppose Licencing. **1692** R. L'ESTRANGE *Fables* xv. (1708) 20 Under the Allegory of the Ass is Insinuated the License of a Buffoon. **1719** YOUNG *Busiris* II. i, Your heart resents some licence of my youth. *a* **1720** SHEFFIELD (Dk. Buckhm.) *Wks.* (1753) I. 272 They are for licence, not for liberty. **1777** SHERIDAN *Sch. Scand.* I. i, The licence of invention some people take is monstrous indeed. **1797** BURKE *Regic. Peace* iii. Wks. VIII. 366 The intolerable licence with which the newspapers break..the rules of decorum. **1813** SCOTT *Rokeby* I. xvii, Thy license shook his sober dome. **1840** THIRLWALL *Greece* VIII. 315 The license which he gave to his troops to enrich themselves with the spoil of the country. **1850** ROBERTSON *Serm.* Ser. III. i. (1864) 3 The first license given to the tongue is slander. **1867** EMERSON *Lett. & Soc. Aims, Prog. Cult.* Wks. (Bohn) III. 226 The freedom of action goes to the brink..of license. **1881** WESTCOTT & HORT *Grk. N.T.* Introd. §13 The mixture has been accompanied or preceded by such licence in transcription.

c. Licentiousness, libertinism.

1713 STEELE *Guardian* No. 18 ¶3 The cause of much license and riot. **1823** SCOTT *Peveril* xvii. His unlimited license..has disgusted the minds of all sober and thinking men. **1841** TREVELYAN *Life Macaulay* (1876) I. ii. 84 The reaction from Puritanic rigour into the license of the Restoration. **1847** JAMES *J. Marston Hall* ix, The license of every kind that then existed in the city no tongue can tell nor pen can describe. **1901** *Expositor* May 367 These implements of license were originally made by God.

4. Deviation from recognized form or rule, indulged in by a writer or artist for the sake of effect; an instance of this. Frequent in phrase ***poetic (poetical,** etc.) **licence.***

1530 PALSGR. 44 Which auctors do rather by a lycence poetycall. **1657** J. SMITH *Myst. Rhet.* 49 By the licence of this figure we give names to many things which lack names, &c. **1697** DRYDEN *Æneid* Ded. (f), I generally join these two Licenses together. **1727–41** CHAMBERS *Cycl.* s.v., *Licence*, in painting, are the liberties which the painter takes in dispensing with the rules of perspective, and the other laws of his art. *a* **1771** GRAY *Corr.* (1843) 260 As to any license in the feet, it is only permitted in the beginning of a long verse. **1819** BYRON *Juan* I. cxx, This liberty is a poetic licence. **1859** KINGSLEY *Misc.* (1860) I. 227 The poem..allows a metrical licence. **1877** L. TOLLEMACHE in *Fortn. Rev.* Dec. 846 By a prophetic license, *perpetual* means *transitory*. **1899** F. T. BULLEN *Log Sea-waif* 179 Coleridge's simile of 'A painted ship upon a painted ocean' is only a poet's licence.

5. *attrib.* and *Comb.*, as ***licence-duty, -fee, -holder, -money, number, plate, -tax.***

1859 K. CORNWALLIS *New World* I. 137 The infliction of the *license fee..tended very much to exasperate the miners. **1897** *Westm. Gaz.* 7 Sept. 3/3 The old *licence-holders are going to the wall, and the brewers are stepping in. **1692** *Ann. Albany* (1850) 121 Ordered that the sheriffe have a warrant to levy the *lycence money. **1900** *Daily News* 4 June 3/4 The Boers collected licence money from all the shops. **1937** D. & H. TEILHET *Feather Cloak Murder* ii. 48 'Did you get the *licence number?'..the grey car had vanished. **1972** L. LAMB *Picture Frame* xx. 178 We found his van... It was Mallender's licence number. **1926** *Amer. Speech* I. 686/1 American: Number plates. English: *License plates. **1962** 'E. MCBAIN' *Like Love* (1964) xiv. 189 You didn't happen to notice the licence plate number, did you? **1974** R. C. DENNIS *Conversations with Corpse* xiv. 140, I..landed..a 1968 license plate. **1885** *Pop. Sci. Monthly* XXVIII. 464 (Cent.) The *license-tax, as it is called there [in Wisconsin] applies to railroads, insurance, telegraph, and telephone companies. **1888** BRYCE *Amer. Commw.* II. II. xliii. 135 Licence taxes..are directly levied by..State officials.

'licenceless, *a.* [f. LICENCE *sb.* 2.] Not possessing a licence.

1906 *Daily Chron.* 22 May 7/7 Six licenseless motorists on the Oxford to Birmingham highway were..discovered. **1923** *Glasgow Herald* 10 Oct. 7/1 Licenceless owners will make themselves liable to prosecution if discovered by the Post Office inspectors.

licensable ('laɪsənsəb(ə)l), *a.* [f. LICENSE *v.* + -ABLE.] †**a.** That may be dismissed. *Obs.* **b.** That may be licensed.

1611 COTGR., *Congeable*,..licensable. **1641** *Downfall Tempor. Poets* 5 (L.), I now have another copy to sell, but nobody will buy it, because it is not licensable. **1896** *List Explosives* 18 Explosives which have passed the tests and therefore become licensable.

license, licence ('laɪsəns), *v.* Forms: 4–6 lycence, 5–6 lyc-, lysense, (7 lycens), 9 *Sc.* leeshance, 4– licence, 6– license. [f. LICENCE *sb.*, q.v. for the question of spelling. In sense 2, ad. F. *licencier*, f. *licence*.]

1. *trans.* To give (a person) permission *to* (do something). Now *rare.* (In early use the personal obj. may be interpreted as *dative*, and *occas.* appears preceded by *to*.)

c **1430** *Syr Gener.* (Roxb.) 2983 If it be your will to licence me to tel my tale. *c* **1460** G. ASHBY *Dicta Philos.* 739 in *Poems* (E.E.T.S.) 76 If ye be to any man licencyng To set his fote vpon youres areryng, He wol after set his fote vppon your nekke. **1555** LATIMER in Foxe *A. & M.* (1563) 1366/1, I beseche your Lordshyp license me to sytte downe. **1577–87** HOLINSHED *Chron.* I. 175/2 The dead bodies of both armies are licenced to be buried. **1590** GREENE *Orl. Fur.* (1599) D4b, King Marsillus licenst thee depart. **1618** EARL SUFFOLK in *Fortesc. Papers* (Camden) 50 But I pray your Lordship to lycens me truly to acquaynt you what mesery yt hath produced unto me. *a* **1639** W. WHATELEY *Prototypes* I. xix. (1640) 212 To license ourselves to commit any sinne out of a conceit that it is small. **1676** TOWERSON *Decalogue* 75 Our friendship with God..licenceth us to come with assurance. **1684** BUNYAN *Pilgr.* II. 193 Therefore they were licensed to make bold with any of his things. **1863** KINGLAKE *Crimea* (1876) I. viii. 127 Lord Stratford was licensed to do no more than send a message to an Admiral.

b. To permit (a thing) to be done; sometimes with *dat.* of the person. Now *rare.*

1477 J. PASTON in *Paston Lett.* III. 191 The Pope will suffre a thyng to be usyd, but he will nott lycence nor grant it to be usyd nor don, and soo I. **1555** RIDLEY in Foxe *A. & M.* (1563) 928/2 At the last I was contente to take it for lycenced, and so began to talk. **1561** T. NORTON *Calvin's Inst.* I. xiii. (1634) 45 To attempt things not licenced. **1598** GRENEWEY *Tacitus' Ann.* III. ii. (1622) 66 Neuer shewing themselues more attentiue, nor at any time licencing themselues a more secret speech of the Prince. **1633** J. DONE *Hist. Septuagint* 99 Hee hath licensed us eating the flesh of foure-footed beasts. **1861** M. PATTISON *Ess.* (1889) I. 40 A patent of Henry II, in which he..licenses the sale of Rhenish wine at the same price as French is sold at. **1869** BROWNING *Ring & Bk.* VIII. 554 If this were..Allowed in the Spring rawness of our kind, What may be licenced in the Autumn dry? *Ibid.* 712 The divorce allowed by Christ, in lieu Of lapidation Moses licenced me.

†**c.** with *clause* as obj. *Obs.*

1398 TREVISA *Barth. De P.R.* IX. xxvi. (1495) 363 It was lycencyd that seruauntes and wymmen and bestes shold reste in the Saturday. **1586** J. HOOKER *Hist. Irel.* in *Holinshed* II. 96/2 The governor licenced that it [the corps] should be buried.

†**2.** [After F. *licencier*.] To give leave of departure to; to dismiss, set free *from* (something); to send away *to* (a place). *Obs.*

1483 CAXTON *G. de la Tour* Bjb, The kyng thenne lycencyd them and gaf to them fayr gyftes. **1551** ROBINSON tr. *More's Utopia* II. (1895) 143 Beynge then lycensed from the laboure of theyr owne occupacyons. *a* **1586** SIDNEY *Arcadia* III. (1629) 276 Amphialus licenced the gentleman, telling him, that by next morning he should have an answer. **1594** SOUTHWELL *M. Magd. Funeral Teares* 188 Licence from thee that needlesse suspition. **1598** BARRET *Theor. Warres* IV. i. 103 He..comming vnto the companies, do licence them to their lodgings. **1603** FLORIO *Montaigne* II. iii. 210 I wil now departe, and licence the remainder of my soule [F. *donner congé aux restes de mon ame*]. **1630** WADSWORTH *Pilgr.* 17 Tuesdayes and Thursdayes..on the after noones they are licenced to the recreation of the open fields. **1632** J. HAYWARD tr. *Biondi's Eromena* 74 Having then taken instructions for the way, and licenced himselfe from the King, he set him forwards on his journey. *a* **1639** WOTTON *Parallel* in *Reliq.* (1651) 17 When he listed he could licence his thoughts. **1676** DRYDEN *Aurengz.* I. i. 333 Sir, you were pleas'd your self to License me. **1814** SCOTT *Waverley* xl, Thus licensed, the chief and Waverley left the presence chamber.

3. To grant (a person) a licence or authoritative permission to hold a certain status or to do certain things, *e.g.* to practise some trade or profession, to hold a curacy, to preach, to use armorial bearings, to keep a dog, to carry a gun, etc. Const. *for, to,* and *to* with *inf.*

c **1400** *Rom. Rose* 7692, I am licenced boldely In divinitee to rede. *c* **1450** *St. Cuthbert* (Surtees) 7598 And besoght his reuerence þat he walde þaim lycence In his diocise to haue place. **1450–1530** *Myrr. our Ladye* 102 None oughte in holy chyrche to..preche openly the worde of god but yf he be specially lycensed therto. **1481** CAXTON *Reynard* (Arb.) 62, I am lycensyd in bothe lawes. **1555** EDEN *Decades* 125 Beyng therto lycenced by the kynge of castile. **1638** *Penit. Conf.* viii. (1657) 277 So licensing them (as it were) for Priestly power. **1764** BURN *Poor Laws* 72 Poor folks licensed to beg out of the limits of any city or town corporate. **1796** MORSE *Amer. Geog.* I. 270 Licensing candidates for the ministry. **1828** MISS MITFORD *Village* Ser. III. 178 Judith Kent, widow, 'Licenced'—as the legend imported, 'to vend tea, coffee, tobacco, and snuff.' **1830** GALT *Lawrie T.* IV. ix. II. 78 Amos Bell..had not been leeshanced above a week. **1878** SIMPSON *Sch. Shaks.* I. 23 The proclamation of July 8, 1557, licensing all English subjects to fit out ships to molest the French and Scots. **1901** *Durh. Dioc. Cal.* 215 Curates licensed.

b. To grant a licence permitting (a house, theatre, etc.) to be used for some specified purpose.

1777 PARSONS *Let.* in *15th Rep. Hist. MSS. Comm.* App. I. (1896) 232 A petition..for leave to bring in a bill to license a theatre at Birmingham. **1868** [see LICENSED *ppl. a.*]. **1874** [see LICENSER]. **1882** MISS BRADDON *Mt. Royal* iii, In which there is..not even a cottage licensed for the sale of ale.

4. To authorize the publication of (a book), or the acting of (a play).

1628 WITHER *Brit. Rememb.* Pref. 279 Were my writing As true as that of holy Iohns inditing, They would not licence it. **1634** *Documents agst. Prynne* (Camden) 23 Mr. Buckner did lycence 64 pages of the booke. **1644** MILTON *Areop.* (Arb.) 39 That no Book..should be Printed..unlesse it were approv'd and licenc't under the hands of 2 or 3 glutton Friers. **1667** POOLE *Dial. betw. Protest. & Papist* 155 Books Licensed by the Approbation..of your Church. **1858** HALLIWELL *Dict. Old Plays* 264 This play was licensed on June 6th, 1634.

†**b.** To vouch for. *Obs. rare.*

1694 R. BURTHOGGE *Reason* 216 A Story Licensed by a Person of Quality and of Great worth.

5. To allow liberty, free range, or scope to; to privilege, tolerate. *Obs.* exc. in *ppl. a.*

1605 BACON *Adv. Learn.* II. iv. §1. 17 Poesie is..in measure of words for the most part restrained: but in all other points extreamely licensed. **1640** LD. J. DIGBY *Sp. in Ho. Com.* 9 Nov. 4, I shall..with your Permission licence my Thoughts too, a little. **1704** STEELE *Lying Lover* I. i. 9 Licence my innocent Flames, and give me leave to love such charming Sweetness.

licensed ('laɪsənst), *ppl. a.* [f. LICENSE *v.* + -ED[1] or LICENCE *sb.* + -ED[2].]

1. To whom or for which a licence has been granted; provided with a licence. Now often *spec.* (of a house, etc.) licensed for the sale of alcoholic liquor. ***licensed victualler***: see VICTUALLER.

1632 SHERWOOD, Licenced, *licencié*. **1645** MILTON *Colast.* Wks. (1847) 222 The reasons of your licensed pamphlet are good. **1765** BLACKSTONE *Comm.* I. viii. 325 There are now eight hundred licensed coaches. **1817** W. SELWYN *Law Nisi Prius* (ed. 4) II. 926 For the purpose of the licensed act of trading..the person licensed was to be considered as virtually an adopted subject of this country. **1868** *Nat. Encycl.* I. 414 A constable may at all times enter licensed premises.

2. To whom or which liberty or free scope is allowed; privileged, recognized, regular, tolerated.

1593 DONNE *Sat.* iv. 228 He..Iests like a licens'd fool, commands the law. **1640** H. MILL *Nights Search* 123 He..turn'd her out; now she's a licenst whore. **1742** POPE *Dunc.* IV. 587 From Stage to Stage the licens'd Earl may run. **1809–10** COLERIDGE *Friend* (1865) 32 The established professions were..licensed modes of witchcraft. **1828** SCOTT *F.M. Perth* xxiii, Some, doubtless, [retired] to the licensed freedoms of some tavern. **1850** TENNYSON *In Mem.* cxiii, Should licensed boldness gather force. **1859** GEO. ELIOT *A. Bede* vi, Imagination is a licensed trespasser. **1879** FROUDE *Cæsar* xv. 229 Clodius was a licensed libertine.

licensee (laɪsən'siː). [f. LICENSE *v.* + -EE.] One to whom a licence is granted.

1868 *Nat. Encycl.* I. 411 A licensee who obliterates any record upon his license is liable to a fine of 5*l.* **1879** CASTLE *Law Rating* 82 A lodger within his own apartment is more than a mere licensee.

licenser ('laɪsənsə(r)). [f. LICENSE *v.* + -ER[1].] One who licenses or gives authoritative permission for something; esp. an official whose function it is to license the publication of books or papers (***licenser of the press***), or the performance of plays (***licenser of plays***), on being satisfied that they contain nothing contrary to law or to public morals or decency.

1644 MILTON *Areop.* (Arb.) 47 Those books must be permitted untoucht by the licencer. **1691** WOOD *Ath. Oxon.* II. 133 He was appointed by the Presbyterians a Licenser of the Press in London. **1737** CHESTERF. *Sp. on Licensing Bill* in Hansard *Parl. Hist.* (1812) X. 334 By good luck he was not the licenser, otherwise the kingdom of France had never had the pleasure..of seeing that play acted. **1755** JOHNSON, *Licenser*, a granter of permission; commonly a tool of power. **1812** SIR F. BURDETT in *Examiner* 21 Dec. 816/1 Much had been said of the tyranny of having a supervisor and licenser of the press. **1855** MACAULAY *Hist. Eng.* xix. IV. 348 Sir Roger Lestrange..had been licenser under the last two Kings. **1874** BUCKNILL & TUKE *Psych. Med.* (ed. 3) 2 The College of Physicians, whose licensers were required to visit the houses which they had licensed. **1884** W. J. COURTHOPE *Addison* v. 83 For a long time the evanescent character of the newspaper allowed it to escape the attention of the licenser.

licensing ('laɪsənsɪŋ), *vbl. sb.* [f. LICENSE *v.* + -ING[1].] The action of LICENSE *v.* in its various senses.

1588 J. UDALL *Demonstr. Discip.* (Arb.) 25 Licencing of wandring preachers, is contrary to the word of God. **1761** *Mem. to Ld. Mayor* in Entick *London* (1766) IV. 369 The licencing public-houses by the county magistrates. **1777** PARSONS *Let.* in *15th Rep. Hist. MSS. Comm.* App. I (1896) 232 The inhabitants..dread the licensing of a theatre as an evil which they would wish to prevent. **1827** in Picton *L'pool Munic. Rec.* (1886) II. 317 Regulations for the licensing of Alehouses.

attrib. **1825** MACAULAY *Ess., Milton* (1887) 28 With a view to the same great object, he attacked the licensing system. **1870** *Daily News* 5 Dec., Reformatories, and licensing bills, and trades unions, and municipal reforms. **1880** *Athenæum* 18 Sept 372/1 The multiplicity of universities and licensing boards is the greatest evil in British and Irish medicine.

licensure (ˈlaɪsənsjʊə(r)). *U.S.* [f. LICENSE *v.* + -URE.] A licensing; esp. the granting of a licence to preach.

1846 in WORCESTER (citing Godwin). **1870–4** ANDERSON *Missions Amer. Bd.* IV. xlii. 411 Seven young men, just graduated from the Seminary, were carefully examined for licensure.

† **ˈlicent,** *sb. Sc. Obs. rare*$^{-1}$. [Precise formation uncertain; cf. the following words.] = LICENCE *sb.*; in quot. *attrib.*

1676 in *Rec. Convent. Roy. Burghs* (1878) III. 694 Without paying any toll or custom as is here called incoming convoy, licent money and vijeil-gilt money, and last gilt.

† **ˈlicent,** *a. Obs. rare.* [? ad. L. *licent-em*, pr. pple. of *licēre* to be permitted: see LICENCE *sb.* (But cf. the note on next word.)] Permitted.

1606 DAY *Ile of Guls* IV. ii. (1881) 79 The eldest day of our licent abode at Court, is run out.

† **licent,** *v. Sc. Obs.* Only in *pa. t.* and *pa. pple.* licent. [? f. prec. (But perh. cf. Eng. dial. *licen'd* = *licensed.*)] *trans.* To license, permit. Also *absol.*

1536 BELLENDEN *Cron. Scot.* (1821) I. 104 The nobillis of Pichtis..war licent to returne hame. **1560** ROLLAND *Crt. Venus* III. 362 Thocht sa had bene his wife had bene on liue The law licent..for to haif ane Concubine.

licentiate (laɪˈsɛnʃɪət), *sb.* Forms: 4–5 licenciat, -cyat, 6–7 licenciate, -tiat, 6– licentiate. [ad. med.L. *licentiātus* (see next) used *absol.* as *sb.*]

1. One who has obtained a licence or authoritative permission to exercise some function.

† **a.** (See quot.) *Obs.*

c **1386** CHAUCER *Prol.* 220 He [the frere] hadde power of confessioun..moore than a Curat, For of his ordre he was licenciat.

b. One who has received a 'licence' from a university, college, or the like. In early use sometimes *gen.* = 'graduate'; more commonly *spec.* the holder of a particular degree between bachelor and master or doctor, still preserved in certain foreign universities (cf. Sp. *licenciato*, F. *licencié*); the latest use in England was in the Cambridge degree of Licentiate of Medicine (*Medicinæ licentiatus*, abbreviated M.L.) which was abolished in 1859. In current British use, almost exclusively in certain designations indicating that the bearer of them has received a formal attestation of professional competence or of a certain degree of proficiency in some art from some collegiate or other examining body: e.g. in *Licentiate of the Royal College of Physicians* (abbreviated L.R.C.P.), *Licentiate in Dental Surgery* (L.D.S.), *Licentiate of the Royal Academy of Music* (L.R.A.M.), *Licentiate of the College of Preceptors* (L.C.P.). The University of Durham grants the title of *Licentiate in Theology* (L.Th.) to those who pass a certain examination, open both to graduates and non-graduates.

1489 CAXTON *Faytes of A.* III. xix. 210 A scoler licencyat atte Cambryge in Englande is come to the unyuersyte of parys. **1555** EDEN *Decades* 80 In the Ilande of saynte Iohn.. Alfonsus Mansus a licenciate [is bysshop]. **1595** A. COPLEY *Wits Fits & Fanices* 82 A reuerend Licentiate at law was a suter to a fair Gentlewoman. **1604** E. G[RIMSTONE] *D'Acosta's Hist. Indies* IV. vii. 225 Whenas the licentiate Pollo governed that Province. *a* **1639** SPOTTISWOOD *Hist. Ch. Scotl.* (Spottiswoode Soc. 1847) I. 211 Alexander Barre, licenciate in the laws succeeded..and died..1397. **1669** WOODHEAD *St. Teresa* II. xxxv. 240 The next day..comes the Priest with the Licentiate. **1691** WOOD *Ath. Oxon.* I. 345 He was made a Licentiat of Divinity. **1726** AYLIFFE *Parergon* 54 The Degree of a Licentiate or Master in this Faculty. **1727–41** CHAMBERS *Cycl.* s.v., Most of the officers of judicature in Spain are known by no other name than that of licentiates. Licentiate among us, is usually understood of a physician, who has a licence to practice. **1779–81** JOHNSON *L.P., Garth*, The College of Physicians, in July, 1687, published an edict, requiring all the fellows, candidates, and licentiates, to give gratuitous advice to the neighbouring poor. **1789** GIBBON *Autobiog.* (1854) 29, I should applaud the institution, if the degrees of bachelor or licentiate were bestowed as the reward of manly and successful study. **1805** *Med. Jrnl.* XIV. 550 A member or licentiate of the College of Physicians. **1826** MISS MITFORD *Village* Ser. II. 188 As fatal as any prescription of licentiate or quack. **1850** PRESCOTT *Peru* II. 304 The licentiate, thus commissioned.. embarked at Seville. **1857** LIVINGSTONE *Trav.* Introd. 7, I was admitted a Licentiate of Faculty of Physicians and Surgeons. **1901** *Whitaker's Almanac* 268 Royal Academy of Music. There are..1,361 Licentiates (L.R.A.M.). *Ibid.*, College of Preceptors. Teachers..are granted diplomas of F.C.P., L.C.P. and A.C.P.

c. In the Presbyterian and some other churches: One who holds a licence to preach but as yet has no appointment; a probationer.

1854 H. MILLER *Sch. & Schm.* ii. (1860) 16 Four of the Presbytery..repaired to the parish church to conduct the settlement of the obnoxious Licentiate. **1866** CARLYLE *Remin.* I. 118 Irving's preachings as a licentiate (or probationer waiting for fixed appointment) were always interesting.

2. *nonce-use.* One who claims or uses licence; one who is not precise in the observance of rules.

1605 CAMDEN *Rem., Anagrams* (1657) 168 The licentiats somewhat licentiously, lest they should prejudice poeticall liberty, will pardon themselves for doubling or rejecting a letter, if the sence fall aptly.

Hence **liˈcentiateship**, the dignity or condition of a licentiate.

1881 *Macm. Mag.* XLIV. 202/1 Then he..proceeded to pass the more difficult examination for the 'licentiate-ship' in his special subject.

† **liˈcentiate,** *pa. pple.* (and *a.*). *Obs.* Forms: 4, 5 licenciat, -cyat, 6 liscenciat, 6–7 licenciate, -tiat, 6– licentiate. [ad. med.L. *licentiāt-us*, pa. pple. of *licentiāre*: see LICENTIATE *v.*]

1. *Sc.* Used as pa. pple. of LICENTIATE *v.*; equivalent to the later *licentiated.* **a.** Allowed, permitted. **b.** Licensed (to preach).

a. *c* **1500** *Bk. Precedence* in *Q. Eliz. Acad.* (1869) 101 All thingis be takin treuly as thai attest, ay liscenciat and lovit with al ledis. **1565** CALFHILL *Treat. Crosse* ii. 52 Louain hath licenciate you, to make what lies ye lust. **1582–8** *Hist. James VI* (1804) 283 The nobillmen..are for the maist part licentiat to liue a libertine life in thair youth. **1639** DRUMM. OF HAWTH. *Mem. State* Wks. (1711) 133 Certain verses.. being afterwards licentiate to be read,..they were forgotten. *a* **1651** CALDERWOOD *Hist. Kirk* (1843) II. 2 The bands of Scotish men of warre..sall be brokin, and the men of warre licentiat to depart.

b. *a* **1660** HAMMOND in *Colet's Serm. Conf. & Ref.* (1661) 29 Those that are..to be licentiate for publick preachers. **1676** W. ROW *Contn. Blair's Autobiog.* xii. (1848) 530 Some ministers were licentiate by the Council.

2. *adj.* Freed from rules; assuming licence, unrestrained, licentious.

1593 NASHE *Christ's T.* (1613) 163 The world would count me the most licentiat loose straier vnder heauen, if [etc.]. **1597** BP. HALL *Sat.* I. ix, Our epigrammatarians, old and late, Were wont be blamed for too licentiate. **1602** T. CAMPION *Art Eng. Poetrie* 41 Neither let any man cavill at this licentiate abbreuiating of sillables. **1656** S. H. *Golden Law* 39 All these miseries..your licentiate liberty, your freedom hath brought us to.

Hence † **liˈcentiateness.**

1656 S. H. *Golden Law* 21 Licentiateness is not a liberty.

licentiate (laɪˈsɛnʃɪeɪt), *v.* Also 6–8 -iat. [f. med.L. *licentiāt-*, ppl. stem of *licentiāre*, f. *licentia* LICENCE.]

1. *trans.* To give liberty to; to allow, permit (something) *to* (a person); to allow (a person) *to* (do something) or *that* (etc.). ? *Obs.*

1560 ROLLAND *Crt. Venus* III. 138, I ȝow protest, ȝe wald me licenciat..That I may [etc.]. **1637** GILLESPIE *Eng. Pop. Cerem.* II. iv. 22 Faithfull men..have neither a doore of enterance, nor a doore of utterance licentiated to them. **1650** DURYE *Just Re-prop.* 21 They rashly licentiat them-selves unto many things. **1660** N. INGELO *Bentivolio & Urania* I. (1682) 84 Their Chief Office is to licentiate Hypocrisie. *a* **1693** *Urquhart's Rabelais* III. xiii. 101 The Nurses..are licentiated to recreate their Fancies. **1706** MAULE *Hist. Picts* in *Misc. Scot.* I. 28 The Scots willingly licenciat them that habitation. *a* **1711** KEN *Hymnotheo* Poet. Wks. 1721 III. 47 'Tis Jesus Will that Angel to ordain, The Tyrant to licentiate or restrain. **1791–1823** D'ISRAELI *Cur. Lit.* (1866) 293/1 They were licentiated to go a begging.

† **b.** To give a licence to; to license. *Obs.*

1632 LITHGOW *Trav.* VIII. 367 They openly Lycentiat three thousand common Stewes.

† **2.** To grant (a person) a licence or faculty, e.g. to practise medicine. *Obs.*

1650 H. BROOKE *Conserv. Health* To Rdr. A iij, Bred up in ..that Faculty and licentiated in the practise theroff.

3. *nonce-use.* [After F. *licencier* or It. *licenziare.*] To discharge (a servant).

1820 BYRON *Let.* in *Eng. Stud.* XXV. 149 You may give up the house immediately, and licentiate the Servitors.

Hence **liˈcentiating** *vbl. sb.*

1676 W. ROW *Contn. Blair's Autobiog.* xii. (1848) 528 He spoke against the way of licentiating. **1694** R. L'ESTRANGE *Fables* xxxviii. (1714) 48 The Licentiating of any thing that is Course and Vulgar.

licentiation (ˌlaɪsɛnʃɪˈeɪʃən). [f. LICENTIATE *v.*: see -ATION.] The action of licensing; now only, the granting of a licence, e.g. to a medical practitioner.

1643 J. FREEMAN *Serm.* 35 There is a tacite licentiation or permission of errour. **1880** E. ROBERTSON in *Encycl. Brit.* XI. 19/2 The system of medical licentiation is year by year becoming more stringent and more centralized.

licentious (laɪˈsɛnʃəs), *a.* Also 5–6 licencious. [ad. med.L. *licentiōsus*, f. *licentia* LICENCE: see -OUS. Cf. OF. *licentieux* (F. *licencieux*).] Characterized by licence or excessive assumption of liberty.

1. Disregarding commonly accepted rules, deviating freely from correctness, esp. in matters of grammar or literary style; overstepping customary limits.

1589 PUTTENHAM *Eng. Poesie* II. viii. (Arb.) 95 Our maker must not be too licentious in his concords. **1597** HOOKER *Eccl. Pol.* V. lix. §2 This licentious and deluding arte, which changeth the meaning of words. **1667** DENHAM *Direct. Paint.* IV. xiii. 4 Poets and Painters are Licentious Youths. **1680** ROSCOMMON *Horace's Art Poet.* 82 The Tyber (whose licentious Waves, So often overflow'd the neighbouring Fields), Now runs a smooth and inoffensive course. *a* **1701** SEDLEY *Venus & Ad.* Wks. 1722 II. 315 If, Alas! thy too licentious Mind Is still to vig'rous Sylvan Sports inclined. **1751** JOHNSON *Rambler* No. 86 ¶ 12 The rest are more or less licentious with respect to the accent. **1785** T. BALGUY *Disc.* 174 It is hard to say whether there be greater inconvenience in too literal or too licentious an interpretation of Scripture. **1837–9** HALLAM *Hist. Lit.* I. I. i. §34. 30 Verse..somewhat licentious in number of syllables. **1850** GLADSTONE *Glean.* V. cxliv. 256 To speak of a treaty as subsisting between the State..and the Church..appears a licentious use of terms. **1881** WESTCOTT & HORT *Gk. N.T.* Introd. §186 Licentious as distinguished from inaccurate transcription.

2. Unrestrained by law, decorum, or morality; lawless, lax, immoral. Now *rare* on account of the prevalence of the specific use 3.

1535 *Act 27 Hen. VIII*, c. 19 Vpon trust of sainctuaries and the licencious liberties that heretofore haue ben..vsed in the same. *c* **1555** HARPSFIELD *Divorce Hen. VIII* (Camden) 272 What should I speak of the licentious liberty that divers princes have usurped. **1607** SHAKS. *Timon* V. iv. 4 You haue..fill'd the time With all Licentious measure, making your willes The scope of Iustice. **1683** *Brit. Spec.* 61 Rights and Priviledges, which licentious people make their pretence of contesting with their Soveraigns. **1687** T. BROWN *Saints in Uproar* Wks. 1730 I. 79 There's no stopping your licentious tongue. **1715** POPE *Iliad* II. 261 But chief he gloried with licentious style, To lash the great. **1733** NEAL *Hist. Purit.* II. 161 The licentious printing of Popish books. **1737** CHESTERF. *Sp. on Licensing Bill* in Hansard *Parl. Hist.* (1812) X. 338 The only place where they [Courtiers] can meet with any just reproof is a free though not a licentious stage. **1767** T. HUTCHINSON *Hist. Mass.* II. ii. 147 The licentious practice..of making depredations upon foreign nations. **1788** GIBBON *Decl. & F.* xxvii. (1875) 441/1 A loud and licentious murmur was echoed through the camps and garrisons of the west. **1803** *Med. Jrnl.* IX. 472 Led astray by the premature illusions of a licentious fancy. **1809** JEFFERSON *Writ.* (1830) IV. 127 The lying and licentious character of our newspapers. **1859** J. CUMMING *Ruth* x. 160 It leaves not one peg for the Antinomian to hang his licentious crotchets upon.

absol. **1595** DANIEL *Civ. Wars* V. lxxvi, In the Licentious yet it bred Despite.

3. Disregarding the restraints of chastity; libertine, lascivious, lewd. In modern usage the prevailing sense.

1555 EDEN *Decades* (Arb.) 53 Dissolute lyuynge, licentious talke, & such other vicious behauours. **1590** SHAKS. *Com. Err.* II. i. 133 How deerely would it touch thee to the quicke, Shouldst thou but heare I were licencious? **1602** WARNER *Alb. Eng.* XII. lxxv. 313 The pompious Prelacie of Rome, and liues lycentious thear. **1682** BURNET *Rights Princes* V. 177 This licentious Prince was, by reason of those scandals of his Life, less able or willing to grapple with the Ecclesiastical Power. **1769** ROBERTSON *Chas. V*, VII. Wks. 1813 III. 54 Whose licentious morals all good men detested. **1835** LYTTON *Rienzi* I. iv, Seeking occasion for a licentious gallantry among the cowering citizens. **1840** DICKENS *Barn. Rudge* xvi, A spectre at their licentious feasts. **1864** D. G. MITCHELL *Sev. Stor.* 226 He indulged freely in the licentious intrigues of Venice.

absol. **1837** HT. MARTINEAU *Soc. Amer.* III. 148 The pleasures of the licentious are chiefly supplied from that class.

† **4.** quasi-*adv.* With licence or liberty; freely.

c **1425** *Found. St. Bartholomew's* 31 More licencyous we may passe yn-to othir.

licentiously (laɪˈsɛnʃəslɪ), *adv.* [f. prec. + -LY^2.] In a licentious manner.

1. Without regard to limit or rule; loosely.

1561 T. NORTON *Calvin's Inst.* Pref., If they will haue the boundes of the same Fathers..to be stedfastly kept: why doo they..so licentiously passe them? **1577** tr. *Bullinger's Decades* (1592) 380 The Nazarites..had heretofore liued too lycenciously. **1589** PUTTENHAM *Eng. Poesie* II. iv. (Arb.) 89 Our auncient rymers..vsed these Cesures either very seldome..or else very licentiously. **1625** K. LONG tr. *Barclay's Argenis* II. i. 67 Lycogenes uttered this sparingly ..but his fellowes did more licenciously presse the King's dishonour. **1751** EARL ORRERY *Remarks Swift* (1752) 177 When I am writing to you..I..wander licentiously out of my sphere. **1804** *Ann. Rev.* II. 19/2 No poem was ever so licentiously translated as the English Lusiad. **1894** *Westm. Gaz.* 3 Jan. 1/2 Discussion..would otherwise have been licentiously prolonged.

2. Without regard to law, decorum, or morality; lawlessly, outrageously. Now *rare.*

1581 SAVILE *Tacitus' Hist.* IV. x. (1612) 153 Licentiously to commit all enormities. **1643** PRYNNE *Sov. Power Parl.* App. 58 That no man should aspire to the Crowne licentiously. **1652** NEEDHAM tr. *Selden's Mare Cl.* 14 That every one might do therein licentiously, all that which it pleaseth him. **1736** BUTLER *Anal.* I. ii. 61 Let them act as licentiously as they will. **1781** S. PETERS *Hist. Connecticut* 12 Without shewing their right to the spot: they licentiously chose it.

3. Lasciviously, lewdly.

1561 T. NORTON *Calvin's Inst.* I. 26 b, I speake not..how licentiously painters and caruers haue in this point shewed their wantonnesse. **1571** GOLDING *Calvin on Ps.* xxx. 7 They licentiously folow their owne lusts. **1665** BRATHWAIT *Comment. Two Tales* (1901) 36 It is not good to touch a woman. To which she answers; not inordinately or licentiously. **1882–3** SCHAFF *Encycl. Relig. Encycl.* I. 159/2 The Phoenician and Syrian female divinities were worshipped licentiously.

licentiousness (laɪˈsɛnʃəsnɪs). [f. as prec. + -NESS.] The quality of being licentious.

1. Assumption of undue freedom; disregard of rule or correctness; laxity, looseness.

1568 H. B. tr. *P. Martyr's Rom.* 441 b, Neither let him with overmuche licentiousnes vse what meates he list. **1612** tr. *Benvenuto's Passenger* I. ii. §92. 165 It is too great licentiousnesse for a servant to goe out without leaue. **1650**

R. STAPYLTON *Strada's Low C. Warres* I. 15 They sometimes come nearer to licentiousness, then liberty. **1684** tr. *Bonet's Merc. Compit.* XVIII. 610 Nor can this new Licentiousness of Bleeding be any way defended. **1778** BP. LOWTH *Transl. Isaiah* Prel. Dissert. (ed. 12) 45 The difference..is not to be imputed to the licentiousness of the translator. **1788** H. WALPOLE *Lett.* iv. 127 Corneille, Racine, Pope, exploded the licentiousness that reigned before them. **1817** BENTHAM *Parl. Ref. Catech.* (1818) 76 The inconsistency between the licentiousness on this point in this situation, and the comparative strictness in other public situations. **1883** BURGON *Revision Revised* 31 Nothing else but depravations of the text, the result of inattention or licentiousness.

2. Disregard of law, morality, or propriety; outrageous conduct. Now *rare*.

1553 EDEN *Treat. Newe Ind.* (Arb.) 31 By which theyr licentiousnes, the people of the Iland beyng prouoked. **1652** NEEDHAM tr. *Selden's Mare Cl.* 14 Such licentiousness or Anarchie is abhorred both of God and nature. **1701** SWIFT *Contests Nobles & Commons* Wks. 1755 II. I. 38 The custom of accusing the nobles to the people..having been always looked upon..as an effect of licentiousness. **1796** MORSE *Amer. Geog.* I. 325 That licentiousness and anarchy which always follow a relaxation of the moral principles. **1815** MACKINTOSH *France in* 1815 Wks. 1846 III. 187 The licentiousness with which they had exercised their saturnalian privileges. *a* **1852** WEBSTER *Wks.* (1877) II. 392 That authorized licentiousness that trespasses on right.

3. Lasciviousness, lewdness.

1586 W. WEBBE *Eng. Poetrie* (Arb.) 88 The licenciousnesse of theyr songes..is hurtfull to discipline and good manners. *a* **1631** DONNE in *Select.* (1840) 24 Though thou haue no farther taste of licentiousness in thy middle age. **1631** GOUGE *God's Arrows* III. xxviii. 233 Gods wrath against..prophanenesse, lewdnesse, and licentiousnesse. **1727** SWIFT *Let. Eng. Tongue* Wks. 1755 II. I. 187 That licentiousness which entered with the restoration. **1763** J. BROWN *Poetry & Mus.* xi. 191 Poem..was now declared to be the Bawd of Licentiousness. **1838** DICKENS *Nich. Nick.* xix, The licentiousness and brutality of so old a hand as you. **1856** FROUDE *Hist. Eng.* (1858) I. iii. 194 Among the clergy properly so called..the prevailing offence was not crime, but licentiousness. **1873** SYMONDS *Grk. Poets* viii. 244 Aristophanes accepts licentiousness as a fact which needs no apology.

lich (lɪtʃ). *Obs.* exc. *arch.* and in *Comb.* Forms: α. 1–2 **líc**, 4–5 **liche, lyche**, 6 **lytche**, 7, 9 **litch**, 3–7, 9 **lich, lych**; in comb. 5 **lege-**, 6–9 **leech-**, 9 **leach-** (see also LICH-GATE, LICH-OWL). *Pl.* 1 **líc**, 3, 5 **liches**. β. 2–5 **lik(e**, (4 **lijk**), 7, 9 **like, lyke**. *Pl.* 9 **likes**. [OE. *líc* str. neut. = OFris. *lîk*, OS. *lîc* (LG. *liche, like*, Du. *lijk*), OHG. *lîh* neut. and fem. (MHG. *lîch* fem., also weak *lîche*, G. *leiche* dead body), ON. *lík* (Sw. *lik*, Da. *lig*), Goth. *leik*:—OTeut. **lîkom* neut. Comparison with the cognate words (see LICHE, LIKE *a.*, LIKE *v.*) suggests that the original sense was prob. 'form, shape'.

The OE. *líc* became by normal development *lich(e* in the south and *like* in the north; hence the diversity of forms above. Cf. *ditch, dike*.]

1. = BODY *sb.* **a.** The living body. Also the trunk, as opposed to the limbs.

Beowulf 733 þæt he ȝedælde..anra ȝehwylces lif wið lice. *a* **900** CYNEWULF *Crist* 1326 þendan bu somod lic & sawle lifȝan mote. *c* **1205** LAY. 17694 For an his bare liche he weorede ane burne. *a* **1225** *Juliana* 16 He het..beten hire swa luðere þat hire leofliche lich liðeri al oblode. *a* **1275** *Prov. Ælfred* 471 in *O.E. Misc.* 131 So deð þe salit on fles, suket þuru is liche. *c* **1300** *Beket* 259 The here he dude next his liche his fleisches maister to beo. **1340–70** *Alisaunder* 195 Liliwhite was hur liche. **1362** LANGL. *P. Pl.* A. XI. 2 A wyf ..þat lene was of lich and of louh chere. *a* **1400–50** *Alexander* 2931 þe litillaike of his like lathely þat þai spyse. *Ibid.* 141 He..him..clethis All his liche in lyn claþe.

b. A dead body; a corpse.

Beowulf 2127 Hio þæt lic ætbær feondes fæðmum under firȝenstream. *c* **893** K. ÆLFRED *Oros.* I. i. §23 Ealle þa hwile þe þæt lic bið inne, þær sceal beon ȝedrync & pleȝa. **1154** *O.E. Chron.* an. 1135 (Laud MS.) Þa namen his sune & his frend & brohten his lic to Engle lande. *c* **1205** LAY. 3862 Heo nomen Morganus liche & leide hit on vrþen. *c* **1250** *Gen. & Ex.* 2447 Egipte folc..first .ix. niȝt ðe liches beðen. *a* **1300** *Cursor M.* 19785 Tilward þat like he turnd his face. ? *a* **1300** *XI Pains Hell* 78 in *O.E. Misc.* 149 A water..þat..stynkeþ so for holde lych. *c* **1440** *Promp. Parv.* 302/2 Lyche, dede body. *c* **1470** HENRY *Wallace* II. 332 Quha aw this lik he bad hir nocht deny. **1806** *Sir Oluf* in Jamieson *Ballads* I. 222 Three likes were ta'en frae the castle away. **1895** BARING-GOULD in *Minster Mag.* 239 'Thomas maketh a beautiful lych, that her do.'

2. *Comb.*: † **lich-bell**, ? a hand-bell rung before a corpse; † **lich-fowl** = LICH-OWL; † **lich-holm**, a shrub of some kind; **lich-house** [cf. Du. *lijkenhuis*], a dead-house, a mortuary; † **lich-lay**, a rate levied to provide a church-yard (cf. LAY *sb.*[7] 4); **lich-path** = *lich-way*; † **lich-rest**, a place for a corpse to rest, a burial-place; † **lich-song**, ? singing at a lyke-wake; **lich-stone**, a stone to place the coffin on at the lich-gate; † **lich-wal, -wale**, a plant (see quots.); † **lich-way**, a path along which a corpse has been carried to burial (this in some districts being supposed to establish a right of way); † **lich-wort**, a plant (see quots.). Also LICH-GATE, LICH-OWL, LYKE-WAKE.

1421 in Warner *Hist. Abb. Glaston.* (1826) App. 99, j processional, j old gradual, iij new *lychebells. **1449** *Yatton Churchw. Acc.* (Som. Rec. Soc.) 90 For a lege bell and the mendyng of another ij[s]. ij[d]. **1552** in W. Money *Ch. Goods Berksh.* (1879) 19 Two lytchebelles of bell metalle. **1611** COTGR., *Effraye*, a Scricheowle, or *Lychefowle. **1614** *Sco. Venus* (1876) 30 These goblins, lich-fouls, Owls, and night-crows to At murthers raile. *a* **1387** *Sinon. Barthol.* (Anecd. Oxon.) 13 Bruscus, frutex est *licheholm. *c* **1200** *Trin. Coll. Hom.* 169 Alswo ofte swo prest singeð þis bede at *lich huse he [etc.]. **1559** *Extracts Aberd. Reg.* (1844) I. 324 Ane tenement of land within the yard and lichowss thairof [*sc.* of the parish church]. **1850** *Ecclesiologist* X. 339 We..propose ..with some degree of confidence,—Lich-House. **1898** *Pall Mall Mag.* Mar. 430/2 He had it [the corpse] brought up and laid in his lych-house. **1753** in Picton *L'pool Munic. Rec.* (1886) II. 170 To purchase a church yard on a *Lych Ley for St. Thomas's Church. **1862** *Church Builder* Apr. 48 That path up which you came..used formally to be called the *Lich-path because all the funerals came along that path. *c* **1000** *St. Mildreds* in *Sax. Leechd.* III. 430 Heo ða hyre *licreste ȝeceas on eliȝ byriȝ. *c* **1205** LAY. 17225 And swa þu hit scalt leden to þere lich-raste. **1558** *Yatton Churchw. Acc.* (Som. Rec. Soc.) 170 Of Wyllam Worthe for the lyche-reste of Ione his wyf vi[s]. viii[d]. *c* **1675** in *Rec. Presbyt. Inverness & Dingwall* (Sc. Hist. Soc.) 121 *note*, Discharging..all ..*Lyksongs, fidling and dancing. **1862** *Athenæum* 30 Aug. 279 [In North Devon] Passing through the lich-gate, the corpse is placed upon the *lich-stone. *c* **1450** *Alphita* (Anecd. Oxon.) 72/2 Granum diureticum, anglice *lichewal. **1597** GERARDE *Herbal* II. clxxx. 487 In English Gromell: of some Pearle plant, and of others Lichwale. **1863** PRIOR *Plant-n.*, *Lichwale*,..the gromwell, *Lithospermum officinale*, L. **1587** FLEMING *Contn. Holinshed* III. 303/2 Aduertised of ..a *leech waie to be made ouer his land, with-out his leaue or consent. **1787** in GROSE *Prov. Gloss.*, *Leech-way*, the path in which the dead are carried to be buried. Exm. *c* **1450** *Alphita* (Anecd. Oxon.) 51/2 Ebulus uel Ebula gall. eble angl. welle-uort uel *licheuart. ? *a* **1500** *MS. Bodl.* 536 in *Sax. Leechd.* III. 336/1 Peritoria .i. peritory or lychewort. **1597** GERARDE *Herbal* App., Lichwort is Pellitorie of the wall. **1880** BRITTEN & HOLLAND *Plant-n.*, Lichwort, *Parietaria officinalis, L.*

Hence † **'lichless** *a. Obs.*, without a dead body.

c **1250** *Gen. & Ex.* 3164 Ðo was non biging of al egipte lich-les, so maniȝe dead ðor kipte.

lich, obs. form of LIKE; LITCH *dial.*, bundle.

† **licham.** *Obs.* Forms: 1–2 **líchama, -homa**, 2 **licama**, 2–4 **licome, lic(c)-, lich-, lick-, likham(e, likame**, 4–5 **lyc-, lygh-, lykam(e**, 5–6 *Sc.* **lec-, lekame**, (5 **licaym**), ? 7 (*ballad corruption*) **lingcan**. [OE. *líchama, -homa* = OFris. *liccoma, lîchama, lîkma*, OS. *likhamo* (MDu. *lichame*, Du. *lichaam*), OHG. *lîhhamo, lîhmo* (MHG. *lîchame, lîcham*), ON. *líkame*, more commonly in str. form *líkam-r* (Sw. *lekam*, Da. *legeme*):—OTeut. type **lîko-hamon-* wk. masc., f. **lîko-* LICH, body + **hamon-*, OE. *hama* shape, covering, garment. (OHG. had also a syntactical combination of the same meaning, *lîhhinamo*, **lîhhin-hamo*, from the genitive of a wk. sb. *lîhha* = LICHE; hence MHG. *lîchnam(e*, mod.G. *leichnam*.)

It has been suggested that the word was originally poetical, describing the body as the 'fleshly garment' of the soul. Cf. OE. *feðerhama* FEATHERHAM.]

The body; the living body; also, the body as the seat of desire and appetite.

c **888** K. ÆLFRED *Boeth.* xxxiv. §9 Se lichoma bið lichoma þa hwile þe he his limu ealle hæfð. *c* **1000** *Ags. Gosp.* Matt. vi. 22 Ðines lichaman leohtfæt is ðin eaȝe. *a* **1175** *Cott. Hom.* 229 Drihten..astah to heofene..mid þan ilce licama þe he onþrowode. *c* **1175** *Lamb. Hom.* 47 Þa bi-com his licome swiðe feble. *a* **1250** *Owl & Night.* 1052 An lerdest hi to don shome An un-riȝt of hire licome. *a* **1300** *Cursor M.* 635 Bath war naked þar licam, Bot þar for thoght þam þen na scham. *Ibid.* 22324 Wit-vten last al his licam [*Edin. MS.* liccame]. **1393** LANGL. *P. Pl.* C. I. 32 For no lykerouse lyflode hure lykame to plese. ? *a* **1400** *Morte Arth.* 3282 His lire and his lyghame lamede fulle sore. **1426** AUDELAY *Poems* 17 To sle the lust of hore lycam, and hore lykyng. *c* **1440** *York Myst.* v. 110 A! Eue, þou art to blame..me shames with my lyghame. *c* **1450** HOLLAND *Howlat* 900 He lukit to his lykame that lemyt so licht. *a* **1510** DOUGLAS *K. Hart* I. 11 In all his lusty lecam nocht ane spot. *a* **1783** *K. Henry* v. in Child *Ballads* I. 299 He's thrown to her his gay mantle Says 'Lady, hap your lingcan'.

b. A dead body; a corpse.

a **1225** *Ancr. R.* 106 Þer leien ofte licomes iroted buuen eorðe. *a* **1300** *Cursor M.* 12295 Dun o þis loft he yod, Til he com þar þat licam lai. *Ibid.* 24599 Quen his licam in stan was laid, Allas! allas! ful oft was said. *c* **1470** HENRY *Wallace* VII. 281 With a claith I couerit his licaym.

† **'lichamly**, *a. Obs.* [OE. *líchamlic*: see LICHAM and -LY[1]. Cf. Du. *lichamelijk*, Icel. *líkamligr*.] Bodily; of the nature of the body; of or pertaining to the body, carnal.

c **888** K. ÆLFRED *Boeth.* xi. §2 Hi wilnodon ðæs lichomlican deaðes..wið þæm ecan life. *c* **1000** *Ags. Gosp.* Luke iii. 22 Se haleȝa gast astah lichamlicre ansyne. *c* **1175** *Lamb. Hom.* 97 Hi neren aferede of nane licamliche pinunge. *a* **1225** *Leg. Kath.* 42 Wið stronge tintreohen and licomliche pinen. *a* **1225** *Ancr. R.* 4 þe oðer riwle..riwleð þe licome & licomliche deden. *c* **1230** *Hali Meid.* 3 Fleschliche þohtes þat leadeð þe & drahen..to licomliche lustes. *c* **1275** *Passion our Lord* 51 in *O.E. Misc.* 38 Mvchel volk hym vulede..Summe for been yuedde of lykamlyche vode.

† **'lichamly**, *adv. Obs.* [OE. *líchamlíce*: see LICHAM and -LY[2].] Bodily (= BODILY *adv.* 1 and 2); in a bodily manner or form; in the flesh.

c **900** tr. *Bæda's Hist.* III. xiii. [xv.] (1890) 200 Þeah þe he lichomlice þær æfweard wære. *c* **1175** *Lamb. Hom.* 89 We ne moten halden moyses e licamliche. *a* **1225** *Ancr. R.* 40 Ȝif me ..stien nu heortliche, & hwon ich stie gostliche, a domesdeie al licomliche, into ðe blisse of heouene. *a* **1240** *Ureisun* in *Cott. Hom.* 185 Ase þu licomliche iwend iwend me from the worlde.

† **liche.** *Obs.* Also 3 **like**, 4–5 **lyke**. [OE. (*man-, swín-*)*líca* = Goth. (*man-*)*leika*, OHG. (*man-*)*lîcha*; cogn. w. LICH.] Form, figure, guise.

c **1175** *Lamb. Hom.* 29 Al swa eða þu mihtest..smiten of þin aȝen heaueð, and gan eft to þin aȝene liche. *c* **1200** *Trin. Coll. Hom.* 59 þe deuel com on neddre liche to adam. *c* **1200** ORMIN 5813 An der off þa fowwre der Wass inn an manness like. *a* **1225** *Ancr. R.* 224 þe þet is com to in one wildernesse in one wummone liche. **1387** TREVISA *Higden* (Rolls) II. 283 þerfore sche [Semiramis] desgised hir self in þe childes liche. *Ibid.* V. 239 þe devel appered to þe Iewes..in Moyses his liche. **1390** GOWER *Conf.* I. 143 In stede of man a bestes lyke He syh. *c* **1470** *Golagros & Gaw.* 858 Thai lufly ledis in lyke, thai layid on in ane ling.

liche, obs. form of LEECH, LIKE.

lichee, variant of LITCHI.

lichen ('laɪkən), *sb.* [a. L. *līchēn*, ad. Gr. λειχήν in all the senses below. Cf. F. *lichen*, Sp. *liquen*, It. *lichene*.

Not in Johnson. The pronunciation ('lɪtʃən) is given in Smart without alternative, and most of the later Dicts. allow it a second place; but it is now rare in educated use.]

† **1.** = LIVERWORT; the lichens and liverworts having formerly been included in the same group.

1601 HOLLAND *Pliny* II. 245 Another kind of Lichen or Liuerwort there is, cleauing wholly fast vpon rockes and stones in manner of moss. **1753** CHAMBERS *Cycl. Supp.*, *Lichen*, liverwort in botany, the name of a genus of mosses. **1759** STILLINGFL. *Gedner's Use Curiosity* Misc. Tracts (1762) 180 The vertues of the lichenes or liverworts upon animate bodies..are not inconsiderable.

2. One of a class of cellular cryptogamic plants, often of a green, grey, or yellow tint, which grow on the surface of rocks, trees, etc. Also *collect.*

According to the modern theory, now generally accepted, the lichen is a fungus parasitic upon an algal, whose form is somewhat modified by the influence of the parasite.

[**1601** HOLLAND *Pliny* II. 169 As well in this wild kind as in planted Plum trees of the hortyard, there is to be found a certain skinny gum, in Greek called Lichen, which hath a wonderfull operation to cure the rhagadies or chaps.] **1715** DELACOSTE tr. *Boerhaave's Aphorisms* 313 The famous earthy ash-colour'd moss call'd Lichen. **1789** E. DARWIN *Bot. Gard.* II. (1791) 29 Where frowning Snowden bends his dizzy brow..Retiring lichen climbs the topmost stone. **1796** COLERIDGE *To Yng. Friend on Domestic. with Author* 4 Where..coloured lichens with slow oosing weep. **1830** LINDLEY *Nat. Syst. Bot.* 325 Lichens are distinguished by their want of a distinct axis of growth. **1856** STANLEY *Sinai & Pal.* viii. (1858) 320 Aged trees covered with lichen, as if the relics of a primeval forest long since cleared away. **1887** ALGIE *Guide to Forres* 66 The coral-like gray lichen. **1893** BRIDGES *Shorter Poems* v. *Winnowers* 8 The red roofs nestle, oversprent With lichen yellow as gold.

3. *Path.* **a.** A skin disease, characterized by an eruption of reddish solid papules over a more or less limited area.

1657 *Physical Dict.*, *Lichen*, a tetter, or ringworm. **1727–41** CHAMBERS *Cycl.*, *Lichen*, a cutaneous distemper, other-wise called *impetigo*. **1842** BURGESS *Man. Dis. Skin* 189 Lichen is not confined to any period of life, or to either sex. **1888** *Syd. Soc. Lex.* s.v., Many authors regard lichen, strophulus, and eczema, as forms of the same disease.

b. With mod.L. adjs., as **lichen planus**, a skin disease characterized by an eruption of wide, flat-topped, shiny, purple-coloured papules; **lichen simplex**, (*a*) a type of eczema characterized by the presence of small red papules; (*b*) (***lichen simplex chronicus***) a disorder characterized by areas of lichenification.

1798 R. WILLAN *Descr. & Treatm. Cutaneous Dis.* I. ii. 41 The extent of the disease being thus limited, I shall proceed to describe the varieties of it, which have occurred to my observation, under the denominations of Lichen simplex, Lichen agrius, Lichen pilaris, Lichen lividus, and Lichen tropicus. **1842** T. H. BURGESS tr. *Cazenave & Schedel's Man. Dis. Skin* 191 Acute lichen simplex requires no other treatment than diluents and tepid baths. **1866** E. WILSON in *Brit. Med. Jrnl.* 13 Oct. 399/1 (*heading*) On lichen planus: the lichen ruber of Hebra. **1910** C. F. MARSHALL tr. *Gaucher's Dis. Skin.* 101 Lichen simplex may occur on all parts of the body, but it chiefly affects the forearms and dorsal surface of the hands, the neck and shoulders, the external and posterior surfaces of the legs, and the internal surface of the thighs. **1934** DORE & FRANKLIN *Dis. Skin* viii. 121 Lichen planus is generally a chronic complaint. **1966** W. D. STEWART et al. *Synopsis Dermatol.* xxvi. 485 Lichen simplex chronicus..is a common pruritic disorder resulting in a localized patch of dermatitis that has a characteristic lichenification. **1971** *Acta Dermato-Venereol.* LII. 216/1 In an epidemiologic house-to-house survey..in Kerala in South India, 7639 individuals were examined for oral lichen planus.

† **4.** After a L. use in Pliny: A callous excrescence on the leg of a horse or ass (? = CHESTNUT *sb.* 6). *Obs.*

1607 TOPSELL *Four-f. Beasts* (1658) 22 There is a collection of certain hard matter about an asses legs, called 'lichen', which if it be burned and beaten, and put into old oil, will cause hairs to grow out of baldness. **1661** LOVELL *Hist. Anim. & Min.* 81 The fume of the lichens, helps the falling sickness.

5. *attrib.* and *Comb.* **a.** simple attributive, as (sense 2) *lichen-dust, -flora, -fungus, -moss, -spot, -thallus, -tuft*; (sense 3) *lichen-eczema, -spot*; **lichen-acid**, any lichen substance which

is an acid; **lichen substance**, any of about 65 compounds, most of which are acids, which are found uniquely in lichens; **b.** instrumental, as *lichen-clad, -clothed, -crusted, -laden, -matted, -tasselled* adjs.; **c.** similative, as *lichen-green, -like* adjs.; **lichen-starch**, a kind of starch associated with lichenin in Iceland-moss.

1893 *Jrnl. R. Microsc. Soc.* 497 (*heading*) New *lichen-acid. **1967** M. E. HALE *Biol. Lichens* viii. 119 Lichen acids and pigments increase the opacity of the upper cortex. **1848** *Chambers' Inform.* I. 563/2 A stunted *lichen-clad bole. **1859** JEPHSON *Brittany* vii. 95 An immense *lichen-clothed menhir. **1886** H. F. LESTER *Under two Fig Trees* 232 An old boundary stone *lichen-crusted. **1880** G. MEREDITH *Trag. Com.* (1881) 117 He snapped the *lichen-dust from his fingers. **1900** J. HUTCHINSON *Archives Surg.* XI. 195 The patient had suffered from *lichen-eczema from the age of 20. **1857** W. A. LEIGHTON (*title*) The *Lichen-Flora of Great Britain. **1875** BENNETT & DYER *Sachs' Bot.* 273 Algæ.. known as the hosts of *Lichen-fungi. **1898** *Daily News* 8 Oct. 6/4 Folds of *lichen-green velvet about the shoulders. **1889** HISSEY *Tour in Phaeton* 49 The old buildings..with ..*lichen-laden roofs. **1885** H. O. FORBES *Nat. Wand. E. Archip.* 101 Blocks of weather-beaten, *lichen-matted trachyte. **1860** RUSKIN *Mod. Paint.* V. VI. x. §25 The silver *lichen-spots rest, star-like, on the stone. **1897** J. HUTCHINSON *Archives Surg.* VIII. 223 The initial stage was a lichen spot, of which there were many around the patches. **1900** *Jrnl. R. Microsc. Soc.* 235 (*heading*) *Lichen-substances. **1954** ASAHINA & SHIBATA (*title*) Chemistry of lichen substances. **1967** Lichen substance [see DEPSIDE]. **1897** MARY KINGSLEY *W. Africa* 572 The heavily *lichen-tasselled fringe of the forest-belt. **1856** W. L. LINDSAY *Pop. Hist. Brit. Lichens* 39 The..tissues of the *Lichen-thallus. **1832** R. CATTERMOLE *Becket* etc. 191 Ashes..gray with *lichen-tufts.

Hence **'lichenless** *a.*, destitute of lichens.

1843 RUSKIN *Mod. Paint.* I. II. I. vii. §36 His very rocks are lichenless.

lichen ('laɪkən), *v.* [f. LICHEN *sb.*] *trans.* To cover with lichens.

1859 TENNYSON *Elaine* 44 There they lay till all their bones were..lichen'd into colour with the crags. **1862** *Macm. Mag.* Sept. 426 How was it [island] lichened and mossed? **1864** SIR J. K. JAMES *Tasso* III. xiii. *note*, Turrets lichened with gold.

fig. **1883** *Harper's Mag.* Feb. 438/2 Popular superstition has not had time yet to lichen over the familiar objects of his country-side.

Hence **'lichened** *ppl. a.*, **'lichening** *vbl. sb.*

1823 PRAED *Poems* (1865) II. 274 O'er the natural tomb The lichened pine rears up its form of gloom. **1887** RUSKIN *Præterita* II. 401 The deeply lichened stones of its low churchyard wall. **1892** *Cornh. Mag.* Sept. 230 The rudeness of the masonry and the lichening of the stones were no real indications of antiquity.

lichenaceous (laɪkə'neɪʃəs), *a.* [f. LICHEN *sb.* + -ACEOUS.] Having the character of a lichen.

1881 GRIFFITH & HENFREY *Microgr. Dict.* (ed. 4), *Opegrapha*, a genus of Graphideæ (Lichenaceous Lichens).

lichenal ('laɪkənal), *a.* and *sb.* [ad. mod.L. *līchēnālis*, f. L. *līchēn* LICHEN *sb.*] **a.** *adj.* Of or pertaining to a lichen. *Lichenal Alliance*: Lindley's name for the group of lichens. **b.** *sb.* A member of the 'Lichenal Alliance', a lichen.

1846 LINDLEY *Veg. Kingdom* 45 Alliance III. *Lichenales.*—The Lichenal Alliance. **1854** A. ADAMS, etc. *Man. Nat. Hist.* 532 Lichenals (*Lichenales*).

lichenian (laɪ'kiːnɪən), *a.* [see -IAN.] = next.

1889 *Amer. Naturalist* XXIII. 5 The 'Lichenian reaction' is seen in all lichens and in none of the fungi.

lichenic (laɪ'kɛnɪk), *a. Chem.* [see -IC.] Of or pertaining to lichens. *lichenic acid*, an organic acid obtained from lichens; its salts are **'lichenates.**

1836–41 BRANDE *Chem.* (ed. 5) 1198 Lichenic Acid apparently much resembles the boletic.. The lichenates of ammonia, potassa, and soda, are soluble and crystallizable. **1871** W. L. LINDSAY in *Q. Jrnl. Microscop. Sci.* XI. 39 Certain true Lichens,..giving lichenic reactions with iodine.

lichenicolous (laɪkə'nɪkələs), *a.* [f. LICHEN *sb.* + L. *col-ĕre* to inhabit + -OUS.] Inhabiting lichens.

1855 in MAYNE *Expos. Lex.* **1871** W. L. LINDSAY in *Q. Jrnl. Microscop. Sci.* XI. 28 This group of Lichenicolous Microscopic Parasites has been little studied.

lichenification (laɪˌkɛnɪ-, ˌlaɪkənɪfɪ'keɪʃən). *Med.* [ad. F. *lichénification* (L. Brocq 1892, in *II. Internat. Dermatol. Congr.* 522), f. F. *lichen* LICHEN *sb.*: see -IFICATION.] Hardening and thickening of the skin caused by scratching or other continued irritation; an area of skin so affected.

1892 L. BROCQ in *Brit. Jrnl. Dermatol.* IV. 326 At a certain time the skin shows quite a peculiar aspect, with a great exaggeration of its natural lines, representing a sort of network with meshes more or less large and regular, and a decided infiltration of the integuments... Such is the morbid process which I call Lichenification. *Ibid.* 329 In the second group..we only meet with the cutaneous lesions we have described as primary lichenifications. **1934** DORE & FRANKLIN *Dis. Skin* iii. 41 The lichenification itself may be painted with crude coal-tar. **1968** A. J. ROOK et al. *Textbk. Dermatol.* I. xii. 222/2 In all forms of lichenification pruritus is the predominant symptom. **1971** *Jrnl. Investigative Dermatol.* LVII. 299/2 Lichenification involves a change in the epidermis, characterized by hyperkeratosis, acanthosis and scattered parakeratosis.

lichenified (laɪ'kɛnɪfaɪd, 'laɪkənɪfaɪd), *ppl. a. Med.* [f. LICHEN *sb.* + -IF(Y + -ED[1] (to parallel LICHENIFICATION).] Showing lichenification.

1892 *Brit. Jrnl. Dermatol.* IV. 327 The cases entering into the second group, which we have called Secondary Lichenifications, are not of the nature of real and true lichens, but are simply lichenified dermatoses. **1927** R. C. LOW *Common Dis. Skin* xii. 161 The situation of these lichenified areas, usually on the back of the neck, is a rare one in lichen planus. **1967** H. MONTGOMERY *Dermatopath.* I. ix. 190/2 In my experience, one cannot distinguish between chronic lichenified disseminate neurodermatitis and localized forms of neurodermatitis histologically.

licheniform ('laɪkənɪfɔːm), *a.* [f. LICHEN *sb.* + -(I)FORM.] Having the form of a lichen.

1855 in MAYNE *Expos. Lex.* **1867** H. SPENCER *Princ. Biol.* §186 II. 24 Some of the inferior liverworts are quite licheniform, and are often mistaken for lichens.

lichenin ('laɪkənɪn). *Chem.* Also **lichenine**. [f. LICHEN *sb.* + -IN.] A kind of starch obtained from Iceland moss and other lichens.

1836–41 BRANDE *Chem.* (ed. 5) 1090 Lichen Starch. Lichenin. **1838** T. THOMSON *Chem. Org. Bodies* 658 Lichenin. **1861–93** COOKE *Struct. Bot.* 9 Lichenine. **1885** GOODALE *Physiol. Bot.* 358 Lichenin is abundant in certain lichens.

lichenism ('laɪkənɪz(ə)m). [f. LICHEN *sb.* + -ISM.] The special symbiosis between alga and fungus occurring in lichens.

1887 GARNSEY & BALFOUR tr. *De Bary's Fungi* 419 Species of Algae..so adapted to lichenism that they can no longer attain their full development outside the Lichen-combination. **1895** OLIVER tr. *Kerner's Nat. Hist. Plants* II. 692.

lichenist ('laɪkənɪst). [f. LICHEN *sb.* + -IST.] = LICHENOLOGIST.

1833 W. J. HOOKER *Smith's Eng. Flora* V. 144 The great Swedish Lichenist. **1861** H. MACMILLAN *Footn. fr. Page Nature* 73 The French lichenists, Tulasne and Itzigsohn. **1862** ANSTED *Channel Isl.* II. viii. (ed. 2) 189 A glance at a few of the more obscure genera,..will convince every lichenist that much yet remains to be done.

lichenivorous (laɪkə'nɪvərəs), *a.* [f. L. *līchēn* + *-(i)vor-us* devouring + -OUS.] Lichen-eating.

1854 *Zoologist* XII. 4377 Lichenivorous or herbivorous ruminants.

lichenized ('laɪkənaɪzd) *ppl. a.* [f. LICHEN *sb.* + -IZE.] **a.** Covered with lichens.

1839 MURCHISON *Silur. Syst.* I. xxiii. 297 Above the weathered and lichenized surfaces of the sandstone.

b. Of a fungus or an alga: living in association with (respectively) an alga or a fungus so as to form a lichen; adapted or evolved to live as a component of a lichen.

1942 *Proc. Sect. Sci. Kon. Akad. Wetensch. Amsterdam* XLV. 276 We believe to have found in the lichenized algal covers of Pleurococcus, Apatococcus and allied species, a better object of study in this respect. **1952** *Symbolae Bot. Upsalienses* XII. 10 It is certainly difficult in many cases to establish whether or not an organism should be regarded as a lichen. One type of questionable or easily misinterpreted cases is provided by such lichen-fungi as are sometimes lichenized and sometimes live without algae. *Ibid.*, A lichenized fungus means in the present paper always a fungus which lives in symbiosis (s. str.) with an alga and which is not a parasymbiont. **1960** *Amer. Jrnl. Bot.* XLVII. 677 (*heading*) Some new and interesting species of Trebouxia, a genus of lichenized algae. **1973** *Nature* 4 May p. xv (Advt.), Taxonomic research in the ascomycetous fungi or their lichenised relatives.

licheno- ('laɪkənəʊ), combining form used (with hyphen) to form adjs. signifying the presence of the disease LICHEN in connexion with some other.

1897 J. HUTCHINSON *Archives Surg.* VIII. 222 Symmetrical licheno-lupoid eruption on the calves of the legs. *Ibid.* 223 The patches..being not a mere pigmentation, but distinctly a licheno-lupoid thickening.

lichenographer (laɪkə'nɒgrəfə(r)). [LICHEN *sb.* + -(O)GRAPHER.] = next.

In mod. Dicts.

lichenographist (laɪkə'nɒgrəfist). [f. LICHEN *sb.* + -(O)GRAPHIST.] One who describes lichens; one who is versed in lichenography.

1848 in CRAIG. **1863** HITCHCOCK *Remin. Amherst Coll.* 42.

lichenography (ˌlaɪkə'nɒgrəfɪ). [f. LICHEN *sb.* + -(O)GRAPHY.] The systematic description or study of lichens. Hence **ˌlicheno'graphic**, **licheno'graphical** *adjs.*, of or pertaining to lichenography.

1824 WATT *Bibl. Brit.* Subjects, *Lichenography.* **1828** WEBSTER, *Lichenographic, Lichenographical.* **1848** in CRAIG; and in later Dicts.

lichenoid ('laɪkənɔɪd), *a.* [f. LICHEN *sb.* + -OID.]

1. *Bot.* Resembling a lichen; lichen-like.

1830 LINDLEY *Nat. Syst. Bot.* 332 Opegrapha and other Lichenoid..genera. **1866** *Intell. Observ.* No. 53. 340 Corrugated or lichenoid ball. **1882** P. GEDDES in *Nature* No. 642. 361 The hypothesis of the lichenoid nature of the alliance between alga and animal.

2. *Path.* Resembling the disease lichen (see LICHEN *sb.* 3).

1859 SEMPLE *Diphtheria* 97 A whitish, lichenoid, pellicular exudation..covered a third of the surface of the left tonsil. **1899** J. HUTCHINSON *Archives Surg.* X. 175 His forehead and some other parts were covered with a form of lichenoid eczema.

lichenologist (ˌlaɪkə'nɒlədʒɪst). [f. LICHEN *sb.* + -(O)LOGIST.] One versed in lichenology.

1830 LINDLEY *Nat. Syst. Bot.* 332 The arrangement..of Acharius has been adopted by lichenologists of this country and of most others. **1874** COOKE *Fungi* 11 No lichenologist of repute has as yet accepted the theory.

lichenology (laɪkə'nɒlədʒɪ). [f. LICHEN *sb.* + -(O)LOGY.] The science that treats of lichens. Hence **liche'nologic**, **licheno'logical** *adjs.*, of or pertaining to lichenology.

1855 in MAYNE *Expos. Lex.* **1856** W. L. LINDSAY *Pop. Hist. Brit. Lichens* 3 The lichenological student requires no cumbrous or expensive apparatus. *Ibid.* 7 A sufficient basis whereupon to found our plea for the study of Lichenology. **1881** *Jrnl. Bot.* X. 128 He was an excellent lichenologist and published many lichenological papers. **1887** GARNSEY & BALFOUR tr. *De Bary's Fungi* 419 The Regensburg 'Flora' is a rich repertory of Lichenology since 1855.

lichenometry (laɪkə'nɒmɪtrɪ). *Geol.* [f. LICHEN *sb.* + -O + -METRY.] The dating of moraines or other surfaces recently exposed for lichen colonization by measurement of the size of lichens growing on them.

1957 R. E. BESCHEL in *Arctic* (Montreal) X. 60/1 This method that I call lichenometry works well for the last 1,000 years under alpine conditions. **1967** *Jrnl. Glaciol.* VI. 818 The basic premise of lichenometry is that the diameter of the largest lichen thallus growing on a moraine, rock glacier or other surface is proportional to the length of time that the surface has been exposed to colonization and growth. **1973** *Oxford Times* 27 July 6/5 There will also be a botanical study of the glaciers and a lichenometry survey to assist the dating of withdrawal of ice.

Hence **licheno'metric**, **-'metrical** *adjs.*

1958 *Arctic* (Montreal) XI. 254/1 (*heading*) Lichenometrical studies in West Greenland. **1959** *Biol. Abstr.* XXXIV. 861/2 In several glaciers of the group, a lichenometric study was performed. **1964** *Geogr. Bull.* (Ottawa) Nov. 80 (*heading*) A lichenometrical study of the north-western margin of the Barnes Ice Cap: a geomorphological technique. **1967** *Jrnl. Glaciol.* VI. 819 The wide geographic distribution of the species, together with its long life span and consistent size-age relationship make *R[hizocarpon] geographicum* ideal for lichenometric dating.

lichenose ('laɪkənəʊs), *a.* [f. LICHEN *sb.* + -OSE.] Having the character of lichens; lichen-like.

1855 in MAYNE *Expos. Lex.* **1874** COOKE *Fungi* 13 It may be affirmed that they have a lichenose nature. **1882** CROMBIE in *Encycl. Brit.* XIV. 552/2 The simplest form under which lichenose vegetation occurs.

lichenous ('laɪkənəs), *a.* [f. LICHEN *sb.* + -OUS.]

1. Of, pertaining to, or consisting of lichens; of the nature of or resembling lichens; overgrown with lichens.

1843 RUSKIN *Mod. Paint.* I. II. I. vii. §35 The..crumbling and lichenous texture of the Roslin stone. **1876** GEO. ELIOT *Dan. Der.* v. xxxvi, An effect something like that of a fine flower against a lichenous branch. **1893** RUSKIN *Poetry Archit.* I. vi. 85 The grey roof is warmed with lichenous vegetation.

2. Pertaining to, or of the nature of, the skin-disease Lichen.

1822–34 *Good's Study Med.* (ed. 4) IV. 125 Opium.. threw out a most distressing lichenous rash. **1872** F. THOMAS *Dis. Women* (ed. 3) 152 A lichenous eruption about the pubes. **1879** *St. George's Hosp. Rep.* IX. 742 The skin being dotted all about with hard lichenous elevations.

licheny ('laɪkənɪ), *a.* [f. LICHEN *sb.* + -Y.] Overgrown with lichens; lichen-clad.

1826 *Blackw. Mag.* XIX. 382 The licheny cliff-stones, and the hollow-rhinded woods. **1856** R. SHIELD *Pract. Hints Moths* 40 The licheny trunks of the trees.

lich-gate, lych-gate ('lɪtʃgeɪt). *arch.* [f. LICH corpse + GATE.] The roofed gateway to a churchyard under which the corpse is set down, to await the clergyman's arrival.

1482–3 in Swayne *Sarum Churchw. Acc.* (1896) 30 Et sol'. Will'o Sariant Carpent' pro emend' le lycheyate, iiijd. **1681** ASHMOLE in *Lilly's Life* (1774) 162 His coarse was..received by the minister (in his surplice) at the Litch-Gates. **1846** *Guide Archit. Antiq. Oxford* 375 A handsome lich-gate of carved oak has been erected at the entrance of the Church-yard. **1864** TENNYSON *Aylmer's F.* 824 Yet to the lychgate, where his chariot stood, [He] Strode from the porch. **1875** JAS. GRANT *One of the '600'* xviii. 138 The ivy-clad lyke-gate of the village church.

lichi, variant of LITCHI.

lichless: see after LICH.

lichlie, lichliness *Sc.*: see LIGHT-.

lichness, obs. form of LYCHNIS.

lichorous, obs. form of LICKEROUS.

'lich-owl. Also 6–7 like-owle. [f. LICH + OWL.] The screech-owl, so called because its cry was supposed to portend death in the house.

1585 HIGINS *Junius' Nomenclator* 56 *Bubo*, a shrichowle: a likeowle. **1601** HOLLAND *Pliny* I. 283 The Otis is a bird lesse than the Like-Owle,.. hauing two plumed ears standing vp aloft. **1604** DRAYTON *Owle* 302 The shreeking Litch-Owle that doth never cry, But boding death. **1688** R. HOLME *Armoury* II. 268/1 The little Horn-Owle.. termed Lich Owls.. because Prognosticaters of Peoples death, when they scrietch about there Houses. **1898** WATTS-DUNTON *Aylwin* (1900) 32/2 Then came the shadow of a lich-owl, as it whisked past us towards the apple-trees.

licht, Sc. form of LIGHT.

lichurie, variant of LECHERY.

†**'lichy**, *a. Obs.* [f. *lich* LIKE *a.* + -Y.] Like.
1370–80 *XI Pains of Hell* 78 in *O.E. Misc.* 225 Byndeþ hem in knucchenus forþi To brenne lyk to licchi, Spousbrekers wiþ lechours [etc.]. **1382** WYCLIF *Matt.* xi. 16 But to whom shal I gesse this generacion lichy [*v. rr.* lyche, lyke]? It is lichi to children sittynge in cheepynge [etc.]. [In six other passages in Wyclif *lic(c)hi, lic(c)hy, lychi, lychy* occur as variant readings for *lich, lyke*, etc.]

licible: see LISIBLE *Obs.*, permissible.

licience, obs. form of LICENCE.

†**licious**, *a. Obs. rare.* Also 5 licius. [aphetic form of DELICIOUS. Cf. LUSCIOUS.] = DELICIOUS.
c **1420** *Sir Amadace* (Camden) xxvii, Mete and drinke y-nuȝhe thay hade With licius drinke and clere. *a* **1670** HACKET *Cent. Serm.* (1675) 515 He that lives by the Allegorie, feeds upon licious Quails.

licit ('lɪsɪt), *a.* Also 5 licyte, lycite, -yte, 7 licite. [ad. L. *licit-us* (pa. pple. of *licēre* to be lawful, either directly, or through F. *licite*).] Allowable, permitted, lawful.
1483 CAXTON *Cato* A v b, She [the wife] ought to.. obeye to hym in al thynges lycite and honeste. **1490** —— *Eneydos* xix. 70 To a peple yssued out of strange lande, is licyte to seke strange places for theyr dwellynge. **1587** FLEMING *Contn. Holinshed* III. 388/1 Such a thing is not licit to a particular. **1656** BLOUNT *Glossogr.*, *Licite*, lawful, granted. **1757** *Herald* No. 4 (1758) I. 54 Whether in our exchange commodities with Holland, the ballance is for or against us in licit trade. **1826** LAMB *Let.* xvi. *To B. Barton* 147 A friend's wife, whom I really love (.. I mean in a licit way). **1864** R. F. BURTON *Dahome* I. 116 The natives of Whydah give the licit dealer scanty encouragement. **1884** *Contemp. Rev.* Feb. 259 Abstinence.. from things in themselves licit. **1892** *Times* 11 Feb. 9/4 The consumption of licit or duty-paid opium. **1897** BARING-GOULD in *Expositor* Sept. 203 To obtain the recognition of Christianity apart from Judaism as a licit religion in the empire.

Hence **'licitly**, in a licit manner, lawfully; **'licitness**, the quality of being licit, lawfulness.
1483 CAXTON *Cato* B ij, Thow oughtest to thynke ofte how .. lycytly thou shalt mowe come to thyn intention. **1788** R. HARRIS (*title*) Scriptural Researches on the Licitness of the Slave Trade. **1806** THROCKMORTON *Consid.* 38 The question may be licitly discussed on the ground of expediency. **1855** R. BOYLE *Case with Wiseman* 27 Whether he could deprive me of saying Mass licitly. **1881** SALA in *Illustr. Lond. News* 7 May 443 Not so much as a glass of lager beer could the privates licitly obtain. **1884** *Catholic Dict.* 629/2 To receive holy orders.. licitly, it is necessary to be in a state of grace.

†**licitate**, *v. Obs. rare*⁻¹. [f. L. *licitāt-*, ppl. stem of *licitārī* to bid at an auction, f. *licit-us*, pa. pple. of *licērī* of the same meaning.] *trans.* To make a bid for, put a price upon.
1601 *Imp. Consid. Sec. Priests* (1675) 85 Ecclesiastical persons.. are.. not to study how to murder Princes, nor to licitate Kingdoms.

lici'tation. *rare*⁻⁰. [ad. L. *licitātiōn-em*, f. *licitārī*: see prec.] (See quots.)
1623 COCKERAM, *Licitation*, an inhauncing of a price set vpon any thing that is sold. **1656** BLOUNT *Glossogr.*, *Licitation*, a setting out to sale; a prizing or cheapening. **1848** WHARTON *Law Lex.*, *Licitation*, the act of exposing to sale to the highest bidder.

†**lici'tator**. *Obs. rare*⁻⁰. [a. alleged L. *licitātor*, agent-n. f. *licitārī*: see prec. (But the L. word exists only as a misreading for *illicitator*.)] One who bids to raise prices at an auction.
1623 COCKERAM, *Licitator*, an inhauncer.

lick (lɪk), *sb.* [f. LICK *v.*]
1. a. An act of licking. Hence quasi-*concr.* a small quantity, so much as may be had by licking; also ***lick-up***. ***a lick of goodwill*** (Sc.), 'a small portion of meal given for grinding corn, in addition to the fixed multure' (Jam.). Also (*U.S. colloq.*) ***a lick***, somewhat, a bit (usu. in neg. contexts).
1603 DEKKER *Grissil* (Shaks. Soc.) 16, I knock'd you once, for offering to have a lick at her lips. **1662** R. MATHEW *Unl. Alch.* lxxxix. 129 This Woman with one lick of my Antidote (which was mixed with hony).. received ease all over her body. *a* **1688** BUNYAN *Jerus. Sinner Saved* (1886) 113 Many love Christ with nothing but the lick of the tongue. **1690** DRYDEN *Amphitryon* II. ii. (1691) 21 He could.. come galloping home at Midnight to have a lick at the Honey-pot. *a* **1733** R. NORTH *Life F. North* 219 He [Jeffries] could not reprehend without scolding; and in such Billingsgate Language, as [etc.]... He call'd it *giving a Lick with the rough Side of his Tongue.* **1814** *Abstract Proof respecting Mill of Inveramsay* 3 (Jam.) P. Wilson depones, that he did not measure or weigh the lick of goodwill. *a* **1825** FORBY *Voc. E. Anglia*, *Lick-up*, a miserably small pittance of any thing. **1826** J. WILSON *Noct. Ambr.* Wks. 1855 I. 255 'Ae wee bit spare rib o' flesh.. to be sent roun' lick and lick about'. **1841** GEN. P. THOMPSON *Exerc.* (1842) VI. 62 The polar man.. shall not have a lick of oil on Christmas Day. **1853** P. B. ST. JOHN *Amy Moss* 50 Everybody brought 'sunthin'—some a lick of meal, some a punkin' [etc.]. **1902** W. N. HARBEN *Abner Daniel* 94 But all day yesterday an' to-day he hain't worked a lick. **1919** H. L. WILSON *Ma Pettengill* vii. 215, I was fool enough to argue with him a bit, trying to see if he didn't have a lick of sense. **1938** C. H. MATSCHAT *Suwannee River* vii. 110, I knocked him loose an' hit him a lick. **1939** JOYCE *Finnegans Wake* 415 Seven bolls of sapo, a lick of lime, two spurts of fussfor. **1957** W. C. HANDY *Father of Blues* v. 66 We had been complaining violently against an Irishman who couldn't cook a lick. **1971** *Black Scholar* Sept. 37/2 His grandfather was a preacher and he couldn't read a lick. **1973** *Black World* Jan. 63/2 His wife Fanny can't cook a lick. **1973** M. & G. GORDON *Informant* xlix. 188 If you've got a lick of sense, you'll mosey back into the woodwork.

b. *colloq.* A slight and hasty wash (usually ***a lick and a promise***). Also, a dab of paint, etc; a hasty tidying up, a casual amount of work.
c **1648** in Maidment *Pasquils* (1868) 154 We'll mark them with a lick of tarre. *a* **1771** GRAY *Candidate* 2 When sly Jemmy Twitcher had smugg'd up his face With a lick of court white-wash, and pious grimace. **1855** ROBINSON *Whitby Gloss.*, *A Lick and a Slake.* **1860** W. WHITE *All round the Wrekin* xx. 207 We only gives the cheap ones a lick and a promise. **1899** E. F. HEDDLE *Marget at Manse* 43 That lassie gi'es a lick and a promise when I tell her to sweep! **1922** A. BENNETT *Lilian* I. vi. 57 The dirty kitchenmaid was giving the stone floor of the porch a lick and a promise. **1934** L. A. G. STRONG *Corporal Tune* III. ii. 230 The room, instead of its usual vigorous cleaning, got what Nelly would have called a lick and a promise. **1942** C. MORLEY *Thorofare* xl. 355 You ought to be writing the Adventures of a Crustacean. You've only done a lick and a promise. There's six more inches to fill. **1948** M. MCCARTHY in *Partisan Rev.* May–June 325 The Dublin Gate players.. had a slapdash style of acting that suggested an Irish house-maid flailing about with a dust-cloth—they gave their roles a lick and a promise and trusted to the audience's good-nature to take the will for the deed. **1967** V. LINCOLN *Private Disgrace* (1968) xi. 91 She had only a basin of water and a rag with which to give the insides of the windows a lick and a promise. **1969** D. CLARK *Death after Evensong* vi. 142 A pale sun gave Rooksby a lick and a promise of better things to come. **1972** J. BURMEISTER *Running Scared* iii. 51 The isolation ward.. was given a lick and a promise once a month by an unsupervised maid.

2. *N. Amer.* **a.** A spot to which animals resort to lick the salt or salt earth found there. Also ***buffalo-lick, salt-lick***.
1747 *Virginia Land Patents & Grants* in *Amer. Speech* (1940) XV. 280/2 Crossing the said Run above a Lick. **1750** T. WALKER *Jrnl. Explor.* (1888) 51 At the mouth of a Creek .. is a Lick, and I believe there was a hundred Buffaloes at it. **1751** C. GIST *Jrnls.* (1893) 42 Salt Licks, or Ponds, formed by little Streams or Dreins of Water. **1784** J. F. D. SMYTH *Tour U.S.A.* I. xviii. 141 Licks are particular places .. where the clay or earth is impregnated with saline particles. **1796** MORSE *Amer. Geog.* I. 663 Salt Lick and Salt Spring are used synonymously, but improperly, as the former differs from the latter in that it is dry. **1807** P. GASS *Jrnl.* 219 One of our sergeants shot a deer at a lick close to our camp. *a* **1816** B. HAWKINS *Sk. Creek Country* (1848) 29 Parallel with this, are some licks in post and red oak saplin flats. **1825** J. PICKERING *Jrnl.* 21 Dec. in *Emigration* (1830) v. 49 Deer will go miles to the salt spring, or 'licks' as they are called. **1827** J. F. COOPER *Prairie* I. v. 78 To rout the unlawful settlers who had gathered nigh the Buffaloe lick in old Kentucky. **1832** J. MCGREGOR *Brit. Amer.* II. 556 Both buffalo and deer resort to them for the purpose of licking the salt off the shrubs hence the name *lick.* **1841** J. F. COOPER *Deerslayer* iv, Like deer standing at a lick. **1877** N. S. SHALER *App. to I. A. Allen's Amer. Bison* 458 The springs at Big-Bone Lick, as at all the other licks of Kentucky are sources of saline waters derived from the older Palaeozoic rocks. **1957** *Beaver* Summer 37/2 The goat evidently was headed for the same lick from which the sheep were returning.

b. = *lick-log.*
1920 WEBSTER *Lick*, an artificial saline preparation given to sheep and cattle to lick. *c* **1920** W. D. POWDRELL *Dairy Farming N.Z.* v. 38 A lick of rock-salt should be provided. **1950** *N.Z. Jrnl. Agric.* July 67/3 By using cobalt either as a topdressing, as a drench, or in licks all classes of stock could be run without any trouble [on this cobalt-deficient country]. **1963** *Times* 4 Feb. 4/7 A large feed block or lick is made available to cattle.

3. A complaint in horses (see quot.).
1827 *Sporting Mag.* XX. 162 Coach horses are subject to symptoms known by the appellation of 'the Lick'... They lick each other's skins, and gnaw their halters into pieces.

4. a. A smart blow. (Cf. *to lick on the whip*, cited from *c* 1460.) Also *pl.* (*Sc.* and *north.*), a beating, in phr. ***to get one's licks, give*** (one) ***his licks.***
1678 J. PHILLIPS *Tavernier's Trav.* vi. 77 [He] gave the fellow half a dozen good licks with his cane. **1724** SWIFT *Wood's Execution* Wks. 1755 V. II. 155, *3rd Cook.* I'll give him a lick in the chops. **1725** RAMSAY *Gentle Sheph.* I. ii, To lend his loving wife a loundering lick. **1785** BURNS *To W. Simpson* Postscr. vii, An' monie a fallow gat his licks, Wi' hearty crunt. **1810** *Sporting Mag.* XXXVI. 79 Unless either of them gave him a lick on the head. **1820** SCOTT *Abbot* vii, The dread of a lick should not hold me back. **1826** J. WILSON *Noct. Ambr.* Wks. 1855 I. 165 Every callant in the class could gie him his licks. **1837** S. LOVER *Rory O'More* (1849) 13 We're used to a lick of a stick every day. **1887** *Schoolmaster* 15 Jan. 104/1 The boy.. deponed that the master gave him twa licks in the lug. **1894** CROCKETT *Lilac Sunbonnet* 103 The yin that got his licks fell down and bit the dust.

b. *transf.* and *fig.*
1739 CIBBER *Apol.* (1756) I. 28 A lick at the Laureat will always be sure bait.. to catch him little readers. **1794** WOLCOT (P. Pindar) *Ode to For. Soldiers* Wks. 1812 III. 247 A Lick at the French Convention. **1803** *Naval Chron.* X. 258 The tars are wishing for a lick, as they call it, at the Spanish galleons. **1883** STEVENSON *Treas. Isl.* IV. xviii, 'I wish I had had a lick at them with the gun first', he replied.

5. *Sc.* 'A wag, one who plays upon another' (Jam.).
1725 *Willie was a wanton Wag* in Whitelaw *Bk. Sc. Songs* (1844) 20/1 And was na Willie a great loun, As shyre a lick as e'er was seen. *a* **1758** RAMSAY *Grub-street* 5 He's naething but a shire daft lick.

6. *dial., colloq., U.S., Austral.*, and *N.Z.* A spurt at racing, a short brisk spin; a 'spell' of work. ***big licks*** = hard work. Also speed, in phr. ***at full lick, at a great lick***, etc.
The phr. ***to go*** (or ***run***, etc.) ***for the lick of one's life*** appears to be restricted to Australia and N.Z.
1809 T. DONALDSON *Poems* 135 Ere I get a pick, In comes young *Nannie* wi' a lick. **1835** *Gent's. Vade Mecum* (Philadelphia) 14 Feb. 3/4 When you come to put in the scientific licks, I squat. **1837** HALIBURTON *Clockm.* Ser. I. xv, That are colt can beat him for a lick of a quarter of a mile. **1847** W. T. PORTER *Quarter Race* 104 He went up the opposite bank at the same lick, and disappeared. **1847** J. S. ROBB *Streaks of Squatter Life* 106 He was puttin' in the biggest kind a licks in the way of courtin'. **1851** —— in T. A. Burke *Polly Peablossom's Wedding* 111, I saw comin' my gray mule, puttin' in her best licks, and a few yards behind her was a grizzly. **1861** BRYANT *Songs from Dixie's Land* 26 At length I went to mining, put in my biggest licks. **1868** *Putnam's Mag.* June 715/1 The father.. did an occasional 'lick of work' for some well-to-do neighbor. **1882** MISS BRADDON *Mt. Royal* II. iv. 79, I.. made up my mind to stay in America, till I'd done some big licks in the sporting line. **1889** P. H. EMERSON *Eng. Idyls* 26 Down the river.. came sailing the.. whery.. ay! going at full lick too. **1889** 'ROLF BOLDREWOOD' *Robbery under Arms* 82 It'll be a short life and a merry one, though, dad, if we go on big licks like this. **1892** *Dialect Notes* I. 230 *To mend one's licks*, to quicken one's steps. 'When the dog got after me, I mended my licks.' **1898** F. T. BULLEN *Cruise Cachalot* 218 The recipient, thoroughly roused by this, starting off at a great lick. **1905** *Dialect Notes* III. 86 You'll have to hit a different lick, if you expect to accomplish anything. **1906** H. D. PITTMAN *Belle of Bluegrass Country* xv. 224 I'll have to take care of the whole gang, and never get a lick of work out of one of them. **1932** W. FAULKNER *Light in August* (1933) i. 7 She's hitting that lick like she's been at it for a right smart while. **1934** J. MASEFIELD *Taking of Gry* 43 'They're [ships] going a good lick, sir,' I said. **1938** *Amer. Speech* XIII. 6/1 *Lick* n., an easy job. 'None of these jobs is a lick.' **1944** J. H. FULLARTON *Troop Target* I. v. 46 'Go for the lick of your life down the lane,' commanded Rangi. **1946** F. SARGESON *That Summer* 84 With all of us going for lick of our lives, there'd only be time for a wisecrack now and then. **1948** D. BALLANTYNE *Cunninghams* (1963) xviii. 203 Clive ran.. full lick into the sea. **1949** *Marshfield* (Wisconsin) *News-Herald* 19 July 4/1 The power lobby got in its licks through a subcommittee of the Senate Appropriations Committee passing on the bill for funds for the Department of Interior. **1951** L. MACNEICE tr. *Goethe's Faust* I. 33 Lord, these strapping wenches they go a lick! **1966** *Sunday Mail Mag.* (Brisbane) 3 Apr. 6/3 A section of the miners agreed that the happiest solution to the sorry affair would be to lynch Mr. Chapple. The little Cornishman got wind of this thinking and, treating it seriously.. went for the lick of his life. **1974** P. RUELL *Death takes Low Road* x. 127 Caroline contrived to be first down the gangway and set off along the quay at a good lick.

7. a. In jazz, dance-music, etc.: a short solo or phrase, usu. improvised and often interpolated into a piece of written music; = BREAK *sb.*¹ 9 c; freq. in phr. ***hot lick*** (cf. HOT *a.* 8 g).
1932 *Melody Maker* June 509 They manage to steal a 'lick' from an American record. **1933** *Metronome* Apr. 29 Please do not.. think I want 'hot licks' to memorize in all keys. **1933** *Fortune* Aug. 47/1 His licks (musical phrases) are original. **1935** [see GO *v.* 22 b]. **1935** [see AD LIB. B *adj.*]. **1935** *Vanity Fair* (N.Y.) Nov. 38/3 Hot artists.. add their licks to the exciting music that flourishes there. **1952** B. ULANOV *Hist. Jazz in Amer.* (1958) xix. 237 The panic was on to push vibrato aside, pick up his licks, and produce his sound. **1970** *Globe & Mail* (Toronto) 26 Sept. 27/3 The blues riff is even better, full of Charlie Parker-like bebop licks.

b. Plan, idea. *U.S. colloq.*
1955 S. ALLEN *Bop Fables* 54 So here's the lick. Take this beat-up bovine to market. **1970** C. MAJOR *Dict. Afro-Amer. Slang* 76 *Lick*, plan, idea, outline of a situation.

lick (lɪk), *v.* Forms: 1 liccian, 2–6 lik, 4–5 like, lyke, 3–7 licke(n, 4–6 likke, 5–6 lycke, lykke, (5 lykkyn), 6– lick. [OE. *liccian* = OS. *liccôn, leccôn* (Du. *likken*), OHG. *leckôn* (MHG., mod.G. *lecken*):—OTeut. **likkôn* (whence It. *leccare*, F. *lécher*), prob. repr. pre-Teut. **lighnā-*, f. OAryan root **ligh-* (: *leigh-*: *loigh-*), found in Goth. (*bi*)*laigôn*, Gr. *λείχειν* to lick, *λίχνος* dainty, L. *lingĕre*, OIrish *ligim*, OSl. *ližati*, Lith. *lëžti*, Skr. *rih, lih* to lick.]
1. *trans.* **a.** To pass the tongue over (something), e.g. with the object of tasting, moistening the surface, or removing something from it.
c **1000** ÆLFRIC *Saints' Lives* (1885) I. 114 Ða reðan deor.. heora liða liccodon mid liðra tungan. *c* **1290** *S. Eng. Leg.* I. 270. 320 þo he i-saiȝ ane leon licke þat bodi. *c* **1375** *Sc. Leg. Saints* xlv. (*Cristine*) 261 þe serpentis hire fete can lyke. *a* **1450** *Knt. de la Tour* (1868) 29 Thei [dogges] were about her mouthe and liked it. **1484** CAXTON *Fables of Æsop* I. xvii, [The asse] beganne to kysse and to lykke hym. **1592** G. HARVEY *Four Lett.* Wks. (Grosart) I. 206 To seek his dinner in poules with Duke humfrey: to licke dishes, to be a beggar. *a* **1617** HIERON *Wks.* II. 456 Must God then lacke the due attendance of the people in His house, while they are licking of thy trenchers? **1712** STEELE *Spect.* No. 431 ¶3, I left off eating of Pipes, and fell to licking of Chalk. **1732** POPE *Ess. Man* I. 84 Pleas'd to the last, he crops the flow'ry food, And licks the hand just rais'd to shed his blood. **1792** WOLCOT (P. Pindar) *Wks.* III. 4 The man I hate.. Who, to complete his dinner, licks his plate. **1798** SIR M. EDEN in *Ld. Auckland's Corr.* (1862) III. 423 They continue to cringe and to lick the hand that strikes them. **1880** MISS BRADDON *Just as I am* i,

Tim stands on end, and licks the wanderer's face. **1885** *Truth* 28 May 844/1 The danger of licking adhesive stamps and envelopes.

absol. c **1460** J. Russell *Bk. Nurture* 295 Lik not with þy tonge in a disch. **1583** *Leg. Bp. St. Androis* 1091 While ane pat doun his hand and lickit. a **1592** H. Smith *Serm.* (1637) 462 When Jonathan saw honey dropping, he must needs be licking. **1694** Salmon *Bate's Dispens.* (1713) 128/2 Mix for a Dose..and to be lick'd of..as need requires. **1890** L. C. D'Oyle *Notches* 60 The elk..was now 'licking' in the little side-valley.

b. Frequent in phrases expressive of actions referred to *allusively* or *fig.*, as *to lick one's fingers*, *to lick one's lips*, an action indicating keen relish or delighted anticipation of some dainty morsel; † *to lick* (another's) *fingers*, *to lick the fat from* (one's) *beard*, to cheat (him) of his gains; † *to lick one's knife*, said of a parsimonious person; *to lick the ground*, *to lick* (another's) *boots* or *shoe* or *spittle* (cf. lick-spittle *sb.*), actions expressive of abject servility; † *to lick* (a patron's) *trencher*, said of a parasite; *to lick the dust*, † *the earth* [a Hebraism: Vulg. *terram lingere*], to fall prostrate, to suffer defeat; *to lick the* (or *one's*, etc.) *chops* (*Jazz slang*), to tune up or warm up before a 'session'.

a **1000** *Ags. Ps.* (Th.) lxxi[i]. 9 His feondas foldan liccizeað. **1382** Wyclif *Ps.* lxxi[i]. 9 His enemys the erthe shul licken. —— *Micah* vii. 17 Thei shuln lick dust as the serpent. c **1400** *Rom. Rose* 6502 What shulde he yeve that likketh his knyf. **1500** Kennedie *Flyting w. Dunbar* 396 Thou sall lik thy lippis, and suere thou leis. **1530** Palsgr. 609/2, I lycke my lippes or fyngers after swete meate. **1548** Hall *Chron.*, *Hen. VI* 169 b, Marchantes within the citee, sore abhorryng the Italian nation, for lickyng the fat from their beardes, and taking from them their livyng. **1555** Eden *Decades* 104 [They] with no lesse confydence licke their lippes secreately in hope of their praye. **1602** *Withals' Dict.* 263 A fellow that can licke his Lordes or his ladies trencher in one smooth tale or merrie lie, and picke their purses in another. **1610** Shaks. *Temp.* III. ii. 27 How does thy honour? Let me licke thy shooe. **1646** J. Whitaker *Uzziah* 24 Have you not known some in a low condition, to bow and scrape, lick the spittle on the ground. **1656** Ld. Hatton in *Nicholas Papers* (Camden) III. 284 He purposeth not to deale at all with my cosen Kertons frends, vnless it be for mault, and that too in an honorable and considerable way without licking my fingars. **1667** Milton *P.L.* ix. 526 Oft he [the serpent] bowd His turret Crest..and lick'd the ground whereon she trod. **1711** Addison *Spect.* No. 5 ⁋2 Sparrows for the Opera, says his Friend, licking his Lips, what, are they to be roasted? **1808** Cobbett *Pol. Reg.* XIII. 1009 He should have learnt to lick spittle, and have drilled himself to crawl upon his belly. **1860** Reade *Cloister & H.* lv. (1896) 162 He found the surly inn-keepers licked the very ground before him now. **1890** Kipling *Barrack-Room Ballads* (1892) 23 An' you'll lick the bloomin' boots of 'im that's got it. **1909** G. B. Shaw *Press Cuttings* 9 And now comes this unmannerly young whelp Chubbs-Jenkinson, the only son of what they call a soda-king, and orders a curate to lick his boots. **1930** —— *Apple Cart* I. 34, I had rather be a dog than the Prime Minister of a country where the only things the inhabitants can be serious about are football and refreshments. Lick the king's boots: that is all you are fit for. **1937** [see cat *sb.*[1] 2 c]. **1937** *Étude* Dec. 835/1 *Licking their chops*, getting warmed up to swing. **1959** J. Braine *Vodi* x. 138 He had to use his.. willingness to lick anyone's boots, no matter how dirty, to get the money. **1970** C. Major *Dict. Afro-Amer. Slang* 77 *Licking the chops*, the tuning up musicians do before a jam session. **1974** *Guardian* 19 Dec. 10/2 If Lifestyle (BBC-2) keeps licking boots like this, Cherry Blossom will sprout out of its ears.

c. in proverbial sayings.

1523 Skelton *Garl. Laurel* 1438 Wele wotith the cat whos berde she likkith. **1539** Taverner *Erasm. Prov.* (1545) 19 He is an euyll cooke that can not lycke his owne fyngers. **1619** Hollybande *Fr. Schoolem.* 100 b. **1822** Scott *Nigel* vi, They say, a good cook knows how to lick his own fingers.

d. With adverbs, e.g. *over*; to take *in* or *up* by licking. With *away*, †*forth*, *off*, *out*, and with prep. *off*: To remove by licking.

a **1240** *Ureisun* in *Cott. Hom.* 185 Huni þer in beoþ liked of þornes. a **1300** *Cursor M.* 2858 þan es sco [Lot's wife, or the pillar of salt] liked al a-way. **1387** Trevisa *Higden* (Rolls) IV. 93 Hanibal likked venym of his owne rynge. c **1440** *Jacob's Well* 247 þe bysschop wyth his tunge lykkyd it out lowly. **1567** *Gude & Godlie Ball.* (S.T.S.) 40 And oft thay [the doggis] did this catiue man refresche Lickand the fylth furth of his laithlie flesche. **1667** Milton *P.L.* x. 632 My Hell-hounds, to lick up the draff and filth. **1721** Ramsay *Prospect Plenty* ix, O'er lang, in troth, have we by-standers been, And loot fowk lick the white out of our een. **1774** Goldsm. *Nat. Hist.* (1776) III. 77 Their [cows] practice of licking off their hair. *Ibid.* VII. 175 The serpent..was seen to lick the whole body over. **1822** Lamb *Elia* Ser. I. *Praise Chimneysw.*, It was a pleasure to see the sable younkers lick in the unctuous meat.

e. With complementary adj. expressing the result, e.g. *to lick clean*. † *to lick whole*: to heal of wounds or sores by licking; in quots. *fig.*

c **1550** *Disc. Common Weal Eng.* (1893) 32 If anie men haue licked theim selues whole youe be the same. **1596** Bp. W. Barlow *Three Serm.* i. 129 Who vnder a shew of licking them whole, suck out euen their hart blood. **1607** Hieron *Wks.* I. 366 It is not a limme of Satan which is wounded; he might then licke himselfe whole. **1670** Ray *Prov.* 211 And yet betwixt them both, they lick't the platters clean. **1681** Dryden *Sp. Fryar* II. iii, If there were no more in Excommunication than the Church's Censure, a wise Man wou'd lick his Conscience whole with a wet Finger. **1712** Arbuthnot *John Bull* IV. vi, He would quickly lick him-self whole again, by his vails.

†**2.** To lap with the tongue; to drink, sip. Also *intr.* constr. *of*, *on*. *Obs.*

13.. *E.E. Allit. P.* B. 1521 So long likked þise lordes þise lykores swete. **1382** Wyclif *1 Kings* xxi. 19 In this place, in the which houndis lickiden the blood of Naboth, shulen lick and thi blood. a **1400–50** *Alexander* 3826 Sum of his awen vryn & sum on Iren lickid. **1513** Douglas *Æneis* VIII. Prol. 139 Sum langis for the liffyr ill to lik of ane quart. **1535** Coverdale *Judg.* vii. 5 Whosoeuer licketh of the water with his tunge, as a dogg licketh. **1583** Melbancke *Philotimus* 100 The Cat would licke milke, but she will not wette her feete. **1791** Cowper *Iliad* xxi. 148 Lie there, and feed the fishes, which shall lick Thy blood secure.

3. *transf.* and *fig.* (from 1 and 2). **a.** Of persons and animals. Formerly in many specialized uses. † *to lick up* (an enemy's forces): to destroy, 'annihilate' (after Num. xxii. 4). † *to lick* (a person) *of* something: to cheat, 'fleece'. † *to lick the letter*: to use alliteration. † *to lick of the whip*: to have a taste of punishment.

c **1460** *Towneley Myst.* iii. 378 In fayth and for youre long taryyng Ye shal lik on the whyp. [**1535** Coverdale *Num.* xxii. 4 Now shal this heape licke vp all that is aboute vs, euen as an oxe licketh vp the grasse in the field.] **1548** Hall *Chron.*, *Hen. VI* 126 Yet sometyme thei wer slain, taken, and licked vp, or thei were ware. **1557** in Tytler *Hist. Scot.* (1864) III. 388 Three hundred of them [Gascons] be licked up by the way. **1560** Daus tr. *Sleidane's Comm.* 259 b, They confesse the craft themselues, wherby they licked vs of our money. **1599** Marston *Sco. Villanie* I. iv. 188 A crewe.. That lick the tail of greatnesse with their lips. **1605** Camden *Rem.* (1637) 34 The English and Welsh delighted much in licking the letter. **1642** Fuller *Holy & Prof. St.* v. ix. 391 Hypocrites rather then they will lose a drop of praise will lick it up with their own tongue. **1647** Trapp *Comm. Ep. & Rev.* App. 690 Till he had licked of the whip, and learned better language. **1726** *Life Penn* in Wks. 1782 I. 136 Those very lies ..which himself had now licked up afresh.

b. Of inanimate agents (chiefly waves, flame, etc.): To lap, play lightly over, etc.; to take *up* (moisture, etc.) in passing over. Sometimes with personification.

c **1000** *Sax. Leechd.* III. 276 Seo lyft liccað and atyhð ðone wætan of ealre eorþan. **1635** Swan *Spec. M.* v. §2 (1643) 149 Untill the sunne or the wind have licked the tops of the grasse and flowers. **1697** Dryden *Virg. Georg.* III. 698 Feavers..rack their Limbs, and lick the vital Heat. **1827** Pollok *Course T.* III, Consumption licked her blood. **1856** J. H. Newman *Callista* 154 The tide of human beings.. licking the base of the hill, rushed vehemently on one side. **1885–94** R. Bridges *Eros & Psyche* Dec. xxvi, An upleaping jet Of cold Cocytus, which for ever licks Earth's base. **1891** T. Hardy *Tess* II. xxiv, The wheels..licked up the pulverized surface of the highway. **1893** Earl Dunmore *Pamirs* I. 45 The flames..ruthlessly licked up everything in their path of destruction. **1900** *Blackw. Mag.* July 59/2 Fires had consumed the underbrush and licked the branches off the giant trees.

c. Sc. *to lick one's winning(s*: To make the best of one's bargain.

1776 C. Keith *Farmer's Ha'* (1796) 144 But now let us our winning lick (He cry'd in pet). **1794** Burns *'O merry hae I been'* 9 Bitter in dool I lickit my winnins, O' marrying Bess, to gie her a slave.

4. *to lick (a person or thing) into (shape*, etc.), also † *to lick over*: To give form and regularity to; to mould, make presentable. Alluding to the alleged practice of bears with their young (see quots.).

[**1413** *Pilgr. Sowle* (Caxton 1483) IV. xxiv. 70 Beres ben brought forthe al fowle and transformyd and after that by lyckynge of the fader and the moder they ben brought in to theyr kyndely shap.] **1612** Chapman *Widowes T.* Wks. 1873 III. 31 He has not licked his whelp into full shape yet. **1621** Burton *Anat. Mel.* Democr. to Rdr. (1676) 7/2 Enforced, as a Bear doth her Whelps, to bring forth this confused lump, I had not time to lick it into form. a **1639** Wotton in *Reliq.* (1685) 444 The Author hath licked them [verses] over. **1699** Burnet *39 Art.* xxviii. (1700) 339 Men did not know how to mould and frame it; but at last it was licked into shape. **1702** *Eng. Theophrast.* 4 The play is writ, the Players upon the recommendation of those that lick'd it over, like their parts to a Fondness. **1780** Wesley *Wks.* (1872) IX. 509 Mr. Law, by taking immense pains, has licked it into some shape. **1862** Mrs. Carlyle *Lett.* III. 132, I shall have trouble enough in licking her [a young servant] into shape. **1891** *Spectator* 12 Dec. 837 Their proposals..would be licked, by debate.. into practicable shape.

5. Contemptuously used for: To smear with cosmetics; to varnish, to smarten with paint; to 'sleek', give smooth finish to (a picture).

1596 Nashe *Saffron Walden* Wks. (Grosart) III. 99 Spending a whole forenoone euerie day in spunging and licking himselfe by the glasse. a **1700** B. E. *Dict. Cant. Crew*, *Lickt*, Pictures new Varnished, Houses new Whitened, or Women's Faces with a Wash. **1853** T. Taylor *Life B.R. Haydon* III. 212 Modern cartoons with few exceptions are licked (smoothed) and polished intentionally.

6. *slang.* **a.** To beat, thrash. Also, to drive (something) *out of* (a person) by thrashing. † *to lick off*: to cut off clean, to slice off.

1535 Stewart *Cron. Scot.* (1858) I. 144 Leggis war likkit of hard of at the kne. **1567** Harman *Caveat* s.v. (Farmer), *Lycke*, to beate. **1719** Ramsay *To Hamilton* vi, May I be licket wi' a bittle, Gin of your numbers I think little. **1732** Fielding *Mock Doctor* I. ii, Suppose I've a mind he should drub, Whose bones are they, Sir, he's to lick? **1775** Mad. D'Arblay *Diary*, *Let. to Mr. Crisp* 19 Nov., As for..your father, I could lick him for his affected coolness and moderation. **1828** Darwin in *Life & Lett.* (1888) I. 167 How these poor dogs must have been licked. **1857** Hughes *Tom Brown* I. viii. (1871) 109 Say you won't fag—they'll soon get tired of licking you. **1879** Spurgeon *Serm.* XXV. 542 Almost as free as America in the olden time, when every man was free to lick his own nigger. **1881** *Atlantic Monthly* XLIX. 41 Well, I've tried to lick the badness out of him... You can, out of some boys, you know.

b. To overcome, get the better of; to excel, surpass. *it licks me*: I cannot explain it. Also *to lick into fits*: to defeat thoroughly.

1800 in *Spirit Pub. Jrnls.* IV. 232 By Dane, Saxon, or Pict We had never been lick'd Had we stuck to the king of the island. **1836** F. B. Head *Let.* in Smiles *Mem. J. Murray* (1891) II. xxxi. 366, I believe we shall lick the radicals. **1847** De Quincey *Milton v. Southey & Landor* Wks. (1859) XII. 179 Greece was..proud..of having licked him [an enemy]. **1879** E. Walford *Londiniana* I. 37 If we have a war and beat Russia or lick Abyssinia into fits. **1889** 'Rolf Boldrewood' *Robbery under Arms* xxiv, It licked me to think it had been hid away all the time. **1890** —— *Col. Reformer* (1891) 195 As a seller of unparalleled generosity, we can't be licked. **1900** *Speaker* 8 Sept. 618 We must either lick and rule these savages or run away.

absol. **1861** Hughes *Tom Brown at Oxf.* xii. (1889) 114, I believe that a gentleman will always lick in a fair fight.

7. *slang.*, (orig. *dial.*: widespread outside the U.K.). *intr.* To run, ride, or move at full speed. Also in the U.S., *to lick it.*

1850 L. H. Garrard *Wah-to-Yah* i. 16 The mad animal ..charged. How they did 'lick it' over the ground! **1856** J. Collie *Poems* 124 Sae aff gaed Death what he cou'd lick. **1886** *Outing* Dec. 198/1 He'd nothin' ter do but ter lick it like blazes, with the little dog a-follerin' along. **1889** 'Rolf Boldrewood' *Robbery under Arms* xxi, A horseman.. rattled down the stony track as hard as he could lick. **1903** J. Lumsden *Toorle* iv. i. 76 Jock! lick awa' in, an' blaw up. **1947** 'A. P. Gaskell' *Big Game* 80 He sped her [*sc.* a car] along. Boy, she can lick. **1953** M. Traynor *Eng. Dial. Donegal* 169/1 *As hard as one can lick*, as fast as one can go. *To lick along*, to go fast. **1966** W. S. Ramson *Austral. Eng.* iv. 65 *To lick*, meaning 'to travel fast' and common in..*as hard as one can lick*.

8. Combs.: **lick-box** *nonce-wd.* ? = lick-dish; **lick-fingers**, one who licks his fingers (used as a term of abuse); **lick-foot** *nonce-wd.*, the action of licking the feet, servility; † **lick-halter** (see quot.); **lick-hole** *Austral.*, a place where lick-logs are placed for stock to lick; **lick-ladle**, a parasite; **lick-log**, a block of salt for cattle to lick; *to stand up to one's lick-logs*, to make a firm stand; **lick-ma-dowp** *Sc. nonce-wd.*, a sycophant; **lick-platter**, a parasite; **lick-sauce** = lick-dish; **lick-spit** = lick-spittle; **lick-trencher** = *lick-platter*; **lick-up**, (*a*) something that licks up (see quot. 1844); (*b*) something 'licked' into shape (see quot. 1851–61); (*c*) used *attrib.* to designate a type of paper-making machine (see quots.). Also lick-dish, lick-penny, lick-pot, lick-spigot, lick-spittle.

1611 Cotgr., *Liche-casse*, a *lick-box, a sweet-lips. **1653** Urquhart *Rabelais* II. xxx, Achilles was a scauld pated maker of hay bundles, Agamemnon a lick-box. **1595** *Locrine* III. iv. F 2 b, You stopsauce, *lickfingers, will you not heare? [**1625** B. Jonson *Staple News*, The Persons of the Play, *Lick-finger*, a Master Cooke, and parcell Poet.] **1630** —— *New Inn* II. ii, No flattery for't, No *lick-foot, pain of losing your proboscis. **1611** Florio, *Lecca fune*, a *licke-halter, a knauish wag, a gallowes-clapper. **1928** 'Brent of Bin Bin' *Up Country* ix. 143 No horse..was safe..in the *lick-hole country of its myriad spring-heads. Pool found a way with rock-salt to make the lick-holes a trap. **1936** M. Franklin *All that Swagger* xvi. 148 A hint without evidence is a snake in the grass, like that boomer you dispatched to-day at the lickhole. **1849** James *Woodman* ii, 'Who and what is he?' 'A *lickladle of the court, lady'. **1834** D. Crockett *Narr. Life* 170, I was determined to stand up to my *lick-log, salt or no salt. **1840** Haliburton *Clockm.* Ser. III. xii, I like a man to be up to the notch, and stand to his lick-log. **1852** G. W. L. Bickley *Hist. Tazewell County* 226 Capt. Moore..was at a lick log..salting his horses of which he had many. **1948** E. N. Dick *Dixie Frontier* 105 Small troughs were cut in the trunk of a fallen tree and occasionally salt was placed there, making what was known as a 'lick log'. **1724** Ramsay *Vision* xxiii, Quhen thus redust to howps, They dander, and wander About pure *lickmadowps. **1853** Lytton *My Novel* VI. xxiii. II. 186 No *lick-platter, no parasite, no toadeater. **1822** T. Mitchell *Aristoph.* II. 302 Him..who has A smutty tale for ev'ry rich man's table? *Lickspit and flatterer both! **1833** Sarah Austin *Charac. Goethe* II. 35 To play..the lickspit about the court of Weimar. **1571** Golding *Calvin on Ps.* To Rdr. 9 Not onely *licktrenchers but also claw backs, which curry fauour with great men by their false appeachings. **1787** Wolcot (P. Pindar) *Ode upon Ode* Wks. 1816 I. 298 Butlers and lick-trenchers. **1844** *Mech. Mag.* XL. 47 [Of Silver plating.] When cool the hammer is allowed to fall upon the lead, to which it firmly adheres by means of a plate roughed as a rasp, which is called the **lick-up.* **1851–61** Mayhew *Lond. Labour* II. 34 A 'lick-up' is a boot or shoe re-lasted to take the wrinkles out..and then blacked up to hide blemishes. **1929** Clapperton & Henderson *Mod. Paper-Making* xv. 212 The 'lick-up' machine may have either a vat or Fourdrinier wet end, but it does not possess a wet press... On this type of machine the underside of the web sticks to the cylinder and receives the polished surface. **1952** F. H. Norris *Paper & Paper Making* xv. 208 The 'lick up' type of machine..may have either a cylinder mould to pick up the stuff out of a vat and form the paper as on a board machine, or it may have the normal Fourdrinier wet end. On a 'lick up' machine, the wet felt also acts as an over-felt, and as there is no wet press, the web is transferred to the wet felt at the top couch roll.

† **ˈlick-dish.** *Obs.* [f. lick *v.* + dish *sb.*]

1. A parasite.

c **1440** *Promp. Parv.* 304/2 Lykdysshe, *scurra.* **1519** Horman *Vulg.* 77 Smellefyestes, lyckedysshes, and franchars come vncalled. **1681** W. Robertson *Phraseol. Gen.* (1693) 824 A lick-dish, *catillo.*

2. Used allusively (see quot. 1562).

[**1562** J. Heywood *Prov. & Epigr.* (1867) 64 She will lie as fast as a dogge will licke a dishe.] **1575** *Gamm. Gurton* v. ii.

252 Thou lier lickdish, didst not say the neele wold be gitten? **1631** [see LIAR (*Proverbs*)].

licked (lɪkt), *ppl. a.* [f. LICK *v.* + -ED[1].] In senses of the vb.

1763 *Brit. Mag.* July 337/2 Went cutting away with that fork and his licked knife. **1896** DU MAURIER *Martian* (1897) 43 The licked one..dabbed his swollen eye with a wet pocket-handkerchief.

lickell, *Obs.* jocular or colloq. form of LITTLE.

licken, *v. Obs.* exc. *dial.* [altered form of LIPPEN *v.*] *intr.* To trust *to*.

1535 COVERDALE *Hos.* xi. 5 The stoare that they haue lickened vnto, shall be destroyed and eaten vp. **1888** in *Sheffield Gloss.* s.v. *Lippen*, 'I know what to likken to'. 'He's nowt to likken to'.

lickenesse, obs. form of LIKENESS.

licker ('lɪkə(r)). [f. LICK *v.* + -ER[1].] **a.** One who or something which licks; *spec.* in sense 6 of the verb. Also ***licker-up***; in *silver-plating* = *lick-up* (see LICK *v.* 8).

1440 *Promp. Parv.* 305/1 Lykkare, or he þat lykkythe, *lecator.* **1552** HULOET, Licker, *lictor.* **1839** URE *Dict. Arts* 999 Plated manufacture..The under face of the stamp-hammer has a plate of iron called the *licker-up* fitted into it. **1860** GEN. P. THOMPSON *Audi Alt.* III. cxxxviii. III Being acquiescent lickers-up of ministerial dishonour. **1894** A. MORRISON *Martin Hewitt* ii. 66 'There's no footprint here nor outside.'.. 'That's a licker,' he said. **1895** J. T. CLEGG *Works* I. 375 Iv that's ony credit to Walsden it's a licker to me! **1898** *Daily News* 4 Apr. 8/3 The licker of red-hot irons was briskly following his profession. **1902** *Eng. Dial. Dict.* III. 587/1 Fatther, this sum is a licker; will yo' du it for mha? **1907** *Daily Chron.* 31 July 4/7 The licking his Majesty once suffered..[and] the half-crown the late Queen gave the licker for his pluck. **1908** A. S. M. HUTCHINSON *Once aboard Lugger* VI. viii. 456 Into a chair Bill collapsed... He gasped 'George, this is a licker, a fair licker.'

b. ***licker-in***, the cylinder in a carding-machine which receives the cotton, wool, etc., from the feed-rollers and passes it on to the main cylinder. Also *attrib.*

1850 *Rep. Comm. Patents 1849* (U.S.) 198, I do not claim a licker-in, nor the first main cylinder as such. **1884** [see BURRING *vbl. sb.*[1]]. **1884** W. S. B. MCLAREN *Spinning* 84 To assist the process..the licker-in rollers are sometimes made hollow, and steam is allowed to fill them. **1888** [see BREAST *sb.* 9 h]. **1892** [see GARNETT *sb.*]. **1946** A. J. HALL *Stand. Handbk. Textiles* iii. 101 The cotton in lap form from the scutching machine is fed on to one of the small rollers (termed the licker-in).

†**lickering**, *a. Obs. rare*$^{-1}$. ? = LICKERISH.

1578 T. P. *Gorg. Gal. Gall. Inventions* K, My lust alluers my lickering lyppes to taste.

lickerish, liquorish ('lɪkərɪʃ), *a.* Forms: 5 liccoris, 6 licoryce, likerishe, -yshe, 6–7 licourish, 7 liccorish, li(c)korish, liquerish, liquourish, licquo(u)rish, 8 likerish, 6–9 lickerish, licorish, liquorish. [Altered form of LICKEROUS, with substitution of suffix -ISH for *-ous*.]

†**1.** Pleasant to the palate; *gen.* sweet, tempting, attractive; = LICKEROUS 1. Of a cook: Skilful in preparing dainties. *Obs.*

1579–80 NORTH *Plutarch* (1595) 50 The deuises of lickerish cookes. **1607** SHAKS. *Timon* IV. iii. 194 With Licourish draughts And Morsels Vnctious. **1615** tr. *De Monfart's Surv. E. Indies* 20 There is another very licquorish fruit. **1634** MILTON *Comus* 700 And wouldst thou seek again to trap me here With lickerish baits fit to ensnare a brute? **1653** A. WILSON *Jas. I*, 37 He [Bacon] was one of those that smoothed his way to a full ripeness by liquorish and pleasing passages. **1728** TICKELL *Horn Bk.* 18 Or if to Ginger Bread thou shalt descend, And Liquorish Learning to thy Babes extend.

2. Of persons, etc.: Fond of delicious fare; = LICKEROUS 2. †Const. *after*, *of*.

?*a* **1500** *Chester Pl.* II. 199 And of that tree of Paradise she shall eate through my coyntice; For women are full liccoris [*v.r.* licorous]. **1553** T. WILSON *Rhet.* 66 Likeryshe of tongue, lighte of taile. **1561** AWDELAY *Frat. Vacab.* 13 This is a licoryce knaue that will swill his Maisters drink. *a* **1632** T. TAYLOR *God's Judgem.* vii. II. (1642) 102 Yet was he lickerish also after any..rarity that was sent into his Table. **1664** EVELYN *Sylva* 42 Cattel being excessively licorish of their leaves and tender buds. **1690** LOCKE *Govt.* I. vi. §57 (1694) 55 They were so liquorish after Mans Flesh, that [etc.]. **1719** LONDON & WISE *Compl. Gard.* 283 Green Peas are ready to satisfie the longing Appetite of the likerish Palate. **1802** G. COLMAN *Br. Grins, Knight & Friar* I. lx, A liquorish black rat Lured by the cook to sniff and smell her bacon. **1828** SOUTHEY in *Q. Rev.* XXXVIII. 201 The holy man..had a licorish tooth. **1879** W. E. HEITLAND *Q. Curtius* Introd. 29 He [Alexander] drank..rather by way of good-fellowship than from a liquorish appetite.

b. *gen.* and *fig.* Eagerly desirous, longing, greedy; = LICKEROUS 2 b.

1579 TOMSON *Calvin's Serm. Tim.* 384/1 The people.. must not bee so lickerish to desire vnprofitable things. **1627** J. CARTER *Expos.* 3 This propertie every one is most liquorish of, taking after their great grand-mother Eve. *a* **1639** WOTTON *Life Dk. Buckhm.* in *Reliq.* (1651) 99 Certain rare Manuscripts..were upon sale to the Jesuits at Antwerp, licourish Chapmen of such Ware. **1658** OSBORN *Adv. Son* (1673) 77 Be not therefore licorish after Fame. **1704** SWIFT *T. Tub* Wks. 1760 I. 60 Their own liquorish affection to gold. **1834** BENTHAM *Deontol.* in *Westm. Rev.* XXI. 9 He might have a lickerish leaning towards the trade of Cacus. **1873** H. ROGERS *Orig. Bible* (1875) 11 Jewish human nature..showed so intense a sympathy with the general tendency to idolatry, as to cast a liquorish eye on every wandering form of it that came near them.

3. Lecherous, lustful; = LICKEROUS 3.

1600 HEYWOOD *1st Pt. Edw. IV*, Wks. 1874 I. 51 Go to, Nell..ye may be caught, I tell ye: these be liquorish lads. **1700** DRYDEN *Wife of Bath* 319 The liquorish hag rejects the pelf with scorn. **1749** FIELDING *Tom Jones* v. xii, Thou art a liquorish dog. **1828** LAMB *Wife's Trial*, The lickerish culprit, almost dead with fear. **1881** SWINBURNE in *Fortn. Rev.* Feb. 133 The smirk of a liquorish fribble.

4. *Comb.*, as ***lickerish-lipped*** adj.

1577 tr. *Bullinger's Decades* (1592) 154 Let euery young man be..not licorish lipped, nor dainty toothed.

Hence **'lickerishly** *adv.*

a **1661** FULLER *Worthies* I. (1662) 116 His expression *licking the Chancery* hath left Posterity to interpret it.. liquorishly longing for that Place.

'lickerishness. [f. LICKERISH *a.* + -NESS.] Love of good fare; *gen.* keen appetite or desire.

1580 HOLLYBAND *Treas. Fr. Tong, Friandise*, licorous thinges, licourishnesse. **1594** T. B. *La Primaud. Fr. Acad.* II. 293 Meere lickerishnes causeth vs to eate such meats as we know are contrary to our health. **1656** J. HARRINGTON *Oceana* (1700) 152 Where there is a liquorishness in a popular Assembly to debate. **1658** OSBORN *Jas. I*, 134 Their Governours licorishnesse after the choyce morsells of the Church. **1733** CHEYNE *Eng. Malady* II. v. §10 (1734) 168 The Snare and Temptation that Liquorishness and high Relish throws many into. **1827** HONE *Every-day Bk.* II. 35 The boy..moved by lickerishness, began to eat.

†**'lickerous**, *a. Obs.* Forms: 3–6 li-, lykerous, (4 lykerus, 5 lykerowse, lykorous, lykkerwys, lekerous, likerose, licrus, likrus), 5–7 licorous, licourous, lycorous(e, (5 lycourous, lycours, lycoruse, 6 lycoures, licoras, likorous, 7 likresse), 6–7 liquorous, lickerous, -orous. [a. AF. **likerous*, **lekerous*, repr. a northern var. of OF. *lecheros* LECHEROUS; cf. ONF. *liquerie* = Central OF. *lecherie* lechery.

In Eng. use this form of the word has chiefly retained its etymological sense (cf., however, sense 3), while *lecherous* has been almost confined to a transferred application.]

1. Pleasing or tempting to the palate. Also *gen.* and *fig.*: Sweet, pleasant, delightful.

c **1275** *XI Pains Hell* 172 in *O.E. Misc.* 228 þo weore þeose þat..hedden of mony metes de-deyn, But hit weore likerous be certeyn. *a* **1310** in Wright *Lyric P.* xxv. 68 Noht may be feled lykerusere, Then thou so suete alumere. **1340** *Ayenb.* 47 þe zofte bed cloþes likerouses. *c* **1380** WYCLIF *Wks.* (1880) 216 Lekerous metis & drynkis. *a* **1450** *Knt. de la Tour* (1868) 22 No woman shulde ete no lycorous morcelles in the absens..of her husbond. **1549** LATIMER *5th Serm. bef. Edw. VI* (Arb.) 139 *marg.*, Lucre is so lickorous that he that once lyckes of it, leketh it. **1577–87** HOLINSHED *Chron.* I. 19/2, I would not be his ghest, vnlesse I tooke his table to be furnisht with more wholesome and licorous viands. **1597** BEARD *Theatre God's Judgem.* li. (1631) 536 Beeing fed with the licorous and deceitfull sweetnesse of their owne lusts. **1603** H. CROSSE *Vertues Commw.* (1878) 47 O tis an amiable diuel, a sweete sinne, a lycorous poyson.

2. Of persons, the appetite, etc.: Fond of choice or delicious food; dainty in eating; greedy of good fare. Const. *of*, *after*.

c **1315** SHOREHAM 160 And et throf dame lykerouse. **1362** LANGL. *P. Pl.* A. VII. 253 Let not sir Surfet sitten at thi bord; ..for he is a lechour and likerous of tonge. *c* **1380** WYCLIF *Serm.* Sel. Wks. I. 2 For þis riche man was boastful in speche and likerous in foode. *a* **1450** *Knt. de la Tour* (1868) 53 There be..other that be lykerous of moche mete and drinke. **1530** PALSGR. 317/1 Lycorouse or daynty mouthed, *friant.* **1599** NASHE *Lenten Stuffe* 54 The Popes caterer casting a licorous glaunce that way. *a* **1632** G. HERBERT *Priest to Temple* xxvi. Wks. (Grosart) III. 183 He that..for quality is licorous after dainties, is a glutton. **1632** LITHGOW *Trav.* v. 182 These Iarres are..interlarded with pitch to preserue the ..Wine; yet making the taste thereof vnpleasant to liquorous lips. **1653** URQUHART *Rabelais* II. xiv. 98 These devils are very lickorous of lardons.

b. *gen.* and *fig.* Having a keen relish or desire for something pleasant. Const. *of*; also, eager *to do* something.

c **1386** CHAUCER *Frankl. T.* 391 Yonge clerkes that been lykerous To reden Artes than been curious. *c* **1400** *Destr. Troy* 444 Syn wemen are..so likrus of loue in likyng of yowthe. **1555** W. WATREMAN *Fardle Facions* II. viii. 178 Whiche..liue a pure and simple life, led with no likerous lustes of other mennes vanitie. *a* **1586** SIDNEY *Arcadia* I. (1622) 82 Fit commendation (whereof womankind is so likerous). **1598** E. GUILPIN *Skial* (1878) 32 For though it be no cates sharpe sauce it is, To lickerous vanitie. *a* **1632** G. HERBERT *Temple, Discharge* i, Busy inquiring heart, what wouldst thou know Why dost thou pry, And turn and leer, and with a licorous eye Look high and low.

3. Lecherous, lustful, wanton.

1377 LANGL. *P. Pl.* B. x. 161 The likerouse launde that Leccherye hatte. *c* **1386** CHAUCER *Miller's T.* 58 And sikerly she hadde a likerous eye. *a* **1420** HOCCLEVE *De Reg. Princ.* 1762 This likerous dampnable errour [adultery]. **1470–85** MALORY *Arthur* XVIII. xxv, Men and wymmen coude loue to gyders seuen yeres and no lycours lustes were bitwene them. **1587** TURBERV. *Trag. T.* 15 Whilst thus Nastagio sought his owne decay, By liquorous lust. **1604** DRAYTON *Owl* 369 There in soft Downe the liquorous Sparrow sat. **1611** COTGR. s.v. *Femme*, From women light, and lickorous, good fortune still deliuer vs.

4. *Comb.*, as ***lickerous-mouthed***, ***-toothed*** adjs.

c **1579–80** NORTH *Plutarch* (1595) 285 Like vnto lickerous mouthed men, who..desire meates with a greedy appetite. **1598** E. GUILPIN *Skial.* (1878) 9 Once Rinus saw a pretty lasse, And liquorous tooth'd desir'd to tast.

Hence †**'lickerously** *adv.*

c **1315** SHOREHAM 114 To meche fode devoury; and to lykerouslyche. *c* **1386** CHAUCER *Monk's T.* 567 Oloferne, which fortune ay kiste So likerously. **1426** LYDG. *De Guil. Pilgr.* 12915 Fatte mussellys large and Rounde, I threste hem in ffu l lykerously. **1580** HOLLYBAND *Treas. Fr. Tong. Friander*, to feed licorously.

†**'lickeroushead.** *Obs. rare*$^{-1}$. In 5 likeroushed. [f. LICKEROUS *a.* + -HEAD.] Lickerousness.

c **1440** *Jacob's Well* 144 Vsyng of mete..no3t only in likeroushed [*printed* liberoushed], but for pompe, to make manye messys.

†**lickerousness.** *Obs.* [f. LICKEROUS + -NESS.] Fondness for good fare; *gen.* keen appetite or desire. Const. *of*, *after*, *inf.* with *to*. Also, lecherousness.

c **1380** WYCLIF *Wks.* (1880) 61 Likerousnesse & lustis of here bely. *c* **1386** CHAUCER *Wife's Prol.* 611 Venus me yaf my lust, my likerousnesse. *c* **1386** —— *Pars. T.* ¶667 Auarice.. is likerousnesse in herte to haue erthely thynges. *c* **1440** *Promp. Parv.* 304/2 Lykerowsnesse, *delicacia.* *a* **1586** SIDNEY *Arcadia* v. (1622) 450 Whether..the likerousnesse of dominion [can] make you beyond iustice. *a* **1638** MEDE *Wks.* I. (1672) 128 As perhaps licorousness of Wine before had caused many of them to do. **1657** REEVE *God's Plea* 129 A people..so given over to licorousnesse, that it is an hard thing to get a Cook to please them. **1665** J. SPENCER *Vulg. Proph.* 119 That natural liquorousness in the minds of men after the knowledg of things to come.

lickety ('lɪkətɪ), *adv. colloq.* (chiefly *U.S.*). Also 9 lickitie; lickerty, licketty, -ity, -oty. [Fanciful; cf. LICK *sb.* 6, LICK *v.* 7.] Usu. prefixed to another word, as **lickety-split**, at full speed; headlong. Also (nonce-wd.) as *vb.* Also ***lickety-cut***, ***-smash***, ***-wallop***, etc.

1817 D. MCKILLOP *Poems* 33, I rattl'd owre the A, B, C, as fast as lickitie An' read like hickitie. **1831** *Boston Even. Transcript* 4 June 2/2 He ran down the street licketty cut, and is probably at home by this time. **1847** J. S. ROBB *Streaks of Squatter Life* 116 Away they started, 'lickety-click', and arrived at the winning-post within touching distance of each other. **1848** in *Amer. Speech* (1935) X. 40 *Lickoty liner*, going very fast. **1858** *Harper's Mag.* May 766/2 There they had it, lickety-switch, rough-and-tumble. **1859** BARTLETT *Dict. Amer.* (ed. 2) *Lickety Split*, very fast, headlong; synonymous with the equally elegant phrase 'full chisel'. 'He went lickety split down hill.' **1863** L. M. ALCOTT *Hospital Sk.* iii. 40 When my mate, Eph Sylvester, caved, with a bullet through his head, I got mad, and pitched in, licketty cut. **1869** MRS. STOWE *Oldtown Folks* xxviii. 358, I tell you if they didn't whip up an' go lickety-split down that 'ere hill. **1886** [see BUMP *v.*[1] 2 e]. **1897** [see BAND *sb.*[3] 4 b]. **1911** R. D. SAUNDERS *Col. Todhunter* ix. 122 You're worse'n a old huntin' dog that goes sky-hootin' off lickety-split after a rabbit. **1928** 'BRENT OF BIN BIN' *Up Country* ix. 141 They rattled the vehicle lickety-smash at a hand-gallop across the flower-strewn plains. **1934** W. SAROYAN *Daring Young Man* (1935) 131 And then he was running lickety split across the school grounds. **1949** O. NASH *Versus* 111 Firemen, what is your destination?.. You have lickety-splitted by so often that my thoughts Are utterly split-licketed. **1949** POWYS & BOLTON tr. *Guitry's Don't Listen Ladies* in *Plays of Year* I. 566, I was coming along the street not thinking of anything, and suddenly you came out and shot past me, lickerty-split. **1949** WODEHOUSE *Uncle Dynamite* iii. 48 If I was you, I'd hop into that car of yours and drive lickerty-split to London and get another bust. **1955** E. POUND *Classic Anthol.* II. 87 We took out our cars lickety-clickety at the call. **1960** V. NABOKOV *Bend Sinister* ii. 17 The old men overtook him in their turn, clattering lickety-split through the mist. **1961** B. FERGUSSON *Watery Maze* x. 245 While going lickety-spit.. they had come up against the formidable 15th Panzer Grenadier Division.., and they were lucky not to have been chased into the sea. **1972** A. FOWLES *Double Feature* xiii. 240 If one of his outriders radios in that Chau Chieu is there he'll come licketty split. **1972** *Last Whole Earth Catalog* (Portola Inst.) 305/3 Just like that. Stopped in here a few minutes, then took off up that creek lickety-split.

lickham(e, variant of LICHAM *Obs.*

licking ('lɪkɪŋ), *vbl. sb.* [f. LICK *v.* + -ING[1].]

1. The action of the vb. LICK; the action of passing the tongue over something, of fashioning into shape, etc.; †also, the action of daubing or smearing the face with paint.

1387 TREVISA *Higden* (Rolls) IV. 435 Bestes..among hem self þey useþ cusses and likkynge and strokynge. *c* **1440** *Promp. Parv.* 305/1 Lykky[n]ge of howndys, or other beestis, *lictus.* **1549** COVERDALE *Erasm. Par.* Ded. 2 What costly deckyng, lyckinge, censinge, and worshipping of ymages. **1623** BP. HALL *Serm.* v. 154 It scorneth to woo favour with farding and licking and counterfeisance. **1631** GOUGE *God's Arrows* III. xcv. 363 By the daily licking of his rankling wounds with the tongue of lady Elenor his wife, he is said to be cured. *a* **1635** NAUNTON *Fragm. Reg.* (Arb.) 27 Besides the licking of his own fingers, he [Dudley] got the King a masse of riches. *a* **1656** BP. HALL *Sel. Th.* §13 Jezebel, for all the licking, is cast out of the window and trodden to dirt in the streets. **1737** FIELDING *Hist. Reg.* III. Wks. 1882 X. 227 Shakespeare was a pretty fellow, and said some things which only want a little of my licking to do well enough. *Mod.* He is somewhat uncouth; he wants licking into shape.

b. *concr.* in pl. (See quot.)

1851 *Illustr. Catal. Gt. Exhib.* 207 Coarse broad salt; exported for the fisheries... Pickings, or cattle lickings.

2. *colloq.* A beating, thrashing. *lit.* and *fig.*

1756 TOLDERVY *Hist. 2 Orphans* II. 151, I gave him such a licking, I question whether he didn't carry some of the bruises with'n to the grave. **1780** in F. Moore *Songs & Ball. Amer. Rev.* (1856) 307 The fray assum'd, the generals thought, The color of a lickin'. **1806–7** J. BERESFORD *Miseries Hum. Life* (1826) III. xiii, Obliged to take a severe licking from a boy twice as big..as yourself. **1818** KEATS *Let.* Wks. 1889 III. 115 He praised Thomson and Cowper, but he gave Crabbe a most unmerciful licking. **1831** PALMERSTON 29 May in H. L. Bulwer *Life* II. VIII. 81 The moment they [the Belgians] stir a step to attack Holland, they will get a most exemplary licking. **1879** G. MEREDITH

Egoist ix. (1889) 74 The power to take a licking is better worth having than the power to administer one.

3. *attrib.*, as *licking-bout*; † **licking-medicine**, an electuary; **licking-place** *U.S.* = LICK *sb.* 2; so *licking-pond*.

1597 GERARDE *Herbal* I. lxxxv. 137 This rosted.. Onion.. is used in a licking medicine against an old rotten cough. **1652** CULPEPPER *Eng. Physic* (1656) 144 The juyce [of Liquoris] dissolved in Rose-water with some Gum-Tragacanth is a fine licking Medicine for Hoarsness, Wheesings, &c. **1751** J. BARTRAM *Observ. Trav. Pennsylv.* etc. 27 The back parts of our country are full of these licking [*printed* liching] ponds; some are.. of pale clay, the deer.. are fond of licking this clay. *Ibid.* 68 We.. travelled along a rich hill side,.. then down to a Licking-place. **1762** P. COLLINSON in W. Darlington *Mem.* (1849) 238 Their bones or skeletons are now standing in a licking-place, not far from the Ohio. **1775** MAD. D'ARBLAY *Diary, Let. to Mr. Crisp* Dec., Times are much alter'd since I gave him such a thorough licking-bout at back gammon.

licking (ˈlɪkɪŋ), *ppl. a.* [f. LICK *v.* + -ING².] That licks. Of a flame: = LAMBENT. Also *slang*, first-rate, 'splendid' (cf. *thumping*, *whacking*).

1648 [see GENTLE *a.* 10]. **1680** COTTON *Compl. Gamester* xiv. 91, I will briefly describe it [Bone-Ace], and the rather because it is a licking Game for Money. **1899** E. PHILLPOTTS *Human Boy* 182 The thing was, to make a licking big frame of light wood.

lickle, childish or illiterate form of LITTLE.

lickly, obs. form of LIKELY.

licknesse, obs. form of LIKENESS.

† **ˈlickpenny.** *Obs.* [f. LICK *v.*] One who or that which 'licks up' the pennies; something that 'makes the money go'. Also *attrib.*

14.. ? LYDG. (*title*) London Lyckpeny. *c* **1600** DAY *Begg. Bednall Gr.* II. ii. (1881) 34 London lick penny call ye it,—t'as lick'd me with a witness. **1607** DEKKER *Sir T. Wyatt* Wks. 1873 III. 116 *Wiat.* Sweet musicke, gallant fellow Londoners. *Clo.* Y faith we are the madcaps, we are the lickpennies. **1648** GAGE *West Ind.* xix. (1655) 151 Their Religion is a dear and lick-penny religion for such poor Indians. **1694** DRYDEN *Love Triumphant* I. i, She has two devils in her eyes; that last ogle was a lick-penny. **1824** SCOTT *St. Ronan's* xxviii, Law is a lick-penny, Mr. Tyrrel.

† **ˈlickpot.** *Obs.* [f. LICK *v.* + POT *sb.*]

1. A name for the first finger.

1387 TREVISA *Higden* (Rolls) VII. 73 Whiche fynger som men clepeþ likpot þat is þe fynger next þe thombe. *c* **1440** *Promp. Parv.* 305/1 Lykpot fyngyr, *index.* *c* **1475** *Pict. Voc.* in Wr.-Wülcker 752/36 *Hic index*, a lykpot.

2. A pot out of which medicine may be licked.

1665 NEEDHAM *Med. Medicinæ* 283 Their Nutritive Messes, Lick-pots, and Pectorals.

licksome, dial. variant of LIKESOME.

† **ˈlick-spigot.** *Obs.* [f. LICK *v.* + SPIGOT.] One who licks the spigot; a contemptuous name for a tapster or drawer; also, a parasite.

1599 NASHE *Lenten Stuffe* Wks. (Grosart) V. 300–1 Let the cunningest licke-spiggot swelt his heart out, the beere shal neuer foame or froath in the cupp. **1599** MIDDLETON, etc. *Old Law* IV. i, *Cook* (*to the Drawer*) Fill, lick-spiggot! **1607** TOPSELL *Four-f. Beasts* 509 Parasites.. whom the Germans call *Schmorotzer* and *Tellerlecker*, that is, smell-feasts and lick-spickets. **1611** CHAPMAN *May Day* Plays 1873 II. 362, I know the old lickspiggot will be nibling a little when he can come too't. **1700** E. WARD *Lond. Spy* II. iii. 4 He that salutes the old Lick-spiggot with other Title than that of Mr. Church-Warden runs the hazard of Paying double Taxes.

ˈlick-spittle. [f. LICK *v.* + SPITTLE.] **a.** An abject parasite or sycophant; a toady.

[**1629** DAVENANT *Albovine* III. Gib, Lick her spittle From the ground. This disguiz'd humilitie Is both the swift, and safest way to pride.] **1825** J. WILSON *Noct. Ambr.* Wks. 1855 I. 40 To hear his lickspittles speak you would think that a man of great and versatile talents was a miracle. **1851** BORROW *Lavengro* III. 319 It is only in England that literary men are invariably lick-spittles. **1883** J. HAWTHORNE *Dust* I. 4 Stage-coachmen were.. comrades to gentlemen, lickspittles to lords. **1890** C. MARTYR *W. Phillips* 76 The South omnipotent and imperious, the North its errand-boy and lick-spittle.

attrib. **1840** THACKERAY *Catherine* ii. Wks. 1869 XXII. 36 A cringing baseness, and lickspittle awe of rank.

b. The practice of toadying.

1914 A. HARRISON *Kaiser's War* 112 A social system of formality, lick-spittle, bullying, and brutality.

Hence (or as a back-formation from the *vbl. sb.*) as *v. trans.*, to toady to (a person). **ˈlickspittling** *vbl. sb.*, toadying.

1839 *Blackw. Mag.* XLV. 767 Such more than oriental prostration, such lick-spittling,.. you never saw in your life. **1886** *Tinsley's Mag.* July 54 Demagogues who have not the chance of lick-spittling princes. **1927** *Daily Express* 2 May 12/3 Christ criticised the sins of the Church His mother attended, and got His reward. He did not lickspittle the wealthy.

† **ˈlickster.** *Obs. rare*⁻¹. In 4 lyckestre. [f. LICK *v.* + -STER.] A female who licks; used to translate OF. *lecheresse*, fem. of *lecheor* LECHER.

1340 *Ayenb.* 56 Þe tonge þe lyckestre him ansuereþ.

licli, licly, obs. forms of LIKELY.

licnen, licnesse, obs. ff. of LIKEN, LIKENESS.

licome, variant of LICHAM *Obs.*

licorice, alternative form of LIQUORICE.

licorish, variant of LICKERISH.

† **licorn.** *Obs.* [a. F. *licorne*, lit. unicorn.] 'An old name for the howitzer of the last century, then but a kind of mortar fitted on a field-carriage to fire shells at low angles' (Adm. Smyth).

1825 in BURN *Nav. & Milit. Dict.*

licorous, licourous, variants of LICKEROUS.

licour, -ish, obs. ff. LIQUOR, LICKERISH.

lict, obs. form of LIGHT.

licter, lictier, obs. forms of LITTER.

lictor (ˈlɪktə(r)). *Rom. Antiq.* Also 4 littour. [L.; perh. agent-n. f. *lig-*, root of *ligāre* to bind.] An officer whose functions were to attend upon a magistrate, bearing the fasces before him, and to execute sentence of judgement upon offenders.

A dictator had twenty-four lictors, a consul twelve.

1382 WYCLIF *Acts* xvi. 35 The magistratis senten littoures, that ben mynistris of ponysching, seyinge, Dismitte, or delyuere, ȝe tho men. **1586** SIR E. HOBY *Polit. Disc. Truth* xxiv. 114 *marg.*, The fagots of the licturs. **1606** SHAKS. *Ant. & Cl.* v. ii. 214 Sawcie Lictors Will catch at vs like Strumpets. **1623** COCKERAM, *Lictor*, a Serieant, a Hangman. **1674** MILTON *P.R.* IV. 65. **1838** ARNOLD *Hist. Rome* I. xv. 302 Each [decemvir] was attended by his twelve lictors, who carried not the rods only but the axe. **1843** MACAULAY *Lake Regillus* i, Ho, lictors, clear the way!

b. *transf.*

1638 *Penit. Conf.* viii. (1657) 223 God shall not greatly need any Lictors or Tormenters. **1667** *Causes Decay Chr. Piety* ii. 31 They.. become their own Lictors and make that their choice which is their extremest punishment. **1686** J. SCOTT *Chr. Life* (1747) III. 352 Satan, as the Lictor or Executioner of our Saviour, immediately seized the Criminal, and inflicted on him some bodily Disease or Torment. **1883** R. W. DIXON *Mano* III. ii. 120 A thousand justices in judgment sit, A thousand lictors deal most righteous blows.

Hence † **licˈtorian** *a.*, pertaining to a lictor.

1656 in BLOUNT *Glossogr.*

licture, licure, obs. ff. LITTER *sb.*, LIQUOR.

licuala (lɪkjʊˈwɑːlə). [mod.L. (C. P. Thunberg 1782, in *Kungl. Svenska Vetenskapsakad. Handl.* III. 284), f. Makassar *lekowala*.] A small palm tree of the genus so called, belonging to the family Palmaceæ, native to Malaysia, New Guinea, and northern Australia, and having fan-shaped leaves and prickly stalks.

1872 *Gardeners' Chronicle* 14 Dec. 1657/2 The Licualas are Fan Palms of Asiatic origin, requiring hothouse cultivation. **1900** L. H. BAILEY *Cycl. Amer. Hort.* II. 911/1 The large fan-shaped leaves of the Licualas are somewhat tender and easily injured. **1930** *Discovery* Nov. 380/1 A few *Licuala* and *Pinanga* palms were seen. **1952** 'W. MARCH' *October Island* x. 125 Zalacca, pinanga, licuala, corypha, And the sealing-wax palm. **1966** E. J. H. CORNER *Nat. Hist. Palms* xiii. 310 When the forest is cleared, the thickets of *Licuala* may be left, and they catch the eye with their striking foliage and long sprays of pink, orange, and red berries.

licval, licwurðe: see LIKEFUL, LIKEWORTH.

lid (lɪd), *sb.* Forms: 1 hlid(d, 2 hlyd, 3–4 lid(e, 4–6 lidd(e, lydde, 5 led(e, lyd(e, 3– lid. [OE. *hlid* neut. = Du. *lid*, OHG. *hlit* (MHG. *lit*, mod.G. in comb. *augenlid* eyelid) lid, ON. *hlið* gate, gateway, gap:—OTeut. **hlido*ᵐ f. wk.-grade of root **hlīđ*-to cover, in OE. *be-hlīdan*, OS. *bihlīdan* to cover, OE. *on-hlīdan*, OS. *anhlīdan* to open.]

1. a. That which covers the opening at the top of a vessel or closes the mouth of an aperture; the upper part of a receptacle, which may be detached or turned upon a hinge in order to give access to the interior.

c **1000** ÆLFRIC *Hom.* II. 262 Ða ledon ða þeȝenas ðone Hælend ðæron, and mid hlide belucon ure ealra Alysend. *c* **1290** *S. Eng. Leg.* I. 53/213 So huy openeden þat lid of is swete toumbe þere. *a* **1300** *Cursor M.* 5618 In þis kist þe barn sco did Quen it spird was wit þe lid [*Fairf.* lidde]. *a* **1375** *Joseph Arim.* 41 Make a luytel whucche, Forte do in þat ilke blod.. whon þe lust speke with me lift þe lide sone. *c* **1410** *Sir Cleges* 272 The porter to the panere went, And the led vppe he hentt. *c* **1450** *Two Cookery-bks.* 73 Hele the potte with a close led, and stoppe hit aboutȝte with dogh or bater. **1483** CAXTON *Gold. Leg.* 437/2 The preest taketh the lydde of the chalys on whyche is the hoost. **1535** COVERDALE *Num.* xix. 15 And euery open vessel that hath no lydd nor couerynge, is vncleane. **1611** BIBLE *2 Kings* xii. 9 Iehoiada the priest tooke a chest, and bored a hole in the lid of it. **1712** ADDISON *Spect.* No. 471 ¶8 Upon his lifting up the Lid of it [Pandora's Box].. there flew out all the Calamities and Distempers incident to Men. **1840** BROWNING *Sordello* I. 589 Meantime some pyx to screen The full-grown pest, some lid to shut upon The goblin! **1841–71** T. R. JONES *Anim. Kingd.* (ed. 4) 417 The outer layer of the lid is formed of earth precisely similar to that which surrounds the hole. **1865** KINGSLEY *Herew.* x. 159 'Lift the lid of this box for me', she said.

b. Applied to a door, shutter, board, or the like, closing an aperture. Now *dial.* or *slang.* Cf. PORT-LID s.v. PORT *sb.*³ 6.

1535 COVERDALE *1 Kings* vi. 4 In yᵉ house he made wyndowes, which might be opened and shut with lyddes. **1593** G. HARVEY *Pierce's Supererog.* Wks. (Grosart) II. 231 Stop thy oven-mouth with a lidde of butter. **1686–7** AUBREY *Rem. Gentilism & Judaism* (1881) 48 Whereas his former Physitian shutt up his windowes and kept him in utter darknesse, he did open his windowe-lids and let in the light. **1890** *Glouc. Gloss.*, *Lid*, a cupboard door. **1942** 'B. J. ELLAN' *Spitfire!* p. x, Shut the *lid*, i.e., close the hood [over the pilot's cockpit].

c. The top crust of a pie. *dial.*

1615 MARKHAM *Eng. Housewife* 68 At a vent in the top of the lid put in the same, and then set it into the Oven again. **1747** MRS. GLASSE *Cookery* 73 A Yorkshire Christmas-Pye. First make a good Standing Crust... Then lay on your Lid, which must be a very thick one.

† **d.** *lid of the knee*: the patella, knee-cap. *Obs.*

1632 LITHGOW *Trav.* x. 462 The lids of my knees beeing crushed.

e. In various slang or colloq. phrases with *down*, *off*, *on*, esp. *to put the lid on*, to bring to a close or climax; to conceal or 'clamp down on'.

1915 *Lit. Digest* 4 Sept. 467/1 In fact, excepting the ordinary saloons,.. the 'lid' is down, secure and tight. **1964** J. P. CLARK *Three Plays* 13, I hope he keeps The lid down on his wife for I fear She is fretting already.

1873 M. F. MAHONY *Chron. Fermors* I. xii. 225 What wonder if the lid was constantly getting off her temper. **1904** *Public Ledger* (Philadelphia) 12 Sept. 16 Commissioner of Police McAdoo.. has taken frequent occasions to deny that the 'lid' was off, to use the slang definition of a lax police administration. **1910** W. M. RAINE *Bucky O'Connor* 96 'Playing with the lid off back there, ain't they?' The sheriff's nod indicated the distant faro-table. *Ibid.* 218 I'll back that opinion with the lid off. **1926** A. HUXLEY *Let.* 14 Nov. (1969) 276 Then a vast book by the Italian Sociologist Vilfredo Pareto, very good.. he really does take the lid off and show you the works. **1927** R. A. FREEMAN *Certain Dr. Thorndyke* II. xviii. 272 'My eye,' exclaimed Miller... 'This puts the lid on it—or rather takes the lid off.' **1951** E. PAUL *Springtime in Paris* ii. 17 A few jubilant days when the lid was off following Liberation. **1962** *Which?* May 160 (*heading*), 14 cars with the lid off. **1968** *Listener* 19 Dec. 819/2 Are you the Editor of the *Sunday Blast*, the paper that 'rips the lid off'? **1973** *N.Y. Law Jrnl.* 4 Sept. 5/3 Inevitably when the lid blows off and riots and bloodshed and vandalism begin, the courts will be called on to do something effective about it. **1974** 'M. INNES' *Appleby's Other Story* ii. 15 What will happen, I ask myself, when the police take the lid off? What.. will be the resulting smell?

1909 *Punch* 30 June 452/2 Your astonishing letter puts the lid on it. **1914** 'HIGH JINKS, JR.' *Choice Slang* 14 *Lid* (*to put on*), to put the lid on a town means to close the saloons, gambling houses and all other resorts except summer resorts. **1914** G. B. SHAW *Misalliance* 77 *Tarleton...* Young man: youre a fool; but youve just put the lid on this job in a masterly manner. **1914** H. A. VACHELL *Quinneys'* II. xx. 288 'Blackmail!' gasped Quinney. 'I prefer to call it a weapon, sir, which you are forcing me, sorely against my will, to use.' 'This puts the lid on.' **1922** C. SIDGWICK *Victorian* ix. 69 'That puts the lid on,' said Jane... 'You've done for yourself now.' **1928** T. GANN *Discoveries Cent. Amer.* xii. 168 Then came the earthquake, which must fairly have put the lid on, as far as Uk was concerned. *a* **1930** D. H. LAWRENCE *Phoenix II* (1968) 236 Inland, in the isolation, the lid is on, and the intense watchful malice of neighbours is infinitely worse than any police system. **1930** J. BUCHAN *Castle Gay* xiv. 216 You can see for yourself how that would put the lid on it. **1966** MRS. L. B. JOHNSON *White House Diary* 6 Aug. (1970) 410 Liz came in with a harried look, wanting to know what she could tell the press. She needed to 'put the lid on' if Luci had departed. **1974** *Times* 6 Feb. 19/4 (*heading*) Putting the lid on distributors' profits.

f. A hat, a cap. *slang.* (Cf. FLIP *v.* 9.)

1896 [see GLAD *a.* 4 e]. **1916** *Story-Teller* Feb. 828/2 'Dash my wig—where's my lid...' He snatched his cap up off the bunk. **1916** C. J. DENNIS *Songs Sentimental Bloke* 21, I dips me lid. *Ibid.* Gloss. 125 *Lid*, the hat. *To dip the lid*, to raise the hat. **1929** WODEHOUSE *Mr. Mulliner Speaking* ix. 304 You've no idea what a blister you look in that lid. **1946** B. MARSHALL *George Brown's Schooldays* xlvi. 178 Keep that lid of yours off your bloody ears if you don't want to look like a rotten sheeny. **1956** B. HOLIDAY *Lady sings Blues* (1973) i. 11 All the big-time whores wore big red velvet hats then with bird-of-paradise feathers on them. These lids were the thing. **1960** WODEHOUSE *Jeeves in Offing* xii. 132 It is almost as foul as Uncle Tom's Sherlock Holmes deerstalker, which has frightened more crows than any other lid in Worcestershire.

g. (See quot. 1971.) *slang.*

1967 *Time* 8 Sept. 18 The high price of 'commercial' marijuana ($10 to $15 for a 'lid' from which some 40 cigarettes can be rolled). **1968** J. D. MACDONALD *Pale Grey for Guilt* (1969) xii. 152 We had almost two lids of Acapulco Gold. **1969** *Rolling Stone* 17 May 6/3 We've got this guy from Sand City we just caught with a lid. **1970** K. PLATT *Pushbutton Butterfly* (1971) iv. 43 He would be selling grass, meth, acid, lids, match boxes,.. or mescaline. **1971** E. G. LANDY *Underground Dict.* 120 *Lid*, one ounce of marijuana, a quantity by which it is sold.

2. *lid* (*of the eye*) = EYELID.

c **1220** *Bestiary* 26 Ðe leun ðanne he lieð to slepen Sal he neure luken ðe lides of hise eȝen. **1398** TREVISA *Barth. De P.R.* v. viii. (1495) 114 Euery byrde closyth the eye wyth the nether lydde. *c* **1400** *Destr. Troy* 3759 His loke was full louely, when ledys were opyn. **1412–20** LYDG. *Chron. Troy* IV. xxxv, And of her eyen held the ledes downe. **1548–77** VICARY *Anat.* ii. (1888) 19 It is needefull that some members be holden vp with a grystle, as the liddes of the eyes. **1605** SHAKS. *Macb.* I. iii. 20 Sleepe shall neyther Night nor Day Hang vpon his Pent-house Lid. **1719** YOUNG *Job* 378 When his [Leviathan's] burnish'd eyes Lift their broad lids, the morning seems to rise. **1798** COLERIDGE *Anc. Mar.* IV. vii, I closed my lids, and kept them close, And the balls like pulses beat. **1830** TENNYSON *Poems* 122, I straightly would commend the tears to creep From my charged lids. **1879** HARLAN *Eyesight* ii. 23 The skin of the lids contains no fat.

fig. **1602** MARSTON *Antonio's Rev.* IV. v. Wks. 1856 I. 131 Ere night shall close the lids of yon bright stars. **1646**

CRASHAW *Sopetto d'Herode* I. xlviii, The fields..saw no more, But shut their flowry lids for ever.

3. Each of the two sides or covers (of a book). Chiefly *dial.* and *U.S.*

1585 HIGINS *Junius' Nomenclator* 7/1 *Inuolucrum, operculum libri, sittybus*,..the couer or lid of a booke. **1854** A. E. BAKER *Northampt. Gloss.*, *Lid*, the boarded cover of a book. **1864** GROSART *Lambs all Safe* (1865) 85, I might close the lids of the Bible. **1881** *Leicester Gloss.* s.v. *Hilling*, In Leicestershire generally, however, the covers of a book are the 'lids'. **1896** *N.Y. Sun* in *Catholic News* 29 Feb. 2/7, I have never yet found 'a good Catholic' who would deny anything in 'The Word of God' from lid to lid.

4. *Bot.* and *Conch.* = OPERCULUM.

1681 GREW *Musæum* 130 That little Shell called Blatta Byzantia, is the Operculum or Lid of the Purple. **1774** GOLDSM. *Nat. Hist.* (1776) VII. 34 Many of them [sea snails] are also furnished with a lid, which covers the mouth of the shell, and which opens and shuts at the animal's pleasure. **1776** WITHERING *Brit. Plants* 799 *Lid*, a cover to the tips of several of the Mosses; as in the Bogmoss. **1839** LINDLEY *Introd. Bot.* I. ii. (ed. 3) 141 The singular form of leaf..which has been called a pitcher..consists of a fistular green body..closed at its extremity by a lid, termed the *operculum*. **1840** *Penny Cycl.* XVI. 9/2 The urn itself [*sc.* of a moss] is closed by a lid, or *operculum*, and contains the spores. **1863** BERKELEY *Brit. Mosses* Gloss. 312 *Lid*, the terminal portion of the sporangium, which usually separates by a circular horizontal fissure.

5. *Mining.* **a.** The roof or roof-stone covering a 'pipe'; a *lid-stone* (q.v.). **b.** A flat piece of wood placed between the roof and the prop supporting it.

a. 1747 HOOSON *Miner's Dict.* Liv b, Pipes never fail of Lids, it is that by which they are distinguished from Flats.

b. 1847 in HALLIWELL. **1860** *Mining Gloss.* (ed. 2), *Derbysh. Terms*, *Cap* or *Lid*, a flat piece of wood placed between the top of the punch and the roof of the mine.

6. *attrib.* and *Comb.*, as ***lid-elevator***, ***-lash***; **lid-cells** *Bot.* (see quot.); **lid-flower**, a tree or shrub of the genus *Calyptranthes* (N.O. *Myrtaceæ*), in which the upper part of the calyx forms a lid; **lid-stone** *Mining* (see quot. 1858).

1887 GARNSEY tr. *Goebel's Morphol. Plants* 482 *Lid-cells of archegonium [of a cryptogam], terminal cells of neck closing for a time canal of neck. Same as stigmatic cells. **1827** *Gentl. Mag.* XCVII. II. 490 The knob, or *lid-elevator, is a pine attached to the lid by a brass pin. **1866** *Treas. Bot.*, *Lid-flower, *Calyptranthes*. **1820** KEATS *Lamia* I. 151 Her eyes..Hot, glazed, and wide, with *lid-lashes all sear. **1653** MANLOVE *Lead-Mines* 265 *Lid-Stones. **1851** TAPPING *Derbysh. Lead-Mining Terms* (E.D.S.), *Rake*,..that species of metallic vein which..is not covered with a lid-stone. **1858** A. C. RAMSAY *Catal. Rock Specimens* (1862) 63 (E.D.D.), Locally called 'lid-stone', from its lying on the top of the iron ore which occurs in the limestone of the Forest of Dean.

lid (lɪd), *v.* Also 3 lide. [f. LID *sb.*] *trans.* To cover with a lid.

a **1225** *Ancr. R.* 84 And he heleð hit & wrihð [*v.rr.* lides, liðeð] so þet he hit nout ne istinckeð. **1750** E. SMITH *Compl. Housew.* (ed. 14) 151 Then lid your pye and bake it. **1913** *Chambers's Jrnl.* Oct. 729/2 The cans..then move along to be lidded. **1950** *N.Z. Jrnl. Agric.* Nov. 429 (*caption*) A case packed to the correct height is shown in the illustration. Severe damage may occur to fruit on the lidding press unless the pack is crowned correctly. **1959** *Listener* 22 Jan. 191/2 Lid the flan with pastry. **1960** *Encounter* Mar. 21/1 They lidded that box again.

lidar ('laɪdɑː(r)). [f. LI(GHT *sb.* + RA)DAR.] A system for detecting the presence of objects or ascertaining their position or motion which works on the principle of radar, but uses laser radiation instead of microwaves.

1963 *Bull. Amer. Meteorol. Soc.* XLIV. 568/1 Scattering at 180°, or back-scattering, is the basis for both the microwave radar and the lidar (laser radar). **1963** *New Scientist* 20 June 673/3 The difficulties already encountered in detecting lidar pulses from the Moon will make astronomers wary of attempting to use such methods on the planets. **1968** *McGraw-Hill Yearbk. Sci. & Technol.* 228/1 The purpose of the lidar was to determine where the spray cloud drifted after release by the aircraft, so that the area of forest 'treated' could be accurately determined. **1970** *Daily Tel.* (Colour Suppl.) 28 Aug. 19/1 At Duisberg in the Ruhr a £20,000 laser system—called 'Lidar'..—which was supplied by a British firm, Laser Associates, monitors the pollution coming from industrial chimneys.

lidded ('lɪdɪd), *ppl. a.* Also 1 **ʒehlidad, -od, ʒehleodad, ilided.** [OE. **ʒehlidod* as if pa. pple. of a vb. **hlidian* or **ʒehlidian*, f. *hlid* (*ʒehlid*) LID *sb.* In mod. use a new formation on LID *sb.* and *v.* + -ED.]

1. Having a lid; covered with or as with a lid.

c **900** *Bæda's Hist.* IV. xxi. [xix.] (1890) 320 Seo [*sc.* þruh] wæs swilce eac ʒerisenlice ʒehleodad [*v.r.* ʒehlidod, -ad] mid ʒelice stane. *a* **1225** *Ancr. R.* 58 Þes put he hat þat heo beo euer ilided & iwrien. **1675** EVELYN *Terra* (1676) 146 Woodden-Cases made like Coffins (but not contracted at the extreams nor lidded). **1821** COLERIDGE *Lett., Convers. &c.* II. 21 The tropical trees..produce their own lidded vessels full of water from air and dew. **1890** J. SERVICE *Thir Notandums* xi. 78 Maist o' the gentlemen wore dark blue..coats.., their waistcoats deep in the lidded pooch.

b. *Mining.* (Cf. LID *sb.* 5.)

1747 HOOSON *Miner's Dict.* Liv b, Though we may in some Parts of this Work seem to assert that Veins are not Lidded, yet..they may be so, but more especially on their Dip. **1847** HALLIWELL s.v., The top of the bearing part of a pipe is said to be lidded when its usual space is contracted to a small compass or width. A mining term.

c. *Bot.* and *Zool.* (Cf. LID *sb.* 4.)

1776–96 WITHERING *Brit. Plants* (ed. 3) I. 357 Capsule..lidded, and opening transversely. **1899** CAGNEY *Jaksch's Clin. Diagn.* vi. (ed. 4) 224 The eggs [of *Distoma sinense*] are oval, lidded, and spiked at the opposite end.

2. Of the eyes: Having lids, covered with lids. Chiefly with adj. or adv. prefixed, as ***half-***, ***heavy-***, ***high-lidded***.

1818 KEATS *Lines written in Highlands* 21 But the forgotten eye is still fast lidded to the ground. **1820** —— *Cap & Bells* xx. Poems (1889) 527 One minute's while his eyes remain'd Half lidded, piteous, languid, innocent. **1879** G. MACDONALD *Sir Gibbie* III. ix. 151 Duff gave him a high-lidded glance, vouchsafing no reply. **1886** J. W. GRAHAM *Neæra* (1887) II. iii. 146 [Eyes] somewhat heavy lidded and slow moving.

lidder, -ness, variants of LITHER, -NESS.

†**'lidderon.** *Obs.* Forms: 4 **ledron**, 5 **lyd(e)ron, -eryn, lydrun, lidrone**, 5–6 **lidderon**, 6 **lydderyn, lydderne, liddurn.** [Perh. a. OF. *ladron* (see LADRONE), influenced by *lidder* LITHER *a.*] A rascal, blackguard.

13.. *K. Alis.* 3210 Mony ledron, mony schrewe. *c* **1440** *Promp. Parv.* 303/2 Lydron, or lyderon (*MS. H.* and *Pynson* lydrun, or lyderyn), *lidorus* [? = Gr. λοίδορος railer]. *Hec quedam glosa super correctione Biblie.* *c* **1440** *York Myst.* xxxi. 167 To se nowe þis lidderon her he leggis oure lawes. *Ibid.* 187 Say..whare ledde ȝe þis lidrone. **1523** SKELTON *Garl. Laurel* 188 Some lidderons [*MS.* liddurns], some losels, some noughty packis. **1526** —— *Magnyf.* 1945 Lydderyns so lytell set by Goddes lawes. *a* **1529** —— *Agst. Venemous Tongues* Wks. 1843 I. 133 To taunt theim like liddrous [*sic*], lewde as thei bee. **1553** BALE *Vocacyon* Pref. 3 b, It is better (they saye in Northfolke) that yonge lyddernes wepe, than olde men.

liddle ('lɪd(ə)l), *a.* Representing a foreign or dialectal pronunciation of, or used hypocoristically for, LITTLE *a.* So **'liddly** *sb.*, a little child.

1906 KIPLING *Puck of Pook's Hill* 224 Come along o' me while I lock up my liddle hen-house. **1929** R. HUGHES *High Wind in Jamaica* i. 8 Rachel, Edward, and Laura, the little ones (or Liddlies, as they came to be known in the family). **1941** M. TREADGOLD *We couldn't leave Dinah* vi. 106 They are nice liddle horses, *nicht wahr*, Karl? **1945** [see CHUTZPAH]. **1970** C. DRUMMOND *Stab in Back* vii. 165 She takes 'er delicate liddle tray and bird-like appetite to one of the upstairs rooms. **1973** K. GILES *File on Death* v. 144 P'raps we could 'ave a liddle natter.

Lide (laɪd). *Obs.* exc. *dial.* Forms: 1 **hlýda**, 3 **lud(e**, 4 **lyde**, 7 **leed(e, leid**, 7– **lide.** [OE. *hlýda*; perh. *lit.* 'noisly', cogn. w. *hlúd* LOUD.] The month of March.

c **1000** *Sax. Leechd.* III. 152 Þone monað martius þe menne hatað hlyda. *Ibid.* 228 Se æresta friȝedæȝ þe man sceal fæsten is on hlydan. **1297** R. GLOUC. (Rolls) 11990 And þe teþe day of lud in to londone he drou. *Ibid.* 12040 In þe monþe of lude. *c* **1325** *Poem times Edw. II* (Percy) xxxv, Cattel cometh & goth As wederis don in Lyde. **1616** BULLOKAR, *Leede*, an olde name of the moneth of March. **1686–7** AUBREY *Rem. Gentilism & Judaism* (1881) 13 The vulgar in the West of England doe call the month of March, Lide. **1866** *Jrnl. R. Instit. Cornw.* Oct. II. 132 *Friday in Lide* is the name given to the first Friday in March... I have heard this archaism only among tinners, where it exists in such sayings as this: 'Ducks wan't lay till they've drink'd lide water'. **1880** *E. Cornwall Gloss.*

b. *attrib.* and *Comb.*, as ***lide-month***, ***-water***; **lide-flower, -lily**, the Lent lily, *Narcissus Pseudo-Narcissus* (Britten & Holland *Plant-n.* 1886).

1609 C. BUTLER *Fem. Mon.* vi. G vij b. Daffadil, *lide-flowre [**1623** *Lide-lilie, **1634** Lide-lilli], blackthorne, &c. **1696** PHILLIPS (ed. 5), *Leed*, or **Leid-moneth*, so called, saith Somner, *quasi Loud-moneth*, from the old Saxon word *Hyld*, a noise or tumult. **1866** *Lide water [see above].

†**'lidgate.** *Obs.* exc. *dial.* Forms: 1 **hlið-, hlidȝeat**, 5 **lidyate, lyde ȝate**, 6 **lydyate**, 9 **lidgitt**, *Sc.* and *north. dial.* **liggat(e, ligget.** [OE. *hlidȝeat*: see LID *sb.* and GATE *sb.*[1] The pronunciation is in some dialects ('lɪdʒɪt), from the ME. *lidȝate*, *-yate*.] A swing-gate; a gate set up between meadow or pasture and ploughed land or across the highway to prevent cattle from straying.

854 in Birch *Cartul. Sax.* (1887) II. 63 Ærest on dic: þonne upp uuið hliðȝeatas. **909** in Earle *Land Charters* (1888) 290 Ærest on icenan æt brombrigce up & lang weȝes to hlidȝeate. **1441** *Plumpton Corr.* (Camden) lix, Parte went into the towne of Helperby..and their festned a lid--yate in the highway at the towne end of Helperby toward Yorke, with stoks, thorns, and otherwise. *a* **1450** MYRC. 1497 Hast þow ay cast vp lyde ȝate þere bestus haue go in ate? **1557** *Scotter Manor Roll* in *Archæologia* (1817) XLVI. 379 That euery man shall sufficiently make their Lydyates in time convenient. **1790** J. FISHER *Poems* 107 They brak' the liggat o' the yard, Ay, a' in smash. **1847** HALLIWELL, *Lidgitts*, ..[Isle of Axholme]. *Linc.* **1874** A. HISLOP *Sc. Anecd.* 325 At another time when 'right about wheel' was required, he attained his object by asking them to 'come round like a ligget, lads!' **1881** J. YOUNGER *Autobiog.* iv. 35 Her an' the bits o' lasses were out list'ning for us at the head o' the liggate as we came up.

ledger, -ier, obs. forms of LEDGER.

‖**lidia** ('liðja). [Sp., lit. 'fight'.] A bull-fight, esp. the earlier stages in which the cuadrilla prepare the bull for the faena; the process whereby the torero obliges the bull to conform to his movements. So **lidiador** ('liðjaðor), a torero considered as controlling his art and the actions of his picadors, and the responses of the bull.

1893 CHAPMAN & BUCK *Wild Spain* v. 57 It was a gay and imposing scene..when the *lidia*, or tournament, took place. *Ibid.* 59 De Bedoya's 'Historia del Toréo'..gives Francisco de Romera as the first professional *lidiador* of the modern epoch. **1932** E. HEMINGWAY *Death in Afternoon* 445 *Lidia*, the fight... *Lidiador*, one who fights bulls. **1952** J. MARKS *To Bullfight* iv. 50 This task consists in calling the toreros to order if they infringe any of the rules that govern the course of *la lidia*, which is the actual conduct of the fight. **1957** A. MACNAB *Bulls of Iberia* i. 11 After a while they start learning to distinguish the cloth from the body. Some breeds..learn quickly, and unless the man knows his stuff properly ('gives correct *lidia*' is the technical expression), he is apt to find himself hanging on a horn. *Ibid.* xv. 230 Antonio is far too good a *lidiador* to..request the President to change the Act. **1967** MCCORMICK & MASCARENAS *Compl. Aficionado* i. 25 As with tragedy, the lidia to the noble bull has about it an aura of inevitability. *Ibid.* viii. 240 He wants the bull to follow the muleta smoothly, as he educated the animal to do throughout his entire lidia.

lidless ('lɪdlɪs), *a.* [f. LID *sb.* + -LESS.] Without a lid.

1522 *Bury Wills* (Camden) 116 A potell pewter pott ledles. **1867** G. MACDONALD *Poems* 119 Lidless coffins. **1894** H. NISBET *Bush Girl's Rom.* 138 Tea which had been boiled over the smoky logs in the lidless billies.

b. Of the eyes: Having no lids; not covered with the lids. Chiefly *poet.* = 'ever-watchful'.

1796 COLERIDGE *Ode Departing Yr.* 145 Her lidless dragon-eyes. **1820** SHELLEY *Ode Liberty* iv, Philosophy did strain Her lidless eyes for thee. **1847** TENNYSON *Princess* IV. 306 Not less to an eye like mine A lidless watcher of the public weal.

c. *Comb.*, as ***lidless-eyed -looking*** adjs.

1818 KEATS *Endym.* I. 598 The lidless-eyed train Of planets. **1878** *N. Amer. Rev.* CXXVII. 153 Lidless-looking eyes.

Lido ('liːdəʊ). [Venetian It. *lido*:—L. *litus* shore.] The name of a spit of land, a famous beach resort near Venice, now used *gen.* for: such a spit enclosing a lagoon; a bathing-beach or resort; a public open-air swimming-pool.

[**1611** CORYATE *Crudities* 160 Venice..is distant from the maine Sea about the space of 3 miles. From the which it is deuided by a certaine great banke called *litto maggior*, which is at the least fifty miles in length.] **1673** J. RAY *Observations Journey Low-Countries* 149 These Lagune are..separated from the main Gulf or Adriatic Sea by a bank of earth (il Lito or Lido they call it). *a* **1680** EVELYN *Diary* an. 1645 (1955) II. 433 A loud acclamation is Echod by the greate Guns of the Arsenale, and at the *Liddo*. **1860** E. HALL *Diary* 17 Oct. in O. A. Sherrard *Two Victorian Girls* (1966) II. 273 We took the boat to the Lido..and caught our first view of the Adriatic. **1930** *Morning Post* 16 July 5/4 The question of the safety of bathers in the Serpentine 'Lido' was raised at an inquest..yesterday. **1931** *Daily Express* 16 Oct. 8/2 £60,000 lido for England. The bathing pool and sun-bathing beach which the Hastings Corporation has just decided to construct [etc.]. **1934** *Discovery* Aug. 215/1 The broad sandspit or *lido* separating the lagoons from the sea. **1935** 'N. BLAKE' *Question of Proof* xiii. 259 What are you doing with all those deck-chairs..? Going to set up as a Lido proprietor? **1953** B. GOOLDEN *Truth is Fallen* xi. 175 'I haven't got any bathing things here.' 'Why on earth should we want them? It is not a Lido.' **1961** *Guardian* 24 Apr. 7/3 The Lido deck. **1969** V. CANNING *Queen's Pawn* xiii. 231 He went..out on to the One Deck Lido. **1971** *Country Life* 6 May 1106/3 Luino is a clean and pleasant place with several hotels, a lido and camping. **1975** M. KENYON *Mr Big* xxi. 204 All his free time was spent..semi-nude at the Serpentine lido.

lidocaine ('lɪdəʊkeɪn). *Pharm.* [f. ACETANI)-LID(E (from which the compound is derived) + -O + *-caine*, after COCAINE.] = LIGNOCAINE.

1949 *Q. Cumulative Index Medicus* XLV. 105/1 Lidocaine, caudal anesthesia in delivery. **1954** *Jrnl. Pharmacol. & Exper. Therap.* CXII. 432 In spite of the wide application of lidocaine in dentistry and medicine, the physiological disposition of this drug has received only limited attention. **1972** *Sci. Amer.* Aug. 45/3 For heart-attack patients with normal or higher-than-normal heart rates lidocaine (a drug without any influence on the heart rate) is given intravenously almost universally in coronary-care units to suppress ventricular ectopic activity. **1972** *Chest* LXI. 682/1 We discuss and emphasize the danger of administering lidocaine in the presence of atrial tachyarrhythmias with rapid ventricular response.

lidrone, variant of LIDDERON.

lie (laɪ), *sb.*[1] Forms: 1 **lyȝe, liȝe**, 3–4 **leȝe, leye, lighe, liyhe** (*pl.* **leis**), 3–5 **legh(e**, 4 **lyȝe**, 4–8 **lye**, 5–6, 9 (*Sc.* and *north. dial.*) **lee** (*pl.* **lees**, 6 **leis**), 5 **le**, 5, 7 **ly**, 6 *Sc.* **ley**, 4– **lie.** [OE. *lyȝe* str. masc. = OHG. *lug* (MHG. *luc*, inflected *lug-*; mod.G. *lug*):—OTeut. type **lugi-z*, f. **lug-* wk.-grade of **leug-*, OE. *léoȝan*: see LIE *v.*[2] Cf. the synonymous OHG. *lugîn* fem. (MHG., mod.G. *lüge*), ON. *lygi* fem. The formal identity between the sb. and the vb. is a result of convergent sound-change. In northern dialects the plural *lees* is liable to confusion with LEASE *sb.*[2]]

1. a. An act or instance of lying; a false statement made with intent to deceive; a criminal falsehood. Phrase, ***to tell*** (†formerly ***to make***) ***a lie***. †Also, ***without lie***, ***no lie***, truly (often as an expletive in ME. poetry; cf. *without fable*).

In mod. use, the word is normally a violent expression of moral reprobation, which in polite conversation tends to be avoided, the synonyms *falsehood* and *untruth* being often substituted as relatively euphemistic.

c **900** tr. *Bæda's Hist.* III. xiv. [xix.] (1890) 212 An is ærest lyȝes [*v.r.* liȝes] fyr [L. *unum* (sc. *ignem*) *mendacii*]. *a* **1000** *Cædmon's Christ & Satan* 53 (Gr.-Wülk. II. 525) Þu us ȝelær-dæst þurh lyȝe ðinne. *a* **1300** *E.E. Psalter* v. 7 That lighe [*MS. Harl.* liyhe] spekes leses tou mare and lesse. *Ibid.* lviii. 13 Of legh, and of cursinge, Sal þai be schewed in endinge. *a* **1300** *Cursor M.* 13941 (Cott.) Sal yee na leis here o mi toth. *c* **1300** *Havelok* 2117 Mo þan an hundred, withuten leye. *c* **1330** R. BRUNNE *Chron.* (Rolls) 10587 Of Arthure ys seid many selcouþ.. Al ys nougt soþ, ne nought al lye. *a* **1340** HAMPOLE *Psalter* xxvi. 18 A wicked spekere delited is in his leghe. **13..** *E.E. Allit. P.* A. 304 Much to blame.. þat louez [*read* leuez] oure lorde wolde make a lyȝe. *c* **1385** CHAUCER *L.G.W.* Prol. 12 Men schal nat wenyn euery thyng a lye For that he say it nat of ȝore a-go. *c* **1400** *Destr. Troy* 12594 Thies foure in hor falshode had forget a lie. *c* **1470** HARDING *Chron.* VII. vii, Iubiter gate Dardanus no lee. **1500–20** DUNBAR *Poems* lix. 13 [Who] in my name all leis recordis. *a* **1533** LD. BERNERS *Huon* xlvi. 155 Oberon neuer as yet made any lye to you. **1596** SHAKS. *Merch. V.* III. iv. 74 And twentie of these punie lies Ile tell. *a* **1618** RALEIGH *Mahomet* (1637) 146 He was never known to make a Ly. *a* **1651** CALDERWOOD *Hist. Kirk* (1843) II. 153 They doe receave but the lees of men for the truthe of God. **1651** HOBBES *Leviath.* I. xi. 51 Able to make a man both to believe lyes, and tell them. **1727** DE FOE *Hist. Appar.* i. (1840) 11 Sarah was the first.. that ever told God a lie to his face. *a* **1764** LLOYD *Ep. to C. Churchill* Poet. Wks. 1774 I. 88 Shrewd Suspicion.. To truth declar'd, prefers a whisper'd lye. **1791** BOSWELL *Johnson* an. 1781 (1848) 670/1 Johnson had accustomed himself to use the word *lie*, to express a mistake or an errour in relation.. though the relater did not mean to deceive. **1796** NELSON 24 July in Nicolas *Disp.* (1846) VII. xciii, The lie of the day is, that Archduke Charles has requested an Armistice, which the French General positively refused. **1816** SCOTT *Antiq.* xxi, For they were queer hands the monks, unless mony lees is made on them. **1820** COLERIDGE *Lett., Convers.*, etc. I. 119, I am almost inclined to reverse the proverb and say 'What every one says must be a lie'. **1879** FROUDE *Cæsar* xx. 339 It was perhaps a lie invented by political malignity.

b. ***white lie***: a consciously untrue statement which is not considered criminal; a falsehood rendered venial or praiseworthy by its motive.

1741 in *Gentl. Mag.* XI. 647 A certain Lady of the highest Quality.. makes a judicious Distinction between a white Lie and a black Lie. A white Lie is That which is not intended to injure any Body in his Fortune, Interest, or Reputation but only to gratify a garrulous Disposition and the Itch of amusing People by telling Them wonderful Stories. **1785** PALEY *Mor. Philos.* (1818) I. 187 White lies always introduce others of a darker complexion. **1833** MARRYAT *P. Simple* xxxiv, All lies disgrace a gentleman, white or black. **1857** C. READE (*title*) White Lies.

c. *transf.* Something grossly deceptive; an imposture.

1560 BIBLE (Geneva) *Ps.* lxii. 9 Yet the children of men are vanitie, the chief men are lies [**1611** men of high degree are a lie]. **1649** BP. REYNOLDS *Hosea* iv. 59 The very formality of an Idol is to be a lye, to stand for that which it is not. **1749** FIELDING *Tom Jones* XI. v, How is it possible for a Man to maintain a constant Lie in his Appearance [etc.]? **1842** MIALL in *Nonconf.* II. 177 Homage the most indirect paid to the state church is.. the worship of a lie. **1851** RUSKIN *Stones Ven.* (1874) I. i. 28 The sculptor of this base and senseless lie [the Vendramin statue].

2. a. ***to give the lie*** (*to*): to accuse (a person) to his face of lying. Also *transf.* of facts, actions, etc.: to prove the falsity of, to contradict (appearances, professions).

1593 ABP. BANCROFT *Daung. Posit.* I. iii. 13 They gaue the Queene the lie. **1599** H. BUTTES *Dyets drie Dinner* C ij, Though Galen saith,.. yet experience gives him the lye. **1610** SHAKS. *Temp.* III. ii. 85 Giue me the lye another time. *c* **1600** RALEIGH *The Farewell* 6 Go, since I needs must die, And give them all the lie. **1638** BAKER tr. *Balzac's Lett.* (vol. II.) 83 Tertullian.. therein gives the lie to all antiquitie. **1711** ADDISON *Spect.* No. 99 ¶7 The great Violation of the Point of Honour from Man to Man, is giving the Lye. **1768** W. DONALDSON *Life Sir B. Sapskull* II. 110 She gave him the lie for his civility, by assuring him she eat very hearty. **1805** T. LINDLEY *Voy. Brasil* (1808) 115 Replies.. that nearly gave the lie to his pretended superior knowledge. **1823** SCOTT *Quentin D.* xxvi, Francis the First, and the Emperor Charles, gave each other the lie direct. **1856** READE *Never too Late* xxiv, Am I to understand that you give Mr. Hawes the lie?

b. Hence occas. ***the lie*** is used for: The action of giving the lie; the charge of falsehood.

1593 SHAKS. *Rich. II*, IV. i. 66 That Lye, shall lie so heauy on my Sword, That [etc.]. **1600** ROWLANDS *Lett. Humours Blood* iii. 61 Astronomers.. By common censure somtimes meete the lie. **1705** HICKERINGILL *Priest-cr.* I. (1721) 17 The other gives him the Lye.. and follows his Lye with a Stab. **1732** BERKELEY *Alciphr.* III. §2 He abhors to take the Lye but not to tell it.

3. *attrib.* and *Comb.*; chiefly objective, as in ***lie-giving***, ***-hater***, ***-monger***, ***-teller***, ***-writer***; ***lie-consuming*** adj.; †**lie-bill** *nonce-wd.*, a distortion of LIBEL *sb.*; **lie-detector** orig. *U.S.*, an instrument intended to indicate when a person is lying by detecting changes in his physiological characteristics; **lie-tea**, said to be a transl. of the name given by the Chinese to teas coloured for the European market.

1620 MELTON *Astrolog.* 61 Pasquil and Morphirius, on whose brests were written no *Lie-Bills, as the Popes called them, but True-Bills of their villanies. **1822** SHELLEY *Hellas* 985 Thy *lie-consuming mirror. **1909** C. E. WALK *Yellow Circle* iv. 69 It is a *lie detector.. You set some wheels going. **1922** *Rep. 45th Ann. Meeting Amer. Bar Assoc.* 619 (*heading*) The Berkeley Lie Detector and other deception tests. **1933** *PMLA* XLVIII. 609 These views lead to such revolting pseudo-scientific nonsense as the use.. of a *lie detector* apparatus in order to convict defendants. **1962** [see GALVANIC *a.* a]. **1971** *Daily Tel.* 28 July 4/8 About 30 employees.. have been given lie-detector tests in the fight against pilfering. It is believed to be the first use of 'polygraph interviews', as the tests are called, in New York shops. **1974** 'A. GARVE' *File on Lester* ii. 9 When a politician talks of frankness most voters reach for their lie-detectors. **1848** THACKERAY *Bk. Snobs* xxxix, *Lie-givings, challenges, retractations. **1900** YORK POWELL in *St. George* III. 66 We at least will be a people of truth-lovers and *lie-haters. **1830** JAMES *Darnley* xxxiv, The tales that were circulated by the *liemongers of the court. **1876** A. H. HASSALL *Food* 114 This article has received the name of '*lie-tea' because it is spurious, and for the most part, not tea at all. **1552** HULOET, *Lye teller, or liynge knaue or queane. *a* **1641** BP. MOUNTAGU *Acts & Mon.* (1642) 215 The end and purpose of the lye-teller. **1863** *N. & Q.* 3rd Ser. III. 300 We would advise him to give more attention to the contemporary libellers and *lie-writers.

lie (laɪ), *sb.*² Also 7 lye. [f. LIE *v.*¹]

1. a. Manner of lying; direction or position in which something lies; direction and amount of slope or inclination. Also *fig.* the state, position, or aspect (of affairs, etc.). Phr. ***the lie of the land***.

1697 *Collect. Connect. Hist. Soc.* (1897) VI. 248 Nott to alter the proper lye of the Land. **1843** RUSKIN *Mod. Paint.* (1851) I. II. VI. i. §30. 399 The general lie and disposition of the boughs. **1849** J. F. JOHNSTON *Exper. Agric.* 101 On what geological formation the land rests—its physical position or lie. **1850** J. H. NEWMAN *Diffic. Anglic.* 325 To map out the field of thought.. and to ascertain its lie and its characteristics. **1862** TROLLOPE *N. Amer.* II. 2 Washington, from the lie of the land, can hardly have been said to be centrical at any time. **1865** CARLYLE *Fredk. Gt.* XX. iii. (1872) IX. 44 Friedrich understands well enough.. from the lie of matters, what his plan will be. **1894** BARING-GOULD *Deserts S. France* I. 15 The horizontal lie of the chalk beds. **1894** BESANT *In Deacon's Orders* 83 The lie of his hair, his pose [etc.]. **1950** E. H. GOMBRICH *Story of Art* 1 To show the newcomer the lie of the land without confusing him with details. **1956** M. LOWRY *Let.* 13 Nov. (1967) 392 If anyone is to blame it is I, for not giving you the lie of the land before. **1966** D. VARADAY *Gara-Yaka's Domain* xi. 123 The quick powers of grasping a situation with which all game are endowed, showed themselves in the speedy summing-up by the leading boar, as he got the lie of the land.

b. *Golf.* (*a*) 'The inclination of a club when held on the ground in the natural position for striking'. (*b*) 'The situation of a ball—good or bad'. (*Badm. Libr.*, *Golf* Gloss.)

1857 H. B. FARNIE *Golfer's Manual* in *Golfiana Misc.* (1887) 126 The precise *lie* [of the ball] it [the niblick] is intended for so seldom occurs. *Ibid.* 141 The lie of these spoons should be rather upright. **1887** SIR W. G. SIMPSON *Art Golf* 152 From a bad lie it is the only way I know of to loft a ball. **1890** HUTCHINSON *Golf* 58 An important consideration is the 'lie' of the driving club.

2. *concr.* A mass that lies; a stratum, layer.

a **1728** WOODWARD *Nat. Hist. Fossils* I. (1729) I. 12 Not in regular orderly Strata.. as Stone-lies, and various sorts of Earth which are in their original State. **1865** SWINBURNE *Phaedra* 153 The heifer.. sleek under shaggy and speckled lies of hair.

3. The place where an animal, etc. is accustomed to lie; to haunt. Also, room for lying.

1869 BLACKMORE *Lorna D.* vii, There were very fine loaches here, having more lie and harbourage than in the rough Lynn stream. **1886** *Q. Rev.* Oct. 359 *note*, At other times he [a salmon] is usually resting in his 'stand' or 'lie'. **1888** RIDER HAGGARD *Maiwa's Rev.* i. 2 A long narrow spinney which was a very favourite 'lie' for woodcock.

4. *Railways.* 'A siding or short offset from the main line, into which trucks may be run for the purpose of loading and unloading' (*Cent. Dict.*). (See also LYE *sb.*²)

5. A period of resting or lying (esp. in bed). See also *lie-down*, *-in*, *-up* below.

1930 L. COOPER *Ship of Truth* i. 30 Sunday was their one chance of a long lie. **1938** D. DU MAURIER *Rebecca* xvii. 271 Have a good long lie tomorrow morning. Don't attempt to get up.

6. lie-about, an idle person, one of no fixed occupation, a disreputable 'character'; = LAYABOUT; **lie-down** *colloq.*, a rest (on a bed, etc.); a form of protest in which the participants lie on the ground and refuse to move; **lie-in** *colloq.* = sense 5; also, as a form of protest, = prec.; **lie-up**, the fact of lying inactive in a place.

1937 M. ALLINGHAM *Dancers in Mourning* ii. 27 He took out a wallet which would have disgraced a lie-about. **1956** *Daily Mail* 26 Apr. 1/1 They are called champions of the prize ring but on Tuesday they appeared as two fat and horizontal lie-abouts. **1961** *Guardian* 27 Jan. 9/4 This former lie-about has got himself married. **1840** H. MOZLEY *Let.* 13 Oct. in D. Mozley *Newman Family Lett.* (1962) 93, I should be very glad of a lie down but cannot. **1850** C. KINGSLEY *Alton Locke* I. v. 80 You must keep moving all night.. or else you goes to a twopenny-rope shop and gets a lie down. **1919** W. S. MAUGHAM *Moon & Sixpence* xlvii. 202 When.. we hadn't even got the price of a lie down at the Chink's, he'd be as lively as a cricket. **1928** ST. JOHN ERVINE *Four One-Act Plays* 65 Yes, Aggie, you go an' 'ave a lie-down, see, and you'll be all right. **1936** *Time* 7 Dec., Second Sit-Down, Lie-Down... Twelve women and forty-five men, picketing the Berkshire Knitting Mills in Reading, Pennsylvania, by lying flat on its ice-covered front walk.. were arrested. **1970** D. BALSDON *Oxf. Then & Now* III. v. 114 It is.. the small body of demonstrators with whom we are here concerned—in particular the sit-down or lie-down to impede the Vice-Chancellor and Proctors in the exercise of their proper duties on November 5th, 1968. **1974** M. BIRMINGHAM *You can help Me* ii. 43, I won't risk our clients to you in your concussed state... Why don't you go and have a little lie-down? **1867** T. WRIGHT *Some Habits Working Classes* III. 206 The luxury of 'a long lie in', is the earliest and most universal of the delights of a working man's Sunday. **1916** 'TAFFRAIL' *Pincher Martin* xvi. 300 Lucky dogs!.. You've got a lie in. I envy you. This is a night for poor old Peter to be at sea. **1932** C. L. MORGAN *Fountain* II. iv. 120 He left orders you was both to have a lie-in this morning. **1959** G. FREEMAN *Jack would be Gent.* ix. 192 I'm going to 'ave a bit of a lie in.. seeing I'm on 'oliday. **1964** *Tuscaloosa* (Alabama) *News* 20 Apr. 1/8 The reported demonstration plans grew—from an auto stall-in on access roads to the fair to sit-ins, lie-ins and alike on other major highways, bridges and in tunnels throughout the city. **1971** *Time* 27 Dec. 40 Last week pollution protesters staged a lie-in at government offices in Tokyo. **1908** J. W. TYRRELL *Across Sub-Arctics of Canada* (ed. 3) 222 The two hundred mile tramp.. had hardened our muscles so much that, with the ten days' 'lie-up' on the bank of the Nelson River,.. we were now in first-class walking trim. **1926** *Blackw. Mag.* Dec. 850/2 We settled ourselves down for a happy four months of 'lie-up'.

Lie (liː), *sb.*³ The name of Sophus *Lie* (1842–99), Norwegian mathematician, used *attrib.* to denote certain concepts investigated by him, as **Lie algebra**, a vector space extending over a field in which a product operation (×) is defined such that for all x, y, z in the space $x \times y$ is bilinear, $x \times x = 0$, and $(x \times y) \times z + (y \times z) \times x + (z \times x) \times y = 0$; **Lie group**, a topological group in which it is possible to label the group elements by a finite number of coordinates in such a way that the coordinates of the product of two elements are analytic functions of the coordinates of the two elements and the coordinates of the inverse of an element are analytic functions of the coordinates of that element.

1935 *Bull. Amer. Math. Soc.* XLI. 344 A Lie algebra L over a non-modular field F will be called normal simple over F if H is an algebraically closed extension of F and L_H is a simple algebra. **1939** H. WEYL *Classical Groups* vii. 188 The process of averaging over a compact Lie group presupposes our ability to compare volume elements at different points of the group manifold. **1965** H. J. LIPKIN *Lie Groups for Pedestrians* i. 14 The use of the Lie algebra therefore simplifies the solution of the eigenvalue problem for the Hamiltonian by defining a number of integrals of the motion. **1967** G. STEINER *Lang. & Silence* 33 One cannot 'translate' the conventions and notations governing the operations of Lie groups.. into any words or grammar outside mathematics. **1969** *Sci. News* 31 May 538 The mathematical name of these patterns is Lie groups or unitary symmetry groups. They have been used to predict the existence of new [subatomic] particles.

†**lie**, *a.*¹ *Obs.* [OE. *lyȝe*, cogn. w. *lyȝe* LIE *sb.*¹] Lying, false.

c **975** *Rushw. Gosp.* Matt. xxvi. 60 Moniȝe lyȝe ȝewitu. *c* **1290** *S. Eng. Leg.* I. 319/688 Hinderful and of bost I-nouȝ, hardi and ofte lie.

‖**lié** (lie), *a.*² [Fr., pa. pple. of *lier* to bind.] Connected with, intimately acquainted with, attached to (a person or group of persons).

1855 E. TWISLETON *Let.* 1 May (1928) xiv. 264 Milnes.. has always been *lié* with Lord Palmerston. **1897** E. DOWSON *Let.* c 14 Nov. (1967) 397, I gather he is rather *lié* with Whibley whom I greatly dislike & do not want to meet. **1906** W. DE MORGAN *Joseph Vance* xi. 86 In case it should strike you that I have said.. very little about Nolly, I hereby declare that this is not because I did not love him, for we soon became very *liés*. **1947** E. JENKINS *Young Enthusiasts* 50 Alex and I.. each had a young man... Alex was *liée* with a naval officer. **1955** A. L. ROWSE *Expansion Eliz. Eng.* i. 22 Esmé Stuart was a danger: he was a Catholic and *lié* with the Guises.

lie (laɪ), *v.*¹ Forms and inflexions: see below. [A Com. Teut. str. vb.: OE. *licgan* = OFris. *liga*, *lidsa*, *lidzia*, OS. *liggian* (Du., LG. *liggen*), OHG. and MHG. *liggen*, *licken*, *ligen* (mod.G. *liegen*), ON. *liggia* (Sw. *ligga*, Da. *ligge*), Goth. *ligan*:—OTeut. **ligjan* (the Goth. *ligan* is abnormal), f. Teut. root **leg-* (:*lag-*:*læg-*) :—West Aryan **legh-* (:*logh-*:*lēgh-*) to lie; cf. Gr. λέχος bed, ἄλοχος bedfellow, wife, λόχος lying in wait, ambush, L. *lectus* bed, OSl. *ležati* to lie.

As in OTeut. **sitjan* SIT *v.*, the present-stem has a *j* suffix, though the pa. t. and pa. pple. are strong. In WGer. and consequently in OE., the pres.-stem has two forms, due to the diversity in the phonetic character of the flexional suffixes: (1) The WGer. *lig-*, OE. *liȝ-*, appears in the 2nd and 3rd pers. sing. pres. ind. and the sing. imp., and is the source of the mod.Eng. *lie*; (2) the WGer. *ligg-*, OE. *licȝ-*, appears in the inf., the 1st pers. sing. and the pl. pres. ind., the pres. subj., and the pl. imp.; it is represented in mod. northern dialects by *lig*; the southern *lidge* has been found only in the Wexford dialect, though the ME. *ligge* in southern texts can only represent the pronunciation (lɪdʒə).]

A. Inflexional Forms.

1. *Infinitive* lie. Forms: α. 1 licgan, licgean, *Northumb.* licga, 2 liggan, 2–5 ligge-n, 3 ligen, luggen (ü), 4–5 lyge, lygge, 4–6 (7–9 *dial.*) lig, ligg, 5 ligyn, lyggyn, lyg, lyegge. β. 2 lien, 3 liȝen, 3 lin, 4 lii, lij, li, lyen, (? *erron.* ley-n, leȝe, lai), 4–5 lyn(e, lyȝe, 4–8 ly, 4–9 lye, 5 liyn, lyyn, lyin, 4– lie. See also LIG *v.*

α. *Beowulf* 3082 (Gr.) Lete hyne licgean, þær he longe wæs. *c* **1160** *Hatton Gosp.* John v. 6 þa se hælend ȝe-seah

þisne liggan. c1175 *Lamb. Hom.* 79 Ho..letten hine liggen half quic. c1205 Lay. 22836 þer he scal liggen [c1275 luggen]. a1275 *Prov. Ælfred* 467 in *O.E. Misc.* 131 He sal ligen long anicht. a1275 *Death* 118 ibid. 174 Nu þu schalt wrecche liggen ful stille. 1297 R. Glouc. (Rolls) 3169 He bad him ligge and slepe wel. a1300 *Cursor M.* 5309, I will me lig to dei. a1340 Hampole *Psalter* v. 4, I sall noght lige in fleschy lustis. c1400 Maundev. (Roxb.) xxv. 118 Whare þe emperour schall ligge on þe morue. 1425 *Ord. Whittington's Alms-house* in Entick *London* (1766) IV. 354 A ..little house..in which he shall lyegge and rest. c1440 [see β]. 1483 *Cath. Angl.* 216/1 To Lyg in wayte. 1579 Spenser *Sheph. Cal.* Sept. 254 There mayst thou ligge in a vetchy bed. 1651 Randolph, etc. *Hey for Honesty* iii. i. Wks. (1875) 431 Liggen in strommel. a1652 Brome *Eng. Moor* i. iii. Wks. (1873) II. 13 Make thy bed fine and soft I'le lig with thee. 1674 Ray *N.C. Words* 30 To Lig: to lye, Var. Dial.

β. 1154 *O.E. Chron.* an. 1137 (Laud MS.) He ne myhte..ne sitten ne lien ne slepen. c1200 Ormin 6020, & nile he nohht tærinne lin. a1300 *Cursor M.* 3778 (Cott.) He..þar-on laid his hefd to li [*Fairf.* ly]. c1375 *Sc. Leg. Saints* vii. (*Jacobus minor*) 482, & þare wele foure dais can þai ley but met & drink. 1382 Wyclif *Isa.* xi. 6 The parde with the kide shal leyn. c1400 *Lanfranc's Cirurg.* 68, I lete it lie still. 1426 Lydg. *De Guil. Pilgr.* 13554 Lat hym lyn a whyle stylle. c1440 *Promp. Parv.* 304/2 Lyyn or lyggyn (*K.* lyin or ligyn), *jaceo*. 1480 Caxton *Chron. Eng.* ccxlii. 277 They..charged hym to lye still. 1849 Macaulay *Hist. Eng.* ix. II. 446 He might lie many years in a prison.

2. *Indicative Present.*

a. *1st pers. sing.* lie. Forms: α. 1 licge, 3-4 ligge, 4-6 (7-9 *dial.*) lig, 5 lige. β. 4 liy, 4-9 lye, 6 ly, 4- lie.

a1240 *Lofsong* in *Cott. Hom.* 211 Ase ich ligge lowe. c1275 Lay. 14137 Ihc ligge faste bi-clused in on castle. a1300-1400 *Cursor M.* 3612 (Gött.) Here..i liy [*other texts* lig, lye] in bed of care. 1377 Langl. *P. Pl.* B. v. 417, I..ligge abedde in lenten. 1432 *Test. Ebor.* II. 22, j matres yt I lige on. 1530 Palsgr. 610/1, I lye a bedde. c1586 C'tess Pembroke *Ps.* lvii. i, On thee I ly. 1688 Levinz in Keble *Life Bp. Wilson* iii. (1863) 99 When I lye under the confinement of my melancholy retreat. 1719 D'Urfey *Pills* (1872) II. 148 Thinking that I lig so nigh. 1801 R. Anderson *Cumb. Ball.* 17 At neet I lig me down. 1802 Coleridge *Ode to Rain* 5 O Rain! that I lie listening to.

b. *2nd pers. sing.* liest ('laɪɪst). Forms: α. 1 liȝest, liȝst, líst, 3-5 list, lyst, 4-9 lyest, 6-7 ly'st, 4- liest. Also *north.* 4 lyis, 5 lise, lyes. β. 5 lyggest, lyggyst.

a1000 *Cædmon's Gen.* 734 (Gr.) þær þu ȝebunden ligst. c1000 Ælfric *Josh.* vii. 10 Aris nu..hwi list ðu neowel on eorþan. c1200 *Trin. Coll. Hom.* 103 Wi list þu turnd on þe eorðe? a1275 *Death* 84 in *O.E. Misc.* 172 Nu þu list [*v.r.* lyst] on bere. c1386 Chaucer *Manciple's T.* 172 Now listow deed [*v.rr.* lyst thow, liest thou, lyes thou]. c1450 *Cov. Myst.* (Shaks. Soc.) 159 Heyl, Lord over lordys, that lyggyst ful lowe. 1470-85 Malory *Arthur* xxi. ii, Here now thow lyggest. 1596 Shaks. *Tam. Shr.* v. ii. 151 Whil'st thou ly'st warme at home. 1671 Milton *Samson* 1663 Thou..now ly'st victorious Among thy slain. 1877 C. Patmore *Unknown Eros* i. ix. (*Eurydice*), Where..On pallet poor Thou lyest, stricken sick.

c. *3rd pers. sing.* lies (laɪz). Forms: α. 1 liȝeþ, liȝþ, líþ, 2-5 liþ, 3 liȝið, 3-6 lyth, 4 lyþe, leiþ, lyhth, liȝth, lyȝt, liht, 4-5 lijth, lithe, 4-6 lythe, 4-7 lyeth, 5-6 lyith, 3- (now *arch.*) lieth. Also (with ending orig. *north.*) 1 liȝes, 4 lyse, lijs, 4-5 lis(e, 4-6 liis, 4-8 lyes, 5-6 lyis, lyese, 6 *Sc.* lysz, lisz, lyisz, 4- lies. β. 2-6 liggeþ, -eth, 4-5 liggith. Also 4 liggus, 4-5 ligus, -es, lygges, -ys, -ez, 5 ligis, 6 (7-9 *dial.*) lig(g)s.

α. a900 *O.E. Chron.* an. 893 (Parker MS.) Seo ea..lið ut of þæm wealda. c950 *Lindisf. Gosp.* Matt. viii. 6 Cnaeht min liȝes in hus eorð-cryppel. a1100 *O.E. Chron.* an. 675 (Laud MS.) Medeshamstede..& eal þ þær to liggeð. *Ibid.* an. 792 His lic ligð æt Tinan muþe. c1220 *Bestiary* 24 Ðanne he lieð to slepen. c1250 *Gen. & Ex.* 889 In ðe weie ðe liȝið to salem. a1300 *Cursor M.* 2117 þis land lies mast vnto þe south. 1362 Langl. *P. Pl.* A. i. 115 Lucifer louwest liȝth of hem alle. c1369 Chaucer *Dethe Blaunche* 181 A-wake..who lyeth there [*v.rr.* lythe, liþe]. 1382 Wyclif *Matt.* viii. 6 My child lyeth [*v.r.* liggeth, 1388 lijth]..sike. c1400 *Destr. Troy* 5369 Teutra..here in tombe lis. c1425 *Hampole's Psalter* Metr. Pref. 26 This same sauter..is þe self..That lyȝt at hampole. c1475 *Rauf Coilȝear* 246, I haue na knawledge quhair the Court lyis. 1533 Gau *Richt Vay* 84 To say..that thair lisz mair pardone to ony oder prayer. c1560 A. Scott *Poems* (S.T.S.) iv. 76 Sum can nocht keip hir gap Fra lansing, as scho lyiss. 1579 Lyly *Euphues* (Arb.) 86 As much as in me lyeth. 1611 Bible *Neh.* ii. 3 When the city..lyeth waste. 1660 Barrow *Euclid* i. xxvi, That side which lyeth betwixt the equal angles. 1666 Milton *2nd Epit. University Carrier* 1 Here lieth one who [etc.]. 1675 Earl Essex *Lett.* (1770) 88 That part of the town which..lyes to the water. 1711 Hearne *Collect.* (O.H.S.) III. 133 His skill indeed chiefly lyes in Coyns.

β. a1300 *Cursor M.* 2033 þi fader slepand..Liggus [*Gött.* lis, *Fairf.* lyse, *Trin.* liþ] here-oute. 13.. *E.E. Allit. P.* B. 1792 A dogge..þat in a dych lygges. a1400-50 *Alexander* 5173 A cabayne quare þe kyng liggis. c1460 *Towneley Plays* ii. 220 Gif hym that that ligis thore. 1597 Tofte *Laura* in Arb. *Garner* VIII. 298 Ah, happy thrice, that ligs in love with thee! 1605 Camden *Rem., Epitaphs* 59 Iohn Bell broken-brow Ligs vnder this steän. a1774 Fergusson *Hallowfair* Poems (1845) 15 When Phœbus ligs in Thetis' lap. 1849 James *Woodman* xxxix, I can find out for him where liggs the pretty lass. 1865 S. Evans *Bro. Fabian* 52 Bold Robin he liggeth here.

d. *plural* lie. Forms: α. 1 licgaþ, licgeaþ, 2-3 liggeð, 4 liggiþ, 2-4 (6 *arch.*) liggen, 5 liggyn, 4 ligge, 5 lygge. Also *north.* 4 ligges, 5 liggez, liggis. β. 2-4 lien, 2-3 lin, 4-6 lyen, 5 lyȝn, lyun, 4-9 ly(e, 4- lie. Also *north.* 4 lijs, *Sc.* 4-6 lyis, lyes.

α. a1000 *Andreas* 1426 (Gr.) Licgað æfter lande loccas todrifene. c1175 *Lamb. Hom.* 49 We liggeð in heueð sunnen. 1297 R. Glouc. (Rolls) 6355 þere hii liggeþ. a1300 *Cursor M.* 25965 Al ur sin þat we..ligges in [*Fairf.* lien]. 1362 Langl. *P. Pl.* A. ii. 105 Thei liggen to-gedere. 1387 Trevisa *Higden* (Rolls) I. 403 They..Stondeþ, sitteþ, liggeþ, and slepeþ. *Ibid.* II. 193 þey ligge [*Caxton* lygge] vpriȝt. a1400-50 *Alexander* 772* þar liggez lymmes of laddes. *Ibid.* 4845 þai seȝe doun sodanly slane of þaire blonkis..& in þe strete liggis. 1486 *Bk. St. Albans* E vij b, The Forchers that liggyn euen between The ij theys of the beest. 1579 Spenser *Sheph. Cal.* May 217 Many wyld beastes liggen in waite.

β. a1100 *O.E. Chron.* an. 963 (Laud MS.) Ealle þa þorpes þe ðærto lin. 1154 *Ibid.* an. 1137 þe landes þe lien to þe circe wican. c1230 *Hali Meid.* 3 Al þat bitter bale þat ter lieð under. a1300 *Cursor M.* 5340 þar lijs [*Fairf.* lyes] our heldres. c1350 *Will. Palerne* 2266 In caue þei lyen, & slepen samen y-fere. c1374 Chaucer *Compl. Mars* 5 Ye lovers that lye [*v.r.* ben] in eny drede. c1375 *Sc. Leg. Saints* xiv. (*Lucas*) 80, & ger thame ryse þat lyis law. c1400 Maundev. (1839) xxiv. 255 Thei lyȝn in Tentes. c1400 *Destr. Troy* 7966 þe grekes, þat on oure ground lyun. 1448 in Willis & Clark *Cambridge* (1886) II. 8 All the bemes that lyen by hemself. 1513 Bradshaw *St. Werburge* i. 284 Whiche Ladyes were buryed..and now there lyen in shryne. 1596 Dalrymple tr. *Leslie's Hist. Scot.* I. 54 Sum monstruous gret amang thame lyis to the cost of Carrik. *Ibid.* 148 In tyme of neid lyes the Pechtis abak wt thair supporte. c1614 Sir W. Mure *Dido & Æ.* i. 101 Troy..Whose ruines poore, which low in ashes lye. 1711 J. Greenwood *Eng. Gram.* 197 Place and Things that ly upward. 1756-7 tr. *Keysler's Trav.* (1760) III. 104 Here lie the remains of Giacomo Sanseverini. 1808 A. Parsons *Trav.* i. 12 Pebbles, which have been dug up..and now lye in heaps.

3. *Indicative Past* lay (leɪ). Forms: α. (strong) *1st and 3rd pers. sing.* 1 læȝ, læiȝ, 2 læi, 2-3 lei, 2-4 lai, leie, 3 læi(ȝ)e, leai, leiȝe, *Ormin* laȝȝ, 3-6 laie, 4 leȝ, leye, 4-5 leyȝe, leghe, 4-6 *Sc.* la, 4-7 ley, (5 lye, leȝe), 5-6 laye, 3- lay. *2nd pers.* 1 lǽȝe, 3 læiȝe, 3-4 lay, lai, etc.; 7 laist, 9 lay'st. *Plural.* 1 lǽȝon, láȝon, *Northumb.* léȝon, 3-4 leien, laien, leiȝen, etc.; also 3- *uninflected*. β. (weak) 6-7 *dial.*, 8-9 *arch.* ligged, 6 *Sc.* liggit, 9 lied, *dial.* lig'd.

α. *Beowulf* 1532 (Gr.) Hit on eorðan læȝ. c950 *Lindisf. Gosp.* Matt. ix. 36 Leȝon suæ scip næfdon hiorde. 11.. *O.E. Chron.* an. 1052 (Cotton MS.) þætte on Sandwic læiȝ. c1160 *Hatton Gosp.* Mark ii. 4 þæt bed þe se lame on laiȝ. c1200 Ormin 3692 He laȝȝ..i cribbe. c1205 Lay. 5030 þa wombe þe þu læie inne swa longe. *Ibid.* 9766 Vaspasien mid his monnen læiȝe [c1275 lay] at Exchæstre. c1220 *Bestiary* 42 In a ston stille he lai til it kam ðe dridde dai. a1275 *Passion Lord* 195 in *O.E. Misc.* 42 þe Gywes vp asturte þat leyen in þe grunde. 1297 R. Glouc. (Rolls) 3830 Boþe stede & king leye sone atte grounde. a1300 *Cursor M.* 10571 þar efterson þai samen lai. *Ibid.* 23500 Quat þou did and in credel lai [*other texts* lay]. 13.. *Gaw. & Gr. Knt.* 2006 þe leude lystened ful wel, þat leȝ in his bedde. 13.. *E.E. Allit. P.* A. 214 Her fax..On schylderez þat leghe. 1387 Trevisa *Higden* (Rolls) V. 107 His body lay in þe streete..unburied. c1400 *Destr. Troy* 8243 The ladies o lofte leghen to waite. c1420 *Chron. Vilod.* 4459 (Horstm.) He lye euery-presonede stylle in þat castelle. a1548 Hall *Chron., Hen. VI*, 173 b, His seignorie and power laie in those partes. 1560 Daus tr. *Sleidane's Comm.* 57 b, His Purse..laye upon his bed. 1596 Dalrymple tr. *Leslie's Hist. Scot.* ix. 86 To ly hidd as he la. 1671 Milton *P.R.* i. 247 The Manger where thou lais't. 1749 Fielding *Tom Jones* xviii. vi, I lay Seven years in Winchester jail. 1847 L. Hunt *Jar Honey* x. (1848) 131 Sicily lay at our feet.

β. 1560 Rolland *Crt. Venus* i. 56 Behind the Bus..I liggit law. a1641 Bp. Mountagu *Acts & Mon.* (1642) 456 Their Cels and Commoratories where they ligged. 1748 Thomson *Cast. Indol.* 595 Here whilom ligg'd th' Esopus of the age. 1813 T. Busby tr. *Lucretius* I. Dissert. 14 Bright eminences and fertile vallies lied in his way. *Ibid.* vi. Comm. 25 Those who, by death or desertion, were deprived of their friends and domestics, lied unburied in their houses. 1879 E. Arnold *Lt. Asia* iii. 2 In which calm home of happy life and love Ligged our Lord Buddha.

4. *Subjunctive Present* lie. Forms: 1 licge, 3-4 ligge, 4 lyg, ligg, 6 lig, 6-7 ly(e, 5- lie.

c1000 *Laws of Wihtræd* c. 25 (Schmid) Licge butan wyrȝelde. a1225 *Ancr. R.* 424 Nenne mon ne leten heo in..ne ne ligge ute. 1340 Hampole *Pr. Consc.* 3507 If any fal in dedly syn Ryse he up, and ligg noght lang þar-in. c1374 Chaucer *Troylus* v. 411 If þow þus ligge a day or two or þre. c1375 *Lay Folks Mass Bk.* (MS. B.) 593 Wheþer we ryde, or be goande, lyg, or sitt. c1449 Pecock *Repr.* ii. xx. 272 That he lie with the lord in oon bed. 1508 Dunbar *Tua mariit wemen* 500 That he be lost or with me lig. 1596 Dalrymple tr. *Leslie's Hist. Scot.* I. 31 How lang saevir the frost ly. 1596 Shaks. *Merch. V.* ii. vii. 61 If my forme lye there.

5. *Subjunctive Past* lay (leɪ). Forms: 1 lǽȝe, (*pl.* lǽȝen), 3 leie, læie, 3-5 leye, 4 laye, 5 leyȝe, 7 ley (etc., as in pa. ind.), 5- lay.

c893 K. Ælfred *Oros.* i. i. §14 He sæde þæt he..wolde fandian hu longe þæt land norþryhte læȝe. a1175 *Lamb. Hom.* 33 þah þu leie in ane prisune. c1205 Lay. 22254 þat his folc gode aswunden ne læie þere [c1275 leye]. c1374 Chaucer *Troylus* iv. 1532 (1560) If þis were wist my lif lay [*v.r.* leye] in balaunce. c1400 *Lanfranc's Cirurg.* 16 It were good þat he lay [*Add. MS.* leyȝe] & traueilide wiþ hise hondis. 1596 Shaks. *1 Hen. IV*, v. ii. 48 O, would the quarrell lay vpon our heads. 1684 T. Burnet *Theory Earth* i. 195 If the ballast ley more at one end, it would dip towards that pole.

6. *Imperative* lie (laɪ). Forms: *sing.* 1 liȝ(e, 3 liȝ(e, 3-5 li, ly, 5-9 *north.* lig, ligg, 6-8 lye, 3- lie. *plur.* 4 liggeth; 4- lie.

c1000 *Sax. Leechd.* II. 118 Liȝe on þa sidan þe [etc.]. c1205 Lay. 18097 Passent liȝ [c1275 ly] nu þer. *Ibid.* 28724 Liȝe þer. a1225 *Ancr. R.* 290 Ne lie þu nout stille. a1275 *Death* 137 in *O.E. Misc.* 176 Li [*v.r.* ly] awariede bali þat neauer þu ne arise. c1374 Chaucer *Troylus* ii. 904 (953) Li stil and lat me slepe. *Ibid.* iii. 899 (948) Liggeth stille and taketh hym right here. c1460 *Towneley Myst.* ii. 326 Lig down ther and take thi rest. c1650 *Christopher White* iv. in Child *Ballads* II. 439 Come, sweet wench, and ligg thy loue on mee. 1680 Otway *Orphan* i. iv. 276 Lye still! my Heart.

7. *Present Participle* lying ('laɪɪŋ). Forms: 1 licgende, *Northumb.* lic(c)end, 2-3 liggend, 4 liynge, lyng, liging, ligand(e, -onde, liende, lyende, liggonde, -ande, lyggynde, 4-5 ligging, -yng(e, 5 liggeng, lieng, lyynge, leing, liend, 4-6 lyeng(e, liand(e, lyand(e, 5 lyond, lyggande, 5-6 lyggyng(e, -ing(e, lyinge, 6 liyng, 7 lyeing, 5- lying, 9 ligging *dial.*

c950 *Lindisf. Gosp.* John v. 6 Ðionne miððy ȝesæh se hælend licgende [*Rushw.* licende]. c1200 *Trin. Coll. Hom.* 183 þus doð þe libbende frend to-ȝenes þe liggende. a1300 *Cursor M.* 6130 (Cott.) For was na hus in al þat land þat þar ne was ded man ligand [*other texts* liggande, ligond]. c1315 Shoreham 122 Lyggynde ine hare forage. c1325 *Song Mercy* 57 in *E.E.P.* (1862) 120 In harde prisoun lyng. c1375 *Cursor M.* 3384 (Fairf.) þe landes lyand towarde þe est. 1382 Wyclif *Matt.* viii. 14 He say his wyues moder liggynge [*v.r.* lyende, 1388 liggynge]. c1400 *Destr. Troy* 12666 þe buernes ..Left hym þer lyond. 1436 *Rolls of Parlt.* IV. 498/1 As Felons..in awayte lyggyng. c1440 *Generydes* 3027 In the feld he left hym liggeng. c1450 Holland *Howlat* 227 Lyand in lichory, laith, vnloveable. 1470-85 Malory *Arthur* xviii. xx, The fayrest corps lyenge in a ryche bedde. 1496 *Naval Acc. Hen. VII* (1896) 175 The Soueraigne leing in the dokke. 1533 Gau *Richt Vay* 64 Liand in his bed. 1553 Brende *Q. Curtius* F viij, The fore front alwayes defended the rest of the work lying behinde. 1596 Dalrymple tr. *Leslie's Hist. Scot.* I. 5 The vthir syd lyeng toward Spane. *Ibid.* 9 The mid parte lyeing betuene that and Cheuott hillis. 1849 Macaulay *Hist. Eng.* v. I. 597 A merchantman lying at the quay took fire. 1864 Tennyson *Northern Farmer* i. i, Wheer 'asta beän saw long and meä liggin' 'ere aloän?

8. *Past Participle* lain (leɪn). Forms: α. (strong) 1 (ȝe)leȝen, 3 i-læien, i-leien, i-leye, i-lei, 3-4 y-leye(n, lei(e)n, 4 y-leine, y-leie, y-lay, y-leighe, yleiȝe, y-lie, leye(n, leie, leiȝen, ligen, lygyn, lin(e, *Sc.* lyin, 4-5 leyn(e, liggen, 4-6 lyn, 4-7 layn(e, laine, lyne, 4-8 layen, lyen, lien (also 9 *arch.*), 5 y-ly, lye, ? loy(e)n, 6 lyene, 7 li'n, lay, 7- lain. β. (weak) 6 *Sc.* liggit, 7 lied, 9 *dial.* lig'd.

α. c893 K. Ælfred *Oros.* v. xiii. §3 þa heo þæron ȝeleȝen wæs. c1200 *Trin. Coll. Hom.* 7 Longe we habben lein on ure fule synnes. 1297 R. Glouc. (Rolls) 1711 He adde ileye sik. a1300 *Cursor M.* 10084 Vte o prisun strang þat þai had ligen [*other texts* liggen, leyn, leyne] in sua lang. *Ibid.* 11297 Efter þat sco suld ha lin [*other texts* lyne, lien, lyn] Fourti dais in hir gisin. c1320 *Sir Beues* 2001 (MS. A.) In is prisoun.. Ichaue leie þis seuen ȝare. c1325 *Lai le Freine* 98 Tvay men han y-ly me by. c1330 *Arth. & Merl.* 4188 (Kölbing) Bi hir he wald haue yleiȝe. 1340 Hampole *Pr. Consc.* 3162 Som ..þat..has..lang lygyn in þair syn. 1362 Langl. *P. Pl.* A. v. 259 He haþ leiȝen [C. vii. 330 leye] bi latro, lucifers brother. *Ibid.* xi. 276 þat hadde leyn [B. x. 419 yleine] with lucifer manye longe ȝeris. c1380 Wyclif *Wks.* (1880) 286 þei han so longe leyen in so gret cursinge. c1440 Capgrave *Life St. Kath.* iv. 2090 It were as good thei had loyn in bedde. a1450 *Le Morte Arth.* 525 How þat he had woundyd bene, And seke he had lye fulle sore. c1450 *Merlin* 86 How a man hadde lyen with her in semblaunce of the Duke. 1463 *Bury Wills* (Camden) 23 Ye bedde that she hath loyen in. c1560 R. Morice in *Lett. Lit. Men* (Camden) 25, I wolde yt hadd byn my fortune to have lyn in London. a1586 Sidney *Arcadia* ii. (1590) 101 b, Those flames which had so long layn deade in me. 1611 Bible *John* xx. 12 Where the body of Iesus had layen. 1624 Heywood *Gunaik.* ii. 67 Oft in one shade the hare and hound hath lyne. 1650 Baxter *Saints' R.* iii. vi. §24 (1651) 125 What if you had lien in Hell but one year? 1675 Earl Essex *Lett.* (1770) 207 An order of Council which had several months lay by me. 1676 Hobbes *Iliad* (1677) 380, I..rolling on the soiled grass have li'n Perpetually, and..wept. 1681 T. Flatman *Heraclitus Ridens* No. 25 (1713) I. 161 If my Life had lain never so much at stake. 1703 T. N. *City & C. Purch.* 43 Bricks..had layen in the Place to dry. 1722 De Foe *Plague* (1756) 227 We ..found it had lyen much longer conceal'd. 1788 Beattie *Burns' Wks.* II. 141 Lang had she lien wi' buffe and flegs. 1871 G. Macdonald *Bk. Sonnets* in *Wks. Fancy & Imag.* II. 176 At thy holy feet I should have lien. 1871 Smiles *Charac.* iii. (1876) 69, I have lain awake all night.

β. 1500-20 Dunbar *Poems* lv. 28, I saw cowclinkis..Had better liggit in the stockis. 1670 Barrow in Rigaud *Corr. Sci. Men* (1841) II. 75 It hath lied by me without looking on for many years. 1832 *Specim. Yorksh. Dial.* 11 Had she lig'd theer lang?

B. Signification and uses.

I. In senses expressive of bodily posture, and developments of these.

1. a. *intr.* Of persons or animals: To be in a prostrate or recumbent position. Formerly also with refl. pronoun.

c1000 Ælfric *Hom.* I. 246 Se witeȝa læȝ and slep. *Ibid.* 328 þa læȝ sum wædla æt his ȝeate, and his nama wæs Lazarus. c1175 *Lamb. Hom.* 81 þes oðer Mon..luueð his sunnen alse deð þet fette swin þet fule fen to liggen in. a1300 *Cursor M.* 690 Bi þe dere þat now es wild, Als lambe him lai þe leon mild. c1300 *Havelok* 475 þe children..Leyen and sprauleden in þe blod. c1330 R. Brunne *Chron.* (1810) 55 'A ha!' said þe erle, 'had þat schank ne bien, þou had liggen þer stille, þe risen suld non haf sene.' 1362 Langl. *P. Pl.* A. Prol. 9 As I lay and leonede and lokede on þe watres. 1382 Wyclif *Gen.* xxix. 2 He sawȝ a pit in the feeld and thre flockis of sheep liggynge bisidis it. c1440 *Gesta Rom.* ii. 6 (Harl. MS.) To ligge ny þe fire. 1551 Robinson *More's Utop.* ii. (1895) 295 When they haue lien a little space on the grounde, the priest giueth them a signe for to ryse. 1607 Dekker *Knt.'s Conjur.* (1842) p. vi, They that haue once or twice lyen vpon the rack of publicke censure. 1809 *Med. Jrnl.* XXI. 385 The woman having lain during the labour upon her left side. 1850 Tennyson *In Mem.* lxxxix. 23 To hear him, as he lay and read The Tuscan poets on the lawn.

b. with predicative complement expressing condition; e.g. *to lie asleep, sick, dead, blind, in a fever*. †Also with inf. (e.g. *to lie to die*).

c1000 *Ags. Gosp.* Matt. viii. 6 Min cnapa lið on minum huse lama. 1154 *O.E. Chron.* an. 1135 (Laud MS.) He lai an

slep in scip. c 1175 *Lamb. Hom.* 81 And efre lei þes wreche for-wunden. a 1225 *Leg. Kath.* 2286 Nalde nawt godd leoten his martirs licomes liggen to forleosen. a 1340 HAMPOLE *Psalter Cant.* 496 A man þat liggys in a strayte fifere. a 1425 *Cursor M.* 14172 (Trin.) He liþ to deȝe þat lele & trewe. c 1440 *Gesta Rom.* lxi. 253 (Harl. MS.) The suster of the Emperoure, þat now lithe in childebed. 1470–85 MALORY *Arthur* XVII. xviii. 715 And anon the kynge sawe hym the whiche had leyne blynd of long tyme. 1526 *Pilgr. Perf.* (W. de W. 1531) 72 b, And so sayd saynt Laurence whan he laye rostynge on the yren crate. 1530 PALSGR. 610/1, I lye at the poynte of dethe. 1560 DAUS tr. *Sleidane's Comm.* 24 b, For the duke of Saxonie lay sicke at Collen. 1564 GRINDAL *Funeral Serm. Ferdinand* A iv b, Aeschilus the Poete lieng on slepe bare headed nere the sea. 1669 PEPYS *Let.* 2 Nov. in *Diary* (1879) VI. 112 My wife..hath layn under a fever so severe, as [etc.]. 1711 SWIFT *Jrnl. to Stella* 31 Aug., Ophy Butler's wife there lies very ill of an ague. 1870 E. PEACOCK *Ralf Skirl.* III. 81 For hours she lay awake. 1887 E. BERDOE *St. Bernard* 68 The..room where she lay a cripple for so many years.

†c. Used *simply* = to 'lie sick', keep one's bed.

a 1300 *Cursor M.* 8942 War his sekenes neuer sa strang, Ne had he lin neuer sua lang. 1470–85 MALORY *Arthur* II. xiii. 91 They..told hym how her lady was seke & had layne many yeres. 1596 DALRYMPLE tr. *Leslie's Hist. Scot.* x. 408 Quhen bot schort he had lyne the x of July he departed this lyfe.

d. Expressing the posture of a dead body: To be extended on a bier or the like; to be buried (in a specified place). *to lie in state*: see STATE. †In OE. and early ME. also, To be dead.

Beowulf 2745 (Gr.) Nu se wyrm liȝeð. a 1000 *O.E. Chron.* an. 901 (Parker MS.) Æðelwald..sæde þæt he wolde oðer oððe þær libban oððe þær licgan. c 1175 *Lamb. Hom.* 35 Ga to þine feder burinesse oðer þer eni of þine cunne lið in. c 1205 LAY. 5869 We eow wulleð bi-foren libben oðer liggen. c 1250 *Gen. & Ex.* 3892 Ðor he [Aaron] lið doluen on ðat wold. a 1300 *Cursor M.* 5340 Þar lijs our heldres, þar sal i li. c 1470 HARDING *Chron.* CLXXIX. ii, Thyrty thousande with theim liggand ly. 1501 *Bury Wills* (Camden) 83 The holy place where the blyssyd and holy Apostyll Seynt Jamys lyth. 1695 SIBBALD *Autobiog.* (1834) 126 He was buried at Edinburgh in the Gray Frier churchyard, where our other relations lye. 1711 ADDISON *Spect.* No. 164 ¶12 Here lie the Bodies of Father Francis and Sister Constance. 1798 WORDSW. *We are seven* 21 Two of us in the church-yard lie, My sister and my brother.

e. To be in one's bed for the purpose of sleeping or resting. Also (now *rarely*) with qualifying word or phrase, e.g. *to lie soft(ly*.

c 1290 *S. Eng. Leg.* I. 102/37 Þare heo leien In heore beden. 1362 LANGL. *P. Pl.* A. VII. 14 The Neodi and the Nakede nym ȝeeme hou thei liggen. c 1375 *Sc. Leg. Saints* xvi. (*Magdalene*) 312 Þu in chuchis & silkine clathis lyis ful softe. c 1386 CHAUCER *Sir Thopas* 200 He nolde slepen in noon hous But liggen in his hoode. c 1440 *Gesta Rom.* lxiii. 274 (Harl. MS.) Certenly he desirith wele to ete, swetly to drinke, softely to ligge. 1579 SPENSER *Sheph. Cal.* May 125 Tho gan shepheards swaines to looke aloft, And leave to live hard, and learne to ligge soft. 1651 HOBBES *Leviath.* (1839) 8 Hence it is that lying cold breedeth dreams of fear. 1710 MRS. CENTLIVRE *Man's Bewitched* v. 68 Leave the London Dames..To lig in their Beds till Noon. 1742 CHESTERF. *Lett.* (1792) I. xc. 250 The people are extremely rude and barbarous, living chiefly upon raw flesh, and lying generally upon the ground, or at best in tents. 1850 THACKERAY *Pendennis* ix, You must lie on the bed which you have made for yourself.

f. Hence *to lie with* (or *†by*): to have sexual intercourse with. Somewhat *arch.*

a 1300 *Cursor M.* 27943 Incest, þat es for to lij Bi þat þi sibman has line bi. c 1330 *Arth. & Merl.* 852 (Kölbing) Þis maiden..feled al so bi her þi, þat sche was yleyen bi. c 1400 MAUNDEV. (1839) xxvii. 276 He wille not lyȝe with his Wyfes but 4 sithes in the ȝeer. 1470–85 MALORY *Arthur* v. xii, That none of his lyege men shold defoule ne lygge by no lady. 1504 *Plumpton Corr.* (Camden) p. lxiv, That they shuld not ligg togedder till she came to the age of xvi yeres. 1533 GAU *Richt Vay* 16 Thay that lysz wit thair kine and bluid. 1611 BIBLE *Jer.* iii. 2 Lift vp thine eyes vnto the high places, and see where thou hast not bene lien with. a 1652 BROME *Mad Couple* I. i. Wks. 1873 I. 16 You have unlawfully lyen with some woman. 1711 STEELE *Spect.* No. 51 ¶7 Tho' he betrays the Honour and Bed of his Neighbour and Friend, and lies with half the Women in the Play. 1750 G. JEFFREYS in *Duncombe's Letters* (1773) II. 250 He was only beforehand with his double-dealing brother in lying with a prostitute.

2. To assume a recumbent or prostrate position. Chiefly in *lie down*, *lie back*, etc., for which see branch IV. †Also with refl. pronoun. †Also, to lean or hang *over* (a wall).

a 1300 *Cursor M.* 20487 To hir bedd son scho ȝod & lay Abutte þe time al of midday. c 1320 *Sir Tristr.* 70 Þat maidens miȝt him se And ouer þe walles to lye. c 1435 *Torr. Portugal* 1166 Ladyes lay over and beheld. c 1440 *Gesta Rom.* xix. 67 (Harl. MS.) And þerfore let vs make him, þat settith such a dyet in vs, to rise with vs, and lig with vs. 1484 CAXTON *Fables of Alfonce* v, We shalle go and lye vs for to slepe. 1530 PALSGR. 610/1, I lye me to slepe, *je me mets a dormir.* a 1828 *Leesome Brand* xxxiii. in Child *Ballads* I. 183 His mother lay ower her castle wa, And she beheld baith dale and down. 1832 TENNYSON *Miller's Dau.* 111 From off the wold I came, and lay Upon the freshly-flower'd slope.

3. a. To be or remain in a specified position of subjection, helplessness, misery, degradation, or captivity; to be kept *in* prison; to continue *in* sin, etc. †Also *simply* = 'to lie in prison'; sometimes idiomatically *to lie by it*. *to lie by the heels* (arch.): see HEEL *sb.*[1] 19. *to lie open (to)*: see OPEN.

c 893 K. ÆLFRED *Oros.* v. i, On carcernum lægon. c 1200 *Vices & Virtues* (1888) 37 ȝif he..lið on sume heaued-senne. c 1300 *Havelok* 1374 He haueth me do..ofte in sorwe and pine ligge. c 1350 *Will. Palerne* 4307 Alle oþer of þe lordes of þat lond þat þere leie in hold. c 1380 WYCLIF *Serm.* (Sel. Wks.) I. 39 A long custom to ligge in synne. 1470–85 MALORY *Arthur* IV. vii, We ben here xx knyghtes prysoners ..& some of vs haue layne here seuen yere. 1483 CAXTON *Gold. Leg.* 239 b/1 And yet he entended to be his pledge and to lye for him, his charite was so grete. 1530 PALSGR. 610/1, I lye bounde in chaynes. 1567 *Gude & Godlie Ball.* (S.T.S.) 133 Sa lang in Sin as thow dois ly. 1586 EARL LEICESTER *Corr.* (Camden) 277 The auditour also..is worthy to lye by the heeles. 1618 E. ELTON *Rom.* vii. (1622) 90 Any particular sinne wherein thou hast liued and lyen. 1631 MASSINGER *Emperor East* III. i, To free all such as lie for debt. 1644 QUARLES *Barnabas & B.* 16, I must be paid, or he lie by it, until I have my utmost farthing or his bones. a 1670 HACKET *Abp. Williams* II. (1692) 138 Lincoln was like to lye by it, and to be shut out of mercy by an irreversible decree. 1692 R. L'ESTRANGE *Fables, Life Æsop* (1708) 7 From Lying at the Mercy of Fire, Water, and a Wicked Woman, Good Lord deliver us. 1849 MACAULAY *Hist. Eng.* iv. I. 482 The defendant..was lying in prison as a debtor. 1882 STEVENSON *Fam. Stud.* 265 His brother still lay by the heels for an unpatriotic treaty with England.

b. *to lie under*: to be subject to (some disadvantage or obligation).

1599 SHAKS. *Much Ado* IV. i. 171 If this sweet Ladie lye not guiltlesse heere, Vnder some biting error. 1682 COUNT KÖNIGSMARK in *Buccleuch MSS.* (Hist. MSS. Comm.) I. 336 The misfortune which I lay under. 1701 W. WOTTON *Hist. Rome* vi. 105 He lay under a sort of a Vow. 1710 ADDISON *Whig Exam.* No. 4 ¶9 Any one who reads this letter will lye under the same delusion. 1748 *Anson's Voy.* II. x. 236 Manila..lies under some disadvantage, from the difficulty there is in getting to sea to the eastward. 1849 MACAULAY *Hist. Eng.* vii. II. 202 In spite of all the restraints under which the press lay. 1866 DK. ARGYLL *Reign Law* vii. (1871) 331 The bondage under which all Science lies to fact.

4. a. To remain in a state of inactivity or concealment (not necessarily prone or reclining). Chiefly with complementary adj. or pa. pple. (For *to lie close*, *low*, *perdu*, etc., see those adjs.)

Cf. sense 8, where the subj. is a thing.

c 1374 CHAUCER *Boeth.* II. Metr. vii. 47 (Camb. MS.) Liggeth thanne stille al owtrely vnknowable. 1538 STARKEY *England* II. i. 174 By the reson wherof our owne marynerys oft-tymys lye idul. 1604 E. G[RIMSTONE] tr. *D'Acosta's Hist. Indies* I. xvii. 57 That these nations of the Indies, which have lyen so long hidden, should bee knowne and discovered. 1679 DRYDEN *Troilus & Cr.* III. i, We'll none of him: but let him like an Engine Not portable, lye lagg of all the Camp. 1745 in *Col. Rec. Pennsylv.* V. 12 We have in this part of the country lain still, both the last Summer and this. 1769 FALCONER *Dict. Marine* (1780), *Tout le monde bas*,..the order to the ship's crew to lie snug upon deck or below. 1838 DICKENS *O. Twist* xlviii, He..resolved to lie concealed within a short distance of the metropolis. *Ibid.* l, Do you mean to sell me, or to let me lie here till this hunt is over? 1885 U. S. GRANT *Mem.* I. xx. 269 They were growing impatient at lying idle so long, almost in hearing of the guns of the enemy.

b. *to lie in ambush*, *in wait*, *† in await* (see the sbs.). *† to lie for* = to lie in wait for. *to lie at catch* or *upon the catch* (? arch. or dial.): to set oneself to entrap a person, to be captious. (For *to lie at lurch*, *at ward*, *on one's guard*, see the sbs.)

1605 T. RYVES *Vicar's Plea* (1620) 141 That hee seeme not to lie at catch for an aduantage against his inferiour fellow minister. 1611 COTGR., *Aguetté*, dogged; watched, waited; lien for. 1655 FULLER *Ch. Hist.* III. i. §11 Lie at catch, and wait advantages one against another. 1671 SHADWELL *Humourists* III. 38 *Dryb*... That's stole out of a Play. *Craz.* What then, that's lawful; 'tis a shifting age for wit, and every body lies upon the Catch. a 1715 BURNET *Own Time* (1724) I. 307 The Dutch had a rich fleet coming from Smyrna.. Holmes was ordered to lye for them..with eight men of war. 1802–12 BENTHAM *Ration. Judic. Evid.* (1827) I. 588 *note*, Since he lay upon the watch and catch, only to see what the plaintiff proved. 1879 SPURGEON *Serm.* XXV. 329 He only asks the question because it ought to be asked, and does not lie upon the catch.

c. *Shooting.* Of game-birds: To remain crouching upon the ground. (Also *to lie dead.*) *to lie to the dogs*, *to the gun*: to permit the approach of a dog or the sportsman without 'rising'.

1797 *Encycl. Brit.* (ed. 3) XVII. 441/1 After the birds have been sprung many times, they lie so dead that they will suffer him [the sportsman] almost to tread upon them before they will rise. *Ibid.* 441/2 Partridges lie much better to dogs that wind them, than to those that follow them by the track. *Ibid.* 443/1 When..the sportsman perceives the birds running with their heads erect, he must run after them..for he may be pretty certain they will not lie well that day. 1848 *Zoologist* VI. 1964 The Spanish snipe would much less frequently 'lie' to the gun. 1886 *Badm. Libr., Shooting* 6 In Scotland grouse are usually walked up with dogs. The birds in that country lie well... If grouse lie well to dogs..they give easy marks to the gunner.

d. *to lie on* or *upon one's arms*, *oars*, *sculls*, *to lie upon wing*: see the sbs.

5. a. To dwell or sojourn; *esp.* to sleep or pass the night (in a place), to lodge temporarily. Now *rare* or *arch.*

c 1330 R. BRUNNE *Chron.* (1810) 312 At Sant Katerine hous þe erle Marschalle lay. c 1350 *Will. Palerne* 166 Þe king edwardes newe at glouseter þat ligges. 1415 SIR T. GREY in 43 *Deputy Keeper's Rep.* 584 And yat neghte I lay at Kengston. 1547 BOORDE *Introd. Knowl.* xvii. (1870) 167 Prage, wher the king of Boeme doth ly much whan he is in the countre. 1632 LITHGOW *Trav.* IV. 141 [He] kept a better house, than any Ambassadour did, that euer lay at Constantinople. 1695 CONGREVE *Love for L.* I. xi, I think your father lies at Foresight's. 1721 *Lond. Gaz.* No. 5980/3 The Exeter Carrier has lain at the Saracen's Head Inn..for many Years past. 1766 GOLDSM. *Vic. W.* vi. (Globe) 12 He refused, as he was to lie that night at a neighbour's. 1776 H. WALPOLE *Let. to Mason* 16 Apr., She lay at home..or according to the chaste modern phrase, slept there. 1849 MACAULAY *Hist. Eng.* viii. II. 295 He lay that night at the deanery.

b. *spec.* of a host or army (or its leader): To be encamped, to have or take up a position in a field. *† to lie in leaguer*: see LEAGUER.

c 1205 LAY. 650 He..leai þer abuten & abat his balesiðes. c 1450 *Merlin* 239 The saisnes..laye that nyght stille armed. 1470–85 MALORY *Arthur* II. vi, For the kyng Ryons lyeth at a syege atte castel Tarabil. a 1533 LD. BERNERS *Huon* lxi. 213 Yᵉ admyrall that lay at sege before yᵉ castell. a 1548 HALL *Chron., Hen. VIII*, 259 The kyng laie before Bullein, and was like to have conquered the same. 1644 VICARS *God in Mount* 146 Their Forces which had lyen so long before Sherborne. a 1671 LD. FAIRFAX *Mem.* (1699) 28 At Wakefield, six miles off, lay three thousand of the enemy. 1724 DE FOE *Mem. Cavalier* (1840) 68 The army lay under their arms all night. 1849 MACAULAY *Hist. Eng.* iii. I. 294 Near the capital lay also the corps which is now designated as the first regiment of dragoons.

†c. To live under specified circumstances or engaged in some specified occupation. (With *at*, *about.*) *Obs.*

1546 LANGLEY *Pol. Verg. De Invent.* VIII. iii. 146 b, It cost hym his life in Areciæ, where he laye at Surgery for the healyng of his legge. 1599 HAKLUYT *Voy.* II. I. 176 An Englishman called Thomas Williams..lieth about trade of merchandize in the streete called The Soca of the Iewes. 1623 MASSINGER *Bondman* II. i, To lie at rack and manger. 1694 MOTTEUX *Rabelais* v. vii. (1737) 27 There he lay at Rack and Manger. 1719 DE FOE *Crusoe* II. vi, The men lying ..at victuals and wages upon the owners' account.

†d. To be quartered *on*. *Obs.*

1669 *Ormonde MSS.* in *10th Rep. Hist. MSS. Comm.* App. v. 101 Five of the horsemen are lying on the tenants of your petitioner.

6. In various idiomatic uses (with preps., etc.), expressive of steady and continuous action. (Cf. L. *incumbere operi.*)

†a. *to lie at*, *upon*: to importune, urge. *Obs.*

1535 COVERDALE *1 Macc.* xi. 40 He..laye sore vpon him, to delyuer him this yonge Antiochus. 1566 GASCOIGNE *Supposes* I. i. Poems 1869 I. 204 The olde dotarde, he that so instantly dothe lye vpon my father for me [i.e. as a suitor for her hand]. 1568 *MS. Depos. Canterbury Cath. Libr.* Bk. 16. 24 Sept., Shee hath layne at me a good while to have your good will in maryage with her. 1600 HOLLAND *Livy* I. 32 Dame Tullia lay ever upon him, & pricked forward his distempered & troubled mind. 1619 W. WHATELEY *God's Husb.* ii. (1622) 114 To lie at him with vncessant and vehement sollicitations to commit such and such foule deeds. 1673 JANWAY *Heaven on E.* (1847) 155 Shall they lie at you day and night, to give your consent,..and are you still unwilling? a 1688 W. CLAGETT *17 Serm.* (1699) 358 The judge in the parable granted the widow's suit merely because she lay upon him, and was troublesome to him. 1737 WHISTON *Josephus, Hist.* III. viii. §3 Nicanor lay hard at Josephus to comply.

†b. *to lie heavy upon*: to oppress, harass. (Cf. 7 c.) *Obs.*

c 1586 C'TESS PEMBROKE *Ps.* CXLVI. iii, He orphans doth support: But heavy lies upon the godlesse sort. 1611 BIBLE *1 Esdras* v. 72 The heathen of the land lying heauy vpon the inhabitants of Iudea. 1676 HOBBES *Iliad* (1677) 181 This said, the Lycians heavier than before (To please their prince) upon the Argives lay.

c. *to lie †at*, *to*: to apply oneself vigorously and steadily to.

1583 STOCKER *Civ. Warres Lowe C.* III. 87 b, Citizens, Souldiers, Souldiers Wiues, and Pages, laye at it daye and night: insomuch that it was quickly dispatcht. 1656 BAXTER *Reformed Pastor* 58 This is the work that we should lie at with them night and day. 1833 L. RITCHIE *Wand. by Loire* 160 The men..lay desperately to their oars, and the skiff sprang through the water. 1837 CARLYLE *Fr. Rev.* II. xi. 78 No mercenary mock-workers, but real ones that lie freely to it.

†d. with gerund: To keep on or continue *doing* something. *Obs. rare.*

1692 R. L'ESTRANGE *Fables* xi. (1708) 13 Why will you lie Pining and Pinching your self in such a Lonesome, Starving Course of Life? *Ibid.* lxii. 77 The Generality of Mankind lye Pecking at One Another, till One by One they are all Torn to Pieces. 1692 —— *Josephus* iv. (1733) 892 Here's an obscure, mean Wretch, that has the Face to lie tutoring me upon a Subject he knows nothing at all of himself.

II. Said of things, material or immaterial.

7. a. Of material things: To be placed or set horizontally or lengthwise or at rest on the ground or other surface.

c 1000 *Ags. Gosp.* John xx. 5 He ȝeseah þa linwæda licȝan. c 1290 *S. Eng. Leg.* I. 9/296 Þat treo ne scholde nouȝt ligge þere. a 1300 *Cursor M.* 1129 His blod on erth sced lijs. 1362 LANGL. *P. Pl.* A. v. 65 As a leek þat hedde I-leiȝen longe In þe sonne. c 1400 MAUNDEV. (Roxb.) iii. 9 Apon þat body lay a grete plate of gold. c 1450 *St. Cuthbert* (Surtees) 6603 Alle þe clathes lay him aboute. a 1548 HALL *Chron., Hen. VIII* 262 b, On all the bankes by the water side, laie peces of ordinaunce whiche shot of. 1590 GREENE *Mourn. Garm.* (1616) 12 A bottle full of Country whigge, By the Shepheards side did ligge. 1747 WESLEY *Prim. Physic* (1762) 75 Take as much as lies on a shilling of Calcin'd Eggshells. 1754 CHATHAM *Lett. Nephew* vi. 42, I hear with great pleasure, that Jocke lay before you, when you writ last to me. 1776–96 WITHERING *Brit. Plants* (ed. 3) II. 436 Corn fields and sandy places, especially where water has lain. 1849 MACAULAY *Hist. Eng.* iii. I. 345 The ruins of an old fort were to be seen lying among the pebbles and seaweed on the beach.

b. To be deposited, remain permanently in a specified place.

c 1400 MAUNDEV. (Roxb.) ii. 6 Þe coroune lyes in a vessell of cristall. 1459 *Test. Ebor.* (Surtees) II. 227 A Sawter..and an Hympner..lyggynge in his saide closet. 1463 *Bury Wills* (Camden) 22 The gardeyn assigned..for woode to lye in.

1535 COVERDALE *Judith* xii. 1 Then commaunded he her to go in, where his treasure laye. **1609** SKENE *Reg. Maj.* 1 b, Al the grains and cornes lyand in bings. **1804** *Europ. Mag.* XLV. 65/1 A Petition from J. Macleod..was ordered to lie on the table. **1849** MACAULAY *Hist. Eng.* iii. I. 393 An esquire passed among his neighbours for a great scholar, if Hudibras and Baker's Chronicle [etc.]..lay in his hall window among the fishing rods and fowling pieces. **1891** *Law Times* XCI. 411/2 Jeune, J. made the order, but directed that it should lie in the office for a week.

c. Of a building, etc.: To be overthrown or fallen; with complement, as ***to lie in ruins, in the dust. to lie heavy***: to be a heavy load *upon* (*lit.* and *fig.*: see HEAVY *a.*). Of food, etc., ***to lie heavy, cold***, etc. (†formerly, simply ***to lie***) ***on the stomach***: to be felt as oppressive.

c **1330** *Arth. & Merl.* 544 (Kölbing) Foundement & werk þai founde Ligge vp so & doun op þe grounde. *a* **1592** H. SMITH *God's Arrow agst. Atheists* v. (1593) K 3 b, If it bee not builded vpon a good foundation..the whole building is like to lie in the dust. **1711** SWIFT *Jrnl. to Stella* 5 Sept., I ate sturgeon, and it lies on my stomach. *c* **1726** [see HEAVY 1 b]. **1884** W. C. SMITH *Kildrostan* 43 One sidewall long had in ruins lain. **1897** *Allbutt's Syst. Med.* III. 704 Delicate persons, in whom the cold water tends to lie heavy on the stomach.

8. To remain unworked, unused, untouched, or undiscovered. Often with complement, as ***to lie barren, hid, waste*** (see also FALLOW *a.*^{2}, LEA *a.*); also in phr. ***to lie on one's hands, to lie at a stand.***

(Cf. sense 4, where the subj. is a person or a personification.)

a **1300** *Cursor M.* 6841 Your land yee sal sau seuen [*sic*] yeir... þe seuend ye sal it lat lij still. **1377** LANGL. *P. Pl.* B. VI. 165 Worth neuere plente amonge þe poeple þer-while my plow liggeth. *a* **1548** HALL *Chron., Hen. VIII*, 173 b, Wherfore all brode Clothes, Kerseis, and Cottons, laye on their handes. **1560** DAUS tr. *Sleidane's Comm.* 150 b, Through our mens wrytinges, sondrye articles are called agayne to lyght, whiche laye before hidde in darkenes. *c* **1590** MARLOWE *Faustus* (1604) D 3 b, Letts goe and make cleane our bootes which lie foule vpon our handes. **1622** in *Buccleuch MSS.* (Hist. MSS. Comm.) I. 211 This hath made matters to lie a little at a stand. **1628** DIGBY *Voyage Medit.* (1868) 68 To make them buy their currantes (which lay vpon their handes). **1641** HINDE *J. Bruen* To Rdr. 7 This worke hath lyen above twice five [years]. **1653** HOLCROFT *Procopius* III. 88 Turris, an ancient City..which had been sack'd by Barbarians, and layen long wast. **1671** FLAVEL *Fount. of Life* I. 3 'Tis pity that anything in Christ should ly hid from his People. **1879** GLADSTONE *Glean.* I. i. 2 Rarely within the living memory has so much of skill lain barren.

†9. Of the wind, the tongue: To be or become still, be at rest, subside. *Obs.*

a **1000** *Phœnix* 182 Ðonne wind liȝeð weder bið fæȝer. **1600** HOLLAND *Livy* XXV. xxvii. 569 When the East wind began to lie, which for certeine daies had blustred and raged. **1611** COTGR., *Languarde*,..a wench whose tongue neuer lyes. **1647** TRAPP *Comm. 1 Thess.* v. 3 When the winde lies, the great rain fals. **1689** PRIOR *Ep. to F. Shephard* 110 Fancies flow in, and Muse flies high; So God knows when my Clack will lye.

10. a. To be situated (in space), to have a (specified) position. Often with adj. (or quasi-adv.) complement.

c **1121** *O.E. Chron.* an. 656 (Laud MS.) Ealle þa landes þa þær abuton liggeð. *a* **1300** *Cursor M.* 2469 þe land o gommor þar-bi lijs. **1377** LANGL. *P. Pl.* B. x. 316 Ac þei leten hem as lordes her londe lith so brode. *c* **1400** *Lanfranc's Cirurg.* 161 In þe holownes þat is aboue liggiþ þe herte & þe lungis. **1455** *Rolls of Parlt.* V. 313/1, vii acres of Mede, liggyng in the Mede beside the Brigge of Chartesey. **1577** HANMER *Anc. Eccl. Hist.* (1619) 508 The citie, which lay wonderfull commodious for the Romanes. **1597** BACON *Coulers Good & Evill* v. Ess. (Arb.) 144 Men whose liuing lieth together in one Shire. **1605** SHAKS. *Lear* III. iv. 21 O that way madnesse lies, let me shun that. **1648** *Hamilton Papers* (Camden) 184, I believe the sceane of disorder may lye heere. **1657** R. LIGON *Barbadoes* (1673) 3 So much is the eye deceived in Land which lies high. **1695** WOODWARD *Nat. Hist. Earth* II. (1723) 77 Those Strata that ly deepest. **1711** ADDISON *Spect.* No. 170 ⁋13 It is a Misfortune for a Woman to be born between the Tropicks; for there lie the hottest Regions of Jealousy. **1793** SMEATON *Edystone L.* §204 A small sea-port of Somersetshire, lying upon the Bristol Channel. **1818** CRUISE *Digest* (ed. 2) V. 606 Within the manor of Collingham, where the lands lay. **1883** *Eng. Illustr. Mag.* Nov. 72/1 The wild beauty of Wicken Fen is in striking contrast with the cultivated land lying around it.

b. To be spread out or extended to the view.

1764 GOLDSM. *Trav.* 100 But let us try these truths with closer eyes, And trace them through the prospect as it lies. **1792** *Gentl. Mag.* 9/2 A spacious field now lies before the Christian world for the introduction of a better policy. **1836** J. H. NEWMAN *Par. Serm.* (1837) III. x. 141 It is remarkable that such difficulties as these should lie on the face of Scripture. **1848** W. H. BARTLETT *Egypt to Pal.* v. (1879) 99 We could not for a moment expect such indications to lie upon the surface. **1860** PUSEY *Min. Proph.* 181 Samaria.. unfenced and unconcealed by walls, lay open, unsheltered in every part from the gaze of the besiegers. **1890** J. PAYN *Burnt Million* II. xxx. 248 What a future seemed to lie before him!

c. Of a road, way, journey, etc.: To extend, have a (specified) direction.

c **1000** ÆLFRIC *Gen.* xxxv. 19 On þam weȝe, þe lið to Euphrate. **1596** SHAKS. *Tam. Shr.* III. ii. 212 There lies your way. **1605** —— *Lear* III. iv. 10 If thy flight lay toward the roaring Sea. **1648** GAGE *West Ind.* 114, I found it not so hard to overcome, as I had conceited, the way lying with windings. **1849** MACAULAY *Hist. Eng.* x. II. 567 The counties through which the road to London lay. **1851** CARLYLE *Sterling* II. vii. (1872) 142 Our course lay along the Valley of the Rhone. **1883** R. W. DIXON *Mano* III. viii. 136 Nor doubt I where my voyage next must lie.

d. Of the wind: To remain in a specified quarter.

1604 E. G[RIMSTONE] *D'Acosta's Hist. Indies* IV. v. 218 Small furnaces vpon the sides of the mountaines, built expresly where the winde lies. **1704** RAY *Creation* I. (ed. 4) 96 The wind lying in that corner at least three quarters of the Year. **1876** 'MARK TWAIN' *Tom Sawyer* i. 4 But in spite of her, Tom knew where the wind lay, now. **1886** F. T. ELWORTHY *West Somerset Word-Bk.* 434 Which way do the wind lie 'smornin?

e. Of horses, yachts, etc., in a race: to occupy a specified ordinal position. Also *transf.*

1951 E. RICKMAN *Come Racing with Me* iii. 24 What is that with the light blue sleeves lying fourth? **1955** J. CHRISTOPHER *Year of Comet* ii. 49 Who's lying fourth? **1972** D. FRANCIS *Smokescreen* iv. 55 He took the first half mile without apparent effort, lying about sixth. **1974** *Country Life* 24 Oct. 1189/3 Busted is lying third in this year's table of sire's winnings.

11. *Naut.* **a.** Of a ship: To be stationed in a berth or anchorage.

c **1121** *O.E. Chron.* an. 1009 (Laud MS.) And þær [þa scipu] sceoldan licgan. *c* **1470** HENRY *Wallace* VII. 1068 A hundreth schippys..in hawyn was lyand thar. **1495** *Naval Acc. Hen. VII* (1896) 254 The seid ship lying at Rode in the Kynges haven. **1530** PALSGR. 610/1, I lye at an anker, as a shyppe dothe. **1775** R. CHANDLER *Trav. Asia Minor* (1825) I. 35 They lay at anchor near Tenedos. *a* **1812** A. CHERRY *Song, Bay of Biscay* 7 Our poor devoted bark, Till next day, there she lay, In the Bay of Biscay O! **1849** MACAULAY *Hist. Eng.* iii. I. 302 He..lay in port when he was ordered to chase a Sallee rover. **1851** D. G. MITCHELL *Fresh Glean.* 12 The Zebra lay just off the pier.

b. To steer in a (specified) direction. Also (quasi-*trans.*) ***to lie the course***: (of a ship) to have her head in the direction wished. ***to lie at hull***: see HULL *sb.*^{2} 2.

1574 BOURNE *Regiment for Sea* xix. (1577) 51 a, If the ship haue had often trauerse by the meanes of contrary windes, so that she could not lie hir course. **1597–8** BP. HALL *Sat.* IV. v. 121 Whiles his false broker lyeth in the wind. **1719** DE FOE *Crusoe* II. ii. (1840) 27 They could not lie near the wind. **1748** *Anson's Voy.* III. v. 342 The proas..are capable of lying much nearer the wind than any other vessel hitherto known. **1769** FALCONER *Dict. Marine* (1780) G gg, The ship cannot lie her course without being close-hauled. **1800** NELSON in Nicolas *Disp.* (1845) IV. 189 The Success being to leeward, Captain Peard..lay across his hawse. **1892** H. M. DOUGHTY *Our Wherry in Wendish Lands* 123 The waterway we now entered..was scarcely four feet deep..and that only in the middle. Luckily we could just lie it. *Ibid.* 301 A turn enabled us to lie our course, and up the sail went.

12. *fig.* **a.** Of immaterial things: To exist, be found, have place, reside (in some specified place or quarter); to be set, fixed, or arranged in some specified position or order. † ***to lie fair***: to be just or reasonable. † ***to lie in common***: to be common *to* or *among* several possessors. *spec.* const. *against, for, to*, in legal use.

c **1250** *Gen. & Ex.* 1916 For-ði wexem wið gret nið And hate, for it in ille (herte) lið. *a* **1300** *Cursor M.* 22280 Al falshed and feluni, And al tresun sal in him lii. **1380** WYCLIF *Wks.* (1880) 334 And þus popes & prelates kepen to hem silf assoylyng, in which lyþe wynnyng. *c* **1449** PECOCK *Repr.* II. xiv. 233 Whiche ij. textis, if thei ben considered as thei liggen to gidere in rewe. **1523** SKELTON *Garl. Laurel* 1200 Therby lyith a tale. **1538** STARKEY *England* I. ii. 33 Herin, me semyth lyth a dowte. **1566** ADLINGTON *Apuleius* To Rdr., I have not..so absolutely translated every word as it lieth in the prose. **1641** MILTON *Animadv.* v. Wks. 1851 III. 223 If the words lay thus in order. **1662** STILLINGFL. *Orig. Sacr.* I. i. §15 This defect..of those histories is either more general, which lies in common to them all, or [etc.]. *Ibid.* II. iv. §1 If the opposition did not lie between the order of true Prophets..and the false Prophets. **1672** R. MONTAGU in *Buccleuch MSS.* (Hist. MSS. Comm.) I. 520 Methinks it is natural and lies fair enough that..I should have some share in [etc.]. **1704** SWIFT *T. Tub* Wks. 1760 I. 67 Their father.. commanded, that whatever they got should lie in common among them all. **1711** ADDISON *Spect.* No. 170 ⁋12 Their Acquaintance and Conversation has lain wholly among the vicious Part of Womankind. **1719** J. T. PHILIPPS tr. *Thirty four Confer.* 43 The fault lies at their own doors. **1845** McCULLOCH *Taxation* I. iv. (1852) 109 If the choice lay only between a tax on property and a tax on income. **1848** J. H. NEWMAN *Loss & Gain* 147 He..holds many profound truths in detail, but is quite unable to see how they lie to each other. **1861** M. PATTISON *Ess.* (1889) I. 33 The people themselves, incapable of discerning where their true interest lay. **1868** FREEMAN *Norm. Conq.* (1876) II. vii. 112 Their sympathies lay wholly with Gruffydd. **1883** R. W. DIXON *Mano* I. viii. 23 And told him all the truth, how all things lay. **1958** *Times* 26 Apr. 6/7 If a chief constable is dismissed by a county council an appeal lies to the Home Secretary. **1964** *Mod. Law Rev.* XXVII. III. 322 Nowadays, after the revival of certiorari as a remedy lying for intra-jurisdictional defects, the scope of review on habeas corpus must be defined with more accuracy. **1970** *Internat. & Compar. Law Q.* 4th Ser. XIX. II. 306 The *Erbersatzanspruch* lies against the heirs, and consists of a sum equal to half the value of the portion, to which a legitimate intestate heir would be entitled. **1971** *Mod. Law Rev.* XXXIV. VI. 691 Where X and Y have a regular course of dealing and are likely to make contracts in the future, a *quia timet* injunction will lie to prevent Z, a third party, from inducing breaches of such contracts as may be made in the future.

†b. Of thoughts, inclinations, activities, etc.: To have a specified direction. *Obs.*

1633 BP. HALL *Hard Texts, N.T.* 281 Our fight doth not lye against flesh and blood. **1641** J. JACKSON *True Evang. T.* III. 189 The Elench here lyes directly, and point-blanck against the Papists. **1666** BOYLE *Orig. Formes & Qual.* (1667) 2 The..Prejudices that lye against them. **1672** VILLIERS (Dk. Buckhm.) *Rehearsal* I. i. (Arb.) 25 My humour lyes another way. **1692** R. L'ESTRANGE *Fables, Life Æsop* (1708) 22 Æsop's Faculty lay notably that way. **1825** *New Monthly Mag.* XIII. 17 My inclinations have not lain towards prose.

c. ***to lie in*** (a person): to rest or centre in him; to depend upon him, be in his power (to do). Now chiefly in phr. ***as far as in*** (***me***, etc.) ***lies***. Also, ***to lie in one's power, to lie in*** (or †***on***) ***one's hands***.

c **1350** *Will. Palerne* 965 þer-for loueliche ladi in þe lis al min hope. *c* **1374** CHAUCER *Compl. Mars* 184 Sith hit lythe in his myght. **1393** LANGL. *P. Pl.* C. XXI. 431 Hit lyth in my grace, Wheþer þei deye oþer deye nat. *c* **1440** *Generydes* 3109, I wote right wele it lithe in me The Sowdon to destroye. **1470–85** MALORY *Arthur* II. iii, Aske what ye wil and ye shall haue it, and hit lye in my power to yeue hit. *a* **1533** LD. BERNERS *Huon* lxxxi. 243 It lyeth now in you to do with hym at your pleasure. *a* **1548** HALL *Chron., Hen. VIII*, 255 b, Thei promised the kyng, to doo all that in theim laie with their frendes. **1590** MARLOWE *Edw. II* (1598) H 2 b, Fauour him my Lord, as much as lieth in you. **1593** SHAKS. *Rich. II*, I. ii. 4 Correction lyeth in those hands Which made the fault that wee cannot correct. **1597** HOOKER *Eccl. Pol.* V. lx. §7 The Church, as much as in her lieth, wilfully casteth away their soules. **1605** BACON *Adv. Learn.* II. vii. §2 (1873) 113 To me..that do desire as much as lieth in my pen [etc.]. **1613** OVERBURY *A Wife* Wks. (1856) 44 Women though they weaker be..yet on their hands The chastity of men doth often lye. **1642** ROGERS *Naaman* 176 As much as in you hath lyen. **1662** CHAS. II in Julia Cartwright *Henrietta of Orleans* (1894) 121, I am sure I have done all that lies in my power. **1720** OZELL *Vertot's Rom. Rep.* I. IV. 226 All the Hopes of the Republic lay in an old Man just taken from the Plough. **1875** SCRIVENER *Lect. Text N.T.* 9 Resolved, so far as in him lay, to root out the Christian Faith. **1885** TENNYSON *Tiresias*, Only in thy virtue lies The saving of our Thebes.

†d. To belong or pertain *to* a person (to do); to pertain, be attached or incident *to* a thing. Also, ***to lie*** (one) ***in hand to do***. *Obs.*

a **1225** *Leg. Kath.* 779 Ne lið hit nawt to þe to leggen lahe upon me. **13..** *Minor Poems fr. Vernon MS.* (E.E.T.S.) 505/453 þer-to liht muche mede. *c* **1430** *Hymns Virg.* 42 To me, maistir deuel, it lijs; To ihesu wole y take hede. **1577** tr. *Bullinger's Decades* (1592) 73 He cannot choose..but..do all things, that lie God a King and Prieste in hande to doe. **1657** W. RAND tr. *Gassendi's Life Peiresc* I. 59 Contrarily, it lies me in hand, I suppose, to take heed, least [etc.].

e. ***to lie with***: to be the office or province of (some one) *to do* something.

1885 *Manch. Exam.* 22 Sept. 5/1 It lies now with Turkey to take the initiative.

f. To rest or be imposed as a burden, charge, obligation, etc. *upon* a person; to be incumbent or obligatory *upon*; to press or weigh upon (one's mind or heart).

a **1300** *Cursor M.* 8348 (Cott.) He tald þat him lai apon hert. *Ibid.* 13385 (Gött.) On vs ligges noght þe nede. **1526** TINDALE *Acts* xxvii. 20 Noo smale tempest laye apon vs. **1551** RECORDE *Pathw. Knowl.* Ep. to King, Sundrie occasions which may lye them on. **1596** SHAKS. *1 Hen. IV*, V. ii. 48 O, would the quarrell lay vpon our heads. **1630** SANDERSON *Serm.* II. 255 It lieth us upon, to employ it to the best advantage we can. **1666** BUNYAN *Grace Ab.* ⁋86 That Scripture lay much upon me, *without shedding of Blood is no remission*. **1676** W. HUBBARD *Happiness of People* 49 The present distress of the war that hath lyen so long upon us. *a* **1715** BURNET *Own Time* (1724) I. 62 It was a duty lying on them by the Covenant. **1722** DE FOE *Plague* (Rtldg.) 94 These Things..lay upon my Mind. **1794** BURKE *Sp. agst. W. Hastings* Wks. XVI. 74 With those charges lying upon him. **1804** CASTLEREAGH in Owen *Wellesley's Desp.* 258 It lay upon them to offer terms to us. **1873** *Act 36 & 37 Vict.* c. 86 §24 It shall lie on the defendant to prove that the child is not of such age.

g. To be set *at stake*; to hang or depend *on* or *upon* a hazard, doubtful issue, etc.

1590 SPENSER *F.Q.* I. iii. 12 Full fast she fled..As if her life upon the wager lay. **1601** SHAKS. *All's Well* III. vii. 43 He persists As if his life lay on't. **1606** —— *Ant. & Cl.* III. viii. 5 Our fortune lyes Vpon this iumpe. **1668** R. STEELE *Husbandman's Calling* iv. (1672) 52 Nor..can he reform sin, if his life lay on it. **1760–72** H. BROOKE *Fool of Qual.* (1809) II. 142 We entered as warmly into it [the question], as though a province had lain at stake.

h. ***to lie in***: to consist in, to have its ground or basis in. †Also with *inf.* instead of *in* and object.

1589 PUTTENHAM *Eng. Poesie* III. xxii. (Arb.) 265 Another point of surplusage lieth not so much in superfluitie of your words. **1633** G. HERBERT *Temple, Faith* vii, If blisse had lien in art or strength, None but the wise or strong had gained it. **1644** MILTON *Areop.* (Arb.) 51 But here the great art lyes to discern in what [etc.]. **1724** A. COLLINS *Gr. Chr. Relig.* 75 The argument lies in the word Netser. *a* **1770** JORTIN *Serm.* (1771) VII. ii. 29 The perfection of every being must lie in its best part. **1871** B. STEWART *Heat* §84 Our only chance of success lies in abstracting heat from this liquid. **1881** GARDINER & MULLINGER *Eng. Hist.* I. iii. 48 The true remedy lay..in female education. *Ibid.* x. 178 Pitt's strength lay in his character.

i. ***to lie in, within***: to be contained or comprised in (a specified room or compass); †to admit of being expressed in (rhyme).

a **1300** *Cursor M.* 9240 (Gött.) Of abiud [cam] Elyachim, Of quam Asor, sadoch of him, þat loth er for to lig in rim. **1712** ADDISON *Spect.* No. 414 ⁋1 The Beauties of the most stately Garden or Palace lie in a narrow Compass. **1771** *Junius Lett.* lviii. 301 The question..lies within a very narrow compass.

†j. ***to lie at one's heart***: to be the object of one's affection or desire. Similarly, ***to lie heavy at*** or ***to one's heart***: to give one grave anxiety. *Obs.*

1607 SHAKS. *Cor.* IV. ii. 48 It would vnclogge my heart Of what lyes heauy too't. **1638** R. BAKER tr. *Balzac's Lett.* (vol. II.) 32, I have something, I know not what, lies heavy at my heart. **1673** SIR W. TEMPLE *To Dk. Ormond* Wks. 1720 I. 123 The Spaniards have but one Temptation to quarrel with Us, which is an occasion of recovering Jamaica, for that has ever lien at their hearts.

13. (Chiefly in *Law.*) Of an action, charge, claim, etc.: To be admissible or sustainable.

c **1320** *Sir Tristr.* 853 Certes, þi fader þan slouȝ y. Seþþen þou so hast sayd, Amendes þer ouȝt to ly. *c* **1385** CHAUCER *L.G.W.* Prol. 409 For sythe no cause of deth lyth in this cace, ȝow oughte to ben the lyghtere merciable. **1495** *Act 11 Hen. VII*, c. 24 §1 None essoyne or proteccion to lye nor to be allowed in the same. **1621** ELSING *Debates Ho. Lords* (Camden) 108 To consider what appeales out of the Chancery to this Courte doe lye. **1651** HOBBES *Leviath.* III. xlii. 277 There lyeth Excommunication for Injustice. **1712** PRIDEAUX *Direc. Ch.-wardens* (ed. 4) 75 There doth lye an Appeal to the Bishop. **1745** WESLEY *Answ. Ch.* 5, I should rejoice if there lay no other Objection against them, than that of Erroneous Opinions. **1748** RICHARDSON *Clarissa* (1811) VIII. 253 If not, then indeed is thy conscience seared, and no hopes will lie for thee. **1756** BURKE *Subl. & B.* II. ix, Some or all of these objections will lie against every figure of a cross. **1818** CRUISE *Digest* (ed. 2) V. 430 A writ of error did not lie after he attained his full age. **1850** ROBERTSON *Serm.* Ser. III. ix. (1853) 121 One from whose knowledge..there lies almost no appeal. **1865** LIGHTFOOT *Galat.* (1874) 124 Still more serious objections lie against identifying it with any later visit in the Acts. **1866** CRUMP *Banking* iv. 93 In which case no action for damages would lie.

†**14.** Of land, landed possessions: To appertain *to*. *Obs.*

839 in Birch *Cartul. Sax.* I. 599, xiiii aeceras & ða mæde þe þær to lið. *c* **1050** in Kemble *Cod. Dipl.* IV. 232 Ælc ðara landa ðe on mines fæder dæȝe læȝ into Cristes cyrcean. *a* **1225** *Leg. Kath.* 28 King of þat lond þat lei into Rome. *a* **1225** *Juliana* 13 Alle þe londes þe þerto liggeð. *c* **1420** *Chron. Vilod.* st. 983 A parcell of lond..þe wheche ryȝtwyslyche to þat Abbay lay. **1583** STUBBES *Anat. Abus.* II. (1882) 29 A house, with pasture lieng to it. **1618** BOLTON *Florus* I. ix. (1636) 24 Whereas they had in the beginning no Land of their owne lying to their City.

¶ **III. 15.** *trans.* Used causatively or by mistake for LAY *v.*[1] Now *rare.*

1387 TREVISA *Higden* (Rolls) VII. 369 He was wont to legge [*MS. γ* lygge] his heed uppon a forme. *a* **1400–50** *Alexander* 2101 He comands To gedire þam vp ilka gome & þam in grauys ligg. **1402** *Jack Upland* (Skeat) 46–7 And whan ye liggen it [your habit] besyde you, than lig ye youre religion besyde you, and ben apostatas. *c* **1485** *Digby Myst.* (1882) IV. 549 We shall..ly hym in the mold. *a* **1500** MEDWALL *Nature* (Brandl) II. 1088 Thy sores whyche be mortall Onles that thys medycyns to theym be layn. **1641** BEST *Farm. Bks.* (Surtees) 48 That in mowinge hee neauer lye out his sheaues beyonde the balkes but rather within the balkes. *c* **1648–50** BRATHWAIT *Barnabees Jrnl.* III. P. iv, I saw a Tombe one had beene laine in. **1699** GARTH *Dispens.* II. (1706) 16 Whilst Seas of melted oar lye waste the Plains. *a* **1703** BURKITT *On N.T.* Mark iv. 41 Christ, as God, lies a law upon the most lawless creatures. **1708** J. C. *Compl. Collier* (1845) 18 Would they but lye their groundless pretences by. **1749** FIELDING *Tom Jones* XII. xii, The whole furniture of the infernal regions hath long been appropriated to the managers of play-houses, who seem lately to have lain them by as rubbish. **1802** *Med. Jrnl.* VIII. 507, I dressed the wound, lying down as much of the scalp as [etc.]. **1809** MALKIN *Gil Blas* I. xvi. ¶5 The cloth was lain. Down we sat at table. **1880** F. G. LEE *Church under Eliz.* II. 245 As God had lain this peer's honour in the dust.

IV. Combined with adverbs.

†**16. lie aback. a.** To be backward, reluctant, or shy. *Obs.*

1560 in Tytler *Hist. Scot.* (1864) III. 397 Not only shall any of his own pretend to disobey or ly aback in this action, but [etc.]. **1596** DALRYMPLE tr. *Leslie's Hist. Scot.* II. 148 Nathir..in tyme of neid lyes the Pechtis abak wt thair supporte.

†**b.** as *sb.* Shyness, timidity. *Obs.*

c **1600** MONTGOMERIE *Cherrie & Slae* 1423 Sir, I have sein them baith, In braidieness and lye aback, Escape and cum to skaith.

17. lie about, to lie here and there; to be left lying carelessly or in disorder.

1852 C. KINGSLEY *Hypatia* (1853) I. xiii. 274 Why, these poor blackguards lying about are very fair specimens of humanity. **1891** R. BUCHANAN *Come live with Me* II. xiii. 168 Ye might leave it [*sc.* poison] lying about, and mischief might happen. **1891** W. MORRIS *News from Nowhere* v. 31 Most children, seeing books lying about, manage to read by the time they are four years old. **1934** G. B. SHAW *Simpleton of Unexpected Isles* i. 4, I hate to see dust lying about. Look! You could write your name in it.

†**18. lie abroad.** To lodge out of one's house or abode; to reside in a foreign country (in quot. 1651 with pun on LIE *v.*[2]). *Obs.*

c **1645** HOWELL *Lett.* (1650) III. 13 We might go barefoot, and ly abroad as beasts having no other canopy than the wild air. **1651** WALTON *Life Sir H. Wotton* Reliq. W. c 1 b, An Embassadour is an honest man, sent to lie abroad for the good of his Countrey. **1653** HOLCROFT *Procopius* II. 39 He.. being said to be sent to ly abroad, to prevent mischief to the Camp. **1675** *Collect. Sev. Treat. Penal Laws* Pref. A iv, The Popes Ambassadors..lye abroad for his..advantage.

19. lie along. a. To be prostrate at full length, to lie outstretched on the ground (now *arch.*); to extend along a surface.

1530 PALSGR. 601/1, I lye..as one lyeth alonge upon the grounde. **1600** SHAKS. *A. Y. L.* II. i. 30 As he lay along Vnder an oake. **1734** J. WARD *Introd. Math.* App. Gauging 455 To find what Quantity of Liquor is in any Cask, when its Axis is Parallel to the Horizon, viz. when it lies along. **1737** WHISTON *Josephus, Antiq.* VI. i. §1 Dagon..lay along, as having fallen down from the basis whereon he had stood. **1771** GOLDSM. *Hist. Eng.* I. 91 A cell so small, that he could neither stand erect, nor lie along in it. **1803** BEDDOES *Hygëia* x. 21 Few persons, suddenly stimulated to anger as they were lying along, would continue to repose in the same easy manner. **1883** R. W. DIXON *Mano* III. vi. 129 Him who there lay dead along. **1885–94** R. BRIDGES *Eros & Psyche* July xxii, The..wings, That from his shoulders lay along at rest.

b. *Naut.* Of a ship: To incline to one side under the pressure of a wind abeam.

1769 FALCONER *Dict. Marine* (1780) s.v. *Along*, *Lying-Along*, the state of being pressed down sideways by a weight of sail in a fresh wind that crosses the ship's course. **1781** ARCHER in *Naval Chron.* XI. 288 The Ship lay very much along, by the pressure of the wind. **1838** POE *A. G. Pym* xiii. Wks. (1865) IV. 109 The hulk lay more along than ever, so that we could not stand an instant without lashing ourselves.

20. lie back. To lean backwards against some support.

1894 CROCKETT *Raiders* 14, I shipped the oars and lay back thinking.

21. lie by. †**a.** To have a concubine. (Cf. LIE-BY I.) *Obs.*

1571 *Satir. Poems Reform.* xxviii. 28 My Father..had ane wyfe, Thocht he abusit his body, and lay by.

b. *Naut.* = *lie to* 29a: see BY *adv.* 2b.

1613 [see BY *adv.* 2b]. **1666** *Lond. Gaz.* No. 60/1 Our Fregats received some damage in their sails, and..were forced to ly by to mend them. **1748** *Anson's Voy.* II. v. 177 We lay by all the night..for Captain Saunders..to join us. **1769** FALCONER *Dict. Marine* (1780) Aaa4, To make sail, after having lain-by for some time.

c. To remain unused, be laid up in store.

1642 ROGERS *Naaman* 59 Let his carnall favour, and erroneous conceits ly by, let him empty himselfe of a worldly heart. *Ibid.* 441 Peters nets lay by when the season was. **1692** R. L'ESTRANGE *Fables* cccclviii. 434 The..Wretchedness of Avarice, that rather then make use of the Bounties of Providence in their Seasons, suffers them to lye by and Perish. **1719** W. WOOD *Surv. Trade* 74 Thriving Nations have..great Stores lying by of their own Manufactures. **1843** MRS. CARLYLE *Lett.* I. 254, I had..pillows lying by of no use.

d. To keep quiet, withdraw from observation; to remain inactive, rest.

1709 ADDISON *Tatler* No. 133 ¶5 To lie by for some Time in Silence and Obscurity. **1754** RICHARDSON *Grandison* II. 53 *Sir H.* 'What a plague—you did not cane him?' *Sir Ch.* 'He got well after a fortnight's lying by'. **1809** MALKIN *Gil Blas* x. i. ¶6 We determined on lying by for a day at Valladolid, as well to rest our mules, as to call on Signor Sangrado. **1824** SCOTT *St. Ronan's* xxv, I lay by on the watch for some opportunity when I might mend my own situation with my father. **1840** R. H. DANA *Bef. Mast* xxxi. 117, I must go below, and lie-by for a day or two. **1892** *Law Times* XCIII. 414/1 The plaintiff had lain by, whereas he should have taken the earliest opportunity of coming to the court.

22. lie down. a. (ME. also *lie adown.*) See sense 2 and DOWN *adv.* 5. Also *refl.* (now *arch.*). Also in pregnant senses: †To fall in battle; †to die; to go to bed; to give up; to be remiss or lazy.

c **1205** LAY. 6864 Seoððen he dun læi [*c* 1275 deaȝede]. **1297** R. GLOUC. (Rolls) 1145 þe romeins leie sone adoun; he made ampti place, & þe brutons arise vaste. *Ibid.* 2204 Oþer ligge adoun & be aslawe. *a* **1300** *Cursor M.* 10711 þan lai þai all in kneling dun. **1340–70** *Alex. & Dind.* 446 We liggen down in our den. *c* **1460** *Towneley Myst.* ii. 326 So lig down ther and take thi rest. **1535** COVERDALE *Ruth* iii. *contents*, Ruth lyeth her downe in the barne at Boos fete. —— *Isa.* xi. 6 The leoparde shal lye downe by the gote. *a* **1631** DONNE *Poems* (1650) 17 Why should we rise, because 'tis light? Did we lie downe, because 'twas night? **1774** FOOTE *Cozeners* III. Wks. 1799 II. 185 *Mrs. Air.* Pray, Madam, is the young lady at home? *Mrs. Fl.* Just lain down for a little. **1815** SCOTT *Guy M.* ii, They rose early and lay down late. **1847** MARRYAT *Childr. N. Forest* iv, There may be another [stag] lying down in the fern close to us. **1860** TYNDALL *Glac.* I. xvi. 113, I lay down and had five minutes sleep. **1861** DASENT *Burnt Njal* II. 312 Kari lay him down. **1904** W. H. SMITH *Promoters* i. 21 When they finally lie down, we'll just say, 'All right, we'll go ahead alone.' **1916** *Lit. Digest* 8 Jan. 87/1 It is natural enough that the accusation of 'lying down' and quitting has been cast up in turn at each of the participants in the conference. **1918** E. POUND *Let.* 3 Apr. (1971) 134 It is the best that can be done. Hope Kahn won't think I am lying down on the job. **1926** J. BLACK *You can't Win* xiv. 193 An ambitious fighting young lawyer who never 'laid down' on a client.

†**b.** To be brought to bed *of* a child. *Obs.*

c **1450** *Merlin* 89 The kynge sawgh that the quene was redy to ly down. **1580** LYLY *Euphues* Ep. Ded. (Arb.) 214 Of the second I went a whole yeare big, and yet when euerye one thought me ready to lye downe, I did then quicken. **1620** J. PYPER tr. *Hist. Astrea* I. vi. 171 His wife lay downe, but it was of a daughter. **1654** tr. *Martini's Conq. China* 212 Matrons with Child and ready to lye down. **1692** R. L'ESTRANGE *Fables* xxii. (1708) 29 A Wolf came to a Sow that was just lying down, and very kindly offer'd to take care of her Litter. **1818** W. GODWIN in Kegan Paul *Life* (1876) II. 256 He says..that Eliza was expected to lie down in two days after he sailed.

†**c.** Of an army: To take up a position *before*.

1693 *Mem. Cnt. Teckely* I. 82 This obliged Heister to demand Cannon and Foot, with whom he lay down before the Castle of Kus.

d. *to take* (a beating, defeat, etc.) *lying down*: to receive it with abject submission.

1888 *Sat. Rev.* 4 Aug. 133/1 Those who..profess themselves willing to take, 'lying down', any and every inconvenience that the victorious Irish may inflict. **1914** G. B. SHAW *Androcles* (1916) I. 17 You know, I should feel ashamed if I let myself be struck like that, and took it lying down. **1931** E. F. BENSON *Mapp & Lucia* viii. 229 She had to swallow her medicine... I had no idea.. that she would take it lying down like that. **1974** M. GILBERT *Flash Point* viii. 64, I heard what the beak said to you. I had an idea you weren't going to take it lying down.

†**23. lie forth.** Of bees: To settle outside the hive. (Cf. *lie out*, 27b.) *Obs.*

1609 C. BUTLER *Fem. Mon.* (1634) 47 Those [hives] that have lyen forth, or otherwise be very full, you may let alone.

24. lie in. a. To be brought to bed *of* a child (†also const. *with*); to be 'confined'. Also *fig.*

c **1440** *Promp. Parv.* 304/2 Lyyn' yn or yn chylde bedde ..*decubo.* *c* **1530** LD. BERNERS *Arth. Lyt. Bryt.* (1814) 42 As yet I am not determyned in what place she shall lye in. **1602** ROWLANDS *Tis Merrie when Gossips meete* 35 When I lay in of my first Boy. **1607** SHAKS. *Cor.* I. iii. 86 You must go visit the good Lady that lies in. **1626** BACON *Sylva* §899 The Shee-Beare breedeth, and lyeth in with her Young. **1729–30** BOLINGBROKE in *Swift's Lett.* (1766) II. 105 His wife lies-in with one child. **1749** FIELDING *Tom Jones* XII. xiv, Five hungry children, and a wife lying in of a sixth. **1762** GOLDSM. *Cit. W.* xc, They regularly retire every year at proper intervals to lie in of the spleen. **1825** *New Monthly Mag.* XIII. 51 Learning then ordinarily lay-in of folio volumes. **1871** TYLOR *Prim. Cult.* 76, 'Tis like a Koravan eating asafœtida when his wife lies in.

†**b.** To amount to, cost (a certain sum); 'to stand (a person) in' so much. *Obs.*

1622 in Picton *L'pool Munic. Rec.* (1883) I. 212 Soe much money..as the tendinge and keepinge of the said clocke shall lye in. **1660** WILLSFORD *Scales Comm.* I A Grocer bought 5¾ C grosse weight of Wares, which lay him in ..£163 13s. 8d. **1677** YARRANTON *Eng. Improv.* 134 The Corn will lye the Mum-Brewers in Two Shillings Six-pence per Bushel. **1755** JOHNSON *Lie* 21, To cost: as, it lies me in more money.

c. *Naut.* (See quot.)

1867 SMYTH *Sailor's Word-bk.*, *Lie in!* the order to come in from the yards when reefing, furling, or other duty is performed.

d. To remain in bed (after one's usual hour of rising). Cf. *lie-in* (LIE *sb.*[2] 6).

1893–4 R. O. HESLOP *Northumb. Words* II. 449 *Lie*, in the combination *lie-in*, to sleep longer than intended. **1911** E. M. CLOWES *On Wallaby* v. 144 On Sundays her husband and son 'lay in', as she called it, till midday, while she gave them their breakfast in bed.

25. lie off. a. *Naut.* Of a ship or boat: To stand some distance away from the shore or from some other craft.

1596 SHAKS. *1 Hen. IV*, III. i. 79 The remnant Northward, lying off from Trent. **1726** G. ROBERTS *Four Years Voy.* 26 As I lay off at an Anchor. **1867** SMYTH *Sailor's Word-bk.*, *Lie off!* an order given to a boat to remain off on her oars till permission is given for her to come alongside. **1890** HALL CAINE *Bondman* I. ix, [The schooner] intending to lie off at Ramsey for contraband rum.

b. To cease work temporarily; to take a rest.

1891 R. KIPLING *City Dreadf. Nt.* 81 As soon as he makes a little money he lies off and spends it. **1899** *Nation* (N.Y.) 21 Dec. 467/1 If McKinley would lie off for the next four years, he might make a very good free-trade candidate for the Presidency in 1904.

c. *Racing slang.* 'To make a waiting race' (Farmer *Slang* 1896).

26. lie on. †**a.** To be laid on. *Obs.*

1641–2 SHUTE *Sarah & Hagar* (1649) 109 Upon the first laying on of the rod, it may be, we will stamp and chafe; but when it still lies on..we lie quiet, and then our spirit comes down.

b. Of a vessel: To be bound *for*.

1850 *Tait's Mag.* XVII. 38/1 Not one [vessel] was, just then, 'lying on' for the Baltic way, the season being so late.

27. lie out. †**a.** To stretch out, extend. *Obs.*

1601 HOLLAND *Pliny* I. 54 Spaine and France..lying out with their promontories into two contrary seas. *Ibid.* 61 Corsica..lyeth out from the North into the South, and containeth in length an hundred and fiftie miles.

b. †To rest or settle outside (*obs.*); to sleep out, now *dial.* of cattle, to be left unhoused at night. *Obs.*

1630 J. LEVETT *Ord. Bees* (1634) 34 Their Bees haue exceedingly lyen out upon the Hiue and board. **1712** ARBUTHNOT *John Bull* III. i, The witnesses farther made oath, that the said Timothy lay out a-nights. **1886** ELWORTHY *W. Somerset Word-bk.*, *Lie in*, *Lie out*, said of horses or cows. If they are kept housed at night, they are said to lie in, if not they lie out. Do your 'oss lie in or out?

c. *Sc.* To delay; *spec.* to delay in entering upon property as heir.

1640–1 *Kirkcudbr. War-Comm. Min. Bk.* (1855) 42 For his lying sae lang out in not subscryveing of the covenant. **1673–88** FOUNTAINHALL in M. P. Brown *Suppl. Decis.* (1826) III. 146 A man is married on a woman, that is apparent heir to lands.—She, to defraud her husband either of the *jus mariti* or the courtesy, lies out and will not enter. **1868** *Act 31 & 32 Vict.* c. 101 §6 The rights and remedies competent to a superior against his vassal lying out unentered.

d. *to lie it out*: to sleep on late into the morning. ? *Obs.*

1748 RICHARDSON *Clarissa* (1811) V. 2 The dear creature was so frightened, and so fatigued, last night, no wonder she lies it out this morning.

e. *to lie out of one's money*: to remain unpaid. *to lie out of one's ground* (Racing slang): see quot. 1896.

1860 GEO. ELIOT *Mill on Floss* I. viii. I. 151, I can't lie out o' my money any longer. You must raise it as quick as you can. **1892** *Daily Chron.* 19 Apr. 9/2 How can zealous discharge of this duty be expected, when the officer..has to advance the cost of the summons, and lie out of his money for a year at a time, if not for ever? **1896** FARMER *Slang*, *To lie out of one's ground* = to 'lie off' too long, so as to be unable to recover lost ground.

28. lie over. a. To be held over or deferred to a future occasion.

1856 MRS. CARLYLE *Lett.* II. 294, I have a strange story to tell you..but that must lie over, or I shall miss the omnibus.

b. 'To remain unpaid after the time when payment is due' (Craig 1848).

c. *Naut.* (See quot.)

1867 SMYTH *Sailor's Word-bk.*, *Lie over*, a ship heeling to it with the wind abeam.

d. *U.S.* To suspend travelling; to stop.

1849 *Ex. Doc. 31st U.S. Congress 1 Sess. Senate* No. 64. 186 But I shall make an early drive and 'lie over' tomorrow at the first water. **1903** A. ADAMS *Log of Cowboy* 181 We overtook a number of wagons loaded with wool, lying over, as it was Sunday.

29. lie to. a. *Naut.* Of a ship: To come almost to a standstill, with her head as near the wind as possible, by backing or shortening sail.

1711 LITTLETON *Let.* 13 Aug. in *Lond. Gaz.* No. 4906/3 The largest of them lay too a long time. **1748** *Anson's Voy.* I. viii. 79 Another storm.. reduced us to the necessity of lying to under our bare poles. **1760–72** H. BROOKE *Fool of Qual.* (1809) III. 81 We shortened sail, and lay to till morning. **1800** *Asiatic Ann. Reg., Chron.* 117/2 It blew a strong gale.. on which Lieut. Roper handed all his sails, except the mizen, which he balanced, and lay to. **1883** STEVENSON *Treas. Isl.* (1886) 212 Take a turn round the capstan, and lie-to for the tide.

b. *Sc.* To come to be fond of a person.

1768 ROSS *Helenore* 79, I do like him sair, An' that he wad ly too [ed. 1789, p. 85 like me], I hae nae fear.

30. lie up. †**a.** To be laid out for burial.

1553 BECON *Reliques of Rome* (1563) 253 Vilanye and synne y^t weren vsed & done about dead bodyes ligging vp & yet is vsed about in many places, or the body be borne to church.

b. To go into or remain in retirement or retreat; to take to one's bed or keep one's room as an invalid; (of a ship) to go into dock.

1699 DAMPIER *Voy.* II. III. 24 There they [ships] must lye up, or be 3 or 4 Years in their return from a place which may be sailed in 6 Weeks. *a* **1868** DICKENS in *Househ. Words* (Cent.), He has a bad cold—rheumatism—he must lie up for a day or two. **1881** GREENER *Gun* 595 The black bear lies up during the day in caves and amongst rocks. **1893** R. KIPLING *Many Invent.* 26 When there's nothing going on, there is nothing going on, and you lie up. **1897** *Allbutt's Syst. Med.* II. 443 Some days the patient may feel comparatively well and fit for work, on other days he is languid and lies up.

c. *to lie up in lavender*: to be in safe keeping or custody. (Cf. LAVENDER *sb.*² 2.)

1822 SCOTT *Nigel* xxv, Alas! the good gentleman lies up in lavender.. himself.

d. To lay or shape one's course.

1779 FORREST *Voy. N. Guinea* 169 The land wind veered to the northward, and we lay up no better than west. **1868** ATKINSON *Cleveland Gloss., Lig up to*, to proceed towards, to lay or shape one's course to, a given place.

lie (laɪ), *v.*² Inflected lying ('laɪɪŋ), lied (laɪd). Forms: *Infin.* 1 léoȝan, 2 leioȝen, 2–5 liȝe-n, 3 lege, (*imper.* lih), 4 ley(e, lei, lije, li, 3–7 ly, 3–8 lye, 4 leighe, leiȝe, lyghe, lyeȝe, leie, 4–5 leȝe, 4–6 ley, *Sc.* le, 5 ly(ȝ)yn, 5–6, 9 *Sc.* and *north.* lee, 4– lie. *Ind. Pres. 2nd sing. α.* 3 *Orm.* leȝhesst, 4 liȝest, leyest, lex(s)t, lixt(e, 4–5 lyest, 3– liest. *β. north.* and *Sc.* 4 lighes, leies, lies, 4–5 lyes, 4–6 leis. *3rd sing. α.* 1 léoȝeþ, líhþ, 3 lih(e)ð, ligeð, leȝeð, legheþ, *Orm.* leȝheþþ, 4 liȝ(e)þ, lyeþ, leiþ, leighth, leȝth, lyeȝ(e)th, lihth, likth, 5 lith(e, 3– lieth. *β.* 4 liges, leies, leyes, 5 lijs, leghes, 6 *Sc.* leis, 4– lies, *3rd pl.* 6 *Sc.* lene, leyne. *Pa. t. α.* 1 léah, léaȝ, (*pl.* luȝon), 2–3 luȝe, 3 leh, læh, lighgh, 3–4 lowe, 4 leigh, legh, ligh, lygh. *β.* 4 liȝed(e, leiȝede, leeȝide, liede, lyede, leghed, lei(e)d, lieid, 4–6 *Sc.* leit, leyt, 4–7 lyed, leid, 7 *Sc.* leed, 4– lied. *Pa. pple. α.* 1 loȝen, 2–3 i-loȝe(n, loȝen, 3 i-lowe, 3–4 y-low(e, loun, 4 lowe(n, leiȝen. *β.* 4 liȝed, *Sc.* leyt, 5 lyet, 4– lied. [A Com. Teut. str. vb. (in Eng. conjugated weak from the 14th c.): OE. *léoȝan* (*léah, luȝon, loȝen*) corresponds to OFris. **liaga*, **liatza* (recorded in 3rd sing. pres. ind. *liucht*, pa. t. sing. subj. *lege*), OS. *liogan, liagan* (Du. *liegen, loog, gelogen*), OHG. *liogan, loug, lugun, gelogen* (MHG. *liegen, louc, gelogen*, mod.G. *lügen, log, gelogen*), Goth. *liugan*, ON. *ljúga* (Sw. *ljuga*, Da. *lyve*), f. Teut. root **leug-* (:*laug-*: *lug-*), whence LIE *sb.*¹; cogn. w. OSl. *lŭža* lie.]

1. *intr.* To tell a lie or lies; to utter falsehood; to speak falsely.

971 *Blickl. Hom.* 29 Se awerȝda gast.. sona leah. *c* **1050** *Voc.* in Wr.-Wülcker 401/1 *Fefellisset*, þa þa he leaȝ. *c* **1175** *Lamb. Hom.* 91 þu hauest iloȝen þan halie gaste. *Ibid.* 93 Ne luȝe þu na monnum! *Ibid.* 153 Hwenne þe muð is open for to liȝe. *c* **1200** *Vices & Virtues* (1888) 9 Ðar ðu luȝe, ðu lease dieuel. *c* **1200** *Trin. Coll. Hom.* 131 He þe neure ne lihgh ne lige ne wile. *c* **1200** ORMIN 5190 þu leȝhesst, & beswikesst swa þin aȝhen wrecche sawle. *c* **1205** LAY. 17684 þus læh [*c* **1275** leh] þe laðe mon. *a* **1225** *Leg. Kath.* 1431 Mit se swiðe lufsome leores ha leien. *a* **1225** *Ancr. R.* 236 þu liest, cweð heo, fule þing. **1297** R. GLOUC. (Rolls) 3348 He adde so foule ilowe. *a* **1300** *Cursor M.* 5143 (Cott.) þou lighes [*Gött.* lies, *Fairf.* lyes, *Trin.* lyest] now, eber pantener! **1340** *Ayenb.* 63 Kvead þing hit is to lyeȝe. *c* **1375** *Sc. Leg. Saints* xxv. (*Julian*) 206 My gud brethyre, quhy lest ȝou le? *c* **1380** WYCLIF *Wks.* (1880) 264 In whiche autorite he seide soþ & in whiche he leiȝede. **1393** LANGL. *P. Pl.* C. XXI. 351 þow lowe tyl eue. *c* **1394** *P. Pl. Crede* 542 þou leyest, & þou lext. *c* **1400** *Gamelyn* 297 Thou lixt, seid Gamelyn, so broke I my chyn. **1483** *Cath. Angl.* 216/1 To Lye (*A.* Lee), *commentari*. **1513** DOUGLAS *Æneis* I. Prol. 233 Les than wyse autouris lene [*ed.* 1553 leyne]. **1567** *Gude & Godlie Ball.* (S.T.S.) 193, I say, ȝe leit euerie one. **1581** SIDNEY *Apol. Poetrie* (Arb.) 52 As I take it, to lye, is to affirme that to be true which is false. **1678** BUNYAN *Pilgr.* I. 7 It was made by him that cannot lye. *a* **1784** JOHNSON in *Boswell* an. 1781 (1848) 670/1 He lies, and he knows he lies. **1885** BURTON *Arab. Nts.* (1886) I. 263, I lied against myself and confessed the theft, albeit I am altogether innocent of it.

b. *to lie of* (arch.), †*on*, †*upon*: to tell lies about.

a **1200** *Moral Ode* 287 Of þo þine þe þere bued nelle ic hou nout leioȝen. *a* **1225** *Ancr. R.* 68 An te unwreste bliðeliche lieð on þe gode. *c* **1230** *Hali Meid.* 39 Forȝet ti folc þat liheð þe of weres & worldes wunne. *c* **1275** *Passion of Our Lord* 241 in *O.E. Misc.* 44 A ueole kunne wise hi lowen him vp-on. *c* **1305** *St. Andrew* 28 in *E.E.P.* (1862) 99 þu wost wel mid alle þat þu þerof loude lixt. *c* **1330** *Amis & Amil.* 838 He leighth on ous, withouten fail. *c* **1400** *Lanfranc's Cirurg.* 142 Manye men liȝen of þe wounde of þe nose. **1508** DUNBAR *Flyting w. Kennedie* 138 Thocht thow.. thus vpoun me leid. **1559** AYLMER *Harborowe* L 2 The smarts of the tormentes made him to confesse it, and lye of him self. **1580** J. HAY *Demandes* in *Cath. Tractates* (1901) 59 Quhy ar ye nocht esscheamed.. to lie on wss in your preachings, saying [etc.]. **1629** EARLE *Microcosm., Modest Man* (Arb.) 80 Whosoeuer dare lye on him hath power ouer him. **1864** CARLYLE *Fredk. Gt.* IV. 409 Nobody was more lied of. **1871** R. ELLIS tr. *Catullus* lxvii. 20 They lie on her [L. *falsum est*].

c. Proverbial expressions. For *to lie in one's teeth, throat, to lie like a trooper*, see the sbs.

a **1400** *Pistill of Susan* 317 Nou þou lyest in þin hed. *a* **1529** SKELTON *Merie Tales* v. Wks. 1843 I. p. lx, He.. woulde lye as fast as a horse woulde trotte. **1530** PALSGR. 610/2 He wyll lye as fast as a dogge wyll trotte. **1588** *Marprel. Epist.* (Arb.) 21 Bishops will lye like dogs.

2. *fig.* Chiefly of inanimate objects: To present false statements; to convey a false impression; to make a deceitful show.

c **1220** *Bestiary* 451 Ðe boc ne leȝeð noȝt of ðis. *a* **1300** *Cursor M.* 5054 For quen þe tan þe toþer sei Na wight moght þair blodes lei. *Ibid.* 14702 þe hali writte lies [*Trin.* lyeþ] na wight. **1426** LYDG. *De Guil. Pilgr.* 22376 The merour lyed verily. **1483** CAXTON *Gold. Leg.* 320 b/2 The Philosophers were brought to this that they sayd.. that the elementys lyeden or god of nature suffred. **1513** DOUGLAS *Æneis* I. Prol. 270 This wther buik.. So frenschlie leis, oneth twa wourdis gais richt. **1697** DRYDEN *Virg. Georg.* I. 587 The Sun, who never lies, Foretels the Change of Weather in the Skies. **1732** POPE *Ep. Bathurst* 340 Where London's column, pointing at the skies, Like a tall bully, lifts the head, and lies.

3. quasi-*trans.* †**a.** with cogn. obj. *Obs.*

a **1300** *Cursor M.* 16067 Mani lesing had þai loun again iesu þat dai. **1377** LANGL. *P. Pl.* B. XVIII. 400 þi lesynge.. þat þow lowe [*v.rr.* leighe, leyȝ] til Eue. *c* **1449** PECOCK *Repr.* II. iii. 150 Many lesingis y haue herd him lie. *c* **1500** *Wyl Bucke's Test.* (Copland) A ij b, My tounge that neuer lied lesinge.

†**b.** To say or allege falsely. *Obs.*

a **1300** *Seven Sins* ix. in *E.E.P.* (1862) 18 O worde ic ȝou lie nelle. *c* **1375** *Sc. Leg. Saints* i. (*Petrus*) 512 þu leis all þat þou sais. *c* **1450** *Merlin* i. 11 How sholde I.. enioyne the penance for thynges which I wene thow lyest veryly.

c. With *adv.* or phrase: To take *away* by lying; to get (a person, etc.) *into* or *out of* by lying.

1720 T. GORDON *Humourist* I. 175, I have known great Ministers rail'd and ly'd out of their Places. **1755** J. SHEBBEARE *Lydia* (1769) II. 44 Slandering women of reputation, and endeavouring to lye away their characters. **1762** FOOTE *Lyar* I. Wks. 1799 I. 290 If you don't one time or another.. lye yourself into some confounded scrape, I will consent to be hanged. **1784** R. BAGE *Barham Downs* I. 48 Every one would tell his story, his own way, and combine to lye an honest lawyer out of his bread. **1858** SIR J. KAYE *Hist. Afghan War* I. 204 The character of Dost Mohamed was lied away. **1865** CARLYLE *Fredk. Gt.* XII. vii. (1872) IV. 177 The tragically earnest meaning of your Life, is quite lied out of you, by a world sunk in lies. **1884** *Punch* 6 Dec. 276/2 Go on tamely to allow yourself to be lied into Party blindness.

†**4.** *trans.* To give the lie to. *Obs.*

1389 in *Eng. Gilds* (1870) 87 If any broþer or syster dispyse or mysconsel or lye his broþer. *c* **1450** *Robin Hood & Monk* xiv. in Child *Ballads* III. 97/2 With þat Robyn Hode lyed Litul Jon. **1464** *Waterford Arch.* in *10th Rep. Hist. MSS. Comm.* App. v. 331 He lied and rebuked the balif, to the great contempt of the King.

lie-abed ('laɪəbɛd). [f. LIE *v.*¹ + ABED.] One who lies late in bed; a late riser; a sluggard.

1764 FOOTE *Mayor of G.* I. Wks. 1799 I. 173 You are a lazy lie-a-bed. **1832** W. IRVING *Alhambra* (1851) 249 She was a little of a slattern, something more of a lie-a-bed, and, above all, a gossip of the first water. **1881** BLACKMORE *Christowell* xlviii, What has made a lark of such a lie-a-bed?

lieand, lieare, obs. ff. LYING *ppl. a.*, LAIR *sb.*¹

‖**Liebchen, liebchen** ('liːpçən, 'liːbçən). [G.] A person who is very dear to another; a sweetheart, a 'pet', darling. Commonly used as a term of endearing address.

1876 GEO. ELIOT *Dan. Der.* IV. VIII. lxii. 232 'Stay a minute, *Liebchen*,' said Lapidoth. **1941** M. TREADGOLD *We couldn't leave Dinah* xv. 226 How providential that there should be this trustworthy boy to keep the *liebchen* so contented. **1972** G. BAXT *Burning Sappho* iv. 71 You are no fool, *liebchen*. You are the most clever woman in the world. **1972** J. ROSSITER *Rope for General Dietz* xiii. 185 'Thank you, *Liebchen*,' she said softly.

liebenerite ('liːbənəraɪt). *Min.* Also liebnerite. [Named, 1847, by J. C. Marignac in honour of L. *Liebener*: see -ITE.] A pinite-like mineral resulting from the alteration of nephelite (Chester).

1865 WATTS *Dict. Chem.* III. 589 Liebenerite. **1878** LAWRENCE tr. *Cotta's Rocks Class.* 38 Liebnerite.

‖**lieber Gott** ('liːbə gɔt). [G.] Dear God, chiefly as *int.*

1898 M. A. VON ARNIM *Elizabeth & her German Garden* 50 The April baby came.. to ask about the *lieber Gott*, it being Sunday. **1912** R. BROOKE *Old Vicarage Grantchester* (1916) 7 And I know How the May fields all golden show.. Gild gloriously the bare feet That run to bathe... *Du lieber Gott!* **1929** R. HUGHES *High Wind in Jamaica* v. 120 Lieber Gott! What do you think I am, eh? **1954** M. STEWART *Madam, will you Talk?* xxi. 160 Kramer snarled: '*Lieber Gott*, will you listen to me?' **1969** A. MARIN *Rise with Wind* vi. 75 Weber said grimly, '*Lieber Gott*, what a profession to be in.'

Lieberkühn ('liːbəkyːn). *Optics.* Also -kuehn. [Named after the inventor J. N. *Lieberkühn* (1711–56), an anatomist of Berlin.] **1.** A silver concave reflector fixed on the object-glass end of a microscope to bring the light to focus on an opaque object.

1867 J. HOGG *Microsc.* I. ii. 58 Illuminated by a combination of the parabola and a flat Lieberkuhn.

2. *Anat.* The name of *Lieberkühn* used with *of*-adjunct, or occas. in the possessive, to designate the Lieberkühnian follicles or glands, as ***crypts, follicles,*** or ***glands of Lieberkühn.***

1844 DUNGLISON *Dict. Med. Sci.* (ed. 4) 420/2 Lieberkuehn's glands or follicles. **1859** R. B. TODD *Cycl. Anat. & Physiol.* V. 346/2 The intestinal tubes—or, as they are commonly called, the follicles of Lieberkuehn—are the first to demand our notice. **1866** G. HARLEY *Histol. Demonstr.* 114 The arrangements of the various coats, and also the villi and Lieberkühn's follicles, can be seen under a low power. **1949** ADAMS & EDDY *Compar. Anat.* xi. 278 The glands of Lieberkühn, which supply the succus entericus, have their openings at the bases of the villi. **1970** C. K. WEICHERT *Anat. Chordates* (ed. 4) v. 189/2 The intestinal wall contains myriads of intestinal glands which are of two main types. The first of these are the simple tubular glands, or crypts, of Lieberkühn, found throughout the entire length of the small and large intestines.

Lieberkühnian (ˌliːbə'kyːnɪən), *a. Anat.* [f. *Lieberkühn* (see prec.) + -IAN.] ***Lieberkühnian follicles*** or ***glands***: minute tubular cavities thickly distributed over the small intestines.

1852 BRANDE *Dict. Sci.* Suppl., Lieberkuhnian [*sic*] glands. **1897** *Allbutt's Syst. Med.* II. 761 Amœbæ are found in the borders of the ulcers, chiefly in the Lieberkühnian follicles.

Liebermann-Burchard (ˌliːbəmæn'bʊəkɑːt). *Biochem.* [The names of Carl *Liebermann* (1842–1914) and H. *Burchard*, German chemists.] ***Liebermann-Burchard reaction***, the reaction of unsaturated sterols with acetic anhydride and sulphuric acid in chloroform, which produces various coloured solutions; used esp. as a test for cholesterol, when a blue-green colour is produced; so ***Liebermann-Burchard test.***

1904 W. R. ORNDORFF tr. *Salkowski's Lab. Man. Physiol. & Path. Chem.* ix. 92 (*heading*) Liebermann-Burchard reaction. **1915** STEDMAN *Med. Dict.* (ed. 3) 509/2 Liebermann-Burchard test. **1934** *Jrnl. Biol. Chem.* CVI. 746 The very weak color produced by digitonin with the modified Liebermann-Burchard reaction. **1956** E. V. TRUTER *Wool Wax* vii. 185 At present, the only technique for quantitatively determining alcohols of the isocholesterol group is based upon the spectrophotometric measurement of the colour developed in the Liebermann-Burchardt test. **1968** *Indian Jrnl. Med. Res.* LVI. 1776 A method for the estimation of total cholesterol in whole blood, serum or plasma, based on the Liebermann-Burchard reaction is presented.

‖**Liebestod, liebestod** ('liːbəstoːt). [G., lit. 'love's death'.] An aria or a duet proclaiming the suicide of lovers (see also quot. 1964); hence, such a suicide; also *fig.*

1889 G. B. SHAW *London Music 1888–89* (1937) 249 Isolde's Liebestod was a failure. **1928** in D. McCarthy *Drama* (1940) 112 Each pair sinks into the euthanasia of a matter-of-fact liebes-tod. **1947** A. EINSTEIN *Mus. Romantic Era* xvi. 283 Yet this festival opera [*sc.* Aïda] ends *pianissimo* and *con sordini* with a *Liebestod*, which is not Romantically philosophical, but purely human. **1959** *Listener* 20 Aug. 280/2 Would the imagination.. not die a *Liebestod* at the very moment it attains its goal? **1964** *Conc. Oxf. Dict. Opera* 223/2 *Liebestod*, the title used today for Isolde's death scene in Wagner's *Tristan und Isolde*, but used by Wagner of the mystic love duet in Act 2. **1971** G. STEINER *In Bluebeard's Castle* i. 25 It is permissible to see.. in the Wagnerian *Liebestod* surrogates for the lost dangers of revolutionary action.

Liebfraumilch ('liːpfraʊmɪlç, 'liːb-). Also **Liebfrauenmilch.** [G., lit. 'milk of Our Lady'.] A white wine orig. produced at Worms; also loosely applied to German white wines.

1833 C. REDDING *Hist. Mod. Wines* vii. 204 The Liebfrauenmilch.. is a well-bodied wine, grown at Worms. **1846** TENNYSON *Let.* 12 Nov. in H. Tennyson *Alfred Lord Tennyson* (1897) II. i. 6 Dickens.. was very hospitable, and gave us biscuits.. and a flask of Liebfraumilch. **1930** W. S. MAUGHAM *Cakes & Ale* ii. 21 We want some of the Liebfraumilch, the '21. **1951** *Good Housek. Home Encycl.* 508/2 The best Hock, which is sold under a number of well-known names, e.g. Johannisberger,.. Liebfraumilch. **1967** A. LICHINE *Encycl. Wines* 323/1 Rheinhessen wines, distinctive in their own right, are so named; the remainder call themselves Liebfraumilch. **1973** *Guardian* 28 June 11/6 Liebfraumilch is an invented name for almost any ordinary German white wine not worthy of its own district label.

Liebig ('liːbɪg). [From the name of the inventor, Baron Justus von *Liebig* (1803–1873).]

a. More fully, ***Liebig's extract*** (*of beef*): A preparation obtained from beef, containing the

salts and extractive principles of the meat in highly concentrated form, without the albumen, gelatin, or fat.

1869 E. A. PARKES *Pract. Hygiene* (ed. 3) 246 When Liebig's extract is taken during fatigue, it is found to be remarkably restorative. **1870** *Daily News* 27 Dec., This [rice] with the chocolate and Liebig which he has in hand will last him for about three weeks. **1873** TRISTRAM *Moab* x. 176 Meat and Liebig, without bread.. was trying diet.
fig. **1874** L. TOLLEMACHE in *Fortn. Rev.* Feb. 247 They do not contain the moral Liebig which would alone satisfy descendants of the Platonic guardians. **1890** *Spectator* 9 Aug., If there is to be a Supreme Parliament in future, it must be a Liebig's extract of Parliament.
attrib. **1893** F. F. MOORE *I Forbid Banns* (1899) 24 Love-making on the Liebig principle.. as much love-making as would do duty for six months compressed into half an hour.

b. ***Liebig('s) condenser***, a device for condensing vapour, consisting of two concentric tubes, the vapour and condensate passing through the inner one and a cooling liquid through the outer one.

1861 *Phil. Mag.* XXI. 179 The liquid.. is.. poured into a retort provided with a Liebig's condenser. **1867** BLOXAM *Chem.* 46, A is a stoppered retort, the neck of which fits into the tube of a Liebig's condenser. **1903** S. YOUNG *Fractional Distillation* i. 6 When a Liebig's condenser is used there is no advantage in having either the inner or the outer tube very wide. **1963** J. W. DAVIS *Adv. Level Pract. Chem.* 158 For preparations in an advanced level course the most suitable water-condensers are short Liebig condensers.

liebigite ('li:bɪgaɪt). *Min.* [Named by J. L. Smith, 1848, after Baron Justus von *Liebig*: see -ITE.] Hydrous carbonate of uranium and calcium, found in thin, yellow incrustations (Chester).

1848 *Amer. Jrnl. Sci.* V. 336. **1868** DANA *Min.* (ed. 5) 308.

‖**Liebling, liebling** ('li:plɪŋ, 'li:blɪŋ). [G.] = LIEBCHEN, LIEBCHEN.

1868 C. M. YONGE *Chaplet of Pearls* I. vii. 79 She is a good little *Liebling*. **1970** J. CLEARY *Helga's Web* iv. 60 'And you're not servile?' 'No, *liebling*.' **1972** J. AIKEN *Butterfly Picnic* vi. 105 Is that you, Liebling?

lie-by. [f. phr. *to lie by*: see LIE *v.*[1] 21.]

1. A concubine, mistress. Now *dial.* (Cf. LIG-BY.)

a **1656** USSHER *Ann.* vi. (1658) 132 He obtained this favour.. by the means of his Lie-by; which was a wench of Eretria. **1825–80** JAMIESON, *Ly-by*.. 2. A mistress, a concubine. *Fife.* **1886** ELWORTHY *W. Somerset Word-bk.* s.v., Why, her wad'n never no better'n Squire ——'s lie by, and now her's anybody's.

†**2.** A neutral. (Cf. *by-lier* s.v. BY- B. 2 a.)

16.. *Postscript to Rutherford's Lett.* (1857) 569 Their Master [Satan] fearing little, or finding little damage to his dominion, by these lazy ly-byes and idle loiterers. **1723** M^cWARD *Earnest Contend.* 354 (Jam.) Such an heroick appearance,.. would make you live and die ornaments to your profession, while ly-bys will stink away in their sockets.

3. (See quot.)

1840 *Evid. Hull Docks Comm.* 31 What is called a lie-by, or recess, to enable vessels to pass.

‖**Lied, lied** (li:t). Pl. Lieder ('li:də(r)). [G.] A song, esp. one characteristic of the German Romantic period. So **lieder-singer**; **lieder-singing** *vbl. sb.*

1852 J. C. PATTESON *Let.* in C. M. Yonge *Life J. C. Patteson* (1874) I. iv. 89 He sang some of Medelssohn's [*sic*] Lieder very pleasantly. *Ibid. Let.* 115 As soon as a Lied or Sonata began, away would go my books. **1854** [see SEGUIDILLA]. **1876** STAINER & BARRETT *Dict. Mus. Terms* 274/2 The German lied, the sacred lied or chorale.. was founded upon the ecclesiastical modes and remained unchanged until the days of the Minnesingers. **1924** M. KENNEDY *Constant Nymph* xvi. 222 She listened sadly to German Lieder. **1936** H. READ *Meaning of Art* (ed. 2) 53 Thus we read in our newspaper that Miss X 'is too deficient in variety of *tone-colour* to make a good lieder singer'. **1937** *Sunday Times* 21 Feb. 7/1 In Lieder singing the words, or rather what is at the back of the words, play a large part in determining the appropriate musical style. **1947** A. EINSTEIN *Mus. Romantic Era* xiv. 184 Berlioz, of course, also wrote lieder and various other kinds of songs. **1955** *Times* 16 May 11/5 Programme included operatic arias,.. two groups of lieder and English and Italian songs. **1959** *Times* 27 Apr. 5/6 (*heading*) Miss Gerda Lammas: a great Lieder singer. **1960** *Guardian* 22 Apr. 9/2 An intimate tone and style are.. essential, to lieder singing. **1963** AUDEN *Dyer's Hand* 505 If one takes, say, a sea-shanty out of its proper context and listens to it on the gramophone as one might to a *lied* by Schubert, one is very soon bored. **1970** *New Yorker* 3 Oct. 36/1 Mother had a nice repertory of the more assailable lieder.

lied, variant of LYED *ppl. a. U.S.*

liedge, liedger, obs. ff. LIEGE, LEDGER.

lief (li:f), *a.* (*sb.*), and *adv.* Forms: 1 léof, líof, 3–4 leof (*inflected* leove, leofve), 3 lof, 4–5 luf, luef, lueve, 2–4 lef (*inflected* leve), 4–6 lef(f)e, 6–9 leve, (4 levef, lewe), 4–6 leefe, (5 leeff), 4–8 leeve, 6, 9– (chiefly *U.S.*) leave, 9 leaf, 4–7 leif, 5 leyf, 6–7 leife, leiv(e, 4 *Sc.* lyfe, 4, 6–8 live, 5 lyve, 4–6 lif(e, (4 lijf), 7–8 liff, 4–6 lyefe, 4–7 liefe, 2– lief. Also *U.S.* 8, 9 leaves, lieves, lives. *Compar.* 1 lé-, líofra (fem. and neut. -re), 2 leofere, 3 leover, 3–6 lever, 4–5 lefer, (4 *Sc.* lyfar), 4–6 levir, -yr, (6 leffer, leir), 5–6 *Sc.* levar, 5–7 leefer, -ir, leever, 6–7 lieffer, 6 leaver, 5–7 liever, leyf(f)er, 7 leif(f)er, 6 *Sc.* loor, 6– liefer. Also 8 lieverer. *Superl.* 1 léof-, líofast, -est, -ust, 3 lefest, 3–4 leovest, 3–6 levest, 4–6 lievest, (6 leif-, lifest), 6– liefest. Also 6 leverest. [OE. *léof, líof* = OFris. *liaf*, OS. *liob, liof* (Du *lief*), OHG. *liub, liup, liob, liab, lieb* (MHG. *lieb, liep*, mod.G. *lieb*), ON. *liúf-r* (Sw. *ljuf*), Goth. *liuf-s* (*liub*-):—OTeut. **leubo*-:—pre-Teut. **leubho*- (whence OSl. *ljubŭ*), f. Aryan root **leubh*- (:*loubh*-: *lubh*-, whence BELIEVE, LOVE).]

A. *adj.*

1. Beloved, dear, agreeable, acceptable, precious. Also ***lief and dear***. **a.** In attrib. use. *Obs.* exc. *arch.*

Beowulf 34 Aledon þa leofne þeoden.. on bearm scipes. *c* **1000** *Ags. Gosp.* Matt. xvii. 5 Her ys min leofa sunu. *c* **1250** *Gen. & Ex.* 4136 In to lef reste his sowle wond. *a* **1300** *Cursor M.* 17 Of tristrem and hys leif ysote. **1362** LANGL. *P. Pl.* A. I. 136 Loue is þe leuest þing þat vr lord askeþ. **1387** TREVISA *Higden* (Rolls) II. 279 Men made ymages to her leue frendes. *a* **1541** WYATT *Poet. Wks.* (1831) 57 For all that can no man bring Lieffer jewel unto his lady dear. **1575** G. HARVEY *Letter-bk.* (Camden) 145 She should not neede to care for ye leefist frende she had. **1590** SPENSER *F.Q.* II. i. 52 My lifest Lord she thus beguiled had. **1601** MUNDAY *Death Earl Huntington* III. i. in Hazl. *Dodsley* VIII. 273 Welcome to Guildford, Salisbury's liefest lord. **1742** SHENSTONE *Schoolmistress* 139 In which, when he receives his diadem, Our sov'reign prince and liefest liege is plac'd. **1844** LD. HOUGHTON *Mem. Many Scenes, Valentia* 198 Here the sun is pleased to cast Liefest smiles.

†**b.** Used in addressing a person. *Obs.*

Beowulf 1216 Bruc ðisses beaȝes, Beowulf leofa, hyse mid hæle. *c* **897** K. ÆLFRED *Gregory's Past.* xxxvi. 253 Ðu leofesta broður. *c* **1175** *Lamb. Hom.* 19 Nimað ȝeme nu leofemon hwilche ȝife he us ȝefeð. *a* **1225** *Leg. Kath.* 1375 O, leue feren, feire is us i-fallen. *c* **1330** *King of Tars* 656 Leove sire, trouwe on this. *c* **1385** CHAUCER *L.G.W.* 1170 *Dido*, Now leue sistyr myn what may it be. **1426** BP. BEAUFORT in Ellis *Orig. Lett.* Ser. II. I. 101 *note*, Levest earthly Lorde. **1481** CAXTON *Reynard* xx. (Arb.) 50 Lief bellyn wherfore be ye angry. **1513** DOUGLAS *Æneis* IV. Prol. 91 Thar bene bot few example takis of vther, Bot wilfully fallis in the fyre, leif brother. **1575** *Gamm. Gurton* II. iv, Who was it leiue son? speke, ich pray the. **1620** QUARLES *Jonah* K 3 b, Deare liefest Lord, that feast'st the world with Grace. **1632** HOLLAND *Cyrupædia* 207 Children mine, liefe and deare, I love you both alike.

c. In predicative use. Const. *dat.* or *to, unto*, esp. in ***liefer was, were, to me, him***, etc. with *inf.* or clause as subject [= 'I had rather']. Also Sc. ***liefis me*** = dear is to me (see also LEEZE ME). *Obs.* exc. *arch.* and *dial.*

a **900** *O.E. Chron.* an. 755 (Parker MS.) þa cuædon hie þæt him nænig mæg leofra nære þonne hiera hlaford. *c* **1000** ÆLFRIC *Gen.* xxix. 19 Leofre me ys þæt ic hig sylle þe þonne oðrum men. *c* **1175** *Lamb. Hom.* 35 Swilche pine ic habbe þet me were leofere þenne al world.. most ic habben an alpi þraȝe summe lisse. *c* **1200** *Trin. Coll. Hom.* 29 Þu shalt ben lef and wurð and liken alle men. *c* **1200** ORMIN 14701 To lakenn himm wiþþ þatt tatt himm Iss lefesst off þin ahhte. *a* **1250** *Owl & Night.* 202 Þeȝ.. leof [*v.r.* lof] him were nihtegale. *a* **1300** *Cursor M.* 23936 Þis ilk praier leuedi þou here, For þaa þat ar me lijfe and dere. **13..** *E.E. Allit. P.* A. 266 Bot Iueler gente if þou schal lose þy Ioy for a gemme þat þe was lef. **1340–70** *Alex & Dind.* 562 Hure was lecherie luf. *c* **1380** *Sir Ferumb.* 1143 Leuere me were by my fay he were to-drawe wyþ hors. **1390** GOWER *Conf.* II. 205 Now ches and tak which you is levere. *c* **1394** *P. Pl. Crede* 16 Þerfor lerne þe byleue leuest me were. *c* **1422** HOCCLEVE *Jonathas* 170 This man to folkes alle was so leef. **1470–85** MALORY *Arthur* IV. xx, Ye haue lefte me the yongest and the fayrest, and she is moost leuest to me. **1500–20** DUNBAR *Poems* lxxv. 42 Full leifis me ȝour graceles gane. **1513** DOUGLAS *Æneis* III. vii. 37 O levis me! the lykest thing leving, And verray ymage of my Astianax ȝing! **1513** MORE *Rich. III*, Wks. 63/1 Them wer leuer to leese all that thei haue besyde, then [etc.]. **1596** SPENSER *F.Q.* IV. iii. 52 Cambel tooke Cambina to his fere, The which as life were each to other liefe. **1597–8** BP. HALL *Sat.* IV. ii. 81 Thy fathers odious name, Whose mention were alike to thee as leeue As a catch-pols fist unto a bankrupts sleeue. **1609** HOLLAND *Amm. Marcell.* 147 Those who are most leife and deere unto us shall bee slaves. **1614** W. BROWNE *Sheph. Pipe* B 7 Leuer me were be slaine in this place.. Then purpose againe you any fallace. **1647** H. MORE *Song of Soul* Lines 8/2 But all are deaf Vnto my Muse, that is most lief To mine own self. **1842** TENNYSON *Morte D'Arthur* 80, I charge thee, quickly go again As thou art lief and dear.

d. In various constructions with ***have*** (see HAVE 22, and cf. G. *lieb haben*, Du. *liefhebben*): ***I*** (etc.) ***had*** (occas. ***have***) ***as lief as, I had*** (occas. †***have***) ***liefer*** (***than***), †***liefest***, with object a *sb.*, *inf.* phrase (with or without *to*), or subordinate clause. †Also in catachrestic constructions (see HAVE 22 c).

In *I'd, you'd, he'd* (etc.) *as lief*, the ambiguous contraction is prob. taken to represent *would* rather than *had*; the examples are therefore placed under the adv. Actual instances with *had* might still occur, but only as *arch.* or *dial.*

c **1290** *S. Eng. Leg.* I. 94/79 For ich habbe leouere þat ȝe hire ouer-come. *Ibid.* 471/321 Ʒuyt hadde ich leouere ich were i-huld. **13..** *K. Alis.* 21 Feole & fille.. hadde lever a ribaudye Than to here of God. *Ibid.* 1234 Theo riche.. saide they hadden, sikirliche, Leovere steorve.. than [etc]. *c* **1350** *Will. Palerne* 453, I have lever that love than lac al mi harmes. *c* **1375** *Sc. Leg. Saints* xxix. (*Placidas*) 390 He had als lef be ded as lef his wyf but remed. *c* **1380** WYCLIF *Sel. Wks.* III. 19 Þei han levere to dien in pryde and in malice þan to lyve in mekenes and charite. *c* **1386** CHAUCER *Merch. T.* 919 Leuere ich hadde to dyen on a knyf, Than thee offende trewe deere wif. —— *Monk's Prol.* 5, I hadde leuere than a barel ale That gode lief my wyf hadde herd this tale. **1390** GOWER *Conf.* II. 130, I hadde hir levere than a Myn of Gold. **1413** *Pilgr. Sowle* (Caxton) v. ii. (1859) 75 Of these thre worldes,.. I hadde leuer here speke, than ony thynge elles. **1609** HOLLAND *Amm. Marcell.* A 4 He had leifer save one citizen and subjects life than kill a thousand enemies. **1643** TRAPP *Comm. Gen.* xxxi. 2 He had as lief have parted with his very heart-blood. **1750** FIELDING *Tom Jones* VII. vii, One had lieverer touch a toad than the flesh of some people. **1756** TOLDERVY *Hist. 2 Orphans* I. 121 With all my heart,.. for I had as liff sit with Lucy or Marget as either of you, and at any time whatsomever. *a* **1766** MRS. F. SHERIDAN *Sidney Biddulph* IV. 311, I had as lief have let it alone.

†**2.** Desirous, wishful, willing, glad. Const. *of*, *to* with *inf.* *Obs.*

[This use app. resulted from a conversion of the construction with dative, *him is lief* (see 1 c) becoming *he is lief*.]

c **1325** *Poem times Edw. II* (Percy) xliii, The gode-man schal have never a mossel, Be he never so lef. *c* **1330** *Arth. & Merl.* (Kölbing) 3072 With five hundred noble kniȝtes Hardi & strong, & leue to fiȝtes. *a* **1340** HAMPOLE *Psalter* cxliii. 4 Man.. þat is leuer to lose his saule þan his lust. *c* **1380** WYCLIF *Sel. Wks.* II. 298 Þes newe ordris ech on þat ben so lef to lye. *Ibid.* III. 173 And thus us ow not to be lefe of jugement of men. *c* **1400** *Songs Costume* (Percy Soc.) 51, I was lefe for to escape. *c* **1430** *Syr Gener.* (Roxb.) 5428 To saue his londes he was lefe. *c* **1460** J. RUSSELL *Bk. Nurture* 487 With a spone lightely to ete your souerayne may be leeff. ?*c* **1475** *Sqr. lowe Degre* 593 That my father so leve he be That wyll profer me to thee. *c* **1500** *Yng. Childr. Bk.* 70 in *Babees Bk.* (1868) 21 Be not lefe to telle tydinge.

3. Antithetically to *loath*, in senses 1 and 2. Also *absol.*, esp. in ***for lief or loath***. *Obs.* exc. *arch.*

Beowulf 511 Ne inc æniȝ mon, ne leof ne lað belean mihte sorhfullne sið. *c* **1200** *Trin. Coll. Hom.* 183 Al þat me was leof, hit was þe loð. *c* **1300** *Havelok* 2379 Ne leten he nouth for lef ne loth. *c* **1385** CHAUCER *L.G.W.* 1639 *Hypsip. & Medea*, That he for lef or loth Ne shulde neuere hire false. **1412–20** LYDG. *Chron. Troy* I. vi, Other for lyef or lothe. *c* **1460** J. RUSSELL *Bk. Nurture* 1182 The Cooke, be he loothe or leeff. **1526** SKELTON *Magnyf.* 2544 Nowe leue, nowe lothe. **1584** PEELE *Arraignm. Paris* II. ii, Well, Juno, whether we be lief or loth, Venus hath got the apple from us both. **1647** H. MORE *Song of Soul* II. i. IV. iv, Our adversaries, loth or lief Must needs confesse that [etc.]. **1870** MORRIS *Earthly Par.* III. IV. 363 An oath To do my bidding once, if lieve or loath It were to thee. **1883** R. W. DIXON *Mano* III. viii. 136 Now hence must I.. be I loth or lief.

†**4.** *absol.* **a.** (When used in addressing a superior = Sir! Sire! Lord!) *Obs.*

c **907** *Mem.* in Earle *Land Charters* (1888) 162 Leof ic ðe cyðe hu hit wæs ymb ðæt lond æt funtial. *c* **1000** ÆLFRIC *Hom.* I. 314 Hi.. cwædon to ðam apostolon, La leof, hwæt is us to donne. *a* **1175** *Cott. Hom.* 235 La lief maȝie wiman forȝeten his oȝe cild. *c* **1300** *Havelok* 2606 'Ye lef ye', couth þe erl gunter. *c* **1330** R. BRUNNE *Chron.* (1810) 44 Lefe & dere, My lond is at þi wille. *c* **1380** WYCLIF *Sel. Wks.* III. 257 But leve take heed to Cristis wordis. —— *Wks.* (1880) 454 Ʒif he do good to þe chirche in preiyng or in studiynge, leve, what is þis to herdis offis. *a* **1400** *Sir Perc.* 1 Lef, lythes to me Two wordes or thre Off one that was faire and fre.

†**b.** quasi-*sb.* A beloved, a dear one; a friend, sweetheart, mistress; occas. a wife. Similarly in the compar., one who is dearer. *Obs.*

971 *Blickl. Hom.* 21 Ne biþ he Godes leof on þæm nehstan dæge. *c* **1250** *Lutelsoth Serm.* 63 in *O.E. Misc.* 188 Hwenne heo to chirche comeþ to þe haliday Eueruch wile his leof iseon. *a* **1300** *Cursor M.* 4352 Þat þou mi lefe wald be. **13..** *E.E. Allit. P.* B. 939 Þo wern Loth & his lef, his luflyche deȝter. **13..** *Gaw. & Gr. Knt.* 1782 Bot if ȝe haf a lemman, a leuer, þat yow lykez better. **1382** WYCLIF *Song Sol.* i. 8 To my riding in charis of Farao, I licnede thee O my leef. *c* **1386** CHAUCER *Miller's T.* 207 Alwey the nye slye Maketh the ferre leve to be looth. **1390** GOWER *Conf.* II. 221 Bot natheles sche hadde a levere. *c* **1430** *Syr Gener.* (Roxb.) 6576 Nou wel I wote this fals theef Hath thus led a-way my leef. *c* **1483** CAXTON *Dialogues* viii. 29 Amand, your cosen alyed Hath a fairer lyef Than ye haue. **1595** SPENSER *Col. Clout* 16 Colin my liefe, my life. **1621** AINSWORTH *Song Sol.* v. 9 What is thy Lief more then another Lief? **1633** P. FLETCHER *Poet. Misc.* 67 Thomalin my lief, thy musick strains to heare More raps my soul, then [etc.].

B. *adv.* Dearly, gladly, willingly. Chiefly with *would*, pa. subj. (occas. *Sc.* with omission of *would*). Also in ***as lief*** (***as***), ***the liefer***; ***lief I were*** = I would gladly be.

The advb. use originated chiefly from the misinterpretation of phrases like *I had as lief, I had liever* (see A. 1 d), in which *would* appears instead of *had* as early as the 13th c.

c **1250** *Gen. & Ex.* 49 And of hem two ðat leue luuen, ðe welden al her and abuuen. **1297** R. GLOUC. (Rolls) 5302 He ches leuere to deye him sulf, þan such sorwe yse. *a* **1300** *Cursor M.* 3135 Þat he ne wald leuer his child cole þan of his lauerd wrath to thole. **1390** GOWER *Conf.* I. 96 Alle wommen lievest wolde Be soverein of mannes love. **1393** LANGL. *P. Pl.* C. II. 143 For to louye þy lord leuest of alle. *a* **1400–50** *Alexander* 1082 Þare lengis him lefe þe kynge & logis all a neuen [= an even]. *c* **1450** *Erle Tolous* 365 Leve y were so worthy a knyght. **1450–1530** *Myrr. our Ladye* 29 They that wolde leuer be in the quier. *c* **1454** *Paston Lett.* I. 285 So, withoute your better avyse, I & my brothyr purpose us to be with you ther at that tyme; for, the sonner, the levyr me. *a* **1500** *Cov. Myst.* (Shaks. Soc.) 267 The trewth wolde I knowe as leff as ye. **1530** TINDALE *Pract. Prelates* C viij b, The Pope.. sendeth him [the Emperoure] his coronacyon home to him oftymes moch leuer than that he shuld come any neare. *c* **1560** A. SCOTT *Poems* (S.T.S.) iv. 79 Scho leir be japit thryiss. **1567** TURBERV. *Ovid's Ep.* 83 b, More leffer shoulde it lurcke, if I might have my will. **1598** R. BERNARD tr. *Terence* 213 Now see whether of these two conditions you would leaver have. **1724** RAMSAY *Tea-t. Misc.* (1733) I. 20 But I loor chuse in highland glens To herd the kid. **1800** COLERIDGE *Piccolom.* IV. v, Far liever would I face about, and step Back to my Emperor. **1814** JEFFERSON *Writ.* (1830) IV. 223 He might spare such a force.. as I would as lieve not have to encounter. **1840** *Southern Lit. Messenger* VI. 508/1

Never mind..I'd as leave be here as anywheres else. **1837** HOWITT *Rur. Life* III. iii. (1862) 242 She would as lieve part with the skin off her back as with her money. **1852** THACKERAY *Esmond* I. vi, I would as lief go there as anywhere. **1855** MRS. GASKELL *North & S.* xxxvii, I'd liefer sweep th' streets, if paupers had na' got hold on that work. **1876** TENNYSON *Q. Mary* III. i, Far liefer had I in my country hall Been reading some old book. **1896** A. E. HOUSMAN *Shropsh. Lad* I, Where shall one halt to deliver This luggage I'd lief set down? **1898** *Pall Mall Mag.* June 220 To strip was to confess her sex, than which she would liefer have died. **1898** M. DELAND *Old Chester Tales* 80, I would just as leave. **1902** A. D. MCFAUL *Ike Glidden* xviii. 144, I would's leave git fired. **1921** D. H. LAWRENCE *Sea & Sardinia* 121 They would fetch you a bang over the head as leave as look at you. **1935** G. INGRAM *'Stir' Train* i. 16 'I've got a little instrument here,' Margot showed him a thin scalpel.., 'and..I would as leave stick it into anyone's belly as any surgeon.'

1771 J. S. COPLEY *Let.* 17 Aug. in *Mass. Hist. Soc. Coll.* (1914) LXXI. 142 If Mr. Joy would as leaves wainscott the ..Room as plaister,.. I should prefer it. *Ibid.* 20 Sept. 160, I had as leaves Miller should paper as any one, provided he does it as Cheep. **1772** M. MASCARENE *Let.* 14 Sept. in *Mass. Hist. Soc. Coll.* (1914) LXXI. 189, I had full as lives have it [*sc.* the portrait] on a larger [plate]. **1856** A. CARY *Married* 22, I would just as lives stand here as not. **1858** J. R. LOWELL *Two Gunners* in *Poetical Wks.* II. 126 I'd jest ez lives eat tripe. **1863** 'G. HAMILTON' *Gala-Days* 241 We'd just as lieves work out of doors..as not. **1891** *Harper's Mag.* Oct. 820/1, I will get Provided Usher to watch with me. He'd just as lives.

lief, obs. form of LEAF, LIFE.

‖ **'lief-hebber.** *Obs. rare.* [a. Du. *liefhebber*, agent-n. f. *liefhebben* to hold dear, f. *lief* dear + *hebben* to have.] An amateur.

1654 BRAMHALL *Answ. to Militiere* 134 Put a *Liefhebber*, or *Virtuoso*, among a company of rare pictures, and he will pick out the best pieces for their proper value. **1656** BLOUNT *Glossogr.*, *Liefhebber*, a lover. [Citing Bramhall. Hence prob. the misuse in the next quot.] **1791** LEARMONT *Poems* 13 Her fause lief hebber owre the ling Did wale his nichtly way.

† **'liefly,** *a. Obs.* Forms: 1–3 léoflic, 3 leoflich, 4 leflich, leveli, 4–5 lefly. [OE. *léoflic* = OFris. *liaflik*, OS. *liof-*, *lioblic* (Du. *liefelijk*), OHG. *liuplich* (MHG. *lieplich*, mod.G. *lieblich*, Goth. *liubaleiks*): see LIEF *a.* and -LY[1].] Lovable, lovely, delightful, beautiful, pleasant, dear, glad. Applied both to persons and things.

Beowulf 1809 Sunu ecglafes heht his sweord niman leoflic iren. *a* **900** CYNEWULF *Crist* 400 [Hi] lofiað leof-licne. *c* **1175** *Lamb. Hom.* 183 Ihesu teke þet tu art se softe and se swete, ȝette to swa leoflic..þet [etc.]. *c* **1205** LAY. 31787 Swiðe leoflic wes þe mon. *a* **1225** *Juliana* 17 Leggeð so luðerliche on hire leofliche lich þat hit liðeri o blode. *a* **1225** *Ancr. R.* 90 Leoflich þing nis hit nout þet ancre bere swuch muð. *a* **1240** *Ureisun* in *Cott. Hom.* 187 Uor alle þinge swetest, alre þinge leoflucest. **1340–70** *Alisaunder* 427 þei..With a leflich lust lachte togeder. *c* **1460** *Launfal* 858 Gawayn, my lefly frende.

† **'liefly,** *adv. Obs.* Also 1 léoflíce, 2–3 leofliche, 3 lefliche, (*Orm.* lefliȝ), levelike, 4 leoflyche. [OE. *léoflíce* = OHG. *liublîhho* (MHG. *liepliche*, mod.G. *lieblich*), ON. *liúflega*: see LIEF *a.* and -LY[2].] Beautifully; dearly, kindly; willingly, gladly.

c **900** tr. *Bæda's Hist.* IV. xxv. (1890) 350 þeah þe ic sceole ealle wican fæstan, ic þæt leoflice do. *a* **1175** *Cott. Hom.* 257 Ich iseo a sonde cumen, swide gledd icheret, feier ant freolich, and leofliche aturnet. *c* **1200** ORMIN 4950 Lefliȝ to þeowwtenn oþre menn. *c* **1205** LAY. 17747 Gingiuere & licoriz he hom lefliche ȝef. *a* **1225** *Leg. Kath.* 2223 And at þes lefdis licome leofliche smirede. *c* **1250** *Gen. & Ex.* 3434 Ðis red ðhuȝte moyses ful god, And leuelike it under-stod. *c* **1275** *On Serving Christ* 59 in *O.E. Misc.* 92 For he wolde þe lawe leoflyche holde. [**1888** *Sat. Rev.* 14 Jan. 55/2 But if Mr. Max Müller will suggest any other word, we will as liefly use it.]

† **'liefness.** *Obs.*$^{-0}$ In 6 lefenesse. [f. LIEF *a.* + -NESS.] Dearness.

1530 PALSGR. 238/1 Lefenesse, *chereté*.

liefsome, variant of LEESOME *Obs.*

a **1547** EARL SURREY in *Tottel's Misc.* (Arb.) 19 So forth I go apace to se that leefsom sight. **1819** W. TENNANT *Papistry Storm'd* (1827) 17 That temple's flures and wa's are lined Wi leifsam pictures a' kinkind.

lieftel, lieful(l, var. ff. LEEFTAIL, LEEFUL.

liege (liːdʒ), *a.* and *sb.* Forms: 3–5 lige, 4–5 lyge; 3–6 lege, (4 leyge), 4–6 leege, (5 lech(e, lyche, lysch; legge, ligge, lygge; lieg), 5–6 lyege, 5–7 leig(e, 6 leag(e, (leighe), 6 liedge, (7 leidge), 4– liege. [a. OF. *lige*, *liege* (med.L. *ligius*, *legius*) = Pr. *litge*, It. *ligio*; the ultimate derivation is disputed.

The prevailing view that the word represents an adoption of OHG. *ledig* free (mod.G. *ledig* unoccupied) is supported by a passage in a charter of 1253 (Du Cange, s.v. *Ledighman*), which contains the words 'ligius homo, quod Teutonice dicitur Ledigh-man'. The assumption of 'free' as the primary sense also seems in accord with the meaning of the med.L. *ligia potestas* (LIEGE POUSTIE), *ligia voluntas*.]

A. *adj.*

1. The characteristic epithet of persons in the relation of feudal superior and vassal.

a. Of the superior: Entitled to feudal allegiance and service. Now rare exc. in *liege lord*, which is also used *fig.*

[**1292** BRITTON III. iv. §18 Si aucun deive fere homage a autre seignur lige qe a nous.] **1297** R. GLOUC. (Rolls) 9376 Vr lige louerd þat yeled is And ismered to ihesu crist. **13..** *Gaw. & Gr. Knt.* 346 þat my leyge lady lyked not ille. **1386** *Rolls of Parlt.* III. 225/1 Owre lige Lorde the Kyng. **1390** GOWER *Conf.* III. 144 Men schull don him reverence As to here liege soverein. **1422** tr. *Secreta Secret.*, *Priv. Priv.* 248 Oure lyge lorde, kynge henry the Fyfte. **1481** CAXTON *Reynard* (Arb.) 30 Not so my liege lorde. **1549** LATIMER *1st Serm. bef. Edw. VI* (Arb.) 30 It hath pleased God to graunt vs a naturall liege kynge and Lorde. *c* **1620** T. ROBINSON *M. Magd.* II. 1566 Shee..followes her Liege-Lorde yᵉ villages throughout. **1770** *Junius Lett.* xli. 209 You deserted the fortune of your liege lord. **1814** SCOTT *Ld. of Isles* II. xx. Who, vassals sworn, 'Gainst their liege lord had weapon borne. **1844** H. H. WILSON *Brit. India* I. 97 Originally a feudatory of Jaypur, the Raja had taken advantage of the enfeebled condition of his liege lord. **1865** KINGSLEY *Herew.* xxi, That is the rule of our liege lord, William.

b. Of the vassal: Bound to render feudal service and allegiance. (Cf. LIEGE MAN.) †Also, owing allegiance *to* (law).

13.. *E.E. Allit. P.* B. 1174 þe lawe þat he was lege tylle. **1362** LANGL. *P. Pl.* A. IV. 147 Al my lige leodes. *c* **1380** WYCLIF *Wks.* (1880) 290 Kyngis schulde constreyne..here lyge freris & here oþere clerkis. **1470–85** MALORY *Arthur* II. i, [They] brente and slewe the kynges true liege peple. **1538** WRIOTHESLEY *Chron.* (1875) I. 80 A false traitor to his Praynce..and a seditious person to the kinges leighe people. **1577** NORTHBROOKE *Dicing* (1843) 137 They shoulde be arrested by the King's liege people as vagabondes. **1689** S. JOHNSON *Rem. Sherlock's Bk.* 19 Every Leige-Subject of England has a Legal Property in his Life. **1823** SCOTT *Peveril* xiii, I had..a right to call on every liege subject to render assistance. **1848** WHARTON *Law Lex.*, *Liege*, bound by some feudal tenure; subject.

†c. *transf.* of persons in other relationships: Entitled and bound to mutual fidelity. *Obs.*

c **1350** *Will. Palerne* 4128, I schal loue him lelli as my lege broþer. *c* **1555** PHILPOT in Coverdale *Lett. Mart.* (1564) 236 The lyuyng lord, which..hath begotten you to be my liege syster, geue you grace so to grow in that generation, that [etc.].

¶ d. Used for: Loyal, faithful. *rare.*

1478 *Certificate* in *Surtees Misc.* (1888) 37 He is a trewe, lige Inglis man. **1890** C. A. ANSELL tr. *A. da Montefeltro's Confer. in Rome* 46 The materialist, liege to his own system, is incapable of doing anything but put one after another the results of his observations.

2. Of or pertaining to the bond between superior and vassal.

1399 *Rolls of Parlt.* IV. 424/2 Homage liege and Feaute. **1750** CARTE *Hist. Eng.* II. 401 The French maintaining it was a lige homage. **1765** BLACKSTONE *Comm.* I. 367 Land held by this exalted species of fealty was called *feudum ligium*, a liege fee. **1818** HALLAM *Mid. Ages* (1872) I. 99 They..always refused to pay liege-homage, which implied an obligation of service to the lord.

B. *sb.*

1. The superior to whom one owes feudal allegiance and service; = *liege lord.*

c **1400** *Destr. Troy* 134 þe lege þat hom lede shuld. *c* **1440** *Promp. Parv.* 302/2 Lyche, lady or lorde,..*ligius*. **1513** MORE *Rich. III*, Wks. 42/2 Ye my liege quod the Duke of Buckingham thei haue [etc.]. **1513** DOUGLAS *Æneis* XII. Prol. 247 The larkis..Lovys thar lege with tonys curyus. **1590** SPENSER *F.Q.* II. iii. 8 The Miser threw him selfe..Streight at his foot in base humilitee, And cleeped him his liege, to hold of him in fee. **1599** SHAKS. *Much Ado* I. i. 291 My Liege, your Highnesse now may doe mee good. **1609** C. BUTLER *Fem. Mon.* v. (1623) Lj, Shee..Most humbly begging in hir Dorik straines Of hir dear Liege leaue to be gone. **1637** R. HUMPHREY tr. *St. Ambrose* II. 41 He would not be profuse and prodigall of another mans good, much lesse of his Leiges. **1705** J. PHILIPS *Blenheim* 396 The Natives, dubious whom They must Obey, in Consternation wait, Till rigid Conquest will pronounce their Liege. **1706** ADDISON *Rosamond* I. vi, Nay, good my Liege, with patience hear. **1785** PALEY *Mor. Philos.* (1818) I. 191 The form of doing homage at this day, by putting the hands between the knees, and within the hands of the liege. **1788** WOLCOT (P. Pindar) *Peter's Pension* Wks. 1812 II. 5 No less, my royal liege, than you and me. **1823** SCOTT *Peveril* xlvi, 'In the name of God, my liege,' said the Duke of Ormond, 'let' [etc.]. **1837** BROWNING *Strafford* II. ii. 35 My liege, do not believe it! I am yours.

2. A vassal bound to serve his superior, a liege man. Hence in a wider sense: A loyal subject of the king.

1377 LANGL. *P. Pl.* B. XIX. 56 Alle his lele lyges. **1390** GOWER *Conf.* I. 338 The kinges founde here oghne liege.. That hem forsoke and desobeide. **1414** *Rolls of Parlt.* IV. 22/2 Youre humble and trewe lieges that ben come for the Co[mmun]e of youre lond. *c* **1440** *Promp. Parv.* 303/1 Lyche, man or womann (P. *ligius*). **1450–80** tr. *Secreta Secret.* 47 God almyȝty kepe oure kynge to ioye of his ligeys. *c* **1470** HENRY *Wallace* IX. 533 Xxᵗʸ thousand off lele legis off France. **1549** *Extracts Aberd. Reg.* (1844) I. 271 Tha had offendit..to the quenis grace of Scotland, in the taking,..of the said William..he beand hir fre liege and subdict. **1648** D. JENKINS *Wks.* Table, His Leidges are bound by Oath to remove the King. **1649** JER. TAYLOR *Gt. Exemp.* II. Disc. xi. 148 For kings and all that are in authority we may..pray for peaceable reign, true lieges, strong armies [etc.]. **1821** SCOTT *Kenilw.* xxvii, Her Majesty, being detained by her gracious desire to receive the homage of her lieges. **1845** S. AUSTIN *Ranke's Hist. Ref.* I. 97 The emperor's lieges. **1880** KINGLAKE *Crimea* VI. ix. 380 In future campaigns the lieges shall not be the marplots they were in the days of Lord Raglan.

† **liege**, *v. Obs. rare.* [f. LIEGE *sb.*] *trans.* To render (homage) as a liege.

1563–87 FOXE *A. & M.* (1596) 348/1 You are entred into our homage by you lieged unto us, acknowledging your selfe ..a liege man unto the King of France.

liegedom ('liːdʒdəm). [f. LIEGE *sb.* + -DOM.] The condition of being a liege.

1813 SCOTT *Trierm.* III. xxxvi, These foremost maidens.. profferr'd sceptre, robe, and crown, Liegedom, and seignorie, O'er many a region wide and fair.

liegeful ('liːdʒfʊl), *a. rare.* [f. LIEGE *sb.* + -FUL.] Loyal, faithful.

1872 A. DE VERE *Legends St. Patrick* 72 If ye be liegeful, sirs, decree the day. *Ibid.* 155 Pure of heart, and liegeful unto Christ. **1887** —— *Legends & Rec. Church & Empire* 264 Liegeful I know hath been your wedded life.

liegefully ('liːdʒfʊlɪ), *adv. rare.* [f. **liegeful* (f. LIEGE *sb.* + -FUL) + -LY[2].] Faithfully, loyally.

1887 SIR A. DE VERE *Ess. on Poetry* I. 53 Her heart was liegefully given to heavenly things.

liegeless ('liːdʒlɪs), *a.* [f. LIEGE *sb.* + -LESS.]

1. Not subject to a superior; free.

1820 KEATS *Hyperion* III. 91 O why should I Feel.. thwarted, when the liegeless air Yields to my step aspirant.

2. Disregardful of obligations to a superior.

In recent Dicts.

liege man, 'liegeman.

1. *Feudal Law.* A vassal sworn to the service and support of his superior lord, who in return was obliged to afford him protection, etc.

c **1350** *Will. Palerne* 2663 Lordinges ȝe ben my lege men þat gode ben & trewe. **1387** TREVISA *Higden* (Rolls) VII. 285 Kyng William wente into Scotland..and kyng Malcolyn bycam his leege man, and swoor hym homage and fewte. ? *a* **1400** *Morte Arth.* 1768 Alle his lele lige mene. **1420** H. STAFFORD in Ellis *Orig. Lett.* Ser. IV. I. 66 The kyngys liche men..han y fetaylid hym well and nothyng vs. **1494** FABYAN *Chron.* V. cxxv. 105 They wolde become his liege-men, and holde theyr lande of hym for euer. **1523** FITZHERB. *Bk. Surv.* 20 b, I shall true liegeman be and true faythe beare to kyng Henry..and to his heyres. **1579** J. STUBBES *Gaping Gulf* F iij b, A true Englishman, a sworne liegeman to hir Maiestie. **1612** DAVIES *Why Ireland*, etc. (1787) 109 If the Irish were receiued into the King's protection, and made liege men and free subjects. **1692** WASHINGTON tr. *Milton's Def. Pop.* viii. (1851) 189 They swear therefore to William, to be his Liege-men. **1813** SCOTT *Trierm.* II. vi, When Arthur..Spoke of his liegemen and his throne. **1839** KEIGHTLEY *Hist. Eng.* I. 35 The princes of Cornwall, Wales, Cumbria and Strath-clyde became his liege men. **1855** MILMAN *Lat. Chr.* VII. ii. (1864) IV. 88 Building fortresses to reduce his freeborn liege men to slavery.

2. *transf.* and *fig.* One who serves as though sworn to do so, a faithful follower or subject.

1823 SCOTT *Peveril* xvii, A faithful liegeman to the law as well as the King. **1827** KEBLE *Chr. Y.* 1 Sunday Advent ii, Sworn liegemen of the Cross. **1862** MERIVALE *Rom. Emp.* (1865) III. xxiv. 98 Liegemen of Death and fares of the Stygian ferryman. **1864** BURTON *Scot Abr.* I. v. 259 When the dispute lay between the liegemen of the university and those of the state the university haughtily arrogated the authority over both. **1865** PARKMAN *Huguenots* vii. (1875) 89 The trespassers, too, were heretics, foes of God and liegemen of the Devil. **1876** BANCROFT *Hist. U.S.* I. iii. 86 Raleigh..sent..at five several times, to search for his liege-men.

Hence † **'liegemanship.**

1611 COTGR., *Lige*, allegiance, or liegemanship.

liege poustie (liːdʒ'paʊstɪ). Chiefly *Sc.* Forms: 4 lege pouste, legge pouste, 5 leg(is po(u)ste, 6 leg powster, liege pouste, 7– liege poustie. [a OF. *lige poesté*, med.L. *ligia potestas*: see LIEGE *a.* and POUSTIE.] The state of being in health and full possession of one's faculties. Now only in *Sc. Law* (see quot. 1882).

1340 HAMPOLE *Pr. Consc.* 5606 þai wrethed God in þair legge pousté. **1375** BARBOUR *Bruce* v. 165 Bot and I lif in lege pouste, Thair ded sall rycht weill vengit be. **1458** *Burgh Rec. Peebles* (1872) 129 Scho had cofit fra hir son in his leg poste qwyl he was lewand. **1462** *Ibid.* 143 The quhylkis scho alegit was gevyn to her by..her fadyr in his legis pouste. **15..** *Bk. Alexander* (Bannatyne Club) 361 Gif I leif lang in liege pouste. *c* **1560** *Aberd. Reg.* XXIV. (Jam.), Ane testament maid be vmquhill Alexʳ. Kay baxter in his leg powster. **1609** SKENE *Reg. Maj.* II. xviii. §7 It is lesome to ilk man to give ane reasonabill portion of his lands, to quhom he pleases, induring his lifetime, in his liege poustie. *a* **1768** ERSKINE *Instit. Law Scot.* III. Tit. viii. §97 (1773) I. 595 Where the ancestor has validly obliged himself in liege poustie to grant a deed. **1882** *Bell's Dict. Law Scot.*, *Liege poustie*, is that state of health which gives a person full power to dispose *mortis causa*, or otherwise, of his heritable property.

lieger, obs. form of LEDGER, LEGER.

liegewoman. *rare.* [Cf. LIEGE MAN.] A woman who is a liege vassal.

1464 *Rolls of Parlt.* V. 544/1 Oure..true Liegewoman.

liegier, obs. form of LEDGER.

lien[1] ('liːən, liːn, 'laɪən) Also 6 lyen. [a. F. *lien*:—L. *ligāmen* bond, f. *ligāre* to bind, tie.

The usual pronunciation in England is ('liːən), though the others are sometimes heard. According to Funk's *Standard Dict.*, the usual pronunciation in the U.S. is (liːn).]

†1. *Anat.* A tendon. *Obs.*

1541 COPLAND *Guydon's Quest. Chirurg.* D j, The lyens or strynges.. be of the nature of synewes.

2. *Law.* A right to retain possession of property (whether land, goods, or money) until a debt due in respect of it to the person detaining it is satisfied.

1531 *Dial. on Laws Eng.* II. vii. (1532) 20 The tenaunt hathe a true cause of a voucher, and of lyen. **1741** T.

ROBINSON *Gavelkind* vi. 125 A Diversity is to to observed between a Lien Real and a Lien Personal. **1809** R. LANGFORD *Introd. Trade* 133 *Lien*, attachment on property in your possession for a debt due to you from the owner of them. **1845** R. W. HAMILTON *Pop. Educ.* vii. (ed. 2) 165 Vermont possesses, also, its literary fund,—a lien of six per cent. on the profits of the banks. **1866** CRUMP *Banking* iii. 83 It is only necessary for the borrower to give a lien to the banker. **1883** SIR E. E. KAY in *Law Times Rep.* XLIX. 77/2 It was hardly said that he was entitled to any charge, or lien, or equity on this particular fund.

fig. **1879** H. GEORGE *Progr. & Pov.* v. ii. (1881) 260 A few thousand of the people of England hold a lien upon the labor of the rest. **1883** J. HAWTHORNE *Dust* I. 168 The chance which had brought Lancaster into relations with the family .. gave him a lien upon the interest and gratitude of the two women. **1922** A. BENNETT *Lilian* II. v. 107 She had no lien, no attachment. **1925** *New Statesman* 3 Oct. 687/1 They desire two sets of negotiations to proceed simultaneously, and if they admit they may be pursued separately, there will nevertheless be so many liens between them, that the success of one will be dependent on the success of the other.

b. *attrib.*, as in ***lien bond, creditor, holder.***

1870 PINKERTON *Guide to Admin.* 19 A widow cannot claim as against a mechanic's lien creditor. **1898** *Westm. Gaz.* 20 June 10/1 A first mortgage on all property not covered by the prior lien bonds.

Hence **'lienor** *U.S. Law*, one who holds a lien.

1890 *Law Times* LXXXIX. 165/1 If the lienors may insure, so may the owners of the injured ship and cargo.

† **'lien²**. *Obs.* In 7 liene. [a. L. *liēn*: ? cogn. w. Skr. *plīhan* and Gr. σπλήν (Brugmann).] The spleen.

1651 *Raleigh's Ghost* 80 The Liene, or Splene conduceth that it may attract to it the more gross .. parts of blood.

lien, obs. pa. pple. of LIE *v.*

lienal (laɪ'iːnəl), *a. Anat.* [f. L. *liēn* LIEN² + -AL¹.] Of or pertaining to the spleen; splenic.

1879 J. R. REYNOLDS *Syst. Med.* V. 221 Thus we have 'splenic' or 'lienal' .. forms [of leucocythæmia].

† **lienary**, *a. Anat. Obs.* [f. L. *liēn* LIEN² + -ARY.] = prec.

1684 tr. *Bonet's Merc. Compit.* VIII. 291 Bloud must be let out of some lienary Vein.

‖ **lienculus** (laɪ'ɛŋkjʊləs). *Anat.* [mod.L., dim. of L. *liēn* the spleen.] One of the small masses of splenic tissue found in the neighbourhood of the spleen; an accessory spleen.

1897 *Allbutt's Syst. Med.* IV. 527 Accessory spleens, splenunculi or lienculi, are common.

liendely, lieng(e, obs. ff. LYINGLY, LYING.

‖ **lienitis** (laɪə'naɪtɪs). *Path.* [mod.L., f. L. *liēn* the spleen + -ITIS.] Inflammation of the spleen; = SPLENITIS.

1845 G. E. DAY tr. *Simon's Anim. Chem.* I. 269 The serum has been observed .. to be turbid in lienitis.

lieno- (laɪ'iːnəʊ), used as comb. form of L. *liēn* spleen, in adjs. signifying 'pertaining to the spleen and ——', as **lieno-gastric** *a.*, pertaining to the spleen and the stomach; **lieno-intestinal** *a.*, pertaining to the spleen and to the intestines; **lieno-renal** *a.*, pertaining to the spleen and the kidneys: applied *spec.* to a short ligament connecting the spleen and the left kidney.

1875 HUXLEY & MARTIN *Elem. Biol.* 172 The system of the *vena portæ* formed by the union of two veins; one *gastric* .., the other *lieno-intestinal*. **1887** A. M. MARSHALL *Pract. Zool.* 232 The lieno-gastric artery. **1887** G. D. THANE *Ellis's Demonstrations Anat.* (ed. 10) viii. 475 The peritoneum may be followed .. to the outer part of the left kidney, where it is reflected along the back of the splenic vessels to the spleen, forming one layer of the lieno-renal ligament. **1932** W. WRIGHT in E. P. Stibbe *Pract. Anat.* 301 To the left it [*sc.* the cavity] is closed by the gastro-splenic omentum, the spleen, and a fold passing from the spleen to the left kidney, the lieno-renal ligament. **1967** G. M. WYBURN et al. *Conc. Anat.* i. 32/2 The lieno-renal ligament, which contains the splenic vessels.

† **lienous**, *a. Obs. rare*⁻¹. [f. LIEN² + -OUS.] = LIENAL.

1657 TOMLINSON *Renou's Disp.* 336 It is good against the lienous, hepatical .. and convulsive dolours.

‖ **lienteria** (laɪən'tɪərɪə). *Path.* [mod.L.: see LIENTERY.] = Lientery.

1398 TREVISA *Barth. De P.R.* VII. li. (1495) 264 Lienteria is a flyxe of the wombe wythout passynge of meete & drynke withoute dygestyon. **1527** ANDREW *Brunswyke's Distyll. Waters* D j, The same water dronke in the forsayde maner stoppeth the whyte laskys named Lienteria. **1625** HART *Anat. Ur.* II. iv. 69 A Citizen .. fell into that kind of laske which we commonly call Lienteria. **1875** H. WALTON *Dis. Eye* 92 Begbie has found many suffering from lienteria, the food being only partially digested.

lienteric (laɪən'tɛrɪk), *a. Path.* [f. next + -IC.] Of or pertaining to lientery.

1681 GREW *Musæum* 333 To strengthen the Tone of the parts, as in Lienterick and other like Cases. **1727** BRADLEY *Fam. Dict.* s.v. *Flux*, There are three sorts of Fluxes of the Belly, viz. the Lienterick, humoral or Diarrhœa, and Dysenterick Flux. **1822–34** *Good's Study Med.* (ed. 4) I. 206 Lienteric diarrhœa. **1866** A. FLINT *Princ. Med.* (1880) 525 The dejections are called lienteric when they contain undigested aliment.

So † **lien'terical** *a.* = prec.

1676 T. DE GARENCIERES *Coral* 24 Hepatical fluxes, lienterical, menstrual, spermatical.

lientery ('laɪəntərɪ). *Path.* Also 6 lyentery, 7 lienterie, lyantery, 7–8 lientary, 8 -ory; and in L. form LIENTERIA. [ad. F. *lienterie*, ad. mod.L. *līenteria*, ad. Gr. λειεντερία, f. λεῖος smooth + ἔντερα bowels.] A form of diarrhœa, in which the food passes through the bowels partially or wholly undigested; an instance or kind of this.

1547 BOORDE *Brev. Health* cciv. 70b, The lyentery or imperfyte dygestion. **1647** A. ROSS *Mystagogus Poet.* ii. (1675) 49 They [Harpies] are troubled with a continual flux or lientary. **1650** H. BROOKE *Conserv. Health* 176 Lienteries and all other Laskes. **1663** BOYLE *Usef. Exp. Nat. Philos.* II. ii. 38 The slimy excretions voided in the lyantery. **1766** AMORY *Buncle* (1770) IV. 87 He has that flux of the belly, which is called a lientery. **1878** KINGZETT *Anim. Chem.* 72 In lientery, also, the pancreas appears to be affected.

lier ('laɪə(r)). [f. LIE *v.*¹ + -ER¹.]

a. One who lies, in senses of the vb.

1596 DALRYMPLE tr. *Leslie's Hist. Scot.* v. 292 The Scotis sa blyth of that Victorie and proud .. heidet thair the deid lyeris. **1737** BRACKEN *Farriery Impr.* (1757) II. 72 Chusing a Horse that is a good Lier, or such a one as lays himself down often... There is a great Difference in Horses, with relation to their being good or bad Liers.

b. With advs. or advb. phrases. † **lier-by**, a kept mistress (cf. LIE-BY 1, LIG-BY). *Obs.*

1583 MELBANCKE *Philotimus* Aa iij, It is a Prouerbe in Englande that the men of Tiuidal borderers on yᵉ english midle marches, haue likers, lemmons, and lyerbies. **1608** WILLET *Hexapla Exod.* 394 These whom the Apostle calls ἀρσενοκοῖται, liers with men. **1611** BIBLE *Joshua* viii. 14 There were liers in ambush against him. —— *Judg.* ix. 25 And the men of Shechem set lyers in wait for him. **1657** FULLER *Serm., Best Employment* 10 He [our Saviour] was no large lier on bed. **1827** CARLYLE *Germ. Rom.* I. 25 She turned the corner with her, and escaped the eyes of the lier-in-wait. **1844** MARY HOWITT *My Own Story* x. 101 The old squire was a late lier in bed.

lier(e, obs. form of LIAR.

lier, obs. var. LEER *sb.*³

lierne (lɪ'ɜːn). *Arch.* Also 5 leyrn. [ad. F. *lierne* (Delorme, 16th c.), of doubtful etym.] In vaulting, a short rib which neither springs from an impost nor runs along the ridge, but connects the bosses and intersections of the principal ribs.

1842 WILLIS in *Trans. Instit. Brit. Architects* I. II. 31 The Liernes connect the ribs at other points [than the crowns] or may connect the crown of one rib with some intermediate point between the crown and springing of another rib. *Ibid.*, The term *Lierne* is applied by De l'Orme 'Inventions pour bien bastir' to the short-ridge ribs which form a cross at the summit of the vault which he has given as an example. **1879** SIR G. SCOTT *Lect. Archit.* II. 212 Liernes are not placed at right angles to the surface of the vaulting, but in a vertical plane. **1886** MRS. CADDY *Footsteps Jeanne D'Arc* 226 The roof branched with liernes, clustering into stars in its vaulting.

b. *attrib.* in † ***lierne-stud, -vault.***

1466 in Willis & Clark *Cambridge* (1886) III. 93 From euery beme a leyrn stood with .ij. braces into the beme and .ij. into the crownetree which shal lye vpon the said studdes. **1850** PARKER *Gloss. Archit.* s.v., Vaults in which such liernes are employed are termed *lierne vaults*. **1896** W. B. WILDMAN *Hist. Sherborne* iv. 20 A lierne vault of the same sort as that of the Nave Aisles.

lierne, obs. form of LEARN.

lierwit, variant of LAIRWITE.

1617 MINSHEU, *Lierwit* est mulcta adulteriorum.

lies(e, obs. pl. of LEE *sb.*² and of LOUSE.

liese, variant of LEESE *v.*¹

Liesegang ('liːzəgæŋ). *Physical Chem.* The name of Raphael Eduard *Liesegang* (1869–1947), German chemist, used *attrib.* (esp. in ***Liesegang ring***) and in the possessive to designate (the formation of) concentric rings or parallel bands of precipitate following the diffusion, one into the other, of two dissolved substances that react to form a slightly soluble precipitate.

1913 *Chem. Abstr.* VII. 3797 The Liesegang figures produced on gelatin plates. **1917** M. H. FISCHER tr. *Ostwald's Introd. Theoret. & Appl. Colloid Chem.* v. 215 A colloid-chemical method for discovering the addition of agar to fruit jellies and marmalades makes use of the influence which such addition has upon the form and the structure of Liesegang rings when formed in such jellies. **1932** *Jrnl. Physical Chem.* XXXVI. 299 The concentric rings in the 'common gall stones' of inflammatory origin are .. a manifestation of the Liesegang phenomenon. **1944** A. VAN HOOK in J. Alexander *Colloid Chem., Theoret. & Appl.* V. 517 Bucher .. has devised a new method of blood analysis depending on the sensitiveness of Liesegang Ring formation to very slight variations in blood composition and quality. **1946** *Thorpe's Dict. Appl. Chem.* (ed. 4) VII. 307/2 A large number of stratified deposits occur in nature, and a study of Liesegang's rings has suggested explanations for some of these structures. **1953** *New Biol.* XV. 123 Periodic precipitations of the Liesegang type may occur. **1959** *Science* 15 May 1366/2 The best way to avoid the formation of multiple macroscopical Liesegang bands is to operate with equivalent concentrations of reagents. **1971** *Jrnl. Colloid & Interface Sci.* XXV. 591/2 The membrane-like behavior of the $PbCrO_4$ Liesegang ring system in agar gel has been confirmed .. with a wide variety of inorganic ions.

liethwake, obs. variant of LEATHWAKE.

lieu (ljuː, luː). Forms: 3 liue, 6 leu, 6–7 lue, 7 le(i)w, 7–8 liew(e, 6– lieu. [a. F. *lieu*:—L. *locum*, acc. of *locus* place.] Place, 'stead'.

1. In phrases. **a.** ***in (the) lieu of***: in the place, room, or stead of (cf. INSTEAD 1); in exchange or return for, as a payment, penalty, or reward for.

c **1290** *S. Eng. Leg.* I. 237/620 And noupe In liue of Aungele ane man ich i-seo. **1534** *Acts 26 Hen. VIII*, c. 15 §2 Any other demaunde or duetie, in the name or lue of the same. **1548** UDALL *Erasm. Par. Luke* Pref. 11 b, In the lieu and place of Goddes innumerable, all their song .. is now of Jesus Christe alone. **1589** NASHE *Anat. Absurd.* 24 In lieu of their crueltie, they were plagued with this calamitie. **1620** SIR R. BOYLE in *Lismore Papers* (1886) I. 239, I .. am to paie him 3 tonnes of yron in lew of 40ˡⁱ. **1640** S. D. EWES in *Lett. Lit. Men* (Camden) 166 Two subsidies granted in leiw of it. **1675** *N. Riding Rec.* VI. 237 Ordᵈ. That £7 be paid unto the said Jane Watson in lue of her money and cloathes. **1680** COTTON *Gamester* 82 He takes in those four Cards and lays out four others in their lieu. **1719** YOUNG *Busiris* I. i, I receive thee from the gods, in lieu Of all that happiness they ravish'd from me. **1793** SMEATON *Edystone L.* §101 A durable stone building in lieu of a perishable wooden one. **1866** CRUMP *Banking* ix. 195 The amount to be paid in lieu of stamp duty. **1891** *Law Times* XCII. 80/1 The plaintiff sued the defendant for a quarter's rent in lieu of notice.

b. ***in lieu***: used *absol.* = INSTEAD 2. *arch.*

1599 in Fowler *Hist. C.C.C.* (O.H.S.) 351 We thought that in Leu to recompense hereof .. we might lawfully take part of the fine for ourselves. *a* **1650** MAY *Old Couple* I. (1658) 2 Keep out the Sun, and do bestow in lieu A greater benefit, a safe concealment. **1768–74** TUCKER *Lt. Nat.* (1834) II. 432 God will not give us the thing we desire, but a better in lieu. **1869** BROWNING *Ring & Bk.* IX. 1195 Quit the gay range o' the world Enter in lieu the penitential pound.

2. Used without preceding prep. for: † **a.** ? Something given 'in lieu' of another thing (*obs. rare*⁻¹). **b.** Stead, room (*rare*).

1592 BP. ANDREWES *Wonderful Combat* vi. (1627) 95 One would thinke it a very large offer to giue so great a lieu for so small a seruice. **1832** AUSTIN *Jurispr.* (1879) II. xlvi. 807 A fungible or representable thing is a thing whose place, lieu or room may be supplied by a thing of the same kind.

† **lieutenance.** *Obs. rare*⁻¹. [a. F. *lieutenance*, f. *lieutenant.*] = LIEUTENANCY 1.

1523 WOLSEY in Fiddes *Life* (1726) II. 114 The kings grace .. either in person or by Livetenance advance thether an Army.

lieutenancy (lɛf-, lɪf'tɛnənsɪ, *U.S.* ljuː'tɛnənsɪ). Also less correctly **lieutenantcy**. [f. LIEUTENANT: see -ANCY.] The office of a lieutenant.

† **1.** Delegated authority or command. *Obs.*

a **1631** DONNE in *Select.* (1840) 255 He that resists his [God's] commission, his lieutenancy, his authority, in law-makers appointed by him, resists himself.

2. The office of a lieutenant, in various senses; e.g. that of deputy governor of a kingdom, etc., of LORD-LIEUTENANT of a county; also, the commission of lieutenant in the army or navy.

1450 *Rolls of Parlt.* V. 186/2 Graunte to hym made, of eny Revenuez .. for his seid Lieutenauncie there. **1675** OGILBY *Brit.* Introd. 3 The Regiments .. upon a Commission of Lieutenancy .. were settled. **1703** *Lond. Gaz.* No. 3886/4 The Earl of Rochester having desired to be discharged from the Lieutenancy of Ireland. **1711** SWIFT *Jrnl. to Stella* 4 Apr., Her husband bought a lieutenancy of foot, and is gone to Portugal. **1712** —— *Let. to Whig Lord* Wks. 1824 IV. 108 All your lordship can hope for, is only the lieutenancy of a county. **1799** WASHINGTON *Lett.* Writ. (1893) XIV. 177 A lieutenancy was considered a handsome appointment for him. **1828** SCOTT *F.M. Perth* xiii, When I was intrusted with the lieutenancy of the kingdom. **1841** J. T. HEWLETT *Parish Clerk* III. 7 The appointment to a coast-guard lieutenancy. **1849** MACAULAY *Hist. Eng.* ix. II. 423 The Earl of Abingdon .. had recently been turned out of the lieutenancy of the county. **1875** STUBBS *Const. Hist.* III. xviii. 140 Edmund Beaufort was ordered to undertake the lieutenancy in France and Normandy.

3. The term of a lieutenant's office.

1632 LE GRYS tr. *Velleius Paterc.* 109 In his Lievetenancie under Marius in France .. hee [Sylla] had routed some of the most esteemed Captaines. **1673** *Essex Papers* (Camden) I. 108 In yᵉ time of my Lord Berkeley's Lieutenancy. **1842** DE QUINCEY *Cicero* Wks. VI. 226 The prolongation of these lieutenantcies beyond the legitimate year was one source of enormous evil.

† **4.** The district or province governed by a lieutenant. *Obs.*

1588 Q. ELIZ. in Ellis *Orig. Lett.* Ser. II. III. 138 The preparinge of our Subjectes within your Lievetennauncies to be in readines for defence againste any attempte. **1687** in Picton *L'pool Munic. Rec.* (1883) I. 258 The list of Deputie Lievetenants .. throughout the said Lievetanancie. **1726** SHELVOCKE *Voy. round World* 266, I mention'd the surprisal of that place [Iquique], it being but a small Lieutenancy.

5. The body of deputy-lieutenants in a county. Also, in the city of London, the body of commissioners (sometimes incorrectly called 'deputy-lieutenants'), now usually appointed annually, who perform the duties of a Lord-lieutenant with regard to the militia and volunteers.

1679 in *Proceed. Guildhall Sept. 13th* 3 He would cause the Lieutenancy to meet on Thursday next. **1683** in *Lond. Gaz.* No. 1859/1 The late Addresses from the Lieutenancy, Grand-Juries, and Corporations in our County. **1708** Q. ANNE *ibid.* No. 4496/1, I Thank the Lieutenancy for their

Address. **1709** H. Felton *Classics* (1718) 115 The List of Undisputed Masters, is hardly so long as the List of the Court of Aldermen and Lieutenancy of our famous Metropolis. **1727** Boyer *Fr. Dict.* s.v., The Lieutenancy of London (the Officers of the Artillery-Men). **1873** *Act 36 & 37 Vict.* c. 84 §2 The commissioners of lieutenancy of the city of London.

b. *pl.* The bodies of troops under the command of the Lord-lieutenants and commissioners of lieutenancy.

1709 Steele *Tatler* No. 28 ¶5 Our Militia and Lieutenancies, the most ancient Corps of Soldiers, perhaps in the Universe.

lieutenant (lɛf-, lɪfˈtɛnənt, *U.S.* ljuːˈtɛnənt). Forms: α. 4–5 lutenand, -a(u)nt; 5 leu(e)-, leuȝ-, lyeu-, 5–7 lieu-, 6 lyue-, liue-, lieue-, leaue-, lew-, 7 leiu-; 4–7 -tenante, -aunt, 5–6 -aunte, 5–7 -ant, 6–7 -ent, -tennent, -ante; 6 *Sc.* lewtennand, 4– lieutenant. β. 4 leef-, 4–5 leyf-, lyef-, 4–6 leve-, 5–6 lyff(e)-, 5–8 lief-, 6 lefe-, lyffe-, lyve-, lieuf-, 6–7 live-, liefe-, leive-, leif-, 7 liev-, life-, + second element as in α. ; 5 luf-tenand, luff tenande, 6 leftenaunt, -tennant, -tenant. [a. F. *lieutenant*, f. *lieu* place + *tenant* holding (see tenant); cf. locum tenens.

The origin of the β. type of forms (which survives in the usual British pronunciation, though the spelling represents the α. type) is difficult to explain. The hypothesis of a mere misinterpretation of the graphic form (*u* read as *v*), at first sight plausible, does not accord with the facts. In view of the rare OF. form *luef* for *lieu* (with which cf. esp. the 15th c. Sc. forms *luf-*, *lufftenand* above) it seems likely that the labial glide at the end of OF. *lieu* as the first element of a compound was sometimes apprehended by Englishmen as a *v* or *f*. Possibly some of the forms may be due to association with leave *sb.*[1] or lief *a.*

In 1793 Walker gives the actual pronunciations as (lɛv-, lɪvˈtɛnənt), but expresses the hope that 'the regular sound, *lewtenant*' will in time become current. In England this pronunciation (ljuːˈtɛnənt) is almost unknown. A newspaper quot. of 1893 in Funk's *Standard Dictionary* says that (lɛfˈtɛnənt) is in the U.S. 'almost confined to the retired list of the navy'.]

1. a. One who takes the place of another; usually, an officer civil or military who acts for a superior; a representative, substitute, vicegerent.

c **1375** *Sc. Leg. Saints* xxxi. (*Eugenia*) 40 To quham..þe hale senat gef þe cure of Alysandir þe cyte þar lutenand þar-of to be. **1375** [*MS.* **1489**] Barbour *Bruce* xiv. 139 Schir Richard of Clare, That..luf-tenand Was off the king of Yngland. **1387** Trevisa *Higden* (Rolls) VIII. 143 Hubert archebisshop of Caunterbury was leeftenaunt [*v.rr.* lutenant, levetenaunt] of þe pope and of the kyng of Engelond. **1390** Gower *Conf.* I. 73, I his grace have so poursuied, That I was mad his lieutenant. **14..** Lydg. & Burgh *Secrees* 2194 Oon singuler man to make thy leyf tenaunt, To the ne thyne is not avayllable. **1480** Caxton *Chron. Eng.* ccli. (1482) 322 He beyng that tyme lyeutenaunt of the kyng in Normandye. *c* **1500** *Melusine* lxii. 369 Sersuell ..held the said Fortres as lieuftenaunt & Captayne there for the kyng of England. **1534** *Act 26 Hen. VIII*, c. 4 §1 Any Justiciar, Steward, Lieuetenaunte, or other officer within wales or the marches of the same. **1552** Lyndesay *Monarche* 4271 To Christe he [the Pope] is gret Lewtennand. **1583** Stubbes *Anat. Abus.* ii. (1882) 106 They are his Liefetenants, his vicegerents in his Church. **1610** Shaks. *Temp.* iii. ii. 20 By this light thou shalt bee my Lieutenant Monster, or my Standard. **1651** Hobbes *Leviath.* (1839) 400 God was king, and the high-priest was to be, after the death of Moses, his sole viceroy or lieutenant. **1703** J. Logan in *Pa. Hist. Soc. Mem.* IX. 192 It will be extremely necessary to procure a lieutenant for some time at least in thy interest. **1788** Gibbon *Decl. & F.* (1869) III. lxvii. 698 His lieutenants were permitted to negociate a truce. **1845** S. Austin *Ranke's Hist. Ref.* III. 231 Though called king, he was in fact only a lieutenant of the sultan. **1869** Freeman *Norm. Conq.* (1876) III. xi. 49 He had the trustiest of lieutenants in his brothers.

†**b.** *fig.* (Now not used, on account of the specific associations of the word.)

1377 Langl. *P. Pl.* B. xvi. 47 *Ac liberum arbitrium* letteth hym some tyme, þat is lieutenant to loken it wel by leue of myselue. *c* **1425** Lydg. *Assembly of Gods* 1254 Then made Vertu Reson hys lyeftenaunt. **1461** *Liber Pluscardensis* xi. viii, He [God] maid Natur to be his luff tenande. *a* **1586** Sidney *Arcadia* iii. (1633) 303 Where..Fore-sight, with his Lievtenant Resolution, had made readie defence. **1621** Quarles *Argalus & P.* (1678) 110 Parthenia (whose tears Are turn'd Lieutenants to her tongue). *a* **1708** Beveridge *Thes. Theol.* (1711) III. 241 The Holy Ghost, Christ's Lieutenant, that supplies the place of the absent Captain.

c. As a formal title of office, usually with defining phrase indicating the object or locality of delegated command, as in ***Lieutenant of the Tower*** (of London), the acting commandant delegated by the Constable; ***Lieutenant of Ireland, of a county*** (now always Lord-lieutenant), and in various other designations now only *Hist.*

1423 *Rolls of Parlt.* IV. 198/2 He beyng the Kynges Lieutenaunt in the said Londe [of Ireland]. **1454** *Ibid.* V. 240/2 The Duk of York, the Kynges Lieutenant of his Parlement. **1481** Caxton *Myrr.* iii. xxiv. 192 Lieutenaunt of the toun of Calays. **1495** *Act 11 Hen. VII*, c. 35 *Preamble*, His Lyeutenaunte of Ireland and Gardeyn of the.. Marches. **1596** Dalrymple tr. *Leslie's Hist. Scot.* ix. 206 Henrie Stuart, quhom the king..maid leauetennant of the gret Gunis. **1596** Sir J. Smythe in *Lett. Lit. Men* (Camden) 89 Mr. Leivetenant of the Tower. *a* **1604** Hanmer *Chron. Irel.* (1633) 140 Whereupon he made Reimond Lievetenant of the forces. *a* **1613** Overbury *A Wife* (1638) 187 He doe's not feare the Lieutenant o' th' Shire. *c* **1667** Cotton in *N. & Q.* 9th Ser. VIII. 41/1, I am through his Magestyes gratyouse Favor lieutennant off yᵉ Forrest. **1679** Wood *Life* 30 Apr., He was lieftenant of the ordinance. **1702** *Lond. Gaz.* No. 3810/8 Her Majesty has been pleased to appoint Sir George Rooke..Lieutenant of the Navies and Seas of this Kingdom. **1864** Burton *Scot Abr.* I. ii. 61 King Robert III had a younger brother Alexander, who was made lieutenant of the northern part of the kingdom.

†**d.** Used as an equivalent for L. *legatus*, *proconsul*, *suffectus*, Gr. ἡγεμών. *Obs.*

1388 Wyclif *2 Macc.* iv. 31 Suffectus..ether lutenaunt. **1526** Tindale *Luke* ii. 2 Syrenus was leftenaunt in Siria. **1553** Eden *Treat. Newe Ind.* (Arb.) 9 *Metellus celer*, proconsull or leauetenaunte of Fraunce. **1557** N. T. (Genev.) *Luke* iii. 1 Lieutenant of Jurie. **1636** E. Dacres tr. *Machiavel's Disc. Livy* II. 639 Fulvius remaining Lieftenant in the army..for that the Consull was gon to Rome. **1658** Sir T. Browne *Hydriot.* i. (1736) 9 A great Overthrow was given unto the Iceni by the Roman Lieutenant Ostorius. **1741** Middleton *Cicero* I. vi. 408 The whole administration of the corn and provisions of the Republic was to be granted to Pompey for five years, with a power of chusing fifteen Lieutenants to assist him in it.

†**e.** (See quot.) *Obs.*

1654 H. L'Estrange *Chas. I* (1655) 72 That Christmas the Temple Sparks had enstalled a Lieutenant, a thing we Country folk call a Lord of Misrule.

2. *Mil.* and *Naval.* (As a prefixed title, often abbreviated *Lieut.*, and in combs. *Lt.*) **a.** In the army: The officer next in rank to the captain. †Also in ***captain-lieutenant*** (see quot. 1727–51; cf. *lieutenant captain* in 3). **b.** In the navy: The officer next in rank and power below the commander. †Also ***lieutenant at arms*** (see quot. 1769).

a. **1578** T. N. tr. *Conq. W. India* 1 Who in his youth applied himselfe to the warres, and was lieutenant to a companie of horsemen. **1642** *Althorp MS.* in Simpkinson *Washington* (1860) p. lxxxii, To liefetennant Scotts horse of oates j. pecke. **1647** Clarendon *Hist. Reb.* i. §52 A lievtenant of a foot company. **1653** Baxter *Chr. Concord* 82 The Lieutenant of the Troop..needs no new Commission. **1727–51** Chambers *Cycl.* s.v. *Captain*, *Captain-lieutenant* is he who commands a troop, or company, in the name and place of some other person, who has the commission, with the title, honour, and pay thereof; but is dispensed withal, on account of his quality, from performing the functions of his post. **1844** *Regul. & Ord. Army* 3 Second Lieutenants take rank of Cornets and Ensigns. **1876** Voyle & Stevenson *Milit. Dict.* (ed. 3) s.v., In the footguards 24 of the lieutenants have the rank of captain in the army, and are called lieutenants and captains.

b. **1626** Capt. Smith *Accid. Yng. Sea-men* 6 The Lieutenant is to associate the Captaine, and in his absence to execute his place. **1757** Smollett *Reprisal* ii. ix, Lieftenant Lyon commands a tender of twelve guns. **1769** Falconer *Dict. Marine* (1780) Z 4 b, The youngest lieutenant of the ship, who is also stiled lieutenant at arms,..is particularly ordered..to train the seamen to the use of small arms. **1833** Marryat *P. Simple* xxi, The Admiralty..had..promoted him to the rank of lieutenant.

c. An officer in the Salvation Army.

1884 [see captain *sb.* 5 b]. *c* **1897** A. E. Housman *Lett.* (1971) 45 Lieutenant Isabella..comes Dealing blows with her umbrella. **1970** *Guardian* 2 May 10/4, I love the Salvation Army through which I found my Saviour... Yours faithfully, Lars Juhlin. Lieutenant.

3. *attrib.* and in *Comb.*, signifying generally one who acts as deputy to the superior officer designated, as in † ***lieutenant-admiral*** (in the Dutch navy), ***lieutenant-bailiff*** (in Guernsey), † ***lieutenant-fire-worker***; † **lieutenant-captain** (see quot.); **lieutenant-colonel**, an army officer of rank next below that of a colonel, having the actual command of a regiment; hence **lieutenant-colonelcy**, the office or rank of lieutenant-colonel; **lieutenant-commander**, a naval officer who is in rank next below a commander and next above a lieutenant; **lieutenant-governor**, the deputy of a governor, *esp.* (*a*) in the British colonies, the actual governor of a district or province in subordination to a governor-general; (*b*) in the United States, the deputy-governor of a state with certain independent duties and the right of succession to the governorship, in case of its becoming vacant; hence † **lieutenant-governancy**, **lieutenant-governorship**, (*a*) the office of a lieutenant-governor; (*b*) the province under his government; † **lieutenant-prætor** = L. *proprætor*. Also lieutenant-general.

1693 *Lond. Gaz.* No. 2867/3 On Sunday last *Lieutenant Admiral Allemond passed by Dover with 4 great Dutch Men of War. **1682** Warburton *Hist. Guernsey* (1822) 49 The Bailiff..is the chief judge of the royal court; his office may be executed by deputy, who is called the *lieutenant-bailiff. **1727–51** Chambers *Cycl.* s.v. *Captain*, **Lieutenant-Captain* is the *captain's* second; or the officer who commands the company under the captain, and in his absence... In some companies, &c. he is also called *Captain-lieutenant*. **1598** B. Jonson *Ev. Man in Hum.* iii. v, He might haue beene Serieant-Maior, if not *Lieutenant-Coronell to the regiment. **1707** *Vulpone* 8 Collonels, Lieutenant Collonels, Majors, Captains. **1876** Bancroft *Hist. U.S.* V. xix. 549 The subject was referred on the part of Howe to Lieutenant-colonel Walcott. **1797** Nelson in Nicolas *Disp.* (1845) II. 446 Your good father tells me you are in great hopes of the *Lieutenant-Colonelcy. **1842** Thackeray *Fitz-B. Pap.* Pref. (1887) 14 His papa would have purchased him..a lieutenant-colonelcy. **1878** *N. Amer. Rev.* CXXVII. 224 *Lieutenant-Commander J. G. Walker had been sent in the iron-clad Baron de Kalb. **1800** *Asiatic Ann. Reg.*, *Char.* 51/2 Mr. Harris was soon after appointed a *Lieutenant Fire-worker. **1595** Maynarde *Drake's Voy.* (Hakluyt Soc.) 13 The *Leiftenant-governor and some others were taken prisoners. **1707** *Lond. Gaz.* No. 4341/3 Colonel Richard Sutton is made Lieutenant-Governor of Hull. **1849** Cobden *Speeches* 72 If we take the case of our North American colonies: we have five colonial and five lieutenant-governors. **1880** V. Ball *Jungle Life India* i. 47 The official residence of the Lieutenant-Governor of Bengal. **1784** *Laura & Augustus* (1794) II. 50 *Lieutenant Governancy. **1745** *Observ. conc. Navy* 44 Many have either had Governments or *Lieutenant-Governorships. **1886** *Athenæum* 24 Apr. 556/1 The Reports on Public Instruction in Bengal and the North-Western Provinces..show considerable difference in the state of education in the two lieutenant-governorships. **1618** Bolton *Florus* ii. xiii. (1636) 130 Anicius, *Lieutenant-Praetor, subdued them in an instant.

lieu'tenant-'general. [After F. *lieutenant-général*, in which the second word is historically an adj. qualifying the preceding sb. In Eng., however, and app. also in Fr., *general* has been commonly apprehended as a sb.]

† **1.** *gen.* One who exercises a delegated rule or command over some extensive region or department; the vicegerent of a kingdom, etc. (Cf. F. *lieutenant général du royaume*.) *Obs.*

c **1489** Caxton *Blanchardyn* xlvi. 176 Made hym seneschall & his leeftenaunt generall of the royalme. *a* **1548** Hall *Chron.*, *Edw. IV*, 244 Duke of Glocester, leuetenaunt generall, and chiefetayne for ye kyng of Englande. *Ibid.*, *Hen. VI*, 161 b, Longvile, lieuetenant generall for the Frenche kyng. **1701** *Lond. Gaz.* No. 3709/4 The King of Spain..has made the Count d'Estrees Lieutenant General of Spain at Sea.

transf. **1583** Stubbes *Anat. Abus.* ii. (1882) 104 The Deuill himselfe, whose vicegerent or Liefetenant generall in his kingedome of impietie he [the Pope] shewes himselfe to be.

2. One who acts as deputy to a general. In the British army, an officer in rank next below a general, and next above a major-general. †Also ***lieutenant-general of the ordnance***.

In the U.S. army the office has been held by only a few distinguished individuals beginning with Washington, and is now in abeyance.

1589 [T. Cates] *Sir F. Drake's W. Ind. Voy.* 5 We descried another tall ship..vpon whom Maister Carleill, the Lieutenant Generall, being in the Tiger, vndertooke the chase. [C. 'commanded the land forces against the Spanish West Indies' (Dict. Nat. Biog.).] **1618** Bolton *Florus* ii. viii. (1636) 120 Scipio Africanus..serving voluntary under him [his brother] there, as Lieutenant General. **1647** Clarendon *Hist. Reb.* ii. §26 The Earl of Essex was made lievetenant-general of the army. *a* **1671** Ld. Fairfax *Mem.* (1699) 84 Lieutenant General Cromwell commanded the left wing of the horse. **1691–2** in *Wood's Life* 23 Jan., Commissions are under the seale to make the duke of Ormond and Sir John Lanier lieutenant generalls. **1702** *Lond. Gaz.* No. 3822/4 Her Majesty has been pleased to constitute..the Rt. Hon. John Granville Esq.; Lieutenant-General..of the Ordnance. **1781** Gibbon *Decl. & F.* xvii. II. 37 The lieutenant-generals of the Roman armies, the military counts and dukes..were allowed the rank and title of *Respectable*. **1798** J. Adams *Wks.* (1854) IX. 159, I..congratulate them and the public on this great event, the General's [*sc.* Washington] acceptance of his appointment as Lieutenant-General and Commander-in-chief of the army. **1808** Wellington in Gurw. *Desp.* (1837) IV. 73, I shall be the junior of the Lieutenant Generals; however I am ready to serve the government wherever and as they please. **1855** W. Sargent *Braddock's Exped.* 290 On 26th February, 1755, he was made..a lieutenant-general. **1878** J. A. Garfield in *N. Amer. Rev.* CXXVI. 452 The office of lieutenant-general was virtually stripped of all authority.

transf. *c* **1620** Day *Parlt. of Bees*, Char. i. (1641), 'Gainst all these outlaws, Martin, bee thou Lievetenant Generall.

†**lieu'tenantry.** *Obs.* Also 7 lieutennendrie, lieutenandry. [f. lieutenant + -ry.]

= lieutenancy in various senses.

1604 in *Reg. Priv. Counc. Scotl.* VII. 19 To command and chairge all..leigis and subjectis within the bounds of the said lieutennendrie to rise. **1604** Shaks. *Oth.* ii. i. 173 If such tricks as these strip you out of your Lieutenantrie. **1606** —— *Ant. & Cl.* iii. xi. 39 He alone Dealt on Lieutenantry, and no practise had In the braue squares of Warre. *a* **1639** Spottiswood *Hist. Ch. Scot.* vi. (1677) 286 A Commission of Lieutenandry was given to the Earl of Angus for convocating the subjects and pursuing the Rebels. **1676** W. Row *Suppl. Blair's Autobiog.* xii. (1848) 461 He is discharged of his lieutenantry over the forces in Scotland.

lieu'tenantship. [f. lieutenant + -ship.] The office of a lieutenant. Now *rare*.

1467–8 *Rolls of Parlt.* V. 588/1 The Office of Stuardeship or Lieftenauntship of oure Lordeship and Maner of Wodestoke. **1581** Savile *Tacitus' Agric.* (1591) 242 In that Lieutenantship hauing spent scarsely three years, he was called home to bee Consull. **1626** in *Crt. & Times Chas. I* (1848) I. 149 The Earl of Warwick is put out of his lieutenantship, and, which is more, out of the commission for the peace. *a* **1641** Bp. Mountagu *Acts & Mon.* (1642) 226 Antipater..having succeeded Antipas his Father in the Lieutenantship of Idumœa. **1721** Strype *Eccl. Mem.* (1822) II. xxxiv. 445 The King gave him [the Marquis of Northampton]..the lieutenantship of the chase of Hampton Court. **1870** *Pall Mall G.* 18 Aug. 4 He had been proposed for a lieutenantship, when..he deserted.

lieve, obs. form of leave *sb.*[1]

liever, var. *liefer*, compar. of lief.

lievrite (ˈliːvraɪt). *Min.* [Named by Werner, 1812, in honour of C. H. Lelièvre, who first described it: see -ite.] A synonym of ilvaite.

1814 T. Allan *Min. Nomen.* 29 Lievrit. **1816** P. Cleaveland *Min.* (1822) 393 Lievrite. **1861** Bristow *Gloss. Min.*

lif, obs. form of LIEF.

life (laɪf), *sb.* Forms: 1 lif, 3–5 lif, lijf, (4 liif, leve, liuf), 4–5 live, 4–6 lyf(f, lyif(f, liff, lyve, 4–7 lyfe, 5 lyyf, 5–6 lief, liffe, lyffe, 4– life. *Gen. sing.* 1 lifes, 2–7 lives, 3 lifves, 4–5 lyfes, lyvis, -ys, 4–6 -es, 5 -ez, lyfes, 6 liffis. *Dat. sing.* 1 life, 2–5 live, 3 liwe, 4–5 lyve; see also ALIVE. *Plural.* 4 lyfis, 4–6 lyves, -is, 4–7 lifes, 5 lywes, lijfis, lyvis, -ess, 6 lyffes, lyfes, lieves, 4– lives. [OE. *líf* str. neut., corresponds to OFris. *lîf* neut., life, person, body, OS. *lîf* neut., life, person (MDu. *lijf* life, body, Du. *lijf* body), OHG. *lîb* masc. and neut., life (MHG. *lîp*, inflected *lîb-*, masc., life, body, mod.G. *leib* masc., body), ON. *líf* neut., life, occas. body (Sw. *lif*, Da. *liv* life, body):—OTeut. **lîbo^m*, f. Teut. root **lîb-*, whence LIVE *v.*, OE. *belīfan* BELIVE *v.*, to remain; the ablaut-var. **laib-* appears in LEAVE *v.* The general meaning of the root (Aryan **leip-*, *loip-*, *lip-*) is 'to continue, last, endure'; cf. Gr. λιπαρής persistent.]

I. The condition or attribute of living or being alive; animate existence. Opposed to *death*.

1. a. Primarily, the condition, quality, or fact of being a living person or animal. Phrases: † ***to bring (out) of life*** (see BRING *v.* 8 b); † ***to do*** or ***draw of live***, to kill, destroy; † ***to go of live***, to die; ***while there is life there is hope*** (and similar phrases); ***there is life in the old dog yet*** (and variants): an assertion of continuing competence, strength, etc., notwithstanding evidence to the contrary.

Beowulf 2471 Þa he of life ʒewat. *c* **1200** *Trin. Coll. Hom.* 197 And te londes men hire.. lacheð, and doð of liue. *c* **1200** Ormin 9776 Profetess all wiþþutenn gilt þeʒʒ haffdenn brohht off life. *a* **1225** *Leg. Kath.* 252 Blodles & banles & leomen buten liue. *c* **1250** *Gen. & Ex.* 201 His licham of erðe he nam, And blew ðor-in a liues blast. *Ibid.* 3806, .xiiii. ðhusent it haueð slaʒen, And .iiii. score of liue draʒen. *Ibid.* 3884 Aaron ðo wente of liwe ðor. *c* **1330** *Spec. Gy Warw.* 252 Vp he ros þe þridde day From deþ to liue wid-oute nay. *c* **1374** Chaucer *Troylus* II. 1559 (1608) Ioue.. bryng hym soone of lyue. *c* **1400** *Destr. Troy* 11038 Phylmen, þe freke, .. Lut to þe lady, & of his lyff þanket. *c* **1400** Maundev. (Roxb.) Pref. 1 In þe whilk land it lyked him to take lief and blude of oure Lady Saint Marie. *a* **1400–50** *Alexander* 2162 If any life lenge in oure brestis. **1539** R. Taverner *Erasmus's Proverbs* f. 36^v, The sycke person whyle he hath lyfe, hath hope. **1560** Daus tr. *Sleidane's Comm.* 415 [He is] so sicke and diseased, that they can hardlye kepe life in him. **1611** Bible *Gen.* ii. 20 The mouing creature that hath life. *a* **1638** Mede *Wks.* 401 The fire is known by its burning; the life of the body is known by its moving. **1671** J. Crowne *Juliana* v. 56 Madam, he breathes, and whilst there's life, there's hope. **1676** Dryden *Aurengz.* I. i. 150 Proof of my Life my Royal Signet made. **1697** Collier *Immor. Stage* 288 As long as there's Life there's Hope. **1727** J. Gay *Fables* xxvii. 93 While there is life, there's hope, he cry'd. **1738** Pope *Universal Prayer* 44 Oh lead me whereso'er I go, Thro' this day's Life or Death. **1765** Blackstone *Comm.* I. i. 94 Life is the immediate gift of God. **1803** *Med. Jrnl.* X. 516 Deep inspiration, sighing, and other strong symptoms of life. **1808** *Monthly Pantheon* I. 366/1 Whilst there is *life* you know there *are hopes*! **1859** S. Allen *Let.* 1 Dec. in D. Ayerst *Guardian* (1971) x. 134 'Are not the advertisements grand?'.. 'There is life in the old dog yet.' **1880** L. Morris *Ode Life* 138 Life! what is life, that it ceases with ceasing of breath? **1908** E. J. Banfield *Confessions of Beachcomber* II. ii. 301 While there is life there is hope is evidently Nelly's creed. **1940** *Time* 15 July 49/1 Tallulah Bankhead demonstrated that there's life in Pinero's old girl yet.

b. In a wider sense: The property which constitutes the essential difference between a living animal or plant, or a living portion of organic tissue, and dead or non-living matter; the assemblage of the functional activities by which the presence of this property is manifested. Often with defining word, as in *animal*, *vegetable*, *psychical life*.

1567 Maplet *Gr. Forest* 25 b, In Plantes.. is the life vegetative. *Ibid.* 26 To apprehende the other life above this [*i.e.* life in the womb] called sensitive. **1678** Cudworth *Intell. Syst.* I. i. §27. **1813** Sir H. Davy *Agric. Chem.* (1814) 54 Life gives a peculiar character to all its productions; the power of attraction and repulsion, combination and decomposition, are subservient to it. **1830** R. Knox *Béclard's Anat.* 4 Life is seen in organized bodies only, and it is in living bodies only that organization is seen. **1874** Carpenter *Ment. Phys.* I. ii. §4 (1879) 120 The Cerebrum, —the instrument of our Psychical or inner life. **1884** F. Temple *Relat. Relig. & Sci.* vi. (1885) 170 There could have been no life when the earth was nothing but a mass of intensely heated fluid. **1889** Burdon-Sanderson in *Nature* 26 Sept. 523 Life is a state of ceaseless change.

c. Continuance or prolongation of animate existence; opposed to *death*. (For *tree*, *water*, *elixir*, etc. *of life*, see these sbs.) (***a matter,*** etc.) ***of life and*** (also ***or***) ***death***: (something) on which it depends whether a person shall live or die; hence *fig.* (a matter) of 'vital' importance.

c **1000** Ælfric *Gen.* ii. 9 Lifes treow omiddan neorxena wange and treow inʒehydes godes and yfeles. *a* **1200** *Moral Ode* 115 Ech Mon scal hin solf demen to deðe oðer to liue. *c* **1450** *ME. Med. Bk.* (Heinrich) 138 Ȝef þe netle be alyue, hit is a synge of lyf. **1690** W. Walker *Idiomat. Anglo-Lat.* 135 To sit upon life and death on a man, *De capite alicujus quærere.* **1837** Dickens *Let.* c 20 Apr. (1965) I. 249 It is matter of life or death to us, to know whether you have got Ainsworth's MS yet. **1887** *Spectator* 3 Sept. 1174 A thoroughly workable mobilisation scheme.. is a matter of life and death to the French. **1898** W. J. Locke *Idols* x. 134 The marriage could be concealed no longer. It was a matter of life or death. **1950** K. Winsor *Star Money* III. xxix. 249, I never have made any man a matter of life or death to me.

d. Animate existence viewed as dependent on sustenance or favourable physical conditions. (For *necessary of life*, *staff of life*, see those words.) †Hence, that which is necessary to sustain life; a livelihood, one's living. *Obs.*

c **1250** *Gen. & Ex.* 176 To fode, and srud, to helpen ðe lif. **1387** Trevisa *Higden* (Rolls) I. 399 Al þat nedeþ to þe lyue þat lond bryngeþ forþ ful ryue. **1553** R. Ascham in *Lett. Lit. Men* (Camden) 14, I trust I cold applie my self to mo Kyndes of liffe than I hope any need shall ever drive me to seeke. **1571** *Satir. Poems Reform.* xxviii. 88 Of all the barnis my Lady Seltoun bure, Scho me constranit to make Ilk ane a lyfe. **1604** E. G[rimstone] *D'Acosta's Hist. Indies* II. ii. 84 Of necessitie it must be contrarie and vnfit for mans life. **1611** Bible *Deut.* xx. 19 The tree of the field is mans life. **1615** W. Lawson *Country Housew. Garden* (1626) 3 And by this meanes your plot shall be fertile for your life. **1655** tr. *Com. Hist. Francion* IX. 7 You.. are so afraid to lay forth your money, that you dare not buy that which is most necessary for life. **1699** Dampier *Voy.* II. I. 15 Cachao is the only place of Trade in the Country, and Trade is the Life of a Chinese.

e. Attributed hyperbolically to products of plastic or graphic art.

1638 F. Junius *Paint. Ancients* 77 He shall shew you.. what marble got life by the carving-iron of the laborious Praxiteles. **1644** Evelyn *Diary* 1 Mar. (1819) I. 46 The *Ecce Homo*.. for the life and accurate finishing exceeding all description.

f. ***to come to life***: to recover as from apparent death; to regain consciousness after a swoon. So ***to bring to life***.

1672 Wiseman *Treat. Wounds* I. ix. 113 We bled him till he came to life. **1678** Lady Chaworth in *12th Rep. Hist. MSS. Comm.* App. v. 52 They saw a man drowning... After some howers he came to lyfe.

2. *fig.* Used to designate a condition of power, activity, or happiness, in contrast to a condition conceived hyperbolically or metaphorically as 'death'. Chiefly in biblical and religious use: The condition of those who are raised from the 'death of sin' and are 'alive unto righteousness'; the divinely implanted power or principle by which this condition is produced; also, the state of existence of the souls of the blessed departed, in contrast with that of the lost.

c **950** *Lindisf. Gosp.* John iii. 15 Eȝhuelc seðe ʒelefeð in ðæm ne losað ah he hæfeð lif ece. *c* **1200** *Vices & Virtues* (1888) 9 Ðat we.. swa cumeð forð in to ðe eche liue ðe he hafð us behoten. *c* **1220** *Bestiary* 46 Ure driȝten.. ros fro dede ðo, vs to lif holden. **1382** Wyclif *Col.* iii. 3 Ȝour lyf is hid with Crist in God. *c* **1430** *Hymns Virg.* 9 To lastynge lijf it wole us lede. *c* **1449** Pecock *Repr.* v. xi. 539 It is bettir to a man forto entre sureli into lijf with oon yȝe, oon hond, oon foot, et cætera. **1585** Fetherstone tr. *Calvin on Acts* viii. 25 The seede of life began to be sowen throughout the whole region. **1829** Carlyle in *Foreign Rev.* IV. 129 If our Bodily Life is a burning, our Spiritual Life is a being-burnt, a Combustion.

3. a. Animate existence (esp. that of a human being) viewed as a possession of which one is deprived by death, esp. in ***to lose, save, lay down one's life***, and similar expressions. Formerly † ***the life*** = one's, his (etc.) life. Often idiomatically conjoined with other sbs., as ***life and limb*** (formerly † ***life and member***), ***life and soul***. ***life for life***: one of the phrases expressing the principle of *lex talionis*.

Beowulf 2751 Þæt ic.. mæȝe æfter maððumwelan min alætan lif and leodscipe. *c* **1000** Ælfric *Exod.* xxi. 23 Sylle lif wið life, eaȝe wið eaȝe [etc.]. ? *a* **1100** *O.E. Chron.* an. 978 (Laud MS.) Sume hit ne ʒedyȝdan mid þam life. *c* **1175** *Lamb. Hom.* 71 Þet lif and saule beon iborȝen. *a* **1200** *Moral Ode* 120 Al his lif scal bon suilch boð his endinge. *a* **1225** *Leg. Kath.* 2441 Þet lif of mi licome. *a* **1300** *Cursor M.* 1970 Þar gas na ransun bot liue for lijf. *c* **1350** *Will. Palerne* 994 A manes liif to saue. *c* **1375** *Sc. Leg. Saints* ii. (*Paulus*) 702 Nero gert hym lose þe lyf. *a* **1400–50** *Alexander* 1918 Of life & o lym my lege men I charge [etc.]. **1477** Earl Rivers (Caxton) *Dictes* 1 To dispose my recouered lyf to his seruyce. **1556** *Chron. Gr. Friars* (Camden) 47 The kynge gave them alle there lyffes & pardynd them. **1632** Lithgow *Trav.* 357 Our lives and liberty is granted. *c* **1645** Howell *Lett.* (1650) I. 335 The Turk.. meddles not with life and limb to prevent the sense of compassion which may arise that way. **1658–9** *Burton's Diary* (1828) III. 235 It is not enough to serve you in those offices, unless they venture life and member. **1685** Evelyn *Diary* 8 July, [They] sold their lives very dearely. **1719** De Foe *Crusoe* II. vi. 140 You have .. sav'd my Life. **1743** Bulkeley & Cummins *Voy. S. Seas* 75 Because he who does not value his own Life, has another Man's in his Power. **1836** Lady W. de Eresby in *C. K. Sharpe's Corr.* (1888) II. 495 Mrs. V.. was pitched off.. but mercifully escaped with life and limb. **1849** James *Woodman* iii, It must.. always be a terrible thing to take a life. **1890** Saintsbury in *New Rev.* Feb. 136 You take your life in your hands, you rebel, and you win or you don't.

b. In generalized or collective sense.

1841 Lane *Arab. Nts.* I. 92 He will not be appeased with money, nor with anything but life. **1847** Marryat *Childr. N. Forest* xx, We must not take more life than is necessary. *Mod.* The sacrifice of life was enormous. These savages have no regard for human life.

c. † ***in, upon, under pain of life***: subject to the penalty of death. † ***for, upon one's life***: on a capital charge. ***for (one's) life, for dear life***, etc., so as to save, or, as if to save, one's life. Also *hyperbolically* in trivial use, ***(I cannot) for my life, for the life of me*** (see FOR *prep.* 9 c).

c **1250** [see FOR A. 9 c]. **1513** Bradshaw *St. Werburge* I. 1022 Cease of suche busynesse, in peyne of thy lyue. **1613** Sherley *Trav. Persia* 50 Enioyning them vpon paine of life to take no other sort of reward. **1632** Lithgow *Trav.* II. 76 For my life I could neuer attaine to any perfect knowledge thereof. **1650** Howell *Giraffi's Rev. Naples* I. 77 That all Cavaliers, under paine of life should deliver their Armes. **1667** Pepys *Diary* 10 Apr., How Sir Thomas Allen.. was tried for his life. *a* **1715** Burnet *Own Time* (1724) I. 586 He was not, as they said, now in a criminal Court upon his life. **1726** Swift *Gulliver* II. i. 6, I saw our Men.. rowing for Life to the Ship. **1809** Malkin *Gil Blas* XI. ii. ¶ 10 Not knowing how for the life of him to part with those flattering hopes. **1813, 1831** [see FOR A. 9 c]. **1842** S. Lover *Handy Andy* xxi, He kept Reddy.. singing away for the bare life. **1843** W. T. Thompson *Major Jones' Chron. Pineville* 93 He.. was climbing for dear life. **1849** [see FOR A. 9 c]. **1872** B. Jerrold *London* ii. 23 Hard-visaged men, breathlessly competing for 'dear life'. **1880** Gladstone in *Daily News* 16 Mar. 2/8, I cannot, for the life of me, see why it should be struck out. **1887** [see FOR A. 9 c]. **1921** H. Crane *Let.* 17 Oct. (1965) 68 The man who would preserve them [sc. feelings] must duck and camouflage for dear life.

d. In asseverative phrases and oaths, as † ***by, for, of my life***; ***God's life***, shortened to 'SLIFE, *life*. †Also in oath-words formed with diminutive suffixes, **lifekins**, **lifelikins**, **lifelings**. Phr. ***not on your life***, not on any account, by no means.

a **1400** *Cursor M.* 2719 (Gött.) At mi gaincum, bi mi lyf [*earlier text* (Cott.), if I haue lijf; *vita comite*, Vulg.] A son sal haue sare þi wijf. **1590** Marlowe *Edw. II*, I. iv. (1598) C, She smiles, now for my life, his minde is chang'd. **1599** Porter *Angry Wom. Abingt.* vi. (Percy Soc.) 34 Ile holde my life, Your minde was to change maidenhead for wife. **1600** Shaks. *A. Y. L.* IV. i. 159 By my life, she will doe as I doe. **1601** —— *Twel. N.* v. i. 188 Odd's lifelings. **1604** Gods life [see GOD *sb.* 14 a]. **1606** Day *Ile of Guls* G, Of my life we are come to the birth of some notable knauery. **1611** Middleton & Dekker *Roaring Girl* D 1 b, Life, sh'as the Spirit of foure great parishes. **1668** Shadwell *Sullen Lovers* IV. Wks. (1720) I. 72 Cods my life-kins! **1692** R. L'Estrange *Fables* ccccxxviii. 404 Lifelikins, says she, I know no more Reason I have to Obey my Husband, then my Husband has to Obey me. **1777** Sheridan *Sch. Scand.* v. ii, Gad's life, ma'am, not at all. **1896** W. C. Gore in *Inlander* Jan. 149 'Say, Jack, are you going to bolt?' 'Not on your life.' **1905** *N. Y. Even. Post* 19 Aug. 2 The congressman was asked if there had been any gambling during the trip. 'Not on your life,' he said. **1913** Kipling *Divers. Creatures* (1917) 294 'Not on your life!' says Lundie. **1944** *Living off Land* iv. 62 Say that you are lost, properly bushed. You come across a river. Well, that river is not bushed—not on your life it isn't. **1962** F. Norman *Guntz* i. 7 My life (I thought) what chance am I going to have if I produce this letter. **1972** H. Carmichael *Naked to Grave* v. 56 'Why not get in touch with your lawyer?' 'Not on your life!.. It would be a tacit admission of my guilt.'

e. A vital or vulnerable point of an animal's body; the 'life-spot'.

1850 Scoresby *Cheever's Whalem. Adv.* iii. (1859) 35 This he did so well as to hit the 'fish's life' at once.

4. a. Energy in action, thought, or expression; liveliness in feeling, manner, or aspect; animation, vivacity, spirit. *spec.* in *Cricket*, that quality in the pitch which causes the ball to rise abruptly or unevenly after pitching.

1583 Stocker *Civ. Warres Lowe C.* III. 96 a, The rest, full of lyfe in the heeles, saued themselues. **1593** Shaks. *Lucr.* 1346 When, seelie Groome (God wot) it was defect Of spirite, life, and bold audacitie. **1597** Morley *Introd. Mus.* 166 Those songs which are made for the high key be made for more life, the other in the low key with more grauetie and staidnesse. **1598** R. Bernard tr. *Terence* 26 *Rem negligenter agit.* He goes carelesslie about the matter. He puts no life into the matter. **1669** Bunyan *Holy Citie* Pref. A iij, I thought I should not have been able to speak.. five words of Truth with Life and Evidence. **1692** Burnet *Past. Care* ix. 115 That a Discourse he heard with any Life, it must be spoken with some. *a* **1715** —— *Own Time* III. (1724) I. 392 His preaching was without much life or learning. **1838** Lytton *Alice* XI. ii, There was no lustre in her eye, no life in her step. **1858** Hawthorne *Fr. & It. Jrnls.* II. 59 The most picturesque aspect of the scene was the life given to it by the many faces. **1884** *Manch. Exam.* 28 Oct. 5/6 The comedy.. is heavy, and all the briskness of actor and actress is exerted in vain to give life to it. **1888** A. G. Steel in Steel & Lyttelton *Cricket* iii. 148 On wet hard wickets.. there is still life and pace in the ground; but in the sodden dead state, directly the ball touches the ground it.. loses all life and pace. **1906** A. E. Knight *Compl. Cricketer* 348 'Life' from the pitch implies the pitch and sting at or with which the ball leaves the ground.

† **b.** ***to give life to***: to bring into active use; to impart an impetus to. *Obs.*

1622 G. Wither *Christmas Carol* iii, *Fair Virtue* O 3 b, Young Men and Mayds, and Girles & Boyes, Giue life, to one anothers Ioyes. **1622** *Lett. to Conde Gondomar* in Rushw. *Hist. Collections* (1659) I. 69 To give life and execution to all Penal Laws now hanging over the heads of Catholicks. **1625** Burges *Pers. Tithes* 48 The Statute of 32. Hen. 8. was principally intended both to giue life to the former Statute. **1631** T. Adams in *Lett. Lit. Men* (Camden) 150 To give life and beginning to the publick Lecture. **1721** R. Bradley *Philos. Acc. Wks. Nat.* 139 The late Dutchess.. whose Curiosity and Skill in Natural Knowledge gave Life to many Discoveries which, without her happy Influence, would have lain uncultivated.

5. a. The cause or source of living; the vivifying or animating principle; he who or that

which makes or keeps a thing alive (in various senses); 'soul'; 'essence'. Hence (*poet. nonce-use*) = 'life-blood'. Also in collocation ***life and soul***.

1340 HAMPOLE *Pr. Consc.* 1692 Als þe saule es lyf of þe body, Swa þe lyfe of þe saule es God allmyghty. **1382** WYCLIF *Prov.* iv. 13 Hold discipline..kep it, for it is thi lyf. **1606** SHAKS. *Tr. & Cr.* II. ii. 194 Why? there you toucht the life of our designe. **1607–12** BACON *Ess., Despatch* (Arb.) 249 Order, & distribution is the life of dispatche. **1611** BIBLE *Gen.* ix. 4 But flesh with the life thereof, which is the blood thereof, shall you not eate. *a* **1618** RALEIGH *Disc. Invent. Ships* Wks. 1829 VIII. 323 The length of the cable is the life of the ship in all extremities. **1683** TRYON *Way to Health* iv. (1697) 79 Water and Air are the true Life and Power of every Being. **1712** J. JAMES tr. *Le Blond's Gardening* 198 'Tis the Life of fine Water-works to be well fed. *Ibid.* 201 Water-Works are the Life of a Garden. **1715–20** POPE *Iliad* IV. 609 The warm Life came issuing from the Wound. **1720** DEFOE *Capt. Singleton* 73 These indeed were the Life and Soul of all the rest, and it was to their Courage that all the rest ow'd the Resolution they shewd. **1797** R. M. ROCHE *Children of Abbey* I. xvii. 309 They had assembled a number of their neighbours, among whom were a little fat priest, called Father O'Gallaghan, considered the life of every party, and a blind piper. **1809** MALKIN *Gil Blas* VII. xiii. (Rtldg.) 14 Ballets incidental to the piece are the very life and soul of the play. **1814** JANE AUSTEN *Mansf. Park* II. i. 9 Sir Thomas was indeed the life of the party. **1844** DICKENS *Mart. Chuz.* xliii, Mr. Pecksniff's young gentlemen were the life and soul of the Dragon. **1861** HUGHES *Tom Brown at Oxf.* iv. (1889) 33 At this very wine-party he was the life of everything. **1897** M. CORELLI *Ziska* xv. 324 Armand Gervase..was making himself the life and soul of everything at the Mena House Hotel. **1932** L. GOLDING *Magnolia St.* III. ix. 595 He's very much the official life-and-soul-of-the-party. **1939** [see BORSCH]. **1965** *Melody Maker* 17 July 9 Offstage..Dudley doesn't strike you as being the life and soul of the party. **1970** G. GREER *Female Eunuch* 33 When the life of the party wants to express the idea of a pretty woman in mime, he undulates his two hands.

b. ***my life***: my beloved, my dearest. Not now in familiar use.

[*a* **1225** *Leg. Kath.* 1531 He is mi lif & mi luue. *Ibid.* 2478 Mi lif, and mi leofmon, Iesu Crist, mi lauerd.] **1540** PALSGR. *Acolastus* III. v. R j b, I can not but I must neede or algates enbrace the my lyfe. **1595** SPENSER *Colin Clout* 16 Colin, my liefe, my life. **1611** SHAKS. *Cymb.* v. v. 226 O Imogen! My Queen, my life, my wife. **1706** ADDISON *Rosamond* I. vi. (1707) 12 Where is my Life! my Rosamond! [**1731** SWIFT *Strephon & Chloe* 208 On Box of Cedar sits the Wife, And makes it warm for Dearest Life.] **1766** GOLDSM. *Vic. W.* xvii, Let us have one bottle more, Deborah, my life. **1837** DICKENS *Pickw.* xiii, 'P. my dear—' said Mrs. Pott. 'My life', said Mr. Pott. **1847** TENNYSON *Princess* VII. 339 My bride, My wife, my life.

6. In various concrete applications.

†**a.** A living being, a person. [So OS., OFris. *lîf*.] *Obs.*

c **1330** R. BRUNNE *Chron.* (1810) 27 Sex sonnes and auht douhtres, þo were faire lyues. **13..** *Gaw. & Gr. Knt.* 1780 ȝif ȝe luf not þat lyf þat ȝe lye nexte. **1390** GOWER *Conf.* II. 204 Tuo cofres..So lich that no lif..That on mai fro that other knowe. *c* **1400** *Destr. Troy* 1499 The last of þos lefe children was a lyffe [*printed* lysse] faire. **1423** JAS. I *Kingis Q.* xxviii, Ane wofull wreche that..of euery lyvis help hath nede. **14..** *Sir Beues* 1963 + 1 (MS. E.) Iosyan, þat ffayre lyff. *c* **1450** *Erle Tolous* 562 Than answeryd that lovely lyfe.

†**b.** One's family or line. *Obs.*

a **1400–50** *Alexander* 599 Bot of þe lyfe þat he liȝt off he like was to nane. *a* **1450** *Knt. de la Tour* 59 And there [in Hell] she [Eve] and her husbonde and all thaire lyff [F. *leur lignée*] was in prison unto the tyme that God deied on the crosse.

c. *nonce uses*. Vitality as embodied in an individual person or thing.

1587 GOLDING *De Mornay* v. 51 Euery life (if I may so speake) begetteth..issue..in it selfe afore it send it out. **1605** SHAKS. *Macb.* v. viii. 2 Why should I play the Roman Foole, and dye On mine owne sword? whiles I see liues, the gashes Do better vpon them. **1850** TENNYSON *In Mem.* xiii, An awful thought, a life removed, The human-hearted man I loved. **1864** —— *En. Ard.* 75 Philip..like a wounded life Crept down into the hollows of the wood.

d. Vitality or activity embodied in material forms; living things in the aggregate.

1728–46 THOMSON *Spring* 187 Well-shower'd earth Is deep enrich'd with vegetable life. **1732** POPE *Ess. Man* I. 215 From the life that fills the Flood, To that which warbles thro' the vernal wood. **1850** TENNYSON *In Mem.* vii, The noise of life begins again. **1858** HAWTHORNE *Fr. & It. Jrnls.* (1872) I. 11 The life of the scene, too, is infinitely more picturesque than that of London. **1865** DICKENS *Mut. Fr.* I. xiv, Very little life was to be seen on either bank.

7. a. (In early use commonly ***the life***.) The living form or model; living semblance; life-size figure or presentation. Also ***life itself***. ***after, from*** (or †***by***) ***the life***: (drawn) from the living model. ***as large as*** (†***the***) ***life***, life-size; hence *humorously*, implying that a person's figure or aspect is not lacking in any point. Hence ***larger-than-life***; ***larger-than-lifeness*** (nonce). ***small life***: ? somewhat less than life-size.

1599 SHAKS. *Much Ado* III. i. 110 There was neuer counterfeit of passion, came so neere the life of passion as she discouers it. **1607** BEAUM. & FL. *Woman-hater* II. i, It doth shew So neere the life as it were naturall. **1607–12** BACON *Ess. Beauty* (Arb.) 210 That is the best part of beauty which a picture cannott expresse, noe nor the first sight of the life. **1625** —— *Ess., Friendship* (Arb.) 179 The best Way, to represent to life the manifold vse of Frendship. **1634** PEACHAM *Gentl. Exerc.* 24 Which shadow..if you draw by the life must be hit at an haires breadth. **1641** EVELYN *Mem.* (1857) I. 36 A glorious crucifix..greater than the life. **1689** *Lond. Gaz.* No. 2420/4 Two Medals, One of his Highness the Prince of Orange, done by the Life. **1758** JOHNSON *Idler* No. 50 ¶9 The picture is..bigger than the life. **1762–71** H. WALPOLE *Vertue's Anecd. Paint.* (1786) I. 229 The figures are less than life, and about half lengths. *Ibid.* IV. 24 A light flimsy kind of fan-painting as large as the life. **1802** C. WILMOT *Let.* 17 Dec. in *Irish Peer* (1920) 129 A beautiful piece of clockwork representing Apollo with his lyre... It was as large as life. **1807** SIR R. C. HOARE *Tour Irel.* 235 Two curious old portraits..the one of King Henry VIII, the other of Anna Bullen, small life. **1816** W. HOLLAR *Dance Death* 7 He was drawing a figure after the life. **1822** M. EDGEWORTH *Let.* 9 Mar. (1971) 368 We 6 went together to see Belzonis tomb—the model first and afterwards the tomb as large as life. **1836** T. C. HALIBURTON *Clockmaker* (1837) 1st Ser. 143 As large as life and twice as nateral. *c* **1840** LADY WILTON *Art of Needlework* xxi. 334 Birds..being, in proportion to other figures, certainly *larger* than life, and 'twice as natural'. **1853** 'C. BEDE' *Verdant Green* I. vi, An imposing-looking Don, as large as life, and quite as natural. **1859** GULLICK & TIMBS *Paint.* 312 The study from 'the Life'. **1871** 'L. CARROLL' *Through Looking-Glass* vii. 150 It's as large as life, and twice as natural! **1891** G. MOORE *Impressions & Opinions* 89 The illusion is complete; it is just, as the phrase goes, like life itself. **1898** G. B. SHAW *Mrs. Warren's Profession* II. i. 176 This is George Crofts, as large as life and twice as natural. **1926** G. HUNTING *Vicarion* i. 21 What she had seen and heard had been life itself! **1930** J. DOS PASSOS *42nd Parallel* 46 Doc Bingham was sitting as large as life in a rocking chair. **1937** M. ALLINGHAM *Dancers in Mourning* i. 12 A larger-than-life edition of his stage self. **1947** L. MACNEICE *Dark Tower* 70 Larger-than-lifeness need not be part of the recipe. **1953** K. AMIS *Lucky Jim* i. 7 Anyway, there it was in the *Post* as large as life. **1959** *Viewpoint* July 12 Larger-than-life faces on television. **1966** R. A. DOWNIE tr. *O. del Buono's Bond Affair* 18 Allen Dulles insisted on regarding James Bond as a larger-than-life character.

b. ***to the life***: with life-like presentation of or resemblance to the original (said of a drawing or painting); with fidelity to nature; with exact reproduction of every point or detail; †Formerly const. *of*. † ***to set oneself out to the life***: to adorn oneself with the utmost pains.

1603 B. JONSON *K. Jas's. Entertain.* Wks. (1616) 848 Where-in..the very site, fabricke, strength, policie, dignitie, and affections of the citie were all laid downe to life. **1626** MASSINGER *Rom. Actor* II. (1629) D 2, A Tragedie..in which a murther Was acted to the life. **1641** MILTON *Ch. Gov.* v. Wks. 1851 III. 119 To frame out of their own heads as it were with wax a kinde of Mimick Bishop limm'd out to the life of a dead Priesthood. **1647** N. BACON *Disc. Govt. Eng.* To Consideration, I propound not this Discourse as a pattern drawn up to the life of the thing. **1662** STILLINGFL. *Orig. Sacr.* II. vii. §12 The shadow or dark representation of that which was to be drawn afterwards to the greatest life. **1703** *Rules Civility* 195 To reflect upon a Lady..for having set her self out to the Life in order to some evil Design. *a* **1758** RAMSAY *Some of Contents Evergreen* vii, The girnand wyfe, Fleming and Scot haif painted to the lyfe. **1809** MALKIN *Gil Blas* II. vii. ¶20, I can take off a cat to the life. **1825** LAMB *Elia* II, *Stage Illusion*, They please by being done under the life, or beside it; not to the life. **1860** READE *Cloister & H.* xxxvii. (1896) 107 Where is the coquette that cannot scream to the life? **1863** COWDEN CLARKE *Shaks. Char.* xvii. 427 The several characteristics of the men are set forth to the very life.

II. With reference to duration.

8. a. The animate terrestrial existence of an individual viewed with regard to its duration; the period from birth to death. Also adverbially, ***all my*** (***his***, etc.) ***life***: = in or during all my (etc.) life; †formerly sometimes without *all*. ***of one's life***, denoting the most important event of its kind in one's life. See also TIME *sb.* 6. Phr. ***for once in my*** (etc.) ***life***.

c **1020** *Rule St. Benet* (Logeman) i. 10 On eallon heora life. *a* **1175** *Cott. Hom.* 225 Noe lefede on all his life niȝon hund ȝeare and fifti. **1297** R. GLOUC. (Rolls) 6125 Febleiche he liuede al is lif & deyde in feble deþe. *a* **1300** *Cursor M.* 12246 For sagh i neuer nan swilk mi liue. *c* **1384** WYCLIF *Sel. Wks.* III. 443 Aftur a man deserves while he lyves here schal he be rewardid aftur his lyife. *c* **1385** CHAUCER *L.G.W.* Prol. 59 Ther loved no wight hotter in his lyve [*other texts* lyfe]. **1433** *Rolls of Parlt.* IV. 472/1 [To] receive the saide annuitee, terme of his lyve. **1460** CAPGRAVE *Chron.* (Rolls) 176 That he schuld..nevir his live dwelle in no soile longing to the Kyng of Ynglond. *c* **1470** G. ASHBY *Dicta Philos.* 680 Poems (E.E.T.S.) 73 Considre that your liff is shorte. **1561** T. HOBY tr. *Castiglione's Courtyer* I. A ij b, So did he end his lief with glorye. **1611** BIBLE *Prov.* xxxi. 12 She will doe him good, and not euill, all the dayes of her life. **1650** TRAPP *Comm. Num.* 50 They would..live all their lives-long in Dalilah's lap. **1718** J. CHAMBERLAYNE *Relig. Philos.* I. xii. §25 This Globe..would be quite dis-peopled in the Life of one Man. **1791** MRS. RADCLIFFE *Rom. Forest* i, Early in life he had married Constance Valentia. **1846** 'MRS. MARKHAM' *Hist. Eng.* (ed. 12) xxxvi. 402 *George*. I think, mamma, that the fire of London was a happy event for the king, as it made him exert himself, for once in his life, to do some good. **1849** MACAULAY *Hist. Eng.* i. I. 47 There is a season in the life both of an individual and of a society, at which [etc.]. **1872** MORLEY *Voltaire* 8 Every day of our lives. **1887** A. M. SULLIVAN *Let.* 13 Nov. in H. Keller *Story my Life* (1903) III. iii. 340 We took Helen to the circus, and had 'the time of our lives'! **1895** *Bookman* Oct. 23/1 The disastrous effects of the blunders of his middle life. **1936** *Discovery* Jan. 14/2 They got the shock of their lives. **1939** W. SAROYAN (*title*) The time of your life. **1961** L. VAN DER POST *Heart of Hunter* i. 25 The men sat with their heads bowed over arms clasped round their knees like long-distance runners recovering from the race of their lives.

b. ***for life***: for the remaining period of the person's life. ***a lease, grant,*** etc. ***for*** (***two, three,*** etc.) ***lives***: one which is to remain in force during the life of the longest liver of (two, three, etc.) specified persons. Hence occas. the persons on whose length of life the duration of a lease depends are called the *lives*.

1470 in Fortescue *Abs. & Lim. Mon.* (1885) 351 That no patente be made..for terme of lyfe, or yeres countervailing terme of lyffe. **1576** *Act 18 Eliz.* c. 6 §1 That no Master, Provoste [etc.]..shall make anye Lease for lief lieves or yeeres, of anie ferme [etc.]. **1641** MILTON *Ch. Govt.* II. Introd. Wks. (1847) 43/1 As men buy Leases, for three lives and down-ward. **1692** R. L'ESTRANGE *Fables* xci. (1708) 106 A Gentle-man that had an Estate for Lives, and two of his Tenants in the Lease... The Man..had Poyson'd himself, and the Revenge upon his Landlord was the Defeating him of his Estate by Destroying the Last Life in the Lease. **1705** ADDISON *Italy* Wks. 1856 I. 363 The administration of this bank is for life. **1712–14** POPE *Rape Lock* I. 80 Nymphs.. For Life predestin'd to the Gnomes Embrace. **1818** CRUISE *Digest* (ed. 2) IV. 211 To the use of himself for life, remainder to his wife for life. **1834** MACAULAY *Pitt* Ess. (1887) 321 Newcastle offered him..the Duchy of Lancaster for life. **1849** —— *Hist. Eng.* vi. II. 156 Four thousand pounds a year for two lives. **1885** *Act 48 & 49 Vict.* c. 77 §7 If any land is comprised in a lease for a life or lives.

c. The term of duration of an inanimate thing; the time that a manufactured object lasts. In *Physics* applied *spec.* to the average duration of existence of the members of a population of identical particles or states (equal to the period in which the population decreases by a factor *e*).

The half-life is equal to the (mean) life multiplied by $\log_e 2$ (about 0·693).

1703 T. N. *City & C. Purchaser* 210 Mosaick,..an Ornament of much Beauty, and long Life. **1876** PREECE & SIVEWRIGHT *Telegraphy* 37 From eighteen to twenty months is the average life assigned to them [battery cells]. **1889** *Scribner's Mag.* Aug. 219/2 The average life of the steel rails. **1892** SIR A. KEKEWICH in *Law Times Rep.* LXVII. 141/1 The short life of the company, and the subsequent liquidation. **1903** RUTHERFORD & SODDY in *Phil. Mag.* V. 607 In one gram of these elements less than a milligram would change in a million years. In the case of radium, however, the same amount must be changing per gram *per year*. The 'life' of the radium cannot be in consequence more than a few thousand years. **1926** R. W. LAWSON tr. *Hevesy & Paneth's Man. Radioactivity* vii. 64 In this so-called 'normal state' the hydrogen atom can persist permanently, whereas the 'life' of all other stationary states is very short. *Ibid.* xii. 111 Each group [of radioactive substances] is arranged in the order of diminishing half-value period, and begins with the member of longest life. **1926** *Sci. Abstr.* A. XXIX. 170 Using the observation that so long as these lines are absorbed, atoms must be in the s_3 and s_5 states, a determination is made of the mean life of these states. **1942** J. D. STRANATHAN *'Particles' of Mod. Physics* xiii. 535 There is some indication that the mean free path may be longer, and the mean life correspondingly longer, for high energy mesotrons than it is for low energy mesotrons. **1947** *Forum* (Johannesburg) 12 Apr. 15/3 Even with the aid of boreholes, which have yet to be sunk, the 'life' of the dam can be extended only until the end of September. **1958** *Times* 23 July 5/2 Its..turbo-jet engines will be permitted an initial 'life' between overhauls of 1,000 hours. **1968** M. S. LIVINGSTON *Particle Physics* x. 178 The quantity $2\pi\Gamma/h$ is the probability of decay per unit time, or the reciprocal of the mean life τ of the state. Mean life is defined as the time for the population of the state to be reduced to $1/e$ of its initial value... This means that, because of the finite lifetime of an excited state, the energy of the state cannot be sharply defined but is intermediate within the energy spread Γ. **1971** *Gloss. Electrotechnical Power Terms (B.S.I.)* IV. i. 26 *Life*, of a lamp. Time during which a lamp has been operated before becoming useless.

d. Imprisonment for life; a life sentence. *slang.*

1903 [see CELL *v.* b]. **1924** E. WALLACE *Room 13* i. 10 He shot a copper and got life. **1967** [see BLOW *v.*[1] 27 b]. **1975** *Times* 29 Apr. 4/6 Although the sentence is life, they all want parole.

9. ***Life assurance*. a.** A person considered with regard to the probable future duration of his life. ***a good life***: one whose life is exposed to no exceptional risks, and who is likely to live at least to the term assigned as the average 'expectation' at his age. So ***a bad life, a first-class life***. **b.** Any particular amount of expectation of life. **c.** 'An insurance on a person's life; a life insurance policy' (Ogilvie, 1882).

1692–3 HALLEY in *Phil. Trans.* XVII. 601 How to make a certain Estimate of the value of Annuities for Lives. *Ibid.* 602 The Price of Insurance upon Lives ought to be regulated. **1777** SHERIDAN *Sch. Scand.* III. iii, I suppose you're afraid that Sir Oliver is too good a life? **1838** DE MORGAN *Ess. Probab.* 212 The rules in the preceding chapter, though the status mentioned are technically called lives, are equally true for any species of circumstances. **1896** *Allbutt's Syst. Med.* I. 476 [An applicant for insurance] was ..called upon to state on oath that he believed himself to be a good life. **1921** A. HUXLEY *Let.* 23 Mar. (1969) 194 This perpetual lack of perfect physical health is intolerable. This was brought home to me more acutely than usual today by the refusal of the London Life Association to insure me... It is..humiliating to be a Bad Life. **1938** *Times Lit. Suppl.* 24 Sept. 618/2 Elizabeth all her days was reckoned a 'bad life'. **1970** *Times* 5 Dec. 9/3 If one is not accepted as a first class life, the most common procedure is for an insurance company to increase the premium.

10. *pl.* in proverbial expressions referring to tenacity of life.

1562 [see CAT *sb.*[1] 13 b]. **1599** MASSINGER, etc. *Old Law* v. i, I believe now a father Hath as many lives as a mother! **1859** MCCLINTOCK *Voy. 'Fox' Arct. Seas* x. 176 We are only now to commence the interesting part of our voyage. It is to be hoped the poor 'Fox' has many more lives to spare.

11. Transferred uses in various games. *Cards* (*'Commerce'*). One of three counters, which each player has; so called because, when he has lost all of them, he falls out of the game. *Pool.* One of three chances which each player has. *Cricket.* The continuation of a batsman's

innings after a chance has been missed of getting him out. Similarly in *Baseball*.

1806–7 J. Beresford *Miseries Hum. Life* (1826) III. xxiii, At the game of commerce losing your life in fishing..for aces. **1840** T. Hook *Fitzherbert* II. viii. 199 All the old people are at whist, and all the young ones at commerce; I have just lost my last life and my only shilling. **1856** 'Capt. Crawley' *Billiards* (1858) 120 The first player who loses his three lives has the privilege of purchasing what is called a star. **1865** *Bell's Life* 24 June 7/1 Mr. Voules (who had 'a life' when he had made but a single) was first to leave. **1868** *Cincinnati Commercial* 24 May 8/2 Meagher had a life given him by Gould not accepting the grounder Meagher hit to him, and Brainard's wild throw to first gave him his second. **1883** *Daily Tel.* 15 May 2/7 The captain..received a life..in the slips. **1955** *Times* 9 July 4/5 Immediately after luncheon Goddard was given a life when he slashed at Tyson and Evans dropped a fast head-high catch. **1974** *Times* 25 Nov. 10/2 Ali also had a life from Barrett at mid-off.

III. Course, condition, or manner of living.

12. a. The series of actions and occurrences constituting the history of an individual (esp. a human being) from birth to death. In generalized sense, the course of human existence from birth to death. ***(anything, nothing) in life***: 'in the world', at all; ***such is life!***: see SUCH *dem. adj.* and *pron.* 2; similarly ***that's life, life's like that***; ***to live one's (own) life***: to conduct oneself without reference to the opinions of others; ***this is the life***: an expression of satisfaction; ***it's a great life (if you don't weaken)***: an ironic comment on the difficulties of one's situation; ***what a life!***: an expression of discontent; ***how's life?*** : how are you faring?

c **900** tr. *Bæda's Hist.* IV. xxxi. [xxx.] (1890) 378 Ða sume we ȝeare for ȝemynde awriton in ðære bec Cuðbertes lifes. ?*a* **1100** *O.E. Chron.* an. 1016 (Laud. MS.) He ȝeendode his daȝas..æfter mycclum ȝeswince..his lifes. *c* **1175**, etc. [see LEAD *v.*[1] 12]. *a* **1300–1400** *Cursor M.* 252 (Gött.) Till þaim ..þat ledis þair liues [*a.* **1425** *Trin.* lyues] in mekil wast. **1513** Douglas *Æneis* III. v. 66, I leif..and ledis life as ȝe se. **1540** Hyrde tr. *Vives' Instr. Chr. Wom.* (1592) N ij, They that marry for love, shall lead their life in sorrow. *a* **1598** Spenser *Hymn Heavenly Love* 183 He our life hath left unto us free. **1667** Milton *P.L.* VII. 193 To know That which before us lies in daily life. *Ibid.* XI. 606 Studious they appere Of Arts that polish Life. **1736** Butler *Anal.* I. iii. Wks. 1874 I. 50 Those persons, whose course of life from their youth up has been blameless. **1796** W. J. Temple *Diary* 7 Apr. (1929) 167 This interruption is very teasing; but such is Life. **1837** Dickens *Pickw.* l, 'Hallo!' responded that gentleman, looking over the side of the chaise with all the coolness in life. **1843** Dickens *Mart. Chuzz.* (1844) xxix. 347 'Sairey,' says Mrs. Harris, 'sech is life. Vich likeways is the hend of all things!' **1849** N. Kingsley *Diary* (1914) 52 For my part [I] could almost wish myself in the same Latitude..but such is life. **1853** C. Brontë *Villette* I. xiii. 229 Thinking meantime my own thoughts, living my own life, in my own still shadow-world. **1865** [see SUCH *pron.* 2]. **1868** M. Pattison *Academ. Org.* 5 One who owes to College endowments all that he has and is in life. **1872** Morley *Voltaire* 2 They realised life as a long wrestling with unseen and invincible forces of grace, election, and fore-destiny. **1875** Jowett *Plato* (ed. 2) I. 221 There is nothing in life that would be a greater gain to me than that. **1879** Mallock (*title*) Is Life worth living? **1903** 'T. Collins' (*title*) Such is life. **1911** D. H. Lawrence *White Peacock* III. iii. 397 At home you cannot live your own life. **1917** *Ladies' Home Jrnl.* Mar. 46 (Advt.), *This is the life*. There are two ways to live nowadays. One way is the life that is daily chock full of healthy activity, wholesome fun and lots of fresh air. **1919** J. Buchan *Mr. Standfast* v. 105 'Back to Glasgow to do some work for the cause,' I said lightly. 'Just so,' he said, with a grin. 'It's a great life if you don't weaken.' **1919** Wodehouse *My Man Jeeves* 234 She's glued to a chair, with this-is-the-life written all over her, taking it in through the pores. **1924** J. Buchan *Three Hostages* xvi. 227 That's life, my dear. We've got to go on to the finish anyhow, trusting that luck will turn. **1926** S. Jameson *Three Kingdoms* x. 301 After all, she had chosen to stand apart from him and to live her own life, as the moderns have it. **1926** R. Macaulay *Crewe Train* xi. 213 This was the life. **1930** J. B. Priestley *Angel Pavement* i. 49 She groaned as she stuck another sheet of paper into the typewriter. 'What a life!' **1933** D. L. Sayers *Murder must Advertise* i. 10 There goes my thousand quid! Oh, well, that's life. **1935** N. L. McClung *Clearing in West* xxv. 205 Still Will had his own life to live and must make his own choice. **1935** N. Mitchison *We have been Warned* v. 511 I've been very busy... How's life? **1943** K. Tennant *Ride on Stranger* xviii. 202 Oh, it was a great life, if you liked that sort of a life. **1959** M. Gilbert *Blood & Judgement* ix. 102 We weren't sharing rooms... She was living her life, I was living mine. **1968** P. Dickinson *Skin Deep* vii. 140 No, it's..not the sort of thing that makes the newspapers... Ah well, life's like that. **1970** *New Statesman* 26 June 924/3 Whatever Ned Kelly was really like..he can scarcely have been like Mr Jagger... The famous last words 'Such is life'—could as well have been 'Pass the salt'. **1972** G. Bell *Villains Galore* viii. 104 'Nothing ventured, nothing lost either,' muttered Boote miserably. 'Gawd! What a life!' **1973** J. McClure *Four & Twenty Virgins* ii. 22 The sports car accelerated away before she reached the end of the path. 'That's life,' said Kegg.

b. The Biblical phrase ***this life*** (Vulg. *hæc vita*, Gr. ἡ ζωὴ αὕτη, 1 Cor. xv. 19) is used (as also ***the*** or ***this present life***) to denote the earthly state of human existence in contradistinction to ***the future life*** (occas. ***another life***, etc.), the state of existence after death. (Phr. *to depart this life, from this life*: see DEPART *v.* 7, 8.) Hence arises an occasional use of *life* for: Either of the two states of human existence separated by death.

c **1000** *Ags. Gosp.* Luke viii. 14 þa ðe..of carum..þiss lifes synt for-þrysmede. *c* **1175** *Lamb. Hom.* 9 Er ure drihten come to þisse liue. *c* **1375** *Sc. Leg. Saints* ii. (*Paulus*) 219 Eftire þis lyfe transitore euire-lestand lyfe is me before. *c* **1380** Wyclif *Serm.* Sel. Wks. II. 229 Here in þis liif. **1549** *Bk. Com. Prayer, Communion* (*Prayer Ch. Milit.*), All them, whyche in thys transytory life be in trouble, sorowe, nede [etc.]. **1579** Fenton *Guicciard.* VII. 363 King Phillip..had chaunged this life for a better within the towne of Burgos. **1751** Jortin *Serm.* (1771) II. xix. 376 This was an effectual confutation of Sadducean notion that there was no life besides the present. **1852** H. Rogers *Ecl. Faith* (1853) 98 Regard this life—as what it is..a pilgrimage to a better.

c. A particular manner or course of living: characterized as *good, bad, happy, wretched*, etc. Phr. ***anything for a quiet life***.

a **1025** Wulfstan *Hom.* (Napier) 270 Ealle hiȝ wæron haliȝes lifes menn. *c* **1200** Ormin 4516 þatt mann..maȝȝ..cwemenn Godd wiþþ haliȝ lif. *c* **1230** *Hali Meid.* 5 Heo stont þurh heh lif iþe tur of ierusalem. *a* **1300** *Cursor M.* 13830 þe lijf he ledes mai nan lede. **1377** Langl. *P. Pl.* B. IX. 62 That lyueth synful lyf here her soule is liche the deuel. ?*a* **1400** *Arthur* 554 He toke þe qwene, Arthourez wyff, Aȝenst goddes lawe & gode lyff. *c* **1400** *Destr. Troy* 8939 To discharge me as cheftain, & chaunge my lif. *c* **1400** Maundev. (Roxb.) viii. 30 þai er deuote men and ledez pure lyf. **1536** Wriothesley *Chron.* (1875) I. 33 Queene Katherin..departed from her worldlie lief at Bugden. **1594** Hooker *Eccl. Pol.* I. x. §2 All men desire to lead in this world a happy life. **1611** Tourneur *Ath. Trag.* v. ii. Wks. 1878 I. 139 My powertie compels My life to a condition lower than My birth or breeding. **1624** T. Heywood *Captives* (1885) III. iii. 169 Anythinge For a quiett lyfe. **1638** Baker tr. *Balzac's Lett.* (vol. II.) 213 One that partakes of the life of a schollar and of a Courtier. **1754** Earl Chatham *Lett. Nephew* iv. 20 Be sure to associate..with men of decent and honourable lives. **1759** Townley (*title of play*) High life below stairs. **1800** M. Edgeworth *Parent's Assistant* (ed. 3) VI. 123 Any thing for a quiet life. **1837** Dickens *Pickw.* xlii. 463 Anythin' for a quiet life, as the man said ven he took the sitivation at the light-house. **1847** Marryat *Childr. N. Forest* xiii, They live a roving life. **1859** Tennyson *Idylls* Ded. 24 Wearing the white flower of a blameless life. **1875** Jowett *Plato* (ed. 2) III. 151 The life of Sparta was the life of a camp. **1968** 'L. Marshall' *Blood on Blotter* v. 40 I'm a born appeaser... Anything for a quiet life.

d. In mod. use: The conspicuously active or practical part of human existence; the business, active pleasures, or pursuits of the world. Often with reference to social gaieties or vicious pleasures, esp. in phr. *to see life*. Also, the position of participating in the affairs of the world, of being a recognized member of society; esp. in phrases ***to begin*** or ***enter life, to be settled in life***.

1771 Mackenzie *Man Feel.* (1886) 26 She had been ushered into life (as that word is used in the dialect of St. James's) at seventeen. **1784** *Unfort. Sensib.* II. 182 The disadvantages of entering life without money. **1809** Malkin *Gil Blas* I. i. ¶5, I was dying to see a little of life. **1819** *Sporting Mag.* V. 123 All the frolic, fun, lark, gig, life, gammon, and trying-it-on are depicted. **1851** H. Mayhew *Mayhew's Characters* (1951) 309, I liked to see 'life', as it was called, and fond of the company of women. **1874** Dasent *Half a Life* III. 123 To see me happily settled in life. **1885** E. Garrett *At Any Cost* vii. 112 Does a man want..to 'see life' in metropolitan boulevards and continental spas? **1918** C. Mackenzie *Early Life Sylvia Scarlett* II. iv. 332 I've got a fancy..to show you a bit of life. **1937** A. Christie *Death on Nile* II. i. 41 He's made a good deal of money and he's seeing life, I fancy. **1972** L. Meynell *Death by Arrangement* i. 9 The spires of Oxford could go on dreaming..for all he cared; he set about getting himself a degree in the university of life.

e. ***the life of the mind***: intellectual or aesthetic pursuits, scholarship; meditation, the realm of the imagination.

1926 E. Hemingway *Men without Women* (1927) 216 Live the full life of the mind, exhilarated by new ideas. **1950** P. Bottome *Under Skin* xxiii. 204 If we try to escape into the life of the mind we find you there before us. **1972** G. Wigg *George Wigg* i. 28 He was an inspired teacher..arousing in us a feeling for literature and poetry and the life of the mind. **1972** *Guardian* 1 Nov. 14/5 Universities exist to promote the life of the mind... They should create and discover knowledge.

13. A written account of a person's 'life' (sense 12); a biography. So ***Life and Times***, a biography combined with a study of the public events of the character's lifetime; ***life-and-work(s***, a biography combined with a study of the writings of the subject.

[*c* **900**: see 12.] *a* **1225** *St. Marher.* 317 Hit were god thet hi radde hire lyf. *c* **1375** *Sc. Leg. Saints* Prol. 28, I writ þe lyf of sanctis sere. *c* **1386** Chaucer *Manciple's T.* 50 Thus writen olde clerkes in hir lyves. *c* **1450** *St. Cuthbert* (Surtees) 967 Saint cuthbert lyfe may he rede. **1641** J. Jackson *True Evang. T.* I. 42 Many for feare fled into desarts and caves, witnesseth S. Ierome in the life of Paul the Eremite. **1758** Johnson *Idler* No. 102 ¶2 Few authors write their own lives. **1849** Macaulay *Hist. Eng.* vi. II. 203 The fifty poets whose lives Johnson has written. **1850** L. Hunt *Autobiog.* I. Pref. 6 Coleridge's Literary Life is professedly autocritical. *c* **1889** W. Pater *Let.* 30 Apr. (1970) 94, I wish I could undertake a life for your admirable Series. **1933** J. Thurber (*title*) My life and hard times. **1951** G. Greene *End of Affair* v. v. 204 'You seem interested in General Gordon.' 'They want me to do a Life.' **1957** *Times Lit. Suppl.* 25 Oct. 640/2 Mr. Wilson's life-and-work summaries are excellent. **1959** *Listener* 9 Apr. 643/2 This is to be a life-and-works, not pure biography. *Ibid.* 3 Dec. 1005/1 It is a 'Life', not a 'Life and Times', that he has written. **1962** *Ibid.* 15 Nov. 804/1 To use a man's letters and all related correspondence to produce a reasonably short life and times. **1975** *Listener* 16 Jan. 93/1 *Cavafy* is..more biographical than critical, but a 'life' was needed and this is the fullest so far.

†**IV. 14.** Phrases formed with preps. with the meaning 'alive'. **a.** ***on live*** (OE. *on life*), ***o live***, etc.: see ALIVE. **b.** ***upon live***.

c **1374** Chaucer *Troylus* II. 981 (1030) þe beste harpour vpon lyue. *c* **1400** *Destr. Troy* 11275 Ne ȝou sechis no socour ..Of no lede vppon lyue. *c* **1420** *Anturs of Arth.* 279 Es noghte a lorde in þat lande appone lyfe leuede.

c. ***of live***, later ***of life***.

c **1375** *Cursor M.* 7934 (Fairf.) Be god of liue [*Cott.* o-liue, *Gött.* a-liue] he square his aþ. **1375** Barbour *Bruce* I. 293 Wes nane off lyve that hym ne dred. *c* **1435** *Torr. Portugal* 299 Alle men of lyve wayte hym nowght. **1444** *Rolls of Parlt.* V. 70/1 If they ben of lyff. *a* **1658** *Little Musgrave* x. in Child *Ballads* II. 244 As thou art a man of life.

d. ***to live*** (OE. *tō life*), north. ***atte live***.

c **1000** Ælfric *Num.* xxxi. 15 Moises..axode hwi hiȝ heoldon þa wifmennn to life. *c* **1250** *Gen. & Ex.* 629 And leten [weren] ðe oðre to liue gon. *c* **1320** *Sir Tristr.* 1022 Wheþer our to liue go, He haþ anouȝ of þis. *c* **1375** *Cursor M.* 5180 (Fairf.) Bot I ne kepped na langer atte liue.

e. ***in live, in lif(e, with life***.

c **1250** *Gen. & Ex.* 1364 To sechen ysaac hom a wif, Of his kinde ðe ðor was in lif. *a* **1300** *Cursor M.* 1839 Na creatur in liue [*Fairf.* on liue]. *c* **1375** *Ibid.* 6492 (Fairf.) Atte he was liuande and in life sulde be. *a* **1425** *Ibid.* 11834 (Trin.) Miȝt no mon wiþ lif [*Fairf.* in life, *Gött* on lijf] haue more.

f. ***of lives, on lives, in lives***. [Cf. ALIVES.]

c **1250** *Gen. & Ex.* 2834 If hise breðere of liues ben. *a* **1300** *Cursor M.* 8373 þou has in liues Mani childer wit þi wiues. *Ibid.* 9676 In all þis world left [na] ma in liues [*Trin.* on lyues]. *Ibid.* 6794 ȝour barns haf na faders in liues [*c* **1375** *Fairf.* on liuis].

†**V. 15.** Lives (OE. *lífes*), the gen. sing. used **a.** predicatively = alive; *occas.* as *sb.*, those who are alive, the living.

c **900** tr. *Bæda's Hist.* v. xvii. [xix.] (1890) 462 He..nemne ðynre eðunge anre ætywde þæt he lifes wæs. *c* **1175** *Lamb. Hom.* 31 He nat to soðe þet heo beoð liues. *c* **1250** *Gen. & Ex.* 3802 He..Ran and stod tuen liues and dead. *c* **1300** *Havelok* 1307 Al..That euere was in Denemark lyues. **13..** *Guy Warw.* (A.) 5459 Niȝt no day swiken Y nille, Liues or deþes þat ich him se. *c* **1380** *Sir Ferumb.* 3685 Y nolde þe lete lyues bee.

b. attributively = live, living.

c **1200** *Trin. Coll. Hom.* 67 Habbe nu sehtnesse and luue to ech liues man. *c* **1320** *Cast. Love* 1422 Heo seȝen him alyue a lyues-mon. *c* **1386** Chaucer *Merch. T.* 620 No lyues creature Be it of fyssh, or bryd, or beest, or man. *c* **1450** Lonelich *Grail* xxxix. 373 Non lyves body there-Inne he say. **1548** Udall *Erasm. Par. Luke* xi. 110 The yearth shal yelde hym again a liuesman on the third daie. ?*a* **1550** in *Dunbar's Poems* (1893) 324 Now glaidith euery liffis creature. **1600** Holland *Livy* XL. viii. 1064 It is the..gift..of God that I am a livesman [L. *vivus*] at this houre.

VI. Combinations.

16. General combs. **a.** simple attrib., as ***life-activity, -air, -anger, -bark, -battle, -beauty, -body, -centre, -chance, -course, -current, -demand, -drama, -electron, -experience, -flame, -flow, -food, -germ, -group, -guidance, -habit, -idea, -instinct, -journey, -mate, -meaning, -mystery, -orientation, -path, -pattern, -phase, -plan, -principle, -process, -quick, -responsibility, -situation, -space, -story, -stream, -stuff, -tackle, -thread, -transit, -urge, -vein , -wish, -wreck***, etc.

1914 R. M. Jones *Spiritual Reformers 16th & 17th Cent.* p. xvii, Undivided faith attitudes always liberate within the field of consciousness energy for *life-activity. **1937** R. A. Wilson *Birth of Lang.* 83 The modern error..of characterizing life-activity as mechanism. **1820** Keats *Hyperion* I. 119 Space regioned with *life-air. **1924** Lawrence & Skinner *Boy in Bush* 203 It was the anger, the deep, burning *life-anger which was the kinship. **1847** Cardl. Wiseman *Unreality Anglican Belief* Ess. 1853 II. 421 Seated at the helm of his *life-bark, that defies every storm. **1837** Carlyle *Fr. Rev.* I. I. ii, He marches and fights, with victorious assurance, in this *life-battle. *a* **1843** Southey *Comm.-pl. Bk.* IV. 274 The trees in their full *life-beauty. **1920** S. Alexander *Space, Time & Deity* II. 355 Hunger and thirst..are the affections of its *life-body. **1923** D. H. Lawrence *Birds, Beasts & Flowers* 54 Fragile-tender, fragile-tender life-body, More fearless than iron all the time. **1902** *Westm. Gaz.* 2 Apr. 10/2 As a *life-centre Lake Eyre has long lost its importance. **1942** R. A. Knox *In Soft Garments* xi. 85 We have got to go back to the life of Jesus of Nazareth, isolating the life-centre from which this vast organism of Christianity has sprung. **1944** *Politics* I. 273/2 However strongly *life chances may be differentiated, this fact in itself..by no means gives birth to 'class action'. **1958** W. J. H. Sprott *Human Groups* 60 The life-chances of children..are almost entirely determined by their position in the kinship scheme. *a* **1930** D. H. Lawrence *Phoenix* (1936) v. i. 609 This reversal of the *life-course. **1970** R. J. Hollingdale tr. *Schopenhauer's Ess. & Aphorisms* 144 The entire life-course, i.e., the inner and outer history, of each one [*sc.* man] differs..from that of all the others. **1899** W. James *Talks to Teachers* 257 The occasion and the experience..are nothing. It all depends on the capacity of the soul to be grasped, to have its *life-currents absorbed by what is given. **1929** D. H. Lawrence *Pansies* 21 A new demand on his intelligence, A new *life-demand. **1872** *Porcupine* 12 Oct. 443/2 He wanted to be left to work out his own *Life-Drama. **1915** D. H. Lawrence *Rainbow* x. 262 On Easter Sunday the life-drama was as good as finished. *a* **1930** —— *Etruscan Places* (1932) 58 So within each man is the quick of him..some spark, some unborn and undying vivid *life-electron. **1852** Robertson *Serm.* Ser. III. xiii. 160 Blessed is the man..whose *life-experience has taught a confiding belief. **1906** *Macm. Mag.* Apr. 436 Two of these *life-flames were burning brightly..in the adjacent theatre. **1960** *Spectator* 14 Oct. 556 English is the true education of the life-flame. **1903** *Ibid.* 11 Apr. 565 The *life-flow of justice..ceased to course through her heart. *a* **1930** D. H. Lawrence *Last Poems* (1932) 107 People who complain of loneliness must have lost..their life-flow Like a plant whose

roots are cut. c1475 Pict. Voc. in Wr.-Wülcker 788/20 Hic victus, *lyfefode. 1875 E. White Life in Christ i. (1876) 12 *Life-germs, which are all born together, do not die together. 1849 Murchison Siluria ii. (1867) 24 Clearly developed and abundant *life-groups. 1891 C. L. Morgan Animal Sk. 214 To watch his *life-habits with sympathetic interest. 1923 D. H. Lawrence Kangaroo xvi. 338 As some great *life-idea cools down and sets upon them. 1908 E. F. Benson Blotting Bk. i. 22 His was the hot blood that could do any deed when the *life-instinct commanded it. 1922 Life instinct [see death-instinct (death sb. 19)]. 1831 Carlyle Sart. Res. (1858) 182 Some months of our *Life-journey. 1906 Westm. Gaz. 17 Feb. 6/3 Each with the *life-mate who should guide his way. 1922 Joyce Ulysses 413 Faithful lifemate. 1923 D. H. Lawrence Kangaroo xii. 283 It is gruesome, with no *life-meaning. 1927 —— Lovely Lady (1932) 230 He deemed it [sc. sex], as the Chinese do, one of the great *life-mysteries. 1936 Wirth & Shils tr. Mannheim's Ideology & Utopia i. i. 22 The point of view of *life-orientation and conduct. 1966 G. E. Evans Pattern under Plough xii. 124 Only tremendous transformations of life-orientation have succeeded in tearing them away from this universal form of religiosity. 1950 Psychiatry XIII. 2 He [sc. Freud] provides the texts.. for contradictory *life-paths and social policies. 1955 Auden Shield of Achilles iii. 76 A fortuitous intersection of life-paths. 1920 T. P. Nunn Education i. 6 There is no limit to the number of *life-patterns into which good or blameless actions may be woven. 1972 Sci. Amer. Jan. 39/1 Although sex-role ideology may be developed in early childhood, it is usually not until adolescence that a girl begins to apply her system of beliefs to her life pattern. 1849 Miss Mulock Ogilvies (1875) 28 The real nature of the *life-phase which was opening upon her. 1849 Robertson Serm. Ser. i. xv. (1866) 257 Each man.. must take up his *life-plan alone. 1851 H. Melville Moby Dick III. xxi. 146 This same.. cunning *life-principle in him. 1950 L. S. Thornton Revelation & Mod. World iii. 90 Totality and identity are two aspects of one life-principle by which the creative Word calls into himself that response which he creates. 1889 Mivart Truth 389 Our merely organic *life-processes. 1923 D. H. Lawrence Stud. Classic Amer. Lit. vi. 119 Nowadays society is evil. It finds subtle ways of torture, to destroy the *life-quick, to get at the life-quick in a man. 1928 —— Lady Chatterley x. 131 What man with a spark of honour would put this ghastly burden of *life-responsibility upon a woman. 1936 Wirth & Shils tr. Mannheim's Ideology & Utopia i. i. 10 Constantly varying social strata and *life-situations. 1969 America 5 July 17/2 The mass media have formed many of our responses to life situations. 1935 Psychol. Abstr. Jan. 3/2 The psychological *life-space (Lebensraum) is a general hodological space, which shows certain relativities. 1957 R. K. Merton Social Theory (rev. ed.) 384 The social life-space of an individual. 1853 Jerdan Autobiog. III. 51 The self-revelations I have deemed essential to my *life-story. 1930 C. Beaton Diary Dec. in Wandering Yrs. (1961) 200 Buy her Life Story for three dollars. 1960 'R. Simons' Frame for Murder xiii. 165 Squere .. produced a bundle of papers. 'This is him. His entire life story.' 1879 Browning Dramatic Idyls 128 'Look unto me and be ye saved!' saith God: 'I strike the rock, outstreats the *life-stream at my rod!' 1941 Wyndham Lewis Let. 10 Aug. (1963) 295 The character.. is so deeply stained with the deposits on the obscure bed of the life-stream. 1880 Wesleyan-Methodist Mag. Aug. 621/1 To say that the *life-stuff of the lowest fungus and that of the most powerful human brain are identical, is absurd. 1956 A. H. Compton Atomic Quest 160 The life-stuff of intense effort. 1831 Carlyle Sart. Res. (1858) 38 The same viscera, tissues, livers, lights, and other *Life-tackle. 1862 Merivale Rom. Emp. (1865) VI. l. 210 The *life-thread.. had been severed by the fatal shears. 1843 Carlyle Past & Pr. iv. iv, In this your brief *Life-transit. 1922 D. H. Lawrence Let. 21 Sept. (1962) II. 717 But I won't mention the *life-urge any more. 1926 W. de la Mare Connoisseur 18, I had become an automaton—little better than a beetle obeying the secret dictates of what I believe they call the Life-Urge. c1530 Hickscorner 117 Death.. Taketh his swerde and smyteth asonder the *lyfe vayne. 1944 R. Lehmann Ballad & Source 13 A *life-wish so crackling with energy that it could overcome no matter what minatory fate. 1890 'Rolf Boldrewood' Miner's Right (1899) 166/1 Failures and *life-wrecks.

b. Objective and obj. gen., as *life-abhorring, -affirming, -bearing, -begetting, -breathing, -bringing, -creating, -denying, -destroying, -devouring, -enhancing, -hugging, -outfetching, -poisoning, -preserving, -quelling, -reaving, -rendering, -renewing, -restoring, -sapping, -sustaining, -working*, (etc.) adjs.; *life-brightener, -denier, -enhancer, -lover*.

1812 Byron Ch. Har. i. lxxxiii, *Life-abhorring gloom. 1947 A. Einstein Mus. Romantic Era xii. 165 He became a priest, the 'Abbé Liszt', who sought in Rome a sort of defense against his overflowing, *life-affirming virtuosity. 1966 Observer 6 Nov. 27/4 This instinctual, familial, life-affirming note of Tolstoy's. 1867 G. Macdonald Poems 13 This old *life-bearing earth. 1648 Herrick Hesper. (1869) 175 Stay but till my Julia close The *life-begetting eye. 1819 Shelley Prometh. Unb. ii. i, The folded depth of her *life-breathing bosom. 1906 W. de Morgan Joseph Vance xxviii. 268 'Come, Joe, some news this time I hope!' I should have liked to be able to say yes, for he looked.. as if he sadly wanted a *life-brightener. 1922 Joyce Ulysses 497 It's a lifebrightener, sure. 1561 T. Norton Calvin's Inst. iv. 121 Yt *lifebringing worde of the Father. 1868 J. H. Newman Verses Var. Occas. 187 *Life-creating Paraclete. 1955 L. P. Hartley Perfect Woman xxiii. 202 Jeremy, with his insistence on rules and regulations, his instinct for decorum in all things, seemed to her a spoil-sport and a *life-denier. 1962 J. B. Priestley Margin Released ii. v. 137 He would be twisted.. malevolent, *life-denying. 1973 Times Lit. Suppl. 21 Dec. 1554/1 Dame Rebecca's Augustine is.. introspective and life-denying, disgusted by physical existence... He bequeathed to posterity a complex of life-denying and art-denying ideas. a1600 in Farr S.P. Eliz. (1845) II. 437 More strong then *life-destroying death. 1590 Spenser F.Q. ii. vii. 17 Avarice.. kindled *life-devouring fire. 1955 S. Spender Making of Poem ii. vi. 102 The golden Romantic poet then is more than *life-enhancer.. He is the magician who.. turns all his experience.. into molten imagination. 1964 Economist 8 Aug. 530/2 That purely modern life-enhancer, the private car. 1896 B. Berenson Florentine Painters xi. 67 The contemplation of his [sc. Leonardo da Vinci's] personality is *life-enhancing as that of scarcely any other man. 1960 Guardian 18 Nov. 7/6 His passionately serious novel.. is a life-enhancing work. 1971 Ibid. 4 Jan. 10/2 The search for safer life-enhancing drugs. 1633 Ford Love's Sacr. v. iii, Let *life-hugging slaves.. be loath to die! 1597 Middleton Wisd. Sol. i. 1 Her *life-infusing speech doth thus begin. 1675 Brooks Gold. Key Wks. 1867 V. 203 Making good the philosopher's notion, that man is a *life-lover. 1647 H. More Oracle 79 In friendly feasts, and *life-outfetching kisse. 1592 Shaks. Ven. & Ad. cxxiii, *Life-poisoning pestilence. 1590 —— Com. Err. v. i. 83 *Life-preseruing rest. 1895 S. R. Hole Tour Amer. 24 Life-preserving belts. 1632 Lithgow Trav. x. 10 Each halfe houre a hell of infernall paine, and betweene each torment, a long distance of *life-quelling time. 1602 Carew Cornwall 58 *Lif-reauing knocks. 1602 Shaks. Ham. iv. v. 146 Like the kinde *Life-rend'ring Politician. 1781 Cowper Conversat. 504 Your heart shall yield a *life-renewing stream. 1781 —— Hope 456 The trumpet of a *life-restoring day. 1909 Daily Chron. 3 Sept. 1/1 The weather improved, but there still remained a light *life-sapping wind which drove despair to its lowest recess. 1928 A. Huxley in Sunday Dispatch 16 Dec. 12/6 No people, it seems to me, has suffered more than the English from that life-sapping malady of too much machinery. 1645 Quarles Sol. Recant. v. 17 His very *life-sustaining diet. 1862 H. Spencer First Princ. ii. ix. §80 (1875) 241 Life-sustaining power. 1613 Jackson Creed ii. ii. iii. §8 The silliest soule among them, might sooner bee partaker of their *life-working sense. 1855 Pusey Doctr. Real Presence Note S. 638 Although the nature of the flesh is in itself powerless to give life, yet it will inwork this when it has the life-working Word.

c. Instrumental and parasynthetic, as *life-clouded, -crowded, -deserted, -eyed, -oriented, -penetrated, -sentenced, -teeming*, adjs.

1921 D. H. Lawrence Tortoises 18 Life establishing the first eternal mathematical tablet, Not in stone.. or bronze, but in *life-clouded.. tortoise-shell. 1839 Bailey Festus (1852) 132 Its seas *life-crowded. 1727–46 Thomson Summer 818 Solitary tracts Of *life-deserted sand. 1839 Bailey Festus (1852) 170 O beauty, holy and divine, *Life-eyed, soul-crowned. 1968 Sun (Baltimore) 4 July A 16/3 Speakers were using such terms.. as *life-oriented curriculum.. and multi-media and multi-mode curriculum. 1893 Month Jan. 52 A potent and *life-penetrated organism. 1901 Chambers's Jrnl. Nov. 744/2 This hapless man had completed seventeen of the twenty years which all *life-sentenced prisoners must serve before release on license. 1847 Herschel tr. Schiller's Spaziergang 3 *Life-teeming fields.

d. In adverbial relations of various kinds, chiefly with adjs. and pples. = 'in, of, for, with, or as life'; as *life-bereft, -blissful, -divine, -empty, -lengthened, -lorn, -lost, -old, -spent, -stupid, -sweet, -thirsting, -weary, (-weariness); life-struggle*. †Also *occas.* = lifelike, as *life expression*.

1896 Sir T. Martin Virgil vi. 219 The bodies *life-bereft Of heroes of renown. 1923 D. H. Lawrence Birds, Beasts & Flowers 54 Flaked out and come unpromised, The tree being life-divine, Fearing nothing, *life-blissful at the core Within iron and earth. 1921 —— Let. c8 May (1962) II. 653 Everybody nice, but rather spent, rather *life-empty. 1621–31 Laud Serm. (1847) 98 Another King, but the same *life expression of all the royal and religious virtues of his father. a1770 Chatterton in Europ. Mag. (1804) XLV. 86 The drowning, *life-infatuate fool. 1608 Sylvester Du Bartas ii. iv. iv. Decay 10 *Life-lengthned Ezechiah. 1871 Palgrave Lyr. Poems 80 The *life-lorn hillside. 1598 S. Rowlands Betray. Christ G ij, His *life-lost blood. 1859 H. Kingsley G. Hamlyn (1900) 87/2 The rupture of *life-old associations. 1633 Ford Broken H. iv. ii, *Life-spent Penthea. 1898 Q. Rev. July 103 The bitter *life-struggle of primitive society. 1922 D. H. Lawrence Fantasia of Unconscious vii. 115 We are really far, far more *life-stupid than the dead Greeks. 1871–4 J. Thomson City Dreadf. Nt. x. vii, Deathstill, *lifesweet, with folded palms she lay. 1859 Dickens T. Two Cities iii. ix. (1872) II. 174 A *life-thirsting ..juryman. 1870 E. Peacock Ralf Skirl. III. 168 His illness had been more *life-weariness than organic disease. 1592 Shaks. Rom. & Jul. v. i. 62 The *life-wearie taker may fall dead. 1866 Carlyle Remin. (1881) I. 112 The most life-weary looking mortal I ever saw.

e. In adj. or advb. relation: Lasting for a lifetime, lifelong; during one's whole life, for life.

1648 Herrick Hesper. (1869) 117 Though hourely comforts from the Gods we see, No life is yet life-proofe from miserie. 1773 Gentl. Mag. XLIII. 618 A bill for raising 265,000l. by life-annuities. 1791 Gibbon Autobiog. (1896) 341 The heir most gratefully subscribed an agreement which rendered my life-possession more perfect. 1813 J. Forsyth Excurs. Italy 85 Extending the livelli, or life-leases. 1840 Carlyle Heroes (1858) 224 Working-out his life-task in the depths of the Desert there. 1849 Grote Greece ii. xlvi. V. 483 The life-sitting elders at Athens. 1868 M. Pattison Academ. Org. v. 127 Colleges were homes for the life-study of the highest and most abstruse parts of knowledge. 1884 Symonds Shaks. Predecess. Pref. 9 Elizabethan Dramatic Literature is.. important enough to occupy a man's life-labours. 1893 Pall Mall Mag. Christmas No. 224 He.. had received a life sentence.

f. In senses relating to *Art*: = 'from the life or living model', as *life-drawing, -study*; 'for the study of the life', as *life academy, -class, -school*; or 'imparting life', as *life-touch*.

1849 Chambers's Inform. II. 638/2 In London and elsewhere there are *life academies. 1891 A. Beardsley Let. 13 Oct. (1971) 30, I eventually selected the Impressionist Academy as my school of art... It will not be so very long before I get into the *life class. 1897 Mag. Art. Sept. 252 The life class should be confined to the study of the figure for purposes of design only. 1967 'L. Egan' Nameless Ones iv. 43 He was built like Tarzan, and could have earned a living posing for life classes. 1915 W. Owen Let. 4 Apr. (1967) 329 Great talent in *Life-Drawings and Oil Portraits; studied in Paris. 1956 K. Clark Nude iv. 117 A splendid drawing of a nude model, one of the first 'life drawings' of a woman. 1899 Mary Deane Bk. Dene, etc., 85 The difficulty of obtaining a *life-study of a.. phœnix. 1668 Dryden Evening's Love Pref., It is fancy that gives the *life-touches. 1678 Norris Coll. Misc. (1699) 173 Moses drew out the main Lineaments, the Skeleton of the Picture,.. but Christ ..gave it all it's Graces, Air, and Life-touches.

17. Special combinations: **life-arrow**, a barbed arrow with a line attached, which is fired from a gun in order to establish communication with a ship in distress (Cassell 1884); **life-assurance** (see assurance 5); **life-belt**, a belt of inflated indiarubber, of cork, or other buoyant material, used to support the body in the water; **life-breath**, the breath which supports life; also *fig.*; **life-buoy** (see buoy *sb.* 1 b); **life-company**, a life-insurance company; †**life-cord** = *life-string*; **life-craft**, a small craft, carried on board a larger one, by which escape may be made in an emergency; †**life-dead**, suffering a living death; **life-drop**, a drop of one's heart's-blood; **life-estate**, an estate, the tenure of which is measured by a person's life: **life expectancy**, expectation of life; also *transf.* and *attrib.*; **life-force**, vital energy; so **life-forcer**, a believer in a philosophy of the *élan vital*; **life-gun**, a gun used for sending life-saving apparatus to ships; **life-history** (*a*) *Biol.*, = life cycle; also *transf.* with reference to inanimate things; (*b*) life-story, the narrative of the career of a person; **life-hold**, applied to property which is held for a life or lives; hence **life-holder**, one who holds such property; **life-index** (see quot. 1915); **life-insurance** (see insurance 4); so *life-insurance policy* [policy *sb.*[2]]; also *fig*; **life-interest**, an interest or estate which terminates with the life of the holder or some other person; **life-jacket**, a life-saving contrivance in the form of a jacket; **life-knot** (see quot.); **life-member**, one who has acquired lifelong membership of a library, society, etc; so **life membership**; **life-mortar**, a mortar for discharging a life-rocket (Ogilvie, 1882); **life net** *U.S.* (see quot. 1969); **life-office**, 'an office or institution where life-insurances can be effected' (Cassell); **life-peer**, a peer whose title lapses at his death; so ***life-peerage***; also **life-peeress**; **life-plant**, a name for plants of the genus *Bryophyllum* (N.O. *Crassulaceæ*), which will grow without being rooted in soil; **life-policy** = *life-insurance policy*; **life-raft**, a kind of raft for saving life in a shipwreck; **life-rate**, 'the rate or amount for which a life is insured' (Ogilvie); †**life-regiment**, ? a regiment of life-guards; **life-ring** *N. Amer.*, a life-buoy; **life-rocket**, a rocket which carries with it a rope to establish communication with those on board a ship in distress (Ogilvie); **life-root**, the Golden Ragwort, *Senecio aureus* (*Syd. Soc. Lex.* 1888); **life science**, any of the sciences (such as zoology, bacteriology, or sociology) which deal with living organisms; such sciences collectively; **life-seat**, a seat contrived to be a life-saving appliance in case of a boat being capsized; **life-shot**, 'a shot carrying a line, and used for the same purpose as a life-arrow' (Cassell); †**life-sin**, actual sin; †**life-sith**, lifetime; **life-span** [span *sb.*[1] 4], lifetime; period of duration (of an animate or inanimate thing); †**life-spencer**, a cork jacket for saving life at sea; **life-spot** *Whaling*, the vulnerable point behind the fin of the whale into which the lance is thrust to kill the animal (*Cent. Dict.*); **life-spring**, the spring or source of life; **life-string**, a string or nerve supposed to be essential to life; *pl.* what is essential to the support of life; **life-support** *a.*, applied to equipment designed to make possible the continued normal functioning of the body in hostile or dangerous environments; **life-table**, 'a statistical table exhibiting statistics as to the probability of life at different ages' (Webster 1864); **life-tenant** = *life-holder*; so **life-tenancy**; **life test**, a test made on a sample of components in specified operating conditions, either for a certain length of time or until failure occurs, to determine the reliability of the components; hence (with hyphen) as *vb. trans.*, to perform a life test on; **life-testing** *vbl. sb.*; †**life-thraw**, lifetime; **life-tide**, †(*a*) ? lifetime; (*b*) the tide or stream of life; **life-token** = *life-index*; **life-tree** = 'tree of life'; **life vest** *U.S.* = *life-jacket*; **life-while** *arch.*, lifetime; **life-work**, the work of a lifetime; the work which is the object of a person's whole life; **life-world** *Philos.* [tr. G. *lebenswelt*], all the immediate experiences,

activities, and contacts that make up the world of an individual, or of a corporate, life; **life-writer**, a biographer; so **life-writing** *sb.*, biography; *adj.* writing biographies.

1830 HERSCHEL *Stud. Nat. Phil.* 58 The institution of *life-assurances. **1866** CRUMP *Banking* iii. 84 Life-assurance policies. **1858** SIMMONDS *Dict. Trade*, **Life-belt*. **1875** BEDFORD *Sailor's Pocket Bk.* viii. (ed. 2) 286 The Life Belts supplied to men-of-war weigh 5 pounds. **1597** J. KING *Jonas* (1618) 87 This is the band wherby the common wealth hangeth together, the *life-breath which these many thousand creatures draw. **1875** STUBBS *Const. Hist.* II. xvii. 621 That constitutional spirit which was the life-breath of parliamentary growth. **1801** *Naval Chron.* VI. 342 The *life buoy being caught hold of. **1875** BEDFORD *Sailor's Pocket Bk.* viii. (ed. 2) 283 The Service Life Buoy is supposed to be capable of keeping four men afloat. **1907** *Westm. Gaz.* 10 Apr. 10/1 That is sufficient justification for the *life-company amalgamation. *a* **1631** DONNE *Progr. Soul* 394 This mouse..to the brain..went, And gnaw'd the *life-cords there. **1840** BROWNING *Sordello* VI. 733 Fate shears The life-cord prompt enough. **1970** *Sci. Jrnl.* June 9/1 Plastic *lifecrafts carried aboard spaceships much as lifeboats are carried by ocean liners, have been advocated. **1970** *New Scientist* 22 Oct. 178/1 A computer would calculate the position of the lifecraft with an accuracy of one to ten miles. *a* **1586** SIDNEY *Arcadia* II. (1629) 222 This *life-deadman in this old dungeon flong. **1807** BYRON *Nisus & Euryalus* 48 And hostile *life-drops dim my gory spear. **1753** CHAMBERS *Cycl. Supp.*, **Life estates*..are either for the life of the owner, or for the life of another, or others. **1935** *Jrnl. Amer. Med. Assoc.* 17 Aug. 514/2 Today, *life expectancy at birth is 57 years. **1956** A. H. COMPTON *Atomic Quest* 330 Life expectancy in our country increased by 50 per cent, from 46 years to 69 years. **1962** *Daily Tel.* 30 Apr. 24/3 Details of the Board's plans for closures in Scotland.. await completion of a 'life-expectancy' survey. **1972** *Guardian* 15 Aug. 4/5 One of the reasons for higher life expectancy in India today is a better public health system. **1896** W. CALDWELL *Schopenhauer's Syst.* ix. 500 The will is the *life-force that pulsates through man's nature. **1903** G. B. SHAW *Man & Superman* III. 109 And these are the creatures in whom you discover what you call a Life Force! *Ibid.* 137 Wagner once drifted into Life Force worship, and invented a Superman called Siegfried. **1920** D. H. LAWRENCE *Lost Girl* xii. 309 Even the will of God is a life-force. **1952** C. DAY LEWIS tr. *Virgil's Aeneid* VI. 137 The life-force of those seeds is fire, their source celestial. **1975** A. FRASER *Whistler's Lane* x. 160 The relentless, uncheckable advent of spring..this all-powerful life force which flowed so strongly. **1931** T. S. ELIOT *Thoughts after Lambeth* 9 These two depressing *life-forcers [*sc.* Bertrand Russell and Aldous Huxley]. **1935** AUDEN & ISHERWOOD *Dog beneath Skin* I. (chorus betw. sc. ii & iii) 43 The naughty life-forcer in the norfolk jacket Was the rebels' only uncle. **1910** *Chambers's Jrnl.* Mar. 159/2 The *life-gun which is used by the rescuers for shooting lines to the vessel. **1870** D. J. KIRWAN *Palace & Hovel* xxvi. 393 Those street hawkers.. will relate their checkered *life-histories with great eagerness. **1873** *Monthly Microsc. Jrnl.* X. 53 (*title*) Researches on the life history of a cercomonad. **1879** DALLINGER *Lett. Min. Forms Life*, We were able in the course of four years' steady work to complete the life history of six distinct forms. **1898** *Allbutt's Syst. Med.* V. 401 The life-history of the white corpuscles. **1909** 'MARK TWAIN' *Is Shakes. Dead?* 141 Philosophers, burglars..surgeons—you can get the life-histories of all of them but one [*sc.* Shakespeare]. **1920** *Discovery* Apr. 111/2 The average value of the uranium present during the life-history of the mineral. **1927** R. FRY *Let.* 31 Aug. (1972) II. 609 The old man..poured out his whole life-history. **1935** B. MALINOWSKI *Coral Gardens* II. VI. 232 The development of speech within the life history of the individual. **1950** K. A. BISSET (*title*) The cytology and life-history of bacteria. **1962** Life history [see ASTROPHYSICS]. *a* **1843** SOUTHEY *Comm.-pl. Bk.* IV. 359 My father's Aunt Hannah had a *life-hold estate. **1813** VANCOUVER *Agric. Devon* 428 Lifehold tenures. **1887** *Athenæum* 31 Dec. 883/2 A small lifehold farm. **1802–12** BENTHAM *Ration. Judic. Evid.* (1827) IV. 635 The axe of the..malicious *life-holder is levelling to the ground the lofty oaks. **1884** STEEL & TEMPLE *Wide-Awake Stories* 404 Outside a person's life is an object which faithfully reflects the conditions of his life: this *life-index is always very difficult of access. **1915** *Encycl. Relig. & Ethics* VIII. 44/2 'Life-token' or 'life-index' is the technical name given to an object the condition of which is in popular belief bound up with that of some person, which indicates his state of health or safety. **1809** R. LANGFORD *Introd. Trade* 51 *Life Insurances are contracts to pay the assured a specified sum of money upon the death of the person or persons named in the contract. **1862** R. H. NEWELL *Orpheus C. Kerr Papers* 1st Ser. 360 He's not an economical man if he don't destroy his life-insurance policy. **1891** E. G. WHITE in *Seventh-Day Adventist Bible Commentary* (1915) VI. 1070/2, I reprieve him from the condemnation of death giving him My life insurance policy—eternal life—because I have taken his place and have suffered for his sins. **1955** *Granta* 26 Nov. 20/2 I'm gonna sell 'em a life insurance policy. **1970** T. HUGHES *Crow* 29 Words came with Life Insurance policies —Crow feigned dead. **1849** MACAULAY *Hist. Eng.* v. I. 657 He had only a *life interest in his property. **1868** FREEMAN *Norm. Conq.* (1876) II. App. 564 His life-interest in his prebend was forfeited. **1883** *Fisheries Exhib. Catal.* 38 Cork *Life Jackets. **1855** MAYNE *Expos. Lex.*, **Life-knot*, a term applied to the neck, or point between the root and stem of plants, because if this part in a young plant be seriously injured it will die, whereas the root or stem may be removed without detriment. **1867** *Harper's Mag.* Aug. 349/2 These *life-members of my charity. **1907** R. FRY *Let.* 5 Mar. (1972) I. 282 I'm so glad they've made you a life member of the museum. **1926** A. E. HOUSMAN *Let.* 15 Jan. (1971) 233 You may be perplexed by communications from the London Library. I am taking steps to have you made a life member. **1972** H. KEMELMAN *Monday the Rabbi took Off* ii. 22 The by-laws made all past presidents life members of the board. **1859** in H. R. Fletcher *Story R. Hort. Soc.* (1969) xii. 187 It is proposed to raise the money by Donation, by *Life Memberships of 40 Guineas and 20 Guineas. **1867** *Harper's Mag.* Aug. 349/1 A most laudable charity—put me down for a life-membership by all means. **1909** *Daily Chron.* 11 Mar. 6/3 New York... Many leapt from the windows and were caught in the *life nets. **1947** *Chicago Tribune* 20 July (Comics) 4 Let's see some action—grab that life net! **1969** *Publ. Amer. Dial. Soc.* LII. 33 *Life net*, a net used to catch people who must jump from a building. **1879** *Life-office [see *experience table*]. **1972** *Accountant* 28 Sept. 388/2 Rates of interest quoted by life offices at the moment are not so attractive as they were when borrow-all policies were popular. **1869** EARL RUSSELL in Hansard *Parl. Deb.* 3rd Ser. CXCV. 454 That a great number of *life Peers may be created. **1948** H. NICOLSON *Diary* 28 May (1968) 141 If they reform the House of Lords, they are certain to make me a life-peer. **1961** *Spectator* 20 Jan. 63 Six new life peers were created. **1973** *Times* 16 May 18/5 The making of life peers rather than hereditary peers (the present Conservative Government has given no hereditary titles) will gradually leave the Crown in increasing isolation as an hereditary institution. **1863** H. COX *Instit.* I. vii. 68 No *life-peerages had been created for several centuries. **1869** EARL RUSSELL in Hansard *Parl. Deb.* 3rd Ser. CXCV. 454 A life peerage had been granted to Lord Wensleydale. **1958** *Times* 24 July 8/7 (*heading*) Life peerages for four women. **1967** *Listener* 20 Apr. 533/1 Her Labour Party allegiance..took her through local government..to a life peerage. **1958** *Times* 24 July 8/7 The wives..of life peers, and the sons and daughters of..life peers and *life peeresses shall be treated ..in the same way as the wives..and children of hereditary barons. **1851** GOSSE *Nat. in Jamaica* 61 The Leaf of Life, or the *Life Plant. **1881** *Harper's Mag.* Jan. 274/2 Most of their bargains with the public are made in the shape of *life policies. **1907** 'MARK TWAIN' in *North Amer. Rev.* Jan. 14 If I hadn't taken out a life policy on this one the premiums would have bankrupted me long ago. **1942** *Mind* LI. 288 His watchword, in thinking not only of the means but of the ends of a life-policy, is 'here, or nowhere, is my America'. **1972** *Accountant* 28 Sept. 388/1 There are various schemes by which funds can be borrowed to buy shares at the outset, with a life policy being used to repay the loan in due course. **1819** *Trans. Soc. Arts* XXXVII. 110 The Gold Medal of the Society was this Session voted to Mr. Thomas Cook, Lieut. R.N. for a *Life Raft. **1903**, **1922** Life-raft [see CARLEY]. **1958** [see *air-sea rescue* (AIR *sb.*[1] III. 1)]. **1962** S. CARPENTER in *Into Orbit* 60, I had a smaller version of it in my liferaft as part of the emergency kit. **1973** *Times* 9 Mar. 26/8 In emergency situations, such as aircrashes, liferafts are automatically inflated. **1723** *Lond. Gaz.* No. 6199/1 The Squadron of Life-Guards, two Squadrons of the *Life-Regiment. **1912** L. J. VANCE *Destroying Angel* xiv. 189 He managed..to jam the *life-ring over her head and under one arm before the next wave bore down upon them. **1972** *Daily Colonist* (Victoria, B.C.) 11 Jan. 7/1 The aircraft sighted.. a life-ring bearing the ship's name. **1941** G. W. HUNTER (*title*) *Life science. A social biology. **1958** M. A. GRAUBARD (*title*) The foundations of life science. **1959** *Vistas in Astronautics* II. 139 (*heading*) The utilization of a satellite laboratory for life science studies. **1970** C. J. & O. B. GOIN (*title*) Man and the natural world: an introduction to life science. **1973** *Freedom* 2 June 3/4, I regard my own specialism, psychology, as a continuing part of the Darwinian revolution in the Life Sciences. **1857** THOREAU *Maine W.* (1894) 121 She was a well-appointed little boat,.. with patent *life-seats and metallic life-boat. *a* **1641** BP. MOUNTAGU *Acts & Mon.* (1642) 532 Concerning actuall, or *life-sinne. *c* **1230** *Hali Meid.* 45 Al hare *lifsiðe. *a* **1240** *Sawles Warde* in *Cott. Hom.* 249 Euch sunne..þat he.. wrahtte in al his lif siðe. **1918** W. B. YEATS *Per Amica Silentia Lunae* 38 Some..have foreknown the event and pricked upon the calendar the *life-span of a Christ, a Buddha, a Napoleon. **1937** B. H. L. HART *Europe in Arms* xxii. 290 He [*sc.* Napoleon] took short views, since his horizon was his own life-span. **1953** J. S. HUXLEY *Evolution in Action* iv. 103 Their life-span..may extend over several decades. **1957** G. E. HUTCHINSON *Treat. Limnol.* I. ii. 177 The life span of the lake. **1966** C. R. TOTTLE *Sci. Engin. Materials* x. 235 The life-span of the neutron depends on its kinetic energy, and on the material through which it passes. **1974** A. HUXLEY *Plant & Planet* xviii. 189 Plants are too varied to have an average lifespan. *Ibid.*, As soon as we move to multi-cellular plants the lifespans increase. **1820** *Trans. Soc. Arts* XXXVIII. 164 *Life-spencer. **1794** MATHIAS *Purs. Lit.* (1798) 310 The *life-springs of taste and of good conduct. **1859** K. CORNWALLIS *New World* I. 14 Hope is the life-spring of enterprise. *c* **1522** MORE *De quat. noviss.* Wks. 77/2 Breaking thy vaines & thy *life stringes w[t] like pain & grief. **1767** G. S. CAREY *Hills Hybla* 39 Thy words have cut my life-string thro'. **1827** KEBLE *Chr. Y.* Tuesday bef. Easter, One by one The life-strings of that tender heart gave way. **1959** *Adv. Space Sci. & Technol.* I. 174 (*heading*) *Life support system. **1962** F. I. ORDWAY et al. *Basic Astronautics* xiii. 509 A life support system for a manned base on the Moon..will be exceedingly complex. **1962** D. SLAYTON in *Into Orbit* 20 NASA decided we would adopt the U.S. Navy pressure suit for our spacesuit, so Wally Schirra..started work on the life-support system which we would need to keep the pilot alive and comfortable. **1969** *Guardian* 21 July 1/6 Before take-off the spacecraft's pressurisation system is tested while the astronauts are still in their life-support suits. **1970** *McGraw-Hill Yearbk. Sci. & Technol.* 280/2 All submersibles require life-support systems. **1865** *Reader* 25 Feb. 213/1 Every insurance office bases its transactions upon an instrument which is called a '*Life Table'. **1908** *Westm. Gaz.* 24 Nov. 4/1 The *life-tenancy individualism which Mr. Carnegie recommends to us is sharply distinguished from the feudal individualism which obtains in old countries. **1962** H. R. LOYN *Anglo-Saxon Eng.* iv. 178 An abbey or church..could receive estates as a gift, and then yield them back to the donor on a life-tenancy. **1837** SYD. SMITH *Let. to Archd. Singleton* Wks. 1859 II. 264/2 An Ecclesiastical Corporation..can sell a next presentation as legally as a lay *life-tenant can do. **1973** *N.Y. Law Jrnl.* 4 Sept. 17/1 Ordinarily a life tenant of real property is entitled to collect all the income but must pay real estate taxes, mortgage interest if any, insurance cost and routine maintenance expenses. **1893** G. S. RAM *Incandescent Lamp* xv. 196 A great many carefully-ascertained *life tests of different lamps have..been reported. **1911** *Chem. Abstr.* V. 1371 (*heading*) Life test of metallic filament lamps. **1929** *Jrnl. Sci. Instrum.* VI. 247 The life test load accommodated by this regulator consists of twenty 2-volt 1-ampere miners' lamps screwed into bus bars. **1958** *Biometrika* XLV. 521 A second difficulty encountered in using conventional experimental methods in industrial life tests is the expense and time involved in waiting for all of the test items to fail. **1959** *Engineering* 20 Feb. 256/2 First on the market, some months ago, was the Hamilton electric watch, which was life tested for several years before the first one was sold, and which has proven itself a most reliable and accurate timekeeper. **1961** *Times* 31 May 18/4 Yet another machine life-tests switches. **1972** R. C. WINANS in D. Baker et al. *Physical Design Electronic Syst.* IV. viii. 368 As a control on time-dependent characteristics, life tests are made on samples from each production lot. These life tests are usually for periods ranging from 100 to 1000 hours, under maximum rated power, temperature, and/or voltage conditions. **1926** J. W. T. WALSH *Photometry* xvi. 449 An important branch of the work of a photometric laboratory is, frequently, the *life testing of lamps. **1957** *Ann. Math. Statistics* XXVIII. 432 Life-testing situations where population properties are of greater interest than sample properties usually involve inanimate objects such as automobile tires, light bulbs, etc. *c* **1375** *Sc. Leg. Saints* xli. (*Agnes*) 332 A lame quhytare þane ony snaw þat euir þai schaw of þe *lif-thraw. **1610** HOLLAND *Camden's Brit.* I. 245 [She] endowed the same with her owne Patrimonie and *Livetide. **1859** DICKENS *T. Two Cities* III. xiii, The life-tide of the city. **1899** R. C. TEMPLE in *Folk-Lore* X. 403 It now seems to have found a definite place among the recognized technicalities of writers on folklore under the guise of the *life-token. **1915** Life-token [see *life-index*]. **1649** J. ELLISTONE tr. *Behmen's Epist.* (1886) vij/2 A Christian.. desire after the same *life-tree of Christ. **1821** BYRON *Cain* I. i. 292 Wherefore pluck'd he not The life-tree? **1962** S. CARPENTER in *Into Orbit* 155 A tiny *life vest which weighed less than a pound and could be folded up into a package not much bigger than a man's hand. **1970** *Washington Post* 30 Sept. D6/1 (Advt.), Fiber-glas hardtop,..2 wipers, 6 life vests, 2 fire ext. and bell. *a* **1300** *Siriz* in Wright *Anecd. Lit.* (1844) 5 Never more his *lif wile. *a* **1849** J. C. MANGAN *Poems* (1859) 321 The life-while of a world. **1871** E. F. BURR *Ad Fidem* iii. 43 Your great *life-work. **1879** PATTISON *Milton* xiii. 167 In 1638..Milton has already determined that this lifework shall be a poem, an epic poem. **1940** A. SCHUETZ in M. Farber *Philos. Ess. in Memory E. Husserl* 173 Human existence itself is referred to an existent *life-world as a realm of practical activity. **1960** D. CAIRNS tr. *Husserl's Cartesian Meditations* §8. 19 Not just corporeal Nature but the whole concrete surrounding life-world is for me..only a phenomenon of being, instead of something that is. **1964** *Philos. Rev.* LXXIII. 418 Merleau-Ponty analyzes what.. Husserl had termed the 'life-world' ('Lebenswelt'). **1969** M. FARBER in R. Klibansky *Contemp. Philos.* III. 167 There are life-worlds for ordinary experience, varying from person to person, from group to group, and from time to time. There are also life-worlds as viewed on the basis of the sciences. **1972** D. FØLLESDAL in Olson & Raul *Contemp. Philos. Scandinavia* 426 We all live in a 'life-world' which is constituted by everyone in community. The term 'life-world' ('*Lebenswelt*') first appeared in an unpublished article on Kant which he [*sc.* Husserl] wrote in 1924, and the life-world became the main theme of his last major work, *The Crisis of the European Sciences* (1936). **1737** WARBURTON *Let. to Birch* 24 Nov. in Boswell *Johnson* (1831) I. Introd. 50 Almost all the *life-writers we have had before Toland and Desmaiseaux are indeed strange insipid creatures. **1772** *Ann. Reg., Misc. Ess.* 193 Of all the fantastic amusements in which modern genius indulges itself, the most whimsical is *Life-writing. *Ibid.* 169/1 This life-writing part of the world. **1889** LOWELL *Latest Lit. Ess.* (1891) 76 It..comes nearer to him [Plutarch] than any life-writing I can think of.

18. The gen. sing. *life's* (12–17th c. *lives*) was formerly much used in certain syntactical combs., as ***lives book, life's day*** (= LIFE-DAY), ***lives food, life's time*** (OE. *lífes tíd*; = LIFETIME), etc.; now *rare* exc. in ***life's end*** (somewhat *arch.*); also † **lives-wet** = blood.

c **900** tr. *Bæda's Hist.* III. xiv. [xix.] (1890) 216 Ealle his lifes tiid. *c* **1205** LAY. 229 þis lond he hire lende, þat come hir lifes ende. *c* **1220** *Bestiary* 287 Seke we ure liues fod. *a* **1225** *Leg. Kath.* 707 þu schalt..libben liues ende wið Iesu Crist. *a* **1225** *Ancr. R.* 246 God hat writen o liues boc al þet heo seið. *a* **1300** *Cursor M.* 28889 Men agh noght warn him liues fode. *c* **1381** CHAUCER *Parl. Foules* 53 Oure present wordis lyuys space Nys but a maner deth. *c* **1385** —— *L.G.W.* 1624 *Medea*, I wot wel that..myn labour May nat disserue it in myn lyuys day. *c* **1420** *Anturs of Arth.* 702 A kniȝte of þe table ronde, To his lyues ende. *c* **1430** LYDG. *Compl. Bl. Knt.* 674 (*Lenvoy*) Go, litel quayre, vnto my lyues queen. *c* **1449** PECOCK *Repr.* 536 For eny certein while or for al hir lyuys tyme. *a* **1533** LD. BERNERS *Gold. Bk. M. Aurel.* (1546) Ccjb, We can never passe one good lyves daie. **1599** MARSTON *Sco. Villanie* I. iv. 187 Cold, writhled Eld, his liues-wet almost spent. **1600** *Certain Prayers* in *Liturg. Serv. Q. Eliz.* (1847) 692 On whose life dependeth the life and life's-joy of so many thousands! **1637** *Sc. Prayer Bk.*, *Catechism*, That I may continue in the same unto my lives end. **1654** GAYTON *Pleas. Notes* III. xii. 156 In the lives-time of their dearly Beloveds deceas'd. **1683** TRYON *Way to Health* 613 There is but little Sand left in their Lives Glass. **1830** *Song in praise of beer*, And I'll contend to my life's end There's nothing to tipple like Beer.

life, *v. rare.* [f. LIFE *sb.*] *trans.* To give life to. Hence **'lifing** *ppl. a.*

1880 G. MACDONALD *Diary Old Soul* Jan. 9, I see him all in all, the lifing mind, Or nowhere. *Ibid.* Mar. 27 As to our mothers came help in our birth—Not lost in lifing us, but saved and blest.

life, obs. form of LIEF.

life-and-death, *a.* [LIFE *sb.* 1 c.] Involving life and death; vitally important.

1822 MILL *Let.* 14 Nov. in *Works* (1963) XII. 14 The life-and-death style in which I speak and write about it [*sc.* the Utilitarian Society]. **1824** BYRON *Def. Transf.* III. i, No bugle awakes him with life-and-death call. **1834** HOOD *Tylney Hall* I. iii. 24 Joe made shift to explain that he was charged with what he called a life and death letter to Sir Mark. **1857** *Edin. Rev.* CVI. 198 The third, the part he assigned to himself in the life-and-death struggle of his country. **1857** *Chambers's Jrnl.* Nov. 338/1 These are really a life and death matter to our neighbours. **1888** MRS. H. WARD *R. Elsmere* II. III. xxiii. 226, I go about haunted by the *seriousness*, the life-and-death interest people throw into

music. **1939** DYLAN THOMAS *Let.* 11 Sept. (1966) 236 If you look at *Tropic of Cancer*..not as a universal life-&-death book,..you must enjoy..it. **1951** S. SPENDER *World within World* ii. 97 At once I was aware of nature as a life-and-death force. **1973** *Times* 21 Dec. 4/2 On Christmas Day and Boxing Day..all inland telegram deliveries..will be suspended. Special arrangements will be made to deliver 'life and death' messages.

ˈlife-blood.

1. The blood necessary to life; vital blood.

1590 SPENSER *F.Q.* I. xi. 53 The weapon..deepe emperst his darksom hollow maw, And, back retyrd, his life blood forth with all did draw. **1596** SHAKS. *Merch. V.* III. ii. 269. **1667** MILTON *P.L.* VIII. 467. **1789** COWPER *Cockfighter's Garland* vii, Nor e'er had fought but he made flow The life-blood of his fiercest foe. **1827** KEBLE *Chr. Y., Good Friday*, With the Saviour's life-blood wet.

2. *transf.* and *fig.* That which gives life to a man's mind, thought, action, etc.; the vital part or vitalizing influence.

1596 SHAKS. *1 Hen. IV*, IV. i. 29 This sicknes doth infect The very Life-blood of our Enterprise. **1601** B. JONSON *Poetaster* IV. vii, [Ovid addressing Julia] Be gon, sweete Life-bloode. **1602** MARSTON *Ant. & Mel.* II. Wks. 1856 I. 29 His love (life blood of all his hopes). **1644** MILTON *Areop.* (Arb.) 35 A good Booke is the pretious life-blood of a master spirit. **1770** *Junius Lett.* xxxvii. 180 The noble spirit of the metropolis is the life-blood of the state. **1857** WILLMOTT *Pleas. Lit.* xx. 110 The poetic element is the life-blood of the narrative.

b. *attrib.* as *adj.* Vital, essential. *rare*$^{-1}$.

1641 MILTON *Reform.* II. Wks. (1847) 16/1 All the most sacred and lifeblood laws.

3. (Also *live-blood.*) The popular name for an involuntary twitching of the lip or eyelid.

1733 CHEYNE *Eng. Malady* II. xi. §2 (1734) 229 Pulsations from Flatulency, like what is vulgarly called the Life-Blood, in several Parts of the Body. **1754** RICHARDSON *Grandison* VI. 221 My upper-lip had the motion in it, throbbing, like the pulsation which we call the life-blood. **1855** J. DIXON *Dis. Eye* 271 The orbicularis palpebrarum muscle is subject to a spasmodic twitching..popularly termed the live-blood.

ˈlife-boat. A boat specially constructed for saving lives in cases of loss of a vessel at sea.

In 1785 a patent was granted to Mr. Lukin for an 'insubmergible boat,' but the word *life-boat* is not used in the specification.

1801 *Ann. Reg., Chron.* 14 Two life boats have been finished by Mr. Greathead of Shields. **1802** *Trans. Soc. Arts* XX. 283 The Gold Medal and Fifty Guineas were..voted ..to Mr. Henry Greathead..for a Boat of peculiar construction, named a Life-Boat, in consequence of the lives of many persons shipwrecked having been preserved by it. **1811** MOORE *'Tis sweet to behold* ii, Yet who would not turn with a fonder emotion, To gaze on the life-boat, though rugged and worn. **1860** *All Year Round* No. 65. 344 The life-boat can brave storms in which a coast-guard boat or fisher boat could not venture to put out.

b. *attrib.*: **life-boat day**, a day on which collections are made for the maintenance of life-boats; **lifeboat-man**, a member of a life-boat's crew.

1858 HOMANS *Dict. Comm.* 1215/2 The National Life-Boat Institution. *Ibid.* 1216/1 A member of the Life-boat Committee. **1860** *All Year Round* No. 65. 345 The life-boat-men's pay. **1864** ATKINSON *Stanton Grange* 40 Shoes on the lifeboat principle, selfacting dischargers of all extra water. **1898** *Daily News* 20 Apr. 4/5 A meeting..for the purpose of establishing a lifeboat day in the town.

life cycle. Also life-cycle. [f. LIFE *sb.* + CYCLE *sb.*] **1.** *Biol.* The series of developments which an organism undergoes in the course of its progress from the egg to the adult state. Also, an account of these developments.

1873 *Monthly Microsc. Jrnl.* X. 57 Thus the entire life cycle of this form is seen. **1894** *Pop. Sci. Monthly* June 272 Each species has two generations in its life-cycle. **1967** M. E. HALE *Biol. Lichens* ii. 27 The life cycle of fungi is completed when the vegetative thallus produces fruiting bodies that contain spores.

b. The course of human, cultural, etc., existence from birth or beginning through development and productivity to decay and death or ending.

1938 H. READ *Coll. Ess. Lit. Crit.* I. i. 19 The classical and romantic periods are related to each other in a 'life-cycle' which is the recurring cycle of the growth, maturity, and decay of culture. **1949** M. MEAD *Male & Female* xvi. 339 Here he is, only in middle age, and his life is over—..no new fields to conquer... So while he is not out of a job..the very nature of the life-cycle in America is such that he feels like an old man. **1959** G. D. MITCHELL *Sociol.* vi. 103 Religion is mostly important to mankind at times of personal crisis or when new and socially significant stages of the life-cycle are approached: at birth, initiation, marriage, death. **1967** B. S. COHN in P. Bohannan *Law & Warfare* 145 The general rule is that, when a household is celebrating a life-cycle rite, all adult males from the *khandan* and at least one adult male.. from every other household in the hamlet is invited. **1969** W. E. MOORE in Lindzey & Aronson *Handbk. Social Psychol.* (ed. 2) IV. xxxii. 316 A rather different perspective on social organization and social process results from dealing with the entire human life cycle.

2. *transf.*, esp. in *Econ.* and *Comm.*

1965 H. I. ANSOFF *Corporate Strategy* (1968) ii. 31 Objectives..will vary from one type of firm to another depending on the firm's past profitability, its prospects, and its stage in the life cycle. **1969** J. ARGENTI *Managem. Techniques* 70 Many product life-cycles are declining. **1971** *Nature* 12 Feb. 486/2 The photo-oxidation of sulphur dioxide to sulphuric acid in the atmosphere is relevant both to the formation of aerosols in polluted air and to the life cycle of sulphur compounds in the atmosphere. **1971** *Daily Tel.* 21 June 17/6 The four-stage life-cycle of every [manufactured] product—exploration, growth, maturity, decline. *Ibid.* 17/8 Companies usually have a range of products at various stages of the life-cycle.

life-day. *Obs.* exc. *arch.* Forms: see LIFE *sb.* and DAY *sb.* A day or some period of a man's life; chiefly *pl.* (occas. *sing.*), a man's life or lifetime, '(all) the days of (one's) life'. † *to bring, do of life-day*, to kill; † *to leese one's life-dawes*, to die.

Beowulf 1622 (Gr.) Se ellor-gast oflet lifdaȝas. *a* **900** CYNEWULF *Crist* 1224 On hyra lif-daȝum. *c* **1175** *Lamb. Hom.* 129 Her heo leueden al heore lifdaȝes on kare. *a* **1250** *Owl & Night.* 1139 Þe while þu art on lif-day. *c* **1250** *Gen. & Ex.* 4119 Quiles him lesten liue daȝes. *c* **1275** *Passion Our Lord* 84 in *O.E. Misc.* 39 Þet heo hyne myhte wreye and don of lyf-daȝe. *c* **1300** *Vox & Wolf* 49 in Hazl. *E.P.P.* I. 59 Thine lif-dayes beth al a-go. **13..** *Sir Beues* (A.) 4456 Beues ..was islawe And ibrouȝt of his lif dawe. *c* **1325** *Chron. Eng.* 1006 in Ritson *Metr. Rom.* II. 312 Therfore he les his lyf-dawes. **1375** BARBOUR *Bruce* III. 293 And haiff he lyff-dayis. *a* **1400-50** *Alexander* 880 He..leues louely with hir all hys lyue days. **1454** *Paston Lett.* I. 278 Which affray shorttyd the lyffdayes of the sayd Phillippe. **1525** LD. BERNERS *Froiss.* II. ccx. [ccvi.] 650 These lordes..acorded well toguyder all their lyue dayes. **1538** DUCHESS NORFOLK in Miss M. A. E. Wood *Lett. R. & Illustr. Ladies* (1852) II. 368 As for my lord my husband, for his liveday I will never trust him. **1568** *Hist. Jacob & Esau* V. ix. G ij, Ye know that now our life daies are but short. **1876** MORRIS *Sigurd* (1887) 25 As a picture all of gold thy life-days shalt thou see. **1893** 'MARK TWAIN' *Lett.* (1917) II. 592, I shall tackle Adam once more. .. I've been thinking out his first life-days today. **1940** AUDEN *Another Time* 61 And we The life-day long shall part no more.

life-everlasting. American cudweed, *Antennaria margaritacea.*

1656 PARKINSON *Paradisi* (ed. 2) 374 *Argyrocome sive Gnaphalium Americanum.* Live long or Life everlasting. **1753** in CHAMBERS *Cycl.* Suppl. App. **1854** THOREAU *Walden* iv. (1886) 111 Life-everlasting grows under the table, and blackberry vines run round its legs.

ˈlife-form. Also life form. [f. LIFE *sb.* + FORM *sb.*] **1.** *Biol.* A habit or vegetative form exhibited by any particular plant or which characterizes a group of plants.

Various life-form classifications have been proposed. That of C. Raunkiær (or a modification of his system) based upon the position of the buds relative to the soil surface during the unfavourable season is the one generally employed.

1899 *Natural Sci.* XIV. 109 Hence groups of similar adaptational form, 'Lebensform' of German authors, need by no means coincide with natural families or groups of species. For example, *Empetrum* and *Erica*, or *Aloe* and *Agave*, possess similar 'life-forms',..yet their floral characters indicate widely separate genetic affinities. **1913** *Jrnl. Ecol.* I. 16 (*heading*) Raunkiær's 'life-forms' and statistical methods. **1926** TANSLEY & CHIPP *Study of Vegetation* ii. 11 Life form is the characteristic vegetative form of a species; in the first place whether it is a tree, shrub, herb, or a member of one of the lower group of the plant kingdom. **1960** [see *growth-form* s.v. GROWTH[1] 5]. **1964** V. J. CHAPMAN *Coastal Vegetation* i. 9 There is no generally recognized life-form system for the algae. **1971** D. W. SHIMWELL *Descr. & Classification of Vegetation* iii. 74 Raunkiær..recognized fifteen main types of life form.

2. A living creature; any kind of living thing.

1905 *Daily Chron.* 17 Aug. 5/7 In the beginning, before life forms appeared, the sun shone on the ocean. **1908** *Lit. Guide* 1 Aug. 115/2 Proof..of an unbroken chain of psychical continuity between the lowest and highest life-forms. **1971** *Daily Tel.* (Colour Suppl.) 30 Apr. 17/3 If only ..it were possible to introduce some terrestrial life-form on to Venus. **1971** I. G. GASS et al. *Understanding Earth* ix. 139/2 Once life had become universally distributed over the face of the globe, it must have prevented the further generation of new life-forms.

lifeful (ˈlaɪffʊl), *sb. rare*$^{-1}$. [f. LIFE *sb.* + -FUL.] An amount sufficient to fill a lifetime.

1866 BLACKMORE *Cradock Nowell* xxvii. (1881) 139 A manuscript containing a lifeful of learning.

lifeful (ˈlaɪffʊl), *a.* Now *rare.* Also 3 liflul, 6 livefull, lifull, lyfull. [f. LIFE *sb.* + -FUL.] Full of life; having much vitality or animation; giving or bestowing life or vitality.

a **1225** *Leg. Kath.* 834 Þe liflule leaue of hali chirche. **1570** T. NORTON tr. *Nowel's Catech.* (1853) 199 We pray to have the daily meat..to be made lifeful and healthful to us. **1595** SPENSER *Epithal.* 118. **1596** —— *F.Q.* VI. xi. 46 Like lyfull heat to nummed senses brought. **1606** MARSTON *Parasitaster* I. ii. B2, Tiberio's life-full eyes and well fild vaines. **1818** KEATS *Endym.* I. 768 A colour grew Upon his cheek, while thus he lifeful spake. **1862** R. H. PATTERSON *Ess. Hist. & Art* 108 Nothing is too lifeful for sculpture, if so be it be beautiful.

Hence **ˈlifefully** *adv.*, **ˈlifefulness.**

a **1470** TIPTOFT *Decl. P.C. Scipio* (Caxton 1481) D iv, In theyr children nature hath lyeffully emprynted..the same. **1832** J. WILSON in *Blackw. Mag.* XXXI. 865 In their lifefulness forgetting all thoughts..that appertain to death. **1864** MRS. CLIVE *John Greswold* II. 179 The..garb which had been worn so lifefully in the morning. **1870** H. MACMILLAN *Bible Teach.* iii. 54 Human hope and lifefulness.

life-giver. One who or that which gives life.

1598 S. ROWLANDS *Betray. Christ* G ib, O..deaths victor, true life-giuer. **1862** LYTTON *Str. Story* I. 98 The air—which is the kindest life-giver. **1875** MANNING *Mission H. Ghost* i. 3 The Holy Ghost, the Lord and Life-Giver.

So **life-giving** *sb.* and *a.*

1561 DAUS tr. *Bullinger on Apoc.* (1573) 133b, This creation and lifegiving, is not communicated to others. **1596** SPENSER *Hymn Hon. Love* 65 Heavens life-giving fyre. **1667** MILTON *P.L.* IV. 199 The vertue..Of that life-giving Plant. *a* **1761** LAW *Comf. Weary Pilgr.* (1809) 31 The life-giving power of his holy presence in our souls. **1855** KINGSLEY *Glaucus* (1878) 201 The life-giving oxygen of the air. **1899** E. G. JONES *Ascent through Christ* II. iii. 295 All life-giving is costly.

ˈlife-guard. [Perh. suggested by Du. *lijfgarde* (obs.), G. *leibgarde* (in both of which, however, the first element = 'body').]

1. a. A body-guard of soldiers; now *pl.* (written *Life Guards*), in the British army, two regiments of cavalry, forming, together with the Royal Horse Guards, the household cavalry.

1648 *Declar. Commons, Reb. Ireland* 63 Most of the King's life-guard are Irish. **1648** *Hamilton Papers* (Camden) 161 One of Sir Tho. Fairefax lief-guard. **1650** FULLER *Pisgah* II. x. 217 The Cherethites were a kind of lifegard to King David. **1702** *Lond. Gaz.* No. 3822/3 A stronger Party of French Horse, drawn out of their Life-Guard. **1828** SCOTT *F.M. Perth* x, A thousand horse mount with him as his daily lifeguard. **1849** ALB. SMITH *Pottleton Leg.* xxiv. 244 He had been passing the evening with an officer—one of the Life-guards Blue. **1884** *Regul. & Ord. Army* 9 Her Majesty's Regiments of Life Guards, and the Royal Regiment of Horse Guards, have the Precedence of all other Corps whatever.

b. *attrib.*, as † *life-guard oath*; **life-guard-man**, a member of a life-guard; also *Life Guardsman*, a soldier belonging to the Life Guards.

1662 JESSEY *Mirab. Ann. Secundus* 84 The biggest life-guard oaths. **1681-2** WOOD *Life* 12 Feb., Three men habited like life-guard men. **1771** SMOLLETT *Humph. Cl.* 23 June, I am resolved to make you my life-guard-man on the highway. **1840** DICKENS *Barn. Rudge* i, His large boots resembled..those worn by our Life Guardsmen at the present day. **1877** MRS. FORRESTER *Mignon* I. 11 You are big enough for a Life Guardsman!

2. The guard or protection of a person's life; a protecting agent or influence. ? *Obs.*

1648 SANDERSON *Serm.* II. 226 Our spirits within us, which should be as our life-guard to secure us against all attempts from without. **1652** S. PATRICK *Funeral Serm.* in *J. Smith's Sel. Disc.* 531 Good men are the lifeguard of the world. **1683** TRYON *Way to Health* iii. (1697) 423 Modesty, the Life-guard of Chastity. *a* **1711** KEN *Hymnotheo* Poet. Wks. 1721 III. 317 All the Heav'nly Host your Life-guard are. **1800** WEEMS *Washington* xiv. (1877) 208 This noble quality was the life-guard of his reason.

3. A device attached to the front of a locomotive for sweeping small obstructions from the track.

1864 *Morn. Star* 9 Sept., Had not the life-guard.. protected the wheels of the engine as it did the train would ..have been thrown off the line.

4. orig. *U.S.* A person employed to watch against accidents to bathers.

1896 HOWELLS *Impressions & Exp.* 217, I came out almost before the life-guard could get ready to throw me a life-preserver. *Ibid.* 223 The life-guard of the bathing-beach. **1921** *Daily Tel.* 29 Aug. 9/6 They were sustained by this means until the life guards arrived to take the women ashore. **1933** *Boy's Mag.* XLVII. 122/1 When a party bathe, one or two of the best swimmers should be posted as life-guards. **1974** HAWKEY & BINGHAM *Wild Card* xiii. 119 A guy who's drowning..who, if he's not subdued, will take the lifeguard down with him.

Hence † **life-guard** *v. trans.*, to protect as a life-guard; to preserve, safeguard.

1690 *Mor. Ess. & Disc.* xii. 209 'Tis not a Man's great Parts..can Life-guard him from Censure, which is a-kin to Death.

† **life-holy,** *a.* Of holy life. Hence † **life-holiness.**

c **1200** *Trin. Coll. Hom.* 133 Þe lif holie prest zacharie. *a* **1225** *Ancr. R.* 142 Þet..heo holden hire up mid hore lif holinesse. *Ibid.* 346 To hire owune schrift feder, oðer to summe oðre lif-holie monne. *a* **1240** *Lofsong* in *Cott. Hom.* 207 His ariste arere me in lif holinesse. **1393** LANGL. *P. Pl.* C. x. 195 Lyf-holy as eremites. *Ibid.* VI. 80 Lyf-holynesse and loue han ben longe hennes. *c* **1440** *Promp. Parv.* 303/2 Lyyf holy, *devotus, sanctus.*

† **life-honey, live-honey.** *Obs.* (See quots. 1609, 1729.)

c **1450** *ME. Med. Bk.* (Heinrich) 111 Tak halue apynt of lyf hony. **1584** COGAN *Haven Health* ccxxxiii. 234 Let it boyle vntill it come to the thicknesse of Liue Honie. **1601** HOLLAND *Pliny* I. 317 Such..as..will not run like life-hony. **1609** C. BUTLER *Fem. Mon.* vi. §27 The other [hony] so soft that it will runne, which therefore is called liue-hony. **1729** *Evelyn's Pomona* Gen. Advt. 96 Live-Honey that which drops freely out of the Combs.

† **ˈlifehood, ˈlivehood.** *Obs.* [f. LIFE *sb.* + -HOOD.] Means of maintaining life, livelihood, sustenance.

c **1440** *Promp. Parv.* 308/2 Lyvelode, or lyfhode (*K.* liyflode), *victus.* **1664** *N. Riding Rec.* VI. 76 If the said inhabitants shall provide for a sufficient lifehood for the said children.

life-in-death. A phantom state, a condition of being or seeming to be neither alive nor dead; something having the form or appearance of the supernatural, an apparition, a spectre. Also, = *death-in-life* s.v. DEATH *sb.* 2.

1817 COLERIDGE *Anc. Mar.* in *Sibylline Leaves* 14 Her skin was as white as leprosy, The Night-Mair Life-in-Death was she, Who thicks man's blood with cold. **1901** *Daily Chron.*

27 Dec. 3/1 They lie in a sort of life-in-death until the touch of a mighty hand grants them their full development. **1904** *Ibid.* 22 Sept. 3/4 In a life-in-death existence she still languishes as an almost forgotten link with the past of forty years ago. **1925** R. W. KETTON-CREMER in *Oxf. Poetry* 22 From something not of earth, nor quite of Death—Some phantom Life-in-Death. **1932** W. B. YEATS *Words for Music* i, I hail the Superhuman; I call it Death-in-Life and Life-in-Death.

lifekins: see LIFE *sb.* 3 d.

lifeless (ˈlaɪflɪs), *a.* Also 5–6 **lyveles**, 6–8 **liveles**, **-less(e**. [OE. *lífléas*, f. *líf* LIFE *sb.* + *-léas* -LESS.] Having no life.

1. That has ceased to live; deprived of life; dead.

c **1000** ÆLFRIC *Gen.* xx. 7 þu bist dead for-raðe, and þa þe þe to lociað beoð liflease eac. *a* **1225** *Leg. Kath.* 1045 He.. mid his worde awahte þe liflese liches to lif. *c* **1400** *Destr. Troy* 8668 The Myrmaidons.. Bere hym.. to his big tent, There left hym as lyueles. *c* **1586** C'TESS PEMBROKE *Ps.* LXXIX. ii, The livelesse carcasses of those That liv'd thy servants, serve the crowes. **1650** W. SAUNDERSON *Aul. Coquin.* 19 He fear'd, that within few daies the Laird would be landlesse and livelesse. **1791** COWPER *Iliad* XVII. 286 He many a lifeless Trojan heap'd On slain Patroclus. **1841** LONGF. *Excelsior* ix, There in the twilight cold and grey, Lifeless, but beautiful, he lay. **1851** RUSKIN *Stones Ven.* (1874) I. App. 351 A blank level of lifeless grass.

Proverb. **1546** J. HEYWOOD *Prov.* (1867) 29 He is liueles, that is faultes. **1629** GAULE *Holy Madn.* 309.

b. *hyperbolically.* Said, e.g., of a person in a swoon; insensible, senseless.

1651 CHARLETON *Ephes. & Cimm. Matrons* II. (1668) 67 Consuming themselves in greedy looks, leave their bodies faint and liveless. **1671** H. M. tr. *Erasm. Colloq.* 517 If the Scorpion by chance creep by the herb Wolfsbane, it grows pale and liveless. **1795** MRS. PARSONS *Myst. Warning* I. iii. 51 His senses fled, and he fell extended on the floor. Happily a servant was passing.. and beheld the lifeless body... He was soon restored to his senses. **1826** DISRAELI *Viv. Grey* III. vi, Mrs. Felix Lorraine sank lifeless into his arms.

2. Not endowed with or possessing life; inanimate.

c **1000** ÆLFRIC *Hom.* II. 574 Fela templa arærdon and mid .. lifleasum anlicnyssum afyldon. **1553** GRIMALDE *Cicero's Offices* II. (1558) 79 What so in things liueless and what so in the use.. of beastes is done profitablie to man's life. **1600** SHAKS. *A. Y. L.* I. ii. 263 That which here stands vp Is but a quintine, a mere liuelesse blocke. **1612** HEYWOOD *Apol. Actors* I. 29 To.. stande in his place like a livelesse image. **1686** J. SCOTT *Chr. Life* (1747) III. 624 They conjur'd their Demons into their consecrated Images, and made the liveless Stocks to move and speak. **1851** ROBERTSON *Serm.* Ser. IV. x. (1876) 124 A collection of lifeless forces. **1887** BOWEN *Virg. Æneid* I. 464 Then on the lifeless painting he feeds his heart to the fill.

3. Wanting vital quality; destitute of animation, vigour, or activity. Also of food: containing no 'life' or nourishment.

a **1225** *Leg. Kath.* 896 þe wrenchfule feont.. weorp ham ut sone of paraises selhðen into þis liflese lif. *a* **1420** HOCCLEVE *De Reg. Princ.* 3894 Aftir moot he rowne with a pilwe His lyfles resouns þere to despende. **1561** DAUS tr. *Bullinger on Apoc.* (1573) 170 b, For Vespasian.. did soone releeve the worlde that had long beene liuelesse and forlorne. **1586** MARLOWE *1st Pt. Tamburl.* III. ii, Ceaseless and disconsolate conceits Which dye my looks so liveless as they are. **1633** BP. HALL *Hard Texts, N.T.* 194 Feeding on hearbs and rootes, and such other liveless nourishment. **1642** *View Print. Bk. int. Observat.* 20 They are livelesse conventions without all vertue and power. **1849** RUSKIN *Sev. Lamps* v. xxi. (1880) 310 The effect of the whole, as compared with the same design cut by a machine or a lifeless hand. **1890** *Daily News* 6 Dec. 2/5 This market is lagging again... Flax lifeless.

4. Devoid of life or living beings.

1728–46 THOMSON *Summer* 748 A wild expanse of lifeless sand and sky. **1762–71** H. WALPOLE *Vertue's Anecd. Paint.* IV. vii. 124 Statues furnished the lifeless spot with mimic representations of the excluded sons of men. **1879** BROWNING *Pheidippides* 53 Treeless, herbless, lifeless mountain.

Hence ˈ**lifelessly** *adv.*, ˈ**lifelessness**.

1727 BAILEY vol. II, *Lifeleness* [sic]. **1814** BYRON *Corsair* III. xx, Each extended tress Long—fair—but spread in utter lifelessness. **1833** L. RITCHIE *Wand. by Loire* 7 Antique-looking vessels, whose white sails hang in utter lifelessness from the mast. **1856** OLMSTED *Slave States* 59 A few negro children.. posed as lifelessly as if they were really figures 'carved in ebony'. **1896** *Academy* 5 Dec. 485/2 [His] style is lifelessly correct and drab with Latinisms.

life-like, lifelike (ˈlaɪflaɪk), *a.*

1. Likely to live. Only in *phrase*. Cf. ALIVE-LIKE.

1613 J. DAY *Diall* (1614) 321 But what neede we take so long a Day as to see what they will say on their Death-beds, we shall heare some of them confesse it somewhat sooner, even while they are aliue, and liue-like. **1881** MISS YONGE *Lads & Lasses Langley* ii. 96 Here, mother.. I'm living and lifelike, thank God.

2. Like or resembling life; exactly like a living original or something in real life.

1725 POPE *Odyss.* IV. 1047 Minerva, life-like on embody'd air, Impressed the form of Iphthima the fair. **1836** H. ROGERS *J. Howe* i. (1863) 15 The life-like forms of the painter or the sculptor. **1875** JOWETT *Plato* (ed. 2) III. 188 As we read this lifelike fiction.

3. as *adv.* With animation or liveliness.

1839 BAILEY *Festus* xx. (1848) 237 He went Life-like through all things.

Hence ˈ**lifelikeness**.

1857 GLADSTONE in *Oxford Ess.* 10 This freshness and genuineness, this life-likeness, are almost wholly wanting. **1862** R. H. PATTERSON *Ess. Hist. & Art* 87 In all the distinctness of objective reality—with all the life-likeness of flesh and blood. **1884** SWINBURNE in *19th Cent.* May 788 The piteous and perfect lifelikeness of these magnificent lines every heart.. may recognize.

lifelikins, lifelings: see LIFE *sb.* 3 d.

ˈ**life-line.** [f. LIFE *sb.* + LINE *sb.*[2]] **1. a.** A line or rope which is intended to be instrumental in saving life, such as the rope attached to a life-buoy, or used by firemen. **b.** A diver's signalling line.

1700 in *N. & Q.* (1941) 12 July 22/2 Lyfline. **1790** *Gentl. Mag.* LX. in *N. & Q.* (1962) Jan. 17/1 A line.. which was called his *Life-line*, as it was found.. to have been serviceable in preserving ships and men. **1794** *Rigging & Seamanship* I. 169 *Life-lines*, for the preservation of the seamen. **1840** R. H. DANA *Bef. Mast* Gloss., *Life-lines*, ropes carried along yards, etc., for men to hold on by. **1877** *Encycl. Brit.* VII. 297/2, *e* is the 'life' or 'signal' line, which is attached to the diver's waist, and by which he makes signals and is hauled to the surface. **1895** *Daily News* 2 Jan. 3/3 He observed a rocket, and informed the coastguard, who arrived with the lifelines. **1896** *Strand Mag.* XII. 351/1 As the strain of the air-pipe was downward, and that of the life-line upward, I concluded that the pipe must be fast below. **1904** *Daily Chron.* 26 Oct. 6/7 Fireman Herbert White lashed a branch hose to his body with a life-line. **1968** *Globe & Mail* (Toronto) 3 Feb. 11/4 Firemen.. used a life-line gun to reach the boat and Mr. MacAdam. **1975** *Times* 6 Jan. 4/4 Lifelines used on Mr Heath's ill-fated yacht.. were yesterday called sub-standard by the British Safety Council.

2. In *Palmistry*: a mark on the palm of the hand supposed to indicate one's length of life.

1890 L. COTTON *Palmistry* II. 36 If the head line is separated, at its departure, from the life line, it indicates great self-confidence. **1894** [see HEAD-LINE 5]. **1919** BEERBOHM *Seven Men* 154, I had seen in my own hand.. a clean break in the life-line. **1971** M. MCCARTHY *Birds of America* 312 He felt a sharp pain in.. his palm, the part bounded by his life line.

3. *fig.* **a.** The line of life: see LINE *sb.*[2] 1 g. **b.** An essential supply route, a line of communication, etc.

1860 HAWTHORNE *Transformation* II. xiii. 209 If there were one of those friends whose life-line was twisted with your own, I am enough of a fatalist to feel assured that [etc.]. **1891** E. S. UFFORD in I. D. Sankey *Gospel Hymns No. 6* 30 Throw out the Life-Line a-cross the dark wave, There is a brother whom some one should save. **1905** *Daily Chron.* 13 Feb. 3/1 Every man who has lived so long.. and kept the life-line so straight and true as Mr. Holyoake. **1936** *Lit. Digest* 17 Oct. 13c Cut what Britain calls her 'life line'. **1941** *Times* (Weekly ed.) 15 Oct. 8 The King spent Wednesday at Liverpool seeing what is being done to hold this end of the Atlantic lifeline. **1963** *Times Lit. Suppl.* 1 Mar. 149/1 Liberals who keep a life-line open between the actual world .. and the one they would like to see exist. **1970** *Daily Tel.* 7 Oct. 1/1 A £54-million 'lifeline' was thrown by the Government yesterday to the farming industry, which has been faced with having to cut back production because of rising costs. **1975** D. RAMSAY *Descent into Dark* ii. 60 Who the hell thinks about honour when her lifeline's being cut?

lifelod(e, obs. form of LIVELIHOOD.

lifelong (ˈlaɪflɒŋ), *sb. rare.* [Evolved from the advb. phrase 'all my (his, etc.) life long': see LONG *adv.*] The duration of a life; a lifetime.

a **1836** R. H. FROUDE *Mem.* (1849) 47 For the making of a single rich man, we make a thousand whose life-long is one flood-tide of misery. **1856** LEVER *Martins of Cro' M.* 119 A spot wherein a student might have passed a lifelong.

lifelong (ˈlaɪflɒŋ), *a.* [f. LIFE *sb.* + LONG.]

†**1.** = LIVELONG. *Obs. rare*[−1].

1757 MRS. GRIFFITH *Lett. Henry & Frances* (1767) I. 84, I wished for you.. in vain all night, the life-long night.

2. Lasting or continuing for a lifetime.

1855 *Ess. Intuitive Morals* 151 The glorious thirst after Knowledge never finds its life-long draught sweet enough. **1866** J. H. NEWMAN *Gerontius* §2 The history of that dreary, lifelong fray. **1875** JOWETT *Plato* (ed. 2) I. 267 Plato.. in his life-long effort to work out the great intellectual puzzle of his age.

3. as *adv.* During the whole length of life.

1875 LOWELL *Poem at Cambridge* (*Mass.*) *Centennial*, The boy feels deeper meanings thrill his ear, That tingling through his pulse life-long shall run.

lifemanship (ˈlaɪfmənʃɪp). [f. LIFE *sb.* + -MANSHIP.] Skill in getting the edge over, or acquiring an advantage over, another person or persons. So (as a back-formation) ˈ**lifeman**.

1950 S. POTTER (*title*) Some notes on lifemanship. *Ibid.* 14 Day by day our centres send out young men, yes and women too, to assess the lifemanship approach. *Ibid.*, The Lifeman is never caddish himself. **1952** *Granta* 29 Nov. 8/2 They are the men who thought Lifemanship was something to practise rather than detect. **1953** *Encounter* Oct. 62/2 'Phoney' and 'corney'.. are concepts, categories for criticising a whole school of bad 'lifemanship'. **1958** *Spectator* 29 Aug. 285/1 His narrative abounds in bashful lifemanship. **1959** *Times* 9 Apr. 15/3 You mean, don't you, that he was nearly the greatest European lifeman? **1964** *Discovery* Oct. 35/1 Lifemanship consists largely of a surreptitious and diplomatic control of what is ordinarily non-verbal and unconscious communication.

†**lifen**, *v. Obs. rare*[−1]. In 7 **lyfen**. [f. LIFE *sb.* + -EN[5].] *trans.* To make lifelike.

1602 MARSTON *Antonio's Rev.* II. v, And with such sighs, Laments, and acclamations lyfen it, As if [etc.].

†ˈ**lifeness.** *Obs. rare*[−1]. [irreg. f. LIFE *sb.* + -NESS.] Lifetime.

1534 LADY ELIZ. DACRES in Miss M. A. E. Wood *Lett. R. & Illustr. Ladies* (1852) II. 127 That the peace shall be concluded during the Princes lyfnes, and a year longer.

life-or-death, *a.* [See LIFE *sb.* 1 c.] = LIFE-AND-DEATH *a.*

1897 G. B. SHAW *Our Theatres in Nineties* (1932) III. 146 We should have had the ablest manager of the day driven by life-or-death necessity to extract from contemporary literature the proper food for the modern side of his talent. **1932** —— *Platform & Pulpit* (1962) 241 They will finally get rid of Parliament because they have a life-or-death pressure of necessity behind them. **1973** J. WAINWRIGHT *Touch of Malice* 134 The impression of life-or-death efficiency.

life-preserver.

1. One who preserves life.

1638 SIR T. HERBERT *Trav.* (ed. 2) 234 The Doctors are nam'd *Hackeems* (it may be radically from the Hebrew word *Hachajim*, that is, a life-preserver).

2. A life-buoy, life-belt, or other contrivance used in saving life at sea.

1804 *Naval Chron.* XII. 189 The plan of the 'Life Preserver' here mentioned is borrowed from that of Commissary Bosquet. **1825** HOOD *Ode to Mr. Dymoke*, Nor would even the best of his earthly inventions, 'Life preservers', have floated him out of this gore. **1850** SCORESBY *Cheever's Whalem. Adv.* ii. (1859) 18 Taking.. a life-preserver, I ventured into one of the little canoes.

3. A stick or bludgeon loaded with lead, intended for self-defence. Often referred to as a frequent weapon of burglars.

1837 *Ann. Reg.* 11 The prisoner was given in charge to the police, a life-preserver having been found upon him. **1851** *Illustr. Catal. Gt. Exhib.* 1056 Life-preservers, of whale-bone and cane, covered with leather. **1887** *Spectator* 26 Feb. 285/1 When a burglar is armed with a bludgeon or a life-preserver.

4. *transf.* and *fig.*

1851 *London at Table* i. 8 The 'life preserver', as the half-pint bottle has been termed. **1852** GEO. ELIOT *Let.* 27 Mar. (1954) II. 15 Your cordial assurance.. is one of those pleasant things—those life-preservers—which relenting destiny sends me now and then to buoy me up. **1941** J. SMILEY *Hash House Lingo* 35 *Life preservers*, doughnuts. **1953** *Manch. Guardian Weekly* 14 May 11 Chambers admits that.. he was busy preparing a 'life preserver' in the form of stolen documents he could use later to silence anyone who might rat on him.

lifer (ˈlaɪfə(r)). *slang.* [f. LIFE *sb.* + -ER[1].]

1. One sentenced to penal servitude (or earlier, transportation) for life.

1830 R. DAWSON *Pres. State Australia* 201 Some were seven years' men, and others were what they call 'lifers'. **1838** DICKENS *O. Twist* xliii, 'They'll make the Artful nothing less than a lifer'. **1872** MISS BRADDON *To the bitter End* III. 266 'I'm a lifer', said Richard grimly.

2. A sentence for life.

1832 *Fraser's Mag.* V. 530 Is it not a shame to give me a lifer, and they only a month each? **1886** BESANT *Childr. Gibeon* II. xi, He got five-and-twenty years, which Joe said was as good as a lifer.

3. One who leads a life of a specified character. Properly the second element of a compound.

1906 *Daily Chron.* 11 May 6/4 The Gospel did not commend itself to the simple lifers of the country-side, but spread like wildfire among the complex lifers of the Greek cities.

4. A life-peer.

1959 *Economist* 31 Jan. 397/1 An infusion of 'lifers'' half blue blood. **1969** *Sunday Tel.* 30 Mar. 2/8, I will not.. turn out for Lifers.

liferent (ˈlaɪfrɛnt). *Sc. Law.* Also 5 **lifrent**, 6 **lyf(e)rent, lyverent**, 7 **liffrent**. A rent which one is entitled to receive for life, usually for support; a right to use and enjoy property during one's life.

1491 *Sc. Acts Jas. IV* (1814) II. 225/1 Landis gevin in coniunctfeftment or lifrent. **1535** *Ibid.* 344/2 þe wardatouris of sik landis [*marg. add.* ladyis of coniunct fee or lyfrent]. **1535** Q. MARGARET in *St. Papers Hen. VIII* (1836) V. 22 *note*, Ye maist partie of oure landis and lyverent lyis apoune ye Bordouris of Ingland. **1591** *Charter* in A. McKay *Hist. Kilmarnock* (ed. 4) 359 We have given.. to our beloved cousin, Thomas, Lord Boyd, in free-holding, or life-rent [etc.]. **1754** ERSKINE *Princ. Sc. Law* (1809) 510 If the person prosecuted for this crime shall be denounced for not appearing, his liferent.. falls upon the denunciation. **1832** AUSTIN *Jurispr.* (1879) II. l. 858 Like the usufruct of the old jus civile liferent is personal to the liferenter. **1837** LOCKHART *Scott* 6 Feb. an. 1826 They would have had a right to his liferent at Abbotsford among other things.

b. *attrib.* and *Comb.*, as ***liferent-infeftment, right, tack***; **liferent-escheat** (see ESCHEAT 1 b).

1681 *Sc. Act* in *Lond. Gaz.* No. 1649/3 They shall be.. punished with the loss of their Moveables and *liferent Escheat. **1754** ERSKINE *Princ. Sc. Law* (1809) 173 A *liferent-infeftment.. or a liferent-tack, when assigned falls not under the assignee's liferent-escheat, but his single. **1842** J. AITON *Domest. Econ.* (1857) 156 A minister had only a *liferent right to his glebe. **1637–50** ROW *Hist. Kirk* (1842) 218 That the licence granted to beneficed persons to sett tacks be restrained either to a *liferent tack, or to a nineteen yeare tack allanerlie.

Hence **life-rented** *a.*, charged with a liferent.

1720 *Lond. Gaz.* No. 5890/3 Part of Calder, not Life-rented.

life-rent, *v.* [f. the sb.] *trans.* To assign in liferent; to use and enjoy property during one's life.

1700 *Edin. Gaz.* 2–5 Sept., The Lands of Hiltoun.. presently Life-rented by the Lady Rosyth, are to be Set in

Tack by way of publick Roup. **1819** SCOTT *Let.* 25 Nov. (1934) VI. 28 My wife's brother has left my children a considerable fortune which is at present life-rented by his lady. **1890** J. RANKINE *Erskine's Princ. Law Scot.* (ed. 18) 218 And money may be liferented, the interest..being due to the liferenter. **1937** *St. Andrews Citizen* 6 Mar. 2 The residue of his estate be life-rented to his sister.

liferenter ('laɪfˌrɛntə(r)). *Sc.* [f. LIFERENT + -ER[1].] A person who is entitled to or enjoys a liferent.

1594 *Sc. Acts Jas. VI* (1816) IV. 73/1 The heretouris and lyfrentaris of landis w[th]in townis and suburbis þeroff. **1599** JAS. I *Βασιλ. Δωρον* (1603) 83 Kingdomes are euer at God's disposition, and in that case we are but liue-rentars. **1685** *Sc. Proclam.* in *Lond. Gaz.* No. 2032/2 All the Heretors, Liferenters, Feuars and Wodsetters in the Shires of Air [etc.]. **1790** BURKE *Fr. Rev.* Wks. V. 181 The temporary possessors and life-renters in it. **1832** AUSTIN *Jurispr.* (1879) II. l. 858 Liferent is personal to the liferenter. **1842** J. AITON *Domest. Econ.* (1857) 124 A minister is but a liferenter.

So **liferentrix**, a woman who enjoys a liferent.

1692 *Inv.* in *Scot. N. & Q.* (1900) Dec. 92/1 Issobel Hackat..lyverentrix thereof. **1816** SCOTT *Old Mort.* ii, Lady Margaret Bellenden liferentrix of the Barony of Tillietudlem. **1825** *Law Reports* 9 App. Cases 329/2 The fee vested..to Anne Niblie, for her own interest, and in her or the liferentrix for behoof of the children *nasrituri*.

'life-saver. [See LIFE *sb.* 16b.] **1.** Something that may save one's life.

1883 *Daily News* 5 July 3/1 Minor life-savers, such as mattresses, deck furniture, belts, dresses, buoys, &c. **1944** *Living off Land* v. 112 Failure to take a life-saver [*sc.* quinine or atebrine] on account of the bitter taste sounds childish yet there are such childish persons.

2. A person assigned to watch against accidents to bathers (at a beach resort, etc.). orig. *U.S.* (The customary term in Australia and N.Z.).

1887 *Courier-Jrnl.* (Louisville, Kentucky) 10 Feb. 8/3 The Police and the Life-Savers still prying into the mystery of Smyser's Pond. **1903** *Boston Even. Transcript* 20 Aug., According to a decision of the Election Commissioners a City Point life saver cannot vote. **1931** V. PALMER *Separate Lives* 99 'It's the life-savers!' he shouted. 'They're practising! Come on.' **1934** T. WOOD *Cobbers* 169 You bask in the sun and watch the life-savers, picked volunteers. **1958** *Observer* 16 Nov. 27/2 He is a handsome cove, in the Australian surf life-saver tradition. **1963** V. B. CRANLEY *27,000 Miles through Austral.* xi. 78 A new life-boat donated to the local surf life-savers. Their performance of swimming and rescue work was really outstanding. **1967** C. O. SKINNER *Madame Sarah* ix. 176 Madame Sarah was presented with a Life Saver's certificate. **1968** W. WARWICK *Surfriding in N.Z.* 1 Since life-saving was practised in and around the sea, it was only natural that lifesavers were the first to try surfriding.

3. *fig.* Some quality, characteristic, or circumstance that helps a person to endure adversity.

1909 *N.Y. Herald* in *Daily Chron.* 8 Mar. 5/2 Both have that great life-saver for men who have to endure periods of stress and storm—a sense of humour. **1934** F. SCOTT FITZGERALD *Let.* 18 Dec. (1964) 258 Again thanks for the money. It was a life-saver. **1973** C. EGLETON *Seven Days to Killing* ix. 101 He spotted a Falk street plan of Paris. It cost him six francs but it proved to be a life-saver.

'life-saving, *a.* [See LIFE *sb.* 16b.] Of or pertaining to the saving of life from drowning, shipwreck, etc. Hence ***life-saving station***, a coastal or beach building with life-saving equipment and life-savers. Also as *vbl. sb.*, the saving of life (from drowning).

1858 *Statutes at Large U.S.A.* XI. 320 Twenty-eight life-saving stations on the coast of New Jersey. **1877** *Harper's Mag.* Dec. 50/2 The life-saving car is passing from the vessel to the shore with living freight. *Ibid.*, The life-saving station. **1903** *N.Y. Times* 25 Sept. 14 The plight of the sloop had been signalled at the life-saving station at Sandy Hook. **1906** *Daily Colonist* (Victoria, B.C.) 30 Jan. 4/1 There should be somewhere within reach adequate life-saving stations. **1915** W. E. DOMMETT *Submarine Vessels* vii. 80 (*caption*) Bluejacket wearing life-saving helmet. **1931** V. PALMER *Separate Lives* 101 Dot and Peter were playing life-saving in the sand: Dot, lying flat on her back with her frock rucked up over her knees, and Peter restoring circulation the way he had seen the men do. **1932** N. PALMER *Talking it Over* 139 The same short stretch of surf..usually marked off short to give the life-saving patrol a chance of handling the crowd. **1933** *Boys' Mag.* XLVII. 122/1 Learn methods of life-saving as soon as possible. **1967** C. O. SKINNER *Madame Sarah* ix. 175 Then came a delegation from the Life-Saving Society of Havre. **1973** A. MANN *Tiara* ii. 14 McCarthy had won prizes for swimming and life-saving.

Hence (as a back-formation) **'life-save** *v. trans.*, to rescue from death by drowning; to act towards as a life-saver. Also *intr.*

1938 'J. BELL' *Port of London Murders* x. 180 You mind what you're about. I'm not going to life-save you a second time. **1968** P. DICKINSON *Weathermonger* i. 11 Geoffrey thought he might possibly be able to swim round to the harbour... But he couldn't do it if he had to lifesave Sally all the way. **1973** 'M. HEBDEN' *Dark Side of Island* iii. 32 Can you life-save?.. Are you a good swimmer?

life-size, *a.* (*sb.*) **A.** *adj.* Of the size of life; (of a picture or statue) equal in size to the original.

1841 *Penny Cycl.* XXI. 139/1 The figures are life-size. **1865** J. H. INGRAHAM *Pillar of Fire* (1872) 340 Here..is a life-size image of Apis, when he was a calf. **1878** BROWNING *Poets of Croisic* Epil. xiii, So he made himself a statue: Marble stood, life-size. **1891** T. HARDY *Tess* (1900) 81/1 Two life-size portraits on panels.

B. as *sb.* The size of life; a life-size portrait or statue. Also *fig.*

1850 *Art Jrnl.* 1 Mar. 95/2 A figure of life-size. **1864** *Illustr. London News* 16 July 55/1 Certain technical shortcomings are revealed by this first attempt by Mr. Mount in the life-size. **1885** W. M. ROSSETTI in *Encycl. Brit.* XVIII. 681/2 Cato as the emblem of wisdom, and (in life-size) numerous figures of classic worthies, prophets, and sibyls. **1959** *Spectator* 14 Aug. 181/2 This reduces M. Debré from the more-than-lifesize proper to all prime ministers..to more normal dimensions.

life-sized, *a.* [LIFE *sb.* 16c.] = LIFE-SIZE *a.*

1847 *Art Union* 1 May 149/2 A life-sized half-length figure. *Ibid.* 1 June 203/2 A life-sized cartoon. **1879** CLEMENT & HUTTON *Artists 19th Cent.* I. 26 'The Birds of America'..was completed in 1839.., containing 448 plates, life-sized and colored. **1898** H. A. GUERBER *Story of Greeks* xxix. 69 The temple and grove [at Olympia] were..adorned, with a great many statues representing the other gods and all the prize-winners, for it was customary to place a life-sized statue of each of them in this beautiful place. **1969** *Harper's Mag.* Feb. 106 Stuffed life-sized dolls drop to the floor of the stage.

lifesome ('laɪfsəm), *a.* Also 6 livesome. [f. LIFE *sb.* + -SOME.]

†**1.** Fraught with life. *Obs.*

1583 T. WATSON *Centurie of Loue* v, O liuesome death, O sweete and pleasant ill.

2. Full of life or animation, lively.

1688 R. HOLME *Armoury* II. 414/1 Joy is depicted with a lifsome merry aspect. **1797–1809** COLERIDGE *Three Graves* III. xii, I wish for your sake I could be More lifesome and more gay. *a* **1849** H. COLERIDGE *Ess.* (1851) II. 11 The speeches of Momus..are very witty and lifesome.

Hence **'lifesomely** *adv.*, **'lifesomeness.**

1674 N. FAIRFAX *Bulk & Selv.* 111 A..plastick spring of lifesomness or animality. **1845** SARA COLERIDGE *Mem. & Lett.* I. 321 What he does see clearly he expresses with great energy and lifesomeness. **1848** —— in *Q. Rev.* Mar. 430 His latest poems..are not so lifesomely evolved from a central idea as those of his morning and noon-day.

lifest, obs. superl. of LIEF *a.*

'life-style. [f. LIFE *sb.* + STYLE *sb.* 24.] **a.** A term originally used by Alfred Adler (1870–1937) to denote a person's basic character as established early in childhood which governs his reactions and behaviour. **b.** *gen.* A way or style of living.

1929 A. ADLER *Probl. Neurosis* [i. 7 The style of life is founded in the first four or five years of childhood.] *Ibid.* 8 This fragment of memory records the two typical motives of the main life-style. **1939** H. ORGLER *Alfred Adler* i. 35 We have only really understood an individual when we have revealed the unitary life-style behind this ostensible duplicity. **1946** 'G. ORWELL' *Crit. Ess.* 137 True to his life style, Koestler was..promptly arrested and interned by the Daladier Government. **1947** M. MCLUHAN in *Sewanee Rev.* LV. 11. 80 While ostensibly setting about the freeing of the slaves, they became enslaved, and found in the wailing self-pity and crooning of the Negro the substitute for any life-style of their own. **1950** COLE & BRUCE *Educational Psychol.* i. 2 The teacher is confronted with such unique individuals, already shaped into recognizable life styles. **1952** M. MACKENZIE *Contrast Psychol.* p. iii, The Freudian believes that the unconscious conflict, underlying an Anxiety State, springs from frustrated 'sexuality'; the Adlerian from an obstructed 'life style'. **1961** *Guardian* 22 Mar. 10/5 The mass-media..continually tell their audience what life-styles are 'modern' and 'smart'. **1972** *Jrnl. Social Psychol.* LXXXVI. 121 When a man's life style is incongruent with the demands of a task he must perform he will experience stress. **1972** M. MEAD *Blackberry Winter* vii. 82 But in other ways those years in Bucks County gave me a view of a much earlier life-style, one that corresponded with my grandmother's girlhood. **1973** T. TOBIN in Ade *Lett.* 7 His commercial successes in the theater enabled him to become financially independent, and Ade chose the lifestyle with which he was most comfortable. **1973** *Times* 11 Apr. 18/4 (*heading*) Council of churches want freedom for students to create their own life-styles.

lifetenant, -aunt, obs. ff. LIEUTENANT.

lifetime ('laɪftaɪm). Forms: see LIFE and TIME.

1. The time that one's life continues, duration of life. Also *attrib.* or as *adj.*, for the duration of a life, during one's life, while one is alive. Phrases: ***all in a*** (or ***one's***) ***lifetime***, implying resignation to whatever happens; ***of a lifetime***, implying that an event, situation, or thing will never be equalled or repeated.

c **1220** *Bestiary* 696 Wu laȝelike ȝe [ðe turtre] holdeð luue al hire lif time. *c* **1350** *Will. Palerne* 999, I graunt him greþli ..mi loue for euer al mi lif time. **1480** CAXTON *Chron. Eng.* ccxxxii. 251 Alle these forsayd thynges trewelych for to kepe ..alle his lyf time. **1553** EDEN *Treat. Newe Ind.* (Arb.) 5 In hys lyfe tyme by hys owne marcial affayres. **1642** tr. *Perkins' Prof. Bk.* viii. §571. 248 Cause them to be given or delivered unto them in their live times. **1732** LEDIARD *Sethos* II. VII. 80 Unless they..restore..them to their favour in their life-time. **1849** N. KINGSLEY *Diary* (1914) 44 My consolation is that it is all in my lifetime and thus make myself quite contented. *Ibid.* 52 This must count as 'all in my lifetime'. **1875** JOWETT *Plato* (ed. 2) III. 183 A lifetime might be passed happily in such pursuits. **1898** F. P. DUNNE *Mr. Dooley in Peace & War* 187 Well, tubby sure, 'tis thryin' to be dhrivin' a coal wagon or a sthreet-car; but 'tis all in a lifetime. **1929** WODEHOUSE *Mr. Mulliner Speaking* vii. 222 But let me tell you, my lad, that you're throwing away the laugh of a lifetime. *Ibid.* ix. 314 It must be a cocktail. The cocktail of a lifetime. **1961** —— *Ice in Bedroom* xxiii. 188 You take one step in its direction and you're going to get the headache of a lifetime. **1962** *Amer. Speech* XXXVII. 16 New England did contribute the largest number of white lifetime migrants to the state of New York. **1974** *Country Life* 2 May 1065/2 The gifts tax..would be a tax on lifetime gifts.

2. = LIFE *sb.* 8c.

1858 HAWTHORNE *Fr. & It. Jrnls.* I. 167 Durable for whatever may be the lifetime of the world. **1920** *Discovery* Apr. 111/1 The helium now found in a mineral can be only a fraction..of the total amount which has been generated within it, and which alone could give a true estimate of its life-time. **1939** *Physical Rev.* LV. 506/1 The lifetime for a mesotron at rest has been estimated..to be of the order 2–4 × 10⁻⁶ sec. **1950** *Ibid.* LXXVII. 153/1 (*heading*) Lifetimes of mercury and potassium atoms in excited states. **1965** H. I. ANSOFF *Corporate Strategy* (1968) ii. 24 If it turns out that the lifetime of some projects exceeds the budget period, the period is extended for purpose of analysis. **1968** [see LIFE *sb.* 8c]. **1968** *Times* 29 Nov. 13/3 The running-down rate of the pulsar implies that it has a lifetime of the same order as the Crab nebula. **1972** *Sci. Amer.* May 50/1 The Viking spacecraft will consist of an orbiter and a lander, each with a lifetime of many months. **1974** *Daily Tel.* 17 Apr. 17/4 There is no possibility of action on the lines of the group's proposals in the lifetime of the present Parliament.

life-timer. [f. LIFETIME.] One serving a life-sentence. (In quot. *fig.*)

1926 J. BLACK *You can't Win* v. 48 Life-timers of society, they were slowly sinking without a straw to grasp at.

'lifeward, *adv.* [See -WARD.] In the direction of life, towards life.

1865 *Daily Tel.* 7 Nov. 8/1 A chance lifeward this way, deathward that. **1897** H. DRUMMOND *Ideal Life* 258 We want a principle life-ward as well as God-ward.

'life-way. orig. *N. Amer.* [f. LIFE *sb.* + WAY *sb.*[1]] Way or manner of life.

1961 in WEBSTER. **1969** *Beaver* (Winnipeg) Spring 62/2 Wouldn't it be expected to contribute notably to an interpretation of their [*sc.* Eskimos'] life-ways in art? **1973** J. M. ANDERSON *Structural Aspects of Language Change* 203 Especially in regard to human lifeways and institutions, [etc.]. **1975** *Nature* 22 May 280/2 He [*sc.* Professor John Bowker (University of Lancaster)] drew attention to the extent to which religions function as bounded systems of information process, in which resources are made available to human beings for the construction of a life-way from birth to death.

lifey ('laɪfɪ), *a.* Also 5 livi, lyfy, 9 lifie. [f. LIFE *sb.* + -Y.] †**a.** Characteristic of or belonging to life (*obs.*). **b.** Lively, spirited.

c **1400** *Lanfranc's Cirurg.* 119 Not oonly animal vertues.. ben I-chaungid, also naturel & liui vertues [*Add. MS.* lyfy]. **1741** RICHARDSON *Pamela* (1824) I. xxxix. 359 A tenderness ..that..runs through one's heart, in the same lifey current. **1808–25** JAMIESON, *Lifey*, lively, spirited. **1819** W. TENNANT *Papistry Storm'd* (1827) 64 There never march'd for open weir A troop sae lifey and sae jolly. **1910** *Chambers's Jrnl.* Nov. 706/2 Those [sapphires] found in Ceylon, which are lighter in colour and 'lifier' than any of the others.

liff(e, obs. forms of LIEF, LIFE, LIVE.

liffleod, obs. form of LIVELIHOOD.

liffrent, obs. form of LIFERENT.

lifful, variant of LEEFUL; obs. f. LIFEFUL *a.*

liffyr, Sc. form of LIVER *sb.*[1]

liflod(e, obs. form of LIVELIHOOD.

lift (lɪft), *sb.*[1] *Obs.* exc. *Sc.* and *poet.* Forms: 1 lyft, 2–3 luft(e (*ü*), 3 leoft, 4 lefte, lifte, lijft, 5–6 lyft, 4– lift. [OE. *lyft* masc., neut., fem., corresponds to OS., OHG., MHG. *luft* masc., fem. (Du. *lucht*, G. *luft* fem.), ON. *lopt* neut. (see LOFT), Goth. *luftus* masc., fem.] The sky, upper regions; †in early use also, the air, atmosphere. Also *pl.*, the (seven) heavens.

Beowulf 2832 Se widfloȝa..nalles æfter lyfte lacende hwearf. *c* **1000** *Sax. Leechd.* II. 146 Romane him..worhton eorþ hus for þære lyfte wylme & æternesse. *c* **1175** *Lamb. Hom.* 79 Of þe uisces iþe wetere and fuȝeles iþe lufte. *c* **1205** LAY. 25585 Com an wunderlic deor, æst in þan leofte [*c* **1275** in þan lufte]. *a* **1225** *Leg. Kath.* 2124 Ich schal..beon toluken þi flesch þe fuheles of þe lufte. **1297** R. GLOUC. (Rolls) 5685 Þo hurde he..angles singe..Vpe in þe luft a murye song. *a* **1300** *Cursor M.* 10479 Sco lift hir hend vn-to þe lift And þus to prai sco gaf a scift. *Ibid.* 12871 Als he loked vp til heuen Open he sagh þe liftes seuen. **1340** HAMPOLE *Pr. Consc.* 1444 Now se we þe lyfte clere and faire. *a* **1375** *Sc. Leg. Saints* xxviii. (*Margaret*) 316 Crist..þat..with mony sternis sere payntyt þe lyft. **1390** GOWER *Conf.* I. 276 A vois was herd on hih the lifte Of which al Rome was adrad. *c* **1475** *Rauf Coilȝear* 326 The lyft lemit vp beliue, and licht was the day. **1500–20** DUNBAR *Poems* xxxv. 49 Quhill that twa monis wer sene vp in the lift. *a* **1600** MONTGOMERIE *Misc. Poems* xlviii. 182 The lift begouth for to ouercast with shours. **1759** *Rural Love* 10 The dearest lass beneath the lift. **1785** BURNS *Winter Night* 4 When Phœbus gies a short-liv'd glow'r, Far south the lift. **1826** J. WILSON *Noct. Ambr.* Wks. 1855 I. 130 The sweet calm moon in the midnight lift. **1862** HISLOP *Prov. Scot.* 107 If the lift fa' the laverocks will be smoored. **1870** MORRIS *Earthly Par.* III. IV. 40 The moon shines dolorous From out the rainy lift.

b. *attrib.* and *Comb.*, as † ***lift-fowl***; **lift-like** *a.*, heaven-like.

a **1225** *Leg. Kath.* 2245 Fode to wilde deor, & to luftfuheles. **1839** BAILEY *Festus* xxi. 274 Long shroud-like lights Lit up its lift-like dome.

lift (lɪft), *sb.*[2] [f. LIFT *v.*]

I. The action or an act of lifting. (See also DEAD LIFT.)

1. a. The action or an act of lifting, in various senses of the vb.; a raising or rising; the distance through which anything is lifted and moved. †*to have the lift*: to be hanged. *to be on the lift* (Southern *U.S.*): to be on the point of removing; also *fig.* to be at the point of death (*Cent. Dict.*).

1470–85 MALORY *Arthur* XXI. v. 848 In the lyftyng the kyng sowned and syr Lucan fyl in a sowne wyth the lyfte. **1494** FABYAN *Chron.* VII. 536 After many showtis & lyftis at the gatis. **1570** *Durham Depos.* (Surtees) 190 He saith that he was comandyd by Brian to gyve a lifft at the aulter ston. **1604** TERILO *Friar Bacon's Proph.* 486 in Hazl. *E.P.P.* IV. 285 And thiefes must hang, and knaves must shift, And silly fooles must have the lift. **1626** BACON *Sylva* §731 In the Lift of the Feet when a Man Goeth up the Hill, the Weight of the Body beareth most upon the Knees. **1632** LITHGOW *Trav.* I. 29 [It] was transported miraculously..from Nazareth..17. hundred Italian miles, O! a long lift for so scuruie a Cell. **1692** R. L'ESTRANGE *Fables* lxxxiii. (1708) 99 The Goat.. gives the Fox a Lift, and so Out [of the Well] he Springs. **1704** F. FULLER *Med. Gymn.* (1711) 128 We must give an equal Lift to all the Parts. **1853** KANE *Grinnell Exp.* xliii. (1856) 397 We continue perched up, just as we were after our great lift of last December. **1857** C. GRIBBLE in *Merc. Marine Mag.* (1858) V. 8 There was so much lift of sea. **1870** LOWELL *Among my Bks.* Ser. I. (1873) 132 An almost imperceptible lift of the eyebrow. **1872** BROWNING *Fifine* lxxxi, No lift of ripple to o'erlap Keel, much less, prow. **1878** B. TAYLOR *Deukalion* I. v, The broader lift of this gray vault o'erhead.

b. A help on the way given to a foot passenger by allowing him to travel some distance in a vehicle. Cf. LIFT *v.* 11 e.

1712 SWIFT *Jrnl. to Stella* 17 June, I generally get a lift in a coach to town. **1825** *Sporting Mag.* XVI. 331 Instead of money for frequent 'lifts,' the driver receives..presents of game. **1844** DICKENS *Mart. Chuz.* xxxv, To get a lift when we can. To walk when we can't. **1876** GEO. ELIOT *Dan. Der.* IV. l. 8 Giving patience a lift over a weary road. **1929** M. DE LA ROCHE *Whiteoaks* v. 70 'Don't they ever send a car for you?' 'Good Lord, no. Sometimes I get a lift.' **1944** J. S. HUXLEY *On Living in Revolution* ix. 106 We found that a bus recorded on the time-table was in reality non-existent; cadged a lift on a road foreman's car to Denness. **1955** *Times* 26 Aug. 7/4 After giving a 'lift' to a hitch-hiker one will have lost only a tablespoonful or two of petrol, perhaps a teaspoonful of oil, and a saltspoonful or two of rubber off the car's tires. **1974** 'J. LE CARRÉ' *Tinker, Tailor* xxxiii. 293 Declining a lift, Smiley said the walk would do him good.

c. *Sc.* and *north. dial.* The removal of a corpse from the house for burial; the starting of a funeral procession.

1887 in *Eng. Dial. Dict.*, s.v. **1897** G. NEASHAM *Joshua Lax* 7 The lift was announced to take place at 11 a.m.

2. *fig.* **a.** In various immaterial applications, e.g.: A 'rise' in station, prosperity, etc.; promotion; a rise in price; an act of helping, or a circumstance that helps, to a higher or more advanced position. *to give* (†*lend*) *a lift*: to 'give a helping hand' *to*. †*to give a lift at*: to attack. †*to have* (*one*) *on the lift*: ? to have at a disadvantage.

1622 MABBE tr. *Aleman's Guzman d'Alf.* II. 123, I did suffer them now and then to draw my money, but neither much, nor often, lest when they had me on the lift, they might haue left off. **1633** G. HERBERT *Temple, Communion* v, Another lift like this will make Them both [body and soul] to be together. **1641** 'SMECTYMNUUS' *Vind. Answ.* v. 66 We would intreat him to lend Bellarmine a lift in answering the famous Doctor Whitakers. **1651** N. BACON *Disc. Govt. Eng.* II. vi. (1739) 32 It is no wonder if the King feeling the incumbrance, gave a lift at the Pope's power, by stopping the current of Money from England, Rome-wards. **1667** PEPYS *Diary* 24 Apr., The only lift to set him upon his legs. **1674** N. FAIRFAX *Bulk & Selv.* 69 To give the objection all the lifts we can. **1676** OTWAY *Don Carlos* IV. i. Plays (1888) 53 Thy foes are tottering, and the day's thy own, Give them but one lift now, and they go down. **1711** H. LAMP *Autobiog.* iii. (1895) 29, I..enter'd my cadet or voluntier in the King's Life Guard of Swissers, in order to get thereby a little lift. **1770** BURKE *Shortening Parlts.* Wks. X. 82 A living was to be got for one,.. a lift in the Navy for a third. **1794** GODWIN *Cal. Williams* 288 You have given the finishing lift to the misfortune that was already destroying him. **1809** MALKIN *Gil Blas* II. i. ¶2 My memory wants a lift. **1832** L. HUNT *Sir R. Esher* (1850) 120, I shall set myself more on a level with these gentry..by a lift in my fortunes. **1885** *Manch. Exam.* 14 Oct. 5/4 The extension of the franchise..has given an incalculable forward lift to the principles of the Alliance. **1897** *Trans. Highld. Agric. Soc.* 142 His spirit, action and style gave him a great 'lift' in the show-yard.

b. An elevating influence or effect. Also, a cheering or encouraging influence or effect, or a sense of elation.

1861 T. HUGHES *Tom Brown at Oxf.* I. xiv. 281 He heard Drysdale's view halloa above all the din; it seemed to give him a lift. **1873** A. G. MURDOCH *Lilts on Doric Lyre* 10 Sae jist to gie their hearts a lift..They cannilie put owre a dram. **1875** LOWELL *Spenser* Prose Wks. 1890 IV. 308 The language and verse of Spenser at his best have an ideal lift in them. **1876** —— *Among my Bks.* Ser. II. 3 The traveller feels the ennobling lift of such society. **1887** [see ASPIRATIONAL *a.*]. **1936** J. DOS PASSOS *Big Money* 498 Dick put down three bourbons in rapid succession but he wasn't getting any lift from them. **1951** E. PAUL *Springtime in Paris* i. 12 Raoul realized that Katya got an enormous lift from secrecy and mystery, and helped her enjoy it. **1957** *Sat. Even. Post* 30 Mar. 102/2 The girl had to rush back to the pusher and complain that it didn't give her a lift. **1975** T. ALLBEURY *Palomino Blonde* xxiii. 135 Hallet had been demented with worry..and the 'lift' that he had got from his talk with Farrow had melted away.

†**c.** A crisis or emergency; = DEAD LIFT. *Obs.*

1624 BP. MOUNTAGU *Immed. Addr.* 6 In Extremitie, when my life is at a lift, or my state set vpon a desperate Cast. **1632** BROME *Novella* IV. i. Wks. 1873 I. 145 Fear it not, Mistris, she is as sure at such a lift.

3. An act of lifting or stealing; in older use, †a shift, trick. *Obs.* exc. *dial.*

1592 GREENE *Upst. Courtier* D, Such yoong youths..fall then to priuy lifts & cosenages. **1594** *2nd Rep. Faustus* in Thoms *E.E. Prose Rom.* (1858) III. 338 Such cranks, such lifts, careers and gambalds as he plaid there. **1621** B. JONSON *Gipsies Metam.* Wks. (1640) 54 If for our Linnen we still us'd the lift, And with the hedge..made shift. **1852** JUDSON *Myst. & Mis. New York* I. iv. 40 When I hear of the boys making a large lift, I always envy them. **1894** LAING *Poems* 12 (E.D.D.) For remember a' villains began wi' a lift That by some folk wad scarcely be reckoned a theft.

4. The act or habit of carrying (the head, neck, eyes, etc.) aloft; elevated carriage.

1835 WILLIS *Pencillings* I. vii. 47 She is a little above middle height, with a fine lift to her head and neck. **1869** BLACKMORE *Lorna D.* xix, The proud lift of her neck was gone. **1870** SWINBURNE *Ess. & Stud.* (1875) 320 The head set firm on it without any droop or lift of the chin. **1889** ADELINE SERGEANT *Esther Denison* I. II. xii. 159 There was a happy expectancy in the lift of her eyes as she walked up the country road.

5. Technical uses.

a. *Engineering.* The action of lifting a load through a vertical distance, or one of several successive distances. Hence, in *Coal-mining*, 'a series of workings being prosecuted to the rise at one time' (Gresley *Gloss. Coal-mining*, p. 201).

1702 SAVERY *Miner's Friend* 59 If you have but one Lift one Station or Engine-Room will be sufficient. *Ibid.* 63 A Custom used in very deep Mines..of raising their Water by several Lifts from Cistern to Cistern. **1860** E. HULL *Coalfields* Introd. (1861) 5 The 'Cannel' seam is reached by means of two 'lifts' at a depth of 600 yards. **1867** SMYTH *Coal* 100 The mines are from 300 to 500 feet deep, sunk in lifts of 40 to 50 feet at a time.

b. *Horology.* The amount of motion of a watch-balance produced by each impulse of vibration.

1884 F. J. BRITTEN *Watch & Clockm.* 73 If it is found that the lift is unequal from the point of rest the balance spring collet must be shifted in the direction of the least lift till the lift be equal.

†**c.** *Card-playing.* The action of lifting or 'cutting' a pack of cards; also quasi-*concr.* one of the portions into which the pack is so divided. *Obs.*

1674–80 COTTON *Compl. Gamester* 84 When they [fraudulent gamesters] deal..to their Partner they place in the second lift next the top, 1, 2, 3, or four Aces. **1728** YOUNG *Love of Fame* VI. 545 When you're enamour'd of a lift or cast, What can the preacher more, to make us chast?

d. The distance or extent to which anything rises, e.g. a safety valve, the pestle of an ore stamp, the water in a canal-lock.

1829 J. MACAULEY *Nat. & Civil Hist. N.Y.* I. 170 This.. lock has an extent within the gates of one hundred and fourteen feet, with a breadth of thirty—the lift is nine feet. **1837** J. T. SMITH tr. *Vicat's Mortars* 306 Length of lift 3·937 inches. **1840** H. S. TANNER *Canals & Railr. U.S.* 252 The difference between the levels is termed the *lift of the lock*, which ranges from 3 to 30 feet. **1851** *Illustr. Catal. Gt. Exhib.* 232 Centrifugal pump for draining marshes.. adapted for a large quantity of water, with a low lift.

e. (i) The upward force acting on an aircraft or other body in the air; *spec.* that produced by its motion through the air; the force on an aerofoil that acts at right angles to its direction of motion through a fluid.

1902 *Encycl. Brit.* XXV. 104/1 The sustaining power, or 'lift',..in horizontal flight must be equal to the weight. *Ibid.*, The present data indicate that, with concave surfaces, angles of 2° to 5° will produce adequate 'lift'. **1919** H. SHAW *Text-bk. Aeronaut.* iii. 43 The upper surface of an aerofoil is considerably more important than the lower surface from the point of view of lift, as the suction over the top surface is numerically much greater than the pressure beneath. **1937** DODGE & THOMPSON *Fluid Mech.* vii. 127 Usually the component opposing the motion is referred to as the drag, while the cross-stream component is called the lift, even though it may not always be acting vertically upward. **1948** *Sci. News* VII. 23 In aerodynamics it is customary to resolve the reaction of the air on a surface into two components, namely lift, which is that part of the force acting upwards.. and is thus desirable, and drag, which is the component at right angles to the lift and..resists the forward motion of the surface through the air. **1959** *Chambers's Encycl.* I. 110/2 In straight level flight the lift equals the weight. **1973** *Nature* 28 Sept. 182/1 Most flying insects depend, for their lift and thrust, on conventional aerofoil action which sets up a bound vertex around the moving wing to create a steady-state flow of air. **1974** *Encycl. Brit. Macropædia* I. 371/1 An airship derives lift from two sources: (1) by displacement of air as a balloon (static lift) and (2) from the reaction of airflow over its envelope and control surfaces when it is under way (dynamic lift).

(ii) The (maximum) weight that an aircraft can raise (including or, more commonly, excluding its own weight).

1910 *Blackw. Mag.* July 4/1 The compartments [of the Zeppelin] contained 351,150 cubic feet of hydrogen, giving a lift of eleven tons. **1929** *Nature* 14 Dec. 916/2 Recourse to the Servo-motor gear was not found necessary (if this holds good at full speed the gear may be removed, and then about ½ ton will be added to the useful 'lift'). **1971** *Daily Tel.* 19 Aug. 2/6 It is much lighter and can be lifted by the Puma tactical transport helicopter, which has a total lift of up to 5,500 lb.

f. *Pros.* An element of high intensity in an alliterative measure, marked by stress or tone. (G. *hebung.*) Cf. DIP *sb.* 1 g.

1894 [see DIP *sb.* 1 g]. **1927** E. V. GORDON *Introd. Old Norse* 293 The rhythm consists of regular alternation of strong and weak metrical elements, known as lift and sinking respectively. **1953** C. L. WRENN *Beowulf* p. xxxvii, [Alliteration] is never repeated on the last lift. **1961** [see DIP *sb.* 1 g].

g. *Dance.* A movement in which a dancer lifts his partner in the air.

1921 *Dancing Times* Aug. 867/2 Miss Jules Andre..filled the roll [*sic*] of 'boy' in..many..numbers. Her lifts and adage work were delightful. **1943** K. AMBROSE *Ballet-Lover's Pocket-Bk.* 40 With the invention of each new ballet, new lifts are devised. **1944** 'BRAHMS' & 'SIMON' *Titania has Mother* ii. 11 'He's a frightfully bad dancer, mother. His lifts!' She shuddered. **1950** *Ballet Ann.* IV. 69 She is equally at home in the most intricate acrobatic lifts..as [her body] is swung upwards in the air by her attendant cavaliers.

h. Transport by air (cf. AIR-LIFT 2); also, a number of persons or an amount of supplies so transported. Cf. LIFT *v.* 11 i.

1942 F. D. ROOSEVELT in W. S. Churchill *Second World War* (1951) IV. xxx. 481 The following shipping can be made available by the United States..: Transports, other than combat leaders, with a lift of 52,000 men. **1947** VISCT. MONTGOMERY *Normandy to Baltic* 137 Our resources.. made it impossible to fly in the whole of the Airborne Corps in one lift. **1947** M. NEWNHAM *Prelude to Glory* ixiv. 350 The entire force was carried in one lift. **1949** *Flight* 15 Dec. 756/1 We eventually had sixteen crews, consisting of three members each, engaged whole-time on the Lift.

i. The establishment by a sheepdog of control over a flock of sheep. Cf. LIFT *v.* 11 g.

1942 R. B. KELLEY *Animal Breeding* xi. 115 A little 'eye' ..can be associated meritoriously with a steady 'lift' and.. restricts the dog from over-running a cast. **1946** F. DAVISON *Dusty* ix. 117 The [sheepdog] trial had four phases; the cast, ..the lift, when the dog, having found them [*sc.* his sheep], established control over them; the fetch,..and the carry. **1955** *Galloway Gaz.* 1 Oct. 6 His dog 'Garry' won the Rosebowl for the best outrun and lift. **1964** *Weekly News* (Auckland) 29 Apr. 37/3 Fleet is losing points hand over fist now. He has failed to obtain a good 'lift': in other words he hasn't been able to head them unobserved and then start them moving gently and firmly. **1973** *Country Life* 25 Oct. 1292/1 From its position at 12 o'clock, the dog begins the critical 'lift', with a quiet authority that brooks neither refusal nor panic in the sheep.

II. A person who lifts.

†**6.** *slang.* One who lifts or takes away and appropriates (something); a thief. (Cf. LIFT *v.* 8)

1592 GREENE *Art Conny Catch.* II. 22 The Lift is he that stealeth or prowleth any plate, iewels,..or such parcels from any place by a sleight conueance vnder his cloke. *c* **1600** *Nobody & Somebody* D 3 b, Talke not of the Gayle, 'tis full of limetwigs, lifts, and pickpockets. **1602** ROWLANDS *Greenes Ghost* 16 Richard Farrie a notable Lift of sixtie yeares of age. **1630** J. TAYLOR (Water P.) *Trav. Twelvepence* I. 71/1 Lifts, Foysts, Cheats, Stands, Decoyes.

III. A device or apparatus for lifting.

7. *Naut.* pl. 'Ropes which reach from each mast-head to their respective yard-arms to steady and suspend the ends' (Smyth *Sailor's Word-bk.*).

1485 *Naval Acc. Hen. VII* (1896) 36 Mayne lyftes..ij. **1611** COTGR., *Balancines*, the lifts. **1627** SMITH *Seaman's Gram.* v. 24 The top-sail Lifts doe serue for sheats to the top gallant yards, the haling them is called the Topping the Lifts. **1762** FALCONER *Shipwr.* II. 260 The parrels, lifts, and clue-lines soon are gone. **1860** *Merc. Marine Mag.* VII. 114 The yard is down on the lifts.

8. a. *Shoemaking.* One of the layers of leather used to form a heel. †**b.** *Wool-carding* (see quot. 1688).

1677 PLOT *Oxfordsh.* 139 The other [stone] in the shape of the heel of an old shoo, with the Lifts plainly to be distinguish'd. **1688** R. HOLME *Armoury* III. 92/2 The Lifts are the narrow pieces of Leather which are Nailed about to hold the Leaf on the Board. **1735** DYCHE & PARDON *Dict.*, *Lifts*,..among the Shoe-makers they are Pieces of Sole Leather put upon the Heels if wooden, or several of 'em one upon another if Leather, in order to make 'em higher or lower. **1880** *Times* 21 Sept. 4/4 The heels are built architecturally by selecting lifts of diminishing size.

†**9.** In a windmill: ? = *lift-tenter*. *Obs.*

1688 R. HOLME *Armoury* III. 340/2 The Parts of a Wind-Mill..the Lift, that which raiseth the Mill-stones higher or lower.

10. a. An apparatus for raising or lowering persons or things from one floor or level to another; an ascending chamber or compartment; a hoist; = ELEVATOR 3 d. Also, the well or vertical opening in which the apparatus works.

1851 *Illustr. Catal. Gt. Exhib.* 230 The principle is applicable to dinner-lifts for hotels and mansions. **1858** SIMMONDS *Dict. Trade*, *Lift*,..an elevator for sending dishes, &c., up or down from a kitchen. **1861** BERESF. HOPE *Eng. Cathedr. 19th C.* 128 Great central hotels with their machinery of lifts. **1861** *Ann. Reg.* 168 Throwing a quantity of waste paper, which he had collected on the upper floors, down the 'lift'. **1878** BLACK *Green Past.* xxxii, We entered the lift to be conveyed to the floors above.

b. chair-lift, a device for transporting people up a mountain slope, usually consisting of seats suspended from a continuously moving overhead cable; **ski-lift**, a chair-lift, or any of various types of apparatus for hauling skiers uphill. Also absol. *lift*.

1940 F. ELKINS *Compl. Ski Guide* II. 161 New 3500-foot 'T-bar' lift to connect with top of chair lift. **1947** *Penguin New Writing* XXX. 27 Dory found himself going up on the ski-lift with a Frenchwoman. **1953** C. J. ALLEN *Switzerland's Amazing Railways* viii. 93 A simpler

application of the *téléphérique* principle is found in the chair-lift, known in French as a *télésiège* and in German as a *Sesselbahn*. **1955** W. PLOMER *Shot in Park* 50 The ski-lift smoothly moves. **1958** *Times* 18 July 11/7 Skiing is also popular..in the Thredbo Valley, where Australia's first chair lift, a mile long, began to work this winter. **1970** *Country Life* 17–24 Dec. 1214/3 Recently, Norway has been developing 'Alpine' resorts where the ski-lifts, the equipment and the ski-schools closely resemble good centres in the Alps. **1972** M. YORKE *Silent Witness* ii. 12 The lifts, and even the cable-car..had stopped, for the snow..had been falling steadily. **1972** D. HASTON *In High Places* vii. 82 Once above the ski-lift level it was still possible to have the whole of a range to one's self on a certain day.

11. A contrivance on a canal serving as a substitute for a lock. Also = LOCK *sb.*² 9 c.

1825 [see LOCK *sb.*² 9 c]. **1875** in KNIGHT *Dict. Mech.*

12. A set of pumps in a mine; also, the section of a shaft occupied by one set.

1849 GREENWELL *Coal-trade Gloss.* (1851), *Lift*,..a column, or parallel columns, of pumps. **1855** *Cornwall* 255 A steam-engine..works nine lifts of pumps, and lifts thirty-six tons six cwt. per stroke.

13. In various applications: see *shoe-lift* (a shoe-horn), *window-lift*.

IV. The thing lifted.

14. The quantity or weight that can be lifted at one time. *spec.* of paper. Also *Sc.* a large quantity.

13.. *Coer de L.* 3352 Off gold well twenty mennys lyffte. **1755** JOHNSON, *Lift*, in Scotland, denotes a load or surcharge of any thing. **1785** BURNS *2nd Ep. J. Lapraik* 74 Gie me o' wit an' sense a lift. **1808** C. STOWER *Printer's Gram.* xvi. 405 Having thus doubled the first lift on the peel, he [*sc.* the warehouseman] raises it, holding it aslant, that the shorter fold of the sheets may open from the peel, in order to convey it over the pole. **1841** W. SAVAGE *Dict. Art of Printing* 444 In the warehouse, each separate portion of printed paper, whether it consists of five or six sheets or more, that is placed upon the poles to dry, is termed a lift. **1861** TROLLOPE *Framley P.* II. ii. 35, I have used up three lifts of notepaper already in telling people that there is no vacancy for a lobby messenger in the Petty Bag office. **1871** R. BROWNING *Pr. Hohenst.* 100 To find..from handlift and from barrow load, What salts and silts may constitute the earth. **1882** OGILVIE (Annandale) s.v., 2 cwt. is a good lift. **1888** C. T. JACOBI *Printers' Vocab.* 75 *Lift*, applied to a handful of printed work in the warehouse. **1967** V. STRAUSS *Printing Industry* x. 632 (*caption*) You see the lift of stock to be cut on the bed or table of the cutter. On the left the lift is lined up with one edge, in the rear it is lined up with another edge. **1971** D. POTTER *Brit. Eliz. Stamps* xv. 175 Batches of 1,000 sheets are broken down into 'lifts' of 25.

15. *dial.* A gate without hinges, that must be lifted in order to remove or open it.

1674 RAY *S. & E.C. Word* 70 A *Lift*: i.e. a Stile that may be opened like a gate, *Norf.* *a* **1825** FORBY *Voc. E. Anglia*, *Lift*, a sort of coarse rough gate..not hung, but [etc.]. **1898** RIDER HAGGARD in *Longm. Mag.* Nov. 25 The stouter undergrowth is split for hurdles and the rest of less substance twisted into another form of hurdle which is known as a 'lift'.

16. *dial.* A particular joint or cut of meat, usually of beef. (The precise application varies according to locality: see quots.)

1688 R. HOLME *Armoury* III. 87/2 The Lift, or Buttock, is the Fleshy part of the Thigh of a Cow or Ox. **1790** A. WILSON *To the Famishing Bard* Poet. Wks. (1846) 55 A sirloin huge—a smoking lift, To feed thy keen devouring eye. **1854** A. E. BAKER *Northamptonsh. Gloss.*, *Lift*, 2. The meat taken out of a flitch of bacon, when the ham is left in; ..the fleshy part of the leg. **1888** *Sheffield Gloss.*, *Lift*, the upper part of the thigh of an ox. **1889** *N.W. Linc. Gloss.*, *Lift*, half a round of beef.

17. A rising ground.

1825 SCOTT *Let. to Mrs. W. Scott* 23 Mar. in *Lockhart*, He started the topic of our intended railroad... I had at my finger end every cut, every lift, every degree of elevation or depression, every pass in the country. **1874** GREEN *Short Hist.* i. §2. 7 A mere lift of higher ground with a few grey cottages dotted over it. **1885** *Century Mag.* Nov. 108 Here and there in the land were sharp lifts where rocks cropped out, making miniature cliffs overhanging some portions of the brook's course.

V. 18. *attrib.* and *Comb.* (several of these combs. should perh. be referred to the vb. stem), as (sense 1) *lift-capstan*, *-pulley*, (sense 10) *lift-attendant*, *-boy*, *-button*, *-cage*, *-man*, *-railway*, *-shaft*, *-well*; also **lift-bridge**, a bridge that may be raised to allow the passage of a boat, e.g. on a canal; **lift coefficient** *Aerodynamics*, a ratio representing the lift developed by unit area of an aerofoil in relation to the air speed, and defined as the lift divided by the product of the aerofoil area (in plan) and the square of the air speed (and, in mod. use, by half the air density also); **lift-drag** *a. Aerodynamics*, relating to both lift and drag; applied *spec.* to the ratio of the lift to the drag; **lift-fan**, a fan in a hovercraft which provides the air-cushion; **lift-gate** (*a*) = sense 15 (Knight); (*b*) a gate opening on to a lift (sense 10); (*c*) *U.S.* in a motor vehicle, a hinged back panel that opens upwards; **lift-hammer** = tilt-hammer; **lift-latch**, a latch that does not slide, but rises and falls; **lift-lock**, a canal lock; **lift-pump**, any pump other than a force-pump; **lift-slab** *attrib.*, applied to a labour-saving system of building whereby pre-cast components are raised by jacks to the position desired; **lift-tenter**, in windmills, a governor for regulating the speed, by adjusting the sails, or for adjusting the action of grinding machinery according to the speed; **lift truck** = *fork-lift truck*; **lift valve**, a valve which opens by the valve head moving (vertically) out of its (horizontal) seat; **lift-wall** (see quot.); **lift-web**, a strip of webbing joining the harness and the rigging lines of a parachute; **lift wire** *Aeronaut.*, a wire on a biplane or light monoplane that extends from the wing to the fuselage and is designed to transmit part of the lift to the latter during flight.

1900 *Westm. Gaz.* 28 June 6/2 The *lift attendant had sustained terrible injuries. **1904** 'SAKI' *Reginald* 15 *Lift-boys always have aged mothers. **1967** L. MEYNELL *Mauve Front Door* vi. 82 Chauffeurs, waiters, lift-boys..they are the operators. **1850** *Proc. Inst. Civ. Engin.* IX. 203 Description of a Vertical *Lift Bridge. **1883** G. C. DAVIES *Norfolk Broads & Rivers* xxv. (1884) 190 At Haddiscoe is a lift-bridge, where a road crosses the Cut. **1955** W. TUCKER *Wild Talent* xiv. 186 The man punched the *lift button. **1970** P. GEDDES *November Wind* vi. 64 Havill watched him press the lift button. **1951** R. SENHOUSE tr. *Colette's Last of Chéri* 213 The *lift-cage heavily splashed with as much lacquer and gold as a sedan-chair. **1971** R. PETRIE *Thorne in Flesh* xi. 145 A boy lounged on a stool in the silent lift-cage. **1495** *Naval Acc. Hen. VII* (1896) 202 *Lyfte Capsteynes. **1919** H. SHAW *Text-bk. Aeronaut.* iii. 39 As the angle of incidence increases the *lift coefficient also increases rapidly, until an angle of about 13° is reached, beyond which the coefficient increases less rapidly, and reaches its maximum value in the neighbourhood of 15°. **1933** *Techn. Rep. U.S. Nat. Advisory Comm. Aeronaut.* No. 463. 18 As speeds above half the velocity of sound are exceeded..the flow breaks down as shown by a drop in the lift coefficient. **1966** *McGraw-Hill Encycl. Sci. & Technol.* I. 85/2 The maximum lift coefficient (the stall value) of the wing is 1·1–1·5. **1919** *Lift-drag ratio [see CEILING *vbl. sb.* 6 b]. **1935** P. W. F. MILLS *Elem. Pract. Flying* i. 6 Variations in incidence..affect lift and drag disproportionately, and thus produce variations in the quantitative relation between lift and drag—that is to say, in what is called the lift-drag ratio. **1960** *Times Rev. Industry* Oct. 58/3 [The] airstream direction detector system..enables an aircraft to be flown on the best lift-drag curve to maintain economic flight conditions. **1962** *Flight Handbk.* (ed. 6) v. 98 The Republic AP-100, in which six J85 engines feed three *lift fans. **1967** *Jane's Surface Skimmer Systems 1967–68* 49/2 A drive-shaft runs vertically upward to the 12-blade lift-fan. **1948** G. V. GALWEY *Lift & Drop* i. 14 The crowd gathered at the *lift gates. **1951** J. WYNDHAM *Day of Triffids* i. 19, I found a large '5' painted on the wall opposite the lift gate. **1961** WEBSTER *Lift gate*, an upper rear panel (as on a station wagon) that opens upward as a tail gate opens downward. **1963** *Aerospace-Automotive Drawing Standards* (Soc. Automotive Engin.) 1 *Liftgate*, a hinged backwindow. **1970** *Motor Trend World Automotive Yearbk. 1971 Buyer's Guide* 112/3 The rear seat for a Gremlin is an optional extra along with the counter-balanced 'lift-gate' that comes with it. **1974** E. MCGIRR *Murderous Journey* 33 The liftman..was fiddling with the lift gate. **1858** SIMMONDS *Dict. Trade*, **Lift-hammer*, a large hammer. **1875** KNIGHT *Dict. Mech.*, **Lift-latch lock*. **1840** H. S. TANNER *Canals & Railr. U.S.* 100 The Wisconisco Canal..has..6 *lift locks. **1883** *Daily Tel.* 26 Feb. 7/8 Honest..man wants a situation..as *liftman. **1485** *Naval Acc. Hen. VII* (1896) 37 *Left poles with iiij sheves of brasse..ij, left poles with ij sheves of brasse..ij. **1858** SIMMONDS *Dict. Trade*, **Lift-pump*, a pump acting by the pressure of the atmosphere on the external body of water. **1893** *Daily News* 13 Mar. 3/7 The Clifton Rocks Railway, a *lift railway cut in a tunnel from the Gorge of the Avon to the summit of Clifton Rocks. **1894** *Times* 14 Feb. 14/1 The door leading from the *liftshaft on to the next floor. **1951** (*title*) Youtz-Slick *lift-slab building method (Inst. Inventive Res., San Antonio, Texas). **1960** *Economist* 22 Oct. 378/3 The 'lift slab' principle..was developed in America, the columns are first cast and erected, then pre-cast floor slabs are lifted by synchronised hydraulic jacks. **1962** *Daily Tel.* 30 Nov. 25/4 A 400,000-gallon watertank resting at the base of a tower before being raised 110 ft by the Lift Slab method... The 95 ft-diameter watertank was raised..in about 40 hours. **1824** R. STUART *Steam Engine* 133 The attached balls, which were called a *lift-tenter, by their centrifugal force either raised or lowered a stage in which the arbour of the spindle revolved, and brought the mill-stones nearer, or removed them farther from each other, as they might be adjusted. **1963** H. GARNER in R. Weaver *Canad. Short Stories* (1968) 2nd Ser. 56 Even with a *lift truck hurrying the parts to the forge we were falling behind. **1971** [see DOZER²]. **1887** *Encycl. Brit.* XXII. 505/1 In many stationary engines *lift or disk valves are used, worked by tappets, cams, or eccentrics. **1898** *Engineering Mag.* XVI. 108/1 Compression has been on the increase ever since the adoption of the lift valve. **1971** B. SCHARF *Engin. & its Lang.* xii. 178 Poppet valves. These are spring loaded lift valves which are commonly used, e.g. in internal combustion engines. **1841** BREES *Gloss. Civ. Engin.*, **Lift-wall*, the cross wall of a lock chamber. **1942** *Tee Emm* (Air Ministry) II. 134 Pass the left hand *in between* the left harness *lift web and the body and grasp the right harness lift web. **1947** M. NEWNHAM *Prelude to Glory* viii. 33 To reduce the risk of backward landings men were told..if necessary to turn their bodies by manipulation of the parachute lift-webs. **1958** P. KEMP *No Colours or Crest* iii. 41, I took a frantic pull on my liftwebs to ease the impact. **1897** *Daily News* 3 Dec. 8/3 The deceased was found..at the bottom of the *lift-well. **1915** W. E. DOMMETT *Aeroplanes & Airships* ii. 26 When the machine is in flight, the upward pressure on the wings is taken by '*lift' wires or stays passing to a framework under the fuselage. **1942** C. C. REDMAN in R. A. Beaumont *Aeronaut. Engin.* xvii. 482/1 Wires running..inwards from the tip portions of the upper surfaces to inboard points of the lower surfaces adjacent to the fuselage—are known as 'flying' or 'lift' wires.

lift (lɪft), *v.* Forms: 4 leftyn, 4–5 lifte(n, 4–6 lyft(e, 5 lyften, -yn, 4– lift. *Pa. t.* 4–5 left(e, lyft(e, 4–5 lifte, 4–7, 9 lift, 4 liftd, -id, -ud, 4– lifted. *Pa. pple.* 4–6 lifte, lyfte, 5–8 (9 *poet.*) lift, 4– lifted. Also 5 i-lift. [a. ON. *lypta* (Sw. *lyfta*, Da. *løfte*) = MHG., mod.G. *lüften*:—OTeut. type **luftjan*, f. **luft-us* (ON. *lopt* air, sky = LIFT *sb.*¹). The etymological sense is therefore to move up into the air.

The verb which occurs in the phrase *lutenn and lefften* (see LOUT *v.*), very frequent in the Ormulum, but not found elsewhere, has been commonly identified with this vb., but neither the form nor the sense favours the identification. Apparently the phrase (which is followed by a dat. of person) means 'to show respect to' (a superior), 'to condescend graciously to' (an inferior). It does not seem possible to connect *lefften* with OE. *lyffettan* to flatter.]

1. a. *trans.* To raise into the air from the ground, or to a higher position; to elevate, heave, hoist. †Also, to erect, rear on high (a building). †*to lift (a child) from the font*: to stand godfather to. Occas., to lower after raising from an elevated position.

a **1300** *Cursor M.* 2388 Abram..Bi betel lifted an auter neu. *Ibid.* 8963 Sco lift hir skirt wit-vten scurn And barfote wode sco þat burn. *c* **1440** *Jacob's Well* 78 In wrast-lyng, whan a chaumpyoun may lyften an-oþerys foot, þanne he throwyth hym doun. **1460** CAPGRAVE *Chron.* (Rolls) 224 A child..whom the kyng..left fro the funt. **1590** SPENSER *F.Q.* I. iv. 4 High lifted up were many loftie towres. **1697** DRYDEN *Virg. Georg.* IV. 499 Arethusa leaping from her Bed, First lifts above the Waves her beauteous Head. **1709** STEELE *Tatler* No. 58 ¶2 Lifting his Legs higher than the ordinary Way of Stepping. **1712** ADDISON *Spect.* No. 433 ¶6 One who could lift Five hundred Weight. **1816** SCOTT *Antiq.* xx, He lifted his cane *in terrorem*. **1839** YEOWELL *Anc. Brit. Ch.* x. (1847) 104 They had no inclination to lift the sword, except against each other. **1841** LANE *Arab. Nts.* I. 91 The Prince..lifted her from his horse. **1851** *Illustr. Catal. Gt. Exhib.* 1147 A..magnet capable of lifting a weight of 500 pounds. **1860** TYNDALL *Glac.* I. xx. 137 The clouds were slowly lifted above the tallest peaks. **1873** BLACK *Pr. Thule* xviii. 282 Lavender made no further sign of surprise..than to lift his eyebrows, and say—'Indeed!' **1920** E. O'NEILL *Beyond Horizon* II. i. 73 Lifting Mary to the floor.

b. with *up*, *aloft*, *away*, *down*, *off*, *out*, and advb. phrases. *to lift up*: †occas. to install in a high seat.

a **1300** *Cursor M.* 14332 þe lid o tumbe awai þai lift. **1362** LANGL. *P. Pl.* A. v. 203 For to lyfte hym aloft [he] leide hym on his knees. **1387** TREVISA *Higden* (Rolls) VII. 349 A whirle-wynd..lefte up sixe rafters of þe cherche. *a* **1400** *Pistill of Susan* 229 He lyft [*v.r.* left] vp þe lach. *c* **1450** *Merlin* 38 Than yede the peple to oon of the stones, and leften it vp. **1460** *Lybeaus Disc.* (Kaluza) 2057 Our on schall other lifte þe bedde of þe chinne. **1509** HAWES *Past. Pleas.* xxxv. (Percy Soc.) 182 He stretched hym up and lyft his axe a lofte. *a* **1533** LD. BERNERS *Huon* lxi. 213 They weyed vp theyr ancres & lyft vp theyr saylles. **1535** COVERDALE *Ps.* cvii. 25 The stormy wynde aryseth, and lifteth vp the wawes therof. **1567** *Gude & Godlie Ball.* (S.T.S.) 44 That Prince on Croce thay lyftit on hicht. **1611** BIBLE *Gen.* xxxvii. 28 They..lift vp Ioseph out of the pit. **1640** tr. *Verdere's Rom. of Rom.* III. xxx. 129 The Knight of the Eagles presently lift up his Bever. **1686** WOOD *Life* 29 Dec., Mr John Massy installed in his deane's place..first his patent was read: then his dispensation..and then he was lifted up. **1725** T. LEWIS *Antiq. Hebr. Rep.* III. 270 When she had lift it [a shoe] up. **1772** HUTTON *Bridges* 99 A large ram of iron..being lift up to the top of them. **1838** DICKENS *O. Twist* II. xxi. 25 Sikes dismounted..holding Oliver by the hand..and, lifting him down directly, bestowed a furious look on him. **1871** R. ELLIS tr. *Catullus* lxi. 121 Lift the torches aloft in air, Boys. **1887** *Times* (weekly ed.) 11 Nov. 7/4 The girls sang as if they wanted to lift themselves off the ground. **1890** A. CONAN DOYLE *Sign of Four* viii. 138 'He acted according to his lights,' said Holmes, lifting him [*sc.* a dog] down from the barrel. **1898** G. B. SHAW *Candida* I. 106, I cant lift a heavy trunk down from the top of a cab. **1920** E. O'NEILL *Beyond Horizon* II. ii. 95 He lifts her down to the grass. **1940** W. FAULKNER *Hamlet* III. i. 212 He finds the basket by smell and lifts it down from the limb and sets it before her.

†**c.** To bear, support. *Obs. rare*⁻¹.

1590 SPENSER *F.Q.* I. xi. 54 Th' earth him underneath Did grone, as feeble so great load to lift.

d. *Sc.* To take up, pick up. Hence in *Golf*: To take up the ball.

1596 DALRYMPLE tr. *Leslie's Hist. Scot.* IV. 206 Dionethie haueng receiued a gret..wound, he is lyfted be his awne. **1830** GALT *Lawrie T.* VII. ii. (1849) 309, I happened..to lift a newspaper. **1840** BLAINE *Encycl. Rural Sports* 117 The ball nearest the hole must be lifted till the other is played. **1842** G. F. CARNEGIE *Golfiana* in *Golfiana Misc.* (1887) 81 Now, lift the stones, but do not touch the ball. **1890** HUTCHINSON *Golf* 447 Gloss. *s.v.*, To lift a ball is to take it out of a hazard and drop or tee it behind.

e. In occasional uses, = RAISE: † (*a*) in *passive*, to rise (*obs.*); (*b*) *colloq.* to bring (a constellation) above the horizon in sailing, etc.

c **1420** *Pallad. on Husb.* IV. 813 Ybrestid brode, and al the body lift In brawnys grete. *c* **1477** CAXTON *Jason* 69 Thenne sodainly rose and was lift a tempeste. **1891** R. KIPLING *Light that failed* vii, She'll [the steamer on her way to Australia] lift the Southern Cross in a week.

f. To help (sick or weak cattle) to stand up. Cf. LIFTING *vbl. sb.* 1 b.

1899 H. G. GRAHAM *Social Life Scot. 18th Cent.* I. 155 Cattle..after the long confinement and starving of winter, were mere skeletons, and required to be lifted on their legs when put into the grass.

g. = *face-lift* vb. (FACE *sb.* 27). Also *transf.*

1922 *Ladies' Home Jrnl.* Sept. 28/2 For a skillful surgeon to 'lift' a woman's face—that is, to remove crescent-shaped pieces of skin, near the ears, and at the hair line, thus lifting the cheeks that have begun to sag and so removing the lines of age about the mouth—is actually a simple operation and practically without danger. **1931** *Daily Express* 2 Sept. 3/5 A woman can now have her face lifted one day and appear among her friends the next. **1934** R. MACAULAY *Going*

Abroad I. 12 Mrs. Aubrey, bored, felt that they wanted her to have her face lifted, de-wrinkled..and given a lick of paint. **1951** G. MIKES *Down with Everybody* 71 Modern nationalism is an attempt to see ourselves without the warts; and many historians, writers and poets are the masseurs and cosmeticians of the national beauty parlours, trying to dye our greying hair golden-blonde and trying to lift our faces. **1959** *Cambr. Rev.* 30 May 549/2 Whole courts have had their faces lifted, with stonework freshly dressed or replaced, stucco renewed. **1974** M. CECIL *Heroines in Love* vi. 149 She ..could cling on to her youth..by having her face lifted.

h. (*not*) ***to lift a finger***: see FINGER *sb.* 3 a.

2. a. In immaterial sense and *fig.*: To elevate, raise. Also with *out*, *up*, and advb. phrases. †***to lift*** (a person) ***out***: to get (him) displaced. †Also (? *nonce-use*), to raise, excite (wonder).

a **1300** *Cursor M.* 25743 Penance sothfast and schrifte.. quen we fall vp mai vs lifte. *a* **1340** HAMPOLE *Psalter* xxii. 6 Þou has purged my hert, and liftid vp to haf þe ioy of contemplacioun. **13..** *E.E. Allit. P.* B. 586 If he has losed þe lysten hit lyftez meruayle. **1497** BP. ALCOCK *Mons Perfect.* C ij, Lyfte fro the erth, refresshed wt ghostly contemplacion. *a* **1533** LD. BERNERS *Gold. Bk. M. Aurel.* (1546) B b, Philosophers..who fyrste lyfted theim selues to regarde the sterres of the heuen. **1581** E. CAMPION in *Confer.* III. (1584) Q iij b, It is our affection..that must be lift vp. **1659** WOOD *Life* Dec. (O.H.S.) I. 299 Carrying tales to the great persons and endeavouring to lift one another out. **1711** STEELE *Spect.* No. 51 ¶4 It lifts an heavy empty Sentence, when there is added to it a lascivious Gesture of Body. **1817** CHALMERS *Astron. Disc.* i. (1852) 19 There is much in the scenery of a nocturnal sky to lift the soul to pious contemplation. **1864** MRS. CARLYLE *Lett.* III. 224 With so rich a husband she would be able to lift them out of all their difficulties. **1893** LIDDON, etc. *Life Pusey* I. iv. 327 Pusey's paper..lifted it [the subject] at once into the region of principle.

b. To raise in dignity, rank, or estimation; to elevate, exalt. Also with *up* and advb. phrases. Now *rare.*

c **1330** R. BRUNNE *Chron.* (1810) 10 Whan þe kyng Kynwolf had don his endyng, Brittrik his kosyn þei lift him to kyng. *a* **1340** HAMPOLE *Psalter* viii. 2 For liftid is þi worship abouen heuens. *c* **1440** *Gesta Rom.* lxv. 280 (Add. MS.) Whan he was thus I-lifte up, his herte was enhaunsed in pride. *c* **1450** tr. *De Imitatione* III. lxiii. 145 Sonne, be war þat þou dispute not..why þis is so gretly peyned, & he is so excellently lifte up. **1526** *Pilgr. Perf.* (W. de W. 1531) 6 b, Whom they moost extoll and lyfte vp moost heye, they forsake soonest. **1591** SYLVESTER *Du Bartas* I. vii. 233 His envious brethren's trecherous drift, Him [Joseph] to the Stern of Memphian State had lift. **1597** HOOKER *Eccl. Pol.* v. xx. §12 Neither can it be reasonablie thought..that we thereby do offer disgrace to the word of God, or lift vp the writings of men aboue it. **1639** FULLER *Holy War* II. ii. (1647) 45 Arnulphus..was by popular faction lifted up into the Patriarchs chair. **1883** R. W. DIXON *Mano* I. xv. 48 Then was he lifted to his former style, Archbishop of Ravenna he became.

absol. **1611** BIBLE *1 Sam.* ii. 7 The Lord..bringeth low, and lifteth vp.

c. Chiefly with *up*: To cheer, encourage. Also, To elate, puff up (with pride). †***to lift up oneself of*** (something): to pride oneself upon. Now *dial.* and *arch.*

c **1450** tr. *De Imitatione* I. ii. 3 Be not lifte up þerfore for eny crafte or eny kunnyng. *Ibid.* vii. 8 Lifte not up þiself of gretnes. **1572** R. H. tr. *Lauaterus' Ghostes* (1596) 108 Gabriel with comfortable words did lift up the blessed Virgin which before was sore troubled by this Salutation. **1586** T. B. *La Primaud. Fr. Acad.* I. (1594) 50 He should not be cast downe too much in adversitie, nor lift up beyond measure in prosperitie. **1611** BIBLE *2 Chron.* xxvi. 16 But when he was strong, his heart was lifted vp to his destruction. **1875** JOWETT *Plato* (ed. 2) V. 62 He who is lifted up with pride,..is soon deserted by God. **1890** HALL CAINE *Bondman* II. ii, It had lifted up his heart that Greeta had chosen poverty..before plenty. **1896** 'IAN MACLAREN' *Kate Carnegie* 207 Gin ye juist jined the fouk..the auctioneer would be lifted.

d. To raise in price, value, or amount. Also *ellipt.*

1907 *Daily Chron.* 7 Nov. 1/7 Home Rails were lifted all round..several rises being substantial. **1928** *Chambers's Jrnl.* Feb. 99/2 He kept on lifting the betting, merely to increase his plunder. *Ibid.* 115/2 Jackson..opened the pot for a pound. The American..raised it five, and Captain Reginald lifted another five. **1962** A. NISBETT *Technique Sound Studio* 272 To lift programme level 'a stop' is to increase it by turning the fader (potentiometer) from one stud to the next.

3. *intr.* for *refl.* (also with *up*). **a.** To rise. Said *esp.* of a vessel riding on the waves, occas. of the waves themselves. Also in quasi-*passive* sense (e.g. of a window): To admit of being raised.

a **1400–50** *Alexander* 1942 We þan lift vp a lite & lent him a-gayne. **1526** *Pilgr. Perf.* (W. de W. 1531) 20 b, So that his body lyfted aboue his bedde foure fote or more. **1757** CAPT. RANDALL in *Naval Chron.* XIV. 95 Although there was a great Sea running, she did not lift. **1807** COLERIDGE *Lett.* (1895) 515 This most morbid and oppressive weight is gradually lifting up. **1844** W. H. MAXWELL *Sports & Adv Scot.* xxxiii. (1855) 262 The windows would not lift. **1861** THORNBURY *Turner* II. 319 Rough days, when..he sat..in boats lifting over enormous waves. **1876** BLACKMORE *Cripps* I. ii. 19 The water..instead of ruffling lifted. **1887** BOWEN *Virg. Æneid* III. 205 Not till the fourth day broke was the land seen lifting afar. **1892** *Blackw. Mag.* CLI. 78/2 Fowl lift only a few inches from the water. **1897** R. KIPLING *Captains Courageous* i, The big liner rolled and lifted.

(ii) Of an aircraft: to rise *off* the ground.

1879 *English Mechanic* 4 July 410/3 The small flying model..only just lifted off the pavement. **1899** H. G. WELLS *When Sleeper Wakes* xxiv. 327 The aëropile..was running down its guides to launch. It lifted clean and rose. **1907** *Daily Chron.* 9 Oct. 4/5 She will have to get rid of at least 250 lb. of ballast before she will lift. **1973** J. DRUMMOND *Bang! Bang! You're Dead!* xliv. 151 By the time Sorensen and Pittaway were lifting off the Wapping tarmac, certain constables..were already deploying... They saw the helicopter about the same time as Mariner did.

(iii) Hence in recent use *off* has changed from being a preposition to being an adverb in Astronautical contexts.

1959 W. A. HEFLIN *Aerospace Gloss.* 57/2 *To lift off*, to take off in a vertical ascent. **1961** BURCHETT & PURDY *Cosmonaut Yuri Gagarin* ii. 27 The giant ship lifts off..in a hurricane of white-hot flames. **1971** *Sci. Amer.* Oct. 49/2 On July 21, 1969, *Eagle* lifted off from the moon with its 22-kilogram cargo of lunar rocks and soil.

b. Of a sail (see quot. 1867).

1810 CAPT. TUCKER in *Naval Chron.* XXIV. 337 By keeping the sails lifting,..we contrived to drift in. **1860** *Merc. Marine Mag.* VII. 114 This must not be hauled too taut so as to hinder the sail from lifting. **1867** SMYTH *Sailor's Word-bk.*, *Lift*, a term applied to the sails when the wind catches them on the leeches and causes them to ruffle slightly.

c. Of clouds, fog, etc.: To rise and disperse. Also (*U.S.*) of rain: To cease temporarily.

1834 M. SCOTT *Cruise Midge* vi. (1842) 102 The clouds.. lifted from the eastern horizon majestically slow. **1858** FROUDE *Hist. Eng.* III. 349 One morning when the darkness lifted, sixty strange sail were found at anchor in the Downs. **1870** E. PEACOCK *Ralf Skirl.* II. 178 The thick fog had lifted. **1901** [see LIFTING *vbl. sb.*].

fig. **1897** MARY KINGSLEY *W. Africa* 232 My..head-ache ..soon lifted.

d. Of a floor, etc.: To swell or warp and rise.

1793 SMEATON *Edystone L.* §268 Those four stones.. should be provided..with trenails to hinder them from lifting. **1840** *Jrnl. R. Agric. Soc.* I. III. 272 A limestone road ..lifts more in frost than a gravel one. **1874** THEARLE *Naval Archit.* 116 The great tendency of the deck to lift..when these heavy guns are fired over it. **1899** *Daily News* 13 Nov. 7/5 The concrete platforms..lifted when test guns were fired.

†**e.** Of a horse: To rear, to raise the feet (high).

1607 [see LIFTING *vbl. sb.*].

f. To rise in tone or volume of sound.

1912 GALSWORTHY *Inn of Tranquility* 157 He seemed to enjoy the sounds of conversation lifting round him. **1918** —— *Five Tales* 340 The wayward music lifted up again.

g. *Printing. intr.* Of a forme of type, to stay in one piece when raised from the surface on which it has been assembled; = RISE *v.* 13 c. Also *trans.*, to raise (lines of type), esp. in moving them from a composing stick to a galley, or in preparation for the distribution of used type.

1854 T. FORD *Compositor's Handbk.* 247 *Lift*, this term applies to the raising of a form from the stone. It is said to Lift when no letters drop out. The same term is applied at press when the pressmen are required to Lift a form before it is worked off. **1884** J. GOULD *Letter-Press Printer* (ed. 3) 34 Before lifting the forme off the stone, raise it a little and observe carefully if any letters, &c., are loose and likely to fall out. If the forme 'lifts', take it from the imposing-stone to the proof-press. **1892** A. POWELL *Southward's Pract. Printing* (ed. 4) xxi. 184 Lock up finally, so that the forme will lift. *Ibid.* 185 The next thing to be done is to 'see if it [*sc.* the forme] will lift'; that is, if it can be raised up from the imposing surface without any letters falling out. **1932** SAYERS & SMART in W. Atkins *Art & Pract. Printing* I. iv. 48 If the job contains lines interspersed of the same size and fount (as in display) 'lift' these and place together. **1961** H. W. LARKEN *Compositor's Work in Printing* viii. 95 When type matter is being lifted, it should be handled firmly. *Ibid.* 96 When lifting single lines from a galley or forme, use the side of the galley or the furniture. *Ibid.* 97 Type that is to be distributed should..be lifted in the same manner as that employed for removing it from the stick... The lifted type is allowed to rest on the third finger of the left hand. **1967** KARCH & BUBER *Offset Processes* 544 When each piece of type in a form stays in place after being locked in a chase, it is said to 'lift'.

†**4.** ***to lift at***: **a.** To pull at (something) in the attempt to raise it. *lit.* and *fig.* **b.** To rise in opposition to. Also in *indirect passive. Obs.*

1530 PALSGR. 611/1, I have lyfted at this same this halfe hour: *jay hallé a cecy ceste demye heure.* **1573** TUSSER *Husb.* li. (1878) 115 Lift at their [*viz.* cattle's] tailes er an Winter be past. **1607** DRAYTON *Leg. T. Cromwell* Wks. (1748) 222 Secret foes..lifted at my state. **1647** MAY *Hist. Parl.* I. ix. 113 Bishops had been much lifted at, though not yet taken away. **1658** GURNALL *Chr. in Arm.* verse 14 (1669) 76/1 The principle of holiness..makes him lift at that duty which he can little more than stirr. **1690** *Andros Tracts* II. 39 Some others..have lifted at the Fourth [commandment]. *a* **1704** LOCKE *Cond. Und.* §27 Like the Body strain'd by lifting at a Weight too heavy.

5. *trans.* In various phrases chiefly Hebraisms, or in the Hebrew manner. **a.** ***to lift*** (***up***) ***one's eyes, brow, face, visage***: to give an upward direction to the eyes, etc.; to look up. *lit.* and *fig.* †Hence ***to lift up one's ears***: to listen attentively.

a **1300** *Cursor M.* 17837 Til heuen þai lifted þair eien brade. *c* **1420** *Anturs of Arth.* 408 He lyfte vpe his vesage fro þe ventalle. **1535** COVERDALE *Ps.* cxxi. 1, I lift vp myne eyes vnto the hilles. **1550** CROWLEY *Inform. & Petit.* 5 Herken you possessioners, and you rich men lyfte vp your ears. **1611** BIBLE *Job* xxii. 26 For then shalt thou haue thy delight in the Almightie, and shalt lift vp thy face vnto God. **1854** S. DOBELL *Balder* xxv. 176 With brow Lift to the glowing sun. **1855** MACAULAY *Hist. Eng.* xii. III. 151 It was whispered that he had dared to lift his eyes to an exalted lady.

b. ***to lift*** (***up***) ***the hand(s***, (occas. ***one's arm***): (*a*) *gen.*; (*b*) in prayer, thanksgiving, etc.; (*c*) in taking an oath; (*d*) in hostility *against* (a person); (*e*) to do a stroke of work (*mod. slang*).

(*a*) *a* **1340** HAMPOLE *Pr. Consc.* 7976 Ne myght have anes to lyft þair hand To wype þe teres fra þair eghen oway. **1758** JOHNSON *Idler* No. 57 ¶9 He lifts up his hands with astonishment.

(*b*) *a* **1300** *Cursor M.* 4767 Oft he liftud vp his hend To godd, þat he helpe þam wald send. **1382** WYCLIF *1 Tim.* ii. 8, I wole..men for to preie in al place, liftynge up clene hondis with oute wraththe. *c* **1435** *Torr. Portugal* 1274 To God, he did his hondys lifte, And thankid hym of his sond. **1634** SIR T. HERBERT *Trav.* 24 A Negro..lift up his hands, invocating Mahomet or the Devil. **1807** ROBINSON *Archæol. Græca* III. v. 222 In praying it was likewise customary to lift up the hands towards heaven.

(*c*) **1535** COVERDALE *Gen.* xiv. 22, I lift vp my honde vnto the Lorde, the most hye God. *a* **1626** BACON *New Atl.* (1900) 4 At which Answear the said Person lift up his Right Hand towards Heaven. **1845** M. PATTISON *Ess.* (1889) I. 22 Chilperic lifted his hands, and calling the Almighty to witness, swore that, etc. **1897** R. KIPLING *Captains Courageous* 52 Seventeen brass-bound officers, all gen'elmen, lift their hand to it that [etc.].

(*d*) **1535** COVERDALE *Ps.* cv[i]. 26 Then lift he vp his honde agaynst them, to ouerthrowe them in the wildernes. **1654–66** EARL ORRERY *Parthen.* (1676) 180 He has lift up his prophane Arm against his generous Deliverer. **1804** J. GRAHAME *Sabbath* 340 The murderer—let him die, And him who lifts his arm against his parent.

(*e*) **1889** 'ROLF BOLDREWOOD' *Robbery under Arms* xlviii, He would not lift his hand for any one that day.

c. ***to lift up one's head***: (*a*) *literally*; (*b*) *fig.* to regain courage or energy; to renew one's efforts, to rally. †***to lift up the head of*** (a person); used in the Bible for: to bring out from prison; restore to liberty or position of dignity.

a **1300** *Cursor M.* 22522 All bestes..Vp þan sal þair hefds lift Apon vr lauerd for to cri. *c* **1385** CHAUCER *L.G.W.* 882 *Thisbe*, And therwithal he leftyth vp his hed. *c* **1400** MAUNDEV. (1839) iv. 24 The Dragoun lifte up hire Hed aȝenst him. **1535** COVERDALE *2 Kings* xxv. 27 The kynge of Babilon..lifte vp the heade of Ioachim yᵉ kynge of Iuda out of preson. **1560** BIBLE (Genev.) *Judg.* viii. 28 Thus was Midian broght lowe..so that they lift vp their heads nomore. **1611** BIBLE *Luke* xxi. 28 **1838** THIRLWALL *Greece* V. 185 Olynthus..in the decline of the Spartan power had begun to lift up her head again.

d. ***to lift up one's heart, mind, soul***: to raise one's thoughts or desires; to encourage, exalt oneself (with pride).

1535 COVERDALE *Ps.* xxv. 1 Vnto the (o Lorde) I lift vp my soule. **1548–9** (Mar.) *Bk. Com. Prayer, Communion*, Lift vp your heartes. **1611** BIBLE *2 Chron.* xvii. 6 His heart was lift vp in the wayes of the Lord. —— *Dan.* v. 20 When his heart was lifted vp, and his minde hardened in pride. **1719** DE FOE *Crusoe* I. xviii. (1840) 327, I forgot not to lift up my heart in thankfulness to heaven.

e. ***to lift*** (***up***) ***a cry, one's voice***, etc.: to cry out loudly. Also *fig.*

1382 WYCLIF *Luke* xvii. 12 Ten leprouse men..reyside [*v.r.* lifteden, liften] the vois, seiynge. **1413** *Pilgr. Sowle* (Caxton 1483) III. iii. 52 Thenne sawe I two spirites that liften vp a wondre hidous crye. **14..** *Tundale's Vis.* (1843) 2302 And or he spake any thyng He lyfte up a greyt sykyng. **1535** COVERDALE *Judg.* ii. 4 The people lifte vp their voyce, & wepte. **1581** SIDNEY *Apol. Poetrie* (Arb.) 65 Fit to lift vp a loude laughter, and nothing els. **1742** WESLEY *Wks.* (1872) I. 351 A rude rout lift up their voice on high. **1845** M. PATTISON *Ess.* (1889) I. 28 The voice of the dauntless Gregory was lifted in behalf of the deserted and friendless Praetextatus. **1873** BURTON *Hist. Scot.* V. liv. 82 He had.. an opportunity of lifting his protest against the greatest crime of his age. **1887** BOWEN *Virg. Eclog.* v. 62 Lo! with joy to the heavens they lift their glorious voice.

f. ***to lift up one's heel, horn*** (see those sbs.).

6. To bear or carry in an elevated position; to 'hold high'. (With some attributed notion of sense 1.)

1671 MILTON *P.R.* IV. 48 There the Capitol thou seest Above the rest lifting his stately head On the Tarpeian rock. **1732** POPE *Ep. Bathurst* 340 Where London's column, pointing at the skies, Like a tall bully, lifts the head, and lies. **1764** GOLDSM. *Trav.* 204 Dear [is] that hill which lifts him to the storms. **1805** WORDSW. *Prelude* III. 4 We saw The long-roofed Chapel of King's College lift Turrets and pinnacles in answering files.

7. To take up or collect (rents or moneys due); to levy (contributions, fines, etc.); to draw (wages, the amount of profits, etc.). Now *dial.*

1413 *Pilgr. Sowle* (Caxton 1483) IV. xxxiii. 81 They haue for to sene that his rentes and revenues and suche other auantages rightwysly to be lyfte. **1473** in *Laing Charters* (1899) 43, viij markis..be ws to be lyftyt ande rasit as for oure saide tairs. **1491** *Act 7 Hen. VII*, c. 18 If the seid fyne had never be lifte. *a* **1639** SPOTTISWOOD *Hist. Ch. Scot.* II. (1677) 59 His person arrested, his Rents lifted by the Kings Officers. **1722** RAMSAY *Three Bonnets* IV. 79 He's sent To Fairyland to lift the rent. **1748** SMOLLETT *Rod. Rand.* xvi. (1760) I. 106 Entitling that person to lift his wages when they should become due. **1799** in J. Smith *Hist. Jefferson Coll.* (1857) 165 That a collection be lifted for the purpose of purchasing such a Dictionary as may be thought necessary for the Society. **1814** BYRON *To Moore* 3 Aug., Whose 'bills' are never 'lifted'. **1869** GIBBON *R. Gray* v, The Laird lifted his rent.

8. *slang.* To take up (a portable object; cf. 1 d) or drive away (cattle) with dishonest intentions; in wider sense, to steal; to steal something from (a shop, etc.); to rob. Cf. *shop-lifting.*

1526 SKELTON *Magnyf.* 1373 Conuey it be crafte, lyft & lay asyde. **1592** GREENE *Upst. Courtier* G 3, It is reported you can lift, or nip a bounge, like a guire [*sic*] Coue. **1595** RECORDER FLEETWOOD in Ellis *Orig. Lett.* Ser. I. II. 303 Lyfte is to robbe a shoppe or a gentilmans chamber. **1666** DRYDEN *Ann. Mirab.* ccxxviii, But if night-robbers lift the well-stored hive, An humming through their waxen city grows. *a* **1670** SPALDING *Troub. Chas. I.* (Bannatyne Club) I. 25 Ther came a company of highlanders, and lifted out of Frendraucht's ground, ane number of goods. **1722** RAMSAY *Three Bonnets* I. 78 Thieves that came to lift their cattle.

1814 SCOTT *Wav.* xviii, Donald Bean Lean never lifted less than a drove in his life. **1840** THACKERAY *Paris Sk. Bk.* (1869) 74 He took to his old courses, and lifted a purse here, and a watch there. **1873** DIXON *Two Queens* I. VI. ii. 307 More [Scots] were bent on lifting kine and sheep. **1881** A. LANG *Library* 52 He used to tell how he had lifted a book.. from a stall on the Pont-Neuf. **1892** R. KIPLING *East & West* in *Barrack-r. Ballads* 75 He has lifted the Colonel's mare that is the Colonel's pride. **1905** E. WALLACE *Four Just Men* ix. 165 They was waitin' to cross towards Charing Cross Road when I lifted the clock. **1968** J. LOCK *Lady Policeman* xix. 159 Goods from three or four stores would be found in them. Others would 'lift' a shopping bag first in which to put all the other 'lifted' goods. **1973** J. WAINWRIGHT *Devil you Don't* 107 Lift a bleedin' gun from somewhere.

transf. **1885** *Spectator* 10 Jan. 51/2 In painting-in his background, he is, therefore, reasonably entitled to 'lift' his materials wherever he finds them. **1892** *Nation* (N.Y.) 15 Dec. 456/3 All that is vitally concerned with Lincoln, is lifted bodily from Herndon's book.

†**9.** The technical word for: To carve (a swan). (The text of quot. *c* 1500 app. contains some error.)

c **1500** *For to serve a Lord* in *Babees Bk.* (1868) 374 Begynne at the lifte legge first of a Swan; and lyfte a gose y-reared at the right legge first. **1513** *Bk. Keruynge* ibid. 266 Lyfte that swanne. **1804** FARLEY *Lond. Art Cookery* (ed. 10) 293 To lift a swan, you must slit it quite down the middle of the breast.

10. *Card-playing. intr.* To cut (for deal). ? *Obs.*

1599 MINSHEU *Span. Dial.* (1623) 26, I lift to see who shall deale, it must be a coat card. **1608** MACHIN & MARKHAM *Dumb Knt.* IV. i. H 3 b, But come, lift for the dealing, it is my chance to deale. **1674–80** COTTON *Compl. Gamester* 86 At French-Ruff you must lift for deal.

11. *trans.* **a.** To take up and remove, take away; to drive (cattle) away or to market, to strike (a tent); *Sc.* to remove (a corpse) for burial; also *absol. fig.*, to remove, discontinue (restrictions, an embargo, etc.).

a **1670** SPALDING *Troubl.* (Bannatyne Club) I. 236 The said day Monro lifts his camp frae Strathbogie. **1816** SCOTT *Bl. Dwarf* xiii, We seem to be met at a funeral.. Ellieslaw, when will you lift. **1832** HT. MARTINEAU *Ireland* i. 11 That's better than seeing them lifted to the pound. **1835** JAMES *Gipsy* ii, I fear that we shall be obliged to lift our tents, and quit this pleasant nook. **1836** MRS. BROWNING *Poet's Vow* v. xv, They came at dawn of day To lift the lady's corpse away. **1840** *Edin. Even. Courant* 19 Sept., We anticipate rather dull sales now, for a week or two, until the St Faith's droves are lifted. **1856** KANE *Arct. Expl.* II. vii. 79 Nearly all my hopes of lifting the sick.. rest upon these dogs. **1882** *Macm. Mag.* XLVI. 164 When an invitation is being given verbally to a funeral in Scotland, the person invited usually asks, 'When do you lift?' **1886** C. SCOTT *Sheep-Farming* 118 If.. a good ewe requires a lamb [her own being dead], it may be advisable to lift a small gimmer's lamb, and put it to her. **1890** *Pall Mall G.* 18 Sept. 7/1 A large number of families went to the church and lifted their books. **1890** 'R. BOLDREWOOD' *Squatter's Dream* iv. 45, I haven't lifted a finer mob this season. **1890** *Argus* (Melbourne) 14 June 4/2 We lifted 7000 sheep. **1891** *Newcastle Even. Chron.* 31 Jan. 2/1 Interment on Sunday; to lift at Two o'clock. **1896** *Daily News* 4 Sept. 3/4 Some hot-headed proposals were made, one being to lift tools at once. **1936** A. RUSSELL *Gone Nomad* I. ii. 11, I hope his droving mission, that of 'lifting' a thousand head of cattle for the markets of the south, was attended with the success it merited. **1941** I. L. IDRIESS *Great Boomerang* x. 75 Red Bill and his gang lifted their cattle. They headed south-west and got safely across to the Paroo.

fig. **1906** *Daily Chron.* 12 Sept. 5/7 It was freely said that if we only applied the suspensions would be lifted. **1974** *Nature* 25 Jan. 171/3 Even if the embargo is suddenly lifted, it will take several weeks for the oil to reach United States ports. **1974** *Daily Tel.* 4 Apr. 17/1 The university authorities yesterday lifted the temporary suspension on deliveries of supplies to the campus.

b. *U.S. to lift (a person's) hair*: to scalp.

1848 RUXTON *Life in Far West* 37 'We'll lift the hair, any how', continued the first, 'afore the scalps cold'.

c. *U.S.* To get rid of, pay off (a mortgage).

1879 J. BURROUGHS *Locusts & W. Honey* 79 The weather must lift the mortgage on his farm, and pay his taxes. **1886** STOCKTON *Lady or the Tiger* 74 So then the spectral mortgage could never be lifted.

d. *Hunting.* (See quot. 1968.) Also, to disperse (scent).

1781 P. BECKFORD *Thoughts on Hunting* x. 147 By lifting his hounds too much, he will teach them to shuffle. **1843** *Ainsworth's Mag.* IV. 125, I seldom allow hounds to be lifted, except to a beaten fox. *Ibid.*, To lift, in that case, is proper and justifiable. **1863** C. MORDAUNT *Diary* 6 Mar. in Mordaunt & Verney *Ann. Warwickshire Hunt* (1896) I. 264 [The hounds] had to be lifted several times to holloas. **1919** J. MASEFIELD *Reynard* II. 85 He heard the sounds Of a cantering huntsman, lifting hounds; The ploughman had raised his hat for a sign, And the hounds were lifted and on his line. **1929** *St. Andrews Citizen* 16 Mar. 7 Fife Foxhounds had three poor days last week. Although the weather was good, the bright, warm sunshine 'lifted' scent. **1968** J. GORDON *Beagle Guide* 172 *Lift*, to remove hounds from a lost scent with the idea of trying to hit the line further on.

e. To give a lift to (in a carriage, motor vehicle, etc.). Cf. LIFT *sb.*[2] 1 b.

1884 E. W. HAMILTON *Diary* 17 Aug. (1972) II. 672 A very hot walk. We got 'lifted' back in a carriage; and afterwards played lawn tennis. **1954** M. SHARP *Gipsy in Parlour* xxii. 211 Up she drove, lifted by Mr Simnel the chemist, Taunton-bound. **1959** I. JEFFERIES *Thirteen Days* vii. 87 He'd like to lift me back to Richon fairly soon as the roads were likely to tighten up during the day. **1960** *Sunday Express* 13 Nov. 14/5 A young R.A.F. hitch-hiker I 'lifted' from Shepherd's Bush to High Wycombe. **1965** I. FLEMING *Man with Golden Gun* vi. 90 Get in the back. Lift you down to your car. **1971** M. RUSSELL *Deadline* ii. 22 Can you lift me in your wagon, Wally?

f. *Artillery. trans.* and *intr.* To increase the range of fire from that being used at a given point in an attack.

1916 in A. Farrar-Hockley *Somme* (1964) iii. 94 Avoid a pause at 0000, at minus three in each field battery, where one section will lift on to the support line. **1917** J. MASEFIELD *Old Front Line* ii. 30 The flash of our shells, breaking a little further off as the gunners 'lifted'. **1922** *Encycl. Brit.* XXX. 255/2 The bombardment is 'lifted' from the first line to reinforce that on the second line. **1962** *Ordnance Technical Terminol.* (U.S. Army Ordnance School) (AD 660 112) 176/2 *Lift fire*, to advance the range of fire by elevating the muzzle of a weapon. **1964** A. FARRAR-HOCKLEY *Somme* iii. 96 The 18-pounders lifted on time as they passed the wire. *Ibid.* 98 Some aghast to see the supporting artillery fire already lifting ahead of them.

g. Of a sheepdog: to establish control over a flock of sheep. Cf. LIFT *sb.*[2] 5 i.

1921 *Kelso Chron.* 12 Aug. 2 This bitch started well... Her haulding, lifting, and penning were good, her bringing and driving very fair. **1942** R. B. KELLEY *Animal Breeding* xiii. 127 When he [*sc.* a pup] has reached this point sit him down and make him lift the flock quietly. **1946** F. D. DAVISON *Dusty* ix. 90 The paddock, what with hills, broken ground and patches of scrub, was not the easiest in the world to lift sheep from. **1949** C. W. G. HARTLEY *Shepherd's Dogs* v. 33 Much will depend upon the manner in which the sheep are 'lifted'.

h. To arrest, take into custody.

1923 G. WATSON *Roxburghshire Word-Bk.* 200 Tam's gruppen an' liftit. **1934** D. ALLAN *Hunger March* III. ii. 208 They've lifted Smith. **1968** 'J. ROSS' *Diminished by Death* ii. 27 The youth stood. 'Am I being lifted?' 'Not at the moment. You are helping us with our inquiries.' **1972** *Times* 24 Jan. 2/1 If you have a father who is lifted, he has sons and cousins who will take his place. **1973** 'J. PATRICK' *Glasgow Gang Observed* iii. 32 A fund.. to raise ten pounds bail money for two of their number who had been 'lifted' the night before for fighting.

i. To evacuate (soldiers) from a beach; to air-lift. Also *transf.* Cf. LIFT *sb.*[2] 5 h.

1941 J. MASEFIELD *Nine Days Wonder* 19 The first men lifted were not always soldiers. **1963** *Times* 24 Jan. 10/3 An emergency rail freighter service ordered by Lord Robens, chairman of the National Coal Board, is lifting thousands of tons of coal into the worst snowbound areas of south-east and south-west England. **1972** *Daily Tel.* 11 Apr. 17 Medical supplies, tents and food were being lifted in by helicopter last night.

12. a. To take up out of the ground (*Sc.* in general sense); *Hort.* to dig up (potatoes, bulbs, etc.). Also occas. *intr.*, in phr. ***to lift well***, of the crops or plants concerned: to produce a good yield or be in good condition when lifted.

1844 STEPHENS *Bk. Farm* III. 1125 When lifted for shipment to the London market, they [potatoes] are first riddled into sizes, then [etc.]. **1883** J. PURVES in *Contemp. Rev.* Sept. 354 The tall, strong farm-women 'lifting' the potatoes. **1883** STEVENSON *Treas. Isl.* I. i, There is still treasure not yet lifted. **1888** L. CASTLE *Flower Gardening* 232 November... Lift Gladioli corms, storing them in a dry place; also Dahlia tubers. **1888** HARDY *Wessex Tales* II. 67 The next day went about his swede-lifting and storing. **1891** 'H. HALIBURTON' *Ochil Idylls* 106 The dreels [of potatoes] are to lift, An' the neeps are to pu'. **1892** E. REEVES *Homeward Bound* 334 She had come over to Paris to lift his remains and remove them to another place. **1892** E. P. DIXON *Seed Catalogue* 25 Fifty-fold [potato].. which may be lifted July and August. **1931** *Morning Post* 19 July 5/1 What to do with the bulbs at this season when, apparently, they are sleeping, has for long been a rather controversial point. Should they be left or lifted? **1959** *Times* 7 Sept. 19/2 Some crops [of potatoes] in Lincolnshire are lifting well, others are below average. **1971** 'L. BLACK' *Death has Green Fingers* vii. 83 Suppose whoever it was had lifted the roses already. **1973** *Times* 20 Oct. 14/6 Nurseries.. cannot lift and pack all their orders in a month.

b. *Sc.* To carry (a crop), clear (a cornfield).

1876 A. LAING *Lindores Abbey* xxiv. 309 He went and searched the ground after the crop was lifted. **1883** [see LIFTED *ppl. a.*].

13. To hit (the ball) into the air; esp. in *Cricket*: often with the bowler as object.

1874 *Times* 5 Oct. 11/2 When the [golf] ball must be 'skied', or lifted over some swell of the ground. **1882** *Daily Tel.* 24 June, W. G. lifted Spofforth round to the leg boundary. **1894** N. GALE *Cricket Songs* 31 He lifts you o'er the Baths for six. **1897** *Daily News* 16 June 3/4 Hill, as is his custom, lifted the ball a good deal.

14. *Comb.*: **Liftback**, the name of a type of hatchback car manufactured by the Toyota motor corporation; occas. (with small initial) applied to other makes of car, = *hatchback* s.v. HATCH *sb.*[1] 9; †**lift-leg**, a name for strong ale; **lift-on, lift-off**, used esp. *attrib.*, a method of hoisting containers from one vessel or vehicle to another; also **lift-on** *attrib.*; **lift-out** *attrib.*, made to lift out; **lift-up** *attrib.*, made to lift up.

1973 *Motor* 5 May 42/3 Toyota have launched two new models in Japan. One is.. a 2-litre fastback with opening tailgate... The 2-litre car is an addition to the Celica range and is called The Liftback. **1977** *Belfast Tel.* 17 Jan. 14/6 (Advt.), Kadett City. A stylish Lift Back that combines good passenger accommodation along with economical and practical motoring. **1979** *Arizona Daily Star* 1 Apr. (Advt. Section) 6/7 Chevette—liftback—economy 4 cylinder with auto. trans. **1985** *Daily Tel.* 26 June 13 (Advt.), The Celica is one of two models (you can also have a liftback). **1587** HARRISON *England* II. xviii. (1877) I. 295 There is such headie ale and beere in most of them, as.. is commonlie called huffecap,.. stride wide, and lift leg. **1956** *Sun* (Baltimore) 16 Oct. 18/3 The relative merits of 'roll-on, roll-off' shipping, where trailers would be rolled aboard, and of 'lift-on, lift-off' service involving only a truck van. **1967** *Freight Management* Jan. 15/1 (Advt.), Last year Southampton handled thousands of containers by lift-on/lift-off. *Ibid.* 46/3 Basically roll-on is more expensive than lift-on. *Ibid.* 47/3 (*caption*) The tanks.. can be used on both roll-on or lift-on vessels. **1968** *Economist* 14 Sept. p. xxxiv/1 The North Sea is now the focal point of a fight between two new forms of transport, the roll-on, roll-off ferry services.. and lift-on, lift-off container services. **1969** *Jane's Freight Containers 1968–69* 73 (*caption*) Simultaneous roll-on and lift-on of trailers make possible a trip a week to Puerto Rico. *Ibid.* 160/3 Lift-on Lift-off Unitised Loads. **1926–7** *Army & Navy Stores Catal.* 314/2 These boilers are.. fitted with a shaking grating and lift-out ashes pan. **1968** *Harrods Christmas Catal.* 3/4 Beauty case with inside pockets and lift-out tray. **1974** *Country Life* 14 Mar. (Suppl.) 41/1 Arm Chair with lift out seat covered in green velvet. **1917** *Installation News* Jan. 5/1 The Cabinets comprise a substantially constructed stained box, fitted with lift-up lid, lock and key. **1950** *N.Z. Jrnl. Agric.* Aug. 132/1 The lift-up gate opens by sliding up between guides fixed to uprights. **1956** *Railway Mag.* Feb. 121/1 There is a separate sheet steel case with lift-up cover containing the engineman's telephone. **1970** *Guardian* 19 Nov. 11/6 Two swing-out drawers, one with a lift-up mirror.

†**lift,** *ppl. a. Obs.* [pa. pple. of LIFT *v.*] = LIFTED *ppl. a.* Also with *up*.

1413 *Pilgr. Sowle* (Caxton 1483) IV. xxxii. 81 Ne neither of them shalle be the lift hand to mayntenaunce of wrong. **1617** A. NEWMAN *Pleas. Vis.* 18 Then seem'd his lookes, and lift-vp hands to say, 'Take heed by me'. **1679** 'T. TICKLEFOOT' *Trial Wakeman* 7 He replyed with lift up hands, God forbid.. that [etc.]. **1724** M. DAVYS *Reformed Coquet* 163 With lift-up Hands.. imploring help.

liftable ('lɪftəb(ə)l), *a.* [f. LIFT *v.* + -ABLE.]

1856 FERRIER *Inst. Metaph.* Introd. 62 To divide the ponderable into the liftable by us.. and the still liftable, though not by us. **1871** CARLYLE in *Mrs. Carlyle's Lett.* III. 194, I was to remove thither with my work (so soon as liftable). **1893** *Field* 4 Mar. 335/1 The centre-plate is so fitted as to be liftable into or out of the boat.

lifted ('lɪftɪd), *ppl. a.* [f. LIFT *v.* + -ED[1].] In senses of the vb.: Raised aloft, upreared, elevated, exalted; stolen, etc. Also with *up*.

1559 AYLMER *Harborowe* R 3 Let vs daylye call to God with lifted vp heartes and handes. *c* **1586** C'TESS PEMBROKE *Ps.* LXXXIX. v, Thy lifted hand a might of wonder showeth. **1654–66** EARL ORRERY *Parthen.* (1676) 725 She endeavour'd to stop his lifted-up Arm from falling on me. **1667** MILTON *P.L.* XI. 866 In the Cloud a Bow, Conspicuous with three lifted colours gay. **1703** ROWE *Ulysses* IV. i. 1803 Provoke the lifted Sword and pointed Spear. *c* **1730** BURT *Lett. Gentl. N. Scot.* (1754) II. 93 His Grandfather.. is therein assured of the immediate Restitution of his Lifted, that is, stolen Cows. **1819** WORDSW. *Waggoner* IV. 151 The morning light in grace Strikes upon his lifted face. **1859** RUSKIN *Two Paths* iv. (1891) 184 All their changing grace of depressed or lifted pinnacle. **1859** GEO. ELIOT (*title*) The Lifted Veil. **1883** MRS. HOPKINS *Autumn Swallows, Bormus*, Down from the lifted cornfield trips The child. **1885–94** R. BRIDGES *Eros & Psyche* Apr. xxv, The last red ray Fled from her lifted arm. **1928** G. B. SHAW *Let.* 31 May in *To a Young Actress* (1960) 127 How will you face old age: With a 'lifted' face, with grease paints and an iceball and rouge, with peroxided hair, an old hag.. pretending to be a young witch.

lifter ('lɪftə(r)). [f. LIFT *v.* + -ER[1].] One who or that which lifts in senses of the vb.

1. a. One who lifts or raises, in either a material or an immaterial sense. Also with *up*.

1535 COVERDALE *Ps.* iii. 3 Thou (o Lorde) art.. the lifter vp of my heade. **1552** HULOET, Lifter wyth leuere, *phalangarius.* **1591** PERCIVALL *Sp. Dict.*, *Llevador*, a bearer, a lifter. **1649** PRYNNE *Demurrer to Jews' Remitter* 83 The greatest designers, plotters and lifters up of themselves against the interest of Christ. **1688** R. HOLME *Armoury* III. 156/2 Musick.. is a lifter of Dead, Drowsie and Melancholly Spirits. **1775** JOHNSON *Western Isl.* Wks. X. 401 Long pieces of wood.. to which the action of a long line of lifters might be applied. **1839** URE *Dict. Arts* 927 Two men at a vat, and a boy as a layer or lifter can make about 6 or 8 reams in 10 hours. **1873** M. ARNOLD *Lit. & Dogma* (1876) 366 The lifter-up to the nations of the banner of righteousness.

b. One who takes up dishonestly; a thief. Cf. *cattle-lifter*, *shop-lifter*.

a **1592** GREENE *Jas. IV*, III. i, Why, I am a lifter, maister, by occupation. **1606** SHAKS. *Tr. & Cr.* I. ii. 129 **1674–80** COTTON *Compl. Gamester* 5 Pads, Biters, Divers, Lifters.. these may all pass under the general.. appellation of Rooks. **1818** SCOTT *Rob Roy* xxix, Ye needna ask whae Rob Roy is, the reiving lifter that he is. **1862** *Athenæum* 30 Aug. 278 While in the 'lifter's' possession.. they [books] had been enriched by numerous annotations. **1885** *Erminie* 11 We are shifters, we are lifters, Working skilfully together.

c. One of a sect of Scottish presbyterians who considered it essential that the officiating minister should 'lift' a piece of sacramental bread while uttering the prayer of consecration.

1805 FORSYTH *Beauties Scotl.* II. 520 Hence.. originated a schism, and the two parties were distinguished by the name of lifters and anti-lifters.

2. Something which lifts or is used for lifting.

a. Something which elevates or raises, in either a material or an immaterial sense; applied also to any simple implement, e.g. †a crutch, †a fork, a curved piece of iron for lifting a stove-lid, and in mod. slang to a heavy blow. Also with *up*.

1570 LEVINS *Manip.* 76/36 A Lifter, forke, *fuscina.* *a* **1700** B. E. *Dict. Cant. Crew*, *Lifter*, a Crutch. **1706** A. BEDFORD *Temple Mus.* viii. 158 *Sakeph Gadol*, or the Greater Lifter up; as if it designed the Musick to be very Loud. **1867** W. W. SMYTH *Coal & Coal-mining* 7 Used as a lifter of water to the top of water-wheels. **1882–3** SCHAFF *Encycl. Relig. Knowl.* 665 Dreams.. in antiquity, were thought to be of

importance as lifters of the veil. **1889** 'MARK TWAIN' *Yankee at Crt. K. Arthur* xxxiii. 383 As long as I'm going to hit him at all, I'm going to hit him a lifter.

b. Technical uses: †(*a*) *Anat.* = LEVATOR 2. (*b*) *Mining.* The wooden beams used as stems for stamps in old-fashioned stamp-mills (Raymond *Mining Gloss.*) (*c*) *Magnetism.* The cross-piece of soft iron applied to the poles of a horse-shoe magnet. (*d*) *Weaving.* ? An appliance for raising and depressing the leaves of the heddles. (*e*) *Steam-engine.* The arm on a lifting-rod that raises the puppet-valve (Webster, 1864). (*f*) *Paper-making.* A bucket-wheel for raising the pulp from the reservoir to the trough. (*g*) *Founding.* 'A tool for dressing the mould; also a contrivance attached to a cope to hold the sand together when the cope is lifted' (Webster, 1864). (*h*) *Surg.* = ELEVATOR 2. (*i*) = *lifting-cam.*

(*a*) **1649** BULWER *Pathomyot.* II. i. 86 That Muscle of the shoulder-blade, from its office commonly called the Levator, or the Lifter.

(*b*) **1671** *Phil. Trans.* VI. 2108 Suffering the Lifters to fall with great force on the Ore, thereby breaking it into small sand. **1860** *Eng. & For. Mining Gloss.* (Cornwall Terms), *Lifters*, wood beams, to which the iron heads of a stamping mill are fastened.

(*c*) **1794** G. ADAMS *Nat. & Exper. Phil.* IV. l. 387 The contact or lifter of soft iron to be placed at the other end of the bars. **1849** NOAD *Electricity* 396 The soft iron lifter of a horse-shoe magnet.

(*d*) **1865** BEN BRIERLEY *Irkdale* I. 236 A weaver..upon a 'jacquard' loom, had the misfortune to break one of the irons of her lifter.

(*f*) **1839** URE *Dict. Arts* 938 The pressure of the pulp and water in the vat forces the pulp up the pipe into the lifter-box, whence it is taken by rotatory lifters, and discharged into a trough, where it runs down and mixes with the thick pulp from the chest.

(*i*) **1852** BURN *Nav. & Milit. Dict.* 11, Lifter or Lifting-cog, cam or wiper. **1884** *Pall Mall G.* 28 Aug. 5/1 The lifter raises the central lever or pawl.

c. *Cricket.* A ball, usu. one from a fast bowler, that rises sharply after striking the pitch.

1959 *Times* 28 July 4/7 He was caught off almost the only lifter of the day in his second [over]. **1974** *Daily Tel.* 12 June 34/1 Gavaskar got an awkward lifter from Old and gave a soft catch to the gully.

lifting ('lɪftɪŋ), *vbl. sb.* [f. LIFT *v.* + -ING^1.]

1. a. The action of the vb. LIFT in various senses. Also ***lifting up***. †Also *concr.* in ***hand-lifting***: so much as can be taken up by the hand. †***at the lifting***: on the point of removal.

1362 LANGL. *P. Pl.* A. v. 204 Glotoun was a gret cherl and grym in þe lyftynge. *a* **1400–50** *Alexander* 567 Stanys [which] Fell fra þe fyrmament as a hand lyftyng. **1482** *Monk of Evesham* (Arb.) 107 The lyftyngys vppe of the crosse. **1551** BIBLE *Gen.* xxiv. *marg. note*, The exercise of the spirit & lyftynge vp of the mind to God, ar called medytacions. **1590** JAS. VI *Sp. Gen. Assembly* Aug., As for our Neighbour Kirk in England..they want nothing of the Masse, but the liftings. **1607** TOPSELL *Four-f. Beasts* (1658) 322 Surbating ..cometh..sometime by the hardness of the ground, and high lifting of the horse. *a* **1662** HEYLIN *Laud* I. 170 There had been some liftings at him in the Court by Sir John Cook. *a* **1670** SPALDING *Troub. Chas. I* (Bannatyne Club) I. 240 This army..by and attour 10000 baggage men is now at the lifting. **1674–80** COTTON *Compl. Gamester* 92 In the lifting for dealing the least deals. *c* **1730** BURT *Lett. Gentl. N. Scotl.* (1754) II. 230 The stealing of their Cows they call Lifting, a soft'ning Word for Theft. **1856** KANE *Arct. Expl.* I. xxiii. 285 A sudden lifting of the fog showed them the cape. **1872** HARDWICK *Trad. Lanc.* 74 The 'lifting' of women by men on Easter Monday. **1884** PAE *Eustace* xix. 244 The cargo is ours for the lifting. **1901** W. D. HOWELLS *Lit. Friends* II. vi. 89 In a lifting of the rain he walked with me down to the village.

b. The raising of sick or weak cattle to enable them to stand. Cf. LIFT *v.* 1 f. So ***at the lifting***, very weak.

1812 W. SINGER *Agric. County of Dumfries* 220 They become quite lean, almost 'at the lifting', as the farmers say. **1899** H. G. GRAHAM *Social Life Scotl. 18th Cent.* I. 155 This period and this annual operation when all neighbours were summoned to carry and support the poor beasts, were known as the 'Lifting'. **1901** M. FRANKLIN *My Brilliant Career* (1966) v. 18 My mother and father and I spent the day in lifting our cows... This cow-lifting became quite a trade.

c. In competitive walking, the raising of the rear heel before the front foot touches the ground.

1867 *Athlete 1866* 119 Lifting, the usual method of walking unfairly, is done by getting a spring from the toe of one foot on to the heel of the other. **1898** F. A. COHEN in W. A. Morgan *'House' on Sport* 433 What is technically called 'lifting' is, except perhaps in a final burst, seldom of any real advantage.

2. *attrib.* and *Comb.* **a.** *gen.*, as ***lifting power***, ***trade***; **b.** a contrivance or portion of a machine adapted for lifting, as ***lifting-bar***, ***-blade***, ***-cog***, ***-crane***, ***-gear***, ***-hitch***, ***-hook***, ***-pallet***, ***-piece***, ***-rod***, ***-screw***, ***-tongs***, ***-wire***; **lifting beam**, a beam, fitted to a crane hook, to which a load may be attached in two or more places; **lifting-cam**, a cam or projection by which a lifting movement is effected, e.g. in firearms; **lifting-day** *local* = *heaving-day*; **lifting-dog**, (*a*) = *lifting-cam*; (*b*) (see quot. 1881^2); **lifting-jack** (see JACK *sb.*^{1} 10); **lifting plate** (see quot. 1888); **lifting screw**, a hook with a threaded shank which can be screwed into an object to facilitate its lifting (see also LIFTING *ppl. a.*).

1831 G. R. PORTER *Silk Manuf.* 247 The *lifting bars which in shape are something like blunted knife blades. **1963** R. HAMMOND *Mobile & Movable Cranes* vi. 167 Aluminium-alloy *lifting beams are very useful for getting the most out of crane-lifting capacity. **1969** *Jane's Freight Containers 1968–69* 130/1 There are new lifting beams used with existing straddle cranes to handle 24 ft. and 20 ft. containers. **1881** GREENER *Gun* 359 The *lifting-cams or 'dogs', are dispensed with. **1852** *Lifting-cog [see LIFTER 2 b (*i*)]. **1879** *Cassell's Techn. Educ.* I. 206/2 These three requisites are very beautifully combined..in the *lifting crane. **1881** GREENER *Gun* 264 Knock the wire pivot right through the *lifting dogs. **1881** RAYMOND *Mining Gloss.*, *Lifting-dog*, a claw-hook for grasping a column of bore-rods while raising or lowering them. **1887** *Daily News* 22 Oct. 2/7 The pinnace was crushed through the breaking of the *lifting gear. **1831** G. R. PORTER *Silk Manuf.* 247 Half the number of *lifting hooks are attached to the lifting bars. **1825** J. NICHOLSON *Operat. Mechanic* 513 That the end of the..spring..may project a little way over the point of the *lifting-pallet. **1704** HARRIS *Lex. Techn.*, **Lifting-pieces*, are Parts of a Clock, which do lift up and unlock the Detents in the Clock-part. **1884** F. J. BRITTEN *Watch & Clockm.* 217 There are four pins in the minute wheel for raising the quarter lifting piece. **1888** *Lockwood's Dict. Mech. Engin.* 208 **Lifting plates*, plates of wrought or malleable cast iron furnished with holes both for rapping and screwing, and let into or screwed on the faces of patterns; and by which they are lifted from the sand, a lifting screw being inserted into the tapped hole in the plate. **1925** J. G. HORNER *Pattern Making* (ed. 5) iii. 56 Screws..either twisted into the wood of the pattern or..fitting into corresponding tapped holes in the lifting plates attached to the pattern face, are used. **1849** NOAD *Electricity* 357 A much greater *lifting power has.. been obtained with other varieties of the electro-magnet. **1885** J. G. HORNER *Pattern Making* xxii. 158 Figs. 206, 207 show two different forms of these [*sc.* rapping] plates, *a* being the plain hole for rapping, *b* the tapped hole for the reception of a *lifting-screw. **1925** —— *Pattern Making* (ed. 5) iii. 59 A central hole bored through the boss for the lifting screw. **1944** E. D. HOWARD *Mod. Foundry Practice* 383/1 (Index), Lifting screw. **1709** HEARNE *Collect.* (O.H.S.) II. 185 This Gentleman..is remarkable for carrying on the *lifting Trade.

lifting ('lɪftɪŋ), *ppl. a.* [f. LIFT *v.* + -ING^2.] That lifts, in senses of the vb., *spec.* in **lifting-bridge**, a bridge of which either a part or the whole may be drawn up at one end when needful; **lifting-gate** = LIFT *sb.*^{2} 15; **lifting-pump**, any pump other than a force-pump; **lifting-sail**, a sail whose action tends to lift the bows out of the water; **lifting-set**, 'the series of pumps by which water is raised from the bottom of a mine by successive lifts' (Knight *Dict. Mech.* 1875). Also, in *Aeronaut.*, providing lift; **lifting body**, a (wingless) spacecraft with a shape designed to produce lift, so that some aerodynamic control of its flight is possible within the atmosphere; **lifting screw**, a rotor operating in a horizontal plane so as to provide lift for a flying machine (see also LIFTING *vbl. sb.*).

13.. *E.E. Allit. P.* B. 443 After harde dayez wern out an hundreth & fyfte, As þat lyftande lome [the ark] luged aboute. **1686** J. DUNTON *Lett. fr. New-Eng.* (1867) 8 Even the Parson himselfe..gave me a lifting hand. **1797** *Encycl. Brit.* (ed. 3) IX. 17/2 Of lifting-pumps there are several sorts. **1839** R. S. ROBINSON *Naut. Steam Eng.* 65 On the top of the air bucket fits the lifting valve. **1851** *Illustr. Catal. Gt. Exhib.* 1148 Swing, lifting, or rolling bridges are..in such cases indispensable. **1875** *Carpentry & Join.* 135 These double-legged tables are very generally made with a rack to allow of their rising by the application of a lifting force. **1882** NARES *Seamanship* (ed. 6) 205 The jib and flying-jib are ..lifting sails. **1894** *Daily News* 19 June 6/5 The supremely interesting feature of this really great work are the lifting bascules. **1895–6** *Cal. Univ. Nebraska* 215 By its use the extensor or lifting muscles are developed. **1898** *Daily News* 16 Nov. 7/1 The mechanism of the lifting roadway is so perfect in its action. **1902** F. WALKER *Aërial Navigation* v. 79 The lifting screws. **1908** *Jrnl. R. Soc. Arts* LVII. 53/1 The Helicoptère, or lifting-screw flying machine. **1919** H. SHAW *Textbk. Aeronaut.* ix. 111 In some machines it is arranged that the tail carries a portion of the load, when it is known as a 'lifting' tail. **1923** *Daily Mail* 12 Feb. 7 While aloft the pilot can change the action of his planes so that they cease to act as vertical lifting-screws and function like the surfaces of an aeroplane. **1935** P. W. F. MILLS *Elem. Pract. Flying* i. 1 Aeroplanes..cannot fly backwards owing to their fixed thrust direction and the arrangement of their lifting surfaces. **1964** *Britannica Bk. of Year* 868/1 *Lifting body*, a wingless, somewhat bathtub-shaped vehicle for aerospace travel that combines some of the heat-handling capacity of a capsule with some of the maneuverability of a wingless aircraft. **1966** *McGraw-Hill Encycl. Sci. & Technol.* VI. 388/2 The disk loading [of a helicopter]..expresses the design gross weight as a function of the swept areas of the lifting rotor. **1969** K. MUNSON *Pioneer Aircraft 1903–14* 104/2 The Blériot III was also a floatplane, with annular lifting surfaces fore and aft. **1972** A. C. KERMODE *Mech. of Flight* (ed. 8) xii. 390 These lifting bodies are but a step towards a shuttle service operating to and from a space station orbiting the earth.

'liftless, *a.* [f. LIFT *sb.*^{2} 10 + -LESS.] Not provided with a lift.

1916 W. J. LOCKE *Wonderful Year* xvii. 245 She was living ..on the fifth floor of a liftless block of flats in Wandsworth. **1921** *Spectator* 16 Apr. 484/2 In a liftless household.

lift-off, *a.* and *sb.* Also liftoff, lift off. [f. vbl. phr. *to lift off* (LIFT *v.* 1 b, 3).] **A.** *adj.* Removable by lifting.

1907 *Yesterday's Shopping* (1969) 385/3 Art cloth box, with lift off lid. **1960** *Farmer & Stockbreeder* 16 Feb. 140/1 (Advt.), Lift-off wide doors..give remarkably easy access. **1970** *Gloss. Industrial Furnace Terms* (*B.S.I.*) 9 *Lift-off* cover furnace, a base over which a cover is placed for heating the charge; separate bases are normally available so that the same cover can be used for several charges. **1974** *Country Life* 6 June 1500 George III Decanter Stand... The lift off tray is divided into nine crenellated compartments.

B. *sb.* **1.** *Parachuting.* A method of leaving an aircraft by opening the parachute while standing on a wing, so as to be carried away by the air current.

1930 P. WHITE *How to fly Airplane* xxii. 303 Two men are about to execute what is known as a 'lift-off' from the wings of a bombing plane. **1946** W. F. BURBIDGE *From Balloon to Bomber* iii. 46 There are two main methods of leaving aircraft. One is known as the 'lift-off' and in using this method the airman climbs on to the wing..and, by releasing his parachute, is lifted off. But this method has been superseded by the 'fall free'. **1957** *Encycl. Brit.* XVII. 252/2 In general use, there are two ways of leaving an aeroplane by parachute: (1) the drag-off or lift-off method, and (2) the jump or free-fall method.

2. [after BLAST-OFF, TAKE-OFF.] The vertical take-off of a rocket, helicopter, or the like; the moment at which an aircraft begins to leave the ground.

1956 in W. A. HEFLIN *U.S. Air Force Dict.* 299. **1958** *Time* 8 Dec. 15/2 With great restraint, Shotwell and his 40-man launch team quietly waited in their bunker a full seven minutes after the lift-off before they dared shout. **1961** *Aeroplane* CI. 92/1 Lift-off took place at Cape Canaveral at 07.20 hrs. local time. **1962** *New Scientist* 22 Feb. 426/3 A plate in 10-gauge aluminium weighed 6·1 lb complete with nine-inch peg and gave adequate protection for fully 50 lift-offs [of VTOL aircraft] on grass. **1962** *Engineering* 27 July 99/1 The flow characteristic..is designed to facilitate part power operation and easy 'lift off' [of hovercraft] from the surface. **1966** J. A. MORRIS *Bird Watcher* (1968) ii. 27 The launch vehicle exploded soon after lift-off. **1967** D. P. DAVIES *Handling Big Jets* vii. 177 Take care when operating in cross winds. On take-off set in a little into-wind aileron control..; this will stop the down wind roll which will otherwise occur just before lift off. **1967** *New Scientist* 16 Nov. 406/1 From lift-off at Cape Kennedy..to splash-down in the Pacific Ocean northwest of Hawaii..the entire operation appears to have been an almost flawless performance. **1970** N. ARMSTRONG et al. *First on Moon* xi. 245 If a serious malfunction should be detected, either by the men in Eagle or by the men on the ground, an immediate liftoff could be ordered.

b. *fig.* Initiation or commencement of activity; 'getting off the ground' (of a project or scheme).

1967 *Oxford Computer Explained* 7 Prior to lift-off on 1 August it was necessary that the actual stock in the warehouse be counted and the stock figures loaded to the computer. **1970** *Daily Tel.* 25 Apr. 17 (*heading*) Shell has lift-off with its space promotion. *Ibid.*, After weeks of harrowing doubt, the..'biggest, most widespread promotion the world has yet seen' achieves lift-off next week.

lifull, obs. form of LIFEFUL.

†**lig**, *sb. Obs.* Also 7 ligge. [Origin obscure; the identity of the word in the two quots. is not certain.] **a.** A projection. **b.** A band, stripe.

1610 GUILLIM *Heraldry* III. xiii. (1611) 125 When any part is thus born with ligges, like peeces of the flesh or skinne, depending, it is termed erasing. **1686** GOAD *Celest. Bodies* II. vii. 252, I cannot..empale each Page of this Discourse with a Black mourning Lig.

lig (lɪg), *v.* [f. dial. var. of LIE *v.*^{1}] To idle or lie about (*colloq.*); also (*slang*), to sponge, to 'freeload'; to gatecrash or attend parties.

1960 *20th Cent.* Feb. 154 The ponce's air of having a function, an occupation..which totally distinguishes him from the mere 'ligging' layabout. **1967** *Melody Maker* 21 Jan. 6 When I was demobbed in 1960 I had no intention of going back to my trade as a fitter. I ligged around and joined Mike Peters. **1967** *Sun* 22 Feb. 6/6 *Lig, loon*, to kick one's heels or lounge about. **1969** *It* 4–17 July 10/2 It's a time for ligging in the streets and doing your thing, man. **1976** *Zigzag* Apr. 32/2 The Feelgoods, now ligging and gigging around America. **1981** *New Standard* 2 June 23/3 *Ligging*, partying. **1985** *Radio Times* 6 Apr. 16/2 [I] suddenly twigged what ligging was all about when I got my first job as a researcher on *Aquarius*. I found..I could get free tickets for everything, everywhere. **1985** *Times* 9 Apr. 8/5 A penniless young man who begins in Trafalgar Square with nothing but a pair of underpants and ligs his way onward and upward with clean-cut charm.

lig, obs. and dial var. LIE *v.*^{1} (see also LIG *v.*).

†**'ligable**, *a. Mus. Obs.* [ad. L. type **ligābilis*, f. *ligāre* to bind: see -ABLE.] Of two or more notes: That may be 'tied' together.

1597 MORLEY *Introd. Mus.* Annot., Minimes..cannot be tied or enter in ligature. But that defect might be supplyed by dashing the signe of the degree either with one stroke, or two, and so cause the Ligable figures serue to any small quantitie of time we list. **1609** DOULAND *Ornith. Microl.* 40 There are foure ligable Notes, that is, a Large, a Long, a Breefe, and a Semibreefe.

ligament ('lɪgəmənt). [ad. L. *ligāment-um*, f. *ligāre* to bind.]

†**1.** Anything used in binding or tying; a band, tie; *Surg.* a bandage, ligature. *Obs.* in lit. sense.

1599 A. M. tr. *Gabelhouer's Bk. Physicke* 344/1 Cut of linnen ligamentes the breadth of three fingers, grease them in this salve... Tye then these ligamentes theron. **1626** BACON *Sylva* §66 The Prince of Aurange..could finde no meanes to stanch the Bloud, either by Medicine or Ligament. **1671** GREW *Anat. Plants* I. iii. App. §4 (1682) 27 The Gardener, with his Ligaments of Leather, secures the main Branches. **1735** J. PRICE *Stone-Br. Thames* 7 All the Work well cemented and join'd together with proper Ligaments. **1753** HANWAY *Trav.* (1762) I. III. I. 228 Their drawers..are more convenient than breeches..being without any tight ligaments.

b. *fig.* Chiefly, a tie, bond of union.

1426 LYDG. *De Guil. Pilgr.* 22595 My boondes and my lygamentys Ben dyuerse comaundementys, To holden in subieccyoun ffolkes off relygyoun. **1596** BELL *Surv. Popery* III. v. 280 The bishoppe of Rome..might have released or pardoned..such ligaments, mults, or canonicall corrections as he had inioyned to publike offenders. **1643** SIR T. BROWNE *Relig. Med.* I. §38, I have not those strait ligaments, or narrow obligations to the World, as to dote on life. **1762** STERNE *Tr. Shandy* VI. x, He looked up..in my uncle Toby's face; then cast a look upon his boy;—and that ligament, fine as it was,—was never broken. **1796** BURKE *Reg. Peace* I. (1892) 70 The law of nations, the great ligament of mankind. **1841** TRENCH *Parables* xvii. (1877) 326 The Sacraments have been often called the ligaments for the wounds of the soul. **1850** HAWTHORNE *Scarlet L.* iv. (1852) 69, I find here a woman, a man, a child, amongst whom and myself there exist the closest ligaments. No matter whether of love or hate;..of right or wrong.

2. *Anat.* One of the numerous short bands of tough, flexible, fibrous tissue which bind the bones of the body together. By extension applied to any membranous fold which supports an organ and keeps it in position.

c **1400** *Lanfranc's Cirurg.* 20 Ne leeue we nouȝt þat ech brood ligament is a skyn, & ech round ligament to be a senewe. **1599** MASSINGER etc. *Old Law* I. i, I might have gently lost it in my cradle, Before my nerves and ligaments grew strong. **1741** MONRO *Anat. Bones* (ed. 3) 213 The Ligament of the Thigh-bone, which is commonly..called the round one. **1802** PALEY *Nat. Theol.* viii. 120 A..flexible ligament, inserted, by one end into the head of the ball, by the other into the bottom of the cup [of a ball and socket joint]; which ligament keeps the two parts of the joint..in their place. **1838** DICKENS *Nich. Nick.* xxi, The ligament which unites the Siamese twins. **1858** LEWES *Sea-side Stud.* 275 To Goethe, bones and ligaments were not less beautiful and full of interest than flowers and streams.

b. A similar part in lower organisms.

1797 *Encycl. Brit.* XIII. 537 A ligament placed at the summit of the [oyster] shell serves as an arm to its operations. **1802** BINGLEY *Anim. Biog.* (1813) I. 42 They [insects] are cut, as it were, into two parts. These parts are in general connected by a slender ligament or hollow thread. **1826** KIRBY & SP. *Entomol.* IV. 185 In those with a sessile one [*sc.* abdomen] the base is attached to the metaphragm by strong ligaments.

c. *spec.* in *Conch.* The elastic substance which holds together the valves of a bivalve shell.

1816 T. BROWN *Elem. Conchol.* 155 **1837** *Penny Cycl.* VII. 433/1 To this hinge is superadded a ligament. **1851** RICHARDSON *Geol.* viii. (1855) 242. **1875** BUCKLAND *Log-bk.* 123 The ligament which holds the two shells together.

3. *Comb.*, as *ligament-wise* adv.

1615 CROOKE *Body of Man* 389 These..are knit to the proper membrane of euery gristle by the interposition as it were of a Periostion Ligament-wise.

Hence †'**ligament** *v. rare* to bind *together*.

1658–9 *Burton's Diary* (1828) III. 210 There was great wisdom..in framing that oath; to ligament the single person and people together.

ligamental (lɪgəˈmɛntəl), *a.* [f. LIGAMENT + -AL[1].] Of the nature of a ligament; composed of the fibrous tissue of which ligaments consist.

1578 BANISTER *Hist. Man* I. 2 Muscles often spryng out of Ligamentall Cartilages. **1615** CROOKE *Body of Man* 628 The Tongue..hath no Ligamentall Fibres to strengthen it as Muscles haue. **1646** SIR T. BROWNE *Pseud. Ep.* v. v. 239 The Urachos or ligamentall passage derived from the bottome of the bladder.

b. Pertaining to the ligament (of a bivalve).

1850 J. D. SOWERBY in *Dana's Geol.* App. i. 699 Equivalve, suborbicular, thin,..ligamental area elongate. **1854** WOODWARD *Mollusca* II. 247 The internal ligament, or cartilage, is lodged in furrows formed by the ligamental plates. *Ibid.* 286 A distinct ligamental ridge in each valve.

ligamentary (lɪgəˈmɛntərɪ), *a.* [f. LIGAMENT + -ARY.] **a.** Of the nature of or composing a ligament; consisting of the tissue proper to ligaments. **b.** Of or pertaining to a ligament.

1744 tr. *Boerhaave's Inst.* III. 411 Besides these ligamentary Fasciæ, there are also others more broad and muscular. **1783** H. WATSON in *Med. Commun.* I. 188 The ligamentary periosteum, which covers the vertebræ. **1816** D. P. BLAINE *Veterinary Art* 411 Ossifications and ligamentary enlargements. **1832** *Westm. Rev.* XVII. 312 Flax..is applied by the natives to almost every purpose of clothing, building, packing, or wherever ligamentary structure can be turned to account. **1850** H. MILLER *Footpr. Creat.* v. 87 In some of the nail-heads..there appear well-marked ligamentary impressions.

ligamen'tiferous, *a.* *Conch.* [See -FEROUS.] (See quot.)

1839 SOWERBY *Conch. Man.* 56 *Ligamentiferous*, having or containing the ligament, as the cardinal pit in Mya.

ligamento- (lɪgəˈmɛntəʊ), used as a pseudo-L. comb. form, with the meaning 'ligamentous and ...', as *ligamento-cartilaginous*, *-muscular* adjs.

1782 A. MONRO *Anat. Bones, Nerves*, etc. 67 This flexible ligamento-cartilaginous substance. **1835–6** TODD *Cycl. Anat.* I. 519/1 A large ligamento-muscular plate.

ligamentous (lɪgəˈmɛntəs), *a.* [f. LIGAMENT + -OUS.] Of the nature of, or characteristic of, a ligament; composed of the tissue proper to ligaments.

1683 A. SNAPE *Anat. Horse* I. vi. (1686) 9 A Muscle, which is one while ligamentous and nervous, and otherwhiles fleshy. **1725** BRADLEY *Fam. Dict.* s.v. *Plants*, Those [plants] that are not woody may be reduced to six Sorts, viz. the fibrous, ligamentous, bulbous [etc.]. **1796** *Phil. Trans.* LXXXVII. 23 All ligamentous parts..are weak in their vital powers. **1804** ABERNETHY *Surg. Obs.* 32 It had unfortunately acquired a ligamentous adhesion to the orbicular ligament of the hip. **1826** KIRBY & SP. *Entomol.* III. 409 The second kind of articulation, the ligamentous, he affirms takes place only in orthopterous and some neuropterous insects. **1872** MIVART *Elem. Anat.* 28 Ligamentous fibres bind together the margins of the apposed articular surfaces. **1880** GÜNTHER *Fishes* 119 The tongue consists merely of ligamentous or cellular substance.

b. Pertaining to the ligaments of the body.

1804 *Med. Jrnl.* XII. 563 Gouty, or ligamentous and tendinous inflammation.

Hence **liga'mentously** *adv.*, by ligaments.

1883 *Encycl. Brit.* XVI. 609 Being also connected ligamentously with the scapulæ.

ligamentum (ˌlɪgəˈmɛntəm). *Anat.* Pl. **-menta.** [L. *ligāmentum* band, tie, bandage.] Used in numerous mod.L. collocations to designate ligaments of the body.

1713 W. CHESELDEN *Anat. Humane Body* I. ix. 30 One large Gland..seated in a Sinus at the bottom of the Acetabulum of the Os Innominatum, which is compress'd by the Ligamentum *Teres*. **1840** G. V. ELLIS *Demonstrations Anat.* 128 The ligamentum nuchæ is a narrow ligamentous structure situated in the cervical region between the trapezius muscle of each side. **1877** W. TURNER *Introd. Human Anat.* II. vi. 335 By its circumference or ciliary border the iris is not only continuous with the ciliary processes, but is connected by fibres, termed *ligamentum pectinatum*, with the posterior elastic lamina of the cornea. **1913** *Cunningham's Text-bk. Anat.* (ed. 4) 308 The laminæ of adjoining vertebræ are bound together by the ligamenta flava (O.T. subflava).., which consist of yellow elastic fibres. **1956** *Nature* 10 Mar. 467/2 Elastic fibres from ox ligamentum nuchæ, when treated with..acetic acid solution .., are apparently devoid of collagen.

ligan, obs. form of LAGAN, wreckage.

ligance, obs. form of LIGEANCE.

ligand (ˈlɪgənd). *Chem.* [f. L. *ligand-us*, gerundive of *ligāre* to bind.] **1.** Each of the atoms or groups attached to the central (usually the metal) atom of a co-ordination complex.

1952 *Jrnl. Chem. Soc.* 4757 Inferences from spectral absorption to thermochemical stability are therefore very speculative, particularly if different types of ligand, say ions and neutral dipoles, are being compared. **1964** J. W. LINNETT *Electronic Struct. Molecules* viii. 138 This implies that..the tendency to form a multiple bond is about the same for the PF_3 ligand as for CO. **1964** *Oceanogr. & Marine Biol.* II. 250 The relative accumulation factors for metals in marine organisms are related, in general, to the stability of the metal ions with ligands. **1971** *Arch. Biochem. & Biophysics* CXLVII. 226/1 At each monomer active site the two iron atoms can be bridged by two small, inorganic ligands.

2. Special Comb.: **ligand exchange**, exchange of ligands between complexes; **ligand field**, the electrostatic field produced by the ligands in the vicinity of the central atom; so ***ligand field theory***, the branch of chemical theory which deals with the effect of ligands on the energy levels of the central atom or ion; *spec.* a theory based on an electrostatic model modified by molecular orbital considerations.

1964 *Jrnl. Amer. Chem. Soc.* LXXXVI. 765 (*heading*) Rates of rapid ligand exchange reactions by nuclear magnetic resonance line broadening studies. **1973** *Jrnl. Chromatogr.* LXXXVII. 513 A rapid ligand-exchange chromatographic method for the separation of α-amino acids from peptides is presented. **1956** *Nature* 18 Feb. 305/2 A proper consideration of the effect of the ligand-field explains why the six-coordinate complexes of nickel are equally stable with the cupric complexes. **1960** L. PAULING *Nature Chem. Bond* (ed. 3) v. 174 In some respects the ligand field theory is closely related..to the valence bond theory. **1966** COTTON & WILKINSON *Adv. Inorg. Chem.* (ed. 2) xxvi. 661 This modified CFT [*sc.* crystal field theory] is often called ligand field theory, LFT. However, LFT is sometimes also used as a general name for the whole gradation of theories from the electrostatic CFT to the MO [*sc.* molecular orbital] formulation. **1970** W. L. JOLLY *Synthesis & Characterization Inorg. Compounds* xxii. 324 If we were able gradually to decrease the ligand field strength to zero, we would find that each term would gradually approach an energy corresponding to one of the states of the free ion. **1971** ORCHIN & JAFFÉ *Symmetry, Orbitals & Spectra* vii. 170 Interpretation of the spectra of inorganic complexes is greatly simplified and successfully integrated by the use of ligand field theory.

So **'ligancy** = *co-ordination number* s.v. CO-ORDINATION 5; **'liganded** *a.*, bound to a ligand or ligands.

1960 L. PAULING *Nature Chem. Bond* (ed. 3) ii. 63 A sharp distinction is to be made between the number of atoms bonded to a central atom (the ligancy or coordination number of the central atom) and the number of covalent bonds formed by the central atom (its covalence). *Ibid.* xiii. 538 The changes from the standard sodium chloride and rutile arrangements, with ligancy 6, to cesium chloride and fluorite, respectively, with ligancy 8, are nearly the same. **1965** PHILLIPS & WILLIAMS *Inorg. Chem.* I. v. 157 The presence of shared edges and especially of shared faces in a coordinated structure decreases its stability; this effect is large for cations with large valence and small ligancy. **1967** *Jrnl. Biol. Chem.* CCXLII. 3705/2 If the αβ dimer that reacts with ligand is free in solution, the now liganded dimer, $\alpha^*\beta^*$, can associate with another liganded dimer to produce a liganded tetramer, $\alpha_2^*\beta_2^*$. **1968** *Inorg. Chem.* VII. 1945/2 There are certain bonding situations common in boron chemistry and uncommon elsewhere that lead to unusual nomenclature problems. These include..excess connectivity or ligancy. **1973** *Jrnl. Molecular Biol.* LXXVI. 238 Hybrids formed in a mixture of HbS and CN met-Hb A would, upon deoxygenation, contain one liganded α chain and one liganded β chain.

ligase (ˈlɪgeɪz, -eɪs). *Biochem.* [f. L. *lig-āre* to bind + -ASE.] (See quot. 1961.)

1961 *Rep. Comm. Enzymes Internat. Union Biochem.* vi. 39 Enzymes catalysing the linking together of two molecules, coupled with the breaking of a pyrophosphate link in ATP, etc., will be known as ligases (pronounced with a short 'i' in English). These enzymes have hitherto been known as synthetases... A new systematic name was necessary. **1965** *Canad. Jrnl. Biochem.* XLIII. 1605 Succinate: CoA ligase (ADP)..catalyzes the formation of succinyl CoA. **1972** *Sci. Amer.* Jan. 31/1 The most unusual of them is an enzyme that is named polynucleotide ligase, which repairs breaks in DNA molecules.

†**ligate**, *a.* *Obs. rare*[−0]. [ad. L. *ligāt-us*, pa. pple. of *ligāre* to bind.] 'Bound, tied'.

1604 in R. CAWDREY *Table Alph.*

ligate (ˈlaɪgeɪt), *v.* Chiefly *Surg.* [f. L. *ligāt-*, ppl. stem of *ligāre* to bind.] *trans.* To bind with a ligature or bandage; *spec.* in *Surg.*, to tie up (a bleeding artery or vessel).

1599 A. M. tr. *Gabelhouer's Bk. Physicke* 37/1 Open a blacke Henne on her backe, applye and also ligate her on his head. **1775** *New Hampsh. Prov. Papers* (1873) VII. 652 He ..was at that time even destitute of a needle to ligate a bleeding vessell. **1896** TREVES *Syst. Surg.* I. 540 When a surgeon is ligating an artery. **1899** *Allbutt's Syst. Med.* VI. 244 If..the superior mesenteric artery be ligated.

fig. *c* **1600** *Timon* III. v, Let it be lawfull for me..to ligate and obligate your eares with my words.

Hence **'ligated** *ppl. a.*, tied with a ligature; (of letters) united in a ligature; **'ligating** *vbl. sb.* Also **li'gator**, 'an instrument to place and fasten a ligature' (Knight *Dict. Mech.* Suppl. 1884).

1597 A. M. tr. *Guillemeau's Fr. Chirurg.* 31 b/1 That nature may have time to close the cutt and ligated vayne. **1866** T. WRIGHT in *Intell. Observ.* No. 50. 108 The Roman ligated letters. **1875** KNIGHT *Dict. Mech.*, Ligating-forceps. **1899** *Allbutt's Syst. Med.* VI. 165 The formation of a thrombus is of no assistance in securing obliteration of a ligated vessel.

ligation (laɪˈgeɪʃən). [ad. L. *ligātiōn-em*, n. of action f. *ligāre* to bind.]

†**1.** The action or process of binding; a connecting or binding fast; also, the condition of being bound; suspension (of the faculties). *Obs.*

1597 A. M. tr. *Guillemeau's Fr. Chirurg.* *iij, To bring to passe in this wretched worlde, in our bodye, a shorte and breefe ligatione [of us and Heaven]. **1612** J. COTTA *Disc. Dang. Pract. Physicke* I. vii. 68 To them that sleep in their clothes..there is not so true a ligation of their senses. **1638** *Penit. Conf.* viii. (1657) 237 He that hath not the power of absolution hath not the power of ligation. **1643** SIR T. BROWNE *Relig. Med.* II. §11 The slumber of the body seems to be but the waking of the soul. It is the ligation of sense, but the liberty of reason. **1656** BLOUNT *Glossogr.*, *Ligation*, a binding, also the tongue-tying in children especially. **1664** H. MORE *Myst. Iniq.* 291 They having no coherence or ligation with the time of the Prophet, but onely with one another. **1684** T. BURNET *Theory of Earth* I. 196 The ligation of Satan proves this point effectually: for so long as Antichrist reigns, Satan cannot be said to be bound.

2. The action of binding with a ligature; *esp.* in *Surg.*, the operation of tying up (a bleeding artery, etc.). Also, an instance of this.

1597 A. M. tr. *Guillemeau's Fr. Chirurg.* 27/2 The ligatione or tyinge of the teeth, to ioyn them together. **1634** T. JOHNSON *Parey's Chirurg.* XIV. iii. 556 The habit of the body ought to prescribe a measure in ligation: for tender bodies cannot away with so hard binding as hard. *a* **1659** OSBORN *Queries* Wks. (1673) 588 Swathing, and the rest of the ligations used by Nurses to Infants. **1689** MOYLE *Sea Chyrurg.* II. v. 39 If such a Wound should happen in the joint of the Hip, where such Ligation cannot be made. **1899** *Allbutt's Syst. Med.* VI. 165 It is this angeiitis which leads to the closure of a vessel after ligation.

3. Something used in binding; a ligature, bandage, bond, tie; also, the place of tying. *arch.*

1597 A. M. tr. *Guillemeau's Fr. Chirurg.* 44 b/2 Reducinge both the endes of the ligatione which we have in our hands above on the wounde. **1633** J. DONE *Hist. Septuagint* 48 There was also an enrichment of Precious stones, strung through a ligation of Cords. *c* **1645** HOWELL *Lett.* II. xlvii, Ther is a peculiar Religion attends frendship, ther is according to the Etymologie of the word, a ligation and solemne tie. **1815** SCOTT *Guy M.* xxxviii, A bundle tied with tape, and sealed at each fold and ligation with black wax.

†**ligatory**, *a.* *Obs.* [ad. L. type **ligātōrius*, f. *ligāre* to bind: see -ORY.] **a.** Serving to bind or tie up. **b.** That has binding force, obligatory.

1610 HEYWOOD *Lanc. Witches* IV. (1634) H 3, *Dough.* Now do I thinke upon the codpeece point the young jade gave him at the wedding... *Arth.* A ligatory point. *Bant.* Alas poore

Lawrence. **1625** W. B. *True School War* 4 It is cleere amongst..Professors of Cases of Conscience, That the errour..which..is called an erronious Conscience, is ligatorie.

ligature (ˈlɪgətjʊə(r)), *sb.* Also 7 ligator. [ad. L. *ligātūra*, f. *ligāre* to bind. Cf. F. *ligature*.]

1. Anything used in binding or tying; a band, bandage, tie. Chiefly *spec.* in *Surgery*, a thread or cord used to tie up a bleeding artery, to strangulate a tumour, etc.

c **1400** *Lanfranc's Cirurg.* 82 Also it is good to..streyne þi ligature at þe ground of þi wounde, & bynde it losely at þe mouþ of þe wounde. **1541** R. Copland *Guydon's Quest. Chirurg.* H iij b, Let it..be cut in the myddes of the lygature and let the nether parte be left. **1621** Burton *Anat. Mel.* II. i. I. i, Whether..by spells,..ligatures, philtures, incantations, &c. this Disease..may be cured. **1624** Wotton *Archit.* in *Reliq.* (1651) 269 The Cover is..a kind of Band or Ligature to the whole Fabrick. **1650** Bulwer *Anthropomet.* 102 The fillets and ligatures that..Nurses use to bind them flat unto the Head. **1726** Swift *Gulliver* I. i, I likewise felt several slender ligatures across my body. **1805** Foster *Ess.* II. ii. 132 The ligatures which the Olympic pugilists bound on their hands and wrists. **1825** Scott *Betrothed* xvii, It is impossible that my bandage or ligature, knit by these fingers, should have started. **1846** J. Baxter *Libr. Pract. Agric.* (ed. 4) II. 277 The ligature [for the artery of a sheep] should generally be made of waxed silk. **1896** Treves *Syst. Surg.* I. 217 The finest sulpho-chromic catgut forms a trustworthy ligature.

b. *fig.* Anything binding or uniting; a bond, tie.

1627 H. Burton *Baiting Pope's Bull* Ep. Ded. 9 No ligatures of lawes can long hold them. **1633** T. Stafford *Pac. Hib.* To Rdr. (1821) 1 History..the common bond and ligature, which unites present time with all ages past. **1642** Jer. Taylor *Episc.* (1647) 329 The Bishop is the band, and ligature of the Churches Unity. **1827** *Examiner* 689/1 The ligatures which connect him with the narrative which he delivers are very artificial.

2. = ligament 2. Not now in good use.

c **1400** *Lanfranc's Cirurg.* 177 Þis hipe boon..is maad fast aboue wiþ ligaturis & pannyclis & nerues. **1641** Wilkins *Math. Magick* I. v. (1648) 29 The Ligatures for the strengthning of them [nerves], that they may not flag and languish in their motions. **1648** Sanderson *Serm.* II. 225 It is said of Belshazzar, Dan. 5..that the joynts (bindings or ligatures) of his loyns were loosed. **1875** Buckland *Log-bk.* 175 The [snake's] eggs were not held by a ligature, but appeared pasted together by some strong adhesive gum.

3. The action of tying; an instance of this. Also, the result of the action or operation; a tie or the place where it is made. **a.** *Surg.*

1541 R. Copland *Guydon's Quest. Chirurg.* L j b, Howe many maners of lygatures or rollynges ben there and howe ought they to be made? **1597** Lowe *Chirurg.* (1634) 93 In amputation..I finde the ligator reasonable sure, providing it be quickly done. **1793** Beddoes *Calculus* 212 Mr. Hamilton made three ligatures in the jugular vein of a cat. **1846** Brittan tr. *Malgaigne's Man. Oper. Surg.* iii. 17 Ligature was known amongst the ancients for the removal of pedunculated tumours. **1896** Treves *Syst. Surg.* I. 540 The ligature of a main artery in its continuity.

b. *gen.* The action of binding up or tying.

1651 Wittie *Primrose's Pop. Err.* IV. xlviii. 406 Some doe annoint the weapon, and binde it up carefully... Neverthelesse, some say, that by the onely dipping of the weapon into the box of ointment, without any ligature, they have performed a cure. **1712** Arbuthnot *John Bull* III. iii, The fatal noose..with the most strict ligature squeezed the blood into his face. **1872** Baker *Nile Tribut.* viii. 137 A tight ligature was made behind each stone.

4. *Mus.* A method of indicating the connexion or binding of notes into groups, as a guide to their rendering by the executant. In ancient notation, a compound note-form expressing two or more tones to be sung to one syllable. †*in ligature*: (of notes) connected in this way. In mod. notation: a tie or slur. In *Counterpoint*: a syncopation.

1597 Morley *Introd. Mus.* 9 *Phi.* But how if it haue a tayle on the right side? *Ma.* Then it is as though it were not in Ligature and is a Long. *Ibid.*, Annot., Ligatures were deuised for the Ditties sake, so that how manye notes serued for one syllable, so many notes were tied together. **1609** Douland *Ornithop. Microl.* 40 A Ligature is the conioyning of simple Figures [notes] by fit strokes. **1753** Chambers *Cycl. Supp.* s.v., Hence syncopes are often called ligatures, because they are made by the ligature of many notes. **1782** Burney *Hist. Mus.* (1789) II. iii. 183 Ligatures or binding notes. **1848** Craig, *Ligature*, in Music, a binding indicated by a curved line. **1880** Rockstro in Grove *Dict. Mus.* II. 136 *Ligature*, a passage of two or more notes, sung to a single syllable. *Ibid.* 138 In some old printed books, the last note of a Ligature is placed obliquely, in which case it is always to be sung as a Breve.

5. In *Writing* and *Printing*. Two or more letters joined together and forming one character or type; a monogram. Also, a stroke connecting two letters. ***in ligature***, combined in one character or type.

1693 *Phil. Trans.* XVII. 887 These Ligatures have been a long time Thorns in the Eyes of all that first learn Greek. **1731** Bailey vol. II, *Ligatures* [with Printers], types consisting of two letters, as *ff*, *fi*, *fl*, &c. **1773** Swinton in *Phil. Trans.* LXIV. 326 As for the Greeks, nothing is more common than ligatures, or monograms, on their coins. **1880** Warren *Book-plates* xii. 137 The two initials..are in ligature. **1883** I. Taylor *Alphabet* I. v. 263 In the earlier monumental scripts the letters are separate, but in some of the Egyptian papyri certain letters are united by ligatures. **1885** Cook tr. *Sievers' O.E. Gram.* (1887) 5 The ligatures and diphthongs..are never geminated. **1896** J. C. Egbert *Lat. Inscript.* 67 Ligatures..are common in Gallic inscriptions from the first century A.D... Ligatures of Three Letters.

†**6.** Binding quality; also *concr.*, that which has this quality. *Obs.*

1675 Evelyn *Terra* (1676) 100 Salt it is which gives ligature, weight, and constitution to things. **1727** Bradley *Fam. Dict.* s.v. *Fir tree*, They grow in moist or barren Gravel, and poor Ground, if not over sandy and light, without any loamy Ligature.

†**7.** The state of being bound; suspension of the intellectual or physical powers (see quots.). *Obs.*

1727–41 Chambers *Cycl.*, *Ligature*, among mystic divines, signifies a total suspension of the superior faculties, or intellectual powers of the soul... This passive state of these contemplative people they call their ligature. *Ligature*, is also used for a state of impotency, in respect to venery, caused by some charm, or witchcraft.

ligature (ˈlɪgətjʊə(r)), *v.* [f. ligature *sb.*] *trans.* To bind with a ligature or bandage; *spec.* in *Surg.* to tie up (an artery, etc.).

1716–20 *Lett. Mist's Jrnl.* (1722) I. 297 All Things were prepared, her Leg ligatured, and..plunged in the warm Bath. *a* **1734** North *Lives* (1826) III. 43 Goat skins..blown full and ligatured, are put under the corners that appear most to sink. **1878** T. Bryant *Pract. Surg.* (1879) II. 19 A wounded artery or vein should be ligatured above and below the wound. **1882** Carpenter in *Standard* 28 Sept. 3/3 The way in which infants were clothed and ligatured. **1896** Treves *Syst. Surg.* I. 217 One does not require to ligature many vessels in a wound now that we have such excellent pressure forceps.

fig. **1821** *Tales of my Landlord, Witch of Glas Llyn* II. 194 By ligaturing his energies and cooling his friends, prudence would have ruined the cause which rashness saved.

Hence ˈ**ligatured** *ppl. a.*

1859 *Nat. Encycl.* I. 150 The ligatured vessel. **1899** *Allbutt's Syst. Med.* VI. 298 A ligatured artery.

lig-by (ˈlɪgbaɪ). *Obs.* exc. *north. dial.* [f. *lig*, northern f. lie *v.*[1] + by *adv.*] A bedfellow; a mistress, concubine; = lie-by 1.

1610 Holland *Camden's Brit.* I. 379 Edith his wife, who before time had beene one of King Henrie the First his sweet hearts and lig-bies. **1632** Brome *North Lasse* v. i. Wks. 1873 III. 85 I'le be none of his Ligby for twice so mickle. **1698** Lacy *Sauny the Scot* II. i. 9 He means to make one of your Lasses his Wench—that is, his Love and his Ligby. **1876** *Whitby Gloss.*, *Lig-beside*, or *Lig-by*, a concubine.

ˈ**ligdur.** *dial.* Also 7 lig-dewe. [Possibly a corruption of F. *ligature* ligature, which occurs in the somewhat similar sense 'belt of coarse cloth worn by peasants and carters'.] (See quot. 1902.)

1617 *MS. Visitations Archd. Canterbury* (Cathedral Libr.) 148 We present Francis Tresse for laying of..a dirty paire of lig-dewes in the chest where the church ornaments do usually lie. **1902** *Eng. Dial. Dict.*, *Ligdur*, long gaiters reaching to the thighs [*Kent*].

lige, obs. form of league, lie *v.*[1], liege.

ligeance (ˈlaɪdʒəns, ˈliːdʒəns). Forms: 4 legg(e)aunce, lygeaunce, ligence, lygiauns, liegance, 4–5 ligeaunce, leg(e)aunce, lygaunce, 4–6 liegeaunce, 4–7 lege-, legiance, ligance, 5 legiaunce, legauns, legence, liegiance, lyeg(e)aunce, lygeance, lygeauns, 6 legyaunce, 6–7 liegeance, 7–8 leigeance, ligiance, 5–9 ligeance. [a. OF. *ligeance*, *legiance*, etc. (latinized *ligentia*, *ligantia*, *legiancia*), f. *lige* liege: see -ance. Cf. allegiance.]

1. The obligation of a liege man to his liege lord; the duty of fidelity of a subject to his sovereign or government; = allegiance 2. *Obs.* exc. *arch.*

1377 *Pol. Poems* (Rolls) I. 217 And in his leggaunce worthily He abod mony a bitter brayd. *c* **1382** Wyclif *Sel. Wks.* III. 503 Þat..alle þo ordiris of freris, in peyne of lesynge of alle hor legeaunce, telle þo kynge..what is þis sacrament. *c* **1400** *Sowdone Bab.* 105 Comaundinge hem vppon legeaunce To come in al hast. **1471** *Arriv. Edw. IV* (Camden) 39 [They] became his true liegemen, with as straight promyse of trew legiaunce as cowthe be devised. **1489** *Plumpton Corr.* (Camden) p. xcviii, Wee understand.. your true mind & faithful liegiance towards us. *c* **1500** *Melusine* lvii. 338 'By god', said geffray, 'gramercy, Fayre lordes, and I am redy to receyue you to your lygeauns.' And þenne they dyde to hym hommage. **1589** Puttenham *Eng. Poesie* II. xi. (Arb.) 112 She enuirons her people round, Retaining them by oth and liegeance. *a* **1641** Bp. Mountagu *Acts & Mon.* (1642) 93 They owe him no leigance, nor obedience. **1660** R. Coke *Justice Vind.* 49 How vile would this man make Majesty! how light the ligeance which is due not only by nature, but by oath from all subjects to their rightful Soveraigns? *a* **1670** Hacket *Abp. Williams* II. (1692) 191 None sate there before he had taken an oath to bear true ligance to him and his heirs, and to defend his Majesty against all perils. **1689** *Consid. conc. Succession & Alleg.* 19 Allegiance or Ligeance with respect to the King (for anciently even Inferiour Lords had their Liege-men) imports..That [etc.] . **1839–44** Tupper *Proverb. Philos.* (1852) 134 Ligeance we swear to our God, and ligeance well we have kept.

occas. in *pl.* **1523** Ld. Berners *Froiss.* I. ccxii. 258 The frenche kynge..shall rendre and delyuer to the..kynge of Englande..the honours, regalities, obeisaunces, homages, liegeaunces..that apperteyneth..to the crowne of Fraunce. **1658** Cleveland *Rustick Rampant* Wks. (1687) 471 By the Faith and Liegances which to us ye owe.

†**b.** Phr. *to do* or *make* (one's) *ligeance*. *Obs.*

1387 Trevisa *Higden* (Rolls) VIII. 55 Þat he and his successoures and men of Scotlond schulde doo homage legeaunce and feaute to the kynges of Engelond. **1395** Purvey *Remonstr.* (1851) 80 Agens here ligeaunce and solempne ooth maad to king Jon. *c* **1440** *Partonope* 2680 The king of fraunce To whom he had made his lyegeaunce. *c* **1450** Lonelich *Grail* xlvi. 446 Therto ben ȝe bownden Echon be the legaunce ȝe han me don. **1651** G. W. tr. *Cowel's Inst.* 23 The next capitall Lord to whom her Ancestors had done legiance.

2. The sway or jurisdiction of a sovereign over his subjects or 'lieges'; the territories subject to a sovereign. Now only in legal use.

c **1380** *Sir Ferumb.* 1270 We..buþ Charlis men þe Emperere & vnder his liegeaunce. **1390** Gower *Conf.* III. 176 What is a king in his ligance, Wher that ther is no lawe in londe? **1447** *Act 25 Hen. VI* in Bolton *Stat. Irel.* (1621) 9 Any such Irish enemies so received to the legeance of our Souveraigne Lord. **1609** Ld.-Chanc. Ellesmere *Sp. on Post-nati* 5 Hee was borne..within the ligeance of his said Maiestie. **1628** Coke *On Litt.* 129 He may be born out of the realm of England yet within the liegeance. **1652** Needham tr. *Selden's Mare Cl.* Ep. Ded., The Seas of Engl. were ever under the Legiance of our Kings. **1765** Blackstone *Comm.* I. 366 Such as are born within the dominions of the crown of England, that is, within the ligeance, or as it is generally called, the allegiance of the king. **1818** Cruise *Digest* (ed. 2) III. 341 All persons born out of the ligeance of the Crown of England. **1832** Austin *Jurispr.* (1879) II. xxxi. 570 An alien enemy living within the ligeance of our king.

†ˈ**ligeancy.** *Obs.* Also legeancy. [f. as prec.: see -ancy.] = prec.

1647 Digges *Unlawf. Taking Arms* iii. 82 The definition of Legeancy is set down in the great customary of Normandy, *Ligeantia est quâ domino tenentur vassalli sui.* **1656** Blount *Glossogr.* s.v. *Liege*, Liege-man is he that owes ligeancy to his Liege Lord. **1660** Sheringham *King's Suprem. Asserted* v. (1682) 36 Allegiance or ligeancy is due to the King, and none but the King.

lige(a)r, ligence, obs. ff. ledger, ligeance.

liger (ˈlaɪgə(r)). [f. li(on *sb.* + ti)ger *sb.*] The offspring of a lion and a tigress. Cf. tigon.

1938 *Times* 28 May 7/7 Two young Whipsnade-bred tigresses have been sent to London with the intention that they shall be paired with lions to produce the so-called ligers. **1948** *Time* 17 May 27 Daisy, a Salt Lake City zoo tigress, gave birth to the first known liger..ever born in the U.S. **1964** *Sunday Mail Mag.* (Brisbane) 8 Nov. 4/6 A 'Liger' is the term applied to the result of a cross between a lion and a tigress. **1975** *Times* 17 Sept. 7/3 The world's only living liger, the cross-breed of a male lion and a female tiger, has died at a Japanese zoo. It was the last of a litter of three born on September 8.

ligeretie, ligeritie, variants of legerity.

1652 Earl Monm. tr. *Bentivoglio's Hist. Relat.* 153 It was rather his ambition and ligeretie..which made him take so sudden and unexpected a resolution.

ligg(en, obs. and dial. form of lie *v.*[1]

liggat(e, ligget, dial. var. lidgate.

ligge, obs. f. lie *v.*[1], liege; var. lig *sb. Obs.*

ligger (ˈlɪgə(r)), *sb.*[1] *dial.* [f. *lig*, northern var. lie *v.*[1] + -er[1]. Cf. ledger *sb.*, which is a doublet of this word, and occurs in several of its senses.]

1. A coverlet.

a **1483** *Liber Niger* in *Househ. Ord.* (1790) 85 Hangers, liggers, and all that is the Kinge's stuffe. **1847** Halliwell, *Ligger*, a coverlet for a bed. *Linc.*

2. a. †A scaffolding-timber; = ledger *sb.* 2 (*obs.*). Also, see quot. 1895.

1500–18 *Acc. Louth Steeple* in *Archæologia* X. 83 For middle scaffolds two pieces going through, 16d, eight smaller liggers 4d. **1895** *E. Anglian Gloss.*, *Ligger*, a pole nailed horizontally from stud to stud to support the splints before receiving a coat of clay or loam.

b. (See quots.) *dial.*

1828 W. Carr *Dial. Craven* (ed. 2) I. 289 *Ligger*.., a branch cut or laid down horizontally in a hedge. **1869** R. B. Peacock *Gloss. Lonsdale* 51 *Ligger*.., a branch of thorn or other tree cut half through and laid along the top of a plashed hedge. **1898** B. Kirkby *Lakeland Words* 92 *Liggers*, long branches which a diker cuts partly through and ligs down to form a dike.

c. = ledger *sb.* 2 b.

1953 J. Arnold *Countryman's Workshop* 160 *Liggers*, hazel strips which hold down thatch. **1965** J. G. Jenkins *Trad. Country Craftsmen* ii. 36 The method of making liggers is somewhat similar to that of spar making but the ends are bevelled for neat joining rather than pointed. **1966** *Punch* 10 Aug. facing p. 216 (Advt.), The ridge..is thickly capped with sedge grass..and is gaily embellished with diamond and herring-bone patterns of 'liggers'. **1971** *Country Life* 18 Nov. 1403/3 The finish [of a thatch] that is visible consists of cleft hazel rods called liggers about four feet long neatly secured by spars, which gives a tidy and attractive appearance.

†**3.** The nether millstone. (Cf. ledger *sb.* 4.)

1781 Pegge in *Archæologia* (1785) VII. 20 The stones which composed these primitive.. mills..were two; an upper stone or runner, and a nether, called in Derbyshire a ligger.

4. (See quots.)

1840 Spurdens *Suppl. to Forby*, *Ligger*, an extemporaneous bridge over a 'mash-deek' [marsh-dike] usually formed of an aldern pole lain over it. **1865** W. White *E. Eng.* I. 162 Ligger or, in native pronunciation, Ligga, is the plank across a ditch or drain. **1887** W. Rye *Norfolk Broads* 67 We crossed a 'ligger', or plank bridge, over a little beck.

5. *Angling.* A line with a float and bait which is left in the water, used chiefly in pike-fishing in the Norfolk Broads. (Cf. LEDGER *sb.* 5.)

a **1825** in FORBY *Voc. E. Anglia.* **1883** G. C. DAVIES *Norfolk Broads* 130 You will see numerous bundles of reeds, each the size of a rolling-pin... These are the Broadman's 'liggers', or trimmers, which he sets for pike all over the Broad. The line is rolled round the ligger with a foot or two free, and the double hook is baited with a roach.

Comb. **1895** P. H. EMERSON *Birds, etc. Norfolk Broadlands* 317 Liggermen detest them [grebes]; for they will clear their liggers of fish.

6. *Worsted-manuf.* One who puts the material on to a carding machine. Also ***ligger on*** (Eng. Dial. Dict.).

1881 *Census Instructions* (1885) 107 Bobbin Ligger. **1899** *Daily News* 12 Jan. 2/1.

ligger ('lɪgə(r)), *sb.*² *slang.* [f. LIG *v.* + -ER¹.] One who gatecrashes parties, a 'free-loader'.

1977 *New Wave Mag.* No. 7. 3 Us: Who actually writes the numbers—you and Billy? (Scuffles from liggers...) TJ: Ignore them—they're just journalists! **1982** *Soundmaker* 4 Dec The usual droves of music biz liggers. **1985** *Observer* 14 Apr. 16/9, I went to a party on Wednesday that was a liggers' dream. **1985** *Legal Times* 29 July 7/4 British reporters compiled lists for 'liggers'..showing how one could eat and drink all day and most of the night at various breakfasts.

ligger ('lɪgə(r)), *v.* [f. LIGGER *sb.* Cf. LEDGER *v.*] *intr.* To fish with a 'ligger'. Hence **'liggering** *vbl. sb.*

1834 *New Monthly Mag.* XLII. 23 Our supreme sport, liggering for pike. **1883** G. C. DAVIES *Norfolk Broads* 130 The liggering on Rockland, therefore, does not interfere with the pike-fishing in the river.

ligging, obs. form of LYING.

ligh(e, ligher, obs. forms of LIE, LIAR.

light (laɪt), *sb.* Forms: 1-2 léoht, 1 líoht, *Anglian* lēht, 2-3 leocht, 2-5 liht, (4 lyht), 3-4 lict, lit(t, liȝt, 3-5 liȝt(e, lyȝt, (liȝht, lyȝhte, lyȝght), lith, 4 lyth(e, 4-6 lyght(e, (5 lyghth, 6 lyghtt), *Sc.* lycht, (4 lyicht), 4, 6 lyte, (4 ?leyt, 6 lytt), 5 leght, 2-3, 4- *Sc.* licht, 3- light. [OE. *léoht* str. neut. (later *lĕoht*, Anglian *lēht*, early ME. *līht*) corresponds to OFris. *liacht*, OS. *lioht* (Du. *licht*), OHG. *lioht* (MHG. *lieht*, mod.G. *licht*):—OTeut. **leuhtoᵐ*:—pre-Teut. **leuktom* (also **leukotom*, whence Goth. *liuhaþ*; for the suffix cf. NAKED *a.*), f. Aryan root **leuk-* to shine, be white. (Not in ON., which has instead a parallel formation on the same root, *liós*:—**leuhs-*.) According to some scholars, the sb. is the neuter of the adj. **leuhto-* LIGHT *a.*²; on this view the primary sense would be 'that which is bright'.

The Aryan root **leuk-* (: **louk-*: **lŭk-*) is represented in a great number of words. In Teut., besides the words mentioned above and their derivatives, there are those mentioned under LAIT *v.*, LEAM *sb.*¹, LEYE; also OE. *líxan* to lighten. Outside Teut. the root appears in Skr. *ruc* to shine, *rōcas*, *rōcis* neut., brightness, *rukma* shining, Gr. λευκός white, λεύσσειν to see, L. *lūx*, *lūmen* light, *lūcēre* to shine, *lūna* (:—**louknā*) moon, OIrish *lón*, *lúan* moon, *lóche* lightning, Welsh *llûg* light, *lluched* lightning, *lleufer* (OWelsh *louber*) light, OSl. *luča* beam of light.]

1. That natural agent or influence which (emanating from the sun, bodies intensely heated or burning, and various other sources) evokes the functional activity of the organ of sight.

a. Viewed as the medium of visual perception generally. Also, the condition of space in which light is present, and in which therefore vision is possible. Opposed to *darkness*.

c **1000** ÆLFRIC *Gen.* i. 3 God cwæð þa: ȝeweorðe leoht, and leoht wearð ȝeworht. *c* **1250** *Gen. & Ex.* 44 Al was ðat firme ðrosing in niȝt, Til he wit hise word made liȝt. **1398** TREVISA *Barth. De P.R.* VIII. xxviii. (1495) 339 Lyghte shedyth itselfe fro the hyghest heuen anone to the mydle of the worlde. *c* **1460** *Towneley Myst.* i. 23 Darknes from light we parte on two. **1593** SHAKS. *Lucr.* 674 Light and lust are deadlie enemies. **1671** MILTON *Samson* 90 Since light so necessary is to life. **1679** DRYDEN *Troilus & Cr.* IV. ii, Now shine, sweet moon! let them have just light enough to make their passes. **1756** BURKE *Subl. & B.* XXI. xiv, All colours depend on light. **1860** TYNDALL *Glac.* I. vi. 45 Beyond a certain intensity..light ceases to be light, and becomes mere pain.

b. Viewed as being itself an object of perception, cognized by means of the specific visual sensation indicated by the use of words like 'bright', 'shining', etc. Also, in particularized sense, an individual shining or appearance of light.

For *northern*, *southern lights* (= AURORA *Borealis*, *Australis*), *zodiacal light*, see the adjs.

Beowulf 727 Him of eaȝum stod liȝe ȝelicost leoht unfæȝer. *?a* **1100** *O.E. Chron.* an. 789 (Laud MS.) Heofenlic leoht [*MS. F.* lioht] wæs ȝelome seoȝen ðær þer he ofslaȝen wæs. *a* **1225** *Leg. Kath.* 1594 Swuch leome & liht leitede þrinne. *c* **1300** *Havelok* 588 She saw þer-inne a lith ful shir, Also brith so it were day, Aboute þe knaue þer he lay. **1567** MAPLET *Gr. Forest* 3 A Gem..in whose Centre..a certaine light is seene shining..like to the Moone. **1596** SHAKS. *Merch. V.* v. i. 89 That light we see is burning in my hall. **1634** MILTON *Comus* 340 With thy long levell'd rule of streaming light. **1846** RUSKIN *Mod. Paint.* II. III. I. v. §4 Whatever beauty there may result from effects of light on foreground objects. **1847** TENNYSON *Princess* IV. 3 The long light shakes across the lakes. **1866** M. ARNOLD *Thyrsis* xvii, And in the scatter'd farms the lights come out.

c. Viewed as residing in or emanating from a luminary. Phr. ***to give light*** (said of a luminary).

c **1000** *Ags. Gosp.* Matt. xxiv. 29 Se mona hys leoht ne sylð. *a* **1300** *Cursor M.* 1771 Sun and mone had tint þair light. **1340-70** *Alex. & Dind.* 122 His [the sun's] lem on þe loft liȝht ȝaf aboute. **1362** LANGL. *P. Pl.* A. I. 163 Chastite withouten Charite.. Is as lewed as a Laumpe þat no liht is inne. **1530** TINDALE *Answ. More* 24 The air is dark of itself, & receiveth all her light of the sun. **1548** HALL *Chron., Hen. VIII*, 22 On the top stode a goodly Bekon gevyng light. **1592** SHAKS. *Rom. & Jul.* v. iii. 125 What Torch is yond that vainely lends his light To grubs and eyelesse Sculles? **1634** MILTON *Comus* 199 And fill'd their Lamps With everlasting oil, to give due light To the misled and lonely Travailer. **1716** POPE *Iliad* VIII. 688 As when the Moon..O'er Heav'ns pure Azure sheds her sacred Light. **1814** SCOTT *Wav.* ii, The sun..poured..its chequered light through the stained window.

d. In scientific use.

The word *light* has been used in six special senses: (*a*) the thing (variously conceived as matter or energy) which is communicated from a luminous body to the body illuminated by it; (*b*) this thing regarded as producing sensation; (*c*) the sensation produced; (*d*) the process (variously conceived as rectilinear motion of corpuscles, undulatory motion of the ether, or periodic change of electrical and magnetic states) by which the communication is made; (*e*) certain characteristics of such processes (rays or waves); (*f*) physical energies and processes of the same type as those involved in the production of vision, but having possibly a different range of periods (e.g. Röntgen rays). The sense (*c*) (rare in actual use, though not uncommonly expressed in definitions) agrees with an occasional use of the word in popular language: we should, e.g., usually apply the name *light* to the sensation experienced when the optic nerve is excited mechanically without the intervention of a luminous body. In the sense (*d*) the word *light* is equivalent to *the process of transmission of light*; in the sense (*e*) it is equivalent to *rays of light* or *waves of light*.

(*a*) **1704** NEWTON *Opticks* I. 18 The Light of the Sun consists of Rays differently refrangible. **1811** A. T. THOMSON *Lond. Disp.* (1818) p. xxxvi, Light is a substance consisting of very subtle particles which are constantly emanating in straight lines from luminous bodies. **1876** TAIT *Rec. Adv. Phys. Sci.* iii. (ed. 2) 66 It necessarily followed that light is a form of energy.

(*b*) **1704** NEWTON (*title*) Opticks: or, a Treatise of the Reflections, Refractions, Inflections and Colours of Light. **1807** T. YOUNG *Lect. Nat. Philos.* II. 629 Radiant Light consists in Undulations of the luminiferous Ether.

(*c*) **1800** HERSCHEL in *Phil. Trans.* XC. 295 Light, both solar and terrestrial, is a sensation occasioned by rays emanating from luminous bodies.

(*d*) **1875** W. K. CLIFFORD in *Fortn. Rev.* XVII. 785 Thus light is described as a vibration and such properties of light as are also properties of vibrations are thereby explained.

(*e*) **1900** LARMOR *Aether & Matter* xii. 205 Waves of high period (much higher however than ordinary light).

(*f*) **1865** MAXWELL in *Phil. Trans.* CLV. 466 We have strong reason to conclude that light itself including radiant heat, (and other radiations if any), is an electromagnetic disturbance in the form of waves. **1897** S. P. THOMPSON (*title*) Light visible and invisible.

e. The portion or quantity of light which comes through a window, or which is otherwise regulated so as to illuminate a given space. ***in a good*** (or ***bad***) ***light***: situated so as to be clearly visible (or the reverse).

In the early 17th c. ***false*** or ***deceiving lights*** are often mentioned as a kind of trickery practised by shopkeepers. See, e.g. *a* **1616** BEAUM. & FL. *Phylaster* v. iii. (1620) 58; *a* **1626** MIDDLETON *Wom. beware Wom.* II. ii. (1657) 120 and *Anyth. for quiet Life* II. ii. (1662) C 3 b.

a **1533** LD. BERNERS *Huon* clxiii. 643 Other wyndowes there were..the whiche gaue great lyght into the house. **1625** BACON *Ess. Building* (Arb.) 551 A double House, without Thorow Lights, on the Sides. **1658** W. SANDERSON *Graphice* 26 Place your best Pieces, to be seen with single lights. *Ibid.* 61 Choose your Light Northwards towards the East, one single Light only, great and fair, without any reflection of Trees or Walls. **1797** HOLCROFT tr. *Stolberg's Trav.* (ed. 2) II. xlii. 69 The picture..is in a bad light. **1854** THACKERAY *Newcomes* xvii, Bed-rooms where Lady Betty has had her hair powdered, and where the painter's northlight now takes possession of the place which her toilet-table occupied a hundred years ago.

f. ***in light***: exposed to rays of light, lighted up.

1847 TENNYSON *Princess* Concl. 41 The happy valleys, half in light and half Far-shadowing from the west.

g. ***one's light***: the ordinary measure of light which a person enjoys, or expects to enjoy, for seeing around him. ***to stand in a person's light*** = to cut him off from the enjoyment of it; hence this and similar phrases are used *fig.* to express injury done to a person's interests; so ***to stand*** (Sc. also ***to sit***) ***in one's own light***. † ***to lay in*** (***a person's***) ***light***: to bring as an objection against.

c **1386** CHAUCER *Miller's T.* 210 Bycause that he fer was from hir sighte, This nye Nicholas stood in his lighte. **1528** MORE *Dialogue Heresyes* IV. Wks. 252/1 He could shewe a fayre law,..which lawe if it wer laied in their light that would take vpon them the defence of any worship to be done to ymages, would make al theyr eyen dase. **1535** STEWART *Cron. Scot.* (1858) II. 73 We sat our fair into oure awin licht. **1538** BALE *God's Promises* v. 21 What tho' fearce Pharao wrought myschef in thy syght, He was a pagan, lay not that in our lyght. **1546** J. HEYWOOD *Prov.* II. iv. Wks. (1562) G ij, How blindly ye stand in your owne light. **1601** DENT *Pathw. Heaven* 222 They [the wicked] be much their owne foes, and stand in their owne light. **1633** B. JONSON *Tale Tub* II. i, Take a vool's Counsel, and do not stand in your own light. **1637** RUTHERFORD *Lett.* (1862) I. 226 And do we not sit far in our own light, to make it a matter of bairn's play. **1848** DICKENS *Dombey* xxxix, To take away the character of a lad that's been a good servant to you, because he can't afford to stand in his own light for your good. **1856** READE *Never too Late* lxx, Don't stand in the poor girl's light. *Mod. colloq.* Please move a little farther that way; you are in my light.

h. A gleam or sparkle in the eye, expressive of animated feeling or the like.

1593 SHAKS. *Lucr.* 1378 And dying eyes gleem'd forth their ashie lights. **1833** H. COLERIDGE *Song*, '*She is not fair*' 10, I cease not to behold The love-light in her eye. **1852** MRS. STOWE *Uncle Tom's C.* xxxix, He was followed by Cassy, pale, calm..and with that same fearful light in her eye. **1893** *Pall Mall Mag.* Christm. No. 249 He had..an eye without light, a voice without charm.

i. ***to put out*** or ***quench*** (one's) ***light***: to extinguish his 'vital spark'.

1604 SHAKS. *Oth.* v. ii. 10-13. *a* **1616** BEAUM. & FL. *Maid's Trag.* IV. i. (1619) G 4 b, *Evad.* You will not murther me? *Mel.* No, tis a iustice and a noble one, To put the light out of such base offenders. **1810** SCOTT *Lady of L.* III. xi, Quench thou his light, Destruction dark! **1866** 'MARK TWAIN' *Lett. from Hawaii* (1967) 152 The sick Portyghee watched his chance..harnessed the provisions and ate up nearly a quarter of a bar'l of bread before the old man caught him, and he had more than two notions to put his lights out. **1891** *Star* 10 Feb. 3/6 He had been heard to say, 'I should like to put her light out,' and had fired at her bed-room window. **1910** W. M. RAINE *Bucky O'Connor* 25 Mebbe I'd a-put his lights out for good and all. **1935** A. J. POLLOCK *Underworld Speaks* 92/2 *Put his lights out*, to kill. **1955** 'A. GILBERT' *Is she Dead Too?* vii. 133 Say she put out the old girl's light, that ain't going to encourage the widower to pay his addresses to her.

j. *pl.* [after L. *lumina.*] Graces of style. *rare*⁻¹.

1710 ADDISON *Tatler* No. 267 ¶4 Bacon..had the..comprehensive Knowledge of Aristotle, with all the beautiful Lights, Graces, and Embellishments of Cicero.

k. fig. ***light of*** one's ***eye(s***: applied to a loved object.

a **1000** *Juliana* 95 Ðu eart dohtor min..minra eaȝna leoht. **1636** MASSINGER *Gt. Dk. Florence* IV. ii, She was the light of my eyes, and comfort of My feeble age. **1841** LANE *Arab. Nts.* I. 108 O my beloved! O light of mine eye.

l. ***the light of God's countenance***: in Ps. iv. 6, etc. = Divine favour. In allusion to this, ***the light of*** (***a person's***) ***countenance*** is often sarcastically used for: (his) sanction, approving presence.

1890 HALL CAINE *Bondman* I. i, Count Trollop was in Iceland at this celebration of the ancient festival, and he was induced by Jorgen to give it the light of his countenance.

2. *spec.* The illumination which proceeds from the sun in day-time; daylight. Also, the time of daylight; day-time, day-break. (Usually ***the light***. Also ***the light of day***.)

c **1000** *Ags. Ps.* (Th.) lxxvii. 33 Ǽr leohte [L. *ante lucem*]. *c* **1020** *Rule St. Benet* viii. (Logeman) 37 Onginnendum leohte [L. *incipiente luce*]. *a* **1175** *Cott. Hom.* 233 Hwat deð si moder hire bearn, formes hi hit cheteð and blissið be þe lichte. *a* **1300** *Cursor M.* 14195 Qua has to wenden ani wai, God es to go bi light o dai. *c* **1300** *Proverbs of Hending* xxxvi. in *Salomon & Sat.* (1848) 279 Drynk eft lasse, and go by lyhte hom, quoþ Hendyng. *a* **1340** HAMPOLE *Psalter* cxviii. 148 As a goed werk man þat rysis bifor light til his werk. **1526** *Pilgr. Perf.* (W. de W. 1531) 138 Lyke as the precyous stone, the more it is polyshed or rubbed, the more perfytly it receyueth the lyght. *a* **1600** MONTGOMERIE *Misc. P.* v. 26 All day I wot not what to do, I loth to sie the licht. **1697** DRYDEN *Virg. Georg.* III. 613 Their Morning Milk, the Peasants press at Night: Their Evening Meal before the rising Light To Market bear. *Ibid.* IV. 274 Then having spent the last Remains of Light, They give their Bodies due Repose at Night. **1813** SIR H. DAVY *Agric. Chem.* (1814) 230 Plants grow vigorously only when supplied with light. **1860-1** FLO. NIGHTINGALE *Nursing* 59 Almost all patients lie with their faces turned to the light exactly as plants always make their way towards the light. **1875** JOWETT *Plato* (ed. 2) I. 134 The appointed hour was approaching when man in his turn was to go forth into the light of day.

b. In the asseverative phrase ***by this*** (***good***) ***light***. Also ***by God's light***: see GOD 14 a and 'SLIGHT. *arch.*

c **1510** *Interl. Four Elem.* (Percy Soc.) 23 Thou art a mad gest, be this lyght! **1599** SHAKS. *Much Ado* v. iv. 93 Come, I will haue thee, but by this light I take thee for pittie. **1610** —— *Temp.* II. ii. 147 By this good light. **1625** FLETCHER *Noble Gent.* v. i, *Beau.* Catcht, by this light! **1821** SCOTT *Kenilw.* iv, By this light, Anthony, thou art mad.

c. ***to see the light***, to come into the world; to be brought forth or published. Now also, to reach a full understanding or realization; to be converted (esp. to Christianity).

a **1687** PETTY *Pol. Arith.* (1690) Ded., Had not the Doctrins offended France, they had long since seen the light. **1705** HEARNE *Collect.* 20 July (O.H.S.) I. 10 He is resolv'd it [a book] shall see yᵉ Light. **1752** HUME *Ess. & Treat.* (1777) I. 175 As soon as the helpless infant sees the light. **1812** *Niles' Reg.* III. 195/2 It is indispensably necessary that every man should 'see the light'. **1889** *Kansas City* (Missouri) *Times & Star* 14 Oct., Up to a few weeks ago, he was opposed to a revival of navigation on the Missouri, but now he has seen the light and says he's for it strong. **1903** *N.Y. Even. Post* 10 Sept., It is altogether likely that they, too, will see the light before another week has passed. **1933** H. G. WELLS *Shape of Things to Come* III. iv. 275 Men who saw the light and spoke were only one species of a larger genus of human beings whose minds worked differently from the common man's. **1944** H. JAMES et al. (*song-title*) I'm beginning to see the light. **1966** 'L. LANE' *ABZ of Scouse* 94 *See ther light*, to plead guilty or to reform.

3. The state of being visible or exposed to view. ***to come to light*** (in early use †***in, on light***): to be revealed, disclosed, made visible or made known. ***to bring*** (rarely †***put***) ***to light*** (cf. F. *mettre en lumière*): to reveal, make known, publish.

a **1000** *Elene* 1123 (Gr.) Nu is in leoht cymen, onwrigen wyrda bigang. *a* **1300** *Cursor M.* 15892 He drogh him bak behind þe men Wald he noght cum in light. **1535** COVERDALE *Ezek.* xvi. 57 When thou wast in thy pryde, and before thy wickednesse came to light. **1549** T. SOME *Latimer's 7 Serm.* Ep. Ded. (Arb.) 19, I haue gathered, writ, and brought into lyght the famous fryday sermons of Mayster Hugh Latimer. **1567** *Gude & Godlie Ball.* (S.T.S.) 44 Thairby it sall cum to lycht That ze ar my Disciples rycht. **1597** MORLEY *Introd. Mus.* Ded., It is necessary for him who shall put to light any such thing as this is, to choose such a patron [etc.]. **1611** BIBLE *Job* xxviii. 11 The thing that is hid, bringeth he foorth to light. **1643** *Declar. Comm., Reb. Irel.* 57 Their devillish designes and devices are come to light, and brought to our Knowledge. **1765** PARSONS in *Phil. Trans.* LV. 48 A worthy family who..had lived in Virginia several years in a conspicuous light. **1870** MAX MÜLLER *Sci. Relig.* (1873) 285 Everybody wished..to bring to light some of the treasures. **1871** FREEMAN *Norm. Conq.* (1876) IV. xviii. 224 Its history is shrouded in the darkness which surrounds all the doings of its Earl till he breaks forth into full light in the course of the next year. **1891** *Law Times* XCII. 18/2 Another defect in the Rules of Court 1883 has come to light.

4. Power of vision, eyesight (now *poet.* or *rhet.*). Also *pl.* = the eyes (now only *slang*).

971 *Blickl. Hom.* 19 Gehyran we nu forwhon se blinda leoht onfeng. *Ibid.* 21 Se blinda..bæd his eagena leohtes. *c* **1250** *Meid Maregrete* 42 Nis no tonge an erþe ne non eyen litt Ðat mai telle þe ioie. **1580** LYLY *Euphues* (Arb.) 340 Hir eyes hasill, yet bright, and such were the lyghtes of Venus. **1599** *Broughton's Let.* vii. 21 The weakning of his [Samson's] strength lost his libertie and his light. **1607** WILKINS *Mis. Enforced Marr.* II. D 1 b, Lift vp thine eyes.. They were not borne to loose their light so soone. **1815** *Sporting Mag.* XLV. 161 He mill'd the stout Caleb and darken'd his lights. **1883** R. W. DIXON *Mano* I. xii. 38 His ministers with point of piercing sword Put out my light for ever.

5. A body which emits illuminating rays.

a. The sun or other heavenly body (after Gen. i. 16).

c **1000** *Sax. Leechd.* III. 234 On ðam feorðan dæge gesceop God twa miccle leoht, þæt is sunne and mona. *c* **1460** *Towneley Myst.* i. 21 Make we heuen & erth..and lyghtys fayre to se. **1574** BOURNE *Regiment for Sea* ix. (1577) 34 b, You may knowe it by the Arke or bearing of the Starres and lyghtes rounde about you. **1608** SHAKS. *Per.* II. ii. 41 And hee the Sunne for them to reuerence; None that beheld him, but, like lesser lights, Did vaile their Crownes to his supremacie. **1819** J. WILSON *Dict. Astrol.*, *Lights*, the luminaries. **1871** R. ELLIS tr. *Catullus* lxii. 26 Hesper, shineth in heaven a light more genial ever?

b. An ignited candle, lamp, gas-jet, or the like. Hence ***wax lights*** = wax candles for lighting (now *rare* in this use: cf. 14 b); ***bright lights***: see BRIGHT *a.* 10 b; ***lights out*** (Mil.): the last bugle-call of the day, giving the signal for all lights to be extinguished. Hence in non-military use.

c **1000** ÆLFRIC *Hom.* (Th.) I. 150 We sceolan on ðisum dæge beran ure leoht to cyrcan, and lætan hi ðær bletsian. *a* **1400-50** *Alexander* 4231 Many liȝtis of a liȝt is liȝtid othire-quile. *c* **1420** *St. Editha* 1276 (Horstm.) þis mayde toke hit [*sc.* þe cerge] þo from þat place & blewe ouȝt þe leyȝt anone sodanly. *c* **1449** PECOCK *Repr.* II. vi. 169 Sette liȝtis or laumpis bifore hem [images]. **1537** *Bury Wills* (Camden) 128, I wyll have a lyte brynnyng yn the chansell before the sacrement. *a* **1548** HALL *Chron., Hen. VIII*, 207 b, In this chamber was hanged a great braunche of silver percell gilte, to beare lightes. **1593** SHAKS. *Lucr.* 673 This said, he sets his foote vppon the light. **1604** E. G[RIMSTONE] *D'Acosta's Hist. Indies* IV. xxxiii. 301 Both rich and poor vse this tallowe for lightes. **1849** JAMES *Woodman* ii, The lights were lighted in a large, comfortable, well-furnished room. **1861** C. READE *Cloister & H.* lvii. (1896) 174 A Tuscan noble promised ten pounds of wax lights to our lady of Ravenna. **1868** *Queen's Regulations Army* §845 Between tattoo and reveille no trumpet or bugle is to be sounded,..with the exception of the call 'lights out'. **1888** *Pall Mall G.* 23 July 6/2 The common practice of seeking for an escape of gas with a light caused a serious explosion yesterday morning. **1905** *Captain* XIII. 42/2 It's off... We aren't allowed to talk after lights-out! **1914** R. BROOKE *Let.* 3 Oct. (1968) 621 Faint lights burning through the ghostly tents, and a distant bugler blowing *Lights Out.* **1922** C. E. MONTAGUE *Disenchantment* iv. 56 They would argue after Lights Out. **1942** *R.A.F. Jrnl.* 13 June 14 There would be no lights-out time, no check-up to ensure every man was in. **1950** A. BARON *There's no Home* ii. 19 The wooden gates..could be closed every evening at Lights Out. **1965** G. JACKSON *Let.* June in *Soledad Brother* (1971) 78 One of those tall ultrabright electrical fixtures used to illuminate the walls and surrounding area at night casts a direct beam of light in my cell at night... Consequently I have enough light, even after the usual twelve o'clock lights-out, to read or study by. **1969** I. & P. OPIE *Children's Games* viii. 246 The statues have to come to life, and do the things they think monsters or fairies..would do... The puller then commands 'Lights out'..and they have to close their eyes.

c. *collect.* The candles or other illuminants used to light a particular place; lights collectively. †Also, material to be burnt for lighting.

a **1023** WULFSTAN *Hom.*, *Sermo Lupi* (Napier) 308 Godes cyrcan..mid leohte and lacum hy gelome gegretan. **1297** R. GLOUC. (Rolls) 7806 Vor me ne miȝte no chirchegong wiþoute liȝte do. *c* **1300** *Havelok* 576 Grim bad Leue bringen lict, For to don on his cloþes. **1387** TREVISA *Higden* (Rolls) VI. 317 An hondred mark to Seynt Peter his liȝt. **1389** in *Eng. Gilds* (1870) 7 Eueri quarter for to meyntene þe liȝt & þe almesse of þe broþerhede .iij.*d.* **1430** *E.E. Wills* (1882) 85 To our lady lyght, vj*d.*.. Item to seint Mergret lyght, iiij*d.* *c* **1449** PECOCK *Repr.* II. vi. 170 Forto knele and preie and bere liȝt and sette up candelis bifore an ymage. *c* **1470** HENRY *Wallace* II. 281 Scho gert graith wp a burd.. honowryt with gret lycht. **1520** *Carpenters' Accts.* in Sharp *Cov. Myst.* (1825) 186 Payd for lyght for the Cressetts *xd.* **1561** *Ibid.*, For carryinge ij cressites and iij stone of lyght.. iijs. **1609** SKENE *Reg. Maj.*, *Stat. Robt. I*, 27 b, Lands given and disponed for singing, or for licht in the kirk.

d. A signal-fire or beacon-lamp, esp. on a ship or in a lighthouse; often with prefixed qualification as ***fixed, flashing, intermittent, revolving light.*** Hence, used for the lighthouse itself.

1604 E. G[RIMSTONE] *D'Acosta's Hist. Indies* III. xi. 155 In the beginning of the night the Admiralls light failed so, as the other shippe never see them after. **1790** BEATSON *Nav. & Mil. Mem.* 253 On the evening of the 3rd of April, Sir Edward 'made the light' of the Baleines on the Isle of Rhée. **1793** SMEATON *Edystone L.* Introd. 5 The original lantern for the light was of a diameter somewhat exceeding five feet. **1793, 1858** [see FLOATING LIGHT]. **1798** COLERIDGE *Anc. Mar.* VI. xxi, They stood as signals to the land, Each one a lovely light. **1850** A. STEVENSON *Treat. Lighthouses* I. 106 The succession of *red* and *white* lights is caused by the revolution of a frame whose different sides present red and white lights... The *flashing* light is produced in the same manner as the *revolving* light. *Ibid.* 107 The *intermittent* light is distinguished by bursting suddenly into view, and continuing steady for a short time, after which it is suddenly eclipsed for half a minute... This distinction, as well as that called the *flashing* light, is peculiar to the Scotch coast. **1863** *Murray's Handbk. Kent & Sussex* 157 The wall, like that of its sister light at Gessoriacum.., is composed of [etc.]. **1894** A. ROBERTSON *Nuggets* 44 Revealing the object he was in search of, as a harbour light reveals the port. **1896** HOUSMAN *Shropsh. Lad* lix, Black towers above the Portland light The felon-quarried stone.

†**e.** A linkman. *Obs.*

1712 STEELE *Spect.* No. 454 ¶7, I went to my Lodging, led by a Light,..and made him give me an Account of the Charge [etc.].

f. ***out like a light*** (with preceding verb or auxiliary): having lost consciousness, having fainted, or gone to sleep, at once.

1934 [see GO *v.* 87 u]. **1956** B. HOLIDAY *Lady sings Blues* (1973) xix. 155 When it came time to come out for the third curtain call I said, 'Bobby, I just can't make it no further,' and I passed out like a light. **1964** R. BRADDON *Year Angry Rabbit* ii. 17 The Prof's out like a light. **1970** *Women's Household* July 10/3 That first night he came dashing in the house, made a running leap at the couch, and was out like a light! **1973** J. PHILIPS *Larkspur Conspiracy* I. iv. 75 He..lay down on his bed. He went out like a light.

g. Usu. *pl.* Traffic lights. Also *fig.*

1938 E. BOWEN *Death of Heart* III. vi. 439 The driver twitched his head once or twice. Then the lights went against him; he pulled up. **1963** A. HUNTER *Gently Floating* ii. 29 They came to the bridge, were halted by lights... The lights changed. Gently drove over. **1970** M. KENYON *100,000 Welcomes* i. 8 I'll drop you at the next lights. **1971** *Daily Tel.* (Colour Suppl.) 22 Oct. 7/2 That's right, you bumbling old fool, slow down as we come to the next lights and we'll miss the green. **1972** *Accountant* 19 Oct. 495/1 Stock markets have been in neutral waiting for the lights to change.

6. Used *fig.* with reference to mental illumination or elucidation.

a. In phrases, as ***to give*** (***carry, bring***) ***light*** (†*to* or *into* a subject). Also ***to get*** or ***receive light.*** Now usually ***to throw*** (***cast, shed***) ***light upon.*** †***to have need of light,*** to need explanation.

c **1449** PECOCK *Repr.* I. iii. 16 Ech man having to do with suche questiouns mai soone se that Holi Writt ȝeueth litil or noon liȝt therto at al. **1559** W. CUNNINGHAM *Cosmogr. Glasse* 127 This carde should seme to giue a great light and knowledge vnto Nauigation. **1581** LAMBARDE *Eiren.* I. ix. (1602) 42 The Salutation of the Queene is but a Catologue of all the names of the Iustices, and contayneth nothing that hath neede of light. **1657-8** *Burton's Diary* (1828) II. 423, I have received great light from him, and hope for much more. *c* **1680** BEVERIDGE *Serm.* (1729) I. 116 Thus I have given you what light I could into both these expressions. **1696** WHISTON *Theory Earth* II. (1722) 102 This Matter will ..give light and strength to some of the former Testimonies. **1706** HEARNE *Collect.* 19 Jan. (O.H.S.) I. 165 Mr. Hugh Broughton..had ye chief Hand and gave light to y^t Work. **1719** DE FOE *Crusoe* II. xi. (1840) 235 Can you give me no further light into it? **1732** BERKELEY *Alciphr.* IV. §2 Arguments..which carry light have their effect, even against an opponent who shuts his eyes. **1793** SMEATON *Edystone L.* §192, I was very desirous to get some light into some of the sensible qualities, that might probably occasion the difference. **1841** CARLYLE *On Heroes* v. 309 When he did speak, it was to throw new light on the matter. **1855** BAIN *Senses & Int.* I. ii. §10 (1864) 38 The experimental enquiries of recent years have thrown much light upon this obscure and mysterious subject. **1860** ADLER *Fauriel's Prov. Poetry* xvi. 351 It is on these antecedents that I shall first endeavor to shed some light. **1884** D. HUNTER tr. *Reuss's Hist. Canon* iv. 57 The various aberrations of heresy are well suited for casting some light on the history of the canon.

b. Illumination or enlightenment, as a possession of the mind, or as derivable from some particular source. ***light of nature,*** the capacity given to man of discerning certain divine truths without the help of revelation.

1422 tr. *Secreta Secret., Priv. Priv.* 134 Thes maner thynges a man may not do wythout wysdome and vndyrstondynge and lyght of connynge. **1595** SHAKS. *John* IV. iii. 61 We had a kinde of light, what would ensue. **1599** [CARTWRIGHT] *Christian Let.* 7 Yet you infer that the light of nature teacheth some knowledge naturall whiche is necessarie to saluation. **1630** PRYNNE *God No Impostor* 12 It is a greater good or happinesse then man by all the light of Art or Nature can attaine vnto. **1669** BUNYAN *Holy Citie* 195 These words do, in my present Light, point [etc.]. **1710** BERKELEY *Princ. Hum. Knowl.* §72 If we follow the light of reason. **1732** —— *Alciphr.* I. §2 Having spread so much light and knowledge over the land. **1790** BURKE *Fr. Rev.* Wks. V. 191 The men of England, the men, I mean, of light and leading in England. **1821** LAMB *Elia* Ser. I. *Old Benchers*, Lovel..was a quick little fellow, and would despatch it [business] out of hand by the light of natural understanding. **1852** H. ROGERS *Ecl. Faith* (1853) 108 That is the point on which I want light! **1871** MORLEY *Condorcet* in *Crit. Misc.* Ser. I. (1878) 87 Less read through-out Europe by men of superior light. **1894** JESSOPP *Random Roaming*, etc., iv. 145 The Rector..doing his duty according to his light as a country parson.

c. *pl.* (*a*) Pieces of information or instruction; facts, discoveries, or suggestions which explain a subject. (*b*) The opinions, information, and capacities, natural or acquired, of an individual intellect. (Cf. F. *lumières*.) Often in phr. ***according to*** (***one's***) ***lights.***

1526 *Pilgr. Perf.* (W. de W. 1531) 125 He hath his suggestyons, felynges, & lyghtes. **1634** SIR T. HERBERT *Trav.* 217 We may entertaine some lights out of authentique Story. **1683** TEMPLE *Mem.* Wks. 1731 I. 387, I had long Conversations with the Pensioner, by which I gain'd the Lights necessary to discover the whole present Scene of Affairs. **1748** *Anson's Voy.* III. vii. 354 The Governor.. might be expected to give us the best lights for avoiding this perplexity. **1793** W. ROY *Milit. Antiq. Rom. Brit.* Introd., Many new lights concerning the Roman history and geography of Britain. **1831** BREWSTER *Newton* (1855) II. xxi. 262 The most distinguished of his successors, with all the lights of a century and a half, could not have stated more correctly [etc.]. **1861** THACKERAY *Four Georges* iii. (1876) 83 He did his best; he worked according to his lights. **1867** TROLLOPE *Chron. Barset* II. lvii. 140 He trusted that Grace would understand this by her own natural lights. **1875** JOWETT *Plato* (ed. 2) III. 503 We may love and honour the intentions of these excellent people, as far as their lights extend. **1879** TROLLOPE *Thackeray* 112 To Pen and to Pen's mother he is beneficent after his lights.

d. ***new light***(***s***: novel doctrines (esp. theological and ecclesiastical) the partisans of which lay claim to superior enlightenment; hence by antithesis ***old light***(***s***, the traditional doctrines to which the 'new lights' are opposed. Also *attrib.* as in ***new light, old light men, teachers, doctrines,*** etc., whence ***New Lights, Old Lights,*** as designations for persons holding 'New Light' and 'Old Light' views.

In Scotland the appellations *New Lights, Old Lights* (Sc. *Auld Lichts*) have been current in two different applications: (*a*) as occasional names for the Moderate and the Evangelical party in the Established Church (so used e.g. by Burns); (*b*) as the usual popular names for the two bodies into which the Associate (or Burgher) Synod was divided in 1799, and the two into which the General Associate (or Antiburgher) Synod was divided in 1806; in each case the 'Old Light' minority (adhering to the 'covenanted reformation' and to the principle of a national church) formed themselves into a separate presbytery, and in 1842 the few remaining Old Light Burghers and Old Light Antiburghers joined to form the Synod of United Original Seceders, to which the name 'Auld Lichts' is still frequently applied.

1650 HUBBERT *Pill Formality* 67 Those that dare even in their Pulpits, mock, and cry out against new lights. **1659** BP. WALTON *Consid. Considered* 176 Give greater occasion to those, who brag of their new lights,..to reject all Scripture as useless. *c* **1665** SOUTH *Serm. 1 Kings* xiii. 33 Serm. (1715) 151 Against which New Lights, sudden Impulses of the Spirit, Extraordinary Calls, will be but weak Arguments. **1722** SEWELL *Hist. Quakers* (1795) I. 19 He was afraid of Fox, for going after new lights. **1744** JON. EDWARDS *Wks.* 1834 I. p. cxviii/1 To attend the ministry of those that are called New Light Ministers. **1785** BURNS *Ep. W. Simpson* xxvii, An' some their new-light fair avow, Just quite barefac't. *Ibid.* xxx, Some auld-light herds in neebor towns Are mind't [etc.]. **1806** R. FORSYTH *Beauties Scotl.* III. 429 The burgher associate clergy..have..resolved to expunge the offending passage from the Confession of Faith. Twelve or thirteen of their clergy..have wished to retain the Confession of Faith unaltered... They are called the adherents of the old light, in opposition to the majority of their brethren, whom they term new light men. **1874** BLUNT *Dict. Sects* s.v. *Burghers*, On Sept. 5th 1799..the Burgher body split into two parties, called respectively the Old-Light and the New-Light. On October 2nd the Old-Light minority constituted themselves into a separate Presbytery. *Ibid.* In 1820 the New-Light Burghers united with the New-Light Antiburghers, and took the name of the United Secession. **1888** BARRIE (*title*) Auld Licht Idylls.

e. A suggestion or help to the solution of a problem or enigma. Now *spec.* in an acrostic puzzle, each of the words which are to be guessed, their initials (or initials and finals) forming the word or words in which the answer to the puzzle consists.

1854 MRS. GASKELL *Company Manners* in *Househ. Words* 20 May 330/1 Why have we not oftener recourse to games of some kind. Wit, Advice, Bout-rimés, Lights..—every one knows these..if they would only not think it beneath them to be called upon..to play at them. **1894** *World* 3 Jan. XL. 37/1 Acrostics... When 'second thoughts' are sent, the whole answer should be forwarded, not corrections to separate lights only. **1937** H. G. WELLS *Brynhild* vii. 108 Valliant Chevrell was generally the director of his scenes [in a charade], but the direction of the first light was taken out of his hands. **1945** H. PHILLIPS *Word Play* xiv. 84 It is permissible to play tricks of this kind with the Lights—beheading or curtailing the words.

f. The answer to a clue in a crossword puzzle.

1925 'TORQUEMADA' *Cross-Words in Rhyme* Introd. Those who wish a separate entertainment..from each Light in their cross-words. **1965** *Listener* 16 Sept. 435/1 Some of the clues are two lines of verse, each by a different author. The names of the two authors have three or more consecutive letters in common and these letters form the light. **1967** *Sci. Amer.* Sept. 268/2 The horizontal words..are called the cross-lights or simply the lights.

7. a. Often with spiritual reference (said of the brightness of Heaven, the illumination of the

soul by divine truth or love, etc.). ***angel*** (or ***spirit***) ***of light***, one who dwells in Heaven.

971 *Blickl. Hom.* 17 Se þe ne can þa beorhtnesse þæs ecan leohtes. c1200 *Trin. Coll. Hom.* 13 Ðese six werkes of brictnesse..he ben nemned lichtes wapne. a1225 *Ancr. R.* 92 God wule..ȝiuen on liht wiðinnen, him uorto iseonne, ant icnowen. c1340 HAMPOLE *Wks.* (Horstm.) I. 13 Mare priuilyer he [Satan] transfigurs hym in þe forme of an awngel of lyght. a1400 *Prymer* (1891) 73 That thou sette the soule of thy seruant..in the Kyngdom of pees and of liȝt. 1588 J. UDALL *Demonstr. Discipl.* (Arb.) 18 The light of the Gospell is (at the least) as cleare as that of the law. 1588 SHAKS. *L.L.L.* IV. iii. 257 Diuels soonest tempt resembling spirits of light. 1732 LAW *Serious C.* v. (ed. 2) 71 To walk in the light of Religion. 1738 WESLEY *Psalms* LXXXVIII. i, Thou art the God of Light! 1827 HARE *Guesses* (1859) 28 Beware, ye who walk in light, lest ye turn your light into a curse. 1854 FABER *Oratory Hymns* lxvii. '*Hark! hark! my soul*' i, Angels of Jesus! Angels of light!

b. *spec.* Among Quakers, the inward revelation of Christ in the soul.

1656 G. FOX *Jrnl.* I. 271 That which is called life in Christ the Word, was called light in us. 1706 [E. WARD] *Wooden World Dissected* (1708) 89 Tho' he's more beholden to Sol, than a Quaker to his inward Light. a1713 ELLWOOD *Autobiog.* (1714) 45, I now saw, in and by the farther Openings of the Divine Light in me. 1765 MACLAINE tr. *Mosheim's Eccl. Hist.* (1768) V. 25 They [Quakers] prefer..to be called, in allusion to that doctrine that is the fundamental principle of their association, Children or Confessors of Light.

c. Applied to God as the source of divine light, and to men who manifest it.

c1000 *Ags. Gosp.* Matt. v. 14 Ge synt middaneardes leoht. c1375 *Sc. Leg. Saints* Prol. 129 God..of þis warld callit þame þe lichte. 1567 *Gude & Godlie Ball.* (S.T.S.) 45 Call on the Lord, our gyde and lycht. 1859 FITZGERALD tr. *Omar* lvi. (1899) 87 Whether the one True Light Kindle to Love, or Wrath consume me quite. 1860 PUSEY *Min. Proph.* 588 In the presence of God Who is Light, all earthly light shall fail.

8. In figurative uses of sense 5:

a. One who is eminent or conspicuous for virtue, intellect, or other excellence; a luminary.

[1526 TINDALE *John* v. 35 He was a brennynge and a shynynge light.] 1592 DAVIES *Immort. Soul* VI. i. (1714) 43 Some who were great Lights of old, And in their Hands the Lamp of God did bear. 1613 SHAKS. *Hen. VIII*, I. i. 6 Those Sunnes of Glory, those two Lights of Men. 1630 PRYNNE *Anti-Armin.* 82 He was..a worthy light of our Church. 1693 J. EDWARDS *Author. O. & N. Test.* 78 Those eminent lights of the Latin church, Rufinus, Jerom, Hilary. a1700 DRYDEN *Iliad* I. 370 If both the Lights Of Greece their private Int'rest disunites. 1832 TENNYSON *Dream Fair W.* 268 Joan of Arc, A light of ancient France. 1837 DISRAELI *Venetia* I. iv, He had been one of the shining lights of his university. 1868 HELPS *Realmah* xiii. (1876) 367 The great lights of the Bench. 1887 *Lantern* (New Orleans) 7 May 3/1 Some of the leading lights of the National League. 1894 JESSOPP *Random Roaming, etc.* v. 189, I know of one eminent man of science, who was a burning and shining light in his day. 1915 T. DREISER *Genius* II. xl. 469 What Eugene thought and what White thought of this prospective situation was that the other would naturally be the minor figure, and that he under Colfax would be the shining light. 1942 BERREY & VAN DEN BARK *Amer. Thes. Slang* §388/4 *Principal or most important person*,..leading card or light. 1943 K. TENNANT *Ride on Stranger* xvi. 180 An eminent legal light. 1974 E. AMBLER *Dr. Frigo* III. 240 The procession could..move off. I was among the least of the lesser lights and so was among the first out.

b. A bright example.

1550 CROWLEY *Waie to Wealth* (1872) 139 Fingered ladies, whose womanlike behauiour and motherlike housewifry ought to be a lighte to al women.

9. In figurative uses of sense 1e: A consideration which elucidates or which suggests a particular (true or false) view of a subject. Hence, the aspect in which anything is viewed or judged. ***in the light of***: (*a*) with the help afforded by knowledge of (some fact); (*b*) in the aspect or character of, viewed as being (so and so).

1689–90 TEMPLE *Ess., Gardening* Wks. 1731 I. 174 Cæsar, if considered in all Lights. 1705 ADDISON *Italy* Pref., I have mention'd but few Things in common with others, that are not either set in a new Light or accompany'd with different Reflections. 1712 STEELE *Spect.* No. 518 ¶9 As you have considered human nature in all its lights. 1719 W. WOOD *Surv. Trade* p. v, Should we consider your Majesty under this Light. 1748 *Anson's Voy.* II. v. 182 In this light it will easily appear, how much more intense the same degree of heat may prove. 1749 FIELDING *Tom Jones* v. i, Those great judges whose vast strength of genius hath placed them in the light of legislators. 1793 SMEATON *Edystone L.* §163 In the light of a foremast seaman, he appeared to be quite a Genius. 1834 MACAULAY in Trevelyan *Life* I. 373, I quite enjoy the thought of appearing in the light of an old hunks who knows on which side his bread is buttered. 1891 E. PEACOCK *N. Brendon* I. 289 In what light did she strike you? 1893 *Times* 1 June 9/5 In the light of all that has been said and done.

10. a. A window or other opening in a wall for the admission of light; *spec.* one of the perpendicular divisions of a mullioned window.

14.. in Willis *Archit. Nomencl. Mid. Ages* (1844) 51 Three windowes, every windowe conteineth vj lights... Item ij hiest small lights. a1490 BOTONER *Itin.* (Nasmith 1778) 287 Sunt in qualibet bay-wyndow septem lyghtis. 1523 *Test. Ebor.* (Surtees) 174 A wynddoo of thre lightes to be placed in the north ile. a1586 SIDNEY *Arcadia* I. (1590) 8 The lightes, doores and staires, rather directed to the vse of the guest, then to the eye of the Artificer. 1608 TOPSELL *Serpents* (1658) 720 They shut their dooes against them [Frogs], and stopped up all their lights to exclude them out of their houses. 1683 MOXON *Mech. Exerc. Printing* ii. ¶1 For the making the height of his Lights to bear a rational proportion to the capacity of the Room. 1723 CHAMBERS tr. *Le Clerc's Treat. Archit.* I. 133 Round or Oval Lights..make a very beautiful Diversity with the larger Windows. 1727 A. HAMILTON *New Acc. E. Ind.* I. xxi. 254 Clear Oyster-shell Lights, that are far inferior to Lights of Glass. 1760 RAPER in *Phil. Trans.* LI. 804 The diameter of the circular light at top is 27 feet 5 inches. 1823 RUTTER *Fonthill* 55 The third window..two lights high, and four wide. 1879 SIR G. SCOTT *Lect. Archit.* I. 182 The east and west windows, of five lights each.

b. *Gardening.* One of the glazed compartments (usually admitting of being opened) forming the roof or side of a greenhouse or the top of a frame.

1733 MILLER *Gardener's Dict.* (ed. 2) s.v. *Hot-bed*, Some have them [Frames] to contain but two Lights, which is very handy for raising Cucumber and Melon Plants. 1821 W. COBBETT *Amer. Gardener* §106 Air is given by pushing up, or drawing down, the Lights, which form the top or roof of the green-house. 1829 —— *Eng. Gardener* §49 Upon this frame, glazed sashes are put, which are called lights. 1847 MRS. LOUDON *Amateur Gard. Cal.* (1857) 208 A frame with glass lights like those used for melon and cucumber beds. 1859 R. THOMPSON *Gardener's Assist.* 625 The soil should be watered about ten a.m., shutting down the lights for a short time, in order to prevent a chill taking place.

11. *Mech.* An aperture or clear space. (Cf. F. *lumière*.)

1776 G. SEMPLE *Building in Water* 12 These Arches consist of a Semi-circle, and the Depth of their Archivolte is a tenth Part of the light or void of the greater, and an eighth Part of the light of the lesser ones. 1884 F. J. BRITTEN *Watch & Clockm. Handbk.* 59 See that the 'lights' between the wheel teeth and the edge of the roller are equal on both sides when the wheel is locked.

12. *Painting.* Light or illuminated surface, as represented in a picture, or considered in regard to such representation; any portion of a picture represented as lighted up. Also *fig.*: usu. opp. to *shade*.

In this sense perh. mixed with an absolute use of LIGHT *a.*[2] Fr. has both *lumière* and *clair* in similar applications.

1622 MABBE tr. *Aleman's Guzman d'Alf.* I. 3 With this onely did he fill and finish his Table, giuing in the rest Lights and shadowes, as might sute best with each seuerall part. 1658 W. SANDERSON *Graphice* 66 In what places you will have those strong and high lights, and reflections to fall, which are seen in satten and velvet. *Ibid.*, Lay your light with thinne and waterish Lake. 1709 FELTON *Classics* (1718) 69 It is in Writing, as in Picture, in which the Art is to observe where the Lights will fall. 1748 *Anson's Voy.* III. x. 412 It is very unusual to see the light and shade justly and naturally handled [in Chinese pictures]. 1811 *Self Instructor* 513 Giving the lights their proper value. c1816 FUSELI in *Lect. Paint.* viii. (1848) 505 One point is the brightest in the eye, as on the object; this is the point of light. 1821 CRAIG *Lect. Drawing* iii. 153 A light is made brighter by being opposed to a dark. 1843 RUSKIN *Arrows of Chace* (1880) I. 5 The Italian masters universally make the horizon the chief light of their picture. 1859 GULLICK & TIMBS *Paint.* 204 Selecting some point of 'highest light'. 1867 TENNYSON *Window* 1 The lights and shadows fly! Yonder it brightens and darkens down on the plain.

fig. 1732 POPE *Ess. Man* II. 121 The lights and shades, whose well-accorded strife Gives all the strength and colour of our life. 1812 *Dramatic Censor 1811* 182 This may be what our modern playmakers call *light* and *shade*. 1937 *Printers' Ink Monthly* May 39/1 *Light and shade*, variations from quietness to tenseness, softness to shouting and which has a tendency to keep a production from a dull sameness. 1952 GRANVILLE *Dict. Theatr. Terms* 110 *Light and shade*, the niceties of intonation, inflection, modulation, etc., in the reading of a part.

13. *Law.* The light which falls on the windows of a house from the heavens, and which the owner claims to enjoy unobscured by obstructions erected by his neighbours. Usu. in *pl.*

In England the inscription 'Ancient Lights' was frequently put on the face or side of a house adjacent to a site on which lofty buildings may be erected; the object being to give warning that the owner would have ground of action against any person who should obstruct the access of light to his windows. (Cf. sense 10 above.)

1768 BLACKSTONE *Comm.* III. 5 If a house or wall is erected so near to mine that it stops my antient lights,..I may enter my neighbour's land, and peaceably pull it down. 1858 LD. ST. LEONARDS *Handy-Bk. Prop. Law* vii. 48 If a house is sold with all the lights belonging to it, and it is intended to build upon the adjoining ground..so as to interfere with the lights, the right to build in that manner should be expressly reserved. *Ibid.* xxv. 187 You should keep in view this distinction between the right to light, and rights of common and of way, or the like.

14. a. A flame or spark serving to ignite any combustible substance. ***to strike a light***, to produce a flame or spark with flint and steel or with a match (see STRIKE *v.*). **b.** Something used for igniting; e.g. a spill, taper, match.

1684 BUNYAN *Pilgr.* II. (1900) 277 Wherefore he strook a Light (for he never goes also without his Tinder-box). 1835 W. IRVING *Tour Prairies* 281 We had implements to strike a light. 1835 MARRYAT *Three Cutters* i, Tell Mr. Simpson to bring me a light for my cigar. 1852 DICKENS *Bleak Ho.* xi, Krook takes it [a candle], goes to the fire, stoops over the red embers, and tries to get a light. 1889 BESANT *Bell St. Paul's* I. 170 A jar of tobacco, and a box of lights. *Mod.* Go and put a light to the fire in the dining-room.

15. *attrib.* and *Comb.* **a.** simple attrib., as ***light-beam, -effect, -glare, -output, -ray, -scatter, -signal, -socket, -song, -source, -spot, -switch, -wave***; **b.** objective, as ***light-absorber, -absorbing, -absorptive, -avoiding, -bearer, -bringer, -creating, -emitting, -gathering, -giver, -giving, -grasping, -hating, -loving, -maker, -making, -passing, -producing, -reflecting, -reflective, -refracting, -throwing*** adjs.; instrumental, etc., as ***light-actuated, -embroidered, -gilded, -sensitive, -stilled*** adjs.

1957 *Technology* Dec. 361/2 *Light absorbers for use in products affected by ultra-violet radiations from the sun. 1967 E. CHAMBERS *Photolitho-Offset* vii. 85 The term *density* refers to the *light-absorbing ability of the [silver] layer. 1963 R. R. A. HIGHAM *Handbk. Papermaking* viii. 210 Opacity is dependent on the number of *light-absorptive or -reflective fibre surfaces in a sheet. 1936 *Discovery* Nov. 358/1 *Light-actuated apparatus for home use is now on the market. 1924 J. A. THOMSON *Sci. Old & New* xxvi. 142 The Fierasfer..is a *light-avoiding fish, related to the sand-eel. 1965 B. E. FREEMAN tr. *Vandel's Biospeleol.* iv. 39 The light-avoiding planarians are simple to keep in captivity. 1398 TREVISA *Barth. De P.R.* VIII. xliii. (Tollem. MS.), A *lyȝt bem [L. *radius*] is a bryȝte strem of a body of lyȝte. 1845 CARLYLE *Cromwell* (1871) IV. 119 Straggling accidental light beams. 1526 *Pilgr. Perf.* (W. de W. 1531) 67b, The sterre called lucifer: that is to say the *lyght berer. 1852 JAMES *Agnes Sorel* (1860) I. 257 Two of the light-bearers cast down their torches and fled. 1831 CARLYLE *Sart. Res.* II. v. (1838) 170 By this fairest of Orient *Light-bringers must our Friend be blandished. 1781 COWPER *Truth* 390 The *light-creating God. 1902 *Westm. Gaz.* 29 Sept. 3/1 The energy required for producing pendulous movements of atoms and molecules giving *light-effects must be very small as compared with the total energy employed. 1962 R. G. HAGGAR *Dict. Art Terms* 192/1 J. M. W. Turner..carried research into light effects further than any previous artist. 1745–6 COLLINS *Ode Liberty* iv. 16 Clouds, that lie Paving the *light-embroider'd Sky. 1964 *Oceanogr. & Marine Biol.* II. 351 The decrease in *light-emitting capacity of a methanol solution of..luciferin. 1869 *Chambers's Jrnl.* 10 Apr. 231/1 Under the high power and vast *light-gathering capacity of Sir W. Herschel's four-foot reflector. 1960 *Farmer & Stockbreeder* 8 Mar. 134 The Meopta 12 × 60 has the rare combination of high magnification and brilliant light-gathering power even at night and under bad climatic conditions. c1670 H. ANDERSON *Crt. Convert* 7 We must..Leave the fair Train, and the *light-guilded Room. 1382 WYCLIF *Gen.* i. 16 And God made two greet *liȝt ȝyuerys [Vulg. *luminaria*]. 1581 SIDNEY *Apol. Poetrie* (Arb.) 20 Poetry..hath been the first light-giuer to ignorance. 1883 *Cassell's Fam. Mag.* July 464/1 It consists of a wick or light-giver, formed of vegetable carbon bent in the form of a loop. 1427–9 *Rolls of Parlt.* IV. 364/2 A redy Bekyn, wheryn shall be *light gevyng by nyht, to alle the Vessellx that [etc.]. 1863 I. WILLIAMS *Baptistery* I. v. (1874) 54 The light-giving face That lights the heavens. 1856 MRS. BROWNING *Aur. Leigh* VI. 572 He had been covered overmuch To keep him from the *light-glare. 1889 *Tablet* 2 Nov. 688 The most powerful *light-grasping instruments as yet used. 1647 H. MORE *Song of Soul* III. App. xxxvii, *Light-hating ghosts. 1895 J. H. & A. COMSTOCK *Man. Study Insects* xxi. 562 The *Light-loving Anomala, *Anomala lucicola*..also feeds on the leaves of grape. 1974 A. HUXLEY *Plant & Planet* viii. 99 During the twelve-hour period of the average night..the plant is regarded as 'dark-loving', while in the other twelve-hour period it is 'light-loving'. 1382 WYCLIF *Ezek.* xxxii. 8, Y shal make alle *liȝtmakers [Vulg. *luminaria*] of heuen for to mourne vpon thee. 1800 HERSCHEL in *Phil. Trans.* XC. 528 *Light-making rays. 1950 *Sci. News* XV. 43 The brightnesses thus catalogued are, however, only apparent... So, in order to compare the *light-outputs of the stars, we introduce the idea of Absolute Magnitude. 1958 *Newnes Compl. Amat. Photogr.* 120 Recent developments have been in the direction of maintaining high efficiency and light-output operating at lower voltages. 1961 G. MILLERSON *Technique Television Production* iii. 38 Construction differences [in lenses] ..can vary their respective *light-passing abilities, although their stop numbers may be measurably identical. 1845 *Harmony of Comprehensible World* Essay II. XIII. 221 Between some bodies there may be no *light-producing sympathy, because the mutual relations of their constituent molecules may not be such as to develope light. 1964 V. B. WIGGLESWORTH *Life of Insects* viii. 126 It is among the insects that some of the most brilliant and certainly the most complex types of light-producing organs are to be found. 1880 'MARK TWAIN' *Tramp Abroad* I. xvi. 129 Of *Light-rays was the Figure wove. 1950 *Sci. News* XV. 17 Light rays cannot bring about a photo-chemical change unless they are absorbed. 1854 GEO. ELIOT tr. *Feuerbach's Essence Christianity* v. 61 Tears are the *light-reflecting drops which mirror the nature of the Christian's God. 1951 S. SPENDER *World within World* iii. 180 Their minds like little caves of calculating darkness which the light-reflecting snow has never penetrated. 1963 *Light-reflective [see *light-absorptive* above]. 1889 E. CARPENTER *Civilization* 88 It [*sc.* modern science] takes the emerald, and breaks it up; treats of its color and *light-refracting qualities. 1957 PARTRIDGE *English gone Wrong* ii. 29 The light-refracting heads of the Communist philosophers and propagandists. 1958 *A.M.A. Arch. Industr. Health* XVIII. 29/1 A plot of the *light-scatter decay was divided into exponential portions by a slope-analysis method. 1961 G. MILLERSON *Technique Television Production* iii. 43 Optically speaking, there are several obvious causes for lack of clarity: dirty lenses, light-scatter in the lens. 1936 *Discovery* May 151/1 It was not until the appearance of a new type of *light-sensitive cell, known as the rectifier or semi-conducting cell, that photo-electric exposure meters became popular. 1946 *Nature* 28 Sept. 454/2 *N. texana* also contains strains which have light-sensitive seeds. 1962 *Science Survey* III. 240 The retina is light-sensitive because it contains one or more photosensitive pigments located in its visual receptors. 1920 A. S. EDDINGTON *Space, Time & Gravitation* iii. 50 It would, in fact, be possible for an observer travelling along *NP* to receive a *light-signal..announcing the event *O*, just as he reached *N*. 1930 *Morning Post* 19 July 13/6 An extension of the system of light signals for road traffic. 1964 *Amer. Jrnl. Physics* XXXII. 262/2 At an arbitrary instant *t* ..a light signal *S* is emitted at the origin *A* of the coordinate system. 1960 H. PINTER *Caretaker* II. 48 There used to be a wall plug..but it doesn't work. I had to fit it in the *light socket. 1935 A. H. HAFFENDEN (*title*) *Light-song. 1946 L. B. LYON *Rough Walk Home* 27 Our anguish has a hand, that gropes For melody, for the light-song of the sun. 1903 *Edin. Rev.* July 113 Because a spectrum line changes with change of..velocity of *light source and other disturbing causes,

the value of its record is thereby increased. **1961** G. MILLERSON *Technique Television Production* iii. 49 Prolonged static captions, and visible light-sources in the scene, are the worst offenders. **1884** EARLE *Ags. Lit.* 98 Anglia became for a century the *light-spot of European history. **1938** W. DE LA MARE *Memory* 81 Peace beyond telling share with the *light-stilled eye. **1892** F. C. ALLSOP *Pract. Electr.-Light Fitting* iii. 39 Lamp or branch switches are designated either by the number of lamps they are intended to control, or..by their current-carrying capacity. They are thus called 1, 2, or 3 *light, or 1, 2, or 3 ampère switches. **1926** G. HUNTING *Vicarion* iv. 63 He went back to his light-switch, closed the closet door which stood ajar, and brought his chair toward them again. **1972** 'H. CARMICHAEL' *Naked to Grave* i. 14 He heard the click of a light switch in the bedroom. **1894** 'MARK TWAIN' in *Century Mag.* Jan. 336 He asked questions that would have brought *light-throwing answers. **1902** *Westm. Gaz.* 1 July 2/1 An excellent translation of a light-throwing and thought-provoking book. **1871** TYNDALL *Fragm. Sci.* (1879) II. viii. 110 Different *light-waves produce different colours.

16. Special Comb.: **light-adaptation**, self-adjustment of the eye to increased intensity of light by means of a decrease in the sensitivity of the retina; also, in extended use, any reversible change in an organism that occurs in response to increased light; so **light-adapted** *pa. pple.* and *ppl. a.*, in the state that results from light-adaptation; **light-ball** *Mil.*, a combustible fired from a mortar at night, to throw light on the operations of the enemy; **light barrier**, (*a*) a limit to the resolution possible with an optical microscope arising out of the finite length of light waves (*nonce-use*); (*b*) the speed of light as the limiting speed attainable by any object; **light-boat** = LIGHT-SHIP; †**light-bolt**, a thunderbolt; also *fig.*; **light-box**, †(*a*) a certain apparatus for striking a light by chemical means; (*b*) *Naut.* = *light-room* (Cent. Dict.); (*c*) a box-like piece of equipment containing a light and usu. having translucent glass on one side which provides an evenly lighted surface; **light bucket** *Astr.* (*colloq.*), a telescope, regarded as a device for collecting and focusing a large quantity of low-intensity radiation; **light bulb** = BULB *sb.* 4; **light-buoy**, a buoy equipped with a warning light which flashes intermittently; **light button**, a knob or disc which, when pressed, turns a light on or off; **light-change** *Astr.*, a change in the amount of light received from a variable star; **light check** *Theatr.* (see quot. 1952); **light cone** *Physics*, a surface in space-time which appears conical when represented in three dimensions and comprises all the world-points from which a light signal would reach a given point (defining the apex) simultaneously (and which therefore appear simultaneous to an observer at the apex); **light cord**, a cord which hangs from a ceiling or lamp stand and operates an electric light when pulled; **light cue**, (*a*) *Broadcasting*, a cue indicated by a light being switched on; (*b*) *Theatr.* (see quot. 1961); **light-cure** *rare* or *Obs.*, a cure effected by sunlight or artificial light; also *attrib.*; **light curve** *Astr.*, a graph showing the variation in the light received over a period of time from a variable star or other heavenly body; **light-demander**, a tree that will not tolerate shade; so **light-demanding** *a.*, of trees or, occas., other plants, needing full light; **light-due, -duty**, a toll levied on ships for the maintenance of lights in lighthouses and lightships; **light-fastness**, resistance to discoloration by light; so **light-fast** *a.*; †**light-fat**, a lamp; **light-filter** *Photogr.* = *colour-filter* (see COLOUR *sb.*[1] 19); **light-fixture**, the flex, socket, and other equipment which is used with a light bulb; **light fog** *Photogr.* (see quot. 1940 and FOG *sb.*[2] 4); **light-grasp** *Astr.*, light-gathering power (of a telescope); **light guide**, a cylinder or strip of transparent material, or a bundle of them, along which light can travel with little loss, by means of total internal reflection; **light gun** = *light pen*; **light-head**, the top portion of a 'light' (sense 10); **light-keeper**, one who has charge of the light in a lighthouse or lightship; **light-land** (*Hist.*), land given for the maintenance of light at an altar or shrine; **light-man**, (*a*) one who attends to the light (in a lighthouse, etc.); a light-keeper; (*b*) a linkman; hence **lightmanship**, the office or duty of a lightman; **light meter**, an instrument for measuring the intensity of light; *esp.* an exposure meter; **light microscope**, a conventional microscope, in which ordinary light is used; **light-money** = *light-due*; **light organ**, in luminescent animals, the structure emitting light; **light pen**, a hand-held, pen-like device that incorporates a lens, photoelectric cell, and amplifier and may be used to feed information by wire to a data-processing system by placing or moving the tip on the screen of a cathode-ray tube or other surface so that electrical impulses are transmitted to the system; **light-picture**, a photograph; **light pipe** = *light guide*; **light-port** (see quot. 1867); **light-pressure**, pressure exerted on a body by light incident on it; **light quantum** *Physics* = PHOTON; **light-room**, (*a*) a small chamber next to the magazine in a war-ship, in which lights are placed behind thick glass windows for illuminating the magazine; (*b*) the room at the top of a lighthouse containing the lighting apparatus; **light-scattering**, scattering of light, *spec.* of monochromatic light by a solution as a method of determining the molecular weight of dissolved polymers and investigating their conformation; **light-sensation**, in the study of visual perception, the sensation produced by light; **light-shot** *Hist.*, a due levied for furnishing the church with lights [= OE. *leoht-ȝesceot*]; **light show**, a display of changing coloured lights or varied film strips, freq. accompanying popular music; also *attrib.*; **light-stand**, a stand to support a light; **light station**, a group of buildings which includes a lighthouse and associated buildings for housing personnel, supplies, and equipment; **light-struck** *a.*, (*a*) ? thunderstruck; (*b*) *Photogr.*, injured by exposure to actinic light; **light-tight** *a.*, impervious to light; **light-time** *Astr.*, the time taken by light to travel from a distant source to the observer; **light-tower**, a lighthouse; **light trap**, (*a*) *Photogr.*, a device for excluding light from a room or other space without preventing access into it; (*b*) a device for attracting, catching, and sometimes killing, night-flying insects; so **light-trapped** *a.*, provided with a light trap; **light value** *Photogr.*, a number representing on an arbitrary scale the intensity of light from a particular direction; ***light-value shutter***, a shutter having the aperture and shutter speed settings linked so that they can be altered together in such a way as to keep the amount of light admitted during an exposure constant; **light valve**, a device which regulates the amount of light passing through it according to the magnitude of an applied electrical signal; **light-vessel** = LIGHTSHIP; **light-well**, a shaft designed to admit light from above into inner rooms or a staircase of a building; **light-year** (see quot. 1890); it is approximately equal to $9{\cdot}46 \times 10^{12}$ km. ($5{\cdot}87 \times 10^{12}$ miles); also *fig.*

1900 W. H. RIVERS in E. A. Schäfer *Textbk. Physiol.* II. 1080 If the eye remained in a condition of *light-adaptation, red and blue..became gradually blacker. **1962** H. C. WESTON *Sight, Light & Work* (ed. 2) i. 8 Thus, after full light-adaptation, complete dark-adaptation may require about an hour. **1964** *Oceanogr. & Marine Biol.* II. 352 Prolonged laboratory culture, starvation, and light- or dark-adaptation had relatively little effect on luminescent ability [of the copepod *Metridia lucens*]. **1900** W. H. RIVERS in E. A. Schäfer *Textbk. Physiol.* II. 1073 He found that in complete dark-adaptation the recurrent image followed the original immediately and was brighter than to the *light-adapted eye. **1935** *Discovery* May 138/1 A source of light which is almost or quite invisible to a light-adapted eye, that is to one coming in from daylight, is quite obvious to a dark-adapted eye. **1950** *Sci. News* XV. 25 A [spontaneous] change in fixation direction is quite possible, particularly when the eye is not fully light-adapted or where there is too large an object for precise fixation. **1797** *Encycl. Brit.* (ed. 3) II. 766/2 Fire-balls, *light-balls, smoke-balls, [etc.]. **1859** F. A. GRIFFITHS *Artil. Man.* (1862) 86 Light balls burn from 10 to 20 minutes. **1959** *Listener* 31 Dec. 1161/1 When one gets down to sizes round about the wavelength of light..one runs into a barrier, which might be called the *light barrier, that no microscope working by means of light can break through. **1964** M. MCLUHAN *Understanding Media* (1967) I. vi. 68 No further acceleration is possible this side of the light barrier. **1968** A. DIMENT *Great Spy Race* x. 180 The faster than light spaceships will bring the stars down into our backyard, for once one has broken the so-called 'light-barrier' there is no limit to speed. **1858** HOMANS *Cycl. Commerce* 1237 *Light-Boats and their Accessories. **1582** STANYHURST *Æneis* III. (Arb.) 76 Thundring *lightbolts from torne clowds fyrye be flasshing. **a1603** BREWER *Lingua* IV. i. (1607) H, Therefore more murthering art thou then the light bolt. **1647** TRAPP *Comm. Rev.* xii. 8 Whatsoever the pope with his bulls, or the emperor with his light-bolts, did to hinder it, still the gospel ran and was glorified. **1849** THACKERAY *Pendennis* I. xix. 173 Helen..went for a *light-box and his cigar-case. **1853** H. KNIGHT *Once upon a Time* II. 273 By-and-by the light-box was sold as low as a shilling. **1940** J. O. KRAEHENBUEHL *Electr. Illumination* viii. 108/2 The light boxes commonly used may be divided into two classes: those which are covered with some form of transmitting medium which is translucent.., and those which have prismatic lens plates. **1943** J. S. HUXLEY *TVA* 98 Note the flush light boxes with patent lenses at the side of the stairway. **1957** *Screen Printer & Display Producer* July 16/3 Pin-holes were spotted out over a lightbox before printing. **1962** H. C. WESTON *Sight, Light & Work* (ed. 2) vi. 195 These devices consist of a light-box of suitable size, the cover-glass or vizor of which allows the emission of light in a regular pattern. **1968** *New Scientist* 31 Oct. 260/2 One piece of equipment is a 34-ft '*light bucket' for seeking out point sources of gamma rays in the universe. **1970** *Nature* 7 Feb. 492/2 Infrared telescopes, more properly called flux collectors—light buckets in the language of astronomy—are cheap compared with similar equipment for the visible spectrum. **1884** *Light bulb [see BULB *sb.* 4]. **1946** E. HODGINS *Mr. Blandings builds his Dream House* (1947) I. v. 78 The cost of your house doesn't get you moved into it with light bulbs in all the sockets. **1975** M. KENYON *Mr Big* xix. 185 His muscled black tangled limbs trailing flex and popping lightbulbs from the overhead fixtures. **1894** W. LE QUEUX *Gt. War in Eng. in 1897* xxix. 236 A cruiser..was lying near the Herwit *light-buoy. **1930** W. DE LA MARE *Desert Islands* 19 Light-ship or beacon or winking light-buoy rocked in the cradle of the deep. **1951** *Oxf. Jun. Encycl.* IV. 71/2 The older light buoys exhibit their light day and night; but they are gradually being superseded by buoys which automatically light up at sunset and extinguish themselves at dawn. **1929** D. HAMMETT *Dain Curse* x. 95 [My] hand touched the *light button. I had sense enough to push it. Light scorched my eyes. **1970** R. BUSBY *Frighteners* xvii. 172 The time-switch light-button on the wall. **1890** A. M. CLERKE *Syst. Stars* ix. 139 The *light-change of S. Cancri, the second of the Algol variables, was discovered by Mr. Hind in 1848. **1928** *Publ. Washburn Observatory Univ. Wisconsin* XV. I. iv. 29 Ellipsoidal figure of the bodies would account for most of the light-change. **1933** P. GODFREY *Back-Stage* i. 18 '*Light checks' are any alterations to the opening lighting of the scene. **1952** GRANVILLE *Dict. Theatr. Terms* 110 *Light check*, a dimming of lights. **1922** E. P. ADAMS tr. *Einstein's Meaning of Relativity* ii. 42 *P'* lies outside the '*light-cone'. **1964** A. O. BARUT *Electrodynamics* i. 8 All time-like vectors are inside the light cone and the space-like ones are outside. **1964** *Listener* 17 Dec. 976/2 Encouragement also comes from the usual diagrams in physics text books representing such relativistic ideas as the 'light cone'. **1968** M. LOCKWOOD *Accessory* (1969) iii. 74 She reached accurately for the hanging *light cord. **1972** E. PAGE *Family & Friends* viii. 124 He pulled at the light cord, glanced at the clock. **1929** *Radio Times* 8 Nov. 389/1 They will sit at the [control] panel, flashing '*light cues', fading and cross-fading studios. **1930** L. HARTMANN *Theatre Lighting* iii. 37 Light cues are written down during the progress of a rehearsal. **1961** BOWMAN & BALL *Theatre Lang.* 201 *Light cue*.., the cue for the commencement of some planned change in illumination. **1901** *Chambers's Jrnl.* Dec. 844/2 Hospitals..have already obtained apparatus for the *light-cure of lupus. **1904** *Daily Chron.* 11 Apr. 5/3 Yesterday morning King Edward..paid a lengthy visit to Professor Finsen's light-cure institution. **1890** A. M. CLERKE *Syst. Stars* viii. 116 The *light-curve [of U Geminorum] takes more or less the form of a double peak with a saddle between. **1956** *Astrophysical Jrnl.* CXXIII. 12 The light-curve for the 1952 eclipse, as measured in the Sudan, is much flatter than the curves..from the 1947 observations. **1968** *Project Icarus* (Mass. Inst. Technol.) i. 7 The rate of rotation of an asteroid and the axis of its rotation can be found approximately by careful analysis of the shape and variation of its light curve. **1975** *Sci. Amer.* Mar. 26/3 The X-ray light curve of Centaurus X-3 is the curve of a typical eclipsing binary system. **1891** W. SCHLICH *Man. Forestry* II. iv. 306 As regards light-requirement it [*sc.* the Weymouth Pine] stands half-way between *light-demanders and shade-bearers. **1928** R. S. TROUP *Silvicultural Syst.* v. 67 If the group system is applied to strong light-demanders, larger gaps would be necessary. **1966** *Times* 21 Apr. 16/6 Some trees are such emphatic light-demanders..that they will not thrive if there is any overhead shade. **1889** W. SCHLICH *Man. Forestry* I. ii. 117 Certain species [which] cannot thrive unless they enjoy a large measure of light throughout life..are called '*light demanding'. **1952** H. L. EDLIN *Forester's Handbk.* viii. 113 Trees described as light-demanding will only succeed if grown in the open. **1964** *Oceanogr. & Marine Biol.* II. 213 In his [*sc.* Ernst's] opinion *Udotea* is a light demanding species [of green algae]. **1839** *Penny Cycl.* XIII. 479/1 *Light-dues are collected..upon ships frequenting our ports. **1860** R. BURSELL in *Merc. Marine Mag.* VII. 4 The Light dues..are one shilling per ton. **1793** SMEATON *Edystone L.* §84 The condition of their receiving the *light duties was that of maintaining a light. **1957** M. B. PICKEN *Fashion Dict.* 213/1 *Lightfast. **1971** *Jrnl. Oil & Colour Chemists' Assoc.* LIV. 847 Bright red paints based on cadmium sulpho-selenide pigments, which are highly light-fast. **1913** C. E. PELLEW *Dyes & Dyeing* iii. 63 The test for *light-fastness is usually made by partially covering a dyed skein with a piece of wood..and exposing it to direct sunlight. **1959** *B.S.I. News* June 4/1 The colour, colour-strength, transparency and light-fastness of these inks in terms of comparison with master standard inks. **1962** J. T. MARSH *Self-Smoothing Fabrics* vi. 75 Dimethylol dihydroxy ethylene urea appears to be quite outstanding in its effect on the light-fastness of dyed goods in general and those containing reactive dyes in particular. **1971** *Jrnl. Oil & Colour Chemists' Assoc.* LIV. 857 Better light-fastness of pigments, non-yellowing media..are thus seen to be important requirements. **c1000** *Ags. Gosp.* John v. 35 He wæs byrnende *leoht-fæt [Vulg *lucerna*] & lyhtende. **c1200** ORMIN 13399 Þurrh Filippe onn Ennglissh iss Lihhtfattess muþ bitacnedd. **1901** *Chambers's Jrnl.* June 367/2 For use either in ortho-chromatic or colour photography, *light-filters..are now commercially produced. **1958** *Newnes Compl. Amat. Photogr.* iv. 83 The smaller increases in exposure needed when light-filters are employed. **1923** *T. Eaton & Co. Catal.* Spring & Summer 357/5 *Light fixture, for dining-room or living-room. **1939** D. PARKER *Here Lies* 27 He bought..storm-windows, and light-fixtures. **1889** E. J. WALL *Dict. Photogr.* 77 **Light fog* makes its appearance generally all over the plate. **1915** *Photo-Era* XXXV. 170/1 Plate and films must be loaded..with the utmost care to avoid light-fog. **1940** *Chambers's Techn. Dict.* 449/1 *Light-fog* (Photog.), fog in an emulsion, caused by intrusion of extraneous light into a camera or other apparatus which is intended to be light-tight. **1946** *Nature* 6 July 18/1 Wood.. used the instrument in his charge for those types of astronomical observation for which it was eminently suitable by virtue of its short focal-length, large field of good definition and powerful *light-grasp. **1961** *Listener* 7 Sept. 353/3 For televising relatively faint objects, such as planets, it is necessary to use a powerful telescope with considerable light-grasp. **1951** *Jrnl. Sci. Instrum.* XXVIII 188/1 (*heading*) A divided *light guide for coincidence counting of scintillations due to alpha particles. *Ibid.*, A forked light guide was constructed from..Perspex rod. **1972** *Science* 9

June 1128/1 Luminescence was detected through a fiber-optic light guide. **1970** O. Dopping *Computers & Data Processing* xi. 179 An extension of the CRT terminal is the light pen, or *light gun, which can be used for identifying details in the picture displayed by the computer and even for making sketches which the computer can record. **1972** *Computers & Humanities* VII. 5 With the use of a light gun the linguist can select from alternative expansions in phrase structure trees. **1886** Willis & Clark *Cambridge* III. 554 A monial which branches over the *light-heads. **1793** Smeaton *Edystone L.* §310 They would fully instruct the person entered as *Light-keeper. **1860** *Merc. Marine Mag.* VII. 94 Its base is surrounded by the light-keepers' dwellings. **1879** E. Waterton *Pietas Mariana* 85 Lands given for this purpose were called lamp-lands and *light-lands. **1457** *Churchw. Acc. Yatton* (Som. Rec. Soc.) 99 For the *lytemen of Cleve..yrecevede iiii marke iis. *a* **1704** T. Brown *Wks.* (1760) IV. 255 The midwife moon might mind her calling, And noisy lightman leave his bawling. **1889** A. T. Pask *Eyes Thames* 68 Box-making, for which the Nore lightmen have been famous for years past. **1534** *Churchw. Acc. Yatton* (Som. Rec. Soc.) 148 Of John Wassborowe for *lygthmanshepe... vis. viijs. **1921** *Gas Jrnl.* CLVI. 563/2 Mr. Haydn T. Harrison next interested the members with a description of the 'Benjamin' *Lightmeter, which is a simple portable apparatus to measure illumination, and enable one to give intelligent and expert advice on factory lighting. **1943** D. Baker *Trio* II. 92 A light-meter on a cord, some photographic lenses, an envelope full of negatives. **1973** A. Broinowski *Take one Ambassador* xiii. 211 Peering at the light-meter reading on his Asahi Pentax. **1941** *Light microscope [see *electron microscope* s.v. electron[2] 2 b]. **1961** *Lancet* 5 Aug. 295/1 There are great difficulties in interpreting the shapes of these small chromosomes because they are almost at the limit of light-microscope resolution. **1672** Marvell *Corr.* cci. Wks. 1872–5 II. 399 He will on his part give you the best security..from the time that the *light-mony shall begin to be payd. **1755** Magens *Insurances* I. 518 For Pilotage and Light-Money £10 10. **1886** E. Schuyler *Amer. Diplom.* 308 Apart from the Sound dues themselves, there were charges of light-money, pass-money, etc., which caused a delay at Elsinore. **1899** D. Sharp in *Cambr. Nat. Hist.* VI. v. 259 The structure of the *light organs [of *Pyrophorus*] is essentially similar to that of the Lampyridæ. **1928** Russell & Yonge *Seas* 192 Some of these cuttlefish from the deep sea have over twenty light organs in various parts of the body. **1954** N. B. Marshall *Aspects Deep Sea Biol.* xi. 273 May not some of the light organs which stud the body [of certain fishes] also attract prey? **1969** R. F. Chapman *Insects* vi. 86 In most beetles the light organs are relatively compact. **1958** *Proc. IRE* XLVI. 1123/1 Narrow-based germanium photodiodes have been fabricated with intrinsic response times of less than 75 mμsec... They have been used with success in many applications among which are:..detector in a transistorized '*light pen' for high-speed oscilloscope readout. **1964** *Discovery* Oct. 53/2 (*caption*) Display console of a computer which illustrates actual graphs, characters and drawings stored within the machine in digital form. The operator can make corrections to the display with a 'light pen' which automatically corrects the stored information. **1966** *Sci. Amer.* Sept. 95/2 The stylus-photocell arrangement called the light pen can be used to make the cathode-ray-tube display serve for the manual input of sketches and diagrams. **1973** *Courier & Advertiser* (Dundee) 21 Feb. 7/1 The 280's light pen will 'read' information from colour bar coded tags and data from 48 terminals can be fed into a central data unit and recorded on magnetic tape ready for computer processing. **1885** Agnes M. Clerke *Pop. Hist. Astron.* 199 By its means the first solar *light-pictures of real value were taken. **1951** *Nucleonics* Aug. 47/2 The counter was made with a long *light pipe. **1961** *Physical Rev.* CXXIII. 1150/2 A dielectric rod constitutes a waveguide (light pipe) and thus additional modes of propagation..are introduced. **1970** *New Scientist* 13 Aug. 340/1 Light can travel along a bundle of certain glass fibres—a light pipe. **1972** *Sci. Amer.* Sept. 112/2 Although light can be conducted through carefully fabricated pipes a centimeter or so in diameter with an attenuation of only a few decibels per kilometer..light pipes have the drawback that they must either be perfectly straight or be provided with optical means for bending the rays wherever the pipe bends. **1769** Falconer *Dict. Marine* (1780) Y y, *Cantanettes*, the *light-ports in the stern of a galley. **1867** Smyth *Sailor's Word-bk.*, *Light-port*, a scuttle made for showing a light through. Also, a port in timber ships kept open until brought deep by cargo. It is then secured and caulked in. **1903** *Encycl. Brit.* Index, *Light-pressure. **1908** *Westm. Gaz.* 23 Oct. 5/3 There is also a small and sharply curved envelope on the side of the nucleus [of the comet] towards the sun, the presumption being that the matter ejected from the head in this direction is quickly turned back by the 'light-pressure' exerted by the sun. **1968** R. A. Lyttleton *Mysteries Solar Syst.* v. 178 With comminution of cometary particles occurring mainly on the perihelion side of the orbit, light-pressure will automatically select all those of appropriate size and expel them from the comet. **1925** D. L. Thomson in J. A. Thomson *Sci. & Relig.* 211 It follows from the modern 'Quantum Theory'..that there are 'smallest-possible' amounts of light, which we might call..*light-quanta. **1938** R. W. Lawson tr. *Hevesy & Paneth's Man. Radioactivity* (ed. 2) ix. 105 According to this hypothesis, the emission of β-radiation is not a unitary elementary process like the emission of a light quantum, but a dual process consisting of the simultaneous emission of an electron and a neutrino. **1948** *Sci. News* VI. 75 In the quantum theory a light signal cannot be sub-divided indefinitely, but consists of finite units, so-called light quanta, or 'photons'. **1974** *Sci. Amer.* Oct. 68/1 Carbohydrates are the direct result of the photosynthetic activity of green plants... The energy needed to promote this reaction is provided by light quanta from the sun. **1769** Falconer *Dict. Marine* (1780), **Light-room*,..it is used to contain the lights by which the gunner, and his assistants, are enabled to fill the cartridges with powder. **1803** *Naval Chron.* XV. 59 Coppered the light room. **1825** J. Nicholson *Operat. Mechanic* 805 The Light-Room Floor, the 86th course of the building. **1875** W. McIlwraith *Guide Wigtownshire* 112 The light-room at the top [of the lighthouse]. **1926** H. C. Macpherson *Mod. Astron.* iv. 64 Dr. Wright, photographing Mars,..concluded that the Martian atmosphere was at least 120 miles in depth and possessed appreciable absorbing and *light-scattering power. **1935** *Trans. Faraday Soc.* XXXI. 1324 We may therefore conclude that the main factor in the light-scattering of an isotropic protein is the molecular weight of the protein and that its scattering power is a true measure of its molecular dimensions. **1965** Peacocke & Drysdale *Molecular Basis Heredity* iv. 34 The hydrodynamic and light-scattering measurements both indicate that in solution its configuration is that of a stiffened coil, rather than that of a rigid rod or of a completely random coil. **1972** Billingham & Jenkins in A. D. Jenkins *Polymer Sci.* I. ii. 147 Despite the complexity and expense of the technique, light scattering remains one of the most useful techniques for the determination of weight average molecular weights of polymers. **1895** E. B. Titchener in *Amer. Jrnl. Psychol.* VII. 82 *Lichtempfindung*, *light sensation. **1914** Williams & Waterlow tr. *Mach's Analysis of Sensations* x. 211 The habit of..giving attention to a large and spatially cohering mass of light-sensations. **1924** R. M. Ogden tr. *Koffka's Growth of Mind* iii. §13. 134 The most varied light-, dark-, and colour-sensations. **1937** *Discovery* July 216/1 The nature of light-sensation, colour-tone, colour-blindness. **1853** Rock *Ch. of Fathers* III. II. 110 Each one according to the extent of land he had, should pay into his parish church ..a certain quantity of wax under the name of *light-shot. **1966** E. Denson in *Berkeley Barb* 1 Apr. 4/1 Led by Tony Martin's *light show, which fills the huge wall behind the bands and their 30 foot row of amplifiers and electronics with red shapes shifting in time to the music, the hall is filled with swaying, writhing people. **1967** *Ramparts* 9 Mar. 12/1 The light show atmospheric technique of projecting slides and wild colors on the walls during rock dances. **1969** *It* 11–24 Apr. 13/1 If it is regarded that lightshows began when the 'underground' or 'psychedelic' revolutions began, then it is doubtful that lightshows will ever recover from the damage inflicted during the capitalists' rape of those movements. **1971** E. E. Landy *Underground Dict.* 120 Light shows are given in auditoriums, coffeehouses, etc. They are put on for the purpose of simulating a hallucinogenic experience. **1836** N. P. Willis *Inklings of Adventure* I. 206 In another moment the *light stand was swept from between us, and he struck me down with a blow that would have felled a giant. **1867** A. D. Whitney *Summer in L. Goldthwaite's Life* vi. 119 On this little green stood.. a round white-pine light-stand with her work-basket and a few books. **1966** A. Feininger *Compl. Photographer* iv. 154 A boom extension arm that fits on a light stand is invaluable. **1953** *Aids to Navigation Manual* (U.S. Coast Guard) xxix. 3/1 The mission of a *light station is to service, tend, and maintain a light on a fixed structure. **1956** *Navigation Dict.* (U.S. Naval Oceanogr. Office) 124/1 *Light station*, a group of buildings including a lighthouse and additional buildings housing personnel, fog signal, radiobeacon, and any other equipment associated with the lighthouse. **1969** *Islander* (Victoria, B.C.) 21 Dec. 16/1 It was December 1934 at Pachena Point, a lonely lightstation on Vancouver Island's stormy west coast. **1971** *Bahamian Rev.* Nov. 5/3 Mrs. Pierre grew up on light stations, as her father was a light-keeper. **1884** J. Parker *Apost. Life* III. 177 *Light-struck, stunned, dazed, disabled. **1890** *Anthony's Photogr. Bull.* III. 105 Five or six [plates]..were too badly light-struck to show whether they had ever been exposed in the camera or not. **1884** *Athenæum* 27 Dec. 864/3 We..were doubtful whether the chamber [of the camera] was *light-tight. **1911** T. E. Lawrence *Let.* 31 Mar. (1938) 101 How to render light-tight a dark slide. **1942** *R.A.F. Jrnl.* 2 May 13 One of the.. operators had just completed a spool, and my guide took it from her when she had fitted it into its light-tight case. **1970** *Jrnl. General Psychol.* LXXXII. 208 Behind the opening were a slide holder and a 12 volt d.c. light, both enclosed in a light-tight housing. **1920** A. S. Eddington *Space, Time & Gravitation* 12 But then you must know the speed of the earth through the aether. It may have shortened the *light-time by going some way to meet the light coming from Arcturus. **1952** *Astrophysical Jrnl.* CXVI. 211 The problem of the determination of the light-time orbit will occur with increasing frequency as the observational data become more accurate and extend over greater stretches of time. **1968** P. R. Escobal *Methods Astrodynamics* vi. 185 (*heading*) Light time correction. **1677** R. Cary *Chronol.* II. I. xi. 120 A Pharos or *Light-Tower. **1834** L. Ritchie *Wand. by Seine* 39 The light-towers of the Heve. **1906** R. C. Bayley *Compl. Photographer* ix. 99 Many otherwise efficient ventilating systems are rendered almost useless by the *light trap. **1931** A. D. Imms *Recent Adv. Entomol.* vi. 141 In many countries practical entomologists have made use of light traps as a means for the quantitative attraction and destruction of noxious species of Lepidoptera. **1935** H. W. & M. Miles *Insect Pests Glasshouse Crops* iii. 54 Light-traps also attract the moths and might be used with advantage in cases of persistent infestation. **1965** M. J. Langford *Basic Photogr.* xv. 266 If..the darkroom is designed for entry or exit of staff without introducing light, some form of 'light trap' is essential. **1973** *Entomologist's Rec.* LXXXV. 95 On the night of May 19th I had an unusual, yet unfortunate, bonus of moths in my light trap. **1956** *Focal Encycl. Photogr.* 677/1 Many darkrooms..have *light-trapped entrances so that the staff can pass freely in and out while sensitized materials are being handled. **1958** *Newnes Compl. Amat. Photogr.* iv. 75 The leading end of the film projects through a light-trapped slit, ready for loading into the camera. **1956** *Focal Encycl. Photogr.* 680/1 Exposure values, as used on shutters, are also frequently referred to as *light values. **1957** T. L. J. Bentley *Man. Miniature Camera* (ed. 5) iv. 46 As the latest development in the between-lens type of shutter has come the so-called light-value shutter. **1958** *Newnes Compl. Amat. Photogr.* ii. 38 The light-value shutter is a modern device.. designed to make speed and aperture setting more easy, and making use of the light value system. **1970** *Which?* June 186/2 You then point the meter at the subject and the needle will move along the light value scale... On some meters, instead of transferring the light value from one scale to another, you move a pointer until it overlaps the needle. **1928** *Trans. Soc. Motion Pict. Engin.* XII. 730 (*heading*) Sound recording with the *light valve. **1932** *Discovery* July 234/2 Three light valves (each a specially developed form of Kerr cell) modulated the beams from the arcs. **1971** L. B. Happé *Basic Motion Pict. Technol.* v. 165 In variable density recording the intensity of illumination passing into this lens system from a lamp and condenser lens is modulated by a light valve consisting of a pair of narrow metal ribbons mounted under tension in a magnetic field at right angles to the direction of the film movement. **1858** *Merc. Marine Mag.* V. 126 A *Light-vessel has been moored in 3 fathoms. **1925** V. G. Childe *Dawn European Civilization* v. 82 The palace was probably provided with a *light-well and decorated with frescoes. **1958** *Listener* 23 Oct. 644/1 The nineteenth-century office block, with the quiet internal lawn shrunk to the scale of the light-well. **1888** *Athenæum* 27 Oct. 558/2 The distances in *light-years of the last two stars. **1890** C. A. Young *Elem. Astron.* xii. §433 It is better, and now usual, to take as the unit of stellar distance the so-called 'light year'; i.e. the distance light travels in a year, which is about 63,000 times the distance of the earth from the sun. **1949** A. Huxley *Let.* 26 Feb. (1969) 593 Hubble..showed us the first pictures taken by the 200 inch telescope... On the random sample selected, the nebulae went on with uniform density to a billion lightyears. **1957** I. Asimov *Naked Sun* (1958) i. 22 That..momentary transition through hyperspace that transferred a ship and all it contained from one point in space to another, light-years away. **1962** F. I. Ordway et al. *Basic Astronautics* vi. 289 (*caption*) Known stars within five parsecs (16½ light years) of the Sun. **1971** *Guardian* 22 July 11/4 Professor Peter Hungerford..said..abortions should be the decision of the mother alone. This is light years from FPA policy. **1973** A. Holden *Girl on Beach* 143 He really is..a spare-time amateur art critic, light-years removed from a creative artist.

b. *Astr.* Combs. modelled on *light-year*, denoting the distance travelled by light in the time specified; so ***light-day***, ***-minute***, etc.

1923 G. D. Birkhoff *Relativity & Mod. Physics* ii. 20 Since it required $(t_2 - t_1)/2$ seconds for the light to travel from the one particle to the other, *B* must have been at a distance of $x = (t_2 - t_1)/2$ 'light-seconds' from *A* at the time *t*. **1925** D. L. Thomson in J. A. Thomson *Sci. & Relig.* 215 A light year is over five million million miles, and the sun is only eight-and-a-half light minutes from the earth. **1963** *Nature* 18 May 651/2 If the flashes are real, either the optical source itself is of the order of light-days in size, or..it must contain substructures of this scale. **1964** *Astrophysical Jrnl.* CXL. 15 Consider a region one light-month, i.e., 7×10^{16} cm, in radius. *Ibid.*, A maximum flash duration of only a few hours is possible for a region a light-month in radius. **1970** *Sci. Amer.* Dec. 25/3 The rapid changes in flux imply that if quasi-stellar objects are as remote as their red shifts indicate, they must have diameters reckoned in light-months, or even less. This means that such objects are on a scale only slightly larger than that of our solar system, which is about one light-day in diameter.

light (lait), *a.*[1] Forms: 1 léoht, liht, *Northumb.* leht, 2–4 liht(e, 3 *Orm.* lihht, (4 lixt, lyht, lit), 4–5 liȝt(e, lyȝt(e, 4–6 lyght(e, 4–7 *Sc.* licht, lycht, (5 leyȝt, 6 leicht, lyȝt, lyȝth, liht), 4– light. [OE. *léoht*, *līht*, Northumb. *lēht* = OFris. *li(u)cht*, OS. **līht* implied in derivatives (Du. *licht*), OHG. *līht(i* (MHG. *līht*, mod. G. *leicht*), ON. *léttr* (Da. *let*, Sw. *lätt*), Goth. *leihts*:—OTeut. **liŋhto-(-tjo-)*, f. Teut. root **liŋgw-*:—pre-Teut. **lenghw-*, as in Lith. *leŋgvas* light; the ablaut-var. pre-Teut. **l̥nghw-*, Teut. **luŋgw-*, appears in Skr. *laghu*, Gr. ἐλαφρός light, ἐλαχύς small, OHG. *lungar* light; cf. also lung.]

I. In the primary physical sense and uses connected therewith.

1. a. Of little weight, not ponderous. The opposite of *heavy*. Also in *to lie light* (cf. heavy 1 b, c). ***light ice***, ***sails*** (see quots. 1867).

a **1000** *Riddles* xli. 76 (Gr.) Leohtre ic eom micle þonne þes lytla wyrm. *c* **1205** Lay. 5903 Heore wepnen weoren lihte. **1393** Langl. *P. Pl.* C. II. 152 Was neuere lef vp-on lynde lyghter þer-after. *c* **1470** Henry *Wallace* III. 85 Gude lycht harnes, fra that tyme, wsyt he euir. **14..** *Promp. Parv.* 304/1 (*MS. K.*) Liht of wyhte, (*P.*) light of weight or mesure. **1534** Tindale *Matt.* xi. 30 My yoke is easy, and my burden is light. **1596** Dalrymple tr. *Leslie's Hist. Scot.* I. 90 Al thair harnesse was lycht. **1613** J. Dennis *Secrets Angling* I. C 2 b, Rods [were made] of lightest Cane and Hazell plant. **1642** Fuller *Holy & Prof. St.* II. xix. 121 Watches have been made as light and little, as many that wore them make of their time. **1697** Dryden *Virg. Past.* x. 51 How light wou'd lye the Turf upon my Breast, If [etc.]. **1762** Falconer *Shipwr.* II. 97 The lighter sails, for summer winds and seas, Are now dismiss'd. **1795** Burke *Corr.* IV. 325 It [wheat] will be very light in the ear. **1867** Smyth *Sailor's Word-bk.*, *Light ice*, that which has but little depth in the water; it is not considered dangerous to shipping, as not being heavy. *Ibid.*, *Light sails*, all above the topgallant-sails; also the studding sails and flying jib. **1871** R. Ellis tr. *Catullus* lxiv. 64 Veils not her hidden breast light brede of drapery woven.

absol. **1509** Hawes *Past. Pleas.* xxiv. (Percy Soc.) 108 Of the eyen the offyce only is the syght, To se.. The whyte, or blacke, the hevy, or the lyght. **1659** Stanley *Hist. Philos.* III. II. 105 Touching judgeth many things, Heavy, Leight, and those that are between them. **1875** Jowett *Plato* (ed. 2) I. 24 The art of weighing, again, has to do with lighter and heavier.

Proverb. **1562** J. Heywood *Prov. & Epigr.* (1867) 151 Light geynes make heuy purses. **1775** S. J. Pratt *Liberal Opin.* cxvi. (1783) IV. 82 He..swore..that I should not leave him till his purse was as light as eleven-pence.

b. Deficient in weight ('*too* light'); below the standard or legal weight.

1589 *Nottingham Rec.* IV. 226 For chaungeinge of fowre light French Crownes. **1596** Shaks. *Merch. V.* IV. i. 328 Be it so much As makes it light or heauy in the substance Or the deuision of the twentieth part of one poore scruple. **1622** Malynes *Anc. Law-Merch.* 115 Light Gold taken for merchandises sold. **1700** Tyrrell *Hist. Eng.* II. 947 All Clipt and Light Money was called in. **1727** Boyer *Fr. Dict.* s.v., This Guinea is light. **1869** Tennyson *Holy Grail* 26 For good ye are and bad, and like to coins, Some true, some light. **1887** T. E. Thorpe in *Gd. Words* 400 There is about £50,000,000 of light gold in circulation.

2. a. Possessing little weight in proportion to bulk; of small specific gravity. In the 17th and 18th centuries often applied to water.

1559 W. Cunningham *Cosmogr. Glasse* 41 It is a generall maior among Philosophers, that al light thynges contend

upwarde. **1621** BURTON *Anat. Mel.* II. ii. I. i. (1651) 232 Pure, thin, light water by all means use. **1632** LITHGOW *Trav.* VI. 260 It is the lightest water the earth yeelds.. I found it so light, that I had no weight.. in the bearing of it. **1683** MOXON *Mech. Exerc., Printing* 383 Founders call their Ashes Lean, if they are Light; because then they have little Mettle in them. **1683** TRYON *Way to Health* vi. (1697) 100 This is the lightest of all Waters, it cools and heats quickly. **1726** LEONI *Alberti's Archit.* I. 6/1 The best Water is clear, transparent and light. *a* **1728** WOODWARD *Fossils* I. (1729) I. 13 The Earthy matter, that was softer and lighter, would be easily washed away. **1838** T. THOMSON *Chem. Org. Bodies* 504 The charcoal is light and brilliant. **1846** J. BAXTER *Libr. Pract. Agric.* (ed. 4) I. 373 The seeds of the different grasses naturally divide themselves into light and heavy seeds. **1868** LOCKYER *Elem. Astron.* iii. §10 (1879) 59 Hydrogen, the lightest gas. **1876** HARLEY *Mat. Med.* (ed. 6) 184 Light magnesia is obtained by the same process from the light carbonate of magnesia.

absol. *a* **1619** FOTHERBY *Atheom.* II. xi. §1. 309 Æqually compounded of Light, and Heauie.

b. Applied to elements whose specific gravity (or atomic number) is relatively low; ***light metal***, a metal of low specific gravity, esp. aluminium or magnesium; so ***light alloy***, an alloy based on such a metal.

1912 ROSENHAIN & ARCHBUTT in *Proc. Inst. Mech. Engin.* Apr. 323 It was decided in the first place to confine the investigations to alloys consisting principally of aluminium, which may be conveniently grouped under the term 'light alloys'. **1924** *Proc. Physical Soc.* XXXVI. 418 The other light elements, hydrogen, helium, lithium, carbon and oxygen gave no detectable effect beyond 7 cm. **1926** *Industr. & Engin. Chem.* Oct. 1016/1 The production of the light metals has only been rendered possible by the comparatively recent work of chemists and chemical engineers. **1936** R. P. BELL tr. *Bjerrum's Inorg. Chem.* 213 The metals fall naturally into two groups: the light metals with densities below four, and the heavy metals with densities above seven. The light metals are the most electropositive, i.e., they have a specially great tendency to form positive ions. *Ibid.*, The light metals react readily with many substances. **1948** 'N. SHUTE' *No Highway* i. 12, I couldn't find anything about light alloy structures in fatigue prior to the year 1927. **1949** A. J. FIELD tr. *A. von Zeerleder's Technol. Light Metals* i. 1 There is at the present time no standard value of this property [*sc.* specific gravity] recognized as a qualification for the title 'light metal'. **1959** *Times Rev. Industry* Apr. 55/1 Reorganization within the light-metal industries. **1962** *Appl. Spectrosc.* XVI. 162/1 The data.. show the great advantage of using a chromium target tube for light element analysis. *Ibid.* 159/1 Light elements are defined as those elements having an atomic number less than 25. **1969** *Jane's Freight Containers 1968–69* 533/1 Containers: non-standard collapsible light-alloy.

†**3.** In comparative: Delivered (*of* a child).

a **1300** *Cursor M.* 8593 On a night bath lighter war þai. *c* **1330** R. BRUNNE *Chron.* (1810) 310 On wherfe þer scho was & lighter of a sonne. *c* **1560** in *Depos. Rebell.* 1569 (Surtees) 61 The morrow after the said Charles wyf was lighter. **1596** DALRYMPLE tr. *Leslie's Hist. Scot.* II. 138 Our quene is instantlie lychter of a bony barne. *a* **1783** *Willie's Lady* viii. in Child *Ballads* I. 86 Of her young bairn she'll neer be lighter.

4. a. Bearing a small or comparatively small load. Of a vessel: Having a small burthen, or (the usual sense) unladen, without cargo. (Cf. HEAVY *a.* 4.) ***light engine*** (see quot. 1881). ***light line*** = ***light water-line***. ***light railway***: a railway constructed for light traffic. ***light porter***: one who carries only light packages. ***light water-draught, water-line*** (see quot. 1867).

1602 in *Rec. Convent. R. Burghs* (1870) II. 133 Quither the schip be laydnit or licht. *c* **1630** MILTON *On the University Carrier* 22 He di'd for heavines that his Cart went light. **1665** *Lond. Gaz.* No. 11/1 The Norwich sent in one of near Three hundred Tuns, a light Ship. **1703** *Lond. Gaz.* No. 3968/1 The Privateer being light and clean, came up with her about 4 in the afternoon. **1729** MORETON *Apparit.* 213 The Ship was sent light as they call it to Virginia for a loading of tobacco. **1794** NELSON in Nicolas *Disp.* (1845) II. 220 To allow light Swedes to leave the Port of Leghorn. **1835** *Mech. Mag.* XXII. 275 When the vessel is light, the speed of the wheels is increased. **1854** DICKENS *Hard T.* II. i. 135 A deaf serving-woman, and the light porter completed Mrs. Sparsit's empire. **1867** SMYTH *Sailor's Word-bk., Light water-draught*, the depth of water, which a vessel draws when she is empty, or nearly so. *Light water-line*, the line showing the depression of the ship's body in the water, when just launched, or quite unladen. **1868** *Act 31 & 32 Vict.* c. 119 §28 A light Railway shall be constructed and.. the Regulations.. shall not authorize a greater Weight than Eight Tons to be brought upon the Rails by any One Pair of Wheels. **1881** M. REYNOLDS *Engine-Driving Life* 111 A 'light engine'—a phrase in railway circles that means an engine alone, without a train. **1894** W. H. WHITE *Man. Naval Archit.* (ed. 3) 47 The displacement of a ship between her light and load lines could be estimated, and would give the true 'dead-weight capability'. **1923** *Man. Seamanship* (Admiralty) II. 270 The portion of the ship's bottom, between the light and loadline, termed the *tapboot*, is difficult to protect from corrosion. **1948** R. DE KERCHOVE *Internat. Maritime Dict.* 416/2 *Light line*, the line of immersion at which a vessel floats when in ballast draft or light trim.

b. *fig.* or in figurative context.

1768 HUME *Balance of Power* Ess. 198 The Athenians always threw themselves into the lighter scale, and endeavoured to preserve the balance. *a* **1774** GOLDSM. tr. *Scarron's Com. Romance* (1775) I. 321 Laden with years, and so extremely light of honesty, that [etc.].

c. ***light industry***: an industry making use of relatively light and therefore easily handled materials. (Cf. HEAVY *a.*[1] 5 b)

1921 *San Francisco Chron.* 20 Sept. 22/1 There may be maintained in a Commercial District.. Light Industries, clearly incidental to the operation of an Amusement Park. **1930** *Economist* 1 Nov. (Russ. Suppl.) 8/2 Only 22 per cent. is allotted to the building and equipment of factories devoted to 'light' industries. **1944** J. S. HUXLEY *On Living in Revolution* 128 Encouragement must be given to light and secondary industries, for only so can a reasonably balanced economy grow up in colonial areas. **1957** [see HEAVY *a.*[1] 5 b]. **1961** E. A. POWDRILL *Vocab. Land Planning* iv. 66 'Light industry' is any industry which does not commit a nuisance by noise, smell, fumes, soot or grit. **1974** E. AMBLER *Dr. Frigo* III. 156 The transformation he envisaged—roads, housing,.. hydro-electric schemes, light industry, fertiliser plants.

5. Chiefly *Mil.* Lightly armed or equipped. †Also, lightly clad. ***light marching order*** (see quot. 1825). Also LIGHT HORSE, HORSEMAN.

c **1386** CHAUCER *Can. Yeom. Prol. & T.* 15 Al light for somer rood this worthy man. **1600** HOLLAND *Livy* VII. x. 255 A light footmans shield he takes unto him. **1633** T. STAFFORD *Pac. Hib.* III. iii. (1810) 527 Captaine Taffes troop of Horse with certaine light foote were sent from the campe. **1781** GIBBON *Decl. & F.* xviii. II. 111 He was overtaken.. by a party of light cavalry. **1808** *Med. Jrnl.* XIX. 305 His Majesty's 13th Regiment of Light Dragoons. **1813** WELLINGTON in Gurw. *Desp.* X. 527, I shall be with the Light division in the morning. **1825** G. R. GLEIG *Subaltern* iii. 48 The division was to enter the trenches.. in what is called light marching order; that is, leaving their knapsacks, blankets, &c., behind, and carrying with them only their arms and ammunition. **1838** THIRLWALL *Greece* xx. III. 161 To send a body of Thracian cavalry and light troops to the aid of the Athenians. **1846** GREENER *Sci. Gunnery* 393 Carbines, for some light infantry regiments. **1871** R. ELLIS tr. *Catullus* xxviii. 2 Starving company, troop of hungry Piso, Light of luggage, of outfit expeditious. **1879** FROUDE *Cæsar* xvi. 265 The legions had come light, without tents or baggage. **1891** C. ROBERTS *Adrift Amer.* 49 To travel in America one must travel light.

6. a. Of a vehicle or vessel: Lightly constructed; adapted for light loads and for swift movement. ***light cart*** = 'spring cart' (see CART *sb.* 3). ***light car***, a small economical car made from light materials.

c **893** K. ÆLFRED *Oros.* I. i. §19 Hy habbað swyðe lytle scypa & swyðe leohte. **1579** FENTON *Guicciard.* I. (1599) 28 It contayned xxxv. light or suttle gallies. **1694** *Lond. Gaz.* No. 3008/1 The Mareschal de Tourville had sent out divers light Frigats.. to get Intelligence. **1716** *Ibid.* No. 5473/1 The lighter part of the.. Fleet, viz. Gallies &c. was in the Port. **1844** DISRAELI *Coningsby* VII. i, The arrival of a first-rate light coach in a country town. **1849** MACAULAY *Hist. Eng.* ix. II. 480 Light vessels sent out by the English admiral for the purpose of obtaining intelligence. **1852** THACKERAY *Esmond* I. xiii, My Lord Mohun sent to London for a light chaise he had. **1882** MISS BRADDON *Mt. Royal* III. i. 15 You had better go in the light cart. **1908** *Westm. Gaz.* 16 Mar. 5/2 This being essentially a light-car year, more than ordinary interest is manifested in the 8-h.p. two-cylindered polished chassis. **1914** *Light Car Manual* 1 Manufacturers have.. solved the difficulty of how to produce a car which shall give all the comfort anyone could desire, and yet.. compare favourably with the cost.. of a motorcycle and side-car. The whole secret of this solution is summed up in the words 'light car'. **1963** [see *fore-car* (FORE- 5)]. **1970** C. F. CAUNTER *Light Car* (ed. 2) p. xv, The popularity of the light car, particularly in its minicar form, had the effect in the 1960's of reducing the average size of motor cars in general.

b. Applied to small, relatively light-weight aeroplanes, such as most private (non-commercial) passenger aeroplanes.

1923 *Flight* XV. 168/1 For want of a better term we have referred to the machine as a 'light plane', much as in the automobile world cars below a certain size and weight are termed light cars. **1933** *Meccano Mag.* Mar. 192/1 Light aeroplanes will fly to and from these places from the main routes. **1965** NAYLER & OWER *Aviation* v. 56/1 The Piper Aircraft Corporation led the world in the sales of light aircraft in 1959. **1971** P. J. MCMAHON *Aircraft Propulsion* xi. 331 Occasionally designers of light aircraft look to the possibilities of using automobile type engines as power units. **1971** *Flying* (N.Y.) Apr. 39/2 In fact, it may well be the best all-around lightplane in the world.

7. Of a building: Having an appearance suggestive of lightness; graceful and elegant in form.

1762 H. WALPOLE *Vertue's Anecd. Paint.* (1765) II. i. 37 *note*, One of the lightest and most beautiful parish churches I have seen. **1818** [see HEAVY *a.* 15]. **1837** *Penny Cycl.* VII. 218/1 Unless [etc.].. such timber model would have given rise to a much lighter style of architecture. **1850** *Gloss. Archit.* (ed. 5) 439 Small light spires.

II. Having the operation or properties of things of little physical weight.

8. Having little momentum or force; gentle, not violent; acting gently; moving, impelling, or manipulating something without heavy pressure or violence. Said esp. of the hand, a step, the wind, †a medicine, or medical appliance (*obs.*), and occas. of immaterial agencies. Also ***light of touch***.

a **1000** *Widsith* 72 (Gr.) Se hæfde moncynnes.. leohteste hond. *a* **1225** *Ancr. R.* 220 Uour dolen, þus todeled—uondunge liht & derne—uondunge liht & openliche—uondunge strong & derne—uondunge strong & openliche. *c* **1400** *Lanfranc's Cirurg.* 88 Þese ben liȝt medicyns.. & þese medicyns ben strongere. *Ibid.* 92 Þer is noon oþer wey, but a liȝt cauterizacion of þe senewe þat is hurt. **1591** SHAKS. 1 *Hen. VI*, I. iv. 69 This Citie must be famisht, or with light Skirmishes enfeebled. **1592** —— *Ven. & Ad.* 566 Waxe.. yeelds at last to euerie light impression. **1765** FOOTE *Commissary* II. Wks. 1799 II. 22 There are risings and sinkings.. as light as a cork. **1797** MRS. RADCLIFFE *Italian* xii, Ellena fled with lighter steps along the alley. **1833** HT. MARTINEAU *Loom & Lugger* I. iv. 51 The lightest of her shriller tones made itself heard. **1836** MARRYAT *Midsh. Easy* xxvii, A tedious passage, from baffling and light winds. **1849** RUSKIN *Sev. Lamps* v. §8. 144 A painter's light execution of a background. **1856** WHYTE MELVILLE *Kate Cov.* iii, Gertrude.. brushing away.. at my back hair, and pulling it unnecessarily hard: no maid ever yet had a 'light' hand. **1863** WOOLNER *My beautiful Lady* 16 Though her hand be airy light Of touch. **1876** GEO. ELIOT *Dan. Der.* IV. lxii. 229 His light walk. **1885** *Law Times Rep.* LIII. 54/1 There was a light breeze from about S.W. by S. **1897** *Allbutt's Syst. Med.* IV. 413 Inter-current inflammations should be treated on general principles but with a light hand. **1901** *Brit. Med. Jrnl.* 5 Jan. 8 When the extent of the cardiac dulness has been determined by careful light percussion [etc.].

9. a. Having little density, tenacity, or cohesive force. Of soil: Friable, porous, workable. Of a cloud: Fleecy, vaporous, evanescent.

1523 FITZHERB. *Husb.* §4 They [wheel-ploughs] be good on euen grounde that lyeth lyghte. **1707** MORTIMER *Husb.* 106 The common sort of white Pea doth best in a light Land that is somewhat rich. **1806** *Gazetteer Scot.* (ed. 2) 262 The district of Glenlivet is remarkably fertile, the soil being a light loam. **1816** BYRON *Siege Cor.* xxi, There is a light cloud by the moon. **1823** J. BADCOCK *Dom. Amusem.* 60 Sand.. generally prevails to the amount of one half in light soils. **1860** TYNDALL *Glac.* I. xxvii. 208 Some of the lighter clouds doubled round the summit of the mountain. **1897** MARY KINGSLEY *W. Africa* 606 A dull roar which made the light friable earth quiver under our feet.

b. Of bread, pastry, etc.: That has 'risen' properly, not 'heavy' or dense.

c **1460** J. RUSSELL *Bk. Nurture* 339 Þan take youre loof of light payne. **1578** BULLEIN *Dial.* (1888) 51 Eate light leauened breade. **1620** VENNER *Via Recta* i. 20 The fourth property is, that it [bread] be light, and somewhat open. **1747** MRS. GLASSE *Cookery* (1767) 145 Make it up into a light paste with cold water..; then roll it out. *Ibid.*, Skim off.. as much of the liquor as will make it a light good crust. **1864** MRS. STOWE *House & Home Papers* x. (1865) 112 Bread: What ought it to be? It should be light, sweet, and tender. *c* **1895** *N. Midl. School Cookery Bk.* 44 To make a light dough.

10. Of food or drink: That does not lie heavy on the stomach; easy of digestion. Of wine, beer, etc.: Containing little alcohol.

c **1000** *Ags. Voc.* in Wr.-Wülcker 282/6 *Melle dulci*, leoht beor. *c* **1000** *Sax. Leechd.* III. 122 Drince leoht wyn. **1422** tr. *Secreta Secret., Priv. Priv.* 241 For yf a man ette fryste grete mettes and sethyn lyght mettis, the lyght mettis shal be annone defyet. *c* **1510** *Interl. Four Elem.* (Percy) 23 Canst get my mayster a dyshe of quales, Smal byrdes, swalowes or wagtayles. They be lyght of dygestyon? **1542** UDALL *Erasm. Apoph.* 9 A light repaste, suche as the bodie maye easyly and without incommoditee awaye withall. **1620** VENNER *Via Recta* iii. 69 The lights are of light digestion. **1693** CONGREVE *Dryden's Juvenal* XI. 128 Apples.. Mellow'd by Winter, from their cruder Juice, Light of Digestion now, and fit for Use. **1707** J. STEVENS tr. *Quevedo's Com. Wks.* (1709) 82 Don Diego took a light Supper. **1822–34** *Good's Study Med.* (ed. 4) I. 675 *note*, The lighter preparations of bark.. are often found to be eligible tonics in hectic cases. **1832** LYTTON *Eugene A.* I. xi, The little family were assembled at the last and lightest meal of the day. **1880** MCCARTHY *Own Times* III. xli. 238 The light wines of Bordeaux began to be familiar to almost every table. **1896** *Allbutt's Syst. Med.* I. 418 Rice and sago and such like puddings are not light or easily digestible foods. **1898** J. HUTCHINSON in *Arch. Surg.* IX. 316 Beer, which you would think was lighter [than stout].

11. ***light in the mouth*** (of a horse): sensitive to the bit. (Cf. HEAVY *a.* 11.)

1727 BAILEY vol. II, *Light upon the Hand* [in Horsemanship] is said of a Horse that has a good tractable Mouth, and does not rest too heavy upon the Bit. **1884** E. L. ANDERSON *Mod. Horsemanship* I. iv. 11 The beginner should be mounted upon a quiet horse that is light in the mouth.

12. Of a syllable: Unemphatic, of little weight or sonorousness. Hence, of rhythm, consisting largely of such syllables.

1887 COLVIN *Keats* v. 109 A perverse persistency in ending his heroic lines with the lightest syllables—prepositions, adverbs and conjunctions—on which neither pause nor emphasis is possible. **1901** BRIDGES *Milton's Prosody* 90 Keeping therefore the term *short*, as it is used in the prosody of the Greeks, for the very shortest syllables, it is necessary to make two classes of their *long* syllables; and these I shall distinguish into *heavy* and *light*. *Ibid.* 96 The greater part of the poem is in a lighter rhythm.

III. Of little gravity or moment.

13. a. Of small importance or consequence, not weighty; slight, trivial. Of a sin: Venial.

c **897** K. ÆLFRED *Gregory's Past.* lxii. (*heading*), Ðætte hwilum ða leohtan scylda bioð beteran to forlætenne. *a* **1300** *Cursor M.* 23021 Þai þat has bot sinnes light sal clengid be. *a* **1340** HAMPOLE *Psalter* xxiv. 4 Godis wayes he calles his lightere biddyngis. *c* **1400** *Destr. Troy* 1424 Light harmes Let ouer-passe. *c* **1430** *Life St. Kath.* (Gibbs MS.) lf. 100 Presume not to blaber aȝenst oure goddes by lythe repreef. **1500–20** DUNBAR *Poems* xxii. 51, I grant my seruice is bot licht. **1563** WINȜET *Four Scoir Thre Quest.* Wks. 1888 I. 52 Breuelie considering the first part of thair titill to this thair supreme auctoritie, I fand it nocht only sclinder and licht, bot planelie inglorius. **1570** G. HARVEY *Letter-bk.* (Camden) 8, I made but smal & liht account of mi fellowship. **1603** KNOLLES *Hist. Turks* (1621) 51 Proscribing.. whole families together, yea and that for light occasions. *a* **1661** FULLER *Worthies* (1840) III. 308 Not only all evil doing, but even the lightest suspicions thereof. **1742** COLLINS *Ode Poet. Char.* 1, If not with light regard, I read aright that gifted bard. **1753** N. TORRIANO *Gangr. Sore Throat* 89 The Disease began with a light Shivering. **1772** *Junius Lett.* lxviii. 338 This is no light matter. **1849** MACAULAY *Hist. Eng.* ii. I. 161 Against the lighter vices the ruling faction waged war. **1866** B. NORTH *Yes or No!* xii. 269 It was what the world calls a venial or light sin. **1871** SMILES *Charac.* i. (1876) 25 They will be held in light esteem by other nations. **1897** *Allbutt's Syst. Med.* III. 476 Windy tumidities.. and therewith light diarrhœas are often associated.

†**b.** Of small value, cheap. Of a price: Low. Also *light cheap* = CHEAP *a.* and *adv.* (Cf. CHEAP *sb.* 8, 9.) *Obs.*

c 1330 R. BRUNNE *Chron.* (1810) 246 This Rescamiraduk . . His letter gan rebuk, sette it at light prise. c 1460 *Towneley Myst.* ii. 236 That cam hym full light chepe. c 1470 *Golagros & Gaw.* 158 Thare come ane laithles leid air to this place, With ane girdill ourgilt, and vthir light gere. 1609 BIBLE (Douay) *1 Kings* x. 15 Al that sold light wares. 1641 TRAPP *Theol. Theol.* 267 That it comes to us so light cheap, is cause of thankfullnesse. 1647 —— *Comm. 1 John* iii. 18 Words are light-cheap, and there is a great deal of mouth-mercy abroad.

†**c.** Of persons: Not commanding respect by position or character; of small account. *Obs.*

1529 MORE *Dyaloge* I. Wks. 175/1, I might by a light person somtime knowe a muche more substanciall man. 1548 HALL *Chron., Hen. VI*, 169 b, Diverse other light marchantes within the citee. 1548 —— *Chron., Hen. VII*, 19 He set more by vile borne vileyns and light persones, then by the princes and nobles.

d. Used *predicatively* or *absol.* in various phrases: † (*a*) *to set* (a person or thing) *light, at light*; *to set light by* or *of* (a person or thing): to account of small value, to despise, slight, undervalue. *to let light of* (see LET *v.*[1] 16). *Obs.*

c 1475 *Rauf Coilȝear* 635 Be Christ, said the Coilȝear, I set that bot licht. *Ibid.* 740 He was ludgeit and led, and set at sa licht. 1540 HYRDE tr. *Vives' Instr. Chr. Wom.* (1592) Z vj, Nor set at light a childes yeeres and age. 1547 *Homilies* I. *Fear Death* II. (1859) 98 Let us not set at light the chastising of the Lord. 1594 T. B. *La Primaud. Fr. Acad.* II. 132 We ought not to set light by that knowledge of it [the soule] which wee may attaine vnto. 1612 SIR H. MOUNTAGU in *Buccleuch MSS.* (Hist. MSS. Comm.) I. 244 My Lord of Exeter chafes; I tell them we set it as light. 1633 G. HERBERT *Temple, Sacrifice* xx, Herod and all his bands do set me light. 1642 J. EATON *Honey-c. Free Justif.* 240 Thereby the words of the Scripture may be extenuated and set light of. 1771 WESLEY *Wks.* (1872) V. 317 It is no other than betraying him . . to set light by any part of his law. 1810 SCOTT *Lady of L.* I. xxiii, Light I held his prophecy.

(*b*) *to make light of*: to treat, consider or represent as of small or no importance.

1526 TINDALE *Matt.* xxii. 5 They made light of it and went their wayes. 1531 ELYOT *Gov.* I. xiii, Or if he be stungen he maketh lite of it and shortly forgetteth it. 1597 BACON *Coulers Good & Euil* in *Ess.* (Arb.) 150 If it appeare to be done by a sonne, or by a wife, or by a neere friend, then it is made light of. 1698 FRYER *Acc. E. India & P.* 311 The Natives make light of such things as we call Colds. 1736 BUTLER *Anal.* II. i. Wks. 1874 I. 170 How great presumption it is, to make light of any institutions of Divine appointment. 1767 GOOCH *Treat. Wounds* I. 236 A Barber-Surgeon was called to her, who made very light of it [a slight wound]. 1815 JANE AUSTEN *Emma* I. xvi. 116 Making light of what ought to be serious. 1898 H. CALDERWOOD *Hume* iii. 31 A tendency to make light of reason.

14. a. Characterized by levity, frivolous, unthinking. Const. †*of*.

a 1225 *Leg. Kath.* 106 þeos lufsume lefdi . . ne luuede heo nane lihte plohen. a 1300 *Cursor M.* 3285 Ne was sco not o letes light. *Ibid.* 28568 Laghter light þat cums of gle. 1340 HAMPOLE *Pr. Consc.* 3346 Sum dros of syn, Als light speche, or thoght in vayn. 1375 BARBOUR *Bruce* VII. 112 Licht men and vauerand. 1461 *Paston Lett.* No. 405 II. 31 The Commynnes throw all the schyer be movyd agayn hym, for cause of his lyght demeanyng towards them. 1483 CAXTON *Gold. Leg.* 256/2 A monke moche Joly and lyght of his lyuyng. 1536 D. BEERLEY *Let. to Ld. Cromwell* in Strype *Eccl. Mem.* I. xxxv. 257 Lyzth and foolish ceremonies made . . [by] lyzth and undiscrete faders. 1554 T. MARTIN *Treat. Marriage Priestes* LI iij, Being (as some were), light braines, runnagates, vnthriftes and riotours. 1571 GRINDAL *Injunct. York* I. §1 Being circumspect, that you offende no man eyther by light behauiour or by light apparell. 1610 GUILLIM *Heraldry* I. viii. (1660) 45 If light eares incline to light lips, harm ensueth. 1631 SANDERSON *Serm.* II. 3 A sober grave matron . . will never be light and garish. 1641 *Vind. Smectymnuus* 31 It never came into our thoughts to use a light expression. 1692 WASHINGTON tr. *Milton's Def. Pop.* M.'s Wks. 1738 I. 469 Was there ever any thing more light and mad than this Man is? 1713 STEELE *Englishman* No. 27. 176 Publick Faith is now commonly talked of in the lightest manner. 1754 RICHARDSON *Grandison* IV. xxxv. 245 The light wretch's as light expression. 1823 SCOTT *Peveril* x, The disposition of the young Earl was lighter and more volatile than that of Julian. 1834 J. H. NEWMAN *Par. Serm.* (1837) I. xxiii. 354 That light perpetual talk about him. 1856 MRS. BROWNING *Aur. Leigh* III. 319, I wrote tales beside . . To suit light readers. 1875 JOWETT *Plato* (ed. 2) I. 58 They speak of friends in no light or trivial manner. 1882 STEVENSON *New Arab. Nts.* (1901) 86/2, I made some light rejoinder.

b. Of persons (chiefly of women) and their behaviour: Wanton, unchaste.

c 1375 *Sc. Leg. Saints* xxxv. (*Thadee*) 3 Thadee . . licht women wes & richt brukil of hyre flesche. 1422 tr. *Secreta Secret., Priv. Priv.* 144 Vntrewe men and light women of body. 1581 LYLY *Euphues* To Schollers Oxf. (Arb.) 208 Did not Iupiters egge bring forth . . Helen a light huswife. 1676 WYCHERLEY *Pl. Dealer* IV. i, To give up her Honour to save her Jointure; and seem to be a light Woman, rather than marry. 1826 SCOTT *Woodst.* iii, Lewd men and light women. 1883 R. W. DIXON *Mano* II. v. 82 For nought beside vain dalliance cared they, And their light folly was before our eyes. 1895 T. HARDY *Jude the Obscure* II. vi. 144 Jude . . found the room full of . . soldiers . . and light women.

IV. Having the quick action that results from lightness.

15. Moving readily; active, nimble, quick, swift. So *light of foot, of person*; † *light-fingers* (cf. LIGHT-FINGERED); † *light to run* (cf. LIGHT-FOOTED). Now only *arch.*

a 1000 *Phœnix* 317 (Gr.) He [se fuȝel] is snel and swift & swiþe leoht. c 1200 *Trin. Coll. Hom.* 13 þat man be waker, and liht, and snel. 1297 R. GLOUC. (Rolls) 9277 Welssemen . . þat liȝte were & hardi. a 1300 *Cursor M.* 3730 Moght i not be sua light o fote. 1375 BARBOUR *Bruce* XIII. 56 Fiff hundreth armyt weill in steill, That on licht horss war [horsyt] weill. 14.. *Voc.* in Wr.-Wülcker 577/14 *Currax*, lyght to renne. 1470–85 MALORY *Arthur* IV. ix. 130 Syr Accolon lost not a dele of blood, therfor he waxt passynge lyghte. 1480 CAXTON *Chron. Eng.* cxxi. 102 He was so lyght of fote that men callyd hym comenlych harold hare foote. 1503 DUNBAR *Thistle & Rose* 95 Lusty of schaip, lycht of deliuerance. a 1548 HALL *Chron., Edw. IV*, 213 b, That diverse persones havyng light horses, should skoure the countrey. 1567 *Satir. Poems Reform.* iii. 70 To dance that nycht thay said sho sould not slak, With leggis lycht to hald the wedow walkane. 1583 STOCKER *Civ. Warres Lowe C.* IV. 54 He that was in the watch, saued himself with a light paire of heeles. 1596 SHAKS. *Tam. Shr.* II. i. 205 Too light for such a swaine as you to catch. 1604 E. G[RIMSTONE] *D'Acosta's Hist. Indies* V. v. 342 He required the Cacique . . to give him an Indian that were light, to carry him a Letter. 1669 WORLIDGE *Syst. Agric.* vii. § 11 (1681) 135 The more remote the Branches are from the Earth, the less are they subject to the injuries of Cattle, or the Fruit to light Fingers. 1706 PHILLIPS (ed. Kersey) s.v., Among Astrologers, a Planet is said To be light, i.e. nimble, compared to another that moves slower. 1801 W. HUNTINGTON *Bank of Faith* Ded. 15 It is common among horse-jockies to cry a horse down if his heels are too light. 1883 R. W. DIXON *Mano* I. ix. 25 Well coloured was she, tall and debonair, And light and very swift.

16. That moves or is moved easily or with slight pressure; pliant, fickle, shifty, unsteady; facile, ready (of belief, etc.). Const. *of, to* with *inf.* Now *rare.* (See also LIGHT OF LOVE.)

c 1320 *Sir Tristr.* 1062 þer to icham al liȝt. 1382 WYCLIF *Prov.* xviii. 14 The spirit forsothe liȝt to wrathen. c 1385 CHAUCER *L.G.W.* 1699 *Lucrece*, He was lyght of tunge. c 1400 *Destr. Troy* 1229 He . . Launches euyn to Lamydon with a light wille. 1483 CAXTON *Cato* C vij b, For euery man oughte to be lyght to heeryng and slowe to speke. 1513 DOUGLAS *Æneis* X. ii. 57 Set in stead of that man, licht as lynd, Ouder a cloud or a waist puft of wynd. 1523 LD. BERNERS *Froiss.* I. xxiii. 32 The kyng, who gaue lyght credence to thaym causedde his vncle . . to be beheeded. 1526 *Pilgr. Perf.* (W. de W. 1531) 40 b, Be not lyght to byleue euery spiryte. a 1529 SKELTON *Dethe Erle Northumberlande* 175 Be not lyght of credence in no case. 1538 BALE *God's Promises* IV. (1744) 21 Thynkest thu that I wyll so sone change my decre? No, no, frynde Moses; so lyght thu shalt not fynde me. 1539 TAVERNER *Erasm. Prov.* (1552) 6 The Lyon, lyght of credite, forthwith ranne upon the wolfe and slewe hym. c 1570 FOXE *Serm. 2 Cor.* v. 52 Some . . use to giue light eare to such whisperers. 1576 TURBERV. *Bk. Venerie* 174 When hounds are hunted with in this sorte, they become so light of beliefe that [etc.]. 1597 BEARD *Theatre God's Judgem.* (1612) 367 To whom the chast Matron gaue light credence. 1603 KNOLLES *Hist. Turks* (1621) 80 At this exaction . . the light Constantinopolitans grievously murmured. 1627 tr. *Bacon's Life & Death* (1651) 56 A young man is light and moveable, an old man more grave and constant. 1748 RICHARDSON *Clarissa* (1811) VII. 410 Were he not to have been so light of belief. 1853 M. ARNOLD *Scholar-Gipsy* xviii, We Light half-believers of our casual creeds. 1890 LECKY *Eng. in 18th C.* VII. 46 A light man, in whom no person can place any confidence.

V. That weighs or presses but little on the powers, senses, or feelings.

17. Easy to bear or endure. Of an expense or impost: Easy to pay. (Cf. HEAVY *a.* 23.)

c 950 *Lindisf. Gosp.* Matt. x. 15 Lihtro bið tuoeȝe burgas in dæȝ domes ðon ðær ceastre. c 1000 *Ags. Gosp.* Matt. xi. 30 Min byrþyn is leoht. c 1320 *Cast. Love* 958 My burþene [is] liȝt i-nouh to beren. 1375 BARBOUR *Bruce* II. 521 Luff . . all paynys maks licht. c 1430 *Two Cookery-bks.* 17 3if þou wolt haue it a-forsyd with lyȝt coste, Take milk [etc.]. 1523 LD. BERNERS *Froiss.* I. ci. 121, I am content ye shall come to a lyght ransome, for the loue of my cosyn of Derby. 1562 WINȜET *Cert. Tractates* iii. Wks. 1888 I. 23 The office of all potestatis is lycht to thaim and plesand to the subiectis. 1567 *Gude & Godlie Ball.* (S.T.S.) 33 The paine, that is now present, schort and licht. 1605 SHAKS. *Lear* III. vi. 115 (Qos. 1608) How light and portable my paine seemes now! 1611 BIBLE *1 Kings* xii. 4 Make thou . . his heauy yoke which he put vpon us, lighter. 1772 PRIESTLEY *Inst. Relig.* (1782) II. 126 The afflictions of this present life will seem light. 1800–24 CAMPBELL *Martial Elegy* iii, Deeming light the cost Of life itself in glorious battle lost. 1882 B. D. W. RAMSAY *Recoll. Mil. Serv.* I. iv. 74 All that we had endured was light compared to the discomfort on board. 1896 MRS. CAFFYN *Quaker Grandmother* 226 Your seeing me has been no light punishment.

18. a. Easy to perform or accomplish, requiring little exertion; now only qualifying a sb. such as *task, work*, etc.; formerly often as predicate with clause as subj. †Also, easy to obtain. †Of speech: Easy to utter; plain. (Cf. HEAVY *a.* 24.) Phr. *light duty*: military service which does not entail full-time work.

c 1000 *Sax. Leechd.* I. 342 Hy habbaþ þæs þe leohtran gang. a 1200 *Moral Ode* 312 It is strong to stonde longe, and liht it is to falle hard. c 1200 ORMIN 4500 Acc witt tu þatt itt niss nohht lihht To berenn hefiȝ sinne. a 1225 *Ancr. R.* 428 þe leaue beo liht in alle þeo þinges þer nis sunne. c 1330 R. BRUNNE *Chron.* Prol. (1810) Pref. 99 In symple speche . . þat is lightest in manne's mouthe. 1340 *Ayenb.* 99 Liȝt to zigge an sotil to onderstonde. a 1375 *Lay Folks Mass Bk.* App iv. 78 þe nexte þing to here, And þe lihtest for to lere. c 1391 CHAUCER *Astrol.* Prol., Ful lihte rewles. c 1400 *Lanfranc's Cirurg.* 229 Glandule comeþ þe most part of fleume, & ben liȝter to resolue. c 1440 *Promp. Parv.* 304/1 Lyght of knowing or werking, *facilis.* c 1449 PECOCK *Repr.* I. xvii. 100 It is liȝt for to answere. 1450–1530 *Myrr. our Ladye* 7 Yt is not lyght for euery man to drawe eny longe thyng from latyn into oure Englyshe tongue. a 1555 PHILPOT *Exam. & Writ.* (Parker Soc.) 335 It is not more lighter for him to slide and fall. 1610 SHAKS. *Temp.* I. ii. 451 Least too light winning Make the prize light. a 1700 DRYDEN *Theod. & Hon.* 247 Well pleas'd were all his Friends, The Task was light. 1788 FRANKLIN *Autobiog.* Wks. 1840 I. 186 The service will be light and easy. 1832 HT. MARTINEAU *Demerara* i. 7 Invalids who were sufficiently recovered to do light work. 1849 MACAULAY *Hist. Eng.* i. I. 123 To keep down the English people was no light task even for that army. 1875 JOWETT *Plato* (ed. 2) III. 239, I cannot promise you that the task will be a light one. 1916 A. HUXLEY *Let.* 13 Feb. (1969) 91 He is still on light duty—so gets plenty of leave from Salisbury Plain. 1953 A. BARON *Human Kind* xiii. 100, I shouldn't be here by rights. I'm a light-duty man.

†**b.** Phrase. *of light* [tr. OF. *de legier*]: lightly, easily. *Obs.*

c 1489 CAXTON *Sonnes of Aymon* iii. 106 A man that is well garnysshed is not of lighte overthrowe. 1490 —— *Eneydos* xii. 45 All this people . . Whiche shall mowe of lyght, aryse, and make werre ayenst the.

19. a. Of literature, dramatic works, music, etc.: Requiring little mental effort; amusing, entertaining. *light comedian*: An actor of light comedy. (Cf. HEAVY *a.* 20, 21.)

1597 MORLEY *Introd. Mus.* 150 Madrigals, Canzonets, and such like light musicke. 1809 MALKIN *Gil Blas* X. vii. (Rtldg.) 355 The library abounded in romances. Don Cæsar seemed to give the preference to that light reading. 1827 L. T. REDE *Road to Stage* 16 In small theatres, the light comedian must play the seconds in tragedy. *Ibid.* 60 In light comedy it is continually requisite to execute music. 1838 THIRLWALL *Greece* xviii. III. 79 Æschylus was accounted no less a master of the light than of the serious drama. 1841 MACAULAY in *Edin. Rev.* Jan. 524 A great and rapid reform in . . our lighter literature was the effect of his [*sc.* Collier's] labours. 1844 J. COWELL *30 Yrs. among Players* 43 The light and low comedy. 1849 *Blackw. Mag.* Jan. 40 Light reading does not do when the heart is really heavy. 1872 D. G. ROSSETTI *Let.* 20 Sept. (1967) III. 1064 Your idea of George's possibly finding an outlet in light literature does not seem promising to me. 1874 W. LENNOX *My Recoll.* I. 186 The highest walks of light tragedy. 1878 BROWNING *Poets of Croisic* xcv, From out your desk Hand me some lighter sample. 1880 *Daily Tel.* 20 Dec., The old-fashioned plan of ending a symphony with a light and brilliant rondo, that lays no tax upon the hearer's wearied faculties. 1885 W. C. DAY *Behind Footlights* 118 The light comedian will complete the list of our company. 1885 J. K. JEROME *On the Stage* 33, I remember the first time our light comedy attempted to sit down on one of these chairs. 1888 BRYCE *Amer. Commw.* (1890) III. iii. 604 What may be called the lighter ornamental style, such as the after-dinner speech. 1888 G. O. SEILHAMER *Hist. Amer. Theatre* I. 23 Comedy parts or light tragedy roles. 1897 *National Police Gaz.* (U.S.) 26 May 6/4 Miss Blanche is, perhaps, the cleverest little lady on the burlesque and light comedy stage. 1929 *Radio Times* 8 Nov. 406/3 *Journey's End* . . is not a memorial service; nor, at the other extreme, is it light entertainment. 1958 *Times Lit. Suppl.* 5 Dec. 701/3 The climax, both exciting and comic, just succeeds in lifting this novel out of the light-entertainment class. 1961 *John o' London's* 18 May 567/4 A more profitable career as a light-comedy lead. 1974 P. DE VRIES *Glory of Hummingbird* iii. 27 Some more pretty good nature lyrics and then a batch of light verse. 1975 *Times* 10 Feb. 3/7 Any programme of cuts . . would have to be closely vetted by the IBA to ensure that they maintain a balance between light entertainment programmes and more serious productions.

b. ***Light Programme***, one of the regular programme services of the B.B.C., chiefly featuring popular music and light entertainment. Also *ellipt.* as ***the Light.*** (On 30 Sept. 1967 its name was changed to 'Radio 2'.)

1945 *Radio Times* 27 July 1/1 Alongside these six regionalised Home Services there is to be available a new alternative, the BBC Light Programme. . . It will be built for the civilian listener. 1956 'M. INNES' *Old Hall, New Hall* III. iii. 205 No *real* American professor could be *quite* like that —not outside the Light Programme. 1959 S. GIBBONS *Pink Front Door* iii. 37 He had missed a particularly good boxing match on the Light. 1962 L. DEIGHTON *Ipcress File* xxviii. 180, I kept the radio tuned to the Light for the 6.30 bulletin. 1966 *B.B.C. Handbk.* 45 The Light Programme seeks to provide a friendly and companionable service for those who are in the mood for entertainment and relaxation. 1968 S. E. ELLACOTT *Everyday Things in Eng. 1914–68* xi. 162 At the end of the war the Home Service and the Light Programme were established (1945).

20. Of sleep: Not oppressive to the bodily sense; easily shaken off. Hence also ***light sleeper.***

c 900 tr. *Bæda's Hist.* V. ix. (1890) 410 Me liht slep oferorn. 1827 KEBLE *Chr. Y., Evening* xiii, Be every mourner's sleep to-night, Like infant's slumbers, pure and light. 1844 DICKENS *Mart. Chuz.* xxxviii, I am a light sleeper; and it's better to be up than lying awake. 1894 HON. EMILY LAWLESS *Maelcho* II. ii. 21 A man who at all times was a light sleeper.

VI. 21. Free from the weight of care or sorrow; cheerful, merry. *Obs.* exc. in ***light heart.*** †Also ***glad and light***, etc. †Const. *of*.

13.. in *Pol. Rel. & L. Poems* 239 þou waxist heui þat was wel lit. ? a 1366 CHAUCER *Rom. Rose* 77 They mote singen and be light. c 1400 *Destr. Troy* 1411 All þere lordes were light þat þai lyffe hade. a 1400–50 *Alexander* 5332 3it be liȝt & lete of þi sorowe. 1430–40 LYDG. *Bochas* I. x. (1554) 21 b, The people were full glad and lyght. c 1430 *Syr Gener.* (Roxb.) 448 He was so light Of hir talking and of hir sight. 1500–20 DUNBAR *Poems* xxvii. 23 Na ferly thocht his hart wes licht. 1778 MAD. D'ARBLAY *Diary* 23 Aug., I have rarely seen a very rich man with a light heart and light spirits. 1844 A. WELBY *Poems* (1867) 1 When my heart was as light as a blossom in June. 1884 W. C. SMITH *Kildrostan* 55 Now my heart is light again, and I Could laugh like children at a pantomime. 1893 F. ADAMS *New Egypt* 146 He broke into a light laugh.

VII. 22. Of the head: Dizzy, giddy. Also of persons: Wandering in mind, delirious = LIGHT-HEADED 1 (now *dial.*: see *Eng. Dial. Dict.*).

[Cf. sense 16; but there appears to be here a reference to a subjective sensation of physical levity.]

1590 SHAKS. *Com. Err.* v. i. 72 And thereof comes it that his head is light. **1604** —— *Oth.* IV. i. 280 Are his wits safe? Is he not light of Braine? **1662** R. MATHEW *Unl. Alch.* §89. 141 He..continued very light eight dayes. **1791** J. LEARMONT *Poems* 8 Light grew her head, her breast did beat. *Mod.* (*Donegal*) 'He's a bit light at the full and the change' (H. C. Hart).

VIII. 23. *Comb.*: **a.** in syntactical combs. used attrib. or as adjs., as ***light-density, -draught, -heart, -land, -marching***; **b.** in parasynthetic derivatives, as ***light-bellied, -bodied, -boned, -brained, -built, †-disposed, -legged, -mouthed, -pointed, -robed, -spirited, -thoughted, -tongued, -winged, -witted*** adjs.; **†light-eared** *a.*, ready to listen, credulous; **†light-poised** *a.*, of light weight; **†light-skirted** *a.* (of a woman: cf. LIGHT-SKIRTS), light in conduct, wanton (hence *†lightskirtedness*); **†light-tailed** *a.* = prec.; **light-timbered** *a.*, (of a horse) lightly-built, active. Also LIGHT-ARMED, LIGHT-FINGERED, etc.

1823 CRABB *Technol. Dict.*, **Light-bellied*, an epithet for a horse that has flat, narrow, and contracted sides. **1686** *Lond. Gaz.* No. 2136/4 A white sanded gray Mare..*light-bodied. **1951** AUDEN *Nones* (1952) 14 Of *light-boned children under great green oaks. **1974** J. STUBBS *Painted Face* ii. 48 She was light-boned and well-fleshed. **1590** MARLOWE *Edw. II*, v. ii. (1598) H 2 b, The proud corrupters of the *light-brained king. **1953** J. CARY *Except the Lord* v. 15 He was a *light-built man, very dark in complexion, with a somewhat hollow face, and a long sharp chin. **1956** E. MUIR *One Foot in Eden* 18 The crescent shadow Of the light-built bridge. **1967** *Times* 28 Feb. (Canada Suppl.) 35/3 This method of operation has implications..for *light-density branch lines. **1967** *Jane's Surface Skimmer Systems 1967–68* 30/1 The H.M.2 is designed for ferry services on light density routes of short stage lengths. **1870** T. W. HIGGINSON *Army Life in Black Regim.* 169 We could then ascend the smaller stream with two *light-draft boats. **1897** *Daily News* 3 Mar. 5/2 Eight light-draught steamers for special service. *a* **1552** LD. SOMERSET in Foxe *A. & M.* (1563) 736 b, When one is ouer *light eared, the one way, and deafe on the other side. **1845** G. MURRAY *Islaford* 37 There was a *light-heart briskness in the air. **1812** *Examiner* 7 Sept. 563/2 *Light-land wheat, almost everywhere good. **1960** *Farmer & Stockbreeder* 29 Mar. 73/1 The only complaint—a little rain needed on some of the light-land farms. **1974** *Times* 15 Apr. 8/3 Dry weather over the past three weeks, rather too long a period for some light-land farmers, has made possible some catching up on the delays of March. *a* **1586** SIDNEY *Arcadia* I. (1622) 87 *Light-legged Pas had got the middle space. **1888** M. MORRIS *Claverhouse* x. 186 The active *light-marching Highlanders. **1884** E. A. ANDERSON *Mod. Horsemanship* v. 18 It is dangerous to have a severe bit upon a *light-mouthed horse. **1824** MISS MITFORD *Village* Ser. I. 263 Its *light-pointed roof, its clustered chimneys. **1615** BRATHWAIT *Strappado* (1878) 205 Swift is't [the water of the Kent] in pace, *light-poiz'd, to looke in cleere. **1876** HUMPHREYS *Coin Coll. Man.* xxiv. 326 A *light-robed female presenting her hand to three soldiers. *a* **1758** RAMSAY *Some of the Contents* vii, *Licht skirted lasses, and the girnand wyfe. **1607** R. C[AREW] tr. *Estienne's World of Wonders* 101 *Light skirtednesse and leuitie. **1600** J. LANE *Tom Tel-troth* (1876) 133 *Light-taylde huswiues. **1777** R. POTTER *Æschylus, Prometheus chain'd* 26 Unfruitfull labour and *light-thoughted folly. **1683** *Lond. Gaz.* No. 1871/4 A *light timbered bright bay Gelding. *a* **1825** FORBY *Voc. E. Anglia, Light-timbered*, light-limbed; active and alert. **1828** SCOTT *F.M. Perth* xvii, To keep *light-tongued companions out of the way. **1604** SHAKS. *Oth.* I. iii. 269 *Light-wing'd Toyes Of feather'd Cupid seele with wanton dulnesse My..offic'd Instrument. **1763** MASON *Sonn. to Earl Holdernesse* 6 Here, as the light wing'd moments glide serene. **1577** H. RHODES *Bk. Nurture* in *Babees Bk.* (1868) 82 For *lyght-witted or dronken, sure, men will name thee in talke. **1699** BENTLEY *Phal.* 86 A foolish light witted fellow.

c. Special Comb.: **light bread** *U.S.* (see quot. 1966); **light fantastic** (see FANTASTIC *a.* and *sb.* A. 6 b), as noun phr., the movements of dancing; **light-heavyweight** (see quot. 1954); also *attrib.*; also *ellipt.* as *light-heavy*; **light oil**, any of various fractions of relatively low specific gravity obtained by the distillation of coal-tar, wood-tar, petroleum, etc.; **light water**, (*a*) water containing the normal (about 0·02%) or less than the normal proportion of deuterium oxide (so ***light water reactor***, a nuclear reactor in which the moderator is light water); (*b*) a foam formed by water and a fluorocarbon surfactant which floats on flammable liquids lighter than water and is used in fire-fighting.

1821 *Western Carolinian* (Salisbury, N. Carolina) 27 Mar., Crackers and *light Bread will always be found in his shop. **1880** 'MARK TWAIN' *Tramp Abroad* II. xlix. 225 Hot light-bread, Southern style. **1966** *Publ. Amer. Dial. Soc. 1964* XLII. 20 *Lightbread*, any yeast-raised bread, to distinguish it from biscuit. **1970** C. MAJOR *Dict. Afro-Amer. Slang* 77 *Light bread*, white bread. **1974** *Amer. Speech 1971* XLVI. 62 The notion that *light bread* is a recessive term is especially plausible because baking is rarely done at home and because supermarkets sell *white bread* or simply *bread*. *c* **1843** J. S. COYNE *Binks the Bagman* (1852) i. 10 Then you're fond of sporting on the *light fantastic? **1892** A. C. GUNTER *Miss Dividends* ix. 128 'You dance very nicely,' she murmurs. 'Yes, for a man who has not tripped the light fantastic for years.' **1913** GALSWORTHY *Dark Flower* I. vii. 34 When I was your age I twirled the light fantastic with the best. **1953** K. AMIS *Lucky Jim* x. 114, I thought you'd all be on the floor by now... I'm not going to permit any more of this skulking about in here. It's the light fantastic for you. **1974** L. DEIGHTON *Spy Story* vi. 57 The inlaid sprung floor would still have supported a light fantastic or two. **1973** R. L. SIMON *Big Fix* (1974) xv. 104 It was the guy..who looked like a promising *light-heavy. **1975** M. KENYON *Mr Big* vii. 63 'These the heavyweights?' 'Light-heavy. Watch Hudson, in the blue trunks.' **1903** *National Police Gaz.* (U.S.) 18 July 3/1 And now there is a new champion in a new class—George Gardiner, of Lowell, Mass., the holder of the *light-heavyweight title. **1913** J. G. B. LYNCH *Compl. Amat. Boxer* (App.) 234 Standard weights... Light-heavy weight, 12 stone 7 pounds and under. **1954** F. C. AVIS *Boxing Reference Dict.* 77 *Light-Heavyweight*, a standard weight division for professional boxers weighing more than 11 st. 6 lb. but not more than 12 st. 7 lb.; for amateurs 11 st. 11 lb. and 12 st. 10 lb. respectively. **1960** M. GOLESWORTHY *Encycl. Boxing* 210/2 Light-heavyweight—Started in America in 1903 by Lou Houseman, manager of Jack Root, who had outgrown the middleweight division. The limit was set at 12 st. 7 lbs. (175 lbs.) and it remains at that figure today. The division was first recognised in Britain in 1913. **1968** *Encycl. Brit.* IV. 43/1 In 1920 light heavyweight competition was added. **1867** BLOXAM *Chem.* 452 The *light oil which first passed over is rectified by a second distillation, and is then sent into commerce under the name of coal naphtha. **1898** F. H. THORP *Outl. Industr. Chem.* 264 The distillate collected [from wood-tar] below 150°C. is called 'light oil', and is chiefly used as a substitute for oil of turpentine in varnish and paints. **1936** *Economist* 22 Feb. 399/2 Increasing demand for the heavier oils has enabled a higher proportion of refinery production to be marketed in that form, and has reduced the proportion subjected to 'cracking' to obtain light oils, such as motor spirit. **1964** N. G. CLARK *Mod. Org. Chem.* xviii. 372 When light oil and crude benzole are distilled to give 'Benzole' for internal-combustion engines—over 70 per cent are treated in this way —a fraction embracing benzene, toluene, and the xylenes is collected. **1933** *Light water [see HEAVY *a.*[1] 2 d]. **1947** CROWTHER & WHIDDINGTON *Science at War* iii. 142 Vast quantities of water have been electrolysed, and separated into 'light water' and 'heavy water', the former containing hydrogen atoms of mass 1 only. **1956** *Nature* 4 Feb. 204/1 Studies have been made of the pressurized light-water reactor and of the sodium-graphite reactor. **1968** *Guardian* 21 Aug. 1/4 The air show's special fire brigade—using helicopters carrying 'light water'. **1971** *Sunday Times* 12 Dec. 45/6 American light water reactors are simple and in some ways cruder. **1972** *Aircraft Engineering* Jan. 28/1 Using Light Water aqueous film forming foam, the team cut a knock-down path to the cockpit within five seconds of reaching the fire. **1973** *Daily Colonist* (Victoria, B.C.) 7 June 42/2 The cost of a solar steam generating plant would now be about double the cost of light-water nuclear plants.

light (lait), *a.*[2] Forms: 1 **léoht**, *Anglian* **leht**, 3 **liht**, 4 **lith**, **ly3t**, 4–5 **li3t**, 4–6 **lyght**, 5 **ley3t**, **licht**, 6 **lighte**, **lycht**, 4– **light**. [OE. *léoht* (Anglian *lĕht*) = OFris. *li(a)cht*, OS., OHG. *lioht* (MHG. *lieht*, mod.G. and Du. *licht*): see LIGHT *sb.*]

1. †a. Bright, shining, luminous. Of a fire: Burning brightly. Phrase, ***on (of, in) a light fire***: in a blaze (very common in 16–18th c.). *Obs.*

c **825** *Vesp. Psalter* xviii. 9 Bibod dryhtnes leht [Vulg. *lucidum*] inlihtende eȝan. *c* **1000** *Sax. Leechd.* II. 30 Seoð þonne æt leohtum fyre. *a* **1400–50** *Alexander* 4464 Gods.. Sum of latoun & of lede & sum of li3t siluir. *c* **1400** *Destr. Troy* 8742 Ymages..Lokend full lyuely as any light angels. **14..** *Tundale's Vis.* 2120 (MS. A.) Bryghtter..Then ever schon sonne that was soo ly3t. *c* **1420** *Chron. Vilod.* 1300 (Horstm.), To stanche þat feyre þat was so ley3t. **1583** STOCKER *Civ. Warres Lowe C.* IV. 57 b, At that tyme also was fire cried at Giethorne, and soone after, many houses were seene on a light fire. **1609** HOLLAND *Amm. Marcell.* 113 Now ..we might discover smoke and light fires all the way along. **1643** TRAPP *Comm. Gen.* xx. 3 For methought, I saw all Heidelberg on a thick smoke, but the Prince his Pallace all on a light fire. **1652** WARREN *Unbelievers* (1654) 24 All Sodome was of a light fire. **1737** *Mem. G. di Lucca* 110 The Flashes were so thick the Sky was almost in a light Fire. **1760** JORTIN *Life of Erasmus* II. 717 He piled those ancient books together and set them all on a light fire.

absol. *c* **1380** WYCLIF *Wks.* (1880) 269 It is a foul lesynge to chese wittingly & meyntene þe lesse perfit, & forsake þe li3ttere, sikerere, & perfitere.

b. Of a place, the time of day, etc.: Having a considerable or sufficient amount of light, not dark. †In early use also with stronger sense: Brightly illuminated; *fig.* enlightened mentally.

c **900** *Bæda's Hist.* I. i. (1890) 26 Ðis ealond..leohte nihte on sumera hafað. *c* **1200** *Trin. Coll. Hom.* 103 *Illuminacio mentis*..þat is heorte be liht. *c* **1205** LAY. 7238 Hit wes an ane time, þat þe dæi wes liht, and þe sunne wes swiðe briht. *c* **1300** *Havelok* 593 Also lith was it þer-inne, So þer brenden cerges inne. *c* **1320** *Seuyn Sag.* (W.) 2064 And to morewen, whan it is light, Sire, thou schalt have thine wille. *a* **1340** HAMPOLE *Psalter* xxxvi. 9 Charite þat makis þe eghen of oure saule lyght & lufly. *c* **1470** HENRYSON *Mor. Fab.* x. (*Fox & Wolf*) xxiii, The nicht was licht, and penny full the mone. **1560** DAUS tr. *Sleidane's Comm.* 235 a/2 By and by commeth he with the letters, and delyuereth them: it was skarce lyght daye. **1596** DALRYMPLE tr. *Leslie's Hist. Scot.* I. 90 Nocht be the day was lycht, nathir at noneday bot at evin. **1611** BIBLE *Micah* ii. 1 When the morning is light, they practise it [euill]. **1704** NORRIS *Ideal World* II. Pref. 8 A man that has a light shop had need sell good ware. **1844** J. T. HEWLETT *Parsons & W.* ix, The boy..got up before it was light on the following morning. **1861** FLO. NIGHTINGALE *Nursing* 56 A patient's bed should always be in the lightest spot in the room. *Mod.* The morning-room is a nice light room.

†c. Clean, pure. *Obs.*

13.. *E.E. Allit. P.* A. 681 þat is of hert boþe clene & ly3t. *Ibid.* B. 987 Wyth ly3t louez vp-lyfte þay loued hym swyþe.

2. a. Pale in hue. Also = *light-coloured*.

1548 TURNER *Names of Herbes* (1881) 73 Siligo..is a kynde of ryghte wheate... Therfore let it be called in englishe lyght wheate. **1686** *Lond. Gaz.* No. 2182/4 He had a light bob Periwig. **1727** BOYER *Fr. Dict.*, Light Hair, *des Cheveux blonds.* **1799** G. SMITH *Laboratory* I. 394 Draw your stuff quickly through, three or four times, according as you would have it deeper or lighter. *Ibid.* 305 Body [of artificial fly] light fur of an old fox. **1873** *Act 36 & 37 Vict.* c. 85 §3 Her name..shall be marked on her stern..on a light ground in black letters. **1898** *Pall Mall G.* 3 Feb. 9/1 Never back a bird which has a light or yellow eye.

b. Prefixed, as a qualification, to other adjectives of colour. (Usually hyphened with the adj. when the latter is used attributively.) ***light red***, (*a*) pale red; (*b*) a pale red or reddish orange pigment produced from iron oxides.

c **1420** *Durham Acc. Rolls* (Surtees) 617, 7 pannis integris de lyghtgrene. *a* **1450** *Fysshynge w. Angle* (1883) 10 A lyght plunket colour. *a* **1500** [see GLAD *a.* 1]. **1530** PALSGR. 239/1 Lyght grene popyngay coloure, *uertgay.* **1729** SAVAGE *Wanderer* I. 71 The dawn in light-grey mists arose. **1803** J. C. IBBETSON *Accidence of Painting in Oil* 17 *Light red*, so called, is either calcined green vitriol mixed with a quantity of other substance, and called Venetian red; or calcined yellow oker. **1863** I. WILLIAMS *Baptistery* II. xix. (1874) 25 Beneath an ash-tree's light-green shade, There side by side The three are laid. **1885** MISS BRADDON *Wyllard's Weird* i. 14 A back-ground of light-drab cloth. **1934** H. HILER *Notes Technique Painting* ii. 125 *Light red, burnt ochre*... It is quite opaque, and may be defined as a scarlet modified by the addition of a little yellow and grey. **1958** M. L. WOLF *Dict. Painting* 142 The red iron oxides found as natural deposits include Indian red, light red,..and others of lesser importance. **1970** R. D. HARLEY *Artists' Pigments* ix. 109 Light red came into current use as a colour name during the eighteenth century, when it was generally used to indicate a brownish red prepared by burning yellow ochre.

3. *Comb.*: parasynthetic, as ***light-coloured, -complexioned, -haired, -leaved, -veined, -waved*** adjs. **Light Sussex**, a white variety of hen.

1631 SANDERSON *Serm.* (1681) II. 2 A too-too *light-coloured habit certainly suteth not well with the gravity of a sermon. **1686** *Lond. Gaz.* No. 2136/4 Left in a Hackney Coach..a light-colour'd gray cloth Sur-toute Coat. **1882** *Garden* 4 Feb. 78/1 The American Ash is, as a rule, lighter coloured both in foliage and bark than ours. **1861** WAUGH *Goblin's Grave* 11 Her *light-complexioned face beamed with..good nature. **1843** MILL *Logic* II. III. xxiii. 149 The probability..that any given inhabitant of Stockholm is *light-haired. **1870** BRYANT *Iliad* I. x. 302 The husband of the light-haired queen of heaven. **1896** HOUSMAN *Shropsh. Lad* lxiii, And fields will yearly bear them As *light-leaved spring comes on. **1909** T. W. STURGES *Poultry Manual* xiii. 359 The *Light Sussex and the Buff Orpington are both blended in the White Orpington. **1938** L. PEARCE-GERVIS *Compl. Poultry Keeper & Farmer* vi. 153 The top prices.. are still made by the Surrey Chicken... For this market either Pure Light Sussex or a cross in which there is a Sussex strain is necessary, for the white flesh must be maintained. **1965** P. WAYRE *Wind in Reeds* xv. 224 A flock of four hundred Silky crossed with Light Sussex bantams. **1613–39** I. JONES in Leoni *Palladio's Archit.* (1742) II. 50 *Light-vein'd marble. **1824** T. FENBY *Hymn to May* iv. 5 Yon *light-wav'd clouds thy tresses show.

†light, *ppl. a. Obs.* [Pa. pple. of LIGHT *v.*[2]] Lighted, kindled, illuminated.

1495 *Act 11 Hen. VII*, c. 27 Take a light candell and sette in the Fustyan brennyng. **1579** FULKE *Refut. Rastel* 722 Neither was it the custome..to sett light candels on the aultars. **1601** HOLLAND *Pliny* I. 45 It quencheth..light torches dipped therein. **1606** CHAPMAN *Mons. D'Olive* I. i, Me thinks through the encourtaind windowes..I see light Tapers. **1632** LITHGOW *Trav.* VI. 274 With light candles in our hands.

light (lait), *adv.*[1] Forms: 1 **léohte**, 3 **lihte**, 3–5 **li3t**, 5 **lyghte**, 6 *Sc.* **licht**, 4– **light**. [OE. *léohte* = OS. *lihto* (Du. *licht*), OHG. *lîhto* (MHG. *lîhte*, mod.G. *leicht*), f. OTeut. **liŋhto-* LIGHT *a.*[1]]

1. In a light manner (cf. senses of the adj.); lightly as opposed to heavily; nimbly, †quickly; †easily, comfortably.

In the phrases ***to think light of, † to care light for***, etc., there may be confusion with LITE, little.

c **900** tr. *Bæda's Hist.* IV. xix. (1890) 320 þa wæs heo ȝeseȝen þurh tweȝen daȝas, þæt hire leohtor & wel wære. *a* **1250** *Prov. Ælfred* 290 in *O.E. Misc.* 120 þene vnþev lihte leten heo myhte. *a* **1300** *Cursor M.* 18059 Fra hus he lepe selcutli light. *c* **1330** R. BRUNNE *Chron.* (1810) 272 He wend haf had fulle light, Edward at his wille. *c* **1420** *Anturs of Arth.* 653 And þane to þe lystis þe lordis leppis fulle lyghte. *c* **1449** PECOCK *Repr.* 268 Euery thing lijk to an other thing bringith into ymaginacioun and into mynde better and li3tir and esier the thing to him lijk, than the thing to him lasse lijk. **1483** CAXTON *G. de la Tour* L ij, Blessed be the houre that my suster clothed her so light. **1573** *Satir. Poems Reform.* xlii. 432 Thocht of the matter thay pas licht. **1590** GREENE *Never too Late* (1600) N 1 b, So light the Ferriman for loue doth care, As Venus passe not if she pay no fare. **1590** SPENSER *F.Q.* I. viii. 10 His boystrous club, so buried in the ground, He could not rearen up againe so light. **1590** SHAKS. *Mids. N.* v. i. 401 Euerie Elfe and Fairie spright, Hop as light as bird from brier. **1592** —— *Ven. & Ad.* 1028 The grasse stoops not, she treads on it so light. **1697** DRYDEN *Virg. Georg.* III. 308 He..treads so light he scarcely prints the Plains. **1807** WORDSW. *Song at Feast Brougham Castle* 75 Thoughts that pass Light as the wind along the grass. **1871** ROSSETTI *Last Confession* 401 She went with.. hands held light before her. **1896** HOUSMAN *Shropshire Lad* lix, Lie you easy, dream you light.

Proverb. **1546** J. HEYWOOD *Prov.* (1867) 77 Light come, light go. **1712** ARBUTHNOT *John Bull* III. iv, Light come, light go, he cares not a farthing. **1857** HUGHES *Tom Brown* I. ix, Light come, light go; they wouldn't have been comfortable with money in their pockets in the middle of the half.

2. *Comb.* (with pres. and pa. pples.) as ***light-bounding, -charged, -clad, -disposed, -harnessed, -loaded, -poised***, etc.

1533–4 *Act 25 Hen. VIII*, c. 17 Many wilfull and light disposed persons..haue attempted the..violacion of the same statutes. **1561** T. NORTON *Calvin's Inst.* (1634) Pref., The light-beleeving and ignorant multitude. **1596** *Edw. III*, I. ii, Nor rusting canker have the time to eat Their light-borne snaffles. **1598** GRENEWEY *Tacitus' Ann.* I. xiii. (1622) 24 The Bructeri..Stertinius ouerthrew with a company of

light harnessed soldiers. **1725** POPE *Odyss.* VIII. 303 Light-bounding from the earth, at once they rise. **1726–46** THOMSON *Winter* 645 The fop light-fluttering spreads his mealy wings. **1742** YOUNG *Nt. Th.* v. 463 Earth's inchanted cup With cool reserve light-touching. **1750** CHATHAM in Seward *Anecd.* (1796) III. 386 'Midst all the tumults of the warring sphere, My light-charg'd bark may haply glide. **1751** *Act 24 Geo. II*, c. 8 §17 Damages do often happen to light-loaded Barges.. by deep-loaded Barges.. lying across ..in the said Rivers. **1776** MICKLE tr. *Camoens' Lusiad* 227 The dancers' heels light-quivering beat the ground. **1777** R. POTTER *Æschylus, Agamem.* 236 Fond as a boy to chace The winged bird light-flitting round. **1798** SOTHEBY tr. *Wieland's Oberon* (1826) II. 152 A veil, light-shadowing each voluptuous charm. **1812** BYRON *Ch. Har.* I. lxxiii, With milk-white crest, gold spur, and light-pois'd lance. **1823** ROSCOE *Sismondi's Lit. Eur.* (1846) II. xxxi. 329 Our light-swung hammocks answering to the breeze. **1876** GEO. ELIOT *Dan. Der.* III. xliv. 269 Lighter-clad intelligence. **1883** F. M. WALLEM *Fish Supply Norway* 31 (Fish. Exhib. Publ.) Add.. a few light-fried truffles or mushrooms. **1883** R. W. DIXON *Mano* II. vi. 84 The Saracen's curved sword and light-wrought mail.

†**light**, *adv.*² *Obs.* Forms: 1 léohte, 3 liht(e, 4–5 liȝt(e, 5 lighte, lyth, 4– light. [OE. *léohte* (= OHG. *liohto*, MHG. *liehte*), f. *léoht* LIGHT *a.*²] Brightly, clearly.

a **900** CYNEWULF *Crist* 1239 (Gr.) þæt hy fore leodum leohte blicaþ. **971** *Blickl. Hom.* 127 [Leohtfatu] leohte & beorhte scinaþ ælce niht. *c* **1230** *Hali Meid.* 43 Euch heate of þe hali gast þat bearneð se lihte wiðute wastinde. *c* **1275** *XI Pains of Hell* 68 in *O.E. Misc.* 149 A hwel of stele is furþer mo And berneþ lihte and turneþ o. *a* **1310** in Wright *Lyric P.* 33 In uche londe heo leometh liht. *c* **1384** CHAUCER *H. Fame* III. 199 These walles of berile.. shoone ful lyghter than a glas. *c* **1470** *Golagros & Gaw.* 485 With fel lans on loft, lemand ful light. **14..** LYDG. *Siege Harfleur* in Arb. *Garner* VIII. 17 With men of arms that lyth did leme. *c* **1710** C. FIENNES *Diary* (1888) 137 Its [*sc.* coal] in great pieces and so Cloven burns light so as the poorer sort works by it.

Comb. *a* **1400–50** *Alexander* 553 Þe liȝt lemand late laschis fra þe heuyn.

light (laɪt), *v.*¹ Forms: 1 líhtan, lýhtan, léhtan, 3 lihte(n, liȝten, 3–4 liht, lyht, 4 liȝt, lyȝt, lith, 4–5 liȝte, 4–6 lyght, *Sc.* licht, lycht, 5 lyghte, leyȝt, lyhte, lyȝte, 5–6 lighte, 6–7 lite, 8–9 *dial.* leet, 4– light. *Pa. t.* α. 1 lihte, 2–3 lihte, 4 liht, lyht(e, lyȝte, licte, *north.* licht, 4–5 liȝt(e, lyȝt, lyghte, 4–8 light, 5 leyt, 5–6 lyght, 8–9 *dial.* leet. β. 4 lihtid, lited, lithed, liȝtid, 4–6 *Sc.* lichtit, lychtit, -yt, 5–6 lyghted(e, 4– lighted; 7– lit. *Pa. pple.* α. 3–5 liȝt, 4 lyȝt, liht, y-lyeght, 5 lyght, 5–8 light. β. 5 y-lyghted, -id, 5–6 lyghted, 6 lyȝthed, 8 lited, 6– lighted; 8– lit. Also 7 lighten. [OE. *líhtan* = OFris. *lichta*, MDu. *liichten* (Du. *lichten*), OHG. (*gi*)*lîhten*, (MHG. *lîhten*, mod.G. *leichten*, now rare; also *lichten*, Naut. from Du.), ON. *létta*:—OTeut. type **līhtjan*, **liŋhtjan*, f. **līhto-*, **liŋhto-*, LIGHT *a.*¹ The senses in branch II app. originate in an absol. use of the vb. in sense 2 ('to relieve a horse or vehicle of one's weight'); cf. ON. *létta* to dismount, halt on a journey.]

I. To lighten.

†**1.** *trans.* To make light, lessen the weight of. Also *fig.* to reduce; to mitigate, assuage. *Obs.*

c **1000** in *Narrat. Angl. Conscrip.* (Cockayne) 8 Ða wolde ic minne þurst lehtan. **1422** tr. *Secreta Secret., Priv. Priv.* 214 Thou shalte lyght the trauaillis of thy baronage. *c* **1440** *Promp. Parv.* 304/1 Lyghtyn chargys or byrdenys, *deonero.* *Ibid.*, Lyghteyn, or make wyghtys more esy (*P.* lightyn burdens, heuy weightis) *allevio.* **1552** HULOET, Lyghten or make easye, *læuigo, leuo.* **1578** BANISTER *Hist. Man* I. 34 We finde the same [bone] here, and there, attenuated, and lighted with long lynes, and flatted sides. **1582** STANYHURST *Æneis* II. (Arb.) 67 Nor backward skewd I myn eyesight, In graue of holy Ceres tyl that my burden I lighted. *a* **1600** MONTGOMERIE *Sonn.* li. 6 Vhilk slaiks my sorou.. And lights my louing largour at the leist.

2. a. To relieve *of* a (material) load or burden; to unload (a ship). Also, to 'relieve' (a person) *of* his property by plundering. ? *Obs.*

a **1225** *Ancr. R.* 422 Ȝe schulen been i-dodded four siðen iðe ȝere, uorto lihten ower heaued. **13..** *E.E. Allit. P.* C. 160 To lyȝten þat lome, ȝif leþe wolde schape. **1375** BARBOUR *Bruce* III. 624 Thar schip thai lychtyt sone. **1545** RAYNOLD *Byrth Mankynde* 34 They can not.. containe or draw any moore, tyll they be lighted and dischargyd of that that is drawen already. **1590** SPENSER *F.Q.* I. xii. 42 Where we must land some of our passengers, And light this weary vessell of her lode. **1623** BINGHAM *Xenophon* 127 Tereus.. was lighted of all his baggage by these men. **1637** B. JONSON *Sad Sheph.* I. ii, The wash'd Flocks are lighted of their wooll. **1715–20** POPE *Iliad* XI. 208 Many a car, now lighted of its lord. **1756** in *R. Rogers's Jrnls.* (1883) 51 *note*, They saw a schooner at anchor some distance from ye shore.. and, upon this intelligence, lighted our boats and intended to board them.

b. To deliver *of* a child. Now *dial.*

c **1394** *P. Pl. Crede* 79 Þat þe lace of oure ladie smok liȝteþ hem of children. *c* **1400** MAUNDEV. (1839) vi. 71 Where oure Lady rested hire, aftre sche was lyghted of oure Lord. *c* **1460** *Towneley Myst.* xiii. 337, I shall say thou was lyght Of a knaue childe this nyght. **1494** FABYAN *Chron.* VII. 339 Leuynge his wyfe with hir modyr tyll she were lyghted of chylde. **1542** *Will of R. Slanye* (Somerset Ho.) Yf.. she be lighted of a childe wherw^t^ she goeth nowe. **1774** *Churchw. Acc. Norton & Lenchwick, Worcestersh.* (MS.) P^d^ Mrs. Sanders for liting Ben Turner wife. **1886** *Chesh. Gloss.* s.v., Is your wife lighted?

†**3. a.** To relieve (*of* pain, sorrow, etc.); to comfort, gladden, cheer (a person, his heart, etc.). *Obs.*

c **1000** *Sax. Leechd.* II. 186 þicge þæt seofon niht, þonne liht þæt þone ȝeswencedan maȝan. *c* **1220** *Bestiary* 375 Liȝten him of his birdene. *a* **1225** *Ancr. R.* 356 Worp awei urom me alle mine gultes, þet ich beo ilihted of hore heuinesse. *a* **1300** *Cursor M.* 5727 He light þam o þair wa. *c* **1384** CHAUCER *H. Fame* I. 467 Venue, The whiche I prey ..vs ay of oure sorwes lyghte. **1388** WYCLIF *Isa.* ix. i, The lond of Zabulon and the lond of Neptalym was releessid [*v. rr.* aliȝted, liȝtid]. *a* **1400–50** *Alexander* 2814, I shall lefe & be lightyd; ȝarfore be ȝe light. *c* **1440** *Jacob's Well* xl. 249 Of oþeris charge þou art lyȝthed. *c* **1470** HENRYSON *Mor. Fab.* Prol. iii, Ane mery sport To licht the spreit. **1473** M. PASTON in *P. Lett.* III. 77 Ye have lyghtyd myne hert therin by a pound. **1529** MORE *Dyaloge* II. Wks. 1171/1 A merye tale wyth a frende, refresheth a manne muche, and.. lyghteth his mynd. **1530** PALSGR. 611/2 This tydynges lyghteth me well. **1597** A. M. tr. *Guillemeau's Fr. Chirurg.* 10/1 She voyded matter, by the which she seemed to be lighted and easyed.

†**b.** *intr.* Of the heart: To grow light or cheerful. Of sickness: To be alleviated. *Obs.*

a **1300** *Cursor M.* 5163 Þan bigan his ert to light. *c* **1386** CHAUCER *Sqr.'s T.* 388 It was so fair a sighte That it made alle hire hertes for to lighte. **1398** TREVISA *Barth. De P.R.* IX. xxii. (Tollem. MS.), In þe dawenynge siknesse of bestes lyȝteþ [*ed.* 1535 is lyghted] and abateþ. *a* **1400–50** *Alexander* 5255 Sire Alexander hire a-vises & all his hert liȝtis. *c* **1460** *Towneley Myst.* xiii. 138 Me thynk my hart lyghtys.

†**4.** *trans.* To make of less effect, deprive of weight or influence. Also *Sc.*, to slight, undervalue.

a **1619** FOTHERBY *Atheom.* I. viii. §2 (1622) 56 Though he were very witty.. yet by his inconstancy, he lighted his authority. [L. *levatur authoritas*]. **1822** GALT *Entail* III. viii. 81 When the Laird lights the Leddy, so does a' the kitchen boys.

5. a. *Naut.* (*trans.* and *absol.*) (See quot. 1867.)

1841 DANA *Seaman's Man.* 114 *Light*, to move or lift anything along; as, to 'Light out to windward!' that is, haul the sail over to windward. *c* **1860** H. STUART *Seaman's Catech.* 45 The men on the yard.. light out on their respective sides. **1867** SMYTH *Sailor's Word-bk.*, *Light, To.* To move or lift anything along; as 'light over to windward', the cry for helping the men at the weather-earing when taking in a reef. *Light along!* Lend assistance in hauling cables, hawsers, or large ropes along, and lifting some parts in a required direction. **1882** NARES *Seamanship* (ed. 6) 132 All.. light the sail out to windward together.

b. ? Hence *to light out* (*U.S. slang*): to decamp, 'make tracks'. *to light in* (or *into*): to attack; to go at. (*U.S. colloq.*)

1866 'MARK TWAIN' *Lett. from Hawaii* (1967) 32 And you want to know what made me light out of bed so sudden last night? Only a 'santipede'. **1878** J. H. BEADLE *Western Wilds* xii. 187 They double-quicked into town and lit in generally. **1884** 'MARK TWAIN' *Huck. Finn* i. 2 And so when I couldn't stand it no longer, I lit out. **1888** *Cornh. Mag.* Oct. 373 He may light out for the country, railing West to a young city yet on the boom. **1889** K. MUNROE *Golden Days* xiv. 156 You've got the levellest head of any man that ever lit into the diggings. **1890** *Century Mag.* Feb. 525/2 We'll light out an' find your brother. **1917** FREEMAN & KINGSLEY *Alabaster Box* i. 3 He'll light into those hot doughnuts. **1948** 'J. TEY' *Franchise Affair* xxii. 262 The girl had lit out... She had dressed in a hurry and gone. **1967** *Boston Sunday Herald* 7 May IV. 5/5 Chris did demonstrate he is prepared for a scrap in the coming campaign when he lit into Mrs. Hicks' proposals. **1969** *Listener* 27 Mar. 433/2 Like a latter-day Huck Finn, he lights out for the territory. **1969** *New Yorker* 19 Apr. 81/1 If the astronaut missed mentioning a rock I knew was there, I'd light into him afterward, just like a football coach critiquing a fumble on a film of a game. **1973** *Observer* 15 Apr. 13/2 Inveighing against that new parliamentary building.. lighting into.. the proposed gymnasium.

II. To descend. Cf. ALIGHT *v.*¹

6. a. *intr.* To descend *from* a horse or vehicle; to dismount; to bring one's ride to an end. Also with *off*, *down*, *adown*, (arch.). †Sometimes conjugated with *to be*.

c **900** tr. *Bæda's Hist.* III. xvi. [xxii.] (1890) 228 He.. lyhte of his horse & feoll him to fotum. *c* **1205** LAY. 5862 Lihteð of eowre blanken and stondeð on eowre sconken. *a* **1300** *Cursor M.* 3256 Biside a well he lighted [*Gött.* lithed, *Trin.* liȝt] dun. **1375** BARBOUR *Bruce* XIV. 121 The erll of Murreff ..Lichtit on fut with his menȝhe. *c* **1470** *Golagros & Gaw.* 130 The knyght.. Reynit his palfray of pride, Quhen he ves lightit doune. **1470–85** MALORY *Arthur* IX. iii, They haue desdayne.. to lyghte of their horses to fyghte with suche a lewde knyght as thou arte. *a* **1592** GREENE *Orpharion* (1599) 19 Set a Begger on horsebacke, and they say he will neuer light. **1596** DANETT tr. *Comines* (1614) 188 All the nobilitie of Fraunce lighted on foot to fight with the English men. **1691** J. WILSON *Belphegor* III. i. Dram. Wks. (1874) 330 Sir, the company are now lighting at door! *a* **1766** MRS. F. SHERIDAN *Mem. Sidn. Biddulph* V. 175, I immediately lit off my horse. **1813** BYRON *Giaour* 587 Stern Hassan.. from his horse Disdains to light. **1868–70** MORRIS *Earthly Par.* I. 158 While from the horse he lit adown.

†**b.** *trans.* (causal) *to light* (*down*): to cause to descend; to help to dismount. *Obs.*

a **1300** *Cursor M.* 22020 He sal þam smett, and dun þam light. *c* **1420** *Anturs of Arth.* 214 Þat is luf paramour.. Þat has me liȝte [*Thornton MS.* gerse me lyghte and lenge] and laft loȝ in a lake.

†**7. a.** Of persons: To descend, go down from a high place or to a low one. Often in ME. used to describe the Incarnation and the Descent into Hell. Occas. *refl.* *Obs.*

c **1175** *Lamb. Hom.* 79 A mon lihte [L. *descendebat*] from ierusalem into ierico. *c* **1220** *Bestiary* 32 Vre louerd is te leun, ðe liueð ðer abuuen;.. him likede to liȝten her on erðe. *c* **1225** *Leg. Kath.* 2494 Te engles lihten of heuene & heuen hire on heh up. *a* **1240** *Lofsong* in *Cott. Hom.* 217 He lihte in to helle. *a* **1300** *Cursor M.* 20531, I lighted doun and man be-cam. *a* **1310** in Wright *Lyric P.* 73 For sunful folk, suete Jesus, Thou lihtest from the heȝe hous. **1377** LANGL. *P. Pl.* B. XI. 240 Ihesu cryste on a iewes douȝter alyȝte [*MS. W.* liȝte], gentil woman þough she were. *c* **1400** MAUNDEV. (Roxb.) xv. 68 How.. Godd sent wisdom in til erthe and lightid in Virgin Mary. *c* **1420** *Anturs of Arth.* 164 (Douce MS.) Withe lucyfer in a lake loȝ am I lighte. *c* **1460** *Towneley Myst.* vii. 115 He will lyght fro heuen towre ffor to be mans saueyoure. **1533** GAU *Richt Vay* 54 The angel said to the virgine maria ye halie spreit sal licht in the.

†**b.** *to light low*: to be brought to the ground; to be degraded or humiliated. *Obs.*

a **1225** *Leg. Kath.* 1011 Leaf þi lease wit þæt tu wlenchest te in & liht to ure lare. *c* **1230** *Hali Meid.* 5 Þat fram se muchel hehschipe & se seli freodom schal lihte se lahe. *c* **1320** *Sir Tristr.* 3340 Wel louwe he dede hem liȝt Wiþ diolful dintes sare. *a* **1400–50** *Alexander* 2362 Ȝit liȝt he law at þe last for all his lethire prid. **1535** STEWART *Cron. Scot.* (1858) I. 395 Scho makis ane man rycht lawlie for to lycht, Quhome of befoir scho set so hie on hicht. **1570** *Satir. Poems Reform.* xxiv. 64 Law sall he lycht downe.

†**8.** *fig.* To descend, emanate, proceed. Const. *from*, *of*. *Obs.*

a **1225** *Ancr. R.* 96 Ȝif eni mon bit fort iseon ou, askeð of him hwat god þerof muhte lihten. *a* **1225** *Leg. Kath.* 1791 Te hali gast, hare beire luue, þe lihteð of ham baðe [*sc.* the Father and the Son]. *a* **1400–50** *Alexander* 599 Of þe lyfe þat he liȝt off he like was to nane. *Ibid.* 4494 Ilk lede þat liȝt is of ȝour lede.

9. To fall and settle on a surface, as a bird, a snowflake, a person leaping upon the ground, or the like. Also with *down*. Phr. *to light on one's feet* or *legs* (fig.): to be fortunate or successful (cf. FALL *v.* 65 h, LEG *sb.* 2 c).

a **1225** *Ancr. R.* 132 Brid.. uorte sechen his mete.. lihteð adun to þer eorðe. *c* **1250** *Hymn to Virgin* 26 in *Trin. Coll. Hom.* App. 256 Þu ert eorþe to gode sede, on þe liȝte þe heouene deuȝ. *a* **1300** *Cursor M.* 1896 Sco [*sc.* the dove].. fand na sted quare-on to light [*Gött.* lith]. *Ibid.* 11612 Quen iesus sagh þam glopnid be, He lighted of his moderkne. **13..** *E.E. Allit. P.* A. 988, I syȝe.. Ierusalem so nwe & ryally dyȝt, As hit was lyȝt fro þe heuen adoun. **1423** JAS. I. *Kingis Q.* clxxvii, A turture.. vpon my hand gan lyght. **1490** CAXTON *Eneydos* lix. 158 That egle that lighted amonge the hepe of swannes. **1530** PALSGR. 611/1 Loke welle where yonder fesante lyghteth. *a* **1541** WYATT *Poet. Wks.* (1831) 109 It is possible.. to fall highest, yet to light soft. *a* **1584** MONTGOMERIE *Cherrie & Slae* 463 Luik quhair to licht before thou loup. **1592** WARNER *Alb. Eng.* VIII. xxxix. (1612) 193 Snow, that lights & lies a moysture moystles. **1642** FULLER *Holy & Prof. St.* IV. i. 244 If he must down, he seeks to fall easily, and if possible, to light on his legs. **1667** MILTON *P.L.* IV. 182 Th' arch fellon.. overleap'd all bound Of Hill or highest Wall, and sheer within Lights on his feet. **1759** BROWN *Compl. Farmer* 95 If the swarms part, and light in sight of one another. **1828** SCOTT *Jrnl.* 6 Mar., A feather just lighted on the ground can scarce be less concerned where the next blast may carry it. **1832** TENNYSON *Œnone* 102 On the tree-tops a crested peacock lit. **1852** THACKERAY *Lett.* 23 Dec., I have made scores of new acquaintances and lighted on my legs as usual. **1871** L. STEPHEN *Playgr. Eur.* iv. (1894) 97 You made a.. spring, and lighted upon another rock.

10. To have a particular place of incidence or arrival. **a.** Of a blow, a weapon: To fall and strike; to fall (short, etc.). Now *rare*.

c **1375** *Sc. Leg. Saints* xix. (*Cristofore*) 657 Ane arow done cane lycht & rewyt þe king of ane ee-sycht. **1489** CAXTON *Faytes of A.* III. xxi. 218 His arowe lighte upon caym and slew hym. **1532** CRANMER *Let. to Hen. VIII* in *Misc. Writ.* (Parker Soc.) II. 234 If the stroke [of an halberd] had not light short. ? *a* **1550** in *Dunbar's Poems* (1893) 305 Fra he begyn to schute his schot, Thow wat nocht quhen that it will licht. **1590** SPENSER *F.Q.* I. viii. 18 The stroke upon his shield so heavie lites. **1604** ROWLANDS *Looke to it* 41 There flies my Dart, light where it will. **1667** MILTON *P.L.* IX. 173, I reck not, so it [Revenge] light well aim'd. **1710** ADDISON *Tatler* No. 155 ¶2 But why in the Heel?.. Because, says I, the Bullet chanced to light there. **1784** R. BAGE *Barham Downs* II. 277 Some of the blows had light upon Lord Somerfort's head and face. **1855** STANLEY *Mem. Canterb.* ii. (1857) 76 The sword lighted on the arm of the monk, which fell wounded.

†**b.** To come to or arrive in a place; to lodge in some position; to arrive *at* a point; to fall *into* a condition; to fall or 'land' in a particular place or position. *Obs.*

a **1240** *Sawles Warde* in *Cott. Hom.* 249 Ha [*i.e.* Death] lihteð hwer se ha eauer kimeð wið a þusent deoflen. *c* **1320** R. BRUNNE *Medit.* 47 And on a þursday þedyr he lyȝt Wyþ hys dycyplys aȝens nyȝt. **13..** *E.E. Allit P.* A. 247, I am forpayned, & þou in a lyf of lykyng lyȝte In paradys erde. *a* **1400–50** *Alexander* 4785 Quare it [the fire] liȝt on his like it lichid him for euir. *c* **1400** *Destr. Troy* 13686 A longyng vnlefful light in his hert. **1545** BRINKLOW *Compl.* i. (1874) 8 If ye wil seke such ways, than wil the Holy Gost lyght in your councel. **1551** RECORDE *Pathw. Knowl.* I. v, Sette the one foote of the compas in the pricke, where you would haue the plumme line to lighte. **1577–87** HOLINSHED *Chron.* (1807–8) III. 37 Let us drinke togither in signe of agreement, that the people.. may.. know that it is true, that we be light at a point. **1627** *Lisander & Cal.* III. 54 Lidian ..entring with a point upon his enemy, lighted just betweene his arme and the curats [= cuirass]. **1629** DRAYTON *Verses* 11 in *Sir J. Beaumont's Bosworth F.* 14 We are light, After those glorious Days, into the Night Of these base Times. **1651** T. BARKER *Art of Angling* (1653) 8 The Pearch feeds well, if you light where they be. **1697** J. SERGEANT *Solid Philos.* a 2, To make you aware of the way you have either chosen, or light into for want of a better.

c. *to light on, upon*: to fall or descend upon, as a piece of good or ill fortune, or the like; to descend upon the head of; to fall to the lot of, to be the 'portion' of: *occas.* conjugated with *to be*,

as in the ME. phrase ***my love is light upon*** (a person). †Also, rarely, to happen *to* a person.

a **1310** in Wright *Lyric P.* 30 Levedi..My love is on the liht. **13..** *E.E. Allit. P.* B. 213 With þis worde þat he warp, þe wrake on hym ly3t. *a* **1440** *Sir Degrev.* 513 My love is leliche y-lyeght One a worthly wyeght. **1526** TINDALE *Matt.* xxiii. 36 All these thinges shall light apon this generacion. **1556** LAUDER *Tractate* 149 Quhat wo and miserie Sall lycht on 3ow. **1579–80** NORTH *Plutarch* (1595) 236 Honour and reputation lighting on yong men before their time. **1602** SHAKS. *Ham.* v. ii. 366 But I do prophesie th' election lights On Fortinbras. **1607** E. SHARPHAM *Cupid's Whirligig* II. D 3 b, The plague of Egypt light vppon you all. **1642** FULLER *Holy & Prof. St.* III. xxv. 233 The best livings light not alwayes on the ablest men. **1667** MILTON *P.L.* x. 833 On mee..all the blame lights due. **1697** J. SERGEANT *Solid Philos.* 447 'Tis evident, that this Eternal Loss of Happiness lights to such Men thro' their acting contrary to their Reason. **1720–21** *Lett. Mist's Jrnl.* (1722) II. 111 The Infamy and Reward must then have light on their Heads. **1832** HT. MARTINEAU *Ireland* iii. 56 A final and overwhelming curse had lighted upon the land.

d. Of persons. ***to light on*** or ***upon*** (or †***of***): to happen to come upon, chance upon; to meet with or discover, esp. unexpectedly or by accident; to come across, whether as the result of search or not.

c **1470** HENRY *Wallace* v. 1068 Ner hand..thai lychtyt apon Clyd. **1579** SPENSER *Sheph. Cal.* Sept. 259 Diggon on fewe such freends did euer lite. **1583** BABINGTON *Commandm.* viii. (1637) 82 Where may we live and not light of false forgers. **1603** KNOLLES *Hist. Turks* (1621) 109 Making spoile of whatsoever they light upon. **1655** STANLEY *Hist. Philos.* II. (1701) 62/1 Not taking heed to the place, he lighted upon a precipice and fell down. **1659** FULLER *App. Inj. Innoc.* I. 34, I thought he had lighten on some rare Evidence, out of the ordinary road. **1687** SEDLEY *Bellamira* IV. i. Wks. (1766) 162 If I light of him I'll tear his goatish eyes out. **1738** WESLEY *Wks.* (1830) I. 38, I called at Alringham, and there lit upon a Quaker. **1779** JOHNSON *Let. to Mrs. Thrale* 16 Oct., How did you light on your specifick for the tooth-ach? **1839–41** S. WARREN *Ten Thous. a Year* I. i. 7 His eye lit on his ring. **1849** C. BRONTË *Shirley* I. iv. 76 He..opened it [a Bible] like at a chance, and was sure to light of a verse..that set all straight. **1867** FREEMAN *Norm. Conq.* (1876) I. App. (1876) 547, I have as yet only once lighted on the word in the singular.

e. To come or fall *into* a person's hands; to chance *into* a person's company. Now *rare* or *Obs.*

1562 COOPER *Answ. Priv. Masse* Pref., One of the Copies of this answere by occasion, as it fortuned..lighted into my hands. **1651** tr. *De-las-Coveras' Don Fenise* 75 The letters which Teodore had sent were read, the which light in her hands unknowne to her father. **1672** MARVELL *Corr.* ccv. Wks. 1872–5 II. 405 Upon Thursday last I accidentally did light into Sir Philip Frowd's company. **1684–5** SOUTH *Serm.* (1823) I. 221 A man by mere peradventure lights into company. **1833** HT. MARTINEAU *Briery Creek* iv. 77 A philosopher suddenly lighting in an infant community instead of having grown up out of it.

f. To turn out (well, happily); also *simply*, to fall out, happen, occur. Now *dial.*

1607–12 BACON *Ess., Beauty* (Arb.) 212 Beautie..for the most part it makes a dissolute youth, and an age a litle out of countenance: But yet certainlie againe if it light well, it maketh vertues shyne, and vices blushe. *a* **1661** FULLER *Worthies, Oxford* (1840) III. 6 To return to our English proverb, ('He looks as the devil over Lincoln') it is conceived of more antiquity than either of the fore-named colleges, though the secondary sense thereof lighted not unhappily, and that it related originally to the cathedral church in Lincoln. *c* **1746** J. COLLIER (Tim Bobbin) *View Lanc. Dial* To Rdr., Wks. (1862) 34 Let't leet heaw't will. **1790** MRS. WHEELER *Westmld. Dial.* (1821) 62 Haw leet it preia, dud it ivver run oway afore? **1844** DISRAELI *Coningsby* VII. ii, Whatever lights, we will stand together.

III. †**11.** *intr.* The analogy of the phrase 'to light *from* a horse' (see 6) suggested the use of the same vb. with preps. of opposite meaning to express the notion antithetic to this. Hence arose the sense: To mount *on* horseback, *into* the saddle, etc. *Obs.*

a **1450** *Le Morte Arth.* 3355 Wrothely in-to hys sadylle he lyght. *c* **1489** CAXTON *Sonnes of Aymon* i. 36 Soo lyghted anone on horsebak the goode duke Aymon. **1509** HAWES *Past. Pleas.* xxxv. (Percy Soc.) 178, I toke my leave and on my stede I lyght. *c* **1555** MACHYN *Diary* (Camden) 54 He lycted be-hynd a gentleman unto the cowrte. **1570** LEVINS *Manip.* 119/28 To Light on horse, *ascendere.*

light (laɪt), *v.*[2] Pa. t. and pa. pple. lighted, lit. Forms: 1 líhtan, lýhtan, 3 lihte(n, li3te, leiten, *Orm.* lihhtenn, 4 li3t, liht, lith, 4–5 lighte, 4–6 lyght, *Sc.* licht, lycht, 5 lyghteyn, (9 *dial.* leet), 4– light. *3rd sing. pres. ind.* 1 líht, lýht, 3 liht, licht, 4 *Kent.* let. *Pa. t. α.* 1 líhte, lýhte, 3 lihte. *β.* 2 lihtede 4 li3tede, 4–6 *Sc.* lychtit, -yt, 4– lighted; 8 litt, 6– lit. *Pa. pple. α.* 3 liht, 3–4 ili3t, 4 i-ly3ht, li3t, 4–5 lyght, (5 lyghth), 4–8 light. *β.* 3 *Orm.* lihhtedd, 4–5 li3tid, 6 lyghted, -yd, *Sc.* lychtet, lichtit, 4– lighted; 6– lit. *γ.* 9 pseudo-*arch.* litten. [OE. *líhtan* = OS. *liuhtian* (MDu. *lichten, luchten*, Du. *lichten*), OHG. *liuhten* (mod.G. *leuchten*), Goth. *liuhtjan*:—OTeut. **liuhtjan*, f. **leuhto-* LIGHT *sb.* or *a.*[2]]

†**1. a.** *intr.* To give or shed light; to shine; to be alight or burning. Also, to lighten. *Obs.*

c **1000** *Ags. Gosp.* John i. 5 þæt leoht lyht on ðystrum. *c* **1000** ÆLFRIC *Gram.* xxii. (Z.) 128 *Fulminat*, hit liht. *c* **1250** *Kent. Serm.* in *O.E. Misc.* 27 Si gode beleaue licht and is bricht ine þo herte of þo gode Manne ase gold. *c* **1290** *Beket* 1382 þe cloudene hire [*sc.* þe sonne] ouer-cast þat-heo ne mai no leng li3te. *c* **1300** *Cursor M.* 24942 þe lem can light, þe storm it fel. *c* **1374** CHAUCER *Boeth.* III. metr. xi. 79 (Camb. MS.) Thilke thing that the blake cloude of errour whilom hadde y-couered, shal lyhten more clerly thanne phebus hym self ne shyneth. *c* **1386** —— *Pars. T.* ⁋963 Right so shal youre light lighten bifore men. **14..** *Ave Regina* in *Tundale's Vis.* (1843) 146 Heyle tho lampe that euer is lyghtand To hye and lowe to ryche and pore. **1646** CRASHAW *Steps, Ps.* xxiii. 66 A beame that falls, Fresh from the pure glance of Thine eye, Lighting to Eternity. *a* **1774** GOLDSM. tr. *Scarron's Com. Romance* (1775) II. 185 And that instant the taper which was lighting in the room was burnt out.

†**b.** Of day, etc.: To grow light. Sometimes conjugated with *to be*. *Obs.*

a **1000** *Cædmon's Dan.* 158 (Gr.) þa dæ3 lyte. *c* **1205** LAY. 28314 Ase þe dæi gon lihte heo bigunnen to fihten. **1382** WYCLIF *2 Sam.* xvii. 22 To the tyme that the dai were li3tid [Vulg. *donec dilucesceret*]. **1596** SHAKS. *1 Hen. IV*, III. ii. 138 And that shall be the Day, when ere it lights [etc.].

2. a. *trans.* To set burning (a candle, lamp, torch); to kindle (a fire); to apply a light to (a combustible); to ignite. (Pa. pple. *lighted, lit*, †*light* = alight.) Also with *up*. † ***to light off***: to ignite as an explosive.

1154 *O.E. Chron.* an. 1140 (Laud MS.) Me lihtede candles to æten bi. *a* **1225** *Leg. Kath.* 1411 And tis ferliche fur schal lihten in ow þe halwende lei of þe hali gast. *c* **1300** *Havelok* 585 Blou the fir, and lith a kandel. *c* **1375** *Sc. Leg. Saints* xvii. (*Martha*) 176 þe sergis al scho lychtyt, bathe gret & smal. *a* **1400–50** *Alexander* 4231–2 Many li3tis of a li3t is li3tid othire-quile, And 3 it þe li3t at þam li3tis is li3tid as before. *c* **1400** *Destr. Troy* 11792 No fyre wold be light; þat assait was full sothely of sere men full ofte. *a* **1450** *Knt. de la Tour* (1868) 23 He fonde..the candelle light. **1506** in *Mem. Hen. VII* (Rolls) 282 Having great torches lit in his and divers other ships. *a* **1547** BALE *Image both Ch.* xiii. (1550) f 1, The candle that he lyght vs to se ouer the house. **1590** SPENSER *F.Q.* I. v. 19 Shyning lampes in Joves high house were light. **1604** E. GRIMSTONE *Hist. Siege Ostend* 219 With ..their matches light, Bullet in the mouth. **1645** WALLER *Of the Queen* 14 Thither my Muse, like bold Prometheus, flyes To light her torch at Gloriana's eyes. **1649** ROBERTS *Clavis Bibl.* Introd. ii. 29 What brightnesse is this I see? Have you light up any Candles? **1711** ADDISON *Spect.* No. 46 ⁋4, I twisted it into a kind of Match, and litt my Pipe with it. **1717** *Entertainer* No. 5 (1718) 28 Like Gunpowder, when they are lighted off, they [the mob] scatter Ruin and Destruction around them. **1763** in Brand *Hist. Newcastle* (1789) I. 20 *note*, The lamps put up in the streets..were lighted up for the first time. **1852** MRS. STOWE *Uncle Tom's C.* xxxvi, How would ye like to be tied to a tree, and have a slow fire lit up around ye? **1854** W. COLLINS *Hide & Seek* II. ix. (1861) 235 'He's the most generous fellow in the world', continued Zack, lighting a cigar. **1856** EMERSON *Eng. Traits, Universities* Wks. (Bohn) II. 91 No candle or fire is ever lighted in the Bodleian. **1890** HAGGARD & LANG *World's Desire* 128 A lamp for our feet the Lord hath litten.

b. *transf.* and *fig.*

1679 DRYDEN & LEE *Œdipus* II. 28 If an immodest thought, or low desire, Inflam'd my breast, since first our Loves were lighted. **1752** YOUNG *Brothers* IV. i, Each morn my life I lighted at her eye. **1866** B. TAYLOR *Anastasia* Poems 267 Thine eyes were lit from other skies. **1883** B. W. RICHARDSON *Field of Disease* 211 It [Phthisis]..in nine cases out of ten is first lighted up by cold.

c. absol. ***to light up***: to light one's pipe, cigar, etc. *colloq.*

1861 HUGHES *Tom Brown at Oxf.* xlix, 'I suppose I may light up', said Drysdale..pulling out his cigar-case. **1943** J. B. PRIESTLEY *Daylight on Saturday* ix. 55 Blandford opened ..a very fine silver cigarette-box, and both men lit up and were then silent. **1959** C. WILLIAMS *Man in Motion* i. 6, I ripped open a packet of the cigarettes, found some matches ..and lighted up. **1970** H. E. ROBERTS *Third Ear* 9/2 *Light up*, to light a marijuana cigarette.

d. *intr.* To take fire, be lighted; *transf.* to 'kindle', become suffused with light.

c **1400** MAUNDEV. (1839) v. 60 His Lampe schal lighte.. withouten touchinge of ony Man. **1820–71** MISS CARY *Poems* (1876) 94 The eve had just begun to light, Along the lovely west. **1845** MRS. S. C. HALL *Whiteboy* xi. 97 A sky, just lighting into a pale, bright gray—an intimation of the first dawn of morning.

fig. **1860** GEO. ELIOT *Mill on Fl.* II. iv. 'You poor-spirited imp,' said Tom, lighting up immediately at Philip's fire.

3. a. *trans.* To give light to (a room or the like); to make light or luminous; to illuminate; *esp.* to furnish with the ordinary means of illumination. (Rarely with *up*.)

c **1200** ORMIN 7279 Crist iss ec soþ sunnebæm þatt all þiss werelld lihhteþþ. *c* **1205** LAY. 25595 Mid his feure he lihte al þis lond-riche. *c* **1250** *Hymn Virgin* 12 in *Trin. Coll. Hom.* App. 255 A leome newe þat al þis world haueð ili3t. *c* **1385** CHAUCER *L.G.W.* 2506 *Phillis*, The mone hath..Syn that thylke day..foure tymes lyght the worlde ageyn. *c* **1400** *Destr. Troy* 6038 Torchis and tendlis the tenttes to light. **1509** HAWES *Past. Pleas.* I. x, Cleare Dyana..Gan for to ryse, lyghtyng our emispery. **1593** SHAKS. *Rich. II*, III. ii. 38 When the searching Eye of Heauen is hid Behind the Globe, that lights the lower world. **1715** *Notice* in *Lond. Gaz.* No. 5351/3 They intend to..grant Liberty for Lighting the City of London. **1802** CAMPBELL *Hohenlinden* ii, Commanding fires of death to light The darkness of her scenery. **1840** *Penny Cycl.* XVIII. 292/1 St. Andrew's church..is lighted with gas. **1849** MACAULAY *Hist. Eng.* iii. I. 362 Letters patent conveying to him for a term of years, the exclusive right of lighting up London. **1860** *Merc. Marine Mag.* VII. 216 The Irish Channel is well lighted. **1870** MORRIS *Earthly Par.* II. III. 184 When the Had..reached the hut now litten bright. **1875** HOWELLS *Foregone Concl.* 3 An apartment so brightly lit by a window looking on the sunny canal.

b. ***to light up***: to furnish or fill with abundance of light; to illuminate in a special manner; to bring into prominence by means of light.

1711 ADDISON *Spect.* No. 50 ⁋7 A huge Room lighted up with abundance of Candles. *Ibid.* No. 90 ⁋7 The Room was lighted up on all Sides. **1824** W. IRVING *T. Trav.* II. 146 Lit up by the rising moon. **1855** MACAULAY *Hist. Eng.* xi. III. 1 In the evening every window from Whitechapel to Piccadilly was lighted up. **1884** 'RITA' *Vivienne* II. iii, The spring sunshine lit up the grey towers.

fig. **1859** JEPHSON *Brittany* xi. 180 Once you can succeed in lighting up their imaginations.

c. *transf.* (Chiefly with ***up***.) To cause (the eyes, features) as it were to gleam with animation or lively expression. Also, to brighten up (writing). Also *intr.* for *refl.* or *passive.*

a **1766** MRS. F. SHERIDAN *Mem. Sidn. Biddulph* IV. 77 Her expressive features all lit up with Joy. **1787** MAD. D'ARBLAY *Diary* 13 July, A ray of genius..instantly lights up his whole countenance. **1800** MRS. HERVEY *Mourtray Fam.* I. 269 Her eyes lighted with pleasure. **1826** DISRAELI *Viv. Grey* v. viii, A smile, rather of pity than derision, lighted up her face. **1854** H. ROGERS *Ess.* (1860) II. 20 The style of Locke is..perpetually lighted up with vivacious illustration. **1855** A. MANNING *Old Chelsea Bun-house* vii. 110, I never saw a Face light up with Joy as Gatty's did, that Moment. **1867** FREEMAN *Norm. Conq.* (1876) I. App. 694 He lights up and gives us a spirited account. **1888** BESANT *Inner House* ii. 34, I see the faces of all light up with satisfaction. **1888** BURGON *Lives 12 Gd. Men* II. xii. 349 All his face [would] become lighted up with the fun of the story.

4. To give light to (a person) so as to enable him to see what he is doing; hence, to show the way to. *lit.* and *fig.* Also *absol.*

c **1200** ORMIN 19089 Soþ lihht..þat lihhteþ all þatt lihhtedd iss, To gan þe rihhte we33e. **1422** tr. *Secreta Secret., Priv. Priv.* 206 Prayer..lightyth a man to the lowe of god. **1551** RECORDE *Pathw. Knowl.* To Rdr., If my light may so light some other, to espie and marke my faultes. **1565** COOPER *Thesaurus*, s.v. *Fax, Præferre facem adolescentulo ad libidinem*, To be an example or sterer of a yonge man to lecherie..as it were to light him the way. **1604** E. G[RIMSTONE] *D'Acosta's Hist. Indies* IV. viii. 230 Those that labour therein, vse candles to light them. **1605** SHAKS. *Macb.* v. v. 22. **1609** T. COCKS *Diary* (1901) 83 Given the Sonne [inn] boye Pawle for lightinge mee home j^d. **1664** BUTLER *Hud.* II. iii. 817 Were the Stars only made to light Robbers and Burglarers by night? **1665** BOYLE *Occas. Refl.* III. ii, Methinks the blaze of this Fire should light me to discern something instructive in it. *c* **1700** EARL MONTAGU in *Buccleuch MSS.* (Hist. MSS. Comm.) I. 350 A Dutch lanthorn of horn upon a great stick, to light before a coach when it is dark. *a* **1766** MRS. F. SHERIDAN *Mem. Sidn. Biddulph* V. 267 A little spark of that virtue which..might have lit me to happiness and honour. **18..** *Oranges & Lemons* in Mrs. Gomme *Tradit. Games* (1898) II. 27 Here comes a candle to light you to bed. **1858** HAWTHORNE *Fr. & It. Jrnls.* I. 121 Poetical faith enough to light her cheerfully through all these mists of incredulity.

5. To enlighten or illumine spiritually or intellectually. ? *Obs.* or *arch.*

c **1175** *Lamb. Hom.* 63 þet he..mid his halie gast us lihte. *c* **1200** ORMIN 18990 All mannkinn iss lihhtedd þurrh fulluhht & þurrh Crisstenndom. *c* **1320** *Cast. Love* 793 That is the clere love and bry3ht That heo is alle with i-ly3ht. *c* **1386** CHAUCER *Sec. Nun's T.* 71 And of thy light my soule in prison lighte. **1422** tr. *Secreta Secret., Priv. Priv.* 133 God ..light 3oure resoun, and make cleer 3oure vnderstondynge. **1535** COVERDALE *Heb.* vi. 4 They which were once lighted & haue taisted of the heauenly gyfte. **1552** ABP. HAMILTON *Catech.* (1884) 42 Your hartis salbe lichtit with the licht of grace. **1819** HEBER *Hymn, 'From Greenland's icy mountains'*, We, whose souls are lighted With Wisdom from on high.

6. *absol.* To dispose the light in a picture.

1889 *Pall Mall G.* 18 Jan. 3/1 Rembrandt lighted falsely for the sake of effect.

light, erroneous spelling of *lite*, LEET *sb.*[2]

1833 *Rep. Sel. Committee on Municipal Corporations* 304 [At Hull] the mayor and alderman put out two names called lights, on a vacancy for alderman. *Ibid.* 305 The chamberlains [of Hull]..are chosen by the burgesses out of four lights.

lightable (ˈlaɪtəb(ə)l), *a.* [f. LIGHT *v.*[2] + -ABLE.] That can be lighted.

1882 in OGILVIE.

lightage (ˈlaɪtɪdʒ). [f. LIGHT *sb.*[2] + -AGE.]

†**1.** A toll paid by a ship coming to a port where there is a lighthouse. *Obs.*

1606 *Charter* in Brand *Hist. Newcastle* (1789) II. 701 Two ..Light Houses att the North Sheiles..and for lights to be kept in them..an ancient..duetie called Lightage..of every English shipp..4*d*. **1789** BRAND *ibid.* II. 714 *note*, Lightage, six-pence for an English vessel.

2. Provision of (artificial) light.

1862 *Edin. Rev.* Jan. 184 On the whole there exists a tolerably efficient system of lightage, buoyage, and beaconage.

light-armed, *a.* [LIGHT *adv.*[1]] Bearing light armour or arms.

1618 BOLTON *Florus* III. x. (1630) 205 Hee with light armed bands of Souldiers got into Gall. **1772** *Ann. Reg.* 234 We..Are but the light-arm'd rangers on the scout. **1814** SCOTT *Ld. of Isles* III. x, England's light-arm'd vessels ride, Not distant far, the waves of Clyde.

fig. **1645** MILTON *Colast.* 2, I still was waiting, when these light-arm'd refuters would have don pelting. **1728** POPE *Dunc.* I. 306 Lead on my sons, Light-arm'd with Points, Antitheses, and Puns.

†ˈ**light-bed,** *v.* *Obs.* *rare*[−1]. [f. LIGHT *adv.*[1] + BED *sb.*] *intr.* Of a vessel: To ground lightly as on a bed of earth.

1611 SPEED *Theat. Gt. Brit.* xiv. (1614) 27/1 He flying before Cæsar..light-bedded upon a shelfe in the Sea.

ˈ**light-bob.** [BOB *sb.*[7]] (See quot. 1785.)

1785 GROSE *Dict. Vulgar Tongue, Light bob*, a soldier of the light infantry company. **1802** in C. JAMES *Milit. Dict.* **1821** *Blackw. Mag.* X. 618 Our active light-bobs, and our bold

grenadiers. **1828** *Ibid.* XXXIII. 189 On then we went,.. great guns and small, lightbob and grenadier.

light cheap: see LIGHT *a.*[1] 13 b.

lighted ('laɪtɪd), *ppl. a.* [f. LIGHT *v.*[2] + -ED[1].] Kindled; illuminated.

1616 J. LANE *Cont. Sqr.'s T.* VII. 530 Hee vsd this stratagem or warr, to sticke vp lighted mattches, which [etc.]. **1706** [E. WARD] *Wooden World Dissected* (1708) 64 Searching.. with a lyghted Candle. **1832** TENNYSON *Lady of Shalott* iv, In the lighted palace near Died the sound of royal cheer. **1884** J. C. SHAIRP *Sketches* (1887) 339 Every one with his lighted torch.

† **'lighten**, *sb. Obs.* In 4-5 **leighten**, 8 *Sc.* **lichten**. [f. LIGHTEN *v.*[2]] Lightning.

c **1400** MAUNDEV. (Roxb.) xiv. 65 In somer es þer grete thundres and leightens [*ed.* 1839 Leytes]. **1791** LEARMONT *Poems* 12 (E.D.D.) Swift as the lichtens fly, Whan thunners crash the clouds aboon.

lighten ('laɪt(ə)n), *v.*[1] Forms: 4 **lihtne**, 4-5 **lyghtyn**, 5 **lightyn**, **liten**, 4- **lighten**. [f. LIGHT *a.*[1] + -EN[5]; in sense 5 perh. rather an extension of LIGHT *v.*[1], the inf. termination *-en* being taken as part of the stem.]

I. 1. *trans.* To reduce or remove the load of (a ship, etc.); to relieve *of* a burden, or something regarded as a burden. Also *intr.* for *pass.*

a **1375** *Joseph Arim.* 644 Heo was lihtned of hire euel in a luytel stounde. **1435** MISYN *Fire of Love* II. xi. 100 Lufe.. is a lyght byrdyn, þe berar not chargeand bot lightynand. **1535** COVERDALE *Jonah* i. 5 The goodes that were in the shippe, they cast in to the see, to lighten it off them. **1590** SPENSER *F.Q.* I. x. 16 She of late is lightned of her wombe. **1615** W. LAWSON *Country Housew. Garden* (1626) 2 In Winter your yong trees and herbs would be lightned of Snow, and your Allyes cleansed. *a* **1700** DRYDEN *Ovid's Met.* xv. *Pythag. Philos.* 606 He lightens of its Load the Tree. **1760-72** H. BROOKE *Fool of Qual.* (1809) II. 114 Clement, with his young pupil, came home, quite lightened of the money they had taken abroad. **1807** E. S. BARRETT *Rising Sun* III. 88 We ought to return our grateful thanks to heaven, for having lightened us from so horrid a charge. **1871** L. STEPHEN *Playgr. Europe* iv. III. 236 To lighten the cart.. I descended and walked on ahead. **1885** *Law Rep.* 14 Q. Bench Div. 517 When vessels.. were of too heavy a burthen to come up the canal they were lightened at Sharpness. **1891** *Daily News* 3 Nov. 3/7 The steamer Amaryllis.. is ashore at Savannah. She will have to lighten before she can get off.

2. To remove a burden from, relieve (the heart or mind); †to cheer, comfort (*obs.*). Now *rare.*

c **1430** *Syr Gener.* (Roxb.) 2410 Whos comyng lightned his hert somdele. **1590** SHAKS. *Com. Err.* I. ii. 21 A trustie vilaine.. that.. Lightens my humour with his merry iests. **1666** BUNYAN *Grace Ab.* ¶258, I was greatly lightened in my mind. **1855** MACAULAY *Hist. Eng.* xvii. IV. 61 To lighten his conscience.

b. *intr.* for *refl.* or *pass.* Somewhat *rare.*

a **1400** *Sir Perc.* 2219 His hert lightened in hy Blythe for to bee. *a* **1450** *Knt. de la Tour* (1863) Prol. 1 Thaire suete songe made my herte to lighten. **1860** TYNDALL *Glac.* I. xi. 74 As I looked aloft.. my heart lightened.

3. *trans.* To reduce the weight of; to make lighter or less heavy (in various senses of the adjs.); to alleviate, mitigate.

1483 *Cath. Angl.* 216/2 To Lyghtyn, *alleuiare*, or to make lightt. **1570** LEVINS *Manip.* 61/27 To Lighten, *leuigare.* **1576** *Act 18 Eliz.* c. 1 §1 Yf any person.. deminishe.. or lighten the proper Moneys.. of this Realme. **1665** BOYLE *Occas. Refl.* I. v, His fellow's Burthen lightens not his Load. **1667** MILTON *P.L.* x. 960 How we may light'n Each others burden in our share of woe. **1670** MARVELL *Corr.* cxlvii. Wks. 1872-5 II. 325 The King.. resolved.. to weigh up and lighten the Duke's efficacy, by coming himself in person. **1781** C. JOHNSTON *Hist. Juniper Jack* II. I. vii. 57 The manner of this address was far from lightening Juniper's embarrassment. **1793** *Trans. Soc. Arts* XI. 114 A stiff loam, lightened with rotten sawdust. **1833** HT. MARTINEAU *Vanderput & S.* ii. 26 He lightens their labour. **1843** LEVER *J. Hinton* xxi. (1878) 144 To lighten the road by song and story. **1860** TYNDALL *Glac.* I. xvi. 110 We.. paused to lighten our burdens and to refresh ourselves. **1871** R. ELLIS tr. *Catullus* ii. 8 Heavier ache perhaps to lighten. **1879** *Cassell's Techn. Educ.* IV. 48/2 This has the effect of lightening the appearance. **1885** *Manch. Exam.* 28 Mar. 5/5 The task of lightening the burdens of the.. ratepayers.

†**b.** To remove the weight of; to lessen the pressure of. *Obs.*

1611 BIBLE *1 Sam.* vi. 5 Peraduenture hee will lighten his hand from off you. [A literalism of translation.] **1797** *Encycl. Brit.* (ed. 3) VI. 670/2 By lightening or sinking the graver with the hand, according to the occasion. *Ibid.* 671/1 The hand should be lightened in such a manner, that [etc.].

c. To make agile or nimble. *rare.*

1599 SHAKS. *Much Ado* v. iv. 120 Let's haue a dance.. that we may lighten our own hearts, and our wiues heeles. **1727** BAILEY vol. II, To *Lighten a Horse*.. is to make a Horse light in the Fore-hand, i.e. to make him freer and lighter in the Fore-hand than behind.

4. *intr.* To grow lighter.

1720 DE FOE *Capt. Singleton* v. (1840) 85 Their luggage.. lightened every day. **1862** TYNDALL *Mountaineer.* iv. 28 Until the rain seemed to lighten.

†**II. 5.** To descend, alight; to light *upon. Obs.*

The well-known passage in the *Te Deum* (quot. 1548-9) is perh. now commonly understood as containing LIGHTEN *v.*[2]

a **1425** *Cursor M.* 11258 (Trin.) While þis aungel tiþing tolde Oþere li3ten [*Cott.* lighted] doun mony folde. *c* **1440** *Gesta Rom.* xliv. 172 (Harl. MS.) þe holy gost shalle liten in the as a shadow. **1548-9** (Mar.) *Bk. Com. Prayer, Te Deum*, O Lorde, let thy mercy lighten upon us [L. *fiat, Domine, misericordia super nos*]. **1704** RAY *Creation* I. 150 They fly out of Italy into Africk: lightning many times on Ships in the midst of the Sea, to rest themselves when tir'd and spent with flying.

lighten ('laɪt(ə)n), *v.*[2] Forms: 4 **li3tne**, **ly3tne**, **li3ten**, **-on**, **-yn**, 5 **ly3tnyn**, **lyghtenyn**, (**lithnyn**), **li3tny**, **lighton**, **li3thon**, **lyten**, 4-6 **lyghten**, 6 *Sc.* **lichtin**, **lychtin**, 3- **lighten**. [f. LIGHT *a.*[2] + -EN[5].]

1. *trans.* To shed light upon; to give light to; to make bright or luminous; to light up, brighten. Also *fig.* or in fig. context.

a **1300** *Cursor M.* 18600 þe dai bitakens þe ded of him þat lightend [*Fairf.* li3tened] has ur ded sa dim. *a* **1340** HAMPOLE *Ps.* lxvi. 1 God.. lighten his face on vs [Vulg. *illuminet vultum suum*]. **1382** WYCLIF *Rev.* xxi. 23 The cleerte of God shal li3ten [**1388** li3tne] it. *c* **1386** CHAUCER *Frankl. T.* 322 Hir desir Is to be quyked and lightned of youre fir [*v.rr.* lyghtenyd, li3tned, lighted]. *c* **1400** MAUNDEV. (Roxb.) xxv. 117 þis charbuncle lightnez all þe chaumbre on þe nyght. **1502** ATKINSON tr. *De Imitatione* III. xlviii. 235 Than shall Iherusalem be lyghtened & enserched with lanternes & lyghtes. **1530** PALSGR. 611/2, I lyghten, I fyll or store a place with lyght, *je enlumine.* **1563** WINȜET *Wks.* (1890) II. 77 Sanct Xistus the Pape, quha now rycht wirschepful lychtnis [L. *illustrat*] the Roman Kirk. **1588** SPENSER *Virg. Gnat* 341 Lightned with deadly lamps on everie post. **1666** DRYDEN *Ann. Mirab.* ccxxxi, A key of fire ran all along the shore And lightened all the river with a blaze. **1766** ENTICK *London* IV. 7 The body of the church is lightened by a series of.. arched windows. **1860** PUSEY *Min. Proph.* 348 The darkness of the captivity was lightened by the light of the prophetic grace which shone through Daniel and Ezekiel. **1880** E. WHITE *Cert. Relig.* 32 That Lord of theirs who lightens the earth with his glory. **1887** HALL CAINE *Deemster* x. 65 Pavement of deep black, lightened only by the image of a star.

b. To cause (the countenance or looks) to light up with lively expression, etc. Also *intr.* for *pass.* of the face, eyes, etc.

1795 *Gentl. Mag.* 544/1 To lighten up the clouded countenances of a dull society. **1856** KANE *Arct. Expl.* II. xvi. 175 The gloom of several countenances was perceptibly lightened. **1867** OUIDA *C. Castlemaine* (1879) 9 The beauty, whose eyes he had seen lighten and proud brow flush. **1890** 'ROLF BOLDREWOOD' *Col. Reformer* (1891) 168 His eye lightened, and the old gleam of pride.. spoke from it.

†**2.** In Biblical lang.: To remove blindness or dimness from (the eyes); to restore sight to. *Obs.*

a **1340** HAMPOLE *Psalter* xviii. 9 þe comaundment of lord shynand, lightenand eghen. *c* **1374** CHAUCER *Boeth.* IV. pr. iv. 99 (Camb. MS.) They ben lyke to bryddes of which the nyht lyhtneth hir lookynge. **1388** WYCLIF *Tobit* xiv. 1 Aftir that he was li3tned he lyuede two and fourti 3eer. *c* **1440** *Gesta Rom.* xlvi. 195 (Harl. MS.) þenne whenne þou ert vp Risen fro slepe of synne, and art I-litenyd, & mayste see. **1535** COVERDALE *Ps.* xii[i]. 3 Lighten myne eyes, that I slepe not in death.

3. To shed spiritual light upon; to enlighten or illuminate spiritually. *arch.*

1395 PURVEY *Remonstr.* (1851) 63 Othere bisshopis ben more lightnid of God in kunnynge and holynesse. *c* **1440** HYLTON *Scala Perf.* (W. de W. 1494) II. xxx, He lyghtned her reason & kyndeled her affeccion. **1502** ATKINSON tr. *De Imitatione* I. xiv. 163 It shalbe longe or thou be gostly lyghtned. **1548-9** (Mar.) *Bk. Com. Prayer, Collect St. John Evang.*, Beeyng lyghtened by the doctryne of thy blessed Apostle and Euangelyste John. **1549** COVERDALE, etc. *Erasm. Par. Rom.* 23 The holy psalme wryter Dauid lightened with the spirite of god. **1550** HUTCHINSON *Image of God* xviii. (1560) 94 The man which falleth after he is lightened, is not without al possibilitie of amendement. **1597** SHAKS. *2 Hen. IV*, II. i. 208 Now the Lord lighten thee, thou art a great Foole. **1609** BIBLE (Douay) *Ezek.* xliii. comm., Al the world is lightned by the preaching of Christs Apostles. **1682** BUNYAN *Holy War* 180 Oh! how they were lightened! they saw what they never saw. **1840** I. WILLIAMS *Hymn*, 'O *heavenly Jerusalem*', To Christ the Sun that lightens His Church above, below.

†**4.** To kindle, ignite; = LIGHT *v.*[2] 2. *Obs.*

a **1340** HAMPOLE *Psalter* xvii. 31 þou lightnys my lantern. *a* **1400** *Prymer* (1891) 46 Li3tne the fier of thi loue in hem. **1490** CAXTON *Eneydos* xv. 58 Venus lyghtened the torches for to receyue hiemen the god of weddynge. *a* **1568** ASCHAM *Scholem.* (Arb.) 56 Who haue had in so fewe yeares the Candel of Goddes worde so oft lightned, so oft put out. *c* **1645** HOWELL *Lett.* (1650) III. 8 As one Taper lightneth another.

5. *intr.* To shine, flash, burn brightly; to be or grow luminous, to glow with light.

1382 WYCLIF *Gen.* i. 15 And li3tne thei in the firmament of heuene and li3tne thei the erthe. *c* **1400** *Destr. Troy* 4630 With a launchant laite lightonyd the water. *a* **1611** BEAUM. & FL. *Maid's Trag.* I. ii, The east begins to lighten. **1665** BOYLE *Occas. Refl.* 222 The Blood that lightens in their Cheeks. **1715-20** POPE *Iliad* x. 155 His steely lance, that lighten'd as he pass'd. **1813** SCOTT *Rokeby* I. xxix, He will wait the hour, When her lamp lightens in the tower. **1854** H. MILLER *Sch. & Schm.* (1858) 350 The low-browed clouds.. that lightened and darkened by fits as the flames rose and fell. **1871** SWINBURNE *Songs bef. Sunrise, Prelude* 120 Her mystic face Lightened along the streams of Thrace.

b. To shine like light *on.* (Cf. quot. 1548-9 under LIGHTEN *v.*[1] 5.)

1814 CARY *Dante, Par.* xxvii. 88 From her radiant smiles, ..pleasure so divine Did lighten on me [orig. 95 *lo piacer divin che mi rifulse*].

6. To flash lightning, to emit flashes of lightning. Chiefly *impers.*

c **1440** *Promp. Parv.* 304/1 Lyghtenyn, or leuenyn (*K.* lithnyn, *as* levyn), *coruscat.* **1470-85** MALORY *Arthur* VII. xxxi, It lyghtned and thondred as it had ben woode. **1555** EDEN *Decades* 244 The heauen neuer ceased thunderyng rorynge & lyghtenynge with terrible noyse. **1611** BIBLE *Luke* xvii. 24 As the lightning that lighteneth out of the one part vnder heauen, shineth vnto the other part vnder heauen. *a* **1637** B. JONSON *Underwoods, Elegy*, ''*Tis true, I'm broke*', God lightens not at mans each fraile offence. **1725** DE FOE *Voy. round World* (1840) 351 Two of the men.. cried out, it lightened. One said, he saw the flash. **1814** SCOTT *Wav.* xviii, It may thunder and lighten before the close of evening. **1819** BYRON *Juan* I. clviii, Her dark eyes flashing through their tears Like skies that rain and lighten. **1896** A. E. HOUSMAN *Shropsh. Lad* l, Where doomsday may thunder and lighten And little 'twill matter to one.

fig. **1722** MRS. E. HAYWOOD *Brit. Recluse* (ed. 2) 132 Scorn lighten'd in her Glances!

7. *trans.* To cause to flash *out* or *forth*; to send *down* as lightning. (*lit.* and *fig.*)

c **1586** C'TESS PEMBROKE *Ps.* LXIX. x, Lighten indignation downe. **1589** GREENE *Menaphon* (Arb.) 27 Shee lightened out smiles from those cheekes. *c* **1590** —— *Fr. Bacon* (1630) A 2, Her sparkling eyes Doe lighten forth sweet Loues alluring fire. **1592** DANIEL *Compl. Rosamond* 11 Wks. (1717) 44 How that thy King.. Lightens forth Glory on thy dark Estate. **1593** SHAKS. *Rich. II*, III. iii. 69. **1627** *Lisander & Cal.* v. 87 Calista nourished an enemy in her house, who lightened forth.. miserable effects in small time after.

lighten, obs. pa. pple. of LIGHT *v.*[1]

lightened ('laɪt(ə)nd), *ppl. a.*[1] [f. LIGHTEN *v.*[1] + -ED[1].] Made light; relieved of a burden.

1700 DRYDEN *Flower & L.* 297 Some tumbled Horse and Man; Around the Fields the lighten'd Coursers ran. **1886** MISS BROUGHTON *Dr. Cupid* III. viii. 171 Peggy returns from it with a considerably lightened heart.

lightened ('laɪt(ə)nd), *ppl. a.*[2] [f. LIGHTEN *v.*[2] + -ED[1].] Enlightened.

1578 J. HOCKWOOD *Serm.* 24 Aug. 28 Moste lighthened, I woulde saye, most Seraphicall Doctors. **1742** YOUNG *Nt. Th.* III. 383 On lighten'd Minds, that bask in Virtue's Beams. **1900** BULLEN *With Christ at Sea* v. 94 To help a fellow wayfarer out of darkness into the Lightened Way of Life.

lightener[1] ('laɪt(ə)nə(r)). [f. LIGHTEN *v.*[1] + -ER[1].]

1. One who lightens, makes light, easy, or less grievous; an alleviator.

c **1611** CHAPMAN *Iliad* Ep. Ded. 78 Learning and her lightener Poesy. **1760-72** H. BROOKE *Fool of Qual.* (1809) II. 108 A sweet lightener of my afflictions. **1789** MAD. D'ARBLAY *Diary* 9 Jan., What a lightener.. would it not be, to this burthening period. **1884** SALA *Journ. due South* I. iv. (1887) 55 An accomplished lightener of the traveller's purse.

†**2.** = LIGHTER *sb.*[1] *Obs.* (*north. dial.*)

1558 *Wills & Inv. N.C.* (Surtees 1835) 168, ij kealles & a half a lightner & a botte. **1592** *Ibid.* 252 My clinkere lightner, with all her geare. **1789** BRAND *Hist. Newcastle* II. 261 *note*, Their [the keelmen's] vessels are called keels or lightners.

lightener[2] ('laɪt(ə)nə(r)). [f. LIGHTEN *v.*[2] + -ER[1].] One who lightens or illuminates; an illuminator; one who flashes lightning.

1382 WYCLIF *Prov.* xxix. 13 The pore and the creaunsour metten togidere; of either the li3tnere is the Lord. **1513** DOUGLAS *Æneis* I. Prol. 63 Phebus lychtnar of the planetis all. **1587** GOLDING *De Mornay* ii. 20 The same Sunne is the lightner of our eyes. **1678** CUDWORTH *Intell. Syst.* I. iv. §32. 482 The Thunderer and Lightner. **1898** *Academy* 26 Nov. 337/1 Aryan speech could express agents only—rainers, not rain; lighteners, not lightning.

lightening ('laɪt(ə)nɪŋ), *vbl. sb.*[1] [f. LIGHTEN *v.*[1] + -ING[1].]

1. The rendering light or lighter; alleviation (of pain, sorrow); †comforting, cheering.

1530 PALSGR. 239/2 Lightnyng of burdayne, *alegement.* **1561** HOLLYBUSH *Hom. Apoth.* 44 b, He falleth to an amendement and lightening. **1625** *Gonsalvio's Sp. Inquis.* 80 To relieue his pensiue and heauie heart with some kind of lightning. **1655** BRINSLEY *Groan for Israel* 24 The lightning and saving of the Ship. **1796** MORSE *Amer. Geog.* I. 605 The Frier Rodrigue.. carrying 50 [guns], went there without lightening. **1890** *Athenæum* 6 Dec. 769/1 The volumes, which would seem to need no lightening, are further brightened by some amusing letters.

2. *concr.* Leaven. *Obs.* exc. *dial.* (see *E.D.D.*).

1720 GIBSON *Dispensatory* III. §8 (1721) 195 Knead it up with Barm or Lightning, and bake it.

lightening ('laɪt(ə)nɪŋ), *vbl. sb.*[2] See also LIGHTNING *sb.* [f. LIGHTEN *v.*[2] + -ING[1].] The shedding or shining of light; suffusion with light, lighting up; *fig.* enlightenment, illumination.

a **1340** HAMPOLE *Psalter* xxvi. 1 Lord my ly3tnynge: and my heel. *c* **1420** *Prymer* (1895) 14 God, þat tau3test þe hertes of þi trewe seruauntis bi li3tnyng of þe holi goost. *c* **1430** *Hymns Virg.* 45 Bi þe li3tnynge of a sterre To ihesu alle þre presentis þei brou3te. **1526** *Pilgr. Perf.* (W. de W. 1531) 74 Grace is an illumynacyon or lyghtnynge of the soule. **1667** MILTON *P.L.* v. 734 The Son with calm aspect and cleer Light'ning Divine. **1814** SCOTT *Fam. Lett.* (1894) I. x. 318 A lightening in the domestic horizon. **1864** SWINBURNE *Atalanta* 1448 This lightening of clear weather. **1873** MISS BROUGHTON *Nancy* III. 228 A kindling of the eye, and godly lightening of all her gentle face.

b. *a lightening before death*: that exhilaration or revival of the spirits which is supposed to occur in some instances just before death.

Cf. 'a glimmering before death' (Fletcher *Sp. Curate*, IV. v.).

1592 SHAKS. *Rom. & Jul.* v. iii. 90 How oft when men are at the point of death, Haue they beene merrie? Which their Keepers call A lightning before death. *c* **1611** CHAPMAN *Iliad* xv. 213 This lightning flew before his death; which Pallas was to giue. **1641** BROME *Joviall Crew* v. Wks. 1873 III. 441 If it be a lightning before death, the best is, I am his heir. **1654** GAYTON *Pleas. Notes* III. viii. 125 Not that I Lightning or fell Thunder feare, (Unless that Lightning before death appear). **1712** ADDISON *Spect.* No. 517 ¶2 We

were once in great Hopes of his Recovery..but this only proved a Light'ning before Death. **1840** Hood *Up Rhine* 7 The old saying about a lightening before death.

c. *attrib.*: **lightening-column**, ? *nonce-wd.*, a beacon-pillar (*fig.*).

1767 S. Paterson *Another Trav.* I. 413 The first emporium of commerce—the lightening-column of navigation to all the world.

'lightening (ˈlaɪt(ə)nɪŋ), *ppl. a.* [f. lighten *v.*² + -ing².] That lightens, shines, flashes, etc.

1592 Constable *Poems* (1859) 1 As my heart shall aye remaine A patient object to thy lightning eyes. **1594** R. Ashley tr. *Loys le Roy* 121 Alexander..who like a lightening thunder leaped into diuers parts. **1609** Daniel *Civ. Wars* vii. xciv. 197 This..Queene; Whose Victories..Haue but as onely lightning motions beene Before the ruine that ensu'd thereon. [Cf. lightening *vbl. sb.*² b.] **1694** Salmon *Bate's Dispens.* (1713) 317/1 *Aurum Fulminans*: Lightning or Thundering Gold. **1877** L. Morris *Epic Hades* iii. 48 As I went Across the lightening fields.

lighter (ˈlaɪtə(r)), *sb.*¹ Forms: (5 lightor, 6 -ur), 6 lyghter, 6–8 lyter, 7 liter, 7–8 leighter, loiter, (7 loyter), 5– lighter. [f. light *v.*¹ (sense 2) + -er¹, or ad. Du. *lichter* of equivalent formation.] A boat or vessel, usually a flat-bottomed barge, used in lightening or unloading (sometimes loading) ships that cannot be discharged (or loaded) at a wharf, etc., and for transporting goods of any kind, usually in a harbour.

1487 in Arnolde *Chron.* (1811) 113 R. A. shall haue free choise..for the said tonne wyne to be taken in the lighter at his plesur. **1545** in R. G. Marsden *Sel. Pl. Crt. Adm.* I. (1894) 137 Suche goodes wares or merchandises which is [laden] into any suche lyghter or lyghters to thintent to cary the same..from land aborde any shyppe or from borde any shippe to land. **1634** W. Wood *New Eng. Prosp.* (1865) 47 These flatts make it unnavigable for shippes, yet at high water great Boates, Loiters, and Pinnaces of 20, and 30 tun, may saile up to the plantation. **1728** Pope *Dunc.* ii. 275 He said, and climb'd a stranded Lighter's height. **1776** Adam Smith *W.N.* v. i. (1869) II. 307 The lighters which sail upon a navigable canal. **1878** Huxley *Physiogr.* 2 Barges, lighters, and other boats are thus enabled..to float up or down the river.

transf. **1831** Lamb *Elia* Ser. ii. *To Shade of Elliston*, What tearing off of histrionic robes..before the surly Ferryman will admit you to set a foot within his battered lighter.

b. *attrib.* and *Comb.*, as ***lighter-boat, -builder, -master***. Also lighterman.

1610 Guillim *Heraldry* iv. ii. (1611) 216 He beareth or a lighter boat in fesse gules. **1638** *Plymouth Col. Rec.* (1855) I. 94 The leighter master shall haue tenn shillings for his man & his leighter for xxiiij howers. **1640** in *T. Lechford's Note-Bk.* (1885) 375 One Lighter boate of the burthen of twenty tunnes. **1722** De Foe *Plague* (1754) 112 Lighter-builders [were] idle, and laid by.

lighter (ˈlaɪtə(r)), *sb.*² [f. light *v.*² + -er¹.]

1. One who lights or kindles. Also ***lighter-up*** (see quot. 1921).

1553 Becon *Reliques of Rome* (1563) 26* A lighter and carier of candels. **1753, 1853** [see candle-lighter 1]. **1885** *Pall Mall G.* 3 Nov. 4/2 The display [of fireworks]..costs about £300. Twelve lighters are stationed at different points, and obey the signal at the same moment. **1909** *Westm. Gaz.* 21 Apr. 8/1 Robert Brown, lighter-up [at locomotive shed] slight cut on left eyebrow. **1921** *Dict. Occup. Terms* (1927) §709 Lighter-up, carries live coals from fire hearth in shed to engine fire box.

2. a. An instrument for lighting; *esp.* a piece of twisted or folded paper used for lighting a pipe, etc.

1851 J. H. Newman *Cath. in Eng.* 247 He evidently thinks there is something religious about this lighter and extinguisher. **1856** Mrs. Browning *Aur. Leigh* viii. 177 This..letter, which Sir Blaise Has twisted to a lighter..To fire some holy taper. **1893** Lloyd & Hadcock *Artillery* 222 Without a 'lighter' it [cordite] does not readily ignite.

b. = *cigarette lighter* (see cigarette 2); also any similar mechanical contrivance for lighting a gas-fire, etc. So ***lighter-fluid, -fuel***, the fuel used to work a lighter.

1895 *Montgomery Ward Catal.* Spring & Summer 554/2 There are two lighters, to be used with alcohol. **1907** *Yesterday's Shopping* (1969) 243/3 The 'Telescopic' Gas Lighter. The best substitute for matches. **1913** Kipling *Divers. Creatures* (1917) 274 He smelt of rare soaps and cigarettes—such cigarettes as he handed me from a golden box with an automatic lighter. **1930** Sayers & 'Eustace' *Documents in Case* xxxvii. 105, I came in to retrieve a garment or lighter that he had borrowed. **1947** 'N. Blake' *Minute for Murder* ii. 47 A thin cylindrical object..rather like a lighter-fuel container. **1955** W. Gaddis *Recognitions* ii. i. 317 Setting fire to his hand dipped in lighter fluid. **1956** E. Ambler *Night-Comers* iv. 85 She had a box of Kleenex and a can of lighter fluid... She began to wipe off the grease. **1959** *New Statesman* 19 Sept. 354/2 The pipe had an aircooled aluminium stem, the lighter was butane-fuelled and had a Cadillac 'V' on the side. **1960** 'H. Carmichael' *Seeds of Hate* xix. 157 There had been a stain on the sleeve ..and he had removed it with lighter fuel. **1961** *Esquire* Aug. 59/2 He kept the bottles on a shelf in a clump of lighter fluid and Never-Leak cans. **1974** M. Gilbert *Flash Point* xii. 102 'You haven't got a cigarette by any chance?'..Patrick got out his case. The girl..took one, and got out her own lighter.

lighter (ˈlaɪtə(r)), *v.* [f. lighter *sb.*¹] *trans.* To remove or transport (goods) in a lighter, or as in a lighter. Also *absol.* or *intr.*

1840 *Evid. Hull Docks Comm.* 212 Whenever you lighter goods from this new contemplated dock. **1861** Smiles *Engineers* II. 195 Their cargoes were lightered to the warehouses higher up the Thames. **1885** *Century Mag.* XXX. 739 Our effects..were lightered ashore by means of the Indian canoes. **1885** *Law Times* LXXIX. 143/2 A standing agreement..that he should not lighter as a common carrier.

Hence **'lightering** *vbl. sb.*

1840 *Evid. Hull Docks Comm.* 18 Would not that very considerably increase the expense of your lightering? **1858** T. Dalton in *Merc. Marine Mag.* V. 337 The lightering to ships in the roads is done..by American..brigs.

lighterage (ˈlaɪtərɪdʒ). Forms: see lighter *sb.*¹; also 7 lightradge. [f. lighter *sb.*¹ + -age.] Transhipment or unloading of cargo by means of a lighter or lighters; the charges made for this.

1481–90 *Howard Househ. Bks.* (Roxb.) 370 Item, to Sergeaunt for lyterage vj. d. **1488** *Naval Acc. Hen. VII* (1896) 32 Bote hire lighterage & portage of the same stuff. **1583** *Rept. to Ld. Burleigh* in Arb. *Garner* I. 46 The lighterage, carriage and porters' due 0 2 8. **1621** Sir R. Boyle in *Lismore Papers* (1886) II. 13 The custome Lyteradg and imposeicons to be all born and defraied by me. **1755** Magens *Insurances* I. 66 Lighterage for the unloading and Demorage. **1798** R. Dodd *Let. on Port Lond.* 14 There will be no necessity for lighterage, shipping, reshipping, &c. **1885** *Law Rep. 15 Q. Bench Div.* 370 He had ever since done the plaintiffs' lighterage. **1886** *Pall Mall G.* 9 Dec. 12/2 Freight to Odessa, insurance, lighterage, and shipping charges.

'lighterman. [f. lighter *sb.*¹ + man *sb.*]

1. One employed on or owning a lighter.

1558 *Act 1 Eliz.* c. 11 §6 Any Wharfinger,..Lyghterman, Weigter or other Officer. **1608** H. Wright in *Lismore Papers* Ser. ii. (1887) I. 126 To paye the lyter men for caryinge downe the plancks. **1766** Entick *London* IV. 145 Lightermen..are to be of the society of watermen and wherrymen. **1861** Hughes *Tom Brown at Oxf.* xxi. (1889) 198 He believes that the men of the uppermost bank [of a trireme] rowed somehow like lightermen on the Thames. **1865** Dickens *Mut. Fr.* i. i, He could not be a lighterman or river-carrier.

2. ? = lighter *sb.*¹ (Cf. *Indiaman*; also lightman.)

1769 *Ann. Reg.* 132 The flames..destroyed..two large lightermen on the river.

ˌlighter-than-ˈair, *attrib. phr. Aeronautics.* Designating a flying machine whose weight is less than the weight of the air which it displaces and which rises as a result of its own buoyancy; also applied to the use of such a machine or machines in flight.

[**1869** J. B. Pettigrew in *Notices Proc. R. Inst. Gt. Brit.* V. 103 A machine lighter than the air must necessarily rise through it. **1887** tr. *J. Verne's Clipper of Clouds* vii. 60 The first inventors did not think of apparatus lighter than air. *Ibid.* viii. 78, I solved the problem of aviation. That is what a balloon will never do, nor will any machine that is lighter than air.] **1903** *Work* 11 Apr. 155/1 The Barton Air Ship..is a combination of the 'lighter than air' and 'heavier than air' system—that is to say, it is a machine in which a system of movable aero-planes is interposed between the car and the balloon. **1907** *Daily Mail* 19 Mar. 5/6 The Berlin 'Zentralblatt für Bauverwaltung'..protests against the subsidising with State funds of airships, dirigible balloons, and other 'lighter-than-air' vehicles. **1912** S. F. Walker *Aviation* i. 7 'Lighter than Air' apparatus which we call balloons. **1923** Hart & Laidler *Elem. Aeronaut. Sci.* i. 8 The problem of 'lighter-than-air' flight. **1953** S. Spender *Creative Element* i. 28 Tennyson was thinking of a battle of lighter-than-air dirigibles. **1963** *Ann. Reg. 1962* 539 [Auguste Piccard.] He and his twin, Jean Félix, were intensely interested in lighter-than-air flight. **1974** *Times* 13 Feb. 14/3 The role of lighter-than-air craft as cargo carriers.

ellipt. **1887** tr. *J. Verne's Clipper of Clouds* v. 39 To these enthusiasts for 'lighter than air' a no less enthusiast for 'heavier than air' had said things absolutely abhorrent. *Ibid.* x. 94 In spite of all the jealousy of the two enemies of 'lighter than air', they could not help being surprised at the perfection of this engine of aerial locomotion. **1910** *Blackw. Mag.* Feb. 206/1 Neglecting the lighter than air as a military auxiliary.

light face. *Typogr.* [f. light *a.*¹ + face *sb.* 22.] A kind of type in which the letters are made up of thin strokes. Also *attrib.* Hence **light-faced** *a.* Cf. *heavy face* (face *sb.* 22, heavy *a.*¹ 15).

1871 *Amer. Encycl. Printing* 275 *Light-Faces*, numerous varieties of job type, in which the lines of the letters are unusually light or thin. **1898** J. Southward *Mod. Printing* I. xxii. 140 The first would be called a *light face*, and the second a *heavy face*. *Ibid.* xxiv. 155 In the case of light-faced letters, they are spoiled for good work after the first time of using. **1917** F. S. Henry *Printing for School & Shop* vii. 90 Dainty, light-faced type. **1962** Corson & Lorrain *Introd. Electromagn. Fields* i. 1 Lightface type will indicate either a scalar quantity or the magnitude of a vector quantity. **1963** Kenneison & Spilman *Dict. Printing* 115 *Light face*, descriptive of a type-face of fine appearance as opposed to medium and bold lines. **1970** W. P. Jaspert et al. *Encycl. Type Faces* (ed. 4) p. ix, We speak also of bold-faced and light-faced types, referring to the thickness or thinness of the strokes of the letter.

light-fingered, *a.* Having light and nimble fingers. **a.** *gen.* **b.** Having fingers quick and dexterous at pilfering; thievish, dishonest. †**c.** Prompt in giving or returning a blow; pugnacious. *Obs.*

a. 1804 *Edin. Rev.* V. 152 The..solemn gravity of the premier affords a fine contrast to the light-fingered agility of his brother. **1890** *Century Dict.*, *Light-fingered*, light in touch with the fingers, as in playing the piano.

b. 1547 Boorde *Introd. Knowl.* xxxviii. (1870) 217 They be lyght fyngerd and vse pyking. **1579–80** North *Plutarch, Aristides* (1595) 351 Themistocles..was a wise man..but yet somewhat light fingered. **1624** Gataker *Transubst.* 148 Some light-fingered person having pickt his purse. **1699** Dampier *Voy.* II. i. 14 Our men contented themselves with looking after their goods (the Tonquinese being very light-finger'd). **1758** Johnson *Idler* No. 26 ¶11 Sharp girls were apt to be light-fingered. **1823** Scott *Let.* 18 June in *Lockhart*, The light-fingered gentry melt plate so soon as it comes into their possession. **1860** Thackeray *Round. Papers, Round Christm. tree* 105 The light-fingered gentry pick pockets furiously in the darkness.

c. 1581 Lambarde *Eiren.* ii. vii. (1588) 220 Youth..whether brawling, quarrelous, lightfingred or bloudie-handed. **1589** R. Harvey *Pl. Perc.* (1860) 3 Light-fingred Younkers, which make euery word a blow. **1607** Topsell *Four-f. Beasts* (1658) 370 Angry men are light-fingered and apt to strike.

Hence **light'fingeredness**.

1881 *Nation* (N.Y.) XXXIII. 358/1 The general persuasion of their [*sc.* Gipsies'] propensity to light-fingeredness.

lightfoot (ˈlaɪtfʊt), *a.* [light *a.*¹]

1. *poet.* = light-footed. (Very common in 16th c.)

c **1440** *Promp. Parv.* 304/1 Lyght foote (*MS. K. c* 1490 liht fotyd), *levipes.* **1579** Spenser *Sheph. Cal.* June 26 And lightfoote Nymphes can chace the lingring night. **1580** Sidney *Ps.* xviii. ix, To match with lightfoote staggs, he made my foote so light. **1594** Shaks. *Rich. III*, iv. iv. 440 Some light-foot friend post to yᵉ Duke of Norfolk. **1600** Fairfax *Tasso* vi. xxxvi. 100 The victor spurr'd againe his light-foot stead. **1832** Tennyson *Œnone* 81 Light-foot Iris. **1896** A. E. Housman *Shropsh. Lad* liv, By brooks too broad for leaping The lightfoot boys are laid.

fig. **1624** Quarles *Sion's Elegies* Poems (1717) 391 Hours, chac'd with lightfoot-minutes, end. **1871** Swinburne *Songs bef. Sunrise, Prelude* 185 By rose-hung river and light-foot rill. **1880** Miss Broughton *Sec. Th.* II. iii. x. 275 The lightfoot hours dance by.

†**2.** quasi-*sb.* A name for the hare, and the deer. *Obs.*

a **1325** *Names of Hare* in *Rel. Ant.* I. 134 He shal seien on oreisoun In the worshipe of the hare..The liȝt-fot, the fernsittere. **15..** *Kinge & Miller* 85 in Furnivall *Percy Folio* (1868) II. 151 'Wiffe' quoth the Miller, 'feitch me forth lightfoote, that wee of his sweetnesse a litle may taste'. A faire venson pasty shee feiched forth presentlye. **1815** *Sporting Mag.* XLV. 169 If light-foot elude the snare, not less than half a dozen of Chanticleer's family can compensate for the disappointment.

light-footed, *a.* Having a light foot; treading lightly, active, nimble.

c **1490** [see lightfoot 1, quot. *c* 1440]. **1552** Huloet, Lyght foted, *aeripes.* **1633** T. Stafford *Pac. Hib.* ii. xiv. (1810) 378 This lightfooted Generall could not bee overtaken. **1795** *Fate of Sedley* II. 88 The ravenous and light-footed pursuers of innocence. **1850** Prescott *Peru* II. 33 The light-footed vicuña. **1859** Geo. Eliot *A. Bede* vi, A good-looking woman..well-shapen, light-footed.

fig. **1727–46** Thomson *Summer* 124 Of bloom ethereal the light-footed dews.

Hence **light'footedly** *adv.*

1887 *Athenæum* 17 Sept. 381/2 Florizel dancing light-footedly among her rustic associates.

lightful (ˈlaɪtfʊl), *a.* [f. light *sb.* + -ful.] Full of light (*lit.* and *fig.*); luminous, bright.

1382 Wyclif *Luke* xi. 34 Al thi body schal be liȝtful. *a* **1450** *Cov. Myst.* (Shaks. Soc.) 20 Aungelle in hevyn evyrmore xal be, In lythful clere bryth as ble. **1587** Golding *De Mornay* iii. 35 Mortall sight, Too weake to see the lightfull Iove that ruleth all with right. **1605** Sylvester *Du Bartas* ii. iii. iv. *Captaines* 199 The lightful ark, God's sacred cabinet. **1650** Earl Monm. tr. *Senault's Man bec. Guilty* 348 Chrystall becomes lightfull without softning it's hardnesse. **1860** Pusey *Min. Proph.* 526 What in the Body of the Lord can be more lightful than those five Wounds? **1889** Doyle *Micah Clarke* 164 The hall within was lightful and airy.

Hence **'lightfulness**.

a **1586** Sidney *Arcadia* iii. (1622) 265 No more then the Sunne wants waxe to bee the fewell of his glorious lightfulnesse. **1587** Golding *De Mornay* vi. (1617) 78 He calleth him the First beginner, Lightfulnesse, or altogether Light. **1839** Bailey *Festus* xxv. (1848) 313 Watery lightfulness of ghostly eyes.

light-handed, *a.* Having a light hand. **a.** Having a light touch; handling objects deftly and quickly. Said of persons and their actions. *lit.* and *fig.* **b.** Having the hand lightly laden; carrying little. **c.** Of a vessel or factory = short-handed.

c **1440** *Promp. Parv.* 304/1 Lyghte handyd, *manulevis.* **1562–3** Sir W. Cecil in *Abp. Parker's Corr.* (Parker Soc.) 172, I beseech your Grace be not too light-handed in licences to every person. **1798** Ld. Clare in *Ld. Auckland's Corr.* (1862) III. 396 The town..was disarmed..by a body of light-handed rebels. **1830** Galt *Lawrie T.* ii. i. (1849) 82 It was agreed..that..we should set out as light-handed as possible. **1846** Young *Naut. Dict.*, *Light-handed*, a term implying that a vessel is short of her complement of men. **1876** T. Hardy *Ethelberta* (1890) 211 She was one of the cleverest and lightest-handed women we ever had about us. **1891** *Spectator* 21 Mar., Light-handed treatment of the trifles of life.

Hence **light-'handedness**.

1613 R. Cawdrey *Table Alph.* (ed. 3), *Legeirdemaine*, light-handednesse, craftie slights, and conueiance. **1879** Black *Macleod of D.* I. 152 What you want is..the dexterous light-handedness of a woman.

†**'lighthead**¹. *Obs.* [f. light *a.*¹ + -head.] Lightness, folly, levity; an instance of this.

1340 *Ayenb.* 207 Ine zuyche liȝthedes [hi] wasteþ hare time. **1382** Wyclif *Jer.* iii. 9 Thurȝ liȝthed of hir fornycacioun [she] defoulede the lond. *c* **1400** *Cato's Morals* 196 Loke for na liȝthede, at þat þing in ani stide of þe haue blaming.

'lighthead². [f. LIGHT *a.*¹ + HEAD *sb.*¹] A light-headed person. Also quasi-*adj.*, light-headed.

[**1587** FLEMING *Contn. Holinshed* III. 1954/1 He was induced to attempt such follie..by some light heads that were then about him. **1609** W. BIDDULPH in Lavendar *Trav.* (1612) 44 This thiefe [Mahomet] perswadeth light heads.. how he is the messenger of God.] **1751** FIELDING *Amelia* II. iv. (1898) I. 98 Whilst I sat by her in her lighthead fits, she repeated scarce any other name but mine. **1825** J. WILSON *Noct. Ambr.* Wks. 1855 I. 9 Thou canst make lubbard and lighthead agree.

light-headed, *a.*

1. Disordered in the head; giddy, delirious. †Of a fever: Characterized by delirium.

?**1537** LATIMER *Let.* in *Serm. & Rem.* (Parker Soc.) 391, I am light-headed for lack of sleep. **1603** *North's Plutarch* (1612) 1204 If they be light headed and distraught of their wits. **1663** PEPYS *Diary* 31 Oct., The Queene continues light-headed, but in hopes to recover. **1747** *Mem. Nutrebian Crt.* I. v. 89, I was carried home senseless and extremely bruised, which caused me to fall into a light-headed fever. **1870** MORRIS *Earthly Par.* I. I. 234 Some..were sore afeard That she had grown light-headed with her woe.

2. Of persons and their actions: Frivolous, injudicious, thoughtless; changeful, fickle.

1579–80 NORTH *Plutarch, J. Cæsar* (1595) 764 These.. were speaches fitter for a rash light headed youth, then for his [Cæsar's] Person. **1590** R. HICHCOCK *Quintess. Wit* 89 He is ouer-light-headed, to change himselfe firste into one parte, then into another. **1632** LITHGOW *Trav.* IX. 388 He was no suppressour of the subiects..to inrich light-headed flatterers. *a* **1674** CLARENDON *Hist. Reb.* XIV. §120 A light-headed Nuntio, who did much mischief to his Majesty's service. **1828** CARLYLE *Misc.* (1857) I. 144 The poor light-headed cicada-swarm of a Chorus. **1864** BURTON *Scot Abr.* I. iii. 144 Such thoughts were in the meantime counteracted by the light-headed doings of the Queen Dowager.

†**3.** quasi-*adv. Obs.*

1639 FULLER *Holy War* I. v. (1640) 6 We see how light-headed this Pagan did talk, being stark drunk with pride.

Hence **light-'headedly** *adv.*, **light-'headedness.**

1722 DE FOE *Plague* (1754) 187 Diliriums, and what we call Lightheadedness. **1813** L. HUNT in *Examiner* 31 May 350/1 A fit of religious light-headedness. **1817** COLERIDGE *Biog. Lit.* 291 A sort of intermittent fever with fits of light-headedness off and on. **1844** DICKENS *Mart. Chuz.* xxiv, As to lightheadedness, there never was such a feather of a head as mine. **1886** STEVENSON *Dr. Jekyll* x. (ed. 2) 128 Gloating on my crime, light-headedly devising others in the future.

light-hearted, *a.*

1. Having a light heart; not oppressed by care or sorrow; cheerful, gay.

a **1400–50** *Alexander* 2814, I sall leue & be lechid, forþi be liȝt-herted. **1530** PALSGR. 317/1 Lyght herted or mery, *alaigre.* **1719** DE FOE *Crusoe* II. xiii. (1840) 279, I was now light-hearted. **1784** COWPER *Task* IV. 12 He whistles as he goes, light-hearted wretch, Cold and yet cheerful. **1817** MOORE *Lalla R.* (1824) 215 Light-hearted maid. **1859** W. COLLINS *Q. of Hearts* (1862) 58 Mrs. K. began to make jokes about it, in her lighthearted way.

2. Proceeding from a light heart.

1841 JAMES *Brigand* i, The light-hearted song in the porch. **1891** T. K. CHEYNE *Psalter* vi. 290 The light-hearted freedom of antiquity.

Hence **light-'heartedly** *adv.*, **light-'heartedness.**

1826 LONGF. in *Life* (1891) I. vii. 89 The joy and light-heartedness which a foot-traveller feels. **1847** DE QUINCEY *Sp. Mil. Nun* Wks. 1862 III. 14 As light-heartedly as the Duke. **1882** *Macm. Mag.* XLVI. 207/1 He considers light-heartedness, and a turn for making the best of things, as a proof of intellectual strength. **1897** MAUDE *Voluntary v. Compulsory Service* 131 Those who..would now light-heartedly plunge us into war with the whole of Europe.

light-heeled, *a.*

1. Having light heels; brisk in walking or running; nimble.

1590 SHAKS. *Mids. N.* III. ii. 415 The villaine is much lighter heel'd then I. **1647** WARD *Simp. Cobler* 29 Light-heel'd beagles that lead the chase. **1742** BLAIR *Grave* 24 Light-heel'd ghosts and visionary shades. **1811** *Sporting Mag.* XXXVIII. 99 Prizes had been distributed to the most light-heeled damsels of either county, for their speed in running. **1829** H. HAWTHORN *Visit Babylon* 18, I followed the light-heeled girl.

†**2.** Of a woman: Loose, unchaste. *Obs.*

a **1613** OVERBURY *Charac., Foote-man* Wks. (1856) 14 His mother..was a light-heeled wench. **1637** NABBES *Microcosm.* II. C 2 b, My mother a light-heel'd madame that kept a vaulting-schoole at the signe of Virgo. **1638** —— *Bride* IV. ii. (1640) G 1 b, She is sure a light heeld wench. **1796** MRS. M. ROBINSON *Angelina* II. 26 Has not Mr. Amathist espoused the venerable remains of a light-heeled Calypso?

So †**light-heels**, a loose woman.

1602 J. COOKE *How to choose a Good Wife* III. ii, I'll tell my mistress as soon as I come home that mistress light-heels comes to dinner to-morrow.

light horse.

1. †**a.** *collect. sing.* Light horsemen; a body of light cavalry (*obs.*). **b.** = LIGHT HORSEMAN. (Cf. F. *chevau-léger.*)

1532 [see HUSSAR 1]. *a* **1548** HALL *Chron., Hen. VI*, 124 b, With .vi. m. archers, and .xiij. hundred light horses. **1611** COTGR., *Estradiot*, a light-horse, an Albanian horseman. **1625** MARKHAM *Souldiers Accid.* 40 The third sort of auncient Horsemen, were called Light-horse. **1759** *Ann. Reg.* 7 England for the first time saw light horse and light foot. **1876** BANCROFT *Hist. U.S.* IV. xx. 462 Three regiments of infantry with one of light-horse from Ireland. *attrib.* **1768–74** TUCKER *Lt. Nat.* (1834) II. 475 Cases..of close combat or light-horse skirmish. **1898** *59th Rep. Deputy Keeper* 5 Books and Papers relating to the Light Horse Volunteers 1779–1831.

†**2.** A courtesan. *Obs.*

a **1627** MIDDLETON *Witch* V. i. (1778) 96 *An.* Florida. *Gas.* She: I know no other, Sir, You were nev'r at charge yet but with one light-horse.

light horseman.

1. A light-armed cavalry soldier.

1548 PATTEN *Exped. Scotl.* A ij b, Suche..lighte horsemen as were comen. **1558** *Nottingham Rec.* IV. 118 Consernyng the light horsse men settyng furthe. **1600** R. CHURCHE tr. *Fumée's Hist. Hungary* 32 Certaine of his light horsemen (who are commonly called Vssarons). **1787** M. CUTLER in *Life*, etc. (1888) I. 226 A light-horseman..was discovered near the bridge on the American side. *fig.* **1899** *Q. Rev.* Apr. 461 It countenanced all the unscrupulous light-horsemen of debate.

2. A slang name for one of a class of Thames thieves. (Cf. HORSEMAN 5.)

1800 COLQUHOUN *Comm. Thames* 59 The gangs, denominated Light Horsemen were generally composed of one or more Receivers, together with Coopers, Watermen, and Lumpers. **1849** [see HORSEMAN 5]. **1899** *Daily News* 9 Jan. 6/1 'Light Horsemen' would look out for a lighter having valuable goods on board, and at night, stealing up quietly, would cut her adrift: then following her, as she floated down with the tide, would by-and-by rescue her, and bring her back, claiming salvage.

†**3.** 'An old name for the light boat, since called a gig' (Smyth *Sailor's Word-bk.*). *Obs.*

1600 J. JANE in Hakluyt *Voy.* III. 843 His long boat and light-horseman were lost at sea. **1634** BRERETON *Trav.* (1844) 1 We came to Gravesend..in a light-horseman. **1656** FINETT *For. Ambass.* 220 Leaving a Light-horseman to be taken up for their baggage at Gravesend.

†**4.** A variety of fancy pigeons. (Cf. HORSEMAN 3.) *Obs.*

1688 R. HOLME *Armoury* II. 244/2 Light Horse-men, a Bastard kind [of Pigeons] between a Cropper and a Carrier.

5. †**a.** An early name of an Australian sea-fish, according to Morris prob. the Sweep, *Scorpis æquipennis.* **b.** A West-Indian fish of the genus *Ephippus.*

1789 W. TENCH *Exp. Botany Bay* xv. 129 A species of grouper, to which, from the form of a bone in the head resembling a helmet, we have given the name of light horseman. **1793** —— *Acc. Settlement Port Jackson* 176 At the top of the list [of fish], as an article of food, stands a fish, which we named light-horseman. **1854** R. OWEN in *Circ. Sci.* (*c* 1865) II. 51/1 The median crest is developed to an extreme height in some fishes, as, e.g. the dolphin and light-horseman fish (*Ephippus*). **1881** *Cassell's Nat. Hist.* V. 5 Sometimes the crest of the bone is exceedingly lofty, as in the Light Horseman fish (*Ephippus*) and sometimes absent, as in the sucking fish Remora.

'lighthouse. [f. LIGHT *sb.*: see HOUSE *sb.*¹ 2.]

a. A tower or other structure, with a powerful light or lights (originally a beacon) at the top, erected at some important or dangerous point on or near the sea-coast for the guidance of mariners. (The earlier name was *pharos.*)

1622 BACON *Hist. Hen. VII* 142 They..were executed.. at diuers places vpon the Sea-Coast..for Sea-markes or Light-houses, to teach Perkins People to auoid the Coast. **1662–3** MARVELL *Corr.* xxxvii. Wks. 1872–5 II. 83, I have herewith sent you an account of your expenses about the Light-house. **1703** *Lond. Gaz.* No. 3971/3 The Light-House upon the Edistone was blown down. **1708** *Ibid.* No 4459/4 The 28th of July last, a Light was placed on the Light-House, Rebuilt on the Edistone-Rock off Plimouth. **1841** W. SPALDING *Italy & It. Isl.* III. 167 In approaching from Turin, we pass along the seaside to the immense lighthouse. **1856** MRS. BROWNING *Aur. Leigh* (1857) 56 Perhaps I darkened, as the light-house will That turns upon the sea.

b. *attrib.* and *Comb.*, as ***lighthouse-keeper, -man, service, -tender, -top, -tower.***

1672 EVELYN *Diary* 14 May, From the North Foreland Light-house-top..we could see our fleete. **1738** *Mass. Bay Acts & Resolves* (1904) XII. 513 That the sum of Fifty one Pounds..be paid..for his services as Light House Keeper. **1798** COLERIDGE *Anc. Mar.* VI. xiv, Is this indeed The light-house top I see? **1831** SCOTT *Pirate* Introd., The author was invited to join a party of Commissioners for the Northern Light-House Service. **1851** KINGSLEY *Three Fishers* ii, Three wives sat up in the lighthouse tower. **1866** CARLYLE *Remin.* (1881) I. 112 Lighthouse-keeper too..by far the most life-weary looking mortal I ever saw. **1889** *Athenæum* 23 Feb. 257 (Advt.), The manners and ways of coastguardsmen, lighthousemen, and other amphibious creatures. **1901** *Daily Colonist* (Victoria, B.C.) 1 Nov. 3/2 The lighthouse-tender Manzanita called in yesterday morning for a short stay. **1921** *Ibid.* 16 Oct. 16/1 The lighthouse tender Berens then took up the search and.. discovered the small boat sheltering behind Mouatt Reef. **1958** W. ARMSTRONG *True Bk. Lighthouses & Lightships* xiv. 142, I remembered, too, stories of how two lighthouse tenders and a pilot-cutter were sunk by mines in World War I. **1969** *Times* 19 Dec. 2/5 (*heading*) Lighthouse man missing.

lighting ('laɪtɪŋ), *vbl. sb.*¹ [f. LIGHT *v.*¹ + -ING¹. In OE. *lihting.*]

†**1.** Alleviation, relief. *Obs.*

c **1000** *Laws of Edgar* III. c. 2 (Schmid) Gif þæt riht to hefiȝ sy, sece siððan þa lihtinge to þam cynge. *a* **1300** *Cursor M.* 27066 Þat strength es o gret ligthing, quen man has casten his birthing o sin. *c* **1460** *Play Sacram.* 789 Yᵘ haste sent me lyghtyng yᵗ late was lame. **1502** *Ord. Crysten Men* (W. de W. 1506) V. iii. 385 Nor truste not for euer to haue socours ne lyghtynge.

2. Descent; dismounting; alighting: also with *down.*

1350–1425 *Cursor M.* 13822 (Trin.) þe aungels liȝtyng [*Cott.* þe angel lightand; *Gött.* þe angel lighting (*vbl. sb., not pple.*)] þere bood I. *c* **1430** *Syr Gener.* (Roxb.) 6373 Mirabel ..made hir ladie forto light. Of that lighting Jewel was woo. *c* **1470** HENRY *Wallace* II. 399 Wallace with that, at his lychtin, him drew. **1506** in *Paston Lett.* III. 405 At the lyghtyng the Kyng of Castylle was of his hors a good space or owr Kyng was a lyght. **1611** BIBLE *Isa.* xxx. 30 The Lord shall..shew the lighting downe of his arme. **1615** W. LAWSON *Country Housew. Garden* (1626) 22 To auoid the lighting of Crowes, Pyes, &c. vpon your grafts. **1665** BOYLE *Occas. Refl.* Table Contents, Upon the Mounting, Singing, and Lighting of Larks. **1746** HERVEY *Medit.* (1818) 41 The lighting down of the grasshopper is a burden on the bending shoulders.

3. *attrib.*, as ***lighting-place*** (used *spec.* with reference to bees).

1609 C. BUTLER *Fem. Mon.* i. A 2 b, If..she [the queen-bee] dislike the weather, or lighting place, they quickly returne home againe. **1727** BRADLEY *Fam. Dict.* s.v. *Bee.* **1759** BROWN *Compleat Farmer* 94 When your swarm hath made choice of a lighting-place.

lighting ('laɪtɪŋ), *vbl. sb.*² [f. LIGHT *v.*² + -ING¹. In OE. *lihting.*]

1. Illumination. †In quot. *c* 1175 = Dawn.

c **1000** ÆLFRIC *Gen.* i. 16 God ȝeworhte..þæt mare leoht to þæs dæȝes lihtinge. *c* **1175** *Lamb. Hom.* 45 Ic ham ȝeue reste..from non on saterdei a þa cume monedeis lihting. **1718** LADY M. W. MONTAGU *Let. to Mr. Thistlethwayte* 16 Oct., Paris has the advantage of London, in the neat pavement of the streets, and the regular lighting of them at nights. **1851** *Illustr. Catal. Gt. Exhib.* 1176 Chemical products, obtained by purifying gas used for lighting. **1874** MICKLETHWAITE *Mod. Par. Churches* 26 The lighting should be mainly from the clerestory. **1876** BLACK *Madcap V.* xlvi. 390 The silver lighting of the restless..sea.

b. *attrib.* and *Comb.*: ***lighting man, power, rate, socket, wire***; **lighting bridge** *Theatr.*, a narrow platform, suspended over a stage, on which lights are operated; **lighting cameraman** *Cinemat.* and *Television* (see quot. 1960); **lighting plot** *Theatr.* (see quot. 1961); **lighting tower** *Theatr.*, a tall structure on which lights are fixed.

1928 C. H. RIDGE *Stage Lighting* vii. 111 The roof and lighting bridge are all built in reinforced concrete. **1933** P. GODFREY *Back-Stage* iv. 43 Above the proscenium arch is the lighting bridge, which will accommodate as many as ten electricians with 'spotting lanterns'. **1967** *Punch* 16 Aug. 242/3 For *Figaro* and Verdi's *Macbeth* at the first [Edinburgh] festival twenty-one years ago, John Christie had to bring in a lighting bridge and sixty floods and perches from Glyndebourne. **1960** O. SKILBECK *ABC of Film & TV* 78 *Lighting Cameraman*, chief cameraman of a unit, who is responsible for ordering the illumination which gives pictorial quality to a shot. **1966** *Listener* 15 Dec. 889/3 The lighting cameraman can earn £1,000 a week on a major picture. **1972** A. FOWLES *Double Feature* iv. 67 I'd been Richard Powell, lighting cameraman. **1972** I. HAMILTON *Thrill Machine* vii. 30 For difficult interiors he should have had a lighting man, for interviews he should have had an audio man as well. **1931** C. S. PARSONS *Amat. Stage Managem. & Production* ii. 18 Lighting plots should always be well rehearsed. **1933** P. GODFREY *Back-Stage* iv. 44 The lighting-plot shows the position of every lamp, the colour of the medium, and the varying intensity of the light required. **1961** BOWMAN & BALL *Theatre Lang.* 201 *Lighting plot*,..a list, with diagrams, showing the lighting to be used in each scene of a production. **1884** F. KROHN tr. *Glaser de Cew's Magneto- & Dynamo-Electr. Machines* 183 A greater part of its lighting-power is due to the incandescence of the electrodes. **1928** *Chambers's Jrnl.* Jan. 21/1 An automatic regulator wherewith to make..and supply lighting power to the lamps. **1858** SIMMONDS *Dict. Trade, Lighting-rate*, a public rate for maintaining the lamps or gas-lights in a parish. **1928** *Chambers's Jrnl.* Jan. 79/1 All that has to be done to start charging is to insert the charger-plug in the nearest lighting socket. **1935** *Discovery* Nov. 326/2 A new power-driven spray-painting outfit which..can be run from an ordinary lighting socket. **1933** P. GODFREY *Back-Stage* iv. 43 In the wings stand a number of lighting towers twelve feet high, each capable of carrying a dozen 1000-watt flood lamps. **1967** R. COURTNEY *Drama Studio* ix. 76 At least one Lighting Tower is needed on the floor area. **1889** *Daily News* 2 Dec. 5/4 A conductor of the fluid from the lighting wire.

†**2.** *concr.* Lightning. *Obs.*

1297 R. GLOUC. (Rolls) 7763 Tempestes þer come þondringe & liȝtinge ek. *a* **1300** *Fragm. Pop. Sci.* (Wright) 146 The liȝting That schut abrod into al the worlde. *a* **1400** *Tokens Doomsday* 25 (E.E.T.S. 1878) Oure lord schal come & smyte adoun, as liȝttyng doþ to ground. *c* **1425** *Seven Sag.* (P.) 2191 Lyghtyn, thondyr, and rayne. **1618** BOLTON *Florus* I. xvii. (1636) 51 As if volleyes of Lighting, and Thunder had beene discharged from the Clouds of Heaven upon the old earth-borne Gyants.

3. a. Kindling, ignition. Also with *up* (see LIGHT *v.*² 2 c).

1389 in *Eng. Gilds* (1870) 35 The sexteyn..ssal han, for lythynge of the lythe, viijᵈ. **1499–1500** in Swayne *Sarum Churchw. Acc.* (1896) 51 Paid..for lyghtyng of the Rode light. **1652** NEEDHAM *Selden's Mare Cl.* 124 The lighting of one Candle by another. **1807** SOUTHEY *Lett. from Eng.* I. viii. 89 Between eight and nine the lighting-up began.., every window being filled with candles. **1855** MACAULAY *Hist. Eng.* xviii. IV. 223 At the first lighting of the beacons. **1897** OUIDA *Massarenes* ix, Do you mind my lighting up, Pater?

b. lighting-up time, the time when lights are switched on, esp. the time when lights on vehicles are required by law to be switched on.

1900 J. K. JEROME *Three Men on Bummel* iii. 55 On sunny afternoons you used to ride about with that lamp shining for all it was worth. When lighting-up time came it was naturally tired, and wanted a rest. **1935** H. G. WELLS *Things*

to Come iii. 23 It [*sc.* a newspaper] should show the customary insets beside the title of the weather forecast and the lighting-up time. **1947** *Whitaker's Almanack* 150/2 The legal importance of *Sunrise* and *Sunset* is that the Road Transport Lighting Act, 1927 defines Lighting-up Time for vehicles as being from one hour after sunset to one hour before sunrise. **1957** *Times* 11 May 7/1 Lighting-up time, 9.8 p.m. **1963** *Times* 20 May 3/3 M.C.C., going in with three-quarters of an hour left, lost Atkinson before the umpires decided it was lighting-up time.

4. The incidence of light upon the features, etc.; the disposition of light in a picture.

1861 *Sat. Rev.* 21 Dec. 648 In a statue by an Italian master, what he notices chiefly are the various effects which various lightings produce upon its features. **1869** *Athenæum* 18 Dec. 826 As a study in colour and lighting the work is a model. **1879** *Cassell's Techn. Educ.* III. 142 The colour and lighting of the object to be photographed.

5. = ANNEALING 3 (Knight *Dict. Mech.* 1875).

lightish ('laɪtɪʃ), *a.* [f. LIGHT *a.*² + -ISH.] Somewhat light, in the senses of the adj. Also *Comb.*, as ***lightish-coloured*** adj.

1656 W. D. tr. *Comenius' Gate Lat. Unl.* §25. 13 The Moon..maketh the night, one while light, another while lightish. **1688** *Lond. Gaz.* No. 2312/4 A loose lightish coloured Camblet Coat. **1723** *Ibid.* No. 6217/3 He..wears a lightish Wig. **1767** S. PATERSON *Another Trav.* II. 14 A lay-habit of lightish gray. **1872** G. MACDONALD *Wilf. Cumb.* I. xv. 237 His hair [was] a lightish brown.

lightless ('laɪtlɪs), *a.* [OE. *léohtléas*, f. *léoht* LIGHT *sb.* + *-léas* -LESS.] Without light.

1. Receiving no light; unillumined, dark.

c **1000** ÆLFRIC *Hom.* (Th.) II. 504 He..sæde ðæt he wære ʒelæd to leohtleasre stowe. **1340** HAMPOLE *Pr. Consc.* 6819 For-þi þat helle es ay lightles, It es cald þe land of myrkenes. **1593** SHAKS. *Lucr.* 1555 Such Deuils steale effects from lightlesse Hell. **1601** W. PARRY *Trav. Sir A. Sherley* (1863) 4 A man from his birth confined in a dungeon or lightlesse cave. **1819** CRABBE *T. of Hall* III. 275 A lightless closet, in a room Hired at small rate. **1843** RUSKIN *Mod. Paint.* I. II. III. iii. §14 Not in her most ponderous and lightless masses will nature ever leave us without some evidence of transmitted sunshine. **1870** MORRIS *Earthly Par.* I. I. 410 Into some nigh lightless prison cast. **1877** BLACKIE *Wise Men* 102 An owl, a bat, Blindworm, or mole, or any lightless thing.

fig. **1387-8** T. USK *Test. Love* I. i. (Skeat) l. 20 Thynke on his disease, howe lightles he lyueth, sithe the beames brennende in loue of thin eien arn so bewet. **1790** R. MERRY *Laurel Liberty* (ed. 2) 13 All..who drew their profit from the lightless crowd.

2. Giving or shedding no light.

1340 HAMPOLE *Pr. Consc.* 4729 Þe son sal be turned in-til mirknes, And þe mone in-til blode, and be lyghtles. **1593** SHAKS *Lucr.* 4 Lust-breathed Tarqvin..to Colatium beares the lightlesse fire. **1639** RUTHERFORD *Lett.* (1881) II. 415 O dim and dark and lightless Sun. **1809** W. TAYLOR in *Monthly Mag.* XXVII. 456 Earth is but earth a dull and lightless body. **1860** PUSEY *Min. Proph.* 130 There will be.. the lightless fire, retaining in darkness the power to burn, but reft of its rays. **1869** TYNDALL *Notes Lect. Light* 43 The almost lightless flame of a Bunsen's burner.

Hence **'lightlessness**.

1865 *Cornh. Mag.* Aug. 186 Something horrible there was too in the lightlessness of the red. **1892** W. E. HENLEY *Song of Sword, Lond. Voluntaries* iii. 16 By a jealous lightlessness oppressed.

light-limbed, *a.* Having light limbs; agile; nimble.

1695 *Lond. Gaz.* No. 3119/4 Lost.., a brown bay Mare,.. pretty light limb'd. **1812** BYRON *Ch. Har.* I. lxxiv, The light-limbed Matadore. **1855** KINGSLEY *Heroes* II. (1868) 20 A young man more light-limbed than the stag.

lightliwode, obs. form of LIKELIHOOD.

† **'lightly**, *a.*¹ *Obs. rare.* [OE. *léohtlic*, f. *léoht* LIGHT *sb.* + *-lic* -LY¹.] Brilliant, lightsome.

a **1000** *Riddles* xxx. 3 (Gr.) Lyhtfæt leohtlic listum ʒeʒierwed. *c* **1440** HYLTON *Scala Perf.* (W. de W. 1494) II. xxvii, This hundreth folde that a soule shall haue..ys noughte but the profyte of this lightly derkenes.

† **'lightly**, *a.*² *Obs.* Forms: 1 **léohtlic**, 3 **lihtlic(h)e**, 4 **lightli**, 5 **liȝtli**, **lyghtly**, 6 **lichtlie**, 4, 7 **lightly**. [OE. *léohtlic*, f. *léoht* LIGHT *a.*¹ + *-lic*, -LY¹.] Frivolous, trifling, fickle; to be slighted, contemptible; also contemptuous, slighting; easy, easy to be persuaded. Cf. the senses of LIGHT *a.*¹ ***lightly cheap*** = ***light cheap*** (see LIGHT *a.*¹ 13 b).

c **897** K. ÆLFRED *Gregory's Past.* xliii. 309 Ond eft ðæm ʒifrum suiðe hrædlice him willað fylʒan leohtlicu weorc & unnyt. *a* **1225** *Leg. Kath.* 1320 Ah nis nawt lihtliche of þis meidenes mot. *a* **1240** *Wohunge* in *Cott. Hom.* 273 Ah noble men and gentile and of heh burðe ofte winnen luue lihtlice cheape. *a* **1300** *Cursor M.* 7222 Þis wijf alsua, þat þou has now, If þou ne war sua lightli to tru! *Ibid.* 28087 To men and wemmen bath i wate, þat oft i helde my lightly late. **1422** tr. *Secreta Secret., Priv. Priv.* 241 Al tymes ette they mettis, wyche ben moiste, lyghtly to defye. *c* **1450** tr. *De Imitatione* I. xx. 24 It is liȝtlier a man ay to be still þan to not excede in wordes. **1533** GAU *Richt Vay* 15 Ony lichtlie takine of ir quhilk men wsis to schaw. **1608** J. KING *Serm. St. Mary's* 13 Dauid the sonne of Isai reigned, whose person was not so lightly.

Hence †**'lightliful** *a.*, slighting, contemptuous; †**'lightliness**, contemptuous manner or treatment; contempt.

1596 DALRYMPLE tr. *Leslie's Hist. Scot.* III. 192 Contemneng his requeistes wᵗ cruel and lychtliful anssers. *c* **1470** HENRY *Wallace* XI. 166 In lychtlynes thai maid answer him till. **1533** GAU *Richt Vay* 13 Thay that..turnis the halie writ to lichtlines and scorne. **1560** ROLLAND *Crt. Venus* IV. 67 Thay wald not thoill Venus haif lichtlines, Nor repudie.

lightly ('laɪtlɪ), *adv.* For forms see LIGHT *a.*¹ and -LY². Also *comparative* 1 **léohtlecor**, 3 **lihtluker**, 4 **lihtloker**, 5 **leyȝtlocure**. [OE. *léohtlíce* (= OFris. *lichtelik*, OHG. *lîhtlîhho*, MHG. *lîhtelîche*, mod.G. *leichtlich*, ON. *léttlega*), f. *léoht* LIGHT *a.*¹ + -LY².] In a light manner.

1. With little weight, so as not to be heavy; with little pressure, force, or violence; not strongly or severely; gently, superficially; in both material and immaterial applications.

c **897** K. ÆLFRED *Gregory's Past.* xxiv. 179 Ða weras mon sceal hefiȝlecor & stiðlecor læran, & ða wif leohtlecor. *a* **1300** *Cursor M.* 29419 If clerkes..Smites oþer lightli in gamen. *a* **1400** *Pistill of Susan* (MS. I) 227 [He] lifte lyhtly þe lache, and lepe ouer þe lake. **1483** CAXTON *G. de la Tour* lv. E v b, Whiche caused the deuyll fyrst to tempte them lyghtlyer. **1503** HAWES *Examp. Virtue* XII. ii, Come on she sayd and walke on lyghtly. **1611** BIBLE *Isa.* ix. 1 At the first he lightly afflicted the land of Zebulun. **1635-56** COWLEY *Davideis* I. 718 Some [Letters] cut in wood, some lightlier traced on slates. **1680** MOXON *Mech. Exerc.* 208 Try how the Centers are pitcht, by Treading the Treddle lightly down. **1747** WESLEY *Prim. Physic* (1762) 62 Boil very lightly one spoonful of white Copperas scrap'd. **1812** J. WILSON *Isle of Palms* II. 452 So lightly doth this little boat Upon the scarce-touch'd billows float. **1818** J. W. CROKER in *C. Papers* (1884) 13 July, I must now mention to you..what I have heretofore touched lightly upon. **1857** H. B. FARNIE *Golfer's Manual* in *Golfiana Misc.* (1887) 143 The cleek again is still more lightly shafted. **1874** SYMONDS *Sk. Italy & Greece* (1898) I. ix. 182 Crimes of bloodshed..sat lightly on the adventurer's conscience. **1883** S. C. HALL *Retrospect* II. 333 The fact must not be passed too lightly over.

b. With reference to sleep (see LIGHT *a.*¹ 20).

c **900** tr. *Bæda's Hist.* IV. xiv. [xi.] (1890) 296 Swa swa he leohtlice onslepte. **1852** MRS. CARLYLE *Lett.* II. 207, I sleep lightly enough for such emergency.

2. In no great quantity or thickness; to no great amount.

c **1000** *Sax. Leechd.* II. 36 Awringe þa wyrta..& ʒeswet swiþe leohtlice mid huniʒe. **1588** SHAKS. *L.L.L.* I. ii. 157 They are but lightly rewarded. **1664** EVELYN *Kal. Hort.* Aug. (1679) 23 You may sow Anemony seeds..&c. lightly cover'd with fit mold in Cases. **1682** SIR T. BROWNE *Chr. Mor.* I. §9 Persons lightly dipt, not grain'd in generous Honesty. **1828** SCOTT *F.M. Perth* xii, I fear me this traveller hath dined but lightly. **1830** LYELL *Princ. Geol.* I. 204 Moulds..rubbed lightly over with a solution of soap. **1875** JOWETT *Plato* (ed. 2) III. 27 They are lightly clad in summer while at their work. **1898** *Westm. Gaz.* 16 Sept. 4/3 Birds are so scarce in some districts that they will need to be lightly shot.

†**b.** In no great degree, slightly. *Obs.*

1594 SHAKS. *Rich. III*, I. iii. 45 They loue his Grace but lightly. **1631** A. CRAIGE *Pilgrime & Hermite* 9 For hee that loues lightliest, Bee sure hee shall speede best. **1659** HAMMOND *On Ps.* xliii. Paraphr. 227 The Forty third Psalm is exactly of the same mournfull subject..with the former, but perhaps lightly varied from thence. **1668** CULPEPPER & COLE *Barthol. Anat. Man* I. i. 302 If he be at least but lightly skilled in Anatomy. **1697** DRYDEN *Virg. Georg.* I. 425 While yet the Head is Green, or lightly swell'd With Milky-moisture.

3. Without depression or heaviness; in lightsome mood; cheerfully, gaily, merrily.

c **1386** CHAUCER *Knt.'s T.* 1012 Who looketh lightly now but Palamon. *c* **1475** *Rauf Coilȝear* 521 'It is lyke', said Schir Rolland, and lichtly he leuch. **1596** HARINGTON *Metam. Ajax* Advt. to Rdr., The first begins grauely and ends lightlye. **1606** SHAKS. *Ant. & Cl.* IV. xiv. 138 Bid that welcome Which comes to punish vs, and we punish it Seeming to beare it lightly. **1875** JOWETT *Plato* (ed. 2) I. 497 Try to bear lightly what must needs be. **1891** E. PEACOCK *N. Brendon* II. 313 The old man..chatted lightly with Basil.

4. Easily, readily. *Obs.* exc. *arch.* † ***one cannot lightly***, etc. = 'one cannot well', etc. *Obs.*

c **1175** *Lamb. Hom.* 49 Þe put ne tuneð noht lihtliche his muð ouer us. *a* **1225** *Ancr. R.* 254 Euerichon to dealen from oðer lihtluker to bersteð. *a* **1340** HAMPOLE *Psalter* ix. 30 Whare men may noght lyghtly see whilk way þai sall take. **1390** GOWER *Conf.* II. 461 Whil ther is oyle forto fyre, The lampe is lyhtly set afyre. *c* **1425** *Eng. Conq. Irel.* 28 Þay.. seiden that lyghtly that myght be done, yf [etc.]. **1485** CAXTON *Chas. Gt.* 27 He wold take a knyght al armed and lyfte hym vp to the heyght of hys breste lyghtly. **1570-6** LAMBARDE *Peramb. Kent* (1826) 331 It could not lightly blowe more boisterously out of any quarter. **1578** LYTE *Dodoens* I. lxix. 103 A man shall not lightly finde it in this countrey. **1653** H. COGAN tr. *Pinto's Trav.* xvii. 53 As we see them play away a piece of Damask at one cast at die, as those that come lightly by them. **1740** CHESTERF. *Lett.* (1792) I. lxii. 175 Credulous people believe lightly whatever they hear. **1818** SCOTT *Hrt. Midl.* xx, That's lightly said, but no sae lightly credited. **1870** MORRIS *Earthly Par.* I. II. 458 As fair was he As any king's son you might lightly see.

Proverb. **1624** SANDERSON *Serm.* I. 251 The ding-thrift's proverb is, 'Lightly come, lightly go'. **1898** BESANT *Orange Girl* II. iv, Lightly got, lightly spent.

5. With facile movement, nimbly. †In early use, quickly, swiftly; *occas.* immediately, at once.

c **1220** *Bestiary* 416 Liȝtlike ȝe lepeð up. *a* **1225** *Ancr. R.* 60 Þe earewen of þe liht eien..fleoð lichtliche uorð. **13..** *E.E. Allit. P.* B. 853 Lyȝtly he ryseʒ & bowez forth fro þe bench in-to þe brode ȝates. *c* **1420** *Chron. Vilod.* 4366 (Horstm.), Ouȝte off his bedde leyȝtlyche he lepe. *c* **1430** *Syr Gener.* (Roxb.) 2245 Lightlie she did hir redie make. *c* **1500** *Melusine* xxxvi. 251 Fayre lordes, now lightly on horsback. **15..** *Helyas* in Thoms *Prose Rom.* (1828) III. 81, I pray you my lord and lady that ye will lightly come... And incontinent the kynge and the queene descended. **1509** HAWES *Past. Pleas.* XXIX. (Percy Soc.) 143 This Godfrey Gobilyve went lightly Unto dame Sapience. *c* **1530** *Hickscorner* 624 When you them mete, lyghtly them arest. **1632** J. HAYWARD tr. *Biondi's Eromena* 75 Which said, he lightly vaulting off his saddle, drew out his sword.

†**6.** As may easily happen; probably, perhaps. *Obs.* [Cf. G. *vielleicht*, Du. *wellicht*, perhaps.]

13.. *E.E. Allit. P.* C. 88 Lyȝtly, when I am lest, he letes me alone. **1393** LANGL. *P. Pl.* C. xx. 321 And lightliche oure lorde at here lyues ende Haþ mercy of suche men. *c* **1460** J. RUSSELL *Bk. Nurture* 487 With a spone lightely to ete your souerayne may be leeff. *c* **1491** *Chast. Goddes Chyld.* 2 Some other maters that lightly wyll falle to purpose. **1615** T. ADAMS *White Devil* 16 Lightly there is one Judas in the congregation to crie 'Why is this waste?' **1672** MARVELL *Reh. Transp.* I. 105 There happens lightly some ugly little contrary accident.

†**b.** As is apt to happen; commonly, often. *Obs.*

c **1380** WYCLIF *Serm.* Sel. Wks. I. 1 Richessis ben perilouse, for liȝtli wole a riche man use hem unto moche lust. **1398** TREVISA *Barth. De P.R.* V. xi. (1495) 116 A beest stryken in the place of the temples dethe lyghtly folowyth. **1535** in *Lett. R. & Illustr. Ladies* (1846) II. 150 He goes to market lightly, one week with another, three times a-week. **1553** T. WILSON *Rhet.* (1580) 219 The beddes heade which lightly is the appointed place for all mens purses. **1601** HOLLAND *Pliny* II. 153 Such as vse ordinarily to be drunk, & are lightly neuer sober. **1615** G. SANDYS *Trav.* 75 When he goeth abroad—which is lightly every other Friday. **1637** R. HUMPHREY tr. *St. Ambrose* I. 44 Where there is leannes, there lightly is pensivenes. **1670** RAY *Prov.* 114 There's lightning lightly before thunder. **1676** ALLEN *Address Nonconf.* 20 They lightly do in the total..but frustrate and disappoint those ends.

7. a. With indifference or unconcern; carelessly, thoughtlessly, indifferently. **b.** Depreciatingly, slightingly.

a **1225** *Leg. Kath.* 942 In his hali nome ich schal leten lihtlice of al þat ȝe cunnen kasten aȝein me. *c* **1250** *Gen. & Ex.* 1218 Ȝhe bi-mente hire to abraham, And sumdel liȝtlike he it nam. *a* **1300** *Cursor M.* 1650, I sal do þam lij ful lau þat letes sua lightly on min au. **1393** LANGL. *P. Pl.* C. v. 168 The kynge..lourede vp-on men of lawe and lightliche seide. **1535** COVERDALE *Ps.* cvi. 11 They..but lightly regarded the councell of the most hyest. **1577-87** HOLINSHED *Chron., Scot.* (1808) V. 437 Offended..that such wandering theeues should so lightlie dare to contemne his power. **1611** BIBLE *1 Sam.* ii. 30 They that despise me, shall be lightly esteemed. **1746** HERVEY *Medit.* (1818) 13 Seriousness and devotion become this house for ever. May I never enter it lightly or irreverently. **1828** D'ISRAELI *Chas. I*, I. v. 119 The Pope lighlty appreciated the bare word of an heretical sovereign. **1832** HT. MARTINEAU *Demerara* i. 11 Her sister stared to hear her speak so lightly of being whipped. **1855** MACAULAY *Hist. Eng.* xx. IV. 419 The Judges treated this argument very lightly. **1875** JOWETT *Plato* (ed. 2) III. 702 Thinking lightly of the possession of gold.

Proverb. *a* **1200** *Moral Ode* 145 Ful wombe mei lihtliche speken of hunger and of festen. *c* **1400** *Apol. Loll.* 49 Þe fulle womb disputiþ litly of fastyng.

8. For a slight cause; without careful consideration, without strong reason.

c **1122** *O.E. Chron.* an. 1009 (Laud MS.) Se cyng..& þa ealdor menn..forleton þa scipo þus leohtlice. *c* **1400** *Melayne* 212 Lyghtly walde þey it [the city] noghte ȝelde. *c* **1420** *Anturs of Arth.* 176 Thane wille þay leue the lyghtely, þat nowe wille the lowte. **1535** COVERDALE *Prov.* iii. 30 Stryue not lightly with eny man, where as he hath done yᵉ no harme. **1751** *Affecting Narr. of Wager* 9 An Asylum that must not lightly be violated. **1790** BURKE *Corr.* (1844) III. 177 These are opinions I have not lightly formed, or that I can lightly quit. **1855** MACAULAY *Hist. Eng.* xv. III. 555 He was not a prince against whom men lightly venture to set up a standard of rebellion. **1883** *Manch. Exam.* 17 Dec. 5/1 A warning to judges not lightly to send such suits to be retried.

†**9.** 'Not chastely' (J.). *Obs.*

a **1745** SWIFT *Story of an injured Lady* (1746) 10 If I were lightly disposed, I could still perhaps have Offers, that some, who hold their Heads higher, would be glad to accept.

10. *Comb.*

1687 *Lond. Gaz.* No. 2274/4 Lost..a dark grey Gelding.. lightly handled. **1798** SOTHEBY tr. *Wieland's Oberon* (1826) I. 76 And clasp'd her lightly-shaded breast beneath. **1860** RUSKIN *Mod. Paint.* V. VIII. iii. 180 Some lightly-budding philosophers. **1863** WOOLNER *My Beautiful Lady* 39 Her beauty walks in happier grace Than lightly-moving fawns. **1883** 'ANNIE THOMAS' *Mod. Housewife* 53 Butter a flat dish and put a layer of lightly-fried bread-crumbs.

lightly ('laɪtlɪ), *v.* Chiefly *Sc.* For forms see LIGHT *a.*¹ [f. LIGHTLY *a.*²] *trans.* To make light of, despise, disparage, disdain.

c **1375** *Sc. Leg. Saints* xxx. (*Theodora*) 218 Na heis [þu] þe for riches, to lichtly othyr mare or lese. *c* **1470** HENRYSON *Mor. Fab.* XI. (*Wolf & Sheep*) xxii, Thay will lichtlie lordis in to thair deidis. **1513** DOUGLAS *Æneis* IV. i. 70 Suppois thow lychtlyit thame of Lybie land. **1584** HUDSON *Du Bartas' Judith* I. (1608) 16 His house..That lightlied earth and seem'd to threat the heaven. **1588** A. KING tr. *Canisius' Catech.* 4 To lychtlie thame for that thay ar poore. **1650** Row *Hist. Kirk* Coronis (1842) 422 We doe not lightlie pearls though gathered out of a dung-hill. **1788** BURNS *Whistle & I'll come to you*, Whiles ye may lightly my beauty a wee. **1814** SCOTT *Wav.* lxvii, It's best no to lightly them that have that character. **1880** MRS. L. B. WALFORD *Troublesome Dau.* I. ix. 192, I'd no' hae my ae bairn gang whaur she was lichtlied. **1892** *Sat. Rev.* 9 Jan. 32/1 Of which trinity two at least are to be lightlied by no man.

Hence **'lightlied** *ppl. a.*, **'lightlying** *vbl. sb.*

1470 *Extracts Aberd. Reg.* (1844) I. 30 In gret lychtlying and contemnyng of our auctorite. **1528** JAS. V in *St. Papers Hen. VIII* (1836) IV. 500 To be confortit and ressavit within his Realme to our hurt lychtlying and displesour. **1826** G. BEATTIE *John o' Arnha'* (ed. 5) 19 They'd gar'd a lightliet lover greet.

†**'lightman.** *Obs.* [? f. LIGHT *a.*[1] + MAN, as in *Indiaman*, etc.] ? An unladen ship. (But cf. LIGHTERMAN.)

1665 *Lond. Gaz.* No. 16/1 On Friday last, 20 sail of Lightmen weighed Anchor.

lightman, lightmanship: see LIGHT *sb.* 16.

'lightmans. *Thieves' cant.* [f. LIGHT *a.*[2]: for the second element cf. DARKMANS.] The day.

1567 HARMAN *Caveat* (1869) 84 Bene Lightmans to thy quarromes. **1611** MIDDLETON & DEKKER *Roaring Girl* K 4 b, I wud lib all the lightmans. *a* **1700** B. E. *Dict. Cant. Crew*, *Light-mans*, the Day or Day-break. **1785** in GROSE *Dict. Vulgar Tongue*.

light-minded, *a.* Having a light or trifling mind; frivolous. Hence **light-'mindedness**.

1611 BIBLE *Eccl.* xix. 4 He that is hasty to giue credit is light minded. **1661** G. RUST *Origen* in *Phenix* (1721) I. 24 Tossed about like feathers with light-mindedness and admiration of trifles. **1833** J. H. NEWMAN *Arians* v. ii. (1876) 387 The light-minded multitude clamorously required it. **1870** EMERSON *Soc. & Solit.* ix. 120 Among the light-minded men and women who make up society. **1884** H. GERSONI tr. *Turgenieff's Diary Superfluous Man* 26 Mar. 97 The sad consequences of light-mindedness.

Lightmonger ('laɪtmʌŋgə(r)). [f. LIGHT *sb.* + MONGER.] A member of the Worshipful Company (formerly the Guild) of Lightmongers, a City of London Livery Company, which represents the lighting industry. Usu. *pl.* in the name of the Company.

1962 *Lightmongers Rules* (Guildhall Libr.) 1 The Society of 'Lightmongers' was formed at a Meeting held on Tuesday the 3rd day of November, 1953, at 'Ye Olde Cock Tavern', Fleet Street. **1970** *City Press* 16 Apr. 9/6 In 1966 the society changed its name to the 'Guild of Lightmongers'. **1974** *Ibid.* 14 Nov. 15/4 (*heading*) New officers for Lightmongers. **1975** *Lightmonger* Winter 5 This year Great Britain was the host country to an international lighting conference—the CIE—and the Lightmongers joined with the Guild of Tallowchandlers to entertain some of the distinguished delegates from overseas. **1984** *City Recorder* 30 Aug. 9/5 The Dragon holds the particular kind of lamp..which has often been kindled ceremonially at functions held by The Lightmongers. **1985** *Times* 1 Feb. 14/2 The Lord Mayor..presented letters patent confirming the grant of livery to the Master of the Lightmongers' Company.

lightner: see LIGHTENER.

lightness[1] ('laɪtnɪs). For forms see LIGHT *a.*[1] [f. LIGHT *a.*[1] + -NESS.] The quality or fact of being light, in various senses.

1. The quality or fact of having little weight. Of a vessel: The fact of being lightly laden. Of a crop: Smallness of the quantity present.

c **1175** *Lamb. Hom.* 83 Oli haueð huppen him lihtnesse and softnesse and hele. *c* **1374** CHAUCER *Boeth.* III. pr. xi. 77 (Camb. MS.) Wher-for elles berith Lythnesse the flaumbes vp. *c* **1586** C'TESS PEMBROKE *Ps.* LXII. iv, Ev'n he that seemeth most of might With lightnesse self if him you weigh, Then lightnesse self will weigh more light. **1590** SIR H. LEE in *Archæologia* (1888) LI. 171 A new brest [plate].. of gret litenes and strengthe. **1667** *Lond. Gaz.* No. 140/1 A Holland Vessel..unable because of her lightness to bear sail. **1765** A. DICKSON *Treat. Agric.* (ed. 2) 231 The lightness of it, and particularly the shortness of the share.. make it go very unsteadily. **1831** SIR J. SINCLAIR *Corr.* II. 86 The different kinds of air, and the superior lightness by which some of them were distinguished. **1848** MILL *Pol. Econ.* I. xii. §2 (1876) 110 It is long..before an English eye becomes reconciled to the lightness of the crops [in the United States]. **1875** JOWETT *Plato* (ed. 2) V. 194 The lightness of bows and arrows is convenient for running.

b. Of bread, pastry, etc.: (see LIGHT *a.*[1] 9 b).

1836 *Penny Cycl.* V. 372/2 To give the bread..porous texture and lightness. **1864** MRS. STOWE *House & Home Papers* x. (1865) 112 The matter of lightness is the distinctive line between savage and civilized bread.

†**2.** The condition of being lightened or relieved; alleviation. *Obs.*

a **1300** *Cursor M.* 24480 Her-wit come me son succur And sum lightnes o mi langur. **1357** *Lay Folks Catech.* 332 In lightenes and alegeaunce of their sekenesse.

3. Absence of heaviness or pressure in action or movement; want of force or moment. Said both of material and immaterial things.

1795 NELSON in Nicolas *Disp.* (1845) II. 15 From the lightness of the air of wind, the Enemy's Fleet and our Fleet were a very long time in passing. **1833** *Regul. Instr. Cavalry* I. 48 Lightness of hand consists in an almost imperceptible feeling and alternate easing of the bridle. **1885** *Spectator* 30 May 704/2 The lightness of touch that so charmingly characterises the literature of the seventeenth and eighteenth centuries. **1893** *Westm. Gaz.* 17 June 5/2 The lightness of the weather spoiled yesterday's race. **1893** *Law Times* XCIV. 600/2 The tax falls with..undue severity upon one class, and with unreasonable lightness upon others.

4. Of form or outline: Freedom from heaviness or clumsiness, graceful slenderness.

1808 SCOTT *Prose Wks.* IV. *Biographies* II. (1870) 35 She had lost much of the lightness of her figure. **1837** *Penny Cycl.* VII. 218/1 In them we observe a progressive change from heaviness to lightness—from columns less than four diameters in height to those of nearly seven. **1885** *Truth* 28 May 848/2 The spray is rendered with much lightness and delicacy.

5. The quality of moving lightly; agility, nimbleness, swiftness. Also in immaterial sense.

c **1386** CHAUCER *Miller's T.* 198 To shewe his lightnesse and maistrye He pleyeth Herodes vp on a Scaffold hye. **1398** TREVISA *Barth. De P.R.* V. lvii. (1495) 172 The bones are holowe for the more lyghtnesse of mouynge. **1483** *Cath. Angl.* 216/2 A Lightenes, *agilitas*. **1530** PALSGR. 239/1 Lightnesse of understandinge, *facilité d'entendre*. **1604** E. G[RIMSTONE] *D'Acosta's Hist. Indies* IV. xxxiv. 304 All these beasts for their lightnesse..have passed from one world to an other. **1859** J. BROWN *Rab & Friends* (1862) 26 Rab.. trotted up the stair with much lightness. **1860** TYNDALL *Glac.* I. xxv. 187 The contemplation of the brightening east ..seemed to lend lightness to our muscles.

†**6.** Ease, facility, readiness, esp. of belief. *Obs.*

a **1300** *Cursor M.* 27735 Lightness o rage. **1549** COVERDALE, etc. *Erasm. Par. Gal.* 8, I..blame your lightenes to beleue, & easynes to be persuaded. **1572** R. H. tr. *Lauaterus' Ghostes* (1596) 152 Oftentimes these men, through their too muche lightnesse of beleefe, fall into great daungers. **1620** VENNER *Via Recta* iii. 63 Linnets are both for lightnesse of digestion, and goodnesse of meate better then Sparrowes. **1741** RICHARDSON *Pamela* I. Introd. 24 Note with what Lightness even Men of good-natur'd Intention fall into Mistakes.

7. Levity in behaviour; fickleness, unsteadiness, frivolity, thoughtlessness, unconcern.

1340 HAMPOLE *Pr. Consc.* 308 Lightnes of hert reves þam drede. *c* **1449** PECOCK *Repr.* 344 Forto forsake God in a liȝtnes and in a rechelesnes. **1579** LYLY *Euphues* (Arb.) 95 This chaunge will..double thy lyghtnesse in tourning so often. **1679** BURNET *Hist. Ref.* I. 424 Imputing this insurrection..to their folly and lightness. **1760** *Ann. Reg.* 52 The general lightness of his faith with regard to his former allies. **1828** SCOTT *F.M. Perth* vii, My Catharine hath not by any lightness or folly of hers afforded grounds for this great scandal. **1887** E. J. GOODMAN *Too Curious* iii, The lightness of tone with which I uttered such serious words.

†**b.** Wantonness, lewdness, incontinence. *Obs.*

1516 *Life Birgette* in *Myrr. our Ladye* (1873) p. xlviii, She somwhat suspectynge the lyghtnesse of the virgyn commaundyd a rod to be brought vnto hir. **1541** *Act 33 Hen. VIII*, c. 21 If they..perceive any wil acte or condicion of lightnes of bodie in hir, which for the time being shall be queene of this realme. **1601** ? MARSTON *Pasquil & Kath.* II. 11 Women of leuitie and lightnesse. **1652** C. B. STAPYLTON *Herodian* III. 18 With him of lightnesse she was much suspected.

8. Freedom from depression or dullness, esp. in ***lightness of heart***; high spirits, joy, mirth.

1398 TREVISA *Barth. De P.R.* III. xix. (1495) 66 The instrument of smellyng is not in a beest onely for lightnes and fayrnesse. *a* **1420** HOCCLEVE *De Reg. Princ.* 1244 Myn hert is al nakid of lightnesse. **1526** *Pilgr. Perf.* (W. de W. 1531) 64 b, And this lyghtnesse or myrth may come somtyme of the clerenes of mannes conscyence. **1653** R. SANDERS *Physiogn.* 55 They signifie Quarrels picked out of lightness of heart. **1828** R. NESBIT in *Mem.* iii. (1858) 83, I am able to pursue my proper work with my usual lightness of spirit. **1861** HUGHES *Tom Brown at Oxf.* xxi. (1889) 195 He really hardly knew what to do to give vent to his lightness of heart.

lightness[2] ('laɪtnɪs). [OE. *líhtnes* (= OHG. *liuchtnisse*), f. *líht, léoht* LIGHT *a.*[2] + -NESS.]

†**1.** Brightness, light (*lit.* and *fig.*). *Obs.*

a **1023** WULFSTAN *Hom.* (Napier) 230 Se sunnandæȝ is restendæȝ and wuldorlic dæȝ and lihtnesse dæȝ. *a* **1325** in Horstm. *Altengl. Leg.* (1878) 145 Alle þe liȝtnesse was aleyd. Sonne & mone lorn her liȝt. *c* **1430** *Pilgr. Lyf Manhode* II. xl. (1869) 91 The sunne..maketh his lightnesse passe thoruh the cloude. *c* **1531** LATIMER *1st Let. to Baynton* in Foxe *A. & M.* (1563) 1322/2 They were vnapte to receyue the bryghte lyghtnes of the truthe. *c* **1532** DU WES *Introd. Fr.* in Palsgr. 922 We knowe selfely the soveraygne lyghtnesse to be darked of a lyght cloude. **1824** SCOTT *Red-gauntlet* let. xiii, His countenance..is now..rendered wild by an insane lightness about the eyes.

2. The condition or state of being illuminated; illumination. Now only *lit.*

c **1250** *Gen. & Ex.* 1559 In ðat dred his ðoȝt was led In to liȝtnesse for to sen, Quow god wulde it sulde ben. *a* **1300** *Cursor M.* 13543 To-quils i in þis werld be, It has na lightnes bot o me. **1591** SPARRY tr. *Cattan's Geomancie* (1599) 29 By the lightnesse and darkenesse which shee receiueth of him. **1651–7** T. BARKER *Art of Angling* (1820) 2 Thus must you to work with your flyes, light for darkness, and dark for lightness. **1832** LYTTON *Eugene A.* II. vii, The first thing that struck Walter in this apartment was its remarkable lightness.

lightning ('laɪtnɪŋ), *sb.* Also 4–5 **liȝtnynge**, 4, 6 **lyghtnyng**, 5–6 **lightnyng**, **lyght(e)nynge**, **lyt(e)nynge**, (5 **litynnynge**, 6 **lyghteling**), 6–8 **lightening**, 7–8 **light'ning**. [Special use of LIGHTENING *vbl. sb.*[2]; now differentiated in spelling.]

1. The visible discharge of electricity between one group of clouds and another, or between the clouds and the ground. Also in particularized sense (now *rare*), A flash of lightning. ***like lightning***, with the swiftness of lightning. Also in phr. † ***in less than***, †***to last no longer than a lightning***.

forked lightning, ***chain*** or ***chained lightning***: designations applied (usu. indiscriminately) to lightning which assumes the form of a zigzag or divided line. ***sheet lightning***: that in which a wide surface is equally illuminated at once. ***summer*** or ***heat lightning***: sheet lightning without thunder, the result of a storm at a great distance.

1377 LANGL. *P. Pl.* B. xix. 197 Thanne come..One *spiritus paraclitus* to Pieres and to his felawes In lyknesse of a liȝtnynge, he lyȝte on hem alle. **1388** WYCLIF *Ps.* lxxvi. 19 Thi liȝtnyngis schyneden to the world. *c* **1425** CAPGRAVE *Chron.* (Rolls) 314 The moost horribil thunderes and litynnyngis that evyr ony man herd. *a* **1470** *Gregory's Chron.* in *Hist. Coll. Citizen Lond.* (Camden) 185 The bones yere was Syn Poulys stypylle fyryd..whythe the lyghtenynge. **1555** EDEN *Decades* 98 He shall rewarde yowe whiche sendeth thunderynge and lyghtelyng to the destruction of myscheuous men. **1591** FLORIO *2nd Fruites* 49 It shall be readie in les than a lightning. **1651** tr. *De-las-Coveras' Don Fenise* 257 A beame of her eyes..which lasted no longer than a lightning. **1718** POPE *Iliad* xv. 725 He..drives him, like a Light'ning, on the Foe. **1722** DE FOE *Plague* (1754) 261 This Notion ran like Lightening thro' the City. **1841** MARRYAT *Poacher* xxvii, Our hero..ran like lightning to the gap. **1859** *All Year Round* No. 17. 400 The lightning..was chiefly 'sheet lightning', though now and then 'chained' or 'forked' was visible. **1880** *Nature* XXI. 407 A few lightnings and rather more auroras were seen.

transf. and *fig.* **1686** tr. *Chardin's Coron. Solyman* 149 The Lightning of Royal disfavour afterwards fell on Mirza Sadee. **1771** MACKENIZE *Man Feel.* xxviii. (1803) 48 His eyes lost the lightning of their fury. **1821** SHELLEY *Death Napoleon* iii, The lightning of scorn laughed forth As she sung [etc.]. **1859** TENNYSON *Guinevere* 516 She..Makes wicked lightnings of her eyes.

2. a. *slang.* Gin. Also, any strong, freq. low-quality, alcoholic spirit. Chiefly *U.S.* Cf. *chain-lightning* (s.v. CHAIN *sb.* 19).

1781 G. PARKER *Life's Painter* 140 Noggin of lightning, a quartern of gin. **1851** MAYHEW *Lond. Labour* I. 160 The stimulant of a 'flash of lightning'. **1858** *Calif. Spirit of Times* (San Francisco) 7 Aug. 1/4 Having in his possession a few kegs of liquid lightning upon which he was avariciously desirous of reaping a speedy profit. **1873** J. MILLER *Life amongst Modocs* viii. 94 In one of the saloons where men were wont to..drink lightning. **1945** L. SHELLY *Jive Talk Dict.* 28/2 *Lightning and thunder*, whisky and soda. **1958** L. VAN DER POST *Lost World of Kalahari* ii. 53 The fiery Cape brandy known to us children as 'Blitz' or Lightning.

b. *pl.* One of the top grades of white jute.

1929 WOODHOUSE & KILGOUR *Spinning Flax & Jute* i. 2 (*caption*) Jute bale marks... Lightnings. **1929** *Observer* 17 Nov. 4/3 Jute... Lightnings November-December quoted £25. **1964** R. R. ATKINSON *Jute* i. 23 White jute is assorted into three main classes... The top class is sub-divided into Firsts, Lightnings, and Hearts.

3. *attrib.* and *Comb.*: **a.** simple attributive, as ***lightning-flame***, ***-flash***, ***-glimpse***; **b.** instrumental, as ***lightning-blackened***, ***-blasted***, ***-struck*** adjs.; **c.** similative and parasynthetic, as ***lightning-footed***, ***-quick***, ***-rapid***, ***-swift***, ***-winged*** adjs.; ***lightning-like*** adj. and adv.

1897 CLARK RUSSELL *Noble Haul* 80 Abaft she was naked, withered, and *lightning-blackened. **1821** SHELLEY *Prometh. Unb.* II. i. 135 Yon *lightning-blasted almond-tree. **1561** T. NORTON *Calvin's Inst.* I. 8 To set the aire on fier with *lightning flames. **1588** SHAKS. *Tit. A.* II. i. 3 Secure of Thunders cracke or *lightning flash. **1866** J. H. NEWMAN *Gerontius* §4 Then sight..As by a lightning-flash, will come to thee. **1870** BRYANT *Iliad* I. VIII. 247 Mars, the *lightning-footed. **1667** MILTON *P.L.* VI. 642 Light as the *Lightning glimps they ran. *a* **1822** SHELLEY *Prose Wks.* (1880) III. 323 *Lightning-like the vigorous maiden strides. **1841** KEBLE *Serm.* xii. (1848) 311 The clear, the indisputable, the lightning-like evidence. **1925** V. WOOLF *Common Reader* 41 That is the quality that first strikes us in Greek literature, the *lightning-quick, sneering, out-of-doors manner. **1947** C. S. LEWIS *Miracles* xii. 118 What they painfully reconstruct from a million dots..he really produced with a single lightning-quick turn of the wrist. **1961** *Times* 25 Mar. 4/7 That strangely reluctant take-away of the club and the lightning-quick swing caused plenty of trouble yesterday. **1922** D. H. LAWRENCE *England, my England* 45 The officer was giving the last *lightning-rapid orders to fire. *c* **1820** S. ROGERS *Italy* (1839) 157 An oak.. Now *lightning-struck. **1857** C. BRONTE *Professor* II. xix. 48 So *lightning-swift is thought. **1646** CRASHAW *Sospetto d'Herode* xxx, The nimblest of the *lightning-winged loves.

d. passing into an *adj.*: Moving or flashing by with the rapidity of lightning; done, produced, or acting with the speed of lightning; spec. ***lightning artist***, an artist who paints or draws pictures very quickly as an entertainment; ***lightning-change***, a rapid change of costume made by an actor or performer; also *attrib.*; ***lightning strike***, a sudden strike (STRIKE *sb.* 9) which takes place without any warning; ***lightning tournament***, a Chess tournament in which each player must make his move within a prescribed few seconds; also ***lightning chess***, ***player***, etc.

1640 BP. REYNOLDS *Passions* iv, To have a vanishing and lightning Fancie that knoweth not how to stay and fasten upon any particular. **1847** DISRAELI *Tancred* IV. xi, He gazed with admiration on her lightning glance. **1873** W. MATHEWS *Getting on in World* 242 Now..people travel by 'lightning lines', going from New York to Chicago in twenty-nine hours. **1875** 'MARK TWAIN' in *Atlantic Monthly* Aug. XXXVI. 192/1 If one of the boats has a 'lightning' pilot, whose 'partner' is a trifle inferior, you can tell which one is on watch by noting whether that boat has gained ground or lost. **1889** G. O. SEILHAMER *Hist. Amer. Theatre* II. xxiii. 299 He may..be accorded the distinction of being the first 'lightning change artist' on the American stage. **1908** *Sears, Roebuck Catal.* 342/5 Silver Dip. The new lightning cleaner. **1910** *Year-Bk. Chess* 143 (*heading*) Two special lightning tournaments were held. **1920** *Radiograph* July p. ix/1 The first step was an endeavour to try to stigmatise the ..action as 'A Lightning Strike'. **1927** W. E. COLLINSON *Contemp. Eng.* 70 A few technical expressions of the Halls which are commonly known to English townsfolk, but not likely to find their way into all the dictionaries, e.g... lightning artists (*caricaturists working at great speed*). **1927** E. GLYN *'It'* 240 She had promised to sit for him just for a lightning sketch. **1928** G. B. SHAW *Intelligent Woman's Guide Socialism* lxxxiii. 448 A lightning strike of waitresses in a restaurant. **1940** E. C. SHEPHERD *Britain's Air Power* 5

In the German 'Lightning War' on Poland the aeroplane was used to the full as an offensive weapon. **1945** *Tee Emm* (Air Ministry) V. 33 Fields, hedges and houses flash past at lightning speed under your wings. **1946** *Happy Landings* (Air Ministry) July 7/2 In addition to making a lightning survey of local air safety measures..a..lecture was given. **1948** C. DAY LEWIS *Otterbury Incident* iv. 39 Lightning sketches by Miss E. Toppingham. *Ibid.* 48 Toppy's sister, the lightning artist, had done particularly well. **1949** H. GOLOMBEK *World Chess Championship 1948* 24 He is..one of the world's best lightning players. **1951** 'ASSIAC' *Adventure in Chess* III. iii. 99 Most proficient at 'lightning Chess'. **1952** GRANVILLE *Dict. Theatr. Terms* 111 *Lightning-change artiste*, the (more usual) quick-change artiste, one who imitates..a number of well-known personalities. **1955** *Times* 3 Aug. 8/7 A shortage of labour caused a lightning strike of about 200 men at the Albert and William Wright docks at Hull to-day. **1971** E. PRITCHARD *Chess for Pleasure* xii. 148 In the evenings there may be *lightning* tournaments, when games are played at 10 seconds a move.

e. Special combs.: **lightning-arrester**, a device to protect telegraphic apparatus, etc. from lightning; **lightning beetle** = *lightning-bug*; **lightning-bone**, ? = FULGURITE 1; **lightning box**, a box used in producing stage-lightning; **lightning-bug** = FIRE-FLY 1; **lightning-catarrh** (see quot.); **lightning conductor**, a metallic rod or wire fixed to the summit (or other exposed point) of a building, or the mast of a ship, to convey lightning harmlessly into the earth or sea; **lightning-discharger** = *lightning-arrester*; **lightning express** *U.S.*, a designation given to certain very rapid trains; **lightning-pains** *pl.*, sharp, shooting pains of momentary duration, felt by patients suffering from locomotor ataxy (*Syd. Soc. Lex.* 1888); **lightning-paper**, a kind of firework giving off flashes of coloured light; **lightning-print**, an appearance sometimes found on the skin of men and animals and on clothing struck by lightning, popularly supposed to be photographs of surrounding objects; **lightning-proof** *a.*, protected from lightning; **lightning-rod** = *lightning-conductor*; **lightning-stone, -tube** = FULGURITE 1.

1870 F. L. POPE *Electr. Tel.* iv. (1872) 44 *Lightning-arresters must always be kept free from dampness and dirt. **1854** B. JAEGER *Life of N. Amer. Insects* 75 Some months since a lady..presented me two of these living *Lightning beetles. **1865** TYLOR *Early Hist. Man.* viii. 223 The name of '*lightning-bones', or 'thunder-bones', given to fossil bones. **1825** P. EGAN *Life of Actor* ii. 67 *Lightning boxes, sheep hooks, and three harlequin's bats. **1855** 'Q. K. P. DOESTICKS' *Doesticks, what he Says* xxvi. 237 The prompter was stretched on the top of a canvas volcano, with the bell-rope in his hand, and his hair full of resin, from the 'lightnin-box'. **1928** A. ROSE *Stage Effects* 26 Fig. 20 is a simple but useful and convenient form of lightning box... One or more electric lights are to be in the centre of the box. **1778** J. CARVER *Trav. N. Amer.* xviii. 491 The *Lightning Bug or Fire Fly is about the size of a bee. **1806** MOORE *Song* iv. Poems 166 Gleam then like the lightning-bug. **1842** *Southern Lit. Messenger* VIII. 199/2 It will never do to tell *us* that there is any humbug in this business, or even that it is a mere *lightning-bug*. **1850** LYELL *2nd Visit U.S.* II. 206 The elegant fire-fly is called a lightning-bug. **1936** T. S. ELIOT *Coll. Poems 1909–1935* 138 The small flare of the firefly or lightning bug. **1947** *Chicago Tribune* 21 June 2/4 He asserted that to 'talk about Henry Wallace intimidating Harry Truman on the veto is like describing a lightning bug as blotting out the rays of the sun'. **1971** *Lebende Sprachen* XVI. 10/1 US lightning bug—BE/US firefly. **1883** B. W. RICHARDSON *Field of Disease* 52 A suddenly developed and intensely severe cold or catarrh, hence sometimes called '*lightning catarrh.' [**1791** E. DARWIN *Bot. Garden* i. Additional Notes 25 The design of these conductors is to permit the electric matter accumulated in the clouds to pass through them into the earth..and it would seem that the finer the point..the better, as it would take off the lightning while it was still at a greater distance.] **1814** W. BENTLEY *Diary* (1914) IV. 262 The post remained, retained on the side of the steeple by the *Lightning conductors. **1832** *2nd Rep. Brit. Assoc.* (1833) 564 This ship had not a lightning conductor up at the time. **1967** *Everyman's Encycl.* V. 429/1 He [*sc.* B. Franklin] estab. the identity of lightning with electricity.. and suggested the use of lightning conductors on large buildings. **1875** KNIGHT *Dict. Mech.*, *Lightning-discharger. **1860** O. W. HOLMES *Prof. Breakf.-t.* vi, The *lightning-express-train *whishes* by. **1896** *Allbutt's Syst. Med.* I. 346 In organic nervous diseases they [i.e. baths] are not to be recommended, unless it be to relieve the *lightning pains of tabes. **1873** SPON *Workshop Rec.* 137 *Lightning Paper. **1876** *Chamb. Jrnl.* 15 Jan. 36/1 Signor Orioli brought before a scientific congress at Naples four narratives relating to *lightning-prints. **1855** HYDE CLARKE *Dict.*, **Lightning-proof.* **1790** in *Trans. Amer. Philos. Soc.* (1793) III. 323 After a *lightening rod has been erected. **1860** EMERSON *Cond. Life, Worship* Wks. (Bohn) II. 407 The lightning-rod that disarms the cloud of its threat. **1865** TYLOR *Early Hist. Man.* viii. 208 The *lightning-stones are metals, stones, pebbles, which the fire of the thunder has metamorphosed. **1831** *Literary Gaz.* 15 Jan. 44/2 *Lightning Tubes—In the neigbourhood of the old castle of Remstein..there have been found this summer very firm and long vitreous tubes.

lightning ('laɪtnɪŋ), *v.* [f. the sb.] = LIGHTEN *v.*[2] 6. Also *fig.*

1903 *Westm. Gaz.* 16 Nov. 8/2 The two metal balls.. thundered and lightninged as they delivered the message. **1926** H. CAINE in *Strand Mag.* Jan. 20/1 Mr. Gladstone leapt to his feet, whereupon the air of the House thundered and lightninged for a short ten minutes. **1935** in Z. N. Hurston *Mules & Men* (1970) I. i. 27 You know, when it lightnings, de angels is peepin' in de lookin' glass.

lightningy ('laɪtnɪŋɪ), *a.* [f. LIGHTNING + -Y[1].] Suggestive of lightning. (In comb. with *thunder.*)

1906 GALSWORTHY *Man of Property* II. ii. 141 They had never seen anyone look so thunder and lightningy as that little June!

light of love, light o' love. Also 6 **light a love, lightilove.** [See LIGHT *a.*[1] 16.]

1. As predicative phr.: Inconstant in love.

1579 LYLY *Euphues* (Arb.) 89 Ah wretched wench, canst thou be so lyght of loue, as to chaunge with euery winde? **1592** HYRDE tr. *Vives' Instruct. Chr. Woman* N j, And if he should mary her, he wil thinke shee will have as good mind to other, as himselfe, when she is so light of love.

2. As *sb.* †**a.** Inconstancy in love. *Obs.*

1578 T. PROCTOR *Gorg. Gallery* E iij b, The fickle are blamed: Their lightiloue shamed.

b. A woman capricious or inconstant in love; also, in more unfavourable sense, a wanton, a harlot.

1599 PORTER *Angry Wom. Abingt.* (Percy Soc.) 35 Foule strumpet, Light a loue, shorte heeles! **1618** FLETCHER *Chances* I. iii, Sure he has encountered Some light-o-love or other. **1828** SCOTT *F.M. Perth* xxi, You and I must part sooner than perhaps a light o' love such as you expected to part with—a likely young fellow. **1892** J. PAYN *Mod. Whittington* II. 167 'My Kitty a light-o'-love—a trollop—' and the wretched father burst into tears.

attrib. **1589** NASHE *Anat. Absurditie* A ij, As there was a loyall Lucretia, so there was a light a loue Lais. **1592** GREENE *Upst. Courtier* B 2 b, To warne such light a loue wenches, not to trust euery faire promise that such amorous Batchelers make them. **1843** JAMES *Forest Days* (1847) 25 Following..his light-o'-love sweetheart to the dance.

†**3.** The name of an old dance-tune. *Obs.*

1591 SHAKS. *Two Gent.* I. ii. 83. **1599** —— *Much Ado* III. iv. 44. **1612** *Two Noble K.* v. iv.

lightradge, obs. form of LIGHTERAGE.

lights (laɪts), *pl.* Forms: 2–3 **lihte**, 4 **liȝtes**, 4–6 **lightes, -is, -ys**, 6 **lyght(e)s**, *Sc.* **lichtis, lychtis, -es**, 6– **lites**, 6– **lights.** [Subst. use of LIGHT *a.*[1]

The word LUNG has the same etymological meaning, the lungs being distinguished from the other internal parts by their lightness.]

a. The lungs. Now only applied to the lungs of beasts (sheep, pigs, bullocks), used as food (chiefly for cats and dogs).

?*a* **1200** *Homily* in Phillipps *Fragm. Ælfric's Gramm.*, *&c.* (1838) 6 þine þermes..lifre & þine lihte. *c* **1205** LAY. 6499 þat deor..ræsde o þene stede, and for-bat him þa breste ..þat þa lihte [*c* 1275 longene] and þa liuere feollen on eorðen. *c* **1320** *Sir Tristr.* 498 þe left schulder ȝaf he, Wiþ hert, liuer and liȝtes And blod tille his quirre. *c* **1400** *Destr. Troy* 10705 With a big arow he Rut þurgh his rybbes.. Betwene the lyuer & the lightes launchit hym þurghe. *c* **1460** *Towneley Myst.* xxxi. 131 Then wofully sich wightys Shall gnawe thise gay knyghtys, Thare lunges and thare lightys. **1513** DOUGLAS *Æneis* IX. xi. 80 So deip the grundin steyll heyd owt of sycht is, Ful hait and warm it festnyt in his lychtis. **1578** LYTE *Dodoens* VI. xli. 711 Bitter Almondes doo open the stopping of the lunges or lightes. **1596** SPENSER *F. Q.* VI. iii. 26 As if his lungs and lites were nigh asunder brast. **1665** WOOD *Life* 12 May, The lights of a bullock or yong oxe. **1671** SALMON *Syn. Med.* I. xliii. 94 The Difficulty of Breathing shews the Lights [to be affected]. **1797** *Lond. Art Cookery* 133 To dress a Calf's Pluck. Boil the lights and part of the liver. **1835** MARRYAT *Jac. Faithf.* xli, It is a piece of lights reserved for the dinner of the cat to-morrow. **1873** E. SMITH *Foods* 79 The lungs, or as they are vulgarly termed lights, are eaten as a part of the pluck or fry. **1963** B. VESEY-FITZGERALD *Cat Owner's Encycl.* 69 Lungs (commonly known as 'lites'), whether of cow, sheep or horses, are strongly to be recommended.

b. Colloq. phr. ***to scare the (liver and) lights out of*** (someone): to scare (someone) greatly.

1884 'MARK TWAIN' *Huck. Finn* xxix. 307 It most scared the liver and lights out of me. **1956** E. POUND tr. *Sophocles' Women of Trachis* 18 You might start by questioning Likhas, scare the lights out of him, and he might tell you.

'lightship. [f. LIGHT *sb.*] A vessel bearing a light, *esp.* one with a warning light or lights moored where a lighthouse cannot conveniently be placed; a floating light.

1837 HT. MARTINEAU *Soc. Amer.* II. 11 The office of the light-ship is to tow vessels in the dark through the strait. **1870** *Daily News* 2 Sept. 3 The visitors to Ramsgate..have had an opportunity afforded them of seeing the far-famed Goodwin lightship at close quarters.

attrib. and *Comb.*

1887 *Chambers's Jrnl.* 1 Jan. 1 (*title*) The lightshipman. **1904** *Westm. Gaz.* 8 Oct. 9/2 The light-ship men were unable to come on shore. **1905** *Daily Chron.* 10 Oct. 4/5 Such strictures upon the lightship keepers' employment would hold equally with reference to the crews of say the light vessels off the Scilly Islands. **1958** W. ARMSTRONG *True Bk. Lighthouses & Lightships* xiii. 131 'Better be safe than sorry' was always the unspoken motto of lighthouse and lightship men.

'light-skirts. A woman of light character.

1597–8 BP. HALL *Sat.* I. viii, Solomon..Singing his love, the holy spouse of Christ, Like as she were some light-skirts of the East. **1602** *2nd Pt. Return Parnass.* I. ii. 310 Hath not Shor's wife, although a light skirts she, Giuen him a chast long lasting memory? **1616** T. TUKE *Treat. agst. Paint.* 39 Actions..becomming onely light-skirts, and idle women. **1632** QUARLES *Div. Fancies* IV. xii. (1660) 145 I'le tell thee, Light-skirts, whosoever taught Thy feet to dance, thy dancing had a Fault. **1834** SIR H. TAYLOR *2nd Pt. Artevelde* III. iii. 114 She's a light skirts! **1898** *Lit. World* 4 Feb. 103 To consider her [Highland Mary's] story..either (1) she was something of a light-skirts, or (2) she is a kind of Scottish Mrs. Harris.

b. *attrib.* (in form *light-skirt*).

1602 *2nd Pt. Return fr. Parnass.* I. vi. 468 You light skirt starres, this is your wonted guise, By glomy light perke out your doutfull heads. **1619** W. SCLATER *Exp. 1 Thess.* (1630) 49 Any light-skirt Dame, or Courtly Herodias shall rather be imitated. **1891** W. A. CLOUSTON in *Athenæum* 3 Oct. 452/1 [The parrot] told tales to its master of his light-skirt wife.

lightsome ('laɪtsəm), *a.*[1] [f. LIGHT *a.*[1] + -SOME. Cf. MHG. *lîhtsam.*]

1. Having the effect or appearance of lightness; now chiefly with reference to form, light, graceful, elegant. †Also, in early use, easy. Somewhat *rare.*

c **1440** *Promp. Parv.* 304/2 Lyghtesum, or esy (*K.* lihtsum), *facilis.* **1578** *Chr. Prayers* 77 b, Let thy yoke become sweete and thy burthen lightsom to me through thy crosse. **1634–5** BRERETON *Trav.* (1844) 179 The pillars as strong as any I have seen..but nothing neat or lightsome. **1737** BRACKEN *Farriery Impr.* (1757) II. 19 Nothing contributes more to a Horse's being easy upon the Rider's Hand, than a lightsome Fore-End, and thin Shoulders. **1759** B. MARTIN *Nat. Hist. Eng.* I, I. of Wight 123 The Air of Newport is lightsome and pleasant. **1824** MISS MITFORD *Village* Ser. I. 14 Snowy blossoms..so lightsome, and yet so rich! *a* **1851** MOIR *Poems, Angler* ii, His hat of whitest straw, Lightsome of wear. **1877** MRS. OLIPHANT *Makers Flor.* iv. 116 The lofty tower, straight and lightsome as a lily.

2. Not weighed down by care, pain, or sorrow; light-hearted, cheerful, merry; also, enlivening, entertaining.

?*a* **1366** CHAUCER *Rom. Rose* 956 With ladies and with bacheleres, Ful lightsom and [ful] glad of cheres. *c* **1400** *Beryn* 2973 Hir thouȝtis..did hir peyn to make liȝtsom chere. **1590** T. WATSON *Eclog. Death Walsingham* 121 That lightsome vaine is changd from youth to aged grauitie. **1657** SPARROW *Bk. Com. Prayer* (1661) 389 White garments.. suit fitly with that lightsome affection of joy. **1679** C. NESSE *Antid. agst. Popery* 202 A lightsome story of a French gentleman..being asked merrily [etc.]. **1712** STEELE *Spect.* No. 547 ⁋ 12, I now find myself cheerful, lightsome and easy. **1812** BYRON *Ch. Har.* II. xcii, Greece is no lightsome land of social mirth. **1818** SCOTT *Hrt. Midl.* xvii, Lightsome sangs make merry gate. **1877** MRS. OLIPHANT *Makers Flor.* ii. 39 The merry-makers were dancing..a lightsome crowd, with garlands and greenery.

b. Flighty, frivolous.

1533 SIR T. MORE in Ellis *Orig. Lett.* Ser. I. II. 52 Not uppon the fallible opinion or sone spoken words of lightsome chaungeable peple. **1800** A. CARLYLE *Autobiog.* 524 The neighbours..were all very agreeable, even the clergyman's wife, who was a little lightsome. **1890** W. A. WALLACE *Only a Sister?* 77 She was as good-living a woman as ever stepped; but lightsome like, as foreign folks are.

3. Moving lightly; lively, nimble, quick.

1601 HOLLAND *Pliny* I. 37 Their sences cleare and lightsome, their wits pregnant. **1683** TRYON *Way to Health* xi. (1697) 193 The Body will feel itself more airy and lightsomer. **1737** BRACKEN *Farriery Impr.* (1756) I. 157 Matter is drawn off, and the Head rendered brisk and lightsome. **1798** FRERE, etc. *Anti-Jacobin* No. 31 (1852) 171 Thy limber and lightsome spirit bounds up against affliction. **1805** WORDSW. *Prelude* XIII. 133 As lightsome as a bird. **1815** L. HUNT *Feast of Poets* 65 Mr. Scott..has a lightsome fancy. **1850** TENNYSON *In Mem.* lxv, There flutters up a happy thought, Self-balanced on a lightsome wing. **1879** J. HAWTHORNE *Laugh. M.* etc. 315 His lofty figure was as alert and lightsome as it was majestic.

lightsome ('laɪtsəm), *a.*[2] For forms see LIGHT *sb.* and -SOME. [f. LIGHT *sb.* + -SOME.]

1. Radiant with light; light-giving, luminous.

c **1440** *Promp. Parv.* 304/2 Lyghtesum, or fulle of lyghte, *luminosus.* **1530** RASTELL *Bk. Purgat.* III. ii, The sonne & the other sterres..we see them so lyghtsom, so pure and clene. **1655** GURNALL *Chr. in Arm.* I. 3 Dark Lanthorn, lightsome one way, and dark another. **1813** SHELLEY *Q. Mab* 102 Lightsome clouds and shining seas.

b. *fig.*

1382 WYCLIF *Ps.* xviii[i]. 10 The heste of the Lord [is] liȝtsum, liȝtende eȝen. **1548** UDALL, etc. *Erasm. Par. John* 12 God the father, the fountain of all light; from whence what soeuer is lightsome in heauen and earth, boroweth his light. **1570–6** LAMBARDE *Peramb. Kent* (1826) 3 Master Camden, the most lightsome antiquarie of this age. **1615** BP. HALL *Contempl.*, *O.T.* XI. vii, The lights of Israel..should be succeeded with one, much more lightsome than they. **1728** SWIFT *Two Lett. to Publ. Dubl. Wkly. Jrnl.* i. Wks. 1824 VII. 206 You must grow from chaos and darkness, to the little glimmerings of existence first, and then proceed to more lightsome appearances afterwards. **1883** R. W. DIXON *Mano* I. viii. 21 Those lightsome words that warm like summer days.

2. Chiefly of an apartment, a building: Permeated with light; well-lighted, bright, illumined.

1538 LELAND *Itin.* VII. 110 The Paroche Chirche is faire and lyghtesom. **1625** BACON *Ess., Building* (Arb.) 548 His Stately Galleries, and Roomes, so Large and Lightsome. **1654** COKAINE *Dianea* I. 44 The Princesse was full of wonder ..That this habitation being under ground was so lightsome. **1726** LEONI *Designs* 2/2 The Ground-floor is.. above the level of the Street, which..makes the offices beneath more lightsome. **1798** WORDSW. *Goody Blake & H. Gill* v, The long, warm, lightsome summer-day. **1873** SYMONDS *Grk. Poets* xii. 407 Beneath the lightsome vault of heaven he stands and prays.

b. *fig.*

c **1425** *St. Mary of Oignies* I. v. in *Anglia* VIII. 138 þey [make] lightsum þe soule with a shynynge. **1587** GOLDING *De Mornay* viii. 101 Beyond the first Olimpiade, there is nothing but a thicke cloud of ignorance, euen in the lightsomest places of all Greece. **1641** M. FRANK *Serm.* (1672) 255 The times of the Gospel are the only lightsome

day. **1863** W. G. BLAIKIE *Better Days Work. People* ii. 48 Will the six days of labour be none the lightsomer for the sunshine of the day of rest?

3. Clear, perspicuous, manifest. Now *rare*.

1532 MORE *Confut. Tindale* Wks. 355/1 So shall I..make you that matter so lightsome and so clere. **1670** MILTON *Hist. Eng.* I. Wks. 1738 II. 2, I..shall endeavour..with plain and lightsome Brevity, to relate..things worth the noting. **1859** I. TAYLOR *Logic in Theol.* 269 But were not ancient schemes of human nature..far more lightsome, and easy of apprehension.

†**4.** Light-hued. *Obs.*

a **1586** SIDNEY *Arcadia* III. (1633) 312 The lightsome colours of affection, shaded with the deepest shadowes of sorrow. **1608** TOPSELL *Serpents* (1658) 767 Black, and not lightsome, only about the edges of it there was some palenesse apparent. **1674** N. FAIRFAX *Bulk & Selv.* 52 It must be a bright lightsom colour.

lightsomely (ˈlaɪtsəmlɪ), *adv.*[1] [f. LIGHTSOME *a.*[1] + -LY[2].] Lightly, nimbly; gaily, merrily.

1561 T. HOBY tr. *Castiglione's Courtyer* I. (1577) E i b, He settleth himselfe lightsomly (not thinking vpon it) in a readie aptnesse. **1668** H. MORE *Div. Dial.* III. xvi. (1713) 214 Though the Phancy of Cuphophron may seem more than ordinary ludibund and lightsomely sportful. **1808** SCOTT *Marm.* II. Introd., The bugles ringing lightsomely. **1837** HAWTHORNE *Twice-Told T.* (1851) II. ix. 131, I perceive a flock of snow birds, skimming lightsomely through the tempest. **1877** MRS. OLIPHANT *Makers Flor.* iii. 88 They now most lightsomely live in that happiness to which there comes no end.

† **ˈlightsomely**, *adv.*[2] *Obs.* [f. LIGHTSOME *a.*[2] + -LY[2].] Clearly, lucidly, manifestly.

c **1510** MORE *Picus* Wks. 7/1 The same thing also in his boke, which he entitled *de Ente & Vno*, lightsomely he treateth. **1610** HOLLAND *Camden's Brit.* I. 381 Gods favour shining more lightsomly had scattered away the clouds of contention. **1662** J. CHANDLER *Van Helmont's Oriat.* 23 It is not as yet..made lightsomely famous.

lightsomeness[1] (ˈlaɪtsəmnɪs). [f. LIGHTSOME *a.*[1] + -NESS.] The quality of being lightsome or not heavy; † easiness (*obs.*), liveliness, cheerfulness, etc.

c **1440** *Promp. Parv.* 304/2 Lyghtesumnesse, or esynesse, *facilitas.* **1581** MULCASTER *Positions* xxxvii. (1887) 154 By lightsomnesse or heauinesse in learning, by easinesse or hardnesse in retaining. **1617** J. MOORE *Mappe Mans Mortalitie* II. vii. 148 Though the heavy burden of our sinfull flesh doe load vs, yet lightsomnesse it is to a Christian to thinke that the way is not long. **1632** tr. *Bruel's Praxis Med.* 200 There is no paine, but rather a lightsomnes of the body. **1668** G. C. in H. More *Div. Dial.* Pref. (1713) vi, That versatility of Wit, and lightsomeness of Humour. **1829** *Westm. Rev.* X. 428 The 'Misfortunes of Elphin'..lacks lightsomeness, grace, and invention. **1876** LOWELL *Among my Bks.* Ser. II. 138 Drayton..had an agreeable lightsomeness of fancy. **1880** J. FOTHERGILL *Wellfields* III. xi. 250 She..was astonished at the sudden lightsomeness of heart which she felt. **1885** PATER *Marius the Epicur.* II. 69 Dainty as that old divinely constructed armour of which Homer speaks, but without its miraculous lightsomeness.

lightsomeness[2] (ˈlaɪtsəmnɪs). [f. LIGHTSOME *a.*[2] + -NESS.] The quality of being lightsome, luminous, or well-lighted; brightness; †clearness.

c **1440** *Promp. Parv.* 304/2 Lyghtesumnesse, *luminositas.* **1532** MORE *Confut. Tindale* Wks. 583/1 The faith is not ordinarily with..open, ineuitable, and invincible lyghtsomenesse inspired into the soule. **1581** J. BELL *Haddon's Answ. Osor.* 182 b, Spoken..with a farre more playne lightsomnesse by our expositors. **1591** HARINGTON *Orl. Fur.* III. xvi, A darksome place with lightsomnes to fill. **1617** COLLINS *Def. Bp. Ely* I. iv. 170 Paul..was dazeled with the exceeding lightsomenesse. **1754** EDWARDS *Freed. Will* IV. ix. (1762) 259 The Sun's being the Cause of the Lightsomeness and Warmth of the Atmosphere. **1791** BENTHAM *Panopt.* I. 14 Airiness, lightsomeness, economy.. are the evident results. **1892** MACLAREN *Paul's Prayers* etc. 173 There are some of you, grovelling down at the bottom of the ocean, to whom..the lightness and lighsomeness of the pure life..would seem miraculous.

ˈlight-ˈtouch, *v. Obs. rare*[−1]. [f. LIGHT *a.* + TOUCH *sb.*] *trans.* To paint with a light touch.

1748 THOMSON *Cast. Indol.* I. xxxviii, Whate'er Lorrain light-touched with softening hue.

lightwards (ˈlaɪtwədz), *adv.* [f. LIGHT *sb.* + -WARD(S.] Towards the light.

1891 L. KEITH *Lost Illusion* II. xix. 219 The geraniums turned lightwards at the window.

ˈlight-weight, light weight, *sb.* and *a.* Also (without hyphen) **lightweight**. [f. LIGHT *a.*[1]]

A. *sb.* **a.** *Sporting.* A man or animal under the average weight; esp. in *Boxing*, now usually a competitor weighing between 126 and 135 pounds. Also in *Racing* handicaps, one of the horses carrying light weights, or a jockey riding at a low weight. Also anything (e.g. a motorcycle) that is relatively light in weight.

1773 BURKE *Corr.* (1844) I. 431 Send him a clever lad who can ride light weights. **1823** EGAN *Grose's Dict. Vulg. Tongue*, *Light weights*, a pugilistic expression for gentlemen under twelve stone. **1823** 'JON BEE' *Dict. Turf*, *Light weight*, in affairs connected with the ring, persons of 11 stone and under are light weights. **1848** THACKERAY *Bk. Snobs* xxxvi, As a light-weight, his skill is of the..highest order. **1871** M. COLLINS *Mrq. & Merch.* III. iv. 112 Presently entered the landlord,..a light weight of five-and-thirty. **1897** *Outing* (U.S.) XXIX. 542/2 Some breeders of the..lightweights [dogs] have gone a trifle too far. **1898** *Pearson's Mag.* Feb. 165/1 The torpedo-boat and the destroyer may fairly be called the light-weights of naval warfare. **1908** *Daily Report* 20 July 9/1 Light-weights of 2 h.p. are quite capable of averaging well over 20 m.p.h. **1960** M. GOLESWORTHY *Encycl. Boxing* 211/1 *Weight Divisions*... Lightweight—1868 at 9 st. 7 lbs. (133 lbs.). 1912 raised to present limit of 9 st. 9 lbs. (135 lbs.) by Willie Ritchie.

attrib. **1857** LAWRENCE *Guy Livingstone* ix. 80 Having her [a mare] broken into a perfect light-weight hunter. **1896** *Daily News* 12 June 6/3 His engagement as a light-weight jockey.

b. *fig.* A person or thing of little importance, profundity, or intelligence.

1885 A. EDWARDES *Girton Girl* III. xi. 205, I am not good at these high passions!..In everything I am a light weight. .. In life I walk gently. **1902** G. H. LORIMER *Lett. Self-Made Merchant* (1903) ii. 19 That is the spot where a young man has the chance to show that he is not a light-weight. **1951** A. L. ROWSE *Eng. Past* 24 Harington was the Queen's godson—clever,..naughty, a light-weight, perpetrator of puns and practical jokes. **1962** *Listener* 25 Jan. 185/2 Of the other stories in this book, those by the long-established writers..are light-weights. **1965** *English Studies* XLVI. 209 After Holiness or Justice, Courtesy may seem as something of a light-weight.

c. A garment, usu. a suit, made from lightweight material.

1972 J. QUARTERMAIN *Rock of Diamond* v. 26 He stood five ten clad in a dark-blue lightweight. **1973** R. BUSBY *Pattern of Violence* v. 80 He..picked up a man's suit jacket from the floor. It was a grey lightweight.

B. *adj.* Light in weight; said *esp.* of coins = LIGHT, *a.*[1] 1 b. Also of clothes, fabrics, etc. Also *fig.*

1809 E. S. BARRETT *Setting Sun* I. 39 May we not see in them the handwriting on the wall,..the end of the government of light-weight princes? **1892–3** *T. Eaton & Co. Catal.* Fall & Winter 31/2 Light weight overcoats in grey, brown, fawn. **1898** *Westm. Gaz.* 24 June 1/3 Some light-weight Colonial gold coins. **1898** *Pall Mall G.* 3 Feb. 9/1 It is customary to start with the lightest-weight birds—say 4 lb. 2 oz. and rising 2 oz. each bird. **1902** *Daily Chron.* 8 Nov. 8/3 Every woman who walks much clings to a light-weight Russian blouse. **1930** J. T. HATFIELD et al. *Curme Vol. Ling. Stud.* 52 The intervening verbs are chiefly light-weight grammatical words. **1940** *Chambers's Techn. Dict.* 499/2 *Light-weight concrete* (Build.), concrete of low unit weight .., made by using aggregates such as pumice, sawdust, and cork, with cellular concrete. **1953** *News Chron.* 2 June 2/2 Squatting to drink it [*sc.* tea] in the light-weight (six pound) proofed cotton nylon tents. **1957** *Times Lit. Suppl.* 13 Dec. 751/2 One cannot reproach him with having produced a rather lightweight book. **1958** *Times* 10 Nov. 14/5 An entertaining, light-weight lecture recital by Mr. Antony Hopkins. **1963** A. J. HALL *Textile Sci.* iii. 158 In these days when light-weight apparel is much favoured the density of a textile fibre is important. **1968** M. WOODHOUSE *Rock Baby* xi. 109 He'd been..wearing a lightweight raincoat. **1973** *Nation Rev.* (Melbourne) 31 Aug. 1443/3 A recent column attacking Whitlam for appearing on TV with 'a lightweight variety performer'.

Hence **light-weighted** *a.*, of light weight; carrying a light weight.

1867 J. R. LOWELL in *Atlantic Monthly* Nov. 625/2 We.. see the rather light-weighted great man wheeled round the room..to converse with his guests. **1905** *Westm. Gaz.* 21 Mar. 8/2 The London and Brighton Handicap Steeplechase on Friday may be won by the light-weighted Dam.

lightwood[1] (ˈlaɪtwʊd). [f. LIGHT *a.*[1]] A name given to various trees from the lightness of their wood; in Australia chiefly applied to *Acacia Melanoxylon*.

(The first quot. may belong to the next word: the writer perh. mistook the reasons for the appellation.)

1685 L. WAFER *Voy. & Descr. Isthmus Amer.* (1699) 95 A Tree about the bigness of an Elm, the Wood of which is very light, and we therefore call it Light-wood. **1843** J. BACKHOUSE *Visit. Austral. Col.* iv. 48 Light-wood..derives this name from swimming in water, while the other woods of V.D. Land, except the pines, generally sink. **1859** H. KINGSLEY *G. Hamlyn* II. 193 A solitary dark-foliaged lightwood. **1866** H. SIMCOX *Rustic Rambles* 54 The numerous lightwood trees. **1866** *Treas. Bot.* 681/1 Light-wood, *Ceratopetalum apetalum.*

ˈlightwood[2]. *North Amer.* & *W. Indian.* [f. LIGHT *sb.* (or LIGHT *v.*[2]).] **a.** Any wood used in lighting a fire; in the southern states, resinous pine-wood. **b.** Used as a name for various trees (e.g. *Amyris balsamifera* CANDLE-WOOD) which burn with a brilliant flame.

[**1685**: see prec.] **1693** *Phil. Trans.* XVII. 620 The *Lignum Rhodium* Tree, called by the Planters of Barbados Lightwood. **1705** R. BEVERLEY *Virginia* III. iii. §11 (1855) 136 They [Indians] generally burn pine or lightwood (that is, the fat knots of dead pine). **1763** W. ROBINSON in W. Roberts *Nat. Hist. Florida* 99 Oak,..cabbage, lightwood, and mangrove trees. **1859** BARTLETT *Dict. Amer.*, *Light-wood*, pine wood as opposed to slower burning wood. **1888** *Century Mag.* XXIX. 880/2 The bright-blazing pitch-pine, called..'lightwood' at the South.

attrib. **1856** OLMSTED *Slave States* 450 Carrying light-wood torches. **1859** K. CORNWALLIS *New World* I. 176 The lightwood tree grew to a height of a hundred feet.

† **ˈlightwort.** *Obs.* [f. LIGHT(S) + WORT.] = LUNGWORT. **sea lightwort**, ? *Mertensia maritima.*

1587 MASCALL *Govt. Cattle* (1596) 18 Mixe the pouder of light wort (which growes among stones or on Okes, like a dried turfe nigh the ground) with [etc.]. *Ibid.* 267 Pomelle, so called in French, in Latin Consiligo, which I take to be the hearb called lightwort or comphere. **1770** SIR J. HILL *Herb. Brit.* II. 163 *Pneumaria Maritima*, Sea Lightwort.

† **ˈlighty**, *a. Obs.* [f. LIGHT *sb.* or *a.*[1] + -Y.]

1. Full of light, bright, shining.

1382 WYCLIF *Matt.* xvii. 5 Loo! a liȝty cloude shadewid hem. —— *Luke* xi. 34 If thin yȝe schal be symple, al thi body schal be liȝtful [*v.r.* liȝti; **1388** liȝti].

2. Enlightened, well-informed.

1562 TURNER *Bathes* I In this our lightye and learned tyme.

† **ˈligialty.** *Obs. rare*[−1]. [ad. OF. *ligeauté* (Godefroy) obligation to homage, f. *lige* LIEGE.] ? A district or province in which one is a liege-lord.

1651 N. BACON *Disc. Govt. Eng.* II. xv. 134 Kings..must act, *Per deputatum*, when their Persons are absent in another Ligialty.

† **ligiament.** *Obs. rare*[−1]. [ad. med.L. *ligiamentum*, f. *ligius* LIEGE.] An act of allegiance.

1432–50 tr. *Higden* (Rolls) VIII. 55 That he, his successours, and men of Scotlonde awe to make homage, ligiament [**1387** *Trevisa* legeaunce], and fidelite to kynges of Ynglonde.

ligiance, ligier, obs. ff. LIGEANCE, LEDGER.

liging, lignage, obs. ff. LYING, LINEAGE.

lign-aloes (laɪnˈæləʊz). Also 4–5 **ligne aloes**, 6–9 **lignaloe**, 9 (sense c) **linaloa, -aloe**. [ad. late L. *lignum aloēs* 'wood of the aloe' (*aloēs* genitive of *aloē*).] **a.** The bitter drug aloes; = ALOE 3. **b.** Aloes-wood; = ALOE 1. **c.** [= Sp. *linaloe*.] An aromatic wood obtained from a Mexican tree of the genus *Bursera*.

c **1374** CHAUCER *Troylus* IV. 1109 (1137) The woful teris.. As bittre weren..as is ligne Aloes or galle. **1577** FRAMPTON *Joyfull Newes* 84 b, Making a Pomander of it, mingled with Muske, Lignaloe, it doeth comfort the braine. **1611** BIBLE *Num.* xxiv. 6 The trees of Lign-Aloes which the Lord hath planted. **1721** BAILEY, *Lign-Aloes*, the Wood of Aloes, a Drug of great Price. **1859** HOOKER in *Man. Sci. Enq.* 428 Lign aloe.—The name of a remarkably aromatic wood sent to the Paris Exhibition of 1855 from the department of Vera Cruz in Mexico. **1867** JEAN INGELOW *Story Doom* I. 18 Where the dew distilled All night from leaves of old lign aloe trees. **1883** OGILVIE Suppl., *Linaloa*, A Mexican wood [etc.].

lignate, obs. Sc. variant of LINGOT.

lignatile (ˈlɪgnətɪl, -aɪl), *a. Bot.* [ad. mod.L. *lignātilis* (cf. L. *saxātilis*), f. L. *lignum* wood.] 'Living or growing upon wood, as certain mushrooms' (Mayne *Expos. Lex.* 1855).

† **ligˈnation.** *Obs.*[−0] [ad. L. *lignātiōn-em*, f. *lignārī* to fetch or procure wood, f. *lignum* wood.]

1623 COCKERAM, *Lignation*, a hewing or purueying of wood. **1721** in BAILEY.

† **ligˈnator.** *Obs.*[−0] [L., f. *lignārī* (see prec.).]

1623 COCKERAM, *Lignator*, he which doth it [*sc.* lignation].

ligne, obs. form of LINE.

† **ligneal**, *a. Obs. rare*[−1]. [f. L. *ligne-us* LIGNEOUS + -AL[1].] Ligneous; (in quot.) obtained from wood. So † **lignean** *a. Obs.*[−0]

1599 A. M. tr. *Gabelhouer's Bk. Physicke* 190/2 He may vse this ligneal water: Take of the best *Ligni Guaiaci* [etc.]. **1656** BLOUNT *Glossogr.*, *Ligneous*, *Lignean*, of wood or timber, wooden, or full of wood.

† **ˈlignee.** *Obs.* In 5 **lignye, lygnee, -nye, lynee.** [a. F. *lignée*, f. *ligne* LINE *sb.*[2] Cf. Pr. *linhada.*] = LINEAGE. (Freq. in Caxton.)

a **1450** *Knt. de la Tour* (1868) 109 Iacob and Alia praied that God wolde yeue his children lynee and generacion and multiplicacion. *c* **1477** CAXTON *Jason* 68 b, Salathiel whiche was of the lignye of the Hebrews. **1490** —— *Eneydos* vi. 29 To thende that their name perysshe not wythoute remembraunce for faulte of lygnee. *c* **1500** *Melusine* i. 6 The noble lynee whiche yssued of the said woman.

ligneous (ˈlɪgniːəs), *a.* [f. L. *ligne-us* (f. *lign-um* wood) + -OUS. Cf. F. *ligneux.*]

1. Of the nature of wood; woody: said *esp.* of plants and their texture (opposed to *herbaceous*).

1626 BACON *Sylva* §504 They being of a more Ligneous Nature, will incorporate with the Tree it selfe. **1646** SIR T. BROWNE *Pseud. Ep.* VI. xii. 334 The exhalations from ligneous and lean bodies, as bones, hair, and the like. **1725** BRADLEY *Fam. Dict.* s.v. *Plants*, Under-Shrubs or ligneous Plants, are those that are less than Shrubs. **1792** BELKNAP *Hist. New Hampsh.* III. 118 That fossil, ligneous substance called peat. **1802** BINGLEY *Anim. Biog.* (1813) III. 247 Towards the centre the galls are hard and ligneous. **1834** MRS. SOMERVILLE *Connex. Phys. Sci.* xxvii. (1849) 365 In approaching the equator, the ligneous exceed the number of herbaceous plants. **1884** BOWER & SCOTT *De Bary's Phaner.* 176 The..secondary bast of ligneous Dicotyledons.

2. (A mod. use, chiefly *jocular.*) Made or consisting of wood, wooden. Also *fig.*

ligneous marble, 'wood coated or prepared so as to resemble marble' (Ogilvie 1882).

1812 H. & J. SMITH *Rej. Addr.* x. (1873) 94 That ligneous barricado, which..now serves as the entrance of the lowly cottage. **1859** SALA *Tw. round Clock* (1861) 62 The ligneous charger..painted bright cream-colour [etc.]. **1865** *Daily Tel.* 18 Oct. 7/5 Fraschini, who is ligneous as ever, and looks as if he were cut out of serviceable oak.

lignescent (lɪɡˈnɛsənt), *a. rare.* [f. L. *lign-um* wood + -ESCENT.] Tending to be ligneous or woody.

a **1706** EVELYN *Sylva* I. ii. (1776) 66 Suffrutices are shrubs lower than the former, lignescent, and more approaching to the stalky herbs Lavender, Rue &c. **1731** BAILEY vol. II, *Lignescent*, growing wooden, becoming wood. [In some mod. Dicts.]

ligni- (ˈlɪɡnɪ), comb. form of L. *lignum* wood, as in **ˈlignicole, ligˈnicoline** *adjs.* [L. *colĕre* to inhabit], growing on wood, as some mosses, lichens, and fungi (*Cent. Dict.*). **lignicolous** (-ˈɪkələs) *a.* [f. as prec. + -OUS], living in wood; 'applied to certain bivalve shells which establish themselves in wood' (Mayne *Expos. Lex.* 1855). **ligniferous** (-ˈɪfərəs) *a.* [see -FEROUS], bearing or producing wood (ibid.). **ligniform** *a.* [see -FORM], of the form or appearance of wood. **ligniperdous** (-ˈpɜːdəs) *a.* [L. *perdĕre* to destroy], wood-destroying. **lignivorous** (-ˈɪvərəs) *a.* [L. *-vorus* devouring], wood-devouring.

1796 KIRWAN *Elem. Min.* (ed. 2) II. 60 *Ligniform Carbonated Wood. **1832** LYELL *Princ. Geol.* II. vii. 122 Beetles, and many other kinds of *ligniperdous insects have been introduced into Great Britain in timber. **1826** KIRBY & SP. *Entomol.* xlix. (1828) IV. 492 In the saprophaga, the *lignivorous tribes form more than a half. **1863** BATES *Nat. Amazon* v. (1864) 128 The felled timber attracts lignivorous insects.

† **ˈlignicide.** *Obs.*$^{-0}$ [ad. L. *lignicīd-a*, f. *lignum* wood + *-cīdĕre, cædere* to cut.] A woodcutter (Blount *Glossogr.* 1656).

lignification (lɪɡnɪfɪˈkeɪʃən). [f. next: see -FICATION.] The process of becoming ligneous.

1808 GOOD in *Ann. Reg., Char.* etc. 112 We can trace the age of a tree with a considerable degree of certainty, by allowing a year for every outer circle, and about two or three years for the complete lignification of the innermost. **1877** BENNETT tr. *Thomé's Bot.* 22 The lignification or conversion into cork of cell-walls. **1885** GOODALE *Physiol. Bot.* 62 Lignification may increase the thickness of the cell-wall.

lignify (ˈlɪɡnɪfaɪ), *v.* [f. L. *lign-um* wood + -(I)FY.] **a.** *trans.* To convert into wood; to make ligneous. Chiefly in *pa. pple.* and *ppl. a.* **ˈlignified. b.** *intr.* To become wood.

1828 in WEBSTER [*trans.* and *intr.*]. **1830** LINDLEY *Nat. Syst. Bot.* 133 Lignified vessels. **1875** BENNETT & DYER *Sachs' Bot.* 33 The corky and lignified scales of the cell-wall. **1884** SOPHIE HERRICK *Wonders of Plant Life* i. 6 The protoplasm disappears, the cellulose lignifies. **1884** BLACKMORE *Tommy Upm.* I. xvii. 265 A lignified turnip.

lignin (ˈlɪɡnɪn). *Chem.* Also **-ine.** [f. L. *lign-um* wood + -IN¹.] An organic substance, forming the essential part of woody fibre.

1822 IMISON *Sci. & Art* II. 131 When a piece of wood has been boiled in water and in alkohol.. what remains insoluble is the woody fibre, or lignin. **1859** *Fownes' Chem.* 360 Pure lignin is tasteless, insoluble in water and alcohol, and absolutely innutritious. **1894** D. H. SCOTT *Struct. Bot.* I. *Flowering Pl.* 56 The woody character of the cell-walls of the xylem is due to the presence of a substance called lignine.

b. *Comb.*: **lignin-dynamite** (see quot.).

1883 *Fortn. Rev.* May 645 'Lignin-dynamite', as the wood sawdust saturated with nitro-glycerine.. is called.

lignite (ˈlɪɡnaɪt). *Min.* [a. F. *lignite* (A. Brongniart in 1807), f. L. *lign-um* wood: see -ITE.] A variety of brown coal bearing visible traces of its ligneous structure.

1808 T. ALLAN *Names Min.* 42. **1849** MURCHISON *Siluria* xii. 307 The pitch-lakes of Trinidad.. are known to exude from Tertiary lignites. **1872** NICHOLSON *Palæont.* 501 The lignites of Austria have yielded very numerous plant-remains.

attrib. **1839** *Penny Cycl.* XIII. 480/2 In the Isle of Wight (Alum Bay) lignite beds.. occur. **1851** *Illustr. Catal. Gt. Exhib.* 1125 Lignite blocks.. used as a combustible.

lignitic (lɪɡˈnɪtɪk), *a.* [f. LIGNITE + -IC.] Pertaining to, or of the nature of, lignite.

1843 in HUMBLE *Dict. Geol. etc.* **1862** DANA *Man. Geol.* iii. 507 A Lignitic formation. **1884** *Manch. Exam.* 20 Aug. 6/3 Large masses of peat, lignitic branches.. and animal remains.

lignitiferous (lɪɡnɪˈtɪfərəs), *a.* [f. LIGNITE + -(I)FEROUS.] Producing lignite.

1859 PAGE *Handbk. Geol. Terms, Lignitiferous*, applied to strata or formations which contain subordinate beds of lignite or brown-coal. **1882** *Pop. Sci. Monthly* XX. 431 The lignitiferous beds of France.

lignitize (ˈlɪɡnɪtaɪz), *v.* [f. LIGNITE + -IZE.] *trans.* To convert into lignite.

1886 *Amer. Jrnl. Sci.* Ser. III. XXXI. 203 A large log two feet in diameter, and completely lignitized was also seen.

ligno- (ˈlɪɡnəʊ), used as a combining form of L. *lignum* wood (cf. LIGNI-) in a few scientific and technical terms. **lignoˈcellulose, lignoˈceric** *a.* [L. *cera* wax] (see quots.). † **ˈlignograph** [-GRAPH], a wood-engraving. † **ligˈnography,** wood engraving. **ˌlignoˈsulphonate,** any of the salts or esters of the lignosulphonic acids, some of which are used as adhesive binders, as pigment dispersants, in the tanning industry, and in the manufacture of vanillin. **ˌlignosulˈphonic acid,** any of various compounds in which sulphonic acid groups are attached to lignin molecules, formed in the sulphite process for producing wood pulp. **ˌligno-sulˈphuric** *a.* = SULPHOLIGNIC *a.*

1900 JACKSON *Gloss. Bot. Terms* 47 *Lignocelluloses, lignin combined with cellulose, as in Jute fibre. **1888** *Syd. Soc. Lex.*, *Lignoceric acid, $C_{24}H_{48}O_2 = C_{23}H_{47}{\cdot}CO_2H$. A fatty acid contained in paraffin and in beech-wood tar. **1844** MANTELL *Medals Creation* I. xviii. Contents, The excellent artists by whom the *lignographs or wood-cuts were engraven. **1849** *Chambers's Inform.* II. 721/1 The art of Wood-Engraving, or, as it is sometimes more learnedly termed.. Xylography and *Lignography. **1908** *Jrnl. Chem. Soc.* XCIV. I. 717 From the liquid obtained by boiling pine-wood with calcium hydrogen sulphite, the author has prepared barium *lignosulphonate, $C_{40}H_{44}O_{17}S_2Ba$. **1952** F. E. BRAUNS *Chem. Lignin* v. 113 The isolation of a basic calcium lignosulfonate from a commercial spent liquor on a technical scale is carried out in the 'Howard process'. **1963** J. F. HARRIS et al. in B. L. Browning *Chem. Wood* xi. 578 Lignosulfonates, in particular the carbohydrate-free products, have found a variety of profitable applications. The most notable of these are their uses in oil well-drilling muds and in the production of synthetic rubber. **1908** *Jrnl. Chem. Soc.* XCIV. I. 717 In *lignosulphonic acid, part of the sulphonic acid is tightly and part loosely bound. **1931** *Canad. Jrnl. Res.* V. 42 The first lignosulphonic acids studied were obtained by heating benzene-alcohol extracted spruce meal with sulphurous acid. **1967** KIRK & OTHMER *Encycl. Chem. Technol.* (ed. 2) XII. 369 The sulfite process for producing pulp can lead to products which consist of lignosulfonic acids, or various lignosulfonates. These are commonly referred to in the trade as lignin sulfonic acids and lignin sulfonates. **1855** OGILVIE Suppl., **Ligno-sulphuric acid*, sulpholignic acid, obtained by the action of sulphuric acid on lignine.

lignocaine (ˈlɪɡnəʊkeɪn). *Pharm.* [f. LIGNO- (as the L. equivalent of XYLO-, the compound having been orig. named *xylocaine* because of its chemical relationship to xylene) + *-caine*, after COCAINE.] A white crystalline aromatic amide, $(CH_3)_2C_6H_3NH{\cdot}CO{\cdot}CH_2{\cdot}N(C_2H_5)_2$, used as a local anæsthetic for the gums and mucous membranes, usually in the form of its hydrochloride and by injection, but also as tablets, sprays, or creams.

1954 *Anaesthesia* IX. 96 The development of a technique utilising the short acting relaxant suxamethonium chloride .. and the analgesic lignocaine hydrochloride (Xylocaine). **1959** *Brit. Dental Jrnl.* CVI. 48/2 Extensive clinical experience has shown that procaine and, probably more so, lignocaine are really very satisfactory as local anæsthetic agents in dental practice. **1970** PASSMORE & ROBSON *Compan. Med. Stud.* II. viii. 6/1 Lignocaine.. is therefore the safest drug in the treatment of acute ventricular arrhythmias even though it is toxic in high dosage.

lignoin (ˈlɪɡnəʊɪn). *Chem.* [f. L. *lign-um* wood + *o* (? after *benzoin* or *aloin*) + -IN¹.] A brown substance ($C_{20}H_{23}NO_8$) obtained by Reichel from old Huanuco bark.

1865 WATTS *Dict. Chem.* III. 695.

lignone (ˈlɪɡnəʊn). *Chem.* [f. as prec. + -ONE.] (See quots.)

1844 FOWNES *Chem.* 421 A specimen of wood-spirit.. was found by Gmelin to contain a volatile liquid, differing in some respects from acetone, to which he gave the term *lignone*. **1865** WATTS *Dict. Chem.* III. 695 *Lignone* or *Xylite*. These names were applied to a volatile liquid of variable composition.. obtained from crude wood-spirit by treatment with chloride of calcium, and subsequent rectification. **1885** GOODALE *Physiol. Bot.* 36 *note*, Lignone, insoluble in water, alcohol and ether; soluble in ammonia, potassa and soda.

lignose (ˈlɪɡnəʊs), *a.* and *sb.* [ad. L. *lignōs-us*, f. *lignum* wood: see -OSE.] **A.** *adj.* = LIGNEOUS.

1698 *Phil. Trans.* XX. 465 Those Plants are more fit for dying Cloth, which are Lignose. **1855** in MAYNE *Expos. Lex.* In mod. Dicts.

B. *sb.* **a.** *Chem.* One of the constituents of lignin. **b.** 'A Silesian blasting powder made of woody fibre charged with nitro-glycerine' (Knight *Dict. Mech.* Suppl. 1884).

1878 A. H. GREEN *Coal* v. 165 The lignose in its turn can be changed into cellulose. **1885** GOODALE *Physiol. Bot.* 36 *note*, Lignose, insoluble in water, alcohol, ether, and ammonia; soluble in solutions of potassa or soda.

lignosity (lɪɡˈnɒsɪtɪ). *rare*$^{-0}$. [f. LIGNOUS or LIGNOSE + -ITY.] The condition of being ligneous or woody.

1888 in *Syd. Soc. Lex.*

lignot, obs. Sc. variant of LINGOT.

lignous (ˈlɪɡnəs), *a. rare* or *Obs.* [ad. L. *lignōs-us*, f. *lign-um* wood: see -OUS.] = LIGNEOUS.

1664 EVELYN *Kal. Hort.* July (1679) 21 Slip Stocks, and other lignous Plants and Flowers. **1673** *Phil. Trans.* VIII. 6133 Its [the Skin of a Root] compounding parts, likewise Parenchymous, and Lignous. **1707** *Curios. in Husb. & Gard.* 38 The Lignous Body is a Substance whose Contexture is more.. close than that of the Bark. **1756** P. BROWNE *Jamaica* 229 The nut or shell appears as if it had been composed of lignous fibres strongly interwoven. **1831** J. DAVIES *Man. Mat. Med.* 75 The remainder is a lignous substance. **1855** MAYNE *Expos. Lex.* s.v. *Lignosus.*

lignum¹ (ˈlɪɡnəm). [L. *lignum* wood.]

‖ **1.** *Bot.* The wood of exogenous plants, comprising both alburnum and duramen.

1826 GOOD *Bk. Nat.* I. 190 The whole of the liber of one year.. becoming the alburnum of the next, and the alburnum becoming the lignum. **1866** in *Treas. Bot.*

‖ **2.** Occurring, with qualification, in the names of various trees and woods: **lignum aloes** (†occas. *aloe*) = LIGNALOES; † **lignum aquilæ,** aloes-wood; † **lignum rhodium,** candle-wood, *Amyris balsamifera*; † **lignum sanctum,** a name for LIGNUM VITÆ.

c **1400** MAUNDEV. (Roxb.) xxxiii. 150 Þe tree þat es called lignum aloes. **1525** tr. *Jerome of Brunswick's Surg.* T iij a/2 Take lignum aloes .ij. ounces. **1529** *Doctors' Commons Wills* (Camden) 14 My beades of lignum alweys dressed with goulde. **1553** Lignum Sanctum [see GUAIACUM 1]. **1555** EDEN *Decades* 239 Lignum aloe, blacke, heauy and fine. **1558, 1604** [see GUAIAC]. **1600** J. PORY tr. *Leo's Africa* Introd. 41 Here groweth the right Lignum Aquilæ, which is of so excellent vertue in phisick. **1669** DRYDEN *Tyrannic Love* IV. i. Wks. 1883 III. 421 The chalks and chips of lignum aloes. **1693** Lignum Rhodium [see LIGHTWOOD²]. **1741** *Compl. Fam.-Piece* I. i. 56 The Powder of Lignum Aloes.

3. Short for LIGNUM VITÆ.

1899 *Sheffield manufacturer's list*, Braces, Beech and Lignum Head.

lignum² (ˈlɪɡnəm). *Austral.* [Corruption of mod.L. *polygonum*.] 'A bushman's contraction for any species of the wiry plants called polygonum' (Morris *Austral Eng.*).

1880 MRS. MEREDITH *Tasmanian Friends & Foes* xxviii. 180 The poor emus had got down into the creek amongst the lignum bushes for a little shade. **1896** H. LAWSON *When World was Wide* 135 (Morris) By mulga scrub and lignum plain. **1903** 'T. COLLINS' *Such is Life* 79 When a certain class of bushman says 'mallee', he means any sort of scrub except lignum. **1933** *Bulletin* (Sydney) 13 Dec. 29/4 Beneath the surface is a mass of lignum roots. **1941** I. L. IDRIESS *Great Boomerang* xiii. 92 Carpeted with yellowish-green lignum —huge bunches of cane-like shrubs like man-high beehives.

‖ **lignum vitæ** (ˈlɪɡnəm ˈvaɪtiː). [L. = wood of life.]

1. A tree; = GUAIACUM 1. Applied also to several other trees having wood of similar properties.

1597 GERARDE *Herbal* III. cxviii. 1309 Italian Lignum vitæ, or woode of Life, groweth to a faire and beautiful tree. **1655** J. S. *Jrnl. Eng. Army in W. Indies* 18 Of.. Mastick and Lignum vitæ trees there are good plenty. **1712** E. COOKE *Voy. S. Sea* 326 The Trees I observ'd here, were Lignum Vitæ, Birch.. and many more. **1792** [see GUAIACUM 1]. **1866** *Morning Star* 17 Mar., The lignum vitæ is putting forth its blossoms. **1866** *Treas. Bot.*, Lignum vitæ of New South Wales, *Acacia falcata*. Lignum vitæ of New Zealand, *Metrosideros buxifolia*. Bastard lignum vitæ, *Badiera diversifolia*.

2. The wood of this tree; = GUAIACUM 2.

1594 BLUNDEVIL *Exerc.* v. xii. (1636) 556 Wood of Brasill, wood of Guaicum, called Lignum vitæ. **1660** PEPYS *Diary* 21 Nov., This morning my cozen Thomas Pepys, the turner, sent me a cupp of lignum vitæ for a token. **1703** MOXON *Mech. Exerc.* 74 If it be very hard Wood you are to Plane upon, as Box, Ebony, Lignum Vitæ, &c. **1817** J. ADAMS *Let.* 5 June Wks. 1856 X. 263 Mr. Adams was born and tempered a wedge of steel to split the knot of *lignum vitæ*, which tied North America to Great Britain. **1886** RUSKIN *Præterita* I. iii. 85 My toy-bricks of lignum vitæ had been constant companions.

3. The resin obtained from this tree; = GUAIACUM 3.

1611 COTGR., *Gayac*, Gwacum, Lignum vitæ, Pockewood. **1616** BULLOKAR, *Guaiacum*, a wood called by some *Lignum vitae*. It is much vsed in physicke against the French disease. **1686** S. SEWALL *Diary* 2 Jan. (1878) I. 116 Discoursed with Ralf Carter about Lignum Vitae.

lignye, variant of LIGNEE. *Obs.*

ligoustre, variant of LIGUSTRE. *Obs.*

ligroin (ˈlɪɡrəʊɪn). *Chem.* Also **ligroïn.** [Etym. unknown: in quot. 1881 a. G. *ligroin*.] Any of various naphtha fractions with ranges of boiling points between 90 and 150°C, used as solvents.

1881 *Jrnl. Chem. Soc.* XL. 1181 The author has investigated the causes of explosions resulting from the products of the distillation of mineral naphtha when used for burning purposes. These products are known as 'gasoline', 'benzoline', 'ligroin', and 'lubricating oil'. **1942** H. BARRON *Mod. Synthetic Rubbers* vii. 82 Straightforward rectification of petroleum yields: Petrol... Benzine... Ligroïn... Kerosene [etc.]. **1965** *Biol. Abstr.* XLVI. 680/2 Experimental solvent extractions of wood rosin from pine stump chips were carried out in ligroin at 0, 20, 50, and 80°C. **1968** B. J. HAZZARD tr. *Asinger's Paraffins* iv. 402 Ligroin with a boiling range of 95–150°C (density = 0·745) containing 3·2 per cent of aromatics, 24·2 per cent of naphthenes, and 72·6 per cent of paraffins.. can be 60–65 per cent nitrated in a single pass through the reactor.

‖ **ligula** (ˈlɪɡjʊlə). [L. *ligula* strap, spoon, by-form of *lingula*, f. *lingua* tongue.]

1. A narrow tongue-like strip or fillet.

a. *Bot.* A narrow strap-shaped part in a plant, as the 'limb' of a ray floret in composite flowers, a projection from the top of a leaf-sheath in grasses, 'an appendage at the base of some forms of Corona' (Henslow 1856). **b.** *Ent.* (*a*) The 'tongue' of Crustaceans, Arachnids, and Insects, being a horny, membranous, or fleshy anterior part of the labium. (*b*) A tongue-like process on the elytra of certain aquatic beetles (*Cent. Dict.*). **c.** *Anat.* 'A thin lamina occupying the angle

between the cerebellum and the restiform body' (*Syd. Soc. Lex.* 1888).

a. **1760** J. LEE *Introd. Bot.* I. xix. (1765) 50 *Ligula*, a narrow Tongue, or Fillet. **1845** LINDLEY *Sch. Bot.* i. (1858) 10 [In grasses] there is often a thin membrane called a ligula, at the upper end of the sheath. **1876** HARLEY *Mat. Med.* (ed. 6) 371 Narrow leaves, with a long slit sheath and stipules adherent, forming a membranous ligula. **1882** VINES *Sachs' Bot.* 392 Lycopodiaceæ... The leaves have no ligula.

b. **1826** KIRBY & SP. *Entomol.* III. 363 *Ligula*, a capillary instrument between the lancets; probably representing the tongue of the perfect mouth. **1828** STARK *Elem. Nat. Hist.* II. 218 The labium..is formed of two parts; one inferior..is the chin (*mentum*), the other membranous [etc.]..is termed *ligula*. **1834** MCMURTRIE *Cuvier's Anim. Kingd.* 424 Their antennæ are always geniculate, and the ligula is small, rounded and concave, or cochleariform.

c. **1848** *Quain's Anat.* (ed. 5) II. 724 The diverging posterior pyramids and restiform bodies surmounted along their margin by a band of nervous substance called the *ligula*.

2. A genus of cestoid worms, typical of the family *Ligulidæ*; a worm of this genus.

1840 E. BLYTH, etc. *Cuvier's Anim. Kingd.* (1849) 649 The fourth Family of the Parenchymata—the Cestoidea—consists of only a single genus,—Ligula. These are the simplest in their organization of all the Entozoa. **1876** *Beneden's Anim. Parasites* Introd., When Rudolphi spoke of the ligulæ of fishes which could continue to live in birds.

3. A genus of molluscs (*Cent. Dict.*).

1839 SOWERBY *Conch. Manual* 56.

ligular (ˈlɪgjʊlə(r)), *a.* [f. LIGULA + -AR. Cf. F. *ligulaire.*] Pertaining to or resembling a ligula.

1875 BENNETT & DYER *Sachs' Bot.* 471 At the point where the lamina bends back from the unguis, ligular structures are often formed on the inner or upper side.

ligularia (lɪgjʊˈlɛərɪə). [mod.L. (H. Cassini 1816, in *Bull. Sci. Soc. Philomatique* 198), f. L. *ligula* strap, referring to the shape of the ray-florets.] A herbaceous perennial plant of the genus so called, belonging to the family Compositæ, often native to China or Japan, and bearing yellow flowers.

1839 G. DON *Sweet's Hortus Britannicus* (ed. 3) 382 (*heading*) *Ligularia DC.* Ligularia (*ligula*, a little tongue; ray-flowers ligulate). **1862** *Curtis's Bot. Mag.* LXXXVIII. 5302 (*heading*) Kæmpfer's Ligularia. **1886** G. NICHOLSON *Illustr. Dict. Gardening* II. 263/1 Ligularias require generally a free, moist soil, and prefer a rather peaty one. **1966** J. BERRISFORD *Wild Garden* II. 149 The ligularias are handsome plants for rich moist soil. **1971** *Country Life* 2 Sept. 567/2 My biggest colour splodges are..various yellow composites: heleniums..ligularias, [etc.].

ligulate (ˈlɪgjʊlət), *a.* [f. LIGULA + -ATE².]

1. Having the form of, or furnished with, a ligula; strap-shaped; *Bot.* applied *esp.* to the ray florets of some composite flowers, and to flowers having a monopetalous corolla slit on one side and opened flat.

1760 J. LEE *Introd. Bot.* I. xix. (1765) 49 Ligulate, when all the Corollulæ..of the Florets are plane, flat,..and expanded towards the outer Side. **1785** MARTYN *Rousseau's Bot.* x. (1794) 101 He calls..the semi-florets, ligulate floscules. **1830** LINDLEY *Nat. Syst. Bot.* 187 The 5 segments that make up the ligulate floret of a Composita. **1839** *Penny Cycl.* XIII. 480/2 *Ligulate flowers*, are such as have a monopetalous corolla slit on one side and opened flat, as in the Dandelion Lilac. **1846** DANA *Zooph.* (1848) 580 Axis..of the branchlets ligulate. **1870** HOOKER *Stud. Flora* 196 Daisy,..Ray-flowers many, 1-seriate, female, ligulate. **1875** BENNETT & DYER *Sachs' Bot.* 547 When the leaf is ligulate and its insertion broad. **1877** COUES & ALLEN *N. Amer. Rodentia* 239 The rudimentary pollex of *Myodes* bears a large ligulate nail.

2. Of letters: Connected by a band.

1851 D. WILSON *Preh. Ann.* (1863) II. 75 A good example of ligulate letters, which English antiquaries are familiar with, not only on the pottery, but also on the altars and inscribed tablets of the Anglo-Roman period.

So **ˈligulated** *a.*, in the same senses.

1753 CHAMBERS *Cycl. Supp.*, *Ligulated floscules.* **1777** G. FORSTER *Voy. round World* II. 15 Some wore round coronets of the small ligulated feathers of the man of war bird. **1855** MAYNE *Expos. Lex.* (s.v. *Liguliformis*), Ligulated corols. **1864** T. WRIGHT in *Intell. Observ.* No. 34. 231 Doubled or ligulated letters.

ligule (ˈlɪgjuːl). [ad. L. LIGULA; cf. F. *ligule.*]

1. = LIGULA 1.

1862 in COOKE *Man. Bot. Terms.* **1870** HOOKER *Stud. Flora* 184 Compositæ,..Corolla..ligulate, lobes elongate and connate into a strap-shaped or elliptic ligule. **1872** OLIVER *Elem. Bot.* II. 277 Observe, in any common Grass..the ligule, a scale-like stipular projection at the base of the blade of the leaf, where it passes into the sheath. **1877** COUES & ALLEN *N. Amer. Rodentia* 528 The end of this ligule or girdle of bone thus encircling the tympanic.

†**2.** 'A small (Romane) measure containing about a spoonefull; and in weight three drammes, and a scruple' (Cotgr.). *Obs.*

1601 HOLLAND *Pliny* II. 41 If it be taken to the weight or quantitie of two or three Ligules, it cures those who [etc.].

liguli- (ˈlɪgjʊlɪ), comb. form of LIGULA in botanical terms, as ***liguliferous*** (see -FEROUS), ***liguliflorate***, ***-florous*** (L. *flōr-*, *flōs* flower), ***ligulifolius*** (L. *folium* leaf), ***liguliform*** (see -FORM).

1855 MAYNE *Expos. Lex.*, *Liguliferus*... Applied by De Candolle to compound flowers which become double by the change of their corols into elongated little tongues or ligules; *liguliferous... *Liguliflorus*..*liguliflorous. *Ligulæfolius*... Having linear leaves, as the *Eryngium ligulæfolium*: *ligulifolious. **1888** *Syd. Soc. Lex.*, **Liguliflorate*, same as *Liguliflorous. Liguliflorous*, applied to the corona of the Compositæ when it is entirely composed of ligulate florets. **1826** KIRBY & SP. *Entomol.* IV. 312 **Liguliform*, When it [tongue] emerges from the labium, is short, flat, and not concealed within the mouth. **1880** GRAY *Struct. Bot.* 418/2.

†**ligurate**, *v. Obs.*⁻⁰ [Badly f. L. *ligurīre.*]

1623 COCKERAM II, To Feed daintily, *ligurate.*

ligure (ˈlɪgjʊə(r)). Also 4 lugre, ligurie, -y, 7 lygure. Also in Lat. form ligurius, 6 *erron.* ligurios. [ad. L. *ligūrius* (Vulgate), ad. Gr. λιγύριον (Exod. xxviii, LXX), app. a variant of a word which appears in many different forms, as λαγούριον, λαγγούριον, λυγγούριον, λυγκούριον; the last of these (adopted in late L. as *lyncūrius*) is connected with the mediæval notion that the stone was a concretion of the urine of the lynx (Gr. λυγκ-, λύγξ lynx, οὖρον urine). The word may conceivably have some connexion with the source of AZURE, LAZULI.] Some precious stone.

c **1305** *Land Cokayne* 91 Smaragde lugre and prassiune. **1382** WYCLIF *Exod.* xxxix. 13 He putte in it foure ordres of gemmes..in the thridde [was] ligury [**1388** ligurie], achatese, amatist. **1398** TREVISA *Barth. De P.R.* XVI. lix. (1495) 572 Ligurius is a stone lyke to Electrum in colour. **1535** COVERDALE *Exod.* xxviii. 19 A Ligurios, an Achatt and an Ametyst. [**1611** a Lygure, an Agate, and an Amethist.] **1567** MAPLET *Gr. Forest* 13 b, Ligurius, is a stone in colour lyke to Tin. **1737** WHISTON *Josephus, Antiq.* III. vii. §5 I. 80. **1750** tr. *Leonardus' Mirr. Stones* 118 Ligurius, as some fancy, is like the Electorius, and draws Straws. **1855** E. SMEDLEY *Occult Sci.* 357 Ligure. Said to attract straws like amber.

Ligurian (laɪˈgjʊərɪən, lɪg-), *a.* and *sb.* [f. L. *Liguria* (f. *Ligur-*, nom. *Ligur*, *Ligus* = Gr. Λίγυς, pl. Λίγυες Ligurian) + -AN.] **a.** *adj.* Belonging to the country anciently called *Liguria* in Cisalpine Gaul, including Genoa, parts of Piedmont and Savoy, etc. Now sometimes used by ethnologists as the distinctive epithet of a race of mankind supposed to be typically represented by the ancient Ligurians or their modern descendants. **b.** *sb.* An inhabitant or native of Liguria; a person belonging to the Ligurian race; also, a Ligurian bee. Also, the Indo-European language of the ancient Ligurians; the Gallo-Italian dialect of this region.

Ligurian bee: a kind of honey-bee, *Apis ligustrica*, indigenous in southern Europe. ***Ligurian republic***: the republic of Genoa, 1797–1805.

1601 HOLLAND *Pliny* I. 57 Of the Ligurians, the most renowned beyond the Alpes, are the Sallij, Deceates, and Oxubij. **1632** LITHGOW *Trav.* I. 11 [I am] vnwilling to make relation of my passing through..the Sauoyean, and Ligurian Alpes. **1795** GIFFORD *Mæviad* (1796) 58 Together we explored the stoic page Of the Ligurian, stern tho' beardless sage [Persius]. **1797** *Encycl. Brit.* (ed. 3) X. 72/2 There is a great disagreement among authors concerning the origin of the Ligurians, though most probably they were descended from the Gauls. **1813** SOUTHEY *Life Nelson* vi, About seventy sail of vessels belonging to the Ligurian republic. **1835** G. C. LEWIS *Ess. Romance Lang.* i. 50 The diffusion of the Latin over Italy, in the place of the Etruscan, the Oscan, the Ligurian, and other native dialects, has been already noted. **1841** W. SPALDING *Italy & It. Isl.* III. 54 It is best exemplified by the constitution of the Italian Republic, which was closely copied in the Ligurian. **1875** J. HUNTER *Bee-keeping* 141 (*heading*) Ligurian bees and the methods of Ligurianizing an apiary. *Ibid.*, The name 'Ligurian' appears to have been given by Spinola, who described it in 1805. *Ibid.*, On the 19th of July, 1859, the Ligurian Bee was introduced to England. *Ibid.* 143 Many Bee-keepers..have successfully replaced their Black Queens with Ligurians, and so eventually succeeded in Ligurianizing their whole apiary. **1888** [see IAPYGIAN *a.* and *sb.*]. **1889** I. TAYLOR *Origin Aryans* 214 The primitive Aryans must be sought for among the four European races—Scandinavian, Celtic, Ligurian, and Iberian. **1909** *Trans. Amer. Philol. Assoc.* XL. 81 The net result of the study is that by far the greater part of what is called Ligurian is strictly Gallic. **1927** C. H. GRANDGENT *From Latin to Italian* 6 In the northwest of Italy we find the Piedmontese dialect, and, to the south, along the Gulf of Genoa from Monaco to Carrara, the Ligurian. **1933** R. S. CONWAY et al. *Prae-Italic Dial. Italy* II. ii. 70 Of Ligurian properly so called very little can be said to be known. **1939** L. H. GRAY *Foundations of Lang.* xi. 335 In the general area of Lago Maggiore, some seventy-two inscriptions..have been discovered... Their language may well represent the sole known remnants of Ligurian, which would seem to have stood midway between Italic and Celtic. **1968** *Encycl. Brit.* XII. 711/2 The dialects may be divided into six major classes: 1. Gallo-Italian: (*a*) Piedmontese; (*b*) Ligurian; (*c*) Lombard; (*d*) Emilian [etc.]. **1974** R. A. HALL *External Hist. Romance Lang.* iii. 51 Ligurian, used along what is now the Italian and French Riviera [*sic*], and perhaps to the north of this area in present-day Piedmont and Savoy.

Hence **Liˈgurianize** *v. trans.*, to make (a colony of bees) Ligurian.

1875 [see above].

ligurie: see LIGURE, LIGURY.

†**ligurine.** *Obs. rare*⁻¹. [ad. mod.L. *ligurīnus*, app. a subst. use of L. *Ligurīnus* Ligurian.] ? Some fringilline bird.

1572 BOSSEWELL *Armorie* II. 105 A Ligurine's head rassed vert, bearing a thistel Or... The birde *Ligurinus* feedeth muche vpon thistles.

†**liˈgurion.** *Obs.*⁻⁰ [ad. late L. *ligūriōn-em* (Du Cange), f. *ligūrīre* to be dainty, greedy.]

1656 BLOUNT *Glossogr.*, *Ligurion*, a devourer, a spend-thrift.

ligurite (ˈlɪgjʊəraɪt). *Min.* [Named by D. Viriani in 1813 from *Liguria*: see LIGURIAN and -ITE.] An apple-green variety of titanite.

1816 W. PHILLIPS *Introd. Min.* (1823) 207 Ligurite..occurs in a sort of talcose rocks..in the Appennines. **1839** *Penny Cycl.* XIII. 481/1 *Ligurite*, this mineral occurs crystallized; the primary form is an oblique rhombic prism. **1865** WATTS *Dict. Chem.* III. 695 *Ligurite*, a mineral having the angles and character of sphene (Dufrenoy) found in a talcose rock in the Appennines.

ligur(r)ition (lɪgjʊəˈrɪʃən). *rare.* [a. L. *ligur(r)itiōn-em*, f. *ligur(r)īre* to be dainty, to lick up.] Gluttonous devouring, licking.

1623 COCKERAM, *Ligurition*, greedinesse, lycorousnesse. **1644** *Vindex Anglicus* 6 (in list of 'inkhorn' terms). **1656** BLOUNT *Glossogr.*, *Ligurition*, a gluttonous devouring; immoderate appetite. **1859** FARRAR *J. Home* 94 Slovenly servants employed in the emptying of wine-glasses and the ligurrition of dishes.

†**ˈligury.** *Obs.*⁻⁰ = LIGURINE.

1598 FLORIO, *Spino*,..the bird Ligurie or a Siskin. **1659** TORRIANO, *Spino*,..a Ligury or Siskin-bird.

ligury: see LIGURE.

†**liˈgustre.** *Obs.* In 5 lygoustre. [a. OF. *ligustre* or ad. L. *ligustr-um* privet.] Privet.

1480 CAXTON *Ovid's Met.* XIII. xv, O Galathee, more whyte than the floure of lygoustre or of lylye.

ligustrin (lɪˈgʌstrɪn). *Chem.* [f. L. *ligustrum* privet + -IN¹. Cf. F. *ligustrine.*] The bitter principle of privet.

1865 WATTS *Dict. Chem.* III. 695 The leaves of privet yield, according to Polex..a yellow, hygroscopic bitter extract, called ligustrin.

ligustrum (lɪˈgʌstrəm). [L. *ligustrum* privet, adopted by Linnæus (*Hortus Cliffortianus* (1737) 6) and earlier botanists as the name of a genus.] = PRIVET¹.

1664 EVELYN *Kalendarium Hortense* in *Sylva* 71 July... Flowers in Prime, or yet lasting... Oleanders red and white, Agnus Castus, Arbutus, Yucca, Olive, Ligustrum, Tilia, &c. **1900** M. THORN in W. D. Drury *Bk. Gardening* xi. 441 Ligustrums (Privets) are represented in many gardens only by *L. ovalifolium* (oval-leaved) and its golden-leaved form. **1957** *New Yorker* 23 Nov. 46/3 I've put four pyramid ligustrums on the sculpture balconies. We always use plants to bring out an exhibition. **1973** W. J. BEAN *Trees & Shrubs Hardy in Brit. Is.* (ed. 8) II. 570 L[*igustrum*] *confusum* is..represented at Kew by a plant 10 ft high in the Ligustrum collection.

ligynge, ligyor, obs. ff. LYING, LEDGER.

lih-: see LIE *v.*¹ and *v.*²

lihȝen, lihȝere, obs. ff. LAUGH *v.*, LIAR.

lihinde, obs. form of LYING *ppl. a.*

liht, obs. f. LIGHT; var. LITE *Obs.*, delay.

Lihyanic (liːˈjɑːnɪk), *sb.* Also **Lihyanite, Lihyanian; Lihyani** (liːˈjɑːniː). [f. Arab. *liḥyān* + -IC.] The name of an ancient Semitic language known only from north Arabian inscriptions of the 2nd and 1st centuries B.C. Also (all forms), as *adj.*

1911 *Encycl. Brit.* XXIV. 626/1 A more commendable proposal is to call the inscriptions Liḥyānī, since the tribe of Liḥyān is sometimes mentioned in them... Other brief inscriptions..have been discovered... Their writing is a somewhat later form of the Liḥyānī, and the dialect..seems to be very similar to Liḥyānī. **1932** W. L. GRAFF *Lang.* xi. 402 From North Arabia we have a certain number of inscriptions dating from the 2d or 1st century B.C. and revealing a language, called Lihyanite, closely related to Arabic proper. **1936** *Encycl. Islam* III. 27/1 The Ṯhamūdaean graffiti..are a development (later or parallel) of the Liḥyānī script. **1937** F. V. WINNETT *Study of Lihyanite & Thamudic Inscriptions* 51 The earlier supplanting of Dedanite by Lihyanite points to a Lihyanite conquest of Dedan (al-'Ula) in the early 5th century B.C. **1939** L. H. GRAY *Foundations of Lang.* 363 North Arabic is first recorded in Liḥyānian and Thamūdian inscriptions (the former between the second or first century B.C. and the fourth or sixth A.D...) and in Ṣafāitic graffiti. **1948** D. DIRINGER *Alphabet* II. ii. 227 The Lihyanite inscriptions can be divided into two groups. **1968** *Encycl. Brit.* I. 663/2 The four South Semitic alphabets..are known as Sabaean, Lihyanic, Thamudenic and Safahitic.

lij-: see LIE *v.*¹ and *v.*²

lijf, obs. form of LIFE, LIEF.

lijk, obs. form of LICH (body, corpse), LIKE.

lijt, variant of LITE *Obs.*, delay; obs. f. LIGHT.

lik: see LICH, LICK, LIKE.

likable, likame: see LIKEABLE, LICHAM.

†**ˈlikance.** *Obs. rare*⁻¹. In 5 lykance. [f. LIKE *v.* + -ANCE.] Liking; pleasure.

c **1460** *Towneley Myst.* xxiv. 56 Loke that ye lowte to my lykance..dilygently ply to my plesance.

likcour, obs. form of LIQUOR.

like (laɪk), *sb.*[1] [f. LIKE *v.*]

†**1.** (One's) good pleasure. (Also *pl.*) *Obs.*

? *a* **1425** *Cursor M.* 2997 (Trin.) What haue I done aȝeyn þi like [*Fairf.* þe to myslike]? **1615** LATHAM *Falconry* (1633) 75 Shee may doe all things at her owne likes.

†**2.** A liking (for). Const. *of. Obs.*

1589 NASHE *Anat. Absurd.* E ij b, Being wonne to haue a fauourable like of Poets wanton lines.

3. In mod. use *pl.* (rarely *sing.*), *likes* (coupled with *dislikes*): Feelings of affection or preference for particular things; predilections.

1851 MAYHEW *Lond. Labour* (1861) II. 495 She used to say, 'It was not her likes, but her husband's, or she'd have had me back.' **1873** BLACK *Pr. Thule* xii. 180 Her odd likes and dislikes. **1889** F. M. CRAWFORD *Greifenstein* III. xxii. 41, I do not care a straw for his like or dislike.

like (laɪk), *a.*, *adv.* (*conj.*), and *sb.*[2] Forms: α. 4–5 liche, lyche, (also 6 *arch.*) lich, (4 liche, 5 lych, leyge). β. 3–4 lic, 3–5 lik, 4 liik, lijc, 4–5 lijk(e, lick(e, 4–7 lyke, *Sc.* lyk, 5 lek(e, lyek, 6 leeke, lyeke, *Sc.* lyik, 4– like. *Comparative.* α. 3–4 licchere, lichyr, ? lecho(u)re. β. 3–4 lickor, lyckore, 4 lykker, 4–6 lyker, (*Sc.* -ar), 5 licker, likkir, 6– liker. *Superlative.* 4 lickest, 4–6 likkest, lykest, 4– likest. [Early ME. *līch*, *līk* (? late OE. **līc*), shortened form (= ON. *līk-r*, Sw. *lik*, Da. *lig*) of OE. *ȝelíc* = OFris. *gelīk*, OS. *gilīk* (Du. *gelijk*), OHG. *gilīh* (MHG. *gelīch*, mod.G. *gleich*), ON. *glīk-r*, Goth. *galeiks*:—OTeut. **galīko-* f. pref. *ga-* (corresponding in meaning to L. *com-*) + **līko-* body, form; the word is thus etymologically analogous to L. *conformis* CONFORM *a.* The OE. *ȝelíc* survived into early mod.Eng. as Y-LIKE: see also ALIKE *a.*

The OE. **lic* yields normally *līch* in Southern and *līk* in Northern ME. The former type did not survive after the 14th c.; the prevalence of the β form may be partly due to the analogy of the comparative, where the *k* is normal in all dialects, though the forms with *ch* were not uncommon.

The inflected comparative and superlative are now rare in educated use exc. *poet.* or *rhetorical*.]

A. *adj.*

1. Having the same characteristics or qualities as some other person or thing; of approximately identical shape, size, colour, character, etc., with something else; similar; resembling; analogous. (In the negative phrases, ***there is none*** or ***nothing like*** ——, the adj. assumes a pregnant sense = 'so good or wonderful as'.)

a. Const. *to*, *unto* (now arch.), north. †*till*, †*of*, *with* (arch.), †*as*.

c **1200** ORMIN 7931 Þeȝȝre sang iss lic wiþþ wop. *a* **1300** *Cursor M.* 9524 And algat til his fader like [*Gött.* of his fader liche; *Trin.* his fadir liche]. *Ibid.* 18861 Þe tane es to þe toþer like. **1377** LANGL. *P. Pl.* B. IX. 33 He..made man likkest [*v.r.* I-likest] to hym-self one. *c* **1380** WYCLIF *Serm.* Sel. Wks. II. 245 Þe wille of God mut nedis be good, licke to þe Fadir of hevene. *c* **1420** *Chron. Vilod.* st. 108 He hadde a gret hedde leyge to a gret blok. *c* **1430** *Hymns Virg.* 47 Lijk to him y neuere noon knewe. *c* **1449** PECOCK *Repr.* IV. vii. 458 The ..seid principal governauncis ben of lijk state, condicioun, nature, and merit with this present..principal gouernaunce. **1514** BARCLAY *Cyt. & Uplondyshm.* (Percy Soc.) 28 What is more folysshe, or lyker to madnesse, Than to spend the lyfe for glory, & rychesse? **1559** W. CUNNINGHAM *Cosmogr. Glasse* 17 A sphere of rounde fourme, like unto a Ball. **1571** *MS. Depos. Canterb. Cathedral Libr.* XVIII. lf. 60 b, You did say that one of Agnes Fullagor's children ys leeke vnto me. **16..** *Ballad, Mary Ambree* 32 (Percy MS.) There was neuer none like to Mary Aumbree. **1604** E. G[RIMSTONE] *D'Acosta's Hist. Indies* IV. xxxviii. 314 It is in face like to a monkie. **1611** BIBLE *Acts* xiv. 15 Wee also are men of like passions with you. **1670** BAXTER *Cure Ch. Div.* 238 You would shew yourselves much liker to God who is love, and unliker to Satan the accuser. **1709** MRS. MANLEY *Secret Mem.* (1736) II. 68 Are not these Shrieks like as those from a Woman in Distress? **1736** BUTLER *Anal.* I. iii. 101 A state of trial..analogous or like to our moral or religious trial. **1796** MRS. GLASSE *Cookery* x. 161 Dried herring..should be steeped the like time as the Whiting in small beer. **1819** SHELLEY *Cenci* V. iii. (Song), Sweet sleep, were death like to thee. **1859** MASSON *Brit. Novelists* ii. 94 Swift..the likest author we have to Rabelais. **1870** M. ARNOLD *Paul & Prot.* 17 Laud..held, on this point, a like opinion with him. **1871** FREEMAN *Hist. Ess.* Ser. II. 97 An old Greek was a being of like passions with a modern Englishman.

b. Const. simple dative. (In early use often placed after its regimen: cf. -LIKE *suffix* 1 a.) In this construction the adj. when attributive follows the sb.

c **1200** ORMIN 3572 Hire sune wass himm lic O fele kinne wise. **1297** R. GLOUC. (Rolls) 5680 No licchere is broþer him was þane wolf is a lomb [*v.rr.* he nas no lechore his broþer: lyker, lichyr, lechoure, lyckore, lickor]. **1340** HAMPOLE *Pr. Consc.* 830–1 Whiles a man lyves he is lyke a man; When he es dede what es he lyke þan? *c* **1380** WYCLIF *Serm.* Sel. Wks. II. 92 3if Y seie, Y knowe him not, I shal be liik 3ou, a lyere. *c* **1386** CHAUCER *Sqr.'s T.* 54 In this world was ther noon it lyche. *c* **1400** MAUNDEV. (1839) xviii. 199 Lymons, that is a manere of Fruyt, lyche smale Pesen. *c* **1470** *Golagros & Gaw.* 404 Thare is na leid on life of lordschip hym like. *a* **1548** HALL *Chron., Hen. VI*, 84 The Parisians..like the Wethercocke be variable and inconstaunt. **1601** SHAKS. *Twel. N.* III. i. 39 Fooles are as like husbands, as Pilchers are to Herrings. **1710** SWIFT *Jrnl. to Stella* 25 Oct., Addison's sister is a sort of a wit, very like him. **1782** PRIESTLEY *Corrupt. Chr.* I. I. 93 There was nothing like it in the philosophy of Plato. **1827** KEBLE *Chr. Y., Restor. R. Family*, Be some kind spirit, likest thine, Ever at hand. **1835** DICKENS *Sk. Boz, Tales* xi. (1892) 446 'Now, uncle', said Mr. Kitterbell, lifting up that part of the mantle which covered the infant's face,..'Who do you think he's like?' **1850** TENNYSON *In Mem.* lv. 4 What we have The likest God within the soul. **1854** BREWSTER *More Worlds* xv. 226 The fixed stars are like our sun in every point in which it is possible to compare them.

¶ Some phrasal uses of the adj. in this construction have a special idiomatic force. The question ***What is he*** (or *it*) ***like?*** means 'What sort of a man is he?', 'What sort of a thing is it?', the expected answer being a description, and not at all the mention of a resembling person or thing. (Cf. WHAT-LIKE.) ***to look like*** (occas. ***to be like***) sometimes means 'to have the appearance of being' so and so; e.g. in 'He looks like a clever man'. (Cf. sense 7.) ***like that***, used predicatively (perh. a Gallicism = F. *comme cela*): of the nature, character, or habit indicated; spec. (usu. accompanying the crossing of the speaker's fingers) as an indication that two people described are very friendly or intimate; ***like another*** [cf. Fr. *comme un autre*]: that is ordinary or unexceptional; that is only one of a number of similar things, possibilities, etc.

1684 tr. *Bonet's Merc. Compit.* XVIII. 647 The unskilfulness of the Dissector, who was liker a Butcher than an Anatomist. **1692** R. L'ESTRANGE *Fables* clxxxi. (1708) 194 The Hypocrite is never so far from being a Good Christian, as when he looks Likest One. **1816** J. WILSON *City of Plague* I. i. 124 Do not I Look, as I feel, most like thy murderer? **1835** MARRYAT *Three Cutters* i, It is Lord B——; he looks like a sailor, and he does not much belie his looks. **1878** PATMORE *Amelia*, She ask'd what Millicent was like. **1889** A. LANG *Prince Prigio* xviii. 139 He refused to keep his royal promise..! Kings are like that. **1899** NEWNHAM-DAVIS *Dinners & Diners* 194, I found myself wondering what an infant incubator could be like. **1904** H. JAMES *Golden Bowl* I. xiii. 236 Isn't the whole thing.. perhaps but a way like another for their gaining time? **1926** F. SCOTT FITZGERALD *Great Gatsby* ix. 206 'We were so thick like that in everything'—he held up two bulbous fingers—'always together.' **1929** D. HAMMETT *Red Harvest* xxii. 219 'You're a friend of Whisper's?' 'You bet.' He held up two thin fingers pressed tightly together. 'Just like that, me and him.' **1936** D. POWELL *Turn, Magic Wheel* I. 37 Theatrical people..just got here from London—they're like that with Cochrane—they know Dame Sybil Thorndike personally. **1966** I. MURDOCH *Time of Angels* xviii. 193, I suppose it's a skill like another. **1971** M. RUSSELL *Deadline* xv. 182 'Of course you had to get on terms with Gregory.' 'Now we're like *that*.'

c. In mod. use (with following dat.) often = 'such as', introducing a particular example of a class respecting which something is predicated.

1886 STEVENSON *Lett.* (1899) II. 41 A critic like you is one who fights the good fight, contending with stupidity. **1887** COLVIN *Keats* i. 1 A birth like that of Keats presents to the ordinary mind a striking instance of nature's inscrutability.

d. Without construction, chiefly in attributive relation: Resembling something already indicated or implied. ***the like***: such as have been mentioned (cf. C. 3); formerly often preceded by an adj. of quantity, as †***many the like***. See also SUCH-LIKE, formerly also †***such a like***. For ***in like manner***, see MANNER; for ***in like wise***, see LIKEWISE.

a **1300** *Cursor M.* 6382 Of honi it had likest sauur [*Gött.* lickest, *Fairf.* likkest]. *c* **1375** *Sc. Leg. Saints* vi. (*Thomas*) 130 A lyk dreme dremyt þai bath. *c* **1400** *Apol. Loll.* 19 For þe honor of God, & profit of himsilf & of þe peple, wiþ mani filal leful leke causis. **14..** *Sir Beues* (MS. C.) 801 In lyke case was þe wylde bore. **1564** in *Vicary's Anat.* (1888) App. III. iii. 166 A proclamacion of lyke substaunce & effect shall furthwith be drawen. **1590** SPENSER *F.Q.* III. vii. 29 For both to be and seeme to him was labour lich. **1591** —— *M. Hubberd* 199 Be you the Souldier, for you likest are For manly semblance, and small skill in warre. **1608** TOPSELL *Serpents* (1658) 601 Solinus reporteth of such a like Wood in a part of Africa. **1611** BIBLE *Transl. Pref.* 2 Wee shall finde many the like examples of such kind, or rather vnkind acceptance. *Ibid.* 3 An Heretike of the like stampe. **1651** HOBBES *Leviath.* I. iii. 10 Like events will follow like actions. **1711** ADDISON *Spect.* No. 69 ⁋ 5 Hips and Haws, Acorns and Pig-nuts, with other Delicacies of the like Nature. **1840** L. HUNT in *Dram. Wks. Wycherley* etc. *Farquhar* p. lxxxvii, Equally profound is..Mr. Lamb in whatever he says at all times on the like subjects. **1865** TYLOR *Early Hist. Man.* i. 5 The like working of men's minds under like conditions. **1875** JOWETT *Plato* (ed. 2) I. 169 They cause disease and poverty and other like evils.

e. Of two or more persons or things: Having the same or closely resembling characteristics; mutually similar; in predicative use = alike (now *rare*). Prov. ***as like as two peas***: see PEA *sb.*

c **1375** *Sc. Leg. Saints* iii. (*Andreas*) 1037 All are lyk, and ȝet..In like face..men fyndis diuersyte. *c* **1400** *Lanfranc's Cirurg.* 14, ij lymes..þat ben lich in complexioun. *c* **1530** LD. BERNERS *Arth. Lyt. Bryt.* 471 They war al goodly persones and moche lyke of stature. **1604** H. JACOB *Reasons Reform.* 9 Al these..are exceeding divers and no way like. *a* **1641** BP. MOUNTAGU *Acts & Mon.* (1642) 355 The two letters of *b* and *m* being in manuscripts very like. **1757** MRS. GRIFFITH *Lett. Henry & Frances* (1767) I. 181, I always looked upon them as twin-sisters, and so very like, that it was difficult to know one from t'other. **1832** TENNYSON *Dream Fair Wom.* 280 No two dreams are like. **1872** BAGEHOT *Physics & Pol.* i. 21 A nation means a *like* body of men, because of that likeness capable of acting together. **1876** JEVONS *Logic Prim.* 9 Things which seem to be like may be different.

¶ **f.** Inaccurately const. dative (etc.) instead of ellipt. possessive.

(Cf. κόμαι χαρίτεσσιν ὁμοῖαι *Iliad* xvii. 51.)

a **1300** *Cursor M.* 18408 Quat ert þou þat es here, þat has to theif so like a chere? *c* **1460** *Towneley Myst.* xxv. 72 The fader voyce, oure myrthes to amende, Was made to me lyke as a man. **1567** *Satir. Poems Reform.* iii. 169 Hir lauchter lycht be lyke to trim Thysbie. **1890** FREEMAN in W. R. W. Stephens *Life* (1895) II. 414 His domestic arrangements.. are rather like a steamer.

2. In phraseological and proverbial expressions.

†**a.** ***all like***: in all cases the same. *Obs.*

1477 EARL RIVERS (Caxton) *Dictes* 21 Whersomeuer one deye, the weye to the other worlde is all like.

†**b.** ***like case*** (advb. phr.): in the same way, likewise. *Obs.* exc. *dial.*

1534 *Kirton-in-Lindsey Churchw. Acc.* in *N.W. Linc. Gloss.* s.v., Paid wytsonday for ij ponde sope for weching cherche clothes iij d. Paid at lammes lyke case iii d. **1552** HULOET, Like case and likewyse, *idem.* **1579** W. A. *Speciall Remedie* f iij b (Roxburghe Club), Yet haue I yeelded like a coward thoe, And followed his pleasures vaine like case. **1889** *N.W. Linc. Gloss.* s.v., Thaay chuckt th' watter tub oher, like caase thaay brok th' tap on it.

†**c.** Alike; in phr. ***share and share like***, ***portion and portion like***. *Obs.*

1540 in R. G. Marsden *Sel. Pl. Crt. Adm.* (1894) 96 To be compelled to bere and pay their partes and porcions of the same averyge after the rate of their said goods porcion and porcion lyke. **1692** R. L'ESTRANGE *Fables* vii. 6 Every one to go share and share-like in what they took.

d. In proverbial formulæ of the type ***like master like man*** (as the master, so the man).

1548 UDALL *Erasm. Par. Luke* xxiii. 177 Beeyng lyke men lyke maister accordyng to the prouerbe. *c* **1550** BALE *K. Johan* (Camden) 73 Lyke Lorde, lyke chaplayne. **1611** BIBLE *Hosea* iv. 9 And there shall be like people, like priest [WYCLIF as the peple so the prest]. **1632** MASSINGER *City Madam* I. i, Like lady, like chicken. *Ibid.* II. ii, Like bitch, like whelps. **1655** FULLER *Ch. Hist.* IX. ii. §20 Like cup, like cover. **1835** MARRYAT *Jac. Faithf.* xxiii, But like mother like child, they say. **1842** TENNYSON *Walking to Mail* 55 Like men, like manners.

e. ***anything like***, ***nothing like***, ***something like***: anything, nothing, something nearly as great, good, effective (etc.) as (another thing), or approaching it in size or quality. Also ellipt. ***something like*** = something like what he, it (etc.) should be, or what is desired or aimed at (chiefly *colloq.*, and serving as an emphatic expression of satisfaction).

1666 BUNYAN *Grace Ab.* §32 My great Conversion from prodigious Profaneness to something like a Moral Life. **1702** S. PARKER tr. *Cicero's De Finibus* IV. 247 This is something-like! **1791** 'G. GAMBADO' *Ann. Horsem.* i. (1809) 67, I have had nothing like a bad fall lately. **1798** *Geraldina* I. 176 'This looks something like, Sir,' said she. **1883** *Manch. Exam.* 22 Nov. 5/4 The Parcel Post is being conducted at a loss of something like £10,000 a week. **1884** *Ibid.* 17 June 4/7 There is nothing like giving a nickname to anything you wish to denounce. **1885** J. PAYN *Talk of Town* II. 117 Not that Pye is an archangel, nor anything like it. **1901** *Expositor* Nov. 396 In the 'Times' the other day, a description of the largest steam-hammer yet made was headed 'Something like a hammer'.

f. The phrases in sense e are also used *adverbially*, conveying the notion of an approximation to what would be expressed by the predicate (vb. or adj.) or its accompanying adv. Also ellipt. ***something like***: in a tolerably adequate manner; † at a fairly reasonable price.

1590 SHAKS. *Com. Err.* III. ii. 105 *Anti.* What complexion is she of? *Dro.* Swart like my shoo, but her face nothing like so cleane kept. *a* **1620** J. DYKE *Serm.* (1640) 379 If a man will sell a commodity, hee will sell it somewhat like, or hee will keepe it. **1748** RICHARDSON *Clarissa* (1811) VI. 241 Why this is talking somewhat like. **1782** ELIZ. BLOWER *Geo. Bateman* III. 111[She sits her horse] nothing like so well as you used to do. **1793** BENTHAM *Wks.* (1843) x. 239 The £600 a-year ..I do not look upon as anything like adequate. **1798** T. TWINING *Recreat. & Stud.* (1882) 237 Often have I heard you something like blamed for these voluntary labours. **1851** WHEWELL in Todhunter *Acc. Writings* (1876) II. 371, I have not any thing like got through the work. **1874** RUSKIN *Fors Clav.* xlvii. 253 No; not so well done; or anything like so well done.

g. Colloq. phr. (***a bit***) ***more like*** (***it***): nearer what it (etc.) should be or what is desired; better; also, closer to the truth. Cf. MORE *adv.* 1 h.

1888 KIPLING *Phantom 'Rickshaw* (1889) 81 'That's more like,' said Carnehan. 'If you could think us a little more mad we would be more pleased.' **1891** S. WEYMAN *New Rector* II. xv. 12 'This is better than No. 383, Mrs. Baxter?' 'Well, sir,..it is a bit more like.' **1907** D. H. LAWRENCE *Phoenix II* (1968) 8 'Ah,' said Beelzebub, ' this is a bit more like it, a bit hotter. The Devils feel at home here.' **1962** D. MAYO *Island of Sin* viii. 63 Paid companion, hell. Whipping-boy was more like it. **1964** A. WILSON *Late Call* iv. 141 Shopping in the Town Centre provided something more like, and she ambled around, taking her time. **1968** P. DURST *Badge of Infamy* vii. 61 'Would you like some coffee?' 'Now that's more like it. Sure why not?'

3. Of a portrait, etc.: Bearing a faithful resemblance to the original. Now only *predicative*.

1561 T. HOBY tr. *Castiglione's Courtyer* IV. (1577) T iij a, A muche more liker Image of God are those good Princes that loue and worshippe him. **1591** SPENSER *Tears Muses* 201 All these, and all that els the Comick Stage With seasoned wit and goodly pleasaunce graced, By which mans life in his likest image Was limned forth. **1638** BAKER tr.

Balzac's Lett. (vol. II.) 167 Those painters, that care not for making a face like, so they make it faire. **1705** Hickeringill *Priest-cr.* ii. Wks. 1716 III. 68 Its own Picture drawn so very like, that it has not patience to behold its own Physiognomy. **1756** Mrs. F. Brooke *Old Maid* No. 36. 295, I have myself seen the camps at Clapham and in Hyde-park, and must own my Correspondent's picture of the last to be like. **1775** Dk. Richmond in *Burke Corr.* (1844) II. 87, I believe you will think it a good and a like portrait when you see it. **1850** E. FitzGerald *Lett.* (1889) I. 203, I got your photograph at last: it is a beastly thing: not a bit like. **1854** Hawthorne *Eng. Note-Bks.* (1879) I. 103 It was very like and very laughable, but hardly caricatured.

4. *Math.* (See quot. 1706.) Now superseded by *similar*, exc. in ***like quantities*** and ***like signs***.

1557 Recorde *Whetst.* D i, When the sides of one plat forme, beareth like proportion together as the sides of any other flatte forme of the same kinde doeth, then are those formes called *like flattes*..and their numbers, that declare their quantities, in like sorte are named *like flattes.* **1660** Barrow *Euclid* vi. iv. Schol., If in a triangle *FBE* there be drawn *AC* a parallel to one side *FE*, the triangle *ABC* shall be like to the whole *FBE.* **1706** Phillips (ed. Kersey), *Like Arches* or *Arks* (in the Projection of the Sphere) are Parts of lesser Circles that contain an equal Number of Degrees with the corresponding Arches of great Ones. *Like Figures* (in Geom.) are such as have their Angles equal, and the Sides about those Angles proportional. *Like solid Figures*, such as are comprehended under Planes that are like, and equal in Number. *Ibid.*, *Like Quantities* (in Algebra), such as are expressed by the same Letters, equally repeated in each Quantity. Thus 2*a* and 3*a*, 6*dd* and 4*dd*, are like Quantities; but 2*a* and 3*aa*, and 6 *f* and 4 *fff* are unlike. *Like Signs*, are when both are Affirmative, or both Negative . . Thus + 16 *c* and + 4 *c*, have like Signs. **1709** J. Ward *Introd. Math.* ii. ii. §4 (1734) 154 Like Signs give + and Unlike Signs give − in the Quotient. **1797** *Encycl. Brit.* (ed. 3) I. 401/1 To add terms that are like and have like signs. **1859** Barn. Smith *Arith. & Algebra* (ed. 6) 201.

5. *Golf.* (See quot.)

1887 Donaldson *Suppl. to Jam.* s.v., When both parties have played the same number of strokes they are said to be *like.*

6. †**a.** Apt, suitable, befitting. Chiefly predicative. *Obs.*

a **1450** *Cov. Myst.* xl. (Shaks. Soc.) 394 This observaunce is most like you to do dewly, Wherfore tak it upon you, brother, we pray. **1477** *Paston Lett.* III. 196 An C *li.*..is no money lyek for syche a joyntore as is desyred of my son. **1592** C'tess Shrewsbury in Ellis *Orig. Lett.* Ser. ii. III. 167 They are the likest instruments to put a bad matter in execution.

b. Characteristic of; such as one might expect from.

1667 Pepys *Diary* 4 Apr., It was pretty to hear the Duke of Albemarle himself to wish that they would come on our ground, meaning the French, for that he would pay them..; which was like a general, but not like an admiral. **1703** *Rules of Civility* 98 That would be liker a Drunkard than a Gentleman. **1711** Swift *Jrnl. to Stella* 8 Sept., It is like your Irish politeness, raffling for tea-kettles. **1840** Dickens *Barn. Rudge* xxvii, It would be like his impudence..to dare to think of such a thing.

7. *predicatively*, in certain idiomatic uses, chiefly with the vbs. *feel, look, sound*: †**a.** With gerund as regimen: Having the appearance of (doing something). **b.** Giving promise of (doing something); indicating the probable presence of (something). **c.** *colloq.* In recent use (orig. U.S.), ***to feel like***: to have an inclination for, be in the humour for.

1654–66 Earl Orrery *Parthen.* (1676) 690 They look'd rather like going to triumph after a Victory, than to win one. **1741** Lady Pomfret *Corr.* (1805) III. 30 The music.. sounds so like being accompanied by an organ, that [etc.]. **1850** Carlyle *Latter-d. Pamph.* III. 2 The Forty Colonies ..are all pretty like rebelling just now. **1863** R. B. Kimball *Was he successful?* ii. xii. 278 He did not feel like returning to his solitary room with his mind unsettled. **1868** Yates *Rock Ahead* II. 245 Wooded uplands suggested good cover-shooting; broad expanse of heath looked very like rabbits. **1894** Du Maurier *Trilby* (1895) 111 Bother work this morning! I feel much more like a stroll in the Luxembourg Gardens.

8. In accordance with appearances, probable, likely. Now only *dial.*

c **1375** Barbour *Bruce* xvi. 324 It wes weill lik..That he mycht haff conquerit..The land of Irland. *c* **1400** *Destr. Troy* 10440 Hit was not lik þat þe lede..Shuld haue killit þis kyng. **1432–50** tr. *Higden* (Rolls) I. 17 Thynges incredible and not lyke [L. *incredibilia..et non verisimilia*]. **1541** Wyatt *Defence* Wks. (1861) p. xxxiii, It was not like that I should get the Knowledge being in Spain. **1545** Brinklow *Compl.* ii. (1874) 14 Who hath the vantage, God knowyth; wether the King, or..the officers..which is most lykest. **1592** Shaks. *Rom. & Jul.* iv. iii. 45 Is it not like that I..run mad? **1603** —— *Meas. for M.* v. i. 104. *c* **1635** W. Scot *Apol. Narr.* (Wodrow Soc.) 27, I know not if it came to Mr. Knox befor his death..as it is like it did. **1664** Butler *Hud.* ii. iii. 835 And is it like they have not still In their old Practices some skill? *a* **1717** Blackall *Wks.* (1723) I. 560 He only desired time, and would, 'tis like, have been able to pay thee. **1733** E. Erskine *Serm.* Wks. 1871 II. 152 The temple where it is like Isaiah got the manifestation. **1816** Scott *Antiq.* xv, 'It's like we maun wait then till the gudeman comes hame'.

9. *predicatively*, const. *to* with *inf.*: **a.** That may reasonably be expected *to* (do, etc.), likely *to*. Now somewhat *rare* in literary use; still common *colloq.*

a **1300** *Cursor M.* 3452 Hir lijf was lickest to be ded. *c* **1380** Wyclif *Wks.* (1880) 372 It is ful like for to stonde in þe same wise wiþ-in a few ȝeris in ynglonde. *c* **1400** *Destr. Troy* 2254 Licker at þe last end in langore to bide. *c* **1420** *Pallad. on Husb.* vi. 199 For that [brik] is maad in somer heete To sone is drie, and forto chyne is like. **1508** Dunbar *Poems* iv. 11 Now dansand mirry, now like to dee. **1573** Tusser *Husb.* xxxv. (1878) 82 Those of the fairest and likest to thriue. **1592** Shaks. *Rom. & Jul.* i. v. 187 My graue is like to be my wedding bed. **1641** J. Jackson *True Evang. T.* iii. 224 Lay a good foundation, and then the superstructure is like to stand. **1704** Swift *Batt. Bks.* Misc. (1711) 239 Discovering how high the Quarrel was like to proceed. *a* **1715** Burnet *Own Time* (1724) I. 368 A man much liker to spoil business than to carry it on dextrously. *a* **1806** C. J. Fox *Jas. II* (1808) 194 He thought himself like to get rid of them. **1873** Ruskin *Fors Clav.* IV. xlviii. 268 But we are in hard times, now, for all men's wits; for men who know the truth are like to go mad from isolation. **1886** Bynner *A. Surriage* iii. 34 The two or three places I am like to have business relations with. **1896** A. E. Housman *Shropsh. Lad* xxii, Such leagues apart the world's ends are, We're like to meet no more.

b. (Now *colloq.* or *dial.*) Apparently on the point of. Sometimes (? by anacoluthon) with ellipsis of the vb. substantive, so that *like* becomes = 'was (or were) like' (now chiefly *U.S., colloq.*). Also in confused use, ***had like to*** (for *was like to*), chiefly with perf. inf.: = 'had come near to, narrowly missed (——ing)'. (A further grammatical confusion appears in the form *had liked to*: see like *v.*² 2 b.)

c **1560** Wriothesley *Chron.* (1875) II. 135 Wherefore that plee would not serve, and so [they] had like to haue had judgment without triall. **1565** J. Sparke in *Hawkins' Voy.* (1878) 26 Which had like to haue turned vs to great displeasure. **1586** A. Day *Eng. Secretary* ii. (1625) 80 That he had like to haue knockt his head against the gallowes. **1600** Shaks. *A.Y.L.* v. iv. 48, I haue had foure quarrels, and like to haue fought one. **1657** W. Rand tr. *Gassendi's Peiresc* i. 20 And these digressions..had like to cost him dear. **1709** Strype *Ann. Ref.* (1824) I. xx. 367 After the treaty had been like to have been broken off. **1709** Mrs. Manley *Secret Mem.* (1736) IV. 160 She advanced toward the Land of Coquetry, and like to have arrived there. **1711** Steele *Spect.* No. 78 ⁋4 The young Lady was amorous, and had like to have run away with her Father's Coachman. **1760–72** H. Brooke *Fool of Qual.* (1809) II. 28, I had like to murder poor Mr. Vindex. **1808** L. Summer in *Southern Hist. Mag.* (1892) I. 52 Strother was 150 votes behind Roberts & like to have lost his election in consequence of his opposing Madison. **1823** Scott *Quentin D.* ii, The eldest man seemed like to choke with laughter. **1826** —— *Jrnl.* I. 124, I had like to have been too hasty. **1830** in *Jrnl. Illinois State Hist. Soc.* (1930–1) XXIII. 214 The boat went under a tree top and like to took me off. **1836** F. A. Chardon *Jrnl. Fort Clark* (1932) 70 Michael Belhumeres horse fell with him, had like to have broken his neck. **1853** Mrs. Carlyle *Lett.* II. 241, I am like to cry whenever I think of her. **1854** in *Southwestern Hist. Q.* (1931–2) XXXV. 217 The supper—I had like to have said table-spread, for I can call it by no other name—it is a dirty old wagon cover sp[r]ead on the ground. **1855** in *Calif. Hist. Soc. Q.* (1929) VIII. 340 Like to never got back myself. **1873** Ruskin *Fors Clav.* xxvii. 7, I had like to have said something else. **1884** 'Mark Twain' *Huck. Finn* xxxix. 396 We like to got a hornet's nest, but we didn't. **1889** 'C. E. Craddock' *Despot of Broomsedge Cove* xviii. 327 That's what like to have happened to me. **1916** 'B. M. Bower' *Phantom Herd* vi. 100, I like to died a-laughing. **1930** G. B. Johnson in B. A. Botkin *Treas. S. Folklore* (1949) iv. iii. 608 'I like to have got killed' means 'I almost got killed'. It is surprising how many phrases used by Negroes are exactly the phrases used by English folk. **1973** *Black World* Apr. 63 Damn brim like to covered broad street.

c. *dial.* (north. and north midland): Constrained, obliged, having no option but *to* (do so-and-so). Also with ellipsis of the inf. (Cf. *fain.*)

1828 *Trial W. Dyon at York Assizes* 11, I promised him I would not tell: I was like for fear of losing my life. *Mod.* (*Sheffield*) You'll be like to let him have his own way.

10. *Comb.*, as ***like-minded*** (whence ***likemindedness***), ***-natured***, ***-seeming***, ***-shaped***, ***-sized*** adjs.

1526 Tindale *Rom.* xv. 5 That ye be *lyke mynded won towardes another. **1841** E. Miall in *Nonconf.* I. 248 Sir Robert Peel will find thousands likeminded with us. **1888** Burgon *Lives 12 Gd. Men* I. iv. 381 They were devoted to one another, inseparable, and entirely like-minded. **1638** Sanderson *Serm.* (1681) II. 120 Our *like-mindedness.. must be according to Christ Jesus. **1579** Fulke *Heskins's Parl.* 192 That this rude and earthly body by a *like natured taste, touching, and meate, should be brought to immortalitie. **1839** Bailey *Festus* (1852) 26 Like-natured with them. **1590** Spenser *F.Q.* i. iii. 26 By his *like-seeming shield her knight by name Shee weend it was. **1897** *Daily News* 5 Feb. 11/1 *Like-shaped and *like-sized balls.

b. In proposed mathematical terms: †***like-jamb***, a parallelogram; †***like-side***, a rhombus.

1551 Recorde *Pathw. Knowl.* i. Defin., Those squares which haue their sides al equal, may be called..likesides,.. and those that haue only the contrary sydes equal,..those wyll I call likeiammys, for a difference.

B. *adv.* (quasi-*prep.*, *conj.*).

1. a. In or after the manner of; in the same manner or to the same extent as; as in the case of. Const. as in A. 1 a, b: also *rarely*, †const. *after*. Also (const. *dat.*), in the manner characteristic of. *like that*: in that manner (cf. A. 1 b ¶).

a **1300** *Cursor M.* 5133 Þai com ham noght as prisuns like [*Gött.* lick, *Trin.* liche] Bot als þai war knigthes rik. ? **1370** *Robt. Cicyle* 58 He rode non odur lyke. *c* **1380** Wyclif *Wks.* (1880) 253 Þan schulden prestis lyue lich to angels. *c* **1386** Chaucer *Prol.* 590 His top was dokked lyk a preest biforn. —— *Frankl. T.* 517 Phebus wax old, and hewed lyke latoun. *c* **1400** *Destr. Troy* 1613 Rome.. Tild vpon Tiber after Troy like. **1432–50** tr. *Higden* (Rolls) II. 187 Floenge like to the water, ȝiffenge place like to the aier. *c* **1500** *Lancelot* 3170 Ful lyk o knycht one to the feld he raid. **1508** Dunbar *Flyting w. Kennedie* 174 Ay loungand, lyk ane loikman on ane ledder. —— *Tua mariit Wemen* 273, I hatit him like a hund. *c* **1590** Marlowe *Faust.* xi. (1604) E 2, Like an asse as I was, I would not be ruled by him. **1594** T. Bedingfield tr. *Machiavelli's Florent. Hist.* (1595) 221 The disorder of his ministers (who liued liker Princes, then priuate men). *c* **1600** Shaks. *Sonn.* xxix, Featur'd like him, like him with friends possest. **1601** —— *Twel. N.* v. i. 275 Thou neuer should'st loue woman like to me. **1654** Earl Monm. tr. *Bentivoglio's Warrs Flanders* 133 Fearing their Town would fare like Oudwater. **1713** Addison *Guardian* No. 97 ⁋1 This ..is using a man like a fool. **1732** Berkeley *Alciphr.* ii. §23 Working like moles under ground. **1779** Mad. D'Arblay *Diary & Lett.* (1842–6) I. 256 She sings like her, laughs like her, talks like her. **1821** Keats *Lamia* i. 49 Striped like a zebra, freckled like a pard. **1854** Mrs. Jameson *Bk. of Th.* (1877) 270 A lecture should not read like an essay. **1871** Morley *Voltaire* (1886) 1 The name of Voltaire will stand out like the names of the great decisive movements in the European advance. **1872** *Punch* 2 Mar. 88/2 What was the use of his talking like that? **1879** McCarthy *Donna Quixote* xxi, But I never was good like that.

b. In colloquial phrases denoting vigour or rapidity of action, as ***like anything***, ***like a shot***, ***like fun***, ***blazes***, etc.

1681 T. Flatman *Heraclitus Ridens* No. 48 (1713) II. 53 He storms and sputters like ——*Jest.* What I prithee? *Earn.* Why—like any think. **1695** Congreve *Love for L.* v. iv. (ed. 2) 76, I have been looking up and down for you like any thing. **1778** Miss Burney *Evelina* xxi. (1784) 157 All the people in the pit are without hats, dressed like anything. **1848** Like fun [see fun *sb.* 1 b]. **1872** L. Carroll *Through Looking-gl.* 73 They wept like anything to see Such quantities of sand. **1885** *Illustr. Lond. News* 18 Apr. 392/3 If she doesn't know anything about it, she'll say so like a shot.

c. ***to know*** or ***read*** (someone or something) ***like a book***: to know very well, understand perfectly; ***to speak*** or ***talk like a book***: (*a*) to talk elegantly; to use literary or pedantic language in conversation; (*b*) to speak knowledgeably and accurately. *colloq.*

1825 J. Neal *Bro. Jonathan* II. xxvi. 444 I can.. read you off, like a book. **1829** *Mass. Spy* 28 Jan. (Th.), You talk like a book, Mr. Bond. **1833** J. Neal *Down-Easters* 26 An educated and travelled Yankee..talking like a book, even to his washerwoman. **1839** 'H. Franco' *Adventures H. Franco* I. xi. 73 'Know him like a book,' replied Mr. Lummucks. **1843** W. T. Thompson *Major Jones' Chron. Pineville* 74, I knows the Curloos like a book. **1844** T. C. Haliburton *Attaché* 2nd Ser. II. 176 Let a man or woman come and talk to me..and I'll tell you all about 'em right off as easy as big print. I can read 'em like a book. **1853** Lytton *My Novel* II. vii. xxi. 281 'If you can contrive to affect to be angry with him for his extravagance, it will do good.' 'You speak like a book, and I'll try my best.' **1875** [see speak *v.* 1 d]. **1933** Wodehouse *Mulliner Nights* 101 That terrible old woman saw through my subterfuge last night. She read me like a book. **1940** H. G. Wells *Babes in Darkling Wood* i. i. 25 Don't you talk like a book, Mr. Jimmy... Don't you go using long words. **1960** *Sunday Times* 27 Nov. 11 'Speaks Welsh like a book, the professor'—and, what's more, he also writes it like a book though he learnt it late in life.

d. *N. Amer. colloq.* Followed by an adj.: in the manner of one who is ——. Cf. *like crazy* (crazy *a.* 4 c), *like mad* (mad *a.* 1 c). Also in less analysable constructions.

1959 *She* May 21/2 Like wow...wonderful. **1961** G. Smith *Business of Loving* xi. 231 Sometimes we get rather soppy about each other..and laugh like young. **1962** [see blow *v.*[1] 14 e]. **1970** *Time* 31 Aug. 19 Afterward, a girl came up to me and said, 'You kinda look interested in this; did you know there are civil rights for women?' And I thought like wow, this is for me.

2. = alike. **a.** In a like degree; equally. Now *arch.* or *poet.* (only qualifying an adj. or adv.).

1340–70 *Alex. & Dind.* 105 Whan eueri lud liche wel lyuede up-on erþe. *c* **1384** Chaucer *H. Fame* i. 10 Why this [is] a dreme, why that is swevene And noght to euery man lyche euene. **1393** Langl. *P. Pl.* C. xvii. 20 Men of grete welþe, And liche witty and wys. *c* **1400** *Rom. Rose* 4160 It was al liche longe & wyde. *c* **1400** *Lanfranc's Cirurg.* 158 Whanne þat alle þe brawnys traueilen liche myche. **1496** *Dives & Paup.* (W. de W.) i. xxvii. 64/2 The sonne in hymselfe is alwaye aite one and shyneth alwaye all lyke. **1584** Cogan *Haven Health* cxxxi. (1636) 131 [Mutton] is.. not like good in all places in England. **1611** Shaks. *Cymb.* iii. iii. 41 Subtle as the Fox for prey, Like warlike as the Wolfe, for what we eate. **1650** Trapp *Comm. Num.* xxi. 1 In our late troubles, it was a like difficult thing, to finde among our enemies, a wicked man in their prisons, or a godly man out of them. **1695** Hickeringill *Lay-Clergy* Wks. 1716 I. 326 That other like ill-advised expression. **1812** Byron *Ch. Har.* i. xvii, Hut and palace show like filthily. **1839** Bailey *Festus* (1852) 337 All His gifts Like wondrous, like unlimited, like fair, As when the wind first blew.

†**b.** In like manner. *Obs. rare.*

1542 Udall *Erasm. Apoph.* 317 b (marg.), Quoque the coniunction, & coce the vocatiue of cocus, sounded both like in Cicero his tyme. **1545** Ascham *Toxoph.* (Arb.) 107 To shote compasse, to draw euermore lyke, to lowse euermore lyke.

†**3.** Followed by an adj. or adjectival phrase: In the manner of one who (or that which) is ——. *Obs.* exc. in *like mad* (see mad *a.*).

1500–20 Dunbar *Poems* xix. 19 Ȝon man is lyke out of his mynd. **1596** Spenser *F.Q.* iv. x. 56 All looking on, and like astonisht staring. **1682** Creech tr. *Lucretius* (1683) 87 The look is vivid still, nor seems like dead, Till every Particle of Soul is fled. **1801** tr. *Gabrielli's Myst. Husb.* III. 211 Being his tenant, he was like in his power.

†**4.** In accordance with, according *to*. *Obs.*

1422 tr. *Secreta Secret., Priv. Priv.* 131 And to ham yeue thow lyke har deserte. **1426** Lydg. *De Guil. Pilgr.* 14281 The ffox, lyk hys entente, Took the chese, and forth he wente. *c* **1430** —— *Chichev. & Byc.* ii. *Min. Poems* 130 These bestis..Be fatte, or lene, or plente,.. Like lak, or plente, of theyr vitaile. —— *Reas. & Sens.* 5784 Arrayed lyche to hir degre. *a* **1586** Sidney *Arcadia* ii. (1622) 209 She..vsed him much liker his birth, then his fortune.

5. *like as.* **a.** Introducing a clause: In the same way as, even as; (just) as if. Also, *like as if* (now somewhat *rare*, occas. † *like as and*).

c **1380** WYCLIF *Wks.* (1880) 368 þai cowde not schake away þis bonde by a contrari glose, lijke as oure prestis kan nowe. *c* **1450** *Merlin* iii. 41 He..tolde hym alle thynges like as were beffalle. **1457** in *10th Rep. Hist. MSS. Comm.* App. v. 298 The pleyntif shall declare..licke as the defendant were present. **1523** FITZHERB. *Surv.* xiii. (1539) 31 Lyke as and it were extortion. **1526** *Pilgr. Perf.* (W. de W. 1531) 139 b, Lyke as whan the wyndowe is opened, the..beames of the sonne foloweth in..so [etc.]. **1535** COVERDALE *Ps.* cii[i]. 13 Like as a father pitieth his owne children, euen so is the Lord mercifull vnto them that feare him. **1609** HOLLAND *Amm. Marcell.* 53 Hee came to Augustudunum aforesaid; like as if he had beene a leader of long continuance. **1611** BIBLE *Job* v. 26. **1616** R. C. *Times' Whistle* IV. 1235 And now our lawes for Mammons cursed golde Like as at open mart are bought and solde. **1691** tr. *Emilianne's Frauds Rom. Monks* (ed. 3) 194 They are all of dry'd Flesh, like as her Heart is. **1717** *Wodrow Corr.* (1843) II. 347 Likeas the Synod did, and hereby do, approve thereof. **1799** COLERIDGE *Lett.* (1895) 272, I held the letter in my hand like as if I was stupid. **1881** FORGAN *Golfer's Handbk.* 34 *Like-as-we-lie*, when both parties have played the same number of strokes. **1888** W. E. HENLEY *Bk. Verses, In Hospital* vi, Likeas a flamelet blanketed in smoke, So through the anæsthetic shows my life.

b. With ellipsis of the vb. of the clause. *Obs.* exc. *poet.*

c **1489** CAXTON *Sonnes of Aymon* ix. 222 Lete vs goo there like as prue and worthy knyghtes. **1500–20** DUNBAR *Poems* xi. 5 For as thow come sa sall thow pass, Lyk as ane schadow in ane glass. **1535** STEWART *Cron. Scot.* (1858) II. 34 Thair semelie schroud likeas siluer schene. **1559** ABP. HETHE *Speech in Parlt.* 21 Feb. in Strype *Ann. Ref.* I. App. vi. 9 Kinge Davyd did..leappe before the arke of God, lyke as his other subjectes. **1704** J. PITTS *Acc. Mahometans* viii. (1738) 149 They travel four Cammels in a breast..tied one after the other, like as in Teams. **1800** COLERIDGE *Piccolom.* IV. i, She's now rising: Like as a sun, so shines she in the east.

6. Used as *conj.*: = 'like as', as. Now generally condemned as vulgar or slovenly, though examples may be found in many recent writers of standing.

This use originated partly in an ellipsis of *as* or an extension of the quasi-prepositional function of the adv. (sense 1) to govern a clause instead of a sb., and partly in an anacoluthic use (somewhat common in the 16th c.) by which the sb. or pronoun which is primarily a dative governed by *like* is used as the subj. or obj. of a following clause. A good example of this anacoluthon (but with *to* instead of simple dative) is the following: **1596** SPENSER *F.Q.* v. iv. 42 Like to an Eagle, in his kingly pride Soring through his wide Empire of the aire..by chaunce hath spide A Goshauke.

a. Introducing an unabridged clause.

c **1530** LD. BERNERS *Arth. Lyt. Bryt.* 520 Ye have said lyke a noble lady ought to say. **1531** ELYOT *Gov.* III. viii, Lyke an excellent Phisitioun cureth moste daungerous diseases, so doth a man that is valyant [etc.]. **1608** SHAKS. *Per.* I. i. 163 Like an arrow shot from a well experienst Archer hits the marke his eye doth leuell at. **1658** A. FOX *Wurtz' Surg.* III. xix. 280 The patient still moveth the wounded joint, like the jack of a watch doth move. **1715** M. DAVIES *Athen. Brit.* I. 253 To act like Judith did with Holofernes. **1792** SOUTHEY *Lett.* (1856) I. 12 He talks like Brunswick did. **1866** DARWIN in *Life & Lett.* III. 58 Unfortunately few have observed like you have done. **1867** H. MAUDSLEY *Phys. & Path. Mind* 18 They are strange and startling, like the products of a dream ofttimes are, to the mind which has actually produced them. **1869** BONAMY PRICE *Princ. Currency* v. 162 Is the demand of the cotton and of the iron for money so real and specific, that the coin is produced, like wine is produced in bottles for the drinkers who desire to drink wine? **1873** MORRIS in Mackail *Life* (1899) I. 301 Dreading the model day like I used to dread Sunday. **1882** J. C. MORISON *Macaulay* (1889) 169 Those assemblies were not wise like the English parliament was. **1886** J. K. JEROME *Idle Thoughts* (1889) 5 Did he [Robinson Crusoe] wear trousers? I forget. Or did he go about like he does in the pantomime? **1941** *Coast to Coast* 192 She made a challenge of it, like she always does. **1961** *Word Study* Apr. 7/1 Like I said... The Beatnik School of Language Degradation must be responsible for the sudden mushrooming of the above expression. **1966** *New Yorker* 10 Dec. 149 Murray the K tells it like it really is. **1968** *Globe & Mail* (Toronto) 17 Feb. 34 (Advt.), Send for your copy now. Like we said, it's free. **1973** *New Society* 6 Dec. 608/1 His successors can build their modest, unpretentious monuments, like the British have been doing for years. **1974** 'E. LATHEN' *Sweet & Low* xviii. 174 Like I said, it was one o'clock... Everybody claims they were asleep.

b. Introducing a clause with vb. suppressed.

Many apparent instances of this use may belong to 1, what is suppressed being a pple. or adj. and not a vb.

1604 T. WRIGHT *Passions* (1620) 194 Did not David thirst after thee, like the thirstie hart the fountaines of cleaere water? **1654–66** EARL ORRERY *Parthen.* (1676) 219 Do not you think me past recovery, and in that faith, do like Physitians to Patients, which are so, permit them anything? **1803** *Spirit Pub. Jrnls.* (1804) 140 The servants..stare upon me like the deer On Selkirk, in Fernandez. **1839** BAILEY *Festus* (1852) 129 Ere yet we have shed our locks like trees their leaves.

c. Followed by a noun or pron. (virtually the subj. or obj. of a suppressed clause) or a phrase.

15.. *Smyth & his Dame* I. 54 in Hazl. *E.P.P.* III. 203, I sawe hym never wyth myne eye That could werke lyke I. **1723** *Pres. State Russia* I. 343 They are not kept in Fishpools and Stews, like in other Places. **1749** SMOLLETT *Gil Blas* (1797) I. 120 A few who like thou and I drink nothing but water. **1833** J. H. NEWMAN *Lett.* (1891) I. 324 Stalls, like in cathedrals. **1840** W. IRVING in *Life & Lett.* (1866) III. 155 There is more of morning visiting, like in country life in England. **1895** MISS BALFOUR *1200 Miles in Waggon* ix. 98 The strain is causing opening of the boards like in a ship after a storm. **1896** *Daily News* 24 Oct. 7/4 Snow..is descending in thick flakes like in January.

†**d.** As well as: as also. *Obs. rare.*

1594 SHAKS. *Rich. III*, III. v. 9 Gastly Lookes Are at my seruice, like enforced Smiles. **1663** GERBIER *Counsel* e v a, You that know what good Building is both by a Genius.. infused into your spirit, like by your particular applications to all things answerable thereunto.

e. As if, 'like as'. Also (now *dial.*) *as like*.

1493 *Festivall* (W. de W. 1515) 89 b, To..bere a candell brennynge in procession [on Candlemas Day] as lyke they wente bodely with our lady. *c* **1530** LD. BERNERS *Arthur Lyt. Bryt.* 338 He was bygge and hye above all other, and coloured like the rede rose had been set on the whyte lyly. **1860** in Bartlett *Dict. Amer.* (ed. 3) 244 The old fellow drank of the brandy like he was used to it. **1886** *Harper's Mag.* June 109/2 None of them act like they belonged to the hotel. **1895** J. PRIOR *Renie* xvii. 191 'E made a noise like 'e were sorry or summat. **1898** H. S. CANFIELD *Maid of Frontier* 100, I sprung from the chair like a man had shot me through the head. **1932** T. S. ELIOT *Sweeney Agonistes* 30 When you're alone in the middle of the bed and you wake like someone hit you on the head. **1940** W. FAULKNER *Hamlet* I. i. 7 For a while it looked like I was going to get shut of it. *Ibid.* ii. 52 It seemed like we begun to hear it right away. **1969** *Observer* (Colour Suppl.) 23 Mar. 23/2 They look at me like I'm dirt. **1973** 'H. HOWARD' *Highway to Murder* vii. 76 That sounded like I was being left to hold the baby.

7. *dial.* and *vulgar.* Used parenthetically to qualify a preceding statement: = 'as it were', 'so to speak'. Also, *colloq.* (orig. *U.S.*), as a meaningless interjection or expletive.

1778 F. BURNEY *Evelina* II. xxiii. 222 Father grew quite uneasy, like, for fear of his Lordship's taking offence. **1801** tr. *Gabrielli's Myst. Husb.* III. 252 Of a sudden like. **1815** SCOTT *Guy M.* vi, The leddy, on ilka Christmas night..gae twelve siller pennies to ilka puir body about, in honour of the twelve apostles like. **1826** J. WILSON *Noct. Ambr.* Wks. 1855 I. 179 In an ordinar way like. **1838** LYTTON *Alice* II. iii, If your honour were more amongst us, there might be more discipline like. **1840–41** DE QUINCEY *Style* II. Wks. 1862 X. 224 'Why like, it's gaily nigh like to four mile like'. **1870** E. PEACOCK *Ralf Skirl.* I. 112 Might I be so bold as just to ax, by way of talk like, if [etc.]. **1911** A. BENNETT *Hilda Lessways* I. vi. 49 He hasn't passed his examinations like... He has that Mr. Karkeek to cover him like. **1929** 'H. GREEN' *Living* vi. 57 'E went to the side like and looked. **1950** *Neurotica* Autumn 45 Like how much can you lay on [*i.e.* give] me? **1961** *New Statesman* 22 Sept. 382/2 'You're a chauvinist,' Danny said. 'Oh, yeah. Is that bad like?' **1966** *Lancet* 17 Sept. 635/2 As we say pragmatically in Huddersfield, 'C'est la vie, like!' **1971** [see *fighting chance* s.v. FIGHTING *vbl. sb.* 3 b]. **1971** *Black Scholar* Apr.–May 26/1 Man like the dude really flashed his hole card. **1973** *Black Panther* 17 Nov. 9/4 What will be the contradictions that produce further change? Like, it seems to me that it would be virtually impossible to avoid some contradictions.

8. Likely, probably. Rare exc. in phr. *like enough*, *very like*, (*as*) *like as not* (colloq. or dial.).

1563–83 FOXE *A. & M.* II. 1219/1 Some sayd it was his wife, some sayd the keeper. Like inough (my lord) quoth Symons, for he is one of the same sort. **1610** SHAKS. *Temp.* v. i. 265 Will money buy em? *Ant.* Very like. **1611** —— *Cymb.* v. v. 259 Most like I did. **1681** HICKERINGILL *Black Non-Conf.* Postscr., Wks. 1716 II. 169 He may fire a Canon, and kill a Friend as like as an Enemy. **1749** FIELDING *Tom Jones* VII. ix, 'Like enough,' cries the 'squire, 'it may be so in London.' **1823** BENTHAM *Not Paul* 285 When I was yet with you I told you these things. Like enough. **1883** STEVENSON *Treas. Isl.* III. xiv, Like enough, to judge from the sound, his back was broken on the spot. **1890** 'ROLF BOLDREWOOD' *Col. Reformer* (1891) 321, I was much deceived in them... Very like... It takes a smart man to be up to chaps of their sort. **1897** *Outing* (U.S.) XXX. 479/2 The players, like as not, handling the ribbons. **1898** G. MEREDITH *Odes Fr. Hist.* 29 No more at midway heaven, but liker, midway to the pit.

†**9.** As if about *to.* (Cf. A. 9 b.) *Obs.*

c **1530** LD. BERNERS *Arth. Lyt. Bryt.* 143 The paleys trembled like to haue gone all to peces.

10. *Comb.*, as *like fashioned* (adj.), *-feelingly* (adv.), *-made*, *-persuaded* (adjs.); **like-dealers**, the designation assumed by certain pirates about 1400.

1401 *Petition to Hen. IV* in Rymer *Fœdera* (1709) VIII. 193 Publicos Dei & omnium Mercatorum bonorum Inimicos, Pyratas, alio Vocabulo Likedelers Nominatos. **1540** COVERDALE *Fruitful Less.* (1593) M m 4, Yet is God of this nature, that he maketh his chosen to bee like fashioned vnto the image of his sonne. **1621** LADY M. WROTH *Urania* 489 Wedded to a vow I made to one, whose breach of his like-made-one to me cannot yet vnmarry me. **1691** NORRIS *Pract. Disc.* 57 The warm influence of a like-persuaded Princes Favour. **1839** BAILEY *Festus* xxxvi. (1848) 363 He Yet feels the frailties of the things He has made And therefore can, like-feelingly, judge them. [**1849** *Sidonia Sorc.* II. 144 That brotherhood who..lived like brothers amongst themselves, dividing all goods alike, so that they were called 'Like-dealers'. (These Like-dealers were the Communists of the Northern Middle Ages.)]

C. *absol.* and *sb.*

1. With qualifying poss. pron. or its analogue: Counterpart, equal, match, analogue, etc.

Sometimes in *pl.*, (*his*, etc.) *likes*, though a collective or typical sing. often occurs where a pl. might be used.

a **1300** *Floriz & Bl.* 483 (Hausknecht) Faire hi habbe here in inome At on palais, nas non his liche. *c* **1374** CHAUCER *Anel. & Arc.* 76 Of trouth is ther non her lich Of all these wymmen. *c* **1400** *Sowdone Bab.* 44 Whan ffrith and felde wexen gaye, And every wight desirith his like. *a* **1533** LD. BERNERS *Huon* lvii. 193 His lyke is not in al yᵉ world. **1579** SPENSER *Sheph. Cal.* Nov. 40 Her like shee has not left behinde. **1597** J. KING *On Jonas* (1618) 65 Socrates was a man excellent for humane wisdome, the like to whom could not be found among thousands of men. **1602** SHAKS. *Ham.* I. ii. 188. **1618** BOLTON *Florus* IV. xii. (1636) 321 A man of a barbarous blunt wit, but which did well enough among his likes. **1656** EARL MONM. *Boccalini's Advt. fr. Parnass.* 105 He rendred his Family as famous..as the like of the greatest Princes. **1667** MILTON *P.L.* VIII. 418. **1802** PALEY *Nat. Theol.* iv. (ed. 2) 55 Producing their like, without understanding or design. **1847** TENNYSON *Princess* VI. 321 Pass, and mingle with your likes. **1875** WHITNEY *Life Lang.* ii. 13 When he first begins to employ preterits and plurals and their like. **1879** JAS. GRANT in *Cassell's Techn. Educ.* IV. 96/1 Two men, whose like will scarcely ever be found in the world.

2. Something considered in respect of its likeness to something else; an instance of similarity; chiefly in proverbial expressions, as: *like* (*will*) *to like*, *like draws to like*, *like begets like*, etc.; *like for like*; *like cures like*.

c **1375** *Sc. Leg. Saints* i. (*Petrus*) 543 Lyk to lyk accordis wele. *Ibid.* xii. (*Mathias*) 134 Lyk to lyk drawis ay. **1470–85** MALORY *Arthur* IX. xxxi, A good knyght wylle fauoure another and lyke wille drawe to lyke. **1528** PAYNEL *Salerne's Regim.* (1535) 68 b, Lyke ioyned to lyke maketh one the more furious. **1539** TAVERNER *Erasm. Prov.* (1552) 8 Lyke wyll to lyke. **1581** DERRICKE *Image Irel.* II. F j b, *marg.*, Like vnto like saide the Deuill to the Collier. **1591** SPENSER *M. Hubberd* 48 The Foxe and th' Ape..determined to seeke Their fortunes farre abroad, lyeke with his lyeke. **1601** SHAKS. *Jul. C.* II. ii. 128 Euery like is not the same. **1607** W. SCLATER *Funeral Serm.* (1629) 2 Illustrated by a comparison of likes. **1631** GOUGE *God's Arrows* III. lx. 296 In case of *talio*, or requiting like for like. **1633** T. ADAMS *Exp. 2 Peter* iii. 10. 1304 No like is the same; Similitude and Identitie are different things. **1692** R. L'ESTRANGE *Fables* ccccxix. 395 Two Likes may be mistaken. **1696** TRYON *Misc.* i. 4 Every Like works upon its Likeness. **1842** TENNYSON *Walking to Mail* 55 Like breeds like, they say. —— *Two Voices* 357 For those two likes might meet and touch. **1856** R. A. VAUGHAN *Mystics* (1860) I. III. ii. 61 Only like can know like.

3. a. *the like*: something or anything similar; the same kind of thing.

Now chiefly in negative contexts, as 'I never saw the like.'

1553 EDEN *Decades* (Arb.) 375 Sum doo wysshe he had doonne the lyke by theyrs. **1556** ROBINSON tr. *More's Utop.* (Arb.) 77 *margin*, The verie like in England in the riuer of Thamys. **1588** PARKE tr. *Mendoza's Hist. China* 388 Which is the like as we have said of the kingdome of China. **1598** SHAKS. *Merry W.* II. i. 70. **16..** *Ballad, Mary Ambree* 79 (Percy MS.) The like in my liffe I neuer did see. **1606** G. W[OODCOCKE] *Hist. Ivstine* IV. 21 The like to this may be accounted of the continuall fire burning in the mountaine of Ætna. *a* **1626** BACON *New Atl.* (1900) 34 His Under Garments were the like that we saw him weare in the Chariott. **1678** WANLEY *Wond. Lit. World* v. i. §87. 467/1 Henry the seventh..having composed matters in Germany ..hastened to do the like in Italy. **1772–84** COOK *Voy.* (1790) IV. 1242 The drops were such as no experienced seaman on board had seen the like. **1820** SHELLEY *Œdipus* II. i. 85 She never can commit the like again. **1878** SIMPSON *Sch. Shaks.* I. 35 It is confessed that Hawkins and Cobham were meant to be buccaneers, and it is absurd to deny the like of Stucley.

†**b.** Preceded by *any*, *many*, *other*. *Obs.*

1573 G. HARVEY *Letter-bk.* (Camden) 7, I prai you let this on suffice in stead of a mani the like. *a* **1592** H. SMITH *Wks.* (1867) II. 97 As for these objections, or any the like. **1599** HAKLUYT *Voy.* II. 118 Had not Q. Curtius or some other like ..revived the remembrance of him. **1631** T. POWELL *Tom All Trades* (1876) 145 And very many other the like.

c. *and the like*, *or the like*: a formula used to avoid further enumeration of an indicated class; = 'and so forth'. See also SUCH-LIKE.

1592 WEST *1st Pt. Symbol.* §100 With these words following, or the like in effect. **1612** BACON *Ess.*, *Studies* (Arb.) 13 Bowling is good for the Stone and Raines; Shooting for the longs and breast; gentle walking for the stomacke; riding for the head; and the like. **1657–83** EVELYN *Hist. Relig.* (1850) I. 3 Everybody agrees that there is in our very nature sentiments of right and wrong; to do as we would be done by;..to clothe our bodies, and the like. **1711** STEELE *Spect.* No. 155 ¶1 In travelling together in the same hired Coach, sitting near each other in any publick Assembly, or the like. **1773** MRS. CHAPONE *Improv. Mind* (1774) II. 43 If you have any acquired talent..such as music, painting, or the like. **1833** S. AUSTIN *Charact. Goethe* I. ii. 30 Questions concerning time, space, mind, matter, God, immortality, and the like. **1852** GLADSTONE *Glean.* (1879) IV. 146 The mundane, earthy, instruments of taxation, police, soldiery..and the like.

†**d.** Used as a mere demonstrative pronoun: = *that* or *those* (followed by *of*). *Obs. rare.*

1650 EARL MONM. tr. *Senault's Man bec. Guilty* 146, I doubt not but that 'twas ambition which kept Scipio chast, that was the sweetnesse of glory which charmed the like of Pleasure. **1653** *Nissena* 145 He had changed his love affections into the like of Friendship, or rather of obsequiousness. **1654** EARL MONM. tr. *Bentivoglio's Warrs Flanders* 214 His death was accompanied by the like of Orange.

e. *the like*(*s of* (rarely *to*): such a person or thing as; now often depreciatory. *colloq.*

1637 RUTHERFORD *Lett.* (1862) I. 384 Many of God's children beleiue that there is something in a broken reed the like of me. **1787** *Minor* 171 Never more presume for to speak to the likes of me. **1825** COBBETT *Rur. Rides* 185, I never saw, nor heard of the like of this before. **1826** JAS. MILL in *Westm. Rev.* VI. 270 The like of which exists in no other spot on the surface of the earth. **1850** MRS. CARLYLE *Lett.* II. 137 This is the best school that the like of me was ever put to. **1872** BROWNING in *Life & Lett.* (1891) 292 The second edition is in the press,..2,500 in five months is a good sale for the likes of me. **1894** DU MAURIER *Trilby* (1895) 210 Are there no harems still left in Stamboul for the likes of thee to sweep and clean?

4. *Golf.* (See quot. 1881.)

1863 *Macm. Mag.* Sept. VIII. 411/2 The Captain hookit his ba' into the Principal's Nose, and the Laird lay snug on the green at the *like*. **1878** 'CAPT. CRAWLEY' *Football* etc. 89 (Golf) The reckoning of the game is made by the terms *odds* and *like*, and *one more*, *two more*, &c. **1881** FORGAN *Golfer's Handbk.* 35 If your opponent has played one stroke more than you—i.e., 'the odd', your next stroke will be 'the like'.

†**5.** Likelihood, probability. *Obs.* $rare^{-1}$.

1609 YONGE *Diary* 19 There is like of war between them.

6. In phrases formed with preps.

†**a.** ***with like***: as is (was, etc.) fitting, in a fitting manner. *Obs.*

c **1200** ORMIN 8190 þatt oþerr follc all ȝede bun, Swa summ itt birrþ, wiþþ like. *a* **1240** *Wohunge* in *Cott. Hom.* 285 Ihesu þus tu faht for me aȝaines mine sawle fan þu me derennedes wið like.

†**b.** ***in like*** (also Sc. ***in to like***), ***in liche***: = ALIKE. Also, without change. *Obs.*

13.. etc. [see INLIKE]. *c* **1375** *Sc. Leg. Saints* ii. (*Paulus*) 210 His ryk þat euire lestis in to lyk. *Ibid.* xxxv. (*Thadee*) 70 His ryke Is stedfaste lestand ay in lyke. *c* **1430** *Syr. Tryam.* 1571 Hedd and fete lay bothe in lyke, To grounde was he caste! **1540** HYRDE tr. *Vives' Instr. Chr. Wom.* (1592) U ij, She.. which ought to count all in like faire & foul, saving her husband. *a* **1555** RIDLEY *Pit. Lament.* (1566) B v b, All sped in lyke. **1557** PAYNEL *Barclay's Jugurth* 75 His ennemies and his owne subiectes he dreeded and suspected both in lyke and after one maner.

†**c.** ***of (a) like, by (the) like***: probably, BELIKE.

1542 UDALL *Erasm. Apoph.* 337 b, Harpalus (who by like had a good insight in suche matiers). **1570–6** LAMBARDE *Peramb. Kent* (1826) 215 In which respect (of like) he gave to the hundreth, the name of the same Towne. **1573** G. HARVEY *Letter-bk.* (Camden) 50 Of a like thai purpose to pluck Jupiter out of heaven. **1577–87** HOLINSHED *Chron.* III. 24/2 King William..conceiued displeasure against Urban..and alledged by the like, that no..bishop within his realme should haue respect..to anie pope. **1579** [see BELIKE]. **1605** VERSTEGAN *Dec. Intell.* iv. (1628) 89 The white rocks or clifs (by like about Douer).

like (laɪk), *v.*[1] Forms: 1–2 **lícian**, 2–3 **likie(n**, 3 **lykyen**, 3–5 **li-**, **lyken**, **-i(n**, **-y(n**, (4 **likke**, **lykky**), 4–7 **lyke**, *Sc.* and *north.* **lik**, (5 **lykey**, **lijk**, **leke**), 6–7 **leeke**, (7 **lyk**), 4– **like**. Also Y-LIKE. [OE. *lícian* = OFris. *likia*, OS. *lîkôn* (Du. *lijken*), OHG. *lîhhên*, *lîchên*, ON. *líka*, Goth. *leikan*:—OTeut. **līkǣjan*, **līkōjan*, f. **līko-* body (*orig.* appearance, form): see LICH *sb.*]

1. *intr.* **a.** To please, be pleasing, suit a person. Chiefly quasi-*trans.* with *dative*; †in early use also const. *to, till.* Also *impers.* as in ***it likes me*** = I am pleased, it is my pleasure *to* do so-and-so. Now only *arch.* and *dial.*

971 *Blickl. Hom.* 129 Æghwylc man, sy þær eorðan þær he sy, þurh gode dæda God lician sceal. *c* **1000** ÆLFRIC *Gen.* xxvii. 14 Heo hit ȝearwode, swa heo wiste þæt his fæder licode. *c* **1175** *Lamb. Hom.* 63 God..ȝife us swa his wil to donne þet we gode likie and monne. *c* **1200** *Trin. Coll. Hom.* 29 þanne he wile don oðer queðen hwat him þanne licað after defles lore. *c* **1205** LAY. 8746 Hit þe likede wel þat þu us adun læidest. **1340** *Ayenb.* 187 Efterward ase merci likeþ to god alsuo hit ne likeþ noþing to þe dyeule. *c* **1374** CHAUCER *Boeth.* IV. pr. vi. 108 (Camb. MS.) The victories cawse lykede to the goddes and the cause ouer-comen lykede to catoun. **1375** BARBOUR *Bruce* I. 505 It likit till his will. **1413** *Pilgr. Sowle* (Caxton 1483) v. xii. 103 This is my loued sone that lyketh me. *c* **1430** *Two Cookery-bks.* 31 Take Porke or Beef, wheþer þe lykey, & leche it þinne þwerte. *c* **1449** PECOCK *Repr.* II. xix. 267 Chese the seers which of tho answers to hem lijkith. **1535** COVERDALE *Esther* i. 8 The kynge had commaunded..that euery one shulde do as it lyked him. **1577** HARRISON *England* II. ix. (1877) I. 201 To give his roiall consent to such statutes as him liketh of. **1613** SHAKS. *Hen. VIII*, I. i. 100 Like it your Grace, The State takes notice. **1627** E. F. *Hist. Edw. II* (1680) 87 How that way may like you, that I know not. **1784** COWPER *Task* VI. 405 There they are free, And howl and war as likes them, uncontroul'd. *a* **1850** ROSSETTI *Dante & Circ.* (1874) I. 41, I rode sullenly Upon a certain path that liked me not.

†**b.** *simply.* To be pleasing, be liked or approved. *Obs.*

c **888** K. ÆLFRED *Boeth.* xviii. §3 (Sedgefield) Forðy sceolde ælc mon bion on ðæm wel ȝehealden þæt he on his aȝnum earde licode. *c* **1315** SHOREHAM *Poems* (E.E.T.S.) 98/13 Senne hys swete and lykeþ, Wanne a man hi dep. **1388** WYCLIF *Gen.* xvi. 6 Lo! thi seruantesse is in thin hond; vse thou hir as it likith. **1616** B. JONSON *Devil an Ass* Prol., If this Play doe not like, the Diuell is in 't.

c. ***to like well*** or ***ill***: to be pleasing or the reverse.

c **1250** *Gen. & Ex.* 4029 Ille liked ðanne balaac Euerilc word ðe prest balaam spac. **1297** R. GLOUC. (Rolls) 11829 Him þoȝte þe wide contreie wolde him liki bet. *c* **1380** *Sir Ferumb.* 76 Wan he was war of þe frenschemen on h[ert] him likid ille. *a* **1450** *Knt. de la Tour* (1868) 18 My fader asked me 'how likithe you?'..And y tolde my fader how me liked. **1590** MARLOWE *2nd Pt. Tamburl.* IV. i. I. 5, Ile dispose them [women] as it likes me best. **1596** DANETT tr. *Comines* (1614) 61 They sallied foorth where liked them best by the breaches thereof. **1608** *Yorksh. Trag.* I. iii, Good Sir, keep but in patience, and I hope my words shall like you well. **1667** MILTON *P.L.* VI. 353 They..colour, shape or size Assume, as likes them best. **1668** PEPYS *Diary* 22 Nov., My boy's livery is come home..and it likes me well enough. **1680** MOXON *Mech. Exerc.* 222 Either with Moldings or other Work upon it, as best likes them. **1799** WORDSW. *Ruth* 209 Where it liked her best she sought Her shelter. **1808** SCOTT *Marm.* VI. xv, At first in heart it liked me ill. **1832** ARNOLD *Serm.* II. 320 If there be no God,..let us eat and drink, or follow what likes us best. **1848** THACKERAY *Van. Fair* xii. 103, I wish any respected bachelor that reads this may take the sort that best likes him.

†**2.** *refl.* and *intr.* for *refl.* To please oneself, take pleasure, delight *in* (something). *Obs.*

a **1300** *E.E. Psalter* xxxvi. 4 Like in Laverd. *a* **1300** *Cursor M.* 19231 Ilk suik it-self bisuikes, And lethes mast þat þar-in likes. *Ibid.* 28336, I ha me liked ai vm-quile In vnnait wordes. **1340** *Ayenb.* 177 Me zeneȝeþ wel ofte..be þe nase ine to moche him to liky in guode smelles. **1549** CHALONER *Erasm. on Folly* F ij b, Yet dooe these my old gurles not a little lyke their selves herein.

3. *intr.* To be pleased or glad. ***to like ill***: to be displeased or sad. Now only *Sc.*

13.. *Guy Warw.* (A.) 500 Þerl for him sori was, Ther liked non in that plas. *c* **1320** *Sir Tristrem* 1151 Þei marke liked ille. *c* **1400** *Gamelyn* 618 And Adam Spencer liked right ille. *c* **1460** *Towneley Myst.* xxvii. 114 Ye ar all heuy and lykyt yll here in this way. *c* **1475** *Rauf Coilȝear* 39 Be that it drew to the nicht, The King lykit ill. **1896** J. BALFOUR PAUL in *N. & Q.* Ser. VIII. X. 485/2, I should like if Mr. Reid would be good enough to inform us if the note-book states [etc.].

†**4.** To be in good condition; to get on, do well, thrive. Chiefly with adv., *well, better*, etc.

c **1325** *Poem times Edw. II* (Percy) xliv, Thi maystre is i-wonne And lyketh. **1523** FITZHERB. *Husb.* §53 It may fortune there be some [sheep] that like not and be weike. **1567** MAPLET *Gr. Forest* 33 It [the beech tree]..liketh best being sowne in moyst grounds. **1584** COGAN *Haven Health* cxciv. (1636) 176 Children..live and like better with that [milk], than with any other thing. **1597** SHAKS. *2 Hen. IV*, III. ii. 92 (Qo. 1600) By my troth, you like [1623 looke] well, and beare your yeeres very well. **1601** HOLLAND *Pliny* I. 500 Trees generally do like best that stand to the Northeast wind. **1615** W. LAWSON *Country Housew. Garden* (1626) 3 We meddle not with Apricocks nor Peaches, nor scarcely with Quinches, which will not like in our cold parts, vnlesse [etc.]. **1634** W. WOOD *New Eng. Prosp.* I. iv, The Cattle.. like as well with it. **1673** RAY *Journ. Low C., Malta* 296 Indigo..agrees with the soil, and likes and thrives there very well. **1681** CHETHAM *Angler's Vade-m.* xxxviii. §4 (1689) 245 The Ponds where they like well.

5. To derive pleasure *of*, occas. *by, with* (a person or thing); to approve *of*, become fond *of*. Also with adv. (*well* or *ill*). *Obs.* exc. *dial.*

c **1430** *Syr Gener.* (Roxb.) 3124 Of this message he liked yll. **1465** *Paston Lett.* II. 186, I understode he lykyd not by hys dysposicyon. **1579–80** NORTH *Plutarch, Lycurgus* (1595) 63 To see his notable lawes..so well established and liked of by experience. **1590** GREENE *Orl. Fur.* (1599) A 4 b, Daughter like of whome thou please. **1611** BIBLE *Transl. Pref.* ¶2 But was that his magnificence liked of by all? **1643** SLINGSBY *Diary* (1836) 98 He..began to like better of his employment. **1672** SIR C. LYTTELTON in *Hatton Corr.* (1878) 100 Yᵉ King likes soe well of Sʳ T. L. that [etc.]. **1709** STRYPE *Ann. Ref.* I. xxv. (1824) 419 Opinions, by no means liked of by the Bishop Cheney. *Ibid.* II. xliv. (1824) 167 They hoped..that their prince..would like well with this their doing. **1764** BURN *Poor Laws* 77 If any beggar's child ..shall be liked of by any subject of this realm of honest calling. *a* **1825** FORBY *Voc. E. Anglia, Like of*, to approve. 'My master will not like of it.' **1854** MISS BAKER *Northamptonsh. Gloss.* I. 397, I daredn't do't; my master wouldn't like of it.

6. a. *trans.* (The current sense.) To find agreeable or congenial; to feel attracted to or favourably impressed by (a person); to have a taste or fancy for, take pleasure in (a thing, an action, a condition, etc.). In early use often ***to like well*** (now *arch.* in this form, though we say freely *to like very, pretty well*, and *to like better or best*), and antithetically ***to like ill*** (arch.) = to dislike. Colloq. phrases: ***I like that!***, an ironical expression of surprise or disgust at someone's impudence, conceit, untruthfulness, etc.; (***to do***, etc., something) ***and like it***, (to endure or perform something unpleasant) with a good grace, without complaint; ***to like it or lump it***, see LUMP *v.*[2] 2. For *to know what one likes* see KNOW *v.* 11 f.

As used with reference to persons, the vb. is often contrasted (as expressing a weaker sentiment) with *love*.

The two earliest quots. may belong to sense 1.

c **1200** *Trin. Coll. Hom.* 95 Mildheorted beð þe man þe reouþ his nehȝebures unselðe, and likeð here alre selðe. **1297** R. GLOUC. (Rolls) 2039 Conan þe kinges neueu ne likede noȝt þis game. *c* **1385** CHAUCER *L.G.W.* 1076 *Dido*, And for he was a straunger sumwhat sche Likede hym the bet. *c* **1470** *Golagros & Gaw.* 1015 Be that schir Wawane the wy likit the wer. **1530** PALSGR. 611/2, I can nat lyke hym better than I do. **1581** T. HOWELL *Deuises* (1879) 200 Wante makes the Lyon stowte, a slender pray to leeke. **1590** SPENSER *F.Q.* III. ix. 24 Yet every one her likte, and every one her lov'd. *a* **1592** H. SMITH *Serm.* (1637) 338 He which would have chosen the best, yet liked another before him. **1602** WARNER *Alb. Eng.* XI. lxvii. (1612) 285 With women, that no lesse attract our senses them to leeke. **1671** MILTON *P.R.* IV. 171, I never lik'd thy talk, thy offers less, Now both abhor. **1711** STEELE *Spect.* No. 79 ¶4 My Lover does not know I like him. *a* **1716** SOUTH *Serm.* (1823) III. 237 Where a man neither loves nor likes the thing he believes. **1741** LADY M. W. MONTAGU *Let. to Mr. Wortley* 5 Nov., The people here [Geneva] are very well to be liked. **1781** COWPER *Truth* 210 He likes your house, your housemaid, and your pay. **1818** SCOTT *Hrt. Midl.* xxxviii, Maybe ye may like the ewe-milk..cheese better. **1852** MRS. STOWE *Uncle Tom's C.* xxiii, I may *like* him well enough; but you don't *love* your servants. *c* **1869** TAYLOR & DUBOURG in M. R. Booth *Eng. Plays of 19th Cent.* (1973) III. 255 *Lilian.* Bertie, you are a duffer. In these [arithmetic] questions the strength is always presumed to be equal. *Fitz-Urse.* I like that. As if one fellow was ever just as strong as another fellow. **1875** JOWETT *Plato* (ed. 2) V. 50 Most persons say that lawgivers should make such laws as the people like. **1902** J. BRYNILDSEN *Dict. Eng. & Dano-Norwegian Lang.* s.v. *like*, I ~ *that*..! det var jo rart! **1927** A. B. COX *Mr. Priestley's Problem* ix. 146 'George, go and send them away.' 'Oh come,' protested George. 'I like that.' *a* **1930** D. H. LAWRENCE *Phoenix II* (1968) 182 'I feel so bare and brazen without a whiff of powder on my nose.' He gave a shout of laughter. 'I like that!' he said. **1941** H. G. WELLS *You can't be too Careful* III. vii. 138 'You *made* me.' 'I like that.' **1943** HUNT & PRINGLE *Service Slang* 11 *And like it!* A Naval expression anticipating a grouse and added to any instruction for an awkward or unwanted job. **1955** J. BINGHAM *Paton Street Case* vi. 97 'I'll have a pint.'..'You won't,' said Stan. 'It's May's birthday. You'll have a double Scotch, Len, and like it.' **1971** 'D. HALLIDAY' *Dolly & Doctor Bird* ii. 21 I'll do it again, and you'll stand by and like it. **1974** I. MURDOCH *Sacred & Profane Love Machine* 73 'If we didn't stupefy ourselves with drink we wouldn't get so comatose.' 'I like that. You taught me to drink.'

b. *absol.* Phr. ***if you like***: if you wish to phrase or consider something in a particular manner; often used as a vaguely intensive expression, = 'indeed', 'perhaps'. *colloq.*

1590 SHAKS. *Com. Err.* III. ii. 7 If you like elsewhere doe it by stealth. **1595** —— *John* II. i. 511 If he see ought in you that makes him like. **1667** MILTON *P.L.* XI. 583 Till in the Amorous Net Fast caught, they lik'd, and each his liking chose. *a* **1742** J. HAMMOND *Love Elegies* vii, They met, they lik'd, they stay'd but till alone. **1808** SCOTT *Marm.* v. Introd., Looking [he] liked, and liking loved. **1875** T. E. BRIDGETT *Our Lady's Dowry* II. xi. 336 They were placed in churches by simple faith, or credulity if you like, but not by wilful fraud. **1909** W. H. HUDSON *Afoot in Eng.* ii. 20 'What!' I exclaimed. 'Lady Y——: that funny old woman!' 'No—middle-aged,' he corrected... 'Very well, middle-aged if you like.' **1955** L. P. HARTLEY *Perfect Woman* xxxvi. 325 Eighteen years faithful to an unfaithful man: there was a proof of staunchness, if you like! **1968** 'A. GILBERT' *Night Encounter* iii. 37 That was a surprise, if you like, you wouldn't have thought Mr. Nicholas had enough humanity in him to give her a child. **1970** *Sunday Times* (Colour Suppl.) 15 Mar. 25/1, I could tell you some stories about Max [Miller], but I won't. Used to make me laugh, though. He was real blue if you like. **1973** *Listener* 15 Nov. 664/1 *Princess Anne*: We're shown the best, if you like. But nonetheless it's life.

c. With direct obj. and inf. or complementary pa. pple. or adj., or (now *rarely*) a clause introduced by *that*.

1534 MORE *On the Passion* Wks. 1290/2 Such as are lerned, will like also, that [etc.]. **1805** SCOTT *Last Minstr.* v. xxx, Less lik'd he still, that scornful jeer Mispris'd the land he lov'd so dear. **1842** J. H. NEWMAN *Lett.* (1891) II. 393 Would he like the subject discussed in newspapers? **1849** THACKERAY *Pendennis* xlv, It was Blanche who..asked him ..whether he liked women to hunt? **1887** COLVIN *Keats* viii. 207 The sonatas of Haydn were the music he liked Severn best to play to him.

d. With *inf.* as obj.: To find it agreeable, feel inclined *to do* or *be* so and so. Often somewhat idiomatically in conditional use, to express a desire, as ***I should like*** (= F. *je voudrais bien*, G. *ich möchte gern*); often derisively in ***I should like to see***—(intimating that what is referred to is impossible), ***I should like to know*** (implying that the question has no natural answer). Also with ellipsis of inf., as in ***to do as one likes***.

c **1350** *Will. Palerne* 5528 Ȝe þat liken in loue swiche þinges to here. *c* **1440** *Generydes* 2010 Do as ȝe leke, for this is my councell. *c* **1450** *St. Cuthbert* (Surtees) 11 Who so lykes to luk it oure. *c* **1470** HENRY *Wallace* I. 33 Quha likis till haif mar knawlage in that part. **1528** GARDINER in Pocock *Rec. Ref.* I. l. 112 His holiness for pastime liked well to hear thereof. **1568** *Satir. Poems Reform.* xlviii. 1 Off cullouris cleir quha lykis to weir, Ar sindry sortis in to this toun. **1596** DALRYMPLE tr. *Leslie's Hist. Scot.* II. 152 Euerie ane mycht marie how mony wyfes he lyket. **1611** BIBLE *Rom.* i. 28 They did not like [Gr. οὐκ ἐδοκίμασαν] to retaine God in their knowledge. **1662** PEPYS *Diary* 22 Aug., I had liked to have begged a parrot for my wife. **1690** LOCKE *Hum. Und.* II. xxi. §50 He may either go or stay, as he best likes. **1694** ATTERBURY *Serm.* (1726) I. 191 He is already under the Dominion and Power of his own Lusts, and perhaps likes to be so. **1819** SHELLEY *Julian & Mad.* 199 If you would like to go, We'll visit him. **1830** MACAULAY *Rob. Montgomery* Ess. (1872) 130 What, we should like to know, is the difference between the two operations which Mr. Robert Montgomery so accurately distinguishes from each other..? **1831** —— in *Life* I. 233, I should have liked to have sate through so tremendous a storm. **1837** DICKENS *Pickw.* xxxii, [Mr. Gunter threatens to throw Mr. Noddy out of window] 'I should like to see you do it, sir,' said Mr. Noddy. **1859** MILL *Liberty* v. 187 A person should be free to do as he likes in his own concerns. **1868** BAIN *Ment. & Mor. Sci.* IV. xi. 406 To say we can be virtuous if we like, is [etc.]. **1874** RUSKIN *Fors Clav.* xxxix. 68, I should like to have somebody for a help. **1884** *Manch. Exam.* 28 May 5/2 Those critics.. who maintain that we are free to do as we like in Egypt.

e. Often used, esp. with conditional auxiliary, for ***like to have***.

1822 SHELLEY *Faust* ii. 1 Would you not like a broomstick? *Mod.* I should like more time to consider the matter. Would you like the arm-chair?

f. The neutral sense inferable from the qualified uses, *to like well* or *ill* (see above), survives in the interrogative use with *how*, as in 'How do you like my new gown?', 'How would *you* like to be called a fool to your face?', etc.

1596 SHAKS. *Merch. V.* III. v. 77 How dost thou like the Lord Bassanio's wife? **1606** DAY *Ile of Guls* B 4 b, Boy, how doost like me in this attyre? **1727** BOYER *Fr. Dict.* s.v. *Trouver, Comment le trouvez-vous?* How do you like it? **1819** SHELLEY *Cyclops* 532 How does the God like living in a skin? **1860** TENNYSON *Sea Dreams* 194 How like you this old satire?

¶**g.** In the colloquial half-jocular expression, used of an article of food or the like, 'I like it, but it does not like me' (i.e. does not suit my health), the use seems to be a mere perversion of sense 6, and not directly connected with sense 1.

1899 H. FREDERIC *Market-place* xxiii. 307 He liked the water, and the water liked him..He decided that he would have a yacht.

like, *v.*[2] Also 5–6 **lyke.** [f. LIKE *a.*]

†**1.** *trans.* **a.** To fashion in a certain likeness. **b.** To represent as like *to*; to compare *to*. **c.** To make a likeness of; to imitate. *Obs.*

c **1450** *St. Cuthbert* (Surtees) 1460 In haly speche he lyked [Bæda *assimilavit*] his lunde. **1591** SHAKS. *1 Hen. VI*, IV. vi.

48 Like me to the pesant Boyes of France. **1613** W. BROWNE *Brit. Past.* I. v. 489 Her lily hand (not to be lik'd by Art) A pair of pincers held. **1622** WITHER *Mistr. Philar.* F 7 b, If to gold I like her Haire.

2. *intr.* (Const. *inf.*) †a. To seem, pretend. *Obs.* b. To look like or be near *to* doing (something) or *to* being treated (in a specified manner). Now *vulgar* and *dial.* (*U.S.*), chiefly in compound tenses, *had* (rarely *were*) *liked to*, or (dial.) *am* (*is*, etc.) *liken* (for *liking*) *to*, etc. (Cf. *had like* s.v. LIKE *a.*)

1426 *Paston Lett.* I. 24 The gret tendrenesse ye lyke to have of the salvacion of my symple honeste. **1598** PARSONS *Archpriest Controv.* (Camden) I. 32 The other disorders that I have signified..were liked to have receved a severe sentence & punishment. **1599** SHAKS. *Much Ado* v. i. 115 Wee had likt to haue had our two noses snapt off with two old men without teeth. *a* **1622** R. HAWKINS *Voy.* (1878) 91 Her old leake..had liked to have drowned all those which were in her. **1654–66** EARL ORRERY *Parthen.* (1676) 18 Joy had lik'd to have performed what grief but begun. *a* **1689** MRS. BEHN *Novels* (1722) I. 282 The Rabble had lik'd to have pulled him to pieces. **1716** ABP. NICHOLSON in Ellis *Orig. Lett.* Ser. I. III. 396 The judges, whom he had liked to have provoked by his clownish behaviour at the bar. **1724** RAMSAY *Tea-t. Misc.* (1733) II. 119 My heart alake, is liken to break When I think on my winsome John. **1760** H. WALPOLE *Let. to G. Montagu* 25 Oct., He probably got his death, as he liked to have done two years ago, by [etc.]. **1781** BENTHAM *Wks.* (1843) X. 92 He..was once what I had liked to have been, a methodist. **1800** A. M. THORNTON in *Rec. Columbia Hist. Soc.* (1907) X. 117 Joe..said they had liked to have been lost in Pohick run. **1802** BENTHAM *Wks.* 390, I would not serve you as X. Y. Bellamy had liked to have served us. **1853** J. A. BENTON *California Pilgr.* 127 The evening liked to have been a tedious evening. **1854** J. E. COOKE *Virginia Comedians* I. xlix. 282 She liked to fainted just now.

-like, *suffix*, forming adjs. and advs. In strictness, the words containing this suffix are compounds of LIKE *a.* and *adv.*, in the senses in which these words govern a dative or are followed by an adj. (see LIKE *a.* 1 b, LIKE *adv.* 1, 3). The compounds so formed not unfrequently resemble in sense the derivatives formed with *-lik(e*, ME. dial. form of -LY[1], -LY[2], but the two formations are entirely distinct: thus ME. *gredilike* adv. (= greedily) is not the same word as the mod. Sc. *greedy-like*.

1. Appended to sbs. a. Forming adjs. with the general sense 'similar to —', 'characteristic of, befitting —'. Early examples are *circlelyk* (*a*1420), *chieftainlike* (*c*1470 Henry *Wallace* VI. 489), *devil-like* (*c*1470), *godlike* (1513), *bishoplike* (1544), *flesh-like* (1552). The suffix may now be appended to almost all sbs., including proper names; in formations intended as nonce-words, or not generally current, the hyphen is ordinarily used.

Some particular writers have shown an extraordinary fondness for words of this formation; e.g. more than 60 occur in Bailey's *Festus*.

1598 DALLINGTON *Meth. Trav.* S iij b, Making Hidalgo-like Rhodomontades. **1603** DEKKER *Grissil* (Shaks. Soc.) 5 Then can you blame me to be hunter like, When I must get a wife? **1607** R. C[AREW] tr. *Estienne's World of Wonders* 188 The testimonies which themselves giue of their Sardanapale-like sobriety. **1784** R. BAGE *Barham Downs* I. 100 An unaccountable unquality-like fit of the spleen. **1823** in *Spirit Pub. Jrnls.* 151 The professor thought this conduct extremely rude and ungoldsmithlike. **1825** *Greenhouse Comp.* II. 38 Their leaves and habits are so salad- and kitchen-garden-like, that we cannot recommend them. *Ibid.* II. 84 A low shrub, with heath- or fir-like leaves. **1834** *Tait's Mag.* I. 758/1 He gave an Egan-like description of a pugilistic encounter. **1839** BAILEY *Festus* (1852) 286 And swore to make all souls Believe alike in clockworklike content. **1849** NOAD *Electricity* 189 That plumbago-like substance found lining the interior of long-used coal-gas retorts. **1857** E. FITZGERALD *Lett.* (1889) I. 263 June over! A thing I think of with Omar-like sorrow. **1866** W. AITKEN *Sci. & Pract. Med.* II. 578 If the noise..is that of a friction-murmur, soft and bellows-like. **1901** *Academy* 13 July 29/2 Strong, cudgel-like Anglo-Saxon words.

b. Forming advs. with the sense 'in or after the manner of —', 'so as to resemble —'. Early instances are *fellowlike* (*c*1530), *gentlemanlike* (1542), *phraselike* (1549), *bishoplike* (1555). These advs., and the method of formation, are now perh. to be regarded as obsolete or at least archaistic, the apparent examples in recent use being explicable as quasi-advb. uses of the adj.; at least, the advs. or quasi-advs. are now employed only to characterize the subject of the sentence, not, as formerly, to indicate the manner of an action. In accordance with this change of signification, *-like* in the quasi-adverbial use now takes optionally a second principal stress, and is nearly always hyphened.

1564–78 BULLEIN *Dial. agst. Pest.* (1888) 80 This is a comely parlour, very netly and trimely apparrelled, London like. **1576** GASCOIGNE *Philomene* (Arb.) 104 She..drest hir Bacchus like. **1624** D. CAWDREY *Humilitie* 39 How vainely and garishly (popingaye-like) are our men and women attired? **1719** DE FOE *Crusoe* II. xii. (1840) 255 How..coward-like they had behaved. [**1768** W. DONALDSON *Life Sir B. Sapskull* I. 71 His father..(dotard like) seem'd fully satisfy'd. **1834** *Tait's Mag.* I. 768/2 Mr. Justice Rivers, Brutus-like, was constrained in justice to condemn. **1871** BROWNING *Prince Hohenst.* 97 Only continue patient while I throw Delver-like, spadeful after spadeful up.]

2. Appended to adjs. a. Forming adjs. In Sc. the suffix is added freely to almost any descriptive adj., esp. those relating to mental qualities, conditions of temper, or the like; the general sense of the compounds is 'having the appearance of being —'. In Eng. use the formation is not common, and the sense is usually 'resembling, or characteristic of, one who is —', as in *genteel-like*, *human-like*.

c **1470** HENRY *Wallace* VI. 694 Schir Rawff Gray saw at thai war Sotheron leik. *Ibid.* x. 210 'Allace', he said, 'the warld is contrar lik!' **1587** FLEMING *Cont. Holinshed* III. 1355/1 Of countenance amiable, and complexion English like. **1621** LADY M. WROTH *Urania* 182 Twas not sillines he saw, that made that innocent-like fashion shew in me. **1632** LITHGOW *Trav.* VI. 264 Wee found twelue Venerable like Turkes, ready to receiue vs. **1639** [see ALIVE-LIKE]. **1724** RAMSAY *Vision* iv, A man..Richt auld lyke, and bauld lyke. **1789** A. WILSON *Let.* in *Poems & Lit. Prose* (1876) I. 48 John's grim-like smile. **1825** LD. COCKBURN *Mem.* ii. 110 It was a low square-like room. **1825** *Greenhouse Comp.* II. 15 A low herbaceous-like shrub. **1827** J. WILSON *Noct. Ambr.* Wks. 1855 I. 357, I think Peter's looking auld-like. **1839** BAILEY *Festus* (1852) 389 Their sublime-like beauty. **1866** AITKEN *Sci. & Pract. Med.* II. 719 A gluey-like material. **1910** A. H. ADAMS *Galahad Jones* 208 I'd be useful-like to keep a look out. **1937** M. SCOTT *Barbara Prospers* 214 Her bein' shaky-like. **1953** 'N. BLAKE' *Dreadful Hollow* 38 We have a stronger parson now—more active-like.

b. Forming advs. With the sense 'like one who is —'. *Obs.* exc. in *Sc.*, where the sense of the advs. is rather 'so as to appear —'.

Chiefly in contexts where the word might admit of being taken as adj.; cf. 1 b.

c **1470** HENRY *Wallace* v. 577 All his four men bar thaim quietlik. **1548** UDALL *Erasm. Par. Luke* 154 b, With suche pompe as this, triumphaunt lyke, and with such a trayne about him, did the Lord Iesus goe vnto Hierusalem. **1594** *Warres Cyrus* 1646 The Goddesse turnde her face, offending-like, frowning with angrie brows. **1681** RYCAUT *Critick* 182 You, Phrygian, or inconsiderate like, replied Critilo, propound late Remedies. **1682** *Songs & Ball.* (Percy Soc.) 126 When thundering like we strike about. *a* **1903** *Mod. Sc.* Dinna rug at it sae rochlike [= roughly], or ye'll brak it. **1895** A. A. GRACE *Maoriland Stories* 105, I suppose you won't care to stop the night with a chap, friendly-like. **1907** W. H. KOEBEL *Return of Joe* 50 Things seemed panning out so strange-like. **1967** *Observer* 10 Sept. 17/3, I went out with her, but all the coloured girls began to look at me weird-like: I had to pack it up quick.

like, obs. f. LICK *v.*; var. LICH, LICHE.

likeable, likable ('laɪkəb(ə)l), *a.* [f. LIKE *v.*[1] + -ABLE.] That can be liked; pleasing; agreeable.

1730 GAY in *Swift's Lett.* (1766) II. 119, I would fain know you; for I often hear more good likeable things than 'tis possible any one can deserve. **1780** MAD. D'ARBLAY *Diary* May, We made a long visit here, as the people were mighty likeable. **1834–43** SOUTHEY *Doctor* xxxiv. (1862) 82 It is a very likeable place, being one of the most comfortable towns in England. **1882** STEVENSON *Fam. Stud.* 389 The most likable utterance of Knox's that I can quote.

Hence **likea'bility** *rare* = next.

1823 SOUTHEY in *Life & Corr.* V. 144 My civilities to them are regulated..a little more perhaps by their likeability.

likeableness ('laɪkəb(ə)lnɪs). [f. LIKEABLE *a.* + -NESS.] The quality of being likeable.

1860 RUSKIN in *Cornh. Mag.* II. 545 The agreeableness of a thing depends not merely on its own likeableness, but on the number of people who can be got to like it. **1879** H. SPENCER *Data of Ethics* ix. §60. 164 The different opinions concerning the likeableness of this or that occupation.

†**liked**, *ppl. a. Obs.* [f. LIKE *v.*[1] + -ED[1].] Regarded with predilection or affection; beloved.

1577–87 HOLINSHED *Chron.* I. 133/2 When the bride Alfreda vnderstood the death of hir liked make and bride-grome..she curssed father and mother. **1583** BABINGTON *Commandm.* ix. (1637) 87 How stealeth it the love of man from his wife,..a friend from his long and liked acquaintance? **1627–77** FELTHAM *Resolves* I. xii. 19 It shall either induce me to a new good, or confirm me in my liked old.

†'**likeful**, *a. Obs.* Also 4 licvol, likful, 6 likefull. [f. LIKE *v.*[1] + -FUL.] Pleasing, acceptable, agreeable.

c **1305** *Land Cokayne* 80 in *E.E.P.* (1862) 158 Þer beþ rosis of rede ble And lilie likful for to se. **1340** *Ayenb.* 217 To þan þet þe bene by parfitliche licuol to gode and worthi to bi y-herd. **1340–70** *Alex. & Dind.* 498 Vs is likful and lef in landus to walke. **1592** WYRLEY *Armorie* 158 How loathsome now that earst so likefull seemd.

†'**likehood**. *Obs. rare.* [f. LIKE *a.* + -HOOD.] Likelihood, probability.

1579 G. HARVEY *Letter-bk.* (Camden) 75 So utterlye beyounde all expectation and likehood.

†'**likeless**, *a. Obs.* [-LESS.] Unlike.

c **1250** *Gen. & Ex.* 1726 Sep or got, haswed, arled, or grei, Ben don fro iacob fer a-wei; ðo3 him boren ðes ones bles Vn-like mani3e and likeles.

†'**likelihead**. *Obs.* exc. *arch.* Also 4 liklih(i)ede, 5 likelehede, 5–6 lyk(e)lyhed(e. [f. LIKELY *a.* + -HEAD.]

1. Probability. Chiefly in phr. *by* or *of likelihead*: probably, in all probability (cf. LIKELIHOOD, 2 b).

c **1386** CHAUCER *Prioress' T.* 144 She gooth..To euery place, where she hath supposed By liklihede hir litel child to fynde. **1495** *Act 11 Hen. VII*, c. 2 Preamble, Extreme rigour ..wherby by likelehede many of theym shuld lose their lives. **1501** *Plumpton Corr.* (Camden) 151 Ye may have trial by lyklyhed what ther answere shalbe. **1533** MORE *Apol.* 151 Certayne letters whyche some of the bretherne lette fall of late, and lost them of lykelyhed as some good fyshe leseth her kayes. **1867** MORRIS *Jason* v. 96 Fellows, what have we done? by likelyhead An evil deed and luckless. **1870** —— *Earthly Par.* I. II. 553 Alas! full little likelihead That he should live for ever there.

2. Likeness; resemblance.

1390 GOWER *Conf.* II. 147 Men mai wel make a liklihiede Betwen him which is averous Of gold and him that is jelous Of love. **1413** *Pilgr. Sowle* (Caxton) II. xli. (1859) 46 Though it passe my wytte, and myn abylete, for to counterfeten it in veray trouthe of lykelyhede, yet [etc.].

likelihood ('laɪklɪhʊd). Forms as those of LIKELY *a.* + 4–6 -hode, 5–6 -hod, 6– -hood. Also 5 lykeleod, 6 lightliwode, likeloode, lykelhood. [f. LIKELY *a.* + -HOOD.]

†1. Likeness; resemblance; similarity. Also an instance of this; a semblance, similitude. *Obs.*

1398 TREVISA *Barth. De P.R.* I. (1495) 3 Parables & semblaunces or liklihodes of thynges naturelles and artyfycyelles. **1548** GEST *Pr. Masse* B iiij, Sacramentes (sayth Augustin) vnlesse they haue certayne lykelyhode wyth the thynges wherof they be sygnes, they be no sacramentes at al. **1567** MAPLET *Gr. Forest* 11 It is called Iris for likeloode to the Rainebow. *a* **1591** R. GREENHAM *Serm.* i. (1599) 96 Thus wee see what likelihood there is betweene the spirit and fire. **1614** RALEIGH *Hist. World* I. (1634) 23 There is no likelihood between pure light and black darkness. **1642** J. BALL *Answ. Canne* ii. 9 It hath too much likelihood to the masse-book. **1688** R. HOLME *Armoury* III. 200/1 Fables [are] Tales of Untruth, yet have a likelyhood of Truth.

2. a. The quality or fact of being likely or probable; probability; an instance of this. Const. *of*; †occas. *to* with *inf.* † *to take likelihood*: to infer as a probability.

c **1449** PECOCK *Repr.* I. xiv. 78 Principlis openest in probabilitie or likelihode to treuthis. **1472–3** *Rolls of Parlt.* VI. 54/1 Seyng..theym selfe in likelyhode to be endamaged. **1488** *Paston Lett.* III. 344 They sey [= saw] no lykeleod that they schuld have lycens. **1509** FISHER *Funeral Serm. C'tess Richmond* Wks. (1876) 309 Who may not nowe take euydent lyklyhode & coniecture vpon this, that [etc.]. **1583** STUBBES *Anat. Abus.* II. (1882) 14 The prince may pardon the offender, if there appeere likelyhoode of amendment in him. **1611** BIBLE *Transl. Pref.* 2 Neither is there any likelihood, that [etc.]. **1630** J. LEVETT *Ord. Bees* (1634) 38 In May or June..there is no great likelihood of a second or third swarm. *a* **1656** BP. HALL *Rem. Wks.* (1660) 9 Hearing of the likelyhood of my removal. **1717** *Entertainer* No. 7 (1718) 39 The State may be in great Likelihood to suffer Shipwreck. **1758** JOHNSON *Idler* No. 67 ¶6 There was a likelihood of rain. **1856** FROUDE *Hist. Eng.* (1858) II. ix. 397 That he really might be too late appeared an immediate likelihood. **1867** FREEMAN *Norm. Conq.* (1876) I. v. 301 The story has strong internal likelihood in its favour.

b. In phrases (mostly obsolete) † ***by likelihood***, † ***by all*** or ***most likelihood***, † ***in, in all likelihood***, † ***of likelihood***: in all probability, probably.

1433 *Rolls of Parlt.* IV. 423/1 Ye which had ellys by liklyhode be lost. **1486** C'TESS OXFORD in *Four C. Eng. Lett.* 7 To the entente by alle lykelyhod, to finde the waies and meanes to gete shipping. **1491** *Act 7 Hen. VII*, c. 5 §1 Every quinzime..of liklyhode shalbe gretly mynysshed and lessed. **1525** LD. BERNERS *Froiss.* II. clxviii. [clxiv.] 270 Their speres grated nat; if they had, by moost lykelhod they had taken hurte. **1585** ABP. SANDYS *Serm.* xvi. 287 The eldest, & therefore by likelyhoode the discreetest seruant of his house. **1599** SHAKS. *Much Ado* IV. i. 238 Then I can lay it downe in likelihood. **1600** W. WATSON *Decacordon* (1602) 121 Who of likelihood..was possessed..with so affectionate an opinion of his brothers aduancement, that [etc.]. **1631** WEEVER *Anc. Funeral Mon.* 812 It hath no Inscription, but in likelyhood it is the Tombe of Sir Roger. **1664** POWER *Exp. Philos.* III. 189 In all likelihood, he that made this great Automaton of the world, will not destroy it, till [etc.]. **1697** DAMPIER *Voy.* I. 95 By all likelihood these ridges of Mountains do run in a continued Chain from one end of Peru and Chili to the other. **1762–71** H. WALPOLE *Vertue's Anecd. Paint.* (1786) I. 259 Oliver..was in all likelihood of French extraction. **1862** MRS. CARLYLE *Lett.* III. 102 In all likelihood we will go home together on Monday.

c. ***the likelihood***: the probable fact, or the probable amount. Now *rare* exc. *Sc.*

1455 *Rolls of Parlt.* V. 287/1 The lyklyhode of the costes and expenses..weyed and considered. **1542–5** BRINKLOW *Lament.* (1874) 85 Yea & yet knowe not you whether they heare you or not, as the likelyhode is they do not. **1894** G. MEREDITH *Ld. Ormont* III. xii. 241 The likelihood is, she'll feel bound in honour to serve him faithfully for the rest of their wedded days. *Mod. Sc.* The likelihood is I'll not be able to go.

†3. Something that is likely, a probability; hence, a ground of probable inference, an indication, sign. Frequent in *pl. Obs.*

1541 *Act 33 Hen. VIII*, c. 21 §1 The likelihoodes and apparances being so far contrarie to that, which..is nowe founde true. **1576** TURBERV. *Venerie* 23 If there be two [dewclaws] it is an euill likelyhoode. **1591** SHAKS. *Two Gent.* v. ii. 43 These likelihoods confirme her flight from hence. **1601** SIR W. CORNWALLIS *Disc. Seneca* (1631) 63 Man cannot divine what end followeth beginning, the nearest is a likelyhood. **1611** SPEED *Theat. Gt. Brit.* xliii. (1614) 85/2 Which..by high-wayes paved leading unto it, and other likelihoods, seems to have beene a worke of the Romanes. *a* **1641** SUCKLING *Lett.* (1646) 64 Thrusting upon your judgment impossibilities for likelyhoods. **1649** MILTON *Eikon.* 119 Against which testimonies, likelyhoods, evidences, the bare denyall of one man cannot countervaile. **1656** EARL MONM. tr. *Boccalini's Advts. fr. Parnass.* I. xxiii.

(1674) 24 This last is a suspition grounded only upon likelihoods.

4. The quality of offering a prospect of success; 'promise'. Now only as an echo of Shakespeare.

1596 SHAKS. *1 Hen. IV*, III. ii. 45 A fellow of no marke, nor likelyhood. **1606** G. W[ODCOCKE] *Hist. Ivstine* VI. 31 Amongst all the..Captaines..there was none of greater likelihood. **1818** LAMB *Lett.* xi. 104 There are actresses of greater merit and likelihood than you. **1847** L. HUNT *Men, Women & B.* II. x. 232 An individual of no mark or likelihood.

likeliness ('laɪklɪnɪs). [f. LIKELY *a.* + -NESS.]

†**1.** Resemblance, similarity; a semblance, similitude; = LIKELIHOOD 1. *Obs.*

1375 BARBOUR *Bruce* III. 88 But at the last thar slayne he wes: In that failȝeit the liklynes. *c* **1375** *Sc. Leg. Saints* xxxviii. (*Adrian*) 608 þe feynd in-[to] þe lyklynes..of a marynare one þe sey to þame can apere. **1412-20** LYDG. *Chron. Troy* I. iii, Jupiter..Takyng lykelynesse of Amphitrion. **1571** GOLDING *Calvin on Ps.* xlix. 14 They chaunge the letter (Beth) into (Caph) the mark of likelynesse. **1596** SPENSER *F.Q.* V. vii. 29 She knew not his favours likelynesse, For many scarres and many hoary heares. **1600** HAMILTON *Facile Traictise* in *Cath. Tractates* (1901) 242 The halie spirit discendit vpon Christ in lyklines of ane whyt dow. **1604** T. WRIGHT *Passions* III. iv. 97 The similitude of inclinations, And likelinesse of passions. **1680** H. DODWELL *Two Lett.* (1691) 117 Books conjectured by Erasmus to be his from the likeliness of their Style. **1702** C. MATHER *Magn. Chr.* III. II. xix. (1852) 442 There is frequently..much likeliness between a Plinyism and a fable.

2. Probability; = LIKELIHOOD 2. Now *rare.* †Also in phrases *by, of likeliness* (cf. LIKELIHOOD 2b). †Also, probable amount = LIKELIHOOD 2c.

?*c* **1370** CHAUCER *Amorous Compleint* 15 Sooth is, that wel I woot, by lyklinesse, If that [etc.]. *c* **1375** *Sc. Leg. Saints* xxvii. (*Machor*) 997 God is mychty to helpe; dred nocht; quhar man na liklines ma se. *c* **1400** *Rom. Rose* 7544 For thing that may have no preving, But lyklinesse, and contriving. **1436** *Rolls of Parlt.* IV. 511/1 By the whiche alienes..by liklynesse, the Counseall..of oure saide Souverayn Lord..is discovered. **1447** BOKENHAM *Seyntys* (Roxb.) 32 Seyng no lyklynesse to ben amendyd Of his host he took his leve that nyht. *c* **1470** HENRY *Wallace* v. 620 'Maister', he said, 'as fer as I haiff feyll, Off lyklynes it may be wondyr weill'. *Ibid.* IX. 1010 Be lyklynes Wallace suld wyn the land. **1475** *Bk. Noblesse* 55 As by possibilite and alle liklinesse may be honourable and truly vanquisshid and wonne bye armes. **1530** PALSGR. 239/2 Likelynesse of a thyng that maye happen, *possibilité.* **1632** SHERWOOD, Likelihood, likelinesse,..*probabilité.*

†**3.** An indication, sign; = LIKELIHOOD 3. *Obs.*

c **1450** LYDG. & BURGH *Secrees* 2671 Shuldrys sharpe..Off evyl feith is lyklynesse.

4. = LIKELIHOOD 4. ? *Obs.*

c **1470** HARDING *Chron.* CLXXXII. iii, There was no king Christen had such sonnes fiue Of lyklynesse. **1530** PALSGR. 239/2 Likelynesse or towardness, *indole.* **1735** DYCHE & PARDON *Dict.*, *Likeliness*, Handsomness or Worthiness.

likely ('laɪklɪ), *a.* and *adv.* Forms: 4 licly, lickli, likliche, 4-6 likly, lyk(e)ly, 5-6 lik(e)li, 5-7 *Sc.* likl(i)e, 4- likely. [a. ON. *líklig-r* (also *glíklig-r*), f. *lík-r* (*glík-r*) LIKE *a.* + *-lig-r* -LY[1]. (OE. had the equivalent *ȝelíclic.*)]

A. *adj.*

†**1.** Having a resemblance, like, similar. Const. *till, to.* Also, resembling the original, portraying accurately. *Obs.*

c **1400** *Rom. Rose* 4852 For he shulde setten al his wil To geten a likly thing him til. ?*a* **1425** *Cursor M.* 21132 (Trin.) þei were likely eiþer to oþer. **1513** DOUGLAS *Æneis* II. xii[i]. 64 Mast liklie a waverand sweving or dreyme [L. *simillima somno*]. **1530** PALSGR. 317/2 Lykly of countenance, *semblable.* **1596** SPENSER *Hymne Beautie* 198 For Love is a celestiall harmonie Of likely harts composed of starres concent. **1657-61** HEYLIN *Hist. Ref.* I. II. iv. 38 Hath not the Father given us..a most excellent Mirrour, wherein to see the ill complexion of the present times? Doth not he set them forth in such likely colours, as if [etc.].

2. a. Having an appearance of truth or fact; that looks as if it would happen, be realized, or prove to be what is alleged or suggested; probable. †Also in advb. phrase *by likely.*

c **1380** WYCLIF *Serm.* Sel. Wks. I. 44 Sum men þenken licly þat [etc.]. **1426** *Paston Lett.* I. 25, I herde..no maner lykly ne credible evidence. **1436** *Rolls of Parlt.* IV. 501/2 To the grettest likly myschief y[t] may falle to the said Roialme. **1545** ASCHAM *Toxoph.* (Arb.) 101 By likely to hit the pricke alwayes is vnpossible. *a* **1592** H. SMITH *Four Serm.* (1612) I 3, Hee would rather content himselfe with his present ease, then commit himselfe to so likely misery. **1605** SHAKS. *Lear* II. i. 11 Have you heard of no likely Warres toward? **1648** MILTON *Tenure Kings* (1650) 25 No likelier cause can be alleg'd. **1814** CHALMERS *Evid. Chr. Revel.* iii. 81 The apparent contradictions admit of a likely..reconciliation. **1856** KANE *Arct. Expl.* II. xxix. 291 The green spots.. would be the likely camping-ground of wayfarers. **1879** FROUDE *Cæsar* xvii. 275 The story told by Ambiorix was likely in itself. **1897** *Allbutt's Syst. Med.* II. 780 A likely source of infection.

b. As predicate to a quasi-impersonal vb., with complement †an *inf.*, or *clause*; also in parenthetical phrase, *as (it) is likely* or *it is likely*. Colloq. phr. *not likely*: certainly not; I refuse.

c **1380** WYCLIF *Wks.* (1880) 475 But it is licly, to many men, that siluestre synnede in his hiyng. *c* **1386** CHAUCER *Doctor's T.* 64 For that she wolde fleen the compaignye Where likly was to treten of folye. **1395** PURVEY *Remonstr.* (1851) 82 We supposen, as it is licli, that King Jon [etc.]. *c* **1450** *St. Cuthbert* (Surtees) 6639 It was likly he was made preste At fyue and twenty ȝere at neste. **1526** *Pilgr. Perf.* (W. de W. 1531) 254 b, It semeth..more lykely that he ascended up certayne steppes to y[e] crosse. *c* **1530** LD. BERNERS *Arth. Lyt. Bryt.* 152 It was likely there to have been a great fray. **1583** STUBBES *Anat. Abus.* II. (1882) 37 It is verie likelie they doe so. **1670** MILTON *Hist. Eng.* Wks. 1738 II. 116 King Edward, by force, as is likeliest, though it be not said how, reduc'd him to Peace. **1695** LD. PRESTON *Boeth.* III. 106 *note*, It is the likelier also that Catullus did intend a Reflection upon Nonius. **1696** BP. PATRICK *Comm. Exod.* i. 10 They had heard the Israelites discourse, it is likely, that they never meant always to stay there. **1710** LADY M. W. MONTAGU *Let. to Wortley Montagu* 25 Apr., 'Tis very likely you will never receive this. **1776** LD. STIRLING in Sparks *Corr. Amer. Rev.* (1853) I. 173 It was not likely any more British troops would be sent out. **1863** FR. A. KEMBLE *Resid. in Georgia* 16 It will be more likely that I should see things extenuate. **1893** G. B. SHAW *Widowers' Houses* II. iv. 47 Catch him going down to collect his own rents! Not likely! **1914** —— *Pygmalion* (1916) III. 153 Walk! Not bloody likely... I am going in a taxi. **1922** C. E. MONTAGUE *Disenchantment* x. 139 The German sentries said, 'Go back, or we shall have to shoot.' The Englishmen said 'Not likely!' advanced to the German wire, and asked again for an officer. **1934** G. B. SHAW *On Rocks* II. 240 Take the land with one hand and give back its cash value to the landlords with the other! Not likely. I ask you again, do you take us for fools?

c. As predicate to a personal vb., followed by *to* with *inf.*, where *he* (etc.) *is likely to* = 'it is likely that he will'. †Also (*rarely*) const. *of* with gerund.

a **1300** *Cursor M.* 4878, I sai it noght for-qui þat yee Ne ern lickli lel men to be. *c* **1374** CHAUCER *Troylus* III. 1221 (1270) þou me..Hast holpin þere I likly was to steruyn. **1406** HOCCLEVE *Misrule* 74 Ful seelde is seen, þat yowthe takith heede of perils, þat been likly for to fall. *c* **1450** *St. Cuthbert* (Surtees) 1138 þai were likly lost to be. **1513** MORE in Grafton *Chron.* (1568) II. 759 He was not likely to speake it of naught. *a* **1548** HALL *Chron.*, *Edw. IV*, 210 Kyng Henry the VI, thus readepted..his croune & dignitie Royall,.. lykely within short space to fall agayn. *a* **1592** H. SMITH *Four Serm.* (1612) I 6 b, Thou art much weaker then a Prophet,..and the likelier to haue a most greeuous fall. **1622** DONNE *Serm.* (*Judg.* v. 20) 24 Men exercised in Judgement are likeliest to thinke of the last Judgement. **1653** WALTON *Angler* vii. 154 A hole where a Pike is, or is likely to lye. **1701** W. PENN in *Pa. Hist. Soc. Mem.* IX. 79 The war is likely, and goods bear a price. **1712** STEELE *Spect.* No. 515 ¶2, I am glad to find you are likely to be disposed of in marriage so much to your approbation. **1747** SARAH FIELDING *Fam. Lett.* 90 Putting themselves to a very unnecessary Trouble to prevent that Pain which seemed not likely of befalling them. **1793** SMEATON *Edystone L.* §123 The heavy expence they were likely to be at. **1849** MACAULAY *Hist. Eng.* i. I. 144 Lambert seemed likely to be the first of these rulers. **1896** *Law Times* C. 466/2 The coronet..did not so closely resemble a Royal Crown as to be likely to be taken for it.

3. Apparently suitable or qualified (*for* a purpose or an action); apparently able or fitted (*to do* or *to be* something expressed or implied).

c **1375** *St. Leg. Saints* xxxvi. (*Ioh. Baptista*) 837 A basare ..stark & likly als but let to strik in twa his als. *c* **1385** CHAUCER *L.G.W.* 1174 *Dido*, Me thynkith that he is..likli for to ben a man. *c* **1393** —— *Scogan* 32 That ben so lykly folk in love to spede. *c* **1440** *Generydes* 2107 In euery wise He was a likely knyght for that Office. *c* **1470** HENRY *Wallace* II. 364 Haile he [Wallace] was, likly to gang and ryd. **1543** *Act 35 Hen. VIII*, c. 17 §1 Standils or Storers, likely to prove and to be Timber-trees. **1557** *Act 4 & 5 Ph. & Mary* c. 3 §1 Suche as were most able and lykelyest to serve well in the same. **1591** H. SMITH *Affin. Faithf.* A 3 b, Deuising the likeliest policie to frustrate & disgrace but one of his Sermons. **1593** SHAKS. *3 Hen. VI*, IV. vi. 74 Himselfe Likely in time to blesse a Regall Throne. **1614** RALEIGH *Hist. World* v. ii. §6 (1634) 597 The best and likeliest means of their common safety. **1653** WALTON *Angler* ii. 45 We are not yet come to a likely place. **1692** R. L'ESTRANGE *Fables, Life Æsop* (1708) 4 He..Carry'd them [slaves] to Samos, as the Likeliest Place for a Chapman. **1712** BUDGELL *Spect.* No. 283 ¶9, I regard Trade..as the most natural and likely Method of making a Man's Fortune. **1748** *Anson's Voy.* II. ii. 131 This Island was the likeliest place..to meet with us. **1789** BURNEY *Hist. Mus.* (ed. 2) III. vii. 410 Lely gave me these papers as the likelyest person to get them perfected. **1796** MORSE *Amer. Geog.* I. 365 The most likely rocks have been tried with *aqua fortis.* **1851** MAYHEW *Lond. Labour* (1861) I. 380, I call at every likely house in the towns or villages.

4. a. Having the appearance, or giving evidence, of vigour or capacity; strong or capable looking. **b.** (Now chiefly *U.S.*) Of young persons (occas. of animals): Giving promise of success or excellence; promising, hopeful.

1454 *Paston Lett.* I. 265 The Duke of York..wole come with his houshold meynee, clenly beseen and likly men. *a* **1548** HALL *Chron.*, *Edw. IV*, 211 b, The kyng had.. marked bothe his wit and his likely towardnes. **1601** R. JOHNSON *Kingd. & Commw.* (1603) 48 The likeliest and ablest springals are chosen. **1686** *Lond. Gaz.* No. 2128/4 Tall, well-set, likely Fellows. **1725** S. WILLARD in *Rec. Lancaster, Mass.* (1884) 235, I arrived at Dunstable with a Company of very good, likely, effective men. **1793** WASHINGTON *Lett.* Writings 1891 XII. 381, I am very sorry to hear that so likely a young fellow..should addict himself to such courses. **1863** *Advt.* in Dicey *Federal St.* I. 254 He [a fugitive slave] is..stout and well built; very likely. **1883** GILMOUR *Mongols* xviii. 226 Chinamen go to Mongolia in spring, buy up likely animals.

5. [? Influenced by LIKE *v.*] Of seemly or comely appearance; good-looking, handsome. ?Now *U.S.* and *dial.*

1470-85 MALORY *Arthur* II. ii. 77 The damoysel beheld the poure knyght, and sawe he was a lykely man. *a* **1586** SIDNEY *Arcadia* I. (1590) 66 b, These young companions make themselues beleeue they love at the first liking of a likely beautie. **1728** VANBR. & CIB. *Prov. Husb.* IV. i, You looked a good likely woman last night. **1748** RICHARDSON *Clarissa* (1811) III. 325 She is very likely and genteel. **1802** H. MARTIN *Helen of Glenross* I. 69 You are white, and she is brown; but you are both likely. **1807** P. GASS *Jrnl.* 32 The women are homely..but the young men likely and active. **1852** MRS. STOWE *Uncle Tom's C.* xii, You'll soon get another husband—such a likely gal as you. **1859** GEO. ELIOT *A. Bede* xxv, That is Hetty Sorrel..a very likely young person. **1863** J. G. MURPHY *Comm. Gen.* ii. 16-17 All the others that were likely for sight and good for food.

†**6.** Seemly, becoming, appropriate. *Obs.*

c **1470** HENRY *Wallace* VI. 379 Be wryt or word quhilk likis yow best till haiff? 'In wryt', thai said 'it war the liklyast'. *a* **1674** MILTON *Wks.* (1738) I. Life 44 After likely Discourses [Lot] præpares for thire entertainment. **1742** *Col. Rec. Pennsylv.* IV. 587 The Vessel had been cleansed and Aired in the likeliest Manner.

†**7.** ***was likely***, also catachr. ***had likely***: came near *to do* or *be* (etc.); = *was* or *had like. Obs.*

1494 FABYAN *Chron.* II. xxxi. 24 The..Gallis..came into y[e] Capitoill & were lykely to haue wonne it. *c* **1503** J. FLAMANK in *Lett. Rich. III & Hen. VII* (Rolls) I. 235 Els, I hade lykly to be putt to a grett plonge for my trothe. **1652** LD. MONM. *Hist. Warrs Flanders* (1654) 274 A very hot skirmish had likely to have been, had not the King [etc.].

8. *Comb.*, as ***likely*** †***-looked, -looking*** adjs.

1709 *Brit. Apollo* II. No. 6. 4/2 He must be a likely-look'd Fellow. **1887** *Spectator* 1 Oct. 1305 The United States' Navy Board..are ready to try any likely-looking invention. **1897** MARY KINGSLEY *W. Africa* 406 Big Eloby is a fine, likely-looking island.

B. *adv.*

†**1. a.** In a like or similar manner; similarly. **b.** With close resemblance (in portraiture). *Obs.*

c **1450** *Mirour Saluacioun* 3348 The faderes redemyd fro helle ioyned he til aungels likely. **1552** HULOET s.v. *Sc.*, Sc. and Sk. bene very likely vsed. **1571** DIGGES *Pantom.* III. xi. S b, Then are those vessels likely proportionall. ?*a* **1600** in *Montgomerie's Poems* (1887) 274 Not abill, in tabill, With colours competent, So quiklie or liklie A form to represent.

2. Probably, in all probability.

Now chiefly ***most likely, very likely***; otherwise rare exc. *Sc. dial.*, or (freq.) *N. Amer.*

c **1380** WYCLIF *Sel. Wks.* III. 434 Likliche hem wantiþ to be þe leeste membre þat Crist haþ ordeyned to be of his Chirche. *a* **1420** HOCCLEVE *De Reg. Princ.* 412 And likly, þat þou demest for folye Is gretter wysdom þan þou canst espye. **1601** R. JOHNSON *Kingd. & Commw.* (1603) 104 When of one house there be three or fower brethren, likely one or two of them give themselves to trafique and merchandize. **1650** TRAPP *Comm. Deut.* 159 And were ready to wish (likely) as the Romanes did of Augustus, that [etc.]. **1683** MOXON *Mech. Exerc.*, *Printing* xxii. ¶9 That part of his Copy.. being such as his whole Copy..will likeliest Come-in alike with. **1692** E. WALKER *Epictetus' Mor.* (1737) lvi, You're likely in the right, when blam'd by them. **1754** J. SHEBBEARE *Matrimony* (1766) I. 15 The young Man who is to succeed him may likely spend his Fortune. **1812** P. DEALTRY *Let. to Parr* 17 Dec. in *P.'s Wks.* (1828) VIII. 363, I shall most likely say a good deal on the subject when we meet. **1859** CORNWALLIS *New World* I. 124 A quartz reef had been.. abandoned, likely as unprofitable. **1875** JOWETT *Plato* (ed. 2) I. 21 You may be very likely right in that. **1883** GILMOUR *Mongols* xviii. 211 Ask him where he is going..and likely he will tell you he is going to some shrine to worship. **1895** *Leeds Mercury* 12 Sept. 4/8 He will likely be asked afresh whether [etc.]. **1919** E. O'NEILL *Ile* in *Moon of Caribbees, etc.* (1923) 10 I'm afeard there'll be trouble with the hands by the look o' things. They'll likely turn ugly...if you don't put her about. **1931** —— *Mourning becomes Electra* I. I. 37 You've likely heard gossip. **1963** *Monsanto Mag.* Mar. 10/2 Beams of different frequencies likely could be obtained by varying the lasing material slightly. **1964** *Amer. N. & Q.* Jan. 76/2 The American public never has understood, and likely never will, the chaotic and complex character of the Indian problem during the 19th century. **1970** *Toronto Daily Star* 24 Sept. 12/8 The heroin addict likely will retrace or repeat many strokes of the pen, showing he is not in full control of his neuromuscular functions. **1971** *Publishers' Weekly* 22 Nov. 14/1 It is possible to predict that within a few years the microfiche likely will move from the library into the study and home.

†**3.** In a fit manner, fitly, suitably, reasonably.

c **1380** WYCLIF *Serm.* Sel. Wks. II. 335 þus in þes fyve figuris many men licly suppose þat [etc.]. *c* **1420** LYDG. *Assembly of Gods* 1442 So was that Lord receuyd..Lykly to hys plesure. **1674** N. FAIRFAX *Bulk & Selv.* 48 The knowledge of heat that we have from the feeling of it, is far more off from the right knowledge of it, or such as may likeliest become God, than [etc.].

Hence †'**likely** *v. trans.*, to make 'likely' or attractive; to adorn, embellish.

1513 DOUGLAS *Æneis* I. Prol. 124 Or than to mak my sang schort sum tyme, Mair compendious, or to liklie my ryme.

†'**likement.** *Obs. rare*[−1]. [f. LIKE *v.* + -MENT.] Liking; pleasure.

1649 J. E[LLISTONE] tr. *Behmen's Epist.* (1886) 27 Take likement and delight therein.

liken ('laɪk(ə)n), *v.* Forms: 4 licne(n, (likkin), 4-5 li(c)kne, lykne(n, -nyn, 4-6 licken, -yn, 5 lycken, lykeny, lykyne, (leccon, legeny, lekyn, likon, -yn), 4-6 lyken, 4- liken. [f. LIKE *a.* + -EN[5]; cf. OHG. *ki-lîhinôn* (MHG. *gelîchenen*), MLG. *lîkenen*, Sw. *likna*, Da. *ligne.*]

1. *trans.* To represent as like; to compare. Const. †*into, to, unto, with.* Also ***to liken together.***

1303 R. BRUNNE *Handl. Synne* 4759 And to þe croys by gode skylle Ys þe harpe lykenede weyle. *c* **1380** WYCLIF *Wks.* (1880) 97 þei may be wel licned to swolwis of þe see & helle. **1393** LANGL. *P. Pl.* C. xx. 168 To a torche oþer to a taper the trinite is likened. *a* **1400-50** *Alexander* 3095 It limps noȝt all-way þe last to licken with þe first. *c* **1420** *Chron. Vilod.* (Horstm.) 1128 Dowuys..ben legenyd to þe holy gost. *c* **1430** *Hymns Virg.* 22 Loue y likne in-to a fier þat slakeen

may for no þing. **c1485** E.E. Misc. (Warton Club) 9, I leccone my lyfe unto the morrow-tyde. **1549** LATIMER Serm. Ploughers (Arb.) 19 Wel may the preacher and the ploughman be lykened together. **1597** SHAKS. 2 Hen. IV, II. i. 97 The Prince broke thy head for lik'ning him to a singing man of Windsor. **1667** MILTON P.L. v. 573 By likening spiritual to corporal forms. **1748** RICHARDSON Clarissa (1811) II. l. 375 Every good servant, for the future, will be proud to be likened to honest Joseph Leman. **1751** HARRIS Hermes Wks. (1841) 147 The world has been likened to a variety of things. **1808** SOUTHEY Lett. (1856) II. 90 You liken her to Henry. **1851** CARLYLE Sterling I. i. (1872) 5, I likened him often..to sheet-lightning. **1884** W. C. SMITH Kildrostan 93 You must not liken her To your wild-eyed Aspasias.

†**b.** To make imputations on (a person). *Obs. rare.*

1377 LANGL. P. Pl. B. x. 42 Þo þat..Lickne men and lye on hem that leneth hem no ʒiftes. Ibid. 277 Lewed men may likne ʒow þus þat þe beem lithe in ʒowre eyghen.

†**c.** *to liken* (a person) *to do* (something): to represent as doing. *Obs.*

1520 Caxton's Chron. Eng. I. 6/1 Athlas..ye whiche is lykened to bere up heven on his sholders.

†**d.** *passive.* To be assigned by repute *to* (a person) as a lover or a future husband or wife; also, to be reputed *to be* (so-and-so). *Obs.*

c1570 Durham Depos. (Surtees) 59 They haith bein likned to-gither more and 2 yere. **1575** Ibid. 304 He saith that the said Janet was never by any report lykned to any man for the getting of the said child, but only the said Robert... The said Robert is lykened to be the father of the said child.

2. To make like. *rare.*

a1400-50 Alexander 4350 To sett him in-to seruituute ..þat god has fourmed to be free & to his face licknud. **1483** Cath. Angl. 216/2 To make lyke (A. to Lykyne), assimilare, conformare. **1720** Duncan Fraser in Evans O.B. (1784) III. xvii. 172, I will liken her to a laidley worm, That warps about the stone. **18..** LD. BROUGHAM (Ogilvie), The occasional deviations from its fundamental principles in a free constitution, and the temporary introduction of arbitrary power, liken it to the worst despotisms.

†**3.** *intr.* To be like, to resemble; also, to become like. Const. *to* or *dative.* Also *trans.* to symbolize, represent. *Obs.*

13.. E.E. Allit. P. B. 1064 If þou wyrkkes on þis wyse, þaʒ ho wyk were, Hir schal lyke þat layk þat lyknes hir tylle. **1340** Ayenb. 88 Þe more he him loueþ þe stranglaker, þe more he him likneþ propreliche. **a1400-50** Alexander 666 Þi fourme Is lickenand on na lym ne like to my selfe. **a1450** Knt. de la Tour (1868) 11 The plater drawen oute of the donge likenithe [Fr. signifie] the soule in the bodi. **1809** BIANCHI Levity & Sorrow I. 70 Her own conduct towards Braunau had much likened to coquetry. Ibid. II. 200, I once knew a lady..that likened surprisingly to you. **1838** CHALMERS On Rom. II. 87 We are daily likening unto Christ in superiority over the world.

Hence †'**likener**, one who likens.

c1440 Promp. Parv. 305/1 Lykenare, or he þat lykenythe.

likeness ('laɪknɪs). For forms see LIKE *a.* and -NESS. [OE. (Northumb.) *lícnes*, shortened form of *ʒelícness* I-LIKENESS.]

1. The quality or fact of being like; resemblance, similarity; an instance of this. Const. *to*; †formerly in the same sense, const. *of* (or genitive of pron.), *with.*

1297 R. GLOUC. (Rolls) 9515 Wite cloþes heo dude hire on ..ilich þe snowe, þat me ne ssolde hire uor þe liknesse ise ne iknowe. **a1300** Cursor M. 3332 Licknes to corbin had he nan. **1398** TREVISA Barth. De P.R. II. xv. (1495) 40 The lykenesse of god is shewed in a lower maner in the lowest ordres of angels. **1470-85** MALORY Arthur VII. xxviii, The vertu of my rynge..that is reed it wil torne in lykenes to grene. **1551** TURNER Herbal I. K v b, It may be called..ciste sage, of the lyknes that it hath with sage. **1596** SHAKS. 1 Hen. IV, v. iii. 8 The Lord of Stafford deere to day hath bought Thy likenesse. **1601** SIR W. CORNWALLIS Ess. (1632) ix, Confounding a Gentleman, and a Peasant with the likenesse of salutation. **1612** W. COLSON Gen. Treasury title, The practise..to adde and substract all vsuall Fractions vnlike, without reduction into likenesse. **1651** HOWELL Venice Pref., Moreover if likenes may beget love, England hath reason to affect Venice more than any other. **a1715** BURNET Own Time (1724) I. 51 His other writings being such that no man from a likeness of style would think him capable of writing so extraordinary a book. **1818** J. C. HOBHOUSE Hist. Illustr. (ed. 2) 386 Neither of them has a shadow of likeness with the lyric poetry of Petrarch. **1850** TENNYSON In Mem. lxxiii, As sometimes in a dead man's face,..A likeness,.. Comes out—to some one of his race. **1855** BAIN Senses & Int. III. ii. §23 (1864) 499 There is scope for the detection of likenesses in the midst of diversity. **1866** G. MACDONALD Ann. Q. Neighb. vii. (1878) 103 It was a likeness to her little boy that had affected me so pleasantly.

2. That which resembles an object; a like shape or form, a semblance. Hence *gen.* form, shape, esp. in phrase *in likeness of.* †In OE. = figure, stature.

c950 Lindisf. Gosp. Matt. vi. 27 Huælc..iurre ʒeðences mæʒe to-ece to licnesse [c1000 anlicnesse] his elne enne. **a1300** Cursor M. 18823 Bot of his licknes þat he bar Quils he went prechand here and þare þan mai we sai. **1340** HAMPOLE Pr. Consc. 332 Þan may men his liknes se Chaunged, als it had never bene he. **c1385** CHAUCER L.G.W. 1142 Dido, Cupido..Hadde the liknesse of the child I-take. **c1400** Lanfranc's Cirurg. 27 Þe fleisch is not hoot, but it is moist & haþ þre maner lijknes. **c1450** Mirour Saluacioun 1861 In liknes of brede and wyne gaf crist his blode and flesshe. **1500-20** DUNBAR Poems xxx. 47 Ane fieind he wes in liknes of ane freir. **1592** SHAKS. Rom. & Jul. IV. i. 104 In this borrowed likenesse of shrunke death Thou shalt continue two and forty houres. **1611** BIBLE Ezek. i. 5 Out of the midst thereof came the likenesse of foure liuing creatures. **1634** MILTON Comus 84, I must..take the Weeds and likenes of a Swain. **1692** R. L'ESTRANGE Fables ccccxix. 395 It is safer yet to stand upon our Guard against an Enemy in the likeness of a Friend, then [etc.]. **1815** SHELLEY Demon World 270 The likeness of a throned king came by. **1881** FREEMAN Subj. Venice 180 Spalato is putting on the likeness of a busy modern town.

3. The representation of an object; a copy, counterpart, image, portrait. Phr. *to take a person's likeness*: to make a portrait of him. Also of persons: One who closely resembles another.

c950 Lindisf. Gosp. Matt. Contents (Sk.) 21/10 Imaginis licnessa. **c1250** Gen. & Ex. 2641 Hamones liknes was ðor-on. **1340** Ayenb. 49 Prelas, þet ssolden bi licnesse and uorbysne of holynesse..to al þe wordle. **1414** BRAMPTON Penit. Ps. (Percy Soc.) 4 Turne the, Lord, and tarye nowʒt, Thin owen lyknes to helpe and save. **1593** SHAKS. Rich. II, III. iv. 73 Thou old Adams likenesse, set to dresse this Garden. **1611** BIBLE Deut. iv. 16 Lest yee..make you a grauen image..the likenes of male, or female. **1647** COWLEY Mistress, My Picture (1687) 50 Here, take my Likeness with you, whilst 'tis so. **1667** MILTON P.L. VIII. 450 What next I bring shall please thee, be assur'd, Thy likeness, thy fit help, thy other self. **1683** TRYON Way to Health xix. (1697) 412 All creatures do vehemently desire to bring forth their Likenesses. **1729** T. COOKE Tales, Proposals, &c. 22 Whose Sire..Had all bequeath'd..To the dear Likeness of himself his Son. **1762-71** H. WALPOLE Vertue's Anecd. Paint. IV. (1786) 2 At most he gave himself the trouble of taking the likeness of the person who sat to him. **1781** COWPER Charity 434 Such was the portrait an apostle drew,..Heaven held his hand, the likeness must be true. **1815** JANE AUSTEN Emma I. vi. 34 Did you ever have your likeness taken? **1857** WILLMOTT Pleas. Lit. xx. 115 History's..portraits ought to be likenesses. **1885** CLODD Myths & Dr. II. xii. 223 They believe that their names and likenesses are integral parts of themselves. **1889** PATER G. de Latour (1896) 32 Her sacred veil.., which kings and princes came to visit, returning with a likeness thereof..for their own wearing.

†**b.** A sculptured image, a statue. *Obs.*

c1200 ORMIN 1057 Off þatt an, off Cherubyn, þeʒʒ haffdenn liccness metedd Uppo þatt oferrwerrc þatt wass Abufenn þarrke timmbredd. **c1205** LAY. 1267 He wolde.. wrchen hire..on licnesse of ræde golde. **c1250** Gen. & Ex. 678 Nilus king Made likenesse, for muni[gin]g After his fader.

†**4.** A comparison; hence, a parable. *Obs.*

1382 WYCLIF Luke v. 36 He seide to hem also a liknesse [Vulg. similitudinem]. **c1386** CHAUCER Knt.'s T. 1984 And shewed hem ensamples and lyknesse. **1413** Pilgr. Sowle (Caxton) II. lviii. (1859) 56 'What reson hath the fyre to pleyne vpon the wode, which..hit brenneth in to asshes?' ..'No cause', quod I..'but between the and me this maner of lykenes is not comparable'. 'Sothly', qwod this body, 'this lykenes is accordaunt'.

†**5.** Probable amount; = LIKELIHOOD 2 c. *Obs.*

c1460 FORTESCUE Abs. & Lim. Mon. x. (1885) 131 Now that the lykennes off the kynges charges ordinarie and extraordinarie bith shewid [etc.].

likening ('laɪk(ə)nɪŋ), *vbl. sb.* [f. LIKEN *v.* + -ING¹.]

1. The action of making like, or representing as like; assimilation, comparison.

c1440 Promp. Parv. 305/1 Lyknynge, assimilacio. **1632** SHERWOOD, A likening,..assimilation. **1832** HT. MARTINEAU Ireland vi. 104 Protestant likenings of the pope and his flock to the devil and his crew. **1894** Athenæum 30 June 835/1 [There is] an unconscious likening of all things to the flowers and hills she loves so well.

†**2.** A figure of speech; a comparison, simile. *at (the) likening of*: under the similitude of.

a1340 HAMPOLE Psalter xxiii. 1 Þe prophet at þe likynynge of a bedel..cries þat [etc.]. **1561** DAUS tr. Bullinger on Apoc. (1573) 94 b, A likening is agayne annexed, as bloud. **1587** GOLDING De Mornay xxvi. 398 What..are the similitudes of Cicero himselfe in his treatise of old age, but liknings taken from husbandry and Vines?

liker ('laɪkə(r)). Now *rare.* [f. LIKE *v.* + -ER¹.] One who likes.

1532 MORE Confut. Tindale Wks. 443/1 To abhore and burne vp hys bookes and the likers of them with them. **1583** [see LIER b]. **1658** COKAINE Poems (1669) 202 Beauty is but opinion of the Liker. **1871** M. ARNOLD Let. 18 Aug. (1895) II. 62, I am one of the true likers of the Continent. **1890** W. C. GANNETT Blessed be Drudgery 41 Each of us is ringed about by two circles.. The outer circle is the circle of our Likers, the inner is the circle of our Lovers.

liker, obs. form of LIQUOR.

likerish, -ose, -ous: see LICKERISH, -OUS.

likesome, *a. Obs.* exc. *dial.* Also *dial.* licksome. [f. LIKE *v.* + -SOME.] Agreeable, pleasant.

c1563 SIR T. CHALLONER tr. Boethius I. metr. i. in Q. Eliz.'s Englishings (E.E.T.S.) App. 150 Theis, of my happie lyksome yougthe yᵉ glorye long ago. **1577-87** HOLINSHED Chron. (1807-8) III. 163 Of favour was she counted likesome. **a1650** Will Stewart & Iohn v. in Child Ballads II. 433/1 Or doe you mourne for a likesome ladye. **1801** Sporting Mag. XIX. 87 He had looked rather gloomy before, but now he appeared quite licksome. **1876** Whitby Gloss., Likesome, that which may be loved or desired. **1877** E. LEIGH Cheshire Gloss. 124 'Charly loves a licksome girl, as sweet as sugar candy.'

likewarm, obs. form of LUKEWARM.

†'**likeways**, *adv. Obs.* [f. LIKE *a.* + *ways*: see WAY.] = LIKEWISE 2 and 3.

1551 RECORDE Pathw. Knowl. I. vii, Like waies I set one foote of the compas steddily in C. **1588** A. KING tr. Canisius' Catech. 81 Our..faith..confirmit lykuayis according to his commandiment. **c1620** A. HUME Brit. Tongue (1865) 20 Lykwayes we sould keep the vouales of the original. **1625** in Ellis Orig. Lett. Ser. I. III. 211 And lykwayes I think I have done you no wrong. **1712** ADDISON Spect. No. 542 ¶2 There are others who have likeways done me a very particular honour. [**1865** DICKENS Mut. Fr. II. xii, Likeways when I went to them two governors.]

likewise ('laɪkwaɪz). [abbreviated from *in like wise*: see LIKE *a.* and WISE *sb.*]

†**1.** (The full phrase.) *in like wise*: in the same manner. *Obs.*

1449 Rolls of Parlt. V. 148/1 As we have..besought the Kyngs Highnesse..in lyke wyse tenderly we desire all youre wysdomes. **c1489** CAXTON Sonnes of Aymon ix. 225 Alarde began to synge..a new song..& Richarde dide in lykewyse. **1509** Bury Wills (Camden) 109 To yᵉ chyrch of All Seyntys in yᵉ same town in lykwyse xs. **1582** STANYHURST Æneis I. (Arb.) 22 In lykewise Neptun thee God..apeered. **1673** RAY Journ. Low C. 183 If any be not present, he is searched out and brought in like wise.

2. In the like or same manner, similarly; = 1. *Obs.* exc. *arch.* in *to do likewise* (after Luke x. 37).

a1460 Gregory's Chron. in Hist. Coll. Citizen Lond. (Camden) 133 Also lyke wyse al maner of personys of Hooly Chyrche obedyente unto us..shalle swere for too kepe thys present acorde. **1489** CAXTON Faytes of A. II. xxxv. 150 Item they..may yssue out.. that owre whan the enemyes be not aware of..and likwyse to sawte them as they be sawted. **1534** TINDALE Luke x. 37 Goo and do thou lyke wyse. **1535** JOYE Apol. Tindale (Arb.) 9 And lyke wyse he plaith with the verb in Luke and in Marke. **1611** BIBLE Judg. vii. 17 Hee said vnto them, Looke on mee, and doe likewise. **c1625** MILTON Death Fair Infant ii, He thought it toucht his Deitie full neer, If likewise he some fair one wedded not. **1828** J. H. MOORE Pract. Navig. (ed. 20) p. xiv, Multiplication of Decimals is performed likewise as that of whole numbers.

3. Also, as well, moreover, too.

1509 FISHER Funeral Serm. C'tess Richmond Wks. (1876) 290 Wherfore let vs consyder lyke wise whether [etc.]. **1604** E. G[RIMSTONE] D'Acosta's Hist. Indies IV. xxxviii. 314 There is likewise a small beast very common which they call Cuyes. **1747** WESLEY Prim. Physic (1762) 84 It is good likewise..in all Hypocondriacal cases. **1816** J. WILSON City of Plague II. iii. 188, I had forgot to mention that his wife Was likewise lying dead. **1850** TENNYSON In Mem. lxxxv. 53 Likewise the imaginative woe..Diffused the shock thro' all my life. **1880** GEIKIE Phys. Geog. Introd. 7 As there is a geographical distribution of climates, so likewise is there one of plants and animals.

Hence †'**likewisely** *adv.*, similarly. †'**likewiseness**, a similar method or manner.

1598 SYLVESTER Du Bartas II. ii. IV. Columnes 327 Th'other, which cuts this equi-distantly..is (like-wisely) The second Colure. **1674** N. FAIRFAX Bulk & Selv. To Rdr., We..may either find better words..or at least coin fitter.. in a likewiseness to the old, than [etc.].

†**likeworth**, *a. Obs.* Forms: 1 lícwyrðe, 3 licwurðe. [OE. *lícwyrðe*, f. stem of *lícian* to LIKE + *wyrðe* WORTH *a.*] Agreeable, acceptable, pleasing. So †**likeworthy** *a.* in the same sense.

c888 K. ÆLFRED Boeth. xvi. §1 (Sedgefield) 35 Hwæt bið þær þonne licwyrðes buton his god & his weorðscipe. **c1200** ORMIN 15918 Acc itt niss nohht biforenn Godd Licwurþiʒ lif, ne cweme. **c1200** Trin. Coll. Hom. 7 His oðer dieliche tocume is softe and swiðe milde and licwurðe. **c1230** Hali Meid. 11 Hit is se heh þing & se swiðe leof godd & se licwurðe.

likham(e, variant of LICHAM *Obs.*

likie(n, obs. form of LIKE *v.*

‖**likin** (liː'kiːn). Also lekin. [Chinese *li-kin*, f. *li* LI² + *kin* money.] A Chinese provincial transit duty.

1876 Agreement of Chefoo (Y.), The amount of likin to be collected will be decided by the different Provincial Governments. **1901** Scotsman 11 Mar. 8/4 Sheng..has memorialised the Court in favour of the abolition of likin duties.

liking ('laɪkɪŋ), *vbl. sb.*¹ [OE. *lícung*, f. *lícian*: see LIKE *v.*¹ and -ING¹.]

†**1.** The fact of being to one's taste (cf. LIKE *v.*¹ 1), or of being liked. *Obs.*

c897 K. ÆLFRED Gregory's Past. xli. 303 Ðætte hie for ðære licunga ðære heringe..ðe hie lufiʒeað eac ʒeðafiʒen ða tælinge. **c1175** Paternoster 247 in Lamb. Hom. 69 On oðer wise ic habbe ifunde hu me mei in sunne bon ibunde. Þet forme is to beon underling and þet oðer is liking. **c1400** Apol. Loll. 26 Þings were in desesse to him, þat now are in mikil leking. **1570-6** LAMBARDE Peramb. Kent (1826) 297 The greatest personages, helde Monkes, Friars, and Nonnes, in such veneration and liking, that [etc.]. **1579** TOMSON Calvin's Serm. Tim. 218/1 The man [must] exhort the woman, and the woman the man, to be out of liking with themselues before God.

†**2.** Pleasure, enjoyment; an instance of this. *at liking*: in a suitable position, at one's ease. *ill liking*: discomfort, unhappiness. *Obs.*

a1225 Ancr. R. 110 Forte, wenden us urommard þe licunge þet flesches lustes askeð. **c1230** Hali Meid. 7 Habbeð mare delit þrin þen anie oðre habbeð ilikinge [= in likinge] of þe worlde. **a1300** Cursor M. 28080 In vayn glory haue i likyng. **c1330** R. BRUNNE Chron. (1810) 132 William þe Scottis kyng therfor was fulle blithe, þat Henry had ille likyng. **1340-70** Alex. & Dind. 956 We lachen likinge y-now of þe lof[t] briddus. **c1350** Will. Palerne 2023 Sche miʒt lede hire lif in liking & murþe. **1375** BARBOUR Bruce I. 226 Fredome mayss man to haiff liking. Ibid. III. 250 Quhen men oucht at liking ar. **1398** TREVISA Barth. De P.R. XVII. cxcii. (1495) 730 This tree is not at lykyng in rough places and mountayns. **a1440** Sir Degrev. 831 Thane durste I saffly syng, Was never emporoure ne kyng More at hys lykyng. **c1470** Golagros & Gaw. 1065 The lordis on the tothir side for liking thay leugh. **c1491** Chast. Goddes Chyld. II. 8 This likynge is more delectable to the body and saule than all the myrthe and likyng that all the worlde myghte gyue. **1548**

HALL *Chron., Hen. VIII*, 80b, And sought..for the delicacie of viandes: well was that man rewarded that could bryng any thyng of likyng or pleasure.

†**b.** In bad sense, more fully ***flesh's*** or ***fleshly liking***: Sensuality, sexual desire, lust. *Obs.*

a **1240** *Ureisun* in *Cott. Hom.* 189 þi deaþ adeadi in me flehces licunge. *a* **1340** HAMPOLE *Psalter* xiii. 1 All þe lust and lykynge of þaire flesch and þis warld. *c* **1400** tr. *Secreta Secret., Gov. Lordsh.* 73 Vse lytel fleshly likyng. *c* **1430** *Hymns Virg.* 92/49 For likinge blindiþ many oon. **1575** TURBERV. *Faulconrie* 269 A man shall knowe when they fall to lyking and laying by this. *a* **1711** KEN *Edmund* Poet. Wks. 1721 II. 96 To Sensuality his Flesh propends, Propension up to Liking straight ascends.

3. The bent of the will; what one wishes or prefers, (a person's) pleasure. Also *pl.* †***of free liking***: of free will. Now *rare.*

c **1375** *XI Pains Hell* 147 in *O.E. Misc.* 215 Moch froyt þer was here face be-fore, To ete þer-of was here lykyng. *c* **1386** CHAUCER *Pard. Prol.* 127 Youre lykyng is that I shal telle a tale. *c* **1400** *Rom. Rose* 1975, I wol ben hool at your devys For to fulfille your lyking. *c* **1400** tr. *Secreta Secret., Gov. Lordsh.* 48 With þe helpe of god þay all shall be subgitz to þy likynges. *c* **1590** GREENE *Fr. Bacon* x. (1630) F 3b, I leaue thee to thine own liking. **1601** SHAKS. *All's Well* III. v. 60 The King had married him Against his liking. *c* **1630** RISDON *Surv. Devon* §12 (1810) 23 This I leave to the liking of others. **1742** RICHARDSON *Pamela* III. 290 Of all Men he is the least to follow his own Liking. **1859** MILL *Liberty* i. 15 No one, indeed, acknowledges to himself that his standard of judgment is his own liking.

b. In phrases †***at, to,*** (rarely ***after, in***) ***one's liking***: according to one's wish, to one's taste.

13.. *Minor Poems fr. Vernon MS.* (E.E.T.S.) 497/133 þouh he be nouȝt at þi lykynge, þe prest þat schal þy masse synge, þerfore lette þou nouht. **1480** CAXTON *Chron. Eng.* ccxlvi. (1482) 311 He spared no thyng of his lustes ne desyres but accomplysshed them after his lykyng. **1551** CROWLEY *Pleas. & Pain* 165 You..spent all at your owne lykynge In wantones and banketynge. **1587** FLEMING *Contn. Holinshed* III. 401/2 Finding a place to his liking, he esconsed himself in despite of the Spaniards. **1633** BP. HALL *Hard Texts, N.T.* 138 Liberty to dispose of thy-selfe to thine owne best liking. **1710** STEELE *Tatler* No. 228 ¶7 A Gentleman, who would willingly marry, if he could find a Wife to his Liking. **1796** MRS. GLASSE *Cookery* v. 41 Season with pepper and salt to your liking. **1869** EADIE *Galatians* 123 It might not be in all points to their perfect liking..but they could not set themselves against it.

4. The condition of being fond of or not averse to (a person or thing); favourable regard; 'fancy' for or inclination to (some object).

1340 *Ayenb.* 23 þe uifte boȝ of prede is ydele blisse þet is fole likinge of fole heryinge. *c* **1350** *Will. Palerne* 452 So gret liking & loue i haue þat lud to bi-hold. **1362** LANGL. *P. Pl.* A. I. 27 Lot..for lyking of drinke, Dude bi his douhtren þat þe deuel louede. **1570** *Henry's Wallace* VIII. 1411 To tak ane lyking [*the MS. has* lak] and syne get na plesance, Sic lufe as that is nathing to avance. **1587** HARRISON *England* II. i. (1877) I. 6 For nothing could be obteined from him, of which the Normans had no liking. **1590** SPENSER *F.Q.* III. xii. 13 She..did great liking sheowe, Great liking unto many, but true love to feowe. **1600** SHAKS. *A.Y.L.* I. iii. 28 Is it possible..you should fall into so strong a liking with old Sir Roulands yongest sonne? **1607** TOPSELL *Four-f. Beasts* (1658) 523 Afterward they grew out of liking of this vain custom. **1655** DIGGES *Compl. Ambass.* 50, I heare secretly that there is not the best liking between the two Queens. *a* **1716** SOUTH *Serm.* (1823) II. 8 Scarce any man passes to a liking of sin in others, but by first practising it himself. **1719** W. WOOD *Surv. Trade* 271 For the improvement of their Manufactures, and..bringing the Europeans to the greater Liking of them. **1742** RICHARDSON *Pamela* III. 294 The Earl has taken a great Liking to him. **1809** MALKIN *Gil Blas* IV. viii. ¶7 Though not dainty in her likings. **1825** HEBER *Journ. Upper Prov. India* (1828) II. 377, I have no liking for all this train. **1832** MISS WORDSWORTH *Loving & Liking* in *Wordsw. Poet. Wks.* I. 251 Likings come, and pass away; 'Tis love that remains till our latest day. **1847–9** HELPS *Friends in C.* (1851) I. 63, I have a lawyer's liking for the best evidence. **1876** GEO. ELIOT *Dan. Der.* xxxii. II. 313 Friendships begin with liking or gratitude.

attrib. **1701** CIBBER *Love makes Man* Epil., And know, that while the liking Fit has seiz'd you, She cannot look, he write, too ill to please you.

†**b.** Approval, consent. (See also GOOD-LIKING 2.) *Obs.*

1607 *Statutes* in *Hist. Wakefield Gram. Sch.* (1892) 59 With the consent or likinge of the Scholemaster.

c. ***on*** or ***upon liking***: on approval or trial. Now *rare* in educated use.

1615 in Picton *L'pool Munic. Rec.* (1883) I. 190 This lycence to continue noe longer then untill Michaelmas..but upon lykeinge. **1685** DRYDEN *Thren. August.* iv, The Royal Soul..Came but a while on liking here. **1727** GAY *Beggar's Op.* I. viii. Are you really bound Wife or are you only upon liking? **1812** W. TAYLOR in *Monthly Mag.* XXXIII. 25 He did not stay..the entire month, which he was to pass on liking. **1834** *Autobiog. Dissenting Minister* 157 After spending a few months on liking, I was unanimously chosen. **1865** DICKENS *Mut. Fr.* IV. iv. He [the waiter] is a very young man on liking, and we *don't* like him.

†**5.** An object liked, (one's) beloved. *Obs.*

c **1450** HOLLAND *Howlat* 496, I sall followe the in faith.. my lyking thow art. *a* **1550** *Christis Kirke Gr.* xiv, The wyffis cam furth with cryis and clappis, Lo, quhair my lyking ligs! Quo thay. **1667** MILTON *P.L.* XI. 587 In the amorous Net Fast caught, they lik'd, and each his liking chose.

†**6.** Bodily condition, esp. good or healthy condition. Cf. GOOD-LIKING 4. *Obs.*

c **1320** *Sir Tristr.* 1279 So gode likeing he fand þat hole he was and fere. *c* **1420** *Pallad. on Husb.* I. 46 Yf contrey-men in likyng hele endure. *c* **1440** *Generydes* 6760 All pale and wanne, owt of likeng he was. **1539** TAVERNER *Erasm. Prov.* (1552) 7 This ought not to seeme any marvayle..yf he were in better lykynge than hys horse. *a* **1568** ASCHAM *Scholem.* (Arb.) 131 If God do lend me..free laysure and libertie, with good likyng and a merrie heart. **1584** COGAN *Haven Health* i. (1612) 2 These..labors..do make a good state or liking of the body. **1590** GREENE *Never too Late* Bb, I have one sheepe in my fold that's quite out of liking. **1611, 1656** [see GOOD-LIKING 4]. **1662** MASCAL *Gov. Cattle* 16 Which will cause the beast to become lean and of ill liking. **1705** *Lond. Gaz.* No. 4145/4 Strayed or stolen.., a bay Mare.., in good Liking. **1737** BRACKEN *Farriery Impr.* (1749) I. 9 They have been observed to eat plentifully and not become fatter or in better liking. **1768–74** TUCKER *Lt. Nat.* (1834) II. 616 To keep it [the child] plump in good liking.

†**'liking,** *vbl. sb.*[2] [f. LIKE *v.*[2] + -ING[1].] The condition of being like or likely. **a.** quasi-*concr.* Something that is like; a resemblance. **b.** Phr. ***in liking***: likely *to* (do something).

1340 *Ayenb.* 47 þe likynges [*F. figures*] and þe ymaginacions of zenne. **1599** *Let.* in Harington *Nugæ Ant.* 47, I am in liking to get Erasmus for your Entertainmente.

†**liking,** *ppl. a.*[1] *Obs.* Also 4–7 *Sc.* **likand.** [f. LIKE *v.*[1] + -ING[2].]

1. Pleasing, pleasant, agreeable, attractive. Of food: Dainty. Of the weather, wind, an opinion: Favourable. Const. *till, to.*

1340–70 *Alex. & Dind.* 949 Summe þat longen to a lud of likinge smellus. **1375** BARBOUR *Bruce* I. 9 And suth thyngis that ar likand Tyll mannys heryng ar plesand. **1387** TREVISA *Higden* (Rolls) VII. 237 Anon likynge wynd filled the sailles. **1401** *Pol. Poems* (Rolls) II. 31 In..delicious and liking feeding..freers passen lords. *c* **1470** HENRY *Wallace* VI. 95 Him thow our threw out off his likand rest. **1513** DOUGLAS *Æneis* IV. xii. 15 O sweit habit, and likand bed, quod sche. *a* **1548** HALL *Chron., Hen. VIII*, 72b, The wynd to hym was likyng, wherby he sayled into Flaunders. **1560** DAUS tr. *Sleidane's Comm.* 244 He appointed hym and his fellowes to come and declare hys lykyng opinion touchyng the same. **1596** J. NORDEN *Progr. Pietie* (1847) 62 Grant that..I may watchfully avoid what thou loathest, howsoever liking it be unto me. **1610** HEALEY *St. Aug. Citie of God* XIX. iii. (1620) 709 Making a liking vse of all. [*a* **1643** W. CARTWRIGHT *Ordinary* III. i, Thou art mine pleasure, by dame Venus brent; So fresh thou art, and therewith so lycand.]

2. 'In condition'; healthy, plump; in a specified condition (e.g. *well, ill liking*). Of a soil: Rich.

c **1325** *Song of Yesterday* 75 in *E.E.P.* (1862) 135 An hounde þat is likyng and Ioly. ? *a* **1366** CHAUCER *Rom. Rose* 1564 Abouten it is gras springing, For moiste so thikke and wel lyking, That it ne may in winter dye. *c* **1380** WYCLIF *Wks.* (1880) 7 It semeþ þe devyl gedreþ siche lumpis of ȝonge men, fatte, and lykynge and ydyl. **1426** LYDG. *De Guil. Pilgr.* 8963 Thow wer to fat, and to lykynge. *c* **1475** *Rauf Coilȝear* 40 Euill lykand was the King. **1523** FITZHERB. *Husb.* §48 It taketh mooste commonly the fattest and best lykynge. **1535** COVERDALE *Dan.* i. 10, I am afrayed off my lorde the kynge,..lest he spye youre faces to be worse lykynge then the other spryngaldes of youre age. **1611** BIBLE *Dan.* i. 10. **1656** HEYLIN *Surv. France* 7 The Countrey of Normandie is enriched with a fat and liking soil.

†**'liking,** *ppl. a.*[2] *Obs. rare* [f. LIKE *v.*[2] + -ING[2].] Likely, probable.

1611 SPEED *Hist. Gt. Brit.* IX. xvii. (1623) 879 A liking report was brought to the towne, that Warwick had prepared foure thousand valiant men.

†**'likingly,** *adv.*[1] *Obs.* [f. LIKING *ppl. a.*[1] + -LY[2].] In a pleasing manner; pleasantly, daintily, attractively; also, to one's liking, with pleasure.

1387 TREVISA *Higden* (Rolls) VII. 405 þe man þouȝte þat he hadde be likyngly i-norsched. **1393** LANGL. *P. Pl.* C. xx. 241 Lordliche for to lyuen and likyngliche be cloþed. *c* **1410** LOVE *Bonavent. Mirr.* iii, Takynge hede and byholdynge likyngely hir shamefast sembland. *c* **1460** *Towneley Myst.* xxiii. 234 You..That lede youre lyfe so lykandly. **1513** DOUGLAS *Æneis* VIII. vi. 31 Sa likandly, in pece and libertie, At eis his commoun peple gouernit he.

†**'likingly,** *adv.*[2] *Obs.* [f. LIKING *ppl. a.*[2] + -LY[2].] In a probable manner; probably.

1388 WYCLIF *Isa.* 2nd Prol., Ellis it wole as likyngli be applied to falsnesse as to treuthe. *c* **1449** PECOCK *Repr.* III. v. 305 Prechours ȝauen hem to flaterie..for to the more likingli fille her wombis and her pursis.

†**'likingness.** *Obs.* [f. LIKING *ppl. a.*[1] + -NESS.] Attractiveness.

c **1430** *Hymns Virg.* 93 þis feisaunt hen is likingnes, And euere folewiþ hir þese ȝonge men.

likke, obs. form of LICK, LIKE.

likkewaan ('lɪkəvɑːn). Also **lagavaan, likawaan.** [Afrikaans.] = LEGUAN. Cf. IGUANA 2.

1907 P. FITZPATRICK *Jock of Bushveld* 315 There was not even a lagavaan slide, a game path, or a drinking place. **1914** *Farmer's Annual* (S. Afr.) 334 Likavaan Skin. How to cure it. Take a quantity of alum and place it along with a small quantity of water in an old iron pot. **1936** WILLIAMS & MAY *I am Black* xviii. 187 That boy was Shabala. It was he who had captured the likkewan [*in 1949 edition corrected to* likkewaan]. **1949** *Cape Argus Mag.* 14 May 10 The dour old likkewaan with his whip-lash of a tail, can still be seen creeping through the shadows in search of birds' eggs to suck. **1971** H. C. BOSMAN *Bekkersdal Marathon* 123 'What I mean is all right, for instance,' Chris Welman continued, 'is to push a small likkewaan down the back of a visitor's neck, and to pretend to him that it's a mamba.'

likli(e, likly, obs. forms of LIKELY.

likorice, likour, obs. ff. LIQUORICE, LIQUOR.

likresse, -rus, variants of LICKEROUS *Obs.*

likth, obs. 3rd sing. pres. ind. of LIE *v.*[2]

Likud (lɪ'kuːd, lɪ'kʊd). [Heb. union, combination; (mod.) coalition, alliance.] A nationalist coalition party in the State of Israel, formed in 1973 to oppose Labour monopoly government.

1973 *Times* 14 Sept. 9/2 The 'Likud', a new nationalist political union which aspires to become an alternative to Mrs Meir's Labour-dominated government..broadened its base today. *Ibid.*, Later today the Likud was joined by a group of prominent Labour Party members. **1974** *Ann. Reg. 1973* 199 Perhaps the most significant party political event..was the success in September of..General Ariel Sharon in forming a united election front known as 'Likud' from the 'Gahal' (Herut-Liberal coalition) and various right-of-centre splinter parties. **1977** *Irish Times* 8 June 5/2 The differences between Likud and the DMC centre on issues of defence and foreign affairs, and mainly on the Likud's insistence on keeping all of the occupied West Bank of the Jordan and the Gaza Strip. **1981** *Economist* 30 May 46/1 Because Likud has kept a better ethnic balance than Labour, it will be less hurt by the fledgling Tami party. **1985** *Ann. Reg. 1984* 183 Early in September, the Labour Party gave its leader, Shimon Peres, the right to form a 'national' coalition with Likud.

likuta (lɪ'kuːta). Pl. **makuta.** [Native word; etym. uncertain; perh. f. Nupe *kuta* stone.] A coin and monetary unit introduced in the Democratic Republic of the Congo (now Zaïre) in June 1967, whose value is one hundredth of a zaïre.

1967 in WEBSTER Add. **1971** *N.Y. Times* 27 June 5 The monetary unit [of the Democratic Republic of the Congo] is the Zaire (Z.) divided into 100 makuta (K.) each worth two American cents. 'Makuta' is the plural form of the word 'likuta'. One Z. equals two U.S. dollars. **1972** *Times* 6 Dec. (Europe & Third World Suppl.) p. iii/2 (Advt.), The Zaire is divided into 100 Makuta and the Likuta (the singular of Makuta) in turn consists of 100 Sengi.

lil, lill (lɪl), *sb.* [Romany.] ‖**a.** As a gipsy word: A book. **b.** *slang.* (See quots.); also 'a five-pound note' (Farmer).

1812 J. H. VAUX *Flash Dict.*, Lill, a pocket-book. **1851** BORROW *Lavengro* I. xvii. 219 Then the more shame for you —a snake-fellow—a horse-witch—and a lil-reader—yet you can't shift for yourself. **1857** —— *Romany Rye* ix. (1900) 58 Lor', brother! how learned in lils you are! **1859** MATSELL *Vocab.* (Farmer), *Lil*, a pocket-book. *Lill*, a bad bill.

lil (lɪl), *a.* Also **li'l.** Colloq. contraction of LITTLE *a.*

1881 J. C. HARRIS *Nights with Uncle Remus* (1884) lx. 258 One ole Bear..hab one, two lilly Bear... Lil boy Bear, 'e des lahff'..Lil gal Bear, 'e look skeer. **1894** HALL CAINE *Manxman* 200 Nice lil thing, too. **1912** C. E. MULFORD in *Pearson's Mag.* May 627/1 Purty, all right. Brown hair an' I reckon brown eyes. Nice li'l girl. **1912** C. MACKENZIE *Carnival* v. 54 Would you like him to give you a lil girl like me? **1932** L. GOLDING *Magnolia St.* III. iii. 516 Good ole Mick!.. Plucky lil bastard! **1953** K. TENNANT *Joyful Condemned* xxxix. 391 We'll go out and see your Mom. Take her a lil present, maybe. **1967** K. ALLSOP *Hard Travellin'* xxiii. 274, I can fiddle a li'l bit. **1967** PERRY & ALDRIDGE *Penguin Bk. Comics* iii. 99 Much of Li'l Abner has been absorbed into American folk-lore. **1969** 'I. DRUMMOND' *Man with Tiny Head* 7 Where's girl? Where's lil girl? **1975** M. KENYON *Mr Big* xviii. 165 Phoebe said, 'That's a helluva greeting for a li'l ladykin.'

lil, var. LILL *v. Obs.*, and LILE *a. dial.*

lila ('liːla). *India.* [ad. Skr. *līlā* play, sport, amusement.] In Hindu mythology, the cosmic dance or playful activity of the Supreme Spirit manifested in the Universe (see quots.); also, the name of an Indian dance representing this.

1828 H. H. WILSON in *Asiatick Researches* XVI. 115 His [*sc.* Krishna's] feats, in which his juvenile characters are regarded, are his *Lilá*, or sport. **1861** —— *Ess. & Lect. Relig. Hindus* I. 124 In this description of creation..the deity [*sc.* Krishna] is still spoken of as a young man... The acts of divinity are his *Lilá*, or sport. **1917** L. L. P. NOBLE in A. Coomaraswamy *Dance of Siva* (1924) 63 The Spirit..is all rapture, all bliss, in this play (*līlā*) Free, divine, in this love struggle. **1924** A. COOMARASWAMY *Dance of Siva* 62 The conception of the world process as the Lord's pastime or amusement (*līlā*) is also prominent in the Saiva scriptures. **1926** *Indian Art & Lett.* II. 78 The *Svabhāva*, or nature of Being-Power, is *Līlā*, or Play, a term which means free spontaneous activity. **1962** A. HUXLEY *Island* x. 167 Shiva-Nataraja dances the dance of endless becoming and passing away. It's his *lila*, his cosmic play. **1967** SINGHA & MASSEY *Indian Dances* xi. 109 Their dance is the *lila* or play of cosmic forces and serves as a preface to the drama which is to follow. **1972** N. HEIN *Miracle Plays of Mathurā* iv. 70 Not only Vishnu's creation of the cosmos is viewed as līlā, but also his actions within the cosmos when he enters his creation in the form of his various incarnations.

lilac ('laɪlək). Forms: 7 lelack(e, 7–8 (9) lilach, 8–9 (now chiefly *dial.* or *U.S.*) laylock, (9 layloc, *U.S. vulgar* lalock), 8 lylac, 7– lilac. [a. F. *lilac* (Cotgr.; now *lilas*), a. Sp. *lilac*, a. Arab. *līlāk*, app. ad. Pers. *līlak*, var. of *nīlak* bluish, f. Pers. *nīl* blue, indigo (Skr. *nīla*, Hindī *līl*); cf. various Pers. words for indigo, *līlah, līlanj*, etc., which have parallel forms with initial *n.* Other forms are Pg. *lilaz* (from Sp. or Arab.), Turkish *leilaq* (whence possibly the early 17th c. *lelacke*, mod. *laylock*.]

1. a. A shrub, *Syringa vulgaris*, cultivated for its fragrant blossoms, which are of a pale pinkish

violet colour; a variety has white blossoms. Also, the flower of this shrub.

1625 [see *lilac-tree* below]. **1658** SIR T. BROWNE *Gard. Cyrus* iii. 128 The Autumnal budds..making little Rhombuses, and network figures, as in the Sycamore and Lilac. **1664** EVELYN *Kal. Hort.* Nov. 79 Plant Roses..Lilac, Syringas [etc.]. **1763** *Brit. Mag.* IV. 605 And gather'd laylocks perish, as they blow. **1777** T. WARTON *Ode* x. *1st Apr.* 25 The lilac hangs to view Its bursting gems in clusters blue. **1844** LADY G. FULLERTON *Ellen Middleton* (1854) II. xii. 69 A large nosegay of lilacs and seringa. **1860** O. W. HOLMES *Prof. Breakf.-t.* ii, Lalocks flowered late. **1865** TENNYSON *On a Mourner* ii, Nature..makes the purple lilac ripe. **1881** BESANT & RICE *Chapl. of Fleet* I. 3 The yellow laburnum, and the laylock were at their best.

b. Applied to other species of *Syringa* (see quots.).

1712 J. JAMES tr. *Le Blond's Gardening* 28 Rose-Trees, Honey-suckles, Persian Lilachs, &c. **1842** *Penny Cycl.* XXIII. 478/2 *Syringa Josikea*, Josika's lilac..is a native of Transylvania, and was discovered by the Baroness von Josika, after whom it was named by Jacquin. *S. Chinensis*, Chinese lilac... In characters it is intermediate between *S. vulgaris* and *S. Persica*, and agrees with a hybrid plant produced at Rouen by M. Vain, and called *S. Rotomagensis*, the Rouen lilac. **1861** DELAMER *Fl. Gard.* 124 *S. Persica*, the Persian Lilac, is a smaller and slenderer shrub, with looser, more drooping heads of flowers, more aromatically perfumed. This also has a white variety.

c. Applied to plants of other genera (see quots.).

1839 *Penny Cycl.* XV. 80/1 *Melia Azedarak*, sometimes called Persian Lilac, Pride of India, and Common Bead-tree. **1860** G. BENNETT *Gatherings Nat. Austral.* xvii. 326 The White Cedar-tree, or Australian Lilac (*Melia Australis*). **1866** *Treas. Bot.* 681/2 African Lilac, *Melia Azedarach*. Australian Lilac, a name used by the settlers for *Hardenbergia monophylla*; also *Prostanthera violacea*. Indian Lilac, *Melia semperflorens*. **1881** J. S. GAMBLE *Indian Timbers* 70 *Melia Azedarach*, Linn... The Persian Lilac. **1898** MORRIS *Austral Eng.*, *Lilac*, name given in Australia to the tree *Melia composita*..called Cape Lilac. It is not endemic in Australia, and is called 'Persian Lilac' in India. In Tasmania the name of Native Lilac is given to *Prostanthera rotundifolia*.

2. a. The colour of lilac blossom.

1791 HAMILTON *Berthollet's Dyeing* II. II. III. xi. 258 The colour was more or less inclined to red, from lilac to violet. **1796** STEDMAN *Surinam* II. xvii. 32 The breast [of the paroquet] is of a leaden hue, the belly lilac. **1816** C'TESS HARDWICKE in *Two Noble Lives* I. 53 Elizabeth wore white and silver, I wore layloc and silver. **1847** TENNYSON *Princess* II. 3 She brought us Academic silks, in hue The lilac.

b. *attrib.*, passing into *adj.* Of the colour of lilac blossom.

1801 MAR. EDGEWORTH *Contrast* (1832) 114 It will spoil my lilac ribbons. **1854–6** PATMORE *Angel in Ho.* x. i. 5 The little lilac glove. **1864** TENNYSON *Grandmother* xv, So Willy and I were wedded: I wore a lilac gown. **1882** *Garden* 1 Apr. 210/1 A beautiful alpine Crowfoot, with delicate lilac flowers.

c. The scent of lilac, esp. as used in cosmetics, etc.

1895 *Montgomery Ward Catal.* 259/3 Perfumes... White Lilac. **1898** *Illustr. London News* 1 Jan. 34 (Advt.), Lance Perfumes..acacia, violet, lilac..price one shilling. *c* **1938** *Fortnum & Mason Price List* 54/1 Soaps..Lilac. **1951** A. LANGENBACH *Wines Germany* xxviii. 126 The finest Rheingau growths..have a delicious lilac-like bouquet. **1972** *Guardian* 22 Aug. 9/4 Jackson's have revived the floral perfumes... The current range comprises sweetpea..purple lilac, and jonquil.

3. *attrib.* and *Comb.*, as ***lilac-ambush***, ***-blossom***, ***-bush***, ***-flower***, ***-shade***, ***-time***, ***-tree***; also, qualifying the names of colours, as ***lilac-blue***, ***-grey***, ***-mauve***, ***-pink***, ***-purple***; parasynthetic, as ***lilac-coloured***, ***-headed***, ***-tinted*** adjs.; **lilac-breasted roller**, *Coracias caudata*, a bird found in the southern half of Africa; **lilac moth** (see quot.); **lilac-tide** *nonce-use*, the time when lilac is in bloom.

1842 TENNYSON *Gardener's Dau.* 111 This, yielding, gave into a grassy walk Thro' crowded *lilac-ambush trimly pruned. **1890** O. WILDE *Dorian Gray* ii. 15 Lord Henry..found Dorian Gray burying his face in the great cool *lilac-blossoms. **1974** A. GOODARD *Vienna Pursuit* III. 115 Some lilac blossom had been blown..across the pavement. **1851** *B'ham & Midl. Gardener's Mag.* May 52 Bunches of delicate *lilac-blue..flowers. **1908** HAAGNER & IVY *Sk. S. Afr. Bird-Life* 29 The beautiful *Lilac-breasted Roller (*C[oracias] caudatus*) is green, blue and brown, with the breast of a purplish-lilac tinge with white shaft-streaks, and the abdomen blue... This bird is not uncommon in the Transvaal bushveld. **1947** J. STEVENSON-HAMILTON *Wild Life S. Afr.* xxxiv. 293 The bright plumage..of the lilac-breasted roller. **1971** *Country Life* 28 Oct. 1126/2 [In Ethiopia] I first saw those gorgeously-coloured birds, the lilac-breasted rollers. **1862** LOWELL *Biglow P.* Ser. II, vi. 87 The catbird in the *laylock-bush is loud. **1766** AMORY *Buncle* (1770) IV. 97 You must write with this *lilach-coloured liquor. **1880** BLACK *White Wings* xx, The silent, glassy, *lilac-grey sea. **1802** G. BARRINGTON *Hist. N.S. Wales* ix. 344 The beautiful *lilac-headed parroquet. **1868** WOOD *Homes without H.* xiv. 296 The little chocolate-coloured moth called the *Lilac Moth (*Lazotænia ribeana*). **1882** *Garden* 7 Oct. 307/3 Pelargoniums..Lady Sheffield, *lilac-pink. *Ibid.* 1 Apr. 223/2 A compact rosette of a rich *lilac-purple. **1849** M. ARNOLD *Modern Sappho* i, Nothing stirs on the lawn but the quick *lilac-shade. **1765** H. WALPOLE *Let. to Earl Hertford* 12 May, Though in all the bloom of my passion, *lilac-tide, I have not been at Strawberry this fortnight. **1906** W. ROBINSON *Eng. Flower Garden* (ed. 10) 881/1 To have a good *Lilac-time it is essential to have the newer varieties raised in France. **1910** A. NOYES *Barrel Organ* in *Coll. Poems* I. 129 Go down to Kew in lilac-time (it isn't far from London!). **1847–9** TODD *Cycl. Anat.* IV. 126/2 *Lilac-tinted spots. **1625** BACON *Ess.*, *Gardens* (Arb.) 556 The *Lelacke Tree. **1650** *Surv. Non-such Palace*, *Archæol.* V. 434 A fountaine of white marble..set round with six trees called lelack trees.

lilaceous (laɪˈleɪʃəs), *a.* [f. LILAC + -EOUS.] Of or belonging to a lilac colour.

1855 in MAYNE *Expos. Lex.* **1890** *Harper's Mag.* Nov. 862/1 A beautiful lilaceous blue. *Ibid.* 864/2.

lilacine (ˈlaɪləsɪn). *Chem.* Also **lilacin**. [f. LILAC + -INE. Cf. F. *lilacine.*] A crystalline substance obtained from the lilac, *Syringa vulgaris*; now called SYRINGIN.

1842 *Pharmaceutical Jrnl.* I. 557 The lilacine appears to be combined in the lilac with malic acid. **1844** in HOBLYN *Dict. Med. Terms*; and in recent Dicts.

lilacky (ˈlaɪləkɪ), *a.* Also **lilacy**. [f. LILAC 2.] Of a lilac colour.

1863 QUEEN VICTORIA *Let.* 23 Dec. in R. Fulford *Dearest Mama* (1968) 281 The sky is a leaden, lilacy blue—with no white clouds. **1910** *Westm. Gaz.* 19 Feb. 2/2 Walls on walls of lilacky limestone.

lilalite. *Min.* [f. F. *lilas* lilac + -LITE.] An obsolete synonym of LEPIDOLITE.

1796 KIRWAN *Elem. Min.* (ed. 2) I. 208 Lepidolite—Lilalite of some.

†**lilburne.** *Obs. rare*⁻¹. A lubber.

a **1553** UDALL *Royster D.* III. iii. (Arb.) 44 Ye are suche a calfe, suche an asse, suche a blocke, Such a lilburne, such a hoball, such a lobcocke.

†**lile**, *sb. Obs.* [f. name of *Lille* in France. Cf. LISLE.] ?A kind of grogram (more fully ***lile grogram***).

1640 in Noorthouck *Lond.* (1773) 843/1 Stuffs, liles, broad or narrow, the piece not above 15 yards, 2*d.* **1660** *Act 12 Chas. II*, c. 4 Sched. s.v. *Buffin*, Buffins, Mocadoes, & Lile Grograns narrow the single peece..iij. *li.* **1674** JEAKE *Arith.* (1696) 65 Lile Grograins.

lile (laɪl), *a.* and *adv. dial.* [app. repr. a contraction of ON. *lītell*, *lītl-* LITTLE: cf. mod.Sw. *lilla*, Da. *lille.*] Little.

1633 *King & Poore N. Man* 89 Full lile we know his hard griefe of mind. **1848** MRS. GASKELL *M. Barton* vii. (1882) 17/1 He'll have a hard death, poor lile fellow. **1863** —— *Sylvia's L.* Novels (1874) 127, I trust to thee to look after the lile lass.

lile: see LILLE *v.* and LILY.

liliaceous (lɪlɪˈeɪʃəs), *a.* Also 8 *erron.* **lilaceous**. [f. L. *līliāceus*, f. *līlium* lily: see -ACEOUS.] Pertaining to, or characteristic of, lilies or the order *Liliaceæ*; lily-like.

1731 BAILEY vol. II, *Liliaceous*, of, pertaining to, or like lilies, of the lily kind. **1775** MASSON in *Phil. Trans.* LXVI. 285 [A flower] of the lilaceous kind, with a long spike of pendulous flowers, of a greenish azure colour..(this is *ixia viridis*). **1785** MARTYN *Rousseau's Bot.* i. (1794) 25 The calyx..is wanting in the greater part of the liliaceous tribe. **1845** DARWIN *Voy. Nat.* ii. (1852) 32 The large liliaceous plants which shaded the streamlets. *a* **1856** H. MILLER *Test. Rocks* ii. (1857) 95 Aquatic plants and liliaceous roots.

lilial (ˈlɪlɪəl), *a.* and *sb. Bot.* [ad. mod.L. *līliālis*, f. *līlium* LILY.] **a.** *adj.* Only in ***lilial alliance***: In Lindley's classification, the 'alliance' or group of orders which includes the *Liliaceæ*. **b.** *sb.* A member of this alliance.

1846 LINDLEY *Veg. Kingd.* 195 [Endogens.] Alliance XVI. Liliales.—The Lilial Alliance... Natural Orders of Lilials. **1854** A. ADAMS, etc. *Man. Nat. Hist.* 501, II. Order—Lilials (Liliales).

†**liliated**, *a.* [f. L. *līlium* LILY + -ATE³ + -ED¹.] Embellished with the fleur-de-lis of France.

1643 PRYNNE *Sov. Power Parl.* App. 156 When he is girded by the King [of France] with the Liliated sword.

Lilibolaro, obs. form of LILLIBULLERO.

lilie, obs. form of LILY.

lilied (ˈlɪlɪd), *a.* Also 6–7 **lillied**, 7 **lily'd**. [f. LILY + -ED².]

1. Resembling a lily in fairness of complexion.

1614 SYLVESTER *Bethulia's Rescue* IV. 372 Her ruddy round Cheeks seem'd to be composed Of Roses Lillied, or of Lillies Rosed. **1627–77** FELTHAM *Resolves* I. xxxvii. 62 The modest sweetness of a lilied face. **1652** BENLOWES *Theoph.* To my *Jamie*, The lily'd breasts with violets vein'd. **1761** *Poetry* in *Ann. Reg.* 234 Did they..Wear ruffs too small..Or, over lilied, add a little rose. **1822** J. WILSON *Lights & Shadows Scott. Life* 4 She was like the fairest of all the lilied brood. **1840** BROWNING *Sordello* I. 266 Of just-tinged marble, like Eve's lilied flesh.

2. Covered with or abounding with lilies.

a **1633** MILTON *Arcades* 97 Nymphs and Shepherds dance no more By sandy Ladons Lillied banks. **1744** AKENSIDE *Pleas. Imag.* II. 287 O'er the lilied vale Clearer than glass it flow'd. *a* **1803** BEATTIE *Ode to Peace* III. iii, Along the lilied lawn the nymphs advance. **1876** GEO. ELIOT *Dan. Der.* I. ix. 65 Its lilied pool and grassy acres specked with deer.

b. Bearing or embellished with the heraldic lilies or fleur-de-lis.

1795 SOUTHEY *Joan of Arc* VIII. 617 And plant the lilied flag Victorious on yon tower. **1814** S. ROGERS *Jacquel.* 88 The lilied banners streaming bright. **1814** CARY *Dante*, *Par.* VI. 116 The fond belief, that heav'n Will truck its armour for his lilied shield. **1884** GARDINER *Hist. Eng.* VII. lxx. 195 The lilied banner of France.

liliform (ˈlɪlɪfɔːm), *a.* [f. LILY + -FORM.] Having the form or shape of a lily.

1856 *Jrnl. Brit. Archæol. Assoc.* XII. 73 Pateræ of red glazed ware..with broad flattened rims of tasselled or liliform patterns were discovered at the same time.

lilipi (ˈlɪlɪpɪ). Chiefly *N.Z. Hist.* Also **lilipu**, **lillipe**, **lillip(p)ee**. [Origin unknown.] (See quot. 1861.)

In quot. 1830, from a W. African context, *lilipee* may be some other word.

1830 H. CROW *Mem.* ix. 146 For the sick we provided strong soups and middle messes, prepared from mutton, goats'-flesh, fowls, &c. to which were added sago and lilipees. **1860** *Taranaki Punch* I. IV. 8 Something..that, although it is *not* lilipi yet, when pronounced by our old friend.., sounds very like it, namely 'lilly pay'. **1861** J. VON HAAST *Rep. Topogr. & Geol. Explor. Nelson Province* i. 22 [We confined] ourselves to a small pot of lillipe (or boiled flour) twice a day. **1874** L. J. KENNAWAY *Crusts* 147 The poor children..lived principally on heavy bread and '*lillippee*', (a mixture nothing more nor less than paper-hanging paste). **1880** J. C. CRAWFORD *Recoll. Trav. N.Z. & Austral.* 99 One old lady..presented us with a dish of *lillipee*, which is simply flour and water. **1915** J. HAY *Reminisc. Earliest Canterbury* i. 34 They [*sc.* the Maoris] were very fond..of wheat and sugar boiled together, to which they gave the name of 'Lilipu'.

Liliput, Liliputian: see LILLIPUT, -IAN.

lilium (ˈlɪlɪəm). [L. *līlium*: see LILY. Adopted by Linnæus in his *Species Plantarum* (1753) I. 302 as the name of a genus.] = LILY 1.

1902 *Westm. Gaz.* 10 Dec. 10/1 Of all flowers none are affected by frost so much as roses,..violets, and liliums. **1903** *Ibid.* 26 Nov. 12/1 White liliums are fetching 4s. a bunch. **1923** *Chambers's Jrnl.* Dec. 786/2 The finest liliums and choice gladioli grow superbly. **1958** M. WEST *Second Victory* vi. 91 Hot-house blooms that must have come from a dozen private homes—cyclamen, orchids, liliums and azaleas. **1970** *Lily Year Bk.* XXXIII. 88 [In Australia] at least four leading lilium nurserymen of a decade ago no longer distribute lilium bulbs in appreciable numbers.

lill (lɪl), *sb.*¹ *Sc.* [Cf. Du. *lul.*] = LILT *sb.* 4.

1721 RAMSAY *Poems* Gloss. (1760), *Lills*, the holes of a wind-instrument of music. **1788** in *R. Galloway's Poems* 154 Go on, then, Galloway, go on, To touch the lill, and sound the drone. **1824** SCOTT *Redgauntlet* Let. xi, He..could play weel on the pipes;..and he had the finest finger for the back-lill [*c*1832 back-lilt] between Berwick and Carlisle.

lill (lɪl), *sb.*² A pin of a very small size.

1882 BECK *Draper's Dict.*, *Lills*, a very small pin; probably an abbreviation of Lilliputian. *Mod. Advt.*, Lills... Pins with perfect Solid Heads.

lill, *sb.*³ *slang.* See LIL *sb.*

†**lill**, *v. Obs.* Forms: 6 lil, lylle, 6–7 lill, (7 lell). [Onomatopœic: cf. LOLL *v.*] *trans.* To loll or hang (the tongue) *out* (rarely *forth*). Also (*rarely*) *intr.* said of the tongue.

1530 PALSGR. 611/1, I lylle out the tonge, as a beest dothe that is chafed, *je hallette*. **1587** MASCALL *Govt. Cattle* (1627) 15 Ye shall see him lil and hold out his tongue. **1590** SPENSER *F.Q.* I. v. 34 Cerberus..lilled forth his bloody flaming tong. **1591** SYLVESTER *Du Bartas* I. v. 228 As the Wood-pecker, his long tongue doth lill Out of the clov'n pipe of his horny bill To catch the Emets. **1600** HOLLAND *Livy* VII. x. 255 Scornfully lelling and blaring out his tongue. **1611** FLORIO, *Lucerna*..Also the Lantern-fish, which lilling foorth his tongue, yeelds a great blaze or light. *Ibid.* s.v. *Lingua*, Like a tongue lilling out of the mouth. **1622** MABBE tr. *Aleman's Guzman d'Alf.* II. 219 They shall..lill out their tongue, like a Calfe. **1656** W. D. tr. *Comenius' Gate Lat. Unl.* ¶651 A scorner sheweth his slightings and scorns..by distorting his lips, lilling out his tongue [etc.]. **1893** *Wiltsh. Gloss.*, *Lill*, to pant as a dog.

lilla-, lillebullero: see LILLIBULLERO.

†**lille**, *v. Obs.* In 3 lylle, 5 lile. [Cf. Du. *lillen* to tremble, quiver.] *intr.* ? To quiver.

13.. *E.E. Allit. P.* C. 447 Þe wyz..Loked alofte on þe lef þat lylled grene.

Lille (liːl), *sb.* The name of a city in the Nord department of France, used *attrib.* to designate a kind of pillow or bobbin lace.

1865 F. B. PALLISER *Hist. Lace* xvi. 211 The semé of little square dots on the ground—one of the characteristics of Lille lace—is still retained. **1900** E. JACKSON *Hist. Hand-Made Lace* 176 Lille laces have always been favourites in England, the black especially. **1953** M. POWYS *Lace & Lace-Making* iv. 31 The Lille lace edgings generally have a straight edge. **1960** *Connoisseur's Handbk. Antique Collecting* 164/1 *Lille lace*, pillow lace very popular in later 18th cent. England, made sometimes in black, but never as a dress lace.

Lillet (ˈliːleɪ). Also **Kina Lillet**. The proprietary name of a French aperitif; also, a glass of this wine.

1930 H. CRADDOCK *Savoy Cocktail Bk.* 41 *Campden Cocktail*, ½ Dry Gin. ¼ Cointreau. ¼ Kina Lillet. **1951** R. POSTGATE *Plain Man's Guide to Wine* iii. 59 St. Raphael is slightly sweeter, Byrrh and Lillet slightly sharper. **1960** *New Yorker* 29 Oct. 51/2 Sipping a Lillet-and-gin. **1972** N. FREELING *Long Silence* I. 59 Now—Campari, Lillet, Chambéry? **1973** *Vogue* Jan. 85/2 A twist of orange with Lillet.

†**lill for loll**, *phr. Obs.* Also 5 lyl for lal, 6 lill for law. [Possibly a jingling perversion of some phrase containing the OE. *læl* bruise; see quot.

*c*1000. For the jingle cf. *tit for tat*.] ***to give***, etc. ***lill for loll***: to retaliate.

[*c* **1000** ÆLFRIC *Exod.* xxi. 25 Sylle lif wið life.. wunde wið wunde, læl wið læle.] *c* **1425** WYNTOUN *Cron.* III. ii. 263 Thai come onone To bind and led away Sampsone, And to quyt hym lyl for lal [*v.r.* lill for law]. **1535** STEWART *Cron. Scot.* (1858) II. 336 Scho murdreist this ilk king: And so that tyme scho plaid him lill for law. **1581** J. BELL *Haddon's Answ. Osor.* 277 b, Why may not I as well wt the like lavishnes of tongue, geve lill for loll? **1639** SMYTH *Hund. Berkeley* (1885) III. 33 Lill for loll. Id est, one for another: as good as hee brought.

lillianite ('lɪlɪənaɪt). *Min.* [Named by Keller, 1889, from the *Lillian* mine, Colorado, its locality: see -ITE.] A steel-coloured sulphide of bismuth and lead.

1892 DANA *Min.* 130.

Lillibullero (lɪlɪbə'lɪərəʊ). Forms: 7 **lilli burlero, Lilly Burleighre**, 8 **lilibolaro, lille-, lilla-**, 8– **lillibullero**. [Unmeaning.] Part of the refrain (hence, the name and the tune) of a song ridiculing the Irish, popular about 1688.

1688 *Pol. Ballads* (1860) I. 275 Ho! broder Teague, dost hear de decree? Lilli Burlero, bullen a-la Dat we shall have a new deputie. **1689** *Diary* in *Topographer* (1790) 32 The Chimes at St. Michaels.. haveing for some time been made to strike Lilli Burlero. **1697** VANBRUGH *Æsop* v. 66 Dol, de tol dol, dol dol, de tol dol: Lilly Burleighre's lodg'd in a Bough. **1714** GAY *Sheph. Week* Sat. 116 He sung of Taffey Welch. and Sawney Scot, Lille-bullero, and the Irish Trot. **1759** STERNE *Tr. Shandy* II. ii, He.. accustomed himself.. to whistle the *Lillabullero*. **1760** H. WALPOLE *Let. to Sir D. Dalrymple* 3 Feb., The mob will never sing lillibullero but in opposition to some other mob. **1849** MACAULAY *Hist. Eng.* ix. (ed. 5) II. 428 One of the characteristics of the good old soldier is his trick of whistling Lillibullero.

Hence **lillibu'llero** *v.*, *trans.* (*nonce-wd.*) to sing 'lillibullero' over.

1762 STERNE *Tr. Shandy* V. iii, My father managed his affliction otherwise.. for he neither wept it away.. nor did he.. rhyme it, or lillabullero it.

lillie, lillied, obs. forms of LILY, LILIED.

lillipe, lillip(p)ee, varr. LILIPI.

Lilliput ('lɪlɪpʌt). The name of an imaginary country in *Gulliver's Travels* (1726), peopled by pygmies six inches high. Used *attrib.* = diminutive. Occas. *sb.*, a person of diminutive size, a child.

1867 WHITMAN *Carol of Harvest* 3 The lilliput, countless armies of the grass. **1879** J. BURROUGHS *Locusts and W. Honey* (1884) 69 One of these Lilliput frogs.. leaped near me. **1890** *Daily News* 17 Dec. 2/1 It is easy enough to decide on what to give the Lilliputs [*sc.* children].

Lilliputian (lɪlɪpjuːʃ(ɪ)ən), *sb.* and *a.* Also **Liliputian.** [f. LILLIPUT + -IAN.]

A. *sb.* An inhabitant of LILLIPUT; hence, a person of diminutive size, character, or mind.

1726 SWIFT *Gulliver* I. iii, etc. **1727** FIELDING *Love Sev. Masques* III. x, Oh, gemini! would I had been born a Lilliputian! **1808** SCOTT *Dryden's Wks.* (1883) IV. 5 The other personages of the drama sink into Lilliputians beside the gigantic Almanzor. **1884** *Fortn. Rev.* Mar. 326 The antics of these official Lilliputians.

B. *adj.* Of or pertaining to Lilliput or its inhabitants; hence, of diminutive size; petty.

1726 SWIFT *Gulliver* I. v, The Lilliputian tongue. **1728** MORGAN *Algiers* II. v. 319 Good substantial Leagues dwindling into even Liliputian Furlongs. *a* **1764** LLOYD *New-River Head* Poet. Wks. 1774 II. 64 The Lilliputian Statesmen rise To malice of gigantic size. **1808** SCOTT in Lockhart *Life* (1869) III. xviii. 150 Petty conquests or Liliputian expeditions. **1842** DICKENS *Amer. Notes* (1850) 33/1 The stairs are of lilliputian measurement, fitted to their tiny strides. **1878** EMERSON *Misc. Papers, Sov. Ethics* Wks. (Bohn) III. 383 In America.. our institutions, our politics.. have fostered a self-reliance which is small, liliputian, full of fuss and bustle. **1884** *Garden. Illustr.* 8 Nov. 427/1 The charming little *Erysimum pumilum*.. is often called the Lilliputian Wallflower.

Hence **Lilli'putianize** *v.*, to dwarf. **Lilliputianized** *ppl. a.*, **Lilliputianizing** *vbl. sb.*

1885 CLARK RUSSELL *Strange Voy.* I. xix. 282 The satirical Lilliputianizing of the stately Margaret Edwards went against the grain. **1889** *Macm. Mag.* Oct. 419/2 The Liliputianized figures of her crew making a very toy of the little fabric. **1890** CLARK RUSSELL *Ocean Trag.* I. xi. 230 Liliputianised as he was [by distance].

lillite ('lɪlaɪt). *Min.* [Named by Reuss, 1857, after —— von *Lill*: see -ITE.] A hydrous silicate of iron, similar in appearance to glauconite.

1865 WATTS *Dict. Chem.* III. 695 *Lillite*, a silicate of iron from Przibram in Bohemia... It is a dull, amorphous, earthy substance of blackish-green colour.

lilly, obs. form of LILY.

lilly-low ('lɪlɪləʊ). *dial.* A playful variation (used in speaking to children) of LOW *sb.*, blaze.

1674–91 RAY *N.C. Words* 47 A *Lilly-low*,.. a comfortable Blaze. **1877** *N.W. Linc. Gloss.*, *Lillylow*, a bright flame. 'When we got there, there was five corn-stacks all in a lilly-low'. **1890** W. A. WALLACE *Only a Sister?* 360 For lily-lows is nought to it for burning.

lilly-pilly. Also **lilli-pilli.** An Australian evergreen tree, *Eugenia* (or *Acmena*) *smithii*, of the family Myrtaceæ, or the timber obtained from it. Also *attrib.*

1860 G. BENNETT *Gatherings Nat. Austral.* xvii. 327 The Lillipilly-trees, as they are named by the colonists, consist of several species of Acmena. **1879** J. E. TENISON-WOODS in *Proc. Linnean Soc. N.S. Wales* IV. 134 *Eugenia Smithii*, or Lillipilli. **1881** *Off. Rec. Sydney Internat. Exhib. 1879* 723 Lilly Pilly. *Eugenia Smithii*... Forms a beautiful shrub when cut back... The wood makes good axe handles. **1890** 'LYTH' *Golden South* 201 Luxurious foliage of.. lily-pilly, and other native trees. **1936** F. CLUNE *Roaming round Darling* iii. 26 In 1881 King George V planted a lillipilli-tree. **1944** *Living off Land* ii. 45 Lilly-pilly or Brush Cherry. **1946** *Coast to Coast 1945* 56 A tree-fern, maidenhair in the mossy banks, and a clump of lilli-pillis marked the dell. **1965** *Austral. Encycl.* III. 412/1 *Acmena* is a small genus containing the common lilly-pilly (*A. smithii*), which is widely spread in eastern Australia along rivers and streams and in the rain-forests... It has small terminal sprays of insignificant greenish flowers followed by purplish to white fruits, and is much cultivated as a hedge plant. **1965** *Courier-Mail* (Brisbane) 16 Nov. 20 The feathered folk in the lilipillies of the great gully below began to welcome Piccaninny Daylight.

Li-Lo ('laɪləʊ). Also **Lilo, lilo.** [f. *to lie low*.] The proprietary name of a type of air-bed or inflatable rubber mattress. Also *fig.*

1936 *Trade Marks Jrnl.* 16 Sept. 1150 Li-Lo... Air-beds, air-pillows and air-pillow-bags, all made principally of india-rubber. P. B. Cow & Company Limited,.. London,.. manufacturers. **1939** 'N. SHUTE' *What happened to Corbetts* i. 1 Sophie their nurse was lying on a Li-Lo on the oil-stained floor, covered with an eiderdown. **1949** O. LANCASTER *Drayneflete Revealed* 63 And Dido on her lilo à sa proie attachée. **1954** W. NOYCE *South Col* iv. 58 The really experienced expeditioners, Ed and George Lowe, had their Li-Los inflated. **1960** V. GIELGUD *To Bed at Noon* I. iv. 27 If the chairs were no more than adequate there were lilos and cushions in abundance. **1969** *Listener* 24 July 114/3 We've been looking at grand pianos... This is one likely spot where a nudist with an eye to the main chance might well secrete himself. A lilo across the wires. **1972** N. BENTLEY *Events of that Week* 39, I left Theresa on a Li-lo and put my sandals on. **1973** *Guardian* 13 Oct. 10/1 The social service Lilo has become too easy to loll on.

lilt (lɪlt), *sb.* [app. f. LILT *v.*]

1. A song or tune, *esp.* one of a cheerful or merry character. Chiefly *Sc.*

1728 RAMSAY *Ep. to W. Starrat* 26 The blythest lilts that e'er my lugs heard sung. **17..** *Jacobite Relics* (1821) II. 193 Is't some words ye've learnt by rote, Or a lilt o' dool and sorrow? **1842** S. LOVER *Handy Andy* v. 52 To the tune of a well known rollicking Irish lilt. **1850** KINGSLEY *Alt. Locke* xli. (1874) 308 Hark to the grand lilt of the 'Good Time Coming!' **1874** BURNAND *My time* xvi. 133 A peasant.. suddenly takes up a pipe.. and commences to play a lilt.

2. The rhythmical cadence or 'swing' of a tune or of verse. Chiefly *literary*.

1840 CARLYLE *Heroes* (1858) 253 It proceeds as by a chant. .. One reads along naturally with a sort of *lilt*. **1869** FARRAR *Fam. Speech* iii. (1873) 91 The sonorous lilt of the Greek Epic verse contrasts.. with the grave unbending stateliness of the Hebrew. **1882** STEVENSON *Fam. Stud.* 289 The lines go with a lilt, and sing themselves to music of their own.

fig. **1870** LOWELL *Study Wind.* 336 This faculty of hitting the precise lilt of thought is a rare gift. **1879** TROLLOPE *Thackeray* 75 An eagerness of description, a lilt, if I may so call it, in the progress of the narrative.

3. A springing action; a light, springing step.

1869 A. C. GIBSON *Folk-sp. Cumberld.* 37 Wid a lilt iv her step an' a glent iv her e'e. **1884** *Daily News* 23 Sept. 6/1 A sort of 'lilt' in the gait, which is by no means graceful.

4. (See quot.) ? *Obs.* Cf. LILL *sb.*[1]

1776 HERD *Coll. Songs* II. 258 Gloss., *Lilts*, the holes of a wind instrument of musick; hence Lilt up a spring. *c* **1832** [see LILL *sb.*[1] quot. 1824].

5. *Comb.*, as ***lilt-like*** adj.

1866 *Daily Tel.* 10 Mar. 246/3 Many of the songs have that lilt-like quality which almost makes them sing themselves.

lilt (lɪlt), *v. Sc.*, *north. dial.*, and *literary*. Also 4 **lulte**, 6 **lylt.** [ME. *lulte* (ü), of obscure origin; perh. cogn. w. Du., LG. *lul*, pipe (cf. LILT-PIPE); Skeat compares Norw. *lilla* to sing.]

1. *trans.* †**a.** To sound (an alarum); to lift up (the voice). *Obs.* **b.** To sing cheerfully or merrily. Also, to strike *up* (a song); to 'tune *up*' (the pipes). Also with *out*.

13.. *E.E. Allit. P.* A. 1207 Loude alarom vpon launde lulted was þenne. **1513** DOUGLAS *Æneis* VII. ix. 88 In ane bowand horne.. A feindlych hellis voce scho lyltis schyll [L. *Tartaream intendit vocem*]. **17..** RAMSAY *Ep. Mr. Gay*, Lilt up your pipes, and rise aboon Your *Trivia* and your moorland tune. **1722** —— *Three Bonnets* IV. 192 Lilt up a sang. **1725** —— *Gent. Sheph.* II. iv, Rosie lilts sweetly the 'Milking the ewes'. *Ibid.* IV. i, Weel liltet, Bauldy, that's a dainty sang. *Ibid.* V. iii, What shepherd's whistle winna lilt the spring? **1847** EMILY BRONTE *Wuthering Heights* xxi. 182 She tripped merrily on, lilting a tune to supply the lack of conversation. **1878** MISS TYTLER *Scotch Firs* 136 An old song lilted in a clear shrill voice. **1883** G. C. DAVIES *Norfolk Broads & Rivers* vi. (1884) 47 Reed-wrens lilting some sweet fragment of song. **1916** A. BENNETT *Lion's Share* xxv. 191 Musa lilted out the delicate, gay phrases of Debussy.

2. *intr.* To sing cheerfully or merrily; to sing with a lilt or merry 'swing'.

1786 BURNS *Ordination* iii, Mak haste an' turn king David owre, An' lilt wi' holy clangor. **1816** SCOTT *Antiq.* xxii, Jenny, whose shrill voice I have heard this half hour lilting in the Tartarean regions of the kitchen. **1842** S. LOVER *Handy Andy* xviii, Murphy, who presided in the cart full of fiddlers like a leader in an orchestra.. shouted 'Now.. rasp and lilt away, boys!' **1901** *Blackw. Mag.* July 24/1 A voice came lilting up the den very sweetly.

3. *north. dial.* 'To move with a lively action' (Dickinson & Prevost *Cumbld. Gloss.* 1899).

1834 WORDSW. *Redbreast* 70 Whether the bird flit here or there, O'er table *lilt*, or perch on chair. **1847** HALLIWELL, *Lilt*, to jerk or spring; to do anything cleverly or quickly. *North.* **1901** KIPLING *Traffics & Discov.* (1904) 79 He lilted a little on his feet when he was pleased. *Ibid.* 80 He went to England, and he became a young man, and back he came, lilting a little in his walk.

4. ***to lilt it out*** (Sc.): to toss off one's liquor.

1721 RAMSAY *Up in Air* iv, Tilt it, lads, and lilt it out.

lilting ('lɪltɪŋ), *vbl. sb.* [f. LILT *v.* + -ING[1].] The action of LILT *v*; cheerful or merry singing.

1719 D'URFEY *Pills* VI. 350 Let's awa' to the Wedding, For there will be Lilting there. *c* **1750** MISS ELIOT *Song, Flowers of Forest* i, I've heard the lilting at our yowe-milking, Lasses a lilting before the dawn of day.

Hence †**lilting-horn**, a kind of trumpet. *Obs.*

c **1384** CHAUCER *H. Fame* III. 133 (Fairfax MS.) And many flowte and liltyng horne [*v.rr.* lytelyng, lyltyng, litelynge]. **14..** *Voc.* in Wr.-Wülcker 593/21 *Lituus*, a lyltynghorn [*printed* lylkynghorn].

'lilting, *ppl. a.* [f. LILT *v.* + -ING[2].] Cheerfully singing; (of song, metre, etc.) characterized by a rhythmical 'swing' or cadence. Also of one's gait: (sense 3 of vb.).

1800 S. T. COLERIDGE *Death Wallenst.* Transl. Pref., This is written.. in the same *lilting* metre (if that expression may be permitted) with the second Eclogue of Spencer's Shepherd's Calendar. **1862** MERIVALE *Rom. Emp.* (1865) VI. liv. 409 He was a proficient in the lilting metre.. of his tutor. **1865** *Daily Tel.* 8 Nov. 4/5 The lilting burden of 'Lero, lero, lillibullero, lero, lero, bullen-a-la'. **1900** J. G. FRAZER *Pausanias* etc. 380 The flute broke into a light lilting air. **1903** *Longman's Mag.* Jan. 271 Swinging down the street with an easy lilting stride.. marched two Englishmen, soldiers both. **1965** E. BHAVNANI *Dance in India* xvi. 208 In a lilting change of movements, boys and girls hold hands or link arms and dance round and round in a circle.

Hence **'liltingness.**

1884 J. BURROUGHS *Birds & Poets* 121 The bobolink.. has .. on the high grass lands.. quite a different strain.. running off with more sparkle and liltingness.

†**lilt-pipe.** *Obs.* [? f. LILT *v.*; cf. Du. *lullepijp* bagpipe.] ? A bagpipe.

c **1450** HOLLAND *Howlat* 761 The lilt pype, and the lute.

lily ('lɪlɪ). Forms: 1, 3–5 **lilie**, 4 **lely, leli, lilye, luly**, 4–5 **lylye, lyle**, 4–6 **lely**, 5 **lylie, lylle, lelly, lele**, 5–6 **lyl(l)y**, 5–8 **lilly**, 6 **lile**, 6–7 **lillie, lyllie**, 8– **lily.** *Plural.* 1 **lilian**, 2 **lilien**, 5 **lilijs, -iis, lylly(e)s, lylyes, lelyes**, 6 *Sc.* **lilleis**, 6–8 **lillies**, 7 **lyllies**, 8 **lilys**, 4– **lilies.** [OE. *lilie* wk. fem., ad. L. *līlium*, a. Gr. *λείριον*.

The L. word has passed into nearly all the European langs.: OS. *lilli*, Du. *lelie*, OHG. *lilja, liljo* (MHG. *lilje, gilge*, mod.G. *lilie*), ON. *lilia* (Sw. *lilja*, Da. *lilie*; F. *lis* (cf. *fleur-de-lis*), Pr. *lilis, liris* (:—popular L. **līlius*), Sp., Pg. *lirio*, It. *giglio*.]

A. *sb.* **1. a.** Any plant (or its flower) of the genus *Lilium* (N.O. *Liliaceæ*) of bulbous herbs bearing at the top of a tall slender stem large showy flowers of white, reddish, or purplish colour, often marked with dark spots on the inside; *esp.* (without qualification) *L. candidum*, the White or Madonna Lily (cf. b), which grows wild in some Eastern countries, and has from early times been cultivated in gardens; it is a type of whiteness or purity.

971 *Blickl. Hom.* 7 Seo hwitnes þære lilian scineþ on þe. *c* **1000** *Sax. Leechd.* II. 90 Drince he lilian wyrttruman awylledne on wine oððe on ealað. *a* **1225** *Leg. Kath.* 1433 Se rudie & se reade ilitet eauereach leor as lilie ileid to rose. *c* **1386** CHAUCER *Doctor's T.* 32 As she [Nature] kan peynte a lilie whit And reed a Rose. **1398** TREVISA *Barth. De P.R.* XVII. xci. (1495) 658 The lely is an herbe wyth a whyte flour and though the leuys of the floure be whyte yet wythin shyneth the lyknesse of golde. *a* **1400–50** *Alexander* 3902 Leons quyte as lylly. *c* **1400** *Lanfranc's Cirurg.* 200 þou schalt make þe lyme neische wiþ oile of lilie. *c* **1420** *Anturs of Arth.* xiii, I was radder of rode þene rose in þe rone, My lere as þe lele, louched one highte. **1562** TURNER *Herbal* II. 38 The Lily hath a long stalk... The flour is excedyng white. **1634** MILTON *Comus* 862 In twisted braids of Lillies knitting The loose train of thy amber-dropping hair. **1704** POPE *Autumn* 26 For her, the lillies hang their heads and die. **1820** SHELLEY *Sensit. Plant* 33 The wand-like lily, which lifted up,.. its moonlight-coloured cup.

b. With qualification, applied to: (*a*) various other plants of the genus *Lilium* or N.O. *Liliaceæ*, the qualifying word indicating the colour, appearance, habitat, etc.; e.g. *flax, martagon, orange, panther, Persian, St. Bruno's, tiger, Turk's cap lily* (see the first element); (*b*) certain allied plants, esp. of N.O. *Amaryllidaceæ*, e.g. *belladonna calla, gold, Guernsey, ixia, Jacobæa(n, knight's star, lent, lide, Mexican, pond, sword lily* (see the first element); also DAY-LILY, WATER-LILY.

African lily, *Agapanthus umbellatus* (Treas. Bot.). **Atamasco lily**, *Zephyranthes Atamasco*. **yellow lily**, † (*a*) the yellow iris, *Iris Pseudacorus*; (*b*) the daffodil, *Narcissus Pseudonarcissus* (dial.).

1555 EDEN *Decades* 200 An herbe much lyke vnto a yelowe lyllie. **1578** LYTE *Dodoens* II. xlii. 200 The white Lillies be very common not only in this Countrie, but in all places els where in gardens. *Ibid.* xliii. 201 Of the Orenge colour, and redde purple Lillies. *Ibid.* xliv. 202 The wilde Lillie hath a straight rounde stemme set full of long leaues, at the toppe

whereof there grow fayre pleasant floures . . of an old purple or dimme incarnate colour, poudered or dashte with small spottes. *Ibid.* xlvi. 204 The yellowe Lillie non bulbus, his leaues be long and narrow . . flowers much lyke to the other Lillies, of a fainte or Ochre colour yellowe. . . The darke red and purple Lillie non bulbus. **1597** GERARDE *Herbal* I. xciii. 150 *Lilium montanum maius*, the great mountaine Lilly. **1633** JOHNSON *Gerarde's Herbal* I. cvi. 199 The Yellow Mountain Lilly with the spotted floure. **1741** *Compl. Fam.-Piece* II. iii. 374 Fiery Lilly, . . Yellow Asphodel Lilly. **1760** J. LEE *Introd. Bot.* App. 317 African Scarlet Lily, *Amaryllis.* Atamasco Lily, *Amaryllis.* **1882** *Garden* 20 May 356/2 A variety of the African Lily, in which the leaves are marked longitudinally with stripes of yellow.

c. Used in all versions of the Bible to render Heb. *shūshan, shōshan, shōshannāh*, LXX and NT. *κρίνον*.

The Heb. words were prob. used, as the corresponding Arab. *sūsan* still is in Palestine, for all the conspicuous species of lily, lotus (*Nymphæa Lotus*), anemone, ranunculus, tulip, etc. In Cant. v. 13 a red flower appears to be meant. The 'lilies of the field' of Matt. vi. 28 have been variously identified with the red *Anemone coronaria* and with the scarlet Martagon or Turk's Cap lily, both of which are common in Galilee. The herbalists of the 16–17th c. took 'the lily among the thorns' (*lilium inter spinas*) of Cant. ii. 2 to be the honeysuckle: see Coles *Art of Simpling* (1656) 7.

2. lily of (or †**in**) **the valley** († *lily convally, convall lily*, † *May*, † *great park*, or † *wood lily*), a beautiful spring flower, *Convallaria majalis*, having two largish leaves and racemes of white, bell-shaped, fragrant flowers.

The name *lily of the valley* represents the Vulgate *lilium convallium*, a literal translation from the Heb. of Cant. ii. 1. The application to this particular plant is app. due to the German herbalists of the early 16th c.

1538 TURNER *Libellus, Ephimeron* est lilium conuallium grandius, quod angli uocant Great parke lyly. **1548** —— *Names of Herbes* 35 The Poticaries in Germany do name it *Lilium conuallium*; it maye be called in englishe May Lilies. **1563** HYLL *Art Garden.* (1593) 98 The wood Lillie or Lillie of the valley, is a flour meruailous sweete. **1579**, etc. [see CONVALLY]. **1597** GERARD *Herbal* II. lxxxvii. 331 Of Lilly in the valley, or May Lillie. **1728–46** THOMSON *Spring* 444 Where scatter'd wild the lily of the vale Its balmy essence breathes. **1729** [see *lily-bell* in 6]. **1814** WORDSW. *Excursion* IX, That shy plant . . the lily of the vale, That loves the ground. **1840** HOOD *Up Rhine* 221 A wreath of artificial lilies-of-the-valley on her head.

b. *lily-of-the-valley tree* (see quot.).

1885 LADY BRASSEY *The Trades* 30 The beautiful lily-of-the-valley tree (*Clethra arborea*) which bears branches of white flowers, like five or six sprays of lilies-of-the-valley growing from one stalk, and emitting the most delicious scent.

c. The scent of lily of the valley, esp. as used in cosmetics, etc.

1890–91 *T. Eaton & Co. Catal.* Fall & Winter 42/2 Morse's perfumes . . new-mown hay, lily of the valley, 25c. per bottle. **1970** *Guardian* 12 May 9/3 This . . sprightly fragrance with . . notes of carnation, . . lily-of-the-valley and roses.

3. *fig.* **a.** Applied to persons or things of exceptional whiteness, fairness, or purity; e.g. a fair lady; the white of a beautiful complexion (*sing.* and *pl.*; cf. *rose*).

c **1386** CHAUCER *Sec. Nun's T.* 87 The name of seinte Cecile . . It is to seye in englissh heuenes lilie, For pure chastnesse of virginitee. *c* **1440** *York Myst.* xxv. 520 [To Jesus] Hayll! lylly lufsome lemyd with lyght! **1498** ALCOCK *Mons Perfect.* a ii b, The beuteous lylyes of chastyte in body and soule. **1613** SHAKS. *Hen. VIII*, v. v. 62 A Virgin, A most vnspotted Lilly. **1622** WITHER *Fair Virtue* D 7 b, The Lillies oft obtaine Greatest sway, vnlesse a blush Helpe the Roses at a push. **1713** STEELE *Guardian* No. 174 ¶ 5 The gamester-ladies . . wear away their lilies and roses in tedious watching. **1859** TENNYSON *Elaine* 1388 Farewell, fair lily.

b. Used as a term of abuse, esp. of a man to imply lack of masculinity.

1923 G. SAINTSBURY *Second Scrap Bk.* v. 39 But in order once more to consider and console that lily, the Educational Expert, let us turn to 'grind'. **1929** HOSTETTER & BEESLEY *It's a Racket!* 231 *Lily*, an easy victim, exceptionally gullible person. **1930** D. H. LAWRENCE *Nettles* 19 And Mr. Mead, that old old lily Said: 'Gross! coarse! hideous!' **1933** S. SPENDER *Poems* 28 Here the pale lily boys flaunt their bright lips. **1958** J. RAYMOND *England's on Anvil!* 142 In this he differed from men like William ('Cory') Johnson, Oscar Browning, A. C. Benson and the rest of the Eton-and-King's lilies who were such a lush feature of the period.

4. A figure or representation of the flower. **a.** *gen.*

1459 in *Paston Lett.* I. 478, j. pellow of silk the growund white wyth lyllys of blewe. **1464** *Ibid.* III. 433 Item, one box of silver . . chased with liliis. *a* **1586** SIDNEY *Arcadia* III. (1629) 260 Pamela . . was working vpon a purse certaine roses & lillies. **1596** DALRYMPLE tr. *Leslie's Hist. Scot.* II. 134 He eiket to the circle of the croune four lillies of golde wt four goldne signes of the croce. **1714** GAY *Sheph. Week* v. 60 Sometimes, like Wax, she rolls the Butter round, Or with the wooden Lilly prints the Pound.

b. The heraldic fleur-de-lis, esp. with reference to the arms of the old French monarchy (also *golden lilies*); hence, the royal arms of France, the French (Bourbon) dynasty.

a **1352** MINOT *Poems* x. 3 Both þe lely and þe lipard suld gader on a grene. [See note, ed. J. Hall.] **1535** STEWART *Cron. Scot.* (1858) II. 357 In thair armes to weir the reid lillie, Quhilk hes bene ay the king of Frances flour. **1660** DRYDEN *Astræa Redux* 18 We sighed to hear the fair Iberian bride [the Infanta Maria Theresa] Must grow a lily to the Lily's side. **1738** F. WISE *Let. conc. Antiq. Berks* 27 The Emperor of Germany is sometimes stiled The Eagle, and the King of France The Lilly, from the Arms they bear. **1769** GRAY *Ode for Music* iv. 39 Great Edward, with the lilies on his brow From haughty Gallia torn. **1815** J. SCOTT *Vis. Paris* (ed. 2) 48 [A Frenchman—faithful adherent of the Bourbons], took the strangers home to his small cottage, to talk fondly of the reviving lilies. **1843** MACAULAY *Ivry* iv, Fair gentlemen of France, Charge for the golden lilies.

†**c.** The fleur-de-lis which is used to mark the north on a compass. *Obs.*

1613 M. RIDLEY *Magn. Bodies* 12 The Lilly of their compasses was turned alwaies towards the North-pole. **1646** SIR T. BROWNE *Pseud. Ep.* II. ii. 60 If wee place a Needle touched at the foote of tongues or andirons it will obvert . . its lyllie or North point. **1661** PHILIPOTT *Disc. Navig.* in *Harl. Misc.* (1744) II. 328 But, sailing farther, it veers its Lilly towards the West.

d. *pl.* The bound feet of Chinese women, in allusion to their Chinese designation *kin-leen* 'golden water-lilies'. Also (in sing.) *attrib.* So **lily-footed** *a.*

1841 W. B. LANGDON *Descr. Catal. Chinese Collection in Philadelphia* 15 The footstools upon which their 'golden lilies' rest, are covered with embroidered silk. **1886** C. M. YONGE *Chantry House* II. xx. 188 Is he going to wed a fair Chinese with lily feet? **1922** W. S. MAUGHAM *On Chinese Screen* xviii. 72 They rest there for a while on their small feet, their golden lilies, gossiping elegantly. **1933** N. WALN *House of Exile* I. i. 26 We could not walk, as . . Mai-da's mother . . had 'lily' feet. **1937** E. SNOW *Red Star over China* I. ii. 26 Yang Hu-Cheng . . was a two-wife man. The first was the lily-footed wife of his youth.

5. Phr. to *paint* (or *to gild*) *the lily*: to embellish excessively, to add ornament where none is needed.

1595 SHAKS. *John* IV. ii. 11 To gilde refined Gold, to paint the Lilly; To throw a perfume on the Violet, . . Is wastefull, and ridiculous excesse. **1919** H. JENKINS *John Dene of Toronto* vii. 113 'Where's Finlay?' asked Colonel Walton. 'He's painting the lily. . . Seeing how near he can get to this Bergen fellow.' **1928** *Manch. Guardian Weekly* 28 Sept. 243/3 Nature and history have already been so kind to that ancient and charming townlet on the Dart that improvement would be a gilding of the lily. **1935** J. BUCHAN *House of Four Winds* 22 It's rather like painting the lily, you know. **1953** *Manch. Guardian Weekly* 19 Feb. 13/2 While it may seem to be painting the lily, I should like to add somewhat to Mr Alistair Cooke's excellent article. **1958** J. RAYMOND *England's on Anvil!* 15 In Englishing the passage, Peter Motteux . . contrives at once splendidly to gild the lily and tone down the anti-Protestantism. **1968** *Encycl. Brit.* XII. 842/1 The favourite technique of decoration of Mogul jades is insetting with gold and precious stones . . an example of painting the lily that would hardly have commended itself to the Chinese jade carver.

6. *attrib.* and *Comb.*: simple attrib., as *lily-avenue, -bank, -bed, -bloom, -bud, -bulb*, † *crop, -crown, family, -garth, group, -honey, -root, shade*; similative, as *lily-clear, -coloured, -green, -scented, -shaped, -shining, -sweet, -whitening, -yellow* adjs.; *lily-like* adj. and adv.; instrumental and locative, as *lily-cradled, -crowned, -paved, -paven, -robed, -silvered, -strangled* adjs. Special combs.: **lily-beetle**, the beetle *Crioceris merdigera*, parasitic on lilies; **lily-bell, lily cup**, the flower of the lily-of-the-valley; **lily-encrinite**, an encrinite resembling a lily in shape; **lily-iron**, a harpoon having a detachable head used in killing sword-fish; **lily-pad** orig. *U.S.*, the broad flat leaf of a water-lily as it lies on the water; **lily-pond**, a pond in which water-lilies are grown; **lily-star**, (*a*) = *feather-star*, a crinoid of the family *Comatulidæ*; (*b*) the star-like flower of the water-lily; **lily-trotter**, a water-bird of the family Jacanidæ, esp. *Actophilornis africana*, found in tropical Africa, or *Microparra capensis*, the lesser lily-trotter, found in east Africa; also = JACANA; † **lily-water**, a 'water' distilled from lilies; **lily-work**, architectural decoration containing designs of lilies. Also LILY-FLOWER, LILY-POT, LILY-WHITE.

1864 TENNYSON *Aylmer's F.* 162 A *lily-avenue climbing to the doors. **1723** RAMSAY *Fair Assembly* x, Like *lily-banks see how they rise. **1606** SHAKS. *Tr. & Cr.* III. ii. 13 Where I may wallow in the *Lily beds Propos'd for the deseruer. **1854** A. ADAMS, etc. *Man. Nat. Hist.* 204 *Lily-Beetles (Crioceridæ). **1729** T. COOKE *Tales, Proposals, &c.* 82 The Poet . . To render his Melissa vain, Calls her the Lilly of the Vale . . The Tears, with which her Eyelids swell, Are Dewdrops on the *Lillybell. **1854** F. TENNYSON *Days & Hours* 87 Some lilybells Pluckt ere the flush of dawn. **1870** MORRIS *Earthly Par.* III. IV. 84 White *lily-blooms. **1877** BRYANT *Poems, Sella* 344 She laid The light-brown tresses smooth, and in them twined The *lily-buds. *c* **1420** *Pallad. on Husb.* III. 538 Now *lilly bulbes sowe Or sette. **1850** MRS. BROWNING *Poems* II. 309 Her face is *lily-clear—Lily-shaped. *c* **1866** G. M. HOPKINS *Poems* (1918) 9 *Lily-coloured clothes provide Your spouse not laboured-at nor spun. **1875** BROWNING *Inn Album* ii. 72 My big and bony, here, against the bunch Of lily-coloured five with signet-ring. **1832** TENNYSON *Œnone* 29 The golden bee Is *lily-cradled. **1390** GOWER *Conf.* III. 249 The *lilie croppes on and on . . He smot of. *c* **1375** *Sc. Leg. Saints* i. (*Peter*) 708 His angelis . . with *lely and rose-cronis in hand. **1746** J. WARTON *Ode to Fancy* 55 Nodding their *lily-crowned heads. **1826** HOOD '*I remember*' 11 The violets and the *lily-cups, Those flowers made of light. **1808** PARKINSON *Organic Rem.* II. 174 The *Lily Encrinite [described]. **1570** LEVINS *Manip.* 34/13 Ye *Lilygarth, *lilietum.* **1739** tr. *Art of Painting in Miniature* (ed. 4) 13 *Lilly-Green, Sap-Green, and Gamboge . . must be temper'd with fair Water only. **1965** S. GIBBONS in J. Gibb *Light on C. S. Lewis* v. 87 Here she was, the right descendant of Grendel, with her lily-green complexion. **1658** ROWLAND *Moufet's Theat. Ins.* 908 It takes the name of Grasse-honey, . . *Lilly-honey, Violet-honey, &c., respect being had to those things from which it is collected. **1852** M. H. PERLEY *Rep. Fisheries New Brunswick* (ed. 2) 187 They [sword-fish] are captured by means of an instrument called a '*lily-iron', from the form of its shaft, or wings, which resemble the leaves of a lily. **1883** *Fisheries Exhib. Catal.* 195 Sword-fish lily-irons and lances and harpoons. **1652** KIRKMAN *Clerio & Lozia* 23 That Rose and *Lilly-like colour mingled together. **1847** TENNYSON *Princess* IV. 143 The lilylike Melissa droop'd her brows. **1843** *Knickerbocker* XXII. 1 Huge moccasin darting away beneath the dense reeds and *lily-pads of the swamp. **1868** LOWELL *Willows* Poet. Wks. (1879) 373/2 A pike lurks balanced 'neath the lily-pads. **1875** J. G. HOLLAND *Sevenoaks* v. 65 A deer, feeding among the lily-pads. **1888** *Nation* (N.Y.) 19 July 57/2 The trout breaking at the edge of the lily-pads. **1946** K. TENNANT *Lost Haven* (1947) 2 Shallow blue water from which the great white paper-barks tower shadowing the lily-pads. **1958** G. DURRELL *Encounters with Animals* I. 38, I had watched her standing on the lily-pads. **1598** SYLVESTER *Du Bartas* II. i. I. *Eden* 531 By some cleer River's *lilly-paved side. **1822** SHELLEY *Tri. Life* 368 O'er *lily-paven lakes. **1901** G. JEKYLL *Wall & Water Gardens* xx. 161 Such a scene as Mr. Robinson's *Lily pond in North Sussex . . could scarcely be bettered. **1974** R. HARRIS *Double Snare* iv. 27 From the direction of the lily pond comes the croak of little frogs. *c* **1450** *ME. Med. Bk.* (Heinrich) 211 Tak *lylie rote. **1796** COLERIDGE *Poems* 18 Summer's *lily-scented plume. **1869** BROWNING *Ring & Bk.* III. vii. 50 The sword I wear shall pink His lily-scented cassock through and through. **1936** R. CAMPBELL *Mithraic Emblems* 31 Out of a wound that never heals Rills forth the lily-scented blood. **1650** H. VAUGHAN *Silex Scint., Relapse* 25 Sweet downie thoughts, soft *lilly-shades, calm streams. **1821** J. S. MILLER (*title*) A Natural History of the Crinoidea, or *Lily-shaped Animals. **1847** TENNYSON *Princess* IV. 268 Half-naked . . lay The *lily-shining child. **1742** POPE *Dunc.* IV. 303 To Isles of fragrance, *lily-silver'd vales. **1854** A. ADAMS, etc. *Man. Nat. Hist.* 334 Pedunculated *Lily-stars (Pentacrinitidæ). **1863** WOOLNER *My Beautiful Lady* 121 Mid splashing waters, sedge, and lily stars. **1887** BROWNING *Parleyings* Wks. 1896 II. 722/1 Some *lily-strangled pool. **1931** V. WOOLF *Waves* 290 Let us commit any blasphemy of laughter and criticism rather than exude this *lily-sweet glue. **1920** *Blackw. Mag.* May 649/2 The busy *lily trotter, hurrying across the broad flat water-lily leaves. **1951** R. CAMPBELL *Light on Dark Horse* 82 Those strange little birds, the lily-trotters. **1958** G. DURRELL *Encounters with Animals* I. 35 It is with the aid of these long toes and the even distribution of weight that they give that the jacana manages to walk across water, using the water-lily leaves and other water-plants as its path-ways. It has thus earned its name of lily-trotter. **1971** *Country Life* 30 Sept. 830/1 The lakes [in Tanzania] give you close views of ibises, egrets, . . lily trotters. **1599** A. M. tr. *Gabelhouer's Bk. Physicke* 254/1 Take *Lillyewater, Rosewater, and water of Mayflowers. *a* **1743** SAVAGE *Employm. of Beauty* 44 The well-rang'd teeth in lily-whitening rows. **1611** BIBLE *1 Kings* vii. 19 The chapiters . . were of *lillie worke in the porch. *c* **1865** G. M. HOPKINS *Poems* (1948) 123 *Lily-yellow is the west.

b. In plant-names (of little currency): **lily asphodel, daffodil**, names for the genus *Amaryllis*; **lily-bind, -bine** *dial.*, bindweed; † **lily-grass**, Gerarde's name for an aquatic species of corn-flag (*Gladiolus*); **lily hyacinth**, † **jacinth**, the genus *Scilla*, esp. *S. Liliohyacinthus*; † **lily leek**, Gerarde's name for MOLY[1]; † **lily narcissus**, a proposed name for the tulip; **lily pink**, the genus *Aphyllanthes*; **lily thorn**, the genus *Catesbæa*; **lilyworts**, Lindley's name for the N.O. *Liliaceæ*.

1753 CHAMBERS *Cycl. Supp.* s.v. Lilio-asphodelus. . . The common yellow flowered *lilly-asphodel. **1760** J. LEE *Introd. Bot.* App. 317 Lily Asphodel, *Amaryllis.* **1828** MISS MITFORD *Village* Ser. III. 244 Snow-white *lily-bines, and light fragile hare-bells. **1733** MILLER *Gard. Dict.*, *Lilio-narcissus* (is so called, because it resembles both these Plants), *Lily-Daffodil. **1760** J. LEE *Introd. Bot.* App. 317 Lily Daffodil, *Amaryllis.* **1597** GERARDE *Herbal* I. xxi. 27 Water Gladiole . . hath on the top of every rushie stalke a fine vmble . . of small flowers, in fashion of the Lillie of Alexandria, the which it is very like, and therefore I had rather call it *Lillie grasse. *Ibid.* lxx. 97 *Hyacinthus stellatus Lilifolius*, *Lillie Iacinth. *Ibid.* 98 The *Lillie Hyacinth is called *Hyacinthus Germanicus liliflorus*, or Germanie Hyacinth, taken from the countrie where it naturally groweth wilde. *Ibid.* Table Eng. Names, *Lillie Leeke, that is Moly. **1578** LYTE *Dodoens* II. lii. 213 The greater is called both *Tulpia*, and *Tulpian*, and of some *Tulipa*, . . we may call it *Lillynarcissus. **1848** CRAIG s.v., **Lily pink*, the plant *Aphyllanthes monspeliensis.* **1816–20** GREEN *Univ. Herbal* I. 267/2 *Catesbæa Spinosa*; *Lily Thorn. . . Discovered near Nassau Town in Providence. **1845** LINDLEY *Sch. Bot.* 135 Liliaceæ—— *Lilyworts.

B. as *adj.* **a.** White or fair as a lily; lily-white; lily-like. Also in parasynthetic comb., as *lily-cheeked, -fingered, -handed, -wristed* adjs.

15.. *Crt. of Love* 781 And lily forhede had this creature. *a* **1553** UDALL *Royster D.* IV. vii. (Arb.) 72 It shall be euen so, by his lily woundes. **1590** SPENSER *F.Q.* I. iii. 6 He . . lickt her lilly hands with fawning tong. **1590** GREENE *Neuer too Late* (1600) 31 Lilly cheekes whereon beside Buds of roses shew their pride. *c* **1590** —— *Fr. Bacon* i. (1630) A 3, She turn'd her smocke ouer her lilly armes. **1591** SHAKS. *Two Gent.* IV. iv. 160 The ayre hath . . pinch'd the lilly-tincture of her face. *a* **1618** SYLVESTER *Sonn.* xxii. Wks. (Grosart) II. 325/2 Thy brow . . Fairer then snow, or the most lilly thing. **1648** HERRICK *Hesper., Country Life* 246 The lilly-wristed morne. **1649** DRYDEN *On Death Ld. Hastings* 58 Blisters . . Like rosebuds, stuck in the lily-skin about. **1720** GAY *Sweet William's Farew.* 48 Adieu, she cries! and wav'd her lilly hand. *a* **1810** SURTEES *Barthram's Dirge* v, They rowed him in a lily-sheet, And bare him to his earth. **1847** TENNYSON *Princess* Concl. 84 No little lily-handed Baronet he. **1859** —— *Elaine* 2 Elaine, the lily maid of Astolat. **1873** BLACK *Pr. Thule* v. 69 He was no mere lily-fingered idler about town. **1877** BRYANT *Poems, Little People of Snow* 110 She saw a little creature, lily-cheeked.

b. Pale, pallid, colourless, bloodless; **lily-livered** *a.*, white-livered, cowardly; so **lily-liver**, a 'lily-livered' person; **lily-liveredly** *adv.*

1590 SHAKS. *Mids. N.* v. i. 337 These Lilly Lips, this cherry nose, These yellow Cowslip cheekes. **1605** —— *Macb.* v. iii. 15 Go pricke thy face, and ouer-red thy feare, Thou Lilly-liuer'd Boy. **1805** JOANNA BAILLIE *Rayner* I. i. 9 That plain word Still makes Sebastian, like a squeamish dame, Shrink and look lily-fac'd. **1857** TROLLOPE *Barchester T.* xiv, Surely..you will not be so lily-livered as to fall into this trap which he has baited for you. **1860** THACKERAY *Roundabout Papers* xii. (1869) 130 When people were yet afraid of me..I always knew that I was a lily-liver. **1929** D. H. LAWRENCE *Pansies* 48 It's either you fight or you die, Die, die, lily-liveredly die. **1934** DYLAN THOMAS *Let.* 14 Jan. (1966) 92 As the black man must have first regarded the features of his lily-faced brother.

Hence **'lilyfy** *v. trans.*, to make lily-like.

1866 READE *Griff. Gaunt* (1887) 109 The full moon's silvery beams shone on her rose-like cheeks and lilyfied chem.

'lily-flower. The flower of the (white) lily; *occas.* the heraldic fleur-de-lis.

a **1300–1400** *Cursor M.* 25630 (Gött.) Þar þu lay in þi bright boure, Leuedi! quite als leli floure. **1340** *Ayenb.* 230 My lemman is ase þe lylye amang þe þornes.. Þis lilye flour lokeþ his uayrhede amang þe þornes of uondingges of þe ulesse. *c* **1385** CHAUCER *L.G.W.* Prol. 161 A garlond..of rose leuys Stekid al with lylye flourys newe. *c* **1440** *York Myst.* xii. 91 Þe lelly floure full faire of hewe. **1612** WEBSTER *Wh. Devil* v. Stage Direction L 2 *marg.*, A pot of lilly flowers. **1833** TENNYSON *Œnone* 94 Poems 56 The smooth-swarded bower, Lustrous with lilyflower.

'lilying, *vbl. sb. rare*⁻¹. = *lily-work* (LILY A. 5).

1874 G. M. HOPKINS *Jrnls. & Papers* (1959) 248 The touching and passionate curves of the lilyings in the iron-work.

'lily-pot.

1. A flower-pot with a lily growing in it; a representation of this, commonly occurring as a symbolic accessory in pictures of the Annunciation, and hence frequent as a religious emblem.

1540 *Invent. Ch. Goods* in *Gentl. Mag. Libr., Ecclesiology* 157 A single vestment of white damask imbroidrede with lily pots. **1578–9** *New Year's Gifts* in Nichols *Progr. Eliz.* (1823) II. 251 A lylly pot of agathe, a lylly flower going owte of it garnesshed with roses of rubyes. **1898** *Archæol. Jrnl.* LV. 172 On the brass of Bishop Andreas at Posen, dated 1479,.. the lily-pot forms the central upright band of the episcopal mitre.

2. An ornamental vase imitating the 'lily-pot' of sacred art; in the early 17th c. app. *spec.* a tobacco-jar.

1610 B. JONSON *Alch.* I. iii, He keepes it [Tobacco] in fine Lilly-pots, that open'd, Smell like conserue of Roses, or French Beanes. *c* **1618** FLETCHER *Q. Corinth* II. iv, *Vintner*: Look into the Lilly-pot. *a* **1652** BROME *Weeding Covent-Gard.* II. ii. (1658) 34 *Vint.* Y'are welcome, Gentlemen, take up the lillie-pot.

b. *Her.* (See quot.: the use seems incorrect.)

1780 EDMONDSON *Her.* II. Gloss., *Lily-pot* see Covered Cup.

†**3.** A size of writing paper distinguished by the 'lily-pot' as a water-mark. *Obs.*

1589 G. HARVEY *Pierce's Supererog.* (1592) 138 Stationers ..find more gain in the lillypot blank than in the lilly-pot Euphued.

lily-white, *a.* (Stress variable.) Also 4 **luly-**.

1. a. White as a lily.

a **1310** in Wright *Lyric P.* vii. 30 Lylie-whyt hue is..that reveth me mi rest. **13..** *E.E. Allit. P.* B. 977 Loth & þo luly-whit his lefly two deȝter. *a* **1400** *Pistill of Susan* 16 Heo was ..Loueliche & lilie whit. **1513** DOUGLAS *Æneis* I. Prol. 453 In loifing of thir ladyis lilly quhyte. **1590** SPENSER *F.Q.* II. iii. 26 A silken Camus lilly whight. **1749** FIELDING *Tom Jones* I. xi, Cherry Cheeks, small Lily-white Hands. **1818** COBBETT *Pol. Reg.* XXXIII. 280 As to despotism, your lily-white hands must never touch it. **1820** SCOTT *Abbot* vii, With..ten lily-white groats in his pouch.

b. as *sb.* (*a*) Lily-white colour. †(*b*) *Old Cant.* A chimney-sweep.

a **1700** B. E. *Dict. Cant. Crew, Lilly-white*, a Chimney-sweeper. **1713** *Eng. Gratitude* 7 See how my Flowers are.. dy'd in Lilly-white or Rosy-red.

2. a. In favour of, committed to, or pertaining to a policy of racial segregation. orig. *U.S.*

1903 *N.Y. Times* 23 Sept., The report that the President was seeking reconciliation with the 'Lilywhite' faction, which eliminated the negro from the last State Convention. **1909** *Westm. Gaz.* 13 Feb. 2/2 That..is what they call the lily-white policy!.. It is the unprincipled white politician who finds anti-negro agitation a popular plank in his platform. **1953** *Manch. Guardian Weekly* 8 Oct. 5/1 Before 1948 groups of landlords had managed to maintain 'lily-white' communities by signing 'restrictive covenants'. **1968** *Morning Star* 10 Aug. 1/1 While the lilywhite Republican convention was nominating Richard Nixon in an atmosphere of ballyhoo and frenzied hysteria, the same city of Miami saw Negroes demonstrating for their rights.

b. Irreproachable, lacking faults or imperfections.

1961 in WEBSTER. **1970** *New Yorker* 9 May 33/3, I think the city should be lily-white on this, so the first thing I'm going to try to do is convert all our city vehicles to low-pollution engines. **1973** *Times* 18 Jan. 2/7 Robert Mark [the commissioner] is determined to have a lily-white police force. He will have a lily-white police force looking pretty in the street.

So †**lily-whited** *a.* in same sense; hence **lily-whiteness**.

1560 PHAER *Æneid* IX. (1562) Ee iij, Some lylywhyted swan. **1885–94** R. BRIDGES *Eros & Psyche* Apr. xxii, Psyche, all in lily-whiteness veil'd.

lim, obs. form of LIMB, LIME *sb.*¹, LIMN.

Lima ('liːmə), the name of the capital of Peru, used *attrib.* in the following names of products of that locality: **Lima bark**, the bark of certain species of *Cinchona*; a kind of Peruvian bark; **Lima bean**, *Phaseolus lunatus*; see also quot. 1858; **Lima-wood**, a kind of Brazil-wood.

1819 [see BUTTER-BEAN]. **1831** M. HOLLEY *Texas* (1833) xi. 123 He had known winters here so mild, as not to kill the Lima bean. **1834** M. G. LEWIS *Jrnl. W. Ind.* 152 The Lima Bean is said to be more like a pea than a bean. **1855** MAYNE *Expos. Lex., Lima Bark*, common name for the *Cinchona pallida*, or pale Peruvian bark. **1858** SIMMONDS *Dict. Trade, Lima-bean*, the *Phaseolus Limensis*, an esteemed kind of pulse cultivated in the tropics; the perennial kidney-bean, *P. perennis*. **1864** CRAIG, Suppl., *Lima-wood* is a fine kind of Nicaragua wood, produced in South America. **1886** A. H. CHURCH *Food Grains Ind.* 155 The Lima or Duffin bean.. is cultivated almost everywhere throughout India. **1969** *Northwest* (*Sunday Oregonian Mag.*) 14 Dec. 19/1 The pulp [of pawpaw] is yellow or orange and contains several brown seeds about the size and shape of a Lima Bean.

b. *ellipt.* = Lima bean. *U.S.*

1856 F. S. COZZENS *Sparrowgrass Papers* vii. 85 Put the Limas to the right..and as for the rest of the seeds sweep them into the refuse basket. **1865** *Trans. Illinois Agric. Soc.* V. 758 Pole Beans—Amongst these the Limas deservedly rank the highest. **1942** E. PAUL *Narrow St.* vi. 51 The Épicerie Danton had limas, normal-sized and 'baby', Canterbury, scarlet runners, pintos, [etc.].

†**limace.** *Obs. rare.* [a. F. *limace* (:—L. **līmācea*) slug, formerly also shell-snail, or ad. L. *līmāc-em*, *līmāx* slug, snail.] A shell-snail.

1491 CAXTON *Vitas Patr.* (W. de W. 1495) I. xlviii. 93 a/2 His skynne was as harde as the shelle of a lymace. **1592** LODGE *Euphues Shadow* (1882) 32 The Limace stayeth what shee toucheth.

limaceous (laɪ'meɪʃəs), *a.* [f. L. *līmāc-*, *līmāx* slug, snail + -EOUS (cf. -ACEOUS).] Pertaining to slugs or snails; snail-like; also in mod. use, pertaining to the genus *Limax* of slugs.

1656 BLOUNT *Glossogr., Limaceous*, snaily, snail-like. **1855** MAYNE *Expos. Lex, Limaceus*... Applied by Mencke to a Family..of the *Gasteropoda cœlopnœa*, having the *Limax* for their type: limaceous. **1861** WILSON & GEIKIE *Mem. E. Forbes* XIV. 490 Delicacies suited to the limaceous appetite. [In mod. Dicts.]

limacian (laɪ'meɪʃən). *Zool.* [f. L. *līmāc-* LIMAX + -IAN. Cf. F. *limacien.*] A limacid or slug.

1839 *Penny Cycl.* XIII. 485/1 Lamarck..concludes by comprehending under his *Limacians* the..five genera: *Onchidium, Parmacella, Limax, Testacella*, and *Vitrina*.

limacid ('laɪməsɪd). *Zool.* [ad. mod.L. *Limacid-æ*, f. LIMAX: see -ID.] A gastropod of the family *Limacidæ*; a slug.

1890 in *Century Dict.*

limaciform (laɪ'meɪsɪfɔːm), *a.* [f. L. *līmāc-*, *līmāx* slug, snail + -(I)FORM.] Having the form of a slug; limaceous.

1826 KIRBY & SP. *Entomol.* III. 185 It is probable that the other limaciform larvæ are similarly circumstanced. **1851–6** WOODWARD *Mollusca* 197 C[*enia*] *Cocksii.* Animal limaciform, back elevated.

limacin ('laɪməsɪn). *Chem.* [ad. F. *limacine*, f. L. *līmāc-* LIMAX: see -IN.] (See quot.)

1865 WATTS *Dict. Chem.* III. 696 *Limacin*, a substance obtained by Braconnot..from the garden-snail (*Limax agrestis*).

limacine ('laɪməsaɪn, -ɪn), *a.* and *sb.* [ad. mod.L. *Limacinæ* (see below), f. L. *līmāc-*, *līmāx* slug: see -INE.] **a.** *adj.* Pertaining to the sub-family *Limacinæ* or family *Limacidæ* of land-snails, typified by the genus *Limax*; limaceous. **b.** *sb.* A slug of the sub-family *Limacinæ* or family *Limacidæ* (Cent. Dict.).

1888 *Syd. Soc. Lex., Limacine*, viscous or slimy, like a snail.

limacinean (laɪmə'sɪnɪən). [f. mod.L. *Limacinea*, f. L. *līmāc-* (see prec.) + -AN.] In De Blainville's classification, a slug belonging to the third family, *Limacinea*, of his *Pulmobranchiata*.

1839 *Penny Cycl.* XIII. 485/1 The second section of the Limacineans of M. de Blainville, or those which have the border of the mantle enlarged into a species of buckler.

limacinid (laɪ'meɪsɪnɪd). [f. mod.L. *Limacinid-æ*: see -ID.] A pteropod of the family *Limacinidæ*, typified by the genus *Limacina*.

1890 in *Century Dict.*

limacoid ('laɪməkɔɪd), *a.* and *sb.* [ad. mod.L. *Limacoid-ea*, f. L. *līmāc-*, *līmāx* slug: see -OID.] **a.** *adj.* Pertaining to the *Limacoidea*, a family of gastropods typified by the genus *Limax*. **b.** *sb.* A slug of the family *Limacoidea*.

1855 MAYNE *Expos. Lex., Limacoides*,..applied by Goldfuss, Ficinus, and Carus to an Order (*Limacoidea*, more correctly *Limacoides*) of the *Enthelmintha*, comprehending the intestinal flat worms which have some resemblance to the *Limaces* or slugs: limacoid.

‖**limaçon** (limasɔ̃). Also 6 **li-**, **lymasson**. [Fr. = shell-snail, spiral staircase, snail-wheel, etc., f. *limace* (see LIMACE).]

†**1.** A kind of military manœuvre. [So in OFr.]

1581 STYWARD *Mart. Discipl.* I. 68 You shall bring them in this proportion of a ring, otherwise called a limasson. **1591** *Garrard's Art Warre* 207 To the end they may assure themselues the better, it is necessarie they make Lymassons when they are in simple and single aray.

2. (See quot.; some Dicts. give the sense as Eng.)

1839 *Penny Cycl.* XIV. 315/2 The Univalve Shells, as they were then [1757] called, or as Adanson denominates them, the *Limaçons*.

3. *Math.* (See quot. 1877.)

1874 SYLVESTER in *Proc. Roy. Instit.* VII. 186 *note*, The Limaçon of Pascal. **1877** CAYLEY in *Encycl. Brit.* VI. 723/1 A form which presents itself is when two ovals, one inside the other, unite, so as to give rise to a crunode—in default of a better name this may be called, after the curve of that name, a limaçon. **1879** SALMON *Higher Plane Curves* (ed. 3) 44 In like manner on the radius vector to a fixed circle from a fixed point on it a portion of fixed length is taken on either side of the circle. The curve is called Pascal's limaçon.

4. A metallic gimp (*Funk's Stand. Dict.* 1893).

limail, lemel ('liːməl). *Now only techn.* Forms: 4–5 **limail(le**, **lymail(le**, **-ayl(e**, **lemaille**, 5 **limayle**, **lymayll**, 6 **limall**, 7 **limaile**, **limmell**, 9 **lemel**, *Sc.* **lummle**. [a. F. *limaille*, f. *limer*:—L. *līmāre* to file.] Metal filings.

c **1386** CHAUCER *Can. Yeom. Prol. & T.* 1267 An Ounce.. Of siluer lemaille. **14..** *Voc.* in Wr.-Wülcker 592/45 *Limatorium*, lytarge or lymayle. **1460–70** *Bk. Quintessence* 9 If ȝe wole not make lymayl of gold, þanne make þerof a sotil þinne plate. **1555** W. WATREMAN *Fardle Facions* II. i. 115 Limall of golde. **1615** MARKHAM *Eng. Housew.* (1660) 105 Take Limmell of Gold, Silver, Lattin, Copper, Iron [etc.]. **1825–80** JAMIESON, *Lummle*, the filings of metal. **1893** *B'ham Gaz.* 12 Jan. 3/3 The waste comprised wire-ends, called gold scrap, and gold dust, called lemel.

‖**liman** (liː'mɑːn). [Russian *liman* estuary; applied to the salt-marshes at the mouths of the Dnieper (cf. Turkish *liman* harbour, mod.Gr. λίμανι, ? Gr. λιμήν).] (See quots.)

1858 SIMMONDS *Dict. Trade, Liman*, a shallow narrow lagoon, at the mouth of rivers, where salt is made. **1859** RAWLINSON *Herod.* III. IV. liii. 48 *note*, The word in the Greek..is rather 'marsh' than 'lake', and the liman of the Dniepr is in point of fact so shallow as almost to deserve the name. **1879** WEBSTER Suppl., *Liman*, the deposit of slime at the mouth of a river.

limasson, obs. form of LIMAÇON.

†**limate,** *v. Obs.*⁻⁰ [f. L. *līmāt-*, ppl. stem of *līmāre*, f. *līma* file.] To file.

1721 in BAILEY.

limation (laɪ'meɪʃən). Now *rare.* [ad. late L. *līmātiōn-em*, used by Cælius Aurelianus, in sense 'diminishing (of the body)', n. of action f. *līmāre*: see prec.] Filing; *fig.* 'polishing up'.

1612 WOODALL *Surg. Mate* Wks. (1653) 272 Limation proper to Metals..is a preparation with a file, whereby they yeeld dust for divers uses. **1656** in BLOUNT *Glossogr.* **1706** PHILLIPS (ed. Kersey), *Limation*..In Surgery, the filing of the Bones, or hard Parts of the Body. **1852** S. R. MAITLAND *Eight Ess.* 197 Two years..during which the new commissioners were employed in the limation of the work [preparation of a book] committed to them.

†**b.** *Astron.* Correction of errors in calculation or observation. *Obs.*

1669 FLAMSTEED in Rigaud *Corr. Sci. Men* (1841) II. 77 You know how much it may conduce to the limation of astronomy, and the correction of our canons, to have the celestial phænomena accurately observed. **1669** —— in *Phil. Trans.* IV. 1109 How the Motion of the Moon's Latitudes, which shall need its limations, is to be reform'd.

limature ('laɪmətjʊə(r)). Now *rare* or *Obs.* [ad. late L. *līmātūra*, f. *līmā-re* to LIMATE: see -URE. Cf. obs. F. *limature.*] Metal filings.

c **1400** *Lanfranc's Cirurg.* 99 Limature of iren... Limature of bras. **1658** tr. *Porta's Nat. Magic* VI. iv. 180 Take three or four pounds of the limature of Iron, wash it well [etc.]. **1721** in BAILEY. (In mod. Dicts., which, however, give as the first sense 'The act of filing', without quot. or reference.)

‖**limax** ('laɪmæks). Pl. **limaces** (laɪ'meɪsiːz). [L. *līmāx* snail, slug.]

1. The typical genus of the *Limacidæ* or slugs; a member of this genus, a slug.

1398 TREVISA *Barth. De P.R.* XVIII. lxx. (1495) 825 Limax ..hathe that name for he bredith in lyme other of slyme. **1706** PHILLIPS (ed. Kersey), *Limax*, a Snail without a Shell; a Dew Snail, a Slug. **1752** SIR J. HILL *Hist. Anim.* 87 The body of the Limax is of a figure approaching to cylindric. *Ibid.*, *Limax ater*, the black Limax. **1834** MCMURTRIE *Cuvier's Anim. Kingd.* III. 31 *Limax Rufus*, L. (the Red Limax). *Ibid.* 32 These Mollusca..closely resemble the common Limaces. **1851–6** WOODWARD *Mollusca* 103 Some of the limaces lower themselves to the ground by a thread.

2. (See quot.; the sense is recognized as Eng. in some modern Dicts.)

1839 *Penny Cycl.* XIII. 484/1 Linnæus uses the word Limax to designate the soft parts of most of the genera of his (*Vermes*) *Testacea*.

limb (lɪm), *sb.*¹ Forms: *sing.* 1–8 **lim**, 3–4 **leome**, **leme**, **lime**, 3–7 **lym**, 4–6 **lyme**, **lymme**, (5 **leyme**),

6–7 **limme, limbe,** 6– **limb.** *pl.* 1 **limu, leomu, -o, -a,** *Northumb.* **lioma,** 1–3 **lime,** (2 **leoman**), 2–3 **limen, lemen,** 3 **leome(n, lumen, (lemman), leomes;** also 2– regularly inflected in *-s.* [OE. *lim* str. neut. = ON. *lim-r* str. masc. (Sw., Da. *lem*):—OTeut. type **limo-*; according to Kluge from a root **li-* in OTeut. **lipu-* LITH *sb.*; cf. also Lith. *lëmů*(:—**loimen-*) trunk, stature.]

1. Any organ or part of the body. *Obs.* exc. *dial.*

c **1000** ÆLFRIC *Hom.* I. 274 Gif an lim bið untrum, ealle ða oðre ðrowiað mid þam anum. *a* **1300** *Cursor M.* 2023 Naked o þat lime lai he þat man think mast scham to see. *a* **1340** HAMPOLE *Psalter* xvi. 9 A man has na lym þat he is warere wiþ þan wiþ his eghe. **1387** TREVISA *Higden* (Rolls) II. 195 We sighe..a mayde..i-torned into a man, and was i-berded anon, and anoon hadde alle lymes as a man schulde haue [L. *barbamque et cetera virilia produxisse*]. **1398** —— *Barth. De P.R.* III. xvii. (Tollem. MS.) þlyme of syȝte [L. *organum visus*]. **1484** CAXTON *Fables of Poge* v, The lymmes of generacion were shewed manyfestly. **1642** ROGERS *Naaman* 166 Self is overspread in all the lims and faculties of thy body and soule. **1880** *W. Cornw. Gloss.* s.v. *Limb*, 'Your daughter looks well'. 'No, she's but slight; her face is her best limb'.

2. a. A part or member of an animal body distinct from the head or the trunk, e.g. a leg, arm, wing.

971 *Blickl. Hom.* 13 þa clænan leomu þære halȝan fæmnan. **1154** *O.E. Chron.* an. 1137 (Laud MS.) [Hi] þrengde þe man þær inne ðet him bræcon alle þe limes. *c* **1175** *Lamb. Hom.* 23 þu sunegest mid summe of þisse limen ofter þenne þu scoldest. *c* **1205** LAY. 19501 Sa me scal lacnien his leomes þat beoð sare. *a* **1225** *Leg. Kath.* 252 Leomen buten liue. *c* **1290** *S. Eng. Leg.* I. 6/164 þe strencþe him failede in is limes. **13..** *Gaw. & Gr. Knt.* 139 His lyndes & his lymes so longe & so grete. **1375** BARBOUR *Bruce* I. 385 Off lymmys he wes weill maid. *c* **1386** CHAUCER *Reeve's Prol.* 32 Oure old lemes mowe wel been vnweelde. *c* **1400** *Destr. Troy* 3762 A large man of lenght with limis full brode. *c* **1440** *York Myst.* xxviii. 21 My lymmys are heuy as any leede. **1470–85** MALORY *Arthur* XXI. iii, He felle amonge the serpentys, & euery beest took hym by a lymme. **1508** FISHER 7 *Penit. Ps.* cxlii. Wks. (1876) 239 Beddes to refresshe theyr wery lymmes. **1558** G. CAVENDISH *Poems* (1825) II. 80 *The Earle of Surrey*, In dewe proportion she [nature] wrought hathe every lyme [*rimes*, tyme, clyme]. **1581** MULCASTER *Positions* vi. (1887) 41 Their weake limmes and failing ioyntes. **1649** JER. TAYLOR *Gt. Exemp.* II. Disc. xiii. 163 He made crooked limmes become straight. **1747** WESLEY *Prim. Physic* (1762) 37 This will stop the bleeding of an amputated Limb. **1814** SCOTT *Ld. of Isles* v. xx, His trembling limbs their aid refuse. **1872** MIVART *Elem. Anat.* iv. 152 A vertebrate animal may exist without limbs, as we see..in most serpents.

fig. **1580** LYLY *Euphues* (Arb.) 417 There is..no birde that flyeth with one winge, no loue that lasteth with one lym. **1615** CROOKE *Body of Man* 728 Through the three Regions, Naturall, Vitall & Animal, we haue carried our Story..it followeth now that we prosecute our History vnto the Limmes. **1664** H. MORE *Myst. Iniq.* iv. 10 The very body of Antichristianism, with the distinct Limbs and Articulations thereof.

b. = LEG. Now only (esp. *U.S.*) in mock-modest or prudish use.

c **1400** MAUNDEV. (1839) lxvi. 175 Summe han here Armes or here Lymes alle to broken, and somme the sydes. **1508** DUNBAR *Flyting w. Kennedie* 182 Thy hanchis hirklis, with hukebanis harth and haw, Thy laithly lymis ar lene as ony treis. ?*a* **1550** in *Dunbar's Poems* (1893) 316 The hingand brayis on adir syde Scho powtterit with hir lymmis wyde. *a* **1550** *Christis Kirke Gr.* iv, His lymis wer lyk two rokkis. **17..** RAMSAY *Scribblers Lash'd* 116 If Nellie's hoop be twice as wide As her two pretty limbs can stride. **1785** BURNS *Jolly Beggars* 1st Air iv, I lastly was with Curtis, among the floating batt'ries, And there I left for witness an arm and a limb. **1837** S. KNOWLES *Love-Chase* II. i. Dram. Wks. 1856 II. 15 I'll show a limb with any of them! Silks I'll wear, nor keep my legs in cases more! **1839** MARRYAT *Diary Amer.* Ser. I. II. 245, I am not so particular as some people are, for I know those who always say limb of a table, or limb of a piano-forte. **1858** *Pittsburg Chron.* June (Bartlett), The poor brute [a horse]..fell..fracturing his limb. **1860** O. W. HOLMES *Elsie V.* vii. 1861) 83 'A bit of the wing, Roxy, or the —under limb?' **1885** in Farmer *Slang* (1891) II. 18/2 Between you'n me, red stockings ain't becomin' to all—ahem—limbs. **1898** M. DELAND *Old Chester Tales* 237 But it was she who informed him that he might stay until his 'limb' permitted him to walk. **1902** H. L. WILSON *Spenders* xxxi. 369 One of my maids who slipped on the avenue yesterday and fractured one of her—er—limbs. **1904** *Courier-Jrnl.* (Louisville, Kentucky) 5 Sept. 1 Her limbs were void of shoes or stockings. **1924** W. M. RAINE *Troubled Waters* i. 12 She dexterously arranged the skirt without being able to conceal some inches of slender limb rising from a well-turned ankle.

†**c.** *pl.* The pieces of a suit of armour.

1651 DAVENANT *Gondibert* I. VI. xliv, Some, who once were steadfast foot,..snatch those limbs which only horse-men wore.

d. Phrases. ***life and limb,*** †***limb and lith,*** †***limb and head,*** †***limb and bone, limb and carcase, limb and wind,*** expressions intended to refer inclusively to all the bodily faculties employed in certain connexions. †***limb and land,*** body or life and property. †***ilk(a) limb, ich a limb,*** used advb. in sense 'in every limb, in every part of the body, all over'. ***to tear*** or ***pull*** (one) ***limb from limb.***

c **1205** LAY. 702 Ȝe sculen habben lif & leomen [*c* **1275** lime]. *Ibid.* 2817 He hehte hælden grið & frið vppe leome & vppe lif. *a* **1300** *Cursor M.* 24619 Sua lam in lime and lith. *c* **1300** *Havelok* 2555 Als he louede leme or lif. *a* **1330** *Roland & V.* 493 He bi-held him ich a lim. **1362** LANGL. *P. Pl.* A. v. 81 Boþe his lyf and his lemes was lost þorw my tonge. *c* **1430** *Hymns Virg.* 43 Saue þee harmelees, lyme & heed. *c* **1440** *York Myst.* xix. 2 Peyne of lyme and lande, Stente of youre steuenes stoute. *c* **1460** *Towneley Myst.* v. 26 He is blyssyd, ich a lym. **1480** CAXTON *Chron. Eng.* lxxvi. 62 He had pyte of hem and yaf hem lyf and lymme. *a* **1548** HALL *Chron., Hen. VI*, 132 That their lifes and lymmes should be saved. **1567** *Satir. Poems Reform.* xi. 23 Lym nor lyth I may not steir. **1584** HUDSON *Du Bartas' Judith* v. (1608) 71 That Duke whose name alone Hath made great warriours quake both lim and bone. **1599** NASHE *Lenten Stuffe* Wks. 1883–4 V. 297 Hee will..tear him limbe from limbe, but hee will extract some capitall confession from him. **1697** DRYDEN *Virg. Georg.* III. 120 Of able Body, sound of Limb and Wind. **1719** DE FOE *Crusoe* II. iii. (1840) 51 They pulled down..their houses, and pulled them..limb from limb. **1840** DICKENS *Barn. Rudge* ii, The traveller..examined him in limb and carcass. **1888** *Times* (weekly ed.) 9 Nov. 16/2 Young men, strong of limb and wind.

3. In uses originally *fig.* (cf. MEMBER).

a. A member (e.g. of the church as 'the body of Christ', of Christ, of Antichrist); a branch or section; an element or component part. *Obs.* exc. in nonce-uses, with distinct reference to a metaphorical ' body'.

c **1000** ÆLFRIC *Hom.* II. 276 Ge..sindon Cristes lichama and leomu. [*c* **1200** *Vices & Virtues* (1888) 27 Hie sculen bien mine lemen, and ich here heaued. *a* **1225** *Ancr. R.* 360 Nis God ure heaued, and we alle his limes?] *c* **1315** SHOREHAM *Poems* (E.E.T.S.) 23 Ȝef þat þou art A lyme of holy cherche. **1340** *Ayenb.* 182 þe kueades þet byeþ ine þise wordle þet byeþ þe lemes of anticrist. *c* **1380** WYCLIF *Wks.* (1880) 412 God haþ ordeyned dyuerse lemes of hooly chirche. *c* **1386** CHAUCER *Pars. T.* ¶62 Ye were the children of God, and lymme of the regne of God. **1547–64** BAULDWIN *Mor. Philos.* (Palfr.) 91 In the soules of men is ingenerate a limbe of science, which with the mixture of a terrestriall substance is darkened. **1550** VERON *Godly Sayings* (1846) 19 His Christian brethren, whom he heareth alsoo to be the lymmes of Christ. **1565** JEWEL *Def. Apol.* (1611) 402 Your Schoolemasters and you are a limme of Antichrist. *c* **1586** C'TESS PEMBROKE *Ps.* LXVI. I, All lands, the lymms of earthy round. **1597** HOOKER *Eccl. Pol.* v. lxviii. §9 A part of the house of God, a limme of the visible church of Christ. **1607** HIERON *Wks.* I. 115 The whole order thereof in euery part and limme set downe in His eternall wisedome and prouidence. **1661** MARVELL *Corr.* xxv. Wks. 1872–5 II. 61 So considerable a body in yourselves and so honourable a limb of the towne. **1679** DRYDEN *Troilus & Cr.* Pref. b 3 b, Fletcher..was a Limb of Shakespear. **1773** BURKE *Corr.* (1844) I. 441, I never can forget that I am an Irishman..I think I would shed my blood, rather than see the limb I belong to oppressed. **1853** KANE *Grinnell Exp.* ii. (1856) 22 Our little corps of officers..including that non-effective limb, the doctor. **1863** KINGLAKE *Crimea* (1876) I. vi. 83 An army is but the limb of a nation.

b. †***the devil's*** or ***the fiend's limb, limb of the devil, of Satan, of hell***: an agent or scion of the evil one; an imp of Satan; hence, a mischievous wicked person (now *dial.*). †So also ***thieves' limb.***

971 *Blickl. Hom.* 33 Cuþ is þæt se awyrȝda gast is heafod ealra unrihtwisra dæda, swylce unrihtwise syndon deofles leomo. *c* **1290** *S. Eng. Leg.* I. 78/20 Zaroen and Arphaxat þat þe deueles limes were. *a* **1340** HAMPOLE *Psalter* iii. 1 Many, þat is, fendes & þe fendes lymmys, rises agayns me. *c* **1350** *St. Mary Magd.* 212 in Horstm. *Altengl. Leg.* (1881) 83 A, lym of Satenas, þi sire! *c* **1380** WYCLIF *Wks.* (1880) 109 þe deuelis lyms maden discencion..aȝenst hem. **1434** *Rolls of Parlt.* V. 435 A disciple and lyme of the feende called the Pucelle. *c* **1450** *Mirour Saluacioun* 2763 Judas yt thevis lymme. *a* **1540** BARNES *Wks.* (1573) 189/2 Such a vyllayne, and lymme of ye deuell. **1607** HIERON *Wks.* I. 201 The gift of regeneration, which is that whereby a man, of a limme of Sathan, is made a member of Christ. **1645** RUTHERFORD *Tryal & Tri. Faith* (1845) 45 He hath made many black limbs of hell fair saints in heaven. **1660** DICKSON *Job* x. Sel. Writ. (1845) I. 71 Ye may as well say, 'I am naturally a devil's limb'. **1833** J. S. SANDS *Poems* 86 (E.D.D.) Divide my game, ye devil's limbs!

c. Hence *limb* alone is used for: A mischievous person (now applied mostly to children); a young imp or rascal. *colloq.*

1625 B. JONSON *Staple of N.* III. Intermeane (1631) 49, I had it from my maid Joane Heare-say: shee had it from a limbe o' the schoole, shee saies, a little limbe of nine yeere old. **1735** DYCHE & PARDON *Dict., Limb*,..sometimes 'tis a Term of Reproach, signifying a Scold, or very turbulent Woman. **1760** FOOTE *Minor* II. Wks. 1799 I. 269 Ah, Foote's a precious limb! Old Nick will soon a football make of him! **1838** DICKENS *O. Twist* xxii, Now listen, you young limb. **1852** MRS. STOWE *Uncle Tom's C.* xx, 'See there!..don't that show she's a limb?' **1862** CALVERLEY *Verses & Transl.* 7 He was what nurses call a 'limb'.

d. ***limb of the law***: a derisive name for a legal functionary of any kind, e.g. a lawyer, a police officer. Also occas. ***limb of the bar***: a barrister.

1730 *Portland Papers* (Hist. MSS. Comm.) VI. 35 He is a Limb of the Law and will be over here [at York] at our Assizes. **1753** *School of Man* 149 There's another Limb of the Law starting from his bed to peruse a case recommended to him. **1770** FOOTE *Lame Lover* III. Wks. 1799 II. 92 Well said, my young limb of the law. **1809** *Gil Blas* I. v. ¶7 A limb of the law, who had hitherto taken us under his protection. **1815** W. H. IRELAND *Scribbleomania* 260 As a limb of the Bar, I with honour renown 'em.

†**e.** applied to things. *Obs.*

1593 Q. ELIZ. *Boeth.* III. pr. x. 64 What tho' all these good thinges, sufficiency, powre, all be but lyms of blissidnes. *c* **1640** *New Serm. of newest fashion* (1877) 37 That Heathenish Structure, the lim of Idolatry Cheapside Crosse. **1661** *Merry Drollery* I. 2 But she a Babe of grace..Thought kissing a disgrace A Limbe of prophanation In that place.

4. Transferred senses.

a. A main branch of a tree.

Beowulf 97 (Gr.) Se ælmihtiȝa..ȝefrætwade foldan sceatas leomum and leafum. **1578** LYTE *Dodoens* VI. lxxxiii. 764 His [the cedar's] limmes and branches be long and stretched out. **1664** EVELYN *Kal. Hort.* Jan. (1706) 5 In taking off an whole Branch or Limb, cut close to the Stem. **1719** DE FOE *Crusoe* I. xx. (1840) 354 A large limb of the tree. **1863** WOOLNER *My Beautiful Lady* 114 Giant shadows trenched the frosty ground From bole and limb. **1879** JEFFERIES *Wild Life in S. Co.* 271 Elms are often stripped..to make the timber..free from the great branches called 'limbs'.

b. In various uses, chiefly of material things and more or less technical: A projecting section of a building, e.g. the outworks of a castle; one of the four branches composing a cross; a member or clause of a sentence, or the like; a spur of a mountain range; one of the pieces which compose the lock of a gun; the part of a compound core of a transformer, electromagnet, etc., on which a coil is wound.

1577 HOLINSHED *Chron.* I. *Hist. Scot.* 477/1 They wanne the lims of the house vpon them, forcing the capitayne..to retire within the dongeon. **1577–87** *Ibid.* III. 593/1 After that all the lymmes of the Castell had beene reuersed and throwne downe, they kept the maister Tower. **1609** HIERON *Wks.* I. 411 Now followeth that limme of the prayer, which concernes the man. **1612** WEBSTER *White Devil* I 3 b, I haue heard you say, giuing my brother sucke, Hee tooke the Crucifix betweene his hands, And broke a limbe off. **1793** SMEATON *Edystone L.* §97 A carpenter's square, having a spirit-level fixed upon one of its Limbs. **1810** SCOTT *Lady of L.* III. viii, A slender crosslet..The shaft and limbs were rods of yew. **1832** J. HODGSON in Raine *Mem.* (1858) II. 258 The outer gateway and court which stood on the most northerly limb of the hill. **1858** HAWTHORNE *Fr. & It. Jrnls.* (1872) I. 20 There is a spiral stair-case within one of its [an arch's] immense limbs. **1859** *Musketry Instruct.* III. 11 Name the limbs of the lock, and the other principal parts of the rifle. **1863** KINGLAKE *Crimea* (1876) I. xv. 355 In another limb of the same sentence. **1868** FREEMAN *Norm. Conq.* (1876) II. x. 515 A short eastern limb, ending in an apse, contained the high altar. **1898** *Allbutt's Syst. Med.* V. 845 So great an increase of arterial pressure as to rupture a limb of the aortic valve. **1902** *Encycl. Brit.* XXVII. 584/1 These [portions] are: (1) the magnet 'cores' or 'limbs', carrying the exciting coils whereby the inert iron is converted into an electro-magnet; (2) the yoke, which joins the limbs together and conducts the flux between them; and (3) the pole-pieces. **1934** H. COTTON *Design Electr. Machinery* viii. 162 With core-type transformers the cross-section of the limbs may be rectangular in the case of small transformers, but it is more usual to adopt for all sizes a cross-section which fits as closely as possible into a circumscribing circle. **1943** *Gloss. Terms Electr. Engin.* (*B.S.I.*) 40 Those parts of the [transformer] core surrounded by windings are termed legs or limbs and those not so surrounded are termed yokes.

†**c.** [tr. med.L. *membrum.*] An estate, etc. dependent on another. *Obs.*

[**1442** in Madox *Formul. Anglic.* (1702) 147 Manerium de Raskell cum omnibus suis membris & pertinenciis suis.] **1605–47** HABINGTON *Surv. Worcs.* in *Worcs. Hist. Soc. Proc.* III. 403 Thys chappell is a lym of Suckley, havinge neyther buryall nor Armes. *Ibid.* 405 Escelie, Wolscote and Wolaston are but lyms of the Manor of Swineford.

d. ***out on a limb,*** in an isolated or stranded position; at a disadvantage. orig. *U.S.*

1897 A. H. LEWIS *Wolfville* 59 Seven of us..seein' whatever can we tie down an' brand, when some Mexicans gets us out on a limb. **1934** *Amer. Speech* IX. 11/2 A player is *out on a limb* when he is allowed to play a hand at an overambitious contract. **1939** F. SCOTT FITZGERALD *Let.* Winter (1964) 50 She might not consider the rearrangement of someone else's words a literary composition, which would leave you out on a limb. **1943** J. B. PRIESTLEY *Daylight on Saturday* xxvii. 210 Somebody does something dam' silly, which probably means that some poor devils somewhere are left out on a limb. **1948** J. STEINBECK *Russ. Jrnl.* (1949) iii. 41 No one is willing to go out on any limb. No one is willing to say yes or no to a proposition. He must always go to someone higher. **1959** *Economist* 18 Apr. 214/2 President Nasser is out on a bit of a limb, but in this uncomfortable situation he can take comfort from the thought that there is still no other pan-Arab leader in sight. **1972** *Guardian* 7 Feb. 10/6 Once in the Commission, the British Civil Servant will feel out on a limb, away from the main-stream of his department. **1973** *Times* 23 May 16/5 At the international law of the sea conference Britain could find herself isolated and out on a limb.

5. *attrib.* and *Comb.*, as ***limb arch, -bone, -dance, -ease, -fitter, -fitting, -muscle, -nerve, -vessel; limb-numbing, -strewn*** adjs.; †**limb-broken** *a.*, affected with hernia, ruptured; **limb-bud** *Embryol.*, in an embryo, a small protuberance from which a limb develops; **limb-girdle** *Anat.* (see GIRDLE *sb.*[1] 4 b); **limb-guard,** defensive armour for the arm or leg; **limb-kinetic** *a. Path.*, denoting a form of apraxia (see quot. 1966); **limb-length** *advb. phr.*, with limbs stretched out to their full length; †**limb-lifter,** a fornicator; †**limb-take** *a.*, crippled; **limb-wood** (see quot.). Also LIMB-MEAL.

1883 MARTIN & MOALE *Vertebr. Dissect.* 102 The general arrangement of the skeleton; its..*limb arches and limbs. **1854** OWEN *Skel. & Teeth* (1855) 6 The strength and lightness of the *limb-bones. **1398** TREVISA *Barth. De P.R.* XVII. xix. (Tollem. MS.), It helep hem at þe beste þat beþ *lyme broke [ed. 1535 limme broken L. *herniosis*]. **1906** G. R. SATTERLEE *Outl. Human Embryol.* v. 55 Outgrowths of mesenchyme occur from the lateral portion of the trunk. These projections are called the *limb-buds, and are the *anlages* for the arms and legs. **1926** [see CULTIVATE *v.* 2 b]. **1965** L. B. AREY *Developmental Anat.* (ed. 7) xii. 210 The limb buds appear late in the fourth week as lateral swellings. *a* **1885** G. M. HOPKINS *Poems* (1918) 79 While cripples are, while lepers, dancers in dismal *limb-dance. **1654** GAYTON *Pleas. Notes* I. i. 6 Longing for *limb-ease, and tooth motion. **1967** *Economist* 8 Apr. 121/3 Hangers granted a rise..to its

*limb-fitters from the start of this year. 1920 *Glasgow Herald* 3 Dec. 8 The *limb-fitting centres in the United Kingdom have been increased from 6 to 20. 1959 *Chambers's Encycl.* I. 652/1 Roehampton, the chief limb-fitting centre in England. 1870 ROLLESTON *Anim. Life* 33 Possessed of no functional limbs nor *limb-girdles. 1869 BOUTELL *Arms & Arm.* viii. (1874) 125 At this time [*c* 1350] the *limb-guards were made to enclose the limbs within back and front pieces, hinged and buckled together. 1914, 1933 *Limb-kinetic [see *ideokinetic* adj. s.v. IDEO-]. 1966 *McGraw-Hill Encycl. Sci. & Technol.* I. 494/1 Several forms of apraxia are usually distinguished. The lowest order apraxia is called limb-kinetic or motor... Limb-kinetic apraxia refers to a loss of coordination usually affecting one upper limb only. Gross movements may be performed fairly well, whereas fine individual movements of the fingers are lost. 1873 SYMONDS *Grk. Poets* vii. 211 Where the Bacchantes lie *limb-length beneath the silver-firs. 1579 GOSSON *Sch. Abuse* (Arb.) 33 Better might they say them selues to be .. perfect *Limme lifters for teaching the trickes of euery strumpet. 1608 MIDDLETON *Fam. Love* v. iii, Abroad thou'rt like a stone horse, you old limb lifter. 1611 FLORIO, *Leuante*,.. a lim-lifter, an vp-taker, a bold pilfrer. 1898 P. MANSON *Trop. Diseases* xiv. 231 Atrophied *limb-muscles. 1897 *Allbutt's Syst. Med.* III. 309 The sweat-nerves, although ultimately in the *limb-nerves, do not leave the cervical or lumbar regions of the cord in the anterior roots of these nerves. 1598 SYLVESTER *Du Bartas* II. i. III. *Furies* 173 The stifning Carpese, th'eyes-foe Hemlock stinking, *Limb-numming belching, and the sinew-shrinking Dead-laughing Apium. 1813 SHELLEY *Q. Mab* v. 101 Amid the horrors of the *limb-strewn field. 1519 HORMAN *Vulg.* 106 Brute beestis cherisshe vp theyr kynde: thoughe they be *lymtake, or be nummed. 1898 J. HUTCHINSON *Archives Surg.* IX. 333 All the larger *limb-vessels must also be simultaneously affected. 1901 J. BLACK *Illustr. Carpenter & Builder Ser.: Home Handicrafts* 62 [For mosaic work] black is obtained by using ebony or bog oak .. green, by .. a species of native green oak, known as '*limb wood'.

limb (lɪm), *sb.*² Also 6–7 lymb(e, limbe, (7 lembe). [ad. L. *limb-us* hem, border, edge, fringe, zodiac, of F. *limbe* (= It., Sp., Pg. *limbo*). Cf. LIMBUS, LIMBO.]

†**1.** *Sc.* = LIMBO 1, LIMBUS 1. *Obs.*

c 1450 *Mirour Saluacioun* 492 (1888) 18 For sawles fro helles Lymbe shuld passe maugre thaire foos. 1513 DOUGLAS *Æneis* VI. Prol. 92 The Lymb of faderis auld, With *Lymbus puerorum*. 1528 LYNDESAY *Dreme* 360 That was the Lymbe, in the quhilk did remaine Our Fore-fatheris, because Adam offendit. 1588 A. KING tr. *Canisius' Catech.* 8 The fatheris, quha war abyddand, in the limbe and place of rest. 1600 J. HAMILTON *Facile Traictise* X 3, To hyd the deliuerance of the patriarches and vthers Iust men, in the auld law out of the lymbe of the fathers. 1797 *Encycl. Brit.* (ed. 3) X. s.v. *Limb, Limbus*... The limb of the patriarchs. .. The limb of infants dying without baptism.

†**2.** A border or edging. *Obs. rare*$^{-1}$.

1644 DIGBY *Nat. Bodies* xxx. (1645) 321 There must appeare at the bottom of the paper, a Lembe of deepe blew.

3. In scientific use; The edge or boundary of a surface. **a.** *gen.*

1704 NEWTON *Optics* (1721) 209 The violet and blue at the exterior Limbs of each Ring, and the red and yellow at the interior. 1791 W. BARTRAM *Carolina* 501 Their ears are lacerated, separating the border or cartelaginous limb. 1826 KIRBY & SP. *Entomol.* IV. 268 *Disk*, the middle of a surface. *Limb*, the circumference. *Margin*, the extreme sides. 1831 *Literary Gaz.* 15 Jan. 40/3 The points thus formed being carefully marked on the limb of the circle, the intervals are then subdivided [etc.].

b. The graduated edge of a quadrant or similar instrument.

1593 FALE *Dialling* 50 b, The 63ᵈ. 30ᵐ. of the limbe of the Quadrant. 1594 BLUNDEVIL *Exerc.* VII. xx. (1636) 677 The limbe of the Mariners Astrolabe is traced .. with three Circles, making two spaces to containe therein the degrees and numbers of altitude. 1690 LEYBOURN *Curs. Math.* 715 b, The Limb of the Quadrant is divided into 90 .. Degrees. 1774 M. MACKENZIE *Maritime Surv.* 34 Mark down the Degrees and Minutes shewn on the Limb. 1837 WHEWELL *Hist. Induct. Sci.* (1857) I. 154.

c. The edge of the disk of a heavenly body, esp. of the sun and moon.

a 1677 HALE *Prim. Orig. Man.* IV. viii. 364 The perception of Sense .. judgeth .. the Limb of the Heavenly Horizon to be contiguous to the Earth. 1726 tr. *Gregory's Astron.* I. 39 The Eastern Limb of the Moon will first cover the Western of the Sun, and the Western of the Moon will last uncover the Eastern Limb of the Sun. 1768–74 TUCKER *Lt. Nat.* (1834) I. 305 When astronomers, in describing an eclipse, talk of the shadow of the earth touching the outer limb of the moon. 1812 WOODHOUSE *Astron.* xi. 90 The lower limb of the Sun when setting. 1879 NEWCOMB & HOLDEN *Astron.* 301 Similar prominences were seen about the sun's limb. 1891 T. HARDY *Tess* I. ix, The sun's lower limb was just free of the hill.

d. *Bot.* The lamina or expanded portion of a monopetalous corolla, of a petal or sepal. Also, the lamina or blade of a leaf.

1735 DYCHE & PARDON *Dict.*, *Limb*, .. among the Florists, 'tis the Edge of Leaves, Flowers, &c. 1760 J. LEE *Introd. Bot.* I. iii. (1765) 7 One Petal; it consists of two Parts, viz... the Limb, or upper Part, which usually spreads wider. 1861 MISS PRATT *Flower. Pl.* I. 6 The upper large part of the petal is termed the limb, and the lower the claw. 1872 OLIVER *Elem. Bot.* I. vii. 85 In a gamopetalous corolla .. the lower united portion is called the tube; the free divisions, which indicate the number of parts cohering, the limb.

e. *Zool.* In trilobites (see quot.)

1877 HUXLEY *Anat. Inv. Anim.* vi. 258 The limb, or lateral area on either side [of the glabellum] answers to a thoracic *pleuron*. *Ibid.* 259 The limb is thus divided into two parts —one fixed .., attached to the glabellum; the other separable .., on which the eye is placed.

4. Special Comb.: **limb-darkening** *Astr.*, the apparent darkening of the face of the sun towards its edges.

1931 *Monthly Notices R. Astr. Soc.* XCI. 893, I(*x*) is of the form *a* – *mx* (limb darkening linearly proportional to distance from the centre). 1938 *Astrophysical Jrnl.* LXXXVII. 45 (*heading*) The effect of an adiabatic layer upon solar limb darkening. 1962 *Science Survey* III. 103 Visual observations .. show that the sun's disc is brightest at the centre, becoming gradually dimmer towards the outer edge, or limb. This phenomenon is known as limb darkening, and is due to the fact that we look less and less deeply into the hotter layers of the sun as we view its surface more obliquely.

limb (lɪm), *v.* [f. LIMB *sb.*¹]

1. *trans.* **a.** To pull limb from limb; to dismember. Also with *up*.

1674 N. FAIRFAX *Bulk & Selv.* To Rdr., As the one had wrackt and limm'd my thoughts .. so had the other nipt in my soul and shrivell'd up my thoughts. 1693 SMALLRIDGE *Jul. Cæsar* in *Dryden's Plutarch* IV. 482 They .. ran .. up and down the city, to find out the men, and limb them. 1731 BAILEY vol. II, *To limb*, to pull limb from limb. 1885 TROMHOLT *Aurora Borealis* I. 172 The intestines being taken out, the trunk is limbed up .. each joint being skilfully dissected. 1888 *Daily News* 10 Sept. 7/1 As to hearing the defendant threaten to 'limb' the complainant.

b. To remove branches from (a tree).

1835 H. EVANS *Jrnl.* 2 July in *Mississippi Valley Hist. Rev.* (1927) XIV. 202 Weather beaten cotton wood trees limbed and shattered by the storms of the prairies. 1839 E. HOLMES *Rep. Explor. Aroostook River* 53 The best mode undoubtedly is to fall the trees and '*limb*' them (that is, cut off the limbs,) in June. 1889 *Harper's Mag.* Jan. 231/1 It seemed to be built principally of alder poles well limbed off and placed, roughly speaking, side by side. 1971 *Timber Trades Jrnl.* 3 Apr. 58/2 The chainsaw has long been used for limbing hardwoods.

†**2.** *refl.* To provide oneself with limbs. *Obs.*

1667 MILTON *P.L.* VI. 352 As they please, They Limb themselves, and colour, shape or size Assume, as likes them best.

limb, obs. form of LIMN.

Limba¹ (ˈlɪmbə), *sb.* and *a.* Also **Limbah**. [Native name.] **A.** *sb.* **a.** A member of a West African people inhabiting Sierra Leone. **b.** The language of the Limbas. **B.** *adj.* Of or pertaining to this people or their language.

1902 *Encycl. Brit.* XX. 624/1 Sierra Leone is inhabited by about a dozen distinct African peoples, the most important being the Mende, Temne, Limba [etc.]. 1925 T. N. GODDARD *Handbk. Sierra Leone* III. 55 The Limbas may be found in the north of the Temne country. 1925 H. C. LUKE *Bibliogr. Sierra Leone* (ed. 2) 149 The Wesleyan Methodist Catechism in Limbah. 1951 K. L. LITTLE *Mende of Sierra Leone* 71 The Limba wear gowns of native cloth and tight shorts of the same material. 1954 R. LEWIS *Sierra Leone* xii. 118 When a Limba chief dies, weird moans issue from it [*sc.* a cave]. Limbas can hear the dead man being brought to Kumba the Krifi. 1964 C. FYFE *Sierra Leone Inheritance* 20 He killed the Limbas and sold them.

limba² (ˈlɪmbə). [f. Gabon name *limbo*.] The West African tree *Terminalia superba* or the hardwood obtained from it; = AFARA.

[1937 J. M. DALZIEL *Useful Plants W. Trop. Afr.* 83 The timber [of *Terminalia superba*] from the Belgian Congo is known as 'limbo (or limba) clair' when at least two-thirds of the diameter is light-coloured.] 1955 *Times* 6 May 12/6 Limba, a light honey-coloured hardwood from Africa. 1960 *House & Garden* Nov. 34/1 The new limba furniture has all the charm and grace one expects. *Ibid.*, An abundance of good designs in limba, tola, lacquer or oak.

limbachite (ˈlɪmbəxaɪt). *Min.* [Named by A. Frenzel, 1873, from *Limbach* in Saxony, its locality: see -ITE.] 'A hydrous silicate of aluminum and magnesium, resembling cerolite' (A. H. Chester *Dict. Min.* 1896).

1882 DANA *Man. Min. & Lithol.* 309.

limbal (ˈlɪmbəl), *a.* *Ophthalm.* [f. LIMB(US + -AL.] Of or pertaining to the limbus of the cornea.

1947 F. H. ADLER *Gifford's Textbk. Ophthalm.* (ed. 4) xi. 221 Fine capillary loops from the anterior ciliary vessels pass into the cornea, forming the limbal arcades. 1958 H. B. STALLARD *Eye Surg.* (ed. 3) viii. 570 The limbal incision covered by a conjunctival flap is preferable, for adjacent blood-supply is better and the firm closure of the wound is quicker than in the corneal section. 1972 *Virchows Archiv* A. CCCLV. 277 The limbal region of the bulbar conjunctiva was covered by a stratified squamous epithelium.

limbate (ˈlɪmbeɪt), *a.* *Biol.* [ad. late L. *limbāt-us*, f. *limbus* LIMB *sb.*², LIMBUS.] Of a part or organ: Having a limb or border; bordered; *Bot.* said esp. of a flower having an edging of a different colour from the rest.

1826 KIRBY & SP. *Entomol.* IV. 291 *Limbate*, when the disk is surrounded by a margin of a different colour. 1836 LOUDON *Encycl. Plants* Gloss., *Limbate*, having a colored or dilated surface. 1866 *Treas. Bot.*, *Limbate*, having one colour, surrounded by an edging of another. 1880 GRAY *Struct. Bot.* 418/2 *Limbate*, bordered.

limbation (lɪmˈbeɪʃən). *Biol.* [f. prec.: see -ATION.] The formation of a border; a border distinguished by colour or structure.

1881 H. B. BRADY in *Jrnl. Microsc. Sci.* Jan. 59 Sutures limbate, the limbation taking the form of raised beads. 1894 in GOULD *Illustr. Dict. Med.*

limbeck (ˈlɪmbɛk), *sb. arch.* Forms: 4 **lambyke**, 5–6 **lembike**, **-byke**, 6 **lembyck**, **-beck**, **lymbeke**, 6–7 **lim-**, **lymbeck(e**, **-bique**, 7 **limbek**, **-bic(ke**, 6–9 **limbec(k**. [aphetized f. ALEMBIC.] = ALEMBIC.

c 1350 *Med. MS.* in *Archæologia* XXX. 409 Lambyke. 1460–70 *Bk. Quintessence* 11 þanne putte it in a lembike and distille it at a good fier. 1529 *Test. Ebor.* (Surtees) V. 277 A lymbeke for stilling of watters. *a* 1599 SPENSER *F.Q.* VII. vii. 31 The dull drops, that from his purpled bill, As from a limbeck, did adown distill. 1667 MILTON *P.L.* III. 605 1667 DRYDEN *Secr. Love* I. iii, I feel my Strength each Day and Hour consume, Like Lillies wasting in a Lymbeck's Heat. 1713 POPE *Guardian* No. 92 ¶4 Like a limbeck that gives you, drop by drop, an extract of the simples in it. 1829 CARLYLE *Misc.* (1857) I. 277 Let the distiller pass it and repass it through his limbecs.

Comb. 1650 FULLER *Pisgah* IV. i. 16 An engine, which limbecklike extracted sweet water out of the brackish Ocean.

b. *fig.*

1593 LODGE *Phillis* (1875) 54 My loue doth serue for fire, my hart the fornace is, The aperries of my sighes augment the burning flame, The Limbique is mine eye that doth distill the same. 1598 TOFTE *Alba* (1880) 3 What my sad eye Distils from Lymbeck of a bleeding Hart. 1605 SHAKS. *Macb.* I. vii. 67. 1660 JER. TAYLOR *Duct. Dubit.* II. iii. rule xiv. §29 (1676) 372 The remaining part [of the books of the Fathers] have passed through the limbecks and strainers of Hereticks [etc.]. 1840 HOOD *Miss Kilmansegg, Her Misery* ix, The waters that down her visage rilled Were drops of unrectified spirit distilled From the Limbeck of Pride and Vanity. 1887 *Athenæum* 20 Aug. 243/2 There are [in the translation] French forms of expression .. which ought to have been passed through the limbeck.

†ˈ**limbeck**, *v.* *Obs.* [f. the sb. Cf. OF. *lambiquer* (16th c.), It. *lambiccare*.]

1. *trans.* To treat as in an alembic; to subject to the process of distillation or extraction of essence, etc. Chiefly *fig.*; esp. to rack or fatigue (the brain) in the effort to extract ideas.

1599 SANDYS *Europæ Spec.* (1632) 162 Where the greater doe nothing but limbicke their braines in the Arts of Alchymy and Ballancing. 1622 MABBE tr. *Aleman's Guzman d'Alf.* II. 50 Wasting my wits, and Limbeking my braines, without drawing any iuice or substance thence at all. *a* 1652 BROME *Songs*, etc. (1661) 255 His Patients grow impatient, and the fear Of death, lymbeck'd their bodies into tears. 1661 FELTHAM *Resolves, Disc. Eccl.* ii. 11 (1677) 346 And when he had try'd and Lymbeck'd all, the spirit and Extract comes forth, Vanity, Vexation.

2. To distil or extract (an essence, etc.) as by an alembic.

1598 FLORIO, *Lambicare*, to distill, to limbecke. 1648 EARL WESTMORELAND *Otia Sacra* (1879) 139 The spring-head, where Crystall is Lymbeckt all the yeere. 1657 W. MORICE *Coena quasi Κοινὴ* Diat. iii. 140 The quintessence to be limbeck'd and distilled [etc.].

Hence ˈ**limbecked** *ppl. a.*, ˈ**limbecking** *vbl. sb.*

a 1618 SYLVESTER *Tobacco battered* 233 The stench and Stuff Extracted from their limbeckt Lips and Nose. 1647 WARD *Simp. Cobler* 18 Metaphysicall Limbeckings.

limbed (lɪmd), *a.* Also 4–5 **i-limed**, **ilymed**. [f. LIMB *sb.* + -ED².] Having limbs. Nearly always with adv. or adj. prefixed, as ***well-limbed***, ***straight-limbed***.

c 1320 *Cast. Love* 624 Hose now I-seȝe heere A child þat riht I-limed nere, þat þreo ffeet and þreo honden beere. 1412–20 LYDG. *Chron. Troy* I. v, So well Ilymed and compact by measure Well growe on heyght and of good stature. 1555 EDEN *Decades* 105 Thinhabitantes are .. well lymmed and proportioned. 1598 GRENEWEY *Tacitus' Ann.* I. xiii. (1622) 26 The Cheruscians being a great limmed people. 1611 SPEED *Hist. Gt. Brit.* IX. xviii. (1623) 898 Little of stature, ill-limmed, and crook-backed. 1667 MILTON *P.L.* VII. 456 Innumerous living Creatures, perfet formes, Limb'd and full grown. 1697 DRYDEN *Virg. Georg.* II. 231 Strong limb'd and stout, and to the Wars inclin'd. 1748 *Anson's Voy.* III. v. 339 These Indians are a bold well-limbed people. 1835 W. IRVING *Tour Prairies* 173 It was a colt about two years old, well grown, finely limbed. 1873 BLACK *Pr. Thule* (1874) 4 A man .. straight-limbed, and sinewy in frame. 1899 *Echo* 9 Mar. 1/4 Every reader of Dickens remembers the frail ex-prisoner of the Bastille, white-haired and feeble-limbed. 1954 T. GUNN *Fighting Terms* 44 My hate throbs yet but I am feeble-limbed.

limbekill, obs. form of LIME-KILN.

†**limbelite**. *Min. Obs.* [Named (*limbilite*) by H. B. de Saussure, 1794, from Limburg, its locality: see -LITE.] A synonym of chrysolite.

1837 DANA *Min.* 335 The minerals Chusite and Limbelite of Saussure, from the volcanic district of Limbourg, appear to be decomposed varieties of this species [Chrysolite]. 1865 WATTS *Dict. Chem.* III. 696.

limber (ˈlɪmbə(r)), *sb.*¹ Forms: 5 **lymor(e**, 5–6 **lymour**, 6 **lymowr**, **lym(m)er**, *Sc.* **lymnar**, 6–7, 9 **limmer**, 9 **limber**. [Of obscure origin. The F. *limon* = sense 1 below; the derivative *limonière* means 'the shafts and connected framework of a vehicle'. If the form *lymnar* in Douglas be genuine, it may be an adoption of *limonière*, and perh. the forms *lymour*, etc., though recorded earlier, may be corruptions of this.]

1. a. The shaft of a cart or carriage. *Obs.* exc. *dial.*

1480 *Wardr. Acc. Edw. IV* (1830) 123 A crouper for the lymour, price iiijs. 1501 DOUGLAS *Pal. Hon.* xxxiii, The lymnaris [of the chariot] wer of birneist gold. 1513 —— *Æneis* IX. vi. 23 The cartis stand with lymowris bendyt strek. 1579–80 NORTH *Plutarch, Coriol.* (1595) 248 They made him carrie a limmer on his shoulders that is fastened to the

Axeltree of a couch [= coach]. **1611** FLORIO, *Timóne*,..the limmer or beame of a Wagon or Waine. **1839** URE *Dict. Arts* 982 (*Pitcoal*) The rolley horses have a peculiar kind of shafts, commonly made of iron, named limbers, the purpose of which is to prevent the carriage from overrunning them. **1860** *Eng. & For. Mining Gloss.* (Newcastle Terms), *Limmer's*, the shafts by which the horses draw.

†**b.** Short for *limber-horse*.

1632 SHERWOOD, A limmer, *limonier*. *Voyez* a Thill-horse.

2. *Mil.* (In early use *pl.*) The detachable fore part of a gun-carriage, consisting of two wheels and an axle, a pole for the horses, and a frame which holds one or two ammunition-chests. It is attached to the trail of the gun-carriage proper by a hook.

Quot. 1628 seems to be an erroneous explanation.

1497 *Naval Acc. Hen. VII* (1896) 84, ij paire lymores with boltes forlokkes kayes lynces and a taile pynne for the said Curtowe. **1578** BOURNE *Invent. & Devices* xcvi. 85 The Lymers that the horses doth draw in. **1628** R. NORTON *Gunner* lix. 130 The sides and Cheekes [of the Cariage] called Limbers. **1801** WELLINGTON in Gurw. *Desp.* (1837) I. 325 A six-pounder, its carriage and limber, and ammunition in the limber box. **1851** *Ord. & Regul. R. Engineers* xix. 96 Twelve pieces of Field Artillery, with their Carriages and Limbers. **1859** F. A. GRIFFITHS *Artil. Man.* (1862) 103 No. 7 attends the limber and serves ammunition.

3. *attrib.*, as (sense 1 b) †*limber croup*, †*hame*, *pillow*; **limber-box**, **-chest** *Mil.*, the ammunition box carried by a limber; **limber-hook** (see quot.); **limber-horse** *dial.*, the horse which is placed between the shafts; †**limber-plank** *Mil.* (see quot.); **limber-saddle**, a cart-saddle.

1801 *Limber-box [see sense 2]. **1876** JAS. GRANT *Hist. India* I. xxiv. 129/1 Wood's field-guns had only five rounds left in the limber-boxes. **1888** *Century Mag.* May 103/2 Some of whom [the enemy], springing nimbly on his *limber-chests, shot down his horses and then his men. **1483** *Wardr. Acc.* in Grose *Antiq. Repert.* (1807) I. 47 *Lymour crowps..*Lymour pilows. **1876** VOYLE *Milit. Dict.* (ed. 3) s.v. *Limber*, At the back of the limber is an iron hook or pintle, termed a *limber-hook, to which the trail of the gun carriage is attached... The limber-hook is stated to have been invented..in 1804. **1628** R. NORTON *Gunner* lx. 131 The *Limber Planks or sides of the Cariage must be 4 and a halfe, or 5 dyametres broad, one thicke. **1480** *Wardr. Acc. Edw. IV* (1830) 123 For a *lymour sadell price *vs.*; for a payre *lymour hamys garnissht xviij*d*. **1806–7** J. BERESFORD *Miseries Hum. Life* (1826) VI. vii, The flap of a limber saddle rolling up and galling and pinching your calf.

limber (ˈlɪmbə(r)), *sb.*² *Naut.* [? a corruption of F. *lumière* hole, perforation (lit. 'light'), used *Naut.* in the same application.]

1. One of a series of holes cut through the floor-timbers on each side of the keelson to form a passage for water to the pump-well.

1626, **1711**, etc. [see *limber-hole*, *-board* in 2]. **1729** CAPT. W. WRIGLESWORTH *MS. Log-bk of the 'Lyell'* 6 Sept., Cleared the Limbers in the Forehold. *c* **1860** H. STUART *Seaman's Catech.* 63 See the limbers are clear, and limber boards shipped. **1898** F. T. BULLEN *Cruise Cachalot* 326 The ship..never made a drop of water more than just sufficient to sweeten the limbers.

2. *attrib.* in spec. combinations: **limber-board** (see quots.); **limber-chain**, a chain used like a limber-rope (Webster, 1864); **limber-hole** *Naut.* = sense 1; **limber-passage** *Naut.*, the passage or channel formed by the limber-strakes on each side of the keelson; **limber-rope** *Naut.*, a rope passing through the limber-holes, by which they may be cleared of dirt; **limber-strake** (or **-streak**) *Naut.* (see quots. and STRAKE); **limber-tar** (see quot.).

1711 W. SUTHERLAND *Shipbuild. Assist.* 70 One Strake next the *Limber Boards. **1769** FALCONER *Dict. Marine* (1780), *Limber-boards*, short pieces of plank, which form a part of the ceiling, or lining of a ship's floor, close to the kelson, and immediately above the limbers. They are.. removed, when it becomes necessary to..clear the limber-holes of any filth,..or gravel, by which they may be clogged. *c* **1860** H. STUART *Seaman's Catech.* 69 The limber boards.. cover these channels or 'limbers', and serve to keep dirt out, which would soon choke the pumps. **1626** CAPT. SMITH *Accid. Yng. Seamen* 8 Then lay all the Flore timbers, and cut your *Limber holes aboue the keele, to bring the water to the well for the pumpe. **1769** FALCONER *Dict. Marine* (1780) s.v. *Limbers*, Every floor-timber has two limber-holes cut through it, viz. one on each side of the kelson. **1869** SIR E. J. REED *Shipbuild.* v. 79 The limber-holes in the floor-plates are, as a general rule, cut above the frame angle-iron. *c* **1850** *Rudim. Navig.* (Weale) 129 **Limber-passage*, a passage or channel formed throughout the whole length of the floor, on each side of the kelson, for giving water a free communication to the pumps. **1769** FALCONER *Dict. Marine* (1780), **Limber-Rope*, a long rope, frequently retained in the limber-holes..in order to clear them by pulling the rope backwards and forwards. **1841** DANA *Seaman's Man.* 114. **1797** *Encycl. Brit.* (ed. 3) XVII. 404/2 The *limber strake. **1841** DANA *Seaman's Man.* 114 *Limber-streak*, the streak of foot-waling nearest the keelson. **1874** THEARLE *Naval Archit.* 55 The limber strakes, while constituting a longitudinal tie over the floors, served also to form watercourses on each side of the keel, leading to the pumps. **1858** SIMMONDS *Dict. Trade*, **Limber Tar*, the bilge-water or refuse found in the hold of a ship that imports tar, which has drained from the casks during the voyage.

limber (ˈlɪmbə(r)), *a.* Also 6 limmer, lymmer, 6–7 lymber. [Of obscure origin; Skeat suggests connexion with LIMP *a.*, which, however, has not been found before 1706; it may perh. be some compound of LIMB *sb.* (cf. the derivation of LEATHWAKE from LITH, limb). Cf. also the synonymous *limmock* dial.]

1. a. Easily bent (without damage to shape or structure); flexible, pliant, supple.

1565 COOPER *Thesaurus*, *Lentus*, softe, tender, pliant, that boweth easely, limber [etc.]. **1567** TURBERV. *Epit.* etc. 87 The Bargeman that doth rowe with long and limber Oare. **1578** LYTE *Dodoens* IV. lxxx. 543 The roote..tough and limmer, and harde to breake. *Ibid.* V. xxxii. 591 The Gourde hath long limmer stalkes. **1657** AUSTEN *Fruit Trees* I. 50 Do not prune off the side branches, lest the body of the plant be too small and limber to beare his head. **1667** MILTON *P.L.* VII. 476 Those wav'd thir limber fans For wings. **1684** BOYLE *Porousn. Anim. & Solid Bod.* v. 46 With another piece of the same Bladder, made limber by being a little wetted in common water. **1713** CHESELDEN *Anat.* I. i. (1726) 12, I..found..in one instance several of the bones as limber as leather. **1738** [G. SMITH] *Curious Relat.* II. 108 A Sort of Paper..as fine and limber as Silk. **1787** J. FARLEY *Lond. Art Cookery* (ed. 4) 7 The feet [of a goose] will be limber, if it be fresh, but stiff and dry if old. **1840** R. H. DANA *Bef. Mast* xxx. 111 That the [new] ropes might have time to stretch and become limber. **1872** BLACKIE *Lays Highl.* 73 Ye Norsemen brave That ply the limber oar.

b. Of persons, their bodies, movements, etc.: Bending or moving easily; lithe and nimble.

1582 STANYHURST *Æneis* IV. (Arb.) 100 Limber in her whisking..shee soars vp nimblye toe skyward. **1603** DRAYTON *Bar. Wars* VI. xxxviii, In Postures strange, their limber Bodies bending. **1605** B. JONSON *Volpone* III. i, I could skip Out of my skin, now, like a subtill snake, I am so limber. **1635** FOXE & JAMES *Voy. N.W.* (Hakluyt Soc.) II. 378 The sunne shone, and thawed our men and made them more limber. **1694** CROWNE *Married Beau* II. 20 Methinks you are As limber in your tongue as in your hams. **1736** CARTE *Ormonde* II. 549 At getting up, he took notice..that his legs were more limber and bended with greater ease. **1751** SMOLLETT *Per. Pic.* (1779) II. xliv. 71 The Italian..a thin limber creature. **1817** COLERIDGE *Christabel* II. 1 A little child, a limber elf. **1844** DISRAELI *Coningsby* I. i, A limber and graceful figure. **1859** WRAXALL tr. *R. Houdin* iii. 27 The fingers remaining perfectly free and limber. **1885–94** R. BRIDGES *Eros & Psyche* Mar. xiv, Her comely boy, The limber scion of the God of War.

†**c.** In unfavourable sense, of things which are properly firm or crisp: Limp, flaccid, flabby.

1592 WARNER *Alb. Eng.* VII. xxxvii. (1612) 182 My limber wings were Leather-like vnplum'de. **1602** MIDDLETON *Blurt* II. i, Limber like the skin of a white pudding when the meat is out. **1658** tr. *Porta's Nat. Magic* I. xv. 20 Flowers are ..to be gathered..before they wax limber. **1736** BAILEY *Housh. Dict.* 195 Observe to clap very quick and very hard, for if you let them dry they will be limber. **1747** MRS. GLASSE *Cookery* (1767) 323 A rabbit, if stale, will be limber and slimy; if new, white and stiff.

2. *fig.*

1602 MARSTON *Ant. & Mel.* I. Wks. 1856 I. 11 Confusion to these limber sycophants. **1611** SHAKS. *Wint. T.* I. ii. 47 You put me off with limber Vowes. *a* **1639** WOTTON in Gutch *Coll. Cur.* I. 219 He had tryed and found him a Prince of limber virtues. **1695** *Remarks Late Serm.* (ed. 2) 2 Men of limber and pliable Consciences can easily do this. **1719** D'URFEY *Pills* (1872) II. 244 Tho' both in his sense, and his Loyalty limber. **1858** BUSHNELL *Serm. New Life* 250 His whole nature becomes limber and quick to his love. **1887** BETHAM-EDWARDS *Next of Kin wanted* I. xx. 272 [He] proved limber as a withy in her hands.

†**3.** quasi-*sb.* Limber quality, limberness. *Obs.*

1786 MRS. A. M. BENNETT *Juvenile Indiscretions* I. 12 The whole depth of his talents laying in the mere limber of his tongue.

4. *Comb.*, as *limber-backed*, *-footed*, *-legged* adjs.; **limber-neck**, a kind of botulism affecting poultry, caused by the toxin produced by a type of the bacterium *Clostridium botulinum*.

1601 HOLLAND *Pliny* I. 96 The Himantopodes be some of them limber legged and tender. **1720** *Humourist* 162 A poor limber-back'd Beau. **1747** MRS. GLASSE *Cookery* (1767) 322 The duck..if new, limber-footed; if stale, dry-footed. **1904** *Westm. Gaz.* 8 May 14/2 Here leaps the limber-footed, listening hare. **1910** C. S. VALENTINE *How to keep Hens for Profit* 271 The disease called '*limberneck', in which the affected bird is unable to control the head, which droops to the ground, is said by many who have had large experience with it to be the result of stomach irritation brought on by eating maggots. **1927** E. T. BROWN *'How to do it' Poultry Bk.* xxiii. 242 Limberneck or false cholera..is due entirely to a form of poisoning. **1931** DICKINSON & LEWIS *Poultry Enterprises* ix. 216 When flies and maggots infest putrid meat and other spoiled feeds, fowls eating them are likely to show symptoms of limber neck disease. **1964** M. HYNES *Med. Bacteriol.* (ed. 8) xx. 296 These types [of botulism toxin] are also most often responsible for 'limber-neck' of chickens and ducks.

Hence ˈ**limberness**.

1565 COOPER *Thesaurus*, *Lentitia*, softenesse, pliantnesse, limbernesse. **1669** BOYLE *Contn. New Exp.* I. 160 The limberness of them [the sides of a bladder] would permit the Air to accommodate it self and the Bladder to the Figure of a Cylindrical vessel. **1743** *Lond. & Country Brew.* IV. (ed. 2) 278 In this [trough] oaken Planks are laid for the confin'd Steam of hot Water..to impregnate and reduce them to a Limberness. **1835** M. SCOTT in *Blackw. Mag.* XXXVII. 460 The extreme pliancy and eel-like limberness, if I may so speak, of the whole body. **1889** F. M. CRAWFORD *Greifenstein* I. viii, 236 He has the most surprising limberness of wrist.

limber (ˈlɪmbə(r)), *v.*¹ [f. LIMBER *a.*] *trans.* To make limber, pliant, or supple. Also with *up*, and *intr.* Hence ˈ**limbering** *ppl. a.* and *vbl. sb.*, **limbering-up** *vbl. sb.*

1748 RICHARDSON *Clarissa* III. 356 Her stiff hams..are now limbered into courtesies three deep at every word. **1753** *Ess. Celibacy* 39 They exempt themselves from the free and limbering situations and circumstances of action. **1872** O. W. HOLMES *Poet Breakf.-t.* iii. (1885) 60 She worked her wrists..to limber 'em. **1883** F. M. CRAWFORD *Mr. Isaacs* viii. 164 The stiffest arms can be limbered. **1901** *Daily Colonist* (Victoria, B.C.) 8 Oct. 3/2 When her machinery is limbered up after it has been used a while she will do much better. **1921** *Ibid.* 5 Apr. 10/2 During the recent fine weather several of the [tennis club] members have been out limbering up after the inactivities of the Winter months. **1921** *Blackw. Mag.* Aug. 262/1 Dempsey had passed the afternoon in a 'limbering-up hike'. **1927** *Dancing Times* Dec. 301/1 Most dance students know that limbering is the basis for every kind of dance work. **1929** WODEHOUSE *Mr. Mulliner Speaking* ii. 64 He waggled his right leg for a moment to limber it up, backed a pace or two and crept forward. **1957** *Oxf. Pocket Bk. Athletic Training* (ed. 2) 27 An athlete who fails to limber-up properly deliberately handicaps himself. **1962** *Listener* 29 March 566/1 As images and figures in compositions..they limber or stretch or occasionally pose. **1963** H. GARNER in R. Weaver *Canad. Short Stories* (1968) 2nd Ser. 23 The limbering up we were getting from our work. **1971** R. DENTRY *Encounter at Kharmel* i. 1 He did twenty four half knee-bends to limber up.

limber (ˈlɪmbə(r)), *v.*² *Mil.* [f. LIMBER *sb.*¹] *trans.* To attach the limber to (a gun). Hence *absol.* to fasten together the two parts of a gun-carriage, as a preparation for moving away. Usually ***to limber up***.

1843 LEVER *J. Hinton* vi. (1878) 34 The heavy artillery was seen to limber up, and move slowly across the field. **1851** *Ord. & Regul. R. Engineers* xix. 95 Breadth of Shed, Guns limbered up..40 ft. 0 in. **1861** *Man. Field Exercise Artillery* 50 Limbering is always done at a trot. **1868** KINGLAKE *Crimea* (1877) III. i. 278 The guns of Turner's battery were limbered up and pushed forward.

limbered (ˈlɪmbəd), *a.* [f. LIMBER *sb.*¹] Having a limber.

1920 *Blackw. Mag.* Feb. 279/2, I lent him some men and a limbered waggon. **1942** *R.A.F. Jrnl.* 3 Oct. 18 The officers saw a German gun-team galloping their limbered gun away.

†ˈ**limberˌham.** *Obs.* [f. LIMBER *a.* + HAM.

The quot. from Wycherley shows that Dryden did not, as is generally supposed, invent the name; whether Wycherley invented it, or whether it was already current as an appellative or a nickname, remains at present uncertain.]

a. In etymological sense: One who has 'limber hams', a supple-jointed person; *fig.* an obsequious person, 'lackey'. **b.** A character like that represented in Dryden's play, a 'kind keeper'.

[**1675** WYCHERLEY *Country-wife* II. 27 There can be no more scandal to go with him, than with Mr. Tatle, or Master Limberham. *Lad.* With that nasty Fellow! no—no. **1678** DRYDEN *Limberham* (1680) Pers. Dram., *Limberham*, a tame, foolish keeper, persuaded by what is last said to him, and changing next word.] **1689** HICKERINGILL *Ceremony-monger* i. Wks. 1716 II. 390 If I were a Papist..I profess I would bow and cringe as well as any Ecclesiastical Limber-ham of them all. *a* **1704** T. BROWN *Praise Poverty* Wks. 1730 I. 99 He's a true limberham, a prodigal cully to the jilt he keeps for the use of the public. **1755** SMOLLETT *Quix.* (1803) IV. 251 When the challenger was asked how the weight of both should be made equal, he insisted on the other's carrying the difference in bars of iron, by which means, Limberham would be upon a footing with Loggerhead. **1756–66** AMORY *Buncle* IV. xiii. §3. 249 She lives..to ruin..the miserable man, who is dunce enough to become a Limberham to the execrable wretch.

†**limberly**, *a.* *Obs. rare*⁻¹. ? = LIMBER *a.*¹

1782 ELPHINSTON tr. *Martial* I. xliii. 47 Not the pears, that are bound by the limberly broom.

limberly (ˈlɪmbəlɪ), *adv.* [f. LIMBER *a.*] In a limber or supple manner.

1891 *Harper's Mag.* Nov. 891/2 His long spare arms swing limberly before a long spare body. **1909** 'O. HENRY' *Roads of Destiny* xii. 186 They..slouched limberly over to the railroad eating-house. **1964** *N.Y. Times Mag.* 23 Aug. 30 It was sculpted to Chanel's small, athletic figure and moves with it as limberly as a leopard's own leopard skin.

limbic (ˈlɪmbɪk), *a.* *Anat.* [ad. F. *limbique* (see quot. 1901), f. *limbe*, LIMB *sb.*² + *-ique*, -IC.] Pertaining to, or having the character of, a border; in ***limbic lobe*** (of cerebrum), 'term applied by Broca to the gyrus fornicatus and its prolongation, constituting the anterior part of the uncinate gyrus, because they are marked off in nearly all mammals from the surrounding convolutions' (*Syd. Soc. Lex.*); also ***limbic fissure***, the fissure surrounding this lobe. Also, of or pertaining to the limbic lobe or limbic system; ***limbic system***, a region of the brain comprising the limbic lobe and certain neighbouring areas (see quot. 1967¹).

1882 *Quain's Anat.* (ed. 9) II. 341 The two ends of the limbic lobe of Broca, which are separated by the deep part of the Sylvian fissure. **1894** GOULD *Illustr. Dict. Med.* s.v. *Fissure*, *Limbic Fissure* (of Broca), the fissure surrounding Broca's great limbic lobe. It includes the supercallosal, precuneal, and part of the collateral fissures. **1899** W. B. LEWIS *Mental Dis.* (ed. 2) 102 The limbic fissure, which here separates the lower limbic arc from the extra-limbic mass. **1901** *Gray's Anat.* (ed. 15) 631 The term limbic lobe (*grande lobe limbique*) was introduced by Broca in 1878, and under it he included two convolutions, viz. the callosal and hippocampal. **1952** *Electroencephalogr. & Clin. Neurophysiol.* IV. 407 The limbic system is comprised of the cortex contained in the great limbic lobe of Broca..together with subcortical cell stations. **1957** H. H. JASPER et al. *Reticular Formation Brain* 665 There is no doubt that all the

varied elementary somatomotor and vegetative mechanisms so clearly influenced by limbic stimulation remain essentially undisturbed after bilateral limbic lesions. **1967** C. R. Noback *Human Nervous Syst.* viii. 224/1 The difficult-to-define limbic system consists of the limbic lobe ..some subcortical nuclei (septal nuclei and amygdala), and neural pathways to other nuclear stations of the brain... Some investigators include the 'other' nuclei (habenular nucleus, hypothalamus, midbrain tegmentum, thalamus, and interpeduncular nucleus) in the limbic system. *Ibid.* 226/2 The midbrain and thalamic reticular nuclei receive inputs from several limbic pathways. **1970** *Nature* 28 Feb. 797/1 Other behaviour patterns..have been elicited by stimulating hypothalamic and limbic regions in many species. **1971** J. Z. Young *Introd. Study Man* x. 136 Sohilder's interpretation of the limbic system is as 'a mechanism for emotion'.

limbie ('lɪmɪ). *Sc.* [f. LIMB *sb.*[1] + -IE dim. suffix.] A little leg.

1789 Burns *To Dr. Blacklock* (21 Oct.) v, Ye glaiket, gleesome, dainty damies, Wha by Castalia's wimplin' streamies, Lowp, sing, and lave your pretty limbies.

limbless ('lɪmlɪs), *a.* [f. LIMB *sb.*[1] + -LESS.] Having no limbs, deprived of a limb or limbs.

1594 R. Wilson *Cobler's Proph.* v. ii. 52 So flies the murderer from the mangled lims Left limles on the ground by his fell hand. **1624** Massinger *Renegado* iv. i. (1630) H 2 b, Till nought were left me But this poore, bleeding limblesse Truncke. **1624** Gataker *Transubst.* 162 Whereas that which is given and received in the Eucharist, is (as Epiphanius well observeth) livelesse and limmelesse. **1770** Foote *Lame Lover* iii. Wks. 1799 II. 86 A tree not only limbless and leafless, but very near lifeless. **1881** Mivart *Cat* 459 The class also contains certain limbless creatures which look like something between snakes and earthworms.

limb-meal ('lɪmmi:l), *adv. Obs.* exc. *arch.* and *dial.* Forms: see LIMB *sb.*[1]; also 3 **-mele, -meel(e,** 5–7 **-meale,** 9 *dial.* **limb-mull, limmel.** [OE. *limmælum*: see LIMB *sb.*[1] and -MEAL.] Limb from limb, limb by limb; piecemeal.

c **1050** *Voc.* in Wr.-Wülcker 440/36 *Membratim*, limmælum. *c* **1205** Lay. 25618 He þer þene beore of-sloh, and hine lim-mele [*c* 1275 leome-mele] to-droh. *a* **1225** *Juliana* 79 þer ase wilde deor limmel to luken ham. *c* **1290** *Beket* 1779 in *S. Eng. Leg.*, þei ich beo drawe lime mele. **1387** Trevisa *Higden* (Rolls) V. 281 Maximus..was alto hakked..and i-þrowe lyme meele into Tyber. **1470–85** Malory *Arthur* viii. xxxvii. 330 He was drawen lymme meale. **1590** Fenne *Frutes* 41 Readie to teare in peeces, and plucke lim-meale the bodie of the bloudie tyrant. **1611** Shaks. *Cymb.* ii. iv. 147 O that I had her heere, to teare her Limb-meale. *a* **1680** Butler *Rem.* (1759) II. 399 Tears Cards Limb-meal without Regard of Age, Sex, or Quality, and breaks the Bones of Dice. **1709** tr. *P. de Cieza's Trav.* 78 Putting him to exquisite Torments and tearing his Body Limb-meal. **1860** T. Martin *Horace* 309 Up with their nails the earth they threw, Then limb-meal tore a coal-black ewe. **1894** *S.E. Worcs. Gloss.*, *Limmel.*

Hence †**limbmeally** *adv.*, in same sense.

1569 Underdown *Ovid agst. Ibis* L iij b, He was..torne limmeally, that is to say, each peece from other.

limbo[1] ('lɪmbəʊ). [L., abl. sing. of *limbus* (see LIMBUS), occurring in such phrases as *in* or *e* (= in or out of) *limbo.* Cf. It. *limbo* and LIMB *sb.*[2]]

1. a. A region supposed to exist on the border of Hell as the abode of the just who died before Christ's coming, and of unbaptized infants.

More explicitly ***limbo patrum, limbo infantum*** or ***of the infants***: see LIMBUS.

13.. *St. Erkenwolde* 291 in Horstm. *Altengl. Leg.* (1881) 272 Quene þou herghedes helle-hole & hentes hom þer-oute, ..oute of limbo, þou laftes me þer. [**1377** Langl. *P. Pl.* B. xvi. 84 The deuel..Bar hem forth boldely..And made of holy men his horde *in lymbo inferni.*] *c* **1450** *Mirour Saluacioun* 198 How crist entred hell To glad our haly fadres in Lymbo as clerkes tell. *c* **1460** *Towneley Myst.* xxv. 96 Thise lurdans that in lymbo dwell. *Ibid.* 213 Lymbo is lorne, alas! **1483** Caxton *G. de la Tour* D vj b, After her deth she [Eve]..fylle in a derke and obscure pryson..that was the lymbo of helle. **1526** *Pilgr. Perf.* (W. de W. 1531) 53 b, After theyr deth they went to lymbo patrum a place of derkenes nye to hell. **1528** Tindale *Obed. Chr. Man* To Rdr. 19 Of what texte thou provest hell, will a nother prove purgatory, a nother lymbo patrum. **1605** Heywood *Troub. Q. Eliz.* Wks. 1874 I. 221, I am freed from limbo, to be sent to hell. *a* **1658** Cleveland *Wks.* (1687) 81 'Tis a just Idea of a Limbo of the Infants. **1749** Wesley *Wks.* (1872) X. 101 In what condition were they [the Old Testament Saints] while thus detained in limbo? **1818** Moore *Fudge Fam. Paris* 57 Souls in Limbo, damn'd half way. **1857–8** Sears *Athan.* xviii. 163 If a spiritual body is desirable at all, why are the saints kept waiting for it in limbo?

b. in extended use (see quots.).

1643 Sir T. Browne *Relig. Med.* i. § 54 Methinks amongst those many subdivisions of Hell, there might have been one Limbo left for these. **1667** Milton *P.L.* iii. 495 All these upwhirld aloft Fly o're the backside of the World farr off Into a Limbo large and broad, since calld The Paradise of Fools. **1712** Addison *Spect.* No. 297 ¶7 The Picture which he [Milton] draws of the Limbo of Vanity. **1851** Carlyle *Sterling* iii. i. (1872) 163 As yet my books are lying as ghost books, in a limbo on the banks of a certain Bristolian Styx.

†**c.** used *gen.* for: Hell, Hades. *Obs.*

1581 T. Howell *Devises* D iij b, And let my Ghost in Lymbo lowe be led, To Tantals thyrst, or prowde Ixions wheele. **1582** Stanyhurst *Æneis* ii. (Arb.) 56 And with hoat assalting too Limbo we plunged a number [L. *multos demittimus Orco*]. **1612** *Proceedings of Virginia* v. 30 in *Capt. Smith's Wks.* (Arb.) 111 These vninhabited Iles; which (for the extremitie of gusts, thunder, raine, stormes, and ill weather) we called Limbo. **1634** W. Tirwhyt tr. *Balzac's Lett.* 270 She hath filled Limbo with her paricidall leachery. *a* **1637** B. Jonson *Baccanall Tri.* 50 in T. Morton's *New Eng. Canaan* (1637) 147 Minos, Eacus and Radamand, Princes of Limbo.

2. *transf.* and *fig.* **a.** Prison, confinement, durance; also, †pawn. *slang.*

1590 Greene *Neuer too Late* (1600) 56 If coyne want, then eyther to Limbo, or else clap vp a commodity. **1590** Shaks. *Com. Err.* iv. ii. 32. **1613**—— etc. *Hen. VIII*, v. iv. 67, I haue some of 'em in *Limbo Patrum.* **1649** Evelyn *Mem.* (1857) III. 51 So that John is now faster in Limbo than Ever. **1664** Butler *Hud.* ii. i. 100 On she went, To find the Knight in Limbo pent. **1687** Congreve *Old Bach.* ii. i, I let him have all my ready Mony to redeem his great Sword from Limbo. **1798** Beresford in *Ld. Auckland's Corr.* (1862) III. 441–2 We have colonels and lieutenant-colonels, and majors and captains enough in limbo. **1843** Carlyle *Past & Pr.* ii. viii, Monks..must not speak too loud, under penalty of foot-gyves, limbo, and bread and water. **1849** Cobden *Speeches* 84 Men of bad character, who have been put into limbo, or flogged. **1881** Besant & Rice *Chapl. of Fleet* i. x. (1883) 79 There were, besides the residents.., poets not yet in limbo.

b. Any unfavourable place or condition, likened to Limbo; *esp.* a condition of neglect or oblivion to which persons or things are consigned when regarded as outworn, useless, or absurd.

1642 Milton *Apol. Smect.* Wks. 1851 III. 275, I am met with a whole ging of words and phrases not mine, for he hath ..mangl'd them in this his wicked Limbo. **1728** Pope *Dunc.* i. 238 O! pass more innocent, in infant state, To the mild Limbo of our Father Tate. **1828** Moore (*title*) Limbo of Lost Reputations. **1866** J. Martineau *Ess.* I. 60 Comte.. dismisses religion into limbo. **1874** Motley *Barneveld* II. xiii. 89 To send the Golden Bull itself to the limbo of worn out constitutional devices. **1894** J. Knight *Garrick* ix. 164 The piece..ran for eleven nights before descending into the limbo of oblivion.

c. A type of anti-submarine mortar. Also *attrib.* or as *adj.*

1955 *Times* 20 June 4/6 The frigate Grenville fired live projectiles from her Limbo anti-submarine weapon. *Ibid.*, The Limbo..is a multi-barrelled mortar of large calibre, linked automatically with a submarine detector of advanced design. **1956** *Jane's Fighting Ships 1956–57* 240/2 Have some side armour as well as deck protection; limbo type anti-submarine rocket throwers. **1957** *Jane's Fighting Ships 1957–58* 42/1 The two Limbos can each fire a pattern of large depth bombs with great accuracy. **1961** T. D. Manning *Brit. Destroyer* 24 The Squid has been improved on by Limbo which..is not fitted in destroyers but only in frigates.

3. *attrib.*, as †***limbo-dungeon***; ***limbo-like*** adj.; †**limbo-lake**, the 'pit' of Hell (cf. LAKE *sb.*[4] 3).

1555–8 Phaer *Æneid* iii. G iv b, For Cyrces yle must furst be seen, and lands of Lymbo lake [L. *infernique lacus*]. **1590** Spenser *F.Q.* i. ii. 32 What voice of damned Ghost from Limbo lake. **1696** Toland *Christianity not Myst.* 27 They should not say they are in Limbo-Dungeon. **1748** Thomson *Cast. Indol.* 458 His father's ghost from limbo-lake, the while, Sees this. **1820** Scott *Abbot* xvi, From haunted spring and grassy ring, Troop goblin, elf, and fairy;..To Limbo-lake, Their way they take. **1848** Geo. Eliot in Cross *Life* (1885) I. 179, I am even now..in a very shattered, limbo-like mental condition.

‖**limbo**[2]. [Zulu: see quot. 1899.] A South African name for a kind of coarse calico.

1891 *Pall Mall G.* 9 Nov. 6/2 This present is accompanied by a quantity of limbo (a coarse quality of calico). **1896** A. B. Balfour *1200 Miles in Waggon* 62 Bright-coloured cotton stuff, limbo, as it is called here. **1899** B. Mitford *J. Ames* ii. 14 A dark blue fabric, commonly called by the whites 'limbo', being a corruption of the native name 'ulembu', which signifieth 'web'.

limbo[3] ('lɪmbəʊ). [W. Indian name.] A dance in which the dancer bends backwards and passes under a horizontal bar raised only a few inches off the ground. Also *attrib.*

1956 *Caribbean Q.* IV. iii. & iv. 204 The firemen also had a characteristic dance similar to the 'limbo', with the body bent sharply backward, knees projecting, and lower legs almost on the pavement. **1958** *Daily Express* 22 Apr. 7/3 The Princess should take home with her memories of gay calypsos and limbos. **1963** *Pix* 2 Mar. 38 Peters said that he first encountered the Limbo on his Pacific cruise..when it was merely known as 'going under the pole'. **1966** *Observer* 13 Feb. 40/4 Trinidad's champion limbo dancer..can ease himself blindfold under a bar which is only 8 in. from the floor and is sometimes soaked in spirit and set alight. **1971** *Country Life* 18 Feb. 372 And watching limbo ladies slither and men blow fire. **1972** E. Hargreaves *Fair Green Weed* i. 12 He..found the pair of them sitting on the patio, watching some limbo dancers on the beach. **1973** *Sunday Advocate-News* (Barbados) 21 Jan. 11/3 More variety should be introduced into these shows, including more steelband music, limbo dancing and folk dancing.

limbric ('lɪmbrɪk). (See quot. 1960.)

1930 *Economist* 18 Oct. 713/1 There is still some business to be done in other lines, such as mercerised cotton brocades and limbrics. **1940** *Chambers's Techn. Dict.* 500/2 *Limbric*, a plain grey cotton cloth of medium quality; used for curtains, etc. after being piece-dyed or printed. **1940** *Manch. Guardian Weekly* 25 Oct. 307 It seems unlikely..that the restrictions of silk piece-goods and made-up goods will cause a larger trade to be done in cotton poplins, cambrics, limbrics, etc. **1960** *Textile Terms & Definitions* (Textile Inst.) (ed. 4) 91 *Limbric*, a light-to-medium weight, closely woven, plain-weave cotton cloth made from good quality yarns.

Limbu ('lɪmbu:), *sb.* and *a.* Also **Limboo.** [Native name.] **A.** *sb.* **a.** A member of a Mongoloid people of eastern Nepal; this people collectively. **b.** The Tibeto-Burman language of the Limbu people. **B.** *adj.* Of or pertaining to the Limbu people or their language.

1819 F. Hamilton *Acct. Kingdom Nepal* i. 54 Among the Kirats was settled a tribe called Limbu... Their languages are said to be different. **1840** *Jrnl. R. Asiatic Soc. Bengal* IX. 495 The Limboos form a large portion of the inhabitants in the mountainous country lying between the Dood-Koosi and the Kanki rivers, in Nipal. **1854** J. D. Hooker *Himalayan Journals* I. v. 138 The Limboo language is totally different from the Lepcha, with less of the *z* in it, and more labials and palatals, hence more pleasing. **1880** H. A. Oldfield *Sk. from Nipal* I. iii. 53 The country of the Kirantis and Limbus at the present time is divided into fifty-two small subahships. **1909** G. A. Grierson *Ling. Surv. India* III. i. 283 The Limbus are one of the principal tribes of Eastern Nepal... We have no information about the number of speakers of Limbu in Nepal. **1928** Northey & Morris *Gurkhas* xv. 217 The Limbu race is now divided into a large number of tribes. These tribes were formerly centred, in groups, in ten different districts of the Limbu country. **1939** R. Godden *Black Narcissus* v. 54 She was learning to distinguish between the State natives and the hill clans, the Lepchas and Bhotiyas and Limbus. **1970** Rose & Fisher *Politics Nepal* i. 12 The Limbus,..are making a serious effort to revive their local language as a literary medium after long years of its suppression under Gorkha rule. **1971** K. Kent in C. Bonington *Annapurna South Face* App. H. 310 Later, the Eastern tribes (Rais and Limbus) were also recruited, and, together with some lesser-known but other martial tribes, also became known under the general title of Gurkhas.

Limburger ('lɪmbɜ:gə(r)). [a. Du. and G. *Limburger.*] **1.** *attrib.* with *cheese*, or *ellipt.* A soft strong-smelling cheese made in the province of Limburg in Belgium. Also ***Limburg cheese.***

1817 C. Campbell *Traveller's Compl. Guide through Belgium & Holland* (ed. 2) iv. 92 The disagreeable smell of the Limburg cheese, called *Herve*, though unpleasant to many, is justly ranked among the delicacies of the rich. **1859** W. H. J. Weale *Belgium* p. xxvii, *Limburg* and *Herve cheese* are also very good, but their odour is intolerable. *c* **1870** *More Yankee Drolleries* ii. 15 Limburger cheese, an abomination guilty of the most powerful odour. **1883** *Authors & Publishers* (G. P. Putnam's Sons) 45 The cheese-monger may not like either Stilton or Roquefort, he may even have his doubts as to the absolute wholesomeness of the more athletic brands of Limburger. **1887** *Harper's Mag.* Mar. 644/1 The obese Teuton delights in 'loud' Limburger and Gruyere. **1905** W. H. Simmonds *Pract. Grocer* III. 88 Limburger is a Belgian cheese of the soft class, which is allowed to ripen before use. **1908** [see Hamburger 2]. **1966** Marquis & Haskell *Cheese Bk.* iii. 197 Strong cheeses like Limburger and Liederkranz are not for cocktail parties because after an hour or so at warm temperatures they will all but clear the room.

2. a. A native or inhabitant of Limburg. **b.** (Also **Lim'burgerish.**) The dialect of the Limburgers. Also as *adj.*

1932 *Times Lit. Suppl.* 16 June 446/4 But this Limburgerish would not be a living language if it could be reduced to simple rules. *Ibid.*, Something for which Limburger grammarians have no doubt an appropriate name. **1963** N. Freeling *Gun before Butter* 51 He was no fool. A Limburger... The people from 'below the rivers' are quicker..than the Dutch of Holland.

limburgite ('lɪmbɜ:gaɪt). *Min.* Also **-yte.** [f. *Limburg*, a Belgian province + -ITE.] A semi-glassy rock consisting of olivin and augite with some magnetite and apatite.

1882 Dana *Man. Min. & Lithol.* 453 Limburgyte. **1897** Geikie *Anc. Volcanoes Gt. Brit.* I. 31 The basic series includes Dolerites,..Limburgites..and Pierites.

‖**limbus** ('lɪmbəs). [L. = edge, border; in med.L., a region on the border of Hell.]

1. a. Occas. used (as the normal form for English adoption) = LIMBO 1. ***limbus patrum*** = 'the limbo of the fathers', i.e. of the just who died before Christ's coming. ***limbus infantum*** = 'the limbo of infants': see LIMBO 1. Also *transf.*

c **1440** *York Myst.* xxxvii. 198 What þanne, is lymbus lorne, allas! **1532** More *Confut. Tindale* Wks. 514/1 The state of soules, both in heauen, hell, purgatory, paradyse, & *Limbus patrum.* **1581** J. Bell *Haddon's Answ. Osor.* 418 b, There be sayd to be 4. Mansions in hell... The second Lymbus, a place for such as are not Baptised. *a* **1623** Pemble *On Zach.* (1629) 148 He..had ransomed the Fathers out of their Purgatory, or infernall Limbus. **1626** Bacon *Sylva* § 1000 As if all Spirits and Soules of Men, came forth out of one Divine Limbus. **1651** Biggs *New Disp.* § 264. 194 The Limbus or Physitians purgatory. *a* **1679** T. Goodwin *Expos. Ephes.* Wks. 1681 I. ii. 121 The Papists..put Children..into a state call'd *Limbus Infantum*, wherein they do as it were eternally sleep. **1790** Burke *Fr. Rev.* (C.P.S.) 224 By the new French constitution, the best and the wisest representatives go equally with the worst into this *Limbus Patrum.*

†**b.** A prison; = LIMBO 2 a. *Obs.*

1583 *Leg. Bp. St. Androis* 349 Laich in a lymbus, whair thay lay, Then Lowrie lowsit them long or day.

2. Used *techn.* in lit. sense of 'border' or 'edge'; e.g. the ridge which borders the crater of a volcano; in *Antiq.* the rim of a crater or wine-bowl; in *Bot.* = LIMB *sb.*[2] 3 d; in *Conch.* 'the circumference of the valves of a bivalve shell from the disc to the border or margin' (*Syd. Soc. Lex.* 1888); also in *Anat.*

1671 Willoughby in *Phil. Trans.* VI. 2126 Having tipp'd the ends, inverted them, and fasten'd a Limbus or ring of soft wax to the great ends. **1697** T. Smith *Voy. Constantinople, Misc. Cur.* (1708) III. 23 Now we see plainly the Smoke briskly issuing out of the Crater, the Limbus of

which was all black. **1699** M. LISTER *Journey to Paris* 71 The Membrane or Valve on the Left side of the *Foramen Ovale* . . extended almost over the hole, without any *Limbus* round its edges. **1727–52** CHAMBERS *Cycl.*, *Limb*, *Limbus*, the outermost border, or graduated edge, of an astrolabe, quadrant, or the like mathematical instrument. **1793** MARTYN *Lang. Bot.*, *Limbus*, the border or upper dilated part of a monopetalous corolla. **1806** GALPINE *Brit. Bot.* 62 Primula. 1. . . limbus of the cor. flat. . . 3. . . limbus of the cor. concave. **1857** BIRCH *Anc. Pottery* (1858) II. 272 Round the crater is the limbus, which is a decorated border of floral or other ornaments. **1877** W. TURNER *Introd. Human Anat.* vi. 368 Another membrane . . arises from a denticulated spiral crest, the limbus or crista spiralis. **1954** S. DUKE-ELDER *Parsons' Dis. Eye* (ed. 12) i. 3 The cornea is set into the sclera like a watch glass so that the latter overlaps the cornea all round the periphery; the junction of the two tissues is known as the limbus. **1961** *Lancet* 22 July 166/2 The blade of the knife emerges 0·5–1·0 mm. on the corneal side of the limbus when the section is complete.

lime (laɪm), *sb.*[1] Forms: 1 lím, 1, 3 liim, 3, 7 lim, 3–7 lym, 3–8 lyme, (4 liym), 3– lime. [OE. *lím* str. masc. = MDu. *lîm* masc. (mod.Du. *lijm* fem.), OHG. *lîm* (MHG. *lîm*, mod.G. *leim*) masc., ON. *lím* neut.:—OTeut. **līmo-* = L. *līmus* mud, f. WAryan root **lī-* in L. *li-nēre* to smear; another grade of the root occurs in LOAM, LAIR *sb.*[2]]

1. a. A viscous sticky substance prepared from the bark of the holly and used for catching small birds; = BIRDLIME. Now only *poet.* (In OE. any adhesive substance, e.g. glue, paste.)

a **700** *Epinal Gloss.* 133 *Bitumen*, lim. *a* **1000** ÆLFRIC *Colloq.* in Wr.-Wülcker 95 Ic beswice fuȝelas hwilon mid neton mid grinum mid lime. *c* **1000** —— *Gram.* (Z.) 258 Swaswa lim ȝefæstnað fel to sumum brede. *a* **1250** *O. & N.* 1056 (Jesus MS.) þe louerd . . Lym [*Cott.* liim] and grune . . Sette and leyde þe for to lacche. *a* **1300** *Cursor M.* 29082 Mani man . . perist was als fuxl in lime. *c* **1440** *Promp. Parv.* 305/1 Lyme, to take wythe byrdys, *viscus*. **1565–6** *Churchw. Acc. St. Martin's, Leicester* (1866) 166 For Lyme to catche yᵉ sterlyngs in yᵉ churche, vijᵈ. *a* **1600** MONTGOMERIE *Misc. P.* xxi. 34, I fand My fethers in the lyme. **1697** DRYDEN *Virg. Georg.* I. 211 Toils for Beasts, and Lime for Birds were found. **1697** *Phil. Trans.* XIX. 377 The Bark [of Holly] begins to be full of Lime. *a* **1850** WORDSW. (W.), Like the lime That foolish birds are caught with.

b. in allusive phrases (cf. LIME *v.*[1] 2, 3).

13.. *K. Alis.* 419 Heo bylevith in folie So in the lym doth the flye. **1477** NORTON *Ord. Alch.* v. in Ashm. (1652) 83 For Fier with Erth hath most concord of all; Because that siccitie is the lyme of heate. **1591** SHAKS. *Two Gent.* III. ii. 68 You must lay lime to tangle her desires By walefull Sonnets. **1592** LODGE *Euphues Shadow* (1882) 20 Philamour that was first caught in the lime, was most of all tormented in his loue. **1604** EARL STIRLING *Paraenesis to Pr. Henry* xxviii, While fancies are not glu'de with pleasures lime. **1610** SHAKS. *Temp.* IV. i. 246 Monster, come put some Lime vpon your fingers, and away with the rest.

2. Usually coupled with *stone*: Mortar or cement used in building. In quot. *a* 1225 *fig.* Now *Sc.*

c **725** *Corpus Gloss.* C 320 *Cementum*: liim, *lapidum*. *a* **1100** *Voc.* in Wr.-Wülcker 314/23 *Cementum*, lim to wealle. *c* **1200** ORMIN 16284 þatt draȝhenn swerd wass inn an hannd, & lim & stan inn oþerr. *c* **1205** LAY. 15818 Ich habbe lim & stan on leode nis betere nan. *a* **1225** *Ancr. R.* 226 So ueste ilimed mid lim of ancre luue euerichon of on to oðer. *c* **1250** *Gen. & Ex.* 2552 Ðo sette sundri hem to waken His tiȝel and lim, and walles maken. *a* **1300** *Cursor M.* 25468 Castel mad o lime and stane. *c* **1380** WYCLIF *Serm.* Sel. Wks. II. 209 þe churche is taken . . for þe hous of liym and stoon, þat conteyneþ sich men. *a* **1400–50** *Alexander* 5088 þar was a cite in þat side asisid all with gemmes, With-outen lyme or laire. *c* **1470** HENRY *Wallace* XI. 680 Mudwall werk with-outyn lym or stayn. **1593** SHAKS. *Rich. II*, III. iii. 26 King Richard lyes Within the limits of yond Lime and Stone. **1745** SIR J. WARE *Wks. conc. Irel.* I. 127 Those slender round Towers of Lime and Stone, which are seen spread through divers Parts of the Country. **1786** BURNS *Twa Brigs* 101 Your ruin'd, formless bulk o' stane and lime. **1827** TENNANT *Papistry Storm'd* I. 25 Throu' the thick stane and the lime, He slippit like a beam throu' glass. *Mod. Sc.* A stane-an'-lime wa' is better nor a dry-stane dyke.

3. a. The alkaline earth which is the chief constituent of mortar; calcium oxide (CaO). It is obtained by submitting limestone (carbonate of lime) to a red heat, by which the carbonic acid is driven off, leaving a brittle white solid, which is pure lime (or QUICK-LIME). It is powerfully caustic and combines readily with water, evolving great heat in the process, and forming hydrate of lime (*slaked lime*).

The designations *carbonate*, *phosphate* etc. *of lime* are still current in popular use, though in technical language they have given place to the more systematic terms *calcium carbonate* (or *carbonate of calcium*), etc. *chloride of lime*: see CHLORIDE 2.

a **1000** *Voc.* in Wr.-Wülcker 197/16 *Calcis uiua*, ȝebærnd lim. **1398** TREVISA *Barth. De P.R.* XVI. xxiii. (1495) 560 Whyle lyme is colde in handlyng it conteyneth preuely wythin fyre and grete hete. *c* **1400** *Lanfranc's Cirurg.* 122 Caste aboue þe wounde þe poudre of lym tofore seid. *c* **1450** *ME. Med. Bk.* (Heinrich) 217 Tak arpment, & slekyd lyme, & argoyle. **1535** COVERDALE *Isa.* xxxiii. 11 The people shal be burnt like lyme. **1596** SHAKS. *1 Hen. IV*, II. iv. 137 You Rogue, heere's Lime in this Sacke too. **1622** R. HAWKINS *Voy. S. Sea* xliii. 103 Since the Spanish Sacks haue beene common in our Tauernes, which (for conservation) is mingled with Lyme in its making, our Nation complaineth of Calenturas, of the Stone [etc.]. **1622** BACON *Hen. VII*, 137 They were now (like Sand without Lyme), ill bound together. **1787** WINTER *Syst. Husb.* 32 Lime, when properly and judiciously applied, ranks first amongst the class of manures. **1816** J. SMITH *Panorama Sci. & Art* II. 488 Lime is detected most effectually by the oxalic acid, which . . forms with it an insoluble precipitate. **1837** WHITTOCK, etc. *Bk. Trades* (1842) 130 Lime is found in chalk, marble, &c., and is the basis of animal bones. **1839** *Penny Cycl.* XIII. 489/1 Phosphate of lime has been recommended in rickets.

†**b.** = *lime-wash*. *Obs.*

? **1593** *Rites of Durham* (Lawson MS. 1656) xxxix, Which pictures have been washed over wᵗʰ Lime, and yet do appear through the Lime.

c. ***lime and hair***: a kind of plasterer's cement to which hair is added to bind the mixture closely together. Also *attrib.*

1626 *Vestry Bks.* (Surtees) 181 For lyme and haire for lymeinge the wyndowes, viijd. **1663** GERBIER *Counsel* 46 Lime and Haire Birdcage-like-Buildings. **1825** J. NICHOLSON *Operat. Mechanic* 640 Cements . . used by plasterers for inside work. The first is called lime and hair, or coarse stuff.

†**d.** ***oil of lime*** [F. *huile de chaux*]: an old name for the so-called 'chloride of lime' in a state of deliquescence.

1471 RIPLEY *Comp. Alch.* Adm. vii. in Ashm. (1652) 191 Oyle of Lime [*printed* Lune] and water. **1742** *Phil. Trans.* XLII. 76. **1800** tr. *Lagrange's Chem.* I. 275.

e. A vat containing a solution of lime for removing the hair from skins; the solution itself.

1885 C. T. DAVIS *Manuf. Leather* xxxii. 525 When sufficiently softened the skins are next placed in the 'limes'. . . The goat-skins remain in the 'limes' about 14 days. **1903** L. A. FLEMMING *Pract. Tanning* 6 When vat room is scarce, it is good practice to haul the skins out after they have been in the lime a few days. **1946** J. W. WATERER *Leather* II. ii. 137 The practice of passing the 'packs' of hides . . through a series of liquors, commencing with an old or 'mellow' lime. **1969** T. C. THORSTENSEN *Pract. Leather Technol.* vi. 87 When the hide is introduced into the lime.

†**4. a.** The CALX of metals. **b.** Used generically for: An alkaline earth. *Obs.*

1707 *Curios. in Husb. & Gard.* 225 Metals, after they are reduc'd into Lime. **1796** KIRWAN *Elem. Min.* (ed. 2) I. 5 When this [aerial, *i.e.* carbonic] acid is expelled, the earth . . is then called lime, or common or calcareous lime, to distinguish it from other earths, which also form limes, when free from all combinations, viz. the Barytic and Scottish earths.

5. a. *attrib.* and *Comb.*, as ***lime-basket***, ***-burn***, ***-burning***, ***-cask***, †***-coop*** (dial.), ***-crag***, †***-fat***, ***-grout***, ***-hater*** (so ***-hating*** adj.), ***-keeve***, ***-lover*** (so ***-loving*** adj.), ***-maker***, ***-man***, ***-merchant***, ***-mortar***, ***-ooze***, ***-process***, †***quarrel***, ***quarrier***, ***quarry***, ***-salt***, ***-scow***, ***-scuttle***; ***lime-daubed***, ***-dressed***, ***-free***, ***-like*** adjs.; **lime-ash** *dial.*, a composition of ashes and lime used as a rough kind of flooring for kitchens, etc.; **lime-ball (light)**, limelight; †**lime-bush**, a bush dressed with birdlime; hence, a means of entanglement; **lime-cartridge** (see quot.); **lime-cast**, a covering or layer of lime mortar; also *attrib.*; †**lime-chalk**, quicklime; **lime-coal** (see quot.); †**lime-core**, unslakable lumps in quick-lime; **lime-cylinder**, a cylinder of lime used in the production of limelight; **lime-liniment** (see quot.); **lime-liquid**, liquid grout of lime; **lime-marl** (see quot.); **lime-milk**, milk of lime, slaked lime diffused in water; **lime ointment**, an ointment consisting of slaked lime, lard, and olive oil (*Syd. Soc. Lex.* 1888); **lime-phial** *Antiq.*, a phial filled with quicklime, fixed at the end of an arrow, used in mediæval warfare for the purpose of blinding the enemy (Hewitt *Anc. Armour* III. 759, *Index*; cf. Strutt *Horda Angelcynnan* I. 98); **lime-putty**, (*a*) (see quot.); (*b*) = *lime-slab*; **lime-rock**, limestone (? now *N. Amer.*); **lime-rubbish**, broken mortar from old walls, etc., used as a dressing for land; **lime-shells**, burnt lime before it is slaked; **lime-silicate** *a. Petrol.*, applied to a rock which was originally an impure limestone or dolomite and has been thermally metamorphosed, with the result that the lime has combined with silica present as impurities to form calcium silicates; **lime-sink**, a rounded depression in the earth found in limestone districts; **lime-slab**, a pasty smooth composition of slaked lime and water used in plastering; **lime soap**, a mixture of insoluble calcium salts of fatty acids formed as a precipitate when soap is used in hard water and manufactured for various industrial purposes; **lime-soda** *attrib.*, applied to a process for softening water by treatment with lime and sodium carbonate; **lime-sour** = *grey sour*, see GREY *a.* 8 (*Cent. Dict.*); **lime-sulphur**, an insecticide and fungicide containing calcium polysulphides which is made by boiling lime and sulphur in water; **lime-wash** *sb.*, a mixture of lime and water, used for coating walls, etc.; *vb.*, to whitewash with such a mixture; **lime-white**, **-whiten** *vbs.*, to lime-wash; **lime-work**, †(*a*) stucco (quot. 1589); (*b*) a place where lime is made (also *pl.*); †**lime-yard** = LIME-TWIG. Also LIME-BURNER, LIME-FINGERED *a.*, LIME-KILN, LIMELIGHT *sb.*, LIME-PIT, LIME-POT, LIME-ROD, LIMESTONE, LIME-TWIG, LIME-WATER, LIME-WORT[1], etc.

1813 VANCOUVER *Agric. Devon* 96 The *lime ash-floor . . costs 6*d.* in the square yard, tempering and laying down. **1893** QUILLER-COUCH *Delect. Duchy* 195 Their clothes dripping pools of water on the sanded lime-ash. **1830** DRUMMOND in *Phil. Trans.* CXX. 391 The intensity of the *lime-ball being therefore 264 times that of the Argand lamp. **1835** *Edin. Rev.* LXI. 238 The lime-ball light of Lieutenant Drummond. **1838** DICKENS *O. Twist* xviii, Mr. Chitling wished he might be busted if he warn't as dry as a *lime-basket. **1879** *St. George's Hosp. Rep.* IX. 538 The 2 *lime-burns occurred in plasterers. **1860** J. S. C. ABBOTT *South & North* 196 [Slaves] employed . . in *lime-burning or fishing. **1577** FENTON *Gold. Epist.* 91 No other things are the riches of the worlde, but . . a stumbling blocke for the wicked, a *limebush for the good. *a* **1640** DAY *Peregr. Schol.* (1881) 53 Like a fishe in a net or a selie bird in a limebushe. **1883** GRESLEY *Gloss. Coal-mining*, **Lime cartridge*, a charge or measured quantity of compressed dry caustic lime made up into a cartridge, and used instead of gunpowder and in a somewhat similar manner for breaking down coal. **1865** MRS. STOWE *House & Home Papers* 94 Seating himself on a *lime-cask which the plasterers had left. **1861** NEALE *Notes Dalmatia*, etc. 96 Here, much hidden by *lime-cast, I made out the inscription. **1873** O'CURRY *Manners Anc. Irish* III. 16 Many lofty lime-cast castles, built of limestone. **1637** HEYWOOD *Dial.*, *Anna & Phillis* Wks. 1874 VI. 320 Water doth make the *lime-chalk scortch with heat. **1883** GRESLEY *Gloss. Coal-mining*, **Lime coal*, small coal suitable for lime burning. **1674–91** RAY *Collect. Words* 38 *Coop*, as, a muck-coop, a *lime-coop; a cart, or wain, made close with boards, to carry anything that otherwise would fall out. **1679** MOXON *Mech. Exerc.* 128 Good dry Earth, *Lime-Core, Rubbish, &c. **1649** *Burgh. Rec. Glasgow* (1881) II. 177 Anent the coall and *lymecraig it is ordourit [etc.]. **1871** tr. *Schellen's Spectr. Anal.* ix. 64 Let the *lime-cylinders then be raised to incandescence by means of the oxyhydrogen gas. **1861** W. F. COLLIER *Hist. Eng. Lit.* 105 As sorry makeshifts for scenery as the *lime-daubed tinker who acted Wall. **1899** J. W. MACKAIL *Life W. Morris* I. 279 The English *lime-dressed vellum had been found almost useless for fine work. **1494** *Act 11 Hen. VII*, c. 19 Cussions, stuffed with horse here [etc.], which is wrought in *lyme fattes. **1935** A. G. L. HELLYER *Pract. Gardening* iii. 34 It is wise to make enquiry when ordering rock plants and shrubs as to whether any of those supplied are likely to require *lime-free soil. **1974** *Country Life* 28 Nov. 1639/1 *V*[*iburnum*] *furcatum* . . needs a lime-free soil. **1875** R. R. BRASH *Eccl. Archit. Ireland* 8 The interior of the walls is filled with small stones and *lime-grout. **1907** R. FARRER *My Rock-Garden* x. 148 The plant [*sc. Cenisia excisa*] . . is a real *lime-hater. **1935** A. G. L. HELLYER *Pract. Gardening* xv. 112 The best plan is to set aside a portion of the rock-garden for lime-haters. *Ibid.* 284/1 (*index*) *Lime hating plants. **1971** *Country Life* 18 Feb. 368/1 For some reason, many of the lime-hating shrubs have only white flowers. **1574** in Worth *Tavistock Par. Acc.* (1887) 30 For mending of the *lyme Keve, vjd. **1756** C. LUCAS *Ess. Waters* I. 141 A salt taste, with something *lime-like or lixivial. **1876** HARLEY *Mat. Med.* (ed. 6) 173 *Lime Liniment is an emulsion of calcareous soap and free oil. **1776** G. SEMPLE *Building in Water* 78 Filling . . the inside with small Stones, and *Lime-liquid. **1907** R. FARRER *My Rock-Garden* i. 12 At this point I will not embark on the awful question of *lime-lovers and peat-lovers. **1971** MRS. D. UNDERWOOD *Grey & Silver Plants* iv. 35 The root fibres of the lime-lovers will wrap themselves round individual [limestone] chippings. **1916** *Nature* 2 Nov. 172/2 It seems probable from the evidence now before us that some of Forrest's newly discovered Chinese rhododendrons . . must be reckoned as *lime-loving species. **1956** MCCLINTOCK & FITTER *Collins' Pocket Guide Wild Flowers* 306 Limestone Polypody . . is the lime-loving counterpart of the Oak Fern. **1974** *Country Life* 28 Nov. 1660/1 Used mushroom compost . . is greatly appreciated by lime-loving cherries. **1573** BARET *Alv.* L 441 A *limemaker, *calcarius*. **1723** *Lond. Gaz.* No. 6128/3 Edward Brent, Lime-maker. **1839** URE *Dict. Arts*, etc. 772 This true limestone must not be confounded with the *lime-marl, composed of calcareous matter and clay. **1703** T. N. *City & C. Purchaser* 208 Many *Lime-men, (and some of those Bricklayers that are in Fee with 'em) may speak against this Practice. **1710** *Lond. Gaz.* No. 4789/4 William Ball, . . *Lyme-Merchant. **1703** T. S. *Art's Improv.* I. 10 Whiten it Three or Four times together with *Lime-Milk. **1839** URE *Dict. Arts* 275 Smeared over with common *lime mortar. **1867** J. N. EDWARDS *Shelby* xxix. 498 He . . disappeared for a moment beneath *lime ooze, half tanned hides and the smell of a charnel house. **1883** GRESLEY *Gloss. Coal-mining*, **Lime process*, the method of getting coal by the use of the lime cartridge. **1888** *Syd. Soc. Lex.*, Lime process of sewage purification. **1892** *Labour Commission* Gloss., **Lime-putty*, ordinary lime run through a fine sieve. **1641** *Sc. Acts Chas. I* (1870) V. 452/1 To haue and win Lymestones in the *lyme quarrells, pairtis and boundis of the Toune and Landis of Paistoun [etc.]. **1753** *Scots Mag.* XV. 52/1 John Potty, a *lime-quarrier. *a* **1649** DRUMM. OF HAWTH. *Consid. to Parlt.* Wks. (1711) 187 That coal-pits, *lime-quarries, within fourty foots of the king's high-ways, be filled up. **1882** OUIDA *Maremma* I. 34 The lime quarries of Alberese. **1665** in *Early Rec. Providence* (Rhode Island) (1893) III. 66 Those *Lime Rocks about Hackletons lime Killne shal be perpetually Common. **1799** J. ROBERTSON *Agric. Perth* 547 A dry sharp soil to work upon mostly covering lime rock. **1969** *Islander* (Victoria, B.C.) 22 June 7/1 He had to tow empty scows from the cement works to Tod Inlet and back with full scows of limerock for making cement. **1805** R. W. DICKSON *Pract. Agric.* I. 270 *Lime rubbish from the pulling down of old houses. **1884** SUTTON *Cult. Veget. & Fl.* (1885) 88 Old gardens should be refreshed with a dressing of lime occasionally, or of lime rubbish from old buildings. **1849** D. CAMPBELL *Inorg. Chem.* 71 A salt of this acid gives, in *lime salts, a semi-solid precipitate. **1823** J. F. COOPER *Pioneer* xxiii. (1869) 99/2 Did'ee ever see a ship, man? or any craft bigger than a *lime-scow, or a wood-boat, on this here small bit of fresh water? **1865** F. MARTIN *Life J. Clare* 62 He sat down upon his *lime-scuttle. **1793** *Statist. Acc. Scot.* VI. 202 To strong land they give from 40 to 70 bolls of *lime shells to the Scotch acre. **1888** J. J. H. TEALL *Brit. Petrogr.* 464/2 *Lime-silicate hornfels. **1902** A. HARKER *Petrol.* (ed. 3) xx. 306 The carbonic acid is completely eliminated, and the whole converted into a lime-silicate-rock (the German

'Kalksilikathornfels' or 'Kalkhornfels'). **1965** G. J. WILLIAMS *Econ. Geol. N.Z.* x. 153/1 Lime-silicate dyke rocks in the ultramafic rocks of southern Westland. **1837** J. L. WILLIAMS *Territory of Florida* 9 Ponds and *lime sinks are numerous between the..rivers. **1845** LYELL *Trav. N. Amer.* I. 176 Lime-sinks or funnel-shaped cavities, are frequent in this country arising from natural tunnels and cavities in the subjacent limestone. **1608–9** in Swayne *Churchw. Acc. Sarum* (1896) 305 Barrowefull *lyme slabb 6*d.* **1857** W. A. MILLER *Elem. Chem.* III. vi. 373 The tallow is melted by injecting hot steam into the vat which contains it, and milk of lime is added... An insoluble *lime soap is thus formed. **1884** [see SOAP *sb.* 2]. **1918** C. M. WHITTAKER *Applic. Coal Tar Dyestuffs* iii. 36 Lime soaps may be removed by treatment with spirits of salts. **1952** KIRK & OTHMER *Encycl. Chem. Technol.* VIII. 524 The use of lime-soap thickened lubricants for the wheels of chariots dates back as far as 1400 B.C... In modern times, however, the manufacture of lubricating greases—also by means of lime soaps—started about 1854. **1961** COHEN & LINTON *Chem. & Textiles for Laundry Industry* iii. 46 Pure lime soap is more or less white when it is formed... If we accept a laundryman's concept of lime soap, on the other hand, we are talking about a dingy, gray, boardy impregnation that builds up in fabrics and defies all efforts to attain good whiteness. **1930** *Engineering* 15 Aug. 219/1 It [*sc.* the base exchange method] gives rise to no precipitate whatever, and this avoids what in the *lime-soda process is often a cause of difficulty. **1950** B. E. HARTSUCH *Introd. Textile Chem.* iv. 92 The lime-soda method for softening water is the oldest and is still most used for very large softening plants. **1970** KIRK & OTHMER *Encycl. Chem. Technol.* (ed. 2) XXII. 98 The lime or lime-soda process is based upon precipitation of calcium as calcium carbonate and magnesium as magnesium hydroxide. **1907** *Bull. Bureau Chem., U.S. Dept. Agric.* No. 101. 12 The next set of experiments was to determine the composition of *lime-sulphur mixtures boiled the same length of time.., but containing varying quantities of lime and sulphur. **1913** *Jrnl. R. Hort. Soc.* XXXIX. 378 It appears unsafe to spray many varieties of gooseberries with either lime-sulphur or liver of sulphur. **1937** A. M. MASSEE *Pests of Fruits & Hops* xiv. 266 In the post-blossom sprays ..lime-sulphur is used as an acaricide as well as a fungicide, and it is then used at a strength of 1 per cent..for the control of the Fruit Tree Red Spider and Apple Scab. **1968** R. HAY *Gardening Year* 472/3 Lime sulphur can also be used against big bud mites on black currants, American gooseberry mildew and peach leaf curl. **1541** *Extracts Aberd. Reg.* (1844) I. 176 Ane skep, ane schod schuill, with ane *lym tub. **1823** J. BADCOCK *Dom. Amusem.* 168 Old Fruit Trees..may be restored..by the application of a good strong *lime-wash. **1847** SMEATON *Builder's Man.* 126 In using lime-wash, it is better to put two thin coats on a wall than one thick one. **1869** E. A. PARKES *Pract. Hygiene* (ed. 3) 305 The walls and ceilings are ordered to be *lime-washed twice a-year. **1777** HOWARD *Prisons Eng.* (1780) 359 It was scraped and *lime-whited once a year. **1861** *Eng. Wom. Dom. Mag.* III. 221 The walls were *lime-whitened. **1589** RIDER *Bibl. Scholast.* 870 *Lime-worke, *albarium opus, albarium.* **1692** *Lond. Gaz.* No. 2819/1 Since the destroying of the Lime-Works by our Dragoons. **1808** J. ROBERTSON *Agric. Surv. Inverness* i. 41 A lime-work belonging to Sir James Grant of Grant. **1971** *Country Life* 1 Apr. 743/3 We struck east across the A515..to re-cross the road farther north by a limeworks. **1377** LANGL. *P. Pl.* B. IX. 179 Leccherye in likyng is *lymeȝerde of helle. *c* **1440** *Promp. Parv.* 305/1 Lyme ȝerde, *viminarium, viscarium.*

b. In names of minerals, denoting the presence of lime or calcium, e.g. *lime-marl, -slate*; **lime-epidote**, zoisite; **lime-feldspar**, triclinic feldspar containing calcium; †**lime-harmotome**, phillipsite; **lime-malachite**, an impure malachite containing calcite; †**lime-mesotype**, scolecite; †**lime-uranite**, autunite; **lime-wavellite**, 'a variety of wavellite, supposed to contain lime as an essential ingredient' (A. H. Chester *Dict. Min.* 1896).

1862 DANA *Man. Geol.* 56 Labradorite, or *lime-feldspar. **1896** CHESTER *Names Min.* 157 *Lime-feldspar*, a syn. of anorthite. **1839** URE *Dict. Arts* 772 This true limestone must not be confounded with the *lime-marl, composed of calcareous matter and clay. **1811** PINKERTON *Petral.* II. 192 Saussure has minutely described a singular transition from granite to *limeslate.

lime (laɪm), *sb.*[2] Also 7 lyme. [a. F. *lime* = mod.Pr. *limo*, ad. Sp. *lima*, a. Arab. *līmaʰ*: see LEMON.]

1. a. The globular fruit of the tree *Citrus Medica*, var. *acida*, smaller than the lemon and of a more acid taste; more explicitly ***sour lime***. Its juice is much used as a beverage. **sweet lime**, *Citrus Medica*, var. *Limetta*.

1638 SIR T. HERBERT *Trav.* (ed. 2) 28 The Ile [Mohelia] inricht us with many good things;..Oranges, Lemons, Lymes. **1697** DAMPIER *Voy.* (1729) I. 296 The Lime is a sort of bastard or Crab-limon. The Tree, or Bush that bears it, is prickly, like a Thorn, growing full of small boughs. **1727–46** THOMSON *Summer* 664 To where the lemon and the piercing lime,..Their lighter glories blend. **1784** COWPER *Task* III. 573 The ruddier orange and the paler lime. **1857** HENFREY *Bot.* 260 *Citrus Limetta*, the cultivated Sweet Lime.

b. Applied with qualification to fruits of trees of other genera. **Ogeechee lime**, the sour tupelo, *Nyssa capitata*, of which a conserve is made. **wild lime**, *Atalantia monophylla* (*Treas. Bot.* 1866), *Xanthoxylum Pterota* (*Cent. Dict.* 1890), and (in Jamaica) *Rheedia lateriflora* (Fawcett in *Bulletin Bot. Dept. Jamaica*, 1896); also, in Australia, = KUMQUAT 2.

1767 P. COLLINSON *Let.* 31 July in W. Darlington *Mem. J. Bartram & H. Marshall* (1849) 292 The Wild Lime..is a singular plant. **1832** D. J. BROWNE *Sylva Amer.* 221 In Georgia this tree is known by the name of Sour Tupelo and Wild Lime. **1863** R. HENNING *Let.* 26 Nov. (1966) 147 We went out to pick some wild limes for preserving. They are a little fruit about the size of a large gooseberry, but in colour, taste, smell and shape exactly like a small lemon. **1965** [see KUMQUAT 2]. **1969** T. H. EVERETT *Living Trees of World* xxi. 209/1 The wild-lime (*Zanthoxylum fagara*) of Florida, Mexico, the West Indies..is an evergreen species.

c. *ellipt.* for *lime-green sb.* and *adj.* (LIME *sb.*[2] 2); also for LIME-JUICE, as in phr. ***gin and lime.***

1923 *Daily Mail* 19 Feb. 1 (Advt.), Smart skirt... Colours: navy,..gold, lime, cardinal and black. **1937** *Discovery* July 217/2 Dresses are burgundy, pine-blue, lime. **1938** L. MACNEICE *Earth Compels* 23 A gin and lime or a double Scotch. **1972** *Vogue* Jan. 12/2 The colours..are remarkable—lime and raspberry, lemon, orange, rose.

2. *attrib.* and *Comb.*, as ***lime-green*** sb. and adj., *lime-tree*; **lime-marmalade**, marmalade made from limes; **lime-myrtle**, the West-Indian name for *Triphasia trifoliata* (Grisebach *Flora Brit. W. Indies*, 1864); **lime-plant**, the May-apple, *Podophyllum peltatum*; **lime-punch**, punch made with lime-juice instead of lemon-juice; **lime-squash**, a drink made with the juice of the lime (cf. *lemon-squash*). Also LIME-JUICE.

1890 *Daily News* 14 July 3/4 The scene was gay with white gowns, pale heliotrope, citron, *lime-green. *c* **1938** *Fortnum & Mason Price List* 44/1 Marmalade..*Lime—per glass 1/3. **1968** 'J. FRASER' *Evergreen Death* x. 80 He did like that lime marmalade they used to get. **1972** *New Statesman* 26 May 709/1 Coffee, bread and lime-marmalade. **1844** C. JOHNSON *Farmer's Encycl.* (Worc.), **Lime-plant*, the May-apple, or wild mandrake; *Podophyllum peltatum.* **1774** P. V. FITHIAN *Jrnl.* (1900) 206 We had after Dinner, *Lime Punch and Madaira. **1834** *Tait's Mag.* I. 299/2, 'I dine with a turtle-party at Bleaden's'. 'Nothing like Bleaden's lime-punch, Sir Jacob, eh?' **1909** *Daily Chron.* 15 June 4/4 For drinking, *lime-squash is superior to lemon squash. **1939–40** *Army & Navy Stores Catal.* 28/2 Lime squash. **1748** *Anson's Voy.* II. viii. 216 We found there abundance of cassia, and a few *lime-trees.

lime (laɪm), *sb.*[3] Also 8 lyme. [App. an altered form of *line* LIND.]

1. A tree of the genus *Tilia* (N.O. *Tiliaceæ*), esp. *T. europæa*, a common ornamental tree having heart-shaped leaves and many small fragrant yellowish flowers; the linden.

red lime, *T. grandifolia* Ehrh.

1625, 1649, 1667 [see 3]. **1697** DRYDEN *Virg. Georg.* IV. 209 His Limes were first in Flow'rs. **1704** POPE *Autumn* 25 The lymes their pleasing shades deny. *a* **1705** RAY *Synopsis Plant. Angl.* (1724) 473 *Tilia foliis molliter hirsutis, viminibus rubris...* 'Tis known by the name of the Red Lime, and grows naturally in Stoken-church Wood. **1711** SWIFT *Jrnl. to Stella* 27 Aug., It is autumn this good while in St. James's Park; the limes have been losing their leaves. **1784** COWPER *Task* I. 316 The lime at dewy eve Diffusing odours. **1842** *Penny Cycl.* XXIV. 447/1 *T[ilia] rubra*, Red Lime... The young branches are of a beautiful coral-red colour, thence it has been called *T. corallina.* **1849** AYTOUN *Buried Flower* 176 Ere the bees had ceased to murmur Through the umbrage of the lime. **1861** DELAMER *Fl. Gard.* 10 The Lime is a good town tree, leafing early in spring, and perfuming the air with its blossoms in August.

2. The seed of the lime-tree.

1747 MRS. GLASSE *Cookery* (1767) 269 To pickle stertion-buds and limes; you pick them off the lime-trees in the summer. Take new stertion-seeds or limes, pickle them when large.

3. *attrib.* and *Comb.*, as ***lime-avenue, -bark, -flower, -gall, -grove, -tree, -walk, -wood***; **lime bug**, an insect that infests lime-trees; **lime hawk-moth**, *Smerinthus tiliæ*, whose larva feeds on the lime (1869 E. Newman *Brit. Moths* 5).

1899 J. W. MACKAIL *Life W. Morris* II. 348 Up the short *lime-avenue to the tiny church. **1894** GLADSTONE *Horace's Odes* I. xxxviii. 2 The wreaths with *limebark bound. **1832** *Planting* vi. 72 (L.U.K.) *Coccus tiliæ*, *lime bug. **1888** *Syd. Soc. Lex.*, **Lime flower oil*, a colourless or yellowish volatile oil obtained by distillation from the flowers of *Tilia europæa* and other species. **1753** CHAMBERS *Cycl. Supp.*, **Lime galls*, ..a sort of galls or vegetable protuberances, formed on the edges of the leaves of the lime tree in spring time. **1667** DRYDEN & DAVENANT *Tempest* III. iii, In the *lime-grove, which weather-fends your cell. **1798** NEMNICH *Polyglotten-Lex.* v. 817 *Lime hawk moth, *Sphinx tiliae.* **1625** BACON *Ess., Gardens* (Arb.) 558 The Flowers of the *Lime Tree. **1649** BLITHE *Eng. Improv. Impr.* (1653) 172 The Lime Tree is also newly discovered as useful in our English plantations. **1797** COLERIDGE '*This lime-tree bower*' 2 Here must I remain, This lime-tree bower my prison! *c* **1662** T. BROWNE *Let.* in *Works* (1931) VI. 307 Uncertain it is whether in any *Tilicetum*, or *Lime-walk, abroad it be considerably exceeded. **1816** JANE AUSTEN *Emma* III. vi. 103 Some are gone to the ponds, and some to the lime walk. **1860** *Murray's Berks, Bucks & Oxon* 172/2 There is a pleasant garden attached to Trinity, with a trellised lime-walk of great celebrity. **1731** *Lunenburg (Mass.) Proprietors' Rec.* (1897) 209 It begins at a red oak and runs east..to a *Limewood. **1832** TENNYSON *Miller's Dau.* 211 Poems (1833) 45 When in the breezy limewood-shade, I found the blue forget-me-not. **1885** F. MILLER *Wood-Carving* iv. 27 Lime-wood was almost exclusively used by Gibbons in his drops and festoons of fruit. **1932** O. EVAN-THOMAS *Domestic Utensils of Wood* 118 Chrism spoon, limewood, entirely carved with sacred objects. **1965** J. ARONSON *Encycl. Furnit.* (1966) 285/1 *Limewood*, light-colored, close-grained wood that cuts as well across as with the grain, rendering it excellent for carving.

†**lime**, *sb.*[4] *Obs. rare*[−1]. In 5 lyme. [? ad. L. *līmes* LIMIT.] Limit, end.

c **1420** *Chron. Vilod.* 109 And þus Englonde toke first his name Fro þe gode kyng Egbertys tyme, Ryȝt as we clepe ȝet þe same And herrafter shulde wᵗ-ouȝte lyme.

lime (laɪm), *sb.*[5] Colloq. abbrev. of LIMELIGHT. Freq. in *pl.* Also (in sing.) *attrib.* Phr. ***in the lime*** (Austral.), in the limelight.

1892 J. NIE *Robinson Crusoe* 6 Here! Where's the limelight man? Of course, used up all his limes for Crusoe. **1895** B. DALY in Chevalier & Daly *A. Chevalier* II. 248 The footlights are turned low, and the hissing noise behind explains that Sam Pennett, the carpenter, is getting his limes ready for use. **1931** *Daily Express* 22 Sept. 17/1 She..used to keep in her shop a working model of a theatre, complete to the last 'lime' and 'float'. **1935** RIDGE & ALDRED *Stage Lighting* iii. 18/2 Producers will frequently ask for the 'limes' when they mean front-of-house arc lanterns. **1941** BAKER *Dict. Austral. Slang* 43, *Lime, in the*, in the limelight. **1958** B. NICHOLS *Sweet & Twenties* xiii. 177 There was one figure which the limes should have picked out. **1961** PARTRIDGE *Dict. Slang* Suppl. 1169/2 *Lime, in the*, popular; much publicised: Australian... I.e. 'in the limelight'. **1966** *Guardian* 18 Feb. 10/5 At 16 he was a lime boy, looking after the lights.

lime (laɪm), *v.*[1] Also 4–7 lyme, 5 lymyn; *pa. pple.* 3 i-limed, 4 ylymed. [f. LIME *sb.*[1]; OE. **līmian* seems to be implied by the vbl. sb. *līming.*]

1. *trans.* To cement. Chiefly *fig.*

a **1225** [see LIME *sb.*[1] 2]. *a* **1225** *Leg. Kath.* 1792 Ant te hali gast, hare beire luue, þe lihteð of ham baðe, & limeð togederes, swa þæt nan ne mei sundrin from oðere. **1593** SHAKS. *3 Hen. VI*, v. i. 84, I will not ruinate my Fathers House, Who gaue his blood to lyme the stones together. *a* **1617** BAYNE *Lect.* (1634) 302 The wicked confidence where-with our hearts are limed to the creature. **1855** BAILEY *Mystic* 115 That cruel tower..Of living souls impacted, limed with blood.

2. a. To smear (twigs or the like) with bird-lime, for the purpose of catching birds. Also *allusively*.

1413 *Pilgr. Sowle* (Caxton 1483) III. v. 54 Ye haue had handes lymed euer redy for to catche. *c* **1440** *Promp. Parv.* 305/2 Lymyn wythe bryd lyme, *visco.* **1547** BOORDE *Introd. Knowl.* ii. (1870) 126 My fyngers be lymed lyke a lyme twyg [*sc.* in order to pilfer]. **1593** SHAKS. *2 Hen. VI*, I. iii. 91 My selfe haue lym'd a Bush for her. **1692** R. L'ESTRANGE *Fables* ccclxxix. 350 Those Twigs in time will come to be Lim'd, and then you're all Lost if you do but touch 'em. **1816** SCOTT *Antiquary* xlii, But he would have found twigs limed for him at Edinburgh.

b. To smear with a sticky substance. *rare.*

c **1250** *Gen. & Ex.* 562 Ðat arche was a feteles good, set and limed a-gen ðe flood. **1483** CAXTON *Gold. Leg.* 39 b/1 Make ther dyverse places and lyme it with cleye and pitche within and without. **1814** CARY *Dante, Inf.* xxi. 18 A glutinous thick mass, that round Lim'd all the shore beneath.

3. To catch with birdlime. Often *fig.*

13.. *K. Alis.* 5701 Hy maden her armes envenymed; He that was take of deth was lymed. *c* **1374** CHAUCER *Troylus* I. 353 Loue he gan hyse federis so to lyme. *c* **1386** —— *Wife's T.* 78 A man shal winne us best with flaterye, And with attendance and with bisynesse Been we ylymed bothe moore and lesse. *c* **1440** CAPGRAVE *Life St. Kath.* v. 115 His demonstracyons coude vs not trappe ne lyme. **1575** CHURCHYARD *Chippes* (1817) 193 When birde is limde, farewell faire feathers all. **1593** SHAKS. *Lucr.* 88. ? *c* **1600** *Distracted Emp.* v. i. in Bullen *O. Pl.* III. 240 Am I then noosd!..am I lymed! **1680** CROWNE *Misery Civ. War* v. 70 The bird that sees the bush where once itself Was lim'd. **1791** E. DARWIN *Bot. Gard.* I. 74 Fine as the spider's flimsy thread he wove The immortal toil to lime illicit love. **1806–7** J. BERESFORD *Miseries Hum. Life* (1826) XI. xxxi, The buzz of a struggling insect who has limed himself in your ear. *a* **1822** SHELLEY *Ess., Def. Poetry* (1840) I. 39 Lucretius had limed the wings of his swift spirit in the dregs of the sensible world. **1868** BROWNING *Ring & Bk.* v. 364 Vittiano—one limes flocks of thrushes there. **1870** MISS BRIDGMAN *Rob. Lynne* II. iii. 64 He was..limed this time [matrimonially].

†**4.** To foul, defile. *Obs.*

1390 GOWER *Conf.* I. 179 For who so wole his handes lime, Thei mosten be the more unclene. *c* **1450** *Cov. Myst.* (Shaks. Soc.) 63 Off handys and dede be trewe evyrmore, ffor yf thin handys lymyd be, Thou art but shent. **1549** CHALONER *Erasm. on Folly* D j, No witte maie be founde not lymed with some great vices. **1592** G. HARVEY *Pierce's Super.* (1593) 37 Who is not limed with some default.

5. To treat or dress with lime.

†**a.** To put lime into (wine). In quot. *absol.* (Cf. LIME *sb.*[1] 3, quots. 1596, 1622.) *Obs.*

1598 SHAKS. *Merry W.* I. iii. 15 (Qo. 1602) *Host*... Let me see thee froth, and lyme [*Fo.* liue].

b. To dress (land, etc.) with lime. Also *absol.* Also to give (wood) a bleached effect by treating it with lime. Cf. LIMED *ppl. a.* 2 b.

1649 BLITHE *Eng. Improv. Impr.* (1653) 135 About twelve or fourteen quarters of Lime will very wel Lime an Acre, you may also over-Lime it, as well as under-Lime it. **1674–91** RAY *Collect. Words* (E.D.S.) 15 The most effectual way to prevent smutting or burning of any corn, is to lime it before you sow it. *a* **1698** W. BLUNDELL *Cavalier's Note-bk.* (1880) 87 Sir Roger Bradshaigh limed the hall croft with lime from Clitheroe. **1757** MRS. GRIFFITH *Lett. Henry & Frances* (1767) I. 158 Sixty-three acres of corn,..all limed, at eighty barrels to an acre. **1765** *Museum Rust.* IV. 245 Where I limed, there seems now a pretty deal of grass. **1796** J. ADAMS *Diary* 27 July, Wks. 1851 III. 421 Making and liming a heap of manure. **1799** J. ROBERTSON *Agric. Perth* 266 Then lime and sow with oats. **1880** *Daily News* 10 Dec. 5/8 The farmer has expended not less than £6000 in building, and in draining, and liming four hundred acres. **1966** M. M. PEGLER *Dict. Interior Design* (1967) 266 Woods other than oak can be limed.

†**c.** To smear or coat with lime-wash. *Obs.* (Also WHITE-LIME.)

c **1440** *Promp. Parv.* 305/2 Lyme wythe lyme, *idem quod* whyton wythe lyme. **1530** PALSGR. 611/2, I lyme a wall, or rofe with whyte lyme to make it whyte. **1574** *Ludlow Churchw. Acc.* (Camden) 161 For lymynge over the vestrye. **1591** LODGE *Catharos* (1875) 30 Thou tylest thy house

against stormes and lymest it well. **1615** CROOKE *Body of Man* 387 Houses newly limed.

d. To steep (skins) in lime and water.

1688–1844 [cf. LIMING *vbl. sb.*[1] 2 c]. **1707** *Rhode Island Col. Rec.* (1859) IV. 7 Leather, which shall be insufficiently tanned, or which hath been over-limed or burnt in lime. **1903** L. A. FLEMMING *Pract. Tanning* 6 The length of time to thoroughly lime the skins depends on the thickness of the skins. *Ibid.* 7 The best results accrue when only skins of like nature and size are limed..together. **1925** J. R. ARNOLD *Hides & Skins* 553 Hides and skins which are prepared for dehairing by sweating or painting..are also limed.

e. (See quot.)

1891 *Lancet* 3 Oct. 783 The sludge..is limed—that is, a small quantity of lime is added to it so as to facilitate the operation of pressing.

†**lime**, *v.*[2] *Obs. rare*—[0]. In 7 limme. [a. F. *lime-r* (13th c. in Littré):—L. *līmāre* (see LIMATE).] *trans.* To file, polish.

Some Dicts. cite a supposed example from Chaucer *H. Fame* 1124, 'A lymed glas'; but the true reading is 'Alym-de-glas' = F. *alun de glace*, crystallized alum.

1613 R. C[AWDREY] *Table Alph.* (ed. 3), *Limme*, pollish, amend.

†**lime**, *v.*[3] *Obs.* [Of obscure origin; cf. the synonymous LINE *v.*[3]] *trans.* To impregnate (a bitch). Also *pass.* and *intr.*, to copulate *with*, to be coupled *to*.

1555 W. WATREMAN *Fardle Facions* App. 317 Yf anye manne require eyther thy dogge for the folde, or for the chace to lime his bitche. **1579–80** NORTH *Plutarch, Lycurgus* (1595) 54 They caused their bitches..to bee limed..with fayrest dogges. **1607** TOPSELL *Four-f. Beasts* (1658) 370 A Mastive Dog was limed to a she Wolf. **1674** N. FAIRFAX *Bulk & Selv.* 130 Why earthworms are limed so much to the headward. **1682** *Roxb. Ballads* IV. 281/71 But France is for thy Lust too kind a Clime, In Africk with some Wolf or Tyger lime.

lime, *v.*[4]: see LIMER[3].

lime, obs. f. or var. LEAM *sb.*[1], LIMB *sb.*[1], LYAM.

limeade (laɪˈmeɪd). [f. LIME *sb.*[2] 1 + -ADE 1 c.] A drink made from lime-juice sweetened with sugar.

1892 F. DAVIES *Temperance Drinks* 81 *Limeade*, plain syrup one gallon, lime-juice a quart, essence of lemon two ounces, essence of lime one ounce. **1936** J. DOS PASSOS *Big Money* 313 Give me a limeade and no sweetnin' in it. **1953** R. CHANDLER *Long Good-bye* xiii. 79 She had finished her limeade. **1966** *Guardian* 28 Dec. 4/6 The abbot and I.. shared a bottle of fizzy limeade.

Limean: see LIMENIAN.

ˈ**lime-burner.** [LIME *sb.*[1]] One whose occupation it is to make lime by burning limestone.

1329 *Petition* in Riley *Mem. Lond.* (1868) 174 Hugh de Hecham, lymbrennere. **1497–8** in Swayne *Churchw. Acc. Sarum* 49 Diuersis lymebrenners pro lyme. *c* **1515** *Cocke Lorell's B.* 10 Parys plasterers, daubers, and lyme borners. **1624–5** in Swayne *Churchw. Acc. Sarum* (1896) 181, 15 quarters of Lyme to Snowe the Lymeburner. **1749** BRACKEN *Farriery Impr.* (ed. 6) xxxiv. 287 The Lime-burners Horses are very subject to the scab. **1808** J. WALKER *Hist. Hebrides* I. 165 A skillful limeburner..who has had full experience in burning limestone with peat, turf, and wood. **1842** S. LOVER *Handy Andy* xxv, My mouth is as dry as a limeburner's wig.

limed (laɪmd), *ppl. a.* [f. LIME *v.*[1] + -ED[1].]

1. Smeared with birdlime (or other sticky substance); †*fig.* said of hands given to pilfering.

c **13..** *Seuyn Sages* (W.) 1280 The wise man dede make a dich Ful of lim and of pich, The fader lep in bifore, Into the limed diche. **1399** LANGL. *Rich. Redeles* II. 186 Lymed leues were leyde all aboute. **1563** B. GOOGE *Eglogs* vi. (Arb.) 54 Somtime I wold betraye the Byrds, that lyght on lymed tree. **1583** STUBBES *Anat. Abus.* II. (1882) 38 Men..who haue limed fingers, liuing vpon pilfering. **1602** SHAKS. *Ham.* III. iii. 68 Oh limed soule, that strugling to be free, Art more ingag'd. **1720** GAY *Dione* II. v. Poems II. 467 On the lim'd twig thus finches beat their wings. **1849** JAMES *Woodman* ii, There are limed twigs about them, my child.

2. a. Dressed or treated with lime.

1707–12 MORTIMER *Husb.* II. Suppl. I. vii. 36 All sort of Peas love limed or marled Land. **1770–4** A. HUNTER *Georg. Ess.* (1803) I. 30 Clay, well limed, will fall in winter. **1898** *Trans. Highl. & Agric. Soc. Scotl.* 91 On limed land, too, Agrostis is eaten by stock.

b. Of wood, esp. oak, that is treated with lime to give it a bleached effect.

1930 *Heal & Son Catal.* 17 Twin Bedsteads in Limed Oak. **1933** *Archit. Rev.* LXXIII. June 230 The Holy Table is in waxed and limed oak. **1952** J. GLOAG *Short Dict. Furnit.* 311 *Limed oak*, oak that has been pickled with a coating of lime... Limed oak surfaces are generally left unpolished. **1957** *N.Z. Timber Jrnl.* Oct. 73/1 *Limed oak*, chloride of lime and water applied to oak furniture to produce a bleached effect. **1973** A. ROOS *Dunfermline Affair* 162 The limed-oak furniture was all built in. Wardrobe, vanity units, dressing-tables.

†**lime-fingered**, *a. Obs.* [Cf. LIME *sb.*[1] 1, LIMED *ppl. a.* (sense 1).] Given to pilfering.

1546 J. HEYWOOD *Prov.* (1867) 21 A cleane fingred huswyfe, and an ydell,..wyll be lyme-fyngerd. **1613** PURCHAS *Pilgrimage* VIII. iv. 629 They are light-footed and lime fingred. **1624** BP. HALL *True Peace-Maker* Wks. (1625) 542 Carelesse, slothfull, false, lime-fingred seruants.

So †**lime-fingers**, thievish propensities.

1613 PURCHAS *Pilgrimage* VII. x. (1614) 700 It is secured from the lime-fingers of any passenger.

limehound, variant of LYAM-HOUND.

Limehouse (ˈlaɪmhaʊs), *v.* [*Limehouse*, a district in the east of London.] *intr.* To make fiery (political) speeches such as Mr. Lloyd George made at Limehouse in 1909. Also as *sb.* and ˈ**Limehousing** *vbl. sb.*

1913 *Daily Mail* 1 Aug. 5 (*heading*) Mr. Lloyd George himself again... Limehousing at Carnarvon. **1914** *National Rev.* June 543 Mr. Lloyd George went to Ipswich and Limehoused on the eve of the poll. **1920** *Glasgow Herald* 20 Mar. 7 It is exactly what he used to say in the old Limehouse days, though his Limehousing now is of a different kind. **1920** *Punch* 31 Mar. 259/1 Guerrilla tactics in the House, suspension, recognition, pacifism, office, original budgeting, limehousing.., social reform. **1932** *Times Lit. Suppl.* 9 June 426/2 He [*sc.* Bonar Law] introduced..a 'new acerbity' into Front Bench debating, or what his opponents might have called the Conservative counterpart of 'Limehouse'. **1937** PARTRIDGE *Dict. Slang* 484/1 *Limehouse*, 'to use coarse, abusive language in a speech'. **1963** *Punch* 16 Jan. 96/1 Enough of the actor to wallow in invective—'Limehousing' they called it.

ˈ**lime-juice.** [f. LIME *sb.*[2]] The juice of the lime used as a beverage and as an antiscorbutic.

1704 *Lond. Gaz.* No. 4074/4 A Parcel of extraordinary good Rum and Lime-juice, to be sold. **1853** KANE *Grinnell Exp.* xxxvi. (1856) 326 Three times a day did these high-spirited fellows drink a wine glass of olive-oil and lime-juice. **1854** *Act 17 & 18 Vict.* c. 104 §224 The master of every such Ship..shall serve out the Lime or Lemon Juice ..and Sugar and Vinegar to the Crew, whenever they have consumed Salt Provisions for Ten Days. **1859** CORNWALLIS *New World* I. 49 Some that had not yet 'got the lime-juice off them', i.e. unmistakable new chums.

b. *attrib.* in ***lime-juice writing***, writing with lime-juice as a sympathetic ink.

1877 OWEN *Surv. Wellesley's Adminstr.* 43 in *Desp*, [He] may seem, by a sort of lime-juice writing, to have invalidated much which he does not repudiate.

Hence ˈ**lime-juicer. a.** *Australian.* One who has lately made the voyage from England; a 'new chum' (cf. quot. 1859 under prec.). **b.** *U.S.*, a British sailor or ship, so called because in the British navy the consumption of lime-juice is enforced (as an antiscorbutic). **c.** An advocate of the use of lime-juice.

1859 CORNWALLIS *New World* I. 58 Turn that lime-juicer out. **1884** *Pall Mall G.* 26 Aug. 11/1 They would not go on a 'lime-juicer', they said, for anything. **1891** C. CREIGHTON *Hist. Epidemics* I. 596 Hawkins, it will have been remarked, was no bigoted 'lime-juicer'.

lime-kiln (ˈlaɪmkɪln). Forms: see LIME *sb.*[1] and KILN; also 6 **lyme kylme**, 7 **limbekill**. A kiln in which lime is made by calcining limestone.

1296 *Durham Halmote Rolls* (Surtees) 6 Septem acras terræ apud limkilne. **1355–6** *Durham Acc. Rolls* (Surtees) 557 Et in 1 Lymkilne comburend. apud Pytingdon, 14*s.* 6*d.* **1509** *Bury Wills* (Camden) 112 Yᵉ hygheway from yᵉ lyme kylle. **1580** FRAMPTON *Dial. Yron & Steele* in *Joyful News* (1596) 145 Put them into an Ouen, like to a lyme keele. **1598** SHAKS. *Merry W.* III. iii. 86 As hatefull to me, as the reeke of a Lime-kill. **1608** BONHAM in Topsell *Serpents* 314 Wormes..which are wont to doe much hurt to Fornaces and Limbekills where they make Limbe. **1692** *Lond. Gaz.* No. 2828/2 They destroyed their famous Lime Kill. **1703** MAUNDRELL *Journ. Jerus.* (1732) 83 Resembling those places in England where there have been anciently Lime-kilns. **1876** ALICE CARY *Pict. Country Life* i. 16 A pile of dry stones that had once been a lime-kiln. **1892** HUME NISBET *Bush-ranger's Sweetheart* xviii. 136 'That infernal "swanky" has left me as dry as a lime-kiln', cried out my companion.

attrib. *c* **1547** in Willis and Clark *Cambridge* (1886) II. 726 A key of yᵉ lyme kylne doore.

b. *transf.* and *fig.*

1606 SHAKS. *Tr. & Cr.* v. i. 25 (Qo. 1609) Now the rotten diseases of the south..Sciaticaes, limekills ith' palme,..take and take againe such preposterous discoueries! **1845** E. B. BARRETT in *Lett. R. Browning* (1899) I. 289 The great Law lime-kiln dries human souls all to one colour.

limeless (ˈlaɪmlɪs), *a.* [f. LIME *sb.*[1] + -LESS.] Having or containing no lime.

1729 SAVAGE *Wanderer* I. 165 Yon limeless Sands loose-driving with the Wind. **1881** *Standard* 22 Jan. 5/2 The limeless mortar and half-burnt bricks of the speculative architect. **1897** *Allbutt's Syst. Med.* III. 120 The degree of calcification from spongy, limeless tissue to normal osseous structure.

limelight (ˈlaɪmlaɪt), *sb.* [f. LIME *sb.*[1]]

1. The intense white light produced by heating a piece of lime in an oxyhydrogen flame. Called also DRUMMOND LIGHT. Formerly much used in theatres to light up important actors and scenes, and so direct attention to them. Hence freq. *fig.*

1826 DRUMMOND in *Phil. Trans.* CXVI. 336 Applied to a revolving light, where four sides are illuminated, each with four reflectors, one reflector, with the lime light, might be substituted on each side. **1860** TYNDALL *Glac.* I. vi. 46 The naked eye can detect no difference in brightness between the electric light and the lime light. **1877** G. B. SMITH *Shelley* I. 45 Transcendent as were his virtues when compared with his faults, the lime-light of a malevolent scrutiny has been turned on the latter. **1881** P. FITZGERALD *World behind Scenes* I. 48 The use of so intense a light as the limelight has favoured the introduction of a new effect in the shape of transparent scenery. **1882** F. HARRISON *Choice Bks.* (1886) 433 When Shakespeare played Hamlet and Macbeth, he had neither limelight, footlights, scenery, costumes, nor stage machinery. **1908** *Daily Chron.* 25 Jan. 3/2 The beauty of his person..helped to throw the limelight upon him. **1922** *Blackw. Mag.* Aug. 150/1 He did not..pose in the limelight to the same extent as his respected chief. **1934** A. HUXLEY *Let.* 1 Oct. (1969) 384 The town hardly gets its full share of the limelight because of the hero. **1952** GRANVILLE *Dict. Theatr. Terms* 111 *Fond of limelight*, greedy for notice. One who claims the centre of the stage. **1955** *Times* 5 May 16/2 German bonds took the limelight in the foreign bond market. *Ibid.* 17 June 9/3 The publicity given to the submission of identical tenders for public authorities' contracts has brought the question into the limelight. **1967** *Guardian* 3 Feb. 7/3 [He] did more than his bit of backing in to the limelight, and his declarations of his own genius aren't to everyone's taste. **1975** R. LEWIS *Double Take* iv. 127 In our business exposure to the limelight of the courts is like the kiss of death.

2. *attrib.*

1874 *Porcupine* 11 Apr. 26/3 And [he], with the willing aid of the stage-carpenter, scenic artist, and limelight man, has made our blood curdle. **1874** *Cassell's Mag.* May 432/1 The lime-light splendour of the tropics. **1876** *Porcupine* 22 Apr. 59/1 There is plenty of bustle and 'business', and lots of pistol-shots and obliging limelight rays. **1892** J. NIE *Robinson Crusoe* 6 Here! Where's the lime-light man? **1897** G. B. SHAW *Let.* 11 June (1965) 774 A ten inch moon, a limelight sky. **1938** W. LORAINE *Robert Loraine* 31 And recount the events of the evening—the mistakes of the limelight man, the hacking cough from the third row.

limelight, *v.* [f. the sb.] *trans.* To illuminate by limelight. Usu. *fig.* Also ˈ**limelighted, -lit** *ppl. a.*; ˈ**limelighting** *vbl. sb.*

1909 *Daily Chron.* 10 Apr. 4/6 The most limelighted person in Europe this morning is Queen Wilhelmina of Holland. **1909** *Westm. Gaz.* 10 Apr. 2/3 We had sympathised with the beautiful lime-lit heroine. **1927** *Daily Express* 21 Feb. 2/4 Unfeminine modern women go limelighting their way through the world. **1927** *Observer* 10 Apr. 29 This is not an occasion when the interests of motorists can be served by limelighting. **1940** *Nation* (N.Y.) 28 Sept. 263/1 What are the facts that justify these limelighted conferences in Berlin and Rome? **1964** *Punch* 12 Aug. 213/1 This keenness to pin something on the limelit.

‖**limen** (ˈlaɪmɛn). *Psychol.* [L. *līmen* = 'threshold'; introduced as an equivalent for G. *schwelle* (a term first used by Herbart *Psychol.* 1824).] The limit below which a given stimulus ceases to be perceptible; the minimum amount of stimulus or nerve-excitation required to produce a sensation. Also called THRESHOLD *sb.*

1895 TITCHENER *Külpe's Outl. Psychol.* 48 The just noticeable stimulus is technically termed the ***stimulus limen*** [G. *Reizschwelle*], and the just noticeable stimulus-difference the ***difference limen*** [G. *Unterschiedsschwelle*]. **1901** —— *Exper. Psychol.* I. 140 The method given for the determination of the limen.

limen, obs. pl. LIMB *sb.*[1]

†**limenarch.** *Obs.* In 7 limenark. [ad. late L. *limenarch-a* ad. Gr. λιμενάρχης, f. λιμεν-, λιμήν harbour + -άρχης ruling, ἄρχειν to rule.] A harbour-master.

1656 BLOUNT *Glossogr.*, *Limenark*, the Warden or Governor of a Port.

Limenian (lɪˈmiːnɪən). Also **Limean** (lɪˈmiːən). [f. *Lima*, capital of Peru: see below.] A native or inhabitant of Lima. Also *attrib.* Also the Spanish forms **limeño** (lɪˈmeɲo) a male, and **limeña** a female, native or inhabitant of Lima.

1824 B. HALL *Extracts Jrnl. Coasts Chili, Peru & Mexico* (ed. 2) I. iii. 90 San Martin's expedition took the Limenians quite by surprise; for they had always held Chili in contempt. **1856** C. R. MARKHAM *Cuzco & Lima* ix. 302 The Limenians, with all their indolence,..bore themselves towards the Creoles with insolent pride. **1891** E. B. CLARK *Twelve Months Peru* iii. 55 It is considered highly improper for a Limeña, either married or single, to walk the streets alone. **1927** T. WILDER *Bridge San Luis Rey* I. 4 It was rather strange that this event should have so impressed the Limeans. *Ibid.* III. 49 Limean gossips..declared them to be Castilian. **1962** N. MAXWELL *Witch-Doctor's Apprentice* ii. 13 Any place with no roads..and only one good hotel is not apt to be frequented by Limeños. **1971** *Guardian* 18 Aug. 3/2 [A] cynical Limeño lawyer. **1974** 'A. HAIG' *Peruvian Printout* 122 The car was a hired Cadillac... Few Limeños ever hired those vehicles; they were strictly for tourists.

ˈ**lime-pit.** [f. LIME *sb.*[1]]

1. a. A limestone quarry. **b.** A pit in which lime is burnt.

c **1440** *Gesta Rom.* lxx. 324 (Harl. MS.) Men that havith great plente of fire, for stonys to be brent in your lyme-pyttis. **1489–90** in Swayne *Churchw. Acc. Sarum* (1896) 371 Cariage of Rubrish fro the lymepittes to the ch., 6*d.*

2. A pit in which tanners dress skins with lime to remove the hair, etc.

1591 PERCIVALL *Sp. Dict.*, *Pelambrera*, a tanners lime pit, *depilatorium*. **1768** BLACKSTONE *Comm.* III. xiii. 218 It is a nusance..to corrupt or poison a water-course by erecting a dyehouse or a lime-pit for the use of trade, in the upper part of the stream. **1839** URE *Dict. Arts* 764 They [skins] are left in the lime-pits for about twelve days, when they are stripped of their hair [etc.].

ˈ**lime-pot.** [f. LIME *sb.*[1]] A pot to contain lime or birdlime; a vessel of lime to pour upon assailants in a fight (*Hist.*); †a pot or furnace in which limestone is burnt; a lime-wash pot.

14.. *Nom.* in Wr.-Wülcker 703/5, *Hoc viscerium*, a lyme-pott. **1483** *Cath. Angl.* 217/1 A Lyme pott or brusche, *viscarium, viminarium*. **1549** *Compl. Scot.* vi. 41 Boitis man, bayr stanis & lyme pottis ful of lyme in the craklene pokis to the top. **1596** *Reg. Mag. Sig.* (1890) 160/1 Vastam caudam terre cum lie vorkhousis et lymepottis ad australem partem.

1692 in *Rec. Convent. R. Burghs* (1880) IV. 571 Item, a years rent of lim potts and grass at the east port 3 8 8. **1860** HEWITT *Anc. Armour* III. 489 Both fire-pots and lime-pots were employed at the siege of Harfleur in 1415. **1860** *Ecclesiologist* XXI. 218 A man armed with a fire-pot, or lime-pot.

ˈlimer[1]. *Obs.* (exc. *arch.*) Also 4–5 **lymer(e**, 5 **lemer, lymour, -eer**, 5–6 **lymmer, limmer**, 5, 7 **lemor**, (*corrupt forms* 6–8 **levyner, -iner, lyemmer**), 7–9 **leamer**. [a. AF. *limer* = OF. *liemier* (mod.F. *limier*), f. OF. *liem* (F. *lien*) leash: see LIEN[1] and LYAM.] A kind of hound, *properly* a leash-hound; in early use (and now *arch.*) a bloodhound; later, a mongrel.

c **1369** CHAUCER *Dethe Blaunche* 362 There ouertoke I a grete route Of hunters and eke of foresters, And many relayes and lymers. *c* **1400** *Sowdone Bab.* 56 With Alauntes, Lymmeris and Racches free. **1426** LYDG. *De Guil. Pilgr.* 21444 They berke, they byte, ryht felly,.. The grete lemerys wer so strong. *c* **1440** *Partonope* 530 Fayre Grehoundes and grete lymours. *a* **1450** *Knt. de la Tour* (1868) 15 Hauithe youre loke and holdithe youre hede ferme as a best that is called a lymer. **1486** *Bk. St. Albans* F iv b, Theis be the namys of houndes.. a Mastyfe, a Lemor, a Spanyell. **1538** ELYOT *Dict.*, *Hybrida*, is a dogge, ingendred betwyxte a hounde and a mastyue, called a lymmar, or mongrell. [**1570** CAIUS *De Canibus Brit.* 11 b, *A leuitate*, Leuyner, *à loro* Lyemmer *appelatur is quem Leuinarium & Lorarium latine nominauimus.*] **1576** FLEMING tr. *Caius' Dogs* in Arb. *Garner* III. 264 Of the Levyner or the Lyemmer. **1688** R. HOLME *Armoury* II. 185/1 The Leviner, or Lyemmer, or Leamer; so called from the Leam, or Lyne wherewith they are led. **1706** PHILLIPS (ed. Kersey), *Limer*, a great Dog to hunt the wild Boar. **1828** WEBSTER, *Leamer*, a dog, a kind of hound. **1897** D. H. MADDEN *Diary Wm. Silence* 65 The bloodhound, or limer, would have been entitled to the first share [of the hart's paunch].

limer[2] (ˈlaɪmə(r)). [f. LIME *v.*[1] + -ER[1].] One who limes; one who snares with bird-lime; one who limewashes. Also a brush used for lime-washing. (See also WHITE-LIMER.)

1611 COTGR., *Blanchisseur*, a white dauber, or white limer. *a* **1642** SIR W. MONSON *Naval Tracts* III. (1704) 347/1 Hair, such as the White Limers use. **1655** *Speymouth Session Rec.* 20 David Dunbar was desyred to agree with some lymers for as much lyme as would serve. **1872** *Daily News* 8 June, She was only furnishing the Whitechapel trappers and limers with a new and valuable kind of quarry. **1894** P. N. HASLUCK *House Decoration* 67 In some parts of the country this 'limer' is the principal ceiling-brush used... Limers of the best kind are as expensive as distemper brushes.

limer[3] (ˈlaɪmə(r)). *West Indies.* [Etym. unknown.] A person who hangs about the streets. Hence (as a back-formation) **lime** *v.*[4] *intr.*, to hang about the streets; also **ˈliming** *vbl. sb.*[3]

Said to have been used in the 1940s but printed evidence is lacking.

1970 *Express* (Trinidad & Tobago) 6 Jan. 4 'Limers' are a menace on High Street at night. **1972** *Ibid.* 4 Feb. 21 One ride in a route taxi and a little liming in Frederick Street.. would uncover whatever the wooding group may have forgotten. **1973** *Sunday Express* (Trinidad & Tobago) 1 Apr. (Suppl.) 13/1 Staying a minute more to lime. *Ibid.* 8 Apr. 13/3 Now I confess that in the past I have often had cause to voice a complaint about his penchant for ole talking and liming. **1974** *Sunday Advocate-News* (Barbados) 3 Mar. 16/6 The limers' attire ranges from the sophisticated to the ridiculous.

Limerick (ˈlɪmərɪk). [The chief town of the county of Limerick in Ireland.] **1.** [Said to be from a custom at convivial parties, according to which each member sang an extemporized 'nonsense-verse', which was followed by a chorus containing the words 'Will you come up to Limerick?'] A form of 'nonsense-verse'.

1896 A. BEARDSLEY *Let. c* 1 May (1971) 128 I have tried to amuse myself by writing limericks on my troubles. *Ibid.* 2 May 129 Your continuation of the limerick is superb. **1898** *Cantab* 6 Oct., *Contents*, Illustrated Limericks. **1898** M. H. in *N. & Q.* 19 Nov. 408 When and why did the non-sense verse as written by Lear acquire the name of 'Limerick'? **1898** J. H. MURRAY *ibid.* 10 Dec. 470 *Limerick*. A nonsense verse such as was written by Lear is wrongfully so called.. Who applied this name to the indecent nonsense verse first it is hard to say. **1899** R. KIPLING *Stalky* 201 Make up a good catchy Limerick, and let the fags sing it.

2. Used *attrib.* to designate: **a.** Gloves of fine leather made originally at Limerick (see quot. 1960).

1804 M. EDGEWORTH *Pop. Tales* I. 245 Are you blind Mr. Hill? Don't you see that they are Limerick gloves? **1842** J. P. LAWSON *Gazetteer Ireland* 607/2 The glove trade ..has now declined, and those articles sold as Limerick gloves are actually manufactured at Cork. **1853** MRS. GASKELL *Ruth* II. vii. 173 She..brought down a pair of Limerick ones, which had been long treasured up in a walnut-shell. 'They say them gloves is made of chicken's-skins,' said Sally. **1960** CUNNINGTON & BEARD *Dict. Eng. Costume, Limerick gloves*, 2nd half 18th and 1st half 19th c... made of very fine leather, said to be made from the skins of unborn lambs.

b. A particular bend or pattern of fish-hook or a fish-hook with such a bend (said to have been orig. made in the town of Limerick) in which the wire of the hook is bent abruptly through a large angle behind the barb but thereafter is bent more shallowly to the point at which it continues as the straight shank. Also *ellipt.* as *sb.*, a Limerick hook.

1828 H. DAVY *Salmonia* 141, I have even made a hook, which..I think, I could boast as equal to the Limerick hooks. **1835** T. T. STODDART *Art of Angling in Scotl.* iii. 16 O'Shaughnessy's Limericks..are not always exactly the thing, excepting those used for salmon..which are really excellent. **1856** 'STONEHENGE' *Man. Brit. Rural Sports* 235/1 The round-bend hook is that which is most used in England, the Limerick pattern being chiefly in vogue in Ireland. **1928** *Chambers's Jrnl.* Jan. 2/2 He..picked out his lure without hesitation—a Number 5, Limerick-bend, double-hooked 'Blue Charm'. **1956** L. V. BATES *Artificial Flies* iii. 55 The Limerick is probably stronger but the fine elegant proportions of the Dee hook make for better hooking.

c. A type of embroidered lace made originally at Limerick. Also *ellipt.* as *sb.*

1842 J. P. LAWSON *Gazetteer Ireland* 607/2 Limerick lace has now obtained a high celebrity. This beautiful manufacture was introduced into the city in 1829 by Mr Walker, an English gentleman. **1886** B. LINDSEY *Irish Lace* ii. 9 A spirit of enterprise and commercial adventure.. originated the Limerick manufacture. **1905** N. H. MOORE *Lace Bk.* 196 Limerick lace is a combination..of cut-work and embroidery, and hardly comes under our definition of lace. **1953** M. POWYS *Lace & Lace-Making* iv. 35 *Limerick lace*, embroidered net, Irish, 19th century... This type of lace is made in all the countries, including America and India. It is light, pretty and easy to produce. Limerick remains the finest of the kind. **1959** *Times* 21 Sept. 12/4 Her old family Limerick lace veil was held in place by a mother-of-pearl coronet. **1967** C. GASKIN *Edge of Glass* iv. 86 [Her] long ancient gown collared in yellowed Limerick lace.

†**lime-rod.** *Obs.* [f. LIME *sb.*[1]] = LIME-TWIG.

c **1386** CHAUCER *Monk's T.* 394 The feeld of snow, with thegle of blak ther-Inne Caught with the lymerod, coloured as the gleede. **1550** COVERDALE *Spir. Perle* xxxi. 260 Like as yᵉ birde yᵗ is caught with the lyme rode. **1617** MINSHEU, *Lime twigges*, or lime roddes. **1626** BRETON *Fantastickes* Jan. (Grosart) 7 The Currier and the Lime-rod are the death of the fowle.

‖**limes** (ˈlaɪmiːz). Pl. **limites** (ˈlaɪmɪtiːz). [L. = LIMIT.] Boundary.

1538 LELAND *Itin.* I. 1 A mile from Eltesle towards Neotes in the limes of Cambridgshire. **1577–87** HARRISON *England* I. xiv. in *Holinshed*, The Twede..is a noble streame and the limes or bound betweene England and Scotland.

limestone (ˈlaɪmstəʊn). [f. LIME *sb.*[1] + STONE.] **a.** A rock which consists chiefly of carbonate of lime, and yields lime when burnt. (The crystalline variety of limestone is marble.)

1523 FITZHERB. *Surv.* 6 b, Yet may he laufully..selle..fre stonne, lyme stone, chalke,..or tynne, to his owne vse. **1695** WOODWARD *Nat. Hist. Earth* (1723) 10 Free-stone, Ragg-stone, Lime-stone. **1707** MORTIMER *Husb.* vi. 95 Any soft Stone as Firestone, Limestone, etc., if broke small, and laid on cold Lands, must be of advantage. **1813** BAKEWELL *Introd. Geol.* (1815) 86 No organic remains are found in the crystalline lime-stone.

b. A species (or †a specimen) of this rock.

1664 EVELYN *Kal. Hort.* May (1679) 17 Having before put some rubbish of Lime-stones, pebbles, shells..or the like at the bottom of the Cases, to make the moisture passage. **1742** *Lond. & Country Brew.* I. (ed. 4) 57 Others are said to make Use of Lime-stones to fine and preserve the Drink. **1813** SIR H. DAVY *Agric. Chem.* (1814) 6 By simple chemical tests the nature of a limestone is discovered in a few minutes. **1833** LYELL *Elem. Geol.* (1865) 395 One of the limestones of the Middle Oolite. **1839** URE *Dict. Arts* 774 When the kiln is to be set in action, it is filled with rough limestones. **1878** HUXLEY *Physiogr.* 118 All limestones from the softest chalk to the hardest marble consists essentially of carbonate of lime.

c. *attrib.* and *Comb.*, as ***limestone-cliff, -crag, -gravel, -land, -region, -slab, -water***; ***limestone-encased*** adj.; **limestone-bead** (see quot.); **limestone-fern** (Britten & Holland), **-polypody**, a fern, *Gymnocarpium robertianum*, restricted to areas of limestone rock.

1793 D. URE *Hist. Rutherglen* 319 The Entrochi..by workmen in Kilbride they are more commonly called *Limestone-beads. **1699** M. LISTER *Journey to Paris* 88 The high Ragstone Mountains and *Lime Stone Cliffs. **1880** HAUGHTON *Phys. Geogr.* v. 243 The yucca grew on the limestone cliffs. **1863** KINGSLEY *Water-Bab.* 14 A low cave of rock at the foot of a *limestone crag. **1889** N. S. SHALER *Aspects of Earth* 102 The North Atlantic where minute *limestone-encased creatures float in the water while they live. **1764** *Museum Rust.* III. xvii. 75 Others fallow, and manure with a very happy provision they have in the thinly-inhabited and interior parts of the kingdom, called *lime-stone gravel. **1805** R. W. DICKSON *Pract. Agric.* I. 236 Lime-stone gravel..has been successfully laid upon land in Ireland. **1685** BOYLE *Salub. Air* 10 A large tract of *Limestone land was so warm (as they speak) as to dissolve the Snow that fell on it. **1811** *Niles' Reg.* 12 Oct. 101/1 Our steepest lime stone lands are very favorable to sheep. **1861** MISS PRATT *Flower Pl.* VI. 164 *Limestone Polypody. **1888** C. T. DRUERY *Choice Brit. Ferns* 118 The young fronds [of the Oak Fern] also, when unfolding, exactly resemble the pawnbroker's sign of three balls, which those of the Limestone Polypody do not. **1908** E. STEP *Wayside & Woodland Ferns* 87 The Limestone Polypody..will be found nowhere except on lime-stone rocks. **1960** P. TAYLOR *Brit. Ferns & Mosses* 164 The Limestone Polypody occurs in the mountains of Europe, temperate Asia and North America. **1865** GOSSE *Land & Sea* (1874) 321 A *limestone region is essential to the abundance of these animals. **1839** URE *Dict. Arts* 774 The several stones are formed of groined arches *o*, and platforms *p*, covered over with *limestone slabs. **1831** J. M. PECK *Guide for Emigrants* 233 Those persons who have been unaccustomed to *lime stone water ..frequently have eruptions of the skin. **1872** E. EGGLESTON *End of World* ix. 65 Having..quaffed the hard limestone water.

ˈlime-twig. [f. LIME *sb.*[1]]

1. A twig smeared with birdlime for catching birds.

? *a* **1400** LYDG. *Chorle & Byrde* (Roxb.) 13 Thy lyme twigges and panters I deffye. **1616** SURFL. & MARKH. *Country Farme* 705 Such as bring vs Hawkes, doe take them for the most part with lime-twigges. **1678** BUNYAN *Pilgr.* Apol. A iv, The Fowler His Gun, his Nets, his Lime-twigs. *a* **1711** KEN *Edmund* Poet. Wks. 1721 II. 113 As Birds unwary on the Lime-twigs tread. *c* **1820** S. ROGERS *Italy* (1839) 136 To catch a thrush on every lime-twig there.

b. *fig.*

1581 J. BELL *Haddon's Answ. Osor.* 457 b, A lymetwygg layed by Hypocrytes to gett money withall. **1593** SHAKS. *2 Hen. VI*, III. iii. 16. **1607** DEKKER *Sir T. Wyatt* Wks. 1873 III. 112 Catch Fooles with Lime-twigs dipt with pardons. **1634** MILTON *Comus* 646. **1771** SMOLLETT *Humph. Cl.* 11 June, There are so many lime-twigs laid in his way, that I'll bet a cool hundred he swings before Christmas. **1821** BYRON *Juan* v. xxii, Ambition, Avarice, Vengeance, Glory, glue The glittering lime-twigs of our latter days.

Prov. **1670** RAY *Prov.* 175 His fingers are lime-twigs. Spoken of a thievish person.

†**2.** One whose fingers are 'limed'; a thief. *Obs.*

c **1600** *Nobody & Someb.* D 3 b, Talke not of the Gayle, 'tis full of limetwigs, lifts, and pickpockets.

†**3.** *attrib.* or as *adj.* Ensnaring; pilfering. *Obs.*

1602 *2nd Pt. Return fr. Parnass.* I. iv. 428 Let vs run through all the lewd formes of lime-twig purloyning villanyes. *c* **1730** *Royal Remarks* 44 The Lime-twigg Titles of their own [the Booksellers'] composing, to catch the curious Birds of Life..Momus wanting that Lime-twigg Faculty.

Hence †**ˈlime-twig** *v. trans.*, to catch as with a lime-twig; to entangle, ensnare.

1646 J. HALL *Horæ Vac.* 87 You may be Lyme-twig'd with their errours and loose the Truth for a friend. **1671** L. ADDISON *W. Barbary* To Rdr., That the Ottoman Empire.. reckon it among their Happinesses not to have their Consultations lime-twigg'd with Quirks and Sophisms of Philosophical Persons. **1681** GLANVILL *Sadducismus* I. (1726) 85 Their Mind is so illaqueated or lime-twigged, as it were, with the Ideas and Properties of Corporeal Things. **1815** LAMB *Lett., to Wordsworth* (1852) 246/1 Lord bless me! these 'merchants and their spicy drugs'.. they lime-twig up my poor soul and body. **1829** LANDOR *Imag. Conv., Barrow & Newton* Wks. 1853 I. 484/1 He allowed his mind to be lime-twigged and ruffled and discomposed by words.

ˈlime-water. [f. LIME *sb.*[1]] A solution of lime in water, used medicinally and in the clarification of sugar.

1677 GREW *Colours Plants* iii. in *Anat. Plants* (1682) 277 Other Alkalies, and particularly Lime-Water. **1794** KIRWAN *Elem. Min.* (ed. 2) I. 5 The strongest lime-water contains no more than about one grain per ounce troy. **1849** D. CAMPBELL *Inorg. Chem.* 136 Lime-water soon becomes covered with a pellicle of carbonate when exposed to the air.

ˈlime-wort[1]. [f. LIME *sb.*[1] + WORT.]

†**1.** The Catchfly, *Silene Armeria*. [So called because covered with a sticky substance.] *Obs.*

1597 GERARDE *Herbal* II. clxxxvi. (1633) 600 This plant called *viscaria* or Lyme-woort.

2. The Childing Pink, *Dianthus prolifer*. [So called from often growing on old mortar.]

1777 ROBSON *Brit. Flora* 99.

ˈlime-wort[2], **limpwort.** [f. **lime*, **lempe* (OE. *hleomece*) in BROOKLIME, *brooklempe*.] The Brooklime, *Veronica Beccabunga*.

1666 MERRETT *Pinax* 6 *Anagallis, sive Becabunga* Brooklime..*ab Herefordensibus* Limpwort. **1851** *Eliza Cook's Jrnl.* 5 July 149 The knapweed..the willow-herb and the lime-wort unfolding their simple many-coloured beauties.

Limey (ˈlaɪmɪ). *colloq.* and *derogatory*. Also **limey.** [abbrev. LIME-JUICER.] **a.** In the former British colonies (esp. Austral., N.Z., and S. Afr.), an English immigrant. Also *attrib.*

The later examples prob. reflect the U.S. use in b.

1888 D. SLADEN *Austral. Ballads & Rhymes* 31 They'd seen old stagers and limey new chums. **1947** J. BERTRAM *Shadow of War* 251, I can remember scores of fights among the 'Limeys'. **1954** T. S. ELIOT *Elder Statesman* III. 93 Everyone would sneer at the fellow from London, The limey remittance man for whom a job was made. **1962** *Times* 6 Jan. 7/1 The [English] boys [at Sasolburg, Orange Free State] were constantly taunted by school-mates as 'Pommie', 'Limey', and 'Rooinek'. **1964** O. E. MIDDLETON in C. K. Stead *N.Z. Short Stories* (1966) 198 We'd all be drawing the dole like every other mother-loving beachcomber in this..Limey hole!

b. *U.S.* An English ship; an English (or British) sailor; hence *gen.*, an Englishman, a Briton. Also *attrib.*

1918 A. N. DEPEW *Gunner Depew* 18 So, all over the world, British ships are called 'Lime-juicers' and their sailors 'Limeys'. *Ibid.* 48 Ask any Limey soldier and he will tell you the same. **1918** R. D. PAINE *Fighting Fleets* v. 87 Squads of the American navy patrol began to stroll about.. displaying no sympathy..for the shipmate who..loudly announced that he could whip any three 'Limies' that ever trod a British deck. **1919** *Texas Rev.* IV. 86 In our fleet a British ship is regularly called a 'limey', from the old lime-juicers. The British seaman is likewise a 'limey'. **1924** *Chicago Tribune* 18 Oct. 1/5 (*heading*) Midway Signs Limey Prof. to Dope Yank Talk. **1930** J. DOS PASSOS *42nd Parallel* II. 169, I..shipped out East on a limey, on an English boat. **1931** E. LINKLATER *Juan in Amer.* II. vii. 115 'An Englishman,' he marvelled, 'the first limey I ever saw shot in Chicago.' **1933** 'J. SPENSER' *Limey* i. 4 'English, eh?' said the manager. 'I ain't too keen on you Limey's.' **1952** J. STEINBECK *East of Eden* lii. 498 Fights in the bar-rooms with the goddam Limeys. **1954** M. BRUCE *Tramp Royal* II. ix.

121 This ship differed from a Limey vessel in the way the watch bells are struck. **1955** G. GREENE *Quiet American* IV. ii. 241, I don't like Limies. **1968** M. PYKE *Food & Society* iii. 32 The pejorative identification of foreigners with unfamiliar foods. This makes.. the English limies. **1969** *Listener* 26 June 881/3 Was it my limey accent that called it forth or did they say it to every customer? **1973** 'D. JORDAN' *Nile Green* xi. 49 Guy always plays up the limey accent when he's in the States.

limicole (ˈlaɪmɪkəʊl). [f. mod.L. group-name *Limicolæ* (see quot. 1930), f. L. *līmus* mud + *colere* to inhabit.] An oligochæte worm living in mud or water.

[**1930** J. STEPHENSON *Oligochaeta* xvi. 607 Oligochaeta may be divided roughly into Terricolae and Limicolae—the earth-dwellers and the mud- and water-dwellers respectively.] **1963** R. P. DALES *Annelids* ix. 180 The common division of the Oligochaeta into the Microdrili or Limicoles (the aquatic families) and the Megadrili or Terricoles (the earthworms) is mainly one of convenience. **1965** B. E. FREEMAN tr. *Vandel's Biospeleol.* vii. 73 The limicoles are more interesting to the biospeleologist.

limicoline (laɪˈmɪkəlaɪn, -ɪn), *a.* [f. L. *līmicola* (f. *līmus* mud + *colĕre* to inhabit) + -INE².] Of or pertaining to the *Limicolæ*, a family of shore or wading birds.

1874 COUES *Birds N.W.* 454 There are numerous exceptions to the rule of four eggs among the limicoline birds. **1896** NEWTON *Dict. Birds* 811 The [Sandpiper's] nest, in which four eggs are laid with their pointed ends meeting in its centre (as is usual among limicoline birds).

limicolous (laɪˈmɪkələs), *a.* [f. as prec. + -OUS.] Living in mud.

1888 BEDDARD in *Encycl. Brit.* XXIV. 678/2 In many limicolous forms, as in earthworms, the setæ are simple in form.

liminal (ˈlɪmɪnəl), *a.* [f. L. *līmin-*, *līmen* threshold + -AL¹.] **a.** *gen.* Of or pertaining to the threshold or initial stage of a process. *rare.* **b.** *spec.* in *Psychol.* Of or pertaining to a 'limen' or 'threshold.'

1884 *Mind* July 428 The liminal difficulties cannot be evaded without the most disastrous consequences to the body of the exposition. **1884** J. SULLY *Outlines Psychol.* v. 114 Every stimulus must reach a certain intensity before any appreciable sensation results. This point is known as the threshold or liminal intensity. **1895** TITCHENER *Külpe's Outl. Psychol.* 243 We may also introduce the concept of the limen, defining the just noticeable deviation from indifference as a liminal pleasantness or unpleasantness.

liminary (ˈlɪmɪnərɪ), *a.* ? *Obs.* [ad. F. *liminaire*, ad. L. *līmināris*, f. *līmin-*, *līmen*: see -ARY².] Introductory, preparatory; = PRELIMINARY.

1603 FLORIO *Montaigne* III. xii. (1632) 595, I need but the liminary epistle [= F. *epistre liminaire*] of a Germane to store me with allegations. **1661** BLOUNT *Glossogr.*, *Liminarie.* **1663** *Flagellum or O. Cromwell* 188 As the grand and Liminary work to Oliver's Regality. **1898** *Blackw. Mag.* Oct. 518/2 With.. its epistles liminary and ultimate.

liminess (ˈlaɪmɪnɪs). [f. LIMY *a.*] The quality of being limy.

1902 E. A. WOODRUFFE-PEACOCK *Thoroughbreds & their Grass-Land* II. 7 Among plants.. a score of species that could be named, suddenly appearing in a turf at once demonstrate a growing liminess in a clay soil.

liming (ˈlaɪmɪŋ), *vbl. sb.*¹ [f. LIME *v.*¹ + -ING¹.]

†**1.** Gluing or cementing together. In quot. *fig.*

c **1050** *Voc.* in Wr.-Wülcker 436/13 Liture, liming. *a* **1225** *Ancr. R.* 138 þet.. monnes soule.. schal beon so ueste iueied to þe flesche, þet nis bute uen & ful eorðe, & þuruh þet ilke limunge luuien hit so swuðe, þet [etc.].

2. The action or process of treating things with lime. **a.** Whitewashing with lime. (See also WHITE-LIMING.) **b.** Dressing earth with lime, in cultivation. **c.** Steeping skins in lime and water.

a. 1552 ELYOT *Dict.*, *Albarium opus*, pargettyng, white limyng. **1591** PERCIVALL *Sp. Dict.*, *Encaladura*, the liming, the plaistering of an house. **1626** *Vestry Bks.* (Surtees) 181 For lymeinge the windowes about that were glased, and other that neaded lymeinge aboute xij d.

b. 1620 MARKHAM *Farew. Husb.* II. ii. (1668) 7 The Liming of your ground will take at least half so much time as the sanding. **1798** *Trans. Soc. Arts* XVI. 122 We have never found that a second liming has produced any good effect. **1856** OLMSTED *Slave States* 13 Deep plowing and limeing, and the judicious use of manures. **1875** *Act 38 & 39 Vict.* c. 92 §5 Claying of land, liming of land, marling of land.

c. 1688 R. HOLME *Armoury* III. 86/2 Lyming, piting the skins with Lime and Water. **1778** *Projects* in *Ann. Reg.* 118/1 Steeping the hides for a short time in a mixture of lime and water, which is called liming. **1844** G. DODD *Textile Manuf.* ii. 50.

†**liming**, *vbl. sb.*² *Obs.* [f. LIME *v.*³ + -ING¹.] Copulation.

1607 TOPSELL *Four-f. Beasts* 138 Sometime she bringeth forth but one, which is a good argument to proue that she is filled at the first lyming. **1674** N. FAIRFAX *Bulk & Selv.* 130 Why Slugs or Dodmans ingender in the neck, and are so many hours, if not days, in the limeing.

liming, *vbl. sb.*³: see LIMER³.

liming, obs. form of LIMNING.

limis, obs. pl. of LIMB *sb.*¹

limit (ˈlɪmɪt), *sb.* Forms: 4-6 **lymyte**, 5-7 **lymit(te**, (5 **-ytt**), 6 **limitt**, **li-**, **lymmet**, **limete**, **lymet(e**, **lemyet**, 6-7 **limite**, 7 **limmit**, 6- **limit**. [ad. F. *limite*, ad. L. *līmit-em*, *līmes* boundary.]

1. a. A boundary, frontier; an object serving to define a boundary, a landmark. Now only in narrower sense: A boundary or terminal point considered as confining or restricting; chiefly *pl.* bounds.

c **1375** [see *limit-stead* in 5]. *a* **1400-50** *Alexander* 5069 Qua list þis lymit ouir-lende, lene to þe left hand. **1474** CAXTON *Chesse* 144 Wyth in the lymytes and space of the royame. *a* **1529** SKELTON *Bk. 3 Foles* Wks. (1568) X v b, Romulus.. dyd Instytute lymittes or markes aboute the citie. **1550** CROWLEY *Last Trump.* 1482 Let it suffice the, to defende thy limites from inuasion. **1555** EDEN *Decades* 83 That twoo such seas haue enuironed any lande with soo narowe lymittes. **1570** BILLINGSLEY *Euclid* I. def. iii, The endes or limites of a lyne, are pointes. **1587** *Mirr. Mag.*, *Forrex* vi, T'inlarge the limetes of our kingdome wide. **1598** in *Egerton Papers* (Camden) 278 Chiveat Hill, being the lemyet of the Easte Marche. **1624** WOTTON *Elem. Archit.* I. 24 When they haue chosen the Floore, or Plot, and laid out the Limits of the Worke, wee should first of all Digge Wels and Cesternes [etc.]. **1625** N. CARPENTER *Geog. Del.* II. ix. (1635) 154 Hence is the Water enforced to enlarge his limits. **1641** J. JACKSON *True Evang. T.* III. 201 Peter Heywood Esquire, one of the Kings Justices of the Peace within the limits of Westminster. **1655** FULLER *Ch. Hist.* I. v. §14 The Picts Wall.. being a better Limit then Fortification, served rather to define then defend the Roman Empire. **1711** STEELE *Spect.* No. 54 ⁋2 To be confined within the Limits of a good handsome convenient Chamber. **1734** BERKELEY *Analyst* Wks. III. 279 A point may be the limit of a line. **1823** F. CLISSOLD *Ascent Mt. Blanc* 23 A circle of thin haze.. marked dimly the limits between heaven and earth.

†**b.** Contour (of the human form). *Obs. rare*⁻¹.

1636 W. BETTIE *Titana & Theseus* B 3 He stept into a greene Arbour.. where he first viewed each limit, or proportraiture of her body. *Ibid.* B 3 b, Theseus.. thought it very strange, that Nature should endow.. such comely limmits with such peruerse conditions.

2. a. One of the fixed points between which the possible or permitted extent, amount, duration, range of action, or variation of anything is confined; a bound which may not be passed, or beyond which something ceases to be possible or allowable.

superior limit: the earlier of the two dates, or the higher of the two quantitative extremes, between which the possible range of something is confined; contrariwise ***inferior limit***.

c **1380** WYCLIF *Sel. Wks.* III. 362 þanne Goddis lawe myȝte freeli renne bi þe lymytis þat Crist haþ ordeyned. **1502** ATKYNSON tr. *De Imitatione* III. viii. 203 Nat ponderinge theyr exyle & pore lymytes of reson. **1579-80** NORTH *Plutarch*, *Theseus* (1595) 2 They range.. out of the boundes or limites of true apparance. **1594** SHAKS. *Rich. III*, III. iii. 8 Dispatch, the limit of your Liues is out. *c* **1600** —— *Sonn.* lxxxii, Finding thy worth a limmit past my praise. **1651** HOBBES *Leviath.* II. xxii. 121 For the limits of how farre such a Body shall represent the whole People. **1693** CONGREVE in *Dryden's Juvenal* (1697) 282 A Wise Man's Pow'r's the Limit of his Will. **1725** WATTS *Logic* I. vi. §5 To leave Obscurities in the Sentence, by confining it within too narrow Limits. **1785** REID *Intell. Powers* II. xxi. 279 Nature has set limits to the pleasures of sense. **1818** JAS. MILL *Brit. India* II. v. v. 505 For six hours.. every part of the English army was engaged to the utmost limit of exertion. **1860** TYNDALL *Glac.* I. vi. 46 The limit at which the eye can appreciate differences of brightness. **1874** MICKLETHWAITE *Mod. Par. Churches* 183 That subject is beyond our present limits. **1878** HUXLEY *Physiogr.* 59 A crystal however has absolutely no limit to its growth. **1878** BROWNING *La Saisiaz* 23 Would I shrink to learn my life-time's limit. **1894** *Current Hist.* (U.S.) IV. 355 Rear Admiral.. B... retired from the active list of the navy under the limit-of-age law. **1895** J. A. BEET *New Life in Christ* I. vi. 45 All men have.. transgressed limits marked out by an authority which none can question. **1895** LD. ESHER in *Law Times Rep.* LXXIII. 702/1 The section does not deal with salvage beyond the three miles limit.

b. *Math.* In various applications. (*a*) A finite quantity to which the sum of a converging series progressively approximates, but to which it cannot become equal in a finite number of terms. (*b*) A fixed value to which a function can be made to approach continually, so as to differ from it by less than any assignable quantity, by making the independent variable approach some assigned value. (*c*) Each of the two values of a variable, between which a definite integral is taken. (*d*) The ultimate position of the point of intersection of two lines which, by their relative motion, are tending to coalescence.

Doctrine or ***Method of Limits***: a term chiefly used to designate that mode of expounding the principles of the Differential and Integral Calculus, according to which the conception of 'limits' or 'limiting values' forms the basis of the system.

[*a* **1727** NEWTON *Opuscula* I. 53 Quibus Terminis, sive Limitibus respondent semicirculi Limites, sive Termini.] **1753** in CHAMBERS *Cycl. Supp.* **1797** *Encycl. Brit.* (ed. 3) X. 78/2 *Limit*, in a restrained sense, is used by mathematicians for a determined quantity to which a variable one continually approaches; in which sense, the circle may be said to be the limit of its circumscribed and inscribed polygons. In algebra the term *limit* is applied to two quantities, one of which is greater and the other less than another quantity; and in this sense it is used in speaking of the limits of equations, whereby their solution is much facilitated. **1839** *Penny Cycl.* XIII. 496/2 There are two conditions which must be fulfilled before *A* can be called the limit of *P*; first, *P* must never become equal to *A*; secondly *P* must be capable of being made as nearly equal to *A* as we please. **1842** DE MORGAN *Diff. Calc.* Pref., The idea of limits being absolutely necessary even to the proper conception of a convergent series. *Ibid.* Introd. Chap. 32 A case will be found in which the limit of an intersection is deduced. **1844** HYMERS *Integral Calc.* 122 Integrals are usually required between limits. **1857** WOOD *Algebra* 168 This quantity, which we call the *sum* of the series, is the *limit* to which the sum of the terms approaches, but never actually attains.

c. *Astron.* ***limit of a planet***: its greatest heliocentric latitude.

1704 HARRIS *Lex. Techn.*, *Limit* of a Planet is the greatest Heliocentrick Latitude. **1727-41** CHAMBERS *Cycl.*, *Limits* of a planet, its greatest excursions or distances from the ecliptic. **1797** *Encycl. Brit.* (ed. 3) II. 507/2 Suppose Venus to be in the point *C* in her utmost north limit.

d. *Comm.* In various applications, e.g. the amount up to which a particular customer of a bank is not permitted to overdraw, the price given by a principal to an agent as the highest at which he will buy, or the lowest at which he will sell. ***founder's limit*** (see quot. 1872-6).

1866 CRUMP *Banking* iii. 76 The banker gives him [his customer] a 'limit', beyond which he must not draw. **1872-6** VOYLE *Milit. Dict.* (ed. 3), *Limit, Founder's.* In the manufacture of ordnance, the limitation of error for guns, shot, &c. allowed to the founder.

e. In generalized sense: Limitation, restriction within limits. Chiefly in phr. ***without limit***.

1599 SHAKS. *Much Ado* I. iii. 5 The sadnesse is without limit. **1742** YOUNG *Nt. Th.* VI. 463 Souls.. Disdaining Limit, or from Place, or Time. **1875** JOWETT *Plato* (ed. 2) IV. 22 Pain is the violation, and pleasure the restoration of limit.

¶**f.** Used by Shaks. for: Prescribed time; the prescribed period of repose after child-bearing.

1603 SHAKS. *Meas. for M.* III. i. 224 Between which time of the contract, and limit of the solemnitie. **1611** —— *Wint. T.* III. ii. 107 Lastly, hurried Here, to this place, i' th' open ayre, before I haue got strength of limit.

g. In various card games, as (*a*) *Poker*, an agreed maximum stake or bet; so *attrib.*, as ***limit game***; (*b*) *Bridge*, a call which shows that the strength of the caller's hand does not exceed a certain value; usu. *attrib.*, as ***limit bid***, ***raise***.

(*a*) **1892** W. J. FLORENCE *Handbk. Poker* 90 Before a game is commenced it is agreed that so many chips shall be the limit... No game ever should be played without a limit. **1928** *Chambers's Jrnl.* Jan. 116/1 Once again the betting came to Poker Jack, and this was his chance. He coolly raised Rymington the limit, and left his two opponents half-stupefied. **1963** *Esquire's Bk. Gambling* II. iv. 109 It is virtually impossible to bluff in a limit game. With a limit, poker is more like Screeno... Big Poker.. as any unlimited-stakes player will be happy to tell you.. requires the most brutality.

(*b*) **1959** REESE & DORMER *Bridge Player's Dict.* 138 A limit-bid is one that describes the strength of a player's hand within fairly narrow limits. *Ibid.*, A raise of partner's suit is generally a limit-raise, expressing the full value of the hand. **1959** *Listener* 24 Dec. 1118/2 Three Spades was a limit bid, which East might have passed. **1964** *Official Encycl. Bridge* 331/1 *Limit*, (1) the highest stake permitted in a bridge club. .. (2) A bid which shows a maximum as well as a minimum range of values in the bidder's hand. **1974** *Times* 23 Feb. 11/1 A player must take the decision whether.. to go straight for a limit bid.

h. *colloq.* The very extreme; the last point or stage; the worst (etc.) imaginable or endurable; the maximum penalty. Phr.: ***go the limit***, to behave in an extreme way; to last the stated number of rounds or the full time, as in a boxing match; to allow sexual intercourse; ***over the limit***, having exceeded a stated bound or point. orig. *U.S.* (Apparently a fig. use of 2 g.) Cf. ***the frozen limit*** (FROZEN *ppl. a.* 1 b).

1904 *Montgomery* (Alabama) *Weekly Advertiser* 26 Aug. 4 We can always depend on Kansas to go the limit in the freak line. **1906** *N.Y. Even. Post* 7 May 1 Desertion is bad enough .. but to fire at one's comrades while in the act of turning against them is—well, the limit. **1907** *Westm. Gaz.* 16 Aug. 2/1 They [*sc.* wages] are low everywhere.. but Belfast is what Americans would call 'the limit'. **1908** A. J. DAWSON *Finn* xxiii. 353 I'll be teetotally damned if that ain't the limit! *a* **1911** D. G. PHILLIPS *Susan Lenox* (1917) I. 389 We've made the plunge. We'll go—the limit. **1914** W. G. LAWRENCE in T. E. Lawrence *Home Lett.* (1954) 502 Bankers and business people of all sorts are the real limit. **1916** 'TAFFRAIL' *Pincher Martin* v. 79 Oh, to hell with you and your rotten excuses!.. You're about the frozen limit! **1919** G. B. SHAW *Heartbreak House* I. 18 Really! your father does seem to be about the limit. **1925** E. F. NORTON *Fight for Everest, 1924* 110 If vitality is low in the early hours at Camp III at 21,000 feet, it can be guessed how near the limit 6 a.m. found us at 27,000. **1925** G. MALLORY in *Ibid.* 237 That cutting against time at the end after such a day just about brought me to my limit. **1925** L. J. SMITS *Spring Flight* viii. 89 I'd marry a girl who had gone the limit just as willingly as I would a strict one, perhaps a little sooner. **1927** *Amer. Speech* III. 29 The boxer 'goes the limit' if he succeeds in lasting the specified number of rounds. **1947** 'N. SHUTE' *Chequer Board* iii. 68 If you get anything to go before court martial, for example, I'll see they get the limit. **1949** A. CHRISTIE *Crooked House* xvi. 126 This house is the absolute limit!.. I don't see why I should have to be burdened with such peculiar parents. **1966** *Daily Tel.* 11 Aug. 26/6 Attempting to drive while over the 80 mg/100 ml. limit can be punished... Being in charge of a vehicle while 'over the limit' can lead.. to up to four months' imprisonment. **1968** N. BENCHLEY *Welcome to Xanadu* iii. 52 She'd heard girls in school talk about going the limit, or all the way.

†**3. a.** The tract or region defined by a boundary; *pl.* the bounds, territories. *Obs.*

1494 FABYAN *Chron.* VI. clxiii. 156 The sayd two bretherne,..entryd the lymyttys of Kynge Charlys. **1581** LAMBARDE *Eiren.* IV. xx. (1588) 619 Those Sessions were to be holden in euery limite of the Shire. **1596** SHAKS. *1 Hen. IV*, III. i. 75 The Arch-Deacon hath diuided it Into three Limits, very equally. *c* **1600** —— *Sonn.* xliv, I would be brought From limits farre remote, where thou doost stay. **1603** OWEN *Pembrokeshire* (1891) 161 In everye Parishe or Lymitte. **1611** BIBLE *Ezek.* xliii. 12 Vpon the top of the mountaine, the whole limit thereof round about shall be most holy. *a* **1649** WINTHROP *Hist. New Eng.* (1826) II. 314 The Dutch governour..pretended to seize the ship as forfeit to the West India Company by trading in their limits without leave. **1667** MILTON *P.L.* v. 755 At length into the limits of the North They came. **1792** S. ROGERS *Pleas. Mem.* I. 290 Great Navarre, when France and freedom bled Sought the lone limits of a forest shed.

†**b.** ? A division or part of the territory (in quot., of one of the Cinque Ports). *Obs.*

c **1692** R. GIBSON in Gardiner *1st Dutch War* (1899) I. 40 The sea government at all those places by courts of Lode manage at each, and the lesser seaports adjacent to be made limits to the greater.

c. *U.S.* and *Canada.* A tract of woodland of defined extent, a timber allotment.

1887 S. CUMBERLAND *Queen's Highw. fr. Ocean to O.* (1887) 5 Timber limits of inexhaustible extent. **1888** *Harper's Mag.* Mar. 550/2 The voyageur..reports the quality and quantity of timber in certain 'limits' or lots.

†**4.** *Logic.* = TERM (med.L. *terminus*). *Obs.*

1599 BLUNDEVILLE *Art of Logic* v. i. 116 Why are they [*sc.* material principles] called tearmes or limites? Because they lymmet a proposition..and bee the vttermost partes or bondes whereunto any proposition is to bee resolved, as for example in this proposition, euery man is a sensible bodie: these two wordes, man and sensible bodie, are the tearmes, limmetes, or boundes, whereof as the saide proposition is compounded, so into the same it is to be resolued, as into his vttermost parts that haue any signification.

5. *attrib.*, as *limit-law, -line*; **limit dog**, one shown in a class limited to dogs having certain required qualifications; **limit gauge** *Engin.*, a gauge used for determining whether a dimension of a manufactured item falls within the specified tolerance; so **limit gauging**, the use of limit gauges to ensure the interchangeability of parts; **limit load** *Aeronaut.*, the maximum load that an aircraft or part of one is expected to bear in particular conditions of operation; so ***limit load factor***, the load factor corresponding to this load; **limit point** *Math.*, a point every neighbourhood of which contains a point (usu., a point other than the limit point) belonging to a given set; †**limit-stead**, a place on a boundary; **limit switch** *Engin.*, a switch that prevents the travel of an object past some predetermined point and is mechanically operated by the motion of the object itself.

1903 *Forest & Stream* 21 Feb. 151/2 *Limit dogs was won by St. Elvan. **1909** *Daily Chron.* 11 Feb. 5/6 The first prize for limit dogs over 45 lb. **1905** A. PARR *Machine Tools & Workshop Pract.* i. 10 (*caption*) *Limit gauge. **1909** *Westm. Gaz.* 7 Dec. 5/1 When it comes to be measured in a special limit-gauge, the slightest discrepancy is discovered. **1970** W. J. PATTON *Mod. Manuf.* xvii. 454 Instead of measuring actual dimensions, we usually check conformity to tolerance specifications in a production run by fixed limit gauges, often termed 'GO' and 'NOT GO' gauges. **1920** *Proc. Inst. Mech. Engin.* Nov. 1076 *Limit gauging may be applied to many kinds of fit. **1964** S. CRAWFORD *Basic Engin. Processes* xiv. 296 Limit-gauging systems have played an essential part in the development of the technique of quantity production. **1849** R. V. DIXON *Heat* I. 139 Boyle's and Mariotte's law may be considered a '*limit law'. **1864** BROWNING *Dram. Pers., James Lee* viii. 14 'As like as a Hand to another Hand:' Who said that, never..followed, like me, an hour, The beauty in this..of the *limit-line! **1889** *Boy's Own Paper* 7 Sept. 780/1 At a given distance from the limit-line of the square in putting the weight..a rectangular pit is prepared. **1950** D. J. PEERY *Aircraft Struct.* iii. 69 The maximum loads which an airplane may be expected to encounter at any time in service are designated as *limit loads or applied loads. The load factors associated with these loads are known as limit load factors... For loads which are under the control of the pilot, flight restrictions are used so that the limit load factor is never exceeded. **1967** *Technology Week* 23 Jan. 66/2 As an industry, we have done remarkably well, from a safety point of view, operating large aircraft with limit load factors of only 2·5 in rough air. **1972** T. H. G. MEGSON *Aircraft Struct.* xii. 413 Having decided on an ultimate load then the limit load may be fixed. **1905** *Trans. Amer. Math. Soc.* VI. 90 A geometrically closed set of points is a set that includes all its geometrical *limit points. **1926** C. WALMSLEY *Introd. Course Math. Analysis* i. 44 For general sequences we define a limit (or limit point, limiting point, limiting value, limiting number) of any sequence $s_1, s_2, s_3,$.. as any number *L*, within an arbitrarily small neighbourhood of which..there lie numbers of the sequence; a number of the sequence itself not being a limit of the sequence unless it is repeated indefinitely often as a term of the sequence or there are other terms of the sequence within the arbitrarily small neighbourhood. **1959** E. M. PATTERSON *Topology* (ed. 2) ii. 29 The points $x = 0$ and $x = 1$ are limit points of the set $0 < x < 1$ on the Euclidean line; and in this case every point of *X* itself is also a limit point. *c* **1375** *Sc. Leg. Saints* xliii. (*Cecile*) 448 Þane ware þe brethire one led, til þai come til þe *lymmyt-stede. **1930** *Engineering* 9 May 595/2 Automatic control at the end of travel is provided by geared *limit switches, and intermediate positions are signalled by a travelling nut on the limit switch. **1956** *Railway Mag.* May 338/1 Limit switches are provided in the hoisting motion, and in the derricking motion, to limit the amount of travel in both directions. **1974** *BP Shield Internat.* Oct. 2 (*caption*) The computerised electronic requirement that operates all valves, limit switches, pressure transducers.

limit ('lɪmɪt), *v.* Forms: 4–6 **lymyt(e**, 6–7 **limite**, **limmit**, **lymit**, (6 **lemyt**, **limitte**, 7 **limytt**), 5– **limit**. Also *pa. t.* 5 **lymett**; *pa. pple.* 4 **lemete**, 5–6 **lemett**, **lymyt**, 6 **lymmit**, **-yt**. [ad. F. *limiter*, ad. L. *līmitāre*, f. *līmit-*, *līmes* LIMIT *sb.*]

1. *trans.* To assign within limits (also *to limit and assign*, *limit and ordain*); to appoint, fix definitely; to specify. Also with *away*, *over*. Const. *dat.* or *to*, (*till*), *upon*, and *to* with *inf.* *Obs.* exc. in legal language.

138.. WYCLIF *Wks.* (1880) 298 As tyme & oþer circumstaunce þat limiten peyne for a dede ben aȝen þe fredom þat crist wole haue in hise lawe. *c* **1400** MAUNDEV. (Roxb.) xxv. 118 Ilkane of þer ostez hase þaire iourneez limited. *a* **1400–50** *Alexander* 4283 Oure lord has lemett vs elike þe lenthe of oure days. **1413** *Pilgr. Sowle* (Caxton) v. i. (1859) 72 Of endeles thynge maye no proporcion be lymyted, ne accounted. **1444** *Rolls of Parlt.* V. 125/1 Thoo peynes that ben speciallі lymyted upon the seid Baillifs. *c* **1460** *Towneley Myst.* xix. 6 Apon the erth he send lightnes, Both son and moyne lymett thertyll. **1494** FABYAN *Chron.* VI. clxxxv. 184 At the daye before lymytted and assygned. **1525** LD. BERNERS *Froiss.* II. xliv. 143 The Lady Elyanoure had it lymytted to her for her dowry. **1536** WRIOTHESLEY *Chron.* (1875) I. 55 Under a certaine paine lymitted for the same for the said cleargie. **1581** W. STAFFORD *Exam. Compl.* iii. (1876) 91 Euery Artificer dwelling out of all townes.. should bee limitted to bee vnder the direction of one good Towne or other. *c* **1590** MARLOWE *Faust* xiv. (1604) F 2 b, O, no end is limited to damned soules! **1603** OWEN *Pembrokeshire* i. (1891) 1 The Center or middle of the same Shere which I limytt to be aboute Heythoch moore. **1603** FLORIO *Montaigne* III. xi. (1632) 578 Astrology could not yet limit the motion of the Moone. **1668** MARVELL *Corr.* Wks. 1872–5 II. 250 Neither do I believe we can finish it and the rest within the time limited us by his Majesty. **1750** BEAWES *Lex Mercat.* (1752) 266 The time limitted in the bottomry bond. **1767** BLACKSTONE *Comm.* II. 155 If..the estate be limited over to a third person. **1795** BENTHAM *Supply without Burden* 32 When an estate in England has been limited away from a man altogether, he never looks at it. **1818** CRUISE *Digest* (ed. 2) IV. 175 In the release there was a power..to revoke the uses contained therein, and to limit other uses.

†**b.** To appoint (a person) to an office; to assign (a duty) to a person. *Obs.*

c **1380** WYCLIF *Serm.* Sel. Wks. I. 140 Þree offices of heerdis þat Crist haþ lymytid to hem. *c* **1380** —— *Wks.* (1880) 331 As if a pope make a lawe þat who euer he lymytiþ to here confessioun of þis man or confession of þis comunatee, he shal here þise mennes shrifte. **1420** *Searchers Verdicts* in *Surtees Misc.* (1888) 16 Sercheours..assigned and lymyt by Thomas of Gare. **1482** *M. Paston's Will* in *P. Lett.* III. 286 After the stipend of the preste lymyted to synge for me be yerly levied. *c* **1505** in *Plumpton Corr.* 189, I had the keyes levered me..& had a fellow lemett to keep the said schawnter with me, & he faylled me in my most neede. **1557** PAYNEL *Barclay's Jugurth* 42 He had lymitted hym in Numidy in his stede to be captayne of the army. **1638** HEYWOOD *Wise Woman* IV. i. Wks. 1874 V. 319, I limit you to be a welcome guest unto my Table.

†**c.** To lot or plot *out*; to allot, apportion. *Obs.*

1530 PALSGR. 612/1 Our grounds were lymyted afore our fathers dayes. **1559** W. CUNNINGHAM *Cosmogr. Glasse* Pref. A vj, And by..th'equinoctiall, polary circles, and altitude of the pole, to limite out the Zones, Climates, and Paralleles. **1577** HARRISON *England* II. iv. (1877) I. 91 England was limited out by families and hidelands. **1579** TOMSON *Calvin's Serm. Tim.* 765/2 God..hath limited out all our life. **1605** VERSTEGAN *Dec. Intell.* vi. (1628) 157 Markenryc, that is the country or Kingdome, marked or limited out. *a* **1619** FOTHERBY *Atheom.* II. i. §8 (1622) 190 He had all his learning and knowledge limited out vnto him: yea, and that by a scant scantling. *a* **1649** *Prayers* in *Chas. I's Wks.* (1662) 197 Let thy infinite Power vouchsafe to limit out some proportion of deliverance unto Me.

†**d.** *Math.* To lay down, 'give' in the hypothesis of a proposition. *Obs.*

1551 RECORDE *Pathw. Knowl.* I. xv, The likeiamme..hath one angle..like to *D.* the angle that was limitted. *Ibid.* II. iii, This triangle..hath two corners equal eche to other, that is *A* and *B*, as I do by supposition limite.

†**e.** *pass.* of proportions or contour: To be outlined or drawn (in a specified manner). *Obs.*

1636 W. BETTIE *Titana & Theseus* B 2, Seeing his face so perfectly featured, and viewing each limb, the portraiture of his body so well limited, that [etc.].

2. To confine within limits, to set bounds to (*rarely* in material sense); to bound, restrict. Const. *to.* †Also, to prohibit (a person) *from* (something).

?*a* **1400** *Morte Arth.* 457 Thy lycence es lemete in presence of lordys. **1508** FISHER *7 Penit. Ps.* cxxx. Wks. (1876) 226 The mercy of god..can neuer be lymyt to ony creature. *c* **1530** MORE *Answ. Frith* Wks. 841/1 Than must he limitte Gods power howe farre he will geue God leaue to stretche it. **1555** EDEN *Decades* 11 They haue lymyted and enclosed certeyne grounde to make gardeynes and orchiardes. **1585** ABP. SANDYS *Serm.* xvii. 298 He limiteth and restraineth his permission, saying, Rest a while. **1597** HOOKER *Eccl. Pol.* v. lxix. §1 If in continuance also limited, they all haue..their set..termes. **1631** *Star Chamb. Cases* (Camden) 80 Sr Francis Leake..made a deed limitting the use to my Lady Leake. **1662** EARL ORRERY *State Lett.* (1743) I. 77 His Hylas was not limited to numbers and rhyme, as mine is. **1670** G. H. *Hist. Cardinals* II. III. 186 He was limited in his Victuals, and ty'd up to a certain allowance every day. *a* **1715** BURNET *Own Time* (1724) I. 557 He thought a government limited by law was only a name. **1722** DE FOE *Moll Flanders* (ed. 3) 62, I had a Husband and no Husband..: Thus I say, I was limited from Marriage, what Offer soever might be made me. **1732** LEDIARD *Sethos* II. x. 362 He limited his number of cavalry to six thousand men. **1786** BURKE *W. Hastings* Wks. 1842 II. 143 The act of parliament..did expressly limit the duration of their office to the term of five years. **1813** LADY HAMILTON in *G. Rose's Diaries* (1860) I. 272 You do not know how limited I am. I have left everything to be sold for the creditors. **1818** CRUISE *Digest* (ed. 2) I. 418 A man cannot by any conveyance at common law limit an estate to his wife. **1828** D'ISRAELI *Chas. I*, I. vii. 216 The philosophical inquirer will not limit his researches by simple dates. **1844** LD. BROUGHAM *Brit. Const.* xvi. (1862) 249 And it [the succession] was afterwards further limited to the descendants of James I.'s daughter. **1856** KANE *Arct. Expl.* II. xxviii. 282 Our draft on the stores ..had been limited for some days to..eggs [etc.]. **1874** GREEN *Short Hist.* v. §1. 218 The commerce..was still mainly limited to the exportation of wool to Flanders. **1900** F. ANSTEY *Brass Bottle* iii. 35 If you remember, sir, you strictly limited me to the sums you marked.

b. To serve as a limit or boundary to; to bound; to mark off *from*. Also *to limit in*. Now *rare*.

1582 STANYHURST *Æneis* I. (Arb.) 26 This rule thus fixed no tyme shal limit, or hazard. **1594** BLUNDEVIL *Exerc.* v. (1636) 560 The Provinces that..are limited with the Provinces of China. **1601** WEEVER *Mirr. Mart.* E v, Limits there be for euery thing beside, No banks can limit in the sea of pride. **1601** HOLLAND *Pliny* I. 122 The kingdome of the Parthians..is limited and separat by these mountaines and streights. **1625** K. LONG tr. *Barclay's Argenis* I. xx. 60 The souldiers reached to the doore of the Temple, in two rankes, limiting the way to them that came to the Princesse. **1633** EARL MANCH. *Al Mondo* (1636) 185 God cannot bee God, if Nature limit him. **1889** GEDDES & THOMSON *Evolution of Sex* xi. 146 Round the chromatin rods vacuoles are formed, limiting them from the surrounding protoplasm.

†**3.** *intr.* To border *upon* (a country). *Obs.*

1613 SHERLEY *Trav. Persia* 4 Those countries limitting upon the King of Spaines vniall partes.

†**4.** To beg within specified limits. [A back-formation from LIMITER (sense 1).] *Obs. rare*$^{-1}$.

1577 NORTHBROOKE *Dicing* (1843) 57 They [Popishe friers] go ydelly a limiting abrode.

limitable ('lɪmɪtəb(ə)l), *a.* [f. LIMIT *v.* + -ABLE.] That may be limited.

1581 MULCASTER *Positions* xliv. (1887) 287 When the childe knoweth his certainetie in all limitable circumstances. **1643** HERLE *Answ. Ferne* 29 A power..limitable..not to be exercised within fifty dayes. **1686** J. SCOTT *Chr. Life* (1747) III. 363 If they are limitable by any other Power, they are Subjects to that Power.

Hence **'limitableness**.

1644 HUNTON *Vind. Treat. Monarchy* iv. 22 Neither its being supreme doth hinder its limitablenesse. **1684–5** H. MORE *Let.* 19 Jan. in Norris *Theory Love* (1688) 154 Those terms *Totum* and *Omne*..imply also a comprehensibleness, limitableness, or exhaustibleness of the number of those parts.

†**'limitage.** *Obs. rare*$^{-1}$. [f. LIMIT *v.* + -AGE.] That which is limited or allotted to a person or persons; an allotment.

1634 RAINBOW *Labour* (1635) 29 Their limitage were fallen to them in a goodly ground.

limital ('lɪmɪtəl), *a.* [f. LIMIT *sb.* + -AL^{1}.] Of or pertaining to a limit or boundary.

1877 GILBERT *Rep. Geol. Henry Mts.* iv. 90 A laccolite of small volume will not exceed the limital area, but will grow by lifting its cover.

limitanean (lɪmɪ'teɪnɪən), *a.* *Rom. Antiq.* [f. late L. *līmitāne-us* (f. *līmit-*, *līmes* LIMIT *sb.*) + -AN.] Stationed on the border.

1839 KEIGHTLEY *Hist. Eng.* I. 129 Lands given to those who were named the Limitanean and Ripuarian soldiery.

†**limi'taneous**, *a.* *Obs. rare*$^{-0}$. [f. as prec. + -OUS.] Of or pertaining to bounds or frontiers.

1721 in BAILEY. Hence **1755** in JOHNSON.

†**'limitany**, *a.* *Obs. rare*$^{-1}$. [f. as prec. + -Y^{1}.] Dwelling on the border.

1611 SPEED *Hist. Gt. Brit.* IX. ix. §66 The Poictouines.. were the limitanie or border-subjects of the English Dominions in Aquitaine.

Limitarian (lɪmɪ'tɛərɪən), *a.* and *sb.* [f. LIMIT *sb.* + *-arian* as in *unitarian*, etc.] A designation applied by adversaries to those theologians who hold the doctrine of 'limited redemption'.

1844 J. CAIRNS *Let.* in *Life* x. (1895) 228 Graham is somewhat delayed in licence by a limitarian presbytery. **1848** CRAIG, *Limitarian*, one who limits, one who maintains the doctrine, that only a part of the human race are to be saved. **1852** J. B. JOHNSTONE (*title*) Who are the Limitarians?

limitary ('lɪmɪtərɪ), *a.* and *sb.* [ad. L. *līmitāris*, f. *līmes* LIMIT: see -ARY^{2}.] **A.** *adj.*

1. Subject to limits; limited in action, range, etc. †Const. *to*.

1620 BRATHWAIT *Five Senses* iv. 46 Delights momentany and limitarie to an instant, may for the present yeeld a satisfaction. **1673** DRYDEN *State Innocence* III. i. Wks. 1808 V. 143 Let me with Him contend, On whom your limitary powers depend. **1727** C. PITT *Callimachus' Hymn to Jupiter* 119 What no inferior Limitary King Could in a length of Years to Ripeness bring. **1814** SCOTT *Ess. Drama*, etc. (1874) 143 The synod of Olympus..were themselves but limitary deities. **1822–56** DE QUINCEY *Confess.* (1862) 169 The poor limitary creature calling himself a man of the world. **1838** SIR W. HAMILTON *Logic* xxix. (1866) II. 107 We cannot, indeed, rise superior to our limitary nature. **1850** *Fraser's Mag.* XLI. 328 The Stuarts looked abroad for models of king-craft, and repined at their limitary right-divine.

b. Of a friar: Licensed to beg within certain limits. (Cf. LIMITER 1.)

1830 SCOTT *Demonol.* vi. 175 Chaucer..ascribes the exile of the fairies..to the warmth and zeal of the devotion of the limitary friars.

2. Of or pertaining to a limit or boundary; situate on the boundary. †Of a sentinel: Stationed on the boundary.

In quot. 1667 the sense is doubtful: it may be 1.

1650 FULLER *Pisgah* II. v. 125 All the former were limitary places in the tribe of Asher. *a* **1661** —— *Worthies, Cumberland* I. (1662) 216 This County (because a Limitary) did abound with Fortifications. **1667** MILTON *P.L.* IV. 969 Then when I am thy captive talk of chaines, Proud limitarie cherub! **1731** BAILEY vol. II, *Limitary*, belonging to the limits or bounds. **1819** *Banquet* 57 Visit your limitary huts, and see Where cleanliness reside, and industry. **1885** W. T. WATKIN in *Academy* 1 Aug. 77/3 We have another limitary mark on a centurial stone at Manchester.

3. Serving as a limit or boundary; limiting, confining, containing. Const. *of*.

1807 ANNA SEWARD in *Athenæum* Mar. (1895) 282/1 Where the horizon's limitary line Meets the gloom'd sea. **1822** B. CORNWALL *Dram. Scenes, Julian the Apostate* ii, A limitary power, Which strikes and circumscribes the soul. **1845** TRENCH *Huls. Lect.* Ser. I. v. 98 Refusing the Scriptures as..authoritative in and limitary of the Truth. **1847** W. R. HAMILTON *Let. to De Morgan, Ess. Analytic Logical Forms* 3 The once formidable array of limitary rules has vanished. The science now shines out in the true character of beauty. **1847–9** TODD *Cycl. Anat.* IV. 451/2 The hepatic cells are enclosed in a limitary membrane. **1899** J. HUTCHINSON *Archives Surg.* X. 151 There was deep erosion of the nails..presenting an abrupt limitary margin.

B. *sb.* = LIMITER 1. (Cf. A. 1 b.)

a **1662** HEYLIN *Laud* (1668) 210 Great were the Sums of Money which the Piety of the Design, and the Diligence of their Limitaries brought in from their several Walks.

limitate ('lɪmɪteɪt), *pa. pple.* and *ppl. a.* In 6 *Sc.* limitat. [ad. L. *līmitāt-us*, pa. pple. of *līmitāre* to LIMIT.] †**A.** *pa. pple.* = LIMITED. *Obs.*

1581 N. BURNE in *Cath. Tractates* (S.T.S.) 164 As gif..his pouar of virking miraclis var limitat to the pairtis onlie quhair your Sanctis var bureit. **1585** JAS. I *Ess. Poesie* (Arb.) 21 Translations are limitat, and restraind in some things, more than free inuentions are.

B. *ppl. a.* **a.** Of land: Parted off by limits or boundaries. *rare.*

1853 WHEWELL tr. *Grotius' De Jure Belli* I. 407 Land.. determined by its measured quantity, is governed by the same rule as limitate land.

b. *Bot.* Bounded by a distinct line, as the hypothallus in some lichens.

1871 W. A. LEIGHTON *Lichen-flora* 401 *Arthonia ilicina*,.. smooth, shining, scaly, limitate.

†'**limitate,** *v. Obs.* [f. L. *līmitāt-*, ppl. stem of *līmitāre* to LIMIT.] *trans.* To put limits or bounds to; to limit. Hence †'**limitated** *ppl. a.*

1560–78 *Bk. Discipl. Ch. Scot.* (1621) 3 The persons nominate..to..define and limitate the jurisdiction of the Kirk. **1563** WINȜET *Four Scoir Thre Quest.* Wks. 1888 I. 125 Gif we..limitatis and determinatis nocht the wisdom of God be our phantasie. **1654** EARL MONM. tr. *Bentivoglio's Warrs Flanders* 457 A clause so general and so limitated, would be interpreted rather in favour of them.

limitation (lɪmɪ'teɪʃən). [ad. L. *līmitātiōn-em*, f. *līmitāre* to LIMIT. Cf. F. *limitation*.]

1. The action of limiting (in senses of the vb.); an instance of this.

c **1380** WYCLIF *Wks.* (1880) 70 þei commaunden þat no man schal preche þe gospel but at here wille & lymytacion. **1483** *Cath. Angl.* 217/1 A Lymytacion, *limitacio*. **1533** MORE *Apol.* ix. Wks. 865/2 They..leaue not one man for Goddes parte thys eyghte hundred yeare paste by theyr owne lymitacion. **1542–3** *Act 34 & 35 Hen. VIII*, c. 20 §1 Their heires inheritable by the limitacion of suche giftes. **1608** WILLET *Hexapla Exod.* 76 This absolute limitation and restraint of Satan. **1683** *Brit. Spec.* 63 The Monarch himself must be Judge, and then farewel Limitation. **1720** WATERLAND *Eight Serm.* 250 It is here, without any restriction or limitation, applied, by the inspired Writer, to our Saviour Christ. **1833** HT. MARTINEAU *Berkeley* I. viii. 159 Some objected to this, that mere convertibility was not enough without limitation. **1845** MAURICE *Mor. & Met. Philos.* in *Encycl. Metr.* II. 610/1 The proper limitation of mathematical accuracy to things without matter. **1863** H. COX *Instit.* III. iii. 623 A fresh limitation of the succession to the throne was made towards the end of the reign of William III.

†**b.** *spec.* The action of determining the boundaries of (a country) or the contour of (a figure). *Obs.*

1677 W. HUBBARD *Narrative* II. 5 Letters Patent granted by the King for the Limitation of Virginia. **1726** LEONI *Alberti's Archit.* III. 31/2 Limitation we call the determining or fixing the sweeps of all the lines, the projections of the angles..and the depression of every hollow.

†**2. a.** An allotted space; the district or circuit of an itinerant officer or preaching friar; the region belonging to a particular nation; *fig.* one's allotted sphere. *Obs.*

c **1380** WYCLIF *Serm.* Sel. Wks. II. 182 Oo frere grutchiþ aȝens anoþer, and fiȝtiþ wiþ him, whanne he prechiþ treuþe in his lymytacioun. *c* **1386** CHAUCER *Wife's T.* 21 The lymytour..seyth his matyns and his hooly thynges As he gooth in his lymytacioun. **1401** *Pol. Poems* (Rolls) II. 21 Your limitors..will not suffer one in anothers limitation. **1426** LYDG. *De Guil. Pilgr.* 12620 Whyl thow the holdest by resoun Wyth-Inne thy lymytacioun, Nat to erryn, nyh nor ffer. **1527** R. THORNE in Hakluyt *Voy.* (1589) 256 The saide Islands fall all without the limitation of Portingall. **1535** *Act 27 Hen. VIII*, c. 27 Auditours..yerely ridinge their seueral circuites and limittacions. **1552** B. GILPIN *Serm. bef. Edw. VI* (1630) 25 Some [pulpits] have not had foure Sermons these fifteene or sixteene yeares, since Friers left their limitations.

†**b.** An allotted time. *Obs.*

1607 SHAKS. *Cor.* II. iii. 146 You haue stood your Limitation.

3. The condition of being limited; limitedness.

1597 HOOKER *Eccl. Pol.* v. lxix. §1 As the substance of God is infinite, and hath no kinde of limitation. **1601** SHAKS. *Jul. C.* II. i. 283 Am I your Selfe But as it were in sort, or limitation? **1710** BERKELEY *Princ. Hum. Knowl.* §4 The natural dulness and limitation of our faculties. **1755** YOUNG *Centaur* i. Wks. 1757 IV. 123 Through the limitation of the human intellect. **1871** R. H. HUTTON *Ess.* I. 109 What seems to us limitation, may be, not limitation, but a mode of divine power. **1875** LYELL *Princ. Geol.* II. III. xxxviii. 331 The limitation of groups of distinct species to regions separated from the rest of the globe by certain natural barriers. **1880** HAUGHTON *Phys. Geog.* vi. 272 The limitation of special families and sub-orders to special Continents.

4. A point or respect in which something is limited; a limiting provision, rule, or circumstance.

1523 FITZHERB. *Surv.* 12 The lymytacyon expressed in the statute of Westmynster. **1590** H. SWINBURNE *Testaments* 134 This limitation is suspected of some not to bee sounde. **1642** MILTON *Apol. Smect.* Wks. 1851 III. 295 That limitation therefore of after settling is a meere tautology. **1664** H. MORE *Myst. Iniq.* x. 33 Let him mince it as well as he can with mental limitations and restrictions. **1667** PEPYS *Diary* 10 Apr., So as that he that goes there may go with limitations and rules to follow. **1733** CHEYNE *Eng. Malady* II. viii. §1 (1734) 193, I shall have little further to add, but some Limitations..with regard to particular Cases. **1790** BURKE *Fr. Rev.* Wks. V. 63 This limitation was made by parliament, that [etc.]. **1855** PRESCOTT *Philip II*, I. II. xi. 261 Most of the provinces coupled their acquiescence with limitations which rendered it of little worth. **1875** MAINE *Hist. Inst.* ii. 53 He was heir to the earldom of Tyrone according to the limitations of the patent.

5. *Law.* **a.** The statutory specification of a period, or the period specified by statute, within which an action must be brought. ***Statute of Limitations***: any of the statutes (now esp. 3 & 4 Will. IV, c. 27) fixing a period of limitation for actions of certain kinds. **b.** The specification of a period or the period specified for the continuance of an estate, or the operation of a law. **c.** The settlement of an estate by a special provision or with a special modification or modifications; the modification or provision itself.

a. **1641** *Termes de la Ley* 196 Limitation is an assignement of a space or time, within which hee that will sue..ought to prove, that he or his ancestor was seised of the thing demanded, or otherwise he shall not maintaine his suit or action. **1768** BLACKSTONE *Comm.* III. 178 It is enacted by the statute of limitations, 21 Jac. I. c. 16. that no entry shall be made by any man upon lands, unless within twenty years after his right shall accrue. *Ibid.* 188 In all these possessory actions there is a time of limitation settled, beyond which no man shall avail himself of the possession of himself or his ancestors. *Ibid.* 250 Sixty years..is the longest period of limitation assigned by the statute of Henry VIII. **1818** CRUISE *Digest* (ed. 2) V. 313 If it be a legal debt, this Court being applied to for a discovery, will not prevent the statute of limitations from running. **1852** LD. PALMERSTON in *Croker Papers* 17 June (1884) I. i. 18 There is..no statute of limitation as to epistolary debts.

b. **1767** BLACKSTONE *Comm.* II. 155 When an estate is so expressly confined and limited by the words of it's creation, that it cannot endure for any longer time than till the contingency happens upon which the estate is to fail, this is denominated a limitation. **1818** CRUISE *Digest* (ed. 2) VI. 495 The future limitation being only for the life of a person *in esse*. **1821** J. Q. ADAMS in C. Davies *Metr. Syst.* III. (1871) 245 The limitation of the act was to three years, or the end of the next general assembly.

c. **1767** BLACKSTONE *Comm.* II. 193 A tenancy in common may..be created by express limitation in a deed. **1818** CRUISE *Digest* (ed. 2) VI. 291 By the limitation of the will, he was to make a grant of the rent. **1827** JARMAN *Powell's Devises* (ed. 3) II. 73 The..failure of the objects of the several limitations. **1868** E. EDWARDS *Raleigh* I. iv. 66 Most grants of this kind were attended by conditions and limitations.

6. = LIMIT 1 and 2. Also *pl.* bounds, boundaries.

1523 LD. BERNERS *Froiss.* I. ccxxxviii. 344 They of the.. marches and lymitacions of the realme of Castell, Came.. and made homage. **1533** ELYOT *Cast. Helthe* (1541) 1 To the conservation of the body of mankynde within the lymitation of helth. **1602** FULBECKE *Pandectes* 61 Numa Pompilius.. did cause as well a publik perambulation to be made throughout his whole kingdom as priuate limitations & bounds betwixt partie & partie. **1616** CAPT. J. SMITH *Descr. New Engl.* 23 The Gouernment, Religion, Territories and Limitations. **1815** JANE AUSTEN *Emma* II. viii. 193 She knew the limitations of her own powers too well to attempt more than she could perform with credit. **1824** L. MURRAY *Eng. Gram.* (ed. 5) I. 319 The supposed exceptions..do not come within the reason and limitation of the rule. **1864** BOWEN *Logic* i. 25 When the use of words is not checked by a frequent recurrence in thought to the precise limitations of their meaning.

limitative ('lɪmɪtətɪv), *a.* and *sb.* [ad. F. *limitatif, -ive* (16th c. in Hatzf.), ad. med.L. *līmitātīvus*, f. L. *līmitāre* to LIMIT: see -ATIVE.]

A. *adj.*

1. Tending to limit; limiting, restrictive.

† ***limitative place***: in Scholastic philosophy, 'place' in the sense in which it is predicable of things that do not occupy space; = DEFINITIVE *a.* 3. ***limitative judgement*** (Logic): used by Kant to denote judgements of the type 'Every A is a not-B', which he regarded as a class co-ordinate with affirmative and negative judgements; also *occas.* used for a judgement serving to limit or modify another.

1530 RASTELL *Purgatory* III. xi. g 4 Therfore purgatory can be no place contynentyue but purgatorye maye be a place lymytatyue, and also a place operatyue. For where so euer that god doth lymyt the soule of man after it is separate from the body to be purged, there is yᵉ place lymytatyue of the soule. **1657** J. SERGEANT *Schism Dispach't* 464 Without using the limitative particle (onely) or (alone) to restrain his extravagant interpretation. **1825** BENTHAM *Offic. Apt. Maximized, Observ. Peel's Sp.* (1830) 53 Before the words 'every other country' stands..the limitative word 'almost'. **1864** BOWEN *Logic* v. 143 The incidental Judgment expressed in an additional word or clause may be either explicative or limitative. **1877** E. CAIRD *Philos. Kant* II. vi. 307 Nor need Logic regard the infinite or limitative judgment as distinct from the affirmative. **1886** *Sat. Rev.* 31 July 151 Their several undertakings should be co-extensive and mutually limitative. **1892** *Athenæum* 4 June 722/3 Being essentially negative and limitative, it can only end in negative conclusions.

†**2.** Subject to a limit or condition, conditional.

1682 SCARLETT *Exchanges* 67 A prudent Possessor of the Bill will accept of no conditional or limitative Acceptance.

B. *sb. Logic.* A limitative judgement.

1864 BOWEN *Logic* v. 144 In respect to Limitatives, no question can arise concerning the truth or falsity of the incidental Proposition.

limited ('lɪmɪtɪd), *ppl. a.* [f. LIMIT *v.* + -ED[1].] In senses of the vb.

†**1.** Appointed, fixed. *Obs.*

1551 ROBINSON tr. *More's Utop.* I. (1895) 67 He..hiereth some of them for meate and drynke, and a certeyne limityd wayges by the daye. **1577–87** HOLINSHED *Chron.* III. 882/1 That euerie man..should paie the whole subsidie..out of hand, not tarrieng till the daies of paiment limited. **1633** T. STAFFORD *Pac. Hib.* II. i. (1810) 225 They did somewhat exceede the time limited.

2. a. Circumscribed within definite limits, bounded, restricted. Of circumstances: Narrow. ***limited edition***, an edition of a book, or reproduction of an object, limited to some specific number of copies. ***limited express*** or ***train*** (U.S.): cf. next. ***limited mail***: a mail train in which only a limited number of passengers is conveyed. ***limited monarchy***: one in which the functions of the monarch are exercised under conditions prescribed by the constitution; so ***limited government, monarch, royalty***. ***limited war***, one in which the weapons used, the nations or territory involved, or the objectives pursued, are limited or restricted.

1610 WILLET *Hexapla Dan.* 259 The knowledge of angels is limited. **1648** R. FILMER (*title*) The anarchy of a limited or mixed monarchy. **1651** HOBBES *Leviath.* II. xix. 98 That King whose power is limited, is not superiour to him, or them that have the power to limit it. **1674** *Essex Papers* (Camden) I. 265, I cannot imagine what it is makes men in England believe yᵉ Govermᵗ of Ireland to be for a Limited Time of Three Years. **1710** in T. B. Howell *State Trials* (1812) XV. 62 The nature of our constitution is that of a limited monarchy. **1736** CHANDLER *Hist. Persec.* Introd. 5 The blessings of a limited government. **1789** GOUV. MORRIS in Sparks *Life & Writ.* (1832) II. 72 The King of France must soon be one of the most limited monarchs in Europe. *a* **1792** BURKE *Address Brit. Colonists N. Amer.* in *Works* (1812) V. 148 England has been great and happy under the present limited Monarchy. **1828** SCOTT *F.M. Perth* xxi, I thank your Highness,..for your cautious and limited testimony in my behalf. **1832** AUSTIN *Jurispr.* (1879) I. vi. 247 In limited monarchies a single individual shares the sovereign powers with an aggregate or aggregates of individuals. **1833** MYLNE & KEEN *Reports* II. 244 His co-executor..was in narrow and limited circumstances. **1853** BRONTE *Villette* viii. (1876) 68 That school offered for her powers too limited a sphere. **1860** TYNDALL *Glac.* I. ii. 15 A limited number of images only will be seen. **1865** MOZLEY *Mirac.* iv. 86 A limited Deity was a recognised conception of antiquity. **1866** DICKENS *Mugby Junction* in *All Year Round* Extra Christmas No. 10 Dec. 17 Driving..at limited-mail speed. **1879** F. R. STOCKTON *Rudder Grange* ix. 93 Time flew like a limited express train. **1883** P. FITZGERALD *Recreat. Lit. Man* 80 He started for Dublin by the mid-day limited mail. **1890** *Harper's Mag.* Aug. 409/1 Coming up by the limited train, Miss Lee was not favorably impressed. **1903** *Connoisseur* VI. 252/2 This library has the trail of the 'Limited Edition' serpent over it all. **1904** *Dial* (Chicago) 16 Oct. 238 It is not a book for the limited express. **1920** H. CRANE *Let.* 28 Jan. (1965) 32 A limited edition hastily gathered up would be the only possible method of presentation. **1930** Limited edition [see HOG-WASH]. **1944** H. TREECE *Herbert Read* 41 The Quixote in him that writes prefaces to Limited editions. **1948** H. J. MORGENTHAU *Politics among Nations* xx. 291 Another variety of a limited war..has been well described. **1955** *Times* 4 July 9/7 Britain, then, has to be prepared for both nuclear and limited war. *Ibid.* 8 July 9/5 The recent war in Korea is an example of a major limited war, and the present operations in Kenya of a minor limited war. **1966** MRS. L. B. JOHNSON *White House Diary* 20 Aug. (1970) 413 It was a good speech [by Lyndon]..'Perhaps it reflects poorly on our world that men must fight limited wars in order to keep from fighting larger wars.' **1971** *Ideal Home* Apr. 143 This Piccadilly mug is produced by Wedgwood in a limited edition of 4,000. **1972** *Country Life* 16 Nov. (Suppl.) 57/1 Pure silk 36 inch hand-rolled head-scarves, in four designs..and in limited editions for £12.50. **1973** *Daily Tel.* 27 Apr. 18 The National Maritime Museum..is adding two new clocks to its collection of historic timepieces next month. The two, however, are replicas of 18th-century clocks which.. Thwaites and Reed are producing in limited editions.

b. ***limited company***: short for ***limited liability company*** (see LIABILITY). ***limited partnership***, inactive partnership, where liability is limited to the value of the capital contribution; so ***limited partner***.

1855 *Act 18 & 19 Vict.* c. 133 §1 The Word 'Limited' shall be the last Word of the Name of the Company. **1872** RAYMOND *Statist. Mines & Mining* 107 The Nevada Land and Mining Company, (limited). **1907** *Act 7 Edw. VII* c. 24 §1 This Act may be cited for all purposes as the Limited Partnerships Act, 1907. *Ibid.* §4 Limited partners, who shall at the time of entering into such partnership contribute thereto a sum..valued at a stated amount and who shall not be liable for the debts or obligations of the firm beyond the amount contributed. **1931** *Pitman's Business Man's Guide* (ed. 9) 372/1 There is a further division into 'general' and 'limited' partners. The former correspond to the 'active' partners, and the latter to the 'sleeping' or 'nominal' partners. **1951** R. W. JONES *Thomson's Dict. Banking* (ed. 10) 381/1 The idea of the limited partnership has not appealed to the business world and..only some 1,300 such partnerships have been registered. **1970** *New Yorker* 10 Oct. 37/2 Richard Roth, Jr., a limited partner, joined the firm. **1973** *N.Y. Law Jrnl.* 31 Aug. 1/4 It omitted compensation agreements between Empire and its counsel..with whom Mr. Goldberg was then associated as a limited partner.

3. a. In *absol.* use = *limited mail* in 2. (*U.S. colloq.*)

1887 *Pop. Sci. Monthly* Mar. 577 Let the great steamship founder, the limited crash through a trestle—living or dead, these men will be found at their posts. **1910** KIPLING *Rewards & Fairies* 145 If you're off to Philadelphia..the Limited will take you there. **1913** E. WHARTON *Custom of Country* v. xliii. 556 A bigger and brighter blur ahead, into which they were plunging as the 'Limited' plunged into the sunset. **1938** S. V. BENÉT *Thirteen o'Clock* IV. 295 'Jerry Pye!' she said, 'I don't know what's come over you. You never take me on any limiteds!'

b. = *limited company.*

1905 *Westm. Gaz.* 20 Nov. 8/1 Company floaters have gone very fast indeed, some limiteds, it is said, not having sufficient capital. **1907** *Daily Chron.* 26 July 3/4 This is my experience in a West-end house..classed with the Limiteds.

Hence **'limitedly** *adv.*, **'limitedness.**

a **1614** DONNE *Βιαθανατος* (1644) 74 You see nothing is delivered by him against it, but modestly, limitedly, and perplexedly. **1656** [J. SERGEANT] tr. *T. White's Peripat. Inst.* 288 A difference of Substance distinct from corporeity and limitednesse. **1812** SHELLEY in Hogg *Life* (1858) II. 91, I assume a character which is..unadapted to the limitedness of my experience. **1891** H. JONES *Browning* 235 He pushes the limitedness of human knowledge into a disqualification of it to reach truth at all. **1895** *Q. Rev.* July 76 We in London need such limitedly local relaxations.

limiter ('lɪmɪtə(r)). Forms: 4-6 lim-, lymitour(e, -ytour(e, (7-9 limitour), 6 lim-, lymiter, -yter, limmeter, 7 limitor, 6- limiter. [f. LIMIT *v.* + -ER[1].]

1. (Also *friar limiter.*) A friar licensed to beg within certain limits. *Obs.* exc. *Hist.*

1377 LANGL. *P. Pl.* B. v. 138 On limitoures and listres lesynges I ymped. *c* **1386** CHAUCER *Wife's T.* 10 The grete charitee and prayeres Of lymytours and othere hooly freres. **1516** *Will of R. Peke of Wakefield* 4 June (MS.), To every lymyter of the iiij orders of freers—xxd. **1552** LATIMER *Serm.* (1562) 94 A limitoure of the graye fryers, in the tyme of his limitation preached manye tymes and hadde but one Sermon. **1556** J. HEYWOOD *Spider & F.* ix. 1 There neuer was Fryer limiter, that duckt So low, where beggyng woon him twenty cheeses. **1591** SPENSER *M. Hubberd* 85, I meane me to disguize..like a Pilgrim, or a Lymiter.

transf. or *allusive.* **1624** BP. MOUNTAGU *Gagg* To Rdr. 2 Some of our Catholique Limitors had beene roming in the countrey and brake into my pale secretly.

2. a. One who or that which limits (in senses of the vb.).

1483 *Cath. Angl.* 217/1 A Lymytour, *limitator.* **1570** LEVINS *Manip.* 80/2 A Limiter, *limitator.* ? **1612** *Two Noble K.* v. i. 30 So hoyst we The sayles, that must these vessells port even where The heavenly lymiter pleases. *a* **1619** FOTHERBY *Atheom.* II. i. §5 (1622) 180 The Sunne is not that infinite limitour, which..setteth seuerall bounds, vnto all other things. **1639** LD. G. DIGBY *Lett. conc. Relig.* (1651) 27, I am sure they are the best declarers and limiters of their own [doctrines]. **1645** MILTON *Tetrach.* Wks. 1851 IV. 222 Abolishing a law so good and moral, the limiter of sin.

b. *Electronics.* A device whose output is restricted to a certain range of values irrespective of the size of the input.

1919 R. STANLEY *Text-bk. Wireless Telegr.* (new ed.) II. xiv. 274 To a certain extent the H.F. amplifying valves of the Marconi Co., known as the V.24 type, are limiters, since their characteristic curves are of short range. **1930** H. M. DOWSETT *Handbk. Technical Instruction for Wireless Telegraphists* (ed. 4) xx. 297 Short wave signals vary greatly in intensity due to various causes, and the use of the limiter makes the signal currents more suitable for operating relays or recording apparatus. **1962** A. NISBETT *Technique Sound Studio* 258 Limiters are necessary in AM transmitters, and in the input to disc recorders in situations where overmodulation may occur by accident. **1972** *Sci. Amer.* Sept. 101/3 Since the amplitude of the FM carrier is constant, limiters can be used to reduce impulse noise.

limiting ('lɪmɪtɪŋ), *vbl. sb.* [f. LIMIT *v.* + -ING[1].] The action of the vb. LIMIT; an instance of this.

1580 HOLLYBAND *Treas. Fr. Tong, Modification*...a qualifying, moderating, limiting, or releasing. **1608** HIERON *Wks.* I. *To Chr. Rdr.* (ante 689) Forms of prayer..are aiudged to be a kind of..limiting of Gods Spirit. **1677** GILPIN *Demonol.* (1867) 405 A bold limiting of the time of forty days.

limiting ('lɪmɪtɪŋ), *ppl. a.* [f. LIMIT *v.* + -ING[2].] That limits, in senses of the vb. *limiting angle* (see quot. 1873). *limiting parallels* (see quot. 1867).

1849 RUSKIN *Sev. Lamps* vii. §7. 192 It would be needful to accept some well known examples..for final and limiting authorities. **1864** BOWEN *Logic* v. 131 The Condition..can always be expressed by a limiting adjective. **1865** M. ARNOLD *Ess. Crit.* i. 33 Even with well-meant efforts of the practical spirit it [*sc.* criticism] must express dissatisfaction, if in the sphere of the ideal they seem impoverishing and limiting. **1867** SMYTH *Sailor's Word-bk., Limiting parallels,* the parallels of latitude upon the earth's surface, within which occultations of stars or planets by the moon are possible. **1873** W. LEES *Acoustics* II. iii. 53 In order that a ray may pass from a dense medium into a rarer, the angle of incidence must not exceed a certain limit,..this angle is called the limiting or critical angle of refraction. **1884** BOWER & SCOTT *De Bary's Phaner.* 539 The limiting zone between the external cortex and the bast-layer.

limitless ('lɪmɪtlɪs), *a.* [f. LIMIT *sb.* + -LESS.] Having or admitting of no limits; unlimited, illimitable; unbounded, unrestricted.

1581 SIDNEY *Astr. & Stella* (1591) G 4 b, Say, whether thou wilt crowne With limitlesse renowne. **1612** J. DAVIES *Wit's Pilgrimage* civ. (Grosart) 20 To this Sea of Cittie-Common-wealth (Lymittlesse London). *a* **1628** F. GREVIL *Sidney* x. (1652) 129 Sir Philip..observed this limitless ambition of the Spaniard. **1760-72** H. BROOKE *Fool of Qual.* (1809) III. 57 While the king acts in consent with the parliament..he is limitless, irresistible. **1868** LOCKYER *Guillemin's Heavens* (ed. 3) 436 In the depths of limitless space, exist numerous assemblages of stars. **1891** E. PEACOCK *N. Brendon* II. 58 Almost limitless power of giving pain.

Hence **'limitlessly** *adv.*, **'limitlessness.**

1865 RUSKIN *Sesame* (ed. 2) 145 When the affection has become wholly and limitlessly our own. **1865** *Spectator* 4 Mar. 239/2 The Imperial throne..the power *solutus a legibus* which in its limitlessness could redress all wrongs.

limitor, -our, obs. forms of LIMITER.

limitrophe ('lɪmɪtrəʊf), *a.* and *sb.* [a. F. *limitrophe*, ad. late L. *līmitrophus*, *līmitotrophus* (a hybrid f. L. *līmit-*, *līmes* + Gr. -τρόφος supporting), applied to lands set apart for the support of troops on the frontier.]

A. *adj.* Situated on the frontier; bordering on, adjacent *to* (another country).

1763 EARL OF BUCKINGHAMSHIRE *Let.* 6 Dec. in *Despatches & Corr.* (1902) II. 113 The inconveniences which might arise if a country limitroph to Russia was governed by a sovereign allied and connected with the great European Powers. **1826** [J. R. BEST] *4 Years France* 129 Russia has already absorbed, within its empire, that great limitrophe nation which might have been a barrier against further progress. **1845** FORD *Handbk. Spain* VI. 503 Like many of these limitrophe Pyrenean districts it became independent soon after..731. **1881** *Daily News* 22 Feb. 5/3 The policy of a limitrophe frontier with Russia revived. **1885** *Pall Mall G.* 1 Apr. 1/2 England..was perfectly free to enter into any relations she pleased with the States limitrophe to India.

†**B.** *sb.* A border-land. *Obs.*

1589 A. M[UNDAY] *Hist. Palmendos* v. (1653) 32 He..became..famous through all the neighbour Marches and limitrophes of Tharsus. **1598** DALLINGTON *Meth. Trav.* C ij b, The Prince ought to have of them [*sc.* castles] in his frontier places, and Lymitrophes (as they call them). **1963** V. NABOKOV *Gift* iii. 155 Thus 'France' corresponded to his warningly raised eyebrows; some kind of 'limitrophes' to the hairs in his nostrils.

Hence †**limitrophing** *ppl. a.*, bordering, adjacent; †**limitrophous** *a.* (see quot.).

1623 tr. *Favine's Theat. Hon.* IV. vii. 29 The Counties of Boulougne, Saint Paule, and other limitrophing Seigneuries. **1727-51** CHAMBERS *Cycl.* s.v. *Column*, Limitrophous or boundary Column, is that which shews the limits of a kingdom, or country conquered.

†**limity.** *Obs.* Also 6 lymytee. [Formation uncertain; possibly *limities*, *-tees*, represents L. *limites*; but cf. OF. *limité*.] = LIMIT.

1525 LD. BERNERS *Froiss.* II. ccx. [ccvi.] 648 There shulde be in their company of the lymytees of Fraunce, mo then fyue hundred knightes. **1545** JOYE *Exp. Dan.* Ded. A iij b, The very limities & boundes of the world. **1553** EDEN *Treat. Newe Ind.* (Arb.) 29 They go not out of ye limities of their own contrie.

limm, obs. form of LIMN.

‖**limma** ('lɪmə). [Late L., a. Gr. λεῖμμα remnant, part left, semitone, f. λείπειν to leave.]

1. *Mus.* The semitone of the Pythagorean scale (see quot. 1694).

1694 W. HOLDER *Harmony* vi. 152 The Pythagoreans, not using Tone Minor, but two Equal Tones Major, in a Fourth, were forced to take a lesser Interval for the Hemitone; which is call'd their Limma, or Pythagorean Hemitone; and, which added to those two Tones, makes up the Fourth; it is a Comma less than Hemitone Major (16 to 15) and the Ration of it, is 256 to 243. **1887** W. S. ROCKSTRO in *Grove's Dict. Mus.* IV. 503 The Ditonic Diatonic Tetrachord, consisting of two greater Tones and a Limma, as set forth by Pythagoras.

2. *Gr. Pros.* A time or mora in a line required by the rhythm but not expressed by a syllable in the words: indicated in schemes by the sign ∧.

limme, obs. form of LIMB *sb.*[1]

limmeal, -ly, obs. vars. LIMB-MEAL, -MEALLY.

limmell, variant of LIMAIL, metal filings.

limmer ('lɪmə(r)), *sb.* and *a.* *Sc.* and *north. dial.* Also 5 lymmare, 6 lymare, -er, lymmar, 6-7 limmar, lymber, lymmer. [Of obscure origin; connexion with LIMB *sb.* is possible.]

A. *sb.*

†**1.** A rogue, scoundrel. *Obs.*

1456 SIR G. HAYE *Law of Armys* (S.T.S.) 233/24 Ane unworthy lymmare, that settis nocht for honour bot for pillery. *c* **1470** HENRYSON *Mor. Fab.* v. (*Parl. Beasts*) xli, [To the fox] 'Byde', quod the lioun; 'limmer, let ws see Gif it be suthe the sillie ȝow hes said.' **1536** BELLENDEN *Cron. Scot.* (1821) I. p. lxiv, He causit hir to be schamfully defowlit with rebaldis and limmaris of his cuntre. **1596** DALRYMPLE tr. *Leslie's Hist. Scot.* IX. 219 Adam Scot special bordirer and limmer, commounlie calit king of traytouris. **1602** JAS. VI *Let. to Eliz.* (Camden) 147 The repreasing of fugitiues and lymmeries [*sic*]. **1607** *Sc. Acts Jas. VI* (1816) IV. 379/2 That Insolent and wicked race and name of the glengregour and notorious lymberis and malefactouris. **1637** B. JONSON *Sad Sheph.* II. i, Fowle Limmer! drittie Louwne! **1828** SCOTT *F.M. Perth* iv, There have been a proper set of limmers about to scale your windows, father Simon.

2. Applied to a woman. **a.** A light woman; a strumpet. **b.** In weaker sense: A jade, hussy, minx.

1566 *Durham Depos.* (Surtees) 83 In causa diffamacionis, viz. that his wyf was a lymer. **1728** RAMSAY *Last Sp. Miser* viii, I wore nae frizzl'd limmer's hair. **1786** BURNS *Twa Dogs* 182 Except for breakin o' their timmer Or speakin lightly o' their limmer. **1814** SCOTT *Wav.* lxiii, Kate and Matty, the limmers, gaed aff wi' twa o' Hawley's dragoons, and I hae twa new queans instead o' them. **1851** BORROW *Lavengro* lxxxv. (1900) 460 Leave my husband in the hands of you and that limmer, who has never been true to us. **1897** CROCKETT *Lad's Love* xiii. 141 'Oh—the limmer—how dared she', cried my mother, on fire instantly at the hint of an insult or rejection to her eldest son.

B. *adj.* Knavish, scoundrelly.

1500-20 DUNBAR *Poems* xxvii. 9 With mony lymmar loun. **1562** A. SCOTT *Poems* (S.T.S.) i. 53 For lymmer lawdis and litle lassis lo. **1637** B. JONSON *Sad Sheph.* II. i, Hence with 'hem, limmer lowne, Thy vermin, and thy selfe, thy selfe art one. *a* **1785** *Rookhope Ryde* iv. in Child *Ballads* III. 439 Limmer thieves drives them away.

Hence †**limmerful** *a.*, knavish; †**limmery,** knavery.

1500-20 DUNBAR *Poems* xvi. 152 Thy lymmerfull luke wald fle thame. **1567** *Gude & Godlie Ball.* (S.T.S.) 206 The lymmerie lang hes lestit.

limmeter, obs. form of LIMITER.

limming, obs. form of LIMNING.

‖**limmu, limu** ('lɪmuː). *Assyriology.* [Assyrian *limmu* period, circuit, administrative year.] The year of office to which the holder gave his name; hence, the office itself. Cf. EPONYM 2.

1862 H. C. RAWLINSON in *Athenæum* 19 July 83/1, I am quite ready to abandon this notion if any more suitable explanation can be found of the office of *Limu*, from which the Assyrians commonly dated; but in the mean time I cannot accept of the unmeaning title of Eponymy, nor can I admit of the etymology which would make the *Limu* merely the 'seer' of the new moon. **1888** Z. A. RAGOZIN *Assyria* (ed. 2) v. 146 The year was then designated as the 'Limmu' of So-and-So. It is thought..that the magistrates themselves, in their capacity of time-keepers, had the special title of Limmu... Every king was *limmu* at least once, generally the second full year of his reign. **1901** R. W. ROGERS *Hist. Babylonia & Assyria* I. xii. 323 Historical inscriptions..often mention the *limmu* or eponym of a certain year, just as they give the name of the king who was reigning. **1956** A. TOYNBEE *Historian's Approach to Relig.* I. v. 57 The Assyrian list of holders of the office of *limmu*. **1963** F. S. LEIGH-BROWNE tr. *Læssøe's People Anc. Assyria* iii. 40 The Assyrians named the year after the official who (for that one year) occupied the office of *limmu*.

limn (lɪm), *v.* Now *literary* and *arch.* Also 5 limyne, lymm, 5-7 lymn(e, 6-7 limm(e, limb(e, limne. [Altered form of LUMINE *v.*]

†**1.** *trans.* To illuminate (letters, manuscripts, books). Also *absol.* *Obs.*

14.. *Trevisa's Higden* (Rolls) VII. 295 Þis bisshop hymself schonede not to write and lumine [*MS. β* (early 15th c.) lymne] and bynde bookes. *c* **1440** *Promp. Parv.* 317/1 Lymnyd, as bookys (*K.* limynid), *elucidatus.* **1499** *Churchw. Acc. Croscombe* (Som. Rec. Soc.) 24 A mass boke of veln lymmyde. **1531** ELYOT *Gov.* I. v, Their fyrst letters to be paynted or lymned. **1534** RICH *Let. to T. Cromwell* in Strype *Eccl. Mem.* I. xxxiv. 179 A certain tale of M. Magdalen, delivering her a letter from heaven, that was limned with golden letters. **1566** DRANT *Horace, Sat.* I. iv. B viij b, And if their toyes, in letters lymde, be printed once in booke, Then [etc.]. **1573** *Art of Limming* title-p., Diuerse kyndes of colours to write or to limme withall vppon velym. **1588** PARKE tr. *Mendoza's Hist. China* 94 When they write letters vnto anie principall person, they gilde the margent of the paper, and limbe it.

†**2.** To adorn or embellish with gold or bright colour; to depict *in* (gold, etc.). Also (*rare*), to lay on (colour). *Obs.*

a **1548** HALL *Chron., Hen. VIII* 73 Images..rychely lymned wyth golde and Albyn colours. **1573** *Art of Limming* title-p., How siluer or golde shalbe layed or limmed vppon the sise. **1587** FLEMING *Contn. Holinshed* III. 490/1 Their bannerols displaied, and richlie limmed with my lords armes. **1653** H. COGAN tr. *Pinto's Trav.* xxiii. 84 The Royal Arms of Portugal were limned in Gold.

3. To paint (a picture or portrait); to portray, depict (a subject). †Formerly *spec.* to paint in water-colour or distemper (see LIMNING *vbl. sb.* 2). †Also with *forth*, *out*.

1592 SHAKS. *Ven. & Ad.* 290 Looke, when a Painter would surpasse the life, In limming out a well-proportioned steed. **1594** CAREW *Huarte's Exam. Wits* vi. (1596) 83 Pictures which are lymned in oyle. **1607** TOPSELL *Four-f. Beasts* (1658) 222 Nicon that famous painter of Greece, when he had most curiously limbed forth a Horses perfection [etc.]. **1622** WITHER *Fair Virtue* M, Where Apelles limb'd to life Loathed Vulcans louely wife. **1641** MILTON *Animadv.* Wks. 1851 III. 230 He may be the

competent Judge of a neat picture, or elegant poem, that cannot limne the like. **1813** SCOTT *Trierm.* III. xxxvii, For there by magic skill, I wis, Form of each thing that living is Was limn'd in proper dye. **1854** MRS. OLIPHANT *Magd. Hepburn* II. 55 The dim chapel..with Scripture stories limned in its ancient glass. **1866** *Cornh. Mag.* Sept. 335 If he be limned aright in the canvas which has descended to us.

b. *transf.* and *fig.*

1593 NASHE *4 Lett. Confut.* 30 With life and spirit to limne deadnes it selfe *Hoc est Oratoris proprium.* **1600** SHAKS. *A.Y.L.* II. vii. 194 As mine eye doth his effigies witnesse Most truly limn'd, and liuing in your face. **1602** MARSTON *Ant. & Mel.* Induct., I fear it is not possible to limme so many persons in so small a tablet as the compasse of our playes afford. **1645** FULLER *Good Th. in Bad T.*, *Mixt Contempl.* xxi. (1649) 83 It is easie for one to endure an affliction, as he limns it out in his own fancie. **1653** MIDDLETON & ROWLEY *Sp. Gipsy* III. iii, What's beauty but a perfect white and red? Both here well mix'd limn truth so beautiful. **1661** FELTHAM *Lusoria* xxxvii. in *Resolves* (1709) 601 He must limb Spirits never tir'd. **1856** SPURGEON *New Park St. Pulpit* I. 56 Instances of persons going to the house of God, and having their characters limned out to perfection. **1871** SMILES *Charac.* x. (1876) 284 Perhaps the most complete picture of a great man ever limned in words. **1878** GLADSTONE *Prim. Homer* 130 The Odusseus is limned with..incomparable art.

4. Prov. ***to limn the water, limn*** (something) ***on water***: said of something transient or futile.

1620 BACON *Poems* (Grosart) 49 Who then to fraile Mortality shall trust, But limmes the Water, or but writes in dust. **1692** *Vindiciæ Carolinæ* ix. 73 All he had done was but a kind of Limming the Water, to them. **1871** R. ELLIS tr. *Catullus* lxx. 4 A woman's words..Limn them on ebbing floods, write on a wintery gale [L. *In vento et rapida scribere oportet aqua*].

†**5.** *absol.* or *intr.* To paint; *esp.* to paint in water-colour or distemper. *Obs.*

1594 PLAT *Jewell-ho.* III. 44 To paint or limne with the colours that are taken from hearbs or flowers. **1622** PEACHAM *Compl. Gent.* xiii. (1634) 126 The vertuous Margaret Queene of Navarre beside her excellent veine in Poesie could draw and limne excellently. **1665** PEPYS *Diary* 7 May, Yesterday begun my wife to learn to limn of one Browne. **1675** CROWNE *Country Wit* IV. 57 *Merry.* Cannot you Limne, Sir? *Rambler.* Limne, what dost thou mean? *Merry.* Why Limne, Sir, draw Pictures in little. **1678** CUDWORTH *Intell. Syst.* I. iii. §30. 136 If Oxen, Lions, Horses and Asses ..were able to limn and paint.

limnacean (lɪm'neɪsɪən), *a.* and *sb.* [f. mod.L. *Limnacea* (see below), for **Limnæacea*, f. LIMNÆA: see -ACEAN.] **a.** *adj.* Pertaining to the *Limnacea*, one of the three families of *Pulmobranchiata* in De Blainville's classification. **b.** *sb.* A gasteropod of the family *Limnacea*; a pond-snail (*Cent. Dict.*). Also **lim'naceous** *a.* = prec. adj. (Mayne *Expos. Lex.* 1855).

‖**limnæa** (lɪm'niːə). *Zool.* Also *erron.* **lymn-**. [mod.L., ad. Gr. λιμναία, fem. of λιμναῖος, f. λίμνη pool, marsh.] A genus of the family *Limnæidæ* or pond-snails, typical of the sub-family *Limnæinæ*; a pond-snail of this genus. Hence **lim'næan**, a gasteropod of the genus *Limnæa*; **lim'næid** (also **limneid**), a gasteropod of the family *Limnæidæ*; a pond-snail; **lim'næine** *a.*, pertaining to the sub-family *Limnæinæ* (Cent. Dict.).

1834 MᶜMURTRIE tr. *Cuvier's Anim. Kingd.* III. 38 Having a shell very similar to that of a Lymnæa. **1851** WOODWARD *Mollusca* 11 The air-breathing limneids live in fresh water. **1856** *Ibid.* III. 361 The Litorinæ and Limnæans are found living together.

limnanth ('lɪmnænθ). *Bot.* [f. Gr. λίμνη lake, marsh + ἄνθος flower.] **a.** A plant of the genus *Limnanthemum* (N.O. *Gentianaceæ*) of perennial water-herbs. **b.** A plant of the genus *Limnanthes* or tribe *Limnantheæ*, N.O. *Geraniaceæ* (Cassell).

1872 OLIVER *Elem. Bot.* II. 209 The..orbicular floating leaves of Common Limnanth (*Limnanthemum nymphœoides*).

limned (lɪmd), *ppl. a.* [f. LIMN *v.* + -ED[1].] †Illuminated (*obs.*); painted, depicted, portrayed.

1538 ELYOT *Dict.*, *Miniati libri*, limned bokes, hauyng letters of dyuers colours. **1573** in Willis & Clark *Cambridge* (1886) III. 26 The lymned letters and pictures. **1595** MARKHAM *Sir R. Grinvile, To the fayrest* vii, Ill limn'd memorials of diuinest rage. **1605** BACON *Adv. Learn.* I. iv. §3. 18 Like the first Letter of a Patent, or limmed Booke. *a* **1628** F. GREVIL *Sidney* Ep. Ded. (1652) 1 Both your Bloud and Vertues do so strongly Intitle you to this well-limb'd Piece. **1648** *Bury Wills* (Camden) 216 The limned picture of my wife. **1814** CARY *Dante, Par.* xxvii. 90 The human flesh Or..its limn'd resemblance.

limner ('lɪmnə(r)). Now *literary* or *arch.* Forms: 4-5 **lymnour**, 4-6 **lymenor(e**, 5 **lymnore**, **lympner**, 6 **lymmer**, 6-7 **lymner**, **limmer**, 7 **limbner**, **limpner**, 6- **limner**. [Altered form of LUMINER: see LIMN *v.* and -ER[1].]

1. An illuminator of manuscripts. *Hist.*

1389 in *Eng. Gilds* (1870) 9 Johannes Dancastre, lymenoʳ. **1398** TREVISA *Barth. De P.R.* XVII. cxli. (1495) 698 Grauours, lymnours and payntours eteth Rewe to sharpe theyr syghte. *c* **1440** *Promp. Parv.* 317/1 Lymnore (*K. c* 1490 luminour), *elucidator, miniographus.* **1483** *Act 1 Rich. III*, c. 9 §1 That this Acte..in no wise extende..to any writer lympner bynder or imprynter. *c* **1515** *Cocke Lorell's B.* 10 Barbers, boke bynders, and lymners. **1555** EDEN *Decades* 188 The lyttle byrdes whiche the lymmers of bookes are accustomed to paynte on the margentes of churche bookes. **1607** R. C[AREW] tr. *Estienne's World of Wonders* 334 A limmer..had drawne S. Peter and S. Paul so liuely. **1859** C. BARKER *Associat. Princ.* i. 18 The *Rector Chori*..had..the charge of the writing materials..and of the colours for the limners.

2. A painter, esp. a portrait painter. †Sometimes *spec.*, a water-colour artist.

1594 PLAT *Jewell-ho.* II. 23 The fine and subtil earth of the hearbe or flower, out of the which some curious Limner may draw some excellent colour. **1607** TOPSELL *Four-f. Beasts* (1658) 10 The Poets (with their apes, the painters, limmers, and carvers). **1638** USSHER *Immanuel* (1645) 16 A curious limmer draweth his own sons pourtraicture to the life. **1659** J. ARROWSMITH *Chain Princ.* 137 The limbner drew it as he was an artist, not as one of this or that nation. **1661-2** PEPYS *Diary* 2 Jan., Cooper, the great limner in little. **1688** R. HOLME *Armoury* III. 147/2 A Limner, a Painter in Water colours. **1752** FOOTE *Taste* I. i, Pray now, Mr. Carmine, how do you Limners contrive to overlook the Ugliness, and yet preserve the Likeness? **1830** D'ISRAELI *Chas. I*, III. viii. 186 Many refined strokes show that the limner had studied his original by her side. **1875** JOWETT *Plato* (ed. 2) III. 250 The drawing of a limner which has not the shadow of a likeness to the truth.

Hence '**limnery**, the work of a limner.

c **1831** H. COLERIDGE *Ess.* (1851) I. 199 The few remnants of church-limnery that have escaped the fanatics and the modernisers.

limnetic (lɪm'nɛtɪk), *a.* [f. Gr. λιμνήτ-ης living in marshes + -IC.] Of, pertaining to, or living in the open part of a freshwater lake or pond, away from the margin or bottom.

1899 G. C. WHIPPLE *Microsc. Drinking-Water* viii. 105 The limnetic or pelagic organisms are those that make their home in the open water. They float or swim freely and are drifted about by every current... Then there are organisms that may be said to be facultative limnetic forms, that is, they are sedentary or free-swimming at will. **1903** *Amer. Naturalist* XXXVII. 503 This work is in the main an extension of Häcker's earlier papers.. on the autonomy of the male and female pronuclei and of their derivatives in the development of limnetic Copepods. **1923** *Ecology* IV. 372 (*heading*) Limnetic A[ssociation]. **1955** C. C. DAVIS *Marine & Fresh-Water Plankton* i. 11 Horizontally, the relatively shallow area close to shore, characterized by rooted emergent or floating vegetation, is called the littoral region, while the region of open water is known as the limnetic (or pelagic) region... The limnetic region is much more extensive than the littoral in most lakes. **1957** G. E. HUTCHINSON *Treat. Limnol.* I. i. 19 The region has had a long limnetic history and has contained large tectonic lakes since the middle Tertiary.

'**limniad.** *rare.* [Erroneously for **limnad*, ad. Gr. λιμναδ-, λιμνάς fem. adj., 'pertaining to lakes,' f. λίμνη lake.] A lake-nymph.

1818 L. HUNT *Foliage, The Nymphs* p. xii, The Limniad takes Her pleasure in the lakes.

limnic ('lɪmnɪk), *a. Geol.* [ad. G. *limnisch* (C. F. Naumann *Lehrb. d. Geognosie* (1850) I. II. iii. 814), f. Gr. λίμνη pool of standing water, marshy lake: see -IC.] Formed or laid down in an inland body of standing fresh water such as a lake or a swamp.

[**1911** *Proc. Amer. Philos. Soc.* L. 28 Naumann recognized the distinction between deposits formed on the sea border and those in fresh-water lakes... These types he terms paralisch and limnisch. *Ibid.* 29 The causes in paralisch areas are different from those in limnisch basins.] **1940** A. C. NOÉ tr. *Stutzer's Geol. Coal* vi. 159 Coal basins which have originated near the sea are called 'paralic basins'; and coal deposits which were formed inland..'limnic deposits'. This classification goes back to Naumann. Recent peat bogs can also be similarly classified. In the interior of a country—for instance, on the northern edge of the Alps—are found limnic moors, while the paralic moors are situated on the coast, as in Friesland. **1968** M.-TH. MACKOWSKY in Murchison & Westoll *Coal* xiv. 327 In the Upper Carboniferous large paralic coal deposits formed along the northern border of the Variscan mountains. Somewhat later the limnic coals of the Saar, Lorraine and central and south-eastern France developed in troughs between the mountains. **1971** *Nature* 30 Apr. 561/1 Tobien *et al.* have excavated a primitive, forest-adapted *Hipparion* fauna..from tuffaceous and limnic beds on the flank of the Höwenegg volcanic centre in southern Germany.

limning ('lɪmɪŋ, 'lɪmnɪŋ), *vbl. sb.* [f. LIMN *v.* + -ING[1].]

1. Illuminating of manuscripts, etc. Also *concr.*

c **1485** *E.E. Misc.* (Warton Club) 72 There begynnyth the crafte of lymnynge of bokys. **1573** (*title*) A very proper treatise, wherein is briefly sett forthe the arte of limming, which teacheth how siluer or golde shalbe layed or limmed vppon the sise [etc.]. **1591** PERCIVALL *Sp. Dict.*, *Luminacion de libros*, lymning, *miniculatio.* **1612** PEACHAM *Gentl. Exerc.* title-p., The making of all kinds of colours, to be vsed in Lymming, Painting, Tricking, and Blason of Coates, and Armes. **1762-71** H. WALPOLE *Vertue's Anecd. Paint.* (1786) I. 39 Of the third Edward, says Mr. Vertue, many portraits are preserved..in illuminated MSS... He has not marked where these limnings exist. **1859** GULLICK & TIMES *Paint.* 100 The art of illuminating, or limning, as it was formerly called.

2. Painting (†formerly *spec.* in water-colour or distemper).

1606 G. W[OODCOCKE] *Lives Emperors* in *Hist. Ivstine* G g 1 b, Singing, playing, and phisick, geometry, painting, and liming. **1675** SALMON *Polygraph.* II. xv. 73 Limning is an Art whereby in Water Colours, we strive to resemble Nature in every thing to the life. **1688** R. HOLME *Armoury* III. 147/2 Limning, Painting in Water colours with Gum or Size. **1712** ADDISON *Spect.* No. 328 Limning, one would think, is no expensive Diversion, but..she paints Fans for all her Female Acquaintance, and draws all her Relations Pictures in Miniature. **1884** B. B. WARFIELD in *Chr. Treasury* Feb. 92/1 The skilled limning of a Michael Angelo.

b. An instance of this; *concr.* a painting.

1689 *Lond. Gaz.* No. 2511/4 A Collection of Paintings and fine Limnings by the best Masters. **1711** SHAFTESB. *Charac.* (1737) III. 295 E'er you attempt those accurate and refin'd limnings or portraitures of mankind, or offer to bring gentlemen on the stage. **1816** SINGER *Hist. Cards* 67 A great many limnings in rather a rude style of art. **1861** *Our Eng. Home* 145 The limnings of early painters on the walls.

3. *attrib.*, as †***limning gold***, †***picture***, ***-skill***.

1420 *Nottingham Rec.* II. 120 *Pro auro vocato* 'lymnyng gold'. **1617** I. OLIVER in *Wills Doctors Com.* (Camden) 84 All my drawings..and lymning pictures, or any thing of lymning whatsoever..as yet unfinished. **1737** MATT. GREEN *Spleen* 450 When fancy tries her limning skill To draw and colour at her will.

'**limning,** *ppl. a.* [f. as prec. + -ING[2].] Painting.

1782 WOLCOT (P. Pindar) *3rd Ode to R.A.'s* iv, Thus should young limning lads themselves demean.

limnite ('lɪmnaɪt). Also **lymnite**. [f. Gr. λίμνη lake + -ITE.]

1. *Palæontology.* A fossil species of the genus *Limnæa.*

1864 WEBSTER, *Lymnite.* **1882** OGILVIE, *Limnite.*

2. *Min.* Bog iron ore, containing more water than limonite.

1868 in DANA *Min.* 178.

limno- ('lɪmnəʊ), comb. form of Gr. λίμνη lake, marsh, as in ˌ**limnobi'ology** *rare*, the biology of lakes and ponds; so ˌ**limnobio'logic, -bio'logical** *adjs.*

1899 *Ann. Rep. Board of Regents Smithsonian Inst. 1897-98* 505 Switzerland has furnished perhaps the greatest number of investigators and stations for limnobiology. *Ibid.* 510 The Mount Prospect Laboratory,..placed under the direction of Mr. G. C. Whipple, whose contributions to limnobiologic questions are well known. **1909** *Cent. Dict.* Suppl., Limnobiological. **1957** G. E. HUTCHINSON *Treat. Limnol.* I. p. x, The first volume is intended to cover geographical and physico-chemical limnology, the second will deal with limnobiology and the ecological, typological, and stratigraphic problems of lake development.

limnograph ('lɪmnəgrɑːf, -æ-). [f. Gr. λίμνη lake, marsh + -GRAPH.] An apparatus for automatically recording the variations of level in a lake.

1880 *Nature* 4 Mar. 427 Beside the fixed limnograph of M. Plantamour.

limnology (lɪm'nɒlədʒɪ). [f. Gr. λίμνη lake, marsh + -λογία -LOGY.] (The study of) the physical, chemical, geological, and biological aspects of lakes and other bodies of fresh stagnant (sometimes also of fresh flowing) water.

1893 *Geogr. Jrnl.* I. 353 He [*sc.* Friedrich Simony].. became the founder of the special branch of science termed by Forel, Limnology, or the scientific study of lakes. **1895** *Athenæum* 10 Aug. 195/3 Limnology was dealt with [at the Geographical Congress] by Dr. F. A. Forel. **1899** *Pop. Sci. Monthly* Sept. 709 The study of microscopic aquatic life and general limnology. **1929** *Jrnl. Ecol.* XVII. 106 A generation or so ago the general conception of the word limnology was that it covered the subject of the physiography of lakes, and that freshwater biology..was more or less a separate science... As the biology of fresh waters developed this branch of science was fairly often included within the range of the word limnology, but still the term continued to be frequently used for the physiographical aspect of lake investigations only, and the notion of limnology as a mere branch of physical geography separated from the biological side of the question persisted. That definition must now be entirely abandoned... The subject of limnology, then, is the study of everything connected with fresh waters—both stagnant and running—their geography, physical features, chemistry, biology, geology of the substrata and basins, in short the Natural History of fresh waters in the broadest sense of the word. **1938** *Jrnl. Wildlife Managem.* II. 94 (*heading*) Fish biology and limnology of Crater Lake, Oregon. **1946** *Nature* 21 Sept. 421/1 Up-to-date knowledge and theory of limnology—the freshwater equivalent of oceanography—has been combined with practical experience of waterworks. **1971** *New Scientist* 4 Feb. 236/1 The professor of limnology at the University of Lund.

So **limno'logical** *a.*, of or pertaining to limnology; **limno'logically** *adv.*; **lim'nologist**, one who studies lakes.

1896 *Rep. 6th Internat. Geogr. Congr. 1895* 601 Such study [of British lakes] has been for the most part occasional and unsystematic, being only in rare cases worthy of being termed limnological. **1909** WEBSTER, Limnologically. **1910** MURRAY & PULLAR *Bathymetrical Survey Scottish Fresh-Water Lochs* I. 9 Several foreign limnologists have visited the Scottish lochs. **1933** *Geogr. Jrnl.* LXXXI. 380 A German limnological expedition was at work in the Dutch East Indies. **1957** G. E. HUTCHINSON *Treat. Limnol.* I. i. 22 Limnologically, this difference is not of any particular significance. *Ibid.* 27 The Lago di Nemi, famous in antiquity.., is also a lake of considerable limnological interest. **1967** *Economist* 29 July 414/3 The Lake Tahoe Area Council..has spent thousands of dollars on engineering and limnological studies. **1970** *Nature* 25 July 420/2 The English Lake District has been and is still a mecca for limnologists.

limnometer (lɪm'nɒmɪtə(r)). Also *erron.* limni-. [f. Gr. λίμνη lake + -METER.] An apparatus for measuring the variations of level in lakes.

1852 TH. ROSS *Humboldt's Trav.* II. xvi. 14 The Marquis del Toro has undertaken to put this design into execution.. establishing limnometers, on a bottom of gneiss rock, so common in the lake of Valencia. **1879** *Nature* 23 Oct. 615/2 M. Edouard Sarasin has recently established a registering limnimeter..near the eastern extremity of the Lake of Geneva.

limnophilous (lɪm'nɒfɪləs), *a.* [f. Gr. λίμνη marsh, pool + φίλ-ος loving + -OUS. Cf. F. *limnophile.*] Fond of or living in marshes or pools, as certain molluscs, etc.

1855 in MAYNE *Expos. Lex.*

limnoplankton (ˌlɪmnəʊ'plæŋktən). [a. G. *limnoplankton* (E. Hæckel 1891, in *Jenaische Zeitschr. Naturwiss.* XXV. 253), f. LIMNO- + PLANKTON.] Plankton found in fresh water.

1893 G. W. FIELD tr. *Hæckel's Planktonic Stud.* in *Rep. U.S. Comm. Fisheries 1889–91* 580 The totality of the swimming and floating population of the fresh water may be called limnoplankton. **1909** GROOM & BALFOUR tr. *Warming's Oecol. Plants* xxxviii. 161 Limnoplankton appears to be one of the most cosmopolitan of formations. **1955** C. C. DAVIS *Marine & Fresh-Water Plankton* i. 28 The limnoplankton is the plankton of lakes.

limnoria (lɪm'nɔərɪə). [mod.L. (W. E. Leach 1815, in *Trans. Linn. Soc. Lond.* XI. 370), ad. Gr. Λιμνορεια a water-nymph.] A marine isopod crustacean of the genus so called, which includes *L. lignorum*, a borer that attacks timber (= GRIBBLE[2]).

1868 BATE & WESTWOOD *Hist. Brit. Sessile-Eyed Crustacea* II. 353 Many kinds of wood, including old oak, are devoured by the *Limnoria.* **1936** *Times Lit. Suppl.* 18 Apr. 325/3 Against teredo's rival limnoria, luckily less widespread, no poison is effective. **1967** J. A. C. NICOL *Biol. Marine Animals* (ed. 2) v. 231 The gribble *Limnoria* is an isopod which tunnels into wood and feeds on wood particles.

limo ('lɪməʊ), colloq. abbrev. of LIMOUSINE. *U.S.*

1968 *New Yorker* 23 Nov. 96 'You ride in the limo, dear,' he said,..helping her out of the Daimler. **1972** R. K. SMITH *Ransom* i. 18 If there's traffic too close to the limo, we forget it. **1972** *New Yorker* 23 Dec. 36/2 Just at the moment when the heavy groups freaking out in rented limos seemed to have wiped everybody out, this sing-song music..began to flower. **1973** R. MOORE *Fifth Estate* i. 16 The company should be sending a limo for me. I'd be happy to drop you off. **1975** *New Yorker* 24 Mar. 32/3 This place has got a laser beam on the perimeter to keep out marauders, as well as free Rolls-Royce and Mercedes limo service.

limo- ('laɪməʊ), taken as comb. form of L. *līmus* mud, in the sense 'clayey and...'

1756 C. LUCAS *Ess. Waters* I. 13 A certain earth of the limo-cretaceous kind.

Limoges (lɪ'məʊʒ). The name of a city in central France used (freq. *attrib.*) to designate painted enamels, porcelain, etc., made there.

1844 DISRAELI *Coningsby* II. v. viii. 310 He has..a collection of Limoges ware that is the despair of the dilettanti. **1856, 1861** [see CHAMPLEVÉ *sb.* and *a.*]. **1870** C. SCHREIBER *Jrnl.* (1911) I. 77 Some beautiful Limoges enamels. **1938** [see CHAMPLEVÉ *sb.* and *a.*]. **1963** L. DEIGHTON *Horse under Water* xvii. 71 Coffee came..in a silver pot attended by Limoges cups and saucers. **1966** MRS. L. B. JOHNSON *White House Diary* 23 Jan. (1970) 356 Exquisite Limoges—white with a chaste gold border—for her formal china. **1966** J. LAVER *Victoriana* 157 Royal Worcester patera of 1867 decorated in the 'Limoges enamel' style..suggested by the painted enamel work on copper which was carried out at Limoges during the Renaissance. **1973** *Country Life* 11 Oct. 1063 French lamp in white Limoges porcelain with sumptuous gold decorations ..£14.95.

‖**limon** (limɔ̃). *Geol.* [Fr., = (*a*) silt, alluvium, (*b*) *limon*, loess:—L. *līmus* mud.] A fine sandy soil, probably of similar origin to loess, which is widespread in northern France and Belgium.

1890 *Rep. Brit. Assoc. Adv. Sci. 1889* 560 At the foot of the Alps,..the löss is dark grey; but west of the secondary chain the same deposit is yellowish, and composed almost entirely of silicious materials, with only a very little carbonate of lime. This *limon* or löss..is very generally modified towards the top by the chemical action of rain. **1931** H. ORMSBY *France* v. 168 Where the covering of *limon* was thick, on the lower slopes the farmer has been able to cover the scars of war with fields of grain. **1972** MANSFIELD & POWRIE *France & Benelux* viii. 137 The most typical of these chalklands is Picardy,..remarkably fertile, owing to the thick covering of *limon.*

limon(e, obs. form of LEMON.

†**limoneer.** *Obs.* In 6 lymoner, -eer. [a. F. *limonier*, f. *limon* shaft: see -EER[1].] A horse which is attached to the shafts of a vehicle.

1523 WOLSEY in Fiddes *Life* (1726) II. 112 That new Lymoneers and horses for draught and carriage should be recovered. **1524** —— in *St. Papers Hen. VIII* (1836) IV. 120 Provision of lymoners, cariages and drawghtes.

limonin ('lɪmənɪn). *Chem.* Also -ine. [f. mod.L. *limonum* (F. *limon*) + -IN.] (See quot.) Also (*rare*) limone [as in Fr.].

1845 GREGORY *Organic Chem.* 459 Limonine, or Limone, a bitter crystalline matter found in the seeds of oranges, lemons, &c. **1864** WATTS *Dict. Chem.* III. 699 *Limonin*, the bitter principle contained in the pips of oranges and lemons.

limonite ('laɪmənaɪt). *Min.* [Named by Hausmann, 1813, probably from Gr. λειμών meadow, a rendering of its earlier Ger. name *wiesenerz*, meadow-ore: see -ITE.] A name at first confined to bog iron ore, but now extended to include all forms of hydrous sesqui-oxide of iron, containing about 15 per cent. of water.

1823 H. J. BROOKE *Introd. Crystallogr.* 472 Bog, Meadow, &c.; Iron ore, Limonite. **1852** C. U. SHEPARD *Min.* (ed. 3) 276 Limonite occurs in beds and veins. **1879** RUTLEY *Study Rocks* x. 156 Limonite occurs in stalactitic, mammillated, pisolitic, or earthy, conditions.

attrib. **1874** RAYMOND *Statist. Mines & Mining* 308 A deposit of limonite-iron ore.

Hence **limo'nitic** *a.*, consisting of or resembling limonite (*Cent. Dict.*).

‖**li'monium.** *Obs.* [mod.L. *līmōnium* = L. *līmōnion* (Pliny), a. Gr. λειμώνιον, neut. of λειμώνιος, f. λειμών meadow.] Any plant of the genus *Pyrola*, esp. *P. rotundifolia*; wintergreen.

1548 TURNER *Names of Herbes* 48 Limonium named of the Herbaries Pyrola, is named in duch wintergrowen... It maye be called in englishe wyntergrene. **1562** —— *Herbal* II. 39 The sede of Limonium..is good agaynst all kyndes of flyxes. **1664** EVELYN *Kal. Hort.* July (1679) 21 Flowers in Prime, or yet Lasting... Indian Tuberous Jacynth, Limonium [etc.]. **1741** *Compl. Fam.-Piece* II. iii. 386 You have besides the scarlet Lichnis,..divers kinds of Limoniums.

limose ('laɪməʊs), *a. Geol.* and *Bot. rare.* [ad. L. *līmōs-us*, f. *līmus* mud.] Pertaining to, of the nature of mud; growing in mud.

1855 MAYNE *Expos. Lex.*, s.v. *Limosus.*

†**li'mosity.** *Obs.* [ad. mod.L. *līmōsitās*, f. *līmōs-us.*] 'Muddiness' (Blount *Glossogr.* 1656).

limo'therapy. *Med. rare.* [f. Gr. λῑμό-ς hunger + θεραπεία medical treatment.] Treatment of disease by fasting; the hunger cure.

1893 in *Dunglison's Dict. Med.* (ed. 21).

limous ('laɪməs), *a.* ? *Obs.* Also 5 lymous, -ows. [ad. L. *līmōs-us*, f. *līmus* mud, slime.] Muddy; slimy.

c **1420** *Pallad. on Husb.* IX. 139 Yf water ther be lymous or enfecte, Admyxtion of salt wol hit correcte. *c* **1440** *Promp. Parv.* 198/2 Gleymows, or lymows, *limosus, viscosus, glutinosus.* **1646** SIR T. BROWNE *Pseud. Ep.* VI. i. 275 The mud and limous matter brought downe by the river Nilus. **1656** in BLOUNT *Glossogr.* *a* **1734** SIR J. FLOYER (J.), They esteemed this natural melancholick acidity to be the limous or slimy fœculent part of the blood. **1794** SULLIVAN *View Nat.* II. 157 A limous lava..which consists of argillaceous and siliceous earths mixed with iron.

Hence †**limousness**, sliminess.

c **1440** *Promp. Parv.* 198/2 Gleymowsenesse, or lymow(s)nesse, *limositas, viscositas.*

Limousin (limuzæ̃). Also 8 **Lemosine, Limosine.** [Name of an old province in central France.] **1.** A native or inhabitant of the former province of Limousin or of the region round Limoges; also, the dialect of this region. Also *attrib.* or as *adj.*, of or pertaining to this region, its inhabitants, or their dialect.

1653 T. URQUHART tr. *Rabelais's Works* (1664) II. vi. 33 When all comes to all, thou art a Limousin, and thou wilt here by the affected speech counterfeit the Parisiens. **1706** J. STEVENS *New Spanish & Eng. Dict.* Pref., In Catalonia.. they have besides a peculiar language of their own... This is a sort of Limosine, or that of the Country of Limoges, being an old barbarous French, formerly brought into this Country out of France. **1716** C. CAMPBELL tr. *Dameto's Hist. Balearick Islands* I. v. 64 That which is in use at this time commonly called the Lemosine Language being originally from Limosin a Province of France, whose Capital is Limoge. **1787** A. YOUNG *Jrnl.* 10 June in *Trav. France* (1792) I. 18 Chestnuts on a calcareous soil, contrary to the Limosin maxim. **1911** S. M. HOGAN *St. Vincent Ferrer* iv. 29 St. Vincent himself tells us that he preached in his mother-tongue—Limousin. **1932** W. L. GRAFF *Lang.* 377 Provençal group, with different varieties: Provençal.. Limousin, Gascon. **1964** *Archivum Linguisticum* XVI. 34 In quoting this dialect [*sc.* North Occitan] I give Limousin forms. **1968** F. WHITE *Ways of Aquitaine* IV. 55 The churches of the Limousin abbeys form a school of their own, deeply impressive because of their darkness and their strength. **1973** J. WAINWRIGHT *Devil you Don't* 62 The V.S.O.P. Cognac—pale, liquid ecstasy with a bouquet of Limousin oak.

2. An animal belonging to the French breed of beef cattle so called. Also *attrib.*

1970 *Times* 6 Apr. 10/7 The Limousin, a hardy, deep fawn coloured animal, is a beef breed which has impressed many visitors to Paris shows. **1971** *Country Life* 30 Dec. 1857/3 Limousins from the Limoges area..are the most recent invaders of the northern English counties. **1973** *Ibid.* 1 Mar. 548/1 A German Zimmenthal bull, and..a Limousin bull in France.

limousine ('lɪmuːziːn). [Fr., f. prec.] A (luxury) motor car with a compartment for the passengers and a separate compartment for the driver. Also *attrib.*

Orig. the driver's seat was outside though covered with a roof. Since the 1930s the word has been more usual in North America than in the U.K.; recently it has been used, esp. in the U.S., for vehicles conveying passengers to and from large airports.

1902 A. C. HARMSWORTH et al. *Motors* 55 With certain kinds of engines, too, it is difficult to adopt any other form of car than the Tonneau, or for the wet weather the Limousine. **1905** *Westm. Gaz.* 22 Nov. 9/2 A touring car.. fitted with a brougham or limousine body. **1916** A. BENNETT *Lion's Share* xxx. 217 A few days later an automobile—not Audrey's but a large limousine—bumped, with slow and soft dignity, across the railway lines. **1920** *Chambers's Jrnl.* May 279/2 He heard the purring of limousines gliding into Pall Mall. **1922** W. J. LOCKE *Tale of Triona* v. 47 Whom she saw drive away in luxurious limousines. **1960** I. WALLACH *Absence of Cello* (1961) 27 Marian..struggled to the bus [at N.Y. airport] that was known for some reason as a 'limousine'. **1968** *Globe & Mail* (Toronto) 3 Feb. 3/4 Limousine service..to take them to the nearest city bus stop. **1970** *Toronto Daily Star* 24 Sept. 38/1 Jones and most of the borough education directors—who are paid the same salary—are given chauffeur driven limousines. **1972** *Daily Tel.* 16 May 9/3 The open limousine was followed by one in which Prince Philip travelled with Mme Pompidou. **1972** *Times* 27 June (Tokyo Suppl.) p. vi/2 There are regular limousine services from the airport. **1973** V. CANNING *Finger of Saturn* i. 10 The people from the limousine got out. .. The limousine driver watched them go. **1973** *Country Life* 13 Sept. 686 If the terms 'limousine' and '1½ litre' appear incompatible, see, sit in, and drive the Triumph 1500... In the generous luxury you get in a well-padded limousine..long-distance travelling is limousine-smooth. All the other limousine touches are there too.

b. limousine liberal: a wealthy liberal. *U.S.*

1969 *Times* 4 Nov. 10/5 The little man truly representing the ordinary people, hitting out strongly at Mr. Lindsay's 'limousine liberal' appeal. **1970** *N.Y. Times* 26 Oct. 36 Canada is most fortunate to have a Premier who is willing to tell the bleeding hearts and limousine liberals what he thinks of them.

†**limp**, *sb.*[1] *Obs. rare*[−1]. [f. LIMP *v.*[1] Cf. OE. *ȝelimp*, f. *ȝelimpan.*] An occurrence.

c **1200** *Trin. Coll. Hom.* 197 On alle þose limpes ne untrowede neure Iob to-genes ure drihten.

limp (lɪmp), *sb.*[2] [f. LIMP *v.*[2]] The action of limping; a limping gait or walk.

1818 TODD s.v., He has a limp in his walking. **1870** DICKENS *E. Drood* iii, The sun-browned tramps..quicken their limp a little. **1876** *Chamb. Jrnl.* 15 Jan. 35/1 The Grecian bend and the Alexandra limp—both positive and practical imitations of physical affliction.

limp (lɪmp), *sb.*[3] *Mining.* An instrument used for throwing off the refuse from the ore in the operation of jigging (see quots.).

1747 HOOSON *Miner's Dict.*, *Limp* [is] a very small and thin Piece of Board, shaped almost half round, and it is Shod on the circular edge with Iron. **1778** PRYCE *Min. Cornub.* 323 The uppermost light stony waste may be easily separated and skimmed off by a piece of semicircular board, called a Limp. **1875** in J. H. COLLINS *Metal Mining* Gloss. **1881** in RAYMOND *Mining Gloss.*

limp (lɪmp), *a.* [Of obscure origin; G. *lampen*, 'to hang limp', has been compared.]

1. a. Wanting in firmness or stiffness, flaccid; flexible, pliant. Of a textile fabric: Unstiffened.

1706 PHILLIPS (ed. Kersey), *Limp*, limber, supple. **1750** M. BROWNE *Walton's Angler* iii. 42 The Chub..eats waterish, and..the Flesh of him is not firm, but limp [*earlier edd.* short] and tasteless. *a* **1825** FORBY *Voc. E. Anglia*, *Limp, limpsy*, flaccid. **1840** DICKENS *Old C. Shop* xvi, His [Punch's] body was dangling in a most uncomfortable position, all loose and limp, and shapeless. **1866** *Cornh. Mag.* Mar. 348 A female with a heap of limp veil thrown up over an obsolete bonnet. **1884** *Bazaar* 19 Dec. 658/1 Scarf arrangements..are made in almost any limp material. **1897** *Bookman* Jan. 116/1 Strangling in our starch we can rally him [Byron] familiarly on his limp collars.

b. *Bookbinding.* Used to designate a kind of binding in which no mill-board is used.

1863 *Parker's Catal. Bks. printed for Univ. Oxf.* 2 Sophoclis Tragœdiæ..each Play separately, limp cloth. 2*s.* 6*d.* **1882** *Clar. Press List New Bks.* 40 The Oxford Bible for Teachers..Turkey Morocco, limp, 22*s.* 6*d.*

c. ***limp wrist*** (see quot. 1960); also *transf.* and (usu. with hyphen) as *attrib. phr.*

1960 WENTWORTH & FLEXNER *Dict. Amer. Slang* 319/2 *Limp wrist* adj., homosexual; said of male homosexuals; effeminate... A homosexual or effeminate man. **1963** *Amer. Speech* XXXVIII. 171 An effeminate young man, a sissy ..*limp wrist.* **1969** *Guardian* 18 Mar. 1/3 Washington..has concluded that if Britain continues to follow a 'limp wrist' policy after the open affront of the shooting affair, the gambling interests would draw obvious conclusions. **1970** C. MAJOR *Dict. Afro-Amer. Slang* 77 *Limp wrist*, having latent homosexual tendencies.

2. *transf.* and *fig.* Wanting in firmness, strictness, nervous energy, or the like.

1853 G. J. CAYLEY *Las Alforjas* I. 196 We told them that our nation had no taste or genius for dancing,..preferring to imitate in a limp and spiritless manner, the dances of foreign countries. **1872** BAGEHOT *Physics & Pol.* (1876) 76 Creeds or systems that conduce to a soft limp mind tend to perish. **1880** VERN. LEE *Stud. Italy* II. ii. 24 His contemporaries composed in loose, limp rhymes. **1885** DOBSON *At Sign of Lyre* 141 Whether..the limp Matron on the Hill Woke from her novel-reading trance.

†**limp**, *v.*[1] *Obs.* Forms: 1 **limpan**, *pa. t.* **lomp**, *pa. pple.* **lumpen**, 2–5 **limpe(n**, 4–5 **lympe(n**; *pa. t.* 5 **lympede, -ide**, *pa. pple.* 4 **lumpen.** [OE. *limpan* str. = OHG. *limphan, limpfan, limfan, limfen*; also *limpan* (MHG. *limpfen*); cf. OHG. *gilimpf*

suitableness, fitness, mod.G. *glimpf* moderation, lenity.]

1. *intr.* To befall, happen. Const. *dative.* Chiefly *impers.* or quasi-*impers.*

Beowulf 1987 Hu lomp eow on lade leofa Biowulf. *c* **888** K. ÆLFRED *Boeth.* xxxix. §2 (Sedgefield) þa yflan habbað ȝesælða, & him limpð oft æfter hiora aȝnum willan. *a* **1225** *Ancr. R.* 412 ȝif out limpeð misliche þet [etc.]. **13..** *E.E. Allit. P.* B. 424 Nyf oure lorde hade ben her lodez-mon hem had lumpen harde. **13..** *Gaw. & Gr. Knt.* 907 Hit was Wawen hym-self þat in þat won syttez, Comen to þat krystmasse, as case hym þen lymped. *a* **1400–50** *Alexander* 3095 It lympys nott allway þe last be lykkynd to þe first. *c* **1420** *Anturs of Arth.* 615 Bot him lympede þe werse, and þat me wele lykis.

2. To belong, pertain, relate *to.*

858 *Charter* in *O.E. Texts* 438 Butan ðem wioda ðe to ðem sealtern limpð. *c* **1175** *Lamb. Hom.* 41 We eow wulleð suteliche seggen of þa fredome þe limpeð to þan deie. *a* **1225** *Ancr. R.* 50 þet hwite creoiz limpeð to ou.

3. *trans.* To incur, meet with.

13.. *E.E. Allit. P.* C. 174 And who-so lympes þe losse, lay hym þer-oute. ?*a* **1400** *Morte Arth.* 875, I hadde lefte my lyfe are cho hade harme lymppyde.

limp (lɪmp), *v.*[2] [cogn. w. MHG. *limphin* (rare) of the same meaning. Cf. also LIMPHALT *a.*]

1. a. *intr.* To walk lamely, to halt. Also with *about, along, away.* Occas. with cognate object.

1570 LEVINS *Manip.* 132/11 To Limp, *claudicare.* **1596** SHAKS. *Tam. Shr.* II. i. 254 Why does the world report that Kate doth limpe? **1601** HOLLAND *Pliny* I. 274 Of Hawks.. the Circos.. is lame and limpeth of one leg. **1648** BP. HALL *Breathings Devout Soul* xxii. 34 That holy servant of thine.. went limping away. **1709** STEELE *Tatler* No. 80 ¶7, I must therefore humbly beg Leave to limp along the Streets after my own Way. **1787** BURNS *Tam Samson's Elegy* x, Owre mony a weary hag he limpit. **1806–7** J. BERESFORD *Miseries Hum. Life* (1826) II. i, Limp along like a pig in a string. **1837** W. IRVING *Capt. Bonneville* III. 259 His trail was followed for a long distance, which he must have limped alone. **1867** DICKENS *Lett.* (1880) II. 275 He limps about and does his work.

b. *fig.*; in quot. *c* 1400, to fall short *of.*

c **1400** *Destr. Troy* 36 Sum lokyt ouer litle and lympit of the sothe. **1586** STANYHURST *Descr. Irel.* i. 11/2 in *Holinshed*, And if anie of these three [*sc.* marks of the subjection of a country] lacke, doubtlesse the conquest limpeth. **1586** J. HOOKER *Hist. Irel.* 105/1 (*ibid.*) Sir John Alen.. was found to limpe in this controuersie. **1596** SHAKS. *Merch. V.* III. ii. 130 So farre this shadow Doth limpe behinde the substance. **1768–74** TUCKER *Lt. Nat.* (1834) I. 566 The whole chain will become a rope of sand, and the consequence limp lame behind. **1821** LAMB *Elia* Ser. I. *My Relations*, I must limp often in my poor antithetical manner. **1887** FREEMAN *Exeter* iv. 90 The pentameter might perhaps have limped less if [etc.].

c. *spec.* Of a damaged ship, aircraft, etc.: to proceed slowly or with difficulty.

1920 *Conquest* Apr. 291/3 The 'standard patch' has rendered invaluable assistance in helping stricken ships to limp into port. **1935** C. DAY LEWIS *Time to Dance* 37 But he tinkered and coaxed, and they limped Over the Adriatic on into warmer regions. **1971** *E. Afr. Standard* (Nairobi) 10 Apr. 1/1 Mr. Sprinzel, driving car No. 16, a Range Rover, with his co-driver David Benson, limped back to Nairobi yesterday afternoon. **1973** *Daily Tel.* 1 Jan. 1/4 The Fleetwood trawler Wyre Captain, 490 tons, limped into port at Thorshavn, Faroe Islands, yesterday, with a damaged bridge and no navigation instruments.

2. *Comb.*, as ***limp-verse***; ***limp-legged*** adj.

1523 SKELTON *Garl. Laurel* 625 With that I herd gunnis russhe out at ones,.. It made sum lympe legged, and broisid there bones. *c* **1648–50** BRATHWAIT *Barnabees Jrnl.*, *Vpon the Errata's*, What tho my limpe-verse be maimed?

†'limpard. *Obs.* [f. LIMP *v.*[2] + -ARD.] A contemptuous name for one who limps, a cripple.

1653 URQUHART *Rabelais* I. xxxix, What could that gouty Limpard have done with so fine a dog?

limper ('lɪmpə(r)). [f. LIMP *v.*[2] + -ER[1].] One who limps.

1632 SHERWOOD, A limper, *vn boisteux.* **1709** STEELE *Tatler* No. 77 ¶1 Before the Limpers came in, I remember a Race of Lispers. *a* **1868** WHITMAN *Boston Town* iii, Back! back to the hills, old limpers!

limpet ('lɪmpɪt). Forms: 1 lempedu, 4–7 lempet(t, (7 lampert, lympit, -pot), 7–9 limpit, (8 limpid), 8–9 *Sc.* lampit, lempeck, 7– limpet. See also LIMPIN. [OE. *lempedu*, a. late L. *lamprēda* limpet, also LAMPREY.]

1. a. A gasteropod mollusc of the genus *Patella*, having an open tent-shaped shell and found adhering tightly to the rock which it makes its resting-place.

c **1050** *Voc.* in Wr.-Wülcker 438/17 *Lemprida*, lempedu. **1312–13** *Durham Acc. Rolls* (Surtees) 10 In lempetis. *c* **1560** A. SCOTT *Poems* (S.T.S.) v. 33 Lapstaris, lempettis, mussillis in schellis. **1602** CAREW *Cornwall* 30 Of shell fish, there are Wrinkles, Limpets, Cockles [etc.]. **1673** SIR W. SCROGGS *Let. to Ld. Hatton* in *H. Corr.* (1878) 117 Those lympitts y[t] wer never seene in England lack wine to make 'em tast. **1684** *Bucaniers Amer.* (1698) II. 155 Every day we had plenty of Lamperts and Mussels of a very large size. **1685** *Phil. Trans.* XV. 1284 And tast as well as Lympots or Winkles. **1726** SWIFT *Gulliver* IV. xi. 168, I continued three Days feeding on Oysters and Limpits, to save my own Provisions. **1748** H. ELLIS *Hudson's Bay* 171 Shells are seldom met with; the only ones I saw were Limpids, Muscles, and Periwincles. **1842** JOHNSTON in *Proc. Berw. Nat. Club* II. No. 10. 36 The Limpet or Lempecks. These have a rather thin shell of a greenish colour.

b. *fig.* and *allusive*, esp. of officials alleged to be superfluous but clinging to their offices. Also *attrib.*

1824 SCOTT *St. Ronan's* xxxi, He.. stuck like a lampit to a rock. **1875** TENNYSON *Q. Mary* III. i, Be limpets to this pillar, or we are torn Down the strong wave of brawlers. **1905** *Westm. Gaz.* 9 Mar. 2/2 Lord Spencer.. had some pertinent criticisms to make of the Limpet Government. **1922** *Daily Mail* 22 Nov. 8 He is rationing the departments and ejecting the 'limpets'. *Ibid.* 23 Nov. 10 Ministries are multiplying their accumulation of limpets and paying them too well. **1927** CARR-SAUNDERS & JONES *Survey Social Struct. Eng. & Wales* 54 After the war, attempts were made to rouse our animosity against 'limpets'.

c. *attrib.* and *Comb.*, as ***limpet rock, shell***; ***limpet-shaped, -shelled*** adjs. **limpet-hammer**, a stone tool believed to have been used by prehistoric peoples to knock limpets off rocks.

1577 HARRISON *England* II. xiii. (1877) I. 255 The workemen happened oftentimes upon lempet shels. **1786** BURNS *Earnest Cry & Prayer* vii, Triumphant crushin't like a mussel Or lampit shell. **1818** KEATS *Ep. to Reynolds* 88 The first page I read Upon a Lampit rock of green sea-weed Among the breakers. **1822–34** *Good's Study Med.* (ed. 4) IV. 477 Limpet-shelled blain. **1885** S. GRIEVE *Great Auk* 57 We were puzzling ourselves as to what could be the use of the numerous oblong stones we met with among the [limpet] shells, and.. he.. informed us they were limpet-hammers. *Ibid.*, Subsequent enquiries have only helped to confirm us in the opinion that the large oblong stones found at Caistealnan-Gillean are really limpet-hammers. **1897** MARY KINGSLEY *W. Africa* 17 The hat.. a large limpet-shaped affair made of palm leaves.

2. A type of explosive device that is attached magnetically to a ship's hull; so ***limpet bomb, charge, mine.***

1942 W. S. CHURCHILL *Secret Session Speeches* (1946) 50 Explosions occurred in the bottoms of the *Valiant* and *Queen Elizabeth*, produced by limpet bombs fixed with extraordinary courage and ingenuity. **1949** F. MACLEAN *Eastern Approaches* II. iii. 202 We fixed a couple of 'limpets' to her stern. These were half-spheres of metal, made to contain a pound or so of high explosive and fitted with a magnetic device to hold them to the side of the ship. **1955** J. THOMAS *No Banners* xix. 175 He wanted permission to use six limpet charges. **1959** *Chambers's Encycl.* IX. 428 Midget submarines placed these limpet mines which, being magnetized, clung to the hull and were fired by a time fuze. **1962** G. WELLER *All about Submarines* (1963) viii. 115 The German officers were sure that limpet mines had been attached to the keel of their battleship. **1971** D. BAGLEY *Freedom Trap* ix. 198 What do we use instead of a limpet?.. I can't invade her in the middle of the Grand Harbour.

†limphalt, *a. Obs.* Also 1 læmpihalt, lemphald, -h(e)alt, 6 lympe hault. [OE. *lęmphealt*, f. **lamp-*, abl.-var. of **limp-*: see LIMP *v.*[2]] Lame, limping. Hence **†limphalting** *vbl. sb.*, limping.

a **700** *Epinal Gloss.* 589 *Lurdus*, læmpihalt [*Erfurt* lemphihalt; *Corpus* lemphalt; *Leiden* lemphald]. *c* **1050** *Voc.* in Wr.-Wülcker 433/17 *Lurdus*, lemphealt. **1530** PALSGR. 317/2 Lympe hault, *boiteux.* **1549** CHALONER *Erasm. on Folly* A iij, Vulcane, that lymphault smithe. *Ibid.* C ij, But when the Gods are sette at bankette, he plaieth the jester, now wyth hys lymphaultynge, now with his skoffinge.

limphatic, obs. form of LYMPHATIC.

limpid ('lɪmpɪd), *a.* Also 7 limpidde. [ad. F. *limpide*, or L. *limpidus*, prob. related to early *lumpa*, class.L. *lympha* clear liquid: see LYMPH.] Chiefly of fluids: Free from turbidity or suspended matter; pellucid, clear.

1613 R. CAWDREY *Table Alph.* (ed. 3), *Limpidde*, cleere, pure. **1646** SIR T. BROWNE *Pseud. Ep.* II. i. 54 Chrystall.. is a minerall body.. made of a lentous colament of earth, drawne from the most pure and limpid juyce thereof. **1682** DRYDEN *Religio Laici* 341 And still the nearer to the spring we go, More limpid, more unsoiled, the waters flow. **1784** COWPER *Task* I. 374 Winds from all quarters agitate the air, And fit the limpid element for use. **1834** MRS. SOMERVILLE *Connex. Phys. Sci.* xiv. (1849) 127 The pure and limpid crystal of Iceland spar. **1860** W. COLLINS *Wom. White* I. viii. 34 The eyes are of that soft, limpid, turquoise blue, so often sung by the poets.

b. of immaterial things and *fig.*

1649 NEEDHAM *Case Commw.* 16 It were vaine to raise more dust out of the Cobwebs of Antiquity in so limpid a case. *a* **1734** NORTH *Lives* (1826) III. 389 Death the only means to free a limpid soul.. from that dungeon of flesh. **1847** *Illustr. Lond. News* 10 July 27/1 She possesses a pure and limpid soprano of considerable compass. **1848** DICKENS *Dombey* xv, Devoutly hoping that his limpid intellect might not be brought to bear on his difficulties until they were quite settled. **1878** GLADSTONE *Prim. Homer* 6 There is a singular transparency in the mind, as there is also in the limpid language, of Homer.

limpidity (lɪm'pɪdɪtɪ). [ad. F. *limpidité* or late L. *limpiditāt-em*, f. *limpidus* LIMPID.] Clearness, transparence, with reference to both material and immaterial things.

1656 in BLOUNT *Glossogr.* **1664** H. MORE *Myst. Iniq.* 245 Rivers what they signifie.. in respect of their limpidity. **1758** REID tr. *Macquer's Chym.* I. 133 We are surprised to observe the solution of copper.. retain its limpidity. **1870** LOWELL *Among my Bks.* Ser. I. (1873) 178 The limpidity of its expression allows us to measure it at a glance. **1886** RUSKIN *Præterita* I. 294 Waters, of a perfect limpidity.

limpidly ('lɪmpɪdlɪ), *adv.* [f. LIMPID + -LY[2].] In a limpid manner.

1870 LOWELL *Among my Bks.* Ser. I. 280 Goethe himself, limpidly perfect as are many of his shorter poems, often fails in giving artistic coherence to his longer works. **1875** BROWNING *Inn Album* III. 84 He's.. Limpidly truthful.

limpidness ('lɪmpɪdnɪs). [f. LIMPID + -NESS.] The quality of being limpid; = LIMPIDITY.

1664 H. MORE *Synops. Proph.* 248 The other consideration of rivers is their limpidness and irrigation. **1758** *Elaboratory Laid Open* Introd. 75 Having that greater degree of lightness, volatility, and limpidness, which brings it to what is called the ethereal state. **1870** LOWELL *Study Wind.* 198 Nothing can be finer than the delicious limpidness of his phrase. **1885** G. MEREDITH *Diana of Crossways* II. i. 8 Lake waters under rock, unfathomable in limpidness.

'limpin. *Obs.* exc. *dial.* Also 7 lympyne. = LIMPET.

1585 HIGINS tr. *Junius' Nomenclator* 70 *Tellina, mytulus*, a limpin. **1601** HOLLAND *Pliny* I. 265 The Limpins, Muskles, and Scallops. **1611** COTGR., *Berdin*, the shell-fish called a Lympyne, or a Lempet. **1745** P. THOMAS *Jrnl. Anson's Voy.* 120 There are.. the largest Limpins that perhaps are anywhere to be met with. **1891** *Owen's Pembrokeshire* 126 *note*, Limpin is still the local name for Limpet.

limping ('lɪmpɪŋ), *vbl. sb.* [f. LIMP *v.*[2] + -ING[1].] The action of LIMP *v.*[2]

1555 W. WATREMAN *Fardle Facions* I. vi. 91 The Claudians: which they so terme of claudicacion or limping. **1604** F. HERING *Def. Caveat* 15 The extreme limping and halting thereof will easily appeare.

limping ('lɪmpɪŋ), *ppl. a.* [f. LIMP *v.*[2] + -ING[2].]

a. That limps.

1592 SHAKS. *Rom. & Jul.* I. ii. 28 Well apparreld April on the heele Of limping Winter treads. **1607** —— *Timon* IV. i. 14 Sonne [*printed* Some] of sixteen, Plucke the lyn'd Crutch from thy old limping Sire. **1724** RAMSAY *Vision* xix, Limpand Vulcan. **1791** COWPER *Odyss.* VIII. 430 The limping smith far-famed replied. **1891** A. WELCKER *Wild West* 18 They.. were followed by limping,.. mangy Indian dogs.

b. *fig.* (Cf. *halting, lame.*)

1577–87 HOLINSHED *Chron.* I. 164/1 The Danes had.. a lame and limping rule in this land. **1599** MARSTON *Sco. Villanie* II. v. 195 Rude limping lines fits this lewd halting age. **1603** FLORIO *Montaigne* (1634) 490 Nothing wrested, nothing limping: all marcheth with like tenour. **1702** DENNIS *Monument* xxv, She to new Slaughter lash'd on limping Fate. **1858** J. MARTINEAU *Stud. Chr.* 146 To give.. the vigor of an athlete to our limping wills. **1876** SPURGEON *Commenting* 113 His prophetic work has been reprinted, but not this limping poetry.

Comb. **1577** GOSSON in Kirton *Mirr. Mans Life* K vij b, A lame and lothsome lymping legged wight.

c. *transf.* Of certain relationships that are held to be legal in one country but not in another.

1963 *Listener* 17 Jan. 122/1 There is probably no more embarrassing experience for a couple than to find that they are regarded as validly married in one country, but living in sin in another. Even worse, perhaps, is the position of a man regarded by one country's laws as divorced and therefore single, but by another country as married and liable to be convicted for bigamy if he remarries. This situation, vividly called 'the limping marriage', is deplored by most systems of law including our own. *Ibid.* 123/2 It goes some way towards mitigating the evil of the 'limping marriage'. **1970** *Internat. & Compar. Law Q.* XIX. I. 12 It was scarcely in the child's interests to make her a 'limping infant' by pronouncing an order which would be refused recognition in a country with which she had significant links. *Ibid.* 17 There was the particular danger.. that the adoption order would not be recognised in some countries, producing a 'limping' adoption.

Hence **'limpingly** *adv.*, **'limpingness.**

1579 TOMSON *Calvin's Serm. Tim.* 826/1 Though wee goe limpingly, yet.. we striue with our selues to go forward. **1611** COTGR., *Boistément*, limpingly. **1754** RICHARDSON *Grandison* (1781) VI. liii. 345 Both were applauded; the time of life of the Lady, the limpingness of my Lord, considered. **1787** BECKFORD *Italy* (1834) II. 38 Our conversation was limpingly carried on in a great variety of broken languages.

†'limpish, *a.*[1] [f. LIMP *v.*[2] + -ISH.] Somewhat limping; inclined to limp.

1570 LEVINS *Manip.* 146/10 Lympish, *claudus.*

limpish ('lɪmpɪʃ), *a.*[2] [f. LIMP *a.* + -ISH.] Somewhat limp (in quot *fig.*: cf. LIMP *a.* 2).

1883 *Harper's Mag.* Sept. 509/1 He was trying to cut a limpish figure.

†'limpitude. *Obs. rare*[−0]. [ad. L. *limpitūdo*, f. *limpidus* LIMPID.] = LIMPIDITY.

1623 in COCKERAM. **1656** in BLOUNT *Glossogr.*

limpkin ('lɪmpkɪn). [f. LIMP *v.*[2] + -KIN; the bird's movements resemble those of a limping man.] A name for the genus *Aramus* of birds, holding a place midway between the Cranes and the Rails; called also COURLAN. (See quot.)

1885 *Riverside Nat. Hist.* (1888) IV. 127 The family of the limpkins or courlans is a very small one, consisting only of one genus of two species... *Aramus pictus* is restricted to Central America, the West Indies, and southern Florida. *A. scolopaceus* inhabits eastern South America.

†limply, *a. Obs.* In 3 limpliche. [OE. *limplic* (Sweet), f. *limp-an* to befit (= LIMP *v.*[1]) + *-lic*, -LY[1].] Suitable, appropriate.

c **1200** *Trin. Coll. Hom.* 25 Ure fader feide.. to elche lime limpliche mihte.

limply ('lɪmplɪ), *adv.* [f. LIMP *a.* + -LY[2].] In a limp manner.

1869 *Latest News* 10 Oct. 6 The legs dangling limply on either flank. **1887** *Scribner's Mag.* I. 630/1 He shook hands somewhat limply.

limpness ('lɪmpnɪs). [f. LIMP *a.* + -NESS.] The quality or condition of being limp.
1731 in BAILEY vol. II. **1873** BLACK *Pr. Thule* xv. 241 Gentle and obedient, not through any timidity or limpness of character. **1877** D. M. WALLACE *Russia* xxxii. 545 The moral laxity and limpness which may be remarked in the lower classes of Russia.

limpsy ('lɪmpsɪ), *a. dial.* and *U.S.* Also **-sey**. [f. LIMP *a.* For the ending, see FLIMSY.] Limp.
a **1825** [see LIMP *a.* 1]. **1865** E. BURRITT *Walk Land's End* viii. 284 That child..makes two steps forward before its limpsy body loses its balance. **1868** WHITMAN *Sel. Poems* 119 The death-howl, the limpsey tumbling body, the rush of friend and foe thither. **1869** MRS. STOWE *Oldtown Folks* xlviii. (1870) 525 She..looked sort o' limpsy, as if there wa'n't no starch left in her.

limpwort: see LIME-WORT[2].

limstock, obs. variant of LINSTOCK.

limu, var. LIMMU.

limuloid ('lɪmjʊlɔɪd), *a.* and *sb.* [f. next + -OID.] **a.** *adj.* Of or pertaining to or resembling the genus *Limulus*. **b.** *sb.* A limuloid crustacean.
1859 PAGE *Handbk. Geol. Terms* s.v. *Limulus*, Several limuloid crustaceans have been discovered in the coal-measures. **1877** LE CONTE *Elem. Geol.* (1879) 313 In general appearance they [Trilobites] certainly approach Limuloids.

‖**limulus** ('lɪmjʊləs). *Zool.* Pl. **-i**. [mod.L. use of L. *līmulus* somewhat askance, f. *līmus* askew.] A genus of *Merostomata* (Order *Limulidæ*); the king-crab or horse-shoe crab.
1837 BUCKLAND *Geol. & Min.* I. 393 A second approximation to the character of Trilobites occurs in the Limulus or King crab. **1859** PAGE *Handbk. Geol. Terms*, *Limulus*, the Molucca-crab, king-crab, or horse-shoe crab. **1873** DAWSON *Earth & Man* v. 94 The Limuli, or horse-shoe crabs.

‖ **'limus.** *Obs.* [L. *līmus*.] Mud, slime.
1649 J. E[LLISTOWE] tr. *Behmen's Epist.* i. §64 Being out of the *limus* of the earth.

limy ('laɪmɪ), *a.* [f. LIME *sb.*[1] + -Y.]
1. Besmeared with birdlime.
1552 HULOET, Lymye or clammye, *viscidus*. **1591** SPENSER *Muiopot.* 429 He..wrapt his winges twaine In lymie snares the subtill loupes among. [In mod. Dicts.]
2. Consisting of or containing lime.
1676 *Phil. Trans.* XI. 615 Some bolar, some sandy, some talky, some limy. **1681** GREW *Musæum* 7 A human Skull cover'd all over with the Skin. Having been buried..in some Limy..soil, by which it was tann'd. **1813** J. C. EUSTACE *Italy* I. xi. (1815) 387 Its limy ruins spread over the surface, burn the soil and check its natural fertility. **1876** PAGE *Adv. Text-Bk. Geol.* iii. 66 Their flinty and limy cases ..being aggregated in countless myriads. **1893** *Black & White* 15 Apr. 464/2 Limy dust..fills the eyes.
3. Of the nature of lime, resembling lime.
1775 A. BURNABY *Trav.* 34 There is peculiarity in the water at Winchester, owing..to the soil's being of a limy quality.

†**lin**, *v. Obs.* Forms: 1 linnan, 2 linnen, 3-7 lynn(e, 5-7 lyn(e, (6 lenne, 7 *Sc.* lein), 6-7 linne, 6-8 lin, 8 *Sc.* lean, leen. *Pa. t.* 1 lann, 4 lan, 5 lyne, 6 lin; *weak* 6 linde, 7 lind, lynned. [OE. *linnan* = OHG. *(bi-)linnan* (cf. BLIN *v.*), ON. *linna* (Da. *linne, linde*), Goth. *(af-)linnan*:—OTeut. **linnan* (?:—**linw-*), cogn. w. ON. *lin-r* soft, yielding, OE. *līðe* (:—**linþjo-*) gentle: see LITHE *a.*
The Sc. forms, *lein, leen, lean*, seem to be due to association with *leend*, LEND *v.*[2]]
1. *intr.* To cease, leave off; desist *from* (something; in OE. const. *dative*); also const. *to* with *inf.* Of the wind: To drop, lull. Also as a command, 'Leave off!' 'Let go!'
Beowulf 1478 Gif ic æt þearfe þinre scolde aldre linnan. *c* **1175** *Lamb. Hom.* 67 For ure fond nefre ne linnen for to fonden us mid sunnen. *a* **1225** *Leg. Kath.* 1717 Þe neauer ne linneð nowðer ne lesseð, ah leaseð aa mare. *a* **1300** *K. Horn* 354 Rymenhild ȝef he cuþe Gan lynne wiþ hire Muþe. *c* **1320** *Sir Tristr.* 38 Þat never þai no lan Þe pouer to wirche wo. **1539** CRANMER *Pref. to Bible*, Which thyng [i.e. reading the Bible at home] also I neuer lynne to beate into the eares of them that bene my famyliers. **1559** *Mirr. Mag.*, *Clifford* i, Couer fire, and it wil neuer linne. **1560** in Nichols *Progr. Q. Eliz.* III. 473 My lippes shall never lenne To power thye prayses to my penne. **1590** GREENE *Mourn. Garm.* (1616) 63 All things did from their weary labour linne. **1601** HOLLAND *Pliny* I. 315 If one pluck off the wings from a drone, and put him again within the hiue, he will neuer lin vntill he haue done the like by all the rest of the same kind. **1625** B. JONSON *Staple of N.* IV. Intermeane (1631) 62 Set a beggar on horse-backe, hee'll neuer linne till hee be a gallop. **1644** Z. BOYD *Gard. Zion* 26 (Jam.) For th' uncle and the nephew never lin, Till out of Canaan they have chac't them clean. **1652** C. B. STAPYLTON *Herodian* II. 85 On both sides to Assayle they never lin. **1693** R. LYDE *Acc. Retaking a Ship* 23 At two in the Afternoon, the wind was at N.N.W. and Lynn'd a little. *Ibid.* 25, I bore away..thinking to go in over the Bar in the Morning tide, but by five the Wind Lin'd. **1697** W. CLELAND *Poems* 96 (Jam.) Pareing time, and all the year, Is one to them, they never lein [*rime* keen]. [**1710** SWIFT *Jrnl. to Stella* 31 Dec., When the year with MD 'gins, It without MD never lins. (These Proverbs have always old words in them; *lins* is leaves off.)] **1725** RAMSAY *Gentle Sheph.* IV. i. (1728), Let gang your Grips, fy, Madge!—howt, Bauldy leen [*rime* seen].
¶**b.** Misused for: To fail, omit.
c **1720** PRIOR *Wand. Pilgr.* 20 They seldom miss to bake and brew, Or lin to break their fast.
2. *trans.* To cease from, leave off, discontinue.
a **1300** *K. Horn* 319 Þi tale nu þu lynne, For Horn nis noȝt her-inne. *c* **1485** *Digby Myst.* (1882) III. 558 Þe lavdabyll lyfe of lecherry let hur neuer lynne. **1548** PATTEN *Exped. Scot.* Livb, Our Northern prikkers..sum hoopynge, sum whistelyng.. never linde these troublous..noyses all yͤ night long. **1610** *Cruel Shrew* 9 in *Roxb. Ball.* (1871) I. 95 She never linnes her bauling Her tongue it is so loud.
b. with vbl. sb. as obj., or *intr.* with pr. pple. as complement.
13.. *Guy Warw.* (A.) 5950 His leman lan neuer wepeing Aniȝt, when sche alon was. **1549** COVERDALE, etc. *Erasm. Par. Tim.* 5, I was so cruell a persecutour, that I coulde neuer lynne doynge of vyolence. **1579-80** NORTH *Plutarch, Aristides* (1595) 358 He [a horse] neuer lin flinging till he cast his maister on the ground. **1607** MIDDLETON *Your Five Gallants* I. i. 292 A ruby that ne'er lins blushing for the party that pawned it. **1643** MILTON *Divorce* I. Pref., We should never lin hammering out of our own hearts, as it were out of a flint, the..sparkles of new misery to ourselves.

lin, obs. inf., pres. pl., and pa. pple. of LIE *v.*[1]

lin, obs. variant of LINE *sb.*[1], LINN, waterfall.

linable, lineable ('laɪnəb(ə)l), *a.* [f. LINE *sb.*[2] or *v.*[2] + -ABLE.] Ranged in a straight line.
1698 in Picton *L'pool Munic. Rec.* (1883) I. 289 Buildings running linable from that and an old howse. **1700** *Ibid.* 290 Yͤ building some time since intended for a Chapell and linable to yͤ southward. **1708** *Ibid.* (1886) II. 60 That a bridge be made..lineable with the new intended street. **1737** BRACKEN *Farriery Impr.* (1757) II. 75 His Feet.. should be carried lineable. **1890** *Pall Mall G.* 24 Nov. 7/2 By opening a valve the slide..becomes lineable with the barrel of the gun.

linac ('lɪnæk). *Physics.* [f. *lin*ear *ac*celerator.] A linear (i.e. straight) particle accelerator.
1950 *Amer. Jrnl. Physics* XVIII. 126/1 At Berkeley, L. W. Alvarez was the chief supporter of the 'linac', and he supervised the construction of the present 40-ft. machine. **1966** *New Scientist* 17 Nov. 359/2 Above the underground linac are two Van der Graaff accelerators. **1969** *Sci. Jrnl.* Jan. 55/1 Although many linear radio-frequency accelerators (called linacs) have been built, the more usual construction is circular so that the same field element can be used many times in the complete acceleration cycle.

linage ('laɪnɪdʒ). Also **lineage**. [f. LINE *sb.*[2] + -AGE.] **a.** Position (of figures) in line. **b.** Quantity of printed or written matter estimated in number of lines. **c.** Payment according to the number of lines; also, the charge made (by a newspaper, etc.) according to the number of lines occupied by an advertisement, etc.
a. **1883** in *Are we to read backwards?* 39 The modern Arabic figures—uniform in linage—were more legible than the 'old style' figures.
b. **1884** *Nonconf. & Indep.* 9 May 446/1 Fair progress was made, though no great amount of lineage of the Bill was disposed of.
c. **1888** *Globe* 27 Oct. 6/5 An editor..offered him [Mr. Swinburne] 'lineage' for a poem. **1898** *Kendal Mercury* 7 Jan. 5/6 One of the terms of the engagement was that he [a reporter] was to have half the 'lineage'. **1961** in WEBSTER. **1968** *Listener* 20 June 818/2 (Advt.), Linage 6s. 6d. a line. **1971** *Timber Trades Jrnl.* 14 Aug. 61 Linage. Minimum 20 words. 10p per word.

linage, obs. form of LINEAGE.

linaloa, -aloe: see LIGN-ALOES.

linalool (lɪ'næləʊʊl). *Chem.* [a. G. *linalool* (F. W. Semmler 1891, in *Ber. d. Deut. Chem. Ges.* XXIV. 207), f. G. *linalo(ëol* linaloe oil + *-ol* -OL.] An optically active tertiary alcohol, $(CH_3)_2C{:}CH{\cdot}CH_2{\cdot}CH_2{\cdot}C(CH_3)OH{\cdot}CH{:}CH_2$, found in linaloe oil and used in perfumery: the *d*-isomer is CORIANDROL and the *l*-isomer also occurs in the oils of rose, bergamot, lavender, and thyme.
1891 *Jrnl. Chem. Soc.* LX. I. 540 Linaloe oil appears to be a mixture of several compounds... The principal constituent which is termed linaloöl, boils at about 195–190° [*sic*]. **1922** *Jrnl. Amer. Chem. Soc.* XLIV. 2966 The odorous constituents of the peach consist chiefly of esters of the aliphatic terpene alcohol linalool. **1951** P. Z. BEDOUKIAN *Perfumery Synthetics & Isolates* 292 Commercial linalool is obtained from several sources, principally from oil of bois de rose, linaloe, shiu and coriander... Linalool occurs to the extent of about 80 per cent in the first two oils. **1968** *Times* 5 Nov. 17/2 Linalool and linalyl isobutyrate..are both fragrant oils found in coriander and lavender.
Hence **'linalyl**, the radical $C_{10}H_{17}$—present in ethers and esters of linalool.
1900 *Jrnl. Chem. Soc.* LXXVIII. II. 101 Analyses of two samples of essence of bergamot..show that during the process of ripening..the linalyl acetate increases from 33·8 to 37·3 per cent. **1964** *Economist* 26 Dec. 1448/1 Linalyl acetate goes into colognes to provide the lavender notes.

linamarin (lɪnə'mærɪn). *Chem.* [a. G. *linamarin* (Jorissen & Hairs 1891, in *Pharmaceut. Post* XXIV. 659), f. L. *līn-um* flax + *amār-us* bitter + -IN[1].] A bitter crystalline compound, $C_{10}H_{17}NO_6$, which occurs in flax; the glucoside of acetone cyanohydrin.
1892 *Jrnl. Chem. Soc.* LXII. I. 502 Linamarin forms groups of colourless needles having a cool and bitter taste. **1934** *Onderstepoort Jrnl. Vet. Sci. & Animal Industry* III. 116 The toxic substance present in the plant *Dimorphotheca cuneata* has been isolated and identified as the cyanogenetic glucoside 'linamarin'. **1964** D. D. DAVIES et al. *Plant Biochem.* x. 385 Feeding experiments have shown that the synthesis of the cyanogenetic glucosides, lotaustralin and linamarin, in *Trifolium repens* is related to the metabolism of isoleucine and valine. **1973** *Daily Colonist* (Victoria, B.C.) 18 July 18/4 Cassava's toxicity takes on a new importance. This toxicity is caused by a substance called linamarin.. together with small amounts of a closely related substance, lotaustralin.

†**'linament.** *Surg. Obs.* [ad. L. *līnāment-um*, f. *līnum* flax.] Lint rolled into a tent for surgical use.
1623 in COCKERAM. **1721** in BAILEY. Hence in mod. Dicts.

‖**linaria** (laɪ'nɛərɪə). *Bot.* Pl. **-as**. [mod.L., f. *līnum* flax.] Toad-flax (*Linaria vulgaris*).
1579 LANGHAM *Gard. Health* (1633) 376 Linaria: wilde flaxe, or tode flaxe. **1741** *Compl. Fam.-Piece* II. iii. 367 Double Violets yet remain, Linaria's. **1758** MRS. DELANY in *Life & Corr.* (1861) III. 509 A little yellow and white flower we found, like linaria.

linarite ('laɪnəraɪt). *Min.* [Named by Glocker, 1837, from *Linares*, Spain, where it is alleged to be found.] Sulphate of lead and copper, found in brilliant blue crystals.
1844 ALGER *Phillips' Min.* 552. **1852** BROOKE & MILLER *Min.* 554 *Linarite.* Cupreous sulphate of lead. **1868** DANA *Min.* (ed. 5) 664 Linarite occurs altered to cerussite.

†**'linary.** *Obs.* In 6 lynary, linari. [Anglicized form of LINARIA.] Toad-flax.
1548 TURNER *Names of Herbes* 58 If it [Osyris] haue no name it maye be called in englishe Lynary or todes flax. **1562** —— *Herbal* II. 93 Pinespourge hathe much milck which linari lacketh in hyr lefe.

linative, corruption of LENITIVE.
1601 *M. Magd. Lament.* Concl. 139 in *Fuller Worthies' Miscell.* (1871) II, Thy linative applide, did ease my paine.

lince, dial. f. LINCH; obs. f. LYNX.

lincean, linceus: see LYNCEAN, -EOUS.

lince(y), obs. variants of LINSEY.

linch (lɪnʃ), *sb.*[1] *Obs.* exc. in *Comb.* Forms: α. 1 lynis, 4 lins, 5 lynce, 4, 8-9 *dial.* lince. β. 6 linche, 9 linch. [OE. *lynis* masc. = OS. *lunisa* fem. (Du. *luns, lens*, late MHG. *luns, lunse*, mod.G. *lünse*). A shorter form *lin* (? OE. **lyne*:—**luni-*) corresponding to OHG. *lun* fem., mod.G. dial. *lunn, lon*, appears in LIN-NAIL and LINPIN.]
†**1.** = LINCH-PIN. *Obs.*
a **700** *Epinal Gloss.* 8 Axedones, lynisas. *c* **1000** *Ags. Voc.* in Wr.-Wülcker 267/29 *Axedo*, lynis. *c* **1315** SHOREHAM iv. 223 (E.E.T.S.) Þer-fore me makeþ prynses þe host to gouerni, And ase whewelen þe linses To-gadere heldeþ hy. **1497** *Naval Acc. Hen. VII* (1896) 84 Boltes forlokkes kayes lynces and a taile pynne for the said Curtowe.
†**b.** *Naut* ? A belaying-pin. *Obs.*
1549 *Compl. Scot.* vi. 41 Haile the linche and the scheitis.
2. *Comb.*: †**linch-box**, ? = *axle-box*; **linch-clout** (see quot.); **linch-drawer** *dial.*, a tool for drawing out linch-pins; **linch-hoop**, 'a ring on the spindle of a carriage-axle, held in place by the linch-pin' (*Cent. Dict.*). Also LINCH-PIN.
1711 *Lond. Gaz.* No. 4935/4 One other sort with both Edges Cyphered off, commonly call'd the Lince-box. **1782** *Rees's Cycl.*, *Linch-clout*, in Artillery, the flat iron under the ends of the arms of an axle-tree to strengthen them, and diminish the friction of the wheels. **1892** *Auctioneer's Catal. Farm Sale* (*Kent*), Lince drawer and grease pots.

linch (lɪnʃ), *sb.*[2] *dial.* Also 9 lynch, lince. [repr. OE. *hlinc*: see LINK *sb.*[1]] A rising ground; a ridge; a ledge, esp. one on the side of a chalk down; an unploughed strip serving as a boundary between fields.
1591 in *Wiltsh. Archæol., etc., Mag.* VI. (1860) 195 There leadinge westwarde..to a linche; there contynuinge the same linch to Maddington Waie. **1670** BLOUNT *Glossogr.* (ed. 3), *Linch* (Sax.), a Bank, Wall, or Causey between land and land, or Parish, and Parish, to distinguish the bounds. **1787** *Survey* in *N.W. Linc. Gloss.* s.v., The lands in the fields are called dales and the linches or green strips on each side are called marfurs or meerfurrows. **1797** MATON *West. Counties* II. 186 Those singular natural terraces..the linches or linchets, as they are called. **1883** SEEBOHM *Eng. Village Community* i. 5 A..peculiar feature of the open field system in hilly districts is the 'lynch'. *Ibid.* 6 These banks between the plough-made terraces are generally called lynches, or linces. **1895** *Edin. Rev.* Apr. 350 'Linches' naturally formed by the action of the plough on a hillside.

linch, *v.*[1] *Obs.* exc. *Sc. intr.* To limp.
1570 LEVINS *Manip.* 134/34 To linche, *claudicare.* **1825-80** in JAMIESON.

†**linch**, *v.*[2] *Obs.* [? Cf. LINK *v.*[2]] *intr.* ? To prance. Only in *ppl. a.*
1593 HOLLYBAND *Fr. Dict.*, s.v. *Coquelineux*, *Cheval Coquelineux*, a linching horse.

linch (lɪnʃ), *v.*[3] [f. LINCH *sb.*[1]] *trans.* To fasten with or as with a linch-pin.
1898 VISCOUNT DILLON in *Archæol. Jrnl.* Ser. II. V. 313 The pasguard is also linched on a pin standing out of the elbow-piece.

linch, variant of LINGE *dial.*, to beat.

linchet: var. of LYNCHET.

'linch-pin. Also 4 lyns-, 7–9 lince, lins(e, 9 (*doubtfully genuine*) link-. See also LINPIN. [f. LINCH *sb.*[1] + PIN.] A pin passed through the end of an axle-tree to keep the wheel in its place.

1376–7 *Compotus Roll Hyde Manor* (*MS. Deeds Westmr. Abbey*), In ij camellis ferri vocatis lynspins emptis pro carectis iiij[d]. **1627** CAPT. SMITH *Seaman's Gram.* xiv. 65 The pins at the ends of the Axeltree is called Linch pins. **1682** *Providence Rec.* (1894) VI. 93 Jn ye Parlor 3 Cart boxes, i lince pinn & a washer 00-01-00. **1696** PHILLIPS, *Lins-pin.* See *Linch-pin.* **1760–72** H. BROOKE *Fool of Qual.* (1809) II. 5 One of the linch-pins that kept the wheel on the axletree. **1780** COWPER *Progr. Err.* 441 If the rogue.. Left out his linchpin, or forgot his tar. **1847** HALLIWELL, *Link-pins.* Linch-pins are called also *link-pins* and *lin-pins* in the provinces. **1857** HUGHES *Tom Brown* I. vi. (ed. 3) 137 There was the good old custom of taking the linchpins out of the farmers' and bagmen's gigs at the fairs. **1860** EMERSON *Cond. Life Consid.* Wks. (Bohn) II. 418 But who dares draw out the linchpin from the wagon-wheel.

Hence **linch-pinned** *a.*, having linch-pins.

1893 H. J. MOULE *Old Dorset* 109 Rough little cars, with wheels loosely linch-pinned.

lincious, linck, obs. ff. LYNCEOUS, LINK.

† **'lincloth.** *Obs.* [f. LINE *sb.*[1] + CLOTH; the vowel of the first element underwent the shortening usual in compounds.

In the first quot. however *linne* seems to represent the accus. of LINEN *a.*]

a. Linen cloth; a piece of the same. **b.** *pl.* Sheets for a bed.

c **1290** *S. Eng. Leg.* I. 171/2261 Fastinge for to make, And .. Linne cloth and schurte of selk for is sunnes forsake. **1340** *Ayenb.* 178 Vor to zeche þe more grace of clennesse, ase þet line cloþ þet is y-huyted be ofte wessinge. *a* **1400–50** *Alexander* 140 And þar him eft clethis, All his liche in lyn claþe. *c* **1450** *Douce MS.* 55 (Bodl.) xxix, Ley hem in a feyre lyncloth. **1506** *Inv.* in *Paston Lett.* III. 408 Item, ij. payre of lyncloys viij*d.* *Ibid.*, Item, ij. schertis and a quarter of lynclothe ijs. vj*d.* *Ibid.* 409 Item, a stomaker of lenclothe viij*d.* *Ibid.* 410 Item, a yerd of lynclothe viij*d.* *Ibid.*, John Keduray, a payre of lynclothys. **1519** HORMAN *Vulg.* 242 Paper, or lyn clothe.. make fenestrals in stede of glasen wyndowes. **1581** *Acc. Bk. W. Wray* in *Antiquary* XXXII. 117, i pece of harborow lynne clothe, *vs.* vj*d.* **1603** OWEN *Pembrokeshire* i. (1891) 5 Well serued of manye forraine Comodities.. as with Wynes,.. Iron Lincloth &c.

Lincoln[1] ('lɪŋkən). Also 6 **lyncolne, -cum, -kome, lincome,** 8 **linkome.** [The name of an English city, the county town of Lincolnshire.]

1. a. Used *attrib.* or *adj.* in the following: † **Lincoln farthing**, a hearth-tax payable at Lincoln; **Lincoln green**, a bright green stuff made at Lincoln; **Lincoln imp**, a grotesque carving in Lincoln cathedral; a door-knocker, ornament, or trinket modelled on this; also *attrib.*; **Lincoln Longwool**, a sheep of the breed so called, characterized by its large size and long fleece; **Lincoln Red**, an animal belonging to a breed of red shorthorn cattle so called, used as producers of both milk and beef; † **Lincoln say**, a say or fine serge made at Lincoln; † **Lincoln twine**, (*a*) a twine or thread made at Lincoln; (*b*) a material woven from this; **Lincoln wool**, wool from a Lincoln Longwool.

1444 *Bp. Alnwick's Reg.* in Wordsw. *Lincoln Stat.* II. (1897) 487 Commissio ad leuand' le smoke ffardyngis alias dict' *Lincoln farthinges. *c* **1510** *Gest R. Hode* ccccxxii. in Child *Ballads* III. 77 Whan they were clothed in *Lyncolne grene, They keste away theyr graye. **1596** SPENSER *F.Q.* VI. ii. 5 All in a woodman's jacket he was clad Of Lincolne green. *a* **1845** HOOD *Forge* I. xiii, With little jackets.. Of Lincoln green. **1926–7** *Army & Navy Stores Catal.* 156/3 Bedroom door knockers.. *Lincoln Imp, 3¼ in., 1/6. **1941** E. BOWEN *Look at Roses* 245 They were mementoes—photos.. a Lincoln Imp, a merry-thought pen-wiper. **1967** *Listener* 13 July 48/3 Lincoln Cathedral has its world famous devil—the Lincoln imp. **1894** *CGA Catal.* 46/1 Sheep. *Lincoln Long Wool Shearling Rams, bred by owner; 1st and 2nd, £10. **1919** W. C. COFFEY *Productive Sheep Husbandry* xix. 163 Breeders in England organized the Lincoln Long-wool Sheep Breeders' Association in 1892. **1972** *Country Life* 16 Mar. 606/2 Lincoln Longwool and some of the white-faced breeds are used for crossing. **1903** *Farmer & Stockbreeder* 20 July 1195/3 The *Lincoln Red is a profitable farmer's beast, growing to great weight. **1966** *Guardian* 13 July 18/1 Cockerington Earl.. won the supreme championship of the Lincoln Red cattle. Lincoln Reds are the heftiest of the beef cattle. **1974** *Country Life* 17 Jan. 65/3 The stocky, sturdy, thick-coated Lincoln reds... Lincoln red cattle are.. most attractive animals. **1310–11** *Durham Acc. Rolls* (Surtees) 506 In xvij ulnis de *Lincolnesaye empt. pro Priore et sociis suis, xliijs. j*d.* **1566** in Hay Fleming *Mary Q. of Scots* (1897) 506 Item of *lyncum tuyne to schew the Quens curges tua unce. **1724** RAMSAY *Tea-t. Misc.* (1733) II. 183 A sark made of the linkome twine. **1930** L. G. D. ACLAND *Early Canterbury Runs* vii. 177 They cut over twelve hundred bales of *Lincoln wool.

† **b.** Short for *Lincoln green.*

a **1568** *Christis Kirke Gr.* 14 Thair kirtillis wer of lynkome licht.

2. *ellipt.* as *sb.* in *pl.* A variety of sheep originally bred in Lincolnshire.

1837 YOUATT *Sheep* viii. 332 The Lincolns were decidedly inferior—they were fen sheep. **1886** C. SCOTT *Sheep-Farming* 155 Lincolns made some good figures. **1897** *Trans. Highl. & Agric. Soc.* 61 The Teeswaters themselves were descended from the same stock as the Lincolns.

Lincoln[2] ('lɪŋkən). Name of Abraham *Lincoln* (1809–65), sixteenth President of the U.S., in **Lincoln rocker**, a type of rocking-chair with straight upholstered back and seat and open arms, popular in the mid-19th c.

1952 J. GLOAG *Short Dict. Furnit.* 311 *Lincoln rocker*, a name occasionally used in the United States for a mid-19th century type of rocking chair. **1967** *Boston Sunday Herald* 26 Mar. I. 51/3 (Advt.), Grape carved Lincoln rocker.

Lincolnesque (lɪŋkə'nɛsk), *a.* [f. the name of Abraham *Lincoln* (1809–65), 16th president of the U.S. + -ESQUE.] Resembling or having the qualities of Abraham Lincoln. So **Lincolnian** (lɪŋ'kəʊnɪən), *a.*

1910 H. P. WILLIS *Stephen A. Douglas* xiii. 283 A characteristic Lincolnian anecdote which the speaker applied to the repetition of the 'state fraud' of the Springfield resolutions. **1923** *Public Opinion* 15 June 565/3 That is Lincolnesque in its homeliness. **1962** E. AMES *Daughter of House* (1963) I. i. 30 The two long Lincolnesque furrows of the cheeks. **1963** *Economist* 20 July 257/2 The [Republican] party's Lincolnian heritage. **1968** MRS. L. B. JOHNSON *White House Diary* 9 Apr. (1970) 659 The star of that day was Hector Legge, of Dublin, Ireland, 'Dean' of the traveling journalists, a towering figure.. with a Lincolnesque face.

Lincolniana (ˌlɪŋkənɪ'ɑːnə). [f. the name of Abraham *Lincoln* (see prec.) + -IANA.] Matter such as books, objects, and writings, relating to or characteristic of Abraham Lincoln.

1921 *Double-Dealer* Feb. 67/1 Another notable essay in Lincolniana appears with the imprint of Walter M. Hill of Chicago—'The Assassination of Lincoln' by E. W. Coggeshall. **1932** *N. & Q.* 19 Nov. 366/2 A considerable amount of hitherto unprinted Lincolniana. **1949** *Jrnl. Illinois State Hist. Soc.* June 137 The volume is one of the few in the vast area of Lincolniana that influenced later research and publications. **1959** *Listener* 19 Feb. 326/1 That vast body of ephemeral Lincolniana.

Lincolnshire ('lɪŋkənʃə(r)). The name of a county on the east coast of England, used *attrib.* in **Lincolnshire Curly-Coat(ed)**, a pig of the extinct breed so called; **Lincolnshire limestone**, a bed of oolitic limestone of Upper Jurassic (Bajocian) age, extensively developed in Lincolnshire and adjoining counties; **Lincolnshire Longwool** = *Lincoln Longwool*; **Lincolnshire Red** = *Lincoln Red.*

[**1847** H. D. RICHARDSON *Pigs* iii. 36 The old Lincolnshire breed was light coloured, or even white, with, in most specimens, a curly and woolly coat.] **1917** W. POWELL-OWEN *Pig-Keeping* xi. 130 Lincoln Curly Coated. This Eastern counties breed is.. most useful for crossing purposes. **1921** H. A. DAY *Pig-Keeping* 13 The Lincolnshire Curly-Coated. I see no reason why this breed should not be given a trial in districts where it is seldom met. **1972** *Country Life* 16 Mar. 606/2 Oxford Sandy and Black.. are only one of five breeds of pigs that have become extinct, the others being the Cumberland, the Dorset Gold Tip, the Lincolnshire Curly Coat and the Yorkshire Blue and White. **1873** *Q. Jrnl. Geol. Soc.* XXIX. 226 The main feature of my Second Part will be the description and consideration of a series of beds grouped by Mr. Judd under the name of the 'Lincolnshire Limestone'. *Ibid.* 284 A few words as to the extent of the area occupied by the Lincolnshire Limestone. It ranges through the whole of the county of Lincoln, stretching into South Yorkshire on the north, and through Rutland into Northamptonshire on the south. **1969** BENNISON & WRIGHT *Geol. Hist. Brit. Isles* xiii. 301 The latter [*sc.* Collyweston Slate] forms a transition to the Lincolnshire Limestone which, appearing in Northamptonshire, thickens northwards to form the conspicuous west-facing escarpment on which Lincoln Cathedral stands. **1874** R. O. PRINGLE *Live-Stock of Farm* vii. 251 The old Lincolnshire long-wools were ungainly animals. **1897** W. HOUSMAN *Cattle* iii. 96 The excellence and purity of the Lincolnshire Red Shorthorn breed.

lincomycin (lɪŋkəʊ'maɪsɪn). *Pharm.* [f. mod.L. *linco(lnensis*, specific epithet (see def.) + -MYCIN.] An antibiotic, $C_{18}H_{34}N_2O_6S$, produced by cultures of the bacterium *Streptomyces lincolnensis* var. *lincolnensis* and given orally or by injection (usu. as the hydrate of the hydrochloride) to combat various Gram-positive bacteria, esp. staphylococci and streptococci.

1963 *Bacteriol. Proc. 1963* 94/1 Lincomycin, developed by The Upjohn Co., is a new antibiotic, chemically distinct from others now in use. **1966** *Practitioner* July 90 Lincomycin hydrochloride should prove useful in general practice against the common gram-positive infections. **1969** *New Scientist* 8 May 277/1 The group A haemolytic streptococci.. are becoming increasingly resistant to tetracycline, erythromycin, and lincomycin. **1973** *Brit. Pharmacopœia 1973* 266/2 Lincomycin Hydrochloride is the monohydrate of the hydrochloride of methyl 6,8-dideoxy-6-(1-methyl-4-propyl-2-pyrrolidinecarboxamido)-1-thio-D-*erythro*-D-*galacto*-octapyranoside. **1975** *Daily Colonist* (Victoria, B.C.) 31 Jan. 3/6 Lee Smith said.. that United States reports on the drugs clindamycin and lincomycin.. were 'wildly exaggerated' in the news media.

lincrusta (lɪn'krʌstə). Also **Lincrusta.** [f. L. *līnum* flax + *crusta* rind, bark: after LINOLEUM.] A special type of thick embossed wall-paper.

1882 *Encycl. Brit.* XIV. 676/2 Mr. Walton, the original patentee of linoleum, has adapted a preparation of oxidized oil and cork or other thickening material embossed with patterns for wall decorations under the name of 'Lincrusta Walton'. **1891** *Jrnl. Soc. Chem. Industry* X. 150/2 Improvements in the Manufacture of Linoleum, Lincrusta, Cere-Cloth, and the like. **1921** *Spectator* 9 Apr. 464/1 'Lincrusta' wears so well that it seemed a sin to take it off. **1923** U. L. SILBERRAD *Lett. J. Armiter* i. 29 Semi-detached house, lincrusta dadoes, basement kitchen—it would suit him. **1939** *Archit. Rev.* LXXXVI. 258 *Lincrusta.* This is a plastic material from which a relief ornament is pressed. **1963** *Punch* 25 Sept. 457/1 He rolled his eyes.. towards the lincrusta ceiling. **1973** M. BENCE-JONES *Palaces of Raj* viii. 142 Lord Curzon replaced some of the Lincrusta with damask.

lincture ('lɪŋktjʊə(r)). [ad. L. type **linctūra*, f. *lingĕre* to lick: see -URE.] = next.

1621 BURTON *Anat. Mel.* II. iv. I. v. (1624) 306 Confection, Treacle,.. Eclegmes or Linctures. **1818** in TODD. **1888** in *Syd. Soc. Lex.*

linctus ('lɪŋktəs). Pl. **linctuses.** [a. L. *linctus* a licking, f. *lingĕre* to lick.] A medicine to be licked up with the tongue.

1681 tr. *Willis' Rem. Med. Wks.* Vocab., Linctus, a medicine that is to be lick'd with the tongue. **1704** F. FULLER *Med. Gymn.* (1718) 78 The Lozenge and Linctus are in every Bodies hand. **1741** *Compl. Fam.-Piece* I. i. 2 Balsams, Linctus's, Pectorals. **1749** SHORT *Hist. Air*, etc. I. 222 Slippery, thickening, Linctuses were found of most Service. **1812** CRABBE *Flirtation* Wks. 1834 V. 276 I've heard of pangs that tender folks endure But not that linctuses and blisters cure.

† **lind.** *Obs.* Forms: α. 1 **lind, linde,** 3–5 **linde,** 3–6 **lynde,** (5 **lyynde**), 5–6 **lynd,** 3– **lind.** β. 6–8 **lyne, line.** See also LINN[2]. [OE. *lind* str. fem. and *linde* wk. fem. (Du. *linde*), OHG. *linda, linta* (MHG. *linde, linte*, G. *linde*), ON. (Sw. and Da.) *lind*:—OTeut. **lendā*, perh.:—pre-Teut. **lentā*, cogn. w. WAryan **lntā*, represented by Gr. ἐλάτη silver fir.]

1. The lime or linden (*Tilia Europæa*). In ME. poetry often used for a tree of any kind, esp. in phr. ***under*** (***the***) ***lind.***

α. *a* **700** *Epinal Gloss.* 1004 *Tilia*, lind. **972** in Bond *Facs. Charters Brit. Mus.* (1877) III. xxx, Of steapan leahe in ða greatan lindan. *a* **1250** *Owl & Night.* 1750 þe wrenne sat in hore lynde. *a* **1310** in Wright *Lyric P.* xiv. 45 In May hit murgeth when hit dawes,.. ant lef is lyght on lynde. *c* **1314** *Guy Warw.* 1205 (A.) And to pleyn vnder þe linde, þe hert to chacen and þe hinde. *c* **1320** *Sir Tristr.* 513 þe king.. teld him vnder linde þe best, hou it was boun And brouȝt. **1377** LANGL. *P. Pl.* B. I. 154 Was neuere leef vpon lynde liȝter ther-after. *c* **1386** CHAUCER *Clerk's T.* 1155 Be ay of chere as light as leef on linde. ? *a* **1400** *Morte Arth.* 454 Lugge þi-selfe undyre lynde, as þe leefe thynkes. *c* **1460** *Play Sacram.* 389 Iason as Ientylle as euer was the lynde. **1535** STEWART *Cron. Scot.* II. 525 Syne vp and doun, als lycht as leif of lynd. **1546** PHAER *Bk. Childr.* (1553) R v a, Ye may still a water, of the floures of lind, it is a tree called in latin tilia. **1796** MORSE *Amer. Geog.* I. 538 Elms, and linds are not here so stately as further north.

β. *c* **1510** *Lytell Geste R. Hode* cccxcviii. in Child *Ballads* III. 75 On euery syde a rose-garlonde They shot vnder the lyne. [*Cf.* ccclxxiv, vnder the lynde.] **1587** HARRISON *England* II. xxii. (1877) I. 342 We haue verie great plentie.. of these [trees].. so are we not without the chesnut, the line [etc.]. **1601** HOLLAND *Pliny* I. 541 As for the Line or Linden tree. **16..** *R. Hood & Guy of Gisbourne* xxii. in Child *Ballads* III. 92 How these two yeomen together they mett, Vnder the leaues of lyne.

¶ **2.** ? Used erroneously for 'wood'.

a **1400** *Stockh. Med. MS.* ii. 572 in *Anglia* XVIII. 321 In an harys skyn do it bynde, And lete it so lyn in feld or lynde.

3. *attrib.*, as ***lind-grove, -tree***; **lind-coal,** charcoal made of the wood of the lime.

c **1450** *Voc.* in Wr.-Wülcker 569/34 *Calea*, a lyndtre. **14..** *MS. Soc. Antiq.* 101 lf. 76 (Halliw. s.v. *lyndecole*) Half an unce of lyndecole. **1577–87** HOLINSHED *Chron.* I. 53/2 Euerie euening he would write twelue tables, such as they vsed to make on the lind tree. **1610** SHAKS. *Temp.* v. i. 12 All prisoners Sir In the Line-grove which weather-fends your Cell. **1621** G. SANDYS *Ovid's Met.* VIII. (1632) 279 On Phrygian hills there growes An Oke by a Line-tree.

Lindabrides (lɪn'dæbrɪdiːz). *arch.* The name of a lady in the romance 'Mirror of Knighthood,' used allusively for: A lady-love, a mistress.

[**1585** R. P. tr. *Mirr. Knighthd.* I. II. xxi. (1599) 75 Beeing with childe by the Emperour [Alicandro].. she was delyuered at one birth of a sonne and a daughter,.. the Damsell is called Lindabrides, and the Knight Meridian.] **1599** B. JONSON *Cynthia's Rev.* III. iii, *Amo.* Lindabrides! *Aso.* I, sir, the Emperour Alicandroes daughter. **1633** ROWLEY *Match at Midnight* II. E.] **1640** SHIRLEY *Love's Cruelty* II. i, One that I would love and honour above all, my lady-paramount and superintendent Lindabrides. **1663** KILLIGREW *Parson's Wedd.* IV. i, Such a woman is my wife, and no Lindabrides. **1670** *Moral State Eng.* 29 When he is laid to sleep, his Landabrides and his dear friend divide the spoil. **1821** SCOTT *Kenilw.* ii, I will visit his Lindabrides, by Saint George, be he willing or no.

lindackerite (lɪn'dækəraɪt). *Min.* [Named by Haidinger, 1853, after J. *Lindacker*, who first analysed it.] Hydrous sulph-arsenate of copper and nickel, found in oblong green crystals.

1857 C. U. SHEPARD *Min.* (ed. 3) II. 427 Lindackerite [occurs].. in oblong, rhombohedral tables. **1868** DANA *Min.*

(ed. 5) 590 Lindackerite..on charcoal gives alliaceous fumes.

lindane ('lɪndeɪn). [f. the name of Teunis van der *Lind*en (b. 1884), Dutch chemist, who investigated the isomers of benzene hexachloride + *-ane* (perh. after CHLORDANE).] The gamma isomer of benzene hexachloride, $C_6H_6Cl_6$, used as an insecticide; it is a colourless crystalline compound that is toxic to mammals but relatively harmless to plant life, and is used in the form of dusts, sprays, and aerosols.

1949 *Lindane* (Interdepartmental Comm. Pest Control, Bureau Entomol. & Plant Quarantine, U.S. Dept. Agric.) 3 The coined name, 'Lindane', is established for the gamma isomer of the chemical 1,2,3,4,5,6-hexachloro-cyclohexane of a purity not less than 99 percent. **1956** *Nature* 25 Feb. 367/1 In solid form 'Dieldrin' and 'Lindane' were the most effective toxicants against the larvæ of *Aedes aegypti* and *Culex fatigans*. **1961** *New Scientist* 6 July 26/3 A new liquid seed dressing..is based on lindane (a very pure form of gamma-BHC), which is considered to be the insecticide least hazardous to wild life. **1970** *Nature* 31 Oct. 403/2 Fresh and rain water in Britain contains small but not insignificant amounts of the chief persistent organochlorine pesticides, DDT, lindane and dieldrin.

Linde ('lɪndə). The name of Carl P. G. R. von *Linde* (1842–1934), German physicist, used *attrib.* to designate a process for liquefying gases by means of repeated cycles of compression, cooling, and expansion, used in the extraction of nitrogen and oxygen from air by exploiting the difference in their boiling points.

1902 *Encycl. Brit.* XXX. 283/2 The efficiency of the Linde process is small, but it is easily conducted and only requires plenty of cheap power. **1928** J. K. ROBERTS *Heat & Thermodynamics* v. 111 Much less preliminary cooling is necessary to liquefy a gas by the Linde method than by the Cascade process. **1937** M. W. ZEMANSKY *Heat & Thermodynamics* xiv. 251 In the Linde process for the production of liquid air, the initial temperature, initial pressure and final pressure are chosen so that, after passing through a throttling valve, a drop in temperature is produced. **1968** B. J. HAZZARD tr. *Asinger's Paraffins* ii. 105 After the removal of carbon dioxide and benzene by washing, coke-oven gas is liquefied by the Linde process, all the constituents except the hydrogen and some nitrogen condensing.

linden ('lɪndən), *sb.* [LINDEN *a.* used subst.

The recent currency of the word is prob. due to its use in translations of German romance, as an adoption of G. *linden* pl. of *linde*, or as the first element in the comb. *lindenbaum* = 'linden-tree'.]

1. The lime-tree (see LIME *sb.*³).

1577 B. GOOGE *Heresbach's Husb.* II. 106 b, The Lynden [*printed* Lynder], in Greeke φιλλυρία, and so in Italian, in Spanish Latera, in Dutch Lynden. **1578** LYTE *Dodoens* VI. lxxiii. 754 The broth of the leaves of Lynden sodde in water cureth the noughtie ulcers and blisters of the mouthes of young children. *a* **1785** T. POTTER *Moralist* II. 20 A majestic Linden reared its towering branches over the mouldering battlements. **1814** BYRON *Lara* II. xxv, Herself would..seat her down upon some linden's root. **1853** M. ARNOLD *Scholar-Gipsy* iii, Air-swept lindens yield Their scent. **1889** COOK in *Nature* 3 Oct. 559 When the linden was in bloom a single hive of bees would sometimes store up 15 lbs. of honey in the day.

2. *Antiq.* Used to render the OE. *lind*, shield of lime-tree wood.

1855 J. HEWITT *Anc. Armour* I. 78 The shields placed in the graves were the ordinary 'lindens', of which no part commonly remains but the metal-boss and handle.

3. *attrib.* and *Comb.*, as ***linden-tree***; ***linden-shaded*** adj.

a **1849** J. C. MANGAN *Poems* (1859) 102 The *linden shaded courtyard. **1579** LANGHAM *Gard. Health* (1633) 373 *Linden tree: for filthy sores of childrens mouthes. **1591** PERCIVALL *Sp. Dict.*, *Teja*, a linden tree. **1760** J. LEE *Introd. Bot.* App. 817 Linden-tree, *Tilia*. **1818** SCOTT *Battle of Sempach* 1 'Twas when among our linden-trees The bees had housed in swarms.

†**'linden,** *a. Obs.* [OE. *linden*, f. *lind*: see LIND.] Made of the wood of the lime-tree.

a **1000** *Gnomic Verses* (Exeter MS.) 95 (Gr.) Scip sceal ʒenæʒled, scyld ʒebunden, leoht linden bord. *c* **1320** *Sir Tristr.* 2039 Bi water he sent adoun Liȝt linden spon.

linder ('lɪndə(r)). *Sc.* A woollen waistcoat or undershirt.

1768 A. ROSS in Whitelaw *Bk. Sc. Song* (1875) 360/2 He'll sell his jerkin for a groat His linder for another o't. **1841** *Fraser's Mag.* XXIV. 142 They wear waistcoats, or linders, reaching no farther down than the waistband of the petticoat. **1897** *Aberd. Weekly Free Press* 26 Feb. (E.D.D.), Charged with having..stolen..a linder.

lindgrenite ('lɪndgrənaɪt). *Min.* [f. the name of Waldemar *Lindgren* (1860–1939), U.S. geologist + -ITE¹.] A basic copper molybdate, $Cu_3(MoO_4)_2(OH)_2$, found as transparent, green, monoclinic, platy or tabular crystals.

1935 C. PALACHE in *Amer. Mineralogist* XX. 491/2 The author takes great pleasure in designating this well-defined mineral lindgrenite in honor of Professor Waldemar Lindgren. His great contributions to the knowledge of the ore deposits and their paragenesis makes it peculiarly fitting that his name should appear in the special literature of mineralogy. **1953** *Amer. Mineralogist* XXXVIII. 905 The physical and optical properties of the Idaho lindgrenite are virtually identical with those of the Chilean material. **1955** *Mineral. Mag.* XXX. 726 This occurrence of lindgrenite at Brandy Gill is perhaps one of the most interesting additions to the remarkable number of rare and unusual minerals..in the Caldbeck district.

lindiform ('lɪndɪfɔːm), *a. Zool.* [f. mod.L. *Lindi-a* + -FORM.] Resembling the genus *Lindia*, said of certain apodous insect larvæ (Webster 1890).

lindsayite ('lɪndzɪaɪt). *Min.* [f. the surname *Lindsay* + -ITE. Named by Nordenskiöld, 1843, but the reference has not been traced.] An altered variety of anorthite.

1850 *Amer. Jrnl. Sci.* IX. 411 Lepolite and Lindseyite. **1892** DANA *Min.* 339 Lindseyite..is a somewhat altered variety.

lindworm ('lɪndwɜːm). Also **lindorm.** [ad. Da. and Sw. *lindorm*. Cf. LINGWORM.] A monstrous and evil serpent, common in Scandinavian legend.

1814 H. WEBER *Illustrations of Northern Antiquities* 60 The terms worm, drake, dragon, and serpent, are indiscriminately applied to these monsters, as well as lind-drake and lind-worm; probably from their haunt being generally under a linden or lime tree. **1896** W. A. CRAIGIE *Scandinavian Folk-Lore* 439 The lindorm is a favourite monster in Swedish as well as Danish tradition. **1910** F. BOND *Wood Carvings Eng. Churches* I. 63 When a wyvern has no wings as at Limerick, he is, in heraldry, a lindworm. *Ibid.*, No rigid distinction can be made between the dragon, wyvern, and lindworm. **1971** BARBER & RICHES *Dict. Fabulous Beasts* 97 *Lindorm*, a snake-like creature, which devoured cattle and ate bodies... The lindworm is a heraldic dragon or wyvern without wings, presumably the same as the lindorm.

Lindy Hop ('lɪndɪ hɒp). Also **lindy-hop.** [f. *Lindy*, nickname of C. A. Lindbergh (1902–74), the American pilot who in 1927 was the first to make a solo non-stop transatlantic flight + HOP *sb.*² 2.] A Negro dance originating in Harlem (New York); also *attrib.* Also *ellipt.* **Lindy.** Hence **Lindy** *v. intr.*, to dance the Lindy Hop; **'lindyhopper,** one who dances the Lindy Hop.

1931 *Zit's Theatrical Newspaper* 2 May 11 The winners of the all-Harlem Lindy Hop contest..drew rounds of applause nightly. **1936** *Life* 14 Dec. 64 The Lindy Hop originated at the Savoy. **1946** MEZZROW & WOLFE *Really Blues* (1957) xvi. 286 We'd get five teams of lindyhoppers from the Savoy Ballroom. **1948** K. DAVIS *Human Soc.* 79 The late and unlamented dance step called the 'Lindy Hop' was a fad. **1951** [see JITTERBUG *sb.* 2]. **1959** *Sears, Roebuck Catal.* Spring & Summer 831/2 Betty White's Teen-Age Dance Book... Clear instructions for fox trot, lindy, mambo, cha cha, etc. **1969** *New Yorker* 15 Feb. 31/3 Their feet began to tap, and they tore into the Lindy. **1969** DISCH & SLADEK *Black Alice* ii. 19 No one could challenge his tango, but when he heard fast music his impulse was to lindy rather than to twist. **1970** G. GREER *Female Eunuch* 108 Here I am, a negro who cannot do the lindy-hop or sing the Blues! **1970** A. MILLER in A. Chapman *New Black Voices* (1972) 538 Few can ignore the effects of the cake walk, fox trot, lindy hop, the twist on the movement habits of people in the States. **1973** *Guardian* 7 Aug. 8/4 When I was a kid I would go and dance for the white folks. Do the splits and the Lindy Hop, and they would throw me pennies.

line (laɪn), *sb.*¹ Now chiefly *dial.* Forms: 1 **lín,** 4–5 **lynne,** 4–6 **lyn,** 4–7 **lyne,** 5–7, 8–9 *dial.* **lin,** 6–7 **linne,** 3– **line.** [OE. *lín* neut. = OS. *lîn* (Du. *lijn* in comb.), OHG. *lîn* (MHG. *lîn*, mod.G. *lein-* in comb.), ON. *lín* (Sw. *lin*), Goth. *lein*:—Com. Teut. type **lînom*, a. or cognate with L. *līnum* flax (whence F. *lin*), cognate with Gr. λίνον (ῐ), and perh. with λῑτί dat., λῖτα accus., linen cloth. The mod. dial. form *lin* (with the antecedent *lynne, linne*) is app. a back-formation from compounds like LINCLOTH, LINSEED.]

1. = FLAX. †**a.** The fibre of flax. *Obs.* exc. as in b.

In the 16–17th c. asbestos was often described as a kind of 'line' or flax (cf. LINEN B. 1 c, L. *linum indicum, linum fossile*).

c **975** *Rushw. Gosp.* Matt. xii. 20 Hread þæt waʒende ne to breceþ & lin smikende ne adwæscet. *c* **1300** *Havelok* 539 The bondes..weren of ful strong line. *c* **1400** MAUNDEV. (Roxb.) xi. 49 þat ressayued þe messangers of Israel..and feled þam in hir hous amang towe of lyne. *c* **1475** *Pict. Voc.* in Wr.-Wülcker 795/18 *Hoc asperum*, a stryke of lyne. **1548** ELYOT *Dict.*, *Asbestinum*, a kynde of lyne which can not be burned. *Ibid.*, *Linum*, lyne or flaxe. **1611** COTGR., *Lin*, line, flax. *Lin vif*, a Kind of Indian line, or linnen, which the fire purifies, but consumes not. **1659** C. HOOLE tr. *Comenius' Orbis Sensual.* (1672) 121 Line and Hemp, being rated in water and dried again, are braked with a wooden Brake.

b. In mod. technical use, flax of a fine and long staple, which has been separated by the hackle from the tow. Occasionally applied to the similar fibre of other plants.

1835 URE *Philos. Manuf.* 215 The heckled flax, called *line*, when freed from the *tow*, is carried away to be sorted. **1851** *Illustr. Catal. Gt. Exhib.* 198 China grass..half-bleached and full-bleached line from this grass. *Ibid.* 278 The long fibres called line, which remains in the hand of the heckler.

c. The plant itself.

c **1420** *Pallad. on Husb.* XII. 28 Now lyne and puls is sowe. *c* **1470** HENRYSON *Mor. Fab.* VIII. (*Preach. Swallow*) xxx, The lint rypit, the carle pullit the lyne. **1548** TURNER *Names of Herbes* 49 Linum is called in englishe Flax, lyne or lynte. **1603** HOLLAND *Plutarch's Mor.* 1289 The herbe Line.. furnisheth us wherewith to make a simple, plaine, and slender vestment. **1616** SURFL. & MARKH. *Country Farme* 37 In August he shall pull his Line and Hempe. **1839** STONEHOUSE *Axholme* 28 Fields of hemp are now no longer to be seen; but line or flax is still grown.

2. Flax spun or woven; linen thread or cloth. †Also, a napkin of linen; and in *pl.* linen vestments.

a **700** *Epinal Gl.* 634 *Manitergium*, liin [*a* **800** *Corpus Gl.* 1270 lin]. *c* **975** *Rushw. Gosp.* John xx. 6 Simon petrus.. ineode in ða byrʒenne & ʒesæh ða lin ʒisetedo. *c* **1200** *Trin. Coll. Hom.* 163 þe haued line sward, and hire winpel wit. *a* **1300** *Cursor M.* 11112 He..wered noþer wol ne line. **13..** *E.E. Allit. P.* A. 730 [He] solde alle his goud boþe wolen and lynne. *c* **1400** tr. *Secreta Secret.*, *Gov. Lordsh.* 82 A fair towaille of lyn. *c* **1420** *Liber Cocorum* (1862) 30 Fars hit thurghe a clothe of lyne. **1558** *Act 1 Eliz.* c. 17 §1 No person ..withe any Devise or Engyne made of Heere, Wooll, Lyne or Canvas..shall take and kyll..Spawne or Frye of Eeles, Salmon, Pyke or Pyckerell. **1591** SPENSER *Muiopot.* 364 Nor anie weauer, which his worke doth boast In dieper, in damaske, or in lyne. *c* **1611** CHAPMAN *Iliad* II. 459 Little he was, and euer wore a breastplate made of linne. **1631** *Vestry Bks.* (Surtees) 299 Ten yeardes of line for a sirptcloth. **1641** BEST *Farm. Bk.* (1857) 106 The kindes of linnes or huswife-cloath are brought aboute of peddlers. **1807** ROBINSON *Archæol. Græca* IV. iii. 342 Some of the thoraces were made of line, or hemp twisted into small cords, and set close together. **1868** ATKINSON *Cleveland Gloss.*, *Lin*, linen; the fabric made with the fibre of flax; in contradistinction to the plant itself, which is sounded Line.

†**b.** Phr. ***under line*** (occas. ***in line***), in one's clothes; used in ME. poetry as a mere expletive. Cf. *under gore* (see GORE *sb.*² 2). *Obs.*

a **1310** in Wright *Lyric P.* xiv. 46 Ah wolde lylie leor in lyn Y-here lovely lores myn. **13..** *Gaw. & Gr. Knt.* 1814 þat lufsum vnder lyne. *c* **1320** *Sir Tristr.* 1202 þe quene, Louesom vnder line. *c* **1400** *Rowland & O.* 846 He.. drissede hym in his worthy wede, þat lofesome vnder lyne.

†**3.** The seed of flax; LINSEED. *Obs.*

1545 RAYNOLD *Byrth Mankynde* 78 Take camomell and lyne of eche lyke much. **1558–68** WARDE tr. *Alexis' Secr.* 90 b, Take thre pounde of the Oyle of lyne. **1577** B. GOOGE *Heresbach's Husb.* (1586) 38 b, They call the seede Lin, and the plant Flaxe.

4. *attrib.* and *Comb.*, as (sense 1) † ***line beat*** (cf. BEAT *sb.*²), †***-beater***, †***-boll*** (cf. BOLL *sb.*¹ 3), ***-dresser***, †***-house***, ***-sorter***, ***-spinner***, ***-spreader***, ***stump***, ***tow***, ***-weaver***, †***-webber***, ***weft***, ***-wick***, ***work***, ***-yard***, ***yarn***; (sense 2) ***line bed***, ***clout***, †***-draper***, †***sock***, †***stock***, ***table-cloth***; †**line-finch**, ? a linnet (cf. *flax-finch*); **line-gout**, some plant which hinders flax in its growth; †**line-spurge**, a proposed name for *Euphorbia Esula*; †**line-strike**, a hank of flax.

1483 *Cath. Ang.* 217/2 A *Lyne bete, *linitorium*. *Ibid.*, A *Lyne beter, *linifex, linificator*. **1418** *E.E. Wills* (1882) 37, ij. remenauntz of the *Lynne bed. **1483** *Cath. Angl.* 217/2 A *Lyne bolle, *linodium*. *c* **1450** *Two Cookery-bks.* 112 Tak a fare *lynne cloute, & do therynne a disshful of ote-mele. **1855** ROBINSON *Whitby Gloss.*, *Lin-clout*, linen rag. **1436** *Close Roll 15 Hen. VI*, *Lynnedraper. *c* **1515** *Cocke Lorell's B.* 9 Lyne webbers, setters, with lyne drapers. **1720** *Lond. Gaz.* No. 5909/4 John Northropp, late of Leeds, *Line dresser. **1483** *Cath. Angl.* 217/2 A *Lyne fynche, *linosa*. **1616** SURFL. & MARKH. *Country Farme* 568 The good hus-wife must be careful when the line is growne, to free it from being intangled with the weed using to wind about it which of some is called *line gout. **1483** *Cath. Angl.* 217/2 A *Lyne howse, *linatorium*. *Ibid.* 218/1 A *Lyne soke (*A.* *Lynstoke), *linipedium*. **1835** URE *Philos. Manuf.* 215 *Line-sorters. **1723** *Lond. Gaz.* No. 6186/10 Corbort Roman,..*Line-Spinner. **1835** URE *Philos. Manuf.* 216 Girls, termed *line-spreaders, are employed to unite the locks of line into one sliver. **1562** TURNER *Herbal* II. 93 Pitiusa..may be called *lynespourge of the lyknes yᵗ it hath with linaria. **1483** *Cath. Angl.* 217/2 A *Lyne stryke, *linipulus*. **1851** *Illustr. Catal. Gt. Exhib.* 198 *Line stumps, or the raw flax plant with the seed..as pulled and dried. **1619** *Vestry Bks.* (Surtees) 75 One *lin tablecloth..for the communion table. **1897** *Daily News* 6 Mar. 8/6 *Line tow and jute yarns in buyers' favour. **1415** in *York Myst.* Introd. 27 *Lynweuers. *c* **1483** CAXTON *Dialogues* viii. 38 Gabriel the lynwevar. **1890** *Daily News* 20 Aug. 2/7 Some stocks of *line wefts are almost nil. **1856** KANE *Arct. Expl.* II. i. 10 With a *line-wick, another Esquimaux plan, we could bake bread. **1483** *Cath. Angl.* 218/1 *Lyne warke, *linificium*. **1611** COTGR., *Lignerage*, a *line-yard, or flax-yard. **1886** *Daily News* 4 Sept. 6/7 *Line yarns quiet.

line (laɪn), *sb.*² Forms: 1 **líne,** 3–7 **lyne,** 4 **lin,** **lingne,** 4–6 **ligne, lygne,** 5 **lyn, lynye,** 3– **line.** *β. Sc.* 4 **lynge,** 4–6 **ling.** [Two words, ultimately of the same etymology, have coalesced. (1) OE. *líne* wk. fem. = MDu. *lîne* (mod.Du. *lijn*), OHG. *lîna* (MHG. *lîne* cord, line, mod.G. *leine* cord), ON. *lína* (Sw. *lina*, Da. *line*); either a native Teut. formation on **lîno-* flax, LINE *sb.*¹, or (more probably) an early Teut. adoption of L. *līnea* (see below); (2) ME. *ligne, line*, a. F. *ligne* = Pr. *ligna*, Pg. *linha* (Sp. and It. in learned form *linea*):—popular L. **linja* repr. classical L. *līnea* (earlier *līnia*), orig. 'linen thread', a subst. use of *līnea* fem. of *līneus* (**līnius*) adj., flaxen, f. *līnum* flax = LINE *sb.*¹; the subst. use of the adj. is due to ellipsis of some fem. sb., possibly *fibra* FIBRE.

In continental Teut. the popular L. **linja* was adopted as OHG. *linia* (MHG., mod.G., Du., Da. *linie*).]

I. Cord or string (and derived senses).

1. a. A rope, cord, string; †a leash for dogs or for hawks. Chiefly *Naut.* or as short for *clothes-line*, etc. Also applied with words prefixed to particular 'makes' of rope, e.g. *cod-line*, *house-*

line, *whale-line*. *spec.* as used by climbers (usu. opp. *rope*).

a **1000** *Sal. & Sat.* 294 (Gr.) Yldo..ræceð wide langre linan, lisseð eall ðæt heo wile. *c* **1050** *Suppl. Ælfric's Gloss.* in Wr.-Wülcker 182/24 *Spirae*, linan. [**1390–1** *Earl Derby's Exped.* (Camden) 40 Pro..v lynes parvis pro les ankeres et seyles.] *a* **1400** *Cursor M.* 29532 (Cott. Galba) Cursing es þe fendes lyne þat harles a man to hell pine. *c* **1470** HENRY *Wallace* IX. 52 The seymen..Thair lynys kest, and waytyt weyll the tyd. *c* **1520** *Mem. Ripon* (Surtees) III. 206 Pro vj^{xx} fawdom long lyne for the convaans of the schryne with ij lytyll lynys callyd syde ropes. **1535** COVERDALE *Josh.* ii. 21 She knyt the rose coloured lyne in the wyndowe. **1589** RIDER *Bibl. Scholost.* 1727 The gesses, *lemniscus*. The lines, *tænia*. **1590** SPENSER *F.Q.* I. i. 4 And by her in a line a milkewhite lambe she lad. **1688** R. HOLME *Armoury* II. 186/2 The string wherewith we lead them;..for a Spaniel [it is called] a Line. **1700** MOXON *Mech. Exerc.* (1703) 247 A Line seldom holding to strein..above 50 or 60 feet. **1753** CHAMBERS *Cycl. Supp.*, *Lines*, among fowlers, is used to express the strings by which they catch birds. **1758** JOHNSON *Idler* No. 8 ¶7 Shirts waving upon lines. **1867** SMYTH *Sailor's Word-bk.* s.v., Deep-sea soundings for scientific purposes are recorded in thousands of fathoms, in which case the line is sometimes made of silk. **1889** A. B. GOULDEN *Mission of St. Alphege* 51 Family washing is hung on lines stretched across the lane. **1907** *Yesterday's Shopping* (1969) 700/2 Fine alpine line. **1923** G. D. ABRAHAM *First Steps to Climbing* ii. 35 A light Alpine line is also supplied but that is mostly used by experts on exceptionally difficult courses... For the beginner the ordinary rope is advisable. **1935** D. PILLEY *Climbing Days* xi. 224 We set aside the ordinary Alpine rope, and used 120 feet of Alpine line. **1950** *Mountaineering Handbk.* (Assoc. Brit. Members Swiss Alpine Club) ii. 27 Line can be used on ice or rock..or for rappel slings... Doubled, it can be used as a light rope. **1957** CLARK & PYATT *Mountaineering in Brit.* ix. 160 One development in technique was..the increasing use of line in preference to full size rope.

b. In generalized sense, as a material: Cord.

1797 *Encycl. Brit.* (ed. 3) XVI. 487/1 The making of two strand and three strand line.

†**c.** A 'cord' in the body. *Obs. rare.*

1611 FLORIO, *Linéa álba*, the white line, the vmbellical veine, the line or hollow tying from the nauel. **1780** COWPER *Table T.* 487 She pours a sensibility divine Along the nerve of every feeling line.

d. Applied to a spider's thread. *poet.*

1732 POPE *Ess. Man* I. 218 The spider's touch, how exquisitely fine! Feels at each thread, and lives along the line. **1780** COWPER *Progr. Err.* 495 Spun as fine As bloated spiders draw the flimsy line. **1839** BAILEY *Festus* (1852) 72 A gossamer line sighing itself along The air.

e. (i) A telegraph or telephone wire or cable. Also (with mixture of sense 26), a telegraph route, a telegraphic system connecting two or more stations; a telephonic connection; an individual 'number' or extension. Cf. *hold the line* (HOLD *v.* 6 h), *hot line* (HOT *a.* 12 c). Also *fig.*, esp. in phr. ***to get the lines crossed***, to become confused.

1847 *Handbk. to Electric Telegraph* 11 So rapid is the transmission of the electric current along the lines of wire, that..to carry the wires eight times round the earth..would occupy but one second of time. **1851** *Illustr. Catal. Gt. Exhib.* 1191 Five great electric telegraphic lines... The extent of line thus served appears to be about fifteen hundred miles. **1854** [see CABLE *sb.* 3]. **1900** C. H. CHAMBERS *Tyranny of Tears* I. 2 Miss Woodward. (*Speaking into telephone—very sweetly.*)..Mr. Parbury's just coming in now—he'll speak to you—keep the line. **1901** *Scotsman* 9 Mar. 9/3 The American trans-Pacific line. **1921** *Conquest* Jan. 127/2 The 'busy tone' is sent back to the calling subscriber if the line he wants is busy. **1934** *Punch* 21 Mar. 332/1 The notepaper should carry—(1) The name of the firm. (2) Its address. (3) Fictitious address for creditors. (4) Telephone number (at least ten lines). **1944** H. MCCLOY *Panic* (1972) 15 Ronnie showed the doctor how to get an outside line and he dialled a number. **1951** *Oxf. Jun. Encycl.* IV. 448/1 The Post Office took over all 'trunk' long-distance lines in 1896, and 6 years later opened the first of several large London exchanges, the 'Central', with 14,000 lines. **1970** B. KNOX *Children of Mist* iv. 77 Thane lifted the telephone. When the desk constable answered he asked for a line... Then he began dialling. **1972** J. WILSON *Hide & Seek* iii. 61 What? I can't hear you. It's a terrible line. **1973** *Times* 16 Apr. 14/6 It clearly has the advantage of keeping all the lines from getting crossed and establishing the priorities of policy. **1973** K. ROYCE *Spider Underground* iii. 50 He told me he couldn't see me then and to get off the line. **1974** *Times* 15 Mar. 8/2 Mr Nixon has admitted that he ordered a cover-up of the plumbers' activities, but suggested that his staff got their lines crossed and took this to be an order to cover up the Watergate affair as well.

(ii) Hence, any wire or cable that serves as a conductor of electric current, for whatever purpose.

1886 G. KAPP *Electr. Transmission of Energy* viii. 205 Overhead lines, whether used for electric lighting or transmission of energy, are exposed to the effects of lightning. **1902** *Encycl. Brit.* XXV. 35/2 Alternate current is used for lighting and continuous current for the tramway line. **1920** *Whittaker's Electr. Engineer's Pocket-Bk.* (ed. 4) 407 Since the induced voltages due to lightning are the same whatever the working voltage of the line, the heavier insulation on extra high voltage lines renders them less subject to lightning trouble. **1930** *Engineering* 25 Apr. 548/2 Minimum expenditure on the transmission and distribution systems from those points, connoting the use of overhead lines. **1957** *Encycl. Brit.* XXI. 887/1 On the teleprinter at the other end of the line, the responses of the armature of a single electromagnet..cause the corresponding character to be printed. **1962** A. NISBETT *Technique Sound Studio* iv. 79 In a building the size of a broadcasting studio centre there is a danger not only of high frequency losses due to capacitance, but also induction of programme signals, hum, etc., from other lines.

f. *pl.* Reins. *dial.* and *U.S.*

1852 BRISTED *Upper Ten Thousand* 67 Handing the lines to Ashburner, as he stopped his team, Masters leaped out. **1895** RYDINGS *Manx Tales* 77 He'd jus' puk up the lines on the hosses back. **1901** G. W. CABLE *Cavalier* x, He stepped into the carry-all and took the lines.

†**g.** *fig.* ***line of life***: the thread fabled to be spun by the Fates, determining the duration of a person's life. *Obs.* Cf. sense 27.

c **1580** SIDNEY *Ps.* XXXIX. iii, Lo, thou a spanns length mad'st my living line. **1600** *Cert. Prayers* in *Liturg. Serv. Q. Eliz.* (1847) 694 That the line of thy mercies and the line of her life may be lengthened and run forth together. **1601** YARINGTON *Two Lament. Traj.* III. ii. E3b, This fatall instrument, Was mark'd by heauen to cut his line of life, And must supplie the knife of Atropos. **1623** HUGH HOLLAND *Pref. Verses* in *Shaks. 1st Folio*, Though his line of life went soone about, The life yet of his lines shall neuer out. **1681** FLAVEL *Meth. Grace* ix. 188 Our troubles about sin are short, though they should run parallel with the line of life.

2. a. A cord bearing a hook or hooks, used in fishing. (Also *fishing-line*.)

a **1300** *Cursor M.* 13285 At see sant Iohn and Iam he fand, Quils þai pair lines war waitand. *c* **1374** CHAUCER *Troylus* v. 777 To fysshen here, he leyde out hook and lyne. *a* **1450** *Fysshynge w. angle* (1883) 8 Arme ʒowr crop at þe ovir ende down to the frete with a lyn of vi herys & double the lyne. **1484** CAXTON *Fables of Avian* xvi, Of a fyssher whiche with his lyne toke a lytyll fysshe. **1590** L. M[ASCALL] (*title*) A Booke of Fishing with Hooke & Line. *a* **1613** J. DENNYS *Secr. Angling* I. xx. B4 The Line to lead the Fish with wary skill. **1653** WALTON *Angler* ii. 55 Put it [a grasshopper] on your hook, with your line about two yards long. **1827** PRAED *Red Fisherm.* 97 The line the Abbot saw him throw Had been fashioned and formed long ages ago. **1884** W. C. SMITH *Kildrostan* 50, I thought you never left your books except To trim the boat and set the lines.

b. In allusive phrases referring to the 'playing' of a hooked fish at the end of the line; esp. ***to give line***: to allow full play, scope, or latitude.

1597 SHAKS. *2 Hen. IV*, IV. iv. 39 Giue him Line, and scope, Till that his passions (like a Whale on ground) Confound themselues with working. **1611** —— *Winter's T.* I. ii. 181, I am angling now, (Though you perceiue me not how I giue Lyne). **1622** MABBE tr. *Aleman's Guzman d'Alf.* II. 124 We began to play, and I went wearying of them out by little and little, giving them line enough to runne themselues out of breath. **1670** EACHARD *Cont. Clergy* 34 So soon as he gets hold of a text, he..falls a flinging it out of one hand into the other, tossing it this way and that; lets it run a little upon the line, then 'tanutus, high jingo, come again'. *a* **1687** WALLER *Pride* 7 The meanest wretch, if Heaven should give him line, Would never stop till he were thought divine. *a* **1715** BP. BURNET *Own Time* (1724) I. 435 The King was willing to give Oates line enough, as he expressed it to me. **1854** DICKENS *Hard T.* II. viii, It's policy to give 'em line enough.

†**3.** *pl.* Strings or cords laid for snaring birds. *Obs.*

c **1325** *Song of Yesterday* 130 in *E.E.P.* (1862) 136 þe schadewe cacchen þei ne myht For no lynes þat þei couþe lay. **1362** LANGL. *P. Pl.* A. v. 199 As hose leiþ lynes to lacche wiþ Foules. **1753** CHAMBERS *Cycl. Supp.*, *Lines*, among fowlers, is used to express the strings by which they catch birds... These lines are made of long and small cords, knotted in different places.

4. a. A cord used by builders and others for taking measurements, or for making things level or straight. (Cf. PLUMB-LINE.) ***line-and-plummet*** (attrib.): rigidly methodical.

1340, **1362** [see LEVEL *sb.* 1]. *c* **1440** *York Myst.* viii. 98 To hewe þis burde I will be-gynne, But firste I wille lygge on my lyne. **1525** FITZHERB. *Bk. Husb.* §124 To take a lyne, and set it there as thou wylt haue thy hedge, and to make a trenche after thy lyne. **1552** ABP. HAMILTON *Catech.* (1884) 28 Ane biggare can nocht make ane evin up wal without direction of his lyne. **1611** BIBLE *Ezek.* xl. 3 A man..with a line of flaxe in his hand, & a measuring reed. **1758** J. WATSON *Milit. Dict.* (ed. 5), *Cordeau*, a Line divided into Fathoms, Feet, &c. to mark Out-works on the Ground, used by Engineers. **1848** *Chambers's Inform.* I. 515/2 The gardener measures and marks off all his figures in the ground with his line and spade. **1849** MISS MULOCK *Ogilvies* xii. (1875) 89 There was a line-and-plummet regularity, an angular preciseness, in Mrs. Breynton's mind and person. **1877** BRYANT *Odyss.* v. 297 Trees then he felled..and carefully He smoothed their sides, and wrought them by a line.

fig. *c* **1374** CHAUCER *Troylus* I. 1068 Eueri wight þat hath an hous to founde..wole..send his hertes lyne out fro with Inne Alderfirst his purpos for to wynne. **1589** PUTTENHAM *Eng. Poesie* III. xxiii. (Arb.) 268 This decencie is..the line and leuell for al good makers to do their busines by. **1859** FITZGERALD tr. *Omar* xli. (1899) 82 For 'Is' and 'Is-not' though with Rule and Line And 'Up-and-down' without I could define.

b. Phr. ***by line***: chiefly in figurative contexts, with methodical accuracy. Also ***by line and level***, ***by rule and line***, etc.

c **1420** *Anturs of Arth.* 477 (Douce MS.) þei settene listes by lyne one þe loȝ lande. **1573** TUSSER *Husb.* xlvi. (1878) 101 Through cunning with dible, rake, mattock, and spade, by line and by leuell, trim garden is made. **1578**, **1610** [see LEVEL *sb.* 1 *fig.*]. **1610** B. JONSON *Alch.* II. i. F3, To carry Quarrells As Gallants doe, to manage 'hem, by line. **1655** FULLER *Ch. Hist.* I. i. §10 It [i.e. the matter] is not pudled, but built up by Plummet and Line, with proportion to Time and Place. **1712** ADDISON *Spect.* No. 414 ¶5 Plantations of our Europeans, which are laid out by the Rule and Line. **1781** COWPER *Conversat.* 789 A poet does not work by square or line, As smiths and joiners perfect a design.

c. *pl.* Appointed lot in life. In echoes of Ps. xvi. 6, where the reference seems to be to the marking out of land for a dwelling-place.

1611 BIBLE *Ps.* xvi. 6 The lines are fallen vnto mee in pleasant places; yea, I haue a goodly heritage. **1865** *Daily Tel.* 25 Oct. 7/3 The poor Pope's lines seem just now to have fallen in most unpleasant places, and are indeed hard lines. **1866** WHITTIER *Marg. Smith's Jrnl.* Prose Wks. 1889 I. 175 My brother's lines have indeed fallen unto him in a pleasant place.

†**5.** Rule, canon, precept; standard of life or practice. [Cf. 4 b.] *Obs. rare.*

Line has been used in several places in the A.V. to translate Heb. *qav* (primarily 'cord') in this sense. Cf. *line upon line* (sense 23 h).

1340 *Ayenb.* 124 Uor be þise uirtue al þet man deþ..al he diȝt and let and reuleþ to þe lyne of scele. *Ibid.* 160 þo þet ne zeneȝeþ..ac doþ al be riȝtuolnesse and be lingne. **1538** STARKEY *England* II. iii. 212 Thys thyng apperyth meruelouse straunge—pepul to haue the lyne of theyr lyfe to be wryte in a straunge tong. **1557** N. T. (Genev.) *2 Cor.* x. 13 We wil not reioyce aboue measure..but according to the measure of that line [κατὰ τὸ μέτρον τοῦ κανόνος], wherof God hath distributed vnto vs a measure. **1563** WINȝET *Wks.* (1890) II. 7 An infallibile, as it is a general, reul to al richt, an ewin lyne of lawtay. **1596** SPENSER *F.Q.* V. i. 3 Let none then blame me, if..I doe not forme them to the common line Of present dayes, which are corrupted sore. **1607** MIDDLETON *Michaelmas Term* II. i. Cb, A man must not so much as spit but within line and fashion. **1611** BIBLE *Ps.* xix. 4 Their line is gone out through all the earth, and their words to the end of the world.

6. ***hard lines***: ill luck, bad fortune. (Prob. nautical in origin; now often associated with 4 c.) ***hard line money*** (Naut.): extra pay in consideration of special hardships.

1824 SCOTT *Redgauntlet* ch. iii, The old seaman paused a moment. 'It is hard lines for me,' he said, 'to leave your honour in tribulation.' **1850** SMEDLEY *F. Fairlegh* iii, It will be 'hard lines' upon him. **1857** KINGSLEY *Two Y. Ago* I. iv. 110 'Gad, Sir, that was hard lines! to have all the pretty women one had waltzed with..holding round one's knees, and screaming to the doctor to save them. **1884** PAE *Eustace* 210 You seem to have had hard lines yourselves. **1886** *Pall Mall G.* 19 Aug. 2/1 *On a Torpedo-boat*, Besides, there is hard-line money, which makes up for a good many discomforts.

II. A thread-like mark.

7. a. A stroke or mark, long in proportion to its breadth, traced with a pen, a tool, etc. upon a surface. ***line of burden***, ***floatation***, ***war*** (on the hull of a ship): see the sbs.

1382 WYCLIF *Isa.* xxxviii. 8, I shal make to turne aȝeen the shadewe of lynes, bi the whiche it hadde go doun in the orilоge of Acath, in the sunne, bacward bi ten lynes. *c* **1400** MAUNDEV. (1839) xvii. 184 Be the gret Compas devised be Lines in manye parties; and that alle the Lynes meeten at the Centre. *c* **1440** *Promp. Parv.* 305/2 Lyne, or lynye, *linea*. **1551** RECORDE *Pathw. Knowl.* I. Defin., Euery lyne is drawen betwene twoo prickes, wherof the one is at the beginning, and the other at the ende. **1559** W. CUNNINGHAM *Cosmogr. Glasse* 122 Draw a right line from A unto D. **1599** SHAKS. *Hen. V*, I. ii. 210 As many Lynes close in the Dials center So [etc.]. **1610** GUILLIM *Displ. Her.* (1679) 12 [Gules] is expressed in Graving by Lines drawn streight down the Escucheon... [Azure] is expressed by Lines drawn cross the Shield. **1610** WILLET *Hexapla Dan.* 195 Archimedes..was drawing of his lines. **1691** T. H[ALE] *Acc. New Invent.* 125 The line of Burthen, or fourth Line. **1753** CHAMBERS *Cycl. Supp.*, *Lines*, in heraldry, the figures used in armories to divide the shield into different parts, and to compose different figures. **1781** COWPER *Hope* 607 He draws upon life's map a zigzag line. **1821** CRAIG *Lect. Drawing* ii. 100 An expression of forms only by simple lines. **1875** JOWETT *Plato* (ed. 2) I. 139 The writing-master first draws lines with a style.

fig. **1603** SHAKS. *Meas. for M.* IV. ii. 83 His life is paralel'd Euen with the stroke and line of his great Iustice. **1633** BP. HALL *Occas. Medit.* 5 If thou have drawn in me some lines & notes of able indowments. **1677** TEMPLE *Let. to Chas. II*, Wks. 1731 II. 438, I promised to represent the whole to Your Majesty in the truest Lines and Colours I could possibly. **1878** LECKY *Eng. in 18th C.* I. i. 80 The lines of his character are indeed too broad and clear to be overlooked.

b. *Mus.* One of the horizontal parallel equidistant strokes forming the stave, or placed above or below it (*ledger lines*).

1602 MARSTON *Ant. & Mel.* v. H4 Cantat. Iudgement gentlemen, iudgement. Wast not aboue line? I appeale to your mouthes that heard my song. **1674** PLAYFORD *Skill Mus.* I. i. 4 Five lines is only usual for one of those Parts as being sufficient to contain the Compass of Notes thereto belonging. **1688** R. HOLME *Armoury* III. 157/1. **1818** BUSBY *Gram. Music* 3 The Spaces, as well as the Lines of the Stave, furnish situations for the notes.

c. ***line of lines***, Gunter's line. ***line of numbers***, ***of shadows*** : see NUMBER, SHADOW.

1727–41 CHAMBERS *Cycl.* s.v. *Gunter's Line.*

d. *Fine Art.* Applied *spec.* to the lines employed in a picture; chiefly *collect.* or in generalized sense, character of draughtsmanship, method of rendering form. Also *pl.* (cf. sense 15) the distinctive features of composition in a picture. ***line of beauty***: the curve (resembling a slender elongated letter S), which according to Hogarth is a necessary element in all beauty of form. Also, with reference to engraving (see *line engraving* in 32).

1616 B. JONSON *Forest* xiii. 20, I, that..haue not..so my selfe abandon'd, as..I should..feare to draw true lines, 'cause others paint. **1753** HOGARTH *Anal. Beauty* vii. 38 The waving line, which is a line more productive of beauty..for which reason we shall call it the line of beauty... The..line of beauty..being compos'd of two curves contrasted, becomes still more ornamental. *Ibid.* x. 52 For as..there is but one that truly deserves the name of *the line of beauty*, so there is only one precise serpentine-line that I call *the line of grace*. **1799** G. SMITH *Laboratory* II. 46 A bold stroke with the line of beauty, and well shaped stalks, leaves and flowers ..are the only things a designer has to observe in compleating a well-designed damask pattern. **1824** DIBDIN

Libr. Comp. p. iv, Miniature engravings in the line manner. **1849** *Chambers's Inform.* II. 727/1 To this state of etching.. professional engravers bring their plates to be finished in the line manner. **18..** *Bookseller's Catal.*, First impressions of ..the 27 fine portraits..all beautifully engraved in line. **1895** ZANGWILL *Master* II. i. 126 To translate into colour and line all this huge pageant of life. *Ibid.* II. iii. 154 We praise the mellow Virgilisms in Tennyson, but we are down upon the painter who repeats another's lines.

e. *Geomancy.*

c **1590** MARLOWE *Faust.* I. i. 49 Lines, circles, scenes, letters, and characters.

f. In various games, as tennis, football, etc., ***the line*** denotes a particular line which marks the limit of legitimate or successful play; in *Cricket*, the line of flight of the ball from the bowler's hand. Also in phr. (taken from American football, but influenced by sense 20 b) ***to hold the line***, to maintain, support, a position, viewpoint, etc.

1546 J. HEYWOOD *Prov.* (1867) 35 Thou hast striken the ball, vnder the lyne. *c* **1645** HOWELL *Lett.* (1753) 127 Poor mortalls are so many balls Toss'd som o'r line, som under fortun's walls. **1887** [see DRIBBLE *v.* 4 a]. **1890** HEATHCOTE etc. *Lawn Tennis* (Badm. Libr.) 334 It will often be extremely difficult for him to judge on which side of the line the ball was dropped. **1899** F. MITCHELL in *Football* (Badm. Libr.) 210 When the throw-out belongs to his opponents, every forward on coming up to the line must mark his man. **1956** B. HOLIDAY *Lady sings Blues* (1973) xi. 102 But 52nd Street couldn't hold the line against Negroes forever. **1960** I. WALLACH *Absence of Cello* (1961) 48 Her voice had a factious quaver as she dug in and prepared to hold the line on Perry's team. **1961** *Times* 18 Aug. 3/3 At 18 Pullar was bowled by Davidson, playing across the line. **1962** *Listener* 19 Apr. 672/2 'Holding the line'..of costs, prices, and wages is vital to what he believes to be the continuance of American prosperity. **1963** A. ROSS *Australia 63* iii. 87 He moved solidly behind the line, early in position for anything that kept low. **1968** W. SAFIRE *New Lang. Politics* 190/2 'Holding the line against inflation' remains a cliché, taken from a football metaphor ('Hold-that-line!') which in turn comes from a military expression. **1969** *Times* 25 Aug. 9/2 Harris, eventually, was leg-before, hitting enthusiastically across the line.

g. *Ballet.* The total effect of the disposition of the dancer's limbs, body, and head in movement or repose. (Cf. sense 7 d.)

1912 J. E. C. FLITCH *Mod. Dancing & Dancers* xi. 170 Her purity of line is never broken by..inartistic feats of athletic dexterity. **1922** BEAUMONT & IDZIKOWSKI *Man. Classical Theatr. Dancing* 26 Beauty of line is one of the dancer's greatest assets. **1936** A. HASKELL *Prelude to Ballet* xvii. 85 Fluidity and large movements whose line can be extended indefinitely are the essential characteristics of the Russian School. **1948** *Ballet Ann.* II. 91 He has a fine classical technique and excellent line. **1960** *Times* 7 Mar. 3/7 She is already a dancer of great charm..with a particularly striking sense of line that showed to advantage in lifts.

h. *Mus.* Instrumental or vocal melody; a structured sequence of notes or tones.

1923 R. H. MYERS *Mod. Mus.* vi. 80 His music has line.. and the enormous merit of condensation. **1955** *Times* 26 Aug. 3/5 In spite of the cello's natural inclination to ruminative melancholy..it has plenty of cantilena... But it is line, always line, not harmony, that is the essence of the matter. **1961** *Listener* 14 Dec. 1046/3 What do singers mean when they talk about 'maintaining the line'?.. It means striking a level in the voice from which all expression is controlled. *Ibid.*, This 'line' of the singer is a physical conception. *Ibid.* 21 Dec. 1089/3 The music takes shape by means of a simple recitative-like vocal line, modal, flexible, limpid, with an orchestral part of matching directness and simplicity. **1962** *Radio Times* 22 Feb. 43/1, I was concerned at the time with the idea of inventing melodic line and harmonic texture directly from the fund of the twelve notes available within the octave. **1967** *Melody Maker* 28 Jan. 7/5, I consider jazz to be a lot of horns and one of those top speed bass lines.

i. Each of the narrow strips into which an image is divided for transmission and reproduction by television, corresponding to a single (usually side-to-side) passage of the scanning spot across the camera tube or picture tube: often with prefixed number, as ***625-line(s)***, indicating the number of lines making up a complete picture.

1929 *Proc. IRE* XVII. 1586 He first arrived at a correlation between the number of 'halftone lines per inch' and the corresponding television 'scanning lines'. *Ibid.*, Halftones of letters and photographs were made up, and their appearance compared with the television image on a 48-line system of the same original. **1938** *Encycl. Brit. Bk. of Year* 633/2 The service was continued, using exclusively a standard of 405 lines 50 frames interlaced scanning. **1961** G. MILLERSON *Technique Television Production* ii. 20 To reduce flicker problems, the beam is made to read the odd lines (odd field) of the image first (i.e. lines 1, 3, 5,..) and then return to scan the even lines between them (i.e. lines 2, 4, 6,..). **1963** *Ann. Reg. 1962* 27 They duly authorized the B.B.C. to start a second television channel by 1964 on U.H.F. and with an improved picture of 625 lines. **1974** *Sci. Amer.* Jan. 115/2 Each 1·25-second signal comprises a 'line' of picture data that is analogous to the line of a television picture. About 850 lines..complete a weather-signal picture.

8. a. Something resembling a traced mark, chiefly in natural objects; e.g. a thin band of colour; a suture, seam, furrow, ridge, etc. ***line of growth*** (Conch.): see quot. 1839.

c **1290** *S. Edmund* 96 in *S. Eng. Leg.* I. 299 In al is bodi nas o weom..bote ase is heued was of I-smyte..A smal red line is al-a-boute. *c* **1400** tr. *Secreta Secret., Gov. Lordsh.* 91 Longe leuys..þat hauyn whit lynys yn hem. **1596** DALRYMPLE tr. *Leslie's Hist. Scot.* v. 266 The Lione he settis in the midis; than tua lynes, on the vttir syd, Wouen in threid of gold. **1601** SHAKS. *Jul. C.* II. i. 203 Yon grey Lines, That fret the Clouds, are Messengers of Day. **1615** CROOKE *Body of Man* 476 The lynes it hath are long and almost superficiary, yet diuided manifold..by the thin membrane running betwixt them. **1672** GREW *Anat. Plants, Idea Philos. Hist.* (1682) 6 Those several Lines, by which both the said Varieties [of plants] are determin'd. **1826** KIRBY & SP. *Entomol.* IV. 290 *Line*, a narrow longitudinal stripe. **1839** SOWERBY *Conch. Man.* 57 *Lines of growth*, the eccentric striæ or lines, formed by the edges of the successive layers of shelly matter deposited by the animal, by which it increases the shell. **1860** TYNDALL *Glac.* I. iii. 26 Along the faces of the sections the lines of stratification were clearly shown. **1880** RIMMER *Land & Freshw. Shells* p. xxiii, The line of growth. **1883** F. M. PEARD *Contrad.* xiv, There were black lines under her eyes the next morning. **1895** ZANGWILL *Master* I. x. 111 A thin line of light crept again under the door.

b. A furrow or seam in the face or hands. In *Palmistry*: A mark on the palm of the hand supposed to indicate one's fate, temperament, or abilities; e.g. ***line of life, of fortune, of the head, of the heart, of health*** or ***liver*** (***hepatic line***).

1538 ELYOT *Dict., Incisuræ*,..the lynes in the palme of the hande. **1567** MAPLET *Gr. Forest* 56 The small lynes in our hande. **1596** SHAKS. *Merch. V.* II. ii. 169, I shall haue good fortune; goe too, here's a simple line of life. **1601** —— *Twel. N.* III. ii. 84 He does smile his face into more lynes, then is in the new Mappe. **1621** B. JONSON *Gipsies Metamorph.* (1640) 55 You..meane not to marrie by the line of your life. **1653** R. SANDERS *Physiogn.* 42 The Line of Life or of the Heart... He that hath this entire, long, clear and ruddy, shall live a happy life. *Ibid.*, Line of liver, liver line [see LIVER *sb.*[1] 1 c and 6]. *a* **1716** SOUTH *Serm.* (1823) IV. 7 No more than he can read the future estate of his soul in the lines of his face. **1842** LONGF. *Sp. Stud.* III. v, The line of life is crossed by many marks. **1895** ZANGWILL *Master* III. ii. 290 There were lines of premature age on the handsome face.

c. A narrow region in a spectrum, appearing to the eye as a fine straight black or shining stroke transverse to the length of the spectrum (cf. FRAUNHOFER). Hence in extended use, a component of emitted radiation at what is nominally a single discrete wavelength (in practice, over a narrow range of wavelengths containing one at which the intensity is a maximum).

1831 BREWSTER *Newton* (1855) I. v. 117 Dr. Woollaston.. discovered six fixed dark lines in the spectrum. **1837** *Penny Cycl.* IX. 21/1 The beautiful discovery made by Wollaston and Fraunhofer of the existence of dark spaces, bands transverse to the length of the spectrum, and now generally designated Fraunhofer's lines. **1932** *Sci. Abstr.* A. XXXV. 1561 (*heading*) Line emission in infra-red. **1962** *Science Survey* III. 67 For a normal lamp, emitting a line in the visible spectrum, the width..of the line would be of the order of 10,000 Mc/s. **1971** D. W. SCIAMA *Mod. Cosmol.* ii. 21 He calculated that a sensitive radio receiver should be able to detect the 21 cm line as emitted by clouds of hydrogen gas in the Galaxy. **1971** *Nature* 31 Dec. 505/2 The atoms made up of the smaller mass particles would then radiate their characteristic lines at longer wavelengths.

d. *Jewellery.* (See quot.)

1883 *Daily Tel.* 12 Feb. 5/2 The..cat's-eye..is characterised by possessing a remarkable play of light resulting from a peculiarity in its crystallisation. This ray of light is called 'line' by jewellers.

9. *Math.* **a.** An element of configuration such as must be represented in geometrical figures by a 'line' (sense 7); a continuous extent (whether straight or curved) of length without breadth or thickness; the limit of a surface; the trace of a moving point.

1559 W. CUNNINGHAM *Cosmogr. Glasse* 17 A Circle is a plaine and flat figure comprehended within one line, which is called a circumference. **1570** BILLINGSLEY *Euclid* I. def. ii. 2 A lyne is a magnitude hauing one onely space or dimension. **1660** BARROW *Euclid* I. Def. ii. 2. **1726** tr. *Gregory's Astron.* I. 434 If from any Point *L* of the Ellipse two right Lines *LS*, *LE* be drawn. **1827** HUTTON *Course Math.* I. 280 Lines are either Parallel, Oblique, Perpendicular, or Tangential. **1831** BREWSTER *Newton* (1855) II. xiv. 6 He considers a line as composed of an infinite number of points. **1885** WATSON & BURBURY *Math. Theory Electr. & Magn.* I. 155 The line $x = \kappa \log f$.

b. With various defining words: A curve connecting all points having a common property.

1826 [see ISOTHERMAL]. **1850**, **1873** [see ACLINIC]. **1877** [see ADIABATIC].

10. a. A circle of the terrestrial or celestial sphere; e.g. † ***ecliptic, equinoctial***, † ***tropic line***. Now *rare*.

1387 TREVISA *Higden* (Rolls) II. 9 In Armenia, Macedonia, Italia, and in oþer londes of þe same lyne. *c* **1391** CHAUCER *Astrol.* Prol., The arising of any planete aftur his latitude fro the Ecliptik lyne. **1511**, **1551** [see EQUINOCTIAL A. 1]. **1553** EDEN *Treat. Newe Ind.* (Arb.) 8 The lyne, called *Tropicus Cancri* and the *Equinoctial* lyne. **1667** MILTON *P.L.* IV. 282 Under the Ethiop Line By Nilus head. **1667–8** NEWCASTLE & DRYDEN *Sir Martin Mar-all* v. i. D.'s Wks. 1883 III. 83, I have seen your..ecliptics, and your tropic lines, sir. **1837** [see EQUINOCTIAL A. 1].

b. ***the line***: the equinoctial line; the equator. ***under the line***: at the equator. (Sometimes written with a capital.)

1588 PARKE tr. *Mendoza's Hist. China* 392 (*marg.*) The straight of Malaca is vnder the line. **1598** W. PHILLIPS *Linschoten* I. iii. 5/1 The shippes are at the least two monthes before they can passe the line. **1624** CAPT. SMITH *Virginia* I. 1 Sebastian Cabot..sayled to about forty degrees South-ward of the lyne. **1676** GLANVILL *Ess.* iii. 27 Some of the Indians that live near the heats of the Line. **1728** POPE *Dunc.* III. 62 Where spices smoke beneath the burning Line. **1764** GOLDSM. *Trav.* 69 The naked negro, panting at the line. **1814** WELLINGTON in Gurw. *Desp.* XII. 92 To prohibit all trade in slaves north of the Line. **1864** TENNYSON *En. Ard.* 606 In a darker isle beyond the line.

allusively. **1610** SHAKS. *Temp.* IV. i. 235. **1613** —— *Hen. VIII*, v. iv. 44. *a* **1667** COWLEY *Misc.*, *Account* 42 Cold frozen Loves with which I pine, And parched Loves beneath the Line. **1667** FLAVEL *Saint Indeed* (1754) 125 The Beams of his glory strike it but obliquely and feebly, but shortly it will be under the line, and there the sun shall stand still.

11. a. Often used for 'straight line' (sense 9); esp. in *Physics* and *techn.*, as in ***line of the apsides, of distance, of force, of sight*** (for which see those words). ***line of fire*** (see quot. 1859).

c **1400** MAUNDEV. (Roxb.) xx. 90 Þe lyne þat es betwene þise twa sternez departez all þe firmament in twa partes. **1559** W. CUNNINGHAM *Cosmogr. Glasse* 139 Marking diligentlye that the Center of the second Circle, be in the line of sighte. **1601** DOLMAN *La Primaud. Fr. Acad.* (1618) III. xxiv. 116 By meanes of the shadowes, or visuall lines, representing the saide shadowes. **1816** PLAYFAIR *Nat. Phil.* II. 266 The forces which act upon a body..may be resolved into the directions of three lines or axes. **1825** J. NICHOLSON *Operat. Mechanic* Gloss. 778 *Line of centres*, a line drawn from the centre of one wheel to the centre of another when their circumferences touch each other. **1851** *Illustr. Catal. Gt. Exhib.* 319 Whenever the axis of a single lens comes in the line between the observers and the focus. **1859** 'STONEHENGE' *Shot-gun* 314 The line of fire is the indefinite projection of the axis of the barrel. **1873** MAXWELL *Electr. & Magn.* §82 I. 84 If a line be drawn whose direction at every point of its course coincides with that of the resultant force at that point, the line is called a Line of Force. **1897** *Outing* (U.S.) XXX. 250/1 Any number of players can take part.. so long as they are not so crowded as to get into each other's line of play.

b. *Fencing.* (See quot.)

1727–52 CHAMBERS *Cycl.*, *Line*, in fencing, is that part of the body directly opposite to the enemy, wherein the shoulders, the right arm, and the sword, ought always to be found; and wherein are also to be placed the two feet, at the distance of 18 inches from each other. In this sense, a man is said to be in his line, to go out of his line, &c.

c. ***on the line***: said of a picture in an exhibition which is hung so that its centre is about on a level with the eye.

1859 GULLICK & TIMBS *Paint.* 314 The centre of the picture should not be much above the level of the eye. In an exhibition the pictures in this most favourable situation are said to be on the 'line'. **1873** *Punch* 26 Apr. 169/1 Pictures hung 'upon the line' at the Academy, for reason of their merit. **1895** ZANGWILL *Master* II. ii. 134 And I was also on the line in the big room.

12. In advb. phr. (mostly *obs.*) having reference to the straight line, e.g. ***even as line, even by line, as straight as line*** (now, ***as a line***), ***as line right, right (up) as a*** or ***any line, in (intil) ane ling*** (Sc.): in a direct course, straightforward; also, straightway, at once. (Cf. LINE RIGHT.)

c **1330** R. BRUNNE *Chron.* (1810) 150 After in a while com R. euen as lyne. *c* **1330** *Arth. & Merl.* 6370 (Kölbing) Þurch þe wombe & þurch þe chine þe spere ȝede euen bi line. *c* **1374** CHAUCER *Troylus* II. 1412 (1461) To his Neces hous as Streyt as lyne He com. *Ibid.* III. 179 (228) Pandarus, as faste as he may dryue, To Troylus þo com as lyne right. *c* **1375** *Sc. Leg. Saints* iv. (*Jacobus*) 298 He gert fele knychtis in a lynge pryk efter þame. **1375** BARBOUR *Bruce* XII. 49 Than sprent thai sammyn in-till a lyng. *c* **1422** HOCCLEVE *Learn to Die* 692 To purgatorie y shal as streight as lyne. *c* **1470** HENRYSON *Mor. Fab.* x. (*Fox & Wolf*) xvi, To the wolff he went in to ane ling. **1513** DOUGLAS *Æneis* x. viii. 43 Lyke as ane lyoun..Cummys braidand on the best fast in a lyng. **1535** STEWART *Cron. Scot.* (1858) II. 687 Quhilk causit him go leip furth in ane ling. **1546** J. HEYWOOD *Prov.* (1867) 27 Thou folowest their steppes as right as a lyne. **1889** 'ROLF BOLDREWOOD' *Robbery under Arms* xliii, He..went as straight as a line.

13. a. A direction as traced by marks on a surface or as indicated by a row of persons or objects. ***to bring into (a) line***: to align; *fig.* to cause (persons) to agree, to make unanimous. † ***to draw in a*** or ***one line***: to be unanimous.

a **1500** *MS. Ashmole* 344 lf. 22 b (*Chess rules*), Draw thy kyng..forth in to the lyne ther his kyng goth yn. **1546** J. HEYWOOD *Prov.* (1867) 65 He loued me: We drew both in one line. **1595** SHAKS. *John* IV. iii. 152 Now Powers from home, and discontents at hom[e] Meet in one line. **1600** HOLLAND *Livy* XLII. xxi. 1127 Seeing the LL. of the Senat thus drawing all in a line. **1676** MOXON *Print Lett.* 6 The Bottom-line is the line that bounds the bottom of the Descending Letters. **1763** HOYLE *Chess* 163 When your Adversary has a Bishop and one Pawn on the Rook's Line. **1851** *Illustr. Catal. Gt. Exhib.* 355 As the breech sight, the muzzle sight, and the object aimed at, are..at different distances from the eye, it is difficult to bring them at once into line. **1857** LAWRENCE *Guy Liv.* ix. 89 Livingstone..was going to get the horses in line, to start them for the farmer's Cup. **1860** GEN. P. THOMPSON *Audi Alt.* III. ci. 2 Jonathan, too, is coming into line; his caustic wit is making its way into the press. **1897** *Daily News* 23 Apr. 3/1 It was found a matter of no small difficulty to get all the owners into line.

b. *Mil.* (See quot. 1872–6.) Cf. sense 21.

1796 *Instr. & Reg. Cavalry* (1813) 73 When the open Column, halted on the Ground on which it is to form, wheels up into Line. **1802** C. JAMES *Milit. Dict.* s.v., When the light infantry companies are in line with their battalions. **1872–6** VOYLE & STEVENSON *Milit. Dict.* (ed. 3) s.v., The term *in line* is applied to a battalion when its companies are deployed on the same alignment to their full extent, i.e. in two ranks. Columns are said to be *in line* when their fronts are on the same alignment. **1881** TENNYSON *Charge Heavy Brigade* i, And he call'd 'Left wheel into line!'

c. In *Politics* (orig. *U.S.*), a particular policy or set of policies which a politician may maintain or expect others to follow; = PARTY LINE. Also *transf.*

1892 *San Francisco Examiner* 9 Nov. 1/7 (*heading*) In the line! California joins the Democratic procession by a decisive majority. **1934** H. M. CHEVALIER tr. *Malraux's Man's Fate* 149 He knew, too, that Moscow would maintain its line. *Ibid.* 169 'There's a general line that directs us—must follow it.' 'And give up our arms! A line that leads us to fire on the proletariat is necessarily bad.' **1938** *Ken* (Chicago) 7 Apr. 46/2 The Intelligence Service of the Foreign Office is a state within a state, virtually Britain's second, secret Government as far as foreign policy is concerned. It often pursues a line different from the Government's policy. **1943** *San Francisco Chron.* 25 May 14/2 The Nazis have done Senator Happy Chandler of Kentucky the honor of picking up his line... Chandler's line may not get far in this country, but the Nazis are not slow to appreciate it. **1944** M. LASKI *Love on Supertax* v. 60, I think the line was made perfectly clear. **1955** *Times* 2 June 6/6 The issue before the court is not so much whether Mr. Lattimore is guilty under the indictment as whether such a nebulous charge as following the Communist 'line' is sufficiently defined to enable him to offer an adequate defence. **1958** *Economist* 29 Nov. 767/2 They think that the liberal line—uncontrolled immigration—can be held for a few more years, but not indefinitely. **1960** *News Chron.* 25 Feb. 2/5 Mr. Barber denied that a 'line' had been agreed on as to the shape of the reports to be sent by..British reporters. **1974** HAWKEY & BINGHAM *Wild Card* xxiii. 188 The official line on what had happened was, at best, grossly understated.

d. *transf.* A marked tendency, a policy or trend (in any activity). In weakened use (*slang*): a glib or superficially attractive mode of address or behaviour, plausible talk. So *to do a line with* (Austral. and N.Z.), to (try to) enter into an amorous relationship with.

Not clearly separable from senses 28 a, b. Cf. also *to shoot a line* (sense 13 g below).

1903 'H. MCHUGH' *Out for Coin* vi. 83 Are you handing me a line of bogus conversation? **1920** F. SCOTT FITZGERALD *This Side of Paradise* I. ii. 76 Lordy, Isabelle—this *sounds* like a line, but it isn't. **1923** *Cosmopolitan* Apr. 82/1 'Where have I been all your life, good lookin'?' 'If you think that line will get you anything here, you're crazy!' **1933** J. G. COZZENS *Cure of Flesh* I. 61 He falls in love with Coral and says that some day, when he makes good, he will come back and marry her. Coral thinks it's just a line with him. **1941** *Illustr. London News* CXCVIII. 488/2 The jacket mentions Huckleberry Finn. Mr. Baum is not, of course, on that level; but that's his line. **1941** [see KNOCK *sb.*[1] 5]. **1942** T. RATTIGAN *Flare Path* I. 102 They'll think it's a line, sir. **1944** J. H. FULLARTON *Troop Target* viii. 63 He was doing a heavy line with the saddler's daughter. **1946** F. SARGESON *That Summer* 91, I could do a line with Maggie. **1946** K. TENNANT *Lost Haven* (1947) x. 156 Do you know young Len's doing a line with Gran'pa's little angel? **1953** *Encounter* Oct. 1/2 Appearing at this time, and amidst these problems, *Encounter* seeks to promote no 'line', though its editors have opinions they will not hesitate to express. **1956** A. L. ROWSE *Early Churchills* ii. 33 He has a fine line in Churchillian invective. **1958** D. REEMAN *Prayer for Ship* viii. 202 He gave me a terrific line about the hold-up. Said it was his partner's fault. But he promises definitely it'll be here tomorrow evening. **1967** *Observer* 6 Aug. 4/6 The sect's most telling line—plugged in all its broadcasts and pamphlets—is that the end of the world is due shortly, probably about 1975. The Arab-Israeli war in June was seen as the first step to Armageddon.

e. *to get a line on*, to acquire information about (a thing), to come to know. So *to give* (someone) *a line on. colloq.* (orig. *U.S.*).

1903 *Sun* (N.Y.) 18 Nov. 4 'These dressmakers'..cannot get a line on the styles except at the Horse Show. **1920** B. CRONIN *Timber Wolves* 138 It ain't over wise to give anyone a line on to what's doing. **1923** R. D. PAINE *Comrades of Rolling Ocean* iii. 41 How about these other birds. Give me a line on them. **1928** D. L. SAYERS *Unpleasantness at Bellona Club* xiv. 165, I did tumble to it that you'd got a line on me when you sent me down with that detective fellow to Charing Cross. **1935** WODEHOUSE *Luck of Bodkins* v. 50 If you want to get a line on how she feels, she gave me a letter to give you... Here it is. **1942** *Penguin New Writing* XII. 85 'They got a line on him,' said the R.P. **1947** *Chicago Tribune* 22 July 1/5 If we can find any one who saw her at a dance after 10:30 p.m. we may be able to get a line on whom she was dancing with and whose company she was in when she left.

f. *to lay* (or *put*) *it on the line*: (*a*) to hand over money; (*b*) to state (something) clearly, plainly, or categorically; (*c*) (with direct object) to put (one's career, etc.) at risk. Also with *place*, and the verb *to be*. Chiefly *U.S.*

1929 D. RUNYON in *Hearst's International* Aug. 73/1 My rent is away overdue for the shovel and broom..and I have a hard-hearted landlady... She says she will give me the wind if I do not lay something on the line at once. **1940** J. O'HARA *Pal Joey* 100 You fellows always put it on the line for me every pay day. **1950** J. D. MACDONALD *Brass Cupcake* i. 13 Lay it on the line. You can't take it with you... Put it on the entertainment account. **1954** J. SYMONS *Narrowing Circle* xxxvii. 188 'I'll see you're not the loser. You put it on the line with Jake Beverley and he'll put it on the line with you..' 'Let me lay it on the line then, Jake.' **1956** E. POUND tr. *Sophocles' Women of Trachis* 17 Put it on the line, what do you know? Get it out clearly. **1967** 'E. E. SUMNER' *Chance Encounter* v. 94 I'll lay it on the line for you, if you like. Are you thinking of asking my girl to marry you? **1968** M. LUTHER KING *Trumpet of Conscience* ii. 40 Our lives must be placed on the line if our nation is to survive its own folly. **1968** *Listener* 22 Feb. 244/3 America must fight in Vietnam ..because it has laid its prestige on the line. **1968** *Guardian* 26 July 9/7 Mayor Stokes is putting his career on the line. And the people know it—they won't let him down. **1970** *Ibid.* 9 May 2/4 It was clear to the [American] President that his credibility was on the line with the leaders in Hanoi. **1972** *New Yorker* 26 Aug. 17/2 He had decided to put his artistic reputation as a talented and original director of opera on the line at the outset of his American career with an unorthodox..production of Bizet's 'Carmen'. **1972** J. QUARTERMAIN *Rock of Diamond* xxiv. 153 I'll lay it on the line, Raven. You can say yes or no. **1973** *Black Panther* 7 July 8/3 The situation is as bad as before the takeover and it only serves to give the Indian people more reason to put their life on the line. *Ibid.* 6 Oct. 3/2 Egil Krogh..put it squarely on the line: 'Anyone who opposed us we'll destroy.'

g. *to shoot a line* (cf. SHOOT *v.* 23 g), to 'put on an act', to talk pretentiously, to boast. So ***line-shoot*** vb. (***-shooting*** ppl. a. and vbl. sb.) and sb., ***-shooter***; also ***shooter of lines***. *colloq.*

Cf. sense 13 d above.

1941 N. COWARD *Blithe Spirit* I. ii. 50 The whole thing's a put up job—I must say, though, she shoots a more original line than they generally do. **1942** *Penguin New Writing* XIII. 24 Occasionally..it publishes a serious article... But this is regarded as a 'bind',..while its author is invariably dismissed as a 'line shooter', i.e. a conceited person. *Ibid.*, The other day..our C.O. introduced a discussion on tactical evasion by saying: 'I do not want this to develop into a "line-shooting" competition.' **1942** *R.A.F. Jrnl.* 30 May 17 For keeping up the spirits, line-shooting is at least as good as beer-drinking. *Ibid.*, The man who shoots a heavy line about the work he is doing is probably very keen on his job. **1943** HUNT & PRINGLE *Service Slang* 44 *Lineshoot*, a tall story. **1944** G. NETHERWOOD *Desert Squadron* i. 2 Some of the chaps also came from other well known fighter units. From the 'line-shooting' that ensued, one would think that the squadron which was then in the process of formation could never hope to be as well known as the one they had left —and so on and so forth. **1944** T. H. WISDOM *Triumph over Tunisia* 121 One of the most thorough and decisive of the air operations in the whole campaign was carried out by the Hurri-bombers. And this is no squadron line-shoot. **1946** G. GIBSON *Enemy Coast Ahead* 144 These things were happening every night, so there was nothing to shoot a line about. **1951** M. KENNEDY *Lucy Carmichael* VII. iv. 377 When Melissa shoots a line..don't protest or argue. Take it up and embroider it. **1952** T. RATTIGAN *Deep Blue Sea* I. 38 Funny thing about gongs... They don't mean a damn thing in war—except as a line-shoot, but in peace time they're quite useful. **1958** *Times Lit. Suppl.* 3 Oct. 564/2 A champion shooter of lines. In a party of outstanding climbers and travellers he could be relied on to cap any story. **1960** *Times* 19 July 18/4 One must bear in mind that what his Lordship had called..'shooting a line' was not necessarily inconsistent with a genuine belief. **1960** V. GIELGUD *To Bed at Noon* I. xi. 73 He believed Tom to have been line-shooting as far as his swimming prowess was concerned. **1973** *Listener* 15 Mar. 342/1 [He] was an awful line-shooter. He claimed to have been at Oxford, but..he hadn't been at Oxford. **1973** *Times* 20 Sept. 20/8 He was awarded (his friends thought inadequately) the MBE by the British and by the French the Croix de Guerre. He never shot a line about his escapades but made them into entertaining stories.

14. a. Contour, outline; lineament.

1590 GREENE *Mourn. Garm.* (1616) C 3 b, Seeming him was his wife, Both in line, and in life. **1601** SHAKS. *All's Well* I. i. 107 Euerie line and tricke of his sweet fauour. **1611** —— *Cymb.* IV. i. 10 The Lines of my body are as well drawne as his. **1818** SHELLEY *Lines on Euganean Hills* 19 The dim long line before Of a grey and distant shore. **1844** KINGLAKE *Eöthen* viii. (1878) 122 The line of my features. **1849** MACAULAY *Hist. Eng.* iv. I. 450 The savage lines of his mouth. **1891** *Truth* 10 Dec. 1240/2 The skirt falling in straight, plain lines to the ground. **1894** HALL CAINE *Manxman* v. iii. 286 The round line of the sea was bleared and broken.

b. *Fashion.* The outline or dominant features of composition of a dress or suit. Freq. with qualifying term or preceded by a letter of the alphabet (to indicate the outline shape of the garment). Cf. sense 23 a below.

1918 in C. W. Cunnington *Eng. Women's Clothes* (1952) iv. 141 What was called the '*barrel line*' brought out by Callot two seasons ago..certainly is a lovely line. **1930** *Times* 13 Mar. 11/6 The curved line was seen in all the long coats. *Ibid.* 27 Mar. 11/6 There is a distinguished coat in black matasol, which has a slimming line. **1932** *Punch's Almanack* 7 Nov. 8 (*caption*) The line of to day. **1955** *Britannica Bk. of Year* 489/2 Fashion produced a new 'line' in women's clothes, the *H-line.* **1958** *Woman's Own* 24 Dec. 14/3 Which year brought out the following trends: (*a*) the New Look; (*b*) the Trapeze Line; (*c*) the A-line. **1968** J. IRONSIDE *Fashion Alphabet* 92 *Line*, the silhouette of a garment that makes it look fashionable or unfashionable. **1968, 1970** [see EMPIRE *sb.* 8 b]. **1975** *Vogue* 1 Mar. 84/1 Overall, a clear narrowing of the silhouette, most marked at Saint Laurent, presaging an even sparer line for autumn.

15. *pl.* **a.** The outlines, plan, or draught of a building or other structure; *spec.* in *Ship-building*, the outlines of a vessel as shown in its horizontal, vertical, and oblique sections. (Also *fig.*)

1673 TEMPLE *Ess. Irel.* Wks. 1731 I. 121 The raising such Buildings as I have drawn you here the Lines of. **1691** T. H[ALE] *Acc. New Invent.* p. xiii, Nor have I heard of any other Ship built by the Kings-fisher's Lines. **1776** G. SEMPLE *Building in Water* 66 The principal Lines of my Design of a Bridge suitable to that Place. **1818** JAS. MILL *Brit. India* II. IV. v. 188 Carnac..remained..to lend his countenance and aid to measures, the line of which he had contributed to draw. **1851** *Illustr. Catal. Gt. Exhib.* 336 Model of a ship's hull... The novelty claimed in the uniformity of its lines. **1860** READE *Cloister & H.* lvii. (1896) 174 Her extravagant poop that caught the wind, and her lines like a cocked hat reversed.

b. *fig.* Plan of construction, of action, or procedure: now chiefly in phr. *on* (such and such) *lines*.

1757 BURKE *Abridgm. Eng. Hist.* I. ii. 13 In all very uncultivated countries..there are but obscure lines of any form of government. **1807** S. COOPER (*title*) The First Lines of the Practice of Surgery; being an elementary work for Students [etc.]. **1862** MERIVALE *Rom. Emp.* (1865) VII. lv. 18 The lines of their policy are often to be traced for the most part by conjecture and inference. **1875** —— *Gen. Hist. Rome* li. (1877) 404 He did not live to lay even the first lines of his great work. **1879** FROUDE *Cæsar* viii. 80 He had reorganised the constitution on the most strictly conservative lines. **1888** BRYCE *Amer. Commw.* II. lxi. 432 Nearly all these offices are contested on political lines. **1889** SWINBURNE *Stud. Prose & Poetry* (1894) 286 No later work of Victor Hugo's, written on the same lines or in the same temper, can reasonably be set beside the *Châtiments*.

16. a. [After F. *ligne*.] A measure of length, the twelfth part of an inch.

1665 *Phil. Trans.* I. 61 It did bear but 2 inches and 9 lines French for its greatest Aperture. **1759** ADANSON *Voy. Senegal* 101, I was informed, that there fell two inches three lines of water. **1849** *Sk. Nat. Hist., Mammalia* IV. 62 The Long-tailed Field-Mouse... Length of head and body three inches eight lines. **1863** BERKELEY *Brit. Mosses* i. 3 Varying from less than a line to many inches in length.

b. In recent technical use (see quot.).

1880 *Plain Hints Needlework* 133 Button Gauge... The numbers indicate the quantity of 'lines' in diameter. This 'line' is equal to the French millimetre.

17. a. A limit, boundary; more fully, ***line of demarcation***. Phr. ***to draw the line*** (see DRAW *v.* 59 b); also, with similar meaning, ***to †lay, form a line***. ***to run the lines*** (U.S.): see RUN *v.*

1595 MARKHAM *Sir R. Grinvile* (Arb.) cxii, And now the night grew neere her middle line. *a* **1613** J. DENNYS *Secr. Angling* I. iv. B 1 b, Of Heauen the middle Line That makes of equall length both day and night. **1727–52** [see DEMARCATION]. **1732** POPE *Ess. Man* I. 228 And Middle natures, how they long to join, Yet never pass the insuperable line! **1769** BURKE *Late St. Nation* Wks. 1842 I. 108 Their different principles compose some of the strongest political lines which discriminate the parties even now subsisting amongst us. **1770** SIR J. REYNOLDS *Disc.* iii. (1876) 33 It is this intellectual dignity..that ennobles the Painter's art; that lays the line between him and the mere mechanic. **1818** JAS. MILL *Brit. India* I. iii. (1840) I. 69 To form a line between them and the Company, it was ordained, that [etc.]. **1849** MACAULAY *Hist. Eng.* i. I. 30 The line which bounded the royal prerogative. **1857** HUGHES *Tom Brown* II. vii, Hold on and hit away, only don't hit under the line. **1878** HUXLEY *Physiogr.* xviii. 303 The lines of separation of the great watersheds.

b. ***Mason's and Dixon's line***: the southern boundary of Pennsylvania, so named from the two astronomers who surveyed it (1763–1767), and forming the line of demarcation between the free and the slave States. Also ellipt. ***the line***.

1779 in W. B. Reed *Life & Corr. J. Reed* (1847) II. 134 Perhaps we would be as well off with Mason and Dixon's line continued. **1845** F. DOUGLASS *Narr. Life F. Douglass* xi. 101 We owe something to the slaves south of the line as well as to those north of it. **1850** WHITTIER *Old Portr. & Mod. Sk.* Pr. Wks. 1889 II. 195 Every petty postmaster south of Mason and Dixon's line became *ex officio* a censor of the press. **1861** LOWELL *E Pluribus Unum* Pr. Wks. 1890 V. 51. **1909** 'O. HENRY' *Roads of Destiny* xxi. 358 If you had come from below the line, I reckon I would have liked you right smart. **1949** *Sat. Even. Post* 26 Mar. 38/2 The critic thunders, and below 'the line' the shades of Marse Robert and Jeff Davis inevitably are summoned forth to meet the charge.

c. *Bridge.* A line across a score-card. So ***above the line***, denoting points scored for game, honours, overtricks, or rubber, or for the failure of opponents to fulfil their contract; ***below the line***, denoting points scored for tricks bid and won, and counting towards game.

1905 H. A. VACHELL *Hill* vii. 144 My partner..made the Little Slam, and scored nearly six hundred below the line. **1908, 1927** [see CONTRACT *sb.*[1] 1 g]. **1933** A. G. MACDONELL *England, their England* vi. 78 Gone down 650 points above the line whereas he ought to have made two no-trumps. **1967** P. ANDERTON *Play Bridge* i. 15 They win ten tricks so they score three times the value of Spades below the line, i.e. 90 points plus another 30 points above the line as a bonus for making one more than their contract. **1970** S. HUGHES *Art of Coarse Bridge* i. 12 This kind of spectacular finale happens far more often than one might expect, but it takes an awful lot of scoring above the line before anyone actually has..the right cards to do it with.

d. In phrases indicating the boundary between a debit and a credit in one's account, or between ordinary and extraordinary expenditure. (See also quot. 1973.) Also ***to pay on the line***, to pay promptly.

1934 J. O'HARA *Appointment in Samarra* i. 20 There were only a few of the Lantenengo crowd who could get a favour out of Ed without paying cash on the line for it. **1938** S. V. BENÉT *Thirteen o'Clock* 249, I kept on schedule with the work, but I couldn't with the money. Each week, I'd be just a little over the line. **1940** *Economist* 13 Apr. 683/1 The figures 'below the line' in the Exchequer Return show the result of the issue of the 4 per cent. **1948** *Ibid.* 31 Jan. 195/1 Aggregate Government expenditure, including..the 'below line' expenditure. **1959** N. MAILER *Advts. for Myself* (1961) 66, I paid on the line every time. **1966** A. GILPIN *Dict. Econ. Terms* 1 Since 1947 it has been customary for the British Budget to contain a full statement of the estimated expenditure and revenue for the following year, some items being shown as 'above-the-line'..and others as 'below-the-line'. Most current items appear above the line and most capital items below. **1973** *New Society* 28 June 736/2 The growth of petrol promotions has coincided with a growth of giveaways, gimmicks and competitions in the marketing of a wide range of products... Termed 'below-the-line' marketing, it is encroaching on the 'above-the-line' (advertising) share of manufacturers' marketing budgets.

e. ***bottom line***: see BOTTOM *sb.* 20.

†**18.** Degree, rank, station. *Obs.*

1528 *Extracts Aberd. Reg.* (1844) I. 121 Skiparis and seruandis of euery lyne. **1596** SHAKS. *1 Hen. IV*, I. iii. 168 To shew the Line, and the Predicament Wherein you range vnder this subtill King. *Ibid.* III. ii. 85 And in that very Line, Harry, standest thou. **1782** PAINE *Let. Abbé Raynal* (1791) 37 One whom years, experience, and long established reputation have placed in a superior line. **1785** G. A. BELLAMY *Apol.*, etc. (ed. 3) IV. 46 She..had received a more liberal education than is usually bestowed upon English women in the middle line of life.

III. Applied to things arranged along a (straight) line.

19. a. A row or series of persons or objects. *spec.* = QUEUE *sb.* 3 (*U.S.*).

1557 RECORDE *Whetst.* H ij, Men call a line of Brickes, and a line of Asshelers stones, when many bee laied in a rowe, in lengthe. **1605** SHAKS. *Macb.* IV. i. 117 What will the Line stretch out to'th' cracke of Doome? **1711** ADDISON *Spect.* No. 63 ¶4 The Officers planting themselves in a Line on the left Hand of each Column. **1718** LADY M. W. MONTAGU *Let. to C'tess Mar* 28 Aug., The Street..is perhaps the most beautiful line of building in the world. **1776** *Trial of Nundocomar* 57/2 The bond was wrote obliquely, from right hand to left, the seals in a line, on the margin. **1836** W. IRVING *Astoria* III. 260 A line of trading posts from the Mississippi and the Missouri across the Rocky mountains. **1840** HOOD *Up Rhine* 31 Trees in formal line. **1848** W. H. BARTLETT *Egypt to Pal.* xiv. (1879) 301 The valley.. enclosed by lower lines of hills than [etc.]. **1853** M. ARNOLD *Scholar-Gipsy* xiii, The line of festal light in Christ-Church hall. **1863** MRS. CARLYLE *Lett.* III. 158 In the whole line of the procession. **1930** M. SULLIVAN *Our Times* III. xii. 502 People..were herded by policemen into lines stretching away from the marble entrance. **1969** D. C. HAGUE *Managerial Econ.* xi. 222 The second kind of stock problem is the queueing problem... A queue (what Americans call a 'line')..will form. **1974** *State* (Columbia, S. Carolina) 15 Feb. 1-B/2 At least one employe went as far away as Forest Drive for gasoline and nearby stations, selling gasoline, quickly acquired lines. **1975** *N.Y. Times* 1 Apr. 35/5 It's to stand silently on unemployment lines with other surplus members of America's work force, waiting to sign for your unemployment check.

b. A fancy name for: A flock of geese.

[**1802** DANIEL *Rur. Sports* II. 465 [Geese in flight] form two oblique lines like the letter V, or if their number be small, only one line.] **1882** *Standard* 10 Feb. 5/3 To speak by the book, of a 'line' instead of a 'flock' of geese.

c. A row of machines or work stations where a product is progressively assembled, or a succession of operations performed on it, as it passes from one end to the other during manufacture or processing. Cf. *assembly line*, *production line*.

1926 *Encycl. Brit.* II. 822/1 All of these lines, with their various machines and operations, are converging on the point where the leaves are assembled into springs. **1937** *Times* 13 Apr. p. xii/2 The raw material is delivered at one end of the machining line with the component passing from machine to machine until it reaches the view table. **1940** *War Illustr.* 16 Feb. 113 In one of Britain's 'shadow' factories bombers on the line will soon be ready to take the air. **1971** *Cabinet Maker & Retail Furnisher* 24 Sept. 531/1 Features of the production facilities at the new factory.. include a fully automated machining line and the longest finishing line in the U.K.

d. In business or management organization, the chain of command or responsibility; the persons responsible for the administration and organization of a business (as opposed to the staff). Hence ***line manager***, ***management***.

1960 NANASSY & SELDEN *Business Dict.* 27 Following are the basic types of internal organization of a business: (1) *line*: The owner gives orders directly to the workers. As the business grows, the owner appoints a few executives, who are responsible to him... (3) *line-and-staff*: Authority flows from top to bottom, with responsibility falling on staff supervisors and special experts. **1964** M. ARGYLE *Psychol. & Social Probl.* viii. 111 In several British factories it was found that the division between 'line' supervisors and 'staff' technicians tended to disappear—technologists must have supervisory responsibility. **1967** C. MARGERISON in Wills & Yearsley *Handbk. Managem. Technol.* 25 The accountants considered that they had responsibility for the end-product and sought to control certain actions of line managers. Line managers resented this interference with their authority and started to obstruct the accountants in their ordinary accounting function. **1967** COULTHARD & SMITH in *Ibid.* 206 A good deal of the failure of these techniques stems from the inability of personnel men to convince line management of their own vital role combined with the assumption by line management that the creation of a specialist department covering personnel policies, training, management development, etc., automatically relieves them of responsibility. **1972** *Accountant* 28 Sept. 391/1 If the internal auditor sees himself as a someone who can review and report upon the functions of line management on matters other than security, then there is one fundamental issue that has to be faced. **1974** *Times* 25 Mar. 17/4 It was a pity that so few line managers were present as it was their present and future competence that was being discussed.

20. *Mil.* **a.** A trench or rampart; *pl.* (also *collect. sing.*), a connected series of field-works. Also, one of the rows of huts or tents in a camp or cantonment (see quots. 1872–6 and 1876). ***line of circumvallation***, ***defence***, etc.: see the second sbs.

1665 MANLEY *Grotius' Low C. Warres* 613 The Line that incompassed his Camp was 8 Foot high. **1695** PRIOR *Ballad Taking Namur* 113 Regain the lines the shortest way, Villeroy. **1711** STEELE *Spect.* No. 139 ¶7 He took the French Lines without Bloodshed. **1793** BURNS *Sodger's Return* i, I left the lines and tented field. **1839** KEIGHTLEY *Hist. Eng.* I. 352 Lines were now run from bastille to bastille, and the town was completely shut in. **1844** H. H. WILSON *Brit. India* II. 21 To attack the Gorkha positions at the western extremity of their line. **1859** F. A. GRIFFITHS *Artil. Man.* (1862) 263 *Lines* are formed for the entrenchment of armies, and are composed of a succession of redans, &c. (joined by curtains). **1872–6** VOYLE & STEVENSON *Milit. Dict.* s.v. *Cantonments*, In India..a cantonment contains barracks for European troops, and native huts termed lines for the Sepoys. **1876** *Murray's Handbk. Surrey*, etc. 173 In the North Camp [Aldershot] the buildings are principally of wood, arranged in 'lines'.. which are lettered from A to Q. Each line is an oblong block of about 40 huts.

fig. **1835** I. TAYLOR *Spir. Despot.* v. 220 They hastened to entrench themselves within the lines of absolute despotism.

b. In the war of 1914–18, the trenches collectively; the front line. So ***up the line*** (see quots.).

1916 H. W. FOWLER *Let.* 5 Mar. in *S.P.E. Tract* XLIII. (1935) 136 What may be going on up the line who knows? **1917** W. OWEN *Let.* 4 Feb. (1967) 430, I am now indeed and in truth very far behind the Line; sent down to this old Town [*sc.* Abbeville] for a Course in Transport Duties. **1917** A. G. EMPEY *Over Top* 313 '*Up the line.*' Term generally used in rest billets when Tommy talks about the fire trench or fighting line. **1919** W. H. DOWNING *Digger Dial.* 52 *Up the line*, in action. 'Up the line, with the best of luck'—a satirical phrase applied to men who, after being for some time in a safe occupation, were returned to fighting units. **1964** B. GARDNER (*title*) Up the line to death.

21. *Mil.* and *Naut.* A row or rank of soldiers (distinguished from a *column*); a row of ships in a certain order. Also occas. *collect. sing.* = ships of the line. ***line of battle***: see BATTLE *sb.* 12. ***ship of the line***: a line-of-battle ship.

1704 *Lond. Gaz.* No. 4054/1 Their Line consisted of 52 Ships and 24 Gallies. **1706** *Ibid.* No. 4222/3 He had then 30 Ships of the Line,..besides two or three Frigats. **1769** FALCONER *Dict. Marine* (1780) A a 3 b, The line is said to be formed abreast, when the ships sides are all parallel to each other, on a line which crosses the keels at right angles. **1800** *Asiatic Ann. Reg., Characters* 56/2 Lord Cornwallis put him in command of the second line of the army. **1801** CAMPBELL *Battle of the Baltic* ii, While the sign of battle flew On the lofty British line. **1805** in Duncan *Life of Nelson* (1806) 231 We have only 11 line, 3 frigates, and a sloop. **1813** SOUTHEY *Life of Nelson* vi, The fleet from Cadiz.. consisting of from seventeen to twenty sail of the line. **1815** BYRON *Ode*, '*We do not curse thee, Waterloo*' iii, While the broken line enlarging, Fell or fled along the plain. **1838** LYTTON *Leila* IV. i, Suddenly the lines of the Moors gave way.

b. ***the line***: in the British army, the regular and numbered troops as distinguished from the guards and the auxiliary forces; in the U.S. army, the regular fighting force of all arms.

1802 C. JAMES *Milit. Dict.* **1813** WELLINGTON in Gurw. *Desp.* (1838) XI. 141 To prevent the men from volunteering to serve in the line. **1849** *Chambers's Inform.* II. 184/2 The pay of a private..in the cavalry of the line [is] 1*s.* 4*d.*..in the infantry of the line, 1*s.* 1*d.* **1858** LYTTON *What will he do?* II. v, Then Charlie Haughton sold out of the Guards..[and] went into the line. **1865–6** H. PHILLIPS *Amer. Paper Curr.* II. 148 The Connecticut line..assembled to return to their homes and leave the army to its fate. **1881** J. GRANT *Cameronians* I. iii. 37 The new head-dress for the Line.

c. ***all along the line***, ***all*** (***the way***) ***down the line***: at every point. Also, ***somewhere along the line***, at some point (in time).

1877 SPURGEON *Serm.* XXIII. 246 God will be victorious all along the line in the present battle. **1880** T. HODGKIN *Italy & Invaders* I. I. i. 117 The campaign of 378 opened auspiciously for the interests of Rome along the whole line. **1924** R. FRY *Let.* 27 June (1972) II. 553 Both he and Courbet did elaborate portraits of the same patron... Courbet wins all along the line. **1936** A. HUXLEY *Eyeless in Gaza* xxi. 297 A refugee from Germany... Aryan, but communist—ardently and all along the line. **1962** J. WAIN *Sprightly Running* v. 189 There is always the wistful hope.. that these young will not merely benefit from meeting each other, but will, somewhere along the line, actually be *taught* something. **1965** *Listener* 16 Sept. 402/2 It is difficult to estimate its direct effect, because all along the line there are people working hard to try to make sure that those defects do not come back on the patient. **1965** *New Yorker* 20 Nov. 162/3 Somewhere along the line, the surf and wind went out of his playing. **1969** B. TURNER *Circle of Squares* xviii. 143 I've helped him all along the line, not always knowing why. **1972** *Guardian* 6 July 2/2 It has been clear that they had had to refer to Moscow for instructions all along the line. **1975** N. LUARD *Robespierre Serial* xi. 87 You've lied to me, all the way down the line. *Ibid.* xvi. 146 I'm not going to let that little bastard get away with it. He's screwed us all down the line from Riyadh to Geneva.

22. A regular succession of public conveyances plying between certain places; e.g. the Cunard line (of steamers), the White Star line. orig. *U.S.*

1786 *Mass. Centinel* (Boston) 11 Jan. 3/1 The new arrangement ordered by Congress, for the more safe and regular conveyance of the Mails, by the line of stages. **1818** *Niles' Reg.* XIV. 14/2 A regular line of waggons and packets are established between the city of New-York and Detroit. **1837** W. JENKINS *Ohio Gazetteer* 56 The post office is supplied by daily lines of Coaches from Cincinnati to Dayton. **1848** *Chambers's Inform.* I. 424/2 Lines of large steamers are got up by companies as a speculation. **1900** F. T. BULLEN *Idylls of Sea* 198 The better class of seamen will be found making voyage after voyage in the same vessel or at least in the same line. **1901** *Scotsman* 2 Mar. 10/1 The first vessel of the new direct line to Jamaica from England.

23. A row of written or printed letters.

a. *gen.* One of the rows of letters in any piece of writing or letterpress: often, esp. in *pl.*, put for the contents or sense of what is written or printed.

line by line, ***line for line***: from beginning to end, seriatim; also, with hyphens, *attrib.* (For *line-for-line* in Fashion cf. sense 14 b). ***to read between the lines***: to discover a meaning or purpose not obvious or explicitly expressed in a piece of writing.

a **1000** *Riddles* xliii. 10 (Gr.) Se torhta Æsc an an linan. **1362** LANGL. *P. Pl.* A. VIII. 94 Þe Bulle In two lynes hit lay and not a lettre more. **1375** BARBOUR *Bruce* XVII. 84 Quhen the marschall the cowyne Till bath the lordis lyne be lyne Had tald. **1377** LANGL. *P. Pl.* B. v. 428 In canoun ne in þe decretales I can nouȝte rede a lyne. *a* **1400–50** *Alexander* 1821 Loo 'litill thefe' in ilka lyne his lettir me callis. **1591** SHAKS. *1 Hen. VI*, III. i. 1 Com'st thou with deepe premeditated Lines? With written Pamphlets? **1638** BAKER tr. *Balzac's Lett.* (vol. III.) 100 The good opinion you have of me, which is to be seen in every lyne of your letter. **1709** H. FELTON *Classics* (1718) 80 Two Lines would express all they say in two Pages. **1711** *Lond. Gaz.* No. 4807/4 Let him send a Line or two directed to the Blue Anchor and Crown. **1713** STEELE *Englishman* No. 53. 344 Clerks amongst us make distant Lines, few words in those Lines. **1755** JOHNSON s.v., (In the plural) A letter; as, I read your lines. **1796** JANE AUSTEN *Pride & Prej.* xxvi. (1813) 130 Not a note, not a line, did I receive in the mean time. **1816** C. WOLFE *Burial Sir J. Moore* 31 We carved not a line, and we raised not a stone. **1856** MRS. CARLYLE *Lett.* II. 299 The distance between your lines in the letter just come. **1866** J. MARTINEAU *Ess.* I. 118 No writer..was ever more read between the lines. **1876** J. WEISS *Wit, Humor, & Shakespeare* iii. 78 There was a worthy old deacon, who, repeating Watts's hymn line for line after his clergyman, said, 'Return, ye rancid sinners!' **1879** FROUDE *Cæsar* xiv. 194 In every line that he wrote Cicero was attitudinising for posterity. **1880** SPURGEON *Serm.* XXVI. 327 They do not say as much to their secret selves; but you can read between the lines these words—'What a weariness it is!' **1896** *Moxon's Mech. Exerc.*, *Printing* p. xviii, A line-for-line and page-for-page reprint of the original text. **1934** T. S. ELIOT *Eliz. Ess.* 17 A line-by-line examination of almost any Elizabethan play..would be a fruitful exercise. **1951** L. MACNEICE tr. *Goethe's Faust* 9, I aimed at a line-for-line translation. **1958** [see FASHION *sb.* 9 c]. **1964** E. A. NIDA *Toward Sci. Transl.* ii. 17 Dryden felt that there were three basic types of translation: (1) metaphrase, a word-for-word and line-for-line type of rendering; (2) paraphrase..; and (3) imitation. **1969** *Guardian* 29 July 7/3 Line-for-line copies of his [couture] collection. **1971** *Computers & Humanities* VI. 7 Comparisons are made on a line-for-line basis. **1971** *Gloss. Electrotechnical, Power Terms* (*B.S.I.*) III. iv. 13 *Line by line scanning*, scanning in which the sweep is effected in straight, substantially horizontal strips extending over the entire width of the picture. **1973** *Country Life* 6 Dec. 1970/1 A perfect line-for-line copy of a couture Dior trouser suit.

fig. **1573** L. LLOYD *Pilgr. Princes* (1586) 210 The last line of all thinges is death.

b. *spec.* in *Printing.* A row of types or quads.

1659 C. HOOLE tr. *Comenius' Orbis Sensualium* (1672) 191 The Compositor..composeth words in a composing stick, till a Line be made. **1676** MOXON *Print Lett.* 11 You must indent your Line four *Spaces*. *Ibid.*, It is not graceful to end a Break with a short word onely in a line. **1683** —— *Mech. Exerc.* II. 394 *White-line*, a Line of Quadrats. **1841** W. SAVAGE *Dict. Printing* 310 *Head line*, the top line of a page in which is the running title and folio, but sometimes only a folio.

†**c.** *collect.* A written record, message, etc. *Obs.*

a **1400–50** *Alexander* 1932 [He] Vn-lappis liȝtly þe lefe & þe line [*v.r.* lines] redes. *Ibid.* 2060 And vneth limpid him þe lee þe lyne me recordis. *c* **1400** *Destr. Troy* 9628 The Secund day suyng, sais me the lyne, Þe Troiens full tymli tokyn þe feld.

d. A few words in writing; often applied to a short letter.

1647 H. MARKHAM *Let.* in *12th Rep. Hist. MSS. Comm.* App. v. 3, I..desire a line under your own hand to whom I shall deliver the castle. **1751** BERKELEY *Let. to Johnson* 25 July, Wks. 1871 IV. 326 A line from me in acknowledgment of your letter. **1775** J. ADAMS *Wks.* (1854) IX. 352, I have this morning received a line from Mrs. Warren. **1849** MACAULAY *Hist. Eng.* iii. I. 415 History was too much occupied with courts and camps to spare a line for the hut of the peasant or for the garret of the mechanic. **1865** MRS. CARLYLE *Lett.* III. 279 Dearest,—Just a line to say that all goes well. **1894** MRS. H. WARD *Marcella* II. 307 Marcella scribbled a line on a half sheet of paper, and..despatched Benny with it.

e. The portion of a metrical composition which is usually written in one line: a verse; *pl.* verses, poetry. Also *pl.*, (so many) lines of verse (sometimes, of prose) set to be written out as an imposition in school.

to read the line (Sc.): to give out the words of a metrical psalm or hymn a line at a time (cf. LINE *v.*² 6).

1563–7 BUCHANAN *Reform. St. Andros* Wks. (1892) 8 The regent sal cause thayme to writ twa or thre lynis of Terence. **1599** DRAYTON *Idea* xlii, And in my lines, if shee my loue may see! **1623** B. JONSON *To memory of Shakespeare*, Marlowes mighty line. **1630** MILTON *On Shaks.*, Each heart Hath from the leaves of thy unvalu'd Book, Those Delphick lines with deep impression took. **1709** POPE *Ess. Crit.* 347 And ten low words oft creep in one dull line. **1752** HUME *Ess. & Treat.* (1777) I. 211 Each line, each word, in Catullus, has its merit. **1792** COWPER (*title*) Lines addressed to Dr. Darwin. **1809** BYRON *Eng. Bards & Review.* 390 Lines forty thousand, cantos twenty-five! **1867** A. DICKSON *Rambling Recoil.* (1868) 33 To dispense with reading the line in psalmody was by many held to be profane. **1875** JOWETT *Plato* (ed. 2) I. 252 The lines of Homer which you were reciting. **1894** WILKINS & VIVIAN *Green Bay Tree* I. 72 To commute the punishment to 500 Latin lines. **1907** *Massacre of Innocents* ii. 13 Vardon, do me five hundred lines. **1914** 'I. HAY' *Lighter Side School Life* vii. 182 Mr. Duckworth.. had occasion to set Master Smith fifty lines for inattention. **1959** I. & P. OPIE *Lore & Lang. Schoolch.* xv. 325 At my junior school the boys had different doors from the girls and if a boy went through the girls' door he had a 100 lines to write out. **1961** D. WOODWARD tr. *Simenon's Premier* ii. 36 He took lessons without appearing to see his pupils..and his only reaction was, if one of them grew restless, to give him two hundred lines. **1974** *Age* (Melbourne) 12 Oct. 12/2

Doing lines, being kept in to write out good resolutions, such as 'I must not put squashed frogs in girls' sandwiches'.

f. *pl.* Short for ***marriage lines***, the certificate of marriage. Applied also *dial.* to other kinds of certificates (e.g. of church membership).

1829 J. Hunter *Hallamsh. Gloss., Lines.* Marriage-lines is a certificate of marriage often asked for and kept by the bride. **1840** Marryat *Poor Jack* xi, She could not produce her marriage lines. **1861–2** Thackeray *Adv. Philip* xii. (1869) I. 254 'How should a child like you know that the marriage was irregular?' 'Because I had no lines', cries Caroline quickly. **1890** W. J. Gordon *Foundry* 81 'Lines of admission', or as we should call them letters of recommendation. **1901** *Union Mag.* Mar. 106/1 The old minister fell into a reverie in the very midst of filling in Sandy M'Turk's lines.

g. *pl.* The words of an actor's part.

1882 *Daily Tel.* 7 Dec., He [an actor] said, 'Do let me get in some of my "lines"'.

h. ***line upon line***: now taken as referring to the reiteration of statements in successive lines of writing or print (for the orig. meaning see 5).

1611 Bible *Isa.* xxviii. 10. **1837** Mrs. T. Mortimer *(title)* Line upon line; or, a second series of the earliest religious instruction the infant mind is capable of receiving. **1896** *Home Mission.* (N.Y.) Aug. 218 A line-upon-line presentation of these facts.

IV. Serial succession.

24. a. A continuous series of persons (rarely of things) in chronological succession. Chiefly with reference to family descent, a series in which each member is the parent of the one next following. So ***male, female line, direct line***. For *heir of line*, see heir 1 b.

c **1386** Chaucer *Wife's T.* 279 If gentillesse were planted natureelly vn-to a certeyn linage, doun the lyne. **1426** Lydg. *De Guil. Pilgr.* 14696 'Flatrye'..by dyssent off lyne doun Eldest douhter off Falsnesse. *c* **1440** *Jacob's Well* 48 In þe lyne vpward, þi fadyr is to þe in þe first degre of kynrede. *c* **1470** Henry *Wallace* i. 34 The fyrst rycht lyne of the fyrst Stewart. **1513** *Bk. Keruynge* in *Babees Bk.* 285 A marshall muste take hede of the byrthe, and nexte of the lyne, of the blode royall. **1640** Ld. Digby in Rushw. *Hist. Coll.* iii. (1692) I. 146 By the concentring of all the Royal Lines in his Person. **1705** Addison *Italy* 13 There is no House in Europe that can show a longer Line of Heroes. *a* **1715** Burnet *Own Time* (1724) I. 457 Isaac, Jacob, Judah..and..Solomon, were preferred with-out any regard to the next in line. **1784** Cowper *Task* v. 211 In the line Of his descending progeny. **1809–10** Coleridge *Friend* (1865) 136 The property.. derived from a long line of ancestors. **1818** Cruise *Digest* (ed. 2) III. 358 Purchases in the line of the mother or grandmother. **1862** Stanley *Jew. Ch.* I. xiii. 254 He and his sons founded a long line of Priests. **1895** *Law Times Rep.* LXXII. 817/1 The case is governed by a line of authorities extending over a century.

†**b.** ***by line***: by lineal descent. *Obs.*

c **1374** Chaucer *Troylus* v. 1481 Of þis lord descendede Tydeus By ligne. *c* **1375** *Sc. Leg. Saints* xi. (*Symon & Judas*) 3 Of Symone..& of Iudas..þat brethire ware be lyne of fles to Sancte Iames callit þe les. *c* **1386** Chaucer *Knt.'s T.* 693 Of his lynage am I, and his of spryng By verray ligne. *c* **1400** *Destr. Troy* 1841 Lord of þe londe as be lyne olde. **1470–85** Malory *Arthur* v. x, My fader is lyneally descended of Alysaunder..by ryght lygne. **1596** Dalrymple tr. *Leslie's Hist. Scot.* ii. 134 The lawful ȝouth quha rycht be lyne was sproung of the kingis blude.

c. Phr. ***line of command***.

1930 *Nautical Mag.* Jan. 41 *(title)* The line of command. *Ibid.* 43 When the machinery fails, then the old line of command is called upon to take its full responsibility. **1962** *Rep. Comm. Broadcasting 1960* 161 in *Parl. Papers 1961–2* (Cmnd. 1753) IX. 259 The planning and operation of a national programme of television can never be simple, even when there is a single objective to be pursued, when effective control resides in a single authority, and when there is a direct line of command.

25. Lineage, stock, race. ? Somewhat *arch.*

c **1330** *Arth. & Merl.* 5462 (Kölbing) Aigilin, A wiȝt kniȝt of gentil lin. *c* **1400** *Sowdone Bab.* 357, I trowe, he were a develes sone, Of Belsabubbis lyne. *c* **1440** *Partonope* 7253* He is of the lyne of king Priam. **1474** Caxton *Chesse* 21 They had put out of rome tarquyn and al his lygne. *a* **1548** Hall *Chron., Hen. VII*, 6 Sole heyre male lefte of the ligne of Richarde duke of Yorke. **1634** Milton *Comus* 923 Virgin, daughter of Locrine Sprung of old Anchises line. **1697** Dryden *Virg. Georg.* iv. 303 Th'immortal Line in sure Succession reigns. **1725** Pope *Odyss.* xxiv. 588 Shame not the line whence glorious you descend. **1849** Macaulay *Hist. Eng.* ix. II. 456 The party hostile to his line, his office, and his person. **1865** R. W. Dale *Jew. Temp.* xiii. (1877) 139 He belongs to no consecrated line. **1874** Bancroft *Footpr. Time* i. 78 The line of Cyrus being extinct.

V. A direction or course of movement.

26. a. Track, course, direction; route: e.g. ***line of march, of operations***.

For ***telegraph line*** see 1 e. ***line of communication***: see communication 6 c.

1426 Lydg. *De Guil. Pilgr.* 21779 That lyne ryht shal lede the To the place..Wych thow hast..souht. **1625** N. Carpenter *Geog. Del.* i. ii. (1635) 15 All earthly bodies are by a right line directed to the Center of the Terrestriall Globe. **1626** Bacon *Sylva* §224 Sounds that move in oblique and arcuate lines. **1748** *Anson's Voy.* ii. vii. 213 This would have carried us in a direct line to the Island of Quibo. **1780** Cowper *Progr. Err.* 574 Though..the shaft..err but little from the intended line. **1819** *Blackw. Mag.* V. 737 Lying in a diagonal direction across the line of march. **1859** Bartlett *Dict. Amer., Line*, the route of a stage-coach, railroad, packet, or steamer. **1863** Kinglake *Crimea* II. 193 The neck of country by which he keeps up his communications with the base is called the 'line of operations'. **1872** B. Stewart *Physics* ii. (1876) 3 You must know..the direction or line in which I am moving. **1895** Zangwill *Master* i. vii. 82 They ran on parallel lines that never met.

b. Short for *line of rails, railway line, tram line*. Cf. branch III.

In railway lang. variously applied (*a*) to a single track of rails, as in ***the up line, the down line***; (*b*) to a railway forming one of the parts of a system, as in ***main line, branch line, loop line***; (*c*) sometimes to an entire system of railways under one management, as in ***the Midland line***. ***line clear***, a signal indicating that a line is unoccupied and that a train may therefore proceed; ***line of rail*** (see quot. 1965; cf. *end of steel*, s.v. end *sb.* 6 e).

1825 J. Nicholson *Operat. Mechanic* 643 The numerous projected lines of rail-road for diminishing the friction of carriages. **1841** *Penny Cycl.* XIX. 251/1 Curves on a main line of railway being..objectionable... When the Liverpool and Manchester line was projected. **1848** *Chambers's Inform.* I. 411/2 The plan of laying down continuous lines or tram-ways of smooth pavement for the wheels to roll over. **1851** *Illustr. Catal. Gt. Exhib.* 1148 Model of a patent railway, with a third line of rails, to prevent running off the line. **1861** Musgrave *By-roads* 195 The farmers..use the line to advantage by sending flour to inland and coast consumers by every train. **1869** *Cornh. Mag.* Mar. 282 Signalman at 3 tells signalman at 2, 'line clear, send train.' *c* **1886** R. Kipling *Railway Folk* 56 Naturally a father who has worked for the line expects the line to do something for the son. **1898** Flor. Montgomery *Tony* 11 A few stations down the line. **1907** *Daily Chron.* 16 Oct. 7/4 Martin should have pulled up until he got the line-clear signal. **1936** *Gloss. Terms Railway Signalling (B.S.I.)* 9 The block indicator shows 'Line Blocked' or 'Normal', 'Line Clear' and 'Train on Line'. **1963** Kichenside & Williams *Brit. Railway Signalling* v. 46 The signal controlling entry to the block section can only be cleared..when the block indicator for the section ahead is at 'line clear'. **1965** *Economist* 8 May 655/2 The figure [of unemployed] exceeds 75,000 and.. they are concentrated in the few towns along the so-called line-of-rail, the thin strip of urbanisation in which is concentrated..the country's [*sc.* Zambia's] economic activity. **1971** *E. Afr. Jrnl.* Mar. 17/2 A few co-operatives, along the line-of-rail especially, produce poultry products for sale.

c. U.S. ***to ride the line***: to make the circuit of the boundary of a cattle-drift in order to drive in stray cattle.

1888 T. Roosevelt in *Century Mag.* Mar. 669/1 Those who do not have to look up stray horses, and who are not forced to ride the line day in and day out.

d. *Hunting.* The straight course in the hunting field, esp. in phrases ***to ride the line, to take, keep one's own line***.

1836 *New Sporting Mag.* X. 62 Nothing is so unsportsmanlike or so dangerous as to cross a man at a leap; every one should keep his own line, and if a man when he gets close to it fears the fence before him, he should pull up. **1895** *Outing* (U.S.) XXVII. 196/2 A parson he was, after a sportsman's heart... Though an old man when I knew him, he always rode the line religiously. **1898** *St. James's Gaz.* 15 Nov. 6/1 Hounds drove along after their fox in rare style,.. the line was worked out to Houghton.

e. Chiefly *Canada* and *N.Z.* A settlement road, a bush road.

Such roads often later developed into roads of standard size and quality, and the word *line* appears in many road-names in both countries. The term may be of English dialectal origin.

1828 *Brockville* (Ontario) *Gaz.* 26 Dec. 3/4 A teamster by the name of M'Pherson from the Scotch Line. **1830** W. S. Moorsom *Lett. from Nova Scotia* ix. 344 The greater part of this line is either a rough horse-path, or in the same state as that described under the name of a 'new cut'. **1841** *N.Z. Jrnl.* No. 43. 224/2 Colonel Wakefield is also about to direct a line or bridle road (the basis of the future road) to be cut. **1853** J. M. Richmond in *Richmond-Atkinson Papers* (1960) I. iii. 133 There is what we call a *good* bush road to Rata Nui but beyond it there are two miles of bush walking along what is called a 'line'; a line is made by cutting the supple jacks and small shrubs with a bill-hook. **1863** E. H. Walshe *Cedar Creek* 103 They wished even for the corduroy expedient a little farther on, when the line became encumbered with stumps left from the under-brushing. **1880** W. H. Patterson *Gloss. Words Antrim & Down* 63 *Line*,..(2) a road. The new roads are so called. **1890** E. H. Searle *Angela* i. 2 This track was known to the neighbourhood as 'Mount's Line'. **1933** 'P. Slater' *Yellow Briar* 172 This grain was hauled down the 6th line and stored till the spring in Isaac Chafee's warehouse. **1943** *Amer. Speech* XVIII. 87 In some country districts [in New Zealand] (the Manawatu, for example) the roads are named *lines*—McDonell's Line, Richardson's Line, Union Line—presumably from early boundary or surveyors' lines. **1961** Price & Kennedy *Notes Hist. Renfrew County [Ontario]* 110 McNaughton's Plan of 1836 shows Queen's Line as an opened road. **1971** M. Tak *Truck Talk* 99 *Line*, a road, route or highway.

f. A row of traps or of poison bait.

Widely used in English-speaking areas outside the U.K.

1854 Mayne Reid *Young Voyageurs* 190 Moreover, he [*sc.* the wolverine] will follow the tracks of the trapper from one to another, until he has destroyed the whole line. **1871** R. L. Dashwood *Chiploquorgan* viii. 109 We followed an old 'sable line',..a line of traps set for that animal. **1949** *Sat. Even. Post* 22 Jan. 98/2 It is usually a glum day for the trapper when he pays his periodic visit to his line and sees in the snow the tracks of a wolverine joining the tracks that he made himself on his previous swing around. **1960** B. Crump *Good Keen Man* 31 Working from the same hut at first, we laid cyanide lines up every ridge within reach of the camp. The dodge was to work in pairs, one laying blobs of flour flavoured with oil-of-aniseed for bait, the other adding crushed cyanide to each heap of flour. We'd do this for three days, then go back over the lines cutting the ears off the dead possums for tokens. **1968** K. Weatherley *Roo Shooter* 39 Whenever a fox got on the line they lost about a quarter of their morning's catch. It would go round all the traps killing and tearing the rabbits until it was disturbed or caught in an unsprung trap.

g. A pipe or tube (of great or indefinite length in relation to its thickness).

1862 W. J. M. Rankine *Man. Civil Engin.* iii. ii. 739 From ..reservoir to..town the main pipes may form a double line, so that in the event of a failure of one line, a supply.. may be conveyed through the other line. **1895** W. T. Brannt *Petroleum* vii. 237 Beside the lines leading from the oil region to Baku..there are a number of branches which lead from the 21 principal lines to the refineries. **1921** W. F. Durand *Hydraulics of Pipe Lines* v. 231 The buried line cannot be inspected or repaired or repainted on the outside, and these conditions will..reduce the serviceable life of the line. **1962** F. I. Ordway et al. *Basic Astronautics* x. 411 As the propellants flow through the feed lines to the pump a certain amount of pressure will be lost due to friction. **1966** A. E. C. Vizard in P. Hepple *Natural Gas* 55 By using large diameter lines at relatively high pressures the potential carrying capacity of a single line can be greater. **1974** *Sunday Express* 14 Apr. 1/3 Detectives investigating the death of a diver..have found that his support line was cut. The line carried oxygen and communication cables to two divers 350 feet down.

h. *Golf.* (See quot. 1910.)

1887 W. G. Simpson *Art of Golf* ii. ix. 166 If their advice as to the line and strength be followed, and the putt comes off, it is supposed..that there was no other way of doing it. **1910** *Encycl. Brit.* XII. 223/2 *Line*, the direction in which the hole towards which the player is progressing lies with reference to the present position of his ball. **1971** Trevino & Fraley *I can help your Game* (1972) v. 72 *(caption)* The putt has been stroked but I maintain my immovable body position, concentrating on keeping the blade square to the line.

i. ***up the line***: on leave. *Naut. slang.*

1942 *Gen* 1 Sept. 13/2 When a sailor goes on leave he goes 'up the line'.

j. Phr. ***the end of the line*** (*transf.* and *fig.*). Cf. *the end of the road* (end *sb.* 3 h).

1948 *Amer. Speech* XXIII. 29 Calcutta commandos.. reached the End of the Line [*sc.* China] by flying..over the Hump. **1955** J. Potts *Death of Stray Cat* (1956) vii. 75 Lillian..turned to face Floyd, as a signal that this was the end of the line for him. **1959** E. Burgess *Divided we Fall* xx. 228 It looks like the end of the line for Roylake. Unless he can think up something—fast! **1967** Wodehouse *Company for Henry* v. 79 'Don't tell me we're there already.'.. 'Yes, this is the end of the line.' **1974** 'J. Graham' *Bloody Passage* x. 133 They have nowhere to go. This is—how do the Americans say it?—the end of the line.

27. Course of action, procedure, life, thought, or conduct.

13.. *K. Alis.* 7266 For his barouns and for myne This weore the ryghtest lyne. *c* **1330** *Arth. & Merl.* 6492 (Kölbing) þe king aros by wrongful lines &..He forlay þe stewardes wiif. **1629** N. Carpenter *Achitophel* 39 The same hand of Kingly munificence which..pointed him out the lines of his obliged loyaltie. **1787** Jefferson *Writ.* (1859) II. 112 The line I have observed with him has been [etc.]. **1800** Mrs. Hervey *Mourtray Fam.* III. 57 Promising to consult with him, in regard to what line of life he should pursue. **1826** Disraeli *Viv. Grey* ii. xiv, I should then have inherited some family line of conduct, both moral, and political. **1850** Lewis *Lett.* (1870) 233 The Protectionists, as a party, have taken no line in the matter. **1878** R. W. Dale *Lect. Preach.* v. 131 You should consider by what lines of thought..you would be able to make the truth clear to them. **1882** Pebody *Eng. Journalism* xvi. (1882) 121 The line that shall be taken upon all the questions of the day. **1893** Swinburne *Stud. Prose & Poetry* (1894) 42 Few men.. whose line of life lay so far apart from a naturalist's or a poet's can ever have loved nature or poetry better.

28. a. A department of activity; a kind or branch of business or occupation.

The sense seems to be largely due to the influence of quot. 1611, where, however, *line* (= Gr. κανών, lit. 'measuring rod', R.V. 'province') was prob. meant by the translators in a sense belonging to branch II. The phrase ***line of things***, sometimes used instead of *line* in the sense above explained, certainly arose from misapprehension of this text, where the words 'in another mans line' are parenthetical.

[**1611** Bible *2 Cor.* x. 16 And not to boast in another mans line of things made ready to our hand.] **1638** Rouse *Heav. Univ.* x. (1702) 148 Keep thou especially in thine own line neither trouble thy self for the line of another. **1655** Fuller *Ch. Hist.* ii. iv. §23 It is not out of Curiosity or Busybodinesse, to be meddling in other mens Lines. **1677** Hubbard *Narrative* ii. 86 To intrude our selves into that which is out of our Line, or beyond our Sphere. **1691** Wood *Ath. Oxon.* I. 266 He entred on the Physick line, but took no degree in that Faculty. **1773** Johnson *Let. Mrs. Thrale* 20 Sept., Seeing things in this light I consider every letter as something in the line of duty. **1787** Jefferson *Writ.* (1859) II. 95 If I can be made useful to you in any line whatever here. **1791** Boswell *Johnson* 23 Sept. an. 1777, Johnson was ..prompt to repress colloquial barbarisms..such as *line*, for *department*, or *branch*, as the civil line, the banking line. **1806–7** J. Beresford *Miseries Hum. Life* (1826) iv. Introd., Any thing much worse than usual in that line? **1809** Malkin *Gil Blas* v. i. ¶65, I had got into the matrimonial line. **1820** Byron *Blues* ii. 94 Stick to those of your play, which is quite your own line. **1836–7** Dickens *Sk. Boz, Char.* ix. (1892) 238 Mr. Augustus Cooper was in the oil and colour line. **1887** *Spectator* 16 Apr. 535/2 The line of this story is correctness rather than interest.

b. ***in*** (or ***out of***) ***one's line***: suited (or unsuited) to one's capacity, taste, etc.; ***not one's line***, not one's vocation or calling, not among one's pursuits or interests; ***to step*** (or ***get***, etc.) ***out of line***, to behave in an unconventional or unexpected manner.

1791 J. Lackington *Mem.* xxv. 191, I cannot help noticing that in one of his [*sc.* Wesley's] publications (stepping out of his line) he betray'd extreme weakness and credulity. **1838** Dickens *O. Twist* xxvi, Have you got anything in my line to-night? **1857** C. Kingsley *Two Yrs. Ago* I. p. xviii, 'He..wanted to call me out.' 'Did you go?' .. 'I told him that wasn't my line.' **1886** R. Kipling *Departm. Ditties*, etc. (1899) 35 Her jokes aren't in my line. **1888** *Harper's Mag.* July 183 Store-keeping was not in my line. **1932** D. Runyon *Guys & Dolls* ii. 37 Reasonably safe

for anyone who does not get too far out of line. **1937** M. Sharp *Nutmeg Tree* xix. 249 'Wouldn't you like to be Lady Waring?'.. 'No, I wouldn't..it's not my line.' **1938** D. Runyon *Furthermore* iii. 45 He is out of line in giving Frankie the hot foot. **1943** J. B. Priestley *Daylight on Saturday* xiii. 87 The welfare worker act.. wasn't her line at all. **1962** P. Gregory *Like Tigress at Bay* iii. 28 As long as he doesn't get out of line too often, I'll keep him on. **1962** J. Ludwig in R. Weaver *Canad. Short Stories* (1968) 2nd Ser. 244 Women weren't Sidney's line. **1973** N. Graham *Murder in Dark Room* viii. 58 You do it his way or else. I stepped out of line when I checked on Redman.

c. ***line of business*** : in the 18th- and 19th-century theatre, the kind of parts for which an actor or actress was specifically engaged. Cf. BUSINESS 20.

1775 F. Abington *Let.* in D. Garrick *Private Corr.* (1832) II. 106 Knowing the impossibility of my attempting that line of business while I am necessarily engaged in so many plays. **1807** A. Holbrook *Mem. Actress* 33 Another shocking custom is, that of giving no distinct line of business; for people, let them possess what talent they may, excel more in certain parts than in others. **1831** P. Egan *Show Folks* 27 Waiting in turn to engage young men for different '*lines of business*' to complete their companies. **1845** *Ainsworth's Mag.* VIII. 150, I have alluded to country actors ..acting characters not in their 'line of business'. **1849** *Theatrical Mirror* 17 Sept. 20 We were surprised to see Mrs. W. Daly playing the part of Lady Macbeth, being quite out of her lines of business. **1901** C. Morris *Life on Stage* vii. 40 These were the principal 'lines of business', and in an artistic sense they bound actors both hand and foot.

d. Phr. ***one's line of country***, one's pursuit, field of interest, area of study, etc. (Freq. in neg. contexts.) Also, *line of work*.

1861 T. Hughes *Tom Brown at Oxf.* III. viii. 138 This sort of thing isn't my line of country at all. **1926** R. Macaulay *Crewe Train* II. v. 115, I don't advise you to join it [*sc.* the R.C. church]. I don't think it's your line of country, exactly. **1943** N. Balchin *Small Back Room* viii. 94 What? Pinching strange females?.. That's more his line of country than yours. **1951** W. Empson *Struct. Complex Words* 15 A mistake made by Richards..is a great deal more illuminating than the successes of other writers in this line of country. **1957** G. Faber *Jowett* v. 94 Josephine's absorption in her new 'line of work'. **1966** M. Brewer *Man against Fear* i. 15 I'd like to help... But it's not my line of country. Only the police can catch them. **1972** *News & Observer* (Raleigh, N. Carolina) 30 Dec 4/3 No one lives in the sticks or is asked his line of work very often.

†**29.** Used by Shaks. in *pl.* for: 'Goings on', caprices or fits of temper. [Cf. the Warwickshire dial. phrase *on a line* = in a rage.]

1598 Shaks. *Merry W.* iv. ii. 22 Your husband is in his olde lines againe. **1606** —— *Tr. & Cr.* ii. iii. 139 Yea watch His pettish lines. [*Mod. edd.* lunes *in both places.*]

30. a. *Comm.* An order received by a traveller or agent for goods; the goods so ordered; also, the stock on hand of a particular class of goods, goods of a particular design.

1834 *Chambers's Edin. Jrnl.* III. 9/3 Even those [travelling salesmen] whose *line* seems the most hopeless and frivolous. **1882** *Daily News* 4 Mar., Spinners content themselves with supplying special lines and immediate requirement. **1892** *Money Market Rev.* 6 Feb., Another error committed by some of the Trusts has consisted in taking inordinately large 'lines' of particular Stocks. **1892** *Daily News* 11 Apr. 6/6 In spite of the new French tariff we still continue to receive fair 'lines' for silver goods from Paris. **1930** H. Cousins in V.A. Demant *Just Price* v. 102 No business can expect that all its 'lines' will be successful. **1959** *Punch* 16 Sept. 177/1, I can do a nice line in powder compacts. **1971** *Cabinet Maker & Retail Furnisher* 1 Oct. 15/3 Rather than let a slow selling line stand on the shop floor it is reduced immediately.

b. The amount which one underwriter (or one company) accepts as his share of the total value of the subject matter covered by insurance.

1899 Hooper & Graham *Mod. Business Methods* 144 The names and the amounts on the back of a policy..would appear thus... Each of the above persons is said to 'take a line' in the policy. **1905** [see *front-ranker*]. **1931** *Times* 14 Mar. 12/6 Many of those [*sc.* insurance companies] who have written large lines..are known to have been influenced by a desire [etc.]. **1974** W. L. Catchpole *Business Guide to Insurance* xxiv. 202 If the chosen underwriter.. agrees to accept a substantial line at an equitable risk, he becomes the leading underwriter on the slip.

c. ***line of credit***: a loan by one country to another, to be utilized by the second for buying goods from the first; credit extended by a bank to a commercial concern to a certain amount; the amount so extended.

1958 *Listener* 18 Sept. 407/1 A line of credit for £8,000,000 from Australia will have helped matters. **1971** *Daily Tel.* 1 Jan. 1/1 A total of 41 million Canadian dollars ..was repaid on the Canadian line of credit.

VI. Combinations.

31. a. Simple attrib. and objective, as ***line battalion, end, -guard, -length, -maker, -making, -numbering, -pair, -regiment, -rime, -room***; ***line-numbered, -throwing*** adjs.

1876 Voyle & Stevenson *Milit. Dict.* 50/1, 2 companies from each of the *line battalions assigned to the sub-district. **1748** W. Hardy *Miner's Guide* 184 Your Assistant having made a mark upon the Ground, where the *Line End touched last. **1908** *Daily Chron.* 23 Oct. 9/4 Now he types instead of stamping the last words so as to obtain an even line end. **1930** T. Sasaki *On Lang. R. Bridges' Poetry* I. v. 21 The strongest stress..is the one at the line-end. **1961** T. Landau *Encycl. Librarianship* (ed. 2) 226/1 *Line division mark*, a vertical line or double vertical lines used in bibliographical transcription to indicate the place of the ends of lines... Also called line end stroke, dividing stroke. **1888** 'J. Bickerdyke' *Bk. All-round Angler* ii. 28 A Nottingham reel fitted with a little invention..intended to prevent the line uncoiling..off the reel. This *line-guard has answered beyond my expectations. **1905** *PMLA* XX. 814 The uniform background of the recurrent *line-lengths. **1929** H. Crane *Let.* 30 Aug. (1965) 344 The line-lengths are longer than in any other section. **1897** *Daily News* 13 Sept. 7/3 Some six miles further on, the point where [railway] *line-making was actually in process. **1905** *Academy* 14 Oct. 1072/2 We can see him turning over the page, *line-numbered. **1959** *N. & Q.* Sept. 313/2 The recent line-numbered edition by W. J. B. Owen. **1953** Amos & Birkinshaw *Television Engin.* I. ii. 33 The system of *line numbering must be explained... The lines are numbered according to the positions they occupy in the raster, number 1 being the top line and, in the British system, 405 the bottom line. **1966** *English Studies* XLVII. 296 His marginal references to Folio lines and passages (using the line-numbering of the Globe edition). **1867** Cayley in *Coll. Math. Papers* (1893) VI. 201 A conic is a curve of the second order and second class; *quà* curve of the second order it may degenerate into a pair of lines, or *line-pair. **1864** Trevelyan *Compet. Wallah* (1866) 255 Eighteen months in such a school would have turned the French *line-regiments into Zouaves. **1860** Marsh *Eng. Lang.* xxv. 554 *Line-rhyme is a constituent of all but the most ancient forms of Icelandic verse. *a* **1643** W. Cartwright *Ordinary* iii. ii, To hang up cloaths, or any thing you please, Your Worship cannot want *line-room. **1887** *Daily News* 9 Mar. 6/7 A *Line-throwing Gun.

†**b.** *Bot.* Used = *linear-*. *Obs.*

1787 *Fam. Plants* I. 37 The leaflets line-lanc'd, keel'd, erect. *Ibid.* 41 Seeds one, cover'd, line-oblong. *Ibid.* 105 Filaments five, line-compress'd.

32. Special combs.: **line angle** *Dentistry*, the angle at the junction of two surfaces of a tooth or cavity; † **line-angular** *a.* (see quot.); **line-at-a-time printer** = *line printer*; **line-backer**, in Amer. and Canad. football (see quot. 1961); **line-bait**, bait used in line-fishing; **line-ball**: *Baseball* (see quot.); also in *Lawn Tennis*; **line blanking** *Television*, the suppression of signals that would contribute to the picture during fly-back of the scanning spot between the transmission of successive lines; freq. *attrib.*; **line block**, a block bearing a design in relief from which an illustration made up of lines without variations in tone may be printed; an illustration printed in this way; also *attrib.*; **line-book**, (*a*) *Printing* (*Obs.* exc. *Hist.*), a book in which compositors working in companionships (chiefly 19th c.) kept account of the lines of set type credited and debited to them; (*b*) (also **lines-book**) *R.A.F. slang*, a record of boasts (see 13 g, above); **line-bred** *a.*, produced by line-breeding; **line-breeding** *U.S.*, 'the breeding of animals with reference to securing descent from a particular family, especially in the female line' (Webster *Suppl.* 1879); **line-camp** *N. Amer.*, a camp, esp. a cabin, for ranch hands in an outlying part of a large ranch; **line-casting** *a.*, of a composing machine, casting type a line at a time; so **line-cast** *a.*, **line-caster**; **line-cod**, cod-fish caught with a line; **line-conch**, a large gasteropod of Florida, *Fasciolaria distans*, marked by black lines (*Cent. Dict.*); **line-coordinate** *Math.*, one of a set of quantities defining the position of a line; **line density** (see quot.); also *gen.*, density or concentration of lines; **line drawing**, a drawing done with a pen or pencil; also *fig.*; **line-drawn** *a.*, made by line-drawing; **line-drive** *Baseball*, a ball driven straight and low above the ground; **line drop** *Electr. Engin.*, the voltage drop between two points on a transmission line (as a result of resistance, leakage, or other causes); **line-ending**, (*a*) = *line-filling*; (*b*) the end of a line of poetry; **line-engraved** *ppl. a.*, inscribed with a line engraving; **line-engraver**, one who does line engraving; **line engraving**, the art of engraving 'in line', i.e. by lines incised on the plate, as distinguished from etching and mezzotint; an engraving executed in this manner; **line-fence** *N. Amer.*, a boundary fence between two farms or ranches; **line-filling**, a flourish or ornament serving to fill up a line of writing; **line finder** *Telephony*, a selector which searches for the calling subscriber's line when he lifts his receiver so that the line can be connected to a group of selectors available to any caller; **line-finishing** = *line-filling*; **line-firing** *Mil.*, firing by a body of men in line; **line-fisherman**, a man who fishes with a line; so **line-fishing** *sb.* and *a.*; **line frequency** *Television*, the number of scanning lines produced per second; **line gale** *U.S.* = *line-storm*; **line gauge** *Printing*, a ruler showing the size of a type or types; **line graph** = GRAPH *sb.*[1] 2 (as distinguished from a *bar graph*, in which vertical rectangles represent the values of the dependent variable); **line haul** *U.S. slang* (see quots.); **line-hunter**, a hound which follows its quarry by the line of the scent alone; so **line-hunting** *a.*; **line-integral** *Math.*, the integral, taken along a line, of any differential that has a continuously varying value along that line; **line-integration**, the operation of finding a line-integral; **line-knife**, a knife used on a whaler for cutting the harpoon rope; **line loss** *Electr. Engin.*, loss of electrical energy along a transmission line (as a result of resistance, leakage, or other causes); **line-maker**, 'a manufacturer of rope, sash-lines, clothes-lines, etc.' (Simmonds *Dict. Trade* 1858); **line management, manager**: see sense 19 d above; **line officer**, a military or naval officer of the line; **line pin**, one of the iron pins used to fasten a bricklayer's line (see quot. 1859); **line pipe**, pipe specially manufactured for use in pipelines; **line printer**, a printer that is capable of printing a whole line of characters in each cycle of operation and is usu. operated under the control of a computer; †**line-reel**, a reel upon which a gardener's line is wound; **line-ride** *v. intr. U.S.*, to perform the action of line-riding; **line-rider** *N. Amer.*, one engaged in line-riding; **line-riding** *U.S.*, riding the line (see sense 26 c); **line-rocket**, a small rocket attached to a line or wire along which it is made to run; **line scan**, (*a*) the motion of a scanning beam or spot along a line; (*b*) the electrical signal which causes this; (*c*) an apparatus or technique which scans an object or scene line by line; so **line scanning** *vbl. sb.*; **line-sequential** *a. Television*, applied to a system of colour television in which each line of the picture is in one of the three primary colours, the colour changing for each successive line; **line shaft, shafting**, a shaft, or shafting, of relatively great length from which a number of separate machines are driven by countershafts or endless belts; **line-side** *attrib.*, adjacent to a railway line; **line-soldier**, a soldier of the line, a linesman; **line space**, the space provided for a line of typescript; so ***line-space lever, mechanism***, etc., the device that turns the platen of a typewriter to a new line of writing; **line-spacing**, the space between successive lines of typescript; *attrib.*, of the device that moves the platen to a new line; **line spectrum**, a spectrum containing lines distributed apparently at random (rather than in groups as in a band spectrum); hence, an emission (of light, sound, or other radiation) composed of a number of discrete frequencies or energies; **line-squall**, a squall, consisting of a violent straight blast of cold air with snow or rain, and occurring along the axis of a V-shaped depression; so **line-thunderstorm**; **line-storm** *U.S.*, an equinoctial storm; **line-synchronizing** *a. Television*, applied to a pulse transmitted in a television signal at the end of each line which initiates fly-back of the scanning spot in the receiver, so keeping the scanning process in synchronism with that in the transmitter; also abbreviated to **line-sync**; **line-tub**, a tub in which a whaling line is kept; **line-way**, † (*a*) a tow-path; (*b*) 'a straight direct path' (Halliwell 1847); **line-width** *Physics*, the width of a spectral line as measured by the difference in wavelength, wave number, or frequency between its two sides; **line-wire** *Telegraphy*, the wire which connects the stations of a telegraph-line; **line-work**, (*a*) drawing or designing executed with the pen or pencil (as opposed to wash, etc.); (*b*) (see quot. 1968); (*c*) work as a lineman. Also LINEMAN, LINESMAN, LINE STANDARD.

1908 G. V. Black *Work on Operative Dentistry* I. 295 *Line angles. **1930** W. H. O. McGehee *Text-bk. Operative Dentistry* xi. 338 Flatten the gingival and axial walls, making a definite line angle at their junction. **1963** C. R. Cowell et al. *Inlays, Crowns, & Bridges* iii. 15 Complete the proximal box, using a chisel to plane its vertical walls and to sharpen the line angles. **1774** M. Mackenzie *Maritime Surv.* p. xviii, A *Line-angular Survey is, when the Coast is measured all along with a Chain, or Wheel, and the Angles taken at each Point and Turn of the Land with a Theodolite, or magnetic Needle. **1955** *Jrnl. Assoc. Computing Machinery* II. 294 *Line-at-a-time printer (92 characters per line), operating at a speed of 150 lines per minute. **1963** Gould & Ellis *Digital Computer Technol.* xi. 141 The line-at-a-time printers have, in the main, been adapted from the tabulating machines of punched card practice. **1961** Webster, **Linebacker*, a football player stationed within one to four yards of the line of scrimmage and expected to make quick tackles close to the line of scrimmage on running plays and to protect against short passes. **1968** *Globe & Mail* (Toronto) 13 Feb. 29/1 Darryl Burgess, a 225-pound linebacker from St. Mary's. **1969** *Eugene* (Oregon) *Register-Guard* 3 Dec. 10/2 Oregon linebacker Tom Graham..played well enough to make both UPI and AP All-Coast teams as a rookie. **1970** *Toronto Daily Star* 24 Sept. 18/5 We can always move Corrigall to linebacker. **1973** *Washington Post* 13 Jan. C5/4 The most misguided portion of the show comes during Jones' interviews of Jim Brown, the former football player-turned-actor, and Ray May, a linebacker for the Baltimore Colts. **1895** *Outing* (U.S.) XXX. 432/1 Minnows, frogs, crayfish or

any favorite *line bait. **1874** H. CHADWICK *Base Ball Man.* 55 A '*line ball' or 'liner' is a ball sent swiftly from the bat to the field almost on a horizontal line. **1891** F. C. BURNAND *Miss Decima* 22 Chorus (outside—watching a game of Lawn Tennis)..Ah! 'Line' ball. **1952** HOWE & DUCLOUX tr. *Kerkhof & Werner's Television* iv. 76 The total *line blanking of the picture signal is 0·15 L. **1957** AMOS & BIRKINSHAW *Television Engin.* (rev. ed.) I. ii. 31 The synchronising signals are not the only form of intelligence which must be transmitted between lines; an additional signal, known as the line-blanking signal, must also be inserted. **1966** G. H. HUTSON *Television Receiver Theory* I. iii. 31 The line blanking period is divided into..the front porch, the line sync. pulse and the back porch. **1896** A. BEARDSLEY *Let.* 29 Sept. (1971) 173 The rest of the drawing has come out so hardly and coldly in the *line block. **1924** E. POUND *Let.* 3 Dec. (1971) 191, I think the idea of ten or twelve Blacks of size that cd. go by post, and that cd. be done in line block, might be useful. **1936** *Burlington Mag.* Mar. p. xiv/1 Line-block illustrations from the author's own drawings. **1956** *Nature* 18 Feb. 301/1 The illustrations are well chosen, both the line-blocks and the half-tones. **1972** P. GASKELL *New Introd. Bibliogr.* 272 The detail of all but the very best photographic line blocks tends to be slightly rougher at the edges than that of wood engravings. **1876** J. GOULD *Letter-Press Printer* 33 The system adopted in some of the smaller houses is for each compositor to make up and impose his own pages, the making-up being passed from one compositor to the companion who follows him, accompanied by the *line book. **1942** *Observer* 4 Oct. 7/2 'There I was, upside down, in cloud, ten-tenths, at 1,500 ft. ..' But you never get to the end of your story if you were so foolish as to begin like that. 'Lineshoot!' they would cry. 'Line!' And most squadrons have a Line Book in which such statements are written down, to their authors' perpetual shame. **1943** C. H. WARD-JACKSON *Piece of Cake* 40 *Lines book*, in which are recorded exaggerated statements made at one time or another by Mess members. **1945** E. TAYLOR *At Mrs. Lippincote's* xxiii. 194 Quick, the line-book! **1972** P. GASKELL *New Introd. Bibliogr.* 193 He [*sc.* the clicker] kept an account of the number of lines that each man set, both in a line-book and by marking the copy. **1891** R. WALLACE *Rural Econ. Austral. & N.Z.* xxxi. 400 The impression that tuberculosis is more prevalent among high *line-bred shorthorns than among the ordinary country-bred cattle. **1960** *Times* 19 Sept. 3/4, 20 dams were chosen..these being line-bred. **1971** *Amer. N. & Q.* Apr. 126/2 The quarter horse, developed from cross-breeding Spanish stock imported to America via Florida (Chickasaw horses) and what Nelson Nye calls 'line-bred orientals' from England, was originally a sport animal. **1888** *Century Mag.* Mar. 667/2 But some of the men are out in the *line camps, and the ranchman has occasionally to make the round of these. **1949** *10 Story Western* May 12/2 He had been telling them all how he was going to winter here at the Buffalo Crossing line camp. **1963** R. D. SYMONS *Many Trails* v. 52 Most outfits had what they call 'line camps' strung along the limits of their range, from which 'line riders' operated. **1973** S. JENNETT *Making of Bks.* (ed. 5) xv. 286 The italic [of Linotype Baskerville] is a little loose fitting, its width, as in other *line-cast type-faces, being governed by the roman. **1972** *Phys. Bull.* Sept. 533/1 These 'second generation' photosetters..are reasonably cheap and are considerably faster than the latest *line-casters which are also tape driven. **1913** *Inland Printer* July 486 (Advt.), There are thousands of publishers all over the United States who have been waiting for a *line-casting and composing machine so simple and easy to operate that it would prove practical in the small shop. **1916** LEGROS & GRANT *Typogr. Printing-Surfaces* iv. 15 Line-casting machine type-metal undergoes a wastage or depreciation. **1973** S. JENNETT *Making of Bks.* (ed. 5) v. 83 The Intertype Fotosetter was also an adaptation, of the Intertype line-casting machine. **1877** HOLDSWORTH *Sea Fisheries* 80 Very few *line-cod are caught in the North Sea for the next three months. **1866** CAYLEY in *Coll. Math. Papers* (1892) V. 521 Considered as (what in the theory of *line-coordinates it in fact is) a particular case of the double tangent. **1873** MAXWELL *Electr. & Magn.* §64 I. 68 In this case we may define the *line-density at any point to be the limiting ratio of the electricity on an element of the line to the length of that element when the element is diminished without limit. **1963** *Reshaping of Brit. Railways* (Brit. Railways Board) 65 Line densities are not the only measure of the use made of the railway. **1971** *Fremdsprachen* XV. 276 It can be used to restore old drawings and to improve line density for microfilming. **1891** A. BEARDSLEY *Let.* 25 Dec. (1971) 32, I am anxious to say something somewhere, on the subject of *lines* and *line drawing. **1895** ZANGWILL *Master* II. vii. 205 To undertake wash-drawings, line-drawings, colour-work or lithography. **1959** *Listener* 9 July 76/3 It [*sc.* an overture] is finer line-drawing than the Gordon Jacob work. **1966** *Ibid.* 6 Jan. 36/3 Over 300 [flowers] are illustrated in close-up colour photographs and 100-odd more in line drawings. **1967** E. SHORT *Embroidery & Fabric Collage* ii. 51 There is a tendency to produce line drawings which might just as well have been done with a pencil. **1903** *Westm. Gaz.* 17 Oct. 4/2 An order of the King in Council was published with two *line-drawn illustrations. **1931** *Randolph Enterprise* (Elkins, W. Virginia) 9 July 5/3 Boyles turned in the star catch of the day by racing..to pull down a *line drive with one hand. **1968** *Washington Post* 4 July C1/3 Mantle was safe as Ron Hansen's throw, after snagging a line drive by Andy Kosco, was a trifle tardy. **1894** *Line drop [see *line loss* below]. **1962** *Newnes Conc. Encycl. Electr. Engin.* 86/1 D.C. boosters are normally low-voltage d.c. generators employed for adjusting a supply voltage, in line-drop compensation and as an aid in controlling the charging of large accumulator batteries. **1928** E. G. MILLAR *Eng. Illuminated Manuscripts XIVth & XVth Cent.* i. 9 Many of the *line-endings..were added in the fifteenth century. **1962** W. NOWOTTNY *Lang. Poets Use* v. 120 The method he adopts is the eccentric placing of line-endings. **1802** *Monthly Mag.* XIV. 253/1 The best *line-engraved prints preserved their superiority. **1881** *Stamp-Collector's Ann.* 5 The fall of the penny stamp and all its line-engraved family. **1936** *Discovery* Dec. 386/1 Practically all [18th-century tradesman's cards] are line- or stipple-engraved. **1965** *Stamp Collecting* ('Know the Game' Series) 44/1 Stamps printed from recess-plates are said to be line-engraved. **1873** *Illustr. London News* 15 Mar. 247/3 This eminent *line-engraver. **1965** DOUGHTY & WAHL in D. G. Rossetti *Lett.* I. 9 Charles Warren (1767–1823), line-engraver and a noted illustrator. **1802** *Monthly Mag.* XIV. 253/1 The *line engraving is now attaining its deserved preeminence. **1810** *Trans. Soc. Arts* XXVIII. 14 Line Engravings of Historical Subjects. **1849** *Chambers's Inform.* II. 729/2 Effect is obtained in etching in the same manner as in line-engraving—namely, by depth. **1845** J. COMLY *Reader & Bk. Knowl.* 96 Always keep good *line-fences. **1854** S. H. HAMMOND *Hills, Lakes & Forest Streams* xxv. 250 Later still, the old line fence was pulled away. **1893** E. R. YOUNG *Stories from Indian Wigwams* 34 One morning I..went off to help a couple of Indians about their line fences. **1946** *Chicago Daily News* 23 Mar. 1/8 He got into an argument with the boy's parents over the building of a line fence between their properties. **1954** C. BRUCE *Channel Shore* 12 From there a person could look east and west along..the northern fields ..separated by line fences. **1895** M. R. JAMES *Abbey St. Edmund's at Bury* 93 The small initials..as well as the *line-fillings, are of the most absolutely perfect kind. **1922** GLAZEBROOK *Dict. Appl. Physics* II. 834/2 The *line finder corresponds to the answering plug in a manual exchange. **1950** J. ATKINSON *Herbert & Procter's Telephony* (new ed.) II. i. 19/2 If..the volume of traffic and the number of 1st selectors are considerable, then line-finders may become more expensive than subscribers' uniselectors. **1968** E. H. JOLLEY *Introd. Telephony & Telegr.* viii. 232/2 The subscribers' lines are multiplied over the bank of contacts of the line-finders so that each subscriber's line appears on each line-finder. **1906** E. JOHNSTON *Writing & Illuminating* xii. 205 *Line-finishings are used to preserve the evenness of the text when lines of writing fall short. **1802** C. JAMES *Milit. Dict.*, **Line-firings* are executed separately and independently by each battalion. **1858** GREENER *Gunnery* 405 For close quarters, line-firing, or quickness of loading, the musket will hold its place for centuries to come. **1899** *Daily News* 12 Apr. 6/2 The *line-fishermen off our coasts. **1848** C. A. JOHNS *Week at Lizard* 242 They depend for this supply on *line-fishing. **1897** *Daily News* 10 Feb. 6/2 The screw line-fishing boat George Baird. **1936** O. S. PUCKLE tr. *M. von Ardenne's Television Reception* i. 11 The total number of lines in the complete picture is 240, scanned sequentially and horizontally at 25 picture traversals per second... The *line frequency is thus 6,000 impulses per second. **1973** *Newnes Colour Television Servicing Manual* I. i. 26/1 Sawtooth voltage at line frequency is developed across the inductive network. **1836** *Knickerbocker* VII. 17, I must take the oars myself, for that blamed *line gale has kept me in bilboes..a dog's age. **1948** *Words into Type* 544 **Line gauge*, a printer's measuring rule, marked off in nonpareils and picas, sometimes showing other type measurements also. **1967** KARCH & BUBER *Offset Processes* 544 *Line gauge*, a printer's ruler usually having 6 and 12 point graduations. Sometimes with other point scales, as: agate, 9-point, 10-point, etc. **1956** *Line graph [see DECODE *v.*]. **1972** *Scholarly Publishing* III. 274 Bar graphs, line graphs, pie charts, and other illustrative devices. **1942** BERREY & VAN DEN BARK *Amer. Thes. Slang* §770 **Line haul*, a scheduled truck route. **1971** M. TAK *Truck Talk* 99 *Line haul*, a scheduled truck run or movement of freight between cities. **1852** R. S. SURTEES *Sponge's Sp. Tour* (1893) 355 Many of them [*sc.* hounds] had their heads up... Some few of the *line hunters were persevering with the scent over the greasy ground. **1856** WHYTE MELVILLE *Kate Cov.* xii, They are capital 'line-hunters', so says John. **1890** *Sat. Rev.* 1 Feb. 135/1 In the vast forests of Europe a line-hunter on the scent of an ungalled hart would be lost to all eternity. *Ibid.*, The old slow *line-hunting staghound. **1873** MAXWELL *Electr. & Magn.* § 69 I. 71 *Line-Integral of Electric Force, or Electromotive Force along an Arc of a Curve. *Ibid.* (1881) II. 232 The magnetic potential, as found by a *line-integration of the magnetic force. **1851** H. MELVILLE *Whale* xli. 202 The captain seizing the *line-knife from his broken prow, had dashed at the whale. **1894** A. T. SNELL *Electr. Motive Power* iv. 126 The *line loss remains constant when the percentage of the line drop is kept the same for variations of supply pressure. **1953** C. F. HOCKETT in Saporta & Bastian *Psycholinguistics* (1961) 64/1 To supply one hundred-watt light bulb, a generator must transmit one hundred watts of power, plus a bit more to make up for line-loss. **1970** D. WATERFIELD *Continental Waterboy* iii. 29 And you have line loss, particularly with very long transmission lines. **1667** PEPYS *Diary* 19 July, The pretty woman, the *line-maker's wife that lived in Fenchurch Streete. **1850** R. GLISAN *Jrnl. Army Life* (1874) i. 2 This rank..avails its possessor..in everything except commanding troops when a *line officer is present. **1909** *Westm. Gaz.* 1 Feb. 2/1 Wives of line-officers, engineers, servants. **1925** R. GRAVES *Welchman's Hose* 29 They hadn't one Line-officer left, after Arras. **1688** R. HOLME *Armoury* III. 395/2 Two *Line Pins, with a Line lapped or raped about part of both. **1700** MOXON *Mech. Exerc.* (1703) 247 A Pair of Line Pins of Iron, with a length of Line on them. **1823** P. NICHOLSON *Pract. Build.* 387 The Line Pins, consist of two iron pins, with a line of about sixty feet, fastened by one of its extremities to each. **1859** *Gwilt's Encycl. Archit.* (ed. 4) II. iii. 514 The line pins..for fastening and stretching the line at proper intervals of the wall, that each course may be kept straight in the face and level on the bed. **1923** *Amer. Petroleum Inst. Bull.* 31 Dec. 117/2 The work of this committee has been.. to the end that a specification might be had that would: (1) Minimize losses arising out of the use of casing *line pipe, tubing and drill pipe, in oil field operations. **1930** L. D. BURRITT in Walker & Crocker *Piping Handbk.* xiv. 719 Line-pipe threads are of the same form and taper as American Standard threads, but the pipe is threaded with a longer length of thread than is standard pipe. **1967** *Times Rev. Industry* Feb. 45/3 The rising demand for line pipe made sense of a connexion between South Durham and Stewarts and Lloyds, which has been marketing X60 seamless line pipe up to 18 inches in diameter for many years. **1955** *Jrnl. Assoc. Computing Machinery* II. 294 Output: *Line printer of a BULL tabulating machine. **1962** *Mod. Lang. Rev.* LVII. 171 The Cambridge Mathematical Laboratory possesses a line-printer which is directly operated by EDSAC 2. **1970** O. DOPPING *Computers & Data Processing* iv. 73 A normal speed for a computer line printer is 1,000 lines per minute. *Ibid.* xi. 164 A mechanical line printer has one printing device for each printing position in the line (for each 'column'). The number of printing positions is often between 100 and 160. **1616** SURFL. & MARKH. *Country Farme* 256 When you haue cast your ground, you shall begin to stretch your line with good and firme *line-reeles, to take the bredth and length of your borders round about. **1883** *Rep. Productions Agric. 10th Census 1880* (U.S. Census Office) 971 The cattle-raisers were obliged to fence or to '*line-ride' to keep their cattle from trespassing. *Ibid.*, The cattle of northwest Texas are in a large measure controlled or held on their ranges by a system of 'line-riding'. **1920** Line-rider [see *fence-rider* (FENCE *sb.* 11)]. **1942** E. E. DALE *Cow Country* 119 This by no means did away with the work of the line rider, though it was made somewhat easier. **1963** Line rider [see *line-camp* above]. **1883** *Rep. Productions Agric. 10th Census 1880* (U.S. Census Office) 973 The cowboys engaged in this work are called '*line-riders'. **1888** T. ROOSEVELT in *Century Mag.* Mar. 668/2 Line-riding is very cold work, and dangerous, too, when the men have to be out in a blinding snowstorm. **1799** G. SMITH *Laboratory* I. 19 Charges for the *line rockets. **1938** J. H. REYNER *Testing Television Sets* iv. 46 If the time base is operating the appropriate noise will be heard—a rapid ticking on the frame scan and a high squeal on the *line scan. **1957** D. G. FINK *Television Engin. Handbk.* x. 12 The harmonic components of the line-scan spectrum may thus be thought of as carrier waves, each with a 60-cps modulation envelope. **1962** *Daily Tel.* 28 Aug. 13/5 Line scan is a system for reconnaissance and mapping at low levels. **1966** D. G. BRANDON *Mod. Techniques Metallogr.* 257 The line scans being automatically repeated 50 μm apart. **1971** *Daily Tel.* (Colour Suppl.) 22 Jan. 22/1 False colour photography..does not record gradations of temperatures exactly, and these can be very important. The instrument which does this is the infra-red linescan, which scans the scene line by line like a television scanner, building up a composite picture from the heat records. **1935** *Television Today* I. 300/2 The *line scanning is usually spoken of as the scanning motion. **1971** H. E. ENNES *Television Broadcasting* iii. 125 Picture information is contained in the fundamental and harmonics of the 60-Hz field frequency and the 15,750-Hz line-scanning frequency. **1949** *Electronics* Dec. 68/3 The change of color is introduced between successive lines in the scanning field, that is, the system is in the *line-sequential class. **1965** G. DU CLOUX tr. *Holm's Colour Television Explained* (ed. 2) iii. 55 The R.C.A. appeared to have arrived at the ultimate solution with a line-sequential, or possibly even a dot-sequential system. **1881** *Spon's Dict. Engin.* Suppl. III. 1093 For the bearings of *line shafts cast iron is ..the best. **1936** Line shaft [see *jack shaft* s.v. JACK *sb.*[1] 34 a]. **1974** *Encycl. Brit. Macropædia* XI. 253/2 In the days when all machines in a shop were driven by one large..prime mover, it was necessary to have long lineshafts running the length of the shop and supplying power..to shorter countershafts, jackshafts, or headshafts. **1872** J. RICHARDS *Treat. Wood-Working Machines* 95 Pulleys for *line-shafting running at high speed should be light and true. **1966** *McGraw-Hill Encycl. Sci. & Technol.* XII. 240/2 The delivery of power to the machines in a shop has generally been converted from line shafting to individual electric motors for each machine. **1961** WEBSTER, **Lineside*, adjacent to a railway line. **1967** *Listener* 26 Jan. 123/1 This can be prodigiously expensive if it involves disturbance of lineside property. **1975** *Daily Tel.* 18 July 2/8 By next year it is expected that there will be fewer faults in the 547 lineside signals and 465 points controlled by the new box. **1869** E. A. PARKES *Pract. Hygiene* (ed. 3) 551 Two-thirds of each *line-soldier's service is passed abroad. **1951** *Oxf. Jun. Encycl.* IV. 472/2 When it reaches the end, a *line space lever is pushed to move the paper up to a new line and return the carriage to the right. **1962** *Which?* Dec. 357/1 Some of the models.. had only two positions for their line space selector, the others all had three. **1957** *Encycl. Brit.* XXII. 645/1 The machine was soon renamed the Remington. Among its original features which were still standard..in the 1950s are the paper cylinder with its *line-spacing and carriage-return mechanism. *c* **1961** *Imperial Type Faces* (Imperial Typewriter Co.), The number of words which can be typed on a quarto page..var[ies] according to the pitch of the letter and line-spacings. **1873** *Phil. Mag.* XLVI. 406 When the gas is near atmospheric pressure, the *line-spectrum of nitrogen is brilliant. **1885** [see BAND *sb.*[2] 13]. **1923** GLAZEBROOK *Dict. Appl. Physics* IV. 780/1 Luminous spectra can be divided into two classes, namely continuous spectra..and discontinuous spectra... Discontinuous spectra may be subdivided into line and band spectra. **1955** MILLER & NICELY in Saporta & Bastian *Psycholinguistics* (1961) 165/2 Acoustically, this means that the voiceless consonants are aperiodic or noisy in character, whereas a periodic or line-spectrum component is superimposed on the noise for voiced consonants. **1957** [see BAND *sb.*[2] 13]. **1962** H. D. BUSH *Atomic & Nucl. Physics* iv. 96 There are two main features of a β-particle spectrum, a continuous spectrum with energies ranging from zero to a maximum value..and a line spectrum consisting of a number of discrete energies superimposed on the continuous spectrum. **1962** A. NISBETT *Technique Sound Studio* 254 A sound which is composed of individual frequencies (fundamental and harmonics or partials, or a combination of pure tones) has a line spectrum. Bands of noise have a band spectrum. **1887** R. ABERCROMBY *Weather* 241 This class of atmospheric disturbance, which, for the sake of classification, we will call '*Line-squalls'. **1850** N. KINGSLEY *Diary* (1914) 115 A fine day with a strong West wind; rather think the *line storm is over. **1867** WHITTIER *The Palatine* 63 Along their foam-white curves of shore They heard the line-storm rave and roar. **1939** R. FROST *Coll. Poems* 38 The line-storm clouds fly tattered and swift. **1940** W. T. COCKING *Television Receiving Equipment* xix. 281 When a very large amplitude of *line sync pulse is applied to the line generator it is tripped at half-line intervals during the frame sync pulses. **1969** C. R. G. REED *Princ. Colour Television Syst.* vi. 71 The line sync pulse duration is 4·7 μs. **1935** *Television Today* I. 300 The time duration of the *line synchronising pulse is usually about 10 per cent. of that of each line. **1953** AMOS & BIRKINSHAW *Television Engin.* I. i. 16 A synchronizing signal is sent out every time the scanning beam at the transmitter reaches the end of a line; this signal is termed the line-sychronizing signal (abbreviated to line-sync signal) and has the function of initiating line flyback at the receiver. **1887** R. ABERCROMBY *Weather* 248 We will now give an example of *line-thunderstorms which are not associated with the trough either of a V or a cyclone. **1839** *Knickerbocker* XIII. 382 *Line-tubs, water-kegs, and wafe-poles, were thrown hurriedly into the boats. **1851** H. MELVILLE *Moby Dick* III. xlviii. 287 Reaching out after the revolving line-tubs, oars and other floating furniture. **1464** *Rolls of Parlt.* V. 569/2 A waye on either syde of the seid water called a *lyne weye, to convey the said Trowes, Botes, Cobles and Shutes, on the seid water. **1946** *Nature* 28 Sept. 450/1 Measures of

effective *line-width, made..upon the brilliant reversal of the *Hα* (λ 6563) contour. **1962** *Science Survey* III. 67 The current reports of the line-width of the radiation produced by the helium-neon optical maser show the line-width is approximately one cycle per second. **1971** *New Scientist* 3 June 565/2 Molecular linewidths are of the order of 10^{-3} cm^{-1} at room temperature. **1972** *Physics Bull.* Feb. 83/2 A dye laser tuned to give a sodium linewidth of a hundredth of an ångstrom. **1870** F. L. POPE *Electr. Tel.* iii. (1872) 24 A Telegraphic Circuit consists of one or more batteries, the *line wire, the instruments and the earth. **1895** ZANGWILL *Master* II. vii. 205 Cross-hatching, solid black, *line-work. **1904** *Brit. Printer* Apr. 86/2 Line work negatives are printed on to zinc. **1911** H. QUICK *Yellowstone Nights* ii. 32 I'm just through with a summer's line-work in the West. **1962** *Times* 10 Jan. 13/4 The pen drawing..is admirable..projecting in its free and open linework all the completeness of an oil composition. **1968** *Gloss. Terms Offset Lithogr. Printing* (*B.S.I.*) 10 *Line work*, copy or reproduction consisting of solid elements only, as distinct from half-tone.

†**line**, *sb.*³ *Obs.* In quots. lyne; see also LIQUE. [a. OF. *lin*, *ligne*, *ling(e.*] Some kind of ship.

[*c* **1394** MALVERNE *Contn. Higden* (Rolls) IX. 91 Franci et Hispani in uno balynger et una lyna sulcantes maria circa ora maritima Angliæ.] *c* **1400** T. WALSINGHAM *Hist. Angl.* (Rolls) II. 135 Duæ grandes galeyæ, et aliud genus ratis quod vocatur 'lyne', et una bargia, et septem balingariæ. **1523** LD. BERNERS *Froiss.* I. cccxxviii. 514 He made redy for him a shyp, called the Lyne, the whiche wolde go on the see with all maner of wyndes without perell.

[**line**, *sb.*⁴, 'a hat-maker's pad', given in some Dicts. (as an application of LINE *sb.*¹) seems to be a spurious word, due to a misreading of LURE *sb.*²]

line (laɪn), *v.*¹ Forms: 4–7 lyne, 5 lynyn, 7 loyn, 5– line. [f. LINE *sb.*¹; with primary reference to the frequent use of linen as a lining material for articles of clothing.]

1. *trans.* To apply a second layer of material (usually different from that of the article 'lined') to the inner side of (a garment; in later use, any covering or containing object); to cover on the inside.

c **1386** CHAUCER *Prol.* 440 In sangwyn and in pers he clad was al Lyned with Taffata and with Sendal. **1432** *E.E. Wills* (1882) 91 A russet gounne lynyt with whythe blanket. *a* **1548** HALL *Chron., Hen. VIII* 239 The sleves and brest were cutte, lyned with cloth of golde. **1591** LODGE *Catharos* (1875) 30 Thou buiest a warme gowne against Winter and linest it well. **1607** TOPSELL *Four-f. Beasts* (1658) 575 Then must the inside be lined with boards, to the intent that the beast..make no evasion. **1664** WOOD *Life* 5 Dec. (O.H.S.) II. 24 For loyning and lengthning my new yarn stockings, 3*d.* **1676** WISEMAN *Surg.* VI. v. 423 You may use..Tin-plates lined with soft Linings to receive the fractured Member. **1718** LADY M. W. MONTAGU *Let. to C'tess Mar* 28 Aug., The church of the Annunciation is finely lined with marble. **1795** BURKE *Regic. Peace* iv. Wks. IX. 123 An ambassador, whose robes are lined with a scarlet dyed in the blood of Judges. **1820** SYD. SMITH *Mem.* (1855) II. 197 Lady Granville is nervous on account of her room being lined with Spitalfields silk. **1829** SOUTHEY *Young Dragon* I. v. 8 With amianth he lined the nest, And incombustible asbest. **1845** BUDD *Dis. Liver* 147 Abscesses,..lined by a distinct, but very thin membrane. **1872** YEATS *Techn. Hist. Comm.* 339 A mode of lining culinary..articles with enamel.

b. *transf.* and *fig.*

c **1586** C'TESS PEMBROKE *Ps.* LV. iii, Mischief cloth'd in deceit with treason lin'd. **1608** TOPSELL *Serpents* (1658) 602 Nature hath..lined them [serpents] with a more thick and substantial flesh. **1649** BP. HALL *Cases Consc.* (1650) 132 How can you escape to be involved in a treason, lined with perjury? **1693** DRYDEN *Juvenal* vi. (1697) 161 Unless some Antidote..lines with Balsam all the Noble Parts. **1742** YOUNG *Nt. Th.* VIII. 503 With modest laughter lining loud applause. **1756** C. LUCAS *Ess. Waters* II. 149 In a few minutes..it is lined with bright, small air bubbles. **1780** COWPER *Table T.* 59 The diadem with mighty projects lined. **1784** —— *Task* I. 310 The willow such, And poplar that with silver lines his leaf.

†**2.** To strengthen by placing something along the side of; to reinforce, fortify. Also *fig.* *Obs.*

1599 SHAKS. *Hen. V*, II. iv. 7 To lyne and new repayre our Townes of Warre. **1605** —— *Macb.* I. iii. 112 He..did lyne the Rebell with hidden helpe And vantage. *a* **1626** BACON *Consid. War w. Spain* Misc. Wks. (1629) 43 Two Generals, ..lined and assisted with Subordinate Commanders of great Experience. *a* **1659** OSBORN *Characters &c.* Wks. (1673) 630 Your Resolution is too well lined by Philosophy against the storms of Danger, to admit a Parley with any force but that of Reason. **1665** MANLEY *Grotius' Low C. Warres* 275 The upper part of the Town, where the Walls were not lined with banks, he thought fit to batter. **1704** HARRIS *Lex. Techn.*, To *Line* a Work, is to strengthen a Rampart with a firm Wall, or to encompass a Parapet or Moat with good Turf, &c. **1761** CHURCHILL *Rosciad* Poems (1763) I. 45 Receiv'd, with joyful murmurs of applause, Their darling chief, and lin'd his fav'rite cause.

3. To fill (one's purse, pockets, stomach, etc.) with something that may be spoken of as a lining; to cram, stuff.

1514 BARCLAY *Cyt. & Uplondyshm.* (Percy Soc.) p. lxi, He had a pautner with purses many folde And surely lined with silver and with golde. **1550** CROWLEY *Last Trump.* 820 Thou wylt viset no sicke man that cannot lyne thy pursse with golde. **1597** SHAKS. *2 Hen. IV*, I. iii. 27 Who lin'd himself with hope, Eating the ayre, on promise of Supply. **1600** —— *A.Y.L.* II. vii. 154 The Iustice, In faire round belly, with good Capon lin'd. **1611** —— *Cymb.* II. iii. 72 What If I do line one of their hands, 'tis Gold Which buyes admittance. **1625** MASSINGER *New Way* IV. i, I will not fail my lord... Nor I, to line My Christmas coffer. **1663** DRYDEN *Wild Gallant* I. i. (1725) 97 When I have lined my sides with a good dinner. **1672** —— *Assignation* Prol., You come to plays with your own follies lined. **1731** W. BOWMAN *Serm.* xxix, Tho' such change would line our breeches. **1795** J. O'KEEFFE *Song, 'Friar of Orders Gray'* ii, With old sack wine I'm lin'd within. **1820** COMBE *Dr. Syntax, Consol.* I. (1869) 144 For now I have my purse well lin'd Nor doth a fear assail my mind. **1824** CARR *Craven Dial.* Gloss. 90 *Lined*, drunk. 'He's weel lined'. **1866** WHITTIER *Maids of Attitash* 30 No bridegroom's hand be mine to hold That is not lined with yellow gold.

4. To cover the outside of; to overlay, drape, pad, *lit.* and *fig.*; to face (a turf-slope). *Obs.* exc. *Naut.*, to add a layer of wood to.

1572 GASCOIGNE *Hearbes, Councell to Barthol. Withipoll* (1575) 152 Theyr smoothed tongues are lyned all with guyle. **1626** [see CLARICHORD ‖]. **1663** WOOD *Life* 9 July (O.H.S.) I. 481 The rayles..were loyned in mourning. **1664** POWER *Exp.* 481 *Philos.* I. 5 A fuzzy kinde of substance like little sponges, with which she [Nature] hath lined the soles of her [the fly's] feet. **1712** J. JAMES tr. *Le Blond's Gardening* 67 Slopes..require more Circumspection in the Method of lining them with Turf. **1794** *Rigging & Seamanship* I. 31 Bowsprits made of two trees, are coaked together in the middle, and bolted as masts, and lined to the size. **1796** C. MARSHALL *Garden.* xviii. (1813) 293 If the bed gets over cool, line it, or cover round with straw.

5. In certain technical senses (chiefly *to line up*). **a.** *Bookbinding.* To glue on the back of (a book) a paper covering continuous with the lining of the back of the cover. **b.** *Cabinet-making.* To put a moulding round (the top of a piece of furniture).

1880 ZAEHNSDORF *Bookbinding* xix. 85 This class of work is not lined up. The leather is stuck directly upon the book. **1885** CRANE *Bookbinding* xv. 118 Before lining the back, the headband should be set. **1889** *Work* 22 June I. 234/1 A small toilet table was being lined up.

6. To serve or be used as a lining for. (Cf. senses 1, 3, and 4.)

1726 SWIFT *Bec's Birth-day* 8 Nov. 34 Domestic business never mind Till coffee has her stomach lin'd. **1733** —— *On Poetry* Wks. 1755 IV. I. 188 Your poem sunk, And sent in quires to line a trunk. **1794** COWPER *Needless Alarm* 15 Wide yawns a gulf beside a ragged thorn; Bricks line the sides, but shivered long ago. **1850** TENNYSON *In Mem.* lxxvii. 6 These mortal lullabies of pain May bind a book, may line a box. **1885** *Law Times Rep.* LII. 738/1 Small quantities of gold and silver..became embedded in the bricks lining the furnaces. **1892** *Speaker* 3 Sept. 289/2 Wild rose..falling.. down to the daisied grass that lines the ditches. **1895** ZANGWILL *Master* II. iv. 167 Caricatures of..sensuous faces lined the walls.

line (laɪn), *v.*² Also 4–6 lyne. [f. LINE *sb.*¹ Cf. L. *līneāre*, F. *ligner* (OF. *lignier*), Sp. *linear*, It. *lineare*.]

1. *trans.* To tie with a line, string, or cord (*rare*); †to string (a bow) (*obs.*).

c **1375** *Sc. Leg. Saints* v. (*Johannes*) 478 þe ȝunge man þan his bov bent syne, and vith his hand þare-vith can lyne. **1398** TREVISA *Barth. De P.R.* XVII. xcvii. (1495) 663 The flex is.. gadred all hole and is thenne lyned. **1872** DE VERE *Americanisms* 131 Cunning mules..are *lined*, that is, the forefoot is tied to the hindfoot on the same side.

2. To measure or test with a line, to cut to a line; also *absol.* Occas. *fig.* to reach as with a measuring-line. *Obs.* exc. in technical use.

a **1400** *Burgh Laws* cv. (*Sc. Stat.* I.), þat þai sall leilly lyne in lenth as braidnes baith foir part and back part of þe land. **1466** in Willis & Clark *Cambridge* (1886) III. 93 The bordes shalbe lynyd and leyd on hye on the gistes. **1541** *Aberd. Reg.* XVII. (Jam.), The Baillies ordanit the lynaris to pass to the ground of the said tenement, and lyne and marche the same, &c. *c* **1575** *Balfour's Practicks* (1754) 44, I sall lyne landis lellelie betwix parteis. **1655** H. VAUGHAN *Silex Scint.* 57 A sweet self-privacy in a right soul Out-runs the Earth, and lines the utmost pole. **1708** J. C. *Compl. Collier* (1845) 32 As they line or sound for the depth of a River. **1890** W. J. GORDON *Foundry* 116 Then if the trunk is to be squared it is 'lined'. The string is fastened at one end, and, mounting the tree, the foreman moves the line about until he finds what branches should be cut away to trim the trunk to the best advantage.

3. a. (*U.S.*) To angle with a hook and line. *rare.*

1833 [see LINING *vbl. sb.*¹ 5].

b. *trans.* and *intr.* To guide or control a boat or canoe from the bank or shore of a stretch of inland water by means of a rope or ropes. *N. Amer.*

1907 J. G. MILLAIS *Newfoundland* 305 Several times they packed everything for a mile or two, but negotiated most of the worst rapids by 'lining' down them. **1912** H. FOOTNER *New Rivers of North* 125 No one has ever descended it alive, but there is a tradition that a party of Iroquois Indians in the 'company's' employ once lined a boat up. **1923** L. R. FREEMAN *Colorado River* 356 The low stage.. gave them room to work below instead of lining from a ledge, eighty feet above the water. **1944** T. ONRAET *Down North* ii. 29 The skiff was too heavy for carrying, and to line it down as we had done in the rapids above was impossible. **1969** E. W. MORSE *Fur Trade Canoe Routes* I. i. 5 Provided that the shoreline was reasonably free of snags, the canoe was lined (tracked).

4. To trace with, or as with, a line or lines; to delineate, sketch. Chiefly in combination with advs. *to line in*: to put in with a hard pencil the permanent lines of (a freehand drawing); also, to insert (objects) in the outline of a picture. *to line off*: to mark off by lines. *to line out*: to trace the outlines of (something to be constructed); to prescribe in general outline; to forecast, adumbrate.

1600 SHAKS. *A.Y.L.* III. ii. 97 All the pictures fairest Linde, are but blacke to Rosalinde. **1618** MYNSHUL *Ess. Prison* 1 My purpose is, with dim water-colours to line me out a heart. **1650** BAXTER *Saints' R.* IV. xiii. §1, I have..lined you out the best way that I know for your successful performance. **1677** YARRANTON *Eng. Improv.* 138 Here is a way plainly lined out to cheat the Rats and Mice. **1799** J. ROBERTSON *Agric. Perth* 264 Mr. D...has boldly lined off streets and a market place through the very heart of the moor. **1819** SCOTT *Leg. Montrose* x, He again strongly conjured him to construct a sconce upon the round hill called Drumsnab, and offered his own friendly services in lining out the same. **1880** G. MEREDITH *Tragic Com.* (1881) 197 She had seen them [mountain heights] day after day thinly lined on the dead sky. **1886** MILLIGAN *Revelation* vi. (1887) 231 The picture may not yet be realised in fulness, but every blessing lined in upon its canvas is in principle the believer's now. **1889** *Anthony's Photogr. Bull.* II. 304 Thick or compressed lips, open or sunken eyes, straight or hooked noses, may enable one to roughly line out a disposition.

5. To mark with a line or lines; to impress lines upon; to cover with lines. Also with *off*, *out*. *to line out*: *spec.* to delete, obliterate. *to line through*: to draw a line *through* (an entry), to cross out.

1530 PALSGR. 611/2 Have you lyned your paper yet? *Ibid.* 612/1, I lyne, as a carpenter dothe his tymber with a coloured lyne before he square it. **1703** MOXON *Mech. Exerc.* 100 The Stuff being thus lined is fastned with wedges over the Pit. **1756** P. BROWNE *Jamaica* 130 It [the land] must be lined out into oblong squares. **1819** SHELLEY *Rosalind & Helen* 429 Selfish cares with barren plough, Not age, had lined his narrow brow. **1826** E. IRVING *Babylon* II. v. 64 The chart was lined off..for tracing upon it the rise, and progress. **1837** DICKENS *Pickw.* xiii, This entry was afterwards lined through. **18..** —— (Ogilvie), He had a healthy colour in his cheeks, and his face, though lined, bore few traces of anxiety. **1867** SMYTH *Sailor's Word-bk.*, *To line a ship*, is to strike off with a batten, or otherwise, the directional lines for painting her. *Ibid.*, *Line out stuff*, to mark timber for dressing to shape. **1874** THEARLE *Naval Archit.* 99 The edges and butts of the plates are lined off. **1892** *Daily News* 26 Jan. 3/1 Every piece of wood [should] be correctly lined before being cut or planed. **1900** A. BLACK in *Expositor* Sept. 223 The pale wronged face, lined with melancholy resignation. **1963** S. WEINTRAUB *Private Shaw & Public Shaw* iii. 94 G.B.S...both edited and altered the language of the..contract,..boldly lining out large passages and inserting new ones.

6. To read out (a metrical psalm, a hymn) line by line for the congregation to sing. Also *to line out.*

1853 N. D. GOULD *Ch. Mus. Amer.* 47 This custom..of reading, or lining, or, as it was frequently called, 'deaconing' the hymn or psalm in the churches. **1885** *Century Mag.* XXIX. 549/2 The preacher was lining out a hymn. He lined out two lines, everybody sung it.

7. *U.S.* To follow the line of flight of (bees).

1827 J. F. COOPER *Prairie* I. v. 78, I had lined a beautiful swarm that very day into the hollow of a dead beech. **1833** HT. MARTINEAU *Briery Creek* ii. 32 Girls..lining the wild bees to their haunt in the hollow tree. **1879** J. BURROUGHS *Locusts & W. Honey* 25, I emerged..just in time to see the runaways disappearing over the top of the hill... Lining them as well as I could, I soon reached the hill-top.

8. a. *trans.* To bring (ships, soldiers, etc.) into a line or into line with others; to bring (one's boat) into line with that of (another). Hence *U.S.* to assign (a person) *to* (certain work). Also, to aim in a direct line *upon* an object. *to line up* (orig. *U.S.*): to align, arrange, deploy, produce, or make ready (someone or something); also in various slang uses (see quots.).

1796 *Instr. & Reg. Cavalry* (1813) 193 The pivots being lined, and the wheeling distances being true. *a* **1884** KNIGHT *Dict. Mech.* Suppl. 665/1 *Peep sight*, a form of hind sight for rifles. It has an opening through which the muzzle sight is lined upon the object. **1884** *Mil. Engineering* (ed. 3) I. II. 75 Too much time must not..be lost in lining the gabion accurately. **1886** *Philadelphia Times* 21 Mar. (Cent.), No actor of American birth and training can be lined to this class of work. **1891** *Daily News* 28 Dec. 3/1 The cast iron frames are lined up in place before the concrete is poured in. **1899** *Ibid.* 29 July 8/7 Blackstaffe..crossed over in front of Howell and lined him. **1902** *Westm. Gaz.* 20 Aug. 8/2 (citing a New York newspaper), I..shall not really feel like myself till I get my coat off and line-up a few trust presidents in front of me for special inspection and drill. **1904** 'G. B. LANCASTER' *Sons o' Men* 41 They were fence-making down at the homestead, and there was no man in the district could line up standards in the same day with Muggins. **1906** *Forum* (N.Y.) Oct. 253 The university president must refuse to be lined up by any clique or party. **1910** *Chambers's Jrnl.* May 282/2 After the conflagration, the smaller débris is collected into heaps and reburned, until the ground is sufficiently cleared to admit of being lined up for planting. **1913** G. J. KNEELAND *Commercialized Prostitution N.Y.* 65 She was 'lined up' about a year ago by a gang that 'hangs out' in a cigar store on East 14th Street. Since then she has been a regular prostitute. **1926** J. BLACK *You can't Win* xiii. 181 We located a big poker game in a soft spot and decided to line up the players. **1931** W. G. MCADOO *Crowded Yrs.* x. 142, I did not see how Clark could possibly line up two thirds of the..votes. **1932** E. WALLACE *When Gangs came to London* viii. 58 You can tell the police all about this... But don't tell more'n the truth, or ever try to line me up by my voice. **1934** WODEHOUSE *Right ho, Jeeves* ix. 94, I tell you I have everything nicely lined up. **1939** COFFEE & COWEN *Family Portrait* II. i. 74 But I'd lined up a big job here—(*adds importantly*) with the Romans. **1941** BAKER *Dict. Austral. Slang* 43 *Line up to*, to approach, accost a person. **1953** E. TAYLOR *Sleeping Beauty* x. 175 Don't line up another one [*sc.* drink] for me. **1958** *New Statesman* 6 Sept. 263/1 Mr. Lim soon called for 'a united Socialist front', which would line up his Labour Front party with the right wing against the extreme left. **1962** A. NISBETT *Technique Sound Studio* 270 Sine tones are useful for studying frequency response and for lining up equipment. **1970** *Language* XLVI. 318 All of the sentences have been 'lined up' with respect to the end of phonation. **1973** G. GREENE

Honorary Consul I. i. 26 It pays to be a consul... Permission to import a new car... I suppose he's got a general lined up in the capital to buy it.

b. *intr.* (*a*) To present to the eye a line of a specified kind. (*b*) To form a (good) line with others; to fall into line; also with *out, up*; *fig.* to come *up to* a certain line. (*c*) To run in line *with*; to border upon.

(*a*) **1794** *Rigging & Seamanship* I. 16 Masts that have cheeks differ in this; they line tapering athwartships... The aftsides of top-masts line straight.

(*b*) **1790** *Bystander* 159 This the printers describe by saying a letter does not line well. **1796** *Instr. & Reg. Cavalry* (1813) 34 The men as they come up endeavour to line well on the part already formed. **1864** TROLLOPE *Small Ho. at Allington* xv, She struggled to line up to the spirit of her promises and she succeeded. **1887** SHEARMAN *Football* (Badm. Libr.) 316 The forward must always be ready to line up and face one man, and one only. **1888** *Pall Mall G.* 12 June 5/2 Nearly two hundred 'old students' lined up to receive the Royalties. **1894** *Daily News* 8 Oct. 2/7 The two old birds and the four cygnets then lined out in battle array. **1897** *Outing* (U.S.) XXX. 334/1 These boats..enjoyed a world-wide renown for their speed, anterior to their lining up against boats of another type.

(*c*) **1881** *Harper's Mag.* No. 369. 433/2 Three hundred acres of good fresh land, lining..with the Booker estate.

c. *Baseball.* To hit a line-drive; to hit (a ball) hard and low. Freq. const. *out.*

1887 *Courier-Jrnl.* (Louisville, Kentucky) 26 May 2/6 He smashed the first ball that came over the plate, and lined out a beautiful hit past second base. **1948** *Daily Ardmoreite* (Ardmore, Okla.) 28 Apr., He..lined out to centerfield and walked twice in five trips to the plate. **1970** *Globe & Mail* (Toronto) 25 Sept. 31/3 Bob Robertson lined a double down the rightfield Line. **1972** *N.Y. Times* 4 June v. 2/5 Willie struck out, lined to Carty in left field, popped to second base and walked.

9. a. To arrange a line (orig. of troops) along (a hedge, road, etc.). **b.** To have or take one's place or (of inanimate objects) to have a place in line along (a road, etc.).

In both significations the vb. is now apprehended with a mixture of the sense of LINE *v.*[1]

a. 1647 CLARENDON *Hist. Reb.* VI. §248 They having lined the hedges behind them with their reserve. **1684** *Scanderbeg Rediv.* v. 115 And Lined the Wood on each side of the Narrow Way with several Companies of Musqueteers. **1740** S. SPEED in *Buccleuch MSS.* (Hist. MSS. Comm.) I. 393 Their coasts were lined with soldiers on that account. **1781** GIBBON *Decl. & F.* xliii. (1869) II. 611 The ramparts were lined with trembling spectators. **1809** MALKIN *Gil Blas* x. iii. (Rtldg.) 344 The walks well gravelled and lined with orange trees. **1812** *Ann. Reg., Gen. Hist.* 139 The numerous batteries with which it [the shore] is there lined. **1820** W. IRVING *Sketch Bk.* II. 155 At such times the street is lined with listeners. **1835** LYTTON *Rienzi* VI. ii, He came into a broad and spacious square lined with palaces. **1849** MACAULAY *Hist. Eng.* v. I. 580 The thick hedges which on each side overhung the narrow lanes, were lined with musketeers. **1859** JEPHSON *Brittany* vii. 88 A fine quay lined with shipping. **1878** BOSW. SMITH *Carthage* 8 The Greeks.. lined the southern shores of Italy with that fringe of colonies, which [etc.]. **1895** ZANGWILL *Master* I. x. 112 A cutting in the hill lined with overhanging snow-drifts.

b. 1598 BARRET *Theor. Warres* 48 At that instant have the shot that line the battell, their time to serve. *a* **1671** LD. FAIRFAX *Mem.* (1699) 30 They..had set about five hundred Musketeers to line the hedges about the Town. **1707** *Lond. Gaz.* No. 4345/3 The Streets were lin'd by the Militia. **1746** HERVEY *Medit.* (1818) 126 The violet..condescends to line our edges. **1773–83** HOOLE *Orl. Fur.* xxxv. 496 Not feeble years, nor childhood stay'd, but All Alike impatient throng'd to line the wall. **1800** *Asiatic Ann. Reg., Chron.* 55/2 Council-house-street..was lined by the body guard. **1861** M. PATTISON *Ess.* (1889) I. 45 Broad landing quays covered with cranes lined the river bank. **1869** BOUTELL *Arms & Arm.* viii. (1874) 132 The English archers..lined the pass. **1879** *Cassell's Techn. Educ.* IV. 126/2 For some twenty years he annually dispatched ten or twelve vessels to the ports lining the Mediterranean.

c. ***line out*** (*intr.* and *trans.*), to transplant (seedling trees) from beds into nursery lines, where they are grown on before being moved to their permanent situation.

1931 *Forestry* V. 17 Care in handling between lifting from seed-beds and lining out is of the utmost importance. **1938** C. P. ACKERS *Pract. Brit. Forestry* v. 180 Seedlings may be left for 1, 2, or 3 years in the seed-beds: they are then lined out and become transplants. **1957** *N.Z. Timber Jrnl.* Oct. 73/1 *Line out*, to transplant seedlings from seedbeds to rows in a nursery. This normally takes place after the first or second year in the seedbed; further lining out may take place again in the same or another nursery. **1970** H. L. EDLIN *Collins Guide Tree Planting & Cultivation* vi. 90 Trees are always transplanted in the nursery along straight lines, and the work is therefore often called lining-out.

line (laɪn), *v.*[3] Also 4, 6 lyne. [ad. F. *ligner.*] *trans.* Of a dog, wolf, etc.: To copulate with, to cover.

1398 TREVISA *Barth. De P.R.* XVIII. xxv. (1495) 784 The Yndens teche bytches and leue them in wodes by nyghte for Tygres shold lyne them and gendre wᵗ them. **1535** STEWART *Cron. Scot.* (1858) I. 57 And scho was lynit with ony of that birth, Sic hundis thai said for hunting ar na worth. **1576** TURBERV. *Venerie* ii. 5 From that time they beganne to haue bitches lined by that dogge and so to haue a race of them. **1687** DRYDEN *Hind & P.* I. 179 These last deduce him from the Helvetian kind, Who near the Leman lake his consort lined. **1727** BRADLEY *Fam. Dict.* I. H iv/1 Mongrels, that come from a Hound-bitch, that has been lin'd by a Dog of another Kind. **1889** MIVART *On Truth* 379 Analogous effects are often produced when a thorough-bred bitch has been once lined by a mongrel.

‖**linea** (ˈlɪniːə). *Anat.* Pl. **lineæ.** [L. *līnea*: see LINE *sb.*[2]] Used in numerous L. or mod.L. collocations to designate lines apparent in or on the body, or structures which form a line.

1611 Linea alba [see LINE *sb.*[2] 1 c]. **1713** W. CHESELDEN *Anat. Humane Body* I. vi. 20 From the lesser Trochanter down the back-part of this Bone 'till within Four Inches of the End, is a Ridge call'd Linea Aspera. **1861** *Guy's Hosp. Rep.* VII. 297 Linear atrophy of the skin..refers to a condition resembling the *lineæ gravidarum*, but affecting both sexes, and probably all parts of the body. **1967** G. M. WYBURN et al. *Conc. Anat.* i. 7/2 A slight furrow formed by an underlying fibrous raphe, the linea alba, extends from the xiphoid process to the symphysis pubis. *Ibid.* vi. 159/1 Pectineus..is inserted into the femur above the linea aspera.

lineable, *a.*: see LINABLE.

lineage (ˈlɪnɪdʒ). Now only *literary.* Forms: 4–7 **li(g)n-, ly(g)nage,** (5 **len-, lyne-, lyngnage,** 6 **linn-, lyna(d)ge**), 7– **lineage.** [a. OF. *lignage, linage* = Pr. *linhatge*, Sp. *linaje*, Pg. *linhagem*, It. *lignaggio, legnaggio*:—L. type **līneāticum* (see -AGE), f. *līnea* LINE *sb.*[2] The spelling *lineage*, which appears late in the 17th c., is prob. due to association with LINE *sb.*[2]; the mod. pronunciation is influenced by *lineal* or L. *līnea.*]

1. a. Lineal descent from an ancestor; ancestry, pedigree.

a **1330** *Otuel* 336 Tel me..Of what linage þou art come. *c* **1385** CHAUCER *L.G.W.* 1820 *Lucrece*, Tarquinius that.. sholdist as be lynage & be right Don as a lord & as a worthi knyght. *c* **1440** *Generydes* 3873 The Kyng of Egipte, born of highe lenage. **1489** CAXTON *Faytes of A.* I. vii. 16 The gretenes of his lignage and hye blood of his persone. **1547–64** BAULDWIN *Mor. Philos.* (Palfr.) 64 He, that to his noble linage addeth vertue & good conditions, is highly to be praised. **1586** Q. ELIZ. in Ellis *Orig. Lett.* Ser. I. III. 23, I am not of so base a linage, nor cary so vile a minde. **1606** G. W[OODCOCKE] *Hist. Ivstine* XLI. 129 There was at the same time one Arsaces, though of unknown lynage, yet of approued valor. **1701** ROWE *Amb. Step-Moth.* III. iii. 41 Thou art the Father of our Kings, The stem whence their high lineage springs. **1748** RICHARDSON *Clarissa* (1811) VIII. 209, I have..been thought to disgrace my lineage. **1767** BLACKSTONE *Comm.* II. 233 When the lineage is clearly made out, there is no need of this auxiliary proof. **1835** LYTTON *Rienzi* I. i, The quiet and lowly spirit of my mother's humble lineage. **1852** MRS. STOWE *Uncle Tom's C.* vii. 43 She was..so white as not to be known as of coloured lineage without a critical survey. **1875** STUBBS *Const. Hist.* I. xiii. 546 Norman lineage was vulgarly regarded as the more honourable.

†**b.** said of animals and inanimate objects. *Obs.*

c **1435** *Torr. Portugal* 493 Ther be hawkes, ase I herd seyne, That byn of lenage gene. **1607** TOPSELL *Four-f. Beasts* (1658) 253 These are said to refuse copulation with any other Horses that are not of their own kinde and linage. **1635** SWAN *Spec. M.* v. §2 (1643) 153 White hoar-frost is of the house and linage of dew. **1693** SIR T. P. BLOUNT *Nat. Hist.* 195 They proceed in the Main from the same Stock and Linage, and are all more or less of the Kindred of Salts. **1697** DRYDEN *Virg. Georg.* III. 252 Distinguish all betimes, with branding Fire; To note the Tribe, the Lineage, and the Sire.

2. quasi-*concr.* (Chiefly *collect.*)

†**a.** The persons through whom one's 'lineage' (sense 1) is traced; one's ancestors collectively. [So F. *lignage*, in opposition to *lignée* = descendants.] *Obs.*

13.. *K. Alis.* 3068 Thow woldest geve vyl trowage; So dude never non of thy lynage. **1470–85** MALORY *Arthur* v. x, Duke Iosue and Machabeus were of oure lygnage. **1500–20** DUNBAR *Poems* xxiv. 402 My linage and forebearis war ay lele. **1557** NORTH *Gueuara's Diall Pr.* 46 His linage was not of the lowest sort of the people..but were men that lyved by the swete of their browes.

b. The descendants of a specified ancestor [= F. *lignée*]. †Also *rarely* applied to an individual descendant.

1303 R. BRUNNE *Handl. Synne* 2883 She wepte nat for any outrage But for of here come no lynage; þat no fruyt of here myȝt sprynge [Orig. *pur defaute de ligne*]. *c* **1375** *Sc. Leg. Saints* xxix. (*Placidas*) 254 þat herytag þat to man I hicht & his lynag. ? *a* **1400** *Arthur* 269 Y am þeir Eyr & þeyre lynage. **1430–40** LYDG. *Bochas* I. vii. (1554) 10 Tencrease his lynage ..He toke a wife that was but yong of age. **1485** CAXTON *Chas. Gt.* 21 Pepyn..was chosen kyng of Fraunce when the lygnage of kyng cloys faylled. *a* **1548** HALL *Chron., Hen. VI* 183 With hym died..heires of greate parentage in the Southe parte, whose linages revenged their deaths. **1573** L. LLOYD *Pilgr. Princes* (1586) 167 b, Fully perswaded with himselfe that hee was of the linage of the Gods. **1623** tr. *Favine's Theat. Hon.* VI. iii. 118 Of this Mariage ensued a plenteous lignage, to witt, three Sonnes and foure Daughters. **1750** JOHNSON *Rambler* No. 34 ¶3, I am now arrived at that part of life in which every man is expected to settle and provide for the continuation of his lineage. **1838** THIRLWALL *Greece* II. xii. 154 Callias, a seer sprung from the gifted lineage of Iamus. **1863** H. COX *Instit.* I. vii. 65 The dignity of the peerage..was confined to the lineage of the person ennobled.

fig. **1863** KINGLAKE *Crimea* (1876) I. ii. 37 The 'Eastern Question', as it was called, had become consecrated by its descent through a great lineage of Statesmen.

c. A family or race viewed with reference to its descent; a tribe, clan. *spec.* in *Anthrop.*, patri- or matrilineal descent within a social group traced from a single ancestor; also occas. the traditional line of descent for the handing down of skills and knowledge pertaining to a particular craft or profession.

? *a* **1366** CHAUCER *Rom. Rose* 258 She [Envye] is ful glad, in hir corage, If she see any greet linage Be brought to nought in shamful wise. **1387** TREVISA *Higden* (Rolls) III. 51 þat was þe bygynnynge of þe þraldom of þe ten lynages of Israel. *c* **1400** MAUNDEV. (1839) xxi. 224 The first Nacyoun or Lynage was clept Tartar. **1483** CAXTON *G. de la Tour* d v b, The fait or dede whiche..the humayne lynage bought ful dere. **1532** *Galway Arch.* in *10th Rep. Hist. MSS. Comm.* App. V. 405 Whatsoever man or woman shall make any comperacion betwixt lynadge and [l]inadge..shuld.. forfayte an hundrid shillinges. **1604** E. G[RIMSTONE] *D'Acosta's Hist. Indies* I. xxv. 80 From him sprang two families or linages. **1871** L. H. MORGAN in *Smithsonian Contrib. Knowl.* No. 218. 151 There were but five other nations of the same immediate lineage of whom we have any knowledge. **1877** —— *Anc. Society* ii. 69 The gens came into being upon three principal conceptions, namely; the bond of kin, a pure lineage through descent in the female line, and non-intermarriage in the gens. **1934** R. H. LOWIE *Introd. Cultural Anthropol.* xiv. 254 A clan including only descendants of a single ancestor is a 'lineage'. Commonly it includes members of two or more lineages, but the concept remains the same. **1949** M. FORTES *Social Struct.* 62 Genealogies are cited to show that the founding ancestors of the lineages occupying the townships..came there some ten to twelve generations ago. **1951** R. FIRTH *Elem. Social Organiz.* ii. 53 The Tikopia lineages are patrilineal, membership being traced through the father along the male line to an original male ancestor. **1952** GERTH & MARTINDALE tr. *Weber's Anc. Judaism* I. ii. 28 Cain is the tribal father of the smith and the musician... It may, thus, be assumed that at the time of the establishment of this lineage such artisans, in Palestine as in India, were guest people. **1957** M. BANTON *W. Afr. City* vii. 123 Marriage is an arrangement between two lineages. **1963** *Listener* 7 Feb. 231/1 Arabic documents held by the mosques and the clerical lineages in Northern Nigeria and in Northern Ghana. **1971** *World Archaeol.* III. 217 Each village has a number of smiths of varying degrees of training and competence each assisted by novices who together form a lineage.

attrib. **1949** M. FORTES *Social Struct.* 65 Continuity in the social structure..is maintained by the lineage system. **1951** R. FIRTH *Elem. Social Organiz.* ii. 54 They and their immediate lineage members form a recognized class of 'chiefly houses'. **1957** V. W. TURNER *Schism & Continuity in Afr. Soc.* v. 152 They consolidate the rest of the..lineage membership against them. **1964** GOULD & KOLB *Dict. Social Sci.* 391/2 Relations between the local groups, which may vary in size and locality over time, can none the less be seen as persistent and relatively stable. In this case lineages may compose a total structure or system, the lineage structure or the lineage system.

lineage, var. LINAGE.

lineal (ˈlɪnɪəl), *a.* and *sb.* Forms: 4–7 **lineall,** 5–6 **liniall,** (5 **linealle, -yalle,** 6 **lin-, lyneal(l, -iall, -yall),** 6– **lineal.** [a. F. *lineal*, f. late L. *līneālis*, f. *līnea* LINE *sb.*[2]]

A. *adj.* **1. a.** Of or pertaining to a line or lines; consisting of lines. †***lineal alphabet***: one in which the symbols consist of lines. ***lineal demonstration***: one performed by means of lines. ***lineal translation***: one in which the original is rendered line for line (*rare*). ***lineal number, perspective***: see LINEAR. Of writing: Arranged in regular lines.

1398 TREVISA *Barth. De P.R.* XIX. cxxvi. (1495) 926 The nombre lineall begynnyth fro one and is wryte arowe and lyne vnto endlesse. *c* **1430** *Art Nombryng* 14 Of nombres one is lyneal, anoþer superficialle, anoþer quadrat, anoþer cubike or hoole. **1624** WOTTON *Elem. Arch.* I. 50 Errors euer occurring more easily in the management of grosse Materials, then Lineall Designes. **1709** J. WARD *Introd. Math.* I. ii. (1734) 10, I might have here inserted a Lineal Demonstration of this Rule of Addition. **1792** W. ROBERTS *Looker-On* No. 7 (1794) I. 91 This way of writing may be as swift, lineal, and legible, as the operations of daylight. **1797** HOLCROFT *Stolberg's Trav.* (ed. 2) III. lxxiii. 113 They were not..ignorant of lineal perspective. **1875** E. C. STEDMAN *Victorian Poets* 371 He now is said to be engaged upon a lineal and literal translation of Virgil.

b. Of measures: Relating to a single dimension of space; = LINEAR *a.* 3.

a **1684** SCARBURGH *Euclid* (1705) 92 And let this measure be called the Lineal Unite. **1848** *Gregory's Mathematics* (ed. 3) 120 An inch is the smallest lineal measure to which a name is given. **1872** RAYMOND *Statist. Mines & Mining* 129 The claim is 1,000 feet lineal measurement in length.

2. a. Of descent, ancestry, consanguinity, inheritance, or succession (hence also of a descendant, ancestor, heir, etc.): That is in the direct line; opposed to *collateral.*

1426 *Pol. Poems* (Rolls) II. 132 Henry the sext, is truly borne heir unto the corone of Fraunce by lynyalle successioun. **1466** *Paston Lett.* II. 285 They shewed a lineall discent, how their first ancetor, Wulstan, came out of France. *a* **1548** HALL *Chron., Hen. VI* 178, I am the..lyneall heyre. **1596** SPENSER *F.Q.* IV. xi. 12 And after them the royall issue came Which of them sprung by lineall descent. **1690** LOCKE *Govt.* I. xi. §161 The Prime and Ancient Right of Lineal Succession to any thing. **1751** JOHNSON *Rambler* No. 172 ¶8 Enriched in the common course of lineal descent. **1767** BLACKSTONE *Comm.* II. 203 Lineal consanguinity is that which subsists between persons, of whom one is descended in a direct line from the other. **1817** MOORE *Lalla R.* 1 Abdalla..a lineal descendant from the Great Zingis. **1858** LD. ST. LEONARDS *Handy-Bk. Prop. Law* x. 65 Under recent legislation the father and other lineal ancestors are let in in default of lineal heirs. **1871** L. H. MORGAN in *Smithsonian Contrib. Knowl.* No. 218. 11 Every system of consanguinity must be able to ascend and descend in the lineal line through several degrees from any given person. *Ibid.* 46 If *Ego* is placed between the father

and son the lineal and first collateral lines would become intelligible. **1880** HAUGHTON *Phys. Geog.* vi. 262 Whether they may not both be the lineal descendants of older and extinct king crabs. **1929** *Encycl. Brit.* XIX. 84/1 The collateral kin of a generation were merged with the lineal.

b. Pertaining to or transmitted by lineal descent. ***lineal warranty*** (see quot. 1767).

1486 in *Surtees Misc.* (1888) 54 By course of liniall possession. **1570** T. NORTON tr. *Nowel's Catech.* (1853) 173 The Jews claimed..the Church of God as peculiar and by lineal right due to their nation. **1626** D'EWES in Ellis *Orig. Lett.* Ser. I. III. 217 To whome the crowne of his auncestors and predecessors is now devolved by lineall right. **1719** YOUNG *Busiris* I. i. (1757) 13 Busiris, who now reigns, was first of males In lineal blood, to which this crown descends. **1767** BLACKSTONE *Comm.* II. 301 Lineal warranty was where the heir derived, or might by possibility have derived, his title to the land warranted, either from or through the ancestor who made the warranty. **1839** BAILEY *Festus* viii. (1848) 34 As if they waged some lineal feud with time. **1858** GLADSTONE *Homer* III. 520 In lineal dignity, he [Anchises] was even before Priam.

c. Of persons: Lineally descended (*rare*). †Also, of children, legitimate (*obs.*).

1599 SHAKS. *Hen. V*, I. ii. 82 That faire Queene Isabel.. Was Lineall of the Lady Ermengare. **1647** N. BACON *Disc. Govt. Eng.* I. lvii. 165 Although it was the lot of Henry the first to have many children, yet it was not his happinesse to have many lineal. **1670** MILTON *Hist. Eng.* Wks. 1738 II. 79 In the East-Angles, Edmund lineal from the ancient stock of those Kings,..was..crown'd at Bury. **1693** DRYDEN *To Congreve* 44 For only you are lineal to the throne. **1800** *Asiatic Ann. Reg., Chron.* 35/1 The reestablishment of the ancient and lineal family on the throne. **1821** KEATS *Lamia* I. 332 A real woman, lineal indeed From Pyrrha's pebbles or old Adam's seed.

B. *sb.* †**1.** Genealogy, pedigree. *Obs.*

1426 *Pol. Poems* (Rolls) II. 137 Don in ordre by corious lynealle.

2. One who is related in the direct line. *rare.*

1757 FOOTE *Author* II. Wks. 1799 I. 156 There's seven yards more of lineals, besides three of collaterals. **1881** E. W. HAMILTON *Diary* 3 Apr. (1972) I. 124 The Probate Duty is to be raised ¼% all round, and the 1% (lineals) in the Legacy Duty scale is to be abolished; accordingly lineals will all benefit to the extent of ¼%. **1909** *Hansard Commons* 29 Apr. 515/1 In the cases of spouses and lineals..I propose to exempt from the new..duties all legacies.

lineality (lɪnɪˈælɪtɪ). [f. LINEAL *a.* + -ITY.] The quality of being lineal; chiefly with reference to modes of writing, uniformity of direction.

1828–32 WEBSTER, *Lineality*, the state of being in the form of a line. *Am. Review.* **1876** T. HARDY *Ethelberta* II. xxx. 6 The luxuriant curves departed, a compressed lineality was to be observed everywhere. **1881** I. PITMAN *Phonographic Phrase Bk.* 43 The principal requisites of phraseography are legibility, easy joinings, and lineality in writing. **1888** *Effective Advertiser* No. 42. 45 The system [Taylor's Shorthand] is laborious..but perhaps less so than the Gurney system, because of its better Lineality.

lineally (ˈlɪnɪəlɪ), *adv.* (Forms as in LINEAL.) [f. LINEAL *a.* + -LY².]

1. In the direct line of descent; by lineal descent.

1426 LYDG. *De Guil. Pilgr.* 1121 Folwyng doun of a kynrede Lynealy, fro gre to gre. **1466** EDW. IV in *Paston Lett.* II. 282 Gentlemen descended lineally of worshipfull blood. **1534** MORE *On the Passion* Wks. 1293/2 Moyses gaue theym warning of Christ, that he should be a verye man, comming linially of one of theyr owne tribes. **1590** SPENSER *F.Q.* III. ix. 38 From whose race of old She heard that she was lineally extract. **1631** HEYWOOD *Lond. Jus Hon.* Wks. 1874 IV. 277 Shee was lineally descended from the Roman Emperours. **1779** F. HERVEY *Nav. Hist.* II. III. 138 From Sir Thomas Monson..are lineally descended the two noble families of Monson and Sondes. **1818** CRUISE *Digest* (ed. 2) III. 421 None but those who are lineally descended from him can derive a title to it by descent.

transf. *a* **1619** FOTHERBY *Atheom.* II. ix. §3 (1622) 296 All those so largely extended lines,..doe lineally descend from one onely prick.

2. In a line; in a direct line. Now *rare.*

1536 in *Laing Charters* (1899) 108 Fra the Blakwell and craig lynallie north. **1597** A. M. tr. *Guillemeau's Fr. Chirurg.* 6/2 Commonlye, shotten woundes doe not enter right, or liniallye into the bodye, but turninge. **1607** in Stonehouse *Axholme* (1839) 404 The Lord may at his pleasure drive, as is accustomed, from Dirkness Crook lineally to Callendike. **1610** HEALEY *St. Aug. Citie of God* 127 The shade of the earth falling from ye suns place lineally upon the moone. **1827** *Chron.* in *Ann. Reg.* 169/2 Ten feet lineally from east to west. **1854** *Jrnl. R. Agric. Soc.* XV. I. 43 The sources of the Nene are two springs..about 70 miles lineally distant from its mouth.

3. In various occasional uses: †**a.** By means of lines; graphically. **b.** With regard to the lines or outline of anything. **c.** Line for line.

1607 TOPSELL *Four-f. Beasts* (1658) 264 Amazed at the admirable frame of giants which were lineally deciphered therein. **1647** WARD *Simp. Cobler* 52 The Essentialls..must ..be..lineally sanctioned by Supreme Councels. **1753** HOGARTH *Anal. Beauty* ix. 50 We may..lineally account for the ugliness of the toad, the hog, the bear and the spider, which are totally void of this waving-line. *Ibid.* xvii. 238 If stage-action..was to be studied lineally, it might [etc.]. **1879** SALA in *Daily Tel.* 26 June, The old structure [Blackfriars bridge] designed by Mylne..was not, lineally, unhandsome. **1887** BOWEN *Virg.* Pref. (1889) 7 Virgil ought to be translated more or less lineally, as well as literally.

lineament (ˈlɪnɪəmənt). Forms: 6 **lineamente**, **linyament**, 6–7 **liniament**, **lyniament**, 6– **lineament**. [a. F. *linéament*, ad. L. *līneāmentum*, f. *līneāre* (in the unrecorded sense 'to trace lines': see LINE *v.*¹), f. *līnea* LINE *sb.*²]

†**1.** A line; also, a delineation, diagram, outline, sketch; *pl.* outlines, designs. *lit.* and *fig.* *Obs.*

1570 DEE *Math. Pref.* 41 The whole Feate of Architecture in buildyng, consisteth in Lineamentes, and in Framing. **1587** HARRISON *England* II. ii. (1877) I. 51 Circles, characters, & lineaments of imagerie. *a* **1640** J. BALL *Answ. Canne* I. (1642) 33, I see here a perfect image of the Brownists..but not so much as any lineament of any English Protestant Preacher. **1669** GALE *Crt. Gentiles* I. I. ii. 15 The choicest parts [of Grecian Metaphysics]..received their first lineaments, and configuration from [etc.]. **1675** tr. *Camden's Hist. Eliz.* To Rdr. b 3, A great part of these Annals..lay yet shadowed in their first Lineaments. **1709–29** V. MANDEY *Syst. Math., Geom.* 137 All Magnitude is either a Line, or a Lineament or Diagram. **1752** HUME *Ess. & Treat.* (1777) I. 237 The broken lineaments of the piece ..are carefully studied. **1794** SULLIVAN *View Nat.* V. 395 The imagination, being free in the choice of its colors and lineaments, incessantly passes from object to object. **1811** PINKERTON *Petral.* p. viii, Diversity may be used to imply a still greater difference than the variety presents. A very faint shade of difference might, if necessary, be called a lineament.

†**b.** A minute portion, a trace; *pl.* elements, rudiments. *Obs.*

1686 GOAD *Celest. Bodies* I. x. 38 The first Lineaments of Mist or Fog, we impute to the Influence of ♃. **1686** SNAPE *Anat. Horse* IV. vii. 159 The Muscles of the Ears in..men.. are so very small, that Galen calls them the lineaments of Muscles. **1811** PINKERTON *Petral.* II. 323 The paste.. encloses some lineaments of black mica.

†**2.** A portion of the body, considered with respect to its contour or outline, a distinctive feature. *Obs.*

In the 17–18th c. very frequently applied to the parts of insects.

1432–50 tr. *Higden* (Rolls) IV. 255 The liniamentes of his body and membres. **1526** *Pilgr. Perf.* (W. de W. 1531) 3 God hath no lineamentes nor partes corporall. **1540** MORYSINE *Vives' Introd. Wysd.* B v, Beautie standeth in suche liniamentes, shape, and portrature of the body, as [etc.]. **1605** CAMDEN *Rem.* 7 Equalling the most excellent inhabitants of the earth, both in the endowments of minde and lineaments of bodie. **1611** J. S. *Hooker's Eccl. Pol.* To Rdr., Beholding the goodly Lineaments of their well set Bodies. *a* **1631** DONNE *Serm.* vii. 64 In the Scriptures, those bodily lineaments, head and feet, and hands, and eyes, and eares be ascribed to God. **1650** FULLER *Pisgah* IV. v. 85 Insects, with so many lineaments in a little compass, that [etc.]. **1671** MILTON *P.R.* I. 91 Man he seems In all his lineaments, though in his face The glimpses of his Father's glory shine. **1707** MIEGE *State Gt. Brit.* ii. 50 The Lineaments of their Bodies are..well proportioned. **1733** SWIFT *On Poetry* Wks. 1755 IV. I. 197 What lineaments divine we trace Through all his figure, mien, and face! **1760–72** H. BROOKE *Fool of Qual.* (1809) I. 36 Men are even as their fellow-insects; they rise to life, exert their lineaments, and flutter abroad.

b. *fig.* in *pl.* (Now associated with the narrower sense 3.) Distinctive features or characteristics.

1638 ROUSE *Heav. Univ.* iv. (1702) 29 Yet have we other fruits that by some kindred may seem to counterfeit some Lineaments of that taste. *a* **1680** BUTLER *Rem.* (1759) II. 103 So near of Kin are all fantastic Illusions, that you may discern the same Lineaments in them all. **1709** SWIFT *Advancem. Relig.* Wks. 1755 II. I. 97 Tracing, however imperfectly, some few lineaments in the character of a lady. **1750** G. HUGHES *Barbadoes* Pref. 5 The most beautiful lineaments in the character of Cato are owing to this excellent science. **1796** BURKE *Let. Noble Ld.* Wks. VIII. 52 Complete in all the lineaments of men of honour. **1840** MACAULAY *Clive* Ess. (1887) 526 Some lineaments of the character of the man were early discerned in the child. **1845** STEPHEN *Comm. Laws Eng.* (1874) II. 68 To trace the principal lineaments of the law of contract. **1864** KIRK *Chas. Bold* I. i. 13 The general lineaments of the era that was passing away.

3. In narrower sense, a portion of the face viewed with respect to its outline; a feature.

1513 MORE in Grafton *Chron.* (1568) II. 789 Aswell in all princely behavior, as in the liniamentes and favour of his visage. **1579** SPENSER *Sheph. Cal.* May 212 Shee sawe (in the younglinges face) The old lineaments of his fathers grace. **1600** SHAKS. *A.Y.L.* I. ii. 44 Fortune reignes in gifts of the world, not in the lineaments of Nature. *a* **1665** J. GOODWIN *Filled w. the Spirit* (1867) 462 Every lineament of his face being here represented. **1692** BENTLEY *Boyle Lect.* ix. 328 The same Features, the same Lineaments visible in both. **1702** *Eng. Theophrast.* 208 A single fine lineament cannot make a handsom face. **1726** SWIFT *Gulliver* III. vii, General benevolence for mankind, in every lineament of his countenance. **1812** BYRON *Ch. Har.* II. lxii, In his lineaments ye cannot trace..The deeds that lurk beneath. **1885** J. PAYN *Talk of Town* I. 75 He examined his lineaments, in the hopes of detecting a likeness to the Chandos portrait.

Hence †**'lineament** *v. trans.*, to delineate, trace in outline. †**'lineamental** *a.*, of the nature of a sketch or imperfect outline; pertaining to lineaments. †**linea'mentally** *adv.*, in accordance with a general design. **,lineamen'tation**, representation in form or lineament.

1628 JACKSON *Creed* IX. xxix. §5 The forementioned speculative knowledge, being lineamented in our brains. **1601** DEACON & WALKER *Spirits & Divels* 140 They might ..have cunningly carued or cut out..some lineamentall fashion..or shape of serpents. **1432–50** tr. *Higden* (Rolls) I. 17 In whom alle thinges excerpte of þer men ar broken in to smalle membres, but concorporate here liniamentally [L. *lineamentaliter*]. **1791** J. LEARMONT *Poems* 188 Man's winter day must also come And all his lineamental bloom Be stained. **1890** J. H. STIRLING *Philos. & Theol.* iv. 65 It does not follow..that we must think the νοῦς a merely immanent principle..of lineamentation and proportion in the material mass.

linear (ˈlɪnɪə(r)), *a.* and *sb.* [ad. L. *līneāris*, f. *līnea* LINE. Cf. F. *linéaire.*]

A. *adj.*

1. Of or pertaining to a line or lines. ***linear perspective***: that branch of perspective which is concerned with the apparent form, magnitude, and position of visual objects, as distinguished from ***aerial perspective*** (see AERIAL 4).

1656 in BLOUNT *Glossogr.* **1841** W. SPALDING *Italy & It. Isl.* I. 192 When backgrounds were introduced, they were ill-executed, the linear-perspective being nowhere accurately observed. **1865** *Pall Mall G.* 11 Nov. 9 That linear hardness which never appears in nature. **1869** J. MARTINEAU *Ess.* II. 63 The general rules of linear perspective. **1878** GURNEY *Crystallogr.* 29 This difference between models and crystals must be remembered. The former have linear symmetry.

2. a. Consisting of lines; involving the use of lines.

1840 LARDNER *Geom.* ix. 93 The..extent of space included within the linear boundaries of any figure is called its area. **1884** RUSKIN *Pleas. Eng.* 21 The Celts developing peculiar gifts in linear design, but wholly incapable of drawing animals and figures. **1900** *Contemp. Rev.* Dec. 796 Two systems of writing, pictographic and linear, did, indeed, exist in the early Aegean world.

fig. **1830** CARLYLE *Misc.* (1857) II. 172 Narrative is linear, Action is solid.

b. Linear A, the earlier of two related forms of writing discovered at Knossos in Crete by Sir A. J. Evans between 1894 and 1901; **Linear B**, the later form, found also on the mainland of Greece, and now shown to be a syllabary imperfectly adapted to the writing of Mycenæan Greek.

[**1902–3** A. J. EVANS in *Ann. Brit. School at Athens* IX. 52 This early system of linear script—which may be conveniently termed Class A as opposed to Class B of the latest Palace Period at Knossos—had a wide extension in the island.] **1907** R. M. BURROWS *Discoveries Crete* vi. 84 The linear writing of class A is now in regular use. *Ibid.* 92 The hoard of clay tablets..shows that its linear writing, called by Mr. Evans Class B, is more advanced. **1909** A. J. EVANS *Scripta Minoa* I. I. v. 31 Documents belonging to the Linear Class A only occur in this particular stratum... In deposits clearly belonging to the remodelled building the inscribed documents all belonged to Class B. *Ibid.* 35 Common to both the linear scripts A and B. *Ibid.* 36 The system of numerals..of the Linear Class B. **1948** A. E. KOBER in *Amer. Jrnl. Archaeol.* LII. 89 Inscriptions of Linear A have been found at several sites. **1950** E. L. BENNETT in *Ibid.* LIV. 81/1 Translations of and commentary upon additional Linear-B tablets from Knossos. *Ibid.* 204/1 The Linear A flourished in the rest of Crete.., and the Linear B at Knossos only. *Ibid.* 218/2 The Linear A ideogram L85 appears to have..the same form. *Ibid.* 219/1 The shapes of four other signs of Linear A..are reflected in the Linear B signs. **1952** J. L. MYRES *Evans' Scripta Minoa* II. 1 In this new 'Linear A' script about one-third of the signs are derived from linearized hieroglyphs. *Ibid.* 2 It was doubtless ..local unconformity that provoked the drastic reform of the 'Linear B' script at Knossos. **1953** VENTRIS & CHADWICK in *Jrnl. Hellenic Stud.* LXXIII. 84 Evans believed that Linear *B*..was an administrative revision of Linear *A*, designed to express the same 'Aegean' language. **1966** C. H. GORDON *Evidence for Minoan Lang.* ix. 32 The Linear A and B texts overlap in time. **1972** *Sci. Amer.* Oct. 37/1 The Cretan system of writing, which we call Linear A, was crude but it was adequate for keeping rough accounts.

c. *Mus.* = HORIZONTAL *a.* 4.

1944 W. APEL *Harvard Dict. Mus.* 409/1 *Linear counterpoint*, a term introduced by E. Kurth..in order to emphasize the 'linear', i.e., horizontal aspect of counterpoint... The term is also used..for what the Germans call *rücksichtsloser* (reckless) *Kontrapunkt*, i.e., the modern type of counterpoint which pays little attention to harmonic combination and euphony. **1955** [see HORIZONTAL *a.* 4]. **1958** A. JACOBS *New Dict. Mus.* 211 *Linear counterpoint*, term—senseless, because all counterpoint is a matter of lines—sometimes used for a type of 20th-century counterpoint (e.g. Stravinsky's) held to be musically valid through the value of the separate lines themselves. **1959** *Listener* 8 Jan. 80/2 In the slow movement the orchestral texture begins in linear style, spare and canonic. **1962** *Ibid.* 18 Jan. 147/1 Linear and rhythmic techniques suggested by medieval music. *Ibid.* 147/2 A conscious employment of linear and metrical 'series' derived from Indian ragas and talas.

3. a. Having the direction of a line; extended in a line or in length; *spec.* in *Math.* and *Phys.* involving measurement in one dimension only; capable of being represented by a straight line on a graph (in Cartesian co-ordinates); involving or possessing the property that a change in one quantity is accompanied by or corresponds to a directly proportional change in a related one. ***linear equation***, an equation of the first degree. ***linear numbers***, ***linear problem*** (see quot. 1706).

1706 PHILLIPS (ed. Kersey), *Linear Numbers*, are those that have relation to Length only: For Example, such as represent one Side of a plane Figure; and if the Figure be a Square, the Linear Number is call'd a Root. *Ibid.*, *Linear Problem* (in *Mathem.*), such a Problem as can be solved Geometrically, by the Intersection..of two Right-lines. **1799** J. WOOD *Elem. Optics* iv. (1811) 83 This line is called the diameter, or linear aperture of the lens. **1806** HUTTON *Course Math.* I. 340 Similar Prisms and Cylinders are to each other, as the Cubes of their Altitudes, or of any other Like Linear Dimensions. **1812–16** PLAYFAIR *Nat. Phil.* (1819) I. 201 The superficial breadth of the stream,

expressed in linear inches. **1816** tr. *Lacroix's Diff. & Int. Calculus* 326 We call it from thence, a linear equation of the first order. **1830** LYELL *Princ. Geol.* I. 314 Active volcanic vents.. arranged in a linear direction. **1831** BREWSTER *Optics* xli. 336 The linear magnifying power is the number of times an object is magnified in length. **1867** DENISON *Astron. without Math.* 71 The resistance does diminish the actual or linear speed. **1872** NICHOLSON *Palæont.* 44 It is possible to arrange the animals of any one sub-kingdom in something like a linear series. **1882** MINCHIN *Unipl. Kinemat.* 6 A point *P* moves in a circle with constant linear velocity. *Ibid.* 123 So that (ξ, η) are also linear functions of (ξ', η'); and if the first satisfy a linear equation.. so must the second. **1910** *Encycl. Brit.* IX. 146/2 The limiting tension beyond which the above law of proportionality [between tension and extension] fails to hold is often called the 'limit of linear elasticity'. **1940** *Chambers's Techn. Dict.* 503/1 *Linear amplification*, amplification in which the output current or voltage is strictly proportional to the input voltage. **1941** *Proc. R. Soc.* A. CLXXVII. 382 The disintegration of boron by slow neutrons has been investigated using an ionization chamber filled with boron trichloride in conjunction with a linear amplifier. **1942** *Electronic Engin.* XIV. 711/1 The conversion must be accomplished in a linear manner, i.e., the amplitude change is directly proportional to the frequency change. **1962** D. F. SHAW *Introd. Electronics* vii. 126 The preservation of the shape is a unique property of the sine wave and.. is a feature which it possesses for all linear circuits. *Ibid.* viii. 147 A circuit is linear if the individual components behave in such a manner that the amplitude of the current through each component is directly proportional to the amplitude of the applied voltage and the relationship between the phases of the voltage and current is independent of the current and voltage magnitude. **1973** *Physics Bull.* Oct. 606/1 A linearizer circuit is used to ensure a true linear relationship between conveyor load and indicated reading.

b. *Educ.* Designating or pertaining to programmed learning aimed at step-by-step progress in which the material is broken down into small steps each of which must elicit a correct response before the next one is presented; freq. contrasted with branching methods.

For *linear programming* in a different sense see 7.

1958 B. F. SKINNER in *Science* 24 Oct. 974/2 A first step is to define the field. A second is to collect technical terms, facts, laws, principles, and cases. These must then be arranged in a plausible developmental order—linear if possible, branching if necessary. **1961** *Barron's Nat. Business & Financial Weekly* 30 Oct. 14/2 We are disciples of neither Crowder nor Skinner. Our programs will make use of either branching or linear techniques, depending on which seems best suited to the subject matter. **1962** A. A. LUMSDAINE in J. E. Coulson *Programmed Learning* 135, I believe that linear programs should almost invariably be constructed first, even if branching is later to be introduced. **1964** *Times Rev. Industry* Feb. 100/2 A novel feature is the method it uses—the linear (non-branching) technique of programmed learning. **1969** G. KENT *Blackboard to Computer* viii. 109 The basis of linear programming is that the subject matter to be understood is always presented to the student in small quantities. **1970** W. K. RICHMOND *Concept Educ. Technol.* iii. 103 That the majority of linear programmes are inordinately dull is, of course, a charge which will be strenuously denied by anyone who has laboured to produce one. *Ibid.*, This aseptic dullness is explained by the linear programmer's dependence upon a bird-brained psychology.

4. a. Resembling a line; very narrow in proportion to its length, and of uniform breadth.

1642 H. MORE *Song of Soul* II. I. ii. 42 [The Soul] Girds the swoln earth with linear list. **1828** STARK *Elem. Nat. Hist.* I. 362 Body gray brown, with transverse linear whitish stripes. **1853** G. BIRD *Urin. Deposits* (ed. 3) 357 Minute linear bodies hardly so long as the diameter of a blood-corpuscle. **1854** BREWSTER *More Worlds* xi. 178 These linear nebulæ, which Sir John Herschel thinks are flat ellipsoids seen edgewise. **1885** WATSON & BURBURY *Math. Th. Electr. & Magn.* I. 218 A conductor, two of whose dimensions are very small compared with the third, as for instance a wire, is called a linear conductor. **1923** C. R. STOCKARD in *Amer. Jrnl. Anat.* XXXI. III. 278 The two groups into which almost all ordinary persons fall more or less exactly may.. be termed the Linear Type and the Lateral Type. The linear type is the faster growing high metabolizing thin but not necessarily tall group, while the lateral type is slower in maturing and is stocky and rounder in form. **1932** *Field Archæol.* (Ordnance Survey) 30 This term 'Linear Earthwork' is used to describe earthworks like Wansdyke.. and the numerous Grim's Dykes... They consist of a bank and ditch and may be of any length from a few yards.. to 10 miles. **1959** *Jrnl. Soc. Archit. Historians* XVIII. 40/1 Soria ..customarily described his Linear City as a vertebrate animal. **1964** M. ARGYLE *Psychol. & Social Probl.* v. 62 Fewer of the delinquents are of linear (thin and bony) physique. **1966** *Guardian* 5 Apr. 2/6 A new linear city of half a million people.. near Inverness.. is the ambition of Professor Robert Grieve.

b. spec. *Bot.* and *Zool.* Like a thread, elongated.

1753 CHAMBERS *Cycl. Supp.* s.v. *Leaf*, *Linear Leaf*, one the two sides of which run almost parallel to one another. **1777** ROBSON *Brit. Flora* 15 *Linear*, everywhere of the same breadth, though sometimes narrowing at the extremities only. **1787** *Fam. Plants* I. 2 Anther linear.. Stigma linear. **1828** STARK *Elem. Nat. Hist.* II. 89 Shell equivalve..; hinge, linear, without teeth. **1851** RICHARDSON *Geol.* (1855) 180 Verticillate fringes of linear leaves growing round the joints. **1851** WOODWARD *Mollusca* 106 Muricidæ... Lingual ribbon long, linear. **1870** HOOKER *Stud. Flora* 225 *Campanula rotundifolia*,.. lower cauline leaves lanceolate, upper narrow linear quite entire. **1874** COUES *Birds N.W.* 430 Two narrowly linear feathers. **1880** GRAY *Struct. Bot.* iii. §4. (ed. 6) 95 Linear, when leaf-blades are narrow, several times longer than wide, and of about the same breadth throughout.

c. Having a (more or less) plain outline; not indented or notched; also said of the outline.

1796 C. MARSHALL *Garden.* xii. (1813) 139 A tree may be regular without being linear. **1797** *Encycl. Brit.* (ed. 3) III. 444/1 A Margin.. entire, linear without the least dent or notch.

5. Surg. ***linear extraction*** (***of cataract***): see quot. 1890. ***linear rectotomy***: the operation of dividing a strictured urethra through the rectum.

1874 G. LAWSON *Dis. Eye* 127 Linear Extraction of Cataract. **1878** T. BRYANT *Pract. Surg.* I. 724 M. Verneuil has advocated the operation of 'linear rectotomy' for the cure of stricture. **1890** BILLINGS *Nat. Med. Dict.*, *Linear extraction*, methods of cataract extraction in which the corneal incision approaches to a plane passing through the centre of curvature of the globe.

6. *Comb.* chiefly *Bot.* **a.** Signifying 'linear and ...', 'between linear and...', as ***linear-acute***, ***-attenuate***, ***-awled***, ***-elliptical***, ***-elongate***, ***-ensate***, ***-filiform***, ***-lanceolate***, ***-ligulate***, ***-oblong***, ***-obovate***, ***-setaceous***, ***-spathulate***, ***-subulate*** adjs.; also ***linear-leaved***, ***-shaped*** adjs.

1847 W. E. STEELE *Field Bot.* 9 Hawkweed,.. bracts *linear-attenuate. *a* **1794** SIR W. JONES in *Asiat. Res.* (1795) IV. 269 Leaves *linear-awled, pointed, opposite. **1881–2** W. S. KENT *Man. Infusoria* II. 786 Body.. *linear-elliptical. **1836** LOUDON *Encycl. Plants* Gloss., **Linear-ensate*, long sword-shaped. **1845** LINDLEY *Sch. Bot.* iv. (1858) 42, 1. *A[lsine] rubra.* Leaves *linear-filiform, mucronate, somewhat fleshy. **1793** MARTYN *Lang. Bot.*, *Lineari-lanceolatum*, *linear-lanceolate. **1825** *Greenhouse Comp.* II. 20 *Pharnaceum lineare*, *linear-leaved Pharnaceum. **1870** HOOKER *Stud. Flora* 373 Potamogeton... Leaves.. *linear-ligulate. **1839** JOHNSTON in *Proc. Berw. Nat. Club* I. No. 7. 205 Teeth transverse, *linear-oblong. **1870** HOOKER *Stud. Flora* 312 *Rumex conglomeratus*,.. inner fruiting sepals linear-oblong. **1845** *Florist's Jrnl.* 89 *Styphelia tubiflora*... Leaves which are sometimes *linear-obovate. **1847** W. E. STEELE *Field Bot.* 21 Scales of receptacle *linear-setaceous. **1845** DARWIN *Voy. Nat.* vii. (1879) 126 The view would resemble that of a great lake, if it were not for the *linear-shaped islets. **1870** HOOKER *Stud. Flora* 130 *Saxifraga Andrewsii*... Leaves *linear-spathulate. **1793** MARTYN *Lang. Bot.*, *Lineari-subulatum*, *linear-subulate.

b. In quasi-Latin form, as ***lineari-elongate***, ***-laciniose***, ***-oblong*** adjs.

1871 W. A. LEIGHTON *Lichen-flora* 9 Spores 8, oblong or lineari-elongate or cylindrical. *Ibid.* 12 Spores 8, colourless, lineari-oblong or subfusiform. *Ibid.* 18 Fuscous-black, lineari-laciniose, laciniæ ligulate.

7. Special collocations: ***linear accelerator*** (see ACCELERATOR e); ***linear motor***, a motor (esp. an induction motor) which produces motion directly in a straight line (as opposed to rotary motion); ***linear programming***, a mathematical technique for maximizing or minimizing a linear function (such as output or cost) of several variables (such as resources) when these are required to satisfy a set of linear equations and inequalities; (see also 3 b above).

1957 E. R. LAITHWAITE in *Proc. Inst. Electr. Engin.* CIV. A. 461/1 [The word 'linear' has already been used in connection with particle accelerators, but as there is little likelihood of confusion between these devices and electric motors, there appears to be no objection to the use of the word for the latter.] *Ibid.*, The use of *linear motors as liquid-metal pumps is examined. **1966** *Listener* 13 Oct. 535/3 British Rail were the first to support Laithwaite's work on the linear motor, and suggested to him in 1960 its possible application to rail traction. **1973** *Sci. Amer.* Oct. 21/1 The evolution of electromagnetic flight is inextricably linked to the problem of propulsion. Two types of 'linear motor' are being studied for this application. One is called the linear induction motor, the other the linear synchronous motor. **1949** G. B. DANTZIG in *Econometrica* XVII. 203 It is our purpose now to discuss the kinds of restrictions that fit naturally into *linear programming. **1953** COOPER & HENDERSON in W. W. Cooper et al. *Introd. Linear Programming* I. 1 Linear programming is concerned with the problem of planning a complex of interdependent activities in the best possible (optimal) fashion. **1966** A. BATTERSBY *Math. in Managem.* iv. 85 Transporting coal to power stations or gasworks, allocating cash to local branches, formulating foods and drawing up a maintenance schedule: these are all areas in which linear programming is at work today. **1967** E. DUCKWORTH in Wills & Yearsley *Handbk. Managem. Technol.* vi. 110 When the optimum order quantities have been decided, problems may occur in scheduling these through factories in the optimum manner. .. Quite complex methods of the linear programming or queueing theory type may be needed. **1971** *Sci. Amer.* Feb. 84/2 Among the intended tasks for ILLIAC IV is linear programming, a mathematical technique for allocating the use of limited resources to maximize or minimize a specified objective. *Ibid.* 85/2 In order to apply linear programming to an entire economic sector one must incur considerable expense in gathering the data to be used in the model.

†**B.** *sb.* A linear equation. *Obs.*

1684 T. BAKER *Geometr. Key* title-p., Of linears, qvadratics, cubics, biqvadratics; And the finding of all their Roots.

linearism ('lɪnɪərɪz(ə)m). [f. LINEAR *a.* + -ISM.] Linearity; emphasis upon line or contour as opposed to colour or mass.

1935 *Archit. Rev.* LXXVII. 61 Far less of a constructor than a decorator, his famous 'linearism' was an echo of the same salient characteristic in Aubrey Beardsley's graphic designs. **1941** *Burlington Mag.* July 17/1 His bold method of brush drawing.. is rendered possible by this two-dimensional linearism.

linearistic (lɪnɪə'rɪstɪk), *a.* [f. LINEAR *a.* + -ISTIC.] Pertaining to or characterized by a linear quality; of a linearized character.

1908 A. J. EVANS in R. R. Marett *Anthropol. & Classics* 41 Many of these signs are linearistic degenerations of animal figures.

linearity (lɪnɪ'ærɪtɪ). [f. LINEAR *a.* + -ITY.]

a. The quality or condition of being linear; a linear arrangement or formation.

1748 *Phil. Trans.* XLV. 390 Another Oversight, in this Plan [of Short-Hand], is the Neglect of Beauty and Linearity. **1837** J. MACCULLOCH *Proofs Attributes God* III. xlvii. 284 The Palmetto is beautiful in its radiation, a Grass in its simple linearity. **1891** *Athenæum* 17 Oct. 515/2 Backslopes and upright strokes are practically discarded, linearity is well preserved. **1947** A. EINSTEIN *Mus. Romantic Era* xvi. 245 Wagner wrote a Prelude.. in the 'linearity' of which he seemed to overstep the stylistic limits of his own time. **1955** HOMANS & SCHNEIDER *Marriage, Authority & Final Causes* 20 Almost all the eastern Asian societies in which he finds mother's brother's daughter marriage preferred are organised in patrilineages. He concerns himself with linearity, [etc.]. **1958** *Times* 5 Dec. 8/6 Ectomorphy describes the linearity of the build. **1964** M. MCLUHAN *Understanding Media* xviii. 172 The linearity precision and uniformity of the arrangement of movable types.

b. *spec.* in *Math.* and *Physics*, the property of being linear in sense 3 a of the adj.; proportionality of two related quantities (such as input and output).

1904 [see EXTRAPOLATE *v.* 2 a]. **1943** *Electronic Engin.* XVI. 55/1 The insertion of a valve amplifier between the time base and the cathode-ray tube often involves some sacrifice in linearity. **1946** *Nature* 7 Sept. 330/2 Linearity is also important in the optical pick-up from the record, in the sense that the illumination of the photo-electric cell must be strictly proportional to the width of the white part of the illuminated area of the record. **1962** SIMPSON & RICHARDS *Physical Princ. Junction Transistors* xii. 269 Because the gain is high and the linearity fair, negative feedback may be used to exchange gain for linearity.

linearize ('lɪnɪəraɪz), *v.* Also **linearise**. [f. LINEAR *a.* + -IZE.] *trans.* To represent in a linear form; to transform *into* a linear figure; to make linear.

1895 *Daily News* 2 May 5/1 The Cretans used a symbol of a double axe-head, bipennis. They linearised this into an X with the top and bottom closed. **1895** *Q. Rev.* July 213 When the Northmen used the Tau for the hammer of Thor, they merely linearised a picture of a real hammer. **1957** L. FOX *Numerical Solution Two-Point Boundary Probl.* iii. 48 The only practical method of general application seems to be to 'linearize' the equations and solve them by an iterative process. **1969** *Physics Bull.* Nov. 463/1 Analysis is made difficult by the nonlinearity of the governing equations; any attempt to introduce approximations which linearize them seems to result in a loss of the basic features of the flow. **1969** *Canad. Jrnl. Ling.* XV. 25 It was speculated.. that the reason that languages had embedding transformations.. was to 'linearize' or spread out in linear form the deeply embedded concoctions which the human mind can produce. **1970** J. EARL *Tuners & Amplifiers* iv. 93 This can.. reduce the distortion and linearise the power response. **1973** *Newnes Colour Television Servicing Manual* I. ii. 57/1 One half of the double triode is concerned essentially with linearising the field scan by means of negative feedback.

Hence ˌ**leari'zation**, the action or process of linearizing; '**linearized** *ppl. a.*; '**linearizer**, that which linearizes, *esp.* a device which linearizes the response of a measuring instrument or other mechanism.

1896 A. J. EVANS in *Academy* 13 June 494/1 Characters of a type representing the linearisation of originally pictographic characters. **1938** *Proc. Physico-Math. Soc. Japan* XX. 319 A method of linearization of wave equations for the electron. **1956** E. H. HUTTEN *Lang. Mod. Physics* iii. 94 Linearisation is a familiar trick in physics. **1962** W. B. THOMPSON *Introd. Plasma Physics* ii. 10 Then we obtain the linearized, approximate equations. **1968** CHOMSKY & HALLE *Sound Pattern Eng.* 391 What we have so far defined is simply a linearized version of rules of the form we have been discussing all along. **1973** *Physics Bull.* Oct. 606/1 Since the output from the digital ratemeter is nonlinear with load, it is necessary to use a short integrating time (about 0·1 s) in the ratemeter to obtain a true load signal after linearization. **1973** *Physics Bull.* Dec. 745/1 The system is precalibrated for particular applications and has a built-in linearizer.

linearly ('lɪnɪəlɪ), *adv.* [f. LINEAR *a.* + -LY².]

a. In a linear direction. **b.** By linear measurement. **c.** By means of lines.

1881 *Nature* XXIII. 331 A cell *n* times greater linearly each way. **1887** R. A. ROBERTS *Integral Calculus* I. 316 The arc of the general bicircular quartic can be determined linearly. **1891** W. A. JAMIESON *Dis. Skin* i. (ed. 3) 6 The upper part is marked with prominences called papillæ arranged linearly.

d. In a way that involves only terms of one dimension; in a linear or proportional manner.

1851 *Phil. Mag.* I. 295 If a quadratic function (U) be linearly converted into another (V), any minor determinant of any order of V must be a syzygetic function of all the minor determinants of U of the same order. **1859** G. SALMON *Lessons Introd. Mod. Higher Algebra* vi. 34 From the four equations thus formed we can eliminate linearly the four quantities, x^3, x^2y, xy^2, y^3. **1885** [see LEGENDRE]. **1955** *Bull. Atomic Sci.* June 208/1 The extent of fall-out varies linearly with the fission yield of the bomb. **1963** *Amer. Jrnl. Physics* XXXI. 336/2 A necessary and sufficient condition.. is that θ and T be related linearly. **1969** *Listener* 12 June 831/1 Criminals in human society.. increase more rapidly than linearly with the total number of victims available.

That is to say, if we double the population we more than double the number of criminals.

†**'lineary**, *a.* *Obs.* [ad. L. *līneārius*, f. *līnea* LINE.] = LINEAR *a.* 2 and 3.

1551 RECORDE *Pathw. Knowl.* II. Pref., Euclides woorkes in foure partes, with diuers demonstrations Arithmeticall and Geometricall or Linearie. **1601** HOLLAND *Pliny* II. 525 The linearie portraying or drawing shapes and proportions by lines alone. **1641** W. PRICE in Rigaud *Corr. Sci. Men* (1841) I. 59 Whether all that may be performed by algebraical equations may likewise be wrought geometrically according to a lineary operation. **1652** GAULE *Magastrom.* 93 We speak of such a figure as is not an accident of a body, but a meer lineary and superficiall character. **1664** EVELYN tr. *Freart's Archit.* 118 The more easy and useful principles of those lineary Arts.

lineate ('lɪnɪət), *ppl. a.* and *sb.* [ad. L. *līneātus*, f. *līneāre* to reduce to a line, f. *līnea* LINE.]

a. *ppl. a.* Marked with lines, *spec.* in *Bot.* (see quot. 1866). †**b.** *sb.* A figure formed of lines. *Obs.*

a **1643** W. CARTWRIGHT *Siege* III. vii, I am my self as void Of all [perfections], as Tables not yet lineate. **1674** JEAKE *Arith.* (1696) 334 Species are Quantities or Magnitudes, denoted by Letters, signifying Numbers, Lines, Lineats, Figures Geometrical, &c. **1777** ROBSON *Brit. Flora* 15 *Lineate*, slightly streaked longitudinally with parallel lines, not impressing the surface. **1793** MARTYN *Lang. Bot.*, *Lineatum folium*, a lineate leaf. **1826** KIRBY & SP. *Entomol.* IV. 290 *Lineate*, painted with several such [longitudinal] stripes. **1866** *Treas. Bot.*, *Lineate*, lined, marked by fine parallel lines.

lineate ('lɪnɪeɪt), *v.* Also 6 liniate, 7 lyneate. [f. L. *līneāt-*, ppl. stem of *līneāre* (see prec.).] *trans.*

a. To mark with lines. †**b.** To delineate; to represent either by drawing or by description.

a. 1558 WARDE tr. *Alexis' Secr.* (1568) 114 b, Then with a cutting yron..you shall liniate and make equall the said fourmes. *a* **1728** WOODWARD *Hist. Fossils* (1729) I. I. 37 A Flinty Peble, black without, lineated within with Stripes of white, yellow and red, encircling one another.

b. 16.. SYLVESTER *Mem. Mortalitie* viii, Life, to the life, The Chess-boord lineats. **1614** C. BROOKE *Ghost Rich. III*, H, They seemed in the object of such Glory T'inuite some Pen to lyneate their Story. **1648** EARL WESTMORELAND *Otia Sacra* (1879) 128, I would my Fancy rear, To lineat a day most clear.

Hence '**lineated** *ppl. a.* = LINEATE *ppl. a.*

1677 PLOT *Oxfordsh.* 100 Of these [stones] there are some curiously lineated, and others plain. *a* **1728** WOODWARD *Hist. Fossils* (1729) I. I. 36 Several..lineated or crusted Pebles. **1797** *Encycl. Brit.* (ed. 3) III. 443/2 [Botany.] A Surface is..Lineated, lined, the nerves being depressed. **1819** TURTON *Conchol. Dict.* 17 *Buccinum lineatum*, Lineated Whelk. **1863** REEVE *Land & Freshwater Mollusks* 179 *Acme lineata.* Lineated Acme.

lineation (lɪnɪ'eɪʃən). [ad. L. *līneātiōn-em*, n. of action f. *līneāre*: see LINEATE *a.*]

1. The action or process of drawing lines or marking with lines; an instance of this; also, a contour or outline; quasi-*concr.*, a marking or line on the surface (*e.g.* of the skin).

1398 TREVISA *Barth. De P.R.* II. iii. (1495) 30 Angels haue noo matere nother lyneacions and shappe of body. **1426** LYDG. *De Guil. Pilgr.* 21182 The vysage and the hand also, Vp-on wych Men may..Telle the condycions By dyvers lyneacions Wych ther be set. *a* **1450** *Cov. Myst.* xx. (Shaks. Soc.) 189 Of lynyacion that longyth to jematrye. **1526** *Pilgr. Perf.* (W. de W. 1531) 197 b, Not ymagynynge in the deite ony corporall fygure or liniacyon. **1657** TOMLINSON *Renou's Disp.* 275 It is a..root, which by exsiccation hath contracted wrinkles and lineations. **1816** G. COLMAN *Br. Grins*, *Luminous Historian* Introd. iii. (1872) 304 Nature's lineations plainly tell There's room and room enough to act them well. **1892** F. GALTON *Finger Prints* i. 5 The ridges, whose lineations appear in the finger print.

b. *collect.* A marking with lines; an arrangement or group of lines.

c **1550** *Sympathising Lover* in Evans *Old Ballads* (1784) III. xxx. 226 Her countenaunce with her lynyacion. **1677** PLOT *Oxfordsh.* 101 Conchites..differing in colour, lineation and valves. *a* **1728** WOODWARD *Hist. Fossils* (1729) I. I. 32 There are in the horney Ground two white Lineations, attended with two of a pale Red. **1759** B. MARTIN *Nat. Hist. Eng.* I. *Oxford* 392 Nothing upon it, but somewhat like a Chalice, and crooked Lineation. **1856** W. B. CARPENTER *Microsc.* §339. 596 The peculiar lineation of the surface of nacre. **1884** GEIKIE in *Nature* 13 Nov. 30/2 Striated planes..covered with a fine parallel lineation.

2. A division into lines.

1853 *Ecclesiologist* XIV. 431 There is no authority to assume one lineation [of a hymn] rather than another. **1891** *Pall Mall G.* 2 Nov. 1/3 The large initials..disturb the lineation of the verse.

†**'lineature.** *Obs.* [ad. L. type **līneātūra*, f. *līneāre*: see LINEATE *v.*] **a.** Something having an outline or shape. **b.** An outline; also *Geom.*, a periphery.

1603 HOLLAND *Plutarch's Mor.* 557 There accompanied him a certeine shadowy and dark lineature. **1630** BRATHWAIT *Eng. Gentlem.* (Draught of Frontispiece), Perfection is only shadowed, because in his native lineature hardly to be expressed. **1651** J. F[REAKE] *Agrippa's Occ. Philos.* 253 By its lineature by which it hath within five obtuse angles, and without five acutes.

'line-boat. Also 7 lime-, lymboat. ? A boat used for line-fishing.

1613 BEAUM. & FL. *Honest Man's Fort.* v. iii, I shall see you Serve in a lowsy Lime boat, ere I die, For mouldy cheese and butter Billingsgate Would not endure. **1614** T. GENTLEMAN *Engl. way to wealth* (title), Wealth that is yearely taken out of his Maiesties Seas, by the Hollanders, by their..Busses, Pinkes, and Line-boates. **1662** *Roy. Trade of Fishing* 12 Now I will descend to the particulars of the Hollanders Busses, Pincks, Yagers, Lymboats, and the use of them in their several fishings. **1897** *Westm. Gaz.* 24 Apr. 8/1 He put it to those who were employed on board line boats if they should lose Sunday at their vocation.

lined (laɪnd), *ppl. a.*[1] [f. LINE *v.*[1] + -ED[1].] In various senses of LINE *v.*[1] ***lined blades*** (see quot. 1833). ***lined gold***, gold having a backing of another metal, used for making jewellery and ornaments. Also in *Comb.*, as ***red-lined***, ***silk-lined***, ***tin-lined***, etc., q.v. under their first elements.

c **1440** *Promp. Parv.* 306/1 Lynyd, as clothys, *duplicatus.* **1492** *Bury Wills* (Camden) 75 Item I be quethe to the wyff of Robert Halowe my best lyned gowne and my cloke. **1502** *Privy Purse Exp. Eliz. of York* (1830) 68 Alle the Quenes lyned gownys. **1530** PALSGR. 239/2 Lyned gowne, *robe doublee.* **1602** *2nd Pt. Return fr. Parnass.* II. vi. 968 A pair of lined slippers. **1607** SHAKS. *Timon* IV. i. 14 Plucke the lyn'd Crutch from thy old limping Sire. **1691** tr. *Emilianne's Frauds Romish Monks* (ed. 3) 396 This is that which at this day makes the Monks of Italy so full of Mony and so well Lin'd. **1704** HARRIS *Lex. Techn.* s.v. *Moat*, *Lined Moat*, is that whose Scarp and Counterscarp are cas'd with a Wall of Masons Work lying in Talus or a-sloap. **1833** J. HOLLAND *Manuf. Metal* II. 38 *Lined blades*—Scissors of all the larger sizes are often made entirely of iron, with the exception of a slip of steel welded along the edge of the blade. **1851** *Illustr. Catal. Gt. Exhib.* 1246 Lined gold is merely gold lined with copper. **1881** GREENER *Gun* Index 667 Lined barrels.

b. *Her.* (See quot. 1893.)

1688 R. HOLME *Armoury* II. xvii. 395/2 The ends turned over his head cloathed of the third, Garnished (or Faced or lined) Or. **1828–40** BERRY *Encycl. Her.* I. **1847** *Gloss. Her.* s.v., A mantle gules, lined ermine. **1893** CUSSANS *Her.* 129 *Lined*,..applied to the lining of a Mantle, Chapeau, &c., when borne of a different tincture from the garment itself.

c. ***lined-up*** (see LINE *v.*[1] 5).

1889 *Work* 22 June I. 210/3 The meaning of a 'lined-up' top is..well known among cabinet makers.

lined (laɪnd), *ppl. a.*[2] [f. LINE *v.*[2] and *sb.*[2] + -ED.]

1. Marked with lines, having lines traced or impressed on the surface.

1776 J. LEE *Introd. Bot.* Explan. Terms 385 *Lineatum*, lined, with depressed Nerves or hollow Lines. **1813** T. DAVIS *Agric. Wilts* 260 App., Provincial Terms for Sexes and Ages of Cattle... Colours..brindled, light brown, approaching to dunn; lined, with white back. **1825** *Greenhouse Comp.* II. 82 *Zizyphus lineatus*, lined Zizyphus, a shrub from China. **1837** GORING & PRITCHARD *Microgr.* 122 They [compound magnifiers] do actually exhibit all sorts of lined and ordinary objects better than single ones. **1839** BAILEY *Festus* (1852) 194 If my brow grow lined while young. **1881** D. C. MURRAY *Joseph's Coat* II. xxi. 165 Old George, looking woefully worn and lined, sat up. **1890** W. J. GORDON *Foundry* 215 In the camera the lined negative undergoes a certain amount of shifting.

2. In parasynthetic combs., as ***five-lined***, ***right-lined***, ***straight-lined***, etc., q.v. in their alphabetical places.

3. *Her.* Of an animal: Having a 'line' attached to its collar.

1828–40 BERRY *Encycl. Her.* I. s.v., Lines, as well as chains, are often affixed to the collars of animals..and are then termed collared and lined. **1847** *Gloss. Her.* s.v., A grey-hound gorged and lined. **1864** BOUTELL *Her. Hist. & Pop.* xvii. §3 (ed. 3) 281 A wolf arg., collared and lined or.

lineless ('laɪnlɪs), *a.* [f. LINE *sb.*[2] + -LESS.]

†**1.** Of a person: ? To whom no bounds can be set. *Obs. rare*[−1]. (If not a misprint for *tirelesse.*)

1594 CAREW *Tasso* II. lix, The tother is Circassian Argant cald..Vntreatable, vnpatient, vnappald, In armes linelesse [It. *infaticabile*], and peerlesse valiaunt.

2. Having no impressed or indented lines.

1798 W. TAYLOR in *Monthly Rev.* XXVI. 247 His countenances have the physiognomy of nature, not the vague lineless face of the statuaries. **1878** *Tinsley's Mag.* XXIII. 70 Her face..was smooth and lineless. **1896** R. KIPLING *Seven Seas*, *Coastwise Lights* ii, Through the endless summer evenings, on the lineless, level floors.

lineman ('laɪnmən). [f. LINE *sb.*[2] + MAN.]

1. A man employed to attend to the condition of a railway, telegraph, or telephone line.

1858 SIMMONDS *Dict. Trade*, *Linemen*, men employed on a railway. **1876** PREECE & SIVEWRIGHT *Telegraphy* 138 The lineman placed in charge of a length by road must walk his length. **1890** *Daily News* 5 Feb. 6/1 While a line-man was repairing an electric wire..he received an electric shock.

2. One who carries the line in surveying.

1858 SIMMONDS *Dict. Trade*, *Linemen*,..persons carrying the measuring line for a surveyor.

3. A line fisherman.

1890 in *Century Dict.*

4. *Amer.* and *Canad. Football.* A forward.

1907 *St. Nicholas* Sept. 1013/2 There was some discussion last year as to whether a line man could run from his position in the line and take the ball from the quarter. **1913** *Collier's* 13 Dec. 27/1 He was an aggressive, hard-fighting, and alert lineman, who did his best work under fire. **1959** *Times* 30 Nov. (Canada Suppl.) p. xx/2 There are five back-fielders and seven linemen. **1970** *Globe & Mail* (Toronto) 26 Sept. 35/5 The linemen and linebackers are all experienced. **1971** *New Yorker* 15 May 54/3 He was a forward, or lineman, in Rugby. **1972** *Nature* 2 June 297/3 Our manuscript read 'linemen', a designation for American football players who crouch in a line with hands on the ground prior to the attack.

linen ('lɪnɪn), *a.* and *sb.* Forms: 1 línen, 1–8 linnen, 3–7 lynnen, (3 linn, linin, 4 lenyne, 5 lynand), 4–6 lyn(n)yn(e, (4 lynyng), 5–6 lynen, -ine, -on, 6–7 li-, lyn(n)ing, -yng(e, 3– linen. [OE. *línen*, *línnen* = OFris. *linnen* (Du. *linnen*), OS. and OHG. *lînîn* (G. *leinen*):—OTeut. type **lînîno-* f. **lîno*[m] flax: see LINE *sb.*[1] and -EN[4].]

A. *adj.* Made of flax. In mod. Eng. apprehended chiefly as an attributive use of the sb., with the sense: Made of linen. †*linen wings* = sails.

a **700** *Epinal Gloss.* 1081 Linnin ryhae. *c* **897** K. ÆLFRED *Gregory's Past.* xiv. 82 Ðæt hrægl wæs beboden ðæt sceolde bion ȝeworht of..twispunnenum twine linenum. *c* **1160** *Hatton Gosp.* John xix. 40 Hyo..be-wunden hine mid linene claðe. *a* **1225** *Ancr. R.* 418 Nexst fleshe ne schal mon werien no linene cloð. **1297** R. GLOUC. (Rolls) 8962 Þis gode mold..gurde aboute hire middel a uair linne [*v.r.* linnene] ssete. **1340** *Ayenb.* 236 Linene kertel erþan hi by huyte uelezipe him be-houeþ þet he by ybeate and y-wesse. **1375** BARBOUR *Bruce* XIII. 422 Thai..lynyng clothis had, but mair. *c* **1375** *Sc. Leg. Saints* vii. (*Jacobus Minor*) 59 Lenyne clath he oysit ay. **1413** *Pilgr. Sowle* (Caxton) I. i. (1859) 1 She kevered it lappyng [it] in a clene lynnen clothe. **1466** *Paston Lett.* II. 270 For grey lynen cloth and sylk frenge for the hers. **1508** DUNBAR *Flyting w. Kennedie* 224, I se him want ane sark, I reid ȝow, cummer, tak in your lynning clais. **1535** COVERDALE *Ezek.* xliv. 18 They shal haue fayre lynnynge bonettes vpon their heades. **1571** GRINDAL *Injunc. at York* B iij, A comely and decent table,..with a faire linen clothe to lay vpon the same. *c* **1620** FLETCHER & MASSINGER *Trag. Barnavelt* v. iii, Who Unbard the Havens that the floating Merchant, Might clap his lynnen wings up to the windes. **1660** PEPYS *Diary* 24 May, Up, and made myself as fine as I could, with the linning stockings on, and wide canons. **1676** HOBBES *Iliad* II. 485 A linen armour he wore on his breast. **1678** WANLEY *Wond. Lit. World* v. iii. §8. 474/1 Sextus [I]..ordered..that Priests should minister in Linnen Surplices. **1719** W. WOOD *Surv. Trade* 88 Our Returns are chiefly in Linnen and Linnen Yarn. **1759** GRAINGER *Tibullus* I. v. 17 And I nine Times, in linnen garbs array'd, In silent Night, nine Times to Trivia pray'd. **1808** *Med. Jrnl.* XIX. 328 Some persons..washed their children with cold water by means of a linen cloth. **1858** SIMMONDS *Dict. Trade*, *Linen-yarn*, spun flax.

B. *sb.*

1. a. Cloth woven from flax.

The explanation 'cloth woven from flax *or hemp*', given by Johnson and copied in most subsequent Dicts., appears to be a mere blunder, founded on occasional loose uses (cf. 3).

1362 LANGL. *P. Pl.* A. I. 3 A louely ladi on leor In linnene I-cloþed. **1377** *Ibid.* B. Prol. 219 Wollewebsteres and weueres of lynnen. *c* **1450** CAPGRAVE *Chron.* (Rolls) 62 In this same tyme was Linus Pope, whech ordeyned that women schuld with lynand cure her heer. *c* **1460** J. RUSSELL *Bk. Nurture* 935 Looke þer be blanket cotyn or lynyn to wipe þe neþur ende. **1513** BRADSHAW *St. Werburge* I. 2540 She neuer ware lynon by day or by nyght. **1535** COVERDALE *1 Sam.* ii. 18 The childe was gyrded with an ouer body cote of lynnen. **1557** N. T. (Genev.) *Luke* xvi. 19 There was a certayne ryche man w[e] was clothed in purple and fyne lynnen. **1596** DALRYMPLE tr. *Leslie's Hist. Scot.* I. 93 Of linnine lykwyse thay maid wyd sarkis. **1662** STILLINGFL. *Orig. Sacr.* II. vii. §10 That other precept was made against wearing a garment of linnen and woollen, because [etc.]. **1695** *Lond. Gaz.* No. 3099/2 An Act for Burying in Scotch Linnen. **1747** WESLEY *Prim. Physic* (1762) 69 Apply a Suppository of Linnen. **1768** HUME *Ess.*, *Balance Trade* xxvii. 194 A tax on German linen encourages home manufactures. **1806** FORSYTH *Beauties Scotl.* IV. 309 Large quantities..are..exported..in an unbleached state; that is, under the name of *brown linen*, and *green linen.* **1843** HOOD *Song of the Shirt* iv, It is not linen you're wearing out, But human creatures' lives! **1864** TENNYSON *Aylmer's F.* 659 For thine Fares richly, in fine linen. **1892** *Labour Commission* Gloss., *Linen*, cloth made from flax or tow. **1899** *Daily News* 16 Jan. 3/4 An article described as linen which was partially made of cotton.

b. *pl.* Various kinds of linen; linen goods.

1748 *Anson's Voy.* II. x. 238 The cottons from the Coromandel coast, make the European linnens almost useless. **1851** *Illustr. Catal. Gt. Exhib.* 1158 An assortment of unbleached linens. **1892** *Daily News* 30 Apr. 2/7 Dress linens keep firm in price.

†**c.** ***fossil linen***: a kind of asbestos. (Cf. LINE *sb.*[1] 1 a and FLAX *sb.* 5 b.) *Obs.*

1797 *Encycl. Brit.* (ed. 3) X. 83/2 *Fossile Linen* is a kind of amianthus, which consists of flexible, parallel, soft fibres,.. celebrated for the uses to which it has been applied, of being woven, and forming an incombustible cloth.

2. a. Something made of linen; a linen garment. *Obs.* in *sing.*; the *pl.* is found in Scottish writers.

1566 in Peacock *Eng. Ch. Furniture* (1866) 137 All the Reste off the lenyns that belong to the papishe priste. **1724** R. WODROW *Life J. Wodrow* (1828) 57 Her friend went into another room and put on clean linens. **1773** JOHNSON *Let. to Mrs. Thrale* 6 Sept., A very decent girl in a printed linen. **1864** BURTON *Scot Abr.* II. ii. 184 A little bag, wherein were my linens and some books. **1891** MISS DOWIE *Girl in Karp.* 147 Dressed in..preternaturally unsullied linens, and a short sheepskin.

†**b.** *pl.* The sails of a ship (cf. *linen wings* in A).

1622 FLETCHER *Sea Voy.* I. i, Farle up all her Linnens, and let her ride it out.

3. *collect.* **a.** Garments or other articles made of linen; often by extension applied to garments normally or originally made of linen, even when other materials are actually used. Often *spec.* = undergarments, e.g. shirts; also = bed-linen, table-linen. ***to wash one's dirty linen at home***: to say nothing in public about family affairs, disputes, or scandals. ***to wash one's dirty linen***

in public: to discuss an essentially private matter, esp. a dispute or scandal, in public.

c **1330** R. BRUNNE *Chron.* (1810) 334 Alle þei fled on rowe, in lynen white as milke. *c* **1460** J. RUSSELL *Bk. Nurture* 876 Wayte hys lynnyn þat hit be clene. *c* **1489** CAXTON *Sonnes of Aymon* xxi. 466 Lady, aryse and fette hym suche linnen as he nedeth. **1552** *Bury Wills* (Camden) 140 All my lynnen except my too best shirts. **1590** SHAKS. *Mids. N.* IV. ii. 40 In any case let Thisby haue cleane linnen. **1607** TOURNEUR *Rev. Trag.* II. ii, He and the Duchesse By night meete in their linnen. **1632** LITHGOW *Trav.* x. 449 My Linnen, Letters, and Sacket was lying in my hostery. **1653** WALTON *Angler* iii. 61 Lets go to that house, for the linnen looks white, and smels of Lavender. **1695** CONGREVE *Love for L.* II. x, *Miss Pru.* I'm resolv'd I won't let Nurse put any more Lavender among my Smocks—ha, Cousin? *Frail.* Fie, Miss; amongst your Linnen, you must say—You must never say Smock. **1702** *Lond. Gaz.* No. 3809/5 A Party of 30 of Paul Diack's Hussars..took away the Linnen that was hanged out to dry upon the Palisades. **1731** LD. BATHURST *Let.* 19 Apr. in *Swift's Wks.* (1841) II. 649 Washing your linen and mending it, darning your stockings, &c. **1802** MAR. EDGEWORTH *Moral T.* (1816) I. xvi. 132 He..bespoke a suit of clothes. He bought new linen. **1820** KEATS *Eve St. Agnes* xxx, And still she slept an azure-lidded sleep, In blanched linen, smooth, and lavender'd. **1840** MARRYAT *Poor Jack* xxvi, Take our dirty linen on shore. **1867** TROLLOPE *Last Chron. Barset* II. xliv. 2 There is nothing..so bad as washing one's dirty linen in public. **1877** R. J. MORE *Under the Balkans* xv. 216 The parents of the bride gave a present of homespun linen to the godfather and godmother. **1895** *Globe* 23 May 1 People who ought to wash their dirty linen at home will not be satisfied with a less public laundry than Piccadilly. **1931** *Times* 3 Aug. 9/1 If the Government had made tactful..representations..to the Holy See,..the whole matter could have been quietly settled without any washing of dirty linen in public. **1935** D. L. SAYERS *Gaudy Night* iv. 80 Even if the poison campaign led to no open disaster..a washing of dirty linen in public was not calculated to do Shrewsbury [College] any good. **1972** *Daily Tel.* 3 May 16, I know it is not done to wash dirty medical linen in public.

†**b.** A piece or pieces of linen, *esp.* strips of linen for use as bandages. In *pl.* graveclothes. *Obs.*

1598 SHAKS. *Merry W.* IV. ii. 79 *Mist. Ford.* Go, go, sweet Sir Iohn: Mistriis Page and I will looke some linnen for your head. **1651–3** JER. TAYLOR *Serm. for Year* (1678) 104 In a single Linnen [he] laid his honour'd head. **1653** S. MEWCE *Let. to Lady H.* in *Hatton Corr.* (1878) I. 9 Lynnen to dresse the wounded men was required. **1653** H. MORE *Antid. Ath.* III. viii. (1712) 111 The Family..gave out that he died..got him washed and laid Linens..handsomly about him. **1676** HALE *Contempl.* I. 121 The linnen that wrapped his body in one place, and the linnen that bound his head in another. **1689** BURNET *Tracts* I. 38 They were some of the Linnings in which Christ was wrapped. *a* **1796** BURNS *'O merry hae I been'* 11 Bless'd be the hour she cool'd in her linnens.

c. Abbrev. LINEN-DRAPER b.

1955 J. PHELAN *Tramping the Toby* 223 *Linen*, a newspaper. **1962** R. COOK *Crust on its Uppers* i. 21 Everything they've ever read in a linen or a clever-clever book.

4. *attrib.* and *Comb.*: **a.** simple attrib., as ***linen-closet***, ***†-loom***, ***-manufacture***, ***-paper***, ***-room***, ***-tape***, ***-thread***, ***-work***. **b.** objective, as ***linen-keeper***, ***-printer***, ***-stainer***, ***-weaver***, ***†-webster***; ***linen-darning***; ***linen-making***, ***-wearing*** adjs. **c.** instrumental and parasynthetic, as ***linen-fitted***, ***-suited***, ***-vestured*** adjs.

1885 'M. RUTHERFORD' *M. Rutherford's Deliverance* iii. 41 She cared nothing for the *linen-closet, the spotless bed-hangings,..the true household gods of the respectable women of those days. **1955** W. TUCKER *Wild Talent* xiv. 181 The butler..saw Paul's questioning glance at the other two doors. 'The nearest one is a linen closet, sir,' he said. **1880** *Plain Hints Needlework* 88 An old harden sheet or apron is invaluable as practice for teaching *linen darning and patching. **1896** *Westm. Gaz.* 8 Oct. 3/2 Woman..has purloined for her own use..the *linen-fitted flannel shirt. *Mod. Advt.*, Required, Position as Housekeeper, *Linen-keeper, Matron, or Lady-Help. **1404** *Nottingham Rec.* II. 22 Item, j. *lynyn lome. **1468** *Ripon Ch. Acts* (Surtees) 133 Unum lynnen-lome. **1692** LUTTRELL *Brief Rel.* (1857) II. 382 A great hearing at councill between the islands of Jersey and Guernsey and the *linnen manufacture corporation. **1727–52** CHAMBERS s.v. *Paper*, *Linen or European Paper is chiefly made of linen rags beaten to a pulp. **1875** SCRIVENER *Lect. Text N. Test.* 17 About the twelfth century linen paper came to be substituted. **1772** *Ann. Reg.* 99 The prisoners were *linen-printers. **1900** E. GLYN *Visits of Elizabeth* 33 Aunt Maria..said it was her day for seeing the *linen-room. **1775** J. ADAMS *Fam. Lett.* (1876) 119, I think there is a particular occupation in Europe, called a paper-stainer or *linen-stainer. **1762** *Gentl. Mag.* 185/1 A limpid stream.. Where *linnen-suited Sal for water goes. **1873** *Young Englishwoman* Mar. 150/2 A piece of *linen tape..keeps the buttons securely in place. **1880** E. GLAISTER *Needlework* v. 49 The letters are made in linen tape, unbleached, the yellower the better. **1897** *Sears, Roebuck Catal.* 321/1 Marshall's *Linen Thread (100 yd. spools, black only). **1908** *Westm. Gaz.* 28 Dec. 5/2 The whole front is a mass of hand embroidery done in heavy linen-thread. **1975** *Times* 6 Mar. 7/6 The greatest problem with owning old lace is getting it repaired... An added problem is the difficulty of obtaining the hair-fine linen thread. **1866** J. B. ROSE *Ovid's Metam.* 30 The *linen-vestured race, Hold her in deepest reverence. **1721** STRYPE *Eccl. Mem.* IV. iv. 49 *Linnin-wearing bishops. **1474** in *Cal. Pat. Rolls 14 Edw. IV*, 22 Nov., *Lynnen wever. **1535** COVERDALE *1 Chron.* iv. 21 The kynred of ye lynnenweuers in ye house of Aszbea. **1708** *Lond. Gaz.* No. 4409/4 Thomas Tuttle, a Linen-Weaver. **1642** in Rushw. *Hist. Coll.* III. (1692) I. 680 Richard Parcivall of Kirkman-Shalme in the said County of Lancaster, *Linen-Webster. **1720** *Lond. Gaz.* No. 5889/4 George Malton, late of Woodkirk, Linnen-webster. **1535** COVERDALE *2 Chron.* iii. 14 He made a vayle also of Yalow Sylke, scarlet, purple, *lynenworke.

5. Special combinations: †**linen ball**, some instrument of torture (cf. LAWN *sb.*[1] 3 b); **linen basket**, a receptacle for dirty clothing; **linen crash** = CRASH *sb.*[2] 1; **linen cupboard**, a cupboard designed to hold bed-linen and table-linen; also, the contents of such a cupboard; **linen-decency** *nonce-use* (see quot.); **linen duster**, a duster (see DUSTER 4 a) made of linen; **linen-fold** = *linen scroll*; **linen-hall**, a market-hall for the sale of linens; **linen-horse** = HORSE *sb.* 7 c; **linen lapper** (see quot.); †**linen-lifter**, a man given to adultery; †**linen-man**, a shirt-maker or linen-draper; **linen-mill** (see quot.); **linen-panel**, one decorated with a linen-scroll; **linen-pattern** = *linen-scroll*; **linen-press**, a frame or receptacle for pressing or holding linen; **linen-prover**, a microscope used to determine the fineness of a linen fabric by counting the threads; **linen-scroll** (see quot.); **linen shower** [SHOWER *sb.*[1]] *N. Amer.*, a party at which a bride-to-be is given presents of household linen, etc.; **linen tea**, a tea arranged in order to provide house-linen for a crèche, day nursery, etc.; †**linen-teller** = *linen-prover*; †**linen-wheel**, app. a kind of sewing machine.

a **1630** *Pathomachia* III. iv. 29 Vnlesse thou confesse..the Spanish Strappado, *Linnen Ball, and Peare of Confession shall torment thee. **1907** *Yesterday's Shopping* (1969) 125/3 *Linen baskets. Barrel shape, buff wicker. **1970** G. F. NEWMAN *Sir, You Bastard* viii. 239 He used his shirt to wipe his damp armpits, then threw it out on to the linen basket. **1895** *Montgomery Ward Catal.* 24/2 *Linen crash or toweling. **1904** *Sci. Amer.* 21 May 409/3 The complainant, a manufacturer of linen crash, had adopted as a trade-mark the words 'Stevens Crash'. **1873** *Young Englishwoman* Mar. 155/1 The plain, economical housewife would do well to follow 'Myra's' plan of her *linen-cupboard. **1939** A. THIRKELL *Brandons* ix. 234 She let Miss Morris help Nurse ..to go through the linen cupboard and mark some new sheets. **1972** P. RUELL *Red Christmas* v. 48 The linen cupboard was, forecastably, full of linen. It was more of a room than a cupboard. **1644** MILTON *Areop.* (Arb.) 75, I fear yet this iron yoke of outward conformity hath left a slavish print upon our necks; the ghost of a *linnen decency yet haunts us. **1850** WHIPPLE *Ess. & Rev.* (ed. 3) II. 12 All the conventional proprieties and linen decencies of language, he would find continually violated. **1867** *Galaxy* III. 635 His cloak..or *linen duster..serves as a cover to hide the manipulations of his agile fingers. **1949** *Chicago Daily News* 11 Feb. 21/3 Grandma was a fashion plate in her smart linen duster for Sunday motoring. **1891** *Trans. Soc. Antiquaries* 22 Jan. 225 The panels are ornamented with '*linen-fold' patterns. **1765** WESLEY *Jrnl.* 4 May, I preached in the *Linen-Hall,..a large square, with piazzas on three sides of it. **1780** A. YOUNG *Tour Irel.* I. 167 He..sells it at the linen-hall in Dublin. **1845** R. COBBOLD *Hist. M. Catchpole* II. xxv. 139 The large *linen-horses belonging to the gaol stood in the passage. **1906** *Mrs. Beeton's Bk. Househ. Managem.* lxix. 1810 Silks..should always be dried in the shade, on a linen-horse. **1893** *Labour Commission* Gloss., **Linen Lappers*, men who examine, measure, and fold the linen for the various markets. (Term used in the North of Ireland.) **1652** FELTHAM *Char. Low C.* (1659) 24 They [Dutchwomen] are not so ready at this play as the English..nor are their Men such *linnen-lifters. **1625** B. JONSON *Staple of N.* I. i, O Founder, no such matter, My Spurrier, and my Hatter, My *Linnen-man, and my Taylor. **1631** MASSINGER *Emperor East* I. ii, How low a new stamp'd courtier May vaile to..His linnen-man, and taylor. **1727–52** CHAMBERS *Cycl.* s.v. *Mill*, *Linen-Mills... Their use is, to scour linens, after their having been first cleansed when taken out of the lixivium, or lye. **1886** WILLIS & CLARK *Cambridge* I. 270 *Lignis undulatis*, that is, with undulated or wavy woodwork... The words probably denote what is now termed '*linen panels'. **1850** PARKER *Gloss. Archit.* s.v. *Panel*, One kind of ornament which was introduced towards the end of the Perpendicular style..consists of a series of straight mouldings..so arranged..as to represent the folds of linen, it is usually called the '*linen pattern'. **1851** MRS. STOWE *Uncle Tom's Cabin* (1852) I. xviii. 296 The store-room, the *linen-presses, the china-closet,..all went under an awful review. **1970** *Canad. Antiques Collector* June 4 (Advt.), Exceptional Pennsylvania walnut linen-press.. Circa 1790. **1894** MASKELYNE *Sharps & Flats* 68 The mirror in this case is mounted somewhat after the fashion of a *linen-prover. **1854** FAIRHOLT *Dict. Terms Art*, **Linen-scroll*, a peculiar style of decorative ornament, extensively used to fill panels in the latter part of the fifteenth, and during the sixteenth century; so termed from its resemblance to a small napkin folded in close convolutions all over its surface. **1904** *N.Y. Tribune* 27 Oct. 7 The managers of the Home for the Friendless invite the public to a *linen shower and reception. **1921** *Daily Colonist* (Victoria, B.C.) 3 Apr. 8/3 A delightful linen shower was given in honor of Miss Dorothy Woods, Thursday evening at the home of Mrs. B. E. Lefevre. **1974** *Evening Herald* (Rock Hill, S. Carolina) 18 Apr. 9/4 Hostesses for a linen shower were Mrs. H. D. Long and Mrs. Arthur Snyder. **1916** *Yorks. Post* 19 Apr. 4/7 The first crèche which held such a '*linen tea'... Yesterday's meeting was for the purpose of collecting house linen to furnish the place. **1948** Linen tea [see *kitchen tea* (KITCHEN *sb.* 7)]. **1797** MIERS FISHER in *Mem. Lit. & Philos. Soc. Manchester* (1798) V. 316, I examined the..skin, with a glass which magnified considerably, and which is known in Ireland by the name of a *linen-teller. **1638** J. ROUS *Diary* (Camden) 85 He [a handless man] tooke three stitches in a cloathe with a *linnen-wheele (prepared with a turner's devise for the foote).

linen-armourer. a. *Hist.* A maker of 'linen armour' (i.e. gambesons and similar adjuncts to armour); in mod. renderings of the original title of the guild now known as the Merchant Taylors' Company. †**b.** Allusively used in jest for: A tailor. Hence †**linen-armouress.**

In AF. the guild was called 'La Fraternite des Taillours et Armurers de Lynge Armurie', anglicized as 'The Fraternite of Taillours and Lynge Armurers'; the Latin charters were addressed 'Cissoribus et Armurariis Linearum'. (See Clode *Mem. Guild Mercht. Taylors* 58–9; Herbert *Guilds* II. 385.)

1603 STOW *Surv. Lond.* (ed. 2) 542, I finde that king Edwarde the first, in the 28. of his raigne, confirmed that Guild by the name of Taylors and Linnen Armorers. **1630** J. TAYLOR (Water P.) *Praise Clean Linen* Ded., Wks. II. 165 You are the only Linnen Armouresse, Cap a pie from the declination of the Stocke to the exaltation of the Nightcap. **1687** *Hist. Sir J. Hawkwood* i. §1. 1 The Merchant-Taylors, then called Linnen-Armourers, were eminent not only in Peace, but War. *a* **1700** B. E. *Dict. Cant. Crew*, *Linnen-armorers*, Tailers. So **1785** in GROSE *Dict. Vulgar Tongue.*

'linen-,draper. [f. LINEN *sb.*] **a.** A retail trader who deals in linens, calicos, and the like.

1549 *Nottingham Rec.* IV. 6 Johannes Cleyter, lynen draper. **1600** *Chester Pl.* Banes 86 Cappers and lynnen drapers, see that you fourth bringe In well-decked order that worthy storie of Balaam and his Asse. **1607** ? DEKKER & WEBSTER *Westward Ho!* I. i, Like politic penthouses, which commonly make the shop of a mercer or linen-draper as dark as a room in Bedlam. **1782** COWPER *Gilpin* 21, I am a linnen-draper bold, As all the world doth know. **1858** LYTTON *What will he do?* II. v, Mrs. Haughton was the daughter of a linen draper.

b. A newspaper. *Rhyming slang.*

1857 'DUCANGE ANGLICUS' *Vulgar Tongue* 12 *Linen-draper*, paper. **1936** J. CURTIS *Gilt Kid* xxiv. 234 It might be just as well to keep under cover for a little until perhaps the linen-drapers gave him the office that the chase had not been taken up. **1972** *Lebende Sprachen* XVII. 8/3 *Linen draper*, paper.

Hence **'linen,draperess**, the wife of a linen-draper, a female linen-draper. **'linen,drapery**, the occupation of a linen-draper; goods in which a linen-draper deals.

1868 MISS BRADDON *Dead Sea Fr.* I. vi. 104 The linen-draperess seated herself in one of the holland-covered arm-chairs. **1849** F. J. FOXTON *Pop. Chr.* 16 The heterodox linen-drapery of the Tractarians. **1895** P. WHITE *King's Diary* 4 Colossal linendrapery ending in such a daughter is a glorified trade.

†**'linener.** *Obs.* [f. LINEN *sb.* + -ER[1].] A linen-draper or shirt-maker.

1609 B. JONSON *Sil. Wom.* II. iii, I doe also loue to see her ..haue her counsell of taylors, linneners, lace-women, embroyderers. **1625** —— *Staple of N.* The Persons of the Play, Linener, Haberdasher, Shoomaker.

linenette (lɪnɪˈnɛt). [f. LINEN *sb.* + -ETTE.] A textile fabric made to imitate linen.

1894 *Daily News* 19 Dec. 9/5 Velvet and velveteen, satin and sateen, linen and linenette..were wholly different materials. **1896** *Ibid.* 9 Dec. 10/3 A piece of linenette or dress material purchased of the defendants.

linenless (ˈlɪnɪnlɪs), *a.* Devoid of linen or underclothing; discarding linen. Also *Comb.*

1855 *Chamb. Jrnl.* IV. 290 It was the tall,..buttoned-up, linenless-looking, grisly old Pole. **1887** *Gd. Words* 82/1 The horsehair shirt and linenless rule admits of no exception.

lineo- (ˈlɪnɪəʊ), used as combining form of L. *linea* line; as in **,lineo-'circular** *a. Math.*, said of an apparatus for converting rectilinear into circular movement. **'lineograph** [see -GRAPH], an instrument for drawing lines of a definite character (*Cent. Dict.*). **,lineo-'linear** *a. Math.*, linear with respect to each of two different variables or sets of variables. **,lineo-'polar** *a. Math.*, produced by taking the $(n-1)$-th polar of a locus with respect to a function of the nth order; so called because such a polar of a point is a line (*Cent. Dict.*).

1858 CAYLEY in *Coll. Math. Papers* (1889) II. 517 The lineo-linear covariant becomes the lineo-linear invariant $ab'-a'b$. **1874** SYLVESTER in *Proc. Roy. Instit.* VII. 186 *note*, In the lineo-circular or parallel-motion adjustment imagine the connecters to be detached from the angles of the diamond, and [etc.].

‖**lineola** (lɪˈniːələ). [L. *līneola*, dim. of *līnea* LINE *sb.*[2]] †**a.** *Math.* A line. *Obs.* **b.** *Anat.* and *Zool.* A little line. Hence **'lineolet** *Ent.*, a fine or obscure line (*Cent. Dict.*).

1726 tr. *Gregory's Astron.* I. 77 The Lineola $\beta\rho$, is to the Lineola br, as the Causes producing them. **1888** *Syd. Soc. Lex.*, *Lineola*, a little line.

lineolate (ˈlɪnɪəleɪt), *a.* *Bot.* and *Zool.* [f. LINEOLA + -ATE[2] 2.] Marked with minute lines. Hence **'lineolated** *a.*, in the same sense.

1819 G. SAMOUELLE *Entomol. Compend.* 421 *Noctua lineolata*, the lineolated Dart [moth]. **1852** DANA *Crust.* I. 354 Postero-lateral region faint lineolate. **1880** GRAY *Struct. Bot.* 418/2 *Lineolate*, marked with fine or obscure lines.

'line-out. Pl. line-outs, lines-out. [f. the vbl. phr. *to line out* (LINE *v.*[2] 8 b).] In Rugby football: (see quot. 1900).

1889 [see TOUCH *sb.* 12]. **1900** A. E. T. WATSON *Young Sportsman* 284 *Line out*,..the arrangement of forwards opposite to one another when the ball is about to be thrown in from touch. **1906** GALLAHER & STEAD *Compl. Rugby Footballer* v. 80 The line-out work. **1931** *Times* 16 Feb. 5/2 Barrington made a clever mark from a knock-on in a line-out, but failed with the kick at goal. **1955** *Times* 18 July 12/6 The Province won four scrummages and lines-out out of

five. **1965** *New Statesman* 19 Mar. 465/1 Just before half-time Wales scored, and thereafter dominated the game, winning the line-outs by intelligent forward play. **1973** *Scotsman* 21 Feb. 18/6 He used to prefer being stationed at No. 7 but agrees that, with the new laws tending so to compress the line-out, it is difficult to win much really usable ball from an opponent of markedly superior height.

liner^{1} (ˈlaɪnə(r)). [f. LINE *v.*^{1}]

1. One who lines or fits a lining to anything.

1611 FLORIO, *Foderáro*,..a liner. **1881** *Census Instr.* (1885) 74 Straw Hat and Bonnet Making:..Liner. *Ibid.* 78 Furrier, Working... Liner. **1887** *Pall Mall G.* 7 Sept. 7/2 William Glover, a bucket liner, was thrown forward and struck among the girders. *Mod. Advt.*, Mantle finishers and liners wanted.

2. *Mech.* Something which serves as a lining. **a.** An inside cylinder, or a vessel placed inside another. **b.** A thin slip of metal, etc. placed between two parts to adjust them; a shim. **c.** A slab on which pieces of marble, etc. are fastened for grinding or polishing (Knight *Dict. Mech.* 1875).

a. 1886 *Pall Mall G.* 1 Sept. 2/1 The gun has a thin liner put in from the breech, extending over the powder-chamber ..it is advisable to have thin liners, which can be easily taken out. **1887** D. A. LOW *Machine Draw.* (1892) 58 A is the cast-iron casing or barrel of the pump; B is a brass liner fitting tightly into the former at its ends. **1894** *Times* 28 Feb. 6/6 The trial had to be abandoned owing to the heating of the eccentric strap of the port low-pressure engine and the destruction of the brass liner.

b. 1869 SIR E. J. REED *Shipbuild.* x. 181 On account of the edge-strips being worked inside the plates, liners had to be fitted at each frame. **1874** THEARLE *Naval Archit.* 114 Wide liners are fitted between the bulkhead frames and bottom plating. **1881** GREENER *Gun* 237 The barrels are bored up within three inches of the muzzle with a fine-boring bit, using a spill and liners.

3. The lining of a garment, esp. one made of an artificial fibre. So ***liner suit*** (see quot. 1969).

1947 *Horizon* Sept. 203 They took off their helmet liners. **1962** F. I. ORDWAY et al. *Basic Astronautics* xiii. 517 The inner liner of the suit is of neoprene-coated fabric... The outer liner is an aluminized coverall. **1969** *Guardian* 7 Jan. 7/2 There is an undergarment called a liner suit which makes PVCs more comfortable to wear. It is a two-piece affair made from knitted nylon with the inside of cosy brushed cotton. **1970** *Washington Post* 30 Sept. B5/3 (Advt.), Zip-in-or-out orlon liner. **1971** C. BONINGTON *Annapurna South Face* 241, 4-oz. Dunloprufe nylon with open-cell foam liner. *Ibid.* 242, 1 pair overmitts [made of] proofed nylon with Borg fur liner.

4. In full, ***liner note***. (See quot. 1953.) orig. *U.S.*

1953 *Britannica Bk. of Year* 638/1 *Liner*, the text accompanying an album of gramophone records. **1955** *Sat. Rev.* (U.S.) Jan. 41 The covers of these new jazz albums.. are being covered..with thousands and thousands of words known as 'liner notes'. **1960** D. CERULLI et al. *Jazz Word* (1962) 106 They couldn't come up with any less information than on some liners today. **1968** *Jazz Monthly* Feb. 21/2 The enthusiastic sleeve note by Brian Rust suggests that he may be on the downward path towards acceptance of those degenerate swing bands whom he has damned in nearly all his liner writing! **1969** *Rolling Stone* 17 May 17/3 As Coleman observes in the liner notes, 'Ornette Denardo is hard to keep up with if you don't tell him what to do.'

liner^{2} (ˈlaɪnə(r)). Also 5 **lynnor**, 5, 7 **lyner**, 6 **lynar**. [f. LINE *sb.*^{2} or LINE *v.*^{2}]

I. Of persons.

1. *Sc.* An official whose duty is the tracing of the boundaries of properties in burghs.

14.. *Burgh Laws* cv. (Sc. Stat. I), þe saidis lyneris sall suer þat þai sall leilly lyne in lenth as braidnes baith foir part and back part of þe land according to þe richt and auld merchis withyn þe burgh. **1461** *Extracts Burgh Recs. Peebles* (1872) 139 Thir ar the lynnoris to serf the burgh of Pebillis: + Wylyem Bulle, Rychart Cant [etc.]. **1541** *Extracts Aberd. Reg.* (1844) I. 453 It was fundyn and determynit be the lynaris anence the debatis betuex Iohne Henrisone Culane ..and Iohn Nachty, twcheing thair landis liand in the Gastraw [etc.]. **1894** K. HEWAT *Little Sc. World* i. 20 The Liner has still important duties to perform in tracing the boundaries of properties.

2. One whose business it is to paint lines on the wheels, etc. of carriages. Also ***liner-out***.

1819 *P.O. Lond. Direct.* 299 Salmon, Thos., Springer and Liner, King-street, Clerkenwell. **1884** *B'ham Daily Post* 28 July 3/3 Carriage-painters.—Wanted, two good Liners-out and Varnishers.

3. A writer of miscellaneous items for the newspapers, which are paid for at so much per line. (Cf. PENNY-A-LINER.)

1861 D. COOK *Paul Foster's Dau.* xix. II. 87 Because now and then a liner is found in the gutter, it doesn't do to cry shame on every man that wields a pen. **1865** *Reader* 20 May 567/1 The account in the *New York World* of the pursuit and capture of Booth is by a prince amongst liners.

4. One who 'lines' a tree. (Cf. quot. 1890 s.v. LINE *v.*^{2} 2.)

1880 *Lumberman's Gaz.* Jan. 28 The scorers and liner fell the trees and roughly trim the two opposite sides.

5. = LINESMAN 1.

1870 *Daily News* 27 Sept., Such troops are less likely to commit excesses in a conquered town than regular liners.

II. Of things.

†**6.** (See quot.) *Obs.*

1683 MOXON *Mech. Exerc.*, *Printing* xii. ¶7 The Liner is ..a thin Plate of Iron or Brass..that being applied to the Face of a Punch, or other piece of Work, it may shew whether it be straight or no. *Ibid.* xvi, He examins by applying the Lyner..and holding it so up between his Eye and the Light, tries whether or not the Lyner ride upon the part that was extuberant.

7. a. (See quot.)

1886 MRS. SHARP-AYRES *Mirror Painting* Introd. 4 Take a very fine brush, called a liner, dip it in the colour, and go over the traced outline of the water lily.

b. A cosmetic used for tinting a part of the face; a brush or pencil for applying this; *spec.* = *eye-liner, eyeliner*.

1926 M. SMITH *Bk. Play Production* xi. 182 Liners are smaller sticks of grease paints..used to make lines on the face, such as wrinkles, 'eyebrows', etc. **1958** OSBORNE & CREIGHTON *Epitaph G. Dillon* II. 44, I always touch mine up with a brown liner... The rings under my eyes. **1966** *Harper's Bazaar* Sept. 70/1 Wrapping up lid, indeed eye, in a cocoon of pale grey shadow and liner. **1972** *Daily Tel.* 24 Jan. 11/1 A narrower streak of colour on the lid by the lashes, in place of liner.

8. a. A vessel (now usually a steam-ship) belonging to a 'line' of packets (see LINE *sb.*^{2} 22).

1838 HALIBURTON *Clockm.* Ser. II. v, All they got to do is, to up Hudson like a shot..and home in a liner, and write a book. **1848** KINGSLEY *Yeast* v. (1851) 96 The rail-road, Cunard's liners and the electric telegraph. **1885** *Manch. Exam.* 21 May 4/7 If the bar was silted up 3 ft. it absolutely prohibited large Atlantic liners from entering Liverpool. **1897** R. KIPLING *Captains Courageous* 1 The big liner rolled and lifted, whistling to warn the fishing fleet.

b. A line-of-battle ship.

1829 W. N. GLASCOCK *Sailors & Saints* I. ii. 25 We *liners*, you know, are not in the habit of leading small craft to their anchorage. **1855** *Chambers's Jrnl.* II. 270/2 Not an hour was lost in expediting the fitting out of our liner, for war was raging. **1858** in SIMMONDS *Dict. Trade.* **1859** G. A. LAWRENCE *Sword & Gown* xvii. 228 A huge 'liner', with English colours at the main... close on the enemy's quarter. **1861** *Sat. Rev.* 14 Dec. 602 There was..a fleet in commission of three liners and three or four frigates. **1863** WOOLNER *My Beautiful Lady* 147 The huge liners of the hostile fleet. **1864** *Times* 17 Oct., Wooden liners had become universally acknowledged as useless to compete with ironclad frigates.

c. One of the aircraft of a regular line, esp. one for passenger transport; an air-liner; a space-ship.

1905 KIPLING *Actions & Reactions* (1909) 125 A Planet liner, east bound, heaves up in a superb spiral and takes the air of us humming. **1919** H. GOLDING *Wonder Bk. Aircraft* 69 *(caption)* *Off!* The pilot of the 'liner' is just giving orders to remove the blocks from the wheels of the under-carriage. **1933** *Boys' Mag.* XLVII. 24/1 Mile after mile of seemingly endless country unfurled itself beneath the flying wings of the giant liner. **1951** A. C. CLARKE *Sands of Mars* iii. 24 The observation gallery..completely circled the liner. **1959** *Times Lit. Suppl.* 17 Apr. 230/3 These well-known liners were conceived with the future needs of the air lines in view. **1969** *New Scientist* 2 Oct. 20/2 The Boeing liner will have rather more than twice the capacity of the Concorde.

d. One of a fleet of lorries.

1955 *Times* 29 June 13/3 The commission have offered the trunk service vehicles, which provide regular daily services between certain towns..'liner' services, compared with 'tramps',..in relatively large lots together with their respective terminal depôts.

9. A boat engaged in sea-fishing with lines.

1901 *Scotsman* 4 Mar. 6/2 The want of herring bait is handicapping the steam liners who are working the cod and ling fishing.

10. *Sports.* (? *U.S.*) **a.** *Baseball.* A ball which, when struck, flies through the air in a nearly straight line not far from the ground.

1874 [see *line-ball*, LINE *sb.*^{2} 32].

b. A ball, marble, or other object that rests on a traced line (*Cent. Dict.*).

11. *colloq.* A picture hung 'on the line' at an exhibition (see LINE *sb.*^{2} 11 c).

1887 W. P. FRITH *Autobiog.* I. x. 114 The work..in due time made its appearance in Trafalgar Square, where it was amongst the fortunate 'liners'.

12. 'A threshed sheaf of corn' (*W. Cornwall Gloss.* 1880).

1602 CAREW *Cornwall* 110b, As the threshing lout, Rusheth his Lyners out, So Lyner on his course rusheth.

13. *attrib.*, as **liner train**, a fast through-running freight train made up of detachable containers on permanently coupled wagons.

1962 *Guardian* 30 Oct. 3/2 'Custom built' services..so that customers can..'buy space' on fixed formation trains —'liner trains'—whose wagons can..bear their name and line of business. **1963** *Reshaping of Brit. Railways* (Brit. Railways Board) 142 The description 'Liner Train' is applied to a conception of transport based upon joint use of road and rail for door-to-door transport of containerised merchandise, with special purpose, through-running, scheduled trains providing the trunk haul... The Liner Train..is a train of chassis which will remain continuously coupled... The speed will be a maximum of 75 and an average of 50 miles an hour. **1964** *Observer* 28 June 8/5 If Dr. Beeching's figures are accepted at their face value, the cost of carrying goods by liner trains will be so much less than by heavy lorries..that he should be able to undercut the roads by a comfortable margin. **1970** *Daily Mail* 16 Feb. 1/6 The plant sends rear axles and brake drums by liner trains to other Ford factories.

ˈ**linerboard.** [f. LINER^{1} + BOARD *sb.*] A paper-board used as a facing on fibre-board.

1961 *Paper Technol.* II. II. 145 We have produced virtually every type of paper and board known today, for example, ranging from glassine to kraft liner board. **1969** *Jane's Freight Containers 1968–69* 439/2 Rectangular container, two layers corrugated fibreboard covered by liner-board. **1972** *Evening Telegram* (St. John's, Newfoundland) 28 June 4/3 What venture capital went into the Stephenville Linerboard Mill?

†**line-right**, *a.* and *adv.* *Obs.* [f. LINE *sb.*^{2} + RIGHT *a.* and *adv.*]

A. *adj.* (Situated) in a straight line; straight.

*c***1391** CHAUCER *Astrol.* I. §21 Under which lyne, whan that the Sonne and the Mone ben lyne-riht..than is the Eclips of the Sonne or of the Mone. **1465** *Hist. Doc. Roch.* (E.E.T.S.) 6 Which wall or syde hous is crokyd, and not lyne-ryȝt.

B. *adv.* In a straight line; rectilineally; straight.

*c***1391** CHAUCER *Astrol.* II. §23 Til that any sterre fix sit lyne-riht perpendiculer over the pol Artik. **1412–20** LYDG. *Chron. Troy* I. vi, Line right agayne the wormes heade They holden it tyll that he be deade. **1419** in *Surtees Misc.* (1888) 14 We awarde that a lyne be drawen lyneryght. *c***1430** LYDG. *Reas. & Sens.* 2536 Lyne ryght thy cours to dresse To thilke path. **14..** *Ephyphanye* in *Tundale's Vis.* (1843) 108 The sterre hem browght to Beedlem And lyne ryght the chylde above.

†**lineseat.** *Obs.* In 5 **lyncet, -set.** [f. *line* flax (see LINE *sb.*^{1}) + SEAT.] The stool on which women sit while spinning.

*c***1440** *Promp. Parv.* 305/2 Lyncet, a werkynge stole. **1465** *Mann. & Househ. Exp.* (Roxb.) 484 Item, to Cumberton fore a lynset the same day, viij.*d.*

lineseed: see LINSEED.

†**lineshark.** *Obs. rare*$^{-0}$.

*c***1475** *Pict. Voc.* in Wr.-Wülcker 773/12 *Hec culingna*, a lineshark.

†**line-sharker.** *Obs. rare*$^{-1}$.

1604 MIDDLETON *Father Hubburd's T.* Wks. (Bullen) VIII. 51 Certain line-sharkers that have coursed the countries to seek you out.

linesman (ˈlaɪnzmən). [f. *line's*, genitive of LINE *sb.*^{2} + MAN. Cf. LINEMAN.]

1. A soldier belonging to a regiment of the line.

1856 E. NAPIER *(title)* The Linesman, or Service in the Guards and the Line during England's long peace. **1885** *Mag. of Art* Sept. p. xlii/2 The ugly shako and the coarse red trousers of the French linesman.

2. = LINEMAN 1.

1883 *Standard* 3 May 6/5 James B——,..telegraph linesman. **1884** *Manch. Exam.* 11 Nov. 8/2 A number of linesmen engaged..in unloading a barge of heavy sleepers.

3. a. *Lawn Tennis.* An umpire posted near to one of the 'lines,' whose duty it is to decide whether any particular ball falls within the court or not. **b.** *Football.* In the Association game since 1891, an official whose chief duty is to mark when and where the ball crosses the touch-line or the goal-line.

1890 HEATHCOTE, etc. *Lawn Tennis* (Badm. Libr.) 349 There should certainly be not less than three linesmen (for the further side-line, and the base-lines) in addition to the umpire-in-chief. **1894** *Westm. Gaz.* 27 Mar. 2/3 [*Football*] Any player of the opposite side—selected by the referee and linesmen. **1897** *Whitaker's Alm.* 644/1 [*Football*] Neutral linesmen shall officiate in all games. **1898** *Laws Assoc.* §13 in *Football* (Badm. Libr.) 326 Two linesmen shall be appointed, whose duty..shall be to decide when the ball is out of play and which side is entitled to the corner kick, goal kick or throw in, and to assist the Referee in carrying out the game in accordance with the laws.

c. In *N. Amer. Football*, (*a*) an official on the sideline with certain duties governed by the rules of the game (see quot. 1969^{2}); (*b*) = LINEMAN 4. In *Ice Hockey*, an official whose chief duty is to give offside decisions.

1897 *Encycl. Sport* I. 425/2 Two linesmen..mark the distance gained and lost, and are aids to the umpire. **1935** *Encycl. Sports* 528/1 The officials in this game are referee, umpire, linesman and two assistants, and a field judge. **1947** E. A. MCCOURT *Music at Close* 119 The crash of opposing linesmen, the spirited end runs, the long spiralling kicks awoke in him a strong desire to be a participant. **1955** *Globe & Mail* (Toronto) 31 Jan. 19/1 Flaman tried desperately to break from linesman Bill Roberts, who had put the clutch on the rampaging Bruin defenseman. **1969** *Official Rule Bk. Nat. Hockey League 1969–70* 44 The duty of the linesman is to determine any infractions of the rules concerning off-side play at the blue line, or center line, or any violation of the 'Icing the Puck' rule. **1969** *Official Playing Rules Nat. & Amer. Football Leagues* 93 Linesman is to mark with his foot ..the yard-line touched by forward point of ball at end of each scrimmage down. *Ibid.*, He and the Umpire are to determine whether ineligible linesmen illegally cross line prior to a pass.

4. One who attends to the upkeep of roadside verges.

1888 *Geysers & Gazers* 7 The road was impeded by a land-slip... As soon as we cleared one slip away, another came into view. I asked the driver why the linesman had not attended to the matter. **1971** *Country Life* 18 Nov. 1372/4, I was privileged to spend many hours in the company of a linesman... He was responsible for the upkeep of the roadside verges of some four to five square miles.

line standard. [LINE *sb.*^{2}] **a.** *Metrology.* A standard of length in the form of a metal bar on which are engraved two lines, the distance between which (under specified conditions) is the standard length.

1888 *Encycl. Brit.* XXIV. 478/1 Standards of length are of two types, the defining points being either at a certain part of two parallel lines engraven in one plane (a line-standard), or else points on two parallel surfaces, which can only be observed by contact (an end-standard). **1906** HALLOCK & WADE *Outl. Evolution of Weights & Measures* x. 223 The line standard, of course, can be used with a microscope with

cross-hairs, or a micrometer microscope, much more readily than an end standard. **1966** KAYE & LABY *Tables Physical & Chem. Constants* (ed. 13) 7 The yard equal to 0·9144 metre supersedes the definition in terms of the former imperial standard yard, a bronze line-standard constructed in 1845. **1967** A. J. T. SCARR *Metrology & Precision Engin.* v. 67 The calibration of a line standard is determined by comparison with a master scale.

b. *Television.* The number of lines constituting a complete picture.

1959 C. DANIEL in *Rep. Comm. Broadcasting 1960* (1962) 340 in *Parl. Papers 1961–2* (Cmnd. 1753) IX. 259 We understand that most of the rest of Europe are likely to adopt ..a line standard of 625 lines. **1973** *Newnes Colour Television Servicing Manual* I. i. 2/2 The degaussing action takes place automatically when there is a change in the line standard during push-button selection.

linet, obs. form of LINNET and of LINT[1].

ˈline-up. orig. *U.S.* [f. LINE *v.*[2] 8a.] The assembling of a number of persons in a line, e.g. for inspection or identification; an instance of bringing into a line; a list of players in a game, orchestra, etc.; the players on such a list. Also of things. Also *fig.*

1889 *Kansas City* (Missouri) *Times & Star* 11 Mar., The line-up of the Kansas City ball club this season. **1904** *Springfield* (Mass.) *Weekly Republ.* 3 June 1 Thus we have a line-up of corporations against the people. **1907** J. LONDON *Road* 89 Then came the line-up, forty or fifty of us, naked as Kipling's heroes. **1911** H. S. HARRISON *Queed* xviii. 224 He studied his trustee list now more purposefully than he had ever pored over his faculty line up. **1913** G. J. KNEELAND *Commercialized Prostitution N.Y.* 62 Here they come to make deals for their women..or in vice resorts, to plan line ups when a 'young chicken' is about to be broken into the business. *Ibid.*, A 'line up' is the ruin of a girl who flirts with men and accepts their advances and immoral suggestions. Finally she yields to an invitation to visit a furnished room and the word quickly passes among the 'gang'. One by one the boys and men, perhaps only two or three, perhaps more, visit the room. **1914** J. B. BICKERSTETH *Land of Open Doors* 172 Guess I'm in the line up for hell all right—with no return ticket either. **1915** *Policeman's Monthly* Sept. 5 (*caption*) The famous 'line-up' at New York Police Headquarters. **1926** *Clues* Nov. 161/2 *Lineup*, suspects arrested the night before lined up for police inspection. **1928** A. G. HAYS *Let Freedom Ring* 289 The prisoners were brought before witnesses—not in a line-up with others of the same general type but separately. **1931** E. LINKLATER *Juan in America* II. xviii. 197 But she didn't know the line-up... It's Bauer that knows that, because Bauer's going to do the job. **1934** —— *Magnus Merriman* xxvi. 292 He knew the whole line-up from old man Plato to Bergson. **1938** *Amer. Speech* XIII. 71/1 *Line-up*, a record of all expected train movements for the day in the section where the gang is working. **1952** *Manch. Guardian Weekly* 10 Jan. 3 A police line-up. **1955** A. J. McCARTHY *Jazzbook 1955* 39 The traditional line-up of trumpet, clarinet, trombone, piano, banjo, string bass and drums. **1965** J. POLLARD *Surfrider* ii. 18 The 'lineup' is where the waves line up to break. **1967** *Word Study* Mar. 1/2 To the general public, the English teacher is the witness qualified to identify the felon in a linguistic lineup. **1968** *Radio Times* 28 Nov. 55/4, 11.10. Late Night Line-Up. A last look around the daily scene. **1970** *Language* XLVI. 317 The negative and positive values of time refer to the computer 'line up' point. **1972** *Jazz & Blues* Sept. 11/3 This was the basic line-up which became the Domino band after the success of 'The Fat Man'. **1973** 'J. PATRICK' *Glasgow Gang Observed* v. 52 The phrase 'line-up'..was normally used to describe the queue of boys waiting to have sexual intercourse in one of the 'gang bangs'.

liney: see LINY.

ling (lɪŋ), *sb.*[1] Forms: 3–5 **lenge**, 4 **leyng**, 4–5 **leenge**, 4–7 **lyng(e**, **linge**, 4– **ling**. [ME. *lenge*, *lienge*, later *ling(e* (whence, according to Hatz.-Darm., F. *lingue*); cf. early mod.Du. *lenghe*, *linghe* (now *leng*), G. *leng*, *länge*, *lange*, ON. *langa*, Sw. *långa*, Norw. *langa*, *longa*, Da. *længe*. Connexion with LONG *a.* is probable.]

1. A long slender gadoid fish, *Molva vulgaris* or *Lota molva*, inhabiting the seas of northern Europe. It is largely used for food (usually either salted, or split and dried). †***old ling***: salted ling. ***organ ling***: see ORGAN.

c **1300** *Havelok* 832 Ne he ne mouthe on the se take Neyther lenge, ne thornbake. **1324–5** *Durham Acc. Rolls* (Surtees) 14 In..ij Lenges empt', iiijs. viij*d.* **1377** *Ibid.* 46 In j Turbutt et j leyng emp. xs. vj*d.* **1425** in Kennett *Par. Antiq.* (1818) II. 255 Cum i viridi lynge, cum iii congers. *c* **1430** *Two Cookery-bks.* 43 Nym Milwel or lenge, þat is wel y-wateryd. **1459** in *Paston Lett.* I. 490 Item, ij saltyng tubbes. Item, viij. lynges. **1573** TUSSER *Husb.* lvii. (1878) 133 Ling, Saltfish and Herring, for Lent to provide. **1599** B. JONSON *Ev. Man out of Hum.* IV. iii. (1600) L 4 b, Hee lookes like.. a drie Poule of Ling vpon Easter-eue, that has furnisht the table all Lent. **1601** SHAKS. *All's Well* III. ii. 12, 13 Our old Lings, and our Isbels a'th Country, are nothing like your old Ling and your Isbels a'th Court. **1615** MARKHAM *Eng. Housew.* II. ii. (1668) 78 Take the jole of the best Ling that is not much watered. **1619** *Pasquil's Palm.* (1877) 152 When Flesh doth bid adue for divers weekes, And leaves old Ling to be his deputie. *a* **1661** FULLER *Worthies* viii. (1662) I. 23 Ling, that Noble Fish, corrival in his Joule with the surloin of Beef. **1667** PEPYS *Diary* 20 Mar., Had a good dinner of ling and herring pie. **1712** A. VAN LEEUWENHOEK in *Phil. Trans.* XXVII. 409, I stood by a Fishmongers Shop, whilst they were laying their dry Ling in the Water to soften it. **1747** MRS. GLASSE *Cookery* ix. 91 Old ling, which is the best Sort of Salt Fish, lay it in Water twelve Hours, then [etc.]. **1802** BINGLEY *Anim. Biog.* (1813) III. 22 The Ling in the neighbourhood of Iceland are so bad, that [etc.]. **1823** LAMB *Elia* Ser. II. *Rejoic. New Yr.*, He..protested there was no faith in dried ling. **1836** YARRELL *Brit. Fishes* II. 182 The most usual length of the Ling is from three to four feet.

2. Applied in America, New Zealand, etc. to other fishes, as the burbot (*Lota maculosa*), the cultus-cod (*Ophiodon elongatus*), etc. (see quots.).

c **1850** [see LAWYER 5]. **1885** *Riverside Nat. Hist.* (1888) III. 212 In eastern Florida it [*Elacate canada*] is called the sergeant-fish, and along the western coast of the peninsula it is known as the ling or snooks. *Ibid.* 260 One [fish] living in the sea round New Zealand (*Genypterus blacodes*) is known as the ling or cloudy bay-cod. **1888** [see CULTUS-COD]. **1898** MORRIS *Austral Eng.*, *Ling*..In New Zealand and Tasmania, it is applied to *Genypterus blacodes*, Forst.; also called Cloudy Bay Cod. *Lotella marginata*, Macl., is called Ling, in New South Wales.

3. *attrib.* and *Comb.*, as ***ling fish*** (cf. *cod-fish*), ***fishery***, ***hook***, ***pie***; **ling-cod** *N. Amer.*, a North Pacific species of cod, *Ophiodon elongatus*, also called cultus cod. (Cf. sense 2.)

1955 W. DAWSON *Ahoy There!* 205 Besides salmon, we catch cod..*ling-cod of up to (in our case) twelve pounds. **1964** *Canad. Geogr. Jrnl.* Mar. 91/3 This is particularly true in the case of the ling cod, the spear-fisherman's favourite quarry. **1971** *Islander* (Victoria, B.C.) 21 Mar. 2/3, I have taken in recent years, six species of rockfish..also lingcod. **1489** CAXTON *Faytes of A.* II. xvi. H vj b, Grete foyson of *ling fysshe, and haburden. *c* **1526** *Plumpton Corr.* (Camden) 224 Sir, ye spoke with me that you wold have had som good ling fish. **1836** *Chamb. Jrnl.* Dec. 388 Spain presents a good..market for dried cod and ling fish. **1798** MALTHUS *Popul.* (1878) 222 The *ling fishery. **1896** LYDEKKER *Roy. Nat. Hist.* V. 436 The ling-fishery is an important industry, large quantities of these fish being cured and dried. **1822** HIBBERT *Descr. Shetld. Isl.* 510 The lines are fitted with *ling hooks. **1623** MARKHAM *Eng. Housw.* 100 A *Ling pie.

ling (lɪŋ), *sb.*[2] Also 4–7 **lyng(e**, 5 **lynk**, 5, 7 **lingge**, 6–7 **linge**. [a. ON. *lyng* (Da. *lyng*, Sw. *ljung*):—OTeut. type **lingwo*ᵐ. Cf. Sw. *lingon* cowberry.] A name applied to various ericaceous plants, chiefly *Calluna vulgaris*; see HEATHER.

c **1357** *Durham Acc. Rolls* (Surtees) 559 Et in reparacione stagni molend. Abbathie cum Mos et Lyng pro eadem. *a* **1440** *Sir Degrev.* 336 He laf slawe in a slak fforty score on a pak..Dede in the lyng. *c* **1440** *Promp. Parv.* 305/2 Ly(n)ge of the hethe, *bruera.* **14..** *Arund. MS.* 42, f. 23 b in *Promp. Parv.* 305 *note*, An heth þat groweþ ful..of lynk. *c* **1475** *Rauf Coilȝear* 397 Gif thow meitis ony leid lent on the ling. **1486** *Nottingham Rec.* III. 249 For xiiij. thrave of lyng. **1538** LELAND *Itin.* V. 122 In the Dales of Richemontshire they burne Linge, Petes, and Turffes. **1548** TURNER *Names of Herbes* 35 Erice..is named in english Heth, hather, or ling. **1577–87** HOLINSHED *Chron.*, *Hist. Scot.* 95/1 There was growing in that place..verie much of that kind of heath or ling, which the Scotishmen call hadder. **1603** HOLLAND *Plutarch's Mor.* 1206 Little beds..made of chast tree and of heath or lings. **1607** NORDEN *Surv. Dial.* v. 235 Heath is the generall or common name, whereof there is one kind, called Hather, the other, Ling. **1686** PLOT *Staffordsh.* 357 Sheep will now abide that heath and feed upon Ling all the hardest winter. **1819** CRABBE *Tales Hall* XIX, She..stirr'd the fire of ling, and brush'd the wicker chair. **1822** BEWICK *Mem.* 11 The shepherd might have his hovel thatched with heather and ling. **1882** OUIDA *Maremma* I. 124 Their huts were always..thatched with rushes and ling.

b. *attrib.*, as ***ling-thatch***; **ling-bird**, the meadow-pipit, *Anthus pratensis.*

1814 *Sporting Mag.* XLIV. 245 *note*, The small heath-bird or *ling-bird. **1893** J. WATSON *Confess. Poacher* 110 The 'cheep-cheep' of the awakening ling-birds rises from every brae. **1482–3** *Durham Acc. Rolls* (Surtees) 648 Pro tractacione xl travis (*sic*) del *lyngthake, xx*d.* **1884** *Gd. Words* 21 The heavy ling thatch hung low over window and wall.

ling, *sb.*[3] [Chinese *ling* (Giles).] The water-chestnut of China, *Trapa bicornis*, the seeds of which are much eaten as food.

1860 SCARTH *Twelve Yrs. China* 8 Gathering the rich mould and decayed vegetable matter where the 'ling' has grown in the water. **1866** in *Treas. Bot.*

†**ling**, *v.* ? *dial.* *Obs.* [Cf. *linge*, to put out the tongue (Oxfordshire, *Eng. Dial. Dict.*).] *intr.* Of the tongue: To protrude from the mouth.

1674 WOOD *Life* (O.H.S.) II. 303 Her tongue would ling out of her mouth.

ling, variant of LENG *v.* *Obs.*

-ling (lɪŋ), *suffix*[1], appended to sbs., adjs., vb.-stems, and (rarely) advs., to form sbs., is a Com. Teut. formative (OE., OS., OHG. *-ling*, ON. *-ling-r*, Goth. *-ligg-s* in *gadiliggs*). It doubtless arose from the addition of the suffix *-iŋgo-z* -ING[3] to noun-stems formed with the suffix *-ilo-* (-EL[1], -LE 1), but in all the historical Teut. langs. it has the character of a simple suffix.

1. In OE., *-ling* added to sbs. forms sbs. with the general sense 'a person or thing belonging to or concerned with (what is denoted by the primary sb.), as *hýrling* hireling, *ierðling* ploughman (f. *ierð* ploughing), *rǽpling* prisoner (f. *ráp* rope). The derivatives from adjs. have the sense 'a person or thing that has the quality denoted by the adj.', e.g. *déorling* darling, *efenling* an equal, *feorðling* quarter, farthing, *ʒeongling* youngling, *ʒesibling*, *sibling* kinsman; similarly from an adv., *underling* subordinate. One or two names of birds have this suffix in OE., as *swertling* ? some black bird (? f. *sweart* black), *stærling* starling; here it may possibly have a diminutive force (see 2 below).

In ME. and mod.E. the suffix continued to be freely employed with the same function as in OE.; examples are *atterling*, *deathling*, *fatling*, *firstling*, *grayling*, *nestling*, *nursling*, *sapling*, *suckling*. The personal designations in *-ling* are now always used in a contemptuous or unfavourable sense (though this implication was not fully established before the 17th c.), as *courtling*, *earthling*, *groundling*, †*popeling* (= papist), *vainling*, *worldling*. On the analogy of words like *nursling*, where the grammatical character of the initial element is ambiguous, a few sbs. in *-ling* have been formed on vb.-stems (taken in passive sense), being personal designations of contemptuous import, such as *shaveling*, *starveling*; of similar origin is *stripling*, though it has lost its primary derisive sense.

The suffix is no longer productive in the uses above explained.

2. In ON. the suffix had a diminutive force, of which there are only slight traces in the other Teut. langs. (cf. OE. *stærling* mentioned above, and G. *sperling* sparrow); chiefly in words denoting the young of animals, as *gǽsling-r* gosling, *ketling-r* kitten, *kiðlin-gr* young kid, †'kidling', but also in a few other words, as *bǿkling-r* booklet, *vetling-r* glove, *yrmling-r* little worm. In Eng. the earliest certain instance of this use appears to be *codling*, recorded *c* 1314 (*kitling*, which appears *a* 1300, being of dubious formation), in the 15th c. we find *gosling* (of which the earliest quoted form, *gesling*, points to adoption from ON.), and *duckling*. In the 16th c. and subsequently the suffix has been employed in many new diminutive formations, chiefly contemptuous appellations of persons, as *godling*, *lordling*, *kingling*, *princeling*; in this use it is still a living formative.

In the formation of diminutives expressing merely smallness of size, *-ling* has never been extensively used; a few writers of the 19th c. have so employed it in nonce-wds.

c **1800** LAMB *Lett.* (1837) I. 147 Gentry dipped in Styx all over, whom no paper javelin-lings can touch. **1815** J. GILCHRIST *Labyrinth Demolished* 8 Philosophling. *Ibid.* 22 Thinkling. *Ibid.* 24 Metaphysicling. **1885** HOWELLS in *Century Mag.* XXX. 541 'A pity for you!' cried the hunchbackling.

-ling[2], **-lin(g)s**, *suffix*, forming adverbs, most of which survive only *dial.* The Teut. root **liŋg-*, *laŋg-*, *luŋg-*, to extend, reach, appears in its three ablaut-forms as the terminal element in certain OE. advs. expressive of direction or extent, as in *bæcling* BACKLING; *andlang* (see ALONG, ENDLONG); *nihtlanges* for a night; *grundlunga* (also *grundlinga*) to the ground. In certain instances the suffixes *-linga*, *-lunga*, were already in OE. substituted for *-inga*, *-unga*, advb. terminations originating in some case (? ablative) of sbs. in *-ing*, *-ung* (see -ING[1]); so in *néadlunga*, *níedlinga*, whence, with adverbial (genitival) *es*, the ME. *nedlingis* NEEDLINGS, of necessity. The original OE. use (in which the suffix is added to sbs. to form advs. of direction) is continued in the later formations *grufelyng* (GROVELLING), *headling(s*, *sideling(s*; more numerous, however, are the words in which the suffix forms advs. of condition or situation from adjs., as *blindling(s*, *darkling(s*, *firstlings*, *flatling(s*, *hidlings*, *mostlings*.

lingal, variant of LINGEL.

Lingala (lɪŋˈgɑːlə). Also **Ngala**. [Native name.] A Bantu language spoken by the Bangala people in the Mangala area of Zaïre, widely used in trade and public affairs. Also *attrib.* or as *adj.*

1903 W. H. STAPLETON *Compar. Handbk. Congo Lang.* p. r, Bangala is a name originally given..to a people..from the settlement of Mangala... The dialect chosen and called Ngala is spoken by the Boloki..and Bokomoi on the South bank. **1922** H. H. JOHNSTON *Compar. Study Bantu & Semi-Bantu Lang.* II. vi. 130 At present we can only surmise that Group KK contains the following sub-groups:..KK_4, the Lingala. **1945** C. M. DOKE *Bantu* 27 Ngala..is today called 'Lingala', though it is based on the speech of the Mangala people. **1965** *B.B.C. Handbk.* 103 Moscow radio started transmissions in..Lingala, Nepalese. **1973** *Black World* May 95/1 The Bolinga, the name for the Black Cultural Resources Center at Wright State University in Dayton, Ohio, is a Lingala word meaning 'love'.

‖**lingam** (ˈlɪŋgæm), **linga** (lɪŋgə). Also 8 **lingum**, 8–9 **lingham**. [a. Skr. *liŋga*, nom. case *liŋgam*; the flexional *m* has been preserved in the word as adopted into the non-Aryan langs. of India.]

Among the Hindus, a phallus, worshipped as a symbol of the god Siva.

The first quot. contains some misunderstanding.

1719 I. T. PHILIPPS tr. *Thirty-four Confer.* 326 The third Way of attaining Salvation, is by offering to the *Piratti Lingum*, which is an Image of a Man made of Dung. **1793** W. HODGES *Trav.* v. 94 These Pagodas have each a small chamber in the center..with a lamp hanging over the Lingham. *Ibid. note*, The Lingham is the great object of superstition among the followers of Brahmah. **1799** COLEBROOKE in *Life* v. (1873) 152 A number of little altars, with a *linga* of Mahadeva on them. **1813** J. FORBES *Orient. Mem.* II. 364 Two respectable brahmins..who..had..performed the accustomed ceremonies to the linga. **1857** R. TOMES *Amer. in Japan* v. 120 Several stones, of four feet in height..which appeared to be lingams.

Hence ˈ**lingamism**, the worship of lingams.

1843 MACAULAY *Sp. Ld. Ellenborough's Govt.* Sp. (1853) II. 9 To what religion was it that the offering was made? It was to Lingamism.

lingan, lingat, obs. ff. of LINGEL, LINGOT.

lingberry: see LINGONBERRY.

Lingby, var. LYNGBY.

lingcan: see LICHAM.

linge, lindge (lɪndʒ), *v. Obs.* exc. *dial.* Also 9 *dial.* linch, linse. [Of obscure origin: the *Eng. Dial. Dict.* cites (s.v. *Linch*) from Moisy a mod. Norman *lincher* to whip.] *trans.* To beat, thrash.

1600 HOLLAND *Livy* LVII. Florus' Brev. 1242 Met he with a soldior out of his ranke and file? If he were a Roman, up he went and was well lindged & swaddled with vine-wands by the centurion. **1606** —— *Sueton.* Annot. 27 As if he had beene well lindged with lether thongs. **1824** MACTAGGART *Gallovid. Encycl.* 319 Linged, lashed, beaten, &c. **1825–80** JAMIESON, *Linge, Lynge*, to flog, beat. **1847** HALLIWELL, *Linse*, to beat severely. *Devon.* **1858** *N. & Q.* 2nd Ser. VI. 278/2 The..magistrate..exclaimed, 'Give me a stick, and I'll linge him myself!' **1868** ATKINSON *Cleveland Gloss.*, *Linch*, to flog or thrash, to beat with a whip or flexible cane.

lingel, lingle (ˈlɪŋg(ə)l), *sb.*[1] Now *dial.* Forms: 5 lynyolf, lynolf, (inniolf), 6 lyngell, 6–7 lingell, 7 *Sc.* linyel, 8 lingan, 9 lingal, liniel, 6– lingel, 7– lingle. [a. OF. *lignoel, ligneul*:—popular L. **līneolum*, f. L. *līnea* LINE *sb.*[2]] A shoemaker's waxed thread.

c **1440** *Promp. Parv.* 306/1 Lynyolf, or inniolf [*H., P.* lynolf], threde to sow wythe schone or botys, *indula, licinium.* **1523** FITZHERB. *Husb.* §142 Bodkyn, knyfe, lyngell, gyue thy horse mete, se he be shoed well. **1530** PALSGR. 239/2 Lyngell that souters sowe with, *chefgros, lignier.* **1562** J. HEYWOOD *Prov. & Epigr.* (1867) 110 For may he once get his shooes on my feete, Without last or lingel his woordes make them meete. **1576** TURBERV. *Venerie* 231 And he must have a lyngell in readinesse to sow up the skin, and at euery stitch that he taketh let him knit his threed or lyngell. **1611** BEAUM. & FL. *Knt. Burn. Pestle* v. iii, Whose Master wrought with Lingell and with All. **1635** D. DICKSON *Pract. Writ.* (1845) I. 196 He had his elsin and linyel for sewing of leather. **1721** RAMSAY *Ode to Mr. F——* i, Hinds wi' elson and hemp lingle, Sit soleing shoon out o'er the ingle. **1771** SMOLLETT *Humph. Cl.* 10 July, A little hemp, which he spun into lingels. *c* **1817** HOGG *Tales & Sk.* III. 306 George..scratched his head with the awl, and gave the lingles such a yerk, that he made them both crack in two. **1868** G. MACDONALD *R. Falconer* I. 104 Settling in haste to his awl and his lingel.

b. *attrib.*, as *lingel-* (or †*lingel's*) *end, -tail.*

1589 R. HARVEY *Pl. Perc.* (1590) 25 My shoe shall rend, my nall blade bend, My lingels end, first shall I spend, Before his works goe downe. *c* **1774** C. KEITH *Farmer's Ha'* v. (1801) 48 They pow and rax the lingel tails. **1899** COLVILLE *Vernacular* 16 The sutor..deftly birsed a fresh lingle-end.

Hence ˈ**lingel** *v. trans.*, to bind firmly with cobbler's thread. *Sc.*

1819 HOGG *Jacobite Relics* I. 102 Come like a cobler, Donald Macgillavry, Beat them, and bore them, and lingel them cleverly.

lingel, lingle (ˈlɪŋg(ə)l), *sb.*[2] Now *dial.* Forms: 5 lengell, (lynnell), 5–7 lingell, 6 lyngell, 7 lingal, 7– lingel, 8– lingle. [app. repr. an AF. **lengle*:—L. *lingula* strap, thong, also spoon; dim. of *lingua* tongue. Cf. LANGLE.]

†**1.** *collect. sing.* The leather straps, etc. of a horse's harness. *Obs.*

1460 *Lybeaus Disc.* 1364 (Kaluza) His scheld was blak as pich, Lingell, armes, trappure swich. *Ibid.* 1664 And of þe same painture Was lingell and trappure.

2. A thong or latchet.

1538 ELYOT *Dict.*, *Cohum*, a thonge or lyngell wherwith the oxe bowe & the yoke are bounden togider. *a* **1585** MONTGOMERIE *Flyting w. Polwart* 342 Shame and sorrow on her snout that..louses off thy lingals sa lang as they may last. **1658** PHILLIPS, *Lingel*, a little tongue or thong. **1790** A. WILSON *To E. Picken* Poet. Wks. (1846) 107 This half a year yer funny tales, Ower mosses, mountains, seas and dales, I've carried i' my lingle. **1801** BEATTIE *Parings* (1873) 4 (E.D.D.) Afore the ingle she knit a lingle to swing the roast. **1832** A. HENDERSON *Prov.* 129 It's short while since the sow bore the lingel. **1875** KNIGHT *Dict. Mech.*, *Lingel*, a small thong of leather for sewing or lacing bands. [syn.] Lingle. **1895** CROCKETT *Men of Moss Hags* xxv. 188, I had my sword dangling by a lingel or tag at my right wrist. **1896** —— *Grey Man* xxix. 200, I..saw nothing but some discharged pistols lying with broken lingels abroad on the sand.

†**3.** A flat blade or spoon, a spatula.

1598 FLORIO, *Paletta di spetiale*, a lingell, a spoone, a tenon, a spattle or slice as Apothecaries vse. **1611** COTGR., *Friquette*, a lingell, smalle sklice, little scummer. *Ibid.*, *Palette*, a Lingell, Tenon, Slice, or flat toole wherwith Chirurgians lay salue on plaisters.

Hence **lingel** *v. trans.*, to fasten with a thong. (Cf. LANGLE *v.*) *Sc.*

1879 G. MACDONALD *Sir Gibbie* xlvi. (1880) 293, I never read the ballant aboot the worm lingelt roun' the tree.

lingenberry: see LINGONBERRY.

†**lingence.** *Obs. rare*⁻¹. [f. L. *lingĕre* to lick: see -ENCE.] A linctus.

a **1661** FULLER *Worthies, Nottinghamsh.* II. (1662) 315 A stick hereof [of liquorice] is commonly the spoon prescribed to Patients, to use in any Lingences or Loaches.

linger, *sb.* [f. LINGER *v.*] †**1.** Delay. *Obs.*

1597 J. PAYNE *Royal Exch.* 34 Who but they cowld abyde such hunger and colde,..besydes the lynger of paye, sycknes and mortalitie?

2. *U.S.* (See quot.)

1895 *Nation* (N.Y.) 9 May 358/3 The enervating influence of the climate, giving rise to that which in the south-western United States is called the 'Texas lingers'.

linger (ˈlɪŋgə(r)), *v.* Forms: 4, ? 6 lenger, (4 langer), 6 lyngar, -er, 6– linger. [Northern ME. *lenger*, frequentative of LENG *v.*: see -ER[5].]

†**1.** *intr.* To dwell, abide, stay (in a place). *Obs.*

a **1300** *Cursor M.* 604 þer-for he gafe him to be-gin A luuesum land at lenger in. *a* **1300** *Ibid.* 1411 And leuer was [adam] siþen to lenger [*Fairf.* langer] in hell þan langer in þis liue to duell.

2. a. To stay behind, tarry, loiter on one's way; to stay on or hang about in a place beyond the proper or usual time, esp. from reluctance to leave it.

1530 PALSGR. 612/1, I lyngar behynde my companye, I tarye behynde them, *je targe.* **1553** EDEN *Treat. Newe Ind.* (Arb.) 27 Leaste any linger behynde his companie. **1568** GRAFTON *Chron.* II. 313 A number of the Souldyours..came home agayne vnpayde and lyngered and still hanged vpon the prince. **1593** SHAKS. *2 Hen. VI*, IV. iv. 54 Then linger not, my Lord, away, take horse. **1594** SPENSER *Amoretti* lxxxviii, And, in her songs, sends many a wish-full vow For his returne that seemes to linger late. **1667** PEPYS *Diary* 30 June, They had no orders, and lay lingering upon the way. **1698** FRYER *Acc. E. India & P.* 254 They pretending they had lost their Way, but more truly lingered, not having us to spur them on. **1794** MRS. RADCLIFFE *Myst. Udolpho* i, In scenes like these she would often linger alone. **1816** SHELLEY *Alastor* 98 He would linger long In lonesome vales, making the wild his home. **1838** LYTTON *Alice* 67 Evelyn could have lingered all day in the room. **1864** D. G. MITCHELL *Sev. Stor.* 245 The broken gentle-man lingers for hours beside the portraits of the old Count. **1874** GREEN *Short Hist.* ii. §6. 94 The White Ship in which he had embarked lingered behind the rest of the royal fleet. **1893** G. E. MATHESON *About Holland* 22 The Dutch trains do perhaps seem to linger somewhat on the way.

b. To proceed at a slow pace; to go lingeringly (*down, past*).

1826 MRS. SHELLEY *Last Man* II. 130 Soon the dim orb passed from over the sun, and lingered down the eastern heaven. **1836–9** DICKENS *Sk. Boz, Scenes* iii. (1892) 54 These men linger listlessly past. **1840** —— *Barn. Rudge* xvi, He was never lingering or loitering, but always walking swiftly. **1863** HAWTHORNE *Our Old Home* (1879) 294 Lingering through one of the aisles.

c. *fig.* (with a prep. as *on, over, round*): To dwell upon, give protracted consideration to, be reluctant to quit (a subject).

1843 RUSKIN *Mod. Paint.* (1848) I. II. II. v. §8. 193 Every one of those broad spaces she would linger over in protracted delight. **1844** STANLEY *Arnold* (1858) I. iv. 168, I linger round a subject. **1871** R. ELLIS tr. *Catullus* lxiv. 117 Yet, for again I come to the former story, beseems not Linger on all done there.

3. 'To remain long in languor and pain' (J.); to continue alive, though oppressed by sickness or other distress. (Cf. LINGERING *ppl. a.* b.)

1534 [see LINGERING *vbl. sb.*]. **1570** LEVINS *Manip.* 78/23 To linger, *languere.* **1604** SHAKS. *Oth.* v. ii. 88, I would not haue thee linger in thy paine. **1607** —— *Cor.* III. iii. 89 Pent to linger But with a graine a day. **1819** SCOTT *Prose Wks.* IV. Biographies II. (1870) 320 He lingered a few days, possessed of his senses, reconciled to his fate. **1882** J. H. BLUNT *Ref. Ch. Eng.* II. 251 He lingered as a prisoner of the Inquisition for sixteen years. **1898** RIDER HAGGARD *Dr. Therne* 6 He lingered for nearly two years.

fig. **1781** COWPER *Hope* 723 When hope, long lingering, at last yields the ghost.

4. To be tardy in doing or beginning anything; to hesitate, delay; to dawdle. †Const. *inf.*

1548 UDALL, etc. *Erasm. Par. Matt.* iii. 7–10 As they yᵗ make hast are pertakers of health, so they that linger are al pertakers of peril. **1586** J. HOOKER *Hist. Irel.* in *Holinshed* II. 16/1 The king..differed the time, and lingered to give any answer. **1598** SHAKS. *Merry W.* III. ii. 58 We haue linger'd about a match betweene An Page, and my cozen Slender. **1611** BIBLE *2 Pet.* ii. 3 Whose iudgement now of a long time lingereth not [Gr. οὐκ ἀργεῖ]. **1692** DRYDEN *Cleomenes* II. ii. 17 And if my Eyes have pow'r, He should not sue In vain, nor linger with a long delay. **1812** S. ROGERS *Columbus* IV. 50 Oft the stern Catalan..Muttered dark threats, and linger'd to obey. **1851** GROTE *Greece* VIII. 420 His accuser denounces him as having..designedly lingered in the business, for the purpose of prolonging the period of remuneration. **1855** MACAULAY *Hist. Eng.* xix. IV. 268 By no remonstrance..could he prevail on his allies to be early in the field... Every one of them lingered, and wondered why the rest were lingering. **1871** FREEMAN *Norm. Conq.* (1876) IV. xviii. 186 Either Malcolm lingered in his preparations, or [etc.].

5. *fig.*, chiefly of immaterial things. **a.** To remain, to be slow to pass away or disappear; to stay or persist, though tending to wane and dwindle. *to linger on*, to continue to linger.

1764 GOLDSM. *Trav.* 172 But winter lingering chills the lap of May. **1805** WORDSW. *Waggoner* IV. 189 Nor could the waggon long survive, Which Benjamin had ceased to drive: It lingered on;—guide after guide Ambitiously the office tried. **1855** MACAULAY *Hist. Eng.* xvi. III. 707 It is by no means improbable that this superstition..may still linger in a few obscure farm-houses. **1868** E. EDWARDS *Ralegh* I. xxii. 483 When the Plague had departed from most parts of London, it often lingered in the Tower. **1875** JOWETT *Plato* (ed. 2) I. 110 But he has still a doubt lingering in his mind.

b. To be slow in coming or accruing.

1842 TENNYSON *Locksley Hall* 141 Knowledge comes, but wisdom lingers. **1863** GEO. ELIOT *Romola* I. Introd. (1880) 9 The wages of men's sins often linger in their payment. **1871** FREEMAN *Norm. Conq.* (1876) IV. xx. 593 When the sentence was once passed its execution did not linger.

c. Of actions or conditions: To be protracted (wearisomely or painfully), to drag on. (Cf. LINGERING *ppl. a.*)

[**1591** SHAKS. *1 Hen. VI*, I. i. 74 One would have lingring Warres, with little cost.] **1836** THIRLWALL *Greece* III. xvii. 8 As the siege of Ithome lingered, the Spartans called on their allies for aid.

6. quasi-*trans.* **a.** with advb. compl. (*forth, on, out*): To draw out, prolong, protract by lingering, tarrying, or dallying. *to linger away*: to waste (time) by lingering.

1550 LATIMER *Last Serm. bef. Edw. VI* (1562) 137 It shal cause things to haue good successe, and that matters shal not be lingred forth from daye to daye. **1597** SHAKS. *2 Hen. IV*, I. ii. 265, I can get no remedy against this Consumption of the purse. Borrowing only lingers, and lingers it out, but the disease is incurable. **1606** —— *Tr. & Cr.* v. x. 9 Let your briefe plagues be mercy, And linger not our sure destructions on. **1622** MASSINGER *Virg. Mart.* II. iii, I'll not insult on a base, humbled prey By lingering out thy terrors. **1695** DRYDEN *Death Mr. Purcell* 29 Now live secure, and linger out your days. *a* **1704** T. BROWN *Praise Drunkenness* Wks. 1730 I. 36 The first linger away their lives in perpetual drudgery. **1721** AMHERST *Terræ Fil.* No. 34 (1754) 179 To prevent the scholars from ling'ring away their time, and neglecting their studies. **1829** SCOTT *Diary* 8 Mar. in *Lockhart*, Half measures do but linger out the feud. **1833** LAMB *Elia* Ser. II. *Wedding*, We all began to be afraid that a suit which as yet had abated none of its ardours, might at last be lingered on, till passion had time to cool. **1860** FROUDE *Hist. Eng.* VI. 522 His policy, therefore, was for the present to linger out the negotiations. **1887** LOWELL *Old Eng. Dram.* (1892) 130 Ford lingers-out his heart-breaks too much.

b. To pass (life) sadly or wearily.

1725 POPE *Odyss.* XIV. 411 Far from gay cities, and the ways of men, I linger life. *a* **1774** GOLDSM. *Hist. Greece* II. 239 They..left him to linger in this manner, unattended, the remains of his wretched life.

7. †**a.** *trans.* To cause to linger; to prolong, protract, draw out (the time, a business, etc.); also, to delay, put off, defer. *Obs.*

1543 GRAFTON *Cont. Harding* 18 Edwarde..thoughte he wold not lynger his busines. **1556** T. HOBY tr. *Castiglione's Courtyer* A iij b, I forbare and lingered the time to see if any [etc.]. **1565** JEWEL *Repl. Harding* (1611) 307 The Bread, that our Lord gaue to his Disciples, he lingred it not [tr. L. *non distulit*], nor bad it to be kept vntill the morning. *a* **1568** COVERDALE *Bk. Death* ii. 7 That wee by no occasion should linger ye amendment of our liues vntill age. **1584** COGAN *Haven Health* (1636) 215 Wherefore I advise all men not to linger the time long in eating and drinking superfluously. **1604** SHAKS. *Oth.* IV. ii. 231 He goes into Mauritania..vnlesse his abode be lingred heere by some accident. **1604** EDMONDS *Observ. Cæsar's Comm.* 59 To linger and detract the war. **1614** RALEIGH *Hist. World* IV. ii. §3. 175 The Leigers..could not be perswaded to linger the time and stay their aduantage. **1632** SANDERSON *Serm.* 301 Secure ones may linger their repentance till it be too late. **1633** FORD *Broken H.* IV. iv, To linger Pain, which I strive to cure, were to be cruel.

†**b.** To keep waiting, put off (a person). Also with *off*. *Obs.*

1534 MORE *Let. to Marg. Roper* Wks. 1429/1 They were not lingered nor made to daunce any long attendance..as sutours were sometime wont to be. **1543** GRAFTON *Contn. Harding* 101 Then Henry spedely prepared him selfe because he would lynger his frendes no lenger. **1594** WEST *2nd Pt. Symbol.* §35 Least the parties should..be long lingered with vaine hope of an endlesse end. **1606** G. W[OODCOCKE] *Hist. Ivstine* XXI. 80 Hee sollicited the Affricks and the King of Mauritane for supply, being lingred off with delayes.

c. *Hort.* To delay the blooming of (flowers) by artificial means.

1906 *Daily Chron.* 12 Sept. 4/4 If you force, you exhaust the [rose-]tree; it languishes. I prefer to 'linger' it.

8. *intr.* To have a longing or craving, to hanker. Const. *after*; also (rarely) with infinitive.

1641 BEST *Farm. Bks.* (Surtees) 11 They [*sc.* tups] will beginne to linger after ewes and decline. *a* **1649** WINTHROP *New Eng.* (1853) I. 54 Such as fell into discontent, and lingered after their former condition in England. **1651** N. BACON *Disc. Govt. Eng.* II. xxvii. (1739) 120 The Cardinal finding the King's mind to linger after another Bedfellow. *a* **1682** SIR T. BROWNE *Tracts* 14 More remarkable it seems that they should extoll and linger after the Cucumbers and Leeks, Onions and Garlick in Ægypt. **1718** MOTTEUX *Quix.* (1733) I. 255 Thou lingerest with Impatience to exercise thy talking Faculty. **1893** *Surrey Words* (E.D.S.) s.v., Being used to hay makes them linger more after it.

lingerer (ˈlɪŋgərə(r)). [f. LINGER *v.* + -ER[1].] One who, or that which, lingers, tarries, etc.; †a dawdler, idler; †one who hankers (*after*).

1579 TOMSON *Calvin's Serm. Tim.* 610/2 As oft as we play the lingerers, & cold staruelinges. **1646** GAULE *Cases Consc.* 3 Our late leaners and lingerers after such a kinde of sect.

1713 STEELE *Guardian* No. 131 ¶1 The mighty body of lingerers, persons who.. waste away In gentle inactivity the day. **1740** J. LOVE *Cricket* (1770) 1. 53 O Flee, you Ling'rer, Flee! **1820** SCOTT *Monast.* viii, 'But you, ye lingerers', he added, looking to a knot of beeches which still bore their withered leaves [etc.]. **1891** SMILES *J. Murray* I. i. 11 The book was a lingerer on his shelves and did not sell. **1892** STEVENSON *Wrecker* vii. 122 A waterside prowler, a lingerer on wharves.

‖**lingerie** (lɛ̃ʒri, 'læ̃nʒəriː). [Fr., 'the making or selling of linnen cloth; also, linnen, linnen stuffe, things made of linnen' (Cotgr.), f. *linge* linen.] **a.** Linen articles collectively; all the articles of linen, lace, etc. in a woman's wardrobe or *trousseau*; women's underwear and nightclothes.

1835 *Court Mag.* VI. p. xviii/2 It is expected that lingerie will be this season in very great request, both in morning and half-dress. **1885** *Illustr. Lond. News* 21 Nov. 516/1 A happy bride supplied with 'a handsome lingerie'. **1894** *Daily News* 11 Apr. 3/1 The ribbons of the lingerie are sky-blue.

b. *attrib.*

1866 MRS. GASKELL *Wives & Daughters* II. xxiv. 248 There was a 'lingerie' shop, kept by a Frenchwoman. **1905** *Daily Chron.* 13 Mar. 8/1 The lingerie blouse made a most emphatic appearance in Paris.. this winter. *Ibid.*, It is the lingerie shirt that wins. **1909** *Westm. Gaz.* 22 Feb. 5/2 As to the lingerie gown, its importance in the wardrobe cannot be questioned. **1909** *Public Ledger* (Philadelphia) 24 June 7/7 (Advt.), Fine lingerie waists, trimmed with dainty laces & embroideries. **1909** *Daily Chron.* 10 Sept. 7/2 Embroider.. if the sacque is of piqué or lingerie materials. **1964** *McCall's Sewing* ii. 30/1 *Lingerie hem*, a rolled hem that is caught with two overcast stitches at intervals of ⅛ to ⅜ inch gathering it in puffs. *Ibid.* 30/2 *Lingerie seam*, supposedly 'rip-proof'; made by pressing both edges of a seam to one side and top-stitching with a zigzag stitch along the edge. **1974** *Country Life* 3–10 Jan. 55/1 Harvey Nichols have.. palazzo suits by Mr Dino. In the lingerie department there are things by Iful, Yves Stillman, Leonara. **1974** *Evening Herald* (Rock Hill, S. Carolina) 18 Apr. 9/4 A lingerie shower was given by Mrs. Preston Ramsey and Mrs. Harold Wolfe.

lingering ('lɪŋgərɪŋ), *vbl. sb.* [-ING[1].]

a. The action of the vb. LINGER. Also *rarely* in *pl.*, last remaining traces (of something).

a **1300** *Cursor M.* 16292 And quils þou liues here wit vs þi lengring sal be care. *c* **1375** *Ibid.* 6686 (Fairf.) þe smyter sal quite his leching and make amendis for his lyngering. **1534** MORE *Comf. agst. Trib.* II. Wks. 1172/1, I know my lingering not likely to last longe, but out wil my snuffe sodainly some daye within a while. **1570** SIR T. WILSON *Demosthenes* 45 Lingering is noysome when necessity requires haste. **1582** STANYHURST *Æneis* II. (Arb.) 66 Now, quod he, no lingring, let vs hence. **1667** MILTON *P.L.* II. 702. **1822** W. IRVING in *Life & Lett.* (1864) II. 80, I.. am still troubled with lameness and inflammation in the ankles, the lingerings of my tedious malady. **1864** TENNYSON *En. Ard.* 267 After a lingering,.. The little innocent soul flitted away. **1886** WILLIS & CLARK *Cambridge* I. 625 A delay of three years.. is a striking illustration of.. the lingering of all college work.

†**b.** Hankering (*after*). *Obs.*

1608 HIERON *Wks.* I. 732/1 Remoue from him.. all worldly desires, all lingring after the deceiuing sweetnes of these earthly things. **1642** ROGERS *Naaman* 89 Gods judgements.. crossing their lingring after Caanan.

c. *Hort.* Retarding the time of blooming by artificial means.

1907 *Daily Chron.* 13 Feb. 6/4 Lingering is retardation without frost; it keeps September roses blooming until January.

'**lingering,** *ppl. a.* [-ING[2].] That lingers, delays, loiters, moves slowly, etc.; remaining behind, slow to depart or disappear.

a **1547** SURREY in *Tottel's Misc.* (Arb.) 31 Of lingring doutes such hope is sprong pardie. **1561** SACKVILLE & NORTON *Ferrex & Porrex* I. ii. 194 The lyngering yeres That draw not forth his ende with faster course. **1594** *Warres Cyrus* 289 We'll starue them with a lingring siege. **1631** GOUGE *God's Arrows* I. §63. 105 Whether sudden or lingring judgements. **1697** DRYDEN *Virg. Past.* VIII. 100 Restore, my Charms, My lingring Daphnis to my longing Arms. **1750** GRAY *Elegy* 88 Nor cast one longing ling'ring Look behind. **1859** J. CUMMING *Ruth* vi. 95 Even in the worst and most depraved of mankind, there is a lingering sense of gratitude. **1878** HUXLEY *Physiogr.* 203 The lingering remains of volcanic activity.

b. *esp.* of disease, suffering, or death: Slow, painfully protracted. †Of poisons: Characterized by slow or tardy action. *Obs.*

1593 SHAKS. *2 Hen. VI*, III. ii. 247 They will.. torture him with grieuous lingring death. **1611** —— *Wint. T.* I. ii. 320. **1611** —— *Cymb.* I. v. 34 Strange ling'ring poysons. **1623** WEBSTER *Duchess Malfi* v. ii, 'Tis a secret That (like a lingring poyson) may chance lie Spread in thy vaines, and kill thee seauen yeare hence. **1627** F. LITTLE *Mon. Chr. Munif.* (1871) 67 His lingering disease increasing, and death approaching. **1655** *Nicholas Papers* (Camden) II. 289 He yet is extreame weake, and I feare his sicknes will proue lingering, but I hope not in any daunger of his life. **1671** MILTON *Samson* 618. **1675** BROOKS *Gold. Key* Wks. 1867 V. 81 We see him die with lingering torments. **1677** BARROW *Serm. Passion* 14 And that no stupifying, no transient pain, but one both very acute and lingring. **1712** ADDISON *Spect.* No. 363 ¶13 Lingring and Incurable Distempers. **1762–71** H. WALPOLE *Vertue's Anecd. Paint.* (1786) IV. 22 He retired .. to Richmond, where he died of a lingering illness. **1841** ELPHINSTONE *Hist. Ind.* II. 511 He put the widow of Sêvajî to a painful and lingering death. **1885** GILBERT *Mikado* II. Orig. Plays Ser. III. (1895) 208 Punishment! Yes. Something lingering, with boiling oil in it, I fancy. **1887** *Kent. Gloss.* s.v., He's in a poor lingering way.

lingeringly ('lɪŋgərɪŋlɪ), *adv.* [-LY[2].] In a lingering manner.

1589 RIDER *Bibl. Scholast.* 873 Lingeringly, *tarde*. **1631** R. H. *Arraignm. Whole Creature* v. 38 Not so long, so lingringly, as this macerating, massacring, murthering Famine. *a* **1649** DRUMM. OF HAWTH. *Poems* Wks. (1711) 24/1 As the flow'r which lingringly doth fade. **1657** AUSTEN *Fruit Trees* I. 73 Barke bound disease makes trees live lingringly and poorely. *a* **1687** COTTON *On Tobacco* 72 Poems (1689) 517 Coughs, Astmas, Apoplexies, Fevers, Rhume, All that kill dead; or lingeringly consume. **1827** MOORE *Epicur.* xvi. (1839) 167 Her hand parted lingeringly from mine. **1859** KINGSLEY *Misc.* (1860) I. 270 Even the best of them look lingeringly and longingly back to Europe and her legends. **1871** ROSSETTI *Poems, Last Confession* 244 Her voice was swift, yet ever the last words Fell lingeringly. **1878** SYMONDS *Sonnets M. Angelo* lxxiv, Death.. Who to sad souls alone comes lingeringly.

[**lingerly,** *adv.*, given in Dicts., appears to be a misprint in the later edd. of C. Brontë's *Jane Eyre* iii; ed. 1 (1847) has *lingeringly*.]

†'**linget**[1]. *Sc. Obs.* In full **linget-seed**. Also 6 **lingeat**, 8 **linjet**. [An unexplained var. of *linnet*, earlier form of LINT *sb.*] The seed of 'lint' or flax, linseed. *oly(e lingeat*: linseed oil.

c **1470** HENRYSON *Mor. Fab.* VIII. (*Preach. Swallow*) xviii, Se ye yon churle,.. Fast sawand hemp and gude linget seid? *Ibid.* xxvi, Yone lint heirefter will do gude; For linget is to litill birdis fude. **1477** *Extracts Aberd. Reg.* (1844) I. 408 Thre peckis of lynget, and thre pekkis of hemp sede. **1501** in *Ld. Treas. Acc. Scot.* II. 25 Item, for iiij pointis olye lingeat xiijs. **1505–6** *Ibid.* III. 184 Item, for ane quart oly lingeat viijs. **1609** SKENE *Reg. Maj.* 152 Linget seed. **1655** in *Rec. Convent. Roy. Burghs* (1878) III. 420 Repairing thither with ane bagg of linget. **1794** *Piper of Peebles* 6 (E.D.D.) An' nane but hamit linjet sawn,—Fan lint was beaten wi' the mill.

†**linget**[2]. *Obs. rare*$^{-0}$. Also 6 **lingette**. [Of obscure origin: Halliwell gives *linget* as a Somerset var. of *linnet*, but cites no authority.] Some small bird; perh. = *ling-bird* (see LING *sb.*[2] b).

1552 ELYOT *Dict.*, *Atricapilla*,.. a byrde with blacke fethers on the crowne of his head, muche like our linget [**1565** COOPER *Thesaurus*, Like a lingette or titlynge]. **1611** COTGR., *Fauvette*, a yellowish bird somewhat lesse then the Nightingale, whereunto she resembles both in singing and shape; some call her, a Linget. **1706** PHILLIPS (ed. Kersey), *Linger* or *Linget*, a kind of Bird.

linget, obs. form of LINGOT.

†**lingible,** *a.* *Obs. rare*$^{-1}$. [ad. L. type **lingibil-is*, f. *lingĕre* to lick.] Meant to be licked.

1661 LOVELL *Hist. Anim. & Min.* 515 Others are lingible, as lohochs, syrups, and sublinguale troches.

Lingism ('lɪŋɪz(ə)m). [f. *Ling*, the name of a Swedish physician + -ISM.] 'Ling's mode of treating disease by the use of gymnastics and appropriate movements' (*Syd. Soc. Lex.* 1888); kinesitherapy.

1879 in WEBSTER Suppl.

lingle: see LINGEL.

ling-long, *a.* ? reduplication of *long*.

a **1810** SURTEES *Barthram's Dirge* iii, She tore her ling long yellow hair, And knelt at Barthram's side.

lingo[1] ('lɪŋgəʊ). Also 8–9 **linguo**. [? corrupt form of LINGUA (*franca*): see LINGUA 2, 2 b, and cf. Pg. *lingoa*.] A contemptuous designation for: Foreign speech or language; language which is strange or unintelligible to the person who so designates it; language peculiar to some special subject, or employed (whether properly or affectedly) by some particular class of persons.

1660 *New Haven Col. Rec.* (1858) II. 337 To wch the plant [= plaintiff] answered, that he was not acquainted with Dutch lingo. **1700** CONGREVE *Way of World* IV. iv, Well, Well, I shall understand your Lingo one of these days, Cozen; in the mean while I must answer in plain English. **1702** C. MATHER *Magn. Chr.* III. 193 They are Sesquipedalia Verba of which their [*sc.* the American Indians'] Linguo is composed. **1749** FIELDING *Tom Jones* VI. ii, I have often warned you not to talk the court gibberish to me. I tell you, I don't understand the lingo. **1758** J. CHUBBE *Misc. Tracts* (1770) I. 84 When men speak French, or any Outlandish Linguo. **1778** SHERIDAN *Camp* II. ii, You may swear he is a foreigner by his lingo. **1818** *Blackw. Mag.* III. 407 The linguo of the Virtuoso clan. **1861** GEO. ELIOT in Cross *Life* (1885) II. 312 The good man.. began to pray in a borrowed, washy lingo. **1864** KINGSLEY *Let. to his Wife* in *Life* (1879) II. 168 The Basques speak a lingo utterly different from all European languages. **1866** LOWELL *Biglow P.* Introd. Poems 1890 II. 165, I should be half inclined to name the Yankee a lingo rather than a dialect. **1875** JOWETT *Plato* (ed. 2) II. 470 They come with their barbarous lingo to flatter us. **1875** E. C. STEDMAN *Victorian Poets* 187 To use the lingo of the phrenologists, his locality is better than his individuality.

lingo[2]. *Weaving.* Also 8 **lingoe**. [? variant of LINGOT.] (See quots.)

1731 MORTIMER in *Phil. Trans.* XXXVII. 106 Every Thread of the Warp goes through a small Brass Ring called a Male, or through a Loop in the Leish, and hath a small long Weight or Lingoe hung below, to counter-balance the Packthreads. **1799** G. SMITH *Laboratory* II. 49. **1831** G. R. PORTER *Silk Manuf.* 254 The cords whereby the leaden weights, which are called lingos, are attached to the harness. **1880** *Antrim & Down Gloss.*, *Lingo*, a long, thin weight of wire used in Jacquard looms.

‖**lingo**[3], **lingoa**. [Moluccan *lenggoa*, dial. var. of Malay *līgūh* (Le Clercq *Ternate Vocab.* 1890). The word appears as *linggoa-boom* (Du. *boom* = tree) in Valentyn *Oost-Indien* (1726) III. I. 215.] A large leguminous tree, *Pterocarpus indicus*, or its wood (native in the East Indies), also called *Burmese rosewood*, *Amboyna wood*, *Kyabuka*, etc.

1800 *Asiatic Ann. Reg.*, *Misc. Tracts* 74 *note*, Of the Lingoa-wood Valentyn describes three sorts, the red, the white, and the stone-hard lingoa. **1808** tr. *Stavorinus* in Pinkerton *Voy. & Trav.* XI. 254 The wood which is called Amboyna wood, or properly Lingoa Wood. **1890** *Century Dict.*, *Lingo*.

‖**lingoa geral** (lɪŋ'gəʊə dʒə'rɑːl). Also **lingua geral**. [Pg., ad. *lingua geral*, lit. 'general language'.] A trade language based on Tupi and used as a lingua franca in Brazil.

1856 [see JUPATI]. **1860** MAYNE REID *Odd People* 46 We shall use that [name] by which it is known in the 'Lingoa geral', and call it a *malocca*. **1876** *Encycl. Brit.* IV. 235/1 Most of the semi-civilized Indians of Brazil.. speak the Lingoa-Geral, a language adapted by the Jesuit missionaries from the original idiom of the Tupinambaras. **1932** W. L. GRAFF *Lang.* 431 The whole of Brazil that came into contact with the whites eventually became bilingual, knowing their own dialect and the Guarani *lingoa geral*. **1948** C. NIMUENDAJÚ in J. H. Steward *Handbk. S. Amer. Indians* III. 257 After their pacification, the *Mura* began to adopt the Lingua Geral... Later they substituted Portuguese for the Lingua Geral. *Ibid.* 311 *Tapanyuna* is not an *Apiacá* word, but a Lingua Geral term which means 'negro'. **1973** E. BROOKS et al. *Tribes of Amazon Basin in Brazil 1972* ii. 58 Tukano is still spoken widely among Indians of Santa Isabel .. and many still speak *lingua geral*, the Jesuit's blend of Tupi and Guarani.

lingonberry ('lɪŋənbɛrɪ). *Canad.* Also **lingberry, lingenberry**. [f. Sw. *lingon* mountain cranberry + BERRY *sb.*[1]] A dwarf variety of mountain cranberry, *Vaccinium vitis-idæa* var. *minus*, native to far northern temperate regions; also, another northern species of cranberry, *V. oxycoccus*.

1955 *Arctic Terms* 50/1 Lingberry,.. [a name for] the fruit of the mountain cranberry. **1960** J. J. ROWLANDS *Spindrift* 156 In Sweden the cranberry is known as the lingonberry. *Ibid.* 161 This berry [*sc.* mountain cranberry] is probably close to the lingonberry of Scandinavian countries. **1961** *Harper's Bazaar* May 106/2 Sweden prides itself on.. pancakes.. dressed with lingonberries. **1970** *Beaver* Winter 23 Wild cranberries.. are also known as lingenberries. **1971** D. NABOKOV tr. *Nabokov's Glory* (1972) vi. 24 Supper at the station (hazel hen with lingonberry sauce).

lingot ('lɪŋgət). ? *Obs.* or *arch.* Forms: 5 *pl.* **lingattis**, 7 (**lignot**), **lingat(e**, **linget**, (8 **lignate**), 6– **lingot**. [a. F. *lingot*: see INGOT.]

1. A mould in which metal is cast; = INGOT 1.

1540 *Ld. Treas. Acc. Scot.* in Pitcairn *Crim. Trials* I. 307* With other gold wark, to be meltit in ane grete lingot. **1686** W. HARRIS tr. *Lemery's Course Chym.* (ed. 2) 36 Lingots are Iron molds [etc.]. **1688** [see INGOT 1].

2. A mass of metal shaped like the mould in which it has been cast; = INGOT 2.

1488 *Ld. Treas. Acc. Scot.* I. 84 Twa lingattis of gold. **1584** HUDSON *Du Bartas' Judith* v. (1608) 77 Golden lingots. **1605** CAMDEN *Rem.* (1637) 179 Among the Lacedemonians iron lingets quenched with vinegar that they may serve to no other use [have been used for money]. **1653** H. COGAN tr. *Pinto's Trav.* xiv. (1663) 42 Lingots of silver. **1670** LD. FOUNTAINHALL in M. P. Brown *Suppl. Decis.* (1826) II. 477 Some lignates of copper. **1697** EVELYN *Numism.* i. 13 They paid Sums in France by Lingat as well as in coin. **1776** SWINBURNE *Trav. Spain* xliv. (1779) 409 The port of Cadiz, where the lingots of America are landed. **1801** HEL. M. WILLIAMS *Sk. Fr. Rep.* I. xviii. 226 The vandalic fury that .. melted into lingots the most exquisite pieces of bronze. **1841** C. MACKAY *Mem. Pop. Delusions* III. 187 The Baron.. showed me a lingot of gold made out of pewter.

transf. and *fig.* **1856** MRS. BROWNING *Aur. Leigh* VII. 1124 The house's front Was cased with lingots of ripe Indian corn. **1868** BROWNING *Ring & Bk.* I. 459 Thence bit by bit I dug The lingot truth, that memorable day.

lingster, variant of LINGUISTER.

lingthorn. A local name for the star-fish, *Luidia fragilissima* (see quot. 1841).

1841 E. FORBES *Hist. Brit. Starfishes* 139 The five-armed form is there [at Scarborough] called Lingthorn by the fishermen, and is taken in deep water: but is very rare. **1843** EMBLETON in *Proc. Berw. Nat. Club* II. No. 11. 50.

'**lingtow.** *Sc. Obs.* [? f. Sc. *ling*, LINE *sb.*[2] + TOW.] A rope used by smugglers. Also *Comb.* **lingtow-men**, smugglers.

1857 J. PATERSON *Mem. J. Train* 185 The carriers from the coast to the interior were called lingtowmen, from the coil of ropes or lingtows which they generally wore like a soldier's shoulder-belt, when not employed slinging or carrying their goods. **1894** CROCKETT *Raiders* i. 14 Wondering how long it would be till my father let me have a horse from the stable and a lingtow over my shoulder to go out to the Free Trade among the Manxmen.

‖**lingua** ('lɪŋgwə). [L., = tongue; in sense 2 prob. chiefly from It.]

1. a. The tongue or a tongue-like organ; *spec.* in *Ent.* (*a*) the ligula, or the central well-

developed portion of it; (*b*) a tongue-like prolongation of the hypopharynx; (*c*) 'the tubular proboscis of Lepidoptera' (*Cent. Dict.*).
1826 KIRBY & SP. *Entomol.* III. 358 *Lingua* (the Tongue), the organ situated within the *Labium* or emerging from it, by which insects in many cases collect their food and pass it down to the *Pharynx*. *Ibid.* 359 According to circumstances it might perhaps be denominated *Lingua* or *Ligula*. **1877** HUXLEY *Anat. Inv. Anim.* vii. 410 The anterior surface of the lingua and hypopharynx is beset with fine hairs. **1878** BELL tr. *Gegenbaur's Comp. Anat.* 246 In the Hymenoptera. .. A process, the tongue (lingua), is developed on the surface of the labium turned towards the mouth, and this has two lateral appendages, or secondary tongues (paraglossæ) at its base. **1880** PASCOE *Zool. Classif.* (ed. 2) 280 *Lingua*,..is sometimes applied to a part of the sucking-apparatus of insects, and to the 'inner integument' of the labrum in some Orthoptera, &c.
b. = LINGO².
1797 *Encycl. Brit.* (ed. 3) XVI. 230/2 The linguas are the long pieces of round or square lead tied to the end of each thread of the long-harness to keep them tight.
2. a. A language or 'lingo'.
1675 J. SMITH *Chr. Relig. Appeal* I. 43 In translating out of, and into those Lingua's they had at their Fingers ends. **1678** *Geneva Ball.* ii. in W. W. Wilkins *Pol. Ballads* (1860) I. 203 Was ever such a Beuk-learn'd Clerk That speaks all linguas of the Ark? **1719** D'URFEY *Pills* III. 100 We teach them their Lingua, to Crave and to Cant. *a* **1734** NORTH *Exam.* I. ii. §90 If they could not (in the Lingua of our East Angles) have t'one, they would have none of t'other. **1857** R. TOMES *Amer. in Japan* viii. 179 Many of the women speak a little of the lingua called Chinese English, or, in the cant phrase, *pigeon*.
b. lingua franca [It., = 'Frankish tongue']: a mixed language or jargon used in the Levant, consisting largely of Italian words deprived of their inflexions. Also *transf.* any mixed jargon formed as a medium of intercourse between people speaking different languages.
1678 DRYDEN *Limberham* I. i, 'Tis a kind of *Lingua Franca*, as I have heard the Merchants call it; a certain compound Language, made up of all Tongues, that passes through the Levant. **1737** [S. BERINGTON] *G. di Lucca's Mem.* 28 That mixed Language called *Lingua Franca*, so necessary in Eastern Countries: It is made up of Italian, Turkish, Persian, and Arabian. **1787** BECKFORD *Italy* (1834) II. 224 Addressing himself to me..in a most fluent lingua-franca, half Italian and half Portuguese. **1836** MARRYAT *Midsh. Easy* xiii, One of the men could speak a little Lingua Franca. **1872** BEAMES *Comp. Gram. Aryan Lang.* I. 121 That ..all-expressive Urdu speech, which is even now the *lingua franca* of most parts of India. **1877** F. BURNABY *Through Asia Minor* I. vi. 64 'What do you want?'—he asked in *lingua franca*, that undefined mixture of Italian, French, Greek, and Spanish, which is spoken throughout the Mediterranean. **1971** J. SPENCER *Eng. Lang. W. Afr.* 31 A very complex infrastructure of scores of vernacular languages as well as a number of regional lingue franche. **1974** R. A. HALL *External Hist. Romance Lang.* 21 The distribution of the Romance languages is best treated under four heads:..(3) use as *lingue franche*.
fig. **1870** LOWELL *Among my Bks.* Ser. I. 170 What concern have we with the shades of dialect in Homer or Theocritus, provided they speak the spiritual *lingua franca* that abolishes all alienage of race? **1955** *Times* 2 July 5/2 Cold war recrimination became the east-west *lingua franca*. **1958** *Times* 16 Sept. 3/2 Mr. Morrice handles them [*sc.* motifs] by cunningly intermingling realism with the *lingua franca* of ballet.

lin'guacious, *a. rare.* Also **linguaceous**. [f. L. *linguāci-*, *linguax* loquacious (f. *lingua* tongue) + -OUS.]
1. Talkative, loquacious.
1651 BIGGS *New Disp.* ¶80 We desire the linguacious Chymistry of these heads to tell us. **1727** in BAILEY vol. II. **1827** J. F. COOPER *Prairie* I. xi. 329 On the summit, Obed fully expected to encounter Esther, of whose linguacious powers, he had too often been furnished with the most sinister proofs. **1950** J. Y. T. GREIG *Thackeray* xiii. 142 She needed it [*sc.* the gift of listening] with a witty and linguacious fellow for a husband. *a* **1953** DYLAN THOMAS *Quite Early One Morning* (1954) 64 And see, too, in that linguaceous stream, the tall monocled men..who lecture to women's clubs.
†**2.** Linguistic. (A bad use.) *Obs.*
1814 W. TAYLOR in *Monthly Rev.* LXXIII. 499 The author..appears..after having completed two volumes of selections from the antient writers, to have..acquired a respectable knowledge..of their linguacious peculiarities.
Hence †**lin'guaciousness**.
1727 in BAILEY vol. II.

†**linguacity**. *Obs.*⁻⁰ [f. L. *linguāci-* (see prec.) + -TY; L. type **linguācitātem*.] Loquacity.
1656 BLOUNT *Glossogr.*, *Linguacity*,..talkativeness, verbosity. **1721** in BAILEY.

linguadental: see LINGUO-.

lingua geral: see LINGOA GERAL.

lingual ('lɪŋgwəl), *a.* and *sb.* [ad. med.L. *linguāl-is*, f. *lingua* tongue. Cf. F. *lingual*.]
A. *adj.*
†**1.** Tongue-shaped (see quot.). *Obs.*
c **1400** *Lanfranc's Cirurg.* 308 The .ix. cauterie is clepid lingual [L. *cauterium linguale*]. *Ibid.* 309 Superfluite of fleisch þat is vpon a mannes browis, þou schalt do awei wiþ a cauterie þat is clepid lingual, schape as it were a tunge of a brid.
2. Chiefly *Anat.* and *Zool.* Of or pertaining to the tongue, or to any tongue-like part (see LINGUA I).
lingual artery, a branch of the external carotid, supplying the tongue. ***lingual bone***, the hyoid bone (*Syd. Soc. Lex.* 1889). ***lingual nerve***, a tactile and sensory nerve (a branch of the inferior maxillary division of the fifth cranial pair), supplying the tongue. ***lingual ribbon***, in molluscs, = ODONTOPHORE. ***lingual teeth***, the chitinous band of teeth which is borne upon the odontophore.
1650 BULWER *Anthropomet.* 143 There are men somewhere who have really a double Tongue, with which they better perform the lingual offices then we do with one. **1826** KIRBY & SP. *Entomol.* III. xxxiv. 426 The labial palpi ..might with equal propriety be denominated lingual palpi. **1831** R. KNOX *Cloquet's Anat.* 287 The constrictor medius is covered, in its outer surface, by the hyo-glossus and lingual artery externally. **1848** CARPENTER *Anim. Phys.* 379 The branch of this proceeding to the tongue, is known as the lingual nerve. **1851-6** WOODWARD *Mollusca* iv. 28 The lingual ribbon of the limpet is longer than the whole animal. **1858** OWEN in Murchison *Siluria* App. (1859) 562 Lingual teeth of gasteropods. **1862** J. G. JEFFREYS *Brit. Conchol.* I. 289 The tongue or lingual plate of Cochlicopa. **1880** GÜNTHER *Fishes* 65 The lingual cartilage is large in all cyclostomes. **1880** R. RIMMER *Land & Freshwater Shells* 23 Central lingual tooth minute. **1882** TRYON *Conchol.* I. 94 At the lower posterior end is situated the lingual sheath, enclosing the odontophore.
3. *Phonetics.* Of sounds: Formed by the tongue.
As a term of phonetic classification, the word has been very variously applied: e.g. by Wilkins to most of the vowels, and to all the consonants exc. the labials and gutturals; some have appropriated it to the 'divided' sounds, *l* and *r*. In present use, it hardly survives exc. as a synonym for CEREBRAL (e.g. in Whitney's *Sanskrit Grammar*, 1879).
1668 WILKINS *Real Char.* III. xiv. §2. 374 Then u, o, ꝋ, should be first, as being Labial, and ɑ, a, e, ɩ, next, as Lingual, or Linguapalatal, and y last, as being Guttural. **1773** W. KENRICK *Dict.*, *Rhet. Gram.* §2. 3 He would be at no loss to perceive, that the guttural and nasal modes of enunciation are less pleasant than the labial and lingual. **1860** O. W. HOLMES *Elsie V.* (1861) 167 Not a lisp, certainly, but the least possible imperfection in articulating some of the lingual sounds.
4. a. Pertaining to the tongue as the organ of speech. **b.** Pertaining to language or languages.
1774 *Westm. Mag.* II. 456, I was advised to take a country lodging for the benefit of the air; but as a lingual noise is not the only one I dislike, I was for ever changing my situation. **1813** T. BUSBY *Lucretius* II. v. 1311 If others yet no language knew, Then, tell me, whence their lingual talent grew. **1822-34** *Good's Study Med.* (ed. 4) I. 415 He [a tongueless boy] underwent a strict examination as to..the lingual powers he still possessed. **1837** CARLYLE *Fr. Rev.* II. I. ii, One great difference between our two kinds of civil war; between the modern lingual or Parliamentary-logical kind, and the ancient or manual kind in the steel battle-field. **1855** J. WILSON in Mitchell *Mem. R. Nesbit* (1858) 396 His lingual studies in India were almost altogether confined to the Marathi and to the elements of Sanskrit. **1871** BLACKIE *Four Phases* i. 79 Your talk is not a mere exhibition of lingual dexterity; it means something. **1873** *Contemp. Rev.* XXI. 928 The lingual ingenuities of logic.
B. *sb.* **1.** A lingual sound (see A. 3).
1668 WILKINS *Real Char.* III. xiv. §2. 374 In conformity with the common Alphabets, I begin [in enumerating the vowels] with the Linguals. *a* **1709** W. BAXTER *Let.* in *Gloss. Rom. Antiq.* (1731) 409 The second Sort I call Linguals, which are proper to Mankind, and borrowed by Imitation from animal and other Sounds. **1817** DUPONCEAU in *Trans. Amer. Philos. Soc.* (1818) I. 261 Four linguals, *zhim*, *shal*, *zed*, and *sin*. **1871** W. A. HAMMOND *Dis. Nerv. System* 36 The linguals and labials among letters are particularly troublesome.
2. *Anat.* The lingual nerve (see A. 2).
1877 M. FOSTER *Physiol.* III. i. 345 Here the sensory lingual was evidently the means of causing motor effects.

lin'guality. [f. LINGUAL *a.* + -ITY.] The quality of being lingual. (*Funk's Stand. Dict.* 1893.)

lingualize ('lɪŋgwəlaɪz), *v.* [f. LINGUAL *a.* + -IZE.] *trans.* To make lingual.
1875 F. HALL in *Nation* XX. 116/2 The letters *d*, *n*, and *t*, where lingual, were, we surmise, first dentalized, so as to conform to their character everywhere on the Continent, and these letters on reaching England, where there are no vernacular dentals, were, in turn, lingualized. **1879** WHITNEY *Sanskrit Gram.* 59 The final *i* or *u* of a preposition or other like prefix ordinarily lingualizes the initial *s* of the root to which it is prefixed.

lingually ('lɪŋgwəlɪ), *adv.* [f. LINGUAL *a.* + -LY².] **a.** In a lingual manner; as regards language. (*Cent. Dict.* 1890.)
b. On the lingual side; towards the tongue.
1902 *Dental Digest* VIII. 925, I have seen some cases of compound cavities which started at a point of structural defect perhaps two millimeters distant lingually from the contact. **1910** *Practitioner* Jan. 115 Internally (lingually), the neck of the tooth..is embraced by a thin shallow flap of gum. **1963** J. OSBORNE *Dental Mech.* (ed. 5) viii. 112 During eruption..the facial muscles push the teeth lingually. **1970** *Nature* 25 July 356/2 A crest extends lingually to delineate the extent of the talonid basin. **1971** *Ibid.*, 30 July 311/1 At the incisor sockets the alveolar margin seems to be preserved lingually but is broken labially.

linguapalatal: see LINGUO-.

Linguaphone ('lɪŋgwəfəʊn). Also **linguaphone**. [f. LINGUA 2 + *-phone* after GRAMOPHONE.] The proprietary name of a language-teaching system based on the use of gramophone records in conjunction with textbooks (see quots.). Also *attrib.*
1908 *Westm. Gaz.* 29 Feb. 7/1 (Advt.), The Linguaphone. This machine.. teaches languages by a marvellous system of phonographic records. **1913** *Chambers's Jrnl.* Nov. 830/2 In the linguaphone system..the records are prepared by distinguished speakers of the various languages. **1925** *Trade Marks Jrnl.* 4 Nov. 2397 Linguaphone..instruments and apparatus for teaching. Jacques Roston,..London,.. teacher of languages and translator. **1926** *Glasgow Herald* 28 Feb. 9 The Linguaphone Institute has produced a system by means of which one can, in his own home, from book and gramophone record obtain a working knowledge of languages. **1936** P. FLEMING *News from Tartary* 162, I had left Peking with a minute..Chinese vocabulary, based on the first half-dozen records of a linguaphone course. **1962** L. DEIGHTON *Ipcress File* xxv. 161 Suppose I buy you a Linguaphone course. **1966** A. E. LINDOP *I start Counting* xv. 174 They had bought some Linguaphone records—so everything was 'quel' this and 'quel' that. **1974** *Country Life* 14 Feb. 304/2 Brito e Cunha breaks off the native-tongue chat..for a caution of 'Hold hard!' or 'I say, sta-idy there!' in linguaphone Leicestershire.

linguate ('lɪŋgwət), *a.* [f. L. *linguātus* (not recorded in this sense) or f. LINGU(A I + -ATE².] Tongue-shaped. As *sb.*, a tongue-shaped flint instrument.
1940 *Proc. Prehist. Soc.* VI. 8 Pointed linguates with untrimmed butts. **1963** S. PIGGOTT in Foster & Alcock *Culture & Environment* iv. 84 In Ireland, a fourth distinctive group of linguate daggers can be recognized.

linguatulid, (lɪŋ'gwætjʊlɪd), *sb.* and *a.* [f. mod.L. name of former class *Linguatulida*, f. the generic name *Linguatula* (G. F. von Froelich 1789, in *Naturforscher* XXIV. 148), f. L. *linguātus* 'having a tongue', eloquent.] A parasitic worm-like arthropod of the genus *Linguatula*, the adult form of which attacks the nasal passages of certain carnivorous mammals, esp. canids; also, a member of the group Pentastomida, including parasitic arthropods, most of which attack snakes; = *tongue-worm* (*b*) (TONGUE *sb.* 16). Also as *adj.*
1923 *Nature* 17 Mar. 381/2 (*title*) On the linguatulid arachnid, *Raillietiella furcocerca*. **1929** PATTON & EVANS *Insects, Ticks, Mites* I. 666 *Porocephalus* is the name of a Linguatulid genus. *Ibid.*, It [*sc.* a parasite] can hardly be acquired by eating the flesh of snakes, the commonest final host of these Linguatulids. **1942** *Ann. Trop. Med. & Parasitol.* XXXVI. 60 (*title*) Linguatulid infestations of man. **1961** C. H. POPE *Giant Snakes* (1962) 193 Linguatulids, some fifty species of which have been described, are degenerate arachnids closely related to ticks and mites.

†**lingued**, *ppl. a. Obs.* [f. L. *lingua* tongue + -ED².] Tongued. Only in Comb. ***honey-lingued***.
1620 MIDDLETON & ROWLEY *World Tost at Tennis* C 4 b, Hony-lingued Polihymnia.

linguet, variant of LANGUET.
1644 DIGBY *Nat. Bodies* xix. 166 The body or linguet [*sc.* 'a tongue, or labell of flannen'] by which the water ascendeth, being a dry one. **1875** KNIGHT *Dict. Mech.*, *Linguet*, a tongue; as in some organ-pipes. A languet. *Ibid.*, *Linguet*, the piece of a sword-hilt which turns down over the mouth-piece of a scabbard.

linguiform ('lɪŋgwɪfɔːm), *a. Bot.*, *Anat.* and *Zool.* Also less correctly **lingua-**, **linguæ-**. [ad. L. type **linguiform-is*, f. LINGUA; see -FORM.] Shaped like the tongue.
1753 CHAMBERS *Cycl. Supp.* s.v. *Leaf*, *Linguiform leaf*, a linear leaf in shape of a tongue, which is obtuse, fleshy, depressed, convex on the under side, and usually cartilaginous at the edge. **1760** J. LEE *Introd. Bot.* III. v. (1765) 186 *Linguiform, Tongue-shaped*. **1826** KIRBY & SP. *Entomol.* III. 424 When you look within the mouth, you will find a linguiform organ, which evidently acts the part of a tongue, and therefore ought to have the name. **1835-6** TODD *Cycl. Anat.* I. 703/1 The foot, which is shaped like a tongue, is named linguiform, as in the *Solen strigilatus*. **1848** CRAIG, *Linguaform*. **1854** WOODWARD *Mollusca* II. 304 Veneridæ:.. foot linguiform. **1862** COOKE *Man. Bot. Terms*, *Linguæform*. **1887** *Brit. Med. Jrnl.* 13 Mar. 641 In some instances the gall-bladder projects beyond the apex of the linguiform projection.

linguine (lɪŋ'gwiːneɪ). Also **linguini**. [It., pl. of *linguina*, dim. of *lingua* tongue.] An Italian pasta made of tongue-shaped ribbons.
1948 LO PINTO & MILARADOVICH *Art of Italian Cooking* (1955) i. 24 *Linguini*, narrow, plain noodles cut about ⅛ inch wide. **1954** G. M. LAPOLLA *Good Food from Italy* 85 When peas are used, rarely is the sauce poured over the linguine or fettuccelle. **1965** M. ECHARD *I met Murder* (1967) vii. 59 Dining on fettuccine or linguini or ravioli. **1968** *N.Y. Times* 26 Jan. 22 The kitchen produces first-rate linguine with clam sauce. **1969** R. LOWELL *Notebk.* 1967-68 (1970) 255 The ebb tide flings up wonders: rivers, linguini, Beercans, bloodstreams, eddies. **1972** R. K. SMITH *Ransom* I. 4 Just a little linguine, and a little veal parmigiana.

lin'guipotence. *nonce-wd.* [f. L. *lingua* tongue + *potentia* power. Cf. *armipotence*.] ? Mastery with the tongue, or of languages.
1820 COLERIDGE in *Lit. Rem.* (1839) IV. 108 The New Testament contains not the least proof of the *linguipotence* of the Apostles, but the clearest proof of the contrary.

linguished: see LINGUIST *ppl. a.*

linguism ('lɪŋgwɪz(ə)m). [f. L. *lingua* tongue + -ISM.] **1.** *nonce-wd.* Conversance with, or predilection for, (foreign) languages.
1819 MOORE *Mem.* 4 Mar. (1853) II. 274 The faults of Mr. Fox's writing may perhaps be traced to his linguism, and some of the purest writers of English have been those that knew but little of other languages.

2. Advocacy of languages on a regional basis.
1967 *Economist* 18 Feb. 596/1 A good deal of the criticism heard..of Indian politics—for instance of 'linguism', 'casteism', and so on—is a roundabout way of wishing that human beings were different from what they are.

linguist ('lɪŋgwɪst). [f. L. *lingua* tongue, language + -IST. Cf. F. *linguiste* (from 17th c.).]
1. a. One who is skilled in the use of languages; one who is master of other tongues besides his own. (Often with adj. indicating the degree or extent of the person's skill.)
1591 SHAKS. *Two Gent.* IV. i. 57 Seeing you are beautifide With goodly shape; and by your owne report A Linguist. **1593** G. HARVEY *Pierce's Super.* Answ. Lett. **3 b, Be thou Iohn, the many-tongued Linguist, like Andrewes, or the curious Intelligencer, like Bodley. **1599** THYNNE *Animadv.* 31 Vnleste a manne be a good saxoniste, frenche, and Italyane linguiste. **1602** BOYLE in *Lismore Papers* Ser. II. (1887) I. 39 A generall Linguist and partycular so in insight in the Ierish tungue. **1604** MARSTON *Malcontent* I. i, I study languages. Who doost thinke to be the best linguist of our age? **1673** HICKERINGILL *Gregory Father Greybeard* 256 Clean Latin style..pencill'd whether by himself or any other linguist. **1678** WANLEY *Wond. Lit. World* v. i. §89. 467/1 The Golden Bull..requires Emperours to be Good Linguists to confer themselves with Embassadours. **1715** M. DAVIES *Athen. Brit.* I. 1 The great Linguist, John Minsheu. **1855** MACAULAY *Hist. Eng.* xiii. III. 276 He was a linguist, a mathematician, and a poet. **1859** MAX MÜLLER *Sci. Lang.* (1862) 24 And here I must protest..against the supposition that the student of language must necessarily be a great linguist. **1867** LADY HERBERT *Cradle L.* iii. 81 He is ..a wonderful linguist, speaking not only Hebrew and Greek, but most of the Arabian dialects.
transf. **1604** DRAYTON *Owl* 47 Each Sylvan sound I truly understood, Become a perfect Linguist of the Wood.
¶ **b.** One who speaks a (specified) language.
1672 PETTY *Pol. Anat.* xiii. Tracts (1769) 371 All the names of artificial things brought into use, since the empire of these linguists ceased, are expressed in the language of their conquerors.
2. A student of language; a philologist.
1641 WILKINS *Mercury* iii. (1707) 12 Many of the other [words]..are of such secret Sense, as I think no Linguist can discover. **1695** J. EDWARDS *Perfect. Script.* 3 Here linguists and philologists may find that which is to be found no where else. **1748** HARTLEY *Observ. Man* I. iii. §1. 320 A Light in which Grammarians and Linguists alone consider Words. **1817** J. EVANS *Excurs. Windsor*, etc. 171 And what will be curious to the linguist, here are the Iliad and Odyssey, the very books from which Pope made his translation. **1922** O. JESPERSEN *Lang.* 64, I think I am in accordance with a growing number of scholars in England and America if I.. apply the word 'linguist' by itself to the scientific student of language (or of languages). **1940** *Amer. Speech* XV. 187 The *Handbook* [of the Linguistic Geography of New England].. seems to suggest that American linguists are naïve. **1964** R. H. ROBINS *Gen. Ling.* 2 The general linguist, in the sense of the specialist or the student concerned with general linguistics. **1966** M. R. D. FOOT *SOE in France* viii. 212 He was a young linguist, a research student at Manchester University. **1966** *New Statesman* 11 Nov. 701/1 One or two of my friends even abandoned literature altogether and became fully fledged philologists—'linguists', as my companion at dinner would have said. **1973** A. P. SORENSEN in D. R. Gross *Peoples & Cultures of Native S. Amer.* 331 Some linguists wondered..whether the comparative method could or even should be applied to American Indian languages at all.
† **3.** An interpreter. *Obs.* (Cf. LINGUISTER.)
'Formerly much used in the East. It long survived in China, and is there perhaps not yet obsolete' (Yule).
1711 C. LOCKYER *Trade India* 104 Get it translated without your Linguists Knowledge. **1742** C. MIDDLETON in A. Dobbs *Hudson's Bay* (1744) 192 The Southern Indian, who was Linguist for the Northern ones, returned with the Boat. **1745** P. THOMAS *Jrnl. Anson's Voy.* 300 This Evening came..a Chinese Interpreter or Linguist. **1780** *Ann. Reg.* 204 The persons who acted as linguist, surgeon, and surgeon's mate. **1843** PRESCOTT *Mexico* (1850) I. 251 Marina ..made herself so far mistress of the Castilian as to supersede the necessity of any other linguist. **1882** *'Fan Kwae' at Canton* 50 Other Chinese were closely allied to the foreign community as 'Linguists'... They were appointed by the Hoppo to act as interpreters.
† **4.** One who uses his tongue freely or knows how to talk; a master of language. *Obs.*
1588 T. HARRIOTT *Virginia* (Cent.), Artamockes, the linguist, a bird that imitateth and useth the sounds and tones of almost all the birds in the countrie. **1599** T. M[OUFET] *Silkwormes* 43 All linguists [*marg.* Pies, parrats, stares, &c.] eke that beg what hart would craue Selling your tongues for euery trifle seene As almonds, nuttes [etc.]. **1612** WEBSTER *White Devil* v. i, Ile dispute with him. Hee's a rare linguist. **1691** WOOD *Ath. Oxon.* I. 374 Richard Martin..was a plausible Linguist, and eminent for Speeches spoken in Parliaments.
5. *attrib.* or appositive, as ***linguist-anthropologist, -philologist, -reader.***
1951 S. F. NADEL *Found. Social Anthropol.* 46 The 'virtuosity' of the linguist-anthropologist..is only the fullest preparation for his task. **1960** *Amer. Speech* XXXV. 217 In a treatment of specific historical changes of morphemes and phonemes the linguist-philologist should attempt to recapture what actually happened. **1964** *Language* XL. 203 A sample passage from a 1956 article by Starkweather is enough to boggle the unprepared linguist-reader.

† **'linguist, 'linguished,** *ppl. a. Obs.* [app. evolved from a misunderstanding of prec. (perh. in the phrase 'the best linguist'), the ending being taken for that of a pa. pple.] Skilled in languages, 'languaged'.
1607 BRETON *Murmurer* (Grosart) 7/1 So profoundly read in the rules of the best learning, and so well Linguist in the most necessary Languages. **1630** J. TAYLOR (Water P.) *Elegy Prince Henry* Wks. II. 336/1 Mean time she [my Muse] 'mongst the linguish'd Poets throngs, Although she want the helpe of Forraigne tongs. **1632** LITHGOW *Trav.* x. 499 They are..delicately linguishd, the most part of them, being brought vp in France or Italy.

linguister ('lɪŋgwɪstə(r)). Now only *U.S.* Also 7 **linkister**, 8 **languister**, 9 **lingster, linkster.** [f. prec. + -ER[1].]
1. An interpreter; = LINGUIST 2.
a **1649** WINTHROP *New Eng.* (1826) II. 237 He, being linkister (because he could speak the language). **1713** in G. Sheldon *Hist. Deerfield (Mass.)* (1895) I. 350, J Jmployed my Indian Languister to talk to her. **1760** *Let. to Gov. Fort St. George* in A. Dalrymple *Orient. Repert.* (1793) I. 396, I was no further concerned, than as a Linguister for the King's Officer who commanded the Party. **1840** J. F. COOPER *Pathfinder* xiii, On the Atlantic..where a seafaring-man has occasion sometimes to converse with a pilot or a linguister in that language [French]. **1885** H. M. STANLEY *Congo* I. 123 Massalla, the lingster of Chinsalla village. **1889** F. R. GOULDING *Marooner's Isl.* (1890) 65 Linkster..is a word in common use in many parts [of Georgia and Florida], being a corruption of linguister, and means interpreter.
¶ **2.** *nonce-use.* A linguist, philologist.
1870 LOWELL *Study Wind.* 265 He who writes to be read, does not write for linguisters.

linguistic (lɪŋ'gwɪstɪk), *a.* and *sb.* [f. LINGUIST + -IC. Cf. F. *linguistique.*]
A. *adj.* **a.** Of or pertaining to the knowledge or study of languages. Also used for: Of or pertaining to language or languages; = LINGUAL 4 b.
The latter use is hardly justifiable etymologically; it has arisen because *lingual* suggests irrelevant associations.
1856 C. J. ELLICOTT in *Cambr. Ess.* 187 Orthographies.. and..the veriest *minutiæ* of linguistic differences. **1858** J. M. MITCHELL *Mem. R. Nesbit* i. 12 His linguistic talent was logical as much as philological. **1860** MARSH *Eng. Lang.* i. (1862) 2 The most striking improvement in linguistic study may be dated from the discovery..of the Sanskrit. **1876** C. M. DAVIES *Unorth. Lond.* 31 In a linguistic point of view the peoples were one. **1911** V. WELBY *Significs & Lang.* v. 17 The implicitly false mental image, source of the false linguistic image. **1921** E. SAPIR *Lang.* vi. 156 In a book of this sort it is naturally impossible to give an adequate idea of linguistic structure. **1935** B. MALINOWSKI *Coral Gardens* II. VI. v. 232 Within the linguistic theory of the present book, in which the distinction between 'form' and meaning is in the last instance illusory. **1936** J. R. KANTOR *Objective Psychol. Gram.* xiii. 195 It is undoubtedly necessary to include many other speech parts if we are to cover linguistic phenomena adequately. **1953** J. B. CARROLL *Study of Lang.* i. 5 It was only natural..that the engineer should have perceived the possibilities of developing various sorts of 'linguistic machines', such as a machine for instantly converting human speech into..printed alphabetic symbols. **1957** W. HAAS in *Studies in Ling. Analysis* (Philol. Soc.) 33 'Zero' in Linguistic Description stands for what is acoustically nothing. **1957** G. RYLE in C. A. Mace *Brit. Philos. in Mid-Cent.* 263 Philosophical problems are linguistic problems—only linguistic problems quite unlike any of the problems of philology, grammar, phonetics..etc., since they are..about the logic of the functionings of expressions. **1964** M. A. K. HALLIDAY et al. *Ling. Sci.* i. 18 If language is described according to the version of linguistic theory outlined, the task of the language learner..will be made easier. **1966** *English Studies* XLVII. 270 Instead of adverb transforms we find occasional instances of 'linguistic shortening', which in itself is a means of expressing emotiveness. **1967** R. TEXTOR *Cross-Cultural Summary* 67 The rationale for including linguistic affiliation is..that 'genetic relationships in culture and past historical connections among societies are commonly revealed.. among the languages spoken by the peoples in question'. **1968** D. HYMES in *Internat. Encycl. Social Sci.* 366/2 Linguistic description has focused on the form of languages, neglecting the structuring of their use. **1968** CHOMSKY & HALLE *Sound Pattern Eng.* i. 4 The essential properties of natural language are often referred to as 'linguistic universals'. **1972** L. R. PALMER *Descr. & Compar. Ling.* ix. 227 Sound laws do not enable us to *predict* linguistic events as a law of chemistry predicts material change.
b. Special collocations: ***linguistic analysis***, (*a*) the analysis of language structures in terms of some theory of language; (*b*) *Philos.*, analysis of language as the medium of thought; so ***linguistic analyst***; ***linguistic anthropology***, anthropological research based on the study of the language of a selected group; so ***linguistic-anthropological*** adj.; ***linguistic atlas***, a set of tables or maps recording regional or dialectal variations of pronunciation, vocabulary, or inflexional forms; ***linguistic form***, any unit or pattern of speech that has meaning; ***linguistic geography***, the study of the geographical distribution of languages, dialects, etc.; so ***linguistic geographer***, ***linguistic-geographical*** adj.; ***linguistic map***, a map in a linguistic atlas; a map showing the distribution of linguistic features; ***linguistic philosophy*** = *linguistic analysis* (*b*); so ***linguistic philosopher***; ***linguistic psychology***, the study of human psychology through the data provided by language; cf. PSYCHOLINGUISTICS; ***linguistic science***, the science of language; the systematic study of linguistic phenomena; so ***linguistic scientist***; ***linguistic stock***, the group to which a set of related languages belongs.
1932 A. F. BENTLEY *Let.* 15 Nov. in Ratner & Altman *J. Dewey & A. F. Bentley* (1964) 51, I have at length found a region of investigation in which some tentative results can be secured, and I am permitting myself to send you a copy of the resulting book, **Linguistic Analysis of Mathematics.* **1943** *Amer. Speech* XXVII. 60/1 Outline of linguistic analysis. **1945** *Mind* LIV. 195 Positivists, as is well known, do not search for answers to the philosophical questions; what they try to bring about, in *all* cases, is the disappearance of the questions by means of what they call linguistic analysis. **1949** *Amer. Speech* XXIV. 55 His charts make it possible to suggest the potentialities of 'slur' as a factor in linguistic analysis. **1957** J. R. FIRTH in *Studies in Ling. Analysis* (Philol. Soc.) p. vi, Palatograms, kymograms ..specifically keyed to the linguistic analysis. **1966** J. J. KATZ *Philos. of Lang.* iii. 16 The leading philosophical movements..have concerned themselves with what they call 'linguistic analysis'. **1945** *Aristotelian Soc. Suppl. Vol.* XIX. 7 If anyone was ever a '*linguistic analyst', surely Socrates was. **1957** G. RYLE in C. A. Mace *Brit. Philos. in Mid-Cent.* 263, I gather that at this very moment British philosophy is dominated by some people called 'linguistic analysts'. **1962** *Listener* 17 May 851/1 You might well meet a philosopher described as a linguistic analyst. **1964** E. A. NIDA *Toward Sci. Transl.* iii. 36 The *linguistic-anthropological approach to meaning has in many respects paralleled developments in symbolic logic, though the immediate area of study in the two fields is different and the approach seemingly quite divergent. **1968** D. HYMES in *Internat. Encycl. Social Sci.* 354/2 Through Boas the interest became an intrinsic part of American *linguistic anthropology. **1923** H. R. LANG in *Romanic Rev.* XIV. 264 It will be clear from this that the study of the charts of this *linguistic atlas affords a deep insight into the various phases of the decline of the dialects of Italy. **1930** *Dialect Notes* VI. ii. 67 The Linguistic Atlas of New England will provide an organized collection of the present forms of the spoken language. **1939** *Amer. Speech* XIV. 64/2 Ten sets of 300 phonograph records representing all the present dialects of Germany. Recorded by Telefunken under the auspices of the Linguistic Atlas. **1952** DIETH & ORTON (*title*) A questionnaire for a linguistic atlas of England. **1954** G. BOTTIGLIONI in Martinet & Weinreich *Ling. Today* 261 The way in which the plan of a linguistic atlas is organized and carried out. **1975** *Times* 6 Jan. 4/7 The next project will be the publication of a complete linguistic atlas which will trace on maps not only the use of specific words but of dialect sounds as well. **1921** E. SAPIR *Lang.* iv. 62 *Linguistic form may and should be studied as types of patterning, apart from the associated functions. *Ibid.* vi. 127 In dealing with linguistic form, we have been concerned only with single words and with the relations of words in sentences. **1943** *Amer. Speech* XVIII. 228 The flier forced down in Libya.., would have little interest in the linguistic form of the utterance, 'I am an American', in Arabic but he might forfeit his life by not knowing how to say it. **1964** M. A. K. HALLIDAY *et al. Ling. Sci.* i. 20 The least obvious distinction perhaps is that between grammar and lexis, since these are two aspects of linguistic form. *Ibid.* ii. 21 When we describe linguistic *form*..we are describing the meaningful internal patterns of language. **1952** *Word* VIII. iii. 275 Who but Rohlfs combines a background of solid 19th century German scholarship with a thorough training as a *linguistic geographer? **1948** *Neophilologus* XXXII. 175 In the absence of English *linguistic-geographical data, no more than tentative suggestions regarding the relation between English and its Continental cognates are as yet possible. **1926** *Germanic Rev.* I. iv. 281 *Linguistic geography, as geography, is an aspect of human geography. **1930** *Dialect Notes* VI. ii. 74 A course in the methods and the interpretation of the results of linguistic geography. **1933** Linguistic geography [see HISTORICAL *a.* 2 d]. **1934** H. KURATH in *Proc. Amer. Philos. Soc.* LXXIV. 228 Linguistic geography undertakes to ascertain the distribution of linguistic features (dialectal features). **1939** —— (*title*) Handbook of the linguistic geography of New England. **1954** G. BOTTIGLIONI in Martinet & Weinreich *Ling. Today* 255 Linguistic geography owes its origin to the comparative method. **1968** D. HYMES in *Internat. Encycl. Social Sci.* 359/2 Linguistic geography, or dialectology, and typological comparison, together with general linguistics, often are distinguished as well. **1944** *Amer. Speech* XIX. 135 The book includes sixteen *linguistic maps and nineteen illustrations. **1951** *Mind* LX. 104 These words should rejoice the heart of any present-day *Linguistic Philosopher. **1963** W. H. WALSH *Metaphysics* i. 16 The brief ascendancy of the Logical Positivists came to an end and their place was taken by the so-called Linguistic Philosophers. **1957** J. L. AUSTIN in *Proc. Aristotelian Soc.* LVII. 9 There are, I know, or are supposed to be, snags in '*linguistic' philosophy, which those not very familiar with it find, sometimes not without glee or relief, daunting. **1962** *Listener* 22 Feb. 353/1 He was reputed to be the high priest of linguistic philosophy. **1966** J. J. KATZ *Philos. of Lang.* iii. 15 The leading philosophical movements in twentieth-century philosophy have been referred to..as 'linguistic philosophy'. **1953** J. B. CARROLL *Study of Lang.* iii. 70 The study of verbal behavior..has variously been called the *psychology of language*, **linguistic psychology*, or *psycholinguistics.* **1966** M. PEI *Story of Lang.* (rev. ed.) xii. 286 The number of unsolved problems in the field of linguistic psychology is tremendous. **1922** O. JESPERSEN *Lang.* 21 Nor did *linguistic science advance in the Middle Ages. **1933** L. BLOOMFIELD *Lang.* ii. 21 Linguistic science arose from relatively practical preoccupations, such as the use of writing, the study of literature and especially of older records, and the prescription of elegant speech. **1938** *Year's Work Eng. Stud.* 1936 27 Philology (which scholars tend more and more to call 'linguistic science' or 'linguistics'). **1971** D. CRYSTAL *Ling.* 36 It is also sometimes called linguistic science. **1934** *Amer. Speech* IX. 88/1 *Linguistic scientists will find a rich ground for study if they will stop thinking of the written or printed Standard Language as solely a secondary, or derivative, form of speech. **1921** E. SAPIR *Lang.* x. 221 What are the most inclusive linguistic groupings, the '*linguistic stocks', and what is the distribution of each. **1953** BEALS & HOIJER *Introd. Anthropol.* xvii. 524 As more and more languages are studied and compared intensively with each other, we may expect that the number of linguistic stocks will decrease.

B. *sb.* [-IC 2.] The science of languages; philology. **a.** *sing.* (Cf. F. *linguistique*, G. *linguistik.*) *rare.*

1837 WHEWELL *Hist. Induct. Sci.* (1840) I. p. cxiv, We may call the science of languages linguistic, as it is called by the best German writers. **1870** LOWELL *Study Wind.* 334 Mr. Hooper is always weak in his linguistic.

b. *pl.*

1847 in WEBSTER. **1855** in OGILVIE, Suppl. *a* **1858** S. W. SINGER (Worc.), A work containing a complete chronological account of English lexicography and lexicographers would be a most acceptable addition to linguistics and literary history. **1875** WHITNEY *Life Lang.* x. 191 A fundamental principle in linguistics. **1893** LELAND *Mem.* I. 112 The extreme interest which I take in philology and linguistics. **1902** *PMLA* XVII. 104 Both linguistics and literature are proper university studies. **1908** H. G. WELLS *War in Air* iii. §4 He thought of himself performing feats with the sign language and chance linguistics. **1938** [see *linguistic science* above]. **1953** J. B. CARROLL *Study of Lang.* iv. 113 Linguistics thus appears to have a bearing on all the social sciences. **1964** M. A. K. HALLIDAY et al. *Ling. Sci.* i. 9 The term 'linguistic sciences' covers two closely related but distinct subjects: linguistics and phonetics. **1964** R. H. ROBINS *Gen. Ling.* ii. 66 The linguist.. may have to rely on sciences other than linguistics and on unsystematized 'common sense'. **1972** L. R. PALMER *Descr. & Compar. Ling.* xiii. 300 There are few discussions of this subject [*sc.* etymology].. in modern handbooks of linguistics.

c. appositive and *Comb.*

1958 *College English* XX. 12/2 Linguistics-based metrical analysis. *Ibid.* 17/2 A few linguistics-manufactured accessories. **1965** *Canad. Jrnl. Ling.* Fall 40 The long history of the linguistics-literary study opposition.

linguistical (lɪŋˈgwɪstɪkəl), *a.* [f. LINGUISTIC + -AL[1].] = LINGUISTIC *a.*

1823 T. G. WAINEWRIGHT *Ess. & Crit.* (1880) 311 To.. garnish one's paragraphs with.. outlandish sprigs, not personally plucked from the linguistical trees. **1845** B'NESS BUNSEN in Hare *Life* II. iii. 85 A remarkable linguistical talent. **1882-3** SCHAFF *Encycl. Relig. Knowl.* III. 2308 In this dictionary he does not pretend to give a linguistical explanation of the words occurring in the N.T.

linˈguistically, *adv.* [f. prec. + -LY[2].] In regard or relation to language or linguistics.

1860 MARSH *Eng. Lang.* xxii. 473 It is also linguistically important because [etc.]. **1865** MAX MÜLLER *Chips* (1880) II. xxv. 267 The similarity of customs.. among races linguistically related to each other. **1876** LOWELL *Among my Bks.* Ser. II. 130 Gawain Douglas, whose translation of the Æneid is linguistically valuable. **1921** B. RUSSELL *Analysis of Mind* viii. 141 The subject.. is introduced, not because observation reveals it, but because it is linguistically convenient and apparently demanded by grammar. **1935** B. MALINOWSKI *Coral Gardens* II. VI. iv. 229 The magical word .. has got some affinity with the name which linguistically defines the relation of man as speaker to the object addressed. **1942** *Language* XVIII. 7 Non-distinctive elements.. are no more significant linguistically than is any other concurrent action of a speaker. **1956** E. H. HUTTEN *Lang. Mod. Physics* ii. 26 Truth is said to be linguistically neutral: whatever is true is true in any language. **1971** W. P. ROBINSON in W. H. Whiteley *Lang. Use & Social Change* 78 Linguistically, the code has the possibility of exploiting the full grammatical and lexical potential of the language.

linguistician (lɪŋgwɪˈstɪʃən). [See -ICIAN.] One who is versed in linguistics.

1895 E. W. FAY in *Amer. Jrnl. Philol.* XVI. 10 This identification of the earlier 'linguisticians' has been latterly abandoned. **1897** *Classical Rev.* 94 The earliest linguisticians regarded *vi* in the words for twenty as a by-form of *dvi*. **1949** *Studies in Ling.* VII. 59, I intend to use *linguistician* regularly henceforth instead of *linguist* 'worker in linguistics'. **1950** *Ibid.* VIII. 1 To one of these, *linguistician*, I not only cannot subscribe [etc.]... This meaning, exemplified by such words as *mortician* and *beautician*, implies pretentiousness rather than precision. **1954** *English Studies* XXXV. 91 In the absence of any.. description by native linguisticians, these observations by an experienced teacher of foreign students.. deserve the attention. **1967** C. L. WRENN *Word & Symbol* 7 If.. texts may be properly explained by allegory and symbolism without any exact knowledge of their language, then the English language.. may as well be left to the linguisticians.

linguistics: see LINGUISTIC B. b.

linguistry (ˈlɪŋgwɪstrɪ). *rare.* [f. LINGUIST + -RY.] Study of language.

1794 T. PAINE *Age of Reason* I. 33 But the apology that is now made for continuing to teach the dead languages, could not be the cause at first of cutting down learning to the narrow and humble sphere of linguistry. **1853** G. J. CAYLEY *Las Alforjas* II. 246 To bring down their estimate of my linguistry, I gave them a literal translation of that proverb which defines comparisons as odious.

‖**lingula** (ˈlɪŋgjʊlə). Pl. lingulæ (-liː). [L., dim. of *lingua* tongue. Cf. LIGULA.]

1. A little tongue or tongue-like part.

Now only *spec.* in *Anat.*, short for various mod.L. names of structures, as *l. fistulæ* (the epiglottis), *l. cerebelli*, etc.

1664 EVELYN *Sylva* xvi. (1679) 74 They.. make the Incision with a Chisel in the Body very neatly, in which they stick a Leaf of the Tree, as a lingula to direct it into the appendent Vessel. *a* **1734** NORTH *Life of Guilford* (1742) 298 The ingenious Mr. Hook put this Scheme of Musick into Clock-work, and made Wheels, with small *Lingulæ* in the Manner of Cogs. **1889** in *Syd. Soc. Lex.*

2. A genus of bivalve molluscs, including many fossil species; any shell of the genus.

lingula flags, micaceous flagstones and slates of N. Wales, containing the lingula in large quantities.

1836 *Penny Cycl.* V. 313/2 *Lingula* has been found in a fossil state in the inferior oolite of Yorkshire. **1851-6** WOODWARD *Mollusca* 240 Observations on the living Lingula are much wanted. **1873** DAWSON *Earth & Man* iii. 39 The Lingulæ, from the abundance of which some of the Primordial beds have received in England and Wales the name of Lingula flags.

lingular (ˈlɪŋgjʊlə(r)), *a. Anat.* [f. prec. + -AR.] Of or pertaining to a lingula.

1855 MAYNE *Expos. Lex.*, *Lingularis*, of or belonging to a little tongue: lingular. **1889** *Buck's Handbk. Med. Sci.* VIII. 126 In the child at birth the lingular folia are rounded and distinct.

lingulate (ˈlɪŋgjʊleɪt), *a.* [ad. L. *lingulāt-us*: see LINGULA and -ATE.] Tongue-shaped.

1849 HARDY in *Proc. Berw. Nat. Club* II. No. 7. 361 Antennæ with the third joint parallelogrammic, with its tip rounded (lingulate). **1863** BERKELEY *Brit. Mosses* Gloss. 312 *Lingulate*, tongue-shaped. **1881** *Nature* 4 Aug. 308 In three years.. I found exactly one hundred implements, mostly lingulate examples (a few ovate).

So **ˈlingulated**, in the same sense.

1797 *Encycl. Brit.* (ed. 3) III. 244/2 [Botany.] Lingulated, tongue-shaped.

linguo, obs. form of LINGO.

linguo-, †**lingua-**, used as combining form of L. *lingua* (the correct form would be *lingui-*) in **linguo-**, †**linguaˈdental** *a.*, of or formed by tongue and teeth; also *sb.*, a sound so formed. (Cf. DENTILINGUAL.) **linguo-**, †**linguaˈpalatal** *a.*, formed by the tongue and palate; also *sb.*

1668 WILKINS *Real Char.* III. xiv. §2. 374 M must be the first, as being Labial; N next, as being Dental; and then NG, as being Lingua-palatal. **1669** W. HOLDER *Elem. Speech* 71 T. and D. are Gingival; Th. and Dh. are Lingua-dental. *Ibid.* 138 The Labiodentals *f, v*, which as also the Linguadentals *th, dh*, he will soon learn by the method before directed. **1817** DUPONCEAU in *Trans. Amer. Philos. Soc.* (1818) I. 262 Three linguo-palatals, *lamed, ro, nim. Ibid.*, Four linguo-dentals, as *delta, tar, thick, thence.* **1828** WEBSTER, *Linguadental*, an articulation formed by the tongue and teeth.

†**linˈguosity.** *Obs.*[−0] [ad. L. *linguōsitāt-em*, f. *linguōs-us* talkative (f. *lingua* tongue): see -ITY.] Talkativeness.

1727 in BAILEY vol. II.

ˈlingworm. Also lyngorm. [ad. ON. *lyngormr* 'heatherworm'. Cf. LINDWORM.] A fabulous serpent.

1870 MAGNUSSON & MORRIS tr. *Völsunga Saga* xiii. 45 The fashion and the growth of him is even as of other lingworms. **1883** J. S. STALLYBRASS tr. *J. Grimm's Teutonic Mythol.* II. xxi. 690 The beautiful Thora Borgarhiörtr had a small lŷngorm given her, whom she placed in a casket, with gold under him. **1972** J. SIMPSON *Icelandic Folktales & Legends* iii. 103 The 'Heath Snake' mentioned here, the *lyngorm*, was a mythical creature which, like the dragon, had a particular affinity for gold.

†**lingwort.** *Obs.* [? f. LING *sb.*[2] + WORT; perh. named from the appearance of the root.] White Hellebore (*Veratrum album*).

1538 TURNER *Libellus*, Lyngwort, *Elleborum album.* **1578** LYTE *Dodoens* III. xxiv. 347 This kind of Hellebor is called .. in English White Hellebor, Neseworte, and Ling-wort. **1607** TOPSELL *Four-f. Beasts* (1658) 401 Mingle them together with Ling-wort and Pepper. **1647** LILLY *Chr. Astrol.* x. 68 The Hearbs are as followeth. The Nettle,.. Lingwort, Onions, Scammony [etc.].

lingy (ˈlɪŋɪ), *a.*[1] [f. LING *sb.*[2] + -Y[1].] Abounding in or covered with ling or heather.

1649 BLITHE *Eng. Improv. Impr.* (1653) 133 A Lingy Heath or Common. **1708** T. WARD *Eng. Ref.* IV. (1710) 103 *margin*, His Cell was upon a Lingy Moor, about two miles from Mulgrave Castle. **1845** WATSON in *Jrnl. R. Agric. Soc.* VI. I. 79 Heath land, or, what is generally termed in the North of England 'lingy land'. **1884** *Kendal Mercury & Times* 26 Sept. 2/6 Three beautiful meadow fields, which were a great contrast to the surrounding lingy land.

lingy (ˈlɪndʒɪ), *a.*[2] *dial.* In 7 lingey. [a. OF. *ligne*, *linge* thin, supple.] Limber; supple.

1674-91 RAY *N.C. Words* 44 *Lingey*; Limber. **1850** in OGILVIE. [Common in mod. dials.: see *Eng. Dial. Dict.*]

linhay (ˈlɪnɪ). *s.w. dial.* Also linn(e)y. [Of obscure origin; the first element may possibly be the stem of OE. *hlinian* LEAN *v.*] A shed or other farm building open in front, usually with a lean-to roof.

1695 *Phil. Trans.* XIX. 30 Backward in the Court there was a Linny that rested upon a wall. **1768** TOPLADY *Wks.* (1794) I. 41 The dwelling-house, the barn, the linhays, the stable, &c... were.. all in flames at once. **1800** *Chron.* in *Ann. Reg.* 25/1 Nearly the whole of the dwelling-house, offices, extensive barns, stables, linneys, &c. were consumed. **1837** COTTLE *Remin.* i. 9 The sties for their pigs, and the linnies for their cattle. **1864** T. Q. COUCH *E. Cornw. Gloss.* in *Jrnl. Roy. Inst. Cornw.* I. 17 *Linhay*, a shed consisting of a roof resting on a wall at the back, and supported in front by pillars. **1893** Q. [COUCH] *Delectable Duchy* 291 Run up to the linhay an' fetch a rope.

liniall, liniation, obs. ff. LINEAL, LINEATION.

liniel, variant of LINGEL *sb.*[1]

†**liˈnigerous,** *a. Obs.*[−0] [f. L. *līniger* (f. *līnum* flax + *-ger* bearing) + -OUS.] (See quot.)

1656 BLOUNT *Glossogr.*, *Linigerous*, that beareth flex or linnen. **1721** in BAILEY; and in mod. Dicts.

liniment (ˈlɪnɪmənt). Also 5 lynyment, (7 leniment). [ad. L. *linīment-um*, f. *linīre* to smear, anoint. Cf. F. *liniment.*]

†**1.** Something used for smearing or anointing.

c **1420** *Pallad. on Husb.* XI. 440 In lynyment ffor tonnes best doth askis of sarment. **1691** RAY *Creation* I. (1692) 139 The Bird.. compressing the Glandules, squeezes out and brings away therewith an oily Pap or Liniment, most fit and proper for the inunction of the Feathers.

2. An embrocation, usually made with oil.

1543 TRAHERON *Vigo's Chirurg., Interpr. straunge Wordes*, Liniment is an oyntment. **1593** G. HARVEY *Pierce's Super.* Wks. (Grosart) II. 252 The Artificial Liniment of Doctor Levinus Lemnius for a comely Beard. **1631** BRATHWAIT *Whimzies, Questman* 127 Leniments, emplasters and unctions. **1727** BRADLEY *Fam. Dict.* s.v. *Anemone*, Anemones.. boiled in old Wine, and apply'd in the Form of a Liniment. **1829** LYTTON *Disowned* 19 Bossolton urged the application of liniments and bandages. **1876** HARLEY *Mat. Med.* (ed. 6) 237 Liniment of Verdigris was formerly an article of the Pharmacopœia.

linin (ˈlaɪnɪn). *Chem.* Also -ine. [f. L. *līnum* flax + -IN[1].] **1.** A crystallizable bitter principle obtained from *Linum catharticum* (Purging Flax).

1852 BRANDE *Dict. Sci.* etc., Suppl., *Linine.* **1865** WATTS *Dict. Chem.* III. 700 Linin melts and decomposes when heated.

2. *Cytology* (now chiefly *Hist.*). [a. G. *linin* (F. Schwarz 1887, in *Beitr. z. Biol. d. Pflanzen* V. 9), f. Gr. λίνον (= L. *līnum*) thread.] A substance which composes the fine threads seen in interphase nuclei; a thread or network composed of this substance (see quot. 1932).

1887 *Jrnl. R. Microsc. Soc.* 979 As components of the nucleus, Schwartz [*sic*] distinguishes the following substances:—.. (3) linin and paralinin, the substance respectively of the nuclear threads, the 'nucleo-hyaloplasm' of Strasburger, and of the intermediate matrix or 'nuclear sap'. **1905** *Rep. Brit. Assoc. Adv. Sci.* 567 The nucleus contains an achromatic network—the linin—in which the chromatin granules are embedded. **1925** E. B. WILSON *Cell* (ed. 3) i. 88 The [nuclear] framework itself appears to consist of two constituents, namely, a continuous 'achromatic' basis, and of more or less discontinuous granules or clumps of 'chromatin' suspended in it... The first of these was found to be oxyphilic and was accordingly designated by Strasburger as nucleohyaloplasm, by Carnoy as the plasmatic network (composed of 'plastin') and later by Schwarz ('87) as linin, a term still in common use. **1932** C. D. DARLINGTON *Recent Adv. Cytol.* 498 *Linin*, a structural component of the nucleus. The term has been applied to the descriptions of various artefacts and has no definite meaning. **1948** W. ANDREW tr. *E. D. P. de Robertis's Gen. Cytol.* vii. 137 A fine lightly staining reticulum, the linin. **1969** BROWN & BERTKE *Textbk. Cytol.* 574/1 *Linin*, achromatic material connecting chromioles in the interphase nucleus, in contrast to only one substance, karyotin, composing the lingy land.

lininess (ˈlaɪnɪnɪs). [f. LINY *a.* + -NESS.] The condition of being liny; undue prominence of lines.

1857 *Ecclesiologist* XVIII. 169 The mouldings of these windows are.. composed mainly of a succession of bold rolls, and so entirely free from any lininess.

lining (ˈlaɪnɪŋ), *vbl. sb.*[1] Also 5-6 lynyng(e, -eng, 5-7 lyning, 6 lyenynge, 7 loyning. [f. LINE *v.*[1] + -ING[1].]

1. a. *concr.* The stuff with which garments are lined; the inner or under surface of material stitched into a coat, robe, hat, etc. for protection or warmth.

1401-2 *Durham Acc. Rolls* (Surtees) 393 In.. factura.. trium casularum cum lynynges. **1462** *Mann. & Househ. Exp.* (Roxb.) 149 For lynynge to the sayd jaket, xij.*d.* **1502** *Priv. Purse Exp. Eliz. of York* (1830) 54 Betwene the outside and the lynyng of the Quenes cloke. **1666** WOOD *Life* 26 Feb. (O.H.S.) II. 73 Loynings for my breches and pockets. **1851** *Illustr. Catal. Gt. Exhib.* 1057 Patterns of hat-linings. **1871** M. ARNOLD *Friendship's Garland* 165, I write with a bit of coal on the lining of my hat.

fig. **1588** SHAKS. *L.L.L.* v. ii. 791 As bumbast and as lining to the time. **1647** TRAPP *Marrow Gd. Authors* in *Comm. Ep.* 648 Allin had a Cardinals hat, but with so thin lining (means to support his state) that he was commonly called, *The starveling Cardinall.*

b. *pl.* Drawers; underclothing. *dial.*

1614 B. JONSON *Barth. F.* II. i, I ha' seene as fine outsides, as either o' yours, bring lowsie linings to the Brokers, ere now, twice a weeke. **1655** tr. *Com. Hist. Francion* IV. 1 His lynings hanging out of his Breeches down unto his shoes. **1669** WOOD *Life* 19 Oct. (O.H.S.) II. 174 A pair of flannill loynings, 2*s.* **1693** SOUTHERNE *Maid's Last Prayer* III. iii. 31 *L. Mal.* Drawers, my Lord, you mean. *Ld. Mal.* Jesu! no; you know I never wear Linings. **1866** T. EDMONDSTON *Gloss. Shetl. & Orkn.* s.v., I was standin' i' my bare līnins. **1894** *Hetton-le-Hole Gloss.*, *Linings*, pit-men's drawers, fastened at the knee by strings.

2. a. In extended use: Any material occurring or placed next beneath the outside one (for spec. applications see quots.).

1713 POPE *Guardian* No. 4 ¶3, I have found unvalued repositories of learning in the lining of bandboxes. **1813** EUSTACE *Italy* I. vii. 281 Some fragments of marble linings .. remain to attest the ancient magnificence of this port. **1829** *Glover's Hist. Derby* I. 61 Ironstone of black colour (Black-stone lining). **1830** LINDLEY *Nat. Syst. Bot.* p. xlvi, Placentae covering the whole lining of the carpella. **1834** *Pickering's Catalogue* 1 Biblia Sacra Hebræa... Bound in blue morocco, with morocco linings. **1834** *Cycl. Pract. Med.* III. 300/1 The lining of the abdominal muscles. **1841** BREES

Gloss. Civ. Engin., *Lining*,..a term applied to puddle laid along the bottom and upon the sloping sides of canals, whereby it prevents the water from escaping. 1859 GWILT *Encycl. Archit.* Gloss. s.v., Lining is distinguished from casing, the first being a covering in the interior of the building, whilst the latter is the covering of the exterior part of a building. 1867 SMYTH *Sailor's Word-bk.*, *Linings*, the reef-bands, leech and top linings, bunt-line cloths, and other applied pieces, to prevent the chafing of the sails. 1881 GREENER *Gun* 231 These barrels,..are welded upon a 'chemise', or plain iron lining. 1895 *Cassell's New Techn. Educ.* III. 362/1 The lining of the edges of modern dining-tables is composed of wood similar in age and character..to that of the table-top.

b. Proverb.

[1634 MILTON *Comus* 221 Was I deceived, or did a sable cloud Turn forth her silver lining on the night?] 1871 SMILES *Charac.* viii. (1876) 218 While we see the cloud, let us not shut our eyes to the silver lining. 1885 GILBERT *Mikado* II. Orig. Plays Ser. III. (1895) 198 Don't let's be down-hearted! There's a silver lining to every cloud.

3. *fig.* Contents; that which is inside.

*c*1430 LYDG. *Min. Poems* (Percy Soc.) 52 Ne hath no joie to do no besinesse, Sauff of a tankarde to pluk out the lynyng. *Ibid.* 53, 54, 55. 1580 SIDNEY *Ps.* v. iv, Mischief their soules for inmost lyning have. 1593 SHAKS. *Rich. II*, I. iv. 61 The lining of his coffers shall make Coates To decke our souldiers for these Irish warres. 1632 W. ROWLEY *Woman never vext* IV. i. 64 This leane Gentleman lookes As if he had no lining in 's guts. 1654 H. L'ESTRANGE *Chas. I* (1655) 2 And (whatever the linings were) certain it is there was such a fair outside of love..as eye scarce ever beheld the like. 1738 *Lady's Decoy* 4 in *N. & Q.* Ser. VII. VI. 205 My money is spent; Can I be content With pockets depriv'd of their lining? 1879 J. BURROUGHS *Locusts & W. Honey* (1884) 86, I was sure to return at meal-time with a lining of berries in the top of my straw hat.

4. The action of LINE *v.*¹; providing with a lining. Also ***lining up***. See LINE *v.*¹ 5.

1839 URE *Dict. Arts* 636 [The hat] is then ready for the last operations of lining and binding. 1880 ZAEHNSDORF *Bookbinding* xix. 84 Books that have been over-cast in the sewing should have rather a strong lining up. 1885 CRANE *Bookbinding* xv. 118 This stage of the lining is represented at Fig. 105. 1889 *Work* 22 June I. 234/1 The following directions do not pretend to cover the whole subject of lining up [in cabinet-making]. 1895 ZAEHNSDORF *Sh. Hist. Bookbinding* Gloss. 26 *Lining-up*, *i.e.*, glueing the back to receive the necessary paper, linen, or soft leather before the final cover goes on.

5. *attrib.*, as ***lining cloth***, ***paper***, ***piece***; **lining side**, the inside or under side.

1585 POLWART *Flyting w. Montgomerie* 566 With laidly lips, and lyning side turned out. *c*1860 H. STUART *Seaman's Catech.* 45 On the after part of the sail is a lining cloth for receiving the chafe of the tops. 1880 ZAEHNSDORF *Bookbinding* Gloss., *Lining Papers*, the coloured or marbled papers at each end of the volume. 1889 *Work* 22 June I. 234/2 The lining pieces will be of..3-in. width. 1938 *Burlington Mag.* July 34/2 Pasted inside [a hanging food cupboard] are the remains of a seventeenth-century lining-paper. 1962 F. T. DAY *Introd. to Paper* viii. 87 Rolls of lining papers of all kinds consume a large volume of paper in many grades.

lining ('laɪnɪŋ), *vbl. sb.*² [f. LINE *v.*² + -ING¹.] The action of LINE *v.*²

1. Arranging in line, alignment (chiefly *Mil.*). Also ***lining-up***.

1598 BARRET *Theor. Warres* III. ii. 48 That kind of lining which is vsed in placing a pike and a shot. *Ibid.*, Lyning of battels with shot or bowes. 1632 SHERWOOD, A Lining (or making straight by a line) a thing drawne by line, *alignement*. 1796 *Instr. & Reg. Cavalry* (1813) 50 The looking and lining of the soldier is always towards that point. *Ibid.*, By the men's lining themselves to one hand (inwards). 1940 *Chambers's Techn. Dict.* 503/2 *Lining-up*, the operation of arranging the bearings of an engine crank-shaft, etc. in perfect alignment. 1959 W. S. SHARPS *Dict. Cinematogr.* 107/1 *Lining up*, the setting of camera or other controls, in order to obtain a correctly framed picture. 1967 E. CHAMBERS *Photolitho-Offset* v. 51 Modern layout and lining-up tables are in many respects similar to stripping benches or shiners, with straight edges often in the form of steel rules, and micrometer-adjustable.

2. a. The use of the measuring line or of a stretched cord for alignment.

1823 CRABBE *Technol. Dict.*, *Lining*, the act of marking the length, breadth, or depth of any piece of timber, according to instruction and design, by a cord rubbed with red or white chalk. 1825 J. NICHOLSON *Operat. Mechanic* 625 When the slater has finished the eaves, he strains a line on the face of the upper slates... This lining and laying is continued close to the ridge of the roof. 1860 *Eng. & For. Mining Gloss.* (Newcastle Terms), *Lining*, dialling or surveying underground.

b. In Scottish royal burghs: The authoritative fixing of the boundaries of burghal properties. Now usually short for ***decree of lining***, the permission granted by a Dean of Guild to erect or alter a building according to specified conditions. Before the institution of Dean of Guild Courts, this permission had to be obtained from the Chancery, the instrument being called a ***brieve of lining***.

1574 *Burgh Rec. Glasgow* (1832) 11 The quhilk day the thre Baillies and ane parte of þe counsale past to visie and decyde þe questione of Lyneyng and nyᵗbourheid betuix Thomas Crawfurd..and maister Dauid Conynghame. 1681 VISCT. STAIR *Instit. Law Scot.* IV. iii. §13 (1693) 554 The third Unretourable Brieve, is, the Brieve of Lyning, which is of this Tenor. 1888 *Cases Crt. Session* 4th Ser. XVI. 259 If, for instance, it was proposed to set up a blubber or a glue work in one of the divisions of Princes Street, the Dean of Guild might refuse a lining because [etc.]. 1898 *N.B. Daily Mail* 23 Sept. 3 This year..649 linings having been granted at a valuation of £2,106,760.

3. Tracing of lines. ***lining out***: see quot. 1823.

1823 P. NICHOLSON *Pract. Build.* 587 Lining-out; drawing lines on a piece of timber, &c. so as to cut it into boards, planks, or other figures. 1839 W. A. CHATTO *Wood Engraving* viii. 663 Some wood engravers are but too apt to pride themselves on the delicacy of their lining. 1869 SIR E. REED *Shipbuild.* viii. 144 When the lining-out had been completed the beam-arms were punched out.

4. The giving out of a hymn (by the precentor) line by line. Also ***lining out***.

1863 S. L. J. *Life in South* I. xvii. 355 Next follows a hymn of alternate singing and 'lining'. 1883 G. W. CURTIS in *Harper's Mag.* Dec. 14/2 The ancient leading and lining of the hymn gave way to modern psalmody. 1894 N. DICKSON *Auld Sc. Precentor* 20 This practice was called 'lining out', or 'reading the line'. 1917 *Encycl. Relig. & Ethics* IX. 27/2 In the ordinary parish churches metrical Psalms only were sung. 'Lining out' by the 'clerk', or precentor, was the order, singing in unison without organ accompaniment the rule. 1968 P. OLIVER *Screening Blues* ii. 82 'Lining out' in which a lead singer paces a line and the congregation follows with the same line or a refrain response with a linear reply.

5. Fishing with a line.

1833 J. V. C. SMITH *Fishes Massachusetts* 262 It [Weak-Fish] is taken both by lining and seining. 1897 LD. MAYO in *19th Cent.* Aug. 199 *note*, Cross-lining, a mode of fishing with two boats; a long line dressed with flies is dragged between each boat.

6. *attrib.*: **lining-gauge**, † **lining-stick**, a type-founder's tool for testing the exact evenness of the bottom serifs of the letters.

1683 MOXON *Mech. Exerc.*, *Printing* xvii. ⁋2 The Lining-Stick is about two Inches long for small Letters.

†**lining**, *vbl. sb.*³ In 7 ligning. [f. LINE *v.*³ + -ING¹.] The action of LINE *v.*³

1611 COTGR., *Alignement*,..the ligning of a bitch.

'**lining**, *ppl. a.* [f. LINE *v.*² + -ING².] That lines or forms a lining.

1853 MARKHAM *Skoda's Auscult.* 265 Catarrhal inflammation of the lining-membrane of the bronchial tubes.

lining, obs. form of LINEN.

linition (laɪ'nɪʃən). [ad. late L. *linītiōn-em*, n. of action f. *linīre* to smear, anoint.] The application of a liniment.

1889 in *Syd. Soc. Lex.*

‖**linitis** (lɪ'naɪtɪs). *Path.* [mod.L., f. Gr. λίν-ον flax + -ITIS: see quot.] 'Inflammation of the areolar tissue which surrounds the blood-vessels of the stomach' (*Syd. Soc. Lex.* 1889).

1859 BRINTON *Dis. Stomach* v. 310 Cirrhotic inflammation or plastic linitis. *Ibid.* 321 *note*, I would suggest that the inflammation of the filamentous network of areolar tissue..might be well expressed by some such word as *linitis* (from the Homeric λίνον, rete ex lino factum). *Ibid.* 331 Suppuration of the areolar tissue, or suppurative linitis.

link (lɪŋk), *sb.*¹ Forms: 1 hlinc, 3 lynk, 5 *pl.* linx, 6 lynck, 6– link. See also LINCH. [OE. *hlinc*, possibly a derivative, with *k* suffix, of the root *hlin-* to LEAN.] **a.** Rising ground; a ridge or bank. *Obs.* exc. *dial.* **b.** *pl.* (*Sc.*) Comparatively level or gently undulating sandy ground near the sea-shore, covered with turf, coarse grass, etc. **c.** *pl.* The ground on which golf is played, often resembling that described in b. In mod. usage sometimes treated as a singular.

931 in Earle *Land Charters* 166 Ðonne norð ondlong ðæs hlinces. *c*1000 *Phœnix* 25 (Gr.) Ne dene ne dalu..hlæwas ne hlincas. *c*1250 *Newminster Cartul.* (1878) 57 In lez Lynkys apud Blythemowth. 1487 *Extracts Aberd. Reg.* (1844) I. 42 No catall sale haf pastour of gyrss apone the lynkis. 1514 *Ibid.* 93 That euery man compeir upoun the linx efter noun. 1545 *Ibid.* 221 To find fiue personis..to vaiche thair blokhouse, linkis, and havin nychtlie. 1583 STOCKER *Civ. Warres Lowe C.* III. 86 There were..placed..in the linkes..about two hundred horse. 1649 BP. GUTHRIE *Mem.* (1702) 48 The Marquiss came ashoar..to the Links of Barnbugall at midnight. 1697 DALLAS *Stiles* 595 The saids Lands..with the Castles, Towers,..Links, Cunningares, and whole remanent Pertinentis of the samine. 1728 in Burton *Lives Lovat & Culloden* (1847) 330 This day,..I got the better of my son at the gouf in Musselburgh links. 1769 *De Foe's Tour Gt. Brit.* (ed. 7) IV. 70 Many Millions of Trees are planted in a sandy Down, or Links, as they call them here, between the House and the Sea. 1836 W. D. COOPER *Gloss. Provinc. Sussex*, *Link*, a green or wooded bank, always on the side of a hill between two pieces of cultivated land. 1853 G. JOHNSTON *Nat. Hist. E. Bord.* I. 8 A narrow strip of links formed of sand knolls fixed by means of bent and similar plants. 1861 H. B. FARNIE *Fife Coast* 115 The links lying at the house door, is a very famous one in the annals of golf. 1873 BURTON *Hist. Scot.* VI. lxxii. 259 The Scots army was paraded on the links of Leith by..Leslie. 1882 STEVENSON (*title*) The Pavilion on the Links. 1890 H. G. HUTCHINSON *Golf* xiii. 311 The links of St. Andrews..holds premier place. *Ibid.* 317 It is a good links. 1904 *Daily Chron.* 20 Aug. 9/5 On a suburban links. 1919 WODEHOUSE *Damsel in Distress* x. 122 His first act..had been to ascertain whether there was a links in the neighbourhood. 1933 H. S. COLT in M. A. F. Sutton *Golf Courses* 124 When..the links is stretched..an excellent test of golf is provided. 1972 R. QUIRK et al. *Gram. Contemp. Eng.* iv. 181 The following nouns invariably end in *-s*: alms..innings..links (..a golf-links).

link (lɪŋk), *sb.*² Forms: 5 *pl.* lynx, 5–6 lynk(e, 5–7 linke, 6 lenk, lyncke, 6–7 linck(e, 6– link. [a. ON. *hlenk-r (Icel. *hlekk-r*, OSw. *lænker*, mod.Sw. *länk*, Da. *lænke*):—OTeut. type **hlaŋkio-z*; cogn. w. OE. *hlęncan* pl., armour, OHG. *lancha* FLANK, loins, bend of the body (MHG. *lanke*), whence MHG. *gelenke* (collective) flexible parts of the body, mod.G. *gelenk* articulation, joint, link.]

1. a. One of the series of rings or loops which form a chain. †Also, formerly, *pl.* chains, fetters.

*c*1450 HOLLAND *Howlat* 606 That no creatur Of lokis nor lynx mycht louss worth a lence. *c*1470 HENRYSON *Mor. Fab.* 2433 in *Anglia* IX. 476 Thinkand thairthrow to lok him in his linkis. 1505 *Nottingham Rec.* III. 100 Duo paria de lenks; duo paria de guyvies de ferro. 1535 COVERDALE *Ps.* cxlix. 8 To bynde their kynges in cheynes, & their nobles with lynckes of yron. 1555 EDEN *Decades* 163 Two cheynes of golde, wherof the one conteyned viii. lynkes. *a*1592 H. SMITH *Serm.* (1637) 763 Sins follow one another like linkes in a Chaine. 1601 SHAKS. *Jul. C.* I. iii. 94 Nor ayre lesse Dungeon, nor strong Linkes of Iron, Can be retentiue to the strength of spirit. 1671 MILTON *Samson* 1410, I praise thy resolution, doff these links. 179. BURNS *The lass that made the bed to me*, Her hair was like the links o' gowd. 1796 H. HUNTER tr. *St. Pierre's Stud. Nat.* (1799) III. 17 All truths run into one another like the links of a chain. 1816 BYRON *Pris. Chillon* xi, My broken chain With links unfasten'd did remain. 1879 FROUDE *Cæsar* ix. 93 The strength of a chain is no greater than the strength of its first link.

†**b.** *sing.* A chain. Also *transf.* and *fig.* *Obs.*

1570 LEVINS *Manip.* 138/14 A linke, chaine, *vinculum*. 1609 BIBLE (Douay) *Isa.* v. 18 Woe unto you that draw iniquitie in cordes of vanitie, and sin as the linke of a wayne. 1704 SWIFT *Batt. Bks.* Misc. (1711) 244 Fasten'd to each other like a Link of Gally-slaves, by a light Chain. 1730 —— *Pulteney's Answ. Walpole* Wks. 1841 II. 430/2 A minister..whose whole management hath been a continued link of ignorance, blunders, and mistakes in every article.

c. One of the divisions, each being a hundredth part, of the chain used in surveying (see CHAIN *sb.* 9); used as a measure of length.

In Gunter's chain of 4 poles length (the one in general use) the link is 7·92 inches. In the U.S. engineers and some surveyors use a chain of 100 links of 1 foot each.

1661 S. PARTRIDGE *Double Scale Proportion* 42 Let the breadth given be 7 chains, 50 links. 1828 HUTTON *Course Math.* II. 80 [This] gives 555152 square links, or 5 acres, 2 roods, 8 perches.

d. Short for ***sleeve-link***.

1807 *Self Instructor* 120 [Bill of Parcels] Card of eight points crystal links *ol.* 14*s.* *od.* 1895 *Army & Navy Coöp. Soc. Price List*, Studs, links, solitaires.

e. ***to let out the links***, to act with more power, to put more into something.

1839 *Spirit of Times* 6 Apr. 54/2 The horses came to the post... At this time Oscar began to let out a few additional links, and with a desperate rush parted company with Dandy, and won the heat handily. 1868 H. WOODRUFF *Trotting Horse* xxxiv. 282 Lancet..in the third heat, let out the links in such a manner that he trotted it in 2 m. 25¼ s. 1880 P. H. BURNETT *Recoll. Old Pioneer* 110 [The buffaloes] let out a few more links, and ran much faster. 1942 *Dict. Amer. Eng.* III. 1429/1 *To let out links*, to make increased exertion or effort.

2. Something looped, or forming part of a chain-like arrangement. **a.** A loop; a segment of a cord, etc.; a lock of hair. In *Angling*, one of the segments of which a hair-line is composed. *Mil.* (see quot. 1802¹).

*c*1440 *Jacob's Well* 3 Be þe wyndas of þi mynde, wyth þis roop made myȝty in thre lynkes schal be turnyd vp þe bokett of þi desyre. 1496 *Fysshynge w. Angle* (1883) 12 Whan ye haue as many of the lynkys as ye suppose wol suffyse for the length of a lyne: thenne must ye knytte theym togyder wyth a water knotte or elles a duchys knotte. *c*1515 *Cocke Lorell's B.* 12 Some made knottes of lynkes endes, Some the stay rope suerly byndes. 1597 SHAKS. *2 Hen. IV*, v. i. 23 Sir, a new linke to the Bucket must needes bee had. *a*1613 J. DENNYS *Secr. Angling* I. xi. B 2 b, The linke that holds your Hooke to hang vpon. 1653 WALTON *Angler* iv. 108 The line should not exceed, especially for three or four links towards the hook, I say, not exceed three or four haires. 1802 C. JAMES *Milit. Dict.*, *Links*, in the art of war, are distinct reins, or thongs of leather used by the cavalry to link their horses together, when they dismount, that they may not disperse. 1802 DANIEL *Rur. Sports* II. 149 In the making lines, every hair in every link should be equally big, round, and even. *a*1825 *Twa Sisters* xix. in Child *Ballads* I. 135/2 You'll tak three links of my yellow hair. 1880 *Plain Hints Needlework* 117 We learn to say a stitch in needlework, a loop or link in knitting.

†**b.** Applied to the joints of the body. *Obs.*

*c*1530 REDFORDE *Play Wit & Sci.* (Shaks. Soc.) 8 Thes jontes, thes lynkes, Be ruffe, and halfe rustye. 1818 HOGG *Brownie of Bodsbeck* xii. I. 278 There's the weight of a millstane on aboon the links o' my neck. *Ibid.* xiv. II. 21 He had as mony links an' wimples in his tail as an eel.

c. One of the divisions of a chain of sausages or black puddings. (Chiefly *pl.*) Now *dial.* Also ***links of love***; (dial.) ***link-hide***, ***-meat***.

*c*1440 *Promp. Parv.* 306/1 Lynke, or sawcistre, *hilla*. *a*1529 SKELTON *E. Rummyng* 443 Some podynges and lynkes. 1611 COTGR., *Andouille*, a linke, or chitterling. 1688 R. HOLME *Armoury* III. 83/1 Links, a kind of Pudding, the skin being filled with Pork Flesh..and tied up at distances. *a*1791 GROSE *Olio* (1796) 191 In Suffolk black puddings made in guts are called links. 1822 LAMB *Elia* Ser. I. *Chimney-Sweepers*, Reserving the lengthier links for the seniors. *a*1825 R. FORBY *Vocab. E. Anglia* (1830) II. 197 *Link*,..a sausage... We call two together a *latch of links*. In some other counties, a far more correct expression is used, 'a *link* of sausages'. 1869 R. B. PEACOCK *Gloss. Lonsdale* 51/2 *Links*, black puddings. 1891 'H. HALIBURTON' *Ochil Idylls* 133 An' links o' puddin's, black to see, An' yowe-milk kebbuck. 1895 W. RYE *Gloss. E. Anglia* 129 *Link hides*, sausage skins, the intestines of a pig prepared and stuffed... *Link-meat*, mince-meat. 1922 JOYCE *Ulysses* 58 Shiny links packed with forcemeat fed his gaze. 1942 *Weekly Telegraph*

(Sheffield) 28 Nov. 10/1 A war-time member of the naval service sends the following glossary,..*links of love*, sausages. **1962** GRANVILLE *Dict. Sailors' Slang* 71 *Links of love*, sausages. Cf. *Bags of Mystery* and *Mystery Torpedoes*.

d. *pl.* Windings of a stream; also, the ground lying along such windings. *Sc.*

?*a* **1700** in Nimmo *Hist. Stirlingsh.* (1777) 440 The lairdship of the bonny Links of Forth, Is better than an Earldom in the North. **17..** *Rattling Roaring Willie* i. in Scott *Last Minstr.* Note lxiv, In the links of Ousenam water They fand him sleeping sound. **1810** SCOTT *Lady of L.* II. xxx, The Links of Forth shall hear the knell. **1835** W. IRVING *Tour Prairies* xxxiii. Crayon Misc. (1863) 183 We wandered for some time among the links made by this winding stream.

3. a. A connecting part, whether in material or immaterial sense; a thing (*occas.* a person) serving to establish or maintain a connexion; a member of a series or succession; a means of connexion or communication. ***missing link***: see MISSING *ppl. a.*

a **1548** HALL *Chron., Hen. VIII*, 133 A convenient mariage..whiche should be a lincke necessary, to knit together the realme of Scotlande and England. *a* **1575** GASCOIGNE *Deuise Maske*, Posies *Flowers* liii, Whose brother had like wise your daughter tane to wife, And so by double lynkes enchaynde themselues in louers life. **1667** MILTON *P.L.* IX. 914, I feel The Link of Nature draw me: Flesh of Flesh, Bone of my Bone thou art. **1712** POPE *Spect.* No. 408 ¶4 Man seems to be placed as the middle Link between Angels and Brutes. **1732** BERKELEY *Alciphr.* II. §1 Being able to see no further than one link in a chain of consequences. **1803** T. WINTERBOTTOM *Sierra Leone* I. xii. 202 The connecting link between the homo sapiens and his supposed progenitor the oran outang. **1822** LAMB *Elia* Ser. I. *Distant Correspondents*, A pun, and its recognitory laugh, must be co-instantaneous... A moment's interval, and the link is snapped. **1836** MARRYAT *Japhet* lvi, I had severed the link between myself and my former condition. **1865** R. W. DALE *Jew. Temp.* xx. (1877) 229 Every link in his argument gives way. **1874** L. STEPHEN *Hours in Library* (1892) I. ix. 302 He is a connecting link between two widely different phases of thought. **1905** H. W. NEVINSON *Bks. & Personalities* 172 Link by link from its small beginning we see the fateful chain of character wrought out. **1928** *New Ventures in Broadcasting* (B.B.C.) iv. 36 A link might be established with local groups. *Ibid.* App. B. 104 There is a very close link between the broadcasting company 'Ravag' and the Vienna Society for Popular Education. **1948** *Internat. Road Federation London Bull.* July–Dec. 9/1 When that is done the first link in the United States of Europe will have been forged. **1968** *Times* 19 Feb. 6/6 The contrast between most backbench speakers and the highly professional commentators who did the links was sharp. **1975** *Sunday Times* 23 Feb. 15/3 The major Press conference announcing the link between the kidnapping and the Dudley shooting produced..more than 700 lines of inquiry.

b. 'Any intermediate rod or piece transmitting motive power from one part of a machine to another'. Also = *link-motion* (in recent Dicts.).

1825 J. NICHOLSON *Operat. Mechanic* 30 And E [is] a link to couple the pin A and the crank D together, so that motion may be communicated to the shaft C.

c. *Math.* (See quot. 1894.)

1866 CAYLEY in *Coll. Math. Papers* (1892) V. 521 The ordinary singularities of a plane curve would thus be the node, the cusp, the link, and the flex. **1874** SYLVESTER in *Proc. Roy. Instit.* VII. 182 First conceive a rhomb or diamond formed by four equal links joined to one another. **1894** CAYLEY in *Coll. Math. Papers* (1897) XIII. 506 It will be convenient to speak of the line joining the two given points as the link.

d. *Mus.* (See quot.)

1880 STAINER *Composition* §108. 90 When it is desired to unite two sections by a musical progression of one or more bars,..the added portion is considered as external to the rhythmic form, and has been appropriately termed a link.

e. A means of travel or transport established between two particular places.

1869 *Bradshaw's Railway Manual* XXI. 115 The use of the intervening link from Askerne to Knottingley..is also permanently secured. **1928** *Econ. Geogr.* IV. 221 A river link ..occurs between Tura and Tavda... These links are characteristic of undeveloped regions. **1934** *Highways & Bridges* 10 July 4/1 The opening of this important section.. will prove..a road link of the greatest value. **1950** *Internat. Road Federation London Bull.* Jan. 10/2 A ferry link will cross Cabot Strait. **1961** *Assessment Highway Requirements S. Wales & Monmouthshire* (British Road Federation) 19 It is advised that the link between Haverfordwest..and Milford Haven..should be widened to provide a single 3-lane carriageway. **1975** *Vogue* 1 Mar. 139/2 (Advt.), Air-link services via Barcelona, Genoa, Marseilles.

f. A means of telecommunication established between two particular points.

1911 *World's Work* XVIII. 578/2 Signals had been flashed through the air from Canada to Great Britain and..the Atlantic was spanned by a new and invisible link. **1926** *Encycl. Brit.* III. 1047/2 The superheterodyne method..is sometimes used for the 'wireless link' between studio and transmitting station in place of the land-line. **1928** *Daily Tel.* 23 Oct. 8/3 President Coolidge, speaking over the radio-link between White House and the workshop of the great inventor, lauded Mr. Edison as the embodiment of the finest traditions of American citizenship. **1957** *B.B.C. Handbk.* 59 The vision signals from remote outside broadcast points are carried back to the main television network by BBC microwave or VHF radio links. **1962** A. NISBETT *Technique Sound Studio* i. 18 The links between the various centres may be landlines or radio links. **1964** J. K. S. JOWETT in F. J. D. Taylor *Goonhilly Project* 2 A broadband link to the inland network..is used for demonstration purposes—in particular, transatlantic interchange of television programmes. **1972** *Sci. Amer.* Feb. 15/1 Microwaves do not bend with the curvature of the earth, so that for long links it is necessary to use repeaters that receive, amplify and retransmit the signal.

g. [tr. Russ. *zvenó*.] The name of a small labour unit on a collective farm in the U.S.S.R. Hence ***link leader***; **link system**, a system of organizing collective farming into links.

1939 L. E. HUBBARD *Econ. Soviet Agric.* xvii. 165 Each brigade was further subdivided into a number of detachments known as *svena* or links, often consisting of relations or members of families living in close proximity. **1950** *Times* 22 Feb. 3/5 Mr. A. A. Andreev..was said to have encouraged during the past 10 years the 'link' system of labour, which..is less effective..than the..'brigade' system. The article blamed the 'link' system for a shortfall in grain and sugar beet deliveries. **1950** *Soviet Studies* I. 261 Piece-work for individuals and small groups was introduced and the work of the link came to be planned... 'Link', the smaller regular working group of collective farm members (averaging about ten people). Several 'links' make a 'brigade'. *Ibid.* 290 Much benefit was derived from.. consultations of link leaders. **1958** R. D. LAIRD *Collective Farming Russ.* IV. ix. 125 As a result of the link system, labor discipline amounted to a major problem. *Ibid.* xi. 154 The brigade leader has a much greater opportunity to effect 'labor-discipline' than did the link leader. **1965** *Economist* 18 Dec. 1283/1 The ' links' are a veiled compromise between the American type of large-scale farming and the Soviet collective method.

h. In Hockey and in Association and Rugby Football = LINKMAN² b (*c*). Also *attrib.*

In some examples not a clearly distinguishable technical term.

1958 PELMEAR & MORPURGO *Rugby Football* VIII. 319 Next came the innovation of the stand-off half, thereby making two links. **1962** G. GREEN in B. Glanville *Footballer's Compan.* II. 209 Didi, floating about mysteriously in midfield, was always the master link. **1963** *Rugby World* June 24/3 Which is preferable—the fly-half as a link or as a tactical general and spearhead in attack? *Ibid.* 25/2 Neither ..is primarily in the 'link' category. **1966** *Hockey Coaching* (Hockey Assoc.) II. 111 The half-back line is the link between the forwards and backs. **1969** B. JAMES *England v. Scotland* x. 233 The superiority of Baxter and Law, the Scottish midfield link players, over their English counterparts. **1970** *Cape Times* 28 Oct. 26/3 Finch has improved considerably since he was moved to right-back after filling the left-back and link positions. **1971** *Times* 15 Feb. 9/1 Rest were handicapped by Purdy, playing at link, with a hand which became increasingly painful.

†**4.** ***in link***: in union or connexion. *Obs.*

1581 MULCASTER *Positions* xli. (1887) 232 Seeing the soule and bodye ioyne so freindly in lincke.

†**5.** (See quot.) *Obs.*$^{-0}$

1706 PHILLIPS (ed. Kersey), *Link*,..Also a thin Plate of Metal to solder with.

6. A machine for linking or joining together the loops of fabrics.

1892 [see LINKER].

7. *attrib.* and *Comb.*, as ***link-belt***, ***-chain***, ***pattern***; **link-block** *Steam-engine*, the block actuated by the link-motion and giving motion to a valve-stem; **link buttons**, a pair of buttons linked by a thread, etc.; **link-lever**, 'the reversing lever of a locomotive' (1875 Knight *Dict. Mech.*); **link-motion**, (*a*) *Steam-engine*, a valve-gear for reversing the motion of the engine, etc., consisting of two eccentrics and their rods, which give motion to a slide-valve by means of a 'link'; (*b*) *Geom.*, a linkage in which all the points describe definite curves in the same plane or in parallel planes (*Cent. Dict.*); **link plate**, a plate with the staple of a lock attached, for fastening down upon a surface; **link road**, a road serving to link two or more major roads or centres; **link rod**, (*a*) a rod which joins the levers on the steered stub axles of a motor vehicle; (*b*) each of the rods which connect pistons to wrist pins on the master rod in a radial internal-combustion engine; **link-staff** *Surveying*, = *offset-staff* (see OFFSET); **link-stud** = 1 d; **link-structure** *Math.*, a linkage or link-work; **link-verb** = COPULA 1; **link-word**, any part of speech performing a linking function; **link-work**, (*a*) work composed of or arranged in links; (*b*) see quot. 1855; (*c*) *Geom.*, a system of lines, pivoted together so as to rotate about one another (for Sylvester's restricted use see quot. 1874); **link-worming**, protection of a rope by 'worming' it with chains (1867 Smyth *Sailor's Word-bk.*).

1884 *Cassell's Family Mag.* Feb. 188/2 An endless *link-belt or chain. **1876** *Sci. American* XXXV. 230/1 Improved *Link Block for Locomotives,..an improved adjustable link block, claimed to fit tightly in the link and to wear it equally. [**1834** E. W. BRAYLEY *Graphic & Hist. Illustrator* 125 Linked Cloak Buttons..., of silver, and exactly alike.] **1895** *Montgomery Ward Catal.* 170 All our cuff buttons, except *link buttons, have patent lever backs. *Ibid.*, (*caption*) Gold filled, engraved link buttons... $1.10. **1964** *McCall's Sewing* ii. 30/2 *Link buttons*, two flat buttons held together with several threads covered with blanket stitches. Used as cuff links. **1839** URE *Dict. Arts* 157 The links are then to be riveted on the pivots, each pivot receiving two of them, and thus holding the hinge together, on the principle of a *link-chain or hinge. **1849–50** WEALE *Dict. Terms*, **Link-motion*, a new apparatus for reversing steam-engines. **1875** BEDFORD *Sailor's Pocket Bk.* vi. (ed. 2) 211 Starting ahead or astern is effected by link motion. **1877** [see *link-structure*]. **1877** J. A. EWING in *Encycl. Brit.* XXII. 505/1 In Stephenson's link-motion—the earliest and still the most usual form—the link is [etc.]. **1901** *Scotsman* 1 Mar. 5/5 A *link pattern chain. **1842** J. DONE *Tuner's Comp.* (ed. 4) 15 Lock, key, escutcheon, *link plate... The link plate is let into that part of the case corresponding with the lock. **1934** *Highways & Bridges* 24 July 5/2 New *link road from the Bedford–Hitchin road..to the Bedford–Luton road;..a 60 ft. link road from the Bedford–Ampthill road..to the Luton road. **1948** T. SHARP *Oxf. Replanned* 9 The construction of the new Southern By-pass and the important link-road approximately along the line to Roman Way will make it even better for industrial purposes. **1961** *Assessment Highway Requirements S. Wales & Monmouthshire* (British Road Federation) 18 A similar problem exists on the link road between Treharris and Cardiff. **1970** *Milestones* Spring 35/1 A..link road from the M23 to the A23 near Gatwick airport will start from a roundabout over the motorway at Burstow. **1972** *Times* 26 Oct. 3/1 It was the eighth of 32 spans that make up the M4 link road bridge. **1925** W. DEEPING *Sorrell & Son* xv. 137 The driver of the lorry..was..repeating the same words over and over again. .. 'The bloomin' *link-rod dropped. I can't think 'ow it came to 'appen. Just when they was passin' me—too. The bloomin' link-rod.' **1928** A. L. DYKE *Aircraft Engine Instructor* ii. 14 The master rod connects to the top or No. 1 piston. The other eight pistons are connected to the eight link rods, the other ends of which bear against bronze bushings on the knuckle pins. **1929** H. T. RUTTER *Mod. Motors* II. ix. 333 (*caption*) Front axle of Daimler, showing link rod. **1946** J. W. VALE *Aviation Mechanic's Engine Manual* i. 16 The master rod forms a bearing on the main crankpin and the remaining link rods form a bearing on the knuckle pin arrangement of the master rod assembly. **1970** K. BALL *Fiat 600, 600D Autobook* ix. 108/1 Remove the cotter pins from the nuts securing the head pins of both link rod and nearside track rod. **1828** HUTTON *Course Math.* II. 59 At every chain length, lay the offset-staff, or *link-staff, down in the slope of the chain. **1877** KEMPE *How to draw a straight line* 6 When such a combination is pivoted in any way to a fixed base, the motion of points on it not being necessarily confined to fixed paths, the *link-structure is called a 'link-work': a 'link-work' in which the motion of every point is in some definite path being..termed a 'link-motion'. **1881** C. E. TURNER in *Macm. Mag.* XLIV. 307 Two gold English *link-studs. **1892** H. SWEET *New Eng. Gram.* I. 94 We call such verbs **link-verbs*, because they serve to connect the predicate with its subject. *To be* is a pure link-verb, that is, a pure form-word, devoid of independent meaning. **1933** O. JESPERSEN *Essent. Eng. Gram.* (1939) xiii. 126 It..serves to connect this with the subject as what is technically termed a *copula* or *link-verb*. **1963** F. T. VISSER *Hist. Syntax* I. iii. 191 Link-verbs like *to abide*..differ from the link-verb *to be* in that their original meaning is not entirely lost. **1871** EARLE *Philol. Eng. Tongue* (1880) §520 Under the title of *Link-word I comprise all that vague and flitting host of words..commonly called Prepositions and Conjunctions. **1892** H. SWEET *New Eng. Gram.* I. 95 Other link-words, while having the same grammatical function of connecting subject and predicate, have also definite meanings of their own. **1947** W. S. ALLEN *Living Eng. Struct.* 235 'Who', 'what', 'which',..etc., are very important as link-words. **1968** *Brit. Med. Bull.* XXIV. 200/2 The computer compiles lists of the words used, and nouns, qualifying words and 'link' words can be sorted out by human intervention before retrieval programs are written. **1530** TINDALE *Ex.* xxviii. 14 Thou shalt make hokes off golde and two cheynes off fine golde: *lynkeworke and wrethed. **1855** OGILVIE, Suppl., *Link-work*, the general term applied in mechanics to that species of gearing by which motions are transmitted by links, and not by wheels or bands. **1874** SYLVESTER in *Proc. Roy. Instit.* VII. 182 *note*, A link-work consists of an odd number of bars, a linkage of an even number.

link (lɪŋk), *sb.*³ Also 6–7 linck(e, lynck(e, linke, lynk(e. [Of obscure origin.

The conjecture that it is a corruption of *lint-* in *lintstock*, LINSTOCK (from LUNT) has little plausibility. Perhaps the likeliest hypothesis is that the word is identical with prec.; the material for torches may have been made in long strings, and divided into 'links' or segments. A not impossible source would be the monastic Latin *linchinus* (one instance in Du Cange, others in Diefenbach), an altered form (by a process common in med.L.) of *lichinus*, glossed 'weke' (wick) and 'meche' (match) in the 15th c. (see Wr.-Wülck.), a. Gr. λύχνος light, lamp.]

1. A torch made of tow and pitch (? sometimes of wax or tallow), formerly much in use for lighting people along the streets.

1526 *Househ. Ord.* (1790) 163 The Secretary..[to have] from the last of October unto the first day of Aprill three lynckes by the weeke. **1530** PALSGR. 239/2 Lynke, *torche*. **1580–1** *Act 23 Eliz.* c. 8 §3 Any maner of..Wares wrought with Waxe, as in Lightes Staftorches..Lynckes Greene Waxe Red Waxe or any other worke..wrought with Waxe. **1591** FRAUNCE *Emanuell* 43 in *Fuller Worthies Misc.* (1871) III, Lynkes gaue light to the night, and causd their swoords to be glistring. **1596** SHAKS. *1 Hen. IV*, III. iii. 48. **1608** MIDDLETON *Fam. Love* III. iii, Give me my book, Club, put out thy link, and come behind us. **1609** HOLLAND *Amm. Marcell.* XVIII. vi. 114 To set upon an horse backe a burning lampe,..that the Persians weening it to be a tallow linke giving light before the captaine softly marching, might take their course that way especially. **1685** WOOD *Life* 13 Apr., Twenty-four lyncks burning on Merton Coll. Tower between 9 and 10 at night. **1706** *Lond. Gaz.* No. 4280/5 Whoever shall..presume to..sell any such Links not weighing 14 l. and upwards to the Dozen..will be prosecuted. **1755** J. SHEBBEARE *Lydia* (1769) II. 245 Frank ..without answering, dashed his link in the villain's face, and bade the chairman go on. **1813** COLERIDGE *Remorse* IV. i, Our links burn dimly. **1840** DICKENS *Barn. Rudge* iii, His face and figure were full in the strong glare of the link. **1852** THACKERAY *Esmond* II. ix, Though the links were there, the link-boys had run away.

b. A link-boy.

1845 DISRAELI *Sybil* (1863) 255 'I think I should like to be a link, Jim,' said the young one. **1846** MRS. GORE *Sk. Eng. Charac.* (1852) 64 Corney is sovereign of the elective monarchy of Links.

†**2.** ? The material of 'links' used as blacking.

Johnson suggests that in the Shaks. passage the word may mean 'lamp-black'. The quot. from Pomet may possibly throw light on Shakspere's use; cf. also quot. *c* 1600.

1596 SHAKS. *Tam. Shr.* IV. i. 137 There was no Linke to Colour Peters hat. [*c* **1600** ? GREENE *Mihil Mumchance* D 2, This Cosenage is vsed like wise in selling olde Hats found vpon dunghils, in steede of new, blackt ouer with the smoake of an olde Linke.] **1712** tr. *Pomet's Hist. Drugs* I. VIII. §56. 212/1 They melt black Pitch, and afterwards dip a Wick of Flax, Hemp, or the like, in it, which we sell by the Name of Links [F. *Bougie noire*], and is us'd sometimes to black Shoes withal.

3. *attrib.* and *Comb.*, as ***link-extinguisher, -light; link-burnt, -lighted*** adjs.

1837 WHEELWRIGHT tr. *Aristophanes* II. 123 Give me the beggar's basket *link-burnt through. **1859** NARES *Gloss.*, **Link-extinguishers*, large extinguishers attached to the railings of houses formerly used by the link men for extinguishing their links. **1899** W. CHURCHILL *R. Carvel* 219 Lanthorns and link extinguishers. **1843** CARLYLE *Past & Pr.* II. ix, We have lights, *link-lights and rushlights of an enlightened free Press. **1849** DICKENS *Dav. Copp.* xix, I had been leading a romantic life for ages to a brawling, splashing, *link-lighted..world.

link (lɪŋk), *v.*[1] [f. LINK *sb.*[2] (though recorded somewhat earlier).]

1. *trans.* To couple or join with or as with a link (*in* or *into* a chain, *in* amity, etc.). (Also *absol.*)

a. two or more things *together*.

1387-8 T. USK *Test. Love* I. i. (Skeat) l. 42 Depe in this pinyng pitte, with wo I ligge istocked, with chaines linked of care, and of tene. ? *a* **1412** LYDG. *Two Merchants* 76 In love he lynketh them that be vertuous. *c* **1420** —— *Thebes* II. in *Chaucer's Wks.* (1561) 364 b, Trouth and mercy linked in a Cheine. *c* **1450** HOLLAND *Howlat* 365 Tharwith [*sc.* other armorial bearings] lynkit in a lyng,.. He bure a lyon as lord, of gowlis. **1494** FABYAN *Chron.* 3 In as wordes fewe As I goodly may I shall lynke in fere, The storyes of Englande and Fraunce. **1530** PALSGR. 612/1 They be so faste lynked togyther by maryage that it wyll be harde to sowe a discorde bytwene them. **1597** HOOKER *Eccl. Pol.* v. lii. §2 Two persons linked in amitie. **1627** CAPT. SMITH *Seaman's Gram.* xiii. 62 Sometimes they linke three or foure together. *a* **1674** CLARENDON *Hist. Reb.* XI. §98 Linked together by many promises and professions, and by an entire conjunction in guilt. **1770** BURKE *Pres. Discont.* Wks. II. 329 Whilst men are linked together, they..speedily communicate the alarm of any evil design. **1781** COWPER *Retirement* 398 The boy, who..Sits linking cherry-stones or platting rush. **1811** BUSBY *Dict. Mus.* s.v. *Appogiature*, In bold and energetic movements, a chain of appogiatures.. serve to link the greater intervals. **1837** LANDOR *Pentameron* Wks. 1846 II. 318 The clapping of hands (so lately linked) hath ceased. **1865** KINGSLEY *Herew.* xv, Your fortunes and his are linked together. **1885** GILBERT *Mikado* I. Orig. Plays Ser. III. (1895) 179 That all who flirted, leered or winked (Unless connubially linked) Should forthwith be beheaded. **1928** *New Ventures in Broadcasting* (B.B.C.) iv. 31 The aim of the B.B.C. is to link together the various national systems for the benefit of the Empire. **1935** R. C. WOODTHORPE *Shadow on Downs* ix. 237 Men began to put up pillars of concrete and link them easily by girders of steel. **1959** *Science* 16 Oct. 954/3 Design effort must be directed toward ensuring that records can be linked in spite of such discrepancies. **1962** K. W. GATLAND *Astronautics in Sixties* xi. 344 One proposed method of linking two vehicles in orbit has been outlined.

b. one thing (*in*) *with* or (*on*) *to* another. Also *occas.* (without construction) = to secure with a link or chain.

1412-20 LYDG. *Chron. Troy* I. ii, So was malice linked with innocence. **1532** MORE *Confut. Tindale* Wks. 638/2 Vnto al their olde heresyes to lynke an whole chaine of newe. **1556** J. HEYWOOD *Spider & F.* xxxviii. 125 Our chaine That lingth vs to credence: is not auctoritie. **1585** ABP. SANDYS *Serm.* xvi. 287 Abraham would not linke his sonne with the wicked. **1590** SPENSER *F.Q.* III. ix. 4 Yet is he lincked to a lovely lasse. **1632** LITHGOW *Trav.* v. 175 They [*viz.* certain serpents]..lincke or claspe themselues about their neckes and bodies. **1667** MILTON *P.L.* IX. 133 All this will soon Follow, as to him linkt in weal or woe. **1693** G. STEPNY in *Dryden's Juvenal* (1697) 203 Driving himself a Chariot down the Hill, And (tho a Consul) links himself the Wheel. **1799** JEFFERSON *Writ.* (1859) IV. 268, I am not for linking ourselves by new treaties with the quarrels of Europe. **1810** SOUTHEY *Kehama* XVI. xii, Strong fetters link him to the rock. **1842** BARHAM *Ingol. Leg.*, *Misadv. at Margate* Moral, Don't link yourself with vulgar folks. **1845-6** TRENCH *Huls. Lect.* Ser. I. iii. 43 A Gospel which should link itself on with whatever had occupied the philosophic mind. **1858** HAWTHORNE *Fr. & It. Jrnls.* I. 104 Linked in, indeed, identified with the..swarming life of modern Rome. **1880** MRS. OLIPHANT *He that will not*, etc. xxxviii, Bell linking herself on to his arm, and Marie holding his hand. **1962** *B.B.C. Handbk.* 47 All these studios outside London..can be linked into the network at short notice. **1968** *Globe & Mail* (Toronto) 17 Feb. B4 One of Mercantile's selling points, particularly to the Canadian export-import community, is that we can link into the Citibank international system. **1969** L. JENSEN in J. N. Rosenau *Linkage Politics* v. x. 311 How a state links itself with the external environment depends upon what it believes will maximize its power.

c. *Mil.* To tie (horses) together with 'links' (see quot. 1895). Also *absol.* (See also LINKED b.)

1796 *Instr. & Reg. Cavalry* (1813) 232 The horses..are.. linked to the center under the bridle reins... All officers link at their posts in squadron. **1802** C. JAMES *Milit. Dict.* s.v., The whole go to the left about together, and link. **1895** SIR E. WOOD *Cavalry Waterloo Campaign* v. 119 Most of the riders had slept at the horses' heads with an arm passed through the reins, though in some Regiments they were 'linked'. *Note*, Horses are said to be linked when the collar chains or head-ropes are passed through the links of the head-collars of the horses on either side.

d. To pass (one's arm) *through* or *in* another's.

1843 BROWNING *Ret. Druses* v. (*init.*), Come, old Nasif —link thine arm in mine. **1862** MRS. H. WOOD *Mrs. Hallib.* II. v. 173 Anthony..linking his arm within his lordship's. **1871** 'M. LEGRAND' *Cambr. Freshm.* 349 Mr. Pokyr, linking his arm through that of his friend. **1872** BROWNING *Fifine* i, O trip and skip, Elvire! Link arm in arm with me! **1884** F. M. CRAWFORD *Rom. Singer* I. 29 Nino..linked an arm in his as we went away.

e. *to link in* (fig.): to entice, beguile. Now *dial.*

1592 GREENE *Disput.* etc. 1 Hath your smooth lookes linckt in some Nouice? **1887** *Kentish Gloss.*, *Link*, to entice; beguile; mislead. 'They linked him in along with a passel o' good-for-nothin' runagates'.

2. a. *intr.* To be coupled, joined, or connected (e.g. in friendship, marriage, etc.). Also followed by *together*.

c **1540** J. HEYWOOD *Four P.P.* B ij, Wynking to drynkinge is alwaye lynkinge. **1582** STANYHURST *Æneis* II. (Arb.) 52 A cluster Of theyre companions they let in, thee coompanye lincketh. **1593** SHAKS. *3 Hen. VI*, III. iii. 115, I were loth To linke with him, that were not lawfull chosen. *a* **1618** RALEIGH *To Son* ii. in *Rem.* (1661) 84 Though thou canst not forbear to love, yet forbear to link. *a* **1680** BUTLER *On Drunkenn.* 79 Rem. 1759 I. 116 Fiercest Creatures..In Love and close Alliance link. **1735** DYCHE & PARDON *Dict.*, *Link* (v.),..to enter into a Cabal or Company of Robbers, Rioters, or Rebels. **1790** BURKE *Fr. Rev.* Wks. V. 181 No one generation could link with the other. **1897** *Westm. Gaz.* 2 Oct. 5/1 We ought forthwith to link in with the Cape Railway system on our southern border. **1922** JOYCE *Ulysses* 77 Those two sluts..linked together in the rain. **1962** K. W. GATLAND *Astronautics in Sixties* xi. 341 The ability of two vehicles to match speed and link together in orbit.

b. To go arm in arm, or hand in hand.

1819 R. ANDERSON *Cumberld. Ball., Carel Fair*, Sae we link'd, an' we laugh'd, an' we chatter'd. **1824** SCOTT *St. Ronan's* ii, Clapping palms wi' them, and linking at their dances and daffings. **1871** C. GIBBON *Lack of Gold* x, Linking home arm-in-arm like douce guidman and guidwife.

3. a. *to link up*, to connect, combine, join *up*.

trans. **1897** *Geogr. Jrnl.* IX. 364 The mouth of the valley ..which I visited for the purpose of linking up the rough survey Garwood and I made. **1927** E. O'NEILL *Marco Millions* II. ii. 45 Their necks, waists, and right ankles linked up by chains. **1942** *R.A.F. Jrnl.* 2 May 11 Efforts are being made to link up other countries. **1942** *Tee Emm* (Air Ministry) II. 68 The fundamental method which links up all the information obtained.

intr. **1915** H. G. WELLS *Boon* 211 Every one with ideas.. had to refer to that doctrinal core, had to link up to it. **1925** A. S. M. HUTCHINSON *One Increasing Purpose* I. xxiv. 147 Did I tell you that or has its connection with what you said only linked up in me since we parted? **1929** *Radio Times* 8 Nov. 393/3 Music lines through Belgium to the whole of Germany..are envisaged for..1930, while it may also be possible to link up to Scandinavia through Hamburg. **1974** 'E. LATHEN' *Sweet & Low* xxiii. 217 The Russians and the Americans linked up in space... Every radio in New York was tuned to that docking.

b. *to link up with* (used as in sense 3 a): (*a*) in general contexts.

1899 E. G. WHITE *Testimonies for Church* (1904) VIII. 188 You were willing to link up with them if they would second your propositions. **1903** *Studio* XXVIII. 159/1 To discuss the efforts of the lesser known men who link up the painters of 1830 with those of 1870. **1912** *Q. Rev.* July 231 The limit is entirely a question of alighting—a problem linked up with 'variable speed' aeroplanes. **1915** H. G. WELLS *Boon* 174 Here is the sort of thing that I invite the intelligent reader to link up if he can with the very natural phenomenon of [etc.]. **1922** JOYCE *Ulysses* 385 Our grandam, which we are linked up with by successive anastomosis of navelcords. **1928** *Sweet Shop* Nov. 6/3 The display man..should link up his shop with the advertisement. **1930** *Times* 15 Mar. 19/4 Our company has always been linked up with the trade to.. South America. **1957** E. BOTT *Family & Social Network* viii. 217 Many of the individuals and groups to which an urban family is related are not linked up with one another. **1967** E. SHORT *Embroidery & Fabric Collage* iii. 78 Napkins, tea-cosies, etc., can be designed to link up with the tablecloth or mats.

(*b*) By some means of transport or system of communication.

1907 *Jrnl. Soc. Arts* LV. 374/1 The linking up of railway stations with outlying country districts by means of mechanically propelled road vehicles. **1909** *Chambers's Jrnl.* XII. 658/1 It is freely mooted that Berlin and Munich will also be linked-up with this system [of airships]. **1910** *Ibid.* XIII. 329/1 Switches linked it [*sc.* a monorail system] up with other lengths of line. **1934** *Highways & Bridges* 24 July 4/4 A new road..would be needed..to link up with the main road. **1937** *Discovery* May 163/2 The network of air lines which now links up the United States with Central and South America. **1961** *Assessment Highway Requirements S. Wales & Monmouthshire* (British Road Federation) 3 Wasting money on local improvements which will not in the end link up with an overall system. *Ibid.* 16 It should link up with the by-pass there.

link (lɪŋk), *v.*[2] *Sc.* and *north. dial.* [Cf. Norw. *linka* to give a toss or bending motion with the body (Aasen), to fling, or drive backwards and forwards (Ross). Cf. also LINCH *v.*[2]] *intr.* To move nimbly, pass quickly along; to trip. ***to link off***: to pass away, disappear quickly.

1715 RAMSAY *Christ's Kirk Gr.* II. xxiv, Maidenheads gaed linkin Aff a' that day. **1725** —— *Gentle Sheph.* I. i, I saw my Meg come linkan o'er the lee. **1785** BURNS *Addr. to Deil* xx, Some luckless hour will send him linkin, To your black pit. **1790** —— *Tam o' Shanter* 150 Ilka carlin..linket at it in her sark! **1882** J. WALKER *Jaunt to Auld Reekie*, etc. 21 The hours gaed linking by. **1893** STEVENSON *Catriona* 68 Ha'e.. this billet as fast as ye can link to the captain.

b. *causal.* To cause to move or circulate rapidly.

1721 RAMSAY *To R. H. B.* ii, He disna live that canna link The glass about.

Hence '**linking** *ppl. a.*

1818 SCOTT *Rob Roy* xxvi, A man that can whistle ye up a thousand or feifteen hundred linking lads to do his will.

‖**link** (lɪŋk), *a.* [Yiddish, f. G. *link* left, left-handed, clumsy.] Not pious, not orthodox (in religion).

1889 *Referee* 3 Feb. 2/3 'Dolly', who was a Jewess, but one who was link rather than froom, was about forty years old. **1892** I. ZANGWILL *Childr. Ghetto* II. 90 'Suppose,' she said slowly, 'I wanted to marry a Christian?..if I was to marry a very *link* Jew, you'd think it almost as bad.' **1907** —— *Ghetto Comedies* ii. 380 But I am so *link* (irreligious).

linkage ('lɪŋkɪdʒ). [f. LINK *sb.*[2] or *v.*[1] + -AGE.]

a. The condition or manner of being linked; a system of links. Also, a link; an association or correlation; the process of linking or connecting (see also quots.). Also *attrib.*

Applied e.g. (*Chem.*) to the union of atoms or radicals in a molecule; (*Geom.*) to a system of straight lines, etc. pivoted together so as to rotate about one another (by Sylvester used with restricted application; see quot. 1874 for *link-work*, LINK *sb.*[2] 7).

1874 SYLVESTER in *Proc. Roy. Instit.* VII. 182 *note*, A compass or a pair of scissors is the simplest form of linkage; a set of lazy-tongs is another. **1877** KEMPE (*title*) How to draw a straight line; a lecture on linkages. **1887** *Jrnl. Franklin Inst.* Jan. 74 Brühl showed that in case of 'double-linkage' each such carbon-atom has a refraction equivalent to about 6·1. **1890** *Spectator* 11 Sept. 462/1 Chemists are persuaded that the ethylenic form of linkage is not the equivalent of two paraffinic linkages. **1893** CAYLEY in *Coll. Math. Papers* (1897) XIII. 292 The results given by the MacMahon linkage. **1897** *Standard* 1 Feb. 5/2 The linkage of life to life in Nature. **1899** *Allbutt's Syst. Med.* VI. 512 Such places of linkage of neurons being called 'synapses'. **1904** *Brit. & Colonial Printer* 10 Mar. 14/2 A linkage system transmits the movement to the slide bars. **1928** A. S. EDDINGTON *Nature Physical World* xiv. 306 If the two structures were identifiable then the atom would involve a complete causal connection of the two types of phenomena. But apparently no such causal linkage exists. **1940** *Chambers's Techn. Dict.* 503/2 *Linkage* (Elec. Eng.), a measure of the product of the magnetic flux passing through a closed electric circuit and the number of turns in the circuit, the unit being one line passing through a circuit having one turn. **1957** *Educational & Psychol. Measurement* XVII. 207 (*title*) Elementary linkage analysis for isolating orthogonal and oblique types and typal relevancies. **1959** B. HIGGINS *Econ. Devel.* IV. xvi. 405 Any particular investment project may have both 'forward linkage' (may encourage investment in subsequent stages of production) and 'backward linkage' (may encourage investment in earlier stages of production). The task is to find the projects with the greatest *total* linkage. *Ibid.* xvii. 413 Favoring deliberate unbalancing of the economy to maximize the 'linkage' effects of investment. **1959** *Science* CXXX. 954/1 The term *record linkage* has been used to indicate the bringing together of two or more separately recorded pieces of information. **1962** K. W. GATLAND *Astronautics in Sixties* xi. 344 Radar..may be relied upon to achieve linkage of the spacecraft. **1962** *Which? Car Suppl.* Oct. 143/1 Modified carburettor and linkage to give smoother operation. **1963** F. W. FREY in L. W. Pye *Communications & Political Devel.* xvii. 301 The ratio of the number of existing power linkages ..to the number of theoretically possible linkages. **1969** J. N. ROSENAU (*title*) Linkage politics. **1970** *Nature* 24 Oct. 387/2 There follows a discussion of the linkages between population growth and food supplies.

b. *Genetics.* (An) association between characters in inheritance, such that if one parent has a pair of characters, there is a probability greater than 50% that any offspring inheriting one of the characters will also inherit the other, which effect is due to the two characters being controlled by alleles located on the same chromosome; formerly called (*gametic*) *coupling* (COUPLING *vbl. sb.* 6 e); also, the amount or degree of this association (varying between 50% and 100%). Also *attrib.*

1912 *Biol. Bull.* XXIII. 175 There are no wingless black flies in the F_2 generation, which the Mendelian expectation calls for. Their absence can only be explained by strong linkage of the yellow factor and the factor for wings. *Ibid.* 178 There are actually 1,858 long grey flies to 916 long black, or a ratio of 2 to 1. This is the linkage ratio when two strongly or completely linked factors are concerned. **1915** T. H. MORGAN et al. *Mechanism Mendelian Heredity* iii. 58 In the case of yellow and white just given the linkage between the two factors is very strong. **1928** *Hereditas* X. 126 The linkages P_1–V and B–V have been reported by Wellensiek. **1940** *Chambers's Techn. Dict.* 503/2 *Linkage group*, a group of hereditary characteristics which remain associated with one another through a number of generations. *Ibid.* 504/1 *Linkage map*, a diagram showing the position of the genes in a chromosome or group of chromosomes. **1958** *Oxf. Univ. Gaz.* 23 Apr. 892 Genetic investigations on mice with special reference to evolutionary processes and linkage. **1959** *Listener* 3 Dec. 967/1 We shall need to know how many chromosomes there are, and what may be the importance of the phenomenon called 'linkage' in keeping the genes on one chromosome together. **1970** AMBROSE & EASTY *Cell Biol.* x. 339 The genes [of *Drosophila*] fell into four linkage groups, which corresponded with the haploid number of four chromosomes. *Ibid.* 340 However far apart two genes are,.. they will never show less than 50 per cent linkage due to multiple cross-overs.

'**link-boy.** [LINK *sb.*[3]] A boy employed to carry a link to light passengers along the streets.

1660 PEPYS *Diary* 4 Feb., Thence to Sir Harry Wright's, and after that with a link-boy home. **1716** GAY *Trivia* III. 114 Nor need th' officious Link-Boy's smoaky Light. **1739** J. MOTTLEY *Joe Miller's Jests* No. 239 A Link-Boy cry'd, Have a Light, Gentlemen? **1837** DICKENS *Pickw.* xxxvi, The red glare of the link-boy's torch. **1854** THACKERAY *Newcomes* I. xvii. 161 Link-boys with their torches lighted the beaux over the mud.

fig. **1698** FARQUHAR *Love & Bottle* III. i, This is the page, love's link-boy, that must light me the way.

linked ('lɪŋkt), *ppl. a.* Also 5 lynket, 6 ylincked, 6–7 lincked. [f. LINK *v.*[1] + -ED[1].] **a.** Connected by or as by links; joined, coupled, associated. †Also, made or fashioned with links. † **linked line** *advb. phr.*, in a continued line.

a **1450** *Fysshynge w. Angle* (1883) 8 Make þe yarde mete vn to the hole of the seyd stafe yn to þe halfe stafe lynket lyngh. **1561** T. HOBY tr. *Castiglione's Courtyer* II. Lij, By and by were vices by that lincked contrarietie necessarily accompanied with them. **1590** SPENSER *F.Q.* II. vii. 46 She held a great gold chaine ylincked well. **1632** MILTON *L'Allegro* 140 With many a winding bout Of lincked sweetnes long drawn out. **1667** —— *P.L.* I. 328 His swift pursuers..with linked Thunderbolts Transfix us to the bottom of this Gulfe. **179.** BURNS *Bonie Peg*, Wi' linked hands, we took the sands Adown yon winding river. **1816** COLERIDGE *Lay Serm.* 29 Notions, linked arguments [etc.] ..influence only the comparatively few. **1821** SHELLEY *Prometh. Unb.* III. iii. 136 The dark linked ivy tangling wild. **1825** SCOTT *Talism.* i, His limbs..fitted to wear his linked hauberk, with as much ease as if the meshes had been formed of cobwebs. **1877** BLACK *Green Past.* xxii. (1878) 180 What trouble..could enter into these linked lives? **1966** *Punch* 5 Oct. 506/2 Tiny terrace houses are now considered acceptable, at £12,000 to £20,000 a time, because they are called 'Town' or 'Linked' housing. **1970** P. LAURIE *Scotland Yard* v. 123 Some traffic-light systems, like the linked set in Oxford Street, are extremely complicated.

b. *Mil.* Since 1872 used of two infantry battalions (or regiments) which are coupled together to form a regimental district (see also quot. 1872–6).

1872 LD. E. CECIL in Hansard *Parl. Debates* 3rd Ser. CCIX. 1343 The linked regiments seemed in some instances rather ill-assorted unions. **1872–6** VOYLE & STEVENSON *Milit. Dict.* (ed. 3) 232 These regiments are termed linked, and in the case of one of the regiments going or being on foreign service requiring men to make up its numbers, soldiers are drafted from the regiment remaining at home. **1892** *Daily News* 12 Apr. 6/1 The line battalion in England, which has a linked battalion abroad, is unfit in every way to go into the field.

c. Of industries: allied to and dependent on one another.

1942 S. FLORENCE in H. B. Newbold *Industry & Rural Life* ii. 43 Certain industries may be linked to other industries..and all the linked industries would have to be dispersed together... An instance of such a complex of linked industries is found in Birmingham. **1961** ESTALL & BUCHANAN *Industr. Activity & Econ. Geogr.* v. 108 'Linked' or related industries often require similar types of labour skills... A further advantage is the easy interchange of materials and products between the linked establishments. **1961** E. A. POWDRILL *Vocab. Land Planning* iv. 77 They [*sc.* factories] must be..near some other industry providing supplies or markets (i.e., 'linked').

linkedness ('lɪŋktnɪs). [f. LINKED *ppl. a.*] Interconnection.

1908 E. V. LUCAS *Over Bemerton's* xiv. 137 (*heading*) The linkedness of life is illustrated.

linker ('lɪŋkə(r)). [f. LINK *v.*[1] + -ER[1].] One who or that which links or joins.

1856 F. L. MACKENZIE in Miles *Mem.* 237 The linker of the seasons, The snowdrop,—it shall bring. **1881** *Census Instr.* (1885) Coal miner: Linker, Hitcher. Hosiery Manufacturer: Linker. **1892** *Labour Commission* Gloss., *Linkers*, workers (females) of links, that is machines for joining or linking together the loops of fabrics.

linking ('lɪŋkɪŋ), *vbl. sb.* [f. LINK *v.*[1] + -ING[1].] Connexion by or as by links; coupling together, association.

1545 UDALL *Erasm. Par., Luke* Pref. (1548) ¶v b, For the better lynkyng of one sentence to an other. **1608** HIERON *Wks.* I. 752/1 The linking of my selfe into this wedlocke band. **1837** D. McNICOLL *Wks.* 204 The beautiful linkings by which the New Testament is combined with the Old. **1894** *Times* 19 May 10/1 The occasional linking of the regiments. **1929** C. J. FRIEDRICH *Alfred Weber's Theory of Location of Industries* vi. 206 The connection is based.. upon the linking of the market of the one with the other. **1957** E. BOTT *Family & Social Network* iv. 99 Marriage becomes a linking of kin groups rather than..a union between individuals. **1960** J. H. JONES in E. Davies *Roads* ii. 26 Linking is the interconnection of two or more traffic signals in such a manner that the beginning of the green period at one signal is related to that of the previous signal.

Also **linking-up**.

1908 *Westm. Gaz.* 19 Nov. 10/4 The 'linking-up' Bill... The process provided for by the [Electricity Supply] bill is known as 'linking-up'. **1909** *Daily Chron.* 19 Feb. 6/5 The increase in the traffic was..the natural result of the linking-up policy adopted. **1923** J. S. HUXLEY *Ess. Biologist* iv. 160 This first linking-up of sex with mind produced, eventually, a large proportion of the beauty of the organic world. **1934** *Highways & Bridges* 26 June 11/3 A 'Seven-Province Program' for the linking up of 13,670 miles of road. **1958** *Britannica Bk. of Year* 213/1 This linking-up was welcomed by delegates. **1972** *Radio Times* 7 Dec. 6/1 That's the date which has been set for the linking up in space of a Russian Soyuz with an American Apollo.

'**linking**, *ppl. a.* [f. LINK *v.*[1] + -ING[2].]

a. That links or joins together.

1871 B. TAYLOR *Faust* (1875) II. II. iii. 161 In linking circles wide extending. **1901** *Blackwood's Mag.* June 845/2 There is a linking sonnet, 127, between the series addressed to Herbert and the shorter series..to the Dark Lady.

b. *spec.* in *Gram.* = COPULATIVE *a.* 1. Also *linking verb*.

1935 G. O. CURME *Parts of Speech* IV. 66 *Linking verbs*... The copula..performs..the function of announcing the predicate... Its use spread because there was an absolute need of such a linking word. **1952** A. H. MARCKWARDT *Introd. Eng. Lang.* ii. 115 Adjectives may also be..separated from the nouns they modify by a linking or copulative verb. **1967** W. N. FRANCIS *Eng. Lang.* ii. 58 The construction is called *linking* or *copulative*... The following are typical linking constructions. **1972** R. QUIRK et al. *Gram. Contemp. Eng.* xii. 820 The verb in sentences with subject complement is a 'copula' (or linking verb), which of itself has little meaning but functions as a link between the complement and subject.

c. *spec.* in *Broadcasting* and *Cinemat.*: providing continuity between programmes, scenes, etc., as music, camera shots, commentary.

1941 *B.B.C. Gloss. Broadcasting Terms* 17 *Linking Material*, words or music forming part of a continuity structure. **1960** N. KNEALE *Quatermass & Pit* II. 63 Fade in linking music. **1962** A. NISBETT *Technique Sound Studio* vii. 129 Trimming linking music to length. *Ibid.* viii. 136 Linking narration will..be necessary. **1967** *Listener* 6 Apr. 466/3 All the undeniably pretty pictures in the outdoor location and linking shots cannot breathe life into them.

d. *linking r*: a letter r in word-final position that is normally pronounced before a following vowel but is silent before a following consonant (as in *far, far away*).

1950 J. S. KENYON *Amer. Pronunc.* (ed. 10) 164 Observe that linking *r* is the use between words of an *r* that is spelt and was formerly pronounced. *Ibid.* 165 Linking *r* is sometimes omitted in Southern British. **1956** D. JONES *Outl. Eng. Phonetics* (ed. 8) xxi. 196 When a word ending with the letter *r* is immediately followed by a word beginning with a vowel, then a *r*-sound..is usually inserted in the pronunciation...*r* inserted in this way is called 'linking *r*'.

Hence † '**linkingly** *adv.*, so as to be linked or connected.

1635 PERSON *Varieties* I. vi. 18 Ptolomee his opinion is more true, that the earth and waters, mutually and linkingly embrace one another and make up one Globe.

linkister, corrupt U.S. form of LINGUISTER.

'**linkman**[1]. A man employed to carry a torch.

1716 GAY *Trivia* III. 139 Though thou art tempted by the link-man's Call Yet trust him not along the lonely Wall. **1762** *Gentl. Mag.* 596 A remarkable robbery was committed near Moor-fields by a linkman. **1851** D. JERROLD *St. Giles* v. 44 A ballad-singer may hold his head up with a linkman any day. **1881** *Census Instr.* (1885) 31 Linkman. **1898** *Daily Tel.* 13 Jan. 7/3 To receive two and six each for acting as linkmen at a wedding.

'**linkman**[2]. Also **link man**. [f. LINK *sb.*[2] + MAN *sb.*[1]] A person serving as a link between groups of people, etc.

Quot. 1909 prob. represents an extended use of LINKMAN[1].

1909 J. R. WARE *Passing Eng.* 168 *Linkman* (*W. London*), general servant about kitchen or yard. **1918** *Linkman* Apr. 1 (*title*) The Linkman—a literary and artistic quarterly review of congenial interests. **1969** *Guardian* 29 July 5/5 He is to.. run an advice centre for residents, acting as a day-to-day 'link man' between the people and the available social and welfare services. **1972** *Where* May/June 150/3 We need a scheme which..makes Governors better linkmen between the school and their community. **1972** *Oxford Times* 20 Oct. 24/4 (*heading*) Social services Linkman. *Ibid.*, He will act as linkman between the department and volunteers. **1973** *Times* 20 Oct. 2/3 Mr Heaton, in his closing speech, claimed the prosecution had changed their allegations concerning his role in the burglary from perpetrator of the crime to link man and alibi for Miss Dugdale.

b. *spec.* (*a*) a commissionaire; (*b*) in Broadcasting, a person providing continuity in a radio or television programme consisting of several items; (*c*) in Hockey and Association Football, a player in any of the mid-field positions.

Sense (*a*) is probably an extended use of LINKMAN[1].

1939 H. HODGE *Cab, Sir?* xv. 222 A commissionaire is still a linkman to us. **1947** *Gloss. Technical Theatr. Terms* (Strand Electr. & Engin. Co.) 20 *Link men*, staff engaged at the Entrances and Exits of the theatre to pass the public to and from the street. **1960** *Listener* 23 June 1114/1, I must enter a protest against commentators, interviewers, announcers, link-men..and all the glorious company of contemporary communications. **1963** *Times* 25 May 3/6 McLintock is a foil and Gibson the link man. **1965** *Daily Express* 13 Aug. 15/5 Linkmen. 'They have to sort out the initial problems in defence,' said Wade, 'and then offer themselves as the focus for a pass from defence before going forward in supporting roles to the attack.' **1966** *Observer* 16 Oct. 23/5 There will be little change of format in the 26-week run. No chat, no singing, no dancing. No 'linkman' saying 'good evening' and 'goodnight'. **1968** K. BIRD *Smash Glass Image* v. 59 One of my qualities as newsreader and linkman was that I remained cool in a crisis. **1968** *Listener* 10 Oct. 469/3 They seemed much more like linkmen waiting for tips outside an expensive hotel than dangerous and purposeful revolutionaries. **1970** *F.A. News* Apr. 340/1 In the days before 'sweepers' and 'link men', Clayton was the ideal old-type 'dual-purpose' wing half. **1974** *Listener* 10 Jan. 58/3 'Well..can you answer very briefly..is Britain really on the edge of disaster?'.. Timings, for linkmen, are of course inexorable.

linkster, corrupt U.S. form of LINGUISTER.

Link Trainer ('lɪŋk 'treɪnə(r)). [f. Edward *Link*, its American inventor.] A flight simulator on which pilots are trained. Also *ellipt.* as **Link**.

1937 *Flight* 28 Oct. 416/2 Practice with a Link Trainer invariably results in a light touch upon the controls of a real aircraft whether flying blind or not. **1939** *War Illustr.* 4 Nov. 243 An ingenious apparatus used in the training of R.A.F. pilots is the Link Trainer. **1940** *Flight* 26 Dec. 548/2 After Link Trainer work, dual instruction in the air in turns, landings and spins, and ground instruction in parachutes, the pupil goes on his first solo. **1942** *R.A.F. Jrnl.* 18 Apr. 3 The lessons you learned on the Link Won't help you evade a Gremlin. **1943** *Ibid.* Aug. 36 Link Trainer Instructor. ..*Group* I. **1945** *Tee Emm* (Air Ministry) V. 41 Here's a nice little Link Trainer exercise. **1952** *New Biol.* XIII. 51 In some respects this apparatus resembled the Link Trainer, but for a number of reasons it was constructed so that, unlike the Link, it remained stationary. **1960** C. H. GIBBS-SMITH *Aeroplane* 299 *Link Trainer*, a synthetic training device, comprising a hooded cockpit, for training in instrument flying, radio aids, etc.

link-up ('lɪŋkʌp). Also **linkup, link up**. [f. LINK *v.*[1]] The act or result of linking up; *spec.* (*a*) of troops, or in a military context; (*b*) of spacecraft.

1945 H. NICOLSON *Let.* 29 Apr. (1967) 452 You can imagine what an exhilarating week this has been. The surrounding of Berlin; the link-up with the Russian armies. **1945** W. S. CHURCHILL *Victory* (1946) 121 Russian and American troops made a link-up at Torgau. **1952** C. S. LEWIS *Let.* 2 Oct. (1966) 244 Much later..came the link-up between his..interest in *Arthuriana* and a new interest in Byzantium. **1958** *Time* (Atlantic ed.) 26 May 20/3 Gaillard had moved to prevent any link-up between the insurgents in Algeria and their sympathizers in France. **1965** *New Scientist* 23 Dec. 852/2 In the technique used in the *Gemini* link-up, *Gemini VI* was first placed in an orbit which was.. elliptical. **1968** K. BIRD *Smash Glass Image* v. 64 What..was the link-up between all these events and what had happened before I came away. **1969** *Daily Tel.* 17 Jan. 22 (*caption*) The link-up between the two Russian manned space-craft took place 150 miles above the earth yesterday. **1970** *Globe & Mail* (Toronto) 26 Sept. 10/3 In the Cambodian fighting, less than a mile had to be spanned for a linkup of Government forces. **1972** *Radio Times* 7 Dec. 6/3 It would be nice to believe that the space link-up is co-operation for co-operation's sake. **1973** D. FRANCIS *Slay-Ride* vii. 78 A world-wide racing investigatory link-up, something along the lines of Interpol.

linky ('lɪŋkɪ), *a.* [f. LINK *sb.*[1] + -Y.] Having the character or appearance of links.

1859 PARKER *Misc. Poems* 19 (E.D.D.) The lang linkie lea rig, once pleasant to see. **1893** STEVENSON *Catriona* 127 The linky, boggy muirland that they call the Figgate Whins.

lin-lan-lone. An echoic formation intended to suggest the sound of a chime of three bells.

1889 TENNYSON *Far—far—away* ii, The mellow lin-lan-lone of evening bells. **1954** J. BETJEMAN *Few Late Chrysanthemums* 73 The dear old village! *Lin-lan-lone* the bells (Which should be six) ring over hills and dells.

linn[1] (lɪn). Chiefly *Sc.* Forms: 1 hlynn, 6 lyn(n, 6–8 lin, 8– linn. [Two words seem to have been confused: OE. *hlynn* str. fem., torrent (? related to *hlynn* masc., 'clangor', *hlynnan, hlynian* to resound), and Gaelic *linne* = Irish *linn*, earlier *lind*, Welsh *llyn*, Cornish *lin*, Breton *lenn*.]

1. A torrent running over rocks; a cascade, waterfall.

c **975** *Rushw. Gosp.* John xviii. 1 Se hælend eode..ofer þah hlynne þe mon Cedron nemneþ. **1513** DOUGLAS *Æneis* XI. vii. 9 The ryveris..Brystand on skelleis our thir demmyt lynnis. **1536** [see LEAP *v.* 2 d]. **1567** *Gude & Godlie Ball.* (S.T.S.) 118 Watter [that] fast rinnis ouer ane lin, Dois not returne againe to the awin place. **1725** RAMSAY *Gentle Sheph.* I. ii, Between twa birks out o'er a little lin The water fa's. **1785** BURNS *Halloween* xxv, Whyles owre a linn the burnie plays. *a* **1810** TANNAHILL *Poems* (1846) 99 The roar of the linn On the night breeze is swelling. **1884** Q. VICTORIA *More Leaves* 311 A linn falling from a height to which foot-paths had been made. **1892** *Standard* 8 Jan. 5/2 In Wales and Scotland there are linns which could render Manchester and Dundee independent of the pitmen of the Black Countries.

2. A pool, esp. one into which a cataract falls.

1577–87 HOLINSHED *Chron., Descr. Scot.* xii. 18/1 A loch, lin, or poole there. *a* **1584** MONTGOMERIE *Cherrie & Slae* 80, I saw an river rin Out ouir ane craggie rok of stane, Syne lichtit in ane lin. **1612** DRAYTON *Poly-olb.* v. 118 Toothy, tripping downe from Verwin's rushie Lin [*marg. note*, A Poole or watry Moore]. **1790** A. WILSON *Suicide* Poet. Wks. (1846) 130 Driven by mad despair..To poison, dagger, or the engulphing linn. *a* **1802** *Earl Richard* xxii. in Child *Ballads* II. 153/1 The deepest pot in a' the linn They fand Erl Richard in. **1865** KINGSLEY *Herew.* I. Prel. 3 He..sees nixes in the dark linns as he fishes by night.

3. A precipice, a ravine with precipitous sides.

1799 *Med. Jrnl.* II. 356 It is found at the bottom of a deep and narrow ravine, or linn. **1808** SCOTT *Marm.* I. Introd. 3 Gazing down the steepy linn, That hems our little garden in. **1818** —— *Hrt. Midl.* l, If you come here again, I'll pitch you down the linn like a foot-ball. **1856** BRYANT *Count of Greiers* v, They dance through wood and meadow, they dance across the linn.

linn[2]. Now *dial.* and *U.S.* Also 5 lyn, 8 lin, 8–9 lynn. [Altered form of LIND *sb.*, the vowel being shortened as is usual in the first element of a compound.] The linden or lime; also, the wood of this tree; *attrib.*, in *linn-bark, -board, -tree.*

c **1475** *Cath. Angl.* 217/2 (Addit. MS.) A Lyn tre, *tilia.* **1674** GREW *Veget. Trunks* vii. §4 Some Woods are soft, but not fast; others are both, as Linn. **1787** W. SARGENT in *Mem. Amer. Acad. Arts & Sci.* IX. 158 Lynn,..a light white wood very proper for finishing the inside of dwelling houses. **1796** in Morse *Amer. Geog.* I. 577 The more useful trees are, maple,..lynn tree. **1796** MARSHALL *Yorksh.* (ed. 2) II. 331 Lin; *tilia europæa*, the lime or linden tree. **1799** J. SMITH *Acc. Remark. Occurr.* (1870) 30 A cover was made of lynn bark which will run even in the winter season. **1808** PIKE *Sources Mississ.* (1810) I. App. 54 The banks of the Mississippi are still bordered by the pines of the different species, except a few small bottoms of elm, lynn and maple. **1812** BRACKENRIDGE *Views Louisiana* (1814) 104 The timber is not such as is usually found in swamps, but fine oak, ash, olive, linn, beech, and poplar of enormous growth. **1819** E. DANA *Geogr. Sk. Western Country* 84 Sugar maple, black

and white walnut,..lynn, sycamore, cotton wood. **1819** E. EVANS *Pedestrious Tour* 299 Here are the lynn tree, gum tree, [etc.]. **1833** *Act 3 & 4 Will. IV*, c. 56 Linn Boards, or White Boards for Shoemakers. **1839** in *Trans. Mich. Agric. Soc.* (1855) VI. 263 The table lands are mostly timbered with the varieties of oak, beech, maple, lynn, hickory. **1847** HALLIWELL, *Linn-tree*, a lime-tree. *Derb.* **1849** E. CHAMBERLAIN *Indiana Gazetteer* (ed. 3) 170 The other forest trees..are ash, walnut,..lynn, [etc.]. **1860** M. CURTIS *Woody Plants N. Carolina* 79 Southern Linn. (*T[ilia] pubescens*, Ait.)—This is confined to the Lower Districts of the Southern States. **1884** C. S. SARGENT *Rep. Forests N. Amer.* 514 A good deal of black cherry, lin, and locust. **1886** *Harper's Mag.* June 58/2 Ropes are made of lynn bark.

‖**linnæa** (lɪˈniːə). *Bot.* [mod.L.; so named by Gronovius, 1749, after the Swedish naturalist C. F. Linné, better known by his latinized name Linnæus.] A slender evergreen flowering plant (*L. borealis*, N.O. *Caprifoliaceæ*) of the north temperate and frigid zones.

1862 H. MARRYAT *Year in Sweden* II. 227 The linnæa loads the air with its perfume. *Ibid.* 396 The forest is here carpeted with the linnæa.

Linnæan, Linnean (lɪˈniːən) *a.* and *sb.* [f. *Linnæ-us* (see prec.) + -AN. (The spelling *Linnæan* is the more common, though the Linnean Society adopts the other form.)]

A. *adj.* Of or pertaining to Linnæus or his system; given or instituted by Linnæus; adhering to the system of Linnæus.

1753 CHAMBERS *Cycl. Supp.* s.v. *Botany* Tab. I Characters of the Classes in the Linnæan System. **1759** B. STILLINGFL. *Calendar Flora* Pref., Misc. Tracts (1762) 243, I have retained the Linnæan names of every plant, and animal in the Swedish Calendar. **1807** J. E. SMITH *Phys. Bot.* 491 The Linnæan genera of Mosses are chiefly founded on the situation of the capsule. **1864** BOWEN *Logic* x. 343 The Linnaean Classification of plants.

B. *sb.* A follower of Linnæus; one who adopts his system.

1772 BARRINGTON in *Phil. Trans.* LXII. 300 If..a bird, which is supposed to migrate in the winter, passes almost under the nose of a Linnæan, he pays but little attention to it, because he cannot examine the beak.

Hence **Liˈnnæanism**, the doctrines and practice of Linnæus, or of his school.

1831 *Blackw. Mag.* XXX. 9 Nobody beyond the barriers of Linnaeanism could ever dream of designating any of these ..a natural history.

linnæite (lɪˈniːaɪt). *Min.* [Named by Haidinger, 1845, after Linnæus, who first described it: see -ITE.] Sulphide of cobalt, containing some nickel and copper.

1849 J. NICOL *Min.* 457 Linnæite..occurs in octahedrons and cubes. **1894** *Mineral Mag.* X. 339 Cleavage and density of linnæite and polydymite being the same.

lin-nail. *Sc.* and *north. dial.* [f. *lin (see LINCH *sb.*[1]) + NAIL. Cf. Ger. dial. *lonnagel.*] = LINCH-PIN.

1496 *Ld. Treas. Acc. Scot.* I. 293 Item, for fyfty iij chenȝeis, to the lynnalis of the cartis and the erleddir pynnys ..ixs. **1562** *Wills & Inv. N.C.* (Surtees 1835) 207 One wayne wth yron bound wheilles, axill nailles, lyn nalles. **1855** ROBINSON *Whitby Gloss.*

linnen, obs. form of LINEN.

linnet (ˈlɪnɪt). Forms: 5 linet, 6 lenet, linnette, lynnet, 7-8 lennet, linot, 6- linnet. [a. OF. *linette, linot, linotte* (mod.F. *linotte*), f. *lin* flax, on the seeds of which the bird feeds. OE. had a *línetwíge*, whence LINTWHITE, and there is one example of *línece*, f. *lín* LINE *sb.*[1], flax.]

1. A common and well-known song-bird, *Linota* (or *Linaria*) *cannabina*, of the family *Fringillidæ*. Its plumage is brown or warm grey; but in summer the breast and crown of the cock (when wild, not when caged) become crimson or rose-colour. Allied species are the Mountain-Linnet or Twite (*Linota flavirostris* or *L. montium*) and the Lesser Redpoll (*L. rufescens*).

[*c* **1050** *Ags. Voc.* in Wr.-Wülcker 286/21 *Cardella*, linece.] *c* **1530** *Crt. of Love* 1412 'What meneth this?' Seid than the linet; 'welcome Lord of blisse'. **1562** TURNER *Herbal* II. 134 b, Men fede byrdes wyth the sede of it [sesamum]..namelye syskennes, and linnettes. **1604** DRAYTON *Owl* 109 Fie, quoth the Lennet, tripping on the Spray. **1631** BRATHWAIT *Eng. Gentlew.* (1641) 290 The shee-Lennet flew away and left the male alone. **1678** RAY *Willughby's Ornith.* 261 The Mountain Linnet: *Linaria Montana*. **1850** TENNYSON *In Mem.* xxvii, I envy not in any moods..The linnet born within the cage. **1893** NEWTON *Dict. Birds* 515 According to its sex, or the season of the year, it is known as the Red, Grey or Brown Linnet.

2. Applied, with qualifications, to birds of other genera. ***green linnet***, the greenfinch (see GREEN *a.* 13 b). ***pine linnet***, a siskin of N. America, *Chrysomitris* (or *Spinus*) *pinus*.

1868 WOOD *Homes without H.* xxix. 550 The Indigo Bird or Blue Linnet of America (Spiza cyanea). **1884** BURROUGHS *Fresh Fields* vi. (1895) 140 The greenfinch or green linnet is an abundant bird everywhere. **1886** —— *Signs & Seasons* ii. (1895) 41 The pine grosbeak and the pine linnet are both nurslings of this tree.

3. *Mining. pl.* Oxidized lead ores (Raymond *Mining Gloss.* 1881).

4. *attrib.* and *Comb.*, as ***linnet-bird, -finch***; ***linnet-like*** adj.; **linnet's heads** (see quot. 1727-52).

1570 LEVINS *Manip.* 86/43 A Linnet bird, *acanthis*. **1598** FLORIO, *Lindria*,..a Lenet-bird or Lack-backer. *c* **1650** *Lovelace's 'To Althea'* in *Percy Fol.* II. 20 When Lynett like confined [**1649** *Lucasta* 98 Like committed Linnets] I With shriller note shall sing. **1727-52** CHAMBERS *Cycl.* s.v. *Teazel*, The smaller kind [of teazles] sometimes called linnots heads, are used to draw out the knap from the coarser stuffs, as bays, &c. **1883** OUIDA *Wanda* I. 276 The sweet linnet-like voice of the Princess Ottilie came on her ear. **1890** *Century Dict.*, *Linnet-finch*, same as linnet.

linnet-hole. *Glass-making.* [f. **linnet*, corruption of F. *lunette* + HOLE.] = LUNETTE.

1662 MERRETT *Neri's Art of Glass* 344 And on the two other sides they have their Calcars, into which linnet holes are made for the fire to come from the furnace, to bake and prepare their Frit, and also for the discharge of the smoak. **1875** in KNIGHT *Dict. Mech.*

linney, variant of LINHAY.

linnow, obs. form of LENNOW *a.*, flabby, limp.

1528 PAYNEL *Salerne's Regim.* (1535) 108 b, Baynyng maketh the skynne linnowe or soupulle.

†**linnow,** *v. Obs. rare*—[1]. [f. *linnow*, LENNOW *a.*] *trans.* To make supple (in quot. *absol.*).

1572 J. JONES *Bathes of Bath* II. 19 b, Of the sweete taste, it shall have the power, that it may linnow, smooth, and fynely lewse.

linny, variant of LINHAY.

lino[1], obs. form of LENO.

1780 MAD. D'ARBLAY *Diary* Apr., He..insisted upon presenting me with a complete suite of gauze lino. **1825** *Blackw. Mag.* XVII. 165 Spangles and sprigged 'linos'!

lino[2] (ˈlaɪnəʊ), colloq. abbrev. of LINOLEUM. Also **linoed, lino'd** *adj.*, covered with linoleum.

1907 C. E. DAWSON in *Process Engravers' Monthly* Jan. 15, I at last happened upon some samples of cork lino. **1920** *Glasgow Herald* 10 Apr. 4 The Earl caught the gloves, but the hat fell on the lino. **1933** R. C. HUTCHINSON *Unforgotten Prisoner* III. xiv. 420 He went up the lino'd stairs. **1966** M. PATTEN *Home Making in Colour* 36/2 Lino is easy to lay.. and is a good background for rugs and carpets. **1966** J. CHAMIER *Cannonball* iv. 29 The edges of his coat swept papers skidding onto the linoed floor. **1973** P. DICKINSON *Green Gene* ix. 173 The lino-covered staircase. **1973** J. WAINWRIGHT *Pride of Pigs* 120 The usual collection of household goods..rugs, carpets and lino.

lino[3] (ˈlaɪnəʊ), abbrev. of LINOTYPE.

1907 *Daily Chron.* 3 Dec. 4/4 He gave me a sketch of his paper. It was set up by 'linos'.

linocut (ˈlaɪnəʊkʌt). [f. LINO(LEUM + CUT *sb.*[2]] A design cut in relief on a block of linoleum; a print obtained from this. Hence **lino-cutting** *vbl. sb.*; **lino-cutter**, a person who makes linocuts; also, a tool used in lino-cutting.

1907 C. E. DAWSON in *Process Engravers' Monthly* Jan. 14 (*title*) Lino-cuts. A new method in blockmaking for posters and other bold work. *Ibid.* 16 This work, which I call *lino-cutting*, is..so easy that almost any simple design can be cut double crown size in an evening. *Ibid.* Feb. 28 Old chapbooks..are most usefully suggestive to the lino-cutter. **1919** R. FRY *Let.* 19 Nov. (1972) II. 471 Get Pamela to show you the lino-cut she did of a swan. **1927** C. FLIGHT *Lino-Cuts* iii. 19 The chief difficulties in lino-cut colour printing lie..in the arrangement of the design in form and colour. **1948** H. MISSINGHAM *Student's Guide Commercial Art* 71 *No. 5 lino cutter*, a sharp steel blade on a pen-nib shank, which can either be used in the normal lino tool handle or in a penholder. **1956** J. SYMONS *Paper Chase* xvii. 137 Round the walls were a variety of paintings ranging from *collages* to linocuts. **1972** J. MANN *Mrs Knox's Profession* xv. 116 One of those triangular blades screwed into a thick handle—a lino cutter. **1973** *Times* 6 Oct. 14/7 Miss Enid Lawrence..was a versatile artist, painter, lino-cutter... Her name is particularly associated with that of Claude Flight and the development of the lino-cut.

Linofilm (ˈlaɪnəfɪlm). *Printing.* [= *line o' film*, after LINOTYPE.] The proprietary name of an electronic photo-composing system. (See quots.) Also *attrib.*

1956 *Trade Marks Jrnl.* 5 Dec. 1212/2 Linofilm... Phototypographic machines and tape perforating machines for use in setting and composing type photographically. Mergenthaler Linotype Company.., Brooklyn, City and State of New York, United States of America; manufacturers. **1961** *Spectator* 14 Apr. 509/3 He referred to ..lino-film, and the demarcation problems which must be solved if photo-composing is to continue. **1965** J. MORAN *Composition of Reading Matter* vii. 75 The Linofilm Magnetic-to-Punched Tape Converter accepts magnetic tape from standard computer and data processing equipment, and produced 15-hole Linofilm tape. **1973** S. JENNETT *Making of Bks.* (ed. 5) v. 86 Most electronic photo-composing machines, however, operate from punched tape only about an inch wide, with six to nine levels or rows of perforations..—the Linofilm, taking tape of fifteen levels, is a notable exception.

Linograph[1] (ˈlaɪnəgrɑːf, -æ-). *Printing.* [= *line o'* + -GRAPH, after LINOTYPE.] The proprietary name of an American composing machine which casts type a line at a time.

1913 *Inland Printer* May 240 (Advt.), The Linograph is now ready. **1931** *Brit. Printer* XLIII. 229/1 The author passes in review all the different types such as the Linotype, the Typograph, the Monotype,..the American Linograph [etc.]. **1965** J. MORAN *Composition of Reading Matter* vi. 59 The Linograph closely resembled the Linotype, but differed in the arrangement of the magazine, which was vertical... The Linograph works were bought by Intertype in 1940.

linography (laɪˈnɒgrəfɪ). [f. L. *līn-um* flax (see LINE *sb.*[1]) + -GRAPHY.] (See quots.) Also **linograph**[2], a picture produced by linography.

1888 *Jrnl. Soc. Chem. Industry* VII. 588/1 Linography. This is a name given to photographing on linen or calico, to serve as a basis for painting in oil. **1945** E. EPSTEAN tr. *Eder's Hist. Photogr.* xxxvii. 325 Linography. Photographic reproductions (mostly enlargements) were produced on linen, to be afterwards colored, by a variation of Talbotypy. .. J. Lüttgens, in Hamburg, states that he used this process in 1856. **1970** *Canad. Antiques Collector* Dec. 26/1 Included in the collection were signed linographs, etchings and posters.

linoleic (lɪnəʊˈliːɪk), *a. Chem.* [f. L. *līn-um* + *ole-um* oil + -IC.] ***linoleic acid***: an acid found as a glyceride in linseed and other oils. Hence **liˈnoleate**, a salt of linoleic acid. So **liˈnolein** [-IN[1]] (see quot. 1900).

1857 MILLER *Elem. Chem.* III. 360 The oleic acid furnished by the saponification of linseed oil differs from ordinary oleic acid; Sacc terms it linoleic acid. *Ibid.* 370 The olein of olive oil differs from the olein of linseed oil, or linolein. **1865** WATTS *Dict. Chem.* III. 700 *Linoleic Acid.* Papaverolic acid. *Ibid.*, Linoleate of lead. **1900** B. D. JACKSON *Gloss. Bot. Terms* 148 *Linolein*, the glyceride of linoleic acid found in linseed oil.

linolenic acid (lɪnəˈlɛnɪk, -ˈliːnɪk). *Chem.* [tr. G. *linolensäure* (K. Hazura 1887, in *Sitzungsber. d. K. Akad. d. Wissensch. (Mat.-Nat. Kl.)* XCV. II. 1055), f. *linolsäure* LINOLEIC *acid* with insertion of *-en* -ENE.] A liquid unsaturated carboxylic acid, $C_{18}H_{30}O_2$, which is found as a glyceride in linseed and most other drying oils: 9,12,15-octadecatrienoic acid.

1887 *Jrnl. Chem. Soc.* LII. 913 The acids from drying oils contain both linolic acid, $C_{18}H_{32}O_2$, and linolenic acid, $C_{18}H_{30}O_2$. **1921** *Ibid.* CXIX. 1307 The product of the action of zinc on linolenic acid hexabromide was a mixture of α- and β-linolenic acids, although only the α-modification occurs naturally. **1951** R. MAYER *Artist's Handbk.* iii. 111 Poppy oil..owes its property of yellowing less than linseed oil to the smaller percentage of linolenic acid it contains. **1969** J. I. ROUTH et al. *Essent. Gen., Org. & Biochem.* xxxiii. 643 Unsaturated fatty acids such as linoleic and linolenic are essential components of cellular lipids that must be obtained in the diet, since they cannot be synthesized by the body.

Hence **linoˈlenate**, a salt or ester of linolenic acid.

1909 *Jrnl. Chem. Soc.* XCVI. I. 357 In the mixture of esters used about 22% was ethyl α-linolenate. **1950** *Jrnl. Nutrition* XLI. 485 When fed with suboptimum doses of linoleic acid, the resultant activity of the additional linolenate equalled that of linoleate.

linoleum (lɪˈnəʊlɪəm). [f. L. *līnum* flax + *oleum* oil.] A kind of floor-cloth made by coating canvas with a preparation of oxidized linseed-oil. Hence **linoleumed** (lɪˈnəʊlɪəmd), *ppl. a.*

1878 *Law Rep., Chanc. Div.* VII. 834 A Mr. Walton obtained several patents, the last and principal being in 1863, for preparing floorcloth by means of a certain solidified or oxidised oil to which he gave the name Linoleum, and the floorcloth made by him therewith had been called and known as 'Linoleum Floor Cloth', and apparently also as 'Linoleum'... In 1864 the Linoleum Manufacturing Company..was formed. **1879** in WEBSTER, Suppl. **1892** *Pictorial World* 21 May 104/1 A chilly tiled or linoleumed passage. **1895** *Daily News* 21 Nov. 9/4 Furnishers, upholsterers, carpet and linoleum warehousemen.

‖**linon** (linɔ̃). [F. *linon.*] A trade-name for 'lawn'. (In some mod. Dicts.)

1901 *Westm. Gaz.* 25 Apr. 2/2 *Linon*, by the way, is just the linen batiste of our shops.

†**liˈnosity.** [ad. mod.L. **līnōsitās*, f. *līn-um* flax.] Abundance of flax (Blount *Glossogr.* 1656).

†**ˈlinostole.** [ad. OF. *linostolie*, ad. Gr. λινοστολία, f. λίνον linen + στολή robe.] A surplice.

1694 MOTTEUX *Rabelais* v. iv. 13.

linot, obs. form of LINNET.

Linotype (ˈlaɪnətaɪp). *Printing.* [= *line o' type.*] The proprietary name of a composing machine invented by Ottmar Mergenthaler (1854-99) that sets type line by line (see quot. 1892). Also *attrib.*

1888 [First used in] *Specif. U.S. Patent* No. 393846, 4 Dec. **1889** *Times* (weekly ed.) 28 June 20/1 The linotype.. has been adopted in the offices of several American newspapers. **1892** A. POWELL *Southward's Pract. Printing* (ed. 4) xxxii. 318 The Linotype..sets up not types, but type-matrices, and then, when a line is complete, passes the matrices on to a foundry which forms part of the apparatus, and a full line is cast... Distribution is avoided. The matter once used..is returned to the metal pot and melted ready for fresh work... The advantages of the machine are its great speed and the economy effected by melting instead of distributing. A disadvantage is the fact that..there is no mode of correction other than to reset the whole line... Still, ..the machine has decided merits. It is in use in many newspaper offices. *Ibid.* (Advt.), The result of a contest between four American Composing Machines..showed that on the Linotype the operator averaged 12,250 Ens an

Hour, corrected matter. **1899** *Appleton's Ann. Cycl.* 623 In 1880 he [Mergenthaler] made a complete change of system, and adopted the plan that he brought to perfection in the linotype. **1902** A. W. BICKERTON (*title*) The perils of a pioneer: a protest in linotype proof. **1903** *Stationer, Printer & Fancy Trades' Reg.* 1 Aug. 364/2 At present linotype operators work on piece, that is to say, they are paid according to the work they do. **1926** *Brit. Gaz.* 12 May 2/2 The *Thanet Advertiser*, Ramsgate, reports that its linotype operators have returned to work. **1946** A. MONKMAN in H. Whetton *Pract. Printing & Binding* iii. 33/1 As the name implies, the Linotype..is a slug-casting machine. Introduced about 1886 it is now used in practically every newspaper office and also in many general printing offices. **1951** E. PAUL *Springtime in Paris* xi. 211 Comrade Rappaport, a linotype operator from *L'Humanité*. **1963** W. CLOWES *Guide to Printing* iii. 22 The 'Linotype' machine incorporates both keyboard and caster. **1973** S. JENNETT *Making of Bks.* (ed. 5) iv. 68 The product of the Linotype is not a line of separate letters, but a solid metal strip, or 'slug', bearing on one of the long edges the characters that go to make up the whole line. **1974** *Northern Times* (Golspie, Sutherland) 21 June 5/2 His son..was a Linotype Operator on the 'N. T.' [*sc.* Northern Times].

Hence **'linotyped** *ppl. a.*, of type set in this way; **'linotyper**, **'linotypist**, one who uses a linotype; **'linotyping** *vbl. sb.*, the process of setting type by the use of this machine.

1895 *Daily News* 26 Nov. 10/5 Linotypist wants day work. **1896** *Peterson Mag.* VI. 305/1 Stenographers, typewriters, compositors, and linotypers. **1902** *U.S. Census Bull.* No. 242. 73 A new departure in the art of linotyping. **1908** *Westm. Gaz.* 21 Apr. 7/2 The linotyped calumny of millionaire journalism. **1911** H. S. HARRISON *Queed* vii. 83 The little knot of linotypers and helpers..now listened.

†**'linous**, *a.*[1] *Obs. rare*[−1]. [f. L. *līn-um* flax + -OUS.] Of the nature of flax; flax-like.

1715 tr. *Pancirollus' Rerum Mem.* I. I. v. 14 Pliny mentions another Sort of Linous Substance [orig. *alterius quoque lini cujusdam*], which he calls in the First Chapter of his Nineteenth Book, ξύλον, Wood.

linous ('laɪnəs), *a.*[2] *rare.* [f. LINE *sb.*[2] + -OUS.] Relating to or in a line.

1860 WORCESTER (cites Sir J. Herschel).

linoxyn (lɪ'nɒksɪn). *Chem.* [a. Du. *linoxyne* (G. J. Mulder *Scheikundige Verhand. en Onderzoekingen* (1865) IV. I. 120), f. L. *līn-um* flax (see LINE *sb.*[1]): see OXY- and -IN[1].] Any of various gelatinous or resinous substances obtained by oxidation of linseed oil by air.

1876 J. HARLEY *Royle's Man. Materia Med.* (ed. 6) 714 By saponification linseed oil is resolved into glycerin and linoleic acid... This, when exposed in thin layers to the air, gradually increases in weight, and is converted into.. oxylinoleic acid, $C_{16}H_{26}O_5,H_2O$. At 212° it loses water, becomes of a blood-red colour, and forms linoxyn, $C_{32}H_{54}O_{11}$. **1925** *Jrnl. Soc. Chem. Industry* 7 Aug. 407T/2 When linseed oil is exposed for five or six days of warm weather in films so thin as to contain less than 0·05 g. of oil per 100 sq. cm. area, a linoxyn can be obtained from the dried (autoxidised) product having the formula $C_{57}H_{96}O_{20}$. **1969** R. F. LANG tr. *Henglein's Chem. Technol.* 774 Linoleum serves as floor covering and contains as basic materials linoxyn (oxidized linseed oil), cork flour, and resins. **1972** *Materials & Technol.* V. xiii. 439 The insoluble linoxyn is highly cross-linked and polymerised.

'lin-pin. *Obs.* exc. *dial.* Also 4–6 lynpin, 5 -pyne, linepin, 7 linnpin. [f. *lin* (see LINCH *sb.*[1]) + PIN.] = LINCH-PIN.

c **1330** *Durham Acc. Rolls* (Surtees) 518 In..duobus Lynpinnes. *c* **1425** *Voc.* in Wr.-Wülcker 665/29 *Hoc hunullum*, lynpyne. **1523** FITZHERB. *Husb.* §5 With..ii. lyn pinnes of yren in the axiltre-endes. **1598** BARRET *Theor. Warres* v. iii. 133 Rammers, linepinnes,..and all such other implements. **1659** C. HOOLE tr. *Comenius' Orbis Sensualium* (1672) 173 The Axle-trees..the Lin-pins, and Axletree-staves. **1688** R. HOLME *Armoury* III. 339/2 Linn Pin.

†**'linquish**, *v. Obs.* [f. L. *linqu-ĕre* + -ISH[2], after RELINQUISH *v.*] *trans.* To abandon, forsake.

1591 HARINGTON *Orl. Fur.* XXXIX. xviii, But now awhile I linquish this conflict. **1604** R. C[AWDREY] *Table Alph.*, *Linquish*, to leaue or forsake. **1694** MOTTEUX *Rabelais* (1737) V. 232 Th' Opime you'd linquish for the Macerated.

linsang ('lɪnsæŋ). [a. Javanese *linsang*, *wlinsang*, wrongly rendered 'otter' in Dicts.] A civet-like mammal of the genus *Prionodon*, which includes *P. pardicolor* of south-east Asia and *P. linsang*, found in this region and Sumatra, Java, and Borneo. A related African species is the Guinea Linsang, *Poiana richardsoni*.

1821 T. HARDWICKE in *Trans. Linn. Soc.* XIII. 236 Viverra? Linsang... The general colour of the animal is a yellowish white. **1885** *Riverside Nat. Hist.* (1888) V. 438 The Linsang (*Prionodon gracilis*) of the Malayan regions.. is white, with broad, black cross bands. It occurs in Borneo, Java, and Singapore.... The Guinea Linsang..ranges from Sierra Leone to Fernando Po. **1893** LYDEKKER *Roy. Nat. Hist.* I. 456 The Asiatic linsangs..constitute the genus *Linsang*. The one African linsang..has been made the type of a separate genus—*Poiana*. **1969** LD. MEDWAY *Wild Mammals Malaya* 91/1 Banded linsang... *Prionodon linsang*... In Malaya widespread on the mainland at all elevations but nowhere common.

linse, obs. and dial. form of LINCH.

linseed ('lɪnsiːd). Forms: α. See LINE *sb.*[1] and SEED. β. 6 lint(e)seede, 7 lyntseed, 7–9 *north. dial.* lintseed. [OE. *līn* LINE *sb.*[1] + *sǣd* seed; cf. MHG. *līnsât*, Du. *lijnzaad*.

The form *lint-seed*, which is strictly to be regarded as a distinct word, f. LINT, is in Scotland used of seed intended to be sown, while the ordinary form is current in other applications.]

a. The seed of flax, well known as the source of linseed-oil, and as a medicament. †Occas. the flax-plant. ***oil of linseed(s*** = linseed-oil.

c **1000** *Sax. Leechd.* I. 140 Genim þas ylcan wyrte seoð.. mid linsæde. *a* **1100** *Gerefa* in *Anglia* (1886) IX. 262 Mederan settan, linsed sawan. **13..** *S.E. Leg.* (MS. Bodl. 779) in Herrig's *Archiv* LXXXII. 311/217 Of linsed & of eyrin & of oþer þing men conne al day oyle out bring. **1398** TREVISA *Barth. De P.R.* XVII. xcvii. (1495) 664 Lyne sede nourissheth but lytyll: and is hard to defye. *c* **1420** *Pallad. on Husb.* XI. 15 Now lynseed, yf the liketh, may be sowe. **1532–3** *Act. 24 Hen. VIII*, c. 4 [They shall] till and and sowe ..one roode..with line sede, otherwise called flaxe sede. **1578** LYTE *Dodoens* I. xlix. 71 Lynseede mengled with hony ..appeaseth the cough. **1626** A. SPEED *Adam out of E.* xv. (1659) 114 The drosse or that which is left after the pressing out of Lyntseeds. **1661** LOVELL *Hist. Anim. & Min.* 418 The catarrhe..if from repletion, it's helped by line-seed, with honey. **1686** AGLIONBY *Painting Illustr.* I. 27 The Secret of Oyl Painting, consists in using Colours that are Ground with Oyl of Nut, or Linseed. **1712** tr. *Pomet's Hist. Drugs* I. 37 Leaves, like those of Linseed but larger, greener. and more viscous. **1729** (*title*) Short Rules and Observations for Sowing of Lint-seed and Hemp-seed. **1782** J. MILL *Diary* in *Shetland Minister 18th Cent.* (1897) 112 A decoction of 2 oz. lint seed, 2 do. of Liquorish-stick bruised and boiled [etc.]. **1807** *Med. Jrnl.* XVII. 554 The..barley water, and infusion of linseed were ordered to be continued. **1823** J. BADCOCK *Dom. Amusem.* 30 Having dipped the fore-finger and thumb partially in oil of linseeds. **1847** MARY HOWITT *Ballads* 66 And some they brought the brown lint-seed, And flung it down from the Flax Low. **1872** OLIVER *Elem. Bot.* II. 148 The seeds of the Flax plant, called Linseed, are very largely imported.

b. *attrib.* and *Comb.*, as ***linseed-shaped*** adj.; **linseed cake**, linseed pressed into cakes in the process of extracting the oil, and used as food for cattle; **linseed-earth** (see quot.); **linseed-meal**, linseed ground in a mill; **linseed-oil**, the oil obtained by pressure from linseed; **linseed poultice**, a poultice made of linseed or linseed-meal; **linseed-tea**, an infusion of linseed, used as a demulcent.

1813 SIR H. DAVY *Agric. Chem.* (1814) 365 Cattle at first refuse *Linseed cake. **1883** GRESLEY *Gloss. Coal-mining*, **Linseed Earth*, blackish grey clay suitable for making into firebricks. **1599** A. M. tr. *Gabelhouer's Bk. Physicke* 68/1 With *lintseede meale make a little paest. **1839** *Penny Cycl.* XIII. 384/1 Cataplasms of linseed-meal. **1548** *Privy-Council Acts* (1890) II. 174 *Lyncede oyle, xx galons. **1726** LEONI tr. *Alberti's Archit.* II. 15/2 Colours mixed up with lintseed oyl. **1879** G. GLADSTONE in *Cassell's Techn. Educ.* IV. 192/1 In oil-gilding the size used is made of a mixture of boiled linseed-oil and ochre. **1833** *Cycl. Pract. Med.* II. 813/2 A common bread and water or *lintseed poultice. **1870** T. HOLMES *Syst. Surg.* (ed. 2) I. 703 The knots [of farcy] are small and *linseed-shaped. **1741** BAKER in *Phil. Trans.* XLI. 659 When I went to-bed, drank some *Linseed-tea.

Hence **linseeded** *ppl. a.*, mixed with linseed.

1864 *Spectator* 27 Feb. 228/2 The Bill for allowing linseeded malt to escape duty passed its second reading.

†**'linsel.** *Obs. rare*[−1]. In 6 lynsel. [ad. F. *linceul* sheet, winding sheet:—L. *linteolum*, dim. of *linteum* linen cloth.] A shawl, a wrap.

1594 KYD *Cornelia* III. D 4 b, Casting a thyn course lynsel ore hys shoulders, That..trayl'd vpon the ground.

linsey ('lɪnzɪ). Also 5 lynesey, 6 lince, 7–8 linsy. [Possibly f. LINE *sb.*[1] + SAY.]

1. In early use, perh. some coarse linen fabric. In later use, = LINSEY-WOOLSEY. Also *attrib.*

1435–6 in Heath *Grocers' Comp.* (1869) 419, xx clothis of lynesey. **1583** *Rates Custom-ho.* D j b. Lince called blew lince the doz. **1771** PENNANT *Tour Scotl.* 1769 (1774) 259 Chiefly engaged in manufactures of linsies, worsted stockings [etc.]. *c* **1826** *Erl Richard* xxiv. in Child *Ballads* II. 463 O haud awa thae linen sheets, And bring to me the linsey clouts I hae been best used in. **1881** *Instr. Census Clerks* (1885) 64 Woollen Cloth Manufacture. Linsey Weaver.

2. (See quot.)

1883 GRESLEY *Gloss. Coal-mining*, *Linsey*, strong Bind, also streaky sandstone.

linsey-woolsey ('lɪnzɪ 'wʊlzɪ). Forms: 5 lynsy-, 6 lylse-, lince-, lynse-, 6–8 linsi(e-, -y(e-, 7 lin(t)sie-, lincy-, linzy-, lynsey-, 7–9 lindsey-, 6– linsey-; 5 -wolsye, 6 -wolse, -woolsy(e, -wulse(y, 6–8 -wo(o)lsie, -y, 6–9 -wolsey, 6– woolsey. [f. prec. + WOOL, with jingling ending.]

1. Orig. a textile material, woven from a mixture of wool and flax; now, a dress material of coarse inferior wool, woven upon a cotton warp. Also *pl.* Pieces or kinds of this material.

1483 *Cath. Angl.* 217/2 Lynsy wolsye, *linistema vel linostema*. **1522** SKELTON *Why not to Court* 128 We shall haue a *tot quot* From the Pope of Rome, To weue all in one lome A webbe of lylse wulse. **1591** H. SMITH *Prep. Marriage* 157 God forbad the people to weare linsey wolsey, because it was a signe of inconstancie. **1599** NASHE *Lenten Stuffe* To Rdr., I had as lieue haue..no cloathes rather then wear linsey wolsey. **1670** D. DENTON *Descr. New York* (1845) 18 They make every one Cloth of for their own wearing, as also woollen Cloth, and Linsey-woolsey. *c* **1710** C. FIENNES *Diary* (1888) 159 Kendall Cotton..is much made here and also Linsi-woolseys. **1784** R. BAGE *Barham Downs* I. 169 Martha..delighted to be cloathed in good Linsy Woolsy, the work of her own hands. **1826** MISS MITFORD *Village* Ser. II. 73 Then ensues another set of changes..till gray hairs, wrinkles, and lindsey-woolsey wind up the picture. **1855** W. SARGENT *Braddock's Exped.* 85 Dresses of linsey-woolsey (a cloth, home-woven, of wool and flax).

b. A garment of this material.

1894 MRS. H. WARD *Marcella* I. 18 Marcella..had usually figured..in a linsey-woolsey.

2. *fig.* or in figurative contexts, *esp.* a strange medley in talk or action; confusion, nonsense.

? **1592** GREENE *Vision* Wks. 1881–6 XII. 235 Thou hast write no booke well, but thy *Nunquam sera est*, and that is indifferent Linsey Wolsey. **1594** NASHE *Terrors Nt.* Wks. 1883 III. 229 A man must not..haue his affections linsey wolsey, intermingled with lust, and things worthy of liking. **1601** SHAKS. *All's Well* IV. i. 13 What linsie wolsy hast thou to speake to vs againe. **1628** FORD *Lover's Mel.* V. i, This unfashionable mongrel, this linsey-wolsey of mortality. **1694** S. JOHNSON *Notes Past. Let. Bp. Burnet* I. 52 Far be it from all Mankind to impute such All-to-mall and Linsey-wolsey to the Providence of God.

3. *attrib.* passing into *adj.*

1618 DONNE *Serm.* cxxxiii. V. 394 Out of his word I can preach against Linsey-woolsey garments [*Deut.* xxii. 11]. **1749** FIELDING *Tom Jones* XI. v, [I] have never seen any of your cash, unless for one lindsey woolsey coat. **1777** W. DALRYMPLE *Trav. Sp. & Port.* xxix, The women wore jackets and aprons..with a kind of linsey woolsey petticoat. **1839** STONEHOUSE *Axholme* 47 Forty or fifty years ago..a servant of the best class..was clad chiefly in linsey woolsey garments. **1855** SINGLETON *Virgil* I. Pref. 5 To dress the sovereign in a linsey-woolsey garb would be seen at once to be a very unsuitable investiture.

b. *fig.* Chiefly with sense, 'giving the appearance of a strange medley', 'being neither one thing nor the other'.

1565 T. STAPLETON *Fortr. Faith* 102 b, An asse in a rochet, a lince wolse bishop. **1619** BP. SANDERSON *Serm.* I. 18 The linsey-woolsey Laodicean church, neither hot nor cold. **1663** BUTLER *Hud.* I. iii. 1227 A Lawless Linsy-woolsy Brother, Half of one Order, half another. **1758** J. RUTTY *Spirit. Diary* (ed. 2) 125 Lord take away this linsey-woolsey virtue! **1823** *Examiner* 532/1 A perking, prurient, linsey-wolsey species of composition.

4. *Comb.*, as ***linsey-woolsey-wise*** adv.

1606 SYLVESTER *Du Bartas* II. iv. II. *Magnif.* 32 And also mingle (Linsie-woolsie-wise) This gold-ground Tissue with too-mean supplies.

Linson ('lɪnsən). The proprietary name of a tough fibrous paper fabric used esp. in bookbinding.

1948 *Trade Marks Jrnl.* 18 Feb. 127/2 Linson... Book-binding materials. R. & W. Watson Limited,.. Renfrewshire; manufacturers. **1952** A. W. LEWIS *Basic Bookbinding* ii. 11 Linson is available in numerous colours and surface finishes. **1957** *B.B.C. Handbook* 248 *Mrs. Dale's Diary*..ordinary edition, 6*s.* 3*d.*, Linson bound, 3*s.* 7*d.* **1963** *Times Lit. Suppl.* 26 Apr. 316/1 Bound in Linson or one of its..equivalents. **1967** J. S. HEWITT-BATES *Bookbinding* (ed. 8) iii. 18 Non-woven materials such as Linson are ideal for school work.

linstock ('lɪnstɒk). *Obs.* exc. *Hist.* Also 6 linestoke, lyn(t)stock, (limstock), 6–7 lint stocke, 6–8 lin(t)stock, 9 lent-stock. [In 16th c. *lint-*, *linestocke*, ad. (with assimilation to LINT and LINE *sb.*[1]) Du. *lontstok*, f. *lont* match (see LUNT *sb.*) + *stok* stick.] A staff about three feet long, having a pointed foot to stick in the deck or ground, and a forked head to hold a lighted match.

1575 CHURCHYARD *Chippes* 95 b, He..in his hand, a smoking lyntstock broght And so gaue fier. **1592** STOW *Ann.* (an. 1563) 1116 A linestoke fell into a barrel of powlder, and set it on fire together with the vessell. **1598** B. JONSON *Ev. Man in Hum.* III. i, Their master gunner..confronts me with his linstock, readie to giue fire. **1682** *Lond. Gaz.* No. 1684/1 Then thirty Gunners with their Linstocks.. followed by thirty Negroes..with their Brown-bills. **1769** FALCONER *Dict. Marine* (1780), Lintstock. **1804** *Naval Chron.* XII. 63, 1 lent-stock; 12 handspikes. **1808** SCOTT *Marm.* I. ix, The gunner held his linstock yare. **1840** BARHAM *Ingol. Leg.*, *Hamilton Tighe*, The linstock glows in his bony hand.

fig. **1602** MARSTON *Ant. & Mel.* II. Wks. 1856 I. 19 The match of furie is lighted, fastned to the linstock of rage.

linsy, obs. form of LINSEY.

lint[1] (lɪnt). Forms: 4–7 lynt(e, 5 lyn(n)et, 6 linte, 7 (9 *dial.*) linet, 5– lint. [In ME. *linnet*; related (somewhat obscurely) to LINE *sb.*[1]; perh. a. F. *linette* (recorded only in the sense 'linseed', but possibly of wider meaning in OF.), f. *lin* LINE *sb.*[1]: see -ET[1].]

1. (Now only *Sc.*) The flax-plant.

1458 [see *lint-sown* in 6]. **1548** TURNER *Names of Herbes* 49 Linum is called in englishe Flax, lyne or lynte. **1562** —— *Herbal* II. 39 Flax is called of the Northen men lynt. **1733** P. LINDSAY *Interest Scot.* 154 Our present Way is to sow our Lint on any Ground, which puts us to a great Expence to weed it. **1785** BURNS *Cotter's Sat. Nt.* xi, The frugal wifie garrulous will tell, How 'twas a towmond auld, sin' lint was i' the bell. **1805** FORSYTH *Beauties Scotl.* IV. 29 Flax, or, as it is universally called in Scotland, lint, is sown.

2. (Chiefly *Sc.*) Flax prepared for spinning. Also, the refuse of the same, used as a combustible.

1375 BARBOUR *Bruce* XVII. 612 Pik and ter als haf thai tane, And lynt and hardiss with brynstane. *c* **1375** *Sc. Leg. Saints* iii. (*Andreas*) 593 Lynt to bet þe fyr of hell. *c* **1470** HENRY *Wallace* VII. 423 This trew woman thaim seruit weill in deid, With lynt and fyr, that haistely kendill wald. **1562** *Durham Depos.* (Surtees) 72 To pay the said Isabell every yere one

bonde of lynt. **1591** HARINGTON *Orl. Fur.* XXXIV. lxxxvii, Each roome therein was full of divers fleeces Of wooll, of lint, of silk, or els of cotten. **1741** in A. Laing *Lindores Abbey* xxi. (1876) 272 For one hundred weight of lint to be given out to the poor people of the paroche to spin. **179.** BURNS *Weary Pund o' Tow* 5, I bought my wife a stane o' lint As gude as e'er did grow; And a' that she has made o' that Is ae poor pund o' tow. **1830** SCOTT *Demonol.* ix. 330 It was at different times a brazier's shop, and a magazine for lint.

3. a. A soft material for dressing wounds (formerly also to burn for tinder), prepared by ravelling or scraping linen cloth. †In *pl.*, pieces of this material.

c **1400** *Lanfranc's Cirurg.* 83 Fille þe wounde wiþinneforþ with lynnet of lynnen clooþ. *c* **1440** *Promp. Parv.* 306/1 Lynt, schauynge of lynen clothe, *carpea.* **1578** LYTE *Dodoens* III. xii. 333 The same..layde to with fine linte or lynnen, doth swage and mitigate the payne. ? *c* **1600** *Distracted Emp.* v. iii. in Bullen *O. Pl.* III. 249 May theire sore wast theire lynnen into lynte. **1612** W. PARKES *Curtaine-Dr.* (1876) 55 Let him but finde the least sparke in the lint, hee neuer ceaseth blowing till he haue made it a huge flame. **1622** BEAUM. & FL. *Sea-Voy.* III. i, O that I had my boxes and my lints now. **1670** COTTON *Espernon* III. x. 498 Very much weakened with ten great wounds, and roul'd up with Lints and Plaisters. **1707** FARQUHAR *Beaux Stratagem* v. iv, Do, do, Daughter—while I get the Lint, and the Probe and the Plaister ready. **1767** GOOCH *Treat. Wounds* I. 189 Lint or Puff-ball, moistened in Alcohol Vini..will generally answer the purpose. **1828** SCOTT *F.M. Perth* ii, He..hastily took from his purse some dry lint, to apply to the slight wound. **1833** HT. MARTINEAU *Charmed Sea* iv. 51 To scrape lint and nurse the wounded was proper woman's employment down in Poland yonder. **1884** M. MACKENZIE *Dis. Throat & Nose* II. 63 Drainage [of the abscess] was kept up by means of a strip of lint.

b. Fluff of any material. †Also, a particle of the same. *rare.*

1611 COTGR., *Freluche*,..a small straw, or lint. *a* **1663** HOWARD *Committee* II. i. *Four Plays* (1665) 88 Driving the lint from his black Cloathes With his Wet Thumb. **1898** *Century Mag.* Jan. 372/2 After a little the saws clogged with lint, the wheel stopped, and poor Whitney was in despair.

4. a. Now only *dial.* or *U.S.* Netting for fishing-nets. †**b.** A net for the hair. *Obs. rare*$^{-1}$.

a. 1615 E. S. *Britain's Buss* in Arb. *Garner* III. 629 Which 245 yards of Lint or Netting (ready made or knit) will cost three pence a yard. **1874** HOLDSWORTH *Deep-sea Fishing* ii. 101 That length of line being appropriated to the 30 yards of [drift-]net, so that the 'lint' or netting is set slack. **1884** KNIGHT *Dict. Mech.* Suppl., *Lint* (*Fishing*), a fisherman's name for the netting of a pound or seine. **1892** P. H. EMERSON *Son of Fens* 37 They ligged the ground rope in, and begun pulling in the lint to the cod end.

b. *a* **1828** *Ld. Livingston* xxxii. in Child *Ballads* IV. 433/2 There's never lint gang on my head.

5. The material which forms the bulk of the fibres in the cotton boll (cf. LINTER¹ b), which is separated from the cotton seeds by ginning and which after processing is the ordinary cotton of commerce.

1877 *Encycl. Brit.* VI. 483/1 When this [*sc.* ginning] is done there remains of the bulk, as gathered from the tree, about one-third of clean cotton fit for manufacturing purposes, and two-thirds of seed. The separation of the seed from the lint is accomplished by different methods. **1883** 'MARK TWAIN' *Life on Mississippi* xxxiii. 325 In sixteen hundred pounds crude cotton four hundred are lint, worth, say, ten cents a pound. **1967** SHAW & ECKERSLEY *Cotton* iii. 10 The seed cotton..may be ginned three times but only the 'lint' from the first ginning is used in normal cotton spinning.

6. *attrib.* and *Comb.*, as ***lint-boll*** (***-bow***), ***-mill***, ***-pad***, ***-sheaf***, ***-speck***; ***lint-sown*** ppl. a.; **lint-box** (*U.S.*), the upper part of a cotton-press; **lint-doctor** *Calico-printing* (see quot.); **lint-haired** = *flaxen-haired*; **lint-head** *U.S. dial.*, a worker in a cotton mill; (in contemptuous use) a person of whom one disapproves; **lint-paper**, ? = *linen-paper*; **lint-scraper**, a person employed to scrape lint (for hospital use); also (*slang*), a contemptuous name for a young surgeon; †**lint-spurge**, a name proposed for the plant *Euphorbia Esula*; **lint-top** (Sc. *-tap*), as much flax as is usually laid on a distaff for being spun off. Also LINT-WHITE *a.*

c **1470** HENRYSON *Mor. Fab.* VIII. (*Preach. Swallow*) xxvii, Me think, quhen that yone *lint-bollis ar ryip, To mak ws feist. *a* **1585** POLWART *Flyting w. Montgomerie* 552 Athort his nitty now Ilke louse lyes linkand like a large lint bow. **1901** G. W. CABLE *Cavalier* xxi, The *lint-box of the old cotton-press was covered with wet morning-glories. **1839** URE *Dict. Arts* 217 Another..sharp-edged ruler, called the *lint doctor, whose office it is to remove any fibres which may have come off the calico in the act of printing. **1891** V. C. COTES *2 Girls on Barge* 78 A dirty *lint-haired ragamuffin. **1933** E. CALDWELL *God's Little Acre* vii. 108 I'd rather be a God-forsaken *lint-head and live in a yellow company house. **1940** C. MCCULLERS *Heart is Lonely Hunter* (1943) II. iv. 128, I would have just been a preacher or a linthead or a salesman. **1969** 'J. MORRIS' *Fever Grass* xvi. 138, I didn't kill that big linthead. *You* did! **1805** FORSYTH *Beauties Scotl.* IV. 49 Upon this water there are..two *lint-mills. **1879** *St. George's Hosp. Rep.* IX. 482 Wet *lint-pad and bandage applied. **1794** BLUMENBACH in *Phil. Trans.* LXXXIV. 180 The outward ones had some traces of our common *lint paper. **1861** THACKERAY *Lovel* vi. (1869) 241 If Miss Prior ..prefers this *lint-scraper to me, ought I to baulk her? **1881** *Instr. Census Clerks* (1885) 48 Lint Scraper. **1799** J. ROBERTSON *Agric. Perth* 168 Some persons..recommend to set up the *lint sheaves..in stooks, like grain. **1458** *Extracts Burgh Rec. Peebles* (1872) 128 Al the wast land that was *lynt or corn sawin. **1827–35** WILLIS *Parrhasius* 53 The *lint-specks floated in the twilight air. **1548** TURNER *Names of Herbes* (E.D.S.) 63 Pityusa..oughte to be called..*Lint-spourge, for it hath smal leaues like Flax. **1721** RAMSAY *Bessy Bell & Mary G.* ii, Bessy's hair's like a *lint tap.

lint² (lɪnt). *dial.* [Short for *lintle* LENTIL.] = LENTIL (chiefly in *pl.*).

1888 in *Sheffield Gloss.*

lintan: see LINTER².

†**linte'arious**, *a. Obs. rare*$^{-0}$. [f. L. *linteāri-us* (f. *linteus* linen) + -OUS.] Of or belonging to linen (Blount *Glossogr.* 1656).

lintel ('lɪntəl). Forms: 4–5, 7 lyntel(l, 5, 7 li-, lyntal(l, (6 lyntil, lynttyll, 7 lental, lindal, lintle, 8 lintil, 9 lentil), 7– lintel. [a. OF *lintel* threshold (F. *linteau*):—popular L. **līmitāle* or **līmitellum* (f. *līmit-*, *līmes* LIMIT *sb.*, confused with *līmin-*, *līmen* threshold).]

1. A horizontal piece of timber, stone, etc. placed over a door, window, or other opening to discharge the superincumbent weight.

1388 WYCLIF *Exod.* xii. 22 Sprynge ȝe therof the lyntel [Vulg. *superliminare*], and euer either post. *c* **1450** *Merlin* 436 The Emperor..wrote letteres on the lyntell of the dore in grewe. **1500–20** DUNBAR *Poems* lxix. 39 Albeid that thow were never sa stout, Vndir this lyntall sall thow lowt. **1601–2** in Willis & Clark *Cambridge* (1886) II. 629 Paid for lyntalls at the fountaine iiij^{s} viij^{d}. **1667** PRIMATT *City & C. Build.* 82 One Lintal to discharge the two Windows and Balcony-door, eight foot of Timber. **1725** POPE *Odyss.* VII. 116 The pillars silver, on a brazen base; Silver the lintels deep-projecting o'er. **1839** YEOWELL *Anc. Brit. Ch.* xii. (1847) 139 A moor-stone lintel is placed across the top to support the little roof. **1863** A. FONBLANQUE *Tangled Skein* II. ii. 29 Upon the lentil of No. 7 [he] found painted the name of Mr. C. L.

†**2.** ? A spoke of a wheel. *Obs.*$^{-0}$

1570 LEVINS *Manip.* 125/13 Lyntil of a cart, *radius.*

3. *attrib.*, as ***lintel-piece***, ***-post***, ***-stone***, ***-tree***.

1842–59 GWILT *Encycl. Arch.* Gloss. s.v., If a wall be very thick, more than one *lintel piece will be required. **1874** RAYMOND *Statist. Mines & Mining* 402 The lintel-piece alone weighs about 3,000 pounds. **1806** J. GRAHAME *Birds Scot.* 942 Others [*sc.* birds] sometimes Are driven within our *lintel-posts by storms. **1575** *Burgh Rec. Glasgow* (1832) 50 Item, to James Law, for þe thre *lintall stanes to þe boiss windois, xij *s.* **1879** LUBBOCK *Addr. Pol. & Educ.* x. 197 The lintel stones of the doorway are 40 feet 10 inches in length. **1601** HOLLAND *Pliny* II. 580 The..maine *lintle-tree which lay ouer the..cheekes of the great dore. **1675** HOBBES *Odyssey* (1677) 77 The door-posts silver..The lintle-tree upon them silver too.

Hence **'lintelled** *a.*, furnished with a lintel. **'lintelling, lintling** *vbl. sb.*, the action of providing with lintels; the material used for this purpose.

1703 T. N. *City & C. Purchaser* 98 Lintelling, Guttering .., &c. at so much per Foot. **1827** *Gentl. Mag.* XCVII. II. 9 A doorway with a lintelled architrave. **1833** J. C. LOUDON *Encycl. Cottage, Farm, & Villa Archit.* 526 The cart-sheds to have a joist..built into the wall at each pillar, and chacked to the lintling beams. **1894** DOYLE *Mem. S. Holmes* 111 Over the low, heavy-lintelled door.

lintel(l, obs. form of LENTIL.

linter¹ ('lɪntə(r)). *U.S.* [f. LINT¹ + -ER¹.]

a. A machine for stripping off the short-staple cotton-fibre from the cotton-seed after ginning. Also ***linter-machine***. (In recent U.S. Dicts.)

b. *pl.* A product composed of the short downy hairs or 'fuzz' adhering to the cotton seeds (from which it is removed by the linter), which is unsuitable for spinning into yarn and is used as a source of cellulose, etc.

1903 E. A. POSSELT *Cotton Manuf.* I. 49 The fibres, short or long, thus obtained, are technically known as 'Linters' and are delivered by the condenser of the linting machine as a sheet or film. **1904** L. L. LAMBORN *Cottonseed Products* iv. 50 The purpose of delinting is to remove more completely the short fibres which form the 'linters'... The products of delinting are the linters. **1927** T. WOODHOUSE *Artificial Silk* iii. 13 The short fibres from cotton seeds—to which the name of cotton linters has been given—are utilized for the cellulose solutions. **1967** SHAW & ECKERSLEY *Cotton* iii. 11 The 'linters' from the second and third ginning are used in the waste trade. **1972** *Sci. Amer.* Dec. 48/2 The early man-made fibers were essentially recast molecules of cellulose originating in wood fibers or cotton linters (very short fibers). **1974** *Ibid.* Apr. 52/1 Paper..has been and is made from rags, straw, cotton linters, bagasse..and flax.

linter², †**lintan**, dial. corruptions of LEAN-TO.

1736 *New Hampsh. Prov. Papers* (1870) IV. 714 'Tis judged the cause [of a fire] was from a spark falling out of the lintan chimney (which was lower than the house). **1861** MRS. STOWE *Pearl of Orr's Isl.* 10 A brown house of the kind that the natives call 'lean to' or 'linter'. **1893** ZINCKE *Wherstead* 261 A penthouse is a 'linter' (lean-to).

†**linterel.** *Obs.* [Perh. a corruption of LINTEL; perh. a dim. of OF. *linter* (? :—L. type **līmitārium*), lintel.] = LINTEL.

a **1548** HALL *Chron., Hen. VIII* (1809) 639 A mightie buildyng of tymber..the lynterelles inhaunsed with pillers.

lintern, linton, altered ff. LINTEL; cf. prec. *Obs.* exc. *dial.*

1533 *Repar. Tower* in Bayley *Tower Lond.* (1821) I. App. 22 It'm for ij. lyntons made for the ij. wyndowes. **1611** CORYAT *Crudities* 133, I read this inscription in a peece of stone..directly over the linterne of the dore. **1614** RALEIGH *Hist. World* II. (1634) 212 When every one of the Hebrewes had slaine a Lambe,..and with the bloud thereof coloured the poste and linterne of the doores. **1864** T. Q. COUCH *E. Cornw. Gloss.* in *Jrnl. Roy. Inst. Cornw.* I. 17 Lintern, a lintel.

lintie ('lɪntɪ). *Sc.* Also **linty.** [f. *lint* in LINTWHITE + dim. ending -IE (-Y).] = LINNET.

1795 BURNS *Verses Destr. Woods* 4 Where linties sang and lambkins play'd. *a* **1835** HOGG *Ringan & May* 41 Poet. Wks. 1838 I. 300 She trows..The linty's cheip a ditty tame. **1899** CROCKETT *Kit Kennedy* 198, I heard the linties singing where I was falling asleep.

lintil, lintle, obs. forms of LENTIL.

1621 BURTON *Anat. Mel.* II. i. I. ii. 504 The Burre and the Lintle cannot endure one another [L. *lappa lenti adversatur*].

lintling, var. LINTELLING *vbl. sb.*

lintonite ('lɪntənaɪt). *Min.* [Named after Miss L. A. Linton, who analysed it.] A variety of thomsonite found in green amygdules in trap.

1879 PECKHAM & HALL in *Amer. Jrnl. Sci.* Ser. III. XIX. (1880) 122.

lintseed, lint-stock: see LINSEED, LINSTOCK.

lintwhite ('lɪnthwaɪt), *sb.* Chiefly *Sc.* Forms: 1 **línaethuíȝae, línetuíȝe, -twíȝe,** 4 **lynkwhytte,** 6 **lyntquhit, -yte,** 7– **lintwhite.** [OE. *línetwíȝe*, perh. f. *lín* flax + *-twíȝe* (? cogn. w. OHG. *zwigôn* to pluck, *vellere*, *carpere*), found also in *þisteltwíȝe* thistle finch. Cf. TWITE *sb.*

The etymology involves a difficulty because the first element appears as *line-* (or *linæ-*) instead of *lín*; but the correspondence in sense with the Rom. name of the bird (see LINNET) is in favour of its correctness. Apart from etymology there is no evidence that the first vowel in the O.E. word was long.]

= LINNET.

c **725** *Corpus Gloss.* (Hessels) C 147 *Carduelis*, linetuiȝe. *a* **800** *Erfurt Gloss.* 309 *Carduelis*, linaethuiȝae. *c* **1000** ÆLFRIC *Gloss.* in Wr.-Wülcker 11/26 *Carduelis*, linetuiȝe. ? *a* **1400** *Morte Arth.* 2674 With lowde laghttirs one lofte for lykynge of byrdez, Of larkes, of lynkwhyttez, þat lufflyche songene. **1513** DOUGLAS *Æneis* XII. Prol. 240 Goldspynk and lyntquhyte fordynnand the lyft. **1549** *Compl. Scot.* vi. 39 The lyntquhit sang cuntirpoint quhen the osȝil ȝelpit. *c* **1690** *Roxb. Ballads* (1888) VI. 607 The Lint-white loud, and Progne proud..do sing as sweetly as in Yarow. **1785** BURNS *To William Simpson* xii, When lint-whites chant among the buds. **1830** TENNYSON *Poems* 76 The lintwhite and the throstlecock Have voices sweet and clear.

lint-white ('lɪnthwaɪt), *a. Sc.* [f. LINT¹ + WHITE.] White as lint or flax; flaxen.

1794 BURNS '*Now nature cleeds*', Lassie wi' the lint-white locks. **1866** MISS MULOCK *Noble Life* viii. 148 With the sun shining on the lint-white hair.

†**'lintworm.** *Obs.* [a. MHG. *lintwurm* dragon.] ? A figure of a dragon.

1423 *Rolls of Parlt.* IV. 218 *Inventory Jewels of Hen. V*, Ung Lyntworme d'or ovec 1 Crois. *Ibid.* 219 Item, 111 Lyntewormes.

linty, *sb.*: see LINTIE.

linty ('lɪntɪ), *a.* [f. LINT¹ + -Y¹.] †**a.** Resembling lint; soft like flax or lint (in quot. *fig.*). **b.** Full of lint or fluff.

1607 MIDDLETON *Phœnix* II. iii. F 2, One good bang vppon a Buckler would make moste of our Gentlemen flye a peeces, tis not for these lintie times. **1705** N. TATE tr. *Cowley's Plants* v. (1721) 392 To see such Kernels such strong Armour wear; First with a linty Wad wrapt close about, (Useful to keep green Wounds from gushing out). **1889** GORDON STABLES *Dog Owners' Kennel Comp.* v. §4. 54 Mixture of about two-thirds hardish hair and one-third linty. **1891** *Bazaar* 20 Feb. 261/3 Swansdown..is better than cotton-wool, because it is not so linty.

‖**linum** ('laɪnəm). *Bot.* [mod.L. use of L. *līnum* flax, LINE *sb.*¹] A genus of plants (N.O. *Linaceæ*) of which flax is a well known example. In popular use, applied to the ornamental species of this genus.

1867 LADY HERBERT *Cradle L.* v. 138 The hillsides [on the road to Bethel] were covered with the most lovely spring flowers; dwarf irises, the delicate pink linum [etc.]. **1882** *Garden* 3 June 385/3 Linums have stood the past winter better than heretofore.

linx, obs. pl. LINK *sb.*; obs. form of LYNX.

liny, liney ('laɪnɪ), *a.* [f. LINE *sb.*² + -Y¹.]

1. Of the nature of or resembling a line or streak, thin, meagre.

1807 OPIE in *Lect. Paint.* (Bohn 1848) 254 Somewhat that is stiff, crude, 'liney', and harsh in respect to anatomy. **1826** MISS MITFORD *Village* Ser. II. 207 The narrow liny clouds, which a few minutes ago lay like soft vapoury streaks along the horizon. **1830** *Fraser's Mag.* I. 146 The architraves..are cut away, and made to look weak and liny. **1855** *Ecclesiologist* XVI. 365 It looks thin, 'liney', and attenuated. **1874** T. HARDY *Far fr. Madding Crowd* viii, Shaping their eyes long and liny, partly because of the light.

2. Full of lines, marked with lines.

1817 KEATS *Sleep & Poetry* 364 Then there rose to view a fane Of liny marble. **1835** T. WALKER *Original* vi. (1887) 65 The brooding affections of the mind..make the countenance fallen, pale, and liny. **1849** RUSKIN *Sev. Lamps* iii. §22. 90 The leaf being..rendered liny by bold markings of its ribs. **1872** *Routledge's Ev. Boy's Ann.* 356/2 To give the grounding a liney appearance.

‖**Linzertorte** (ˈlɪntsətɔːtə). [G., f. *Linzer* adj., f. *Linz* the name of an Austrian city + *torte* tart.] A kind of tart with a jam filling, decorated on top with strips of pastry in a lattice pattern.

1906 *Mrs. Beeton's Bk. Househ. Managem.* lii. 1542 Linzertorte. (German Gâteau.) **1936** LUCAS & HUME *Au Petit Cordon Bleu* 153 Linzertorte... Place a flan ring on to a baking sheet. Line carefully with the paste, fill with raspberry jam... Cover the top criss-cross with thin strips of paste. **1961** J. HELLER *Catch-22* (1962) xxiv. 249 *Linzer* and *Dobos Torten* from Vienna, *Strudel* from Hungary [etc.]. **1969** H. MACINNES *Salzburg Connection* iv. 47 What chance had she ever had of being taught how to run a house or bake Linzertorte?

lion (ˈlaɪən), *sb.* Forms: *α.* 1 léa, lío, léo, 3 leo, 3 *Orm.* le (*genitive* leness, leoness, leuness). *β.* 3 leun(e, lyun, 3–4 leoun, liun(e, 3–5 leon, 3–8 lyon, 4 leone, lyen, 4–6 ly-, lione, lioun, 5 lyown, lywn, 5–6 lyoun(e, 6 lionne, 3– lion. [The mod. form represents an adoption (first appearing *c* 1200) of AF. *liun* (F. *lion*), a Com. Rom. word = Pr. *leo*, Sp. *leon*, Pg. *leão*, It. *leone*, *lione*:—L. *leōnem*, nom. *leo*, a. Gr. λέων (stem λεοντ-, perh. altered from an earlier *λεϝον-). The Gr. word was perh. adopted from some foreign lang.; a noteworthy similarity of sound is presented by Heb. *lābī* lion (pl. *lᵉbā'īm*), also occurring in the sense 'lioness' with the vocalization *lᵉbiyyā*; cf. also Egyptian *labai*, *lawai* lioness. The synonymous Gr. λῖς (cf. Heb. *layish*) is not etymologically connected.

Before the adoption of the Fr. word, English possessed forms directly representing the Latin *leo*, *leōnem*. The word was used, with difference of gender and inflexion, both for 'lion' and 'lioness', the L. *leæna* not having been adopted. Owing to the two-fold form of the L. word in the nom. and the oblique case, the declension in OE. is irregular and variable. The recorded forms are: nom. sing. *léo* (Anglian *léa*), gen. sing. *léon* (Northumb. masc. *léas*), dat. sing. *léon*, *léone*, *léonan*, acc. sing. *léon* (fem. also *léo*), nom., acc. pl. *léon*, gen. pl. *léona*, dat. pl. *léoum*, *léom*, *léonum*.

The L. word has been adopted into all the Teut. langs.: cf. OFris. *lawa*, MDu. *leuwe*, *lēwe* (Du. *leeuw*), OHG. *lewo*, *lêwo*, *louwo*, *lio* (MHG. *lēwe*, *leu*, mod.G. *löwe*, *leu*), ON. *león*, *lión* (MSw. *leon*, Sw. *lejon*, Da. *løve* from Ger.). From Gr. or L., but in some cases through Teut. as the immediate source, are the forms in the Balto-Slavic langs.: Lith *lẽvas*, *liutas*, Lettish *lauvas*, OSl. *lĭvŭ*, Russ. *lev*, Polish *lew*, Czech *lev*.]

1. a. A large carnivorous quadruped, *Felis leo*, now found native only in Africa and southern Asia, of a tawny or yellowish brown colour, and having a tufted tail. The male is distinguished by a flowing shaggy mane. (The Maneless Lion of Gujerat is a recognized Asiatic variety with only a slight mane.) It is very powerful, and has a noble and impressive appearance; whence it is sometimes called 'the king of beasts'. In early use the name was applied to both sexes; from the 13th c. the derivative LIONESS has been used for the female.

The young are now commonly called 'lion's *cubs*'; the older designation 'lion's *whelp*' survives in rhetorical applications, owing to its use in the Bible.

α. *c* **825** *Vesp. Psalter* vii. 3 Ðyles æfre ȝeslæcce swe swe lea sawle mine. *c* **893** K. ÆLFRED *Oros.* III. xi. §3 Seo leo bringð his hungreȝum hwelpum hwæt to etanne. *c* **1000** *Sax. Leechd.* I. 364 Ða þe scinlac þrowien etan leonflæsc. *c* **1050** *Voc.* in Wr.-Wülcker 438/22 *Leo*, lio. *c* **1200** ORMIN 5834 And tatt wass rihht tatt le wass sett Onngæn þatt Goddspellwrihhte,.. Forr leness whellp þær þær itt iss Whellpedd, tær liþ itt stille þre daȝhess. *Ibid.* 6026 þatt deor þatt wass i leoness like. *c* **1205** LAY. 28064 þa com an guldene leo liðen ouer dune. *c* **1325** in *Rel. Ant.* I. 125 Gentil ich wes ant freo Wildore then the leo.

β. *c* **1200** *Vices & Virtues* (1888) 139 Ðe lyon ðe gað abuten þe dier hem to forswoleȝen. *c* **1205** LAY. 4085 He liððe ȝeon þeos leoden sulch hit an liun were [*c* **1275** a lion]. *a* **1225** *Juliana* 33 Daniel bimong þe wode liuns. *a* **1300** *Cursor M.* 690 Als lambe him lai þe leon mild. *c* **1330** R. BRUNNE *Chron. Wace* (Rolls) 11255 (Petyt MS.) Ilkon proudere þan þe lion. *c* **1386** CHAUCER *Knt.'s T.* 798 Tho myghtest wene that this Palamon In his fightyng were a wood leon. **1390** GOWER *Conf.* III. 74 As leon is the king of bestes. **1413** *Pilgr. Sowle* (Caxton 1483) II. xlv. 51 Somme hadden longe hoked clawes, lyke as they had ben lyons. *c* **1470** HENRY *Wallace* II. 113 Thus Wallace ferd als fers as a lyoun. **1526** *Pilgr. Perf.* (W. de W. 1531) 129 Rauenynge wolues or rampynge lyons. *a* **1548** HALL *Chron.*, *Rich. III*, 54 b, We must.. fight together like lions, and feare not to dye together lyke men. **1671** MILTON *P.R.* I. 313 The Lion and fierce Tiger glar'd aloof. *a* **1687** WALLER *Summer Isl.* II. 16 They roar'd like Lions caught in toyles, and rag'd. **1727–38** GAY *Fables* II. ix. 73 The Lion is (beyond dispute) Allow'd the most majestic brute. **1839** *Penny Cycl.* XIV. 32/2 The Maneless Lion of Guzerat. **1859** FITZGERALD tr. *Omar* xvii. (1899) 74 They say the Lion and the Lizard keep The Courts where Jamshyd gloried and drank deep.

b. Extended to other animals of the genus *Felis*. ***American mountain lion***, the puma or cougar.

1630 *New-England's Plantation* (1835) 8 For Beasts there are some Bears, and they say some Lyons also; for they haue been seen at Cape Anne. **1649** *Perf. Descr. Virginia* 17 [List of native beasts] Lyons, Beares, Leopards, Elkes. **1774** GOLDSM. *Nat. Hist.* (1824) I. 431 The Puma, which has received the name of the American Lion.

c. Applied ironically (usually with qualification) to certain weak or timid animals: †***lion of Cotswold***, †***Cotswold lion*** (also Sc. ***Lammermoor lion***), a sheep; ***Essex*** or ***Rumford lion***, a calf. See also quots. 1825, 1827.

1537, *a* **1553**, *a* **1612** [see COTSWOLD]. **1546** J. HEYWOOD *Prov.* (1867) 36 She is as fierce, as a Lyon of Cotsolde. **1678** RAY *Proverbs* 307 As valiant as an Essex lion, i.e. a calf. **1699** T. BROWN *Wks.* (1720) I. 216 That Prodigy of a Man that.. so dexterously mimick'd the Harmony of the Essex Lions. *a* **1700** B. E. *Dict. Cant. Crew*, Rumford-Lyon, a Calf. **1721** KELLY *Sc. Prov.* 380 You look like a Lamermoor Lyon. **1825** C. M. WESTMACOTT *Eng. Spy* I. 156 I'll thank you for a cut out of the back of that *lion*, tittered a man opposite. With all the natural timidity of the hare whom he thus particularised, I was proceeding to help him [etc.]. **1827** LYTTON *Pelham* xxxix. (1849) 101 'A lion *is* a hare, sir.' 'What!' 'Yes, sir, it is a hare!—but we call it a lion, because of the Game Laws.'

2. Proverbial and allusive phrases. **a.** Proverbs (chiefly referring to the strength or ferocity of the lion). **b.** ***a lion in the way*** (or ***path***): after Prov. xxvi. 13, applied to a danger or obstacle, esp. an imaginary one. **c.** ***the lion's mouth***: taken as a type of a place of great peril. (Cf. Ps. xxii. 21, 2 Tim. iv. 17.) Similarly, ***in the lion's paws***. **d.** ***the lion's share***: the largest or principal portion. **e.** ***the lion's skin*** occurs chiefly with reference to the fable of the ass that clothed himself in the skin of a lion. (See also quots.) **f.** ***the lion's provider*** = JACKAL *sb.*, *lit.* and *fig.* **g.** ***to twist the lion's tail***: freq. in journalistic use with reference to foreign insults to, or encroachments on the rights of, Great Britain (cf. 5 c).

a. *a* **1382** WYCLIF *Eccl.* ix. 4 Betere is a quyc dogge thanne a leoun dead. *c* **1386** CHAUCER *Sqr.'s T.* 483 As by the whelp chasted is the leon [cf. F. *battre le chien devant le lion*]. —— *Wife's Prol.* 692 Who peynted the leon, tel me who? [See note, ed. Skeat.] **1595** SHAKS. *John* II. i. 138 You are the Hare of whom the Prouerb goes Whose valour plucks dead Lyons by the beard. **1640** HOWELL *Dodona's G.* 10 Like the moneth of March, which entreth like a Lion, but goeth out like a Lamb. **1655** FULLER *Ch. Hist.* VI. ii. 291 As the Proverb saith, The Lion is not so fierce as he is painted. **1749** [see BEARD *v.* 3]. **1808** SCOTT *Marm.* VI. xiv, And dar'st thou then To beard the lion in his den, The Douglas in his hall?

b. **1641** MILTON *Reform.* II. Wks. (1847) 18/1 They fear'd not the bug-bear danger nor the Lyon in the way that the sluggish and timorous Politician thinks he sees. **1647** CLARENDON *Hist. Reb.* VI. §342 There be both Mountains, and Lyons in the way. **1868** BRIGHT *Sp. Ireland* 1 Apr., You have always.. lions in the path. **1869** TENNYSON *Holy Grail* 643, I have been the sluggard, and I ride apace, For now there is a lion in the way.

c. *a* **1225** *St. Marher.* 7 Leose me lauerd ut of þe liunes muð. **1601** DENT *Pathw. Heaven* 62 What doth hee else, but (as it were) put his finger into the Lions mouth. **1629** CAPT. SMITH *True Trav.* xx. (Arb.) 878 But Merham, the old fox, seeing himselfe in the lions pawes, sprung his loufe. **1726** CAVALLIER *Mem.* IV. 289 He wou'd not lay down his Arms, saying it was better to die, than to run into the Lion's Mouth. **1856** EMERSON *Eng. Traits, Truth* Wks. (Bohn) II. 54 In the power of saying rude truth, sometimes in the lion's mouth, no men surpass them.

d. **1790** BURKE *Fr. Rev.* Wks. V. 252 Nor when they were in partnership with the farmer.. have I heard that they had taken the lion's share. **1836** SIR H. TAYLOR *Statesman* xxii. 155 Always.. ready to take the lion's share of responsibility and labour. **1865** LOWELL *Wks.* (1890) V. 251 Attacking a government which they knew only by their lion's share in its offices. **1872** *Punch* 22 June 253/1 The art of finding a rich friend to make a tour with you in autumn, and of leaving him to bear the lion's share of the expenses.

e. [**1484** CAXTON *Fables of Auian* (1889) 219 The fourthe fable is of the asse, and of the skynne of the Lyon.] **1599** SHAKS. *Hen. V*, IV. iii. 93 The man that once did sell the Lyons skin While the beast liu'd, was kill'd with hunting him. **1611** COTGR. s.v. *Lion*, *Il n'y eut iamais bon marché de peaux de lions*,.. a Lyons skinne was neuer bought good cheape. **1636** MASSINGER *Gt. Dk. Florence* v. i, Reason assured me It was not safe to shave a lion's skin. **1700** TYRRELL *Hist. Eng.* II. 847 When the Lyon's Skin alone would not serve turn, he knew how to make it out with that of the Fox. **1711** [see ASS *sb.* 1 c].

f. **1774** GOLDSM. *Hist. Earth* II. 322 This has given rise to the report of the jackall's being the lion's provider. **1808** SCOTT *Let. to W. Gifford* 25 Oct. in *Lockhart*, If you will accept of my services as a sort of jackal or lion's provider. **1823** BYRON *Juan* IX. xxvii, The poor jackals.. (As being the brave lion's keen providers). **1831** CARLYLE *Sart. Res.* (1858) 14 Old Lieschen.. was his.. cook, errand-maid, and general lion's-provider.

3. *fig.* (chiefly after biblical usage; cf. Rev. v. 5). **a.** Taken (in a good sense) as the type of one who is strong, courageous, or fiercely brave.

the Lion of the North, Gustavus Adolphus.

c **1175** *Lamb. Hom.* 131 þa streonge leo þet wes þes liuiȝendes godes sune. [**1297** R. GLOUC. (Rolls) 9384 Is mouþ is as a leon, is herte arn as an hare.] *c* **1325** *Poem Times Edw. II*, 252 in *Pol. Songs* (Camden) 334 Nu ben theih liouns in halle, and hares in the feld. *c* **1470** HENRY *Wallace* VIII. 1225 At the palȝoun, quhar thai the lyoun [*sc.* Wallace] saw. **1579–80** NORTH *Plutarch, Comp. Lys. & Sylla* (1595) 522 Lyons at home, and Foxes abroade. **1589** [see LAMB *sb.* 2 b]. **1590** SPENSER *F.Q.* I. iii. 7 He, my Lyon, and my noble Lord. **1599** KYD *Sol. & Pers.* II. 61 Wks. (1901) 167 English Archers.. Eclipped Lyons of the Westerne worlde. **1607** SHAKS. *Cor.* I. i. 239 He is a Lion That I am proud to hunt. **1632** LITHGOW *Trav.* 504 The Lyon.. whose Sire, was surnam'd Dowglas. **1842** *Penny Cycl.* XXIII. 396/1 The campaigns.. of the Lion of the North, till his fall in the moment of triumph at Lützen. **1863** WOOLNER *My Beautiful Lady* 132 The manliest, and king of English kings, The lion Cromwell, in his dress of war.

b. In a bad sense: A fiercely cruel, tyrannical or 'devouring' creature or person.

Partly after biblical uses: cf. Ps. xxxiv. 17, lvi. 4, 1 Pet. v. 8, etc.

a **1225** *St. Marher.* 6 Ant tu grisliche gra þu luðere liun lað godd. *a* **1225** *Ancr. R.* 120 Wummone wroð is wuluene, & mon wroð is wulf, oðer leun. **1340** *Ayenb.* 17 Prede is king of wyckede þeawes. Hy is þe lioun þet al uorzuelþ. **1589** PUTTENHAM *Eng. Poesie* III. xxiv. (Arb.) 299 A Lyon among sheepe and a sheepe among Lyons. **1683** TRYON *Way to Health* xiv. (1697) 273 All such as would have the bestial, savage Nature strengthen'd.., and have a mind to be Lions and Devils.. to their own kind. **1832** H. BLUNT *Hist. Paul* (ed. 2) I. 40 That the lion had become a lamb, that the persecutor was now a humble and inquiring believer.

†**c.** (See quot.) *Obs.*

1713 ADDISON *Guardian* No. 71 ¶2 We polite men of the town give the name of a lion to any one that is a great man's spy. *Ibid.* ¶7 A lion, or a master-spy, hath several jack-calls under him.

4. a. *pl.* Things of note, celebrity, or curiosity (in a town, etc.); sights worth seeing: esp. in phr. ***to see***, or ***show, the lions***. †In early use, ***to have seen the lions*** often meant to have had experience of life.

This use of the word is derived from the practice of taking visitors to see the lions which used to be kept in the Tower of London. See the introductory quots.

[**1629** CAPT. SMITH *True Trav.* xviii. (Arb.) 872 After, one Master John Bull.., with divers of his friends, went to see the Lyons [in the Tower]. **1731** FIELDING *Lottery* iii. Wks. 1882 VIII. 480, I must see all the curiosities; the Tower, the lions, and Bedlam, and the court, and the opera. **1806–7** J. BERESFORD *Miseries Hum. Life* (1826) VII. lxviii, Escorting two or three coaches full of country-cousins.. to the Lions, the Wax-work, the Monument, &c.]

1590 GREENE *Neuer too Late* (1600) 34 Francesco was no other but a meere nouice, and that so newly, that to vse the olde prouerbe, he had scarce seene the Lions. **1600** B. JONSON *Cynthia's Rev.* v. ii. Wks. 1616 I. 242 *Amo.* You come not to giue vs the scorne, Monsieur? *Mer.* Nor to be frighted with a face, Signior! I haue seene the lyons. **1622** J. TAYLOR (Water-P.) *Water-Cormorant* Wks. 1630 III. 5 Some say [of a Drunkard] hee's bewitcht, or scratcht, or blinde,.. Or seene the Lyons, or his nose is dirty. **1770** JENNER *Placid Man* (1773) I. 119 It made no inconsiderable figure amongst the Lions of Bath. **1782** MAD. D'ARBLAY *Cecilia* I. viii, Mr. Monckton.. asked Morrice why he did not shew the lyons. **1792** T. TWINING *Recr. & Stud.* (1882) 157, I suppose the lions of Nottingham are public, accessible lions, and require no interest to get sight of. **1809** MALKIN *Gil Blas* v. i. ¶6 The churches were the best lions we met with in our way. **1810** SCOTT *Let. to J.B.S. Morritt* 9 Aug. in *Lockhart*, The cavern at Staffa.. is one of the few *lions* which completely maintain an extended reputation. **1840** HOOD *Up Rhine* 96 The rest of the day was spent in seeing the Lions—and first the Cathedral. **1859** JEPHSON *Brittany* viii. 123 He was polite.. and showed the lions very good-naturedly. **1864** 'C. BEDE' in *Lond. Soc.* VI. 27/1 That celebrated collection of lions of which his University can show so complete a menagerie in her College Halls, Bodleian [etc.].

b. Hence: A person of note or celebrity who is much sought after.

1715 LADY M. W. MONTAGU *Town Eclogues, Tuesday*, Fops of all kinds, to see the Lion, run; The beauties stay till the first act's begun. **1774** MAD. D'ARBLAY *Early Diary* (1889) I. 311 The present Lyon of the times, according to the author of 'the Placid Man's' term, is Omy, the native of Otaheite. **1815** LADY GRANVILLE *Lett.* (1894) I. 67 [At a ball.] The King of Prussia is the only Royal lion. **1838** LYTTON *Alice* VI. i, The literary lion who likes to be petted. **1850** THACKERAY *Contrib. to Punch* Wks. 1886 XXIV. 251 What is a lion? A lion is a man or woman one must have at one's parties. **1889** T. A. TROLLOPE *What I remember* III. 131 Longfellow.. largely paid the poet's penalty of being made the lion of all the drawing rooms.

†**c.** *Oxford slang.* A visitor to Oxford. ? *Obs.*

1785 GROSE *Dict. Vulgar Tongue*, *Lion*.. a name given by the gownsmen of Oxford, to inhabitants or visitors. **1785** R. CUMBERLAND *Observer* No. 95 ¶4, I did not excel in any of my academical exercises, save that of circumambulating the colleges and public buildings with strangers..; in this branch of learning I gained such general reputation as to be honoured with the title of *Keeper of the Lions*. **1807** SOUTHEY *Espriella's Lett.* II. xxxii. 60 [The young student] had abstained from visiting many things himself, till he should have a lion to take with him. **1818** T. WARD *Strictures Charac. Barristers* (ed. 2) 45 To the amusement of the Nobility and Gentry visiting Oxford, the latter of whom are known by the University men by the appellation of Lions and Lioness's, when observed in the streets with an Oxford Guide in their hand, or gaping about.

†**d.** (See quot.) *Obs.*

1785 G. A. BELLAMY *Apol.* II. 68 Just under him, in the pit, sat a lion [*Footnote*, A term at that time in vogue for a cit].

5. a. An image or picture of a lion. (A favourite sign for inns and taverns: usually *Red*, *White*, *Golden*, etc. *Lion*.)

? *a* **1366** CHAUCER *Rom. Rose* 894 Y-painted al.. with briddes, libardes, and lyouns. *c* **1400** MAUNDEV. (1839) viii. 86 Lyouns of Gold. **1487** *Will* in *Paston Lett.* III. 464 An hanging bed, with a lyon thereupon. **1534** in W. H. Turner *Select. Rec. Oxford* 118 Ye marke which ye Mayor.. had striken in ye.. butchers waytes,.. which marke was ye lyon and crowne. **1562** in Welch *Tower Bridge* (1894) 83 To one that brought home a lyone blowen downe upon London Bridge, 4*d.* **1564–78** BULLEYN *Dial. agst. Pest.* (1888) 18 Bearyng upon his breast a white Lion. **1611** CORYAT *Crudities* (1776) I. 237 A great red flagge.. with the winged Lyon made in it in gold. **1745** P. THOMAS *Jrnl. Anson's Voy.* 21 The Lion was very loose, and would certainly have been lost but for.. two strong Supporters.. fix'd from the Ship's Bows to secure him. **1838** *Murray's Hand-bk. N. Germ.* 376 A colossal lion, of cast iron. **1855** TENNYSON *Daisy* 55

Porch-pillars on the lion resting, And sombre, old, colonnaded aisles.

b. *spec.* in *Her.*

c **1320** *Sir Tristr.* 1040 Wiþ alaunce.. He smot him in þe lyoun, And tristrem,.. Bar him þurch þe dragoun In þe scheld. *c* **1400** *Destr. Troy* 5927 Thre lions the lord bare all of light goulis. **1449** *Pol. Poems* (Rolls) II. 222 The White Lioun [*i.e.* the Duke of Norfolk] is leyde to slepe. **1591** SHAKS. *1 Hen. VI*, I. v. 28 Hark, countrymen! either renew the fight, Or tear the lions out of England's coat. **1596** DALRYMPLE tr. *Leslie's Hist. Scot.* v. 265 The Lionis, quhilkes the kingis of Scotis weiris in thair armes. **1805** SCOTT *Last Minstr.* IV. xxiii, The lion argent decked his breast. **1813** *Gentl. Mag.* LXXXIII. 37/2 With supporters (lion and unicorn) of the Royal arms. **1868** CUSSANS *Her.* vi. (1882) 84 Three Lions passant-guardant in pale or, on a field gules, constitute the Arms of England.

c. ***British Lion***, the lion as the national emblem of Great Britain; hence often used *fig.* for the British nation. Similarly ***Scottish lion***.

1687 DRYDEN *Hind & P.* I. 289 Such mercy from the British Lyon flows. **1796** BURKE *Regic. Peace* iii. Wks. VIII. 293 He would no longer amuse the British Lion in the chace of mice and rats. **1806** *Naval Chron.* XV. 52 Each [of the seamen] appeared a true-bred cub of the British Lion. **1849** W. E. AYTOUN *Lays Sc. Caval., Heart Bruce* xxv, We'll let the Scottish lion loose Within the fields of Spain! **1853** LYTTON *My Novel* XII. xxv. IV. 174 The British Lion is aroused! **1859** THACKERAY *Virgin.* lxiv, The British Lion, or any other lion, cannot always have a worthy enemy to combat, or a battle royal to deliver.

6. a. A gold coin current in Scotland down to the reign of James VI. **b.** A Scottish copper coin = HARDHEAD². *Obs.* exc. *Hist.*

1451 *Sc. Acts Jas. II* (1814) II. 40/1 Item þ^t^ þare be strikyn ane new penny of golde callit a lyon w^t^ þe prent of þe lyon on þe ta side & the ymage of Sanct Andro on þe toþer side. .. And þat þe said new lyon.. sall ryn for vjs. viij*d.* of the said new mone. *a* **1557** *Diurn. Occurr.* (Bannatyne Club) 344 Lyounis vtherwayes callit hardheidis. *a* **1572** KNOX *Hist. Ref.* Wks. 1846 I. 365 (MS. G) Daylie thair was suche numbers of Lions (alias called Hardheids) prented, that [etc.]. **1899** GRUEBER *Handbk. Coins Gt. Brit. & Irel.* 169, 184.

7. The constellation and zodiacal sign LEO. Also *Little Lion*: the constellation Leo Minor.

c **1386** CHAUCER *Frankl. T.* 330 Next at this opposicion Which in the signe shal be of the leon. **1509** HAWES *Past Pleas.* XLIV. (Percy Soc.) 216 Out of the Lyon to enter the Vyrgyne. **1697** CREECH *Manilius* II. 44 The Lion.. The squeezing Crab, and stinging Scorpion. **1868** LOCKYER *Guillemin's Heavens* (ed. 3) 326 To conclude our examination of the constellations visible on the 22nd of March at midnight, we must notice.. the Little Lion above the Lion.

†**8.** *lion of the sea*: **a.** ? A kind of lobster (cf. F. *lion de mer*). **b.** = SEA-LION. *Obs.*

1598 *Epulario* G iij b, To dresse the fish called the Lion of the sea. **1772** *Ann. Reg.* 92/1 These sea-wolves, which he calls lions.

†**9.** Alchemy. *Green lion*: a 'spirit' of great transmuting power, supposed to be produced by certain processes in alchemy; sometimes identified with the 'philosophical mercury'. *Obs.*

1471 RIPLEY *Comp. Alch.* Recapitulation in Ashmole *Theatr. Chem. Brit.* (1652) 188 The Spottyd Panther wyth the Lyon greene. **15..** A. ANDREWES (title) in *Ibid.*, 278 *Hunting of the Greene Lyon.* **1593** G. HARVEY *Pierce's Super.* Wks. (Grosart) II. 69 He would seeme to haue the Green Lion and the flying Eagle in a box. **1605** TIMME *Quersit.* i. xiii. 53 A greene sharpe spirit... This is that greene lyon which Rypley commendeth so much. **1610** B. JONSON *Alch.* II. ii, Your generall colours, sir, Of the pale citron, the greene lyon, the crow, The peacocks taile.

10. *attrib.* and *Comb.*: **a.** simple attrib., as ***lion-colour, -cub, -kind, -king, -lair, -limb, -mask, -paw, -skin, -whelp***; **b.** objective, as ***lion-keeper, -stalking, -tamer, -taming***; **c.** similative, as ***lion-bold, -coloured, -sick*** adjs. (see also 12); **d.** parasynthetic, as ***lion-faced, -footed, -headed, -hued, -maned, -mettled, -thoughted, -throated*** adjs.; **e.** instrumental, as ***lion-guarded, -haled, -haunted*** adjs.

1669 STURMY *Mariner's Mag.* I. ii. 21 Wisemen stout, and stung, grow *Lion-bold. **1551-2** *Act 5 & 6 Edw. VI*, c. 6 §23 Anye other color or colors then.. *lyon color motteley or iren grey. **1662** MERRETT tr. *Neri's Art of Glass* xlii, In the bottom there will remain a Lion colour. **1920** E. POUND *Hugh Selwyn Mauberley* 25 The coral isle, the *lion-coloured sand. **1964** *Listener* 30 July 163/3 Sun-swept, lion-coloured plains. **1727** GAY *Fables* I. xix. 13-14 A *Lyon-cub, of sordid mind, Avoided all the lyon-kind. **1856** C. M. YONGE *Daisy Chain* II. xix. 551 He leant on his *lion-faced boy's arm, and walked down to the Minster. **1919** W. S. MAUGHAM *Moon & Sixpence* lv. 242 A look—how shall I describe it?—the books call it lion-faced. **1946** R. GRAVES *Poems 1938-45* 35 The Lion-faced Boy at the Fair. **1610** HEALEY *St. Aug. Citie of God* 686 Ausonius makes her [i.e. the Sphynx].. *Lyon-footed. **1898** J. DAVIDSON *Last Ballad* etc. (1899) 149 The trader and the usurer Have passed the *lion-guarded door. **1871** R. ELLIS tr. *Catullus* lxiii. 76 Cybele, the thong relaxing from a *lion-haled yoke. **1870** MORRIS *Earthly Par.* III. IV. 239 The *lion-haunted woods. **1864** PUSEY *Lect. Daniel* iii. 115 The human-headed lions and bulls, and perhaps conversely, the *lion-headed men were religious, not political symbols at all. **1591** PERCIVALL *Sp. Dict.*, *Leonado*, *lion hued, *fuluus.* *a* **1843** SOUTHEY *Comm.-pl. Bk.* Ser. II. 645 If one of these lions enraged is going to assail the spectators, the *lion-keepers hold under his nose the confiture of Gazelles' meat [etc.]. **1711** SHAFTESB. *Charac.* (1737) II. 188 Representations of human victorys over the *lion-kind. **1727** [see *lion-cub*]. **1971** D. BEATY *Temple Tree* 232 Reincarnation. The new *Lion King of Ceylon. **1972** *Times* 29 June 16/4 Their epics extol the 'Lion-king' Sundiata who founded the Manding Empire. **1860** PUSEY *Min. Proph.* 361 Nineveh was still one vast *lion-lair. **1885** G. M. HOPKINS *Poems* (1918) 62 Why wouldst thou.. lay a *lionlimb against me? **1851** H. MELVILLE *Whale* lxxxvii. 428 The *lion-maned buffaloes of the West. **1906** *Westm. Gaz.* 9 May 8/2 A large vase decorated with *lion-masks. **1933** *Burlington Mag.* July 36/1 The cabriole legs with their goats' heads and lion masks. **1605** SHAKS. *Macb.* IV. i. 90 Be *Lyon metled, proud. **1934** *Burlington Mag.* Oct. p. xv/2 The tripod terminates in *lion-paw feet. **1972** *Country Life* 15 June (Suppl.) 43/2 Regency Rosewood Bookcase with.. brass lion paw feet. **1606** SHAKS. *Tr. & Cr.* II. iii. 93 He is not sicke. *Aia.* Yes, *Lyon sicke, sicke of proud heart. **1805** SOUTHEY *Ballads & Metr. Tales* Poet Wks. VI. 267 He could have swallowed Hercules, Club, *lion-skin, and all. **1890** 'ROLF BOLDREWOOD' *Miner's Right* xliv, We are graciously permitted.. to try a little *lion-stalking in Algeria. **1798** SOTHEBY tr. *Wieland's Oberon* v. viii, O'er me the *lion-tamer holds his hand. **1870** O. LOGAN *Before Footlights* 354 After stating that *lion-taming was a gift of nature with him. **1944** *Mind* LIII. 162 Others found it [*sc.* welfare] wholly comprehended in trout-fishing and lion-taming. **1820** KEATS *Hyperion* II. 68 Tiger-passion'd, *lion-thoughted, wroth. **1927** E. SITWELL *Rustic Elegies* 91 Where two *lion-throated fountains fell. **1957** R. CAMPBELL *Coll. Poems* II. 56 From lion-throated blooms ablaze. *a* **1300** *E.E. Psalter* ciii. 22 *Lyoun whelpes.. seke fra god mete vnto þa. **14..** *Wyclif's Gen.* xlix. 9 (MS. S) Judas a lyoun whelp. **1864** TENNYSON *En. Ard.* 98 The portal-warding lion-whelp, And peacock-yewtree of the lonely Hall.

11. a. Special comb.: **lion-ant**, the same as *ant-lion*; †**lion-cat**, an Angora cat; †**lion comique** *Obs.*, a leading comic singer in a music-hall or the like; †**lion-cudweed**, the Edelweiss (see *lion's foot* in b); **lion dance**, a traditional Chinese dance in which the dancers are masked and costumed to resemble lions; so **lion dancer**; **lion dog** [after F. *chien-lion* (Buffon)], a variety of dog having a flowing mane; also, a dog belonging to one of several breeds resembling miniature lions in colour or type of fur, or once used for hunting in country inhabited by lions; **lion-dollar** (see DOLLAR 5): **lion-dragon**, a heraldic beast having the fore-part like a lion and the hind part like a wyvern; **lion forceps** (see quot.); **lion-head**, a variety of goldfish, *Carassius auratus*, having an enlarged head; **lion house**, a building in which lions are kept at a zoo; **lion-hunter**, one who hunts lions; one who is given to lionizing celebrities; **lion-hunting**, the action of a lion-hunter, *lit.* and *fig.* (in quot. †going in quest of the 'lions' of a place); **lion-huntress**, a female 'lion-hunter'; †**lion-leopard** (F. *lion léoparde*), a lion passant guardant; = LEOPARD 3 b; **lion-lizard**, the basilisk, its crest being compared to a lion's mane; **lion marmoset**, a small Brazilian monkey, *Leontideus rosalia*; = *lion-monkey*, MARIKINA; **lion-monkey**, the marikina or silky marmoset; †**lion noble** = 6 a; **lion-poisson** *Her.* [F. *poisson* fish] (see quot. 1868); **lion-show** *jocular*, a gathering of 'lions' or celebrities; **lion-skinned** *a.*, clothed in a lion's skin, *fig.* with allusion to the ass in the fable (cf. 2 e); †**lion-string**, some kind of string for musical instruments; **lion-tailed baboon, monkey**, the wanderoo (*Macacus silenus*); **lion-tawny** *a.*, of the tawny colour characteristic of lions; also *sb.*; **lion-tiger**, used *attrib.* of a cub bred between a lion and a tiger.

1774 GOLDSM. *Nat. Hist.* (1776) VII. 323 Of the Formica Leo, or *Lion-Ant. **1845** DARWIN *Voy. Nat.* xix. (1852) 442 *note*, This Australian pit-fall was only about half the size of that made by the European lion-ant. **1774** GOLDSM. *Nat. Hist.* (1862) I. IV. i. 359 The *lion cat; or as others more properly term it, the cat of Angora. **1899** BEERBOHM *More* 120 The *Lion Comique bawled out.. some such crude, conventional ditty. **1927** *Observer* 11 Dec. 8 When did the music-hall die?.. Where is the 'lion comique'..? **1597** GERARDE *Herbal* II. cxcv. §10. 517 *Leontopodium siue Pes Leoninus*, *Lion Cudweede. **1937** *N.Y. Times* 10 Feb. 2 The parades, according to a spokesman from the Chinese Benevolent Association, will take the form of *lion dances. **1952** W. EBERHARD *Chinese Festivals* i. 57 The 'lion dance'.. we still see in the streets of old Peking—and sometimes even in San Francisco's Chinatown. **1964** *Catal. National Museum Kuala Lumpur* 5/2 (*caption*) Lion dance tableau, authentically North China, is one of several in one main gallery. **1966** D. FORBES *Heart of Malaya* vi. 77 The Boat People of Hong Kong feast.. with roast pig, lion dances and boat races on the twenty-third day of the third moon in our month of April. **1968** *Encycl. Brit.* VII. 33/1 In China itself there may be lotus dances, stilt dances, butterfly dances, lion dances (inspired by Buddhist stories from the parts of India where lions are known). **1927** BREDON & MITROPHANOW *Moon Year* xii. 394 Akin to the strolling players are the '*Lion Dancers' who wander from village to village. Each troupe is composed of two or three mountebanks with rude but picturesque properties. **1975** *Times* 17 Feb. 3/3 London's Chinatown in Soho celebrated the Chinese new year yesterday... Lion Dancers.. wound and jigged all day around Gerrard Street. **1774** GOLDSM. *Nat. Hist.* (1824) II. i. 9 The *Lion Dog greatly resembles that animal, in miniature, from whence it takes the name. **1845** YOUATT *Dog* 50 The Lion Dog.. The origin of this breed is not known; it is, perhaps, an intermediate one between the Maltese and the Turkish dog. **1921** V. W. F. COLLIER *Dogs China & Japan* xii. 183 Tibetan lion-dogs are bred to resemble lions, and they, like the Chinese, appear to be willing to call any shaggy coated dog a lion-dog. **1938** E. C. ASH *New Bk. Dog* x. 430 Tibetan Lhasa Apso... This being the true Tibetan Lion-dog, golden or lion-like colours are preferred. *Ibid.* xi. 466 (*caption*) A Rhodesian Ridgeback (Lion Dog). **1958** *Bk. Dogs* (Nat. Geographic Soc.) 354/2 Ancient ancestors of the Peke were honored dogs of the imperial palace in Peking... At ceremonies two of these Lion Dogs preceded the emperor, two followed. **1971** DANGERFIELD & HOWELL *Internat. Encycl. Dogs* 284/1 Many breeds have been called lion dogs. With the exception of the Rhodesian Ridgeback, these have all been small dogs with a real, or imagined, lion-like aspect. **1697** *Virginia St. Papers* (1875) I. 52 Dollers, comonly called *Lyon or Dog Dollers, have no vallue ascertained whereby they may pass currantly amongst the inhabitants of this County. **1610** GUILLIM *Heraldry* III. xxvi. 183 *Lions-dragons, Lions-Poisons, and whatsoeuer other double shaped animall of any two.. of the ..kinds before handled. **1864** P. HOLME *Syst. Surg.* IV. 1045 The '*lion forceps' of Fergusson.. is a strong straight forceps provided with two sets of teeth.. by which it obtains a firm hold on a bone. **1928** *Daily Express* 5 July 8 Fancy goldfish can be very expensive... I paid £30 each for a *lionhead and an oranda recently. **1972** Y. MATSUI *Goldfish Guide* xi. 176 The premier goldfish is the Ronchū or Lionhead. **1895** C. J. CORNISH *Life at Zoo* 64 The present *Lion House, with its fine outdoor summer palaces, and its indoor winter cages.. seems to leave nothing to be desired. **1909** *Westm. Gaz.* 30 Jan. 7/1 We had better get them to the lion-house. **1974** *Times* 29 Apr. 10/8 Work to replace the outdated Lion House could not be started. **1829** R. C. SANDS *Writings* (1834) II. 199 During the interval.. two *lion-hunters.. came into the box and introduced themselves. **1839** *Penny Cycl.* XIV. 32/1 (art. *Lion*) The dangers and hair-breadth escapes of the lion-hunters. **1840** CARLYLE *Heroes* (1858) 330 These Lion-hunters were the ruin and death of Burns. [Cf. the name 'Mrs. Leo Hunter' in Dickens *Pickwick* (1837).]. **1878** *Athenæum* 19 Jan. 81/2 Keats, the obscure medical student, who died before a single lion-hunter had found him out. **1770** JENNER *Placid Man* (1773) I. 120 *Lion-hunting.. being the whole end and design of travelling. **1828** SCOTT *Jrnl.* 1 July (1941) 271 A professed *lion-huntress, who travels the country to rouse the peaceful beasts out of their lair. **1850** THACKERAY in *Punch* 24 Aug. 89 The Lion-Huntress of Belgravia. Being Lady Nimrod's Journal of the Past Season. **1926** A. HUXLEY *Two or Three Graces* 229 The old familiar stories about that famous lion-huntress were being repeated. **1612** SELDEN *Notes on Drayton's Poly-olb.* xi. 182 Being blazon'd in Hierom de Bara, and other French heralds, *Lion-Leopards. **1707** FUNNELL *Voy.* ii. 35 A large sort of Lizard called a *Lion-lizard. **1738** MORTIMER in *Phil. Trans.* XL. 347 *Lacertus griseus.* The Lion Lizard. **1906** *Westm. Gaz.* 19 Feb. 12/2 Here may be seen the beautiful *lion marmoset from Brazil. **1936** E. G. BOULENGER *Apes & Monkeys* vii. 195 Of the long-tusked marmosets, two of the most ornate are the 'emperor' and the 'lion'... The lion is one of the most vividly coloured of all mammals, the long silky fur being of a flaming orange hue. **1965** *Amer. Jrnl. Physical Anthropol.* XXIII. 261 (*title*) The skull of the lion marmoset, *Leontideus rosalia* Linnaeus. **1803** SARRETT *New Pict. Lond.* 115 In one of the glass cases is a beautiful *lion-monkey. **1586** *Min. Privy C.* 10 Dec. in Burns *Coinage Scot.* (1887) II. 389 *Lyoun noblis. **1887** BURNS *ibid.* 388 Lion nobles or Scottish angels. **1610** *Lion-Poisons [see *lion-dragon*]. **1868** CUSSANS *Her.* vi. (1882) 101 The Lion-poisson, or Sea-lion, which has the head and shoulders of a Lion, with fins for paws, and the *nowed* tail of a Fish for a body. **1839** LOCKHART *Scott* (1869) III. xix. 186 *note*, Mr. Coleridge's own stately account of this *lion-show in Grosvenor Street. **1768-74** TUCKER *Lt. Nat.* (1834) I. 596 Hail, glorious Liberty!.. *Lion-skinned Freethinking, safe affector of thy bravery.. claims to be the sole gatherer up of thy spoils. **1659** HOWELL *Vocab.* l. Sig. Y yyyyyy, Wire strings, gut strings, venice catlings, nimikins, *Lion strings; *Diverse sorti di corde.* **1781** PENNANT *Quadrupeds* I. 183 *Lion-tailed Baboon. *Ibid.* Plate xxii, Lion tailed Monky. **1893** LYDEKKER *Roy. Nat. Hist.* I. 113 The Lion-Tailed Monkey (*Macacus silenus*).. These monkeys inhabit the Malabar, or Western, Coast of India. **1573** *Art of Limming* 8 If you mingle redde Lead and Masticot together, you shal have thereof a *Lyon tawney. **1611** COTGR., *Lionnin*.., of a Lyon-tawnie colour. **1885** BURTON *Arab. Nts.* (1886) I. Foreword 7 The boundless waste of lion-tawny clays and gazelle-brown gravels. **1839** *Penny Cycl.* XIV. 35/1 *Lion-Tiger Cubs.

b. Combinations with *lion's* (mostly plant-names): †**lion's claw**, (*a*) Black Hellebore, *Helleborus niger*; (*b*) a kind of oyster; **lion's ear**, 'a common name in the Andes for some species of *Culcitium*; also *Espeletia* and *Leonotis*' (*Treas. Bot.* 1866); **lion's foot**, (*a*) Lady's Mantle, *Alchemilla vulgaris*; (*b*) Black Hellebore; (*c*) the genus *Leontopodium*, esp. *L. alpinum*, the Edelweiss; **lion's heart**, a plant of the U.S., *Physostegia virginiana*; **lion's leaf**, any plant of the genus *Leontice*, esp. *L. Leontopetalum*; **lion's leap**, an acrobatic leap or somersault; cf. F. *sault du lion* (Cotgr.); **lion's mouth**, a name for *Antirrhinum majus*; **lion's paw** = *lion's foot*; **lion's snap** = *lion's mouth*; **lion's tail**, (*a*) the plant *Leonotis Leonurus*, from the supposed resemblance of the inflorescence to the tuft of a lion's tail; (*b*) Motherwort, *Leonurus Cardiaca*; **lion's tooth** or **teeth**, the Dandelion; †**lion's turnip**, = *lion's leaf*.

1611 COTGR. s.v. *Lion*, *Patte de lion*, *Lyons claw, Setterwort, Settergrasse, bastard blacke Ellebore. **1759** MRS. DELANEY in *Life & Corr.* (1861) III. 560 Kind of oysters called the lion's claw. **1835** BOOTH *Analyt. Dict.* 261 *Leonotis*, *Lion's ear. *c* **1000** *Sax. Leechd.* I. 98 Ðeos wyrt þe man pedem leonis, & oðrum naman *leon-fot nemneð. **1538** TURNER *Libellus*, Lyons fote, *Elleborum nigrum.* **1611** COTGR., *Alchimille*, Lionsfoot, Ladies mantle, great Sanicle. **1845** A. WOOD *Class-Bk. Bot.* 282 *Physostegia Virginiana*... A beautiful plant native in Penn. and southward... **Lion's heart.* **1597** GERARDE *Herbal* II. iv. §4. 182 Plinie doth call it also Leontopetalon, Apuleius Leontopodion... In English *Lyons leafe and Lyons Turnep. **1760** J. LEE *Introd. Bot.* App. 317 Lion's-leaf, *Leontice.* **1882** J. SMITH *Dict. Plants* 247 Lion's-leaf (*Leontice Leontopetalum*), a herbaceous

plant of the Barberry family. **1883** *Chamb. Jrnl.* 131 The *lions-leap, flip-flap, &c., of the acrobat. **1706** PHILLIPS (ed. Kersey), **Lion's-Mouth, Lion's-Paw, Lion's-Tooth*, several sorts of Herbs. **1773** *Hist. Brit. Dom. North Amer.* XI. iii. 189 The flower called the lion's-mouth..forms a sweet nosegay of itself, and is worthy the gardens of kings. **1591** PERCIVALL *Sp. Dict.*, *Pata de Leon*, *Lions pawe, *Leontopetalon.* **1601** HOLLAND *Pliny* II. 262 The leaues of Lions paw. **1597** GERARDE *Herbal* II. clv. §4. 439 Snapdragon is called..in English Calues snout, Snapdragon, and *Lyons snap. **1760** J. LEE *Introd. Bot.* App. 317 *Lion's-tail, *Leonurus.* **1562** BULLEYN *Def. agst. Sickness* (1579) 10 The vertue of Dandelion or *Lyons teeth. **1886** BRITTEN & HOLLAND *Plant-n.*, Lion's teeth, *Leontodon Taraxacum.* **1597** *Lyons Turnep [see *lion's leaf*]. **1611** COTGR. s.v. *Lion*, Some also tearme Lyons leafe, and Lyons Turnep, *pes Lioninus*.

12. *attrib.* passing into *adj.* = 'lion-like; characteristic of a lion; strong, brave, or fierce as a lion'.

1614 JONSON *Barth. Fair* II. iii. (1631) 21 You shall not fright me with your Lyon-chap. **1671** MILTON *Samson* 139 The bold Ascalonite Fled from his Lion ramp. **1681** DRYDEN *Sp. Fryar* I. 1 Pox o' this Lyon-way of wooing though. *Ibid.* IV. 57 Gross Feeders, Lion talkers, Lamb-like fighters. **1752** YOUNG *Brothers* I. i. Wks. 1757 II. 205 We'll seek his lion Sire, Who dares to frown on us, his conquerors. **1757** GRAY *Bard.* 117 Her lion-port, her awe-commanding face. **1795** J. FAWCETT *Art of War* 31 The savage soldier.. Nurs'd in no silken lap, his lion-nerves, Strings strong as steel. **1813** SHELLEY *Q. Mab* viii. 196 The jackal of ambition's lion-rage. **1824** MISS MITFORD *Village* Ser. I. 274 May,..barking in her tremendous lion-note, and putting down the other noises like a clap of thunder. **1842** TENNYSON *Eng. & Amer. in 1782*, 3 Strong mother of a Lion-line. **1849** *Blackw. Mag.* Feb. 156 This true soldier.. had fallen in that lion-rush which Richard made at his foe. **1860** PUSEY *Min. Proph.* 266 Jonah feared not the fierceness of their lion-nature, but God's tenderness.

Lion, Lion Herald, Lion King-at-arms: see LYON.

‖**'lionceau.** *Obs.* Chiefly *Her.* Forms: *pl.* 5 leonnceux, lyonsewes, 6 lionne-sewys, 7 lionceaux. [a. F. *lionceau*, OF. also *leonceau* 'a Lyons whelpe' (Cotgr.), later form of *lioncel* LIONCEL.] A young lion: = LIONCEL.

c **1450** *Merlin* 413 This lyon crowned hadde in his companye xviij lyonsewes crowned. *c* **1450** *Mirour Saluacioun* 1167 Twelve leonnceux ouer sex greces Salomones throne exourned. *c* **1500** *Sc. Poem Heraldry* 147 in *Q. Eliz. Acad.* 99 Twa thingis in armis sal end in schewis a[l]wey;..As lionne-sewys, to sey, and heronne-sewis. **1610** GUILLIM *Heraldry* I. vi. 24 Six..Lionceaux rampant purpure.

lionced, leonced ('laɪənst), *a. Her.* [irreg. f. LION.] (See quot.)

1828–40 BERRY *Encycl. Herald.* I, *Lionced* or *Leonced*, adorned with lions' heads, as a cross, the ends of which terminate in lions' heads. In mod. Dicts.

lioncel ('laɪənsɛl). Also 7 lioncell, lyoncel. [ad. OF. *lioncel*, dim. of *lion* LION. Cf. LIONCEAU.] A small or young lion; chiefly *Her.* (see quots.).

1610 GUILLIM *Heraldry* III. xv. 139 In the Blazoning of Armes consisting of more Lions in a Field then one, you must terme them Lioncels. **1688** R. HOLME *Armoury* II. 134/1 A Lioness Lionseth a Lioncell, or Lions Whelp. **1706** PHILLIPS (ed. Kersey), *Lioncels* is also a Term in *Heraldry* for Lions, when there are more than two of them born in any Coat of Arms, and no Ordinary between them. **1864** MISS YONGE *Trial* I. xi. 225 She was more flattered by the civilities of a lioncel like Harvey Anderson. **1864** BOUTELL *Her. Hist. & Pop.* xiv. §1 (ed. 3) 153 Three chevronels sa., the middle one charged with a lioncel passant of the field.

†**lion-drunk**, *a. Obs.* Said of a man in the second of the proverbial four stages of drunkenness, in which he becomes violent and quarrelsome.

The mediæval saying was that wine makes a man successively resemble a sheep, a lion, an ape, and a sow. (See Skeat's note to Chaucer *Manciple's Prol.* 45.)

1592 NASHE *P. Pennilesse* 23 b. The second [kind of drunkard] is Lion drunke, and he flings the pots about the house, calls his Hostesse whore [etc.]. **1623** MASSINGER *Bondman* III. iii. *a* **1640** DAY *Peregr. Schol.* (1881) 52 When the lions bloode mates with a furious disposition,..it converts to rage, stabbings, and quarrells; and such we call Lion-Drunk.

lionel ('laɪənəl). *Her.* [a. OF. *lionel*, dim. of *lion* LION.] = LIONCEL.

1661 MORGAN *Sph. Gentry* IV. ii. 15 Three demy Lionels passant argent. **1736** SLEECH in *Lett. Lit. Men* (Camden) 366 His Arms (a Chevron between 3 Lionels) carv'd on it.

lionesque (laɪə'nɛsk), *a.* [f. LION + -ESQUE.] Characteristic of a lion.

1882 *Macm. Mag.* XLVI. 245 His profile was that of a Greek statue; the eyes small and piercing; the whole face lionesque. **1894** FENN *In Alpine Valley* II. 166 His lionesque tramp up and down their prison.

lioness ('laɪənɪs). Forms: 4 leoun-, lioun-, (lyenn-), 4–5 leon-, 4–7 lyon-, lyonn-, 4–8 lionn-; 4 -es, 4–7 -ess(e, (5 -asse, -ys); 7– lioness. [a. OF. *lion(n)esse*, *leonesse* (now superseded by *lionne*), f. *lion* LION.]

1. The female of the lion.

a **1300** *Cursor M.* 12336 Right be þat water side lai a leoness [*Fairf.* liones, *Gött.* leones]. **13..** *Sir Beues* (MS.A.) 2465 Stoutliche þe liounesse þan Asailede Beues. *c* **1375** *Sc. Leg. Saints* xlix. (*Tecla*) 210 Ymang þai bestis ves richt stark & fel a lyonnes. *c* **1386** CHAUCER *Wife's Prol.* 637 Stibourne I was as is a Leonesse. **1461** *Rolls of Parlt.* V. 475 The Office of kepyng Lyons, Leonesses and Leopardes, within oure Toure of London. **1588** SHAKS. *Tit. A.* IV. ii. 138 The chafed Bore, the mountaine Lyonesse. **1667** MILTON *P.L.* VIII. 393 They rejoyce Each with thir kinde, Lion with Lioness. **1717** POPE *Iliad* x. 213 The gaunt Lioness, with Hunger bold. **1726** AYLIFFE *Parergon* 46 Lyons do in a very severe manner punish the adulteries of the Lyoness. **1813** BYRON *Giaour* 1215 Go, when the hunter's hand hath wrung From the forest-cave her shrieking young, And calm the lonely lioness.

b. *fig.* Applied to persons.

1413 *Pilgr. Sowle* (Caxton 1483) I. xv. 12 Yet wote I wel that leon is he nought ne thou ne myght no leonesse be. **1595** SHAKS. *John* II. i. 291 Were I at home At your den sirrah, with your Lionnesse, I would set an Oxe-head to your Lyons hide. **1847** TENNYSON *Princess* VI. 147 O fair and strong and terrible! Lioness That with your long locks play the Lion's mane.

2. A female celebrity; a woman who is lionized. †Also (*Oxford University slang*), a lady visitor to a member of the university.

1808 SCOTT *Let. to Lady Louisa Stuart* 19 Jan. in *Lockhart*, Miss Lydia White..is what Oxonians call a lioness of the first order, with stockings nineteen times nine dyed blue. **1824** —— *St. Ronan's* vii, Bring Mr. Springblossom—Winter-blossom—and all the lions and lionesses. **1848** J. H. NEWMAN *Loss & Gain* v. 26 He..had promised him tickets, for some ladies, lionesses of his, who were coming up to the Commemoration. **1861** HUGHES *Tom Brown at Oxf.* xxv, The whole load,..were on the look-out for lady visitors, profanely called lionesses. **1894** FENN *In Alpine Valley* I. 8 She was received in society and petted as the new lioness.

lionet ('laɪənɪt). [a. OF. *lionet*: see LION and -ET[1].] A young lion.

a **1586** SIDNEY *Arcadia* III. (1629) 252 A braue Lion, who taught his young Lionets how in taking of a prey to ioyne courage with cunning. **1633** P. FLETCHER *Purple Isl.* ix. xx, So may we see a little lionet—When newly whelped, a weak and tender thing, Despised by every beast. **1795** SOUTHEY *Joan of Arc* x. 382 Emulous he strove, like the young lionet When first he bathes his murderous jaws in blood. **1819** LAMB *Lett.* xi. *To Miss Wordsworth* 109 The whelps (lionets) he was sorry to find were dead. **1845** HOOD *Remonstr. Ode* 19 All the nine little Lionets are lying Slumbering in milk, and sighing.

lion-heart. †**a.** A heart like that of a lion, i.e. brave, courageous; in quot. 1665 with pun on *hart*. **b.** A lion-hearted, courageous person; commonly used to translate *Cœur de Lion*, the traditional appellation of Richard I of England.

1665 DRYDEN *Ind. Emperor* I. ii, My lion-hart is with love's toils beset. **1682** OTWAY *Venice Preserved* III. ii, Oh! I could tell a Story would rouze thy Lion-Heart out of its Den. **1832** TENNYSON *Margaret* iii, What songs..The lion-heart, Plantagenet, Sang looking thro' his prison bars? **1872** RUSKIN *Eagle's N.* §240 The Christian chivalry which was led in England by the Lion-Heart, and in France by Roland, and in Spain by the Cid.

lion-hearted, *a.* Having the heart or courage of a lion; courageous; magnanimously brave.

1708 J. PHILLIPS *Cyder* II. 563 See Lyon-Hearted Richard, Piously valiant. **1725** POPE *Odyss.* xx. 182 Two dogs of chace, a lion-hearted guard. **1838** DICKENS *Nich. Nick.* xxx, Farewell, my noble, my lion-hearted boy!

Hence **lion'heartedness.**

1885 RUSKIN *Pleasures Eng.* 155 The lion-heartedness which gave the glory and the peace of the gods to Leonidas.

lionhood ('laɪənhʊd). [f. LION + -HOOD.] The state or condition of being a 'lion'.

1833 WHEWELL in Mrs. S. Douglas *Life* iv. (1881) 153 But she [Miss Martineau] is a remarkable person. She is now enjoying the honours of her lionhood in London. **1845** LOWELL *Lett.* (1894) I. 111 Do not understand me as exaggerating the miseries which my lionhood entails on me.

lioning ('laɪənɪŋ), *vbl. sb. nonce-wd.* [f. LION + -ING[1].] The being made a 'lion' of.

1866 CARLYLE *Remin.* (1881) II. 219 My loyal little darling taking no manner of offence not to participate in my lionings.

lionish ('laɪənɪʃ), *a.* Also 6 lyonyshe, 6–7 lyonish. [f. LION + -ISH.] Of or pertaining to a lion; resembling or having the nature of a lion; brave or fierce as a lion.

1549 E. ALLEN *Jude's Par. Rev.* 7 This hath Jesus Christ yᵉ sauiour of yᵉ world, deserued & brought to passe wᵗ his lyonyshe might. **1612** T. TAYLOR *Comm. Titus* i. 16 Promises..of safety from wicked, lyonish, cruell, and blood-thirstie men. **1644** *Answ. Doctr. & Disc. Divorce* 10 The Lionish dispositions shall so be changed that they shall be fit for the society of milder natures. **1864** BOUTELL *Her. Hist. & Pop.* xxx. (ed. 3) 450 Our Lions may be..drawn both thoroughly lionish and thoroughly heraldic.

lionism ('laɪənɪz(ə)m). [f. LION + -ISM.] The practice of lionizing; the condition of being treated as a 'lion' or celebrity.

1835 *Athenæum* 23 May 392/3 Mrs. Hemans..was remarkable for shrinking from the vulgar honours of lionism. **1851** CARLYLE *Sterling* III. i. (1872) 167 Sterling was..vividly awake to what was passing in the world; glanced..into its Puseyisms, Liberalisms, literary Lionisms, or what else the mad hour might be producing.

Lionist, obs. form of LYONIST.

lionite ('laɪənaɪt). *Min.* [Named, 1877, from the Mountain *Lion* Mine in Colorado, its locality.] A variety of native tellurium, containing much silica.

1877 T. BERDELL in *Proc. Amer. Phil. Soc.* 172 (Chester).

lionize ('laɪənaɪz), *v.* [f. LION + -IZE.]

1. *trans.* To visit the 'lions' of (a place); to visit or go over (a place of interest).

1838 TICKNOR *Life, Lett. & Jrnls.* II. viii. 157 Eager to lionize the town with us. **1852** E. LEAR *Jrnls. Painter in S. Calabria* 75 Lionising the church and convent. **1863** OUIDA *Held in Bondage* (1870) 32 The time to lionise Cambridge is May and June. **1883** LD. R. GOWER *My Remin.* II. xxi. 20 The next day..I passed at Northampton, lionising the different buildings of interest in the place.

2. a. To show the 'lions' to (a person). Also *absol.* **b.** To show the 'lions' of (a place).

1830 MACAULAY *Southey's Colloq.* in *Edin. Rev.* L. 535 Mr. Southey very hospitably takes an opportunity to lionize [*Ess.* **1843** I. 228 escort] the ghost round the lakes. **1856** LEVER *Martins of Cro' M.* 135, I want you to lionise an old friend of mine, who has the ambition to 'do' Connemara under your guidance. **1861** HUGHES *Tom Brown at Oxf.* xxv. (1889) 238 I'm not in the humour to be dancing about lionizing. **1870** DISRAELI *Lothair* xxiv, He had lionised the distinguished visitors during the last few days over the University. **1875** BUCKLAND *Log-bk.* 189 The vicar then lionised the church. **1881** E. FITZGERALD *Lett.* (1889) I. 475, I was lionized over some things new to me, and some that I was glad to see again.

3. *intr.* To see the 'lions' of a place.

1825 C. M. WESTMACOTT *Eng. Spy* I. 137 We sallied forth to lionize..which is the Oxford term for gazing about, usually applied to strangers. **1847** R. W. CHURCH *Let.* 6 Feb. in *Life & Lett.* (1897) 80 We got in yesterday [at Malta] at 1.30, and have been lionising since. **1860** TRISTRAM *Gt. Sahara* xviii. 312, I was soon compelled to desist from all attempts to lionize, as ophthalmia rendered the light intolerable.

4. *trans.* To treat (a person) as a 'lion' or celebrity; to make a 'lion' of.

1809 SCOTT in Lockhart *Life* xix, They cannot lionize me without my returning the compliment and learning something from them. **1864** *Spectator* No. 1875. 639 During the height of the Russian War, Russians were as safe in London as in St. Petersburg, were, indeed rather lionized.

5. *intr.* To be a 'lion'.

1834 *Fraser's Mag.* IX. 64 This is quite fame enough for any one, and upon the strength of it he may continue to lionise.

Hence **'lionizing** *vbl. sb.*; **lioni'zation**, the action of the vb.; **'lionizer**, one who lionizes.

1829 FROUDE in *Rem.* (1838) I. 239, I got within the baleful influence of Lionisers, and was pestered out of my wits by humbugging guides. **1837** LOCKHART *Life of Scott* lxxiii, The pernicious and degrading trickery of lionizing. **1841** DICKENS *Let.* in *Life* (1872) I. xv. 229 The horrors of lionization. **1851** R. F. BURTON *Goa* 268 A glimpse of scenery that even a jaded lionizer would admire. **1857** MRS. MATHEWS *Tea-Table T.* I. 100 Her lionizing mania had reached to fever point. **1861** MRS. CLARA BROMLEY *Wom. Wand. West. World* 34 In a hurried journey one gets sadly tired of lionising. **1864** 'C. BEDE' in *Lond. Soc.* VI. 27/1 The country cousins will retain but a very vague remembrance of their Oxford lionizings. **1887** FRITH *Autobiog.* II. xxix. 346 The lion was Tom Moore, the poet; and the lionizers, consisting chiefly of ladies [etc.]. **1890** 'ROLF BOLDREWOOD' *Col. Reformer* (1891) 462 Antonia had to submit to the lionisation of her husband.

'lion-like, *a.* (*adv.*) **a.** *adj.* Resembling a lion or what pertains to a lion.

1556 J. HEYWOOD *Spider & F.* xci. 122 This lionlike spider: erst feerce as could be. **1611** BIBLE *1 Chron.* xi. 22 He slue two Lyon-like men of Moab. **1747** T. SMITH *Jrnl.* (1849) 270 There has been no high winds this month [March]—no lion-like days. **1829** SCOTT *Rob Roy* Introd. App. v, The lion-like mode of wooing practised by the ancient Highlanders. *a* **1849** H. COLERIDGE *Ess.* (1851) II. 51 His [Achilles'] lion-like fury of sorrow for Patroclus.

b. *adv.*

1610 NICCOLS *Ed. Ironside* lxix. *Mirr. Mag.* 600 The anguish arm'd our armes with strength to strike, And made vs both incounter lion-like. **1670** DRYDEN *1st Pt. Conq. Granada* III. i, But, lion-like, has been in deserts bred. **1865** CARLYLE *Fredk. Gt.* II. xiv. (1872) I. 131 Ritterdom fought lionlike, but with insufficient strategic and other wisdom.

lionly ('laɪənlɪ), *a.* Now *rare.* [f. LION + -LY.] Lion-like.

1631 R. H. *Arraignm. Whole Creature* xiv. §2. 242 Sacrifizing to their Pagan Gods..that Lyonly Nazarite Sampson. **1660** GAUDEN *Serm. Brownrig* 236 That which in their Physiognomy is..lupine or leonine (for so we read some men had lionly looks). **1898** G. MEREDITH *Odes Fr. Hist.* 50 Which bring at whiles the lionly far roar.

lionne (ljɔn). [F., fem. of *lion* LION.]

†**1.** A lioness. *Obs.*

a **1400** *Isumbras* 180 So come a lyonne with latys unmylde, And in hir pawes scho hent the childe.

‖**2.** A woman of the highest fashion.

1846 LOUISA S. COSTELLO *Tour Venice* 384, I was much amused at the splendid dresses of the lionnes, and the singularity of that of the lions of the Tyrol. **1856** RUSKIN *Mod. Paint.* III. IV. v. §11 The lionne of the ball-room, whom youth and passion can as easily distinguish as [etc.].

lionne, -esse, obs. forms of LION, LIONESS.

lionne-sew, variant of LIONCEAU.

†**lion-piece.** *Obs.* In 7 lyon-. [Perh. f. vbl. phr. *lie on*; hardly f. LION or LIERNE.] (See quot.)

1611 COTGR., *Filière*,..a Lyon-peece, or Ridge-peece, of timber; a side-wauer. [Hence in Halliwell as *lion*.]

†**lionse**, *v. Obs.* [? A back-formation from LIONCEL.] *trans.* To whelp: said of a lioness.

1562 LEIGH *Armorie* (1597) 44 It is saide that when they are first Lionsed, they sleepe continually three long Egyptian daies. **1688** R. HOLME *Armoury* II. 134/1 A Lioness Lionseth a Lioncell or Lions Whelp.

lionship ('laɪənʃɪp). [f. LION + -SHIP.] The quality or condition of being a 'lion'; also, the personality of a 'lion' (used as a mock title).

1769 GOLDSM. *Epil. to 'Sister'* 32 Strip but this vizor off, and sure I am You'll find his lionship a very lamb. **1837** *New Monthly Mag.* L. 179 The history of poor Byron's lionship lives in all our memories. **1865** F. MARTIN *Life J. Clare* 218 William Hilton, like Clare, was averse to lionship.

lioun, -esse, obs. forms of LION, LIONESS.

liour, variant of LEAR². *Obs.*

lip (lɪp), *sb.* Forms: 1 lippa, 2–7 lippe, (3 leppe), 4–6 lyppe, 5 lyp, (lype), 7 lipp, 4– lip. [OE. *lippa* wk. masc., corresponds to OFris. *lippa* masc., MLG., MDu. *lippe* fem. (whence mod.G. *lippe*, mod.Du. *lip* fem.), MSw. *lippe*, *lippa*, and *läpe*, mod.Sw. *läpp*, Da. *læbe*:—OTeut. type **lipjon-*, cogn. w. the synonymous OSax. *lepor*, OHG. *leffur*, *lefs* masc. (MHG. *lefs* masc., *lefse* fem., mod.Ger. dial. *lefze* fem.):—OTeut. **lepoz-*, **leps*, f. root **lep-*, pre-Teut. **leb-*; ablaut-variants occur in L. *labium*, *labrum*, and Pehlevi *lap* (mod.Persian *lab*) lip. The LG. word was adopted into OF. as *lipe*, whence mod.F. *lippe* thick under-lip.]

I. 1. a. Either of the two fleshy structures which in man and other animals form the edges of the mouth. Distinguished as *upper* and *lower*, also as †*over* (obs.) and *under*, colloq. or dial. *top* and *bottom lip*. Phr. (***immersed, steeped***) ***to the lips***.

c **1000** ÆLFRIC *Gloss.* in Wr.-Wülcker 157/22, *Labium*, ufeweard lippa. *Labrum*, niðera lippe. *Rostrum*, foreweard feng þære lippena togædere. *c* **1000** *Sax. Leechd.* III. 100 Wið lippe sar. *c* **1205** LAY. 29359 Of cnihten he carf þe lippes. **13..** *K. Alis.* 6428 Heo no hath nose, no mouth, no toth, no lippe. *c* **1375** *XI Pains of Hell* 81 in *O.E. Misc.* 213 Þo þat stod vp to þe leppis Be þe seruys of god þai set noȝt by. **1377** LANGL. *P. Pl.* B. XVIII. 52 Poysoun on a pole þei put vp to his lippes. *c* **1400** MAUNDEV. (Roxb.) xxii. 100 Men þat hase þe ouer lippe so grete þat, when þai slepe in þe sonne, þai couer all þe visage with þat lippe. *c* **1470** HENRY *Wallace* IX. 1928 His lyppys round, his noys was squar and tret. **1500–20** DUNBAR *Poems* liii. 39 For lauchter nain mycht hald thair lippis. **1590** SHAKS. *Mids. N.* II. i. 49 When she drinkes, against her lips I bob. **1604** —— *Oth.* IV. ii. 50 Had they.. Steep'd me in pouertie to the very lipes. **1724** R. WODROW *Life J. Wodrow* 166, I observed his lips quivering. **1758** J. S. *Le Dran's Observ. Surg.* (1771) 37 A cancerous Tumour on the Middle of the Under-Lip. **1822** SHELLEY *Fragm. Unfinished Drama* 113 Some said he was.. steeped in bitter infamy to the lips. **1836** YARRELL *Brit. Fishes* (1859) I. 449 [The Loach].. with four barbels or cirri.. on the upper lip in the front. **1883** R. W. DIXON *Mano* I. xvi. 51 To the lips was he in luxury immersed. **1891** T. HARDY *Tess* II. xxii, The little upward lift in the middle of her top lip.

†**b.** Proverbs. (See also LETTUCE 2.) *Obs.*

1546 J. HEYWOOD *Prov.* (1867) 77 He can yll pype, that lackth his vpper lyp. **1577–87** HOLINSHED *Chron.* II. *Hist. Scot.* 464 A man cannot pype without his vpper lip.

†**c.** *transf.* or *fig.* in phr. ***the lip*** (? = point) ***of a lance***. Obs.

c **1400** *Destr. Troy* 10139 With the lippe of þere launsis so launchet þai somyn. *Ibid.* 10147.

d. = EMBOUCHURE 3; the condition or strength of a wind instrumentalist's lips.

1889 in *Cent. Dict.* **1933** *Metronome* July 26 He's got the ideas, but his lip's weak yet. **1960** *Jazz Rev.* Nov. 10 My lip went bad after a year in the Earl Hines band. **1972** *Rolling Stone* 9 Nov. 10/2 Having not played for several months, Miles had lost the eternally fragile trumpeters' lip.

2. In phrases referring to certain actions regarded as indicative of particular states of feeling. ***to bite one's lip*** or † ***on one's lip***, (*a*) to show vexation, (*b*) to repress emotion; ***to carry*** or ***keep a stiff upper lip***, to keep one's courage, not to lose heart; in bad sense, to be hard or obstinate; ***to curl one's lip*** (see CURL *v.* 3 b); † ***to fall a lip of contempt***, to express contempt by the movement of the lip; † ***to hang the lip***, to look vexed (cf. HANG *v.* 4 b); ***to lay*** (a person) ***on the lips***, to kiss (see LAY *v.* 34); ***to lick one's lips*** (see LICK *v.* 1 b); † ***to make*** (***up***) ***a lip***, to frame the lips so as to express vexation or merriment *at*; to pout or poke fun *at* [cf. F. *faire sa lippe*]; ***to smack one's lips***, to express relish for food, *fig.* to express delight.

1330 [see BITE *v.* 16]. **1362** LANGL. *P. Pl.* A. v. 67 For wraþþe he bot his lippes. **1390** GOWER *Conf.* I. 283 And go so forth as I go may, Fulofte bitinge on my lippe. **1546** BP. GARDINER *Declar. Art. Joye* 46 b, Eyther they make a lyppe at it, or yelde with silence to seme to gyue place to auctoritie for the tyme. **1557** SEAGER *Sch. Vertue* 455 in *Babees Bk.*, Not smackyng thy lyppes As comonly do hogges. **1568** GRAFTON *Chron.* II. 846 The Erle.. was therewithall a little vexed, & began somwhat to hang the lip. **1607** SHAKS. *Cor.* II. i. 127, I will make a Lippe at the Physician. **1611** —— *Wint. T.* I. ii. 373 Hee.. falling A Lippe of much contempt, speedes from me. **1781** MAD. D'ARBLAY *Diary* 14 Sept., Was not that a speech to provoke Miss Grizzle herself? However, I only made up a saucy lip. **1833** J. NEAL *Down Easters* I. ii. 15 'What's the use o' boo-hooin'?.. Keep a stiff upper lip; no bones broke—don't I know?' **1837** HALIBURTON *Clockm.* Ser. I. xxv, She used to carry a stiff upper lip, and make him and the broomstick well acquainted together. **1837** DICKENS *Pickwick* xlv, He then drank.. and smacking his lips, held out the tumbler for more. **1840** BROWNING *Sordello* II. 70 He.. Biting his lip to keep down a great smile Of pride. **1969** C. BOOKER *Neophiliacs* vi. 134 The tradition of 'stiff upper lip' epics looking back to wartime greatness. **1973** G. GREENE *Honorary Consul.* I. i. 11 *Machismo*.. the Spanish equivalent of *virtus*.. had little to do with English courage or a stiff upper lip. **1973** *Guardian* 10 Feb. 3/3 Stiff upper lip all round on Mrs Gandhi's taunt. **1973** *Times* 24 Dec. 14/4 (*heading*) How the Italians are facing up to austerity with a stiff upper lip.

3. a. Chiefly *pl.* Considered as one of the organs of speech; often in figurative contexts. (In early examples chiefly in literalisms from the Vulg.) † ***to lift*** or ***move a lip***: to utter even the slightest word ***against***. ***to escape*** (a person's) ***lips***: see ESCAPE *v.* ***to hang on*** (a person's) ***lips***: to listen with rapt attention to his speech.

c **1020** *Rule St. Benet* (Logeman) xxxviii. (1888) 69 Mine lippan þu ȝeopena & min muð. *a* **1225** *Ancr. R.* 158 Ich am a man mid suilede lippen. *c* **1290** *S. Eng. Leg.* I. 266/192 Heo ne wawede leome non bote hire lippene vnneþe 3ware-with heo seide hire oresun. *a* **1310** in Wright *Lyric P.* ix. 34 Heo hath a mury mouht to mele, With lefly rede lippes lele, Romaunz forte rede. *c* **1375** *Sc. Leg. Saints* xxxv. (*Thadee*) 147 Na ȝet þi lyppis suld nocht be opnyt to pray the trinite. **1526** *Pilgr. Perf.* (W. de W. 1531) 132 And the locke of good aduysement shall be set on our lyppes. **1579** TOMSON *Calvin's Serm. Tim.* 42/2 We may not once moue the lippe against them. **1603** SHAKS. *Meas. for M.* II. ii. 78 Mercie then will breathe within your lips. **1606** —— *Tr. & Cr.* I. iii. 240 Peace Troyan, lay thy finger on thy lips. **1625** BACON *Ess., Of Atheism* (Arb.) 333 Atheisme is rather in the Lip, than in the Heart of Man. **1667** MILTON *P.L.* VIII. 56 From his Lip Not Words alone pleas'd her. **1704** *Good Expedient for Innoc. & Peace* in *Harl. Misc.* (1746) VIII. 14/2 It might appear a Crime to lift a Lip against, or return any Answer to this Objection. **1781** COWPER *Expost.* 44 Hypocrisy, formality in prayer, And the dull service of the lip, were there. **1842** TENNYSON *Gardener's Dau.* 50 Not less among us lived Her fame from lip to lip. **1855** MACAULAY *Hist. Eng.* xi. III. 127 John Hampden.. produced a composition.. too vituperative to suit the lips of the Speaker. **1875** JOWETT *Plato* (ed. 2) III. 238 Unless I hear the contrary from your own lips. **1882** FARRAR *Early Chr.* II. 427 If the Christianity of the lips is consistent with anti-Christianity of life.

†**b.** *sing.* Language; chiefly in phrase, ***of one lip*** (a Hebraism); also used for 'agreeing in one story'. *lit.* and *fig. Obs.*

1382 WYCLIF *Gen.* xi. 1 Forsothe the erthe was of oo lip [**1388** langage], and of the same wordis. **1677** YARRANTON *Eng. Improv.* 174 [The poor Clothiers of Worcester] are all of one Lip, a bad Trade, and they do not know when it will mend [etc.]. **1681** *Whole Duty Nations* 15 In parts remote one from another, and of a divers lip or language. **1695** LD. PRESTON *Boeth.* II. 90 This, People of a different Lip doth bind With sacred Cords.

c. *slang.* Saucy talk, impudence.

1821 *D. Haggart's Life* (ed. 2) 20, I was at no loss in vindicating myself and giving him plenty of lip. **1884** 'MARK TWAIN' *Huck. Finn* v. 31 'Don't you give me none o' your lip,' says he. **1895** CROCKETT *Cleg Kelly* xx. (1896) 152 Says Sal to me, 'None of your lip'.

d. A lawyer, esp. a criminal lawyer. *U.S. slang.*

1929 *Sat. Even. Post* 13 Apr. 54/3 A lawyer is a mouthpiece or a shyster or a lip. **1930** *Amer. Mercury* Dec. 456/2 Get a lip for a writ an' I'll lam. **1950** H. E. GOLDIN et al. *Dict. Amer. Underworld Lingo* 127/1 The lip took a hundred skins (dollars) and never showed (appeared) in court.

II. Something resembling the lips of the mouth.

4. a. The margin of a cup or any similar vessel; e.g. of a bell.

1592 R. D. *Hypnerotomachia* 60 And in the bearing out of the lippe of the vessell ouer the perpendicular poynt of the heade there was fastened a rynge. **1660** BOYLE *New Exp. Phys. Mech.* Proem 9 The Orifice [of a vessel] is incircled with a lip of Glass, almost an inch high. **1684** T. BURNET *Th. Earth* I. viii. I. 102 The Sea.. bounded against those Hills.. as the ledges or lips of its Vessel. **1758** REID tr. *Macquer's Chem.* I. 321 Raise the coals quite to the lip of the crucible. **1810** E. D. CLARKE *Trav. Russia* (1839) 31/1 The fracture had taken place.. seven feet high from the lip of the bell. **1830** MISS MITFORD *Village* Ser. IV. 259 A small brown pitcher with the lip broken. **1847** C. BRONTË *J. Eyre* xx, He held out the tiny glass.. 'Now wet the lip of the phial'. **1884** F. J. BRITTEN *Watch & Clockm.* 156 [The] Lips.. [are] the rounded edges of the cylinder in a Cylinder Escapement.

b. The edge of any opening or cavity, esp. of the crater of a volcano.

1726 LEONI tr. *Alberti's Archit.* I. 38/1 The Lips of the Apertures. **1830** LYELL *Princ. Geol.* I. 341 Every stream of lava descending from the lips of the crater. **1855** STEPHENS *Bk. Farm* (ed. 2) II. 575/2 The remainder should be placed on the ditch lip on the headridge. **1878** HUXLEY *Physiogr.* 190 The partially-molten rock.. may eventually run over the lip of the crater. **1879** E. GARRETT *House by Works* II. 106 Crouching.. under the heathery lip of the chasm.

c. In wider sense: Any edge or rim, esp. one that projects; *spec.* in *Coal-mining* (see quot. 1883).

1608 WILLET *Hexapla Exod.* 589 Certaine claspes which.. caught holde of the edge or lip of the table. **1813** *Sporting Mag.* XLII. 130 The lip of the hammer [of a gun] overhangs the upper edge of the inclined plane. **1839** MURCHISON *Silur. Syst.* I. xxix. 379 Round the northern lip of this coal tract. **1883** GRESLEY *Gloss. Coal-mining*, *Lip*,.. the low part of the roof of a gate-road near to the face; taken down or ripped, as it is called, as the face advances. **1890** J. SERVICE *Thir Notandums* xv. 102 The Laird o' Auchinskeich had a bit mailin' on the lip o' the moss.

5. In scientific and technical uses.

a. *Surg.* One of the edges of a wound.

c **1400** *Lanfranc's Cirurg.* 35 Be war þat.. no þing.. þat lettiþ consolidacioun, falle bitwene þe lippis of þe wounde. **1541** R. COPLAND *Galyen's Terap.* 2 F iv, Yf the lyppes of the vlcere appere harde and stony, they must be cutte. **1685** BOYLE *Enq. Notion Nat.* 333 The Chirurgeon does often hinder Nature from closing up the Lips of a Wound. **1758** J. S. *Le Dran's Observ. Surg.* (1771) Introd. 3 The Lips of a Wound must be joined. **1807–26** S. COOPER *First Lines Surg.* (ed. 5) 288 As soon as the bones are reduced, the lips of the wound are to be accurately brought together. **1889** in *Syd. Soc. Lex.*

b. *Anat.* and *Zool.* = LABIUM or LABRUM.

1597 [see LABIUM 1 a]. **1611** COTGR., *Landies*, the two Pterigones, or great wings within the lips of a womans Priuities. **1722** [see LABIUM 1 b]. **1828, 1862** [see LABIUM 2]. **1875** *Encycl. Brit.* (ed. 9) II. 280/2 (*Arachnida*), A rudimentary sternal lip (*labium*). **1880** [see LABRUM]. **1901** *Gray's Anat.* (ed. 15) 631 The central lobe or island of Reil lies deeply in the Sylvian fissure, and can only be seen when the lips of that fissure are widely separated.

c. *Bot.* (*a*) One of the two divisions of a bilabiate corolla or calyx. (*b*) = LABELLUM 1.

1776 J. LEE *Introd. Bot.* Explan. Terms 395 *Ringens*, gaping, irregular, with two lips. **1776–96** WITHERING *Brit. Plants* (ed. 3) II. 41 Lip scolloped, blunt, longer than the petals. **1807** J. E. SMITH *Phys. Bot.* 434 *Ajuga* [has] scarcely any upper lip at all. **1832** LINDLEY *Introd. Bot.* I. ii. §7. 118 The lower lip or labellum, the latter term is chiefly applied to the lower lip of Orchideous plants. **1892** *Garden* 27 Aug. 184 Orchids. *Cattleya Schilleriana*... The lip is three-lobed.

d. *Conch.* One of the edges of the aperture of a spiral shell.

1681 GREW *Musæum* 124 Note, That when I speak of the Right or Left Lip of a Shell, I mean, as it is held with the Mouth downward. **1851** RUSKIN *Stones Ven.* I. xx. 216 One of the innumerable groups of curves at the lip of a paper Nautilus. **1866** TATE *Brit. Mollusks* iii. 45 The outer lip is thin, not thickened or reflected as in the majority of the land shells.

e. *Mech.* In various senses (see quots.).

c **1850** *Rudim. Navig.* (Weale) 130 *Lips of scarphs*. The substance left at the ends, which would otherwise become sharp, and be liable to split, and, in other cases, could not bear caulking. **1884** KNIGHT *Dict. Mech.* Suppl., *Lip*, the helical blade on the end of an auger to cut the chip. **1898** *Cycling* 53 Split bracket; 'lips' compressed by screw bolt.

f. *Organ-building.* (See quot. 1876.)

1727–52 CHAMBERS *Cycl.* s.v. *Organ*, Over this aperture is the mouth BBCC; whose upper lip, CC, being level, cuts the wind as it comes out at the aperture. **1852** SEIDEL *Organ* 79 The good intonation, or speaking of a pipe, depends on the correct position of the lips. **1876** HILES *Catech. Organ* iv. (1878) 24 Above and below [the mouth of an organ pipe] are two edges called the lips. **1881** C. A. EDWARDS *Organs* 128 The opening between the lips of a pipe is called 'the mouth'.

6. *attrib.* and *Comb.* **a.** simple attributive: (*a*) belonging to a lip or lips, as in ***lip-end***, ***-favour***, ***-hair***, ***-position***, ***-quiver***, ***-smile***; also ***lip-like*** adj.

1874 THEARLE *Naval Archit.* 70 Sometimes, only those at the *lip ends of the scarphs are left. **1592** GREENE *Philomela* (1615) E 2, Lutesio kind, gaue the Gentlewoman a kisse: for he thought she valued a *lip fauour more then a peece of gold. **1873** W. CORY *Lett. & Jrnls.* (1897) 325 Snobs and gents, and men with waxed *lip-hair. **1836–9** TODD *Cycl. Anat.* II. 543/1 The *lip-like folds of skin before the membrana tympani. **1870** ROLLESTON *Anim. Life* 128 The upper lip-like portion of the anterior suckers. **1632** MASSINGER *Maid of Hon.* IV. iii, His house full Of children, clyents, servants, flattering friends, Soothing his *lip-positions. **1851** H. MELVILLE *Whale* xxxiv. 167 Dough-Boy's life was one continual *lip-quiver. **1871** G. MEREDITH *H. Richmond* xvii, She had her lips tight in a mere *lip-smile.

(*b*) In uses relating to the lips as the organs of speech (sense 3), chiefly with the implication 'merely from the lips, not heartfelt', as in ***lip-babble***, ***-Christian***, ***-comfort***, ***-comforter***, ***-cozenage***, ***-devotion***, †***-gospeller***, ***-holiness***, ***-homage***, ***-love***, †***-lusciousness***, ***-physic***, ***-religion***, ***-resignation***, ***-revel***, ***-reverence***, ***-reward***, ***-righteousness***, ***-wisdom***; ***lip-†good***, ***-holy***, ***-learned***, ***-wise*** adjs. Freq. in terms of Phonetics, as ***lip-action***, ***-closure***, ***-consonant***, ***-position***, ***-protrusion***, ***-rounded*** adj., ***-rounding***, ***-spreading***.

1933 L. BLOOMFIELD *Lang.* vi. 107 It is relative tenseness, too, which in addition to *lip-action, makes the Italian vowels very different from those of English. **1895** ZANGWILL *Master* I. vi. 70 Were these things, then, merely *lip-babble? **1882** FARRAR *Early Chr.* I. 448 *note*, He is speaking, not of *lip-Christians but, of converts who lapse into 'wretchlessness of unclean living'. **1922** O. JESPERSEN *Lang.* 278 That *lip-closure which is an essential part of the ordinary [m]. **1632** MASSINGER *Maid of Hon.* III. i, *Lip comfort cannot cure me. *a* **1815** SOUTHEY *Soldier's Funeral* 43 Reverend *lip-comforters that once a week Proclaim how blessed are the poor. **1867** *Lip consonant [see BACK *a.* 1 c]. **1877** H. SWEET *Handbk. Phonetics* 32 Lip. S.G. *w* in '*wie*', '*wo*' is an example of a pure lip consonant. **1627** E. F. *Hist. Edw. II* (1680) 40 Pretends himself, with a new strain of *Lip-cousenage, to be the Heir of Edward the First. **1607** HIERON *Wks.* I. 292 There may be somewhat like prayer, which yet is not prayer, but *lip-deuotion. **1603** B. JONSON *Sejanus* I. ii, But, when his Grace is merely but *lip-good, And that [etc.]. **1558** E. P. tr. *Cranmer's Confut. Unwrit. Verities* Pref. A iiij, We were.. *lippe gospellers, from the mouth outeward and no farther. **1624** DAVENPORT *City Nt.-Cap* I. i, She that is *lip-holy Is many times heart-hollow. **1591** GREENE *Maiden's Dream* in *Shaks. Soc. Papers* (1845) II. 141 *Lip-holines in Cleargie men [*Dyce suggests* Lip-holy Clergie men] he could not brooke. **1858** R. A. VAUGHAN *Ess. & Rem.* I. 46 The transcendentalist bestows

upon it [Christianity] his *lip-homage. **1683** TRYON *Way to Health* 531 The fashion which our *Lip-learned Physitians and Apothecaries..practice is this [etc.]. *a* **1703** BURKITT *On N.T.* Philem. 7 There is a frozen charity, and a *lip-love found among many professors, whom Christ will disown at the great day. **1650** FULLER *Pisgah* I. iv. 10 Some conceive voluptuousnesse thereby is forbidden; others *lip-lusciousnesse and hypocrisie in divine service. *a* **1625** BEAUM. & FL. *Lover's Progr.* I. i, This is cold comfort, And, in a friend, *lip-physic. **1929** *Amer. Speech* IV. 414 The *lip position of the Gascon sound was identical with that of the Parisian *b*. **1932** D. JONES *Outl. Eng. Phonetics* (ed. 3) xxi. 177 A correct English ʃ may be acquired by..retracting the tip of the tongue and exaggerating the *lip-protrusion. **1597** J. PAYNE *Royal Exch.* 14 These marchants deceyve moche by there paynted faulshode and *lipp religion. **1876** GEO. ELIOT *Dan. Der.* IV. lxix. 353 The Invisible Power that has been the object of..*lip-resignation. **1815** MILMAN *Fazio* (1821) 42 'Tis an old tale Thy fond *lip-revel on a lady's beauties. *c* **1843** CARLYLE *Hist. Sk. Jas. I & Chas. I* (1898) 204 Not with *lip-reverence but heart-reverence. **1595** MARKHAM *Sir R. Grinvile* l, To euery act shee giues huge *lyp-reward. **1801** SOUTHEY *Thalaba* v. xxxv, For the dupes Of human-kind keep this *lip-righteousness! **1921** E. SAPIR *Lang.* viii. 186 In *foti* 'feet' the long *o* was colored by the following *i* to long *ö*, that is, *o* kept its *lip-rounded quality. **1910** *Mod. Lang. Rev.* V. 93 The *lip-rounding is less energetic. **1950** D. JONES *Phoneme* xxxi. 224 A..case..for representing the Japanese u by w on the ground that it has less lip-rounding than the European u-sounds. **1964** R. H. ROBINS *Gen. Ling.* 97 The English front vowels are mostly accompanied by *lip-spreading. **1964** P. STREVENS in D. Abercrombie et al. *Daniel Jones* 121 Pupils may be exhorted to..'smile a little as you say that', in order to achieve voicing or lip-spreading. *a* **1586** SIDNEY *Arcadia* I. (1629) 65 All is but *lip-wisedom, which wants experience. **1603** FLORIO *Montaigne* I. li. (1632) 166 They only are good Pretors, to do justice in the Citie, that are subtile, cautelous, wily and *lip-wise.

b. objective and obj. genitive, as ***lip-biting***, ***-feeding***, ***-treatment***; ***lip-blushing***, ***-dewing***, adjs.

a **1734** NORTH *Exam.* III. viii. §10 (1740) 589 How they had posted themselves in the View of the Prisoner, and made Signals at all Turns with Winks and *Lipbitings. *c* **1588** KYD *1st Pt. Jeronimo* (1605) B, By this *lip blushing kisse. **1791–3** WORDSW. *Descr. Sk.* 132 *Lip-dewing song. **1647** TRAPP *Comm. Matt.* xiii. 52 God hath purposely put honey and milk under their tongues..that they may look to *lip-feeding. **1897** *Allbutt's Syst. Med.* III. 343 Neglect of this precaution is almost certain to produce failure of the *lip-treatment.

c. instrumental and locative, as ***lip-bearded***, ***-born***, ***-licked*** adjs.

1615 A. NICCHOLES *Marr. & Wiving* vi. 17 Meere Croanes..*lip-bearded, as wiches. **1872** GEO. ELIOT *Middlem.* lxxx. IV. 279 Why had he brought his cheap regard and his *lip-born words to her who had nothing paltry to give in exchange? **1632** LITHGOW *Trav.* I. 4 Clouted complements, stolne Phrases, and *lip-licked labours, of lamp-liuing spirits.

7. Special comb.: **lip-auger** (see quot.); †**lip-berry**, ? any small red berry, *esp.* that of the Arum; **lip-bit** (see quot.); **lip-blossomed** *a.* (*nonce-wd.*), labiate; **lip-bolt** = *lip-head bolt*: **lip-brush**, a small brush used to apply lipstick; **lip-click**, a clicking noise made with the lips; †**lip-clip**, a kiss; **lip-fern** (see quot.); **lip-full** *a. dial.*, full to the lips; †**lip-glass** (see quot.); **lip gloss**, a glossy cosmetic applied to the lips; **lip-head bolt** (see quot.); **lip-hook**, (*a*) the upper hook of several on a line, which is put through the lip of a live bait; (*b*) 'a grapnel for catching in the lip of the whale, to tow it to the vessel' (Knight); **lip-language**, (in the instruction of the deaf and dumb) language communicated by movements of the lips; †**lip-letter**, a labial (see LABIAL *sb.* 1); †**lip-lick**, a kiss; **lip-line**, the outline of a person's lips; **lip microphone** (see quot. 1941); **lip pencil** (see PENCIL *sb.* 2c); **lip-piece**, a plug of wood thrust through the lip and worn as an ornament; **lip-pipe** *Organ-building*, a flue-pipe; **lip-plate**, the hypostome of trilobites (*Cent. Dict.*); **lip-plug** = *lip-piece*; **lip-print**, the imprint made by a person's lips; **lip-read** *v. trans.* and *intr.*, to apprehend (someone, or what someone says) by observing the movement of the lips; so **lip-reader**; **lip-reading**, (in the instruction of the deaf and dumb) the apprehending of what another says by watching the movements of his lips; **lip-ring**, a ring passed through the lip, and worn as an ornament; **lip-rouge**, red cosmetic for the lips; **lip-smacking**, the act of smacking one's lips (see SMACK *v.*[2] 1); also as *ppl. adj.*; **lip-speaking**, speaking to one who is deaf by means of movements of the lips (cf. *lip-reading*); **lip-spine** *Conch.*, a spine on the edge of a shell (*Cent. Dict.*); **lip-strap** (see quot.); **lip-sworn** *a.*, that has taken an oath of secrecy; **lip-sync(h)**, **-synchronization** (see quots.); so **lip-sync** *v. intr.*, **lip-synchronized** *ppl. a.*, **lip-syncing** *vbl. sb.*; **lip-thatch** (*jocular*), a moustache; **lip-tooth**, a tooth on the lip of a shell; **lip-vein**, a labial vein (see LABIAL *a.* 1b); **lip-wing** (*jocular*), a moustache; **lip-work** = LIP-LABOUR (so ***lip-working*** adj.); **lip-wort seed** *nonce-wd.* (*humorous*) = idle talk. Also LIP-DEEP, LIP-LABOUR, LIP-SALVE, LIP-SERVICE, LIP-WORSHIP.

1884 KNIGHT *Dict. Mech.* Suppl. s.v. *Lip*, A *lip auger has pod and lip; in contradistinction to the screw auger. *a* **1613** DENNYS *Secr. Angling* II. xxxv. C8b, *Lip berries from the bryar bush or weede. **1681** CHETHAM *Angler's Vade-mecum* iv. §27 (1689) 27 Lip-berries. Whose true name is Aron berries or Berries of Cookow-pints or Wake-Robin. **1875** KNIGHT *Dict. Mech.*, **Lip-bit*, a boring tool adapted to be used in a brace, and having a cutting lip projecting beyond the end of the barrel. **1876** E. R. LANKESTER *Hist. Creation* I. i. 15 The great natural family of *lip-blossomed plants. **1874** THEARLE *Naval Archit.* 38 These *lip bolts are likewise shown. **1947** *Glamour* Aug. 96 If you're aiming for makeup perfection..you'll naturally want the finest in *lipbrushes. **1958** Lipbrush [see AEROSOL 2]. **1960** *News Chron.* 21 June 6/2 Make the most of the mouth one has... This can only be done skilfully with a lip-brush. **1606** *Wily Beguiled* 21 A Maid cannot loue, or catch a *lip clip or lap clap, but heers such tittle tattle. **1933** E. SITWELL *Eng. Eccentrics* 18 The *lip-clicks of the earthworms which are, it may be, amongst the earliest origins of our language. **1890** *Century Dict.*, **Lip-fern*, a fern of the genus *Cheilanthes*; in allusion to the lip-like indusium. **1822** H. AINSLIE *Land of Burns* 16 The recent rains have..swollen the river *lip full. **1825** T. COSNETT *Footman's Direct.* 128 Two sets of finger-glasses, and *lip-glasses for the company to wash their mouths in. **1939–40** *Army & Navy Stores Catal.* 437/1 Max Factor... *Lip gloss—2/6. **1972** *Country Life* 4 May 1127/3, I have now come to..like lip gloss... These shiny lip colours have several good uses. You can use them alone for a pale, glossy look or you can put them over a lipstick to add gloss. **1972** *Vogue* June Special 90 Blueberry Wine Lipstick matching Lip Gloss. **1875** KNIGHT *Dict. Mech.*, **Lip-head Bolt*, a bolt with a head projecting sideways. **1870** CHOLMONDELEY-PENNELL *Mod. Pract. Angler* 12 The *lip-hook is a very important portion of the spinning-flight. *Ibid.* 208 The single lip-hook is passed through the upper lip of the bait. **1879** H. CALDERWOOD *Mind & Br.* 209 The German method of instructing deaf-mutes by *lip-language. **1591** R. PERCIVALL *Sp. Dict.*, B is a *lip-letter. **1582** STANYHURST *Æneis* I. (Arb.) 40 When she shal embrace thee, when *lyplicks sweetlye she fastneth. **1951** W. SANSOM *Face of Innocence* ii. 21 A smell of coffee and cigars blended with the black perfume and the red *lipline of Eve's presence. **1960** *Farmer & Stockbreeder* 16 Feb. Suppl. 5/3 It is seldom the young who apply their lipstick badly. Their natural lip-line is still clear. **1941** *B.B.C. Gloss. Broadcasting Terms* 17 **Lip microphone*, type of ribbon microphone designed to be held close to the mouth and to eliminate extraneous sounds reaching it from either side. **1949** *Electronic Engin.* XXI. 354 There will be a commentator's box equipped with a lip microphone. **1904** *Lip pencil [see s.v. PENCIL *sb.* 2c]. **1948** *Woman & Beauty* Dec. 57 (*caption*) One of the new Gala lip pencils. **1796** MORSE *Amer. Geog.* I. 111 *note*, This custom of the women's wearing the '*lip-piece' by way of ornament. **1855** HOPKINS *Organ* 354 *Lip, mouth, or flue pipes..are such as have an oblong opening, called the mouth..bounded above and below by two edges called the lips; which are made to sound by the wind first passing through a narrow fissure, flue, or wind-way. **1876** [see LABIAL A. 1c]. **1894** *Nation* (N.Y.) 14 June 451/1 The Suyá are made fun of for their *lip-plug, or *botoco*. **1934** 'J. RHODE' *Poison for One* II. ii. 92 Has it [*sc.* a drinking-glass] been examined for what I may term *lip-prints? **1970** *New Scientist* 3 Sept. 455/2 They have collected lip prints from 280 people, using a technique akin to finger printing. **1892** *Strand Mag.* Mar. 250/2 He..*lip read the advocates who examined him. *Ibid.* 251/1 He would like to test the lad's ability to speak, and to lip read. **1906** *Chambers's Jrnl.* 29 Dec. 80/1 An arithmetic class where questions..were not only heard (or, rather, lip-read) but answered. **1946** *Sat. Even. Post* 9 Mar. 10/2 Tele addicts contend they see football better than from any seat in the stadium, and can lip-read the signals. **1962** A. NISBETT *Technique Sound Studio* x. 170 My deaf friend preferred to switch it off and lip-read. **1973** C. CARFAX *Sleeping Salamander* vii. 66 Watching, I lipread rather than heard his words. **1912** *Strand Mag.* Jan. 15/1 In those days this youthful *lip-reader had no name for her gift of seeing speech. **1941** V. WOOLF *Between Acts* 242 There was Dodge, the lip reader,..a seeker like her after hidden faces. **1974** R. C. DENNIS *Conversations with Corpse* ii. 10 A pity you aren't a lip reader. **1874** CARPENTER *Ment. Phys.* §185 a. 204 It has long been known that individuals among the Deaf-and-Dumb have acquired the power of '*lip-reading'. **1866** LIVINGSTONE *Last Jrnls.* I. i. 24 The teeth are filed to points, and huge *lip-rings are worn by the women. **1926** MAINES & GRANT *Wise-Crack Dict.* 11/1 *Leave a good impression*, use lots of *lip rouge. **1930** J. DOS PASSOS *42nd Parallel* I. 76 She smeared liprouge on his nose. **1947** N. LINDSAY *Halfway to Anywhere* vii. 124 With *lip smacking over swigs of cooking sherry, it was felt that luxury could go no farther. **1958** [see CAPSULIZE *v.*]. **1966** AUDEN *About House* 21 Lip-smacking Imps of mawk and hooey. **1880** *Times* 28 Sept. 9/5 If *lip-speaking could not be taught, the deaf, while they must have continued a community apart, would have [etc.]. **1876** VOYLE & STEVENSON *Milit. Dict.* 232 **Lip-strap*, a small strap with a buckle passing from one cheek of the bit through a ring in the centre of the curb chain to the other cheek, for the purpose of preventing the horse from seizing the cheek of the bit in his mouth. **1602** MIDDLETON *Blurt Master-Const.* III iii. E4b, Your *lip-sworne seruant may there visit you as a Physition. **1957** MANVELL & HUNTLEY *Technique Film Music* ii. 27 *The Jazz Singer*..introduced in certain sequences *lip-synchronized singing by Al Jolson. **1959** W. S. SHARPS *Dict. Cinematogr.* 107/1 *Lip synchronization.* Abbreviated to Lip sync. The recording of sound, usually at the same time as its associated picture, so that on projection of the completed film, the words uttered synchronize exactly with the performer's lip movements as shown in the picture. **1961** A. BERKMAN *Singers' Gloss. Show Business* 55 *Lip sync*, to move the lips in synchronization with a recorded sound; to pantomime with a recording. **1970** M. TORMÉ *Other Side of Rainbow* (1971) iii. 50 A decision was made to prerecord one of Judy's songs, which she would lip-sync on the show. While lip-syncing is anathema to most singers, it was Judy's particular teacup. **1972** *Cinema Rising* Aug. 2/2 A feature-length Western, and a lip-synch musical. **1892** R. KIPLING *Barrack-r. Ballads* 167 For each man knows, ere his *lip-thatch grows, he is master of Art and Truth. **1886** E. D. COPE *Origin Fittest* v. (1887) 178 The *lip-teeth characteristic of the genus *Triodopsis*. **1597** A. M. tr. *Guillemeau's Fr. Chirurg.* 29b/2 The seaventh is the *lippe vayne, whereof on each syde are two. **1825** C. M. WESTMACOTT *Eng. Spy* II. 58 Twirled the dexter side of his *lip-wing. **1616** B. JONSON *Devil an Ass* I. ii, *Fitz*... And I except all kissing..I forbid all *lip-work. **1649** MILTON *Eikon.* i. Wks. 1851 III. 344 Manuals, and Handmaids of Devotion, the lip-work of every Prelatical Liturgist, clapt together, and quilted out of Scripture phrase. **1894** LD. WOLSELEY *Life Marlborough* II. lxix. 231 There can be no doubt..that Marlborough did make these protestations of penitence..But it was all lip-work. **1642** MILTON *Apol. Smect.* Wks. 1851 III. 311 Their office is to pray for others. And not to be the *lip-working deacons of other mens appointed words. **1562** J. HEYWOOD *Prov. & Epigr.* (1867) 211 Lyuerwort I haue none: but *Lipwort seede I haue.

lip (lɪp), *v.*[1] [f. LIP *sb.*]

1. a. *trans.* To touch with the lips, apply the lips to.

1826 E. IRVING *Babylon* I. IV. 262 As it were lipping the cup, whose bitterness this generation shall have to drink. *a* **1839** PRAED *Poems* (1864) II. 166 Or the bubble on the wine, which breaks Before you lip the glass. **1842** S. LOVER *Handy Andy* xviii. 154 After the final adjustment of the mouthpiece lipping the instrument with an affectation exquisitely grotesque. **1869** BLACKMORE *Lorna D.* xlii, No good sheep-dog even so much as lips a sheep to turn it. **1876** STAINER & BARRETT *Dict. Mus. Terms*, *Lip, to*, to adjust the lips so as to produce the proper tone of wind-instruments played by the mouth.

b. To kiss. *poet.*

1604 SHAKS. *Oth.* IV. i. 72 To lip a wanton in a secure Cowch. **1606** —— *Ant. & Cl.* II. v. 30 A hand that Kings Haue lipt, and trembled kissing. **1605** MARSTON *Eastward Hoe* I. i, Lip her, knave, lip her. *a* **1845** HOOD *What can old Men do?* ii, Love will not clip him, Maids will not lip him. **1871** ROSSETTI *Poems, Eden Bower* xix, Lip me and listen. **1888** *Harper's Mag.* Dec. 116 With the traders' wives made merry, Lipped the young and mocked the old.

c. *transf.* Of water: To kiss, to lap.

1842 TENNYSON *Audley Crt.* 11 The dying ebb..faintly lipp'd The flat granite. **1861** WHYTE MELVILLE *Good for Nothing* II. 61 Her cargo was..stowed away by deck and hold, till the waters lipped the gunwale. **1869** BLACKMORE *Lorna D.* i, When the waxing element lips..but a single pebble of the founder's name. **1877** L. MORRIS *Epic Hades* II. 110 The clear cold crystal of a mossy pool Lipped the soft emerald marge. **1889** HERRING & ROSS *Irish Cousin* II. II. iv. 34 The murmur of the sea, slightly lipping the rocks.

absol. **1875** BLACKMORE *A. Lorraine* III. ix. 149 It did not lip, or lap, or ripple,..as all well-meaning rivers do.

2. a. To pronounce with the lips only; to murmur softly. **b.** To take upon one's lips, to utter (? *obs.*); (*slang*) to sing (a song).

1789 G. PARKER *Life's Painter* 113 But come, I'll lip ye a chaunt. **1799** in *Spirit Pub. Jrnls.* III. 353 Sir John lipt us the favourite chaunt of Jerry Abershaw's 'Ye scamps [etc.].' **1818** KEATS *Endym.* I. 965 Salt tears were coming when I heard my name Most fondly lipp'd. **1840** LYTTON *Pilgr. Rhine* v, The..fame..is lipped by the Babel of the..world. **1861** *Temple Bar* I. 169 A respectable British Bacchus..lipping soft lyrics to the blushing Ariadne at his side. **1887** T. HARDY *Woodlanders* III. xiii. 274 'Ah, I thought my memory didn't deceive me!' he lipped silently. **1893** 'B. ABBOTSFORD' *But* 74, I lipped 'Good-morning' to him. **1896** *Punch* 11 Jan. 15/1 There's Arnold and there's Morris, both can lip the laureate line.

c. To insult, abuse, be impudent to (someone). *dial.* or *colloq.*

1898 B. KIRKBY *Lakeland Words* 93 He lipt mi rarely. **1902** *Eng. Dial. Dict.* III. 618/1 He's lipt mi as Ah was never lipt afoor. **1941** *Penguin New Writing* III. 65 Young Ernie was lippin' me just before you come in. **1972** A. DRAPER *Death Penalty* ii. 18 If anyone lips you, just swallow it.

3. (Chiefly *Sc.*) **a.** *intr.* Of water, etc.: To rise to, cover, or flow over the lip or brim of a vessel. Also with *in*, *over*. Also of the vessel: To have the water, etc. flowing over its brim or edge.

1703 D. WILLIAMSON *Serm. bef. Gen. Assembly Edin.* 49 The wrath of God lipping in over their Souls. **1839** R. M. M'CHEYNE in *Mem.* (1872) 334 It [your joy] will be like a bowl lipping over. **1883** STEVENSON *Silverado Sq.* 231 To carry [the waterpail] with the water lipping at the edge. **1883** —— *Treas. Isl.* IV. xvii, The gunwale was lipping astern.

b. *trans.* To serve as a lip or margin to.

1845 DARWIN *Voy. Nat.* xx. (1852) 478 Oval basins of coral-work just lipping the surface of the sea. **1880** BLACKMORE *Mary Anerley* II. xviii. 305 The margin..instead of being rough and rocky, lips the pool with gentleness.

†**c.** To overlay the lip or edge of (a vessel).

1607 TOPSELL *Four-f. Beasts* 722 With the hornes are made drinking Cups, and for that purpose the richer sort of people do edge or lip them ouer with siluer and gold.

d. To notch on the lip or edge.

1821 *Blackw. Mag.* IX. 323 That broth pot ladle, sorely lipped, and riven. **1828** SCOTT *F.M. Perth* viii, It were worth lipping a good blade, before wrong were offered to it.

e. *intr. Path.* Of a bone: To form a lip or morbid outgrowth at the extremity. Also of a casting: To have an irregular projection at the edge.

1891 *Pall Mall G.* 14 May 3/1 When a statue is cast in several pieces and one of the pieces 'lips'. **1894**, **1897** [see LIPPING *vbl. sb.* 1b].

f. *trans. Golf.* To drive the ball just to the lip or edge of (a hole).

1899 *Daily News* 24 Apr. 10/6 At the fourteenth Mr. B. again lipped the hole and lost.

g. *Sc.* To fill the interstices of (a wall) up to the lips or face.

1805 R. W. DICKSON *Pract. Agric.* I. 115 Walls..may frequently be made either more durable, or more ornamental, by being dashed, lipped, or harled with lime.

1845 *Statist. Acc. Scot.* X. 307 He has built stone dikes of more than 9 miles in length lipped and pointed with lime.

†**lip**, *v.*[2] *Obs.* [Of obscure origin: cf. LOP *v.*] *trans.* To cut off (the head of an animal); to cut short, prune (a root); to shear (a sheep).

c **1420** *Avow. Arth.* lxv, Sone the hed fro the hals Hit lyputt fulle euyn. **1601** HOLLAND *Pliny* II. 21 Lightly to barbe and pluck off with a sarcling hook, the beards or strings of the root; that being thus nipped and lipped.. they might [etc.]. **1607** TOPSELL *Four-f. Beasts* 608 Their sheepe bring foorth twice in a yeare, and are likewise twice lipped.

lip, obs. form of LEAP *v.*

lipæmia: see LIPO-.

lipard, obs. form of LEOPARD.

liparite ('lɪpəraɪt). *Min.* [Named, 1847, by Glocker, f. Gr. λιπαρ-ός shining + -ITE.] = FLUORITE.

1865 in WATTS *Dict. Chem.* **1879** RUTLEY *Study Rocks* xi. 177 The vitreous rocks of the first or highly-silicated subclass closely resemble the liparites, trachytes, andesites [etc.].

liparocele ('lɪpərəʊsiːl). *Path.* [f. Gr. λιπαρό-ς oily + κήλη tumour.] A fatty tumour of the scrotum (see quots.)

1830 KNOX tr. *Béclard's Anat.* 90 At the exterior of the peritonæum, this tumour constitutes the adipose hernia or liparocele. **1844** HOBLYN *Dict. Med.*, *Liparocele*, a species of sarcocele, in which the enclosed substance is fat. **1890** BILLINGS *Nat. Med. Dict.*, *Liparocele*, a circumscribed fatty tumour growing from subperitoneal connective tissue, and making its way through the abdominal walls, simulating an abdominal hernia.

Hence ˌliparo'celic *a.* (Mayne *Expos. Lex.* 1855).

lipase ('lɪpeɪz, -s). *Biochem.* [a. F. *lipase* (A. A. M. Hanriot 1896, in *Compt. Rend.* CXXIII. 753), f. Gr. λίπ-ος fat: see -ASE.] Any enzyme which catalyses the hydrolysis of fats and oils to fatty acids and alcohols; *esp.* one present in the pancreatic juice.

1897 *Jrnl. Chem. Soc.* LXXII. II. 150 The active enzyme, for which the name *lipase* is suggested, is also capable of acting.. on the natural oils and fats. **1946** *Nature* 14 Sept. 375/1 It thus appears that there are at least two distinctly different enzymes (or enzyme systems) present in these glycerol extracts: (1) a lipase, hydrolysing esters of glycerol..; and (2) an esterase, hydrolysing esters of lower alcohols than glycerol. **1955** *Sci. Amer.* Oct. 70/2 Some enzymes (e.g., amylase and lipase) work in the digestive system, breaking up the crude food material into simpler parts which can be transported by the bloodstream. **1970** R. W. MCGILVERY *Biochem.* xvi. 342 The globule of stored triglyceride within an adipose tissue cell is not attacked by lipoprotein lipase... Breakdown of the stored material depends on the action of other lipases within the cell.

ˌ**lip-'deep**, *a.* **a.** Immersed to the lips; in quots. *fig.*

1780 COWPER *Progr. Err.* 233 Lip-deep in what he longs for, and yet curst With prohibition and perpetual thirst. **1867** ANDERSON *Rhymes* 129 (E.D.D.) Lip-deep in poverty he strove.

b. Going no deeper than the lip; superficial.

1802 MRS. E. PARSONS *Myst. Visit* I. 257 Sentiments that were merely lip-deep. **1831** TRELAWNY *Adv. Younger Son* I. 288 Their courage is but lip-deep. **1863** COWDEN CLARKE *Shaks. Char.* ii. 36 No cold profession merely,—no lip-deep ostentation. **1897** L. KEITH *Bonnie Lady* ix. 95 The lave of them are bonnie bargains, and their promises but lip deep.

lipe (laɪp), *sb.*[1] *Obs.* exc. *dial.* Forms: 4 lippe, lyppe, 6, 9 lipe, lype. [Cf. OF. *lipee* (F. *lippée*).] **a.** A portion, a slip. **b.** A pleat or fold.

a. 1377 LANGL. *P. Pl.* B. v. 250, I.. lene folke þat lese wol a lyppe at euery noble. **1393** *Ibid.* C. XII. 226 Me were leuere, ..a lippe of godes grace, Than al þe kynde witt þat ȝe can boþe. **1851** *Cumbld. Gloss.*, *Lipe*, a fragment. **1878** *Cumbld. Gloss.*, *Lipe*, a large portion. Usually applied to land.

b. *a* **1600** *Queen's Wardrobe* in Nichols *Progr. Q. Eliz.* III. 508 One peticoate of tawney satten,.. with lypes, lyned with orenge-colour sarconet. **1808–80** JAMIESON, *Lype*, a crease, a fold.

†**lipe**, *sb.*[2] *Obs.* A sudden movement, a jerk.

1545 ASCHAM *Toxoph.* I. (Arb.) 89 You shall se a weake smithe, which wyl wyth a lipe and turnyng of his arme, take vp a barre of yron, yat another man thrise as stronge, cannot stirre.

lipe, var. LYPE.

lipemania, incorrect form of LYPEMANIA.

†'**lipet.** *Obs. rare*$^{-1}$. [f. LIPE *sb.*[1] + diminutive ending -ET[1].] A small piece, a bit.

c **1430** LYDG. *Min. Poems* (Percy Soc.) 52 A boy Checrelik was his sworn brothir, Of every disshe a lipet out to take.

†**li'phæmia**[1]. *Obs.* In 8 leiphæmia. [mod.L., f. Gr. λιπ- weak stem of λείπειν to leave, fail, be lacking + αἷμα blood.] (See quot.)

1753 CHAMBERS *Cycl. Supp.* s.v. *Blood*, An excess in the quantity of blood constitutes what we call a..*plethora*; a defect or want of a competent quantity, a *leiphæmia*.

liphæmia[2], var. LIPOHÆMIA: see LIPO-.

lipic ('lɪpɪk), *a. Chem.* [f. Gr. λίπ-ος fat + -IC.] ***lipic acid***: a crystallizable acid produced by the action of nitric acid upon a fatty acid.

1852 BRANDE *Dict. Sci.* etc. Suppl., *Lipic acid*, an acid formed by acting upon stearic and oleic acid, by means of nitric acid. **1865** in WATTS *Dict. Chem.*

lipid ('lɪpɪd). *Biochem.* Also -ide (-aɪd). [a. F. *lipide* (G. Bertrand 1923, in *Bull. de la Soc. de Chim. biol.* V. 102), f. Gr. λίπ-ος fat: see -IDE. For the origin of the now more common form *lipid* see *Chem. & Engin. News* (1952) 5 May 1910.]

1. Any of the large group of fats and fat-like compounds which occur in living organisms and are characteristically soluble in certain organic solvents but only sparingly soluble in water; it is generally taken to include esters of higher aliphatic acids, together with various groups of related and derived compounds, and freq. also steroids and carotenoids.

1925 W. R. BLOOR in *Chem. Rev.* II. 244 Three terms have been suggested for the group, namely, 'Lipins' by Gies and Rosenbloom, 'Lipides' by the International Congress of Applied Chemistry, and the old term 'Lipoids' by the author. The term lipins has been used in a different sense by Leathes, and was later adopted by McLean in his monograph as a name for a subgroup containing the cerebrosides and the phosphatides. The term lipoids is understood by many to exclude the fats, although used in the wider sense by many workers on the Continent. For these reasons, and for the sake of uniformity, the author recommends the use of the term Lipides as the general group name. **1927** M. BODANSKY *Introd. Physiol. Chem.* iii. 49 The term 'lipides' or 'lipids'.. referring to the fats and fat-like substances. **1937** *Nature* 6 Nov. 787 'Lipides' may be confused with 'lipins', and both these words together with 'lipoids' generally signify substances of a fat-like nature yielding on hydrolysis fatty acids or derivatives of fatty acids, and containing in their molecule either nitrogen or nitrogen and phosphorus... Some confusion may therefore arise since 'lipids' as used by the author signifies not only the above substances but also the simple fats and waxes and even the sterols. **1946** W. R. FEARON *Introd. Biochem.* (ed. 3) x. 172 The third great family of bio-organic compounds, namely, the lipides. **1954** A. WHITE et al. *Princ. Biochem.* xviii. 453 Lipids are the most concentrated source of energy to the organism, yielding per gram over twice as many calories as do carbohydrates and proteins. **1955** J. A. LOVERN *Chem. Lipids* ii. 37 Lipids by definition are soluble in the 'fat' solvents, such as ether, alcohol and chloroform. **1958** G. A. MAW *Aids to Org. Chem. for Med. Students* (ed. 5) p. xxxiv, Substances such as paraffin wax, petroleum jelly and mineral oils, although of a fatty or oily nature, are not classified as lipids since they do not occur in living material. **1961** *Chem. Abstr.* LV. 27470 Chemistry of lipides. **1968** PASSMORE & ROBSON *Compan. Med. Stud.* I. x. 5/2 The steroids form a large class of lipids, which includes the hormones of the adrenal and sex glands, vitamin D and the bile acids. **1973** *Sci. Amer.* Aug. 89/1 Today there are 10 well-characterized human diseases that are known to be caused by the excessive accumulation of lipids in tissue cells.

2. *attrib.* and *Comb.*, as ***lipid storage*** (freq. used *attrib.*, designating a disorder otherwise known as a LIPIDOSIS); ***lipid-soluble*** adj.

1964 G. H. HAGGIS et al. *Introd. Molecular Biol.* vi. 151 Lipid-soluble substances are substances with a relatively high solubility in oils. **1955** H. J. DEUEL *Lipids* II. vi. 623 (*heading*) Lipid storage under abnormal conditions. **1960** *Jrnl. Neurol., Neurosurg. & Psychiatry* XXIII. 211/2 The group of so-called lipid storage disorders.. includes.. Hand-Schuller-Christian disease, gargoylism, Niemann-Pick's disease, Gaucher's disease, and amaurotic family idiocy. **1973** *Sci. Amer.* Aug. 88/1 When the enzyme that catalyzes a particular lipid reaction is inactive or absent, excessive amounts of that lipid begin to accumulate in certain tissues. In human beings lipid-storage disorders often result in mental retardation and enlargement of the spleen and the liver. Most of the known lipid-storage disorders are fatal.

lipidarye, lipken, obs. ff. LAPIDARY, LIBKEN.

lipidosis (lɪpɪ'dəʊsɪs). *Med.* Pl. lipidoses. [f. LIPID + -OSIS.] Any disorder characterized by an excessive accumulation of a lipid in certain tissues.

1941 S. J. THANNHAUSER *Lipidoses* i. 2 A summary of the present knowledge.. of lipid substances is.. an appropriate introduction to the group of diseases, which are called 'lipoidoses' or 'lipidoses'. **1961** R. D. BAKER *Essent. Path.* iv. 47 The lipidoses are conditions in which fatty substances collect in macrophages, sometimes as part of the macrophage (reticulo-endothelial) system, sometimes in ectopic clusters of these cells and rarely in other types of cells. These diseases are also termed lipid-storage diseases. *Ibid.* 49 Niemann-Pick's Disease. This is a truly systemic lipidosis of the macrophage system, occurring typically in infants, with splenomegaly and hepatomegaly. **1966** WRIGHT & SYMMERS *Systemic Path.* I. v. 245/1 Different lipids are concerned in each of the primary lipidoses, a different enzyme failure presumably being characteristic of each disease.

lipin ('lɪpɪn). *Biochem.* Also -ine. [f. Gr. λίπ-ος fat + -IN[1], -INE[5].] †**a.** Any lipid containing nitrogen. (Originally used more specifically: see quot. 1910.) *Obs.* **b.** = LIPID.

1910 J. B. LEATHES *Fats* 3 Lipines [will be used] to denote compounds of fatty acids containing nitrogen but no phosphorus or carbohydrate group. **1911** ROSENBLOOM & GIES in *Biochem. Bull.* I. 51 We venture to propose the accompanying chemical classification of fats and the many substances related to or resembling them, which collectively can be very appropriately and conveniently called lipins. **1937** [see LIPID 1]. **1946** *Q. Jrnl. Microsc. Sci.* LXXXVII. 444 The lipines used in this investigation were lecithin, cephalin, sphingomyelin, and galactolipine, all obtained from the brains of sheep. **1952** *Chem. & Engin. News* 5 May 1910/1 'Lipide', however, has proved popular, replacing the older 'lipoid' and 'lipin', with a better defined meaning.

Lipiodol (lɪ'paɪədɒl). *Med.* Also lipiodol. [f. Gr. λίπ-ος fat + IOD(INE *sb.* + -OL.] A proprietary name of a liquid containing about 40% iodine which is obtained by treating poppy-seed oil with iodine and is used as a contrast medium in radiography.

1923 *Brit. Med. Jrnl.* 4 Aug. 174/1 Between 1 and 2 c.cm. of lipiodol is injected into the spinal theca through a suboccipital puncture. **1925** *Trade Marks Jrnl.* 20 May 1096 Lipiodol... A pharmaceutical preparation for human use. Laurent Lafay,.. Paris, France; chemist. **1928** CHANDLER & WOOD *Lipiodol in Diagn. Thoracic Dis.* i. 1 The properties of lipiodol are opacity to the X-rays, a high specific gravity, an absence of any irritating action on mucous membranes, a reputed antiseptic and analgesic action, lubrication, and so firm a combination of the iodine with the oil that none of the ordinary effects of iodine are experienced. **1972** *Acta Chirurg. Scand.* CXXXVIII. 481/1 Oily contrast medium (lipiodol) injections from 10 to 30 ml were given in an attempt to demonstrate tumours.. in the liver.

Lipizzan, Lippizan ('lɪpɪtsən), *a.* [See -AN.] Of or pertaining to Lipizza or Lippiza, the home of the former Austrian Imperial Stud, esp. designating a strain of horse originally bred there. So **Lipi'zzana, Lippi'zana, -'aner**, a horse of this breed; also *attrib.*

[**1911** M. C. GRIMSGAARD *Orig. Handbk. Riders* Suppl. 320 (*caption*) 'Muestoso-Moschina', a Lipizza stallion, one of the eight famous stallions at the.. Spanish Court Riding-School in Vienna.] **1928** *Observer* 17 June 27/3 Twelve of the famous Lippizaner horses. *Ibid.*, The Lippizana is a perfectly separate and peculiar breed of horse, in appearance much like an Arab, but.. more massive. **1946** P. BOTTOME *Lifeline* x. 100 Each horse was.. a *Lippizaner*. **1954** A. PODHAJSKY *Spanish Riding School* (ed. 2) 4/1 General Patton .. fulfilled the request made to him that the Lipizzan stud.. be brought back to Austria. **1967** A. ARENT *Gravedigger's Funeral* (1968) xii. 189 A Lippizaner, a white stallion from the Spanish Riding Academy in Vienna. **1971** *Islander* (Victoria, B.C.) 30 May 2/4 Those beautiful leaps and dancing steps made by the white Lipizzan stallions of the Spanish Riding School. **1972** *Guardian* 4 Oct. 4/6 The 58 photogenic white Lippizaner stallions of the Spanish Riding School which has just celebrated its four hundredth anniversary.

'**lip-labour.** [See LIP *sb.* 6 a (*b*).] Labour of the lips. **a.** Empty talk; *esp.* vain repetition of words in prayer. Also *attrib.*

1538 BALE *Thre Lawes* 1140 No Sabboth wyl we with Gods worde sanctyfye, But with lyppe labour, and ydle ceremonye. **1599** SANDYS *Europæ Spec.* (1632) 235 Those heathenish repetitions and unnatural lip-labours which our Saviour censured. **1641** *Arminian Nunnery* in *R. Brunne's Chron.* (1810) I. App. Pref. 130 A lip-labour devotion, and a will-worship. *a* **1642** SIR W. MONSON *Naval Tracts* II. (1704) 286/2 They will think it a little Lip-labour for their Tongues to pronounce it. **1679** 'T. TICKLEFOOT' *Trial Wakeman* 6 Marshal not being shye of his lip-labour, fell to impertinent questioning him. **1732** LAW *Serious C.* x. (ed. 2) 152 They [our Prayers] become an empty lip-labour. **1788–92** T. SCOTT *Comm., Pract. Obs. on Eccl.* v. 1 Our wandering imaginations.. render our attendance on divine ordinances little better than a mere lip-labor.

†**b.** Kissing. *Obs.*

1583 STANYHURST *Æneis*, etc. (Arb.) 145 Syth mye nose owtpeaking, good syr, your liplabor hindreth, Hardlye ye may kisse mee, where no such gnomon apeereth. **1665** BRATHWAIT *Comment. 2 Tales* 17 They express their mutual love in Lip-labour.

Hence †**lip-labouring** = LIP-LABOUR; †**lip-laborious** *a.*, given to lip-labour.

1549 LATIMER *Serm. bef. Edw. VI* (Arb.) 124 Many talke of prayer, and make it a lyplabouryngе. *Ibid.* 132 It is no prayer that is wythout fayth, it is but a lyppe labouryng. **1630** LORD *Hist. Banians* xiii. 86 The Bramanes grew hypocriticall and lip-laborious.

†**lip-lap** ('lɪplæp). *Obs.* Also liplap. [Native name.] In the Dutch East Indies, a half-caste or Eurasian; a child born in the East Indies.

1798 S. H. WILCOCKE tr. *Stavorinus's Voy. E. Indies* I. II. v. 315 Children born in the Indies, are nicknamed *lip-laps* by the Europeans, although both parents may have come from Europe. **1893** *Academy* 11 Feb. 122 The acclimatisation.. of liplaps, signos, and mannas, as the Dutch half-castes are variously called.

lipless ('lɪplɪs), *a.* [f. LIP *sb.* + -LESS.] Having no lips.

c **1400** MAUNDEV. (Roxb.) xxii. 100 Þai hafe a platte mouth, lippless. **1613** PURCHAS *Pilgrimage, Descr. India* (1864) 85 Drawing away the cover of their lips, as if they were lipelesse. **1793** HOLCROFT *Lavater's Physiogn.* x. 59 A lipless mouth.. denotes coldness. **1798–1812** JOANNA BAILLIE *Orra* v. ii. Wks. (1851) 259 And lipless jaws that move and clatter round us In mockery of speech. **1849–52** TODD *Cycl. Anat.* IV. 886/2 The lipless mouth of the snake. **1862** GEO. ELIOT *Romola* I. xvi, A.. flat broad face, with high ears, wide lipless mouth [etc.].

liplet ('lɪplɪt). [f. LIP *sb.* + -LET.] A little lip; *spec.* in *Ent.*, a small lip-like projection.

1816 KIRBY & SP. *Entomol.* (1843) I. 333 The case.. terminates in two turgid liplets.

lipne, obs. form of LIPPEN.

lipo- (lɪpəʊ) (before a vowel lip-), combining form of Gr. λίπος fat, used in various pathological terms, chiefly mod. L., in *Biochem.* and other fields. **li'pæmia** *Path.* [Gr. αἷμα blood], prevalence of fatty matter in the circulation; hence **li'pæmic** *a.*; **lipoamide** (lɪpəʊ'eɪmaɪd) *Biochem.*, the amide of lipoic acid; **'lipoate** *Biochem.*, the anion, or a salt or ester, of lipoic acid; **lipocaic** (-'keɪɪk) *Biochem.* [see quot. 1936], a substance extracted from the pancreas which is found to prevent the accumulation of fat in the livers of animals from which the pancreas has been removed; **lipo'cardiac** *a.* [CARDIAC], pertaining to a fatty heart (*Syd. Soc. Lex.* 1899); **lipo'chondrion** (pl. **-'chondria**) *Cytology* [ad. G. *lipochondrie* (E. Ries 1935, in *Zeitschr. f. Zellforschung u. mikrosk. Anat.* XXII. 528), f. Gr. χονδρίον, dim. of χόνδρος granule, prob. after G. *mitochondrie* MITOCHONDRION], a lipoid granule in the cytoplasm, esp. one seen in live preparations and possibly related to the Golgi apparatus; so **lipo'chondrial** *a.*; **'lipochrin** [see OCHRE and -IN], 'a yellow colouring matter obtained by treating the eyes of frogs with ether after removing the retinæ' (*Syd. Soc. Lex.*); **'lipochrome** *Biol.* [ad. G. *lipochrom* (C. F. W. Krukenberg *Vergleichend-physiologische Studien* II. III. 93), f. Gr. χρῶμ-α colour], any of various mainly yellow or red pigments which are found naturally in both plants and animals and which are soluble in fats or fat solvents (see quot. 1951); ‖**,lipofi'broma** *Path.* [FIBROMA], a fibrous lipoma; **lipo'fuscin** [FUSCIN], any of various brownish pigments of animals, esp. those characteristically deposited in the cells during old age; **lipo'genesis** [-GENESIS], the formation of fat; **li'pogenic** *a.* [Gr. γεν- + -IC], tending to produce fat; **li'pogenous** *a.* [Gr. γεν- + -OUS] = prec. (*Syd. Soc. Lex.*); **lipo'hæmia** = *lipæmia* above; **(α-)li'poic acid** *Biochem.*, a carboxylic acid, $\underbrace{S-S-CH_2}CH_2CH(CH_2)_4COOH$, found in yeast and liver extracts which is a cofactor in the decarboxylation of pyruvate *in vivo*; **lipo'lytic** *a.* [Gr. λυτικός loosening], having the property of decomposing or hydrolysing fats; hence **li'polysis**, the hydrolytic breaking down of fat; **lipo'lytically** *adv.*; ‖**,lipomy'xoma** *Path.* [MYXOMA], a tumour composed partly of fatty and partly of mucous tissue (*Syd. Soc. Lex.*); **'lipophile, lipo'philic** *adjs.* [-PHIL, -PHILE], having an affinity for lipids; readily dissolving, or soluble in, lipids; **lipo'phobic** *a.* [-PHOBIC], tending to repel lipids; not readily soluble in lipids; **,lipopoly'saccharide** *Biochem.*, any complex containing lipid and polysaccharide moieties; **lipo'protein** *Biochem.*, any complex containing lipid and protein moieties, *spec.* one which is soluble in water or salt solution (as distinct from a proteolipid); **,liposar'coma** (pl. **-'omata**) *Path.* [SARCOMA], a sarcoma of fatty tissue; **li'positol** *Biochem.* [IN)OSITOL], any phospholipid containing inositol in its molecule, *spec.* the one found in soy-beans; **'lipoyl** *Biochem.* [-YL], the radical $C_7H_{13}S_2 \cdot CO$—which is derived from lipoic acid.

1866 A. FLINT *Princ. Med.* (1880) 72 In diabetes the blood often has a slightly milky appearance from an increased amount of fat. This condition of the blood has been called *lipaemia. **1915** *Jrnl. Biol. Chem.* XXIII. 317 Alimentary lipemia is due to nothing more than the addition of these glycerides. **1961** *Lancet* 26 Aug. 492/2 After fat ingestion, visible lipæmia normally reaches a maximum in about four hours. **1906** *Bio-Chem. Jrnl.* II. 22 Case XV, also not *lipaemic, was allowed a fat-rich diet, but five days later the lipaemic condition was absent, and has remained so. **1961** *Lancet* 26 Aug. 492/2 Sera from 10 patients.. were visibly lipæmic before sodium *d*-thyroxine was given. **1960** *Biochim. & Biophys. Acta* XXXVII. 314 The turnover numbers at 25° vary from 1000 with DL-lipoic acid to about 80,000 with DL-*lipoamide. **1972** *Zeitschr. für physiol. Chem.* CCCLIII. 875/2 We measured the overall reaction of the multi-enzyme complex.., the decarboxylase and the lipoamide oxidoreductase. **1954** V. H. CHELDELIN in Sebrell & Harris *Vitamins* III. xviii. 580 The cyclic disulfide may react to produce an acyl *lipoate. **1970** R. W. MCGILVERY *Biochem.* xi. 215 The oxidizing agent is a coenzyme containing a disulfide bond, lipoate, which is attached to a lysyl residue in the peptide chain of transsuccinylase. **1936** L. R. DRAGSTEDT et al. in *Amer. Jrnl. Physiol.* CXVII. 180 We have chosen the name '*lipocaic' for this substance. It is derived from the Greek words 'λιπος', 'fat' and 'καιω', 'I burn'. A more general term suggesting that the hormone plays a rôle in the utilization of fat was sought but without success. **1955** H. J. DEUEL *Lipids* II. vi. 672 A number of facts lead one to question whether or not lipocaic can be classified as a hormone in the usual sense of the word. **1936** *Biol. Abstr.* X. 219 During differentiation the cells.. are relatively small..; ergastoplasm is absent and the reserve material consists of yolk globules and *lipochondria. **1946** *Jrnl. Exper. Zool.* CI. 361 Apart from finding yolk, pigment granules, and mitochondria, these workers [*sc.* Ries and Fischer] observed large osmiophilic fat granules... These elements were called lipochondria. **1946** [see LIPOSOME 1]. **1950** J. R. BAKER in *Proc. Linn. Soc.* CLXII. 71 Since the particular artifact studied by Golgi represents so badly what is actually present in the living cytoplasm, it no longer seems desirable to connect the great neurologist's name with this cellular constituent. A descriptive name is surely preferable. Ries's name 'Lipochondrien' (Ries, 1935) is convenient, but a Greek ending is more suitable for a word that must be used internationally, I therefore suggest *lipochondrion* (plural *lipochondria*). **1968** [see LIPOSOME 1]. **1971** *Acta Embryol. Exper.* 43 (*heading*) The cytoplasmic inclusions of the salamander oocyte. III. Lipochondria. **1946** *Jrnl. Exper. Zool.* CI. 390 Only *lipochondrial substances were involved. **1887** *Encycl. Brit.* XXII. 420/2 A red pigment of the *lipochrome series. **1928** [see *lipofuscin* below]. **1951** H. J. DEUEL *Lipids* I. vi. 511 The term lipochrome was proposed by Krukenberg to cover a number of animal and plant pigments which had been known by such diverse names as luteins, carotin, zoonerythrin, tetronerythrin, chlorophane, xanthophane, and rhodophane. Although this designation was originally limited to pigments with yellow or reddish tints, by implication it obviously should include any fat-soluble pigment such as chlorophyll. **1968** Lipochrome [see *lipofuscin* below]. **1923** *Chem. Abstr.* XVII. 1667 *Lipofuscin is not limited to ectodermal cells, although it is found there chiefly. **1928** *Amer. Jrnl. Path.* IV. 293 The pigment present in these last organs.. is a yellow to brown granular substance which is frequently tinged with fat stains, and therefore has been called lipochrome in this country, and lipofuscin in Germany. These two names are used to designate the substance in most English and American literature, but they actually represent different pigments. **1964** *Oceanogr. & Marine Biol.* II. 408 Another brown pigment [in the echinoderm *Diadema*] appears to be a lipofuscin. **1968** PASSMORE & ROBSON *Compan. Med. Stud.* I. xiii. 16/1 Lipofuscin, one of the commonest cellular pigments, is known by a variety of names (wear and tear pigment, haemofuscin, lipochrome, brown atrophy and age pigment), a selection which demonstrates its complexity as well as ignorance of its function, and indicates that it contains some lipid and some iron. **1882** QUAIN *Dict. Med.* 1052/1 The current views on *lipogenesis or fat-formation. **1897** *Allbutt's Syst. Med.* IV. 308 They are often obese, and hence the name '*lipogenic glycosuria' has been used in these cases. **1872** THUDICHUM *Chem. Phys.* 24 This particular form of fatty acid emulsion occurs in *lipohæmia. **1951** L. J. REED et al. in *Science* 27 July 93/2 This work has led to the obtaining of a crystalline compound from processed insoluble liver residues, which is highly active for the growth of *Streptococcus lactis* in the absence of acetate... This compound is being called α*-lipoic acid. *Ibid.*, The crystalline compound reported in this paper is designated as α-lipoic acid to indicate that it is the first member to be obtained of a series of chemically related substances which possess acetate-replacing and pyruvate oxidase factor activity. **1962** H. A. KREBS in A. Pirie *Lens Metabolism Rel. Cataract* 351 Cofactors such as.. pyridoxal phosphate, or lipoic acid may play a role in controlling reaction rates by virtue of being shared cofactors. **1968** R. F. STEINER *Life Chem.* vi. 100 The reduced form of lipoic acid contains two sulfhydryl groups.. and can accept an acetyl group from active acetaldehyde. **1903** DORLAND *Med. Dict.* (ed. 3) 380/1 *Lipolysis. **1907** *Science* 27 Sept. 413/1 Since the bile salts are known to increase lipolysis, the effects of the sodium salts of cholic, glycocholic and taurocholic acids in *n*/500 solutions were tested on lipolytic hemolysis. **1972** *Jrnl. Lipid Res.* XIII. 651 (*heading*) Effect of cell size on lipolysis and antilipolytic action of insulin in human fat cells. **1898** LAZARUS-BARLOW *Man. Gen. Pathol.* 507 The *lipolytic ferment of the pancreas (steapsin). **1912** *Jrnl. Amer. Chem. Soc.* XXXIV. 845 Preparations possessing lipolytic activity. **1955** H. J. DEUEL *Lipids* II. ii. 15 No correlation between sex, age, or food intake and lipolytic activity of adipose tissue was observed in rats. **1972** *Jrnl. Lipid Res.* XIII. 325 (*heading*) Hydrolysis of fully esterified alcohols.. by the lipolytic enzymes of rat pancreatic juice. **1912** *Jrnl. Amer. Chem. Soc.* XXXIV. 829 *Lipolytically inactive substances. **1917** *Jrnl. Biol. Chem.* XXIX. p. xxvi, Experiments.. resulted in the production of lipolytically active substances by the action of alkali on castor bean globulin, caesin, and gelatin. **1938** A. D. WHITEHEAD tr. *Jordan's Technol. Solvents* i. 12 The aliphatic.. and aromatic.. hydrocarbons .. are electrically neutral or non-polar since they contain no hydrophile groups. They are therefore hydrophobic or *lipophile. **1950** *Chem. & Engin. News* 26 June 2181 (Advt.), The Atlas HLB System.. is based on the hydrophile-lipophile balance of each emulsifier. **1965** *Acta Endocrinol.* XLIX. 538 Whether these findings can be attributed to the lipophile properties of the sulphatide facilitating its entrance into the cell cannot be decided. **1946** *Arkiv för Kemi, Mineral. och Geol.* XXIIA. XVIII. 29 The *lipophilic end should contain an aromatic structure. **1954** JIRGENSONS & STRAUMANIS *Short Textbk. Colloid Chem.* ii. 16 Substances which, like rubber, polystyrene or polyvinyl-chloride do not contain hydrophilic groups are insoluble in water. They are composed of lipophilic.. groups such as CH_3, $-CH_2-$, and others, which have some affinity for the molecules of fats, fat solvents and other oils. **1971** *Nature* 21 May 186/2 Morphine has a highly lipophilic molecule. **1946** G. M. SUTHEIM *Introd. Emulsions* i. 4 Hydrophilic substances.. are named oleophobic or *lipophobic. **1961** E. O'F. WALSH *Introd. Biochem.* ii. 33 The polar end of the lecithin molecule, here represented as a Zwitterion, is hydrophilic and lipophobic. **1954** *Chem. Abstr.* XLVIII. 9453 Injection of a *lipopolysaccharide from *Salmonella abortivoequina* increases the phagocytic activity of the granulocytes. **1958** *Immunology* I. 181 The stimulation of non-specific immunity by lipopolysaccharides could not be correlated with the serum properdin level at the time of challenge. **1970** W. J. LENNARZ in S. J. Wakil *Lipid Metabolism* v. 164 Lipopolysaccharides, the complex heteropolysaccharides typical of Gram-negative enteric bacteria, are currently under extensive investigation. **1909** *Chem. Abstr.* III. 82 It is probable that in fatty degeneration there is a splitting off of fat from *lipoproteins of this character. **1929** *Jrnl. Immunol.* XVI. 448 The constituents in fowl sera responsible for these non-specific precipitations are indicated to be lipo-proteins and neutral fats. **1955** H. J. DEUEL *Lipids* II. v. 371 The lipoproteins are widely distributed in living matter, where they occur in cell nuclei, mitochondria, cell membranes, chloroplasts, in egg yolk, in milk, and in blood. **1971** L. W. BURLEY in Johnson & Davenport *Biochem. Lipids* iv. 86 'Proteolipids'.. differ from lipoproteins in being soluble in certain organic solvents but insoluble in aqueous solutions. **1893** DUNGLISON *Dict. Med. Sci.* (ed. 21) 637/2 *Liposarcoma. **1916** E. H. KETTLE *Path. Tumours* II. 94 Liposarcomata.. are undoubtedly rare. **1970** PASSMORE & ROBSON *Compan. Med. Studies* II. xxx. 16/2 Liposarcomata are most common in old men. **1943** D. W. WOOLLEY in *Jrnl. Biol. Chem.* CXLVII. 581 It is proposed to call the new substance soybean *lipositol, since it is a lipid which contains inositol. **1949** H. W. FLOREY et al. *Antibiotics* II. xliv. 1386 The antibacterial activity of 50 units of streptomycin in 1 ml. was completely antagonized by as little as 0·2 μg. of lipositol. **1969** S. R. WILLIAMS *Nutrition & Diet Therapy* iii. 29/1 Other important phospholipids are cephalins and lipositols, which are like the lecithins except that they contain other factors in place of choline. **1960** *Biochem. Jrnl.* LXXVII. 347/1 There is a close correlation between the rates of the enzyme-catalysed oxidation of DPNH by the lipoyl derivatives used and the rates of reoxidation of the red intermediate.. by the same *lipoyl derivatives. **1970** R. W. MCGILVERY *Biochem.* xi. 215 The reaction is now complete except for the regeneration of the original disulfide bond in the lipoyl group.

lipodystrophy (,lɪpəʊ'dɪstrəfɪ). *Path.* Also as mod.L. **,lipody'strophia.** [f. LIPO- + DYSTROPHY.] Any of various disorders of fat metabolism; ***intestinal lipodystrophy***, a rare disease (usu. called Whipple's disease) of uncertain ætiology, chiefly of middle-aged men, presenting with joint pains, steatorrhœa, wasting, and lymph node enlargement; ***progressive lipodystrophy*** [tr. mod.L. *lipodystrophia progressiva* (A. Simons 1911, in *Zeitschr. f. d. ges. Neurol. u. Psychiatrie* (*Orig.*) V. 36)], a condition in which there is a progressive loss of subcutaneous fat, usu. from the upper half of the body while the lower half retains its fat. So **,lipody'strophic** *a.*

1907 G. H. WHIPPLE in *Bull. Johns Hopkins Hosp.* XVIII. 391/1 In searching for a name to designate this condition great difficulties were encountered. It would seem that no suitable name can be applied to it until the etiological factor is determined. The term *Intestinal Lipodystrophy* is suggested. **1925** *Q. Jrnl. Med.* XVIII. 224 Progressive lipodystrophy is a rare disease characterized by symmetrical and progressive loss of subcutaneous fat over the face, neck, arms, thorax, and abdomen, with a relative or absolute abundance of subcutaneous fat over the lower limbs. *Ibid.* 231 The active stage having ended, the lipodystrophic process becomes stationary. **1933** *Lancet* 23 Dec. 1417/1 The blood chemistry in lipodystrophia progressiva is normal. **1946** *Ibid.* 18 May 730/2 There is no satisfactory classification of the lipodystrophies. *Ibid.* 731/1, I venture to argue how Ziegler's lipodystrophic case might have a similar disturbance of fat-metabolism without an obvious lipæmia. **1964** *Pediatrics* XXXIII. 609/1 The syndromes of partial and total lipodystrophy have been reviewed... For inclusion in the syndrome of partial lipodystrophy symmetrical loss of fat from the face with or without truncal loss, but with retention of distal adipose depots was required. In total lipodystrophy fat loss was generalized. **1971** *Daily Colonist* (Victoria, B.C.) 28 Dec. 2/1 Lipodystrophy means a disturbance in the metabolism of fatty tissue.

lipogram ('lɪpəgræm). [Back-formation f. Gr. λιπογράμματος *adj.*, wanting a letter, f. λιπ -, weak stem of λείπειν to leave, be wanting + γραμματ-, γράμμα letter. Cf. F. *lipogramme.*] A composition from which the writer rejects all words that contain a certain letter or letters.

1711 ADDISON *Spect.* No. 62 ⁋3 Anagrams, Chronograms, Lipograms and Acrosticks. **1880** W. T. DOBSON *Lit. Frivol.* 58 Lipogram is the name applied to a species of verse in which a certain letter, either vowel or consonant, is altogether omitted.

lipogrammatic (,lɪpəʊgræ'mætɪk), *a.* [f. as prec. + -IC. Cf. F. *lipogrammatique.*] Of or pertaining to a lipogram; of the nature of a lipogram.

1739 J. MERRICK *Triphiodorus* p. xv, Tryphiodorus is said ..to have composed a Lipogrammatick Odyssey, from which he entirely excluded the letter Sigma. **1891** H. MORLEY *Note to Spect.* No. 59 ⁋2 The earliest writer of Lipogrammatic verse is said to have been the Greek poet Lasus, born in Achaia 538 B.C.

So **lipo'grammatism**, the art or practice of writing lipograms. **lipo'grammatist**, a writer of lipograms.

1711 ADDISON *Spect.* No. 59 ⁋2 The first I shall produce are the Lipogrammatists or Letter-droppers of Antiquity. **1816** SOUTHEY *Ess.* vi. (1832) I. 296 No author ever shackled himself by more absurd restrictions (not even the Lipogrammatists). **1862** MARSH *Eng. Lang.* 394 Lipogrammatism.. would not deserve to be noticed, had not distinguished authors.. occasionally practised it.

lipography (lɪ'pɒgrəfɪ). [f. Gr. λιπ-, weak stem of λείπειν to leave, be wanting + -GRAPHY.] The omission of a letter or syllable in writing.

1888 GOW *Compan. to Classics* 55 *Haplography* or *Lipography*, writing once a letter or syllable which should be written twice, is a special and very common case of omission. **1893** *Classical Rev.* Oct. 360/2 The reading.. is invoked as evidence for ancient tradition: is it not simply a case of lipography?

lipoid ('lɪpɔɪd), *a.* and *sb.* [f. Gr. λίπ-ος fat + -OID.] **A.** *adj.* Resembling fat.

1876 tr. *Wagner's Gen. Pathol.* 349 A peculiar 'lipoid transformation' of a fœtus. **1907** *Biochem. Jrnl.* II. 22 The lipöid material being mainly composed of an ester of cholesterin. **1946** *Nature* 13 July 41/1 Solution of the odorous substance in the lipoid or aqueous phase of these flagellæ is, therefore, the point from which all theories of osmic perception must proceed. **1974** *Ibid.* 1 Feb. 301/1 The uterine or milk glands in tsetse flies..release a nutritive liquid of proteinaceous and lipoid nature for the maturing intrauterine larva.

B. *sb.* [a. G. *lipoïd* (E. Overton *Studien über die Narkose* (1901) 54).] **a.** Any fat-like substance other than a true fat. **b.** = LIPID.

1906 *Jrnl. Chem. Soc.* XC. II. 780 (*heading*) The influence of diffusibility and the solubility of lipoids on the rate of intestinal absorption. **1912** *Biochem. Bull.* I. 51 Fats and the substances resembling them ('lipoids'). **1925** [see LIPID 1]. **1932** I. SMEDLEY-MACLEAN in *Ann. Rev. Biochem.* I. 135 The term lipoid is retained..to denote the ether-soluble constituents of a tissue, without regard to their nature. **1946** W. R. FEARON *Introd. Biochem.* (ed. 3) x. 173 Lipoids.—These are biological compounds resembling the lipides in certain physical properties, notably solubility in fats. **1952** [see LIPIN]. **1955** GAIGER & DAVIES *Vet. Path. & Bacteriol.* (ed. 4) i. 6 All the normal body tissues contain fat in one form or another, the chief forms being neutral fat, fatty acids, soaps and lipoids (lecithin, cholesterol and myelin). **1958** *Times Lit. Suppl.* 17 Jan. 34/1 Living matter consists essentially of carbohydrates (or 'sugars'), lipoids (or 'fats') and proteins. **1971** *Nature* 9 July 138/3 'Lipoid' is used instead of the more usual 'lipid' throughout [the book].

lipoidal (lɪ'pɔɪdəl), *a.* [f. prec. + -AL.] Resembling or containing fat.

1919 *Amer. Jrnl. Anat.* XXV. 251 Lipoidal vacuoles are becoming more abundant in the outer and especially the middle cortical zone. **1920** *Proc. R. Soc. Med.* XIII. (Path. Section) 8 The antitrypsin is lipoidal in nature. **1928** P. BAILEY in E. V. Cowdry *Special Cytol.* I. xv. 493 Small globules of lipoidal substances are seen in all the cells. **1954** A. J. MARSHALL *Bower-Birds* ii. 10 Considerable aggregations of heavily lipoidal Leydig cells can now be seen.

lipoidosis (lɪpɔɪ'dəʊsɪs). *Med.* Pl. lipoidoses. [f. as prec. + -OSIS.] = LIPIDOSIS.

1932 *Amer. Jrnl. Dis. Children* XLIV. 1117 Niemann-Pick's disease..is called phosphatide cell lipoidosis. *Ibid.*, Christian's disease..is called cholesterol cell lipoidosis. **1936** *Proc. R. Soc. Med.* XXIX. 585 The three principal types of these lipoidoses are Schüller-Christian's disease, the spleno-hepatomegaly of Gaucher and the spleno-hepatomegaly of Niemann-Pick. **1962** *Lancet* 13 Jan. 64/1 When infections, blood dyscrasias, lipoidoses, reticuloses,..and congenital fibrosis..are excluded there remain some instances in which no obvious disorder can be demonstrated.

‖**lipoma** (lɪ'pəʊmə). *Path.* Pl. lipomata (lɪ'pəʊmətə). [mod.L., f. Gr. λίπ-ος fat + -ωμα: cf. *steatoma*, etc.] A fatty tumour.

1830 R. KNOX *Béclard's Anat.* 91 The lipomata..sometimes present the appearance of the omentum when they are drawn out. **1893** *Brit. Med. Jrnl.* 9 Dec. 1274/1 A large diffuse lipoma.

Hence **li,poma'tosis** [after Gr. words in -ωσις], excessive accumulation of fat in a tissue. **li'pomatoid, li'pomatous** *adjs.* [-OID, -OUS], resembling, or of the nature of, a lipoma.

1847-9 TODD *Cycl. Anat.* IV. 129/2 A lipomatous mass had formed in the pleura. **1855** MAYNE *Expos. Lex.*, *Lipomatoides*..lipomatoid. **1866** A. FLINT *Princ. Med.* (1880) 647 Lipomatosis or development of adipose tissue between the acini which may be thereby obliterated.

lipomorph ('lɪpəmɔːf). *Zool.* [f. Gr. λιπ- (weak stem of λείπειν to leave, be wanting) + μορφ-ή form.] (See quots.)

1897 SCLATER in *Geog. Jrnl.* June IX. 474 'Lipomorph' = a group which characterizes a particular district by its absence from it. *Ibid.* 673 Bears and deer are 'lipomorphs' of Africa south of the Atlas, and cats (*Felis*) of Australia.

liposome ('lɪpəsəʊm). *Biol.* [ad. G. *liposom* (E. Albrecht 1904, in *Verhandl. deutsch. path. Ges.* VI. 64): see LIPO- and -SOME[4].] **1.** A natural globule of fat or lipid suspended in the cytoplasm of a cell.

1910 *Anat. Rec.* IV. 211 The protoplasm of renal cells, muscle fibers, etc., shows usually a large number of small more or less refractive droplets (liposomes) when examined in aqueous humor, or dilute potassium hydroxide. **1946** *Jrnl. Exper. Zool.* CI. 374 In the following discussion, while being aware of the arbitrariness of the choice, the term 'lipochondria' will be used as an alternative for 'lipoprotein bodies'. Their conversion product, the fat droplets, may be termed 'liposomes'. **1968** MCGEE-RUSSELL & ROSS *Cell Struct.* xxvi. 351 The lipid inclusions of amphibian embryo cells have been studied by Holtfreter and Karasaki. Holtfreter called the larger bodies liposomes, and the small ones lipochondria.

2. A minute artificial globule consisting of one or more layers of phospholipid enclosing an aqueous core, used experimentally as a model for biological membranes.

1968 SESSA & WEISSMANN in *Jrnl. Lipid Res.* IX. 310 (*heading*) Phospholipid spherules (liposomes) as a model for biological membranes. *Ibid.*, Throughout this review, the artificial structures will..be referred to as 'spherules'. A. D. Bangham has used the term 'smectic mesophases', and colloquially we have called them 'liposomes' or 'Bangasomes'. As the literature dealing with these structures accumulates, the term 'liposome' is gaining favor, and should win general acceptance. **1970** *New Scientist* 11 June 511/1 In 1965 Alec Bangham..devised the 'liposome'. **1972** M. K. JAIN *Bimolecular Lipid Membrane* iii. 69 A large number of vesicles with cell-like geometry can be produced under suitable conditions by dispersing phospholipids in aqueous salt solutions above the phase-transition temperature of the lipid. These vesicles are generally termed liposomes, spherules, smectic mesophase, and sometimes Bangosomes (after Dr. Bangham).

lipostomous (lɪ'pɒstəməs), *a. Zool.* [f. as LIPOMORPH + Gr. στόμ-α mouth + -OUS.] Having no mouth.

In some mod. Dicts.

lipostomy (lɪ'pɒstəmɪ). *Zool.* [f. as prec. + -Y.] Absence of a mouth or osculum.

1880 F. P. PASCOE *Zool. Classif.* (ed. 2) 280 *Lipostomy*, absence of a mouth. **1888** ROLLESTON & JACKSON *Forms Anim. Life* 793 The absence of an..osculum is known as lipostomy.

lipothymy (lɪ'pɒθɪmɪ), **lipothymia** (lɪpə'θaɪmɪə). Also 7 **leipothymy, lypothimy,** 7-8 **lipothymie,** 7 **lipothymy,** 9 **leipothymia.** [ad. and a. mod.L. *lipothȳmia*, ad. Gr. λιποθυμία, f. λιπ-, weak stem of λείπειν to leave, fail, be lacking + θυμός animation, spirit. Cf. F. *lipothymie* (16th c.).] Fainting, swooning, syncope; an instance of this. †Also *fig.*

1603 F. HERING *Cert. Rules Contagion* (1625) B iij b, The wearers of these Amulets haue fallen into sodaine Lypothimies and soundings. **1654** H. L'ESTRANGE *Chas. I* (1655) 5 This lipothymie, this faint-heartednesse, lost him [James] the reputation and respects of his people. **1660** JER. TAYLOR *Duct. Dubit.* (1676) 807 When nature is in a lipothymie. **1665-6** BOYLE *Let. to Stubbe* 9 Mar., Wks. 1772 I. *Life* 82 Others are freed from lypothymias by being pinched, or having cold water thrown in their faces. **1681** tr. *Willis' Rem. Med. Wks.* Vocab., *Leipothymy*. **1761** PULTENEY in *Phil. Trans.* LII. 351 A faint weak voice, an aptitude to fall into lipothymies from slight causes. **1787** W. FALCONER *Influence Passions* (1791) 90 *note*, He himself was affected with Lipothymia at seeing a criminal broken on the wheel. **1835-6** TODD *Cycl. Anat.* I. 796/1 Syncope occurs without any antecedence of pain or leipothymia.

So **lipo'thymial, lipo'thymic,** †**lipothymous** *adjs.*, of or pertaining to lipothymy; characterized by or tending to lipothymy.

1665 G. HARVEY *Advice agst. Plague* 26 If the patient is surprised with a Lipothymous anguor, jactitation, or great oppression about the stomach or Hypochonders, expect no relief from Cordials. **1689** —— *Curing Dis. by Expect.* iv. 28 Bleeding very oft..doth upon the stopping of the Blood throw them into a long and deep swooning or Leipothymick fit. **1836** I. TAYLOR *Phys. Theory Another Life* 319 All the facts connected with..paralysis and leipothymic states of the system,..will, if fairly considered, either confirm or exclude the theory we adopt. **1898** *Allbutt's Syst. Med.* V. 371 The lipothymial symptoms soon predominate.

lipotropic (lɪpəʊ'trəʊpɪk, -'trɒpɪk), *a. Physiol.* [f. LIPO- + -TROPIC.] Tending to prevent or remove an accumulation of excess fat in the liver. So **lipo'tropism**, lipotropic property or phenomena.

1935 C. H. BEST et al. in *Nature* 18 May 821/2 The term 'lipotropic' is used to describe substances which decrease the rate of deposition and accelerate the rate of removal of liver fat. **1945** *Jrnl. Biol. Chem.* CLX. 601 (*heading*) Growth and lipotropism. I. The dietary requirements of methionine, cystine, and choline. **1951** A. GROLLMAN *Pharmacol. & Therapeutics* xxvii. 607 Because of their lipotropic action, choline and, to a lesser extent, methionine and inositol have been used therapeutically in cirrhosis of the liver, hepatitis, [etc.]. **1953** *Canad. Jrnl. Med. Sci.* XXXI. 474 (*heading*) Further studies on lipotropism in the domestic duck. **1968** A. WHITE et al. *Princ. Biochem.* (ed. 4) xxi. 503 Any material capable of contributing methyl groups for choline synthesis has the property of being lipotropic.

lipotype ('lɪpətaɪp). *Zool.* [f. Gr. λιπ-, λείπειν to leave, be wanting + TYPE.] (See quot.)

1882 *Proc. Zool. Soc.* 21 Mar. 312 Mr. Sclater stated that ..he had found it convenient to coin a term for the designation of a type of animal, the absence of which was characteristic of a particular district or region. This term he proposed should be 'Lipotype'.

lipoxenous (lɪ'pɒksɪnəs), *a. Bot.* [f. as prec. + ξέν-ος a host + -OUS.] Deserting its host; said of certain parasitic fungi which after a time quit the plant which served as a host for them. So **li'poxeny**, the phenomenon of desertion of the 'host' by parasites.

1887 GARNSEY tr. *De Bary's Fungi* 388, 496.

lipp(e, obs. form of LEAP *v.*, LIP *sb.*

lippard, obs. form of LEOPARD.

lippe, variant of LIPE *Obs.*

lipped (lɪpt), *ppl. a.* [f. LIP *sb.* or *v.* + -ED.] **1.** Having or furnished with a lip or lips; having lips of a specified kind. Often in parasynthetic comb., as ***blubber-, red-, thick-lipped.***

1377 onwards [see BABBER, BLABBER, BLOBBER, BLUBBER]. **1604** SHAKS. *Oth.* IV. ii. 63 Thou young and Rose-lip'd Cherubin. **1755** JOHNSON, *Lipped*, having lips. **1820** KEATS *Lamia* I. 189 A virgin purest lipped. **1844** WILLIS *Lady Jane* I. 644 Lamps conceal'd in bells of alabaster, Lipp'd like a lily. **1851** *Beck's Florist* 133 Stalk..inserted in a small, sometimes a lipped, hollow. *c* **1865** J. WYLDE in *Circ. Sci.* I. 403/2 A lipped vessel should..be used. **1897** *Allbutt's Syst. Med.* II. 1058 The *filaridæ* are long filiform worms with a lipped, a papillated, or a simple mouth. **1897** MARY KINGSLEY *W. Africa* 72 Delicate little nostrils, mouths not too heavily lipped. **1902** *Brit. Med. Jrnl.* 12 Apr. 879 The synovial membrane was found rather inflamed, and the edges of the cartilages were lipped.

2. *Bot.* = LABIATE; also, having a labellum.

1836 LOUDON *Encycl. Plants* Gloss., *Lipped*, having a distinct lip or labellum. **1847** W. E. STEELE *Field Bot.* Introd. 16 (*Gloss.*), *Lipped* = Bilabiate. **1854** S. THOMSON *Wild Fl.* III. (ed. 4) 251 Another lipped flower, is the..hemp nettle.

lippen ('lɪpən), *v.* Chiefly *Sc.* Forms: 2 lipnen, -ien, 4, 6 lip-, lypnin, (4 lepnyn, 6 lippne), 5-6 lip-, lyppin, -yn, (7 lipen, 9 lippin), 6- lippen. [Of obscure origin; cf. the synonymous LICKEN *v.* and LITTEN *v.*[1]]

1. *intr.* To confide, rely, trust. Const. *to*, *till*; occas. *in*, *into*, *of*, *on*, *unto*. Also in *indirect pass.* ***to lippen for***: To look confidently for.

c **1175** *Lamb. Hom.* 37 Ne lipnie ȝe no al to eower festene. *a* **1200** *Moral Ode* 22 Ne lipnie na mon to muchel to childe ne to wiue. *c* **1470** *Golagros & Gaw.* 832 Thus may ye lippin on the lake, throu lair that I leir. **1500-20** DUNBAR *Poems* lx. 70 To thy auld schervandis have an E, That lang hes lippinit into the. **1563** DAVIDSON *Confut. Kennedy* in *Wodrow Soc. Misc.* (1844) 208 Thay disseave baith thaim selves and all uthers quha lippinnis in thaim. **1577** BUCHANAN *Let. to Randolph* Wks. (1892) 58 Yf ye gett it not or thys winter be passit, lippin not for it. **1637-50** ROW *Hist. Kirk* (Wodrow Soc.) 456 We must lippen much to the old charter, *Providebit Dominus.* **1685** T. SHARP *Let.* 5 Mar., in *Thoresby's Corr.* (ed. Hunter) I. 68, I lippened, as we say, of you, else [etc.]. **1789** BURNS *To Dr. Blacklock* (21 Oct.) ii, I lippen'd to the chield in trouth. **1816** SCOTT *Old Mort.* ix, I jaloused him..no to be the friend to the government he pretends: the family are not to lippen to. **1868** G. MACDONALD *R. Falconer* I. 49 A gude-hertit crater, but ye cudna lippen till him. **1893** STEVENSON *Catriona* I. ii. 23, I would lippen to Eli's word—ay, if it was the Chevalier, or Appin himsel'.

2. *trans.* To entrust. Const. *dative* or *to*, (*till*), occas. *in*. Also, to trust (a person) *with* (a thing).

c **1375** *Sc. Leg. Saints* xxii. (*Laurentius*) 128 þat þu before lepnyt to me, of godis burd þe priwete. *c* **1450** HOLLAND *Howlat* 456, I loue ȝou mair for that loiss ȝe lippyn me till. **1513** DOUGLAS *Æneis* v. xiv. 46 Or quhat in windis sa dissaitfull to ws,..Wald thow I lipnit the maist noble Enee? **1636** RUTHERFORD *Lett.* (1862) I. 179 Christ will lippen the taking you to heaven, neither to yourself, nor any deputy, but only to Himself. **1883** BLACK *Four Macnicols* v, The people would say I had done wrong in lippening a boat to such a young crew. **1887** *Suppl. to Jamieson* Addenda s.v., I'll lippen ye wi' my siller.

3. To expect with confidence. Also with sentence as obj. † ***to lippen*** (a thing) ***in, upon*** (a person): To expect from.

c **1425** WYNTOUN *Cron.* VII. iv. 554 Than is to lyppyn sum remede. **1535** STEWART *Cron. Scot.* (1858) II. 150 Lyp[n]ing richt lang that tha suld thame reskew. **1552** ABP. HAMILTON *Catech.* (1884) 59 To traist upon God, lippin all gud upon him. **1559** LD. HUME in Sadler *State Papers* (1809) II. 137 To sende to me zour resolut answer,..that I may perfitlie understand quhat I may lyppin. *a* **1572** KNOX *Hist. Ref.* Wks. 1846 I. 74 Your cord and lousie coit and sark, Ye lippin, may bring yow to salvatioun. **1637** RUTHERFORD *Lett.* (1862) I. 444, I can yet lippen that meikle good in Christ as to get a suspension. *c* **1746** J. COLLIER (Tim Bobbin) *View Lanc. Dial.* Wks. (1862) 68 Hoo lippen't her feather wur turned strackling. **1768** ROSS *Helenore* (1789) 51 But some chield ay upon us keeps an ee, And sae we need na lippen to get free.

Hence **'lippening** *vbl. sb.*

1375 BARBOUR *Bruce* XII. 238 Thai ar cummyn heir, For lypnyng in thair gret power. **1535** STEWART *Cron. Scot.* (1858) III. 289 All his beleif and lipning wes in thame. **1565** *Postscr. to Q. Mary's Let.* in Keith *Hist. Ch. Scot.* (1845) II. 328 This we doubt not bot ze will do according to oure lippinnins with all possible haist.

lipper ('lɪpə(r)), *sb.*[1] *Naut.* and *dial.* Also 6 *Sc.* lippir. [Belongs to LIPPER *v.*[1]] A rippling, slight ruffling of the surface of the sea. Often *collect.* Also ***wind-lipper.*** See also quot. 1867.

1513 DOUGLAS *Æneis* VII. ix. 119 Lyk as the see changis fyrst his hew In quhyt lippiris by the wyndis blast. **1789** *Trans. Soc. Arts* II. 221 A deal of sea and wind lipper. **1823** J. F. COOPER *Pioneers* xv. (1869) 67/1 'As to the seas, they russ more in lippers in the Bay of Biscay'. **1855** ROBINSON *Whitby Gloss.* s.v., There's no great sets o' wind, but a great deal of lipper on. **1867** SMYTH *Sailor's Word-bk.*, *Lipper*, a sea which washes over the weather chess-tree, perhaps *leaper*. Also, the spray from small waves breaking against a ship's bows. **1882** *Good Cheer* 33 A light breeze was blowing, making what sailors call a lipper on the surface of the water. **1890** *Pall Mall G.* 7 July 6/2 The approaching torpedo, so clearly identifiable by..the lipper of its 'wake'.

lipper ('lɪpə(r)), *sb.*[2] *Glass-making.* [f. LIP *v.*[1] + -ER[1].] An implement used in forming the lip on a glass vessel.

1869 J. LEICESTER in *Eng. Mech.* 3 Dec. 282/2 The workman then takes his lipper, which is merely a round piece of glass, the shape of a small rolling-pin.

lipper ('lɪpə(r)), *sb.*[3] *Whalefishing.* (See quot.)

1887 G. B. GOODE etc. *Fisheries U.S.* II. 287 In lippering up decks a man takes an oil scoop in one hand and the lipper in the other, with which he brushes the refuse fluid into the receptacles and transfers it to the tubs. [*Note*] A lipper is a piece of thin blubber of an oblong shape, with incisions in one end for the men to grasp... Sometimes a piece of leather may be used. Different vessels employ different utensils of this kind. A large metal ladle used for scooping up the oil from the deck is also called the lipper.

lipper ('lɪpə(r)), *v.*¹ [? frequentative formation related to LAP *v.*¹] *intr.* Of water: To ripple.

1513 DOUGLAS *Æneis* VIII. xi. 73 The lypperand wallis quhyt War pulderit full of fomy froyth mylk quhit. *Ibid.* X. vi. 11 Nor ȝit na land brist lyppering on the wallis. **1853** G. JOHNSTON *Nat. Hist. E. Bord.* I. 107 A little burn, with scarce audible noise, runs lippering in the bottom.

lipper ('lɪpə(r)), *v.*² *dial.* [? freq. of LIP *v.*¹ (cf. LIP *v.*¹ 3).] *intr.* Of a boat: To have its lip or gunwale level *with* (the water).

1822 HIBBERT *Descr. Shetld. Isles* 511 Nor can these lighten the boat so much as that she will not appear, according to the phrase of the fishermen, just lippering with the water. **1844** W. H. MAXWELL *Sports & Adv. Scotl.* xv. (1855) 136 The boat..being..sunk so far as just to *lipper* with the water.

lipper ('lɪpə(r)), *v.*³ *Whalefishing.* [f. LIPPER *sb.*³] *trans.* To wipe (the deck) with a lipper. Chiefly *to lipper up, off.*

1887 G. B. GOODE, etc. *Fisheries U.S.* II. 287 The decks ..are..'lippered up' regularly while boiling, for the sake of cleanliness and economy as well. *Ibid.*, Lippering up [see LIPPER *sb.*³]. **1890** *Century Dict.* s.v., To lipper off the deck.

lipper, var. LEPER *sb.*¹ *Obs.*; obs. f. LEPER *sb.*²

Lippes loop ('lɪpɪz luːp). [f. the name of its inventor, the American physician, Jack *Lippes.*] An intrauterine contraceptive device in the shape of a double s.

[**1962** J. LIPPES in C. Tietze *Intra-Uterine Contraceptive Devices* 71, I wanted a device such that the muscular contractions of the uterus would not press on the entire piece of plastic but on one section at a time only... With this in mind, I designed a device which I call a 'loop'.] **1964** *Lancet* 31 Oct. 958/1 The five types available are: the Margulies spiral, the Lippes loop, the Birnberg bow, the Hall-Stone stainless steel ring, and the Zipper nylon ring. **1966** E. MEARS in M. Pollock *Family Planning* iv. 50 With.. the Lippes loop the inserter is loaded, introduced..beyond the internal os, rotated..and the device expelled by pushing the plunger. **1967** *Time* 7 Apr. 73 From Dr. Jack Lippes' labs in Buffalo came a series of double-S designs, now known as the Lippes loop, which has probably the widest acceptance both in the U.S. (150,000 users) and overseas (up to 4,000,000). **1971** H. J. DAVIS *Intrauterine Devices for Contraception* vi. 95 The shield..conforms most closely to the average uterine cavity size. The Lippes loop is the next most anatomically correct, commercially available device.

†**'lippet.** *Obs. rare*⁻¹. [Cf. LAPPET.] The lobe (of the ear).

1598 R. HAYDOCKE tr. *Lomazzo* I. 29 The lower part whereof [*sc.* the ear] is called the tippe or lippet.

lippie ('lɪpɪ). *Sc.* [f. LIP *sb.* + -IE.] A little lip.

179. BURNS *Song*, *'O, whar did ye get'* 9 My blessin's upon thy sweet wee lippie.

lippie, variant of LIPPY, *sb. Sc.*

lipping ('lɪpɪŋ), *vbl. sb.*¹ [f. LIP *v.* + -ING¹.]

1. a. The action of LIP *v.*¹ in various senses.

1867 SMYTH *Sailor's Word-bk.*, *Lipping*, making notches on the edge of a cutlass or sword. **1887** *Pall Mall G.* 28 Dec. 5/1 Soon the gentle lipping of the tide was replaced by the roar of white-crested waves.

b. *spec.* in *Pathology.*

1894 *Brit. Med. Jrnl.* 2 June 1188/1 The lipping of the articular ends of the bones being characteristic. **1897** *Allbutt's Syst. Med.* III. 106 The presence of bony thickening and lipping about the joints. **1899** E. BLAKE *Study of Hand* (ed. 2) 28 Attacks of chondritis with fibrous degeneration, followed by bulging of the cartilage, known as 'lipping', due to muscular traction, on the opposing articular surfaces.

2. A strip of wood or the like fixed to the edge of a board, door, table-top, etc.; the act of fixing such a strip.

1963 *Gloss. Terms Timber* (*B.S.I.*) 62 *Lipping*, a strip of wood or other material applied to the edge of a flush door, table top, etc. **1966** A. W. LEWIS *Gloss. Woodworking Terms* 53 *Lipping*, fixing a strip of solid wood to the edge of a board, usually by means of a tongue and groove. **1971** *Timber Trades Jrnl.* 14 Aug. 58/2 The pre-glued edging can be either conventional plastics or wood lippings.

lipping ('lɪpɪŋ), *vbl. sb.*² [f. LIP *v.*² + -ING¹.] (See quot.)

1796 C. MARSHALL *Garden.* vii. (1813) 100 Lipping is cutting the slope face of the cion so as to leave a rib down in the middle.

lipping ('lɪpɪŋ), *ppl. a.* [f. LIP *v.*¹ + -ING².] That lips, in senses of the vb.

1843 E. JONES *Sens. & Event* 29 She rose against the lipping wind. **1850** W. MILLER *Songs Nursery* in *Whistle-Binkie* (1890) II. 66 Hairst time's like a lipping cup. **1851** MAYNE REID *Scalp Hunt.* xix. 135 The first little rivulet that trickled forth from their lipping fulness would be the signal of their destruction.

lippir, obs. Sc. form of LIPPER *sb.*¹

lippitude ('lɪpɪtjuːd). Now *rare.* Also 7 lipitude. [ad. L. *lippitūd-o* (f. *lippus* blear-eyed), either directly or through F. *lippitude.*] Soreness of the eyes; blearedness; an instance of this.

1626 BACON *Sylva* §297 Such are Pestilences, Lippitudes, and such like. **1661** LOVELL *Hist. Anim. & Min.* 121 The loines bruised and applied help the dry lippitude. **1680** AUBREY *Lives* (1898) II. 169 His lippitude then was come even to blindnesse. **1788** J. C. SMYTH in *Med. Commun.* II. 217 Ointments..are..useful in cases of lippitude. **1822-34** *Good's Study Med.* II. 573 An unsightly lippitude and excision of the lower eyelid, are hence a very common result of a scrofulous attack on this organ.

Lippizan(a, Lippizaner: see LIPIZZAN *a.*

Lippmann ('lɪpmən). *Photogr.* The name of Gabriel *Lippmann* (1845-1921), French physicist, used *attrib.* with reference to a method of colour photography invented by him in which colours are produced by interference effects in an emulsion containing very fine silver halide particles.

1902 *Westm. Gaz.* 26 Sept. 4/2 Among all experts in this branch of photography it is agreed that the Lippmann interference process is the only one which gives all the colours of Nature in a direct manner, but these experts are unfortunately also agreed that it is an exceedingly difficult process to work. **1908** *Astrophysical Jrnl.* XXVII. 346 This flexible silver mirror is immediately laid, silver surface down, on a wet Lippmann plate. **1936** R. M. FANSTONE *Colour Photogr.* ii. 7 The Lippmann Process presented difficulties, and was somewhat costly to work. **1942** C. E. K. MEES *Theory Photogr. Process* xxi. 872 A Lippmann emulsion..is practically grainless when properly prepared. **1963** F. W. H. MUELLER in *Photographic Theory: Liège Summer School 1962* I. i. 31 Lippmann emulsions, sometimes called grainless emulsions, contain very small silver halide crystals, 10 to 50 mμ in diameter, and are used for scientific purposes... They are chloride or bromide emulsions made by inversed or double jet addition. **1973** F. H. PERRIN in W. Thomas *SPSE Handbk. Photogr. Sci. & Engin.* xvii. 930 The finest grain is produced by procedures devised to make Lippmann color photographs.

lippy, lippie ('lɪpɪ), *sb. Sc.* Also 7 leippie. [dim. of LEAP *sb.*²] The fourth part of a peck; in goods sold by weight usually 1¾ lb.

1612 in *Rec. Convent. Roy. Burghs* (1870) II. 374 To tak na mair for furlett, pek, and leippie, fra the burrowes bot fourty merk in tyme cumming. *a* **1693** *Urquhart's Rabelais* III. xviii, There shall her *justum* both in Peck and Lippy be furnish'd to the full eternally. **1725** *Newburgh Council Rec.* in Laing *Lindores Abbey* etc., xxiv. (1876) 310 All conserned ar to pay the said herd ffor ilk beast off Coū six lippies off good and sufficient bear. **1743** R. MAXWELL *Sel. Trans.* 272 Give each Beast twice a Day, Morning and Evening,..a Lippy and a half..Linlithgow Measure, of the best Oats. **1796** *Statist. Acc. Scot.* XVII. 464 The return of lint is commonly a stone of flax from the lippie. **1868** *Perthsh. Jrnl.* 18 June, We lately heard of some being caught after roosting whose stomachs were found to contain one-fourth of an imperial lippy of grain. **1896** BARRIE *Marg. Ogilvy* iv. (1897) 65, I was sounded as to the advisability of sending him a present of a lippie of shortbread.

b. A measure or vessel holding this quantity.

1847-8 H. MILLER *First Impr.* xi. (1857) 168 A measure, much like what in Scotland we would term a meal lippy.

c. *Comb.*: **lippy('s-bound(s,** the space of ground required for sowing a 'lippy' of flax-seed.

In some districts = 100 square yards.

1876 LAING *Lindores Abbey* etc., xxiii. 300 Domestic servants had a small patch (two lippies-bounds, equal to about five and a half poles) allotted to them.

lippy ('lɪpɪ), *a.* [f. LIP *sb.* + -Y.] **1.** Of a dog (see quot.).

1877 GORDON STABLES *Pract. Kennel Guide* iii. 35 *Lippy* —applied to hanging lips of some dogs where hanging lips should not exist, as in the Bull Terrier.

2. *colloq.* or *dial.* Impertinent, insolent; talkative, verbose.

1875 W. D. PARISH *Dict. Sussex Dial.* 70 *Lippy*, impertinent; apt to answer saucily. **1893** W. K. POST *Harvard Stories* 195 Ain't he getting pretty flip? The lippy dude! **1906** *Punch* 4 Apr. 250/3 'Aughty as teetotallers an' as lippy as Passive Resisters. **1968** V. CANNING *Melting Man* v. 128 You're a lippy bastard. **1971** R. ROBERTS *Classic Slum* 203 Any child who requested a book by title he at once designated as 'forward' or 'lippy'. **1971** R. THOMAS *Backup Men* iv. 32 It might learn them not to be so goddamned lippy.

lipsalve ('lɪpsɑːv, -sælv). [f. LIP *sb.* + SALVE *sb.*] Salve or ointment for the lips; an example of this; also *fig.* flattering speech. *attrib.* in *lipsalve-box.*

1591 PERCIVALL *Sp. Dict.*, *Cerillas*, lip salue, *Vnguentum labiorum.* **1627** E. F. *Hist. Edw. II* (1680) 91 One that.. taught him not to trust a Woman's Lip-salve, when that he knew her breast was fill'd with rancour. **1631** BRATHWAIT *Eng. Gentlew.* (1641) 297 Let not their lip-salve so annoynt you, as it make you forgetfull of him that made you. **1710** STEELE *Tatler* No. 245 ¶2 A Collection of Receipts to make ..Pomatums, Lip-Salves. **1767** MRS. GLASSE *Cookery* 383 A fine lip salve. **1806-7** J. BERESFORD *Miseries Hum. Life* (1826) VI. xxxi, You supply the deficiency of the former with wafers, pocket-pieces, lip-salve-boxes, cut cards, &c. **1826** SCOTT *Jrnl.* 13 May, Praise..costs men nothing, and is usually only lip-salve. **1882** J. ASHTON *Social Life Reign Q. Anne* I. 128 Rose and white lip salves were used as now.

†**lipse**, only in riming phr. *without lipse*, app. = 'without fail'.

a **1380** *S. Paula* 34 in Horstm. *Altengl. Leg.* (1878) 4.

lipse, obs. variant of LISP *v.*

'lip-service. [See LIP *sb.* 6 a (*b*).] Service of the lip; service that is proffered but not performed.

1644 *Direct. Publ. Worship* Pref. 2 Pleasing themselves in their lip-service in bearing a part in it. **1825** J. NEAL *Bro. Jonathan* I. 419 No lip-service for me. **1850** SYD. DOBELL *Roman* i. Poet. Wks. 1875 I. 15 They..subdued the world And with superior scorn heard its lip-service. **1891** HALL CAINE *Scapegoat* xiv, People who had showed him lip-service when he was thought to be rich.

So ˌ**lip-'server**, one whose service is in profession only.

1860 *All Year Round* No. 44. 419 Such a noisy lip-server as that pauper.

lipstick ('lɪpstɪk), *sb.* Also **lip stick, lip-stick.** [f. LIP *sb.* + STICK *sb.*¹ 8.] A stick of cosmetic for colouring the lips, usu. a shade of pink or red; hence, cosmetic for the lips. Also *attrib.*

1880 E. JAMES *Amat. Negro Minstrel's Guide* 4 Prepared burnt cork, ready for use, 25 and 50 cents per box; lip sticks, 25 cts. *Ibid.* 8 An application of lipstick..around the natural part of the lips will extend that feature to a size quite remarkable. **1919** H. L. WILSON *Ma Pettengill* iii. 93 Metta was even using a lip stick! **1922** A. BENNETT *Lilian* II. vii. 116 She also knew what was the best lip-stick. **1926** *Spectator* 18 Sept. 435/2 What is the matter with powder, paint and lipstick? **1942** D. POWELL *Time to be Born* x. 222 She applied a lipstick brush tenderly. **1962** F. I. ORDWAY et al. *Basic Astronautics* xiii. 521 Many are packaged in.. devices resembling lipstick cases. **1966** AUDEN *About House* 46 Spotless rooms..Chill me, so do cups used for ashtrays or smeared With lipstick. **1973** *Country Life* 20 Sept. 831/2, I liked..the clear colours and good texture of the lipsticks. **1974** 'J. ROSS' *Burning of Billy Toober* xii. 113 There were two gilt lipstick cases.

Hence **'lipstick** *v. trans.* and *intr.*, to apply lipstick to (one's lips); **'lipsticked** *ppl. a.*; **'lipsticking** *vbl. sb.*; **'lipsticky** *a.*, covered or sticky with lipstick; also *fig.*

1926 *Ladies' Home Jrnl.* Apr. 24 She..had recently lipsticked a red mouth into startling contrast to her natural pallor. **1928** *Sunday Express* 15 Apr. 15/4 She may be made of wax, with large, liquid eyes, a lipsticked mouth, and real hair. **1931** *Daily Tel.* 21 May 13/3 They chatted, smoked, 'lipsticked', read, sewed, [etc.]. **1931** *Punch* 28 Oct. 476/3 Her chronicle of minor adventures, if occasionally a shade too lip-sticky for all tastes, is thoroughly vivacious and entertaining. **1933** J. B. PRIESTLEY *Wonder Hero* vi. 249 The first thing she did was to give Charlie a large smacking lip-sticky kiss. **1940** A. G. MACDONELL *Crew of Anaconda* xxi. 260 Florinda did a little powdering and lipsticking. **1949** *Landfall* June 183 The lipsticky essays of her daughter into informed adolescence. **1960** *20th Cent.* Oct. 313 She would open her handbag, lipstick her mouth, and go home. **1966** J. B. PRIESTLEY *Salt is Leaving* i. 5 Sheila stopped lipsticking. **1969** *Daily Tel.* (Colour Suppl.) 5 Sept. 46/3 My eyes are still wandering over that lip-sticked mouth. **1974** *Listener* 17 June 69/1 Jonathan Miller used to imagine the BBC as an actual aunt, powdered and lipsticked and getting on in years.

Liptauer, liptauer ('lɪptaʊər). Also **Liptai, Liptau, Liptoi.** [G., f. *Liptó* place-name in Czechoslovakia.] A soft cheese originally made in Hungary, usu. coloured and flavoured with paprika and other seasonings. Also *attrib.*

1902 J. T. LAW *Grocer's Manual* (ed. 2) 143/2 *Bringen* or *Liptau Cheese*, a Continental kind made in Hungary. Constituents:—Water, 34 per cent.; fatty matter, 28; Caseine, 23; salts, 5. **1935** M. MORPHY *Recipes of All Nations* 348 Liptauer cheese..which is extensively made in Germany and Austria, is of Hungarian origin. It is made from sour milk. **1955** G. FREEMAN *Liberty Man* I. ii. 32 The fillings came from a delicatessen. Liverwurst and liptauer cheese. **1964** *Punch* 19 Feb. 262/3 Mortadella, lachscinken, kabanosi or Liptauer cheese. **1964** E. HUXLEY *Back Street New Worlds* vii. 75 In one [supermarket]..you can buy.. Czech braun, gacciatori, or Liptauer cheese. **1967** T. A. LAYTON *Cheese & Cheese Cookery* 228 Liptoi is a goats' milk cream cheese; Liptoi is sold in Hungary packed in small bladders and owes its name to the county of Lipto (now in Czechoslovakia)... The German name of this cheese, *Liptauer*, is often used in shops and restaurants both in Hungary and abroad.

†**liptote.** *Obs.* [ad. mod.L. *liptotēs*, blundered form of *lītotēs*. Cf. MDu. *liptote.*] = LITOTES.

1589 PUTTENHAM *Eng. Poesie* III. xvii. (Arb.) 195 By another [figure] we temper our sence with wordes of such moderation, as in appearaunce it abateth it but not in deede, and is by the figure Liptote. *a* **1661** FULLER *Worthies, Cambridgesh.* I. (1662) 157 Bale beginneth very coldly in his commendation.., *Vir non omnino stupidus*..; but we understand the language of his Liptote.

‖**lipuria** (lɪ'pjʊərɪə). *Path.* [mod.L. *lipūria*, f. Gr. λίπ-ος fat + οὖρον urine.] 'The presence of oily matter in the urine' (*Syd. Soc. Lex.* 1889).

1897 *Allbutt's Syst. Med.* IV. 262 The so-called characteristic symptoms..namely, fatty stools and lipuria.

'lip-worship. [See LIP *sb.* 6 a (*b*).] Worship that consists only in words.

1630 SANDERSON *Serm.* II. 262 The knee-worship, and the cap-worship, and the lip-worship they may have that are in worshipful places and callings. *a* **1716** BLACKALL *Wks.* (1723) I. 216 They worship him in vain, who give him only a Knee, or a Lip-worship. **1862** MERIVALE *Rom. Emp.* (1865) VII. lvi. 75 The lip-worship of courtiers and time-servers.

Hence **'lip-'worshipper**, one whose worship is limited to professions.

1884 SIR A. DE VERE *1st Pt. Mary Tudor* IV. ii, True love Visits not thrones. The lonely sitter there Finds flatterers, lip-worshippers, but not True love.

†**liqua'bility.** *Obs. rare*⁻¹. [f. L. *liquābil-is*: see next and -ITY.] The state of being liquable.

1662 S. P. *Acc. Latitude Men* 17 That softness should signifie liquability, answered just to humidity signifying fluidity. **1731** in BAILEY vol. II.

†**'liquable,** *a.* and *sb. Obs.* Also 5 liquible, 7 liqueable. [ad. L. *liquābil-is*, f. *liquāre*: see LIQUATE *v.* and -ABLE.]

A. *adj.* That can be liquefied; capable of melting. Also, soluble (in a liquid).

1471 RIPLEY *Comp. Alch.* Ep. x. in Ashm. (1652) 111 Such bodies which in nature be liquable. **1567** MAPLET *Gr. Forest* 20 Quicksilver and Brimstone are the..cause of beginning in all thinges liquable or those which melt, which are commonly called Mettals. **1657** G. STARKEY *Helmont's Vind.* 314 A Salt..liquable in water or Wine. **1768** A. CATCOTT *Treat. Deluge* 382 The matter contained within the shell exactly resembled any liquable substance cast fluid into a mould.

B. *sb.* A substance that may be liquefied.

1460–70 *Bk. Quintessence* 7 Wiyn not aloonly holdiþ in it þe propirtees of gold, but myche more þe propirtees of alle liquibles if þei be quenchid þerinne. **1612** STURTEVANT *Metallica* 109 Any kind of liquor or liqueable..which is put into the Furnace, Pot, Kettle, Caldron or Copper, to be further heated, and boyled.

Hence **'liquableness**.

1727 BAILEY vol. II.

‖**liquamen** (lɪ'kweɪmɛn). [L. *liquāmen* a liquid mixture, f. *liquāre*: see LIQUATE *v.*] †**a.** A substance reduced to a liquid state. Also, the name of a kind of fish-sauce used by the ancient Romans; garum. *Obs.*

c **1420** *Pallad. on Husb.* III. 827 And make liquamen castimoniall Of peres thus. **1672** *Phil. Trans.* VII. 5059 That Liquamen or softer pulp (which I took to be Bees-meat). **1770** *Ibid.* LXI. 343, I mixed..six drams of the putrid liquamen, with..this liquor. **1806** A. HUNTER *Culina* (ed. 3) 60 The Romans had a raw salad..made savoury with liquamen, oil, and vinegar. The liquamen was something like our anchovy liquor.

b. 'A fluid for administering medicine' (*Syd. Soc. Lex.* 1889).

†**liquament.** *Obs. rare*⁻¹. [ad. L. *liquāmentum*, f. *liquāre*: cf. prec.] A concoction, liquid mixture.

1657 TOMLINSON *Renou's Disp.* 731 Mix the brayed Lithargie with the liquament.

liquate ('laɪkweɪt), *v.* [f. L. *liquāt-*, ppl. stem of *liquāre* to melt, cogn. w. *liquor* LIQUOR.]

†**1.** *trans.* To make liquid, cause to flow. Also *intr.*, to become liquid, melt.

1669 W. SIMPSON *Hydrol. Chym.* 69 Disenteries, which grating upon the tender tunicles thereof, liquates the blood from them..; at every tormenting liquation puts nature upon the rack. *a* **1728** WOODWARD *Nat. Hist. Fossils* (1729) I. I. 10 If the Salts be not drawn forth before the Clay is baked, they..are apt to liquate afterwards. *Ibid.* 19 Being wet,..the Salts liquating, it becomes soft like Marle.

2. *Metallurgy.* To liquefy metals in order to separate them or to free them from impurities. Also *to liquate out.*

1864 in WEBSTER. **1874** RAYMOND *Statist. Mines & Mining* 424 A liquation-furnace, used for liquating the bullion, in order to free it from such impurities as may not have been eliminated in its passage through the lead-softening furnace. **1882** T. E. THORPE in *Nature* XXVI. 172 Heating disintegrated suet..when a clear yellow oil is (to borrow a term of the metallurgists) 'liquated out'.

Hence **'liquated** *ppl. a.*, **'liquating** *vbl. sb.*

1684 tr. *Bonet's Merc. Compit.* XIX. 700 A Bath promotes the flowing of the Blood, liquating of it. **1874** RAYMOND *Statist. Mines & Mining* 483 The liquated lead is completely desilverized.

liquation (lɪ'kweɪʃən). [ad. L. *liquātiōn-em*, n. of action f. *liquāre*: see prec.]

1. The process of making or of becoming liquid; the condition or capacity of being melted.

1612 WOODALL *Surg. Mate* Wks. (1653) 272 Liquation is when as that which shall be made into one body, is dissolved, that it can flow abroad like waves. **1646** SIR T. BROWNE *Pseud. Ep.* II. i. 49 Crystall is nothing else, but Ice or Snow ..congealed beyond liquation. **1657** TOMLINSON *Renou's Disp.* II. xviii. 74 Liquation differs from Dissolution, in that Liquation is alwayes caused by heat, and seldome or never with any humour; Dissolution alwayes with humours, seldome with heat. **1669** [see LIQUATE *v.* 1]. **1722** QUINCY *Phys. Dict.* (ed. 2) s.v., Such unctuous Substances as are procured by Liquation, or Liquefaction, which signify the same.

2. *Metallurgy.* The action or process of separating metals by fusion.

1471 RIPLEY *Comp. Alch.* VII. v. in Ashm. (1652) 170 As yt [Gold] doth the Fyre doth fele, Lyke Wax yt wylbe redy unto Lyquacyon. **1605** TIMME *Quersit.* I. xiii. 59 In the liquation or melting of gold with other metalls. **1646** SIR T. BROWNE *Pseud. Ep.* III. xxi. 161 Mettals in their liquation, although they intensly heat the air above their surface, arise not yet into a flame. **1839** URE *Dict. Arts* 774 Lead and antimony are the metals most commonly subjected to liquation.

3. *Comb.*, as ***liquation furnace, hearth, tube***; **liquation cake**, a cake, composed of black copper and lead, used in charging a liquation furnace.

1839 URE *Dict. Arts* 775 The flames, after playing round about the sides of the liquation tubes, pass off..into the chimney. *Ibid.* 824 The working area charged with the liquation cakes and charcoal. *Ibid.*, These cakes are..placed in the liquation furnace. **1875** KNIGHT *Dict. Mech.*, *Liquation Hearth*, or *Furnace.*

†**liquative**, *a. Obs. rare*⁻¹. [f. L. *liquāre*: see LIQUATE *v.* and -ATIVE.] Of or pertaining to liquation.

1657 TOMLINSON *Renou's Disp.* II. xvii. 75 The Alcumists ..have invented many things, whereby the liquative or fusitive Art is enriched.

†**liquator.** *Obs. rare*⁻⁰. [a. L. **liquātor*, agent-n. of *liquāre* to melt.] (See quot.)

1623 COCKERAM, *Liquator*, he which melteth.

lique, an alleged name for a kind of small seagoing vessel, is prob. a spurious word: in the Fr. text of Froissart, which Berners followed, *lique* is believed to be a mistake for *ligne*: see LINE *sb.*[3]

1523 LD. BERNERS *Froiss.* I. lxxxiiii. h b/2 A lytell shyppe called Lyque [F. *lique*]. **1847** NICOLAS *Hist. R. Navy* II. 164 Lique was a small, light, swift vessel. Froissart says [etc.]. **1894** C. N. ROBINSON *Brit. Fleet* 210 'Liques' and 'lynes', small swift rowing galleys.

liquefacient (lɪkwɪ'feɪʃ(ɪ)ənt), *a.* and *sb.* [ad. L. *liquefacient-em*, pr. pple. of *liquefacĕre* to LIQUEFY: see -FACIENT.] **a.** *adj.* 'Making liquid' (*Syd. Soc. Lex.* 1889). **b.** *sb.* Something which serves to liquefy; *spec.* in *Med.*, an agent (such as mercury and iodine) supposed to have the power of liquefying solid deposits (Dunglison *Med. Lex.* 1853). Also, an agent which increases the amount of fluid secretions (*Syd. Soc. Lex.* 1889).

†**liquefacted**, *ppl. a.* [f. L. *liquefact-*, ppl. stem of *liquefacĕre* to LIQUEFY + -ED[1].] Liquefied.

1597 A. M. tr. *Guillemeau's Fr. Chirurg.* 22 b/1 With the liqvefacted and moulten corrosive. **1599** —— tr. *Gabelhouer's Bk. Physicke* 90/2 Inungate therwith externallye your Croppe, with liquefactede Bacon.

†**liquefactible**, *a. Obs. rare*⁻¹. [f. as prec. + -IBLE. Cf. OF. *liquefactible.*] That may be liquefied, liquefiable.

1644 DIGBY *Nat. Bodies* xvii. (1658) 191 Those bodies.. which by heat are mollified or are liquefactible.

†**liquefacting**, *ppl. a. Obs. rare*⁻¹. [f. as prec. + -ING[2].] Used in the liquefaction of metals.

1597 A. M. tr. *Guillemeau's Fr. Chirurg.* 41 b/2 We must yet make greater fyer thervnder, with violente flames, as if it were a liqvefactinge fyer.

liquefaction (lɪkwɪ'fækʃən). Also 8–9 *erron.* liquifaction. [a. F. *liquéfaction*, ad. L. *liquefactiōn-em*, n. of action f. *liquefacĕre* to LIQUEFY.]

1. The action or process of liquefying, or the state of being liquefied; reduction to a liquid state.

1477 NORTON *Ord. Alch.* v. in Ashm. (1652) 59 Ayer also with his Coaction, Maketh things to be of light liquefaction: As Wax is and Butter, and Gummes all, A little heate maketh them to melt and fall. **1633** T. ADAMS *Exp. 2 Peter* ii. v. 562 Which [cloudes] were encreased by the liquefaction and distilling of the aire into water. **1768–74** TUCKER *Lt. Nat.* (1834) I. 12 The qualities of fire remain the same, whether you throw gold or clay into it; yet upon casting in the latter no liquefaction will ensue. **1800** HENRY *Epit. Chem.* (1808) 37 Ice, during liquefaction, must absorb much caloric. **1818** FARADAY *Exp. Res.* xxi. (1844) 106 The liquefaction and solidification of gases. **1851** J. H. NEWMAN *Cath. in Eng.* vii. 298, I think it impossible to withstand the evidence which is brought for the liquefaction of the blood of St. Januarius at Naples. **1880** C. & F. DARWIN *Movem. Pl.* 69 The softening or liquefaction of the outer surface of the wall of the hair.

†**2.** *fig.* Said of the 'melting' of the soul by ardour of devotion, etc. (Cf. F. *liquéfaction.*)

1526 *Pilgr. Perf.* (W. de W. 1531) 150 A liquefaction or a meltynge of the soule. *a* **1631** DONNE *Serm.* xxvi. 257 Till thou feele in thy selfe..a liquefaction, a colliquation, a melting of thy bowels under the commination of the Judgements of God upon thy sin. **1633** EARL MANCH. *Al Mondo* (1636) 201 They laboured by a liquefaction of their soules into God, to insoule themselues in God. *a* **1711** KEN *Hymns* Poet. Wks. 1721 I. 228 She rap't at his endearing Eye ..in sweet, am'rous Liquefaction dy'd.

liquefactive (lɪkwɪ'fæktɪv), *a.* [ad. L. type **liquefactīv-us*, f. *liquefacĕre* to LIQUEFY.] Having the effect of liquefying.

1877 ROBERTS *Handbk. Med.* (ed. 3) I. 47 Fatty or liquefactive change..may lead to its absorption. **1899** *Allbutt's Syst. Med.* VI. 164 The liquefactive softenings which may occur in old thrombi.

liquefiable ('lɪkwɪˌfaɪəb(ə)l), *a.* Also liqui-. [f. LIQUEFY *v.* + -ABLE. Cf. F. *liquéfiable.*] That may be liquefied.

1558–66 WARDE tr. *Alexis' Secr.* III. VI. 69 b, To make all metalles liquifiable. **1626** BACON *Sylva* §839 The Consistencies of Bodies are..Liquefiable, Not Liquefiable. **1855** *Jrnl. R. Agric. Soc.* XVI. I. 34 Their more fluid and liquefiable parts. **1865** MANSFIELD *Salts* 298 Both these substances are, at ordinary temperatures, gases, but liquefiable by pressure and cold.

fig. **1829** BENTHAM *Justice & Cod. Petit.* Wks. 1843 V. 485 The penance and the excommunication themselves have been made liquifiable into fees.

liquefier ('lɪkwɪfaɪə(r)). [f. LIQUEFY *v.* + -ER[1].] One who or that which liquefies.

1824 J. WILSON in *Blackw. Mag.* XV. 721 Punch—cold lime and rum punch, I mean—the best liquifier, perhaps, that has yet been invented for this season. **1894** *Daily News* 22 Feb. 3/1 The great liquefier [*sc.* of air and gases], Professor Dewar.

liquefy ('lɪkwɪfaɪ), *v.* Also 6–9 liquify. [a. F. *liquéfier*, ad. L. *liquefacĕre* to make liquid, f. *liquēre* to be fluid: see -FY.]

1. *trans.* To reduce into a liquid condition. With obj. a solid substance; also in *Physics*, air, gases. †Formerly, to dissolve (in a liquid).

1547 BOORDE *Brev. Health* 75, I do lyquifye it in the oyle of Roses. **1599** A. M. tr. *Gabelhouer's Bk. Physicke* 10/2 Liquefye the Suger in Melisse water. **1661** LOVELL *Hist. Anim. & Min.* Introd., Some of them may be Liquefied by liquour, as earths, salt,..&c., some by fire, as metallick fluores. **1756–7** tr. *Keysler's Trav.* (1760) III. 63 The substance in the phial..looks like balsam of Peru, which may be very easy liquefied. **1824–9** LANDOR *Imag. Conv.* Wks. 1846 II. 245 Sweat ran from them liquefying the blood that had..hardened on their hands and feet. **1863** TYNDALL *Heat* ii. §21 (1870) 26 Simply to liquefy a mass of ice an enormous amount of heat is necessary. **1881** LUBBOCK *Addr. Brit. Assoc.* in *Nature* No. 618. 411 Oxygen and nitrogen have been liquefied.

2. *fig.* To 'melt' with spiritual ardour. (Cf. F. *liquéfier.*) Also *intr.* for *passive.*

1483 CAXTON *Gold. Leg.* 313/2 From that houre the sowle of hym lyquefyed and the passion of Jhesu cryst was merueylously infyxed in his herte. **1502** ATKINSON tr. *De Imitatione* III. vi. 201 That I may lerne..what is to man to be lyquyfyed and molten in loue.

3. *intr.* To become liquid; †*rarely* to dissolve (in water).

1583 STUBBES *Anat. Abus.* II. (1882) 29 Othersome will cast wette salt into it [wool], which in time will liquifie. **1626** BACON *Sylva* §840 The Disposition not to Liquefie proceedeth from the Easie Emission of the Spirits, whereby the Grosser Parts contract. **1705** ADDISON *Italy* (1733) 119 Blood..which liquefy'd at the Approach of the Saint's Head, tho'..it was hard congeal'd before. **1750** tr. *Leonardus's Mirr. Stones* 18 Some stones..do not liquify, and also sink in water. **1812** SIR H. DAVY *Chem. Philos.* Wks. 1840 IV. 71 Crystalline muriate of lime and snow, both cooled to 0° Fahrenheit..act upon each other and liquefy. **1860** TYNDALL *Glac.* II. xi. 289 The ice liquefying rapidly.

4. *trans.* To give (a consonant) a 'liquid' or semivocalic pronunciation.

1714 FORTESCUE-ALAND *Notes Fortescue's Abs. & Lim. Mon.* 27 This letter *g* is also liquified in the middle, as in the word sail from the Saxon *saegl.* **1842** M. RUSSELL *Polynesia* i. (1849) 39 They [the consonants] are liquefied to a soft and almost vowel sound.

5. *jocular.* To moisten or 'soak' with liquor or 'drink'. Also *absol.*

1826 SCOTT *Jrnl.* 5 Mar., Something of toddy and cigar in that last quotation, I think. Yet I only smoked two, and liquified with one glass of spirits and water. **1827** HONE *Every-day Bk.* II. 12 When thoroughly liquefied, his loquacity is deluging.

Hence **'liquefied, 'liquefying** *ppl. adjs.*

1599 A. M. tr. *Gabelhouer's Bk. Physicke* 243/1 Which foresayed..paper balle, she must winde in liquefyede waxe. **1731** *Hist. Litteraria* III. 252 Iron melted into a liquified Matter. **1825** J. NICHOLSON *Operat. Mechanic* 741 Liquefied amber..separated from the oily portions which alter its consistence. **1860** TYNDALL *Glac.* I. xi. 83 After we had divided the liquefied snow..amongst us we had nothing to drink. **1898** P. MANSON *Trop. Diseases* xxiii. 365 Some irritating liquefying body derived from the decomposition processes going on on the surface of the dysenteric ulcer.

liqueres, -is(e, obs. forms of LIQUORICE.

liquerish, obs. form of LICKERISH.

liquerous, variant of LICKEROUS.

1609 W. M. *Man in Moone* D 2.

liquesce (lɪ'kwɛs), *v. rare.* [ad. L. *liquescĕre* to become liquid.] *intr.* To become liquid. Also *fig.*, to merge *into.*

1831 T. HOPE *Ess. Origin Man* I. 157 When by degrees.. the heat..penetrates within the ice so as to make it distend and liquesce. **1920** *19th Cent.* Dec. 977 The perpetual tendency of privilege, royal as well as any other, to liquesce into the common stream of humanity.

liquescence (lɪ'kwɛsəns). *rare.* [f. LIQUESCENT *a.*: see -ENCE.] The process or fact of becoming liquid.

1875 *Fam. Herald* 13 Nov. 29/2 If the phial of Januarius were..duly attested to be coagulated human blood..its liquescence periodically would be acknowledged as a miracle. [In some recent Dicts.]

li'quescency. *rare*⁻⁰. [f. next: see -ENCY.] The state or quality of being liquescent; 'aptness to melt' (J.).

1656 in BLOUNT *Glossogr.* **1706** in PHILLIPS (ed. Kersey). **1755** in JOHNSON; whence in later Dicts.

liquescent (lɪ'kwɛsənt), *a.* [ad. L. *liquescent-em*, pr. pple. of *liquescĕre* to become liquid: see -ESCENT.] **a.** That is in process of becoming liquid; apt to become liquid. Also *transf.*

1727 BAILEY vol. II, *Liquescent*, melting, consuming. **1758** REID tr. *Macquer's Chem.* I. 23 They..attract the moisture of the air, and are thereby melted into a liquor. These may be called *Liquescent Salts.* **1822–34** *Good's Study Med.* (ed. 4) II. 486 The spinal marrow..was found disorganised and liquescent.

transf. a **1849** POE *Ulalume* Poems (1859) 69 At the end of our path a liquescent and nebulous lustre was born. **1867** BAILEY *Universal Hymn* 16 Globelets of liquescent flame. **1967** *Listener* 31 Aug. 287/3 Huge eyes fluctuating between fear and wonder and roguish amusement—liquescent, all light suddenly sinking out of them. **1969** *Daily Tel.* 10 Dec. 12/4 Debussy's 'Prélude à l'après-midi d'un faune' could

scarcely have been bettered for delicate dynamic nuances and shapely liquescent phrasing.

b. Of a sound: Tending to a 'liquid' pronunciation.

1755 JOHNSON s.v. *Malign*, The *g* is mute or liquescent.

Hence †**li'quescentness**.

1727 BAILEY vol. II, *Liquescentness*, aptness to melt.

†**li'quescible**, *a. Obs. rare.* [f. L. *liquesc-ĕre* to become liquid: see -IBLE.] Liquefiable.

1657 TOMLINSON *Renou's Disp.* 264 The best [scammony] is nitid, splendic, clear like gum..easily liquescible.

liqueur (‖likœr, lɪ'k(j)ɜː(r), often lɪ'kjʊə(r)), *sb.* [F.; = LIQUOR *sb.*]

1. a. A strong alcoholic liquor sweetened and flavoured with aromatic substances.

1742 POPE *Dunc.* IV. 316 He..Try'd all *hors-d'œ uvres*, all *liqueurs* defin'd, Judicious drank, and greatly-daring din'd. *c* **1750** SHENSTONE *To the Virtuosi* v, Tis you..Know what conserves they chuse to eat And what liqueurs to tipple. **1768** BOSWELL *Corsica* (ed. 2) 280 At dinner we had.. different sorts of wine and a liqueur. **1804** T. TROTTER *Drunkenness* v. (1884) 176 The liqueur called Noyau. **1815** *Sporting Mag.* XLVI. 122 Cafes, where coffee and liqueurs are taken. **1871** LONGF. in *Life* (1891) III. 169 Manufacturers of exquisite liqueurs. **1882** *Encycl. Brit.* XIV. 686/2 Bitters form a class of liqueurs by themselves.

b. A mixture (consisting of sugar and certain wines, or sugar and alcohol) used to sweeten and flavour champagne.

1872 THUDICHUM & DUPRÉ *Treat. Wine* 468.

2. = *liqueur-glass*. Also = *liqueur chocolate*.

1907 *Yesterday's Shopping* (1969) 937 Table glass services... 12 Clarets... 12 Champagnes... 6 Liqueurs... 12 Tumblers. **1925** *Heal & Son Catal.: Glass*, Table glass. ..Champagne..Claret..Sherry..Port..Liqueur..Tumbler. **1965** E. BROWN *Big Man* xi. 96 Andy took from his shoulder bag the box of liqueurs. **1967** K. GILES *Death in Diamonds* iii. 59 Elizabeth was..eating chocolates. 'My present to myself,' she said, 'Austrian Liqueurs and none for pigs.' **1968** G. BEARD *Mod. Glass* ii. 101 (*caption*) Automatic production six sizes of 'Five Star' 1 oz. liqueur to 12½ oz. goblet.

3. *attrib.* and *Comb.*, as ***liqueur manufacturer***, ***merchant***; **liqueur brandy**, a brandy of special bouquet, which is consumed in small quantities as a liqueur; **liqueur chocolate**, a chocolate with a liqueur filling; **liqueur-frame**, a frame for holding liqueur bottles; **liqueur-glass**, a very small drinking glass used for liqueurs; **liqueur-man**, one who adds the liqueur in the process of champagne-making; **liqueur-stand** = *liqueur-frame*; **liqueur-wine** [= F. *vin de liqueur*], one of the strong and delicate-flavoured wines that have the character of liqueurs.

1882 *Encycl. Brit.* XIV. 686/2 Wines and spirits remarkable for their amount of bouquet, such as tokay and *liqueur brandy, &c. **1904** 'SAKI' *Reginald* 84 Some *liqueur chocolates had been turned loose by mistake among the refreshments—really liqueur chocolates, with very little chocolate. **1950** O. BLAKESTON *Pink Ribbon* vii. 76 Some flying beetle, rather like a small liqueur chocolate, zoomed past my ear. **1969** J. ELLIOT *Duel* I. iii. 74 A small box of liqueur chocolates..shaped like miniature bottles. **1875** JAS. GRANT *One of the '600'* iv, Binns appeared..followed by a servant bearing *liqueur-frames, filled with 'mountain dew'. **1850** E. RUSKIN *Let.* 9 Mar. in M. Lutyens *Effie in Venice* (1965) I. 155 The little *Liqueur glasses of Rossolio. **1859** LANG *Wand. India* 18 Two liqueur glasses. **1904** 'SAKI' *Reginald* 16 There are liqueur glasses, and crystallized fruits. **1962** E. O'BRIEN *Lonely Girl* iv. 48 Joanna opened the wine and served it in liqueur glasses to make it go far. **1975** *Sunday Times* (Colour Suppl.) 23 Feb. 11/4, 6 sherry glasses which when half filled double superbly as liqueur glasses. **1872** THUDICHUM & DUPRÉ *Treat. Wine* 468 The liqueur is kept in the atelier in a large can attached to a machine which is under the guidance of the *liqueur-man. **1858** SIMMONDS *Dict. Trade*, **Liqueur manufacturer*. **1800** *Ann. Reg.* 441 An Italian *liqueur merchant. **1858** SIMMONDS *Dict. Trade*, **Liqueur stand*. **1872** THUDICHUM & DUPRÉ *Treat. Wine* 515 *Liqueur Wines.

li'queur, *v.* [f. LIQUEUR *sb.*] *trans.* To flavour (champagne) with a liqueur.

1872 THUDICHUM & DUPRÉ *Treat. Wine* 467 The operation of liqueuring. *Ibid.* 469 It sometimes happens, however, that..the wine which has been disgorged or liqueured undergoes a slight second fermentation. **1876** M. COLLINS *Blacksmith & Scholar* I. ix. 243 The liqueured champagnes for which we give as many shillings as it cost pence.

liquible, variant of LIQUABLE *Obs.*

liquid ('lɪkwɪd), *a.* and *sb.* Forms: 4 liquyd, 5–6 li-, lyquide, -yde, (5 lyquet, 6–7 liqued), 6– liquid. [a. OF. *liquide*, ad. L. *liquid-us*, f. *liquēre* to be liquid, cogn. with *liquāre* LIQUATE *v.*, *līquī* to be liquid, *liquor* LIQUOR.]

A. *adj.*

I. 1. a. Said of a material substance in that condition (familiar as the normal condition of water, oil, alcohol, etc.) in which its particles move freely over each other (so that its masses have no determinate shape), but do not tend to separate as do those of a gas; not solid nor gaseous. Hence, composed of a substance in this condition.

1382 WYCLIF *Ezek.* xliv. 30 Alle liquyd [**1388** moist] sacrifices, or fleetynge, as oyle, and hony, and syche. *c* **1400** *Lanfranc's Cirurg.* 203 Fleuma vitreum was liquide fleuma, & wiþ cooldnes it is congilid. **1494** FABYAN *Chron.* VII. 373 Rosyn, grece, and other lyquet & brynyng stuffe. **1544** PHAER *Regim. Lyfe* (1560) O iv b, Another devine medecine, in a liquide-fourme. **1562** TURNER *Herbal* II. 29 Rosin of yᵉ larche tre..is moyster or more liqued. **1590** SPENSER *F.Q.* II. ii. 6 Which feedes each living plant with liquid sap. **1590** SHAKS. *Mids. N.* I. i. 211 Decking with liquid pearle, the bladed grasse. **1610** WILLET *Hexapla Dan.* 202 Windes doe not blowe so much vpon the solid earth, as vpon the liquid sea. **1697** DRYDEN *Virg. Georg.* IV. 601 Down from his Head the liquid Odours ran. **1760–2** GOLDSM. *Cit. World* cvi. ¶4 The whole is liquid laudanum to my spirits. **1800** tr. *Lagrange's Chem.* II. 113 Add a very small quantity of water, in order that the mixture may form a paste somewhat liquid. **1849** R. V. DIXON *Heat* I. 21 Liquid thermometers, may be applied to measure temperatures considerably above those at which the liquid filling them boils in the open air. **1863** MARY HOWITT *F. Bremer's Greece* II. xi. 1 With the taste of Nectar and colour of liquid gold.

b. In poetical and rhetorical lang. often used for: Watery.

1606 SHAKS. *Tr. & Cr.* I. iii. 40 And anon behold The strong ribb'd Barke through liquid Mountaines cut. **1611** CORYAT *Crudities* 559, I will returne againe to my liquid iourney betwixt Mentz and Franckford vpon the river Mænus. **1657** BP. H. KING *Poems* (1843) III. xiii. 103 All the Ship-wracks, and the liquid graves. **1725** POPE *Odyss.* x. 58 Meanwhile our vessels plough the liquid plain. **1819** WORDSW. *Waggoner* Concl. 36 While Grasmere smoothed her liquid plain The moving image to detain. **1856** EMERSON *Eng. Traits, Voy. Eng.* Wks. (Bohn) II. 11 The good ship..gliding through liquid leagues. **1879** J. BURROUGHS *Locusts & W. Honey* (1884) 82 It [the strawberry] is the product of liquid May touched by the June sun.

c. *occas.* Of the eyes: Filled with tears.

1598 ROWLANDS *Betray. Christ* 57 Her liquid eies stroue each t'exceed the other,..by teares her woe appeares. **1873** BLACK *Pr. Thule* iii. 36 Poems, over which fair eyes had grown full and liquid.

II. In various *transf.* and *fig.* senses.

2. Of light, fire, the air: Clear, transparent, bright (like pure water). [Cf. L. *liquidus* in poetry.]

1590 SPENSER *F.Q.* III. iv. 49 And with her pineons cleaves the liquid firmament. **1653** H. MORE *Antid. Ath.* II. ii. (1712) 41 Though the Earth move floating in the liquid Heavens. **1688** PRIOR *Exodus* III. v, Why does he [the Sun] wake the correspondent Moon, And fill her willing Lamp with liquid Light? **1697** DRYDEN *Virg. Georg.* III. 378 They That wing the liquid Air, or swim the Sea. **1742** GRAY *Ode on Spring* iii, The insect youth are on the wing, Eager to.. float amid the liquid noon. *c* **1800** K. WHITE *Poems* (1837) 73 The liquid lustre of her fine blue eye. **1850** KINGSLEY *Alt. Locke* xiii. (1879) 163 The dark hazel eyes shone with a more liquid lustre. **1884** *St. James's Gaz.* 10 May 6/2 A youthful forehead and a pair of liquid eyes.

3. Of sounds: Flowing, pure and clear in tone; free from harshness or discord. Also in *Phonetics*, Of the nature of a 'liquid' (see B. 2).

a **1637** B. JONSON *Eng. Gram.* (1640) 47 It [R] is sounded firme in the beginning of the words, and more liquid in the middle, and ends: as in *rarer, riper.* **1646** CRASHAW *Steps to Temple*, etc. 105 Bathing in streames of liquid melodie. **1697** DRYDEN *Æneid* Ded., The many Liquid consonants are plac'd so Artfully, that they give a pleasing sound to the Words. **1733** POPE *Hor. Sat.* II. i. 31 Lull with Amelia's liquid name the Nine. **1752** HUME *Ess.* xxi. Wks. 1854 III. 229 The Italian is the most liquid, smooth, and effeminate language that can possibly be imagined. **1797** MRS. RADCLIFFE *Italian* xi. (1824) 586 The liquid cadence, as it trembled and sank away, seemed to tell the dejection of no vulgar feelings. **1847** TENNYSON *Princess* II. 404 Make liquid treble of that bassoon my throat. **1855** H. SPENCER *Princ. Psychol.* (1872) I. II. i. 149 Tones which are alike in pitch.. are distinguishable by their..ringing or their liquid character. **1879** J. BURROUGHS *Locusts & W. Honey* (1884) 86 The liquid and gurgling notes of the bobolink. **1888** SWEET *Eng. Sounds* §21 But those 'vowellike' or 'liquid' voiced consonants which are unaccompanied by buzz are often also syllabic.

†**4. a.** Of proofs, exposition, etc.: Clear, evident, manifest. *Obs.*

1610 DONNE *Pseudo-martyr* 17 With vs it is euident and liquid enough. *a* **1619** FOTHERBY *Atheom.* II. iii. §3. (1622) 219 But vnto those that be learned, it is cleare enough and liquid. **1620** WOTTON in *Reliq.* (1672) 519 You had suspended your Judgement till more liquid proofs. *a* **1657** R. LOVEDAY *Lett.* cxxx. (1659) 236 My most liquid discoveries, as I thought, of undoubted truths, have so oft been confuted. **1657** W. MORICE *Coena quasi Κοινὴ* xxii. 222 S. Augustine impressed himself especially to fight against [the Donatists], as is liquid through the whole torrent of his writings. **1685** H. MORE *Paralip. Prophet.* 462 This is the clear and liquid reason why [etc.]. **1726** AYLIFFE *Parergon* [305], I have robbed my self of liquid Proof by my own Act.

b. Of an account or a debt: Undisputed. Now only in *Scots Law*, said of a debt that has been ascertained and constituted against the debtor, either by a written obligation, or by the decree of a court.

1660 HOWELL *Dict.* s.v., To make accounts liquid, or cleer, *liquider, arrester les comptes.* **1681** RYCAUT tr. *Gracian's Critick* To Rdr., A Debt of One hundred thousand Pieces of Eight, which his Catholic Majesty owed unto my Father: The Demand was unquestionable, for the Account was liquid, and clearly stated by the Council of the Exchequer. **1682** SCARLETT *Exchanges* 120 To Discount..is good and sufficient payment, if it be of a due and liqued Debt. **1726** AYLIFFE *Parergon* 135 Nor does it admit of any delay tho' the Debt be entirely Liquid. **1731** Liquid sum [see LIQUIDATION 1]. **1754** ERSKINE *Princ. Sc. Law* (1809) 253 Inhibition may proceed..upon a liquid obligation. **1884** SIR R. COLLIER in *Law Times Rep.* LI. 581/2 A claim by way of compensation is admissible when it is for a demand which is termed liquid.

5. Not fixed or stable. Of movement: Facile, unconstrained.

1835 I. TAYLOR *Spir. Despot.* iv. 165 The liquid or convertible state in which we find the designations of office in the New Testament. **1867** DEUTSCH *Rem.* (1874) 13 The liquid nature, so to speak, of its technical terms. They mean anything and everything. **1877** PAUER *Pianoforte Playing* 16 The task of rendering the five fingers of each hand fluent, or, as we may say, liquid.

6. Of assets, securities, etc.: Capable of being promptly converted into cash.

1879 *Daily News* 26 May, Liquid Securities, or in other words, those easily convertible into cash when necessity arises. **1884** *Pall Mall G.* 5 May 7/2 A company with sufficient capital to take over the bank's liquid assets. **1930** J. M. KEYNES *Treat. Money* II. xxv. 67 On the other hand, bills and call loans are more 'liquid' than investments. **1962** C. H. KREPS *Money* I. i. 12 The assets categorized as near money are those that are highly liquid; that is, they are convertible into money quickly, easily, and without loss. **1974** *Times* 12 Nov. 14/4 These small engineering businesses..are now..low on liquid assets.

7. *Comb.*: **liquid air**, air in a liquid state; **liquid compass**, a form of magnetic compass used in ships in which the card and needle are mainly supported by floating in a bowl filled with liquid; **liquid controller** *Electr.* = *liquid rheostat*; **liquid crystal** *Physical Chem.* [tr. G. *flüssiger krystall* (O. Lehmann 1890, in *Ann. d. Physik und Chem.* XL. 404)], a turbid liquid that exhibits double refraction (indicative of internal anisotropy and hence some degree of ordering in its structure, as in an ordinary crystal) and exists as a distinct state of certain pure substances between the melting point and some higher temperature, at which it becomes an ordinary liquid; **liquid crystal display**, a visual display, esp. of segmented numbers or letters, in which liquid crystals are made visible by temporarily modifying their birefringence by electrical or other means and hence the way they reflect and scatter ambient light; abbrev. *LCD* s.v. L 7; **liquid extract** (occas. as one word) *Pharm.* = *fluid extract* s.v. FLUID *a.* 1 a; **liquid fire**, any very 'fiery' (in taste) or highly combustible liquid, now *esp.* one that can be sent as a burning jet in warfare; **liquid fuel**, fuel that is a liquid, now esp. as used in rocketry; so **liquid-fuelled** *a.*; **liquid glue**, glue that keeps a liquid form till applied; **liquid lunch** *colloq.*, a midday meal at which drink rather than food is consumed; **liquid manure** *Hort.*, a water extract of manure used as a fertilizer; **liquid oxygen**, oxygen in a liquid state; **liquid paraffin** *Pharm.*, an almost tasteless and odourless oily liquid that consists of hydrocarbons obtained from petroleum and is used as a laxative and in dressings; **liquid petrolatum** *N. Amer.* = *liquid paraffin*; **liquid rheostat** *Electr.*, a rheostat which uses an electrolyte solution as the resistive element; **liquid soap**, soap in liquid form; **liquid-solid** *a.* (see quot.); **liquid starter**, a liquid rheostat used as a starter of an electric motor.

1899 *McClure's Mag.* XII. 397 (*heading*) *Liquid air. A new substance that promises to do the work of coal and ice and gunpowder, at next to no cost. *Ibid.* 399/1 A liquid-air engine, if powerful enough, will compress the air and produce the cold in my liquefying machine exactly as well as a steam engine. **1901** *Daily Colonist* (Victoria, B.C.) 6 Oct. 3/4 The most sensational thing in the scientific world today is liquid air. **1925** E. F. NORTON *Fight for Everest, 1924* 91 Waiting for us with hot soup in a liquid-air flask. **1946** *Nature* 20 July 105/1 A laboratory liquid-air plant utilizing Freon-12 as a pre-cooling fluid has been designed and is now being constructed. **1865** *Rep. Brit. Assoc. Adv. Sci. 1864* 14 The distinctive peculiarities of the *liquid compass are an air-tight metallic case, within which is placed the magnetic needle, and of such size and weight as to be of very nearly the same specific gravity as the liquid in which it is intended to float. **1959** E. C. GOLDSWORTHY *Seamanship & Navigation* iii. 41 This liquid compass is preferred to the dry-card compass where there is much vibration, as the liquid damps the oscillations of the card caused by the movements of the vessel. **1916** C. C. GARRARD *Electr. Switch & Controlling Gear* v. 357 The rating of the *liquid controller is, therefore, based upon the maximum horse-power dissipated. **1957** W. J. JOHN *Mod. Electr. Engin.* II. iii. 58 (*caption*) A liquid controller of the type shown here provides smooth control from normal down to crawling speed. **1891** *Jrnl. Chem. Soc.* LX. I. 250 *Liquid crystals, when heated between cover glasses slightly above the point where they pass into ordinary liquids, retain on cooling the original direction of their optical axes. **1938** *Ann. Reg. 1937* 352 Tobacco mosaic virus is a nucleoprotein of special character, existing as mesomorphic fibres in the cell sap and spontaneously forming liquid crystals of gigantic cell-size when isolated. **1962** *Times* 30 Apr. 7/1 When detergents are mixed with a limited amount of water, several distinct 'mesomorphic' phases may be formed. These phases are also known as 'liquid crystals' because some of their properties are akin to those of a solid while others are characteristic of a liquid. **1972** *Physics Bull.* May 279/1 These fascinating compounds can no longer be regarded as freaks of nature, for out of every two hundred organic compounds at least one may be a liquid crystal. **1968** *Electronics World* Nov. 58/3 Compared with whiteness of bond paper, the *liquid-crystal displays have an efficiency of 50 to 60 percent. **1973** *Electronics* 16 Aug. 33/1 Field-effect liquid-crystal displays may give the electronic watch a big boost. **1983** *Listener* 14 July 38/2 The

Japanese are already working on flat-screen television sets which use a liquid crystal display on a matrix of light-emitting diodes. **1985** *Which Computer?* Apr. 35/1 It has the advantage of being flat, like liquid crystal displays, but is also clear and crisp. **1864** *Brit. Pharmacopœia* 219 *(heading)* *Liquid extract of Bael. **1930** J. W. COOPER *Pharmacy* xiii. 115, 1,000 grm. of couch grass is used to produce 1,000 mil. of liquid extract. **1935** Liquidextract [see FLUID *a.* and *sb.* A. 1 a]. **1968** *Biol. Abstr.* XLIX. 1161/1 This liquid extract [from the bark of *Oroxylon indicum*] lowered the vascular permeability of rats sensitized with egg protein. **1604** SHAKS. *Oth.* v. ii. 280 Whip me ye Diuels..Wash me in steepe-downe gulfes of *Liquid fire. **1667** MILTON *P.L.* I. 229 If it were Land that ever burn'd With solid, as the Lake with liquid fire. **1815** J. SMITH *Panorama Sci. & Art* II. 579 It is in this way that the various kinds of cordial waters are prepared... The term liquid-fire has not unaptly been given them. **1838** E. EDEN *Let.* 28 Nov. in *Up Country* (1866) I. xxvi. 282 Runjeet produced some of his wine, a sort of liquid fire. **1862** *Temple Bar* July 512 Ordinary phosphorus is readily soluble in bisulphide of carbon: when thus in solution constituting the liquid denominated by Captains Disney and Norton 'liquid fire'. **1915** *Illustr. London News* 13 Mar. 321 The enemy attacking a trench into which they had sent liquid fire. **1889** GROVES & THORP *Chem. Technol.* I. 293 *(caption)* *Liquid fuel. **1912** W. S. CHURCHILL *Let.* 11 June in *World Crisis 1911–14* vi. 32 This liquid fuel problem has got to be solved. **1913** *Chem. Abstr.* VII. 3827 One of the principal differences between solid and liquid fuels is in the proportion of C combined with H. **1920** *Conquest* Nov. 47/2 In the near future liquid fuel will have to be 'rationed' again. **1935** *Jrnl. R. Aeronaut. Soc.* XXXIX. 507 Germany consumes two million tons of liquid fuel per year. **1946** *Jrnl. Brit. Interplanetary Soc.* VI. I. 2 At first the research was conducted with powder rockets, but after a few years a change was made to liquid fuel. This was at first tried out on a test bench, and then, in July, 1929, what is claimed to be the first liquid-fuel rocket to take-off was launched near Worcester—but it exploded at 900 feet. **1963** BIRD & HUTTON-STOTT *Veteran Motor Car* 75 Daimler's 'high-speed' liquid-fuel engine. **1966** *Electronics* 17 Oct. 35 For the next decade, at least, liquid fuel will propel United States astronauts into space. **1969** *Times* 3 June (Suppl.) p. ii/4 Goddard launched on March 16, 1926, the world's first liquid fuel rocket. **1960** *Times* 18 Oct. 13/6 The Minuteman cannot carry as large a warhead as the *liquid-fuelled i.c.b.m.s. **1967** *Technology Week* 20 Feb. 3/2 The hardened, storable liquid-fueled *Titan* carries the largest U.S. missile warhead and can also reach targets beyond the range of the current *Minuteman I.* **1875** E. SPON *Workshop Receipts* 41/1 *Liquid glue... Soft water, 1 quart; best pale glue, 2 lbs.; [etc.]. **1927** KNIGHT & WULPI *Veneers & Plywood* xxv. 276 Probably the general public..thinks of liquid glues, whenever glue is mentioned, but such preparations are in no way typical of manufacturing materials or procedures. **1966** *McGraw-Hill Encycl. Sci. & Technol.* VI. 219/2 Liquid glue is commonly made from fish collagen because this has little tendency to gel, but it can also be made from animal glue by treatment with acid or certain salts to inhibit gelation. **1970** G. F. NEWMAN *Sir, You Bastard* ii. 65 The caretaker, aroused from his post-*liquid-lunch slumber, confirmed that the couple had parted. **1972** B. EVERITT *Cold Front* vii. 55 He..refused all offers of liquid lunches and bore me off ..for a great deal of solid pasta. **1837** C. W. JOHNSON *(title)* On *liquid manures. **1842** J. C. LOUDON *Suburban Horticulturist* iii. 59 Arrangements should be made for collecting all the liquid manure into two adjoining tanks. **1869** S. R. HOLE *Bk. about Roses* vi. 83 The rich extract, full of carbonate of ammonia..may be used..as liquid manure in the Rosary. **1911** O. ONIONS *Widdershins* 247 The hares and foxes were down four days ago, and the liquid-manure pumps like a snow man. **1914** J. LONDON *Let.* 21 Sept. (1966) 429, I have a fairly decent brood-barn, with liquid-manure tank attached. **1973** R. GENDERS *Epicure's Garden* II. 167 An occasional application of liquid manure will also prove beneficial. **1878** *Jrnl. Chem. Soc.* XXXIV. 10 A jet of *liquid oxygen escaping from the tube when the pressure was taken off. **1885** [see REFRIGERANT *sb.* 3]. **1919** *Chem. Abstr.* 791 Spontaneous explosion of the charcoal in liquid-oxygen containers. **1954** *Economist* 11 Sept. 12/1 Rocket motors do not need atmospheric oxygen, although they frequently carry liquid oxygen, and rocket power is, unlike jet power, effective in outer space. **1956** *Spaceflight* Oct. 5/1 Propellants which are in common use to-day (e.g. liquid oxygen and petrol) yield exhaust velocities of the order of 2½ km./sec. **1884** *Jrnl. Chem. Soc.* XLVI. 1073 The '*liquid paraffin' of the German Pharmacopœia, is an oily liquid consisting of a mixture of hydrocarbons of the methane series. **1943** J. B. PRIESTLEY *Daylight on Saturday* ii. 6 She was a dark girl with a long sad nose, and dosed herself with liquid paraffin. **1962** *Which?* Jan. 26/2 Liquid paraffin is the only common lubricant laxative. **1905** *Pharmacopœia U.S.* 336 *Liquid Petrolatum, a mixture of hydrocarbons, chiefly of the methane series, obtained by distilling off most of the lighter and more volatile portions from petroleum, and purifying the liquid residue. **1926** *Daily Colonist* (Victoria, B.C.) 20 Jan. 7/3 (Advt.), Liquid petrolatum, heavy, special at 53¢. **1951** A. GROLLMAN *Pharmacol. & Therapeutics* xix. 386 Liquid petrolatum is also available in the form of a flavored emulsion. **1905** P. DAWSON in M. Maclean *Mod. Electr. Pract.* VI. v. iv. 214 Amongst the advantages claimed for *liquid rheostats may be mentioned the gradual variation of the resistance, their compactness and cheap first cost, and the absence of damage from sparking when the current is interrupted. **1957** W. J. JOHN *Mod. Electr. Engin.* II. iii. 59/1 A common method of providing resistance is by means of a liquid rheostat, consisting of a tank of electrolyte containing two electrodes, one fixed and one movable. **1600** *Liquid sope [s.v. SOAP *sb.* 2]. **1907** *Yesterday's Shopping* (1969) 536/3 Moline, a liquid soap, delicately perfumed for the toilet. **1920** A. KEANE tr. *Deite's Man. Toilet Soap-Making* (ed. 2) 236 The liquid soaps are mostly solutions of potash soaps in glycerine, sugar, or alkali and strong alcohol solutions. **1966** J. S. COX *Illustr. Dict. Hairdressing* 90/2 *Liquid soap shampoo.* The base is usually green soft soap and sometimes in addition either cocoanut oil, olive oil or eucalyptus oil. **1862** H. SPENCER *First Princ.* II. xiii. §100 (1875) 292 A *liquid-solid aggregate, or, as we commonly call it, a plastic aggregate, will admit of internal redistribution with comparative facility. **1907** G. W. O. HOWE tr. *Thomälen's Text-bk. Electr. Engin.* 453/1 (Index), *Liquid starter. **1916** C. C. GARRARD *Electr. Switch & Controlling Gear* v. 353 The liquid starter, in which a solution of caustic soda or washing soda replaces the resistance wire or grids as used in the ordinary form of starter, is the most rugged of all forms of starting gear. **1932** E. MOLLOY *Pract. Electr. Engin.* IV. 1319/2 Liquid starters are best suited for medium and large-size motors which require to be started infrequently.

B. *sb.*

1. a. A liquid substance (see A. 1). In *pl.* often = *liquid food.*

Liquids and *gases* are classed together as *fluids*: see FLUID.

1708 J. PHILIPS *Cyder* I. 31 Be it thy Choice..To sit beneath her leafy Canopy, Quaffing rich Liquids. **1725** WATTS *Logic* I. vi. §4 Juice includes both substance and liquid. **1773–83** HOOLE *Orl. Fur.* XXII. 88 E'er his lips essay'd The moistening liquid. **1805** *Med. Jrnl.* XIV. 125 He refused to swallow liquids. **1839** R. S. ROBINSON *Naut. Steam Eng.* 161 Steam when in contact with the liquid from which it is formed. **1842** A. COMBE *Physiol. Digestion* (ed. 4) 36 Thirst, or a desire for liquids. **1875** FORTNUM *Majolica* vi. 58 The liquid of the bath must be thin. **1879** THOMSON & TAIT *Nat. Phil.* I. I. §320 We shall designate a mass which is absolutely incompressible, and absolutely devoid of resistance to change of shape, by the simple appellation of a liquid. **1895** ZANGWILL *Master* II. iii. 157 Popping corks and gurgling liquids.

b. *Dutch liquid*: see DUTCH *a.* 3 b.

2. *Phonetics.* A name applied to the sounds denoted by the letters *l, m, n, r,* or (by some writers) only to those denoted by *l* and *r.*

The name (L. *liquidæ*, sc. *litteræ*) is a literal translation of the Gr. ὑγρά (sc. στοιχεῖα) applied to λ, μ, ν, ρ, on account of their flowing and easy sound as compared with other consonants, or perh. as having an indeterminate or unstable character between consonant and vowel (cf. the application of ὑγρός to a vowel of variable quantity; also the term ἡμίφωνα 'semi-vowels', applied to the 'liquids' and σ). A somewhat analogous term is the F. *mouillé* lit. 'wet', used to denote the palatalized pronunciation of *l* and some other consonants.

1530 PALSGR. Introd. 23 Theyr consonantes be devyded in to mutes & liquides or semivocalles. **1611** FLORIO, *Liquide*, liquids, as L. M. N. R. *a* **1637** B. JONSON *Eng. Gram.* (1640) 47 It [L] melteth in the sounding, and is therefore called a liquid, the tongue striking the root of the palate gently. **1710** ADDISON *Tatler* No. 163 ⁋7 There is scarce a Consonant in it; I took care to make it run upon Liquids. **1751** JOHNSON *Rambler* No. 88 ⁋3 By tempering the mute consonants with liquids and semi-vowels. **1817** BYRON *Beppo* xliv, With syllables which breathe of the sweet South, And gentle liquids gliding all so pat in.

3. *attrib.* and *Comb.*, as ***liquid-cooled, -filled*** adjs.; ***liquid-cooling***; **liquid-drop**, used *attrib.* in *Physics* to denote a theoretical model in which an explanation of the properties and behaviour of the atomic nucleus is sought by likening it to a droplet of liquid, as regards the forces between its constituents; **liquid-liquid** *a.*, pertaining to or involving two different liquids, or liquids in two different ways; **† liquid vessel**, receptacles for liquids.

1931 *Jrnl. R. Aeronaut. Soc.* XXXV. 180 The developments to be described are..applicable to all water or *liquid-cooled engines. **1967** *Jane's Surface Skimmer Systems 1967–68* 25/1 The power plant..comprises a 240 hp Rolls-Royce LV-8 liquid-cooled eight-cylinder engine. **1933** J. D. FRIER *Aero Engines* I. vii. 94 A great advantage of *liquid cooling is that..the engine temperature is limited to the boiling-point of the liquid employed. **1960** *McGraw-Hill Encycl. Sci. & Technol.* IV. 604/2 In liquid cooling, the engine and radiator may be separated and each placed in the optimum location. [**1939** MEITNER & FRISCH in *Nature* 11 Feb. 239/1 On account of their close packing and strong energy exchange, the particles in a heavy nucleus would be expected to move in a collective way which has some resemblance to the movement of a liquid drop.] **1939** BOHR & WHEELER in *Physical Rev.* LVI. 426 On the basis of the *liquid drop model of atomic nuclei, an account is given of the mechanism of nuclear fission. **1955** R. D. EVANS *Atomic Nucleus* xi. 365 The liquid-drop model is the antithesis of the independent-particle models. The interactions between nucleons are assumed to be strong instead of weak. **1970** D. F. JACKSON *Nucl. Reactions* ii. 17 The static liquid drop model of the nucleus..was the first successful nuclear model and was used to describe the bulk properties of nuclei such as nuclear masses and binding energies. **1960** E. L. DELMAR-MORGAN *Cruising Yacht Equipment & Navigation* ii. 33 The *liquid-filled 'dead-beat' instrument [*sc.* compass] has now taken its place. **1967** KARCH & BUBER *Offset Processes* iv. 128 Modification of copy is effected simply by liquid-filled cylindrical lenses or prisms in front of the copy or film. **1940** GLASSTONE *Text-bk. Physical Chem.* x. 725 *(heading)* Distribution in *liquid-liquid systems. **1951, 1952** [see *gas-liquid* adj. (GAS *sb.*[1] 7)]. **1958** *Chambers's Techn. Dict.* 991/1 *Liquid-liquid extraction*, process whereby two non-mixing liquids are brought together for an exchange of substances dissolved in them. **1968** COULSON & RICHARDSON *Chem. Engin.* (ed. 2) II. xii. 486 The separation of the components of a liquid mixture with a solvent in which one or more of the desired components is preferentially soluble is known as liquid-liquid extraction. This process has been..very extensively applied to the separation of hydrocarbons in the petroleum industry. **1649** *New Haven Col. Rec.* (1857) I. 458 The wormes would eat it [timber] so as it would be vnserviceable for making of *liquid vessell.

Hence **'liquidless** *a.*, without liquid.

1826 *Blackw. Mag.* XX. 397 Coleridge's patent inkstand stood liquidless as a sand-bottle.

liquidambar (lɪkwɪˈdæmbə(r)). Also **liquid amber.** [a. mod.L. *liquidambar* (in Renou 1615), app. irreg. f. L. *liquid-us* LIQUID + med.L. *ambar* AMBER.]

1. A resinous gum which exudes from the bark of the tree *Liquidambar styraciflua.* Called also *copalm balsam.*

1598 FLORIO, *Liquidambro*, liquid amber. **1616** BULLOKAR, *Liquid Amber.* A sweete Rosin brought from the West Indies, comfortable to the braine. **1657** TOMLINSON *Renou's Disp.* IV. II. ix. 673 Liquid Amber is a certain oleous Rosine..called from its suaveolence, Liquid Amber, or Oyl of Amber [*orig.* Liquidambar dictum,..quasi ambarum liquidum]. **1727–41** CHAMBERS *Cycl.* s.v. *Amber*, Liquid Amber, is a kind of native balsam, or resin, like turpentine; of a pleasant smell, somewhat like ambergris.

2. *Bot.* A genus of trees, N.O. *Hamamelideæ*, consisting of two species, *L. orientalis* of Asia Minor (which yields the balsam known as liquid storax), and *L. styraciflua*, the Sweet-gum Tree of N. America; a tree of this genus.

1843 PRESCOTT *Mexico* (1854) 2 The rich foliage of the liquid-amber tree. **1846** W. D. COOLEY *Maritime & Inl. Discov.* III. v. xviii. 273 The eastern slope of the Cordilleras of Mexico, covered with thick forests of liquidambar. **1881** *Gard. Chron.* No. 412. 652 Some young Liquidambars. **1884** E. EGGLESTON in *Century Mag.* Jan. 446/2 Carts with truck wheels sawed from the liquid-amber or sweet-gum tree.

liquidate (ˈlɪkwɪdeɪt), *ppl. a. Law. rare.* Also 7 *Sc.* liquidat. [ad. late L. *liquidāt-us*, pa. pple. of *liquidāre*, f. *liquidus* liquid, clear.] Ascertained and fixed in amount. (Cf. LIQUID *a.* 4 b.)

1609 SKENE *Reg. Maj.* 77 The Judge sal take ane pledge fra the defender..to pay the debt, with the skaiths taxat and liquidat in the persewers clame, to the persewer, within space of fiftene dayes. **1868** *Act 31 & 32 Vict.* c. 101 Sched. (FF) No. 1 With a Fifth Part more of the Interest due at each Term of liquidate Penalty.

liquidate (ˈlɪkwɪdeɪt), *v.* Also 7 liquidat. [f. late L. *liquidāt-*, ppl. stem of *liquidāre*, f. *liquidus* LIQUID. Cf. F. *liquider*, Sp. *liquidar*, It. *liquidare* (in sense 4).]

†1. a. *trans.* To make clear or plain (something obscure or confused); to render unambiguous; to settle (differences, disputes). *Obs.*

a **1670** HACKET *Abp. Williams* I. (1692) 19 There he discours'd with that depth of Learning, yet liquidating that depth with such facility of opening it. **1732** *Hist. Litteraria* III. 382 He liquidates many Points. **1765** H. WALPOLE *Vertue's Anecd. Paint.* I. ii. 43 A senseless jumble, soon liquidated by a more egregious act of folly. **1765** —— *Otranto* iii. (1798) 49 Ere we liquidate our differences by the sword. **1779–81** JOHNSON *L.P. Addison* Wks. III. 58 There were these words, 'Britons, arise!'..Addison was frighted, lest he should be thought a promoter of insurrection, and the line was liquidated to 'Britons, attend.' **1780** BENTHAM *Princ. Legisl.* iii. §10 In what other respects our ideas of them [pains and pleasures] may be liquidated will be considered in another place.

b. To clear away, resolve (objections). *rare.*

1620 SIR R. NAUNTON in *Fortesc. Papers* 114 He may liquidat all scruples when he shall come to the Spanish Court. **1865** F. H. LAING in *Ess. Relig. & Lit.* Ser. I. (1865) 202 The same principle of a long preparation liquidates many other objections of the same character.

†2. To determine and apportion by agreement or by litigation; to reduce to order, set out clearly (accounts). *Obs.*

c **1575** *Balfour's Practicks* (1754) 41 Ane Baron, in his awin court, may liquidate the prices of his fermis, auchtand to him be his tenentis. **1622** MABBE tr. *Aleman's Guzman d'Alf.* I. 22 [He] could cleare you any account, could liquidate and divide it to an haire. **1739** CIBBER *Apol.* (1756) II. 45 This pension was to be liquidated into an equal share with us. **1755** *Connect. Col. Rec.* (1856) X. 366 A committee with full power..to examine, liquidate, adjust, settle, and give needful orders for the payment of the several accounts. **1758** J. BLAKE *Plan Mar. Syst.* 41 The commander..will be able to liquidate the amount of his nett wages. **1795** WYTHE *Decis. Virginia* 14 An account of goods not delivered or accepted as a payment nor liquidated between the parties ought not to be accepted as a payment in paper. **1798** BAY *Amer. Law Rep.* (1809) I. 114 Agreed to pay the debt on its being liquidated.

fig. **1759** CHESTERF. *Let. to Son* 27 Feb. (1892) III. 1248 If our epistolary accounts were fairly liquidated, I believe you would be brought in considerably debtor.

3. To clear off, pay (a debt). Also *absol.* in *U.S. slang.*

1755 JOHNSON, *Liquidate*, to clear away; to lessen debts. **1785** LD. MALMESBURY *Diaries & Corr.* II. 122 The King desired the Prince of Wales to send in an Exact Statement of his debts, giving him to understand he would liquidate them. **1786** R. KING in *Life & Corr.* (1894) I. 6 As the debt arose during the circulation of paper, it may probably be more easily liquidated by the scale than in any other way. **1823** LINGARD *Hist. Eng.* VI. 110 Charles..had not wherewith to liquidate the arrears of his victorious army in Italy. **1834** HT. MARTINEAU *Moral* IV. 135 No effort should be spared to liquidate the National Debt. **1835** HALIBURTON *Clockm.* Ser. I. xviii, When I liquidate for my dinner, I like to get about the best that's goin. **1849** GROTE *Hist. Greece* II. lxxi. (1862) VI. 333 The pay which he had offered was never liquidated. **1868** ROGERS *Pol. Econ.* iv. (1876) 6 In the vast majority of instances no money is used to liquidate debts on either side.

4. *Law* and *Comm.* **a.** *trans.* To ascertain and set out clearly the liabilities of (a company or firm) and to arrange the apportioning of the assets; to 'wind up'. **b.** *intr.* To go into liquidation.

1870 *Standard* 16 Nov., A proposal to liquidate by arrangement was resolved upon by the creditors. **1883** *Manch. Exam.* 27 Nov. 4/7 It has been decided to liquidate the Exchange Bank. **1884** *Law Times* 13 Dec. 119/1 The debtor liquidated and a trustee was appointed.

5. a. *trans.* To liquefy, melt. *rare.*

1656 Blount *Glossogr.*, *Liquidate*, to make moist, to clear. **1862** *Jrnl. Soc. Arts* X. 324/2 The heat of the ship's hold being sufficient to partially liquidate its [*sc.* rubber] substance.

b. *fig.* To dissipate, waste.

1702 De Foe *Reform. Manners* Misc. 91 These [*sc.* drunkards] liquidate their Wealth, and covet to be poor.

6. To make (a sound) less harsh or grating.

In some mod. Dicts.

7. [after Russ. *likvidírovat'* to liquidate, wind up.] To put an end to, abolish; to stamp out, wipe out; to kill.

1924 *Yale Rev.* XIII. 477 In this way the 'Labor Opposition', the 'Workers *Pravda*', and a few other recalcitrant groups were all 'liquidated'. **1926** C. Sheridan *Turkish Kaleidoscope* xvi. 125 The evening paper, *L'Akcham*, came out with large headlines: 'How to Liquidate a Strike'. **1930** *Economist* 1 Nov. (Russ. Suppl.) 2/2 Only in 1929, when the growth of the Socialist section of agriculture was enabling the State to become independent of the supplies of the Kulaks, could the Government begin to 'liquidate' them. **1939** V. A. Demant *Relig. Prospect* iv. 90 The Trotskyists..are 'liquidated' as being insufficiently dialectical to see that the policy of the Russian State at any moment has absolute finality. **1943** C. S. Lewis *Abolition of Man* iii. 37 Once we killed bad men: now we liquidate unsocial elements. **1957** Partridge *English gone Wrong* ii. 31 *Liquidate*, therefore, is an erudite synonym of 'to wind up', hence, in its euphemistic transferred sense, it means 'to eradicate in a thoroughly ruthless manner', 'to destroy, especially by mass murder'. **1970** *Nature* 26 Dec. 1248/2 All existing sources of industrial pollution are to be 'liquidated'. **1971** *Sunday Times* 13 June 12/6 When the army units fanned out in Dacca on the evening of March 25..many of them carried lists of people to be liquidated.

Hence **'liquidated** *ppl. a.*, **'liquidating** *vbl. sb.* and *ppl. a.*

1727 Bailey vol. II, *Liquidated*, made moist or clear; also spoken of Bills made current or payable; pay'd off, cleared. **1749** *Connect. Col. Rec.* (1876) IX. 453 That he press forward the liquidating, settling and obtaining final payment for the accounts. **1798** Bay *Amer. Law Rep.* (1809) I. 16 Liquidated accounts. **1848** Arnould *Mar. Insur.* I. iv. (1866) I. 181 Debts in the legal sense, that is, liquidated and ascertained amounts. **1891** *Daily News* 15 Jan. 2/2 A substantial surplus will remain for division among the partners of the liquidated firm. **1895** *Ibid.* 8 May 8/7 Wheat ..declined under the combined control of lower cables, further rains in the West, and active liquidating. **1899** *Ibid.* 2 Feb. 4/7 Liquidating or abortive companies. **1931** *Economist* 20 June 1331/1 The market capitalisation of the common shares of these concerns was equal to only 74 per cent. of the 'liquidating value' of the assets behind them. **1964** *Ann. Reg. 1963* 103 It provided that..the permanent heads of the three territorial Treasuries would constitute a liquidating agency to wind up the affairs of the Federation. **1975** [see liquidator c].

liquidation (lɪkwɪˈdeɪʃən). [n. of action f. late L. *liquidāre* to liquidate. Cf. F. *liquidation.*]

1. *Law.* The action or process of ascertaining and apportioning the amounts of a debt, etc.

c **1575** *Balfour's Practicks* (1754) 41 Liquidation of prices of fermis. **1731** Bailey vol. II, *Liquidation*, an ascertainment of some dubious or disputable sum; or of the respective pretensions which 2 persons may have to the same liquid or clear sum. **1737** *Ibid.*, *Liquidation* [in trade] the order and method which a trader endeavours to establish in his affairs.

2. a. The clearing off or settling (of a debt).

1786 R. King in *Life & Corr.* (1894) I. 6 How far a liquidation by the scale will be equitable or just, in your estimation, I cannot say. **1790** Burke *Fr. Rev.* Wks. V. 226 The national debt, for the liquidation of which there is the one exhaustless fund. **1804** Wellington in Gurw. *Desp.* III. 272 It shall be applied to the liquidation of his debt to the Company. **1850** Merivale *Rom. Emp.* (1865) I. ix. 382 His property was confiscated to the state in liquidation of the fine. **1879** Lubbock *Addr. Pol. & Educ.* vi. 127 The liquidation of Debt is a national duty.

b. *Chess.* The partial clearing of the board, by an exchange of pieces, to obtain an obviously winning position; simplification.

1965 Love & Hodgkins *Further Chess Ideas* xv. 124 Sometimes, too, under pressure of an enemy attack and with good end game prospects if ever one should be reached, wholesale exchanges are most welcome. This is called liquidation. **1965** W. H. Cozens tr. *Euwe & Kramer's Middle Game* II. x. 185 The problem of liquidation is to select the precise moment when pieces, or some particular piece, should be exchanged... Judicious liquidation involves steering a middle course between the one extreme of premature simplification and the other extreme of interminable 'wood shifting'. **1966** *New Statesman* 2 Dec. 854/3 True enough, White is a P up, but the Black heavy artillery is well placed. Yet, hey presto: a miraculous 'liquidation', and a won ending in a few moves.

3. a. The action or process of winding up the affairs of a company, etc.; the state or condition of being wound up; *esp.* in phr. ***to go into liquidation***. Also, the selling of certain assets in order to achieve greater liquidity. (See quot. 1965.)

1869 *Echo* 23 Mar., The..Company (limited) has passed into voluntary liquidation. **1873** *Daily News* 22 Sept. 3/2 The notifications..for the liquidation of ecclesiastical property in Rome number more than 60. **1874** Mrs. Riddell *Mortomley* II. viii. 99 If his own brother had gone into liquidation. **1879** *Daily News* 7 Jan. 5/5 A petition for liquidation in bankruptcy. **1880** *Ibid.* 28 Oct., The vast majority of defaulters have their affairs arranged in liquidation. **1909** *Westm. Gaz.* 2 Mar. 4/2 As many people ..think that the word 'liquidation' must necessarily be associated with bankruptcy.., I am asked to state officially that the liquidation of the old company is only one step in the course of reconstruction for the purpose of obtaining fresh capital. **1929** *Observer* 17 Nov. 4/2 The Rhodesian share market was in a depressed condition, owing to the liquidation taking place on American account. **1939** J. A. Schumpeter *Business Cycles* I. iv. 149 Abnormal liquidation destroys many things which could and would have survived without it. **1965** *McGraw-Hill Dict. Mod. Econ.* 299 *Liquidation*, the process of selling assets, such as inventories or securities in order to achieve a better cash position.

b. [f. liquidate *v.* 7.] The action or process of abolishing or eliminating; the doing away with or killing of unwanted persons.

1925 tr. *L. Trotzky's Whither England?* vi. 145 History is liquidating liberalism and preparing for the liquidation of pseudo-labor pacifism. **1932** *Week-end Rev.* 2 Jan. 24/1 The Russians..took starvation almost as a matter of course, just as they..take as a matter of course the liquidation of unfortunate individuals with contra-revolutionary idealogies. **1949** F. Maclean *Eastern Approaches* I. ii. 24 There was nothing new in the 'liquidation', as it was called, of public figures. For some years past numerous politicians and others had met with the same fate, variously branded as 'Trotskists' [*sic*], 'wreckers',..and so on. **1952** *Sat. Rev.* (U.S.) 20 Sept. 37/1 Liquidation..was extended..to persons in..the Party... The liquidation occurred during the purges (a revolting combination).

4. The action or fact of partaking of an alcoholic drink. *rare.*

1889 F. E. Gretton *Memory's Harkback* 311 As regards *liquidation*, champagne..is now almost as *vin ordinaire*. **1909** 'O. Henry' *Roads of Destiny* vii. 106 His desire for liquidation was expressed so heartily that I went with him to a café..where we had some vile vermouth and bitters.

liquidator (ˈlɪkwɪdeɪtə(r)). [f. liquidate *v.* + -or. Cf. F. *liquidateur.*] **a.** A person appointed to conduct the winding-up of a company.

1858 Ld. St. Leonards *Handy-Bk. Prop. Law* xxii. 170 All executors and administrators, liquidators under the Joint Stock Companies Act. **1870** *Daily News* 23 Apr., The official liquidator..had done all that he could to get in and administer the assets of the company. **1965** Seldon & Pennance *Everyman's Dict. Econ.* 260 The Official Receiver is appointed provisional liquidator, and his appointment may be confirmed or he may be replaced at the first meeting of the creditors. **1971** *Daily Tel.* 9 Feb. 15/5 The creditors' call for a provisional liquidator for Mineral Securities.. followed on intense activity..with leading Australian international financiers. **1971** *Times* 10 Dec. 8/6 The appointment of a provisional liquidator and special manager was essential in order to collect those balances and get the other assets in.

b. ***liquidators of vessels*** (U.S.): a class of officers of the New York custom-house.

1884 R. Wheatley in *Harper's Mag.* June 58/1.

c. A person who implements a policy of liquidation. Cf. liquidate *v.* 7.

1949 [see grave-digger 3]. **1963** *Listener* 24 Jan. 171/1 The psychotic actions of totalitarian liquidators. **1975** J. Gardner *Killer for Song* ii. 16 Special Security had employed him as an agent—a liquidating agent, designed, quite literally, to cut down security risks. They had even called him the Liquidator.

Hence **'liquidatorship**, the office of liquidator.

1869 *Daily News* 5 Nov., That..the official liquidator should be allowed to retire from the provisional liquidatorship.

liquidity (lɪˈkwɪdɪtɪ). [ad. L. *liquiditāt-em*, f. *liquidus* liquid *a.*: see -ity. Cf. F. *liquidité.*]

a. The quality or condition of being liquid.

1620 Venner *Via Recta* viii. 183 They..doe..by reason of their liquiditie, very fitly prepare the way for other meats. **1653** H. More *Conject. Cabbal.* (1713) 83 Air and Water, for their thinness and liquidity, are very like one another. **1758** Borlase *Nat. Hist. Cornwall* 82 Passing from a state of liquidity into a state of solidity. **1794** Kirwan *Elem. Min.* (ed. 2) I. 398 Lavas owe their liquidity to melted bitumen and sulphur. **1813–21** Bentham *Ontology* Wks. 1843 VIII. 200 Of such of them as are in a state of fluidity, liquidity and gaseosity included. **1860** Tyndall *Glac.* I. iii. 29 Heavy rain fell,..but it came from a region high above that of liquidity. **1871** Roscoe *Elem. Chem.* 40 This amount of heat which is necessary to keep the water in the liquid form..is..termed the heat of liquidity. **1881** G. Macdonald *Mary Marston* I. ii. 33 Eyes..with..more than a touch of hardness in the midst of their liquidity.

†**b.** Rarefied condition, subtlety. *Obs.*

1665 Glanvill *Scepsis Sci.* vi. 28 The spirits, for their liquidity, are more uncapable than the fluid Medium, which is the conveyer of Sounds, to persevere in the continued repetition of vocal Ayres.

c. Of sound: Clearness or purity of tone.

1817 Keats *Sleep & Poetry* 371 The wild Thrilling liquidity of dewy piping. **1819** P. Morris in *Blackw. Mag.* VI. 309 The mind wandering abroad rejoices in joining itself with..the soothing liquidity of rivers. **1821** *Examiner* 155/2 Sweet and indefinable liquidity of tone.

d. *Econ.* The interchangeability of assets and money; hence **liquidity preference**, the holding of assets in money or near-money in preference to securities or interest-bearing investments; **liquidity ratio**, that proportion of total assets which is held in liquid or cash form, esp. by a bank.

1923 R. G. Hawtrey *Currency & Credit* (ed. 2) v. 83 The liquidity of the Bank of England is secured by its power of printing notes, and the interchangeability of its deposits with cash is absolute. **1925** G. G. Munn *Bank Credit* i. 9 Gold is the ultimate in liquidity, the ultimate intermediate of exchange, and is *ipso facto* irredeemable. **1936** J. M. Keynes *Gen. Theory Employment* xiii. 168 Liquidity-preference is a potentiality or functional tendency, which fixes the quantity of money which the public will hold when the rate of interest is given. *Ibid.* xvii. 241 Money itself rapidly loses the attribute of 'liquidity' if its future supply is expected to undergo sharp changes. **1940** *Economist* 27 Jan. 152/1 The attainment of a more than adequate liquidity ratio is perhaps the main feature..over the past year. **1940** G. Crowther *Outl. Money* ii. 76 The more highly developed banking systems are more prone to suffer from such a 'liquidity preference' than the less developed countries. **1958** *Economist* 26 July 281/2 The real spark-plug of expansion—improved international liquidity—cannot be discussed in the Commonwealth context alone. **1961** *Ann. Reg. 1960* 488 The 'liquidity ratio' is the proportion of 'liquid assets', i.e. cash, short money and bills, to gross deposits. **1962** C. H. Kreps *Money* I. i. 12 One view of the fundamental nature of interest regards interest as compensation for loss of liquidity. *Ibid.*, Using this liquidity-preference approach, we may say that wealth held in absolutely liquid form—in the form of money, that is—yields its owner no income. **1969** *Times* 5 May (Suppl.) p. iv/3 The market would lose its liquidity... As liquidity declined.., public confidence would lessen considerably. **1972** *Accountant* 23 Mar. 385/1 It was necessary to increase liquidity during the year to finance the continuing substantial capital programme.

liquidize (ˈlɪkwɪdaɪz), *v.* [f. liquid *a.* + -ize.] **a.** *trans.* To make liquid, in various senses. Also *intr.*, to become liquid.

1837 *New Monthly Mag.* L. 72 The coffee-jug, which he at times applied to his lips, seemed to liquidize his imagination. **1840** *Ibid.* LIX. 204 It should be liquidized in a silver saucepan. **1880** *Libr. Univ. Knowl.* (N.Y.) X. 696 This also liquidizes..all broad vowels, when a corresponding termination has dropped. **1887** Mary Linskill *In Exchange for a Soul* III. lv. 113 The bells were ringing softly, the softer for the nearness of the water, which seems always to 'liquidise' the sound. **1969** *Sunday Times* (Colour Suppl.) 9 Feb. 13/2 The lettuce liquidising in the vegetable compartment.

b. [f. liquidizer.] To purée, emulsify, or blend in a liquidizer. Hence **'liquidizing** *ppl. a.* and *vbl. sb.*

1959 *Which?* June 49/1 It was satisfactory in its mixing and liquidizing. **1966** *Punch* 2 Nov. 676/3 A very nice Melde dish is made by heating the vivid green..liquidised leaves with cheese to serve on toast as 'Anglo-Saxon Rarebit'. **1972** S. Atterbury *Waste Not—Want Not* ii. 53 After liquidising, pour the soup into a saucepan. *Ibid.* 54 Do not add too much liquid before the pods are liquidised or the subtle flavour might be swamped. **1972** Beale & Johnston *Mixer & Blender Cookery* xxi. 132 Liquidize ½ or 1 banana and add to thick custard. **1972** *Garde ta Foie!: Cambridge Cookery Bk. for Shelter* (Cambridge Shelter Group) 7 Stew gently with lid on until soft. Sieve or liquidise. **1973** *Daily Tel.* 27 Jan. 1/2 After his thirst and hunger strike ended, MacStiofain was given soups, tea and liquidised vegetables.

liquidizer (ˈlɪkwɪdaɪzə(r)). [f. liquidiz(e *v.* + -er[1].] A machine used in the preparation of food, to make purées, emulsify, etc. Also *attrib.*, as ***liquidizer attachment***.

1950 *Consumers' Res. Bull.* (U.S.) Feb. 9 (*heading*) 'Liquefiers', 'liquidizers', or 'blenders'. **1958** *Observer* 24 Aug. 7/5 The most usual 'extras' are mincers, juice squeezers, and liquidisers—the last consisting of whirling blades inside a glass goblet, to make purées, soups, drinks, etc. **1962** *Which?* May 144/2 All the mixers had liquidiser attachments, and we tested them to see how well they pulped tomatoes, made breadcrumbs, chopped nuts, ground coffee beans, chopped parsley and crushed ice. **1969** H.-P. Pellaprat *Everyday French Cooking* 48 Put through a fine sieve or the liquidiser. **1972** Beale & Johnston *Mixer & Blender Cookery* iv. 20 The liquidizer reduces dried peas, beans, lentils, rice, etc., into powder speedily.

liquidly (ˈlɪkwɪdlɪ), *adv.* [f. liquid *a.* + -ly[2].] **1.** In a liquid manner; after the manner of a liquid.

1652 Sparke *Scintilla Altaris* (1663) 533 That dozen springs did liquidly record The twelve apostles. **1821** *New Monthly Mag.* III. 523 A noble crystal, which..is so liquidly transparent as to shew images truly through its softening medium. **1847** L. Hunt *Men, Women, & B.* I. ix. 175 Tea, between black and green..; something with a body, although most liquidly refreshing.

†**2.** *fig.* Clearly, plainly (= L. *liquido*). *Obs.*

1620 Donne *Serm.* lxxiv. 750 That sense which arises.. evidently, liquidly, and manifestly out of the Originall Text it selfe. **1657** W. Blois *Mod. Policies* F iv, It concerns Christians to be cautelous before swearing, to swear Liquidly, and to observe Conscionably. **1657** W. Morice *Coena quasi Κοινὴ* xv. 199 That the ancient Suspension was attended with such an interdict, appears liquidly enough by the second Councel of Arles. **1662** Pagitt *Heresiogr.* (ed. 6) 283 Which they did..as liquidly, clearly and truly expound and paraphrase, as if [etc.].

liquidness (ˈlɪkwɪdnɪs). [f. liquid *a* + -ness.] The quality or condition of being liquid, liquidity.

1530 Palsgr. 239/2 Lyquednesse, *moystevr*. **1622** Mabbe tr. *Aleman's Guzman d'Alf.* II. 54 The myre, by reason of its liquidnesse, had soked it selfe quite thorow my cloathes. **1675** Sir E. Sherburne *Manilius* Pref. 11 The fluidity and Liquidness of the Heavens. **1710** J. Clarke *Rohault's Nat. Phil.* (1729) I. 119 They are mistaken in their Notion of Hardness and Liquidness. **1836** F. Mahoney *Rel. Father Prout* (1859) 194 The bright river's gliding liquidness. **1839** *Tait's Mag.* VI. 584 With such quivering liquidness of tune, The Gondola draws nigh.

liquidus (ˈlɪkwɪdəs). [L. *liquidus* liquid *a.*, adopted in this sense (in G.) by H. W. B. Roozeboom 1899, in *Zeitschr. f. phys. Chem.* XXX. 387.] A line in a phase diagram, or a temperature (corresponding to a point on the line), above which a mixture is entirely liquid and below which it consists of liquid and solid in equilibrium; freq. *attrib.* as ***liquidus curve***, ***temperature***. Also (more fully *liquidus*

surface), an analogous surface in a three-dimensional phase diagram.

1901 *Proc. R. Soc.* LXVIII. 174 Cooling curves will.. give the approximate moment of complete solidification of an alloy, and enable us to plot in a rough way the 'solidus' curve, as Roozeboom calls it; but the solidus curve thus obtained is not nearly so accurate as the 'liquidus' or freezing-point curve. **1923** GLAZEBROOK *Dict. Appl. Physics* V. 245/2 The liquidus and the solidus meet, in the case under consideration, at the points A and C, which are the melting points of the pure metals, and B, which is known as the eutectic point. **1948** GLASSTONE *Textbk. Physical Chem.* (ed. 2) x. 762 Separation of solid.. commences at *y* and is complete at *z'*; for this reason the liquidus curve is sometimes called the freezing-point curve, and the solidus curve is called the melting-point curve. **1960** C. J. PHILLIPS *Glass: Industr. Applic.* v. 54 The viscosity at the liquidus temperature is high enough to prevent nucleation. **1967** A. H. COTTRELL *Introd. Metall.* xvi. 252 (*caption*) Liquidus surface of a eutectic system. **1972** *Physics Bull.* Nov. 352/3 Glass is a metastable state; it can be brought to the stable state by holding at temperatures near the liquidus.

† **liquidy**, *a. Obs. rare*⁻¹. [f. LIQUID *sb.* + -Y¹.] Of a liquid nature.

c **1400** *Lanfranc's Cirurg.* 78 (Add. MS.) A venemy Vlcus is, in whom habundeþ venym sotyl & liquydy [*v.r.* liquid].

liquiform ('lɪkwɪfɔːm), *a.* [Contracted ad. mod.L. type **liquidiformis*, f. *liquid-um* LIQUID *sb.*: see -FORM.] Having the form or appearance of a liquid. ***liquiform melanosis***, 'a name given by Dr. Carswell to the product of the disintegration of melanotic tumours which are sometimes found in serous cavities' (*Syd. Soc. Lex.* 1889).

1805 T. WEAVER tr. *Werner's Treat. External Char. Fossils* 204 Native-Quicksilver, which is found in globules, and liquiform. **1833** CARSWELL *Pathol. Anat., Melanoma* 3 Liquiform Melanosis.

liquirice, obs. form of LIQUORICE.

liquor ('lɪkə(r)), *sb.* Forms: 3 licur(e, 4 li-, lykour, 4–6 lycour(e, 4–7 licour(e, liquour(e, 5–6 lycor, 5–7 licor, (5 lycure, lycowr, liccore, 6 liquore, lyquor, liker, lickor, likcour, 7 liqor, liquer, licquor, lecker), 6– liquor. [a. OF. *licur, licour, likeur*, mod.F. *liqueur* (Pr. *licor, liquor*, Sp., Pg. *licor*, It. *liquore*), a. L. *liquor* (in Lucretius also *līquor*) liquidity (hence *concr.* a liquid, liquor), cogn. w. *liquāre, liquēre, liquī* (see LIQUATE, LIQUID). The later Eng. forms have been assimilated graphically to the L. word, without change of pronunciation.

The L. root **līqu-* is by some scholars thought to represent a pre-Latin **wliq-*, found also in Celtic (Irish *fliuch*, Welsh *gwlyb*, wet); but this is doubtful.]

† **1. a.** A liquid; matter in a liquid state; *occas.* in wider sense, a fluid. *Obs.* in general sense.

a **1225** *Ancr. R.* 164 Hwo þet bere a deorewurðe licur, oðer a deorewurðe wete, as is bame, in a feble uetles. *a* **1300** *Cursor M.* 21620 Þis cros was men þan wont to se, and it was tald þat a licure þar-of ran. **1357** *Lay Folks Catech.* 289 It [baptisme] be done anely in water, For nanothir licour is leuefull tharfore. **1444** *Rolls of Parlt.* V. 116/2 Vynegre, Oyle, and Hony and all other Lycours gaugeable. **1450–1530** *Myrr. our Ladye* 239 Wyth thre lyquores that ys with wepynge teares, wyth blody swette, and wyth blode. **1508** FISHER *7 Penit. Ps.* xxxii. Wks. (1876) 41 Parte of theyr payne shall be in a pytte full of brennynge lycour. **1604** E. G[RIMSTONE] *D'Acosta's Hist. Indies* IV. x. 234 Although it [quicksilver] be a liquor, yet is it more heavie then any other mettall. **1610** SHAKS. *Temp.* II. ii. 21 Yond same blacke cloud,.. lookes like a foule bumbard that would shed his licquor. **1664** POWER *Exp. Philos.* I. 59 Which Veins and Arteries [in the Louse] are so exceeding little, that both they and their Liquor are insensible. **1701** tr. *Le Clerc's Prim. Fathers* 309 He [Prudentius] would have the Soul to be a very subtle Liquor.

¶ Used in the primary Latin sense: Liquid quality, liquidity. *Obs. rare.*

1477 NORTON *Ord. Alch.* v. in Ashm. (1652) 63 Your principall Agent.. Which I teach you to knowe by signes fowre, By Colour, Odour, Sapor and Liquore.

b. In somewhat specialized uses: The liquid constituent of a secretion or the like; the liquid product of a chemical operation. Also in various phrases (often translating Lat. names of substances), as ***liquor of flints*** = ***liquor silicum*** (see 6); ***liquor of the Hollanders*** (see quot.); ***liquor of Libavius***, bichloride of tin.

1565 in *Satir. Poems Reform.* I. 4, I heave not vpe my handes filled wᵗʰ liquour of gowld, but wᵗʰ water so muche prysed by Artaxerxes. **1800** tr. *Lagrange's Chem.* II. 150 If liquor of flints, siliceous potash, be poured into a solution of gold. **1808** DAVY in *Phil. Trans.* XCIX. 93 The fuming muriate of tin, *the Liquor of Libavius*, is known to contain dry muriatic acid. **1831** J. DAVIES *Manual Mat. Med.* 305 Treat directly the morphia with diluted sulphuric acid and permit the liquor to crystallize. **1838** T. THOMSON *Chem. Org. Bodies* 12 The chloride of olefiant gas, usually called Liquor of the Hollanders. **1879** J. M. DUNCAN *Lect. Dis. Women* xv. (1889) 108 The retained menstrual fluid becomes denser, the liquor being mostly absorbed.

2. a. A liquid or a prepared solution used as a wash or bath, and in many processes in the industrial arts, e.g. in *Tanning*, the ooze or tan-water. ***iron, red, yellow liquor*** (see quot. 1839).

1583 STUBBES *Anat. Abus.* II. (1882) 37 The shoomaker liquoreth his leather, with waterish liquor, kitchen stuffe, and all kinde of baggage mingled togither. **1611** *Vestry Bks.* (Surtees) 161 Paide for wodd and coles for the boylinge of the lecker to the same, xijd. **1691** LUTTRELL *Brief Rel.* (1857) II. 292 The sole invention for dipping of cloth, hats, scarfes, &c. in a certain liquor that shal preserve them to keep out rain. **1730** SOUTHALL *Bugs* 14 My Liquor's being then so strong and oleous, that I durst not venture to liquor the Furniture. **1797** *Encycl. Brit.* (ed. 3) XVIII 307/1 The hides are then put into a pit of strong liquor called ooze or wooze, prepared.. by infusing ground bark in water. **1839** URE *Dict. Arts* 223 The pyrolignite of iron called iron liquor in this country, is the only mordant used in calico-printing for black, violet, puce, and brown colours. The acetate of alumina, prepared from pyroligneous acid, is much used by the calico-printers under the name of red or yellow liquor, being employed for these dyes. *Ibid.* 1209 Some finely clarified syrup, made from loaf sugar, called liquor by the refiners, is poured.. upon the base of each cone. **1883** B. W. RICHARDSON *Field of Disease* 492 In the further process of finishing the snuff.. there is what is called sifting 'the shorts', preparatory to adding the 'liquors', viz. salt and water to make weight, and scents to give perfume.

† **b.** *dial.* Grease or oil (for lubricating purposes). *Obs.* (Cf. LIQUOR *v.* 1.)

1559 *Ludlow Churchw. Acc.* (Camden) 90 Payd for lycor to lycor the chymes.. jd. **1584** *Ibid.* 167 Item, for a pynte of goose liker, to liker the belles.. iijd.

c. *Brewing.* Water.

1741 *Compl. Fam.-Piece* I. vi. 278 The Day before you intend to brew, you should boil a Copper of Liquor, (Water being an improper Term in a Brew-house). **1742** *Lond. & Country Brew.* I. (ed. 4) 22 The Liquor (for it is Six-pence Forfeit in the London Brew-house if the Word Water is named). **1880** *Times* 2 Oct. 6/1 'Liquor' is the word used, because in brewing it is considered a grave solecism to speak of 'water'.

3. a. Liquid for drinking; beverage, drink. Now almost exclusively *spec.*, a drink produced by fermentation or distillation. ***malt liquor***, liquor brewed from malt; ale, beer, porter, etc. ***spirituous liquor***, liquor produced by distillation; spirits. ***vinous liquor***, liquor made from grapes; wine.

a **1300** *Cursor M.* 13405 Dranc he neuer ar sli licur. **13..** *Coer de L.* 3048 To mete hadde he no savour, To wyn, ne watyr, ne no lycour. **1340** HAMPOLE *Pr. Consc.* 6763 Na licour sal þai fynd to fele, þat þair threst mught sleke. **1390** GOWER *Conf.* III. 315 This Maister [a Surgien and Phisicien].. putte a liquour in hire mouth. **1412–20** LYDG. *Chron. Troy* I. vi, For his chiefe socoure She toke to hym a vyoll with lycoure. **1494** FABYAN *Chron.* I. iii. 10 In the whiche they caste wyne, mylke, and other Lycours. **1542** BOORDE *Dyetary* x. (1870) 252 Water.. of the whiche dyuers lycours or drynkes for mannes sustynaunce be made of [*sic*]. **1611** BIBLE *Num.* vi. 3 Neither shal he drinke any liquor of grapes. **1667** MILTON *P.L.* v. 445 Eve.. thir flowing cups With pleasant liquors crown'd. **1687** A. LOVELL tr. *Thevenot's Trav.* I. 33 They call it Coffee,.. This Liquor is made of a Berry. **1698** FRYER *Acc. E. India & P.* 36 A broad Face, from which drops his Proboscis or Trunk..; through its Hollow he sucks his Liquor. **1718** LADY M. W. MONTAGU *Let. to C'tess Mar* 10 Mar., Sherbet.. is the liquor they drink at meals. **1719** DEFOE *Crusoe* I. xiii. (1840) 227 There were some casks of liquor, whether wine or brandy I knew not. **1765** *Phil. Trans.* LV. 227 Beer, cyder, champaign, and other Huffy liquors. **1789** W. BUCHAN *Dom. Med.* (1790) 139 Persons afflicted with low spirits,.. find more benefit from the use of solid food and generous liquors. **1813** SIR H. DAVY *Agric. Chem.* (1814) 141 Fruits for the manufacture of fermented liquors. **1842** M. RUSSELL *Polynesia* iii. (1849) 120 Their own laws were strong enough to prevent the manufacture of spirituous liquors at home.

fig. **1526** *Pilgr. Perf.* (W. de W. 1531) 53 Fruytfull and quycke by the lycour and sappe of charite and grace. **1549** COVERDALE, etc. *Erasm. Par. Gal.* 16 My sonne Isaac by drynkyng the effectuall lickor of the gospel, shal styll.. growe vp, vntill he become a perfite man. **1584** LODGE *Alarum* (1879) 44 They.. are drunken with the lycour of her abhominations. **1859** FITZGERALD tr. *Omar* ii. (1899) 69 Awake, my Little ones, and fill the Cup Before Life's Liquor in its Cup be dry.

b. With reference to intoxicating effect. ***disguised with liquor*** = DISGUISED *ppl. a.* 6. ***in liquor***: in a state of intoxication. ***to be (the) worse for liquor***: to be overcome by drink.

a **1529** SKELTON *Bk. 3 Fools* Wks. 1843 I. 202 Thou hast wylde lycoure, the whiche maketh all thy stomacke to be on a flambe. **1592** NASHE *P. Penilesse* (ed. 2) 23 a, He is reputed.. a boore that will not take his licour profoundly. **1752** HUME *Ess. & Treat.* (1777) I. 229 Though the passion for liquor be more brutal and debasing. **1753** *Scots Mag.* May 260/2 He was in liquor. **1855** MACAULAY *Hist. Eng.* xvii. IV. 110 When he had slept off his liquor. **1871** SMILES *Charac.* ix. (1876) 246 He.. led her across, not observing that she was in liquor at the time. **1893** FORBES-MITCHELL *Remin. Gt. Mutiny* 108 He had never been the worse for liquor in his life.

c. *slang.* (Chiefly *U.S.*) A drink (of an intoxicating beverage). Also, ***a liquor-up***.

1860 LEVER *One of them* xxii, If you choose to come in and take a liquor with me. **1872** *Echo* 23 Aug. (Farmer), To have,.. as the Americans would say, a liquor-up, at the hotel. **1882** *Punch* 29 Apr. 193/2 These 'nips' and 'pegs' and 'liquors'.. at all hours of the day were unknown to us.

† **d.** Used for LIQUEUR. *Obs.*

1797 *Encycl. Brit.* (ed. 3) XII. 259/2 Liquors of various sorts are compounded and distilled at Montpelier.

4. The water in which meat has been boiled; broth, sauce; the fat in which bacon, fish, or the like has been fried; the liquid contained in oysters.

c **1430** *Two Cookery-bks.* 11 Þen take þe lycowr of þe bonys, an þe skyn, an þe brothe þat þe Capoun was sothyn ynne. *c* **1440** *Promp. Parv.* 303/1 Lycure, or brothe of fysche, and oþer lyke, *liquamen*. *c* **1450** *ME. Med. Bk.* (Heinrich) 65 Take and seþe verueyne, and betonye, and wermod.. & þanne.. take þe same erbys.. and grynde hem.. and tempre hem wyþ þe same licour a ȝeyne. *c* **1460** J. RUSSELL *Bk. Nurture* 382 Looke ye haue good mustarde þer-to [bravne] and good licoure. **1514** BARCLAY *Cyt. & Uplandyshm.* (Percy Soc.) p. xlvii, Oft all the broth & licour fat Is spilt on thy gowne. **1719** DE FOE *Crusoe* II. ii. (1840) 30 He.. softened them with the liquor of the meat. **1747** MRS. GLASSE *Cookery* ii. (1767) 49 Take some of the oyster liquor [etc.]. *Ibid.* 59 Let them grow cold in their own liquor before you serve them up. *Ibid.* vi. 125 When you boil a leg of pork or a good piece of beef, save the liquor... Then put in the pork or beef liquor. **1806** A. HUNTER *Culina* (ed. 3) 77 Add a little anchovy liquor. *Ibid.* 115 A few oysters with their liquor. **1896** *Warwicksh. Gloss., Liquor*, gravy, the grease of fried bacon, &c.

5. The liquid produced by infusion (in testing the quality of a tea). ***in liquor***, in the state of an infusion.

1870 E. MONEY *Cultiv. & Manuf. Tea* (1878) 111 They judge from three things, first, the Tea; secondly, the liquor; thirdly, the out-turn... *The Liquor.*—In taste this should be strong, rasping, and pungent. *Ibid.* 136 Its [*sc.* Flowery Pekoe's] strength in liquor is very great. **1882** *Tea Cycl.* 224/1 Poor teas of weak liquor.

‖ **6.** The Latin word, pronounced ('laɪkwɔː(r)) and ('lɪkwɔː(r)), is used (*a*) in *Pharmacy* and *Med.* in the names of various solutions of medicinal substances in water, as ***liquor ammoniæ***, strong solution of ammonia (*Syd. Soc. Lex.* 1889); ***liquor potassæ***, an aqueous solution of hydrate of potash; ***liquor silicum***, 'a compound of silex and salt of tartar, discovered by Van Helmont in 1640, which becomes liquid in a damp moisture' (*Syd. Soc. Lex.* 1889). (*b*) in *Physiol.*, as ***liquor amnii***, the fluid contained in the sac of the amnion; ***liquor sanguinis***, the blood-plasma.

1796 KIRWAN *Elem. Min.* (ed. 2) I. 51 He melted the white sand of Freyenwalde with four times its weight of salt of tartar, and formed a *liquor silicum*. **1839** LINDLEY *Introd. Bot.* I. ii. 220 The fluid matter contained within the nucleus is called the *liquor amnios* [sic]. **1846** G. E. DAY tr. *Simon's Anim. Chem.* II. 360 The liquor amnii at the sixth month was turbid. **1857** G. BIRD *Urin. Deposits* (ed. 5) 184, I dissolved a portion of this concretion in liquor potassæ. **1874** JONES & SIEV. *Pathol. Anat.* (ed. 2) 14 Liquor sanguinis consists of a watery solution of certain inorganic salts.

7. *attrib.* and *Comb.*, as ***liquor-bar, -cistern, -dealer, -gage, glass, house, law, licence, question, -saloon, -seller, -selling, -shop, -store, -tent, trade, traffic, vessel; liquor-fired, -seasoned*** adjs. Also † **liquor-back**, a kind of vat used in brewing; **liquor prescription** *Canad. Hist.*, a doctor's prescription of alcohol for 'medicinal' purposes, to evade the prohibition regulations; **liquor-pump**, 'a portable pump for emptying casks, etc.' (Knight *Dict. Mech.* 1875); also in *Sugar-Manuf.* (see quot.); **liquor-thief**, a tube which is let down through the bung-hole of a cask in sampling spirits (Knight).

1691 T. H[ALE] *Acc. New Invent.* 102 Cisterns, Scuppers, *Liquor-Backs. **1813** W. DUNLAP *Mem. G. F. Cooke* II. xxx. 278 The fountain of mischief, the *liquor-bar, was shut. **1839** URE *Dict. Arts* 765 The cock.. above is left open to maintain a communication with the *liquor cistern [in tanning]. **1859** H. W. BEECHER *Life Thoughts* Ser. II. 70, I can imagine how a *liquor-dealer would feel to own his conversion. **1898** T. HARDY *Wessex Poems* 138 Her *liquor-fired face. **1875** KNIGHT *Dict. Mech.*, **Liquor-gage*. **1830** MARRYAT *King's Own* ix, A bottle of brandy, and a *liquor glass. **1924** W. M. RAINE *Troubled Waters* ii. 21 The postmistress handed him a letter and two circulars from *liquor houses. **1852** *Boston Bee* 29 July, The Life Boat.. takes the Bee to do, for its course in relation to the *Liquor law. **1858** A. LINCOLN *Coll. Works* (1953) II. 493, I do not believe in the right of Illinois to interfere with.. the Liquor Laws of Maine. **1866** G. MEREDITH *Let.* c 27 Nov. (1970) I. 345 You will become a fanatical Retired Admiral advocating Maine Liquor laws for every natural appetite on earth. **1908** *Daily Chron.* 27 Feb. 4/4 Certain liquor-law restrictions which had existed under the second Empire. **1975** *Listener* 16 Jan. 76/1 The counties would have.. their own educational system, their liquor laws. **1850** *Hunt's Merchant's Mag.* XXII. 87 (*caption*) Statistics of *Liquor Licenses in New York City. **1956** B. HOLIDAY *Lady sings Blues* (1973) xix. 157 According to the law.. nobody who has a police record can hold a liquor licence. **1971** *Sunday Express* (Johannesburg) 28 Mar. (Homefinder) 7/2 (Advt.), 1. Dance hall. 2. Restaurant—Liquor licence. **1921** *Daily Colonist* (Victoria, B.C.) 18 Mar. 1/3 The suspension of 19 physicians in Manitoba for unlawfully issuing *liquor prescriptions has resulted from an inquiry. **1839** URE *Dict. Arts* 1196 In Demerara.. it is usual to attach to the [sugar] mill a *liquor-pump. In action, the liquor from the gutter of the mill-bed runs into the cistern of the pump, and is raised.. to the gutter which leads to the clarifier or coppers. **1855** *Liquor question [see *liquor-shop* below]. *c* **1918** C. STELZLE *Why Prohibition!* 291 Michigan was about to vote on the liquor question. **1863** *Daily Even. Bulletin* (San Francisco) 29 Sept. 3/2 At 1 o'clock they went into a *liquor saloon kept by a woman on Kearny Street. **1874** D. MACRAE *Americans at Home* xl. 320 In liquor-saloons and gambling-houses. **1884** *Mag. of Art* Mar. 215/2 Some.. getting *liquor-seasoned as they grow older. **1855** P. T. BARNUM *Life* 359 The *liquor seller, the moderate drinker, and the indifferent man. **1877** *Harper's Mag.* Dec. 146/2 A method which practically makes the government the liquor-seller. *Ibid.*, All *liquor-selling is not equally dangerous to the community. **1809** MALKIN *Gil Blas* VII. xiii. (Rtldg.) 15 A *Liquor-shop. **1855** 'Q. K. P. DOESTICKS' *Doesticks, what he Says* xxxi. 276 The great excitement was on the liquor question; it was Noggs and no liquor shops, or Boggs and a few liquor shops. **1877** J. HABBERTON *Jericho Road* xix. 167 There was not even a streak of light visible under the door of any liquor-shop in the town. **1911** *Encycl. Brit.* XVI.

769/2 The effect has been a very large reduction in the number of liquor shops. **1815** *Ann. Reg., Chron.* 46 Mr. Henry Beer's *liquor-store. **1855** 'Q. K. P. Doesticks' *Doesticks, what he Says* xii. 98 Fire in a liquor-store—hose burst; brandy 'lying round loose'. **1887** *Nation* (N.Y.) 15 Dec. 468/3 To keep a liquor-store in Philadelphia. **1939** F. P. Grove *Two Generations* 39 Take the proceeds to the liquor store. **1964** *Calgary Herald* 24 July 23/2 A liquor store on the site would devalue residential property to the immediate west. **1972** R. Bloch *Night-World* (1974) xi. 72 He passed the lights of the liquor store. **1889** T. Hardy *Mayor of Casterbr.* i, The licensed *liquor-tent. **1908** *Daily Chron.* 12 May 4/4 Unfortunately for the Labour party they have got entangled with the *liquor trade vote. **1848** J. Marsh (*title*) A discourse on the extent and evils of the Sunday *liquor traffic in cities. **1877** *Harper's Mag.* Dec. 146/2 This work is a compilation of evidence on 'the problem of law as applied to the liquor traffic'. **1901** *19th Cent.* Oct. 538 The illicit liquor-traffic had been absolutely stopped. **1915** W. J. Bryan *Mem.* 2 Oct. (1925) 434 The brewers and distillers were connecting them with the liquor traffic to their detriment. **1608** R. Norton tr. *Stevin's Disme* D iij, Of Gaudging, and the measures of all *Liquor vessels.

Hence **'liquordom** *nonce-wd.*

1892 Farrar in *Contemp. Rev.* Oct. 545 In the sense in which it is incessantly used by the defenders of liquordom. **1918** T. H. Walker *Principal J. Denney* 119 His hatred of liquordom..sprang from devotion to his Master.

liquor ('lɪkə(r)), *v.* [f. liquor *sb.*]

1. *trans.* To cover or smear with a liquor; *esp.* to lubricate with grease or oil. *Obs.* exc. as *nonce-use* in ***to liquor over.***

1573 *Churchw. Acc. St. Margaret, Westm.* (Nichols 1797) 19 Paid for netesfoot oil to liquor the belles..2ᵈ. **1577** Fenton *Gold. Epist.* 46 He liquored the earth wyth hys bloude. **1626** Bacon *Sylva* §117 Cart-Wheeles squeak not when they are liquored. **1655** Baxter *Quaker's Catech.* 22 If I had your Spirit to liquor my tongue, I should..preach the people out of the place. *a* **1680** Butler *Rem.* (1759) I. 388 Witches liquor their Staves and fly through the Air. **1718** Motteux *Quix.* (1733) I. 149 That which he fansy'd to be Blood, was only..the Oil of the Lamp that had liquor'd his Hair and Face. **1737** Bracken *Farriery Impr.* (1756) I. 348 Greasing, or Liquoring the Hoofs with Hog's Lard. **1847** Halliwell, *Liquor*, to oil, or anoint. *Glouc.* **1864** *Gd. Words* 80/2 Great knobs of buds on a horse-chestnut.. liquored over with an oily exudation.

2. *esp.* To dress (leather, boots or shoes) with oil or grease.

1502 [see liquoring *vbl. sb.*]. **1598** Shaks. *Merry W.* iv. v. 100 They would melt mee out of my fat drop by drop, and liquor Fishermens boots with me. **1607** Topsell *Four-f. Beasts* (1658) 527 The fat of Swine is very precious to liquor shooes and boots therewithal. **1681** Chetham *Angler's Vade-m.* xxxiv. §31 (1689) 202 Let the Currier very well Liquor them with following Liquor. **1776** Anstey *Election Ball* 29 Polish his Stirrups and liquor his Boots. **1830** G. Colman *Br. Grins, Random Records* (1872) 471 [He] liquored his boots, rubbed down his Highland pony [etc.].

b. *slang*, in phr. ***to liquor*** (a person's) ***boots***: (*a*) to cuckold (him); (*b*) (see quot. 1785).

1702 T. Brown *Wks.* (1720) II. 305 Believing for some Reasons he had an underhand Design of liquoring his boots for him. **1785** Grose *Dict. Vulg. Tongue* s.v., *To liquor one's boots*, to drink before a journey, among Roman Catholicks to administer the extreme unction.

†**c.** *slang.* To thrash, beat; *esp.* in phr. ***to liquor*** (a person's) ***hide***. *Obs.*

a **1689** *R. Hood & Little John* viii. in Child *Ballads* III. 134/2 I'll liquor thy hide, If thou offerst to touch the string. **1719** D'Urfey *Pills* VI. 101 I'll liquor your Hide.

†**3.** *Cookery.* To cover (pie-crust) with a prepared liquor; to glaze. *Obs.*

a **1704** *Compl. Servant-Maid* (ed. 7) 72 Liquor it [a pie] with Claret, Butter, and stript Time. **1751** Smollett *Per. Pickle* II. xlviii. 82 Two pies, one of dormice liquored with syrup of white poppies.

4. In various industrial arts: To steep in or soak with a liquor; to steep (malt) in water; to clear (sugar-loaves) by pouring over them a 'liquor' of fine syrup.

1743 *Lond. & Country Brew.* ii. (ed. 2) 99 While the Malt lies liquored in the Mash-vat. **1833** Ure *Rep. Sugar Refining* 3 in *Parl. Papers* XXXIII. 553, I regret that circumstances did not permit me to adopt as my general practice the clearing the loaves with fine syrup, called liquoring, instead of using clay pap. **1851** Ronalds & Richardson *Chem. Technol.* III. 155 The [tobacco] leaves intended for the production of snuff are sorted and liquored. **1874, 1893** [see liquoring *vbl. sb.*].

b. *transf.* To adulterate (spirits) with water.

1894 *Daily News* 18 Apr. 6/6 They will be obliged to 'liquor' their spirits—that is to say, they will dilute them with water.

5. To supply with liquor to drink; to ply with liquor. Also ***to liquor up.*** Now *slang.*

c **1560** *Misogonus* i. iv. 19 (Brandl *Quellen* 434), I thinke, heis at Alhouse, a likeringe ones brayne. **1577** Fenton *Gold. Epist.* 115 The blynde man, who weening to powre drinke into hys dyshe, powreth it into yᵉ riuer which hath no neede to bee liquored. *c* **1600** *Timon* iii. iv, If that your throates are dry, I'le liquour them. **1642** R. Carpenter *Experience* i. xvii. 118 If wee licker them throughly with strong Beere. **1662** *Rump* I. 336 Unlesse the Brewer doth liquor him home. **1709** E. Ward *Secret Hist. of Clubs* 321 There are several of these Flat-Cap Societies of Female Tatlers, who, as soon as their Business is over, liquor their Weather-beaten Hides at the Taverns adjacent to the Markets which they use. [Cf. 2 c.] **1710** —— *Brit. Hudibras* 5 Some liquor'd well with Foggy Ale. **1852** R. S. Surtees *Sponge's Sp. Tour* (1893) 294 'Call him in', roared Sir Harry, 'and let's liquor him'. **1890** *Boy's Own Paper* 11 Jan. 227/3 I've been liquored up and stroked down till I feel about as shaky as our friend Hugh there.

6. *intr.* (*slang.*) To drink alcoholic liquor. Also ***to liquor up.***

1839 Marryat *Diary Amer.* Ser. i. I. 239 It's a bargain then,..come let's liquor on it. **1845** S. Judd *Margaret* i. xii. 81 The old man called her Mary. 'No, Dad,..it must be Margaret'. 'No! Mary... Besides, that's a Bible name, and we can't liquor up on Margaret'. **1862** *Macm. Mag.* June 146 They..liquored at the bar, and played the mysterious game 'euchre'. **1895** Zangwill *Master* ii. xi. 259 'Will you liquor with me?' he said.

Hence **'liquored** *ppl. a.*; **'liquoring** *vbl. sb.* Also **'liquorer.**

1502 *Privy Purse Exp. Eliz. of York* (1830) 37 A barrell of greese..for the licoryng of the Quenes borehydes. **1611** Cotgr., *Surpoint*,..an oylie grease scummed from peeces of lichored leather. **1667** Lacy *Sauny Scot* iv. (1698) 26 O' my Saul, Sawndy wou'd be Hang'd gin I sud bestow an aw'd Liquor'd Bute. **1681** Dryden *Abs. & Achit.* ii. 460 Og from a treason-tavern rolling home, Round as a globe, and liquored every chink. **1851** Ronalds & Richardson *Chem. Technol.* III. 156 The liquored leaves [of tobacco] are tied up in bundles. **1874** W. Crookes *Dyeing & Calico-pr.* iv. 47 By this alternate steaming and liquoring, the goods are much more thoroughly cleansed than [etc.]. **1885** A. Edgar *Old Ch. Life Scot.* 326 These sobered liquorers. **1893** C. Booth *Life & Labour Lond.* IV. 224 The class of operatives [of a cigar factory] known as 'liquorers' and 'strippers'. *Ibid.*, 'Liquoring' is the preliminary process to which the [tobacco] leaf is subjected, and consists in sprinkling it with pure water by means of a spray [etc.]. **1896** G. M. Stisted *Life Sir R. F. Burton* xi. 267 A stroll..enlivened by an occasional liquoring up with a new acquaintance.

liquoras, obs. form of liquorice.

liquorice, licorice ('lɪkərɪs). Forms: 3 licoriz, 3–5 licorys, lycorys, 4–5 lycorice, -yce, 5 lycuryce, 5–6 li-, lycores(se, 5–7 li-, lycoris(e, (6 -yse, -yze, -isse), 6 likorice, lykorise, lickorise, licquoris, liquerise, lyqueryce, -esse, li-, lycouresse, lycuresse, lykeres, liquoras, 6–7 li-, lycoras, liquoris, 7 lichoras, licorish, liquirice, liqueres, lykyrrhize, licourice, 7–8 liquorish, 9 *dial.* lickerish, 6– licorice, 7– liquorice. [a. AF. *lycorys*, OF. **licorice*, early mod.F. *liquerice* (Cotgr.), ad. late L. *liquiritia* (whence It. *liquirizia, legorizia*, MHG. *lakeritze*, mod.G. *lakritze*, Du. *lakk(e)ris*, Da., Sw. *lakrits*), corruptly a. Gr. *γλυκύρριζα* (latinized *glycyrrhiza* by Pliny), f. *γλυκύς* sweet + *ῥίζα* root. The Rom. langs. in general have metathetic forms of the late L. word: OF. *recolisse, regolisse*, etc. (mod.F. *réglisse*), Pr. *regalicia*, Sp. *regaliz(a*, Pg. *regaliz, regalice*, It. *regolizia*.]

1. The rhizome (also called ***liquorice-root***) of the plant *Glycyrrhiza glabra.* Also, a preparation (used medicinally and as a sweetmeat) made from the evaporated juice of this rhizome, and commonly sold in black cylindrical sticks; also called ***extract of liquorice, stick*** or ***Spanish liquorice, Spanish juice. Italian liquorice***: a similar product obtained from *Glycyrrhiza echinata.*

c **1205** Lay. 17745 And gingiuere & licoriz he hom lefliche ȝef. **13..** *K. Alis.* 428 His love is al so swete, y-wis, So ever is mylk or licoris! *a* **1310** in Wright *Lyric P.* v. 26 Such licoris mai leche from lyve to lone, Such sucre mon secheth that saveth men sone. **1436** *Pol. Poems* (Rolls) II. 160 Commodytés..commynge out of Spayne,..Bene fygues And lycorys, Syvyle oyle, and grayne. **1519** Horman *Vulg.* 39 b, Lycuresse is good for the voyce. **1542** Boorde *Dyetary* xxii. (1870) 287 Lyqueryce..doth loose fleume. **1601** Holland *Pliny* I. 356 Cheese made of Mares or Asses milk, and Licorice. **1611** Beaum. & Fl. *Knt. Burn. Pestle* i. i, Carry him this sticke of Licoras, tell him his Mistresse sent it him, and bid him bite a peece, 'twill open his pipes the better, say. **1613** in *Rec. Convent. Roy. Burghs* (1870) II. 396 Ilk gritt ball of brissell annetseides and liqueres. **1684** tr. *Bonet's Merc. Compit.* xiv. 487 A Lambitive that consists of the Syrups of Lykyrrhize, violets [etc.]. **1685** *Lond. Gaz.* No. 2000/4 The Juyce of Liquorice of Blois..is sold at the two Pestles and Mortars in St. Martins Lane near Charing-Cross. **1747** Wesley *Prim. Physic* (1762) 35 Use Water wherein sliced Liquorice is steeped. **1750** *Phil. Trans.* XLVII. xii. 77 Their poison..has a great deal of resemblance with Spanish liquorice. **1840** Marryat *Poor Jack* viii, Don't eat the stick-liquorice. **1869** Blackmore *Lorna D.* vi, I cough sometimes in the winter-weather, and father gives me lickerish. **1875** Tennyson *Q. Mary* iii. i. 109 He hath a yellow beard... Like a carrot's,..and English carrot's better than Spanish licorice.

fig. **1592** G. Harvey *Pierce's Super.* (1593) 164 O the sugar candy of the delicate bagpipe there: and o the licorise of the diuine dulcimers there.

2. The leguminous plant *Glycyrrhiza glabra*, the dried rhizome of which is the liquorice of commerce. Applied also to other species, esp. *G. echinata.*

1548 Turner *Names of Herbes* 40 Glycyrrhiza called in latin *Radix dulcis* is named in english Lycores, in duch Sueszholtz, or Lycoris or Clarish. **1567** Maplet *Gr. Forest* 50 Of Licorise. Lycorise is so saide, especially through the Greeke word, for that it hath a sweete roote. **1576** *Surv.* in *Antiq. Rep.* (1809) IV. 424 Gardinges and Orchettes wharin growes..Cherries, Wallnutes & also Licores. **1588** Greene *Pandosto* (1607) Ded. 2 Vnicornes being glutted with brousing on rootes of Lycoras. **1654** Evelyn *Mem.* (1857) I. 316 All marsh ground till we came to Brigg, famous for the plantations of licorice. **1760** Brown *Compl. Farmer* ii. 31 You may, if a deep mould, plant them [certain lands] with liquorish. **1811** Lysons *Suppl. Env. Lond.* 448 About ten acres of licorice have lately been planted in the parishes of Barnes and Mortlake. **1830** Lindley *Nat. Syst. Bot.* 91 The roots of the liquorice contain an abundance of a sweet subacrid mucilaginous juice. **1870** Yeats *Nat. Hist. Comm.* 243 Liquorice is a native of Italy, Spain, Sicily, and the southern parts of Europe.

3. Applied, with qualifying epithet, to various plants, the roots of which resemble or are used as substitutes for the true liquorice, as ***English, Indian, mountain, wild liquorice*** (see quots.).

1548 Turner *Names of Herbes* 86 *Regalicum*..It mayе be called in englishe mocke Licores, because the leaues are lyke Licores. **1725** Bradley *Fam. Dict.* II. 6 E ij/1 Put to it as much of the fine Powder of Bole Armoniack and English Liquorish..as will make it up into a stiff Paste. **1760** J. Lee *Introd. Bot.* App. 317 Liquorice, Wild, *Astragalus*; *Caperaria*; *Glycine.* **1866** *Treas. Bot.* II. 687/2 Wild liquorice, *Abrus*; also an American name for *Galium circæzans.*

4. *attrib.* and *Comb.*, as ***liquorice all-sorts*** (see *all-sorts* s.v. all E. 13), ***drop, jujube, lozenge, lump, -planter,*** †***-race*** (= root), ***-root, -runner, -set, -soup, toffee, treasure, -tree, -water, -wood***; **liquorice bootlace** = boot-lace c; **liquorice juice**, the juice extracted from liquorice root, esp. as dried and prepared for use; **liquorice mass, paste**, 'crude liquorice' (*Cent. Dict.*); **liquorice powder**, ground liquorice root, used as an aperient; **liquorice-stick**, (*a*) = *stick-liquorice*, sense 1 above; (*b*) *Jazz slang*, a clarinet. **liquorice vetch**, *Astragalus glycyphyllus*; **liquorice weed**, a tropical plant, *Scoparia dulcis* (*Cent. Dict.*)

1928 *Sweet Shop* Nov. p. ii (Advt.), Original *Liquorice All Sorts. **1931** [see *all-sorts* s.v. all E. 13]. **1946** *R.A.F. Jrnl.* May 162 His C.O...with the broad ring and a row of gongs that reminded Joe of liquorice all-sorts. **1952** *Blackw. Mag.* July 30/2 Lollipops, pincushions, *liquorice boot-laces, bottles of home-made wine. **1956** 'R. Crompton' *William & Space Animal* v. 135 Doughnuts an' trifle an' liqu'rice boot laces. **1906** 'O. Henry' *Four Million* (1916) 173 *Liquorice drops—the kind that make your cheek look like the toothache. **1967** R. Mackay *House & Day* 74 Have you licorice drops? **1657** Tomlinson *Renou's Disp.* i. vi. 392 Of *Liquorice Juyce. **1838** *Penny Cycl.* XI. 279/1 Good liquorice juice is black, dry, easily broken.., with a shining fracture. **1891** *Confectioners' Union* IV. 530 (Advt.), Goods packed in 4 lb. boxes..Bright *liquorice jujubes. **1857** J. A. Symonds *Let.* 25 Jan. (1967) I. 86 Will you send me also another box of *Liquorice Lozenges. **1893** *Official Catal. Internat. Manufacturing Confectioners Exhib.* 60 (Advt.), Linseed Liquorice and Chlorodyne Lozenges. **1926** 'R. Crompton' *William—the Conqueror* iii. 54 Large paper bags of bullseyes, *liquorice lumps, barley sugar and chocolate cigars. **1763** *Museum Rusticum* I. lx. 256 *Liquorice-planters in Yorkshire and Surry. **1712** Steele *Spect.* No. 328 ¶3 When I had occasion to buy Treacle or *Liquorish Power [sic] at the apothecary's shop. *c* **1400** *Lanfranc's Cirurg.* 183 *Liquericie rase ȝ iij. **1530** Palsgr. 239/1 *Lycorice rote, *reclice.* **1789** W. Buchan *Dom. Med.* (1790) 401 Sliced liquorice-root. **1763** *Museum Rusticum* I. lx. 253 Some *liquorice runners, or *sets are to be procured. **1864** *Daily Tel.* 10 Mar., The *liquorice soup and fat pork which constitute the usual diet at the hotel. **1580** Hollyband *Treas. Fr. Tong, Vn friquet*,..also a *lickorous sticke. **1782** J. Mill *Diary* (1889) 67 A decoction of 2 oz. lint-seed, 2 do. of Liquorish-stick bruised and boiled. **1879** Liquorice-stick [see *goose-yoke*]. **1935** *Vanity Fair* (N.Y.) Nov. 71/3 *Agony pipe, wop stick*, and *licorice stick* for clarinet. **1958** N. D. Hinton in *Publ. Amer. Dial. Soc.* xxx. 39, I have found a common belief that jazzmen refer to a clarinet as a 'licorice stick'... Jazz musicians do in fact use these terms..in a very peculiar way. **1967** C. Drummond *Death at Furlong Post* iv. 39 Bee dispensed liquorice sticks..and fizzy drinks. **1930** *Confectioners' Union Directory Trade Marks & Trade Names* 18/2 (Advt.), Buttered *Liquorice Toffee in Dainty Pieces. **1924** 'R. Crompton' *William—the Fourth* viii. 125 'Have a *liquorice treasure?' she said. **1882** A. J. C. Hare in *Gd. Words* Mar. 186 The rich plain sprinkled with *liquorice-trees. **1760** J. Lee *Introd. Bot.* App. 317 *Liquorice Vetch, *Astragalus.* **1882** *Garden* 24 June 439/1 In the hedges you may very occasionally meet with a rare plant..known by the not inappropriate name of Liquorice Vetch. **1860** Dickens *Gt. Expect.* (1861) I. ii. 29 That intoxicating fluid, Spanish-*liquorice-water. **1865** *Athenæum* No. 1984. 614/2 A glass of liquorice-water. **1913** C. Mackenzie *Sinister St.* I. iv. 59 They used to go calling up and down, 'Fine liquorice-water!..Bring out your pins and have a bottle of liquorice-water.' **1960** *Guardian* 6 Dec. 7/2 The bottles of liquorice-water which provided grog for his young games of pirates. **1611** Florio, *Ligoritia*, the *Lycorice-wood.

liquoring ('lɪkərɪŋ), *ppl. a. Comm.* [f. liquor *v.* + -ing².] Of tea: That produces (a specified kind of) liquor. (Cf. liquor *sb.* 5.)

1891 *Times* 13 Oct. 9/3 Tea..Undesirable liquoring sorts were rather lower. **1892** *Pall Mall G.* 22 Aug. 7/1 Useful liquoring teas show an advance of a farthing.

liquorish ('lɪkərɪʃ), *a.* [f. liquor *sb.* + -ish. (An etymologizing sense-perversion of lickerish.)] Fond of or indicating fondness for liquor.

1894 S. R. Keightley *Crimson Sign* 312 A rare seaman, but liquorish... He was born with a thirst. **1899** F. T. Bullen *Log Sea-waif* 270 He turned a liquorish eye upon me.

Hence **'liquorishly** *adv.*; **'liquorishness.**

1789 *Emblems of Mortality* p. xxvii, To contemplate the Liquorishness of one Figure of Death, who is secretly sucking through a Reed the Wine from the emptied Cask. **1852** R. S. Surtees *Sponge's Sp. Tour* (1893) 39 That purpose was to try how many silver foxes' heads full of port-wine Tom could carry off without tumbling, and the old fellow, being rather liquorishly inclined, had never made any objection to the experiment.

liquorish: see LICKERISH, LIQUORICE.

liquorist (ˈlɪkərɪst). [a. F. *liquoriste.*] One who makes liqueurs.

1844 *Fraser's Mag.* XXX. 435/1 The French are our masters in the art of the liquorist. **1879** *Spon's Encycl. Industr. Arts* etc. I. 225 The manufacture of these liqueurs constitutes the trade of the 'compounder' or 'liquorist'.

liquorless (ˈlɪkəlɪs), *a.* [f. LIQUOR *sb.* + -LESS.] Without liquor.

1859 SALA *Gas-light & D.* ii. 27 The haughty Hospodar of Hungary, drinks confusion to the Bold Bandit of Bulgaria in a liquorless cup. **1891** *Voice* (N.Y.) 26 Mar., Cannot the poor man's club be a liquorless club?

†**ˈliquorous**, *a. Obs. rare*⁻¹. [f. LIQUOR *sb.* + -OUS.] Of the nature of liquor; liquid.

1678 R. R[USSELL] *Geber* II. i. IV. xiii. 117 And by that which is made by Filter, We acquire the Clearness of every Liquorous Thing.

†**ˈliquorsome**, *a. Obs.* [f. LIQUOR *sb.* (erroneously supposed to be the source of *liquorous* LICKEROUS *a.*) + -SOME.] = LICKERISH, LICKEROUS. Hence **ˈliquorsomely** *adv.*

1656 H. MORE *Enthus. Tri.* (1712) 27 Men of shallow minds and liquorsome bodies, cleaving to the pleasures of the flesh. **1664** —— *Myst. Iniq.* I. vii. 21 Liquorsomely partaking of the diffused reek of the things Sacrificed.

liquourish, obs. form of LICKERISH.

‖**lira** (ˈlira, ˈlɪərə). *Pl.* ‖**lire** (ˈlire), *rarely* **liras.** Also 7 in anglicized form **lire.** [It. *lira*, a contracted form of L. *lībra* pound: see LIBRA.]

1. The name of an Italian silver coin which is the unit of monetary value in that country.

1617 MORYSON *Itin.* I. 70, I bought..a fat hen for two lires. **1756–7** tr. *Keysler's Trav.* (1760) IV. 118 A *bracera*.. may be hired from Venice to Trieste for fifty or sixty *lire. Note*, A *lira* is about 6*d.* sterling. **1868** BROWNING *Ring & Bk.* I. 39, I found this book, Gave a *lire* for it, eightpence English just. **1877** L. W. M. LOCKHART *Mine is Thine* iv, The money went to the marchioness..who may have fed the hungry and clothed the naked with the *lire* of the angry man. **1884** F. BOYLE *On the Borderland* 237 A baksheesh of two liras.

2. A monetary unit in Turkey.

1871 *Murray's Handbk. Turkey in Asia* (new ed.) 27 The coinage consists of copper, silver, and gold, at the rate of 100 piastres to the Turkish pound or *lira.* **1884** F. BOYLE *On Borderland betwixt Fact & Fancy* 237 The high wall on our left was that of the pasha's grounds. The one-eyed calender informed me that he could get permission to visit them next day, for a baksheesh of two liras. Thirty-six shillings seemed too much to pay for a stroll through a burnt-up garden. **1904** *Daily Chron.* 17 Feb. 3/6 A thousand Turkish liras weigh about 14 lb. **1912** T. E. LAWRENCE *Let.* 10 Feb. (1938) 136 The foot seal must be worth a lira at the least. **1975** J. RATHBONE *Kill Cure* III. vii. 128 'How much?'..'Forty dollars or twenty-five sterling. Turkish lira, much more.'

lirate (ˈlaɪərət), *a.* [f. L. *līra* ridge, furrow: see -ATE².] Of a shell: having ridges. Hence **liˈration**, marking of this kind.

1894 J. W. TAYLOR *Monogr. Land & Freshwater Mollusca Brit. Isles* I. i. 28 Cingulate, or Lirate, when the whorls are furnished with spiral ribs or ridgings. **1901** *Proc. Zool. Soc.* II. 357 *Actis calotropis*... A very delicate species, vitreous, ..delicately spirally lirate. **1904** *Ann. & Mag. Nat. Hist.* 7th Ser. XIII. 459 This liration bears small tubercles connected by short cross-ridges with the dentations of the keel.

lirate, variant of LYRATE.

lircher, obs. form of LURCHER.

lire (laɪə(r)), *sb.*¹ *Obs.* exc. *Sc.* and *north. dial.* Forms: 1 **lira**, 4–7 **lyre**, 4–5 *Sc.* **lyr**, (4 **lere**), 3– **lire.** [OE. *líra* wk. masc., of obscure origin.] Flesh, muscle, brawn.

c **1000** *Sax. Leechd.* II. 216 þa liran þara lendena sariað. *Ibid.* II. 264 Breost ablawen & sar þeoh & lira. *c* **1000** ÆLFRIC *Gloss.* in Wr.-Wülcker 159/8 *Pulpa, uel uiscum*, lira. *a* **1225** *Juliana* 58 As þat istelet irn to limede hire ant te leac lið ba ant lire. *c* **1330** *Arth. & Merl.* 8202 (Kölbing) For he carf man & stiel & ire, So flesche hewer doþ flesches lire. *c* **1375** *Sc. Leg. Saints* xxxviii. (*Adrian*) 504 Scho wald haf ronnyne in þe fire, til half brynt hir bane & lyr. *c* **1386** CHAUCER *Sir Thopas* 146 He didde next his white leere Of clooth of lake fyn and cleere A breech and eek a sherte. ?*c* **1390** *Form of Cury* (1780) 12 Take the lire of Pork and grynd it smal. **1460** *Lybeaus Disc.* 1899 Lybeauus..smot of hys theygh, Fell, and bone, and lyre. **1483** *Cath. Angl.* 218 Lyre of flesche, *pulpa.* **1513** DOUGLAS *Æneis* VI. iv. 35 The haill bowkis of beistis, bane and lyre. **1584** HUDSON *Du Bartas' Judith* VI. (1608) 95 Ther was no sinew, Arter, vaine, nor lyre, That was not mangled with their vulgar rage. **1610** HEALEY *St. Aug. Citie of God* XXI. iv. (1620) 786 A boiled Peacock was serued in and I..tooke some of the Lyre of the breast. *c* **1817** HOGG *Tales & Sk.* VI. 133 He never observed ..the hook, which indeed was buried in the lire. *a* **1835** J. R. WILSON *Tales of Borders* (1837) III. 304/2 He was nae feckless smaik that, either in bane, limb, or lire. **1876** *Whitby Gloss., Lire*, the flesh of an animal, or rather the increasing substance as it grows bulky. 'There's a fair deal o' lire about it.'

Hence **ˈliry** *a. Obs.* exc. *dial.* Fleshy.

1483 *Cath. Angl.* 218/1 Lyrye, *pulposus.* **1876** *Whitby Gloss.* s.v. *Lire*, 'Quite liry', well fleshed.

lire, *sb.*² *rare*⁻¹. [App. due to some mistake on Scott's part, perh. a confused recollection of LITRE.] A supposed old French measure. (The glossaries of recent edd. say 'a pint'.)

1823 SCOTT *Quentin D.* xxxiv, 'If you want a confessor', said Trois-Eschelles—'Or a *lire* of wine', said his facetious companion.

†**lire, lier**, *v. Obs.* [f. **lire*, **lier*, LEAR².] *trans.* To thicken with a 'lear' (see LEAR² 2).

15.. *Wyl Bucke his Test.* (Copland) B ij b, Take blode of a good shepe..& drawe hit with the brede & lier vp thy pot therwith but not to thicke. *Ibid.* Lire him vp with crustes of brede, drawne with wine.

lire, var. LEER *sb.*¹ *Obs.*; obs. form of LYRE.

lire, pl. and obs. sing. form of LIRA.

‖**lirella** (lɪˈrɛlə). *Bot.* [mod.L. = F. *lirelle*, a diminutive f. L. *līra* furrow.] The narrow 'shield' or apothecium, with a furrow along the middle, found in some lichens.

1839 LINDLEY *Introd. Bot.* (ed. 3) 271 *Lirella* is a linear shield, such as is found in Opegrapha, with a channel along its middle. **1861** BENTLEY *Man. Bot.* 383 The more usual forms [of apothecia] are round and linear; in the latter case they are commonly termed lirellæ.

Hence **liˈrellate, liˈrelline, liˈrelliform** (*erron.* **lirellæform**), **liˈrellous** *adjs.*, shaped like a lirella.

1855 MAYNE *Expos. Lex., Lirelliformis*, ..lirelliform. *Lirellosus*, ..lirellous. **1871** W. A. LEIGHTON *Lichen-flora* 162 Apothecia..lirelliform. *Ibid.* 388 Apothecia lirellæform. **1889** *Syd. Soc. Lex., Lirellate.* **1900** JACKSON *Gloss. Bot. Terms, Lirelline.*

liricall, obs. form of LYRICAL.

†**liriconfancy.** *Obs.* Also 6 **liricum-, liriconfancie, lyryconfancy,** 7 **lilly-confancy,** 8 **liricumphancy.** [Corruption of L. *lilium convallium* (see CONVALLY), influenced by FANCY.] The lily of the valley.

1567 MAPLET *Gr. Forest* 49 Liricumfancie, or as other iudge May Lilie. **1578** LYTE *Dodoens* II. xxvi. 178 Lyllie Conuall, is now called..in English..Lyryconfancy. **1597** GERARDE *Herbal* II. lxxxvii. §2. 332 It is called in English Lillie of the valley, or the Conuall Lillie, and May Lillies, and in some places Liriconfancie. **1657** W. COLES *Adam in Eden* xii. 24 It [Lily of the Valley] is called..in some places, Liriconfancy or Lilly-Confancy. **1746** *Poor Robin, an Almanac* A 8 b (May), The Honey-suckle, Rosemary, Liricumphancy, Rose-parsley,...Which do this Month adorn each Field. **1755** JOHNSON, *Liriconfancy*, a flower.

liring, variant of LEARING: see LEAR².

‖**lirio** (ˈlirjo). [Sp. *lirio* iris.] The American Spanish name for the water hyacinth, *Eichhornia crassipes.*

Quot. 1844 refers to a different plant, perhaps the frangipani, *Plumeria rubra.*

[**1844** J. G. F. WURDEMANN *Notes on Cuba* v. 140 The quaint lirio's trumpet-shaped flowers painted yellow and red, and bursting in bunches from the blunt extremities of each leafless branch.] **1926** D. H. LAWRENCE *Plumed Serpent* v. 94 A long canal paved with bright green leaves from which poked the mauve heads of the lirio, the water hyacinth.

liriodendrin (laɪərɪəʊˈdɛndrɪn). *Chem.* [f. next + -IN.] A bitter principle extracted from the bark of the *Liriodendron tulipifera.*

1838 T. THOMSON *Chem. Org. Bodies* 836 The crystals of liriodendrin. **1865** WATTS *Dict. Chem.* s.v.

‖**liriodendron** (laɪərɪəʊˈdɛndrɒn). [mod.L., f. Gr. λείριον lily + δένδρον tree.] A genus of plants, N.O. *Magnoliaceæ*, of which the N. American Tulip-tree is the only representative.

[**1753** CHAMBERS *Cycl. Supp., Liriodendrum*,..a name given by Linnæus to a genus of plants called *tulipifera* by Catesby and others, and by us the *tulip tree.*] **1802** M. CUTLER in *Life* etc. (1888) II. 104 A number of trees, magnolias, bignonias, Liriodendrons, etc. **1847** *Nat. Encycl.* I. 925 The liriodendron.

ˈliripipe, ˈliripoop. *Obs.* ex. *Hist.* Forms: 6–7 **liripoope,** 6 **liripope, lerripoop, leerypoope, liri-, lyri-, leripup,** 7 **lyripoope, lirry-poop(e, leerepoop, luripup, lirripippes,** 9 **(liripipy), liripipe.** [ad. med.L. *liripipium, leropipium*, explained in glosses as 'tippet of a hood', 'cord', 'shoe-lace', and 'inner sole-leather of shoes'. No plausible etymology has been found; connexion of the latter part with F. *pipe* PIPE *sb.* is not unlikely; the form *loripipium*, which suggests L. *lorum* strap, is prob. an etymologizing corruption. Cf. F. *liripipion* (Cotgr.) 'a graduate's hood'.

Ménage's ludicrous guess, that *liripipium* is a corruption of *cleri ephippium*, is repeated seriously in recent Eng. Dicts.]

1. In early academical costume: The long tail of a graduate's hood (see quot. 1860).

[**1350–70** *Eulogium Hist.* (1863) III. 230 Habent etiam.. liripipia usque talum longa modo fatuorum dilacerata.] **1737** OZELL *Rabelais* I. xviii. I. 213 With his Hair cut round as a Dish, his Liripoop on his Head, after the old fashion. **1860** FAIRHOLT *Costume Eng.* (ed. 2) 93 It [the hood] is closed tightly about the head by the liripipe, or long pendent tail of the hood, that hung down the back when the hood was thrown off, and was wound like a bandage about it when placed over the head. **1872** E. L. CUTTS *Scenes & Charac.* 429 The priest is habited in a robe of purple, with a black cap and a black liripipe attached to it.

¶ A passage of Knighton (*c* 1400), well known from being quoted by Du Cange, speaks of certain court ladies as wearing male attire, with 'liripipes'. Hence such mod. examples as the following:

1843 JAMES *Forest Days* (1847) 83 As to her dress, she had a purfled liripipy might have suited a court harlot.

b. (See quot.; perh. a mistaken guess.)

1706 PHILLIPS (ed. Kersey), *Leripoops*, certain old-fashion'd Shoes, tipt with Horn, and ty'd up to the Knees with Silk-Ribbons, or Silver-Chains.

†**2.** Something to be learned and acted or spoken; one's 'lesson', 'rôle', or 'part'; chiefly in phrases ***to know*** or ***have*** (one's) ***liripoop, to teach*** (a person) ***his liripoop.*** *Obs.*

1546 *Supplic. of Poore Commons* (E.E.T.S.) 84 They know their liripope so well that they draw the tayle betwine the legges, and gette them selues streyght to the kennell. **1568** U. FULWELL *Like Will to Like* B iij, I shal teache you bothe your liripup to knowe. **1576** NEWTON *Lemnie's Complex.* vii. 58 A wittold..Who can his lyrypoope, and gaze full mannerly For birdes nestes in the roofe, while others syckerly Dubbes him an horned knight. **1577** STANYHURST *Descr. Irel.* in Holinshed II. 35/1, I will teach thee thy lyrripups after an other fashion than to be thus malepertlie cocking and billing with me that am thy gouernour. **1589** *Pappe w. Hatchet* 30, I am nor al tales, and riddles, and rimes, and iestes, thats but my Liripoope, if Martin knock the bone he shall find marrow. **1591** LYLY *Sappho* I. iii. 163 Thou maist bee skilled in thy logick, but not in thy leerypoope. **1594** —— *Moth. Bomb.* I. iii, Theres a girle that knowes her lerripoope. *c* **1600** DAY *Begg. Bednall Gr.* II. ii. (1881) 35 I'll teach him his leripoop for stealing whilst he hath a day to live again. **1611** COTGR. s.v. *Roulet, Qui scait bien son roulet*, That knowes his liripoope, thats thoroughly prouided to speake. *a* **1625** BEAUM. & FL. *Wit at Sev. Weap.* I. i, So, so, I have my lerrepoop already. **1633** BRETON *Packet Lett.* 60, I see you haue little to doe that haue so much leasure to play your Luripups.

¶ **b.** Used for: A shrewd trick.

1605 *London Prodigal* IV. i. E 3 b, Well, cha a bin zerued many a sluttish tricke, But such a lerripoope as thick ych was nere a sarued.

†**3.** A silly person. *Obs.*

1621 FLETCHER *Pilgrim* II. i, Keepe me this young Lirrypoope within doors. **17..** MILLES *MS. Devon Gloss.* (Halliw.), A *liripoop*, vel *lerripoop*, a silly, empty creature; an old dotard.

†**liripipionated**, *ppl. a. Obs. rare*⁻¹. [ad. F. *liripipionné* (nonce-wd.), f. *liripipion*: see prec.] Furnished with a 'liripipe'.

1653 URQUHART *Rabelais* I. xviii, Master Janotus, with his haire cut round like a dish..in his most antick accoustrement Liripipionated with a graduates hood [etc.].

lirique, obs. form of LYRIC.

lirk (lɜːk). *Sc.* and *north. dial.* Also 5, 9 **lerk,** 9 **lurk.** A fold in the skin; a wrinkle.

c **1400** *Destr. Troy* 3029 Hir forhed [was] full fresshe & fre to be-holde,..Nouþer lynes ne lerkes but full lell streght. **1728** RAMSAY *Last Sp. Miser* xv, Some loo to keep their skins frae lirks. **1737** MESTON *Poet. Wks.* (1767) 145 The Mare.. had no lirk in all her leather. **1880** *Antrim & Down Gloss.* s.v., The child's that fat I can't get dryin' all his lirks.

transf. & *fig.* **1723** MᶜWARD *Contend. for Faith* 307 (Jam.) The Lord..who knows to seek out the lirks of our pretences. **1802** SCOTT *Minstr. Scott. Bord.* (1803) III. 281 The bought i' the lirk o' the hill. *a* **1835** J. M. WILSON *Tales of the Borders* (1857) I. 207 Till I find her dead body in the lirk of the hill. **1849** LD. COCKBURN *Circuit Journeys* (1883) 359 A ..button..was found twisted in what the witness called 'a lurk', or fold, of the sheet. **1894** CROCKETT *Raiders* (ed. 3) 63 The..herds' cothouses in the lirks of the hills.

Hence **lirk** *v.*, to wrinkle.

1680 LAW *Mem.* (1818) 176–7 It [the elephant] has..a rough tannie skin, and lirking throughout all its body; the trunk of it lirks, and it contracts it, and draws it in..as it pleases. **1880** *Antrim & Down Gloss.* s.v., The uppers of your boots is all lerked.

liroconite (laɪəˈrɒkənaɪt). *Min.* Also *erron.* **liriconite.** [f. Gr. λειρός pale + κονία powder: see -ITE.] Hydrous arsenate of aluminum and copper, occurring in bluish-green crystals.

1821 R. JAMESON *Man. Mineral.* 94 Ord. IV. Malachite. Genus II. Liriconite. **1825** HAIDINGER *Mohs' Min.* Index, Liroconite. **1868** DANA *Min.* (ed. 5) 853 Liroconite.

†**lirp.** *Obs. rare.* A snap (of the fingers). So also **lirp** *v.*, **ˈlirping** *vbl. sb.*

1548 THOMAS *Ital. Gram.* (1567), *Chricch*, is the lirpyng that is made with the fingers. **1598** FLORIO, *Frulla*, a flurt or lirp with ones fingers... *Frullare*, to flurt or lirp with ones fingers.

lirrop, dial. var. LARRUP, to beat.

lirry, lirrie: see LURRY.

†**lirt.** *Obs.* [cf. BELIRT *v.*] Deception, trick.

c **1440** *York Myst.* xxvi. 255 For truly þou moste lerne vs That losell to lache, Or of lande, thurgh a lirte, That lurdayne may lepe. **1887** JAMIESON, Suppl. s.v., 'He gied her the lirt', i.e. the slip, go-by.

†**lirylong**, *adv. Obs. rare*⁻¹. [Cf. ALIRY.]

c **1400** *Beryn* 309 He stappid into the tapstry wondir pryuely And fond hir ligging lirylong.

lis¹ (liːs). *Her.* Pl. **lis, lisses.** Also 7 **lize,** 8 **lys.** [a. F. *lis* lily.] = FLEUR-DE-LIS 2.

1611 SPEED *Hist. Gt. Brit.* IX. xii. 572 Hee [Edw. III].. quartered the Flower de Lize with the Leopards..albeit wee see his former Seale also adorned with two Lize or

Lillies. **1707** CHAMBERLAYNE *St. Gt. Brit.* II. ii. 90 Or, within a double Tressure, Counter-flower'd Lys. **1870** H. JENNINGS *Rosicrucians* vii. 45 Now of the 'lisses', as we shall elect to call them. *Ibid.* 46 The three 'Lotuses', or 'Lisses', were the coat of arms. **1888** *Athenæum* 1 Dec. 742/1 A cross fleury with lions and lis in the angles.

lis[2], **liss** (lɪs). *Irish Antiq.* [a. Ir. *lios*, OIr. *liss*, *less* = Welsh *llys*.] A circular enclosure having an earthen wall; often used as a fort.

1845 G. PETRIE in *Trans. R. Irish Acad.* XX. 443 The great Rath or Lis, called Lismor, or the great fort. **1858** B. O'LOONEY in *Trans. Ossianic Soc.* IV. 231 The nobles of this country are said to live in the great and large duns, fortresses, lisses, and raths. **1899** W. B. YEATS *Secret Rose* in *Wind among Reeds* 49 Him who drove the gods out of their liss.

lisarde, obs. form of LIZARD.

Lisbon ('lɪzbən). The name of the capital of Portugal. [= Pg. *Lisboa*.] Hence: **a.** A white wine produced in the province of Estremadura in Portugal and imported from Lisbon; also ***Lisbon wine***. † **b.** A kind of soft sugar. **c.** A kind of lemon.

Lisbon cut, a kind of brilliant cut, the same as 'double brilliant' (1874 Knight *Dict. Mech.* 384/2). ***Lisbon diet-drink*** (see quot. 1854–67 s.v. DIET-DRINK).

1767 MRS. GLASSE *Cookery* 368 Take one pound of the best Lisbon sugar. **1767** H. KELLY *Babler* No. 41 I. 173 A Vintner who owed me a hundred pounds for some Lisbons (for you must know I am a wine-merchant). **1769** MRS. RAFFALD *Eng. Housekpr.* (1778) 42 Put to it a glass of Lisbon wine. **1799** M. UNDERWOOD *Treat. Dis. Children* (ed. 4) III. 125 A little Lisbon sugar may be added to this compound of sugar and milk. **1818** TODD, *Lisbon*. 1. A kind of white wine. 2. A kind of soft sugar. **1897** MISS HARRADEN *Hilda Strafford* 133 Robert went to a lemon-nursery and bought 500 Lisbons, budded on the sour root.

lische, obs. Sc. form of LEASH.

lise, obs. 3rd sing. ind. pres. of LIE *v.*[1]

†**liser**. *Obs.* Also 4 **lyser**, **lesere**, 5 **lysure**. [a. OF. *lisiere*, of unknown origin. Cf. LISIÈRE.] A list, selvage; also, a strip or cutting of cloth.

1377 LANGL. *P. Pl.* B. v. 210 Thanne drowe I me amonges draperes my donet to lerne, To drawe þe lyser [*v.rr.* liser, lesere] alonge þe lenger it semed. *c* **1440** *Promp. Parv.* 307/1 Lyyst, or lysure, *strophium*. Lyyste, lysure, or schrede, or chyppyngys, what so euer hyt be, *presegmen*.

†**li'sette**. *Obs.* [a. F. *Lisette*, dim. of *Élise*, *Élisabeth*. Cf. LISKIN.] A French maidservant.

1774 CHESTERF. *Lett.* (1792) I. xxxvi. 118 Your footman and lisette would be your equals, were as rich as you.

lish (lɪʃ), *a. dial.* Also **leash**, **leish**, **lies(c)h**, **leesh** (see *Eng. Dial. Dict.*) Active, nimble.

1781 J. HUTTON *Tour to Caves* 92 Gloss., *Lish*, stout and active. **1818** HOGG *Brownie of Bodsbeck* I. 39 Twa lang liesch chaps. **1820** *Blackw. Mag.* May 160 He was a leash lad and a leal. **1822** BEWICK *Mem.* 86 Up came a 'lish' clever young man, a Highlander smartly dressed in the garb of his country.

lish, variant of *leish*, LEASH *sb.* (sense 7 a).

1799 G. SMITH *Laboratory* II. 49 The journeyman-weaver.. transfers the lish or cord [etc.].

†**lisible**, *a. Obs.* Also **licible**, **loisible**. [a. F. *loisible* (? OF. **leisible*), f. OF. *loisir*, *leisir* (see LEISURE *sb.*):—L. *licēre* to be lawful: cf. LICENCE.] Lawful, permissible.

a **1420** HOCCLEVE *De Reg. Princ.* 1565 Þi conceyt holdeþ it good and lisible [*Halliwell reads* licible] To doon. *Ibid.* 3119 When he a man y-murdred hath and slawe A man to sle by lawe, it is lisible. **1546** *St. Papers Hen. VIII*, XI. 309 Toching the stay of his fortifications at Portet, which ar alledged by us not loisible by the treaty.

‖**lisière** (lizjɛr). *Fortif.* ? *Obs.* Also 8 **lizier**. [Fr.: cf. LISER.] = BERM, FORELAND 2 b.

1706 PHILLIPS (ed. Kersey), *Lisiere*,..a Term in Fortification, the same as *Berme* and *Fore-land*. **1758** J. WATSON *Milit. Dict.*, *Foreland*, Barm, Berm, or Lizier.

lisk (lɪsk). Now *dial.* Forms: α. 3 *Orm.* **lesske**, 5–7 **leske**, 6 *Sc.* **leisk**, 7– **lesk**. β. 6– **lisk**, (7 **liske**, **lysk**). γ. 5–6 **laske**, 8 **lask**. [Prob. of Scandinavian origin: cf. MSw. *liuske*, *liumske* (mod.Sw. *ljumske*) masc., Da. *lyske*, MDu., Flemish *liesche* fem. (mod.Du. *lies* fem.); a form *lesca* 'inguen' in the Werden Glosses (Gallée *O.S. Texts* 360) may possibly be OE. (for **léosca*), but the *sk* (instead of *sh*) of the ME. and mod. forms shows that they do not descend from this.] The loin or flank; also, the groin.

α. *c* **1200** ORMIN 4776 Lende, & lesske, & shulldre, & bacc. ? *a* **1400** *Morte Arth.* 1097 Lyme and leskes fulle lothyne. *c* **1440** *Promp. Parv.* 298/2 Leske (or flanke), *inguen*. **1483** *Cath. Angl.* 214/1 A Leske, *ypocondria*. **1513** DOUGLAS *Æneis* x. x. 103 At his left flank or leisk [**1553** lisk] persyt tyte. **1615** CROOKE *Body of Man* 32 In the leske or groyne are the Emunctories of the Liuer. **1639** HORN & ROB. *Gate Lang. Unl.* xxi. §255 In the lesk, under the groin or share, are the privities or secrets. **1847** HALLIWELL, *Lesk*, the groin or flank. **1886** *S.W. Linc. Gloss.* s.v. *Lesk*, My husband's broke his body, and it presses on his lesk.

β. **1508** DUNBAR *Flyting w. Kennedie* 121 Lene larbar, loungeour, baith lowsy in lisk and lonȝe. **1603** in Pitcairn *Crim. Trials* II. 417 Be the straik of ane sword in the lisk and tne wambe. **1679** *Lauderdale Papers* (1885) III. xciv. 163 Wounded.. in the groyn or lisk with a partizan. **1690** *Lond. Gaz.* No. 2575/4 A white Mare,..blew Spots about the Lysk, bob-tail'd. **1709** *Jacob. Songs* (1887) 57 Ane proddit her in the lisk Anither aneath the tail. **1857** GEN. P. THOMPSON *Audi Alt.* I. xxiv. 93 There was but one point on which he could not bear being attacked, like a horse which will not stand being touched in the lisk.

γ. ? **14..** *Harl. MS.* 219, lf. 150 (in *Promp. Parv.* 298) *Mes flanks*, my laskes. **1552** HULOET, Laske or flancke, *pyga*. **1781** J. HUTTON *Tour to Caves* 92 Gloss., *Lisk*, or *lask*, the flank.

liskeardite (lɪ'skɑːdaɪt). *Min.* [Named by Maskelyne, 1878, from *Liskeard* in Cornwall: see -ITE.] Hydrous arseniate of iron and aluminium.

1878 *Nature* 15 Aug. 426/2. **1883** *Ibid.* XXVII. 307 Two new aluminous mineral species, Evigtokite and Liskeardite.

†**'liskin**. *Obs.* [a. obs. Du. *Liesken* (= mod.Du. *Liesje*), dim. of *Elisabeth*. Cf. LISETTE.] A Dutch maidservant.

1594 PLAT *Jewell-ho.* I. 55 And this can our duche liskins, and kitchin maides well approue.

Lisle (laɪl). The name of a town in France (now *Lille*), used *attrib.* in ***Lisle glove***, ***lace***, ***thread*** (see quots.).

1851 *Illustr. Catal. Gt. Exhib.* 201 Fast cotton dyeing for Lisle thread gloves. **1858** SIMMONDS *Dict. Trade*, *Lisle-gloves*, fine thread gloves for summer wear. *Lille-lace*, *Lisle-lace*, a light, fine and transparent white thread hand-made lace, sometimes called 'clear foundation'. **1879** WEBSTER Suppl., *Lisle-thread*, a hard twisted cotton thread, originally produced at Lisle, France.

lisne, obs. variant of LISSEN *dial.*, rock-cleft.

lisnisse, variant of LESNESS *Obs.*

c **1305** *St. Christopher* 75 in *E.E.P.* (1862) 61 Þu most in lisnisse [*S. Eng. Leg.* 273/73 lesnesse] of þi synne þer habbe þi woninge.

lisome, variant of LEESOME *a.*[2] *Sc. Obs.*

1653 *Burgh Rec. Glasgow* II. 260 It sall not be lisome to any landwart or countery man to buy [etc.].

†**lisoun**. *Obs.* In 4 **lysoun**. [? a. OF. *luision* shining, light.] ? Glimpse; trace.

13.. *E.E. Allit. P.* B. 887 Þay lest of Lotez logging any lysoun to fynde.

lisp (lɪsp), *sb.*[1] [f. LISP *v.*] The action or an act of lisping.

a **1625** FLETCHER & MASSINGER *Elder Bro.* II. ii, Love those that love good fashions, Good clothes and rich, they invite men to admire'm That speake the lispe of Court, Oh, 'tis great learning! **1676** ETHEREDGE *Man of Mode* I. i, *Bell.* What a pretty lisp he has! *Dor.* Ho, that he affects in imitation of the people of Quality of France. **1709** STEELE *Tatler* No. 27 ¶5 She has naturally a very agreeable Voice and Utterance, which she has chang'd for the prettiest Lisp imaginable. **1716** LADY M. W. MONTAGU *Let. to C'tess Mar* 21 Nov., They all affect a little soft lisp. **1848** DICKENS *Dombey* xxxvi, A young lady of sixty-five,..who spoke with an engaging lisp. **1869** J. EADIE *Galatians* 303 The childlike lisp in the word Abba and its easy labial pronunciation.

b. *transf.* A sound resembling a lisp, e.g. the rippling of water, the rustle of leaves.

1855 BROWNING *Popularity* viii, As if they still the water's lisp heard Through foam the rock-weeds thresh. **1863** LONGF. *Wayside Inn*, *1st Interlude* 55 Wild birds gossiping overhead, And lisp of leaves, and fountain's fall. **1864** SWINBURNE *Atalanta* 68 The mother of months.. Fills the shadows and windy places With lisp of leaves and ripple of rain.

Lisp (lɪsp), *sb.*[2] *Computing.* Also **LISP**. [f. *list processor*: cf. *list processing* s.v. LIST *sb.*[6] d.] A high-level programming language devised for list processing.

1959 *Q. Progr. Rep.* (Mass. Inst. Technol. Res. Lab. Electronics) No. 53. xiii. 122 The purpose of this programming system, called LISP (for LISt Processor), is to facilitate programming manipulations of symbolic expressions. **1969** P. B. JORDAN *Condensed Computer Encycl.* 282 LISP is an interpretive language developed for manipulation of symbolic strings of recursive data. **1983** *Austral. Personal Computer* IV. v. 41/1 The language's underlying strength in symbol handling and the ease with which Lisp programs are modified and extended have led to its use in high precision arithmetic and algebraic manipulation. **1984** J. HILTON *Choosing & using your Home Computer* 159 LISP.. has been widely used in the field of Artificial Intelligence, which involves continually searching and comparing lists of data, relationships and responses.

lisp (lɪsp), *v. Pa. t.* and *pa. pple.* **lisped** (lɪspt). Forms: 1 ***wlispian**, (**áwlyspian**), 4 **wlispe**, 4–6 **lysp(e**, 4–5, ? 7 **lipse**, (5 **lyspyn**), 6–7 **lispe**, 7– **lisp**. (Also 7–9 *jocularly* **lithp.**) [OE. **wlispian* (known only in comb. *áwlyspian*), f. *wlisp*, *wlips* adj., lisping; cf. MLG. *wlispen*, *wilspen*, LG., Du. *lispen*, Sw. *läspa*, Da. *læspe* to lisp, OHG. *lisp* adj., stammering, OHG., MHG. *lispen* to trip in speaking, lisp, mod.G. *lispeln* to lisp.]

1. *intr.* To speak with that defect of utterance which consists in substituting for (s) and (z) sounds approaching (θ) and (ð); either by reason of a defect in the organs of speech or as an affectation. Also, *loosely*, to speak with child-like utterance, falteringly or imperfectly.

a **1100** *MS. Junius* 23, lf. 142 b (in *Mod. Lang. Notes* (1889) May 279/1), And seo tunge awlyspaþ, seo þe ær hæfde ful recene spræce. **1375** BARBOUR *Bruce* I. 393 In spek wlispyt he sum deill. *c* **1386** CHAUCER *Prol.* 264 Somwhat he lipsed, for his wantownesse To make his englissh sweete vp on his tonge. *c* **1440** *Promp. Parv.* 306/2 Lyspyn yn speche, *sibilo*. **1530** PALSGR. 612/2 He lyspeth a lytell, but it becometh hym well. **1588** SHAKS. *L.L.L.* v. ii. 323 He can carue too, and lispe. **1600** —— *A.Y.L.* IV. i. 34 Looke you lispe, and weare strange suites. **1604** MIDDLETON *F. Hubburd's Tales* Wks. (Bullen) VIII. 80 She had a humour to lisp often, like a flattering wanton. *c* **1680** BEVERIDGE *Serm.* (1729) I. 111 As a nurse to a child.. lisps in broken language. **1712** STEELE *Spect.* No. 492 ¶4, I can move with a speaking mien, can look significantly, can lisp, can trip, can loll. **1735** POPE *Prol. Sat.* 128 As yet a child, nor yet a fool to fame, I lisp'd in numbers, for the numbers came. **1786** MAD. D'ARBLAY *Diary* 13 Aug., Lady Charlotte is very handsome,..she unfortunately lisps very much. **1827** KEBLE *Chr. Y.* 3rd Sund. Lent, As little children lisp, and tell of Heaven.

2. *trans.* To utter with a lisp or lispingly (also with *out*). In extended use, to utter with childlike, imperfect, or faltering articulation; to give imperfect utterance or articulation to (*lit.* and *fig.*).

1620 SANDERSON *Serm.* I. 157 As nurses talk half syllables, and lipse out broken language to young children. **1651** N. BACON *Disc. Govt. Eng.* II. xxx. 239 The Statute of Henry the fourth concerning Heresie doth lispe some such Power. **1661** BOYLE *Style of Script.* (1675) 28 Vouchsafing to lisp mysteries to those that would be deterred by any other way of expressing them. **1702** POPE *Dryope* 81 When first his infant voice shall.. lisp his mother's name. **1718** *Freethinker* No. 17 ¶6 Her Maid trips in, and lisps out to me, that her Lady is gone to Bed. **1750** GRAY *Elegy* 23 No Children run to lisp their Sire's Return. **1818** COBBETT *Pol. Reg.* XXXIII. 64 Pray send me the Report that you speak of, in which they begin to lisp their intentions. **1819** *Metropolis* III. 174 Lady tho and tho, lithpth out an Insipid. **1834** MACAULAY *Pitt* Ess. (1887) 319 Newcastle sent for Pitt, hugged him,.. and lisped out the highest compliments. **1838** LYTTON *Alice* 62 'And me, too', lisped Sophia—the youngest hope. **1855** BROWNING *Cleon* 3 The light wave lisps 'Greece'.

Hence **lisped** *ppl. a.*

a **1851** JOANNA BAILLIE *Basil* II. iv. Wks. (1851) 27 The lisp'd flattery of a cunning child.

lisper ('lɪspə(r)). Also 5 **lyspare**, 6 **lispar**, **lypsar**. [f. LISP *v.* + -ER[1].] One who lisps.

c **1440** *Promp. Parv.* 306/2 Lyspare, *blesus..sibilus*. **1519** HORMAN *Vulg.* 31 No man shulde rebuke and scorne a blereyied man or gogylyed, or toungetyed, or lypsar, or a stuttar or fumblar. **1684** tr. *Bonet's Merc. Compit.* II. 42 The disaffection of Lispers consists in Conformation, and not at all in Intemperature. **1709** STEELE *Tatler* No. 77 ¶1, I remember a Race of Lispers, fine Persons, who took an Aversion to particular Letters in our Language. **1823** BYRON *Juan* IX. lxxviii, Each lovely lisper Smiled. **1827** LYTTON *Pelham* iii, 'Ah', said the lisper, carelessly; 'but can he write poetry, and play proverbs?'

lisping ('lɪspɪŋ), *vbl. sb.* [f. LISP *v.* + -ING[1].] The action of the verb LISP (*lit.*, *transf.*, and *fig.*).

c **1440** *Promp. Parv.* 306/2 Lyspynge, *sibilatus*, *blesura*. **1625** J. KING *David's Strait* 5 Plato's crump-shoulder and Aristotle's lisping. **1641** 'SMECTYMNUUS' *Vind. Answ.* §13. 156 For our parts we answer without lisping. **1674** R. GODFREY *Inj. & Ab. Physic* 205 Having some defect in her Speech, to wit, a Lisping. **1768–74** TUCKER *Lt. Nat.* (1834) II. 622 To prevent lisping, stammering, and other such like imperfections. **1820** HAZLITT *Lect. Dram. Lit.* 10 These first crude attempts at poetry and lispings of the Muse. **1839** LONGF. *Voices Nt.* Prelude xiii, Low lispings of the summer rain.

attrib. **1875** TENNYSON *Q. Mary* v. ii, I remember How I would dandle you upon my knee At lisping-age.

'lisping, *ppl. a.* [f. LISP *v.* + -ING[2].] That lisps; (of sounds or utterance) characterized by a lisp or lisping.

1535 COVERDALE *Isa.* xxviii. 11 The Lorde also shal speake with lispinge lippes and with a straunge language vnto this people. **1586** A. DAY *Eng. Secretary* I. (1625) 68 A pleasant lisping sound. **1646** FANSHAWE *Guarino's Pastor Fido* (1676) 142 Thy lithping gibberish. **1669** HOLDER *Elem. Speech* 45 The other pair of Lisping and Sibilant Letters. **1776** S. J. PRATT *Pupil Pleas.* (1777) I. 27 A lisping accent. **1827** LYTTON *Pelham* iii, I heard my own name pronounced by a very soft, lisping voice. **1841** MYERS *Cath. Th.* III. v. 17 The father who should impose the obligations of manhood upon a yet lisping son,.. would be as unjust as he would be unwise.

lispingly ('lɪspɪŋlɪ), *adv.* [f. prec. + -LY[2].] In a lisping manner; with faltering utterance.

1630 J. TAYLOR (Water P.) *Agst. Cursing & Swearing* Wks. I. 50/1 Little children that can scarce.. speake plaine, can make a shift to sweare lispingly. **1660** FULLER *Mixt Contempl.* 62 How lispingly and imperfectly doe we perform the close of this Petition. **1833** *New Monthly Mag.* XXXVII. 419 The affairs which were lispingly discussed in the lady's chamber.

lispound ('lɪspaʊnd). Also 6 **lespund**, **lesh pund**, 7–8 **leispound**, (8 **lispond**), 8–9 **lispund**. [ad. LG. and Du. *lispund*, contr. f. *livsch pund* 'Livonian pound' = med.L. *livonicum talentum*. (An example, in the form *lispunt*, is quoted by Du Cange from a Polish document of 1454.)] A unit of weight used in the Baltic trade, and in Orkney and Shetland, varying at different periods and in different localities from 12 to 30 pounds.

1545 *Rates Custom Ho.* d vj, viii lyspoundes facit .c. li. xx. lispoundes facit a shyp pounde. **1597** SKENE *De Verb. Signif.* s.v. *Serplaith*, Ane stane and twa pound Scottish makis ane lesh pund. **1693** J. WALLACE *Orkney* 92 Leispound a weight of their Victual, which contains 24 of their Merks: it is also called a Setten. This answers to 28 of our pounds. **1793**

Statist. Acc. Scot., Shetl. V. 197 The butter..is delivered to the landlord in certain cases by the lispond. This denomination of weight consisted originally of only 12 Scotch or Dutch pounds. By various acts..it has been gradually raised to 30 lb. **1822** SCOTT *Pirate* i. Eight lispunds of butter. **1837** G. G. MACDOUGALL *Graah's E. Coast Greenland* 33 A tribute of 127 lispounds of walrus-teeth. **1858** HOMANS *Cycl. Commerce* 1635 [At Riga] the lispound = 20 lbs. [= 18·4 lbs. avoirdupois].

lispy (ˈlɪspɪ), *a. nonce-wd.* [f. LISP *sb.*^{1} + -Y.] Characterized by a lisp; inclined to lisp.

1873 DURNFORD *Let.* 25 Oct. *Mem.* (1899) 165 Lord Stanhope reminded me really of what he was years ago, rather prosy and lispy, but sensible and full.

†**liss.** *Obs.* Also 1 líðs, liss, 2–4 lisse, 3 lysse, 4–5 lys. [OE. *líðs, líss*, f. *líðe* gentle, soft: see LITHE *a.*]

1. Remission, release; mitigation, abatement; hence, cessation, end.

c **1000** *Credo* 54 (Gr.) *Remissionem peccatorum.* Lisse ic ȝelyfe leahtra ȝehwylces. *c* **1175** *Lamb. Hom.* 145 Song wiδ-uten lisse. *c* **1200** *Moral Ode* 239 in *Trin. Coll. Hom.*, Eiδer doδ hem wo inoh, nabbeδ hie none lisse. *c* **1384** CHAUCER *H. Fame* I. 220 Ther sawe I Ioues venus kysse And graunted was of the tempest lysse. *c* **1386** —— *Frankl. T.* 510 What for his labour and his hope of blisse His woful herte of penaunce hadde a lisse. **1393** LANGL. *P. Pl.* C. II. 200 Loue is lech of lyue and lysse of alle peyne. *c* **1450** LONELICH *Grail* li. 310 Of his peynes he myhte hauen non lys. **1802** SIBBALD *Chron. Sc. Poetry* IV. Gloss., *Liss*, remission or abatement, especially of any acute disease.

2. Tranquillity, peace, rest; joy, delight.

c **1000** *Phœnix* 672 (Gr.) Lifȝan in lisse lucis et pacis. *a* **1023** WULFSTAN *Hom.* (Napier) 265 þa eadiȝan ceasterwaran þær ȝefeoþ and wynsumiaδ on lisse and on blisse. *c* **1175** *Lamb. Hom.* 15 Blisse and lisse ic sende uppon monnen þe me luuieδ. *c* **1205** LAY. 3261 þat he mihte.. libben on lisse [*later text* ine blisse]. *c* **1275** *Sayings of Bede* 34 in Horstm. *Altengl. Leg.* 505 þer-inne is reste and lisse. *a* **1310** in Wright *Lyric P.* xviii. 57 Suete Ihesu,..Myn huerte love, min huerte lisse. **13..** *Guy Warw.* (A.) 430 Bring me of þis wodenisse And bring me in to sum lisse. **1377** LANGL. *P. Pl.* B. IX. 29 Lorde of lyf and of lyȝte of lysse and of peyne. **1393** *Ibid.* C. VII. 315 Me ys leuere in this lif as a lorel beggen þan in lysse to lyue.

liss: see LIS^2.

Lissajous (ˈlɪsæʒuː). The name of Jules Antoine *Lissajous* (1822–80), French physicist, used *attrib.* and in the possessive to designate the plane figures (mostly crossed loops and simple curves) traced by a point executing two independent simple harmonic motions at right angles to one another and with frequencies in a simple numerical ratio (described by Lissajous in *Compt. Rend.* (1855) XLI. 814).

1877 RAYLEIGH *Theory of Sound* I. p. vii, Lissajous' Figures. **1902** *Encycl. Brit.* XXV. 50/1 If both forks vibrate, an observer looking through the microscope sees the bright point describing Lissajous figures. **1939** *Brit. Jrnl. Psychol.* Oct. 129 The frequency of the tones employed..is checked by obtaining a Lissajous's figure against a constant frequency source applied to the other deflectors of the cathode-ray tube. **1943** *Electronic Engin.* XVI. 170 Two measuring techniques for the Lissajous' figures produced on the oscilloscope screen are described. **1973** *Sci. Amer.* Aug. 76/2 The two tones were next matched precisely on a cathode ray oscilloscope by tuning the generated tone until a clear Lissajous figure with a ratio of 1:1 appeared repeatedly on the screen.

‖**lisse** (liːs), *sb.*^{1} [F. *lisse* smooth (in *crêpe lisse* smooth crape).] A kind of silk gauze.

1852 MRS. STOWE *Uncle Tom's C.* xiii. 113 The snowy lisse crape cap. **1864** *Daily Tel.* 11 Mar., A long white crape lisse veil. **1879** MRS. ELIOT JAMES *Ind. Househ. Managem.* 18 Lisse, if you go to a hot station [in India], would be almost useless. **1884** *Cassell's Fam. Mag.* Feb. 184/2 Edge it with lace plaiting or lisse frilling.

‖**lisse** (liːs), *sb.*^{2} *Weaving.* [a. F. *lisse, lice* (cf. with quot. F. *haute lice*).] = LEASE *sb.*^{4} 2, 3. Also see quots. 1878, 1885.

1782 *Encycl. Brit.* (ed. 2) IX. 6711/1 [Parts of a ribbon-loom] 6 The high-lisses, or lists, are a number of long threads, with platines, or plate-leads, at the bottom [etc.]. **1878** DE CHAMPEAUX *Tapestry* Introd., [Explains the 'lisses' to be the two cylinders of which the loom consists]. **1885** E. MÜNTZ *Tapestry* xvi. 358 Rings of small cord called 'lices' or 'lisses', are fastened to each thread of the front cloth.

†**lisse,** *v. Obs.* (? exc. *Sc.*) Also 4 les, 4–5 lis, lys, 4–6 lysse. [OE. *líssian*:—pre-Eng. *linþisôjan, f. *linþjo- soft, mild: see LITHE *a.*]

1. *trans.* To subdue (only OE.); to mitigate, assuage, relieve (pain, etc.).

a **1000** *Sal. & Sat.* 294 (Gr.) Yldo beoþ on eorþan æȝhwæs cræftiȝ..lisseþ [? *for* lissaδ] eal δæt heo wile. *c* **1320** R. BRUNNE *Medit.* 702, Y prey þe sumdele hys peyne þou lys. *c* **1350** *Will. Palerne* 848 Forto lissen his langour. *c* **1470** *Golagros & Gaw.* 173 Hym likis in land your langour to lis. **1562** TURNER *Herbal* II. 113 Such compositiones as stanche or lysse ake.

2. To relieve (*of* pain, etc.); to comfort.

c **1374** CHAUCER *Troylus* I. 702 Lat vs lyssen wo with oþer speche. *Ibid.* I. 1082 Troylus..is somdel of akynge of his wounde Ilyssed. *c* **1375** *Sc. Leg. Saints* xxxviii. (*Adrian*) 117 As for to les þame of þar payne. *c* **1386** CHAUCER *Frankl. T.* 442 In hope for to been lissed of his care. *c* **1440** *Pol. Rel. & L. Poems* 245/45 This leche lyssyd me, lazars. *c* **1460** J. RUSSELL *Bk. Nurture* 31 Son, open thyn hert for peraventure y cowd the lis. *c* **1470** HARDING *Chron.* XCIV. ii, In water [he] was cast, his fleshe to keele and lisse. **1483** CAXTON *Gold. Leg.* 352 b/1 That..they may be eased and lyssed of theyr paynes.

3. *intr.* To abate, cease, stop; to be relieved *of.*

c **1400** *Rom. Rose* 3758 Than of my peyne I gan to lisse. *Ibid.* 4128, I trowe my peyne shall never lisse. **1825–80** JAMIESON, *To Liss*, to cease, to stop. *It never lisses*, it never ceases, Roxb.

Hence †ˈ**lissing** *vbl. sb.*

? *a* **1412** LYDG. *Two Merchants* 641 Which in to lissyng his langour did leede.

lissen (ˈlɪs(ə)n). *dial.* Also 7 lisne, 7–9 lissom. [Of obscure origin: cf. LIST *sb.*^{3}, which has some affinity in meaning (cf. sense 4 of that word).]

1. A cleft or seam dividing the strata of a rock.

c **1640** J. SMYTH *Hundred of Berkeley* (1885) III. 175 A strange stone..wherein is noe chinke, cracke, chopp, or Lisne at all. *a* **1677** HALE *Prim. Orig. Man.* II. vii. 192 In the Lisne of a Rock at Kingscote in Glocestershire, I found at least a Bushel of Petrified Cockles. **1677** PLOT *Oxfordsh.* 58 We have another fine Earth..found frequently in the lissoms or seams of the Rocks. **1847** HALLIWELL, *Lissen*, a cleft in a rock. Glouc. **1890** *Gloucester Gloss.*, *Lissen*, a cleft in a rock; the parting of stone in a quarry.

2. A layer or stratum; †a support for a beehive.

1790 *Trans. Soc. Arts* VIII. 126 (Let. fr. Faringdon, Berks.) Two [hives]..that I was obliged to raise on lissoms nine inches high. **1879** in MISS JACKSON *Shropsh. Word-bk.* s.v., 'In burnin' lime we putten first a lissom o' coal, an' then a lissom o' lime-stwun'.

3. A strand of rope; 'one of the rows of straw plait in a bonnet' (Devon 1837 in E.D.D.).

1875 KNIGHT *Dict. Mech.*, *Lissens*, the ultimate strands of a rope. **1886** ELWORTHY *W. Somerset Word-bk.*, *Lissom*, the strand of a rope; each lissom may be composed of several yarns.

lissencephalous (ˌlɪsɛnˈsɛfələs), *a. Zool.* [f. mod.L. *Lissencephal-a* (f. λισσός smooth + ἐγκέφαλος brain) + -OUS.] Pertaining to the *Lissencephala*, the second group of mammals in Owen's classification, which have smooth brains.

1859 OWEN *Class. Mammalia* 33 The following Table exemplifies the correspondence of the groups in the Lyencephalous and Lissencephalous series. **1875** BLAKE *Zool.* 53 The lissencephalous or smooth-brained mammals fall naturally into four well-defined orders.

lisses, pl. of LIS^1.

lissoir (liswar). *Archæol.* [Fr.] A smoothing, polishing tool.

1911 W. J. SOLLAS *Ancient Hunters* viii. 214 A small object, about the size and shape of the human tongue, possibly the end of a 'lissoir' (smoothing implement). *Ibid.* xii. 368 The ivory 'lissoir' or smoother of the Eskimo..is represented in the Magdalenian industry. **1932** *Jrnl. R. Anthrop. Inst.* LXII. 265 Skin-rubbers were made from antler of *Dama Mesopotamica*, cut obliquely and smoothed, in the manner of the Magdalenian *lissoir*. **1937** GARROD & BATE *Stone Age Mt. Carmel* I. I. ii. 15 Bone points and pierced animal teeth and a *lissoir* of *Dama Mesopotamica* antler. **1964** *New Scientist* 9 Apr. 88/1 A single, well-used bone-tool came to light; it appears to be a sort of 'lissoir' for working leather thongs.

lissom (ˈlɪsəm), *a.* Also lissome. [Contracted variant of LITHESOME.] **a.** Supple, limber; lithesome; lithe and agile.

a **1800** PEGGE *Suppl. to Grose* (1814) 34 *Lissom*, limber, relaxed, North. **1824** MISS MITFORD *Village* Ser. I. 147 They are..so much more athletic, and yet so much lissomer—to use a Hampshire phrase, which deserves at least to be good English. **1825** BRITTON *Beauties Wiltsh.* III. 375 *Lithesome*, or *Lissome*, soft, pliable; expert in action. *a* **1839** PRAED *Poems* (1864) II. 135 Back flew the bolt of lissom lath. **1855** TENNYSON *Brook* 70 Straight, but as lissome as a hazel wand. **1879** JEFFERIES *Wild Life in S. Co.* 11 The lissom bound of the hare. **1890** 'ROLF BOLDREWOOD' *Miner's Right* (1899) 187/1 The tongues grow lissom under the influence of good fellowship and potent liquor.

fig. **1859** HELPS *Friends in C.* Ser. II. I. viii. 227 His [Ovid's] lissome lines are droned over.

b. That renders supple. *nonce-use.*

1864 LD. DERBY *Iliad* XVIII. 389 They wash'd the corpse, With lissom oils anointing.

Hence ˈ**lissomely** *adv.*; ˈ**lissomness.**

1857 HUGHES *Tom Brown* II. iii. (1871) 264 He..was applauded by all for his lissomness. **1895** SAINTSBURY *Corrected Impressions* xv. 142 His..marvellous lissomeness ..of thought. **1902** W. DE LA MARE *Songs of Childhood* 54 Though danced she lissomely. **1927** M. SADLEIR *Trollope: a Comm.* 322 Trollope worried to find it limping on its way, when usually his stories moved so lissomely.

lissotrichous (lɪˈsɒtrɪkəs), *a. Zool.* [f. Gr. λισσός smooth + τριχ-, θρίξ hair.] Smooth-haired; leiotrichous.

1880 F. P. PASCOE *Zool. Classif.* (ed. 2) 280 *Lissotrichous* or *Liotrichous*, having straight smooth hair.

†**list,** *sb.*^{1} *Obs.* Forms: 1 hlyst, 2–4 lust(e, 3–4 list(e, lyst, 4 lest, 4–6 list. [OE. *hlyst* masc. and fem. = OS. *hlust* fem., ON. *hlust* fem.:—OTeut. *hlusti-z:—OAryan *klusti-s (Skr. *çruṣṭi* obedience), f. root *klus- (:kleus- :klous-), OTeut. *hlŭs- (:hleus- :hlaus-), found also in the vbs. OE. *hlosnian*, OHG. *losên* (MHG. *losen*), OHG. *lûstrên* (mod.G. dial. *laustern*: cf. G. *lüstern*, Sw. *lystra*, Da. *lystre* to 'answer' to a name, 'answer' the helm), MHG. *lûschen* (mod.G. *lauschen*), MHG. *lusemen, lüsenen*, all meaning 'to listen'; also, outside Teut., in OSl. *slyšati* to hear, *sluχŭ* hearing, Lith. *klausà* obedience, *klausýti* to hear, Zend *çraosānē* to hear, Welsh *clûst*, Irish *clúas* fem., ear (:—OCeltic *kloustā). The root OAryan *klus-: kleus-: klous- (Teut. *hlŭs-: hleus-: hlous-) is an extended form of *klu- (Teut. *hlŭ-): see LOUD *a.*]

1. Hearing; the sense of hearing. ***to have*** or ***give a list***: to give ear, be attentive, keep silence.

c **1000** ÆLFRIC *Hom.* II. 550 Ða fif andȝitu ure lichaman, δæt is ȝesihþ and hylst, swæcc and stenc and hrepung. *c* **1000** *Sax. Leechd.* II. 40 Gif [mon] yfelne hlyst hæbbe. *c* **1175** *Lamb. Hom.* 75 Hore lust hore loking hore blawing hore smelling heore feling wes al iattret. *c* **1200** *Trin. Coll. Hom.* 61 Gif he binimeδ us ure sihte oδer ure liste. *c* **1205** LAY. 11577 Mi fader Caredoc makede lust & þus spæc. *a* **1300** *Cursor M.* 13708 All þai gaf him list ilkan. *c* **1330** *Assump. Virg.* (B.M. MS.) 2 Sitteþ stille & haueþ lyst. **1398** TREVISA *Barth. De P.R.* VII. xxi. (1495) 238 Thyckenes of luste and of heryinge. *a* **1400** *Octouian* 60 Fele of hem casted a cry.. That noon of hem that sytte hym by May haue no lest.

2. The ear. (But cf. LIST *sb.*^{3} 1 b.)

c **1380** *Sir Ferumb.* 1900 With ys hond a wolde þe ȝyue a such on on þᵉ luste þat al þy breyn scholde clyue al aboute ys fuste. *c* **1386** CHAUCER *Wife's Prol.* 634 He smoot me ones on the list. *a* **1535** MORE *Howe a Sergeant would learne to play the frere* Wks. D ij b, And with his fist, Upon the lyst, He gaue hym such a blow, That [etc.].

†**list,** *sb.*^{2} *Obs.* Also 3–4 liste, 4–5 lyst(e, lest(e. [Com. Teut.: OE. *list* str. fem. corresponds to OFris. *lest*, OS. *list* art, wisdom (Du. *list* fem., cunning), OHG., MHG. *list* masc., wisdom, art, craft (mod.G. *list* fem., craft, stratagem), ON. *list* fem., art, skill (Sw., Da. *list*), Goth. *lists* fem., stratagem, wile:—OTeut. *listi-z, f. root *lĭs- (:lais- in Goth. *lais* I know): see LEARN *v.*, LORE.] Art, craft, cunning. Also phr. ***by*** or ***with list.***

a **900** CYNEWULF *Christ* 1318 Mid hu micle elne æȝhwylc wille þurh ealle list lifes tiliȝan. *a* **1000** *Cædmon's Gen.* 588 (Gr.) Lædde hie swa mid liȝenum & mid listum speon idese on þæt unriht. *c* **1205** LAY. 17210 Betere is liste [*c* **1275** sleahþe] þene ufel strenδe. *a* **1225** *Leg. Kath.* 1527 Swa þe cnotte is icnut..þæt ne mei hit liste ne luδer strengδe nowδer ..leowsin. *a* **1250** *Owl & Night.* 172 Ich wolde biȝte bet mid liste, Than thu mid al thine strengthe. *a* **1275** *Prov. Ælfred* 638 in *O.E. Misc.* 136 Of him þu miȝt leren listes and fele þeues. **13..** *Seuyn Sag.* (W.) 2046 This was a dede of queint list. *c* **1375** *Sc. Leg. Saints* ix. (*Bartholomaeus*) 322 He crucifyt wes fyrste & [syne] his skyne of flayne with lyste. *c* **1430** *Hymns Virg.* (1867) 42 We ben bigilid alle wiþ oure lyst.

list (lɪst), *sb.*^{3} Also 4–7 lyst(e, liste, 5 liest, lyyst(e. [OE. *líste* wk. fem. = MDu. *lijste* (Du. *lijst*), OHG. *lîsta* (MHG. *lîste*, mod.G. *leiste*); the Teut. word was adopted in Rom. as It. *lista*, F. *liste*; the ON. *lista* (*í*) is prob. from Fr. or ME.]

I. Border, edging, strip.

†**1. a.** *gen.* A border, hem, bordering strip. *Obs.*

a **700** *Epinal Gloss.* 583 *Lembum*, listan *vel* thres. **13..** *E.E. Allit. P.* B. 1761 þe myst dryues þorȝ þe lyst of þe lyfte, bi þe loȝ medoes. **13..** *Guy Warw.* (1887) p. 464 (MS. A) His targe wiþ gold list He carf atvo. *c* **1375** *Sc. Leg. Saints* vii. (*Jacobus Minor*) 48 þai stryfe wald, quha mycht fyrst Of his kirtil nycht þe liste. **1433** *Test. Ebor.* (Surtees) II. 49 Unam tuellam de twill, cum nigris lystez. **1513** DOUGLAS *Æneis* XIII. Prol. 38 The nycht furthspred hyr cloke with sabill lyst. **1591** G. FLETCHER *Russe Commw.* (Hakl. Soc.) 16 In the very farthest part and list of Europe bordering upon Asia. **1597** HOOKER *Eccl. Pol.* V. xx. §10 [They] haue thought it better to let them [the books of the Apocrypha] stand as a list or marginall border vnto the olde Testament. **1650** FULLER *Pisgah* I. vi. 15 Trachonitis, the coursest list and most craggy ground about the countrey of Judea. **1684** R. WALLER *Nat. Exper.* 96 The water begins first to congeal at the top round the edges, and from that List of Ice shoots several small Threads to the middle. **1696** BP. PATRICK *Comm. Exod.* xxv. 11 A Border or List of Gold went round at the Top of it.

†**b.** Applied to the lobe of the ear. *Obs.* [Cf. G. *ohrleiste*, which, however, means the 'helix' of the ear; also LIST *sb.*^{1} 2.]

1530 PALSGR. 239/2 Lyste of the eare, *mol de loraylle.* **1611** COTGR. s.v. *Mol.* **1631** DEKKER *Match me in Lond.* II. 30 They haue giuen it me soundly, I feele it vnder the lists of both eares.

2. a. *spec.* The selvage, border, or edge of a cloth, usually of different material from the body of the cloth. †Phrase, ***within the lists*** (usual in statements of measurement). [So F. *liste* in Cotgr.]

[**1297** *Magna Carta Edw. I*, c. xxv, Una latitudo pannorum tinctorum, russetorum, & haubergettorum scilicet due ulne infra listas.] **1433** *Rolls of Parlt.* IV. 452/1 The lyste at the one ende of all soche Streite Clothes. *c* **1440** *Promp. Parv.* 307/1 Lyyst of clothe, *forago.* **1523** *Act 14 & 15 Hen. VIII*, c. 1 All maner of white brode wollen clothes with crumpil listes, otherwise called bastardes. **1535** *Act 27 Hen. VIII*, c. 12 §2 Euery brode cloth shall conteine in breadth seuen quarters of a yarde within the listes at the least. **1592** NASHE *P. Penilesse* (ed. 2) 8 For his breeches they were made of the lists of broad cloaths. **1603** SHAKS. *Meas. for M.* I. ii. 30. **1677** W. HUBBARD *Narrative* II. 1 The List or Border here being known to be more worth then the whole Cloth. **1700** TYRRELL *Hist. Eng.* II. 716 Woollen-Cloaths that were not two Ells within the Lists, according to King Richard's [1st] late Assize, or Statute. **1835** URE *Philos. Manuf.* 186 A few threads of strong coarse yarn are

placed to form the lists or selvages of the cloth. **1842** BISCHOFF *Woollen Manuf.* II. 396 The list is made in the West of England frequently of goats' hair. **1844** G. DODD *Textile Manuf.* iii. 104 The tenter-hooks were driven into poles and rails, and the cloth hung on them by the 'list' at the edges.

b. *fig.* and proverbial.

1589 *Pappe w. Hatchet* A 2 b, Yet find fault with broad termes, for I haue mesured yours with mine, & I find yours broader iust by the list. **1596** LODGE *Marg. Amer.* (1876) 24 Arsadachus knowing the cloth by the list, the bill by the Item, the steele by the marke [etc.]. **1622** PEACHAM *Compl. Gent.* i. (1634) 15 Which miserable ambition hath so furnished both Towne and Countrey with Coates of a new list, that [etc.]. **1655** H. VAUGHAN *Silex Scint.* II. *Garland*, False joyes,.. Peeces of sackcloth with silk lists. **1677** GILPIN *Demonol.* (1867) 294 Who will reject a fine web of cloth, as one speaks, for a little coarse list at the end.

c. In generalized use: Such selvages collectively; the material of which the selvage of cloth consists.

1567 HARMAN *Caveat* (Shaks. Soc.) 33 Their armes bounde up with kercher or lyste. **1693** EVELYN *De la Quint. Compl. Gard.* II. 62 We must..constrain the Branches of those Fig-Trees, as near as we can to the Walls,..with Nails and List. **1719** D'URFEY *Pills* I. 263 Sissly..Pulls off her Garter of woolen List. **1748** SMOLLETT *Rod. Rand.* lxi. (1804) 438 A dirty rag..tied with two pieces of list. **1772** MRS. DELANY *Lett.* Ser. II. I. 401, I have had list nailed round my doors, and stopping every crack and crevice that let in cold air [etc.]. **1901** *Q. Rev.* Apr. 483 By 1850 india-rubber had superseded list for cushions [of billiard-tables].

d. *attrib.* (quasi-*adj.*) = Made of list.

1661 *Inuentarye* in *MS. Rawl. A.* 182 lf. 311 On rugg, 2 Liste couerlids [etc.]. **1809** JANE AUSTEN *Let.* 24 Jan. (1952) 257 We..could have staid longer but for the arrival of my List shoes to convey me home. **1847** C. BRONTË *J. Eyre* xvii. (1890) 171 Her quiet tread muffled in a list slipper. **1851** *Illustr. Catal. Gt. Exhib.* 1121 List carpet. **1856** DICKENS *Dorrit* (1857) I. xiii. 106 Mr. Casby rose up in his list shoes. **1866** MRS. H. WOOD *St. Martin's Eve* xvii. (1874) 193, I have got on list shoes, ma'am. **1901** *Q. Rev.* Apr. 485 List cushions were abandoned in favour of rubber. **1908** A. BENNETT *Old Wives' Tale* IV. iii. 480 Sophia wore list slippers in the morning. It was a habit which she had formed in the Rue Lord Byron—by accident rather than with an intention to utilize list slippers for the effective supervision of servants.

3. a. A strip of cloth or other fabric.

a **1300** *Birth Jesus* 587 in Horstm. *Altengl. Leg.* (1875) 91 And bond him wiþ aliste. *a* **1300** *Cursor M.* 19845 A mikel linnen clath four squar Laten dun, him thoght was þar, At nokes four, four listes lang, Vnto þe lift þar-wit it hang. **1362** LANGL. *P. Pl.* A. VI. 8 He bar a bordun I-bounde wiþ a brod lyste. **1398** TREVISA *Barth. De P.R.* VI. iv. (1495) 191 Chyldrens..lymmes ben bounde wyth lystes and other couenable bondes that thei ben not crokid. *c* **1450** *ME. Med. Bk.* (Heinrich) 122 Bynde him aboue þe brawon of þe arme wyþ a good lyste. ? *a* **1525** *Treat. Galaunt* 186 in Hazl. *E.P.P.* III. 159 Theyr gownes and theyr cotes shredde all in lystes. **1546** PHAER *Bk. Childr.* (1553) X v b, Make a girdle of a wollen list mete for the midle of the pacient. **1596** SHAKS. *Tam. Shr.* III. ii. 69 With a linnen stock on one leg, and a kersey boot-hose on the other, gartred with a red and blew list. **1713** SWIFT *Elegy on Partridge* Wks. 1755 III. II. 80 A list the cobler's temples ties, To keep the hair out of his eyes. **1727** BRADLEY *Fam. Dict.* s.v. *Amble*, Many fold fine soft Lists about the Gambrels of the Horse. **1796** MORSE *Amer. Geog.* II. 37 The four seams adorned with lists of a different colour from that of the cap. **1855** P. T. BARNUM *Life* 109 Mallet had agreed..to deliver twelve yards of broadcloth 'lists' to Shepard. **1886** F. T. ELWORTHY *West Somerset Word-Bk.* 442 In flannels and in wool-dyed cloths it is usual to have a list or narrow border on each side of the cloth.

transf. **1599** B. JONSON *Cynthia's Rev.* V. ii. Wks. 1616 I. 246 You slaue, you list, you shreds, you—. (*Beats the Tailor*). **1614** —— *Barth. F.* IV. iv. (1631) 67 Those superstitious reliques, those lists of Latin, the very rags of Rome, and patches of Poperie.

†**b.** Formerly often: A strip of cloth used for filtering or for causing a liquid to drip. *Obs.*

1593 T. HYLL *Art Gardening* 152 Putting clothes or lists ..hanging halfe out of the pan..that they may so drop continually water on them in the forme of feltring, as the wise name it. *c* **1623** LODGE *Poor Mans Talent* (1881) 12 Distill them by a filter, which is by a list, or passe them through a cloth or bagg. **1660** BOYLE *New Exp. Phys. Mech.* xxxv. 263 We resolved, instead of a List of Cotton, or the like Filtre, to make use of a Siphon of Glass.

4. a. A band or strip of any material; a line or band conspicuously marked on a surface. ? *Obs.*

1398 TREVISA *Barth. De P.R.* XVII. clxii. (1495) 709 A meete borde is areryd and sette vpon fete: and compassed wyth a lyste abowte. *c* **1575** J. HOOKER *Life Sir P. Carew* (1857) 108 His herse was set up..with list and rail garnished with scutcheons. **1599** R. LINCHE *Anc. Fiction* M ij, A certaine white list and streake, called by the Astrologers *Via lactea.* **1648** GAGE *West Ind.* xii. (1655) 57 Their shooes.. the outside whereof of the profaner sort are plated with a list of silver. **1669** BOYLE *Contn. New Exp.* I. (1682) 55 The divisions of an Inch made on a list of paper. **1686** PLOT *Staffordsh.* 413 There is a list of grass greener than ordinary, call'd St. Kenelms-furrow. **1713** DERHAM *Phys. Theol.* VII. ii. 379 A black List of Something adhering to the Rock— which he found was a great number of Swallows. **1747** *Gentl. Mag.* 310 Their ends [of wire] being fastened to the under parts of the boards at XX, by means of a list of tin, half inch broad, which is nailed over them. **1776** *Phil. Trans.* LXVII. 37, I have glued three wooden lists on the back of the board to prevent its warping.

b. One of the divisions of a head of hair, or a beard. [? Suggested by It. *lista.*]

1859 TENNYSON *Vivien* 242 A comb of pearl to part The lists of such a beard as youth gone out Had left in ashes. **1880** A. J. BUTLER *Dante's Purg.* i. 4 He wore his beard long and mingled with white hair, like to his locks, of which a twofold list [orig. *una doppia lista*] fell to his breast.

5. a. A stripe of colour. ? *Obs.* (Cf. F. *liste.*)

1496 *Fysshynge w. Angle* (1883) 34 The body of blacke wull & a yellow lyste after eyther syde. **1530** PALSGR. 239/2 Lyste on horsebacke, *raye.* *a* **1586** SIDNEY *Arcadia* III. (1629) 273 His horse was of a firie sorrell, with blacke feete, and blacke list on his backe. **1621** AINSWORTH *Annot. Pentat., Exod.* xxviii. 19 There are many colours [of Agate] and some the best, that are greene with a golden list. **1646** SIR T. BROWNE *Pseud. Ep.* VI. xi. 334 The Asse having a peculiar marke of a crosse made by a blacke list downe his backe, and another athwart. **1650** BULWER *Anthropomet.* Pref., Painted with lists, here, naked arms behold. **1772–84** COOK *Voy.* (1790) I. 319 The blue cat..having a fine blue tinge, with a beautiful red list down its back. **1774** GOLDSM. *Nat. Hist.* II. 49 All along the back there runs a white list, which ends at the insertion of the tail. **1846** *P. Parley's Ann.* VII. 35 With some black about the face, and a list of the same down the hind part of the neck.

†**b.** Used for: A mark of a wound, a scar. *Obs. rare*⁻¹.

c **1489** CAXTON *Sonnes of Aymon* xxi. 464 He sholde never have knowen hym, yf it had not be a lityll liste [orig. *cicatrice*] that he had by his right eye.

6. *Arch.* †**a.** (See quot. 1812–16.) *Obs.* **b.** A small square moulding or ring encircling the foot of a column, between the torus below and the shaft above. (Cf. LISTEL.)

Cf. obs. F. *liste*, 'a small square out-iutting brow, or member of a piller' (Cotgr.).

1663 GERBIER *Counsel* 32 The Freese, the List, the Ovolo. **1735** DYCHE & PARDON *Dict., List*,..a Fillet or flat Ring that ornaments the Bottoms of Columns immediately above the Torus. **1745** POCOCKE *Descr. East* II. II. 156 The capital consisting only of a large list or square stone, and a large quarter round under that. **1812–16** J. SMITH *Panorama Sci. & Art* I. 177 The list or spiral line of the volute runs along the face of the abacus. **1842–59** GWILT *Archit.* Gloss.

7. In various technical senses. †**a.** (See quot. 1688.) **b.** *Carpentry.* (? *U.S.*) 'The upper rail of a railing' (Knight *Dict. Mech.* 1875). **c.** *Carpentry.* A strip cut from the edge of a plank. (Cf. LIST *v.*³ 3). **d.** *Tin-plating.* The wire of tin left on the under edge of a tinned plate, which is removed by plunging the plate into the list-pot.

1688 R. HOLME *Armoury* III. 285/1 The Parts of a [Wool-] Card... The List, is that as is nailed to hold the Leaf. **1834** HOLLAND *Manuf. Metal* III. 37 There is always..a list or selvage of tin on the lower edge of every plate... When the list is melted..the boy takes out the plate.

II. Boundary.

†**8. a.** A limit, bound, boundary. Often *pl. Obs.*

1389 in *Eng. Gilds* (1870) 44 Any brother or sister yat duellen wyt-outen ye lystys of thre myle from ye cite. *c* **1400** *Destr. Troy* 10669 All the ledis to the listes on the laund past. *Ibid.* 10018. **1559** *Primer* in *Priv. Prayers* (1851) 90 The miserable captives, which as yet be hedged in within the lists of death. **1579** TOMSON *Calvin's Serm. Tim.* 334/1 God setteth vs barres and listes. **1587** GOLDING *De Mornay* vii. (1617) 94 The Tropicks are his [the Sunnes] vttermost lists. *a* **1592** H. SMITH *Serm.* (1637) 203 As though humility were the bond of all duties, like a list which holdeth men in compasse. **1599** SHAKS. *Hen. V*, V. ii. 295 You and I cannot bee confin'd within the weake Lyst of a Countreyes fashion. **1601** —— *Twel. N.* III. i. 86, I am bound to your Neece sir: I meane she is the list of my voyage. **1638** CHILLINGW. *Relig. Prot.* I. Concl. 411 To keepe my discourse within those very lists and limits which yourself have prescrib'd. **1645** QUARLES *Sol. Recant.* VI. 60 To what strange Lists Is her conceal'd Omnipotence confin'd?

†**b.** Region, territory. *Obs.*

a **1649** DRUMM. OF HAWTH. *Poems* 57 Whateuer foggy Mists Do blind men in these sublunary Lists.

9. a. *spec.* in *pl.* (†sometimes construed as *sing.*) as the equivalent of the like-sounding OF. *lisse* (mod.F. *lice*): The palisades or other barriers enclosing a space set apart for tilting; *hence*, a space so enclosed in which tilting-matches or tournaments were held. †Phr. *in, within* (*the*) *lists.* Sometimes, by extension, the arena in which bulls fight or wrestlers contend, etc. †Also (*rarely*) *sing.* in the same sense.

[The OF. *lisse* (see LYCE, used once by Caxton), which appears to have influenced the application of the Eng. word, is of doubtful etymology; it corresponds to Sp. *liza*, Pg. *liça*, It. *lizza*, med.L. *liciæ* palisades, lists. Hatz.-Darm. suggest a late L. type **listia*, f. OHG. *lista*: see above.]

c **1386** CHAUCER *Sqr.'s T.* 660 Cambalo That faught in listes with the bretheren two For Canacee. *c* **1400** *Rom. Rose* 4199 Without the diche were listes made, With walles batayled large and brade. *c* **1420** *Anturs of Arth.* 497 (Douce MS.) þe lordes by-lyue hom to list ledes With many seriant of mace. **1470–85** MALORY *Arthur* VIII. xxii, Blamor..tooke his hors at the one ende of the lystes, and sire Trystram atte other ende of the lystes. **1475** *Bk. Noblesse* (Roxb.) 77 To doo armes in liestis to the utteraunce. **1523** LD. BERNERS *Froiss.* I. cliv. 183 These two dukes came into the felde, all armed, in a lystes made for yᵉ sayd duke of Almayne, chalenger, and for the duke of Englande, defender. **1589** *Pasquil's Return* C iv b, It fareth with them, as it dooth with the Wrastler within the Lystes. **1593** SHAKS. *Rich. II*, II. iii. 43 On paine of death, no person be so bold..as to touch the Listes, Except the Marshall. **1621** LADY M. WROTH *Urania* 497 Encountering his enemie in a List, made of purpose betweene the Campe, and Castle. **1672** DRYDEN *Conq. Granada* I. i, When the Lists set wide, Gave room to the fierce Bulls. **1812** BYRON *Ch. Har.* I. lxxii, The lists are oped, the spacious area clear'd. **1813** SCOTT *Trierm.* II. vii, A summer-day in lists shall strive My knights. **1842** TENNYSON *Sir Galahad* i, They reel, they roll in clanging lists.

b. *transf.* and *fig.* A place or scene of combat or contest. Phr. *to enter* (*the*) *lists.*

1592 SHAKS. *Ven. & Ad.* xcix, Now is she in the very lists of love, Her champion mounted for the hot encounter. **1612** DRAYTON *Poly-olb.* V. 100 As when his Trytons' trumps doe them to battell call Within his surging lists to combat with the Whale. *a* **1626** BP. ANDREWES 7 *Serm. Wond. Combat* vi. (1627) 88 The lysts where this temptation was vsed, was the Mountaine. **1647** N. BACON *Disc. Govt. Eng.* I. iv. (1739) 9, I hold it both needless and fruitless to enter into the Lists, concerning the original of the Saxons. *Ibid.* lix. 116 The King, loth to enter the List with the Clergy about too many matters. *a* **1649** DRUMM. OF HAWTH. *Poems* Wks. (1711) 22/2 See, Chloris, how the clouds Tilt in the azure lists. **1671** MILTON *Samson* 463 Dagon hath presum'd, Me overthrown, to enter lists with God. **1725** POPE *Odyss.* VIII. 110 Demodocus..Majestic to the lists of Fame repairs. **1831** BREWSTER *Newton* (1855) I. iv. 77 The Royal Society.. contained few individuals..capable of..entering the lists against his..assailants. **1848** KINGSLEY *Saint's Trag.* IV. i. 35 [Let] the spirit Range in free battle lists. **1878** BROWNING *Poets Croisic* lxii, Slight lists Wherein the puppet-champions wage..mimic war.

†**10. a.** *sing.* and *pl.* An encircling palisade; a railed or staked enclosure. **b.** *pl.* The starting-place of a race (= L. *carceres*). Also *sing.* a racecourse or exercising ground for horses. *Obs.*

1581 STYWARD *Mart. Discipl.* I. 59 The citie, pales or lyst or fort where yᵉ campe is lodged. **1598** HAKLUYT *Voy.* I. 68 All these were placed without the lists [L. *extra tabulatum*]. **1601** HOLLAND *Pliny* I. 222 To the Lists they [horses] must not be brought to enter into any mastries there before they be full fiue yeres of age. **1644** EVELYN *Mem.* (1857) I. 101 A list to ride horses in, much frequented by the gallants in summer. **1662** H. MORE *Philos. Writ.* Pref. Gen. (1712) 12 We both setting out from the same Lists, though taking several ways,..meet together..at the same Gaol. **1737** WEST *Let.* (in verse) in *Gray's Poems* (1775) 19 As yet just started from the lists of time.

III. 11. *Comb.*: **list-boy**, in *Tin-plating*, a boy employed to place the plates in the list-pot; **list-pot**, a cast-iron trough containing a small quantity of melted tin, in which the tinned plates are plunged to remove the 'list' (see 7 d); **list-wall** [cf. sense 4], a dry wall with one or more strips or bands of cemented walling.

1818 S. PARKES in *Mem. Lit. & Phil. Soc. Manch.* (1819) Ser. II. III. 369 There is always a wire of tin on the lower edge of every plate, which is..removed..in the following manner. A boy called the *list-boy, takes the plates when they are cool enough to handle, and puts the lower edge of each..into the *list-pot. **1793–1813** *Reports Agric.* 62 (E.D.D.) A wall-fence 'partly dry and partly cemented with mortar, or what is commonly called a *list wall'. **1850** *Jrnl. R. Agric. Soc.* XI. II. 728 The fence is what is called a list wall, alternate layers of dry wall and stone with mortar.

list (lɪst), *sb.*⁴ Also 4–5 lest(e, lyst(e. [f. LIST *v.*² Cf. Icel. *lyst* fem., appetite (for food).]

†**1.** Pleasure, joy, delight. *Obs.*

c **1205** LAY. 13078 þa andswarede þe munec mid muchelere liste [*later text* mid swiþe gode wille]. **13..** *E.E. Allit. P.* A. 467 So fare we alle wyth luf and lyste, To kyng & quene by cortaysye. *c* **1386** CHAUCER *Prol.* 132 In curteisye was set ful muche hir lest [*v.r.* list]. *c* **1440** *Promp. Parv.* 306/2 Lyst, or lykynge,..*delectacio.* *c* **1450** HOLLAND *Howlat* 755 All thus our lady thai lovit, with lyking and lyst. **1573** *Satir. Poems Reform.* xl. 197 How he suld..leaue this lyfe with list for all thair plaid.

2. Appetite, craving; desire, longing; inclination. Const. *to* (with sb. or inf.), rarely *for, of*; †frequently collocated with *leisure.* Now only *arch.*

c **1220** *Bestiary* 544 He doð men hungren and hauen ðrist, and mani oðer sinful list. *c* **1250** *Gen. & Ex.* 1231 Hem wexon ðrist, ðe water sleckede ðe childes list. *a* **1300–1400** *Cursor M.* 24751 (Gött.) þat gifs me list [*other MSS.* lust(e] of hir to rede. *c* **1374** CHAUCER *Troylus* II. 738 (787) Right a-noon as sesed is here lest, So cesseth loue and forth to loue an newe. **1423** JAS. I *Kingis Q.* lvii, Hastow no lest to sing? **1513** DOUGLAS *Æneis* IX. ii. 69 The wyld wolf..Rasys in ire, for the wod hungris list. *a* **1533** LD. BERNERS *Huon* lxvi. 226 The traytoure Gerard had no lyst to slepe. **1563–87** FOXE *A. & M.* (1596) 410/1 He had no leisure, and lesse lyst, to attend unto Wickliffes matters. **1575** TURBERV. *Faulconrie* 278 It is a very good way to..kill the list and lyking of a Spar-hawke, to feede hir..with liquid meates washt in water. **1596** W. SMITH *Chloris* (1877) 29 Since my disgrace I had of them no list. **1613** PURCHAS *Pilgrimage* II. xv. (1614) 195 If he have list to the stoole. **1641** MILTON *Reform.* I. Wks. 1851 III. 9, I have done it, neither out of malice, nor list to speak evill. **1659** FULLER *App. Inj. Innoc.* (1840) 319, I had little list or leisure to write. **1682** BUNYAN *Holy War* 242, I thank you for all things courteous and civil, but for your cordial I have no list thereto. **1825** SCOTT *Talism.* xxvi, I have more list to my bed than to have my ears tickled. **1839** BAILEY *Festus* viii. (1848) 84 To give a loose to all the lists of youth. **1888** P. CUSHING *Blacksmith of Voe* III. x. 216 The divine list of sex, and the sweet ache of soul.

3. (One's) desire or wish; (one's) good pleasure. Phrase **at** (**one's**) **list.** Now only *arch.*

a **1300** *Cursor M.* 22130 Turn þai sal til him titest, And siþen þaas other at his list. *c* **1400** *Rom. Rose* 1957 Pleyn at your list I yelde me. **1579** LYLY *Euphues* (Arb.) 261 Honestie my olde Graundfather called that, when menne lyued by law, not lyst. **1610** G. FLETCHER *Christ's Tri.* I. xxxi, Frail multitude! whose giddy law is list. **1682** BUNYAN *Holy War* 110 He that can of list and will propound what he pleases. **1695** HICKERINGILL *Lay-Clergy* Wks. 1716 I. 326 By the Law of the Land, and not the Arbitrary list or will of any Man living. **1867** J. B. ROSE tr. *Virgil's Æneid* 26 It was a god there working his own list.

list (lɪst), *sb.*⁵ Also 7–8 (*Naut.*) lust. [Of obscure origin: perh. a use of LIST *sb.*⁴]

1. *Naut.* The careening or inclination of a ship to one side.

1633 T. JAMES *Voy.* 82 The Ship at low water had a great lust to the offing. **1658** PHILLIPS, *Lust of a ship.* **1834** M. SCOTT *Cruise Midge* ii. (1842) 30 What a list to port she is

getting! **1881** *Daily News* 11 Nov. 2/6 The cargo shifted giving the ship a list to port. **1883** *Times* 4 Jan. 8 The vessel gave a sudden list to starboard.

2. *transf.* A leaning over (of a building, etc.).

1793 SMEATON *Edystone L.* §85 The whole building had got a considerable List or leaning to the S.W. **1901** *Longm. Mag.* Sept. 396 Two lines of straggling fence running with all sorts of lists and bends.

list (lɪst), *sb.*^{6} [a. F. *liste* = Sp., Pg., It. *lista*; prob. identical with LIST *sb.*^{3}, the special sense being developed from that of 'strip' (of paper): see LIST *sb.*^{3} 4.] **a.** A catalogue or roll consisting of a row or series of names, figures, words, or the like. In early use, *esp.* a catalogue of the names of persons engaged in the same duties or connected with the same object; *spec.* a catalogue of the soldiers of an army or of a particular arm; also in †phr. ***in*** or ***within the list***(*s*, ***in list*** (occas. fig.).

active list, a list of those officers in the army or navy who are liable to be called upon for active service. ***free list***, (*a*) a list of persons who are allowed free admission to a place of entertainment; (*b*) a list of articles which are exempt from duty under the revenue laws. Also *army list*, CIVIL LIST, *retired list*, *sick list*, etc. (see the first words).

1602 SHAKS. *Ham.* I. i. 98 Young Fortinbras.. Hath.. Shark'd vp a List of Landlesse Resolutes. *Ibid.* ii. 32 The Leuies, The Lists, and full proportions are all made Out of his subiect. **1606** —— *Ant. & Cl.* III. vi. 76 The Thracian King Adullas.. The Kings of Mede, and Licoania, With a more larger List of Scepters. **1613** —— *Hen. VIII*, IV. i. 14 'Tis the List Of those that claime their Offices this day. **1622** F. MARKHAM *Bk. War* IV. iii. 130 Pioners.. are not reckoned Souldiers, neither come neere by many degrees either to that list or reputation. **1625** BACON *Ess.*, *Of Youth & Age* (Arb.) 257 He was the Ablest Emperour, almost, of all the List. **1633** T. STAFFORD *Pac. Hib.* I. i. (1810) 3 To bee in list 3000 Foot, and 250 Horse. **1646** EVANCE *Noble Ord.* 20 You will not be out of the List long. **1653** HOLCROFT *Procopius* IV. 157 The Battalion was of eight thousand foot, and the Archers of the List. **1655** FULLER *Ch. Hist.* I. v. §10 Their Fear brought in a false List of their Enemies Number. **1696** PHILLIPS (ed. 5), *List*, a Scrowl of the Names of several Persons of the same Quality with whom we have Business, or with whom we have some Relation. A List of the Slain and Wounded in such a Battel. A List of such a ones Creditors. A List of the Prisoners in such a Prison. **1742** YOUNG *Nt. Th.* I. 284 Endless is the list of human ills. **1797** *Encycl. Brit.* (ed. 3) VII. 383/2 The letter-founders have a kind of list, or tariff, whereby they regulate their founts. **1809** LD. MULGRAVE in *G. Rose's Diaries* (1860) II. 358 His name being removed from the List of the Navy. **1847** MARRYAT *Childr. N. Forest* xx, Edward took a list of the contents. **1865** DICKENS *Mut. Fr.* I. ii, She keeps a little list of her lovers. **1874** GREEN *Short Hist.* iii. §4. 128 The earliest classical revival restored Cæsar and Virgil to the list of monastic studies.

In specific senses: (*a*) the titles of the books (to be) published by a particular publisher. So ***autumn list***, BACKLIST, ***spring list***.

1860 G. H. LEWES *Let.* 4 Jan. in Geo. Eliot *Lett.* (1954) III. 243 It will be well now to begin announcing it in lists—if not the title at any rate the fact of a new novel being in the press. **1919** *Publisher's Let.* Aug. in T. S. Eliot *Waste Land Drafts* (1971) p. xvi, Mr. Eliot's work is no doubt brilliant, but it is not exactly the kind of material we care to add to our list. **1922** T. S. ELIOT *Let.* 25 June in *Waste Land Drafts* (1971) p. xxii, Knopf said that it was too late for his autumn list this year. **1930** E. WAUGH *Vile Bodies* ii. 28, I suppose you could get the book rewritten in time for the Spring List? **1938** H. R. DENT in J. M. & H. R. Dent *House of Dent* xxiii. 300 It used to be said.. that a publisher kept poetry on his lists more for the look of the thing than anything else. **1951** M. SHARP *Lise Lilywhite* xix. 161 Mr Villiers.. published chiefly poetry... He had no list, in the trade sense, nor had he travellers. **1964** R. CHURCH *Voyage Home* viii. 166, I should send the book to the house of Dent, whose list it would suit admirably. **1967** E. GRIERSON *Crime of One's Own* viii. 60 Christmas operated like a guillotine on the Autumn lists, leaving only a bare four weeks of selling time.

(*b*) an official register of buildings of architectural or historical importance that are statutorily protected from demolition or major alteration. Cf. LIST *v.*^{4} 1 e.

1947 *Act 10 & 11 Geo. VI* c. 51 §30 With a view to the guidance of local planning authorities.. in relation to buildings of special architectural or historic interest, the Minister shall compile lists of such buildings, or approve.. such lists compiled by other persons or bodies of persons. *Ibid.*, So long as any building.. is included in any list compiled or approved under this section, no person shall execute.. any works for the demolition of the building or for its alteration or extension in any manner which would seriously affect its character. **1968** P. WARD *Conservation & Devel. Historic Towns & Cities* III. 98 Lansdown Parade.. is also a Grade II listed building on the Ministry of Housing and Local Government's list of architecturally or historically important buildings.

(*c*) In the National Health Service, a general practitioner's register of patients.

1949 *Britannica Bk. of Year* 412/2 Doctors starting their careers.. had few patients on their lists. *Ibid.* 413/1 The doctor was free to accept or reject anyone applying to go on his list. **1971** *Reader's Digest Family Guide to Law* 242 A doctor.. does not have to give reasons for his refusal to accept a patient on his list. **1974** M. BIRMINGHAM *You can help Me* iii. 56, I asked him if he did not sometimes hanker after.. a few wealthy private patients so that he could afford to keep his list shorter.

b. *Racing slang.* Short for: The list of geldings in training. Hence ***to put on the list*** = to castrate.

1890 FARMER *Slang*, *Added to the List*, an abbreviation of 'added to the list of geldings in training'.

†**c.** *American.* The return of particulars of taxable property required to be furnished by the owners. (Cf. LIST *v.*^{4} 1 b.) *Obs.*

1646 *Virginia Stat.* (1823) I. 329 To the prejudice of many who have duely and according to law presented their lists. **1655** *Connect. Col. Rec.* (1850) I. 279 Sea-Brooke is fyned forty shillings for not sending ye Lists of theire estates to the Courte.

d. *Comb.*: **list-betting**, betting on the list of horses displayed in a list shop; **list broker**, a trader in mailing lists; so **list-broking** *vbl. sb.*; **list house** = *list shop*; †**list-maker** = LISTER^{2} 2; **listman**, one who works in a list shop; a bookmaker; **list price**, the price fixed for an article in the printed list issued by the maker, or by the general body of makers of the particular class of goods; **list processing** *Computing*, the manipulation and use of chained lists and of data in them; freq. *attrib.*; so **list processor**, a processing system, language, etc., for use in list processing; cf. LISP *sb.*^{2}; **list shop**, an illegal betting shop where prices on future important races were displayed; **list system** (also ***party list system***), a system of voting, common in continental W. Europe, in which voters cast their vote for a list of candidates rather than for an individual candidate; so **list vote, voting**.

1874 *Porcupine* 18 July 248/2 Mr. Chaplin, M.P., with other horse-owners, have.. chuckled greatly at the prospect of *list-betting no longer interfering with their speculations. **1928** *Daily Express* 24 Mar. 1/1 The.. gaming laws.. were primarily intended only to abolish notorious gaming houses and list-betting in shops and houses. **1959** *Economist* 7 Feb. 498/1 Publishers now send out circulars to people on mailing lists, bought from a growing class of '*list brokers'. **1967** *Guardian* 27 Dec. 4/2 She is a list broker, which means that she trades in names and addresses. *Ibid.* 4/4 The magnitude of *list-broking in the United States. **1970** *Daily Tel.* 12 Oct. 17/3 'List broking' in this country could well develop into the sophisticated service industry it is in America. **1902** 'N. GUBBINS' *Dead Certainties* 71 Most of the '*list-houses' (in Long Acre and elsewhere), whose name was legion, had their shutters up on the morning after Lord Zetland's horse had defeated Pitsford. **1666** *Connect. Col. Rec.* (1852) II. 48 This Court doth order that ye land.. be valued by the *list makers of Stonington. **1922** *Daily Mail* 6 Nov. 11 Most of the *listmen got scared to death over particular animals in these final handicaps. **1937** PARTRIDGE *Dict. Slang* 486/1 *Listman*, a ready-money bookmaker. **1871** *English Mechanic* 10 Nov. 206/2 The *list price for a $\frac{1}{2}$ horse-power engine is £60. *c* **1883** J. MONTAGU *Let.* in Troubridge & Marshall *John Lord Montagu of Beaulieu* (1930) 30 Now my old machine [*sc.* tandem bicycle] cost £26 list price, and we finally got it for £23:10s. owing to discount for ready money. **1928** *Publisher's Weekly* 30 June 2603 The reprint is usually about one-third of the list price of the earlier edition. **1955** *Radio Times* 22 Apr. 51/1 Hand in an old electric shaver.. and claim £2 allowance off the list price of a Remington 60. **1967** *Autocar* 28 Dec. 38/3 All 'list' prices are taken from *Autocar's* 'Recommended New Car prices'. **1959** *Q. Progr. Rep.* (Mass. Inst. Technol. Res. Lab. Electronics) No. 53. 122 A series of programs in *List Processing Language is being written. **1960** *Jrnl. Assoc. Computing Machinery* VII. 87 Statements in the language are written in usual Fortran notation, but with a large set of special list-processing functions appended to the standard Fortran library. **1970** O. DOPPING *Computers & Data Processing* xix. 313 List processing, a type of non-numerical application, can be programmed in Lisp and IPL-V. **1983** *Listener* 10 Feb. 33/2 There is Fortran, Algol, Cobol and Jovial, along with 'string and list processing' languages such as Comit, Lisp and Slip. **1959** *List processor [see LISP *sb.*^{2}]. **1963** *Communications Assoc. Computing Machinery* VI. 524/1 SLIP is a list processing system in which each list cell carries both a forward and a backward link as well as a datum... SLIP is a descendant of at least four earlier list processors. **1875** *Encycl. Brit.* III. 619/1 '*List shops', where the proprietors kept a bank against all comers, and backers could stake their money in advance on a horse.. sprung up.. leading to.. flagrant dishonesty. [**1901** T. R. & H. P. C. ASHWORTH *Proportional Representation* vii. 162 The *Liste Libre*, or Free List system,.. applies the proportional principle not to individual candidates but to parties.] **1908** J. KING *Electoral Reform* vii. 87 In the Party *List System the elector gives his vote for the party list, on which the candidate is enrolled, when he gives a vote to any candidate. **1911** *Encycl. Brit.* XXXIII. 115/2 In the 'list systems'.. candidates are grouped in lists. **1926** HOAG & HALLETT *Proportional Representation* v. 60 Most of the countries which use list systems.. have been successful in securing reasonable accuracy in the assignment of seats to parties. **1971** G. K. ROBERTS *Dict. Political Analysis* 115 *List system*, a system of election, based on proportional representation of parties or similar groups, each of which presents a list of candidates. The voter then casts his vote for one of these lists. **1911** J. H. HUMPHREYS *Proportional Representation* viii. 180 *List votes form a pool from which the candidates of the list draw in succession as many votes as are necessary. **1954** B. & R. NORTH tr. *M. Duverger's Pol. Parties* I. i. 44 The list vote (*scrutin de liste*), operating within the framework of a large constituency, obliges the.. local branches of the party to establish amongst themselves a strong system of articulation within the constituency, so that they can agree upon the composition of the lists. *Ibid.* 45 Belgium, where at the end of the nineteenth century party structure was amongst the strongest in Europe: it coincided with *list-voting. **1958** W. J. M. MACKENZIE *Free Elections* ix. 75 List voting is almost always associated with formulae for distributing seats.

list, *sb.*^{7} *Obs.* exc. *dial.* [Of obscure origin: cf. Du. *lies* pork-fat, G. *leiste* flank, groin.] The flank (of pork); a long piece cut from the gammon.

1623 MARKHAM *Country Content.* I. 71 Take the largest of your Chines of Porke, and that which is called a Liste. **1824** CARR *Craven Dial.*, *Lists*, the flanks.

list, *sb.*^{8}, variant of LISSE *sb.*^{2} = LEASE *sb.*^{4} Also *Comb.* **list-stick** (see quot.).

1782 *Encycl. Brit.* (ed. 2) IX. 6711/1 The list-sticks, to which the high-lisses are tied. The high-lisses, or lists, are a number of long threads, with platines, or plate-leads, at the bottom.

list, *a.* *Obs.* exc. *dial.* [app. connected with LIST *sb.*^{1}] Ready, quick (*esp.* of hearing). Also applied to rooms, etc. in which one hears well.

1813 CULLUM *Suffolk Words* s.v., 'List of hearing', quick of hearing. **1823** GALT *Gilhaize* II. 130 When any of his disciples were not just so list and brisk as they might have been. **1847** HALLIWELL s.v., A list house or room, where sounds are heard easily from one room to another. *Kent.* **1861** *N. Brit. Rev.* Nov. 325 His ear was not list to catch the distant sounds. **1863** *Trans. Essex Archæol. Soc.* II. 185 *List*, quick; as list of speech. **1887** *Kent. Gloss.*, *List*, the condition of the atmosphere when sounds are heard easily. 'It's a wonderful list morning.'

list (lɪst), *v.*^{1} *arch.* Forms: 1 **lystan**, 3–4 **leste(n**, **luste(n**, 4–6 **lyst**, 5 **lyste**, **lest**, **lust**, 6–7 **liste**, 3– **list**. *3rd sing. pres.* (contracted) 1–6 **lyst**, 2–6 **lust**, 3 *Orm.* **lisste**, 3–5 **luste**, 4–5 **lest(e**, 4–6 **lyste**, **liste**, 4–7 **list**. *Pa. t.* 1–5 **lyste**, 2–5 **leste**, 3 *Orm.* **lisste**, 3–6 **lust(e**, 4–6 **liste**, **lyst(e**, 4–7 **list**, (5 **leist**, **lest**). Also 4 **lysted**, 5 **-yd**, etc., 4– **listed**. [OE. *lystan* = OS. *lustian* (Du. *lusten*), OHG. *lusten* (MHG., mod.G. *lüsten*), ON. *lysta* (Sw. *lysta*, Da. *lyste*):—OTeut. **lustjan*, f. **lust-us* pleasure: see LUST *sb.*

It is often somewhat uncertain whether forms in *lust-* should be referred to this verb or to LUST *v.*; in southern and perh. in West Midland ME. the vowel may represent either *u* or *ü*, and the examples are here placed under the one vb. or the other as the sense suggests. In other dialects of ME., and occas. in the 16th c., *lust* occurs in the sense of *list*, and with its peculiar inflexion (e.g. 3rd sing. pres. *lust*), and in these cases it is more convenient to regard it as an altered form of this vb., due to the influence of the sb. or vb. *lust*, than as a special use of the latter.]

1. *impers. trans.* (in OE. with *acc.* or *dat.*) To be pleasing to. ***me list*** (occas. ***listeth***): I please, choose, like, care, or desire.

a. Const. inf.

971 *Blickl. Hom.* 51 Hine ne lyst his willan wyrcean. *c* **1000** ÆLFRIC *Gram.* (Z.) 211 *Lecturio*, me lyst rædan. *c* **1175** *Lamb. Hom.* 103 Þenne þan mon ne lust on his liue nan god don. *c* **1200** ORMIN 8119 Himm lisste þa Wel etenn off an appell. *c* **1205** LAY. 30253 Þam kinge luste slepe. *a* **1300** *Cursor M.* 22601 Na creatur sal þan list [*Trin.* luste, *Edin.* lesten] plai. **13..** *Gaw. & Gr. Knt.* 941 Þenne lyst þe lady to loke on þe knyȝt. *c* **1375** *Sc. Leg. Saints* xxv. (*Julian*) 206 My gud brethyre, quhy lest ȝou le? *c* **1385** CHAUCER *L.G.W.* Prol. 490 The lestyth nat a louere be. *c* **1400** MAUNDEV. (Roxb.) xxiii. 108 Na man es forboden.. to trowe in what lawe þat him list leue on. *c* **1440** *Sir Gowther* 499 Him lystyd nothyng for to play, For he was full weri. *c* **1450** *Merlin* 48, I knowe alle thinges, that me leste to wite. *c* **1491** *Chast. Goddes Chyld* 12 Somme whan they sholde slepe thenne hem list wake and pray. Some whan they sholde wake and pray thenne hem lust to slepe. **1584** PEELE *Arraignm. Paris* I. ii, Me list.. This idle task on me to undertake. **1590** SPENSER *F.Q.* I. vii. 35 When him list the prouder lookes subdew. *a* **1618** RALEIGH *Maxims St.* (1651) 49 When it listeth him to call them to an account. **1633** P. FLETCHER *Poet. Misc.* 64 When me list to sadder tunes apply me. **1808** SCOTT *Marm.* I. viii, When at need Him listed ease his battle-steed.

b. Without dependent inf. (Chiefly in subordinate clauses introduced by *as*, *if*, *what*, *when*, etc.)

c **888** K. ÆLFRED *Boeth.* xxxiii. §2 Ne him eac næfre ȝenoȝ ne þincð ær he hæbbe eal þæt hine lyst. *c* **1205** LAY. 30741 Æiþer gon liðe þider him to liste. *a* **1300** *K. Horn* 918 Nu ȝe reste One while, ef ȝou leste. *c* **1375** *Lay Folks Mass Bk.* (MS. B.) 243 Offer or leeue, wheþer þe lyst. **1375** BARBOUR *Bruce* III. 519 Wemen.. can wet thair chekys, quhen thaim list, with teris. **14..** *Nun* 298 in *E.E.P.* (1862) 146 There we talkeden as vs lest. **1526** TINDALE *Matt.* xx. 15 Ys yt not lawfull ffor me to do as me listeth with myne awne. *a* **1553** UDALL *Royster D.* III. ii. (Arb.) 43 Let hym come when hym lust. **1581** SAVILE *Tacitus' Agric.* (1622) 191 Licence to do what them listed. **1633** BP. HALL *Hard Texts* 518 This proud Antiochus shall doe what him listeth. **1885–94** R. BRIDGES *Eros & Psyche* Aug. xvii, Thy mortal life is but a brittle vase, But as thee list with wine or tears to fill.

¶ With ellipsis of *go*.

c **1330** R. BRUNNE *Chron.* (1810) 87 To þe holy land him list, & þider gan him spede.

†**c.** Const. *of* (= OE. gen.), *after*.

a **1000** *Boeth. Metr.* xxvi. 71 Hi for ðæm yrmðum eardes lyste. *c* **1200** ORMIN 11334 Whanne hiss fasste forþedd wass þa lisste himm affterr fode. *a* **1352** MINOT *Poems* (Hall) i. 71 No thing list þam þan of play. *c* **1400** *Destr. Troy* Prol. 20 He.. has lykyng to lerne þat hym list after.

2. With *personal* construction. **a.** Const. inf.: To desire, like, wish *to do* something.

1340–70 *Alisaunder* 776 Þe Ladie lay on hur bed & lysted too slepe. *c* **1400** MAUNDEV. (1839) xix. 209 Thei bryngen up als many as men list to have. *a* **1510** DOUGLAS *K. Hart* 124 Quhen [that] hir court leist semble fair and clein. **1563–87** FOXE *A. & M.* (1596) 13/2 He either wist not, or list not to shew his cunning therein. **1590** GREENE *Orl. Fur.* (1599) A 4 b, I list not boast in acts of Chiualrie. **1602** SHAKS. *Ham.* I. v. 177 If we list to speake. **1613** JACKSON *Creed* I. xx. §5 Points he listed not meddle withall. **1667** MILTON *P.L.* VIII. 75 If they list to try Conjecture. **1687** TOWERSON *Baptism*

149, I list not to contend about anything, of which I myself am not more strongly perswaded. **1814** Scott *Ld. of Isles* III. xx, If you list to taste our cheer. *Ibid.* xxiii, We little listed think of him.

b. Without dependent inf.: To wish, desire, like, choose. (Chiefly in subordinate clauses, as in 1 b.)

c **1200** *Vices & Virtues* (1888) 13 After ðan ðe here herte leste, ic hem folȝede. *c* **1320** R. Brunne *Medit.* 352 Þy wyl be ydo, ryȝt as þou lest. **1430–40** Lydg. *Bochas* VIII. v. (1558) 4 All worldly thynges chaungyng as she lust. *a* **1450** *Knt. de la Tour* (1868) 3 To that entent that who so luste may kepe hem from harme. *c* **1470** Henry *Wallace* v. 123 Deyme as yhe lest, ye that best can and may. **1535** Coverdale *Ps.* lxxii. 7 They do euen what they lyst. **1563** *Homilies* II. *Agst. Idolatry* II. (1859) 209 The Bishop of Rome..did in all the West Church..what he lust. *a* **1586** Sidney *Arcadia* II. (1629) 199 Your griefes, and desires whatsoeuer and whensoeuer you list, he will consider of. *Ibid.* III. 260 He might returne if he listed. **1611** Bible *John* iii. 8 The winde bloweth where it listeth. **1616** R. C. *Times' Whistle* IV. 1441 Thou mayst make sale of it to whom thou list. **1674** Playford *Skill Mus.* I. 60 By his Musick he could drive men into what Affections he listed. **1741** Richardson *Pamela* (1824) I. xxvii. 42 Let them think what they list. **1823** Scott *Peveril* v, We will, if your ladyship lists, leave him. **1869** Freeman *Norm. Conq.* (1876) III. xiv. 348 The invaders landed and harried where they listed.

†**c.** *to list of*: to care for. *Obs.*

a **1300** *Cursor M.* 1791 Þe leuedis listed [*Fairf.* list] noght o pride. *c* **1400** *Melayne* 1254 One þᵉ lawnde righte þer þay lay..And liste no thynge of playe. **14..** *Women's Horns* in *Rel. Ant.* I. 80 They have despit, and ageyn concyence, Lyst nat of pryde, then hornes cast away. *c* **1450** *St. Cuthbert* (Surtees) 1744 Þe shipmen of na lykyng lyste.

†**3.** *trans.* To desire or wish for (something).

1545 Ascham *Toxoph.* I. (Arb.) 59 And seinge also they haue libertie to lyste what they will, I pray God they haue will to list that which is good. **1587** Golding *De Mornay* v. 55 By our listing of a thing, we may perceiue some alteration in our selues; but the thing it selfe that is listed or willed feeleth nothing thereof.

list (lɪst), *v.*² *arch.* Forms: 1 **hlystan**, 2–3 **lusten**, 2–5 **luste**, 3 **lhisten**, **(h)listen**, **hleste(n**, **lheste**, 3–6 **liste**, **lest(e**, 4–5 **lyst**, (5 **lyston**, **-yn**, **listyn**), 4– **list**. [OE. *hlystan*, f. *hlyst* LIST *sb.*¹ (Cf. mod.Icel. *hlusta*.)]

1. *intr.* = LISTEN *v.* 2.

c **1000** *Instit. Polity* §5 in Thorpe *Anc. Laws* (1840) II. 310 Hlystaþ hwæt ic secge. *c* **1200** *Trin. Coll. Hom.* 141 Lusteð nu þanne, and undernimeð þreo þing. *Ibid.* 185 Eie ne maig swo muchel biholden, ne ere lhisten ne herte þenchen. *a* **1250** *Owl & Night.* 263 Bo nu stille, and lat me speke,.. And lust hu ich con me bi-telle. *a* **1300** *K. Horn* 355 Lust whi [*Harl. MS.* list were fore] ihc wonde Bringe þe horn to honde. *a* **1300–1400** *Cursor M.* 20399 (Gött.) Listes all i ȝu biseke i-wiss. **1549** Latimer *Serm. on Ploughers* (Arb.) 29 But nowe I thynke I se you lysting and hearkening, that I shoulde name him. *c* **1590** Greene *Fr. Bacon* xi. (1630) G, List how they rumble. **1606** Shaks. *Ant. & Cl.* IV. iii. 12 Peace, what noise? 1 [*Sol.*] List, list. 2 [*Sol.*] Hearke. **1637** Milton *Comus* 480 List, list, I hear Som far off hallow break the silent Air. **1765** H. Walpole *Otranto* v. (1798) 89 List, sirs, and may this bloody record be a warning to future tyrants. **1808** Scott *Marm.* II. xxxiii, The stag..Spread his broad nostril to the wind, Listed before, aside, behind. **1847** Emerson *Poems* (1857) 12 Great Napoleon Stops his horse, and lists with delight. **1871** R. Ellis tr. *Catullus* lv. 1 List, I beg, provided you're in humour.

b. Const. *to*, *unto*, *till*; in OE. dat. and gen.

c **897** K. Ælfred *Gregory's Past.* xlix. 385 Ða fundon hie hiene..hlystende hiora worda. *c* **1000** *Ags. Gosp.* Luke xvi. 29 Hiȝ hlyston him. *c* **1200** Ormin 7846 Þatt he Ne lisste nohht wiþþ ære Till naness kinness idellleȝȝc. *a* **1300** *Cursor M.* 13833 Ne till vr laghes will he noght list. *c* **1380** *Sir Ferumb.* 4002 Now lysteþ to þis spelle. *c* **1592** Marlowe *Jew of Malta* I. ii. (1633) C 2, Graue Gouernors, list not to his exclames. **1791** Cowper *Iliad* VII. 54 Wilt then list to me? **1813** Scott *Rokeby* I. i, The warder..Lists to the breeze's boding sound. **1884** Browning *Ferishtah, The Family* 22 List to a tale.

2. *trans.* To listen to, hear; = LISTEN *v.* 1.

c **1175** *Lamb. Hom.* 63 [He] þe luste nulleð þesne red. *c* **1200** *Vices & Virtues* (1888) 67 Hlest hwat se heiȝeste ðe seið. *c* **1200** Ormin 9017 To lisstenn whatt te preost ȝuw seȝȝþ Off ȝure sawle nede. *c* **1200** *Trin. Coll. Hom.* 35 Hie openeden his earen to luste þe defles lore. *a* **1300** *Cursor M.* 20590 Listes þe bon þat scho him badd. *a* **1300** *K. Horn* 505 'Kyng', he sede, 'þu leste [*Laud MS.* wiltu luste] A tale mid þe beste'. *c* **1400** *Destr. Troy* 5083 So is it wit, a wiseman his wordis to listyn. **1598** Shaks. *Merry W.* v. v. 46 Elues, list your names. **1642** T. Hill *Trade of Truth* Ep. Ded., I put it into your Honourable Protection, who have listed it [a sermon]. **1775** Sheridan *Rivals* Epil., But ere the battle should he list her cries, The lover trembles—and the hero dies! **1813** Scott *Rokeby* III. xvii, I list no more the tuck of drum. **1821** Clare *Vill. Minstr.* II. 178, I..list the drone of heavy humble-bees. **1896** A. E. Housman *Shropsh. Lad* iii, And you will list the bugle That blows in lands of morn.

list (lɪst), *v.*³ [f. LIST *sb.*³; cf. OF. *lister* (one example in Godef.) to put a list on (cloth); also It. *listare*, G. *leisten*, Du. *lijsten*.]

†**1.** *trans.* To put a list, border, or edge round (an object); to border, edge. Also, to put as a list or border *upon*. *Obs.*

13.. *Guy Warw.* (A.) xciii. (1887) 454 A targe listed wiþ gold. *c* **1430** *Pilgr. Lyf Manhode* I. xciv. (1869) 51 The scrippe was of greene selk,..Lysted it was wel queyntliche with xii belles of siluer. **1530** Palsgr. 612/2, I lyste a garment, or border it rounde about with a lyst..I have lysted my cote within to make it laste better. **1580** Hollyband *Treas. Fr. Tong*, *Lisier*, to list or border any thing. **1624** Wotton *Archit.* in *Reliq.* (1651) 297 A long straight mossie walk..listed on both sides with an Aquæduct of white stone. *a* **1639** —— *Dk. Buckhm.* ibid. 80 Such an Accumulation of benefits, like a kind of Embroidering or listing of one favour upon another. *c* **1645** Howell *Lett.* (1650) I. i. 2 Trite and trivial phrases..listed with pedantic shreds of School-boy verses. **1670** Milton *Hist. Eng.* VI. Wks. (1847) 553/1 A Danish curtaxe, listed with gold or silver. **1703** Petiver in *Phil. Trans.* XXIII. 1451 The edges [of a fern leaf] are listed with Seed.

b. To fix list upon the edge of (a door).

1860 Worcester, *List*..5. To fix list, or a strip of cloth, to; as, 'To list a door'. **1881** R. T. Cooke *Somebody's Neighbors* 64 Monsieur Leclerc..listed the doors against approaching winter breezes.

†**2.** To enclose; to shut *in* with rails or the like.

1494 Fabyan *Chron.* VII. 463 [He] kepte his daye appoynted for that batayll, in a felde called in Frenshe Lapre Aux Clers, where for theim was ordeyned a place lyestyd and closed in goodly wyse. **1555** W. Watreman *Fardle Facions* II. i. 109 Upon the other thre quarters, it [Asie] is lysted in with the Occean. **1565** Cooper *Thesaurus*, *Cauea*, ..euery place listed or rayled in.

†**b.** To bound, limit. *Obs.*

a **1600** Hooker *Eccl. Pol.* VII. viii. §4 The local compass of a bishop's authority and power was never so straitly listed, as some men would have the world imagine.

3. *Carpentry.* To cut away the sappy edge of a board; to shape a block or stave by chopping.

1635 *Plymouth Col. Rec.* (1855) I. 34 Sawne bords..cut sharp at ye tope, and either listed or shote with a plaine. **1823** P. Nicholson *Pract. Build.* Gloss., *Listing*, the act of cutting away the sap-wood from one or both edges of a board. **1874** *Skyring's Builders' Prices* 22 Floors..For each edge listed, add *os. 2d.* **1875** Knight *Dict. Mech.*

4. *Agric.* To prepare (the land) for the crop (of cotton or Indian corn) by making ridges and furrows with the plough or beds and alleys with the hoe. *local U.S.*

1785 Washington *Writ.* (1891) XII. 224 Some of it..had been twice ploughed, then listed, then twice harrowed before sowing. **1856** Olmsted *Slave States* 432 Boys and girls, 'listing' an old corn-field with hoes.

list (lɪst), *v.*⁴ [f. LIST *sb.*⁶

In senses 3 and 4 the word is now taken chiefly as an aphetic form of *enlist*, and written '*list*.]

1. a. *trans.* To set down together in a list; to make a list of; to catalogue, register.

1614 Raleigh *Hist. World* IV. i. §1 (1634) 457 These kings were of the nation of Argives who are listed as followeth. **1655** H. Vaughan *Silex Scint.*, *Rules & Lessons* xx, When night comes, list thy deeds. **1712** *Official Notice* in *Lond. Gaz.* No. 4994/3 The Persons bringing the said Tickets, are desired to List the same in a Numerical Order, and to write in their List the Name. **1861** O'Curry *Lect. MS. Materials* 271 Of the Forbasa listed in the Book of Leinster there is one more so remarkable, that [etc.]. **1887** *Athenæum* 6 Aug. 171/2 About one hundred species of butterflies have been listed.

b. To set down or enter in a special, formal, or official list (e.g. of persons or property for assessment, of stocks, etc.); *U.S.* to enter or register for taxation.

1658 *Virginia Stat.* (1823) I. 454 All negroes imported.. and Indian servants..being sixteen years of age, to be listed and pay leavies as aforesaid. **1666** *Plymouth Col. Rec.* (1855) IV. 136 Incase they be not accomodated with land amongst them with whom they are listed neare the Bay line. **1687** Rycaut *Contn. Knolles' Hist. Turks* II. 223 There were listed fifty-five thousand, who paid duties of Harach. **1702** *Hawick Kirk Session Rec.* 4 Oct., The Minister..desired such as intended to communicate to list themselves this week. **1787** M. Cutler in *Life*, etc. (1888) I. 324 Spent the day in listing my money for Congress. **1877** Burroughs *Taxation* 214 Assessors are to list such lands only as are situate [etc.]. **1881** *Daily News* 1 Nov. 5/7 Only seven cases were listed for to-day. **1893** *Times* 14 July 4/1 The shrinkage in the value of American securities 'listed' in this market.

c. *U.S.* To place (a property) in the hands of a real-estate agent for sale or rent; to add to the list of properties advertised by a real-estate agent. Cf. LISTING *vbl. sb.*² 3.

1906 W. A. Carney *Real Estate Business* v. 20 A real estate broker..should have listed considerable property. *Ibid.* 21 He can sometimes list a real bargain. **1908** *Amer. Real Estate Seller* July 2 Every real estate dealer should have a form contract and use it. He should not list a property that he has not a contract on. **1909** *Ibid.* Aug. 6 The real estate dealers should combine and pass a resolution to list property exclusively. **1911** *National Realty Jrnl.* Mar. 14/2 The land owner, the investor, will also find it to his interest to recognize an active agent and list property with him. **1921** J. B. Spilker *Real Estate Business* v. 25 Only those properties which in the mind of the sales manager are saleable, and only those properties which are secured at a fair price and reasonable to both the buyer and seller, should be listed for sale. **1945** G. H. Beurhaus *Who handles your Real Estate?* (rev. ed.) vi. 19 The broker..proceeds to list property. **1972** J. L. Gale *Listing Real Estate* p. xix, Once we learn the ground rules for listing residences, we can then go on and successfully list property of any kind.

d. To enter (a name and address) in a telephone directory.

1959 R. Stout *Crime & Again* 91 'I'll see if she's listed.' I went to my desk for the Manhattan phone book. **1971** *Post Office Telephone Directory Section 101: London Postal Area* 12/1 A special Greater London Business directory has been introduced, listing certain businesses within about thirty miles of Charing Cross.

e. To protect (a building, etc.) by placing it on a statutory preservation register. Cf. LIST *sb.*⁶ a (*b*).

1968 *Act Eliz. II* c. 72 §52 A building which, immediately before the date of the compulsory purchase order, was listed. *Ibid.* §54 Matters which may be taken into account by the Minister in listing buildings. **1972** E. Lemarchand *Cyanide with Compliments* vi. 74 The lovely little seventeenth-century timber-framed house... It's recently been listed. *Ibid.* xiii. 170 Some local preservation enthusiasts succeeded in getting the house listed as of architectural and historic interest. **1973** *Daily Tel.* 24 Mar. 14/6 Church House..was listed on Feb. 27 because of its architectural or historic merit. But workmen knocked a hole through the front wall on Tuesday.

†**2.** To comprise in a list or catalogue; to enrol (*among*, *in*, *into* a certain number, *under* a certain head); to include or enrol in the number or membership *of*; to put in the same category *with*. *Obs.*

1622 Mabbe tr. *Aleman's Guzman d'Alf.* II. 142 He that.. desires to be listed into the rolle of those that haue gotten greatest fame. **1637** Massinger *Address to Shirley on his 'Grateful Servant,'* My obscure name, Listed with theirs, who here advance thy fame. **1649** Milton *Eikon.* xxiv. Wks. 1851 III. 489 What are Chaplains? In State perhaps they may be listed among the upper Servingmen of som great houshold. **1668** Pepys *Diary* 5 Feb., The persons therein concerned to be listed of this or that Church. **1675** Traherne *Chr. Ethics* To Rdr., Vertues are listed in the rank of invisible things. **1704** Swift *T. Tub* Wks. 1768 I. 51 It is under this class I have presumed to list my present treatise. **1727** A. Hamilton *New Acc. E. Ind.* I. xxii. 274 All Trades and Occupations being listed into Tribes; none can marry out of their own Tribe. **1777** Sir A. Dick *Let. to Johnson* 17 Feb. in Boswell *Johnson*, I have..listed Dr. Samuel Johnson in some of my memorandums..under a name which [etc.].

3. a. To enter on the list of a military body; to appoint formally (an officer); also in *pass.* with compl., to be appointed or 'gazetted' as (captain, etc.). In later use only in narrower sense, to enrol (private soldiers), to receive as recruits; = ENLIST *v.* 1.

1643 *Declar. Comm., Reb. Irel.* 28 The Parliament..had made choice of, and listed all the Commanders..for that Expedition. **1647** Clarendon *Hist. Reb.* II. §55 Some troops of those who had been listed by them under good officers. **1648** *Eikon Bas.* ix. 61 What Tumults could not do, an Army must, which is but Tumults listed. **1653** Shirley *Crt. Secret* IV. 47, I was listed Captain, before some The Generall knew had been seven years in service. **1706** Farquhar *Recruiting Officer* I. i, I don't beat up for common soldiers; no, I list only grenadiers. **1736** Bolingbroke *Patriot.* (1749) 26 Looking on themselves like volunteers, not like men listed in the service. **1795–7** Southey *Juvenile & Min. Poems* Poet. Wks. II. 82, I was trapp'd by the Sergeant's palavering pretences, He listed me when I was out of my senses.

b. *transf.* and *fig.*

1668 W. Penn *No Cross No Cr.* Wks. 1782 II. 96 Last of all, it lists thee of the company of..Jesus; to fight under his banner. **1701** Swift *Contests Nobles & Comm.* Wks. 1755 II. I. 50 He is listed in a party, where he neither knows the temper, nor designs, nor perhaps the person of his leader. **1742** Young *Nt. Th.* II. 9 He that is born, is listed; life is war. **1750** Chesterf. *Lett.* 5 Feb. (1792) II. ccxvi. 332 You are but just listed in the world, and must be active, diligent, indefatigable. **1776** Bentham *Fragm. Govt.* Wks. 1843 I. 288 Men whose affections are already listed against the law in question. **1882** J. Walker *Jaunt to Auld Reekie* 88 Farmer-folks in politics Wi' Tory lairds are listed.

4. a. *refl.* and *intr.* (for *refl.*) To have one's name entered upon the list of a military body; to engage for military service; = ENLIST *v.* 4. Phr. ***to list (oneself) a soldier*** or ***for a soldier***.

1643 *Declar. Comm., Reb. Irel.* 62 Who..have lysted themselves in the Lord Dillons Troupe. *c* **1665** Mrs. Hutchinson *Mem. Col. Hutchinson* (1846) 162 Secure yourself in some other parliament garrisons, or list into the castle. **1675** tr. *Machiavelli's Prince* viii. (Rtldg. 1883) 57 In his youth [he] listed a soldier. **1702** Sedley *Grumbler* III. i. Wks. (1766) 233 *Catau.* Brillon has listed himself a solder. *Grichard.* Listed himself a soldier! *Catau.* Yes, Sir, listed to go to the war. **1709** Steele *Tatler* No. 89 ¶6 A Drum passing by,..I listed myself for a Soldier. **1765** Blackstone *Comm.* I. 414 If any officer and soldier..shall desert, or list in any other regiment. **1827** Hallam *Const. Hist.* (1876) II. ix. 138 Whether a thoroughly upright and enlightened man would rather have listed under the royal or parliamentary standard. **1893** Stevenson *Catriona* 164 He listed at last for a sodger.

b. *transf.* and *fig.*

1650 Fuller *Pisgah* I. vii. 19 They lost their names by listing themselves under some other people. **1658** *Whole Duty of Man, Private Devotions* (1684) 173 Having now anew listed my self under his banner. **1694** Dryden *Love Triumph.* IV. i, You..who are listing yourself into the honourable company of cuckolds. **1732** Pope *Ess. Man* II. 98 Passions, though selfish, if their means be fair, List under Reason. **1738** Wesley *Psalms* II. ii, The Rulers list themselves his Foes. **1791** Burke *App. Whigs* Wks. VI. 254 To list themselves, and even to take a lead, with the party which they think most likely to prevail. *a* **1845** Hood *Irish Schoolm.* xvii, When first the scholar lists in learning's train. **1845** Stephen *Comm. Laws Eng.* (1874) I. 3 Merely that they [M.P.'s] may list under party banners.

list (lɪst), *v.*⁵ *Naut.* Also 7–8 **lust**. [f. LIST *sb.*⁵] *intr.* Of a ship: To careen, heel, or incline to one side. Also with *off*.

1626 Capt. Smith *Accid. Yng. Sea-men* 29 Cun the ship spoune before the winde, she lusts, she lyes vnder the Sea. *c* **1740** A. Allen *MS. Dict.* s.v. *Lust*, Mariners say the Ship lusteth, when she leans to one side rather than to another. **1880** *Times* 6 Aug. 5/3 When heavily laden she..had a tendency to list, and righted herself with difficulty. *Ibid.* 17 Dec. 5/6 She was moored outside the dock but listed off, and makes a good deal of water. **1885** *Century Mag.* XXIX. 742 She listed to port and filled rapidly.

listable (ˈlɪstəb(ə)l), *a.* *U.S.* [f. LIST *v.*⁴ + -ABLE.] That may be listed or put upon a list

(e.g. of men liable to military service, of property liable to taxation); assessable, rateable.

1665 *Rhode Island Col. Rec.* (1857) II. 115 Their sones and sarvants that are listable, which are to be listed, and to traine. **1688** *New Eng. Hist. & Gen. Reg.* (1880) XXXIV. 371 An Acco^t of the lystable Estates in the towne of Lyme. **1779** *Vermont St. Papers* (1823) 295 A true account of all their listable poles, and all their rateable estate. **1895** *Columbus Disp.* (Ohio) 23 Nov. 13/5 Of a nature and form not listable for taxation.

listed ('lɪstɪd), *a.*¹ [f. LIST *sb.*³ + -ED².]

1. Provided with a list or selvage.

1552 *Act 5 & 6 Edw. VI*, c. 6 §1 Everie White Clothe.. shalbe..lysted accordinge to the auncyent custome. **1691** *Lond. Gaz.* No. 2725/4, 24 yards of white Salisbury Cloth, which was Listed, and some part of it stained Reddish.

2. Bordered, edged; striped. Also (of colours), arranged in bands or stripes.

c **1450** *Merlin* 163 Crownes of goold and asure bendes entrauerse lysted as grene as a mede. **1616** SURFL. & MARKH. *Country Farme* 150 His haire drawing toward the colour of blacke, sleeke, and listed. *Ibid.* 386 The wood of the walnut tree is..listed and smooth of his owne nature. **1659** *Plymouth Col. Rec.* (1855) III. 159 A blew paire of stockings and a gray listed garter. **1667** MILTON *P.L.* XI. 862 A dewie Cloud, and in the Cloud a Bow Conspicuous with three listed colours gay. **1814** CARY *Dante, Par.* xiv. 87 In two listed rays The splendours shot before me. **1876** LONGF. *Dutch Picture* iv, The listed tulips look like Turks.

3. Covered or edged with list.

1827 FARADAY *Chem. Manip.* ii. 43 The listed rings..are easily made out of a slip of thin pliant wood,..the rough ring being covered by rolling list round it. **1866** THOREAU *Yankee in Canada* i. 12 We pushed aside the listed door of this church. **1889** *Anthony's Photogr. Bull.* II. 415 A listed strip fitting the opening.

4. (See quot. and LIST *v.*³ 3.)

1842–59 GWILT *Archit.* Gloss., *Boards, listed*, such as are reduced in their width by taking off the sap from their sides.

listed ('lɪstɪd), *a.*² [f. LIST *sb.*³ II + -ED².]

1. Of ground: Enclosed in or converted into lists for tilting. Of a combat: Fought in the lists.

1671 MILTON *Samson* 1087 Those encounters, where we might have tri'd Each others force in camp or listed field. **1727–46** THOMSON *Summer* 1470 Bold..are thy generous youth,..and first Or on the listed plain or stormy seas. **1793** SOUTHEY *Let.* in Dowden *Life* (1880) 30 The tapestried room—the listed fight—the vassal-filled hall. **1812** JOANNA BAILLIE *Orra* I. i Wks. (1851) 237 In these listed combats. **1818** BYRON *Ch. Har.* IV. cxxxix, On battle-plains or listed spot? **1862** GOULBURN *Pers. Relig.* vii. III. (1873) 216 To fight it out with them inch by inch in a listed field.

2. Engaged in the lists.

1861 LYTTON & FANE *Tannhäuser* 37 The blazon'd urn That held the name-scrolls of the listed bards.

listed ('lɪstɪd), *ppl. a.*¹ [f. LIST *v.*⁴ + -ED¹.]

1. Enlisted for military service.

1649 MILTON *Eikon.* Wks. 1738 I. 390 Their defensive Armies were but listed Tumults. [Cf. quot. 1648 in LIST *v.*⁴ 3.] **1693** W. FREKE *Art of War* viii. 257, I would rathe be a Volunteer, than a Listed Souldier. **1709** *Royal Proclam.* 27 Jan. in *Lond. Gaz.* No. 4510/2 They shall take a Receipt.., acknowledging the Receipt of such Listed Man.

2. Included in a list, directory, or catalogue; ***listed building***, one protected from demolition or major alteration by being included in an official list of buildings of architectural or historical importance.

1907 *Installation News* Jan. 11/1 Conduits have now to be manufactured to exact listed diameters. **1965** H. I. ANSOFF *Corporate Strategy* vi. 117 Investment funds which trade in listed securities have the additional advantage of knowing the full field of choice. **1968** R. H. MCCALL in P. Ward *Conservation & Devel. Historic Towns & Cities* III. 110 Of 439 Listed buildings in the City [*sc.* Winchester], 9 on the Statutory List have been wholly or partly demolished. **1971** P. GRESSWELL *Environment* 150 There are now about 120,000 'listed' buildings in England. *Ibid.*, An owner can also be threatened with compulsory purchase if he fails to keep a listed building in reasonable repair. **1973** *Country Life* 29 Mar. 866/2 The highest price, about £54,000, was paid for the Wealden farmhouse, a listed building that probably dates from the 17th century.

listed ('lɪstɪd), *ppl. a.*² [f. LIST *v.*³ + -ED¹.]

a. (See LIST *v.*³ 4.)

1888 *Sci. American* 12 May 298/1 Being designed..for use on growing check-rowed and listed corn.

b. *Basket-making.* Having an extra (decorative) skein on a handle.

1912 T. OKEY *Introd. Basket-Making* xii. 145, I have carried out a listed handle with skeins of ordinary chair cane. **1953** [see LISTING *vbl. sb.*⁴].

†**'listed**, *a.*³ *Obs.* [f. LIST *sb.*¹ + -ED².] Only in comb. ***thick listed***, hard of hearing.

1579 TWYNE *Phisicke agst. Fort.* II. xcvii. 289 a, They that are thicke listed, seeme in a maner to be out of their wittes, but they that are blinde, are reputed more miserable, and therefore we laugh at the deafe, and pittie the blinde.

listel ('lɪstəl). *Arch.* Also in It. form listello, listella. [a. F. *listel*, ad. It. *listello*, dim. of *lista* = LIST *sb.*³] A small list or fillet.

1598 R. HAYDOCKE tr. *Lomazzo* I. xxv. 89 The vpper rule, called listello. **1664** EVELYN tr. *Freart's Archit.*, etc. 127 Those very small Listellos or Annulets under the Echinus of the Doric Capitel, by the Italians call'd Gradetti, Degrees. **1715** LEONI *Palladio's Archit.* (1742) I. 16 Annulets, or Listellas. **1812–16** J. SMITH *Panorama Sci. & Art* I. 172 A small flat face is called a fillet, or listel. **1848** tr. *Hoffmeister's Trav. Ceylon & Ind.* 339 The roof..is..formed of smooth planks, over the seams of which are laid triangular listels, to prevent the rain from penetrating.

listen ('lɪs(ə)n), *sb.* [f. LISTEN *v.*]

†**1.** Hearing, sense of hearing. *Obs.*

13.. *E.E. Allit. P.* B. 586 He þat fetly in face fettled alle eres If he has losed the lysten hit lyftez meruayle.

2. a. The action or an act of listening; a spell of listening or attentive hearing. Also ***listen-out*** (after *look-out*). Chiefly in phr. ***on*** or ***upon the listen***: in the act of listening.

1788 'ASPASIA' in *Amer. Museum* IV. 565 Every time the door opens, or a foot is on the stairs, you are on the listen. **1803** MARY CHARLTON *Wife & Mistress* II. 151 They are always upon the listen in this house. **1807** tr. *Three Germans* I. 6 Not the faintest..sound..reached their attentive listen. *Ibid.* II. 30 He remained upon the silent listen. **1817–18** COBBETT *Resid. U.S.* (1822) 206 The anxious listen, the wistful look, and the dropping tear, of the disconsolate dams. **1834** J. WILSON in *Blackw. Mag.* XXXVI. 729 They were alarmed, as they kept a listen-out, by an incessant barking. **1840** *New Monthly Mag.* LIX. 397 Mrs. Hawkey is..clearing her throat for a long talk, myself settled down.. for a long listen. **1884** FENN *Sweet Mace* II. xiii. 223 She was often on the watch, and always on the listen. **1935** *World-Radio* 5 July 9/1 People like me, who..are constantly on the listen with half an ear for something. **1968** J. PHILIPS *Hot Summer Killing* (1969) III. ii. 138 Take a listen while I try to find Jerry. **1968** C. WATSON *Charity ends at Home* x. 122 So what I did was to pull off to the side and have a proper listen under the lid. **1970** P. BAIR *Tribunal* II. i. 60 'Did you have a nice talk?' 'I had a long listen.' **1971** *It* 2–16 June 19/3 Give it a listen.

b. listen-in, a period of listening to a broadcast, telephone conversation, etc. Cf. LISTEN *v.* 2 e.

1922 *Daily Mail* 30 Nov. 7 A listen-in. The Queen.. listened to a recitation sent out from Marconi House. **1946** *Philadelphia Bulletin* 1 Aug. 3 An occasional listen-in on the ..[telephone] line later convinced company men.

listen ('lɪs(ə)n), *v.* Forms: 1 *Northumb.* lysna, 3 lustnie, -in, *pa. pple.* i-lustned, 3–4 lustne(n, listne(n, 4 *pa. t.* and *pple.* lisnyt, lesnyt, 4–5 lesten, -yn, -in, li-, lystyn, -in, 4–6 lysten, 5 lystny, 7 lissen, 3– listen. [ONorthumb. *lysna*, **hlysna*, corresp. to MHG. *lüsenen*:—OTeut. type **hlusinôjan*, f. Teut. root **hlus-*: see LIST *sb.*¹ From the same root is OE. *hlosnian* (:—OTeut. type **hlos-*, *hlusnôjan*) to listen. The forms with *t* are due to association with the synonymous LIST *v.*¹]

1. a. *trans.* To hear attentively; to give ear to; to pay attention to (a person speaking or what is said). Now *arch.* and *poet.*

c **950** *Lindisf. Gosp.* Matt. xiii. 18 Gie forðon ȝeheras *vel* lysnas bisena ðæs sauende. *c* **1205** LAY. 25128 þa heo hafden longe i-lustned þan kinge. *c* **1220** *Bestiary* 398 Listneð nu a wunder. *c* **1250** *Gen. & Ex.* 2137 King pharaon listnede hise red. *a* **1300–1400** *Cursor M.* 20590 (Gött.) Listnes þe bone þat scho him bad. *c* **1350** *Will. Palerne* 4607 Ladis & oþer lordes lesteneþ now my sawe! *c* **1400** *Destr. Troy* 8421 Lystyn my wordes. *c* **1476** J. PASTON in *P. Lett.* III. 159 If it lyke you to lystyn him. **1590** GREENE *Orl. Fur.* (1599) 25 What messenger hath Ate sent abroad With idle lookes to listen my laments? **1634** MILTON *Comus* 551 At which I ceas't, and listen'd them a while. **1795** SOUTHEY *Joan of Arc* v. 310 The tale of all the ills she hath endured I listen. **1823** BYRON *Juan* XIII. xlviii, Listening debates not very wise or witty. **1830** TENNYSON *Ode to Memory* iii, Listening the lordly music flowing from The illimitable years.

†**b.** With two objects: To hear (something) from (a person). *Obs.*

c **1330** R. BRUNNE *Chron.* (1810) 288 þe chance listnes me.

2. a. *intr.* To give attention with the ear to some sound or utterance; to make an effort to hear something; to 'give ear'.

c **1205** LAY. 26357 He lustnede [*later text* luste] ȝeorne. *c* **1225** *Leg. Kath.* 785 We schulen lustnin hu þi lauerd & ti leof..wule werien to dei þine leasunges. *a* **1275** *Prov. Ælfred* 212 in *O.E. Misc.* 115 Lustlike lustine [*v.r.* lustnie; *earlier text* Lvsteþ]..lef dere. *c* **1315** SHOREHAM I. 2091 Nou lestne. *c* **1350** *Will. Palerne* 1929 Now listenes, lef lordes, þis lessoun þus i ginne. **1375** BARBOUR *Bruce* VI. 72 He..lisnyt full ententily Gif he oucht herd of thare cummyng. *c* **1400** *Sowdone Bab.* 20 Listinythe a while and ye shall see. **14..** *Voc.* in Wr.-Wülcker 566/1 *Asculto*, to lystny. **1530** PALSGR. 612/2 Lysten at the crevysse if thou cannest here any by [*sic*] steryng. **1667** MILTON *P.L.* v. 627 And in their motions harmonie Divine So smooths her charming tones, that Gods own ear Listens delighted. *a* **1703** BURKITT *On N.T., Mark* i. 45 Christ doth not stay in the crowd with his ear open to listen how men admire the preacher. **1781** COWPER *Retirement* 448 A man..Who..Speaks with reserve, and listens with applause. **1875** DASENT *Vikings* I. xii. 162 Every one listened what he would add to such a clever beginning. **1875** JOWETT *Plato* (ed. 2) I. 323 They will be sure to listen if they find that you are a good speaker.

fig. **1842** TENNYSON *Godiva* 54 The deep air listen'd round her as she rode.

b. Const. *to* (*unto*): to give ear to (= sense 1); also, in extended sense, to give heed to, allow oneself to be persuaded by.

c **1290** *S. Eng. Leg.* I. 462/2 Lustniez nouþe to mi speche. *a* **1300–1400** *Cursor M.* 6451 *heading* (Gött.), Listens nou vnto mi saw. *c* **1450** *Merlin* 11 The holy man lestned well to all hir confession. **1595** SHAKS. *John* III. i. 198 King Philip, listen to the Cardinall. **1611** BIBLE *Isa.* xlix. 1. *a* **1661** FULLER *Worthies, Durham* (1662) I. 295 Lissen to Mr. Cambden his Character of him. **1667** MILTON *P.L.* VI. 908 List'n not to his Temptations. **1748** *Anson's Voy.* I. i. 8 These officers..were much listened to by some considerable persons. **1856** FROUDE *Hist. Eng.* (1858) I. v. 375 Henry must have been compelled to listen to many such invectives. **1883** —— *Short Stud.* IV. I. xi. 139 Boys and girls found him always ready to listen to their small distresses.

c. † ***to listen of***: to hear tell of. † ***to listen on*** = *listen to*. ***to listen for***, † ***after***: to be eager or make an effort to catch the sound of; to endeavour to hear or to hear of. ***to listen out***, to listen for a sound, e.g. on a radio receiver.

a **1300–1400** *Cursor M.* 22431 (Gött.) If ȝe of þaim will listen a trau, I sal ȝu tell of þaim sothsau. *c* **1320** *Sir Tristr.* 402 Of a prince proude in play Listneþ, lordinges dere. ?*a* **1400** LYDG. *Chorle & Byrde* (Roxb.) 14 To heere of wisedom thyn eeres ben half deef Lyke an asse that lystneth on an harpe. **1593** SHAKS. *2 Hen. VI*, I. iii. 152, I will..listen after Humfrey, how he proceedes. **1597** —— *2 Hen. IV*, I. i. 29 Heere comes my Seruant Trauers, whom I sent..to listen after Newes. **1642** R. CARPENTER *Experience* Pref. 15, I beg..that they will so farre listen after me..as to take notice..what becomes of me. **1642** FULLER *Holy & Prof. St.* III. iv. 160 Scholars listen after Libraries, Disputations, and Professours. **1749** FIELDING *Tom Jones* x. vi, She pricks up her ears to listen after the voice of her pursuer. **1859** TENNYSON *Elaine* 862 The sick man..Would listen for her coming. —— *Enid* 184 While they listen'd for the distant hunt. **1871** FARRAR *Witn. Hist.* i. 26 Then must science and civilisation listen for the voice of a new deliverer. **1910** A. BENNETT *Clayhanger* III. v. 362 Don't latch the door. Pull it to. I'll listen out. **1945** *Tee Emm* (Air Ministry) V. 35 Owing to the fact that they were listening out on channel 'A' instead of channel 'B', he failed to make contact. **1946** L. E. O. CHARLTON *R. Air Force July 1943 to Sept. 1944* 21 (*caption*) This photograph..depicts a scene in the flying control room—'listening out' to bring the Lancasters back to base. **1959** *Listener* 16 July 111/3 Initially I was afraid that the work would founder in an over-poetic fog but Mr. Bradnum was worth listening out for. **1971** J. WAINWRIGHT *Last Buccaneer* I. 49 We need receiving equipment to listen-out—to pinpoint every wavelength. **1974** D. KYLE *Raft of Swords* xiii. 140 He searched the air waves... For several days he had 'listened out' to a Russian ship with three operators aboard.

†**d.** ***to listen one's ears*** (or ***an ear***) ***to***: = b. *Obs.*

a **1533** LD. BERNERS *Gold. Bk. M. Aurel.* (1546) Y iv, I neuer..lystened myne eares to murmures. **1579** TOMSON *Calvin's Serm. Tim.* 726/2 If we listen our eares to obey that that is shewed vs here. *a* **1656** USSHER *Ann.* (1658) 559 The Citizens would by no means lissen an eare to the accusation.

e. ***to listen in***, to listen to a broadcast programme, etc.; to listen secretly to a telephone conversation. Also const. *to*, *on*, and *transf.*

1905 *Electrician* 20 Jan. 532/1 At the end of the first section the operator on the ship listened in for a reply. At last he took off the telephone. **1915** A. F. COLLINS *Bk. Wireless* p. vii, A boy sitting..at home with..a telephone receiver to his ear *listening-in* to the news of the world. **1920** *Wireless World* Jan. 594/2 While 'listening-in', the switch.. is placed over to the right. **1926** *Daily Chron.* 13 May 3/1 By the primitive process of passing it from lip to lip the news sped 'like wildfire' amongst the London millions who were not listening in, but were just sitting in their offices or lunching in the restaurants, or walking about the streets. **1928** *Chambers's Jrnl.* Jan. 27/2 None of us could help 'listening in' to the fun that was going on in the kitchen. **1931** *Boys' Mag.* XLV. 99/2 Patients..are able to listen-in to the Radio programmes by means of headphones. **1939** MRS. BELLOC LOWNDES *Diary* 5 Oct. (1971) 180, I asked him if he ever listened in, whereupon he said in an explosive tone: 'never'. I observed that one learnt a great deal from listening in. **1973** 'H. CARMICHAEL' *Too Late for Tears* xv. 175 His wife wasn't involved... If she had been she wouldn't have wanted us to listen-in on that phone conversation. **1973** 'M. INNES' *Appleby's Answer* v. 49 They have forgotten about you and resumed their tittle-tattle. Whereupon you listen in. **1973** *Radio Times* 15 Nov. 73/3 For thousands of children..who 'listened in' each Friday afternoon, Romany *was* the countryside.

f. *spec.* To listen to a broadcast programme.

1929 *Radio Times* 8 Nov. 395/3 We sat listening..with a portable set. **1935** *World-Radio* 5 July 19/3 (Advt.), Below 100 Metres, Listen to the World. **1936** *B.B.C. Empire Broadcasting* 2 Dec. 2/3 Your greeting, Big Ben, and then the National Anthem, moved us profoundly—it took quite a time to listen without real emotion. *Ibid.* 9 Dec. 2/1 Whenever there was a sporting commentary a host of people used to come to my bungalow to listen. **1946** *B.B.C. Year Bk.* 11 With the restoration of peace there was a natural tendency for the citizens of other countries to listen, at first, only to their own newly freed broadcasting services. **1970** *B.B.C. Handbk.* 98 There is magic in ensuring that most people in the world can listen in a language they can really understand.

†**3.** (quasi-*trans.*) ***to listen forth, out***: to obtain tidings of. (Cf. HEARKEN *v.* 8.) *Obs.*

a **1592** GREENE *Geo. a Greene* (1599) A 3, Come, Bonfield, let vs goe, And listen out some bonny lasses here. *Ibid.* D 4 b, Ienkin,..goe to Bradford, And listen out your fellow Wily. **1602** WARNER *Alb. Eng.* XII. lxxiii. (1612) 300 For Mandeuil they seeke, and him at last did listen forth.

4. *intr.* To sound (in a certain way). Freq. with *to* = to strike (one) as. *U.S.*

1908 K. MCGAFFEY *Sorrows of Show Girl* 78 That listened very well indeed, and we all climbed into a cabbage and vamped over. **1912** C. MATHEWSON *Pitching in a Pinch* vii. 143 All is fair in love, war, and baseball except stealing signals dishonestly, which listens like another paradox. **1923** R. D. PAINE *Comrades of Rolling Ocean* xiv. 250 Here's where I slip it out..to help square the repair bill for my joy-ride. How does it listen to you? **1923** L. J. VANCE *Baroque* xxvii. 174 [It] don't listen reasonable to me. **1945** MENCKEN *Amer. Lang.* Suppl. I. 317 It has been suggested ..that *it listens well* may be from *es hört sich gut an.*

listenable ('lɪs(ə)nəb(ə)l), *a.* [f. LISTEN *v.* + -ABLE.] Easy or pleasant to listen to; willing to

listen. Hence **listena'bility**, the quality of being listenable.

1920 C. MORLEY *Haunted Bookshop* vi. 95 He felt very talkative, as most older men do when a young girl looks as delightfully listenable as Titania. **1946** *Newsweek* 18 Feb. 90 In listenability, it is more like the Concerto for Orchestra. **1958** *Oxford Mail* 12 Aug. 6/6 Viewers are invited to.. listen to.. works carefully selected from the classics for their 'listenable' qualities. **1964** *Listener* 31 Dec. 1066/2 Talks producers might take a little more trouble in making them [*sc.* scripted talks] listenable, if they were given credits in *Radio Times*. **1966** G. N. LEECH *Eng. in Advertising* iii. 27 Characteristics of advertising language.. readability (or 'listenability'). **1970** *Guardian* 9 June 8/2 Berta was full of listenable opinions on her father. **1971** *Hi-Fi Sound* Feb. 78/2 It can be seen how singularly useless the THD results are, when attempting to assess the 'listenability' of an amplifier.

listener ('lɪs(ə)nə(r)). Also 7–8 **listner**. [f. LISTEN *v.* + -ER[1].]

1. a. One who listens; an attentive hearer.

1611 COTGR., *Escouteur*, an hearer, hearkener, listener. *a* **1618** RALEIGH *Maxims St.* (1651) 45 To have their Beagles, or listeners in every corner.. of the Realm. **1643** *True Informer* 8 They are great listners after any Court news. **1692** R. L'ESTRANGE *Fables* clxx. (1708) 184 'Tis an Old Saying, That List'ners never hear Well of Themselves. **1711** ADDISON *Spect.* No. 31 ¶1 This gentleman.. was entertaining a whole Table of Listners with the project of an Opera. **1855** MACAULAY *Hist. Eng.* xxi. IV. 592 The streets were stopped up all day by groups of talkers and listeners. **1875** JOWETT *Plato* (ed. 2) IV. 4 The youthful group of listeners.. are.. at last convinced by the arguments of Socrates.

b. *slang.* The ear.

1821 *Sporting Mag.* VII. 274 Sampson was floored from a tremendous wisty-castor, under the listener. **1822** *Blackw. Mag.* XI. 594 A douss on the smeller—a dimmer to the daylights, and a larrup on the listeners. **1827** EGAN *Anecd. Turf* 6 Hooper planted another hit under Wood's listner.

2. *Fortif.* = *listening-gallery* (see LISTENING *vbl. sb.* 18 b).

1828 J. M. SPEARMAN *Brit. Gunner* (ed. 2) 302 From the envelope gallery are run out.. galleries in directions parallel to the capitals of the works... These latter are called *listeners.* **1833** STRAITH *Fortif.* §213. 161 The distance between the listeners depends.. on the nature of the soil that conveys the sound.

3. One who listens to a broadcast. Also *attrib.* Also *listener-in.* Cf. LISTEN *v.* 2 e, f.

1922 *Daily Mail* 21 Nov. 7 The limited service has already established itself in high favour with 'listeners-in'. **1923** *Radio Times* 28 Sept. 12/1 It seems to me that the B.B.C. are mainly catering for the 'listeners' who own expensive sets. **1926** *Daily Chron.* 13 May 3/1 By the magic of wireless it was, perhaps, the listeners-in who heard it first. **1929** *Radio Times* 8 Nov. 388/1 The recent broadcasting of *Aïda* has prompted a Forest Hill listener to send in.. a very delightful story. **1936** *B.B.C. Ann.* 87/2 The BBC has recently established, at its Head Office, a special unit, with the object of co-ordinating information.. and studying new methods of 'listener research'. **1950**, **1951** [see AUDIENCE 7 d]. **1970** *B.B.C. Year Bk.* 23 For the great majority of listeners.. there will be little evidence of sudden upheaval.

Hence **'listenership**, the estimated number of listeners to a broadcast programme or to radio (*spec.* as opp. to television).

1943 *Business Week* 30 Jan. 44 Increased emphasis on news broadcasts and commentators boosted listenership particularly between 5 and 7 p.m. **1958** *New Statesman* 2 Aug. 142/2 In America, reports *Time*, sound-radio is enjoying a 'spectacular comeback'; latest figures of 'listenership' show it 'up 8 per cent over last year, 25 per cent over its pre-TV peak in 1947'. **1971** *Daily Tel.* 17 Apr. 19/2 Listenership levels are still an imponderable. It is unlikely that the British public will listen to local radio as much as, say, the Americans.

listening ('lɪs(ə)nɪŋ), *vbl. sb.* [-ING[1].] **1. a.** The action of the verb LISTEN.

13.. *K. Alis.* 4798 Yif yee willeth yive listnyng, Now yee shullen here gode thing. **1596** SHAKS. *Tam. Shr.* IV. i. 68 This Cuffe was but to knocke at your eare, and beseech listning. **1641** MILTON *Ch. Govt.* II. Pref. Wks. 1738 I. 59 It were a folly to commit any thing elaborately compos'd to the careless and interrupted listening of these tumultuous times. **1847** TENNYSON *Princess* VII. 95 Lonely listenings to my mutter'd dream.

b. listening gallery *Fortif.* (see quot. 1872–6); **listening key** *Teleph.* (see quot. 1940); **listening post** *Mil.*, an advanced position used to discover movements or the disposition of the enemy; also *transf.*

1833 STRAITH *Fortif.* §213. 160 Listening galleries. **1872–6** VOYLE *Milit. Dict.* (ed. 3), *Ecoutes*, listening galleries... These galleries are run out under and beyond the glacis at regular distances in the direction of the besiegers' works, and enable the besieged to hear and estimate how near the besiegers have carried their mining operations. **1906** J. POOLE *Pract. Telephone Handbk.* (ed. 3) x. 159 (*heading*) Kellogg combined listening and ringing key. **1940** *Chambers's Techn. Dict.* 505/1 *Listening key*, the lever key which the operator throws, to put her head-set on to a cord circuit and speak to a subscriber. **1916** *War Illustr.* V. 69/1 At a listening-post. **1928** BLUNDEN *Undertones of War* xv. 167 The men lying at each listening-post were freezing stiff. **1945** *Life* 19 Nov. 119/2 The barbed wire was up everywhere, and the few listening posts that we did have at Vichy, at General Weygand's North African Headquarters—were in perpetual danger of sabotage by the well-meaning but essentially stupid remonstrances of the more emotional Left press. **1961** *Guardian* 29 May 9/5 Vienna is Europe's busiest listening post. **1965** MRS L. B. JOHNSON *White House Diary* 3 Nov. (1970) 335 John Gronouski was seated on my left and I enjoyed hearing him talk about Poland and how it serves as a sort of listening post for what is going on in Red China. **1971** J. TUNSTALL *Journalists at Work* iii. 86 Fairly standard features are centres like Hong Kong and Beirut which are used as 'listening posts' and jumping-off points for covering China and South East Asia, and the Middle East respectively. **1972** *Guardian* 25 Jan. 15/8 Paris uses the Commission mainly as a listening post to find out what the others are up to.

2. (Also *listening-in.*) The action of listening to a radio broadcast, a record-player, etc.; also, the action of listening (esp. secretly) to a telephone conversation. (Cf. LISTEN *v.* 2 e, f.) Also *attrib.* and *transf.*

1904 *Electr. World & Engin.* 7 May 875/2 The removal of the operator's plug, or her 'listening-in', restores the circuits to their proper condition for subsequent use. **1921** *Wireless World* 10 Dec. 581/1 'Listening in' was indulged in. **1925** A. HUXLEY *Those Barren Leaves* II. v. 149 But of what use is leisure, when leisure is occupied with listening-in and going to football matches? **1927** *Sat. Even. Post* 24 Dec. 80/2 These telephones were connected with a listening-in device concealed behind a picture on the wall. **1929** *Radio Times* 8 Nov. 389/3 The sounds heard had emerged from the loud-speaker of the caretaker... The caretaker was extremely annoyed at this interruption to his listening. **1939** *War Illustr.* 21 Oct. p. ii/1 Its [*sc.* the B.B.C.'s] dud programmes have led to a great falling-off in listening. **1940** *Manch. Guardian Weekly* 2 Feb. 83 From South West Germany it is stated that controllers have been appointed in blocks of flats to supervise the listening-in. **1941** *B.B.C. Gloss. Broadcasting Terms* 17 *Listening log*, list, in prescribed form, of the broadcast programmes heard by one person over a period of time. **1951** J. B. PRIESTLEY *Festival at Farbridge* II. ii. 217 Dan Cobbley was another radio personality, although he was on a lower listening figure level. **1957** *Encycl. Brit.* X. 619/2 The new possibilities for continuous listening helped enormously. On the debit side was the tendency especially of solo artists to record whole programs on LP disks, repeating endlessly the same established repertoire. **1969** *John Edwards Mem. Foundation Q.* V. IV. 126 The transcriptions of the songs.. are as nearly accurate as I can make them. After countless listenings I still can't make out some of the words. **1971** *Gloss. Electrotechnical, Power Terms* (*B.S.I.*) III. ii. 31 *Listening-in*, listening to a call in progress.

3. (With qualifying adj.) Broadcast, recorded, or other matter for listening to, esp. with reference to its quality or kind. Cf. READING *vbl. sb.* 7 a.

1938 *Listener* 25 May 1120/2 There must be a great deal of material available on this subject which would make more good listening. **1962** [see COMPULSIVE *a.* 3 b]. **1966** *Listener* 10 Feb. 221/3 The portrayal of.. the jostling and jockeying of the foreign ambassadors, made really good listening. **1985** *Church Times* 19 July 9/3 Other incidents in his life also made interesting listening.

'listening, *ppl. a.* [-ING[2].] **a.** That listens or hears attentively. Also *fig.*

a **1275** *Prov. Ælfred* 654 in *O.E. Misc.*, So deit þe lusninde luþere mon. *c* **1586** C'TESS PEMBROKE *Ps.* LXI. i, Lord, lend my voice a listning eare. **1608** SHAKS. *Per.* I. ii. 87 That I should open to the listning ayre How many worthie Princes' blouds were shed. **1727–46** THOMSON *Summer* 745 Thro' the soft silence of the listening night. **1750** GRAY *Elegy* 61 Th' Applause of list'ning Senates to command. **1820** KEATS *Hyperion* I. 37 There was a listening fear in her regard. **1866** GEO. ELIOT *F. Holt* (1868) 59, I pray for a listening spirit, which is a great mark of grace.

b. (Also *listening-in.*) That listens to a broadcast, recording, etc.

1926 *Punch* 14 July 39 (*caption*) *Husband* (to listening-in Wife). 'What's the matter, dear? Is it bad news or Stravinsky?' **1935** *Discovery* Sept. 277/2 They are providing ever better products and service to enable the listening public to get more enjoyment from the 'audio' programmes. **1941** *B.B.C. Gloss. Broadcasting Terms* 17 *Listening group*, group of listeners meeting regularly with the twofold object of hearing a particular series of broadcast talks.. and engaging in discussion. **1957** *B.B.C. Handbk.* 104 Audience Research set up permanent Listening Panels to report their reactions to the programmes they heard. **1970** *Ibid.* 112 A special listening section keeps track of the activities of foreign radio stations. **1974** *Times* 30 Nov. 10/4 The practitioners [of religious broadcasting].. are impeded by some notion of what the listening public expects their output to be.

†**lister**[1]. *Obs.* Also 4 **listre**, 4–5 **lyster**, 5 **-are**, **-yr**, **-ore**, **lyysterre**. [a. OF. *listre*, altered from *litre*:—L. *lector* (see LECTOR).] A reader or lector. In first quot., app. a preaching friar.

1377 LANGL. *P. Pl.* B. v. 138 On limitoures and listres [*v.rr.* listers, legistreris] lesynges I ymped. *c* **1380** WYCLIF *Wks.* (1880) 298 Somme freris procuren to be bisshopis, somme to be lystris. **1387** TREVISA *Higden* (Rolls) VI. 257 He hadde a lyster at mete. **1430–40** LYDG. *Bochas* I. iv. (1554) 7 Prudent listers, which list in bokes rede. *c* **1440** *Promp. Parv.* 307/1 Lyysterre (*H.* lystyr, *S.* lystore, *P.* listyr), *lector* (S. *delector*). **1460** CAPGRAVE *Chron.* (Rolls) 235 He.. went to Rome and there was he mad lyster of the Paleis, and comensale with the Pope. **1555** W. WATREMAN *Fardle Facions* II. xii. 264 Porters, Scribes, Listers, and many other persones without office.

lister[2] ('lɪstə(r)). [f. LIST *v.*[4] + -ER[1].]

1. An enlister.

1678 *Connect. Col. Rec.* (1859) III. 11 Whither the former immunities were stated upon the Troop as a Troop or upon those whoe were the first listers. *a* **1701** SEDLEY *Grumbler* III. Wks. 1778 II. 234 *Cat.* Sir, they will list me too, the serjeant would have taken me, if I had not been too quick for him... *Gri.* Why these are terrible listers!

2. One who makes out a list, *spec.* (*U.S.*) of taxable property; an assessor.

1716 *Coll. Connect. Hist. Soc.* (1897) VI. 321 Voted that the Listers and Ratemakers distribute the New Law book in this Town. **1858** W. T. MARTIN *Hist. Franklin County* in A. E. Lee *Hist. Columbus* (Ohio) (1892) I. 156 John Blair lister of taxable property in Franklin Township.

lister[3] ('lɪstə(r)). *U.S.* [f. LIST *v.*[3] 4 + -ER[1].] A double-mouldboard plough, used in corn and beet culture, which throws up ridges and at the same time plants and covers seed in the furrows. Also *attrib.*

1887 *Sci. Amer.* LVI. 6/3 When grain is planted by the so-called 'combined lister and drill', the listing forms a ditch or furrow several inches deep, in which the seed is deposited. **1897** *Sears, Roebuck Catal.* 157/2 (*heading*) Subsoil lister with wood beam complete with runners. **1946** *Harper's Mag.* Oct. 307/2 In my day a lister cost $20—a great deal of money, indeed. **1949** *Lubbock* (Texas) *Morn. Avalanche* 23 Feb. II. 6/4 Lister shares for any make tractor $3.50 each.

lister, variant of LEISTER.

listerella (lɪstə'rɛlə). *Bacteriology.* Pl. **-ella**, **-ellæ**. [mod.L., f. the name of Joseph (later Lord) *Lister* (1827–1912), English surgeon + L. *-ella* (see -EL[2]).] = LISTERIA.

[**1927** J. H. PIRIE in *Publ. S. Afr. Inst. Med. Res.* III. xx. 164 The 'Tiger River Disease' is present among gerbilles... The causative organism of this disease is a small Gram-positive bacillus, for which, from its most striking pathogenic effect, I propose the specific name *hepatolytica*, and the generic name, *Listerella*, dedicating it in honour of Lord Lister, one of the most distinguished of those connected with bacteriology whose name has not been commemorated in bacteriological nomenclature.] **1940** *Vet. Jrnl.* XCVI. 330 *Listerella* were recovered from the uteri of the sheep slaughtered immediately after aborting. [**1940**: see LISTERIA.] **1948** *Jrnl. Bacteriol.* LV. 471 (*heading*) A new technique for isolating listerellae from the bovine brain.

Hence ˌ**listere'llosis** [-OSIS] = LISTERIOSIS.

1939 *Science* 6 Oct. 337/1 More recently Biester and Schwarte reported spontaneous bovine listerellosis in Iowa. **1940** [see LISTERIA]. **1948** *Jrnl. Bacteriol.* LV. 473 Listerellosis as manifested in the ovine is extremely acute. **1961** R. D. BAKER *Essent. Path.* ix. 190 Infection with the small gram-positive rod, *Listeria monocytogenes* (listerellosis) is limited largely to meningitis, although it apparently causes abortions and stillbirths.

listeria (lɪ'stɛrɪə). *Bacteriology.* Pl. listeria, -ias. [mod.L., f. LISTER(ELLA + -IA[1] (see quot. 1940).] Any bacterium of the genus *Listeria*, formerly called *Listerella*, esp. *L. monocytogenes* which is a widespread pathogen of man and animals.

[**1940** J. H. PIRIE in *Science* 19 Apr. 383, I have been informed.. that the new name *Listerella* which I proposed for a genus of bacteria in 1927 had already been given to a Mycetozoan by Jahn in 1906 and to one of the Foraminifera by Cushman in 1939. My proposed name, therefore, becomes a homonym, but as the genus has acquired some importance in both human and veterinary pathology and references to 'Listerellosis' are becoming fairly common in literature, I think that a name as near to my original proposal as possible is desirable. I therefore propose *Listeria*, as the name for the genus of bacteria as defined by me in Publication No. XX of the South African Institute for Medical Research.] **1961** *Lancet* 2 Sept. 514/1 The amniotic fluid was examined again.. and listeria grew copiously from it.

Hence **li'sterial**, **li'steric** *adjs.*, caused by or derived from listerias; **listeri'osis**, infection with or disease caused by listerias.

1941 *North Amer. Vet.* XXII. 545 (*heading*) An outbreak of listeriosis in sheep. **1961** *Jrnl. Clin. Path.* XIV. 193 (*heading*) Human listerial meningitis. **1961** tr. *H.P.R. Seeliger's Listeriosis* 144 A generalized listeric septicaemia. *Ibid.* 145 [Seeliger] established that 'Granulomatosis infantiseptica' was a listeric infection. **1961** *Lancet* 2 Sept. 515/1 Listeriosis should no longer be considered a rare disease in man. **1972** *Amer. Jrnl. Vet. Res.* XXXIII. 591 (*heading*) Effects of listerial hemolysin on rabbit heart. **1972** *Obstetr. & Gynecol.* XL. 91 (*heading*) Listeriosis as a cause of fetal wastage. *Ibid.* 96/1 Penicillin or tetracycline.. should be started immediately when the possibility of Listeric infection is entertained.

Listerian (lɪ'stɪərɪən), *a.* [f. *Lister* + -IAN.] Applied to the system of antiseptic surgery invented by Sir Joseph (later Lord) Lister.

1880 MAC CORMAC *Antisept. Surg.* 52 The enormous advantages which are to be derived from the Listerian system of dressing.

Listerine ('lɪstərɪn). [f. *Lister* (see prec.) + -INE.] An antiseptic solution (see quot. 1889).

1889 *Syd. Soc. Lex.*, *Listerine*, a solution containing the antiseptic constituents of thyme, eucalyptus, baptisea, gualtheria, and mentha arvensis, with two grains of benzo-boric acid in each drachm. **1897** *N.Y. Voice* 3 June 7/2 One who rinses her mouth with listerin once a day.

Listerism ('lɪstərɪz(ə)m). [See -ISM.] The system of antiseptic surgery originated by Lister.

1880 MAC CORMAC *Antisept. Surg.* 53 Listerism is destined to become more largely employed.

Listerize ('lɪstəraɪz), *v.* [See -IZE.] *trans.* To treat according to Listerian methods.

1888 *19th Cent.* June 846 In this way the patients are 'Listerized', to use a hospital term. **1902** *19th Cent.* Jan. 102 The English surgeons were 'Listerizing' wounds with great success.

listful ('lɪstfʊl), *a.* *Obs.* exc. *arch.* [f. LIST *v.*[2] + -FUL.] Inclined to listen, attentive.

1595 SPENSER *Col. Clout* 7 The shepheard swaines.. with greedie listfull eares, Did stand astonisht at his curious skill.

1596 —— *F.Q.* v. i. 25. **1860** I. TAYLOR *Ess.* 94 Explicit cautions, as they enter a too listful ear, are likely to be suggestive of evil.

†**listily**, *adv. Obs.* In 5 **lystyly**. [f. LISTY *a.* + -LY^2.] With pleasure or delight, pleasantly.

c **1440** *Promp. Parv.* 318/1 Lustyly, or lystyly, *delectabiliter*.

listing ('lɪstɪŋ), *sb.* [f. LIST *sb.*^{3} + -ING^1.]

1. Selvage; list; border; the material of which the list of cloth is composed.

14.. *Nom.* in Wr.-Wülcker 696/22 *Hec forigo*, a lystynge. **1444** *Test. Ebor.* (Surtees) II. 99, j coverlet de blodio..cum alio coopertorio rubeo habente in lystyng volucres et albas ollas. **1762** GOLDSM. *Cit. W.* xxx, The humid wall, with paltry pictures spread;..The Seasons, framed with listing, found a place. **1823** J. BADCOCK *Dom. Amusem.* 115 Procure two yards..of web, of broad tape, or cloth listing. **1827** CARLYLE *Germ. Rom.* II. 152 A..chamber, hung round with red damask, which was trimmed with golden listings. **1835** URE *Philos. Manuf.* 206 Wool..so coarse that we could use it only in the edging of cloths or listing. **1870** ROCK *Text. Fabr.* i. 178 The listing or border..charged with a..rich ornamentation.

2. *Naut.* (See quot.)

1846 YOUNG *Naut. Dict.*, *Listing*, a narrow strip cut out off the edge of a plank in order to expose the vessel's timbers for examination; or in order to put in a new piece instead of altogether replacing a defective or damaged plank.

3. *Comb.*: **listing-pot** = *list-pot*: see LIST *sb.*^{3} 11.

1818 S. PARKES in *Mem. Lit. & Philos. Soc. Manch.* (1819) Ser. II. III. 362 The listing-pot, with a little melted tin in it.

†'**listing**, *vbl. sb.*^{1} *Obs.* [f. LIST *v.*^{1} + -ING^1.] Desiring, wishing.

1587 GOLDING *De Mornay* v. (1617) 60 Willing or listing is no more an action that passeth into the outward thing, than vnderstanding is.

'**listing**, *vbl. sb.*^{2} [f. LIST *v.*^{4} + -ING^1.]

1. Enrolment, enlistment.

1641 CHAS. I *Declar. to Parlt.* in Rushw. *Hist. Coll.* III. (1692) I. 536 Why the listing of so many Officers..should be misconstrued, We much marvel. **1648** HEYLIN *Relat. & Observ.* I. 134 Skippon's underhand Listing of Schismaticks. *a* **1655** VINES *Lords Supp.* (1677) 204 Baptism may be..for initiation, and listing of souldiers under Christ's colours. **1709** *Royal Proclam.* 27 Jan. in *Lond. Gaz.* No. 4510/3 Any three..of the..Commissioners, who shall be present at the listing of any Person. **1715** M. DAVIES *Athen. Brit.* I. 289 Mr. Medcalf, who plume's himself with the criminal poling and listing of his Winefed-Pilgrims.

attrib. **1763** *Brit. Mag.* IV. 547 And as a clown hates listing-money—So The sign of Serjeant Kite is still his foe. **1786** *Gentl. Mag.* LVI. I. 521 He took from him about six guineas in gold, listing-money.

2. The drawing up of a list (*e.g.* of rateable property). Also *attrib.*

1659 FULLER *App. Inj. Innoc.* (1840) 295 The listing of such faults as have escaped, either in the beginning or end of the book. **1891** K. FIELD *Washington* IV. 371/1 The listing committee of Denver's Mining Exchange is supposed to guard against the fraudulent listing of property. **1899** *Daily News* 5 Dec. 2/5 Lists of the numbers, and forms for listing.

3. *N. Amer.* The placing of a property on the list of a real-estate agent; an estate agent's register of properties that he has for sale; a property so listed. Cf. LIST *v.*^{4} 1 c.

1906 W. A. CARNEY *Real Estate Business* v. 21 Where values are changing it is necessary to confirm and correct the listings every month or two. **1909** *Amer. Real Estate Seller* Aug. 6 It may be well to explain exclusive listing here... When you have a piece of property to sell and you empower one and only one agent to dispose of it for you—your property is being listed exclusively. **1925** P. L. MELBERG *Realty Salesman* 138 Well bought is half sold can be applied to listings also; a good exclusive listing is half sold. **1926** HINMAN & DORAU *Real Estate Merchandising* vii. 95 Every administrator of the policies of a real estate firm will have to make a decision for or against multiple listing. **1950** C. URBAN *Successful Real Estate Practice* 78 Many brokers will take a listing at any price, hoping to get some offer the owner will accept. **1968** *Globe & Mail* (Toronto) 17 Feb. 45 (Advt.), To inspect this new listing please call Viola Roper. **1972** J. L. GALE *Listing Real Estate* p. xix, Listings are the inventory, the stock on the shelves, the merchandise of the real estate broker.

4. An entry in a catalogue, telephone directory, or other list.

1962 K. ORVIS *Damned & Destroyed* v. 443, I..reached out for the telephone directory. Helen Ashton had no listing. **1965** J. CLAPP *(title)* College textbooks, Supplement I: a classified listing of 9,500 textbooks used in 36 colleges. **1969** *John Edwards Mem. Foundation Q.* V. IV. 125 This complete listing of Cash's recordings was compiled by John Smith. **1971** *Amer. N. & Q.* Sept. 10/1 Every Lowe listing [in a bibliography] is found either in the main body or in an appendix. **1971** *Post Office Telephone Directory Section 101: London Postal Area* 6 The alphabetical listings under 'Telephone Service'.

listing, *vbl. sb.*^{3} *U.S.* [f. LIST *v.*^{3} 4 + -ING^1.] The action of LIST *v.*^{3} 4. In **listing-plough**, a double-mouldboard plough used in listing (Knight *Dict. Mech.* Suppl. 1884).

1805 R. PARKINSON *Tour Amer.* 165, I was near two months getting a plough made, therefore I hired for the listing (as they call it). **1887** *Sci. Amer.* LVI. 6/3 The drawback to this listing is due to the fact that close to the edges of the furrow on each side, a row of weeds springs up. **1935** *Nature* 17 Aug. 253/1 One of the processes whereby the drift of loose soil has been to some extent countered. This process, known to farmers as 'listing', consists of specially deep ploughing with the aid of motor-driven tractors... The furrows may be as many as fifteen feet apart.

'**listing**, *vbl. sb.*^{4} *Basket-making.* [f. LIST *v.*^{3} + -ING^1.] (See quots. 1912, 1953.) Hence **listing-skein**. Cf. LISTED *ppl. a.*^{2} b.

1912 T. OKEY *Introd. Basket-Making* 153 *Listing*, an additional skein or skeins worked in with the lapping of skein handles. **1953** A. G. KNOCK *Willow Basket-Work* (ed. 5) 36 *Listing*, a method of adding a raised form of ornamentation to a lapped handle by the use of one or more additional skeins, called listing-skeins... The listing on any handle can be added after the handle has been lapped. *Ibid.*, Diagram 26 shows a simple listed handle employing three listing-skeins. **1961** L. G. ALLBON *Basic Basketry* vii. 53 Another method of decorating a wrapped handle would be with listing. **1972** D. WRIGHT *Baskets & Basketry* ii. 61 Listing is worked over the interwoven No. 3 or 4 cane.

†**listing**, *ppl. a.*^{1} *Obs.* [f. LIST *v.*^{2} + -ING^2.] Listening.

1604 DRAYTON *Owl* 10 To breathe their deare thoughts to the listing Woods.

listing, *ppl. a.*^{2} [f. LIST *v.*^{5} + -ING^2.] Of a ship: heeling, inclining to one side.

1923 *Public Opinion* 30 Mar. 312/3 Six projectiles struck the listing Iowa.

listless ('lɪstlɪs), *a.* [f. LIST *sb.*^{4} + -LESS. Cf. the collateral form LUSTLESS, which occurs in the sense of 'listless' (tr. L. *deses*) as early as 1398.] Of persons, their actions, etc.: †**a.** Destitute of relish or inclination for some specified object or pursuit; const. *of* (*obs.*). **b.** Characterized by unwillingness to move, act, or make any exertion; marked by languid indifference as to what goes on around one, or as to what one has to do.

c **1440** *Promp. Parv.* 307/2 Lystles, *desidiosus, segnis.* **1667** W. FAIRFAX in *Phil. Trans.* II. 549 He was ever a listless, dull and melancholy fellow. **1678** BUNYAN *Pilgr.* Author's Apol., This Book is writ in such a Dialect As may the minds of listless men affect. **1697** DRYDEN *Virg. Georg.* IV. 378 The sick..idle in their empty Hives remain, Benum'd with Cold, and listless of their Gain. **1702** *Eng. Theophrast.* 136 Intemperance and sensuality do make men's minds listless and unactive. **1750** GRAY *Elegy* 103 His listless Length at Noontide wou'd he stretch. **1766** FORDYCE *Serm. Yng. Wom.* (1767) I. Pref. 3 A dull discourse naturally produces a listless audience. **1811** EDGEWORTH *Pract. Educ.* (1822) II. 442 The playthings of children should be calculated to fix their attention, that they may not get a habit of doing any thing in a listless manner. **1860** TYNDALL *Glac.* I. xi. 78 The listless strokes of his axe proclaimed his exhaustion. **1883** SIR T. MARTIN *Ld. Lyndhurst* v. 121 Listless students of law do not make their way at the Bar.

absol. **1758** JOHNSON *Idler* No. 3 ¶7 By what methods the listless may be actuated.

Comb. **1822** [C'TESS BLESSINGTON] *Magic Lantern* 8 A listless looking young man.

Hence †**listlesshede**, listlessness.

c **1440** *Promp. Parv.* 307/2 Lystles-hede, *segnicies, desidia.*

listlessly ('lɪstlɪslɪ), *adv.* [-LY^2.] In a listless manner; with languid indifference.

1693 LOCKE *Educ.* §116. 142 Whether he lazily and listlessly dreams away his time. **1697** DRYDEN *Virg. Georg.* III. 707 Where thou seest a single Sheep..Listlessly to crop the tender Grass. **1836–9** DICKENS *Sk. Boz, Tales* vi. (1892) 354 The cold hands,..when she ceased to hold them, fell listlessly and heavily back on the coverlet. **1876** MISS BRADDON *J. Haggard's Dau.* III. 3 She went about the house listlessly, yet was too restless to sit long at her work.

listlessness ('lɪstlɪsnɪs). [-NESS.] The condition or quality of being listless; † (*a*) want of relish for some particular object or pursuit (const. *of, to*) (*obs.*); (*b*) languid indifference as to one's surroundings, or as to what one has to do.

1646 JENKYN *Remora* 23 There is in the heart, a naturall listlesnes [*pr.* listnesnes] from, and opposition unto a right reformation. **1693** LOCKE *Educ.* §119. 146 If listlesness and dreaming be his natural Disposition. **1705** HICKERINGILL *Priest-cr.* II. vii. 67, I have..*A Third Part of Priest-craft* in my Head, which perhaps may come abroad and take the Air, if not prevented by my Laziness, Listlesness, or Old Age. **1725** BRADLEY *Fam. Dict.* s.v. *Malt Liquor*, Nauseousness at the Stomach, and Lassitude of [*sic*] Listlessness to Motion. **1776** G. MASON in Sparks *Corr. Amer. Rev.* (1853) I. 180 Ill health, and a certain listlessness inseparable from it, have prevented my writing..so often. **1795** *Montford Castle* II. 282 His lovely mistress..without whom felicity was nothing but listlessness and quietism. **1842** PUSEY *Crisis Eng. Ch.* 8 The general listlessness which crept over the Church during the last century. **1869** SEELEY *Lect. & Ess.* ii. 54 The disposition to listlessness which belongs to the military character.

†'**listly**, *adv. Obs.* (or *dial.*) Forms: α. 1 **listelíce**, 3 **listeliche**, 4 **lystyly**, **-yly**, **listely**. β. 4 **listli**, **lystly**, 4–6, (9) **listly**. [OE. *listelíce* (= ON. *listulega* elegantly, cunningly), f. *list* skill, art (? *u* stem: cf. ON. *listug-r* skilled, polite). With reference to the formation see note s.v. GREEDILY.] Cunningly, craftily, deftly.

α. *c* **1000** *Sax. Leechd.* II. 30 Seoð þonne æt leohtum fyre listelice oþ huniȝes þicnesse. *a* **1275** *Prov. Ælfred* 666 in *O.E. Misc.* 137 He wole stelin þin haite and keren, and listeliche on-suerren. **13..** *Gaw. & Gr. Knt.* 1190 He..layde hym doun lystyly, & let as he slepte. *Ibid.* 1334 Þen brek þay þe bale, þe balez out token, Lystily forlancing, & bere of þe knot. *c* **1350** *Will. Palerne* 25 Þat litel child listely looked out of his caue.

β. *c* **1350** *Will. Palerne* 2742 He ful listli hem ledes to þat loueli schippe. *c* **1375** *Sc. Leg. Saints* vi. (*Thomas*) 307 He..lystly lousit sone þe band, þat thomas had in fwte & hand. *Ibid.* xxxviii. (*Adrian*) 296 Scho..softyt hurtis þat ware sare, & listly als kemmyt þare hare. **1503** DUNBAR *Thistle & Rose* 100 This lady..leit him listly lene vpone his kne. [**1847** HALLIWELL, *Listly*,..easily, distinctly.]

listred ('lɪstrɛd). [ad. Welsh *llestraid* lit. vesselful, f. *llestr* vessel.] A Welsh corn-measure, equal to $3\frac{3}{4}$ imperial bushels.

1879 *Parl. Return Corn Weights & Meas.* 52 *note*, Cardiff. Wheat is sold by bushel of a certain weight and by listred. **1883** *Standard* 2 Mar. 3/8 Winchester bushels, bags, listreds, windles, and Carlisle bushels.

†'**listy**, *a. Obs.* [f. LIST *sb.*^{4} or *v.*^{1} + -Y.] ? Pleasant, delightful. Also, pleased or willing *to do* something; hence, ready, quick. (Cf. LIST *a.*)

c **1440** *Promp. Parv.* 307/1 Lysty, or lusty, *delectabilis. Ibid.* 317/2 Lusty, or lysty, *delectuosus* (K. *delectabilis, voluptuosus*). **1539** LATIMER *Serm. & Rem.* (Parker Soc.) 417 If you be listy to hear of Furnes fools. ? *a* **1550** in *Laneham's Let.* (1871) Pref. 130 Haue youe gyffune any drynke vnto your husband to make hyme lystear to occupye with youe? **1570** LEVINS *Manip.* 111/45 Listy, *libens.*

lisz, obs. Sc. 3rd sing. ind. pres. of LIE *v.*^{1}

Lisztian ('lɪstɪən), *a.* (*sb.*) [f. the name of *Liszt* (see below) + -IAN.] Of, pertaining to, or characteristic of the Hungarian pianist and composer Ferencz (Franz) Liszt (1811–86) or his music. Also as *sb.*, an adherent or imitator of Liszt.

1890 G. B. SHAW *London Music 1888–89* (1937) 308 Such Lisztian hero-worshippers as Herr Stavenhagen and the late Walter Bache. **1921** A. HUXLEY *Crome Yellow* xxi. 227 A brilliant Lisztian tremolo. **1934** C. LAMBERT *Music Ho!* III. 163 The Lisztian symphonic poem. **1947** A. EINSTEIN *Mus. Romantic Era* vii. 70 Genuine Lisztians or innovators like Smetana..wrote no more symphonies. **1947** N. CARDUS *Autobiogr.* 208 In the 'Sanctus' we have the original prototype of how many Lisztian and other symphonic-poems. **1963** *Times* 24 Jan. 14/5 The late Lisztian keyboard style. **1971** *Daily Tel.* 26 Apr. 9/1 [He] produced moments of Lisztian abandon in which the whole orchestral palate crowded in on the keyboard.

lit (lɪt), *sb. Obs.* exc. *dial.* Forms: 3, 7, 9 **lit**, 4–5 **litte**, 5 **lyt**, 7, 9 **litt**. [a. ON. *lit-r* colour, also countenance, corresponding etymologically to OE. and early ME. WLITE.]

1. A colour, dye, hue; also, a stain.

c **1250** *Gen. & Ex.* 1968 In kides blod he wenten it, ðo was ðor-on an rewli lit. *a* **1310** in Wright *Lyric P.* 36 Whittore then the moren mylk, with leofly lit on lere. *a* **1400–50** *Alexander* 4336 Nouthire to toly ne to taunde transmitte we na vebbis, To vermylion ne violett ne variant littis. *c* **1425** WYNTOUN *Cron.* v. vii. 1381 Fayr and quhyt, but ony lyt. **1768** A. ROSS in Whitelaw *Bk. Sc. Song* (1844) 361/1 A pair o' grey hoggers weil cluikit benew, Of nae other lit but the hue of the ewe. **1832** A. HENDERSON *Scot. Prov.* 128 It's like Pathhead lit—soon on, soon aff.

2. Dye-stuff; also, a batch of dyeing.

13.. *Childh. Jesus* 677 in *Archiv Stud. neu. Spr.* LXXIV. 336 Bot we vs hame faste nowe hye Alle oure litte thane mone we tyne. **1457** *Sc. Acts Jas. II* (1814) II. 49/1 It is sene speidfull, þat lit be cryit vp, and vsyt as it was wont to be. **1612** *Sc. Bk. Rates* in *Halyburton's Ledger* (1867) 321 Litt, callit orchard litt, the barrell—xii *li.* **1637–50** Row *Hist. Kirk* (Wodrow Soc.) 432 It is excellent litt. **1822** HIBBERT *Descr. Shetld. Isles* 442 The *Lichen tartareus* yields a lit or dye, that was formerly an article of commercial notice. **1884** D. GRANT *Lays & Leg. North* 4 The dyster..lost..a' his claith, His bowies, pots, an' lit.

3. *attrib.* and *Comb.*, as *lit-pot*, *-vat* (see Eng. Dial. Dict.); **lit-house** = DYE-HOUSE 1.

1662 in Pitcairn *Crim. Trials* III. 605 [Confession] M. B. and I went in to A. Cumings litt-hows in Aulderne.

lit (lɪt), *v. Obs.* exc. *dial.* Forms: 3–4 **lite(n**, 4–7 **litte**, 5 **lytt**, **lytyn**, 5–6 **lytte**, 6 **litt**, 9 **let**, 7–9 **lit**. [a. ON. *lita*, f. *lit-r*: see prec.]

1. *trans.* To colour, dye; to stain.

a **1225** *Ancr. R.* 268 He liteð cruelte mid heowe of rihtwisnesse. **13..** *Childh. Jesus* 657 in *Archiv Stud. neu. Spr.* LXXIV. 336 Thies clathis sente he hedire to mee For to litte thayme. *a* **1340** HAMPOLE *Psalter* lxvii. 25 Þat þi fote be littid in blode. *a* **1400** *Burgh Laws* xx. (*Sc. Stat.* I), Na man bot a burges sall by woll to lytt [L. *ad tingendum*] na clathe to mak na schere. **1496** *Fysshynge w. Angle* (1883) 34 The wynges of the redde cocke hakyll & of the drake lyttyd yellow. **1513** DOUGLAS *Æneis* VII. x. 35 New sched blude littis thair armour cleyr. **1557–8** *Act 4 & 5 Phil. & Mary* c. 5 §3 The Wooll [shall]..bee first dyed, litted and coulered withe the coulour blue. **1609** SKENE *Reg. Maj.* Table 107 Wooll to be littid may not be bocht, bot be Burgessis. **1683** G. MERITON *Yorks. Dialogue* 622 (E.D.S.), I heve some Garne to send with thee to Lit. *a* **1823** BEATTIE *John o' Arnha* (1826) 15 Weel dy'd and litit through and through. **1841** R. W. HAMILTON *Nugae Lit.* 359 To let is to dye, but not in fast colours.

2. *intr.* for *refl.* To blush deeply.

1801 BEATTIE *Parings* (1873) 10 (E.D.D.) Wi' this my face began to lit. **1888** D. GRANT *Scotch Stories* 30 Her face littit scarlet.

Hence **lit**, '**litted** *ppl. a.*, dyed.

1483 *Cath. Angl.* 219/1 Littyd, *jnfectus.* **1820** J. HOGG in Whitelaw *Bk. Sc. Song* (1844) 509/2 Wi' littit brogues an' a', lassie, Wow but ye'll be vaunty! **1860** C. INNES *Scot. in Mid. Ages* viii. 237 A stone of litted wool. **1897** *Shetland News* 28 Aug. (E.D.D.), Wi' a hap o' Sibbie 's an' my muckle blue lit froke inunder her head an' shooders.

lit (lɪt), *ppl. a.* [pa. pple. of LIGHT *v.*^{2}]

a. Lighted, illumined; also with *up*. (Also in *comb.*, as *sun-lit*.)

1820 SHELLEY *Cloud* 39 When sunset may breathe, from the lit sea beneath, Its ardours of rest and of love. **1847** MARY HOWITT *Ballads* 62 He looks all round, 'tis drear and dim, Save in the lit-up castle yonder. **1865** SWINBURNE *Atalanta* 1928 My lit eyes Flame with the falling fire that leaves his lids Bloodless. **1922** M. A. VON ARNIM *Enchanted April* i. 17 She listened to her impetuous, odd talk and watched her lit-up face. **1936** R. CAMPBELL *Mithraic Emblems* 18 My own lit heart, its rays of fire.

b. *slang.* Drunk (see also quots. 1933 and 1971). Freq. const. ***up.***

1914 'HIGH JINKS, JR.' *Choice Slang* 14 *Lit up*, intoxicated. **1918** J. M. GRIDER *War Birds* (1927) 82 We walked into the vamp's house. We all got lit and had a hell of a time. **1922** *Daily Mail* 16 Dec. 10, I am afraid I was rather tight—certainly lit up. **1933** *Amer. Speech* VIII. II. 27/1 When one has contracted the habit or is under the immediate influence of the drug, he is *all lit up*. **1938** G. GREENE *Brighton Rock* III. i. 109 If I hadn't been a bit lit this wouldn't have happened. **1939** M. ALLINGHAM *Mr. Campion & Others* I. ii. 37 Driving round the country with a topper over your eyes and a blanket round your neck at three o'clock in the morning... You *must* have been lit. **1948** WODEHOUSE *Spring Fever* xviii. 189 A lit-up Augustus Robb should, he considered, provide a spectacle which nobody ought to miss. **1949** E. HYAMS *Not in our Stars* xvii. 220 Some of the lads a bit lit, eh? Who's this in the hedge? **1971** E. E. LANDY *Underground Dict.* 121 *Lit up*,.. under the influence of a narcotic.

lit, obs. f. LIGHT *sb.*, *a.*[1]; pa. t. LIGHT *v.*[1] and [2].

lit, obs. f. LITE *sb.*[1], LITE *v.*; dial. f. LITE *a.*

lit., Lit., colloq. abbrev. of (*a*) LITERATURE. Cf. ENG. LIT. (*b*) LITERARY *a.* Also used *absol.* = literary student, literary magazine. Also ***lit. crit.***, literary criticism; ***lit. ed.***, literary editor; ***lit. sup.***, literary supplement.

(*a*) **1850** [see ENG. LIT.]. **1870** GEO. ELIOT *Let.* 11 Feb. (1956) V. 77 The lentisc or mastich tree.. figures both in Greek and Roman lit. **1946** L. DURRELL *Let.* 20 Oct. in *Spirit of Place* (1969) 87 In Athens I am going to see Seferis and Katsimbalis and give modern lit a bashing with them. **1959** *Observer* 8 Mar. 22/2 Chadwick's opposition to tacking on 'Lit' to 'Lang', followed by his decision to leave the English Tripos. **1964** W. MARKFIELD *To Early Grave* (1965) xii. 252 Perhaps if I should ever give a regional lit course. **1973** P. GEDDES *Ottawa Allegation* xiii. 173 She.. worked in publishing... She was into Canadian Lit. before he could draw breath. **1975** *New Yorker* 21 Apr. 103/3 You don't get much of that in Russian lit.

(*b*) **1895** W. B. YEATS *Let.* 20 Jan. (1954) II. 245 Not one word was said about the Irish Lit Society and Prof Dowden expressed scorn for the Irish Lit movement. **1895** W. C. GORE in *Inlander* Nov. 64 *Lit*, literary student. **1900** *Dialect Notes* II. 45 *Lit*, n., the Literary Monthly, Quarterly, etc., a student publication. **1930** *English Jrnl.* XIX. 632 Whatever wit or lightness of heart characterizes the magazines appears in the East; the Western 'lits' are in dead earnest. **1932** H. NICOLSON *Diary* 19 Oct. (1966) 122 Kingsley Martin.. wants me to become the literary editor... But I.. could not expect to make more than £1,000 a year as Lit. Ed. **1932** V. WOOLF *Let.* in K. Martin *Editor* (1968) i. 30, I used to try to write regularly for *The Times Lit. Sup.* **1935** N. MITCHISON *We have been Warned* IV. 437 He showed her his reviews... The *Lit. Sup.* had been dull, the *New Statesman* annoying. **1936** L. C. DOUGLAS *White Banners* viii. 171 Naturally the 'Lits' began to view Professor Ward with a new respect. **1962** M. DRABBLE *Summer Bird-Cage* xi. 206 'I could have guessed that from his books. They lack compassion.' 'How beautifully, how lit. critically you put it.' **1963** 'N. BLAKE' *Deadly Joker* ii. 33 The Americans had.. begun to make an industry of lit. crit. **1968** *Lebende Sprachen* XIII. 110/2 Jet-age litcrit. **1968** E. MCGIRR *Lead-Lined Coffin* ii. 44 Rostron sat making derisive noises over the Sunday lit. sups. **1973** *Times Lit. Suppl.* 6 Apr. 401/5 The refingered worry-beads of lit-crit jargon.

litaneutical (lɪtəˈnjuːtɪkəl), *a.* [f. Gr. λιτανευτικός, f. λιτανεύειν to pray, whence λιτανεία LITANY.] Of the nature of a litany.

1839 W. PALMER *Orig. Liturg.* (ed. 3) I. 288 The litaneutical form of praying is visible in all the offices of the eastern churches. **1847** H. BAILEY *Rituale Anglo-Cath.* Pref. 21 The Litaneutical form of praying is itself an example of the same kind.

litany (ˈlɪtənɪ), *sb.* Forms: 3–5 **letanye**, 3–7 **letanie**, (4 **letayne**), 4–7 **letany**, (5 **letony**, **-eny**, **latanie**, 6 **latenie**, **-ony**, **-yny**, 7 **latiny**), 6– **litany**. [ad. med.L. *litania*, *letania* (whence OF. *letanie*, F. *litanie*, Pr., Sp. *letania*, Pg. *ladainha*, It. *litania*, *letania*, *letana*), a. Gr. λιτανεία prayer, entreaty, f. λιτανεύειν to pray, entreat, f. λιτανός suppliant, f. λιτή supplication, related to λίτεσθαι, λίσσεσθαι to supplicate.]

1. *Eccl.* An appointed form of public prayer, usually of a penitential character, consisting of a series of supplications, deprecations, or intercessions in which the clergy lead and the people respond, the same formula of response being repeated for several successive clauses. A litany may be used either as part of a service or by itself, in the latter case often in procession.

Greater and Lesser Litany: see quot. 1885.

The name of 'the Lesser Litany' has also been given to the petitions *Kyrie eleison, Christe eleison, Kyrie eleison*, and 'Lord, have mercy upon us, Christ, have mercy upon us, Lord, have mercy upon us'.

[*a* **900** *O.E. Martyrol.* 3 May 72 Cristes folc mærsiað letanias.] *a* **1225** *Ancr. R.* 22 Seoue psalmes siggeð sittinde oðer cneolinde, mit te Letanie. **1297** R. GLOUC. (Rolls) 8393 Clerkes.. on god gonne crye Wepinde wiþ procession & songe þe letanye. **1387** TREVISA *Higden* (Rolls) I. 375 He schal be housled and i-lad to þe dore of purgatorie wiþ processioun and letanye. *Ibid.* V. 299 Aboute þat tyme Seint Mammertus.. ordeyned solempne letanyes þat beeþ i-cleped þe Rogaciouns,.. and beeþ i-cleped þe lasse letayne for difference of þe more letayne þat Gregorye ordeynede to be seide a Seynt Markes day. **1483** CAXTON *Gold. Leg.* 21 b/2. **1525** LD. BERNERS *Froiss.* II. 753 Whyle he was anoyntynge, the clergy sange the latyny. **1535** STEWART *Cron. Scot.* (1858) II. 63 The sevin psalmis.. to sing and reid, With latony, placebo, and the creid. **1611** SPEED *Hist. Gt. Brit.* IX. i. §4 In their publike Processions, and Letanies of the Church, this Petition was added, From the rage of the Normans, good Lord deliuer vs. **1704** NELSON *Fest. & Fasts* vi. (1739) 514 These earnest Supplications for the Mercy of God, which were called Litanies. **1866** BLUNT *Annot. Bk. C.P.* 22 *note*, The lesser Litany is an ancient and Catholic prefix to the Lords Prayer. **1877** MISS YONGE *Cameos* III. xxxiv. 366 The University of Paris commanded that there should be public litanies. **1883** R. W. DIXON *Mano* II. viii. 95 Through the streets the priests and monks gan pace In their procession, chanting litanies. **1885** *Cath. Dict.* (ed. 2) 519/2 The Litany of the Saints is chanted on the feast of St. Mark (April 25), and on the three Rogation days; on the former occasion it is called the Greater (*litaniæ majores*), and on the Rogation days the Lesser (*litaniæ minores*).

b. ***the Litany***: that form of 'general supplication' appointed for use in the Book of Common Prayer, of similar form to those mentioned above, and consisting of petitions to the Trinity, deprecations, and obsecrations, with concluding suffrages and prayers.

[*c* **1420–30** *Primer* (1895) 47 And here bigynneþ þe letanie.] **1544** *Durham Acc. Rolls* (Surtees) 726 Paid to the chaunter of Westmynster for pryking the new Latyny.. in prykeson. **1548** *Act 2 & 3 Edw. VI*, c. 1 §6 The Mattens, Evensonge, Letanye, and all other prayers. **1548–9** (Mar.) *Bk. Com. Prayer*, *Litany* (heading), The Letany and Suffrages. **1660** R. COKE *Power & Subj.* 244 To have.. the Lords Prayer, Creede and Letany in the English tongue. **1679–1714** BURNET *Hist. Ref.* (1715) III. I. 164 In the Litany they did still [anno 1545] Invocate the Blessed Virgin.. and all the Blessed Company of Heaven to pray for them. *a* **1695** A. WOOD *Life* (1848) 117 Which being all done.. the fellowes went to the letany. **1885** RUSKIN *Pleasures Eng.* 136 Our petition in the Litany, against sudden death.

2. *transf.* A form of supplication (e.g. in non-Christian worship) resembling a litany; also, a continuous repetition or long enumeration resembling those of litanies.

c **1400** MAUNDEV. (1839) xvi. 177 Thei putten his name in hire Letanyes, as a Seynt. **1600** HOLLAND *Livy* VII. xxviii. 268 Not onely the Tribes should go in solemne procession with their praiers and Letanies, but also [etc.]. **1643** SIR T. BROWNE *Relig. Med.* II. §10 Lord deliver me from my self, is a part of my Letany. **1649** JER. TAYLOR *Gt. Exemp.* Ep. Ded. 10, I shall think my returne full of reward if you shall .. put me into your Letanies. **1658** tr. *Bergerac's Satyr. Char.* ix. 28 The passengers Letanies are mixt with the mariner's blasphemies. *a* **1822** SHELLEY *Stud. for Epipsychidion* 56 Hear them mumble Their litany of curses. **1834** L. RITCHIE *Wand. by Seine* 168 Beggars throng the road, chanting their ceaseless litanies. **1881** BESANT & RICE *Chapl. of Fleet* I. viii. (1883) 68 So did these reprobates maintain a perpetual litany of ribaldry.

¶ The form of a parody of the Litany has often been employed as a vehicle for scurrilous political satire.

1659 (*title*) A Free-Parliament-Letany. **1680** (*title*) The Loyal Subjects Litany. **1682** (*title*) The Cavalier's Litany. **1817** (*title*) The Political Litany diligently revised. To be said or sung, until the appointed change come, throughout the Dominion of England and Wales, and the Town of Berwick upon Tweed. **1851** MAYHEW *Lond. Lab.* I. 236 One intelligent man told me properly to work a political litany, which referred to ecclesiastical matters, he 'made himself up', as well as limited means would permit, as a bishop!

3. *attrib.* and *Comb.*, as ***litany-chant***, ***-book***, ***-prayer***; **litany-desk**, **-stool**, a low movable prayer-desk at which a minister kneels while reciting the litany; = FALDSTOOL 3; **litany-wise** *adv.*, after the manner of a litany.

c **1475** *Pict. Voc.* in Wr.-Wülcker 755/9 A *letenyboke, *Hec letenia.* **1844** CARDL. WISEMAN *Minor Rites* Ess. I. 511 It blesses the fields with its solemn procession and *litany-chant. **1725** T. THOMAS in *Portland Papers* VI. (Hist. MSS. Comm.) 130 A large stone, at the East End of the Choir .. (on part of which stands the *Litany desk). **1845** *Ecclesiologist* IV. 162 Let them.. introduce the use of a Litany-desk. **1894** E. BISHOP in *Dublin Rev.* Oct. 452 The fact that these *Litany-prayers are found in the Sundays of Lent is interesting. **1845** *Ecclesiologist* IV. 147 The nave will contain both lettern and *litany-stool. **1659** H. L'ESTRANGE *Alliance Div. Off.* iv. 102 Which versicle was used *Litany-wise (that is, returned by the people) in the service of the Temple.

Hence **'litanying** *vbl. sb.* (*nonce-wd.*), recitation of litanies.

1843 CARLYLE *Past & Pres.* IV. vii, Pause in thy mass-chantings, in thy litanyings, and Calmuck prayings by machinery. **1865** —— *Fredk. Gt.* III. v. (1872) I. 169 Popish litanyings.. and idolatrous stage-performances.

litarge, -i(e, -ik, -yk: see LETHARGY, -ARGIC.

litarge, -y, litargirij, obs. ff. LITHARGE.

†**li'tation.** *Obs.* [ad. L. *litātiōn-em*, n. of action f. *litāre* to offer a successful sacrifice.] The action of sacrificing; a sacrifice.

1623 COCKERAM, *Litation*, a sacrifice. **1658** PHILLIPS, *Litation*, a sacrificing. **1660** STANLEY *Hist. Philos.* IX. (1701) 400/2 The terrestrial gods.. delight in banquets, and mournings, and funeral litations, and costly sacrifices.

litch (lɪtʃ). *Obs.* exc. *dial.* [Of obscure origin: cf. LEECH *sb.*[3] and *sb.*[4]]

1. A handful (of reeds, etc.); a bundle (of cords, yarn, etc.). In mod. use, 'a tangled mass' (*Eng. Dial. Dict.*).

1538 ELYOT *Dict.*, *Thomices*, lyches of hempe wherwith halters are made. **1552** HULOET, Liches or linckes of cordes, halters, or ropes, *thomices.* **1609** C. BUTLER *Fem. Mon.* (1634) 39 Being thus prepared, take out of that wet bundle a litch of 40 or 50 reeds or straws.

2. (See quot.) [Perh. a different word.]

1851 H. NEWLAND *Erne* 59 The Captain who had been baiting a formidable litch with a good sized par. *Footnote*, Litch,.. An arrangement of hooks and swivels calculated to give the appearance of life to a dead bait.

litch, variant of LICH, body.

litchi (ˈliːtʃiː). Forms: 6 **lechia**, **-ya**, 7 **lichea**, 8 **letchee**, 8–9 **lichee**, 9 **lé ché**, **leecha**, **leeche**, **leechee**, **li-chee**, **lichi**, **li-chi**, **lychee**, ? **lychus**, 8– **litchi.** [Chinese *li-chi.* First used as a generic name in P. Sonnerat *Voyage aux Indes Orientales* (1782) III. 255.] The fruit of an evergreen tree, *Litchi chinensis*, of the family Sapindaceæ, native to southern China but widely cultivated in tropical countries elsewhere; the fruit is a large berry with a rough, brown skin and sweet, white flesh, which is eaten fresh or preserved.

1588 PARKE tr. *Mendoza's Hist. China* iii. 6 They haue a kinde of plummes that they doo call Lechias. **1697** DAMPIER *Voy.* (1729) II. I. 24 The Lichea.. is as big as a small Pear, somewhat long shaped, of a reddish Colour. **1727** A. HAMILTON *New Acc. E. Indies* II. xlvi. 156 Delicious Fruits, such as.. Rambostans, Letchees, and Dureans. **1775** *Ann. Reg.* II. 33 Among those plants are the lichees, a very fine fruit of China of several sorts. **1822** HEBER *Journ. Upper Prov. India* (1844) I. iv. 60 Of the fruits which this season offers, the finest are leechees and mangoes. **1841** MACAULAY *W. Hastings* (near end), He tried also to naturalize in Worcestershire the delicious leechee. **1878** P. ROBINSON *In My Indian Garden* 49 The lichi hiding under a shell of ruddy brown its globes of translucent and delicately fragrant flesh. **1887** *Standard* 16 Sept. 5/3 The litchi and the longan. **1908** *Daily Chron.* 12 Nov. 3/4 Lychees, pine-apples, pears, cranberries, dates, figs, medlars and mangos swell the number of fruits. **1933** *Punch* 9 Aug. 142/2 We never dreamed that it [*sc.* tinned fruit] would appear.. in such dazzling variety.. from loquats to li-chees. **1938** *Nature* 14 May 866/2 The litchi has arrived in much larger quantities lately and been much appreciated. **1953** R. CAMPBELL *Mamba's Precipice* 137 Monkeys lived on the beautiful lychees and loquats. **1965** *Listener* 1 July 23/2 You'd never know, looking at me, I had.. eaten lychees in a town called Reading. **1969** *Oxf. Bk. Food Plants* 104/1 Litchis are most usually eaten fresh, but are also sometimes canned for export or preserved in syrup. **1972** A. F. SIMMONS *Growing Unusual Fruit* 175 The litchee can.. be grown in Britain in a large green-house.

attrib. **1876** HARLEY *Mat. Med.* (ed. 6) 707 The delicious 'litchi-nuts'. **1879** MISS MAIVE STOKES *Indian Fairy Tales* xv. 91 Here are a hundred and sixty lichi fruits for you.

litcop: see LYTH-COOP *Obs.*

†**lite**, *sb.*[1] *Obs.* Also 4 **lijt**, **lit**, **litte**, 4–5 **lyte**, **lytt.** [f. LITE *v.* Cf. LET *sb.*] Delay, tardiness; frequent in phr. ***without lite.***

a **1300** *Cursor M.* 4776 Iacob wen he was mast in sijt God lighted him, wit-outen lijt. *Ibid.* 5790 Þar-to sal be now na lang lite. *a* **1350** *St. Cecilia* 353 in Horstm. *Altengl. Leg.* (1881) 163 And at þe last withouten lite All þaire heuides he gert of smite. *c* **1400** *Ywaine & Gaw.* 1620 So lang gaf sho him respite, And thus he haves hir led with lite. *c* **1460** *Towneley Myst.* ix. 225 Fast for to fle outt of my land, Byd thaym, withouten lyte.

†**lite**, *sb.*[2] *Sc.* and *north. dial. Obs.* In 5 **lyit**, **lyte.** [Aphetic var. of ELITE *sb.*[1] Cf. LEET *sb.*[2]]

A bishop-elect; = ELITE *sb.*[1]

c **1425** WYNTOUN *Cron.* VII. v. 741 He stud as Lyte twa yhere owre, And Byschape thretty yhere and foure. *c* **1450** *St. Cuthbert* (Surtees) 6519 And cuthbert to hexham lyte. **1497** HALYBURTON *Ledger* (1867) 83 Johne Fressall, factor to Master John Fressall, lyit of Roys.

†**lite**, *sb.*[3] *Sc. Obs. rare*[−1]. [ad. L. *līt-em*, *līs.*] Strife.

1493 *Sc. Acts Jas. IV* (1814) II. 232/2 Exhorting and praying þame to leif þair contentiounnis, litis and pleyis.

lite, *sb.*[4], *a.*, and *adv.* *Obs.* exc. *arch.* or *dial.* Forms: 1 **lýt**, 2–3 **lutte**, 3–4 **lut**, 3–5 **lute**, **luyte**, 3, 5–6, 8–9 **lit**, 4 **liȝt**, **luite**, 4–7 **lite**, **lyte**, 4, 9 **lyt**, 5–6 **litte**, 6 **lyght**, **lytte**, 8 **loyt**, 9 **leet**, **light**, **loit.** [Partly repr. OE. *lýt* sb., adj., adv. (= OS. *lut* sb.), and partly the synonymous ON. *litt* adv., contraction of *litet*, neut. of *lítell*: see LITTLE.]

A. *sb.*

1. Little, not much. ***unto lite***: very nearly.

a **1000** *Runes* 22 (Gr.) Wen ne bruceþ, ðe can weana lyt, sares and sorge. **12..** *Prayer Our Lady* 24 in *O.E. Misc.* 193 Muchel ich habbe ispened, to lite ich habbe an horde. *c* **1290** *Life of Jesus* 632 Ȝiueth us, heo seiden, of ouwer eoli... Nai, seiden þe oþere, þere were to luyte to us alle. **13..** *Guy Warw.* (A.) 640 Of mi liif is me bot lite. **1377** LANGL. *P. Pl.* B. XIII. 149 He that loueth the lelly lyte of thyne coueiteth. *c* **1386** CHAUCER *Man of Law's T.* 11 Thy neighebore thou wytest synfully And seist thou hast to lite, and he hath al. *a* **1420** HOCCLEVE *De Reg. Princ.* 930 Vpon þis woful thoght I.. muse so, that vn-to lite I madde. **1513** DOUGLAS *Æneis* I. Prol. 38, I knaw tharin full lyte. *a* **1575** *Friar & Boy* 59 in Hazl. *E.P.P.* III. 63 He sayd he wolde ete but lyte, Tyll nyght that he home came. **1867** ROCK *Jim an' Nell* lxv.

(E.D.S. No. 76), And Joe an' Will have each a-bro't A main peart o' the leet they've got, Gosh, 'e'll ha quite a vortin.

b. (*a, by*) ***lite and lite***: (by) little and little. Also erroneously, ***by lithe and lithe***.

c 1290 *S.E. Leg.* I. 313/465 So þat þe sonne bi-fore geth luyte and luyte i-wis. c 1325 *Song of Yesterday* 44 in *E.E.P.* (1862) 134 Heo ne schal fade as a flour Luyte and luyte leosen hir beute. c 1386 CHAUCER *Sompn. T.* 527 (Cambr. MS.) Euere it wastith lyte & lyte awey. 1406 HOCCLEVE *Misrule* 92 A lyte & lyte to withdrawen it. a 1577 GASCOIGNE *Don Barth.* Wks. (1587) 104 By lite and lite his fits away gan flie. 1592 DEE *Comp. Rehears.* (Chetham Soc.) 23 Not long after.. by lithe and lithe I became hindered.

c. ***a lite*** (in early texts often written *alite*): a little. Used also advb.

c 1290 *Beket* 1896 in *S. Eng. Leg.* I. 161 A luyte [*v.r.* lute] bi-fore cristemasse to þe kinge heo come. c 1290 *St. Kenelm* 318 ibid. 354 Huy comen into one wode: a luyte bi este þe toune. c 1330 *Arth. & Merl.* 435 (Kölbing) For þe barouns were hende Bi Salesbiri biside a lite Al redi bataile to smite. c 1369 CHAUCER *Dethe Blaunche* 249 If he wol make me slepe a lyte,.. I wil yive him a fether-bed. a 1420 HOCCLEVE *De Reg. Princ.* 1240, I have but a lite, And likly am herafter to have lesse. c 1430 *Two Cookery-bks.* 17 þe 3olke an þe whyte y-strainyd a lyte. 1513 DOUGLAS *Æneis* VIII. Prol. 3, I slaid on a swevynnyng slummerand a lite. 1530 LYNDESAY *Test. Papyngo* 766 Wyll the deith a lyte withdrawe his darte. 1584 LODGE *Alarum* (1879) 73 Such stately knees as when they bend a lite, All knees doo bend. 1674 RAY *N.C. Words* 30, A *Lite*: a few, a little. 1746 *Exmoor Courtship* 561 (E.D.S.) Es hire ya lick a lit about ma Cozen Magery.

2. (In OE. followed by genit. pl. with sing. vb.; subsequently *ellipt.* as subj. to plural vb.) Few.

Beowulf 2882 Wer3endra to lyt þrong ymbe þeoden. a 1200 *Moral Ode* 104 Hwi boð fole iclepede, and swa lut icorene. c 1200 *Trin. Coll. Hom.* 123 Lit ben þat þus understonden and bishechen god. c 1205 LAY. 4045 Her wes muchel mon-qualm þat lut her quike bi-lefden. a 1300 *K. Horn* 658 (Harl. MS.) Of þat þer were o ryue he lafte lut o lyue. c 1375 *Cursor M.* 8496 (Fairf.) þis write wiþ many was rede and sene bot lite [*Cott.* fa, *Gött.* fone] wiste quat hit walde mene.

B. *adj.* (Uninflected in OE.)

1. Few. Also, *a lite* = *a few* (see FEW 2 a).

a 1000 *Be Domes Dæ3e* 61 He mid lyt wordum ac 3eleaf-fullum his hæle be3eat. c 1200 *Trin. Coll. Hom.* 105 We wilen bi godes wissinge and bi his helpe þerof cuþen 3iu þese lit word. c 1230 *Hali Meid.* 19 þe hehscipe of þe mede þat tis ilke lut wordes bicluppen abuten. c 1375 *Cursor M.* 27864 (Fairf.) þer ar synnis lite [*Cott.* foun].. worre to amende þen is þis. c 1380 WYCLIF *Sel. Wks.* III. 211 Lite prestis or none ben clene of þis symonye. c 1400 *Destr. Troy* 1312 Soght to þe Citie on soppes to-gedur Tho þat left were on lyue þogh þai lite were. c 1420 *Liber Cocorum* (1862) 47 With a lite grotes put hom þer in And sethe hom wele. ? a 1550 *Scotish ffielde* 9 in Furnivall *Percy Folio* I. 212 There were lite Lords in this land: that to that Lord longed. 1860 WAUGH *Yeth-Bobs* iii. 47 'It'll be within a light (few) minutes o' noon, aw'll be bund.' 1870 BRIERLEY *Ab-o'-th' Yate on Times & Things* 48 If anybody had axt me heaw mony friends I had,.. I should ha' bin bothered to ha' said how loit (few).

2. Little in amount; not much of.

c 1175 *Lamb. Hom.* 29 Iþencheð hu lutte hw(i)le 3e beoð here. a 1250 *Owl & Night.* 763 Oft spet wel a lute lyste, Thar muche strengthe sholde miste. c 1290 *S. Eng. Leg.* I. 87/24 Deol and sor and luyte gladnesse. 1297 R. GLOUC. (Rolls) 2041 Is poer lute was vor þe king was euere aboue. a 1300 *K. Horn* 1211 (Cambr. MS.) Wyn nelle ihc, Muche ne lite, Bute of cuppe white. c 1300 *Havelok* 276 Soþlike, in a lite þrawe Al engelond of him stod awe. a 1375 *Joseph Arim.* 554 Luyte wonder hit was so þey wrou3t haden. 1387 TREVISA *Higden* (Rolls) III. 423 Lite fortune and povert and scarste of riches makeþ me a þeef. 1423 JAS. I. *Kingis Q.* xiii, I.. in my tyme more Ink and paper spent To lyte effect. 1508 DUNBAR *Gold. Targe* 71 Your aureate tongis both bene all to lyte, For to compile that paradise complete. 1796 [R. WALKER] *Plebeian Politics* (1801) 31 Hoo.. knokt eawt whot loyt breans he had. 1837 MRS. PALMER *Devon. Dial.* 22 The leet money I've a croop'd up I be a shirk'd out o'.

3. Little in magnitude; small. Often coupled with *great* or *much*.

c 1205 LAY. 22208 þa wes Walwain lute child. a 1225 *Ancr. R.* 280 Holie men þet hielden lutte & of lowe liue. c 1300 *St. Brandan* 184 Tho fle3 ther up a lute fowel. ? a 1366 CHAUCER *Rom. Rose* 532 Upon this dore I gan to smyte, That was [so] fetys and so lyte. c 1384 —— *H. Fame* III. 279 Me thougt she was so lyte That the lengthe of a cubite Was lengere than she. c 1391 —— *Astrol.* Prol., Latin ne canstow yit but smal, my lyte sone. 14.. LYDG. *Temple of Glass* 1291 For al my life it were to lit a space. a 1450 MYRC 1268 Any mon myche or luyte. a 1575 *Friar & Boy* 226 in Hazl. *E.P.P.* III. 71 Though I be lyte, Yonder byrde wyll I smyte. 1600 FAIRFAX *Tasso* IX. lxxxi. 175 Yet blossom'd out her flowres, small or lite. 1802 WOLCOT (P. Pindar) *Middlesex Elect.* Wks. 1816 IV. 172 Vor now I'll screw my fiddle-strings Forsooth, a leet bit higher. 1877 TUGWELL *Hand-bk. N. Devon* 253 Jan, do'e zee the lit woman standing by the bed?

absol. c 1320 *Seuyn Sag.* (W.) 1137 He let of-sende moche and lite, Hise neyebours him to visite. 1600 FAIRFAX *Tasso* XI. xxvi, From this exploit he spar'd nor great nor lite.

C. *adv.* Little; in a small degree, to a small extent.

a 1000 *Cædmon's Gen.* 1566 (Gr.) He lyt on3eat, þæt him on his inne swa earme 3elamp. 1340 *Ayenb.* 31 þe uerste [zenne] is þonneliche, huanne þe man loueþ lite and lheucliche oure lhord. c 1380 *Sir Ferumb.* 708 Charlis wiþ þe hore berde doþ þe lite Auaylle. c 1400 *Lanfranc's Cirurg.* 86 þanne thou nedyste a medycine þat ys lyte dryinge. c 1430 LYDG. *Compl. Bl. Knt.* 413 In straunge lande ryding, ne travayle, Ful lyte or nought in love doth avayle.

lite, *v.*[1] *Obs.* exc. *dial.* Also 4 lit, 5 litte, lytyn, 6 lyte, 8 light. [app. a. ON. *hlíta* to trust.]

1. *intr.* To expect, wait, delay.

a 1300 *Cursor M.* 2821 (Cott.) Quen þai sagh loth be to litand þai tok him-self bi þe hand. a 1300–1400 *Ibid.* 10209 (Gött.) Child to gete þai litid [*Cott. has* littend] lang. a 1400–50 *Alexander* 801 þen littid þai na langer bot laschid out swerdis. 1413 *Pilgr. Sowle* (Caxton 1483) I. xxii. 24 They lyte the redy weyes for to lerne. c 1440 *Promp. Parv.* 308/1 Lytyn, or longe taryyn, *moror*. 1855 ROBINSON *Whitby Gloss.* s.v., To wait in expectation of proceeding. 'I have been liting o' you this half hour'.

2. To rely *on*, to trust to.

1570 LEVINS *Manip.* 151/11 To Lyte, or trust, *fretus esse*. 1674 RAY *N.C. Words* 30 To *Lite* on: to Rely on. 1683 G. MERITON *Yorksh. Dial.* 91 (E.D.S. No. 76), I lited on Hobb, and he lited on me. 1788 W. MARSHALL *Yorksh.* II. 340 Gloss., *Light*, to rest, depend, or rely. 'It is not to light on'; it is not to be depended upon. 1855 ROBINSON *Whitby Gloss.* s.v., 'I suppose, then, I may lite o' you'.

Hence † **liting** *vbl. sb.*, delay.

a 1300 *Cursor M.* 26631 þou sal shriue þe als sone als þou has euer þi synne done,.. for liting is ful selcouþ ille.

† **lite**, *v.*[2] *Obs.* Also lit. [Aphetic f. *delite*, the earlier form of DELIGHT *v.*] *refl.* To delight.

a 1300 *Cursor M.* 1560 Amang kaym kyn þat lited [*Fairf.* delitet, *Trin.* delited] þam noght bot in sin. *Ibid.* 25950 þe thrid [sin] es wers of alle we rede, to lig and lit vs in vr sake, And siþen wil na mendes make.

lite, obs. form of LIGHT *v.*[1]

-lite (= F. *-lite*, G. *-lith*, *-lit*), a frequent ending in names of minerals (also in names of certain fossils, as *coprolite*, and of certain types of mineral structure, as *axiolite* and of some rocks, as *ijolite*, *phonolite*), represents the Gr. λίθος stone; the words in which it occurs are mostly intended to correspond to assumable Gr. formations, so that in actual use the ending is almost always *-olite*, with the thematic or combining *o* usual in Gr. compounds; there are a few exceptions, as *auerlite*, *chesterlite*. The form *-lite*, which was used in some original English formations (*actynolite*, etc.) by Kirwan in 1794, is due to the example of the French geologists, who used *-lite* instead of the older *-lithe*, the two spellings representing one and the same pronunciation in Fr. The adoption of the abnormal form was prob. helped by the analogy of CHRYSOLITE, where the *t* instead of *th* is due to the fact that the Gr. word came at an early period into Eng. by way of med.L. and OF.

litel, obs. form of LITTLE.

liten, var. LEIGHTON *Obs.*; obs. f. LIGHTEN *v.*[1]

liter, obs. f. LIGHTER *sb.*[1]; var. LITRE.

liter, obs. form of LITTER *sb.*

literacy ('lɪtərəsɪ). [f. LITERATE: see -ACY. (Formed as an antithesis to *illiteracy*.)] The quality or state of being literate; knowledge of letters; condition in respect to education, *esp.* ability to read and write. Also *transf.*

1883 *New Eng. Jrnl. Educ.* XVII. 54 Massachusetts is the first state in the Union in literacy in its native population. 1888 *New Princeton Rev.* Dec. 336 Education is more general, our literacy greatly increased, our habits and tastes more refined. 1893 *Athenæum* 19 Aug. 255/3 It was for Mr. Edgar to trace the gradual progress in Scotland from illiteracy to literacy. 1943 *Amer. Mag.* Mar. 103/1 To help many of the poverty-stricken peoples to set their feet on the path of education, manual dexterity, and economic literacy. 1962 *B.B.C. Handbk.* 33 Our skills in the understanding of the medium [*sc.* television] and our own literacy in it are growing all the time. 1969 *Times* 4 Nov. 25/2 A project aimed at raising the level of economic literacy.

literæ humaniores, var. LITTERÆ HUMANIORES.

literal ('lɪtərəl), *a.* and *sb.* Forms: 5–8 litteral, (5, 6 lyt(t)urall, 6 lyt(t)ar-, -erall), 6–7 lit(t)erall, 4– literal. [a. OF. *literal* (F. *littéral*), ad. L. *litterālis*, f. *littera* LETTER *sb.*]

A. *adj.*

1. a. Of or pertaining to letters of the alphabet; of the nature of letters, alphabetical; †expressed by letters, written. †Of a verse = ALLITERATIVE.

c 1475 *Partenay* 6605 And so haue I don, after myne entent, With litterall carectes for your sake. 1585 JAS. I *Ess. Poesie* (Arb.) 63 Be Literall I meane, that the maist pairt of zour lyne, sall rynne vpon a letter, as this tumbling lyne rynnis vpon F. 1621 ELSING *Debates Ho. Lords* (Camden) 15 Whether we shoulde expecte a literall acknowledgment of the charge, or to heare a personall confession of the same. 1632 LITHGOW *Trav.* VIII. 348, I wrot this literal Distich: Glance, Glorious Geneue, Gospell-Guiding Gem; Great God Gouerne, Good Geneues Ghostly Game. 1733–63 N. HOOKE *Rom. Hist.* (ed. 5) I. 8 The art of expressing their thoughts by literal characters. 1793 SMEATON *Edystone L.* Contents 7 Literal References.

b. Of a misprint (*occas.* of a scribal error): Affecting a letter. (Cf. B. 2.)

1606 HOLLAND *Sueton.* To Rdr., If there happen to occur some Errata..ye will..either pass them over with connivency if they be literall or else taxe with some easie censure in case they be materiall. 1699 BENTLEY *Phal.* iii. 112 'Twas a literal fault in that Copy, which Casaubon used. 1748 *Anson's Voy.* Introd. 6, I know of none but literal mistakes, some of which are corrected in the table of Errata. 1841 MYERS *Cath. Th.* III. viii. 26 There are just the same kind of literal imperfections in them [the books of the Bible] that there are in all others. 1880 *Athenæum* 25 Sept. 398/1 It is..vexatious that, through the inattention of the printers, any literal errors should have crept into it.

c. Of mathematical notation and computation: Performed by means of letters. Of a quantity, an equation, etc.: Denoted or expressed by a letter or letters. Opposed to *numerical*.

1673 KERSEY *Algebra* I. i. 2 Algebra is by late Writers divided into two kinds; to wit, Numeral and Literal (or Specious). 1706 W. JONES *Syn. Palmar. Matheseos* A iij b, The First Principles of Literal Computation, usually called Algebra. 1755 JOHNSON s.v., The literal notation of numbers was known to Europeans before the cyphers. 1797 *Encycl. Brit.* (ed. 3) I. 399/2 The literal calculus and the algebraic rules of Harriot. 1842 FRANCIS *Dict. Arts* etc., *Literal Equation*.

2. Of a translation, version, transcript, etc.: Representing the very words of the original; verbally exact. †Also, (the) exact (words of a passage).

1599 MASSINGER etc. *Old Law* I. i, Pray you repeat the literall words expresly. 1692 DRYDEN *Juvenal* Ded. (1697) 87 The common way..is not a literal Translation, but a kind of Paraphrase. a 1753 R. NEWTON *Theophrastus' Char.* (1754) p. viii, I do not say it is necessary, that all Greek Authors should be attended with versions so literal. c 1850 *Arab. Nts.* (Rtldg.) 258, I have had the honour to give you both a literal and a faithful narrative of the conversation. 1853 KANE *Grinnell Exp.* ix. (1856) 67 This may excuse a literal transcript from my diary. 1871 B. TAYLOR *Faust* (1875) I. Notes 227, I shall not imitate Shelley in adding a literal translation.

3. a. *Theol.* Pertaining to the 'letter' (of Scripture); the distinctive epithet of that sense or interpretation (of a text) which is obtained by taking its words in their natural or customary meaning, and applying the ordinary rules of grammar; opposed to *mystical*, *allegorical*, etc. †Also *occas.* of a commandment, law, etc.: That is to be interpreted literally.

1382 WYCLIF *Prol.* 43 Holy scripture hath iiij vndirstondingis; literal, allegorik, moral, and anagogik. 1460 CAPGRAVE *Chron.* (Rolls) 107 Not only with litteral teching, but with many mysti exposiciones. 1502 *Ord. Crysten Men* (W. de W. 1506) II. ix. 108 Unto the lyturall sens, by this commaundement is pryncypally defended manslaughter. c 1530 MORE *Answ. Frith* Wks. 835/1 If he sayd that the wordes of Chryste might beside the lyttarall sence be vnderstanden in an allegorye, I woulde wel agre wyth him. 1561 T. NORTON *Calvin's Inst.* II. 97 The couenant of God made with the auncient people, was voide, bicause it was onely literall. 1597 HOOKER *Eccl. Pol.* v. lix. §2 Where a litterall construction will stand, the farthest from the letter is commonly the worst. 1605 CAMDEN *Rem.* (1674) 8 b, Moses received of God a literal Law..to be imparted to all, and another Mystical. 1664 H. MORE *Myst. Iniq.* 433 The Prophets predicting things of them in reference to the first Completion which is Literal. a 1761 LAW *Comf. Weary Pilgr.* (1809) 114 All these texts, which a learning, merely literal, has thus mistaken, do only prove [etc.]. 1862 STANLEY *Jew. Ch.* (1877) I. vi. 125 The literal meaning of the incident is almost lost in its high spiritual application.

b. Hence, by extension, applied to the etymological or the relatively primary sense of a word, or to the sense expressed by the actual wording of a passage, as distinguished from any metaphorical or merely suggested meaning.

1597 G. HARVEY *Trimming T. Nashe* Wks. (Grosart) III. 36, I giue not euery word their litteral sence. 1638 R. BAKER tr. *Balzac's Lett.* (vol. III.) 12 Never eares were more attentive,..then those of our family when I read your letter ..they were not satisfied to have onely a literal interpretation. 1718 *Freethinker* No. 35. 255 If you mention the *Golden Age* to him, he understands it in a literal sense. 1763 CHESTERF. *Let. to Son* 18 Dec. (1892) III. 1302, I see very few people; and, in the literal sense of the word, I hear nothing. 1809–10 COLERIDGE *Friend* (1865) 156 Advocates for reform in the literal sense of the word. 1902 GREENOUGH & KITTREDGE *Words & their Ways* xvii. 235 *Position* and *situation* are similar to *state* in their literal meaning.

c. Of persons: Apt to take literally what is spoken figuratively or with humorous exaggeration or irony; prosaic, matter-of-fact.

1778 MAD. D'ARBLAY *Evelina* (1791) II. xxxvii. 246, 'I fancy you will find no person..call going about a few places in a morning *seeing Bath*'. 'Mayhap, then,' said the literal Captain, 'you think we should see it better by going about at midnight?' 1837 HT. MARTINEAU *Soc. Amer.* III. 78 Their tendency..to something of the literal dulness which Charles Lamb complains of in relation to the Scotch. 1858 O. W. HOLMES *Aut. Breakf.-t.* iii. 20 One man who is a little too literal can spoil the talk of a whole tableful of men of *esprit*. 1865 M. ARNOLD *Ess. Crit.* Pref. 12 The earnest, prosaic, practical, austerely literal future.

Comb. a 1849 H. COLERIDGE *Ess.* (1851) I. 320 Literal-minded, unimaginative..individuals.

d. Of composition: Free from figures of speech, exaggeration, or allusion.

1736 BUTLER *Anal.* I. iii. 88 They are not to be taken as intended for a literal delineation of what is in fact the particular scheme of the universe. 1887 M. MORRIS *Claverhouse* iv. (1888) 66 His own despatch is singularly literal and straightforward.

e. **literal-minded** *a.*, having a literal mind; characteristic of one who takes a matter-of-fact or unimaginative view of things. Hence ***literal-mindedness***.

1869 *Wesleyan-Methodist Mag.* Jan. 28 An old friend, whom we used to call 'Bacon', because he..was a literal-minded man. 1905 J. L. LOWES in *PMLA* XX. 816 A strangely literal-minded, not to say naïve, interpretation of the charming fiction of the Prologue. 1927 *Glasgow Herald* 31 Oct. 10 The gentleman married the lady on the strength of her literal-mindedness. 1941 [see ANALYST 6]. 1944 *Mind* LIII. 238 One of my aims is..to formulate, in a manner

which is freed from all merely technical literal-mindedness, the epistemological idea and significance of pure semantics. **1957** *Essays & Stud.* X. 18 It delivers us from too much matter-of-fact and from the dreary flats of literal-mindedness. **1974** M. FIDO *R. Kipling* 80/2 'If you won't retract the lies.. I'll blow out your goddam brains!' 'If I don't do certain things, you'll kill me?' Rudyard asked, with infuriating English primness and literal-mindedness.

4. Used to denote that the accompanying sb. has its literal sense, without metaphor, exaggeration, or inaccuracy; literally so called.

1646 SIR T. BROWNE *Pseud. Ep.* I. iii. 11 The literall and downe-right adorement of Cats, Lizards, and Beetles. **1659** PEARSON *Creed* (1839) 385 When we say Christ ascended, we understand a literal and local ascent.. of his humanity. **1679** HARBY *Key Script.* i. 5 The seventh Head also (was not Rome Papal, but) appertained to Rome Literal. **1867** FREEMAN *Norm. Conq.* (1876) I. ii. 18 The literal extirpation of a nation is an impossibility.

†**5.** Of or pertaining to letters or epistles; epistolary. *Obs.*

c **1645** HOWELL *Lett.* (1650) III. 4 To hold this litterall correspondence I desire but the parings of your time.. let our Letters be as Eccho's. *a* **1657** R. LOVEDAY *Lett.* (1663) 168 To.. shorten the distance betwixt us, by a literal intercourse.

†**6.** Of or pertaining to letters or literature; = LITERARY. *Obs.*

c **1485** *Digby Myst.* (1882) II. 658 Lackyng lytturall scyens. **1591** G. FLETCHER *Russe Commw.* (Hakl. Soc.) 63 They excell in no kinde of common arte, much lesse in any learning or litterall kinde of knowledge. **1604** T. WRIGHT *Passions* III. iv. 102 If they be delighted in musicke they present them with instruments,.. if in studie with literall labours.

B. *sb.*

†**1.** A literal interpretation or meaning. *Obs.*

1630 DONNE *Serm.* xiii. 127 S. Gregory hath.. given us many Morals (as he cals them) upon this Booke [Job], but truly not many Literals for.. he bends all the sufferings of Iob figuratively, mystically upon Christ. **1646** SIR T. BROWNE *Pseud. Ep.* IV. x. 204 How dangerous it is in sensible things to use metaphoricall expressions unto the people, and what absurd conceits they will swallow in their literals.

2. *Printing.* A misprint of a letter.

1622 R. HAWKINS *Voy. S. Sea* [170] Errata sic corrige... The litteralls are commended to favour. **1880** *Print. Trades Jrnl.* xxx. 6 We noticed rather a large number of literals.

3. *Computers.* An operand in a program which directly specifies the value of a constant, or defines itself rather than serving as an address or label.

1960 *Nebula: a Programming Lang.* (Ferranti, Ltd.) iii. 5 A literal need not always be a numerical quantity. For example, the item ADDRESS may have a value which is '216 London Road' and this whole phrase (viz., 216 London Road) is then a literal. **1962** D. N. CHORAFAS *Programming Syst. for Electronic Computers* ix. 107 Commercial Translator distinguishes among three different types of constant: defined constants, literals and basic constants. *Ibid.*, A literal is a purely numerical constant which is introduced in a procedure statement as the need arises. **1968** S. M. BERNARD *System/360 COBOL* I. 52 A literal is a self-defining value; that is, it does not have to be separately defined by the programmer. 1. Non-numeric literals... 2. Numeric literals. **1968** N. CHAPIN *360 Programing* ii. 19 The symbolic addresses used by the programmer take four main forms: self-defining values, literals, symbolic names, and relative addresses. **1970** O. DOPPING *Computers & Data Processing* xix. 311 In certain languages.. a literal must be surrounded by quotation marks. In those systems, the literal may even begin with a letter. In that case, we could ..write the instruction PRINT 'SUM' for ordering the computer to print the word SUM. **1971** L. CODDINGTON *Quick COBOL* ii. 16 Literals are: 777, which is a numeric literal.. and alpha-numeric literals (YES, NO, SMITH, ZZZZ) which consist of letters... They are not true data-names: 'SMITH' is not only the name of a location in store, but the contents of that location. The numeric literals need no explanation.

literalism ('lɪtərəlɪz(ə)m). [f. prec. + -ISM. Cf. F. *littéralisme.*]

1. The disposition to accept and interpret the terms of a statement in their literal sense.

1644 MILTON *Divorce* II. xvii, If none of these considerations.. can avail to the dispossessing him of his precious Literalism, let [etc.]. **1845** J. H. NEWMAN *Ess. Developm.* 324 Diodorus and Theodore of Mopsuestia,.. the most eminent masters of literalism in the succeeding generation. **1865** LECKY *Ration.* I. iii. 342 The doctrine was stated with the utmost literalism and precision. **1882** FARRAR *Early Chr.* I. 385 Extravagant literalism has been even more fatal to exegesis than extravagant allegorising.

2. Literality as a principle of translation; a peculiarity of expression due to this.

1883 A. ROBERTS *O.T. Revision* xi. 224 The great characteristic of the translation of Aquila is its extreme literalism. *Mod.* Some of the translator's literalisms are very ungraceful.

3. *Fine Arts.* The disposition to represent objects (occas. to interpret representations) faithfully, without any idealization.

1863 HAWTHORNE *Our Old Home* (1883) I. 208 On considering this face of Charles.. and translating it from the ideal into literalism, I doubt [etc.]. **188.** *Studio* III. 147 (Cent.) He shunned the literalism of both form and color that jarred the ideal vision.

literalist ('lɪtərəlɪst). [f. as prec. + -IST. Cf. F. *littéraliste.*] One who insists upon the literal sense of a text or statement. Also, in art or literature, one who depicts or describes objects exactly as they are; an exact copyist.

1644 MILTON *Divorce* II. xx. 72 Let the extreme literalist sit down now, and revolve whether this in all necessity be not the due result of our Saviours words. **1685** H. MORE *Paralip. Prophet.* xl. 348 The Objector has rather acted the part of a Literalist. **1827** G. S. FABER *Sacr. Calend. Prophecy* (1844) III. 321. **1866** *Contemp. Rev.* II. 548 The merely descriptive writer, the literalist, though he write in verse, is not a poet at all. **1873** M. ARNOLD *Lit. & Dogma* (1876) 139 The veriest literalist will cry out: Everyone knows that this is not to be taken literally!

literalistic (ˌlɪtərə'lɪstɪk), *a.* [f. prec. + -IC.] Pertaining to or characteristic of a literalist; belonging to or having the character of literalism.

1875 POSTE *Gaius* IV. Comm. (ed. 2) 503 Strictum jus adheres to a grammatical or literalistic interpretation of a disposition. **1891** T. K. CHEYNE *Psalter* viii. 387 A literalistic interpretation will not meet the requirements of these psalms.

literality (lɪtə'rælɪtɪ). [f. LITERAL + -ITY.]

1. The quality or fact of being literal; literalness; an instance of this. †Also, a literal meaning.

1646 SIR T. BROWNE *Pseud. Ep.* I. iii. 9 Not attaining the deuteroscopy, and second intention of the words, they.. are not sometime perswaded by fire beyond their literalities. **1650** BP. HALL *Revelation unrev.* §8 Wks. 1808 X. 107 How wild a paradox it is to tie those frequent and large promises of the Prophets.. to a carnal literality of sense. **1818** LAMB *Female Orators* Wks. 635 One her coarse sense by metaphors expounds And one in literalities abounds. **1844** *For. Q. Rev.* XXXIII. 460 It is easy.. to sneer at literality;.. literality is after all the first merit of translation. **1867** H. MACMILLAN *Bible Teach.* xv. (1870) 293 Those to whom the sea has proved cruel, may.. rejoice to accept the announcement in all its literality, that in heaven there shall be no more sea. **1888** BRYCE *Amer. Commw.* I. 375 The same spirit of strictness and literality.

†**2.** Learning, knowledge of letters. *Obs.*

1656 in BLOUNT *Glossogr.*

literalize ('lɪtərəlaɪz), *v.* [f. LITERAL + -IZE.] *trans.* To render literal; to represent or accept as literal.

1826 G. S. FABER *Diffic. Romanism* (1853) 96 If we are to literalise the words of our Lord. **1827** *Examiner* 581/1 Ridicule is poorly employed in literalizing poetical allegory. **1856** R. A. VAUGHAN *Mystics* (1860) I. 90 This disposition to literalize metaphors gave currency to the monkish stories.

Hence **'literalizing** *vbl. sb.* and *ppl. a.* Also **literali'zation**, the action of literalizing (1864 in Webster); **'literalizer**, one who literalizes.

1848 G. S. FABER *Many Mansions* Pref. (1851) 20 The literalising Reveries of the Chiliasts. **1866** *Contemp. Rev.* I. 538 The hierarchical, repressive, and literalizing spirit,.. will be seen to exist in the Free Church of Scotland. **1871** TYLOR *Prim. Cult.* I. 352 Several of the epithets usually applied only need literalizing to turn into the wildest of the legendary monster-stories. **1895** *Thinker Mag.* VIII. 493 Ver. 14.. does not help the literalizers at all.

literally ('lɪtərəlɪ), *adv.* [f. LITERAL + -LY[2].]

†**1.** *nonce-uses.* **a.** By the letters (of a name). **b.** In letters or literature. *Obs.*

1584 R. SCOT *Discov. Witchcr.* XVI. iii. (1886) 399 One T. of Canterburie, whose name I will not litterallie discover. **1593** R. HARVEY *Philad.* 7 And yet I tell you me-thinkes you are very bookishly and literally wise.

2. a. With reference to a report, translation, etc.: In the very words, word for word.

1646 SIR T. BROWNE *Pseud. Ep.* III. xvi. 145 Which are literally thus translated. **1712** STEELE *Spect.* No. 521 ¶5 Others repeat only what they hear from others as literally as their parts or zeal will permit. *a* **1753** R. NEWTON *Theophrastus' Char.* (1754) p. viii, I would.. advise every Scholar.. to translate his Author thus literally, word for word. **1843** MRS. CARLYLE *Lett.* I. 238 Every word of this is literally as the men spoke it.

b. *transf.* With exact fidelity of representation.

1816 BYRON (*title*) Churchill's Grave, a fact literally rendered.

3. a. In the literal sense.

1533 FRITH *Answ. More's Let.* C 3 b, Allthough it were literalye fulfillyd in the childern of Israell.. yet was yt allso ment & verified in Christ hym selfe. **1579** FULKE *Heskin's Parl.* 105 They interprete literally, which the doctors did write figuratively. **1664** H. MORE *Myst. Iniq., Apol.* 481 All those Passages are not to be Literally understood. **1719** DE FOE *Crusoe* II. xiv. (1840) 286 This was a china warehouse indeed, truly and literally to be called so. **1783** HAILES *Antiq. Chr. Ch.* iv. 78 *note*, It may be doubted, whether this was ever literally true. **1876** E. MELLOR *Priesth.* iv. 161 Literally speaking, 'this cup' could never be 'a new covenant'. **1895** SIR A. KEKEWICH in *Law Times Rep.* LXXIII. 663/1 It is found that the Act does not mean literally what it says.

b. Used to indicate that the following word or phrase must be taken in its literal sense.

Now often improperly used to indicate that some conventional metaphorical or hyperbolical phrase is to be taken in the strongest admissible sense. (So, e.g., in quot. 1863.)

1687 DRYDEN *Hind & P.* III. 107 My daily bread is litt'rally implor'd. **1708** POPE *Let. to H. Cromwell* 18 Mar., Euery day with me is literally another yesterday for it is exactly the same. **1761-2** HUME *Hist. Eng.* (1806) V. lxxi. 341 He had the singular fate of dying literally of hunger. **1769** *Junius Lett.* xxx. 137 What punishment has he suffered? Literally none. **1839** MISS MITFORD in L'Estrange *Life* (1870) III. vii. 100 At the last I was incapable of correcting the proofs, literally fainting on the ground. **1863** FR. A. KEMBLE *Resid. in Georgia* 105 For the last four years .. I literally coined money. **1887** I. R. *Lady's Ranche Life Montana* 76 The air is literally scented with them all. **1902** *Daily Chron.* 10 Dec. 7/2 A contemporary states that Kubelik has been 'literally coining money' in England. **1906** *Westm. Gaz.* 15 Nov. 2/1 Mr. Chamberlain literally bubbled over with gratitude. **1922** R. MACAULAY *Mystery at Geneva* xiv. 72 The things 'they' say! They even say.. that 'literally' bears the same meaning as 'metaphorically' ('she was literally a mother to him,' they will say). **1960** V. NABOKOV *Invitation to Beheading* iii. 31 And with his eyes he literally scoured the corners of the cell. **1973** *Good Food Guide* 176 'Crabs and lobsters are literally to be found crawling round the floor waiting for an order,' reports an early nominator.

literalness ('lɪtərəlnɪs). [f. LITERAL + -NESS.] The quality of being literal; literality.

1630 DONNE *Serm.* xiii. 127 Origen.. doth never pretend to much literalnesse in his expositions. **1824** *New Monthly Mag.* X. 246 The same literalness of perception and absence of passion. **1881** WESTCOTT & HORT *Grk. N.T.* II. 8 The greater literalness of later transcription.

literarian (lɪtə'rɛərɪən). [f. as LITERARY + -AN.] One engaged in literary pursuits.

1866 F. HALL in *Reader* 24 Feb. 206/2 Passing to his compatriot Sanskritists, we come upon a brood of literarians. **1887** *Lit. Opinion* 1 Apr. 48/2 When a renowned literarian pauses in his chronicles.

literarily ('lɪtərərɪlɪ), *adv.* [f. LITERARY + -LY[2].] In a literary manner or respect.

1825 *Blackw. Mag.* XVII. 593 Go as.. tutor to a young gentleman literarily disposed. **1895** *Daily News* 10 Apr. 3/5 My education has.. been a good one, classically, literarily, and commercially.

literariness ('lɪtərərɪnɪs). [f. LITERARY + -NESS.] The quality of being literary.

1877 MALLOCK *New Republic* I. III. i. 239 Why, I thought culture was books and literariness, and all that. **1899** *Academy* 16 Dec. 715/2 Most good literary critics, if they have not style, have 'literariness'.

literarism ('lɪtərərɪz(ə)m). [f. LITERAR(Y *a.* + -ISM.] = LITERARYISM.

1942 PARTRIDGE *Usage & Abusage* 173/1 *Literarisms* are either the journalese of the literary (these literarisms might also be stigmatized as high-brow) or such unusual words as are used only by the literary or learned. **1963** A. HUXLEY *Lit. & Sci.* i. 5 Snow or Leavis? The bland scientism of *The Two Cultures* or, violent and ill-mannered, the one-track, moralistic literarism of the Richmond Lecture? **1970** F. R. LEAVIS in *Times Lit. Suppl.* 23 Apr. 441/4 The term 'literarism' was in fact coined by the late Aldous Huxley for use against me.

literary ('lɪtərərɪ), *a.* [ad. L. *litterāri-us*, f. *littera* letter. Cf. F. *littéraire.*] (Not in Johnson 1755-1775.)

†**1.** Pertaining to the letters of the alphabet. *Obs.*

1646 SIR T. BROWNE *Pseud. Ep.* I. ix. 37 Our first and literary apprehensions being commonly instructed in Authors which handle nothing else [but idle fictions]. **1769** *Middlesex Jrnl.* 8-11 July 4/2 A complete set of Literary Cards, for teaching children to read, spell, count. **1793** SMEATON *Edystone L.* §334 *note*, The literary references to Plates Nos. 19, and 20.

†**2.** Carried on by letters; epistolary. *Obs.*

1757-8 SMOLLETT *Hist. Eng.* (1800) II. 252 A literary correspondence was maintained between the English General and the Mareschal de Villars. [**1818** TODD s.v., *Literary* is not properly used of missive letters.]

3. Of or pertaining to, or of the nature of, literature. **a.** Pertaining to letters or polite learning. **b.** Pertaining to books and written compositions; also, in a narrower sense, pertaining to, or having the characteristics of that kind of written composition which has value on account of its qualities of form. ***literary dinner, lunch(eon), party, prize***; also ***literary adviser***: one who gives advice or information on literary matters; ***literary agent*** (see quot. 1960); also ***literary agency***; ***literary circle*** (see CIRCLE *sb.* 21); ***literary criticism*** = CRITICISM 2 (of works of literature); so ***literary critic, literary-critical*** adj.; ***literary editor***: (*a*) the editor of the literary section of a newspaper; (*b*) the editor of a book of collected writings; so ***literary-edit*** vb., ***-editorship***; ***literary executor*** (see EXECUTOR 3); ***literary history*** (e.g. of a legend, a historical personage or event, etc.): the history of the treatment of, and references to, the subject in literature; ***literary property***: (*a*) property which consists in written or printed compositions; (*b*) the exclusive right of publication as recognized and limited by law; ***literary world*** (see WORLD *sb.* 16 b).

1749 L. EVANS *Middle Brit. Col.* (1755) 3 The Seats of some Half a Dozen Gentlemen, noted in the literary Way. **1758** J. G. COOPER *Retreat Aristippus* Epist. i. 198 With these, and some a-kin to these,.. I live in literary ease. **1759** GOLDSM. *Pol. Learn.* vi. Wks. (Globe) 430/1 A man of literary merit is sure of being caressed by the great, though seldom enriched. **1773** JOHNSON in *Boswell* 29 Apr., Mallet had talents enough to keep his literary reputation alive as long as he himself lived. **1779** —— *L.P., Cowley* ¶2 His mother.. struggling earnestly to procure him a literary education. **1831** M. EDGEWORTH *Let.* 6 Jan. (1971) 469 He .. criticises so well—not as a mere literary critic appealing to authorities. **1840** MACAULAY in *Edin. Rev.* Jan. 520 In 1698, Collier published his 'Short View..', a book which threw the whole literary world into commotion. **1845** GRAVES

Canon Law in *Encycl. Metrop.* II. 785/1 The literary history of the early Greek collections has been carefully illustrated by Biener. **1845** H. C. ROBINSON *Diary* 27 Jan. (1967) 234 Mrs. Jameson.. is now received in the highest literary circles. **1851** *N. & Q.* 28 June 527 (Advt.), Literary Agency —Mr. F. G. Tomlins.. is desirous to make it known that a Twenty years' experience with the Press and Literature,.. enables him to give advice and information to Authors, Publishers and Persons wishing to communicate with the Public. **1853** C. M. YONGE *Heir of Redclyffe* I. xv. 251 She was.. the leading lady of the place.., giving literary parties, with a degree of exclusiveness that made admission to them a privilege. **1857** G. H. LEWES *Let.* 11 Feb. in Geo. Eliot *Lett.* (1954) II. 295 When I am no longer here to act as go-between he [*sc.* Geo. Eliot] must, I think, become his own literary Agent. *a* **1859** MACAULAY *Hist. Eng.* xxiii. (1861) V. 7 The parliamentary conflict on the great question of a standing army was preceded by a literary conflict. **1862** G. H. LEWES *Let.* 10 May in Geo. Eliot *Lett.* (1956) IV. 31 Smith again offered me the editorship of the C[ornhill] M[agazine] which I again declined; but accepted the post of Literary Advisor. **1868** Literary executor [see EXECUTOR 3]. **1876** GEO. ELIOT *Let.* 2 May (1956) VI. 244 One cannot escape seeing and hearing something of political and literary criticism. **1883** TROLLOPE *Autobiogr.* II. xiv. 88 Literary criticism.. has become a profession,—but it has ceased to be an art. **1885** Literary circle [see CIRCLE *sb.* 21]. **1898** H. CALDERWOOD *D. Hume* iii. 28 A large measure of literary ability was appearing in Scotland. **1900** J. G. FRAZER *Pausanias*, etc. 68 The writer, it is plain, has exaggerated for the sake of literary effect. **1904** A. BENNETT *Great Man* x. 98 Henry had learnt for the first time what a literary agent was. **1912** R. BROOKE *Let.* 25 Nov. (1968) 408 German literary circles are.. entirely cut off from English. **1919** 'C. DANE' *Legend* 84 You know I'm literary executor? **1919** MRS. BELLOC LOWNDES *Diary* 10 July (1971) 91 The great literary prizes awarded in the last fifty years by the French Academy. **1923** Literary-edit [see *art-edit* v. (ART *sb.* 18)]. **1931** R. CAMPBELL *Georgiad* iii. 51 O Dinners! take my curse upon you all, But literary dinners most of all. **1932** H. NICOLSON *Diary* 23 Feb. (1966) 110 Leonard Woolf has an idea that I should take on the literary editorship of the *New Statesman. Ibid.* 19 Oct. 122 Round to the *New Statesman.* Kingsley Martin indicates that he wants me to become the literary editor when Ellis Roberts goes. **1936** *Discovery* Jan. 28/2 The literary executors of the late Professor Hicks are to be congratulated. **1936** 'E. M. DELAFIELD' *Provincial Lady in Amer.* 116 Literary luncheon really important function will receive wide press publicity letter follows Stop Very sincerely Katherine Ellen Blatt. **1937** F. M. FORD *Let.* 17 Feb. (1965) 271 The eccentric Principal, Brewer, who once humorously subedited—or rather literary-edited the *Spectator* for three weeks. **1940** 'M. INNES' *There came both Mist & Snow* x. 114 The young man.. had just that deference which I am accustomed to meet with from young critics at literary parties. **1941** 'G. ORWELL' in *Listener* 29 May 768/1, I am speaking on literary criticism. **1941** V. NABOKOV *Real Life S. Knight* (1945) i. 6 Last winter at a literary lunch, in South Kensington, a celebrated old critic .. was heard to remark.. 'A dull man.' **1950** 'E. CRISPIN' *Frequent Hearses* i. 12 I'm acting as literary advisor in connexion with a film they're making. **1960** G. A. GLAISTER *Gloss. Bk.* 238/1 *Literary agent*, an agent, paid on a commission basis, who acts for an author by submitting his work to, and dealing with a publisher; and who may arrange the sale of translation or other rights. **1962** J. B. PRIESTLEY *Margin Released* III. ii. 158 Most of my meetings with authors took place.. at literary parties. **1965** *Philos. Rev.* LXXIV. 208 Literary-critical description.. is what is needed. **1965** L. SANDS *Something to Hide* i. 14 She had attended a dull literary luncheon. **1967** *Guardian* 14 Sept. 2/5 A highlight of the literary world.. a Foyles Luncheon. **1968** *Writers' & Artists' Year Bk.* 242 Literary agents exist to sell saleable material. *Ibid.*, Adamastor Press and Literary Agency Ltd. **1968** K. MARTIN *Editor* i. 7 Raymond Mortimer.. was the sort of literary editor with whom I scarcely ever wanted to interfere. **1969** A. G. THOMAS in L. Durrell *Spirit of Place* 11, I have had one advantage not generally available to literary editors. When work on this book was well advanced Durrell came to stay with me.. and I was able to consult him. **1971** D. CRYSTAL *Ling.* 107 An 'objective correlative' (to apply T. S. Eliot's literary critical term in a context where it was never intended). **1972** A. CHRISTIE *Elephants can Remember* i. 11 I'm always being asked to literary lunches. **1972** *Guardian* 1 Dec. 13/2 The Marxist writer, John Berger, had arrived at the National Liberal Club to receive the Guardian literary prize for his novel 'G'. **1973** *Listener* 15 Feb. 211/2 I've never been a great one for going out in literary circles, but I did know Wells very well, and I knew Galsworthy slightly. **1973** J. GOODFIELD *Courier to Peking* ii. 23 There's lots of people I must talk to... I'm his literary executor. **1975** A. CLARKE *My Search for Ruth* xii. 111 A terrifying woman at a literary party.

4. Acquainted with or versed in literature; *spec.* engaged in literature as a profession, occupied in writing books. Of a society, etc.: Consisting of literary men. Also, ***literary gent*** (colloq.): one who prides himself on his literary accomplishments.

1785 *Daily Universal Reg.* 1 Jan. 1/1 This Day is published.. by the Literary Society, *Modern Times*.. a Novel. **1791** BOSWELL *Johnson* an. 1764, That club.. at Mr. Garrick's funeral [an. 1779] became distinguished by the title of The Literary Club. **1809** *Med. Jrnl.* XXI. 192 A few years since, he married Miss Edgeworth, a lady of a respectable literary family in Ireland. **1840** CARLYLE *Heroes* (1858) 302 In the true Literary Man there is thus ever.. a sacredness. **1850** THACKERAY *Pendennis* II. xxxiv. 336 Doctor Johnson has been down the street many a time with ragged shoes... You literary gents are better off now. **1870** J. H. NEWMAN *Gram. Assent* I. iii. 18 The primary duty of a literary man is to have clear conceptions, and to be exact and intelligible in expressing them. **1895** *Bookman* Oct. 14/1 Artistic and literary Glasgow owed much to his genial energy. **1937** 'G. ORWELL' *Road to Wigan Pier* xii. 243 Ten years ago.. the typical literary gent wrote books on baroque architecture. **1967** L. WOOLF *Downhill all Way* I. 106 Being also what I call a literary gent, he [*sc.* James Stephens] used to fill me alternately with depression and irritation.

5. Of painting, sculpture, etc.: that depicts or represents a story.

1928 *Morning Post* 20 Oct. 10/6 The music is too 'literary', but its craftsmanship and imagination are undeniable. **1931** C. HOLMES *Gram. Arts* vii. 118 The intrusion of 'literary' elements into the arts has long been suspect. **1962** R. G. HAGGAR *Dict. Art Terms* 196 *Literary art...* The term is frequently used in a pejorative sense, but most romantic painting is dependent upon a text. **1970** *Daily Tel.* 8 June 12/8 It is accepted by many as a compliment rather than as an insult to describe a painting as literary.

Hence **'literaryism**, addiction to literary forms; an instance of this, a form of expression belonging to literary language.

1879 ELWORTHY *Pref. to Exmoor Scolding* (E.D.S.) 13 The same culture which prompts them to compose at all, binds them in chains of literaryism. *Ibid.* 14 A great many literaryisms are pointed out in the notes. **1891** STEVENSON *Vailima Lett.* i. (1895) 94, I found a lot of slacknesses and (what is worse in this kind of thing) some literaryisms.

Also as *sb.*, a literary club or society; a literary person. *U.S.*

1904 *Dialect Notes* II. 419 We organized a literary at the school-house. **1923** U. L. SILBERRAD *Lett. J. Armiter* vi. 145 Obstacles.. may be a blessing in disguise to half-baked literaries. **1928** *Amer. Speech* IV. 130 In many districts a 'literary' is held every Friday night, when the 'Sandhillers' of this district recite and sing and debate. **1936** E. G. BARNARD *Rider Cherokee Strip* 157 We spent a happy winter at this work and visiting our neighbors and going to the 'literaries' and dances.

‖**litera scripta** ('lɪtərə 'skrɪptə). [L.] The written word.

1864 J. S. LE FANU *Uncle Silas* I. xxi. 256 Henceforward all is circumstantial evidence.. except the *litera scripta*, and to this evidence every note-book, and every scrap of paper.. must contribute.. what it can. **1910** R. BRIDGES in *Essays & Stud.* I. 48 The *litera scripta* has an enormous power.

‖**literata** (lɪtə'reɪtə). *nonce-wd.* In quot. *pl.* [L. fem. of *litterātus*.] A learned or literary lady.

1794 COLERIDGE *Lett.* (1895) I. 87 The young lady is said to be the most literary of the beautiful, and the most beautiful of the literatæ.

literate ('lɪtərət), *a.* and *sb.* Also 5, 7 litterate, 6 litterat. [ad. L. *litterātus*, f. *littera* letter.]

A. *adj.*

1. Acquainted with letters or literature; educated, instructed, learned. In early use, const. *in*.

1432–50 tr. *Higden* (Rolls) IV. 81 The kynge toke to the childe a m. talentes whiche bouȝhte anoon a c. childer litterate. **1560** ROLLAND *Crt. Venus* III. 142 For I in law am not weill litterat. **1603** OWEN *Pembrokeshire* (1891) 176 Done by the witnesses themselves if they were literate. **1631** CHAPMAN *Cæsar & Pompey* v. i. H 2 b, The Ægæan sea, that doth diuide Europe from Asia. (The sweet literate world From the Barbarian). **1636** BRATHWAIT *Rom. Emp.* 150 An enemy of all litterate and learned men. **1680** *Answ. Stillingfleet's Serm.* 7 Re-ordination is an uncouth thing, quite against the hair of the literate World. **1748** CHESTERF. *Lett.* (1792) II. clxxii. 139 You are going to a polite and literate Court. **1768–84** JOHNSON in *Boswell* App. (1848) 812/2 Had my mother been more literate, they had been better companions. **1821** LAMB *Elia, Old Benchers Inner Temple*, He was the Friar Bacon of the less literate portion of the Temple. **1845** R. W. HAMILTON *Pop. Educ.* x. (ed. 2) 267 On the same ground, a Literate qualification for electoral rights in the commonwealth, must be condemned. **1884** D. HUNTER tr. *Reuss's Hist. Canon* ii. 19 When the writings of the first disciples.. came within reach of persons who were literate, they might [etc.].

absol. **1859** T. HARE *Election Representatives* (1865) 90 Reducing.. the literate and the ignorant.. to one dead level. **1859** SMILES *Self-Help* x. (1860) 274 The humblest and least literate must train his sense of duty.

2. a. Of or pertaining to letters, literary men, or literature; literary.

1648 W. MOUNTAGUE *Devout Ess.* I. xix. §3. 348 Surely this is the proper function of literate elegancy, to figure vertue in so lively and fresh colours, that [etc.]. **1651** tr. *Wolton's Panegyr. Chas. I* in *Reliq. W.* 135 To beguile,.. with some literate diversion, the tedious length of those days. **1711** SHAFTESB. *Charac.* (1737) III. Misc. v. ii. 274 Downright Ignorance of all literate Art, or just Poetick Beauty. **1764** SCOTT *Bailey's Dict.* Title-p., Republished with many corrections, additions and literate improvements. **1811** *Antiq.* in *Ann. Reg.* 534/2 His own liberal hand was speedily extended to relieve literate distress. **1837–9** HALLAM *Hist. Lit.* I. v. (1855) I. 352 By the Reformation the number of.. those requiring.. a literate education was greatly reduced. **1851** D. WILSON *Preh. Ann.* (1863) II. IV. ii. 242 Another inscription preserving.. the only authentic literate Memorial. **1872** M. COLLINS *Two Plunges* III. vi. 137 The old town.. has not the first force of either the aristocratic or the literate or the mercantile impulse.

†**b.** = LITERAL 4. *Obs.*

1556 J. HEYWOOD *Spider & F.* Concl. 60, I craue leaue.. one sence tenterpretate: Of apt aplication to sence literate.

3. 'Marked with short, angulated lines resembling letters: applied to the surfaces of shells and insects' (*Cent. Dict.*).

B. *sb.*

1. A liberally educated or learned person.

a **1550** *Image Hypocr.* IV. 80 in *Skelton's Wks.* (1843) II. 440 Advocates, And parum litterates, That eate vpp all estates. **1778** *Learning at a Loss* II. 152 Christopher Hartley, Esquire, a Sir Wou'd-be Literate. **1808** ELEANOR SLEATH *Bristol Heiress* V. 324 Persuading her that she was the most accomplished literate and female wit of the age. **1852** J. H. NEWMAN *Callista* (1856) 238 Callista was a Greek; a literate, or blue-stocking. **1878** LADY HERBERT tr. *Hübner's Ramble* II. ii. 494 The literates in China are all atheists.

2. *spec.* In the Church of England, one who is admitted to holy orders without having obtained a university degree.

1824 BP. JEBB *Sp. Irish Tithe Compos. Amendmt. Bill* 49 In Ireland we have no literates, none of that class, who, in this country, prepare themselves by private study, at a trifling cost, for the profession of the Church. **1861** BERESF. HOPE *Eng. Cathedr. 19th C.* 18 Literates—who enter holy orders without any reasonable hope of any better material position. **1866** S. B. JAMES *Duty & Doctrine* 19 Graduates of the three Universities.. theological-college men and literates. **1868** M. PATTISON *Academ. Org.* iv. 74 To obtain ordination as a literate is something.

3. One who can read and write. Opposed to *illiterate*.

1894 H. C. LEA in *Forum* (U.S.) Aug. 675 Statistics show that literates contribute a larger percentage of their class to the criminal ranks than do the illiterates.

4. (*Lady*) ***Literate in Arts***, the title conferred on the holder of a higher certificate for women issued at St. Andrews University. Abbrev. *L.L.A.*

This diploma was discontinued in 1931.

1881 *St. Andrews Univ. Cal.* 203 Any Candidate who passes in four subjects, [etc.].. will receive the title of Literate in Arts (L.L.A.). **1891** R. F. MURRAY *Scarlet Gown* 122 An L.L.A. is a Lady Literate in Arts. **1901** *Daily Record* 30 July 3 Lady Literates in Arts. **1931** *L.L.A. Examination, Diploma, & Title for Women* (Univ. St. Andrews) 8 There is no limit as to age in the L.L.A. Examination.

†**literated,** *a. Obs.* [f. prec. + -ED[1].] Learned.

1611 FLORIO, *Alletterato*, literated, learned. **1612** WEBSTER *Wh. Devil* III. i. E 2 b, Most literated Iudges, please your Lordships [etc.]. **1647** LILLY *Chr. Astrol.* clxv. 706 Much tugging and shuffling with Atturneys, men witty and literated, cheats in Accompts.

‖**literati** (lɪtə'reɪtaɪ), *sb. pl.* Also 8 litterati. [L. *litterātī*, pl. of *litterātus*: see LITERATE.

In It. the word occurs in the same form (pl. of *literato*, now written *litterato*; also *letterato*). Possibly in the 17–18th c. the Eng. use may have been supposed by some to be derived from It. and not from Latin; early in the 18th c. LITERATO appears as the sing. beside LITERATUS.]

Men of letters; the learned class as a whole.

The earliest application in Eng. use is as the appellation of the learned class of China, which Burton obtained from the Latin version of the letters of the Jesuit M. Ricci, 1606–7. The word is still so employed by writers on China.

1621 BURTON *Anat. Mel.* To Rdr. (1624) 52 To be.. examined & approued as the literati in China. **1664** EVELYN tr. *Freart's Archit.* etc. 132 An industrious searcher of the Sciences, which is the same that a good Philologer is amongst our Literati. *a* **1677** HALE *Prim. Orig. Man.* I. ii. 63 These Sentiments are not confined to the Literati of mankind. **1714** ADDISON *Spect.* No. 581 ⁋33, I shall consult some Litterati on the project. **1787** M. CUTLER in *Life*, etc. (1888) I. 281 The University literati and men of fortune are become proprietors. **1803** SYD. SMITH *Wks.* (1859) I. 63/1 The list of Danish literati will best prove that they have no literati at all. **1809** W. IRVING *Knickerb.* III. iii. (1820) 174 Manifold are the tastes and dispositions of the enlightened literati, who turn over the pages of history. **1830** CARLYLE *Misc.* (1857) II. 137 Certain provincial literati of the Hof-district. **1860** R. D. *Vac. Tour.* 114 The literati of the southern Slaves are not to be found among a higher class than the village clergy, and masters of village-schools.

‖**literatim** (lɪtə'reɪtɪm), *adv.* [L. *litterātim*, f. *littera* letter.] Letter for letter; literally.

1643 *Myst. Iniq.* 36 He wrote this Copy out of his *literatim. a* **1733** R. NORTH *Examen* I. ii. §131 (1740) 102 The Proceedings of the Lower House, which are set forth *literatim* in many Prints. **1813** LD. ERSKINE *Speeches* I. 329 A paper which it sets out literatim on the face of the record. **1901** *Athenæum* 27 July 119/1 This.. does not profess to be an exact reproduction literatim of the text.

literation (lɪtə'reɪʃən). [f. L. *littera* + -ATION.]

a. The action or process of representing (sounds or words) by letters.

1918 HARDY in T. H. Ward *Eng. Poets* V. 174 His aim in the exact literation of Dorset words is not necessarily to exhibit humour and grotesqueness. **1928** J. SYKES *Mary Anne Disraeli* ix. 85 'D'Israeli and Mrs. D'Izzy'—an unusual form of literation of the familiar diminutive.

b. The method or style of making letters.

1926 *Times Lit. Suppl.* 10 June 390/2 To sacrifice.. the exquisite literation that in the old hands delights us like a poem.

literatist ('lɪtərətɪst). [f. LITERATE + -IST.] One engaged in literary pursuits; a writer, author.

1660 FISHER *Rusticks Alarm* Wks. (1679) 469 He was not ashamed, as our Universities Literatists are at this day, to learn of Women. **1830** 'JON BEE' *Ess.* in *Dram. Wks. S. Foote* I. p. xxix, Indeed they are never the most elegant literatists who study longest, at college, the jargon of the schools. **1866** F. HARPER *Peace thro. Truth* Ser. I. 135 It would.. seem as though the greater number of our modern literatists were a sort of inferior caste in English civilization.

'literatize, *v. nonce-wd.* [f. as prec. + -IZE.] *trans.* To pass *away* (time) in literary occupations.

1836 LD. LYTTON in R. R. Madden *Life C'tess Blessington* (1855) II. 41, I literatize away the morning.

‖**literato** (lɪtə'rɑːtəʊ). Also 8 litterato. [It. *litterato*, ad. L. *litterātus*.] One of the literati; a man of letters or erudition; a learned man. Cf. LITERATUS.

1704 N. N. tr. *Boccalini's Advts. fr. Parnass.* I. 91 Every Literato is proud of the Honour of his [Bacon's] Company. **1711** STEELE *Spect.* No. 53 ⁋9 Some may think we descend

from our Imperial Dignity, in holding Correspondence with a private Litterato [*v.r.* Litterati]. ? **1789** COWPER *Let. to W. Bagot* Wks. 1836 VI. 266 A folio edition of the Iliad, published..at Venice, by a literato, who calls himself Villoison. **1851** R. F. BURTON *Goa* 100 You cannot boast of ever having produced a single eminent literato.

literator (ˈlɪtəreɪtə(r)). [a. L. *lit(t)erātor* (1) a teacher of ABC, (2) a grammarian, critic, (3) a smatterer, a sciolist; f. *littera* letter. Cf. F. *littérateur*.]

†**1.** A pretender to learning, a sciolist. *Obs.*

1635 A. STAFFORD *Fem. Glory, Apol.* (1869) p. xcv, Theise Puritanicall Christians will admit of any Church-Mountebanke, any Literator, soe hee can shew him selfe seditious enough. *a* **1641** BP. MOUNTAGU *Acts & Mon.* (1642) 457 Gregory Martin, a Literator, who brawles against us for using sometime the word Congregation for the Church.

2. A literary man; = LITTÉRATEUR.

1791 BURKE *Let. to Member Nat. Assembly* Wks. VI. 36 [French] preceptors..a set of pert petulant literators, to whom..they assign the brilliant part of men of wit and pleasure. **1812** *Brenan's Milesian Mag.* July 87 A history of Ireland..is about to be published by that illustrious literator Jack Squintum [Jn. Lawless: pub. 1814]. **1817** TICKNOR *Lett. & Jrnls.* (1876) I. 128 He..asked me with the eagerness of a hardened literator, whether [etc.]. **1829** LANDOR *Imag. Conv.* Wks. 1853 I. 385/1 They are lawyers, literators, metaphysicians. **1831** *Blackw. Mag.* XXIX. 902 Hume, even as a litterator, was every way superior to the bishop. **1849** THIRLWALL *Lett.* (1881) 196 On the metaphysicians and literators I do not suppose that it would produce the slightest impression. **1872** SWINBURNE *Under Microscope* 58 The men really and naturally dear to them [English reviewers] are the literators of Boston. **1878** BROWNING *Poets Croisic* lxxxi, Literators trudging up to knock At Fame's exalted temple-door. **1890** *Athenæum* 11 Jan. 44/2 No array of circumstances can transmute the born 'literator' into a mere man of action. **1900** *Pall Mall G.* 5 Dec., Mr. Gibb is no mere Orientalist; he is also preeminently a literator.

3. †**a.** A bibliographer (*obs.*). **b.** One who concerns himself with verbal and textual criticism. *rare.*

1727-51 CHAMBERS *Cycl.* s.v. *Book*, The history of a book is either of its contents..or of its appendages and accidents, which is the more immediate province of those called literators, and bibliothecarians. **1826** DE QUINCEY *Lessing's Laocoon* in *Blackw. Mag.* XX. 733 It is impossible from the slight notices of this drama [the *Laocoon* of Sophocles] in the old literators to come to any conclusion about the way in which it was treated. **1858** —— *R. Bentley* Wks. VII. 102 The philological researches of the Greek and Latin literator.

4. *nonce use.* (See quot.)

1785 TRUSLER *Mod. Times* III. 166 Lord W. wished to appoint me his literator, which office was to cull out the pith of every new publication, and retail it to him at breakfast.

†ˈ**literatory**, *a. Obs. rare.* [ad. L. *litterātōrius*, f. *litterātor* (see prec.).] Literary.

1652 URQUHART *Jewel* Wks. (1834) 181 The martial and literatory endowments of some natives of that soyle.

literature (ˈlɪtərətjʊə(r)). Forms: 4 *Sc.* **lateratour**, 5-6 **litt-**, **lytterature**, 6 *Sc.* **literatur**, **-uir**, 6- **literature**. [ad. (either directly or through F. *littérature*) L. *litterātūra* (whence Sp. *literatura*, It. *letteratura*, G. *litteratur*), f. *littera* a letter. Cf. LETTRURE.]

1. Acquaintance with 'letters' or books; polite or humane learning; literary culture. Now *rare* and *obsolescent*. (The only sense in Johnson and in Todd 1818.)

c **1375** *Sc. Leg. Saints* xxxi. (*Eugenia*) 53 Scho had leyryte ..of þe sewine sciens..& part had of al lateratour. *c* **1425** WYNTOUN *Cron.* IX. xxiii. 2227 Cunnand in to litterature, A seymly persone in stature [etc.]. **1432-50** tr. *Higden* (Rolls) VI. 359 Seynte Grimbalde the monke, nobly instructe in litterature and in musyke. **1513** BRADSHAW *St. Werburge* II. 4 The comyn people..Whiche without lytterature and good informacyon Ben lyke to Brute beestes. *a* **1529** SKELTON *Bowge of Courte* 449, I know your vertu and your lytterature. **1581** N. BURNE *Disput.* xxv. 109b, Ane pure man, quha.. hes nocht sufficient literatur to vndirstand the scripture. **1605** BACON *Adv. Learn.* I. To the King §2. 2 There hath not beene..any King..so learned in all literature and erudition, diuine and humane. *c* **1645** HOWELL *Lett.* (1650) I. 346 In comparison of your spacious literature, I have held all the while but a candle to the sun. **1693** J. EDWARDS *Author. O. & N. Test.* 239 Another person of infinite literature [Selden]. **1727** SWIFT *Let. Eng. Tongue* Wks. 1755 II. I. 187 Till better care be taken in the education of our young nobility, that they may set out into the world with some foundation of literature. **1779-81** JOHNSON *L.P., Milton* (1868) 37 He had probably more than common literature, as his son addresses him in one of his most elaborate Latin poems. *Ibid.* 62 His literature was unquestionably great. He read all the languages which are considered either as learned or polite. **1802** MAR. EDGEWORTH *Moral T.* (1816) I. 206 A woman of considerable information and literature. **1862** BORROW *Wild Wales* II. x. 104 The boots [is] a fellow without either wit or literature. **1880** HOWELLS *Undisc. Country* xix. 290 In many things he was grotesquely ignorant; he was a man of very small literature.

2. Literary work or production; the activity or profession of a man of letters; the realm of letters.

1779 JOHNSON *L.P., Cowley* ¶1 An author whose pregnancy of imagination and elegance of language have deservedly set him high in the ranks of literature. **1791-1823** D'ISRAELI *Cur. Lit.* (1859) II. 407 Literature, with us, exists independent of patronage or association. **1830** SCOTT *Introd. to Lay Last Minstr.* Poet. Wks. 1833-4 VI. 17, I determined that literature should be my staff, but not my crutch, and that the profits of my literary labour..should not..become necessary to my ordinary expenses. **1853** LYTTON *My Novel* VII. viii, Ah, you make literature your calling, sir? **1879** MORLEY *Burke* 9 Literature, the most seductive, the most deceiving, the most dangerous of professions.

3. a. Literary productions as a whole; the body of writings produced in a particular country or period, or in the world in general. Now also in a more restricted sense, applied to writing which has claim to consideration on the ground of beauty of form or emotional effect. ***light literature***: see LIGHT *a.*[1] 19.

This sense is of very recent emergence both in Eng. and Fr.

1812 SIR H. DAVY *Chem. Philos.* 6 Their literature, their works of art offer models that have never been excelled. **1838** ARNOLD *Hist. Rome* I. 21 Many common words, which no nation ever derives from the literature of another, are the same in Greek and Latin. **1845** M. PATTISON *Ess.* (1889) I. 1 Such history, almost more than any other branch of literature, varies with the age that produces it. **1856** EMERSON *Eng. Traits, Ability* Wks. (Bohn) II. 41 There is no department of literature, of science, or of useful art, in which they have not produced a first rate book. **1857** BUCKLE *Civiliz.* I. v. 244 Literature, when it is in a healthy and unforced state, is simply the form in which the knowledge of a country is registered. **1874** GREEN *Short Hist.* vii. §7. 413 The full glory of the new literature broke on England with Edmund Spenser. **1879** SEELEY in *Macm. Mag.* XLI. 24 Those who cannot have recourse to foreign literatures are forced to put up with their ignorance.

b. The body of books and writings that treat of a particular subject.

1860 TYNDALL *Glac.* I. vi. 44, I was well acquainted with the literature of the subject. **1879** HARLAN *Eyesight* i. 9 It.. has accumulated a literature of its own which an ordinary lifetime is hardly long enough to master. **1939** [see NORMALIZABLE *a.*]. **1969** [see DÉCOLLEMENT 2]. **1971** *Nature* 25 June 499/1 We have searched the literature for reliable radiometric ages for Late Pre-Cambrian glaciogenic rocks, but they seem to be rare. **1973** *Sci. Amer.* June 55/3 A voluminous scientific literature accumulates each year on the normal vibrational modes of molecules in liquids and on optical phonons in crystals.

c. *colloq.* Printed matter of any kind.

1895 *Daily News* 20 Nov. 5/2 In canvassing, in posters, and in the distribution of what, by a profane perversion of language, is called 'literature'. **1900** *Westm. Gaz.* 12 Oct. 2/1 A more judicious distribution of posters, and what is termed 'literature'. **1938** WODEHOUSE *Code of Woosters* i. 8 It is some literature from the Travel Bureau. **1962** *Observer* 4 Mar. 37/1 (Advt.), Full details and literature from: Yugoslav National Tourist Office. **1973** D. FRANCIS *Slay-Ride* vii. 78, I talked my throat dry, gave away sheaves of persuasive literature.

‖**literatus** (lɪtəˈreɪtəs). *rare* [L. *lit(t)erātus*, f. *littera* letter.] One of the LITERATI; a man of letters or erudition; a learned man. Cf. LITERATO.

1704 HEARNE *Duct. Hist.* (1714) I. 401 It is..not a sufficient Reason to decry it so much as a late Ingenious Literatus has done. **1806** LAMB *Lett.* viii. *To Mr. Rickman* 79 You do not happen to have any place at your disposal which would suit a decayed Literatus? **1823** DE QUINCEY *Lett. Yng. Man* i. Wks. 1890 X. 19 Now we are to consider that our bright ideal of a literatus may chance to be married. **1972** *Times Lit. Suppl.* 19 May 563/3 He had already made himself the universal literatus. *Ibid.* 28 July 880/2, I join with a literatus in conversation about the trash we read in childhood.

litere, obs. form of LITTER.

literose (ˈlɪtərəʊs), *a. rare.* [ad. late L. *litterōsus*, f. *littera* letter.] Studiedly or affectedly literary. Hence **liteˈrosity**.

1888 HOWELLS in *Harper's Mag.* Feb. 479/2 Daudet is always literose. **1891** —— *Introd. to Mrs. Craig's tr. Verga's House by Medlar-tree* 6 He has as completely freed himself from literosity as the most unlettered among them.

lites, var. LIGHTS.

lith (lɪθ), *sb.*[1] *Obs.* exc. *arch.* or *dial.* Forms: 1 **leoð**, 1-4 **lið**, 3-6, 9 **lithe**, 3-6 **lyth**, 4 **liþþe**, 5 **leth**, **lythe**, 5, 7, 9 **leith**, 6 **lethe**, 4- **lith**. [OE. *liþ* neut. = OFris. *lith*, *lid* neut., OS. *lið* masc. (Du. *lid* neut.), OHG. *lid* masc. and neut., ON. *lið-r* masc. (Sw. and Da. *led* masc.), Goth. *liþus* masc.:—OTeut. **liþu-*:—pre-Teut. **litu-* f. root **lĭ-*:—see LIMB *sb.* A compound of this word with the prefix *ga-* (= Y-) is OHG. *gilid* (G. *glied* limb, member).]

1. A limb. ***lith from lith***, †***from lith to lith***: limb from limb.

a **900** CYNEWULF *Crist* 1032 (Gr.) Sceal þonne anra ȝehwylc..leoðum onfon & lichoman. *c* **900** tr. *Bæda's Hist.* IV. xxx[i]. (Schipper) 534 He wæs byȝendlic on þam ȝeþeodnessum his liþa [*v.rr.* leoða, lima]. *c* **1330** *Arth. & Merl.* (Kölbing) 8494 Wawains breþer on & oþer smiten euerich liþ fram oþer. **1390** GOWER *Conf.* I. 99 Sche hath no lith withoute a lak. *c* **1410** *Sir Cleges* 292, I schall the bette euery leth, Hede and body, wythout greth. *c* **1430** *Life St. Kath.* (1884) 53 To make al hir body to be rent lyth from lyth. **1496** *Dives & Paup.* (W. de W.) I. vi. 38/1 The horryble wheles whiche the tyraunt Maxencius ordeyned to rente her from lyth to lyth. **1732** E. ERSKINE *Serm.* Wks. 1871 II. 177 Everything was in its proper joint and lith, subservient unto the great end of their creation.

2. A joint; frequent in *lith and limb*, etc.; also ***lith and bone***. ***out of lith***: out of joint.

c **1000** *Sax. Leechd.* II. 242 On ðone lið þæra eaxla. *c* **1220** *Bestiary* 626 He ne hauen no lið ðat he muȝen risen wið. *a* **1300** *Cursor M.* 12612 Weri was sco bath lith and ban. *c* **1375** *Sc. Leg. Saints* xxiv. (*Alexis*) 518 Quhat sek mane þat twechit hym, His hele he gat in lith and lyme. **1470-85** MALORY *Arthur* III. xiv, Allas syr sayd the lady myn arme is oute of lythe. **15..** *How Gd. Wyfe taught Dau.* 38 in *Q. Eliz. Acad.* 45 Loke þou mekly ansuere hym, And meue hym noþer lyth ne lymme. *c* **1560** A. SCOTT *Poems* (S.T.S.) ii. 135 Thow art moir lerge of lyth and lym Nor I am, be sic thre. **1718** RAMSAY *Christ's Kirk Gr.* III. xxiv, Ilka member, lith and lim. *a* **1782** LD. AUCHINLECK in Croker's *Boswell* (1831) III. 79 *note*, God, doctor! he gart kings ken that they had a lith in their neck. **1828** J. WILSON in *Blackw. Mag.* XXIV. 683, I..finally sunk away into voluptuous diffusion of lith and limb on that celestial sofa. *a* **1828** *Bonny Bows o Lond.* xvii. in Child *Ballads* I. 135/2 He's taen a lith o her little finger bane.

b. *fig.* esp. in phrase ***to hit the lith*** or ***to hit upon the lith***, an expression borrowed from carving.

a **1225** *Ancr. R.* 262 Þus, lo þe articles, þet beoð, ase þauh me seide, þe liðes of ure bileaue onont Godes monheade. **1637** RUTHERFORD *Lett.* (1862) I. 221 To hold off an erroneous conclusion in the least wing or lith of sweet sweet truth. **1727** P. WALKER *Life Peden* in *Biogr. Presb.* I. 122 And seldom hit upon the right lith or joint. *Ibid.* 140 Of late, I have heard some liths and nicks of the Gospel made plain.

c. The last joint or tip (of the finger).

c **1000** *Ags. Gosp.* Luke xvi. 24 Send lazarum þæt he dyppe his fingres lið on wætere & mine tungan ȝehæle. **1815** SCOTT *Guy M.* xxxix, A scar abune the brow, that ye might hae laid the lith of your finger in.

3. *Sc.* A division (of an orange, etc.); one of the rings surrounding the base of a cow's horn.

1795 G. ROBERTSON *Agric. Surv. Mid-Lothian* 155 The horns (of the Mysore cow in particular) are without annulets, or liths as we call them. *a* **1859** J. P. NICHOL (Ogilv.), The reader will at once comprehend the reason by cutting an orange through its centre obliquely to its axis. Each lith is of equal size, but the exposed surface of each on the freshly-cut circle will not be so. **1890** H. DRUMMOND in *Life* xv. (1899) 376 A green banana leaf..wound once round the head after being cut into four or five 'liths'.

†**lith**, *sb.*[2] *Obs.* [OE. *hliþ* neut.:—OTeut. type **hliþo*ᵐ, f. root **hlĭ-* (see LEAN *v.*[1], LADDER):—pre-Teut. **klei-*; cf. the ablaut var. ON. *hlíð* of the same meaning.] A slope.

Beowulf (Z.) 1893 No he mid hearme of hliðes nosan gæstas grette. *a* **1000** *Andreas* 841 (Gr.) Fore burȝȝeatum beorȝas steape, hleoðu hlifodon. *c* **1200** *Trin. Coll. Hom.* 117 Þere weren men of eche londe þat is under heuene liðe. *c* **1205** LAY. 32219 3eond wudes & ȝeond liðen. [**1789** WHITE *Selborne* (1853) 171 A steep abrupt pasture-field..known by the name of Short Lithe. *Ibid.*, Steep pastures are called the Lithe.]

†**lith**, *sb.*[3] *Obs.* Also 3 **lið**, **leoð**. [ON. *lið* a host, also help, f. root of *líða* to go, travel, go on an expedition (see LEAD *v.*[1]).]

1. A body of men.

c **1205** LAY. 5307 We wullet gan a leoðe. **1377** LANGL. *P. Pl.* B. XVI. 181 Þre leodes in o lith non lenger þan other, Of one mochel & myȝte in mesure and in lengthe.

2. Help, remedy.

c **1205** LAY. 5213 Nes þer nan oðer lið ȝif heo nalden ȝernen grið.

†**lith**, *sb.*[4] *Obs.* Also 4-5 **lithe**, **lythe**. [Of somewhat uncertain origin; most prob. a. ON. *lýð-r* people, vassals collectively (see LEDE); but it may wholly or partly be a use of LITH *sb.*[3] 1.] People, subjects, vassals. Only in alliterative phrases. (Cf. LEDE 1 b.)

a **1300** *Cursor M.* 13165 Noþer i ask þe lith na land. *c* **1300** *Havelok* 2515 Lond and lith, and oþer catel. *c* **1330** R. BRUNNE *Chron.* (1810) 194 Þer wille wille not be went, ne lete lond ne lith [Fr. *tere ne tenement*]. **1357** *Lay Folks Catech.* 252 In cas that we have..Wittandly and willfalli gere our euen cristen..falsly be desesed of land or of lithe. *c* **1420** *Anturs of Arth.* liii. (MS. Douce), Here I gif Sir Galerone..Al þe londes and þe lithes fro lauer to layre. *c* **1440** *Bone Flor.* 841 Who schall us now geve londes or lythe, Hawkys, or howndes? **1456** SIR G. HAYE *Law of Arms* (S.T.S.) 148, I am lyke to tyne up all, bathe..land, lythe, and place.

lith, obs. forms of LIGHT *sb.* and *a.*[2]

lith, obs. f. 3rd pers. sing. pres. ind. of LIE.

-lith, a terminal element representing Gr. λίθος stone, in adaptations of actual or assumed Gr. compounds. The words with this ending are chiefly terms of Biology and Pathology, as *coccolith*, *cyatholith*, *discolith*, *helmintholith*, *hippolith*; other examples are *acrolith*, *aerolith*, *laccolith*, *monolith*. In terms of mineralogy -LITE is commonly used instead of *-lith*.

‖**lithæmia** (lɪˈθiːmɪə). *Path.* [mod.L., f. Gr. λίθ-ος stone + αἷμ-α blood.] The condition in which lithic or uric acid is in excess in the blood; formerly called *uricæmia*.

1874 C. MURCHISON *Functional Derangem. Liver* ii. 65 This morbid state of the blood I propose to designate Lithæmia. **1884** F. J. NOTT in *Harper's Mag.* Aug. 442/2 These waters are..efficacious in..lithæmia.

Hence **lithæmic** (lɪˈθiːmɪk) *a.*, of or pertaining to lithæmia; affected with lithæmia.

1889 *Syd. Soc. Lex.*, *Lithæmic insomnia.* **1897** *Allbutt's Syst. Med.* IV. 10 These also are frequently found in lithæmic persons. *Ibid.* 750 The so-called 'lithæmic diathesis' is a..frequent cause of throat disease.

lithagogue ('lɪθəgɒg), *a.* and *sb. Path.* Also 9 *erroneously* lithogogue. [f. Gr. λίθ-ος stone + ἀγωγός drawing forth.]

a. *adj.* Having the power to expel calculi from the kidneys or bladder. **b.** *sb.* A medicine supposed to have this power.

1844 HOBLYN *Dict. Med. Terms, Lithagoga*,.. Lithagogues. **1850** OGILVIE has adj. and sb.

‖**litham** (li:'θɑ:m). Also lisam. [ad. Arab. *liṯām* veil.] A veil of cloth wound round the head leaving only the eyes uncovered and worn by the men of the Tuareg people of the central Sahara desert.

1839 E. W. LANE tr. *Thousand & One Nights* I. vi. 467 The Khaleefeh then put on himself the fishermen's jubbeh and turban, and, having drawn a lithám over his face, said to the fisherman, Go about thy business. **1855** R. F. BURTON *Pilgrimage* I. xii. 346 This veiling the features is technically called *Lisam*: the chiefs generally fight so, and it is the usual disguise when a man fears the avenger of blood, or a woman starts to take the *Sar*. **1879** *Encycl. Brit.* IX. 129/1 The *litham* or shawl-muffler of the Tuareg, wound round the mouth to keep out the blown sand of the desert. **1903** W. J. H. KING *Search for Masked Tawareks* xv. 220 He stood.. slightly raising with his long slender fingers the upper fold of his *litham* or mask. **1966** M. WOODHOUSE *Tree Frog* xxi. 157 Mohammed Jalil al Murzuq sat still..the veil, the *litham* drawn across his face.

lithanode ('lɪθənəʊd). *Electr.* [f. Gr. λίθος stone + ANODE.] A hard compact form of peroxide of lead, used in storage batteries. Also *attrib.*

1887 D. G. FITZGERALD *Patent Specif.* Engl. No. 16608 for 1886 My invention relates to the manufacture of peroxide of lead in porous coherent self-supporting masses (or what is known as 'lithanode'). **1892** *Electrical Engineer* 16 Sept. 283/2 This difficulty, we are told, was soon overcome by utilising some of the small lithanode cells to produce a flashing arc. **1893** *Pall Mall G.* 10 Jan. 4/3 The lamps are worked by Lithanode batteries from the stage.

‖**li'thanthrax.** *Obs.* Also 7 lithanthrix, 8 lithonthrax. [Mod.L., f. Gr. λίθ-ος stone + ἄνθραξ charcoal.] Used as a scientific name for mineral coal (i.e. 'coal' in the mod. sense), in distinction from *xylanthrax* (charcoal).

1611 SPEED *Theat. Gt. Brit.* I. xlvi. 89 The Chiefest commodity..are those Stones Linthancraces [*sic*: ? *read* lithantraces], which wee call Sea-coales. **1696** PHILLIPS (ed. 5), *Lithanthrix*, a stony Coal, being a kind of Gagate. **1706** *Ibid.* (ed. Kersey), *Lithanthrax*, stony Coal, a kind of Jeat; Pit-coal, or Sea-coal. *a* **1728** WOODWARD *Nat. Hist. Fossils* I. (1729) I. 165 Lithonthrax, or Coal. **1802** A. ELLICOTT *Jrnl.* (1803) 24 Mines of pit coal (lithanthrax), are..inexhaustible from Pittsburgh many miles down the river.

litharge ('lɪθɑ:dʒ). Forms: α. 4–6 litarge, 5–6 lytarge, 6 lethargy, lytherge, 6–7 litargy, littarge, 7 lithargie, -y, lytharge, (littorage, lytoridge, lyturgy), 8 litargie, letharge, litherage, (liturge), 5– litharge. β. 5 litargirij, 6 lithargirye, lythurgyry, 7 lithargiry. [a. or ad. OF. *litarge*, *litargire* (F. *litharge*), ad. L. *lithargyrus*, a. Gr. λιθάργυρος, f. λίθ-ος stone + ἄργυρος silver. The β forms are from the mod.L. derivative *litargirium*, *-ia*.]

1. Protoxide of lead (PbO) prepared by exposing melted lead to a current of air. †Also *litharge of lead*.

1322 in *Wardr. Acc. Edw. II* 23/20 Litarge 4*d.* per lb. *c* **1386** CHAUCER *Can. Yeom. Prol. & T.* 222 Oure grounden litarge eek in the P[o]rfurie. **1477** NORTON *Ord. Alch.* iii. in Ashm. (1652) 41 Then we name it our grounde Litharge. **1563** T. GALE *Antidot.* II. 49 Take Litarge of leide in fyne pouder. **1674** RAY *Collect. Words, Smelting Silver* 114 When the furnace is come to a true temper of heat the Lead converted into Litharge is cast off. **1707** *Curios. in Husb. & Gard.* 325 Lead being..burnt into Litargie, retakes also its first Form..if a Lixiviate Salt be..applied to it. **1758** REID tr. *Macquer's Chem.* I. 389 Pure Lead, being exposed to a strong fire without any additament, turns to Litharge. **1860** PIESSE *Lab. Chem. Wonders* 155 Put a few grains of litharge before the blowpipe flame.

†**b.** *litharge of gold*: a name given to litharge when coloured red by mixture of red lead. *litharge of silver*: a name given to it as being a by-product in the separation of silver from lead. *litharge of bismuth*: ? a similar product obtained by the oxidation of bismuth. *Obs.*

c **1400** *Lanfranc's Cirurg.* 99 Take..litarge of gold, litarge of siluir ȝ. viii. **1578** LYTE *Dodoens* VI. lxxxvii. 771 To be pound with the lytarge of sylver and frankencense. **1597** GERARDE *Herbal* II. l. 269 The iuice mixed with oile of roses, ceruse, and littarge of golde, and applied [etc.]. **1601** HOLLAND *Pliny* I. 304 The very root of the right Nard..is mingled..with Litharge of siluer, Antimony, or the rind of Cyperus. **1639** T. DE GRAY *Compl. Horsem.* 208 Take lyturgy of gold and lyturgy of silver..mix well the lyturgys. **1718** QUINCY *Compl. Disp.* (1719) 212 *Lythargyrus Auri*, Litharge of Gold. It generally is call'd thus for its Colour sake. **1727–41** CHAMBERS *Cycl.*, Artificial Litharge, which is of two kinds, *viz.* that of gold, and that of silver; or rather it is the same, with this difference, that the one has undergone a greater degree of fire than the other. **1796** KIRWAN *Elem. Min.* (ed. 2) II. 489 Litharge of Bismuth.

†**2.** Used as equivalent to *white lead* or *red lead* (see LEAD *sb.*[1] 2).

1551 TURNER *Herbal* I. Mj, The iuice of Coriandre with whyte lede or lythurgyry and vinegre. **1660** HOWELL *Lexicon*, Litargie, or white Lead. **1683** PETTUS *Fleta Min.* I. (1686) 26 Of these pibble-stones take one part, and half a part of red Littorage or Littarge..and hete it well. **1796** KIRWAN *Elem. Min.* (ed. 2) II. 368 Litharge or Red Lead. **1800** tr. *Lagrange's Chem.* II. 64 If you expose to heat in a crucible red oxide of lead or litharge.

3. *attrib.*, as *litharge-furnace*; **litharge-plaster** ? = DIACHYLON; **litharge-way**, the opening in a reverberatory furnace through which the litharge flows in the fining of silver.

1887 RAYMOND *Statist. Mines & Mining* 26 We canvassed the..necessity of erecting a *litharge furnace. **1784** M. UNDERWOOD *Dis. Children* (1799) III. 94 Small pieces of the *litharge-plaster may be applied. **1889** *Syd. Soc. Lex.*, Litharge plaster, the *Emplastrum plumbi*. **1797** *Encycl. Brit.* (ed. 3) XI. 464/2 This blast..throws the litharge that is not imbibed by the test towards a channel, called the *litharge-way, through which it flows.

lithargie, obs. form of LETHARGY.

lithate ('lɪθeɪt). *Chem.* Also lithiate. [f. LITH-IC + -ATE.] A salt of lithic acid.

1821 W. PROUT *Gravel, Calculus*, etc. 112 The quantity of lithate of ammonia in the urine is increased above the natural standard. **1823** CRABB *Technol. Dict., Lithiate.* **1862** H. W. FULLER *Dis. Lungs* 248 The urine is generally scanty during the height of the disease, deep-coloured, loaded with lithates. **1876** HARLEY *Mat. Med.* (ed. 6) 119 It is supposed to decompose the insoluble lithate of soda in the system.

Hence **lithatic** (lɪ'θætɪk) *a.*, of or pertaining to, or of the nature of a lithate.

1858 J. H. BENNET *Nutrition* v. 154 The turbidity is owing to the presence of a lithatic deposit.

†**lithe**, *sb.*[1] *Obs.* [f. LITHE *a.*; not connected with LETHE *a.*] A calm, lull; *fig.* respite.

c **1300** *Havelok* 147 Ne he ne mouchte no lyþe gete. *c* **1440** *Promp. Parv.* 310/1 Lyye, or lythe, and calme wedyr, *malacia*.

Hence †'**lithefull** *a.*, calm, gentle.

c **1205** LAY. 1262 He þonkede hire ȝeorne mid liðfulle worden.

lithe, *sb.*[2] *Obs.* exc. *dial.* In 7 lyth, 9 lythe. [? f. LITHE *v.*[2]] (See quots.)

1688 R. HOLME *Armoury* III. 83/1 Lyth, or Lything, is Oatmeal or bruised Groats that thickens Broth. **1899** *Cumbld. Gloss.*, *Lythe*, oatmeal and water mixed smooth and added to broth to thicken it.

lithe (laɪð), *sb.*[3] *Sc.* Also 8–9 lythe. [? variant of LEWTH. (But cf. LITHE *a.* 2 c.)] Warm shelter.

1768 ROSS *Helenore* (1789) 58 She frae ony beeld was far awa', Except stane-sides, and they had little lythe. **1868** G. MACDONALD *R. Falconer* II. 195 Come into the lythe o' the bank here.

lithe (laɪð), *a.* Forms: 1 liðe, lýðe, 2–5 liðe, 4 liȝth, 4–7 lith, lythe, 5–7 lyth, 8–9 *dial.* lyth(e, 4– lithe. Also 3 i-liðe. [OE. *líðe* = OS. *lîthi*, OHG. *lindi* (MHG. *linde*, mod.G. *lind*) soft, gentle, mild:—OTeut. type **linþjo-*, f. Teut. and WAryan root **len-*, whence LIN *v.*, ON. *lin-r* soft, L. *lentus* slow.]

†**1.** Of persons, their actions, dispositions and utterances: Gentle, meek, mild. Const. *dat.* or *to*. *Obs.*

Beowulf 3183 Manna mildust..leodum liðost. *a* **1000** *Apollonius of Tyre* (1834) 2/25 Ða cliopode heo hi hire to mid liðere spræce. *c* **1000** *Ags. Gosp.* Matt. v. 5 Eadiȝe synt þa liðan. *c* **1200** ORMIN 7754 Forr lamb iss soffte & stille deor, & liþe & meoc & milde. *c* **1205** LAY. 4 He wes Leouenaðes sone liðe him beo drihten. *Ibid.* 4917 þu eært me swiðe iliðe [*c* **1275** liþe] & ich þe leouie swiðe. *a* **1225** *Ancr. R.* 428 Swuch ouh wummone lore to beon—luuelich & liðe. *a* **1325** *Prose Psalter* cxliv. [cxlv.] 9 Our Lord is liþe to alle. *c* **1400** *Destr. Troy* 9706 The first of þo fre, þat to þe freike said, Was Vlyxes, the lord, with his lythe wordes.

2. Of things, chiefly material things: Mild, soft; also, agreeable, mellow, pleasant. Of a medicine: Gentle in operation. *Obs.* exc. *dial.*

c **888** K. ÆLFRED *Boeth.* xl. §3 Hwæðer him cume þe reðu w[y]rd þe liðu. *a* **1000** *Cædmon's Gen.* 211 (Gr.) þæt liðe land. *c* **1175** *Lamb. Hom.* 129 Ðet weter of egipte wes liðe and swete. *c* **1320** *Sir Tristr.* 707 Water þai asked swiþe... Wit mete and drink liþe. *c* **1384** CHAUCER *H. Fame* I. 118 To make lythe of that was harde. *c* **1400** *Lanfranc's Cirurg.* 87 If þe quytture be þicke & towȝ, þanne is þe medicyn to liþe. *c* **1400** *Rom. Rose* 3762 The savour soft and lythe Strook to myn herte withoute more. **1642** ROGERS *Naaman* 172 How lythe and cheerfull would the soule be in going to Zoar out of Sodome. **1664** SPELMAN *Gloss.* s.v. *Ledo*, lenis (nobis hodie, Lithe). **1844** THOM *Rhymes of a Weaver* 72 They miss the lythe licht o' their May. **1878** —— *Jock o' Knowe* 56 (E.D.D.) Lithe Time stole away.

†**b.** Of weather: Calm, serene. [Cf. OE. *Líða*, June and July.] Of water: Smooth, still. *Obs.*

c **1205** LAY. 7242 þæt weder wes swiðe liðe. *Ibid.* 24198 þa ..þat gras was riue and þat water wes liðe. *a* **1300** *E.E. Psalter* cvi. 29 His stremes leften lithe. **13..** *Coer de L.* 4859 The wynd gan wexe lythe. *a* **1440** *Sir Eglam.* 1056 To the see they went fulle yare And passyd the watur lythe. *c* **1460** *Emare* 348 The wedur was lythe of le. **1577–87** HOLINSHED *Chron.* II. *Hist. Scot.* 203/2 It prooved as lithe a daie, without appearance of anie tempest to insue.

c. Comfortable, genial, sheltered, warm. *Sc.*

c **1430** *Syr Tryam.* 417 Sche toke up hur sone to hur And lapped hyt fulle lythe. *c* **1470** HENRY *Wallace* II. 276 Syn in a bed thai brocht him fair and lyth. *a* **1774** FERGUSSON *Wks.* (1807) 262 Like thee they scour frae street or field, And hap them in a lyther bield. **1867** G. W. DONALD *Poems* (1879) 66 Licht an' lythe wes Peggie's bosom. **1871** W. ALEXANDER *Johnny Gibb* xi. (1873) 66 They're fine lythe parks, an' ear' tee; beasts mith live o' them throu' the winter naar. **1884** D. GRANT *Lays & Leg. North* 274 Winter drives them o'er the sea To seek the lyther land.

3. Easily bent; flexible, limber, pliant, supple. (The current sense, the only one in Johnson.)

c **1400** *St. Alexius* (Laud 622) 6 Of bodies stronge & liȝth. **1579** SPENSER *Sheph. Cal.* Feb. 74 His dewelap as lythe, as lasse of Kent. **1599** *Withals' Dict.* 109 b, The bills of birds we see full oft, Whiles they bee yong are lith and soft. **1667** MILTON *P.L.* IV. 347 Th' unwieldy Elephant..wreath'd His Lithe Proboscis. **1667** R. NORWOOD in *Phil. Trans.* II. 567 To the Harping-Iron is made fast a strong lythe rope. **1814** CARY *Dante, Par.* XXVI. 85 Like the leaf, That bows its lithe top till the blast is blown. **1833** TENNYSON *Poems* 36 As lithe eels over meadows gray Oft shift their glimmering pool by night. **1856** BRYANT *Poems, Hymn to Death* 37 The perjurer, Whose tongue was lithe, e'en now, and voluble Against his neighbour's life. **1871** R. ELLIS tr. *Catullus* lxi. 106 He more lithe than a vine amid Trees.

4. Of broth, soup, etc.: Smooth, thick. *dial.*

a **1648** DIGBY *Closet Open.* (1669) 259 Stir it up quick with your hands, like a lith pudding. **1805** J. STAGG *Misc. Poems* (1808) 56 Bit swoaps o' drink an' guod lythe keale.

5. *Comb.*

1791 COWPER *Iliad* XV. 839 Or swans lithe-necked grazing the river's verge. **1897** *Daily News* 26 May 9 There are sixteen of them..tall, lithe-looking sun-burnt figures.

†**lithe**, *v.*[1] *Obs.* Forms: 1 líðan, 3 liðen, *Orm.* liþenn. *Pa. t.* 1 láð, 3 læð, lað, *pl.* liðe(n; also *in weak form* lið(e)de. *Pa. pple.* 3 iliðe(n. [OE. *líðan*, *láð*, *liden* = OS. *líðan*, OHG. *lídan* carry (MHG. *lîden*), ON. *líða* to travel (Sw. *lida*, Da. *lide*), Goth. (*af-*, *ga-*, *us-*)*leiþan* to go, f. Teut. root **līþ-* (:**lăd-*, see LOAD *sb.*).] *intr.* To go, pass; in OE. esp. to go by sea, to sail.

Beowulf 221 Ða liðende land ȝesawon. *c* **900** tr. *Bæda's Hist.* III. xiv. [xix.] (1890) 218 þa forlet he þa mæȝðe & ofer sæ lað in Gallia rice. *c* **1200** ORMIN 8434 Inntill whillc ende off all þatt land He badd himm þanne liþenn. *c* **1205–75** LAY. [*passim*: see *Glossary*].

Hence †'**lithing** *ppl. a.*, of a ship, sailing.

c **1205** LAY. 943 Alle þa liðinde scipen þe on his londe beoð.

†**lithe**, *v.*[2] *Obs.* Forms: 1 líþan, líþian, 3 liðen, 4–7 lythe, 3– lithe. [OE. *líð-an*, weak vb. f. *líðe* mild, LITHE *a.*]

1. *trans.* To render 'lithe', i.e. gentle or mild; to influence (a person) gently; to relax (fetters); to assuage, mitigate (grief, pain); to relieve, soothe; to render (a limb) supple; to bend, subdue (persons, their passions).

c **897** K. ÆLFRED *Gregory's Past.* xvii. 124 Ðis is ðearf ðæt se se þe wunde lacnian wille ȝeote win on..& eft ele, ðæt se hie liðe & hæle. *c* **1200** *Trin. Coll. Hom.* 95 Shereðures-daies absolucion liðe þe sinne bendes. **13..** *K. Alis.* 2797 The saut com so thikke and swithe, That no weryng ne myghte heom lithe. **1362** LANGL. *P. Pl.* A. VII. 183 Lome mennes limes weore lyþet þat tyme. *c* **1374** CHAUCER *Troylus* IV. 726 (754) He þat wont here wo was for to lyþe, She mot for-gon. *a* **1400–50** *Alexander* 3754 To lithe vs all if þou limpes na louyng þou gettis. *c* **1430** *Syr Gener.* (Roxb.) 7721 Hir angre she gan ther to lithe. **1552** ABP. HAMILTON *Catech.* (1884) 173 The haly spreit..be his grace lythis and turnis our hart to God. **1614** T. ADAMS *Diuells Banket* vi. 291 England.. hath now suppled, lythed, and stretched their throates. **1642** ROGERS *Naaman* 313 Giue me also faith, Lord,..to lythe, to forme, and to accommodate my spirit and members.

2. To render 'lithe' or thick; to thicken (broth, etc.). Also *transf.*

1674 RAY *N.C. Words* 30 Lithe the pot, i.e. put Oatmeal into it. **1711** W. STORR *Bk. Rem.* in *Yorksh. Arch. Jrnl.* VII. 58 Lithe it with bean meal as hot as can be bidden. **1808** BALD *Coal-trade of Scot.* i. 13 The coalmasters frequently inquired if the sinkers were lything the water, that is, making it of a thick and muddy colour by their operations. **1867** B. BRIERLEY *Marlocks* iii. 69 The old woman was engaged in 'lithing' the broth.

lithe (laɪð), *v.*[3] *Obs.* exc. *arch.* and *dial.* Forms: 3 liðen, -in, 3–7, 9 lythe, 4, 7 lithen, 4 lythen, 4, 6–7 lith, 4–6 lyth, 3– lithe. [ON. *hlýða* (MSw. *lydha* to listen, Sw. *lyda*, Da. *lyde* to obey; the Da. *lytte* to listen, is a different formation), f. *hljóð* neut., listening, sound, corresp. to Goth. *hliuþ* listening attention (ἡσυχία), OHG. *hliudar*, OE. *hléoðor* sense of hearing, music, f. Teut. root **hleu-* to hear: see LIST *sb.*[1]] *intr.* To hearken, listen. Const. *dat*, or *to*, *unto* (*at*, *till*). Also, to hear *of* (a thing). Occas. quasi-*trans.* with obj. a thing.

a **1225** *Juliana* 73 Lvsteð me leoue men & liðeð ane hwile. *c* **1250** *Gen. & Ex.* 2077 Quað ðis bred-wriȝte, 'liðeð nu me'. *c* **1300** *Havelok* 1400 Liþes nou alle to me, Louerdinges. **13 ..** *Gaw. & Gr. Knt.* 1719 Thenne was hit lif vpon list to lyþen þe houndez. *c* **1330** R. BRUNNE *Chron.* (1810) 67 How þe gamen ȝede lithe I salle ȝow seie. *c* **1330** *Amis & Amil.* 429 Hir name was cleped Belisaunt, As ye may lithe at me. **1393** LANGL. *P. Pl.* C. XI. 65 To lithen here laies and here loueliche notes. ? *a* **1400** *Morte Arth.* 1810 Theis newe made knyghttez Lythes vn-to the crye. *c* **1400** *Tale of Gamelyn* 1 Litheth and lesteneth and herkeneth aright. *a* **1400–50** *Alexander* 5023 þan list him lithe of his lyfe & of his last ende. *c* **1470** *Golagros & Gaw.* 1163 Lufly ledis in land, lythis me til! ? *a* **1500** *Ballad, Adam Bell*, etc. I. 17 Now lithe and listen, gentlemen That of mirth loueth to heare! **1500–20** DUNBAR *Poems* l. 1 Now lythis of ane gentill Knycht, Schir Thomas Norray. **1592** in *Vicary's Anat.* (1888) App. ix. 228 Lythe and I shall tell them the. **1615** BRATHWAIT *Strappado* (1878) 132 Thou mun not take petition (lithen me) Nor entertaine him, till thou take thy fee. **1683** G. MERITON *Yorksh. Dial.* 4 Lythe yee, Lythe yee! How fondley you tawke. **1807** STAGG *Poems* 20 Monny a sleepless night she past,..As she lythe'd the lengthnin' blast. **1840** BARHAM *Ingol. Leg.* Ser. I. *Witches' Frolic*, One

tale I remember of mickle dread, Now lithe and listen, my little boy Ned.

lithe, variant of LYTHE, the pollack.

lithe, obs. 3rd sing. ind. pres. of LIE v.^{1} and ^{2}.

†**litheby**, a. Obs. Forms: 1 liþebiȝ(e, 3 leoðebeie, leþebei. [OE. leoþu-biȝe, liþebiȝe :—pre-Engl. *liþubaugjo-, f. liþu- LITH sb.^{1} + *baugjo-, f. root of BOW v.] Supple-jointed, lissome.

c1000 ÆLFRIC Hom. II. 152 Þa wearð þæt haliȝe lic hal on eorðan ȝemet,..liðe biȝe on limum. a1225 St. Marher. 16 Sei me seli meiden hwonne is te ileanet i þine leoðebeie limen so stalewurðe strencðe. a1275 Prov. Ælfred 692 in O.E. Misc. 138 Þe lonke mon is leþe bei.

lithectasy (lɪˈθɛktəsɪ). Surg. [f. Gr. λίθος stone + ἔκτασις: see ECTASIS.] The operation of removing calculi through the urethra, by first extending or dilating it.

1842 R. WILLIS Stone in Bladder Pref., The operation which I have described under the title of Lithectasy. 1876 GROSS Dis. Bladder 236 Professor Dolbeau..has performed the operation, which he terms perineal lithotrity, but which differs only from lithectasy in removing the calculus piecemeal.

lithectomy (lɪˈθɛktəmɪ). Surg. [f. Gr. λίθ-ος stone + ἐκ out + τομία cutting.] A proposed substitute for the inaccurate word LITHOTOMY (Syd. Soc. Lex. 1889).

lithed, obs. pa. t. LIGHT v.^{1}

lithely (ˈlaɪðlɪ), adv. [f. LITHE a. + -LY^{2}.]

†1. Gently, graciously, meekly, mildly. Obs.

c897 K. ÆLFRED Gregory's Past. xxi. 150 Hwilum liðelice to ðreatiȝeanne. a1225 Ancr. R. 428 Techeð ham to holden hore riulen..liðeliche þauh, & luueliche. a1240 Sawles Warde in Cott. Hom. 259 Wel is riht þat we þe liðeliche lustnin.

2. With pliant movement; briskly, nimbly.

1813 HOGG Queen's Wake 69 And quhen we cam to the Lommond height, Se lythlye we lychtid doune. 1854 Fraser's Mag. L. 398 Your line springs lithely into the air, hookless, and of course fishless.

litheness (ˈlaɪðnɪs). [f. LITHE a. + -NESS.]

†a. Gentleness, meekness, mildness. b. Flexibility, suppleness.

c1175 Lamb. Hom. 95 Erest he walde us mid liðnesse isteoren. c1375 Sc. Leg. Saints x. (Mathou) 445 Þe clergy.. with lythnes [had] byde goddis wrake. 1460 CAPGRAVE Chron. (Rolls) 52 Summe men seide that he [Aristotle] was the son of swech a spirit whech thei clepe Incubus, for the lithnes of his body, an the sotilte of his witte. 1530 PALSGR. 239/2 Lythenesse, delyvernesse, souplesse. 1642 ROGERS Naaman 458 Thou canst remove that utter unwillingnesse ..and cause lythnesse, and complying therewith. 1731 BAILEY vol. II, Litheness, suppleness, limberness. 1861 WILSON & GEIKIE Mem. E. Forbes xii. 402 The litheness of his body at this time was altogether surprising. 1877 BLACKIE Wise Men 20 To sinewy grasp and litheness bred.

†**ˈlither**, sb. Obs. [OE. lið(e)re:—prehistoric *liþrjôn-, f. *leþrom LEATHER.] A sling.

c725 Corpus Gloss. (Hessels) F 385 Funda, liðre. c900 tr. Bæda's Hist. IV. xvii. [xiii.] (1890) 304 Swa micelre brædo swa mon mæȝe mid liðeran ȝeweorpan. 1297 R. GLOUC. (Rolls) 8124 Me ne miȝte noȝt ise bote arwen & flon, & stones out of liþeren [v.r. leþeren].

lither (ˈlɪðə(r)), a. and adv. Forms: α. 1 lýðre, (hlýðre), léðre, (2 leoðre), 2–3 luðere, 3 leðere, luðre, (lui-, luyþer), 3–4 liðere, luther(e, 3–5 luðer, 4 luthur, luþur, lyþere, lythyre, 4–5 lethur, 5 lether, lethir(e, lethur, lithur, lythyr, (5 leither, 6 lytheir, liether, 3– lither. β. 5 ledyr, liddyr, lyder, -ir, -yr, 6 lidder, lydder, -ir, -yr. [OE. lýðre:—prehistoric *liuþrjo-; the first element of MHG., G. liederlich lewd (in early use also slight, trifling, pretty), and related by ablaut to LODDER. Some scholars regard the Gr. ἐλεύθερος and L. līber, free, as ultimately connected.]

A. adj.

†1. Of persons, their actions, dispositions, etc.: Bad, wicked; base, rascally unjust. Also of an animal: Ill-tempered. Obs.

c893 K. ÆLFRED Oros. VI. xxxvi, Ac se ealdormon hie betæhte lyþrum monnum to healdonne. c1000 Ags. Gosp. Luke xix. 22 Of þinum muðe ic ðe deme la lyðra þeowa. a1175 Cott. Hom. 241 Iudas and þat leoðre folc hit repen. a1225 Ancr. R. 256 He is umbe, deies & nihtes, uorte unlimen ow mid wreððe, oðer mid luðer onde. 1297 R. GLOUC. (Rolls) 1873 A luþer emperour biuore þat het maximian. 1340–70 Alex. & Dind. 272 Al luþur bi-leue we loþen in herte. 1362 LANGL. P. Pl. A. v. 98 Þus I liue loueles lyk A luþer dogge. a1400–50 Alexander 840 Sa he lost has þe lyfe for his leþer [Dublin MS. lether] wordis. a1529 SKELTON Agst. Garnesche 146 The follest slouen ondyr heuen, Prowde, peuiche, lyddyr, and lewde. 1546 J. HEYWOOD Prov. (1867) 39 All folke thought them..to lyther, To lynger bothe in one house togyther.

†b. absol. (quasi-sb.). sing. Evil in the abstract. pl. Bad men.

a1225 St. Marher 3 Ne ne let tu neauer mi sawle forleosen wiþ the forlorne ne wiþ the luðere mi lif. 13.. E.E. Allit. P. A. 566 Oþer ellez þyn yȝe to lyþer is lyfte. Ibid. B. 163 For alle arn laþed luflyly, þe luþer & þe better. 1340–70 Alex. & Dind. 629 Lede clanly ȝour lif & no luþur wirche. 1393 LANGL. P. Pl. C. XVIII. 82 Thus are þe lithere lykned to lussheborue sterlinges.

†2. Of things: Bad (in various senses, chiefly physical); poor, sorry, ill-conditioned, ill-looking, worthless; hurtful. Of a part of the body: Withered, paralysed, impotent. Obs.

c1000 ÆLFRIC Gen. xli. 27 Þa seofon hlænan oxan and þa seofon hlyðran ear ȝetacniað seofon hungerȝear. c1050 Suppl. Ælfric's Gloss. in Wr.-Wülcker 179/45 Lolium et cetera adulterina genera Boþen and oðre lyðre cynn. a1225 Ancr. R. 258 Þeo ilke reouðfulle garcen of þe luðere skurgen. 1297 R. GLOUC. (Rolls) 621 So þat a luþer beuerege to hare biofþe hii browe. 13.. E.E. Allit. P. C. 156 For be monnes lode neuer so luþer, þe lyf is ay swete. a1330 Otuel 942 Sore he fel oppon þe grounde, & hadde a fol luþer wonde. 1340–70 Alex. & Dind. 868 Þere-fore no like no lud of his luþur fare. 1377 LANGL. P. Pl. B. xv. 342 As in lussheborwes is a lyther alay and ȝet loketh he lyke a sterlynge. c1400 Ywaine & Gaw. 599 He passed..mony a playne, Til he come to that lethir sty, That him byhoved pass by. 1513 DOUGLAS Æneis VI. v. 17 His smotterit habit, our his schulderis lidder. 1549 CHALONER Erasm. on Folly F ij b, They..still daube theyr lither chekes with peintyng. 1556 ABP. PARKER Ps. xxxvi. Argument, He careth and carkth for his lytheir gayne. 1567 GOLDING Ovid's Met. XII. 152 b, And in his lither hand he hilld a potte of wyne. 1622 MABBE tr. Aleman's Guzman d'Alf. II. 7, I like them [radishes] better.. being thus lyther, and withered as you see, then when they are fresh and cripsie.

†b. of the air: Foul, pestilential. Obs.

1393 LANGL. P. Pl. C. XVI. 220 Founde ich þat..hus [the pope's] bulle myghte Letten þis luþer eir..Thenne wolde ich [etc.].

3. Lazy, sluggish, spiritless; also absol. Now dial.

c1460 Towneley Myst. xiii. 147 Crystys curs, my knaue thou art a ledyr hyne! 1501 DOUGLAS Pal. Hon. III. xxxiv, Behald ȝe men that callis ladyis lidder. 1529 LYNDESAY Complaynt 75 Thocht I be, in my askyng, lidder. c1560 A. SCOTT Poems (S.T.S.) ii. 68 Thair lanciss come to lidder & slaw. 1600 Look About You xi. c4 b, Ile bring his lyther legges in better frame. 1611 FLORIO, Badalone,..a lubbard, a lither, a loger head. 1632 J. HAYWARD tr. Biondi's Eromena 143 The qualitie of the Princesse her servants, was not so lither and effeminate..as [etc.]. 1675 HOBBES Odyss. (1677) 217 The man to see to was both great and tall, Though but a lither fellow. 1820 SCOTT Abbot iv, Thine own laziness.. that dost nothing but drink and sleep and leaves that lither lad to do the work. 1884 J. C. EGERTON Sussex Folks & Ways iv. 61 'Lither'..was quite familiar to him in the sense of 'idle, lazy'.

b. **lither lurden**: = 'lazy lout'. Hence **the lither lurden**: the disease of laziness = FEVER-LURDEN.

a1590 Marr. Wit & Wisd. (Shaks. Soc.) 13, I am alwayes troubled with the litherlurden. 1615 BRATHWAIT Strappado (1878) 129 What Iockie (lither lurden) lesse for wea, Thou'st be so tattert.

4. Pliant, supple; (of the air, sky) yielding. arch. Also, in mod. dialects (influenced by LITHE a.): Agile, nimble.

1565 COOPER Thesaurus, s.v. Brachium, Cerea brachia, Nice and liether armes. 1591 SHAKS. 1 Hen. VI, IV. vii. 21 Thou antique Death..Two Talbots winged through the lither Skie, In thy despight shall scape Mortalitie. c1600 DAY Begg. Bednall Gr. IV. ii. (1881) 82 Vanish, I know thou art but lither ayr, Thy hand fell lightly on me. 1643 BURROUGHES Exp. Hosea (1652) 102 They have wide, checker, lyther consciences. 1658 ROWLAND Moufet's Theat. Ins. 957 The Butterfly is a volatile Insect, having.. two lither cornicles growing forth from before his eyes. 1807 HOGG Mount. Bard, Mary of Moril Glen 103 With limbs as lydder and as lythe As duddis hung out to dry. 1860 MAURY Phys. Geog. Sea iv. §239 We see, as in a figure, the lither sky filled with crystal vessels full of life-giving air. 1891 MAXWELL GRAY In Heart of Storm I. 38 Boys..are made that lither and sprack they can't bide quiet long together.

†B. adv. Badly, wickedly; ill, poorly. Obs.

c1000 Christ & Satan 62 (Gr.) Habbað we alle swa for ðinum leasungum lyðre ȝefered. c1205 LAY. 2785 Ah toward his lifes ende him ilomp wel luðere [c1275 luþre]. a1225 Juliana 33 Þu biwistest daniel bimong þe wode liuns ilatet se luðere. c1300 Proverbs of Hendyng in Rel. Ant. I. 114 Lyht chep luthere ȝeldes.

Hence †ˈ**litherback**, a slothful person. †ˈ**litherhead**, wickedness.

1297 R. GLOUC. (Rolls) 9488 Þe godemen of þe lond hire luþerhede iseye. c1305 St. Kenelm 88 in E.E.P. (1862) 50 Heo turnede to folie & to liþerhede al hire þoȝt. 1577 tr. Bullinger's Decades (1592) 269 Hee must be no litherbacke, vnapt, or slothfull fellow.

†ˈ**lither**, v.^{1} Obs. [f. LITHER sb.]

a. trans. To hurl, shoot forth from (or as from) a sling. b. intr. To sling stones, to let fly. Const. to (= at).

a1225 Ancr. R. 290 Liðere to him luðerliche mid te holie rode steue. 1297 R. GLOUC. (Rolls) 11438 Hii wolde sir edward vawe out to hom sende Iliþered wiþ a mangenel, hom wiþ hom to lede. 1393 LANGL. P. Pl. C. XIX. 48 Þese lourdeines litheren þer-to þat alle þe leues fallen, And feccheth a-way this frut.

†ˈ**lither**, v.^{2} Obs. In 3 liðerien, lyþerien. [f. LITHER a.] intr. To act wickedly, to do harm.

a1300 E.E. Psalter xxv. 5 Kirke of liþerand [Vulg. ecclesiam malignantium] hated I. Ibid. xxxvi. 9 For þat liþeres, outend sal þai. Ibid. civ. 15 In mine prophetes nil lithre þou.

lither, liðere, obs. forms of LATHER v.

litherage, obs. form of LITHARGE.

†ˈ**litherby**. Obs. rare^{-1}. [f. LITHER a. + -BY (see -BY^{2}).] (See quot.)

1598 R. BERNARD tr. Terence, Andria I. iii. 19 Thers no time to plaie the litherbie now, or lasie lubber.

†ˈ**litherly**, a. Obs. [f. LITHER a. + -LY^{1}. OE. had lýþerlic in the sense of sordid, mean; cf. G. liederlich (mentioned s.v. LITHER a.).]

a. Spiteful, mischievous. b. Idle, lazy.

1573 TUSSER Husb. lxxxv. (1878) 174 Some litherly lubber more eateth than twoo, yet leaueth vndone that another will doo. a1643 W. CARTWRIGHT Ordinary II. ii. (1651) 25 What wends against the grain is lytherly. 1684 H. MORE Answer 24 To awaken them out of their remissness and litherly formalness. 1805 SCOTT Last Minstr. II. xxxii, He was waspish, arch and litherlie.

†ˈ**litherly**, adv. Obs. For forms see LITHER a. and -LY^{2}. [f. LITHER a. + -LY^{2}.] In a 'lither' manner.

a. Wickedly, deceitfully, viciously. b. Badly, meanly, miserably, wretchedly. c. Idly, lazily.

c1050 Suppl. Ælfric's Gloss. in Wr.-Wülcker 178/27 Pessime, luþerlice. a1225 St. Marher. 4 Thine forðfederes beoð..forloren luðerliche. c1250 Gen. & Ex. 1563 Ðin broðer iacob was her nu And toc ðin bliscing liðer-like. 13.. E.E. Allit. P. B. 36 What vrþly haþel..Wolde lyke, if a ladde com lyþerly attyred. c1350 Will. Palerne 1231 Leþerly as a lyoun he lepes in-to þe prese. c1386 CHAUCER Miller's T. 113 A clerk hadde litherly biset his whyle, But if he koude a Carpenter bigyle. ?a1400 Morte Arth. 1263 To unlordly he wyrkez, Thus letherly agaynes law to lede my pople. c1460 Towneley Myst. xiii. 171 Men say 'lyght chepe letherly for-yeldys'. 1550 COVERDALE Spir. Perle xvii. (1588) 167 Earnestly, manfully, and not litherly or faintly. a1583 ARBUTHNOT in Pinkerton Anc. Sc. Poems (1786) 144 Men wes sueir, and durst not steir; But lurkit lidderlie. 1600 HOLLAND Livy II. lviii. 83 Doing all things that they did, litherly, slowly, rekelesly and stubbornely.

†ˈ**litherness**. Obs. [f. LITHER a. + -NESS.]

1. Wickedness.

a1240 Ureisun in Cott. Hom. 197 Þu ne uorsakest nenne mon uor his luðernesse. 1297 R. GLOUC. (Rolls) 7999 His strengþe and is wisdom..He turnde to luþernesse, þo lanfranc was ded. 1340 HAMPOLE Pr. Consc. 226 Þis worlde .. es ful of pompe and lythernes.

2. Laziness, sloth, listlessness, indifference; want of spirit, cowardice. Also in physical sense, laxity.

c1425 WYNTOUN Cron. VI. iv. 355 He that lay in lythyrnes. 1523 SKELTON Garl. Laurel 733, I am not ladyn of liddyrnes with lumpis. 1570 SIR T. WILSON Demosthenes 17 Things lost by much letherness must be recovered againe by great diligence. 1603 FLORIO Montaigne (1634) 540 It is..uniust that the litherness of our wives, should be fostered with our sweat. 1656 W. D. tr. Comenius' Gate Lat. Unl. §617. 189 Shun both extremities; but sloath and litherness more. 1727 BRADLEY Fam. Dict. s.v. Dropsy, When the Dropsy proceeds from the real Indisposition..of the Liver, its known by.. Litherness or Supinity of the Belly.

lithesome (ˈlaɪðsəm), a. [f. LITHE a. + -SOME.] Pliant, supple, agile; = LISSOM.

1768–74 TUCKER Lt. Nat. (1834) I. 177 Nature may have ..made some of our organs more lithesome..than others. 1812 J. HENRY Camp. agst. Quebec 64 Smith was lithsome and quick afoot. 1863 KINGLAKE Crimea II. 428 The warlike carriage of the men, and their strong, lithesome, resolute step. 1882 SERJT. BALLANTINE Exper. v. (ed. 5) 248 My attention was attracted by an active lithesome old man.

lithia^{1} (ˈlɪθɪə). Chem. [a. mod.L. lithia, altered from LITHION, after soda, potassa. Cf. LITHINA.] The oxide of lithium, LiO.

1818 Jrnl. Sci. & Arts V. 337 Lithia (the name given to the new alkali) was first found in the petalite. 1819 [see LITHIUM]. 1826 HENRY Elem. Chem. I. 573 The acetate of lithia..was converted by calcination into carbonate of lithia. 1875 H. C. WOOD Therap. (1879) 497 Lithia..closely resembles potash in its effects upon the system.

b. attrib. and Comb., as **lithia salt, water; lithia-emerald** (see HIDDENITE); **lithia-mica** = LEPIDOLITE; **lithia-tourmaline** = RUBELLITE.

1854–68 DANA Min. (ed. 5) 314 Lepidolite..*Lithia-mica. 1879 RUTLEY Study Rocks xii. 211 Greisen is a granular-crystalline rock, consisting of quartz and mica, the latter usually lithia-mica. 1842 PARNELL Chem. Anal. (1845) 50 A *lithia salt. 1878 KINGZETT Anim. Chem. 201 *Lithia water is often prescribed to gouty..persons.

c. colloq. Short for lithia water.

1893 SALTUS Sapphira 21 Mr. Snaith..refreshed himself with whisky and lithia.

‖**lithia**^{2} (ˈlɪθɪə). Path. [mod.L., f. Gr. λίθος stone.] The formation of sand or stony concretions in the body, esp. in the Meibomian follicles of the eye. (Cf. LITHIASIS.)

1822–34 Good's Study Med. (ed. 4) IV. 255 Tendency to the separation or production of a morbid superabundance of calcareous earth in Osthexia and Lithia. 1842 DUNGLISON Med. Lex., Lithia, the formation of stone or gravel in the human body. Also, an affection in which the eyelids are edged with small, hard, and stone-like concretions. 1889 in Syd. Soc. Lex.

lithian (ˈlɪθɪən), a. Min. [f. LITH(IUM + -IAN 2.] Of a mineral: having a (small) proportion of a constituent element replaced by lithium.

1930 W. T. SCHALLER in Amer. Mineralogist XV. 571 Lithium—lithian. 1953 Ibid. XXXVIII. 91 The following characteristics of lithian muscovite illustrate its close structural similarity to normal muscovite. 1964 Ibid. XLIX. 398 (heading) Lithian hureaulite from the Black Hills.

‖**lithiasis** (lɪˈθaɪəsɪs). Path. [mod.L. lithiasis, Gr. λιθίασις, f. λιθιᾶν, f. λίθος stone.] The

formation of stony concretions in any part of the body, *esp.* in the bladder and urinary passages.

1657 *Physical Dict.*, Lithiasis, the disease of the stone, engendered in a mans body. **1727-41** CHAMBERS *Cycl.* s.v. *Stone*, The *lithiasis*, or the disposition of the kidneys and bladder to generate stones. **1835** G. GREGORY *Theory & Pract. Med.* (ed. 4) 567 The foundation of our reasonings concerning lithiasis. **1855** MAYNE *Expos. Lex.*, *Lithiasis*. Name given to a disease of the eyelids, in which small hard tumours grow upon their margins. **1866** A. FLINT *Princ. Med.* (1880) 906 The discharge from the body of urinary concretions.. constitutes lithiasis or gravel.

lithiate, *sb.*: see LITHATE.

lithiated (ˈlɪθɪeɪtɪd), *ppl. a.* [Two formations: (1) f. LITH(IC) + -ATE + -ED[1]; (2) f. LITHI-UM + -ATE + -ED[1].] †**a.** Combined with 'lithic' (now called *uric*) acid (*obs.*). **b.** Impregnated with a salt of lithium.

1797 WOLLASTON in *Phil. Trans.* LXXXVII. 389 Gouty matter is lithiated soda. **1884** *Nonconf. & Indep.* 11 Sept. 883/2 Another form of soda is the lithiated compound phosphate. [**1890** *Century Dict.*, *Lithiate*, v., to impregnate with a salt of lithium.]

lithic (ˈlɪθɪk), *a.*[1] and *sb.* [ad. Gr. λιθικός, f. λίθος stone.] **A.** *adj.*

1. *Chem.* and *Path.* Of or pertaining to 'stone' or calculi in the bladder. †*lithic acid*: an obsolete name for uric acid.

1797 WOLLASTON in *Phil. Trans.* LXXXVII. 386 A peculiar concrete acid, which, since his [Scheele's] time has received the name of lithic. *Ibid.* 393 The appearance of the lithic strata.. shews that they are.. an accidental deposit. **1803** *Med. Jrnl.* IX. 350 Small quantities of uncombined lithic, or, as it is now called, uric acid. **1821** W. PROUT *Gravel, Calculus*, etc. 223 A small or moderately sized lithic calculus in the bladder. **1845** BUDD *Dis. Liver* 37 The efficacy of alkalies in preventing the deposit of lithic gravel in the urine. **1851** CARPENTER *Man. Phys.* (ed. 2) 445 Urinary deposits, which consist of the normal elements of the Urine,—namely, Lithic Acid, and the Phosphates. **1876** GROSS *Dis. Bladder* 180 The uric, or lithic, acid calculus.

2. *gen.* Of or pertaining to stone; consisting of stone. *lithic age*, the 'stone age' of Archæology.

1862 LOWELL *Biglow P.* 93 This remarkable example of lithick literature. [Quasi-archaic.] **1865-7** J. FERGUSSON *Hist. Archit.* (1874) I. 35 The best lithic ornaments are those which approach nearest to the grace and pliancy of plants. **1874** *Contemp. Rev.* XXIV. 762 The architecture.. of St. Paul's is lithic, and suitable to no other material than stone. **1883** N. JOLY *Man bef. Metals* I. i. §3. 23 Even in our day groups of men exist who are still in their lithic age. **1946** F. E. ZEUNER *Dating Past* vii. 208 The lithic industries of the Grotte de l'Observatoire were described by Boule. **1971** *Nature* 6 Aug. 383/2 Although other human remains that may be attributed provisionally to *Homo erectus* have been found at Olduvai,.. the discoveries at [site] WK are the first occasion on which a well represented lithic industry has been directly associated. **1971** *World Archaeol.* III. 144 There is a need for studies of lithic technology.

B. *sb.* A medicine given for stone in the bladder (Funk's *Stand. Dict.* 1893).

lithic (ˈlɪθɪk), *a.*[2] *Chem.* [f. LITH-IUM + -IC.] Pertaining to lithium. *lithic paint* (see quot.).

1875 KNIGHT *Dict. Mech.*, *Lithic Paint*, a mastic of petalite (which contains an alkali known as lithia), sand, and litharge, used as a coating for walls. **1878** LOCKYER *Spectrum Analysis* vi. (ed. 2) 160 Lithic Iodide gave the red line of this metal extending all across the spectrum.

lithifaction (lɪθɪˈfækʃən). [f. LITHI(FY *v.* + -FACTION (cf. *petrifaction*).] = LITHIFICATION.

1893 *Compte Rendu 5me Sess. Congrès Géol. Internat.* 160 The formations of the Coastal plain range in age from Pleistocene to early Cretaceous or late Jurassic..; all, indeed, are commonly unconsolidated and lithifaction is local and exceptional. **1971** I. G. GASS et al. *Understanding Earth* xix. 264/1 Sediments in various degrees of lithifaction. **1972** *Islander* (Victoria, B.C.) 1 Oct. 13/3 According to James T. Fyles, geologist with the department of mines, these concretions are formed during the process of lithifaction of sand.

lithification (ˌlɪθɪfɪˈkeɪʃən). [f. next: see -FICATION.] The process of forming into stone.

1872 *Amer. Jrnl. Sci.* Dec. 468 Even the former moderate temperature.. would be sufficient to produce incipient change—at least lithification, if not metamorphism. In fact, lithification of sediments will probably take place under heavy pressure even at ordinary temperature. **1877** LE CONTE *Elem. Geol.* (1879) 221 The cause of joints is probably the shrinkage of the rock in the act of consolidation from sediments (lithification), as in stratified rocks. **1971** I. G. GASS et al. *Understanding Earth* xiii. 165/1 The lithification of the soft sediments after deposition.

lithify (ˈlɪθɪfaɪ), *v.* [f. Gr. λίθ-ος stone + -(I)FY.] *trans.* To form into stone. Chiefly as **ˈlithified** *pa. pple.* and *ppl. a.*

1877 LE CONTE *Elem. Geol.* v. (1879) 478 All these deposits are imperfectly lithified sand and clays in nearly horizontal position. *Ibid.* 480 The rocks of this period.. are mostly imperfectly lithified. **1937** *Geogr. Jrnl.* LXXXIX. 9 This is the normal beach-rock—lithified sands containing a few boulders of coral here and there. **1963** D. W. & E. E. HUMPHRIES tr. *Termier's Erosion & Sedimentation* x. 215 When clays are lithified by compaction and cementation, they become mudstones or limestones with fossil mud cracks on their surfaces. **1971** *Nature* 2 Apr. 287/1 The rock was thus almost certainly lithified during the lower relative sea level of the Pleistocene.

†**lithina.** *Chem. Obs.* [mod.L., altered from the earlier name LITHION; cf. -INE[5]. The Fr. name is still *lithine*.] = LITHIA[1].

1826 [see LITHION].

†**ˈlithion.** *Chem.* [mod.L., as if Gr. λίθειον, neut. of λίθειος adj., stony, f. λίθος stone; the name was proposed in 1818 by Berzelius for the fixed alkali discovered by Arfwedsson in 1817, to designate its *mineral* origin, the two previously known being of vegetable origin.] An earlier name for LITHIA[1].

1818 W. PHILLIPS *Outl. Min. & Geol.* (ed. 3) Advt., Of the new fixed Alkali, Lithion. **1825** *Amer. Jrnl. Sci.* IX. 330 A very useful test for lithion. **1826** HENRY *Elem. Chem.* I. 572 To distinguish it from the two other fixed alkalis, both of vegetable origin, it received the name of lithion, (from λίθειος, *lapideus*;) and this term, to suit the analogy of the other alkalis, was afterwards converted into lithia or lithina.

attrib. **1856** *Qly. Jrnl. Geol. Soc.* XII. II. 11 The metallic base of the lithion-alkali. *Ibid.* Petalite, Lithion-spodumen [etc.].

lithionite (ˈlɪθɪənaɪt). *Min.* [f. LITHION + -ITE.] An obsolete synonym of LEPIDOLITE.

1884 BAUERMAN *Descr. Mineralogy* 201 Zinnwaldite, Lithionite, Cryophyllite—apparent axial angle up to 65°. **1896** in A. H. CHESTER *Names Min.*

lithiophilite (lɪθɪˈɒfɪlaɪt). *Min.* [A name given, 1878, by Brush and Dana; f. LITHI-UM + Gr. φίλ-ος friend + -ITE.] A mineral containing a large proportion of lithium.

1878 *Amer. Jrnl. Sci.* XVI. 118 No crystals of Lithiophilite were found. **1892** DANA *Min.* 757 Lithiophilite occurs at Branchville, Fairfield Co., Conn.

lithiophorite (ˌlɪθɪˈɒfəraɪt). *Min.* [ad. G. *lithiophorit* (O. Breithaupt 1870, in *Jrnl. f. prakt. Chem.* CX. 205): see LITHIUM, -O, and -ITE[1].] A basic oxide of aluminium, lithium, and manganese $(Al,Li)MnO_2(OH)_2$, found as bluish-black monoclinic crystals.

1871 *Jrnl. Chem. Soc.* XXIV. 205 Lithiophorite is amorphous, occurs in compact botryoïdal and reniform masses, in flat shell-like forms, and in pseudomorphs after calcspar. **1932** *Amer. Mineralogist* XVII. 149 Material which in the past has been classified as psilomelane may actually be.. lithiophorite, previously considered as a variety of psilomelane containing lithium and aluminium, but which the *x*-ray pattern shows to be a distinct mineral. **1952** *Acta Crystallogr.* V. 676/2 Lithiophorite has a layer structure with alternate sheets of MnO_6 and $(Al,Li)(OH)_6$ octahedra placed one on top of the other. **1970** *Mineral. Mag.* XXXVII. 618 Lithiophorite.. is one of the major mineral forms of nodular manganese in Australian soils.

lithistid (lɪˈθɪstɪd), *a.* and *sb.* [ad. mod.L. *Lithistida* (O. Schmidt *Grundzüge einer Spongien-fauna des Atlantischen Gebietes* (1870) ii. 21), f. Gr. λίθος stone + ἱστός web: see -ID.]

a. *sb.* A silicious sponge of the group *Lithistida*, in which the spicules are articulated to form a silicious skeleton. **b.** *adj.* Pertaining to or having the character of the *Lithistida*.

1885 J. E. TAYLOR *Our Common Brit. Fossils* i. 26 Sections of it show it to belong to the *lithistids*. **1892** *Athenæum* 13 Feb. 218/2 Tetractinellid, lithistid, and hexactinellid spicules are also present. **1894** *Geol. Mag.* Oct. 467 Lithistid sponges from the Upper Cambrian of the Mingan Islands are better preserved. **1972** P. MEGLITSCH *Invertebr. Zool.* (ed. 2) v. 98/2 Desmas are often cemented together to form a solid meshwork, or lithistid skeleton.

lithistidan (lɪˈθɪstɪdən), *sb.* and *a.* = LITHISTID. In some recent Dicts.

lithium (ˈlɪθɪəm). *Chem.* [f. LITHIA[1]: see -IUM.] A metallic element of the alkaline group occurring in small quantities in various minerals.

1818 *Jrnl. Sci. & Arts* V. 338 The chloride of lithium.. is a white semi-transparent body. **1819** BRANDE *Man. Chem.* 201 A.. substance is separated, which may be called *lithium*, the term *lithia* being applied to its oxide. **1851** RICHARDSON *Geol.* v. 81 Three metallic bases of the alkalis—potassium, sodium, and lithium. **1873** WATTS *Fownes' Chem.* (ed. 11) 69 Lithium shows a bright brilliant line in the red.

attrib. **1871** ROSCOE *Elem. Chem.* 213 The lithium salts were formerly supposed to be very rare. **1873** RALFE *Phys. Chem.* 99 Twenty grains of lithium carbonate.

litho (ˈlɪθəʊ, now more usually ˈlaɪθəʊ). A techn. abbrev. of LITHOGRAPH. Also, abbrev. of LITHOGRAPHIC, LITHOGRAPHY.

1890 in *Century Dict.* **1896** *Daily News* 27 July 4/4 Litho artists jostled the bricklayer, and the bricklayer joined hands with the baker. **1897** *Westm. Gaz.* 5 Apr. 7/3 There was no difference between the ordinary stone lithos and the transfer paper lithos. **1903** *Brit. Printer* Jan. 40/1 The *Gazette* is the organ of the litho trade. **1915** *Southward's Mod. Printing* (ed. 3) II. xxxiii. 284 A number of transfers may be laid down on the stone, and from such litho prints there is, of course, no impression on the back. **1946** A. KIRK in H. Whetton *Pract. Printing & Binding* xvi. 190/1 Part of the very extensive mail-order catalogue business of America.. is printed from the web by litho-offset at very high speeds. **1948** *Sci. News* VII. 100 A simple processing technique resulted in litho printing plates ready for use. *Ibid.*, Litho printers. **1965** S. C. GILMOUR *Paper* (ed. 2) xix. 236 Litho offset ink is normally stiffer than that used for letterpress. **1972** *Nature* 17 Mar. 101/2 This printing is done quite quickly by the Ordnance Survey by litho directly from the typescripts. **1973** *Times Lit. Suppl.* 7 Dec. 1492/2 One other contributory factor has been the growth of film-setting, which composes letters directly on to film, whence they can be directly transferred to a litho printing plate. *Ibid.* 1518/1 Letterpress, although progressively eroded by litho, still prints about 50 per cent of bookwork.

Also (abbrev. of LITHOGRAPH *v.* 1) as *vb.*

1934 J. A. LEE *Children of Poor* (1949) VI. 205, I would print or litho intricate design in varied colour.

litho- (lɪθəʊ), before a vowel **lith-**, combining form of Gr. λίθος stone, in many scientific terms (the more important appear as main words): ‖**lithobiblion** (-ˈbɪblɪɒn) *Geol.* [Gr. βίβλιον book], a laminated schistose rock; a bibliolite (Webster 1828-32); **lithobiotic** (-baɪˈɒtɪk) *a.* [Gr. βιωτικός, f. βίος life], pertaining to the natural state of crystals, minerals, and stones (Mayne *Expos. Lex.* 1856); hence **lithobiotism** (-ˈbaɪətɪz(ə)m), the hidden or undeveloped existence of crystals, etc. (*ibid.*); **ˈlithocarp** (-kɑːp) [Gr. καρπός fruit], 'a fossil or petrified fruit; a carpolite' (Webster 1828-32); **lithochryˈsography** [Gr. χρυσός gold + -GRAPHY], printing in gold on stone; †**ˈlithocol, -colla** [Gr. κόλλα glue]: see quot.; **lithoˈcoralline** [CORALLINE], pertaining to or having the character of the *Lithocorallia* or stone-corals; (in recent Dicts.); **lithocyˈst-otomy** *Surg.* [CYSTOTOMY] = LITHOTOMY (Billings *Nat. Med. Dict.* 1890); ‖**lithodiˈalysis** *Surg.* [DIALYSIS], an operation by which stone in the bladder is dissolved (Mayne); hence ˌ**lithodiaˈlytic** *a.*, pertaining to lithodialysis (*ibid.*); **ˈlithofacies** *Geol.*, a facies (FACIES 2b) distinguished by its lithological character (see quot. 1949[2]); **lithofellic** (-ˈfɛlɪk), **-fellinic** (-fɛˈlɪnɪk) *adjs. Chem.* [L. *fel* gall, bile], the designation of an acid which is a large constituent of bezoars; ‖**lithofracteur** (-ˈfræktœ(r)) [Fr. (L. *fractor* breaker)], an explosive compound of nitroglycerine, used for blasting; **lithoˈfractor** [L. *fractor* breaker] = LITHOCLAST (*Syd. Soc. Lex.* 1889); **lithoˈgenesis, -genesy** (-ˈdʒɛnɪsɪ) [-GENESIS, Gr. -γενεσία], that department of mineralogy which treats of the formation of stones; also, the formation of rock; **lithogenous** (lɪˈθɒdʒɪnəs) *a.* [Gr. -γενής producing + -OUS], stone-producing: applied to those animals which produce coral; **lithogeny** (lɪˈθɒdʒɪnɪ) *Path.* [see -GENY], (*a*) the formation of calculi (*Syd. Soc. Lex.* 1889); (*b*) *Geol.* (*rare*) = *lithogenesis* above; **litholabe** (ˈlɪθəleɪb), also in mod.L. form †**-labon** *Surg.* [late Gr. λιθολάβος, f. λαβ- to seize, take], an instrument for extracting stone from the bladder or for holding it while being operated upon; **litholapaxy** (-ləˈpæksɪ) *Surg.* [Gr. λάπαξις evacuation], an operation for crushing stone in the bladder and evacuating it; **litholatry** (-ˈɒlətrɪ) [see -LATRY], stone-worship (Ogilvie 1882); so **liˈtholatrous** *a.*, stone-worshipping (*Cent. Dict.*); **litholeine** (lɪˈθəʊlɪɪn) [L. *oleum* oil + -INE[5]], 'a yellow oily liquid distilled from petroleum, used in eczema and parasitic skin-diseases' (*Cent. Dict.*); ‖**litholysis** (lɪˈθɒlɪsɪs) *Surg.* [Gr. λύσις solution], the dissolving of stone in the bladder by means of lithotriptic injections (*Syd. Soc. Lex.*); hence **ˈlitholyte** (-laɪt) [G. -λυτης solvent], 'a form of catheter for conveying solvents of calculi into the bladder' (Knight *Dict. Mech.* 1875); **litholytic** (-ˈlɪtɪk) *a.*, pertaining to litholysis (*Syd. Soc. Lex.*); **lithometer** (-ˈɒmɪtə(r)), an instrument for measuring the size of a stone in the bladder (*ibid.*); also *attrib.*; **lithomyl** (ˈlɪθəmɪl) [Gr. μύλη mill], an instrument devised for reducing calculi to powder; hence **lithomyly** (-ˈɒmɪlɪ), the use of the lithomyl (*ibid.*); ‖ˌ**lithoneˈphritis** *Path.* [NEPHRITIS], calculous inflammation of the kidney (*ibid.*); **lithoneˈphrotomy** *Surg.* = NEPHROLITHOTOMY (Billings *Nat. Med. Dict.* 1890); ‖**lithopædion, -ium** (-ˈpiːdɪɒn, -ɪəm) [Gr. παιδίον little child], a dead extra-uterine fœtus, impregnated with calcareous matter; **lithophagous** (-ˈɒfəgəs) *a.* [Gr. -φάγος eating], stone-eating; applied esp. to molluscs which bore through stones; ‖**liˈthophagus**, a stone-eater; pl. (-i), lithophagous animals; **lithophane** (ˈlɪθəfeɪn) [Gr. -φανής appearing], a kind of ornamentation produced by impressing upon porcelain-glass in a soft state figures which are made visible by transmitted light (Ogilvie 1882); so **lithophanic** (-ˈfænɪk) *a.*, pertaining to lithophane or lithophany; **lithophany** (-ˈɒfənɪ) [cf. F. *lithophanie* (also used)], the art of making ornamented glass of this kind; (see also quot. 1904); **ˈlithophil(e, lithoˈphilic** *adjs. Geol.* and

Chem. [ad. G. *lithophil* (V. M. Goldschmidt 1923, in *Skrifter utgit av Videnskapsselsk. I. Mat.-nat. Kl.* III. 5); see -PHIL, -PHILE], applied to elements which are commonly found as silicates and are supposed to have concentrated in the outermost zone when the earth was molten; **lithophilous** (-'ɒfɪləs) *a.* [-φιλος loving], applied to insects living in stony places and to plants growing upon rocks (Mayne *Expos. Lex.* 1856 and *Syd. Soc. Lex.*); **litho'phosphor** [PHOSPHOR], a stone which becomes phosphorescent when heated (Webster 1828–32); hence **,lithophos'phoric** *a.*, becoming phosphorescent when heated (Craig 1848); **,lithopho'tography** = PHOTOLITHOGRAPHY; ‖**litho'phthisis** *Path.* [PHTHISIS], the stage of tubercular phthisis in which calcareous concretions are present in the lungs (Mayne); **lithophyll** ('lɪθəfɪl) *Palæont.* [Gr. φύλλον leaf], a fossil leaf or the impression of a leaf, or a stone containing such a leaf or its impression (*Syd. Soc. Lex.*); ‖**lithophysa** (lɪθəʊ'faɪsə), **lithophyse** ('lɪθəfaɪs) [Gr. φῦσα bellows], a spherulite having a concentrically chambered structure (*Cent. Dict.*); **'lithopone** [Gr. πόνος work, anything produced by work], a mixture of zinc sulphide and barium sulphate used as a white pigment in paint, linoleum, and printing ink, and as a filler in paper; **'lithoscope** *Surg.* [see -SCOPE], an instrument used to determine the size and form of a calculus (Mayne); †**li'thoscopist**, ? one who examines stones; **'lithosere** *Ecol.* [SERE], a plant succession having its origin on bare rock; **'lithosol** *Soil Sci.* [-SOL], any azonal soil consisting largely of imperfectly weathered rock fragments; **lithosphere** ('lɪθəsfɪə(r)) [SPHERE], a term (corresponding to *atmosphere* and *hydrosphere*) used by some to designate the crust of the earth; in mod. use, usu. applied to the crust and the upper part of the mantle; formerly also used for the crust together with the whole interior portion of the earth, or the crust together with the entire mantle; hence **litho'spheric** *a.*; **,lithostra'tigraphy** *Geol.*, stratigraphy based on the physical and petrographic characters of rocks, rather than on fossils; so **,lithostrati'graphic, -'graphical** *adjs.*; **,lithothe'ology**, natural theology as illustrated by the study of stones; **'lithotint** [TINT *sb.*], the art or process of printing tinted pictures from lithographic stones; a picture so printed; so **'lithotinted** *ppl. a.*; ‖**lithu'resis, -'uria** *Path.* [Gr. οὔρησις, -ουρία urination], the passing of small calculi with the urine (Mayne *Expos. Lex.* 1856); ‖**lithuro'rrhœa**, calculous diabetes (*ibid.*).

1845 FORD *Handbk. Sp.* I. II. 361 This new style of printing in Gold and colours on stone, this '*Lithochrysography' and 'Lithocromatography'. **1696** PHILLIPS (ed. 5), **Lithocol*, the Cement with which the Stones are fastned, when they are cut, under the Grindstone; made of Pitch, Resin, and old Brick. **1706** *Ibid.* (ed. Kersey), **Lithocolla*. **1946** M. KAY in *Progr. Rep. Res. Comm. Amer. Assoc. Petroleum Geologists* 15 Jan. 4 The forms present in any population are influenced by age, but also by habitat reflected in lithology (*lithofacies). **1949** R. C. MOORE in *Mem. Geol. Soc. Amer.* XXXIX. 16 It seems clear that 'facies' should not be used in double manner to refer also to this type of differentiation, and I suggest the term 'lithofacies'..as appropriate for such meaning. *Ibid.* 32 The rock record of any sedimentary environment, including both physical and organic characters, is designated by the term 'lithofacies'. **1958** *Bull. Amer. Assoc. Petroleum Geologists* XLII. 2729 The term lithofacies seems to have been introduced by the Russian geologist Eberzin (1940: *fide* Markevich, 1957). When and by whom it was launched in America is not clear from available references. Soon after 1945 it appeared in publications and was used in the sense given above. **1968** R. W. FAIRBRIDGE *Encycl. Geomorphol.* 92/1 (*heading*) Braided stream lithofacies. **1839–47** TODD *Cycl. Anat.* III. 805/1 *Lithofellic acid. **1852** *Fownes' Chem.* (1859) 566 Oriental bezoar stones..consist essentially of a ..*lithofellinic acid. **1875** KNIGHT *Dict. Mech.*, **Lithofracteur*. **1883** *Times* 24 Nov. 7 Dynamite, lithofracteur, or any similar nitro-glycerine compounds. **1909** *Cent. Dict.* Suppl., **Lithogenesis*, the production or origin of minerals or rocks; lithogenesy. **1937** WOOLDRIDGE & MORGAN *Physical Basis Geogr.* vi. 82 The period of lithogenesis, during which the rocks later to form the range are accumulated. **1956** 'H. MACDIARMID' *Stony Limits & Scots Unbound* 42 All is lithogenesis—or lochia,..Stones blacker than any in the Caaba. **1963** D. W. & E. E. HUMPHRIES tr. *Termier's Erosion & Sedimentation* 405 The cycle of geological phenomena comprises lithogenesis or petrogenesis, orogenesis, then glyptogenesis. **1828–32** WEBSTER (citing *Dict. Nat. Hist.*), **Lithogenesy*. **1832** LYELL *Princ. Geol.* II. 288 The operations of *lithogenous polyps. **1888** J. J. H. TEALL *Brit. Petrogr.* 437 **Lithogeny*, that department of petrology which treats of the formation of rocks. **1958** *Contrib. Cushman Found. Foraminiferal Res.* IX. 106/2 The Illinois cyclothem comprises a widely consistent, repetitious succession of rock types whose lithogeny records the environmental changes of the place and time in considerable detail. Various aspects of the lithogenesis, biology, and ecology of the sedimentary units in the Illinois and related kinds of cyclothems have been described. **1846** BRITTAN tr. *Malgaigne's Man. Oper. Surg.* 534 Push the external canula as far forwards as possible on the *litholabe. **1731** BAILEY vol. II, **Litholabon*. **1878** BIGELOW in *Trans. Lond. Clinical Soc.* XII. 24 This method, which I have called *litholapaxy, its peculiar feature being evacuation. **1891** tr. *De La Saussaye's Man. Sci. Relig.* xii. 89 Tree worship is as widely spread as *litholatry. **1856** R. DRUITT *Surgeon's Vade Mecum* IV. xx. (ed. 7) 576 *Litholysis, or solution of stone. **1860** in *Lancet* 25 Aug. 185 (title) Calculus in the Bladder treated by Litholysis. **1876** GROSS *Dis. Bladder* 221 Sect. II. Litholysis. **1842** R. WILLIS *Stone in Bladder* i. 30 The stone in the bladder was caught ..by means of a *lithometer. **1895** ERICHSEN *Sci. & Art Surg.* (ed. 10) II. 1077 Lithometer Sound for measuring Stone. **1822** GOOD *Study Med.* IV. 257 An osseous or almost stony mass, which has been distinguished by the name of osteopædion or *lithopædion. **1896** *Allbutt's Syst. Med.* I. 195 The *lithopædium of extra-uterine gestation. **1828–32** WEBSTER, **Lithophagous*. **1835–6** TODD *Cycl. Anat.* I. 704/1 The lithophagous..Conchifera. **1827** *Mirror* I. 8 There was brought to Avignon a true *lithophagus, or stone-eater. **1833** LYELL *Princ. Geol.* III. Gloss. *Lithophagi*, molluscous animals which bore into solid stones. **1947** M. PENKALA *Europ. Porc.* 32 The *lithophane process..involved the use of white biscuit plaques of varying thickness. **1960** R. G. HAGGAR *Conc. Encycl. Cont. Pott. & Porc.* 269/1 Some of the German porcelain factories made effective use of the lithophane for lamp shades and sconces. **1970** G. SAVAGE *Dict. Antiques* 244/2 Lithophanes were first modelled in translucent wax, the object of the craftsman being to remove sufficient wax to give the desired amount of light transmission, building up his picture from dark and light passages. **1828** *Specif. Patent* No. 5626 *Lithophanic china. **1861** F. JOUBERT in *Jrnl. Soc. Arts* IX. 500/2 A process known as *lithophany, or transparent china, or biscuit slabs. **1866** W. CHAFFERS *Marks Pott. & Porc.* (ed. 2) 431 At the Berlin manufactory *Lithophanie* was invented. **1904** E. DILLON *Porcelain* xvi. 264 Another application of porcelain was to the 'transparencies' or *lithophanie*, in which the design, as seen by transmitted light, was given by variations in the thickness of the paste. **1923** *Mineral. Abstr.* II. 159 Corresponding with the zones of the earth postulated in the preceding papers, the chemical elements are divided into four main groups: (1) Siderophil elements..; (2) Chalcophil elements..; (3) *Lithophil elements of silicate fusions (O, Si, Ti, F, Cl, Al, Ce, Na, K, Be, Mg, Ca, V, &c.); (4) Atmophil elements. **1950** RANKAMA & SAHAMA *Geochem.* iv. 91 The lithophile metals form ions of the noble-gas type having 8 electrons in the outermost shell. **1965** PHILLIPS & WILLIAMS *Inorg. Chem.* I. xvi. 598 Goldschmidt quoted the following elements: Fe Co Ni [etc.]..as concentrating in terrestrial sulphides (chalcophil) rather than in silicates (lithophil). **1973** *Nature* 28 Sept. 204/1 The entry into or rejection of lithophile ions from silicate lattices is dependent on size and valency *inter alia*. **1971** *Ibid.* 27 Aug. 606/1 Elements like Be and Th..are strongly *lithophilic under both crustal and mantle conditions. **1854** FAIRHOLT *Dict. Terms Art*, **Lithophotography*, the modern art of producing prints from lithographic stones, by means of photographic pictures developed on their surface. **1892** *Athenæum* 21 May 670/3 The *Lithophyses in the Obsidian of the Rocche Rosse, Lipari. *a* **1884** KNIGHT *Dict. Mech.* Suppl. 551/2 *Lithopone. **1902** *Jrnl. Soc. Chem. Industry* 31 Mar. 427/1 'Lithopone' is prepared by mixing together solutions of barium sulphide and zinc sulphate, the precipitate of $ZnS,BaSO_4$ being then washed, dried, and ignited. **1923** U. R. EVANS *Metals & Metallic Compounds* II. 156 Lithopone is a comparatively cheap pigment, and is much used for flat wall paints and the cheaper grade of enamel paints. **1961** J. P. CASEY *Pulp & Paper* (ed. 2) III. xx. 1830 Lithopone has been known to cause trouble in coated offset papers by reacting with the acid in the fountain water. **1693** E. LHUYD *Let.* 18 Apr. in *Gentl. Mag.* (1822) XCII. I. 318, I have been all this while expecting the return of our *Lithoscopist. **1916** F. E. CLEMENTS *Plant Succession* ix. 182 While the surfaces of rock and of dune-sand may be almost equally dry, the differences of hardness and stability result in very dissimilar adseres. These may be distinguished as *lithoseres..and psammoseres. **1960** N. POLUNIN *Introd. Plant Geogr.* xi. 325 As a characteristic xerosere we will take a lithosere initiated on bare rock. **1939** *U.S. Dept. Agric. Yearbk. 1938* 1171 **Lithosols* (skeletal soils), an azonal group of soils having no clearly expressed soil morphology and consisting of a freshly and imperfectly weathered mass of rock fragments. **1968** H. C. T. STACE et al. *Handbk. Austral. Soils* iii. 35 Lithosols are found throughout Australia wherever natural erosion has been active enough to maintain a thin soil cover. **1887** *Times* 6 Sept. 11/3 The form of the *lithosphere and the material of its surface. **1893** A. GEIKIE *Text-bk. Geol.* (ed. 3) 38 (*heading*) The solid globe or lithosphere. **1900** *Pop. Sci. Monthly* LVI. 436 Thus were formed the oceanic basin and the continental arches of the lithosphere. **1910** LAKE & RASTALL *Text-bk. Geol.* i. 8 The Lithosphere or solid part of the earth, so far as it is open to our inspection, consists of rocks. **1950** RANKAMA & SAHAMA *Geochem.* ii. 32 The Sial crust, which is the surface layer of the silicate shell of the Earth (the lithosphere), is composed of three groups of rocks of different origin. **1957** G. E. HUTCHINSON *Treat. Limnol.* I. iv. 222 The water content of the major part of the lithosphere, the great mantle of ultrabasic rock which composes most of the earth, is unknown. **1971** I. G. GASS et al. *Understanding Earth* xvi. 248/1 As a result of seismological studies, it has been realised that the Earth's outermost skin, or lithosphere, which exhibits appreciable strength and rigidity, extends well beneath both continental and oceanic crusts to depths of 50 or even 100 km. **1973** M. W. MCELHINNY *Palaeomagnetism & Plate Tectonics* v. 156 In this 'new global tectonics'.., now generally referred to as Plate Tectonics, it is supposed that a mobile, near-surface layer of strength (the lithosphere) plays a key role... The lithosphere, which generally includes the crust and uppermost mantle, has significant strength, and is of the order of 100 km thickness. The asthenosphere, which is a layer of effectively no strength on the appropriate time scale, extends from the base of the lithosphere to a depth of several hundred kilometres. **1970** *Nature* 5 Sept. 1016/1 At ridge crests the *lithospheric plates are thinned by the elevation of the geotherms as a result of mantle upwelling and emplacement. **1971** I. G. GASS et al. *Understanding Earth* xi. 153 (*caption*) Biospheric, lithospheric and atmospheric evolution on the primitive Earth. **1950** *Bull. Amer. Petroleum Geologists* XXXIV. 2365 Our repeated efforts to treat stage and zone as true time-stratigraphic units have met with failure. Since these are biostratigraphic or *lithostratigraphic in character.. we have no logical choice but to place them also in a category by themselves. **1970** *Earth-Sci. Rev.* VI. 270 The formation is the fundamental unit in lithostratigraphic classification. **1964** J. CHALLINOR *Dict. Geol.* (ed. 2) 144/2 *Lithostratigraphical unit. **1969** *Proc. Geol. Soc.* Aug. 141 For the description of stratified rocks lithostratigraphical procedure is already generally agreed. **1956** *Bull. Amer. Assoc. Petroleum Geologists* XL. 2711 (*heading*) Factors in *lithostratigraphy. **1969** *Proc. Geol. Soc.* Aug. 155 The boundaries between stages are based on biostratigraphy where possible, and on lithostratigraphy otherwise. **1869** BARING-GOULD *Orig. Relig. Belief* (1878) II. i. 17 There has been an astrotheology, a *lithotheology, a petinotheology [etc.]. **1892** A. B. BRUCE *Apologetics* I. v. 117 Books appeared on bronto-theology, seismo-theology, litho-theology, phyto-theology. **1843** HARDING & HALL *Baron. Halls Eng.* Pref., The prints which illustrate this work are executed in *Lithotint,..that is to say, they are drawn on stone with the brush. **1853** KANE *Grinnell Exp.* xxii. (1856) 171 Lieutenant Brown, whose admirably artistic sketches I had seen in Haghe's lithotints. **1938** *Archit. Rev.* LXXXIV. 177/3 Hullmandel's lithotint process, patented in 1840,..used a resin solution..which could be painted on to the polished tint stone so that it printed a modulated, instead of a flat tint. **1969** D. BLAND *Hist. Bk. Illustration* (ed. 2) vii. 250 The forerunner of the chromo-lithograph was the lithotint. *Ibid.* 251 One of the best litho-tinted books is *Original Views of London as it is* (1842). **1879** T. BRYANT *Pract. Surg.* II. 90 It is safer to attribute *lithuria to dyspepsia.

lithochromatic (,lɪθəkrəʊ'mætɪk), *a.* and *sb.* [f. LITHO- + Gr. χρωματ-, χρῶμα colour + -IC.]

A. *adj.* Pertaining to lithochromatics; involving or produced by applying oil colours to stone. B. *sb. pl.* The art or process of applying oil colours to stone and taking impressions therefrom.

1846 BUCHANAN *Technol. Dict.*, *Lithochromatics*, the art of painting in oil upon stone, and taking impressions on canvas. **1870** *Eng. Mech.* 7 Jan. 404/3 The influence..of lithography and litho-chromatic printing upon the older arts of engraving..has been such that the processes in..use fifty years ago can scarcely be said to exist.

So **litho'chromic** *a.* and *sb.*, in the same sense.

1850 OGILVIE, *Lithochromics*.

lithochromatography (,lɪθəkrəʊmə'tɒgrəfɪ). [f. LITHO- + Gr. χρωματ-, χρῶμα colour + -GRAPHY.] = CHROMOLITHOGRAPHY. Hence **,lithochromato'graphic** *a.*, chromolithographic (in mod. Dicts.).

1843 F. E. PAGET *Pageant* 37 Blessings on the inventor of an art with such a brief, soft, and euphonious name as that of lithochromotography! **1845** Lithocromatography [see LITHO-].

lithochrome ('lɪθəkrəʊm), *a.* [f. LITHO- + Gr. χρῶμα colour.] Lithochromatic. Also *absol.* Chromolithography; = LITHOCHROMY 2.

1854 FAIRHOLT *Dict. Terms Art*, *Lithocrome*, colour printing by the lithographic process, generally termed chromolithography. **1863** ALCOCK *Capital Tycoon* I. 907 The lithocrome process..has long been familiar to them.. blocks of wood only being used instead of stones. *Ibid.* II. 285 Our lately discovered art of lithochrome printing.

lithochromy ('lɪθəkrəʊmɪ). [f. LITHO- + Gr. χρῶμα colour + -Y. Cf. F. *lithocromie.*]

1. Painting on stone.

1837 *Civ. Engin. & Arch. Jrnl.* I. 72/2 The peripteral temple executed by me in Munich Park, which, to the best of my knowledge, constitutes the first example of lithochromy in the present day. **1850** LEITCH tr. *C. O. Müller's Anc. Art* (ed. 2) §320 A very important application of painting, from an early period, was that for which in our times the term lithochromy has been formed.

2. Chromolithography.

1885 E. C. AGASSIZ *Life L. Agassiz* I. 282 The newly-invented art of lithochromy [*anno* 1838].

lithoclast ('lɪθəklɑːst, -æ-). [f. LITHO- + Gr. -κλάστης breaker, f. κλᾶν to break.]

†1. A stone-breaker. *Obs. rare*⁻¹.

1829 BURCKHARDT *Trav. Arabia* I. 307 A party of horsemen..were ready..to assist the lithoclast, as soon as he should have executed his task.

2. *Surg.* An instrument for breaking up stone in the bladder.

1847 SOUTH tr. *Chelius' Surg.* II. 560 The perforating instruments..have been set aside by Jacobson's lithoclast. **1882** SIR H. THOMPSON *Dis. Urinary Organs* xii. (ed. 6) 81 Urethral lithoclasts.

Hence **litho'clastic** *a.*, pertaining to the lithoclast or to lithoclasty; **'lithoclasty** [cf. F. *lithoclastie*], 'the reduction of a vesical calculus into fragments by the aid of the lithoclast' (*Syd. Soc. Lex.* 1889).

lithocol, -coralline: see LITHO-.

lithocyst ('lɪθəsɪst). [f. LITHO- + CYST.]

1. *Zool.* One of the sacs containing mineral particles found in certain Medusæ, and supposed to be organs of hearing.

1859 HUXLEY *Oceanic Hydrozoa* 24 Every appendage (except the hydrothecæ and lithocysts) commences its existence as a cæcal process of the ectoderm and endoderm. **1870** NICHOLSON *Man. Zool.* 92 The margin of the umbrella is furnished with a series of..'lithocysts'. **1877** HUXLEY *Anat. Inv. Anim.* iii. 126 There can be little doubt that the lithocysts..are of the nature of auditory organs.

2. *Bot.* A cell containing crystals of calcium carbonate formed beneath the surface of the leaves of some plants.

1882 VINES *Sach's Bot.* 88 Transitional forms between the imperfect laticiferous vessels of bulb-scales and simple lithocysts which do not contain latex but only raphides.

lithocystotomy, -dialysis, etc.: see LITHO-.

lithodipyra (ˌlɪθəʊdɪˈpaɪərə). [mod.L., f. LITHO- + DI-² + Gr. πῦρ fire, as repr. 'stone twice fired'.] The name given to a kind of artificial stone by members of the Coade family when in 1769 they took over the factory in Lambeth where it was made (until *c* 1837) which stone (also called *Coade stone*) was claimed to have greater frost and heat resistance than natural stone and was much used for statues, monuments, and decorative work.

c **1778** (*title*) Coade's lithodipyra or artificial stone manufactory. For all kinds of statues, capitals, vases, tombs, coats of arms, & architectural ornaments &c. &c. **1910** *N. & Q.* 2 July 15/1 A monument to Edward Wortley Montagu, made of Coade's Lithodipyra, is in the west walk of the Cloisters of Westminster Abbey. **1928** *Connoisseur* Oct. 81 (*caption*) Plaque in Lithodipyra, from a design by J. Bacon, R.A. installed on the east front of Hooton Hall, Cheshire 1788. **1954** *Archit. Rev.* CXVI. 296/1 George Coade died in 1770 and can, therefore, have had little to do with the development of 'Coade's Lithodipyra Terra-Cotta or Artificial Stone Manufactory'.

lithodome (ˈlɪθədəʊm). Anglicized form of LITHODOMUS.

1848 in CRAIG.

lithodomize (lɪˈθɒdəmaɪz), *v.* [f. as next + -IZE.] *trans.* To burrow in (stone), as a lithodomus.

1864 *Reader* 19 Nov. 644/1 Lithodomized stones.

lithodomous (lɪˈθɒdəməs), *a. Zool.* [f. next + -OUS.] Dwelling in rock or stone; produced by or pertaining to mussels of the genus *Lithodomus*.

1862 DANA *Man. Geol.* 588 Nine feet above this they are penetrated by lithodomous or boring shells. **1875** *Lyell's Princ. Geol.* II. III. xxx. 172 Deposits, which envelop the pillars below the zone of lithodomous perforations.

‖**lithodomus** (lɪˈθɒdəməs). *Zool.* Pl. -i. [mod.L., ad. Gr. λιθοδόμος mason, f. λίθος stone- + -δόμος building, δέμειν to build.] A genus of small mussels which burrow in rock or stone; a mussel of this genus, a date-shell.

1833 LYELL *Princ. Geol.* Gloss., *Lithodomi*, molluscous animals which bore into solid rocks, and lodge themselves in the holes they have formed. **1843** HUMBLE *Dict. Geol.* etc., *Lithodomus.* **1848** CRAIG, *Lithodomes, Lithodomi.* **1851–6** WOODWARD *Mollusca* 11 The shipworm adheres to timber, and the pholas and lithodomus to limestone rocks.

lithofacies, -fellic, -fractor, -genesis, etc.: see LITHO-.

lithoglyph (ˈlɪθəglɪf). [f. LITHO- + Gr. γλύφειν to carve.] An incision or engraving on stone; an incised or engraved stone; also, the art of engraving on precious stones.

1842 FRANCIS *Dict. Arts, Lithoglyph*, the art of engraving on precious stones. **1862** BURTON *Bk. Hunter* 3 If there be any remains of sculpture on the stone, it becomes a lythoglyph or a hieroglyph.

†**lithoglypher.** *Obs.*⁻⁰ = LITHOGLYPHIC *sb.*

1730 BAILEY (folio), A *Lithoglypher*, a Stone-cutter or Mason.

lithoglyphic (lɪθəʊˈglɪfɪk), *a.* and *sb.* [ad. Gr. *λιθογλυφικ-ός, f. λιθογλύφος stone-cutter.]

a. *adj.* Pertaining to the art of engraving on precious stones (Craig 1848). †**b.** *sb.* An engraver on precious stones. *Obs.*⁻⁰

1623 COCKERAM, *Lithoglyphicke*, a grauer or cutter of stones. **1658** in PHILLIPS. **1736** BAILEY (folio), *Lithoglyphick*, of or pertaining to carving or cutting in stone.

lithoglyphite (lɪˈθɒglɪfaɪt). [Formed as LITHOGLYPH + -ITE.] A fossil which bears the appearance of having been artificially cut or engraved.

1828–32 in WEBSTER (who cites LUNIER).

lithograph (ˈlɪθəgrɑːf, -æ-), *sb.* [f. LITHO- + -GRAPH (or a back-formation from LITHOGRAPHY).]

1. A lithographic print. Also *attrib.*

1828 DISRAELI *Voy. Capt. Popanilla* ix. 96 It was a sublime lithograph. **1839** MISS MITFORD in L'Estrange *Life* (1870) III. vii. 98 We have an exquisite lithograph of Lucas's portrait of my father. **1846** N. F. MOORE *Hist. Sk. Columbia Coll.* 23 These streets, probably, like those of many lithograph cities of recent date, existed only upon paper. **1868** G. DUFF *Pol. Surv.* 179 Melancholy lithographs represent to us a long-faced, square-browed man. **1970** *Oxf. Compan. Art.* 666/1 Lithographs have..taken on a number of appearances, ranging from simple linear designs made with pen or crayon to colour prints with the most varied effects of transparency and texture.

2. An inscription on stone. *nonce-use.*

1859 WHITTIER '*The Rock' in El Ghor* iv, The graven wonders pay No tribute to the spoiler, Time! Unchanged the awful lithograph Of power and glory undertrod.

ˈ**lithograph,** *v.* [f. as prec.]

1. *trans.* To print from stone; to produce by a lithographic process; in first quot. to make a lithographic portrait of. Also *absol.* or *intr.*

1825 HONE *Every-day Bk.* I. 1457 This personage has obtained himself to be sketched and lithographed. **1853** SIR H. DOUGLAS *Milit. Bridges* (ed. 3) 93 Of this work, the part relating to bridges was, in 1850, lithographed at the Royal Engineer Establishment at Chatham. **1859** LANG *Wand. India* 235 This native print..was lithographed in the Oordoo language.

2. To write or engrave on stone. *rare.*

1872 J. FERGUSSON *Rude Stone Mon.* 73 If they could have written to any primeval 'Times', they would not have taken such pains to lithograph their victory on the spot.

Hence ˈ**lithographed** *ppl. a.*

1826 DISRAELI *Viv. Grey* I. II. x. 151 A bundle of Stewart Newton's beauties, languishing, and lithographed. **1829** H. C. ROBINSON *Diary* 13 Aug. (1967) 102 Knebel had shown me a lithographed manuscript. **1839–41** S. WARREN *Ten Thous. a Year* III. 407 A lithographed likeness of his odious face. **1851** *Illustr. Catal. Gt. Exhib.* 1213 Specimens of gilt, lithographed, and coloured borders. **1880** V. BALL *Jungle Life India* xii. 535, I bought several lithographed books in the Urdu language. **1890** *Athenæum* 21 June 802/3 It is proposed to publish in lithographed facsimile a manuscript volume of recipes.

lithographer (lɪˈθɒgrəfə(r)). [f. LITHO- + -GRAPHER.]

†**1.** One who writes treatises about stones. *Obs.*

1685 *Phil. Trans.* XV. 1056 Though it be commonly by the Lithographers reckon'd amongst stones. **1686** PLOT *Staffordsh.* 175 The Sardachates of the Lithographers.

2. One who practises lithography; a lithographic draughtsman or printer.

1828–32 in WEBSTER. **1871** *Amer. Encycl. Print.* (ed. Ringwalt) 284 The first attempts at transferring, in lithography, were made in Paris, in 1826, by a lithographer named Motte. **1878** RICHMOND *Gram. Lithography* 3 Many difficulties which do not now confront the Lithographer.

lithographic (lɪθəʊˈgræfɪk), *a.* [f. LITHOGRAPHY + -IC. Cf. F. *lithographique.*]

1. a. Pertaining to, employed in or produced by lithography; engraved on or printed from stone. Cf. LITHOGRAPHY 3.

1813 in *Archæol. Jrnl.* (1894) Ser. II. II. 117 Forty Lithographic impressions from drawings by Thomas Barker. **1816** SINGER *Hist. Cards* 158 *note*, This fac-simile..is curious as being a production of the newly invented Lithographic process. **1819** *Trans. Soc. Arts* XXXVII. 131 A Lithographic Press, the invention of Mr. Alois Senefelder. **1827** DE QUINCEY *Murder* Wks. 1862 IV. 30 No better than..a lithographic print by the side of a fine Volpato. **1839** *Penny Cycl.* XIV. 44/2 The two principal agents used for making designs, writings, &c., on stone, are called lithographic chalk and lithographic ink. **1885** *List of Subscribers, Classified* (United Telephone Co.) (ed. 6) 123 Lithographers and Lithographic Printers. **1892** A. POWELL *Southward's Pract. Printing* (ed. 4) i. 3 Lithographic printing is done with stones, zinc plates, &c. **1915** *Southward's Mod. Printing* (ed. 3) II. xxxiii. 281 Rotary lithographic machines work from zinc or aluminium plates carried on a plate cylinder. **1970** E. A. D. HUTCHINGS *Survey of Printing Processes* v. 75 Lithographic plates are made from both zinc and aluminium. **1972** P. GASKELL *New Introd. Bibliogr.* 269 Nineteenth-century lithography was a separate trade... Towards the end of the century, however, powered lithographic cylinder machines were developed which had a productivity comparable with that of the letterpress machinery of the period, and they were followed around 1900 by lithographic rotaries which ran at yet higher speeds. These new machines, used in conjunction with photographic transfer methods of plate preparation, pointed the way to the integration of lithographic with general letterpress printing which took place during the first half of the twentieth century. **1973** *Brit. Printer* July 68/3 It was only with the increase in lithographic printing that photosetting began to 'find its feet'.

b. ***lithographic limestone, slate, stone***: a compact yellowish slaty limestone used in lithography. Hence the adj. is applied to rocks resembling this.

1836 BUCKLAND *Geol. & Min.* I. (1837) 406 The lithographic limestone of Solenhofen. **1839** URE *Dict. Arts*, etc. 777 The lithographic stones of the best quality are still procured from the quarry of Solenhofen. **1849** MURCHISON *Siluria* iv. 79 Smoother than the finest lithographic stone. **1853** TH. ROSS *Humboldt's Trav.* III. xxix. 165 The chain of hills..which is reddish white, and almost of lithographic nature, like the Jura limestone of Pappenheim. **1876** PAGE *Adv. Text-bk. Geol.* xvii. 322 The lithographic limestones of Germany.

2. Descriptive of stones or rocks. *rare.*

1820 DA COSTA in *Gentl. Mag.* XC. I. 222 A Lithographic view of the several Counties in England.

3. Writing on stone. ? *allusive nonce-use.*

1862 G. WILSON *Relig. Chem.* 32 The records.., which geology has written down with her lithographic pen.

4. lithographic offset = OFFSET *sb.* 10 b; **lithographic paper,** paper suitable for lithographic printing; **lithographic varnish,** a preparation of linseed oil used in inks for lithographic printing.

1915 *Southward's Mod. Printing* (ed. 3) II. xxxiii. 282 *Lithographic Offset Printing. Offset printing is popularly supposed to have owed its introduction to a 'miss' made in printing on a lithographic cylinder machine. **1946** H. WHETTON *Pract. Printing & Binding* 446/1 Lithographic offset printing. **1960** G. A. GLAISTER *Gloss. Bk.* 239/2 Modern lithographic offset printing is mostly done in rotary presses. **1937** E. J. LABARRE *Dict. Paper* 167/1 Since the introduction of the offset printing process, however, all papers have become possible as '*lithographic' papers. **1963** R. R. A. HIGHAM *Handbk. Papermaking* vii. 202 Lithographic papers..are similar to offset cartridge, but generally cheaper and in a lighter substance. **1903** A. SEYMOUR *Pract. Lithogr.* x. 52 The most useful and the commonest form of reducing medium is a linseed oil product, known in its prepared state as a *lithographic varnish. **1951** R. MAYER *Artist's Handbk.* x. 312 Lithographic varnishes, from which many types of inks for other printing purposes are also made, are heat-bodied linseed oils.

lithoˈgraphical, *a.* [f. as prec. + -AL¹.]

1. Pertaining to lithography. *rare*⁻⁰.

1828–32 in WEBSTER.

2. Pertaining to the descriptive science of stones; lithological.

1872 W. S. SYMONDS *Rec. Rocks* vi. 154 The Denbighshire grits are Lower Wenlock strata, changed and altered as regards their lithographical constituents.

Hence **lithoˈgraphically** *adv.*, by means of lithography.

1828–32 in WEBSTER. **1952** in G. H. Bourne *Cytol. & Cell Physiol.* p. iv, (*Imprint*) First edition 1942. Reprinted (with corrections) 1945. Second edition 1951. Reprinted lithographically..at the University Press, Oxford, 1952 from corrected sheets of the second edition. **1965** *Economist* 6 Mar. 1026/2 No model of Picasso can hide in obscurity and the olive-shaped outline of the head of Françoise Gilot is known, lithographically, to millions. **1967** E. CHAMBERS *Photolitho-Offset* xvii. 264 The artist has complete freedom of expression and application to produce an image from which impressions can be obtained lithographically.

†**liˈthographize,** *v. Obs.* [f. next + -IZE.] = LITHOGRAPH *v.*

1821 A. H. ROWAN *Let.* 14 Sept. in *Lady Morgan's Mem.* (1862) II. 151, I am lithographising Mr. Wolff's prayer over the corse of the persecuted—injured Queen of England. **1822** T. G. WAINEWRIGHT *Ess. & Crit.* (1880) 264 An interesting series..might be lithographized by some of his pupils. **1830** BENTHAM *To Pres. Jackson* 10 Jan., Wks. 1843 XI. 41 The author of an address to the French army that, after having been written here, and either printed or lithographized, has been transmitted to..France.

lithography (lɪˈθɒgrəfɪ). [ad. mod.L. *lithographia* or F. (and Ger.) *lithographie*: see LITHO- and -GRAPHY.]

†**1.** A description of stones or rocks. *Obs.*

1708 *Phil. Trans.* XXVI. 161 Having some Years since Publish'd his *Specimen Lithographiæ Helveticæ*, and perhaps designing a Lithography, his Observations on Figur'd Fossils are not so numerous as we should other-wise have wish'd.

†**2.** The art of engraving on precious stones.

1730 BAILEY (folio), *Lithography*, the Art of cutting or engraving in Stone; also a Description of Stones.

3. The art or process of making a drawing, design, or writing on a special kind of stone (called 'lithographic stone'), so that impressions in ink can be taken from it. Also, a planographic printing process using metal or plastic plates with a sensitized coating on which the matter to be printed is fixed chemically, before the non-printing areas of the plates are damped and the remainder printed with greasy inks on flat-bed or cylinder presses. Cf. DRIOGRAPHY, OFFSET *sb.* 10 b, PHOTOLITHOGRAPHY.

Lithography was invented in 1796 by Alois Senefelder of Munich (1771–1833). The term (in Ger. form *lithographie*) was used *c* 1804–5 by Senefelder's associates at Munich.

1813 H. BANKES *Lithography* 8 Mr. P. H. André introduced the art under the title of Polyautography... I have taken the liberty, however, to change this for Lithography. **1819** tr. Senefelder (*title*) A Complete Course of Lithography. **1832** BABBAGE *Econ. Manuf.* xi. (ed. 3) 78 A few years ago one of the Paris newspapers was reprinted at Brussels as soon as it arrived by means of lithography. **1851** RUSKIN *Stones Ven.* I. Pref. 10 Executed in tinted lithography. **1879** *Print. Trades Jrnl.* XXVI. 17 The process of lithography consists essentially in the application of a greasy ink on to a damp stone. **1906** *Brit. Printer* Dec. 296/2 The tendency of the day is undoubtedly towards..the utilization of lithography by typographers doing certain classes of work. **1932** *Jrnl. Soc. Chem. Industry* 9 Sept. T313/1 Lithography is based essentially on the adsorption of fatty acids by the metal. **1946** A. KIRK in H. Whetton *Pract. Printing & Binding* xvi. 190/1 Although the printing of daily newspapers is outside the present scope of lithography, the uninterrupted weekly production of *The Australian*, Melbourne, since 1929 may be instanced as but one outstanding achievement..in this direction. **1973** *Brit. Printer* July 68/3 The radically reduced cost of photosetting machines in recent years, their improved capability, and the continuing growth in the use of lithography have all been instrumental in increasing the demand for photosetting and allied equipment.

lithoid (ˈlɪθɔɪd), *a.* [ad. Gr. λιθοειδ-ής, f. λίθο-ς stone: see -OID.] Of the nature or structure of stone.

1841 W. SPALDING *Italy & It. Isl.* III. 299 A capping of lithoid tuff rising about a hundred feet. **1885** A. GEIKIE *Text-bk. Geol.* (ed. 2) 108 By the progressive development of crystallites or crystals during the cooling and consolidation of a molten rock a glass loses its vitreous character and becomes lithoid; in other words, undergoes devitrification.

So **lithoidal** (lɪˈθɔɪdəl) *a.*, in the same sense.

1833 LYELL *Princ. Geol.* III. 124 At a greater depth the mass assumes a more lithoidal structure. **1852** TH. ROSS *Humboldt's Trav.* I. ii. 93 Lithoidal lavas.

Lithol ('lɪθɒl). *Dye Chem.* Also **lithol**. Any of various azo pigment dyestuffs, many of which are the salts of diazo coupling compounds of β-naphthol and aromatic amino-sulphonic acids. ***Lithol red***, any of various salts of the diazo coupling compound of 2-naphthyl-amine-1-sulphonic acid with β-naphthol, used as red pigments of moderate colour fastness.

Formerly a proprietary name in the U.S.

1903 *Official Gaz.* (U.S. Patent Office) 16 June 1891/1 Dyestuff. Badische Anilin & Soda Fabrik, Ludwigshafen, Germany. Filed April 24, 1903... The word 'Lithol'. Used since June 6, 1901. **1930** A. W. C. HARRISON *Manuf. Lakes & Precipitated Pigments* xii. 146 Lithol red being the most profitable of all the bright pigment reds, as regards such desirable qualities as strength, price and reasonable fastness to light in full shades, it is made in larger quantities than any other pigment red. *Ibid.* xiii. 176 Two cheaper bright yellows which may be used are Pigment Chlorine G.G. and Lithol Fast Yellow G.G., which are formaldehyde condensation products. **1947** L. S. PRATT *Chem. & Physics Org. Pigments* viii. 116 Lithols, as a class, are prepared by coupling the diazonium salts of Tobias acid..with β-naphthol, and then converting the resulting practically insoluble sodium lithols into the corresponding barium, calcium, or strontium products. *Ibid.*, The lithols are the most important single group of organic pigment colors. **1967** KARCH & BUBER *Offset Processes* vii. 269 Lithol reds range in shades from an orange to deep maroon. In between these extremes are some very brilliant and deep shades which are used where extreme permanency to light is not important.

litholabe, -lapaxy, -latry, etc.: see LITHO-.

†**li'thologer.** *Obs. rare*⁻¹. [f. Gr. λίθο-ς stone + *-loger* as in *astrologer*.] A lithologist.

1685 H. MORE *Illustration* 366 That it [chrysolite] strengthens the Intellect..is the opinion of Lithologers.

litho'logic, *a.* [f. LITHOLOGY + -IC.] = next.

1828–32 in WEBSTER. **1860** TYNDALL *Glac.* I. x. 130 If the Houses of Parliament were built up by the forces resident in their own bricks and lithologic blocks [etc.].

lithological (lɪθəʊ'lɒdʒɪkəl), *a.* [f. LITHOLOGY + -IC + -AL¹.] Pertaining to lithology; relating to the nature or composition of stones.

1797 *Monthly Mag.* III. 50 A description of the lithological and mineralogical empire. **1833** LYELL *Princ. Geol.* III. 237 To put the student upon his guard against too implicit a reliance on lithological characters as tests of the relative ages of rocks. *Ibid.*, Gloss., *Lithological*, a term expressing the stony structure or character of a mineral mass. We speak of the lithological character of a stratum as distinguished from its zoological character. **1881** RAMSAY in *Nature* No. 618. 420 The various formations, by help of the fossils they contain, have been correlated in time, often in spite of great differences in their lithological characters.

Hence **litho'logically** *adv.*, in regard to lithology; with respect to the nature of stones.

1845 CAPT. NEWBOLD in *Jrnl. Asiatic Soc. Bengal* XIV. 300 Ferruginous and coloured clays that sometimes, lithologically speaking, resemble laterite. **1872** W. S. SYMONDS *Rec. Rocks* iv. 84 The Aran range, with its mountain peaks,..resembles the rocks of Cader Idris lithologically.

lithologist (lɪ'θɒlədʒɪst). [f. LITHOLOGY + -IST.] One who is versed in lithology.

1746 DA COSTA in *Phil. Trans.* XLIV. 398 A regular jointed conic Body, called by Lithologists the Alveolus of the Belemnites. **1811** W. TAYLOR in *Monthly Mag.* XXXI. 448 Our lithologists would do well to revive this name.

lithology (lɪ'θɒlədʒɪ). [ad. mod.L. *lithologia* or F. *lithologie*: see LITHO- and -LOGY.]

1. That department of mineralogy which treats of the nature and composition of stones and rocks. Also, the lithological characters of rocks, etc.

1716 M. DAVIES *Athen. Brit.* III. 104 Mr. Scheutzer..in his..De Querelis Piscium, seem's to have quite different Fancies of that subterraneous Ichthyologico-Lithology. **1802** PLAYFAIR *Illustr. Hutton. Theory* 82 A specific difference which it is the business of lithology to mark by some appropriate character, annexed to the generic name of granite. **1870** *Athenæum* 22 Jan. 127/3 Considering first the petrology and lithology of rock masses, Prof. Molloy divides the compounds of the earth's crust into..3 groups. **1876** PAGE *Adv. Text-Bk. Geol.* xvi. 287 In different districts the lithology of these groups will be found to vary. **1877** LE CONTE *Elem. Geol.* Introd. (1879) 2 A knowledge of mineralogy and lithology is required to understand structural geology.

2. That department of medical science which is concerned with the study of *calculi* in the human body. Also, a treatise on *calculi*.

1802 HOOPER *Quincy's Lex.-Med.*, *Lithology*, a discourse or treatise on stones. **1828–32** WEBSTER, *Lithology*..2. A treatise on stones found in the body. *Coxe.* **1855** MAYNE *Expos. Lex.*, *Lithologia*... Term for the consideration of the nature and different qualities of stones, or of *calculi*; lithology. **1890** J. S. BILLINGS *Nat. Med. Dict.* II. 76.

litholysis, -lyte, etc.: see LITHO-.

lithomancy ('lɪθəmænsɪ). [f. Gr. λίθος stone + μαντεία divination, -MANCY.] Divination by signs derived from stones.

1646 SIR T. BROWNE *Pseud. Ep.* II. iii. 75 The Lithomancy or divination from this stone, whereby..Helenus the Prophet foretold the destruction of Troy. **1656** BLOUNT *Glossogr.*, *Lithomancy*, divination by casting Pibble stones, or by the Load-stone. **1895** ELWORTHY *Evil Eye* 444 Lithomancy, divination with a precious stone called siderites.

lithomarge ('lɪθəmɑːdʒ). *Geol.* Also in L. form **lithomarga**. [ad. mod.L. *lithomarga*, f. Gr. λίθο-ς stone + L. *marga* marl.] 'An early name for several kinds of soft clay-like minerals, including kaolin' (A. H. Chester 1896).

1753 CHAMBERS *Cycl. Supp.*, *Lithomarga.* **1784** KIRWAN *Min.* 74 Lithomarga or stone marl. **1815** W. PHILLIPS *Outl. Min. & Geol.* (1818) 138 A Quartzose rock..composed of quartz, schorl, beryl and lithomarga. **1820** R. JAMESON *Min.* II. 74 There are two kinds, viz. Friable Lithomarge, and Indurated Lithomarge. **1843** PORTLOCK *Geol.* 210 Lithomarge of greenish-white colour..at Dunluce. **1870** *Athenæum* 14 May 646 Restormelite is a variety of kaolinite, standing nearest to the lithomarge group.

lithometer, -nephritis, etc.: see LITHO-.

lithontriptic (lɪθɒn'trɪptɪk), **lithonthryptic** (-'θrɪptɪk), *a.* and *sb.* *Med.* Also 7–8 **lython-**, 8–9 **-thriptic**. [ad. F. *lithontriptique* or mod.L. *lithontripticus* (in the 17th c. etymologically corrected to *-thrypticus*), repr. the Gr. phrase (φάρμακα τῶν ἐν νεφροῖς) λίθων θρυπτικά '(drugs) comminutive of stones (in the kidneys)' (Galen), where λίθων is genitive pl. of λίθος stone and θρυπτικός (neut. pl. -κά) an adj. f. θρύπ-τειν to crush small, comminute. The inaccurate spelling *-tripticus* gave rise to the notion that the word was derived from Gr. τρῖβ-ειν to rub, wear down, and the *Physical Dict.* 1657 gives a mod.L. *lithontribon* sb., which seems to be meant for a Gr. combination, as if λίθον τρῖβον 'that which rubs down stone'. (Cf. the med.L. *litontripon, litotripon* sb., in glosses.) Some recent writers have substituted the more analogically formed LITHOTRIPTIC.]

A. *adj.* Having the property of breaking up stone in the bladder.

α. **1646** SIR T. BROWNE *Pseud. Ep.* II. v. 83 The Lithontripticke powder of Nicolaus. **1661** LOVELL *Hist. Anim. & Min.* 89 Euonimus mixes lithontriptick herbs with the bloud thereof to wast the stone. **1742** J. PARSONS *(title)* Description of the urinary bladder..with animadversions on lithontriptic medicines. **1830** LINDLEY *Nat. Syst. Bot.* 50 The old idea of their [*viz.* saxifrages] being lithontriptic appears to have been derived from their name rather than their virtues. **1883** HOLMES & HULKE *Syst. Surg.* (ed. 3) III. Index 924 Lithontriptic treatment of calculus.

β. **1850** OGILVIE, *Lithonthriptic* [adj. and sb.].

B. *sb.* A lithontriptic medicine.

α. **1694** WESTMACOTT *Script. Herb.* 30 Conserve of Hips..is said by Authors to be a Lithontriptick. **1774** T. PERCIVAL *Ess.* (1776) III. 138 Lime water has been long and justly celebrated as a lithontriptic. **1845–55** GARROD *Mat. Med.* (ed. 6) 114 Magnesia is at times employed as a lithontriptic. **1876** GROSS *Dis. Bladder* 217 Lithontriptics, or solvents and disintegrators of stone.

β. **1683** *Phil. Trans.* XIV. 533 Some medicines, though they are not Lythonthripticks yet may be good nephriticks. **1693** *Ibid.* XVII. 766 'Tis esteem'd as a great Traumatick and Lithonthriptick. **1727–41** CHAMBERS *Cycl.* s.v. *Stone*, A liquor that will dissolve or break the concrete stone..which is called a lithonthriptic.

lithontriptist, -or: see LITHOTRIPTIST, -OR.

lithophagous, -phane, -phile, -philous, etc.: see LITHO-.

lithophone ('lɪθəfəʊn). *Surg.* [f. LITHO- + Gr. φωνή sound.] An instrument for rendering audible the contact of a sound or probe with a vesical calculus.

1889 in *Syd. Soc. Lex.*

lithophotography, -phyll, -physe: see LITHO-.

lithophyte ('lɪθəfaɪt). [f. Gr. λίθο-ς stone + φυτόν plant. Cf. next.]

1. *Zool.* A polyp the substance of which is stony or calcareous, as some corals.

1774 GOLDSM. *Nat. Hist.* (1824) III. 324 Of the lythophytes and sponges. **1831** BEECHEY *Voy. Pacific*, etc. I. 263 The aversion of the lithophytes to fresh water. **1862** M. HOPKINS *Hawaii* App. 413 It is the general assumption that coral islands are built up from the bottom of the ocean by the unaided labour of lithophytes. **1875** LYELL *Princ. Geol.* II. III. xlix. 594 All were increasing their dimensions by the active operations of the lithophytes.

attrib. **1853** TH. ROSS *Humboldt's Trav.* III. xxvi. 113 Pectens, venuses, and lithophyte polypi.

2. *Bot.* A plant growing upon stone or rock.

1895 OLIVER tr. *Kerner's Nat. Hist. Plants* I. 56 The number of lithophytes is comparatively very small. They include those lichens and mosses which cling in immediate contact to the surface of stones and derive their food in a fluid state direct from the atmosphere.

Hence **litho'phytic, -'phytous** *adjs.*, pertaining to or of the nature of a lithophyte.

1828–32 in WEBSTER. **1836–9** TODD *Cycl. Anat.* II. 408/2 The propagation of some of the lithophytous polypes resembles that of the hydra. **1895** OLIVER tr. *Kerner's Nat. Hist. Plants* I. 81 The atmospheric deposits supply lithophytic plants with a sufficient quantity of nutrient salts. *Ibid.* 82 Many mosses are completely lithophytic in early stages of development whilst later they figure as land-plants.

‖**lithophyton.** *Obs.* Pl. **-phyta**. [mod.L., f. Gr. λίθο-ς stone + φυτόν plant.] Coral.

1646 SIR T. BROWNE *Pseud. Ep.* II. v. 91 That Corall (which is a Lithophyton or stone plant). **1691** RAY *Creation* I. (1692) 74 Not only the Herbaceous and Woody Submarine Plants, but also the Lithophyta themselves affect this manner of growing. **1753** CHAMBERS *Cycl. Supp.* s.v., The white sea lithophyton called shrubby coralline. **1761** ELLIS in *Phil. Trans.* LII. 357 Mr. Mason of Barbadoes..brought me this rare lithophyton.

lithopone: see LITHO-.

'lithoprint, *v.* [f. LITHO(GRAPHY + PRINT *v.*] *trans.* To print by photolithography, usu. in reference to the production of copies of a typescript by this means. Also as *sb.* = LITHOGRAPH *sb.* Hence **'lithoprinting** *vbl. sb.*

1935 *Amer. Botanist* Jan. 39 The book is lithoprinted from type-written copy. **1947** *Amer. Speech* XXII. 136 It is too bad that this most important of volumes on its subject could not have been put in more solid form than lithoprinting. **1957** TRAGER & SMITH *Outl. Eng. Struct.* 7 The preliminary drafts were reproduced in lithoprinted form. **1969** *Sunday Times* 6 Apr. 30 His enchanting drawings (transformed into big, clear-coloured lithoprints in limited editions of 100 each) are in a gallery run by his mother. **1971** *New Scientist* 28 Jan. 206/2 The several hundred local natural history publications, often duplicated or lithoprinted, offer an easy first outlet for young artists.

lithops ('lɪθɒps). [mod.L. (N.E. Brown 1922, in *Gardeners' Chron.* 28 Jan. 44/2), f. Gr. λίθος stone + ὤψ face.] A small succulent plant of the genus so called, belonging to the family Aizoaceæ, native to Namaqualand, South Africa, and resembling small stones.

[**1922** *Gardeners' Chron.* 28 Jan. 44/2 Lithops, N. E. Brown. Very dwarf succulent plants, in nature growing buried in the ground with their tops scarcely, or not at all, rising above the level of the surface. *Ibid.*, Dr. Marloth is quite wrong in his identification of the plant, which I have no doubt whatever is a species of Lithops.] **1938** H. A. DAY *Flowers of Desert* iv. 148 It is most difficult to tell which are plants and which are pebbles when the two are mixed, as they are in the habitat of the *Lithops*, for the plants grow in the stony deserts of South Africa. **1966** E. PALMER *Plains of Camdeboo* xvi. 269 We have never found a Lithops on Cranemere, the nearest species that we know of being Burchell's Lithops to the north and another species, *Lithops terricolor*, to the west.

lithoscope, -sere: see LITHO-.

lithosiid (lɪ'θəʊsɪɪd), *a.* and *sb.* [ad. mod.L. *Lithosiid-æ* (see below), f. generic name *Lithosia* (Fabricius), f. Gr. λίθος stone + -IA¹. See -ID.]

A. *adj.* Pertaining to the family *Lithosiidæ* of bombycid moths, called footmen. **B.** *sb.* A moth of this family; a footman (*Cent. Dict.*).

1863 BATES *Nat. Amazon* xii. (1864) 414 The moth is of a dull slaty colour, and belongs to the Lithosiide group of the silk-worm family (*Bombycidæ*).

lithosol: see LITHO-.

lithosperm ('lɪθəspɜːm). Anglicized f. next.

1865 WATTS *Dict. Chem.* III. 730 The root-bark of *Lithospermum arvense* contains a red colouring matter..the lithosperm-red forms a blue solution with ether. **1893** E. H. BARKER *Wand. South. Waters* 236 A sprig of lithosperm stood like a little tree laden with Dead Sea fruit.

‖**lithospermon, -um** (lɪθəʊ'spɜːmɒn, -əm). [mod.L., a. Gr. λιθόσπερμον, f. λίθο-ς stone + σπέρμα seed; adopted by Linnæus in his *Systema Naturæ* (1735) as the name of a genus.] A herb or sub-shrub of the genus so called, belonging to the family Boraginaceæ, native to Europe, northern Asia, or North America, and bearing white, yellow, or blue flowers.

1646 SIR T. BROWNE *Pseud. Ep.* II. vi. 101 Lithospermon, or grummell. **1727** BAILEY vol. II, *Lithospermon*, the Herb Stone Crop, Gromwell, or Graymil [*printed* Graynul]. **1865** TYLOR *Early Hist. Man.* vi. 123 The virtues of the lithospermum or stone-seed, in curing calculus. **1900** J. M. ABBOTT in W. D. Drury *Bk. Gardening* ix. 295 Lithospermums are showy rockwork plants. **1937** *Daily Express* 10 May 12/4 The lithospermum's name [*sc.* 'Heavenly Blue'] is no exaggeration of its colour. **1966** J. BERRISFORD *Wild Garden* II. 166 With their brilliant blue flowers and evergreen leaves the lithospermums are most desirable garden plants.

lithospermous (lɪθəʊ'spɜːməs), *a.* *Bot.* [f. Gr. λίθο-ς stone + σπέρμα seed + -OUS.] Having hard, stony fruit.

1889 in *Syd. Soc. Lex.*

lithosphere, -stratigraphy: see LITHO-.

lithothamnion (ˌlɪθəʊ'θæmnɪɒn). [mod.L. (R. A. Philippi 1837, in *Arch. Naturgesch.* III. 387), f. LITHO- + Gr. θάμνος shrub.] A calcareous, marine, red alga of the genus so called. Also *attrib.* Hence **litho'thamnic** *a.*

1895 G. MURRAY *Introd. Study Seaweeds* 241 *Lithophyllum* forms thin stony plates of erect habit, while *Lithothamnion* gives rise to massive stony branches. **1935** J. E. TILDEN *Algae* viii. 362 Portions of the *Lithothamnion* crust were kept for many months. **1967** *Oceanogr. & Marine Biol.* V. 551 Both fauna and flora of this lithothamnic bottom are very abundant. **1972** *Sci. Amer.* June 62/1 A hitherto minor group of coralline red algae, the

lithothamnions, now began to play an increasingly important role.

lithotheology, -tint: see LITHO-.

lithotome (ˈlɪθətəʊm). [ad. Gr. λιθοτόμον (in sense 1), neut. of λιθοτόμος adj., stone-cutting, f. λίθο-ς stone + -τόμος cutting, τέμνειν to cut. Cf. F. *lithotome*.]

1. *Surg.* An instrument for cutting the bladder in lithotomy; more properly called a *cystotome*.

1758 J. S. *Le Dran's Observ. Surg.* (1771) 257, I..thrust the Point of the Lithotome cross the *Perinæum* into its *Canula*. **1839–47** TODD *Cycl. Anat.* III. 934/2 Should the blades of the lithotome..be too widely divaricated.. liability to venous hemorrhage..will be the result. **1846** BRITTAN tr. *Malgaigne's Man. Oper. Surg.* 521 It only remains to incise the prostate and neck of the bladder in withdrawing the lithotome.

2. A stone in its natural state which resembles a stone artificially cut.

1828–32 WEBSTER (citing *Dict. Nat. Hist.*).

lithotomic (lɪθəʊˈtɒmɪk), *a.* [ad. Gr. λιθοτομικός, f. λιθοτόμος (see prec.).] Stone-cutting; of or pertaining to lithotomy. So **litho'tomical** *a.*

1825 SOUTHEY *Lett.* (1856) III. 484 Your Butler, when left by forgetfulness four-and-twenty hours in the lithotomic machine. **1828–32** WEBSTER *Lithotomic*, pertaining to or performed by lithotomy. **18..** *Med. Jrnl.* (Worc.), Lithotomical. **1885** A. STEWART *'Twixt Ben Nevis & Glencoe* iv. 27 He had cheek enough..to undertake a lithotomical operation if it came handy.

lithotomist (lɪˈθɒtəmɪst). [f. LITHOTOMY + -IST. Cf. F. *lithotomiste*.]

1. One who practises lithotomy.

1663 BOYLE *Usef. Exp. Nat. Philos.* II. ii. 79, I inquired of him, whether he had met with a remedy that could dissolve the stone, offering him much more for a cure of that kind, then he would require as a lithotomist. **1731** *Gentl. Mag.* I. 78 Dr. Bamber, lithotomist to that [*viz.* St. Bartholomew's] hospital. *a* **1754** R. MEAD *Wks.* (1775) 405 Ammonius, a Greek physician, who..was surnamed Λιθοτόμος, the Lithotomist. **1883** HOLMES & HULKE *Syst. Surg.* (ed. 3) III. 281 Some of the most successful lithotomists have.. advocated sufficient incision as less dangerous than violent extraction.

2. One who cuts inscriptions on stone. *rare.*

1713 *Phil. Trans.* XXVIII. 291 Lithotomists careless in dividing Syllables.

lithotomize (lɪˈθɒtəmaɪz), *v.* [f. next + -IZE.] *trans.* To subject to the operation of lithotomy. Hence **li'thotomized** *ppl. a.* In quot. *absol.*

1836 *Brit. & For. Med. Rev.* II. 467 Of the lithotomized in Paris, at least four out of five recover. **1876** GROSS *Dis. Bladder* 202 Patients are often brought to the surgeon from a distance to be lithotomized.

lithotomy (lɪˈθɒtəmɪ). [ad. late L. *lithotomia*, a. Gr. λιθοτομία, f. λίθο-ς stone + -τομία cutting.]

1. The operation, art, or process of cutting for stone in the bladder.

1721 in BAILEY. **1722** in QUINCY *Lex. Phys.-Med.* (ed. 2). **1783** *Encycl. Brit.* (ed. 2) X. 8431/1 (*marg.*) Lithotomy reckoned exceedingly dangerous by the ancients. **1800** *Med. Jrnl.* III. 193, I was induced to make use of a Bistoire Caché, in the operation of Lithotomy. **1846** BRITTAN tr. *Malgaigne's Man. Oper. Surg.* 508 Three principal methods: perineal lithotomy, recto-vesical lithotomy, hypo-gastric lithotomy. **1875** SIR W. TURNER in *Encycl. Brit.* I. 815/1 The lateral operation of lithotomy.

attrib. **1871** HOLMES *Syst. Surg.* (ed. 2) V. 1083 Surgeons seem still divided in opinion as to whether a lithotomy knife should or should not be beaked. **1878** T. BRYANT *Pract. Surg.* I. 699 Lithotomy scoops or forceps. **1879** *St. George's Hosp. Rep.* IX. 271 The patient was placed in the lithotomy position. *Ibid.* 344 A lithotomy tube was passed into the bladder, and tied in.

†**2.** [After Gr.] A quarry. *Obs.*

1656 BLOUNT *Glossogr.*, *Lithotomy*, a Masons Work-house, or quarry; also a Prison. D. Br. [*i.e.* Sir T. Browne] useth it.

lithotripsy (ˈlɪθətrɪpsɪ). Also in mod.L. form **lithotripsis**. [f. LITHO- + Gr. τρῖψις rubbing, f. τρίβ-ειν to rub. Cf. next.] The operation of rubbing down or crushing stone in the bladder by means of a lithotriptor.

1834 *Good's Study Med.* (ed. 4) IV. 409 *note*, A tribute of praise to the several individuals by whom lithotrity and lithotripsy have been brought to their present state of efficiency. **1846** R. LISTON *Pract. Surg.* xii. (ed. 4) 495 In the year 1827, when lithotripsy was yet in its infancy. **1889** *Syd. Soc. Lex.*, *Lithotripsis*.

lithotriptic (lɪθəʊˈtrɪptɪk), *a.* and *sb.* [Refashioned form of LITHONTRIPTIC, as if f. Gr. λίθο-ς stone + -τριπτικός, f. τρίβειν to rub, wear away.] = LITHONTRIPTIC.

1847 SOUTH tr. *Chelius' Surg.* II. 561 Rigal's chest-like contrivance, which contains all the lithotriptic instruments. *Ibid.* 564 The duration of a lithotriptic sitting depends on the sensibility of the patient.

lithotriptist (lɪθəʊˈtrɪptɪst). *rare*⁻⁰. Also **lithon-**. [f. LITHOTRIPT-IC + -IST.] One who practises lithotripsy.

1836 SMART, *Lithontriptist*. **1850** OGILVIE, *Lithotriptist*, *Lithontriptist*.

‖**lithotriptor** (lɪθəʊˈtrɪptɔː(r)). *Surg.* Also lithon-. [Orig. *lithontriptor*, a quasi-L. agent-noun on the analogy of LITHONTRIPTIC; afterwards refashioned (cf. prec.).] An instrument for rubbing down or crushing stone in the bladder.

1825 in *Patents, Abridgem. Specif. Med.* etc. (1863) 92 A surgical instrument for destroying the stone in the bladder without cutting, which he denominates 'lithontriptor'. **1847** SOUTH tr. *Chelius' Surg.* II. 561 The catheter having been withdrawn, the lithotriptor is introduced.

lithotrite (ˈlɪθətraɪt). *Surg.* [Back-formation from LITHOTRITY.] An instrument for crushing stone in the bladder into minute particles which can be passed through the urethra.

1839 R. DRUITT *Surgeon's Vade Mecum* VI. iv. 401 The instrument which has now superseded the foregoing, is the screw lithotrite of Mr. Weiss. **1876** GROSS *Dis. Bladder* 149 The tumor was seized and torn away with the trilabe, or crushed by a lithotrite.

lithotritic (lɪθəʊˈtrɪtɪk), *a.* [f. LITHOTRITY + -IC.] Relating to lithotrity; having the property of crushing stone in the bladder.

1830 COOPER *Dict. Pract. Surg.* (ed. 6) 1179 It is..alleged, that as lithotomy is very successful upon young subjects, lithotritic attempts are not requisite. **1889** *Syd. Soc. Lex.*, *Lithotritic*.

lithotritist (lɪˈθɒtrɪtɪst). [f. LITHOTRITY + -IST.] One who practises lithotrity.

1836 *Brit. & For. Med. Rev.* II. 470 The road to the lithotritist's success is clevery marked out by M. Amussat. **1846** R. LISTON *Pract. Surg.* xii. (ed. 4) 495 In 1829, a professed lithotritist arrived in this country. **1868** SIR H. THOMPSON *Dis. Urinary Organs* xiii. (1882) 87 The skill of the lithotritist may to some extent be known by the debris he makes.

lithotritize (lɪˈθɒtrɪtaɪz), *v.* [f. LITHOTRITY + -IZE.] *trans.* To subject to lithotrity.

1842 R. WILLIS *Stone in Bladder* iv. 107 The third is perfectly well,—but he has not yet been lithotritized. **1864** T. HOLMES *Syst. Surg.* (1870) IV. 1117 This increases the number of adult patients with stone to 103, of which only 34 were lithotritised.

lithotritor (ˈlɪθətraɪtɒr). *Surg.* Also in Fr. form **-triteur**. [ad. F. *lithotriteur*, an alteration of LITHOTRIPTOR, as if f. L. *tritor*, agent-n. f. *terĕre* to rub.] = LITHOTRIPTOR.

1828–32 in WEBSTER. **1846** BRITTAN tr. *Malgaigne's Man. Oper. Surg.* 534 It is well to move the lithotriteur backwards and forwards to assure yourself that the stone is well seized. **1857** DUNGLISON *Med. Lex.* 550 The instruments employed for this purpose [i.e. Lithotrity] are called, in the abstract, Lithotrites, Lithotriteurs, Lithotritors, Lithotriptors, Lithothryptors, Lithotrypetæ, and Lithoclasts.

lithotrity (lɪˈθɒtrɪtɪ). [Formed after LITHOTRITOR, by substitution of suffix: see -Y.] The operation of crushing a stone in the bladder by means of a lithotrite.

1830 tr. Baron Heurteloup (*title*) Cases of Lithotrity or Examples of the Stone cured without incision. *a* **1862** SIR B. BRODIE *Autobiog.* (1865) 144 After the year 1835..I scarcely ever had recourse to lithotomy at all, substituting for it that of lithotrity. **1878** WALSHAM *Surg. Pathol.* 396 The operations of lithotomy, lithotrity, and puncture.

attrib. **1860** *N. Syd. Soc. Year-bk. Med.* 295 Statistical Analysis of twenty-one Lithotrity Operations.

lithotype (ˈlɪθətaɪp), *sb.* [f. LITHO- + TYPE *sb.*]

1. A stereotype made with gum-shellac, sand, tar, and linseed-oil, and pressed while hot on a plaster mould taken from type.

1875 in KNIGHT *Dict. Mech.*

2. An etched stone surface for printing.

1875 in KNIGHT *Dict. Mech.*

3. A lithographed finger-print.

1890 CONAN DOYLE *Sign of Four* i. 10 Lithotypes of the hands of slaters, sailors, cork-cutters [etc.].

'lithotype, *v.* [Back-formation from LITHOTYPY.] *trans.* To prepare for printing by lithotypy (Ogilvie 1882).

lithotypic (lɪθəʊˈtɪpɪk), *a.* [f. next + -IC.] Relating to lithotypy; printed by the lithotype process.

In mod. Dicts.

lithotypy (lɪˈθɒtɪpɪ). [f. LITHOTYPE *sb.* + -Y.]

1. The process of making lithotypes (see LITHOTYPE *sb.* 1).

1882 in OGILVIE.

2. Printing from etched stone.

In mod. Dicts.

lithoxyl (lɪˈθɒksɪl). *Min.* Also **-yle**. [Orig. *lithoxylon* (J. G. Wallerius 1747); f. Gr. λίθο-ς stone + ξύλον wood.] A synonym of wood-opal.

1828–32 WEBSTER, *Lithoxyle*, petrified wood.

So **li'thoxylite** = prec. (Ogilvie 1882).

†**lithoxy'loidical**, *a. Obs.* [Formed as prec. + -OID + -IC + -AL¹.] Resembling pyritized wood.

1757 tr. *Henckel's Pyritol.* 23 Lithoxiloidical, as if fibrous, or pyritified wood.

lithsman (ˈlɪθsmən). *Hist.* [OE. *liðsmann*, a. ON. *liðsmað-r* (accus. *-mann*), f. *liðs*, genit. of *lið* host + *maðr* MAN.] A sailor in the navy under the Danish kings of England.

11.. *O.E. Chron.* an. 1036 (Laud MS.) þa liðs men on Lunden ȝecuron Harold to healdes ealles Engla landes. **1848** PETRIE & STEV. *Chron.* 95 The thanes..and the 'lithsmen' at London. **1848** LYTTON *Harold* III. ii, 'The lithsmen of London', cried a Saxon thegn, 'are all on his side, and marching already through the gates'. **1865** KINGSLEY *Herew.* (1867) I. 11 He succeeded, by the help of the.. lithsmen of London,..in setting his puppet on the throne. **1867** FREEMAN *Norm. Conq.* (1876) I. vi. 485 A new element, the 'lithsmen', the nautic multitude of London.

Lithuanian (lɪθjuːˈeɪnɪən), *a.* and *sb.* Also 7 **Lituanian**. [f. proper name *Lithuania* + -AN.]

A. *adj.* Belonging or relating to Lithuania, its people or language.

1797 *Encycl. Brit.* (ed. 3) X. 102/2 Another division [of Lithuania] is into Lithuania properly so called, and Lithuanian Russia. **1839** *Penny Cycl.* XIV. 53 The bulk of the Lithuanian nation remained faithful to their idols. **1843** R. GARNETT in *Proc. Philol. Soc.* (1845) I. 147 The Lithuanian *merga*, maiden.

B. *sb.* A native of Lithuania; also, the Lithuanian language, being one of the Lettic group of Aryan languages.

1607 TOPSELL *Four-f. Beasts* (1658) 414 Antonius Schvebergerus, the Lituanian of Vilna. **1839** *Penny Cycl.* XIV. 53 In the twelfth century the Lithuanians began to be more known. **1847** MRS. A. KERR *Hist. Servia* 72 The plague..is considered by..the Lithuanians..to be a personal being.

Lithuanic (lɪθjuːˈænɪk), *a.* and *sb.* [Formed as prec. + -IC.] **a.** *adj.* = LITHUANIAN *a.* Also, in wider sense, applied to the group of languages, (also called *Lettic* and *Baltic*) which includes Lithuanian together with Lettish and Old Prussian. **b.** *sb.* The Lithuanic language or group of languages.

1841 LATHAM *Eng. Lang.* 3 The Livonian,..the Old Prussian, and the Lithuanian of Lithuania, constituting the Lithuanic stock. **1844** —— in *Proc. Philol. Soc.* (1845) I. 235 In Lithuanic the term in use is *one*; as, wiens *wienâ*.

Lit. Hum. Abbrev. of LITTERÆ HUMANIORES.

1939 L. MACNEICE *Autumn Jrnl.* xii. 49 If it were not for Lit. Hum. I might be climbing A ladder with a hod.

lithur, obs. form of LITHER *a.*

lithuresis, lithurorrhœa, etc.: see LITHO-.

lithwayke, variant of LEATHWAKE *Obs.*

†**lithwort**. *Obs.* Also 5 **lyt(h)wort**. [OE. *liðwyrt*, f. *lið* LITH *sb.*¹ + *wyrt* root, plant.] Dwarf elder, *Sambucus Ebulus*.

c **1000** *Sax. Leechd.* I. 124 Ðeos wyrt þe man ostriago, & oðrum naman lyðwyrt nemneð. *a* **1100** *Voc.* in Wr.-Wülcker 299/2 *Erifeon*, liðwyrt, *idem est ostriago*. *c* **1265** *Voc. Plants* ibid. 558/21 *Ostragium*, herbyue, liþewurt. *c* **1450** *ME. Med. Bk.* (Heinrich) 203 Jus of lythwort. *Ibid.* 205 Tak lytwort, bresewort Rybwort.

lithy (ˈlɪðɪ), *a. dial.* Forms: 1 **liðiȝ**, 4 **leoþi**, 4–5 **leþi**, 4–6 **lethy, -ie**, 5–6 **lithie, -ye**, 6 **lythey**, 6–7 **lythy, -ie**, 7– **lithy**. [OE. *liðiȝ* = ON. *liðug-r* yielding, nimble, free, unimpeded, MDu. *ledech* unimpeded, unoccupied (Du. *ledig*, *leeg* empty, vacant, unoccupied), MHG. *ledic* free, unimpeded (mod.G. *ledig* unoccupied, vacant). The ulterior etymology is obscure; see Kluge s.v. *ledig*.] Pliable, flexible, supple; soft, unresisting.

c **1000** ÆLFRIC *Saints' Lives* (1885) I. 224 þa ȝelæhte petrus hire liþian hand. *a* **1023** WULFSTAN *Hom.* xlvi. (1883) 234/22 Heo [*sc.* a man's heart] biþ liðiȝ swa clað..onȝean deofles lare. *c* **1315** SHOREHAM (E.E.T.S.) vii. 590 Ʒef eny loȝ þer leþi were. **1387–8** T. USK *Test. Love* III. vii. (Skeat) l. 101 So oft falleth the lethy water on the harde rocke, till it haue through persed it. **1398** TREVISA *Barth. De P.R.* VI. vi. (Tollem. MS.), Suche children ben nesche of flesche, leþi [*ed.* 1535 lethye, *ed.* 1582 lythie] and pliant of body. *Ibid.* XVII. ii. (1495) N iiij b/2 That stalke is fyrste feble & lethy: and that for defawte of harde humour. *a* **1400** *Disp. Mary & Cross* 483 in *Leg. Rood* (1871) 147, I bar þi fruit leoþi and lene. **14..** *Sir Beues* (MS. M.) 647 All to leþy the spere was wrought. *a* **1425** *Cursor M.* 9779 (Trin.) þenne were he leþyere [*Laud* lethier, *Cott.*, *Gött.* wayker] þen he was ere. **1542** UDALL *Erasm. Apoph.* 121 *marg.*, Yᵗ thei might haue their ioynctes nymble & lithye. **1573** TWYNE *Æneid.* XII. M m ij b, And up shee leapes, and lithie raignes with hand she turneth round. **1598** [R. CAREW] *Herrings Tayle* B, Their lithie bodies bound with limits of a shell. *a* **1618** SYLVESTER *Spectacles* xli, The World's Weapons were but lythie Wax; And Vertue's Shield is of celestiall Fier. **1640** PARKINSON *Theat. Bot.* 227 It hath many small weake, but lithy and tough slender greene stalks. **1843** BORROW *Bible in Spain* x, His limbs were now thoroughly lithy, and he brandished his fore legs in a manner perfectly wondrous. **1848** *Blackw. Mag.* LXIV. 259 A man..in the full active use of his lithy form.

†**b.** *fig.* Weak, feeble. *Obs.*

1377 LANGL. *P. Pl.* B. x. 184 Ac theologie..A ful lethy þinge it were ȝif þat loue nere. **1387** TREVISA *Higden* (Rolls) VII. 157 My cause..may be made lethy [L. *infirmari*], and it may be reysed up. *a* **1533** LD. BERNERS *Gold. Bk. M. Aurel.* (1546) Ll iv, Ye are..in aduersitie feeble and lethy.

lithy-tree. [app. f. prec.] The wayfaring-tree, *Viburnum Lantana*; also *Rhus caustica* (Cent. Dict. 1890).

1866 *Treas. Bot.* 689/1 Lithy-tree, *Viburnum Lantana*.

litigable ('lɪtɪgəb(ə)l), *a.* [f. L. *lītigāre* (see LITIGATE) + -ABLE.] That may become the subject of litigation; disputable.

1764–7 LD. LYTTELTON *Hen. II* (1769) II. 401 The litigable title to Nantes and its earldom. **1824** W. TAYLOR in *Monthly Rev.* CIII. 242 Which last frontier contains much litigable territory. **1897** *Daily News* 7 July 5/1 To add another litigable point to the Bill.

litigant ('lɪtɪgənt), *a.* and *sb.* [ad. F. *litigant*, ad. L. *lītigant-em*, pr. pple. of *lītigāre* (see LITIGATE).] **A.** *adj.* Engaged in a law-suit or in a dispute. Only in connexion with *party*.

1638 CHILLINGW. *Relig. Prot.* I. v. §98. 299 The parties litigant are agreed that many errors were held by many of the ancient Doctors. **168.** in Somers *Tracts* I. 196 Verdicts are found..as the litigant Parties exceed one the other in Power and Practice. **1754** HUME *Hist. Eng.* (1761) I. App. ii. 257 Sometimes the party litigant offered the king a certain portion..payable out of the debts. **1884** SIR J. BACON in *Law Rep.* 26 Ch. Div. 135 The shareholders who are the parties here litigant.

B. *sb.* A person engaged in a lawsuit or dispute.

1659 *Gentl. Calling* (1696) 1 Much greater is the odds between these two Litigants. *a* **1674** CLARENDON *Surv. Leviath.* 102 If the Litigant be not pleased with the opinion of his Judg. **1728** T. SHERIDAN *Persius* iv. (1739) 62 The Judges and Litigants both used to swear at this Altar. **1810** BENTHAM *Packing* (1821) 228 That security, which the aggregate body of litigants..do not enjoy. **1849** MACAULAY *Hist. Eng.* viii. II. 339 Ordinary litigants complained that their business was neglected. **1885** SIR C. S. C. BOWEN in *Law Times Rep.* LIII. 484/2 The great rule is, that poverty is no bar to the litigant.

litigate ('lɪtɪgeɪt), *v.* [f. L. *lītigāt-*, ppl. stem of *lītigāre*, f. *līt-*, *līs* lawsuit.]

1. *intr.* To be a party to, or carry on, a suit at law; to go to law. Also † *gen.* to dispute.

1615 DANIEL *Queen's Arcadia* Poems (1717) 181 Then might they be taught..To litigate perpetually. **1675** BAXTER *Cath. Theol.* I. I. 27 If any will litigate de nomine entis, let them call it Being or No-being as they please. **1726** AYLIFFE *Parergon* 83 The Appellant after the Interposition of an Appeal still litigates in the same Cause before the Judge a Quo. **1834** *Tait's Mag.* I. 697/1 Making the determination of two Justices of Peace final, if the Quaker did not litigate farther. **1881** *Daily News* 29 Dec. 5/3 It was a characteristic of Lord Justice Lush as a Judge to prevent suitors if he could from litigating to the uttermost.

2. *trans.* To make the subject of a lawsuit; to contest at law; to plead for or against.

1741 T. ROBINSON *Gavelkind* II. v. 234 A question formerly much litigated. **1748** RICHARDSON *Clarissa* (1811) I. xiii. 87 If I do not oblige them, my grandfather's estate is to be litigated with me. **1774** *Connect. Col. Rec.* (1887) XIV. 381 A rate of one penny farthing on the pound, to pay their costs in sundry matters litigated before the Assembly. **1791** COWPER *Iliad* XII. 515 Litigating warm Their right in some small portion of the soil. **1818** CRUISE *Digest* (ed. 2) VI. 350 The precise question ought not to be again litigated. **1864** BURTON *Scot Abr.* II. i. 117 The property in 'Anderson's Pills' was litigated in the Court of Session.

b. *gen.* To dispute, contest (a point, etc.).

1739 CIBBER *Apol.* (1756) II. 26 He never cared to litigate anything that did not affect his figure upon the stage. **1758** H. WALPOLE *Catal. Roy. Authors.* (1759) II. 230 The point indeed has been much litigated, but is of little consequence. **1842** G. S. FABER *Prov. Lett.* (1844) I. 91 He..deems it indecorous to litigate the question with his diocesan.

Hence '**litigating** *vbl. sb.* and *ppl. a.*

1760–72 H. BROOKE *Fool of Qual.* (1809) II. 10 Compelling my litigating opponents to an accomodation. **1780** *Newgate Cal.* V. 25 A family estate, the right of which was litigating in the court of chancery. **1884** T. H. GORE in *Law Times* 8 Nov. 29/1 The retailer was the person litigating.

litigated ('lɪtɪgeɪtɪd), *ppl. a.* [f. prec. + -ED^1.]

a. Made the subject of a lawsuit; contested at law. **b.** *gen.* Contested, disputed.

a **1745** SWIFT *Acc. Crt. & Empire Japan* Wks. 1841 I. 559/1 There were two maritime towns..bordering upon Tedsu: of these he purchased a litigated title. **1772** BARRINGTON in *Phil. Trans.* LXII. 266 This litigated point can only receive a satisfactory decision from very accurate observations. *a* **1797** H. WALPOLE *Mem. Geo. II* (1847) II. i. 23 Malone made him great promises..of even acquiescing to the litigated clause of the King's consent. **1813** JEFFERSON *Writ.* (1830) IV. 210 It is a litigated question, whether the circulation of paper, rather than of specie, is a good or an evil. **1835** REEVE *De Tocqueville's Democr.* I. ii. 41 Officers were charged..with the arbitration of litigated landmarks. **1865** CARLYLE *Fredk. Gt.* III. xiv. (1872) I. 231 These litigated Duchies are now the Prussian Province Jülich-Berg-Cleve.

litigation (lɪtɪ'geɪʃən). [ad. late L. *lītigātiōn-em*, n. of action f. *lītigāre* to LITIGATE.]

1. The action or process of carrying on a suit in law or equity; legal proceedings; †in *pl.*, kinds of litigation. ***in litigation***: in process of investigation before a court of law.

1647 CLARENDON *Hist. Reb.* IV. §38, I have never yet spoken with one clergyman who hath had the experience of both litigations that hath not ingenuously confessed he had rather..have three suits depending in Westminister Hall than one in the Arches or any ecclesiastical court. **1661** J. STEPHENS *Procurations* 139, I never heard of any that stood out a suit against this payment..but was alwayes overthrown in the litigation. **1834** LYTTON *Pompeii* 24 My relations threatened me with litigation concerning my inheritance. **1856** FERRIER *Inst. Metaph.* (ed. 2) Introd. 6 A tribunal to which any point in litigation can be referred. **1880** MCCARTHY *Own Times* IV. liv. 176 Litigation means the waste of time and money.

b. The practice of going to law.

1785 PALEY *Mor. Philos.* VI. viii. (1786) 509 Nothing quells a spirit of litigation like despair of success. **1821** SYD. SMITH *Wks.* (1859) I. 349/1 This method would destroy litigation as effectually as the method proposed by Mr. Scarlett. **1862** TROLLOPE *Orley F.* ix. (ed. 4) 62 The spirit of litigation within him told him that the point was to be carried.

2. Disputation. Now *rare*.

1567 *Satir. Poems Reform.* iii. 149 Quha dow abstene fra litigatioun, Or from his paper hald aback the pen, Except he hait our Scottis Natioun? **1677** GALE *Crt. Gentiles* III. 29 Wiclef was much offended at this kind of sophistic litigation in maters of faith. **1749** FIELDING *Tom Jones* XVIII. x, The squire..was, after some litigation, obliged to consent. **1786** BURKE *Articles agst. W. Hastings* Wks. 1842 II. 87 To receive an explanation..of the matter in litigation. **1887** W. JAMES in *Mind* Jan. 1 Whether the 'muscular sense' directly yields us knowledge of space is still a matter of litigation among psychologists.

‖**litigator** ('lɪtɪgeɪtə(r), -ə(r)). [L.; agent-n. f. *lītigāre* (see LITIGATE).] One who litigates.

In mod. Dicts.

†**litigi'ose**, *a.* *Obs.* [ad. L. *lītigiōsus*: see LITIGIOUS.] = LITIGIOUS 1.

1677 GALE *Crt. Gentiles* III. 28 None gave so great an advance and perfection to this Dialectic litigiose mode of Philosophising as Aristotle.

litigiosity (lɪtɪdʒɪ'ɒsɪtɪ). [f. as prec. + -ITY.] The character or quality of being litigious; *esp.* in *Civil* and *Scots Law* (see LITIGIOUS 2 b).

1868 *Act 31 & 32 Vict.* c. 101 §159 *marg.*, Litigiosity as to lands not to begin before date of registration of notice of summons of reduction. **1875** POSTE *Gaius* IV. Comm. (ed. 2) 611 If the purchaser had notice of the litigiosity, he forfeits the purchase money to the fiscus.

litigious (lɪ'tɪdʒəs), *a.* Also 6 **litygyous, lytygious, letigeus**, 7 **la-, letigious, litigeous**. [ad. F. *litigieux*, ad. L. *lītigiōsus*, f. *litigium* litigation, related to *lītigāre* to LITIGATE: see -OUS.]

1. Of persons, their actions, dispositions, and utterances. **a.** Fond of disputes, contentious. Now *rare*. **b.** Fond of litigation; eager to go to law.

1382 WYCLIF *1 Tim.* iii. 3 It bihoueth a byschop for to be ..not litigious, or ful of stryf. **1432–50** tr. *Higden* (Rolls) III. 285 Socrates hade ii. litigious and malicious wifes. **1541** R. COPLAND *Galyen's Terap.* 2 B iij b, The other are all togyther stupydes, sturdy, & lytygious. **1592** [see BARRATOUS]. **1622** BEAUM. & FL. *Sp. Curate* II. ii, 'Tis some honest Client, Rich and litigious, the Curate has brought to me. **1639** FULLER *Holy War* III. xxviii. (1840) 168 A door was opened for her litigious pretenders to the Crown. **1665** GLANVILL *Scepsis Sci.* xix. 118 This Philosophy is litigious, the very spawn of disputations and controversies. **1682** BURNET *Rights Princes* ii. 51 A litigious prosecution of their suits. **1732** BERKELEY *Alciphr.* VII. §13 If the moment of opinions had been by some litigious divines made the measure of their zeal. **1793** BURKE *Observ. Conduct Minority* Wks. VII. 234 Objections which I must ever think litigious and sophistical. **1803** WELLINGTON in Gurw. *Desp.* II. 338 Lieut. Proctor is of a very litigious disposition. **1841** ELPHINSTONE *Hist. Ind.* I. 373 They [Hindus] are very litigious... They will persevere in a law-suit till they are ruined. **1855** MACAULAY *Hist. Eng.* xiii. III. 299 Sir Patrick Hume..had returned from exile, as litigious..as he had been four years before. **1868** E. EDWARDS *Ralegh* I. xxv. 601 Pine's grasping and litigious spirit had..given plenty of trouble in bygone days to Ralegh. **1875** BROWNING *Aristoph. Apol.* Wks. (1896) I. 685/1 Play the litigious fool to stuff the mouth Of dikast with the due three-obol fee.

absol. **1711** ADDISON *Spect.* No. 21 ¶ 3 This prodigious Society of Men may be divided into the Litigious and Peaceable.

†**c.** Engaged in litigation or contention; litigant. *Obs.*

1589 WARNER *Alb. Eng.* VI. xxxii. 143 He of Lancaster, and she of Yorke the heire: Of which letigious Famelies here mapped be the Lines.

absol. **1665** J. WEBB *Stone-Heng* (1725) 155 Gateways..by which the litigious and others had Access.

†**2.** Open to dispute or question; disputable, questionable; productive of litigation or contention. *Obs.*

1520 WHITINTON *Vulg.* (1527) 10 And in especyal that ye haue ended the litygyous mater. *c* **1555** HARPSFIELD *Divorce Hen. VIII* (1878) 41 To determine..dubious, and litigious questions insurging upon Moses' law. **1594** HOOKER *Eccl. Pol.* IV. xi. §12 The feast of Easter being..litigious in the dayes of Constantine. **1598** SIR T. NORREYS in *Lismore Papers* Ser. II. (1887) I. 17, I feare the matter will prove very letigeus. **1615** CROOKE *Body of Man* 336 The time of his birth seemeth to him to be litigious. **1648** BP. HALL *Select Th.* Ded., An age..that hath almost lost piety, in the chase of some litigious truths.

b. Disputable at law; that is or is liable to become the subject of a lawsuit, esp. of a benefice (see quot. 1768). In *Civil* and *Scots Law* said esp. of property respecting which an action is pending, and which therefore may not be alienated.

1568 *Mem. Q. Eliz. to Commissioners* in H. Campbell *Love Lett. Mary Q. Scots* App. 15 The rest, that is litigious and doubtful, to be equally divided. **1611** BEAUM. & FL. *Triumph of Love* ii, Thou hast put so sure a plea, That all my weal's litigious made by thee. **1624** SIR H. BOURGCHIER in *Ussher's Lett.* (1686) 314 Dr. Dee's [library]..hath been long litigious, and by that means unsold. *a* **1648** LD. HERBERT *Hen. VIII* (1683) 417 The Earl of Desmond dying, leaves his Estate litigious betwixt his Brother and Grand-child. **1697** DRYDEN *Virg. Georg.* I. 194 Nor Marks nor Bounds Distinguish'd Acres of litigious Grounds. **1768** BLACKSTONE *Comm.* III. 246 If two presentations be offered to the bishop upon the same avoidance, the church is then said to become litigious. **1868** *Act 31 & 32 Vict.* c. 101 §159 No summons of reduction..shall have any effect in rendering litigious the lands..except [etc.]. **1880** MUIRHEAD *Gaius* Digest 493 If the thing was not known to be litigious when purchased.

3. Of or pertaining to lawsuits or litigation.

1589 PUTTENHAM *Eng. Poesie* III. ii. (Arb.) 153 Certaine Doctours of the ciuil law were heard in a litigious cause betwixt a man and his wife. **1612** DEKKER *It be not good* Wks. 1873 III. 268 The barres of our latigious Courts had wont To crack with thronging pleaders. **1644** MILTON *Educ.* Wks. (1847) 99/1 Pleasing thoughts of litigious terms, fat contentions, and flowing fees. **1705** T. BROWN *To Author of Address* in *Coll. Poems* 95 Scaffolds are rais'd in Litigious Hall, The Maces glitter, and the Serjeants Bawl. **1710** STEELE & ADDISON *Tatler* No. 253 ¶ 13 Your Knowledge in the litigious Parts of the Law. **1780** BURKE *Sp. Œconomic Reform* Wks. III. 261 The fury of litigious war blew her horn on the mountains. **1825** BENTHAM *Ration. Rew.* 71 A defendant, unjustly dragged into the litigious contention.

litigiously (lɪ'tɪdʒəslɪ), *adv.* [f. prec. + -LY^2.] In a litigious manner, after the manner of a litigant; in a contentious spirit; wranglingly.

1608 MIDDLETON *Trick to Catch Old One* IV. iv. 121 Some foolish words..did pass, Which now litigiously he fastens on me. **1674** OWEN *Holy Spirit* (1693) 270 An Acquaintance with the Nature and Course of some Courts proceeding litigiously by Citations. **1719** D'URFEY *Pills* III. 47 From Mad-men, Fools, and Knaves he did Litigiously receive it. **1836** MARRYAT *Japhet* lxxiii, Instead of expressing anxiety to receive his son, he litigiously requires proofs.

litigiousness (lɪ'tɪdʒəsnɪs). [f. as prec. + -NESS.] The quality of being litigious; readiness to go to law.

1655 FULLER *Ch. Hist.* VI. iv. §9 This would minister matter of much litigiousnesse. *a* **1668** DAVENANT *Rutland House* Wks. (1673) 356 Farewel the happiness of the Nation when the populousness of the City argues the litigiousness of the Country. **1707** ATTERBURY *Vind. Doctr.* 37 The Intemperance and Litigiousness, with which he reproaches some of them. **1791** *Gentl. Mag.* 20/2 Promiscuous ridicule and the weapons of litigiousness had been thrown into the crowd. **1841** ELPHINSTONE *Hist. Ind.* I. 467 Strangers are now struck with the litigiousness..of the natives. **1866** *Daily Tel.* 31 Jan. 6/6 The Corporation is notorious for its obstructiveness and litigiousness.

litir, obs. form of LITTER.

litis-contestation (ˌlaɪtɪskɒntɛs'teɪʃən). *Civil* and *Scots Law.* Also 9 in compound form **liticontestation**. [ad. L. *lītis* (gen. of *līs* lawsuit) *contestātiōn-em* (n. of action f. *contestārī* to take or call to witness).] The formal entry of a suit in a court of law.

1456 SIR G. HAYE *Law Arms* (S.T.S.) 276/8 And fra litiscontestacioun be, the plede is begunnyn. *c* **1575** *Balfour's Practicks* (1754) 30 Quhilk day being come, the defendar sall mak litiscontestatioun. **1622** MALYNES *Anc. Law-Merch.* 446 By the common rules of the law, where no litiscontestation is past..no witnesse should be receiued. **1752** J. LOUTHIAN *Form of Process* (ed. 2) 265 Before Litis-contestation, the Defender may crave Protestation against the Pursuer for not insisting. **1802** BENTHAM *Princ. Judic. Proced.* Introd., Wks. 1843 II. 7 Expense of liticontestation, defrayed as far as possible by the public. **1880** MUIRHEAD *Gaius* III. §180 An obligation is extinguished by litiscontestation or joinder of issue.

†**litis'pendence.** *Obs.* *rare*$^{-0}$. [a. OF. *litispendence* (F. *litispendance*), ad. late L. *litispendentia*, f. *litis* (see prec.) + *pendentia*, n. of state f. *pendēre* to hang.] **a.** (See quot. 1706.) **b.** A plea that another action is pending.

1656 BLOUNT *Glossogr.*, *Litispendence*, the hanging of a suit till it be tried or decided. **1706** PHILLIPS (ed. Kersey), *Litispendence*, the time during which a Law-suit is depending. **1728** in BAILEY, and in some mod. Dicts.

†**litis'pendency.** *Obs.* *rare*$^{-1}$. [f. as prec.: see -ENCY.] = prec.

1762 tr. *Busching's Syst. Geog.* VI. 58 The preventing of any violent procedures betwixt the parties during this litispendency.

†**litlum**, *adv.* *Obs.* Forms: 1 **lýtl-, lítlum, lítlan**, 3 **lutlen**, 4 **lytul-, litel-, lutlum**, 4–5 **litlum**. [OE. *lýtlum*, dat. pl. neut. of *lýtel* LITTLE, used advb.] Little by little, gradually: chiefly repeated. ***litlum and litlum***; also (rarely) ***by litlum***.

c **1000** ÆLFRIC *Gram.* xxxviii. (Z.) 228 *Paulatim*, lytlum. *c* **1000** ÆLFRIC *Gen.* xl. 10 Ic ʒeseah þær on weaxende blosman litlum and litlum. *a* **1123** *O.E. Chron.* an. 1110 (Laud MS.) Syððan litlan and litlan his leoht wanode. *c* **1205** LAY. 3569 Makie him god baid..& him blod lete lutlen [*c* 1275 lutel] and ofte. *a* **1225** *St. Marher.* 12 þat liht alei lutlen ant lutlen. **1377** LANGL. *P. Pl.* B. xv. 599 Lere hem litlum & lytlum [**1393** C. XVIII. 320 lytulum and lytulum; *v. rr.* lit(e)lum and lit(e)litlan, litel and (bi) litel]. *a* **1380** *St. Ambrose* 533 in Horstm. *Altengl. Leg.* (1878) 16 A schort fuir ..lutlum and lutlum In to his mouþ crep hole and sum. *c* **1425** *St. Mary of Oignies* I. vi. in *Anglia* VIII. 139/9 Hee þat rekkiþ not smale thinges fallíþ doune by litlum.

litmus ('lɪtməs). Forms: 6 **lyȝtmose, lyt(t)mos(se, litmouce**, 7 **litmas(e, -mouse, litt(i)mus**, 7–8 **litmose**, 8 **litmoss, lytmus**, 7– **litmus**. [Altered from MDu. *leecmos*, *lijcmoes* (mod.Du. *lakmoes*) LACMUS, prob. from

association with LIT *v.*] **a.** A blue colouring matter, obtained from various lichens, esp. archil, *Roccella tinctoria*. Also *fig.*, as in ***litmus test***.

It is turned red by acids, and the blue colour is restored by alkalis.

1502 *Receipt for Corke* in *Arnolde's Chron.* 71 b/1 Take an C. & a q'rt of ly3tmose. **1518** *Will of R. Hoby* (Somerset Ho.), xij bagges of Lytmos otherwise called white Corke. **1546** *Inv. Ch. Goods Surrey* 107 Item for lyttmosse ijli. viijd. **1594** PLAT *Jewell-ho.* III. 37 Dry Litmas scraped in water. **1606** PEACHAM *Art of Drawing* 57 If you put to overmuch Litmose it maketh a deep blew. **1640** *Rates* in Noorthouck *Lond.* (1773) 838/2 Littimus, the cwt. qt. 112 lb. 1*d.* **1722** *Act Encour. Silk Manuf. &c.* in *Lond. Gaz.* No. 6040/7 Litmus the Hundred Weight,..twenty Shillings. **1811** A. T. THOMSON *Lond. Disp.* (1818) 471 This solution.. reddens tincture of litmus. **1898** *Allbutt's Syst. Med.* V. 448 Soak the papers in strong neutral litmus and dry them. **1957** *Essays in Crit.* VII. 80 Their possession is as good a cultural litmus test as any I can think of. **1971** *Daily Tel.* Nov. 13/2 The litmus test comes with the old issue of whether the NUS should re-join the IUS. **1972** *Times* 21 Nov. 21/7 The litmus test will be the effect of the rise from 4p to 10p in the basic charge for an inpayment.

b. *attrib.*, as ***litmus colour, liquor, tincture***; **litmus blue**, a blue pigment prepared from litmus; **litmus paper**, unsized paper stained blue with litmus, to be used as a test for acids; when reddened by an acid, it serves as a test for alkalis.

1612 PEACHAM *Gentl. Exerc.* 83 The principal blewes..are Blew bice, Smalt, *Litmose blew. **1727** W. MATHER *Yng. Man's Comp.* 83 Put the quantity of a Hazel-Nut of Litmose-blue, to three Spoonfuls of Conduit-Water. **1805** W. SAUNDERS *Min. Waters* 30 Another portion of the same *litmus liquor reserved for comparison. **1803** DAVY in *Phil. Trans.* XCIII. 246 A fluid came over, which reddened *litmus-paper. **1827** FARADAY *Chem. Manip.* xii. 270 Two of them [test papers]..surpass the rest, these are litmus and turmeric papers. **1899** CAGNEY tr. *Jaksch's Clin. Diagn.* vii. (ed. 4) 367 May's *litmus tincture.

litnien, variant of LITTEN *v.*[1] *Obs.*

litoptern (lɪˈtɒptɜːn). *Palæont.* Also **litopternan**. [f. mod.L. name of order *Litopterna* (F. Ameghino 1889, in *Actas Acad. Nac. Córdoba* VI. 492), f. Gk. λῑτός smooth + πτέρνη heel-bone.] An extinct South American ungulate mammal of the order so called. Hence **litopternine** (lɪˈtɒptɜːnaɪn) *a.*

[**1891** E. D. COPE in *Amer. Naturalist* XXV. 688 The articulation in the Litopterna is of ungulate character.] **1925** C. R. EASTMAN tr. *Zittel's Text-bk. Palaeontol.* III. 123 The Litopternine suborder of ungulates is restricted to South America. **1927** HALDANE & HUXLEY *Animal Biol.* xi. 243 *(caption)* Extinct South American Litopternan. **1933** A. S. ROMER *Vertebr. Paleontol.* xvi. 316 Small litopterns.. present in the oldest known Tertiary beds of South America, had primitive bunodont cheek teeth. **1971** *Nature* 15 Jan. 172/1 In some mammals, tapirs, elephants, the extinct astropotheres, pyrotheres, and litopterns, the external nares are posterior and large.

†**litorean**, *a. Obs. rare*⁻⁰. [f. L. *lītore-us* (f. *lītor-, lītus, littus*, shore) + -AN.] = LITTORAL *a.*
1656 in BLOUNT *Glossogr.*

†**li'tote.** *Obs. rare*⁻¹. See also LIPTOTE. [a. F. *litote*, ad. Gr. λιτότης: see next.] = next.
1645 RUTHERFORD *Tryal & Tri. Faith* xv. 116, Ps. 23. 4 Yea though I walk [etc.]; its a *Litote*, I will believe good: its a cold and a dark shadow to walke at deaths right side.

‖**litotes** (ˈlaɪtəʊtiːz). *Rhet.* [Gr. λῑτότης, f. λῑτός smooth, plain, small, meagre.] A figure of speech, in which an affirmative is expressed by the negative of the contrary; an instance of this.

Examples of litotes are: 'A citizen of no mean city'; 'When no small tempest lay on us.'

1657 J. SMITH *Myst. Rhet.* 3. **1696** in PHILLIPS (ed. 5). **1727** POPE, etc. *Art of Sinking* 115 The *litotes* or diminution, [is the peculiar talent] of ladies, whisperers, and backbiters. **1883** SCHAFF *Hist. Chr. Ch.* I. v. 291 Pressing into his service ..the litotes and other rhetorical figures.

‖**lit-par-lit** (liparli), *a. Geol.* [Fr., = 'bed by bed'.] Designating the intrusion of innumerable narrow, more or less parallel, sheets or tongues of magma into the bedding of rocks. Also as *adv.*

1896 *Q. Jrnl. Geol. Soc.* LII. 635 In..1890..Mr. Horne obtained confirmatory evidence of the 'lit par lit' introduction of granitic materials into the crystalline schists south-west of Strath Halladale. **1902** *Ibid.* LVIII. p. lxxv, M. Michel Lévy recognizes two types of intermixture: the one taking place by superposition, the other by injection lit par lit... In the latter type the compound rock consists of alternating folia of granite and sedimentary material. **1909** F. H. HATCH *Text-bk. Petrol.* (ed. 5) I. 18 When the intrusion is repeated between many planes of stratification, it is known as *lit-par-lit* intrusion. **1925** B. N. ODELL in E. F. Norton *Fight for Everest 1924* 291 It is composed of dark horizontally banded biotite gneiss alternating with bands of light granite, though in the upper part of the cliff the latter is represented by pegmatite, and the whole appears to represent a large-scale example of *lit-par-lit* injection. **1962** A. E. J. & C. G. ENGEL in A. E. J. Engel et al. *Petrologic Stud.* 42 The amphibolites are only locally shredded, injected *lit-par-lit*, or replaced by granite. **1968** K. R. MEHNERT *Migmatites* ix. 278 Banded gneisses and migmatites of the 'lit-par-lit'-type follow.

litrameter (lɪˈtræmɪtə(r)). [f. Gr. λίτρα a pound + METER.] An instrument for ascertaining the specific gravity of liquids.

1826 R. HARE in *Amer. Jrnl. Sci. & Arts* XI. 183 On the Litrameter. This name..is given to one of the instruments which I have contrived for ascertaining specific gravities. **1858** in SIMMONDS *Dict. Trade.* Hence in mod. Dicts.

†**litre**[1]. *Obs. rare*⁻¹. In 7 lytre. [ad. late L. *litra*, a. Gr. λίτρα a pound.] A pound.
1603 HOLLAND *Plutarch's Mor.* 432 One silver boul, weighing fiue lytres [*marg.* or pounds].

litre[2] (ˈliːtə(r), Fr. litr). Also *U.S.* liter. [a. F. *litre*, first formed in 1793; suggested by *litron*, the name of an obsolete Fr. measure of capacity, app. f. late L. *litra*, a. Gr. λίτρα pound.] **a.** The unit of capacity in the metric system, represented by a cube whose edge is the tenth of a metre, and equivalent to rather more than $1\frac{3}{4}$ pints.

In 1901 the litre was redefined as the volume of a kilogramme of water under specified conditions (see quot. 1957), which made it equal to approximately 1·000,028 cubic decimetres; this definition was abandoned in 1964 in favour of the original one (see quot. 1965).

1797 *Jrnl. Nat. Philos.* Aug. 197 A vessel of a cubical form, having for its side one decimetre, or a cylindrical vessel of the same solid contents, has received the name of litre. It contains about two pounds of water, or twenty-five ounces of wheat. **1810** *Naval Chron.* XXIV. 301 Littre, Decimeter cube. **1839** *Penny Cycl.* XIV. 56/1 Four litres and a half make, roughly speaking, an imperial gallon. **1866** ODLING *Anim. Chem.* 6 If we take..a litre of hydrogen and a litre of chlorine, we obtain exactly two litres of hydrochloric acid. **1886** W. J. TUCKER *E. Europe* 336 The farmers..strike bargains over a couple of 'liters' of wine with the Hebrew corn, cattle, or pig dealer. **1902** *Nature* 10 Apr. 538/1 Annexe iv..recapitulates the decisions of the Troisième Conférence Générale held at Paris last October, as to the definitions of the metric units, metre, kilogramme and litre. **1923** GLAZEBROOK *Dict. Appl. Physics* III. 777/2 The definition of the litre has no reference to the units of length, and the original intention that it should be equal to 1 cubic decimetre has been quite abandoned. *Ibid.* 778/2 In his final résumé of the whole observations M. Benoit gives 1 litre = 1000·027 c.c. as the most probable value. **1957** E. R. COHEN et. al. *Fund. Constants Physics* ii. 5 The liter is defined as the volume of a kilogram of water, at standard atmospheric pressure and at the temperature of its maximum density, approximately 4°C. On a level of sufficient precision this is an ambiguous definition, since it does not specify the isotopic constitution of the water... We adopt..1 liter = 1000·028 ±0·004 cm³. **1965** *Nature* 6 Feb. 553/1 The twelfth General Conference of Weights and Measures was held..during October 6–13, 1964... Resolution 6 (the litre) abolished the definition of the litre established in 1901 by the third General Conference, declared that the word 'litre' can be used as a special name given to the cubic decimetre and recommended that the name 'litre' shall not be used to express the results of volume measurements of high precision... It now reverts to its original meaning. The intention is that this litre shall only be used for ordinary transactions in trade and not for scientific purposes. **1969** *Physics Bull.* Feb. 58/2 It was a regrettable international decision in 1964 which reinstated the name litre for a cubic decimetre.

b. Preceded by a number or a word denoting a number so as to form adjs. denoting the capacity (i.e. the inside volume of the cylinders) of a motor vehicle or its engine, and used *ellipt.* for a vehicle having the specified engine capacity.

1927 A. HUXLEY *Let.* 25 Feb. (1969) 284 We have gone and bought a really rather tremendous car—an Itala six cylinder two-litres. **1951** *Engineering* 26 Oct. 533/2 It is a full six-seater, powered by a new 3-litre six cylinder engine developing 90 brake horse-power at 4,100 r.p.m. **1955** *Times* 3 May 10/5 Bruigi, driving a three-litre Ferrari, crashed into a cement road sign near Teramo. **1974** *Country Life* 17 Jan. (Suppl.) 34/1 Put the Triumph 2000 beside any other 2-litre in its class and there's very little in it for mpg.

‖**litron.** [Fr.; see prec.] (See quot.)
1725 BRADLEY *Fam. Dict.* s.v. *Wig*, Half a Litron or somewhat more than half a pint of wheat flower.

ˈ**litster.** ? *Obs.* Forms: 4 litestere, 4–5 littester, 5 littstar, lystare, -er, lyt(a)ster, lyttester, 5–6 lytster, 6 litstair, 5– litster, (9 *dial.* lister). [f. LIT *v.* + -STER.] A dyer.

c **1374** CHAUCER *Former Age* 17 No mader, welde, or wod no litestere Ne knew. **1428** in *Surtees Misc.* (1888) 6 [He] seld yt furth deceyvabilly to lytsters, and, in especial, to John Kyrkby and Robert Dowfe, lytsters of York. **1432** *Test. Ebor.* (Surtees) II. 21, I wyll..to Kendall wyfe, lyttester, xxvjˢ viijᵈ. **1488** *Nottingham Rec.* III. 12 Et de iijs. pro firma unius gardini nuper in tenura Thomae Parker, litster. **1587** *Sc. Acts Jas. VI*, c. 119 As alsua ane litstair or ma for litting and perfitting of þair saide warkis. **1609** *N. Riding Rec.* I. 165 Tho. Newton, litster, presented for brewing [etc.]. **1649** G. DANIEL *Trinarch., Rich. II*, xcv, As though the state Might weare noe Cloath by Dyed in Litstar's fatt. **1714–26** G. GUTHRIE *Mem.* (1900) 18 He had also two other Sons..both Litsters in Aberdeen. **1819** HUNTER *Hallamsh. Gloss., Lister.* **1887** BULLOCH *Pynours* 85 The burn still runs, but now of small use to any Litster.

litt, littarge, obs. ff. LIGHT, LIT, LITHARGE.

litte, obs. f. or var. LIT, LITE.

ˈ**litten**, *sb. Obs.* exc. *dial.* Forms: 1 líc-tún, 5 lytton(e, letton, 6 lyttyn, 7 litton, 6– litten. [OE. *líc-tún*, f. *líc* corpse, LICH + *tún* enclosure, TOWN.] A churchyard. (Cf. CHURCH-LITTEN.)

c **900** tr. *Bæda's Hist.* III. xvii. (Schipper) 268 His lichama ..wæs..on þæra broþra lictune bebyrized. *c* **1420** *Chron. Vilod.* 4087 Bot when he come in to þat chirche-lyttone þo, Twey wemen he founde þere. **1474–5** in Swayne *Churchw. Acc. Sarum* (1896) 18 It. of the gift of the Bochers for grounds to her Stallys with oute the letton ijs. *Ibid.* 20 It' in cleansyng of the Lytton xj*d.* **1506** *Will of Leer* (Somerset Ho.), To be buried in the cloister or in the lyttyn of the Trynite. **1595** in Swayne *Churchw. Acc. Sarum* (1896) 145 The wale against the litten. **1614–15** *Ibid.* 165 Masonn mendinge the Church litton wale, 5*s.* **1706** PHILLIPS (ed. Kersey), *Litten*, as Church-litten; a word us'd in Wiltshire for a Church-yard. **1798** J. JEFFERSON *Hampsh. Gloss.* (MS.) s.v., The buryᵍ. ground at Holy Ghost Chapel at B'stoke is called the Litten. It is used also at Newbury in Berks. **1818** in TODD; and in mod. Dicts.

litten (lɪt(ə)n), *ppl. a.* [pseudo-archaic pple. of LIGHT *v.*[2]] = LIGHTED. Usually in comb., e.g. ***dim-, gray-, red-litten***.

a **1849** POE *Haunted Palace* vi, And travellers now within that valley, Through red-litten windows, see Vast forms that move fantastically To a discordant melody. **1861** LYTTON & FANE *Tannhäuser* 72 And 'salvum me fac Domine' they sung Sonorous, in the ghostly going out Of the red-litten eve along the land. **1870** MORRIS *Earthly Par.* III. 9 After the weary tossing of the night And close dim-litten chamber. **1896** CROCKETT *Cleg Kelly* 407 Sal Kavannah moved into the gray-litten space. **1899** *Blackw. Mag.* Feb. 319/1 It [yellow hair] sprayed out like a cloud of litten gold.

†ˈ**litten**, *v.*[1] *Obs.* Also 2 litnien, 3 *Orm.* littnenn. [? Extended form (with suffix -EN[5]) of ON. *lita* = OE. *wlitan* to look.] *intr.* To look *to, unto.* Also const. *for to* with *inf*: to rely on.

c **1175** *Lamb. Hom.* 7 Forþi ne litmie [? *read* litnie] namon to swiðe to þisse liue. *c* **1200** ORMIN 6115 Þet birrþ wislike nittenn Uppo þe sellfenn, and o þa þatt I ttnenn to þin fode. *a* **1300** *Cursor M.* 10209 Child for to gett þai littend lang. **1535** COVERDALE *Jer.* xlvi. 25 Pharao, and all them yᵗ litten vnto him.

†ˈ**litten**, *v.*[2] *Obs.* [? f. *lit* LITE: see -EN[5].] *trans.* To diminish.

c **1300** *Havelok* 2701 Hwan Hauelok saw his folk so brittene, And his ferd so swithe littene, He cam driuende upon a stede.

litter (ˈlɪtə(r)), *sb.* Forms: 4–7 liter(e, 4 litir, littar, 5 leter(e, -yr, lyttar, -ere, -ier, -yer, lyter(e, -ier, -our, 5–7 lytter, -tre, 6 litto(u)r, (litre), (6–7 licter, 7 letter, lictier, -ure, litour, littier, littre), 5– litter. [ad. AF. *litere*, OF. *litiere*, (F. *litière*) = Pr. *leitiera*, Sp. *litera*, It. *lettiera*:—med.L. *lectāria*, f. L. *lect-us* (F. *lit*) bed.]

†**1. a.** A bed. *Obs.*

a **1300** *Cursor M.* 13817 Quen he had made me hale and fere, 'Rise vp', he said, 'wit þi litere'. *a* **1400–50** *Alexander* 4910 All lemed of his letere þe loge as of heuen. **1440** J. SHIRLEY *Dethe K. James* (1818) 17 The traitours sought the Kyng..yn the withdrawyng chaumburs, yn the litters, undir the presses. *c* **1460** *Towneley Myst.* xiv. 590 Lo, here a lytter redy cled. **1481** CAXTON *Reynard* (Arb.) 61 Tho laye they doun on a lytier made of strawe, the foxe hys wyf and hys chyldren wente alle to slepe.

b. In technical use: A 'bed' or substratum of various materials.

1848 RONALDS & RICHARDSON *Chem. Technol.* I. 35 Having first made a litter of shingles, planks or billets, with a layer of charcoal powder several inches in thickness.

2. a. A vehicle in use down to recent times, containing a couch shut in by curtains, and carried on men's shoulders or by beasts of burden. **b.** A framework supporting a bed or couch for the transport of the sick and wounded.

c **1330** *Arth. & Merl.* 8541 (Kölbing) Sche akeuered, par ma fay, & was yleyd in liter, Al mast liche an hors bere. **1375** BARBOUR *Bruce* IX. 106 In littar thai [him] lay, And till the slevach held thair vay. **1412–20** LYDG. *Chron. Troy* II. xx, In a lytter made tho full royall..To cary hym softe and easyly. *c* **1450** *Merlin* xviii. 301 Than thei ordeyned hir a litier vpon two palfrayes. **1470–85** MALORY *Arthur* XIX. vii, He ordeyned lyttyers for the wounded knyghtes. **1502** *Privy Purse Exp. Eliz. of York* (1830) 28 Item a covering for a litter of blewe cloth of golde. **1557** GRIMALD in *Tottel's Misc.* (Arb.) 123 In littour layd, they lead him vnkouth wayes. **1606** HOLLAND *Sueton.* 51 A flash of lightning glaunced upon his licter, and struck his servant stone dead. **1634** MILTON *Comus* 554 The drowsie frighted steeds That draw the litter of close-curtain'd sleep. **1663** WOOD *Life* 4 July, The scutcheons on the litter hung on still. **1734** tr. *Rollin's Anc. Hist.* (1827) I. Pref. 50 To keep himself close shut up in his litter. **1808** PIKE *Sources Mississ.* I. 31 Found five litters in which sick or wounded men had been carried. **1839** KEIGHTLEY *Hist. Eng.* I. 429 She was conveyed..in a litter, over which four knights held a canopy of cloth of gold. **1894** A. ROBERTSON *Nuggets*, etc. 153 He soon made a comfortable litter in which to carry Elsie home.

3. Straw, rushes, or the like, serving as bedding.

†**a.** For human beings. *to make litter of* (one's life): to sacrifice lavishly (= F. *faire litière de*). *Obs.*

c **1440** *Promp. Parv.* 307/2 Lytere of a bed, *stratus, stratorium.* *c* **1450** *Bk. Curtasye* 435 in *Babees Bk.*, Gromes palettis shyn fyle and make litere. *a* **1483** *Liber Niger* in *Househ. Ord.* (1790) 41 The groome porter berith wood, strawe, rushes, for the King's chambre, making the King's litters of his bed. **1652** HOWELL *Giraffi's Rev. Naples* II. 119 Whereupon the said Duke offer'd to make litter of his life for the service of his Catholick Majesty the King. **1774** COLLYER *Hist. Eng.* II. 126 John Baldwin held the manor of Oterarsee..by the service of finding litter for the king's bed, viz. in summer grass or herbs, and in winter straw.

b. For animals. In mod. use also, the straw and dung together.

[**1314–15** *Rolls of Parlt.* I. 302/2, xxiii quarters de aveyn & de litter.] *c* **1430** LYDG. *Hors, Shepe, & G.* (Roxb.) 10 As pelows ben to chambres agreable So is harde strawe lytter for the stable. *c* **1440** *Promp. Parv.* 307/2 Lytere, or strowynge of horse, and other beestys, *stramentum*. **1583** STUBBES *Anat. Abus.* II. (1882) 12 A little straw or litter bad inough for a dog to lie in. **1662** GERBIER *Princ.* 35 The space which the Horse doth possess when in the night time he lyeth stretcht on his Litter. **1693** EVELYN *De la Quint. Compl. Gard.* I. 54 To place daily under those Animals..a sufficient quantity of fresh New Straw, well spread, which is call'd making of Litter. **1731** SWIFT *Bro. Protestants* Wks. 1755 IV. I. 181 The gen'rous wheat forgot its pride, And sail'd with litter side by side. **1809** SCOTT *Prose Wks.* IV. *Biographies* II. (1870) 124 There was no wood to burn and no litter or forage to be had for his horses. **1845** *Florist's Jrnl.* 127 Take some long litter from the dung heap. **1849** MACAULAY *Hist. Eng.* iii. I. 320 The litter of a farmyard gathered under the windows of his bed-chamber.

c. Hence applied to straw or similar materials used for other purposes, *e.g.* †as a component of plaster, †for thatch, or for the protection of plants.

1453 *Mem. Ripon* (Surtees) III. 160 Et de 2*d.* solut. pro liter pro dobura ibidem. **1486** *Nottingham Rec.* III. 255 For litter for dawbyng of þe same bothes. **1659** TORRIANO, *Stìpia*,..licture, or thatch for cottages. **1664** EVELYN *Kal. Hort.* Mar. (1679) 12 Take off the Littier from your Kernel-beds. **1706** LONDON & WISE *Retir'd Gard'ner* I. III. xiii. 304 Tulips..are protected..by Coverings of Straw, or long Litter. **1744** PICKERING in *Phil. Trans.* XLIII. 100 Over the Bed, thus prepared, must constantly be kept a Covering of long new Litter..to preserve the Plant from the Frost. **1846** J. BAXTER *Libr. Pract. Agric.* (ed. 4) II. 195 In frosty weather, protect the rows by fern leaves, long litter, or branches of evergreens. **1861** DELAMER *Fl. Garden* 22 Agapanthus..may be permitted to remain throughout the winter in the open ground, under a covering of litter or leaves.

4. Odds and ends, fragments and leavings lying about, rubbish; a state of confusion or untidiness; a disorderly accumulation of things lying about.

1730 SWIFT *Lady's Dressing-r.* 8 Strephon..took a strict survey Of all the litter as it lay. **1742** FIELDING *J. Andrews* IV. ix, She was ashamed to be seen in such a pickle,..her house was in such a litter. **1796** C. MARSHALL *Garden.* xx. 397 Drying flowers, all litter, and everything unsightly, admonish the gardener to trim his plants. **1835** URE *Philos. Manuf.* 232 They [silkworms] must be well cleansed from the litter. **1860** RUSKIN *Mod. Paint.* V. IX. ix. 293 He [Turner]..enjoyed and looked for litter... His pictures are often full of it. **1868** J. H. BLUNT *Ref. Ch. Eng.* I. 347 An old pamphlet among the litter of the abbot's study. **1894** HALL CAINE *Manxman* III. xvii. 182 The kitchen was covered with the litter of dressmakers preparing for the wedding.

5. a. The whole number of young brought forth at a birth.

1486 *Bk. St. Albans* F vj, A Litter of welpis. **1546** J. HEYWOOD *Prov.* (1867) 27 The litter is lyke to the syre and the damme. **1597** SHAKS. *2 Hen. IV*, I. ii. 14, I doe heere walke before thee, like a Sow, that hath o'rewhelm'd all her Litter, but one. **1601** HOLLAND *Pliny* I. 220 The best of the whole litter is that whelpe that is last ere it begin to see. **1604** MIDDLETON *Witch* I. ii, Seven of their young pigs..Of the last litter. **1698** TYSON in *Phil. Trans.* XX. 123 Possibly this Subject never had a Litter. **1731** *Gentl. Mag.* I. 352 A Litter of young Lions was whelp'd at the Tower. **1802** PALEY *Nat. Theol.* xiv. (ed. 2) 276 In the sow, the bitch, the rabbit,.. which have numerous litters, the paps are numerous. **1820** BYRON *Mar. Fal.* III. ii, The hunter may reserve some single cub From out the tiger's litter. **1859** DARWIN *Orig. Spec.* i. (1873) 6 Strongly-marked differences occasionally appear in the young of the same litter.

transf. and *fig.* **1565** HARDING *Confut. Jewels' Apol.* IV. xx. 219 Verely a man might thinke this booke was set forth by some ennemye of our newe english clergy,..had not them selues..acknowledged it for a whelpe of their one littour. *a* **1639** W. WHATELEY *Prototypes* I. xix. (1640) 223 That abhominable litter and broode of sinnes which have their originall in mans heart. **1662** SOUTH *Serm.* 9 Nov. (1663) 35 Let him reflect upon that numerous litter of strange, senselesse absurd Opinions, that crawle about the world. **1664** POWER *Exp. Philos.* Pref. 6 They are as inapprehensive, and of the same litter with the former. **1688** *Vox Cleri Pro Rege* Pref. A ij, In the time when Hawkers were loaded with whole Litters of Pamphlets. *a* **1704** T. BROWN in R. L'Estrange *Colloq. Erasm.* (1711) 358 A servant maid and a litter of children. **1796** BURKE *Regic. Peace* iii. Wks. VIII. 282 To bring into an happy birth her abundant litter of constitutions. **1860** GEO. ELIOT *Mill on Fl.* viii, When a man had married into a family where there was a whole litter of women, he might have plenty to put up with if he choose.

†b. An act of bringing forth young: usually in phr. ***at a*** or ***one litter***. Said of animals only.

c **1440** *Promp. Parv.* 307/2 Lytere or forthe bryngynge of beestys, *fetus, fetura*. **1693** DRYDEN *Juvenal* vi. (1697) 129 The thirty Pigs at one large Litter farrow'd. **1794** S. WILLIAMS *Vermont* 91 The female produces from three to six young ones at a litter.

6. *attrib.* and *Comb.*, as (sense 2) ***litter-bearer***, ***-bier***, ***-car***, ***-gelding***, ***-man***, ***-window***; also ***litter-wise*** adv.; (sense 3) ***litter-cutting***; (sense 4) ***litter-bag***, ***-basket***, ***-bin***, ***-box***, ***-bug*** (BUG *sb.*[2] 3 a), ***-carrier***, ***-cart***, ***-lout***; (sense 5) ***litter-mate***, ***-sister***.

1968 *Punch* 19 June 892/2 Drop it sadly in your heavy white kraft paper car *litterbag. **1958** J. CANNAN *And be a Villain* vii. 160 Oh, the mess they leave on our little common ..in spite of the *litter baskets. **1972** J. BROWN *Chancer* xiv. 191 There's a row of litter baskets each side of the gates. **1552** ELYOT *Dict.*, *Lecticariola*, she that attendeth on a *licter bearer. **1870** MORRIS *Earthly Par.* II. III. 14 He shut his eyes, and now no more could hear His litter-bearers' feet. **1859** TENNYSON *Enid* 1414 Yet raised and laid him on a *litter-bier. **1947** *Archit. Rev.* CII. 198 (*caption*) On the right a typical *litter-bin. **1972** *Guardian* 28 Jan. 5/6 Clerical staff..have been..sweeping up, and emptying litter bins. **1953** *News Chron.* 2 June 4/4 What a mess there will be on Coronation Day unless people use the *litter-boxes. **1947** *N.Y. Herald-Tribune* 16 Feb. 2/7 (*heading*) 47,000 subway '*litterbugs' pay $107,000 in fines in 1946 drive. **1959** *Times* 23 July 7/7, I rate such persons in the same category as litter bugs. **1971** *Guardian* 8 Dec. 24/8 He picks up any litter he can find..and he is apt to give litter-bugs a severe dressing-down. **1812** SIR R. WILSON *Priv. Diary* I. 140 Two of my dragoons..got into the *litter-cars of the country. **1915** J. LONDON *Let.* 26 Jan. (1966) 445 He has no *litter-carriers to carry manure. **1967** *Litter-cart [see *cloth-capped* adj.]. **1851** *Illustr. Catal. Gt. Exhib.* 396 Two-knife cane-top *litter and chaff-cutting machine. **1836** DEVON *Issue Exch. Jas. I* 319 A *litter-gelding for the Queen's litter. **1927** *Children's Newspaper* 25 June 8/2 It is time the *Litter Lout was taken seriously in hand. **1972** *Guardian* 29 Mar. 24/1 The packaging industry had been made a scapegoat for the actions of the litter lout. **1505** *Ld. Treas. Acc. Scot.* III. 97 Item, for ij steikis chamlot to the Quenis tua *littar men.. viij[li]. **1647** HAWARD *Crown Rev.* 33 Six Littermen: Fee a peice 10*l.* **1670–98** LASSELS *Voy. Italy* II. 84 Augustus Cæsar..had escaped a thunderclap which kill'd his litter-man close by him. **1707** CHAMBERLAYNE *St. Gt. Brit.* III. xi. 440 All belonging to the Stables, as Coachmen, Footmen, Littermen, Postilions, &c. **1921** *Genetics* VI. 122 These are assumed to be *litter-mates for whom all or nearly all tangible environmental factors may be assumed to be in common. **1946** *Nature* 24 Aug. 258/2 A biological test of a solution in arachis oil of the vitamin A thus obtained showed growth-promoting activity in rats (ten litter-mate growth comparisons) of the order indicated by spectroscopic assay. **1972** *Sci. Amer.* Feb. 22/3 Rodents are small, inexpensive and bear large litters, so that littermates with the same genetic background can be assigned to different conditions. **1897** *Sketch* 24 Nov. 192 The puppy..is a *litter-sister to the then ten-weeks-old Wayward. **1960** *Farmer & Stockbreeder* 1 Mar. 79/2 Mr. G. H. Lewis was not to be denied in the junior class, litter-sisters from him..taking first and second places. **1973** *Country Life* 15 Feb. 385/1 Miss S. G. Weall's fawn dog..collected two firsts and his litter sister..two seconds. *a* **1661** HOLYDAY *Juvenal* 42 Keep His *litter-window shut, and he can sleep. *a* **1626** BACON *New Atl.* (1900) 32 He was carried in a rich Chariott, without Wheeles, *Litter-wise.

litter ('lɪtə(r)), *v.* [f. LITTER *sb.*]

†1. *trans.* To carry in a litter. *Obs. rare*⁻¹.

1713 ? DARRELL *Gentl. Instructed* I. Suppl. iii. 18 These Pagan Ladies were litter'd to Campus Martius, ours are coach'd to Hide-Park.

2. To furnish (a horse, etc.) with litter or straw for his bed; *humorously*, to provide (a person) with a bed. Also ***to litter down***.

1398 TREVISA *Barth. De P.R.* XVIII. xli. (1495) 802 The colte is not lyttrid wyth strawe nother coryed wyth an horse combe. **1607** TOPSELL *Four-f. Beasts* (1658) 291 It shall be necessary to keep him warm..by littering him up to the belly with fresh straw. *a* **1670** HACKET *Abp. Williams* II. (1693) 30 Tell them how they litter their Jades and exercise Merchandize in the House of God. **1737** BRACKEN *Farriery Impr.* (1749) I. 77 Bedding or littering him down with dry clean Straw. **1799** WASHINGTON *Lett.* Writ. 1893 XIV. 220 That the stock may be well fed,—littered,—and taken care of according to the directions. **1840** HOOD *Kilmansegg* xvi, One is litter'd under a roof Neither wind nor waterproof. **1859** F. A. GRIFFITHS *Artil. Man.* (1862) 221 Let him be returned to the stable, littered down. **1861** SMILES *Engineers* II. 112 Thrashing straw to litter the large stock of cattle he had on hand.

absol. **1577** B. GOOGE *Heresbach's Husb.* I. (1586) 41 b, Al kinde of strawe, is good to litter withall.

transf. or *fig.* **1821** CLARE *Vill. Minstr.* I. 129, I love the browning bough to see That litters autumn's dying bed.

3. *intr.* To lie down on a bed or on litter. *rare.*

1634 HABINGTON *Castara* II. 72 The Inne, Where he and his horse litter'd. **1858** W. ARNOT *Laws fr. Heaven* II. 279 That poor wretch..has a number of children littering in the hovel which they call their home.

4. *trans.* **†a.** To compound (plaster) with or as with litter (*obs.*). (Cf. LITTER *sb.* 3 c.) **b.** *nonce-use.* To plaster.

1559 MORWYNG *Evonym.* 65 Some use pure clay littered with ox heare. **1862** J. SKELTON *Nugæ Crit.* i. 60 The hovels of the natives were built of turf, littered with mud.

5. To cover with litter. Also with *down*.

1700 DRYDEN *Cock & Fox* 226 But, for his ease, well littered was the floor. **1813** *Sporting Mag.* XLII. 55 A loose stable, well littered down with fresh straw. **1831** CARLYLE *Sart. Res.* II. iii. (1891) 73 Mind, which grows, not like a vegetable (by having its roots littered with etymological compost), but like a spirit.

6. a. To cover as with litter, to strew *with* objects scattered in disorder. Also with *round*, *over*, *up*.

1713 SWIFT *Cadenus & Vanessa* Wks. 1755 III. II. 15 They found The room with volumes litter'd round. **1770** FOOTE *Lame Lover* II. Wks. 1799 II. 68 You know how angry your mother is at their rapping, and littering the house. **1784** COWPER *Task* VI. 280 Littering with unfolded silks The polished counter. **1825** SCOTT *Fam. Lett.* 17 May, We need not litter up your house..as we can always get into a hotel. **1859** DICKENS *T. Two Cities* II. v, A dingy room lined with books and littered with papers. **1883** FROUDE *Short Stud.* IV. I. iv. 49 Dinner was over. The floor was littered with rushes and fragments of rolls and broken meat. **1888** MRS. H. WARD *R. Elsmere* I. I. iv. 90 The house was littered over with stanzas from the opening canto of a great poem on Columbus. **1890** A. CONAN DOYLE *Sign of Four* v. 84 The table was littered over with Bunsen burners, test-tubes, and retorts. **1895** E. A. PARKES *Care Health* 35 Serving merely to litter up the surface of the earth.

b. To scatter in disorder *about*, *on*, *over*.

1731 SWIFT *Strephon & Chloe* 289 View them litter'd on the floor, Or strung on pegs behind the door. **1863** FR. A. KEMBLE *Resid. in Georgia* 31 Firewood and shavings lay littered about the floors. **1883** LD. R. GOWER *My Remin.* I. xviii. 358 A room..which we found full of soldiers asleep littered over the floor.

c. Of things: To lie about in disorder upon.

1856 LEVER *Martins of Cro'M.* 14 Pieces of stuccoed tracery..littered the garden and the terrace. **1882** B. D. W. RAMSAY *Recoll. Mil. Serv.* II. xiv. 41 Papers, belonging to our various departments under him, littering his table. **1896** A. E. HOUSMAN *Shropsh. Lad* xli, Or littering far the fields of May Lady-smocks a-bleaching lay.

7. a. Of animals, occas. *transf.* in contemptuous use of human beings: To bring forth (young).

1484 CAXTON *Fables of Æsop* I. ix, Whan the bytche had lyttred her lytyl dogges. **1576** TURBERV. *Venerie* 187 She doth lytter them deepe under the ground and so the wolf doth not. **1607** SHAKS. *Cor.* III. i. 239, I would they were Barbarians, as they are, Though in Rome littered. **1610** —— *Temp.* I. ii. 282 Saue for the Son, that [s]he did littour heere, A frekelld whelpe, hag-borne. **1622** DONNE *Serm.* clvi. VI. 231 Lions are littered perfect but Bear-whelps licked unto their shape. **1867** SMILES *Huguenots Eng.* v. (1880) 84 Wolves littered their young in the deserted farmhouses. **1874** *Supernat. Relig.* I. I. iv. 112 He must take the after-birth of a black cat, which has been littered by a first-born black cat.

fig. *a* **1814** *Orpheus* III. i. in *New Brit. Theatre* III. 299 For now I see Calamity is littering plagues to me.

b. *absol.* or *intr.*

1484 CAXTON *Fables of Æsop* I. ix, A bytche which wold lyttre and be delyuerd of her lytyl dogges. **1607** TOPSELL *Four-f. Beasts* (1658) 30 Pliny precisely affirmeth that they litter the thirtyeth day after their conception. **1733** SWIFT *On Poetry* Wks. 1755 IV. I. 184 Infants dropt, the spurious pledges Of gipsies litt'ring under hedges. **1848** MACAULAY *Hist.* xii. Wks. 1866 II. 504 If ever it [Kerry] was mentioned, it was mentioned as a horrible desert..where the she wolf still littered.

litter, variant of LIGHTER *sb.* and *v.*

Perh. mispr. for *liters, litered.* (The quot. for the vb. is much older than those under LIGHTER *v.*)

1677 YARRANTON *Eng. Improv.* 152 The goods are littered to and from the Ships. *Ibid.* 153 The great charge..by carrying..goods by Litters, to and from the Ships.

‖**litteræ humaniores** ('lɪtəraɪ hjuːmænɪ'ɔəriːz). Also **literæ humaniores**. [L., lit. 'more humane letters'.] The humanities, secular learning as opposed to divinity; esp., at the University of Oxford, the study of Greek and Roman classical literature, philosophy, and ancient history; also, = *Greats* (GREAT C. 10).

1747 CHESTERFIELD *Let.* 24 Nov. (1932) III. 1057 Studies of the *Literæ Humaniores*, especially Greek. **1760** STERNE *Tr. Shandy* (ed. 3) II. xii. 61, I would not depreciate what the study of the *Literæ humaniores*, at the university, have done for me. **1883** *Sat. Rev.* 3 Nov. 581/2 We cannot conceive a better accompaniment to the study of *literæ humaniores*. **1907** 'B. BURKE' *Barbara goes to Oxf.* 43 'Greats', you must know, is a nickname for the school of 'Literae Humaniores'. **1911** BEERBOHM *Zuleika D.* iii. 30 He ..was reading, a little, for Literae Humaniores. **1926** FOWLER *Mod. Eng. Usage* 240/2 *The Humanities*, or *Litteræ humaniores*, as an old-fashioned name for the study of classical literature. **1962** K. CHORLEY *Arthur Hugh Clough* iv. 72 In Clough's day there were but two schools open to men reading for honours—namely, Mathematics and *Literae Humaniores*. **1965** J. A. W. BENNETT in J. Gibb *Light on C. S. Lewis* 48 But *litterae humaniores* were his foundation, and they did in every sense make him more humane, enlarging his responses not restricting them. **1972** *Univ. Oxf. Examination Decrees* I. 120 The Subjects of the Honour School of Literæ Humaniores shall be (I) Greek and Roman History, (II) Philosophy, (III) Greek and Latin Literature.

†'**litterage**. *Obs.* In 7–8 **litteridge**. [f. LITTER *sb.* + -AGE.] **a.** The process of littering or being littered; birth. **b.** (See quot. 1726.)

1601 DOLMAN *La Primaud. Fr. Acad.* III. lxxxvii. (1618) 834 In the same Countrey there are Bores like to others..in their litteridge, which are grown in two moneths, and yet are smaller then conies. **1726** *Nat. Hist. Irel.* 79 The other [sort of ore]..went most away into litteridge or dross.

litterat(e, obs. form of LITERATE.

‖**littérateur** (literatœr). Also **litérateur**. [F. *littérateur*, ad. L. *litterātor*, f. *littera* letter.] A literary man, a writer of literary or critical works.

1806 *Edin. Rev.* VII. 364 During a part of this time he lives with a profligate *literateur* [sic] of the name of Beauvin. **1816** BYRON in Moore *Lett. & Jrnls.* (1830) II. 10 He [Bonstetten] is also a *littérateur* of good repute. **1854** DE QUINCEY *Autobiog. Sk.* Wks. II. 348 Like Gibbon, he [Southey] was the most accomplished *littérateur* amongst the erudite scholars of his time. **1882** P. FITZGERALD *Recreat. Lit. Man* I. ii. 8 For many years now, I have been an industrious *littérateur* of all work. **1895** E. DOWSON *Let.* 22 Dec. (1967) 335, I suppose you have heard of the abortive petition which he started among French littérateurs for the grace of Oscar? **1925** W. STEVENS *Let.* 14 Oct. (1967) 245, I have seen very few litérateurs during the last year or two.

‖**littératrice** (literatris). *rare.* [F. *littératrice*, fem. of *littérateur*.] A literary woman; an authoress.

18.. O. W. HOLMES in *Cornhill Mag.* Apr. (1879) 419 In an inland city, where dwells a *littératrice* of note.

litterature, obs. form of LITERATURE.

littered (ˈlɪtəd), *ppl. a.* [f. LITTER *v.* + -ED[1].] In senses of the vb.

1. Employed or strewn as litter; also, scattered in disorder.

1754 DODSLEY *Public Virtue, Agriculture* II. 231 Strew around Old leaves or litter'd straw, to screen from heat The tender infants. **1863** A. B. GROSART *Small Sins* 67, I remember how the littered concealing straw was raised. **1863** LD. LYTTON *King Amasis* II. 137 See these littered shards upon the sordid earth!

2. Covered or strewn with litter; clogged *up* with litter.

1870 *Evening Standard* 29 Oct., From one of the upper balconies of this littered chateau we looked down upon Paris. **1895** *Educat. Rev.* Sept. 166 The mind is left in a littered-up condition. **1900** *Blackw. Mag.* Aug. 220/1 He looked at the littered table.

3. *nonce-use.* That has produced a litter.

1894 GLADSTONE *Horace, Odes* III. xxvii. 1 With littered fox, and lapwing's call.

ˈlitterer. [f. LITTER *sb.* 4 + -ER[1].] One who throws or drops litter.

1928 *Sunday Dispatch* 29 July 12/2 Every corner of the finest streets in London is disfigured with the..manifold refuse of the litterer. **1958** *Observer* 10 Aug. 8/7 The Act.. includes parish councils among the authorities empowered to proceed against litterers.

†**ˈlittering**, *sb. Obs.*

1706 PHILLIPS (ed. Kersey), *Litterings*, small Sticks that keep the Web stretch'd on a Weaver's Loom.

littering (ˈlɪtərɪŋ), *vbl. sb.* [f. LITTER *v.* + -ING[1].] In senses of the vb.

1. a. The action of furnishing beasts with litter, or covering a floor with litter. **b.** *concr.* The straw of an animal's bed; a layer of litter in a stable. **c.** *collect.* Odds and ends scattered about.

a. 1607 MARKHAM *Caval.* v. iv. 15 This is called littering of Horses; and when you haue thus done, you shall let him rest till the next morning. **1849** STEPHENS *Bk. of the Farm* §955 Mr. Hunter..tried..the littering of the break, occupied by the sheep, with straw.

b. 1382 WYCLIF *Gen.* xxxi. 34 Rachel..hidde the mawmetis under the literyng of a camele. **1856** FERRIER *Inst. Metaph.* Introd. (ed. 2) 9 To add another coating to the infinite litterings of the Augean stable.

c. 1897 *Daily News* 3 May 7/2 Ten times more littering.. is left by the fashionable promenaders on the expensive fête days.

d. The action of throwing or dropping litter.

1960 *Times* 14 Sept. 12/7 There is something of the threat of doom in the perfunctory notice of New York pavements 'Littering 25 dollars'. **1970** D. E. WESTLAKE *Hot Rock* (1971) I. i. 13 He threw the Kleenex on the sidewalk. Littering. **1972** *Jrnl. Soc. Psychol.* LXXXVII. 324 The interview dealt with littering...'should it be everyone's responsibility to pick up litter?'

2. The process of bringing forth (young) or of being brought forth.

1542–5 BRINKLOW *Lament.* 26b, The ionge in the lytteryng, or forth bryngynge. **1607** TOPSELL *Four-f. Beasts* (1658) 110 They [bitches] have milk about five days before the littering. **1646** SIR T. BROWNE *Pseud. Ep.* III. xxv. 174 At the first littering their eyes are fastly closed.

littering (ˈlɪtərɪŋ), *ppl. a.* [f. LITTER *v.* + -ING[2].] That litters, or makes a 'litter'.

1863 ATKINSON *Stanton Grange* xvi. (1864) 172 The first thing I saw..was part of a huge littering jackdaw's nest.

litterure, variant of LETTRURE *Obs.*

littery (ˈlɪtərɪ), *a.* [f. LITTER *sb.* + -Y.] Of or pertaining to litter; marked by the presence of litter; tending to produce litter; untidy.

1805 DICKSON *Pract. Agric.* I. 270 The long littery dung from livery stables. **1847** in *Fraser's Mag.* (1848) XXXVII. 308 The littery practice of serving up the potatoes in their skins. **1858** MISS MULOCK *Th. about Wom.* 275 The rooms are untidy and 'littery'. **1859** R. THOMPSON *Gardener's Assist.* 622 As much short moist dung as will prevent the littery portion from becoming dry. **1866** CARLYLE *Remin.* I. 101 He took me into his library, a rough, littery, but considerable collection. **1882** *Garden* 21 Jan. 43/3 The whole process is troublesome, littery,..and is..uncertain in its results.

littimus, obs. form of LITMUS.

†**ˈlitting**, *vbl. sb. Obs.* [f. LIT *v.* + -ING[1].] The action of colouring, dyeing, or painting. Also *Comb.* †**litting-lead**, a dyer's vat.

a **1225** *Ancr. R.* 392 Ine schelde beoð þreo þinges, þet treo, and þet leðer, & þe peintunge [*v.r.* litinge]. *c* **1440** *Promp. Parv.* 308/2 Lytynge of clothe (*MS. K., P.* littinge), *tinctura.* **1485–6** *Durham Acc. Rolls* (Surtees) 157 Operanti super..et posicione unius lyttyngled. **1543** *Extracts Aberdeen Reg.* (1844) I. 187 Ane gryt litting leid, price twenty poundis, ane litill litting leid, price sax poundis. **1568** *Satir. Poems Reform.* xlviii. 31 Seure, be my witting, not brunt in the litting.

little (ˌlɪt(ə)l), *a.*, *adv.*, and *sb.* Forms: 1 lýtel, lítel, *Northumb.* lyttil, (lýtl-, lítl-), 2–3 lutel, lut(t)l-, lit(t)l-, 3 lutil, luttel, leitel, 3–5 luytel, litelle, -ul, 3–6 lit(t)el, litell, 4 luitel, littil, lytille, -ulle, 4–5 lytul, 4–6 lytel, -il, -yll, litil(l, littill, -ell, 4–7 litle, 5 litull(e, -ille, -yll, littull, lytyle, -elle, 5–6 lyt(t)ell, lyttyll, lytill, -yl(le, 6 lyt(t)le, lyttil, lytel, lityll, (laytell, lickell, 7 lickle), 6– little. See also LEETLE. [OE. *lýtel, lytel*, corresponds to OS. *luttil* (MDu. *luttel, lettel*, Du. *luttel*), OHG. *luzzil*, also *liuzil*, ? *lūzil* (MHG., mod.G. dial. *lützel*):—WGer. **lŭttilo-*, f. **lŭt* (prob. f. the root of OE. *lútan* to bow down: see LOUT *v.*) represented in OE. *lýt, lyt* (and the equivalent forms: see LITE *sb.*), and in OS. *luttik*, OFris. *littich*, OHG. *luzzīg* little. A synonymous and phonetically similar (but radically unconnected) adj. OTeut. **lītilo-* is found as Goth. *leitils*, ON. *lítell* (Sw. *liten, lilla*, Da. *liden, lille*), and possibly in OE. *lítel*, MDu. *lītel*, mod.Flem. *lijter*; the root **līt-*:—pre-Teut. **leid-* may be cogn. with **loid-* in Gr. λοίδορος abuse, L. *lūdus* (:—**loidos*) play; some scholars have compared Lith. *laidau* I let flow, *leidžu* I set free.

The long vowel in OE. *lýtel* is vouched for by metrical evidence (Sievers in *Beiträge* X. 504) and certain features of the declension (Sarrazin *ibid.* IX. 365), as well as by the early ME. *luitel.* On the other hand, the Northumb. *lyttel*, and the widespread early ME. *luttel, littel*, suggest that the *y* may have been short in some dialects, and perh. generally in the syncopated flexional forms. The modern dialects that are marked by a large Scandinavian element in the vocabulary mostly have the vowel long, the pronunciation being (ˈlaːt(ə)l) or the like; this seems to point to influence from the ON. *lítell.*]

A. *adj.* The opposite of *great* or *much.* Compar. LESS, LESSER; superl. LEAST.

These forms, however, are not quite coextensive in application with the positive, so that in certain uses the adj. has no recognized mode of comparison. The difficulty is commonly evaded by resort to a synonym (as *smaller, smallest*); some writers have ventured to employ the unrecognized forms *littler, littlest*, which are otherwise confined to dialect or imitations of childish or illiterate speech.

I. Opposed to *great.* Often synonymous with *small.*

Its customary antithetic association (in mod. Eng.) is with *great* or *big*, not with *large*; on the other hand, *small* is the customary antithesis of *great* or *large*, but not of *big.* One difference between the two synonyms is that *little* is capable of emotional implications, which *small* is not.

1. a. Of material objects, portions of space, etc.: Small in size, not large or big. Of persons: Short in stature.

c **1000** ÆLFRIC *Gram.* i. (Z.) 2 Ic Ælfric wolde þas lytlan boc awendan to engliscum ȝereorde of ðam stæfcræfte. *a* **1225** *Leg. Kath.* 2517 Of þe lutle banes, þe floweð ut wið þe eoile, floweð oðer eoile ut. *c* **1290** *S. Eng. Leg.* I. 407/162 He may here in þe grounde ane luttle worm i-seo. *a* **1300** *Cursor M.* 14939 A littel hill Man calles mont oliuete. **1432–50** tr. *Higden* (Rolls) I. 373 He schewede to hym a lytulle rownd dyche. **1470–85** MALORY *Arthur* I. xvi, The xj kynges.. withdrewe hem to a lytil woode and so ouer a lytyl ryuer. **1567** *Satir. Poems Reform.* iii. 178 War..I ane cat and sho ane lyttill mous. **1596** SHAKS. *Merch. V.* I. ii. 1 By my troth Nerrissa, my little body is wearie of this great world. *a* **1677** HALE *Prim. Orig. Man.* I. i. 4 Even in the very little Insects, there appears the excellent work of the Divine Wisdom. **1735** BOLINGBROKE *Study Hist.* (1777) 335 There is a prejudice in China in favour of little feet. **1818** SCOTT *Rob Roy* xiii, You may bring him to the little back-gate. **1849** THACKERAY *Pendennis* xxi, She was called tall and gawky by some..of her own sex, who prefer littler women.

b. Used to designate animal and vegetable species or varieties which are distinguished by their smallness from others belonging to the same genus or bearing the same name.

c **1450** *ME. Med. Bk.* (Heinrich) 227 þe lytel daysye. **1562** TURNER *Herbal* II. 133 Moustayle or litle stone crop. **1776–96** WITHERING *Brit. Plants* (ed. 3) II. 327 Little Mouse-tail. **1785** J. LATHAM *Gen. Synopsis Birds* III. I. 90 Little Egret... Size of a Fowl: length near a foot: weight one pound. **1802** G. MONTAGU *Ornith. Dict.* I. s.v. *Egret*, Little Egret. **1831** A. WILSON & BONAPARTE *Amer. Ornith.* I. 110 The little owl is seven inches and a half long. **1861** MISS PRATT *Flower. Pl.* V. 295 Little Bulbous Rush. **1876** SMILES *Sc. Natur.* xii. (ed. 4) 247 The Little Auk has a wonderful power of resisting the fury of the waves. **1908** R. LYDEKKER *Sportsman's Brit. Bird Bk.* 248 Of the little egret..sixteen individuals appear to have been recorded from the British Islands during the last century. **1919** Little-smelt [see GRUNION]. **1953** *Calif. Almanac* 36/2 On certain moonlit nights in the spring great numbers of small fish, termed 'grunion' or 'little smelt' appear along the beaches. **1971** *Country Life* 18 Feb. 356/3 Neither the little egret nor the common heron have been proved to breed in the [Ebro] delta, though both are present.

c. Used to characterize the smaller or less important of two countries or places of the same name. †*Little Britain*, Brittany. Similarly in many Eng. village names, as *Little Gidding, Little Malvern*; in river-names; and in names of streets: cf. GREAT *a.* 6e. Also in names of constellations, as ***the Little Bear***: cf. GREAT *a.* 6d. ***Little Witham***: in phrases.

c **1400** MAUNDEV. (1839) xxv. 259 Descendynge toward the litille Armenye. *c* **1450** *King Ponthus & Fair Sidone* xxvi. *heading* (1897) 93 How Ponthus retorned to Litle Bretayn. *c* **1530** [see BRITAIN *sb.*[1] 2]. **1560** J. HEYWOOD *Fourth Hundred Epygrams* sig. A7 Whens come great breeches? from little wittam. **1595** R. WILSON *Pedlers Prophecie* sig. B4[v] At litle Wytham seuen yeares I went to schoole. **1640** YORKE *Union Hon.* 73 Philebert de Chandew, a Baron in his own countrey of little Brittaine in France. *a* **1661** FULLER *Worthies* (1662) Lincs. 153 *He was born at Little Wittham*... It is applyed to such people as are not overstock'd with acutenesse. **1677** F. SANDFORD *Genealog. Hist. Kings Eng.* 62 Conan of Little Britain. **1787** GROSE *Provincial Gloss.* s.v. *Essex*, He was born at Little Wittham. A punning insinuation that the person spoken of wants understanding. Ray places this proverb in Lincolnshire. **1932** E. WEEKLEY *Words & Names* x. 151 The stupid are said to be 'born at Little Witham'.

d. With superl. meaning, in ***little finger, toe.***

a **1000** *Boeth. Metr.* xx. 179 þæt hire [*sc.* of the soul] þy læsse on ðæm lytlan ne bið anum fingre þe hire on eallum bið þæm lichoman. *c* **1290** *S. Eng. Leg.* I. 309/329 ȝif he ne may with is luytel finguer ane man to sunne teche. **1398** TREVISA *Barth. De P.R.* v. xxix. (1495) 140 The fyfthe fyngre is the lytyll fyngre and highte Auricularis. *c* **1400** *Lanfranc's Cirurg.* 36 Ech poynt schal be from oþir bi þe brede of a litil fyngir. **14..** *Nom.* in Wr.-Wülcker 679/10 *Hic articulus*, a lytyle too. **1535** COVERDALE *1 Kings* xii. 10 My litle fynger shall be thicker then my fathers loynes. **1563–83** FOXE *A. & M.* II. 804/1 Openly pronouncing that Luther had more learning in his litle finger, then all ye doctours in England in their whole bodies. **1643** I. STEER tr. *Exp. Chyrurg.* xv. 61 His fore-finger..and little finger were..burnt. **1726** MONRO *Anat. Bones* (1741) 305 *Os metatarsi* of the little Toe is the shortest. **1840** DICKENS *Barn. Rudge* lxxviii, He used the little finger..of his right hand as a tobacco-stopper. **1872** MIVART *Elem. Anat.* 152 The fifth [finger is] the 'little digit'.

e. Often emphasized by being coupled with some other adj. implying smallness. †Also reduplicated ***little little.***

a **1400–50** *Alexander* 507 Scho had layd in his lape a litill tyne egg. **1542** UDALL *Erasm. Apoph.* 189 When he..sawe there a litle litle herthe, & in the same a litle preatie small fyer, he saied [etc.]. **1593** SHAKS. *Rich. II*, III. iii. 153 And my large Kingdome, for a little Graue, A little little Graue, an obscure Graue. **1597** —— *2 Hen. IV*, v. i. 29 Any pretty little tine Kickshawes. **1598** —— *Merry W.* I. iv. 22 He hath but a little wee-face.

2. a. Used *spec.* of young children or animals. ***little one*** (often pl.): child, offspring, young one.

c **893** K. ÆLFRED *Oros.* III. xvii. §1 His ȝingran dohtor.. seo wæs lytel cild. *c* **1200** ORMIN 3217 þiss lif to ledenn he bigann Whann he wass ȝet full litell. *Ibid.* 8053 Whil þatt I wass litell child Icc held o childess þæwess. *c* **1386** CHAUCER *Man of Law's Prol.* 73 Thy litel children hanging by the hals For thy Iason, that was in loue so fals. *c* **1420** *Sir Amadace* (Camden) lxvii, He toke vppe the ladi, and the litulle knaue. **1468** J. PASTON, jun. in *P. Lett.* II. 319 And, modyr, I beseche yow that ye wolbe good mastras to my lytyll man, and to se that he go to scole. **1526** TINDALE *Matt.* xviii. 6 Whosoever offende one of these lytell wons, which beleve in me. **1598** SHAKS. *Merry W.* IV. iv. 47 Nan Page (my daughter) and my little sonne. **1611** COTGR., *Petit*,..the little one, or young one, of a beast. **1641** MARMION *Antiquary* I. i, Well said, little-one, I think thou art wiser than both of them. **1779** T. TWINING in *Recreat. & Stud.* (1882) 71 My sister and her little fellow-traveller. **1819** SHELLEY *Cenci* V. iii. 103 My wife! my little ones! Destitute, helpless. **1849** MACAULAY *Hist. Eng.* vii. II. 172 Through life he continues to regard the little Bentincks with paternal kindness. **1894** H. DRUMMOND *Ascent Man* 377 Among the Carnivora the mothers have frequently to hide their little ones in case the father eats them. **1898** FLO. MONTGOMERY *Tony* 19 The little boy's small back.

¶**b.** ***little language***: Swift's name for the infantine dialect which he used in conversation and correspondence with 'Stella'. (Often quoted in references to Swift's life.) Also *transf.*

1711 SWIFT *Jrnl. to Stella* 4 May (1901) 209 Do you know that every syllable I write I hold my lips just for all the world as if I were talking in our own little language to MD? **1863** *Fraser's Mag.* Feb. 152/1 She carried on hip a prize baby, a most 'doody' thing, to quote the 'little language'. **1866** MRS. GASKELL *Wives & Daughters* II. xxiv. 244 Some innocent sentences of love,..little sentences in 'little language' that went home to the squire's heart. **1922** O. JESPERSEN *Lang.* viii. 144 It would not do, however, for the child's 'little language' and its dreadful mistakes to become fixed. **1944** H. G. WELLS *'42 to '44* 142 The first thing two lovers set about doing is..to devise a little language of their own.

c. In collocations ***little brother, sister***: younger (cf. 2a). Also *fig.*

1611 BIBLE *Song of Solomon* viii. 8 We haue a little sister, and shee hath no breasts. **1799** JANE AUSTEN *Let.* 21 Jan. (1952) 57 Our own particular little brother got a place in the coach last night. **1859** THACKERAY *Virginians* II. xii. 93 Your brother and mine are gone to see our little brother at his school at the Chartreux. **1876** C. M. YONGE *Womankind* xvi. 126 In no case should they go without a more real chaperon than a maid or a little sister's governess. **1940** G. B. SHAW *Geneva* (1946) IV. 123 Ruritania is, so to speak, our little sister, and..if you laid a finger on her..we should be obliged to knock the stuffing out of you. **1949** R. CHANDLER (*title*) The little sister. **1974** *Country Life* 21 Nov. 1573/3 At present this dehydrated food is only available to caterers and food manufacturers, although its little sister Vegex (dehydrated vegetarian version) is on sale in some health-food shops.

d. ***little brother*** (see quot. 1928 and cf. BIG *a.* 3g); also *attrib.* and in extended use.

1928 *Daily Tel.* 10 July 16/2 Ninety-six youths will leave Tilbury to-day to take up farm work in Australia... Captain R. T. Thornton..will visit many of the 1,400 'Little Brothers' who have gone to the Commonwealth. **1962** *Times* 25 Apr. 11/6 'Little brother' organizations formed mostly of young people.

e. Phr. ***to laugh like little Audrey***: to laugh heartily (esp. at a serious situation). Also *attrib.*, of a type of joke, a CRUELLIE.

1939 C. MORLEY *Kitty Foyle* xiv. 143 She laughs like Little Audrey. **1959** I. & P. OPIE *Lore & Lang. Schoolch.* v. 82 Crazes for limericks, Little Audrey jokes, Knock-knocks, and Shaggy Dog stories. **1972** J. AIKEN *Butterfly Picnic* ix. 165 If I choose to..laugh like little Audrey when I'm all knotted up..who the hell's got the right to forbid me?

3. Used to convey an implication of endearment or depreciation, or of tender feeling on the part of the speaker. Also coupled with an

epithet expressing such feelings, e.g. *pretty*, *sweet little*.

1567 *Satir. Poems Reform.* iii. 154 The wois that Ouid in Ibin Into his pretty lytill buik did wryte. **1590** SHAKS. *Mids. N.* III. i. 204 And when she weepes, weepe euerie little flower. **1596** —— *Merch. V.* v. i. 21 In such a night Did pretty Iessica (like a little shrow) Slander her Loue. **1597** —— *2 Hen. IV*, II. iv. 225, I prethee Iack be quiet, the Rascall is gone: ah, you whorson little valiant Villaine, you. **1694** WOOD *Life* 23 June, I returned from London in the company of a little poore thing, Sir Lacy Osbaldeston. **1819** SHELLEY *Cyclops* 246 My dear sweet master, My darling little Cyclops. **1847** TENNYSON *Princess* Prol. 154 A rosebud set with little wilful thorns. **1849** DICKENS *Dav. Copp.* xxvi, She had the most delightful little voice, the gayest little laugh, the pleasantest and most fascinating little ways, that ever led a lost youth into hopeless slavery. **1883** R. W. DIXON *Mano* I. viii. 23 Sweet was her carriage, sweet the little folds Of her fair dress close drawn with meekest care. *Mod.* Bless your little heart!

4. Of collective unities: Having few members, inhabitants, etc.; small in number.

c **1000** *Ags. Gosp.* Luke xii. 32 Ne ondræd þu þe la lytle heord. *c* **1386** CHAUCER *Manciple's Prol.* 1 A litel toun Which þat ycleped is Bobbe up and down. **1513** BRADSHAW *St. Werburge* I. 1845 A lytell vyllage called Exmynge. **1565** STAPLETON tr. *Bæda's Hist. Ch. Eng.* 152 A litle parte of these reliques were at that time in this monasterie. **1588** SHAKS. *L.L.L.* I. i. 13 Our Court shall be a little Achademe. **1591** —— *1 Hen. VI*, IV. ii. 46 A little Heard of Englands timorous Deere. **1611** BIBLE *Exod.* xii. 4 If the houshold be too little [COVERDALE few] for the lambe. **1696** *View Crt. St. Germain* 2 The number of the Consciencious Jacobites.. must be very little. **1754** COWPER *Ep. Rob. Lloyd* 18 A fierce banditti..Make cruel inroads in my brain, And daily threaten to drive thence My little garrison of sense. **1820** KEATS *Ode on Grecian Urn* iv, What little town by river or sea shore..Is emptied of this folk, this pious morn? **1871** MORLEY *Voltaire* (1886) 7 In the realm of mere letters, Voltaire is one of the little band of great monarchs. **1879** WHITNEY *Sanskrit Gram.* 157 In a little class of instances (eight) the root has a preposition prefixed.

5. Of immaterial things, considered in respect of their quantity, length in series, etc.

c **1275** *Passion Our Lord* 1 in *O.E. Misc.* 37 Ihereþ nv one lutele tale þat ich eu wille telle. *c* **1330** *Spec. Gy Warw.* 166 He..halt þerof ful litel prys. **1470–85** MALORY *Arthur* XVIII. xviii, The knyghte..put..a lytel dele of water in his mouthe. **1555** BRADFORTH in Strype *Eccl. Mem.* III. App. xlv. 127 Thoughe yt be never so daungerous to me to sett this lyttell treatys abroad. **1590** SHAKS. *Mids. N.* I. ii. 54 Ile speake in a monstrous little voyce. **1599** —— *Much Ado* V. i. 162, I said thou hadst a fine wit: true saies she, a fine little one. **1598** T. BASTARD *Chrestoleros* 14 The Printer when I askt a little summe, Huckt with me for my booke. **1809** MALKIN *Gil Blas* v. i. ¶66 He was no longer at a loss for his little pocket expenses. **1843** DICKENS *Christmas Carol* iii. 99 Tiny Tim..had a plaintive little voice and sang it very well indeed. **1849** MACAULAY *Hist. Eng.* iii. I. 335 Proprietors, who..derived their subsistence from little freehold estates. **1872** EARLE *Philol. Eng. Tongue* §499 The indefinite article, which is descended from the littlest of the numerals. **1875** E. C. STEDMAN *Victorian Poets* 152 A little poem, 'The Flower'.

6. a. Of dimension, distance, or period of time: Short. † *so little while* (advb. phr.): for so short a time.

Beowulf 2097 (Gr.) He onweȝ losade, lytle hwile lifwynna breac. *c* **1205** LAY. 343 Nes Brutus i þon londe bute lutel ane wile. *Ibid.* 26939 þer heo leien stille ane lutle stunde. *a* **1300–1400** *Cursor M.* 14754 (Gött.) ȝe felle þis kirc dune to þe grund, I sal it raise in littel stound. *c* **1375** *Sc. Leg. Saints* Prol. 28 In lytil space here, I wryt þe lyf of sanctis sere. *c* **1420** LYDG. *Assembly of Gods* 1283 A lytyll tyne hys ey castyng hym besyde. *c* **1440** *Generydes* 148 After soper, withynne a litill space She brought hym to his bedde with torche light. ? *c* **1540** in Strype *Eccl. Mem.* (1721) I. II. App. lxxii. 174 They may think things pas lightly here, that are so little while liked. **1591** HARINGTON *Orl. Fur.* II. xii, When that she a little way had past. **1610** SHAKS. *Temp.* IV. i. 157 Our little life Is rounded with a sleepe. **1667** MILTON *P.L.* x. 320 And now in little space The Confines met of Empyrean Heav'n And of this World. **1675** MARVELL *Corr.* ccxxxvi. Wks. 1872–5 II. 449 Although..the House of Commons hath both days been long and very busy, the relation falls within a litle compasse. **1712** ADDISON *Spect.* No. 475 ¶2 She hopes to be married in a little time. **1859** FITZGERALD tr. *Omar* iii. (1899) 70 You know how little while we have to stay.

b. Qualifying a sb. denoting definite measure of duration or distance, to emphasize its brevity. †Also, in 16–17th c., used for: Bare, scarcely complete.

1523 LD. BERNERS *Froiss.* I. cvii. 128 In the mornyng they wer within two lytell leages of Auberoche. **1568** GRAFTON *Chron.* II. 343 The Abbey of Mauros, which was .ix. little myle from Rosebourgh. **1602** SHAKS. *Ham.* I. ii. 147 A little Month, or ere these shooes were old. **1670** COTTON *Espernon* II. vii. 312 This retirement of the Duke's being but ten little Leagues from Paris. **1697** tr. *Le Comte's Mem. & Rem. China* iv. (1737) 108 It is off of Nankin thirty leagues from the sea, a little half league broad. **1794** COWPER *Moralizer corrected* 17 Distant a little mile he spied A western bank's still sunny side. **1816** J. WILSON *City of Plague* II. i. 98 Your brother died Some little hours before. **1848** BROUGHAM *Of Revolutions* Wks. 1857 VIII. 332 But a little month ago, and ..the Germans would have held the like language of national self-complacency. **1871** R. ELLIS tr. *Catullus* v. 5 We, when sets in a little hour the brief light, Sleep one infinite age, a night for ever.

7. a. Of qualities, emotions, conditions, actions, or occurrences: Small in extent or degree.

c **1205** LAY. 26452 For æuere heo ȝelp makieð heore monscipe is luttel. **1377** LANGL. *P. Pl.* B. Prol. 195 Better is a litel losse þan a longe sorwe. *c* **1380** WYCLIF *Wks.* (1880) 333 No man shuld liȝe a lytel lesyng to saue þe worlde. *c* **1440** *Boctus & Sidrak* (Laud MS. 559 lf. 3), I shall teche yoow a lytill ieste: That befelle oonys in Yᵉ Este. **1513** BRADSHAW *St. Werburge* I. 704 þat litel spirital dede. **1602** SHAKS. *Ham.* III. ii. 182 (1604 Qo.) Where loue is great, the litlest doubts are feare, Where little feares grow great, great loue growes there. *c* **1620** in *Hatton Corr.* (1878) 3 It is a sinn, and that not a lickle one. **1768** GOLDSM. *Good-n. Man* I. i, Upon that I proceed,..though with very little hopes to reclaim him. **1885** J. K. FOWLER in *Daily News* 14 July 2/1 Fowl-growing and egg-selling are distinctly little businesses.

†**b.** Const. *of*: Having the quality or performing the action mentioned to a slight extent only.

c **1380** WYCLIF *Sel. Wks.* I. 195 And siþ þes foulis ben litil of prys. *c* **1381** CHAUCER *Parl. Foules* 513, I am a sede foul.. and litil of cunnynge. **1432** *Rolls of Parlt.* IV. 405/2 Thei [wines] wex all noght or litell of value. *c* **1450** *Bk. Curtasye* 34 in *Babees Bk.*, Loke þou be hynde and lytulle of worde. **1484** CAXTON *Fables of Æsop* IV. xiv, It behoveth not to the yong and lytyl of age to mocke..theyr older. **1508** DUNBAR *Tua mariit wemen* 185 He lukis as he wald luffit be, thocht he be litill of valour.

c. With agent-noun or sb. indicating occupation, etc.: That is such on a small scale.

c **1440** *Promp. Parv.* 308/1 Lytylle lyare, *mendaculus*. **1767** A. YOUNG *Farmer's Lett. to People* 55 A much larger capital than any little farmer can possess. **1834** YOUATT *Cattle* vi. 192 The dairyman and the little farmer clung to the old breed.

d. Now often idiomatically in somewhat playful use, indicating some feeling of amusement on the part of the speaker.

1885 ANSTEY *Tinted Venus* 72 How long do you mean to carry on this little game? **1888** RIDER HAGGARD *Col. Quaritch* ix, How well she managed that little business of the luncheon. *Mod.* I understand his little ways.

8. a. Of things: Not of great importance or interest; trifling, trivial.

a **1100** *O.E. Chron.* an. 656 (Laud MS.) Hit is litel þeos ȝife. *a* **1175** *Cott. Hom.* 221 Hwi wolde god swa litles þinges him forwerne. *c* **1200** *Vices & Virtues* (1888) 17 Ouer litel þing ðu ware trewe; ouer michel þing ic ðe scal setten. *a* **1300** *Cursor M.* 3302 Leue freind..þine asking Es noght bot a litell thing. **1593** SHAKS. *Rich. II*, I. iii. 213 How long a time lyes in one little word. **1606** —— *Ant. & Cl.* II. ii. 134 All little Ielousies which now seeme great..Would then be nothing. **1849** MACAULAY *Hist. Eng.* v. I. 524 Every little discontent appears to him to portend a revolution. **1865** DICKENS *Mut. Fr.* III. v, Constant attention in the littlest things.

b. Of persons: Not distinguished, inferior in rank or condition. Now *rare*.

c **1220** *Bestiary* 689 He ðe is ai in heuene mikel, wurð her man, and tus was litel. *c* **1450** tr. *De Imitatione* III. viii. 75 If þou coudist at all tymes abide meke & litel in þiself. *c* **1477** CAXTON *Jason* 11, I am..litil seruaunt unto the quene of the countre. **1611** BIBLE *1 Sam.* xv. 17 When thou wast litle in thine owne sight. **1744** OZELL tr. *Brantome's Sp. Rhodomontades* 69 Honour'd and esteem'd..both by Gentle and Simple, by Little and Great Folks. **1751** JOHNSON *Rambler* No. 152 ¶5 To learn how to become little without being mean. **1772** MACKENZIE *Man World* I. viii. (1823) 428 There is no Tax so heavy on a little man, as an acquaintance with a great one.

9. Paltry, mean, contemptible; little-minded.

1483 *Cath. Angl.* 218/2 Litille,..*decliuus ad ingenium pertinet*. *Ibid.*, Litille,..*paulus mediocritatis est, paululus, pupus, pusulanimis*. *c* **1665** MRS. HUTCHINSON *Mem. Col. Hutchinson* (1885) II. 43 One of their own members who encouraged all those little men in their wicked persecution of him. *Ibid.* II. 74 Almost all the parliament-garrisons were infested and disturbed with like factious little people. **1693** DRYDEN *Juvenal* xiv. Notes (1697) 367 He dy'd a very little Death..being Martyr'd by the fall of a Tile from a House. **1701** ROWE *Amb. Step-Moth.* II. ii. 804, I hear thee and disdain thy little Malice. **1712** STEELE *Spect.* No. 268 ¶2 [It] renders the Nose-puller odious, and makes the Person pulled by the Nose look little and contemptible. **1766** FORDYCE *Serm. Yng. Wom.* (1767) II. xiii. 246 Haughtiness is always little. **1776** GIBBON *Decl. & F.* xi. I. 308 The little passions which so frequently perplex a female reign. **1829** LYTTON *Devereux* II. viii, The littlest feeling of all is a delight in contemplating the littleness of other people. **1863** COWDEN CLARKE *Shaks. Char.* xix. 484 They do this with the little cunning of little minds.

II. Opposed to *much*.

10. a. Not much; only a slight amount or degree of; barely any. (Often preceded by *but*. Also in phr. *little or no*...).

c **1000** *Ags. Gosp.* Matt. xiv. 31 He..þus cwæð la lytles ȝeleafan hwi twynedest þu? *a* **1300** *Cursor M.* 530 þow may þam find with litul suink. *c* **1320** *Sir Tristr.* 2125 Tristrem, for soþe to say, Y wold þe litel gode. **1377** LANGL. *P. Pl.* B. I. 139 To litel latyn þow lernedest, lede, in þi ȝouthe. *c* **1386** CHAUCER *Shipman's Prol.* 28 Ther is but litil Latin in my mawe. *c* **1449** PECOCK *Repr.* I. iii. 16 Holi Writt ȝeueth litil or noon liȝt therto at al. **1581** MULCASTER *Positions* vi. (1887) 45 To much meat cloyes, to litle faintes. **1591** SHAKS. *Two Gent.* IV. i. 11 Then know that I haue little wealth to loose. **1697** DRYDEN *Virg. Georg.* IV. 703 Strong Desires th' impatient Youth invade; By little Caution and much Love betray'd. **1821** SHELLEY in Lady Shelley *Mem.* (1859) 54 There is little probability of an injunction being granted. **1828** MACAULAY *Hallam* Ess. (1872) 71 He had little money, little patronage, no military establishment. **1871** FREEMAN *Norm. Conq.* (1876) IV. xviii. 213 William..was able to attack the town from the point where it gained little advantage from its site.

b. Forming with its sb. a kind of privative combination, with the sense 'absence or scarcity of' (what the sb. denotes). Now *rare*.

c **1000** *Ags. Ps.* lxxxviii. 40 Gemune, mære God, hwæt si min lytle sped [L. *quæ mea substantia*]. *c* **1532** DU WES *Introd. Fr.* in Palsgr. 905 The lytell corage, *la pusillanimité*. **1606** SHAKS. *Tr. & Cr.* III. iii. 220 They thinke my little stomacke to the warre..restraines you thus. **1654–66** EARL ORRERY *Parthen.* (1676) 535 Surena was constrain'd by his little Victuals. **1752** BURKE *Corr.* (1844) I. 29 Our little curiosity, perhaps, cleared us of that imputation [of being spies]. **1802** WORDSW. *Sailor's Mother* 35 God help me for my little wit!

11. a. *a little*: a small quantity of; some, though not much. Identical in sense with *a little of* (see B. 4) from which it prob. originated by ellipsis.

14.. *Voc.* in Wr.-Wülcker 604/20 *Posse*, a lytyl hauynge, or a lytyl myght. *c* **1430** *Two Cookery-bks.* 16 Caste þer-to a littel Safroun & Salt. *c* **1450** *ME. Med. Bk.* (Heinrich) 134 Take harde spaynessh sepe and a litul stale ale. **1545** RAYNOLD *Byrth Mankynde* 128 The iuyce of quynces with a lyttell cloues and sugre. *a* **1548** HALL *Chron., Hen. VI* 166 b, Whose mother susteyned not a litle slaunder and obloquye of the common people. **1595** SHAKS. *John* III. iv. 176 As a little snow, tumbled about, Anon becomes a Mountaine. **1598** BACON *Ess.*, *Atheisme* (Arb.) 125 A little naturall philosophie..doth dispose the opinion to Atheisme. **1709** POPE *Ess. Crit.* 215 A little learning is a dang'rous thing. **1849** MACAULAY *Hist. Eng.* vi. II. 6 By a little patience, prudence, and justice, such a toleration might have been obtained. **1901** H. BLACK *Culture & Restraint* iii. 88 It takes a great deal of life to make a little art.

†**b.** *Rarely* used without *a* in this sense. *Obs.*

1597 SHAKS. *2 Hen. IV*, III. i. 43 A Body, yet distemper'd, Which to his former strength may be restor'd, With good aduice, and little Medicine. **1601** —— *Twel. N.* v. i. 174 O do not sweare, Hold little faith, though thou hast too much feare.

†**12.** With pl. and collect. sing.: = FEW. *Obs.*

13.. *Guy Warw.* (A.) 2468 þemperour..Wille huntte to morwe..Wiþ litel folk & nouȝt wiþ miche. **1430–40** LYDG. *Bochas* v. iv. (1494) Rj, Cleomenes..with lityll peple made his fone to flee. **1621** LADY M. WROTH *Urania* 541 Desiring to know what accident brought him thither, especially armed, where little Armes was required. **1660** FULLER *Mixt Contempl.* 28 Our late Civil warre which lasted so long in our land; yet left so little signs behind it.

III. 13. Special collocations: **Little American** (cf. *Little Englander*), **Americanism**; **little black dress** (or *frock*, etc.), a simple black garment suitable for a woman to wear at most kinds of relatively formal social engagements; **little chief hare** *N. Amer.* [tr. Chipewyan *bucka-thrae-ggayaze*], a North American pika, *Ochotona princeps*; **little death** [cf. F. *petite mort*], a weakening or loss of consciousness, spec. in sleep, during an orgasm, etc.; †**little Easter Sunday**, ? Low Sunday; **Little Englander**, one who advocated a 'little England', that is, desired to restrict the dimensions and responsibilities of the Empire; so **Little Englandism**, the policy or views of Little Englanders; **Little Entente**: see ENTENTE (quot. 1923); **little fever** ? *U.S.*, typhoid (*Cent. Dict.*); **little giant**, 'a jointed iron nozzle used in hydraulic mining' (Raymond *Mining Gloss.*); cf. GIANT *sb.* 4; **little green man**, an imaginary inhabitant of outer space; an imaginary person of peculiar appearance (in quot. 1906 an actual person tattooed green); **little habit** = *lesser habit* (s.v. HABIT *sb.* 2 b); **little hours**, the 'hours' of prime, terce, sext, and none (= F. *les petites heures*); **little house**, a privy (now *Austral.*, *N.Z.*, and *dial.*); **Little Irelander** (cf. *Little Englander*); †**little Jack**, an irreverent name for the little box (sometimes in the form of a human figure) in which the reserved sacrament was enclosed within the Easter sepulchre during part of Holy Week; **little Joe**, in the game of Craps (see quots.); †**little king** [tr. L. *regulus*, cf. F. *roitelet*], the wren; **little magazine**, a name designating any of various periodicals devoted to serious literary or artistic interests (see also quots.); also *attrib.*; so (as colloq. abbrev.) **little mag**; **Little Mary** *colloq.*, the stomach; **(poor) little me** (†**I**), used to convey the speaker's mock-depreciation of (and the supposed vulnerability of) himself; **little mother**, a young girl who behaves maternally towards her younger brothers or sisters, or her dolls; **little Ned** (also **little Neddy**) [NEDDY 3], one of a number of committees under the National Economic Development Council; **little old** (followed by a pronoun or a name): used as an endearing or mock-depreciatory mode of reference; **little Orphan(t) Annie**, the name of an orphan child in a poem by J. W. Riley and a strip-cartoon by Harold Gray, used allusively in various senses (see quots.); †**little pox**, small-pox; **little review** = *little magazine*; **little science**, term used of scientific and technological investigation that does not require large resources; **little season**, a fashionable season in London in the winter; †**little son** [= F. *petit-fils*], a grandson; **little theatre**, a small playhouse, esp. one used for dramatic experiment (in quot. 1771 the name of an actual theatre); also *attrib.*; **Little Venice**, a name given to various local areas felt to resemble Venice in canal scenery; also *attrib.*; **Little Willie**, a term first used of Crown Prince Friedrich Wilhelm Viktor August Ernst of Germany (1882–1951)

and applied to persons as a term of disparagement and to weapons (see quots.); (quot. 1907 is prob. an unconnected casual use); **little woman**, (*a*) one's wife, freq. with *the*; (*b*) a private dressmaker or odd-job woman. See also *Little* BETHEL, CASSINO, CUSTOM (*sb.* 4), ENTRANCE (1 c), MASS, SEAL, SHILLING, etc.; also the main words below.

1904 *Press* (Philadelphia) 11 Aug. 6 Judge Parker's whole contention is that of the *little American. *Ibid.*, His *little Americanism invites fuller discussion. **1902** H. JAMES *Wings of Dove* xviii. 427 She might fairly have been dressed tonight in the *little black frock..that Milly had laid aside. **1949** D. SMITH *I capture Castle* xi. 192 Perhaps it gives you a glorious, valuable feeling to wear little black suits of fabulous price. **1951** *Woman & Beauty* May 1/2 Invest your all in one good little black dress. **1968** J. IRONSIDE *Fashion Alphabet* 19 *Little black dress.* This highly useful garment was at first almost the trademark of the British designer, Molyneux, who perfected it as an 'after 6' look in the cocktail party era between 1920 and 1939. The ultimate in sophistication then, it is still much in demand. **1973** *Country Life* 13 Dec. 2067/1, I have included a little black dress in my photographs this week, because I think it is the right alternative to glitter for winter '73. **1868** *Proc. Calif. Acad. Sci.* IV. 6 *Lagomys princeps* Richardson—'*Little Chief Hare'; Rat-rabbit. **1898** F. RUSSELL *Explor. Far North* p. vi, The timid squeak of the little chief hare was often heard. **1947** V. H. CAHALANE *Mammals N. Amer.* 581 Some imaginative naturalist has given the animal the title of 'little chief hare'. **1960** *Canad. Audubon* Jan.-Feb. 28/3 The industrious little pika has yet another name, the Indian name, 'Little Chief Hare'. **1932** A. HUXLEY *Brave New World* v. 89 The sexophones wailed like melodious cats under the moon, moaned in the alto and tenor registers as though the *little death were upon them. **1939** —— *After Many a Summer* II. ii. 198 Like all the other addictions, whether to drugs or books, to power or applause, the addiction to pleasure tends to aggravate the condition it temporarily alleviates. The addict goes down into the valley of the shadow of his own particular little death. **1959** W. GOLDING *Free Fall* v. 108 The little death shared or self-inflicted was neither irrelevant nor sinful. **1959** D. KROOK *Three Traditions Moral Thought* x. 275 That other aspect of the sexual act that Augustine finds so disturbing, that oblivion which the poets called the 'little death', the overwhelming of the will and the reason, need have no terror in it. **1969** G. SIMS *Sand Dollar* x. 126 She attained her climax with a deep shudder... Her features took on a delicate nature in the 'little death'. **1971** R. RENDELL *One Across* III. xxi. 166 A little death would make the unbearable present pass... The pubs wouldn't be open yet. **1973** D. BAGLEY *Tightrope Men* i. 9 That everyday miracle of the reintegration of the psyche after the little death of sleep. **1602** CAREW *Cornwall* 137 b, Vpon *little Easter Sunday the Freeholders..did there assemble. **1895** *Westm. Gaz.* 1 Aug. 2/2 Do not let us fall into the error so often made by *Little Englanders and suppose that [etc.]. **1899** *Times* 20 Jan. 9/2 Mr. Morley's proud pronouncement of the faith of '*Little Englandism'. **1874** RAYMOND *Statist. Mines & Mining* 352 In Deer Lodge County..'*little giants'..have been introduced. [**1906** KIPLING *Puck of Pook's Hill* 185 The little green man orated like a—like Cicero.] **1961** PARTRIDGE *Dict. Slang* Suppl. 1170/2 **Little green men*, mysterious beings alleged to have been seen emerging from flying saucers. **1966** K. GILES *Provenance of Death* iv. 121 Are you saying you are being watched perhaps by little green men? **1967** M. KENYON *Whole Hog* iv. 42 There was a desert-island cartoon..and a little-green-men-from-Mars cartoon. **1969** C. HODDER-WILLIAMS *98–4* iv. 46, I wasn't at the Cape, nor Atlantis, nor a lunatic asylum for little green men with antennae. **1971** 'H. CALVIN' *Poison Chasers* iii. 36 We been reading too many books about little green men from Mars. **1972** *Daily Tel.* 25 Sept. 7/7 Neither he, nor I, believes that 'little green men' from Mars..are watching us and closely inspecting our planet. **1720** T. GORDON *Cordial Low Spirits* 64 It was observed that all the while it [Treaty at Utrecht] was making, Her Ministry went frequently to the *Little House. **1789** J. PARKER in *New England Hist. & Geneal. Reg.* (1915) LXIX. 305 Charles worked on my Little house. **1796** WESLEY *Wks.* (1872) XII. 249, I particularly desire wherever you have preaching..that there may be a little-house. **1812** W. TAYLOR in *Monthly Mag.* XXXIII. 228 A privy is called a little house. **1939** L. MANN *Mountain Flat* ii. 23 A gate led from the first yard into another in which were the pig sty, the hen-house, the tool-shed and what they called jocosely 'the little house'. **1939** F. THOMPSON *Lark Rise* i. 10 Later, the place of honour in the 'little house' was occupied by 'Our Political Leaders', two rows of portraits on one print. **1941** BAKER *N.Z. Slang* vi. 53 Other expressions ..to make a sale, to vomit; little house, a privy;..poled for stolen. **1927** *Sunday Times* 13 Feb. 5/1 This may not be pleasing to certain *little Irelanders who wish us to live in complete isolation. **1566** in Peacock *Eng. Ch. Furniture* (1866) 46 Item a sepulker wth *litle Jack..litle Jack was broken in peces this yeare by the said churchwardens. **1890** *Dialect Notes* I. 61 *Big Dick*: 10; **little Joe*: 4. **1926** T. S. STRIBLING *Teeftallow* viii. 67 The shooter..was half drunk, ..chanting at each shot, 'Come up, Little Joe! Don't deceive yo' pappy!' **1968** *Scottish Daily Mail* 16 July 2/1 If you throw crap dice and a combination of seven is showing on top, what is facing down?.. Little Joes? **1450–80** tr. *Secreta Secret.* 35 Rebelle as a *litille kyng, obeyshaunt as a pekok. **1962** *Listener* 24 May 920/2 Shaw had no use for the '*little mag' mentality. **1900** *Book-Lover* (San Francisco) Autumn (recto rear cover), To quote its publishers we may tell our friends *Impressions* is a *little magazine, simply done to tell the truth about books and other matters. **1913** *Writer's Mag.* Oct. 140/1 *The Black Cat* externally is the same little magazine that it has been for years. **1926** *Atlantic Monthly* Mar. 391/2 As these little magazines often contain only thirty-two pages, cost..two or three cents a copy to produce, and sell for fifteen..you can afford to dispense with advertisements. **1947** *Partisan Rev.* XIV. 473 This group formally includes members of the faculties of the universities and the few writers in the larger cities who do independent critical work pitched beyond the level of commercialism. These find their outlet in the little magazines. **1952** *Times Lit. Suppl.* 29 Aug. Suppl. p. xlvii, The birth of the Little Magazine may also now be seen in retrospect as heralding the decline of the greater. **1958** *Spectator* 18 July 116/3 Little-magazine society. **1971** *Ann. Rep. Curators Bodl. Libr. 1969–70* 39 Acquisitions in contemporary literature of the United States and the Commonwealth, including 'little magazines'..continued. **1972** *Guardian* 30 Aug. 8/2 Little magazines have been the pioneers of twentieth-century literature from Wyndham Lewis's Blast in the First World War to F. R. Leavis's Scrutiny in the thirties and forties and on to the present day. **1903** *Punch* 14 Oct. 258/1 And what is the subject of the piece [Barrie's *Little Mary*]? Who is Little Mary? It is nobody: it is simply a nursery name that the child-doctor invents as a kind of polite equivalent to what children ordinarily allude to as their 'tum-tum'. *Ibid.*, Good-natured British audiences have strong *Little Maries. **1905** *Daily Chron.* 8 Nov. 6/5 To wear it over their chest, not to speak of Little Mary, as people all now call their other danger spot. **1923** U. L. SILBERRAD *Lett. J. Armiter* iv. 82 Then I get a cold in Little Mary, my vulnerable spot. **1933** W. H. HARRISON *Humour in East End* 18 'I've got a little Mary too!' Swift as lightning came the reply, with a shrewd glance at a corpulent waistcoat: 'Not arf yer ain't, guv-nor.' **1781** N. MUNDY *Let.* 21 Oct. in A. E. Newdigate-Newdegate *Cheverels* (1898) iii. 48 How very Ill poor *Little I am used kick'd quite out & not allowed room. **1818** M. EDGEWORTH *Let.* 15 Oct. (1971) 126 Could I four years ago have believed if it had been prophecied to me that I poor little i should this day have been driving about London with Honora *alone*? **1895** A. W. PINERO *Second Mrs. Tanqueray* III. 111, I really thought you'd forgotten poor little me. **1899** R. WHITEING *No. 5 John St.* xxx. 267 The wonder why the irresponsible ..powers could not let 'poor little me' alone. **1913** A. BENNETT *Regent* I. iii. 68 'What about poor little me?' cried the driver, who was evidently a ribald socialist. **1923** E. BOWEN *Encounters* 9 *Nobody* takes *any* notice of little me. **1961** M. BEADLE *These Ruins are Inhabited* (1963) ix. 124 A cold snap prompted the writing of some poor-little-me letters home. **1968** A. DIMENT *Bang Bang Birds* viii. 149 He had had instructions from his bosses to liquidate little me. **1828** M. WILMOT *Let.* 23 Apr. (1935) 316 Blanche..is the *little *Mother* of the house upon the occasion. **1897** *Sears, Roebuck Catal.* 333/1 Little Mother's Outfit... Contains.. a 'Little Mother's Fashion Book', showing designs and directions for making dolls' dresses. **1967** A. WILSON *No Laughing Matter* II. 70 Sukey had better deal with them. She likes being the little mother. **1963** *Daily Tel.* 18 Oct. 31/3 The committee will be among the first '*little Neddies' set up under the auspices of the National Economic Development Council. **1964** *Economist* 5 Dec. 1112/1 The 'little Neds' (the separate councils..for different industries). **1967** *Punch* 24 May 766 The Little Neddy for the hotel and catering industry has just published the result of a survey it commissioned among foreign travel agents. **1969** *Times* 13 Jan. 11/3 Even a small shift in the distribution of domestic resources could meet the needs of the expansion postulated by Little Neddy, provided the profits were already there. **1905** *Little old [see MONEY *sb.* 6 a]. **1961** C. COCKBURN *View from West* vii. 71 Iceland..was menacing poor little old England in a truly devilish manner. **1966** J. POTTS *Footsteps on Stairs* (1967) xiv. 177 Why couldn't I have been looking out for little old me? **1968** J. SANGSTER *Touchfeather* vi. 54 He wasn't carrying a gun, probably considering that with just little old me to look after he didn't need to. **1973** A. ROSS *Dunfermline Affair* 80 Askwith and Gibson made polite noises, but little old Abbie refused to dissemble. **1973** *Guardian* 12 Mar. 9/1, I started at 15..and it was three or four years before I got a little old machine of my own. [**1913** J. W. RILEY *Poems* 9 Little Orphant Annie's come to our house to stay. **1924** H. GRAY in *Daily News* (N.Y.) (Pink ed.) 5 Aug. 26 (*title of cartoon strip*) Little Orphan Annie.] **1938** D. SMITH *Dear Octopus* I. 39 You stood there in the doorway..looking exactly like *little Orphan Annie. **1952** M. STEEN *Phoenix Rising* vi. 142, I won't have my friends..made uneasy by your bogey tales. You're worse than Little Orphant Annie! **1960** *Woman* 20 Feb. 6/3 She cast herself in the rôle of Little Orphan Annie. **1965** *Newsweek* 19 July 58/1 A Little Orphan Annie dress by Mary Quant or Caroline Charles will do, or for the male, a set of Mod threads. **1966** M. G. EBERHART *Witness at Large* (1967) i. 13 You'll soon be out of a job, Little Orphan Annie. *Ibid.*, It was true that I was in a position of Little Orphan Annie in my relationship to the Esseven family. **1619** *Notes B. Jonson's Convers. w. Drummond* (Shaks. Soc. 1842) 23 Sir P. Sidneye's Mother, Leicester's sister, after she had the *litle pox, never shew herself in Court therafter bot masked. **1914** (*title*) The *little review. **1958** *Times Lit. Suppl.* 24 Jan. 37/3 As Mr. Granville Hicks has pointed out, the 'little reviews' themselves have become erudite, careful, critical not creative, moved more by the spirit of Sainte-Beuve than by that of Baudelaire. **1961** A. M. WEINBERG in *Science* 21 July 162/1 We must make Big Science flourish without.. allowing it to trample *Little Science—that is, we must nurture small-scale excellence as carefully as we lavish gifts on large-scale spectaculars. **1963** D. J. PRICE (*title*) Little science, big science. **1970** *Sunday Times* (Colour Suppl.) 16 Aug. 22/2 Little Science changed into recognisable Big Science during the Second World War. **1972** *Science* 9 June 1084/1 There is no question that for nearly every scientist the personal joys of little science are greater than those of big science. **1928** *Daily Tel.* 3 Jan. 1/5 Lady Chamberlain's Tuesday afternoon At Homes at the Foreign Office..were one of the features of the '*little season'. **1938** *Burlington Mag.* Feb. p. xvii/1 Highly successful sales..in the so-called 'little season' which ended just before Christmas. **1959** J. FLEMING *Miss Bones* xiv. 150 This..is the Little Season, as it's known. There are numerous Embassy parties..first nights at the theatres..and what have you. **1570** MARY Q. OF SCOTS *Let. to C'tess Lennox* 10 July in H. Campbell *Love Lett. Mary* (1824) 228 The transporting ȝoure *littil son and my onelie child in this country... I have born him,..and of ȝow he is descendit. **1771** SMOLLETT *Humph. Cl.* I. 246 His detestation of the mob..has prevented him from going to the *Little Theatre in the Hay-market. **1813** JANE AUSTEN *Pride & Prej.* III. ix. 166 London was rather thin, but however the little Theatre was open. **1912** M. B. LEAVITT *50 Yrs. Theatr. Managem.* xxxvii. 574 'Little Theatres' have for some time been playing important rôles in the dramatic life of Paris, Berlin and London. **1914** *Writer's Mag.* Jan. 327/2 (*caption*) The 'little' theater movement expanding. **1916** *Stage Year Bk.* 45 Another little theatre, the Portmanteau..opened its doors with a programme of one-act plays. **1929** [see *community theatre*]. **1958** *Listener* 21 Aug. 283/2 The shabby treatment accorded here to our little theatres. **1965** E. O'BRIEN *Aug. is Wicked Month* ii. 22 She worked for a little theatre magazine. **1971** *Author* LXXXII. 118 A trusting author, Mr. X, wrote a 'philosophical' conversation-piece which was staged at a London little theatre. **1973** *Philadelphia Inquirer* (Today Suppl.) 7 Oct. 49/1 There is only one fully funded..little theatre in the Philadelphia area. **1934** M. ALLINGHAM *Death of Ghost* i. 2 *Little Venice [on the Regent's Canal] in 1930... The room ..took up the entire first floor of the old house on the canal. **1951** D. NEWTON *London West of Bars* xxii. 323 Robert Browning, back from Italy, settled for a time in a tall house overlooking 'Little Venice'. **1960** C. MACINNES *Mr. Love & Justice* 21 Edward was sitting with his girl in the park at Little Venice, up by the Harrow road. **1968** *Guardian* 12 July 20/6 The justices granted a provisional restaurant licence for two barges to be moored..near the lock of the Rochdale Canal... It was hoped this section of the canal.. would become a Little Venice patronised by yachtsmen. **1970** *Ibid.* 8 Aug. 7/3 It has taken a solid anniversary to bring the Little Venice Boat Show back to London... The anniversary signals the completion in 1820 of the Regent's Canal. **1907** F. H. BURNETT *Shuttle* xxiii. 229 *Little Willie's not quite as easy as he looks. **1915** D. O. BARNETT *Let.* 27 May (1915) 154 At intervals of about twenty minutes last night they fired a *Little Willie* on to our trench. *Ibid.* 8 June 166 Our fieldgun H.E. shell is a very fine thing, more powerful than the German one (otherwise known as *Little Willie*). **1925** A. CHRISTIE *Secret of Chimneys* xii. 121 That some one unlatched the window..to make it look like an outside job—incidentally with me as Little Willie. **1925** FRASER & GIBBONS *Soldier & Sailor Words* 304 *Big and Little Willie*, names given the Kaiser and German Crown Prince in a series of cartoons... The names soon..were applied to a variety of objects. For instance, two experimental tanks, which were begun on about August, 1915... 'Little Willie' first 'moved' on September 8th. **1927** 'D. YATES' *Blind Corner* iv. 125 'God give it's Little Willie,' said Ellis, and sucked in his breath. 'I'd like to meet him like this.' **1965** BROPHY & PARTRIDGE *Long Trail* 145 *Little Willie, Big Willie*, the Crown Prince and the Kaiser. Journalese. So used occasionally by the troops, who applied the terms to all manner of things: e.g. a long-range naval gun operating on the Western Front. **1624** J. CHAMBERLAIN *Let.* 20 Mar. (1939) II. 551, I send Dr. Bargraves sermon and the *litle womans worke for my Lady. **1795** W. B. STEVENS *Jrnl.* 18 Aug. (1965) III. 280 The Little Woman's passions swell. .. She is expecting her Husband to be her Slave. **1801** M. O'CONNELL *Let.* 6 Nov. in D. O'Connell *Corr.* (1972) I. 63 Complying with the earnest request of your *little woman* whose entire happiness is wrapped up in you. **1852** DICKENS *Bleak Ho.* (1853) xxxii. 314 My little woman will be looking for me, else. **1936** 'R. WEST' *Thinking Reed* viii. 262 We went off to a little woman who does manicures. **1959** *Sunday Express* 26 July 10/5 I've..found a 'little woman'—one of those treasures who will dressmake at home. **1970** G. GREER *Female Eunuch* 286 Loving mockery of the little woman. **1973** G. GREENE *Honorary Consul* IV. i. 175 The material was quite inexpensive, and I had it run up by a little woman.

IV. 14. *Comb.* (chiefly parasynthetic), as ***little-footed***, ***-haired***, ***-headed***, ***-minded*** (whence ***little-mindedness***), ***-statured***; **little-bitty**: see BITTY *a.* 3; **little-boy** *attrib.*, pertaining to, suited to, or resembling a small boy; infantile; so **little-boyish** *a.*; **little-boy-lost**: used (without hyphens) as a title of literary works by William Blake and other writers after him; *attrib.* or as *adj. phr.*, resembling a small boy who has lost his way; also *absol.*; **little boys' room** (cf. *little girls' room*), a genteelism for a gentlemen's lavatory; **little-endian** *a.* and *sb.*, the designation of the orthodox party in the controversy in the state of Lilliput on the question at which end an egg should be opened (Swift *Gulliver* iv); hence used *allusively*; **little-girl** *attrib.*, resembling or characteristic of a little girl, e.g. a type of collar, a voice; so **little-girlish** *a.*; **little-girlhood**, **-girlishness**; **little-girl-lost** (cf. *little-boy-lost*); **little girls' room**, a genteelism for a ladies' lavatory; †**little-sight** *a.*, short-sighted; **little-thrift**, an unthrifty person.

1847 THACKERAY *Van. Fair* (1848) v. 39 Out of the *little-boy class into the middle-sized form. **1923** D. H. LAWRENCE *Stud. Classic Amer. Lit.* (1924) vii. 143 Old-fashioned Nathaniel, with his little-boy charm. **1929** —— *Phoenix II* (1968) 537 Men..spend years training up the little-boy-baby-face type, till they've got her perfect. Then the moment they marry her, they want something else. **1951** M. MCLUHAN *Mech. Bride* (1967) 68/2 The male tends to assume the little-boy role. **1955** E. BLISHEN *Roaring Boys* iv. 182 Two faces, well-washed and *little-boyish. **1968** H. WAUGH *30 Manhattan East* (1969) 149 That little-boy quality that wasn't little-boyish at all. **1789** W. BLAKE *Songs of Innocence* in *Compl. Writings* (1972) 120 (*title*) The *little boy lost. **1905** W. H. HUDSON (*title*) A little boy lost. **1949** M. LASKI (*title*) Little boy lost. **1957** R. HOGGART *Uses of Literacy* ix. 235 An appearance compounded of the metallically-cynical and the little-boy-lost. **1957** *Numbers* VII. 4 The strand of dark hair..made him appear slightly dishevelled and rather little-boy-lost. **1961** J. PUDNEY *Thin Air* viii. 95 The-little-boy-lost look..which..brought out the mother in most women. **1967** V. CANNING *Python Project* ix. 186 Having that little-boy-lost feeling and knowing that all the world is against you. **1973** 'B. MATHER' *Snowline* iv. 51 He was beginning to realize his aloneness. Little boy lost in a big strange country. **1957** A. WILSON *Bit off Map* 145 'Hullo,' said Sylvia, 'I expected Victor.' 'He's gone to the *little boy's room,' said the girl. 'He'll be back in a jiffy.' **1973** W. FAIRCHILD *Swiss Arrangement* vi. 74 He bought me this jumbo cornet... I took it into the little boys' room with me... In case it started to melt while I was having a pee. **1973** M. WOODHOUSE *Blue Bone* ii. 15 Rodway pulled up in a lay-by. 'All out for the little boys' room,' he said. **1832** *Little endian [see BIG *a.* B. 2]. **1888** *Pall Mall G.* 13 Sept. 11/1 A..controversy..between the Big-endians and the Little -endians of female attire. **1847** TENNYSON *Princess* II. 118 She fulmined out her scorn of laws Salique And

*little-footed China. **1864** C. M. YONGE *Trial* I. xiii. 263 Gertrude did not like people in the '*little girl' stage. **1896** E. TURNER *Little Larrikin* xiii. 149 Isn't he a bit like your little-girl ideal man? When you were seventeen.. and had ideals? **1938** *Chatelaine* July 27/1 Last year it was the Little Girl Look. **1939** M. B. PICKEN *Lang. Fashion* 95/3 *Little girl collar*, narrow, round collar, smaller than Peter Pan or Buster Brown. **1949** M. MILLER *Sure Thing* (1950) 69 Her voice was a little-girl voice. **1967** MRS. L. B. JOHNSON *White House Diary* 5 Jan. (1970) 470 In came Lynda.. wearing mesh hose and little-girl flat shoes. **1925** 'R. CROMPTON' *Still—William* viii. 134 His ideal of *little-girlhood was Joan, dark haired and dark-eyed and shy. **1945** 'O. MALET' *My Bird Sings* I. iv. 30 Camille, glad of her still unquestioned little-girlhood, kept out of the way. **1901** A. F. BROWN *Lonesomest Doll* 35 Clotilde soon became *little-girlish again. **1936** C. DAY LEWIS *Friendly Tree* iv. 58 Anna felt absurdly obedient and little-girlish. **1962** I. MURDOCH *Unofficial Rose* xiii. 122 She spoke with a little-girlish satisfaction. **1974** M. HIGGINS *Changeling* xiv. 75 You've done something to your hair.. it's too little-girlish. **1936** J. CURTIS *Gilt Kid* v. 58 It was obvious that she was playing *little girlishness for all that she was worth. **1936** C. DAY LEWIS *Friendly Tree* xiii. 190 You can be the *little girl lost, and I'll be the policeman who finds you. **1963** *Guardian* 18 Jan. 4/6 Her little-girl-lost brand of charm. **1963** 'G. BLACK' *Dragon for Christmas* xi. 173 If ever there was a little girl lost it was Mei Lan. She had known love and the Kiangsi opera and had been cut off from both. **1974** M. HIGGINS *Changeling* ix. 46 That little-girl-lost look you have. **1949** M. MILLER *Sure Thing* (1950) 267 'Look, where are you going?' 'To the *little girls' room.' **1959** P. H. JOHNSON *Humbler Creation* vi. 43 'I wonder where on earth she's gone?'.. 'Probably to the little girls' room.' **1975** A. THACKERAY *One Way Ticket* I. 10, I just saw Maggie disappear into the little girls' room. **14..** *Voc.* in Wr.-Wülcker 574/18 *Comatulus*, *lytyl heryd. **1670** G. H. *Hist. Cardinals* II. i. 122 Two sorry *little-headed Nephews. **1707** HEARNE *Collect.* 25 Oct. (O.H.S.) II. 66 This is *little minded. **1813** *Examiner* 24 May 332/2 The little-minded vanity of a nation. **1824** in *Spir. Pub. Jrnls.* (1825) 342 The *little-mindedness which shrinks from professional satire. **1398** TREVISA *Barth. De P.R.* v. vi. (1495) 112 An eye is *lytyll syght whiche seeth not well aferre. **1702** *Lond. Gaz.* No. 3774/4 Went away from his Mother.., James Bristow, aged about 17 years, *little Statured. **1849** JAMES *Woodman* iv, They cannot be such idle *little-thrifts as you make them out.

B. *absol.* and *sb.*

I. The adj. used *absol.*

1. Chiefly with *the*: Those that are little; little persons.

c **1000** *Ags. Ps.* (Th.) cxiv. 6 Drihten ȝehealdeð dome þa lytlan. *c* **1200** ORMIN 8002 Forrþi let he cwellenn þa þe miccle & ec þe little. *a* **1300** *Cursor M.* 6551 Þai fled a-wai, .. Littel and mikel, less and mare. *c* **1400** *Destr. Troy* 12058 Þe lordis to þo litill þe lyuys han grauntid. **1484** CAXTON *Fables of Æsop* I. xiii, The lytyle ryght ofte may lette and trouble the grete. **1535** COVERDALE *Judith* xiii. 13 They came all to mete her, litle & greate. **1692** R. L'ESTRANGE *Fables* xvi. (1708) 21 The Great and the Little have Need one of Another.

2. *the little*: that which is little; the little qualities, characters, aspects, etc.

1791 COWPER *Yardley Oak* 87 Comparing still The great and little of thy lot. **1806** PRISC. WAKEFIELD *Domestic Recreation* vi. 80 The invention of man has not yet contrived glasses that comprehend either the vast or the little of nature. **1875** BROWNING *Aristoph. Apol.* 5123 Little and Bad exist, are natural.

3. a. Not much; only a small amount or quantity: often preceded by *but*; admitting of being qualified by advs. of degree, as *very*, *rather*. ***little or nothing***: hardly anything. † ***little is me of***: I care little for. † ***to say little***: to make no reply, to be silent. † ***within little***: within a short distance *of*. ***to make*** or †***let little of***, ***set little by***, etc.: see the verbs.

c **1200** ORMIN 6480 Her iss litell oþerr nohht I þiss land off þatt sallfe. *c* **1205** LAY. 3465 Þe mon þe litul ah. *a* **1225** *Juliana* 26 Lutel is me of ower lufe. *c* **1275** *Moral Ode* 12 in *O.E. Misc.* 58 Al to muchel ich habbe i-spend to lutel i-leyd an horde. *a* **1300** *Cursor M.* 26997 Litel he sette be his life. **13..** *Minor Poems fr. Vernon MS.* (E.E.T.S.) 525/51 3if þou haue luytel, luitel ȝiue and do. **1340** HAMPOLE *Pr. Consc.* 1459 Now haf we or litel, now pas we mesur. **1470–85** MALORY *Arthur* IX. iv. 344 Thenne she smote doun her heed and sayd lytel. *a* **1533** LD. BERNERS *Huon* lxvi. 226 He dyd ete & drynke but lytell. **1546** J. HEYWOOD *Prov.* (1867) 67 Though ye spent but lickell. *a* **1548** HALL *Chron., Hen. VII*, 9 Landed for a purpose at the pyle of Fowdrey within lytle of Lancastre. *Ibid., Hen. VIII*, 139 These wordes sore astonied sir Richard Weston, but he said litle. *c* **1580** JEFFERIE *Bugbears* IV. v. in *Archiv Stud. neu. Spr.* (1897), Lyttle sayd, sone amended. **1611** BIBLE *Luke* vii. 47 To whom litle is forgiuen, the same loueth litle. **1635** R. N. *Camden's Hist. Eliz.* II. an. 13. 124 It missed little but hee had been proscribed when he was dead. **1719** DE FOE *Crusoe* II. viii. (1840) 194 (Like me) he came from little at first. **1766** GOLDSM. *Vic. W.* viii. Ballad viii, Man wants but little here below, Nor wants that little long. **1794** BURNS *Song* (first line), Contented wi' little, and cantie wi' mair. **1808** SCOTT *Marm.* I. xxiv, Little he eats and long will wake. **1862** BORROW *Wild Wales* II. xxvi. 295 He was a tall lanikin figure .., and upon the whole appeared to be good for very little. **1869** RUSKIN *Q. of Air* vii, The myth of a simple and ignorant race must necessarily mean little, because a simple and ignorant race have little to mean. **1881** *Med. Temp. Jrnl.* XLIX. 31 We know little or nothing about the truth.

b. Const. *of*.

Now *rare* exc. when the context does not permit the use of *little* adj., e.g. when the sb. is defined by a demonstrative adj. The use with an adj. used *absol.* (as in quots. 1824, 1833) is a Gallicism, and not in common use.

c **1386** CHAUCER *Knt.'s T.* 921 That lord hath litel of discrecion, That in swich cas kan no diuision. *c* **1400** MAUNDEV. (1839) xxv. 259 In that Kyngdom of Medee there ben many grete Hilles, and litille of pleyn Erthe. **1486** *Bk. St. Albans* D iij, Off spare hawkes ther is chooce and lytill of charge of thaym. **1824** LANDOR *Imag. Conv.* Wks. 1853 I. 221/1 There was little of sound and salutary which they did not derive from Democritus or from Pythagoras. **1833** MOORE *Mem.* VI. 337 [Stones like] those at Stonehenge.. have but little of new or marvellous for him who has seen the rocks beyond the Atlantic. *Mod.* Of political sagacity he had very little. He showed little of the amiability which was ascribed to him.

†**c.** In the genitive depending on an indefinite pron., as ***what, somewhat***. ***littles what***, also ***what littles***: little or nothing, a trifling quantity; in first quot., trifles. *Obs.*

a **1100** *O.E. Chron.* an. 1070 (Laud. MS.) Bec & mæsse hakeles & cantelcapas & reafes & swilce litles hwat. *c* **1200** ORMIN 4681 For þatt tu muȝhe winnenn her Wiþþ sinne summwhatt littless. *Ibid.* 6952 Forrþi þatt teȝȝ..Ȝet unnderstodenn littlesswhatt Off all þe rihhte trowwþe. *c* **1305** *St. Edmund* 396 in *E.E.P.* (1862) 81 Hit was what lutles þat he et.

d. Qualified by a demonstrative or possessive: (The) little amount or quantity; (so) small a quantity, a (very) small amount, etc.

c **893** K. ÆLFRED *Oros.* I. i. §17 þæt lytle þæt he erede he erede mid horsan. *a* **1240** *Sawles Warde* in *Cott. Hom.* 265 Þis lutle ich habbe iseid of þat ich iseh in heouene. **1604** E. G[RIMSTONE] *D'Acosta's Hist. Indies* IV. xlii. 325 This little may suffice touching the Bezaars stone. **1633** P. FLETCHER *Poet. Misc.* 71 My little fills my little-wishing minde. **1667** MILTON *P.L.* II. 1000 If all I can will serve, That little which is left so to defend. **1738** JOHNSON *London* 40 Ev'ry moment leaves my little less. **1789** BURNS *Upon seeing a wounded hare*, Go, live, poor wanderer of the wood and field, The bitter little that of life remains. **1842** TENNYSON *Dora* 50 Dora stored what little she could save. **1847** GROTE *Greece* (1862) III. xxix. 73 The little of his poems which remains. **1887** *Times* (weekly ed.) 1 July 13/1 Lord S. spoke of the little.. done for our coast defences during the last 20 years.

II. *sb.* (With *a* or in *plural*.)

4. a. A small quantity, piece, portion; a small thing; a trifle.

c **1220** *Bestiary* 110 Naked falleð in ðe funt-fat, and cumeð ut al newe, buten a litel. *c* **1380** WYCLIF *Sel. Wks.* III. 347 Cristis apostlis.. were not bisie about dymes, but helden hem paied on a litil, þat the puple ȝaf hem redily. *c* **1400** *Destr. Troy* 1449 Lo, how fortune.. of a litill hath likyng a low for to kyndull. **1614** DAY *Festivals* ix. (1615) 267 Contemne not these littles, be they in truth never so little. **1631** FOSBROKE *Solomons Charitie* (1633) 7 Many littles, given unto many,.. is better then much conferred upon one. **1692** R. L'ESTRANGE *Fables* ccccl xviii. 443 A Man may be Happy with a Little, and Miserable in Abundance. **1846** D. JERROLD *St. Giles* xxiii. (1851) 236 When a man's being shaved, what a little will make him laugh. **1865** DICKENS *Mut. Fr.* II. xiv, A debt to pay off by littles.

Prov. **1622** MABBE tr. *Aleman's Guzman d'Alf.* I. 50 Many a little, makes a mickle. **1791** J. O'KEEFFE *Wild Oats* v. iii. 64 It is'n't much, but every little helps. **1840** MARRYAT *Poor Jack* xiii. 90 It's a very old saying, that every little helps. **1872** S. HALE *Lett.* (1918) 84, I get fearfully tired, and a very little Abbey goes a long way with me. **1873** 'MARK TWAIN' in 'Mark Twain' & Warner *Gilded Age* xxiv. 226 Every little helps, you know. **1910** E. M. FORSTER *Howard's End* xxiv. 201 Dolly's a good little woman.. but a little of her goes a long way. **1936** 'G. ORWELL' *Let.* 14 Feb. in *Coll. Ess.* (1968) I. 163, I expect I can either review it or get it reviewed... Not that that gives one much of a boost, but every little helps. **1951** J. MASTERS *Nightrunners Bengal* I. i. 3 A little of Caroline Langford went a long way. **1967** V. CANNING *Python Project* iv. 63 Carry on. Every little helps. You might turn up something.

b. Const. *of*. (In early use with *genitive*.)

For the restriction in mod. use see 3 b.

c **1000** *Sax. Leechd.* II. 336 Nim.. hwerhwette niþewearde an lytel. *c* **1200** ORMIN 4086 þeȝȝ ummbeshærenn þeȝȝreshapp.. A litell off þe fell aweȝȝ. *c* **1205** LAY. 30107 Wið an luttel ȝeren þa uade[re]s dede weoren. *c* **1450** *ME. Med. Bk.* (Heinrich) 68 Do a lytul þer of in þe sore eye. **1460–70** *Bk. Quintessence* 21 Putte þerinne a litil of rubarbe or of summe oþer laxatiue. **1535** COVERDALE *1 Sam.* xiv. 29 Se how lighte myne eyes are become, because I haue taisted a litle of this hony. **1616** T. GODWIN *Moses & Aaron* III. (1641) 92 He drank a little of the wine. **1762–71** H. WALPOLE *Vertue's Anecd. Paint.* (1786) IV. 4 Architecture was perverted to meer house-building, where it retained not a litle of Vanbrugh. **1798** WOLCOT (P. Pindar) *Tales of Hoy* Wks. 1812 IV. 418 Not a bit of a Ballad.. nor a little of a Tale to enliven the evening. **1826** DISRAELI *Viv. Grey* v. xv, Let me recommend you a little of this pike! **1887** *Jrnl. Educ.* Dec. 509 The 'little of everything' theory [of education].

c. Used advb.: To a little or slight extent; in a small degree; somewhat, rather. ***not a little***, a good deal, extremely.

† ***a little of the biggest*** (quot. 1654): rather large.

1382 WYCLIF *Heb.* ii. 7 Thou hast maad him litil, a litil lesse fro aungelis. *c* **1400** *Lanfranc's Cirurg.* 139 In þe ij day he openede a litil hise yȝen. **1413** *Pilgr. Sowle* (Caxton) I. ix. (1859) 7, I was comforted nought a litel. **1470–85** MALORY *Arthur* XVII. xvii, Thenne was not he a lytel sory for launcelot. *a* **1548** HALL *Chron., Hen. VI*, 104 b, Here must I a litle digresse. **1606** G. W[OODCOCKE] *Lives Emperors* in *Hist. Ivstine* G gj, Although himselfe was of smal knowledge, and a little eloquent. **1611** BIBLE *Ps.* ii. 12 When his wrath is kindled but a little. **1644** VICARS *God in Mount* 147 All the enemies Horse began to shogge a little. **1654** DOROTHY OSBORNE *Lett. to Sir W. Temple* (1888) 240 The ring, too, is very well, only a little of the biggest. **1722** DE FOE *Col. Jack* (1840) 159, I was a little afraid. **1847** MARRYAT *Childr. N. Forest* xviii, We are not a little hungry, I can tell you. **1887** *Spectator* 5 Nov. 1494 The Magazines are a little dull this month.

5. a. A short time or distance. Chiefly in ***after a little***, ***for a little***, ***in a little***.

c **1000** *Ags. Gosp.* John xvi. 16 Nu ymbe alytel [*Hatton* an lytel] ȝe me ne ȝeseoð, & eft embe lytel ȝe me ȝeseoþ. **1610** SHAKS. *Temp.* IV. i. 266 For a little Follow, and doe me seruice. **1611** BIBLE *2 Pet.* ii. 18 They allure.. those that were cleane [*marg.* Or, for a little, or a while] escaped from them who liue in errour. *a* **1814** *Hector* III. ii. in *New Brit. Theatre* IV. 345 And death we all must in a little share. **1827** CARLYLE *Germ. Rom.* I. 293 In a little, he and Froda left the inn. **1881** W. H. MALLOCK *Rom. 19th Cent.* II. 290 Be here then and we will go for a little into the garden.

b. Used *advb.* = For or at a short time or distance.

c **1175** *Lamb. Hom.* 93 Ȝe iherden a lutel er on þisse redunge þet ðe halie gast com ofer þa apostlas. *c* **1200** ORMIN 3467 Forr aȝȝ itt flæt upp i þe lifft Biforenn hemm a litel. *a* **1300** *Cursor M.* 14327 Forgeten has þou son þi lare þat i þe said a littel are. *c* **1400** *Destr. Troy* 8421 Lengye here at a litill, lystyn my wordes. *c* **1400** MAUNDEV. (Roxb.) xxii. 101 It rynnez into þe see a lytill fra þe citee. *c* **1475** *Rauf Coilȝear* 800 He lukit ane lytill him fra. *a* **1533** LD. BERNERS *Huon* lxvi. 227 Let me slepe a lytell lenger. **1643** TRAPP *Comm., Gen.* xxii. 9 Mount Moriah.. was a little from Salem, as mount Calvary also, was a little from Jerusalem. **1671** MILTON *Samson* 1 A little onward lend thy guiding hand To these dark steps, a little further on. **1702** ROWE *Tamerl.* I. i, Yet, yet, a little and destructive Slaughter Shall rage around. **1794** COWPER *Moralizer corrected* 21 In hope to bask a little yet. **1825** WATERTON *Wand. S. Amer.* I. i. 107 The tree which thou passedst but a little ago. **1842** TENNYSON *Locksley Hall* 1 Comrades, leave me here a little, while as yet 'tis early morn.

†**6.** ***but a little*** = 'but little' (see 3). *Obs.*

With quot. 1377 cf. 1470–85 and 1548 in 3.

1377 LANGL. *P. Pl.* B. II. 188 Sothenesse seiȝ hym wel and seide but a litel. **1579** LYLY *Euphues* (Arb.) 87 An aunswere which pleased Ferardo but a lyttle. **1596** SHAKS. *Tam. Shr.* I. ii. 61 Thou'dst thank me but a little. **1628** T. SPENCER *Logick* 146, I haue a little to say touching this fourth seate; for, I haue done enough in the last, to satisfie this.

III. Phrases, chiefly formed with prepositions.

7. Forming expressions, chiefly with repetition of *little*, having the sense: By small degrees; a little at a time; gradually.

a. ***by little and little***; also †***by little and by little***, †***by a little and (a) little***.

c **1380** WYCLIF *Sel. Wks.* I. 358 Crist wole teche his disciplis bi litil and litil alle þes. **1413** *Pilgr. Sowle* (Caxton) V. i. (1859) 68 Alwey it decrecyd by a litel and a litel. **1422** tr. *Secreta Secret., Priv. Priv.* 243 Hit sholde not be sodaynly chaungid that wyche is custoumet, but slowly by lytill and by litill. *a* **1548** HALL *Chron., Hen. VI*, 112 b, And so by a litle and litle, the Englishmen recovered again many tounes. **1577** HOLINSHED *Chron.* I. *Hist. Eng.* 112/2 By what wyles and craft he might by little and little settle here, and obteine a kingdome in the Ile. **1611** BIBLE *Exod.* xxiii. 30. **1625** BACON *Ess., Atheism* (Arb.) 337 Custome of Profane Scoffing in Holy Matters; which doth, by little and little, deface the Reuerence of Religion. **1682** DRYDEN *Relig. Laici* Pref. 2 Their Descendants lost by little and little the Primitive and Purer Rites. *a* **1774** GOLDSM. *Hist. Greece* I. 321 Both fleets arrived by little and little. **1823** J. BADCOCK *Dom. Amusem.* 105 Add, by little and little, as much pearl-ash.. as it will take up. **1886** RUSKIN *Præterita* I. 243 All this we knew by little and little.

†**b.** ***a little and (a) little***. *Obs.*

c **1350** *Will. Palerne* 950, I wol a litel and litel laskit in hast. **1482** *Monk of Evesham* (Arb.) 23 Hys spyrite beganne a lytyll and a lytyll to come ageyne. *a* **1548** HALL *Chron., Hen. VI*, 170 This great tumult and sodain fury, was.. a litle and litle appeased and finally quenched. **1655** STAPLETON tr. *Bede's Hist. Ch. Eng.* 75 The companie of faithfull began a litle and litle to encreace againe. **1719** DE FOE *Crusoe* I. ix. (1840) 157 My ink.. I eked out with water a little and a little, till it was so pale. **1751** R. PALTOCK *Peter Wilkins* (1884) I. 50 Stowing them all close together to keep in the moisture, which served us to suck at for two days after, a little and a little at a time.

†**c.** ***little and little***. *Obs.*

c **1380** WYCLIF *Sel. Wks.* III. 302 Litel and litel þei may gete al þe rewme into here owene hondis. **1450–80** tr. *Secreta Secret.* 33 He may not leve it attones, but litille and litille. **1523** LD. BERNERS *Froiss.* I. cxv. 138 And soo lytell and lytell, the dethe of Jaques Dartuell was forgoten. **1546** J. HEYWOOD *Prov.* (1867) 67 Littell and littell the cat eateth the flickell. **1588** PARKE tr. *Mendoza's Hist. China* 294 They shoulde haue a special care vnto their healthes, in trauelling not too fast but little and little.

d. ***little by little***.

1483 *Cath. Angl.* 218/2 Lityile be litille, *diuisim*, *paulatim*. **1586** D. ROWLAND *Lazarillo* II. (1672) Q 2 Weak and dead for hunger, I went little by little up the street. *a* **1643** LD. FALKLAND, etc. *Infallibility* (1646) 16 How many things little by little may have been received under old names, which would not have been so at once under new ones. **1865** *Cornh. Mag.* XI. 643 Little by little, the face of the country began to change. **1892** WESTCOTT *Gospel of Life* 272 Little by little, the revelation of Christ's Nature was made through the events of His intercourse with men.

†**e.** ***by (a) little***. *Obs.*

1577 HANMER *Anc. Eccl. Hist.* (1663) 171 Our affairs began by a little, and as it were by stealth, to grow unto some quiet state. **1579** E. K. in *Spenser's Sheph. Cal.* Ep. Ded. §4 Young birdes.. by little first proue theyr tender wyngs. **1647** W. BROWNE *Polex.* II. 178 That melancholy waxing away by little. **1763** *Ann. Reg., Char.* etc. 106 Sift.. more of the same sand by little upon it. *a* **1814** *Love, Honor & Interest* I. i. in *New Brit. Theatre* 263 Soon by little he began to droop.

†**8.** ***into (right) little***: very nearly. *Obs.*

c **1374** CHAUCER *Troylus* IV. 856 (884) For which we han so sorwed he and I That in-to litel boþe it hadde vs slawe. *c* **1540** LADY BRYAN in Strype *Eccl. Mem.* I. App. lxxi. 173 It wil be (in to right little) as great Profit to the Kings Grace this way, as the t'other way.

†**9.** ***in a little***: in a few words, briefly. *Obs.*

1613 SHAKS. *Hen. VIII*, II. i. 11 But pray how past it? Ile tell you in a little.

10. ***in little***: on a small scale; formerly esp. with reference to *Painting* = in miniature.

1597 SHAKS. *Lover's Compl.* 90 On his visage was in little drawne What largenesse thinkes in parradise was sawne. **1602** —— *Ham.* II. ii. 384 [They] giue twenty, forty, an hundred Ducates a peece, for his picture in Little. **1635** A.

STAFFORD *Fem. Glory* 7, I shall endeavour to limme her soule in little (since in great neither my time, nor ability will let me). **1655** STANLEY *Hist. Philos.* III. (1701) 119/1 The Temple was an imitation in little of that at Ephesus. **1724** A. COLLINS *Gr. Chr. Relig.* Pref. 61 This autority was at first exercised in little by those, who [etc.]. **1762–71** H. WALPOLE *Vertue's Anecd. Paint.* (1786) II. 171 Sir Kenelm Digby.. compares Vandyck and Hoskins, and says the latter pleased the most, by painting in little. **1842** TENNYSON *Gardener's Dau.* 13 A miniature of loveliness, all grace Summ'd up and closed in little. **1873** BROWNING *Red Cott. Nt.-cap* 137 By Boulevard friendships tempted to come taste How Paris lived again in little there.

C. *adv.*

1. a. To only a small extent; in only a slight quantity or degree; but slightly; not much, not very.

The use of the word to qualify adjs. (= 'not very') seems to be a Latinism or Gallicism, and has never been common.

c **1000** *Ags. Ps.* (Th.) cxviii. 87 Hio me lytle læs [L. *pauloninus*] laþe woldan, ðisses eorð-weȝes ende ȝescrifan. *c* **1200** ORMIN 3751 Þatt te birrþ.. lætenn swiþe unnorneliȝ & litell off þe sellfenn. *c* **1380** WYCLIF *Serm.* Sel. Wks. I. 139 Þei loven to litil þe sheep. *c* **1400** *Destr. Troy* 13912 He drof at hym with þe dart, derit hym but litle. *a* **1450** MYRC 21 Luytel ys worthy þy prechynge ȝef thow be of euyle lyuynge. **1484** CAXTON *Fables of Æsop* II. xvii, Who that preyseth hym self lytyll he is ful wyse. *a* **1548** HALL *Chron., Hen. VII*, 17 Remembryng the olde proverbe, love me litle and love me longe. **1601** R. JOHNSON *Kingd. & Commw.* (1603) 82 They.. intermeddle little in the ordinary government of the state. **1710** ADDISON *Tatler* No. 192 ¶2 They liked us as little as they did one another. **1766** GOLDSM. *Vic. W.* iii, He.. found that such friends as benefits had gathered round him were little estimable. **1812** SIR H. DAVY *Chem. Philos.* 4 The most refined doctrines of this enlightened people were little more than a collection of vague speculations. **1849** MACAULAY *Hist. Eng.* ii. I. 161 A zeal little tempered by humanity or by common sense. **1876** GLADSTONE *Homeric Synchr.* 126 But this is little material.

b. When, contrary to the usual order, *little* is placed before the vb. which it qualifies, it becomes an emphatic negative, as in ***he little knows*** = 'he is very far from knowing'. This use is confined to the vbs. *know*, *think*, *care*, and synonyms of these.

c **1200** *Moral Ode* 137 in *Trin. Coll. Hom.* 224 Litel wot he hwat is pine. *a* **1300** *Cursor M.* 1834 Littel roght þam of his manance. *a* **1548** HALL *Chron., Edw. IV*, 227 b, They would littel thynk, that he would so untrewly handle me. **1667** MILTON *P.L.* IV. 86 They little know How dearly I abide that boast so vaine. **1802** MAR. EDGEWORTH *Moral T.* (1816) I. xix. 164 He little imagined of how much consequence it might be. **1819** SHELLEY *Cenci* v. iii, Little cares for a smile or a tear The clay-cold corpse upon the bier!

†**2.** A little time (before); for a little time. *Obs.*

c **1200** ORMIN 463 Alls I seȝȝde nu littlær. *a* **1225** *Leg. Kath.* 1918 For me lauerd, Iesu Crist, mi deorewurðe leofmon, lutel ear me haueð ileaðet. *a* **1300** *Cursor M.* 14188 Ne was þou noght bot littel gan Almast þar wit þe juus slan? *c* **1375** *Sc. Leg. Saints* i. (*Petrus*) 549 Þe vilne.. þat lytil befor tholit he Of thame namyt of galele. **1604** E. G[RIMSTONE] *D'Acosta's Hist. Indies* VII. x. 523 The Mexicaines by this meanes, remained much eased and content, but it lasted little.

3. *Comb.*, as ***little-able***, ***-heard-of***, ***-known***, ***-loved***, ***-travelled***, ***-used*** adjs.; **little-bless** *v.*, *nonce-wd.*, = Heb. *bērēk* ('bless' euphemistically for 'curse').

1825 COLERIDGE *Lett. Convers.*, etc. II. xlv. 225 May God bless you, and your *little-able but most sincere friend. **1610** BROUGHTON *Job* i. 5 It may be my children have sinned, and *little-blessed God in their hart. **1787** BENTHAM *Def. Usury* i. 3 The.. *little-heard-of offence of Maintenance. **1894** *Pop. Sci. Monthly* June 162 That singular and *little-known people the Mosquito Indians. *a* **1586** SIDNEY *Arcadia* II. (1590) 102 Being ridde of this louing, but *little-loued company. **1889** HISSEY *Tour in Phaeton* 211 A *little-travelled land, this. **1900** *Everybody's Mag.* III. 585/1 They went to the *little-used front door.

†**'little**, *v. Obs.* exc. *poet.* Also 3 lutli, -i(e)n, littlin, 3–4 litelen, 4 littel, -yl, lutle, luttul, 5 lytil, -el, letil, lityll. [OE. *lýtlian*, f. *lýtel* LITTLE *a.*]

1. a. *trans.* To make little, diminish; to reduce in size, amount, or importance. Also with *away*.

c **888** K. ÆLFRED *Boeth.* xxix. §1 Þonne lytlað ðæt his anweald, & ecð his ermða. *c* **1200** *Vices & Virtues* (1888) 49 He litlede him seluen to-foren mannes eiȝen. *a* **1250** *Owl & Night.* 539 Oft ich singe for heom þe more For lutli sum of heore sore. *a* **1300** *E.E. Psalter* viii. 6 Þou liteled him a litel wight Lesse fra þine aungeles bright. *a* **1325** *Prose Psalter* xvii[i]. 46 Y shal littelel [*sic*] hem as poudre. *c* **1380** WYCLIF *Sel. Wks.* II. 423 Departing litliþ strengþe. *c* **1400** tr. *Secreta Secret., Gov. Lordsh.* 85 Be it put vpon a softe fyr, to þe þrydde party be lytild away. *a* **1483** *Liber Niger* in *Househ. Ord.* (1790) 38 Nother Marshalls, nother usshers of hall.. owe not to little or withdrawe any hole stuffe of fleshe or fyshe. **1642** ROGERS *Naaman* 75 Oh pray God to little the, to pare off thy superfluities. **1928** HARDY *Winter Words* 194 Can littlest life beneath the sun More littled be? **1957** A. CLARKE *Later Poems* (1961) 61 Yet, littling by itself, I found one That had never run to town.

b. To belittle, extenuate (a sin).

a **1450** *Knt. de la Tour* (1868) 61 She [Eue] wende to haue lytelyd her synne. **1611** W. SCLATER *Key* (1629) 164 Paul stiles himselfe the chiefe of sinners, imputes the crucifying of Christ to the ignorance of the Iewes; so littleing a sinne more grieuous. **1627** —— *Exp. 2 Thess.* (1629) 291 Its natural to most, to litle their sins.

2. *intr.* To become little, be diminished; to dwindle, wane.

c **950** *Lindisf. Gosp.* John iii. 30 Hine ȝedæfnað þætte auexe mec uutudlice þæt ic lytleȝe [*Ags. Gosp.* waniȝe, L. *minui*]. *a* **1225** *St. Marher.* 5 Ne his makelese lufsum lec ne mei neauer littlin ne aliggen. *a* **1240** *Sawles Warde* in *Cott. Hom.* 265 Of þulli blisse, þat hit ne me neauer mare lutlin ne wursin. *c* **1325** *Old Age* in *Rel. Ant.* II. 211, I werne, I lutle, ther-for I murne. *a* **1375** *Joseph Arim.* 145 His Godhede luttulde not þeiȝ he lowe lihte. *c* **1491** *Chast. Goddes Chyld.* 20 They lityll and deye by longe contynuaunce of ghostli siknesse.

Hence †**'littling** *vbl. sb.*

c **1400** tr. *Secreta Secret., Gov. Lordsh.* 102 If he conseille þe to lytelynge of þi þinges þat þou hauys in tresour.

little-ease. *Now Hist.* or *arch.* A place in which there is little ease for him who occupies it; a narrow place of confinement; *spec.* the name of a dungeon in the Tower of London, and of an ancient place of punishment for unruly apprentices at the Guildhall, London. Also, the pillory or stocks.

a **1529** SKELTON *Col. Cloute* 1171 Lodge hym in Lytell Ease Fede hym with beanes and pease! **1548** ELYOT *Dict.* s.v. *Arca*, A streicte place in a prisone, called littell ease. **1550** LATIMER *Last Serm. bef. Edw. VI* (1562) 115 Was he not worthy to be cast in bocardo or lytle ease? **1608** MIDDLETON *Family of Love* III. i. D 1 b, How dost thou brooke thy little ease, thy Trunk? [To a person who has been carried in a trunk.] *a* **1623** W. PEMBLE *Wks.* (1635) 548 As a prisoner of the Jayle, or one that is in little ease. **1663** DRYDEN *Wild Gallant* I. ii, I sweat to think of that garret.. why 'tis a kind of little ease, to cramp thy rebellious prentices in. **1688** R. HOLME *Armoury* III. 312/1 There is another like place of punishment in our House of Correction in Chester.. it is called the Little Ease, a place cut into a Rock, with a Grate Door before it. **1738** *Curiosity, or Gentl. & Lady's Libr.* (1739) 54 Here ev'ry Creditor has Right to teize, And make his Home a real Little-Ease [*Note.* A Place of Punishment in Guildhall, London, for unruly 'Prentices]. **1752** CARTE *Hist. Eng.* III. 736 A loathsome filthy hole or dungeon in the Tower, called Little Ease. **1840** H. AINSWORTH *Tower Lond.* xiii, The walls of the cell, which was called the Little Ease, were so low, and so contrived, that the wretched inmate could neither stand, walk, sit, nor lie at full length within them. **1899** F. T. BULLEN *Log Sea-waif* 10 The pantry: a sort of little-ease in a corner of the cuddy.

transf. **1638** FEATLY *Strict. Lyndom.* II. 58 In the Romish Purgatory all soules are in little-ease. **1681** *Whole Duty Nations* 6 To grant nothing to this consideration, is rather to crowd men into a Little-ease in Religion, than to unite them.

little-go. [f. LITTLE *a.* + GO *sb.*[1] Cf. GREAT-GO.]

1. A private and illegal lottery. *Now Hist.*

See also quot. 1867; but no authority for the statement has been discovered.

[? *c* **1710**: cf. quot. 1867.] **1795** *Sporting Mag.* VI. 274 A private lottery, or little go, was drawing at a house in Islington. **1796** COLQUHOUN *Police Metropolis* 149 The Keepers of unlicensed Insurance Offices.. have recently invented and set up private Lotteries, or Wheels, called by the nick-name of Little Go's. **1798** EDGEWORTH *Pract. Educ.* (1811) I. 315 Unlicensed lottery-wheels are called little-goes. **1802** *Act 42 Geo. III*, c. 119 § 1 All such Games or Lotteries, called Little Goes, shall.. be deemed.. common and publick Nuisances, and against Law. **1806** *Ann. Reg.* 388 An unlawful game of chance,.. formerly known by the name of the Little Go, but now distinguished, to avoid the penalty, by the name of Ivory. **1830** GEN. P. THOMPSON *Exerc.* (1842) I. 195 It is a political little-go, in which everybody knows the concern to be ruinous in the main. **1867** C. WALFORD *Insur. Guide* (ed. 2) 25 About this date [1710].. commenced a system of speculative assurances known as 'the little goes'. A number of persons combined, and each subscribed 5*s.* fortnightly, inclusive of policy stamps and entrance money, on condition of £200 being paid to his heirs and executors. In another of these schemes 5*s.* a quarter entitled the subscriber's representatives to receive £120 on his demise. **1887** PROCTOR *Chance & Luck* 133 At illegal [lottery] offices, commonly known as 'little goes', any sum, however small, could be risked.

2. *Univ. colloq.* The popular name (later superseded at Oxford by 'smalls') for the first examination for the degree of B.A., officially called 'Responsions' at Oxford and 'The Previous Examination' at Cambridge (discontinued in the 20th c.).

1820 *Gentl. Mag.* XC. I. 32 At present the Examination [at Oxford] is divided into a Little-go and a Great-go; colloquial appellations of the facetious great children sucking at the bosom of Alma Mater. **1824** *Blackw. Mag.* Oct. 461 *note*, The little-go is a new classical examination lately instituted at Cambridge. **1838** F. W. ROBERTSON *Lett.* 23 May (1882) I. 37 [dated 'Brazenose, Oxford'], I have to take.. my 'little go' this term. **1849** THACKERAY *Pendennis* iii, He's coaching me and some other men for the little go. **1860** M. BURROWS *Pass & Class* i. (1866) 11 Responsions, commonly called 'Little go' or, still more familiarly, 'Smalls'. **1876** DARWIN *Life & Lett.* (1887) I. 47 In my second year I had to work for a month or two to pass the Little Go, which I did easily.

attrib. **1882** L. CAMPBELL *Life Clerk Maxwell* vi. 152 Some time before the little-go examination. **1889** *Boy's Own Paper* 3 Aug. 693/3 First came the three answers given to the 'Little Go' question.

3. *transf.* (various senses).

1852 MRS. GASKELL *Let.* 19 May (1966) 191, I (boldly) asked them all to come here.. so we had an impromptu *little-go* last night. **1858** *Leisure Hour* 15 July 448/1 This preliminary spread, or 'little go'. **1909** J. R. WARE *Passing Eng.* 169/1 *Little go*, first imprisonment, first invented by a fallen university man. **1960** WENTWORTH & FLEXNER *Dict. Amer. Slang* 321/1 *Little go*, an unimportant, unexciting, or incomplete attempt, effort, task, or performance.

little-good.

1. *Sc.* The devil.

1821 GALT *Ann. Parish* xlix. 384 All this running here and riding there as if the littlegude was at his heels. **1822** —— *Entail* II. 284 The mim maidens now-a-days hae delivered themselves up to the Little-gude in the shape and glamour o' novelles and Thomson's Seasons.

2. *dial.* The sun-spurge, *Euphorbia Helioscopia*. Also the sour dock, *Rumex acetosa*.

1808–80 in JAMIESON. **1831** W. PATRICK *Plants Lanark.* 210 Sun Spurge, *Euphorbia Helioscopia*... Called Devil's Kirnstaff and Little-good. **1876** *Hardwicke's Science Gossip* 39 *Rumex acetosa* gets [the name of] 'little guid'.

†**littlehead.** *Obs.* [See -HEAD.] Littleness.

a **1300** *E.E. Psalter* liv. [lv.] 8, I a-bade him þat sauf me made Fra littelhed of gast. *c* **1440** *Jacob's Well* 106 Arwenesse, þat may be clepyd lytelhed of trust of good dede. *c* **1489** CAXTON *Faytes of A.* I. i. 1 The lytylhed of my persone.

†**littlelaik.** *Obs.* [a. ON. *lítil-leik-r*: see LITTLE *a.* and -LAIK.] Littleness.

a **1400–50** *Alexander* 1709 As he lenes & lokis on his fourme, His litillaike [*Dublin MS.* litilayke] & his licknes he laythly dispiced. *Ibid.* 2706 How þi lawnes & þi litillaike [*Dublin MS.* lityllake] þou lickyns to my hiȝt.

little man.

1. The little finger. *Obs.* exc. *dial.*

c **1290** *S. Eng. Leg.* I. 308/310 Þe deuel.. wolde fain henten heom bi þe polle with 'luttle man', is leste finguer. *c* **1475** *Pict. Voc.* in Wr.-Wülcker 753/3 *Hic auricularis*, the lythylman. **1888** in *Sheffield Gloss.*

2. a. A small landowner or capitalist; a person working or producing on a small scale; a small craftsman or tradesman; a local man available to do light work.

1811 in W. Marshall *Review Repts. Board Agric., East.* 88 A little man may as well have nothing allotted to him as have it so far off. **1820** LAMB *Elia* Ser. I. *Two Races of Men*, I grudge the saving of a few idle ducats, and think I am fallen into the society of lenders, and little men. **1825** H. WILSON *Mem.* IV. 103 That little man in St. James's Street, who sells box-combs. **1890** W. BOOTH *In Darkest Eng.* vi. 214 Would it not be possible.. to establish.. a Poor Man's Bank.. doing for the 'little man' what all the banks should do for the 'big man'? **1891** S. C. SCRIVENER *Our Fields & Cities* 29 They have a very strong objection to a 'little man' getting three acres, or less, with or without a cow. **1937** *Ann. Reg. 1936* II. 63 The potential customers being most numerous among the 'little men', *i.e.*, small shopkeepers and owners of one-man businesses. **1952** *Economist* 30 Aug. 514/1 Diversified investment buying by the general public, especially by the 'little man'. **1959** *Motor Manual* (ed. 36) xiii. 269 For cars so built it is seldom possible to have an adequate towing bracket made up by the 'little man round the corner' who happens to have a welding plant and some iron. **1962** *Guardian* 12 Dec. 4/4 What most of us have to do is to find a 'little man' who will oblige with a bit of painting in his spare time. **1966** *Listener* 15 Sept. 382/2 The Bideford 'little man' who fears competition.

b. The undistinguished and ordinary 'man in the street'.

1933 E. SUTTON tr. H. Fallada (*title*) Little man, what now? **1935** *New Statesman* 8 June 857/1 The old *noli-me-tangere* John Bull has disappeared, and his place has been taken by the all-enduring Little Man. **1936** 'G. ORWELL' *Keep Aspidistra Flying* iii. 64 To turn into the typical little bowler-hatted sneak—Strube's 'little man'. **1941** AUDEN *New Year Let.* III. 52 The hitherto-unconscious creed Of little men who half succeed. **1946** *R.A.F. Jrnl.* May 162 Joe represents the typical 'little man' in blue, doomed to a lowly rank. **1952** M. LASKI *Village* xiii. 187 The element of the ordinary man, the little man, taking matters into his own hands. **1960** *Times* 28 Sept. 15/4 Its central episode is the rebellion of a 'little man' against the anonymity and dreariness of his life. **1975** *Times* 2 Jan. 13/3 Mr [Charlie] Chaplin's indomitable little man beset by adversity.

3. *Sc.* **a.** (See quot. 1835.) **b.** (See quot. *c* 1880).

1835 CARRICK *Laird of Logan* (1841) 153 Amongst the servants in the employment of our Scottish farmers. There is the 'muckle man' and the 'little man'. *c* **1880** *Sketchy Mem. Eton* 16 (Barrère) He called the footman (or little man, as was the generic term for this class of domestic at my tutor's).

4. *pl.* Fairies, 'little folk'.

1850 ALLINGHAM *Poems* 87 Up the airy mountain Down the rushy glen, We daren't go a hunting For fear of little men.

5. A young male child: see MAN *sb.*[1] 4 f.

little master.

†**1.** An inferior master. *Obs.*

1382 WYCLIF *Gal.* iii. 25 Now we ben not vndir the litil maistir [**1388** vndurmaistir, Vulg. *sub pædagogo*].

2. *pl.* A group of German engravers of the sixteenth century, followers of Dürer, so called from the smallness of their prints. [G. *die kleinen meister*, *die Kleinmeister*; F. *les petits maîtres*.]

1837 *Penny Cycl.* IX. 440/1. **1879** W. B. SCOTT *Little Masters* iii. 16 Dürer, the reputed teacher of the Little Masters.

3. (See quots.)

1870 L. BRENTANO *Introd. to Toulmin Smith's Eng. Gilds* 178 In this [viz. the hat-] trade prevailed, early in the eighteenth century, the system of carrying on industry by means of sub-contractors (*alias* sweaters), who were called Little Masters. **1888** *Sheffield Gloss.*, *Little master*, a manufacturer in a small way of business, who works as a journeyman.

†**'littlemeal**, *adv. Obs.* In 4 -mele, melome. [f. LITTLE *sb.* + -MEAL.] Little by little.

1382 WYCLIF *Gen.* xxxiii. 14 Y shal folwe litil mele the steppis of hym. —— *Deut.* vii. 22 He shal waste thes nacious in thi siȝt, litilmele [1388 litil and litil] and bi partees. —— *Judg.* xx. 33 The busshementis.. litil melome hem seluen bigunnen to opne.

Little Neck. *U.S.* The name of a locality in Long Island, used *attrib.* in **little neck clam** to designate small specimens of the quahog, *Mercenaria mercenaria*, or other similar clams. Also *absol.*

1884 *Bull. U.S. Nat. Mus.* No. 27. 234 Another name [for the small round clam] is 'Little Neck', derived originally from a neck of land on the north shore of Long Island, known as Little Neck, whose clams had a superior flavour. **1899** J. HATTON in *People* 17 Dec. 2 Regret was expressed that New York did not possess the English sole..but there was good compensation in the little-neck clam and the bass. **1910** *Chambers's Jrnl.* July 430/2 In the restaurants the British visitor will invariably be confronted with the possibilities contained in 'little neck clams',..and so on. **1935** J. C. LINCOLN *Cape Cod Yesterdays* 49 Everyone eats oysters and Little Necks *au naturel.* **1972** *Guardian* 1 Sept. 9/1 Clams from the Maine coast, Quahogs, 'steamers', Littlenecks.

littleness ('lɪt(ə)lnɪs). [OE. *lýtelnes*: see LITTLE *a.* and -NESS.] The attribute of being little.

1. Smallness of quantity, amount, bulk, stature, degree, or extent.

c **1000** ÆLFRIC *Gram.* xxxviii. (Z.) 228 Sume syndon *quantitatis*, ðа ȝetacniað mycelnysse oð ðe lytelnesse [*v.r.* lutelnesse]. **1398** TREVISA *Barth. De P.R.* XIII. xxvi. (1495) 460 Affocius is a lytyll fysshe and for lytylnes it not may be tak with hoke. **1526** *Pilgr. Perf.* (W. de W. 1531) 63 b, His vylenes, lytelnes, or other deformite of nature. ? *a* **1550** in *Dunbar's Poems* (1893) 317 For littilnes scho was forlorne, Siche ane kemp to beir. **1642** FULLER *Holy & Prof. St.* II. ix. 86 Those of unusuall littlenesse are made ladies dwarfs. **1655** —— *Hist. Camb.* 83 Lowness of endowment, and littlenesse of Receit, is all [that] can be cavilled at in this foundation. *a* **1667** COWLEY *Greatness* in *Verses & Ess.* (1674) 121, I confess, I love Littleness almost in all things, A little convenient Estate, a little chearful House, a little Company, and a very little Feast. **1726** SWIFT *Gulliver* II. viii, Observing the littleness of the houses, the trees, the cattle, and the people, I began to think myself in Lilliput. **1828** CHALMERS in Watson *Life A. Thomson* (1882) 81, I thought not of the littleness of time, I recklessly thought not of the greatness of eternity. **1883** *Harper's Mag.* Nov. 902/1 A marvellous littleness of hand and foot.

2. Want of greatness, grandeur, or importance; insignificance, triviality, meanness, pettiness; smallness of mind.

1388 WYCLIF *Ps.* liv. 9 [lv. 8], I abood hym, that made me saaf fro the litilnesse [Vulg. *pusillanimitate*], ether drede of spirit. **1483** *Cath. Angl.* 219/1 A Litilnes, *decliuitas ingenij est, modicitas, paruitas, paucitas.* **1502** *Ord. Crysten Men* (W. de W. 1506) II. i. 84 Knowynge the lytylnesse & fray[l]te of humayne nature. **1694** SOUTH *Serm.* II. Ep. Ded., If the supposed Littleness of these matters should be a sufficient Reason for the laying them aside. **1710** STEELE *Tatler* No. 197 Ƿ4 There is a Sort of Littleness in the Minds of Men of wrong Sense. **1779** MAD. D'ARBLAY *Diary* 20 Oct., Mrs. Thrale..is so enraged with him for his littleness of soul in this respect. **1822** HAZLITT *Table-t.* Ser. II. iii. (1869) 78 Littleness is their element, and they give a character of meanness to whatever they touch. **1871** L. STEPHEN *Playgr. Eur.* xi. (1894) 262 The mountains..speak to man of his littleness and his ephemeral existence. **1896** W. WARD *Talks with Tennyson* in *New Rev.* July 81 Contemptuousness.. was, he said, a sure sign of intellectual littleness.

b. An instance of this; a mean, petty quality or action.

1660 INGELO *Bentiv. & Ur.* II. (1682) 110 Neither are our minds troubled with those Limitations and Littlenesses which we meet with in our preception of other things. *a* **1797** H. WALPOLE *Mem. Geo. II* (1847) III. xi. 292 One of those vainglorious littlenesses which too often entered into his composition. **1832** CARLYLE *Misc.* (1857) III. 38 Pitiful Littlenesses as we are. **1859** TENNYSON *Idylls* Ded. 25 Wearing the white flower of a blameless life, Before a thousand peering littlenesses. **1865** MERIVALE *Rom. Emp.* VIII. lxiii. 66 The greatness of their general character overshadowed their littlenesses.

little people. **1.** Fairies, gremlins. Cf. LITTLE MAN 4.

1726-31 WALDRON *Descr. Isle of Man* (1865) 27 As they confidently assert that the first inhabitants of their Island were fairies, so do they maintain that these little people have still their residence among them. **1897** E. PHILLPOTTS *Lying Prophets* x. 101 The li'l people takes all manner o' shaapes. **1941** [see GREMLIN 1]. **1973** *Times* 17 Mar. 14/8 The two larger clovers..were said to afford protection against 'unkind Little People'. **1973** *Stornoway Gazette* 19 May 6/2 As a writer, and collector of unusual information, I would be interested to hear from people who have seen the 'little people' or any strange, apparently non-human beings, under any circumstances whatever.

2. Children.

1752 M. W. MONTAGU *Let.* 22 July (1967) III. 15 How often do I fancy to my selfe the pleasure I should take in seeing you in the midst of your little people! **1876** C. M. YONGE *Three Brides* I. xvii. 282 My little people are so anxious to have me with them. **1934** H. G. WELLS *Exper. Autobiogr.* II. viii. 602 The Bastable family she created is still a joy to little people between ten and seventeen. **1972** A. ROUDYBUSH *Sybaritic Death* (1974) ii. 7 Tiled Beatrix Potter bunnies still scampered around the frieze..and windows, barred to prevent accidents to little people. **1975** *Sunday Times* 30 Mar. 8/1 (Advt.), Big savings for little people from Boots.

3. The poor; ordinary or undistinguished people.

1827 LYTTON *Pelham* ii, There was in it..no cringing to great, and no patronising condescension to little people. **1901** C. MORRIS *Life on Stage* xxiv. 195, I hear many tales of the insolence of stars—of their..injustice to 'little people' as the term goes. **1951** M. MCLUHAN *Mech. Bride* (1967) 66/1 Her allies are the little people, who..have to contend with the frustrations brought about by bureaucratic bungling.

Littler ('lɪtlə(r)). The name of William *Littler* (1724–84), English potter, used in the possessive to denote a rich blue colour applied to porcelain or stoneware.

1957 MANKOWITZ & HAGGAR *Conc. Encycl. Eng. Pott. & Porc.* 130/2 *Littler's blue*, a brilliant 'royal' blue or lapis-lazuli found on porcelain attributed to Longton Hall, and on salt-glazed stoneware believed to have been made by William Littler & Aaron Wedgwood, c. 1750. **1971** *Country Life* 28 Oct. 1124/1 William Littler..was the originator of a rich blue enamel which has come down in collectors' jargon as 'Littler's blue'.

Little's disease. *Med.* [Named after William John *Little* (1810–94), English physician, who described it.] Cerebral spastic paralysis of infants.

1885 *Boston Med. & Surg. Jrnl.* CXII. 217/1 (*heading*) Cases of congenital muscular rigidity, or Little's disease. *Ibid.*, This 'congenital muscular rigidity' was first described as an affection by Little, of London, in 1853, and Rupprecht ..suggested that the name of Little's disease be applied to it. **1887** *Buck's Handbk. Med. Sci.* V. 200/2 Little's disease. Spasmodic tabes of children. **1938** *Times Lit. Suppl.* 22 Jan. 50/2 Recent researches would appear to have established that the trouble from which Byron suffered was not an ordinary club-foot: that he was the victim of some obscure nervous malady—Little's disease, otherwise spastic paraplegia, has been suggested. **1964** S. DUKE-ELDER *Parsons' Dis. Eye* (ed. 14) xxxiv. 549 Congenital spastic diplegia (*Little's disease*), a bilateral spastic paralysis present from birth, considered at one time to be due to meningeal hæmorrhage as a result of birth injury, is probably a degenerative cerebral process of obscure ætiology.

† **little-what.** *Obs.* [f. LITTLE + WHAT. Cf. *littles what* s.v. LITTLE B. 3 c.] A small portion or quantity (*of*); somewhat. Also ***a little what*** (advb.): in some degree, somewhat.

c **1380** WYCLIF *Serm.* Sel Wks. I. 62 So þat ech on myȝte take a litil what of breed. **1387** TREVISA *Higden* (Rolls) II. 99 Twenty ȝere and a litelwhat more. *Ibid.* V. 191 And so he reste a litel what sittynge [L. *modicum sedendo*]. **1398** —— *Barth. De P.R.* IV. ix. (Tollem. MS.), A litill what swete in sauoure [L. *in sapore parum dulce*]. *a* **1400-50** *Alexander* 4392 Of þi lare a litill-quat likis me to write.

† **little world.** *Obs.* A literal rendering of MICROCOSM.

c **1200** ORMIN 17597 Mycrocossmos, þatt nemnedd iss Affterr Ennglisshe spæche þe little werelld. **1450-80** tr. *Secreta Secret.* 35 The philesofre callith man the litille world. **1603** H. CROSSE *Vertues Commw.* (1878) 124 If the bodie be not set on worke, the minde goeth astray, whereby this litle world is soone ouerthrowne. **1605** SHAKS. *Lear* III. i. 10 (Qo. 1608). **1614** SYLVESTER *Little Bartas* 28 The Little-World, wherein the Great is shown. **1649** G. DANIEL *Trinarch., Hen. IV*, cclix, The Little World thus Circumscribes a Nation.

little-worth, *a.* (*sb.*) Now *arch.* and *Sc.* Of little worth; *esp. Sc.* = of worthless character.

c **1200** ORMIN 16518 All swa summ itt wass litell wurrþ Till þeȝȝre sawle nede. *c* **1386** CHAUCER *Pars. T.* Ƿ236 Right so as contricion auailleth noght with-outen sad purpos of shrifte..right so litel worth is shrifte or satisfaccion with-outen contricion. **1565** JEWEL *Def. Apol.* (1611) 41 M. Harding saith, all this that I haue heere alleged..is Little-worth stuffe. **1611** BIBLE *Prov.* x. 20 The heart of the wicked is little worth. **1733** E. ERSKINE *Serm.* Wks. 1871 II. 189 Lax little-worth young men. **1785** BOSWELL *Tour Hebrides* 75 He had once come to a stranger who sent for him; and he found him 'a little-worth person!' **1825-80** JAMIESON s.v., He's a littleworth body. **1850** TENNYSON *In Mem.* lxxxv. 30, I..Whose life, whose thoughts were little worth.

b. *sb.* A 'little-worth' person.

1825-80 JAMIESON, *Little worth.* This term is used substantively in Dumfr[ies]; as, He's a littleworth.

'**littling.** *dial.* [OE. *lýtling*: see LITTLE *a.* and -ING³.] A little child or young animal.

c **975** *Rushw. Gosp.* Matt. xix. 14 Leteþ þa lytlingan cuman to me. *c* **1000** *Ags. Gosp.* Matt. xi. 25 þu þe be-hyddyst þas þing fram wisun and gleawun, and onwruge þa lytlingun. **1721** BAILEY, *Litteling*, a little one. **1852** ALEX. ROBB *Poems & S.* 187 Twa or three Curs o' littlins baulin'. **1888** *Sheffield Gloss.*, *Littling*, the smallest pup, &c., of a litter. **1889** BARRIE *Window in Thrums* 104 But never no sign o' a murdered litlin'.

littlish ('lɪtlɪʃ), *a. dial.* Also **littleish.** [f. LITTLE *a.* + -ISH.] Rather little.

1860 GEO. ELIOT *Mill on Fl.* III. vi, This littlish blade's broke. *c* **1865** —— in *Pall Mall G.* 18 Nov. (1883) 1/2 Their [*sc.* servants'] standard measures too are of a private kind; a good lump, a handful, a tea-cup, a littleish basin [etc.].

littly, littlie ('lɪtlɪ), *sb.* [f. LITTLE *a.* + -Y⁶, -IE]. A small child or person; *pl.*, small children, the younger children of a family, etc.

1893-4 R. O. HESLOP *Northumb. Words* II. 453 *Littlie*, a smaller person than others. **1961** A. UPFIELD *Bony & White Savage* v. 41 How's she? How's the littlies? **1967** B. JEFFERIS *One Black Summer* vi. 122 Can you see Hilary instructing the littlies at Sunday school?

littly ('lɪtlɪ), *adv.* [f. LITT(LE *a.* + -LY².] In a small, modest, undistinguished way.

1897 F. THOMPSON *New Poems* 137 Littly he sets him to the daily way. **1905** BEERBOHM *Around Theatres* (1924) II. 177 To strut agreeably, littly, as in the average production.

litton, obs. form of LITTEN *sb.*, churchyard.

littor, littorage, obs. ff. LITTER, LITHARGE.

littoral ('lɪtərəl), *a.* and *sb.* Also 7 **litorall, litteral,** 7–9 **litoral.** [ad. L. *littorālis*, better *lītorālis*, f. *lītor-*, *lītus* (often written *littus*) shore. Cf. F. *littoral.*]

A. *adj.* Of or pertaining to the shore; existing, taking place upon, or adjacent to the shore.

1656 in BLOUNT *Glossogr.* **1657** W. RAND tr. *Gassendi's Life Peiresc* II. 125 The litteral parts when they are just against the rising Sun are sooner inlightned. **1803** *Edin. Rev.* I. 378 The British forces would only attack by sea, or by a littoral warfare. **1833** LYELL *Princ. Geol.* III. 346 The littoral Cordillera of Brazil. **1853** PHILLIPS *Rivers Yorksh.* v. 151 The beneficial action of the sea air is apparent on our littoral climate. **1869** RAWLINSON *Anc. Hist.* 320 The littoral extent of Italy is, in proportion to its area, very considerable. **1875** *Wonders Phys. World* II. ii. 223 The ice of littoral glaciers exhibits a green colour. **1895** HOFFMAN *Begin. Writing* 44 The Innuit of littoral Alaska.

b. *Zool.*, *Geol.*, etc.: Growing, living, or deposited on the 'littoral zone' (see quot. 1876).

1661 LOVELL *Hist. Anim. & Min.* Introd., Fishes..are either pelagious, living in the main sea,..or litorall, living neer the shore. **1731** BAILEY vol. II, *Litoral shells.* **1776** DA COSTA *Conchology* 66 Some [Shell-fish] are even littoral, or inhabit the shores. **1830** LYELL *Princ. Geol.* I. 151 There were then also littoral formations in progress, such as are indicated by the English*Crag.* **1845** DARWIN *Voy. Nat.* xiii. (1879) 285 The islands were here..composed of a stratified, soft, littoral deposit. **1866** TATE *Brit. Mollusks* iv. 82 *Limax gagates* is a littoral animal. **1876** PAGE *Adv. Text-Bk. Geol.* iii. 76 The Littoral [zone] lies between high and low water mark. **1880** GRAY *Struct. Bot.* 419/1 *Litoral, Littoral*, Belonging to or growing on the seashore or rivershore.

B. *sb.* A littoral district; the region lying along the shore. [After It. *littorale*, F. *littoral.*]

[**1815** WELLINGTON in Gurw. *Desp.* (1838) XII. 287 By the cession to Geneva of part of the *littorale* of the lake by the King of Sardinia.] **1828** [J. R. BEST] *Italy* 54 He has obtained a littoral, or sea-coast, stretching along the whole of his continental territory. **1859** W. H. GREGORY *Egypt* II. 193 The towns along the Mediterranean littoral. **1868** E. P. WRIGHT *Ocean World* iv. 79 The sand of the littoral of all existing seas is so full of these minute but elegant shells. **1882** O'DONOVAN *Merv Oasis* Pref. 7 The Russian settlements on the Eastern Caspian littoral. **1894** *Pop. Sci. Monthly* June 162 The portion of the Caribbean littoral commonly known as the Mosquito Coast.

Littorina (lɪtəˈraɪnə, -iːnə). [mod.L. (A. d'A. de Férussac *Tableaux Systématiques des Animaux Mollusques* (1822) p. xxxiv), f. L. *lītus* shore.]

1. A gastropod mollusc of the genus so called; = PERIWINKLE² 1.

[**1820-5** J. & G. B. SOWERBY *Genera Recent & Fossil Shells* plate 211 As the name implies, the Littorinæ are found on and near the shore.] **1857** L. REEVE *Conchologia Iconica* X. s.v. *Littorina*, plate 1, species 1 (*heading*) The bubbled Littorina. **1963** D. W. & E. E. HUMPHRIES tr. *Termier's Erosion & Sedimentation* iii. 64 The Littorinas of California ..have each been able to dislodge 0·3 gm of grains in twenty-four hours.

2. Littorina (or **Litorina**) **sea,** the Baltic sea at the end of the Boreal period. Also ***Littorina beach, minimum, period, stage, transgression*** (see quots.).

1921 R. A. S. MACALISTER *Text-bk. European Archæol.* I. ii. 43 The Baltic Sea became of much the same configuration as at present, but rather larger in extent and more salt; the name given to this stage of its history, once more derived from the name of its mollusc, is *Littorina Sea.* The greatest depression of this phase of land-movement may be called the *Littorina Minimum.* The Littorina period is also known as the *Tapes* period. **1928** C. DAWSON *Age of Gods* iii. 48 The climate of Scandinavia became much warmer, owing perhaps to a change in the ocean currents... This is the Litorina stage, named after the periwinkle which now inhabited the warmer waters of the Baltic. **1949** W. F. ALBRIGHT *Archaeol. of Palestine* iii. 62 Pottery came into use in an early phase, scarcely later than about 4500 B.C., at the height of the Litorina period. **1954** S. PIGGOTT *Neolithic Cultures* i. 2 The Littorina Transgression of the Baltic. **1963** D. W. & E. E. HUMPHRIES tr. *Termier's Erosion & Sedimentation* i. 26 Corresponding to the Calaisian are the *Littorina* beaches.

littorinid (lɪˈtɒrɪnɪd). [f. mod.L. family name *Littorinidæ*, f. generic name *Littorina* (see prec.).] A marine snail of the family Littorinidæ.

1948 *Austral. Jrnl. Sci. Res.* B. I. 191 The Supralittoral is the region above high-water spring tide levels which has been invaded by only a few typically marine animals, chiefly gastropods. The species are Littorinids, and one might call this the Littorinid zone. **1952** *Jrnl. Ecol.* XL. 87 We agree.. in defining the upper limit of the littoral..as the region where littorinids become dominant. **1964** V. J. CHAPMAN *Coastal Vegetation* ii. 37 The littorinids do not penetrate them [*sc.* lichen zones] under normal conditions. **1974** *Nature* 3 May 11/3 Littorinids are present on the rock shores of all continents.

littour, early form of LICTOR; obs. f. LITTER *sb.*

littress ('lɪtrɪs). (See quot.)

1875 KNIGHT *Dict. Mech.*, *Littress*, a smooth kind of cartridge-paper, used in the manufacture of cards.

littuit, variant of LITUIT *Obs.*

Lituanian, obs. form of LITHUANIAN.

lituate ('lɪtjʊeɪt), *a. Bot.* [f. L. *litu-us* clarion + -ATE² 2.] Forked with the points turned a little outwards.
1866 in *Treas. Bot.* **1889** in *Syd. Soc. Lex.*

li'tuiform, *a. rare*⁻⁰. [f. L. *litu-us* clarion + -(I)FORM.] Shaped like a clarion.
1840 in SMART; and hence in mod. Dicts.

†**lituit**. *Her. Obs.* Also 7 littuit, lytuite. [variant of LETTICE.] (See quots.)
1562 LEIGH *Armorie* (1597) 75 b, The second [fur] is called Argent, and is vsed for a doubling, and taken for the Littuit's skin. **1610** GUILLIM *Heraldry* I. iii. 9 The skinne or furre of a litle beast called a Lytuite, so named (as I conceiue) [of] Lithuania. **1731** in BAILEY vol. II.

lituite ('lɪtju:aɪt). *Geol.* [ad. mod.L. *Lituites*, f. *lituus*: see LITUUS; so called from its shape.] A fossil cephalopod shell of the genus *Lituites*.
1828-32 in WEBSTER. **1837** BUCKLAND *Geol. & Min.* I. 365 *Lituite*. Together with the Orthoceratite,.. there occurs a cognate genus of chambered shells, called Lituites. **1859** in PAGE *Handbk. Geol. Terms.*

lituolite ('lɪtju:əlaɪt). *Geol.* [f. mod.L. *Lituol-a*, dim. of L. *lituus* (see LITUUS: the name refers to the shape of the shell) + -ITE.] A microscopic fossil foraminifer of the genus *Lituola*.
1843 HUMBLE *Dict. Geol.* etc., *Lituolite*, a fossil lituola. **1859** in PAGE *Handbk. Geol. Terms.*

‖**litura** (lɪ'tjʊərə). *Ent.* [L.] (See quot.) Hence '**liturate** *a. Ent.* and *Bot.* (see quots.).
1826 KIRBY & SP. *Entomol.* IV. 285 *Litura*, an indeterminate spot growing paler at one end, as if daubed or blotted. *Ibid.*, *Liturate*, a surface painted with one or more such spots [Lituræ]. **1866** *Treas. Bot.*, *Liturate*, when spots are formed by the abrasion of the surface.

†**liturate**, *v. Obs. rare*⁻⁰. [f. L. *litūrāt-*, ppl. stem of *litūrāre*, f. *litūra* an erasure, f. *lit-*, ppl. stem of *linĕre* to blot out.] *trans.* To blot out, erase.
1656 in BLOUNT *Glossogr.*

liturge (lɪ'tɜ:dʒ). *rare*⁻¹. In 8 liturg. [ad. L. *lītūrg-us*, Gr. λειτουργ-ός (see LITURGY).] A priest or minister; = LITURGIST 3.
1737 WATERLAND *Eucharist* 478 In these three ways, the Christian Officers are Priests, or Liturgs to very excellent Purposes, far above the Legal ones. [In some recent Dicts.]

liturge, obs. form of LITHARGE.

liturgic (lɪ'tɜ:dʒɪk), *a.* and *sb.* [ad. late L. *lītūrgic-us*, a. Gr. λειτουργικ-ός, f. λειτουργ-ός: see LITURGY.] **A.** *adj.* = LITURGICAL.
1656 BLOUNT *Glossogr.*, Liturgick, pertaining to such a Liturgy; ministerial. *a* **1763** BYROM *Expost. with Sectarist* 11 Misc. Poems 1773 II. 280 At all liturgic Pray'r and Praise it storms, As Man's Inventions. **1781** WARTON *Hist. Eng. Poetry* III. xxvii. 166 The *Te Deum, Benedictus*,.. and the rest of the liturgic hymns. **1880** T. C. MURRAY *Orig. & Growth Ps.* ix. 282 We saw that it [Ps. cviii] was a purely liturgic cento.

b. *Gr. Antiq.* (Cf. LITURGY 3.)
1849 GROTE *Greece* II. lxi. (1862) V. 318 The Athenians abridged the costly splendour of their choric and liturgic ceremonies at home.

B. *sb. pl.* † **1.** ? Liturgical books. *Obs.*
a **1677** BARROW *Pope's Suprem.* (1680) 81 The like may be said for Saint James, if he (as the Roman church doth in its Liturgicks suppose) were an Apostle.

2. a. The study of liturgies, their form, origin, etc. **b.** That part of pastoral theology which deals with the conduct of public worship.
1855 OGILVIE, Suppl., *Liturgics*, the doctrine or theory of liturgies. **1860** WORCESTER (citing *Eclectic Rev.*). **1882** W. BLAIKIE *Ministry of Word* 296 Ample treatises on Homiletics, Liturgics, etc. **1882-3** SCHAFF *Encycl. Relig. Knowl.* 2127 His principal writings relate to liturgics.

liturgical (lɪ'tɜ:dʒɪkəl), *a.* [Formed as prec. + -AL¹.] Pertaining to or connected with public worship; having to do with liturgies or forms of public worship, or *spec.* with the Liturgy or Eucharistic service. Also, pertaining to liturgics.
liturgical colours: the colours used in ecclesiastical vestments, hangings for the altar, etc., varying according to the season, festival, or kind of service. *liturgical day*: a day on which mass was celebrated. *Liturgical Movement* (see quot. 1957).
1641 MILTON *Animadv.* Wks. 1851 III. 202 The time is taken up with a tedious number of Liturgicall tautologies, and impertinencies. **1704** NELSON *Fest. & Fasts* ix. (1739) 581 There being no less than five liturgical Words in that Text. **1849** ROCK *Ch. of Fathers* I. ii. 106 The greatest Liturgical scholars are divided on the meaning of this ordinance. *Ibid.* 172 The Anglo-Saxons got all their liturgical books from Rome. **1861** PEARSON *Early & Mid. Ages Eng.* 135 A liturgical service like that of the missal. **1875** *Chamb. Jrnl.* No. 133. 54 The impressive pomp of liturgical ceremonial. **1894** O. J. REICHEL in *Trans. Exeter Diocesan Archit. Soc.* I. 30 That Pope writing to Decentius informs him that on ordinary liturgical days the presbyters consecrated with their bishop. **1929** *Tablet* 17 Aug. 197/2 The proficiency of these youngsters has been acquired in our Catholic schools, the grand hope of the Liturgical Movement, and Catholic girls are not lagging behind Catholic boys. **1935** A. G. HEBERT *Liturgy & Society* v. 126 The so-called Liturgical Movement is concerned with things vastly more important than mere ritualism. **1957** *Oxf. Dict. Chr. Ch.* 815/1 *Liturgical Movement*, a Movement of which the object is the restoration of the active participation by the people in the official worship of the Church. **1959** *Times Lit. Suppl.* 29 May 325/3 Since the war the landscape of Christianity has been unmistakably changing.. under the gradual pressures of that climate of opinion generally called the Liturgical Movement.

Hence **li'turgically** *adv.*, from a liturgical point of view; in a liturgy, in liturgical worship.
1864 GOULBURN *Communion Office* I. 77 Liturgically considered the Decalogue is to be regarded as a lesson from the Law. **1899** T. K. CHEYNE *Chr. Use Psalms* i. 18 The Psalms are all used liturgically.

liturgician (lɪtɜ:'dʒɪʃən). [f. LITURGIC: see -ICIAN.] One skilled in liturgics.
1889 CHR. WORDSWORTH in *Guardian* 13 Nov. 1767/1 Henry Bradshaw (who had naturally yet more of the liturgician's spirit).

liturgiological (lɪˌtɜ:dʒɪə'lɒdʒɪkəl), *a.* [f. LITURGIOLOGY + -IC + -AL¹.] Pertaining to or connected with liturgiology.
1887 *Athenæum* 16 July 80/1 What is to be thought of the liturgiological attainments of a writer who cites as an authority 'the Catholic Prayer Book'? **1894** *Westm. Gaz.* 20 Nov. 3/3 The book, 'The Hours of the Virgin Mary', was published by the society for its liturgiological interest.'

liturgiologist (lɪtɜ:dʒɪ'ɒlədʒɪst). [f. next + -IST.] One who is skilled in liturgiology.
1866 *Ch. Times* 27 Jan. 30/3 Ninety-nine out of a hundred liturgiologists,.. would have.. replaced the old Roman names so unnecessarily laid aside. **1882** T. F. SIMMONS *Alms & Oblations* 18 By the offering of the oblations and prayers, *sub uno*, as liturgiologists express it.

liturgiology (lɪtɜ:dʒɪ'ɒlədʒɪ). [f. LITURGY + -OLOGY.] The science which treats of liturgies.
1863 NEALE (*title*) Essays on Liturgiology. **1866** *Ch. Times* 27 Jan. 30/1 Liturgiology is passing out of the stage of private investigation and theory into a salient feature in the daily work of the clergy. **1889** *Q. Rev.* Jan. 188 The Science of Comparative Liturgiology.

liturgism ('lɪtədʒɪz(ə)m). [f. LITURGY + -ISM.] Excessive concentration on liturgy; a disproportionate concern with liturgical detail.
1926 *Q. Register* Feb. 117 With this prevailing liturgism, religion ceased to be an important force in common life. **1953** E. L. MASCALL *Corpus Christi* iii. 79 It is possible to point to parishes whose priest is an enthusiastic amateur liturgiologist, where the layfolk have to adapt themselves at regular intervals to fresh modifications in the rite and ceremonies of the Mass in agreement with the stage now reached by their pastor in his researches. Liturgism of this kind is simply individualism run riot.

liturgist ('lɪtədʒɪst). [f. LITURGY + -IST. Cf. F. *liturgiste* (1752, Dict. de Trévoux).]
1. One who uses or advocates the use of a liturgy.
1649 MILTON *Eikon.* i. Wks. 1851 III. 344 Manuals, and Handmaids of Devotion, the lip-work of every Prelatical Liturgist, clapt together, and quilted out of Scripture phrases. **16..** *Harl. MS.* 6612, If. 2 The Catholick Lyturgist to his rightly religious frend. **1812** *Religionism* 54 Keep your distance, caitiff wretches, do, Vile liturgists!

2. A student of or authority on liturgies; a compiler of a liturgy or liturgies.
1657 SPARROW *Bk. Com. Prayer* (1664) 218 It comes down to us from ancient times, as appears by S. Hieromes Lectionarius.. and other old Liturgists and Expositors. **1712** SIR G. WHELER *Liturgy after the Anc.* 202 (MS.) Our Apostolic and Primitive Liturgists. **1849** ROCK *Ch. of Fathers* I. 450 Dionigi, the liturgist. **1894** *Tablet* 24 Mar. 443 In.. the works of mediaeval liturgists.. Holy Week is called *Hebdomada Authentica*.

3. One who celebrates divine worship; a minister.
1848 R. I. WILBERFORCE *Doct. Incarnation* xii. (1852) 327 The Minister ought not to be considered as merely a preacher, but also as a real Liturgist, i.e. as the organ through which the devotion of the congregation is conveyed. **1890** in *Century Dict.*

Hence **litur'gistical** *a.*, of or pertaining to a liturgist.
1889 CHR. WORDSWORTH in *Guardian* 13 Nov. 1767/1 A Bishop.. has an inherent liturgistical character by our ancient custom.

liturgize ('lɪtədʒaɪz), *v. rare*⁻¹. [f. LITURGY + -IZE.] *intr.* To perform a liturgical act.
1826 G. S. FABER *Diffic. Romanism* (1853) 245 They, who bring these oblations in remembrance of the Lord, approach not to the dogmas of the Jews: but, liturgising spiritually, they shall be called the sons of wisdom.

liturgy ('lɪtədʒɪ). Also 6-7 **leitourgie, leiturgie, -y, liturgie.** [ad. med.L. *lītūrgia*, a. Gr. λειτουργία public service, service of the gods, public worship, f. λειτουργός (also ληιτ-, Hesych.) public servant, minister, f. *λεῖτο-ς (believed to be a var. of *λήïτος, public, recorded in the subst. uses λήïτον public hall, λήïτη, λήïτη priestess; app. a derivative of λεώς, λαός people) + -εργος that works. Cf. F. *liturgie* (16th c.).]
1. (With capital initial.) The service of the Holy Eucharist: properly applied to the rite of the Eastern Church. In liturgics, used *spec.* (with qualification) of the different types of Eucharistic service.
1560 BECON *Catech.* v. Wks. 1564 I. 462 b, In the Liturgie of the Ethiopes we reade thus. So soone as the Gospel is ended, the Deacon sayth [etc.]. **1564** HARDING *Answ. to Jewel's Challenge* 105 Basile in his liturgie, that is to saye, seruice of his Masse, sayeth thus in a prayer. **1565** JEWEL *Repl. Harding* 10 St. James Liturgie hath a special prayer for them that liue in Monasteries. **1635** PAGITT *Christianogr.* 73 They use the Liturgie of Saint Chrysostome. **1843** PUSEY *Serm. Holy Euch.* 25 The Liturgies join together, manifoldly, remission of sins and life eternal, as the two great fruits of the Sacrament. **1890** *Ch. Q. Rev.* Jan. 288 The revision of the Scottish 'Liturgy' or Communion Office.

2. A form of public worship, esp. in the Christian Church; a collection of formularies for the conduct of Divine service. †Also, public worship conducted in accordance with a prescribed form.
c **1593** *Exam. H. Barowe*, etc. B j b, Wither he thinketh that any Leitourgies, or prescript formes of prayer, may be imposed vpon the church. **1594** HOOKER *Eccl. Pol.* IV. xi. §9 The Church in her liturgies hath intermingled with readings out of the New Testament lessons taken out of the Law and the Prophets. **1605** BACON *Adv. Learn.* II. xxv. §20 Four main branches of divinity; faith, manners, liturgy, and government. **1640** BP. HALL *Humb. Remonstr.* 9 The prime subjects of their quarrell, and contradiction, Leitourgie and Episcopacy. **1657-61** HEYLIN *Hist. Ref.* II. Pref. 47 The Smectymnian.. rather chose to fell down Liturgie it self as having no authority from the Word of God. **1704** SWIFT *Mech. Operation Spirit* Misc. (1711) 290 Their Discretion in limiting their Devotions and their Deities to their several Districts, nor ever suffering the Liturgy of the white God to cross or interfere with that of the black. **1854** EMERSON *Lett. & Soc. Aims, Quot. & Orig.* Wks. (Bohn) III. 214 The psalms and liturgies of churches, are.. of this slow growth. **1885** A. M. FAIRBAIRN *Catholicism* II. iv. 73 Organs and liturgies have found a home in the land and church of Knox.
fig. **1630** B. JONSON *New Inn* III. ii, The Liturgie of Loue, *Ouid de arte amandi.* **1651** HOBBES *Leviath.* I. xii. 54 Charming, and Conjuring (the Leiturgy of Witches). **1784** COWPER *Task* VI. 679 For Garrick was a worshipper himself; He drew the liturgy, and framed the rites And solemn ceremonial of the day.

b. Chiefly with *the*: The Book of Common Prayer.
1629 PRYNNE *Ch. Eng.* 128 That worthy Arch-Bishop Cranmer caused our Leiturgy to be translated into Latine. *c* **1646** MILTON *Sonnet, On new forcers of Conscience*, Because you have thrown of your Prelate Lord, And with stiff Vowes renounc'd his Liturgie. **1688** PENTON *Guardian's Instruct.* (1897) 35 The simple, full and significant style of the Liturgy. **1704** NELSON *Fest. & Fasts* (1739) Prelim. Instruction 2, K. Charles 2. issued out a Commission for the reviewing of the Liturgy. **1828** MACAULAY *Hallam* Ess. (1887) 64 To this circumstance she [the Church of England] owes.. her noble and pathetic liturgy. **1843** BORROW *Bible in Spain* (ed. 2) III. xii. 222 It was Sunday.. and I happened to be reading the Liturgy.

3. *Gr. Antiq.* At Athens, a public office or duty which the richer citizens discharged at their own expense.
1836 LYTTON *Athens* (1837) II. 461 The State received the aid of.. what were termed liturgies from individuals. **1847** GROTE *Greece* II. xi. III. 159 The Liturgies of the State, as they were called, unpaid functions such as the trierarchy, choregy, gymnasiarchy, which entailed expence and trouble upon the holder of them. **1880** *Sat. Rev.* 25 Dec. 790 It was a species of liturgy—a voluntary contribution to a great public object.

4. *attrib.* and *Comb.*
1641 MILTON *Animadv.* 25 The principall scope of those Liturgie-founders was to prevent either the malice or the weaknesse of the Ministers. **1711** *Countrey-Man's Lett. to Curat* 48 Make him a Church of England or Liturgie-Man, the best way you ever can. **1901** *Westm. Gaz.* 22 Aug. 10/1 The liturgy-melodies.. can now again be given in their original purity.

Hence †**liturgy** *v. rare*⁻¹, *trans.*, to conduct by means of the Liturgy.
1716 M. DAVIES *Athen. Brit.* III. 10 All the Presbyterians .. unanimously agree to go to the Church-Service, to be Liturgy'd into Wedlock and into the Grave.

‖**lituus** ('lɪtju:əs). [L.]
1. *Rom. Antiq.* **a.** The crooked staff borne by an augur; an augural wand. **b.** A curved trumpet, a clarion.
[**1579-80** NORTH *Plutarch, Camillus* (1595) 159 They.. did finde.. Romulus augures crooked staffe.... This staffe is crooked at one of the ends, and.. they call it *Lituus*.] **1611** *Coryat's Crudities, Panegyr. Verses* 11 b, (*Note*) The Augures lituus or bended staffe. **1776** BURNEY *Hist Mus.* I. 518 A double *Lituus*. The lituus was a crooked military instrument, in the form of the augural staff, whence it had its name. It was a species of Clarion, or octave Trumpet. **1801** A. RANKEN *Hist. France* I. I. ii. 234 The lituus of the Roman augurs became the crosier, or bishop's staff. **1851** D. WILSON *Preh. Ann.* (1863) I. II. iii. 368 A lituus or musical wind-instrument found in 1768.

2. *Math.* (See quot. 1839.)
[*a* **1716** R. COTES *Harmonia Mensurarum* (1722) 85 Hujus generis alteram hic adjungam Spiralem, quam Litui Figuram appello propter formæ similitudinem.] **1758** LYONS *Fluxions* iv. §119 If *BF* is inversely as the square of *SP*, the curve is called by Mr. Cotes the *Lituus*. **1839** *Penny Cycl.* XIV. 58 *Lituus*, a name given to a spiral thus described:—Let a variable circular sector always have its centre at one fixed point, and one of its terminal radii in a given direction. Let the area of the sector always remain the same; then the extremity of the other terminal radius describes the lituus. The polar equation of this spiral is $r^2\theta = a$.

3. *Zool.* A genus of cephalopods, now called *Spirula*; a shell of the genus.

1753 CHAMBERS *Cycl. Supp.* s.v., The lituus is always a conic shell, running in a strait line from the mouth, through a great part of the length, and from the end of this strait part to the extremity, twisting into the shape of a cornu ammonis. *Ibid.*, *Lituites*, a name given to the stones formed in the lituus-shell.

Litvak ('lɪtvɒk). Also Litvok. [Yiddish, f. Pol. *Litwak* Lithuanian.] A Jew from Lithuania or its neighbouring regions.

1892 I. ZANGWILL *Childr. Ghetto* I. 38 To a Dutch or Russian Jew, the 'Pullack', or Polish Jew, is a poor creature; and..the 'Pullack' looks down upon the 'Litvok', or Lithuanian. **1970** L. M. FEINSILVER *Taste of Yiddish* 10 Four major dialects developed. Of these, the one spoken by so-called Litvaks, the Jews of Lithuania, White Russia and Northeastern Poland, is essentially 'standard' or literary Yiddish. **1970** I. SIEFF *Mem.* i. 5 'What can you expect? He's a Litvak.' A kind of Scot in Jewry? Whatever the reason, many Litvaks led the way in emigration when the circumstances were most daunting. **1971** B. MALAMUD *Tenants* 209 A middle-aged Litvak, a stocky man in mud-spotted trousers.

Litz (lɪts). *Electr.* Also litz. [f. LITZ(ENDRAHT.] Used *attrib.* to designate wire composed of many fine strands twisted together and individually insulated, so as to reduce the skin effect and the associated increase in resistance at high frequencies.

1927 *Wireless World* 13 Apr. 447/1 (*heading*) Preparing Litz wire. **1928** *Observer* 17 June 26/3 The most efficient inductance to use in a 'tuned anode', radio-frequency amplifying circuit is one wound with 'Litz' wire. **1959** K. HENNEY *Radio Engin. Handbk.* (ed. 5) iii. 2 Since the smaller the conductor, the less the skin effect, if the conductor is broken down into many small strands, twisted..and each strand insulated from the others, the skin effect is lessened. Such wire is known as 'litz' wire. **1968** *Radio Communication Handbk.* (ed. 4) iv. 14/2 Tuned circuits of higher *Q* than can readily be obtained in the conventional type of i.f. transformer (even when wound with Litz multi-stranded wire).

litzendraht ('lɪtsəndrɑːt). *Electr.* [a. G. *litzendraht* Litz wire, f. *litze* braid, cord, lace, strand + *draht* wire.] Litz wire.

1921 J. H. MORECROFT *Princ. Radio Communication* ii. 124 It is..important in getting the stranded wire (sometimes called litzendraht) to see that..it is made up of a great number of well-insulated strands..properly interwoven. **1933** K. HENNEY *Radio Engin. Handbk.* vii. 151 The former [*sc.* skin] effect is minimized by the use of conductors with insulated strands—so-called *litzendraht*. **1962** *Newnes Conc. Encycl. Electr. Engin.* 445/2 *Litzendraht*, stranded cable for high-frequency currents.

liue, liuf, liun(e, obs. ff. LIEU, LIFE, LION.

livability: see LIVEABILITY.

livable: see LIVEABLE.

livanomancy, erron. var. LIBANOMANCY.

livant, var. LEVANT *v.*[1]

livar, obs. form of LIVER *sb.*[2]

live (laɪv), *a.* [An attributive use of *live* in *on live*, ALIVE. Cf. *lives* in LIFE *sb.* 15.]

1. a. That is in the possession or enjoyment of life; living, as opposed to 'dead'. ***live hair, feathers***: hair or feathers pulled from a living animal.

1542 UDALL *Apophth. Erasm.* 256 b, A liue doggue, a cocke, an adder and an ape. **1548** UDALL, etc. *Par. Erasm., Mark* 19 b, A liue carkas liuyng only to his payne & torment. **1590** SHAKS. *Mids. N.* II. i. 172 The iuyce of it on sleeping eye-lids laid, Will make or man or woman madly dote Vpon the next liue creature that it sees. **1597** HOOKER *Eccl. Pol.* v. lxiv. §5. 155 It seemed..not against reason to repute them by a courteous construction of law, as liue-men. **1607** TOPSELL *Four-f. Beasts* (1658) 215 Hairs..pulled off from a live Hare. **1681** *Lond. Gaz.* No. 1656/4 One who pretends to buy Live Hair to make Periwigs. **1692** R. L'ESTRANGE *Fables* cclxxxvi. 250, I had rather be a Live-Begger then a Dead Countess. **1839–41** S. WARREN *Ten Thous. a Yr.* II. iv. 99 The only live things visible. **1848** KINGSLEY *Saint's Trag.* I. i. 126 Shall two hundredweight of hypocrisy bow down to his four-inch wooden saint, and the same weight of honesty not worship his four-foot live one? **1856** MRS. CARLYLE *Lett.* II. 288, I brought two live plants in flower pots. **1864** BROWNING *J. Lee's Wife* VIII. ii, 'Tis a clay cast..From Hand live once, dead long ago. **1875** MAINE *Hist. Inst.* iv. 107 It [i.e. the land] has 'live chattels and dead chattels'. **1897** *Allbutt's Syst. Med.* II. 686 The importation of live cattle from countries in which foot-and-mouth disease exists, has been prohibited.

†**b.** *absol. Obs.*

1565 T. STAPLETON *Fortr. Faith* 125 b, A comfort for the liue, and token of their good heart. **1577** FULKE *Two Treat. agst. Papists* II. 456 One sacrifice for the liue and the deade. **1608** WILLET *Hexapla Exod.* 486 Both the liue and dead should be equally diuided. **1699** BENTLEY *Phal.* xi. 279 This Gentleman..that can put the Dead and the Live together in Dialogue.

c. Somewhat frequent in jocular use, esp. in 'a real live ——' (*slang* occas. of inanimate things).

1887 *Fun* 26 Oct. XLVI. 175/1 A real live glass milk-jug ..given to every lady that buys one pound of our two shilling Bohea. **1890** W. A. WALLACE *Only a Sister* 53 Rosemary had taken a great deal of trouble to catch 'a real live' philosopher.

d. *a live certainty*: app. a nonce-phrase, substituted for *a dead certainty* (see DEAD *a.* 18).

1855 THACKERAY *Newcomes* II. xlii. 374 Then Mrs. Mackenzie would probably be with them to a live certainty.

2. *transf.* and *fig.* in various applications.

a. Of impersonal agencies, conditions, etc.: Full of life or active power; stirring or swarming with living beings; indicating the presence of life; busy, active. (Cf. ALIVE 5, 6.)

1647 H. MORE *Song of Soul* III. II. xxiv, Flush light she sendeth forth, and live Idees. **1853** M. ARNOLD *Scholar-Gipsy* ii, All the live murmur of a summer's day. **1858** KINGSLEY *Parable from Liebig* viii. (1878) 251 The world is too live yet for thee. **1878** DOWDEN *Stud. Lit., Geo. Eliot* ii. 296 Style..so live with breeding imagery.

b. (orig. *U.S.*). Of persons: Full of energy and alertness; 'wide-awake', up-to-date. Of questions, subjects of consideration: Of present interest and importance; not obsolete or exhausted.

1857 *Knickerbocker* L. 456 A neighbouring bath-house, kept by a live Yankee of the name of Martin. **1870** *Scribner's Monthly* I. 71 Quite as likely..the 'advanced' preacher selects a 'live' subject, a theme for the times. **1877** BESANT & RICE *Gold. Butterfly* 147, I shall only get live people to write for me. **1877** TALMAGE 50 *Serm.* 26 In all the world of literature there is no such live book as the Bible. **1888** BRYCE *Amer. Commw.* III. cviii. 565 An enterprising man..created a new type of 'live' newspaper. **1900** *Speaker* 8 Sept. 618/1 The strenuous effort of the Republicans to resurrect the money question and make it a live issue is becoming ludicrous. **1932** E. V. LUCAS *Reading, Writing & Remembering* 45 A varied, learned and very live and amusing book would be the result. **1973** *Times* 26 Apr. 9/8 Bungebah ..could be a 'live' Imperial Cup prospect one day.

c. Corresponding to actual facts.

1927 CARR-SAUNDERS & JONES *Survey Social Struct. Eng. & Wales* 152 The Unemployment figures were obtained by taking an average of the 'live registers' of the employment exchanges in Great Britain. **1931** *Times Educ. Suppl.* 9 May 166/3 The 'live' register has, it is true, dropped from 923 to 757, but these figures are now swollen..by the children who left school at the Easter recess.

d. Of a performance, heard or watched at the time of its occurrence, as distinguished from one recorded on film, tape, etc. Also quasi-*adv.*

1934 *B.B.C. Year-Bk.* 248 Listeners have..complained of the fact that recorded material was too liberally used..but ..transmitting hours to the Canadian and Australasian zones are inconvenient for broadcasting 'live' material. **1937** M. LOWELL *Listen In* 109 People do not like 'canned' entertainment when they can obtain 'live' entertainment just as easily. **1944** *Ann. Reg. 1943* 348 It was still felt..that attendance at concerts and listening to 'live' performances belonged to a better order of things. **1947** *Penguin Music Mag.* II. 21 The standard of playing..has suffered..because ..there was an unprecedented demand for live performances. **1953** [see *3-D, 3 D* (D III. 3)]. **1953** E. SMITH *Guide Eng. Traditions* 11 The development of the gramophone and wireless broadcasting..has made many thousands familiar with the great musical composers and anxious to hear 'live' performances of their works. **1955** *Radio Times* 22 Apr. 15/2 At the moment, Northern Ireland has no means of originating 'live' television programmes. **1958** *Listener* 25 Sept. 463/2 Long experience of the effect of gramophone record sales and broadcasts provides pretty convincing evidence that they have strengthened rather than sapped the general interest of the public in attending live performances. **1970** *New Scientist* 2 July 13/1 We now accept full live coverage of soccer games in Mexico as a matter of course. **1974** *Daily Tel.* 2 May 13/5 Live entertainment is to return to the London Casino,..since 1953 the home of Cinerama. **1974** *Times* 14 Nov. 8/8 The hearing was televised live. **1975** *Daily Tel.* 18 Apr. 13/2 When people spoke 'live' or on tape it was often difficult to hear what they were saying.

3. Of combustibles: Flaming, glowing.

1611 BIBLE *Isa.* vi. 6 Then flew one of the Seraphims vnto mee, hauing a liue-cole in his hand. *a* **1626** W. SCLATER *Exp. 2 Thess.* (1629) 288 Where is any liue sparke or seede of Grace? **1756–7** tr. *Keysler's Trav.* (1760) III. 34 The scorpion, when hemmed in with live coals..stings himself in the head. **1840–2** GEO. ELIOT in *Academy* 20 Jan. (1894) 56/3 Philanthropy, kindled by the live coal of gratitude and devotion to the Author of all things. **1887** BOWEN *Virg. Æneid* v. 103 Under the spits live embers place.

transf. and *fig.* **1658–9** *Burton's Diary* (1828) III. 278 We come to set up votes that are live quarrels, like York and Lancaster. **1728–46** THOMSON *Spring* 964 Now from the virgin's cheek a fresher bloom Shoots less and less the live carnation round. **1873** T. W. HIGGINSON *Oldport Days* 199 There is to-day such a live sparkle on the water, such a luminous freshness on the grass. **1902** *Blackw. Mag.* May 646/1 'Dead' and 'live' were terms used in speaking of dull opal that could be made to flash as if alive by the application of water.

4. Containing unexpended energy. Of a shell, a match, etc.: Unkindled, unexploded. Of a rail, wire, etc.: Connected to a source of electrical potential. In a single-phase supply: being the conductor on which the supply voltage is developed (with respect to the neutral). Also *ellipt.*, a live conductor or terminal. Of a cartridge: Containing a bullet, opposed to *blank*.

1799 *Naval Chron.* I. 440 A quantity of six-inch live shells fired. **1833** ALISON *Hist. Europe* (1849–50) XI. lxxvii. §6. 506 Live shells were placed along the top of the rampart. **1890** *Daily News* 4 Jan. 6/6 Touching a live electric wire somewhere in the city. **1894** *Times* 29 May 6/6, I have repeatedly found matches about the ground... They were 'live' matches. **1897** *Daily News* 10 Mar. 7/4 The accused said, 'You are a —— fine pal to give me a live cartridge'. **1898** *Westm. Gaz.* 11 July 2/1 The rails are said to be 'live' when charged with the electric current. **1898** *Allbutt's Syst. Med.* V. 856 A person for example may be seriously injured.. through an iron tool in his hand by which accidental contact is made with live metal. **1913** D. S. MUNRO *Pract. of Electr. Wiring* xx. 181 When the neutral wire is itself practically at earth potential there are, of course, increased risks, if the live wire be in contact with its metal cover. **1938** J. W. SIMS *Electr. Installations* 148 When the fuse unit is enclosed in an iron case there should be an inch clearance all round any live part. **1966** J. F. WHITFIELD *Electr. Install. & Regulations* vi. 123 Two-pin sockets and plugs. Live and neutral only are catered for in these units. **1970** *Which?* Aug. 256/2 Britain objected to black for the live, since in Britain it was being used for the neutral. **1973** G. BURDETT *Householder's Electr. Guide* vi. 34 Two-core sheathed flex is now made with the new core colours of brown for the 'live' core and blue for the neutral.

5. a. Of a mineral, a rock: Native, unwrought; = L. *vivus*. **b.** Of air: In its native state, pure.

1661 LOVELL *Hist. Anim. & Min.* 22 Live brimstone, boiled to the thicknesse of Honey. **1778** PENNANT *Tour in Wales* II. 307 A well cut in the live rock. **1855** BROWNING *Old Pictures in Flor.* ii, Through the live translucent bath of air. **1855** TENNYSON *Maud* I. xiii. 11 His essences turn'd the live air sick. **1875** BROWNING *Aristoph. Apol.* 1526 The live rock latent under wave and foam.

6. Said of parts of machines or apparatus which either themselves move or impart motion to others. (Cf. DEAD *a.* 23.) Applied *spec.* to an axle.

1825 J. NICHOLSON *Operat. Mechanic* 325 The dead pulley is fixed to the axis and turns with it, and the other, which slips round it, is called the live pulley. *c* **1860** H. STUART *Seaman's Catech.* 74 There is a live sheave for the working top pendant, and a dumb one for the hawser. **1875** KNIGHT *Dict. Mech.*, *Live-axle*, one communicating power; in contradistinction to a dead or blind axle. *Ibid.*, *Live-head*, the head-stock of a lathe, which contains the live-spindle. **1878** LOCKYER *Stargazing* 308 Three conical rollers carried by a loose or 'live' ring. **1882** NARES *Seamanship* (ed. 6) 53 The metal rollers are each made to revolve round their own pins, which are secured to a plate, called the live ring. **1884** KNIGHT *Dict. Mech.* Suppl., *Live Ring*, a circular gang of wheels, as used in the turn-tables of draw-bridges, and in those for locomotives. **1884** F. J. BRITTEN *Watch & Clockm.* 156 [A] Live Spindle..[is] a rotating spindle; applied generally to the rotating mandrel of a lathe. **1903** *Work* XXV. 199/3 The two systems of driving are the live axle and the double sprocket chain. **1904** A. B. F. YOUNG *Compl. Motorist* (ed. 2) iv. 116 The driving of the rear wheels being direct through a powerful chain and live axle. **1929** NEWTON & STEEDS *Motor Vehicle* xxi. 259 A live axle is one that rotates or houses shafts that rotate, while a dead axle is one that does not rotate or house rotating shafts. **1963** BIRD & HUTTON-STOTT *Veteran Motor Car* 8 In modern usage 'live axle transmission' means the combination of propellor shaft and bevel- or worm-geared live axle—but many chain-driven cars also had live axles of a different sort. **1971** *Daily Tel.* 24 Mar. 11/3 It has a water cooled engine driving the rear wheels and a live rear axle.

7. Of or pertaining to a living being. † ***live voice***: the voice of a living man. (Cf. *vivâ voce*.)

1613 JACKSON *Creed* II. 367 For the begetting of true and liuely faith, we suppose the liue voice of an ordinary Ministery as the Organe, whereby [etc.]. **1649** J. H. *Motion to Parl. Adv. Learn.* 32 Ineffectuall..if not quickned with some live-voyce and knowing assistance.

8. *Acoustics.* Of a room or enclosure: having a relatively long reverberation time (opp. DEAD *a.* A. 14 b).

1931 L. COWAN *Recording Sound for Motion Pict.* xviii. 266 The music is reproduced in the live end, which would correspond to the stage of an auditorium, and the microscope is placed in the comparatively deader end, which would correspond with the audience position. **1962** A. NISBETT *Technique Sound Studio* ii. 33 The answer might at first sight appear to be to do away with reverberation entirely and try to create entirely 'dead' studios... But listening tests indicate that most people prefer a moderately 'live' acoustic. **1974** *Which?* Aug. 243/3 In a very live room — one with a lot of hard surfaces that can reflect sound—upper and middle frequencies will stand out more.

9. a. In various collocations and combinations: **live action** (see quot. 1960); also *attrib.*; † **live anatomy**, vivisection (see ANATOMY 1 b); **live-asunder** ? *nonce-wd.*, (torn) apart while living (as a limb from the body); **live-birth**, the fact of a child's being born alive; **live-born** *a.*, born alive; **live-broken** *a.*, broken alive; **live-cannibalism**, the practice of eating the flesh of human victims still living; **live fence** orig. *U.S.*, a hedge; also *live-fencing*; **live-gang** *U.S.* (see quot.); † **live-goods**, ? = LIVE-STOCK; **live-hole** *Brickmaking* (see quot.); † **live-like** *a.*, resembling a living person; **live load** *Engin.*, a temporary or varying load imposed on a structure by its being put to use (cf. *dead load* s.v. DEAD *a.* A. 29); **live matter** (see quot.); † **live-personal** *a.*, made by the person himself; † **live-shape**, living form; **live-steam** (see quot.); **live-thorn** *a.*, constructed of living thorn (cf. *quickthorn* QUICK D); **live-vat** (see quot.); **live weight**, the weight of an animal before it is slaughtered and prepared as a carcase; also *attrib.* and as quasi-*adv.*; † **live-wight**, a living thing; **live wire** (see sense 4) orig. *U.S.*, *fig.* esp. a person full of energy; also (with hyphen) *attrib.*; **live-work** (see quot.). Also LIVE-BAIT, LIVE-OAK, LIVE-STOCK.

1957 MANVELL & HUNTLEY *Technique Film Music* iii. 136 A great deal of Hollywood's comedy music is linked with the cartoon world and..a number of techniques associated with the animation studios are increasingly employed during the making of *live-action scenes. **1960** O. SKILBECK *ABC of Film & T.V.* 79 *Live action*, normal cinematography as opposed to Animation, Titles, etc. **1964** *Listener* 5 Nov. 735/3 There was a very long-drawn-out rescue scene in which live-action and graphics were mingled in a

fashionable but not here very convincing way. a 1834 COLERIDGE in *Lit. Rem.* (1836) II. 248 He has by guilt torn himself *live-asunder from nature, and is, there-fore, himself in a preter-natural state. 1889 *Syd. Soc. Lex.* s.v. *Live-birth*, The aerated condition of the lungs is no proof of *live-birth in the legal sense. 1797 MRS. A. M. BENNETT *Beggar Girl* II. iii. 41 The self same house..where they had nine children *live born and christened. 1824 CAMPBELL *Theodoric* Wks. (1837) 55 A wretch *live-broken on misfortune's wheel. 1804 *Ann. Rev.* II. 199/1 After these atrocities it would seem trifling to speak..of the *live-cannibalism of Tongataboo. 1804 J. ROBERTS *Pennsylvania Farmer* 84 When the hedge is full grown, then there is a perfect *live fence. 1858 J. A. WARDER *Hedges & Evergreens* I. i. 13 Live-fences, or—as they are commonly called—Hedges, are a means of enclosure that belongs to an advanced state of civilization. 1866 *Bull's Wellington* (N.Z.) *Almanack* 28 Sow..furze for live fences. 1882 W. D. HAY *Brighter Britain!* 192 We have done something towards making live-fences. 1958 *Chambers's Techn. Dict.* 991/1 *Live fence* (Highways), a hedge. 1829 *Mass. Spy* 25 Mar. (Th.), Messrs. G. Th. and Son have imported 75,000 hawthorns, for '*live fencing'. 1875 KNIGHT *Dict. Mech.*, **Live-gang*, a gang-saw mill, so arranged as to cut through and through the logs without previous slabbing. 1626 JACKSON *Creed* VIII. xiii. §1 To exercise the like rage upon his person or *live-goods, which did the wrong, could be no satisfaction either to the law, or party wronged. 1836 *Penny Cycl.* V. 408/2 Clamp-bricks are burned in the following manner:—The flues or *live holes—are carried up two courses high through the clamp. 1614 JACKSON *Creed* III. xii. §3 Hauing now met them as *liue-like as they themselues were. 1866 *Live load [see FACTOR *sb.* 8]. 1908 M. S. KETCHUM *Design of Highway Bridges* ii. 41 The live loads on railway bridges are properly a series of moving concentrated loads. 1918 COWLEY & LEVY *Aeronautics* viii. 163 When the aeroplane is just smoothing out from a steep dive the angle of attack is suddenly increased and the loading rapidly attains a value which in practice is several times its normal. This [*sic*] in all essentials a live load is allowed for in the safety factor. 1974 *Sci. Amer.* Feb. 93/1 A building must ordinarily sustain three kinds of force. The first is the 'dead load' of the structure itself and its fixed contents; the second is the 'live load' of the building's occupants and of such movable components as elevators... The third force is produced by the movement of air. 1875 KNIGHT *Dict. Mech.*, **Live-matter* (*Printing*), type in page or column ready for printing. 1614 JACKSON *Creed* III. xvii. §6 Moses' *live-personal proposal. 1851–61 MAYHEW *Lond. Labour* II. 193 Some of the most experienced '*live salesmen' and 'dead salesmen'. 1626 JACKSON *Creed* VIII. x. § 1 The lust of the flesh, the lust of the eyes, and the pride of life, tooke their distinct specificall being, or *live-shape, from the first sinne. 1875 KNIGHT *Dict. Mech.*, **Live-steam*, 1. Steam from the boiler at its full pressure; in contradistinction to dead-steam. 2. Steam from the boiler; in contradistinction to exhaust-steam. 1889 *Pall Mall G.* 21 Oct. 3/2 The heat is supplied by the waste steam, supplemented if necessary by live steam. 1893 *Daily News* 29 June 5/2 Enclosed with a strong *live-thorn palisade impenetrable to arrows. 1852 MORFIT *Tanning & Currying* (1853) 163 The fresh, or *live vat, is that which has not yet been worked. 1852 *Trans. Mich. Agric. Soc.* III. 151 Two hundred lambs..weighing some one hundred pounds..*live weight. 1872 BAKER *Nile Tribut.* xv. 261 The live weight of the male would be about five hundred pounds. 1898 *Trans. Highl. & Agric. Soc.* 286 The live-weights of the individual sheep were ascertained three times during the experiment. 1960 *Farmer & Stockbreeder* 12 Jan. 50 More than 3½ lb. of food to make 1 lb. of liveweight gain. 1971 *Farmers Weekly* 19 Mar. 85/1 The cost per pound of gain would exceed the price per pound liveweight received at slaughter. 1972 *Country Life* 30 Nov. 1504/2 These small birds [*sc.* turkeys]..are killed out..when they achieve liveweights of about 8½ lb. 1657 W. RAND tr. *Gassendi's Life Peiresc* II. 148 All which he possesses, seems to be no lesse common to all learned men, then the Air and Water are to all *Live-wights. 1668 CULPEPPER & COLE *Barthol. Anat.* I. xx. 51 Those Live-wights which have no Lungs, have no bladder. 1903 'H. MCHUGH' *Back to Woods* 12 Bunch went down to the skating pond one day with $18 and picked four *live wires at an average of 8 to 1. 1903 *Everybody's Mag.* IX. 30/1 If you cut 'Browny' you cut a live wire and were socially paralyzed. 1909 *Sat. Even. Post* 13 Mar. 24/1 As a legislator..he was probably known to many people as an aggressive 'comer' of the live-wire kind. a 1911 D. G. PHILLIPS *Susan Lenox* (1917) II. v. 110, I sized you up as a live wire the minute I saw you. 1931 A. CHRISTIE *Sittaford Mystery* xxiv. 197 He appears to be one of the live wires of this investigation. 1935 AUDEN & ISHERWOOD *Dog beneath Skin* I. ii. 39 And I'm the live wire of the *Evening Moon.* 1952 J. C. MASTERMAN *To teach Senators Wisdom* i. 17 He was, if anyone was, the live wire of the Senior Common Room. 1971 *Daily Tel.* 21 Aug. 14/4 The live-wire management here will miss few opportunities given the right political and economic background in which to operate. 1973 D. FRANCIS *Slay-Ride* x. 121 Our Lars was a live wire once himself. Did a lot of motor racing. 1855 *Cornwall* 148 We might distinguish these two kinds of work as dead and *live work—the dead being that which proceeds in the dead rock, and the live that which is concerned in extracting and pulverizing the ores.

b. In the names of various contrivances for holding living objects or for examining them microscopically, as ***live-box, -car, -trap, -well.***

1862 GOSSE in *Pop. Sci. Rev.* I. 41 *note*, Specimens hatched in the same live-box, in the same water, from the same brood, and on the same day. 1875 KNIGHT *Dict. Mech.*, *Live-trap*, a device for imprisoning living microscopic objects. It consists of three parallel glass slips; the middle one has a circular perforation forming the cell, while the other ones constitute the sides. 1883 *Fisheries Exhib. Catal.* 199 Live-car, full size, for keeping fish alive. 1893 *Funk's Stand. Dict.*, *Live-well*, a well in a fishing-boat for keeping fish alive.

live (lɪv), *v.*[1] Pa. t. and *pa. pple.* lived (lɪvd). Forms: *Inf.* α. 1 libban, 2–4 li-, lybben, 3 *Orm.* libbenn. β. 1 lifian, lifiȝean, lyfan, -ian, leofian, -iȝean, *Northumb.* lifiȝa, 2–4 lifen, livien, 3 *Orm.* lifenn, 2–4, 6 liven; 3 leofen, leofven, (lioven, luvien), 4–5 lif(f(e, (4 lijf, lyfve, luf(e), 4–6 lyve(n, lyvie, -yn, *Sc.* leif(f(e, leyff, lyf(f(e, 5 lyf(e, (4–5 liwe, -i, -y, lywe); 2, 4–5 lef(en, 4–5 leven, -yn, (4 levin, loven), 5 lewyn, 5–6 leve, 6–7 *Sc.* leaf, leiv(e, 4– live. *Pa. t.* 1 lifode, -ade, lifde, 2–5 livede, 4– lived. *Pa. pple.* 1 ȝelifd, 3–4 y-lyved, i-lyved, (6 liven, lyven), 3– lived. [A Common Teutonic weak vb.: OE. *libban* (WS.). *lifian*, *lifȝan* (Anglian and in poetical texts), pa. t. *lifode*, *lifde*, corresp. to OFris. *libba*, *liva*, *leva*, OS. *libbian*, pa. t. pl. *libdun* (Du. *leven*), OHG. *lebên* (MHG., mod.G. *leben*) to live, ON. *lifa* to live, remain (Sw. *lefva* to live, *qvar-lefva* to remain, Da. *leve* to live), Goth. *liban*, pa. t. *libaida* to live:—OTeut. stem **libǣ-*, f. root **lĭb-* (: *laib-*) to remain, continue, whence LIFE *sb.*, q.v. for cognate words.]

1. a. *intr.* To be alive; to have life (see LIFE 1 b) either as an animal or as a plant; to be capable of vital functions. † ***to live and look*** (see LOOK *v.*).

In this sense the simple present is now *arch.* or *rhetorical*; the compound present *is living* is the usual form.

c 825 *Vesp. Psalter* cxiii. 18 We ða ðe lifȝað we bledsiað dryhten. 971 *Blickl. Hom.* 57 Se lichoma buton mete & drence leofian ne mæȝ. a 1000 *O.E. Chron.* an. 901 (Parker MS.) He wolde oðer oððe þær libban oððe þær licȝan. c 1175 *Pater Noster* in *Lamb. Hom.* 65 Ure gultes lauerd bon us forȝeuen al swa we doþ alle men þet liuen. c 1205 LAY. 4668 Ich sugge þe to soðe þat ȝet leoueð þi broðer. a 1225 *Leg. Kath.* 2262 Tu schalt libben, & beon leof & wurð me. a 1300 *Cursor M.* 17408 þe lauerd liues yee did on rode. c 1330 R. BRUNNE *Chron.* (1810) 17 þat to þe kyng Egbriht alle were þei gyuen For þer heritage þer to die or lyuen. c 1400 MAUNDEV. (Roxb.) iii. 9 þerfore may na beste ne fewle liffe þare. c 1460 *Towneley Myst.* xiv. 95 And, certys, for to lyf or dy I shall not fayll. 15.. *Interl.* 4 *Elem.* 452, I am for you so necessary Ye can not lyue without me. 1529 RASTELL *Pastyme* (1811) 33 He was crownyd lyuing hys fader by pope Johnn. 1587 GOLDING *De Mornay* v. 51 Now this second Plant liued in the first, ere it liued in itselfe, and al liuing wights do liue, moue, and feele..afore they come forth. 1611 BIBLE *Gen.* xlv. 3 And Ioseph said..Doeth my father yet liue? 1677 GALE *Crt. Gentiles* II. IV. 309 Plants are said by some kind of analogie to live..yet they cannot be said properly to live... Brutes are said properly to live, because they have a true self-motion. 1774 GOLDSM. *Nat. Hist.* (1776) II. 198 Those parts may be said to live no longer when the circulation ceases. 1821 SHELLEY *Adonais* xli, He lives, he wakes—'tis Death is dead, not he. 1838 LYTTON *Leila* I. ii, Yonder stream is of an element in which man cannot live nor breathe. 1862 J. F. STEPHEN *Def. R. Williams* 296 A more eminent or more excellent man hardly ever lived.

b. *fig.* of things: To exist, be found. *poet.*

1593 SHAKS. *Rich. II*, II. ii. 79 We are on the earth Where nothing liues but crosses, care and greefe. 1599 —— *Much Ado* III. i. 110 No glory liues behinde the backe of such. 1850 TENNYSON *In Mem.* xcv[i]. 11 There lives more faith in honest doubt, Believe me, than in half the creeds. 1871 R. ELLIS tr. *Catullus* lxxxvi. 4 In all that bodily largeness, Lives not a grain of salt, breathes not a charm anywhere.

2. a. To supply oneself with food; to feed, subsist. Const. †*by*, †*of*, *on*, *upon*, †*with*, rarely †*in* (either the actual food or the means of providing it). ***to live on a person***: to burden him with one's maintenance. Also in phr. ***to live off the country*** (or ***the land***); to obtain sustenance from the produce of the countryside without payment.

971 *Blickl. Hom.* 51 Godes is þæt yrfe þe we biȝ leofiaþ. c 1000 *Sax. Leechd.* II. 62 Eft ȝenim swines scearn þæs þe on dun lande and wyrtum libbe. c 1200 ORMIN 7775 Cullfre ne lifeþþ nohht bi flessh. c 1250 *Gen. & Ex.* 573 Foueles waren ðer-inne cumen..And mete quorbi ðei miȝten liuen. a 1300 *Cursor M.* 11109 Ion liued wit rotes and wit gress, Wit honi o þe wildernes. c 1380 WYCLIF *Wks.* (1880) 242 Many..þat wolen make hem self gentel men and han litel or nouȝt to lyue on. 1382 —— *Matt.* iv. 4 A man lyueth not in breed aloon. 1393 LANGL. *P. Pl.* C. XXII. 217 Tresour to lyue by to here lyues ende. c 1440 *Gesta Rom.* lxxxix. 411 (Add. MS.) She..leuyd..many yeres with rotes and grasse, and such Frute as she myght gete. c 1470 HENRY *Wallace* IX. 288 Leiff on your awin. 1523 LD. BERNERS *Froiss* I. ccvii. 244 They coude fynde nothynge to lyue by in the playne countrey. a 1548 HALL *Chron.*, *Hen. VIII*, 92 b, To whom the kyng assigned an honest pencion to live on. 1583 STUBBES *Anat. Abus.* II. (1882) 42 [They] are to be compelled to worke, and not to liue vpon other mens labours. 1601 HOLLAND *Pliny* I. 147 The Agriophagi..liue most of panthers and lions flesh. 1651 HOBBES *Leviath.* III. xlii. 294 They that served at the Altar lived on what was offered. 1670 EACHARD *Cont. Clergy* 20 A person, at all thoughtfull of himself and conscience, had much better chuse to live with nothing but beans and pease-pottage. 1712 STEELE *Spect.* No. 264 ¶2 Irus..spent some Time after with Rakes who had lived upon him. 1747 WESLEY *Prim. Physic* (1762) 35 For Asthma..live a fortnight on boiled Carrots. 1802 PALEY *Nat. Theol.* xvi. 5 Wks. 1830 IV. 194 The spider lives upon flies. 1852 R. S. SURTEES *Sponge's Sp. Tour* iii. 9 He then lived on his 'means' for a while. 1884 *Century Mag.* Feb. 503/1 In his marches he had been obliged to live, to a great extent, off the country. 1889 JESSOPP *Coming of Friars* ii. 84 Sometimes they were..living upon their friends. 1913 H. FOOTNER *Jack Chanty* 68 The Indians..live off the land during the summer. 1934 *Discovery* Mar. 63/1 It is possible to 'live off the land' to an extent never dreamed of by earlier explorers. 1949 *Milwaukie* (Oregon) *Rev.* 4 Aug. 1/4 The main cause for the Communist army success was the fact that it was well fed, living off the country as it marched through China. 1966 *Globe & Mail* (Toronto) 5 Jan. 25/3 Eskimos in the area [Boothia Peninsula] live off the land.

b. *fig.*

971 *Blickl. Hom.* 57 þa gastlican lare..þe ure saul biȝ leofaþ. c 1375 *Cursor M.* 15614 (Fairf.), I warne ȝou to..liue a-pon his lare. 1754 SHEBBEARE *Matrimony* (1766) I. 246 They..agreed..to live on Letters, till the painful age should be lapsed which held them apart. 1844 A. B. WELBY *Poems* (1867) 49 To live untill this tender heart On which it lives is dead.

3. a. To procure oneself the means of subsistence. Const. *by*, †*of*, *on* or *upon*, † *with*. Also, *to live from* HAND TO MOUTH. ***to live by one's wits***: see WIT.

c 900 tr. *Bæda's Hist.* IV. iv. (Schipper) 371 [Hi] be heora aȝenum handȝewinne lifiȝeaþ. 1297 R. GLOUC. (Rolls) 964 þe scottes sede þat þet lond noȝt inou be To hom bothe to libbe by as hii miȝte ise. 1362 LANGL. *P. Pl.* A. XI. 272 A feloun was sauid þat hadde lyued al his lyf with lesinges & þeftis. 1387 TREVISA *Higden* (Rolls) IV. 311 He made his douȝtres use hem to wolle craft..þey schulde ȝif hem nedede lyve by þe craft. c 1440 *Jacob's Well* 160 Comoun womman, þat leuyth by here body. c 1450 *ME. Med. Bk.* (Heinrich) 210 Item, þe galle of euery fowl, þat lyueþ by raueyne doþ þe same. 1484 CAXTON *Fables of Alfonce* iii, [He] lyued by the laboure of his handes pourely. 1530 PALSGR. 612/2 Thou lyvest of nothyng but of pollyng. a 1548 HALL *Chron.*, *Hen. VI*, 174 b, Men..had lived by the kynges wages, more then a few yeres. 1602 *2nd Pt. Return fr. Parnass.* III. iii. 1291 A dunce I see is a neighbourlike brute beast, a man may liue by him. 1604 E. G[RIMSTONE] *D'Acosta's Hist. Indies* III. xix. 178 They lived of fishing at sea, and of seeds. 1628 EARLE *Microcosm.*, *Surgeon* (Arb.) 62 His gaines are very ill got, for he liues by the hurts of the Common-wealth. 1675 BROOKS *Gold. Key* Wks. 1867 V. 295 God left man..to live..by his own industry. 1713 STEELE *Englishm.* No. 24. 161 A whimsical Fellow..liv'd upon setting Stones in Wrist-Buttons. 1796 H. HUNTER tr. *St.-Pierre's Stud. Nat.* (1799) II. 428 Every one..must live by his trade. 1865 KINGSLEY *Herew.* Prel., Why should he reverence Nature? Let him use her and live by her. 1887 JESSOPP *Arcady* i. 11 Those luxuries which the big man consumes..the small man lives by.

b. Proverb. ***live and let live***; also *attrib.*

1622 MALYNES *Anc. Law-Merch.* 229 According to the Dutch Prouerbe..*Leuen ende laeten leuen*, To liue and to let others liue. 1687 R. L'ESTRANGE *Answ. Diss.* 43 And what's the Whole Bus'ness at last; but Live, and let Live. 1885 W. MORRIS in Mackail *Life* (1899) II. 136 Two or three people are of no use, and are kept-on on the live-and-let-live principle. 1928 BLUNDEN *Undertones of War* xv. 161 Our future..depended on the observance of the 'Live and Let Live' principle. 1936 'R. WEST' *Thinking Reed* xii. 418 Servants..haven't the live-and-let-live of equals. 1957 L. F. R. WILLIAMS *State of Israel* 217 The belief that he was on the point of reaching some kind of live-and-let-live understanding with Israel. 1959 *Films & Filming* May 22/3 Father, in spite of the live-and-let-live attitude of his brother, persecutes the elderly Dr. Boris Winkler. 1972 J. BROWN *Chancer* iii. 46 What's got into you, love?.. I thought you were always one for live and let live. 1975 J. AIKEN *Voices in Empty House* vi. 161 It takes all sorts, as I always say. Live and let live.

4. To pass life in a specified fashion, indicated by an adv. or advb. phrase (occas. an adj. or compl. sb.) having reference

a. to the manner of regulation of conduct, esp. in a moral aspect.

c 900 tr. *Bæda's Hist.* I. xxvii. (Schipper) 61 Hu hie mid heora ȝeferum drohtian & lifiȝean [*MS. B.* lifian] scylan? c 1200 ORMIN 372 And ȝuw maȝȝ ben þiss ilke word God lare hu ȝuw birrþ libbenn. 1297 R. GLOUC. (Rolls) 4025 Hit is ney vif ȝer þat we abbeþ yliued in such vice. 13.. *E.E. Allit. P.* B. 581 þaȝ þou a sotte lyuie,..by-þenk þe symtyme. 1340–70 *Alex. & Dind.* 288 Leden clanliche our lif & libben as simple. c 1375 *Sc. Leg. Saints* xiv. (*Lucas*) 32 How þai liffyt her but blame. 1426 AUDELAY *Poems* 2 He that levys here ryȝtwysly. 1472 *Presentm. Juries* in *Surtees Misc.* (1890) 24 Thomas Dransfeld..now liffez as a vacabond. 1538 STARKEY *England* I. i. 9 Wych tyme he lyuyd more vertuesly. 1609 SKENE *Reg. Maj.*, *Stat. Robt. II* 39 Ilk ane of them sall leaue leallie and trewlie in their office. 1657–83 EVELYN *Hist. Relig.* (1850) I. 174 They live like goats, and die like asses. 1875 JOWETT *Plato* (ed. 2) V. 63 Living on this wise, we..shall pass our days in good hope.

b. to personal conditions, e.g. degree of happiness, comfort, splendour, repute, or the contrary. † ***to live away***: to lead a life of extravagance. ***to live in clover*** (see CLOVER *sb.* 3). ***to live dangerously***: to take risks habitually; to live with little regard for one's safety. ***to live fast*** (see FAST *adv.* 7).

Beowulf (Z.) 99 Swa ða driht-guman dreamum lifdon eadiȝlice. c 1200 ORMIN 5207 þær he shollde libbenn Wiþþ resste and ro. 1297 R. GLOUC. (Rolls) 535 (MS. *a*) þer abbeþ kinges & mani oþere ofte ilyued in ioie. a 1300 *Cursor M.* 11132 To speke of nedes of þair huse Als dos þe men þat liues in spus. c 1350 *Will. Palerne* 1588 þus þei left in likyng a god while after. 1375 BARBOUR *Bruce* I. 228 He levys at ess that frely levys! c 1375 *Sc. Leg. Saints* iii. (*St. Andrew*) 944 To luf in contemplacione. c 1400 *Destr. Troy* 9760 And fele..fre kynges frusshet to dethe, þat might haue leuyt as lordes in þere lond yet. 1484 CAXTON *Fables of Æsop* I. xi, Better worthe is to lyue in pouerte surely then to lyue rychely beyng euer in daunger. a 1572 KNOX *Hist. Ref.* Wks. 1846 I. 364 To suffer everie man to leaf at libertie of conscience. 1611 BIBLE *Acts* xxiv. 5 After the most straitest sect of our religion, I liued a Pharisee. 1643 TRAPP *Comm.*, *Gen.* xxi. 15 Who erst lived at the full in his fathers house. 1703 COLLIER *Ess. Mor. Subj.* II. 181 He that would have his health hold out must not live too fast. 1719 J. T. PHILLIPS tr. *Thirty-four Confer.* 316 The Inhabitants live very easie and happily in all these Four Provinces. 1767 H. KELLY *Babler* No. III. II. 218 Possessed of such a handsome sum, I considered it as nothing more than a proper compliment to my wife, to live away for some time, and therefore set up a smart post-chaise. 1807 E. S. BARRETT *Rising Sun* II. 80 He set up for an esquire himself, lived away at a most extravagant rate, and neglected his business. 1810 S. GREEN *Reformist* I. 34 Old Mr. Ellingford, though he lived close, known to be immensely rich. 1836 W. E. FORSTER in T. W. Reid *Life*

(1888) I. iii. 79 My parents are as poor as rats..and consequently we live in quite a small way. **1859** G. Meredith *Juggling Jerry* x, I..have lived no gipsy. **1861** Hughes *Tom Brown at Oxf.* i. (1889) 4 They lived very much to them-selves, and scarcely interfered with the dominant party. [**1910** T. Common tr. *Nietzsche's Joyful Wisdom* 219 The greatest enjoyment of existence is to *live in danger*!] **1930** A. Henderson *Contemporary Immortals* 78 The numerous attempts at assassination give point to Mussolini's avowed motto, after Nietzsche: 'To live dangerously!' **1938** L. MacNeice *I crossed Minch* vii. 93 The young people lack spirit... If only they would appreciate 'living dangerously'! **1939** F. Scott Fitzgerald *Let.* 7 Oct. (1964) 407, I have 'lived dangerously' and I may quite possibly have to pay for it. **1962** *Listener* 9 Aug. 226/1 The spectators in the Bridgearama theatre saw the British pair..living dangerously. **1969** *Outdoor Life* Mar. 88/2 To fish the stream when the water is running full pipe is to live dangerously.

c. to the rule or guiding principle, or to the object and purpose of one's life.

971 *Blickl. Hom.* 35 We ealne þysne ʒear lifdon mid ures lichoman willan. *a* **1225** *Juliana* 75 Lusteð writen lare and luuieð þrefter. *a* **1240** *Ureisun* in *Lamb. Hom.* 189 þi deaþ.. do me liuien to þe. *a* **1300** *Cursor M.* 16424 We [*MS.* He] haf vr lagh,..þat we liue wit al in land. **1387** Trevisa *Higden* (Rolls) III. 281 Socrates seide þat meny men wil leve forto ete and drynke. **1533** Gau *Richt Vay* 20 Ane man lwffis notht god ower al thyng..na liffis notht efter his halie wil. **1562** Winȝet *Cert. Tractates* iii. Wks. 1888 I. 23 Giue euerie man mycht leue according to his vocation. **1622** Mabbe tr. *Aleman's Guzman d'Alf.* II. 126 Euery man liue for himselfe. **1656** Stanley *Hist. Philos.* v. (1701) 167/1 Maligned by those who lived after Tyrannical institutions. *a* **1716** Blackall *Wks.* (1723) I. 3 Rules..such as all that call themselves Christ's Disciples are oblig'd to observe and live by. **1840** Carlyle *Heroes* i. 5 It is not easy to understand that sane men could ever..live by such a set of doctrines. **1858–65** —— *Fredk. Gt.* II. i. (1872) IV. 24 They saw no society; lived wholly to their work.

d. ***to live well***: (*a*) to have abundance, to feed luxuriously; (*b*) to be in comfortable circumstances; (*c*) to live a virtuous life.

For *well to live* = 'well to do', prosperous, see Well *adv.*

c **1350** *Will. Palerne* 5393 þus was þe kowherd out of kare kindeli holpen,..wel to liuen for euer. **1530** Palsgr. 612/2, I shal lyue well ynoughe without you. **1620** Shelton *Quix.* III. xx. 141 He preaches well that lives well, quoth Sancho, and I know no other Preaching. **1796** Pegge *Anonym.* (1809) 64 If you would live well for a week, kill a hog; if you would live well for a month, marry; if you would live well all your life, turn priest. **1807–26** S. Cooper *First Lines Surg.* (ed. 5) 68 Carbuncles seem..most common in persons who have lived well.

e. ***to live in*** (or ***within***) ***oneself***: to rely upon oneself for occupation and diversion, opposed to living 'in society'.

a **1674** Clarendon *Tracts* 293 They live to and within themselves. **1762–71** H. Walpole *Vertue's Anecd. Paint.* (1786) II. 125 Living much within himself..his chief amusement was his collection. **1872** J. L. Sanford *Eng. Kings, Chas. I*, 333 His mind had been prepared for the application of these lessons by that early necessity of living very much in himself.

f. With *up*. † (*a*) ***to live up***: *fig.* to live on a high level; to take a high intellectual or moral position. (*b*) ***to live up to***: to act in full accordance with (principles, rules, etc.). Also, to push expenditure to the full limits of (one's fortune). (*c*) ***to live it up***: to live gaily and extravagantly.

1682 Dryden *Relig. Laici* 209 Those who followed Reason's dictates right, Lived up, and lifted high their natural light. **1694** Atterbury *Serm. & Disc.* (1726) I. 72 The Rule is strict indeed; but..there are Great Helps.. enabling us to live up to it. **1709** Steele *Tatler* No. 125 ¶1 All those who do not live up to the Principles of Reason and Virtue. **1711** Addison *Spect.* No. 163 ¶4, I am one of your Disciples, and endeavour to live up to your Rules. **1832** J. S. Knowles *Hunchback* I. i. 9 Your fortune..is ample; And doubtless you live up to't. **1837** G. E. Corrie 17 Sept. in *Mem.* iv. (1890) 90, I had an interesting conversation with the Squire on the duty of living up to one's convictions. **1951** *San Francisco Examiner* 14 Feb. 12 Lieutenant Thumhill is really livin' it up! **1957** P. Frank *Seven Days to Never* vii. 200 They come to Havanna to live it up. They live about two years in two days. **1959** H. Hobson *Mission House Murder* iii. 24 Off-key characters who live it up like crazy. **1961** C. McCullers *Clock without Hands* xiii. 249 Nobody lives for always, but when I live I like to live it up. **1970** N. Armstrong et al. *First on Moon* ii. 39 Those who lived it up in the cocktail lounges that night were also emotionally moved. **1973** C. Bonington *Next Horizon* xiv. 203 We certainly had little chance of living it up on our *Daily Telegraph* expense accounts.

5. a. quasi-*trans.* with cognate *obj.* = 4. spec. ***to live one's own life***: to follow one's own plans or principles; to live independently.

c **1000** Ælfric *Hom.* (Th.) II. 476/16 Se cyning Eglippus leofode his lif on eawfæstre drohtnunge. *c* **1175** *Lamb. Hom.* 115 He scal..for godes eie libban his lif rihtliche. *a* **1300–1400** *Cursor M.* 10175 (Gött.) Sua haly lijf þai liued euer. *c* **1380** *Sir Ferumb.* 686 þou hast y-lyued þy lif to longe to do me such a spyte. *c* **1380** Wyclif *Sel. Wks.* III. 171 How prestis schulde lyfue [*printed* lyfne] a pore lif. *c* **1450** *St. Cuthbert* (Surtees) 40 What lyfe he lyffyd þe treuth ys tald. **1526** *Pilgr. Perf.* (W. de W. 1531) 15 b, They that lyueth the holy lyfe of religyon. **1567** *Gude & Godlie Ball.* (S.T.S.) 72 We suld..Leif in the warld a lyfe perfyte. **1594** Marlowe & Nashe *Dido* IV. iii. E 3, This is no life for men at armes to liue. **1660** Jer. Taylor *Worthy Commun.* 35 To live the life of the spirit. **1712** Addison *Spect.* No. 530 ¶4 It shall be my business hereafter to live the life of an honest man. **1853** M. Arnold *Scholar-Gipsy* xvii, And each half lives a hundred different lives. **1853** C. Brontë *Villette* I. xiii. 229 Thinking meantime my own thoughts, living my own life in my own still, shadow-world. **1871** Morley *Voltaire* (1886) 9 Montaigne,—content to live his life, leaving many questions open. **1893** O. Wilde *Lady Windermere's Fan* II. 56 There are moments when one has to choose between living one's own life..or dragging out some false..existence that the world in its hypocrisy demands. **1895** Zangwill *Master* I. vii. 74 The panorama seemed more varied than when he was living the scenes in all their daily detail of dull routine. **1921** R. Macaulay *Dangerous Ages* iii. 52 Now I must Live my own Life, as the Victorians used to put it. **1933** 'E. Cambridge' *Hostages to Fortune* IV. ii. 221 All Jane's set, with their ceaseless chatter about.. living their own lives,..had that macabre, sullen look.

b. *transf.* in *Hunting.* To keep up (the pace). Also *absol.* in phr. ***to live with hounds***.

1840 *Fraser's Mag.* XXII. 681 We whip and spur, but cannot live the pace. **1898** *St. James's Gaz.* 15 Nov. 6/1 The check..was most welcome to the contingent who still lived with hounds.

6. quasi-*trans.* ***to live down***: † **a.** To defeat by superiority of life (*nonce-use*). **b.** To put down, silence, wear out (prejudice, slander, etc.); to cause (some discreditable incident) to be forgotten by a blameless course of life. **c.** To lose hold of, forget (a fancy) as life goes on.

a **1731** Atterbury (J.), A late prelate, of a remarkable zeal for the church, were religions to be tried by lives, would have lived down the pope, and the whole consistory. **1842** Miall in *Nonconf.* II. 1 It has lived down prejudice. **1884** Rider Haggard *Dawn* xxix, It is very probable that your cousin will live down his fancy. **1893** Gunter *Miss Dividends* 158 How long do you think it will take in New York society for a girl with sixty thousand dollars a year to live anything down?

7. *trans.* To express in one's life; to carry out in one's life the principles of.

1542 Becon *Potation for Lent* L vj b, Not only loue but also lyue yͤ Gospel. **1642** Fuller *Holy & Prof. St.* II. ix. 81 Our Minister lives Sermons. **1650** Trapp *Comm. Lev.* xix. 37 Words not so much to bee read as lived. **1671** Flavel *Fount. of Life* ix. 26 He preached the Doctrine, and Lived the Application. *a* **1708** Beveridge *Thes. Theol.* (1711) III. 147 Hereby you may be sure to live heaven upon earth in time. *a* **1770** Jortin *Serm.* (1771) IV. i. 3 To say who is the Lord..is to deny God..and live a lie. **1874** Blackie *Self-Cult.* 70 To live poetry, indeed, is always better than to write it.

8. a. *intr.* In an emphatic sense: To have life that is worthy of the name; to enjoy or use one's life abundantly.

1606 Day *Ile of Guls* H iv b, They trewly liue, that liue in scorne of spight. *a* **1628** Preston *Breastpl. Love* (1631) 194 One man may liue more in a day than another in twenty. **1673** Shadwell *Epsom Wells* II. i. 19, I have vow'd to spend all my life in London... People do really live no where else. **1726–31** Tindal *Rapin's Hist. Eng.* (1743) II. XVII. 129 Well might I breathe but never think I lived. **1759** Johnson *Rasselas* xxix, While you are making the choice of life, you forget to live. **1827** Keble *Chr. Y.* Ascension Day x, Our wasted frames feel the true sun, and live. **1851** Thackeray *Eng. Hum.* v. (1858) 268 He was living up to the last days of his life. **1889** 'Rolf Boldrewood' *Robbery under Arms* (1890) 317 Jack Dawson..didn't care about anything but horses and dogs, and lived every day of his life.

b. ***where one lives***; at or to the right or vital point. *U.S. slang.*

1860 J. G. Holland *Miss Gilbert's Career* xxii. 386 When that little wife of mine says, 'Tom you're a good fellow, God bless you,' it goes right in where I live. **1878** J. H. Beadle *Western Wilds* xxxvi. 597 The Mormons never got a cent of it. This hurt Brigham—right where he lived. **1886** *Century Mag.* Feb. 511/1 If I could only have reached him where he lives, as our slang says. **1900** 'Flynt' & 'Walton' *Powers that Prey* 122 'Sock it to him!' 'Hit him where he lives!'

9. a. To continue in life; to be alive for a longer or shorter period; to have one's life prolonged. Also in phrases ***to live to*** (be or do so and so); ***Long live*** (formerly simply ***live***) ***the king!***; ***to live and learn***: a catch-phr. used, freq. on the acquisition of some new knowledge, to indicate that one learns through experience; ***I'll*** (or ***he'll***, etc.) ***live***: there is no need for serious worry or concern (freq. used in a trivial way).

831 *Charter* in *O.E. Texts* 445 Gib eadwald leng lifiʒe ðonne cyneðryð, ʒeselle [etc.]. **1154** *O.E. Chron.* an. 1137 (Laud MS.) Ʒif he leng moste liuen. *a* **1175** *Cott. Hom.* 225 He lefede nigon hundred ȝiere and xxx[ti]. *c* **1205** Lay. 252 Ah lut ȝer he leouede. **1297** R. Glouc. (Rolls) 7823 He..biset, ȝif he moste libbe, þat he nolde misdo nammore. *a* **1300** *Cursor M.* 2082 Noe..Liued fourti ȝere after þe flod. **1362** Langl. *P. Pl.* A. VII. 16, I schal leue hem lyflode..As longe as I liue. *c* **1400** *Lanfranc's Cirurg.* 94 If þei ben not curid, þei lyuen þe lengere tyme. *c* **1420** *Anturs of Arth.* 259 (Douce MS.) þou shal leve but a stert. *c* **1450** *ME. Med. Bk.* (Heinrich) 138 Wheþer he shal lyuen or dye of þe seeknesse. *a* **1548** Hall *Chron., Hen. VI*, 130 b, Criyng: sainct Denise, live kyng Charles. **1586** in Hearne *R. Glouc.* (1724) 675/2, I am so unhappy to haue lyuen to see this unhappy daye. **1601** Shaks. *Jul. C.* IV. iii. 114 Hath Cassius liu'd To be but Mirth and Laughter to his Brutus? **1615** W. Lawson *Country Housew. Gard.* (1626) 7 Not suffring a Tree to liue the tenth part of his age. *c* **1620** in *Roxburghe Ballads* (Ballad Soc.) (1871) I. 60 A man may liue and learne. **1653** Walton *Angler* 153 Harme him [a frog] as little as you may possibly, that he may live the longer. **1699** R. L'Estrange *Erasm. Colloq.* (1725) 210 If I live to come back again. **1718** Prior *Solomon* Pref., And in this kind Mr. Philips, had he lived, would have excelled. **1743** Bulkeley & Cummins *Voy. S. Seas* 34 If he lives, I will carry him a Prisoner to the Commodore. **1776** *Trial of Nundocomar* 32/2, I should not have supposed he could live many hours. **1782** Cowper *Gilpin* 253 Now let us sing, Long live the king! And Gilpin, long live he! **1803** M. Wilmot *Let.* 6 Aug. in *Russ. Jrnls.* (1934) I. 32 Humph! thinks I. One must live and learn. **1818** Cruise *Digest* (ed. 2) II. 270 To the use of A. for 99 years, if he should so long live. **1844** Dickens *Mart. Chuz.* xxxiv, Live and learn Mr. Bevan! **1849** Dickens *Dav. Copp.* (1850) xx. 208 Live and learn. I had my doubts, I confess, but now they're cleared up. **1893** *Academy* 13 May 412/1 Lord Carnarvon did not live to put the final touches to his translation. **1956** J. Symons *Paper Chase* xi. 88 'Are you hurt?' 'I shall live.' **1957** A. Huxley *Let.* 12 Dec. (1969) 836 Problems which I have been trying to solve for the last four months, without any success; for they are, so far as I can see, insoluble. So there we are. One lives and learns. **1963** N. Freeling *Gun before Butter* III. 145 'Potato salad..doesn't sound much fun.' 'I'll live.' **1967** O. Hesky *Time for Treason* xviii. 146 'Better, darling?' Miller asked Miriam anxiously. .. 'Yes, she'll live,' Tami said sourly. **1971** M. McCarthy *Birds of America* 111 Well, live and learn! **1972** 'R. Crawford' *Whip Hand* I. vi. 34 The doctor asked him how he felt. 'I'll live.'

fig. **1813** R. Thornton 16 June in Hansard *Parl. Debates* XXVI. 685 A great statesman..had once exclaimed, 'Perish commerce—live the constitution!'

b. with †*forth*, *on*, †*over*.

c **1200** Ormin 17213 Acc ȝiff þatt he þatt fullhtnedd iss Her lifeþþ forþ onn erþe. **1387** Trevisa *Higden* (Rolls) VII. 141 Alfridus forsoþe after his blyndynge sent unto Hely liffed over but fewe dayes. *c* **1400** *Destr. Troy* 13105 Made was this mariage þo mighty betwene,..And [they] lyuet furth in Lykyng a long tyme after. **1611** Shaks. *Wint. T.* II. iii. 155 Shall I liue on, to see this Bastard kneele, And call me Father? **1866** M. Arnold *Thyrsis* iii, While the tree lived, he in these fields lived on. **1896** M. Field *Attila* I. 20, I would rather drop down dead Than live on like my cousin.

c. said of the Deity and of spirits.

971 *Blickl. Hom.* 131 þurh Godes fultum, þe lyfað & rixað a butan ende. *c* **1200** *Trin. Coll. Hom.* 23 And alle men shullen cume to libben echeliche. *a* **1225** *Leg. Kath.* 1771 þer as me liueð aa in blisse buten euch bale. **1447** Bokenham *Seyntys* (Roxb.) 77, I wold wot what it may the avayle To forsakyn the goddys wych leuyn ay. **1604** E. G[rimstone] *D'Acosta's Hist. Indies* v. vii. 345 The Indians of Peru beleeved commonly that the Soules lived after this life.

d. To escape spiritual death.

c **1375** *Sc. Leg. Saints* xvi. (*Magdalena*) 15 þe ded of synful I na wil bot þat he leife his syn & lif. **1435** Misyn *Fire of Love* II. xi. (1896) 99 Lern..to lufe þi makar, if þou desyre to lyfe qwhen þou hens passys. **1508** Fisher *7 Penit. Ps.* li. Wks. (1876) 103, I wyll not the deth of a synner, but that he be tourned from his wyckked lyfe and leue. **1611** Bible *Ezek.* xxxiii. 11.

e. *fig.* (*poet.* and *rhetorical*). Of things: To survive, continue in operation.

1768 Gray *Elegy* 92 E'en in our Ashes live their wonted Fires. **1863** Woolner *My Beautiful Lady* 38 Nothing lives but perfect Love. **1895** Merriman *Sowers* i, What little daylight there was lived on the western horizon. **1896** *Athenæum* 24 Apr. 547/2 Blunders of this sort live long.

f. quasi-*trans.* ***to live out***: to complete (a term of life); also to survive the end of (a period of time). Also *dial.* to survive (a person): see *Eng. Dial. Dict.*

1535 Coverdale *Ps.* lv. 23 The bloudthurstie and disceatfull shal not lyue out half their daies. **1899** Guy Boothby *Dr. Nikola's Experim.* ii. 55 He was as certain as any one possibly could be that the chap could not live out the week. *Mod.* I never thought he would live out the night. (Recent Dicts. give 'to live out a war, a term of office, a century'.)

10. Chiefly of a vessel: To escape destruction; to remain afloat. Also quasi-*trans.* of persons. ***to live out*** (a storm): to escape destruction by.

1601 Shaks. *Twel. N.* I. ii. 14, I saw your brother..binde himselfe..To a strong Maste, that liu'd vpon the sea. **1615** A. Stafford *Heav. Dogge* To Rdr. 17 There are Coltes who will venture to row in waters wherein (to use the sea-faring phrase) they cannot liue. **1671** Narborough in *Acc. Sev. Late Voy.* I. (1694) 190 It was impossible for the Boat to live any longer in that Sea. **1719** De Foe *Crusoe* I. xvi. (1840) 289 The savages in the boat never could live out the storm. **1793** Smeaton *Edystone L.* §142 Carrying out the King's Mooring Barges so far to sea, where they could not live but in fine weather. **1838** Col. Hawker *Diary* (1893) II. 145 A ferocious hurricane..so that nothing could 'live' afloat. **1854** H. Miller *Sch. & Schm.* (1858) 15, I have seen a boat live in as bad a night as this.

11. To continue in the memory of men; to be permanently commemorated; to escape obliteration or oblivion.

c **1586** C'tess Pembroke *Ps.* LXIX. xi, From out the booke [let the wicked] be crossed, Where the good men live engrossed. **1613** Shaks. *Hen. VIII*, IV. ii. 45 Mens euill manners, liue in Brasse, their Vertues We write in Water. **1638** F. Junius *Paint. Ancients* 56 Let..the temples be graced with such sights; worke them out in ivorie; let them live in colours. **1688** Prior *To Countess Exeter* 13 Eliza's glory lives in Spenser's song. **1718** —— *Solomon* III. 264 A fancied kind of being to retrieve, And in a book, or from a building live. *a* **1748** Watts (J.), That which strikes the eye Lives long upon the mind. **1800–24** Campbell *Hallowed Ground* vi, To live in hearts we leave behind, Is not to die. **1855** Macaulay *Hist. Eng.* xviii. IV. 131 One noble passage still lives, and is repeated by thousands who know not whence it comes. *a* **1873** Macready *Remin.* (1875) I. 94 Cooke's representation of the part..lived in my memory in all its sturdy vigour. **1883** R. W. Dixon *Mano* I. viii. 21 So would he..give me those kind looks which live in me.

12. a. To make one's abode; to dwell, reside; *transf.*, to have its place. Also with †*forth*. ***to live in***: to reside in the establishment; opposed to *to live out*. ***to live out*** (U.S. colloq.): to be in domestic service. ***to live together*** spec., to cohabit.

c **1205** Lay. 6235 We wulleð..þe leofuen wið a to ure liue. *c* **1220** *Bestiary* 518 Ðis fis wuneð wið ðe se grund, and liueð ðer eure heil and sund. **1377** Langl. *P. Pl.* B. x. 438 For-þi lyue we forth with lither men. **1430–40** Lydg. *Bochas* VIII. i. (1554) 178 Decius..liued in deserte ferre out in wildernes. *c* **1450** *Pol. Poems* (Rolls) II. 249 That haiit lywith in Lowthe many longe days. **1508** Dunbar *Poems* vii. 30 Welcum, therfor, abufe all livand leyd, Withe us to liue, and to maik

recidence. **1580** LYLY *Euphues* (Arb.) 266 He is not where he liues, but wher he loues. **1600** SHAKS. *A.Y.L.* II. iii. 72 Here liued I, but now liue here no more. **1662** STILLINGFL. *Orig. Sacr.* II. iv. §2 It was their office to teach the people, and therefore it was necessary they should live among them. **1681** FLAVEL *Meth. Grace* xiv. 283 The righteous is more excellent than his neighbour, though he live next doore to a graceless nobleman. **1711** STEELE *Spect.* No. 49 ¶4 The Coffee-house is the Place of Rendezvous to all that live near it. **1731** *Gentl. Mag.* I. 391/1 Bluster..has liv'd in the Country ever since. **1813** JANE AUSTEN *Pride & Prej.* III. xv. 266, I..am only concerned that their living together before the marriage took place, should be so generally known. **1815** *Ann. Reg., Chron.* 49 The family, with whom she lived servant. **1855** MRS. TERHUNE *Hidden Path* vii. 63 She has never lived out before. **1875** JOWETT *Plato* (ed. 2) I. 80 Melesias and I live together, and our two sons live with us. **1879** TROLLOPE *John Caldigate* III. viii. 106 They had not become man and wife... They had lived together. **1890** J. WATSON *Nature & Woodcraft* vi. 71 The farm servants of Cumbria 'live in'. **1891** *Daily News* 14 July 7/3 It was admitted that they lived together. **1895** *Law Times* C. 133/2 The deceased lived in a cottage near the up side of the railway line. **1896** C. BOOTH *Life & Labour Lond.* VII. 217 The majority of grocers' assistants still live in. *Ibid.* 218 Men..who live out not unfrequently help them-selves to food. *a* **1916** H. JAMES *Sense of Past* (1917) IV. iii. 242 A pot of about the size..of that one..with something or other on the cabinet or wherever, the place where it 'lives', as we say, rather branching out on either side of it. **1919** R. FRY *Let.* 6 Oct. (1972) II. 457, I don't think they're married; they've lived together for twelve years. **1938** E. BOWEN *Death of Heart* III. vi. 426 I should like to know how she knew I'd been at her diary. I put it back where it lives. **1953** A. UPFIELD *Murder must Wait* v. 45 The nurse girl..didn't live in... She came every day. **1958** J. CANNAN *And be a Villain* i. 37, I couldn't find any brandy. Do you know where it lives? **1961** N. STREATFEILD *Silent Speaker* iv. 61 Mrs. Simpson had led Olivia into the little room where the vases lived. **1963** M. MCCARTHY *Group* ii. 42 She and Dick had 'lived together' on quite a different basis. **1971** *Woman's Own* 27 Mar. 21/3 One advantage of the permissive society is that it's all right to live together before marriage. **1971** *Daily Tel.* 16 Oct. 2/8 The development is designed..to provide extra accommodation for undergraduates to enable all 400 to 'live in'.

fig. *a* **1340** HAMPOLE *Psalter* xvii. 50 Lord lifes in my hert. **1857** PUSEY *Real Presence* i. (1896) 4 The Fathers, among whom, for these last twenty years, I have lived, as in my home.

b. *to live in* (a room, etc.): to occupy, inhabit; to treat as one's ordinary abode. In quots. in *indirect passive*.

1885 MRS. C. PRAED *Head Station* I. 3 The veranda was more lived in than the sitting-room. **1895** *Pall Mall Mag.* Mar. 407 The drawing-room looked more lived-in than ever. **1975** *New Yorker* 21 Apr. 103/1 Mr. Ritman has a knack for making his sets look lived in.

13. *to live with*: **a.** To live with as if husband and wife; to cohabit with (COHABIT *v.* 2).

1749 J. CLELAND *Mem. Woman Pleasure* II 36. I had now liv'd with Mr. Norbet near a quarter of a year. **1813** JANE AUSTEN *Pride & Prej.* III. viii. 147 She was more alive to the disgrace, which the want of new clothes must reflect on her daughter's nuptials, than to any sense of shame at her eloping and living with Wickham, a fortnight before they took place. **1854** GEO. ELIOT *Let.* 23 Oct. (1954) II. 179 If you hear of anything that I have said..in relation to Mr. Lewes beyond the simple fact that I am attached to him and that I am living with him,..believe that it is false. **1871** [see ALLOW *v.* 7]. **1879** TROLLOPE *John Caldigate* II. iii. 33 Did she ever live with you?.. As your wife? **1923** D. H. LAWRENCE *Stud. Classic Amer. Lit.* vii. 123 Do you imagine Adam had never lived with Eve before that apple episode? **1928** E. WALLACE *Flying Squad* xvi. 159 People are under the impression that you're living with me. **1963** M. MCCARTHY *Group* i. 11 The knowledge..of Kay's having 'lived with' Harald filled them with a sudden sense of the unsanctioned. **1972** M. J. BOSSE *Incident at Naha* 31 'Virgil asked me to live with him two months ago,' I stated.

b. *fig.* To put up with; to come to terms with. *colloq.*

1937 T. S. ELIOT in B. Dobrée *From Anne to Victoria* xliii. 603 Were one a person who liked to have busts about, a bust of Scott would be something one could live with. **1941** F. D. ROOSEVELT *Let.* 1 July in H. L. Ickes *Secret Diary* (1955) III. 567 Both of these are elements that we have to live with whether we like it or not. **1961** *Listener* 2 Nov. 694/2 We know that, on account of the balance of military power, we have got to live with it [*sc.* Communism]. **1964** 'W. HAGGARD' *Antagonists* ii. 16 That was awkward, but the experienced Mr Palliser could live with it. **1965** *Ottawa Jrnl.* 29 Apr. 25/3 Canada is so bound by the General Agreement on Tariffs and Trade that in effect it would have to live with its big auto deficit with the U.S. if there were no U.S.-Canada agreement. **1973** J. PORTER *It's Murder with Dover* vi. 56 Gary was illegitimate... Not that I ever made any secret about it. It was something Gary had to learn to live with.

c. *to live with oneself*: to retain one's self-respect.

1962 P. GREGORY *Like Tigress at Bay* xiv. 143 Would he be able to live with himself, later? **1971** 'J. J. MARRIC' *Gideon's Art* xi. 98, I think he'll find it difficult to live with himself if he's taken off [the job]. **1973** R. PERRY *Ticket to Ride* ii. 32 The note of hysteria in her voice stopped me dead. The sensible thing to do would have been to continue on my way but if I did I knew I'd find it awfully difficult to live with myself.

14. *Comb.* In names of plants: **live (for) ever,** (*a*) = LIVE-LONG 1 and 2; (*b*) Everlasting Flower, *Helichrysum*. **live in idleness** (= *love-in-idleness*), a name for the Heartsease or Pansy.

1597 GERARDE *Herbal* II. cxcv. 517 It..may be kept.. by the space of a whole yeere..wherefore our English women haue called it Liue long, or Liue for euer. *Ibid.* II. ccxcix. 705 Called..in English..Pansies, Liue in Idlenes. *a* **1700** B. E. *Dict. Cant. Crew, Hearts-ease*,..an Herb called..Live in Idleness,..or Pansies. **1715** PETIVER in *Phil. Trans.* XXIX. 355 Round Saddle-leaved Cape Live-ever. *Elichrysum Capense.* **1760** J. LEE *Introd. Bot.* App. 317 Live-ever, *Sedum.* **1763** J. WHEELER *Bot. & Gardener's Dict.*, Liveever, *Crassula.* **1866** *Treas. Bot.*, Livelong or Live-for-ever, *Sedum Telephium.* **1884** BURROUGHS *Fresh Fields* viii. (1895) 171, I did not catch a glimpse of..elecampane, live-for-ever, bladder campion, and others, of which I see acres at home.

†**live,** *v.*[2] *Obs. rare.* [f. *live*, LIFE *sb.* Cf. LIVEN *v.*] *trans.* To give life to; to quicken, vivify.

1413 *Pilgr. Sowle* (Caxton 1483) IV. xxviii. 73 This soule sensitif whiche euery beest beryth in his blood lyueth or quycketh the body to which he is conioyned.

live, variant of LEVE *v.*[2] *Obs.*

liveability, livability (lɪvəˈbɪlɪtɪ). [f. LIV(E)AB(LE *a.* + -ILITY.] **a.** Survival expectancy, *spec.* that of poultry. **b.** Suitability for habitation.

1914 *Springfield* (Mass.) *Republican* 28 June II. 9/2 You increase the egg yield, the fertility of eggs for hatching and the 'livability' of every chick hatched. **1922** E. W. NELSON in V. Stefansson *Northward Course of Empire* p. xviii, He [*sc.* Stefansson] has developed here and elsewhere the story of the 'livability' of the Far North, and shown that this hitherto dreaded region offers a welcome. **1934** W. A. LIPPINCOTT *Poultry Production* (ed. 5) iv. 133 The livability or vigor of a given chick might be looked upon as a part of its individuality. **1945** NELSON & WRIGHT *Tomorrow's House* vi. 75/2 Soft, general illumination which can give this room the same air of livability as the living-room itself. **1950** *N.Z. Jrnl. Agric.* Apr. 331/1 This trial..is..a means of measuring the productive powers, the livability, and the quality of pullets intended as breeding stock. **1960** *Farmer & Stockbreeder* 8 Mar. 158/1 Spinks pullets are uniform, batch after batch, giving high egg production, good size and liveability. **1971** *Farmers Weekly* 19 Mar. 90/2 What about liveability, egg numbers, egg size and feed conversion?

liveable, livable (ˈlɪvəb(ə)l), *a.* [f. LIVE *v.* + -ABLE.]

†**1.** Likely to live. *Obs. rare*$^{-0}$.

1611 in COTGRAVE s.v. *Viable.*

†**2.** Conducive to (comfortable) living. *Obs.*

1664 PEPYS *Diary* 19 Feb., They are counted very rich people, worth at least 10 or 12,000*l.*, and their country house all the yeare long, and all things liveable.

3. Of a house, a room, or locality: That may be lived in; suitable for living in.

1814 JANE AUSTEN *Mansf. Park* xxv, There will be work for five summers at least before the place is liveable. **1827** SCOTT in Lockhart *Life* August, He [Scott] used to say that he did not know a more 'liveable' country [than the vale of Tweed]. **1830** CAMPBELL in *Lady Morgan's Mem.* (1862) II. 310 You will find me in a far more liveable part of London than I lived in before. **1849** LD. CARLISLE *Jrnl.* 12 Feb. in Trevelyan *Life Macaulay* (1889) 479 His rooms at the top of the Albany are very liveable. **1879** MISS BIRD *Rocky Mountains* 202 [South Park] looked to me quite lowland and livable. **1895** *Athenæum* 10 Aug. 195/3 If men had learnt the art of living in Africa, that continent would prove quite as 'livable' as Brazil.

4. Of life: That can be lived; bearable, supportable.

1841 ARNOLD in Stanley *Life* (1844) II. App. C. 436 But not the strongest Tory or Conservative values our Church or Law more than I do, or would find life less liveable without them. **1865** WHEWELL in *Life* 541, I cannot yet see how life is livable. **1896** *Nation* (N.Y.) LXII. 28/3 Who has for three years found life quite livable.

5. Of persons (also *liveable with*): That may be lived with; companionable, sociable.

1860 *Chamb. Jrnl.* XIV. 305 Many men and women are of irreproachable character in all the great essentials, yet are not liveable people. **1888** *Athenæum* 21 Apr. 501/3 Few will leave so pleasant an impression [as Matthew Arnold], few will seem so livable-with as he. **1896** E. F. BENSON *Babe B.A.* 7 They were both..very live-able-with.

Hence **ˈliveableness**, quality of being 'liveable' (in quot. 1895, capability of living, 'viability').

1860 *Chamb. Jrnl.* XIV. 305 Everybody who has ever been a member of a household or a family, must have a ready conception of the quality—liveableness. **1882** STEVENSON *Fam. Stud.* 103 If the poet is to be of any help, he must testify to the liveableness of life. **1895** *Athenæum* 27 July 129/1 The articles..are very fair of their kind. But they have absolutely no independent livableness.

ˈlive-bait. [f. LIVE *a.* + BAIT *sb.*] A living worm, small fish, etc. used as a bait in angling.

1616 SURFL. & MARKH. *Country Farme* 513 Your Liue-baits are wormes of all kinds. **1851** *Illustr. Catal. Gt. Exhib.* 361 Folding live-bait kettle.

Hence **ˈlive-baiting**, fishing with live bait.

1867 F. FRANCIS *Angling* (1880) 132 Live baiting is the next method for discussion.

liveblood: see LIFE-BLOOD 3.

lived (laɪvd), *a.* [f. LIFE *sb.* + -ED[2].] Possessed of or endowed with a certain kind or length of life. Also LONG-LIVED, SHORT-LIVED *adjs.*

1589 R. HARVEY *Pl. Perc.* (1860) 13 If you pearce his hart, you can doo him little harme, for he is liude like a Cat. **1825** COLERIDGE *Lett.* (1895) 743 Nature is a wary wily long-breathed old witch, tough-lived as a turtle.

lived (lɪvd), *ppl. a.* [f. LIVE *v.* + -ED[1].] **a.** That has been lived or passed through. **b.** That is expressed in one's life.

1879 TODHUNTER *Alcestis* 3 Cheapen not the worth of our lived lives. **1882** HINSDALE *Garfield & Education* I. 77 The world demands a lived gospel as well as a preached gospel.

live-day long (Burns): see LIVELONG 1 b.

ˈlived-in, *a.* [Cf. LIVE *v.*[1] 12 b.] Occupied, inhabited.

1873 'S. COOLIDGE' *What Katy did at School* i. 3 The lived-in-look of the best parlor. **1950** C. EDWARDS in M. Cecil *Heroines in Love* (1974) viii. 203 Your home has that wonderful lived-in feeling. **1960** *House & Garden* July 50/1 Halls..can insulate the more lived-in parts of the house. **1970** *Daily Tel.* 19 May 16/4 It [*sc.* a play] has a lived-in look and all the acting is robustly expressive.

livefull, -les, obs. ff. LIFEFUL, LIFELESS.

live-honey: see LIFE-HONEY.

live-in (ˈlɪvɪn), *a.* [f. vbl. phr. *to live in* (LIVE *v.*[1] 12).] Resident, residing in the establishment (as opp. to living out or at home). So **ˈlive-out** *a.*, that lives out.

In quot. 1966 used in the sense 'deliberately living in as a form of protest'. Cf. -IN *suffix*[3].

1955 'C. H. ROLPH' *Women of Streets* 148 Worked for four months as live-in domestic. **1966** *Maclean's Mag.* 18 June 1 The 'live-in' principles used by civil rights workers in the southern United States. **1969** *New Yorker* 18 Jan. 41 He has a live-out cook, but he likes to bend over the stove himself. **1970** *Daily Tel.* (Colour Suppl.) 9 Jan. 19/1 In 1920..the House at Maiden Bradley was run with the help of 26 live-in staff. **1971** H. WAUGH *Shadow Guest* ii. 10 We had a live-in couple to cook and caretake and a live-out woman to clean.

livelich, obs. form of LIVELY.

†**ˈlivelihead.** *Obs.* [f. LIVELY + -HEAD.]

1. Liveliness; vivacity.

c **1440** *Promp. Parv.* 308/2 Levelyheede, or qwyknesse [*MS. K.* liyflines], *vivacitas.* **1647** H. MORE *Song of Soul* II. iii. I. ii, The stronger hope, the stronger feed is fed; One mother both and the like livelyhed. *a* **1717** PARNELL *Poet. Wks.* (1833) 20 With lusty livelyhed he talks.

b. Living form or original. Also, condition of being alive; life.

c **1542** SURREY *Death Sir T. Wyatt* 2 in *Tottel's Misc.* (Arb.) 28 Dyuers thy death doe diuersely bemone: Some, that in presence of thy liuelyhed Lurked. **1590** SPENSER *F.Q.* II. ix. 3 What mote ye weene, if the trew lively-head Of that most glorious visage he did vew! **1596** *Ibid.* VI. vii. 20 But, when he nigh approcht, he mote aread Plaine signes in him of life and livelihead.

2. In senses of LIVELIHOOD[1]: Means of living; also, inheritance.

1471-6 *Plumpton Corr.* (Camden) 27 She hath no other mean to help herself with, unto that a determination be had betwixt T—— I—— & her, of the livelyhed that standeth in travers betwixt them. **1590** SPENSER *F.Q.* II. ii. 2 Full little weenest thou what sorrowes are Left thee for porcion of thy livelyhed.

livelihood[1] (ˈlaɪvlɪhʊd). Forms: α. 1 líflád, 2-5 lif-, 3-6 lyf-, 4 liif-, lyff-, lyif-, 4-6 lyfe-, lyve-, 4-7 live-; 2-4 -lad, 3-7 -lode, 4 -ladd, -laid(e, -late, -led(e, 4-6 -lode, -lood, 4-7 -lod, -loode, 5 -lothe, *Sc.* -lat, 5-7 -load, 6 -lodde, *Sc.* -lait, -lett. β. 5 livelhod, -hud, liffleod, 6 lyveliod, livelihod, livelehood, lyvelyhoode, 7 liveliehood, 6– livelihood. [OE. *líflád*, f. *líf* life + *lád* course, way, also subsistence (see LOAD, LODE). Cf. the corresponding OHG. *lîbleita* provisions, subsistence, f. *lîb* life + *leita* conduct. In the 16th c. the spelling was gradually assimilated (see forms) to that of LIVELIHOOD[2], -HEAD.]

†**1.** Course of life, lifetime; kind or manner of life; conduct. *Obs.*

c **1000** *Benedictine Rule* i. (Schröer-Wülker) 9/20 þæt feorðe muneca cyn is, þe is Widscriþul ʒenæmned, þa ealle heora liflade [L. *tota vita sua*] ʒeond missenlice þeoda farað. *c* **1175** *Lamb. Hom.* 85 Hwet is þet he mei mare spenen of his aȝen feire forbisne of his aȝene liflade. *c* **1230** *Hali Meid.* 5 þurh englene liflade & heuenlich þat leades þah ha licomliche wunie up on eorðe. *a* **1300** *Cursor M.* 1506, I find na term of his [caymes] liuelaid. *a* **1300** *Ibid.* 2009 A neu liuelade cun þai bigin. *c* **1449** PECOCK *Repr.* II. xii. 217 For gouernaunce and reule of her lijflode. *a* **1470** G. ASHBY *Dicta Philos.* 374 Directe his levelode profitably. **1581** J. BELL *Haddon's Answ. Osor.* 344 How is this contrarye to yᵉ auncient custome..of the Elders, If ministers..marry wives for the necessary comfort of theyr livelyhood?

2. Means of living, maintenance, sustenance; esp. in *to earn*, *gain*, *get*, *make*, *seek a livelihood.*

a **1300** *Fall & Passion* 37 in *E.E.P.* (1862) 13 In þe vale of eboir his liuelod he [Adam] most swink sore. *a* **1300** *Cursor M.* 1962 Ete..Na o fouxul þat refes his liuelade. **13..** *Gaw. & Gr. Knt.* 133 þat þe lude myȝt haf leue liflode to cach. **1357** *Lay Folks Catech.* 212 We..withdrawes lyuelade fra tham that nede haues. *c* **1375** *Sc. Leg. Saints* xxiv. (*Alexis*) 169 And Ilke day thigyt his lyf-led At þame þat passage-by þare mad. **1387** TREVISA *Higden* (Rolls) VII. 331 Lanfrank ..was a man þat kouþe doo no grete werkes to gete his liflode þerwiþ. *c* **1449** PECOCK *Repr.* 342 Poul..wrouȝte with hise hondis forto haue his lijflode. *c* **1470** HENRY *Wallace* IX. 376 My lyflat is bot honest chewysance. **1483** CAXTON *Gold. Leg.* 40/2 Noe began to labouer for his lyfelode with his sones. **1581** MARBECK *Bk. of Notes* 1104 Then must it be the Priests wages, which at that time had no other livelode. **1611** BIBLE *Pref. to Rdr.* ¶1 Those nourishing fathers and mothers..that withdraw from them who hang vpon their breasts..liuely-hood and support fit for their estates. **1660** WOOD *Life* Dec. (O.H.S.) I. 360 To gaine a bare livelihood. **1680** AUBREY in *Lett. Eminent Persons* (1813) III. 401 What he did for his delight and recreation only when a boy, proved to be his livelihood when a man. **1702** *Eng. Theophrast.* 117 A hazardous Trade to which they have bound themselves to

get a Livelyhood. **1719** W. WOOD *Surv. Trade* 297 To.. restrain our own Subjects from.. seeking their Livelihoods. **1727** DE FOE *Syst. Magic* I. i. (1840) 4 They made a livelihood or trade of it. **1830** HERSCHEL *Stud. Nat. Phil.* 61 Fishermen who gain their livelihood on its waters. **1875** JOWETT *Plato* (ed. 2) V. 118 Let each man practise one art which is to be his livelihood. **1882** JEAN L. WATSON *Life R. S. Candlish* vii. 87 When Dr. Candlish left the Establishment he did so without any prospect of a livelihood.

†**b.** Corporeal sustenance, food, victuals. *Obs.*

a **1300** *Cursor M.* 19835 Quils þai dight him his liuelade, In orisun he lai and bade. *c* **1375** *Sc. Leg. Saints* xxxvi. (*Baptista*) 280 Wyld hony wes his lyflede, & a thinge callit locusta. **1382** WYCLIF *Deut.* ii. 28 Lyuelodis bi prijs sel to vs, that we eeten. *c* **1400** *Apol. Loll.* 21 Crist.. wold not curse hem þat denoied to Him harborow & lifelod. **1688** R. HOLME *Armoury* II. 122/2 Oaks, Elms, Ashes, Walnuts, Chesnuts, and such Trees, wrong them [Fruit Trees].. of their Livelyhood.

†**c.** In immaterial sense or *fig. Obs.*

1616 HIERON *Wks.* II. 38 Faith is (as it were) the liuelyhood of a Christian: it is the stocke whereon hee liues. **1639** DRUMM. OF HAWTH. *Answ. to Objections* Wks. (1711) 214 We will allow no livelyhood to tender consciences. **1678** BUNYAN *Pilgr.* I. (1900) 118 His livelihood was upon things that were Spiritual [*marg. note*, Little-Faith could not live upon Esaus Pottage].

†**3.** Income, revenue, stipend; *pl.* emoluments.

1422 *E. E. Wills* (1882) 51, I bequeth to two prestes,.. resonable lyuelode. **1433** *Rolls of Parlt.* IV. 424/2 Some withoute any liflode or guerdon. **1439** W. BYNGHAM *Petit. to Hen. VI* in Willis & Clark *Cambridge* (1886) I. Introd. 56 For all liberall sciences used in your seid universitees certein lyflode is ordeyned and endued. *c* **1440** *Promp. Parv.* 308/2 Lyflode, or warysone,.. *donativum*. *c* **1460** FORTESCUE *Abs. & Lim. Mon.* x. (1885) 131 How necessarie it is that he [the King] haue grete livelod aboff the same charges. **1463** *Bury Wills* (Camden) 29 The seid Marie preest to haue the seyd iijs. iiij*d*. to avmentacion of his lifloode. **1475** *Bk. Noblesse* (Roxb.) 32 Rewarded in lifelode of londes and tenementis yoven in the counte of Mayne. **1502** ARNOLDE *Chron.* (1811) 270 The Yerely Stint of the Lyuelod belonging to London Brydge. **1530–1** *Act 22 Hen. VIII*, c. 15 Any spirituall persone.. hauyng any dignitee, benefyce, promocion, or other spirituall lyuelode, within the prouince of Yorke. *a* **1548** HALL *Chron.* (1809) 199 The Cardinall.. gave Elizabeth Beauchampe thre C. markes of Livelod. **1563–83** FOXE *A. & M.* II. 1052, I.. exhorte you to beare your partes of your liuelode & salarie towerd the paiment of this summe graunted. **1621** BP. MOUNTAGU *Diatribæ* 297 There was payed vnto the Sanctuary for them λυτρον, which went to the maintenance of the Priests amongst their other liuely-hoods and Reuenues.

†**4.** Property yielding an income, landed or inherited property; an estate, inheritance, patrimony. Also, ***man of* (*great, small*) *livelihood*.** *Obs.*

1413 *Pilgr. Sowle* (Caxton 1483) IV. xxx. 80 Yf the Chyuetayne were taken of the same countre where that he is enheryted and hath his lyuelode. **1438** *E.E. Wills* (1882) 111 Item all myn owne lyuelode to remeyne to my next heires. *c* **1440** *Partonope* 5013 He was no man of grete lifelode. ? **1465** *Paston Lett.* II. 254 What tyme that I rode oute aboute my litil livelod. **1470–85** MALORY *Arthur* I. iii, Syre Ector.. had grete lyuelode aboute london. **1484** CAXTON *Fables of Poge* iv, [None ought to hunt and hawk] withoute he be moche ryche and man of lyuelode. **1513** *Bk. Keruynge* in *Babees Bk.* (1868) 285 Some lorde is of blode royall & of small lyuelode. **1528** TINDALE *Obed. Chr. Man* 94 b, To byld abbays, to endote them with lyvelode, to be prayd fore for ever. **1545** BRINKLOW *Compl.* xv. (1874) 38 Thei can not be content with the sufficyent lyuelodes that their fathers left them. **1570** *Queen's Councell's Let.* 7 Feb. (in *N. & Q.* 1 Aug. 1857), Such speciall men of lyveliod and worshipp of the said Countie as have interest herein. **1594** CAREW *Tasso* (1881) 15 To this liuelode that from his mother came, Conquests he winned. **1601** HOLLAND *Pliny* I. 411 Being entred once vpon those grounds as his owne liuelode and possession. **1627** SIR R. COTTON in Rushw. *Hist. Coll.* (1659) I. 469 For the Land-forces, if it were for an Offensive War, the men of less livelihood were the best spared.

5. *Comb.*: †**livelod-man**, man of property.

c **1470** HENRY *Wallace* VI. 72 This lyflat man hyr gat in mariage. *c* **1500** *Melusine* vi. 31, I shal make the for to be.. the gretest and best lyuelod man [F. *terrien*] of them all. **1570** *Henry's Wallace* VII. 869 The lyflait men [*c.* 1470 the blessit men], that was off Scotland borne, Fwnde at his faith Wallace gert thaim be sworn.

† **'livelihood**[2]. *Obs.* [f. LIVELY *a.* + -HOOD.] = LIVELINESS in various senses.

1566 PAINTER *Pal. Pleas.* I. 106 How much his [Love's] assaultes can debilitate the livelihoode of the bodies and spirites of men. **1593** *Rites & Mon. Ch. Durh.* (Surtees) 29 The fairness of the wall, the staitlynes of the pictures and the lyvelyhoode of the paynting. **1594** J. KING *Funeral Serm.* in *Jonas* (1618) 673 His spirit departeth; not only his strength, his health, his agility, his liuelihood; but his breath. **1601** SHAKS. *All's Well* I. i. 58 The tirrany of her sorrowes takes all liuelihood from her cheeke. **1616** SURFL. & MARKH. *Country Farme* 638 The red [wines] which are not yet come to their liuelyhood and maturitie. **1619** W. SCLATER *Exp. 1 Thess.* (1630) 13 They are actions operatiue, full of liulihood and efficacy. **1640** C. HARVEY *Synagogue* (1647) 37 Thy Circumcision writ thy death in blood, Baptisme in water seales my livelyhood. *a* **1641** BP. MOUNTAGU *Acts & Mon.* (1642) 93 In the Law-maker and the Law-dispenser, doing their duties, consists the life and livelihood of any State. **1641** *Relat. Answ. Earl Strafford* 3 The Lieutenant.. spake .. with such a measure of Eloquence and Lively-hood, that his very Enemies were affected with it. **1646** J. GREGORY *Notes & Obs.* (1650) 32 The first judged of the Livleyhood and duration.. of the City.

live-like: see LIFE-LIKE and LIVE *a.* 9.

livelily ('laɪvlɪlɪ), *adv.* [f. LIVELY *a.* + -LY[2].] In a lively manner (see the senses of LIVELY *a.*). Briskly, vigorously; keenly; vividly, impressively.

1558 KNOX *Baptism* Sel. Writ. (1845) 253 The promises of Salvation in Christ Jesus are not in the papistical baptism livelily and truly explained to the people. **1634–5** BRERETON *Trav.* (Chetham Soc.) 57 Pictures made in wax most livelyly of the Infanta. **1646** H. LAWRENCE *Comm. Angells* 59 Let them walke livelily and cheerefully. **1697** tr. *C'tess D'Aunoy's Trav.* (1706) 28 Least he should.. appear livelily toucht with the Reproach she made him. **1709** S. SEWALL *Diary* 13 July (1879) II. 258, I found the Deal-Box of Wafers all afire, burning livelily. **1751** ELIZA HEYWOOD *Betsy Thoughtless* III. 132 Those distractions, which her letters to him had so livelily represented. **1825** LAMB *Elia* Ser. II. *Superann. Man*, Livelily expressing the hollowness of a day's pleasuring. *a* **1834** COLERIDGE in *Lit. Rem.* (1836) II. 116 Truths, which it seems almost impossible that any mind should so distinctly, so livelily, and so voluntarily, have presented to itself. **1845** E. WARBURTON *Crescent & Cross* I. 12 [They] bound over the depths of ocean as livelily as if they were all tritons and sea-nymphs. **1865** *Athenæum* No. 1944. 132/1 A fourth, who is livelily talking.

liveliness ('laɪvlɪnɪs). [f. LIVELY *a.* + -NESS.] The quality of being lively (see the senses of LIVELY *a.*); †vitality (*obs.*), activity, vigour, animation, vivacity, vividness.

1398 TREVISA *Barth. De P.R.* III. xvii. (1495) 63 The syȝte hath the name of vivacitas, that is lyflyness. *c* **1440** *Promp. Parv.* 308/2 Levelyheede, or qwyknesse (*MS. K.* lyflines), *vivacitas*. **1545** RAYNOLD *Byrth Mankynde* 139 Ouer muche aboundance of water.. extynguyssheth the lyuelynesse & the naturall power of the grayne and sede. **1584** COGAN *Haven Health* ccxiii. (1636) 224 The Emperour [asked] by what meanes he.. reteined still the vigour or live-linesse of body and minde. **1630** PRYNNE *Anti-Armin.* 82 In present readinesse and liuelinesse of wit he excelled all the men in Europe. **1658** CAPEL *Rem.* To Rdr. §3 The live-linesse of his prayers. **1684** *Contempl. State Man* II. viii. (1699) 212 The Imagination.. encreasing the pains of the Senses, by the liveliness of its Apprehension. **1708** C. MATHER in *New Eng. Hist. & Gen. Reg.* (1879) XXXIII. 186 He continued unto the Ninety Fourth year of his Age, an unusual Instance of Liveliness. **1713** STEELE *Guardian* No. 10 ¶2 Any.. part of her head-dress, which by its darkness or liveliness might too much allay or brighten her complexion. **1727** BRADLEY *Fam. Dict.* s.v. *Florist*, It will be the best way to put 'em all together into Earth, this will preserve their Livelyness. **1736** BAILEY *Househ. Dict.* 12 When the briskness and liveliness of malt liquors in the cask fails.. let them be drawn off and bottled up. **1831** *Society* I. 254 Probably we are indebted to the liveliness of his imagination for the whole cream of the story. **1855** MACAULAY *Hist. Eng.* xiv. III. 457 The perspicuity and liveliness of his [Sherlock's] style have been praised by Prior and Addison. **1875** JOWETT *Plato* (ed. 2) V. 12 There is little of the liveliness of a game in their mode of treating the subject. **1885** DUNCKLEY in *Manch. Exam.* 2 Mar. 6/1 If she [Russia] wishes to exhibit any liveliness it must be at a safe distance from their frontiers.

livelong, live-long ('lɪvlɒŋ), *sb.* Also 6–7 lib-, lyblong. [f. LIVE *v.* + LONG *adv.*] Used as the name of certain plants. Cf. *live-for-ever* (LIVE *v.*[1] 14) and LIFE-EVERLASTING.

1. *Sedum Telephium*, ORPINE.

1578 LYTE *Dodoens* I. xxxi. 43 Like the roote of Orpyn or Lyblong. **1579** LANGHAM *Gard. Health* (1633) 455 Orpin or Liuelong, hath the nature and vertue of Houseleek. **1597** GERARDE *Herbal* II. cxxxviii. 417 In English Orpyne; also Liblong, or Liuelong. **1640** PARKINSON *Theatr. Bot.* 726 In English Orpine, and of some Livelong, because a branch of the greene leaves hung up in any place will keepe the verdure a long time. **1760** J. LEE *Introd. Bot.* App. 317 Live-long. *Sedum.* **1861** MISS PRATT *Flower. Pl.* II. 325.

†**2.** American Cudweed, *Antennaria margaritacea.*

1597 GERARDE *Herbal* II. cxcv. 517 Wherefore our English women haue called it [*Gnaphalium*] Liuelong, or Liue for euer, which name doth aptly answer his effects. **1656** PARKINSON *Parad.* 375 The Live-long was brought out of the West-Indies, and groweth plentifully in our Gardens.

livelong ('lɪvlɒŋ), *a. poet.* and *rhetorical.* Forms: 5 lefe, leve longe, 6 leeue long, 6– livelong, 8–9 *Sc.* lee-lang. [Originally two words = LIEF *a.* and LONG *a.*; cf. the corresponding use in G. *die liebe lange nacht* (lit. 'the dear long night'): see Grimm s.v. *Lieb.* In the latter part of the 16th c. the word was apprehended as if f. LIVE *v.* + LONG *a.*, and altered in form in accordance with this view.]

1. An emotional intensive of *long*, used of periods of time. Chiefly in ***the livelong day, night.***

c **1400** *Sowdone Bab.* 832 Thus thai hurteled to-gedere Alle the lefe longe daye. *c* **1450** LONELICH *Grail* xxxix. 319 Al that leve longe Nyht Into the Se he loked forth Ryht. *c* **1575** LANEHAM *Let.* (1871) 61 Thus haue I told ye most of my trade, al the leeue long daye. **1597** BP. HALL *Sat.* III. vii. 65 He touch't no meat of all this liue-long day. **1602** *2nd Pt. Return fr. Parnass.* III. v. 1462 Where dreary owles do shrike the liue-long night. **1672** MARVELL *Reh. Transp.* I. 263 For though it seems so little a time.. it hath been a whole live-long night. **1709** STEELE *Tatler* No. 2 ¶2 Here I sit moping all the live-long Night. **1758** JOHNSON *Idler* No. 9 ¶4 Vacant of thought.. I indulge the live-long day. **1786** BURNS *Twa Dogs* 295 Or lee-lang nights, wi crabbit leuks, Pore owre the devil's pictur'd beuks. **1787** MAD. D'ARBLAY *Diary* June, This was the last day of freedom for the whole livelong summer. **1806** J. GRAHAME *Birds Scot.* 77 The live long summer day She at the house end sits. **1829** HOGG *Sheph. Cal.* I. 25 He watched there the lee-lang night. **1847** EMERSON *Poems, Good-bye* Wks. (Bohn) I. 416 Where arches green, the live-long day, Echo the blackbird's roundelay. **1870** BRYANT *Iliad* I. II. 35 It ill becomes a chief To sleep the livelong night.

¶**b.** Used by Burns in transposed form.

179. BURNS *Mother's Lament*, So I, for my lost darling's sake, Lament the live-day long.

2. *nonce-use.* That lives long or endures; lasting.

1630 MILTON *On Shakespeare* 8 Thou in our wonder and astonishment Hast built thy self a live-long monument.

¶**3.** Taken as = LIFELONG. (Prob. meant to be pronounced (laɪv-).)

1882 FREEMAN *Reign Will. Rufus* II. vii. 453 He lived.. to meet with a heavy doom, live-long bonds,.. at the hands of his offended cousin and sovereign.

lively ('laɪvlɪ), *a.* Forms: 1 líflic, 3 livelich, 4 life-, liif-, livelich(e, -lyche, 4–6 lif(e-, lyf(e)ly, (6 lyvelycke), 6 live-, lyvelie, -lye, 4– lively. *Comp.* 5 liveloker. [OE. *líflic*, f. *líf* life + *-lic* -LY[1] = OHG. *líblîch*, ON. *lífligr*.]

†**1.** Possessed of life; living, animate; = ALIVE 1, LIVE *a.* 1, LIVING. *Obs.*

c **1000** ÆLFRIC *Hom.* I. 358 He.. wæs.. his Fæder liflic onsægednys on lambes wisan ȝeoffrod. **1430–40** LYDG. *Bochas* (1554) 124 Death assaileth euery liuely thing. **1521** FISHER *Serm. agst. Luther* Wks. (1876) 338 Thou arte christ the sone of the lyuely god. **1534** MORE *On the Passion* Wks. 1334/2 Many lyuelye members in the vnitye of Christes mysticall bodye. **1567** MAPLET *Gr. Forest* 14 The Lodestone.. draweth Iron to it.. The common people therefore.. haue iudged.. yͤ Iron liuely. **1582** BENTLEY *Mon. Matrones* II. 14 It hath pleased thee to humble thy selfe.. in making thy selfe a liuelie man. **1588** SHAKS. *Tit. A.* III. i. 105 Now I behold thy liuely body so? **1601** HOLLAND *Pliny* I. 4 All liuely creatures else [*sc.* other than man] take care onely for their food. *a* **1628** SIR J. BEAUMONT *Bosworth F.* 106 The holy King then offered to his View A lively Tree, on which three Branches grew. **1628** T. SPENCER *Logick* 207 He hath a bodie made lively by his soule. **1638** A. READ *Chirurg.* xxi. 155 The colour of a lively bone is of a whitish colour, mingled with a lively ruddiness.

fig. **1547** *Homilies* I. *Faith* II. (1859) 39 There bee two kinds of faith; a dead and unfruitfull fayth; and a fayth lively.

†**b.** In various transferred applications of L. *vivus*: = LIVE *a.* 3, 5, LIVING. *Obs.*

a **1000** *Ags. Hymnarium* (Surtees) 92 Wyll líflic. *c* **1000** ÆLFRIC *Hom.* II. 202 Ic eom se liflica hlaf, þe of heofenum astah. **1526** *Pilgr. Perf.* (W. de W. 1531) 232, I am yͤ lyuely breed that descended from heuen. **1548** UDALL, etc. *Erasm. Par. Matt.* v. 36 To thurst for that lively water. **1581** PETTIE *Guazzo's Civ. Conv.* I. (1586) 16 b, And as a dead coale, layed to a liuelie, kindleth. **1607** NORDEN *Surv. Dial.* III. 85 And these springs I like well. For a house without liuely water is maymed. **1609** W. BIDDULPH in *Lavender's Trav.* (1612) 30 His house.. being hewed out of the liuely rocke. *c* **1610** *Women Saints* 80 Where she was killed there sprong a lyuelie fountayne. **1632** MASSINGER & FIELD *Fatal Dowry* II. i. D 2 See, the young sonne interd a liuely graue.

†**c.** Of or pertaining to a living person. Of instruction, etc.: Delivered or imparted *vivâ voce*. (Cf. LIVE *a.* 7, LIVING.) *Obs.*

1561 T. NORTON *Calvin's Inst.* I. 13 They do beleue that it is as verily come from heauen as if they heard the liuely voice of God to speak therein. **1570** DEE *Math. Pref.* 5 They which are not liable to atteine to this without lively teaching. **1582** BENTLEY *Mon. Matrones* II. 13 The liuelie voice of God, rebukinglie tooke me vp. **1611** BIBLE *Acts* vii. 38 This [*sc.* Moses] is he.. who receiued the liuely oracles [λόγια ζῶντα], to giue vnto vs. **1709** MANDEY *Syst. Math., Arith.* 10 The Solution.. is learnt much easier by lively instruction, than by deaf and dumb Letters.

†**2.** Of or pertaining to life; necessary to life, vital. *Obs.*

In this sense the spelling *lifely, lyfely* persisted longer than in the others, owing to association with the sb.

a **1000** *Ags. Hymnarium* (Surtees) 80 Lificum mid þinum ..blode [L. *vivido tuo sanguine*]. *c* **1000** *Basil's Hexameron* xi. (1849) 18 God.. ableow on his ansyne líflicne blæd. *c* **1375** *Sc. Leg. Saints* i. (*Petrus*) 484 Gyf he liffis, he ma spek, and ga, and oþir lifly taknis ma. **1382** WYCLIF *Wisd.* xv. 11 That bleȝ in to hym a lifli spirit. **1387–8** T. USK *Test. Love* Prol. (Skeat) l. 121 Utterly these thinges be no dremes ne iapes, to throwe to hogges, it is lyfelych meate for children of trouth. *a* **1420** HOCCLEVE *De Reg. Princ.* 3252 For verray cold, His lyfly myght he loren hadde at moost. **1528** PAYNEL *Salerne's Regim.* (1535) 36 a, Yͤ lifely spirites that procede from the brayne to the other membres. **1530** RASTELL *Bk. Purgat.* II. ii, The soule is no nother thynge but a lyfely power. **1568** GRAFTON *Chron.* II. 755 With a.. maladie.. so grievously taken, that his lively spirites began to faile. *c* **1570** GRINDAL *Dial.* in Foxe *A. & M.* (1583) II. 1390 Turkes, Iewes, and heathen be dead, because they lack yͤ liuely foode of the soule. *c* **1592** MARLOWE *Jew of Malta* III. (1633) F 1 b, Oh that my sighs could turne to liuely breath. **1640** DYKE *Worthy Commun.* Ep. to Rdr., A branch.. hath all lively sap and moisture.. from the root and stocke.

fig. *c* **1380** WYCLIF *Sel. Wks.* III. 265 Spiritual swerdis and lyflyche word of oure God. **1542–5** BRINKLOW *Lament.* (1874) 79 The greate parte of these.. Cytezens will not haue in their howses that lyuely worde of our soules. *c* **1570** GRINDAL *Dial.* in Foxe *A. & M.* (1583) II. 1388 So violently to tread downe the liuely worde of God.

3. Of an image, picture, etc.: Life-like, animated, vivid. (In later use associated with 4 c.)

c **1320** *Sir Tristr.* 2845 So liifliche weren þai alle Ymages semed it nouȝt, To abide. **1568** SKINNER tr. *Montanus' Inquisition* 3 b, But they draw his counterfaite as liuely as may be. **1590** SPENSER *F.Q.* II. ix. 2 Full lively is the semblaunt, though the substance dead. **1604** DEKKER *Kings' Entert.* Wks. 1873 I. 292 The countenaunces of the Marchants being so lively that bargaines seeme to come from their lippes. **1631** WEEVER *Anc. Funeral Mon.* 41 The

liuely Statues and stately Monuments in Westminster Abbey. **1703** MAUNDRELL *Journ. Jerus.* (1732) 72 All the Candles were instantly put out, to yield a livelier Image of the occasion. **1712** ADDISON *Spect.* No. 416 ¶5 A Description often gives us more lively Ideas than the Sight of Things themselves. **1755** (*title*) The Expedition of Major General Braddock to Virginia... Being Extracts of Letters .. Together With many little Incidents, giving A lively Idea of the Nature of the Country. **1762–71** H. WALPOLE *Vertue's Anecd. Paint.* (1786) I. 42 The person of Richard II. is still preserved in the most lively manner, in two different pictures. **1817** J. SCOTT *Paris Revisit.* (ed. 4) 163 The most lively pictures have been given of the hasty flights, the crowded roads [etc.]. **1849** MACAULAY *Hist. Eng.* iii. I. 384 Under the reign of Elizabeth, William Harrison gave a lively description of the plenty and comfort of the great hostelries.

4. Full of life.

a. Of persons (occas. of animals), their faculties and actions: Vigorous, energetic, active, brisk.

a **1225** *Ancr. R.* 6 Sum is ȝung & liuelich, & is neode þe bettere warde. **1398** TREVISA *Barth. De P.R.* v. xii. (1495) 118 Mannes eeres meue leest.. but to here they ben moost able and lyuely. **1422** tr. *Secreta Secret., Priv. Priv.* 237 Tho men whych kepyth reysonabill diette.. bene more hole of body,.. more lyueloker [etc.]. **1526** *Pilgr. Perf.* (W. de W. 1531) 158b, Let vs syng.. with a quycke spiryt, open mouth, and lyuely voyce. **1611** BIBLE *Exod.* i. 19 The Hebrew women.. are liuely, and are deliuered ere the midwiues come in vnto them. *c* **1665** MRS. HUTCHINSON *Mem. Col. Hutchinson* (1846) 31 A truer or more lively valour there never was in any man. *a* **1761** LAW *Comf. Weary Pilgr.* (1809) 17 A man.. of lively parts and much candour. **1780** COWPER *Let.* 18 Mar., Wks. (1876) 42 Men of lively imaginations are not often remarkable for solidity of judgment. **1807** CRABBE *Par. Reg.* III. 833 The strong attack subdued his lively powers. **1850** SCORESBY *Cheever's Whalem. Adv.* v. (1859) 71 The mate, if lively, is soon aloft. **1883** GILMOUR *Mongols* xxxii. 368 Goods are transported on carts drawn by lively horses. **1893** *Law Times* XCV. 268/2 A lively discussion is expected.

b. Of feelings, impressions, sensations, memory: Vivid, intense, strong.

1535 COVERDALE *1 Pet.* i. 3 Blessed be God.. which.. hath begotten vs agayne vnto a lyuely hope by the resurreccion of Iesus Christ. *a* **1548** HALL *Chron., Hen. VII*, 4b, That in the same cytie, the memory of kyng Richard his mortall enemy was yet recent and lyvely. **1592** SHAKS. *Ven. & Ad.* 498 But now I dy'de, and death was liuely ioy. **1660** JER. TAYLOR *Worthy Commun.* II. ii. 131 If we.. pray that we may have lively relish and appetite to the mysteries, it may be well in time. **1734** tr. *Rollin's Anc. Hist.* IV. IX. 297 However lively the father's affliction might be. **1769** ROBERTSON *Chas. V*, III. Wks. 1813 V. 331 The remembrance of their ancient rivalship and hostilities was still lively. **1788** V. KNOX *Winter Even.* III. VII. ii. 11 They are guided too implicitly by their lively sensations. **1816** T. L. PEACOCK *Headlong Hall* xi, In the habit of.. anticipating with the most lively satisfaction. **1821** CRAIG *Lect. Drawing* i. 55 Those impressions are the most lively which are conveyed to the mind in the shortest space of time. **1823** F. CLISSOLD *Ascent Mt. Blanc* 17 The state of the weather excited the liveliest hopes of success. **1859** MILL *Liberty* ii. 33 The clearer perception and livelier impression of truth. **1865** M. ARNOLD *Ess. Crit.* i. 44 An intimate and lively consciousness of the truth of what one is saying. **1873** HAMERTON *Intell. Life* VII. vii. (1875) 261 Taking a lively interest in the small events around them. **1876** GROTE *Eth. Fragm.* iv. 101 A source of the liveliest fear. **1895** ZANGWILL *Master* II. viii. 220 'My dear young ——', she began, in accents of lively affection.

c. Of evidence, illustrations, expressions: Vivid or forcible in effect, convincing, striking, telling.

1604 E. G[RIMSTONE] *D'Acosta's Hist. Indies* v. v. 343 They shew the Indians their blind errors, by lively and plaine reasons. **1647** CLARENDON *Hist. Reb.* III. §49 He could not give a more lively and demonstrable evidence. **1657** R. LIGON *Barbadoes* (1673) 53 A hint of this, I will give you in a lively example. **1713** STEELE *Englishman* No. 41. 265 Example is the liveliest Way of Instruction. **1870** HOWSON *Metaph. St. Paul* iii. 149 A more copious and lively instance of the same kind of illustration. **1875** WHITNEY *Life Lang.* vii. 114 A term becomes.. too directly significant, and we have to devise a new one, less lively.

d. Of physical processes; Active, vigorous, brisk. Of liquor: Brisk, sparkling; opposed to *flat*. Of air: Fresh, invigorating.

1615 MARKHAM *Eng. House-w.* 123 It [beer] may bee drunke at a fortnight's age and will last as long and liuely. **1742** *Lond. & Country Brewer* I. (ed. 4) 66 Its heavy Parts will.. keep it mellow and lively to the last. **1844** KINGLAKE *Eöthen* xvii. (1878) 217 The air.. is much cooler and more lively. **1854** RONALDS & RICHARDSON *Chem. Technol.* (ed. 2) I. 320 Producing a greater amount of heat and a more lively combustion. **1896** A. E. HOUSMAN *Shropshire Lad* lxii, Oh many a peer of England brews Livelier liquor than the Muse.

e. Of a landscape, etc.: Full of bright and interesting objects. Of a narrative, etc.: Full of action and incident.

1697 DRYDEN *Virgil, Life* (1721) I. 68 The liveliest Episode in the whole Æneis. **1756** BURKE *Subl. & B.* II. v Which he has represented in the colours of.. bold and lively poetry. **1839** J. HODGSON in J. Raine *Mem.* (1858) II. 385 To see.. the trees bourgeoning in our lively woods. **1840** DICKENS *Barn. Rudge* xx, It was the liveliest room in the building. **1851** CARLYLE *Sterling* II. vii. (1872) 147 The view from the top is.. remarkably lively and satisfactory. **1883** GILMOUR *Mongols* xxiv. 295 A valley lively with flocks, herds, tents [etc.]. **1887** I. R. *Lady's Ranch Life in Montana* 84 I've been having a pretty lively week of it.

f. In humorously euphemistic use.

1772 FOOTE *Nabob* I. Wks. 1799 II. 290 My Lady's temper's apt to be lively now and then. **1883** *Manch. Guard.* 15 Oct. 5/2 The police had a lively time of it in bundling out the peace-breakers. **1891** *Pall Mall G.* 21 Nov. 2/2 Altogether things are getting lively. **1892** *Law Times* XCII. 197/2 The Press is making things lively for Her Majesty's judges.

†**g.** *humorously.* Of cheese: Teeming with life.

1581 MULCASTER *Positions* xxxix. (1887) 194 Liuely cheese is lusty cheare.

5. Of colour, light, etc.: Vivid, brilliant, fresh.

c **1374** CHAUCER *Boeth.* I. pr. i. 2 (Camb. MS.), I sawh.. a womman.. with a lyfly coloure. **1552** ELYOT *Dict.* s.v. *Color, Floridi colores*, liuely colours. **1593** SHAKS. *Lucr.* 1589 Her liuelie colour kil'd with deadlie cares. **1604** E. G[RIMSTONE] *D'Acosta's Hist. Indies* IV. xv. 251 These oisters within are of the colour of heaven, very lively. **1658** ROWLAND *Moufet's Theat. Ins.* 1013 The green Scarabee.. is of a lively emerald colour. **1711** POPE *Temp. Fame* 252 Bright azure rays from lively sapphyrs stream. *a* **1763** SHENSTONE *Elegies* vii. 19 And livelier far than Tyrian seem'd his vest, That with the glowing purple ting'd the ground. **1810** SCOTT *Lady of L.* I. xiv, And islands that, empurpled bright, Floated amid the livelier light. **1819** G. SAMOUELLE *Entomol. Comp.* 344 Griseus, lively light gray. **1855** MACAULAY *Hist. Eng.* xii. III. 136 The turf is of livelier hue than elsewhere. **1870** ROCK *Text. Fabr.* I. 1 In gold and lively colours.

6. Gay, sprightly, vivacious.

1580 CHURCHYARD (*title*) A light Bondell of liuly discourses called Churchyardes Charge. **1741** MIDDLETON *Cicero* I. vi. 488 A man so lively and entertaining. **1756** J. WARTON *Ess. Pope* (1782) I. ii. 22 Voltaire, in the first volume of his entertaining and lively Essay on General History. **1778** MISS BURNEY *Evelina* (1791) II. xxxi. 191 Never did I see him more lively or more agreeable. **1781** GIBBON *Decl. & F.* xxx. III. 187 He had compared, in a lively epigram, the opposite characters of two Prætorian præfects of Italy. **1790** COWPER *Let.* 7 July *Wks.* (1876) 334 The French.. like all lively folks are extreme in every thing. **1798** FERRIAR *Illustr. Sterne* ii. 31 Sterne even condescended to adopt some of those lively extravagancies. **1838** LYTTON *Alice* 131 But your manner is livelier and younger. **1868** MISS YONGE *Cameos* I. xvi. 124 He was lively in conversation. **1885** *Pall Mall Budget* 19 June 31/1 His account of the *America* is lively reading and will appear very seasonably.

7. *Naut.* Of a vessel: Capable of rising lightly to the sea.

1697 DAMPIER *Voy.* I. 498 We found our Vessel lively enough with that small sail which was then aboard. **1793** SMEATON *Edystone L.* §170 To render them very floaty and lively in a rough hollow sea. **1897** *Daily News* 11 Dec. 8/3 In the sense, therefore, that she rides the waves instead of labouring through them, the Cambria might be described as a lively ship.

8. quasi-*sb.* *colloq.*

1889 CLARK RUSSELL *Marooned* (1890) 171 'Time from me, my livelies!' cried Mole.

9. *Comb.*, as ***lively-foliaged***, ***-looking*** adjs.

1809 MALKIN *Gil Blas* VII. ix. (Rtldg.) 3 He drew from his pocket a phial full of a lively-looking red liquor. **1836** MACGILLIVRAY tr. *Humboldt's Trav.* xxiv. 362 Lively-foliaged poplars generally shadowed their extremities.

lively ('laɪvlɪ), *adv.* Now *rare.* Forms: 1 **líflíce**, 4 **lyfly**, 4–6 **lifly**, (5 **liyfly**, **lyfely**), 5–6 **lyvely**, (5 **lievlie**, **lyvele**), 6 **livelie**, 8 *Sc.* **lyflie**, 6– **lively**. [OE. *líflíce*, f. *líf* LIFE + *-líce* -LY^2.]

†**1.** (OE. only.) So as to impart life.

c **1000** ÆLFRIC *Hom.* II. 244 He ȝenam ða hlaf and hine líflíce ȝehalȝode.

†**2.** As a living person or thing. *Obs.*

1398 TREVISA *Barth. De P.R.* II. xviii. (1495) 44 Though an angel take a body for euery nedefull doyng he may take it Not lyfly, neyther gyuyth therto lyfe. **1590** SPENSER *F.Q.* III. i. 38 A dainty flowre.. Which in that cloth was wrought, as if it lively grew.

3. With animation, actively, briskly, nimbly, vigorously.

c **1400** *Destr. Troy* 2997 There light þai full lyfely, lept into bote. *c* **1450** *Merlin* 355 He lept vp on foote as lifly as he hadde noon harme ne dissese. ? *a* **1500** *Mankind* (Brandl) 41/73 Leppe a-bout lyuely, þou art a wyght man. **1553** BRENDE *Q. Curtius* R viij, Beinge .Lxx. yeares of age, [he] executed the office of a capitaine as lively as though he had bene younge in yeares. **1613** HAYWARD *Norm. Kings, Will. I*, 9 The Normans did liuely charge vpon them in head. **1643** CROMWELL *Let.* 6 Aug. in A. Kingston *East Angl. & Civ. War* (1897) 121 You must act lively; do it without distraction. **1664** POWER *Exp. Philos.* 4 If you divide the Bee .. you shall.. see the heart beat most lively. **1699** SALMON *Bate's Dispens.* (1713) 276/2 It will.. make the Medicine work more lively and briskly. **1883** G. H. BOUGHTON in *Harper's Mag.* Feb. 402/2 We found that it was going on a little livelier than ever.

†**b.** Feelingly; (touched) to the quick. *Obs.*

1579 TOMSON *Calvin's Serm. Tim.* 79/1 The examples.. ought to make vs feele it liuely, and to the quicke. **1625** *Gonsalvio's Sp. Inquis.* 197 Making him.. liuely to lament his owne filthinesse and abomination. **1651** tr. *De-las-Coveras' Don Fenise* 33 Don Louis.. was so lively touched with compassion.. that [etc.]. **1653** *Nissena* 86 She was so lively imprest with what she had heard. *a* **1758** RAMSAY *Some of the Contents* vii, How lyflie he and amorous Stuart sing!

†**c.** Promptly; at once; = BELIVELY. *Obs.*

c **1400** *Destr. Troy* 372 [He] led hom furthe lyuely into a large halle. *Ibid.* 4355 And so the ledis of the lond lyuely hym cald. *Ibid.* 5447 Out of Lyce come lyuele þe lege kyng Glaucon.

4. In a life-like manner; vividly, 'to the life'. Very frequent in the 17th century. ? *Obs.*

c **1386** CHAUCER *Knt.'s T.* 1229 Wel koude he peynten lifly that it wroghte. **1559** BP. SCOT in Strype *Ann. Ref.* I. App. vii. 18 Who so redith the third chapter of the second epistle of St. Paul to Tymothie, may see them there lively described. **1598** F. MERES *Palladis Tamia* 287 Apelles painted a Mare and Dogge so liuelie, that Horses and Dogges passing by woulde neigh and barke at them. **1604** DEKKER *Kings' Entert.* Wks. 1873 I. 293 In a large Table.. is their fishing and shipping lively and sweetely set downe. **1615** T. ADAMS *Spiritual Navig.* 6 This glasse lively represents to us ourselves and our Saviour. **1631** WEEVER *Anc. Funeral Mon.* 14 The funeralls of Misenus, most liuely thus expressed. **1659** EVELYN *Diary* (1827) II. 143 A sheete of paper, on which was very liuely painted ye thing in miniature. **1682** H. MORE *Annot. Glanvill's Lux O.* 30 Meeting with nothing.. that lively resembles these things in our former state. **1687** BURNET *Trav.* i. (1750) 39 The Image also seemed to shed tears; and a Painter had drawn those on her Face so lively, that the People were deceived by it. **1726** *Life of Penn* in *Wks.* I. 28 What Game such Persons play at, may be lively read in the attempts of Dionysius, &c. **1775** S. J. PRATT *Liberal Opin.* lxx. (1783) III. 22 He [Draper] painted himself.. much livelier.. than it was in the power of any other person to depict him.

†**b.** Clearly, plainly. *Obs.*

1548 UDALL *Erasm. Par.* Pref. 17 And liuely to know the ungodly maligners. **1570–6** LAMBARDE *Peramb. Kent* (1826) 171 She seemed.. most liuely to beholde.. with hir eie. **1601** R. JOHNSON *Kingd. & Commw.* (1603) 144 The wisedome of a prince is not livelier discerned, then [etc.]. **1625** GILL *Sacr. Philos.* I. 107 The shape of a man cannot bee more lively seene in a looking glasse, than [etc.]. **1634** CANNE *Necess. Separ.* (1849) 14 The Pope's pontifical, wherein he showeth himself to be Antichrist most lively. **1673** PENN *The Chr. a Quaker* v. 533 It had been utterly impossible for divers weighty Things.. to have been known, and said so lively, had they not been seen by the Light.

†**5.** Of a vessel: (Floating) in a lively manner. (Cf. LIVELY *a.* 7.) *Obs.*

1793 SMEATON *Edystone L.* §171 Remarkably full in their bows; which.. enabled them to float much more lively upon the surface.

6. *Comb.*, as ***lively-expressed***; ***lively-daring***, ***-shining***, ***-skipping***, ***-speaking***, ***-thriving*** adjs.

1622 DRAYTON *Poly-olb.* xxii. 962 The *liuely daring French. **1577** tr. *Bullinger's Decades* (1592) 2 Gods will, first of all vttered in a *liuely expressed voice by the mouth of Christ. **1727–46** THOMSON *Summer* 918 The *lively-shining leopard, speckled o'er With many a spot. **1612** DRAYTON *Poly-olb.* v. 123 The *liuelie skipping Brane along with Gwethrick goes. **1607** TOPSELL *Four-f. Beasts* (1658) 112 Giving as ready obedience.. as they can to any *lively speaking prince of the world. **1618** W. LAWSON *New Orch. & Gard.* (1623) 32 You shall haue for one *liuely thriuing tree, foure.. euill thriuing, rotten and dying trees.

liven ('laɪv(ə)n), *v. colloq.* [f. LIFE + -EN^5. Cf. ENLIVEN.] **a.** *trans.* To put life into; to brighten, cheer. Also with *up*. **b.** *intr.* To grow lively, to brighten; in quot. with *up*.

1884 *Manch. Exam.* 26 Nov. 8/1 Matters will liven up a bit during the day. **1897** J. H. CRAWFORD *Wild Flowers Scot.* Introd. 13 A few typical forms in a natural setting, livened by some incident.. in which I shared.

Hence '**livener**, something that enlivens; *spec.* a drink of beer or spirits; a 'pick-me-up'.

1887 *Pall Mall G.* 2 Aug. 13/2, I think he would want a livener before the time had expired. **1895** *Daily News* 4 Jan. 3/7 He could not get out of bed unless he had two or three 'liveners'.

liven, variant of LEVE *v.*^{2} *Obs.*

†**livenath.** *Obs.* Also 3 **liveneð**, **-oðe**, 4 **lyfnoþ**. [a. ON. *lífnað-r* (only in the sense 'conduct of life') f. root of LIVE *v.*^{1}] Food, means of living.

c **1175** *Lamb. Hom.* 63 Gif us ure livenað. *c* **1220** *Bestiary* 275 Ðe mire muneð us mete to tilen, Long liuenoðe. *c* **1230** *Hali Meid.* 29 Lutel þarf þe carien for þin anes liueneð. **1340** *Ayenb.* 138 He.. ham poruayþ.. have lyfnoþ zuetliche and mid guod savour.

liveness ('laɪvnɪs). [f. LIVE *a.* + -NESS.] The quality or condition of being 'live'. Also *attrib.*

1890 *Sat. Rev.* 22 Mar. 357/2 The 'liveness' of the New Scholarship. **1926** N. M. GUNN *Grey Coast* ii. 21 That liveness of the body with its whirl and suppressed gaiety. **1931** L. COWAN *Recording Sound for Motion Pict.* xviii. 261 (*heading*) Liveness of sets. **1940** *Scrutiny* IX. 94 A translator of Mr. Archer's liveness of interest and taste. **1961** *Jrnl. Acoustical Soc. America* May 604 Liveness effects on the intelligibility of noise-masked speech.

livening ('laɪv(ə)nɪŋ), *ppl. a.* [f. LIVEN *v.* + -ING^2.] **a.** That enlivens or cheers; cheering. **b.** That grows lively or bright.

1705 ELSTOB in Hearne *Collect.* 30 Nov. (O.H.S.) I. 107 Help'd by ye livening Virtue of ye Sun. **1866** BLACKMORE *Cradock Nowell* i. (1873) 2 The blackcocks lift their necks in the livening heather.

live-oak ('laɪv'əʊk). [LIVE *a.*] An American evergreen tree (*Quercus virens*) growing in the southern Atlantic States. The name is applied to some other species in the Pacific States.

The second quotation probably refers to the Ilex.

1610 *True Declar. Col. Virginia* (1844) 22 Ashe, Sarsafrase, liue Oake, greene all the yeare, Cedar and Firre. **1671** tr. *Frejus' Voy. Mauritania* 43 Mountains, whose tops in crossing we found also covered.. with live-Oaks, (which are green all the year,) and wild Pines. **1770** COOK *Jrnl.* 6 May (Wharton 1893) 248 The wood of this is hard and Ponderous, and something of the Nature of America [*sic*] live Oak. **1841** CATLIN *N. Amer. Ind.* (1844) II. xxxvi. 32 The ever-green live oak and lofty magnolia dress the forest in a perpetual mantle of green. **1862** S. L. J. *Life in South* (1863) II. xvi. 306 Valuable timber, such as live oak. **1883** STEVENSON *Treas. Isl.* III. xiv, I crawled under cover of the nearest live-oak.

attrib. **1792** *Descr. Kentucky* 51 The American live-oak and cedar ships cost from 33 to 35 dollars [a ton]. **1863** T. W. HIGGINSON *Army Life* (1870) 40 The great live-oak branches, and their trailing moss.

liver ('lɪvə(r)), *sb.*^{1} Forms: 1 **lifer**, 3–4 **livre**, 3–5 **livere**, **lyvre**, 4 **lyvour**, 4–5 **lyvere**, 4–6 **lyver**, 5

levir, -yr, lyffere, lyvir, -yr, lywer, 5–6 lever, 6 *Sc.* liffyr, luffer, 7 livour, 1, 4– liver. [OE. *lifer* fem. = MDu. *lēver, lēvere* (Du. *lever*), OHG. *libara, lebara, lebera, lepera* (MHG. *leber, lebere*, G. *leber*), ON. *lifr* (Sw. *lefver*, Da. *lever*):—OTeut. **librâ*, ? cogn. w. Armenian *leard*.

Some scholars regard the Teut. word as cogn. w. the Aryan **yeqṛt* (Skr. *yakrt*, Gr. *ἧπαρ*, L. *jecur*), the root being supposed to be **liq*- (:**lyēq*-); but the supposition involves serious difficulties.]

1. a. A large glandular organ in vertebrate animals, serving chiefly to secrete bile and to purify the venous blood. Also in generalized sense, the flesh of a liver or livers, *e.g.* used as food.

In the warm-blooded animals the liver is usually of a dark reddish-brown colour. In man it is situated below the diaphragm, and is divided by fissures into five lobes.

c **888** K. ÆLFRED *Boeth.* xxxv. §6 [7] And se Uultor sceolde forlætan þæt he ne slat þa lifre Tyties [*MSS.* Sticces, Ticcies] ðæs cyninges. *a* **900** *Kentish Glosses* in Wr.-Wülcker 61/33 *Iecor eius*, his lifere. *c* **1205** LAY. 6499 þat deor..forbat him þa breste ban and þa senuwen þat þa lihte and þa liuere feollen on eorðen. *c* **1290** *S.E. Leg.* I. 320/738 In þe Neþemeste bolle þat þe liuere deoth of springue, þare comez o-manere soule. **13..** *K. Alis.* 2156 Alisaundre hutte him, certe, Thorugh livre, and longe, and heorte. *c* **1386** CHAUCER *Sompn. T.* 131 Have I nat of a capon but the livere. *c* **1400** *Lanfranc's Cirurg.* 27 þilke chylum spredeþ þorwe al þe lyffere by mene of veynes Capillares. *c* **1420** *Liber Cocorum* (1862) 41 Take lyver of porke and kerve hit smalle. *c* **1460** *Towneley Myst.* iii. 399 Me thynk my hert ryfis both levyr and long, To se sich stryfis wedmen emong. **1530** LYNDESAY *Test. Papyngo* 1124 ȝe thre my trypes sall haue, for ȝour trauell, With luffer and lowng. **1598** *Epulario* H iv b, To make a Tart of the liuer of fishes. **1606** SHAKS. *Tr. & Cr.* v. iii. 19 They are polluted offrings, more abhord Then spotted Liuers in the sacrifice. **1667** MILTON *P.L.* VI. 346 Spirits that live throughout Vital in every part, not as frail man In Entrailes, Heart or Head, Liver or Reines. **1717** PRIOR *Alma* I. 440 The liver..parts and strains the vital juices. **1771** GOLDSM. *Haunch Venison* 81 A fry'd liver and bacon. **1803** *Med. Jrnl.* X. 1 Abscess of the Liver. **1818** BYRON *Beppo* xcii, I never Saw a man grown so yellow! How's your liver? **1872** HUXLEY *Physiol.* v. 117 The liver is the largest glandular organ in the body, ordinarily weighing about 50, or 60 ounces.

b. Applied to analogous glandular organs or tissues in invertebrates.

1841–71 T. R. JONES *Anim. Kingd.* (ed. 4) 588 The liver is proportionally of very large size in the Mollusca we are now describing. **1861** J. R. GREENE *Man. Anim. Kingd.*, *Cœlent.* 106 Within the roof of the latter [polypite]..is lodged a peculiar brownish mass, the so-called liver.

c. Palmistry. ***line of the liver***: the line which stretches from the wrist (near the 'line of life') to the base of the little finger.

1653 R. SANDERS *Physiogn.* xv. 50 Of the Line of the Liver, or the Hepatique. *Ibid.*, When this line of the Liver is winding up and down, and waving, it signifies Theft, evill Conscience.

2. *fig.* and *allusive.* **a.** Formerly often mentioned *fig.* with allusion to its importance as a vital organ of the body (coupled with *brain* and *heart*); also with allusion to the ancient notion that it was the seat of love and of violent passion generally. (Now only *arch.*) **b.** A *white liver* is spoken of as characterizing a coward: cf. *white-livered.*

1390 GOWER *Conf.* III. 100 The livere makth him forto love. **1593** SHAKS. *Lucr.* 47 To quench the coale which in his liuer glowes. **1596** —— *Merch. V.* III. ii. 86 How manie cowards..Who inward searcht, haue lyuers white as milke. **1599** —— *Much Ado* IV. i. 233. **1601** —— *Twel. N.* I. i. 37. **1602** *Narcissus* (1893) 703 That greives my liver most. **1606** *Sir G. Goosecappe* I. iv. in Bullen *O. Pl.* III. 24 Because I am all liver, and turn'd lover. *Ibid.* II. i. 37 Their livers were too hot,.. and for temper sake they must needs have a cooling carde plaid upon them. **1611** SHAKS. *Cymb.* v. v. 15 To you (the Liuer, Heart, and Braine of Britaine) By whom (I grant) she liues. **1612** CHAPMAN *Widow's Tears* v. Dram. Wks. 1873 III. 66 It will be such a cooler To my Venerean Gentleman's hot liuer. **1623** WEBSTER *Duchess of Malfi* II. iii. E 2 b, By him I'll send A Letter, that shall make her brothers Galls Ore-flowe their Liuours. **1651** N. BACON *Disc. Govt. Eng.* II. xvi. (1739) 84 The Mint is the very Liver of the Nation, and was wont to be the chief Care of the Parliament. **1697** DRYDEN *Virg. Georg.* III. 404 When Love's unerring Dart Transfixt his Liver, and inflam'd his Heart. *a* **1859** MACAULAY *Hist. Eng.* xxv. (1861) V. 304 [an. 1701] In every market place..papers about the brazen forehead..and the white liver of Jack Howe, the French King's buffoon, flew about. **1897** MARY KINGSLEY *W. Africa* 734 He was a great hunter, and his liver grew hot in him for the bush.

†**c.** Disposition, temperament, 'kidney'. *rare.*

1800 *Spirit Public Jrnls.* (1801) IV. 182 John Bull will solemnly and dully sit down to his pipe and bowl with a fellow of the same serious liver.

3. A diseased or disordered condition of the liver; liver-complaint. Also, with qualification specifying the disease, as ***bronze, cirrhotic, hobnailed liver.***

1805 J. LEYDEN in *Scott's Prose Wks.* IV. *Biographies* II. (1870) 179, I had a most terrible attack of the liver. **1826** JEKYLL *Corr. w. Lady Stanley* (1894) 165 Lord Wycombe was dying of liver and dropsy. **1839** *Penny Cycl.* XIV. 60/2 The 'fatty liver' is a frequent attendant on pulmonary phthisis. **1871** SIR T. WATSON *Princ. & Pract. Physic* (ed. 5) II. 670 What used to be called the 'nutmeggy' liver, is simply the result of congestion of its blood-vessels. **1884** A. FORBES *Chinese Gordon* iii. 148 He suffered from ague for the first time since boyhood, and later came liver. **1898** P. MANSON *Trop. Diseases* xxvi. 390 Dyspeptic troubles.. usually attributed to 'liver'.

4. In old chemical terminology applied (tr. L. *hepar*) to certain liver-coloured substances, e.g. metallic sulphides, and compounds of a metal or of sulphur with an 'alkali'.

1694 SALMON *Bate's Dispens.* I. (1699) 436/1 *Hepar Sulphuris*, Liver of Sulphur. **1706** PHILLIPS (ed. Kersey), *Liver of Antimony* (among Chymists), Antimony open'd by Salt-peter and Fire, so as to make it half Glas, and give it a Liver-colour. **1797** *Encycl. Brit.* (ed. 3) X. 104/2 Liver of Arsenic, is a combination of white arsenic with liquid fixed vegetable alkali, or by the humid way. **1799** W. TOOKE *View Russian Emp.* I. 283 Liver-of-sulphate springs; i.e. springs which are impregnated with sulphurate. **1800** tr. *Lagrange's Chem.* I. 174 You fuse together equal parts of sulphur and alkali,..and the result will be a solid mass of a reddish brown colour,..which has a considerable resemblance to the liver of certain animals. It is for this reason that sulphurets have been called Livers. **1876** *Daily Tel.* 27 July 3/5 (E.D.D.) Do you ever use black antimony, or liver of antimony, with any of the horses?

5. *Agric.* 'Livery' soil.

1803 *Annals Agric.* XXXIX. 79 Upon these strong soils, the point..most necessary to attend to is that of avoiding all spring ploughing, which loses a friable surface, and turns up liver.

6. as *adj.* Liver-coloured.

1868 WOOD *Homes without H.* xi. 203 That peculiar brown which is called 'liver' by bird-fanciers. **1892** *Daily News* 31 May 6/1 General D.'s familiar browns [horses] and the chestnuts liver and pale.

7. *attrib.* and *Comb.*, as ***liver abscess, ache, attack, cell, chill, colour, disease, disorder, distome, extract, function, ill, oil, paste, pâté, pudding, pus, trouble; liver-coloured, -helping, hued, rotten, -shaped*** adjs.; **liver-brown** *a.*, of the brown colour of the liver, dark brownish red; **liver-complaining** *a.*, ? complaining of liver disease; **liver-complaint**, disease of the liver; **liver-faced** *a.*, 'mean and cowardly' (Smyth *Sailor's Word-bk.* 1867); **liver-fluke**, a trematoid worm (*Fasicola hepatica*) infesting the liver; †**liver-grown** *a.*, suffering from enlargement of the liver; also, adherent as an enlarged liver (in quot. *fig.*); **liver-hearted** *a.*, cowardly; hence ***liver-heartedness***; †**liver-lap**, a lobe of the liver; †**liver-lask** (see quot.); **liver-leaf** *U.S.*, = LIVERWORT 2; **liver-line**, 'line of the liver' (1 c); **liver money** (see quots.); **liver-opal**, an obsolete synonym of mexilite (Chester *Names Min.* 1896); **liver-ore**, an early name for hepatic cinnabar (*ibid.*); **liver pad**, a pad or plaster to be applied about the region of the liver; †**liver-padding**, ? = *liver-pad*; **liver-pill**, a pill intended to cure disease of the liver; **liver-pyrites**, hepatic pyrites (*Cent. Dict.* 1890); **liver rot**, disease of the liver caused by the liver-fluke; also, a type of anæmia in sheep, cattle, and, occasionally, other animals, caused by the liver fluke; **liver salt**, a powder with purgative properties which is intended to be taken, in solution, for the relief of dyspepsia or a bad 'liver'; usu. short for the proprietary name *Andrews Liver Salt* and used in *pl.*; **liver sausage** [tr. G. *leberwurst*], a soft sausage filled with cooked liver, or a mixture of liver and pork, with various seasonings; cf. LIVERWURST; †**liver-sea**, an imaginary sea in which the water is 'livered' or thick, so as to impede navigation (cf. G. *lebermeer*); **liver-shark**, the basking shark, *Cetorhinus maximus* (Webster 1890); †**liver-shot, -sick** *adjs.*, diseased in the liver; **liver-spot**, 'a popular name for *Chloasma*, or macular pigmentation of the skin; because it was supposed to depend on some disorder of the liver' (*Syd. Soc. Lex.*); also, one of the small brown spots characteristic of this condition; **liver-spotted** *a.*, having liver-coloured spots or liver-spots. **liver-starch** = GLYCOGEN (*Syd. Soc. Lex.*); **liver-stone** = HEPATITE; **liver-sugar**, the sugar derived from glycogen (*Syd. Soc. Lex.*); †**liver-vein**, the basilic vein; also *allusively*, 'the style and manner of men in love' (Schmidt); **liver-weed**, *Hepatica triloba* (Syd. Soc. Lex.); cf. *liver-leaf*; **liver-wing**, the right wing of a fowl, etc. which, when dressed for cooking, has the liver tucked under it; hence *jocularly*, the right arm.

1898 P. MANSON *Trop. Diseases* xxiii. 363, I have many times seen amœbic *liver abscess cases recover completely. *Ibid.* ii. 64 The pain in the loins and the *liver-ache continue. **1897** *Allbutt's Syst. Med.* III. 900 There had been undoubted dyspepsia or a '*liver attack' before the onset of the symptoms. **1794** KIRWAN *Elem. Min.* (ed. 2) I. 30 **Liver brown*—greyish brown. **1849** D. CAMPBELL *Inorg. Chem.* 107 When protosulphide is fused with rather more than its weight of sulphur a liver brown mass is obtained. **1873** T. H. GREEN *Introd. Pathol.* (ed. 2) 273 Atrophy of the *liver-cells. **1897** *Allbutt's Syst. Med.* IV. 46 The vague condition called '*liver-chill' is regarded by some authors as a form of active congestion of the liver. **1686** *Lond. Gaz.* No. 2114/4 A.. Spaniel Bitch,..mark'd all over her body..with specks of *liver-colour. *a* **1728** WOODWARD *Nat. Hist. Fossils* I. (1729) I. 232 A Piece of Iron-Ore, of a dark Liver Colour. **1663** BOYLE *Usef. Exp. Nat. Philos.* II. ii. 166 A clotted and almost *liver-coloured masse. **1810** *Sporting Mag.* XXXV. 261 His ..liver-coloured dog Don. **1787** *Generous Attachment* II. 145 A love writing, love sick, *liver complaining girl. **1809** J. CURRY (*title*) Examination of the prejudices against mercury in *liver complaints. **1867** J. HOGG *Microsc.* II. iii. 563 The excitation of the *liver disease in sheep. **1900** J. HUTCHINSON *Arch. Surg.* XI. No. 41. 2 Foremost amongst the most definite indications of *liver disorder we have the yellow condition of the skin known as Jaundice. **1897** *Allbutt's Syst. Med.* II. 1026 By comparing the figures of these *liver distomes. **1910** MARTINDALE & WESTCOTT *Extra Pharmacopœia* (ed. 14) 820 Early cases of cirrhosis have been well treated with glycerinated *liver extract. **1959** *Brit. Med. Jrnl.* 28 Mar. 833/2 Parenteral liver extracts still enjoy some popularity. **179.** NEMNICH *Polyglotten-Lex.*, **Liver fluke.* Fasciola hepatica. **1836–9** TODD *Cycl. Anat.* II. 121/1 The liver-fluke is extremely rare. **1897** *Allbutt's Syst. Med.* IV. 51 Various general symptoms referable..to disturbances of gastro-intestinal and *liver functions. **1645** MILTON *Tetrach.* Wks. 1851 IV. 159 Unlesse it be the lowest lees of a canonicall infection *liver-grown to their sides. **1658** EVELYN *Mem.* (1857) I. 344, I suffered him to be opened, when they found that he was what is vulgarly called liver-grown. **1748** SMOLLETT *Rod. Rand.* (1812) I. 321 She was only liver-grown and would in a few months be as small in the waist as ever. **1571** GOLDING *Calvin on Ps.* xiii. 1 He complayneth not of the miserie of a fewe dayes, as the tender and *liver-harted sort [L. *pusillanimes*] are wont to doe. **1897** BLACKMORE *Dariel* liii. 468 If thou art too liver-hearted to avenge thy father's wrongs. **1897** O. SCHREINER *Trooper P. Halket* i. 79 'It's not *liver-heartedness', said Peter. **1611** COTGR., *Hepatique*,..*Liuer-helping; comforting a whole, or curing a diseased, liuer. **1678** *Lond. Gaz.* No. 1327/4 White body, with some *liver-hued spots. **1513** DOUGLAS *Æneis* VIII. Prol. 139 Sum langis for the *liffyr ill to lik of ane quart. *a* **1000** *Ags. Voc.* in Wr.-Wülcker 238/30 *Fibra, i. uena, iecoris intestina*, *lifer-læppa. **1596** FITZ GEFFRAY *Sir F. Drake* (1881) 25 Her..turtle-doves,..Whose liver-laps do swell with full-vain'd loves. **1607** TOPSELL *Four-f. Beasts* (1658) 582 The Liver laps of a Wolf. **1597** A. M. tr. *Guillemeau's Fr. Chirurg.* 48/1 The waterye Bloodye flixe is called *Fluxus Hepaticus*, the *Liver laske. **1851** S. JUDD *Margaret* II. i. (1871) 162 *Liver-leaves with cups full of snow-capped threads. **1653** R. SANDERS *Physiogn.* 102 The *Liver line at a distance, and not touching the Vital line. **1935** R. M. *Trawler* 132 Firstly, there is the '*liver-money'. The livers of all fish caught..are taken aft and tried down for the oil they produce... The proceeds of sale are divided among the crew. **1962** J. TUNSTALL *Fishermen* ii. 55 *Liver money*, received for the amount of cod and haddock livers landed. **1875** H. C. WOOD *Therap.* (1879) 407 When a mineral acid..is added to cod-liver oil, the well-known biliary play of colors occurs;..it shows that it is a *liver oil. **1799** G. SMITH *Laboratory* I. 201 The miners find sometimes a matter in the mines they call *liver-ore. **1879** G. W. PECK *Peck's Fun* 38 A boarder at a Leadville hotel investigated his beef-steak and found that it was a fried *liver pad. **1889** *Anthony's Photogr. Bull.* II. 72 Used as a liver pad. **14..** *Voc.* in Wr.-Wülcker 580/16 *Epaticum*, a *lyverpaddyng. *c* **1938** *Fortnum & Mason Price List* 51/1 *Potted meats*..*Liver Paste—per tin 1/-. **1961** M. SPARK *Prime of Miss Jean Brodie* iv. 121 Some sandwiches of liver paste. **1964** S. BELLOW *Herzog* (1965) 70 Cheese, liver paste, crackers. **1935** E. CRAIG *Family Cookery* 50 *Calf's *liver pâté*... Put the liver, uncooked bacon and ham twice or three times through a mincer. **1951** E. DAVID *French Country Cooking* 222 *Liver pâté.* The French Amieux brands are always reliable. **1964** 'J. MELVILLE' *Murderers' Houses* iv. 75 Velia was making a liver pâté for Sunday supper. **1889** J. K. JEROME *Three Men in Boat* 2, I had just been reading a patent *liver-pill circular. **1716** C. LUDWIG *Teutsch-Englisches Lexicon*, *Leberwurst*, a haggass or haggess, a *liver-pudding, a pudding made of liver and lights or lungs. **1723** J. NOTT *Cook's & Confectioner's Dict.* sig. S2ᵛ To make Liver Puddings. Boil a Hog's Liver..; take an equal Quantity of grated Bread, two Pound of Beef-suet. **1887** *Boston Jrnl.* (Mass.) 31 Dec. 2/4 A liver-pudding completed this typical Georgia repast. **1898** P. MANSON *Trop. Diseases* xxiii. 361 The naked-eye appearance of *liver-pus. **1837** YOUATT *Sheep* xi. 452 The river overflows ..The foundation may be laid for foot-rot..but the *liver-rot is out of the question. **1937** A. FRASER *Sheep Farming* xvi. 144 Liver-rot has at one time or another caused tremendous losses among sheep. **1972** *Country Life* 2 Mar. 524/2 In the early 19th century men were still prepared to argue that liver-rot was due to poisonous dew. **1820** COLERIDGE *Lett.* (1895) 707 What avails it..to a man in the last stage of ulcerated lungs, that his neighbour is *liver-rotten as well as consumptive? **1896** *Trade Marks Jrnl.* 10 June 517 Andrews *Liver Salt..purifies & strengthens the whole system... A medicinal preparation for human use. The firm trading as Andrews & Co.,..Newcastle-on-Tyne; manufacturers. **1938** L. MACNEICE *I crossed Minch* x. 140 De Valera's sham industries—putting liver salts into tins. **1951** J. B. PRIESTLEY *Festival at Farbridge* III. iii. 584 The High Street chemist who had sold him shaving soap and liver salts. **1969** M. RUSSELL *Hunt to Kill* II. 116 'I'm fine. Bit of a gut-ache. Too much booze.' 'Get home, take liver-salts.' **1855** GEO. ELIOT in *Fraser's Mag.* June 706/1 He is enthusiastic about the delights of dining on *blaukraut* and *leberwurst* (blue cabbage and *liver sausage). **1868** [see *blood-sausage* (BLOOD *sb.* 21)]. **1965** *House & Garden* Jan. 60 Liver sausage ranges in seasoning from extremely bland to highly spiced and pungent. **1971** *Sunday Times* (Colour Suppl.) 27 June 50/3 Liver sausages are found in every European country. *a* **1600** MONTGOMERIE *Misc. Poems* xlix. 11 The perillous gredy gulfe of Perse, And *levir sees that syndry shippis devoirs. **1942** S. SPENDER *Ruins & Visions* III. 51 A tree..rotted By a *liver-shaped fungus on the bank. **1954** M. RICKERT *Painting in Brit.: Middle Ages* viii. 197 The border.. contains some motifs found earlier in East Anglian manuscripts, as the little round liver- and heart-shaped leaves. **1618** LATHAM *2nd Bk. Falconry* (1633) 7 She [a hawk] is seldome..subiect to be *liuer shot. **1578** LYTE *Dodoens* IV. lviii. 520 The rootes..are good for such as be *liver sicke. **1597** BP. HALL *Sat.* II. vii. 45 Demon my friend once liuer-sicke of loue. **1883** G. HARLEY *Treat. Dis. Liver* xxv. 1061 Among a few practitioners of the old school one hears a good deal about the diagnostic value of what are called *liver-spots. **1964** 'E. MCBAIN' *Axe* vi. 101 He wore a dark black suit and he kept his hands, brown with liver spots, tented in front of his face. **1971** *Physics Bull.* July 410/3 Seborrheic keratosis, commonly called liver spot—a

blemish occurring frequently in the middle aged and aged. **1973** N. GRAHAM *Murder in Dark Room* iv. 24 He had a thin, yellow face dotted with liver spots. **1922** R. LEIGHTON *Compl. Bk. Dog* vi. 86 Prince IV..a *liver-spotted specimen. **1971** V. CANNING *Firecrest* i. 7 Everything about him was contained, precise and impeccable..the fingernails of his liver-spotted hands immaculate. **1975** D. BAGLEY *Snow Tiger* xxiv. 205 Critchell placidly continued to fill his pipe with liver-spotted hands. **1794** KIRWAN *Elem. Min.* (ed. 2) I. 143 *Liverstone. **1861** *New Syd. Soc. Yr.-bk. for 1860*, 88 That *liver sugar is..identical with the sugar of the grape. **1897** *Allbutt's Syst. Med.* II. 430 Signs of *liver-trouble precede..the intestinal disorder. **1528** PAYNEL *Salerne's Regim.* (1535) 105 In Aprile and May, the *lyuer veyne must be lette bloudde. **1588** SHAKS. *L.L.L.* IV. iii. 74 This is the liuer veine, which makes flesh a deity. **1660** CULPEPPER *Two Treat.* (1672) 10 At what time Bleeding is good..In Summer, open still the Liver-vein. *a* **1845** HOOD *United Fam.* xviii, We all prefer the *liver-wing. **1855** BROWNING *De Gustibus* ii, The king Was shot at, touched in the liver-wing. **1861** DICKENS *Gt. Expect.* xix, Mr. Pumblechook helped me to the liver wing.

liver (ˈlɪvə(r)), *sb.*[2] Forms: see LIVE *v.* [f. LIVE *v.* + -ER[1].]

1. One who lives or is alive; a living creature. Now *rare*. Also, an inhabitant, dweller (chiefly *U.S.*).

1377 LANGL. *P. Pl.* B. XII. 132 Lyueres to-forn vs. **1382** WYCLIF *Gen.* iii. 1 The edder was feller than ony lifers of the erthe. **1382** —— *Isa.* xxxviii. 11, I shal not see the Lord God in the lond of lyueres. *c* **1400** *Apol. Loll.* 8 A liuar in þis world. *a* **1533** LD. BERNERS *Gold. Bk. M. Aurel.* (1546) Ff iij b, She that ouercometh all lyuers, shall be vanquished of the alonely by death. **1592** WARNER *Alb. Eng.* VIII. xliii. (1612) 206 When as the wandring Scots and Picthts King Marius had subdude, He gave the Liuers dwellings. **1599** GREENE *Alphonsus* Wks. (Rtldg.) 234 Thou king of heaven, which..Dost see the secret of each livers heart. **1677** CARY *Chronol.* II. ii. III. xiv. 252 They must instantly have been Detected by the present Livers that were upon the Place. **1718** PRIOR *Power* 47 Try if life be worth the liver's care. **1747** in *Col. Rec. Pennsylv.* V. 87 One, John Powle, a Liver on Sasquehanna River. **1817** KEATS '*I stood tiptoe*' 117 Dear delight Of this fair world and all its gentle livers. *a* **1845** HOOD *Stanzas to T. Woodgate* i, Tom;—are you still within this land Of livers? **1863** D. G. MITCHELL *Sev. Stor.*, *My Farm of Edgewood* 289 There is no liver in the country so practical.

b. Qualified by adjs. having advb. force: One who lives (in a specified way, for a long time, etc.).

c **1375** *XI Pains of Hell* 64 in *O.E. Misc.* 212 Cursid leuers with here cumpers. *c* **1386** CHAUCER *Man of Law's T.* 926 So vertuous a lyuere..Ne saugh I neuere as she. **1433** *Rolls of Parlt.* IV. 447/1 Untrewe lyvers, and poeple withoute conscience. **1476** *Paston Lett.* III. 166 The lenger lyver of yow bothe. **1590** SPENSER *F.Q.* II. xii. 6 The damned ghosts doen often creep Backe to the world, bad livers to torment. **1632** LITHGOW *Trav.* x. 429 The Turke, and the Irish-man, are the least industrious, and most sluggish livers vnder the Sunne. *a* **1635** NAUNTON *Fragm. Reg.* (Arb.) 63 As I have placed him last, so was he the last liver of all the Servants of her favour. **1712** SWIFT *Jrnl. to Stella* 28 Apr., The Queen is well, but I fear will be no long liver. **1767** T. HUTCHINSON *Hist. Mass.* II. i. 18 A grave man and a good liver. **1836** W. IRVING *Astoria* III. 197 Though a loose liver among his guests, the governor was a strict disciplinarian among his men. **1896** A. E. HOUSMAN *Shropshire Lad* l, The country for easy livers, The quietest under the sun.

c. [Cf. LIVING *vbl. sb.*] ***good liver***: (*a*) one given to good living; (*b*) *dial.* a well-to-do person.

1602 CAREW *Cornwall* 68 b, The haruest dinners are held by euery wealthy man, or as wee terme it, euery good liuer betweene Michaelmas and Candlemas. **1883** *Cornh. Mag.* Apr. 459 Or it is a group of good-livers round the table of a private house.

2. One who lives a life of pleasure. (Cf. F. *viveur*.)

1852 R. S. SURTEES *Sponge's Sp. Tour* (1893) 133 The sixth earl,..having been a 'liver', had run himself aground by his enormous outlay on this Italian structure.

3. *dial.* The 'quick' of the finger-nail. Also *Comb.* **liver-sick**, an agnail. (See E.D.D.)

liver (ˈlaɪvə(r)), *sb.*[3] Also 7 leaver, 7–9 lever. [A back-formation from the name *Liverpool*.] A name arbitrarily given to the bird figured in the arms of the city of Liverpool.

It was intended for the eagle of St. John the Evangelist, the patron saint of the corporation, but owing to the unskilful delineation there have been many guesses as to the identity of the bird represented. In some ornithological books the name is given to the Glossy Ibis.

1668 in Picton *L'pool Munic. Rec.* (1883) I. 269 The Armes of this towne viz[t] the Leaver. **1688** R. HOLME *Armoury* II. xii. 266/2 He beareth Azure, the Head of a Lever couped proper: of some termed a Shovellers head: this fowl is..in Low Dutch Lepler, or Lepelaer, or Lefler; from the Germane termed Lofler, which we more finely pronounce Lever: Yet Mr. Ray in the translation of the Ornithology terms this Bird, a Spoon Bill. **1873** PICTON *Memor. L'pool* I. 18 Mr. Gough Nichols has..shown..that the so-called liver or cormorant was intended to represent the symbolic eagle of St. John the Evangelist.

†ˈ**liver**, *a. Obs.* Also 4–5 lyvir, 6 lyver. [Aphetic f. DELIVER *a.*]

1. Delivered (*of* a child); = DELIVER *a.* 3. *rare.*

a **1400–50** *Alexander* 3746 And be scho lyuir of a lasse scho lengis in oure burȝe.

2. Free from restraint in motion; active, nimble; = DELIVER *a.* 2.

1530 PALSGR. 317/2 Lyver quyke, *deliure*. **1535** STEWART *Cron. Scot.* (1858) II. 51 Lycht lyuer men to cirkill thame about. *c* **1650** *R. Hood, Beggar & 3 Squires* 46 in Furnivall *Percy Folio* I. 17 Those that saw Robin Hood run, said he was a liver old man. **1664** *Flodden F.* v. 50 With lusty Lads liver and light. **1686** G. STUART *Joco-ser. Disc.* 39 Again speaks out a Lyver lad A trusty Trojan.

liver (ˈlɪvə(r)), *v. Obs.* exc. *dial.* [Partly a. F. *livre-r* (11th c. in Littré):—L. *līberā-re* to LIBERATE; and partly aphetic f. DELIVER *v.*]

= DELIVER *v.*[1] in various senses.

a **1300** *Cursor M.* 15879 (Cott.) Þe fals felun Iudas..liuerd his maister vp. *Ibid.* 20391, I liuerd me of mi sarmon. *a* **1300–1400** *Ibid.* 14418 (Gött.) God..liurd þaim of mekil wa. **13..** *S. Gregory* (Vernon MS.) 72 Liuere me, lord, out of þis pyne. *a* **1400–50** *Alexander* 3152 [Þai] egirly cries On Alexander eftir help & he ham all liuers [*Dubl.* delyuerys]. *c* **1460** *Towneley Myst.* xxiv. 265, I am leuerd a lap is lyke to no lede. *c* **1489** CAXTON *Sonnes of Aymon* i. 33 Yf he haue doon soo I shall neuer leuer hym the value of a peny. *c* **1500** *Melusine* xxxvi. 275 That they be prest redy to lyuere you batayll. **1596** SPENSER *State Irel.* Wks. (Globe) 623/2 The which woord [livery]..is derived of livering or delivering foorth theyr nightlye foode. *c* **1626** BP. MOUNTAGU in *Cosin's Corr.* (Surtees) I. 99 Hath Dr. Wrende livered my letter and effected it? **1672** *Sc. Acts Chas. II* (1814) VIII. 61/1 If any of that victuall shall happin to be livered within their bounds. **1701** in J. Bulloch *Pynours* (1887) 74 If any goods shall be livered at the shoar below the Estler work. *a* **1765** *Northumberland betrayd by Douglas* ix. in Child *Ballads* III. 412/1 For all the gold that's in Loug Leuen, William wold not liuor mee. **1855** ROBINSON *Whitby Gloss.*, *Livver*, to deliver. 'Is the ship livvered,' unloaded. **1883** *Almondb. & Huddersf. Gloss.*, *Liver*, to deliver; so *posit* for deposit. **1887** J. BULLOCH *Pynours* 41 Their industrious wives..were loading or livering some vessel in the 'herborie'.

liver, obs. form of LIVERY, LIVRE.

†**liverage**[1]. *Obs.* [a. OF. *livrage* tax (1395 in Godef.), f. *livrer* LIVER *v.*] (Sense uncertain.)

1544 *Wills & Inv. N.C.* (Surtees 1835) 120 Whils thre score poundes be paid that I am owen for liverage.

†**liverage**[2]. *Obs.* In 6 liv(e)reage. [? f. LIVER *sb.*[2] (sense 3) + -AGE.] An agnail.

1598 FLORIO, *Pipitula*, the skinne growing at the fingers ends about the nayle, called of some the wortwales, or liuereages. *Ibid.*, *Redunia*, a fellon or sore that breedeth betweene the naile and the flesh. Some..call the same wortwales, or liureages.

liverance (ˈlɪvərəns). *Obs.* exc. *dial.* [Partly a. OF. *livrance* delivery, sort of homage, f. *livrer* to DELIVER; partly aphetic f. DELIVERANCE.]

a. Delivery, distribution, LIVERY. **b.** Deliverance, liberation, release.

a **1300** *Cursor M.* 5045 Þai..þe stiward fand At a garner soiurnand, þar he liuerance [*Fairf.* deliueraunce, *Trin.* lyuerey] made of corn. *a* **1375** *Joseph Arim.* 163 Þow schalt haue liueraunce of In and al þat þe neodes. *c* **1380** *Sir Ferumb.* 4299 If y may lyue til moneday non, lyuerance wil y make. **1384** *Charter Lond.* in Arnolde *Chron.* (1811) 17 That no man take hostel within ye wallis of London..by strengthe nor by lyueraunce of the Marchal. **1433** *Rolls of Parlt.* IV. 473/2 A speciall warrant of discharge..for the lyverance ayeen of hir saide londes. **1488** in Arnolde *Chron.* (1811) 233, I haue sett y[e] said Richard to the lyueraunce. **1553** BECON *Reliques of Rome* (1563) 239 All those y[t] their liueraunce purchase against the right of holy Churche. **1737** BRACKEN *Farriery Impr.* (1757) II. 35, I accepted of him at the Price of Seventeen Guineas;..but before I took Liverance of him (as it is called) I had him run along a little in his Halter. **1855** ROBINSON *Whitby Gloss.*, *Livverance*, liberation, departure. **1869** *Lonsdale Gloss.*, *Liverance* delivery.

liveray, livere, obs. forms of LIVERY.

livered (ˈlɪvəd), *a.* Also 3 lyured, 4 liuerd, lyuered, 6 leueryd. [f. LIVER *sb.*[1] + -ED[2].]

†**1.** Coagulated, clotted. ***livered sea*** = *liver sea* (LIVER *sb.*[1] 7); in quot. applied to the Red Sea.

c **1275** *XI Pains of Hell* 47 in *O.E. Misc.* 148 Snov and is and lyured blod. **1297** R. GLOUC. (Rolls) 925 Vor þo þe folc of israhel moyses wiþ him nom & ladde hom out of egipt in to þe liuerede [*v.r.* reed(e, rede] se. *a* **1300** *Cursor M.* 6506 Vr godd..þis ilk es he þat brogh(t) vs thoru þe liuerd se [*Trin.* þe rede see]. **13..** *Minor Poems fr. Vernon MS.* (E.E.T.S.) 645/236 Þer was no thyng bot lyuered blode. **14..** *Siege Jerusalem* (E.E.T.S.) 2/29 Þe lyppe lyþ on a lumpe lyuered on þe cheke.

2. Of bread: Heavy. Now *dial.*

1688 R. HOLME *Armoury* III. 317/1 Bakers Terms ..*Livered*, tough Bread. **1847** HALLIWELL, *Livered*, heavy, or underbaked. *South.*

3. With prefixed adj.: Having a liver of a certain kind. (See also *lily-*, *pigeon-*, *white-livered*.)

1628 FORD *Lover's Mel.* III. ii, What a greene sicknesse-liuer'd Boy is this!

†**liverer.** *Obs.* Also 4 livrere, 6 *Sc.* liverair. [? a. OF. *livreure* delivery, deliverance, f. *livre-r* LIVER *v.*] = LIVERY *sb.* in various senses.

c **1330** *Amis. & Amil.* 1640 He..feched her livrere eueri day, To her liues fode. **1548** W. PATTEN *Exped. Scotl.* Pref. cviij, Their perfit appointment of sure armour,..& their sumptuous sutes of liuerers beside. **1549** *Compl. Scot.* xvii. 148 There is diuerse princis that gyffis..leuerairis, armis ande heretage to them that hes committit vailȝeant actis in the veyris. *c* **1650** *Merline* 306 in Furnivall *Percy Folio* I. 432 That they wold wend to Vortiger & aske him meede & liverr [*read* liverer].

liveried (ˈlɪvərɪd). [f. LIVERY *sb.* + -ED[2].] Dressed in, furnished with, or wearing a livery.

1634 MILTON *Comus* 455 A thousand liveried Angels lacky her. **1641** EVELYN *Mem.* (1857) I. 7 He had 116 servants in liveries, every one liveried in green satin doublets. **1738** POPE *Epil. Sat.* I. 155 Our Youth, all livery'd o'er with foreign Gold, Before her dance: behind her crawl the Old. **1798** WORDSW. *Simon Lee* 28 Old Simon to the world is left In liveried poverty. **1798** JANE AUSTEN *Northang. Abb.* (1833) II. v. 126 A fashionable chaise and four, postilions handsomely liveried. **1837** HT. MARTINEAU *Soc. Amer.* III. App. 327 Aristocratic girls..who grace a ball-room, or loll in a liveried carriage. **1838** DICKENS *Nich. Nick.* x, A liveried footman opened the door.

fig. *a* **1639** WOTTON *Descript. Spring* 24 in *Reliq.* (1651) 524 All look't gay, all full of Chear, To welcome the New-liveri'd yeare. **1750** C. SMART in *Student* I. 225 The livery'd clouds shall on thee wait.

†**livering.** *Obs.* [f. LIVER *sb.*[1] + *-ing*, ? after *pudding*.] A pudding made of liver and rolled up in the form of a sausage.

c **1460** *Towneley Myst.* xii. 217 Oure mete now begyns;.. Two blodyngis, I trow, a leueryng betwene. **1556** WITHALS *Dict.* (1568) 49 a/1 *Tomaculum, ex iecore porcino cibus fit, vt supra*, a lyueryng. **1591** A. W. *Bk. Cookrye* 12 b, To make Liuerings of a Swine. **1611** COTGR., *Fricandeaux*: Short.. daintie puddings..rolled vp into the forme of Liuerings. **1624** CHAPMAN *Homer's Batrachom.* 58 Lyurings (white-skind as Ladies). **1674** N. FAIRFAX *Bulk & Selv.* 159 The Darbyshire huswife..when she makes whitings and blackings, and liverings and hackings. **1694** MOTTEUX *Rabelais* v. xxvii. (1737) 122 Chitterlings, Links,.. Liverings.

†**livering,** *vbl. sb. Obs.* [f. LIVER *v.* + -ING[1].] Delivering, delivery; provision of entertainment.

13.. *K. Alis.* 7171 Ther was fair hostell, and lyvereyng.

liverish (ˈlɪvərɪʃ), *a.* [f. LIVER *sb.*[1] + -ISH.]

1. Resembling liver; of the consistency of liver.

1740 CHEYNE *Regimen* p. xli, The Blood..continues bad, that is, sizy, liverish.

2. *colloq.* Having the symptoms attributed to disordered liver.

1896 *Advt.* in *Daily News* 9 July 9/1 When you begin to feel 'liverish'. **1902** *Daily Chron.* 14 Apr. 3/6 Mr. Alfred Bishop was welcome as the hearty Earl, who is inclined to be testy when 'liverish'.

liverishness. [f. LIVERISH *a.*] Symptoms attributed to disordered condition of the liver.

1904 *Westm. Gaz.* 5 Oct. 10/1 Ordinary attacks of liverishness or biliousness are swiftly dispersed. **1928** *Daily Express* 14 July 15/7 Yellow, perhaps, suggests liverishness. **1930** R. LEHMANN *Note in Music* v. 199 Never, he thought, would he forget..his liverishness.

†**liverison.** *Obs.* In 2 liureisun, 4 liversoon, liuerisoun, 5 lyveresone. [a. OF. *liv(e)reison*, mod.F. *livraison*:—L. *līberātiōn-em*, n. of action f. *līberāre* to deliver, LIBERATE (cf. LIVER *v.*).] Delivery, deliverance, LIVERY.

c **1175** *Lamb. Hom.* 85 In þe deie of liureisun hwense god ..wule windwin þet er wes iporschen. **13..** *K. Alis.* 1011 In a castel heo was y-set, And was deliverid liversoon. *c* **1330** R. BRUNNE *Chron.* (1810) 197 Isaac þe Emperour takes his liuerisoun. *c* **1440** *Promp. Parv.* 309/1 Lyveresone, *corrodium*.

liverless (ˈlɪvəlɪs), *a.* [f. LIVER *sb.*[1] + -LESS.] That has no liver; deprived of the liver; also *fig.* of one whose liver does not perform its functions.

1598 I. M. *Seruingmans Comfort* (1868) 164 My poore masterlesse, and Lyuerylesse, nay Lyuerlesse and Hartlesse brother in Christ. **1864** C. CLARKE *Box for Season* I. 107 Liverless bachelors, all cayenne pepper, turtle, and Peruvian cyanokaita. **1886** 'HUGH CONWAY' *Living or Dead* II. xiv, Such a peppery diet would make me as liverless and heartless as [etc.]. **1897** *Allbutt's Syst. Med.* IV. 37 A healthy frog received 0·016 milligramme [of strychnine] subcutaneously without any ill effect; while a smaller dose (0·012) killed the liverless one with violent convulsions.

Liverpool (ˈlɪvəpuːl). [The name of an English city on the River Mersey.] **1.** Applied *attrib.* to the delftware and porcelain manufactured in Liverpool in the eighteenth century. Also *ellipt.*

1863 W. CHAFFERS *Marks Pott. & Porc.* 130 *Liverpool.* A pottery, called Herculaneum, was established on the Mersey by Richard Abbey, in 1794. **1869** C. SCHREIBER *Jrnl.* 5 Nov. (1911) I. 60 A Liverpool printed mug of Gen. Wolfe. **1957** MANKOWITZ & HAGGAR *Conc. Encycl. Eng. Pott. & Porc.* 131/2 Liverpool is at times difficult to distinguish from Bristol. **1964** M. DRABBLE *Garrick Year* iv. 56 One of my Liverpool ware teapots was broken. **1972** *Country Life* 6 Jan. 21/3 Liverpool or Delft tiles decorate the fireplace surround. **1972** *Collector's Guide* Aug. 9/1 (Advt.), An extremely rare Liverpool Vase, c. 1760 (William Ball's factory).

2. Special combs.: **Liverpool button** (see quot. 1896); **Liverpool house** *Naut.*, a deck-house; **Liverpool pantile**, a hard ship's biscuit; **Liverpool pennant** (see quot. 1933); **Liverpool sound**, the music, popular in the early 1960s, played by pop singers and groups in Liverpool, chiefly the Beatles; **Liverpool weather** *Naut. colloq.*, windy and 'dirty' weather.

1896 FARMER & HENLEY *Slang* IV. 212/1 *Liverpool-button*, a kind of toggle used by sailors when they lose a button. **1908** E. NOBLE *Grain Carriers* III. i. 146 Shanghaied crews are usually persons dressed in a rag and a Liverpool button. **1869** in C. N. Longridge *Cutty Sark* (1933) II. 205 Liverpool house fitted on centre 30 feet long. **1948** R. DE KERCHOVE *Internat. Maritime Dict.* 422 *Liverpool house*, a superstructure extending from side to side and situated amidships in large (steel built) sailing vessels. **1902** B.

LUBBOCK *Round the Horn* viii. 311 He handed me a regular bad-looking Liverpool pantile from the bread-barge. **1925** B. HAYES *Hull Down* iii. 28 The biscuits, commonly called 'Liverpool pantiles', were so hard you could break them only with a hammer. **1933** J. MASEFIELD *Bird of Dawning* 287 *Liverpool pennants*, rope yarns used instead of buttons. **1963** *Daily Mail* 20 Sept. 10/4 It's been boys, boys, boys from Merseyside who have dominated pop music since the 'Liverpool sound' started to carry all before it towards the end of last year. **1963** *Daily Tel.* 10 Dec. 13 A show by the Beatles, the 'Liverpool sound' group, was not typical of 'pop' concerts. **1929** F. C. BOWEN *Sea Slang*, Liverpool weather. **1934** G. H. GRANT *Consigned to Davy Jones* (1935) xviii. 260 If we was on a windbag.. it would be what we calls Liverpool weather.

Liverpudlian (lɪvə'pʌdlɪən), *a.* and *sb.* [f. *Liverpool* (with jocular substitution of *puddle* for *pool*) + -IAN.] **a.** *adj.* Belonging to Liverpool. **b.** *sb.* A native or inhabitant of Liverpool.

1833 *New Sporting Mag.* V. 40 As Mr. Canning said to the Liverpudlians. **1849** CLOUGH *Poems*, etc. (1869) I. 139, I like the Manchester people..better than the Liverpuddlians. **1887** *Pall Mall G.* 26 Jan. 1/1 The division ..is a fairly typical section of the Liverpudlian electorate.

liverwort ('lɪvəwɜːt). [tr. med.L. HEPATICA (applied to plants having liver-shaped parts or used in diseases of the liver). Cf. G. *leberkraut*, Du. *leverkruid*.] A name of various plants.

1. The lichen-like plant *Marchantia polymorpha*; = HEPATICA 2. Sometimes called Stone Liverwort.

a **1100** in *Archiv Stud. neu. Spr.* LXXXIV. 326 Wiþ liferadle. Nim liferwyrt & bere hi man onder cneowe. *a* **1387** *Sinon. Barthol.* (Anecd. Oxon.) 19 *Epatica*, liver-wort. *c* **1450** *Alphita* (Anecd. Oxon.) 57 Epatica..crescit in saxis ..et uidetur quasi frustula membrane inherentia..anglice, a liureuurt. **1533** ELYOT *Cast. Helthe* (1541) 9 b, Thynges good for the Lyver: Lyverworte. **1538** TURNER *Libellus*, Lyverwort, *Lichen*. **1562** —— *Herbal* II. 36 Liuerwurt sodden in wine is good for the diseases of the liuer and longes. **1578** LYTE *Dodoens* III. lxx. 411 Stone Liuerwort spreadeth it selfe abroade vpon the ground, hauing wrinckled, or crimpled leaues layde one vpon another as the scales of fishe. **1718** QUINCY *Compl. Disp.* 130 Liver-wort grows near Springs, Wells, and Watry Places, very low, almost like a Moss. **1858** LEWES *Sea-side Stud.* 74 Springs, glossy with liverwort and feathery with fern. **1867** J. HOGG *Microsc.* II. i. 308 The little group of Hepaticae or Liverworts which is intermediate between Lichens and Mosses. **1875** BENNETT & DYER *Sachs' Bot.* 185 The two flat sides of the gemmæ of this liverwort are identical.

2. *Anemone* (*Hepatica*) *triloba*; = HEPATICA 1. Formerly called Noble Liverwort, Three-leaf Liverwort. (The name in U.S. is *liver-leaf*.)

1578 LYTE *Dodoens* I. xl. 59 [It] maye be called in English Hepatica, Noble Agrimonie, or Three leafe Lyuerwurte. *Ibid.*, The Hepatica or Noble Lyverwurte is a souveraigne medicine against the heate..of the Lyver. **1629** PARKINSON *Parad.* xxix. 226 In English you may call them either Hepatica, after the Latine name, as most doe, or Noble Liuerwort. **1646** SIR T. BROWNE *Pseud. Ep.* II. vi. 101 *Herba Trinitatis*..obtaineth that name onely from the figure of its leaves, and is one kinde of liverworte or Hepatica.

†**3.** Agrimony, *Agrimonia Eupatoria*. *Obs.*

1578 LYTE *Dodoens* I. xxxix. 57 In Latine *Eupatorium*,.. in base Almaigne Agrimonie, and of some Leuercruyt, that is to say, Liuerwurte. **1617** MINSHEU *Ductor* 9 Agrimony,.. called also Liuer-wort because it is good for the liuer.

4. With qualification: **ground liverwort**, *Peltidea canina*; **marsh liverwort**, the genus *Riccia*; **water liverwort**, Water Crowfoot, *Ranunculus aquatilis*; **white liverwort**, Parnassus Grass, *Parnassia palustris*; **wood liverwort**, the lichen *Sticta pulmonacea*.

1597 GERARDE *Herbal* II. ccxciv. 692 Parnassus Grasse or white Liuerwoort. *Ibid.* III. clviii. 1375 *Hepatica terrestris*, Ground Liuerwort. *Ibid.* clix. 1377 Lungwoort, or woode Liuerwoort. **1736** BAILEY *Househ. Dict.* 296 *Lichen cinereus terrestris*,..Ash coloured Ground Liverwort. **1760** J. LEE *Introd. Bot.* App. 317 Liver-wort, Marsh, *Riccia*. **1866** *Treas. Bot.* 858/1 *Peltidea*, a genus of lichens the species of which are vulgarly confounded with *Marchantia* under the name of liverwort. The herbalists, however, distinguish them as Ground Liverwort.

liverwurst ('lɪvəvʊəst, -wɜːst). [Partial tr. of G. *leberwurst*.] = *liver sausage*.

1869 *Atlantic Monthly* Oct. 483/1 Our Dutch neighbors make *liver-wurst* ('woorsht') or meat pudding, omitting the meal, and this compound stuffed into the large intestines, is very popular in Lancaster market. **1929** E. WILSON *I thought of Daisy* iii. 150 The boy-friend's passed out! Too many of those rich liverwurst sandwiches! **1934** H. MILLER *Tropic of Cancer* 41 Throw in some sweetbreads,..Throw in some fried liverwurst. **1945** S. LEWIS *Cass Timberlane* (1946) vi. 39 Coca-Cola, liverwurst, stuffed olives, and chocolate layer cake. **1954** P. HIGHSMITH *Blunderer* (1956) xxii. 139 Kimmel ordered a liverwurst sandwich. **1965** A. ROUDYBUSH *Season for Death* (1966) xix. 111 Spreading two slices of rye bread thickly with liverwurst.

livery ('lɪvərɪ), *sb.* Forms: α. 3 liverei, 4 liveri, 4–5 levere, livere(e, *Sc.* lufre, 4–6 lyvere, -er(e)y, li-, lyveray, 4–7 livre, levery, li-, lyverie, -ye, (5 levore, *Sc.* liffray, luveray, lyvera, lewray), 5–6 leveray, liverey, -erie, (6 li-, lyveraie, -aye, livorie, *Sc.* leifray, lufray(e, 7 livrie, livory, *Sc.* lewerie), 5- livery. β. (?) 6 lyver, 7 liver. [a. AF. *liveré* (1292 in Britton), F. *livrée* (1351 in Du Cange s.v. *Liberare*), fem. pa. pple. of *livrer* LIVER *v.*: see -Y. Cf. It. *livrea*, Sp. *librea* (both from Fr.); med.L. had *liberata*.]

1. a. The dispensing of food, provisions, or clothing (cf. 2) to retainers or servants; hence *gen.*, provision, allowance. **b.** The food or provisions so dispensed; an allowance or ration of food served out. Now *Hist.*

a **1300** *Cursor M.* 2122 Þe thrid part..al on þis side þe greckes see, was Iaphet giuen til his liuere. *Ibid.* 19220 Wit þam i mai ha mete and drinc, Mi liuere haf wit-vten suinc. *c* **1330** R. BRUNNE *Chron.* (1810) 146 To London forto com, whan parlement suld be,..and tak þer his liuere. **13..** *Test. Christi* 376 (MS. Harl. 2382) in *Archiv Stud. neu. Spr.* LXXIX. 431 A cote-armur..the which y toke of thy luyere. **1375** BARBOUR *Bruce* XIV. 233 Tharfor he maid of vyne lufre [*MS. E.* levere, *ed.* 1616 lewerie] Till ilk man. **1399** *Rolls of Parlt.* III. 452/1 That thei..gyf no Liverees of Sygnes, no make no Retenue of men. **1399** LANGL. *Rich. Redeles* II. 2 Moche now me merueileth..Of ȝoure large leuerey to leodis aboute. **1422** tr. *Secreta Secret.*, *Priv. Priv.* 133 Syr Stewyn Serope..Hauynge the gouernaunce of Irlande, many extorcionys did, Lyuerez takynge. *c* **1450** *Bk. Curtasye* 371 in *Babees Bk.*, Lyueray he hase of mete and drynke, And settis with hym who so hym thynke. *Ibid.* 839 Of candel liueray squiyers schalle haue. *a* **1483** *Liber Niger* in S. Pegge *Cur. Misc.* (1782) 79 Taking every of them, for his livery at night, half a chet loaf, one quart of wine, one gallon of ale; and for winter livery, from All-Hallowtide till Easter, one percher wax, one candle wax [etc.]. *c* **1492** *Gest R. Hode* clxi. in Child *Ballads* III. 64/1 There he made large lyueray, Bothe of ale and of wyne. **1573** *Satir. Poems Reform.* xlii. 409 ȝe ar far large of Leueray. **1596** SPENSER *State Irel.* Wks. (Globe) 623/2 In great howses, the liverye is sayd to be served up for all night, that is theyr nyghtes allowaunce for drinke. **1639** DAVENPORT *New Trick to Cheat Devil* I, [Stage-direction. *Ent. with Wine*, Chan.] *Chan.* I have brought your Livery. **1670** BROOKS *Wks.* (1867) VI. 47 They serve God for a livery, for loaves, and not for love. **1707** CHAMBERLAYNE *St. Gt. Brit.* II. x. 140 To whom [the Lord Great Chamberlain] belongs Livery and Lodging in the Kings Court. **1861** *Our Eng. Home* 81 The butler.. dispensed the stores to the cook, and gave out the rations or liveries of meat, wine, and beer. **1875** STUBBS *Const. Hist.* III. xxi. 531.

fig. **1633** FORD *Broken H.* IV. i, Great (faire one) grace my hopes with any instance Of Liuery, from the allowance of your fauour, This little sparke. [mod. ed. *Attempts to take a ring from her finger*.] **1643** SIR T. BROWNE *Relig. Med.* I. §47, I found upon a naturall inclination, and inbred loyalty unto vertue, that I could serve her without a livery.

c. Allowance of provender for horses. *at livery*: (of a horse) kept for the owner, and fed and groomed at a fixed charge. Now *rare* or *obs.* exc. in LIVERY-STABLE.

coynye and livery: see COYNYE.

a **1440** *Sir Degrev.* 1003 A thousaund hors and thre..Ylke nyȝt tok lyvere Off cowrne and off hay. **1481–4** *Paston Lett.* III. 280, I had my horsse with hym at lyvery. **1596** SPENSER *State Irel.* Wks. (Globe) 623/2 What Liverye is, we by common use in England knowe well enough, namelye, that it is allowaunce of horse-meate. **1601** HOLLAND *Pliny* I. 559 Champions and wrestlers, whose allowance was much like to the liurie giuen to laboring horses. **1631** BRATHWAIT *Whimzies, Keeper* 49 A keeper of horses at livery. **1679–88** *Secr. Serv. Money Chas. & Jas.* (Camden) 70 Twelve guineys a year..which King Cha. the 2[d] allowed him for a nagg's livery. **1706** PHILLIPS (ed. Kersey), *Livery of Hay and Oats*, the giving out a certain Quantity for feeding Horses, &c. **1731** BAILEY vol. II. s.v., To stand at Livery is to be kept at livery stables. **1829** SCOTT *Rob Roy* xix, There was a necessity..for arresting the horse, and placing him in Baillie Trumbull's stable, therein to remain at livery, at the rate of twelve shillings (Scotch) per diem.

fig. **1589** *Pappe w. Hatchet* Dij b, They finde all themselues good meales, and stand at liuerie as it were, at other mens tables. **1599** MASSINGER, etc. *Old Law* II. i, To keepe you sixe at Liuery, and still munching. **1611** B. JONSON *Introd. Verses* to Coryat *Crudities*, And here he disdain'd not, in a forraine land, To lie at Livory, while the Horses did stand. **1618** FLETCHER *Chances* III. i, Best hang a signpost up to tell the Signiors Here ye may have lewdnesse at Liverie. **1647** R. STAPYLTON *Juvenal* 157 In whose [Venus'] temple at Corinth two hundred maids daily stood at livery.

†**d.** Stipendiary allowance (for a fellow of a college or the like). *Obs.*

1587 R. HOVENDEN in *Collect.* (O.H.S.) I. 211 We willinglie and thanckfullie acknowledge great benefitt by the statute mentioned... But such benefitte as commethe to each on for his liverye risheth cheflie by fynes and woodsales; which liveryes..are in reazon somewhat increased but not dobbled. **1611** COTGR. s.v. *Livree*, *La Livrée des Chanoines*, their liuerie, or corrodie; their stipend, exhibition, daily allowance in victuals or money.

2. a. A suit of clothes, formerly sometimes a badge or cognizance (e.g. a collar or hood), bestowed by a person upon his retainers or servants and serving as a token by which they may be recognized; in wider sense, a distinctive badge or suit worn by a servant or official, a member of a company, etc.; †formerly, the uniform of a soldier or sailor. In generalized use, the distinctive uniform style of dress worn by a person's servants, etc. (now only men-servants). *in livery*: wearing a particular livery. *out of livery*: (of a servant) not dressed in livery; wearing plain clothes. †In early use also, a set of distinctive badges or suits; in first quot. = garments, clothes.

13.. *E.E. Allit. P.* A. 1107 And alle in sute her liurez wasse. **1375** BARBOUR *Bruce* XIX. 36 Thre hundreth and sexte had he Of squyeris, cled in his liverye. *c* **1386** CHAUCER *Prol.* 363 An haberdasshere and a Carpenter, A Webbe, a Dyere, and a Tapycer, And they were clothed in o lyueree Of a solempne and a greet fraternitee. **1389** in *Eng. Gilds* (1870) 21 Ye bretheren and sisteren of yis gilde..shul han a lyueree of hodes in suyte. **1399** LANGL. *Rich. Redeles* II. 79 That no manere meyntenour shulde merkis bere, Ne haue lordis leuere þe lawe to apeire. *c* **1440** *Gesta Rom.* xv. 51 (Add. MS.), xl[ti] knyghtes of oone leveraye. **1463** *Bury Wills* (Camden) 41 Bothe my colers of silvir, the kyng's lyfre. **1473** WARKW. *Chron.* (Camden) 14 He..wered ane estryche feder, Prynce Edwardes lyvery. **1480** *Wardr. Acc. Edw. IV* (1830) 124 A gowne and a hoode of the liveree of the Garter for the Duke de Ferrare. **1485** CAXTON *Paris & V.* 14 Every baron gaf hys lyverey that they shold be knowen eche fro other. **1522** WRIOTHESLEY *Chron.* (1875) I. 13 The kinge and he ridinge both together in one liverey. *a* **1548** HALL *Chron.*, *Hen. VI*, 173 b, The erle perceiving by the livery of the souldiors, that he was circumvented. ?*a* **1550** in *Dunbar's Poems* (1893) 319 ȝe noble merchandis..Address ȝow furth ..In lusty grene lufraye. *a* **1592** GREENE *Geo. a Greene* (1599) F 1 b, Two liueries will I giue thee euerie yeere, And fortie crownes shall be thy fee. **1622** BACON *Hen. VII* 58 Liveries, tokens, and other badges of factious dependance. **1631** HEYWOOD *Lond. Jus Hon.* Wks. 1874 IV. 273 All this goodly band..in their City Liveries. **1671** MILTON *Samson* 1616 Immediately Was Samson as a public servant brought, In thir state Livery clad. **1684** in *Scott. Antiq.* XV. 18 Skulking and vagrant persons who have hitherto imitated the livery of the king's sojors. **1707** FARQUHAR *Beaux Strat.* III. i. 23 What sort of Livery has the Footman? **1710** *Lond. Gaz.* No. 4710/4 Deserted.., John Stephens, a Serjeant,.. having his Serjeant's Livery on. **1814** MRS. J. WEST *Alicia de Lacy* III. 113 Disguised in the livery of a trooper. **1841** LYTTON *Nt. & Morn.* I. i, A Servant out of livery leaped from the box. **1863** KINGLAKE *Crimea* (1876) I. ii. 28 Hunting the country in the livery of the Salisbury Hunt. **1875** STUBBS *Const. Hist.* II. xvii. 610 The king out of compliment wore the livery of the duke of Lancaster. **1900** *Blackw. Mag.* Dec. 862/2 Servants in claret and yellow livery noiselessly served wine.

β. **1512** HEN. VIII *To Earl Shrewsbury* in Rymer *Foedera* (1710) XIII. 338 Badges, Tokens or Lyvers to Were. **1660** tr. *Amyraldus' Treat. conc. Relig.* III. i. 303 To wear the liver of an enemy to one's King.

b. *transf.* and *fig.*

?*c* **1325** *Earth* ix. in *E.E.P.* (1862) 151 Whan erþ makiþ is liuerei he grauiþ vs in grene. **1412–20** LYDG. *Chron. Troy* II. xiii, When that Flora..Hath euery playne, medowe, hil and vale..clad in lyuery newe. **1494** FABYAN *Chron.* VI. clxxxii. 180 That Rollo shuld..take vpon hym the lyuerey of Cristes baptym. **1563** *Homilies* II. *Rogation Week* IV. (1859) 495 Love and charity, which is the only livery of a Christian man. **1590** SHAKS. *Mids. N.* II. i. 113 The childing Autumne, angry Winter change Their wonted Liueries. **1611** COTGR., *Liripipionné*,..faithfull to the pot, and therefore bearing the red-faced liuerie therof. **1661** BOYLE *Style of Script.* (1675) 192 White (the livery of innocence). **1667** MILTON *P.L.* IV. 599 Now..Twilight gray Had in her sober Livery all things clad. **1697** DRYDEN *Virg. Georg.* III. 665 A Snake..has cast his Slough aside, And in his Summer Liv'ry rouls along. **1722** WOLLASTON *Relig. Nat.* v. 96 Trees receive annually their peculiar liveries, and bear their proper fruits. **1734** BERKELEY *Analyst* §1 Wks. 1871 III. 258 Clothing themselves in the livery of other men's opinions. **1797–1804** BEWICK *Brit. Birds* (1847) II. 112 The females may be seen in the livery either complete or partial, of the past Season. **1813** SCOTT *Rokeby* I. i, Sorrow's livery dims the air. **1835** THIRLWALL *Greece* I. viii. 311 The rustic garb, which was the livery of his servitude.

c. An emblem, device, or distinctive colour on a vehicle, product, etc., indicating its owner or manufacturer.

1938 H. A. VALLANCE *Highland Railway* xiv. 155 He introduced on the Highland Railway the style of painting which was afterwards so well-known on the south coast. Passenger engines were painted yellow... For goods engines a dark green livery was adopted. **1966** J. THOMAS *Callander & Oban Railway* x. 169 The Caledonian 2-4-2 tanks..had the plain conical chimney..and the Prussian-blue passenger livery then standard on the line. **1970** *Guardian* 27 July 16/2 The Antonovs [*sc.* planes] are painted battleship grey, with red hammer and sickle emblems, not the normal livery of Aeroflot passenger aircraft. **1972** *Times* 13 Oct. 17/7 London Transport's intention can be simply stated. It is that the livery of the bus fleet will remain red, with a very strictly limited number offered to advertisers for all-over painted designs. **1973** *Times* 1 Dec. 17/7 As the designers responsible for the BEA livery we were invited, along with two other design groups, to make proposals for 'British Airways'. **1974** P. LOVESEY *Invitation to Dynamite Party* ii. 22 An enormous express locomotive painted in the brilliant golden ochre and dark olive green livery of the London, Brighton and South Coast Railway Company.

3. *collect. sing.* **a.** Retainers or servants in livery. †Also *occas.* a liveried servant. ? *Obs.*

1413 *Pilgr. Sowle* (Caxton 1483) v. xiii. 104 In these ryall festes the kyng yeueth his leuery ful ryche and ryal robes. *a* **1577** SIR T. SMITH *Commw. Eng.* (1609) 106 First of retainers, that no man should haue aboue a number in his Liuery or retinue. **1628** SHIRLEY *Witty Fair One* I. ii. (1633), Her Father..rides..With halfe a douzen wholesome Liueries, To whom he gives Christian wages. *Ibid.* II. ii, My lodging is next to her chambers, it is a confidence in my Master to let his Liuery lye so neere her. **1714** STEELE *Lover* 11 Mar. (1723) 38 Seeing a Place in the second Row of the Queen's Box kept by Mrs. Lucy's Livery, I placed my self in the Pit directly over against her Footman. **1766** CHESTERF. *Let. to C'tess Suffolk* Nov. (1892) III. 1349 If she is a Mrs. with a surname, she is above the livery, and belongs to the upper servants. **1791–1823** D'ISRAELI *Cur. Lit.* (1866) 450/2 As cross-humoured as the livery of this day, in their notices of what we now gently call our 'supplies'.

†**b.** Used for: Following, faction. (Cf. F. *livrée* in the sense of 'party'.) *under* (a person's) *livery*: in dependence on him. *Obs.*

c **1477** CAXTON *Jason* 116 b, As to the regarde of Hercules, Theseus [etc.]..they faylled not to be of the lyuereye of Iason. *a* **1548** HALL *Chron.*, *Hen. VII* 12 To compasse that the duchy of Bryteyne should breuely come vndre their liure and subjeccion. **1613** MILLES tr. *Mexia's Treas. Anc. & Mod. Times* 722/2 All the other Christians, as Maronites.. and others of that Liverie, never used it [circumcision].

c. = *livery company* (see 10 b) or the liverymen of a company. Also, *to take up one's livery* (? orig. in sense 2): to become a liveryman of one of the City companies.

c **1521** *Old City Acc. Bk.* in *Archæol. Jrnl.* XLIII, Receyved of Brether admittid & taken into the lyuerey this yere. **1529** in *Vicary's Anat.* (1888) App. xiv. 252 A Remedye agaynst theym that wyll not be of the lyuerey, nor bere offyce. **1624** Massinger *Renegado* III. ii, I should.. nere be pittied By the liueries of those companies. **1637** *Decree Star Chamb.* in *Milton's Areop.* (Arb.) 17 Euery Master-printer that is of the Liuery of his Company. **1706** Phillips (ed. Kersey) s.v., The Livery or Livery-men of a Company or Corporation, such Members as are advanc'd to a Degree above the Yeomanry, and have a Right to wear a Livery-gown upon solemn Occasions. **1839** *Penny Cycl.* XIV. 119/1 (London) Certain senior members of the livery, who form what is commonly called 'The Court of Assistants'. *Ibid.*, In more modern times..it has frequently been made imperative upon many freemen of the City to take up their livery in one of the Companies. **1854** Thackeray *Newcomes* v, We belong to the same Livery in the City.

†**d.** *slang.* (See quot.) *Obs.*

1680 Betterton *Revenge* I. 8 'Tis..out of fashion now to call things by their right names. Is a Citizen a Cuckold? no, he's one of the Liverie.

†**4.** The lodging provided or appointed for a person. Also, the quarters of a portion of an army. *Obs.*

?*a* **1400** *Morte Arth.* 241 The soueraingne..Assingnyde to the senatour certaygne lordes, To lede to his leuere. *Ibid.* 3078 In iche leuere on lowde the kynge did crye. **1525** Ld. Berners *Froiss.* II. clx. [clvi.] 440 The duke of Berrey was come to Auygnon and was lodged in the popes palais, but he came to Vyle neufe to the kynge, and laye in the lyuere [*footn.* hotel; Fr. *en sa liuree*] of arras, called Amontays, in the way to Mountpellyer.

5. *Law.* **a.** The legal delivery of property into a person's possession; phr. *to have, give, take livery. to sue* (also *sue for, sue out*) *one's livery*: to institute a suit as heir to obtain possession of lands which are in the hands of the court of wards. (Also *fig.*) **b.** The writ by which possession of property is obtained from the court of wards.

1430–31 *Rolls of Parlt.* IV. 372/2 Noght havyng liveree of the saide Wolles. **1460** *Ibid.* V. 388/1 The Sollicitours for the Quene..causid the seid John and Isabell to sue a speciall Livere of the seid Londes and Tenementes. **1465** *Paston Lett.* II. 192 He desyryd me to mak hym levery of the seyd bests so taken. **1531** *Dial. on Laws Eng.* I. vii. 13 b, By way of surrendre..a freholde may passe without lyuerey. **1593** Shaks. *Rich. II*, II. i. 129, I am denyde to sue my Liuerie here, And yet my Letters Patents giue me leaue. **1603** Owen *Pembrokeshire* (1891) 155 The Courte of Wardes and liveries, doeth allso call all Wardes in Wales to sue forth their lyveries there. **1622** Bacon *Hen. VII*, 210 The Kings Wards after they had accomplished their full Age, could not bee suffered to haue Liuerie of their Lands, without paying excessiue Fines. **1635** Quarles *Embl.* v. ix. (1718) 281 What mean these liv'ries and possession keys? **1649** Milton *Eikon.* xi. Wks. 1851 III. 426 It concern'd them first to sue out their Livery from the unjust wardship of his encroaching Prerogative. **1656** Blount *Glossogr., Livery*.. 3. It is the Writ which lies for the heir to obtain the possession or seizin of his lands at the Kings hands. **1660** *Act 12 Chas. II*, c. 24 §1 It is hereby Enacted That the Court of Wardes and Liveries and all Wardships Liveries Primer-Seizins and Ouster-le-mains..be taken away and discharged. **1707** Chamberlayne *State Gt. Brit.* II. vi. 98 He [the king's eldest son] may that Day sue for the Livery of the said Dukedom [of Cornwall] and ought of Right to obtain the same. **1765** *Act 5 Geo. III*, c. 17 §1 Tythes or other incorporeal hereditaments only, which lie in grant and not in livery. **1818** Cruise *Digest* (ed. 2) IV. 318 Sir J. Palmer thought, that in a deed to pass an inheritance, where there was a common in gross, the word *grant* was absolutely necessary; for it could not pass by the livery. **1827** Hallam *Const. Hist.* (1876) III. xviii. 384 The recusants were allowed to sue for livery of their estates in the court of wards. **1875** Poste *Gaius* II. Comm. (ed. 2) 173 In English law conveyance by livery was an older title than conveyance by deed.

c. *livery of seisin* (freq. erron. *livery and seisin*; AF. *livery de seisin*): the delivery of property into the corporal possession of a person; in the case of a house, by giving him the ring, latch, or key of the door; in the case of land, by delivering him a twig, a piece of turf, or the like.

Virtually abolished by 8 & 9 Vict. cap. 106 §2, which provides that after 1 Oct. 1845 'all corporeal Tenements and Hereditaments shall as regards the Conveyance of the immediate Freehold thereof, be deemed to lie in Grant as well as in Livery'.

c **1475** *Partenay* 560 After sette day of lyuerey and season, That men deliuer you possession. **1574** tr. *Littleton's Tenures* 13 a, In a leas for terme of yeares by deede or without deede, it nedeth no lyvery of seisin to be made to the lessee. **1596** Spenser *F.Q.* VI. iv. 37 She gladly did of that same babe accept As of her owne by liuerey and seisin. **1608** Dod & Cleaver *Expos. Prov.* xi–xii. 189 How large demeanes may a man be estated in by taking a turfe in way of liuery and seison? **1652** Evelyn *Mem.* (1857) I. 297, 22nd [Jan.] was perfected the sealing, livery and seisin of my purchase of Sayes Court. **1741** T. Robinson *Gavelkind* II. iii. 195 The Livery of Seisin must be *propriâ manu* of the Infant. **1818** Cruise *Digest* (ed. 2) IV. 57 Livery of seisin is exactly similar to the investiture of the feudal law; it was adopted here..that the proprietor of each piece of land should be publicly known. **1876** Freeman *Norm. Conq.* V. xxii. 24 He who could neither show his writ, nor bring evidence, of personal livery of seisin, was held to have no lawful claim to the lands which he held.

transf. and *fig.* **1628** Jackson *Creed* IX. ix. §5 Abraham in that sacred banquet which the King of Salem exhibited to him did (as we say) take levery de seisin of the promised land. **1651** Biggs *New Disp.* ¶180 The Feaver, who hath now taken livery and seisen. **1659** Hammond *On Ps.* cx. 7. 566 To take livery and seizin of an hostile Countrey.

†**6. a.** *gen.* The action of handing over or conveying into a person's hands; delivery (of goods, money, etc., of a writ). *Obs.*

c **1400** *Beryn* 1896 The marchandise within Is nat in my charge; ye know as wele as I To make therof no lyuery. c **1440** *York Myst.* xxv. 65 What are ȝe þat makis here maistrie, To loose þes bestis with-oute leverie? **1442** *Rolls of Parlt.* V. 64/2 At the tyme of the sale, and tofore the lyvere of hem from the seid Staple. **1444** *Ibid.* 125/2 Upon the levere of him so arrested. **1464** *Ibid.* 560/2 After the lyvere of the said Writte. **1465** *Paston Lett.* II. 192 He desyred me to mak hym levery of the seyd bests so taken. **1579–80** North *Plutarch, Camillus* (1595) 150 He sent an Herauld before to Rome, to demand liuerie of the man that had offended him, that he might punish him accordingly. **1745** *Observ. conc. Navy* 14 Had they arrived in the Ship at her Port of Livery.

†**b.** Delivery or dealing (of blows). *Obs.*

c **1350** *Will. Palerne* 1233 þanne lente he swiche leuere to ledes þat he ofrauȝt, þat [etc.]. *Ibid.* 3822 William..leide on swiche liuere..þat [etc.]. **13..** *Coer de L.* 4029 Swilke levery he hem delte, Al that he hytte anon they swelte. **1399** Langl. *Rich. Redeles* III. 330 They..lente hem leuere of her longe battis. c **1400** *Laud Troy Bk.* 7613 Ector deled about lyueray To alle that euere come In his way.

†**7.** A due or tribute. Cf. med.L. *livrea* (Du Cange). *Obs. rare*⁻¹.

1577 Harrison *England* II. ii. (1877) I. 58 S. Davids hath Penbroke and Caermardine shires, whose liuerie or first fruits to the see of Rome was one thousand and five hundred ducats at the hardest.

8. A particular sort of wool (see quot. 1837).

1837 Youatt *Sheep* iii. 67 The livery—principally the skirtings and edgings, and the short coarse or breech wool, that which comes from the breech of the animal. **1843** *Penny Cycl.* XXVII. 551/1 The [wool] sorter has to make his selection in relation to the fineness, the softness, the strength, the colour, the cleanness, and the weight of the wool; and in reference to these qualities he separates the wool into many parcels, which receive the names of—'prime', 'choice',..'fine abb', 'coarse abb', 'livery', &c. **1875** in Knight *Dict. Mech.* s.v. *Wool-sorting*.

9. *U.S.* = livery-stable. (*Cent. Dict.*) Also *attrib.*

1845 F. Douglass *Narr. Life F. Douglass* 16 His stable and carriage-house presented the appearance of some of our large city livery establishments. **1888** C. D. Ferguson *Experiences Forty-Niner* i. 15 We placed our horses in a livery on Third street. **1902** W. N. Harben *Abner Daniel* 29, I could 'a' gone to a livery an' ordered out a team. **1903** A. Adams *Log of Cowboy* xiii. 81 Long before we reached the Mulberry, a livery rig came down the trail to meet us. **1936** E. G. Barnard *Rider Cherokee Strip* 210 They met a traveling man who was driving a good livery team to a buckboard. **1940** W. Faulkner *Hamlet* ii. 32 The village consisted of a livery barn and lot and a contiguous shady though grassless yard.

10. *attrib.* and *Comb.* **a.** Simple attrib. passing into adj., in various senses: (*a*) †given as or constituting a livery; intended for servants' use (*obs.*), as *livery arrows, bedstead, bow, feather-bed, meal, towel*; (*b*) pertaining to, forming part of, or used as a livery, as *livery beard, button, cloak* (in quot. *fig.*), *cloth, coat, collar, colour, gown, hat, lace, plush, red, suit*; (*c*) kept at livery or for hire, as *livery horse, nag*; transf. *livery friend, mistress, punk*; (*d*) wearing a livery, as *livery attendant*.

1549 *Privy Council Acts* (1890) II. 350 *Lyverey arrowes, xv^c shef. **1599** Nashe *Lenten Stuffe* Ep. Ded., His patient *liuery attendant. **1641** Brome *Joviall Crew* IV. i. Wks. 1873 III. 417 All the Servants wear *Livery-Beards. **1610** *Althorp MS.* in Simpkinson *The Washingtons* App. p. iv, The Butler's Chamber. Impr. a *leverye bedstead, with a tester of buckram. **1566** *Act 8 Eliz.* c. 10 §3 Bowes..of the course sorte, called *Livery Bowes. **1590** Sir J. Smyth *Disc. Weapons* 19 b, All Liueray or warre Bowes. **1848** Thackeray *Bk. Snobs* xxxiv, A *livery-button maker. **1599** Marston *Sco. Villanie* 167 Sirra, *liuorie cloake, you lazie slipper slave. **1791** Learmont *Poems* 179 Ye gie them wage, board, *livery-claith. **1842** Bischoff *Woollen Manuf.* II. 151, I have sold a large quantity of livery cloths for the use of London. **1551** T. Wilson *Logike* 45 b, A *liverie coate garded with velvet. **1575–85** Abp. Sandys *Serm.* v. 83 Loue is the Liuerie-coate of Christ. **1820** Scott *Abbot* vi, Showing you it was your Lady's livery-coat which I spared, and not your flesh and blood, Master Roland. **1473** in *Ld. Treas. Acc. Scotl.* (1877) I. 68 A *leueray colare of the Kingis. **1621** *Bury Wills* (Camden) 167 Two of the ordinarie *lyverie fetherbedes. *a* **1637** B. Jonson *Disc.* (1641) 105 They have *Livery-friends, friends of the dish, and of the Spit. **1462** *Paston Lett.* II. 120, I have but on gowne at Framyngham and an other here, and that is my *levere gowne. **1606** *Progr. Jas. I* (1828) II. 67 The Companies of London, in their lyverie-gownes and hoodes. **1778** *Eng. Gazetteer* (ed. 2) s.v. *Hartford*, The chief bailiff was then allowed by the king 20*s.* a year for his livery-gown. **1890** *Army & Navy Stores Catal.* Mar. 1173 *Livery Hat. **1838** H. Colman *1st Rep. Agric. Mass.* (Mass. Agric. Survey) 17 The number of stage and *livery horses kept in the county cannot fall short of one thousand,..who depend on the purchase of hay. **1865** Mrs. Carlyle *Lett.* III. 301 Putting Mr. C. to the cost of a livery-horse. **1701** *Lond. Gaz.* No. 3716/4 Some new Cloth and *Livery-Lace. **1799** J. Robertson *Agric. Perth* 341 The practise of giving them six and a half bolls of meal..is daily becoming more general. These farmers, who keep any married servants, have them all on this establishment of *livery meal. **1623** Massinger *Dk. Milan* IV. ii, He that at euerie stage keeps liuerie Mistresses. **1784** Cowper *Tiroc.* 901 Wouldst thou with a Gothic hand Pull down the schools..Or throw them up to *liv'ry-nags and grooms? **1851** *Illustr. Catal. Gt. Exhib.* 1055 *Livery plushes, of various qualities. **1624** Massinger *Renegado* III. ii, His ships, his goods, his *liuery-puncks, confiscate. **1708** *Lond. Gaz.* No. 4447/4 Their *Livery Red, lin'd and fac'd with Yellow. **1705** *Ibid.* No. 4162/4 Two *Livery-Suits, of a deep blue. **1888** Wardrop *Poems & Sk.* 232 John, that livery suit and hat, please. **1582** *Wills & Inv. N.C.* (Surtees 1860) 46, vij long table towells, and iiij *liveraye towells.

b. Special comb.: **livery company**, one of the London City companies which had formerly a distinctive costume used for special occasions; †**livery cupboard**, a cupboard in which 'liveries' of food were served out; in later times, app. an ornamental buffet or sideboard; **livery fine**, the payment due from those who become liverymen in a London company; **livery-fish** *Anglo-Irish*, the striped wrasse, *Labrus mixtus*; **livery list**, the list of the liverymen of a company; **livery office** (see quot.); †**livery pot**, a pot in which 'liveries' of wine were served out; **livery servant**, (*a*) a servant who wears livery; (*b*) = *livery-fish*; †**livery table**, a table on which 'liveries' or rations were put; hence, a side table; **livery tavern**, an inn at which horses may be kept at livery. Also livery-man, livery-stable.

1766 Entick *London* IV. 73 This is also a *livery company. **1871** W. H. Ainsworth *Tower Hill* I. ix, The barges of the twelve livery companies. **1571** *Bury Wills* (Camden) 267 A carpet for the *lyvery cubberd. **1632** J. Hayward tr. *Biondi's Eromena* 184 The livery cupbords of gold inlaid with rich pretious stones. **1737** tr. *Le Comte's Mem. & Rem. China* vi. 172 A livery cupboard borne by the officers of the palace. **1821** Scott *Kenilw.* xxxii, The livery cupboards were loaded with plate of the richest description. **1837** *2nd Rep. Munic. Corp. Comm., Lond. Companies* 18 Prior to the 15th December 1796, the *Livery fine was 13*l.* 6*s.* 8*d.* **1880–4** F. Day *Brit. Fishes* I. 258 Cook wrasse, blue-striped wrasse,..Livery-servant and *livery-fish in the north of Ireland. **1861** *Evening Star* 4 Oct., The proceedings in the City Registration Court during the revision of the *Livery lists. **1848** Wharton *Law Lex.*, **Livery-office*, an office appointed for the delivery of lands. **1575** Laneham *Let.* (1871) 8 A payree [*sic*] of great whyte syluer *lyuery Pots for wyne. **1656** Finett *For. Ambass.* 133 An old guilt Livery Pot that had lost its fellow. **1702** *Order in Council* 8 Mar. in *Lond. Gaz.* No. 3791/4 That..all Lords..do.. cloath their *Livery Servants with Black Cloth. **1822** Hazlitt *Table-t.* II. ii. 24 They will go in the character of livery-servants to stand behind the chairs of the great. **1601** Holland *Pliny* II. 297 To remoue the cupboord of plate, & *liuery table [L. *mensam vel repositorium*], whiles one of the guests is a drinking. **1650** Fuller *Pisgah* v. xviii. 173, I conceive therefore the other nine [Tables of Shew Bread], onely as side-cupboards, or Livery tables ministeriall to that principall one. **1787** M. Cutler in *Life, Jrnls. & Corr.* (1888) I. 252 My companion conducted me to..a *livery tavern.

Hence †**liveryless** *a.*

1598 [see liverless].

livery (ˈlɪvərɪ), *a.* [f. liver *sb.*¹ + -y.]

1. Of the consistency or colour of liver; *dial.* (of soil) heavy, tenacious.

1778 [W. Marshall] *Minutes Agric.* 28 Mar. 1775 The surface is..remarkably fine for such a livery, leathery, water-shaken Ley. **1857** *Jrnl. R. Agric. Soc.* XVIII. I. 101 [Potatoes] not heavy, livery balls,..but light and flowery. **1877** *N.W. Linc. Gloss.* s.v., Clay or warp land is said to turn up livery when, on ploughing the soil, it is found to be sad and heavy, without tendency to crumble into mould.

2. *colloq.* = liverish 2.

1937 in Partridge *Dict. Slang* 487/2. **1968** R. Jeffries *Traitor's Crime* iii. 34 You had too much port: port always makes you livery.

†ˈ**livery**, *v.* *Obs. rare.* [f. livery *sb.*] *trans.* To array in a livery: in quot. *fig.*

1597 Shaks. *Lover's Compl.* 105 His rudenesse so with his authoriz'd youth Did liuery falsenesse in a pride of truth. **1611** Florio, *Liureáre*, to liuery, to giue or put into liueries.

ˈ**livery-man,** ˈ**liveryman.**

1. A liveried retainer or servant. ? *Obs.*

1693 *Lond. Gaz.* No. 2877/1 After them Sir William's own Livery-men, to the number of 12, all with their Hats off. **1711** Shaftesb. *Charac.* (1737) III. 340 Some inferiour officer or livery-man of the train. **1821** Scott *Kenilw.* vii, Officers of the Earl's household, liverymen, and retainers, went and came.

b. (See quot.) ? *Obs.*

1743 Zollman in *Phil. Trans.* XLII. 458 Those [Caterpillars] to which Gardeners have given the Name of Livery-men, by reason of the Distribution of their Colours.

2. A freeman of the City of London who is entitled to wear the 'livery' of the company to which he belongs, and to exercise other privileges.

1682 *Enq. Elect. Sheriffs* 21 In the Case of my Lord Mayors imposing a Sheriff upon the City, without the concurrence of the Livery-men. c **1710** C. Fiennes *Diary* (1888) 241 All freemen or Liverymen of this city hath a Right to Choose their sherriffs. **1773** *Gentl. Mag.* XLIII. 149 The lord mayor, at the request of a numerous body of liverymen, having summoned a common-hall. **1861** *Evening Star* 4 Oct., He is a Liveryman—and a member of one of the twelve great companies. **1875** Stubbs *Const. Hist.* III. xx. 416 The franchise was formally transferred to the livery-men of the companies.

3. A keeper of or attendant at a livery-stable.

1841 Lytton *Nt. & Morn.* (1851) 103 Come off, clumsy! you can't manage that 'ere fine animal', cried the livery man. **1853** G. J. Cayley *Las Alforjas* I. 135 We had a slight

altercation with the livery-man,.. who wished to charge us for more days than our ponies had been in pupilage.

livery-stable. A stable where horses are kept at livery, or are let out (with or without carriages) for hire. (Also ***livery and bait stable.***)

1705 *Lond. Gaz.* No. 4182/4 Left at a Livery Stable.., a Chesnut Mare. **1714** MANDEVILLE *Fab. Bees* (1725) I. 95 Houses, in which women are hir'd as publickly as horses at a livery stable. **1839** MRS. CARLYLE *Lett.* I. 114 A fly.. furnished us from a livery-stable. **1840** THACKERAY *Catherine* v, The livery-stable was hard by.

Comb. **1736** *Rhode Island Col. Rec.* (1859) IV. 527 Alexander Thorp, livery stable keeper, and Isaac Cusno, saddler. **1865** DICKENS *Mut. Fr.* I. ii, A livery stable-yard in Duke Street. **1867** TROLLOPE *Chron. Barset* II. lii. 95, I should be so much obliged if I might be allowed to pay the livery-stable keeper's bill.

lives, livesman: see LIFE *sb.* 15, 15 b, 18.

live stock, 'live-stock.

1. Domestic animals generally; animals of any kind kept or dealt in for use or profit.

1777 SHERIDAN *Sch. Scand.* III. iii, Nothing but live stock—and that's only a few pointers and ponies. **1777** ROBERTSON *Hist. Amer.* (1783) III. 420 The number of its live-stock is more than treble. **1828** MISS MITFORD *Village* Ser. III. 264 Trying the great market of Covent-garden for the sale of his live-stock. **1840** R. H. DANA *Bef. Mast* xxix. 105 Our live stock, consisting of four bullocks, a dozen sheep, a dozen or more pigs. **1863** FAWCETT *Pol. Econ.* II. v. (1876) 159 Farmers may also now insure their live-stock.

transf. **1775** SHERIDAN *Rivals* II. i, You talked of independence and a fortune, but not a word of a wife. *Sir A*... Odds life, sir! if you have the estate, you must take it with the live stock on it, as it stands. **1894** W. MORRIS in Mackail *Life* (1899) II. 305 Our suffering the human live-stock of the country to live such a wretched scanty existence as they do.

attrib. **1856** *Farmer's Mag.* Jan. 7 The Council have.. agreed to the Live-Stock Prize-Sheet. **1894** *Daily News* 4 July 5/7 The live-stock trade.

2. Body vermin. *dial.* and *slang.*

1785 GROSE *Dict. Vulg. Tongue, Live stock*, lice, or fleas.

livetenant, obs. form of LIEUTENANT.

live-tide: see LIFE 17.

live time, obs. form of LIFETIME.

livett, var. LIBBET[1].

liveware ('laɪvwɛə(r)). [f. LIVE *a.* + WARE *sb.*[3], after HARDWARE 1 c.] People, personnel, as distinct from the inanimate or abstract things they work with; *spec.* computer personnel.

1966 *Times* 11 Apr. 12/2 The three elements which comprise a working computer system are hardware, the equipment itself; software, the vital programming aids; and the 'liveware', or personnel. **1967** H. COBLANS in de Reuck & Knight *Communication in Science* 80 Indexing devices are less crucial than the 'liveware'—the insight and experience of the men and women who do the indexing. **1978** *Computing Europe* 16 Mar. 15/4 The 1970s have seen a very expensive commodity—computer liveware—coping with a growing load of maintenance. **1984** *Times* 28 July 2/7 We were looking after the 'liveware'—the people. ICL was the leader and supplied hardware.

liveyere ('lɪvjə(r)). *Canad.* Also **liveyer, livier, livyer(e.** [Prob. f. the phr. *live here* (see below).] (See quot. 1909.) Also a permanent resident (as opp. to visiting fishermen, etc.).

Dict. Canadianisms suggests that the term 'may be < *livier* < OF. *livree* (cp. *livery*), formerly in English villages a manorial worker having certain hereditary rights to a cottage and a small piece of land, thus being regarded as a permanent resident'. But cf. LIVIER.

1863 J. MORETON *Life & Work in Newfoundland* iii. 35 It is said of any uninhabited place that there are no *liviers* in it. **1881** EARL OF DUNRAVEN in *19th Cent.* IX. 93 A 'livier' signifies a person who lives all the year around in a locality, in contradistinction to one who visits it during the fishing season. **1895** W. GRENFELL *Vikings of To-day* 57 The summer Labrador settlements are on islands or outside headlands, and here both Newfoundlanders and 'Livyeres' dwell, the latter retiring up the bays and inlets, to be nearer wood and game, when the former return to Newfoundland. **1901** *Chambers's Jrnl.* Jan. 68/2 The residents along this coast are termed 'livyres' (live heres), to distinguish them from the nomadic fisherfolk. **1905** N. DUNCAN *Dr. Grenfell's Parish* i. 12 The shore fishermen of the remoter Newfoundland coasts, the Labrador 'liveyeres', the Indians of the forbidding interior. **1907** D. WALLACE *Long Labrador Trail* xxiii. 273 Even tea and molasses, usually found amongst the 'livyeres' (liveheres) of the coast, were lacking. **1909** *Toilers of Deep* July 176/1 The permanent inhabitants of the Labrador coast, the 'liveyeres' are about three thousand in number. **1925** *Dialect Notes* V. 335 *Livyere*, one who lives here (in Newfoundland), usually an outport man. **1955** *Arctic Terms* 50/1 *Liveyere*, a corruption of 'live here', used in south-eastern Labrador to designate a semisettled inhabitant who customarily has a summer dwelling near coastal fishing grounds and a winter dwelling in an inland valley or in a mission settlement. **1966** A. R. SCAMMELL *My Newfoundland* 47 The steamer had just turned the point, whistled hoarsely a couple of times to alert the livyers. **1969** H. HORWOOD *Newfoundland* xxv. 204 Most of the Livyers today are black-haired and a little darker than most Europeans... But many Livyers with blond hair, blue eyes, and fair skin keep cropping up too.

livi, obs. form of LIFEY.

livid ('lɪvɪd), *a.* [ad. F. *livide* or L. *līvidus*, f. *līvēre* to be livid.] **a.** Of a bluish leaden colour; discoloured as by a bruise; black and blue.

1622 BACON *Hen. VII* 9 There followed no Carbuncle, no purple or liuide Spots. **1663** COWLEY *Christ's Passion*, Verses & Ess. (1669) 2 Dost thou not see the livid traces Of the sharp scourges rude embraces? **1703** POPE *Thebais* I. 83 Thou, sable Styx! whose livid streams are roll'd Thro' dreary coasts. **1720** GAY *Poems* (1745) II. 252 With wan care Sunk are those eyes, and livid with despair. **1786** tr. *Beckford's Vathek* (1883) 143 A voice from the livid lips of the Prophet articulated these words. **1797** MRS. RADCLIFFE *Italian* v, The light glared on the livid face of the corpse. **1808** *Med. Jrnl.* XIX. 345 A livid suffusion like that of erysipelas slightly elevated. **1816** PLAYFAIR *Nat. Phil.* II. 197 In 1607 it [the Comet] was dark and livid. **1828** STARK *Elem. Nat. Hist.* I. 311 Silvery Gull or Herring-Gull of Latham. Mantle bluish-cinereous; legs livid. **1864** BROWNING *Jas. Lee's Wife* VI. v, Her lean fingers shut Close, close, their sharp and livid nails Indent the clammy palm. **1870** HOOKER *Stud. Flora* 220 *Hieracium Lawsoni*.. styles livid. **1882** OUIDA *Maremma* I. 179 Over the water there hung.. a livid fog of heat.

Comb. **1860** J. R. EDKINS *Chinese Scenes & People* (1863) 132 A long-faced livid-looking individual.. rose.

b. Prefixed, as a qualification, to other adjectives or substantives of colour. (Usually hyphened with the adj. when the latter is used attributively.)

In botanical use the form *livido-* (see -O *suffix*) has been employed in compound designations of colour: so *livido-castaneous, -fuscous, -virescent*, etc. (W. A. Leighton *Lichenflora*, 1871.)

1814 SCOTT *Ld. of Isles* V. xxvi, His trembling lips are livid blue. **1827–35** WILLIS *Leper* 53 White scales, Circled with livid purple, cover'd him. **1859** SEMPLE *Diphtheria* 8 The edges of this foul ulcer are swollen, and of a livid-red colour. **1865** DICKENS *Mut. Fr.* I. x, His colour has turned to a livid white. **1887** W. PHILLIPS *Brit. Discomycetes* 218 Disc livid-glaucous.

c. Furiously angry, as if pale with rage. *colloq.*

1912 *Collier's* 9 Mar. 21/1 He sprang to his feet, livid. 'That's a lie,' and he stopped suddenly, startled by his own violence. **1918** C. MACKENZIE *Early Life Sylvia Scarlett* II. ii. 292 He was livid with fury. He asked if I thought he was made of money. **1936** M. KENNEDY *Together & Apart* II. 151 Betsy is *livid*. She says now she will fight to the last ditch to get complete custody of the children. **1949** R. CHANDLER *Little Sister* ii. 10 Orrin would be absolutely livid. Mother would be furious too. **1959** J. VERNEY *Friday's Tunnel* xxiv. 214 Friday's livid because he thinks you've punctured his bike. **1973** 'D. SHANNON' *No Holiday for Crime* (1974) x. 162 Mr. MacFarlane would be livid to have it [*sc.* whisky] impounded as evidence.

Hence **'lividly** *adv.*, in a livid manner, with a livid tinge.

1819 WIFFEN *Aonian Hours* (1820) 58 Tinging the bough till lividly it grew All ashes. **1898** J. HUTCHINSON in *Arch. Surg.* IX. 339 He looked lividly pale, but by no means absolutely blanched.

lividity (lɪ'vɪdɪtɪ). [ad. F. *lividité* or late L. *līviditās*, f. *līvidus*, LIVID.] The quality or condition of being livid; a pale-bluish discoloration.

1477 NORTON *Ord. Alch.* v. in Ashm. (1652) 65 This Waun Colour called Lividitie, In Envious Men useth much to be. **1611** COTGR., *Lividité*, liuiditie, lewnesse [etc.]. **1731** ARBUTHNOT *Aliments* (1735) 207 The Signs of a Tendency to such a State, are Darkness or Lividity of the Countenance [etc.]. **1876** *Trans. Clinical Soc.* IX. 189 There was no lividity of lips or cheeks. **1885** MISS BRADDON *Wyllard's Weird* II. 58 A shade more livid than the normal lividity of the complexion. **1900** J. HUTCHINSON in *Arch. Surg.* V. 207 The lividity of the hands.. was never attended by algidity.

'lividness. [f. LIVID + -NESS.] = prec.

1656 PRYNNE *Demurrer to Jews' Remitter* 26 He is whipped even unto bloud and lividnesse. **1698** MUSGRAVE in *Phil. Trans.* XX. 179 The remarkable Lividness of their Faces. **1762–65** H. WALPOLE *Vertue's Anecd. Paint.* III. 53 He.. caught the roundness of his flesh, but with a disagreeable lividness. **1798** WILSON in *Phil. Trans.* LXXXVIII. 354 This occasional lividness would happen to a child in that state. [In mod. Dicts.]

livido-: see LIVID *a.* b.

†**'lividous**, *a. Obs. rare*$^{-1}$. [f. L. *līvid-us* LIVID + -OUS.] Livid.

1597 A. M. tr. *Guillemeau's Fr. Chirurg.* 3 b/1 The Membrana is blacke, leadish-colourede, and lividouse.

livier ('laɪvɪə(r)). *local.* [? f. *live(s)*, pl. of LIFE + -IER.] One who holds a tenement on a lease for a life or lives.

1883 T. HARDY in *Longm. Mag.* July 269 Many of these families had been life-holders... The 'liviers' (as these half-independent villagers used to be called). **1891** —— *Tess* (1900) 127/2 'Liviers' were disapproved of in villages almost as much as little freeholders.

living ('lɪvɪŋ), *vbl. sb.* [f. LIVE *v.*[1] + -ING[1].]

1. a. The action of the vb. LIVE in various senses; the fact of being alive; the fact of dwelling in a specified place; †the faculty or function of life; course of life; †continuance in life.

a **1325** *Prose Psalter* lxii. 4 Þy mercy is better vp lybbeinges. *c* **1340** HAMPOLE *Prose Tr.* (1866) 25 For wysely and discretely thei departed hir levynge in two. —— *Pr. Consc.* 4130 Ful synful sal be his bygynnyng, And wonderful sal be his lyvyng. And his endying sal be sodayn. *c* **1375** *Sc. Leg. Saints* xviii. (*Egipciane*) 152 Sume of lyfinge mad na forse. *c* **1440** *Gesta Rom.* xxxix. 363 (Add. MS.) [For] the fyrste woman he gafe to the soule weyng [? *read* beyng] and leuyng with trees; for the second he gafe felyng with bestes [etc.]. *c* **1520** GRESHAM in Ellis *Orig. Lett.* Ser. III. I. 236 God.. send your Grace goode helthe and long leyffven. **1601** R. JOHNSON *Kingd. & Commw.* (1603) 127 This long living is the true cause of their propagation. **1631** JORDAN *Nat. Bathes* ii. (1669) 14 There is no living for any creature, where there is no water. **1719** DE FOE *Crusoe* I. v. (1840) 96 There would be no living for me in a cave. **1809** MALKIN *Gil Blas* VII. vii. (Rtldg.) 27 He was.. so jealous, that there was no living for vexation at his un-founded surmises. **1861** FLO. NIGHTINGALE *Nursing* 20 As if living in the country would save them from attending to any of the laws of health. **1897** *Daily News* 15 Nov. 5/4 This [campaigning] is 'living', anyhow, in a sense in which garrison life is not.

†**b.** Duration of life; lifetime. *Obs.*

[**1340** *Ayenb.* 73 Voryet þi body ones a day guo in-to helle ine þine libbinde þet þou ne guo ine þine steruinge.] *c* **1374** CHAUCER *Anel. & Arc.* 188 Sheo ne graunted him in hir lyvynge No grace. *c* **1450** LONELICH *Grail* liii. 263, I schal preyen be my levynge [F. *en mon vivant*], that I.. In that same Abbeye I-beryed to be. *c* **1470** *Golagros & Gaw.* 1076 Than war I woundir vnwis, To purchese proffit for pris, Quhare schame ay euer lyis, All my leuing. *c* **1475** *Partenay* 488 That neuer, dais of your leuing,.. Ye shall not enquere of me the saturday. **1597** SHAKS. *Lover's Compl.* 238 She.. did thence remoue, To spend her liuing in eternall loue.

c. The action of passing or conducting one's life in a particular manner, whether with reference to moral considerations or to food and physical conditions; †manner of life. †Also, a particular (monastic) rule of life.

1340 HAMPOLE *Pr. Consc.* 205 He þat right ordir of lyfyng wil luke Suld bygyn þus. *a* **1400** *Cursor M.* 28943 (Cott. Galba) þam þat has bene haueand, hend, of lifing clene. *a* **1450** MYRC 22 For luytel ys worthy þy prechynge, ȝef thow be of euyle lyuynge. *c* **1450** *St. Cuthbert* (Surtees) 3690 Demys ȝow na better in ȝour doyng þan othir of þe same leuyng. **1485** *Act 1 Hen. VII*, c. 4 Priests.. openly reported of incontinent living in their Bodies. **1513** BRADSHAW *St. Werburge* I. 2474 He forsoke this worlde and chaunged his lyuynge. **1555** EDEN *Decades* (Arb.) 53 Dissolute lyuynge, licentious talke, and such other vicious behauours. **1577** NORTHBROOKE *Dicing* (1843) 15 We.. haue almost minde at no time to repent and amend our liuings. **1650** FULLER *Pisgah* II. 63 Whereas all those in Egypt, though pain-full in their livings, were healthfull in their lives. **1689** W. SHERLOCK *Death* iii. §4 (1731) 114 There is a Living a-pace, as some call it; not to lengthen, but to shorten Life. **1743** BULKELEY & CUMMINS *Voy. S. Seas* 78 Our Living now is very hard. **1802** WORDSW. '*O Friend! I know not*', Plain living and high thinking are no more. **1862** H. SPENCER *First Princ.* II. i. §36 (1875) 129 Under Socrates.. Philosophy became little else than the doctrine of right living. **1874** HELPS *Soc. Press.* ii. 23 There are huge improvements to be made.. in the first requisites for decorous and beautiful living.

d. ***living-in, -out:*** the practice of residing in or out of an employer's premises. Also *attrib.*, ***living-in*** or ***-out system.***

1896 C. BOOTH *Life & Labour Lond.* VII. 505 Index, 'Living-in' system. **1899** *Daily News* 22 June 9/5 The iniquities of the living-in system. **1901** *Daily Chron.* 15 May 2/7 Living out.. would take a great deal of responsibility from the shoulders of employers. **1942** *R.A.F. Jrnl.* 13 June 14 The misunderstanding has arisen.. over the living-out system on which the Commandos work. The men are neither billeted nor fed by the Army. **1955** M. LASKI *Apologies* 59 I'd never have living-in servants again. **1962** L. DEIGHTON *Ipcress File* xi. 71 Murray decided that this was a good time to ask about his living out allowance. **1970** 'J. BELL' *Hydra with Six Heads* vii. 76 There was a living-in cook. **1974** 'P. B. YUILL' *Bornless Keeper* viii. 71 Check with Exeter [Gaol] he isn't on their wonderful living-out rehabilitation scheme.

2. The action, process, or method of gaining one's livelihood.

1538 STARKEY *England* II. i. 152 To.. fynd to them some honest lyvyngs. **1711** ADDISON *Spect.* No. 55 ¶ 1 Most of the Trades, Professions, and Ways of Living among man-kind. **1890** 'ROLF BOLDREWOOD' *Col. Reformer* (1891) 286 That occasional entire dependence upon personal resources which has been roughly translated as 'living by his wits'. **1901** H. BLACK *Culture & Restraint* ii. 35 Men are so concerned about living that they lose sight of life.

3. a. The means of living; livelihood, maintenance, support; †also, an income, an endowment. Now chiefly in ***to earn, get, make a living.***

c **1330** *Arth. & Merl.* 976 (Kölbing) A cabel.. Forto drawen vp al þing, þat nede was to her libbeing. *c* **1375** *Sc. Leg. Saints* xxi. (*Clement*) 122 þat matydiane worthit ga to gat lyfing to þame twa. **1450** in *Exch. Rolls Scotl.* V. 425 *note*, We have.. gevin till oure loved Patrik Lyndesay five markes.. till his living yerly. *c* **1470** HENRY *Wallace* VII. 897 Rycht wichtly wan his lewyng in to wer. **1496** *Act 12 Hen. VII*, c. 6 Woollen Cloth.. by making whereof.. the poor People have most universally their Living. **1536** BELLENDEN *Cron. Scot.* (1821) II. 250 Gawine Dounbar.. biggit ane brig ouir Dee,.. and foundit ane yeirly leving, to sustene the same. **1550** CROWLEY *Last Trumpet* 493 If thou have any lyveyng So that thou nede not to laboure; Se thou apply the to learnynge. **1611** BIBLE *Mark* xii. 44 She.. did cast in all that she had, euen all her liuing. **1632** QUARLES *Div. Fancies* III. lxxxii. (1660) 134 Instead of giving Encrease to her revenues, make a living Upon her ruins. **1724** *Lond. Gaz.* No. 6306/3 Sometimes plays on the Violin for a living. **1764** BURN *Poor Laws* 150 No person will have need to beg or steal; because he may gain his living better by working. **1860** EMERSON *Cond. Life* iii. (1861) 52 Society is barbarous, until every industrious man can get his living without dishonest customs. **1868** HELPS *Realmah* xvii. (1876) 472 He cannot make a living out of it, if [etc.]. **1883** SIR J. BACON in *Law Times Rep.* 1 Mar. (1884) 9/2 The son.. earns his living as a licensed victualler.

b. †Also in narrower sense: Food; *pl.* Victuals (*obs.*).

c **1375** *Sc. Leg. Saints* xx. (*Blasius*) 39 Quhare vthyre lyfynge had he nocht bot as þe foulis til hym brocht. *c* **1450** LONELICH *Grail* xlv. 620 A brid that browhte me my lyveng. **1525** LD. BERNERS *Froiss.* II. ccii. [cxcviii.] 623 The see was closed fro them on all partes, wherby their lyuenges [F. *viures*] and marchaundises myght nat entre into their countreys. **1607** TOPSELL *Four-f. Beasts* (1658) 516 There is scarse any food whereof they do not eat, as also no place wherein they pick not out some living. **1863** FR. A. KEMBLE *Resid. in Georgia* 20 Our living consists very mainly of wild ducks.

†**4. a.** Property in general, esp. landed estate; *pl.* estates, possessions. Phr. ***man of living.*** Obs.

c **1430** *Syr Gener.* (Roxb.) 2280, I haue lost my living A hundreth pound it was worth wele. **1465** in *Exch. Rolls Scotl.* VII. 321 *note*, Cuthbert Colevile..has left his leving and gudis in the said realme. **1566** ASCHAM *Let. to Leicester* 14 Apr., My lease..the whole and only liveing that I have to leave to my wife and children. **1580** HAY *Demandes in Cath. Tractates* (1901) 61 Except onlie the pattimonie and leaving of the kirk. **1581** LAMBARDE *Eiren.* I. vi. (1588) 34 That none be now placed in the Commission, whose Leuings be not answerable to the same proportion. **1588** A. MARTEN *Exhort. Faithf. Subjects* D 2 There be many more great houses alredy, then there be men of liuing able to vphold. **1597** BACON *Coulers Gd. & Evill* Ess. (Arb.) 144 Men whose liuing lieth together in one Shire. **1603** OWEN *Pembrokesh.* (1891) 21 Maintaineinge himselfe upon his owne lyveinges verye noblye. **1633** T. STAFFORD *Pac. Hib.* II. xi. (1810) 351 Hee presented unto him all the men of living and quality in the Province. *c* **1672** *Roxb. Ballads* (1886) VI. 261 My Lands and Livings are but small, For to maintain my Love withal. **1716** B. CHURCH *Hist. Philip's War* (1867) II. 101 Not far from Penobscot, where the main body of our Enemies living was. **1813** SCOTT *Rokeby* I. xxi, Thy kinsman's lands and livings fair.

†**b.** A holding (of land), a tenement. *Obs.*

1583 STUBBES *Anat. Abus.* II. (1882) 28, I would not haue them [parkes] to be made of poore mens liuings. **1605–47** HABINGTON *Surv. Worcestersh.* in *Worc. Hist. Soc. Proc.* I. 139 Thys lord..did fyrst sell to many of the Tenants heere the inheritance of theyre lyvinges. **1617** *N. Riding Rec.* II. 159 J. D. presented for refusing to pay his sessment..of that living on which he now dwelleth. **1819** SCOTT *Noble Moringer* iv, There's many a valiant gentleman of me holds living fair.

5. *Eccl.* A benefice. More fully ***ecclesiastical, spiritual living.***

1426 AUDELAY *Poems* 40 A mon to have iiij. benefyse, anoder no lyvyng, This is not Godys wyl. *c* **1550** *Disc. Common Weal Eng.* (1893) 138 What reason is it that one man should haue ij mens livinges and ij mens charge? **1563–87** FOXE *A. & M.* (1596) 3/2 For the holding and reteining of all other spiritual livings whatsoever. **1577** HARRISON *England* II. v. (1877) I. 110 When a man is to be preferred to an ecclesiastical living. **1650** HUBBERT *Pill Formality* 28 They have two or three Livings apiece. **1680** COUNTESS MANCHESTER in *Hatton Corr.* (1878) 217 He haveing a great many very good liveings in his gifft. *a* **1703** BURKITT *On N.T., 1 Pet.* v. 3 To take a living only to get a living, is an horrid impiety. **1704** NELSON *Fest. & Fasts* x. (1739) 602 Any Person presented to any..Living Ecclesiastical. **1762** GOLDSM. *Cit. W.* xxvii, My father..was possessed of a small living in the Church. **1796** JANE AUSTEN *Pride & Prej.* xvi. (1813) 69 The late Mr. Darcy bequeathed me the next presentation of the best living in his gift. **1849** MACAULAY *Hist. Eng.* v. I. 532 At the time of the Restoration ..he had held a living in Kent. **1884** J. BRIGHT in *Times* 5 Aug. 10/4 The 500 peers are possessors of not less..than 4000 livings of the Church of England.

†**6.** A term in the game of Maw. *Obs.*

c **1570** *Groome-porters lawes at Mawe* in *Coll. Black-Let. Ball. & Broadsides* (1867) 124 If you turne vp the ace of hartes, and thereby make either partie aboue xxvj, the contrary part must haue liuings; but if the contrary parte bee xxv, by meanes whereof liuings sets them out, then is he who turned vp the ace of hartes to make for the set.

7. *attrib.* and *Comb.* **a.** simple attributive, as (sense 1 with reference to dwelling) ***living-dining room, -house, -place, -wagon.*** **b.** objective, as (sense 3) ***living †-giver, †-griper;*** (sense 5) ***living-broker; living-seeking*** adj.; **living area** = *living space* (*c*); †**living-days**, days of life; **living floor** *Archæol.*, the site of a prehistoric camp indicated by bones, tools, etc., found there; **living space**, (*a*) tr. LEBENSRAUM; (*b*) space for accommodation; (*c*) a habitable area in a room or house; **living standard** [cf. STANDARD *sb.* 12 a], the level of consumption in terms of food, accommodation, clothing, services, etc., estimated for a person, group, or nation; **living wage**, a wage on which it is possible for a worker to live; similarly ***living price.***

1962 *Listener* 18 Jan. 135/1 A new house..which I recently visited is centred on a large *living area. **1965** in P. Jennings *Living Village* (1968) 103 The garages are built at road level, and the living areas of the houses are built over the garages. **1969** K. GILES *Death cracks Bottle* vii. 74 The inglenook which the architect had fashioned in the living area. **1765** J. CLUBBE *Misc. Tracts* (1770) II. 44 Now is it not justly to [be] apprehended, that a certain order of men.. may come over hither, and commence *living-brokers? *c* **1440** CAPGRAVE *Life St. Kath.* v. 237 Oure *leuynge dayes ..arn at an ende. **1509** HAWES *Past. Pleas.* v. (Percy Soc.) 22 Whose goodly name..Was called Carmentis in her livyng dayes. **1933** *Archit. Rev.* LXXIV. 20 The exhibit is part of a projected structural unit which includes an entrance hall and kitchen in addition to the *living-dining room. **1945** NELSON & WRIGHT *Tomorrow's House* iv. 41/1 The living-dining-room was a makeshift..but nevertheless an expedient to save space and money. **1968** *Globe & Mail* (Toronto) 17 Feb. 45 (Advt.), Living-dining room with open fireplace. **1946** *Nature* 2 Nov. 637/2 In 1943, further evidence was obtained pointing to the conclusion that on the site, now known as Glorgesailie site 10, there was a series of actual *living floors or camp sites of Acheulean men. **1947** L. S. B. LEAKEY in *E. Afr. Ann.* 1946–7 69/1 On the ancient land surfaces were uncovered the actual 'living floors' or camp sites of ancient Acheulean hunters. **1965** HOLE & HEIZER *Introd. Prehist. Archeol.* iii. 35 The amount of bone and stone tools suggests seasonal, or perhaps permanent year-round camps. In Africa these are called 'living floors'. **1614** R. TAILOR *Hog hath lost Pearl* III. E 2, Is thy *liuing-giuer within, sir? *Ser.* You meane my master, sir? **1600** ROWLANDS *Lett. Humours Blood* ii. 51 A Gentle-man perhaps may chaunce to meete His *Liuing-griper face to face in streete. **1897** MARY KINGSLEY *W. Africa* 624 There are near to the *living-house large, well-built houses with the proper machinery for drying the cocoa. **1889** JESSOPP *Coming of Friars* iii. 124 The cloister was really the *living-place of the monks. **1834** *Congress. Globe* 3 May 362/2 Mr. Forsyth said that..70 to 76 cents was a very *living price for fish oil. **1892** *Nation* (N.Y.) 3 Mar. 168/2 Mr. C. would be glad to be enabled to do, at a living price, a series of prints. **1898** *Daily News* 31 May 6/6 The Premier had much dislike for *living-seeking parsons. **1939** W. S. CHURCHILL *Into Battle* (1941) 127 The Swiss..may rob them of their *living-space. **1944** F. CLUNE *Red Heart* 20 The Australian native..can make a 'living-space' in a country where white people can't. **1959** *Listener* 10 Dec. 1032/1 The 5,000 or so species of pest insects are man's most dangerous competitors for food and living space on this planet. *Ibid.* 17 Dec. 1071/1 The bed-sitting-room was divided by curtains into three living-spaces. **1959** *Chambers's Encycl.* IV. 338/2 Hitler's next objective was to sweep Czechoslovakia out of the road to 'living space' in the east. **1961** L. D. STAMP *Gloss. Geogr. Terms* 296/2 *Living space*, an English translation of the German *Lebensraum* but most authors prefer to use the German word when discussing its geo-political implications. **1961** *Listener* 28 Dec. 1110/1 Architects will be able to plan, on the ground floor, one, two, or three living spaces—for example, a kitchen partially opening into a dining-room, with a separate living-room. **1966** *Ibid.* 19 May 729/3 The average living space per person in Moscow is officially admitted to be eight square metres. **1972** M. JONES *Life on Dole* i. 15 There might have been a couple of lodgers, unmarried men..whose living space was a cot in the corner. **1957** P. WORSLEY *Trumpet shall Sound* vi. 121 The aim of the Government was to raise *living-standards to those of the Europeans. **1964** GOULD & KOLB *Dict. Social Sci.* 690/1 The concept of *living* standards, or levels, would include and perhaps emphasize, 'material' quantitative elements such as the consumption of goods and services. **1968** *Listener* 10 Oct. 469/3 This was the chief reason..why..Western achievements and Western living standards were so consistently lied about. **1974** *Times* 16 Jan. 13/2 Improving personal living standards. **1888** E. BELLAMY *Looking Backward* xxviii. 450 The wonder to me is, not that industries conducted as these are do not pay you *living wages, but that they are able to pay you any wages at all. **1893** *Ch. Times* 6 Oct. 995/2 As firm..as are the miners in standing out for what they call a 'living' wage. **1900** *Westm. Gaz.* 24 Nov. 10/1 Sir Andrew Clarke..used for the first time the phrase 'the living wage'..in 1892. **1967** *Listener* 23 Feb. 248/1 Some of them already have to work up to fifty-six hours a week to make up their weekly pay to a living wage of £20. **1974** *Guardian* 31 Jan. 13/8 Another miner..sounds bitter... 'We are broken down old men; we're limping and we are injured. And all we want is a living wage.' **1851** MAYHEW *Lond. Labour* I. 329 He termed it, as all showmen do—the *living wagon.

Hence **'livingless** *a.*, without a living.

1878 L. WINGFIELD *Lady Grizel* I. viii. 136 They were enjoined to roam..with a livingless parson as a mentor.

living ('lɪvɪŋ), *ppl. a.* [f. LIVE *v.* + -ING².]

1. *Predicatively*, or *attrib.* following the sb.: Alive, or when alive. †Also in the absolute construction, *living* ——, = 'in the lifetime of ——'.

c **825** *Vesp. Psalter* liv. [lv.] 16 Astiȝen hie in helle lifȝende. *c* **900** tr. *Bæda's Hist.* I. viii. (Schipper) 29 Constantius..be Diocletiane lyfȝendum Gallia rice..heold. *a* **1300** *Cursor M.* 4847 Elleuen breþer es we liuand. **1375** BARBOUR *Bruce* II. 547 The wiffis had him till his cuntre, Quhar wes na man leiffand bot he. *c* **1460** *Towneley Myst.* xx. 459 Ye shall se me well certan, and lyfand shall I be. **1535** COVERDALE 2 *Esdras* xii. 33 He shal sett them lyuynge before the iudgment. **1572** *Satir. Poems Reform.* xxxviii. 60 Thou hes left leifand bot few in that land. *c* **1641** BP. MOUNTAGU *Acts & Mon.* (1642) 267 Living his mother Alexandra, he had been with the High Priesthood nine yeares. **1771** *Junius Lett.* xlix. 254 As long as there is one man living who thinks you worthy of his confidence. **1827** JARMAN *Powell's Devises* II. 357 Where a testator..gives to his four children then living. **1830** R. B. PEAKE *Crt. & City* I. ii, You are the only man living that can serve my brother!

2. *attrib.* That lives or has life.

a. said of the Deity (after Biblical use).

c **900** tr. *Bæda's Hist.* IV. xxviii. (Schipper) 523 Ealle.. hine þurh þone lifiȝendan Dryhten halsedon. **1535** COVERDALE *Ps.* xli. 2 My soule is a thurste for God, yee euen for the lyuynge God. **1567** *Satir. Poems Reform.* vii. 231 The Leuing Lord bring thame to this gude end! **1732** BERKELEY *Serm. to S.P.G.* Wks. III. 240 The church of the living God. **1852** DICKENS *Bleak Ho.* liv, By the living Lord it flashed upon me..that she had done it.

b. of human beings, animals, and plants, or their parts. In mod. use sometimes used for 'now (or at the time spoken of) existing or living', 'contemporary'.

living fossil: a plant or animal that has survived the extinction of others of its group. †*living stock* = LIVE STOCK. *living skeleton*: an individual with an extremely emaciated frame.

a **1225** *Leg. Kath.* 1529 þæt ne mei hit..strengðe..of na liuiende mon leowsin. *a* **1240** *Ureisun* in *Cott. Hom.* 193 Ne non liuiinde þing woc þer nis ne ȝeomer. *a* **1300** *Cursor M.* 1689 þou sal tak tuin Of ilk liuand best. **1340–70** *Alisaunder* 790 A libbing lud lay in hur armes. **1362** LANGL. *P. Pl.* A. VIII. 64 Libbinde Laborers þat libben bi heore hondes. *c* **1375** *Sc. Leg. Saints* v. (*Johannes*) 577 þar wes na liffand man þat mycht se hym for þat mekil lycht. *c* **1400** tr. *Secreta Secret., Gov. Lordsh.* 59 Oþer many euelys comyn, þurgh whilk many leuand creatures ar perschyd. **1501** DOUGLAS *Pal. Hon.* Prol. 112 Saw neuer man so faynt a leuand wicht. **1559** W. CUNNINGHAM *Cosmogr. Glasse* 43 Th' Earth..is called..the norishe of lyving creatures,..the sepulchre of the dead. **1567** *Gude & Godlie Ball.* (S.T.S.) 116 All leuing man in to this warld sa round Sall loue thy name. **1611** BIBLE *Gen.* vi. 19. **1690** LUTTRELL *Brief Rel.* (1857) II. 37 Destroying the living stock. **1736** BUTLER *Anal.* I. i. 41 The supposed likeness which is observed between the decay of vegetables and of living creatures. **1791** BURKE *App. Whigs* Wks. VI. 115 That he preferred a dead carcase to his living children. **1825** *Ann. Reg.* (1826) LXVII. 239*/1 The name of the Living Skeleton is C. A. Seurat. **1841–71** R. JONES *Anim. Kingd.* (ed. 4) 733 The Crocodile..likewise kills living prey. **1849** MACAULAY *Hist. Eng.* xiv. II. 457 He was generally esteemed the greatest living master of the art of war. **1859** RUSKIN *Two Paths* ii. (1891) 82 He went to Rome and ordered various works of living artists. **1860** TYNDALL *Glac.* I. xxvii. 197 After this we encountered no living thing. **1875** BENNETT & DYER *Sachs' Bot.* 1 The living succulent parts of plants. **1878** HUXLEY *Physiogr.* 81 A fresh supply of air is constantly required by a living animal. **1935** C. J. CHAMBERLAIN *Gymnosperms* iv. 61 The cycads of today may well be called 'living fossils'. **1953** J. S. HUXLEY *Evolution in Action* v. 127 There is the persistence of a few survivors from a once-abundant group—so-called 'living fossils', like the duckbill platypus; and that of a whole successful group. **1955** *Sci. Amer.* Apr. 108/2 A living fossil is defined as an organism that has survived beyond its era. A standard example is the tuatara of New Zealand, which looks like a lizard but is in fact the 'sole survivor of an order of reptiles which flourished in the great Age of Reptiles and is now extinct except for this one species'. **1966** C. A. W. GUGGISBERG *S.O.S. Rhino* ii. 31 The two-horned Sumatran rhinoceros..has come to us practically unchanged from the Tertiary Age, another 'living fossil'. **1974** *Encycl. Brit. Micropædia* VI. 276/3 Living fossil, an organism long believed extinct that is discovered to be still in existence.

c. absol. ***the living***: those who are alive. ***the land of the living***: see Ps. xxvii. 13, lii. 5; Isaiah xxxviii. 11, liii. 8. See also LAND *sb.* 3 c.

c **825** *Vesp. Hymns* iii. 3 Ic ne ȝesio dryhten god in eorðan lifȝendra. *a* **1175** *Cott. Hom.* 223 Hi is aelra libbinde moder. **13..** *E.E. Allit.* P. A. 699 For non lyuyande to þe is Iustyfyet. *c* **1470** *Golagros & Gaw.* 954 Lord..thow life lent to levand in leid. **1535** COVERDALE *Eccl.* vi. 8 What helpeth it the poore, that he knoweth to walke before the lyuynge? **1611** BIBLE *Ruth* ii. 20 He..hath not left off his kindnesse to the liuing and to the dead. **1672** PETTY *Pol. Anat.* (1691) Ded., Your Generosity..takes all occasions of exerting it self towards the Living. **1708** LADY CAVE *Let.* in M. M. Verney *Verney Lett.* (1930) I. xiv. 266 Sir Thomas is glad to hear Col. Oughton is in the land of the living..having not heard a word from him. **1778** MISS BURNEY *Evelina* (1791) II. xxxvii. 242 I'm glad to see you still in the land of the living. **1793** BURKE *Corr.* (1844) IV. 185 The true way to mourn the dead, is to take care of the living who belong to them. **1859** TENNYSON *Elaine* 1359 If one may judge the living by the dead. **1925** E. PHILLPOTTS *Voice from Dark* ii. 22 And is Mr. Bitton still in the land of the living? **1964** *Roman Breviary* 346 P, You are my refuge, my portion in the land of the living.

d. *transf.* (*a*) In various phrases of biblical origin. Of water: Constantly flowing; also, refreshing. (*b*) Of coals: Burning, flaming. Cf. LIVE *a.* 3. (*c*) Of rock, stone: Native; in its native condition and site, as part of the earth's crust. Cf. LIVELY *a.* 1 b.

1388 WYCLIF *John* vi. 51 Y am lyuynge breed, that cam doun fro heuene. *c* **1400** MAUNDEV. (1839) iv. 29 The Welle of Gardyns and the Dyche of lyvynge Waters. **1483** CAXTON *G. de la Tour* lxxxvii. L j b, [He] made..to..come out of the stone lyuyng and swete water. **1567** *Gude & Godlie Ball.* (S.T.S.) 16 Christis blude..is ane leuand well Celestiall. **1697** DRYDEN *Virg. Æneid* I. 78 In a spacious cave of living stone. *Ibid.* VIII. 547 And living Embers on the Hearth they spred. **1726** LEONI *Alberti's Archit.* I. 64/1 A high bold shore of living craggy Rock. **1735** SOMERVILLE *Chase* I. 59 What remains On living Coals they broil. **1821** JOANNA BAILLIE *Metr. Leg., Wallace* xxxviii, His soldiers firm as living rock. **1837** YOUATT *Sheep* xi. 452 He got another pond of living water, and sustained in that season no loss to his flock. **1843** LE FEVRE *Life Trav. Phys.* II. I. xiv. 45 The fish ponds..were fed by a living stream. **1893** BUDGE *Mummy* 14 The Sphinx is hewn out of the living rock.

e. Of a language: Still in vernacular use. (Cf. *dead language* s.v. LANGUAGE 1.)

1706 A. BEDFORD *Temple Mus.* ii. 45 The Hebrew ceasing to be a Living Language. **1749** *Numbers in Poet. Comp.* 12 Not only in English but French, and..every living Language in Europe. **1807** CRABBE *Library* 66 Here all the living languages abound. **1845** [see LANGUAGE 1].

f. *fig.* in various uses. ***living corpse; living dead***: as *adj. phr.*, having lost hold of life, not using one's life abundantly; as *sb. phr.*, such people. ***living death***: a state of misery not deserving the name of life. ***living pledge*** (see quot. 1767).

1388 WYCLIF *1 Pet.* i. 3 The fadir of oure Lord Ihesu Crist ..bigat vs aȝen in to lyuynge [1382 quik] hope by the aȝen risyng of Ihesu Crist. **1611** SPEED *Hist. Gt. Brit.* VI. xlvi. 261 So Constantines glorious life drew to an end, though his liuing-glory shall be endlesse. **1671** MILTON *Samson* 100 To live a life half-dead, a living death, and buried. **1738** WESLEY *Psalms* LI. xx, Their every Thought, and Word, and Deed, That from a living Faith proceed. **1750** GRAY *Elegy* 48 Or wak'd to Extacy the living Lyre. **1767** BLACKSTONE *Comm.* II. 157 *Vivum vadium*, or living pledge, is when a man borrows a sum (suppose 200*l.*) of another; and grants him an estate, as, of 20*l.* per annum, to hold till the rents and profits shall repay the sum so borrowed. **1853** KINGSLEY *Hypatia* i. 5 Each man had..living trust in the continual care of Almighty God. **1860** J. W. PALMER tr. *Michelet's Love* IV. viii. 243 It may be said that she came out of the asylum a living corpse, and it was not long before she died in reality. **1863** O. W. HOLMES *Old Vol. Life* iii. (1891) 78 It is the living question of the hour, and not the dead story of the

past, which forces itself into all minds. **1869** SEELEY *Lect. & Ess.* (1870) 77 Not that there is anything in a living Christianity incompatible with liberty. **1871** FARRAR *Witn. Hist.* ii. 65 The idea..was created solely by the living fact. **1917** R. GRAVES *Fairies & Fusiliers* 28 You'll find me buried, living-dead In these verses that you've read. *a* **1930** D. H. LAWRENCE *Last Poems* (1932) 168, I know the unliving factory-hand, living-dead millions Is unliving me, living-dead me, I, with them, am living dead. **1958** *Listener* 14 Aug. 225/2 What they thought of 'squares', and the living dead in general.

3. Of or pertaining to a living person or what is living. ***living chess***: a game of chess in which living persons act as the chessmen; †***living-fence***: a fence formed of living wood, esp. hawthorn; ***living force*** = *vis viva* s.v. VIS *sb.*² 2 c; ***within living memory***: in the recollection of persons still alive; ***living newspaper*** (see quot. 1966); ***living theatre***: the theatre, as opposed to the cinema.

1676 GLANVILL *Ess.* iii. 6 Death having overcome that Envy which dog's living Virtue to the Grave. **1686** PLOT *Staffordsh.* 357 For a living-fence, I met with none so.. serviceal as those, made by the planching of Quicksets. **1836** J. H. NEWMAN *Par. Serm.* (1837) III. xxiii. 351 It is as if a living hand were to touch cold iron. **1855** MACAULAY *Hist. Eng.* xiv. III. 438 There had within living memory been no equally serious encounter between the English and French. **1864** *Lond. Rev.* 27 Aug. 247/2 Psychonomy..illustrated by tracings from living hands. **1876** TAIT *Rec. Adv. Phys. Sci.* (1885) 360 That which is denoted by the term Living Force, though it has absolutely no right to be called force, is something as real as matter itself. **1877** W. MORRIS in Mackail *Life* (1899) I. 341 The newly-invented study of living history is the chief joy of so many of our lives. **1888** BURGON *Lives 12 Gd. Men* II. v. 1 No ecclesiastic within living memory..has enjoyed a larger share of personal celebrity. **1905** *Lasker's Chess Mag.* II. III. 131 So that the reader may visualize the phases through which the game has passed we will show two historical cameos of living chess. **1929** *Brit. Chess Mag.* LXIX. 126 A picturesque display of living chess was given by the schoolboys. **1935** *N.Y. Times* 31 Dec. 10/1 Elmer Rice, regional director, announced that ..the Biltmore will open before the end of January with the first topical production of the unit known as the 'Living Newspaper'. The initial show..will offer in graphic terms the background of the Italo-Ethiopian war. **1938** *Times* 28 Dec. 11/3 The 'living' theatre, as it has come to be called in distinction from the cinema, must be in a very healthy condition. **1940** *Ann. Reg. 1939* 40 The Chancellor made the entertainment tax lighter for the 'living theatre'. **1941** J. S. HUXLEY in *Fortnightly* July 11 The theatre project indeed began to create new types of popular drama like the Living Newspaper, which undoubtedly stimulated social self-consciousness. **1963** *Guardian* 12 Mar. 2/6 It was deplorable that Plymouth had no living theatre. **1966** J. R. TAYLOR *Penguin Dict. Theatre* 159 *Living newspaper*, a sort of topical documentary revue in a series of short scenes based on current social and political problems, devised in the 1930s in the U.S.A. by the Federal Theatre, and used elsewhere for propaganda during the war. **1970** A. SUNNUCKS *Encycl. Chess* 291 *Living chess.* During the past 600 years the game played with living pieces has from time to time been presented in different countries. **1971** J. WILLETT in A. Bullock *20th Cent.* 243/1 The Theater Project..evolved a new form of lecture-cum-sketch in the Living Newspaper.

4. With prefixed adv.: That passes life in a specified manner.

c **1380** WYCLIF *Wks.* (1880) 33 Vnkunnynge & euyl leuynge prelatis. **1901** *Daily Chron.* 19 Oct. 3/1 Richardson ..was..a good and virtuous-living man.

5. = LIVELY *a.* in senses 4, 5, and 6. ***living gale*** Naut. (see quot. 1883).

a **1718** PENN *Life* Wks. 1726 I. 231 During her Illness she uttered many Living and Weighty Expressions. **1816** BYRON *Dream* ii, A most living landscape. **1844** STANLEY *Arnold* I. ii. 46 The sight of the city and of the neighbourhood, to which he devoted himself..gave him a living interest in Rome. **1851** RUSKIN *Stones Ven.* (1874) I. App. 370 Bold, and rich, and living architecture. **1876** FREEMAN *Norm. Conq.* V. xxii. 47 The portrait of William is drawn..in living colours, by the Chronicler. **1883** CLARK RUSSELL *Sailors' Lang.*, *Living gale*, a tremendous gale. **1888** BURGON *Lives 12 Gd. Men* I. Pref. 9 Faithfully to commit to paper a living image of the man.

6. ***living picture***, (*a*) = *tableau vivant* (TABLEAU *sb.* 4); (*b*) a motion-picture.

1875 *N.Y. Herald* 24 Nov. 2/4 Mr. Matt Morgan's Classical Tableaux of Living Pictures, illustrated by a Corps of Beautiful Ladies. **1895** G. B. SHAW in *Sat. Rev.* 6 Apr. 443/2, I sat out the entire list of sixteen 'Living Pictures'. Half a dozen represented naiads, mountain sprites, peris, and Lady Godiva, all practically undraped. **1897** *Knowledge* 1 Sept. 216/2 Last winter saw the 'living pictures' adopted as the craze of the season for music-halls, bazaars, and variety entertainments generally. **1897** *Sears, Roebuck Catal.* 342/2 [The book] includes also elaborate directions for exhibiting Living Pictures and Tableaux. **1899** H. V. HOPWOOD *Living Pictures* vi. 207 The first requirement in the projection, as in the taking, of Living Pictures is absolute rigidity of the apparatus. **1906** J. A. MANSON *Indoor Games* 30 Living Pictures, or Tableaux Vivants, if considered as an indoor game, must be placed on the highest level... It need hardly be said that neither acting nor speech is required in a living picture. **1962** E. LARSEN *Film Making* i. 18 Soon nearly every variety show contained 'living pictures' as a programme item.

livingly ('lɪvɪŋlɪ), *adv.* [f. LIVING *ppl. a.* + -LY².] In a living manner; as if living; vitally; livelily, vividly.

a **1470** in *Hist. Collect. Cit. Lond.* (Camd.) 137 We..shalle ordayne for hyr governaunce of the persone of oure sayde fadyr, sykerly, lyvyngly, and honestely, aftyr the askynge of hys ryalle astate and dygnyte, by [etc.]. **1577** KNEWSTUB *Confut.* (1579) 40 b, His children, heauenly, spirituall and liuingly minded. **1638** MAYNE *Lucian* (1664) 157 You have most livingly described the peeces in Orestes Temple. **1661** G. RUST *Origen* 79 That vital temper the Soul requires in the body she will livingly joyn with. **1680** G. KEITH *Rector corrected* i. 9 That word which doth..quicken our Souls unto God, and livingly doth refresh and comfort us. **1769** WOOLMAN *Jrnl.* x. (1840) 141 The doctrine of Christ, 'Take no thought for the morrow', arose livingly before me. **1826** *Blackw. Mag.* XX. 488 The life, yet breathing and livingly remembered, of men. **1835** LYTTON *Rienzi* VI. ii, A fountain still played sparkling and livingly. **1850** MAURICE *Mor. & Met. Philos.* (ed. 2) I. 122 It was absolutely necessary that he [Socrates] should be brought livingly before us. **1881** W. R. NICOLL *Incarnate Saviour* 24 This is not the mere history of the past: it touches us livingly.

livingness ('lɪvɪŋnɪs). [f. LIVING *ppl. a.* + -NESS.] The quality, condition, or fact of being alive or living; vigour, vivacity, vividness.

1688 SANDILANDS *Salut. Endeared Love* 29 Which indisposeth both Body and Mind to serve the Lord even in that livingness and freshness which he requires. **1831** LYTTON *Godolphin* 51 The attitude was even awful in the livingness of its command. **1851** BRIMLEY *Ess.* 113 There has arisen in our country..a sense of the livingness and value of our history. **1871** F. J. A. HORT *Hulsean Lect.* 195 Early sense of life..branches off into self-regarding passions, but thereby loses its own livingness. **1884** MRS. OLIPHANT *Open Door* 43 Signs of the livingness of nature.

living-room. Also **living room**. [LIVING *vbl. sb.* 7.] **1.** A room that is set aside for ordinary social use (as opp. to a bedroom, etc.).

1825 *Greenhouse Comp.* I. 9 No living-room should depend for its ventilation on such of its windows as may communicate with a green-house. **1857** C. VAUX *Villas & Cottages* 119 Under the..living-room is a basement-kitchen. **1867** 'T. LACKLAND' *Homespun* I. 139 The joy with which grand parents welcome us in the great living-room. **1879** F. R. STOCKTON *Rudder Grange* i. 7 There was a kitchen, a living room, a parlor and bedrooms. **1884** *Illustr. Lond. News* 1 Mar. 209/2 From all the living-rooms glimpses were obtainable of soft green hills and white cottages. **1911** C. HARRIS *Eve's Second Husband* 310 She occupied one chair in the living room all day. **1911** H. S. HARRISON *Queed* xix. 239 Queed..went upstairs to the comfortable living-room. **1917–18** *T. Eaton & Co. Catal.* Fall & Winter 416/4 Massive living-room arm chair. **1931** A. J. CRONIN *Hatter's Castle* I. i. 12 The common room, the living room of the house where its inhabitants partook of meals, spent their leisure and congregated in their family life. **1933** *Discovery* July 218/2 The growing popularity of the living-room as the central dominant feature of the modern dwelling..has completely altered the design of the house. **1933** H. WALPOLE *Vanessa* II. 287 The room at the top of the first stairflight that had once been the drawing-room with the fine gilt chairs,..the rosy cupids on the ceiling, was now the general living-room. **1953** G. GREENE (*title*) The living room. **1967** E. SHORT *Embroidery & Fabric Collage* iii. 78 [The cushion] can transform a divan from a bed into an acceptable piece of living-room furniture. **1971** *Daily Tel.* (Colour Suppl.) 12 Nov. 30/1 In the living-room is the Steinway upright.

2. tr. LEBENSRAUM.

1938 *Times* 18 Nov. 17/6 The Danube valley and the Balkans are..the natural 'living-room' of industrial Germany. **1940** 'G. ORWELL' in *New English Weekly* 21 Mar. 321/1 Hitler envisages, a hundred years hence,..a continuous state of 250 million Germans with plenty of 'living room'. **1942** E. PAUL *Narrow St.* xxxiv. 305 The leaders had told them Hitler would behave, if appeased, that he did not want their lands and goods but only 'living room'.

Livingstone ('lɪvɪŋstən). [Origin unknown.] A name used *attrib.* to designate the **Livingstone daisy**, a small, annual, succulent plant, *Dorotheanthus bellidiformis* (*Mesembryanthemum criniflorum*), native to the Cape Province of South Africa, and bearing daisy-like flowers.

1934 B. P. MANSFIELD in *Gardeners' Chronicle* 19 May 330/1 The Livingstone Daisy. From..seed catalogues.., I gather that *Mesembryanthemum criniflorum* is introduced as a 1934 novelty. **1950** W. E. SHEWELL-COOPER *Compl. Gardener* III. 243 The 'Livingstone Daisy' is a delightful annual with fairy-tale flowers in many lovely shades of pink, crimson, pale or golden-yellow or apricot. **1960** *House & Garden* Aug. 53/2 South Africans like..the Livingstone Daisy. **1971** *Daily Colonist* (Victoria, B.C.) 16 May 36/5 There is another Mesembryanthemum, *M. criniflorum*, known as the Livingstone Daisy, which is a delightful little spreading carpeter.

livingstonite ('lɪvɪŋstənaɪt). *Geol.* [named by M. Barcena, 1874, in honour of Dr. David *Livingstone*: see -ITE.] Sulphantimonide of mercury.

1874 *Amer. Jrnl. Sci.* VIII. 145 Livingstonite much resembles, in color and aspect, stibnite. **1892** DANA *Min.* 110 An ill-defined alternative product of livingstonite.

†**'livish**, *a. Obs.* Also 3–4 lifissh, 6 lyvish, -yshe. [f. LIFE *sb.* + -ISH.] = LIVING *ppl. a.*, in various senses.

c **1200** ORMIN 5140 þatt tu Ne do nan ifell dede Forr lufe off nan lifisshe mann. **1390** GOWER *Conf.* III. 93 Air..Of whos kinde his aspirementz Takth every lifissh creature. *c* **1530** tr. *Erasmus' Serm. Child Jesus* (1901) 4 Christ, from whose body flodes of lyuyshe water do renne. *Ibid.* 39 To be a lyuyshe member of the most holy body, the church. **1542** BECON *News out of Heaven* Prol. A iij b, Yf there were true & liuish fayth, than [etc.]. —— *Pathw. Prayer* xxxvi. O vij b, Eueryе houre oughte we to offer a lyuish prayer vnto God.

Hence **'livishly** *adv.*

1530 PALSGR. 839 Lyvysshely, *au vif.* *a* **1560** BECON *Chr. Knt.* Pref., Wks. II. 145 b, These vertues..do liuishly shine in your Lordships daylye behauiour.

livish, obs. variant of LOVAGE.

Livonian (lɪ'vəʊnɪən), *sb.* and *a.* [f. med.L. *Livonia*, Livland, a former Baltic province of Russia.] **A.** *sb.* **a.** A native or inhabitant of Livonia. **b.** The language of the Livonian people. **B.** *adj.* Of or pertaining to Livonia, or to the Livonian people or their language.

1652 HEYLYN *Cosmographie* II. 167 *Derpt* or *Derbren*.. situate on the Beck..in the midst of the Province; and taken at the same time by the Moscovite; who transporting the Livonians into other places, planted these parts with Colonies of his own people. **1677** [see PRUSSIAN *sb.*]. **1757** J. DYER *Fleece* IV. 139 The Livonian gulph Receives her sails. **1824** J. D. COCHRANE *Narr. Journey Russia & Siberian Tartary* I. 23 A young Livonian Baron..gave me letters of recommendation to the frontiers of Siberia. **1841** [see LETTISH *a.* (*sb.*)]. **1872** [see LETTIC *a.* (*sb.*)]. **1882** *Encycl. Brit.* XIV. 723/2 [The] plateaus..of Haanhoff and of the Livonian Aa. *Ibid.* 724/1 The Livonians..have nearly all passed away. **1926** *Spectator* 31 July 176/1 If one of their German servants or retainers wanted to marry a Livonian girl the Lutheran priest would seek to stop him. **1933** L. BLOOMFIELD *Lang.* 68 The other languages of the Baltic branch, Carelian,..Ludian, Vepsian, Livonian, [etc.]. **1936** *Times Lit. Suppl.* 27 June 532/2 Descended, to quote his own words, from 'a middle-class East Prussian, a Westphalian peasant's son, a Livonian *bourgeoise* and a Livonian noblewoman'. **1954** *Trans. Philol. Soc.* 86 In the Livonian dialect of Lettish all gender has vanished, a state of affairs clearly due to the influence of Livonian, a Finno-Ugrian, genderless language. **1972** W. B. LOCKWOOD *Panorama Indo-European Lang.* 140 Languages belonging to the Baltic division of Finnic... The best known of the languages concerned is Livonian which in the thirteenth century still predominated in the area of the Gulf of Riga, i.e., in the historic province of Livonia. It is not yet entirely extinct.

livor ('laɪvɔː(r)). [a. L. *līvor* in both senses.]

1. *Path.* 'The mark of a blow; lividness, lead-colour' (*Syd. Soc. Lex.*). Also, the discoloration of skin in a corpse; *pl.* the parts of skin discoloured.

1656 BLOUNT *Glossogr.*, *Livor*, a black and blew mark in a body, coming of a stroke or blow; also blackness of the eyes coming of humors. **1822–34** *Good's Study Med.* (ed. 4) II. 672 The erysipelatous livor..gained ground. **1873** SYMONDS *Grk. Poets* i. 33 It is the fashion..to praise..even the strange livors of corruption. **1885** SIR R. CHRISTISON *Life* I. *Autobiog.* xiv. 307 Natural cadaveric livor is confined to so thin a layer of tissue that [etc.].

†**2.** Ill-will, malignity, spite. *Obs.*

1607 TOPSELL *Four-f. Beasts* (1658) 74 With unappeaseable wrath and blood-desiring livor, he pressed and trod to pieces the incest marriage-causer. **1621** BURTON *Anat. Mel.* I. ii. III. viii, Out of this roote of envy, spring those ferall branches of faction, hatred, livor, emulation. **1675** BAXTER *Cath. Theol.* I. I. 127 But what a plague livor and faction is [to] the Church and the owners souls, let but these ugly words of his be witness.

livorie, -y, obs. forms of LIVERY *sb.*

Livornese (lɪvɔː'niːz), *sb.* and *a.* [f. name of the Italian city of *Livorno* (Leghorn) + -ESE.] **A.** *sb.* The people of Leghorn. **B.** *adj.* Of or pertaining to Leghorn.

1819 SHELLEY *Let.* 17 Nov. (1964) II. 157 The astonishment of the Livornese when she returns from her cruise. **1821** *Ibid.* 8 June 296 The Livornese merchants, who sell board & lodging. **1912** N. DOUGLAS *Fountains in Sand* vii. 78 The old distinction between Livornese and Tunisian Jews is slowly becoming effaced.

‖**livraison** (livrɛzɔ̃). [F.:—L. *līberātiōn-em*, n. of action f. *līberāre* to deliver (see LIBERATE *v.*).] A part, number, or fascicule (of a work published by instalments).

1816 *Gentl. Mag.* LXXXVI. I. 197 The *livraison* which I hope shortly to lay before the publick. **1824** *Advt.* in Cowper *Priv. Corr.* II. (*at end*) Napoleon's Memoirs... The first three Livraisons, each in two Parts... Editions in French and English. **1882** WALT WHITMAN *Spec. Days* 7 *note*, These soil'd and creas'd livraisons, each composed of a sheet or two of paper.

‖**livre** (livr). Also 7–8 liver. [F.:—L. *lībra* the Roman pound.] An old French money of account, divided into 20 sols (or sous), and approximately equivalent to the franc of *c* 1900.

Besides this livre, called *livre tournois*, there was also at one time a *livre parisis* = $1\frac{1}{4}$ *livres tournois*.

1553 J. LOCKE in *Hakluyt's Voy.* (1599) II. 102 Euery Sechino is of venetian money eight liuers and two soldes. **1604** E. GRIMSTONE *Hist. Siege Ostend* 168 A barrell of.. Beere was worth twenty foure Liures which is eleuen Germaine Dollers. **1611** CORYAT *Crudities* 250 The Liver is Nine pence, the Sol an halfe penny. *Ibid.* 286 That thou maiest be paide all thy money in the exchange coyne, which is this brasse peece called the Liuer. **1679** G. R. tr. *Boaystuau's Theatre World* 195 Eighteen Livers tornoys. **1702** W. J. *Bruyn's Voy. Levant* xxix. 110 This Amounts every Year to Four Piasters, which make about Ten French Livers. **1746** *Acc. French Settlem. N. Amer.* 13 A Captain here has one hundred and twenty livres a month. **1797** *Encycl. Brit.* (ed. 3) XII. 259/2 They had the conscience to charge an English sea officer..300 livres (12 guineas and a half) for eight days lodging. **1886** *Athenæum* 24 Apr. 549/1 Her son, the Duke of Richmond, had left France, and had thereby forfeited the pension of 20,000 livres allowed him.

livre, obs. form of LIVER, LIVERY *sb.*

livreage, variant of LIVERAGE² *Obs.*

‖**livre de chevet** (livr də ʃəvɛ). [Fr., lit. pillow-book.] A bedside book; a favourite book.
1923 A. HUXLEY *On Margin* 122 For some days I made Dr. Legat's book my *livre de chevet*. **1939** *Times Lit. Suppl.* 13 May 284/1 It may also be recommended as a *livre de chevet*. **1958** L. DURRELL *Mountolive* v. 111 It was Darley.. who introduced me to the current Alexandrian *livre de chevet* which is a French novel called *Moeurs*. **1972** *Times Lit. Suppl.* 5 May 529/2 To restore the *Heroides* to its rightful place as a *livre de chevet* for the literary connoisseur.

‖**livre de circonstance** (livr də sirkõstɑ̃s). [Fr.] A book composed or adapted for the occasion.
1945 *Yale Rev.* Winter 356 It is one of those rare *livres de circonstance* with a relevance that may extend far beyond the moment to an entire generation. **1957** C. VEREKER *Devel. Political Theory* iii. 93 Begun as a *livre de circonstance*, Hooker's great work raised most of the abiding problems of political authority. **1973** *Times Lit. Suppl.* 1 June 606/5 Mr Neelkant's *livre de circonstance* provides a good deal of ammunition for defenders of the Indo-Soviet Treaty by setting out in detail the many ways in which Russian aid has contributed to India's industrial development.

‖**livret** (livrɛ). Also 5 lyveret. [F. dim. of *livre* book.] A small book.
c **1450** LONELICH *Grail* xvi. 539 Thanne fonde he there A lytel lyveret Wher-Inne that these names weren set. *Ibid.* xxxix. 267 Al this was wreten In thike lyveret. **1794** *Sporting Mag.* IV. 44 Each ponte is furnished with a livret or book, containing a suit of thirteen cards.

livrie, obs. form of LIVERY.

livyer(e, varr. LIVEYERE.

‖**liwa** (ˈliːwɑː). [Arab. *liwā'*.] A province or large administrative district in any of several Arabic-speaking countries.
1925 S. H. LONGRIGG *Four Centuries Mod. Iraq* 308 In 1872 he was Mutasarrif of his own Liwa. **1931** *Special Rep. Progress of 'Iraq, 1920–1931* (Colonial Office) vi. 49 It has been pointed out above that in 1921 the country was divided into 10 liwas. **1957** *Encycl. Brit.* XII. 590C/2 Tobacco is grown in the Sulaimaniya and Ariba *liwas* [of Iraq]. **1959** *Chambers's Encycl.* VII. 705/2 The administration [of Iraq] is centralized, the *mutasarrifs* of the *liwas*.. being all appointed from Baghdad. **1962** *Times* 14 Aug. 9/7 The main centre of activity has now shifted northwards to the *liwa* of Mosul. **1974** *Internat. Jrnl. Middle East Stud.* V. 165 Stafford at the time was the Administrative Inspector of the *liwas* of Mosul and Arbil.

†**lix.** *Obs. rare.* [ad. L. *lixa*.] A (Roman) camp follower.
1679 J. BROWN *Life of Faith* (1824) II. x. 262 Moderating all that under agents and lixes are doing. *Ibid.* xi. 263 Consider by whom he was put to suffer.. by judges higher and lower, and by lixes, by Jews and Romans.

lixam, obs. dial. f. LIKESOME, pleasant.
1688 R. HOLME *Armoury* III. iii. 69 To be of a Cheerful, and Lixam Countenance.

†**lixive.** *Obs. rare.* [a. F. *lixive* (Cotgr.), ad. L. *lixīvium* LIXIVIUM.] = LIXIVIUM.
1606 DANIEL *Queen's Arcadia* III. i, Then can I.. vse strange speech Of.. Eclegmats, Embrochs, Lixiues, Cataplasmes. **1725** BRADLEY *Fam. Dict.* s.v. *Walnut Tree*, A Dye is also made of this Lixive to colour Wool, Wood, and Hair. **1802** SAMPSON *Surv. Londonderry* 112 To two ounces of the water, were added ten drops of lixive, or lye of tartar.

lixivia: see LIXIVIUM.

lixivial (lɪkˈsɪvɪəl), *a.* (and *sb.*). Now *rare.* [f. L. *lixivi-um* lye + -AL¹. Cf. F. *lixiviel*.]
A. *adj.* Of or pertaining to lixivium or lye; obtained by lixiviation. †Hence formerly used for: Alkaline; sometimes in narrower sense as the distinctive epithet of potash.
1650 CHARLETON *Van Helmont's Ternary of Paradoxes* Proleg. D, A Lixivial Tincture, or Alchahal. **1651** BIGGS *New Disp.* ⁋ 139 Pot-herbs.. for the most part have a lixiviall volatile salt. **1675** *Phil. Trans.* X. 414 All kinds of Alcaly's whether lixivial or alcalisate, fixt or volatile. **1676** HODGSON *ibid.* XI. 765 The Lixivial salt I used, was only Potashes dissolved in Spring-water. **1684–5** BOYLE *Min. Waters* 26 Of the tast of the Mineral Water, as Acid, Ferruginous, Vitriolate, Lixivial, Sulphureous, &c. **1689** HARVEY *Curing Dis. by Expect.* iv. 13 The swelling.. was discussed by a lixivial Fomentation. **1731** ARBUTHNOT *Aliments* i. (1735) 14 The common Symptoms of the Excretion of the Bile being vitiated, are.. a lixivial Urine [etc.]. **1742** H. BAKER *Microsc.* II. xviii. 171 This Distemper.. requires lixivial Washes. **1797** BECKFORD *Pop. Tales Germans* I. 163 Its neighbour [*sc.* stream] at Carlsbad.. announces its entrance into the world by hot lixivial fumes. **1800** W. SAUNDERS *Min. Waters* 343 Carbonated soda.. gives the lixivial taste.
†**B.** *sb.* A lixivium, an alkali. *Obs.*
1684 tr. *Bonet's Merc. Compit.* IV. 129 An Ulcer is an effect of an acid, not of a lixivial. **1698** *Phil. Trans.* XX. 199 A Medicine.. put into a very strong Lixivial.

†**liˈxivian**, *a.* *Obs. rare*⁻¹. [f. L. *lixīvi-um* LIXIVIUM + -AN.] = LIXIVIAL *a.*
1727 BRADLEY *Fam. Dict.* s.v. *Corn setting Engine*, Pigions dung or any other saline or lixivian substance.

†**liˈxiviate**, *a.* and *sb.* *Obs.* Also 7 lixiviat, *erron.* lixivate. [f. LIXIVI-UM + -ATE².]
A. *adj.* Obtained by lixiviation; of or pertaining to a lixivium or to lixivial salts; alkaline.
1657 G. STARKEY *Helmont's Vind.* 318 Their [*sc.* Salts] Lixiviate Acrimony is somewhat hostile. **1663** BOYLE *Usef. Exp. Nat. Philos.* II. App. 381 Those that.. prescribe the lixiviat salts of plants. **1680** —— *Produc. Chem. Princ.* I. 32 Egyptian Niter being acknowledged to be a Native Salt.. is yet of a lixiviate nature. **1694** SALMON *Bate's Dispens.* (1713) 301 The Salt.. will.. have lost all its lixivate Taste. **1718** J. CHAMBERLAYNE *Relig. Philos.* (1730) III. xxviii. §11 A Lixiviate Salt will mix with Oil, and turn it into Soap. **1727** in BAILEY vol. II; and in mod. Dicts.
B. *sb.* A lixivium, alkali.
1677 PLOT *Oxfordsh.* 41 The water turned.. of.. a brisk green colour, the Index of a lixiviate. **1824–8** LANDOR *Imag. Conv.* Wks. 1846 I. 59 He.. washed them in a lixiviate.

lixiviate (lɪkˈsɪvɪeɪt), *v.* [f. ppl. stem of mod.L. *lixīviāre*, f. *lixīvium* LIXIVIUM. Cf. F. *lixivier*.]
1. *trans.* To impregnate with lixivium or lye.
1646–1794 [see LIXIVIATED *ppl. a.*]. **1736** BAILEY *Househ. Dict.* 112 Having been thus lixiviated they [*sc.* linens] are to be returned to the mill. **1791** HAMILTON *Berthollet's Dyeing* I. I. II. i. 153 He directs us to lixiviate the dressed hemp in a solution of soda.
2. To subject to lixiviation.
1758 REID tr. *Macquer's Chem.* I. 140 This coal when burnt falls into ashes, which being lixiviated with water, give a fixed alkali. **1817** J. BRADBURY *Trav. Amer.* 248 In order to obtain the nitre, the earth is collected and lixiviated. **1827** FARADAY *Chem. Manip.* xxiv. 608 Collect some charcoal ashes from the crucible furnace and lixiviate them. **1854** *Chamb. Jrnl.* II. 279 The great ocean lixiviates our earth. **1876** HARLEY *Mat. Med.* 134 By lixiviating the saline soil over a filter of wood-ashes.
fig. **1796** BURKE *Let. Noble Lord* Wks. V. 60 Churches, play-houses, coffee-houses, all alike are destined to be.. well-sifted, and lixiviated, to crystallize into true, democratick, explosive, insurrectionary nitre.
Hence **liˈxiviated** *ppl. a.*, **liˈxiviating** *vbl. sb.* (in quot. *attrib.*).
1646 SIR T. BROWNE *Pseud. Ep.* III. iii. 110 The salt and lixiviated serosity with some portion of choler. **1794** PEARSON in *Phil. Trans.* LXXXIV. 391 The lixiviated carbonaceous matter being mixed with 300 grains of red oxyd of lead. **1839** URE *Dict. Arts* 329 The lixiviated *gahröste* mixed with from ¼ to ⅕ of the lixiviated *dünnsteinrost*. **1881** *Brit. Trade Jrnl.* XIX. 335 It is conveyed from the furnaces.. to the laxiviating-pans [*sic*].. where it is crushed.

lixiviation (ˌlɪksɪvɪˈeɪʃən). [ad. mod.L. **lixīviātiōn-em*, agent-n. f. *lixīviāre*: see prec. Cf. F. *lixiviation*.] The action or process of separating a soluble substance from one that is insoluble by the percolation of water, as salts from wood ashes.
1788 *Trans. Soc. Arts* VI. 145 The Salt extracted from Barilla by lixiviation. **1805** *Useful Projects* in *Ann. Reg.* 860/1 A solution which may be procured by the lixiviation of ashes. **1813** SIR H. DAVY *Agric. Chem.* iv. (1814) 163 The water of lixiviation.. will be found to contain the saline and soluble animal or vegetable matters if any exist in the soil. **1866** LIVINGSTONE *Last Jrnls.* (1873) I. ii. 34 A good deal of salt is made by lixiviation of the soil. **1881** J. DAVIS *Rise & Fall Confed. Govt.* I. 478 The niter was obtained from lixiviation of nitrous earth.

lixivious (lɪkˈsɪvɪəs), *a.* Now *rare.* [f. L. *lixīvi-um* lye + -OUS.] = LIXIVIAL *a.*
1658 SIR T. BROWNE *Hydriot.* 31 The salt and lixivious liquor of the body. **1686** W. HARRIS *Lemery's Course Chym.* Introd. (ed. 3) 5 The Salt of Plants drawn after this manner, is called Lixivious Salt. **1757** A. COOPER *Distiller* I. xxiv. (1760) 99 Impregnated with a lixivious Taste from the alcaline Salts used in Rectification. **1761** *Brit. Mag.* II. 537 Those united Contraries (commixing oily with lixivious particles) compose together a new soluble, and saponaceous body. **1800** W. SAUNDERS *Min. Waters* 227 [Seltzer water] has a gently saline and decidedly alkaline taste. If it be exposed to the air.. it intirely loses its pungency, and the alkaline or lixivious flavour becomes proportionably stronger.

‖**lixivium** (lɪkˈsɪvɪəm). Pl. lixivia (*rare*). [L. *lixīvium* neut. of *lixīvius* (also *lixīvus*) adj., made into lye, f. *lix* ashes, lye. L. had also the fem. *lixīvia*, whence F. *lessive*.] Water impregnated with alkaline salts extracted by lixiviation from wood ashes; lye. Also, a solution obtained from other substances by lixiviation.
1612 WOODALL *Surg. Mate* Wks. (1653) 304 *Aqua vitæ* is also precious in all Lixiviums against Gangrens. **1651** BIGGS *New Disp.* ⁋ 80 His device was, out of the ashes of a Nettle, to draw a weak Lixivium. **1731** ARBUTHNOT *Aliments* iv. (1735) 95 The Urine is a Lixivium of the Salts that are in a Human Body. **1736** BAILEY *Househ. Dict.* 319 Wash it very well with a lixivium of quick lime. **1799** *Med. Jrnl.* II. 469 The application of a lixivium of soap and water proved successful. **1812** SIR H. DAVY *Chem. Philos.* 242 The cloths.. after being treated with alkaline lixivia.. were exposed.. to dew and air. **1885** WATT *Leather Manuf.* xi. 135 A lixivium composed of the dung of pigeons and fowls in water. **1894** SMILES *J. Wedgwood* xviii. 233 Painted colours effected by Prussian lixivium.
¶ Used for: LAVA. In quot. *fig.*
1814 SIR R. WILSON *Diary* II. 383 The whole of Europe is a smothered volcano. If the channels of wisdom, justice, and liberality had been opened, the boiling lixivium would have flowed safely away.

†**lixivye.** *Obs. rare.* [ad. L. LIXIVIUM] = prec.
1597 A. M. tr. *Guillemeau's Fr. Chirurg.* 41 b/2 We may also make goode Lixivye only of Oacken ashes. **1599** —— *Gabelhouer's Bk. Physicke* 7/1 Make this subsequente Lixivye, or lye: Take Zeduaria,.. bayberryes,.. grosselye beaten, seeth or boyle it together with a quarte of wyne.

lixt(e, obs. 2nd sing. ind. pres. of LIE *v.*²

liyhe, -er, -inge, obs. ff. LIE, LIAR, LYING.

liynglye, obs. form of LYINGLY.

liza (ˈlaɪzə). *U.S.* [a. Sp. *liza* (applied to various species of mullet): see Valenciennes *Hist. Nat. Poiss.* (1836) XI. 36, 61–2.] An American species of mullet; according to U.S. Dicts. *Mugil curema*, a different species from *Mugil liza* Val.

lizard (ˈlɪzəd). Forms: 4–5 lesard(e, lisard, 4 liserd, lusarde, 5 lesere, lizart, 6 lisarde, lessert, lucert, lycert, -sert, lyzard, -erd, leazard, *Sc.* lyssard, 7 lyser, lezard, lisart, lyzard, lizzard, 6– lizard. [a. OF. *lesard* masc., *lesarde* fem. (mod.F. *lézard*, *lézarde*) (= Pr. *lazert*, *lauzert*, Sp., Pg. *lagarto*, It. *lacerta*, *lucerta*), repr. L. *lacertus* masc., *lacerta* fem., lizard; the ending in OF. would normally have been *-ert*, *-erte*, but was assimilated to the suffix *-ard*.]
1. a. A name popularly applied to reptiles of the genus *Lacerta*, and to other reptiles resembling these in shape and general appearance, having an elongated body, a long tail, four legs, and a scaly or granulated hide. Ordinarily, the name relates to the small animals of the genus *Lacerta* and other genera of the order *Lacertilia*; by extension, animals like the crocodile, the agama, the iguana, or the great fossil saurians, are often spoken of as lizards. In scientific books, the name is commonly used as coextensive with that of the order *Lacertilia*, which includes many animals which, as lacking either limbs or scales, or both, would not be popularly regarded as 'lizards'.
1377 LANGL. *P. Pl.* B. XVIII. 335 Thus ylyke a lusarde with a lady visage, Theuelich þow [*sc.* Satan] me robbedest. **1382** WYCLIF *Lev.* xi. 30 A lacert, that is a serpent that is clepid a liserd. *c* **1400–50** *Alexander* 3573 Bestis.. As lebards, lesards, & lenxis, lions & tigris. *c* **1420** *Pallad. on Husb.* I. 1056 A floor.. So maad that lisardis may not ascende. *c* **1440** *Promp. Parv.* 298/1 Lesarde wy[r]m, *lacertus*. *c* **1483** CAXTON *Dialogues* (E.E.T.S.) viii. 28 Men ete not.. Of bestes venemous:—Serpentes, lizarts, scorpions. **1501** DOUGLAS *Pal. Hon.* I. xxv, The feild was odious Quhair dragouns, lessertis, askis, edders swatterit. **1575** TURBERV. *Faulconrie* 244 You shall give your hawke two inches of a Lucert's tayle newly cut off. **1578** LYTE *Dodoens* 220 The thirde kinde of Orchios, called in Latine *Hirci testiculus*... Upon the.. stemme groweth a greate many of small floures.. much like.. to a Lezarde. **1593** SHAKS. *2 Hen. VI*, III. ii. 325 Their softest Touch, as smart as Lyzards stings. **1605** SYLVESTER *Du Bartas* II. iii. III. *Law* 450 As starry Lezards in the Summer time Upon the wals of broken houses clime. **1605** SHAKS. *Macb.* IV. i. 17 Adders Forke, and Blindewormes Sting, Lizards legge, and Howlets wing. **1611** BIBLE *Lev.* xi. 30 These also shalbe vncleane vnto you,.. the Cameleon, and the Lyzard. **1648** GAGE *West Ind.* xii. (1655) 45 Mans flesh, which the great Lisarts, or Caimains eat very well. **1663** BOYLE *Usef. Exp. Nat. Philos.* II. i. 18 Of lizards it hath been observed.. that their tails being struck off will grow again. **1728** RAMSAY *Twa Lizards* 14 In Nilus giant Lizards sport, Ca'd Crocodiles. **1774** GOLDSM. *Nat. Hist.* (1776) IV. 119 The scales of the lizard seem stuck upon the body even closer than those of fishes. **1818** BYRON *Ch. Har.* IV. cxvii, Through the grass The quick-eyed lizard rustles. **1856** MRS. BROWNING *Aur. Leigh* 33 Lizards, the green lightenings of the wall. **1864** TENNYSON *En. Ard.* 602 He watch'd.. So still, the golden lizard on him paused.
b. applied, with qualifying word, to many species of the genus *Lacerta* (see quots.).
1688 R. HOLME *Armoury* II. viii. 160/1 This is generally called by the name of a Green Lizard, but in the Summer time they are paler. **1693** RAY *Syn. Meth. Anim. Quadr.* 264 *Lacertus viridis*, the green Lizard. **1751** G. EDWARDS *Nat. Hist. Birds* II 248 Lacertus minor, cinereus maculatus, *Asiaticus*. The small spotted grey Lizard. **1769** PENNANT *Zool.* III. 16 The Brown Lizard. **1801** SOUTHEY *Thalaba* IV. v, And his awaken'd ear Heard the grey Lizard's chirp. **1838** T. BELL *Brit. Reptiles* 17 Sand Lizard. *Lacerta agilis*. Linn. *Ibid.* 32 Viviparous Lizard. Nimble Lizard. Common Lizard. *Zootoca vivipara*. **1883** *Cassell's Nat. Hist.* IV. 274 The other species of Lacerta, which may be seen frequently on the Continent of Europe, are the Green (*Lacerta viridis*) and the Ocellate (*L. ocellata*) Lizards, and the lively little Wall Lizard (*L. muralis*). **1896** *Roy. Nat. Hist.* (ed. Lydekker) V. 159 The pearly lizard (*Lacerta ocellata*) of Southern Europe, may be taken as our first example of the typical genus *Lacerta*. *Ibid.* 161 The.. sand-, or hedge-lizard (*L. agilis*).
c. applied, with qualifying word, to other genera of *Lacertilia* and *Batrachia*. **anguine lizard**, *Chamæsaura anguina*. **croaking lizard** (see quot.). **flying lizard**, *Draco volans*. **water lizard**, (*a*) a tailed batrachian, newt; (*b*) a varanian, monitor. Also FENCE, FRILL or FRILLED, GROUND, LACE, LION, SAIL *lizard*.
1841 *Penny Cycl.* XX. 457/1 The Monodactyle or *Anguine lizard. **1885** *Riverside Nat. Hist.* (1888) III. 408 In the island of Jamaica, the *croaking-lizard, *Thecadactylus lævis*, is a most abundant.. animal. **1693** RAY *Syn. Meth.*

Anim. Quadr. 275 *Lacerta volans Indica*, the *Flying Indian Lizard. **1774** GOLDSM. *Nat. Hist.* (1824) III. 165 The whole race of dragons is dwindled down to the Flying Lizard. **1688** R. HOLME *Armoury* II. viii. 160/1 The Neute, Asker, or *Water Lizard are one and the same Creature. **1883** *Cassell's Nat. Hist.* IV. 277 The largest known Lizards belong to the family of Water Lizards, Monitoridæ, or Platynota.

d. Lizard skin. Also *attrib.*

1895 *Montgomery Ward Catal.* 100/1 Ladies' pocket books... Light American lizard grained leather. **1926–7** *Army & Navy Stores Catal.* 495/3 Manicure cases... Polished lizard with silver gilt fittings. **1957** M. B. PICKEN *Fashion Dict.* 215/1 *Lizard*, leather made from lizard skins. **1968** J. IRONSIDE *Fashion Alphabet* 238 *Lizard*, scaly skin of the lizard from Java and India. Used mainly for shoes and handbags, it is harsh and not pliable. **1974** A. LASKI *Night Music* 134 Her good navy lizard shoes and bag.

2. †**a.** ***lazy lizard***: a term of reproach applied to a slothful person. *Obs.*

1600 J. LANE *Tom Tel-troth* (1876) 128 And there this lazie lizard soundly sleeped. **1629** SYMMER *Spir. Posie* I. ix. 30 The sluggard, the lazie Lizzard, and the luskish Lubby?

b. *Austral.* and *N.Z. slang.* A musterer of sheep; a man employed to maintain boundary fences.

1931 'W. HATFIELD' *Sheepmates* xv. 121 You'd be better out in the camp with me than crawlin' around a fence like a fly-catcher lizard. **1933** L. G. D. ACLAND in *Press* (Christchurch, N.Z.) 4 Nov. 15/7 *Lizard*, slang for musterer, I suppose, because they both crawl over the hills. **1937** A. W. UPFIELD *Winds of Evil* xviii. 175 What bloke wouldn't be depressed at coming down to a fence lizard?.. Come down to fencin' and you want to know why a bloke's depressed. **1945** BAKER *Austral. Lang.* II. iii. 63 Shepherds have been known variously as *lizards, crawlers.*

c. = *lounge lizard.*

1935 E. POUND *Let.* Feb. (1971) 269 Alas, as you are writing English, you can't call *them there bloody* gallants, 'cake-eaters' or 'lizards', 'dudes', 'gigolos', 'young scum' [etc.].

3. a. A figure of a lizard; esp. in *Heraldry.*

1688 R. HOLME *Armoury* II. viii. 160/1 He beareth Argent, a Lizard, Vert, countergoing, a Newte or Asker, proper. **1868** CUSSANS *Her.* (1893) 340 The Ironmongers Crest: Two Lizards erect, combattant, proper, chained and collared or.

¶**b.** ? Confused with LUCERN.

1780 EDMONDSON *Her.* II. Gloss., *Lizard*, or *Lezard*, a beast somewhat like a mountain or wild-cat, with a short tail, and long dark-brown hair, spotted... It is the crest and dexter supporter to the arms of the Skinners' Company of London.

4. A fancy variety of the canary. In full ***lizard canary***.

1865 *Derby Mercury* 25 Jan., The gold and silver spangled lizards were very superior. **1876** R. L. WALLACE *Canary Bk.* xiv. 164 The Lizard... Lizard canaries are more frequently tampered with than any other variety by unprincipled exhibitors.

5. *Naut.* A piece of rope having a thimble or block spliced into one or both ends.

1794 *Rigging & Seamanship* I. 169 *Lizard*, an iron thimble spliced into the main-bowlines, and pointed over to hook a tackle to. *c* **1860** H. STUART *Seaman's Catech.* 19 At the quarters, quarter strops and lizzard. **1882** NARES *Seamanship* (ed. 6) 44 The other end is secured with a lizard to the opposite quarter. *Ibid.* 137 The lizard is sometimes only a pendant.

6. A crotch of timber or a forked limb, used as a sled to support a stone being hauled off a field; a stone-boat (Knight *Dict. Mech.* 1875).

¶**7.** = LACERT[2]. *obs. rare*$^{-1}$.

1574 J. JONES *Nat. Beginning Grow. Things* 24 Sinews, muscles, lizards, tendones, gristles, bones.

8. *attrib.* and *Comb.*, as ***lizard-kind, shape, tribe***; ***lizard-like***, adj.; **lizard-bird, dragon**, animals half lizard and half bird or dragon; **lizard canary** (see 4); †**lizard fish**, (*a*) the horse-mackerel or scad; (*b*) a fish of the genus *Synodus*; **lizard-green**, a colour resembling that of the green lizard; also as *adj.*; **lizard orchis**, the plant *Orchis hircina* (see quot. 1578 in 1); **lizard-seeker**, one of the West Indian genus *Saurothera*, of ground-cuckoos, so called because the birds live much on lizards (Ogilvie *Suppl.* 1855); **lizard-skin** *a.*, made of the skin of a lizard; **lizard wine** (see quot.).

1862 G. WILSON *Relig. Chem.* 39 The heroes of the geological bas-reliefs are ichthyosaurs,.. *lizard-birds, gigantic crocodiles [etc.]. **1911** KIPLING in Fletcher & Kipling *School Hist. Eng.* i. 9, I remember the bat-winged lizard-birds. **1883** R. JEFFERIES *Story Heart* ii. (1891) 19 The *lizard-dragon wallowing in sea foam. **1753** CHAMBERS *Cycl. Supp.*, *Lacertus*.. the *lizard fish,.. a fish of the cuculus kind, much resembling the common mackerel.. and more usually called *trachurus.* **1882** JORDAN & GILBERT *Fishes N. Amer.* (*Bull. U.S. Nat. Mus.* III.) 279 *Synodus.* Lizard-fishes. *Ibid.* 280 *S. foetens*.. Sand Pike; Lizard-fish. **1897** *Daily News* 9 Sept. 6/5 A graduated panel of white cloth braided in *lizard-green. **1899** *Ibid.* 28 Jan. 6/4 Lizard-green satin. **1774** GOLDSM. *Nat. Hist.* (1824) III. vi. 157 The modern salamander is an animal of the *lizard kind. **1876** GEO. ELIOT *Dan. Der.* III. xlviii. 343 His most *lizard-like expression. **179.** NEMNICH *Polyglotten-Lex.*, **Lizard orchis.* Orchis coriophora. **1882** *Garden* 11 Feb. 89/1 That curious and nearly extinct native, the Lizard Orchis. **1753** CHAMBERS *Cycl. Supp.* s.v. *Iguana*, It is an amphibious animal, of the *lizard shape. **1895** ZANGWILL *Master* II. iii. 156 He pulled out a *lizard-skin case. **1774** GOLDSM. *Nat. Hist.* (1824) III. vi. 158 This animal.. differs from the rest of the *lizard tribe. **1894** *Daily News* 15 Sept. 5/4 A curious article of export from Pakhoi (China) is dried lizards.. They are used for making a medicine called '*lizard wine'.

b. with **lizard's**, in the names of plants, as **lizard's herb, tail, tongue** (see quots.).

1866 *Treas. Bot.*, *Lizard's herb, *Goniophlebium trilobium.* **1753** CHAMBERS *Cycl. Supp.* App., **Lizard's tail*, the English name of a genus of plants, described by Linnæus under that of *Saururus.* **1866** *Treas. Bot.*, *Saururus*,.. It has ..small white flowers, nearly sessile in a slender naked terminal spike, from which the plant has derived the popular name of Lizard's-tail. *Ibid.*, *Lizard's tongue, *Sauroglossum.*

lizardite ('lɪzədaɪt). *Min.* [f. *Lizard*, the name of a peninsula in Cornwall + -ITE[1].] A basic silicate of magnesium, $Mg_3Si_2O_5(OH)_4$, which is a variety of serpentine.

1956 WHITTAKER & ZUSSMAN in *Mineral. Mag.* XXXI. 122 A new name is desirable by which specimens [of serpentine] possessing the single-layer ortho-cell can be distinguished from chrysotile and from antigorite. Since a well-known locality for serpentine minerals is the Lizard area of Cornwall, England, and since specimens of the sub-group in question are known to occur there.., the name lizardite would seem appropriate. **1967** *Prof. Papers U.S. Geol. Survey* No. 384B. 101/1 We have further investigated this stability using lizardite from the type locality at The Lizard, Cornwall, England.. and natural admixtures of lizardite and clinochrysotile from Snarum, Parish of Buskerud, Norway, from New Almaden mine, Santa Clara County, Calif., and from Forest Hills, Hartford County, Md. **1968** *Zeitschr. für Kristallogr.* CXXVI. 163 The measured *x* and *z* parameters of single-layer lizardite from Raduša chromite Mine, Yugoslavia, indicate a distortion of the basic serpentine layer similar to that found in chrysotiles.

lizardly ('lɪzədlɪ), *a. rare*[1]. [f. LIZARD + -LY[1].] Resembling a lizard.

1883 G. M. FENN *Sweet Mace* I. xi. 205 That long, lanky, lizardly fellow, Abel Churr.

lizard stone. (See quot. 1858.)

1755 JOHNSON, *Lizardstone*, a kind of stone. **1858** SIMMONDS *Dict. Trade*, *Lizard-stone*, a name for the serpentine marble stone obtained in Cornwall, in the vicinity of the Lizard Point.

†**lizary.** *Obs.* = ALIZARI.

1791 HAMILTON *Berthollet's Dyeing* II. II. III. ii. 154 When we wish to obtain a fine bright colour we mix several kinds of lizary together.

lizier(e, variant of LISIÈRE.

lizor, liz(z)ure, Sc. or dial. ff. LEASOW.

Lizzie ('lɪzɪ). *slang.* Also **lizzie**. [Abbrev. of the female Christian name *Elizabeth.*] **1.** A lesbian. Also, an effeminate young man; also ***lizzie boy***.

1905 *Dialect Notes* III. 87 *Lizzie* (*boy*), an effeminate young man. **1912** N. L. MCCLUNG *Black Creek Stopping-House* xi. 98 She's married to a no-good Englishman, a real lizzie-boy. **1949** A. WILSON *Wrong Set* 98, I wish you wouldn't talk to those Lizzies. **1966** J. B. PRIESTLEY *Salt is Leaving* vi. 75 She has a Lizzie crush on me. **1970** J. SYMONS *Man who lost his Wife* I. x. 70 You'd never have thought I was a lizzie, would you? And butch at that.

2. A motor car, esp. an early model of a 'Ford'. Also *Tin Lizzie.*

1913 'B. L. STANDISH' *The Desert* (Advt. on rear cover), So, when you get tired of rolling around in your Lady Lizzie ..hie yourself to the nearest news dealer. **1915** *Chicago Herald* 2 Nov. 4/2 You're right about the guy who is able to make a tin lizzie out of the cans they tie to him. **1922** *Blackw. Mag.* Jan. 37/2 We then prepared to start for home; but 'Lizzie'.. refused.. to think of starting. *Ibid.* Feb. 253/1 An extra bad pothole put Lizzie's back axle out of action. **1949** D. M. DAVIN *Roads from Home* 233 The pace they drove their old tin lizzies. **1956** J. TICKELL *Moon Squadron* 39 These special duty 'Lizzies' had to be stripped of all guns, armour and wireless equipment—except radio telephones —in order to allow room for the passengers.

3. (See quot.)

1925 FRASER & GIBBONS *Soldier & Sailor Words* 145 *Lizzie*, a big gun: also its shell. A term originating at the Dardanelles and suggested by the firing of the big fifteen-inch guns of H.M.S. *Queen Elizabeth.*

4. Lisbon wine.

1934 M. ELLISON *Sparks beneath Ashes* 182 She drinks 'Lizzie' and methylated spirit. **1936** J. CURTIS *Gilt Kid* v. 48 A glass of cheap Lisbon red wine, lizzie they called it.

LL. Contraction for L. *legum* of laws, in degrees, as LL.B. = *Legum baccalaureus*, Bachelor of Laws, LL.D. = *Legum doctor*, Doctor of Laws. †Also for 'Lords' (see L. III).

-ll (l; after a consonant ((ə)l)), contraction of WILL, after pronouns ending in a vowel, as *I'll, he'll, you'll, who'll*; sometimes, more colloquially, after other words as in *that'll do, John'll go.* Formerly written also **'le**, as in *Ile* or *I'le, youle.*

1576 GASCOIGNE *Steele Gl.* (Arb.) 19 Ile trust unto my wit. **1599** SHAKS. *Much Ado* III. iii. 185 Youle be made bring deformed forth. *Ibid.* iv. 8 Ile weare this. **1700** CONGREVE *Way of World* I. 15 I'll take a turn before Dinner. **1743** EMERSON *Fluxions* 12 Divide the given Equation by *y*, and you'll have [etc.]. **1883** *St. James's Gaz.* 22 Sept. 3 There'll be no more rest for China. **1885** G. MEREDITH *Diana of Crossways* I. viii. 176 The mare'll do it well,.. She has had her feed.

llama ('lɑːmə, Sp. 'ʎama). Also 7–9 **lama**, 8 **glama.** [a. Sp. *llama*, quoted as a Peruvian name of the animal in 1535 (Oviedo *Hist. Peru* ed. 1851 I. 418); in Dom. de S. Thomas *Lexicon de la Lengua del Perú* (1560) it is given (along with *paco, guanaco*, and *vicuña*) as a rendering of *oveja* (sheep).] **a.** A South American ruminant quadruped, *Auchenia llama*, closely allied to the camel, but smaller, humpless, and woolly-haired; used as a beast of burden in the Andes.

1600 HAKLUYT *Voy.* III. 735 An Indian boy driuing 8. Llamas or sheepe of Peru which are as big as asses. **1604** E. G[RIMSTONE] *D'Acosta's Hist. Indies* IV. xli. 319 There is nothing at Peru of greater riches and profit than the cattell of the country, which our men call Indian sheep, and the Indians in their generall language call them Lama. **1752** SIR J. HILL *Hist. Anim.* 574 The glama.. is an extremely singular animal. **1774** GOLDSM. *Nat. Hist.* II. 413 The lama, which may be considered the camel of the new world. **1845** DARWIN *Voy. Nat.* viii. (1852) 166 The guanaco or wild Llama, is the characteristic quadruped of the plains of Patagonia. **1870** EMERSON *Soc. & Solit.*, *Courage* Wks. (Bohn) III. 110 The llama that will carry a load if you caress him, will refuse food and die if he is scourged.

b. The wool of the llama or a material made from this.

1864 'P. PATERSON' *Glimpses Real Life* xxv. 244 The hosier's bill is £70—all kinds of stockings, silk,.. embroidered, striped, llama,.. and otherwise. **1882** *World* 21 June 18/1 A pink llama was made with a wide flounce of coarse white lace coming from under the scarf. **1887** TUER & FAGAN *First Year Silken Reign* iv. 69 Her [the Lady Mayoress's] petticoat was of llama and gold.

c. *attrib.* as ***llama-cloth, -driver, -stuff, -wool.***

1809 CAMPBELL *Gertr. Wyom.* II. xvi, The lama-driver on Peruvia's peak. **1851** *Illustr. Catal. Gt. Exhib.* 1055 Embroidered Llama stuff. *Ibid.* 1083 Llama wool shawls. **1871** W. H. G. KINGSTON *On Banks of Amazon* (1876) 109 The coca-bag.. was made of llama cloth, dyed red and blue.

‖**llano** ('lɑːnəʊ, Sp. 'ʎano). [Sp.:—L. *plānum* PLAIN, PLANE.] A level treeless plain or steppe in the northern parts of South America. Hence **Lla'nero, lla'nero**, an inhabitant of a *llano* (see also quot. 1878).

1613 PURCHAS *Pilgrimage* (1614) 873 Peru is divided into three parts, which they call Llanos, Sierras, and Andes... The Llanos or Plaines on the Sea-coast have ten leagues in bredth. **1868** G. DUFF *Pol. Surv.* 176 The Llanos of the Orinoco, huge intertropical steppes. **1878** A. H. KEANE in H. W. Bates *Cent. Amer.* 519 (*heading*) American tribes and languages... Llaneros... An Apache tribe. **1885** B. HARTE *Maruja* ii, Ten leagues of the llano land. **1908** *Daily Chron.* 27 Oct. 4/6 The llanos,.. on which the llaneros live a precarious life. **1910** *Encycl. Brit.* II. 158/2 The chief divisions of the Apaches were the Arivaipa,.. Llanero, [etc.]. **1960** H. S. FERNS *Brit. & Argentine* iii. 96 Now José Paez, the *llanero*, began to rally the cowboys to the side of the revolution. **1973** *Country Life* 20 Dec. 2114 Simon Bolivar ..was.. one of the greatest horsemen who ever lived... His outstanding skill.. enabled him to control the wild Llaneros of the coastal plains who.. were the backbone of his army.

lliana, erron. form of LIANA.

1863 R. F. BURTON *Abeokuta* I. 24.

Lloyd-Georgian (lɔɪd'dʒɔːdʒɪən), *a.* and *sb.* [f. the name of David *Lloyd George* (1863–1945), British politician.] **A.** *adj.* Of, pertaining to, or associated with Lloyd George. **B.** *sb.* A follower or supporter of Lloyd George or his policy.

1909 *Daily Graphic* 12 Oct. 6/2 The self-sacrificing Ministerial millionaires.. with the Lloyd-Georgian iron entering into their souls. **1928** [see ASQUITHIAN *a.* and *sb.*]. **1928** *Daily Tel.* 25 Sept. 12/2 The kaleidoscopic contortions of Lloyd-Georgian politics. **1963** [see DRESSAGE].

So **Lloyd-Georgeite** = *Lloyd-Georgian* sb.; **Lloyd-Georgery** [-ERY 2], **Lloyd-Georgism**, the political policy of Lloyd George.

1910 *Blackw. Mag.* Dec. 772/2 Lloyd Georgism (not Liberalism) was defeated in the Division last January. **1921** *Spectator* 19 Mar. 352/1 They must now be counted as Lloyd Georgeites rather than as Unionists. **1958** *Ibid.* 11 July 48/1 Most of his time was spent talking.. second-rate Lloyd-georgeries about the opinions of posterity.

lloydia ('lɔɪdɪə). [mod.L. (R. A. Salisbury 1812, in *Trans. Hort. Soc. Lond.* I. 328), f. the name of Edward Lhwyd or *Lloyd* (1660–1709), Welsh antiquary and Keeper of the Ashmolean Museum, who discovered the British species on Snowdon.] A small alpine bulbous plant of the genus so called, belonging to the family Liliaceæ, native to the northern hemisphere, and bearing white or yellow flowers; also called the Snowdon lily or mountain spiderwort.

1850 HOOKER & ARNOTT *Brit. Flora* (ed. 6) 442 Lloydia... *L. serotina* Reich. (Mountain L[loydia])... On the Welsh mountains, rare. **1866** LINDLEY & MOORE *Treas. Bot.* II. 690/2 Lloydia. A liliaceous plant, from five to six inches high. **1956** WALTERS & RAVEN *Mountain Flowers* v. 104 The Devil's Kitchen is well named, and I wish anybody luck who tries to find *Lloydia* in flower there. **1966** W. CONDRY *Snowdonia National Park* vi. 112 Lhuyd found quantities of the tiny lily later called Lloydia in his honour.

Lloyd Morgan's canon (lɔɪd 'mɔːgənz 'kænən). *Psychol.* [f. the name of Conwy *Lloyd Morgan* (1852–1936), British psychologist.] (See quot. 1937.)

[**1894** C. LLOYD MORGAN *Introd. Compar. Psychol.* iii. 53 In no case may we interpret an action as the outcome of the exercise of a higher psychical faculty, if it can be interpreted as the outcome of the exercise of one which stands lower in the psychological scale.] **1937** *Discovery* May 162/1 No action must be interpreted as a higher psychological process if it can be interpreted as one lower in the scale. This is

known as 'the Lloyd Morgan canon'. **1964** A. KOESTLER in *Listener* 14 May 786/2 A principle which became a kind of eleventh commandment for psychologists, known as 'Lloyd Morgan's canon'. **1968** E. BORING in *Internat. Encycl. Social Sciences* X. 495/2 He [*sc.* Lloyd Morgan] is best known for what has come to be called Lloyd Morgan's canon, which demands parsimony in the inference of an animal's place on the scale of mind from its behavior.

Lloyd's (lɔɪdz). [f. the name of Edward *Lloyd* who opened a coffee-house in London in 1688, and supplied shipping information to his clients.] Name of a London association of underwriters and agency for arranging insurance (formerly marine insurance only, but now nearly all kinds); it also issues daily shipping intelligence, as ***Lloyd's List*** (of which the occasional newspaper ***Lloyd's News*** was a precursor). ***Lloyd's Register*** (***of Shipping***), an independent society which surveys ships to ensure compliance with standards of strength and maintenance; its annual classified list of such ships. Also ***Lloyd's policy***, an insurance policy underwritten by Lloyd's; so ***Lloyd's underwriter***.

1819 M. EDGEWORTH *Let.* 4 Mar. (1971) 174 He won £30,000 by a bit of gambling insurance on 2 missing..ships. The ships re-appeared... He never could shew his face at Lloyds afterwards. **1829** G. GRIFFIN *Collegians* (ed. 2) II. xxvi. 248 A more crazy and precarious mode of conveyance could not be found, even among the ships marked with the very last letter in Lloyd's list. **1833** [see UNDERWRITER 2]. **1846** [see REGISTER *sb.*[1] 4 c]. **1876** F. MARTIN (*title*) History of Lloyd's and of marine insurance in Great Britain. **1882** J. ASHTON *Social Life in Reign of Anne* I. xviii. 224 Lloyd's was then in Lombard Street, and indeed to this day, on Lloyd's policies, is stated that this policy should have the same effect as if issued in Lombard Street. **1911** *Encycl. Brit.* XV. 833/2 Lloyd's... Originally a mere gathering of merchants..in a coffee-house kept by..Edward Lloyd in Tower Street, London, the earliest notice of which occurs in the *London Gazette* of the 18th of February 1688. *Ibid.* XIX. 554/2 In 1696 Edward Lloyd..started a thrice-a-week paper, *Lloyd's News*, which..was the precursor of the *Lloyd's List* of the present day. *Ibid.* XXIV. 957/2 *Lloyd's Register*, as at present constituted, has existed since 1834. **1922** *Ibid.* XXXI. 492/1 Lloyd's underwriters have shown a great deal of enterprise in accepting risks of a novel kind. **1959** *Chambers's Encycl.* VIII. 623/2 The incorporation of Lloyd's as a chartered body on 25 May 1871.

lo (ləʊ), *int.*[1] *arch.* Forms: 1 lá, 2-4 la, 3-4 lou, low, 4 lowe, 4-6 loo, 6 loa, 6-7 loe, 3- lo. Also 3-4 (as if imperative pl.) los. See also LEW *int.* [The evidence of rimes in ME. poetry shows that the spelling *lo* or *loo* represents two distinct words. (1) ME. *lǭ*:—OE. *lá*, an exclamation indicating surprise, grief, or joy, and also used (like O!) with vocatives. (2) ME. *lo* with close *ō*, prob. a shortened form of *lōke* (OE. *lóca*), imperative of LOOK *v.*; cf. ME. and mod. dial. *ta* for *take*, *ma* for *make*, also the mod. dial. *loo' thee* = 'look you'. The *los* of the Cursor M., used in addressing a multitude, seems to be imper. pl. The peculiar early ME. forms *lou*, *low(e* may stand for *lo we* = 'look we'. The present pronunciation (ləʊ) would normally represent OE. *lá*, but it may be a mere interpretation of the spelling, as the mod. *lo* corresponds functionally to the second of the two words, which should normally have become **loo* (luː) in mod. Eng.]

†**a.** In early use, an interjection of vague meaning, corresponding approximately to the modern O! or Oh! (*obs.*). **b.** Used to direct attention to the presence or approach of something, or to what is about to be said; = Look! See! Behold! Freq. in phr. ***lo and behold*** (usu. jocular).

Beowulf 1700 þæt la mæȝ secgan, se þe soð and riht fremeð on folce. *c* **1000** *Ags. Gosp.* Matt. iii. 7 He cwæð to him; La næddrena cyn [etc.]. *c* **1175** *Lamb. Hom.* 89 Lahwet scal þis beon? *Ibid.*, La hu ne beað þa þet here specað galileisce? *c* **1200** ORMIN 17964 þiss blisse iss min la fuliwiss. *a* **1225** *Leg. Kath.* 2454 Low, þe ȝete of eche lif abit te al iopenet! *a* **1300** *Cursor M.* 16411 And sua it es, La god it wijt. *Ibid.* 16367 Pilat said, 'los, her yur king!' *c* **1380** WYCLIF *Sel. Wks.* I. 77 Lo, þe loomb of God: lo him þat takiþ awey the synnes of þis world. **1393** LANGL. *P. Pl.* C. xx. 4 Loo, here þe lettere ..in latyn and in ebrew. *a* **1400-50** *Alexander* 399 Lo, maister, slike a myschefe! *c* **1425** *Crafte of Nombryng* (E.E.T.S.) 11 þou schalle do way þe hier figure & write þere a cifer, as lo an Ensampull. *c* **1450** *Merlin* 77 Open: lo, here the duke. **1480** CAXTON *Chron. Eng.* ccliii. (1482) 325 Lo what a mariage was this as to the comparison of that other. **1532** MORE *Confut. Tindale* Wks. 574/1 When they suffer wrong, they cannot forgeue loe, and when men take away their goodes they be angry, so they be lo. **1562** A. SCOTT *Poems* (S.T.S.) i. 53 For lymmer lawdis and litle lassis lo [*rimes* scho, þ'to, do] Will argun bay[t] w[t] bischop, preist, and freir. **1590** SPENSER *F.Q.* I. iv. 42 His dearest loue the faire Fidessa loe Is there possessed of the traytour vile. **1611** BIBLE *Haggai* i. 9 Ye looked for much, and loe it came to litle. **1630** PRYNNE *Anti-Armin.* 167 Loe here wee haue expresse mention of seuerall sorts of worlds. **1735** BERKELEY *Free-think. in Math.* §34 Lo! This is what you call 'so great, so unaccountable'. **1758** C. WESLEY *Hymn*, Lo! He comes with clouds descending. **1807** J. BARLOW *Columb.* III. 177 The prince drew near; where lo! an altar stood. **1808** LADY LYTTELTON *Let.* June in *Corr.* (1912) i. 20 Hartington..had just told us how hard he had worked all the morning..when, lo and behold! M. Deshayes himself appeared. **1841** LYTTON *Night & Morning* II. III. v. 144 The fair bride was skipping down the middle..when, lo and behold! the whiskered gentleman..advanced..and cried—'*La voilà!*' **1849** DICKENS *Dav. Copp.* (1850) xxii. 234 What does he do, but, lo, and behold you, he goes into a perfumer's shop. **1859** FITZGERALD tr. *Omar* vii. (1899) 71 The Bird of Time has but a little way To fly—and Lo! the Bird is on the Wing. **1930** J. B. PRIESTLEY *Angel Pavement* ii. 60 And then—lo and behold—it was there all the time. **1947** T. WILLIAMS *Streetcar Named Desire* x. 151 You come in here and sprinkle the place with powder and spray perfume and cover the light-bulb with a paper lantern, and lo and behold the place has turned into Egypt and you are the Queen of the Nile!

lo, 'lo, *int.*[2] Colloq. abbrev. of HALLO, HALLOA, HELLO, HULLO, HULLOA *ints.*

1921 J. DOS PASSOS *Three Soldiers* I. i. 13 "Lo, buddy,' came a voice beside him... 'Goin' to the movies?' **1922** JOYCE *Ulysses* 287 Lo, Joe, says I. How are you blowing? **1938** F. D. SHARPE *Sharpe of Flying Squad* ii. 16 "Lo,' said Moisher. "Lo,' said Harry. **1968** R. CLAPPERTON *No News on Monday* viii. 99 "Lo, son. You the detective?' he murmured.

Lo, *sb. U.S.* [Humorously from Pope's line '*Lo*, the poor Indian', etc., *Essay on Man* I. 99.] An American Indian. Also ***Mr.*** (or ***Mrs.***) ***Lo***.

1871 *Republican Rev.* (Albuquerque, New Mexico) 2 Sept. 1/4 Cowardly Lo prefers to attack none but very small parties of teamsters, farmers, or lone mail riders. **1873** G. W. PERRIE *Buckskin Mose* vi. 88 This document set forth that the bearer was a good Lo. *Ibid.*, He appeared again at the head of our train, in the company of thirty or forty other Los. **1874** J. G. MCCOY *Hist. Sk. Cattle Trade* 260 Crossing the plains was an undertaking fraught with great danger; especially as Mr. Lo was decidedly fond of horses. **1880** A. A. HAYES *New Colorado* (1881) iii. 40 Colonel Craig..and his men began, not unsuccessfully, the repression and suppression of Mr. Lo. **1885** [see EVOLUTE *v.* 2]. **1904** *Minneapolis Daily Times* 12 June 6 The march of civilization has convinced Lo that fighting is not as profitable as it used to be. **1904** *N.Y. Even. Post* 6 Aug., On Florida's shield stands a placid and buxom Mrs. Lo, with fringed skirt falling to the knee. **1947** R. P. T. COFFIN *Yankee Coast* 220 He..went to join Lo, the Poor Indian on the Happy Hunting Grounds.

lo, obs. form of LOW *sb.* and *a.*

†**Lo.,** obs. abbreviation of LORD.

1610 *True Declar. Virginia* (1844) 13 That noble Gouernour, the Lo. Laware.

‖**loa**[1] ('ləʊə). [Native name in Angola, used as a specific name in *Filaria loa* (T. S. Cobbold *Entozoa* (1864) xiv. 389) and as a generic name in *Loa loa* (C. W. Stiles 1905, in *Bull. U.S. Dept. Agric. Bur. Anim. Ind.* no. 79. 50).] A filarial worm of the monotypic genus so called, found in tropical Africa and infecting the eyes and subcutaneous tissues in man. Also *attrib.*

1864 T. S. COBBOLD *Entozoa* xiv. 389, I had independently arrived at the conviction that the *Loa* was a totally distinct worm from the *Filaria oculi*. *Ibid.*, The parasite in question is rather more than an inch in length, it is..termed *Loa*. **1889** *Syd. Soc. Lex.*, *Loa-worm*. **1898** P. MANSON *Trop. Diseases* xxxiii. 518 The man remembered that when a lad, he had a loa in his eye. *Ibid.* 519 The blood of another patient, known to be the subject of loa infection. **1958** *Ann. Trop. Med. & Parasitol.* LII. 158 (*title*) The relationship between human and simian Loa in the rain-forest zone of the British Cameroons. **1971** PRICE & HOPPS in R. A. Marcial-Rojas *Path. Protozoal & Helminthic Dis.* lii. 917/1 (*heading*) The eye worm, loa worm. *Ibid.*, He [*sc.* Guyot] described the worm under the native name 'loa'.

loa[2] ('ləʊə). Pl. loa or loas. [ad. Haitian Creole *lwa*.] A deity in the voodoo cult of Haiti.

1933 J. H. CRAIGE *Black Bagdad* xv. 267 Thanks to the spells I have made in your behalf, the *loas* have held their hands over you, and you are free. **1937** M. J. HERSKOVITS *Life in Haitian Valley* II. iv. 81 The ordinary plates or calabashes on which food is offered the *loa*, or African deities. **1959** H. CHARTERIS tr. *Métraux's Voodoo in Haiti* iii. 120 A *loa* moves into the head of an individual having first driven out..one of the two souls that everyone carries in himself. **1960** *Spectator* 5 Aug. 218/3 The peculiar congregation, led by the Voodoo Priestess, start summoning up their favourite spirits or 'loas', who—dead on cue—take possession of the celebrants one after another. **1966** *Punch* 10 Aug. 235/3 The 'loa', the demon-gods who take possession of the initiates at Voodoo ceremonies and impose on them their own voice, features, and character.

loac, variant of LAKE *sb.*[1] *Obs.*

loach (ləʊtʃ). Forms: 5 looche, 5-7 loch, 5-9 loche, 6- loach. [a. F. *loche* (13th c.), loach, also *dial.* slug; cf. mod. Norman *loque* loach, slug (Moisy). Sp. *loja* is from Fr.]

1. A small European fish, *Cobitis* (*Nemachilus*) *barbatula* (*-us*), inhabiting small clear streams and highly prized for food; also, any fish of the family *Cobitidæ*. **spinous loach**, *Cobitis tænia*.

1357 [see 4]. **14..** *Voc.* in Wr.-Wülcker 585/18 *Fundulus*, a looche. **14..** *Nom.* ibid. 705/1 *Hec alosa*, a loch. *c* **1420** *Liber Cocorum* (1862) 54 And smalle fysshe thou take.. sperlynges and menwus withal And loches. **1558** *Act 1 Eliz.* c. 17 §4 Places where Smeltes, Loches, Mynneis..hathe been used to bee taken. *c* **1560** A. SCOTT *Poems* (S.T.S.) ii. 108 Thair wes nowdir lad nor loun Mycht eit ane baikin loche Ffor fowness. **1651-7** T. BARKER *Art of Angling* (1820) 31 Bait your hooks with millers thumbes, loaches. **1653** WALTON *Angler* viii. 161 Carps and Loches are observed to breed several months in one year. **1789** G. WHITE *Selborne* xviii, The loach in its general aspect has a pellucid appearance. **1819** CRABBE *T. of Hall* xiii. 6 Where in the shallow stream the loaches play. **1837** M. DONOVAN *Dom. Econ.* II. 33 That ugly little fish the loche. **1869** BLACKMORE *Lorna D.* vii. (ed. 12) 38 A jar of pickled loaches. **1882** J. WALKER *Jaunt to Auld Reekie* 118 The Coachman, sluggish as a bearded loach.

2. Applied to fishes of other genera.

a. The burbot or eel-pout. (In recent U.S. Dicts.) **b.** ***sea-loach***, the whistle-fish.

a **1672** WILLUGHBY *Ichthyogr.* (1686) 121 *Mustela vulgaris*,..A Sea Loche *Cestriæ*. Whistle-fish *in Cornubia*. [So **1769** PENNANT *Brit. Zool.* III. 164.]

†**3.** *fig.* A simpleton. *Obs.*

1605 *Tryall Chev.* III. i. in Bullen *O. Pl.* III. 303 The Loach gets me into a Sutlers bath and there sits me drinking for Joanes best cap. *c* **1620** *Peele's Jests* 17 This Loach spares not for any expence.

4. *attrib.* and *Comb.*

1357 *Act 31 Edw. III, Stat.* iii. c. 2 Le pesson de Doggerefissh & lochefissh. **1587** MASCALL *Govt. Cattle, Oxen* (1596) 43 Some do take a loch fish quick, and put it down the beasts throat. **1869** BLACKMORE *Lorna D.* xv. (ed. 12) 90 Was not I a lout gone by, only fit for loach-sticking? **1883** *Fisheries Exhib. Catal.* 254 Loach Traps,..Loach Hook and Rod.

loach: see LOHOCH.

load (ləʊd), *sb.* Forms: 1 lád, 3-6 lode, 5 lod, 5-6 lood(e, 6-7 loade, 6- load. *β. north.* and *Sc.* 4-9 lade, 5-9 laid, (5 layde). [OE. *lád* fem., way, course, journey, conveyance, corresp. to OHG. *leitâ* course, leading, procession (MHG., mod.G. *leite*), ON. *leið* way, course:—OTeut. **laidā* (whence **laidjan* to LEAD), related to **līpan* to go (OE. *līðan*, ON. *líða*). The development of meaning has been influenced by the association of the sb. with LADE *v.*; in extreme northern dialects this word is not distinguishable from LADE *sb.*[1] The words *load* and LODE are etymologically identical; the present article includes only those senses in which the mod. spelling is *load*, and obs. senses akin to these.]

†**1.** Carriage. Also, an act of loading. *Obs.*

c **1000** *Laws Northumbr. Priests* c. 55 in Schmid *Gesetze* 368 Sunnandæȝes cypinge we forbeodað..and ælc weorc, and ælce lade, æȝðer ȝe on wæne ȝe on horse ȝe on byrdene. *c* **1380** *Sir Ferumb.* 2703 Wanne þe barouns it i-knewe what þay in lode hadde. *c* **1440** *Promp. Parv.* 310/2 Loode, or caryage, *vectura*. **1523** FITZHERB. *Bk. Husb.* §25 The more hey maye be loded at a lode, and the faster it wyll lye.

2. a. That which is laid upon a person, beast, or vehicle to be carried; a burden. Also, the amount which usually is or can be carried; e.g. ***cart-load, horse-load, wagon-load***.

a **1225** *Ancr. R.* 268 Ȝif a miracle nere..heo hefde iturpled mid him, boðe hors & lode, adun into helle grunde. *c* **1290** *S. Eng. Leg.* I. 187/80 He let nime platus of Ire..wel neiȝ ane cartes lode. *a* **1300** [see CART-LOAD]. **1375** BARBOUR *Bruce* VIII. 467 Thai kest thair ladis doun in hy. *c* **1475** *Rauf Coilȝear* 642 My laid war I laith to lois. **1483** *Cath. Angl.* 206 *A layde*, a burdyn. **1582-8** *Hist. James VI* (1804) 125 Sundrie cariers baith of hors and laides. **1593** SHAKS. *2 Hen. VI*, v. ii. 64 Æneas bare a liuing loade; Nothing so heauy as these woes of mine. **1774** GOLDSM. *Nat. Hist.* (1776) II. 113 By strapping the load round the shoulders of the person, who is to bear it. **1840** DICKENS *Old C. Shop* i, Where some halt to rest from heavy loads. **1882** *Rep. to Ho. Repr. Prec. Met. U.S.* 99 In January, 1881, 11 car-loads from the mine yielded $190.

b. The specific quantity of a substance which it is customary to load at one time; hence, taken as a unit of measure or weight for certain substances.

The equivalence of a load varies considerably according to the locality and to the substance. As a measure, a load of wheat is usually 40 bushels, of lime 64 (in some districts 32) bushels, of timber 50 cubic feet, of hay 36 trusses (= 18 cwt.), of bulrushes 63 bundles, of meal 2 bolls (Sc.). A load of lead ore (in the Peak, Derbyshire) = 9 dishes (see DISH *sb.* 6 c).

1384-5 *Durham Acc. Rolls* (Surtees) 390 In iij ladys calcis empt. *c* **1386** CHAUCER *Knt.'s T.* 2060 Of stree first ther was leyd ful many a lode. **1409** *Durham Acc. Roll* in *Eng. Hist. Rev.* XIV. 529, xii lodas continentes cc[m]xl petras ferri. **1458** *Nottingham Rec.* II. 220, xl. lod de Baseford ston. **1497** *Naval Acc. Hen. VII* (1896) 230 A loode of lyme from Havant. *a* **1533** LD. BERNERS *Huon* cxliii. 532 Mo then .x. lode of thornes were caryed out to brenne the noble lady. **1550** CROWLEY *Epigr.* 501 A lode [of coals] that of late yeres for a royall was solde. **1570** *Wills & Inv. N.C.* (Surtees 1835) I. 344 Ane laid of quheit, ane laid of beir, ane laid of aitts. **1622** MALYNES *Anc. Law-Merch.* 50 The Load of Lead is 175 ll. **1709** J. WARD *Introd. Math.* I. iii. (1734) 37 Nine of those Dishes they [*sc.* Derbyshire lead-miners] call Load of Ore. **1747** HOOSON *Miner's Dict.* Mj b, Three Loads five Dishes will be full enough to make up one Ton Weight. **1812** J. SMYTH *Pract. of Customs* (1821) 105 Hay, the Load of 36 Trusses, each Truss 56 lbs. **1825** COBBETT *Rur. Rides* 194 This rick contains..what they call in Hampshire ten loads of wheat, that is to say, fifty quarters, or four hundred bushels. **1887** ROGERS *Agric. & Prices* V. 255 The load..at Appleby..is [*c* 1700] for peas, rye and wheat 4 bushels, of [*sic*] barley and bigg 5 bushels. **1887** *Cunningham's Diary* (Scot. Hist. Soc.) Introd. 18 Though no longer carried on horseback, a load of meal still means two bolls. **1898** *Daily News* 16 June 7/2 Wheat futures are usually dealt with in 'loads'. A load is a thousand quarters.

c. The material carried along by a stream in suspension, by saltation, or by traction (by some

writers material carried in solution is included); the amount of material so carried; hence, by extension, the material carried by various other natural agents of transportation, as glaciers, winds, and ocean currents.

1888 J. W. POWELL in *Science* 16 Nov. 229/2 In erosion and corrasion the material which is transported may be called the 'load'. The load is transported by two methods, a portion floats with the water, and another portion is driven along the bottom. **1907** R. D. SALISBURY *Physiogr.* iv. 122 The sediment moved by a stream, whether in suspension or at the bottom, is its load. **1950** W. H. TWENHOFEL *Princ. Sedimentation* (ed. 2) vi. 226 These figures show that the suspended loads of rivers draining dry areas are larger than the dissolved loads. *Ibid.* 227 The loads of standing bodies of water are small in terms of any unit of volume... There is not a great deal of information respecting loads in the open ocean away from shallow water. **1968** R. W. FAIRBRIDGE *Encycl. Geomorphol.* 627/2 Load is an additional variable which changes together with flow along a stream wherever it is joined by a tributary. **1970** *Jrnl. Glaciol.* IX. 227 (*heading*) Contrast between the debris loads of polar and temperate glaciers.

3. a. A material object or a force, which acts or is conceived as a weight, clog, or the like.

1593 SHAKS. *2 Hen VI*, I. ii. 2 Why droopes my Lord like over-ripen'd Corn, Hanging the head at Ceres plenteous load? **1667** MILTON *P.L.* IV. 972 Farr heavier load thy self expect to feel From my prevailing arme. *Ibid.* v. 59 O fair Plant..with fruit surcharg'd, Deigns none to ease thy load and taste thy sweet? **1698** KEILL *Exam. Th. Earth* (1734) 273 The great River of the Amazons..runs up to the Equator with a vast load of Waters. **1725** N. ROBINSON *Th. Physick* 260 Bleeding..lessens the additional Quantity of Blood, and removes its Load. **1832–52** I. MURRAY in *Whistle-Binkie* (Scot. Songs) Ser. III. 43 The hazle bushes bend nae mair Beneath the lades that crushed them sair. **1842** A. COMBE *Physiol. Digestion* (ed. 4) 361 If we eat more than the system requires, the bowels become..weakened by their load. **1852** *Beck's Florist* Dec. 273 The luxuriance and profusion, I may say the loads of bloom.

b. The charge of a fire-arm.

1692 *Capt. Smith's Seaman's Gram.* II. xii. 108 What quantity of Powder will be a sufficient Load for such a Piece. **1813** *Sporting Mag.* XLII. 141 A gun with but one barrel.. will, by a single operation on the trigger, discharge six or eight loads in succession. **1858** SIMMONDS *Dict. Trade*, *Load*, the charge of a gun.

c. *Electr.* The resistance to a dynamo or motor of the machinery which it drives, apart from its own friction.

1895 THOMPSON & THOMAS *Electr. Tab. & Mem.* 57 If the dynamo is run at constant speed, the motor also will run of itself at nearly constant speed, whatever its load. *Ibid.* 82 Lifting Power of Magnets.—The rule is:—Load = $a \times$ the square of the cube root of the magnet's own weight.

d. *Building.* The pressure caused by gravity upon a structure or any part of it.

1871 R. S. BALL *Exper. Mech.* xi. 172 A structure has to support both its own weight and also any load that may be placed upon it. Thus a railway bridge must at all times sustain what is called a permanent load, and frequently, of course, the weight of one or more trains. **1879** SIR G. SCOTT *Lect. Archit.* I. 49 The columns..are..proportioned in thickness to their load, irrespective of their height.

e. *Phys.* The amount of resistance to be overcome by the contraction of a muscle.

1894 STARLING *Elem. Hum. Physiol.* 94.

f. *Electr. Engin.* The electric power that a generating system is delivering or required to deliver at any given moment; **base load**, the minimum value of the load during any period, generally met (in a grid system) by the continuous operation of the most efficient stations, without the intermittent and varying contribution of the less efficient ones.

In the earliest quots. identical with 3 c.

1888 *Proc. Inst. Mech. Engin.* Oct. 508 The efficiency of its working was limited to a constant load and a uniform speed, as when the dynamo was supplying a constant current with constant pressure. *Ibid.*, In many electric lighting installations..motors were required that would work economically between wide variations of load. **1891** *Min. Proc. Inst. Civil Engin.* CVI. 15 The cost of labour per unit ..would continue to decrease as long as the duration of maximum load increased, up to a certain limit. **1894** [see BOOSTER 2]. **1900** *Westm. Gaz.* 22 May 2/1 Giving a day-load for traction and power and a night-load for light. **1903** *Electr. World & Engin.* 23 May 866/2 It is necessary at times of fall and winter peak loads to operate the steam plants in the three combination sub-station and subsidiary steam plants which the company was operating three years ago. **1928** *Daily Express* 4 June 15/3 We have, in twenty-six years, built up a huge base-load..with an annual output of over 25,000,000 units. **1956** *Nature* 4 Feb. 204/2 The prospect of competitive nuclear power with low operating costs means that this plant will carry the base load. **1966** *Economist* 14 May 734/1 Running charges have, since 1961, differed by day and by night, since costs for the best, base-load stations at night are so much lower than the average running costs in the mixed bag of stations, from good to awful, used by day. **1974** *Times* 15 Jan. 14/3 A mass switch-off..which would record several million watts being wiped off the national energy load.

g. *Electronics.* An impedance or circuit that receives the output of a transistor or other device, or in which the output is developed.

1918 *Physical Rev.* XII. 180 Variations in potential difference are set up between cathode and grid, and these cause variations in the current in the circuit *FPR*, the power developed in the load *R* being greater than that fed into the input circuit. **1931** *Proc. IRE* XIX. 49 With the pentode.. the maximum output was obtained at approximately a 10,000-ohm load. **1943** C. L. BOLTZ *Basic Radio* xv. 243 In a receiver the load on the output is a loudspeaker or telephone. **1957** B. I. & B. BLEANEY *Electr. & Magn.* xiv. 362 In many applications the size of the load is fixed; if, for example, the load is a loud-speaker, its impedance..is generally in the range 5 to 15 ohms. **1962** SIMPSON & RICHARDS *Physical Princ. Junction Transistors* xi. 251 We require a current in the load of 2 mA. *Ibid.*, Since R_{e_1} is assumed to be by-passed by a capacitor, the a.c. load consists of $R_{c_1} + R_{e_1}$.

h. Colloq. phr. ***to take a load off*** (***one's feet***): to sit or lie down; to relax.

1945 A. KOBER *Parm Me* 35 How's about taking a load off your feet? **1968** J. HUDSON *Case of Need* III. i. 175 'Sit down,' she said. 'Take a load off.'

4. *fig.* **a.** A burden (of affliction, sin, responsibility, etc.); something which weighs down, oppresses, or impedes. Esp. in phr. (***to take***) ***a load off one's mind***: (to bring someone) relief from anxiety.

1593 SHAKS. *2 Hen. VI*, III. i. 157 Sharpe Buckingham vnburthens with his tongue, The enuious Load that lyes vpon his heart. **1599** —— *Much Ado* v. i. 28 Those that wring vnder the load of sorrow. *c* **1646** MILTON *Sonnet on Mrs. C. Thomson*, Meekly thou didst resign this earthy load Of Death, call'd Life. **1700** DRYDEN *Pal. & Arc.* II. 265 Our life's a load. **1748** *Anson's Voy.* Introd., When I consider.. of how tedious, and often unintelligible, a load of description it [*sc.* drawing] would rid them. **1764** GOLDSM. *Trav.* 374 And all that freedom's highest aims can reach, Is but to lay proportion'd loads on each. **1766** FORDYCE *Serm. Yng. Wom.* (1767) II. xii. 206 From some people..a favour ..is a load. **1791** BURNS *Lament Earl Glencairn* v, I bear alane my lade o' care. **1818** CRUISE *Digest* (ed. 2) II. 175 So did they give the heir the privilege of laying the load upon the personal estate. **1851** D. JERROLD *St. Giles* xiv. 141 With this thought, a load was lifted from the old man's heart. **1852** LYTTON *My Novel* (1853) III. x. vi. 132 It is a load off one's mind. **1855** MACAULAY *Hist. Eng.* xiv. III. 400 His spirit.. sank down under the load of public abhorrence. **1857** DICKENS *Perils Eng. Prisoners* iii, in *Househ. Words* Extra Christmas No., 7 Dec. 31/2 It takes a load off my mind to leave her in your charge. **1951** E. CALDWELL *Episode in Palmetto* vii. 136 It's a big load off my mind to hear you say that.

b. *slang.* An occurrence of venereal disease; = DOSE *sb.* 2 d. Cf. LOAD *v.* 4 (quots. 1799, 1818).

[**1878** *N. & Q.* 10 Aug. 105/1 *Load*, an eruption, measles, smallpox.] **1937** PARTRIDGE *Dict. Slang* 488/1 *Load*, a venereal infection. **1965** F. SARGESON *Mem. Peon* ii. 28 They displayed their rubber goods, and..were doubly protected against finding themselves landed with either biological consequences or a load.

c. An amount of work, teaching, etc., to be done by one person; freq. with defining word prefixed, as ***case-load***, ***teaching-load***, ***work-load***.

1946 *Nature* 17 Aug. 216/2 The scientific study of conditions affecting the work-load involved in various processes. **1950**, etc. [see *case-load* s.v. CASE *sb.*[1] 14]. **1958** J. C. HEROLD *Mistress to an Age* (1959) III. xiv. 294 His teaching load amounted to three and a half hours daily for five days a week. **1961** *Lancet* 5 Aug. 303/1 He cemented the relationships by careful inquiry into examinations and study load. **1964** in *Rep. Comm. Inquiry Univ. Oxf.* (1966) II. 450 Please give as accurate estimates as you can for your average weekly load this term. **1966** *Ibid.* 465 A quarter were critical of the heavy teaching load with its consequent adverse effects on research. **1971** *Black Scholar* Jan. 64/2 (Advt.), Normal load is 6 courses per year. **1971** *Sat. Rev.* (U.S.) 18 Dec. 56/2 Teaching loads at white schools often are only a fraction the size of those at black schools.

5. a. As much as one can 'carry' of drink; (one's) fill; phr. ***to have*** (or ***have taken***), ***to get one's load***, ***to have a load***, etc. (now esp. with *on*); also, a satisfying amount to eat; (*U.S.*) a dose of narcotics. *slang.* †**b.** ***to give*** (a person) ***his load***: to beat soundly.

1598 LODGE & GREENE *Looking Glass Lond.* H 2 b, Ply it till euery man hath tane his load. **1678** RAY *Prov.* 87 Proverbiall Periphrases of one drunk... He has a jagg or load. **1692** R. L'ESTRANGE *Fables, Life Æsop* (1708) 16 The Cups went round, and Xanthus by this Time had taken his Load, who was mightily given to talk in his Drink. *Ibid.* clvii. 173 There are Those that can never Sleep without their Load. **1694** ECHARD *Plautus* 188 Give him his load so as he shan't b' able to find the way home. **1697** DAMPIER *Voy.* I. 369 Then we drank,..The General leapt about..a little while; but having his Load soon went to sleep. **1890** *Century Dict.* s.v., He went home late with a load on. **1897** BARRÈRE & LELAND *Dict. Slang* II. 22/1 A man who walks unsteadily, owing to intoxication, is said to have a load on. **1902** *Eng. Dial. Dict.* s.v., *To get one's load*, to be drunk. **1922** JOYCE *Ulysses* 160 After their feed with a good load of fat soup under their belts. **1929** J. B. PRIESTLEY *Good Companions* I. i. 26 You've got a load on and no mistake. **1929** [see BANG *sb.*[3]]. **1934** J. O'HARA *Appointment in Samarra* (1935) vii. 202 What a load you had. Did you get home all right? **1942** WODEHOUSE *Money in Bank* (1946) xxvi. 229 Drunk!..He's got a load on that would sink an ocean liner. **1948** V. PALMER *Golconda* ix. 65 We're not to blame if men get a load on and begin to fight. **1968** C. NICOLE *Self Lovers* ii. 38 I'm sorry about last night. I was carrying a load. Else I'd have recognised you.

c. *Mech.* (See quots.)

1855 OGILVIE, Suppl. s.v., In mech. an engine or other prime mover is said to be loaded when it is working to its full power, and the quantity of work it is then doing is called its load. **1875** KNIGHT *Dict. Mech.*, *Load*, the amount of work done by an engine worked up to its capacity. Not to be confounded with *duty*.

6. ***loads*** (also ***a load***): a great number or quantity (esp. *of* something desirable or nonsensical), 'lots', 'heaps'. *colloq.*

With the earlier quots. cf. CART-LOAD b.

1606 SHAKS. *Tr. & Cr.* v. i. 22 Loades a grauell i' th' backe, Lethargies, cold Palsies, and the like. **1655** *Nicholas Papers* (Camden) II. 205 There is a loade of newes. **1852** CLOUGH *Poems*, etc. (1869) I. 183 Sunday.—Loads of talk with Emerson all morning. **1860** EDKINS *Chinese Scenes* (1863) 73, I was very much pleased to get all the home letters on Monday last—This mail I had loads. **1943** C. H. WARD-JACKSON *Piece of Cake* 41 *Load of guff*, a lot of humbug or nonsense. **1964** [see CRAP *sb.*[1] 7 b]. **1965**, etc. [see COD, abbrev. of CODSWALLOP]. **1967** *Jazz Monthly* Dec. 12 Playing a load of rubbish, while sounding quite competent to the casual listener. **1968** [see COBBLER 1 c]. **1974** A. MORICE *Killing with Kindness* iv. 38 No man is an island... That's what Mike used to say. Mind you, I always thought it was a load of rubbish.

7. Phrases. (*Obs.* in a–d.) **a.** ***to lay on load***: to deal heavy blows (occas. ***to lay load about*** or ***about one***); *fig.* to speak with emphasis or exaggeration; to emphasize (the fact) *that*..; to exaggerate, 'lay it on thick'; also, to be extravagant in expenditure. Also, ***to lay on load of reproaches***. **b.** ***to lay load on*** or ***upon***: to belabour with blows; also *fig.* to blame, reproach. **c.** ***to lay*** (or ***cast***) ***the load***: to throw the blame. **d.** ***to lay on by load***: to heap or pile on. **e.** Phr. ***to get a load of*** (freq. *imp.*): to look at, perceive, make oneself aware of, scrutinize; to listen carefully to. *slang* (orig. *U.S.*).

a. *c* **1537** *Thersites* (Roxb. Club) 51, I wyll..laye on a lode with this lustye clubbe. **1579** CHURCHYARD *Gen. Rehearsal Wars* K j b, He strake diuers of the Almaines..and laiyng loade about hym, he made such waie that the gate was free. **1580** FULKE *Dang. Rock* 169 He layeth on lode, that Luther and Caluines authoritie is not like to Christes. **1586** WARNER *Alb. Eng.* I. vi. (1589) 19 The Danter then of Trespassers.. laies lustie lode about. **1587** *Mirr. Mag.*, *Cæsar* xxviii, They fell from wordes to sharpe, and layde on loade amayne. **1589** NASHE *Martins Months Minde* To Rdr., Wks. (Grosart) I. 163 Who being both but newelie come to their Fathers lands and goods,..lay on such loade, and spend al their leudnes so fast. **1596** SPENSER *F.Q.* IV. ix. 22 So dreadfull strokes each did at other drive, And laid on load with all their might and powre. **1598** GRENEWEY *Tacitus' Ann.* II. iv. (1622) 37 They should..lay on thicke load; and strike at their faces with their swords. **1611** COTGR., *Exaggerer*, to exaggerate, aggravate, lay on load. **1613** DAY *Festivals* viii. (1615) 234 They lay on load of bitter Reproaches against it. *a* **1620** J. DYKE *Sel. Serm.* (1640) 211 Satan will be busie to lay on loade, and to affright a man with Hell and damnation. **1652** C. B. STAPYLTON *Herodian* VII. 57 They raile and scoff when er'e he comes abroad, And of his lewd behaviour laies on Load. **1677** MIEGE *Eng.-Fr. Dict.* s.v., They laid much load upon that expression, *ils exaggererent beaucoup cette expression.* **1832** SIR S. FERGUSON *Forging of Anchor* 22 Leap out, my masters; leap out and lay on load.

b. [*c* **1435**: see LADE *sb.*[1]] *c* **1550** WEVER *Lusty Juventus* D ij, Lay lode on the flesshe, what so euer befal You haue strength Inough to do it with all. *c* **1560** INGELEND *Disobed. Child* (? 1570) F j, [Stage direction] Here the wyfe must laye on lode vppon her Husbande. **1577–87** HOLINSHED *Chron. Eng.* (1807) I. 466 They laid load vpon the Romans with their arrowes and darts. **1647** H. MORE *Song of Soul* I. III. v, The vast thumps of massie hammers noise, That on the groning steel laid on such lode. **1679** DRYDEN *Œdipus* I. i. Dram. Wks. 1725 IV. 378 Lay load upon the Court; gull 'em with Freedom. **1683** TEMPLE *Mem.* Wks. 1731 I. 429 The Dutch began to lay Load upon their Allies, for their Backwardness. **1697** DRYDEN *Æneid* IX. 1097 Mnestheus lays hard load upon his Helm.

c. *a* **1715** BURNET *Own Time* (1724) I. 251 The load of that marriage was cast on Lord Clarendon. *Ibid.* (1734) II. 565 It was moved to lay the Load of that Matter on him.

d. **1546** J. HEYWOOD *Prov.* (1562) 64 He makth you beleue, by lies laide on by lode.

e. [**1929** D. HAMMETT *Dain Curse* (1930) xix. 217 The red-head nurse was getting a load at the keyhole.] **1929** D. RUNYON in *Hearst's International* Oct. 64/1, I am not so sure ..Blake will care to be anybody's husband, and especially Madame La Gimp's after he gets a load of her. **1941** I. BAIRD *He rides Sky* 143 What do you think would have happened if Queen Bess had got a load of the Air Force? **1958** E. DUNDY *Dud Avocado* I. ix. 157 Come over here.... Get a load of this script. **1966** [see *casting-couch* s.v. CASTING *vbl. sb.* 4]. **1972** D. BLOODWORTH *Any Number can Play* xxii. 221 Get a load of that chick over there.

8. *attrib.* and *Comb.*, as ***load goods***, ***-hauling***, ***wagon***; ***load-bearing***, ***-carrying*** adjs.; **load-carrier**, a vehicle with the capacity to accommodate a load; **load cast** *Geol.*, a rounded protrusion on the underside of a stratum (usu. one of sandstone), owing to its having sunk before consolidation into the underlying bed (which is usu. shale); so **load-casted** *a.*, modified or covered by a load cast; **load-casting**, the formation of load casts; **load-cell**, an electronic device for weighing large quantities of material; **load displacement**, **draught**, the displacement or draught of a vessel when laden; **load factor**, the ratio of the average to the maximum amount of work, power, etc., of consumption to productive capacity, etc.; also, in *Aeronaut.*, (*a*) the ratio (or its reciprocal) of the weight of an aircraft to the maximum the wings can support, or that of the force exerted on a part of the structure in ordinary horizontal flight to that exerted in some other condition; (*b*) the ratio of the number of passenger seats occupied to the number available; † **load-horse**, a pack-horse; **load line**, (*a*) = LOAD-WATER-LINE; (*b*) *Electronics*, a straight line that crosses the characteristic curves (of output voltage against output current) of a valve or transistor and has a gradient and position determined by

the load, so that it represents the possible operating conditions of the device; †**load-man**, a man who bears or has charge of a load; †**load-mark-line** = *load-line*; **load-penny** *Hist.*, a market due anciently levied on loads; †**load-pin**, a bar inserted into the side of a wagon, to increase its capacity; **load-rail, -tree**, a broad rail fixed across the middle of a certain kind of corn or hay cart; **load-shedding**, a temporary curtailment of the supply of electricity to a specific area to prevent excessive load on the generating plant; also *transf.* and *fig.*; also ***load-spreading***. Also LOAD-SADDLE, -WATER.

1925 HULL & INGBERG *Fire Resistance of Concrete Columns* 658 Pittsburgh gravel concrete was used in the *load-bearing portion and cinder concrete from bituminous cinders in the outer portion. **1947** *Horizon* Oct. 63 No columns or load-bearing walls intervene. **1961** *Architect & Building News* 21 June 822/1 The building has massive load-bearing walls facing on to the Fellows' Garden and the College Park. **1974** *Times* 18 Feb. 12 Facilities include such items as load-bearing ceiling girders. **1962** *Times* 3 May 19/4 The rear seat can be folded flat to convert the car into an exceptionally roomy *load-carrier. **1974** *Country Life* 21 Nov. 1579/3 A very comfortable car and a handy load carrier. **1611** COTGR. (1632) *Sommier*..any toyling, and *load carrying, drudge, or groome. **1895** *Westm. Gaz.* 14 June 1/3 The fire-resisting material and the load-carrying material. **1960** R. W. MARKS *Dymaxion World of B. Fuller* 55/1 For this reason the truss has an enormous load-carrying ability. **1953** P. H. KUENEN in *Bull. Amer. Assoc. Petroleum Geologists* XXXVII. 1048 The base is sharply cut and flat or forms pockets in its substratum, 'flow casts' in Shrock's terminology (1948). As this term tends to cause confusion it is here suggested to call them '*load casts'. **1969** BENNISON & WRIGHT *Geol. Hist. Brit. Isles* v. 101 Sedimentary structures, including flute casts, load casts, graded bedding, etc., have been described from the arenites. **1957** *Jrnl. Geol.* LXV. 248/1 (*heading*) *Load-casted current markings. **1972** F. J. PETTIJOHN et al. *Sand & Sandstone* iv. 123 Load-casted ripples. **1953** *Bull. Amer. Assoc. Petroleum Geologists* XXXVII. 1051 They were not formed after deposition by *load casting. **1972** F. J. PETTIJOHN et al. *Sand & Sandstone* iv. 124 If one turbidite flow follows on the heels of another, conditions are more favorable for load-casting. **1958** *Engineering* 28 Feb. 39 (Advt.), A standard range of *loadcells designed for industrial weighing. **1884** *Daily News* 9 Oct. 5/7 The Rodney..has a *load-displacement of 9,740 tons. **1898** *Ibid.* 12 Apr. 6/6 Her displacement at *load draught will be 15,000 tons. **1891** R. E. B. CROMPTON in *Min. Proc. Inst. Civil Engin.* CVI. 3 What, for want of a better term, is hereafter called the '*load-factor', that is, the relation which the actual output of a plant..bears to what would be its output if worked continuously day and night, at the full load. **1898** *Allbutt's Syst. Med.* V. 916 The load factor of the heart, the ratio between its average and its maximum work, is ample. **1899** *Westm. Gaz.* 15 Feb. 4/1 The 'load factor', the proportion between the hours of daily consumption and the productive power. **1922** *Encycl. Brit.* XXX. 21/2 The 'load factor' is the number of times the weight of the craft which the wings will support; a measure of the strength. **1943** *Jrnl. R. Aeronaut. Soc.* XLVII. 195 Allowing for the 65 per cent. load factor which seems to be about the maximum that can be expected on any commercial service under normal peace-time conditions, that would call for an aircraft providing accommodations for 57 passengers. **1950** Load factor [see *limit load* s.v. LIMIT *sb.* 5]. **1962** *Times* 16 May 15/3 The passenger load factor (the proportion of passenger capacity used) dropped by 1·7 per cent. to 48·1 per cent. **1970** D. WATERFIELD *Continental Waterboy* iii. 29 The B.C. Power Commission has a load factor of around 52%. **1890** *Daily News* 8 Nov. 5/7 When he left the camp of the Rear Guard he told them that they must not lose their *load goods. **1902** *Daily Chron.* 16 Jan. 3/2 *Load-hauling and gradient-climbing. **1568** *Loode horse [see LOADER¹ 1]. **1607** TOPSELL *Four-f. Beasts* (1658) 254 Of *Load or Pack Horses. **1884** H. SPENCER in *Pop. Sci. Monthly* XXIV. 727 A compulsory *load-line for merchant-vessels. **1898** *Westm. Gaz.* 4 June 8/1 The operation of the load-line tables, which was so dear to the late Mr. Plimsoll. **1901** *Scotsman* 5 Mar. 7/8 Light loadline bill. This bill..provided for the marking of a second load-line..to indicate the minimum depth to which a vessel might be immersed in water when she was in ballast. **1931** *Proc. IRE* XIX. 49 The maximum output will be obtained when the slope of the load line equals minus the slope of the plate current curve. **1962** SIMPSON & RICHARDS *Physical Princ. Junction Transistors* vii. 140 The straight line passing through the battery-voltage point..has a slope ($-1/R_l$) corresponding to the resistance R_l of the load and is called the load line. **1375** BARBOUR *Bruce* VIII. 466 The *layd-men that persauit weill, Thai kest thair ladis doun in hy. *c* **1515** *Cocke Lorell's B.* 11 Lode men, and bere brewers. **1711** W. SUTHERLAND *Shipbuild. Assist.* 91 The Line a. d. is termed the deep *Load-mark Line. **1883** GREEN *Conq. Eng.* ix. 440 The gift of its [*sc.* Worcester's] market-dues, wain-shilling and *load-penny, was the costliest among the many boons which Æthelred and Æthelflæd showered on Bishop Werfrith. **1641** BEST *Farm. Bks.* (Surtees) 137 They..putte the shelvinges, and *loade-pinnes, and pike-stowers, of everie waine into her body. **1851** STEPHENS *Bk. Farm.* (ed. 2) II. 357 The *load-rail, 9 inches broad, is convenient to sit upon in driving, and to stand upon when forking the sheaves in unloading. **1947** *Times* 10 Feb. 2/2 If the saving that was essential was not forthcoming the company would have to resort to *load shedding or temporary cuts in supply. **1948** *Ann. Reg. 1947* 8 The cuts in coal and the 'load-shedding'—a term now incorporated into the vocabulary of the citizen—were due to 'the wretched private coal-owners'. **1963** *Guardian* 29 Apr. 8/6 Lord Longford has announced his resignation as chairman... This is part of the load-shedding of some of his extensive social work. **1951** *Engineering* 6 Apr. 402/2 Electricity *load spreading..necessary..owing to heavy demand for electricity. **1851** STEPHENS *Bk. Farm.* (ed. 2) II. 357 The *load-tree or rail. **1659** HOOLE tr. *Comenius' Orbis Sensualium* (1672) 173 A Wagon, which is either a Timber-Wagon or a *Load-Wagon.

load (ləʊd), *v.* Forms: 5–6 lode, 6 loade, 6– load. *Pa. pple.* (6 lode, 7 load), 7– loaded. *strong* 6–7 loden, 6–8, 9 *dial.* loaden. [f. LOAD *sb.* The strong pa. pple. *loaden* was formed on the analogy of LADEN.]

1. a. *trans.* To put a load on or in; to furnish with a burden, cargo, or lading; to charge *with* a load. Freq. in pa. pple. ***loaded*** (†***loaden***) ***with*** = laden with, having a load of. ***loaded down***: weighed down with a load.

1503 S. HAWES *Example of Virtue* i. 19 A shyp..with moche spyces ryght well lode. **1530** PALSGR. 613/1, I lode a carte..This horse is not halfe loden. **1576** GASCOIGNE *Steele Gl.* Ep. Ded. (Arb.) 43, I haue ben streaking me (like a lubber) when the sunne did shine, and now I striue al in vaine to loade the cart when it raineth. **1579** FENTON *Guicciard.* VII. 398 Sundrie boates and lighters loaden with prouisions. **1660** JER. TAYLOR *Duct. Dubit.* (1676) 808 Deploring his condition that his horse being loaden could not run fast. **1775** T. HUTCHINSON *Diary* 1 Jan. I. 339 A large Dutch ship..loaden with tea. **1847** A. M. GILLIAM *Trav. Mexico* 57 The water-carrier loaded down with the weight of his earthen-vessels. **1865** TROLLOPE *Belton Est.* ii. 15 The men were loading another cart. **1867** W. W. SMYTH *Coal & Coal-mining* 154 Trams, weighing when loaded 25 to 32 cwt. each.

b. *intr.* (for *refl.*). Of a vehicle: To fill with passengers.

1832 *Examiner* 346/2 Last week the coach travelled nearly empty..[Now] the coach loads better than ever. **1893** *Times* 4 May 12/2 This coach always loads well.

2. a. To place on or in a vehicle as a load for transport; to put on board as cargo; †to carry (hay, etc.). In quot. 1495 *transf.* †Also with *in*, *out*.

1495 *Trevisa's Barth. De P.R.* XVIII. xxix. 790 Castors..laye one of them vpryght on the grounde..and layeth and lodyth the styckes and wode bytwene his legges and thies and draweth him home to their dennes. **1523** FITZHERB. *Bk. Husb.* §22 He maye well lode oute his dounge before none, and lode heye or corne at after none. **1613** in Picton *L'pool Munic. Rec.* (1883) I. 184 Ev'ie freeman may loade and carry goods from the waterside. **1714** *Fr. Bk. of Rates* 415 The Dutch Ships which are to have Passports to load in France Wines, Brandy, and other Goods. **1720** DE FOE *Capt. Singleton* v. (1840) 89 We..fetched our luggage, and loaded it..into the canoes. **1725** BRADLEY *Fam. Dict.* s.v. *Untry'd Earth*, Dung..is accordingly loaded in at a great Expence, more particularly in making an Asparagus-Bed. **1743** T. JONES in *Buccleuch MSS.* (Hist. MSS. Comm.) I. 402 The whole Army should..have their baggage loaded..in a readiness to march by break of day. **1900** F. T. BULLEN *With Christ at Sea* ii. 32 We were to load mahogany for home.

b. *absol.* or *intr.* To take in one's load or cargo. Also with *up*.

1720 *Lond. Gaz.* No. 5836/4 Who has now a Ship loading thereof at St. Katherine's Dock. **1822** J. FOWLER *Jrnl.* (1898) 98, I then Con Cluded to load up and move on the Road Which We did and on loading up the Horses We find seven Hors loads of meet. **1857** R. TOMES *Amer. in Japan* xvi. 368 The 'Macedonian' sailed for Manila..leaving the 'Suppy' to load with the coal purchased at Formosa.

3. a. To add or affix a weight to, to add to the weight of (something); to be a weight or burden upon; to bear down or oppress *with* a material weight; to weight, *spec.* to weight with lead (see LOADED *ppl. a.*); to increase the resistance in the working of (a machine) by the addition of a weight. ***loaded with*** = supporting the weight of. †***to load with earth***: to bury.

1578 LYTE *Dodoens* II. xlviii. 205 [The stalkes] being loden [with] litle flowers from the middle even up to the very top. *a* **1625** BEAUM. & FL. *Bloody Bro.* v. ii. (1639) I b, When thou hast loaden me with earth for ever. **1627** HAKEWILL *Apol.* (1630) 58 So their trees were more plentifully loaden with fruits. **1642** FULLER *Holy & Prof. St.* III. xiv. 188 Some rich man of mean worth loaden under a tombe big enough for a Prince to bear. **1667** MILTON *P.L.* IV. 147 A circling row Of goodliest Trees loaden with fairest Fruit. **1697** DRYDEN *Virg. Æneid* x. 608 The Phrygian Troops escap'd the Greeks in vain, They, and their mix'd Allies, now load the Plain. **1711** ADDISON *Spect.* No. 15 ¶1 The coach was drawn by six milk-white horses, and loaden behind with the same number of powdered footmen. **1715–20** POPE *Iliad* XVIII. 548 The ponderous hammer loads his better hand. **1748** *Anson's Voy.* III. ii. 313 We were neither disordered nor even loaded by this repletion. **1793** BEDDOES *Lett. Darwin* 52, I eat one-third or one-fourth more than before without feeling my stomach loaded. **1802** MAR. EDGEWORTH *Moral T.* (1816) I. x. 79 A bat loaded with lead. **1825** J. NICHOLSON *Operat. Mechanic* 79 A machine may be so loaded as just to be in equilibrio with its work. **1860** TYNDALL *Glac.* I. x. 67 The fresh snow which loaded the mountain. **1871** R. ELLIS tr. *Catullus* lxiv. 304 Many a feast high-pil'd did load each table about them. **1892** STARLING *Elem. Human Physiol.* 84 The shortening is not very powerful, and can be prevented by loading the muscle moderately.

b. To adulterate by adding something to increase the weight of the article; to make (light or thin wine) appear full-bodied by adulteration.

1860–1 [see LOADED *ppl. a.* 2]. **1887** *Harper's Mag.* June 120/1 If the paper is to be 'loaded', that is, adulterated with clay or cheap fibres.

c. *Electr.* To provide with additional inductance (e.g. by means of a loading coil) in order either to counteract the effect of capacitance and so reduce the distortion and attenuation of signals (in the case of a telephone line or other transmission line), or to reduce the resonant frequency (in the case of an aerial); more widely, to provide with a load (LOAD *sb.* 3 g) consisting of any kind of impedance.

1901 M. I. PUPIN in *Trans. Amer. Inst. Electr. Engin.* XVII. 452 Though a given cord may be properly loaded for some wave-length it will not be properly loaded for shorter wave-lengths. **1922** GLAZEBROOK *Dict. Appl. Physics* II. 852/2 The effect of loading a line in such a way is approximately the same as though inductance were uniformly distributed along the circuit. **1923** E. W. MARCHANT *Radio Telegr.* iii. 26 The frequency of the oscillation in the aerial can be varied by varying its inductance; that is, coils of copper tube may be inserted which will have the effect of 'loading' it, and so bringing down the frequency of the oscillations. **1962** *Newnes Conc. Encycl. Electr. Engin.* 846/1 Some low-frequency lines are 'loaded' with added inductance to give some approximation to the distortionless condition. **1970** J. EARL *Tuners & Amplifiers* iv. 82 Each source, whether it be radio tuner..or ceramic pickup or tape head, requires to be loaded by a specific value of impedance or within a range of impedance.

4. To supply in excess or overwhelming abundance *with*. Chiefly in pa. pple. ***loaded*** (†***loaden***) ***with***: charged, fraught, or heavily laden with; having an abundance of. Also ***to load up with*** (something).

1577–87 HOLINSHED *Chron.* III. 7/1 The Danes, being loden with riches and spoiles..departed to their ships. **1611** BIBLE *Ps.* lxviii. 19 Blessed be the Lord, who daily loadeth vs with benefits. **1674** BREVINT *Saul at Endor* 263 A Rich Noble-Man, notoriously loaden with Crimes. **1709** STEELE *Tatler* No. 69 ¶1 If a Man be loaded with Riches and Honours. **1709** BERKELEY *Th. Vision* §71 The air..may be loaded with a greater quantity of interspersed vapours. **1716** LADY M. W. MONTAGU *Let. to C'tess Bristol* 22 Aug., The shops [are] loaded with merchandise. **1799** M. UNDERWOOD *Dis. Children* (ed. 4) I. 288 When they have slept in the same bed with one loaded with it [i.e. small-pox]. **1818** JAS. MILL *Brit. India* II. IV. v. 212 He returned to Moorshedabad, loaded with disease. **1828** SCOTT *F.M. Perth* xxiv, Old Torquil..loaded him with praises and with blessings. **1869** E. A. PARKES *Pract. Hygiene* (ed. 3) 93 The air of London is so loaded with carbon. **1880** 'MARK TWAIN' *Tramp Abroad* xxxviii. 435, I loaded them up with paragoric and put them to bed. **1882** MISS BRADDON *Mt. Royal* II. vii. 138 He would have loaded her with gifts, had she been willing to accept them. **1892** 'MARK TWAIN' *Amer. Claimant* iii. 21 He loads up the house with cripples and idiots and stray cats. **1943** K. TENNANT *Ride on Stranger* (1968) i. 3 Other men get married without being loaded up with kids, kids, and then more kids.

5. a. To put the charge into (a firearm); also *absol.* ***to be loaded***: (of a body of men) to have their arms charged.

1626 CAPT. SMITH *Accid. Yng. Seamen* 32 To loade a peece. **1688** SHADWELL *Sqr. Alsatia* v. Wks. 1720 IV. 105 [She snaps a pistol at Belfond] *Belfond.* Thank you, Madam; are you not a Devil? 'twas loaden. **1799** *Instr. & Reg. Cavalry* (1813) 271 The same principle of reserving the fire with the front line, till the rear support is loaded. **1804** W. TAYLOR in *Ann. Rev.* II. 262 Several pieces of heavy ordnance, loaden with grape-shot. **1841** THACKERAY *Drum* II. xlv, They load and fire. **1851** *Illustr. Catal. Gt. Exhib.* 1146 At one operation, these caps are loaded with fulminating-powder. **1891** E. PEACOCK *N. Brendon* I. 145 How many barrels are loaded?

b. To insert a photographic film or plate in (a camera); also with the film as object.

1902 *Year Bk. Photogr.* 13 (Advt.), The 'Roll Film' Automan will be preferred by many on account of the ease with which it may be loaded and unloaded in daylight. **1936** *Discovery* Aug. 237/1 This unique camera..weighs 305 pounds when loaded. **1956** A. L. M. SOWERBY *Dict. Photogr.* (ed. 18) 88 A long roll of film..was loaded into the camera at the factory.

c. To fill (a tobacco-pipe).

1927 'F. LONSDALE' *On Approval* II. 66 He crosses to stool down R, and loads his pipe.

6. *fig.* **a.** To weigh down, burden, oppress (*with* something immaterial); to clog, encumber.

1526 *Pilgr. Perf.* (W. de W. 1531) 232 b, He sholde..fixe them in his hert, lodyng & chargynge his memory with them. **1599** *1st Pt. Ret. fr. Parnassus* I. i. 360 And if I live, I'le make a poesie Shall loade thy future's yeares with infamie. **1605** CAMDEN *Rem.* (1637) 39 Neither are we loden with those declensions, flexions, and variations, which are incident to many other tongues. **1625** BACON *Ess., Superstition* (Arb.) 347 Ouer-great Reuerence of Traditions, which cannot but load the Church. **1632** LITHGOW *Trav.* I. 5 Load with the filth of dallying Lust and Sin. **1671** MILTON *P.R.* IV. 418 And sturdiest Oaks Bow'd thir Stiff necks, loaden with stormy blasts. **1777** J. ADAMS in *Fam. Lett.* (1876) 272, I have been now for near ten weeks..constantly loaded with a cold. **1865** J. H. NEWMAN *Gerontius* §4 Lest so stern a solitude should load And break thy being. **1884** A. R. PENNINGTON *Wiclif* viii. 257 The frivolous vanities with which Confirmation was loaded, led him to speak in a disparaging tone of it.

absol. **1593** *Tell-Troth's N.Y. Gift* 9 A frowne lodeth, and a smile lightneth; to frowne therefore kindly, is a barre to Iellocy: but loading crabbedly, men vndoe themselues speedily.

b. To overwhelm *with* abuse, reproaches, etc. †Also, to throw blame upon; to charge *with* something opprobrious.

1662 GURNALL *Chr. in Arm.* (1669) 296/2 A few silly men, loaden with the vilest reproaches that the wit of man could invent. **1692** R. L'ESTRANGE *Fables* xxv. (1708) 31 To be Loaden at every turn with Blows and Reproaches. **1697** DRYDEN *Virg. Æneid* XI. 335 These are the Crimes, with which they load the Name of Turnus. **1709** STANHOPE *Paraphr.* IV. 583 They Load his Doctrine with Imposture and Blasphemy. *a* **1715** BURNET *Own Time* (1734) II. 272 Every thing was acceptable there, that loaded that Treaty, and these Lords. *Ibid.* 564 The Design was now formed, to load the late Administration all that was possible. **1726** SWIFT *Gulliver* III. i, While the Dutchman..loaded me with all the curses and injurious terms his language could afford.

1901 D. SMITH in *Expositor* Oct. 282 An angry brother once loaded him with abuse.

7. a. To heap or pile *on*. *rare*.

1580 SIDNEY *Ps.* IX. viii, Lord,.. Ponder the paines which on me loaden be. **1671** MILTON *Samson* 1243 E're long thou shalt lament These braveries in Irons loaden on thee. **1852** MRS. STOWE *Uncle Tom's C.* iii, The more he sees I can do, the more he loads on.

b. *Painting.* To lay (colour) on thickly in opaque masses.

1859 GULLICK & TIMBS *Paint.* 228 In the foreground.. the 'impasto' should be bold; but in the more brilliant lights, it can scarcely be 'loaded' too much. **18..** *Art Jrnl.* N.S. XI. 10 (Cent.) Masses of white enamel are loaded upon the surface, with a view to further treatment.

8. *intr.* **a.** To collect into a load or heap. **b.** To become loaded or clogged.

1806-7 A. YOUNG *Agric. Essex* (1813) I. 139 The objection to so much concavity or flatness in the fore part of the breast, ..is the loose earth of the furrow loading there. **1890** *Cent. Dict.* s.v., Oysters are apt to load with sand.

9. a. *refl.* and *intr.* (*Stock-exchange.*) To buy heavily of stock. **b.** *pass.* ***to be loaded up***: to have large quantities of a thing in hand as security.

1870 J. K. MEDBERY *Men & Mysteries Wall St.* 136 To 'load' one's self with stocks is to buy heavily. **1885** *Pall Mall G.* 8 June 5/2 One of those cornering cliques which are the curse of legitimate trade across the Atlantic appears to have loaded heavily on the chance of an outbreak. **1893** *Times* 15 Aug. 7/4 No banking system could stand being loaded up with rye year after year.

10. *Life-insurance.* To increase (a premium) by adding a charge (called the 'loading') as a provision against contingencies or for other reasons; to charge (a particular life) with a 'loaded' premium. (Cf. LOADING *vbl. sb.* 3.)

1867 C. WALFORD *Insur. Guide* (ed. 2) 260 Table shewing the process of 'loading' rates of premiums: also affording a comparison between the English and Carlisle Rates loaded, and the Northampton *net* Rates. **1897** *Allbutt's Syst. Med.* IV. 615 If the body-weight bear an undue proportion to the weight of the individual, such cases are either 'loaded' or declined as second or third class lives.

11. *Psychol.* To weight (a result or outcome), to contribute to or be correlated with; also *intr.* (const. *on*), to be correlated (with something else).

1931 *Psychol. Rev.* XXXVIII. 408 The ministry is loaded high for interest in people and in language but low for science. **1952** R. B. CATTELL *Factor Analysis* xviii. 340 The factor loading (situational index) is not a measure of the mean amount of the contribution of the factor to the situation. For example, the discovery that in a certain collection of books, the factor of weight is loaded 0·6 in thickness and only 0·2 in height simply indicates that for a given weight (overall size) these books vary more in thickness than they do in height—as books on a tidy shelf should. **1970** LIEBERT & SPIEGLER *Personality* vi. 132 As part of the factor analysis, the ratings on each of the 50 trait elements, on which the subjects were rated, were correlated with each of the factors which had been found... The elements which loaded (correlated) most highly both in a positive and in a negative direction (recall that the magnitude of a correlation is independent of its sign) are listed in Table 6-3. **1971** *Jrnl. Gen. Psychol.* LXXXIV. 242 Both of these [test variables] were originally predicted to load the insight factor. **1972** *Jrnl. Social Psychol.* LXXXVIII. 190 The items loading on Factor I seem to reflect the parent's interests.

load, obs. form of LODE, LODH.

loadability (ləʊdəˈbɪlɪtɪ). [f. LOAD *v.* + -ABILITY.] The degree of ease with which goods may be loaded or transported.

1945 F. HAMANN *Air Words* 35/1 *Loadability.* (1) Cargo volume of commercial aircraft. (2) Ease of access in aircraft. **1955** *Times* 10 June 3/1 The definition of loadability.. should include other traffic characteristics such as bulk in comparison to weight, stowage potential, [etc.]. **1960** *Economist* 22 Oct. 392/3 Generally, road hauliers would like to charge more for the smaller loads ('loadability' is as important by road as by rail). **1967** *Freight Management* Jan. 46/2 As far as loadability is concerned, roll-on offers many advantages. **1974** *Country Life* 26 Dec. 2019/3 The Citroen Safari for sheer loadability with comfort.

†**loadage.** *Obs.* [f. LOAD *v.* + -AGE.] A toll or due for loading.

1661 [see ANCHORAGE^{1} 5].

loadberry (ˈləʊdbərɪ). *Shetland dial.* Also lodberry. [Cogn. w. Norw. dial. *ladberg*, ON. *hlaðberg* a lading-rock, a natural quay or pier.] A flat rock forming a natural landing-place; *spec.* a small enclosed landing-place for the unloading of boats.

1764 in W. R. Mackintosh *Glimpses Kirkwall* (1887) 173 The said loadberry or north east part of the Ness of Quanterness. **1871** *Black's Picturesque Tourist of Scotl.* (ed. 19) 596 Lerwick is now before us, a great portion of the houses lining the shore, and standing in the sea, with loadberrys and piers attached. **1950** *Menzies' Guide to Shetland* 10 The most interesting feature of this part of the town [*sc.* Lerwick] is the series of lodberries, or enclosed courtyards with wooden doors surmounting steps down to the water. **1975** *Country Life* 13 Feb. 367/1 Many of these houses had their own slipways with stores or lodberrys.

loaded (ˈləʊdɪd), *ppl. a.* [f. LOAD *v.* + -ED^{1}.]

1. a. Charged, burdened, laden, etc. (see the verb).

1661 FELTHAM *Resolves* II. lxxxv. 375 When 'tis ripe..it downward turns its loaded head. **1682** OTWAY *Venice Preserv'd* I. 10 If thou art alter'd, where shall I have harbour? Where ease my loaded Heart? **1693** G. STEPNY in *Dryden's Juvenal* (1697) 195 To turn a Mill, or drag a Loaded Life Beneath two Panniers. **1735** SOMERVILLE *Chase* II. 218 As now in louder Peals the loaded Winds Bring on the gath'ring Storm. **1766** SMOLLETT *Hist. Eng.* (1804) V. 262 Many loaded guns went off while the houses were burning. **1785** MAD. D'ARBLAY *Lett.* 25 Aug., When-ever we are quite alone, she now unburthens her loaded heart. **1821** SYD. SMITH *Wks.* (1867) I. 325 He who sets a loaded gun means it should go off if it is touched. **1830** *Examiner* 107/1 A loaded cart. **1889** RUSKIN *Præterita* III. 107 The loaded apple trees in the orchard.

b. Weighted, esp. with lead, as a ***loaded stick, whip. loaded dice***: dice in which lead is inserted in order to make them fall with a particular face upwards.

1771 WESLEY *Jrnl.* 7 June, With his loaded whip, [he] struck Nancy A—— on the temple. **1781** COWPER *Conversat.* 302 He says but little, and that little said Owes all its weight, like loaded dice, to lead. **1787** WINTER *Syst. Husb.* 27 The surface should be well worked with loaded harrows. **1839** R. S. ROBINSON *Naut. Steam Eng.* 111 The water still driven by the plunger..goes on to the loaded valve. **1858** SIMMONDS *Dict. Trade, Loaded Cushion*, a lady's table pincushion for fastening work to, and which is loaded with lead. **1889** J. M. ROBERTSON *Christ & Krishna* xv. 86 One is flogged to death with loaded whips.

¶**c.** Charged with magnetism, magnetized. [After LOADSTONE.]

1717 PRIOR *Alma* II. 225 Great Kings to Wars are pointed forth, Like loaded Needles to the North.

d. *fig.* Charged with some hidden implication or underlying suggestion; biased, prejudiced.

1942 *College English* Oct. 16 General Semantics..being metaphysical in a particularly partial and dogmatic sense.. can yield us only a vocabulary of 'loaded' general words, calculated to distort rather than to illuminate the writings of any other school. **1957** *Observer* 29 Dec. 9/2 Is our popular preference for plays of less blatant sexuality a mark of higher civilisation or merely of greater hypocrisy? Is the Dionysiac cult..more childish or simply more honest than the religious practices that have succeeded it in the West?.. These are loaded questions, I admit. **1958** *Times* 7 July 13/2 You cannot solve the riddle of the universe by giving the answer 'Yes' or 'No' to a loaded question. **1961** *Listener* 7 Dec. 991/3 He chose to use emotionally loaded words like 'scare' and 'infection'. **1975** D. BAGLEY *Snow Tiger* xi. 96 It is improper of Mr Smithers to ask such a loaded question... He is usurping the function of this commission.

2. In technical use. Of wine: Adulterated so as to appear full-bodied. Of the tongue: Thickly furred. Of the liver: Charged with excess of bile. Of the urine: Surcharged with salts, etc. Of a muscle: Subjected to a 'load' (see LOAD *sb.* 3 e). Of a camera: with a film inserted. Of a film: inserted (in a camera) (cf. LOAD *v.* 5 b). In *Electr.*, of a telephone line, etc. (cf. LOAD *v.* 3 c). In insurance: of a life (cf. LOAD *v.* 10).

1860-1 THACKERAY *Lovel* iii. 193 Loaded claret, and sweet port. **1875** B. MEADOWS *Clin. Observ.* 12 Tongue is now somewhat loaded in a morning. **1888** *Judge* (U.S.) 20 Oct. 27/1 (Advt.), The Kodak Camera..Loaded for 100 instantaneous views. **1897** *Allbutt's Syst. Med.* IV. 17 The stimulation of the intestinal glands..relieves the 'loaded' liver. **1898** P. MANSON *Trop. Diseases* xxi. 339 Furred tongue, scanty, high-coloured, loaded urine. **1898** *Allbutt's Syst. Med.* V. 925 A loaded does more work than an unloaded muscle. **1901** *Trans. Amer. Inst. Electr. Engin.* XVII. 475 Propagation of electrical waves over a periodically loaded loop..is compared to that over a uniform loop. **1903** *Phil. Mag.* V. 313 The loaded line discussed in this paper is an electrical circuit of two long parallel conducting wires having self-induction coils inserted at regular intervals. **1922** *Encycl. Brit.* XXXII. 709/2 In 1911 Messrs. Siemens introduced a form of balata dielectric as a substitute for gutta-percha in loaded submarine cables... The effect was to reduce materially the attenuation constant and increase the range of speech in loaded cables. **1928** *Daily Express* 10 May 11/6 The application was refused in the first instance, and only afterwards accepted as a 'loaded' life. **1937** *Discovery* Apr. 112/2 Little..envelopes, in which glass plates and flat films are sold ready loaded. **1968** *Radio Communication Handbk.* (ed. 4) xvi. 33/1 While the centre loaded aerial may be the best radiator, on the lower frequency bands, particularly 1·8 Mc/s and 3·5 Mc/s, mechanical considerations may have to influence the loading coil position.

3. *U.S. slang.* **a.** Drunk.

1890 in *Century Dict.* **1892** *Voice* (N.Y.) 28 July, A Democrat who stood on the sidewalk made this uncharitable exclamation as S. stepped into a carriage: 'He's loaded'. **1897** in BARRÈRE & LELAND *Slang.*

b. Drugged; under the influence of drugs; containing a drug. (Cf. LOAD *sb.* 5 a.)

1923 J. F. FISHMAN *Crucibles of Crime* vi. 126 It was discovered that each of them [*sc.* handkerchiefs] has a small ink mark in one of the corners..these handkerchiefs had been dipped in cocaine... The mark in the corner notified the 'snowbird' that it was 'loaded'. **1928** J. TULLY *Circus Parade* xviii. 237 When guys are loaded up on heroin it'll give 'em more nerve. **1953** W. BURROUGHS *Junkie* xii. 120 To get really loaded, you would need four papers. *Ibid.* xv. 147 He was loaded on H and goof-balls. **1962** K. ORVIS *Damned & Destroyed* xi. 74 'I'm gorgeous,' she said. 'Loaded and gorgeous.'

4. Rich; extremely wealthy. *slang* (orig. *U.S.*).

[**1910** O. JOHNSON *Varmint* iv. 60 He's just loaded with the spondulix.] **1948** *Call-Bulletin* (San Francisco) 16 July 10/4 Lonely but loaded, a carpenter newly returned from Guam was taken for a ride by six young women. **1949** A. HYND *We are Public Enemies* i. 20 The boys were loaded after the safety deposit opening and the money was burning their pockets. **1952** 'J. TEY' *Singing Sands* xi. 172 He slapped his pocket, 'I'm loaded.' **1957** C. MACINNES *City of Spades* I. iv. 23 'Is your Dad rich?'..'He's reasonably loaded.' **1971** D. O'CONNOR *Eye of Eagle* v. 32 Adriana's a very popular girl and there are guys here who are absolutely loaded.

†**ˈloaden**, *ppl. a. Obs.* [Strong pa. pple. of LOAD *v.*]

1. = HEAVY-LADEN 2. Also *absol.*

1542-5 BRINKLOW *Lament.* (1874) 82 Come vnto me all ye that laboure and are loden (meaninge with sinne). **1653** BINNING *Serm.* (1845) 427 This we preach unto you, that until you be wearied and loaden, you will not cast your burden on Jesus. **1711** SHAFTESB. *Charac.* (1737) II. III. i. 386 Large Creatures; who..go led and loaden thro those dry and barren Places!

2. Loaded, charged, weighted, laden.

1600 SURFLET *Country Farme* v. xviii. 694 You must haue speciall regard to sowe them [Beanes] all about the fifteenth daie after the change of the moone, bicause that in so doing, they will bee the better loaden. **1619** FLETCHER & MASSINGER *False One* IV. iii, Pitty me, Pitty a loaden man. **1639** *Mass. Col. Rec.* (1853) I. 266 A loaden horse carrying a sack of corne. **1704** ADDISON *Italy* (1733) 105 The Seas.. Shove the loaden Vessels into Port. **1725** POPE *Odyss.* IX. 274 The loaden shelves afford us full repast. *a* **1774** GOLDSM. tr. *Scarron's Com. Romance* (1775) I. 289 Certain peasants who attended a loaden cart. **1792** CHARLOTTE SMITH *Desmond* I. 213 Those majestic and deeply-loaden clouds.

loaden (ˈləʊd(ə)n), *v. Obs.* exc. *dial.* Also 6 loden. [f. LOAD *sb.* + -EN^{5}.] *trans.* = LOAD *v.*, in various senses. Hence **ˈloadened** *ppl. a.*

1568 Q. ELIZ. *Let. to Mary Q. Scots* 21 Dec. in H. Campbell *Love Lett. Mary* (1824) App. 55 We did not thynk ..to have seen or heard such matters of so great apparence & moment to charge & loden yow. **1628** GAULE *Pract. Theory* (1629) 167 That they straiten not our Thoughts, ere they loaden our Backes. **1638-48** G. DANIEL *Eclog.* I. 213 Our loadned trees Beare equall Burthens. **1658** BROMHALL *Treat. Specters* I. 96 A loadned and ballasted ship. **1768** STERNE *Sent. Journ.* (1775) I. 52 (*Letter*) He had loaden'd himself in going up stairs with a thousand compliments to Madame. **1790** A. WILSON *Poems & Lit. Prose* (1876) II. 278 With ripe fruit the loaden'd bough Bends to the swaird. **1877** *N.W. Linc. Gloss., Loadened*, loaded. 'I wen't hev loaden'd guns browt into th' hoose'. **1880** *Antrim & Down Gloss.* s.v., I was told to loaden up with flax. **1889** MABEL PEACOCK *Lincs. Tales* 127 When he's tekken his jackit off to help to loäden a cart.

loader^{1} (ˈləʊdə(r)). Also 5-6 loder, 6 looder. [f. LOAD *v.* + -ER^{1}.]

1. a. One who loads (in various senses); a carrier (*obs.* or *dial.*); a man who stands on the top of a wagon, a haystack, etc., and arranges the hay or corn which is forked up.

1476 *Paston Lett.* III. 153 It come home the same daye that I come owte, browght by Herry Berker, loder. **1568** in W. H. Turner *Select. Rec. Oxford* 325 Nether any looder, carye or recarye wth their loode horse or horses..any maner of corne. **1577-87** HOLINSHED *Chron.* III. 1060/2 So were his loders more readie to aggrauate his burthen, than willing to ease him. **1619** DALTON *Country Just.* xliv. (1630) 103 [To] punish the offences of..Badgers Loaders Poulters or other ministers for the King's Majestie. **1641** BEST *Farm. Bks.* (Surtees) 35 The one of the men is a loader, the other a forker, and the woman to rake after the waine. *a* **1661** FULLER *Worthies, Cornw.* (1662) I. 204 The French-man did it out of covetousness, that so two loaders might bring double grists to his Mill. *a* **1722** LISLE *Husb.* (1752) 217 It is good husbandry to have two pitchers to one loader in the field. **1848** THOREAU *Maine W.* (1894) 58 According to Springer, the company consists of choppers, swampers,— who make roads,—barker and loader, teamster, and cook. **1880** *Lumberman's Gaz.* 28 Jan., There are also 'loaders', who assist the teamsters in placing the logs on their sleds. **1880** BOTTRELL *Trad. Cornw.* Ser. III. 158 The 'loader' (miller's boy) having brought the grist to a farmhouse.

b. An attendant whose business it is to load guns for a man who is shooting game.

1869 *Pall Mall G.* 1 Sept. 2 A quick man, with a good loader at his back, will not unfrequently get at least three barrels into a rise of birds. **1895** G. W. SMALLEY *Stud. Men* 198 The killing was done not to his own gun, but to his own three guns, as he had two loaders.

c. (*a*) A loading-machine. (*b*) See quot. 1872-6.

1872-6 VOYLE & STEVENSON *Milit. Dict.* (ed. 3), *Loader*, an instrument used with S. B. siege howitzers to steady the shell in the passage down the bore. The fixed iron band which crosses the hollow hemisphere of the loader has a hole in it which embraces the fuze, and which on reaching the bottom of the bore can be easily disengaged. **1875** KNIGHT *Dict. Mech., Loader*, a machine attached to a wagon, as a *hay-loader* or *stone-loader*. **1884** KNIGHT *Dict. Mech.* Suppl.

†**2.** App. a dicing term; a doublet. (In quots. *fig.*) *Obs.*

1693 DRYDEN *Juvenal* VI. Argt. (1697) 114 Lust is the main Body of the Tree... Every Vice is a Loader; but that's a Ten. **1694** —— *Love Triumphant* IV. i, You will find but one bastard charged upon you: you see I was not for laying loaders.

3. A gun which is loaded in a particular way, always with qualification, e.g. BREECH-LOADER, MUZZLE-LOADER, *single-loader*. Applied similarly to other things, such as agricultural machinery (e.g. *front-end loader*), washing machines (e.g. *front-loader*), etc.; see also *side-loader* s.v. SIDE *sb.*^{1} 27.

1858 [see BREECH-LOADER]. **1868** *Rep. to Govt. U.S. Munitions War* 31 When it is required to be used as a single-loader, and a full magazine held in reserve for a greater emergency. **1968** *Which?* May 149/1 This [washing] machine is a top loader, but has a horizontal stainless steel drum. **1975** *Radio Times* 22-28 Feb. 56/1 Fully automatic top-loader. Takes loads of 4 lbs., 7 lbs., or 10 lbs... 7 programme automatic front loader. Takes load of 9 lbs.

4. Special comb.: **loader gate** *Coal-mining*, a passage along which coal is conveyed away from a long-wall face.

1964 A. NELSON *Dict. Mining* 258 *Loadergate*, a gate road equipped with a gate conveyor or a gate-end loader; the gate to which the face conveyors deliver their coal. **1973** *Times* 3 May 4/1 Then I saw all the loader gate workmen running towards me. Someone shouted 'run, water has broken in.'

† **ˈloader²**. *Obs.* [f. LOAD *sb.* + -ER^1.] = *load-horse.*

1600 N. BRETON *Pasquil's Passion* ix. (Grosart) 26/1 The Sacke, That laide awry may breake the Loaders backe.

loading (ˈləʊdɪŋ), *vbl. sb.* [f. LOAD *v.* + -ING^1.]

1. a. The action of the verb LOAD; the placing of a load or cargo in a vehicle, vessel, etc. † *bill of loading* = bill of lading (see BILL $sb.^3$ 10).

1523 FITZHERB. *Husb.* §22 In lodynge of hey or corne, the cattel is alwaye eatynge or beytynge. **1571** CAMPION *Hist. Irel.* viii. (1633) 102 The Irish impositions of Coyne, Livery, Cartings, carriages, loadings,..and such like. **1626** CAPT. SMITH *Accid. Yng. Sea-men* 25 With your Commission, Cocket, or bills of loading. **1727** A. HAMILTON *New Acc. E. Ind.* II. xxxiii. 17 Perrin must take them, and sign Bills of Loading for good well-conditioned Goods. **1806** *Gazetteer Scot.* (ed. 2) 545 The want of a pier..prevents them from loading or unloading except at low water. **1898** *Allbutt's Syst. Med.* V. 961 The 'loading' indeed, if not excessive, stimulates the organ to stronger contraction.

b. *Arch.* The placing of a 'load'.

1751 LABELYE *Westm. Br.* 80 The further Loading of the settled Pier would be dangerous. **1853** SIR H. DOUGLAS *Milit. Bridges* (ed. 3) 48 In the bridge, without any loading, each large pontoon is immersed to the depth of about $9\frac{1}{2}$ inches.

c. *Painting.* (See LOAD *v.* 7 b.)

1859 GULLICK & TIMBS *Paint.* 228 This loading of thick masses of colour upon the picture. **1882** HAMERTON *Graphic Arts* 230 Loading is the use of opaque colour in heavy masses which actually protrude from the canvas and themselves catch the light as the mountains do on the moon.

d. The use of weights or of some added material for the purpose of falsification or adulteration. *concr.* The material used for this purpose.

1886 *Pall Mall G.* 3 June 4/2 Loading is slipping about an ounce weight of lead down the ears of the horse..No matter how vicious the beast may be it becomes dazed and stupid when the load plugs its ears. **1889** *Ibid.* 16 Nov. 6/3 Into lobsters and crabs which have become by reason of age of lighter weight are introduced portions of fresh haddock or roker... This is technically called 'loading'. **1890** WATT *Paper-making* 114 The very finest qualities of paper are usually made without the addition of any *loading*, as it is called.

e. *Conjuring.* (See quot.)

1872 *Routledge's Ev. Boy's Ann.* 345/2 For the purpose of what is called 'loading', i.e. bringing a rabbit or other article into a hat, etc.

f. *Electr.* Addition of inductance, or the inductance added (see LOAD *v.* 3 c); any impedance that acts as a load (LOAD *sb.* 3 g).

1903 *Phil. Mag.* V. 325 Loading..presents the greatest possibilities upon long cable circuits. **1922** GLAZEBROOK *Dict. Appl. Physics* II. 850/2 The increase in voltage resulting from the increased impedance..increases the leakage losses, and these set a limit to the possible improvement in transmission efficiency by loading. **1959** K. HENNEY *Radio Engin. Handbk.* (ed. 5) xxviii. 29 Uniformly surrounding the conductor with a thin layer of magnetic material of high permeability..is known as continuous loading. This has been used, to some extent, in the construction of some long submarine-cable circuits for telegraphy as well as telephony. However, loading is usually introduced in telephone circuits by connecting loading coils in series with the conductors at intervals. **1968** *Radio Communication Handbk.* (ed. 4) xvi. 34/1 With a centre loaded coil on 3·5 Mc/s it may be possible to vary the transmitter frequency over about 25 kc/s before it becomes essential to re-adjust the loading. **1973** *Physics Bull.* Dec. 716/1 This changes the impedance of the loop and hence it alters the loading of the RF circuit and this can be detected in the RF drive output.

g. The (maximum) current or power that an electrical appliance is designed to take.

1938 E. M. ACKERY *Electr. Heating for Public & Commercial Libraries* iv. 42 The coke-boiler was replaced by a 400 gallon thermal storage tank, fitted with immersion heaters with a total loading of 100 kw. **1951** *Good Housek. Home Encycl.* 310/1, 2 or 3 kilowatts is a sufficient loading for the average-sized tank. **1973** *Daily Tel.* 4 Dec. 11/4 Fan heater with loading of 2 kw: 1·8p an hour (2 units).

2. The putting of the charge in a firearm.

1655 MRQ. WORCESTER *Cent. Inv.* §58 To make a Pistol discharge a dozen times with one loading. **1748** *Anson's Voy.* III. viii. 375 The whole crew..were..quick in loading, all of them good marksmen. **1879** *Cassell's Techn. Educ.* II. 66 The loading was effected almost as easily and rapidly as in a smooth-bore.

3. *Life-insurance.* (See quot. 1881.)

1867 C. WALFORD *Insur. Guide* (ed. 2) 258 Some loading to the pure premiums may be considered as absolutely necessary. *Ibid.* 329 There will still remain..a considerable surplus, after paying all proper expenses, out of the loading of the premiums. **1881** *Encycl. Brit.* XIII. 173/1 With the introduction..of mortality tables which approached more closely the death-rates among assured lives, there revived the practice of making an addition to the pure premiums, in order to provide for expenses, for fluctuations in the death-rate, and for other contingencies. This addition is called the 'loading' or 'margin'... The terms 'loading' and 'margin' have come to bear a somewhat extended meaning. They are now used to designate the difference between the premiums payable by the assured and the net premiums deduced from any table that may be employed for the time. **1896** *Allbutt's Syst. Med.* I. 477 The calculated premium is slightly in excess of the true net premium, and the 'loading' in contingent cases is usually heavy.

4. *concr.* **a.** That with which something is loaded; a load, lading, cargo. Now somewhat *rare.*

1494 FABYAN *Chron.* VII. 620 A Frenshman..beynge a carter, whiche dayly vsed to entre this towne with vytayll & other lodynge of his carte. *c* **1592** MARLOWE *Jew of Malta* I. i. 85 Goe thou thy wayes, discharge thy Ship, And bid my Factor bring his loading in. **1604** SHAKS. *Oth.* V. ii. 363 Looke on the tragic loading of this bed. **1703** *Lond. Gaz.* No. 3917/4 The Loading of the Dorothy..will be exposed to publick Sale. **1720** DE FOE *Capt. Singleton* i. (1840) 11 The ship, having taken in her loading, set sail for Portugal. **1745** ELIZA HEYWOOD *Female Spect.* XVII. (1748) III. 258 The plumb unhandled lost its bloom, the weak stems let fall their loading yet unripe. **1755** *Man* No. 13. 5 In failure of better loading, my wife and my chum might have the first ride in it [*viz.* a cart]. **1804** in Lewis & Clarke *Trav.* (1893) I. 45 No damage was done to the boats or the loading. **1825** J. NICHOLSON *Operat. Mechanic* 656, 21 waggons of five cwt. each, which, with their loading of coals, amounted to 43 tons eight cwt. **1890** 'ROLF BOLDREWOOD' *Col. Reformer* (1891) 245 He had, as early as such loading could be procured, ordered from town great stores of fruit-trees and plants.

b. *pl.* in *Mining.* (See quots.)

1875 J. H. COLLINS *Metal Mining* 96 Blocks, which are mounted upon piers or 'loadings' of masonry. **1883** GRESLEY *Coal-mining Gloss.*, *Loadings*, pillars of masonry carrying a drum or pulley.

5. The weight supported by a wing divided by its area. More fully ***wing loading*** (cf. *power loading*).

1918 [see *live load* s.v. LIVE *a.* 9]. **1919** H. SHAW *Textbk. Aeronaut.* xv. 181 The loading of a machine, which is the weight carried per unit area of surface, varies in different types. **1936** *Discovery* Mar. 73/2 Most birds fly at a loading of $1\frac{1}{2}$ to $2\frac{1}{2}$ lb. per sq. ft. **1973** *Sci. Amer.* Dec. 103/2 The glider can travel much faster than the vulture at a given gliding angle. This is owing partly to..its higher wing loading (the ratio of weight to wing area).

6. *Psychol.* The extent to which any given factor or variable contributes to or is correlated with some resultant quality or overall situation, usu. represented by a number arrived at by statistical analysis of the results of a series of tests.

1931 *Psychol. Rev.* XXXVIII. 407 Our next problem is to assign a weight or loading of each of the general factors to each of the variables... Engineering, for example, has a high loading of interest in science, a rather low loading of interest in language. **1935** L. L. THURSTONE *Vectors of Mind* viii. 201 (*heading*) The elimination of negative factor loadings. **1947** L. E. TYLER *Psychol. Human Differences* xv. 364 The task of the factor analyst then becomes one of determining these weights or loadings. The raw material for the mathematical work in each case is the original table of intercorrelations. **1952** [see LOAD *v.* 11]. **1971** *Jrnl. Gen. Psychol.* LXXXV. 72 The loadings have been rounded to two figures and the order of both factors and variables rearranged to facilitate inspection. *Ibid.* 212 Because many of the memory tests require recall of the items memorized, and because the operations of divergent and convergent production are so much dependent upon retrieval of information from the memory store, it might be expected that..either production tests would have some memory loadings, or memory tests would have some loadings on production factors.

7. *attrib.* and *Comb.* Pertaining to the loading of goods, cargo, etc., as ***loading-berth, -board, -book, -pick, -tool, -tower, -yard***; pertaining to or used in the loading of firearms, as ***loading-bar, -chamber, -funnel, -hammer, -machine, -plug, -tongs, -tray***; **loading bay**, a bay (BAY $sb.^3$) or recess in a building where vehicles, etc., are loaded and unloaded; **loading coil** *Electr.*, an inductance coil used in the loading of telephone lines or aerials (see sense 1 f and LOAD *v.* 3 c); **loading gauge** *Railways*, (*a*) the maximum height and width allowed for rolling stock to ensure adequate clearance under bridges and in tunnels; (*b*) a device suspended over railway lines for checking the dimensions of rolling stock; **loading-rod**, a ramrod; **loading-turn** (see quot. 1858).

1881 WILHELM *Milit. Dict.*, *Loading-bar*, a bar used to carry shot. It is passed through the ring of the shell-hooks; also called *carrying-bar.* **1963** *Listener* 31 Jan. 202/2 The whole street is sometimes used as an open-air *loading bay and temporary warehouse. **1971** R. BUSBY *Deadlock* x. 152 The roller doors of the loading bay were shut. **1900** F. W. BULLEN *With Christ at Sea* iii. 53 We had reached our *loading berth. **1910** W. M. RAINE *Bucky O'Connor* 36 The *loading board was lowered and the horses led from the car. **1812** J. SMYTH *Pract. of Customs* (1821) 407 J. Mann, Cart-follower, kept the *Loading-book. **1867** SMYTH *Sailor's Word-bk.*, *Loading-chamber*, the paterero, or inserting piece in breech-loading. **1901** *Ann. Rep. Amer. Telephone & Telegr. Co.* 4 The efficiency of these lines will be largely increased by the use of '*loading coils'. **1922** GLAZEBROOK *Dict. Appl. Physics* II. 853/1 Loading coils are encased in iron cases and are mounted in manholes—if the circuit..is a cable circuit—or are mounted at the cross-arms of poles if the circuit..is an open-wire line. **1974** *Encycl. Brit. Micropædia* VI. 286/1 Auto radios generally use loading coils because whip antennas are much too short to resonate at broadcast frequencies. **1875** KNIGHT *Dict. Mech.*, *Loading-funnel*, one for charging mortars with loose powder. **1883** F. S. WILLIAMS *Our Iron Roads* (ed. 4) 266 Among the minor appurtenances of a railway station is the wagon *loading gauge. **1901** *Young Engineer* I. 53 The fire-box may be extended to the full width of the loading gauge. **1930** *Engineering* 22 Aug. 230/2 The upper part [of a coke wagon] slopes inward to suit the loading gauge. **1875** KNIGHT *Dict. Mech.*, *Loading-hammer*, one for loading rifles. **1860** *Eng. & For. Mining Gloss.* (Derbysh. Terms), *Loading pick*, a pick made purposely to cleave or rive up coals and prepare them for laying on the corves. **1864** TREVELYAN *Compet. Wallah* (1866) 164, I appeared among them with my *loading-rod. **1881** WILHELM *Milit. Dict.*, *Loading-tongs*, a pair of tongs used with siege howitzers to set the shell home. **1874** J. W. LONG *Amer. Wild-Fowl Shooting* 20, I usually made a practice of reloading as fast as possible between shots, carrying an ammunition-box and *loading-tools with me. **1901** *Chambers's Jrnl.* May 12/1 Steam-cranes and movable *loading-towers..lower the coal into the hold of the vessel. **1858** SIMMONDS *Dict. Trade*, *Loading Turn*, the successive rotation for ships to approach the quays, to take in cargo. **1899** WESTM. GAZ. 20 Apr. 5/3 Many of the collieries have little or nothing to sell for some weeks ahead, while loading turns as a rule are practically full to the end of the month. **1909** *Westm. Gaz.* 9 June 11/1 Between them is a *loading yard 200 ft. by 60 ft.

loading (ˈləʊdɪŋ), *ppl. a.* [f. LOAD *v.* + -ING^2.]

1. That loads.

1891 *Labour Commission* Gloss., *Loading-up Men*, men at the docks who stop the bales from the cranes and pile them up on the trucks.

† **2.** *fig.* Burdening, oppressive, aggravating. *Obs.*

1625 BACON *Ess.*, *Goodness* (Arb.) 205 Such Men, in other mens Calamities, are, as it were, in season, and are euer on the loading Part. **1632** tr. *Bruel's Praxis Med.* 2 The paine that doth seaze thereon [the brain], is farre duller, and more loading. **1642** S. ASHE *Best Refuge* 29 Our Patentees,..may justly be cast under this loading aggravation.

3. That is loaded in a specified way: in comb. with prefixed word, as BREECH-LOADING.

a **1858** [see BREECH-LOADING]. **1889** *Sat. Rev.* 16 Mar. 318/1 The relative effects of breech-loading and muzzle-loading rifle fire. **1902** *Daily Chron.* 15 Apr. 3/1 Daylight-loading cameras.

loadless (ˈləʊdlɪs), *a.* [f. LOAD *sb.* + -LESS.] Having no load.

1876 RUSKIN *Fors Clav.* VI. lxix. 297 It will be simply to me only occasion for the loadless traveller's song.

loadmaster (ˈləʊd,mɑːstə(r), -,mæstə(r)). *Aeronaut.* [f. LOAD *sb.* + MASTER $sb.^1$] The crew member of an aircraft who is responsible for the load or cargo.

1961 *Newsweek* 6 Mar. 9 The United Nations and C-130 loadmasters did most of the work. **1967** *New Scientist* 17 Aug. 328 The aircraft [*sc.* Douglas C-47s] carry a crew of eight—pilot, co-pilot, navigator, flight mechanic, load master (who also drops the flares), two gun loaders, and a Vietnamese Air Force liaison officer. **1973** *Daily Tel.* 2 Oct. 2 If she passes her 14-week officer training course she will join an aircrew as a loadmaster. **1974** *Ibid.* 22 Feb. 14/4 Flying Officer Howard has logged 3,500 flying hours all over the world as an air loadmaster in VC-10s of No. 10 Squadron based at Brize Norton. The job, formerly known as air quartermaster, was given air crew status in 1962.

loadsaddle. *Obs.* exc. *dial.* Also (*north.*) 4 lad-, 5 layd-, 5- lade-, laid-. [f. LOAD *sb.* (or perh. LADE $sb.^1$) + SADDLE *sb.*] A pack-saddle.

1397–8 *Durham Acc. Rolls* (Surtees) 136 In ij ladsadell' et uno panel empt. ixs. iiijd. **1418–19** *Ibid.* 615 In cartesadil-trees et ladesadiltrees empt. ijs. viijd. **1483** *Cath. Angl.* 206/1 A layd sadylle, *gestatorium, gestarium.* **1563** *Richmond. Wills* (Surtees 1853) 169 A lade sadle, ij girths, a halter, and a wanton bodome, xx^d. *a* **1568** *Wowing Jok & Jynny* 52 in *Bannatyne Poems* (1878) 389, I haif..Ane auld pannell of ane laid sadill. **1847** HALLIWELL, *Lade-saddle*, a saddle for a horse carrying a load or burthen on its back. **1855** ROBINSON *Whitby Gloss.*, *Load-saddle*, a wooden pack-saddle.

† **ˈloadsome,** *a. Obs.* or *arch. rare.* [f. LOAD *sb.* + -SOME.] Burdensome.

1578 BANISTER *Hist. Man* I. 2 That therby the reading.. may be more conspicuous..which otherwise would be loadsom, and tedious. **1583** GREENE *Mamillia* 36 The weakest wit & youngest yeeres..is euer forced to bear the lodesom burden of loue. **1850** *Fraser's Mag.* XLII. 139 It has all the charms of idlesse, without the weary, loadsome, and loathsome self-reproachingness of idleness.

loadstar: see LODESTAR.

loadstone, lodestone (ˈləʊdstəʊn). Also 6 (?) lodysshestone. [f. *load*, LODE + STONE *sb.*

Literally 'way-stone', from the use of the magnet in guiding mariners. Cf. LODESTAR.]

1. Magnetic oxide of iron; also, a piece of this used as a magnet.

c **1515** *Cocke Lorell's B.* 12 One kepte ye compas and watched ye our glasse, Some ye lodysshestone dyd seke. **1548** UDALL, etc. *Erasm. Par. Mark* 38 b, Like as the lode-stone draweth vnto it yron, so [etc.]. **1579** *Lanc. Wills* (Chetham Soc.) II. 156 One rynge of gold havinge in it a stone called a lode stone. **1635** SWAN *Spec. M.* vi. (1643) 291 The Loadstone, is coloured like iron, but blewer, and tending to a skie colour. **1716** LADY M. W. MONTAGU *Lett. to Pope* 10 Oct. I. 129 A small piece of loadstone that held up an anchor of steel too heavy for me to lift. **1849** NOAD *Electricity* (ed. 3) 292 The smallest loadstones have generally a greater attractive power, in proportion to their size, than larger ones. **1877** W. JONES *Finger-ring* 304 A loadstone sometimes was set instead of a jewel, indicative of love's attractions. **1891** *Nature* 3 Sept., The property of the magnet or 'loadstone' to point to the north first became known in the eleventh century.

2. *fig.* Something which attracts.

1577 NORTHBROOKE *Dicing* (1843) 102 Such things which are occasions and loade stones to draw people to wickednesse. *a* **1592** GREENE *Alphonsus* Wks. (Rtldg.) 246 To have his absence whom he doth account To be the load-stone of his life! **1630** J. TAYLOR (Water P.) *Bk. Martyrs* Wks. III. 141/1 She was at home, abroad, in euery part,

Loadstar and Loadstone to each eye and heart. *a* **1649** DRUMM. OF HAWTH. *Poems* Wks. (1711) 47/1 Load-star of love, and load-stone of all hearts. **1778** MISS BURNEY *Evelina* xxvii. (1791) II. 172, I find you..the general loadstone of attention. **1857** MAURICE *Mor. & Met. Philos.* III. v. §3. 164 His human sympathy and human sorrow were to be the lodestone of all hearts. **1877** C. GEIKIE *Christ* lx. (1879) 735 Jerusalem was now the loadstone that had drawn the whole Jewish world around it.

† **ˈloadum.** *Obs.* Also lodam(e, loadam, loadem, load him. [Florio (1598 and 1611) identifies the game with one called in It. *carica l'asino* (load the ass), which suggests *load 'em* as the etymological spelling; but the reason for the name is not clear.] A game of cards; in one form, called ***losing loadum***, the loser won the game.

1591 FLORIO *2nd Fruites* 67 At primero, at trump..and at lodam. **1599** *Hist. of Pope Joan* A j b, In which the gamesters like loadam playe and bring them forth last that are of most price. **1601** *2nd Pt. Return fr. Parnass.* Prol. 14 You that have been deepe students at post and paire, saint and Loadam. **1611** COTGR., *Coquimbert qui gaigne pert*, A game at cards, like our loosing Lodam. **1650** BULWER *Anthropomet.* 111 Which must needs be hindred by their practise, which with Rings and Jewels play at such loosing Loadem with their Lips. **1652** URQUHART *Jewel* Wks. (1834) 232 After the nature of Load-him, a game at cards where he that wins loseth. **1695** CONGREVE *Love for L.* I. xi, To converse with Scandal, is to play at Losing Loadum; you must lose a good Name to him, before you can win it for yourself. **1755** *Poor Robin, an Almanac* Dec., At loadum, cribbidge, and all fours.

load-water-line. *Naut.* The line of floatation of a ship when she has her full cargo on board. (Called also † ***load-water-mark***, ***load-line***, and *Plimsoll's mark.*) Hence **load-water-draught**, **-length**, **-section** (see quots.).

1769 FALCONER *Dict. Marine* (1780) D 1 a, The line which determines her depth under the water is usually termed the load-water-line. *Ibid.* D j b, The load-water-mark. **1862** *Q. Rev.* Apr. 570 Admitting that she is now sunk three or four feet below her proper loadwater-line. **1867** SMYTH *Sailor's Word-bk.*, *Load water-section*, a horizontal section at the load water-line in the shipbuilder's draught. **1887** *Daily News* 28 Sept. 5/1 The Thistle has a load-water length of 86ft. 4in. **1895** *Funk's Stand. Dict.*, *Load-water*, pertaining to a loaded vessel; as, load-water draft. **1897** *Outing* (U.S.) XXX. 336 1 By halving the sum of load-water-line length and the square root of the sail-area.

loaf (ləʊf), *sb.*[1] Pl. loaves (ləʊvz). Forms: *sing.* 1 hláf, 3–4 laf, 3–5 lof, 4–5 loof, (4 lhoue), 5 layf, *Sc.* lafe, loofe, looff, 5–6 lofe, loffe, 6–7 loafe, 8 *Sc.* leaf, 7– loaf; *pl.* 1 hláfas, 3 *Orm.* lafess, 3–4, 6 *Sc.* laves, 4 lafes, lavis, -ys, *Sc.* lafis, lawis, 3–7 loves, 4–5 lofes, looves, 4 lofis, lovis, loovys, 5 loofes, looffis, lovys, *Sc.* laffis, 7 loafs, loafes, 6– loaves. [Com. Teut.: OE. *hláf* masc. = OHG. and MHG. *leip*, inflected *leib-*, bread, loaf (mod.G. *laib*, also written *leib*, loaf), ON. *hleif-r* loaf (Da., MSw. *lev*), Goth. *hlaif-s* bread (whence *ga-hlaiba* messmate, comrade, = OHG. *gileipo*, which seems to have suggested the equivalent late L. *compānio* COMPANION):—OTeut. **hlaibo-z*.

Whether the sense of 'bread' or that of 'loaf' is the earlier is uncertain, as the ulterior etymology is obscure. For many doubtful conjectures see Uhlenbeck *Gotische Etymologie* s.v. *hlaifs*. Some have suggested connexion with OE. *hlifian* to rise high, tower, the reference being supposed to be to the 'rising' of leavened bread. Outside Teut. the following synonymous words are certainly in some way connected (most probably adopted from Teut.): OSl. *χlěbŭ* (Russian *khleb*), Lith. *klêpas*, Lettish *klaips*, Finnish *leipä*, Esthonian *leip*. It has been supposed by some that the initial element in G. *lebkuchen*, *lebzelter*, gingerbread, is an ablaut-variant of this word.]

1. Bread. *Obs.* exc. *dial.*

c **950** *Lindisf. Gosp.* Matt. vi. 11 Hlaf userne ofer wistlic sel us todæȝ. *c* **1050** *Byrhtferth's Handboc* in *Anglia* (1885) VIII. 322 And eton hiȝ þeorfne hlaf mid grenum lactucam. *a* **1175** *Cott. Hom.* 227 He hi afedde feortiȝ wintre mid hefenlice hlafe. **1821** *Hunter's MS.* in *Sheffield Gloss.* s.v., People say 'some loaf', as well as 'some bread'.

fig. *c* **950** *Lindisf. Gosp.* John vi. 48 Ic am hlaf lifes.

2. a. A portion of bread baked in one mass; one of the portions, of uniform size and shape, into which a batch of bread is divided. Also with qualifying word, as ***barley***, ***bran***, ***cottage***, ***household***, ***tin***, ***tinned loaf***, for which see the first element. ***brown loaf***, a loaf of BROWN BREAD. ***white loaf***, a loaf made of wheaten flour only.

c **950** *Lindisf. Gosp.* Matt. xiv. 17 Nabbas we her buta fif hlafum & tuoeȝ fisces. *c* **1200** ORMIN 11788 Þurrh þatt te laþe gast himm badd Off staness makenn lafess. *c* **1290** *S. Eng. Leg.* I. 227/283 Ane wel faire ȝwite lof. **1340** *Ayenb.* 82 Þe wyfman grat myd childe þet more hi uynt smak in ane zoure epple þanne ine ane huetene lhoue. *c* **1380** WYCLIF *Serm.* Sel. Wks. II. 69 How many hynen in my fadirs hous ben ful of loves, and Y perishe here for hungre. **1393** LANGL. *P. Pl.* C. x. 150 A loof oþer half a loof oþer a lompe of chese. *a* **1400** *Prymer* (1891) 64 (Ps. cxxxii. 15) His poore y schal fylle wiþ lofes. *c* **1440** *Douce MS.* 55 lf. 6 b, Take a lofe of white brede & stepp hit with the brothe. **1485** in *Descr. Cal. Anc. Deeds* I. (1890) 358 And iiij loves of the secunde brede wekely, every love weyng too pondes. **1562** BULLEYN *Bk. Simples* 13 b, The best bread is that, that is of a daie old and the loves or manchedes, maie neither be great nor little. **1611** BIBLE *2 Kings* iv. 42 Bread of the first fruits, twentie loaues of barley. *a* **1643** W. CARTWRIGHT *Lady-Errant* v. i. Plays (1651) 66 Just as so much Quick-silver Is put into hot loves, to make 'em dance As long as th' heat continues. **1782** PRIESTLEY *Corrupt. Chr.* II. VI. 33 It was the custom to make one great loaf. **1828** SCOTT *F.M. Perth* xxviii, Bread was the scarcest article at the banquet, but the Glover and his patron Niel were served with two small loaves. **1875** JOWETT *Plato* (ed. 2) III. 243 Kneading the flour, making noble puddings and loaves.

fig. **1650** TRAPP *Comm. Num.* xxiii. 1 A loafe of the same leaven, was that resolute Rufus.

Proverbial. **1546** J. HEYWOOD *Prov.* (1867) 30 For better is halfe a lofe than no bread. **1588** SHAKS. *Tit. A.* II. i. 87 Easie it is Of a cut loafe to steale a shiue we know. **1687** *Good Advice* 43 And then she will think that half a Loaf had been better then no Bread. **1758** CHESTERF. *Let. to Son* 13 June (1892) III. 1227 The lady has wanted a man so long, that she now compounds for half a one. Half a loaf——. **1785** GROSE *Dict. Vulgar Tongue* s.v., To be *in bad loaf*, to be in a disagreeable situation, in trouble.

b. † ***assize loaf***, a loaf of the weight fixed by the assize of bread (31 Geo. II. c. 29). † ***church loaf*** = HOLY LOAF. † ***prized loaf***, a loaf of the price fixed by the assize of bread. † ***St. Stephen's loaf***, a stone. Also HOLY LOAF.

1499 *Churchw. Acc. Croscombe* (Sonn. Rec. Soc.) 24 Paid W. Toyt for tyndyng of the lyght and the church loffe. **1694** MOTTEUX *Rabelais* v. ix, He took up one of St. Stephens's Loaves, alias a Stone, and was going to hit him with it. **1762** *Act 3 Geo. III.* c. 11 No Assize Loaves of the Price of three Pence, and prized Loaves called Half Quartern Loaves,.. shall..in any Place be made for Sale [etc.].

c. ***loaves and fishes*** (fig. phr., after John vi. 26): pecuniary advantages as a motive for religious profession (or, *occas.*, for display of public spirit); the emoluments of ecclesiastical office.

1614 BP. HALL *Recoll. Treat.* 954 If it were not for the loaves and fishes, the traine of Christ would bee lesse. **1799** JEFFERSON *Writ.* (1859) IV. 300 Their seducers have wished war..for the loaves and fishes which arise out of war expenses. **1823** BYRON *Age of Bronze* xiv, 'The loaves and fishes', once so high, Are gone. **1867** TROLLOPE *Chron. Barset* I. x, Any clergyman..whose loaves and fishes are scanty.

d. ***oyster***, ***mushroom loaf***: The crust of a loaf or roll of bread filled with a stuffing of oysters or mushrooms.

1747 MRS. GLASSE *Cookery* 99 To make Oyster-Loaves. **1769** MRS. RAFFALD *Eng. Housekpr.* (1778) 287 To make Mushroom Loaves. **1837** DISRAELI *Venetia* I. iv, A dish of oyster loaves.

e. Minced or chopped meat moulded into the shape of a loaf and cooked; generally eaten cold, in slices. Usu. with qualifying word, as ***beef***, ***ham***, ***meat***, ***veal loaf***.

[**1787** LADY NEWDIGATE *Let.* 21 Oct. in A. E. Newdigate-Newdegate *Cheverels* (1898) v. 71 We made an excellent Dinner upon our Cold Loaf.] **1895** 'M. RONALD' *Century Cook Bk.* 308 Liver loaf, or false pâté de foie gras..is better cold with salad, or used like pâté de foie gras. A loaf of any game may be made in the same way. **1902**, **1907** [see *ham loaf* s.v. HAM *sb.*[1] 3]. **1939** AUDEN & ISHERWOOD *Journey to War* 90 We had fruit-juice, meat-loaf, salad and cake. **1964** J. MASTERS *Trial at Monomoy* iv. 140 She stared at rows of Spam, corned beef, meat loaf, ham loaf. **1975** *Times* 7 Mar. 5/2 She recommended home-made vegetable soup and meat loaf, followed by apple or rhubarb crumble.

f. *slang.* [Prob. from *loaf of bread*, rhyming slang for 'head'.] The (human) head; hence, the mind, common sense; *esp.* in phr. to ***use one's loaf***.

1925 FRASER & GIBBONS *Soldier & Sailor Words* 145 *Loaf*, head, *e.g.*, 'Duck your loaf—*i.e.*, keep your head below the parapet'. **1938** J. CURTIS *They Drive by Night* xiv. 155 Bloody seconds counted in a job like this. You certainly had to use your loaf. **1943** HUNT & PRINGLE *Service Slang* 44 *Use your loaf* is the injunction often heard when someone is particularly slow in following orders. But this phrase, in its finer meanings, says: 'Use your common sense. Interpret orders according to the situation as you find it, and don't follow the book of words too literally.' **1949** 'N. BLAKE' *Head of Traveller* ii. 36 Do try to use your loaf. **1957** P. FRANKAU *Bridge* 73 He uses his loaf where you and I just muddle along. **1971** B. W. ALDISS *Soldier Erect* 79 You want to use your bloody loaf, Stubbs, or we'll never win this war the way you're carrying on. **1973** *Jewish Chron.* 2 Feb. 12/1 Use your loaf. Didn't Sir Jack Cohen of Tesco..start the same way?

g. ***loaf o(f) bread***: rhyming slang for 'dead'.

1930 BROPHY & PARTRIDGE *Songs & Slang 1914–18* 137 Loaf o' Bread, dead. **1935** AUDEN & ISHERWOOD *Dog Beneath Skin* III. i. 123 O how I cried when Alice died The day we were to have wed! We never had our Roasted Duck And now she's a Loaf of Bread.

3. A moulded conical mass of sugar; a sugar-loaf. (Cf. LOAF-SUGAR.)

1363–4 *Durham Acc. Rolls* (Surtees) 566 In ix lb. Sucr. de Sipr. empt. in uno laf apud Ebor. **1373–4** *Ibid.* 578 In ij lafes de Sugour ponder. xxiij lib. quarteron empt...xlvijs. iiijd. **1440–41** *Ibid.* 78 Item j layf de suggir, iiijs. vjd. **1556** W. TOWRSON in Hakluyt *Voy.* (1589) 98 The isle of Tenerif, otherwise called the Pike, because it is a very high Island with a pike vpon the toppe like a loafe of Sugar. **1654** EVELYN *Diary* 27 June, Here [at Bristol] I first saw the manner of refining suggar and casting it into loaves. **1835** URE *Philos. Manuf.* Pref. 9 Refined loaves.

† **4.** A mass or lump (of anything). *Obs.*

1598 FLORIO, *Phigethlo*, a little swelling hard and red,.. our chirurgions do call it a little loafe or manchet. **1604** E. G[RIMSTONE] *D'Acosta's Hist. Indies* IV. xii. 244 They put all the mettall into a cloth, which they straine out,..and the rest remaines as a loafe of silver. **1611** COTGR., *Pain de moustarde*, a loafe, or ball, of drie, or dried mustard. **1694** SALMON *Bate's Dispens.* 504/2 The Cakes [*sc.* of corrosive sublimate]..they call Loaves.

5. A 'head' (of a cabbage).

[**1585**: implied in LOAFED.] **1817–18** COBBETT *Resid. U.S.* (1822) 113 All the plants from the English seed produced solid loaves by the 24th of June. **1829** —— *Eng. Gard.* §129 When it [the cabbage] makes its loaf in the summer, you cut the loaf off... In a month after cutting the head, the stump should be taken up.

6. *attrib.* and *Comb.*, as ***loaf basket***, ***-tin***; objective, as ***loaf-giver***; similative, as ***loaf-shaped*** adj.; † **loaf-cabbage**, a cabbage with a 'loaf' or head; **loaf-cake**, a plain cake made in the form of a loaf.

1891 *Daily News* 6 Mar. 3/7 The bread boy bears the *loaf basket. **1727** S. SWITZER *Pract. Gardiner* III. xxiii. 131 That which..comes in just as *loaf cabbages decay. **1733** TULL *Horse-hoeing Husb.* 19 Some have lost their Lives by Toads, being accidentally boil'd in the folds of a Loaf-Cabbage. **1828** E. LESLIE *75 Receipts* 62 *Loaf Cake. **1844** *Knickerbocker* XXIV. 423 The biscuit would not rise, her loaf-cake was heavy. **1906** KIPLING *Puck of Pook's Hill* 195 Hobden said that the loaf-cake..was almost as good as what his wife used to make. **1941** F. M. FARMER *Boston Cooking-School Cook Bk.* (ed. 7) 624 Loaf and layer cakes. **1882** EDNA LYALL *Donovan* ix, A moral song..in which a charitable *loafgiver is represented. **1890** H. LATHAM *Pastor Pastorum* v. 129 Our Lord was hungry, and *loaf-shaped stones were lying all about Him. **1883** *Facts, or Experiences Recent Colonist N.Z.* iii. 30 The materials required are:—..one deep tin-pan, six *loaf tins, one wooden spoon. **1932** E. CRAIG *Cooking with E. Craig* 305 Place..in a greased loaf tin. **1972** K. STEWART *Times Cookery Bk.* xviii. 235 Divide the dough... Place carefully in..two small, greased, 1 lb loaf tins.

loaf (ləʊf), *sb.*[2] *slang.* ? *U.S.* [f. LOAF *v.*[2]] The action of loafing.

1855 WHITMAN *Leaves of Grass* (1884) 39 The farmer stops by the bars as he walks on a First-day loafe and looks at the oats and rye. **1886** *American* XII. 76 A resolution I have made to enjoy a solid old-fashioned loaf this summer. **1897** *Outing* (U.S.) XXX. 374/2 The holiday camp, in which a restful loaf is the principal object. **1900** *Daily News* 21 Apr. 3/1 In those days a Sandhurst instructorship was.. looked upon as a 'comfortable loaf'.

b. *Comb.*: **loaf-day**, a day when no regular work is done. [But cf. Sw. *lofdag*, Du. *verlofdag* leave-day, holiday.]

1881 *Scribner's Mag.* XXII. 217/2 On 'loaf-days' the hands occupy themselves with making the neat cans which it is their..business to fill.

loaf (ləʊf), *v.*[1] [f. LOAF *sb.*[1] (sense 5).] *intr.* To form a loaf or 'head'. Hence **ˈloafing** (in 9 *loaving*), *vbl. sb.*

1578 LYTE *Dodoens* 552 The white cabbage cole..closeth or lofeth in June, July, and August. **1817–8** COBBETT *Year's Resid. Amer.* (1822) 67 The cabbages..were..earlier in loaving, than any of the rest of the plot.

loaf (ləʊf), *v.*[2] Also loafe. [Of obscure origin.

Lowell's conjecture (adopted in recent Dicts.) that the vb. is ad. Ger. dial. *lofen* = *laufen* to run, is without foundation; the Ger. vb. has not the alleged sense 'to saunter up and down'. G. *landläufer* (= LANDLOUPER) has a sense not very remote from that of *loafer*, but connexion is not very probable.]

intr. To spend time idly. Also quasi-*trans.* To idle *away* (time).

1838 J. C. NEAL *Charcoal Sk.* III. ii. 34 One night, Mr. Dabbs came home from his 'loafing' place—for he 'loafs' of an evening like the generality of people—that being the most popular and the cheapest amusement extant. **1844** DICKENS *Mart. Chuz.* xvi, Major Pawkins rather 'loafed' his time away, than otherwise. **1852** MRS. STOWE *Uncle Tom's C.* xii, Men talked, and loafed, and read, and smoked. **1855** WHITMAN *Leaves of Grass* (1884) 29, I loafe and invite my soul, I lean and loafe at my ease. **1857** C. KEENE *Let.* in G. S. Layard *Life* iii. (1892) 62 My friend..fished, and I loafed about sketching. **1864** SALA in *Daily Tel.* 23 Dec., [At Niagara] You may lounge, you may loafe, you may saunter, you may moon,..but you..cannot study. **1885** M. PATTISON *Mem.* 39 He allowed me to waste those two precious years in loafing about at home.

loaf-bread. Now *dial.* Bread made in the form of loaves; ordinary baker's bread as distinguished from cakes or wafers.

1559 FECKNAM in Strype *Ann. Ref.* I. App. ix. 25 The communyon riceyved..in lofe bread, without any reverence. **1563** FOXE *A. & M.* 980/2 Then cake bread and loafe bread are all one with you. **1564** J. RASTELL *Confut. Jewell's Serm.* 162 b, The Sacrament was ministred..some tyme in loeuebread, some tyme in wafers. **1832** W. JAMESON in *Mem. & Lett.* (1845) 93 Bakers don't care for loaf-bread, nor ministers for Sermons. **1899** M. RUSSELL *Irish Farmer's Sunday Morning* in *Idyls of Killowen* 3/4 Before the sire the loaf-bread, too, is laid. *Note.* As contra-distinguished from griddle-bread.

loaf-eater. *Antiq.* [A literal rendering of OE. *hláf-ǣta*. Cf. BEEF-EATER.] One who 'eats the bread' of a master; a household servant.

[*a* **1000** *Laws of Ethelbert* c. 25 in Thorpe *Laws* I. 8 Gif man ceorles hlaf-ætan ofslæhð.] **1844** *Camp of Refuge* I. 54 Frithric..had maintained one score and ten loaf-eaters or serving men in his glorious abbey. **1897** MAITLAND *Domesday & Beyond* 101 A mere ceorl has had..a soke.. over his house and over his loaf-eaters.

loafed, loaved (ləʊft, ləʊvd), *a.* [f. LOAF *sb.*[1] + -ED[2].] Having a 'loaf' or 'head' (see LOAF *sb.*[1] 5).

1578 LYTE *Dodoens* 552 In the steede of the thicke cabbaged or lofed leaves, it [cauliflower] putteth foorth many small white stemmes. **1585** HIGINS tr. *Junius' Nomenclator* 128 *Lactuca sessilis*,..loafed or headed lettice. **1817–8** COBBETT *Year's Resid. Amer.* (1822) 19 We have fine loaved lettuces. **1825** —— *Rural Rides* 26 All [farm animals] like these loaved cabbages.

loafer ('ləʊfə(r)). [? f. LOAF *v.*[2] + -ER[1]; but the sb. may be the source of the vb. by back-formation.] **1.** One who spends his time in idleness.

1830 *Mechanic's Press* (Utica, N.Y.) 10 July 274/1 Nor are they topers at taverns, or *benchers* at groceries, or loafers who 'chase misfortune o'er the towpath'. **1835** *Knickerbocker* VI. 63 The late Ben Smith, Loafer. I present an outline sketch of one of that species of the *genus homo*.. which Custom has christened with the expressive appellation of Loafer! **1840** R. H. DANA *Bef. Mast* vii. 17 The men appeared to be the laziest people upon the face of the earth; and indeed.. there are no people to whom the newly invented Yankee word of 'loafer' is more applicable than to the Spanish Americans. **1842** DICKENS *Amer. Notes* (1850) 130/2 When we stop to change, some two or three half-drunken loafers will come loitering out with their hands in their pockets. **1852** THOREAU *Autumn* (1894) 46 Even insects in my path are not loafers, but have their special errands. **1873** LELAND *Eng. Gipsies & their Lang.* vi. 89 When the term first began to be popular in 1834 or 1835, I can distinctly remember that it meant to *pilfer*. Such, at least, is my earliest recollection, and of hearing school boys ask one another in jest, of their acquisitions or gifts, 'Where did you loaf that from?' A petty pilferer was a loafer, but in a very short time all of the tribe of loungers in the sun, and the disreputable pickers up of unconsidered trifles,.. were called loafers. **1893** LIDDON, etc. *Life of Pusey* I. ii, Older boys knew that he was no loafer: and when he felt unwell he could always get off 'fagging cricket'.

attrib. **1888** BRYCE *Amer. Commw.* II. lvii. 397 Among the 'loafer' class. **1896** J. DAVIDSON *Fleet Street Eclog.* Ser. II. 81, I see the loafer-burnished wall.

2. [cf. Sp. *lobo* wolf.] A timber wolf, *Canis lupus nubilus*, found in the south-western part of North America; = LOBO. Also *attrib.*

1878 MCDANIELD & TAYLOR *Coming Empire* v. v. 314 The Mexicans call these big wolves 'lobos' and the Texans call them 'loafers' which is a corruption of the Mexican word. **1908** *Sat. Even. Post* 4 July 16/3 One of the loafers had run in, leaping out of the black like a streak of gray light. **1948** *Ibid.* 10 July 80/3 With loafers,.. mountain lions or bears, he was absolutely ruthless. **1974** *Islander* (Victoria, B.C.) 16 June 13/2 The lobo wolf derived its name from a word in the Blackfoot Indian language meaning 'buffalo wolf' and sounding like 'lobo', the Spanish word for wolf. They were also known as the buffalo grey or loafer wolf as they followed migrations of bison.

3. a. Usu. *pl.* The proprietary name of a shoe for wearing on informal occasions.

1939 *Trade Marks Jrnl.* 19 Apr. 520/2 *Loafer.* Boots, shoes, slippers, sandals, leggings and gaiters. Fortnum and Mason Ltd.—London. **1948** M. STURGES-JONES *In Wedlock Wake* 11 Pullover sweaters, bobby socks, and leather loafers. **1963** T. PYNCHON *V* vi. 136 Profane kicked off his shoes —old black loafers of Geronimo's—and concentrated on dancing in his socks. **1971** 'V. X. SCOTT' *Surrogate Wife* 161, I saw him standing there in lean slacks.. and suède loafers. **1972** *Last Whole Earth Catalog* (Portola Inst.) 406/2 The big thing for guys is jeans or slacks, button-down shirts or T-shirts and brown loafers without socks.

b. A type of jacket for informal wear.

1959 *Trade Marks Jrnl.* 19 Aug. 688/2 *Loafers*... Jackets. Chas. MacIntosh & Company Limited,.. London. **1969** P. ROTH *Portnoy's Complaint* 125 My clip-on tie and my two-tone 'loafer' jacket.

Hence many nonce-wds., as '**loaferdom**, the state of being a loafer; '**loaferess**, a female loafer; '**loafering**, the practice or 'occupation' of a loafer; in quot. *attrib.*; '**loaferish** *a.*, somewhat of a loafer; pertaining to or characteristic of a loafer; '**loaferism**, the practice of loafing; '**loafery**, (*a*) = LOAFERISM; (*b*) a place where people loaf; '**loafership**, the state of being a loafer.

1842 B. M. NORMAN *Yucatan* iv. (1843) 88 The Casa-real ..was the loafering-place of the Indians. **1861** *Macm. Mag.* IV. 76/1 Encouraging 'loafery' by the instances we are going to adduce of Idleness and Scampishness succeeding where Philosophy has failed. **1866** HOWELLS *Venet. Life* xix, A scene composed of the four pleasant ruffians in the loaferish postures which they have learned as *facchini* waiting for jobs. **1885** *Advance* (Chicago) 16 July 458 Loafers and loaferesses. **1889** *Home Missionary* (N.Y.) Dec. 362 Loaferism and blackguardism. **1889** *Field* 28 Sept. 448/1 The dangers which 'loafership' entails upon the future of any juvenile. **1893** *Scribner's Mag.* Feb. 262/2 A mere loaferish breach of the peace. **1894** *Forum* (U.S.) May 276 The steps from enforced idleness down into loaferdom.. and crime are short and near together. **1898** *Daily Tel.* 10 Feb. 7/3 The Whitechapel Guardians have been considering a proposal to call their workhouse by another name... Perhaps 'House of Repose' or 'The Loaferies' would be appropriate. **1903** *Liberty Rev.* July 7 A new trap is set for it—the free loafery at the corner.

loafing ('ləʊfɪŋ), *vbl. sb.* [f. LOAF *v.*[2] + -ING[1].] The action of the vb. LOAF. Also *attrib.*

1838 [see LOAF *v.*]. **1846** *Simmond's Colonial Mag.* Sept. IX. 41 Practices of this kind come properly under the head of 'loafing' (living idly on other people), as defined in the American vocabulary. **1862** H. KINGSLEY *Ravenshoe* xli, Shoeblacks are compelled to a great deal of unavoidable 'loafing'. **1864** SALA in *Daily Tel.* 13 Oct., There is..a public news-room, and a public loafing-hall. **1883** A. M. GOW *Primer of Politeness* 214 The trouble began with loafing; loafing led to blackguarding.

loafing ('ləʊfɪŋ), *ppl. a.* [f. LOAF *v.*[2] + -ING[2].] That loafs.

1857 HUGHES *Tom Brown* I. ii, A half-gipsey, poaching, loafing fellow. **1873** BLACK *Pr. Thule* xiv. 222 Loafing vagabonds, who would pick your pocket.

Hence '**loafingly** *adv.*, in a loafing manner.

1860 *All Year Round* No. 42. 367 The shop, about which I had all this time been loafingly prowling.

loaflet ('ləʊflɪt). *nonce-wd.* [f. LOAF *sb.*[1] + -LET.] A small loaf.

1876 G. MEREDITH *Beauch. Career* I. xv. 228 Crisp home-made loaflets.

loafs, obs. pl. of LOAF.

loaf-sugar. Sugar refined and moulded into a loaf or conical mass.

c **1440** *Anc. Cookery* in *Househ. Ord.* (1790) 473 And medel therwith two pounde of lofe sugre. **1678** J. PHILLIPS tr. *Tavernier's Trav. India* II. 131 Loaf-Sugar is also made at Amadabat, where they are perfectly skill'd in refining it. **1732** FIELDING *Mock Doctor* ix. Wks. 1882 IX. 267 These look exactly like lumps of loaf-sugar. *c* **1865** J. WYLDE in *Circ. Sci.* I. 356/2 In a purer state.. the cane-sugar is called 'loaf' or 'lump-sugar'.

loaiasis (ləʊə'aɪəsɪs). *Path.* Also **loasis** (ləʊ'eɪsɪs), **loiasis** (ləʊ'aɪəsɪs). [mod.L., f. LOA[1] + -IASIS.] Infection with, or disease caused by, loas.

1913 CASTELLANI & CHALMERS *Man. Trop. Med.* (ed. 2) lx. 1442 (*heading*) Loasis. **1919** *Ibid.* (ed. 3) lxxxviii. 1972 Lŏiasis is a subcutaneous and subconjunctival filariasis caused by *Loa loa*. **1923** E. A. & T. M. NEATBY *Man. Trop. Dis. & Hygiene* 382 The species responsible for the filariases and loasis. **1956** *Nature* 25 Feb. 367/1 Studies on loiasis in the Cameroons and Nigeria. **1961** *Lancet* 5 Aug. 323/2 In 1948 Gordon started an investigation of the African filarial infection, loaiasis. **1963** T. J. BROOKS *Essent. Med. Parasitol.* III. 259 Loaiasis, or eye worm infection.

loa loa (ˌləʊə 'ləʊə). [Taxonomic name of the causative organism: see LOA[1].] = LOAIASIS.

1923 E. A. & T. M. NEATBY *Man. Trop. Dis. & Hygiene* 396 Loa loa is a filarial infection, confined to West Africa, the worm (*Filaria loa*) resembling *F. bancrofti.* **1963** *Times* 8 Feb. 15/7 It was found that exactly the reverse held true for the form of filarial disease in West Africa, known as loa loa. Here the number of microfilariæ in the bloodstream is maximal at noon and minimal at midnight.

loam (ləʊm), *sb.* Forms: 1 *lám*, (laam), 3-4 lam, 3-5, 6-9 *Sc.* lame, 5-8 lome, (4 in comb. lom-), 6-8 loame, 6-7 *Sc.* and *north.* leame, 7 leem, 8-9 loom, (9 laem), 6- loam. [OE. *lám* neut. = MDu., Du. *leem*, MLG. *lêm*, whence mod.G. *lehm* masc.; with different declension the word is found as OHG. *leimo* masc. (MHG. *leime*, mod.HG. dial. *leimen*); the OTeut. forms **laimo-*, **laimon-* are from the root **lai-* (:**lĭ-*) to be sticky, occurring also in LAIR *sb.*[2]; for cognates in other ablaut-grades see LIME *sb.*[1]]

†**1. a.** Clay, clayey earth, mud; *occas.* 'earth' or 'clay' as the material of the human body. *Obs.*

c **725** *Ags. Voc.* in Wr.-Wülcker 6/38 *Argella*, laam. *c* **1000** ÆLFRIC *Gen.* ii. 7 God ʒesceop eornostlice man of þære eorðan lame. *c* **1175** *Cott. Hom.* 221 And god þa ȝeworhte ænne man of lame. *a* **1225** *Leg. Kath.* 991 Ȝe! ne makede he mon of lam to his ilicnesse? *a* **1300** *Cursor M.* 11985 And o lame o þaa lakes selue Wit handes made he sparus tuelue. *c* **1375** *Sc. Leg. Saints* ix. (*Bartholomaeus*) 135 Adame, þat wrocht wes of vmwemmyt lame. **1593** SHAKS. *Rich. II*, I. i. 179 The purest treasure mortall times afford Is spotlesse reputation: that away, Men are but gilded loame, or painted clay. **1600** HOLLAND *Livy* 1376 The name [Argiletus] it taketh of a kind of clay or lome, where of there is plentie in that place. **1610** HEALEY *St. Aug. Citie of God* XIII. xxiv. (1620) 467 This man therefore being framed of dust or lome [L. *de terræ pulvere sive limo*] (for lome is moystned dust). *a* **1633** AUSTIN *Medit.* (1635) 289 My Fathers House is Earth where I must lye: A House of Clay best fits a Guest of Lome. **1655** CULPEPPER *Riverius* IX. iii. 257 Some [*sc.* depraved appetites] desire Clay, Coals, Earth, Loam, Chalk and the like.

fig. **1645** G. DANIEL *Poems* Wks. 1878 II. 72 See to the Politicke Is not Hee partly Sicke? Are his Designes vnmixt with Drosse and Loame? *a* **1657** LOVELACE *Poems* (1864) 192 Thou art become Slave to the spawn of mud and lome.

b. Used loosely for: Earth, ground soil. *arch.*

a **1300** *Cursor M.* 193 þar sal ȝe find.. O lazar ded laid vnder lam. *c* **1440** *York Myst.* xxxix. 5 *Maria.* In lame is it loken all my light, For-thy on grounde on-glad I goo. **1616** *Barbour's Bruce* XIX. 256 (ed. Hart) That time Edward of Carnauerane The King, was dead, and laide in Lame [*MSS.* stane]. **1867** G. MACDONALD *Poems* 160, I'll see the corpse, ere he's laid in the loam. **1871** JOAQUIN MILLER *Songs of Italy* (1878) 12 These skies are Rome! The very loam Lifts up and speaks in Roman pride.

2. Clay moistened with water so as to form a paste capable of being moulded into any shape; *spec.* a composition of moistened clay and sand with an admixture of horse-dung, chopped straw, or the like, used in making bricks and casting-moulds, plastering walls, grafting, etc.

1480 *Ward. Acc. Edw. IV* (1830) 127 Payed.. for borde naill and lome for cering and amending of his chambre flore. **1483** CAXTON *Gold. Leg.* 56/2 In nowyse gyue nomore chaf to the peple forto make lome and claye. **1577** HARRISON *England* II. xii. (1877) I. 234 The claie wherewith our houses are impanelled, is either white, red, or blue,.. the second is called lome. **1587** MASCALL *Govt. Cattle* (1627) 40 Ye may giue him lome of a wall mixt with vrine. **1602** SHAKS. *Ham.* v. i. 233. **1626** BACON *Sylva* §427 You may take off the Barke of any Bough.. and couer the bare Place.. with Loame well tempered with Horse-dung, binding it fast downe. **1683** MOXON *Mech. Exerc.* 11 Make a Loam of three parts Clay and one part Horse-dung. **1684** *Ibid.* 57 By covering Steel [in annealing] with a course Powder of Cow-Horns,.. and so inclosing it in a Loam. **1688** R. HOLME *Armoury* II. 86/2 Lome, a kind of Clay to put about Grafts, made of Clay and Horse-dung. **1694** DRYDEN *Love Triumph.* IV. i. 65 The Lodging Rooms are furnisht with Loam. *c* **1710** C. FIENNES *Diary* (1888) 116 Their buildings are of timber of Loame and Lathes. **1759** ELLIS in *Phil. Trans.* LI. 208 A cake of plaisterers stiff loam, or such as the brewers use to stop their beer barrels. **1789** P. SMYTH tr. *Aldrich's Archit.* (1818) 80 The loom during the winter should be kept steeped, and made into bricks in the spring. **1839** URE *Dict. Arts* 518-19 [*Founding.*] Over the brick dome a pasty layer of loam is applied..; this surface is then coated with a much smoother loam. **1883** T. D. WEST *Amer. Foundry Pract.* (ed. 2) 184 In some places a natural loam can be obtained—but this is rare; most shops have to make their loam of different proportions of sharp and loam sands.

Proverb. phr. **1586** HOOKER *Serm.* ii. §19 Wks. (1888) III. 504 But we wash a wall of loam; we labour in vain.

3. A soil of great fertility composed chiefly of clay and sand with an admixture of decomposed vegetable matter.

It is called *clay loam* or *sandy loam* according as the clay or sand preponderates.

1664 EVELYN *Kal. Hort., May* (1706) 57 A natural Earth, with an Eye of Loam in it (such as is proper for most Flowers). **1727** BRADLEY *Fam. Dict.* s.v. *Flower*, Where the Ground is too stiff, and that you desire a natural Mixture to bring it to the State of Loam, you must add to it a sufficient Quantity of dry or Sea Sand. **1765** A. DICKSON *Treat. Agric.* (ed. 2) 458 Loam, it is probable, is not an original soil, but the earth of rotten vegetables. **1767** A. YOUNG *Farmer's Lett. People* 119 The soil is an exceeding light sandy loam. **1806** *Gazetteer Scotl.* (ed. 2) 16 The soil.. consisting of clay and sand, and in some places of a loam. **1830** LYELL *Princ. Geol.* I. 268 Cliffs, composed.. of alternating strata of blue clay, gravel, loam, and fine sand. **1879** JEFFERIES *Wild Life in S. Co.* 376 The loam discolours the water during a storm for several yards out to sea. **1887** T. HARDY *Woodlanders* II. xii. 228 The fruity district of deep loam.

4. *attrib.* passing into *adj.* Made of or consisting of loam.

1536 BELLENDEN *Cron. Scot.* (1821) I. 108 In Fyndoure.. wes found ane anciant sepulture, in quhilk were ii lame piggis, craftely maid. **1563** DAVIDSON *Confut. Kennedy* in *Wodr. Soc. Misc.* (1844) 214 The leame pote that contenis the medicine. **1606** BIRNIE *Kirk-Buriall* (1833) 2 *Cælo tegitur qui non habet urnam*... And heauens will cover when leame tombes cannot do'ide. **1623** GOAD *Dolef. Euen-Song* 13 They with their Kniues opened the Loame-wall next vnto them. **1637** RUTHERFORD *Lett.* (1664) 66 Are we not Gods leem vessels? **1637-50** ROW *Hist. Kirk* (1842) 260 He dreamed that he was a lame pig. **1655** FULLER *Ch. Hist.* x. vi. §31 To cut their passage out of a lome wall into the next chamber. **1663** *Inv. Ld. J. Gordon's Furniture*, A lame pot for watering chamberes. **1703** *Lond. Gaz.* No. 3953/1 A Manufacture of Lame, Purslaine and Earthen Ware. **1824** MACTAGGART *Gallovid. Encycl.* s.v. *Aschet*, Ashets seem to have been the first things of lame ware. **1884** *Cassell's Fam. Mag.* Feb. 140 Our loam-heap should be free from all vermin.

5. *attrib.* and *Comb.*, *spec.* in *Founding*, *Brickmaking* and *Bricklaying*, as ***loam brick***, ***cake***, ***casting***, ***lute***, ***mould***, ***work***; ***loam-beater***, ***-board***, ***-foot***, ***-hook***, ***-mill***, ***-moulder***, ***-moulding***; **loam-salts**, ? land composed of loam impregnated with salt.

1888 *Lockwood's Dict. Mech. Engin.*, **Loam Board*, a board having an edge cut to the outline of the sectional shape of the work which it is intended to strike up. **1881** C. WYLIE *Iron Founding* 15 Dried loam off castings.. is only used for making *loam bricks for cores. **1875** KNIGHT *Dict. Mech.*, **Loam-cake*. **1881** C. WYLIE *Iron Founding* 49 *Loam castings, as a rule, do not contract so much as sand castings. **1940** T. S. ELIOT *East Coker* i. 8 Lifting heavy feet in clumsy shoes Earth feet, *loam feet, lifted in country mirth. **1955** D. DAVIE *Brides of Reason* 28 Come with me by the self-consuming north (The North is spirit), to the loam-foot west And opulent departures of the south. **1700** MOXON *Mech. Exerc., Bricklayers-Wks.* 14 A *Loame-hook, Beater, Shovel, Pick-Ax, Basket and Hod, which commonly belong to Bricklaiers Labourers, and may be called the Labourers Tools. **1839** URE *Dict. Arts* 1057 It [*sc.* a stoneware pipe] is ..secured at the joints with *loam-lute. *Ibid.* 518 The mould is formed of a pasty mixture of clay, water, sand, and cow's hair.. kneaded together in what is called the *loam mill. *Ibid.* *Loam moulds. **1881** C. WYLIE *Iron Founding* 98 No doubt Hiram, in Solomon's time, was a thorough *loam-moulder. *Ibid.*, *Loam moulding stands distinctly apart from either green-sand or dry-sand moulding. **1852** WIGGINS *Embanking* 100 A piece of silty *loam-salts, near Fossdyke. **18..** *Archit. Publ. Soc. Dict.* s.v., Early *loam work [*sc.* in building] is often stamped in patterns. **1881** C. WYLIE *Iron Founding* 50 In large loam castings this occurs to a greater extent than in small or light loam work.

loam (ləʊm), *v.* [f. LOAM *sb.*]

1. *trans.* To cover or plaster with loam. ? *Obs.*

1600 SURFLET *Country Farme* III. xviii. 460 After.. loming the ioints and seames very well with gum and wax mixt together. **1630** CAPT. SMITH *Trav. & Adv.* 25 With the ashes of bones tempered with oile, Camels haire, and a clay they have; they lome them so well, that no weather will pierce them. **1671** J. WEBSTER *Metallogr.* xi. 157 They diligently lome or daub up the pots with clay, or lute. **1703** MOXON *Mech. Exerc.* 264 Girders which lye in the Walls, must be Loamed all over, to preserve them from the corroding of the Morter.

2. To dress with loam.

? **1842** LANCE *Cottage Farmer* 12 They are grown in the deep sands which have been loamed.

3. *Austral. intr.* and *trans.* To search (a region) for gold by washing the loam from a hill's base until the increasing number of gold grains leads to the lode. So '**loaming** *vbl. sb.*

1916 R. MACKAY *Recoll. Early Gippsland Goldfields* vi. 29/2 The science of loaming was either then unknown, or known to very few. *Ibid.* 30/1 The loaming system will tire the strongest and most wiry man that every swung a pick. **1935** *Bulletin* (Sydney) 13 Feb. 21/1 He'll be loaming up a hill and following a trace, Until he gets above the gold. **1953** *People* (Austral.) 23 Sept. 39/1 Loaming for gold he explains, entails, roughly, taking samples of loam from the topsoil, washing it in a dish, counting the colors and following them in intensity until a likely spot to sink a shaft

is found. **1966** 'J. Hackston' *Father clears Out* 50 Old Tom was to make himself useful about the plant, and loam the surrounding country for the reef.

loamed (ləʊmd), *a. rare.* [f. loam *v.* and *sb.* + -ed.] **a.** Stopped with 'loam' or earth. **b.** In *deep-loamed*, having a great depth of loam.

1819 Keats *Isabella* xxxv, The forest tomb Had..taken the soft lute From his lorn voice, and past his loamed ears Had made a miry channel for his tears. **1900** *Contemp. Rev.* Sept. 347 A deep-loamed field.

loamless ('ləʊmlɪs), *a. nonce-wd.* [f. loam *sb.* + -less.] Without loam; unmixed with loam.

1872 Blackie *Lays Highl.* 183 Even in that thin, and loamless brook The mountain-trout..all nimbly glancing I spied.

† **'loam-pit.** *Obs.* In 1 lámpytt, 4 lompet, 6 lomepitt. A clay pit.

990 in Kemble *Cod. Dipl.* III. 252/24 Swa andlang mearce on ða lampyttas. *c* **1315** Shoreham iv. 134 Þe crokkere myȝte segge: þou proud erþe of lompet, Ine felþe þou schelt lygge. **1596-7** S. Finche in *Ducarel's Hist. Croydon* App. (1783) 157 The lome-pitts beyond Dubbers-hill.

Loamshire ('ləʊmʃə(r)). Name given to an imaginary rural county, muched used in novels and plays; also (*pl.*) a regiment from this county. Also *attrib.*

1859 Geo. Eliot *Adam Bede* I. v. 108 He was only a captain in the Loamshire Militia. *Ibid.* xii. 230 Jolly housekeeping—finest stud in Loamshire. **1866** —— *Felix Holt* I. i. 18 Transome Court was a large mansion..with a park and grounds as fine as any to be seen in Loamshire. **1912** G. W. E. Russell *Afterthoughts* xvii. 158 In Loamshire 'my foot is on my native heath', and I have been renewing my youth by contact with my early friends. **1920** 'Sapper' *Bull-Dog Drummond* i. 24 Captain Hugh Drummond, D.S.O., M.C., late of His Majesty's Royal Loamshires. **1954** K. Tynan in *Observer* 31 Oct. 6/1 Look about you; survey the peculiar nullity of our drama's prevalent *genre*, the Loamshire play. **1962** *Listener* 6 Dec. 959/1 They [*sc.* English novelists] also have to avoid the pitfall of regionalism and dialect. They have to avoid Loamshire. **1974** Green & Hooper *C.S. Lewis* x. 247 In the version which Green read..Digory..stayed in a farm cottage with an old countryman called Piers and his wife, who spoke with a rather laboured 'Loamshire' accent.

loamy ('ləʊmɪ), *a.* [f. loam *sb.* + -y^1.]

† **1.** Formed of earth (see loam *sb.* 1). *Obs. rare*$^{-1}$.

c **1230** *Hali Meid.* 47 Alle þeo þat leauen luue of lami mon; for to beon his leofmon.

2. Of or pertaining to loam; consisting of, or resembling, loam.

1599 *Broughton's Let.* vii. 24 With this Rabbinicall rubbish..haue you laboured a lomie and sandie building. **1607** Topsell *Four-f. Beasts* 495 He [Agricola] ascribeth to the beech-martin, a loamie or red throat. [A mistranslation of *quod guttur eius lutei sit coloris*, G. Agricola *De Re Metall.* (1561) 490.] **1626** Bacon *Sylva* §665 Mellow Earth is the best..Especially if it be not Loamy and Binding. **1720** De Foe *Capt. Singleton* vii. (1840) 118 We found the earth..of a yellowish loamy colour. **1784** Cowper *Task* iv. 437 The farmer's hedge Plash'd neatly, and secured with driven stakes Deep in the loamy bank. **1876** Page *Adv. Text-Bk. Geol.* xx. 432 Its dark loamy aspect renders it readily separable from the 'subsoil' of sand.

† **b.** Built with loam or plaster. *Obs. rare*$^{-1}$.

1658 Hewyt *Last Serm.* 195 The Peasant that from his loamy cottage is carried prisoner to a stately Castle..changes his golden liberty for iron shackles.

Hence **'loamily** *adv.*, (*nonce-wd.*) in the manner of loamy soil; **'loaminess.**

1727 Bailey vol. II, *Loaminess*, fulness of Loam, or loamy Nature. **1841** J. Grey in *Jrnl. R. Agric. Soc.* II. ii. 171 The greater friability and loaminess of the soil. **1869** Blackmore *Lorna D.* vii, The bank is steep..overhanging loamily.

loan (ləʊn), *sb.*^{1} Forms: 3-4 lan(e, 5-6 *Sc.* lane, layne, 3-8 lone, (4 lon, 5 lonne, 7 loyane), 4-6 loon(e, (5 lowne, 6 londe), 6-7 loane, 6- loan. [a. ON. *lán* neut. (Da. *laan*, Sw. *lån*) = OE. *lǽn* fem., MDu. *lêne* (Du. *leen*), OHG. *lêhan* (MHG. *lêhen*, mod.G. *lehn*) neut.:—OTeut. **laihwniz-*, *oz-*, neut.:—OAryan **loiqnes-*, *-os-* (Skr. *rēknas* inheritance, wealth), f. root **loiq-* (:*leiq-*: *liq-*) represented in Gr. λείπειν to leave, Goth. *leihwan*, OHG. *lîhan* (mod.G. *leihen*), OE. *léon* to lend.

The OE. *lǽn* did not survive into ME., being superseded by the Scandinavian form; but its derivative vb. *lǽnan* is the source of lend *v.*^{2}]

† **1.** A gift or grant from a superior. *Obs.*

a **1240** *Sawles Warde* in *Cott. Hom.* 257 Wiit..þonkeð god ȝeorne..of se riche lane [*MS. T.* leane]..þat he haueð ileanet him. *a* **1250** *Prov. Ælfred* 186 in *O.E. Misc.* 114 Ayhte nys non ildre istreon; ac hit is godes lone. *a* **1300** *Cursor M.* 10179 In thrin his godes did he dele þat godd had lent him of his lane. **13..** *Evang. Nicod.* 1530 in *Archiv Stud. neu. Spr.* LIII. 419 Þus all þa saintes þanked him ryght þat slyke lane wald þam len. *a* **1375** *Lay Folks Mass Bk.* App. iv. 640 Vr lord lene vs þat lon. *c* **1386** Chaucer *Sompn. T.* 153 God be thanked of his loone. *c* **1440** *Bone Flor.* 1916 The lady..Dwellyd as nonne..Loveing god of hys loone. *c* **1460** *Towneley Myst.* xix. 271 Thou leyne vs lyffyng on thi lone. *c* **1470** Henryson *Mor. Fab.* xii. (*Wolf & Lamb*) xix, Lordis that hes land be goddis lane [*rimes* tane, gane].

2. a. A thing lent; something the use of which is allowed for a time, on the understanding that it shall be returned or an equivalent given; *esp.* a sum of money lent on these conditions, and usually at interest. Phr. † *to loan*: as a loan.

a **1300** *Cursor M.* 14036 Tua men..asked him penis to lan. *c* **1375** *Sc. Leg. Saints* xxvi. (*Nycholas*) 810 Þe low..gert cal hyme in Iugment, to prowe his lane þat he lent. **1388** Wyclif *Exod.* xxii. 25 If thou ȝyuest money to loone to my pore puple. *c* **1449** Pecock *Repr.* i. iii. 16 Ȝeve ȝe loone, hoping no thing ther of [*Luke* vi. 35]. **1467** in *Eng. Gilds* (1870) 387 Euery man that payeth to such a yefte or lone aboue specificied. **1502** *Ord. Crysten Men* (W. de W. 1506) iv. xxi. 226 He the whiche receyueth that londe of money. **1533** Gau *Richt Vay* 17 Our saluior sais in the vi chaiptur of S. Luc. len ȝour layne traistand no thing thairfor. **1611** Bible *1 Sam.* ii. 20 The Lord giue thee seed of this woman, for the loane which is lent to the Lord. **1740** W. Douglass *Disc. Curr. Brit. Plant. Amer.* 11 Their Money being Loans of Paper Credit called Bills, from their Government to private Persons upon Land Security. **1844** H. H. Wilson *Brit. India* II. 409 Dhar ceded to the British government..as security for a pecuniary loan, the province of Bairsia for five years. **1863** Fawcett *Pol. Econ.* i. iv. (1876) 37 Indian railways have been constructed by loans subscribed almost entirely in England.

b. *fig.* Said, in recent use, of something (as a word, a custom) 'borrowed' or adopted by one people from another.

1891 T. K. Cheyne *Psalter* viii. 405 To regard the conceptions of Isa. lxv. 17, and still more, of Isa. lxvi. 15 as mere loans from Mazdeism is uncritical. **1892** E. P. Barrow *Regni Evangelium* iv. 78 Inward graces and outward opportunities are loans which may be enlarged by use and must be accounted for.

3. a. The action of lending; an instance of this; also in phr. † *at*, †*by*, †*in*, *on* or *upon loan*; and † *to put to loan*, in quot. *fig.*

c **1290** *S. Eng. Leg.* I. 244/136 'Leneth me', he sede, 'Ane hondret quarters of þat corn..þis schipmen seiden ne dorre we make no lone'. *c* **1386** Chaucer *Shipman's T.* 295 No wight in al this world wiste of this loone. **1393** Langl. *P. Pl.* C. v. 194 Lumbardes of lukes þat lyuen by lone as Iewes. **1454** *Rolls of Parlt.* V. 245 2 Ther shal be severally leveide and had by wey of lonne and preste to hym. **1463** *Mann. & Househ. Exp.* (Roxb.) 220 Item, delyveryd to the sayd Straton, by lone, xijd. **1494** Fabyan *Chron.* vii. 496 Any bargeyn or lowne of money by way of vsury. *a* **1548** Hall *Chron., Edw. IV*, 244 Money..prested out in lone. **1646** *Massach. Col. Rec.* 4 Nov. (1853) II. 164 The Corte..formerly granted Maior Nehemia Bourne the loane of sixe great guns. **1712** Hearne *Collect.* (O.H.S.) III. 319, I am promis'd the loan of it [a book]. **1721** *Rhode Island Col. Rec.* (1859) IV. 297 To permit and suffer the said Richard Ward to have and take upon loan as much of said bills..as by them shall be thought needful. **1729** *New Hampsh. Prov. Papers* (1870) IV. 553 The vote of the House..for re-emitting some bills at loan. **1753** Washington *Jrnl.* (1754) 6 The Waters were quite impassable, without swimming our Horses; which obliged us to get the Loan of a Canoe. **1813** J. Adams *Wks.* (1856) X. 36, I am much obliged to you..for the loan of this precious collection of memorials. **1817** W. Selwyn *Law Nisi Prius* (ed. 4) II. 972 If the loan is not upon the vessel, but upon the goods and merchandize. **1845** S. Austin *Ranke's Hist. Ref.* III. 605 He incessantly pressed for a 'brave sum of money' on loan. **1858** W. H. Sumner in *N. Eng. Hist. & Gen. Reg.* XII. 226, I obtained the loan of that Order Book. **1900** Mrs. Carus-Wilson *Irene Petrie* Pref. 12, I am indebted..to many friends for loan of letters, etc.

transf. and *fig.* (*rare*). **1538** Elyot *Dict.* Addit., *Animam debet*..he hath not his lyfe but in lone. **1609** Heywood *Brit. Troy* v. xlix. 118 The blow was put to loane. **1854** Thackeray *Newcomes* I. 297 She gratified Clive by a momentary loan of two knuckly old fingers.

† **b.** *occas.* The action of hiring or letting.

1601 *Exp. Judges riding West. & Oxford Circuit* 49 in *Camden Misc.* (1858) IV, It. the loane of vessells vs. iiijd. **1790** *Weston Rec.* (Massach.) 5 Apr. (1893) 414 The proceeds of the Sale or Loan of the Same [pews] to Discharge the Debts of the Town.

4. *National finance.* **a.** A contribution of money, formerly often a forced one, from private individuals or public bodies, towards the expenses of the state, the amount of which is acknowledged by the government as a debt; sometimes, the sum of money so contributed.

1439 *Rolls of Parlt.* V. 8/2 Ye gret loones and presttes, ye which yei have afore this tyme made unto our said Soverain Lord. **1495** *Act 11 Hen. VII*, c. 8 At the tyme of the same lone or taking of the seid money. **1542-3** *Act 34 & 35 Hen. VIII*, c. 27 §1 Euery high collectour of any .xv. subsidie or other taxe or lone. *a* **1548** Hall *Chron., Hen. VIII*, 102 b, At the last loane some lent the fifth part. **1603** *North's Plutarch, Seneca* (1612) 1217 He..ransacked all Italie with impositions and excessiue lones. **1626** in *Crt. & Times Chas. I* (1848) I. 126 The money which the aldermen gave the king, they neither presented in the name of a loan nor of their own proper gift. **1772** *Junius' Lett.* lxviii. 347 Several persons..refused to contribute to a loan exacted by Charles the First. **1833** Ht. Martineau *Fr. Wines & Pol.* vi. 82 Loans of almost every kind, and under every species of pretence had been raised upon the suffering nation. **1845** S. Austin *Ranke's Hist. Ref.* II. 143 They..obstinately refused to grant a loan which they were called upon to advance, and which was to be repaid out of the proceeds of the tax for the Turkish war. **1868** G. Duff *Pol. Surv.* 162 Since Juarez triumphed, there have been no forced loans, no exactions.

b. An arrangement or contract by which a government receives upon its own credit advances of money on specified conditions, esp. the payment of a stipulated interest.

1765 Blackstone *Comm.* i. viii. 324 The frequent opportunities of conferring particular obligations, by preference in loans [etc.]. **1844** H. H. Wilson *Brit. India* I. 109 It had been thought necessary to offer..ten per cent. per annum, on a loan. **1846** McCulloch *Acc. Brit. Empire* (1854) II. 429 To reduce the charge on account of the loan to 3 or 3 ½ per cent. **1853** Bright *Sp. India* 3 June, The Company has contracted loans to the extent of 16,000,000*l.*

5. *attrib.* and *Comb.* **a.** simple attributive, as *loan-account*, *-act*, *-chest*, *-fund*, *-market*, *-shop*; **b.** objective, as *loan-contractor*, *-jobber*, *-jobbing*; † **loan-bank**, an establishment from which poor people could borrow money at a low rate; † **loan-bill** = *exchequer-bill*; **loan-blend**, a compound word consisting of both native and foreign elements; a hybrid (see hybrid *sb.* 2); **loan capital**, the part of the capital of a company or the like that is borrowed for a specified period; **loan-collection**, a collection of works of art, curiosities, or the like, lent by their owners for exhibition; **loan-farm** *S. Afr.*, land loaned to a farmer by the government; **loan-form**, a form adopted by one language from another; **loan-god**, a god borrowed from another religion; **loan-holder**, one who holds debentures or other acknowledgements of a loan; a mortgagee; † **loan-house** = loan-office 1; **loan-monger**, a contemptuous name for a loan-contractor; so *loan-mongering* vbl. sb., *loan-mongery*; **loan-myth**, a myth borrowed from a foreign mythology; **loan-note**, an acknowledgement of indebtedness signed by an officer of a borrowing society on its behalf; **loan-place** *S. Afr.* = *loan-farm*; † **loan-recusant**, one who refused to contribute to a loan; **loan-shark** orig. *U.S.* (see quot. 1928 and shark *sb.*^{1} 2); so **loan-sharking** *sb.*, lending money at exorbitant rates of interest; **loan-shift**, a change in the meaning of a word resulting from the influence of a foreign language; a word so affected; **loan-society**, an association of persons who pay a periodical subscription in order to form a fund from which loans may be made to members or others; **loan-translation** [= G. *lehnübersetzung*], an expression adopted by one language from another in more or less literally translated form; a calque; **loan-word** [= G. *lehnwort*], a word adopted or borrowed from another language. Also loan-money, loan-office.

1899 *Westm. Gaz.* 22 Aug. 6/3 The customer..is informed that a *loan-account..has been opened in his name. **1743** *New Hampsh. Prov. Papers* (1871) V. 668 The *Loan Act for emitting £25,000 which his Majesty has condescended to approve. **1662** Petty *Taxes* 11 If publick *loan-banks, lombards, or banks of credit..were erected. **1746** *Connect. Col. Rec.* (1876) IX. 250 A certificate..for letting out the loan bank made by this Colony. **1872** Yeats *Growth Comm.* 63 Loan banks lent money. **1722** *Lond. Gaz.* No. 6078/2 The Exchequer Bills, called *Loan Bills. **1950** *Language* XXVI. 215 *Loanblends show morphemic substitution as well as importation. **1974** R. A. Hall *External Hist. Romance Lang.* 9 On occasion, a newly formed word may consist, in part, of a native term..and, in part, of a borrowing. The result is a *loan-blend*, as in Fr[ench] *bar-serveuse* 'bar-maid', with the first part of the loan-compound kept and with the second part replaced by Fr. *serveuse* 'maid, waitress'. **1848** *Bradshaw's Railway Almanack* (ed. 2) 57 The guarantee is extended to the payment of interest on £1,000,000 (the authorized *Loan Capital) at whatever rate it may be borrowed. **1964** *Financial Times* 31 Jan. 19/5 No share or loan capital of the Company or any of its subsidiaries has within two years preceding the date hereof been issued or is proposed to be issued for cash or otherwise. **1886** Willis & Clark *Cambridge* III. 473 There were special *loan-chests, the borrower deposited some object of value as a pledge in the chest out of which his loan had been taken. **1895** H. F. Brown *Biog. J. A. Symonds* I. 100 Symonds saw the first *loan collection of old masters [at Manchester]. **1834** *Tait's Mag.* I. 390/1 The vitals are eaten out of Old England by subsidies, *loan-contractors, and Jew-jobbers. **1804** J. Barrow *Acct. Trav. S. Afr.* II. 380 The number of these *loan farms registered in the office of the receiver of the land revenue, on closing the books in 1798, were..1832. **1955** J. H. Wellington *S. Afr.* II. iii. xiv. 208 To create a stable border farming population in the place of the cattle farmers trekking from loan farm to loan farm, land was offered to settlers on a quit-rent basis. **1966** E. Palmer *Plains of Camdeboo* ii. 21 Probably in the 1770's the land was issued as a loan place and became the temporary property of one farmer. Loan farms were apportioned in the simplest possible way and were held at a nominal rent. **1902** *Amer. Anthropologist* IV. 31 Penobscot *nachigadonkak* is a Passamaquoddy *loan-form. **1835** *Act 5 & 6 Will. IV*, c. 23 §1 Certain Institutions for establishing *Loan funds have been..established..for the Benefit..of the Labouring Classes. **1893** Dk. Argyll *Unseen Foundat. Society* xvi. 521 A loan-fund had been opened. **1901** A. Lang *Magic & Relig.* ii. 15 The Theory of *Loan-Gods; or borrowed Religion. **1823** Byron *To Bowring* 10 Oct. in Moore *Lett. & Jrnls. Byron* (1830) II. 693 It will be requisite for the *loan-holders to set apart..50,000*l.* sterling for that purpose. **1883** *Manch. Exam.* 6 Nov. 5/1 The shareholders and loanholders would have confidence. **1622** T. Scott *Belg. Pismire* 79 Their Lumbards, or *Loane-houses, are principally for the benefit of the poore. **1797** in *Spirit Pub. Jrnls.* (1802) I. 84 *Loan-jobbers and Contractors are quarrelling which shall rob us. **1822** in Cobbett *Rur. Rides* (1885) I. 144 Loan-jobbers, stock-jobbers, Jews. **1831** T. L. Peacock *Crotchet Castle* i. (1887) 15 A junior partner in the eminent *loan-jobbing firm of Catchflat and Company. **1844** Mill in *Westm. Rev.* XLI. 593 The already existing pressure upon the *loan market. **1870** J. K. Medbery *Men & Mysteries Wall St.* 11 Its loan market holds the keys of trade. **1837** Disraeli *Venetia* i. iv, He..turned up his nose at the Walpolian *loanmongers. **1898** *Spectator* 8 Jan. 39 The plunder of conquered States for the benefit of the victor

through the agency of the loan-monger. **1826** in Cobbett *Rur. Rides* (1885) II. 259 Till excises and *loanmongering began, these vermin [the Quakers] were never heard of in England. **1822** *Examiner* 419/2 This must be the case..even if *loan-mongery goes on. **1887** LANG *Myth. Ritual, & Relig.* I. 322 Many Greek myths are '*loan-myths'. **1883** *Law Rep.* 11 Q. Bench Div. 564 The *loan-notes of the Cherry Tree Building Society. **1844** J. BACKHOUSE *Narr. Visit Mauritius & S. Afr.* 585 A **loan place* which is a place obtained from the Government, that has not yet been surveyed, is half-an-hour's walk in every direction from the house or centre. **1939** J. S. MARAIS *Cape Coloured People* iv. 140 During the previous twenty years land had been granted to farmers as 'loan places'. **1654** H. L'ESTRANGE *Chas. I* (1655) 75 The *Loan-Recusants appeared the only men in the peoples affections. **1905** TAYLOR & GIBSON *Log of Water Wagon* 41 *Loan sharks have been following the Lithia all day. **1911** *Collier's* 4 Feb. 8/1 Mr. Ham became interested in the 'World's' lucrative and lengthy list of loan-shark advertisements. **1913** *Munsey's Mag.* Nov. 218/1 In New York the loan-sharks were doing a business of twenty million dollars per annum. *Ibid.* 221/1 At the convention of the Legal Aid Society in Pittsburgh..the loan-shark evil was discussed. **1928** *Daily Tel.* 5 May 9/5 It is hoped by this plan virtually to put out of business the 'loan shark', who exacts usurious rates of interest from the person of small means. **1972** *Sunday Sun* (Brisbane) 27 Aug. 22/1 He was a loan-shark extortionist, and he had a very cute way of making sure customers paid up. **1970** *New Yorker* 15 Aug. 24/1 Other illicit activities engaged in by Cosa Nostra.. included..hijacking, *loan-sharking. **1971** *Daily Colonist* (Victoria, B.C.) 10 Sept. 25/5 We are all aware that narcotics, prostitution, gambling and loansharking make up the bankroll of organized and syndicated crime. **1950** *Language* XXVI. 220 *Loanshifts in general occur most readily when there is both phonetic and semantic resemblance between foreign and native terms. **1964** *Ibid.* XL. 95 The problems of translators and their role in introducing neologisms and loanshifts. **1974** R. A. HALL *External Hist. Romance Lang.* 9 French *réaliser* 'to bring into existence' has..undergone a shift of meaning to 'become aware', under the influence of Eng[lish] *realise.* Such a process of reinterpretation is known as a *loan-shift*, and its result as a *calque.* **1849** *N. & Q.* 1st Ser. I. 5 The Lombard merchants..were the first to open *loan-shops in England. **1835** *Act 5 & 6 Will. IV*, c. 23 An Act for the Establishment of *Loan Societies in England and Wales. **1933** L. BLOOMFIELD *Lang.* xxv. 456 The Slavic languages translate the term [sc. *conscientia*] by 'with' and 'knowledge', as in Russian ['so-*vest*] 'conscience'. This process, called *loan-translation, involves a semantic change: the native terms or the components which are united to create native terms, evidently undergo an extension of meaning. **1958** C. RABIN in *Aspects of Translation* 140 Loan-translation (calque)..is very common [in modern Hebrew]. We find, for example, *gan yeladim* 'garden of children', which (except for the difference in the..order of elements) reproduces G. *Kindergarten* even to the pl. of *Kinder.* **1964** C. BARBER *Ling. Change Present-Day Eng.* IV. 101 Another type of loan from a foreign language is the *calque* or *loan-translation.* **1965** *Ulster Dialect Archive Bull.* (Ulster Folk Museum) IV. 11 Fairy lore appears in *fergorta*..occurring also as a loan-translation *hungry-grass.* **1974** *Verbatim* Dec. 2/1 Hebrew.. has a little series, mostly loan translations,..on a semantically similar pattern. **1874** SAYCE *Compar. Philol.* v. 171 *Loan-words are common to all dialects. **1900** MARGOLIOUTH in *Expositor* Apr. 248 Isaiah's oracles were full of Aramaic loan-words.

loan (ləʊn), *sb.*[2] Now only *Sc.* and *dial.* Also 4, 8-9 lone. [See LANE *sb.*]

1. A lane, a by-road.

1362 LANGL. *P. Pl.* A. II. 192 Lyȝere..Lurkede þorw lones [*B., C.* lanes]. *Ibid.* v. 162 Clarisse of Cokkes lone [*B., C.* lane]. **1785** FORBES *Poems Buchan dial.* 33 Why fear'd he to gang up the lone, and trembled at their swords? **1809** T. DONALDSON *Poems* 94 An' down the loan he took his flight. **1868** ATKINSON *Cleveland Gloss., Lone, loan*, a lane, a narrow passage. **1894** CROCKETT *Lilac Sunbonnet* 36 Maybes he's comin' up the loan this verra meenit.

2. An open uncultivated piece of ground near a farmhouse or village, on which the cows are milked.

1715 RAMSAY *Christ's Kirk Gr.* II. xix, Milk het frae the loan. **1721** —— *Richy & Sandy* 72 Nuckle kye stand rowting in the loans. **1881** W. T. ROSS *Poems* 208 From the woods and loans An answering storm was hurled.

†**loan**, *sb.*[3] *Sc. Obs.* [? a. Gael. *lòn.*] Provisions. Also *attrib.*, **loan-money**, **loan-silver**, board wages.

a **1578** LINDESAY (Pitscottie) *Chron. Scot.* (S.T.S.) II. 289 That thay sould be in reddynes agane the xxj day of Julij instant with fourtie dayes loan. **1639** MRQ. HUNTLEY in Spalding *Troub. Chas. I* (1850) I. 145 That all his Majesteis leges..be in reddiness prepairit with all diligens to repair whair and when he think fitting, vpone 48 houris aduertesement, with 15 dayis lone. *a* **1670** SPALDING *Ibid.* 316 Ilk heretour to furnesh his prest man with 40 dayis loan. *Ibid.* II. 320 Ilk souldiour to haue sex schillinges ilk day, during the space of 40 dayes, of loan siluer..Togidder also with thair hyre or levie or loan money. *a* **1836** W. ROBERTSON in W. Walker *Bards Bon-Accord* (1887) 606 Aft there's ease in dolefu' croon, Tho' little loan lie in the wallet.

loan (ləʊn), *v.* Now chiefly *U.S.* Forms: (? 3-4 **lane(n)**, 6 **loane**, 6, 8 **lone**, 6- **loan**. [f. LOAN *sb.*[1]

The earliest quots. are doubtful, as they may belong to LEND *v.*[2] (*a* miswritten for *æ*); if correct, they indicate an early adoption of ON. *lána* of equivalent etymology.]

trans. To grant the loan of; to lend. Also with *out.*

c **1200** *Vices & Virtues* (1888) 77 Gif ðu him lanst ani þing of ðinen. *c* **1205** LAY. 3680 Ich þe wulle lanen of mine leode-folc fif hundred schipes. *Ibid.* 6247 Ic eow wulle lanen [etc.]. **1542-3** *Act 34 & 35 Hen. VIII*, c. 2 §1 Lonyng or leying out the same for gaines in purchasing landes. *c* **1640** J. SMYTH *Lives Berkeleys* (1883) I. 203 In yeares of dearth and Scarcity, [he] loaned to many of them..wheat and other corne out of his grayneries. **1644** J. LANGLEY *Mournf. Note of Dove* 20 By way of location, or loaning them out. **1729** B. FESSENDEN in *N. Eng. Hist. & Gen. Reg.* (1859) XIII. 32 Gershom Tobey loans Oxen. **1740** *Connect. Col. Rec.* (1874) VIII. 320 The remainder of the said thirty thousand pounds ..shall be loaned out to particular persons. **1785** *Weston Rec.* (Massach.) 19 Sept. (1893) 370 Said sum being Loned to the Treasurer by the Direction of the Town. **1803** FESSENDEN *Terrible Tractorat.* I. (ed. 2) 3 They will not loan me, gratis, Their jingling sing-song apparatus. **1834** CALHOUN *Wks.* II. 328 The power to withdraw the money from the deposit, and loan it to favorite State banks. **1847** BROWNSON *Wks.* V. 541 We once loaned a Protestant lady a pamphlet by an eminent Catholic divine. **1880** BONAMY PRICE in *Fraser's Mag.* May 674 He receives a deposit from one man; he loans it out in part..to another. **1896** NEWNHAM-DAVIS *Three Men*, etc. 172 The stalls..are barrack chairs loaned for the occasion.

absol. or *intr.* *a* **1325** *Prose Psalter* xxxvi[i]. 27 The ryȝtful ys merciful..and laneþ [*MS. Dubl.* leneþ]. **1864** in WEBSTER. **1901** *N. Amer. Rev.* Feb. 262 The limit..within which the executive officers..may loan to a director.

loan, obs. form of LONE *a.*

loanable ('ləʊnəb(ə)l), *a.* [f. LOAN *v.* + -ABLE.] That may be loaned or lent, esp. of capital, etc.: Available for use in loans.

1848 MILL *Pol. Econ.* III. xxiii. §4 (1876) 390 It is therefore so much subtracted from the amount of what may be correctly called loanable capital. **1885** *Manch. Guard.* 20 July 5/5 The accumulation of loanable gold in the banks.. is a proof that gold has not risen in value.

loaned (ləʊnd), *ppl. a.* [f. LOAN *v.* + -ED[1].] That has been lent; that has been issued as a loan.

1553 GRIMALDE *Cicero's Offices* 106 b, Who so..do thinke meete that loned mony be remitted to the debters. **1602** WARNER *Alb. Eng.* XII. lxxiv. (1612) 309 She, the Pawne accepted, did her loned Ring forgoe. **1740** *Connect. Col. Rec.* (1874) VIII. 357 Three thousand pounds of loaned bills were drawn in for interest for the year 1740. **1749** *Ibid.* (1876) IX. 455 Mortgages given for the security and payment of the last loaned moneys. **1883** *Sat. Rev.* LV. 498 An unwarrantably loaned umbrella.

loanee (ləʊ'niː). [f. LOAN *v.* + -EE.] One to whom a loan has been granted; a borrower.

1832 *Fraser's Mag.* V. 157 Having the honour of being the Adam of South American loanees. **1853** WHEWELL tr. *Grotius* II. 65 A loanee is bound to make good the thing lent if it be destroyed.

loaner ('ləʊnə(r)). [f. LOAN *v.* + -ER[1].] One who loans or lends; one who grants a loan.

1884 *Home Mission.* Nov. 285 They loan through agents, and..these agents do not protect the interest of the loaner. **1898** *19th Cent.* Sept. 364 Mr. Joseph Jefferson, who is the loaner of this collection.

†**loange.** *Obs.* Also 4-5 loenge. [a. OF. *loenge* (F. *louange*), f. *loer* (*louer*) to praise.] Commendation, praise.

1390 GOWER *Conf.* III. 223 Al the poeple of his nobleie Loange unto his name seie. *c* **1399** *Pol. Poems* (Rolls) II. 14 To the loenge of perdurable gloire. **1485** CAXTON *Chas. Gt.* 25 He was chosen emperour of Rome wyth grete loange. **1490** —— *Eneydos* xvi. 64 Doo bi suche manere of wyse, that the loeuynge [*sic*] be vnto the attrybuted.

loaning ('ləʊnɪŋ), *vbl. sb.* [f. LOAN *v.* + -ING[1].] The action of the vb. LOAN; lending.

1740 *Connect. Col. Rec.* (1874) VIII. 360 The committee for the loaning the said bills are to take notice hereof. **1889** *Pall Mall G.* 3 Dec. 6/2 The President proceeds to condemn the loaning of public funds to banks without interest. **1901** *N. Amer. Rev.* Feb. 261 The excessive loaning of a bank's funds to its officers and directors.

loaning ('ləʊnɪŋ), *sb. Sc.* and *north.* Forms: 4-5 lon(n)yng(e, 6-7 loning, 8 lownin, 9-lonnin(g, 7-loaning. [f. LOAN *sb.*[2] + -ING[1].]

1. = LOAN *sb.*[2] 1. †*free loaning*: a right of way.

1324 *MS. Charter* (*penes* W. Greenwell of Durham), Le Lonnynge quod ducit usque Charlawe. **1370** *Durham Halm. Rolls* (Surtees) 60 Injunctum est omnibus tenentibus quod faciant les lonyngs. **1475** *Extracts Burgh Rec. Peebles* (1872) I. 175 Accepand a fre lonyng throw the sayde auche to Glentras as efferis to the town to haf of law. **1502** *Will* in *Ripon Ch. Acts* 356 Brakan more lonyng. **1597** *Wills & Inv. N.C.* (Surtees 1860) 341 To the loning that lyethe betwex Lumley parke paile and Lamb felds. **1610** *N. Riding Rec.* I. 199 For not repayring the loning betwene Earbie and West Ronckton. **1808** R. ANDERSON et al. *Ballads in Cumberland Dial.* 23 In dark winter neeghts i' the lonnins. **1832** *Act. 2 & 3 Will. IV*, c. 65 §5 Any distance to be measured along any street, lane, or loaning. **1849** F. T. DINSDALE *Gloss. Teesdale* 81 It's a lang lonnin that has nivver a turn. **1862** M'COSH *Supernatural* I. v. 92 We steal away thro' some green loaning. **1893** CROCKETT *Stickit Minister* 114 Leaning on the gate at the head of the loaning. **1896** F. M. T. PALGRAVE *List Words Hetton-le-Hole* 29 *Lonning*, 'laning', i.e. lane... 'We find swiney up Mousely (Moorsley) lonen.' —Extract from boy's essay on Wild Flowers. **1933** *Times Lit. Suppl.* 6 Apr. 243/2 This is for those whose feet leave the road at the first chance and strike up through lonnins and intakes to untrodden ground. **1971** *Country Life* 9 Sept. 630/1 We came to the lonnin that turns away from the river and leads beside the church towards the dale road.

2. = LOAN *sb.*[2] 2.

c **1750** MISS ELLIOT *Song, The Flowers of the Forest* i, But now they are moaning on ilka green loaning. **1824** SCOTT *Redgauntlet* let. ii, See not a Dulcinea in every slipshod girl, who drives..out the village cows to the loaning. **1882** J. WALKER *Jaunt to Auld Reekie*, etc. 38 Crummies rootin up the loanin' Wi weel-filled baggies.

3. *attrib.*, as ***loaning-end***; **loaning-dike**, a wall dividing the arable land from the pasture.

1383 *Durham Halm. Rolls* (Surtees) 177 De ten. villæ quia noluerunt facere le lonyngdiks juxta Bishoplaw. **1596** *Reg. Mag. Sig.* (1890) 160/2, 6 rudas terrarum..inter..lie Ovir Frankland ex australi, lie loning-dyke ex occidentali. **1895** CROCKETT *Men of Moss Hags* xxxv. 256 Every day the old man passed this loaning-end.

'loan-,money.

†**1.** Money payable as a contribution to a government loan. *Obs.*

1523 in Ellis *Orig. Lett.* Ser. I. I. 221 The ij[e] of the Li of lone money shalbe payed with a good will and with thanke. *c* **1645** HOWELL *Lett.* (1892) I. 249 There is much murmuring about the restraint of those that would not conform to Loan Moneys. **1659** in Rushw. *Hist. Coll.* I. 431 Sir P. H. refusing to part with Loan-money, was called before the Lords of the Council. *a* **1715** BURNET *Own Time* (1724) I. 381 Sir Harbottle's father..lay long in prison, because he would not pay the loan-money.

2. Money advanced as a loan.

1727 T. AMORY 24 May in W. B. Weeden *Econ. & Soc. Hist. New Eng.* (1890) II. 480 We shall soon see if the Loan Money will be continued. The Lower House is for it. **1764** *Rhode Island Col. Rec.* (1861) VI. 393 As fast as gold and silver shall be paid into the said office, for the aforesaid loan money. **1895** *Daily News* 3 May 9/4 A decline in the rate for loan money from 4 to 3 ½.

'loan-,office.

1. An office for lending money to private borrowers.

1720 *Lond. Gaz.* No. 5859/9 Subscriptions for erecting.. Loan-Offices, Publick Treasuries, &c. pretending to assist the Poor. **1732** *New Jersey Archives* (1894) XI. 304 Purchasing New-Jersey Currency and keeping it up till they could make an Advantage of it by imposing upon the Poor, who were in necessity of it to pay into the Loan-Office. **1897** *Daily News* 8 May 4/7 Indictments charging against four prisoners loan-office and turf frauds.

2. An office for receiving subscriptions to a government loan.

1777 J. ADAMS *Wks.* (1854) IX. 45 The design of loan-offices was to prevent the farther depreciation of the bills by avoiding farther emissions. **1779** FRANKLIN *Wks.* (1888) VI. 428 The interest..is payable only at the loan office in America from whence the bills issued. **1865** H. PHILLIPS *Amer. Paper Curr.* II. 55 Congress..erected a Loan Office in each of the United States.

attrib. **1781** FRANKLIN *Wks.* (1888) VII. 178 Accepted a number of loan-office bills this day.

So **'loan-,officer** (*U.S.*), an official charged with the duty of receiving subscriptions to a government loan.

1737 *Col. Laws N. York* (1895) II. 1040 An Act to facilitate and Explain the duty of the Loan officers in this Colony. **1790** J. ADAMS *Wks.* (1854) IX. 571 The loan officers or collectors, or some other known character, will have this additional duty annexed to him.

loansom, obs. form of LONESOME.

loap(e, obs. form of LOPE *v.*

loar(e, obs. form of LORE.

loasaceous (ləʊə'seɪʃəs), *a. Bot.* [f. mod.L. *Loasaceæ*: see next and -ACEOUS.] Of or pertaining to the N.O. *Loasaceæ* or *Loaseæ.*

1856 in MAYNE *Expos. Lex.*; and in some recent Dicts.

loasad ('ləʊəsæd). [f. mod.L. *Loasa* (prob. of S. American origin) + -AD.] A plant of the order *Loaseæ* or *Loasaceæ* (native to tropical America), of which *Loasa* is the typical genus.

1846 LINDLEY *Veg. Kingd.* 744 The resemblance between Loasads and Cucurbits.

loasis, var. LOAIASIS.

†**loath**, *sb. Obs.* Forms: 1 **láð**, (**laað**), 2-4 **lath(e**, 4-6 **loth(e**, 4, 6 *Sc.* and *north.* **laith**, 6- **loath(e**. [OE. *láð*, orig. neut. of *láð* LOATH *a.* In sense 2 from the vb. LOATHE. (Cf. LETH.)]

1. Something hateful or harmful; evil, harm, injury; an annoyance, a trouble.

c **900** tr. *Bæda's Hist.* v. vi. (Schipper) 576 Eala; hwæt þu me mycel yfel and lað dest mid þinre ærninge. *c* **1000** *Sax. Leechd.* I. 74 Ðonne bið þæs innoðes sar settende & liðiȝende, þæt hit sona næniȝ lað ne bið. *c* **1205** LAY. 16073 Nu þu most þat lað on-fon. *c* **1300** *Havelok* 76 Wo so dede hem wrong or lath,..He dede hem sone to hauen ricth. *c* **1375** *Sc. Leg. Saints* xxiv. (*Alexis*) 308 þat na man did hyme lath. *a* **1400** *Sir Perc.* 1935 To do that lady no lothe That pendid to velany. *c* **1460** *Towneley Myst.* xvi. 9 Harmes shall ye hent And lothes you to lap.

2. Dislike, hatred, ill-will; in later use, in physical sense, disgust, loathing. Also ***to have in loath.***

c **1175** *Lamb. Hom.* 157 Men schedden hate teres for laþe of þe worlde. *c* **1200** ORMIN 11887 To shildenn þe wiþþ all hiss laþ. *a* **1240** *Sawles Warde* in *Cott. Hom.* 255 Ich mei.. warnin ow of his lað. *a* **1330** *Otuel* 603 Eyther forȝaf oþer his loþ. ? *a* **1400** *Morte Arth.* 458 Be now lathe or lette, ryghte as þe thynkes. *c* **1420** *Chron. Vilod.* st. 818 Ever bytwyne hem was hate & loth. **1508** DUNBAR *Poems* vi. 28 Det michi modo ad potandum And I forgif him laith et wraith. **1589** R. BRUCE *Serm.* (1843) 129 We are come to such a loath, disdain and off casting of this heavenlie food. **1607** TOPSELL *Four-f. Beasts* (1658) 301 If your Horse..grow to a loath of his meat. **1614** MARKHAM *Cheap Husb.* (1623) 141 They are by experience found to breede loathe in the Birds. **1669** FLAMSTEED in Rigaud *Corr. Sci. Men* (1841) II. 84 What then hath cast us behind them? not our want of wits, but loathe of pains. **1728** P. WALKER *Life Peden* (1827) 113 O Scotland, many long and great shall thy Judgments be of all kinds..for Loth and Contempt of the Gospel.

loath, loth (ləʊθ), *a.* Forms: α. 1 **láð,** (**laad, laath, láth**), 2–3 **lath,** (3 **læð**). β. *Sc.* and *north.* 4–6 **lath(e,** 4–8 **laithe, layth(e,** 6–9 **leath,** 4–9 **laith.** γ. 3–5 **leith,** 5–6 **leyth.** δ. 2–4 **loþ,** (2 **lod**), (3 **leoð, lodt, lothȝ**), 4–6 **lothe,** (4 **lot**), 4–5 **looth(e,** (7 **loathe, lought**), 4– **loth,** 6– **loath.** [Com. Teut.: OE. *láð* = OFris. *leed* (for **lêth*), OS. *lêð* (Du. *leed*), OHG. *leid* (MHG. *leit, leid-*; mod.G., as sb., *leid* sorrow, pain; cf. *leider* unfortunately, which is properly the comparative of the adj.), ON. *leið-r* (Sw., Da. *led*):—OTeut. **laiþo-*, adopted in Rom. as F. *laid*, It. *laido* ugly.

The ulterior etymology is obscure. Apparently cognate are OHG. *lêwes* alas, and possibly OE. *lá* LO *int.*[1]]

†**1.** Hostile, angry, spiteful. *rare* in ME. *Obs.*

Beowulf (Z.) 1506 þæt heo þone fyrd-hom ðurh-fon ne mihte..laþan fingrum. *c* **1400** *Destr. Troy* 3811 He lengit not long in his lothe hate.

†**2.** Repulsive, unpleasant, hateful, loathsome.

Beowulf (Z.) 134 Wæs þæt ȝe-win to strang lað ond longsum. *a* **700** *Epinal Gloss.* 514 *Ingratus*, lath. *c* **1175** *Lamb. Hom.* 71 And kep us from his waning þat laþe gast þet laðe þing. *a* **1200** *Moral Ode* 283 Þer is þe loþe sathanas. *c* **1220** *Bestiary* 458 Seftes sop ure seppande..leiðe and lodlike. *c* **1250** *Gen. & Ex.* 369 And niðful neddre, loð an liðer, sal gliden on hise brest neðer. *a* **1300** *Cursor M.* 7829 To dreri ded þat he be don, Laþer ded þan [*printed* þat] ani in lijf. *c* **1300** *Harrow. Hell* 154 Bring ous of this lothe hous. *a* **1340** HAMPOLE *Psalter* xv. 6 Þof þai seme laith & outkastynge. *c* **1375** *Sc. Leg. Saints* ii. (*Paulus*) 771 A fowle padow..þat wes laythe to se. **1426** AUDELAY *Poems* 31 Thenk on the leyth lazar was borne into Abragus barme. *c* **1460** *Towneley Myst.* x. 63 He was foule and layth to syght. **1513** DOUGLAS *Æneis* II. ii. 128 But mair abaid, As was devisit, the laith worde furth braid. **1583** BABINGTON *Commandm.* viii. (1590) 381 Wee should not take any sure comfort til we haue..altered quite so loath a life. **1592** WYRLEY *Armorie* 155 Relaxment from loth prison strong.

†**b.** Const. *dat.* or *to*, esp. in ***him*** (etc.) ***loath is, were,*** etc. *to* (do so and so); also with clause as subject. *Obs.*

c **893** K. ÆLFRED *Oros.* IV. x. §7 Swa lað wæs Pena folc Scipian..ðæt [etc.]. **11..** *O.E. Chron.* an. 1048 (Laud MS.) Him wæs lað to amyrrene his aȝenne folȝað. *c* **1175** *Lamb. Hom.* 31 He his uniseli ȝif him is lað to donne þis. *c* **1205** LAY. 4000 Þe quike hire wes swa swiðe leoð þat [etc.]. *Ibid.* 7321 Þes tiðende him wes læð. *a* **1225** *Ancr. R.* 200 Þisse unðeauwe..is þauh of alle on loðest [*printed* onloðest] God. *c* **1250** *Gen. & Ex.* 1216 Hir was ysmaeles anger loð. *c* **1290** *S. Eng. Leg.* I. 119/454 Lothȝ vs were any-þing to don. *a* **1300** *Cursor M.* 1102 To blam þe broiþer was þam laith. *c* **1350** *Will Palerne* 1255 Him loþ þouȝt no lenger to striue. *c* **1386** CHAUCER *Manciple's T.* 41 For hym were looth byiaped for to be. *c* **1420** *Anturs of Arth.* 432 To losse swylke a lordschipe me thynke it fulle laythe. *c* **1430** *Syr Gener.* (Roxb.) 1484 Here seruice to him was nat lothe. **1470–85** MALORY *Arthur* I. xxii, That is me loth said the knyght, but sythen I muste nedes I wille dresse me therto. **1513** DOUGLAS *Æneis* I. Prol. 489 Bot laith me war, but other offence or cryme, Ane bruitell body suld intertrike my ryme.

†**3.** Ugly; esp. in phrase ***for fairer, for loather,*** in the marriage service. *Obs.*

c **1400** MAUNDEV. (Roxb.) xvii. 77 Þe wymmen er riȝt layth and ill araid. **1403** *York Manual* (Surtees) p. xvi, I take the, N., to my wedded wyfe..to hold and to haue..for fayrer, for layther. **1484** in *Ripon Ch. Acts* 162 *note*, For farer for lather.

Proverb. **1546** J. HEYWOOD *Prov.* (1867) 49 The lothe stake standeth longe.

4. Averse, disinclined, reluctant, unwilling. Const. (†*for*) *to* with *inf.*, also *for* (a person) *to* (do something), also with sentence as object; occas. with *of, to, unto*, followed by a sb.

c **1374** CHAUCER *Boeth.* II. pr. iv. 27 (Camb. MS.) She lyueth loþ of this lyf. **1398** TREVISA *Barth. De P.R.* I. (1495) 3 Loathe to offende I purpose [etc.]. *a* **1400** *Cursor M.* 27788 (Cott. Galba) Slewth..it makes a man lath for to lere. **1413** *Pilgr. Sowle* (Caxton 1483) IV. xxiv. 70 She fond the so dulle and soo lothe to hir wordes. *c* **1440** *Bone Flor.* 1126 The pope was not lothe To assoyle hym of hys othe. *c* **1475** *Rauf Coilȝear* 702 He was..laith for to stynt. **1523** LD. BERNERS *Froiss.* I. cxciii. 229 The whiche the erle of saynt Powle was lothe vnto. **1535** STEWART *Cron. Scot.* I. 575 Full laith he wes..To put his honour in dame Fortonis handis. *a* **1548** HALL *Chron.*, *Hen. VI*, 93 The duke of Gloucester..beganne to waxe lothe of his supposed wife. **1598** DELONEY *Jacke Newb.* vii. 86 The lother to speake, for that hee could speake but bad English. **1599** HAKLUYT *Voy.* I. 600 The residue shewed themselues unwilling and loath to depart. **1611** SPEED *Hist. Gt. Brit.* (1632) 1023 What king hath be lother to punysh his subjects. *a* **1657** SIR W. MURE *Sonnet* iii. 12 (S.T.S.) I. 49 No greif at all..Sall mack me ewer loath of my estait. **1662** J. BARGRAVE *Pope Alex. VII* (1867) 22 His relations being lought to part with the estate they had got by his supposed death. **1667** PEPYS *Diary* 7 Feb., I..would be loth he should not do well. **1713** BERKELEY *Hylas & Phil.* ii. Wks. 1871 I. 314 You are loath to part with your old prejudice. **1722** SEWEL *Hist. Quakers* (1795) I. III. 169 She found him moderate, and loth to send her to prison. **1724** RAMSAY *Tea-t. Misc.* (1733) I. 114, I am laith that she shou'd tyne. **1811** W. TAYLOR in *Monthly Mag.* XXXI. 5 The Calvinists..are seen to be..loth to military service. **1844** LD. BROUGHAM *Brit. Const.* ix. §1 (1862) 113 Would be loath to risk a shilling of it. **1861** GEO. ELIOT *Silas M.* 62 Lammeter isn't likely to be loth for his daughter to marry into my family. **1890** SIR A. KEKEWICH in *Law Times Rep.* LXIII. 764/1 One is loth to believe the similarity is innocent and unintentional.

b. without construction; sometimes quasi-*adv.* Phr. ***nothing loath***: not at all unwilling.

c **1475** *Lerne or be Lewde* 11 in *Babees Bk.*, To Lothe, ne to Lovyng, ne to Lyberalle of goode. **1608** G. WILKINS *Pericles* vi. (1857) 42 To take a loth and sorrowfull departure of her. **1667** MILTON *P.L.* IX. 1039 Her hand he seis'd, and to a shadie bank..He led her nothing loath. **1702** ROWE *Tamerl.* I. i. 406 As Wretches..Part with their Lives, unwilling, loth and fearful. **1813** SCOTT *Rokeby* v. i, Thus aged men full loth and slow The vanities of life forego. **1836** J. H. NEWMAN in *Lyra Apost.* (1849) 123 See in king's courts loth Jeremiah plead! **1852** THACKERAY *Esmond* I. xi, The children were nothing loth, for the house was splendid, and the welcome kind enough. **1873** BROWNING *Red Cott. Nt.-cap* 227 Give me permission to cry 'Out of bed, You loth rheumatic sluggard!'

†**c.** Displeased. *Obs. rare.*

a **1250** *Prov. Ælfred* 363 in *O.E. Misc.* 124 Þurh lesinge mon is loþ. **1670** DRYDEN *Conq. Granada* I. i. (1725) 38 You are loth, That, like a perjur'd Prince, you broke your Oath.

5. Used antithetically to *lief*, in senses 2 and 4. See LIEF *a.* 3, and quots. there given.

†**6.** quasi-*adv.* Reluctantly, slowly. *Obs.*

a **1340** HAMPOLE *Psalter* lxxvi[i]. 1 Þe laghere is oure voice and þe lathere ere we herd. *c* **1374** CHAUCER *Troylus* II. 1185 (1234) Of þing ful ofte loth bygonne Comth ende good.

7. ***loath to depart***: orig. the tune of a song (prob. containing those words) expressive of regret for departure; *transf.* any tune played as a farewell.

1584 GREENE *Arbasto* Wks. (Grosart) III. 211 With that she cast on me such a louing looke, as she seemed to play loth to depart. **1609** *Ravenscroft's Deuteromelia* in Chappell *Pop. Mus. Old Time* I. 173 Sing with thy mouth, sing with thy heart, Like faithful friends, sing *Loath to depart.* **1657** S. PURCHAS *Pol. Flying-Ins.* 80 Yet againe returning to the Hive, with delightful melody singing a loath to depart, [they] invite all their Sisters to hasten apace, and wait upon their Queen now on her coronation day. **1855–7** CHAPPELL *Pop. Mus. Old. Time* II. 708 It [*sc.* 'The Girl I left behind me'] has also been played for at least seventy years, as a *Loth-to-depart*, when a man-of-war weighs anchor, and when a regiment quits the town in which it has been quartered. **1867** SMYTH *Sailor's Word-bk.*, *Loath to depart*, probably the first line of some favourite song; formerly the air was sounded in men-of-war, when going foreign, for the women and children to quit the ship.

loathe (ləʊð), *v.* Forms: α. 1 **láðian,** 2–3 **laðen, lathen,** 3 **laðien,** 4–6 *Sc.* and *north.* **lath(e,** 5 **laith(e.** β. 3–4 **loðien,** 3–5 **loþe(n,** 3–7 **lothe,** (5 **lothee**), 6–7 **loth,** 5–6 **loothe,** 6–8 **loath,** 6– **loathe.** [OE. *láðian* = OS. *lêthon*, ON. *leiða*:—OTeut. type **laiþôjan*, f. **laiþo-* LOATH *a.* (OE. had *lǽðan* to hate, cause to shun, revile = OHG. *leidan*:—OTeut. type **laiþjan*, f. **laiþo-*.)]

†**1.** *intr.* To be hateful, displeasing, or offensive. Const. *dat.* or *to. Obs.*

c **893** K. ÆLFRED *Oros.* III. xi. §5 Þa Cassander þæt ȝeascade þæt hio ðæm folce laðade, þa ȝegaderade he fird. *c* **1175** *Lamb. Hom.* 101 Þe oferlifa on hete and on wete macað þene mon un-halne, and his saule gode laðeð. *c* **1230** *Hali Meid.* 9 Þat te schal laði þi lif. **1297** R. GLOUC. (Rolls) 750 Þo þis kyng leir eldore was, he bigan to loþe, Vor he so longe liuede, is leue doȝtren boþe. **1390** GOWER *Conf.* III. 217 The barli cake is Gedeon, Which..Schal come and sette such ascry..That it schal to us alle lothe. **1393** LANGL. *P. Pl.* C. I. 173 Þat ous loþeþ þe lyf er he lete ows passe. *c* **1400** *Destr. Troy* 12122 For hit [deth] laithit hir les þen on lyue be. *a* **1547** SURREY *Æneid* IV. 24 If geniall brands and bed me lothed not. **1573** SIR C. HATTON *Let. to Q. Eliz.* (Pearson's 81st Catal., 1900, p. 36), So great Discorde in the sweetness of your most rare & excellent Musike as would lothe you. *a* **1597** PEELE *David & Bethsabe* (1599) E iv b, Let not the voice of Ithay loth thine eares.

†**b.** *impers.*; also quasi-*impers.* with subj. *inf.* simply or with *it.* (*it*) *loathes me* (*of*) = I am disgusted (with). *Obs.*

a **1225** *Ancr. R.* 324 Smit hine so luðerliche þet him loðie to snecchen eft to þe. **1303** R. BRUNNE *Handl. Synne* 686 To þenke on hem, forsoþe me loþys. **1413** *Pilgr. Sowle* III. ix. (Caxton 1483) 56 Now mowe this folke swolewe ynowe of the fyre of helle and lycken til them lothe. *c* **1430** *Hymns Virg.* 85 Thus is þe day come to nyȝt þat me loþith of my lyuynge. **1530** PALSGR. 614/2, I lothe his villanye, or it lotheth me of his villanye. **1581** J. BELL *Haddon's Answ. Osor.* 131 b, It would have loathed me to have rehearsed the same in this place. **1596** DANETT tr. *Comines* (1614) 95 It lotheth mee to make mention of this cruelty.

†**2.** To be or become disgusted, to feel disgust. Const. *at, for, of, with* (something). *Obs.*

c **1400** *Destr. Troy.* 8123 If men laith with þi lyf, lyffyng in erthe. **1422** tr. *Secreta Secret.*, *Priv. Priv.* 136 Al the roialme thanne rumourt and lothit for that rousty Synne. *c* **1430** *Syr. Gener.* (Roxb.) 7718 Of hir life she gan to loothe. *a* **1600** MONTGOMERIE *Misc. Poems* xiii. 4 My maistres hes a man of me, That lothis of euery thing bot love. **1609** BIBLE (Douay) *Num.* xxi. 6 Our soule now lotheth at this most light meate.

†**3.** *trans.* To excite loathing or disgust in (a person, etc.). Const. *of.* Also, to render (a person) loath or reluctant *to* (do something) or averse *from* (something). *Obs.*

1568 ABP. PARKER *Pref. to Bishops' Bible* *1 To lothe christen men from reading, by their couert slaunderous reproches of the scriptures. **1577** NORTHBROOKE *Dicing* (1843) 101 Such matters..as will lothe any honest man or good woman to come neare such playes. **1599** H. BUTTES *Dyets drie Dinner* D ij, Medlers..if you deale much with them, they wil extremely irck, and loath you. *c* **1610** *Women Saints* 75 Such a filthie state, as might lothe the stomacke of the beholder. **1645** BRINSLEY *Church-Remedie* 34 As if one should endeavour to loath a sick man of his portion, before it come at him. **1661** H. D. *Disc. Liturgies* 6 They are..good for nothing but to loath pious souls.

4. To feel aversion or dislike for; to be reluctant or unwilling *to* (do something). Now only with stronger sense: To have an intense aversion for; to regard with utter abhorrence and disgust.

The stronger sense in mod. use may be partly due to association with the idea of nauseation often implied in the specific use 4 b.

a **1200** *Moral Ode* 128 Wel late he latheð uuel werc, þe ne mei hit don ne mare. **1300** *Poem 7 deadly Sins* in Brampton *Penit. Ps.* (Percy Soc.) 62 Good werk he lothith to bigynne. **1393** LANGL. *P. Pl.* C. VII. 142 Alle ladies me loþen þat louen eny worschep. *a* **1400–50** *Alexander* 5115 Forþi like it to ȝour lordschip & lathis noȝt my sawis. *c* **1418** *Pol. Poems* (Rolls) II. 246 Thes Lollardes that lothen ymages most. **1508** DUNBAR *Tua Mariit Wemen* 328 Than I him lichtlyit as a lowne, et lathit his maneris. **1526** *Pilgr. Perf.* (W. de W. 1531) 114 All though it be that thynge that y^u lothest moost. *a* **1586** SIDNEY *Arcadia* III. (1629) 259, I should loath the keeping of my bloud with the losse of my faith. **1697** DRYDEN *Virg. Georg.* IV. 158 The Swarms..loath their empty Hives, and idly stray. **1784** COWPER *Task* II. 416 In my soul I loath All affectation. **1833** HT. MARTINEAU *Charmed Sea* iii. 35 Mother, I loathe him. *a* **1862** BUCKLE *Civiliz.* (1869) III. iii. 148 Whose malignant cruelty made him loathed by his contemporaries. **1888** BRYCE *Amer. Commw.* III. lxxxi. 73 To dictate their terms to statesmen who loathe the necessity of submission.

absol. **1842** TENNYSON *Two Voices* 104 To breathe and loathe, to live and sigh. **1884** BROWNING *Family* 72 Man who..craves and deprecates, and loves and loathes.

b. To feel an aversion or disgust for (food, etc.).

c **1400** *Rom. Rose* 5610 If in syknesse that he falle, And lothe mete & drink withalle. **1602** MARSTON *Antonio's Rev.* III. ii. Wks. 1856 I. 109 Ile force him feede on life Till he shall loath it. **1611** BIBLE *Prov.* xxvii. 7 The full soule loatheth an honie combe. *a* **1677** BARROW *Wks.* (1686) III. Serm. xxxvii. 411 A stomach, surcharg'd with foul, or poisonous matter, which it loaths. **1764** GOLDSM. *Trav.* 182 He sees..No costly lord the sumptuous banquet deal, To make him lothe his vegetable meal. **1866** J. THOMSON *Philosophy* IV. v, Your stomach soon must loathe all drink and meat.

loathed (ləʊðd), *ppl. a.* [f. LOATHE *v.* + -ED[1].] That is an object of loathing or disgust; utterly disliked, abhorred, detested.

a **1420** HOCCLEVE *De Reg. Princ.* 542 His compaignye is vn-to folkis lothid. **1579** SPENSER *Sheph. Cal.* Dec. 70 The grieslie Tode-stoole..And loathed [1611 loathing] Paddocks lording on the same. *a* **1586** SIDNEY *Arcadia* III. (1633) 305 But her waiting Jaylors with cruell pitie brought loathed life unto her. **1602** *2nd Pt. Return fr. Parnass.* II. i. 572 Earth the loathed stage Whereon we act this fained personage. **1667** MILTON *P.L.* XII. 178 Frogs, Lice, and Flies, must all his Palace fill With loath'd intrusion. **1742** COLLINS *Ode on Poet. Charac.* 13 It left unbless'd her loath'd, dishonour'd side. **1885–94** R. BRIDGES *Eros & Psyche* Mar. xiii, Her beauty will I mock with loathèd lust.

Hence **'loathedness.**

a **1859** L. HUNT *Shewe Faire Seeming* xxvii, What first was Love, was now called Loathednesse.

loather ('ləʊðə(r)). [f. LOATHE *v.* + -ER[1].] One who loathes or feels disgust at (anything).

1601 WEEVER *Mirr. Mart.* D ij, Louers of playes, and loathers of good preaching. **1665** BOYLE *Occas. Refl.* V. iii. (1848) 306 The mutinous Loathers of Manna, and lusters after flesh, had their wish severely granted. **1885** TENNYSON *Freedom* viii, Thou loather of the lawless crown As of the lawless crowd.

loathful ('ləʊðfʊl), *a.* Also 6 **lothefull,** 5–6 **lothful(l,** 8–9 *Sc.* **laithfu'.** [f. LOATH *sb.* + -FUL.]

1. That is an object of loathing or disgust; hateful, loathsome. Now *rare.*

a **1450** *Cov. Myst.* (Shaks. Soc.) 75, I lothfolest that levyth. **1481** EARL WORCESTER *Tulle of Old Age* (Caxton) f 3 b, I demaunde you Scipion and Lelius if the olde age of such as delited them in the labourage of londes semyth unto you to be wretched or lothfull. **1561** T. NORTON *Calvin's Inst.* III. 280 Whosoeuer prepareth himself to praye, let hym be lothful to himself in his owne euils. **1591** SPENSER *M. Hubberd* 735 And lothefull idlenes he doth detest. **1892** *Times* 10 Nov. 3/5 Europeans whose presence is so loathful to every right-thinking Mussulman.

2. Reluctant, retiring, bashful. *Obs.* exc. *Sc.*

1561 T. NORTON *Calvin's Inst.* III. xxv. (1634) 485 So that yet we bee not lothfull or wearie of long tarrying. **1591** SPENSER *M. Hubberd* 1314 Which when he did with lothfull eyes beholde. **1785** BURNS *Cotter's Sat. Nt.* 69 But blate and laithfu', scarce can weel behave. **1862** HISLOP *Prov. Scot.* 12 A landward lad is aye laithfu'.

Hence **'loathfully** *adv.*, in a loathful manner, with reluctance. **'loathfulness,** the quality or condition of being loathful; reluctance.

1596 SPENSER *F.Q.* IV. xii. 32 Proteus..reading it with inward loathfulnesse, Was grieved to restore the pledge he did possesse. **1887** HISSEY *Holiday on Road* 57 There was nothing for it but to loathfully walk away.

†**'loathiness.** *Obs. rare*[−1]. [f. LOATHY *a.* + -NESS.] Disinclination; reluctance.

c **1449** PECOCK *Repr.* I. xix. 114 Redinesis into synne and lothinessis into good.

loathing ('ləʊðɪŋ), *vbl. sb.* [f. LOATHE *v.* + -ING[1].] The action of the vb. LOATHE; intense dislike, abhorrence; strong distaste (for food).

c **1340** HAMPOLE *Prose Tr.* (1866) 33 What es þis desire? Now, sothely, na thyng bot a lathynge of all þis werldis blysse. *c* **1440** HYLTON *Scala Perf.* (W. de W. 1494) II. i, But he askyth a lothynge of synne. *c* **1550** LLOYD *Treas. Health* (1585) I iv, Lothing cometh of muche corrupte meate or sum grosse and sharp humor. **1611** BIBLE *Transl. Pref.* ¶ 15 To weane the curious from loathing of them for their euery-where-plainenesse. **1614** W. B. *Philosopher's Banquet* 75 Medlers helpe the loathing of the stomack, being taken in the instant thereof. **1657** SPARROW *Bk. Com. Prayer* (1661) 270 Which..hymn..though it should be said night and day yet could it never breed a loathing. **1713** STEELE *Guardian* No. 17 ¶ 10 Objects..who would now move Horror and

Loathing. 1718 Quincy *Compl. Disp.* 31 It..does often occasion Loathings and Gripes. 1792 *Burns' Prose Wks.* 93 *note*, Burns marked his loathing of remuneration by the use of even a stronger term than this. 1838 Dickens *Nich. Nick.* xxxiii, Your brother's widow and her orphan shun you with disgust and loathing. *a* 1862 Buckle *Civiliz.* (1869) III. ii. 48 It is this loathing at tyranny..which makes it impossible that tyranny should ever finally succeed. 1901 *19th Cent.* Aug. 214 Hunters will tell you of the absolute loathing generated for venison when [etc.].

†**b.** Comb.: **loathing-stock**, an object of loathing. *Obs.*

1622 S. Ward *Woe to Drunkards* (1627) 35 Hee hath.. with Beere made thy body a carkase fit for the Biere, a laughing and lothing-stocke..to men and Angels.

loathing ('ləʊðɪŋ), *ppl. a.* [f. loathe *v.* + -ing[2].] That loathes, in senses of the vb.

†**1.** That causes loathing or disgust; disgusting.

1508 Dunbar *Flyting w. Kennedie* 102 Laithly and lowsy, als lathand as ane leik. 1614 W. B. *Philosopher's Banquet* 52 Goose-egges are loathing; yeelding an euill taste and sauour. 1683 Tryon *Way to Health* xix. (1697) 418 You deliver them [Daughters] up, and force them into loathing Embraces.

2. That feels disgust or is disgusted.

c 1586 C'tess Pembroke *Ps.* cvii. vi, Their lothing soule doth foode refraine. 1599 H. Buttes *Dyets Drie Dinner* P 3 b, Clowding the loathing ayre with foggie fume Of Dock-Tabacco. 1825 Lytton *Falkland* 46, I looked upon the aims of others with a scornful and loathing eye.

Hence **'loathingly** *adv.*, in a loathing manner, as one who feels a loathing or disgust.

1606 Warner *Alb. Eng.* xv. xcv. 380 Yea, let them listen, lothingly, what Iesuites propound Gainst Kings and States. 1824 Lamb *Lett.* (1888) II. 112, I was loathingly in expectation of brencheese. 1862 Lytton *Str. Story* II. 378 Again I recoiled—wrathfully, loathingly.

†**'loathless**, *a. Obs.* [OE. *láðléas*, f. *láð* harm, loath *sb.* + *-léas* -less.] Harmless, innocent.

c 1050 *Voc.* in Wr.-Wülcker 419/2 *Inmunes*, laþlease. *c* 1200 *Trin. Coll. Hom.* 49 Loðles is þe man þe ne doð ne ne quað ne þencð no þing þat he [etc.]. *a* 1225 *Juliana* 45 Godes licome þat he nom of þat laðlese meiden.

Hence †**'loathlessness**, innocence.

c 1200 *Trin. Coll. Hom.* 33 Deflen Ðe bireueden him alle his riche weden þat waren..undeðlicnesse and loðlesnesse.

loathliness ('ləʊðlɪnɪs). [f. loathly *a.* + -ness.] The quality of being loathly; hatefulness, hideousness, loathsomeness. Now *rare.*

1483 Caxton *Gold. Leg.* 371 b/2, I shal cutte of my nose so that euery man shal hate me for my lothelynes. 1531 Elyot *Gov.* iii. xxv, The deformitie and lothelynes of vice. 1587 Golding *De Mornay* xxx. 482, I will none of your sacrifices ..al such things are but smoke and louthlynes in my sight. 1846 G. S. Faber *Lett. Tractar. Secess.* 245 Popery.. through the loathliness of its own corruptions [etc.].

loathly ('ləʊðlɪ), *a.* Forms: 1 **láðlic**, 2–3 **loðlic**, 3 **lad-**, **lað-**, **loð(e)liche**, 3– 4 **lod(e)lich(e**, **-like**, **-lych**, **loþely(ch**, 4 **lat-**, **laþ-**, **loþli**, **loth(e)-**, **loþliche**, 4–6 **lod(e)ly**, **loth(e)lie**, **-ly**, (5 **lathely**, **loodly**, **looþeli**, **lotly**), 5–6 **layth(e)- liche**, **-ly**, 6 *Sc.* **lathly**, **laitlie**, **-ye**, 6– **loathly**. *compar.* 3 **laðluker**, *superl.* 3 **lað-**, **lodlukest**, 4 **lodlakest**. See also laidly. [OE. *láðlic* (= OFris. *lêdlík*, OS. *lêðlîk*, OHG. *leidlîh*, MHG. *leidelich*, *leitlich*, ON. *leiðilig-r*), f. *láð* loath *a.* + *-lic* -ly[1].]

Hateful, disgusting, loathsome, repulsive, hideous, horrible. Rare in 17th and 18th cents.; revived in the 19th c. as a literary word.

c 900 tr. *Bæda's Hist.* iii. xiv. (Schipper) 260 Mon laþlice deaþe þone cyning acwealde. *a* 1175 *Cott. Hom.* 219 Awende ..to loðlice deoflen. *a* 1200 *Moral Ode* 279 þer ligget laðliche fend in stronge raketeie. *a* 1225 *Ancr. R.* 66 Ower greste, & ower lodlukeste sunnen. *c* 1250 *Gen. & Ex.* 3030 So woren he lodelike on to sen. *a* 1300 *Cursor M.* 20420 Lokes ..þat naman of all our fer bi-fore hir mak latli chere. 13.. *Minor Poems fr. Vernon MS.* (E.E.T.S.) 584/383 That forehed is lodly That is calouh and bare. *c* 1386 Chaucer *Wife's T.* 244 Thou art so loothly, and so oold also. 1393 Langl. *P. Pl.* C. xvii. 265 Ypocrisie..is ylikned in latyn to a lothliche dounghep. 1413 *Pilgr. Sowle* (Caxton) i. xiii. (1859) 10 He hath..wesshen in the lothely lake of cursyd luxury. 1483 Caxton *G. de la Tour* cxvii. K vj, My clothyng semeth to yow lothly. 1501 Douglas *Pal. Hon.* ii. xx, Ȝone Catiue..A laithlie ryme dispitefull and subtelle Compylet hes. 1552 in *Vicary's Anat.* (1888) App. xvi. 313 If..ye shall happen to espie any persone infected with any lothelie grief or disease. 1591 Spenser *Tears Muses* 335 Clerks they to loathly idlenes entice. 1610 Shaks. *Temp.* iv. i. 21 Discord shall bestrew The vnion of your bed, with weedes so loathly That you shall hate it both. 1748 Thomson *Cast. Indol.* i. 543 In chamber brooding like a loathly toad. *a* 1839 Praed *Poems* (1864) II. 309 And hide reluctant Truth in Error's loathly veil. 1871 R. Ellis tr. *Catullus* cviii. 1 Loathly Cominius. 1886 Besant *Childr. Gibeon* ii. vi, A knight was sent forth to kill a dragon or a loathly worm. 1896 Barrie *Marg. Ogilvy* vi. (1897) 115 She sighs at sight of her son, dipping and tearing, and chewing the loathly pen.

†**b.** *absol.* or quasi-*sb.* A monster. *Obs.*

c 1400 *Destr. Troy* 934 He laid on þat loodly, lettyd he noght, With dynttes full dregh, till he to dethe paste.

loathly ('ləʊðlɪ), *adv.* Forms: see loath *a.* and -ly[2]. [OE. *lâðlíce*, f. *láð* loath *a.* + *-líce* -ly[2].]

†**1.** In a manner to cause loathing; foully, hideously, dreadfully, shockingly. *Obs.*

a 1000 *Boeth. Metr.* xxvi. 83 (Sedgefield) 196 þa ðe leon wæron on gunnon laðlice yrrenga ryn. *c* 1205 Lay. 7935 Laðliche [*c* 1275 loþliche] heo feohten. *a* 1240 *Lofsong* in *Cott. Hom.* 205 Ich am lodliche i-hurt ine licame and ine soule. *a* 1300 *Cursor M.* 7358 þe find..laithli sal his licam dight. *c* 1320 *Cast. Love* 1136 He..lodliche was bi-lad al for vre sake. *c* 1475 *Rauf Coilȝear* 139 Of ilk airt of the Eist sa laithly it laid. 1483 Caxton *Gold. Leg.* 431 b/1 A cytyzen of parys..lothely sweryng had blasphemyed Jhesu cryste. 1600 Fairfax *Tasso* v. xxxii, With dust and blood his locks were loathly dight.

†**b.** With abhorrence or detestation. *Obs.*

13.. *E.E. Allit. P.* B. 1090 Alle þat longed to luþer ful lodly he hated. 1605 Shaks. *Lear* ii. i. 51 Seeing how lothly opposite I stood To his vnnaturall purpose.

2. Reluctantly, unwillingly. Now *rare.*

1547 J. Harrison *Exhort. Scottes* H vij b, In punishyng you, he did it lothely. 1556 J. Heywood *Spider & F.* xciii. 14 Lothlie he losed his arms, and leete him go. 1624 *Trag. Nero* iv. vi. in Bullen *O. Pl.* I. 78 Thou loathly this imprisoning flesh putst on. 1641 Sanderson *Serm.* (1681) II. 11, I know how lothly men are induced to suspect themselves to be in an error. 1811 Scott *Don Roderick* ii. v, For Roderick told of many a hidden thing Such as are lothly utter'd to the air. 1845 T. W. Coit *Puritanism* 408 Mr. Knowles loathly admits, that [etc.]. 1880 Mrs. C. Reade *Brown Hand & White* III. iv. 102 The child goes, but loathly, and crying that she will come to see them very soon.

Hence †**'loathlihead** *rare*[−1], loathsomeness.

1340 *Ayenb.* 203 þet is apert tokne þet..þe lodlichede byeþ ine þi herte.

†**'loathly**, *v. Obs.* In 3 **loðlichen**, 6 *Sc.* **laithly**. [f. loathly *a.*] **a.** *trans.* To make loathly or repulsive; to disfigure. **b.** To look upon as loathly; to loathe.

a 1225 *Ancr. R.* 256 Vor a lute clut mei lodlichen swuðe a muchel ihol peche. 1508 Dunbar *Tua Mariit Wemen* 381, I him forleit as a lad, and lathlyit him mekle.

loathness ('ləʊθnɪs), *a.* [f. loath *a.* + -ness.] The quality or condition of being loath.

†**1.** In various senses of loath *a.*: Harmfulness, enmity; unpleasantness. *Obs.*

c 1175 *Lamb. Hom.* 95 He wes dreihninde on þissere worlde..mid nane laðnesse and mid sibsumnesse. *a* 1225 *Ancr. R.* 310 He..haueð..loðnesse of ham alle, as Ieremie witneð: *Omnes amici ejus spreverunt eam.* *c* 1400 *Destr. Troy* 2949 It ledis vnto laithnes and vnlefe werkes. 1529 More *Dyaloge* iii. Wks. 1229/1 You tel me the lothnes of the losse, and the comfort of the keeping.

2. Reluctance; disinclination. Const. *to* with *inf.*; rarely *of* with *gerund.*

a 1300 *Cursor M.* 26589 And tell þi sins ilkan bi nam, for lathnes leue þou noght, ne scam. *c* 1528 Hen. VIII in Fiddes *Wolsey* (1726) ii. 140 The other shall declare and shew the loathnes that is in him..to be displeased. 1529 Sir T. More *Suppl. Souls* ii. Wks. 316/2 Diuers doctours allege diuers causes of his heauines and lothnes at yͭ time to depart & die. 1610 Shaks. *Temp.* ii. i. 130 The faire soule her selfe Waigh'd betweene loathnesse and obedience. 1616 Hayward *Sanct. Troub. Soul* i. i. (1620) 16 How doth my resolution sticke betweene loathnesse and necessitie? 1637–50 Row *Hist. Kirk* (1842) 545 A loathnes of running to close without clearnes. 1709 Strype *Ann. Ref.* I. li. 547 The negligence or lothness of the Bishop, to prosecute them.

loathsome ('ləʊðsəm), *a.* Forms: 4 **loþsom**, 4–5 **loothsom**, 4, 6–7 *Sc.* and *north.* **laithsum**, **-some**, 5 **lathesum**, **loth(e)sum**, 6–9 **loth(e)som(e**, 7–8 **loathsom**, 6– **loathsome**. [f. loath *sb.* + -some; = OHG. *leidsam.*]

1. Exciting disgust or loathing. (Now always with emotional implication.) **a.** In physical sense: Exciting nausea; offensive to the senses; noisome, sickening.

a 1300–1400 *Cursor M.* 23229 (Gött) Fell dragons and tadis bath..ful laithsum [*Cott.* wlatsum] on to here and se ..þar sal be. 1398 Trevisa *Barth. De P.R.* v. xvi. (1495) 121 Yf the teeth were bare they were loathsom and nat fayr. *c* 1460 *Pol. Rel. & L. Poems* 172 Man is but lothesum eorthe and claye. 1561 Hoby tr. *Castiglione's Courtyer* iv. (1577) S viij, Unwittinglye otherwhile eate some lothesome and abhorring meate. 1602 Shaks. *Ham.* i. v. 72 A most instant Tetter bak'd about, Most Lazar-like, with vile and loathsome crust, All my smooth Body. 1671 Milton *Samson* 480 Thou must not..Lie in this miserable loathsom plight Neglected. 1703 Maundrell *Journ. Jerus.* (1732) and let. after p. 145 A Gouty scrofulous Substance, very loathsom to look upon. 1748 *Anson's Voy.* iii. viii. 383 The stench of the hold [was] loathsome beyond all conception. 1847 Grote *Greece* (1862) III. xxvii. 42 She died shortly of a loathsome disease. 1849 Macaulay *Hist. Eng.* iv. I. 432 A loathsome volatile salt, extracted from human skulls, was forced into his mouth.

Comb. 1897 *Allbutt's Syst. Med.* II. 671 Covered from head to foot with loathsome-smelling scabs.

b. In a moral sense: Hateful, distasteful, odious, repulsive, shocking.

c 1440 Hylton *Scala Perf.* (W. de W. 1494) i. lxiii, Wyth thy pryde thou defowlest all thy good dedes and makyth hem loothsom in the syghte of thy lorde. 1567 *Gude & Godlie Ball.* (S.T.S.) 218 How lusting lufe, that laithsum sin, The oppin eyis of sum do blind. 1579 Lyly *Euphues* (Arb.) 112 If Lawe seeme loathsome unto thee, searche the secrets of Physicke. 1666 Bunyan *Grace Ab.* ¶84, I was more loathsome in my own Eyes than was a Toad. 1748 Hume *Ess. Mor. & Polit.* xix. 208 The Mind, unexercis'd, finds every Delight insipid and loathsome. 1872 Holland *Marb. Proph.* 93 Death can but loose a loathsome bond. 1874 L. Stephen *Hours in Library* (1892) I. vii. 259 He was free from the errors which make some of Rousseau's confessions loathsome.

†**2.** Affected with loathing or disgust; disgusted. Const. *of. Obs.*

1577 Harrison *England* iii. xv. [ix.] (1877) ii. 61 We, as lothsome of this abundance, or not liking of the plentie. 1579 Twyne *Phisicke agst. Fort.* i. xxiv. 34 a, Thou mayest refresh thy loathsome and weeried minde.

loathsomely ('ləʊðsəmlɪ), *adv.* [f. prec. + -ly[2].] In a loathsome manner.

1. In a manner to excite loathing; disgustingly, foully, repulsively, shockingly.

a 1425 *Cursor M.* 15825 (Trin.) þei..lugged him loþsumly ouer hilles dale & slowȝe. 1547–64 Bauldwin *Mor. Philos.* (Palfr.) 48 No dead carrion so loathsomely stincketh in the nose of any earthly man, as [etc.]. 1577 Dee *Relat. Spir.* i. (1659) 209 Those that are..lothsomely apparelled, may knock long before they enter. 1652 Gaule *Magastrom.* 371 Alexander..rotted lothsomely. 1711 Shaftesb. *Charac.* III. 174 Favourites must be now observ'd, little Engines of Power attended on, and loathsomly caress'd. 1868 Ruskin *Time & Tide* vi. (1891) 35 Our English masks are only stupidly and loathsomely ugly.

†**2.** With reluctance or hesitation, reluctantly.

1561 T. Norton *Calvin's Inst.* iv. 106 Nothing ought to be lothesomely receiued, which [etc.].

loathsomeness ('ləʊðsəmnɪs). [f. loathsome + -ness.]

1. The quality or condition of being loathsome, whether in a physical or moral sense.

a 1300 *Cursor M.* 1641 Al lathsumnes o wikkudhede has filed þe werld on lenth and brede. *a* 1340 Hampole *Psalter* cii. 2 Delite of syn be noght in thi sight: bot lathsumnes of syn. *a* 1529 Skelton *Dk. Albany* Wks. (Dyce) II. 72 Euer to remayne..In lousy lothsumnesse. 1654 T. Hall *(title)* The Loathsomnesse of Long Haire. 1756–7 tr. *Keysler's Trav.* (1760) IV. 373 To observe the sudden change of vain beauty into loathsomeness. 1857–8 Sears *Athan.* xvi. 135 The.. utter loathsomeness of those crimes. 1883 *Contemp. Rev.* Dec. 800 If there is beauty, it is mated with hideousness and loathsomeness.

b. quasi-*concr.* Something loathsome, a loathsome object.

1549 Coverdale, etc. *Erasm. Par. Peter* 7 Those sacrifices of Moses are now all ready growen in to a lothesomenes. 1565 Jewel *Repl. Harding* (1611) 312 For auoiding of putrefaction, or some other lothsomnesse. 1656 Earl Monm. tr. *Boccalini's Advts. fr. Parnass.* i. xiii. (1674) 16 Those enormous and hatefull loathsomnesses, which do so much nauseate good mens eyes. 1867 Bushnell in *Hours at Home* Nov. 6 The very thing now wanted..is a good supply of disfigurements,..loathsomenesses, objects of aversion and disgust.

†**2.** A feeling of loathing, disgust, or repugnance; aversion, dislike, reluctance; nausea. *Obs.*

c 1425 *St. Mary of Oignies* ii. ii. in *Anglia* VIII. 154/28 She receyued no worldes ioye..but forsoke hem wiþ a loþsumnes of herte. 1533 Elyot *Cast. Helthe* (1541) 28 b, Southistel..causeth fastidiousnes or lothsomnesse of the stomake. 1536 Cecil in Froude *Hist. Eng.* (1881) VII. 450 The loathsomeness of the Queen's Majesty to consent thereto. 1560 Daus tr. *Sleidane's Comm.* 190 Neyther that they runne away from them, or fordo them selues for impatientnes and lothsomenes of that estate [slavery]. 1620 Venner *Via Recta* (1650) 132 The sweet Oranges..cause lothsomnesse in the stomack. 1635 Pagitt *Christianogr.* iii. (1636) 108 Loathsomenesse to drinke after others. 1807 E. S. Barrett *Rising Sun* II. 103 We must now, unwillingly, and with a degree of loathsomeness, proceed to give some few examples of it. 1808 Southey *Lett.* (1856) II. 104 No sentiment can be excited except of hatred and disgust, which approaches to loathsomeness.

loathy ('ləʊðɪ), *a. arch.* Also 5–6 **lothy**. [f. loath *sb.* + -y.] = loathsome.

1481 Caxton *Reynard* (Arb.) 16 Neuer man sawe fowller ne lothyer beest. *a* 1529 Skelton *Agst. Garnesche* 29 Wks. (Dyce) I. 117 Your wynde schakyn shankkes, your longe lothy legges. 1587 Golding *De Mornay* xi. (1617) 170 Things which seem most filthy and lothy. 1840 Browning *Sordello* iv. 23 Docks, quitchgrass, loathy mallows no man plants. 1855 Kingsley *Westw. Ho!* xx. (1881) II. 127 The loathy floor of liquid mud lay bare beneath the mangrove forest.

loave, obs. f. lave *sb.*[1] and *a.*; var. love *v.*[2] *Obs.*

loaved, **loaving**: see loafed, loafing *vbl. sb.*[1]

loaver, variant of lower, hire.

†**lob**, *sb.*[1] *Obs.* [OE. *lobbe* wk. fem.; cf. *loppe*, lop *sb.*] A spider.

c 1000 *Lamb. Ps.* lxxxix. 10 (Bosw.) Ure gær swa swa lobbe [Vulg. *sicut aranea*] oððe rynge beoþ asmeade. *a* 1325 *Prose Psalter* xxxviii. 15 þou madest his soule to stumblen as a lob [Vulg. *sicut araneam*]. *Ibid.* lxxxix. 10 Our yeres shal þenchen as þe lob.

lob (lɒb), *sb.*[2] Also 6–7 **lobbe**, 9 **lobb**. [Perh. onomatopœic in origin. Several Teut. words of similar sound express the general notion of something heavy, clumsy, or loosely pendent: cf. e.g. EFris. *lob(be* hanging lump of flesh, MLG. and early mod.Du. *lobbe*, *lubbe* (mod.Du. *lob*, *lubbe*) hanging lip, also ruffle, hanging sleeve, Da. *lobbes* clown, bumpkin, Norw. *lubb*, *lubba* short stout person.]

†**1.** The pollack. *Obs.* (Cf. lob-keeling.)

1357 *Act 31 Edw. III*, Stat. 3 c. 2 Les trois sortz de lob, lyng, & cod. 1607 Cowell *Interpr.*, *Lobbe* is a great kind of north sea fish. 1727 in Bailey vol. II. 1769 Pennant *Zool.* III. 161.

2. A country bumpkin: a clown, lout. Now *dial.*

1533 *Image Ypocr.* 1645 To prove oure prelates goddes And lay men very lobbes. *Ibid.* 2275 Frier bib, ffrier bob, ffrier lib, ffrier lob. 1550 Lever *Serm.* (Arb.) 65 The rude

lobbes of the countrey, whiche be to symple to paynte a lye. **1590** SHAKS. *Mids. N.* II. i. 16 Farewell thou Lob of spirits, Ile be gon. **1603** DEKKER *Wonderfull Yeare* D iij, The sight of a flat-cap was dreadfull to a Lob. **1609** HOLLAND *Amm. Marcell.* XVII. ix. 91 One that, under the shew of wisedome and learning, was a very lob and foole. **1658** CLEVELAND *Rustick Rampant* Wks. (1687) 456 William Greyncob an Hind.. This Lob too was made principal Prolocutor. **1694** MOTTEUX *Rabelais* IV. xlvii, The Country Lob trudg'd home very much concern'd. **1854** W. GASKELL *Lectures Dial.* 13 We sometimes hear a heavy clumsy man called 'a great lob of a felley'.

3. Something pendulous, e.g. the wattles of a fowl, hanging blossoms or ornaments, etc. *rare.*

1688 R. HOLME *Armoury* II. 245/2 The Cock of the Mountain.. hath.. about the cheeks two red fleshy lobs or gills. **1876** BESANT & RICE *Gold. Butterfly* (1877) 3 Immense steel spurs, inlaid with silver filigree, and furnished with 'lobs' attached to them.

4. A lump, a large piece: a nugget (of gold); a 'lump' (of money). Chiefly *dial.*

1825–80 JAMIESON, *Lub*, a thing heavy and unwieldy. *Dumfr.* **1843** W. CARLETON *Traits Irish Peasantry* I. 8 Any how we'll gain a lob by it, I'm thinking. **1847** HALLIWELL, *Lob*.. (2) A very large lump. *Linc.* **1863** *Once a week* III. 535 (Farmer) He must have a regular lob of gold stowed away somewhere. **1884** ROGERS *New Rush* I. 5 Imagine future 'lobs' of which they share.

5. *Brewing.* A thick mixture (see quot.).

For the sense cf. LOBLOLLY, LOBSCOUSE.

1839 URE *Dict. Arts* 103 When the wort is discharged into the gyle-tun, it must receive its dose of yeast, which has been previously mixed with a quantity of wort, and left in a warm place till it has begun to ferment. This mixture, called *lobb*, is then to be put into the tun, and stirred well through the mass.

6. *attrib.* and *Comb.*, as ***lob-like*** adj. and adv.; †**lob-coat** = LOBCOCK; **lob grass** *dial.*, *Bromus mollis*; **lob-tailing** *vbl. sb.* and *ppl. a.* (see quots.); so **lob-tail** *v. intr.*

1604 *Wit of a Woman* (Comedy) G 3 b, My bush and my pot, cares not a groate, for such a *lob-coate, farewell. **1756** LISLE *Observ. Husb.* (1757) 72 The grass which country-people call the hooded-grass, or *lob-grass, is apparently of but little value. **1605** SYLVESTER *Du Bartas* II. iii. I. *Abraham* 589 He yawns; and leaning-on His (*Lob-like) elbow hears This Message don. **1611** COTGR., *Enlourdi*, growne dull, sotish, lumpish, heauie-headed, lob-like. **1933** B. WILLOUGHBY *Alaskans All* 134 Nearby, a third [whale] would pop up and '*lob-tail'—that is stand on its head with its tail out flaying the sea with thundering blows that sent clouds of spray in every direction. **1851** H. MELVILLE *Moby Dick* II. xliv. 298 Five great motions are peculiar to it [*sc.* the tail of a whale]... Fourth, in *lob-tailing. **1867** SMYTH *Sailor's Word-bk.*, *Lob-tailing*, the act of the sperm whale in violently beating the water with its tail. **1899** F. T. BULLEN *Idylls Sea* xii. 75 It sounded.. as if an extra large whale were 'lob-tailing'—i.e. poised in the water head downwards, and striking deliberate blows upon its surface with his mighty flukes. **1937** *Discovery* Oct. 310/1 In 'lobtailing', it [*sc.* the cachalot] stands on its head with its tail some thirty feet out of the sea.

7. *attrib.* passing into *adj.* Rustic; clownish, loutish; clumsy. Also *appos.* as quasi-proper name.

1508 DUNBAR *Tua Mariit Wemen* 387, I wes laith to be loppin with sic a lob avoir. **1593** 'P. FOULFACE' *Bacchus Bountie* A 4, The Beziladistes, those deuout doctors of Lob libers canne. **1603** H. CROSSE *Vertues Commw.* (1878) 82 It is a world of sport to heare how some such clouting beetles rowle in their loblogicke. **1613** BEAUM. & FL. *Knt. Burning Pestle* III. iv, There's a pretty tale of a Witch,.. that had a Giant to her sonne, that was cal'd Lob-lie-by-the-fire. **1653** URQUHART *Rabelais* I. xxv. 116 Grouthead gnat-snappers, lob-dotterels, gaping changelings [etc.]. **1873** MRS. J. H. EWING *Lob Lie-by-the-Fire* Introd. 3 Lob Lie-by-the-fire—the Lubber-fiend, as Milton calls him—is a rough kind of Brownie or House Elf. **1879** G. MEREDITH *Egoist* I. Prelude 4 They lump along like the old lob-legs of Dobbin the horse.

lob (lɒb), *sb.*[3] *Mining.* Also lobb. *pl.* Steps in a mine. Also applied to an irregular vein of ore resembling a flight of steps.

1681 HOUGHTON *Compl. Miner* (E.D.S.), *Lobs*, steps that ascend or descend within the mines, as stairs up to and down from a chamber. **1747** HOOSON *Miner's Dict.* M j b, When we drive Dipping downwards, we go by Stairs or Lobbs so as the diping requires. **1769** *Nat. Hist.* in *Ann. Reg.* 99/1 The descent is about 160 yards, through different lodgments, by ladders, lobs, and cross-pieces of timber let into the rock. **1851** TAPPING *Manlove's Lead Mines* Gloss. 28 Also when the ore in a vein does not go down perpendicularly, but only a few yards at once, then level for a yard or two, and then sets down again, such veins are called *lobbs*.

lob (lɒb), *sb.*[4] *Thieves' slang.* Also lobb. A box; a till.

1718 C. HIGGIN *True Discov.* 15 (Farmer) A wedge lobb, alias gold or silver snuff-box. **1753** *Discov. John Poulter* (ed. 2) 39 A Lobb full of Glibbs, a Box full of Ribbons. **1812** J. H. VAUX *Flash Dict.*, *Lob*, a till or money-drawer. **1868** *Temple Bar* XXIV. 537 'Lob' means the till.

b. *Comb.*: **lob-crawler**, a till-thief; **lob-crawling, -sneaking**, robbing tills.

1887 J. W. HORSLEY *Jottings from Jail* 25 Poor old Jim, the *lob crawler, fell from Racker and got pinched. **1894** A. MORRISON *Tales Mean Streets* 259 Scuddy made a comfortable living in the several branches of *lob-crawling and peter claiming. **1868** *Temple Bar* XXIV. 537 Stealing the till and opening the safe is what we call '*lob-sneaking' and 'Peter-screwing'.

lob (lɒb), *sb.*[5] *Games.* [f. LOB *v.*]

1. *Cricket.* A slow underhand ball.

1851 J. PYCROFT *Cricket Field* ix. 178 Practise high lobs—a most useful variety of ball. **1875** *Times* 29 June 12/1 At 67 Mr. Greenfield tried three overs of lobs. **1882** *Daily Tel.* 20 May, Humphreys tried his lobs once more, and got rid of Garrett almost directly. **1891** W. G. GRACE *Cricket* 250 An article on bowling would not be complete without some reference to slow underhand, or, to use the familiar word, 'lobs'.

attrib. **1865** F. LILLYWHITE *Guide to Cricketers* 59 A good lob-bowler and excellent long-stop. **1871** 'THOMSONBY' *Cricketers in Council* 40 The best lob bowlers by a mere turn of the wrist impart an enormous amount of twist to the ball. *Ibid.*, 'Lob' bowling is, we believe, rather undervalued at the present day. **1883** *Standard* 3 Aug. 6/5 Preston made a very poor show.. against the lob bowling of Mr. Walker. **1888** STEEL & LYTTELTON *Cricket* (Badm. Libr.) 160 Every batsman.. knows the danger of playing wildly at under-hand 'lobs'... Occasional mistakes are made, no doubt, when an unexpected lob bowler appears.

2. *Lawn-tennis.* (See quot.) Also *attrib.* in ***lob-volley***.

1890 HEATHCOTE *Tennis* (Badm. Libr.) 238 When a lob is about to drop near the base-line it is now generally returned either by the 'lob-volley'.., which is a defensive stroke, or the player runs back and returns it again with a lob. *Ibid.* 242 The 'lob' is a ball tossed high in the air, and, if possible, over the opponent's head... As a 'toss' it was known and tolerated long before it was condemned as a 'lob'. *Ibid.* 245 The service, the stroke off the ground, the volley, the half-volley, and the lob.

lob (lɒb), *v.* Inflected **lobbed** (lɒbd), **lobbing**. [f. LOB *sb.*[2]]

†**1.** *intr.* To behave like a 'lob' or lout. *Obs.*

1596 J. SMYTH in *Lett. Lit. Men* (Camden) 92 There is no man that doth well knowe mee, that will beeleeve that I would (if I had not been distempered by surfett and drinke) ryde lobbinge and dawinge to rayle at your Lordship.

2. *trans.* To cause or allow to hang heavily; to droop. ? *Obs.* exc. *slang.*

1599 SHAKS. *Hen. V*, IV. ii. 57 Their poore Iades Lob downe their heads, dropping the hides and hips. **1821** EGAN *Real Life in Lond.* I. 187 The dancing party.. were lobbing their lollys [= heads] on.. the table.

3. a. *intr.* To move heavily or clumsily; to walk *along* with a slow lumbering movement. Of a cabman: To 'crawl' or 'prowl' in search of a fare.

1819 PAUL BOBBIN *Sequel* 21 (E.D.D.) So off I lobb'd. **1843** *Blackw. Mag.* LIII. 81 Keeping a sharp look-out for any night cabman who may be 'lobbing', as the phrase is, off his stand. **1847** HALLIWELL s.v., *To lob along*, to walk loungingly. **1849** E. E. NAPIER *Excurs. S. Africa* II. 363 The lion.. may next be seen lobbing up some open grassy ascent. [**1865**: see LOBBING *vbl. sb.*] **1887** L. OLIPHANT *Episodes* 86 The enemy's shells came lobbing into it [the trench]. **1898** *Blackw. Mag.* Dec. 744/1 Our ponies.. lobbing and lurching through the heavy sand.

b. *to lob (in)*, to arrive. *Austral. slang.*

1916 C. J. DENNIS *Songs Sentimental Bloke* 56 'Twas at a beano where I lobs along To drown them memories o' fancied wrong. *Ibid.* 125 *To lob*, to arrive. **1934** *Bulletin* (Sydney) 12 Dec. 25/2 Scrubby lobs in one sundown while Old Dave is over with the storekeeper. **1950** K. S. PRICHARD *Winged Seeds* ii. 24 You never knew who'd lob into the camp. **1970** *Sunday Truth* (Brisbane) 5 July 30/5 When they had 15 pines on board, the farmer lobbed on the scene.

4. a. *trans.* To throw heavily or clumsily; to toss or bowl with a slow movement. In *Lawn-tennis*, to strike (a ball) well into the air so as to fall at the back of the opponent's court; also *absol.*

1847 HALLIWELL, *Lob.* (1) To throw gently. *Sussex*... (7) To cast or throw. *Durham.* **1880** MAITLAND in *Encycl. Brit.* XI. 313/2 Suppose.. that shell are being lobbed from behind a parapet at high angles into a work. **1884** *Mil. Engineering* (ed. 3) I. II. 70 Sandbags.. which are pulled down one by one, and.. lobbed over the others by hand. **1889** W. M. BROWNLEE *Lawn-Tennis* 141 If you can lob at a good pace just over his head, you may beat him altogether, and score. *Ibid.* 142 Sweet.. lobbed to him six balls in succession. **1891** R. KIPLING *Life's Handicap* 87 Martini-Henri carbines that would lob a bullet into an enemy's camp at one thousand yards.

b. To send (a player) a lobbed ball.

1921 A. W. MYERS *20 Yrs. Lawn Tennis* 135 Having discovered the wisdom of lobbing Barrett, Hackett.. allowed McLoughlin to kill anything smashable. **1928** *Daily Tel.* 5 June 17/1 As soon as one is certain of not being lobbed. **1972** D. DELMAN *Sudden Death* (1973) vi. 170 He lunges for the backhand volley... He is off balance, out of position, and I lob him wickedly.

5. *Brewing.* To add 'lob' (see LOB *sb.*[2] 5) to (wort).

1838 [see LOBBING *vbl. sb.*].

6. *Metallurgy.* (See quot.)

1875 KNIGHT *Dict. Mech.*, *Lobbing* (*Metallurgy*), breaking blocks of ore into pieces with the hammer, for assortment as to quality with such ores as copper, and for more effectual treatment in the preparatory roasting or calcining processes.

Hence **lobbed** *ppl. a.*

1883 *Pall Mall G.* 17 July 4/1 [Champion Lawn Tennis] A lobbed return with a twist.

lobar (ˈləʊbə(r)), *a.* [ad. mod.L. *lobār-is*, f. L. *lobus* LOBE: see -AR[1].] **a.** Pertaining to a lobe.

1856 in MAYNE *Expos. Lex.* **1889** *Syd. Soc. Lex.*, *Lobar arteries*, the arteries which are distributed to the lobes of the brain. *Lobar fissures*, the sulci between the cerebral and cerebellar lobes.

b. *spec.* in *Path.* Applied to an acute form of pneumonia lasting about nine days, most commonly caused by pneumococcal infection, and marked by fever, pains in the chest, coughing, and bloodstained sputum, and by inflammation concentrated in one lobe of the lung.

1858 J. COPLAND *Dict. Pract. Med.* II. 761/2 The French pathologists, and after them some recent English writers, have distinguished the disease [*sc.* pneumonia] into lobar, lobular, and vesicular... Of these the lobar is the most common. **1873** T. H. GREEN *Introd. Pathol.* 287 This form of pneumonia almost invariably affects an extensive portion of the lung, hence the term 'lobar' which is applied to it. **1876** J. S. BRISTOWE *Treat. Theory & Pract. Med.* iii. 406 Lobar pneumonia commences with hyperæmia of the small vessels which are distributed in the walls of the air-cells and bronchial passages. **1961** R. D. BAKER *Essent. Path.* ix. 151 There may be lobar pneumonia in one lung and lobular in another. Lobar pneumonia has this difference, that almost all cases are caused by the pneumococcus, whereas many cases of lobular pneumonia are caused by other bacteria, such as streptococci or staphylococci. **1966** WRIGHT & SYMMERS *Systemic Path.* I. x. 368/2 In most cases the onset of lobar pneumonia is abrupt.

lobate (ˈləʊbeɪt), *a.* [ad. mod.L. *lobātus*, f. L. *lobus* LOBE: see -ATE[2].] Having or characterized by lobes, lobed.

1760 J. LEE *Introd. Bot.* III. v. (1765) 178 *Lobate, lobed*; when they are divided to the Middle into Parts that stand wide from each other, and have their Margins convex. **1785** MARTYN *Rousseau's Bot.* xxi. (1794) 290 The leaves.. so deeply serrate as to be almost lobate. **1816** W. SMITH *Strata Ident.* 23 The lobate Oyster, or Gryphus. **1871** W. A. LEIGHTON *Lichen-flora* 14 Thallus.. crustaceous, granulose or lobate. **1872** OLIVER *Elem. Bot.* II. 140 Sweet Mignonette. An herbaceous (garden) annual, with alternate entire or lobate exstipulate leaves. **1872** NICHOLSON *Palæont.* 323 Fins not lobate. **1875** HUXLEY in *Encycl. Brit.* I. 132/1 The oral and aboral pole, or the oral only, bear lobate appendages. **1890** COUES *Field & Gen. Ornithol.* II. 195 In the lobate foot, a paddle results not from connecting webs, but from a series of lobes or flaps along the sides of the individual toes. **1919** D. W. JOHNSON *Shore Processes* iv. 188 Where the current of a river's distributaries strongly predominate[s] over shore currents and wave attack, the delta shoreline will be of the 'lobate' type, as in the case of the Mississippi delta. **1933** SCHUCHERT & DUNBAR *Textbk. Geol.* (ed. 3) xix. 430 When the ice later retreated northward over the Great Lakes region, its front became deeply lobate. **1957** G. E. HUTCHINSON *Treat. Limnol.* I. i. 85 Genuine morainic dams are probably commoner in regions of moderate preglacial relief that has been covered by continental ice sheets or by large lobate glaciers. **1967** *New Scientist* 2 Feb. 263/2 The hills in the north of the ring define lobate shapes in a manner highly reminiscent of viscous lava flows on Earth.

Hence ˈ**lobately** *adv.*, so as to form lobes.

1846 DANA *Zooph.* (1848) 616 Substipitate, lobately divided.

lobated (ˈləʊbeɪtɪd), *a. Nat. Hist.* [f. as LOBATE + -ED[1].] = LOBATE.

1703 PETIVER in *Phil. Trans.* XXIII. 1425 The twigs and footstalks are Thorny, the Leaves single, sometimes lobated. **1775** JENKINSON *Brit. Plants* Gloss. **1862** C. A. JOHNS *Brit. Birds* (1874) p. xxiv, Toes three or four, more or less connected by a membrane at the base, sometimes lobated.

lobation (ləʊˈbeɪʃən). [f. LOBATE: see -ATION.] The formation of lobes; the condition of being lobate.

1840 BLYTH, etc. *Cuvier's Anim. Kingd.* (1849) 246 The Phalaropes which it [*sc.* the Lobefoot] resembles in the lobation of its toes. **1846** DANA *Zooph.* (1848) 647 The lobations of an oak-leaf. **1880** GRAY *Struct. Bot.* III. iv. 98 Lobation or segmentation. **1889** *Nature* 3 Oct. 558 Suggestions are made upon the subject of progressive lobation [in ice-formations]. **1890** COUES *Field & Gen. Ornithol.* II. 190 This lobation of the hallux is seen.. in all truly lobe-footed birds.

lobato- (ləʊˈbeɪtəʊ), taken as comb. form of LOBATE in the sense 'lobate and..', as ***lobato-digitate, -foliaceous, -ramose***, etc.

1846 DANA *Zooph.* (1848) 618 Branches much compressed, very broad,.. lobato-digitate. *Ibid.* 647 Flabellate and lobato-foliaceous. *Ibid.* 496 Branchlets angular, irregular, lobato-ramulose. **1871** W. A. LEIGHTON *Lichen-flora* 21 Lobato-divided or subradiate. *Ibid.* 26 Lobato-partite at the apex. **1889** *Syd. Soc. Lex.*, *Lobato-sinuate*, applied to a lobate leaf which has curved sinuations between the lobes.

lobb: see LOB.

lobber, obs. f. LUBBER.

†**lobbet.** *Obs. rare*[−1]. [? For *lobet, f. LOBE + -ET[1].] A lobe (of the liver).

1662 J. CHANDLER *Van Helmont's Oriat.* 216 The heart of a Pigeon sits in the four Lobbets of the hollow of his Liver.

lobbing (ˈlɒbɪŋ), *vbl. sb.* [f. LOB *v.* + -ING[1].] The action of the vb. LOB, in various senses.

1824 MISS MITFORD *Village* Ser. I. 160 Samuel Long is a slow bowler, George Simmons a fast one, and the change from Long's lobbing to Simmons's fast balls posed them completely. **1838** T. THOMSON *Chem. Org. Bodies* 1019 The distillers make the specific gravity of their wort as high as from 1·084 to 1·110.. by lobbing, that is, by preparing a strong infusion of the flour of malt, or of barley, and malt, and hot water, and adding this almost saturated solution to the wort, till it has acquired the requisite strength. **1851** PYCROFT *Cricket Field* ix. 179 The old-fashioned underhand lobbing. **1865** *Irish Times* 18 Sept., A number of car drivers were prosecuted for 'lobbing'. **1875** [see LOB *v.* 6]. **1889** W. M. BROWNLEE *Lawn-Tennis* 140 Lobbing has caused more fits of temper than any stroke in the game. *Ibid.*, I had omitted to give him full credit for his lobbing powers.

'lobbing, *ppl. a.* [f. LOB *v.* + -ING².] That lobs (in various senses).

1840 E. E. NAPIER *Scenes and Sports For. Lands* I. ii. 26 The gaunt wolf, whom thou hast before now forced to drop his long lobbing pace, and put his best foot foremost. **1851** PYCROFT *Cricket Field* xi. 223 A lobbing bowler. **1860** RUSSELL *Diary India* I. xvii. 268 Some wounds from lobbing round-shot. **1891** R. WEIR *Riding* (Badm. Libr.) iv. 105 There are.. plenty of horses that from bad riding get into a loose lobbing canter behind the hand.

†**'lobbish,** *a. Obs.* [f. LOB *sb.*² + -ISH.] Characteristic of a 'lob' or rustic: clownish.

1567 *Triall Treas.* (1850) 10 That loute of lobbishe kinde. **1580** HOLLYBAND *Treas. Fr. Tong, Flac*,.. a great lobbish knaue. *a* **1586** SIDNEY *Arcadia* v. (1622) 450 Their lobbish guard (who all night had kept themselues awake, with prating how valiant deeds they had done when they ran away).

lobby ('lɒbɪ), *sb.* [ad. med.L. *lobium* or *lobia*: see LODGE *sb.*

From quot. 1553 it would appear that the word came into Eng. as a monastic term; hence there is no improbability in supposing the med.L. word to be the immediate source.]

†**1.** ? A covered walk, cloister (in a monastery).

1553 BECON *Reliques of Rome* (1563) 53 Our Recluses neuer come out of their lobbeis, sincke or swimme the people.

2. a. A passage or corridor connected with one or more apartments in a building, or attached to a large hall, theatre, or the like; often used as a waiting-place or ante-room.

1593 SHAKS. *2 Hen. VI*, IV. i. 61 How in our voyding Lobby has thou stood, And duly wayted for my comming forth? **1602** —— *Ham.* II. ii. 161 Sometimes He walkes foure houres together, heere in the Lobby. **1603** DRAYTON *Bar. Wars* VI. lxiii. 147 Thus in the Lobby as they freely were Charg'd on the suddaine by this armed trayne. **1607** SHAKS. *Timon* I. i. 80 All those which were his Fellowes but of late, .. Follow his strides, his Lobbies fill with tendance. **1609** B. JONSON *Sil. Wom.* IV. v, Doe you obserue this gallerie? or rather lobby, indeed? **1673** DRYDEN *Marr. à la Mode* III. i. Wks. 1883 IV. 303, I have such a *tendre* for the court, that I love it even from the drawing-room to the lobby. **1726** LEONI *Alberti's Archit.* I. 79/2 All.. shou'd be so joined together by the Roof and by Lobbies, that the Servants.. may not be called as it were out of another House. **1741** RICHARDSON *Pamela* (1824) I. xxviii. 45, I went into the lobby leading to the great hall, and dropt into the first chair. **1806–7** J. BERESFORD *Miseries Hum. Life* (1826) v. v, Fretting and freezing in the outer lobbies and at the street doors of the theatre. **1842** DICKENS *Amer. Notes* (1850) 148/1 The box lobby of a theatre. **1842** TENNYSON *Walking to Mail* 29 A jolly ghost, that shook The curtains, whined in lobbies, tapt at doors. **1863** GEO. ELIOT *Romola* lvi, Passing through a small lobby, they came to another open door. **1882** MISS BRADDON *Mt. Royal* III. i. 18 Christabel ran down to the lobby that opened into the stable yard.

b. *Naut.* (See quots.)

1815 *Falconer's Dict. Marine* (ed. Burney), *Lobby*, in a ship, is a small apartment adjoining the fore part of the bread room, and appropriated to the use of the surgeon. *c* **1850** *Rudim. Navig.* (Weale) 130 *Lobby.* A name sometimes given to an apartment close or next before the great cabin bulk-head.

c. *Agric.* A small enclosure for cattle adjoining the farm-yard.

1777 MARSHALL *Min. Agric.* II. Digest 21 *note, Farmery.* The Slip or Lobby is entered from the Common. **1819** in REES *Cycl.* s.v.

d. A watchman's 'box' in a factory.

1902 *Daily Chron.* 19 June 10/3 [A witness, watchman at Messrs. Doulton's, said:] He then sat in his 'lobby', seventy yards from the gate, till four.

3. *spec.* **a.** In the House of Commons, and other houses of legislature, a large entrance-hall or apartment open to the public, and chiefly serving for interviews between members and persons not belonging to the House; also (more fully ***division lobby***), one of the two corridors to which members retire to vote when the House divides.

1640 in Rushw. *Hist. Coll.* III. (1692) I. 1 The outward Room of the Commons House, called the Lobby,.. where the Cryer of the Chancery first made Proclamation in the King's name. **1648** C. WALKER *Hist. Independ.* I. 40 Refusing to let some Members passe out of the House, or come forth into the Lobby. **1648** NEDHAM *Mercurius Pragmat.* No. 39. 20 Dec., Col. Pride.. caused them [Members] to retreat into the Lobby, where they use to drink Ale and Tobacco. **1695** SHEFFIELD (Dk. Buckhm.) *Sp. Ho. Peers* 18 Apr. *Wks.* 1723 II. 123, I think the first time I propos'd it was here in the bishops lobby. **1772** *Ann. Reg.* 196/1 While I waited in the lobby during the debate. **1798** I. ALLEN *Hist. Vermont* 207 Colonel Allen went into the lobby, and began to write a memorial to the Legislature of New Hampshire. **1845** DISRAELI *Sybil* (1863) 171 The mysteries of the Lobby are only for the initiated. Three quarters of an hour after the division was called, the result was known to the exoteric world. **1865** BRIGHT *Sp. Canada* 23 Mar., If the hon. member divides, I shall go into the same lobby with him. **1887** *Spectator* 6 Aug. 1046/1 Considerations which chiefly determine the lobby into which Members of Parliament go.

b. *collect.* Those who frequent the lobbies of the House or who vote in a particular lobby; *U.S.* the persons who frequent the lobby of the house of legislature for the purpose of influencing its members in their official action; the body of lobbyists.

1808 *Deb. Congress U.S.* 2 Feb. (1852) II. 1536 If we move to Philadelphia we shall have a commanding lobby. **1859** BARTLETT *Dict. Amer.*, *Lobby*, the persons who frequent the lobby of a house of legislature. **1884** *Century Mag.* Mar. 655/1 The lobby and corruption are legitimate subjects for satire. **1888** BRYCE *Amer. Commw.* I. I. App. 555 'The Lobby' is the name given in America to persons, not being members of a legislature, who undertake to influence its members, and thereby to secure the passing of bills. **1892** *Pall Mall G.* 25 Mar. 2/3 The friends of the eight hours movement have great reason to be satisfied not only with the number but the quality of their lobby.

c. In extended use: a sectional interest (see INTEREST *sb.* 4), a business, cause, or principle supported by a group of people; the group of persons supporting such an interest.

1952 *Economist* 26 July 254/2 American.. interests have maintained their effective lobby against the project [*sc.* the St. Lawrence Seaway]. **1954** *Ibid.* 7 Aug. 425/1 M. Mendès-France.. has to face powerful colonial lobbies in parliament. **1958** *Listener* 21 Aug. 273/1 The United States Government, sensitive to the Jewish lobby.. backed the Jews. **1959** *Ibid.* 4 June 968/2 They even tackled the vested privileges and subsidies of the powerful alcohol lobby. **1971** *Daily Tel.* 9 Mar. 10/6 The anti-pollution lobby might claim that a spot of exaggeration is justified in such a cause.

4. *attrib.* and *Comb.*, as ***lobby correspondent, door, fire, -lounger, -lounging, room, stove, -table, -wicket***; **lobby chest** (see quot. 1803); **lobby man,** (*a*) *U.S.* (see quot. 1934); (*b*) a lobbyist; **lobby-member,** a lobbyist.

1803 T. SHERATON *Cabinet Dict.* 261 *Lobby chest, is a kind of half chest of drawers, adapted for the use of a small study, lobby, or small lodging room. **1970** *Canadian Antiques Collector* Nov. 15/2 All sorts of compact, changeling furniture.. lobby chests and Rudd's tables, [etc.]. **1886** *Pall Mall G.* 11 Oct. 8/2 When Mr. L. was *lobby correspondent he was invariably entrusted with the publication of any items of information which Mr. Chamberlain wished to be made known. **1768** *Chron.* in *Ann. Reg.* 151/2 The *lobby door of the King's bench prison. **1799** E. DU BOIS *Piece Family Biog.* III. 73 Chatting in high glee with one of the Cyprian corps before the *lobby fire. **1803** *Sporting Mag.* XXI. 145 The fashionable accoutrements of a *Lobby-Lounger. **1807** tr. *Goede's Trav.* II. 205 Lobby-loungers [at a theatre] make their appearance at 8, 9, and even 10 o'clock. **1894** *Westm. Gaz.* 9 May 1/2 *Lobby-lounging is substituted for fighting in the House. **1934** WEBSTER **Lobbyman*, one who works as attendant or porter, or does chores, in a lobby. **1958** *Times Lit. Suppl.* 21 Feb. 93/4 The high-pressure methods of the United States lobby-men, whose contacts and antecedents are open to inspection. **1848** CRAIG, **Lobby Member.* **1860** WORCESTER (citing GREELEY), *Lobby-member*, one who frequents the lobbies of a house of legislation in order to influence the action of the members. **1650** W. SAUNDERSON *Aul. Coquin.* 10 [He] put the King in a *Lobby Room, next the Chamber. **1842** J. AITON *Domest. Econ.* (1857) 76 Every manse should be kept dry and warm by the help of a *lobby stove. **1843** MRS. CARLYLE *Lett.* I. 190 She clanked it on the *lobby-table. **1876** T. HARDY *Ethelberta* (1890) 314 Her sister Picotee, who came in at the north door, closed the *lobby-wicket softly, and went lightly forward to the choir.

lobby ('lɒbɪ), *v.* orig. *U.S.* [f. LOBBY *sb.*]

1. *trans.* To influence (members of a house of legislature) in the exercise of their legislative functions by frequenting the lobby. Also, to procure the passing of (a measure) *through* Congress by means of such influence. Also *transf.*

1850 LYELL *2nd Visit U.S.* 28 A disappointed place-hunter, who had been lobbying the Houses of Legislature in vain for the whole session. **1862** J. SPENCE *Amer.* 37 How is it to be expected that a needy and ambitious lawyer.. having nothing but his three or four dollars a day.. shall not be open to the influences of those who lobby him? **1864** SALA *Daily Tel.* 29 Sept., The American Emigration Company was cleverly lobbied through Congress. **1868** *Nat. Encycl.* I. 619 *To lobby through*, is to get a bill adopted by such influence. **1887** GOLDW. SMITH in *Contemp. Rev.* July 11 The people, at all events, cannot be lobbied, wheedled, or bull-dozed. **1894** *Yorksh. Post* 4 Apr. 5 To send delegates to London.. to 'lobby' members for their respective constituencies with a view of obtaining the largest possible majority. **1955** *Times* 17 June 4/6 M.P.s were lobbied yesterday by delegates of the Uganda National Congress. **1971** P. GRESSWELL *Environment* 154 We can always lobby our councillors. **1974** *Times* 18 May 8 [Wilberforce] was lobbying heads of state.

2. *intr.* To frequent the lobby of a legislative assembly for the purpose of influencing members' votes; to solicit the votes of members.

1837 *Cleveland* (Ohio) *Herald* (Weekly ed.) 6 Oct. 2/6 Gen. Bronson.. spent a considerable portion of the last winter in Columbus, lobbying to procure the establishment of a Bank at Ohio City. **1855** in OGILVIE Suppl. *a* **1859** *N.Y. Tribune* (Bartlett), There is a quarrel in Philadelphia about Mr. W—'s appointments. Some of the Loco-focos have come out to lobby against him. **1864** E. SARGENT *Peculiar* III. 32 You were biased by the semi-loyal men who were lobbying for slavery. **1879** CATH. & C. TAIT *Mem.* 570 Bishop Williams of Connecticut, whose handsome figure may be seen at most times in the smoking-room, either lobbying or telling good stories. **1888** BRYCE *Amer. Commw.* II. III. lxxv. 619 Manufacturers who have had to lobby in connection with the tariff. **1898** *Westm. Gaz.* 27 Apr. 2/1 The large majority against this Westminster Bill was in part a protest against the way in which its promoters had lobbied in its interests. **1916** GALSWORTHY *Sheaf* iii. 55 Animals.. cannot lobby in the House of Commons, withdraw votes or commit outrages. **1962** *Listener* 20 Dec. 1041/1 In France the planners, being part of the civil service machine, have always been able to lobby from inside.

fig. **1876** LOWELL *Among my Bks.* Ser. II. 98 In the Greek epic, the gods are partisans,.. they lobby and log-roll for their candidates.

Hence **'lobbying** *vbl. sb.* and *ppl. a.*

1855 in OGILVIE Suppl. (s.v. *Lobby v.*) **1862** *Times* 6 Jan., 'Lobbying' as it is termed, is a well known institution at Washington. **1864** *Reader* No. 88. 297/1 *Lobbying*—this is,.. buying votes with money in the lobbies of the Hall of Congress. **1873** *Spectator* 22 Feb. 237/1 They will not knowingly choose the agents of the 'lobbying' Rings. **1888** BRYCE *Amer. Commw.* I. I. App. 556 What is known as lobbying by no means implies in all cases the use of money to affect legislation.

lobbyer ('lɒbɪə(r)). *U.S.* [f. LOBBY + -ER¹.] = LOBBYIST.

1862 J. SPENCE *Amer.* 76 The whole legislation was bribed .. even the lobbyers.. were admitted to a share of the spoil. **1873** *Spectator* 22 Feb. 237/1 There are lobbyers among us, too, but they refrain from putting temptation into that crude form.

lobby-gow (ˌlɒbɪ'gaʊ). *U.S. slang.* [Etym. unknown.] An errand-boy, messenger; a hanger-on, underling, esp. in an opium den or in the Chinese quarter of a town.

1906 I. SWIFT *Sketches of Gotham* 41 The lobbygows—the errand men of the Chinese—the whites, who execute commissions for them,.. saw and noted this Queen also. *a* **1911** D. G. PHILLIPS *Susan Lenox* (1917) II. x. 248 The lobbygows—men who live by lying in wait in the darkness to seize and rob the lonely, friendless fast woman. **1911** C. B. CHRYSLER *White Slavery* xi. 80 A 'lobbygow'—a Chinaman who acts as stool pigeon and informer for the police. **1911** G. BRONSON-HOWARD *Enemy to Society* ix. 295, I 'ain't gunna have her think Stevey's tied up with a bunch of lobby-gows. **1930** D. H. CLARKE *Louis Beretti* ii. 22 He ran errands for the girls, which made him a lobby-gow in the original meaning of the word. **1956** 'T. BETTS' *Across Board* xii. 177 He flung away fortunes in grubstakes to bums, heels, and lobby-gows.

lobbyist ('lɒbɪɪst). Chiefly *U.S.* [f. LOBBY + -IST.] One who frequents the lobbies of the House of Representatives in order to influence members in the exercise of their legislative functions; *occas.*, a journalist or other person who frequents the lobby of the House of Commons. Also, one who promotes a 'lobby' (see LOBBY *sb.* 3 c).

1863 *Cornh. Mag.* Jan. 96 A Representative listening to a lobbyist. **1888** BRYCE *Amer. Commw.* I. xiv. 213 The arrangements of the committee system have produced and sustain the class of professional 'lobbyists',.. who make it their business to 'see' members. **1894** *Sat. Rev.* 14 Apr. 383/2 The excited lobbyists who prattled last Saturday and Monday about a threatened defeat of Ministers. **1945** *Sun* (Baltimore) 23 Oct. 1/4 Hoffman identified Arundel in a House speech as a Washington 'lobbyist' who, he was informed, picked up the $75,000 check which paid for the festivities. **1961** *Encounter* Jan. 6/2 Skilful lobbyists with large funds and a powerful influence on the Algiers administration. **1971** *Nature* 4 June 278/2 The food industry lobbyists convincingly argue that the FDA is not responsibly handling the authority it already has. **1971** *Daily Tel.* 9 Nov. 15/6 Legislative provisions, which are promoted by a group of hysterical lobbyists who are spreading the fear of a world catastrophe because of chemical poisoning. **1974** 'R. B. DOMINIC' *Epitaph for Lobbyist* i. 6, I don't like high-powered lobbyists and their greasy favors.

So **'lobbyism,** the system of lobbying.

1883 *Pall Mall G.* 6 Sept. 3/2 American manners, American lobbyism, and American corruption.

lobcock ('lɒbkɒk). Now *dial.* [f. LOB *sb.*¹ + COCK.] A country bumpkin; a clown, lout, boor; a heavy dull creature; a blundering fool.

a **1553** UDALL *Roister D.* III. iii. (Arb.) 44 Ye are.. Such a lilburne, such a hoball, such a lobcocke. **1594** NASHE *Unfort. Trav.* 76 Seneca and Lucan were lobcockes to choose that death. **1611** COTGR., *Richereau*, a wealthie chuffe, rich lobcocke, well-lined boore. **1694** MOTTEUX *Rabelais* v. xix. (1737) 83 We are a silly sort of Grout-headed Lobcocks. *a* **1700** B. E. *Dict. Cant. Crew, Lobcock*, a heavy, dull Fellow. **1710–11** SWIFT *Lett.* (1767) III. 135 Again at the lobby, like a lobcock, of the house of commons, about your Irish yarn. **1719** D'URFEY *Pills* IV. 171 Ev'ry Lobcock hath his Wench. **1875** *Lancash. Gloss.*, *Lobcock*, a great, idle, young person. **1895** *E. Anglia Gloss.*, *Lobcock*, *Lubbock*, a lout, a lubber.

attrib. and *appos.* **1577** BRETON *Wks. Young Wit* (L.), I now must leave you all, alas, And live with some old lobcock ass! **1577–82** —— *Flourish Fancie* (Grosart) 15/2 The lobcoke Lust. **1606** *Wily Beguiled* (1623) C, Your lubberly legges would not carry your lobcocke body.

Hence †**lobcocked** *a.*, loutish, boorish.

1606 *Wily Beguiled* (1623) G, Such a great, long, large, lobcokt, loseld Lurden.

lobe (ləʊb). Also 6 lobbe. [ad. late L. *lobus*, a. Gr. λοβός lobe of the ear, of the liver, capsule or pod of leguminous plants:—pre-Hellenic **logw*- cogn. with **legw*- in L. *legūmen* pod, *legula* lobe of the ear. Cf. F. *lobe* (16th c.).]

1. A roundish projecting part, usually one of two or more similar portions into which an object is divided by a fissure. **a.** One of the divisions of the liver or lungs formed by the fissures.

[**1525** tr. *Jerome of Brunswick's Surg.* B iv/1 The longues hath .v. lobos or feders.] **1541** R. COPLAND *Guydon's Quest. Chirurg.* Hj b, Demaunde, Howe many lobbes hath the lunges? Answere .v. Thre in the ryght party and two in the lefte. **1578** BANISTER *Hist. Man* v. 75 These eminences are neither to be called Lobes, Fibres, nor wynges. **1646** SIR T. BROWNE *Pseud. Ep.* III. ii. 108 The lobes and severall parcells of the liver. **1667** N. FAIRFAX in *Phil. Trans.* II. 549 The left Lobe of the Lungs almost quite wasted. **1802** PALEY *Nat. Theol.* xi. (ed. 2) 202 The heart lies on the left side; a lobe of the lungs on the right. **1845** BUDD *Dis. Liver* 320 The liver was found of large size, and its left lobe reached over the stomach into the left hypochondrium. **1859** DARWIN *Orig. Spec.* xiv. (1873) 397 In snakes one lobe of the lungs is rudimentary.

b. The lower soft pendulous part of the external ear.

1719 QUINCY *Lex. Physico-Med.* (1722) 124/1 The external [ear] is.. divided into two Parts, of which the upper is called *Pinna*, or the Wing, the lower *Fibra*, or Lobe. **1807–26** S. COOPER *First Lines Surg.* (ed. 5) 393 An incision was begun over the condyloid process, opposite the lobe of the ear. **1844** DICKENS *Mart. Chuz.* ix, Pursued and brought back by the hair of his head, or the lobe of his ear. **1871** G. MEREDITH *H. Richmond* xli. (1889) 370 Her ear.. was of a very pretty shape, with a soft unpierced lobe.

c. *Bot.* † (*a*) A pod, capsule, or fruit-case. *Obs.* (*b*) A rounded projection or division of a leaf (sometimes, of other organs) of a plant.

1671 GREW *Anat. Plants* I. i. (1682) 3 Some very few Seeds are divided, not into two Lobes, but into more. **1681** —— *Musæum* II. v. 211 Of Berrys, Cones, Lobes, and some other Parts of Trees. *Ibid.* 212 A Long Flat Lobe... Its whole Cavity is filled up with one single Fruit. **1731** MILLER *Gard. Dict.* (1733) s.v., A Pea or Bean being committed to the Ground, is first found to cleave into two Parts, which are, as it were, two Leaves or Lobes of the Placenta. **1760** J. LEE *Introd. Bot.* II. viii. (1765) 90 Such as have the Lobes of the Corollæ bent obliquely to the Right. **1784** COWPER *Task* III. 522 Then rise the tender germs, upstarting quick And spreading wide their spongy lobes. **1845** LINDLEY *Sch. Bot.* iv. (1858) 26 c, Leaves divided palmately into many narrow lobes. **1861** BENTLEY *Man. Bot.* 570 Corolla monopetalous, and bearing.. as many stamens as it has lobes. **1875** DARWIN *Insectiv. Pl.* xiii. 292 The immersion of a leaf in pure water sometimes caused the lobes to close. **1880** GRAY *Struct. Bot.* III. iv. 98 Lobe is the common name of one of the parts of a simple blade, especially when there is only one order of incision.

d. One of the divisions of the brain. Also, in the cerebellum, a group of folia marked off by unusually deep fissures.

1672 WISEMAN *Wounds* I. 134 A maid servant was shot into the right side of the Sinciput.. she lived as long, viz. until the Lobe of the Brain was wrought out or corrupted. **1719** QUINCY *Lex. Physico-Med.* (1722) s.v., Bidloo uses the diminutive *Lobellus*, for [*sic*] little Lobe, for the four Processes of the Brain. **1831** R. KNOX *Cloquet's Anat.* 411 The middle lobes of the brain, separated from the posterior by a groove directed obliquely backwards. **1849** NOAD *Electricity* (ed. 3) 461 Of the four lobes of the brain, the fourth only is found to actuate the electric current; it is hence called the electric lobe. **1851** CARPENTER *Man. Phys.* (ed. 2) 558 That the Lobes of the Cerebellum are the parts specially concerned in the regulation of the muscular movements. **1872** HUXLEY *Physiol.* viii. 196 The olfactory lobes which.. form.. a part of the brain.

e. *Zool.* A rounded projection or part of an organ.

1826 KIRBY & SP. *Entomol.* III. 357 *Lobi* (the Lobes), the parts of the Maxilla above the Palpus. **1828** STARK *Elem. Nat. Hist.* I. 352 The Galley Wasp.. Two little lobes before the tympanum. **1843** YARRELL *Brit. Birds* III. 42 The vignette represents the structure of the foot.. one lobe on each side each of the phalanges. **1846** PATTERSON *Zool.* 34 The lobes of the mouth become more or less distended. **1849** MURCHISON *Siluria* xiii. 342 The upper lobe of the tail. **1893** NEWTON *Dict. Birds* 382 Their [*sc.* grebes'] feet.. have the tarsi flattened and elongated toes furnished with broad lobes of skin.

f. The larger or most important and projecting part of a cam-wheel.

1855 OGILVIE Suppl. s.v., The lobe of a cam-wheel is the portion of curve between two minor distances from the centre of rotation, and including a major distance between them. If the wheel has *n* lobes, then $2\pi/n$ is the lobe-angle and there are *n* lobes in a revolution.

g. *Geol.* A great marginal projection from the body of a continental ice sheet.

1889 *Nature* 3 Oct. 558 The moraines can be traced around continuously from one lobe to another.

h. *gen.*

1877 J. WELLS *Bible Echoes* iv. 47 You have often seen little lobes of gum on the bark of such trees as the fir-tree.

i. *Electr.* A portion of the radiation pattern of an aerial which represents a group of directions of stronger radiation and is bounded on each side by directions in which there is minimum radiation.

1926 *Bell Syst. Techn. Jrnl.* V. 297 It is interesting to observe the variation in the diagrams... A lobe starts as a small bud, it grows in size until it reaches the unit circle, it then becomes dented. **1947** J. S. HALL *Radar Aids to Navigation* i. 13 All antennas radiate small amounts of power in directions other than the main lobe. **1959** DAVIES & PALMER *Radio Stud. Universe* iii. 39 In the simplest form of interferometer each narrow lobe of the aerial polar diagram produces its own small drift curve. **1968** *Radio Communication Handbk.* (ed. 4) xiii. 40/2 With increased spacing between the two aerials, more lobes appear... This type of pattern is not very useful, but if the intervening space is filled with aerials spaced $\lambda/2$, one pair of lobes grows at the expense of all the others, giving a sharp main beam with a number of relatively small minor lobes.

j. *Calligraphy.* A curved projecting part of a letter.

1957 N. R. KER *Catal. Manuscripts Containing Anglo-Saxon* p. xxvii, In minuscule of the eighth and ninth centuries **a** is a pointed letter, the back of which projects above the place at which it is joined by the lobe. **1969** M. B. PARKES *Eng. Cursive Bk. Hands 1250–1500* p. xxvi, The letter b comprises a stem or mainstroke which rises above the general level of the other letters and a lobe made with a curved stroke to the right of the stem.

2. *attrib.* and *Comb.*, as *lobe-like* adj.; **lobe-angle** *Mech.* (see quot. 1855 in 1 f); **lobe-berry**, the seaside grape, *Coccoloba uvifera*, of the West Indies (*Treas. Bot.* 1866); **lobe-foot**, a lobe-footed bird; **lobe-footed** *a.*, having lobate feet, as some birds; †**lobe-leaf**, a foliole of a compound leaf; **lobe-plate** (see quot.).

1833 P. J. SELBY *Illustr. Brit. Ornith.* II. 166 In the Orkneys.. the Red *Lobefoot is a common species. **1835** JENYNS *Man. Brit. Vertebr. Anim.* 214 *Lobipes hyperboreus* Steph. (Red Lobefoot). **1890** COUES *Field & Gen. Ornithol.* II. 190 In all truly *lobe-footed birds, as coots,.. grebes,.. and phalaropes. **1758** ELLIS in *Phil. Trans.* L. 446 Because they have an equal number of pinnæ, or *lobe-leaves, on the whole leaf of each tree. **1849–52** TODD *Cycl. Anat.* IV. 1224/2 *Lobe-like expansions. **1875** KNIGHT *Dict. Mech.*, **Lobe-plate*, a strong piece of cast-iron laid upon the keelson, etc., to support the parts of a marine steam-engine.

lobectomy (ləʊˈbɛktəmɪ). *Surg.* [f. LOB(E + -ECTOMY.] Excision of a lobe of some organ, esp. of a lung or the brain.

1911 DORLAND *Med. Dict.* (ed. 6) 464/1 *Lobectomy*, excision of a lobe of a gland, as the thyroid. **1932** *Arch. Surg.* XXV. 898 (*heading*) Lobectomy and pneumectomy in dogs. **1940** *Brit. Jrnl. Psychol.* XXX. 371 Thirty-two cases, each representing a partial lobectomy. **1949** *Amer. Jrnl. Physiol.* CLVII. 135 Liver lobectomy. **1965** [see COMPUTER 2 b]. **1967** S. TAYLOR et al. *Short Textbk. Surg.* xvi. 208 Treatment is wide removal of the tumour with surrounding healthy lung... Lobectomy may suffice, but pneumonectomy may be required.

lobed (ləʊbd), *a.* [f. LOBE + -ED[2].] Having a lobe or lobes; lobated. Chiefly *Nat. Hist.*

In *Bot.* applied to a leaf in which the division extends not more than half-way from the margin to the centre and the segments or the sinuses are rounded.

1787 tr. *Linnæus' Fam. Plants* I. 77 Stigma two-lobed. **1796** WITHERING *Brit. Plants* (ed. 3) III. 781 Leaves... The largest lobes lobed or divided half way down to the mid-rib. **1828** STARK *Elem. Nat. Hist.* II. 450 Proteus... Body very minute,.. diversely lobed instantaneously. **1830** LINDLEY *Nat. Syst. Bot.* 134 Leaves.. deeply lobed. **1843** YARRELL *Brit. Birds* III. 44 The dilated and lobed membranes of the toes. **1849** MURCHISON *Siluria* x. 218 This fossil.. is globular, lobed, branched. **1880** GRAY *Struct. Bot.* VI. v. 245 The calyx or corolla.. is said to be.. lobed, a general term for any considerable separation beyond toothing. **1893** W. H. HUDSON *Patagonia* 138 The wings beating rapidly, the long legs and lobed feet sprawling behind.

Comb. **1832** *Planting* 116 (L.U.K.) The lobed-leaved, or post oak.

lobelacrin (ləʊbɪˈlækrɪn). *Chem.* [f. LOBELIA + L. *ācri-*, *ācer* sharp + -IN.] An acrid principle found in the leaves of *Lobelia inflata*.

1874 FLÜCKIGER & HANBURY *Pharmacographia* 358 This substance which we may term Lobelacrin, is decomposed if merely boiled with water; by the influence of alkalis or acids it is resolved into sugar and Lobelic Acid. **1887** T. L. BRUNTON *Text.-bk. Pharmacol.* 960.

lobeless (ˈləʊblɪs), *a.* [f. LOBE + -LESS.] Without lobes.

1864 SALA in *Daily Tel.* 16 Aug., The straight, coarse black hair,.. lobeless ears, and slightly protruding lips, are all extremely Oriental.

lobelet (ˈləʊblɪt). *rare.* [f. LOBE + -LET.] A small lobe, a lobule.

1850 OGILVIE, *Lobelets*, in *bot.* small lobes. **1880** GRAY *Struct. Bot.* III. iv. 98 Ultimate portions or small lobes may be called Lobules or Lobelets.

lobelia (ləʊˈbiːlɪə). [mod.L., f. name of Matthias de Lobel (1538–1616), botanist and physician to James I: see -IA.] **a.** A genus of herbaceous (rarely shrubby) plants, typical of the N.O. *Lobeliaceæ*, of which many species are cultivated for the beauty of their flowers, which are chiefly blue, scarlet, or purple; they are widely distributed in tropical and subtropical regions and characterized by a deeply-cleft corolla without a spur; a plant of this genus, or its flower.

1739 P. MILLER *Gardeners Dict.* II. s.v., *Lobelia frutescens* .. Shrubby Lobelia, with a purslane Leaf. **1855** HALIBURTON *Nat. & Hum. Nat.* II. 114 He foamed at the mouth like a hoss that has eat lobelia in his hay. **1874** C. GEIKIE *Life in Woods* xiv. 223 The scarlet lobelia.

b. In the Pharmacopœia, the herb *L. inflata*.

1849 N. KINGSLEY *Diary* (1914) 94 Lobelia is the great cure, but some are against it. **1858** COPLAND *Dict. Pract. Med.* III. I. 404 In doses exceeding fifteen or twenty grains, the Lobelia causes speedy and severe vomiting. **1868** *Daily News* 30 July, He had poisoned a dog with lobelia, and it died 48 hours after. **1875** H. C. WOOD *Therap.* (1879) 525 Lobelia is used only when the inflammatory action is complicated with [etc.].

lobeliaceous (ləʊbiːlɪˈeɪʃəs), *a.* *Bot.* [f. mod.L. *Lobeliace-æ* (f. LOBELIA) + -OUS: see -ACEOUS.] Belonging to the N.O. *Lobeliaceæ*.

1830 LINDLEY *Nat. Syst. Bot.* 187 He is also, perhaps, right in considering Jasione more properly a Campanulaceous than a Lobeliaceous plant. **1839** *Penny Cycl.* XIV. 77/1 Isotoma, a lobeliaceous genus.

lobeliad (ləʊˈbiːlɪæd). *Bot.* [f. LOBELIA + -AD.] Lindley's name for: A plant of the N.O. *Lobeliaceæ*.

1845 LINDLEY *Sch. Bot.* (1862) 106.

lobelic (ləʊˈbiːlɪk), *a.* *Chem.* [f. LOBEL-IA + -IC.] *lobelic acid*: an acid existing in *Lobelia inflata*.

1840 PEREIRA *Elem. Mat. Med.* II. 947. **1874** [see LOBELACRIN]. **1887** T. L. BRUNTON *Text-bk. Pharmacol.* 960.

lobeline (ˈləʊbɪlɪn). *Chem.* Also lobeli(i)n and (mod.L.) lobelina. [f. LOBEL-IA + -INE[5].] An oily alkaloid with a pungent tobacco-like taste obtained from *Lobelia inflata* (Indian tobacco).

1844 *Pharmaceut. Jrnl.* III. 128 Analysis of Lobelia inflata. By Reinsch... Analysis gave following results:—Water [etc.].. Peculiar substance (Lobeliin). **1850** W. BASTWICK in *Pharmaceut. Jrnl.* X. 270 *Lobelina.* **1852** BRANDE *Dict. Sci.* etc. Suppl., *Lobeline.* **1856** MAYNE *Expos. Lex.*, *Lobelina*,.. lobelin. **1875** H. C. WOOD *Therap.* (1879) 355 *Lobelina.* **1887** T. L. BRUNTON *Text-bk. Pharmacol.* (ed. 3) 317 Lobeline.

ˈlobellated, *a.* *rare*[−1]. [f. mod.L. **lobellus*, dim. of *lobus* LOBE + -ATE[2] + -ED.] Lobulated.

1809 *Med. Jrnl.* XXI. 395 Oval leaves, either entire, or lobellated.

Lobel's catchfly. [From the name *Lobel*: see LOBELIA.] The plant *Silene Armeria*.

1664 EVELYN *Kal. Hort.* Aug., Flowers in Prime, or yet lasting.. Lobels Catch-fly [etc.]. **1741** [see CATCHFLY]. **1845** LINDLEY *Sch. Bot.* (1862) 42.

lober, obs. form of LUBBER.

†**ˈlobfish.** *Obs.* Also 6–7 lubfysh, 9 lubfish. [f. LOB *sb.*[2]] A kind of stockfish.

[**1421** in Rogers *Agric. & Prices* (1882) III. 312/1 Lob fish.] **1538** FITZHERB. *Just. Peas* 156 Fysshers that actually labour to take Lyng, Haberdine, Lobfyshe. **1545** *Rates Custom ho.* c vj, Stokfyshe called lubfysh. **1660** *Act 12 Chas. II*, c. 4 *Sched. Rates Inwards*, Stockfish *voc.* Cropling.. Lubfish. **1817** SCOTT *Rob Roy* I. ii. 32 Stockfish—Titling —Cropling—Lub-fish.

lobie, obs. form of LOOBY.

†**ˈlobilin.** *Obs.* [? quasi-proper name, f. LOB *sb.*[2], after *Colin*; cf. *Lubin*.] A rustic, boor.

1588 J. HARVEY *Disc. Probl.* 98 Rest you merrie, O ye Colin clowtes: Clap your hands, O ye Lobilins.

lobing (ˈləʊbɪŋ), *vbl. sb.* *Bot.* [f. LOBE + -ING[1].] Formation of lobes; lobation.

1870 HOOKER *Stud. Flora* 8 *Ranunculus hirsutus*... Leaves variable in lobing. **1872** OLIVER *Elem. Bot.* I. iv. 38 The carpels so completely consolidated as to leave no trace of lobing.

lobing (ˈləʊbɪŋ), *ppl. a.* *Bot.* [f. LOBE + -ING[2].] Forming lobes.

1870 HOOKER *Stud. Flora* 169 *Heracleum sphondylium*.. segments.. lobing and toothing.

lobiole (ˈləʊbɪəʊl). *Bot.* [ad. mod.L. *lobiolus* (irreg. after *petiolus* PETIOLE), dim. f. *lobus* LOBE.] One of the small lobes into which the thallus of some lichens is divided (*Treas. Bot.* 1866).

1856 in MAYNE *Expos. Lex.*

lobiped (ˈləʊbɪpɛd), *a.* and *sb.* *Zool.* Also -pede. [ad. mod.L. *lobiped-*, *-pēs*, f. *lobus* LOBE + *pēs* foot.]

A. *adj.* Lobe-footed, as certain birds; having lobate feet.

1856 MAYNE *Expos. Lex.*, *Lobipes*,.. lobipede.

B. *sb.* A lobe-footed bird; a lobe-foot.

1882 in OGILVIE.

lob-keeling. ? *Obs.* or *dial.* [f. LOB *sb.*[2] + KEELING *sb.*[1]] The coalfish.

c **1325** *Metr. Hom.* 136 Riht als sturioun etes merling, And lobbekeling etes sperling. **1880–4** F. DAY *Brit. Fishes* I. 295 *Gadus virens*.. Coal-fish.. lob, lob-keeling [etc.].

loblolly (ˈlɒblɒlɪ). Now *dial.* Also 7 lap-, 8–9 lop-. [perh. onomatopœic: cf. the dialectal *lob* 'to bubble while in process of boiling, said esp. of porridge', also 'to eat or drink up noisily' (E.D.D.), *lolly* (obs. Devon), 'broth, soup, or other food boiled in a pot' (*ibid.*).]

1. a. Thick gruel or spoon-meat, freq. referred to as a rustic or nautical dish or simple medicinal remedy; burgoo. †Hence, a ship-doctor's medicines.

1597 GERARDE *Herbal* II. xxxv. §2. 242 The lowe countreymen.. vse it for their meate called Wermose, and with vs Loblollie. **1620** MARKHAM *Farew. Husb.* (1625) 132 It makes an excellent grewell, or lob-lolly which is very soueraigne at Sea. **1621** BURTON *Anat. Mel.* II. iii. III. (1651) 326 There is a difference (he grumbles) between Laplolly and Phesants. **1657** R. LIGON *Barbadoes* (1673) 31 This we call Lob-lollie. But the Negroes, when they come to be fed with this,.. cry out, O! O! no more Lob-lol. **1694** MOTTEUX *Rabelais* I. iv. 13 What a filthy deal of Lob-lolly was here, to swell and wamble in her Guts. **1746** *Exmoor Scold.* 189 (E.D.S.) And nif et be Loblolly, tha wut slop et oll up. **1750** [see BURGOO]. **1786** [see *loblolly man* in 4].

b. *U.S. colloq.* A mud-hole.

1865 *Memphis* (Tennessee) *Daily Argus* 19 Nov. 3/1 We noticed a party of two or three men attempting to clean off one of them.. but as fast as they cleaned away the lob-lolly, the lob-lolly rolled back again. **1899** ADE *Doc Horne* i. 6 In those days a mud-hole with this deceptive dry crust on top was called a 'loblolly'. **1903** A. ADAMS *Log Cowboy* xi. 164 His ineffectual struggles caused him to sink farther to the flanks in the loblolly which the tramping of the cattle had caused. **1944** in *Publ. Amer. Dial. Soc.* II. 58.

2. A bumpkin, rustic, boor.

1604 BRETON *Grimello's Fort.* (Grosart) 9/2 This Loblollie, with slauering lips, would be making loue. **1675**

COTTON *Scoffer Scoft* 86 He Lies gaping like a great Loblolly. **1694** MOTTEUX *Rabelais* IV. xxi, That jolt-headed Loblolly of a Carter. **1894** R. LEIGHTON *Wreck Golden Fleece* 91 Blest if you aren't worth a dozen o' these Low's-toff loplollies.

3. = *loblolly pine*.

1819 E. DANA *Geogr. Sk. Western Country* 195 Contiguous to the Florida line, a space, occupying in width from 50 to 60 miles, is timbered with cypress, loblolly, and long and short leafed pine. **1849** *Nat. Encycl.* I. 355 The forest trees in..the south [of Alabama are] pine, cypress, and loblolly.

4. *attrib.* and *Comb.*, as ***loblolly feast, -making, -pot***; **loblolly bay**, an ornamental tree, *Gordonia Lasianthus*, of the southern United States; **loblolly boy**, an attendant who assists a ship's surgeon and his mates in their duties; also *dial.* an errand-boy, man of all work; †**loblolly doctor**, a sailor's name for a ship's doctor; †**loblolly lamb** = sense 2; **loblolly man** *Naut.*, a surgeon's mate; **loblolly pine**, the tree *Pinus Tæda*, growing in swamps in the southern United States; **loblolly sweetwood**, a West Indian name for *Sciadophyllum Jacquinii* (*Treas. Bot.* 1866); **loblolly tree** = *loblolly wood*; **loblolly whitewood**, *Nectandra sanguinea*; **loblolly-wood**, *Cupania glabra*; also *Pisonia cordata* (*Treas. Bot.*).

1760 J. LEE *Introd. Bot.* App. 306 Bay, *Loblolly, *Gordonia*. *Ibid.* 317 Loblolly Bay, *Hypericum*. **1770** ELLIS in *Phil. Trans.* LX. 519 That elegant evergreen-tree, called in South Carolina and the Floridas, the Loblolly-bay, or *Alcea Floridana*. **1748** SMOLLETT *Rod. Rand.* xxvii. (1804) 178 Among the sailors I was known as the *Loblolly Boy. **1836** E. HOWARD *R. Reefer* lvi, The loblolly boy, that is, the young man who had charge of the laboratory where all the medicines were kept. **1875** *Fam. Herald* 23 Oct. 415/2 He began life as a 'loblolly boy' on board a barge. **1899** F. T. BULLEN *Log Sea-waif* 273 They were just loblolly boys, at every one's beck and call. **1710** C. SHADWELL *Fair Quaker Deal* I. 15 [Sailor speaks] Our Rogue of a *Loblolly Doctor, being not satisfied with his two Pences, must have a Note for ten Months' Pay for every Cure. **1645** R. BEAKE *Lett. fr. Sommer Isl.* in *Prynne's Discov. Prodig. Blazing Stars* App. 3 A certaine Feast, held every week at severall houses, which Feast they called a *loblolly Feast. **1600** *Hosp. Incur. Fooles* A iij b, Those notted, grosse, and *loblolly-lams. **1706** [E. WARD] *Wooden World Dissected* (1708) 64 The Mystery of *Loblolly-making. **1786** MRS. PIOZZI *Anecd. Johnson* 285 He [Dr. Johnson] asked an officer what some place was called, and received for answer, that it was where the *loplolly man kept his loplolly. **1760** *Acts Gen. Ass. Georgia* (1881) 219 Squared Timber that shall be made of swamp or *loblolly pine. **1637** T. MORTON *New Eng. Canaan* (1883) 342 [He] called to his wife to set on the *loblolly pot. **1806** *Naval Mag.* XV. 241 We found several..girls stewing venison..in a loblolly-pot. **1750** G. HUGHES *Barbadoes* 143 The *Loblolly tree. This is a middle-sized tree. **1756** P. BROWNE *Jamaica* 214 *Loblolly whitewood, or White Sweetwood. *Ibid.* 178 *Loblolly-wood. This shrubby tree..rises generally to the height of 12 or 14 feet.

‖**lobo** ('ləʊbəʊ). [Sp.:—L. *lupus* wolf.] **a.** A large grey wolf of the south-western United States, *Canis lupus occidentalis*.

[**1839** COL. HAMILTON SMITH *Dogs* (Naturalist's Libr.) I. 152 The Spanish wolves congregated formerly in the passes of the Pyrenees in large troops, and even now the lobo will accompany strings of mules as soon as it becomes dusky.] **1859** BAIRD *Mammals N. Amer.* II. 14 *Canis occidentalis*, var. *Mexicanus*, Lobo Wolf. (In recent U.S. Dicts.) **1918** C. E. MULFORD *Man from Bar-20* ix. 88 What you saw was a bear or a lobo or a cougar come up to see th' fire. *Ibid.* 93 The lobo wolf in the canyon. **1973** R. D. SYMONS *Where Wagon Led* I. v. 79 But there were still a few buffalo wolves about. We called them lobos.

b. *transf.*

1907 'O. HENRY' *Heart of West* 220 I'm not one of them lobo wolves..who are always blaming on women the calamities of life.

†**'loboite.** *Min. Obs.* [Named by J. J. Berzelius in 1815, after *Lobo* da Silveira, who first described it: see -ITE.] Vesuvianite.

1816 W. PHILLIPS *Introd. Min.* (1823) 34 Berzelius mentions a 'Magnesian Idocrase' from Gökum and Frugord, under the name of Loboïte. **1837** DANA *Min.* 350 Idocrase..Loboit, Frugardit, Idokras, of the Germans.

‖**lobola** ('ləʊbələ). Also loboler, lobolo. [a. Nguni, f. *ukulobola* to give a dowry.] The South African native custom of marriage by purchase. Also, the price or present given for a bride according to this custom. Also *attrib.*

1825 N. ISAACS *Jrnl.* 25 Oct. in *Trav. E. Afr.* (1836) I. iii. 49 Jacob had become enamoured of Enslopee's sister, and had sent three head of cattle to 'Loloiler'. **1897** *Daily News* 17 July 5/6 Mr. Rhodes..pointed out that the old system of lobola was equivalent to the custom of marriage settlement in vogue with the whites. **1901** *Edin. Rev.* Oct. 302 The custom of lobola—i.e. the marriage gift of cattle to the bride's father—stands in the way of many Kafir marriages. **1905** *Westm. Gaz.* 19 Apr. 9/2 The native custom of passing cattle, known variously as 'lobolo', 'ikazi', and 'bohadi', in connexion with marriage. *Ibid.* 8 Sept. 5/1 Many of the natives are able to find the lobola for the luxury of additional wives. **1953** D. LESSING *Five* v. 248 And when our sister marries, he will have her cattle and her lobola money. **1957** G. MULDOON *Trumpeting Herd* ix. 95 According to the Angoni custom, the aunts and not the parents are responsible for fixing the Lobola, or payment for the bride. **1971** *Weekend World* (Johannesburg) 9 May 9/6, I have since paid part of the lobola to her parents. **1972** *Police Rev.* 24 Nov. 1520/3 [Rhodesia] A man may take, under tribal rites, as many wives as he can afford and he pays a bride price (called lobolo) for each.

lobose ('ləʊbəʊs), *a.* [ad. mod.L. *lobōsus*, f. *lobus* LOBE.] Having many or large lobes; *spec.* pertaining to the *Lobosa*, an order of *Rhizopoda* so characterized.

1885 LANKESTER in *Encycl. Brit.* XIX. 842/2 A certain small number of independent lobose Gymnomyxa.

lobotomy (ləʊ'bɒtəmɪ). *Surg.* [f. LOB(E + -O + -TOMY.] Incision into a lobe; *spec.* incision into the frontal lobe of the brain, esp. in the treatment of mental illness.

1936 FREEMAN & WATTS in *Med. Ann. District of Columbia* V. 326 (*heading*) Prefrontal lobotomy in agitated depression. **1946** *Lancet* 29 June 953/2 Pain of organic disease relieved by prefrontal lobotomy. **1950** [see LEUCOTOMY]. **1972** *Lancet* 8 July 69/2 Schizophrenia is no longer a standard reason for performing any kind of lobotomy. **1973** *Nature* 23 Mar. 222/3 Unlike the classical lobotomy operation, which reached its height of popularity in the 1950s and was used on up to 50,000 people in the US, psychosurgery now rarely involves actually cutting into the brain.

fig. **1959** N. MAILER *Advts. for Myself* (1961) 91 Success had been a lobotomy to my past, there seemed no power from the past which could help me in the present. **1972** *Village Voice* (N.Y.) 1 June 80/2 Even private screenings are not immune to artistic lobotomy, out-of-focus, and other chronic hazards.

Hence **lo'botomize** *v. trans.*, to perform lobotomy on; **lo'botomized** *ppl. a.* (also *fig.*, sluggish, stupefied).

1943 *Jrnl. Amer. Med. Assoc.* 27 Nov. 810/1 The lobotomized individual is friendly, good natured and indifferent to others' opinions. **1952** B. WOLFE *Limbo* (1953) xxii. 368, I can tell you a thing or two about lobotomizing little rapists down to good little pacifists. **1955** *Sci. Amer.* June 34/3 One interesting case was that of a lobotomized patient. When she was given LSD, she reverted to her pre-lobotomy depression. **1963** H. C. SHANDS in H. I. Schneer *Asthmatic Child* vi. 78 Her brother had developed an intractible schizophrenic illness and had been lobotomized. **1971** 'T. COE' *Jade in Aries* (1973) iv. 38 Manzoni can have our unfortunate friend committed, castrated, lobotomized and deported.

fig. **1953** W. BURROUGHS *Junkie* (1972) ix. 84 One night, I got lobotomized drunk in Frank's and went to a queer bar. **1968** *N.Y. Times* 5 Feb. 29 It was the life and times of a tightly clustered and rather faceless group, which ended with a robotlike square dance. Mr. Sheppard's lobotomized shuffle was a joy to watch. **1971** *Atlantic Monthly* Apr. 50 [He] was explaining his reasons for calling the police onto the campus, a speech greeted for the most part with a lobotomized silence.

lobous ('ləʊbəs), *a.* [f. LOBE + -OUS.] Having (many or large) lobes.

a **1722** LISLE *Husb.* (1752) 190 Blossoms, arising from joints with lobous leaves.

lobscouse ('lɒbskaʊs). *Naut.* and *dial.* Also 8–9 **lobscourse**, 9 **lobskous, -scouce, lap's course.** [Of obscure origin: cf. LOBLOLLY. (SCOUSE is now used in the same sense.)] A sailor's dish consisting of meat stewed with vegetables and ship's biscuit, or the like.

1706 [E. WARD] *Wooden World Dissected* (1708) 83 He has sent the Fellow.. to the Devil, that first invented Lobscouse. **1751** SMOLLETT *Per. Pic.* (1779) I. ix. 76 A mess of that savoury composition known by the name of lob's course. **1823** J. F. COOPER *Pioneers* v. (1869) 22/1 He acquired the art of making lobskous. **1835** MARRYAT *Jac. Faithf.* xi, Prepares to revel upon Lobscouse. **1867** SMYTH *Sailor's Word-bk.*, *Lap's Course*, one of the oldest and most savoury of the regular forecastle dishes. **1894** F. F. MOORE *Journalist's Note Bk.* 146 Something like a glorified Irish stew, or perhaps what yachtsmen call 'lobscouce'.

Hence **lobscouser** ('lɒbskaʊsə(r)), a sailor, tar.

1888 CLARK RUSSELL *Marooned* (1890) 18 Plain ginger-haired British lobscousers.

lobsided, variant of LOPSIDED.

Lob's pound. Now *dial.* Also (?*erron.*) 7 **Cobs pound,** 8 **Hob's pound.** [See LOB *sb.*[2] 2.] Prison; jail; the lock-up. Also *fig.*, an entanglement, difficulty.

1597 E. S. *Discov. Knights of Post* B, Knightes of the Poste, Lords of lobs pound, and heires apparant to the pillory. **1612** *Pasquil's Night-Cap* (1877) 64 There is the Woodcocke fall'n into the gin, And in Lobs-pound intangled by a wile. **1639** J. CLARKE *Paroemiologia* 188 Hee's in Cobs pound. **1663** BUTLER *Hud.* I. iii. 910 Crowdero, whom in Irons bound, Thou basely threw'st into Lob's pound Where still he lies. **1667** G. DIGBY *Elvira* II. 23 He hath us faith Fast in Lobb's Pound. **1694** ECHARD *Plautus* 8 If Mr Constable and his Watch shou'd pick m'up and in wi' me to Lobs-Pound? **1796** MAD. D'ARBLAY *Camilla* IV. iii, What! are you all in Hob's pound? **1829** BENTHAM *Justice & Cod. Petit.* Wks. 1843 V. 494 From the sheriff the information would, in course, pass on to the defendant, when the time came for his finding himself in Lob's pound. **1895** *E. Anglia Gloss.*, *Lobspound*, to be in any difficulty or perplexed state.

lobster[1] ('lɒbstə(r)). Forms: 1 **lop(p)estre, lopystre,** 4 **lopister,** 4–7 **lopster,** 5 **loppestere, lopstere,** 5–7 **lobstar,** 6 *Sc.* **lapstar,** 6–7 **lopstar,** 4– **lobster.** [OE. *lopustre, lopystre, loppestre*, corruptly ad. L. *locusta* LOCUST. The L. word orig. denotes a lobster or some similar crustacean, the application to the locust being suggested by the resemblance in shape. In late L. the original sense survived alongside the other: cf. F. *langouste*, OCornish *legast* lobster.

The ending *-stre* of the OE. word is due to assimilation to OE. fem. agent-nouns (see -STER): cf. OE. *myltestre* from L. *meretrix*. The cause of the substitution of *þ* for the L. *c* is obscure.]

1. a. A large marine stalk-eyed ten-footed long-tailed crustacean of the genus *Homarus*, much used for food; it is greenish or bluish black when raw, and of a brilliant red when boiled; the first pair of feet are very large and form the characteristic 'claws'.

a **1000** ÆLFRIC *Colloq.* in Wr.-Wülcker 94/14 Crabban muslan pinewinclan..and lopystran and fela swylces. *a* **1100** *Voc.* ibid. 319/20 *Polipos*, loppestre. **1311–12** *Durham Acc. Rolls* (Surtees) 9 In sperling', creuis, lopisters, et pisc. aque dulcis. **1314–15** *Ibid.* 10 In burbot, sprot et lopsters. **1398** TREVISA *Barth. De P.R.* XIX. lxxviii. (1495) 909 The vertue of gendringe of egges is..in crabbes and lobsters. *c* **1450** *Two Cookery-bks.* 114 Nym ye perch other ye loppestere or drie haddok. *c* **1475** *Pict. Voc.* in Wr.-Wülcker 764/31 *Hic polupus*, a lobstar. *c* **1560** A. SCOTT *Poems* (S.T.S.) v. 33 Lapstaris, lempettis, mussillis in schellis. **1599** MARSTON *Sco. Villanie* I. iii. 181 A Crabs bak'd guts, a Lobsters butterd thigh. **1646** SIR T. BROWNE *Pseud. Ep.* III. xv. 142 Lobsters will swim swiftly backward. **1688** R. HOLME *Armoury* 338/1 A Crefish..a Species of the Lobster, but of a lesser size. **1720** GAY *Poems* (1745) II. 17 On unadulterate wine we here regale, And strip the lobster of his scarlet mail. **1794** C. PIGOT *Female Jockey Club* 139 She faints at the approach of a mouse; if surprised by the sight of a black lobster, she screams unmercifully. **1875** F. W. PAVY *Food* (ed. 2) 174 The flesh of the lobster is mainly found in the tail and claws.

b. Applied with qualification to other crustaceans resembling the above. **Norway lobster**, *Nephrops norvegicus*. **spiny** or **thorny lobster**, *Palinurus vulgaris* = CRAYFISH *sb.* 3 b. Some crayfishes are called ***fresh-water lobsters***.

1778 *Encycl. Brit.* (ed. 2) III. 1610/1 The strigosus, or plated lobster, with a pyramidal spiny snout. **1795** tr. *Thunberg's Trav.* I. 240 The Cape lobster (*Cancer arctos*).. has no large claws, and is craggy all over, and covered with erect prickles. **1819** G. SAMOUELLE *Entomol. Compend.* 92 *Palinurus vulgaris*..is sometimes denominated Spiny-lobster, or sea Cray-fish. **1865** GOSSE *Land & Sea* 81 The sea cray-fish, or thorny lobster. **1883** *Fisheries Exhib. Catal.* (ed. 4) 104 A peculiar pale-blue Lobster from Norway.

c. The flesh of the animal, as food.

1789 CULLEN *Mat. Med.* I. 393, I have known..persons who could not take even a very small quantity of lobster or crab without being affected soon after with a violent colic.

¶ **d.** The construction of jointed plate-armour is often described by comparison to a lobster's tail. Cf. *lobster-tail, -tailed* (in 5 below).

1786 GROSE *Anc. Armour* 22 Gauntlets..were..oftener of small plates of iron rivetted together, in imitation of the lobster's tail, so as to yield to every motion of the hand. *Ibid.* 23 Cuissarts or thigh pieces... They were made flexible at the knees by joints like those in the tail of a lobster.

2. †**a.** An opprobrious name (? for a red-faced man).

1602 MIDDLETON *Blurt Master Constable* D 2 b, Let him goe..an old combe-peckt rascall..hang him, lobster. **1605** *Tryall Chev.* II. i. in Bullen *O. Pl.* III. 289 What a dictionary of proper names hath the Rogue got together!..Ile pearce you for this, you Lobster. *Ibid.* 290 Leere not, Lobster, lest I thump that russeting face of yours with my sword hilt. **1609** B. JONSON *Epicœne* v. iii. Wks. (1616) 593 You whorson Lobster.

b. A slow-witted, awkward, or gullible person; a fool, dupe; a bore. *U.S. slang.*

1896 ADE *Artie* x. 91 Every time I ever see him he was a lobster. **1900** —— *Fables in Slang* 54 He went to College, where he proved to be a Lobster. **1947** T. H. WHITE *Elephant & Kangaroo* (1948) xix. 157 When she was giving breakfast to Father Byrne, after a Station, she used to lean forward whenever the old lobster spoke. **1965** *English Studies* XLVI. 468 The noun 'lob' 'dupe' became the root of *lobster* 'dupe; victim'.

3. a. A contemptuous name for: A British soldier. The name was originally applied to a regiment of Roundhead cuirassiers from their wearing complete suits of armour (cf. 1 d above). In later times it has been referred to the characteristic red coat. Also ***boiled lobster***. ***raw*** (or ***unboiled***) ***lobster***: a policeman: so called in contradistinction to 'boiled lobster', on account of his blue uniform.

c **1643** *Songs Lond. Prentices* (Percy Soc.) 68 When as 'tis but a lobster, whom (men say) Turn him but o're and o're he'll turn to you. **1644–7** CLEVELAND *Char. Lond. Diurn.* 5 Translate but the Scene to Roundway-downe: There Hasleriggs Lobsters were turned into Crabs, and crawl'd backwards. **1647** CLARENDON *Hist. Reb.* VII. §104 [June 1643] Sir William Waller having received from London a fresh regiment of five hundred horse, under the command of sir Arthur Haslerigge, which were so prodigiously armed that they were called by the other side the regiment of lobsters, because of their bright iron shells with which they were covered, being perfect curasseers. **1660** in *Harl. Misc.* (1810) V. 73 Redcoats, lobsters, corporals, troopers, or dragoons. **1687** T. BROWN *Saints in Uproar* Wks. 1730 I. 73 The women..exclaim against lobsters and tatterdemallions, and desire 'em to prove 'twas ever known..that a red-coat died for religion. **1776** S. HAWS in *Milit. Jrnls.* (1855) 89 The Lobsters [*i.e.* British troops] came out almost to copple hill and took 3 cows. **1803** *Sporting Mag.* XXII. 29 He had gained over the lobster, as he called the serjeant. **1829** BUCKSTONE *Billy Taylor* I. iii, I..am no more a dull drab-coated watchman... *Mary*... Thou unboiled lobster, hence! **1830** *Ann. Reg., Chron.* 9 Nov. 191/2 'No Peel—down with the raw lobsters!' **1878** BESANT & RICE *Celia's Arb.* xxxix. (1887) 284 Jack the Sailor, Joe the Marine, and

the Boiled Lobster. **1896** W. W. Jacobs *Many Cargoes* 214 She's married a lobster.. He's a sergeant in the line.

attrib. or *appos.* **1758** L. Lyon in *Milit. Jrnls.* (1855) 40 This afternoon their was a Lobster Corperel married to a Road Island whore. **1779** J. Carpenter in *Proc. Vermont Hist. Soc.* (1872) p. viii, 7 Prisoners broke Prison from the grand Lobster guard at Fortin.

b. slang phr. ***to boil one's lobster***: see quot.

1785 Grose *Dict. Vulg. Tongue* s.v., To boil one's lobster, for a churchman to become a soldier, lobsters which are of a bluish black, being made red by boiling.

4. Short for *lobster-caterpillar, -moth.*

1869 E. Newman *Brit. Moths* 216 The Lobster (*Stauropus Fagi*). *Ibid.* 217 This singular caterpillar, which is known to collectors as 'The Lobster', feeds on oak and birch.

5. *attrib.* and *Comb.*, as ***lobster-catch, -catching, -fishery, -fishing, -hatchery, -man, -red*** adj., ***mayonnaise, patty, -salad, -sauce, -shell, -shop, soup, -supper, -woman***; **lobster bisque**, a thick cream soup made of lobster; hence, the colour of this soup; **lobster-boat**, a boat used in lobster-fishing, fitted with a well in which to keep the lobsters alive; **lobster-box** *slang*, (*a*) a transport ship; (*b*) barracks (*Slang Dict.* 1865); **lobster-car** *U.S.*, 'a box or frame in which lobsters are kept alive under water awaiting sale or transport' (*Cent. Dict.*); **lobster caterpillar**, the larva of the lobster-moth; **lobster-clad** *a.*, clad in jointed armour suggesting a lobster's shell; **lobster-claw**, (*a*) 'a screw jack used in setting rigging' (Knight *Dict. Mech.* Suppl.); (*b*) *pl.* a common marine alga, *Polysiphonia elongata*, so called because it bears tufts of filaments resembling a lobster's claws (*Cent. Dict.*); **lobster-coated** *a.*, red-coated; **lobster cocktail**: see COCKTAIL 4; **lobster-crab**, a crustacean of the family *Porcellanidæ*; a porcelain-crab; **lobster-crawl**, 'a fishing ground for lobsters' (*Cent. Dict.*); **lobster-creel**, = *lobster-pot*; **lobster-flower**, the Barbados flower-fence, *Poinciana pulcherrima* (*Treas. Bot.* Suppl. 1874); **lobster-joint**, a joint in an instrument resembling a joint in a lobster's claws; **lobster-louse**, a parasite of the lobster, *Nicothoe astaci*; **lobster-moth**, the bombycid moth *Stauropus fagi*; **lobster Newburg**, lobster cooked in a thick cream sauce containing sherry or brandy; **lobster-night** *nonce-wd.*, ? a night celebrated by a lobster supper; **lobster-pot**, a basket or similar structure serving as a trap to catch lobsters; **lobster-smack** *jocular*, a military transport; **lobster-tail**, a piece of armour jointed after the manner of a lobster's tail (cf. 1 d); also *attrib.*; **lobster-tailed** *a.*, wearing 'lobster-tail' or jointed armour; **lobster thermidor**, cooked lobster mixed with a cream sauce, returned to its shell, sprinkled with cheese, and browned in the oven; **lobster-trap** = *lobster-pot.*

1895 'M. Ronald' *Century Cook Bk.* 569 *Lobster bisque. **1929** E. Wilson *I thought of Daisy* i. 8 She seemed appetizing in her lobster-bisque dress. **1967** L. Deighton *London Dossier* 49 Bentley's.. sells lobster bisque freshly tinned. **1974** *Times* 15 Jan. 14/8 Their amazing lobster bisque did much to console me. **1777** Pennant *Zool.* IV. 8, I am told.. that when men of war meet a *lobster-boat, a jocular threat is used, That, if the master do not sell them good lobsters, they will salute him. **1833** M. Scott *Tom Cringle* ii. (1842) 64 We landed in the *lobster-box, as Jack loves to designate a transport. **1887** G. B. Goode, etc. *Fisheries U.S.* v. II. 674 Entirely submerged *lobster-cars are used in Norway. **1901** *Q. Rev.* July 48 If the difficulties in reference to the treaties were confined to the *lobster-catch. **1881** *Scribner's Mag.* XXII. 215/1 For *lobster-catching.. two kinds of nets.. are occasionally used. **1859** Gen. P. Thompson *Audi Alt.* II. xciii. 73 The ancient *lobster-clad knights. ? **1794** Burns *Let. to Mrs. Riddel* Wks. (Globe) 539 Those *lobster-coated puppies. **1854** A. Adams, etc. *Man. Nat. Hist.* 290 *Lobster-crabs (*Porcellanidæ*). **1853** Reade *Chr. Johnstone* 320 The periodical laying down, on rocky shoals, and taking up again, of *lobster-creels. **1865** Bertram *Harvest of Sea* 391 In France the *lobster-fishery is to some extent 'regulated'. *Ibid.* 385 *Lobster-fishing. **1884** *Riverside Nat. Hist.* (1888) II. 53 Two methods of lobster fishing are in vogue. **1889** *Nature* 21 Mar. 499 A complete *lobster-hatchery could be established.. on the West coast. **1880** M. Mackenzie *Dis. Throat & Nose* I. 511 The introduction of the inner tube [into the trachea] without employing *lobster-joints. **1863** Wood *Nat. Hist.* III. 640 The *Lobster-louse is sometimes found in considerable numbers, fixed to the gills of the lobster. **1881** *Scribner's Mag.* XXII. 210/2 The typical *lobsterman lives at the bottom of a charming and remote cove. **1889** A. B. Marshall *Cookery Bk.* vi. 100 *Lobster Mayonnaise à l'Osborne. *Ibid.* 101 Lobster Mayonnaise with Aspic. **1913** J. Vaizey *College Girl* xxvii. 368 Iced soup, lobster mayonnaise, salmon and green peas. **1969** *Queen* 17–30 Sept. 50/3, I would not dispute the quality of the lobster mayonnaise at the Marbella Club. **1819** G. Samouelle *Entomol. Compend.* 247 *Lobster moth. **1863** Wood *Nat. Hist.* III. 535 The Lobster-moth derives its name from the grotesque exterior of the caterpillar. [**1895** 'M. Ronald' *Century Cook Bk.* ii. iii. 139 Lobster à la Newburg.] **1914** 'Saki' *Beasts & Super-Beasts* 172 The *lobster Newburg and the egg mayonnaise. **1968** H. Franklin *Crash* vii. 82 We.. had a dozen oysters, Lobster Newburg and Chablis from the barrel. **1715** Pope *Farew. to London* Wks. (Globe 1895) 479 Luxurious *lobster-nights farewell, For sober studious days! **1817** I. D'Israeli *Curiosities of Lit.* III. 240 Keep up the fire, and lively play the flame Beneath those *lobster-patties. **1845** E. Acton *Mod. Cookery* (ed. 2) xvi. 349 For lobster patties, prepare the fish as for a *vol-au-vent*, but cut it smaller. **1942** Mrs. Belloc Lowndes *Let.* 19 Nov. (1971) 235 There were lobster patties, and queer looking Maid of Honour cakes. **1972** C. Drummond *Death at Bar* i. 36 A large tray of lobster patties. **1764** *Ann. Reg.* 92 Tangled in the lines of some *lobster pots. **1862** Ansted *Channel Isl.* iv. xxii. (ed. 2) 508 The number of lobsters taken weekly from the various lobster-pots round the coast of Guernsey is estimated to average 4,000. **1856** Kane *Arct. Expl.* I. xv. 167 The little *lobster-red fury of a stove. **1819** Byron *Juan* i. cxxxv, I'm fond of.. A *lobster salad. **1837** Thackeray *Ravenswing* vi, We had champagne and lobster-salad. **1822** *Blackw. Mag.* XI. 161 Turbot.. which ruddy *lobster-sauce accompanies. **1848** Dickens *Dombey* vi, *Lobster shells. **1823** *Blackw. Mag.* XIV. 508 An occasional crash of oyster-shells cast.. from some *lobster-shop. **1829** Marryat *F. Mildmay* v, I steered for 'the *lobster-smack'. **1723** J. Nott *Cook's & Confectioner's Dict.* sig. S3ᵛ (*heading*) To make *Lobster Soop. **1865** R. Riddell *Indian Domestic Econ.* (ed. 6) 37 Lobster soup. [Recipe.] **1960** *Good Housek. Cookery Bk.* (rev. ed.) 78/1 Simple lobster soup. **1973** J. Cleary *Ransom* iii. 74 Lobster soup—why the hell did I buy that? **1869** C. C. Black tr. *Demmin's Weapons War* (1877) 219 The long '*lobster-tails' which replaced the waist-piece and the tassets. **1880** M. Mackenzie *Dis. Throat & Nose* I. 512 The angular and descending portions of the inner tube of the.. canula.. have to be made with joints on the lobster-tail principle. **1826** Scott *Woodst.* v, Oliver on horseback,.. charging with his *lobster-tailed squadron. **1889** Doyle *Micah Clarke* 376 Old as I am.. I am fit to exchange broadsides with any lobster-tailed piccaroon. **1933** E. A. Robertson *Ordinary Families* xiii. 291 *Lobster thermidor always brings on a sort of gastric aphasia. **1969** R. Airth *Snatch!* ix. 90 She'd made this lobster thermidor. **1865** Bertram *Harvest of Sea* 385 The *lobster-traps and crab-cages, which are not unlike overgrown rat-traps. **1898** G. Parker *Battle of Strong* v. 33 A *lobster-woman.. put on her sabots.

Hence (*nonce-wds.*) **'lobsterdom**, the 'realm' of lobsters; **'lobsterling**, a young lobster.

1863 Kingsley *Water-Bab.* 146 He had live barnacles on his claws, which is a great mark of distinction in lobsterdom. **1901** *Spectator* 27 July 119/2 Sunlight.. brings swarms of lobsterlings to the top of the jars in which they are hatched.

lobster² ('lɒbstə(r)). *East Anglian.* Also 6 **lopster, lobstart,** 6, 9 **lopstart, lobstert** (*E.D.D.*). [f. LOB *sb.*² + *stert*, START, tail. Cf. *clubstart*, CLUBSTER.] A stoat.

? **1490** *Paston Lett.* III. 365 Wesellis, lobsters, polkattys. **1552** Huloet, Lopster vermyn. **1577** Harrison *Descr. Engl.* iii. xiii. in *Holinshed*, Haryers, whose game is the Foxe,.. Lobstart [1586 lopstart], Wesell, Conye, &c. **1787** Marshall *Norf.* (1795) II. 383. *a* **1825** Forby *Voc. E. Anglia.* **1864** C. Elton *Norway* ix. 124 Even now it is said that farmers in England complain of the 'lobsters' sucking the eggs and killing the chickens.

lobster³ ('lɒbstə(r)). [Jocular formation on LOB *v.* + -STER.] One who bowls 'lobs' at cricket.

1889 *Daily Chron.* 8 June 5/4 It is welcome to note the success with the ball of.. Winter, the lobster. **1890** E. Lyttleton *Cricket* 36 The gentle and sensitive 'lobster'.

lobstering ('lɒbstərɪŋ), *vbl. sb.* [f. LOBSTER¹ + -ING¹.] Catching lobsters.

1881 *Scribner's Mag.* XXII. 211/1 [The lobsterman] is a fisherman in other branches and a farmer as well, for lobstering need not take the whole of any one's time. **1957** *Times Lit. Suppl.* 8 Nov. 676/2 The story opens with lobstering in the Orkneys. **1971** *Country Life* 9 Dec. 1643/1 There is good lobstering and mackerel fishing for the retired.

lobsterish ('lɒbstərɪʃ), *a.* [f. LOBSTER¹ + -ISH¹.] Resembling a lobster; red-faced.

1914 Chesterton *Wisdom of Father Brown* x. 259 [He] thrust his laughing, lobsterish face into the room. **1946** G. Millar *Horned Pigeon* x. 140 Clifton, a bald, lobsterish little man with freckles all over his muscle-rounded back.

†**lobsterize**, *v. Obs. nonce-wd.* [f. LOBSTER¹ + -IZE.] *intr.* To move backwards, as a lobster is supposed to do. (Cf. *to crawfish.*)

1605 Sylvester *Du Bartas* ii. iii. iv. *Captaines* 621 Thou makest Rivers the most deafly-deep To lobstarize (back to their source to creep).

lobstick, var. *lop-stick* (LOP *sb.*³ 4).

lobular ('lɒbjʊlə(r)), *a. Phys.*, etc. [f. LOBULE + -AR.] Pertaining to or having the form of a lobule or lobules. Of pneumonia: Affecting the lobules of the lungs.

1822–34 *Good's Study Med.* (ed. 4) I. 389 The substance of the lungs is lobular. **1826** Kirby & Sp. *Entomol.* IV. xl. 116 A lobular substance consisting of granules filling the whole cavity of the body. **1834** J. Forbes *Laennec's Dis. Chest* (ed. 4) 199 Central peripneumonies, and those denominated lobular. **1845** Budd *Dis. Liver* 55 Lobular pneumonia. **1889** *Syd. Soc. Lex.*, *Lobular fissures*, the sulci between the several cerebral and cerebellar lobules. **1892** Woodhead *Pract. Pathol.* (ed. 3) 372 Lobular pneumonia.

Hence **'lobularly** *adv.*

1899 *Allbutt's Syst. Med.* VI. 386 The left lung was.. condensed with.. lobularly disposed lesions throughout.

lobulate ('lɒbjʊlət), *a.* [f. LOBULE + -ATE².] Having or consisting of lobules or small lobes.

1862 in Cooke *Man. Bot. Terms* 52. **1870** Hooker *Stud. Flora* 172 Ivy.. Albumen lobulate.

lobulated ('lɒbjʊleɪtɪd), *a.* [Formed as prec. + -ED¹.] = prec.

1783 W. Keir in *Med. Commun.* I. 130 The.. kidney.. had a lobulated form. **1870** Rolleston *Anim. Life* 79 Lobulated masses of adipose tissue.

lobulation (lɒbjʊ'leɪʃən). [f. LOBULATE: see -ATION.] The formation of lobules or small lobes; a lobulated condition.

1861 Bumstead *Ven. Dis.* (1879) 611 There is no lobulation of the organ.

lobulato-, taken as comb. form of LOBULATE in the sense 'lobulate and..'.

1846 Dana *Zooph.* (1848) 701 Coralla.. lobulato-glomerate. **1871** W. A. Leighton *Lichen-flora* 225 Thalline margin lobulato-crenate.

lobule ('lɒbju:l). Chiefly *Anat.* [ad. mod.L. LOBULUS.] A small lobe.

1682 T. Gibson *Anat.* (1697) 14 The lobules of which the Lungs are composed. **1720** Hale in *Phil. Trans.* XXXI. 5 Every Duct is made of lesser Ducts united, which rise from the Lobules.. which constitute each distinct Lobe. **1800** *Med. Jrnl.* III. 139 Its last adhesion, was to the helix of the left ear, just above the lobule. **1866** Huxley *Preh. Rem. Caithn.* 157 The nose nearly straight and ending in a rounded lobule. **1872** —— *Physiol.* v. 119 The smallest obvious subdivisions of the liver substance.. which are termed the lobules. **1880** [see LOBELET].

lobulization (lɒbjʊlaɪ'zeɪʃən). [f. LOBULE + -IZATION.] 'The passage of a tissue from a uniform to a lobular condition' (*Syd. Soc. Lex.*).

lobulose ('lɒbjʊləʊs), *a.* [f. LOBULE + -OSE.] Having many lobules.

1846 Dana *Zooph.* (1848) 618 Stout lobes which are much and crowdedly lobulose.

lobulous ('lɒbjʊləs), *a.* [f. LOBULE + -OUS.] 'Possessing lobules, or prominences resembling lobules' (*Syd. Soc. Lex.* 1889).

‖**lobulus** ('lɒbjʊləs). Pl. **lobuli** ('lɒbjʊlaɪ). [mod.L., dim. of *lobus* LOBE.] A small lobe, lobule.

1731 Arbuthnot *Nat. Aliments* (1735) 28 A great number of those Air-Bladders form what we call Lobuli, which hang upon the Bronchia, like Bunches of Grapes upon a stalk. **1826** Kirby & Sp. *Entomol.* IV. xl. 117 The result of the approximation of polygonous lobuli. **1842** E. Wilson *Anat. Vade M.* (ed. 2) 461 The lower dependent and fleshy portion of the pinna is the lobulus.

lob-worm ('lɒbwɜ:m). [f. LOB *sb.*²] **a.** A large earthworm used for bait by anglers. **b.** The LUG-WORM (*Arenicola marina*).

a. 1651 T. Barker *Art of Angling* (1653) 7, I baited my hook with two Lob-worms. **1653** Walton *Angler* iv. 94 For the Trout the Dew-worm (which some also call the Lob-worm) and the Brandling are the chief. **1718** G. Jacob *Compl. Sportsman* 119 The Lob or Garden-Worm well scoured is the only Bait. **1867** F. Francis *Angling* i. (1880) 31 The large roach will.. take the tail of a lob-worm very ravenously.

b. 1854 *Eng. Cycl., Nat. Hist.* I. 295 *Arenicola piscatorum*, the Lob or Lug-Worm. **1875** *Encycl. Brit.* (ed. 9) II. 71/1 All round the British and many other coasts the lob-worm (*Arenicola marina*) is used for bait.

loby, obs. form of LOOBY.

loc, variant of LAKE *sb.*¹ *Obs.* (offering, gift).

loc, obs. form of LOCK *sb.*, LOHOCH.

locable ('ləʊkəb(ə)l), *a. rare.* [f. L. *locāre* to place: see -BLE.] Of persons: That can be placed (in a situation or office). As *sb.*, one who is fit to be so placed; hence *attrib.*, as ***locable list.***

a **1816** Bentham *Offic. Apt. Maximized, Introd. View* (1830) 5 Persons locable in the several situations, say in one word, *locables*. **1816–30** *Ibid.*, *Extract Const. Code* 27 Applicants.. demanding admission into the locable list, and to that end presenting themselves for examination.

local ('ləʊkəl), *a.* and *sb.* Also 5–6 **localle**, 5–7 **locall**, 6 **locale**. [a. F. *local* (= Sp., Pg. *local*, It. *locale*), ad. L. *locāl-is*, f. *loc-us* place.]

A. *adj.*

1. a. Pertaining to or concerned with 'place' or position in space. Now chiefly in ***local situation.***

1485 Caxton *Chas. Gt.* 1 And also in recountyng of hye hystoryes the comune vnderstondyng is better content to the ymag[i]nacion local than to symple auctoryte to which it is submysed. *Ibid.* Envoy 250 The ymagynacion locall. **1561** T. Norton *Calvin's Inst.* iv. xvii. (1634) 675 *marg.*, A local presence of the body of Christ. **1590** Shaks. *Mids. N.* v. i. 17 (1st Qo. Fisher 1600) G 3 The Poets penne turnes them to shapes, And giues to ayery nothing, a locall habitation, And a name. **1659** Pearson *Creed* (1839) 335 As to a local descent into the infernal parts they all agree. **1706** W. Jones *Syn. Palmar. Matheseos* 46 Some of these Powers have borrowed their Denominations from Local Extension. **1777** Priestley *Matt. & Spir.* (1782) I. xix. 231 The Cartesians.. maintain.. that spirits have no extension, nor local presence. **1818** Cruise *Digest* (ed. 2) VI. 341 The local situation of the lands devised. **1862** Stanley *Jew. Ch.* (1877) I. v. 109 This change of local situation was at once a change of moral condition.

†**b.** Having the attribute of 'place' or spatial position. *Obs.*

1533 Frith *Answ. More* (1548) 55 Yᵉ Lord, whiche to shewe his humanite to be locall (that is to saye: contained in

one place onely) dyd saye vnto his disciples. I ascende vnto my father. *Ibid.* 55 b, Howe dyd he ascende in to heauen, but because he is locall and a very man. **1565** JEWEL *Replie Harding's Answ.* VI. 348 His [Harding's] answeare is, that Christes bodie is Local onely in one place. **1577** tr. *Bullinger's Decades* (1592) 734 Angels peraduenture at this daie are more aptly saide to bee locall or in place not circumscriptiuely, but definitiuely. **1621** BURTON *Anat. Mel.* II. ii. III. (1651) 246 [They] will have Hell a materiall and local fire in the center of the earth. **1718** PRIOR *Solomon* I. 564 A higher flight the venturous goddess tries, Leaving material worlds, and local skies. **1729** SWIFT *Direct. Birthday Song* 272 That sound divine the truth has spoke all, And pawn'd his word, Hell is not local.

†**c.** ***local motion***, movement from place to place, motion of translation, locomotion. *Obs.*

1561 EDEN *Arte Nauig.* I. viii. 10 The elementes are.. moueable by locall motion. **1644** DIGBY *Nat. Bodies* xxiii. 208 Zoophytes..that is such creatures as though they goe not from place to place, and so cause a locall motion of their whole substance, yet in their partes, they haue a distinct and articulate motion. **1678** CUDWORTH *Intell. Syst.* I. v. 831 It is certain, that cogitation, (phancy, intellection, and volition) are no local motions. **1707** *Curios. in Husb. & Gard.* 34 Plants have no local or progressive Motion.

d. *Grammar.* Relating to place or situation.

1842 JELF *Greek Gram.* II. 230 *[heading]* Local Dative. **1845** *Ibid.* I. 296 [Adverbs] are divided into *a.* Local,..*b.* Temporal,..*c.* Modal [etc.]. *Ibid.* 298 The Local adverbs in ει, as..ἐκεῖ. **1889** E. A. SONNENSCHEIN *Lat. Gram.* §348 Local Clauses. (Clauses of Place.)

e. Psychol. ***local sign*** (after G. *localzeichen*): that element in a sensation which is the basis of our instinctive judgement as to its locality.

1874 SULLY *Sensation & Intuition* 70. **1884** BOSANQUET tr. *Lotze's Metaph.* 490.

2. a. Belonging to a particular place on the earth's surface; pertaining to or existing in a particular region or district.

local time: the time of day or night reckoned from the instant of transit of the mean sun over the local meridian.

?**14..** in *Myrr. our Ladye* p. xxi, Priuileges ordynary iniunccions localle statutes laudable custons decrees & al other ordynaunces. **1612** SELDEN *Illustr. Drayton's Poly-olb.* i. init., If in Prose and Religion it were as iustifiable, as in Poetry and Fiction, to inuoke a Locall power..I would therin ioyne with the Author. **1687** in *Magd. Coll. & Jas. II* (O.H.S.) 112 That College had the Bishop of Winchester for their Visitor Local. **1740** PITT *Æneid* VIII. 461 The Swains the Local Majesty rever'd. **1792** *Aneed. W. Pitt* II. xxix. 125, I have no local attachments; it is indifferent to me, whether a man was rocked in his cradle on this side or that side of the Tweed. **1833** HERSCHEL *Astron.* iii. 139 Two observatories..provided with accurate means of determining their respective local times. **1849** MACAULAY *Hist. Eng.* v. I. 612 *note*, Oldmixon, who was a boy at Bridgewater when the battle was fought,..was so much under the influence of local passions that his local information was useless to him. **1868** GLADSTONE *Juv. Mundi* ii. (1870) 31 The name Γραῖα..is only a local name of a settlement of..Boeotians. **1891** E. PEACOCK *N. Brendon* II. 313 Mr. Yeo, the local lawyer. **1968** H. FRANKLIN *Crash* i. 9 Our estimated time of arrival at Cairo is 17.45 local time, 15.45 G.M.T. **1973** 'E. FERRARS' *Small World of Murder* ii. 20 She had not adjusted her watch to local time. **1974** 'A. HAIG' *Peruvian Printout* 99 Arrive Lima 0730hrs local time.

b. With restrictive force: Limited or peculiar to a particular place or places.

1615 G. SANDYS *Trav.* 170 Those ceremonies that are not locall, I willingly omit. **1781** COWPER *Retirement* 119 Truth is not local, God alike pervades And fills the world of traffic and the shades. **1811** *Henry & Isabella* I. 3 Her ideas were as local as Andrew's; and they neither of them seemed likely to disturb the brain of the other. **1860** MOTLEY *Netherl.* (1868) I. i. 5 The importance of the struggle would have been more local and temporary. **1871** MORLEY *Carlyle* in *Crit. Misc.* Ser. I. (1878) 189 That letter (of the moral law) read in our own casual and local interpretation.

c. Belonging to a town or some comparatively small district, as distinct from the state or country as a whole. ***local government***, the administration of the affairs of a town (or other limited area) by its inhabitants, as distinguished from such administration by the state at large. ***local authority***, an administrative body in local government (cf. AUTHORITY 3). Also *attrib.*

local board: in England and Wales *spec.* (see quots. 1863 and 1901). *Local Government Board*: a department of State established in 1871, to act as the central authority for Local Government in England and Wales.

1688 *Connect. Col. Rec.* (1859) III. 439 The law that doth confirm o[r] locall lawes. **1776** ADAM SMITH *W.N.* v. i. (1869) II. 402 The local or provincial expenses of which the benefit is local or provincial..ought to be no burden upon the general revenue of the Society. **1786** BURKE *W. Hastings* Wks. 1842 II. 191 He the said Warren Hastings hath left the said troops, by his new treaty, without any local controul. **1818** HALLAM *Mid. Ages* (1872) I. 128 Such is the national importance which a merely local privilege may sometimes bestow. **1844** H. H. WILSON *Brit. India* III. 279 The local government was involved in a discussion with the Supreme Court at the Presidency. **1861** MILL *Repr. Govt.* xv. 273 Things..which would be best left to local authorities if there were any whose authority extended to the entire metropolis. **1861** *Ibid.* 278 Among the duties classed as local, or performed by local functionaries, there are many which might with equal propriety be termed national. **1863** H. COX *Instit.* III. ix. 732–3 In the places and districts in which the [Local Government] Act is adopted, it is carried into execution by local Boards..The local Boards have extensive powers of undertaking and regulating the drainage and cleansing of towns, the suppression of nuisances, and similar matters of police. **1880** E. ROBERTSON in *Encycl. Brit.* XI. 21 Local government repeats on a small scale the features of the supreme government, but its business is chiefly judicial and administrative. **1897** *Lancet* 20 Feb. 537/1 [A Bill] which has for its object the superannuation of the officers and servants of local authorities. This latter term has a wide significance, as it includes practically all local bodies having sanitary and parochial functions, outside boards of guardians and other authorities, to which the Poor Law Officers Superannuation Act of last session relates. **1901** FAIRLIE *Munic. Administr.* 69 An important change.. was made by the Local Government Act of 1894..The urban local boards are called Urban District Councils, and the term of office of the councillors is fixed at three years. **1909** *Daily Chron.* 22 July 5/3 There would soon be a growth in the number of local authority training colleges. **1937** *Discovery* Jan. p. viii, The difficulty of persuading local authorities to provide funds. **1956** J. M. RICHARDS in A. Pryce-Jones *New Outl. Mod. Knowl.* 380 The best British local-authority housing. **1972** M. GILBERT *Body of Girl* iv. 40 We put her into a local authority home..and she stayed there until she was fourteen. **1973** *Inverness Courier* 31 July 4/4 It was noted with regret that a teacher from Kingussie High had been offered, but turned down, a local authority house, and it was left with the Clerk to tell the county housing factor.

d. In various specific collocations. ***local call***, a telephone call within a prescribed area around a telephone exchange (opp. a long-distance call); ***local cluster*** Astr., a cluster of stars (within the Galaxy) to which the sun belongs; also = *local group*; ***local examination***, the name given to certain examinations of boys and girls, held in a number of different places under the direction of a central board at one of the Universities; ***local exchange*** (see quot. 1940); ***local group*** (also with capital initials) Astr., the cluster of about twenty galaxies to which our own galaxy belongs; †also = *local cluster*; ***local line***, a railway line used by local or stopping trains (opp. *main line*); ***local paper***, a newspaper distributed only in a certain area and usu. featuring local, as distinct from national, news; ***local preacher*** (among the Methodists), a layman who is authorized to preach in the district in which he resides, as distinguished from the ordained itinerant ministers; ***local radio***, radio that serves a local area only; ***local rank*** (see quot. 1876); ***local room*** U.S., the reporters' room in a newspaper office; ***local supercluster*** or ***supergalaxy*** Astr., a supercluster to which it is thought the 'local group' belongs; ***local talent***, talented people, *spec.* (*colloq.*) the attractive women, in a particular locality; ***local veto***: the prohibition of the sale of liquors in a district, under the system of LOCAL OPTION (see e); hence the nonce-wds. ***local-vetoist, -vetoism.***

1927 E. MURRAY *Post Office* viii. 138 A fixed annual charge for the installation together with a uniform fee for each effective local call. **1975** D. BAGLEY *Snow Tiger* xv. 124 The exchange has a bank of batteries... We're all right for local calls. **1922** H. S. JONES *Gen. Astron.* xiv. 359 We must therefore conclude that our stellar universe has a longest diameter of at least 300,000 light-years... It seems probable that the Sun is near the centre of a large local cluster situated eccentrically in this larger system. **1938** W. M. SMART *Stellar Dynamics* i. 2 There is some evidence that the stars in the neighbourhood of the sun form a loose cluster—known as the local cluster—with characteristics of distribution somewhat different from those of the galactic system as a whole. **1971** *New Scientist* 29 July 245/1 The Supergalaxy is, in turn, composed of smaller clusters of galaxies, including the local cluster of about a dozen members, our Galaxy being one of them. **1858** *Exam. Students Not Members Univ. Camb.* 15 Notice for Local Examinations. **1861** *4th Ann. Rep. Delegacy (Local Exam.)* 1 The Oxford Local Examinations for the year 1861 commenced on Tuesday, May 28. **1940** *Chambers's Techn. Dict.* 507/2 *Local exchange*, the exchange to which a given subscriber has a direct line. **1918** J. C. KAPTEYN in *Astrophysical Jrnl.* XLVII. 106 Within this boundary the B0–B5 stars are about 12 times and the B8–B9 stars about 5·7 times more numerous than in the surrounding regions. This alone proves..that we have to do with a local group which probably does not extend in depth much farther than it does laterally. **1922** H. S. JONES *Gen. Astron.* xiv. 359 On the above hypothesis it must be assumed that the B-type stars belong mainly to the local group, for stars of this type do not increase in number with decreasing apparent magnitude as rapidly as do other types. **1936** E. HUBBLE *Realm of Nebulæ* vi. 125 The known members of the 'local group' are the galactic system with the Magellanic Clouds as its two companions; M31 with M32 and NGC 205 as its companions; M33, NGC 6822 and IC 1613. **1939** SKILLING & RICHARDSON *Astron.* xvii. 543 The two large spirals.., M31 and M33, belong to what Hubble calls the Local Group of nebulae. **1965** *Listener* 2 Dec. 891/2 The Andromeda Spiral and the [Magellanic] Clouds belong to what is termed the 'local group'. **1971** D. W. SCIAMA *Mod. Cosmol.* iii. 40 They [*sc.* galaxies] show considerable clustering, ranging from pairs of galaxies through clusters with fifteen or twenty members like the local group, up to clusters such as the one in Virgo containing several thousand galaxies. **1869** *Bradshaw's Railway Manual* XXI. 86 The question was accordingly referred to the arbitration of Captain Galton, who decided that the Midland might work the local line with Cheltenham..but that it ought not to work the main line. **1967** G. F. FIENNES *I tried to run a Railway* iv. 43 At Seven Kings we went down the local line. **1837** DICKENS *Pickw.* xlix. 532 If it gets into one of the local papers, it will be the making of me. **1883** Local paper [see PAPER *sb.* 8]. **1947** G. GREENE *19 Stories* 78 No book-shops, just *Film Fun* and the local paper. **1967** R. RENDELL *New Lease of Death* ix. 88 Elizabeth Crilling sat..reading the Situations Vacant in last week's local paper. **1772** WESLEY *Wks.* (1872) III. 476 A Justice levied a fine on a Local Preacher, on pretence of the Conventicle Act. **1885** *Min. Wesleyan Confer.* 369 Our supply of Ministers is drawn from our Local-preachers. **1966** *Economist* 1 Oct. 22/2 That aim should be the creation of a legal framework within which it would be possible to establish, without subsidy, a large number of low-powered local radio transmitting stations. **1971** *Guardian* 17 Nov. 10/6 The real question..is whether local radio can make a good profit and still be local radio. **1974** *Ibid.* 23 Mar. 10/1 Capital Radio, the general commercial radio in London..[is] in competition with four BBC networks and BBC Local Radio. **1876** VOYLE & STEVENSON *Milit. Dict.* (ed. 3) 327 *Local rank*, the rank given to an officer in her Majesty's service serving in a foreign land with other troops, whereby he is placed in his proper position, as regards equality of rank, with those officers whose first commissions are of the same date, but who have been more fortunate in promotion. **1890** *Scribner's Monthly* Aug. 157/2 We were all talking about it one night..in the local room. **1903** E. L. SHUMAN *Pract. Journalism* 90 Almost the only open door to the editorial room is through the local room. **1948** *Chicago Tribune* IV. 18 Jan. 2/3 The usual banter that goes on in a local room after presstime. **1958** *Nature* 29 Nov. 1479/2 We assume that the local supercluster is in a state of differential rotation and differential expansion about its centre in the Virgo cluster. **1971** *New Scientist* 29 July 245/1 They analyse the distribution, first of normal bright galaxies known to belong to a local supercluster of galaxies, and then of quasars and some peculiar galaxies. **1953** *Astron. Jrnl.* LVIII. 30 *(heading)* Evidence for a local supergalaxy. **1974** *Encycl. Brit. Macropædia* VII. 830/1 Evidence found in the early 1950s gave strong support to the concept of a 'local supergalaxy'. **1947** M. GILBERT *Close Quarters* xii. 175 You can play darts and engage the local talent in gossip. **1972** R. QUILTY *Tenth Session* 138 He's not the sort who would import local talent just for the hell of it. **1975** *Times* 18 Feb. 13/3 So much 'local' talent, so much unearthed by chance... Is the crafts revival the illustration of the desire for independence and self-sufficiency? **1894** SIR W. LAWSON in *Westm. Rev.* 27 Sept. 4/3 What would happen if they, the Local Vetoists, got their bill? **1900** A. J. BALFOUR in *Daily News* 29 May 2/5 Perhaps the hon. baronet would reverse his opinion about the infallibility of democracies, or even of local vetoism.

e. local option. The right granted by the legislature of a country or state to the inhabitants of each particular district to decide whether the trade in liquor shall be prohibited within the district. Hence occas. by extension, the principle of allowing localities to decide for themselves whether they will accept or reject certain regulations. Hence **local optionism**, the principle of local option; **local optionist**, an advocate of local option.

1878 SAMUELSON *Hist. Drink* 218 *note*, The tendency of legislation seems to be towards 'local option' or 'permissive prohibition'. **1880** *Daily News* 28 Jan. 2/4 The Home Rulers, the Teetotallers, the Local Optionists. **1882** *Encycl. Brit.* XIV. 688/2 Those celebrated 'local option laws' which are in force in some of the United States. *Ibid.* 689/1 Such laws are in force in Massachusetts, New Jersey (which had the Chatham Local Option Law of 1871), New Hampshire, Connecticut, and Vermont. **1882** M. ARNOLD *Irish Ess.* 174 Measures like that for granting Local Option, as it is called, for doing away the addiction of our lower class to their porter and their gin. **1901** *Scotsman* 28 Feb. 6/3 The reluctance of the Welsh and Midland miners to admit the principle of local option.

3. *Law.* (In renderings of the AF. phrases *chose local*, *trespas local*.)

1598 KITCHIN *Courts Leet* 180 b, Pur ceo que le chose est local, & annex al franketeñ. **1607** COWEL *Interpr.* s.v. *Chose*, Chose locall is such a thing as is annexed to a place. For example: a mill is chose locall. [With reference to Kitchin.] **1708** *Termes de la Ley* 419 An Action of Trespass for Battery, is transitory and not local, and therefore the place need not be..set down in the Declaration. **1727–41** CHAMBERS *Cycl.* s.v. *Trespass*, *Trespass local* is that which is so annexed to the place certain, that if the defendant join issue upon a place, and traverse the place mentioned in the declaration, and aver it; it is enough to defeat the action.

4. Pertaining to a particular place in a system, series, etc., or to a particular portion of an object.

a. Pertaining to, or affecting, a particular part or organ of the body. Chiefly *Med.*, of diseases, ailments, etc., and hence of remedies which are applied to such ailments.

1541 R. COPLAND *Guydon's Formul.* R ij b, The fyrste shal be of the locall remedyes of hote apostemes. **1543** TRAHERON *Vigo's Chirurg.* 25 b/2 The doctours make no mention of locale medicines in these diseases. **1606** SHAKS. *Tr. & Cr.* IV. v. 244 Tell me you Heauens, in which part of his body Shall I destroy him? Whether there, or there, or there, That I may giue the locall wound a name. **1667** MILTON *P.L.* XII. 387 Dream not of thir fight, As of a Duel, or the local wounds Of head or heel. **1706** PHILLIPS (ed. Kersey), *Local Medicaments*, those Remedies that are apply'd outwardly to a particular Place, or Part; as Plaisters, Salves, Ointments, etc. **1804** ABERNETHY *Surg. Obs.* 145, I employed only local means for their cure. **1813** J. THOMSON *Lect. Inflam.* 179 The Local or Topical treatment of inflammation. **1834** *Cycl. Pract. Med.* III. 49/1 The symptoms may be considered as local and general, the *local* being, principally, pain, tenderness, and tumefaction; the *general*, fever [etc.]. **1874** SULLY *Sensation & Intuition* 56 The exquisite delicacy of local sensibility, especially that of the retina. **1899** *Allbutt's Syst. Med.* VII. 11 A local inflammation or hæmorrhage.

b. *Electricity* and *Magnetism.* ***local action***, action between different parts of a plate in an electric battery as distinguished from the general action of the battery. ***local attraction*** (see quot. 1867). ***local battery, local circuit*** (see quot. 1868). ***local current***, a current set up by local action; also, a current in a local circuit. ***local oscillator*** (Radio and Television), an

oscillator in a receiver that generates oscillations (*local oscillations*) with which an incoming signal is heterodyned.

1841 BRANDE *Man. Chem.* (ed. 5) 297 In the common battery..much local action takes place upon the zinc plates without contributing to the circulating forces. **1867** SMYTH *Sailor's Word-bk.*, *Local attraction*, the effect of the iron in a ship on her compasses; it varies with the position of a compass in a ship, also with that of a ship on the earth's surface, and with the direction of the ship's head. **1868** CULLEY *Handbk. Telegr.* (ed. 3) 169 *Local circuit*, one which includes only the apparatus in the office, and is closed by a relay... *Local [battery]*, the battery of a local circuit. **1876** PREECE & SIVEWRIGHT *Telegraphy* 101 We then work by local currents. *Ibid.*, A local battery. *Ibid.* 102 In flowing through R' it..completes the local circuit by which the local current flows from L'B' through M'. [**1908** R. A. FESSENDEN in *Electrician* 4 Sept. 787/2 The heterodyne receiver, in which a local field of force actuated by a continuous source of high-frequency oscillations interacts with a field produced by the received oscillations and creates beats of an audible frequency.] **1913** *Proc. IRE* July 102 In the apparatus using a local oscillation generator in combination with a standard rectifier receiver electrical beats are produced and utilized. **1919** R. STANLEY *Text-bk. Wireless Telegr.* (new ed.) II. viii. 143 With an independent local oscillator C.W. reception can take place with very loosely coupled circuits. **1931** [see HETERODYNE *a.*]. **1967** WHARTON & HOWORTH *Princ. Telev. Reception* v. 74 The function of the mixer is to multiply together the received and local oscillator signals so as to produce an output at the intermediate frequency. **1972** *Sci. Amer.* Feb. 76/1 Radio telescopes receive signals that are at too high a frequency to be recorded directly on magnetic tape. Independent local oscillators must therefore be used to 'heterodyne' the radio-frequency signal..to a much lower intermediate frequency.

c. Arith. ***local value***: that value (of a numeral figure) that depends on its place or serial position.

1853 BARN. SMITH *Arith. & Algebra* (1857) 2 All numbers have a simple or intrinsic value, and also a local value.

d. Photogr. ***local reduction*** (see quot.).

1892 BOTHAMLEY *Ilford Man. Photogr.* viii. 68 Local reduction (*i.e.* reduction of parts of the image) can be effected by..applying a very weak solution of the ferricyanide.

e. local colour: (*a*) *Painting.* The colour which is natural to each object or part of a picture independently of the general colour-scheme or the distribution of light and shade. (Now usu. *collect. sing.*: formerly the pl. was used.) (*b*) Hence, in works of art or literature: The representation in vivid detail of the characteristic features of a particular period or country (e.g. manners, dress, scenery, etc.), in order to produce an impression of actuality. (*c*) Something picturesque in itself. Also ***local colouring***, ***colourist***.

1721 BAILEY, *Local Colours*, in painting, are such as are natural and proper for each particular Object in a Picture. **1782** J. T. DILLON tr. *Mengs' Sk. Art Paint.* 76 The local tints of the flesh, in every part are admirably diversified. *Ibid.* 80 If Titian was happy in his tints, and the local colour of his objects, Correggio..exceeded him in [etc.]. **1797** *Encycl. Brit.* (ed. 3) XIII. 599/2 The happy dispositions of colours both proper and local. **1821** CRAIG *Lect. Drawing* i. 15 The objects were all drawn..with a pen and..then thinly washed over with indications of their local colours. **1854** *Chambers's Jrnl.* 7 Jan. 8/2 Local colouring—*couleur locale*—is a modern expression signifying the accordance..of the adjuncts in a work of art..with the..subject. **1859** GULLICK & TIMBS *Paint.* 8 The local colour, which is the self colour of an object, and what we mean when we talk of a 'red coat' or a 'green field'. **1884** *Sat. Rev.* 22 Nov. 666/2 There are [in *Doris*] some capital pictures of the times of landlord shooting..without any-thing Irish in character, or dialogue, or local colour. **1904** F. M. COLBY *Imaginary Obligations* 7 Stupendous 'local color' work going on at every railway junction, and you heed it not. **1912** A. T. SLOSSON (*title*) A local colorist. **1934** *Amer. Speech* IX. 111/2 Villages with 'local color'. **1949** A. HUXLEY *Let.* 6 Mar. (1969) 593 About the country in which they lived you might consult, for local colour, a travel book by..Freya Stark. **1959** *Listener* 15 Oct. 616/1 [Henry] James never needed such ironic advice, since he was not a local colourist.

5. Pertaining to places (in the geographical sense) or to an individual place as such.

1605 CAMDEN *Rem.*, *Surnames* (1614) 112 The most surnames in number, the most ancient, and of best account, haue bene local, deduced from places in Normandie and the coyntries confining. **1857** R. MORRIS (*title*) The Etymology of Local Names. *Mod.* One of the most trustworthy of local etymologists.

6. *Math.* Pertaining to a locus. ***local problem***, a problem in which the object is to determine a geometrical locus.

1704 HARRIS *Lex. Techn.*, *Local Problem.* *a* **1865** SIR W. R. HAMILTON *Elem. Quatern.* (1899) I. 39 The degree of the function *f*, or of the local equation, marks (as before) the order of the curve [etc.].

B. *sb.* (absol. use of the adj.)

1. a. A person who is attached by his occupation, function, etc. to some particular place or district; an inhabitant of a particular locality. Chiefly *pl.*

1835 HOOD *Poetry, Prose, & Worse* xxxv, How sweet to be drawn for the locals By songs setting valour a-gog. **1891** 'H. HALIBURTON' *Ochil Idylls* 148 Gang freely, fishers, by their banks, Baith foreign loons an' locals. **1900** *Westm. Gaz.* 16 Mar. 1/3 He has been what is known in the legal world as a 'local'—that is, he has confined his practice to courts of Lancashire, and has not taken up a professional abode in London. **1901** H. G. HUTCHINSON in *Longm. Mag.* July 236 We go to some 'rough' as the locals call it—ground of long grass..giving fine protection for partridges.

b. *esp.* A local preacher (see A. 2 d).

1824 CARR *Craven Dial.* Gloss. 90 *Local*, a local preacher amongst the Methodists. **1889** T. E. BROWN *Manx Witch*, etc. 121 He cudn go on by the hour Like these Locals.

2. Something local.

a. An item of local interest in a newspaper; *collect.*, local news, matter of local interest.

a **1869** W. CARLETON *Farm Ballads, Editor's Guest* 36 So long as the paper was crowded with 'locals' containing their names. **1888** BARRIE *When a Man's Single* (1900) 17/1 There's a column of local coming in, and a concert in the People's Hall.

b. A postage-stamp current only in a certain district. **c.** *U.S.* Postal matter bearing an address locally used but not known generally.

1870 *Routledge's Ev. Boy's Ann.* Feb. Suppl. 3/1 The apparently interminable Russian locals. **1873** *Ibid.* Jan. Suppl. 4 Russian and Egyptian Locals. **1882** *U.S. Offic. Postal Guide* 681 Locals and nixes. Matter addressed to places which are not post offices is unmailable.

d. *Telegraphy.* A local battery or circuit (see A. 4 b).

1875 KNIGHT *Dict. Mech.*

e. A local train; a train which serves the stations of a particular district, or which stops at all or most of the stations on a line (opp. an *express train*).

1879 WEBSTER Suppl., *Local*..an accommodation railway train, which receives and deposits passengers and freight along the line of the road. **1902** *Strand Mag.* Jan. 74/2 He boarded the local in the morning. **1955** AUDEN *Shield of Achilles* i. 21 Any junction at which you leave the express For a local that swerves off soon into a cutting. **1975** S. JOHNSON *Urbane Guerilla* I. 21 The downtown local was already at the platform.

f. A local examination (see A. 2 d).

1893 *Athenæum* 4 Feb. 157/3 This [book] is intended mainly for students preparing for..the University Locals.

g. A local branch of a trade union. *N. Amer.*

1888 *Nation* (N.Y.) 3 May 356/3 The Knights of Labor have locals of engineers and firemen. **1911** M. W. OVINGTON *Half a Man* 98 Strong organizations in the South, as the bricklayers, send men North with union membership, who easily transfer to New York locals. **1949** *Newsweek* 18 Apr. 29/1 The local announced..miners would refuse to work in the pits with him. **1967** *Boston Herald* 1 Apr. 1/7 Nicholas P. Morrissey, New England regional director of the Teamsters Union, said Boston Local 25 will vote Sunday at 10 a.m. in the Charlestown armory. **1971** D. RAMSAY *Little Murder Music* 121 Statement of Detective Anthony Crawley, deputed to question members of Local 6, American Federation of Musicians. **1972** *Evening Telegram* (St. John's, Newfoundland) 24 June 3/2 A trawler..had taken aboard approximately 100,000 pounds of fish, according to Jack Dodd, president of the fishermen's local.

h. (Usu. ***the local***.) The public house in the immediate neighbourhood. *colloq.*

1934 *Evening News* 11 Sept. 10/1 After a modest beer or two at the 'local', bedtime calls about nine o'clock. **1937** 'T. SHY' in L. RUSSELL *Press Gang!* 178 What about a snort at the local? **1943** *R.A.F. Jrnl.* Aug. 4 Someone..has done him a good turn by..standing him a drink in the 'local'. **1954** L. M. BOSTON *Children of Green Knowe* 120 The story about it is widespread. It has been told me in much the same form in different 'locals' all over the country. **1957** J. BRAINE *Room at Top* x. 92 The Siege Gun was our local. **1970** G. GREER *Female Eunuch* 142 Women don't nip down to the local.

local ('ləʊkəl), *v.* *Scots Law.* [f. LOCAL *a.*] *trans.* 'To apportion an increase of salary to a minister among different landholders' (Jam.); to lay the charge of such stipend *on* or *upon* a landholder or his land.

1593 *Sc. Acts Jas. VI* (1816) IV. 34/1 To locall sufficient stipendis. **1695** J. SAGE *Fund. Charter* Wks. (1844) I. 248 The Earl of Morton..had flattered the Church out of their possession of the thirds of the benefices,..promising instead thereof localled stipends upon the ministers. *a* **1768** [see LOCALITY 5 b]. **1808** *Act 48 Geo. III*, c. 138 §14 The Right of any Heritor to surrender his valued Teind in place of subjecting his Lands, to the Amount of the Stipend localled upon them, shall not be taken away. **1816** SCOTT *Antiq.* xix, A clause, which had occurred in a process for localling his last augmentation of stipend. **1872** *Bell's Princ. Law Scot.* §1162 (ed. 6) 496 The localling or apportioning of the burden on the unexhausted teind is under the jurisdiction of the Court of Session as Commissioners of Teinds. **1877** in *Cases Crt. Session* 4th Ser. IV. 1127 The proceedings shewed that at this time there was sufficient free teind without localling on heritors who had heritable rights. *Ibid.*, The lands were localled on for stipend in an interim locality in 1853. **1880** *Law Rep.*, *App. Cases* V. 249 A scheme of locality was prepared, D lodged objections to the scheme in so far as it localled minister's stipend on eighty-one acres of his land.

locale (ləʊ'kɑːl), *sb.* [f. F. *local* sb., respelt to indicate stress: see LOCAL *a.* and *sb.*] A place or locality; esp. a place considered with reference to some particular event or circumstances connected with it; a quarter in which certain things are done, or which is chosen for particular operations.

1772 SIMES *Mil. Guide* (1781) 7 The Mareschal [de Puysegur] says, he saw a battle lost, because an Aid-de-camp had, upon a false representation of the local made to the General, been sent to him who commanded the right wing, to order him to change his ground. **1783** *Phil. Trans.* LXXIII. 189 Unless they attend..to the nature of the soil of the local where those accidents happened, their reports will generally meet with little credit. **1816** SCOTT *Bl. Dwarf* xi, O, the propriety of the *locale* is easily vindicated. **1842** BARHAM *Ingol. Leg.* Ser. II. *Old Woman in Grey*, But no matter—lay the *locale* where you may. *c* **1844** SYD. SMITH in *Mem.* (1855) II. 539, I hear that Lord Carlisle is wheeled down to the gallery... I know all the *locale* so well that I see him in his transit. **1865** E. BURRITT *Walk Land's End* xi. 381 Feeling that their little thatched cottage would, some day or other, be ranked among the celebrities of English *locales*. **1926** FOWLER *Mod. Eng. Usage* 331/1 The 'erroneous form' (OED) *locale* is recommended... If something happens in a locality, the locality becomes that something's locale, or place of happening. **1957** *New Statesman* 2 Nov. 551/3 Madison Avenue is already associated in the public mind (more than subliminally) with tricky manœuvring, having all but replaced Wall Street as a suspect locale. **1970** S. J. PERELMAN *Baby, it's Cold Inside* 226 My existence would acquire new purpose..if I could visit the actual locale of the movie. **1973** *Nature* 6 July 61/1 These locales were chosen with considerable attention to site safety.

localism ('ləʊkəlɪz(ə)m). [f. LOCAL *a.* + -ISM.]

1. Attachment to a locality, esp. to the place in which one lives; limitation of ideas, sympathies, and interests growing out of such attachment; disposition to favour what is local. Also (with *pl.*), an instance of this state of mind.

1843 BORROW *Bible in Spain* xxvii. (1872) 160, I have never seen the spirit of localism which is so prevalent throughout Spain more strong than at Saint James. *a* **1852** WEBSTER *Wks.* (1877) II. 526, I am one of those who believe that our government is not to be destroyed by localisms, North or South. **1877** S. BOWLES in Merriam *Life* (1885) II. 428 Congress is simply an aggregate seething and struggling of a great number of localisms—rarely or never losing themselves in the stream of national or patriotic feeling. **1883** *Spectator* 30 June 828 Agriculture is more weighted by what we may call the localism of labour than by any other single cause.

2. Something characteristic of a particular locality; a localizing feature; a local idiom, custom, or the like.

1823 E. MOOR (*title*) Suffolk Words and Phrases, or an attempt to collect the Lingual Localisms of that County. **1839** C. CLARK (*title*) John Noakes and Mary Styles... A Poem, exhibiting some of the most striking lingual localisms peculiar to Essex. **1850** FREEMAN in *Ecclesiologist* X. 284 Architectural localisms, as illustrated by the churches of Northamptonshire and Leicestershire. **1858** *Almæ Matres* 38 All talk scandal, gossip, localisms. **1897** *Saga-Bk. Viking Club* Jan. 306 Brushing away many of the most interesting localisms in thought and language.

localist ('ləʊkəlɪst). [f. LOCAL *a.* + -IST.] One who inclines to treat or regard things as local, to subject them to local conditions, etc.; a student of what is local; one who assigns a local origin to (diseases).

1683 O. U. *Parish Churches no Conventicles* 16 The Legislators had more regard to the Duty, than to the Place of it, and had more respect to the Discretion of the Priest, than this Localist hath; he labouring more for the Circumstance of Place, to gratify his own Humour, then the Intention of the Thing to edify the Congregation. **1833** *Cycl. Pract. Med.* II. 163 In our opinion, both essentialists and localists have taken a much too limited view of the etiology of fever. **1860** BERKELEY *Brit. Fungol.* 55 Where species are very difficult to distinguish, it is in general because forms are separated which are too closely allied, an evil which is familiar enough to every practical botanist, though apt to be overlooked or completely ignored by the inexperienced or mere localists. **1901** *Q. Rev.* Oct. 542 The 'Localists' attributed the epidemics to local conditions, atmospheric changes, uncleanliness, and so forth.

localistic (ləʊkə'lɪstɪk), *a.* [f. prec. + -IC.] Of a theory: Attributing a local nature or origin.

1882 *Pop. Sci. Monthly* XX. 336 The localistic theory of cholera. **1896** *Allbutt's Syst. Med.* I. 881 Until now he has defended the 'localistic' view [of the origin of cholera poison] against those of Koch and the contagionists. **1899** E. P. MORRIS in *Amer. Jrnl. Philol.* XX. 323 As long as the conflict between localistic and grammatical theories of the cases is undecided.

localitis (ləʊkə'laɪtɪs). *colloq.* [f. LOCAL *a.* + -ITIS.] (See quots.)

1943 *Newsweek* 12 Apr. 18 The 'Pacific first' strategists are now reduced to those afflicted with *localitis*, a military disease..common to those, usually in remote spots, who see their local areas as the axial hub of all strategic movements. **1961** WEBSTER *Localitis*, undue concern (as on the part of a military commander) with a particular area or the problems of a particular situation resulting in failure to visualize adequately the whole of which it is a part. **1962** *Listener* 8 Nov. 747/1 He was suffering from the complaint known in the Foreign Service as 'localitis'—such an intense obsession with his own particular field that he could not see beyond it. **1964** *Economist* 25 July 396/1 Among the world's occupational diseases, there is one that afflicts ambassadors. Americans call it 'localitis'..when an envoy is so captivated by the country..to whom he is accredited that he keeps urging his home government to follow a policy which that country would favour.

locality (ləʊ'kælɪtɪ). [a. F. *localité*, ad. late L. *locālitātem*, f. *locālis* LOCAL.]

1. The fact or quality of having a place, that is, of having position in space.

1628 BP. HALL *Old Relig.* vii. §3. 69 It destroyes the truth of Christs humane bodie, in that it ascribes quantitie to it, without extension, without localitie. **1661** BLOUNT *Glossogr.*, *Locality*, the being of a thing in a place. **1661** GLANVILL *Van. Dogmatizing* xi. 100 That the Soul and Angels..they have nothing to do with grosser locality, is generally opinion'd. **1772–82** MASON *Eng. Gard.* I. 181 Come then, thou sister Muse, from whom the mind Wins for her airy visions colour, form, And fix'd locality; sweet Painting, come. **1790** HAN. MORE *Relig. Fash. World* (1791) 34 The locality of Hell, and the existence of an Evil Spirit,

are annihilated. **1855** H. Spencer *Princ. Psychol.* vi. xiii. (1872) II. 174 Imagine a solitary point A, in space which has no assignable bounds; and suppose it possible for that point to be known by a being having no locality.

2. The fact of being local, in the sense of belonging to a particular spot. Also *pl.* local characteristics, feelings, or prejudices. *Obs.*

1771 Mrs. Griffith *Hist. Lady Barton* I. 33 And now I talk of coaches, I have never set my foot in ours, since you left London: I begin to think that this is carrying the idea of locality too far, and will therefore order it to set me down at the play-house, this evening. **1791** Burke *Th. Fr. Affairs* Wks. 1802 IV. 14 These factions..weakened and distracted the locality of patriotism. **1802** A. Hamilton *Wks.* (1886) VII. 246 The vast variety of humors, prepossessions and localities which, in the much diversified composition of these States, militate against the weight and authority of the General Government.

3. *pl.* The features or surroundings of a particular place. [So Fr. *localité*, 'particularité ou circonstance locale' (Littré).]

1828 Scott *F.M. Perth* x, Owing to the height to which he was raised, and the depth of the vaulted archway, his eye could but indistinctly reach the opposite and external portal. It is necessary to notice these localities. **1832** G. Downes *Lett. Cont. Countries* I. 61 After nightfall we walked over to Sallenches. The localities about the bridge reminded me of Milltown in the County of Dublin.

4. a. The situation or position of an object; the place in which it is, or is to be found; *esp.* geographical place or situation, e.g. of a plant or mineral.

1836 Buckland *Geol. & Min.* II. Index, Lignite, localities of. *Ibid.* Lituite, locality and character of. **1838** Hawthorne *Amer. Note-Bks.* (1883) 202 A blind man.. feeling all around him with his cane, so as to find out his locality. **1850** Robertson *Serm.* Ser. iii. iv. (1872) 53 The anatomist can tell you that the localities of these powers are different. **1860** Tyndall *Glac.* ii. xiv. 303 He insists upon the power of the glaciers to mould themselves to their localities. **1894** H. Nisbet *Bush Girl's Rom.* 249 The reports that the police were sending down constantly, of his supposed locality and outrages.

b. A place or district, of undefined extent, considered as the site occupied by certain persons or things, or as the scene of certain activities.

1830 Lyell *Princ. Geol.* I. 321 Pallas mentions that, in the same locality, opposite old Temruk, a submarine eruption took place in 1799. **1862** Stanley *Jew. Ch.* (1877) I. xv. 291 The deliverer is to be sought in the locality nearest to the chief scene of the invasion. **1880** Haughton *Phys. Geog.* iv. 185 The tremendous rainfall of the Khasi Hills, amounting in some localities..to 559 inches of annual rainfall.

5. *Sc.* †**a.** An assessment, tax, or levy, esp. one for the support of soldiers or other war-expenses. *Obs.*

1640 in *Minute Bk. War Comm. Kirkcudbright* (1855) 157 Desyering the said Committie to allot and allocate to thame ..ane competent localitie, furthe of the redrest of thair said husbands' rentes, goodes and geir, for aliment of thame and thair said childrene. **1659** in *Clarke Papers* (1901) IV. 161 We are in greate want of monies, to carry on our Locality, for coales and candle, all the six Companies beinge draune into the Cittadell. **1679** in McDowell *Hist. Dumfries* xxxvii. (1873) 426 Ane months locality for sixty horse. **1686** *Corshill Baron-Court Book* in *Ayr & Wigton Arch. Coll.* (1884) IV. 172 James Bichet..persued Robert Lachlane and Johne Wyllie..for the 2 pairte pryce of ane seck,..lost by them in takeing localitie to sojouris with corne. **1687** *Cameronian Soc. Let. to Friends* in Shield *Faithf. Contendings* (1780) 301 Paying any of their wicked impositions, as Militia-money, Cess, Locality, or Fines.

Comb. **1685** J. Renwick *Serm.* (1776) 151 Then shall cess payers and locality-payers be paid home.

b. 'The apportioning of an increase of the parochial stipend on the landholders, according to certain rules' (Jam.); the stipend as apportioned. Also short for ***decree of locality***.

1664 in Morison *Decis. Crt. Session* (1806) XXXIII. 14789 There being but a decreet of modification, and no locality, the Earl alleged locality should be first made. *a* **1768** Erskine *Instit.* ii. x. §47 (1773) 359 Where a determinate quantity of stipend..is modified to a minister out of the tithes of the parish..the decree is called *of modification*: but where that quantum is also localled or proportioned among the different landholders liable in the stipend, it is styled a decree *of modification and locality*. **1870** in *Cases Crt. Session* 3rd Ser. IX. 59 This was a process of augmentation, modification, and locality of the stipend of the parish of Cameron. In the locality.. one of the heritors..objected to the interim scheme of locality prepared by the common agent, on the ground that [etc.]. **1883** Ritchie *St. Baldred* 23 (E.D.D.) The Old Localitie, payable to the minister of Tyninghame, by way of minute.

c. (See quots.)

1807–8 R. Bell *Dict. Law Scot.* (1815) s.v., The term *locality* is also applied to such lands as a widow has secured to her by her contract in liferent. These are said to be her *locality lands*. **1872** *Bell's Princ. Law Scot.* §1947 (ed. 6) 831 In the stipulations of a marriage contract these points are important—1. A provision by jointure, locality, etc., if accepted, discharges the claim of terce... Locality is an appropriation of certain lands to the wife in liferent; her security depending on the completion of her right by infeftment duly recorded.

6. *Law.* Limitation to a county, district, or place.

1768 Blackstone *Comm.* iii. xxiii. 384 The locality of trial required by the common law seems a consequence of the antient locality of jurisdiction. All over the world, actions transitory follow the person of the defendant, territorial suits must be discussed in the territorial tribunal.

7. *Phrenol.* The faculty of recognizing and remembering places.

1815 Spurzheim *Physiognom. Syst.* (ed. 2) 364, xxiv. Organ of locality. *Ibid.* 368 This faculty measures distance, and gives notions of perspective: it makes the traveller, geographer and landscape-painter; it recollects localities and judges of symmetry. Hence it seems to me that it is the faculty of locality in general. **1875** E. C. Stedman *Victorian Poets* 187 To use the lingo of the phrenologists, his locality is better than his individuality.

8. *Psychol.* in phr. ***sense of locality*** (see quots.).

1888 *Encycl. Brit.* XXIII. 480/2 These investigations show not only that the skin is sensitive, but that one is able with great precision to distinguish the part touched. This latter power is usually called the *sense of locality*. **1889** *Syd. Soc. Lex.*, *Locality, sense of*, the faculty of distinguishing the part of a sensory surface to which a stimulus is applied.

localizability (ˌləʊkəlaɪzəˈbɪlɪtɪ). [f. localizable *a.* + -ability.] The quality of being localizable.

1957 *Think* May 10 Whitehead's reference to the fallacy of simple location, the reminder that existence need not be tied to localizability, was useful in its day. **1966** *Amer. Philos. Q.* III. 233/2 Spatial localizability..is not so shared. **1969** *Nature* 21 June 1207/1 Since the early days of quantum theory there has been much discussion concerning the concept of the localizability of a particle. **1972** *Science* 12 May 592/3 The ultimate localizability of space-time measurements.

localizable (ləʊkəˈlaɪzəb(ə)l), *a.* [f. localize *v.* + -able.] That can be localized.

1855 H. Spencer *Princ. Psych.* vii. xvii. (1872) II. 467 Such components of consciousness..being unlocalizable in space, and being but indefinitely localizable in time. **1865** F. H. Laing in *Ess. Relig. & Lit.* Ser. i. 196 It is the same localisable faculty that is supposed in the idea of the name's being 'called upon' one, as a pledge of God's favour. **1879** H. Spencer *Data of Ethics* vi. 78 The feelings classed as emotions, which are not localizable in the bodily framework.

localization (ləʊkəlaɪˈzeɪʃən). [f. localize *v.* + -ation.]

1. The action of making local, fixing in a certain place, or attaching to a certain locality; the fact of being localized. Also, an instance of such action or condition.

1853 Sir E. S. Creasy *Eng. Constit.* (1858) 371 The contrast as to the centralization or localization of administrative power, which exists between England and other civilized countries. **1872** Cardwell in Hansard *Parl. Deb.* 3rd Ser. CCIX. 895 With us, therefore, localization means identification with a locality for the purposes of recruiting, of training, of connecting Regulars with auxiliaries [etc.]. **1885** *Law Times* 14 Feb. 276/1 Nothing tends more strongly than localisation to confirm the despotic instincts in a judge.

b. *Phys.* The process of fixing, or fact of being fixed, in some particular part or organ of the body.

1855 H. Spencer *Princ. Psychol.* v. vi. (1870) I. 573 Localization of function is the law of all organization whatever. **1861** T. J. Graham *Pract. Med.* 214 The inflammation may be stated to be the effect of the localization in the peritoneum of the influence of a specific morbid poison. **1878** Foster *Physiol.* iii. vi. §3. 500 Hence it became very common to deny the existence of any localization of functions in the convolutions of the hemisphere.

2. Assignment (in thought or statement) to a particular place or locality. Also, the ascertaining or determination of the locality of an object.

1816 G. S. Faber *Orig. Pagan Idol.* III. 494 This curious though very natural localization of history. **1832** *Westm. Rev.* XVII. 405 To Bala Lake..there is a legend attached, which might be imagined to be a localization of the Deluge. **1857** *Zoologist* XV. 5479 The determination of the seat of these functions, or in other words their localization, has been attempted in every way. **1881** W. H. Preece in *Nature* No. 620. 465 In order to apply this apparatus to the localisation of a bullet in a wound. **1882** Grosart *Spenser's Wks.* III. p. ciii, The..fact..disproves this attempted localisation of her in the 'Vale of Evesham'. **1884** Bosanquet tr. *Lotze's Metaph.* §275. 481 The psychological genesis of our ideas of space and the localisation of the impressions of sense. **1886** J. Ward in *Encycl. Brit.* XX. 52/1 What has been..called the 'localization and projection' of sensations. **1899** *Allbutt's Syst. Med.* VI. 139 The localisation of the physical signs, and the differences in the mechanical effects produced, will probably make this fact clear.

localize (ˈləʊkəlaɪz), *v.* [f. local *a.* + -ize.]

1. *trans.* To make local in character; to invest or imbue with the characteristics of a particular place or locality.

1792 Mary Wollstonecr. *Rights Wom.* 123 May it not be fairly inferred that their [*sc.* the nobility's] local situation swallowed up the man, and produced a character similar to that of women, who are localized, if I may be allowed the word, by the rank they are placed in, by courtesy? *a* **1796** Burns *Remarks Sc. Songs* Wks. 1834 VIII. 18 Songs are always less or more localised (if I may be allowed the verb) by some of the modifications of time and place.

2. To fix or plant in a particular place or district, or in a particular part or point of any whole or system. Usually with limitative force: To restrict or confine *to* a particular place or area; to make local in range or currency.

1798 W. Taylor in *Monthly Rev.* XXV. 162 Their privileged banks [etc.]..which unnaturally localize and accumulate wealth, that was intended by nature for equal diffusion among the skilful and industrious. *a* **1835** J. MacCulloch *Proofs & Illustr. Attrib. God* (1837) III. xlii. 91 To localize peculiar foods to peculiar climates. **1839** *Spirit Metrop. Conserv. Press* (1840) I. 54 There, on that spot, stands the fatal axe of the revolutionary tribunal, naturalised everywhere, localised everywhere. **1859** G. Wilson *Gateways Knowl.* (ed. 3) 96 Though we are in the habit of speaking of it [*sc.* the sense of touch] as localised in the fingers. **1866** Grove *Contrib. Sci.* in *Corr. Phys. Forces* 201 The power of localising, if the term be permitted, heat which would otherwise be dissipated. **1888** *Daily News* 25 July 5/1 Contributors may subscribe either to the general fund, or, if they prefer it, to the local institute... It would be a matter for general regret if any very large proportion of the contributors localised their money.

b. To identify with a particular locality or localities; to attach to particular districts.

1870 *Daily Tel.* 24 Nov., The advocates for 'localising' the Army give us advice of the most valuable kind. **1872** Cardwell in Hansard *Parl. Deb.* 3rd Ser. CCIX. 895 The principles on which we propose to localize the Army.

c. To concentrate (attention) ***upon*** a particular spot.

1820 W. Taylor in *Monthly Rev.* XCII. 62 Localizing attention on the meritorious parts. **1861** Wynter *Soc. Bees* 493 Thus we may will that a spot in the skin shall itch, and it will itch, if we can only localize our attention upon the point sufficiently.

3. To attribute (in thought or statement) to a particular place or locality; to find or invent a locality for, ascertain or determine the locality of. Occas. const. *to.*

1816 G. S. Faber *Orig. Pagan Idol.* II. 254 The mere vanity of local appropriation, similar to that by which they severally localized the history of the deluge and the appulse of the Ark. **1833** Wordsw. *Fancy & Tradition*, Thus everywhere to truth Tradition clings, Or Fancy localizes Powers we love. *a* **1849** H. Coleridge *Ess.* (1851) II. 270 *note*, The Romans appropriated and localised every tale and tradition. **1855** Bain *Senses & Int.* ii. i. §12 (1864) 97 Part of the agreeable feeling in the exercise of the muscular organs..can be localised, or referred to the muscles actually engaged. **1868** Bain *Ment. & Mor. Sci.* 4 Descartes localized mind in the pineal gland. **1875** H. James *R. Hudson* vii. 232 It seemed to him that he had seen her before, but he was unable to localize her face. **1879** *Cassell's Techn. Educ.* iii. 182 At first it was a somewhat difficult matter to discover the exact place of the fault, or, as it is termed, to 'localise' it. **1879** *St. George's Hosp. Rep.* IX. 664 He was again attacked by intense headache, which could not be localised to any particular part of the head.

Hence **ˈlocalizing** *vbl. sb.* and *ppl. a.*

1816 G. S. Faber *Orig. Pagan Idol.* I. 397 The localizing humour of their religion. **1841** I. Taylor *Anc. Chr.* (1842) II. vii. 841 In every system of polytheistic worship there has been a localizing of divinities. **1870** Ruskin *Lect. Art* ii. (1875) 57 Speaking exclusively of this localising influence as it affects our own faith. **1898** P. Manson *Trop. Diseases* xxiii. 354 Pain on firm pressure with the finger tips in an intercostal space..is a common and valuable localising sign [of liver abscess]. **1899** *Allbutt's Syst. Med.* VI. 762 Any such localising symptoms as have been described.

localized (ˈləʊkəlaɪzd), *ppl. a.* [f. localize *v.* + -ed[1].] In senses of the verb: e.g. made local, invested with local characteristics; fixed in, attached or restricted to, a certain locality.

1816 G. S. Faber *Orig. Pagan Idol.* II. 26 The history of the Argo must have been well known to that southern nation, anterior to its localized adoption by the Greeks. *a* **1849** H. Coleridge *Ess.* (1851) I. 330 A strongly localized religion. **1860** G. H. K. *Vac. Tour* 136 The oak..has vanished altogether,..and I could never hear of or see any in the bogs, so that I expect that even in the old times they were strictly localized. **1869** E. A. Parkes *Pract. Hygiene* (ed. 3) 83 A very sudden and localised outbreak of either typhoid fever or cholera. **1880** *19th Cent.* No. 38. 708 That each native regiment should be composed of men of some distinct nationality, religion, or race, with a localised depôt.

b. Fixed in a particular part (of a system or the like); gathered or concentrated into one point or part; *spec.* in *Path.*, occurring in, or restricted to, some particular part or parts of the body.

1856 Dove *Logic Chr. Faith* ii. ii. 117 All matter is only localised and partial force. **1871** Tyndall *Fragm. Sci.* i. vii. (1876) 237 To produce the spark the heat must be intensely localised. **1880** Mac Cormac *Antisept. Surg.* 18 A localised abscess formed near the drainage tube. **1885** Watson & Burbury *Math. Th. Electr. & Magn.* I. 251 If we had an electric field with given localised charges. **1899** *Allbutt's Syst. Med.* VI. 859 Such localised pain soon becomes merged in the diffuse pain due to pressure on the cord as a whole. *Ibid.* VIII. 15 This form of valgus..is curable by localised faradisation of the muscle.

localizer (ˈləʊkəlaɪzə(r)). [f. localiz(e *v.* + -er[1].] One who or that which localizes; *spec.* in *Aeronaut.*, a device for transmitting a narrow vertical radio beam along a runway by means of which an incoming aircraft can be brought into line with it and any lateral deviation automatically corrected. (In quot. 1872, 'a reporter of local items'.)

1872 *Newton Kansan* 22 Aug. 3/1 This quiet season.. furnishes poor food for localizers. **1889** *Cent. Dict.*, *Localizer*, a small coil of definite resistance placed at each station of an electric fire-alarm system, which is brought into the circuit when the alarm is given, thus enabling the observer at the receiving-station to know the locality from which the alarm is sent. **1892** Mrs. M. Butler *Jrnl.* 26 Jan. in H. Tennyson *Tennyson & his Friends* (1911) 216 He [*sc.* Tennyson]..preferred to believe that Homer's descriptions were entirely imaginary. When I said that I thought that a disappointing view, he called me 'a wretched localizer'. **1942** H. L. Smith *Airways* 364 On the landing field engineers placed a 'localizer', which was a radio device emitting a peculiar beam. **1945** *Aeronautics* Feb. 29/3 The equipment linked up as a whole is then designed to guide the

aircraft steadily along a localiser beam to keep it in dead line with the centre of the runway. **1946** *Jrnl. R. Aeronaut. Soc.* Oct. 750/1 The first radio aid to approach and landing, consisting of a Marconi very high frequency track beacon or 'localiser' with associated marker beacons, was installed at Heston aerodome in 1935. **1965** *Sun* 28 Oct. 8/5 As the plane approaches London Airport it fixes on a 'localiser' beam which brings it into line with the runway.

locally ('ləʊkəlɪ), *adv.* In 5 localliche. [f. LOCAL *a.* + -LY².] In a local manner.

1. In respect to place, or position in space.

c **1430** *Pilgr. Lyf Manhode* I. lxxxvi. (1869) 49 Now lady, ..quod he, vnderstonde ye that localliche, virtualliche, or oother wise? **1551** CRANMER *Answ. to Gardiner* III. 85 The body of Christ was & is all one to yᵉ fathers & to vs, but corporally & locally he was not yet born vnto them. **1621** BURTON *Anat. Mel.* I. i. II. viii, By this faculty therefore we locally move the body. **1659** PEARSON *Creed* (1839) 383 By which that body..became substantially present in heaven, and no longer locally present in earth. **1746–7** *Act 20 Geo. II*, c. 43 §15 The shire [or shires respectively] within which such lands do locally lie. **1796** BURKE *Regic. Peace* iv. Wks. IX. 104 That they look upon us, though locally their countrymen, in reality as enemies. **1857** PUSEY *Real Presence* iii. (1869) 327 To Moses God appeared locally in the flame of fire in a bush. **1868** M. PATTISON *Academ. Org.* iv. 122 These establishments are not subordinate to the University, within which they are locally situated.

†**2.** In regard to a particular 'place' or topic; in particular circumstances. *Obs.*

1638 CHILLINGW. *Relig. Prot.* I. v. §47. 269 A man may Locally and properly depart from the Accident of a subject, and not from the subject it selfe.

†**3.** (Named) after a particular place. *Obs.*

c **1630** RISDON *Surv. Devon* §223 (1810) 233 Soldon had.. lords locally named. *a* **1661** FULLER *Worthies* (1840) III. 375 He was the last clergyman I find..who locally was surnamed.

4. In regard to a particular (geographical) place, or the situation of a particular object; in some particular place, in certain districts; in the particular place or district (specified or alluded to). Also *Comb.*

1860 J. F. THRUPP *Study & Use Psalms* II. 66 Those Jewish opponents of Christianity, still, perhaps, locally, if not generally, formidable. **1862** ANSTED *Channel Isl.* II. ix. (ed. 2) 223 The spiny lobster, locally called crayfish. **1863** H. COX *Instit.* I. i. 7 A further division of the functions of government.. distributes the offices of government locally under the heads of domestic, colonial, and international government. **1885** *Manch. Exam.* 30 Dec. 5/5 Vigorous efforts are being made locally to cope with the distress. **1896** R. S. S. BADEN-POWELL *Jrnl.* 5 Dec. in *Matabele Campaign* (1897) xix. 480 The locally-born children are as healthy..as you could wish. **1955** J. BETJEMAN in R. S. Thomas *Song at Year's Turning* 11 Locally-printed volumes. **1968** *National Fisherman* Aug. 26-A/3 U.S. firms are willing and ready to buy locally caught tuna. **1975** *Country Life* 16 Jan. 143/1 Perhaps Jay was asked..to revise a locally-made design.

5. In respect to some particular part or parts (e.g. of the body).

1800 JENNER in *Med. Jrnl.* III. 295 Dr. Jenner's assertion, that a person may be 'repeatedly affected, both locally and generally, with the Cow-pox'. **1897** *Allbutt's Syst. Med.* IV. 860 Locally a menthol spray may be used.

'localness. *rare*⁻⁰. [-NESS.] The quality of being local.

1731 BAILEY vol. II, *Locality, Localness*, the being of a thing in a place.

‖**locanda** (lo'kanda). [It., ad. med.L. (*camera, domus*) *locanda*, (room, house) to be let. (*Est locanda* is still used in Rome for 'To Let'.)] A lodging-house or inn.

1838 J. STEPHENS *Trav. Greece* etc. (1839) 11/1 When we found ourselves in a neat little locanda. **1844** *Mem. Babylonian P'cess* II. 263, I was carried to a locanda in Leghorn.

locant ('lɒkənt). *Chem.* [f. L. *locant-, locans*, pres. pple. of *locāre* (see LOCATE *v.*).] A number or letter in the name or cipher of a compound that indicates the position in its molecular structure of a constituent atom or group.

1946 G. M. DYSON in *R. Inst. Chem. Lect. New Notation Org. Chem.* 10 A number immediately preceding a symbol is referred to as a locant, as, for example, in '2ZN' or '6, 7QC'; in the second example both 6 and 7 are locants. **1952** *Chem. & Engin. News* 2 June 2337/1 He [*sc.* G. M. Dyson] also thinks that a subscript might be used to indicate a number of identical locants; for example 1,1,1,2,2,3,3,4-octachloro- might be written 1₃,2₂,3₂,4-octachloro-. **1965** *Nomencl. Org. Chem.* (I.U.P.A.C.) C. 29 The starting point and direction of numbering of a compound are chosen so as to give lowest locants to the following structural factors (if present). **1968** R. S. CAHN *Introd. Chem. Nomencl.* (ed. 3) viii. 79 Locants used for the ring system are the usual numerals—the '2' in the examples above refer to the 2-position of the naphthalene nucleus.

Locarno (lə'kɑːnəʊ). The name of a town in Switzerland used to designate the conference held there and the treaties signed as a result in 1925 between Germany and several other European countries for the preservation of peace and the continuation of existing territorial boundaries. So *transf.*, a similar conference, treaty, or agreement. Hence **Lo'carnist** *sb.*, a supporter or advocate of the policy adopted at the Locarno Conference; also as *adj.*; **Lo'carnize** *v. intr.*, to settle disputes by pacific means.

1926 *Glasgow Herald* 19 Feb. 8 Sir Austen had called Locarno only a beginning... Some business men, having settled a quarrel among themselves, said that they had 'Locarnized'. *Ibid.* 5 Mar. 9 We shall go to Geneva to work there as 'Locarnists' in the Locarno spirit. **1927** *Daily Tel.* 21 June 13/3 After Locarno there was..a genuine desire to get on better terms with the Reich. *Ibid.*, The demand for the evacuation of the Rhineland..has met with opposition, even in strongly Locarnist quarters. *Ibid.* 6 Sept. 9/5 All the talk about Eastern or Danubian Locarnos is very much in the air, when even the Western Locarno is seen to be in difficulties already. **1937** *Ann. Reg. 1936* [74] The answers of Germany and Italy to the invitation sent on July 24 to a new 'Locarno' Conference were still being awaited. *Ibid.* [189] The Hitler Government could count on the help of Italy in its negotiations for a new Locarno Pact. **1937** KOESTLER *Spanish Testament* ii. 60 The Europe of the Locarno period..would have reacted..with a storm of indignation. **1971** A. BULLOCK *20th Century* 72/1 Stresemann had refused to conclude an Eastern Locarno which would mean accepting Germany's postwar frontiers with Poland and Czechoslovakia, and in April 1926 he balanced his acceptance of Locarno by a new treaty of friendship with Soviet Russia.

locatable (lə'keɪtəb(ə)l), *a.* Also locateable. [f. LOCAT(E *v.* + -ABLE.] Capable of being located.

1936 *Discovery* Apr. 122/1 Thus we find..four parallel alleys, or 'zones', locatable at the 'wavelength' for the stream. **1964** *English Studies* XLV. 250 Any locatable regional dialect. **1968** E. RUSSENHOLT *Heart of Continent* III. vii. 101 Officials of 'the Company' and some free traders are locateable.

locate ('ləʊkeɪt, ləʊ'keɪt), *v.* [f. L. *locāt-*, ppl. stem of *locāre* to place, let for hire, f. *loc-us* place.]

1. *trans.* To appoint the place or situation of (the lands referred to in a grant); to fix the site of (a building, etc.). Chiefly *U.S.*

1765 C. COLDEN in *C. Papers* (1878) II. 10 Your Lordships Commands to give my assistance in locating their Lands on any part between New York and Albany. **1773** WASHINGTON *Writ.* (1889) II. 375, I have also taken the liberty of writing to the Governor of West Florida expressing my hopes of obtaining this land (and more) in case you should think proper to locate it in that government. **1780** *Virginia Stat.* X. 317 Be it enacted..That the ground to be appropriated to the purpose of building thereon a capitol..shall be located on Shockoe hill.

2. To survey and define the limits of (a tract of land); to lay out (a road); to mark the position or boundaries of, to enter on or take possession of (a land-claim, a gold-mine, etc.). *U.S.*

1739 *Hist. Pelham* (Mass.) (1898) 26 Voted..the Making a Road..and John Gray and James Allexander are appointed a Comittee To see ye same located in the most Suitable place for Publick Advantage. **1754** H. SHARPE *Corr.* (1888) I. 58 The method..of Locating Land Warrants by selecting the most rich and fertil Spots. **1780** *Virginia Stat.* X. 317 An act for locating the publick squares, to enlarge the town of Richmond. *a* **1817** T. DWIGHT *Trav. New Eng.* etc. (1821) I. 192 Such, as attended, drew for their lots; and located them at their pleasure. **1857** THOREAU *Maine W.* (1894) 303 If you want an exact recipe for making such a road,..send a family of musquash through to locate it. **1877** RAYMOND *Statist. Mines & Mining* 332 The Golden Queen Mine was located in the latter part of September, 1873. **1885** F. B. VAN VORST *Without a Compass* 10 He.. located a valuable claim near the Pyramid Mountains.

3. To fix or establish in a place; to settle; *pass.* to be settled, stationed, or situated. Chiefly *U.S.*

1807 R. CUMBERLAND *Mem.* II. 186 This was amongst the motives that led me to locate myself at Tunbridge Wells, &c. **1813** in J. Maclean *Hist. Coll. N. Jersey* (1877) II. 153 The Assembly passed an act locating the Theological Seminary permanently at Princeton. **1819** FRANCES WRIGHT *Views* (1821) 176 The Dutch and the German [emigrants] invariably thrive the best, locate themselves, as the phrase is here, with wonderful sagacity. **1823** *Stat. Massach.* 10 Feb., Said insurance company shall be located and kept in the town of Salem. **1833** HT. MARTINEAU *Charmed Sea* iii. 25 To work in the silver mine by the mouth of which they were located. **1836** MARRYAT *Japhet* I. xi. 133 When the gathering dispersed we packed up and located ourselves about two miles from the common. **1840** W. L. GARRISON in *Life* II. 386, I shall do what I can to locate him [N. P. Rogers] in New York. **1841** MARRYAT *Poacher* xlv, As soon as Mary was located, she wrote a letter. **1844** DICKENS *Pictures fr. Italy* (1846) 38 Albaro, the suburb of Genoa where I am now, as my American friends would say, 'located'. **1853** J. H. NEWMAN *Hist. Sk.* Ser. II. (1873) 216 They suffered themselves to be diffused and widely located through the great empire of the Caliphs. **1856** G. DAVIS *Hist. Sk. Stockbridge & Southbr.* 173 The stocks, which were a terror to evil doers, were located in the rear of the church. **1896** *Century Mag.* Dec. 218 He said he would locate his headquarters near those of Meade.

b. *U.S.* In the Methodist Episcopal Church: To appoint (a minister) to a fixed pastoral charge, as distinguished from the position of a 'circuit-rider'.

a **1814** T. COKE in Southey *Wesley* (1820) II. 464 It is most lamentable to see so many of our able married preachers.. become located merely for the want of support for their families. **1838** HALIBURTON *Clockm.* Ser. II. ii, I never heerd you preach so well, says one, since you was located heer. **1894** H. GARDENER *Unoff. Patriot* 46 He had asked the presiding elder to locate him as a married man for the next year since he was about to marry.

c. To place in an office or position. *rare.*

[**1769**: see LOCATED *ppl. a.*] *a* **1816** BENTHAM *Offic. Apt. Maximized, Introd. View* (1830) 5 His wish will..be, to see located, in each situation, the individual in whose instance the maximum of appropriate aptitude has place. **1828–9** *Ibid., On Militia* (1830) 5 Persons holding command in this body—to whom does it belong to locate them? To the monarch... To whom to dislocate them, and that at pleasure? To the same.

d. *pass.* Of a quality, faculty, etc.: To 'reside', have its 'seat'.

1829 T. L. PEACOCK *Misfort. Elphin* iv. 57 Even the tenth part of those homely virtues..are matters of plebeian admiration in the persons of royalty; and every tangible point in every such virtue so located, becomes [etc.]. **1865** TYLOR *Early Hist. Man.* ii. 32 Placing the hand on the stomach, in accordance with the natural and wide-spread theory that desire and passion are located there.

4. *intr.* for *refl.* To establish oneself in a place; to settle.

This is the earliest recorded use, unless, as is not unlikely, the first quot. is *absol.* from sense 2.

1652 *Virginia Mag. Hist. & Biog.* V. 35 Divers Indians.. have..suffered us to locate upon their land. **1837** DICKENS *Pickw.* xviii, Beneath whatever roof they locate, they disturb the peace of mind and happiness of some confiding female. **1858** *Jrnl. R. Agric. Soc.* XIX. I. 62 Scarcely any have more than two bedrooms, in which the whole family have to locate. **1883** *Harper's Mag.* Jan. 236/2, I..shall be the guest of Molly Porter,..while I'm locating. **1887** *Ibid.* Feb. 458 Their wanderings become more and more restricted, and they locate on the north or northwest faces of the highest mountains.

5. To allocate, allot, apportion.

1816 BENTHAM *Offic. Apt. Maximized, Extract Const. Code* (1830) 13 Remuneration thus located is a premium on inaptitude. **1828** *Edin. Rev.* XLVII. 88 The banks of these rivers are fast filling with settlements,—those of the Hunter ..being, we understand, entirely located.

6. To refer or assign (in thought or statement) to a particular place; to state the locality of.

1807 R. CUMBERLAND *Mem.* 476 Under this roof the biographer of Johnson..passed many jovial joyous hours; here he has located some of the liveliest scenes..in his entertaining anecdotes of..Samuel Johnson. **1842** J. H. NEWMAN tr. *Fleury's Eccl. Hist., Ess. Miracles* p. cxxix, As if inspired Scripture itself were so precise in dating, locating, and naming the sacred persons and sacred things which it introduces. **1852** —— *Scope Univ. Educ.* 153 That large Philosophy which embraces and locates truth of every kind. **1856** THOREAU *Autumn* (1894) 72, I locate there at once all that is simple and admirable in human life. **1865** MORLEY *Mirac.* vii. 157 These extraordinary actions of omnipotence are conveniently located in the past.

7. To discover the exact place or locality of (a person or thing).

1882 B. HARTE *Flip* i, He contented himself..with endeavouring to locate that particular part..from which the voices seemed to rise. **1896** H. S. MERRIMAN in *Cornh. Mag.* July 55 'We had a fire in the hold, and the skipper he would go down alone to locate it'. **1898** *Daily News* 2 Sept. 5/2 The gunboats yesterday made a river reconnaissance and located the enemy's position at Kereri.

¶**8.** *Civil Law.* Used to render L. *locāre* in the sense: To let out, hire out. *rare.*

1880 MUIRHEAD *Gaius* II. §50 A thing that has been lent or located to..the deceased. *Ibid.* III. §145 When a thing is located in perpetuity, as happens in the case of lands belonging to a municipality granted by it in lease.

†**locate,** *pa. pple. Obs.* In 7 locat. [ad. L. *locāt-us*, pa. pple. of *locāre* to LOCATE.] Let or hired out, leased.

1681 VISCT. STAIR *Instit.* I. xv. §5 (1693) 130 The Conductors Obligation is to pay the Hire, and after the end of Location, to restore the thing locat.

located (ləʊ'keɪtɪd), *ppl. a.* [f. LOCATE *v.* + -ED¹.] In senses of the verb; †in first quot. = put in its place (the opposite of *dislocated*).

1689 MOYLE *Sea Chyrurg.* II. vi. 44 Your compound Fracture..will be the more difficult to reduce, because of the new Located Joint. **1764** FRANKLIN *Wks.* (1887) III. 330 A claim that the proprietaries's best and most valuable located uncultivated lands should be taxed no higher than the worst and least valuable of those belonging to the inhabitants. **1769** *Pol. Reg.* IV. 140 Governmental,..200 noble; 300 senatorial; 25,000 located; 40,000 coated, red and blue. **1799** J. SMITH *Acc. Remark. Occurr.* (1870) 121, I took a journey westward, in order to survey some located land I had on or near the Youhogany. **1830** GALT *Lawrie T.* III. i. (1849) 84 Babelmandel,—a newly located town. **1833** C. STURT *South Australia* II. ii. 23 We were now far beyond the acknowledged limits of the located parts of the colony. **1894** H. GARDENER *Unoff. Patriot* 42 The village where he was soon to begin his first year's pastorate as a 'located' preacher.

locatee (lɒkə'tiː). *rare.* [f. LOCATE *v.* + -EE.] One who is located.

1816–30 BENTHAM *Offic. Apt. Maximized, Extract Const. Code* (1830) 46 An appropriate instrument of location, signed by Locator and Locatee.

locater, var. LOCATOR.

locating (ləʊ'keɪtɪŋ), *ppl. a.* [f. LOCATE *v.* + -ING².] That locates.

1816–30 BENTHAM *Offic. Apt. Maximized, Extract Const. Code* (1830) 55 The locating functionaries will..remain in possession of a power of choice, altogether arbitrary. **1898** P. MANSON *Trop. Diseases* xxiii. 356 When limited it [*i.e.* local œdema] is a useful locating symptom.

location (ləʊ'keɪʃən). [ad. L. *locātiōn-em*, n. of action f. *locāre* to LOCATE.]

1. *Civil* and *Sc. Law.* The action of letting for hire (correlative with CONDUCTION): see quot. *a* 1768. ***contract of location***: a contract by which the use of a chattel is agreed to be given for hire,

or by which a person agrees to give his services on the same condition.

1592 WEST *1st Pt. Symbol.* §29 If the partie commaunded haue anything for his paine, it is not then properly commaundement, but Location and Conduction. **1609** SKENE *Reg. Maj.* Table 86 Location (setting for hyre and profite)..Location and conduction of kirk-lands. **1651** HOBBES *Govt. & Soc.* iii. §6. 40 In buying, selling, borrowing, lending, location, and conduction, and other acts whatsoever belonging to Contractors. **1681** VISCT. STAIR *Instit.* I. xv. §1 (1693) 129 Location and Conduction is a Contract, whereby Hire is given for the Fruits, Use, or Work of Persons or Things. *a* **1768** ERSKINE *Instit.* III. iii. §14 (1773) 450 Location is that contract, in which a hire is agreed upon, for the use of any moveable subject, or for the work or service of persons. **1818** JAS. MILL *Brit. India* I. II. iv. 136 Part of the great subject, location, or letting and taking to hire. **1880** MUIRHEAD *Gaius* II. §60 If we have neither taken the thing from our creditor in location, nor on our own request obtained possession of it from him. *Ibid.* III. §14 [see CONDUCTION 7].

2. a. The action of placing; the fact or condition of being placed; settlement in a place.

1623 COCKERAM, *Location*, a placing. **1674** GREW *Anat. Plants, Disc. Mixture* iii. (1682) 226 As Mixture is varied with respect to the Bodies Mixed; so likewise in respect of the Mixture it self, which I call the Location of Principles, or the Modes of their Conjunction. **1799** J. WINTHROP in *N. Eng. Hist. & Gen. Reg.* (1873) XXVII. 354 The location of the camps and the idea of an harbor are mine. **1837** J. D. LANG *New S. Wales* I. 166 For opening new settlements for the location of additional free settlers. **1838** PRESCOTT *Ferd. & Is.* (1846) I. x. 404 The Castilian officers, to whom the location of the camp had been intrusted. **1891** *Month* LXXIII. 433 The location and translocation of spirits. **1901** *Scotsman* 13 Mar. 9/6 A possible location of batches of 1000 Boers at Dehra.

b. Appointment to official positions. *rare.*

a **1816** BENTHAM *Offic. Apt. Maximized, Introd. View* (1830) 7 Remuneration to the intended functionaries..for the time and labour requisite to be expended on their part; before location, in qualifying themselves for rendering their several official services; after location, in the actual rendering of those same services. **1816** *Ibid., Extr. Const. Code* 18 System of official location, or, for shortness, the location system.

3. The fact or condition of occupying a particular place; local position, situation. Also, position in a series or succession.

1597 A. M. tr. *Guillemeau's Fr. Chirurg.* 32 b/1 When the recurved muscles revert to there accustomede locationes. **1610** GUILLIM *Heraldry* I. vii. (1611) 29 The middle Points are those that haue their location in or neere to the Center of the escocheon. **1632** tr. *Bruel's Praxis Med.* 1 The head is more tormented with paine then any other part of the body; which is partly caused by the location of the head. **1653** BAXTER *Chr. Concord* 17 Our Reasons for the location and order of each part and terme. **1674** GREW *Anat. Plants, Disc. Mixture* iii. (1682) 226 Both the Conjugation, Proportion, and Location of Letters is varied in every Word. *a* **1817** T. DWIGHT *Trav. New Eng.* etc. (1821) II. 283 East-Hartford resembles East-Windsor in location, soil, agriculture. **1883** A. BARRATT *Phys. Metempiric* 173 Definite location in space is necessary for an intelligence having varied experience of a world of objects in space. **1883** P. SCHAFF *Hist. Ch.* II. xII. lxxxiii. 709 He knows the location of the praetorium.

4. The marking out or surveying of a tract of land (*esp.* of a 'claim') or a settlement; the laying out of a road or the like. *U.S.*

1718 *New Jersey Archives* (1882) IV. 379 Lands..laid out on Passaiak by name, and Scituate on ye same Passaiak by an actual Survey or location. **1770** WASHINGTON *Lett.* Writ. 1889 II. 275 Sandy Creek (one of the places allotted for the location of our grant). **1785** T. PICKERING in *R. King's Life & Corr.* (1894) I. 72 To explore the country and make locations. **1795** SULLIVAN *Hist. Maine* 159 There was no regularity in the locations of the lands. **1881** RAYMOND *Mining Gloss., Location*, the act of fixing the boundaries of a mining claim, according to law.

5. *concr.* **a.** (*U.S.*) A tract of land marked out or surveyed; *spec.* a mining 'claim'. Also, in South Africa, the quarters or area set apart for Black South Africans; occas. also used of an area in which Coloureds live.

1792 BELKNAP *Hist. New Hampsh.* III. 14 In the map.. those parts are more full and correct, excepting the lines of towns and locations. **1798** I. ALLEN *Hist. Vermont* 14 A few families settled..on locations from and under the Province of Massachusetts. **1809** KENDALL *Trav.* III. 173 Above Conway is Bartlett, the last town on the east side of the mountains, the lands above being at present only called locations. **1833** G. GREIG *S. Afr. Almanac & Directory* 191 The population consists of a mixture of Bastards and Hottentots, who are divided into about 60 parties, each of which has a district location allotted to it. **1835** D'URBAN in W. M. Macmillan *Bantu, Boer, & Briton* (1929) 128 He may be placed in a location in His Majesty's Colony [*sc.* the Cape]. **1848** THOREAU *Maine W.* (1894) 48 They tell a story of a gang of experienced woodmen sent to a location on this stream, who were thus lost in the wilderness of lakes. **1851** J. J. FREEMAN *Tour S. Afr.* xv. 361 They are located by the Government, and on these locations they cultivate lands and build their native huts. **1878** AYLWARD *Transvaal* ii. (1881) 20 They [i.e. the natives] are allowed as much land as they want for their locations. **1882** *Rep. to Ho. Repr. Prec. Met. U.S.* 321 The Grand Dipper is a promising location in the same locality with the Bunker Hill. **1894** M. O'RELL *J. Bull & Co.* 283 A kraal, called a location, where the Kaffirs employed in the town as porters, etc., live in huts. **1926** O. SCHREINER *From Man to Man* II. ix. 316 You..stood looking down at the..little brown huts of the Kaffir Location sleeping at your feet. *Ibid.*, A Kaffir servant might be seen hurrying from the Location to the town. **1945** R. HARGREAVES *Enemy at Gate* 241 The 'location' occupied by the half-breed fraternity. **1961** T. MATSHIKIZA *Chocolates for my Wife* v. 45 Several beasts were sacrificed and thousands of location residents partook of the traditional royal roast. **1971** *Rand Daily Mail* 4 Sept. 5/1 Transkeians were against the establishment of locations in their territory.

b. In Australia, a farm or station.

1828 P. CUNNINGHAM *N.S. Wales* (ed. 3) II. 141 Importation succeeding importation until the distance of the locations required a fresh central farm to be instituted. **1863** M. LEMON *Wait for End* xiii. (1866) 162 She was continually the companion of her father in his rides about the location. **1865** F. H. NIXON *Peter Perfume* 101 This 'location' of Deniliquin is the best place for spreeing I've ever been in.

attrib. **1846** J. L. STOKES *Discov. Austral.* II. vii. 246 A piece of land is obtained by a person who merely performs the location duties, and does nothing to his estate.

c. In the production of motion pictures, an exterior place, away from a film-studio, where a scene is filmed; freq. in phr. ***on location***. Also *attrib.* orig. *U.S.*

1914 *Scribner's Mag.* Mar. 276/1 It was his duty..to pick out 'locations', as are called the scenes and backgrounds of a moving-picture play. **1918** H. CROY *How Motion Pictures are Made* v. 120 If an exterior is chosen for the first scenes it has been selected in advance by the 'location man' and the director. *Ibid.* iv. 148 Now many actors are..in the studio or on location. **1928** 'I. HAY' *Poor Gentleman* iii. 42 They're converting the whole place into what is called a Location, where they can stage dramas of English country life. **1935** *Time* 8 July 32/3 The fault most likely to creep into pictures made on location comes from their producers' natural reluctance to throw away bits of local color even when these impede their story. **1957** M. SUMMERTON *Sunset Hour* iv. 62, I have been working hard... Working out location shots. **1971** *Daily Tel.* (Colour Suppl.) 12 Nov. 51/1 On location in Yugoslavia and at Pinewood Studios I talked to four people deeply involved in the filming of *Fiddler on the Roof*. **1973** J. LEASOR *Host of Extras* iii. 41 I'm hiring them out to a film company. Two weeks guaranteed, on location. Corsica.

6. Place of settlement or residence. Chiefly *U.S.*

1827 G. HIGGINS *Celtic Druids* 57 My theory or system to move the location of the first inhabitants of the earth. **1827** *Examiner* 261/2 [He] changes his character, costume, and location (as the Yankees say). **1839** MARRYAT *Diary Amer.* Ser. I. I. 138 These were students of Schenectady College: would I like to see it? a beautiful location, not half a mile off. **1876** BESANT & RICE *Gold. Butterfly* (1877) 218 They visited Windsor. Mr. Beck said that if he had such a location he should always live there. **1890** 'ROLF BOLDREWOOD' *Col. Reformer* (1891) 221 A..first-class, fattening, plains-country cattle station..having been his ideal location.

7. The action of discovering, or the ability to discover or determine, the position of a person or thing.

1900 *Geogr. Jrnl.* Oct. 382 These birds [*sc.* penguins] must have a wonderful power of location. **1962** A. NISBETT *Technique Sound Studio* 259 The script is also marked..with notes for quick groove location. *Ibid.* 276 These help in the exact location of editing points on tape.

locational (ləʊˈkeɪʃənəl), *a.* [f. LOCATION + -AL.] Of or pertaining to location.

1909 in *Cent. Dict.* Suppl. **1926** *Cleaning & Dyeing World* Oct. 19 He has one advantage, however, which the extensive advertiser does not have, and that is locational identification. **1957** *Economist* 5 Oct. 15/1 These two locational accidents could have served as the theme of the conference. **1960** ROBBINS & TERLECKYJ (*title*) Money metropolis: a locational study of financial activities in the New York region. **1971** *Nature* 18 June 426/2 In the population sector, locational attraction is a function of existing floorspace and available land in a zone.

locative (ˈlɒkətɪv), *a.* and *sb.* [ad. L. *locātīv-us, f. *locāt-*, *locāre* to LOCATE: see -IVE.]

A. *adj.* Pertaining to location.

1. *Gram.* The name of the particular case-form which denotes 'place where'; e.g. L. *domī* = at home. Also, pertaining to this case.

1841 H. H. WILSON *Skr. Gram.* 33 The termination of the locative case. **1862** T. CLARK *Compar. Gram.* 114 This view of the Locative origin of the Latin Genitive in the second declension. **1894** W. M. LINDSAY *Lat. Lang.* ix. §5 Locative Adverb-forms. *Ibid.*, The adverbial Locative cases of Nouns in common use, *hŭmī, dŏmī, militiæ*, &c.

2. Pertaining to appointment to offices.

1816 BENTHAM *Offic. Apt. Maximized, Extract Const. Code* (1830) 53 Of the locative function, the mode of exercise is as follows.

3. Serving to locate or fix the position of something.

1817 CHIEF JUSTICE MARSHALL in H. Wheaton *Rep.* II. 211 Entries made in a wilderness would most generally refer to some prominent and notorious object which might direct the attention to the neighbourhood in which the land was placed; and then to some particular object which should exactly describe it. The first of these has been denominated the general or descriptive call, and the last the particular or locative call, of the entry. *Ibid.*, If, after having reached the neighbourhood, the locative object cannot be found within the limits of the descriptive call, the entry is equally defective.

B. *sb. Gram.* The locative case.

1804 W. CAREY *Skr. Gram.* II. i. 35 There are seven Cases, viz. the Nominative, Accusative, Instrumental, Dative, Ablative, Possessive, and Locative. **1859** MAX MÜLLER *Sci. Lang.* vi. (1861) 206 There was originally in all the Aryan languages a case expressive of locality, which grammarians call the locative. **1867** RAWLINSON *Anc. Mon.* IV. iv. 214 The ordinary sign of the locative (which in Sanscrit and Zend is -i) was in the old Persian -ya or -iya. **1888** KING & COOKSON *Sounds & Inflex. Grk. & Lat.* xii. 341 The adverbs in *-ē* were originally locatives.

locator (ləʊˈkeɪtə(r)). Also locater, 7 -our. [a. L. *locātor*, agent-n. f. *locāre* to LOCATE.]

1. One who lets for hire; esp. in *Civil* and *Sc. Law.*

1607 TOPSELL *Four-f. Beasts* (1658) 55 Some buy kie and let them forth to farm, reserving the Calf to themselves; and if by the negligence of the Cowherd, the Cow cast the Calf, the hirer is bound to answer the value, but if it miscarry without his negligence, then is the loss equall to the Locatour or Farmer. **1652** NEEDHAM tr. *Selden's Mare Cl.* 87 The people was Lord thereof and Letter or Locator. **1681** VISCT. STAIR *Instit.* I. xv. §6 (1693) 130 The Obligation on the part of the Locator, is to deliver the thing locat, and to conti[n]ue it during the time of the Location. **1872** *Bell's Princ. Law Scot.* §133 (ed. 6) 60 The Locator or Letter of the subject or of the labour. **1875** POSTE *Gaius* III. Comm. (ed. 2) 423 The locator supplies a service for which the conductor pays the price.

2. *U.S.* One who 'locates' (see LOCATE *v.* 2); one who takes up a grant of land, opens a mine, etc.

1817 CHIEF JUSTICE MARSHALL in H. Wheaton *Rep.* II. 211 A subsequent locator..must look for the beginning called for in this entry twelve miles below the mouth of Licking. **1882** B. HARTE *Gentl. La Porte*, As one of the original locators of the Eagle Mine he enjoyed a certain income. **1883** *Century Mag.* XXV. 585 Here no locator encroached upon his neighbor's claim. **1883** STEVENSON *Silverado Sq.* 220 The place for the locator's name at the end of the first copy.

3. One who places persons in office. *rare.*

1816-30 BENTHAM *Offic. Apt. Maximized, Extract Const. Code* (1830) 34 Of this scrutiny, as of the other, the result will lie in the view of each locator.

4. Something which locates; *spec.* a device for indicating the position or direction of something. Also *attrib.*

1902 *Cyclists' Touring Club Gaz.* Aug. 359/1 A spicule of flint..pierced my tube, but kindly remained in evidence as a locater. **1919** *Nature* 30 Oct. 182/1 Sound-locators were also used to board anti-submarine craft. **1951** *Gloss. Aeronaut. Terms* (*B.S.I.*) III. 29 *Locator beacon*, a non-directional radio-beacon of low power, associated with a recognized instrument landing system. **1971** J. B. CARROLL et al. *Word Frequency Bk.* p. xix, The editorial outputs prepared from the tape files included..a locator list that can be used to determine the source of every token in the Corpus. **1973** *Black Panther* 21 July p. B, The automatic car locator system.

loc. cit. (lɒk sɪt), abbrev. of L. *loco citato* or *locus citatus*, '(in) the place cited', i.e. in the book, etc., that has previously been quoted.

1854 H. H. MILMAN *Hist. Latin Christianity* I. II. iii. 149 In the words of the ecclesiastical historian,..by such a deed a deep stain was fixed on Cyril and the Church of Alexandria. [fn.] Socrat. loc. cit. **1937** M. LEACH *Amis & Amiloun* p. xc, Kölbing, *loc. cit.*, and also in his edition of *Amis and Amiloun*. **1969** Y. KAMISAR in A. B. Downing *Euthanasia* 132 Chesterton, 'Euthanasia and Murder', loc. cit.

loce, obs. f. or var. LOOSE, LOSE.

locellate (ləʊˈsɛleɪt), *a. Bot.* [ad. mod.L. *locellāt-us*, f. L. LOCELLUS.] Divided into *locelli*.

1880 GRAY *Struct. Bot.* 419/1.

‖**locellus** (ləʊˈsɛləs). *Bot.* [L., dim. of *locus* place.] A secondary cell (see quots.).

1862 in M. C. Cooke *Man. Bot. Terms*. **1866** *Treas. Bot., Locelli, Loculi*, the peridia of certain fungals. **1880** GRAY *Struct. Bot.* 419/1 *Locellus*, a secondary cell, as where a proper cell (*loculus*) of an anther or an ovary is divided by a partition into two cavities.

loch[1] (lɒx). *Sc.* Forms: 4-6 **locht, louch,** (6 **louche**), 6- **loch.** [Gael. (and Irish) *loch*. Cf. the Anglo-Irish LOUGH. The word was adopted in ONorthumbrian as *luh*.] A lake; applied also to an arm of the sea, *esp.* when narrow or partially landlocked.

1375 BARBOUR *Bruce* III. 430 In A nycht and In A day, Cummyn owt our the louch ar thai. *c* **1375** *Sc. Leg. Saints* xx. (*Blasius*) 309 þe tyrand þane gert bynd hym fast & in a depe locht hyme cast. **1501** DOUGLAS *Pal. Honour* III. vi, Bot suddanelie thay fell on sleuthfull sleip, Followand plesance drownit in this loch of cair. *a* **1586** *Satir. Poems Reform.* xxxvi. 84 Quhen that þe Quene wes in the Louche Inclusit. **1596** DALRYMPLE tr. *Leslie's Hist. Scot.* I. 40 Amang the Lochis or bosumis of the Sey. **1609** SKENE *Reg. Maj., Crimes Pecuniall* 146 Na greene lint, suld be laid in lochs, or running burnes. *c* **1730** BURT *Lett. N. Scotl.* (1818) II. 102 Winding hollows between the feet of the mountains whereinto the sea flows..these the natives call lochs. **1791** BOSWELL *Johnson* 13 Sept. an. 1773, Kingsburg conducted us in his boat across one of the lochs, as they call them, or arms of the sea. **1806** *Gazetteer Scotl.* (ed. 2) 22 Extensive arms of the sea which bear the name of lochs. **1847** EMERSON *Poems, Forerunners* Wks. (Bohn) I. 447 On eastern hills I see their smokes, Mixed with mist by distant lochs. **1901** *Longm. Mag.* May 90 You may have heard friendly owls hooting to each other across a loch.

b. *attrib.* and *Comb.*, as *loch-fishing, -foot, -side, -trout*; **loch-leech** *local Sc.*, a leech; **loch-maw**, a species of mew (Jam.); **loch-reed** (see quot.).

1860 G. H. K. *Vac. Tour* 165, I do not care much for *loch-fishing myself. **1895** CROCKETT *Men of Moss Hags* xlvi. 328 The lads..now lay quiet enough down in the copse-wood at the *loch-foot. **1741** *Compl. Fam.-Piece* I. i. 43 In this Case Blood is to be taken at the Arm, or with *Loch-Leeches. **1829** HOGG *Sheph. Calendar* I. 182 The gowk kens what the tittling wants, although it is not aye crying *Give, give*, like the horse loch-leech. **1673**

WEDDERBURN *Vocab.* 16 (Jam.) *Larus*, a *loch-maw. **1777** LIGHTFOOT *Flora Scotica* II. 1131 *Arundo phragmites*. The *Loch-Reed. **1375** BARBOUR *Bruce* III. 109 Ane narow place, Betuix a *louchside and a brae. **1596** DALRYMPLE tr. *Leslie's Hist. Scot.* I. 46 Vpon the loch-syd of the Ness..is situat a verie..ancient hous. **1899** CROCKETT *Kit Kennedy* 224 The household at the farm by the lochsides. **1875** W. MCILWRAITH *Guide Wigtownshire* 21 The grey *loch-trout plays in the depths of the little inland seas.

loch². *Mining.* ? *Obs.* (See quots.)

1789 J. WILLIAMS *Min. Kingd.* I. 288 These open caverns are frequently met with in hard mineral veins, and they are generally called by miners lochs, or loch-holes. **1874** J. H. COLLINS *Metal Mining* Gloss., *Loch*, a cavity in a vein, a vugh. Derbyshire term.

loch, variant of LOHOCH.

Lochaber (lɒx'æbə(r)). Also 7 Loquhabor, Lochwaber. [The name of a district of Inverness-shire.] *attrib.* in ***Lochaber-axe*** (Antiq.): 'a sort of halbert of a large size, having a strong hook behind for laying hold of the object assaulted' (Jam.). Also in ***Lochaber-trump*** Sc., a Jew's-harp (E.D.D.).

1618 J. TAYLOR (Water P.) *Penniless Pilgr.* E 4 b, Harquebusses, Muskets, Durks and Loquhabor Axes. **1643** *Sc. Acts Chas. I* (1819) VI. 43/2 That they be furnisched with halbert, lochwaber axes, or Jedburgh staffes and swordis. **1812** W. TENNANT *Auster F.* II. xxxviii, Claymore and broad-sword and Lochaber-axe. **1814** SCOTT *Wav.* xvi, Two wild Highlanders..one of whom had upon his shoulders a hatchet at the end of a pole, called a Lochaber-axe. **1882** J. WALKER *Jaunt to Auld Reekie* 179 Lochaber-axes of the city guard.

lochage ('ləʊkeɪdʒ). *Gr. Antiq.* Also in quasi-Latin form ‖**lochagus** (lɒ'keɪgəs). [ad. Gr. λοχᾱγός (λοχηγός), f. λόχος LOCHUS + ἀγ-, ἡγ-, ἄγ-ειν to lead.] The commander of a lochus.

1808 MITFORD *Hist. Greece* III. 149 Xenophon..called together the lochages of the troops which had served under Proxenus. **1832** Lochagus [see LOCHUS]. **1849** GROTE *Greece* V. II. xlii. 254 Amompharetus the lochage. **1850** *Ibid.* VII. II. lvi. 112 Each lochagus had the power of dividing his lochus into more or fewer enomoties as he chose.

lochan ('lɒxən). *Sc.* [Gael. *lochan*, dim. of *loch*.] A small loch or lake.

1789 D. DAVIDSON *Seasons* 36 The rumour spreading round the lochan, The cause could not be told for laughin. **1811** MRS. ANNE GRANT *Superstit. Highlanders* I. 266 In the depth of the valley, there is a lochan (the diminutive of loch) of superlative beauty. **1854** H. MILLER *Sch. & Schm.* x. (1857) 205 A little irregular lochan, fringed round with flags and rushes. **1865** J. BROWN *Enterkin* 31 Still there sleep unnumber'd lochans Craig-begirt 'mid deserts dumb.

loche, variant of LOACH.

Loch Fyne (lɒx faɪn). The name of a sea loch in West Scotland, used *attrib.* to designate a type of fishing-boat having a standing lug mainsail.

1906 *Yachting Monthly* II. 15/1 The first boat built on Loch Fyne lines, and approximating in size to the ordinary fishing boat, was the May. *Ibid.* 19 Col. Dunlop's Loch Fyne ketch Marsailidh. **1930** *Ibid.* XLIX. 209/2 More odd rigs have been tried out here than in any other class in existence, including split lugs, Loch Fyne skiff rigs, and sprit sails. **1974** R. SIMPER *Scottish Sail* 31 The Loch Fyne skiffs were rather lightly constructed and seem not to have lasted very long.

‖**lochia** ('lɒkɪə). *pl. Path.* Also anglicized 7 lochies, 8 loches. [mod.L., ad. Gr. λόχια, neut. pl. of λόχιος adj., pertaining to childbirth, f. λόχος a lying in. Cf. F. *lochies*.] The discharge from the uterus and vagina which follows childbirth.

1685 COOKE *Marrow Chirurg.*, *Physic* III. xiv. (ed. 4) 605, If the Lochies flow duly, commit it to Nature. **1706** PHILLIPS (ed. Kersey), *Lochia*. **1722** QUINCY *Lex. Phys.-Med.*, *Lochia*, Loches. **1747** tr. *Astruc's Fevers* 352 The evacuation we call *lochia*. **1789** W. BUCHAN *Dom. Med.* (1790) 537 A suppression of the *lochia*, or usual discharges after delivery. **1857** BULLOCK *Cazeaux' Midwif.* 497 These purulent lochia.

Hence **'lochial** *a.*, of or pertaining to the lochia.

1753 CHAMBERS *Cycl. Supp.* s.v. *Lochia*, The lochial flux. *Ibid.*, Lochial fevers. **1808** *Med. Jrnl.* XIX. 11 She attributed her complaints to the profuseness of the lochial discharge. **1862** *N. Syd. Soc. Year-bk. Med. & Surg.* 382 In eighteen cases the lochial secretion was examined from day to day. **1893** *Brit. Med. Jrnl.* 7 Jan., Mem. 12/2 Between the birth of the two [boys] there was no lochial discharge.

Lochinvar (lɒkɪn'vɑː(r)). The name of the hero of a ballad in Sir Walter Scott's *Marmion*, used allusively for a young male eloper; also *transf.* (see also quot. 1951).

1879 C. M. YONGE *Magnum Bonum* I. xii. 233 His bride.. had had a young Lochinvar, and even in her wedding dress, favoured by sympathising servants, had escaped down the back stairs of a London hotel, and been married at the nearest Church. **1890** 'R. BOLDREWOOD' *Colonial Reformer* III. xxviii. 129 Much he marvelled at this Australian edition of 'Young Lochinvar'. **1906** 'O. HENRY' *Four Million* (1916) 125 He..received the hearty thanks of the backyard Lochinvar. **1936** J. BUCHAN *Island of Sheep* ix. 170 The young Lochinvar business was rather out of my usual line. **1951** E. HILL *Territory* 311 Lochinvars sold the women to the drovers and the stations at £10 a head. *Ibid.* 444 *Lochinvar, the*, old time term for catching lubras to work cattle, etc. **1966** [see EXTRAMURAL *a.* b]. **1970** *New Yorker* 3 Oct. 83/1 The majority of young artistic Lochinvars..have turned..to the tools and processes of modern industrial technology. **1972** 'J. & E. BONETT' *No Time to Kill* iv. 45 She looked..expectant, waiting..for the return of her young Lochinvar. But young Lochinvar..had found another bride, and she had married Eldred.

Lochlann ('lɒxlæn). *Hist.* [a. Irish *Lochlann* Scandinavia, *Lochlannach a.* and *sb.* Scandinavian.] A viking, (ancient) Scandinavian, Norseman.

1857 W. REEVES *Adamnan's Life St. Columba* 332/2 About the same time the Fortrenns and Lochlanns fought a battle. **1861** F. O'CURRY *Lect. Manuscript Materials Anc. Irish Hist.* x. 225 A book for the saints, and a book for the Fomorians, Lochlanns or Danes. **1880** W. F. SKENE *Celtic Scotl.* I. I. vi. 304 Forty-eight of the number of Icolumkill slain by the Lochlanns. **1905** *Westm. Gaz.* 15 Aug. 2/1 The ships of the Lochlanns lie in the river, and never send a man against her. **1922** JOYCE *Ulysses* 46 Galleys of the Lochlanns ran here to beach, in quest of prey.

lochlet ('lɒxlɪt). *rare.* [f. LOCH¹ + -LET.] A little loch.

1925 A. S. ALEXANDER *Tramps across Watersheds* 40 These lochlets with their ancient relics are mostly meadows now.

Loch Ness. [LOCH¹.] The name of a loch in Scotland used *attrib.* of a water-monster alleged to exist in its waters. Also *fig.*

1933 *Inverness Courier* 9 June 5/5 The Loch Ness 'monster' was seen near the west end of the Loch. **1934** *Discovery* Jan. 14/1 That elusive creature the sea-serpent is again in the news, this time in the shape of the Loch Ness 'monster'. **1937** *Ibid.* Nov. 334/2 Though the Loch Ness monster itself were laid before him in all its magnitude, he would still surely find an outlet..for his nervous, driving, shrewish disposition. **1959** A. HARDY *Fish & Fisheries* xiv. 364, I am deliberately not discussing the so-called Loch Ness monster. If there is some strange creature there it is clearly not a sea-beast bigger than a seal which might make its way up the shallow River Ness. **1965** *New Society* 9 Sept. 7/3 Britain's brain drain appears, then, to be something of a Loch Ness monster. It surfaces sporadically, then vanishes from view. **1971** *Stornoway Gaz.* 10 July 1/6 Preparations are now complete and they set off in a few days' time to try and capture that elusive denizen of the deep—the Loch Ness Monster.

lochtris, obs. pl. form of LACHTER.

c **1375** *Sc. Leg. Saints* ix. 219 þe lochtris of hare.

‖**lochus** ('lɒkəs). *Gr. Antiq.* Pl. lochi ('lɒkaɪ). [mod.L., ad. Gr. λόχος.] A division of the army, in Sparta and some other Greek states.

1832 ARNOLD *Thucyd.* v. lxviii. II. 339 The lochus then consisted ordinarily of 100 men, under the command of the lochagus... On extraordinary occasions..the strength of the lochus was doubled..while the number of the lochi themselves was not increased. **1849** W. SMITH *Gk. & Rom. Antiq.* (ed. 2) 483/2 The lochus here is a body of 512 men, and is commanded by a polemarch.

lochy ('lɒxɪ), *a. rare.* [f. LOCH¹ + -Y.] Full of lochs.

1828 J. WILSON in *Blackw. Mag.* XXIV. 302 As woody, as lochy, and as rivery a parish, as ever laughed to scorn Colonel Mudge. **1899** J. LUMSDEN *Edin. Poems & Songs* 6 Duddingston's lone, lochy dell.

† **'locitate**, *v. Obs.*⁻⁰ [f. L. *locitāt-*, ppl. stem of *locitāre*, freq. of *locāre* to let or hire out.] *trans.* To set or let out to hire (Cockeram 1623).

lock (lɒk), *sb.*¹ Forms: 1 loc, locc, 3-7 locke, 4-5 loke, 4-6 lokk(e, 5, 7 lok, look(e, (8-9 *dial.* in sense 2 luck, *Sc.* loake), 5- lock. [OE. *loc* masc. = OS.? *loc* (MS. *loci*, glossing *cesariem*; MDu. *locke*, Du. *lok* fem.), OHG. *loc* masc. (MHG. *loc* masc., pl. *locke*, mod.G. *locke* fem.), ON. *lokk-r* masc. (Sw. *lock*, Da. *lok*):—OTeut. **lokko-z*, **lukko-z*:—pre-Teut. **lugno-s*. Cognate words in Teut. are ON. *lykkja* loop, bend (Norw. *lykke*, Da. *løkke*), mod.Icel. (*h*)*lykkur* a bend.

The pre-Teut. root **lŭg-* (:*leug-* :*loug-*) prob. meant 'to bend' (cf. Gr. λύγος withy, whence λυγοῦν, λυγίζειν to bend; also Lith. *palugnas* compliant); it is formally coincident, or perh. really identical, with the root of LOCK *sb.*², LOUK *v.*]

1. One of the portions into which a head of hair, a beard, etc., naturally divides itself; a tress. In *pl.* often = the hair of the head collectively. †***fickle under her lock***: ? having guile in her head.

a **700** *Epinal Gloss.* 28 *Antiæ*, loccas. *c* **897** K. ÆLFRED *Gregory's Past.* xviii. 138 Eft hie ne sceoldon hiera loccas lætan weaxan. **971** *Blickl. Hom.* 243 Ne an loc of eowrum heafde forwyrð. *c* **1205** LAY. 18449 [Heo] sluȝen ȝeond þan feldes falewe lockes. *c* **1290** *S. Eng. Leg.* I. 330/237 His lockes weren ful hore. **13..** *Seuyn Sag.* (W.) 2207 But sche was fikel, vnder hir lok, And hadde a parti of Eue smok. *c* **1374** CHAUCER *To Scriv.* 3 Vnder þy long lokkes þowe most haue þe scalle. *c* **1400** *Destr. Troy* 459 His lockes full louely lemond as gold. *c* **1430** *Chev. Assigne* 254 And þenne she lepte to hym & kawȝte hym by þe lokke. **1526** *Pilgr. Perf.* (W. de W. 1531) 257 Those blessed lockes of heare..whiche in lyfe moost semely did become that gracyous heed. **1612** CAPT. SMITH *Map Virginia* 37 The lockes of haire with their skinnes be hanged on a line vnto two trees. **1667** MILTON *P.L.* III. 361 With these..the Spirits Elect Bind thir resplendent locks. **1712** POPE (*title*) The Rape of the Lock. **1740** LADY POMFRET *Lett.* (1805) II. 81 They wear..their heads dressed in locks with jewels. **1794** BURNS *Song*, Lassie wi' the lint-white locks. **1839** YEOWELL *Anc. Brit. Ch.* iii. (1847) 30 The hair of his head hanging down in long locks covered his back and shoulders. **1859** W. COLLINS *Q. of Hearts* (1875) 26 She sometimes begged for a lock of his hair.

†**b.** A lovelock; also, a tress of artificial hair.

1600 *Jacke Drums Entert.* (*Pasq. & Kath.*) I. (1601) B 4 b, And when his period comes not roundly off, [he] takes tole of the tenth haire of his Bourbon locke. **1602** *2nd Pt. Return fr. Parnass.* III. ii. 1209 He whose thin sire dwells in a smokye roufe, Must take Tobacco and must weare a locke. **1603** in Brand *Hist. Newcastle* (1789) II. 232 [Apprentices shall not] weare their haire longe nor locks at their ears like ruffians. **1666** PEPYS *Diary* 29 Oct., My wife (who is mighty fine and with a new fair pair of locks). **1676** SHADWELL *Virtuoso* III. Wks. 1720 I. 368, I have..all manner of Tires for the head, Locks, Tours, Frouzes, and so forth. **1688** R. HOLME *Armoury* II. 389/1 Women usually wear such Borders [of Hair], which they call Curls or Locks when they hang over their ears.

c. *transf.* and *fig.* (esp. of the foliage of trees).

1567 MAPLET *Gr. Forest* 56 b, Penroyall..It hath lockes verie like Isope. **1579** SPENSER *Sheph. Cal.* Nov. 125 The faded lockes fall from the loftie oke. **1667** MILTON *P.L.* x. 1066 While the Winds Blow moist and keen, shattering the graceful locks Of those fair spreading Trees. **1819** SHELLEY *Ode to West Wind* ii. 9 The locks of the approaching storm. **1850** MRS. BROWNING *Prometh. Bound* Poems I. 188 Let the locks of the lightning Flash coiling me round! **1851** C. L. SMITH tr. *Tasso* III. lxxvi, The grand oaks Which had a thousand times their locks renewed.

2. Of wool, cotton, etc.: A tuft or flock; a loose fragment, a shred, esp. one 'twisted on the finger of a spinner at the distaff' (Halliwell).

In *pl.* used by wool-dealers for: The lowest class of remnants after the removal of the fleece, consisting of the shortest wool, coming from the legs and belly of the sheep.

c **1300** *Battle Abbey Custumals* (Camden) 56 Et habere lockes de ventre ovium. **1425** in Kennett *Par. Antiq.* (1818) II. 251 De lana fracta, videlicet lokys, collecta in tonsura ovium. **1463-4** *Rolls of Parlt.* V. 503/2 By puttyng in Flecez, lokkes of Wolle, and peces of moche worse Wolle. **1483** *Act 1 Rich. III*, c. 8 Preamb., Great quantitie of Wolls..hath ben sorted..and thereof is made moche Lokkys and Refuse. **1523** FITZHERB. *Husb.* § 146 At the leaste waye, she may haue the lockes of the shepe, eyther to make clothes or blankettes. **1581** J. BELL *Haddon's Answ. Osor.* 477 What a noyse is here, and not so much as a locke of wolle. *c* **1640** J. SMYTH *Lives Berkeleys* (1883) I. 156 Money..yearly made by sale of locks, belts, and tags of Sheep. *a* **1656** BP. HALL *Rem. Wks.* (1660) 81 A lock of wooll falls without noise. **1697** DRYDEN *Virg. Georg.* IV. 476 Their Distaffs full With carded Locks of blue Milesian Wooll. **1710** ADDISON *Tatler* No. 229 ¶ 3 He goes into the next Pool with a little Lock of Wool in his Mouth. **1801** BLOOMFIELD *Rural T.* (1802) 3 She..laid aside her Lucks and Twitches. **1844** G. DODD *Textile Manuf.* i. 25 The clotted locks of cotton..are caught by the various iron pins, and torn open fibre by fibre. *Ibid.* iii. 97 The locks of wool are dissected, and the fibres loosened one from another. **1849** NOAD *Electricity* (ed. 3) 444 He took a lock of cotton two inches long. **1851** S. JUDD *Margaret* I. ii. (1871) 6 There is a bunch of lucks down cellar. **1883** *Leisure Hour* 243/1 The loose fragments of wool..are made up into bales by themselves under the name of 'locks'.

attrib. **1866** ROGERS *Agric. & Prices* I. xvii. 365 Inferior wool, known in the accounts as broken, refuse, or lock wool. **1899** *Daily News* 23 May 10/3 Fur machinists for lock linings wanted.

3. A quantity, usually a small one, of any article, esp. of hay or straw; a handful, armful, a bundle. Now *dial.* Also in Sc. legal phrase ***lock and gowpen***.

c **1440** *Promp. Parv.* 311/1 Lok of hey, or oþer lyke, *vola*. **1563-87** FOXE *A. & M.* (1596) 1879/2 His lying was upon the cold ground, hauing not one lock of straw, nor cloth to couer him. **1575** GASCOIGNE *Posies, Flowers* 38 Fewe men wyll lend a locke of heye, but for to gaine a loade. **1629** *Orkney Witch Trial* in *N. Brit. Advertiser* Oct. 1894 [He] fearing your evill, went to the barne and geve yow ane lock corne. *a* **1635** CORBET *Poems* (1807) 95 So good clothes ne're lay in stable Upon a lock of hay. **1661** D. NORTH in R. North *Lives* (1826) II. 308 Good grass which the adjacent inhabitants in summer cut down and make into locks. **1673** A. WALKER *Leez Lachrymans* 8 A lock or strik of Flax. **1711** ADDISON *Spect.* No. 131 ¶ 9, I suppose this Letter will find thee picking of Daisies, or smelling to a Lock of Hay. **1804** R. ANDERSON *Cumberld. Ball.* 89 Monie went there [Burgh Races] a lock money to bet. **1818** SCOTT *Hrt. Midl.* xiii. *note*, The expression lock for a small quantity..is still preserved ..in a legal description as 'the lock and gowpen' or small quantity and handful. **1823** *New Monthly Mag.* IX. 454/2 Spreading a good lock of tar round the bottom of the bush. **1827** CARLYLE *Germ. Rom.* I. 47 Gleaning, if so were that a lock of wheat might still be gathered from these neglected ears. **1843** LEVER *J. Hinton* xxi. (1844) 142 It isn't a lock of bacon or a bag of meal he cares for. **1847** *Jrnl. R. Agric. Soc.* VIII. II. 283 Children following the waggons to pick the locks of clover left by the pitchers. **1874** T. HARDY *Madding Crowd* iii, I'll curl up to sleep in a lock of straw.

lock (lɒk), *sb.*² Forms: 1-4 loc, 4-6 lok, loke, 4-5 lokk(e, 4-7 locke, 3- lock. [OE. *loc* neut. corresponds to OFris. *lok* lock, OS. *lok* hole, OHG. *loh* (MHG., mod.G. *loch*) hole, ON. *lok* lid, also end, conclusion (Sw. *lock*, Da. *laag* lid):—OTeut. **lokom*, **lukom*, *f.* **luk-*, wk.-grade of the root **lŭk-* (:*leuk-* :*louk-*) to close, enclose (see LOUK *v.*). OE. had also from the same root *loca* wk. masc. (cf. ON. *loka* wk. fem., lock or latch, MDu. *lōke* enclosure): see LOKE.

The great diversity of meanings in the Teut. words seems to indicate two or more independent but formally identical substantival formations from the root.]

I. A contrivance for fastening.

1. a. An appliance for fastening a door, lid, etc., consisting of a bolt (or system of bolts) with mechanism by which it can be propelled and withdrawn by means of a key or similar instrument. (In OE. app. used with wider

meaning, applied, e.g. to a bar, bolt, latch, or the like.)

c **900** tr. *Bæda's Hist.* I. i. (Schipper) 9 Mid þam æðelestum ceastrum..ða þe wæron mid..ȝeatum and þam trumestum locum ȝetimbrade. *c* **1000** ÆLFRIC *Hom.* II. 572 Godes engel undyde ða locu ðæs cwearternes. *c* **1175** *Lamb. Hom.* 127 Þet is þet loc þeðe deofel ne con unlucan. *a* **1300–1400** *Cursor M.* 17357 (Gött.) Þai..vndid þair lock all wid þe kay. *c* **1315** SHOREHAM I. 2146 Seynt Iohan..seȝ a bok was fast ischet Wyþ strong[e] lokes seuene. **1393** LANGL. *P. Pl.* C. VII. 266 Ich..pryuyliche hus pors shok, vnpiked hus lokes. *a* **1420** HOCCLEVE *De Reg. Princ.* 1098 Necessarie vnto him is it Barres and lokkes stronge for to haue. **1500–20** DUNBAR *Poems* lv. 13 Thai brak vp durris, and raeff vp lockis. **1536** *Reg. Riches* in *Antiq. Sarisb.* (1771) 195 Gemmels and locks of silver, containing the Coronation of our Lady. **1562** *Child Marriages* 131 To pull out the nayles of the hindges, and open hit [a chest] on the other side, contrary to the locke. **1611** BIBLE *Song Sol.* v. 5 My hands dropped with myrrhe ..vpon the handles of the locke. *a* **1625** BEAUM. & FL. *Noble Gent.* v. i, A strange locke that opens with Amen. **1796** H. HUNTER tr. *St.-Pierre's Stud. Nat.* (1797) 311 See under how many locks and doors these metals are secured. **1833** J. HOLLAND *Manuf. Metal* II. 263 Early fame of Wolverhampton locks. **1889** G. FINDLAY *Eng. Railway* 94 The Electric lock has been designed to lock and unlock sidings at a distance from the signal box.

transf. and *fig.* **1340** *Ayenb.* 255 Do to þine mouþe a dore and a loc. **1393** LANGL. *P. Pl.* C. II. 198 And þat is þe lok of loue þat vn-loseþ grace. **1526** *Pilgr. Perf.* (W. de W. 1531) 132 The locke of good aduysement shall be set on our lyppes. **1725** RAMSAY *Gentle Sheph.* III. iv, Obedience to your strict command Was the first lock. **1831** CARLYLE *Sart. Res.* II. vi, I kept a lock upon my lips.

¶ App. explained to mean: A wicket or hatch (or perh. a leaf of a door or casement). Cf. LOUK *sb.*

c **1440** *Promp. Parv.* 311/1 Loke, sperynge of a dore or wyndow, *valva*. [See Way's note s.v.]

b. Phrases. ***lock and key*** (rarely † ***key and lock***) occurs freq. as a phraseological combination in the literal sense or as a typical expression for appliances for fastening or securing; also *fig.* (freq. *attrib.*) with allusion to the structural complementarity or mutual specificity of a lock and its key. ***under lock and key***, formerly also † ***under (a) lock*** (cf. KEY *sb.* 1 b): securely locked up. So ***under lock and seal***, † ***under lock and hasp***, etc.

a **1250** *Owl & Night.* 1557 He hire bi-lukþ myd keye and loke. *a* **1300–1400** *Cursor M.* 14711 (Gött.) Ioseph..ȝe lokid vnder lock and sele. *c* **1400** MAUNDEV. (Roxb.) xx. 89 Þare es na thing vnder lokk, and als riche es a man as anoþer. **1413** HOCCLEVE *Min. Poems* (1892) 48 He, of thy soules helthe, is lok and keye. **1432–50** tr. *Higden* (Rolls) I. 373 Kepenge hit with grete diligence vnder a locke. *c* **1485** *Digby Myst.* (1882) I. 389 God, that art both lok and keye of all goodnesse. **1522** *Bury Wills* (Camden) 116 A rownde tabyll of waynskott wᵗ lok and key. *c* **1570** *Marr. Wit & Sci.* II. i. B ij, Althinges must be kept vnder locke and haspe. **1585** T. WASHINGTON tr. *Nicholay's Voy.* IV. xxxi. 154 With great care [they] kept their wyves so closely under lock and key. **1635** J. HAYWARD tr. *Biondi's Banish'd Virg.* 105 The foremost [room] whereof was assured with a good lock and key. *c* **1860** H. STUART *Seaman's Catech.* 62 Under lock and key, in the..store room. [**1894** E. FISCHER in *Ber. d. Deut. Chem. Ges.* XXVII. 2992 Um ein Bild zu gebrauchen, will ich sagen, dass Enzym und Glucosid wie Schloss und Schlüssel zu einander passen müssen, um eine chemische Wirkung auf einander ausüben zu können.] **1899** MARY CHOLMONDELEY *Red Pottage* 224 She has a lock-and-key face. **1901** C. A. MITCHELL tr. *Oppenheimer's Ferments* v. 65 Two haptophore groups coinciding with one another ('lock and key') and a subsequently active zymophore group. **1924** K. G. FALK *Chem. Enzyme Actions* (ed. 2) v. 116 E. Fischer's lock-and-key simile for the mutual getting together of substrate and enzyme, each fitting in with the other, gives a mechanical picture of the action. **1950** *Sci. News* XV. 120 So far, blood group antibodies have been described as having the property of reacting by agglutination with red cells which contain the specific antigen, and with no others, on the lock-and-key principle. **1969** *Times* 25 Apr. 13/6 It seems that some of the proteins in the mixture are able to recognize and bind to certain sites on the RNA molecule by a lock-and-key mechanism. **1974** *Physics Bull.* Dec. 581/1 The lock and key interaction between enzyme and substrate does not usually involve strong covalent bonds.

c. ***locks-and-keys*** (dial.): see quots.

1837 J. F. PALMER *Devon. Gloss.*, *Locks-and-keys*, the seed-pods of the ash and sycamore. **1847** HALLIWELL, *Locks-and-keys.* Ash-keys. *West.*

2. 'A cotter or key; as the one which fastens the cap-square over the trunnion of a mounted cannon; a forelock' (Knight *Dict. Mech.* 1875).

† **3.** A hobble or shackle on a horse's (or other animal's) foot to prevent it from straying. Also HORSE-LOCK. *Obs.*

[**1486** etc.: see HORSE-LOCK.] **1528** LYNDESAY *Dreme* 894 Quho wyll go sers amang sic heirdis scheip, May, habyll, fynd mony pure scabbit crok, And goyng wyll at large, withouttin lok. **1539** *MS. Acc. St. John's Hosp., Canterb.*, Payd for a lock for the mare. **1610** MARKHAM *Masterp.* II. lxxxiv. 364 If a horse be galled in the pastorne, on the heele, or vpon the cronet, either with shackell or locke. **1695** *Lond. Gaz.* No. 3065/4 Stolen or Stray'd.., a Roan..Gelding,.. with a Lock on his Foot.

transf. **1589** HAKLUYT *Voy.* 151 Till at the last, God sent him [John Fox] fauour in the sight of the keeper of the prison, so that he had leaue to goe in and out..wearing a locke about his legge.

4. A contrivance to keep a wheel from revolving, or from turning to right or left. (Cf. *lock-chain.*)

1884 J. G. BOURKE *Snake-Dance Moquis* i. 8 There was no brake, no shoe to the wheels. **1898** *Cycling* 37 Steering Locks are valuable..for preventing the machine from moving when resting against a wall.

5. In fire-arms, the piece of mechanism by means of which the charge is exploded. (See also FIRELOCK, FLINT-LOCK, MATCHLOCK.) Phr. ***lock, stock, and barrel*** = the entirety of anything; also as *advb. phr.* (See also STOCK *sb.*¹ 28 b.)

[Appears first in the comb. FIRELOCK. Prob. the name is due to some resemblance of the mechanism of the original wheel firelock to that of a lock (sense 1). Cf. G. *schloss*, used both for the 'lock' of a door and the 'lock' of a gun.]

1547, etc. [see FIRELOCK 1]. **1681** GREW *Musæum* 366 Under the Breech of the Barrel is one Box for the Powder. A little before the Lock, another for the Bullets; Behind the Cock, a Charger, which carries the Powder to the further end of the Lock. **1725** *Lond. Gaz.* No. 6390/2 They broke some of the Locks of their Pieces. **1833** J. HOLLAND *Manuf. Metal* II. 90 The priming was laid in the hollow at the side of the lock. **1839** MARRYAT *Phant. Ship* iv, I'll put a new flint in my lock. **1842** W. T. THOMPSON *Major Jones' Courtship* (1844) 66 All moved, lock, stock, and barrel. **1855** S. A. HAMMETT *Wonderful Adventures Captain Priest* xii. 76 He sold off his feathered stock, 'lock, stock, and barrel'. **1891** R. KIPLING *Light that failed* v, The whole thing, lock, stock, and barrel, isn't worth one big yellow sea-poppy. **1909** [see CAGEY *a.*]. **1961** B. FERGUSSON *Watery Maze* xii. 292 One of the ministries would take over lock, stock and barrel the administration. **1974** P. ERDMAN *Silver Bears* i. 12, I bought us a Swiss bank: lock, stock and barrel.

6. Short for ROW-LOCK.

1850 SCORESBY *Cheever's Whalem. Adv.* xii. (1859) 178, I had placed my left hand and weight against the oar. Instantly laying hold of his own in like manner, his first effort broke it short at the lock.

II. A barrier, an enclosure. [Cf. OE. *gáta loc* pen for goats.]

† **7.** A barrier on a river, constructed so as to be opened or closed at pleasure. (See quots. 1758, 1793.) *Obs.*

? *c* **1300** *Rolls of Parlt.* I. 475 Il sont desturbeez par Gortz, par Lokes, & par Molins. **1472–5** *Ibid.* VI. 159/1 Milles, Mille dammes, Mille pooles, Lokkes,..and dyvers other ympedymentes. **1531–2** *Act 23 Hen. VIII*, c. 5 §1 Weares.. gores gootes fludgates lockes. **1576** in W. H. Turner *Select. Rec. Oxford* 387 A lock called Rewley lock is to be repayred. **1613–16** W. BROWNE *Brit. Past.* I. ii. Wks. 1772 I. 47 Let no man dare To spoile thy fish, make locke or ware. **1677** PLOT *Oxfordsh.* 233 Provided the fall of water be not great, a Lock will suffice, which is made up only of bars of wood called Rimers, set perpendicularly to the bottom of the passage. **1758** BINNELL *Descr. Thames* 158 The Use of Locks was happily invented, which are a Kind of wooden Machines, placed quite a-cross the River, and so contrived, as totally to obstruct the Current of the Stream, and dam up the Water.

† **8.** The passage or waterway between the piers of a bridge. *Obs.*

1545 in W. H. Turner *Select. Rec. Oxford* 177 A certen lokk..called Ruly myddell lokk shall be stopped upp. **1685** *Lond. Gaz.* No. 2062/4 Vessels..too large to pass through any other Lock of the said Bridge. **1705** *Ibid.* No. 4121/4 The Lock belonging to London-Bridge, commonly called the Draw-Bridge-Lock, will be barrocaded up. **1813** T. FAULKNER *Fulham* 6 The largest opening for the passage of vessels is in the middle,..and is called Walpole's Lock.

9. a. On a canal or river: A portion of the channel shut off above and below by folding gates provided with sluices to let the water out or in, and thus raise or lower boats from one water level to another.

1577 W. VALLANS *Tale two Swannes* in *Leland's Itin.* (1759) V. p. xiii, This locke containes two double doores of wood, Within the same a Cesterne all of Plancke, Which only fills when boates come there to passe. **1677** YARRANTON *Eng. Improv.* 154 Building two great Stone Locks or Sluces to let down and bring up the Ships. **1742** YOUNG *Nt. Th.* VI. 511 O be content, where heav'n can give no more! More, like a flash of water from a lock, Quickens our spirit's movement for an hour. **1794** S. WILLIAMS *Vermont* 34 Except the falls, which the states are now making navigable by locks. *a* **1817** T. DWIGHT *Trav. New Eng.*, etc. (1821) II. 94 The whole number of locks, including a guard lock, is seven. **1831** LARDNER *Hydrost.* iv. 67 The surface of the water in the lock is thus slowly elevated raising the vessel with it. **1866** M. ARNOLD *Thyrsis* xiii, Where is the girl, who by the boatman's door, Above the locks..Unmoor'd our skiff?

b. The quantity of water which fills a lock.

1791 W. JESSOP *Rep. River Witham* 7 The Trade on the Navigation..will take two Locks of water.

† **c.** A 'lift' on a railway, for raising and lowering vehicles from one level to another. *Obs.*

a **1824** DICKSON in *Trans. Highland Soc.* VI. 115 The plans for the locks may be divided into two, one for water, condensed air or steam; one for animal power, wind [etc.]. **1825** NICHOLSON *Operat. Mech.* 659 Where locks or lifts occur [on a railway], the stationary steam-engine should drag up the vehicle..not simply from the one level to the other, but to a platform some feet above the higher level.

d. Short for *lock-keeper*.

1865 DICKENS *Mut. Fr.* III. viii, 'I am the Lock', said the man. 'The Lock?' 'I am the Deputy Lock on job, and this is the Lock-house.'

10. *Engineering.* More fully ***air-lock***. An antechamber giving access to a chamber in which work is carried on in compressed air; also, a similar chamber used between air at atmospheric pressure and either water (e.g. outside a submarine) or a vacuum (e.g. outside a spacecraft).

1874 KNIGHT *Dict. Mech.* I. 49 *Air-lock. Ibid.* 421 s.v. *Caisson.* **1894** *Westm. Gaz.* 16 Oct. 3/1 Entrance is obtained by means of a couple of 'locks', tubular chambers about 6 ft. in diameter. **1899** *Allbutt's Syst. Med.* VII. 41 Perhaps the most frequent exciting cause [of caisson disease] is too rapid a reduction of the pressure in 'locking out', that is, in passing from the caisson to the open air through the lock or antechamber. **1914** S. F. WALKER *Submarine Engin.* iii. 35 The air lock..is a chamber with doors at each end, arranged so that only a small quantity of air or water can enter each time the lock is opened. **1959** 'WYNDHAM' & PARKER *Outward Urge* ii. 66 The duty-man operated the lock, and presently Troon was outside. **1961** E. LEYLAND *Crash Dive* viii. 91 Taking the place of the Twill Trunk..came the Escape Chamber method, a permanent chamber or lock entered by way of a watertight door.

III. Senses derived from LOCK *v.*¹

11. a. A locking together, interlocking; †an unintelligible or ambiguous discourse (*obs.*); an assemblage of objects jammed together, now esp. a crowd of carriages in the streets, a 'block', 'jam'.

1550 GARDINER in Foxe *A. & M.* (1563) 759/1 The worst man of all is that will make him self a locke of wordes and speach, which is knowen not to be my faction,..and how can that be a doubtfull speach in him that professeth to agree with the kinges lawes,..which I did expresly. **1697** DRYDEN *Æneid* v. 265 Sergesthus, eager with his Beak, to press Betwixt the Rival Galley and the Rock, Shuts up th' unwieldy Centaur in the Lock. **1834** DE QUINCEY in *Tait's Mag.* I. 594, I have seen all Albemarle Street closed by a 'lock' of carriages. **1854** THACKERAY *Newcomes* I. 231 Stopped on the road from Epsom in a lock of carriages. **1857** *Abridg. Specif. Patents Sewing*, etc. 17 The stitch produced is termed the 'chain stitch', the two threads having a double lock with each other.

b. ***lock and block (system)***: a system of railway signalling by which a train does not enter a section of line until the preceding train has left it, the signal being locked at 'danger' and only released when the preceding train leaves the section.

1902 *Encycl. Brit.* XXXIII. 146/2 'Lock-and-block' has been used to a limited extent on a good many lines in England and a half-dozen in America. **1905** *Westm. Gaz.* 12 Jan. 7/2 The failure was partly due to faulty line circuits of the lock and block instruments. **1950** *Engineering* 1 Dec. 436/1 Signals..operated mechanically..with the Sykes lock-and-block system. **1956** *Railway Mag.* Nov. 748/1 The Sykes lock-and-block, although old fashioned,..has a long record of reliable service in the operation of dense traffic.

c. *Rugby Football.* A player in the second row of the scrummage (see quots.); this position. Also *attrib.*, as ***lock-forward***, ***-man***.

1906 GALLAHER & STEAD *Compl. Rugby Footballer* vii. 100 Working the [New Zealand] Scrum... The lock [etc.]. *Ibid.* 104 Immediately behind these hookers..is he whom we call the lock man... His duty is to hold or lock the two hookers. *a* **1914** J. E. RAPHAEL *Mod. Rugby Football* (1918) xvii. 225 The middle man in the second row, the 'lock', bound the 'hookers' together, not his own row. **1956** V. JENKINS *Lions Rampant* ii. 23 Mr Siggins..was one of the finest lock-forwards of his day. **1959** *Times* 10 Sept. 4/3 It was strange to see the former hefty England wing, Woodward, at lock in the blues' scrummage. **1971** *Sunday Express* (Johannesburg) 28 Mar. 20/6 Springboks fullback Ian McCallum, prop Hannes Marais and lock Frik du Preez are in the opening fixture.

12. a. A grapple, grip, or trick in wrestling (cf. quot. 1899); hence *fig.* (*a*) a stratagem, trick, dodge; (*b*) a difficulty, dilemma, chiefly in phr. ***(to be, have, put) at, on,*** or ***upon a (the) lock.*** *Obs.* (Cf. DEADLOCK *sb.*)

1608 DEKKER *2nd Pt. Honest Whore* (1630) G 3 b, He and foure of his men drew vpon me, sir..I made no more adoe, but fell to my old locke, and so thrashed my blue Coates, [etc.]. **1616** J. LANE *Cont. Sqr.'s T.* (Chaucer Soc.) 129 *note*, Both closelie graplinge with a mutual locke. **1644** MILTON *Educ.* 7 They must be also practiz'd in all the locks and gripes of wrastling. **1646** FULLER *Wounded Consc.* (1841) 321 If the devil catches us at this lock, he will throw us flat. **1650** CROMWELL in Carlyle *Lett. & Sp.* (1871) III. 40 Being indeed upon this lock, hoping that the disease of your army would render their work more easy. **1651** —— *Let.* 26 July, The Enemy is at his old lock. **1657** R. LIGON *Barbadoes* (1673) 41 At that lock they often were, and some good Planters too, that far'd very hard. **1663** COWLEY *Cutter Coleman St.* IV. iv, Why look you, Colonel, he's at's old Lock, he's at's May-bees again. **1672** MARVELL *Reh. Transp.* I. 159 This, beside all the lock and advantage that I have the Nonconformists upon the since the late times. *Ibid.* 216 Now the Author having got them at this lock cries Victory. **1699** R. L'ESTRANGE *Erasm. Colloq.* (1711) 225 He was now upon the same lock with Balbinus. **1723** *Wodrow Corr.* (1843) III. 39 My inclination is..that you keep the books to yourself rather than put the Colonel upon the lock. **1744** P. WHITEHEAD *Gymnasiad* iii. 42 *note*, The youthful hero, being on the lock, must again inevitably have come to the ground. **1825** J. NEAL *Bro. Jonathan* I. 256 A few heavy tumbles were given without a trip or a lock. **1899** *Cumbld. Gloss.*, *Lock*, a term in wrestling, used when the left (right) leg is passed between the opponent's legs, and then twisted round his right (left) leg by a motion which is first backward, then outward, and finally forward. **1954** E. DOMINY *Teach Yourself Judo* iii. 41 There are only a few basic types of lock and these can be developed by anyone sufficiently interested. **1974** 'J. LE CARRÉ' *Tinker, Tailor* xxii. 189 Guillam selected Tarr's right arm and flung it into a lock against his back, bringing it very near to breaking. **1974** P. ERDMAN *Silver Bears* xiii. 143 He would sooner see the whole bank go down the drain..than get beaten by us. Unless we develop an even better lock on him—and that won't be easy.

b. *slang.* (See quots.)

1725 *New Cant. Dict.*, s.v., *He stood a queer Lock*; i.e. He stood an indifferent Chance. **1735** in DYCHE & PARDON *Dict.* *c* **1780** G. PARKER *Life's Painter* 116 What lock do you cut now? [explained to mean 'by what way do you get your livelihood now?' *Ibid.* 137]. **1785** in GROSE *Dict. Vulg. Tongue* s.v.

13. (*to walk*) ***lock and lock*** = arm in arm.

1837 HALIBURTON *Clockm.* Ser. I. xxiii, She don't wait any more for him to walk lock and lock with her.

14. The occupation of locking (prison-cells). *on the lock*: engage in locking up.

1855 DICKENS *Dorrit* II. xix, Will you go and see if Bob is on the lock?

15. a. The swerving (to right or left) of the wheels of the fore-carriage of a vehicle from the line of direction of the hind-wheels. (Cf. LOCK *v.*[1] 3.)

1851 *Illustr. Catal. Gt. Exhib.* 366 New application..to a caravan, or waggon,..to allow a higher fore wheel, and give a greater amount of lock. **1875** in KNIGHT *Dict. Mech.*

b. The turning of the front wheels of a motor vehicle to change its direction of motion; the full extent of such turning.

1908 *Autocar Handbk.* (ed. 2) xvi. 123 There should be plenty of 'lock' for the wheels, which, with an inconsequence not unusual in our language, means that the wheels shall be quite free to be deflected through a large angle. **1939** L. MACNEICE *Autumn Jrnl.* xxiv. 79 The quick lock of a taxi. **1959** *Observer* 1 Mar. 21/5 From lock to lock it takes $3\frac{3}{8}$ turns, allowing prompt correction if a heavy throttle foot should provoke tail wag on a slippery surface. Turning circle is 37 ft. **1967** *Autocar* 28 Dec. 10/2 The 35 ft 3 in. mean turning circle with 4·25 turns lock-to-lock is not excessive. **1974** L. MEYNELL *Fairly Innocent* xi. 148, I must have got on to the wrong lock... I don't really understand about going backwards.

16. *Plastering* (See quot.)

1875 KNIGHT *Dict. Mech.*, *Lock* (Plastering), the projection of the plaster or cement behind the lath, which keeps it from falling or scaling off.

17. *Thieves' slang.* (App. short for *lock-all-fast*: see first quot.) A receiver of stolen goods; also, a house where stolen goods are received.

a **1700** B. E. *Dict. Cant. Crew*, *Lock all fast*, one that Buys and Conceals Stolen Goods. *The Lock*, the Magazine or Warehouse whither the Thieves carry Stolen Goods. **1718** HIGGIN *True Discov.* 16 (Farmer) That woman they spoke to as they passed by is a Lock, alias Receiver and Buyer of stolen goods. **1727** GAY *Begg. Op.* I. ii, Betty hath brought more goods into our Lock to-year than any five of the Gang. **1804** *Europ. Mag.* XLV. 365/1 We lament that this ancient palace of the Kings of France should become a Lock, (which ..means a repository for stolen goods).

IV. 18. (Now usually with capital L; more fully *Lock-hospital.*) A hospital for the treatment of venereal diseases.

The 'Lock lazar-house' in Southwark, which is mentioned as having received a bequest in 1452, was afterwards employed as a hospital for venereal diseases, and its name came to be used as a general designation for institutions of that kind. The origin of the name is uncertain; it has been conjectured that the 'Lock lazar-house' was so called as being specially isolated or quarantined.

a **1700** B. E. *Dict. Cant. Crew*, *The Lock*,..an Hospital for Pockey Folks in Kent-street. **1720** BECKET in *Phil. Trans.* XXXI. 60 The Lock beyond St. Georges Church, and that at Kingsland, are at this time applyed to no other use than for the entertainment and Cure of such as have the Venereal Malady. **1753** SMOLLETT *Ct. Fathom* (1784) 157/1 To erect an hospital, lock, or infirmary, by the voluntary subscription of his friends. **1755** FLEMING in *Phil. Trans.* XLIX. 263 *note*, Mr. John Clark, now surgeon to the Lock-Hospital, near Hyde-Park Corner. **1766** ENTICK *Lond.* IV. 444 There is a lock hospital for venereal complaints. **1869** E. A. PARKES *Pract. Hygiene* (ed. 3) 501 Certified Lock Hospitals are provided for her treatment. **1922** JOYCE *Ulysses* 509 Mary Shortall that was in the lock with the pox.

V. *attrib.* and *Comb.*

19. a. simple attributive, as (sense 1) *lock-bolt*, *-staple*; (sense 5) *lock-action*, *-cover*, *-lanyard*, *-plate*, *-side*, *-stop*, *-string*; (sense 9) *lock-bank*, *-bar*, *-bridge*, *-canal*, *-charge*, *-cut*, *-duty*, *-gate*, *-hatch*, *-house*, *-man*, *-pen*, *-side*, *-station*, *-thief*, *-wall*. **b.** signifying 'provided with a lock or locks', as (sense 1) †*lock-chest*, †*-cock*, (U.S.), †*-house*; (sense 9) *lock-weir*.

1898 R. KIPLING in *Morn. Post* 7 Nov. 5/1 A Maxim [gun] making sure of its *lock-action. **1773** *Ann. Reg.* 66 Upwards of 600..workmen were entertained upon the *lock-banks with an ox roasted whole. **1923** F. L. PACKARD *Four Stragglers* 312 The *lock-bar worked through the side of the pier wall. **1865** DICKENS *Mut. Fr.* II. iv. i. 162 He crossed back by his plank *lock-bridge to the towing-path side. **1903** *Westm. Gaz.* 2 Jan. 3/1, I imagine that the Panama waterway is to be a *lock canal. **1877** J. HABBERTON *Jericho Road* ii. 20 Dont you b'leeve she could run the dam at Mount Zion, and dodge paying *lock-charges? **1552** *Inventories* (Surtees) II, ij *lok-chestes. **1814** *Sporting Mag.* XLIII. 112 Beer..which stood in a corner of his front parlour, with a *lock-cock to it. **1833** *Regul. Instr. Cavalry* I. 103 Unstrap the Carbine; take off the *lock-cover. **1905** *Westm. Gaz.* 16 Aug. 5/3 Motor boats..probably find their way down *lock-cuts made more difficult and tedious than before. **1908** *Daily Chron.* 30 Apr. 1/2 An assistant lockkeeper..found the body of a child floating in the lock-cut. **1776** ADAM SMITH *W.N.* v. i. (1869) II. 308 The toll or *lock-duty upon a canal. **1677** PLOT *Oxfordsh.* 233 *Lock-gates put down between every two of them. **1795** J. PHILLIPS *Hist. Inland Navig.* 338 The most effectual..method of providing lock-gates. **1710** *Brit. Apollo* III. No. 70. 2/1 Whether tame Rabbits may not be as Good..as the Wild..provided they are kept in a *Lock-house, having the advantage of [etc.]. **1865** [see 9 d]. **1890** *Century Dict.* s.v. *Lanyard*, A *lock-lanyard is the cord fastened to the lock of a gun by which the gun is fired. **1887** *Times* 14 Oct. 3/4 Robinson, *lockman at the South West India Docks. **1907** *Westm. Gaz.* 20 Aug. 12/1 The *lock-pen ..opens and shuts now to let through the *Queen Elizabeth* in solitary state. *c* **1860** H. STUART *Seaman's Catech.* 11 On the stock is a..*lock plate. **1860** *All Year Round* No. 71. 500 The stock is divided into the..*lock-side [etc.]. **1897** *Daily News* 30 July 5/2 At Molesey only a limited number of people are admitted to the lock-side. **1898** *Athenæum* 7 May 594/3 The place where the *lock-staple had once been fitted. **1863** E. E. HALE *If, Yes & Perhaps* (1868) 16, I would start in the morning to walk to the *lock-station at Brockport on the canal. **1883** LD. SALTOUN *Scraps* I. 280 The rifle was loaded and capped, but secured by the *lock-stops. **1885** *Century Mag.* XXIX. 758, I..ran out the gun, and, taking deliberate aim, pulled the *lockstring. **1863** E. E. HALE *If, Yes & Perhaps* (1868) 22 At night I walked the deck till one o'clock..to keep guard against the *lock-thieves. **1885** WARREN & CLEVERLY *Wand. 'Beetle'* 61 He ran along the *lock-wall to open his gates when he saw us coming. **1831** T. L. PEACOCK *Crotchet Castle* iv. 67 Mud, filth, gas-dregs, *lock-weirs..have ruined the fishery.

c. objective, as (sense 1) *lock-filer*, *-maker*, *-picker*; *lock-making*; (sense 9) *lock-keeper*, *-owner*, *-shutter*, *-tender*.

1858 GREENER *Gunnery* 213 They have..obtained a much better price than any other *lock-filers out of London. **1794** RENNIE *Rep. Thames Navig.* 53 Examination..of the *Lock-keeper's books. **1861** HUGHES *Tom Brown at Oxf.* ii. (1889) 12 The lock-keeper again came to the rescue with his boat-hook. **1797** *Encycl. Brit.* (ed. 3) X. 111/2 It is still possible for a mechanic of equal skill with the *lock-maker to open it without the key. **1850** CHUBB *Locks & Keys* 16 The lock-makers of England. **1787** BRAMAH *Locks* 6 The art of *Lock-making. **1882** W. MORRIS in Mackail *Life* (1899) II. 68 Am I doing nothing but make-believe, something like Louis XVI's lock-making? **1731** in *Extracts from Navig. Rolls* 23 Unless Notice hath been..given to the said *Lock-owners. **1882** STEVENSON *Fam. Stud.* (1901) 151 Thieves, cheats and *lockpickers. **1751** in *Extracts from Navig. Rolls* 13 To the *Lock-shutter 6*d.* **1788** *Act 28 Geo. III*, c. 51 §18 Bargemen, Watermen, Lock-Shutters. **1877** BURROUGHS *Taxation* I. 37 Gardens occupied by *lock-tenders..were exempt.

20. Special comb. (in some cases perhaps combinations with the vb. stem): **lock-band**, **-bay** (see quots.); **lock-box** *U.S.*, a delivery letter-box provided with a lock; **lock-chain**, a chain employed to lock the wheels of a vehicle; **lock-chamber**, the space enclosed between the side-walls and gates of a lock; **lock-hole**, †(*a*) a keyhole; (*b*) 'the recess in a musket-stock to receive the lock' (Knight); **lock-in**, the action or fact of locking in a person or thing (see LOCK *v.*[1] 2 and 3 e); also *attrib.*; **lock-net** (see quot.); **Locknit**, the proprietary name (but see quot. 1935) of a fabric knitted with an interlocking stitch; also **lock-knit**; freq. *attrib.*; **lock-nut**, a nut screwed down upon another to prevent its breaking loose, a check-nut; also, a nut specially designed to prevent accidental loosening once it has been tightened; **lock-paddle** (see quot.); **lock-pen** = *lock-chamber*; **lock-piece**, (*a*) 'in guns of the old construction, a lug cast just alongside of the vent for the attachment of the lock' (Knight); (*b*) (see quot. 1860); †**lock-pit**, ? = sense 9; **lock-pool**, ? = LASHER 4 b; **lock-pulley**, two pulleys formed to rotate separately, or together, at will (Knight); **lock-rail** (see quot. 1842); **lock-saw**, a long tapering saw, used to cut the seat for a lock in a door; **lock-seat**, the excavation on a river or canal intended to contain a lock; †**lock-shoe**, **-sill** (see quots.); **lock-spring**, the spring by means of which the case of a watch is opened or closed; **lock-step** *Mil.* (see quot.); also *fig.*, a rigid or unchanging pattern; also *attrib.*, rigid, unchanging; hence *lock-step* adv. and vb.; **lock-stitch**, a sewing-machine stitch, in which two threads are locked firmly together; also *attrib.*; **lock timber** *Mining* (see quot.); **lock-tool** = *lock-cramp*; **lock-work**, (*a*) the manufacture or construction of locks (senses 1 and 9); (*b*) the parts of a lock; (*c*) a series of locks (sense 9); (*d*) *pl.* a factory for the manufacture of locks (sense 1); (*e*) *pl.* operations in progress for the construction of locks (sense 9).

?*c* **1582** DIGGES in *Archæologia* (1794) XI. 233 The hewinge of the stone ashlar, and Endstons, with artyficiall bevelinge, and *lockbands, stone within another, will amounte..for the rodde 16*s.* 6*d.* **1847** HALLIWELL, *Lock-bands*, binding stones in masonry. **1875** KNIGHT *Dict. Mech.*, *Lock-bay*, the pond or space of water between the gates of a canal-lock. **1872** E. CRAPSEY *Nether Side N.Y.* 150 C. H. Chester, M.D., *Lock Box 4, Reading, Pa. **1906** M. E. FREEMAN *By Light of Soul* 384 She saw one letter slanted across the dusty glass of the box. It was not a lock box, and she had to ask the postmaster for the letter. **1955** E. POUND *Section: Rock Drill* lxxxviii. 42 A First Folio (Shx) in his lock-box. **1859** MARCY *Prairie Trav.* iii. 93 If there are no *lock-chains upon wagons, the front and rear wheels on the same side may be tied together with ropes so as to lock them very firmly. **1861** SMILES *Engineers* I. 375 *Lock chamber. **1592** GREENE *Philom.* E 4 b, The Earle..peeping in at the *locke hole, saw them two standing..hand in hand. **1752** J. LOUTHIAN *Form of Process* (ed. 2) 87 Within the Lock-hole of the most patent Door of his Dwelling-house. **1821** CLARE *Vill. Minstr.* I. 7 The mistic tribes of night's unnerving breeze, That through a lock-hole even creep with ease. **1920** *Contemp. Rev.* Dec. 823 To the lock-out of the masters, the workers replied with the '*lock-in' movement—the temporary capture of the factories and work-shops. **1970** *Globe & Mail* (Toronto) 25 Sept. B7/6 There may be some giving in on peripheral items such as reducing the length of lock-in clauses. **1973** *Times* 25 Jan. 23/5 First, there is the 'lock-in' factor. Given additional tax burdens, the first reaction of any jobber is to feel less inclined to sell. **1863** BUCKLAND *Curios. Nat. Hist.* Ser. II. (ed. 4) 251 The '*lock nets'..are simply a large form of the round nets used to catch freshwater crayfish. **1935** *Trade Marks Jrnl.* 8 May 588/2 *Lansil Locknit.* Registration of this Trade Mark shall give no right to the exclusive use of the word '*Locknit'. Knitted piece goods composed wholly or mainly of artificial silk. Cellulose Acetate Silk Company, Ltd...Lancaster. **1936** *Times* 14 Feb. 9/5 A three-piece in pale blue chalk stripe locknit and plain jersey. **1951** *Good Housek. Home Encycl.* 231/1 Lock-knit or open weave articles should be dried flat. **1952** 'J. TEY' *Singing Sands* vi. 93 Hams hung from the roof among strings of locknit undergarments. **1973** R. RENDELL *Some lie & Some Die* ix. 84 Passing her iron across a pair of pink locknit knickers. *a* **1864** GESNER *Coal, Petrol.* etc. (1865) 79 Leakage around the pipe [is] prevented by two *locknuts. **1887** D. A. LOW *Machine Drawing* 20 In practice, the thin nut, called the lock-nut, is often placed on the outside. **1907** *Westm. Gaz.* 21 Nov. 4/2 The steering is ..of the worm and segment type, the adjustment of which is easily effected by releasing a lock-nut and slightly turning the steering column. **1964** S. CRAWFORD *Basic Engin. Processes* xiv. 304 The rollers are secured by tightening the locknut with the special adjusting key. **1972** *Practical Motorist* Oct. 162/3 If this resistance is felt *before* the vertical position of the lever is reached, or if no resistance is felt at all, adjustment can be made by loosening the lock-nut 'C'. **1842** FRANCIS *Dict. Arts*, *Lock Paddles*, the small sluices used in filling and emptying locks. **1891** A. J. FOSTER *Ouse* 170 Most of the *lock-pens will only hold two lighters at a time. **1860** *Eng. & For. Mining Gloss.* (Cornwall Terms), **Lock piece*, a piece of timber used in supporting the workings. **1802** *Hull Dock Act* 1503 With a *lockpit or entrance into the same from the said river Humber. **1772** *Extracts from Navig. Rolls* Remarks p. ix, A strong Breast-work of Piles on the upper Side of the *Lock-pool. **1881** TAUNT *Thames Map* p. xv/1 Caution should always be used when in a weir or lock-pool. **1825** J. NICHOLSON *Operat. Mechanic* 589 On the *lock-rail the lock is either mortised in, or screwed on. **1842–59** GWILT *Archit.* 568 The next are called the lock or middle rails in doors. **1688** R. HOLME *Armoury* III. 365/1 A *Lock Saw..to make Key holes in Doors. **1794** WASHINGTON *Let.* Writ. 1892 XIII. 1 Mr. Weston's opinion, respecting the *lock-seats at the Great Falls of that river. **1785** G. FORSTER tr. *Sparrman's Voy. Cape G.H.* (1786) I. 124 In order that the wheel that is to be locked may not be worn,..a kind of sledge carriage, hollowed out on the inside, and called a *lock-shoe is fitted to it. **1842** FRANCIS *Dict. Arts*, **Lock-sills*, the angular pieces of timber at the bottom of the lock against which the gates shut. **1884** F. J. BRITTEN *Watch & Clockm.* 47 The *lock spring fits in a groove formed in the band of the case. **1802** C. JAMES *Milit. Dict.*, **Lock-step*, this step consist in the heel of one man being brought nearly in contact with the joint of the great toe of another. **1816** J. SCOTT *Vis. Paris* (ed. 5) 55 The men who are now practising the lock-step in front of the window of Louis XVIII. **1828** *Examiner* 630/1 A Sailor toe-and-heels it, and lock-steps and straddles. **1836** T. POWER *Impressions Amer.* I. 379 They [*sc.* convicts] were marched from the building in squads, using what is called the 'lock-step', and were jammed together as closely as they could possibly travel. **1866** THOREAU *Yankee in Canada* ii. 25, I observed one older man..marching lock-step with the rest. **1955** *Sci. News Let.* 16 Apr. 255 A 'what will people think' disease is driving us all, cab driver as well as scientist, toward straitjacketed thinking and lock-step living. **1963** *New Society* 7 Nov. 19/1 The prescribed lock-step of school life. **1971** *New Yorker* 30 Oct. 155 Mrs. Handy's lockstep methods (copy the great novelists, read the 'Masters of the Far East', stay away from girls) produced a handful of published novels. **1972** *Business Week* 18 Mar. 32/1 The break could occur if Ireland did not follow Britain into the EEC. For the republic marches in an economic lockstep with Britain. **1973** *Where* Apr. 109/3 Students working..in their own way, and at their own pace, freed from the 'lock-step' of the classroom. **1973** *Time* 25 June 74/1 The 'whole thing' was an attempt..to break what he calls 'the lockstep'—the educational process that leads in a straight line from kindergarten through graduate school, and often onward into the walled-in offices of academia. **1869** J. WEBSTER in *Eng. Mech.* 17 Dec. 326/3, I do not say one word against *lock-stitch machines. **1881** RAYMOND *Mining Gloss.*, **Lock-timber*, an old plan of putting in stull-pieces in Cornwall and Devon. The pieces were called lock-pieces. **1686** PLOT *Staffordsh.* 376 So curious are they in *Lockwork (indeed beyond all preference). **1794** W. COMBE *Boydell's Thames* I. 47 A successive apparatus of lock-work, to remedy the various levels of the country. **1857–8** *Proc. Inst. Civ. Engin.* (1858) XVII. 389 The construction of the gates was entirely independent of the lock-work. **1890** *Pall Mall G.* 7 Jan. 2/3 The bright steel and very elaborate lock-work was perfect. **1899** *Daily News* 14 Oct. 6/7 The new lock and safe works recently erected..by Messrs. Chubb and Sons. **1901** *19th Cent.* Oct. 550 One finds here..bridge works, lock-works.

lock (lɒk), *v.*[1] Pa. t. and pa. pple. locked (lɒkt). Forms: 4–6 lok(e, 4–5 lokke, 5 lokkyn, 4–6 locke, 5– lock. [f. LOCK *sb.*[2]; cf. ON. *loka*, similarly f. *loka* sb., lock, latch; also ON. *lykja* (Sw. *lycka*, Da. *lukke*.)

The older vb. with this meaning was LOUK, OE. *lúcan*; after the 14th c. this survived mainly in the pa. pple. *loken*, which was probably looked upon as belonging to *lock* vb.]

1. a. *trans.* To fasten (a door, gate, box, drawer, etc.) with a lock and key; occas. with †*to*, *up*. Hence (chiefly with *up*), to secure (a chamber, building, enclosure) by locking the doors.

a **1300** *Cursor M.* 17347 þai..did to sper þe dors fast, Locked bath wit-vte and in. *c* **1375** *Sc. Leg. Saints* vii. (*Jacobus Minor*) 781 þe Iowis..In til a cawe me closit faste, lokit, & celyt at þe laste. *c* **1440** *Promp. Parv.* 311/2 Lokkyn or schette wythe a lokke. **1480** CAXTON *Chron. Eng.* ccxxii. 215 The gates of the castel ben lokked with the lokkes that dame Isabel sent hidder. **1535** COVERDALE *Judg.* iii. 23 Ehud ..put to ye dore after him, and lockte it. **1590** SHAKS. *Com. Err.* IV. iv. 73 Were not my doores lockt vp, and I shut out? **1600** in A. Bisset *Ess. Hist. Truth* v. 218 Maister Alexander locked to the study door behind him. **1651** HOBBES *Leviath.* I. xiii. 62 When going to sleep, he locks his dores. **1726** *Adv.*

Capt. R. Boyle 66 The Hour drawing near, they lock'd up the Doors of the House. **1819** BYRON *Juan* I. clxxxvii, Juan .. liking not the inside, lock'd the out. **1855** MACAULAY *Hist. Eng.* xiii. III. 250 The reformers locked up the church and departed with the keyes. **1900** MACKENZIE *Guide Inverness* 43 The Greyfriars Churchyard is kept locked.

fig. **1526** *Pilgr. Perf.* (W. de W. 1531) 83 b, Yf the gate of yᵉ mouth be not shutte with the dore of scylence, & locked with the key of discrecyon. **1713** GAY *Fan* III. 54 Death blasts his bloom, and locks his frozen eyes. **1859** FITZGERALD tr. *Omar* vi. (1899) 71 And David's Lips are lock't. **1866** B. TAYLOR *Poems, Sorrowful Music* 37 This weight of grief Locks my lips. **1879** BROWNING *Halbert & Hob* 61 His lips were loose not locked.

Proverb. **1855** BOHN *Handbk. Proverbs* 445 Lock the stable-door before the steed is stolen. **1885** *Times* (weekly ed.) 11 Sept. 3/1 This is done probably on the principle of locking the stable door after the horse has been stolen.

b. absol. ***to lock up***: to lock up the house, lock the doors.

1901 A. HOPE *Tristram of Blent* xxvi. 356 'Is her ladyship still out, ma'am?' he [the butler] asked... 'I was going to lock up'... 'Oh, go to bed', she cried.. 'We'll lock up..'.

c. *intr.* Of a door: To be locked; to admit of being locked.

1590 SPENSER *F.Q.* II. ix. 23 Doubly disparted, it did locke and close, That when it locked, none might thorough pas. *Mod.* The door will not lock.

2. *trans.* To shut up or confine with a lock; to put under lock and key. Const. *in, into, within.* Also with advs. *in, up.*

a **1300** *Cursor M.* 17661 In a hus we lokked þe. **13..** *K. Alis.* 3936 The kyng.. bad him loke in prisoun. *c* **1386** CHAUCER *Wife's Prol.* 317, I trowe, thou woldest loke me in thy chiste. *c* **1470** HENRY *Wallace* IV. 775 'To the chawmer, quhar he was vpon chance, Speid fast', he said, 'Wallace is lokit in'. ? *a* **1550** *Freiris Berwik* 221 in *Dunbar's Poems* (1893) 292 Lok vp all in to ȝone almery. **1590** MARLOWE *Edw. II*, II. ii. 54 The lovers of fair Danaë, When she was lock'd up in a brazen tower, Desir'd her more. **1596** SHAKS. *Merch. V.* III. ii. 42 Away then, I am lockt in one of them, If you doe loue me, you will finde me out. **1632** J. HAYWARD tr. *Biondi's Eromena* 17 Some dayes before he had begunne to locke himselfe in his chamber. **1713** SWIFT *Frenzy J. Dennis* Wks. 1755 III. I. 144 We locked his friend into a closet. **1732** POPE *Hor. Sat.* II. ii. 13 Your wine lock'd up, If then plain bread and milk will do the feat, The pleasure lies in you, and not the meat. *a* **1745** SWIFT *Direct. Servants, Butler* 33 Always lock up a Cat in a Closet where you keep your China Plates, for fear the Mice may steal in and break them. **1840** DICKENS *Old C. Shop* lxi, The little cell in which he was locked up for the night. **1891** *Law Times Rep.* LXIII. 690/2 The defendant.. had given distinct orders to Nunney never to lock anyone up.

3. *transf.* **a.** To enclose, hem in, surround. Chiefly with *in.*

c **1400** MAUNDEV. (1839) xxvi. 265 Alle faste y lokked and enclosed with highe Mountaynes. *a* **1400–50** *Alexander* 5495 He lockis in ane ser limy with a laith mey[n]he. **1691** T. H[ALE] *Acc. New Invent.* p. lxii, The great winding of the River.. locks in the Water that it cannot make that haste down to the Sea that it would. **1793** SMEATON *Eddystone L.* §199 Lodged in a dovetail recess, wherein it was locked fast on three sides. **1833** TENNYSON *Pal. Art* 249 A still salt pool, lock'd in with bars of sand. **1837** LOCKHART *Scott* 19 July an. 1821, He and.. his companion, found themselves locked in the crowd, somewhere near Whitehall. **1837** DISRAELI *Venetia* VI. i, So completely is the land locked with hills. **1851** DIXON *W. Penn* xxiii. (1872) 201 The vessel was locked in ice.

b. To keep securely or render inaccessible, as if in a locked receptacle. Chiefly with *up.*

1562 WINȜET *Cert. Tractates* iii. Wks. 1888 I. 27 Worthy to be lokit in the memorie of thaim quha [etc.]. **1646** SIR T. BROWNE *Pseud. Ep.* IV. vi. 194 The seed of plants lockt up and capsulated in their husks. **1646** J. HALL *Horæ Vac.* 92 Keepe your secrets fast lock't up. **1652** NEEDHAM tr. *Selden's Mare Cl.* Ep. Ded. 2 A Jewel.. lockt up in a Language unknown to the greatest part of that Nation. **1666** *Rhode Island Col. Rec.* (1857) II. 159 In the hardest winters when the Massachusetts and others.. are fast locked up with strong doores of ice. *a* **1763** SHENSTONE *Ess.* (1765) 40 Prudent men lock up their motives. **1779** MAD. D'ARBLAY *Diary* 26 May, As censorious a country lady as ever locked up all her ideas in a country town. **1796** MORSE *Amer. Geog.* II. 101 The seaports in Holland and Germany are every winter locked up with ice. **1807–8** SYD. SMITH *Plymley's Lett.* Wks. 1859 II. 163/2 The very same wind.. locks you up in the British Channel. **1838** PRESCOTT *Ferd. & Is.* (1846) I. viii. 376 Their [*sc.* Arabians'] literature.. locked up in a character.. so difficult of access to European scholars. **1855** BAIN *Senses & Int.* III. ii. §26 (1864) 507 Sir Humphrey Davy suggested that metallic substances were locked up in soda, potash, and lime. **1859** GULLICK & TIMBS *Paint.* 222 Some colours.. are perfectly permanent when 'locked up' (to use the painter's phrase) in oil. **1879** STAINER *Music of Bible* 157 Their secrets remain for ever locked up.

c. Comm. and Finance. ***to lock up***: To invest (capital) *in* something that is not easily convertible into money.

1692 LOCKE *Consid. Lower. Interest* 113 If one Third of the Money imploy'd in Trade were locked up,.. must not the Land-holders receive ⅓ less for their Goods. **1833** HT. MARTINEAU *Briery Creek* iv. 73 The money he had locked up in land would never be productive while he remained its owner. **1848** MILL *Pol. Econ.* I. v. §9 (1876) 52 To set free a capital which would be otherwise locked up in a form useless for the support of labour. **1868** ROGERS *Pol. Econ.* xi. (1876) 149 A banker cannot afford.. to have his capital locked up in long advances.

d. Of sleep, stupefying agencies, enchantment: To hold fast, overpower completely. Also with *up.*

1725 POPE *Odyss.* x. 77 Me, lock'd in sleep, my faithless crew bereft Of all the blessings of your god-like gift! **1789** CHARLOTTE SMITH *Ethelinde* (1814) V. 258 He endeavoured to awaken her from the heavy shock which seemed to have locked up her senses. **1860** TYNDALL *Glac.* I. xvi. 119 Went to bed, where I lay fast locked in sleep for eight hours. **1873** W. BRUER *Serm. & Commun. Addr.* 199 His mind may be locked up in insensibility. **1879** GEO. ELIOT *Coll. Breakf. P.* 834 That border-world Of dozing ere the sense is fully locked. **1885–94** R. BRIDGES *Eros & Psyche* Nov. xxvi, 'Art thou the woman of the earth', she said, 'That hast in sorceries mine Eros lockt?'

e. Const. *in.* To trap or fix firmly or irrevocably; to fix in position.

1953 BERREY & VAN DEN BARK *Amer. Thes. Slang* (1954) §623a/7 *Locking in*, adjusting the televised image for a clear picture. *Ibid.* §623a/10 *Locked in*, televised image properly synchronized. **1959** *Economist* 16 May 634/2 This may tend to 'lock in' many traders with their present holdings. **1968** *Sunday Times* 3 Mar. 51 The Extra campaign had to be aggressive because people are so locked in to coupons. **1968** *Telegraph* (Brisbane) 8 Nov. 14/7 Anything I knew.. was too late to help Ford. They already were locked in on their program. **1972** *Sci. Amer.* Nov. 96/3 Lowering its temperature back to normal locks in any deformations due to loadings.

4. To shut off with or as with a lock *from* (a person); to preclude or prevent *from* (something) by or as by locking. Also with *up.*

1601 SHAKS. *Jul. C.* IV. iii. 80 When Marcus Brutus growes so Covetous, To locke such Rascall Counters from his Friends. **1611** —— *Cymb.* IV. iv. 2 To locke it [*sc.* life] From Action and Adventure. **1613** MIDDLETON *Tri. Truth* Wks. (Bullen) VII. 243 He locks his ear from those sweet charms. **1688** *Lond. Gaz.* No. 2378/4 Lost.., a brown bay Filly,.. being locked from taking Horse. **1700** CONGREVE *Way of World* IV. v, Do you lock your self up from me, to make my search more Curious? **1735** POPE *Prol. Sat.* 19 Is there, who, lock'd from ink and paper, scrawls With desp'rate charcoal round his darken'd walls? **1742** YOUNG *Nt. Th.* IX. 285 Angels cannot guess The period; from created beings lock'd In darkness. **1785** J. PHILLIPS *Treat. Inland Navig.* vi, Large tracts of country are locked up from commerce.

5. lock out. a. To turn (a person) out, and lock the door against him. †Also, *to lock forth.* **lock out. b.** To prevent the entrance of (persons) by locking the door; hence, (of an employer) to refuse employment to (a body of operatives) as a means of coercion. (Cf. LOCK-OUT 1)

1590 SHAKS. *Com. Err.* IV. i. 18 For locking me out of my doores by day. *Ibid.* IV. iv. 98 Say wherefore didst thou locke me forth to day? **1592** —— *Rom. & Jul.* I. i. 145 Shuts vp his windows, lockes faire day-light out. **1842** F. E. PAGET *Milford Malv.* 53 When I was being locked out of yonder church. **1861** DUTTON COOK *P. Foster's D.* i, I am locked out. **1868** ROGERS *Pol. Econ.* ix. (1876) 89 Large funds are subscribed, out of which labourers on strike or locked-out are supported.

c. *Electronics* and *Computers.* Temporarily to prevent the operation or use of. Cf. LOCK-OUT 2.

1953 R. C. WALKER *Relays* viii. 222 Voltage selective systems have been devised in which the value of the applied voltage actuates one of a group of thermistors and locks out all the others. **1962** *Gloss. Terms Automatic Data Processing* (*B.S.I.*) 47 During an autonomous peripheral transfer, the storage blocks concerned may be locked out to prevent reference to those blocks until completion of the transfer. **1972** *Computer Jrnl.* XV. 194/2 Another circumstance in which an investigation.. is called for is when a record that has been locked out preparatory to being updated remains locked out for an unreasonable time.

6. a. To fasten, make or set fast, fix; *techn.* to fasten or engage (one part of a machine) *to* another; also in *passive*, (of a joint) to be rendered rigid. ***to lock up a form*** (Printing): to fix the types or pages in a metal frame so as to prepare them for press, etc.

1670–98 LASSELS *Voy. Italy* II. 106, I saw the great chair which locketh fast any man that sitteth down in it. **1674** N. FAIRFAX *Bulk & Selv.* Contents, The world no heap, but a set of Bodies lockt fast together. **1683** MOXON *Mech. Exerc., Printing* viii, The Office of these Quoyns are to Lock up the Form, viz. to wedge it up.. close together. **1816** *Mechanic* I. 370 This scape-wheel is locked on its extreme point, and unlocks in an easy manner. *Ibid.* 411 The wheels are locked, without spring-work, perfectly safe from getting out of order. **1824** J. JOHNSON *Typogr.* II. xiv. 495 It is the business of the person who locks-up the form, to ascertain whether all the pages are of an equal length. **1825** J. NICHOLSON *Operat. Mechanic* 38 A locking clutch is fitted upon the spindle between these two wheels, and can.. be made to lock either one of the wheels to the spindle, at the same time that it leaves the other disengaged. **1841** LANE *Arab. Nts.* I. 80 His teeth were locked together. **1899** *Allbutt's Syst. Med.* VII. 142 Every attempt at movement.. locking the limb in a tetanoid spasm. **1927** R. B. MCKERROW *Introd. Bibliogr.* I. ii. 16 The furniture employed to fill up the chase is 'locked up' by the insertion and driving home of wedges or 'quoins'. **1972** P. GASKELL *New Introd. Bibliogr.* 80 The quoins were driven home with a mallet and 'shooting stick' to lock the forme up tightly.

b. To put a lock on the foot of (a horse); to fasten (a wheel) so as to keep it from turning. Cf. LOCK *sb.*[2] 3, 4.

1694 *Lond. Gaz.* No. 3011/4 An Iron grey Colt.. Lockt on the further Foot before. **1825** COBBETT *Rur. Rides* 19 The descent so steep as to require the wheel of the chaise to be locked. **1884** J. G. BOURKE *Snake-Dance Moquis* i. 8 The driver got out, locked the wheels, and walked.

c. *intr.* for *refl.* Of mechanism, a joint (*e.g.* the knee-joint): To become fixed or set fast. †Of an animal's flanks: To draw together, shrink.

1658 R. WHITE tr. *Digby's Powd. Symp.* (1660) 124 The dog.. not being able to take any nourishment, his flanks do lock up. **1869** W. BLADES *Bks. in Chains* (1892) 219 Our artist.. has put quoins at the head and foot too, making the pages lock up all round the chase— truly a mechanical puzzle. **1901** *Westm. Gaz.* 1 Oct. 5/2 The accident was due to the rudder locking. **1902** *Brit. Med. Jrnl.* 12 Apr. 879 When he attempted to bend the knee it locked.

7. a. To fix or join firmly by interlacing or fitting of parts into each other. Also with *together, up.*

1592 SHAKS. *Ven. & Ad.* 228 And when from thence he struggles to be gone, She locks her lillie fingers one in one. **1598** —— *Merry W.* V. v. 81 Pray you, lock hand in hand. **1608** *Yorksh. Trag.* I. ii, Not as a man repentant, but half mad He sits and sullenly locks up his arms. **1720** DE FOE *Capt. Singleton* xi. (1840) 187 The Portuguese.. ran their bowsprit into the fore part of our main shrouds,.. and so we lay locked after that manner. **1725** POPE *Odyss.* IX. 512 In his deep fleece, my grasping hands I lock. *a* **1728** WOODWARD *Nat. Hist. Fossils* I. (1729) I. 159 The Columns were incorporated with, and lock'd into each other. **1772–84** COOK *Voy.* (1790) IV. 1461 It was required, that.. we should.. have our hands locked together. **1859** TENNYSON *Vivien* 288 Merlin lock'd his hand in hers. **1867** SMYTH *Sailor's Word-bk.*, *Lock*, to entangle the lower yards when tacking. **1893** MCCARTHY *Red Diamonds* III. 233 Granton .. locked his right leg round Bland's leg in an attempt to throw him.

b. *intr.* for *refl.* To interlock, intertwine.

1688 CLAYTON in *Phil. Trans.* XVII. 791 The Heads of the Branches of the Rivers interfere and lock one within another. **1806** *Gazetteer Scot.* (ed. 2) 94 The stones are.. made to lock into one another with grooves and projections. **1858** *Merc. Marine Mag.* V. 227 Until.. you observe the North and Inner South Heads locking.

c. *Fencing.* †(*a*) = ENGAGE *v.* 17 (*obs.*); (*b*) (see quot. 1782).

1579 GOSSON *Sch. Abuse* (Arb.) 46 Teaching the people howe to warde, and how to locke, howe to thrust, and how to strike. **1592** *Arden of Feversham* H 2 b, When he should haue lockt with both his hilts He in a brauery florisht ouer his head. **1782** REES *Chambers's Cycl.*, To Lock, in Fencing, is to seize your adversary's sword-arm, by turning your left arm round it, after closing your parade, shell to shell, in order to disarm him. (So in mod. Dicts.)

d. ***to lock horns***: (of cattle) to entangle the horns mutually in fighting. Hence *fig.* U.S., to engage in combat ***with*** (some one).

1839 *Hist. Virgil A. Stewart* 23 (Th.), They are enemies, and let them lock horns. **1855** *Knickerbocker* XLVI. 95 As neither of the trains stop at way-stations, I expect nothing more than to see the two lock horns at the corner of my kitchen. **1865** SWINBURNE *Atalanta* 942 Then shall the heifer and her mate lock horns. **1888** BRYCE *Amer. Commw.* II. III. lxx. 552 *note*, The Boss of Tammany, with whom Mr. Cleveland had at an earlier period in his career 'locked horns'. **1901** *U.S. Corresp.* in *Academy* 25 Mar. 240/2 We should hardly feel warranted in locking horns with Tammany Hall.

e. To embrace closely; also, to grapple in combat. Now only *passive. lit.* and *fig.*

1611 SHAKS. *Wint. T.* V. ii. 83 Shee.. locks her in embracing, as if shee would pin her to her heart. **1646** EVANCE *Noble Ord.* 15 The Devill thought to have lockt Job upon that hip. **1828** SCOTT *F.M. Perth* xxxii, Catharine.. was locked in the arms of Louise. **1854** M. ARNOLD *Switzerland, Farew.* 11 Lock'd in each other's arms we stood. **1878** BOSW. SMITH *Carthage* 252 Before the two armies became locked in the deadly combat now to be related. **1893** TRAILL *Social Eng.* Introd. 35 The birth and early years of the nineteenth century found our country still locked in the death-grapple with Napoleon.

8. *Mil.* (See quot. 1802.) *absol.* and *passive.*

1802 C. JAMES *Milit. Dict.*, *To Lock up*, to take the closest possible order in line or in file. The expression is derived from the lock-step. **1844** *Regul. & Ord. Army* 264 He is to take care that.. the rear ranks.. are well locked up. **1847** *Infantry Man.* (1854) 56 He will see that the rear rank locks well up. *c* **1860** H. STUART *Seaman's Catech.* 11 In loading what precautions are necessary? To lock close up with the front rank to prevent accident.

9. *Printing.* (See quot.)

1820 SCOTT *Prose Wks.* IV. Biographies II. (1870) 325 A leaf in the former [*sc.* a copy of Caxton's Book of Troy] was what is technically called locked. [*Footnote*] Such is the phrase when, by an error at press, the reverse has been printed on the side of the leaf which should have presented the obverse, so that page 32 precedes 31.

10. *intr.* Of a vehicle: To admit of the forewheels' passing askew under the body of the carriage. Said also of the wheel. (Cf. LOCK *sb.*[2] 15.)

1669 WORLIDGE *Syst. Agric.* (1681) 328 To Lock, is a term used by Drivers in moving the fore wheels of a Waggon to and fro. **1706** PHILLIPS (ed. Kersey), *To lock*, among Drivers, to move the wheels of a Waggon to and fro. **1805** DICKSON *Pract. Agric.* I. 33 A very useful improvement.. is that of leaving the space sufficiently deep in the bed of the waggon for the fore wheels to lock round in the shortest curve. **1851** *Illustr. Catal. Gt. Exhib.* 260 When locking, the carriage draws the lever *b* from its recess. **1873** MISS BROUGHTON *Nancy* III. 148 The road is narrow, and the coach will not lock. **1879** *Cassell's Techn. Educ.* IV. 174 The front wheel.. has to lock or turn under the arch.

11. *Engineering* and *Navigation.* **a.** *intr.* To provide locks for the passage of vessels. **b.** Of a canal: To pass by a lock *into.* Also of the vessel: To pass *down, in,* or *out* through a lock. Of persons: To pass *out* through an air-lock. **c.** *trans.* To pass (a vessel) *down, in, out* or *through* by means of a lock. **d.** *intr.* To take a boat into a lock. **e.** *trans.* To furnish (a canal) with locks; to shut *off* (a portion of a river) by means of a lock.

a. **1769** in Picton *L'pool Munic. Rec.* (1886) II. 245 This Council will.. lock down to the sea shore there at their own expence.

b. **1795** J. PHILLIPS *Hist. Inland Navig.* Add. 168 The canal locks into the river at Beeston Meadow. **1840** *Evid. Hull Docks Comm.* 121 They will have to lock in and out

again. **1857–8** *Proc. Inst. Civ. Engin.* XVII. 397 Two long levels of a canal locking from one into the other. **1897** *Outing* (U.S.) XXX. 364/2 There was less trouble in locking down at the various levels. **1899** *Allbutt's Syst. Med.* VII. 41 Too rapid a reduction of the pressure in 'locking out', that is in passing from the caisson through the lock or ante-chamber in which the pressure should be gradually reduced.

c. **1840** *Evid. Hull Docks Comm.* 121 The small vessels.. would have to be locked in and out. **1857–8** *Proc. Inst. Civ. Engin.* XVII. 397 An up train [of boats], which had been locked through from the lower level. **1876** STEVENSON in *Encycl. Brit.* IV. 788/1 Vessels are locked down from the sea into the [North Holland] canal.

d. **1857** P. COLQUHOUN *Comp. Oarsman's Guide* 18 Care must be taken in locking with a barge to keep astern of her.

e. **1892** *Pall Mall G.* 24 Nov. 2/1 The portion of the river thus diverted would then be locked off.

12. *to lock on to*: **a.** *intr.* Of radar or other equipment: to locate and then to track automatically; to accept as a target or reference object that is thereafter maintained as such (usu. automatically).

1949 *Jrnl. R. Aeronaut. Soc.* May 439/2 The aerial system has been designed to 'lock on' to the responder signal and to 'follow it' during its motion through the atmosphere quite automatically and with great accuracy. **1964** *Discovery* Oct. 7/3 The stabilized instrument platform has been developed ..to lock on to the sun (or moon) within two minutes of lift-off. **1966** *New Scientist* 25 Aug. 405 Stars were often mistaken for aircraft lights. In 27 cases pilots chasing a target aircraft had 'locked on' to a star for periods between one and ten minutes and actually tried to fly up to it. **1968** *Times* 10 Dec. 6/7 The satellite was to have used six star trackers which would lock on to reference stars.

b. *trans.* To cause (a piece of equipment) to lock on to some object.

1954 K. W. GATLAND *Devel. Guided Missile* (ed. 2) iv. 118 After a short period, radar tracking and aiming devices are 'locked on' to target, and from then on the whole attack is automatic. **1964** *Guardian* 1 Dec. 1/4 Their fourth attempt to 'lock' Mariner-4 on to the star Canopus. **1971** *Nature* 8 Oct. 367/3 The flight took place aboard a skylark sounding rocket, which was stabilized and 'locked on' to the strong X-ray source Sco X-1 during the four minutes of observing time.

†**lock**, *v.*^{2} *Obs.* or *arch.* [ad. Du. *lokken* = G. *locken*.] *trans.* To allure, entice. Also *absol.*

1481 CAXTON *Reynard* (Arb.) 110, I am no byrde to be locked ne take by chaf. **1562** TURNER *Baths* Pref., Flockinge byrdes..ceas not locking and calling, if they heare any of their kindes. **1855** KINGSLEY *Westw. Ho!* xv, 'Tis just like that old Lucy, to lock a poor maid into shame.

-lock, *suffix*, in mod. Eng. occurring only in *wedlock*, represents OE. *-lác*, the second element of numerous compounds (usually neuter: rarely masc.) in which the first element is a sb. OE. had about a dozen of these compounds (those in which *-lác* means 'offering', LAKE *sb.*^{1}, are not counted); in all these the second element may be rendered 'actions or proceedings, practice', as *brýdlác* nuptials, *beadolác*, *feohtlác*, *heaðolác* warfare, *hǽmedlác*, *wiflác* carnal intercourse, *réaflác* robbery, *wedlác* pledge-giving, also espousals, nuptials, *wítelác* punishment, *wróhtlác* calumny. The *-lác* of these compounds should probably be identified with *lác* play, sport, LAKE *sb.*^{2}; the words meaning 'warfare', which may have been the earliest examples of this use, may be compared with the synonymous compounds in *-plega* play. Of the OE. compounds of *lác* three (*brýdlác*, *feohtlác*, *réaflác*) survived into early ME., and *wedlác* still survives with altered meaning. In ME. the suffix was sometimes assimilated in form to the etymologically equivalent but functionally distinct Scandinavian -LAIK. A few examples, not recorded in OE., appear in early ME.: *dweomerlak* (DEMERLAYK), FERLAC, SHENDLAC, *treulac*, *wohlac* (cf. WOUHLECHE), the last from a vb.-stem, *woȝ-* to woo; but none of these survived later than the 14th century.

lockable ('lɒkəb(ə)l). [f. LOCK *v.*^{1} + -ABLE.] That can be locked.

1893 *Field* 4 Mar. 335/1 Lockable hatches. **1898** *Century Mag.* Jan. 375/1 Some clever Japanese artisans then made the paper-walls..eye-proof, and the openings cunningly lockable.

lockage ('lɒkɪdʒ). [f. LOCK *sb.* and *v.* + -AGE.]

†**1.** The means of locking or fitting (pieces of timber) together. *Obs.*

1677 PLOT *Oxfordsh.* 272 Whose Lockages [*sc.* of the roof of the Sheldonian Theatre] being so quite different from any before mentioned.

2. (See LOCK *sb.*^{2} 9, 9 c.)

a. The amount of rise or fall effected by a lock or series of locks.

1770 J. BRINDLEY *Surv. Thames* 2 The Length will be about a Mile, and the Fall or Lockage ten Feet. **1795** J. PHILLIPS *Hist. Inland Navig.* Addenda 5 The total lockage is five hundred and forty-four feet, viz. four hundred and ninety-six feet fall, and forty-eight feet rise. **1829** J. MACAULEY *Hist. New York* I. 184 The ascending and descending lockage is about one thousand and thirty-two feet. **1879** *Daily News* 28 Aug. 3/2 From Chicago to Montreal..there are..56 locks, and a total lockage of 564 feet.

b. Toll paid for going through a lock or locks.

1771 *Act 11 Geo. III*, c. 45 §9 Which price or lockage shall be..painted..on Boards, on the said Locks. **1800** COLQUHOUN *Comm. Thames* xv. 483 The price of lockage is not to exceed 4^d per ton per lock. **1819** *Stat. Massach.* 19 June, Toll or lockage at the lock or locks. **1856** *Farmer's Mag.* Nov. 424 The expense of lockage, transhipment, &c.

c. The construction and working of locks; also, the aggregate of locks constructed.

1809 *Chron.* in *Ann. Reg.* 403/1 Nearly 200 feet of lockage. **1824** R. STEVENSON in *Trans. Highland Soc.* VI. 133 The great desideratum in the Railway-system, must doubtless lie in a convenient mode of lockage, for raising the waggons from one level to another. **1830** *Blackw. Mag.* XXVII. 459 To convert the..river by lockage into a channel capable of receiving..vessels. **1839** SOUTHEY in *Q. Rev.* LXIII. 426 This line was..impeded..by an enormous quantity of lockage. **1853–4** *Proc. Inst. Civ. Engin.* (1854) XIII. 218 It was the same thing hydrostatically,..whether the lockage was up or down, or indeed, whether there was any vessel at all in the lock. **1861** SMILES *Engineers* I. iv. 452 Brindley's plan was..to cut the level as flat as possible, in order to avoid lockage. **1883** *Manch. Exam.* 19 Dec. 4/5 The..drainage area of the coal-bearing rocks along the route of the proposed Canal would give a sufficient amount of water for lockage.

d. *attrib.*, as *lockage-system*, *-water*.

1816 *Mechanic* I. 319 (*title*) Method of saving lockage water, in Canals, Docks, and Navigation. **1861** SMILES *Engineers* II. 147 Powerful steam-engines were also erected to pump back the lockage water into the canal above. **1895** *Forum* (N.Y.) Aug. 750 The lockage system of the Welland [canal] is out of date.

e. The passage (of a vessel) through a lock.

1913 J. B. BISHOP *Panama Gateway* v. iv. 375 The average number of lockages through the..Canal..was 39 per day.

'**lockchester.** *Obs.* exc. *dial.* Also 5 lokecheste. [perh. f. LOCK *v.*^{1} + CHEST + -ER^1, in allusion to the creature's habit of rolling itself up tightly.] A woodlouse.

c **1440** *Promp. Parv.* 310/2 *Locchester*, wyrm. *a* **1485** *Ibid.* 316/2 (MS. S.) *Lukchester*, worm. **14..** *Voc.* in Wr.-Wülcker 597/8 *Multipes*, a lokecheste, or a shrympe. **1847–78** HALLIWELL s.v. *Lockchest*, A gardener [in Oxfordshire] used to call the wood-louse *lockchester*.

†**lockdor.** *Obs. rare*$^{-1}$. [f. LOCK *v.*^{1} + DOOR *sb.* or perh. DOR *sb.*^{1}] = prec.

c **1440** *Promp. Parv.* 311/2 Lokdore, wyrme,..*multipes*.

locke, obs. form of LUCK.

locked (lɒkt), *a.*^{1} [f. LOCK *sb.*^{1} + -ED^2.] Having locks or tresses. (Cf. the parasynthetic derivatives *golden-locked*, *long-locked*.)

1871 R. ELLIS tr. *Catullus* lxiv. 98 The maid, for a guest so sunnily lock'd deep sighing.

locked (lɒkt), *a.*^{2} [f. LOCK *sb.*^{2} + -ED^2.]

1. Furnished with a (pad)lock.

1786 BURNS *Twa Dogs* 13 His locked, letter'd, braw brass collar.

2. Of a canal: Provided with locks.

1819 D. THOMAS *Trav. Western Country* 30 The mill-dams on this stream are locked. **1884** *Pall Mall G.* 23 Feb. 8/2 A 'locked' ship canal for large ocean steamers between Runcorn and Manchester.

locked (lɒkt), *ppl. a.* [f. LOCK *v.*^{1} + -ED^1.] **a.** In senses of the vb.: Closed with a lock and key, closely fastened or entwined, etc. Also *fig.*

c **1470** HENRY *Wallace* IV. 234 A loklate [*v.r.* lokkit] bar, was drawyn ourthourth the dur. **1580** *Burgh Rec. Glasgow* (1832) 125 For taking awaye of ane lokit dur, w^t key of ane stabill. **1605** B. JONSON *Volpone* IV. i, Your garbe..must be ..Very reseru'd and lock't. **1606** SHAKS. *Tr. & Cr.* IV. iv. 39 Iniurie of chance..forcibly preuents Our lockt embrasures. **1857** *Abridg. Specif. Patents Sewing*, etc. (1871) 96 A locked tambour stitch having a running thread passed through the loops. **1871** TYNDALL *Fragm. Sci.* (1879) II. v. 63 By the same agent we tear asunder the locked atoms of a chemical compound. **1883** ANNIE THOMAS *Mod. Housewife* 134, I.. left it in a locked drawer in my wardrobe. **1883** R. W. DIXON *Mano* II. iii. 72 Then the locked mountains either hand that stood Met knee to knee. **1895** R. KIPLING in *Pall Mall G.* 30 July 2/3 A locked and swaying mob that moved from right to left and from left to right along the bank. **1895** *Westm. Gaz.* 26 Nov. 2/3 Years of locked and agonised joints. **1902** *Brit. Med. Jrnl.* 12 Apr. 878 Limited movement in knee which becomes locked if moved much.

b. With *up*.

1593 SHAKS. *Lucr.* 446 Shee much amaz'd breakes ope her lockt vp eyes. **1676** MACE *Musick's Monument* title-p., All Its Occult Lock'd-up Secrets Plainly laid Open. **1721** RAMSAY *Morning Interview* 8 He starts with lock'd-up eyes. **1854** DICKENS *Hard T.* II. i, A locked-up iron room with three locks. **1891** *Daily News* 9 Dec. 6/3 Locked-up securities left on the hands of the bank.

c. **locked jaw**: (*a*) a jaw set fast by spasmodic contraction of the muscles; (*b*) = LOCKJAW, and occas. = JAW-FALL 2.

(*a*) **1765** *Phil. Trans.* LV. 86, I was soon convinced she had that terrible symptom, a locked jaw. **1802** JANE WEST *Infidel Father* III. 4 A private ball has been known to save half a county from such an immoderate fit of yawning, that people grew apprehensive of locked jaws. **1822–34** *Good's Study Med.* (ed. 4) II. 269 In some, a locked-jaw takes place about the seventh day from the operation.

(*b*) **1767** GOOCH *Treat. Wounds* I. 331 A convulsive contraction called the locked-jaw came on. **1788** [see JAW-FALL 2]. **1799** M. UNDERWOOD *Dis. of Childr.* (ed. 4) I. 19 *note*, The formidable disease so fatal to new-born children in the West-Indies, called the locked-jaw, or jaw-fallen. **1841** *Penny Cycl.* XXI. 363/2 Locked-Jaw is not an infrequent disease among sheep. **1845** CARLYLE *Cromwell* (1873) I. i. 5 So that no man shall henceforth contemplate them.. without danger of locked-jaw.

d. *locked-coil*: used *attrib.* to denote a rope or cable which has the outer strands of such a shape as to lock together and form a smooth cylindrical surface.

1885 *Cassell's Family Mag.* Dec. 59/1 A new kind of rope, called the locked-coil rope, has recently been brought out. **1952** T. BRYSON *Mining Machinery* (ed. 3) x. 246 The desire to increase further the wearing surface of ropes led to construction of locked-coil ropes.

e. *locked-room*: used *attrib.* to denote a mystery, or a mystery story, involving a locked room.

1942 H. HAYCRAFT *Murder for Pleasure* vi. 104 *The Mystery of the Yellow Room*..remains..the most brilliant of all 'locked room' novels. **1954** J. SYMONS *Narrowing Circle* iii. 14, I listened to the dictabook on my desk, which was a deliberately old-fashioned locked-room style detective story. **1965** 'D. SHANNON' *Death-Bringers* (1966) vii. 83 He'd never believed there were such things as Locked Room mysteries in real life. **1970** —— *Unexpected Death* (1971) xiii. 194 Lock the door on the outside and shove the key under the door. No locked-room puzzle.

f. *locked groove*: on a gramophone record, a circular groove into which the normal spiral groove runs.

1958 in *Chambers's Techn. Dict.* Add. **1962** A. NISBETT *Technique Sound Studio* xii. 207 On disc, using locked grooves to provide rhythmic repetitions.

g. With *in*: of a surfer, enveloped in and being carried along on a wave.

1965 *S. Afr. Surfer* I. III. 7 Its breathlessly fast hollow waves afford the lucky surfer an easy 300 yard locked-in ride. *Ibid.* 33 Each situation, from being locked-in to wiped-out, is entirely dependent on how the surfer uses the wave. **1971** *Studies in English* (Univ. of Cape Town) Feb. 27 If the wave is very hollow, as at Gansbaai, then the wave may arch over the surfer and he will get covered up and enjoy a tube ride. This is called being locked in.

locker ('lɒkə(r)), *sb.*^{1} Also 5–6 loker(e, -yr. [f. LOCK *sb.*^{2} or *v.*^{1} + -ER^1.]

I. One who locks.

1. An officer at the Custom House, in charge of a locked-up warehouse, acting under the warehouse-keeper.

1735 J. CHAMBERLAYNE *St. Gt. Brit.* II. III. 200 (List of Excise Officers), Six Lockers at the Tea Warehouses, each 30*l.* per Ann. **1812** J. SMYTH *Pract. of Customs* (1821) 361 The Locker in attendance at the Warehouse receives notice of the Merchant's intention to ship the Goods. **1858** in SIMMONDS *Dict. Trade.* **1887** *Daily News* 7 Apr. 6/7 Robert Lecky, the prisoner's father,..had been a locker in the service of the Customs.

2. *slang.* (See quot.)

1718 C. HIGGIN *True Discov.* (Farmer), I am a locker, I leave goods at a house and borrow money on them, pretending that they are made in London.

3. With advs.

1751 *Hist. Acc.* 66 *note*, Had it fell into the Hands of one of the Park-Lockers-up. **1887** *Pall Mall G.* 18 Oct. 4/1 Young men may remain out until twelve on leaving their names with the locker-up. **1894** *Athenæum* 30 June 831/2 In several pitched battles between the two parties the lockers-out were successful.

II. A means of locking.

4. **a.** *techn.* Something that locks or closes; †? a stopper, a stop to a bell.

1417 in *Surtees Misc.* (1888) 13 That the water be ledde downe..be a pype of lede closed wyth a loker. **1545** *Ludlow Churchw. Acc.* (Camden) 21 Item, for settynge up of a loker to drawe the corde before the crucifixe. **1569** *Ibid.* 139 Item, a locker and a handell ffor the second bell..iiij*d.* **1844** G. DODD *Textile Manuf.* vii. 211 Bobbins, pushers, lockers, point-bars. **1883** GRESLEY *Gloss. Coal Mining* 159 *Locker*, a short iron or wooden bar for scotching tram wheels on inclined roads.

†**b.** = LOCKET 2. *Obs.*

1660 *Act 12 Chas. II*, c. 4 Sched., Lockers or Chapes for Daggers.

III. A locked or enclosed receptacle.

5. **a.** A box or chest with a lock; also, a small cupboard, e.g. one attached to a bench, or placed under a window-seat.

c **1440** *Promp. Parv.* 311/2 Lokere, *cistella.* **1447** BOKENHAM *Seyntys* (Roxb.) 31 They..trussyd the body in a loker of tre. **1463** *Bury Wills* (Camden) 19 The bulle and the busshoppees seelys..be set in a loker of burde for brekyng of the seelys. **1719** DE FOE *Crusoe* I. ii, Some small Lockers to put in some Bottles of such Liquor as he thought fit to drink. **1754** MRS. DELANY *Lett. to Mrs. Dewes* 296, I have ordered lockers to your windows. **1807** J. E. SMITH *Phys. Bot.* 509 The specimens thus pasted, are conveniently kept in lockers. **1823** P. NICHOLSON *Pract. Build.* 237 Some benches have a locker, or cavity. **1873** J. RICHARDS *Woodworking Factories* 112 The planers, lathes, and drills have their lockers. **1886** W. J. TUCKER *E. Europe* 316 Iliana's trousseau was stored away in the stout old heavy lockers.

b. *Naut.* A chest or compartment for containing clothes, stores, ammunition, etc. Often with word prefixed to indicate its use, as *chain-*, *shot-locker*. *boatswain's locker*: 'a chest in small craft wherein material for working upon rigging is kept' (Smyth *Sailor's Word-bk.* 1867). *(not) a shot in the locker*, used *fig.* for: (no) money in one's pocket, (not) a chance left. *laid in the lockers* fig., dead. For *Davy Jones's locker* see DAVY JONES.

1626 CAPT. SMITH *Accid. Yng. Sea-men* 11 A Hamacke, the lockers, the round-house [etc.]. *a* **1642** SIR W. MONSON *Naval Tracts* III. (1704) 356/2 The Gunner is..to have his

Shot in a Locker near every Piece. **1644** Manwayring *Seamans Dict.* s.v., Any little boxes, or as it were, Cubbords which are made by the Ships-sides to put in shot by the Peeces,.. are (by a common name) called Lockers. **1726** G. Roberts *Four Years Voy.* 41 Heaving the rest into David Jones's Locker. **1793** *Trans. Soc. Arts* XI. 188 Coiling the line in the front locker. **1815** Scott *Guy M.* xxxiii, Brown's dead—shot—laid in the lockers, man. **1835** Marryat *Jac. Faithf.* vii, In front of the bed-places were two lockers, to sit down upon. **1840** R. H. Dana *Bef. Mast* iii. 4 He.. has charge of the boatswain's locker. **1848** Thackeray *Van. Fair* xxvi, As long as there's a shot in the locker, she shall want for nothing. **1865** Livingstone *Zambesi* vi. 151 They made a sudden dash over the lockers and across our faces for the cabin door. **1890** W. E. Norris *Misadventure* xl, He had another shot left in his locker, which he now fired.

6. a. A compartment in a pigeon-house, a pigeon-hole. †Applied also to the cell of bees.

1600 J. Pory tr. *Leo's Africa* III. 146 These doues they keepe in certaine cages or lockers on the tops of their houses. **1608** Topsell *Serpents* (1658) 649 The Lockers or holes of the up-grown Bees, are somewhat too large. *a* **1617** Bayne *On Eph.* (1658) 91 Pigeons flye home to their own lockers. **1639** Horn & Rob. *Gate Lang. Unl.* xiv. §154 In a dove [pigeon-] hovse.. to each pare of tame ones is appointed out a locker. **1727** Bailey vol. II, *Locker*, a Pigeon Hole. **1731** *Gentl. Mag.* I. 451 A Gentleman.. who kept tame pigeons.. discerned something white at the Lockers. **1816** Kirby & Sp. *Entomol.* (1843) I. 130 Which makes it advisable never to have their [Pigeon's] lockers fixed to a dwelling house. **1859** Brent *Pigeon Bk.* 86 Pigeon-houses, or lockers, on a more limited scale, are of various forms.

b. *Eccl.* A cupboard, recess, or niche in a wall usually near an altar, fitted with a door and lock, for the reservation of the Sacrament, the keeping of sacred vessels, etc.

1527 *Extracts Aberd. Reg.* (1844) I. 117 The Egiptiens tuk out of Thomas Watsouns houss tua siluer spounis, liand in the locker of ane schryne. **1552** in *Inv. Ch. Goods Yorksh.*, etc. (Surtees) II. 65 Item, one loker for the sacriment. **1593** *Anc. Rites Durham* (Surtees) 2 The severall lockers or ambers for the safe keepinge of the vestments and ornaments belonginge to everye Altar.

IV. 7. *attrib.* and *Comb.*, as (sense 4) ***locker-bar, -plate***; (sense 5) ***locker-hole, -key, -nipper, -room, -seat***.

1839 Ure *Dict. Arts* 733 In the year 1824, Mr. Morley added another plate to each of the *locker-bars. **1765** *Treat. Dom. Pigeons* 112 The common runt.. kept.. generally in *locker-holes in inn yards. **1894** *Outing* (U.S.) XXIV. 379/1 Here are my *locker keys; you'll find everything open. **1802** J. Anfrey in *Naval Chron.* VII. 48 The yeoman of the *locker-nipper. **1839** Ure *Dict. Arts* 732 Two other long flat bars below, called the *locker plates. **1895–6** *Cal. Univ. Nebraska* 252 The *locker room for young men is fitted with ninety-six lockers. **1906** *Westm. Gaz.* 11 July 8/1 Two extra payments are a penny for a bath, including towel and soap, and 6d. deposit for the use of a large locker in the *locker room. **1931** *Maclean's Mag.* 1 Aug. 28/4 Mere males are lucky to find sanctuary in locker room, grill and bar. **1934** [see bathroom]. **1972** *Newsweek* 10 Jan. 30/2 On one side of the crowded Kansas City locker room, veteran quarterback Lenny Dawson dressed hurriedly and disappeared. **1877** W. Thomson *Voy. Challenger* I. i. 21 The *locker-seat stretches across the forward end of the laboratory.

† **'locker**, *v. Obs.* Chiefly *Sc.* [? f. lock *sb.*¹ + -er⁵.] *intr.* To curl. Only in ppl. adjs. † **'lockered** (***lockard, lokerit, lokkerit***) curled, and † **'lockering** (***lokerand***) curling. Also † **'locker** *sb.* in *pl.* = curled locks. † **'locker** *a.*, curled.

? *a* **1400** *Morte Arth.* 779 Alle with lutterde legges, lokerde unfaire. *c* **1470** Henryson *Mor. Fab.* vii. (*Lion & Mouse*) Prol. v, With lokker hair, quhilk ouer his schulderis lay. **1513** Douglas *Æneis* vii. xii. 63 A felloun bustuus and gret lyoun skyn, Terrible and rouch, wyth taty lokyrand haris. *Ibid.* xiv. 8 His helm.. Wyth cristis thre, lik till ane lokerit mane. *Ibid.* xii. Prol. 127 Hevinly lylleis, with lokerand toppis quhyte. *Ibid.* xii. i. 16 For ire [the lyoun] the lokkerris of his nek vpcastis. **1687** H. More *Contn. Remark. Stor.* (1689) 428 The Daughters lockard hair.

locker, variant of lockyer *Obs.*

lockeram, variant of lockram.

locker-gowlan, -on: see lucken-golland.

locket ('lɒkɪt). Forms: 4 **lokat**, 5 **loket**, 6 **lockett, -itt**, *Sc.* **lokart**, 6– **locket**. [ad. OF. *locquet, loquet, luquet* (mod.F. *loquet* latch), dim. of *loc* latch, lock (recorded chiefly as AF.), of Teut. origin, cognate with lock *sb.*²]

† **1.** One of the iron cross-bars of a window. *Obs.*

1354 *Mem. Ripon* (Surtees) III. 92 In mercede fabri facientis pragges et lokats de ferro suo proprio pro fenestris figendis. **1541** in *Proc. Soc. Antiq. Scotl.* (1862) III. 163 And to put in ilk lycht of the wyndois grete lokartis of irne for binding of glas thareto. **1598** in Willis & Clark *Cambridge* (1886) II. 252 In euery light one vpright barr and fiue Crosse barrs or locketts.

attrib. **1379** *Mem. Ripon* (Surtees) III. 101 Et in C loketnayles 3½*d.* *Ibid.* 102 Et in lxx loketnayles, 2*d.*

2. One of the metal plates or bands on a scabbard.

1562 *Act 5 Eliz.* c. 7 No person.. shall bring.. into this Realme.. Hiltes, Pommeles, Lockettes, Chapes, Dagger Blades [etc.]. **1706** Phillips (ed. Kersey), *Locket*,.. that part of a Sword-scabbard, where the Hook is fastened. **1879** *Unif. Reg.* in *Navy List* (1882) July 487/2 *Scabbard.*—The top and middle lockets to be four and three inches and a half long respectively.

† **3.** A fastening or socket; *Naut.* (see quot. *a* 1642). *Obs.*

a **1642** Sir W. Monson *Naval Tracts* iii. (1704) 346/1 Lockets are the Holes the Pintle of the Murderers goes into. **1664** Butler *Hudibras* ii. i. 808 That other Virtuous School of Lashing; Where Knights are kept in narrow lists, With wooden Lockets 'bout their wrists.

† **4.** A group of small jewels set in a pattern. *Obs.*

1664 Power *Exp. Philos.* i. 12 Like a Locket of Diamonds, or a Sett of round Crystal Beads. **1696** Bp. Patrick *Comm. Exod.* xxviii. (1697) 541 Twelve Ouches, in which every single Stone was set, as we see it now, in our present Lockets. **1704** *Lond. Gaz.* No. 3984/4 Lost,.. a Gold Case of a Watch, set on the outside with nine Lockets, and little Diamonds between. **1706** Phillips, *Locket*, a Set of Diamonds, or other Jewels.

5. † **a.** 'A small lock; any catch or spring to fasten a necklace or other ornament' (J.). *Obs.* Hence the now current sense **b.** A small case of gold or silver, containing a miniature portrait, a lock of hair, etc., and worn (usually, suspended from the neck) as an ornament.

For a passage *c* 1320 often quoted as an example of this sense, see loket.

a. 1727 Bailey vol. II, *Locket*, a little Lock of a Gold Chain. **1765** *Ann. Reg.* 152 The [nabob's] turban.. has a top.. most ingeniously contrived with lockets and springs to take in or let out.

b. 1679 [see hair *sb.* 10]. **1720** Gay *Poems* II. 399 Some by a snip of woven hair In posied lockets bribe the fair. **1838** Dickens *O. Twist* xxxviii, It contained a little gold locket: in which were two locks of hair. **1862** *Catal. Internat. Exhib.* II. xxxiii. 45 Locket, fine brilliant centre and drop, pierced open setting.

Hence **'locketed** *ppl. a.* (*a*) Ornamented with a locket. (*b*) Set in a locket.

1871 G. A. Sala in *Belgravia* XIV. 430 Somebody.. was highly curled, oiled, ringed, chained, pinned, and locketed. **1901** *Academy* 10 Aug. 110/1 His [Geo. IV's] request to be buried in his night-shirt, beneath which was a locketed portrait of Mrs. Fitzherbert.

lockfast ('lɒkfɑːst, -æ-), *a.* [Two formations: (1) f. lock *sb.*² + fast *a.*; (2) f. lock *v.*¹ + fast *adv.*]

1. Chiefly *Sc.* Fastened or secured by a lock.

1453 in *Exch. Rolls Scotl.* V. 556, xxxiiij grotis of xij*d.* grotis and j*d.* in a lokfast box. **1554** *Extracts Aberd. Reg.* (1844) I. 281 The saidis baillies suld tak and apprehend the said John Chalmer, and put him in custodie in stark lokfast hows. **1752** J. Louthian *Form of Process* (ed. 2) 137 That ye make steiked and lockfast Gates and Doors open and patent. **1820** Scott *Monast.* xxiv, Having no sure lock-fast place of my own. **1888** Annie S. Swan *Doris Cheyne* xv. 232 It was not lockfast, of course, but I had no right with what it contained. **1890** *Harper's Mag.* Nov. 882/1 The cemetery was lock-fast now.

fig. **1838** *Blackw. Mag.* XLIII. 440 Psychology will be.. lightened of a useless and unmarketable cargo which has kept her lockfast for many generations.

b. quasi-*sb.* A receptacle that is locked fast.

1851–61 Mayhew *Lond. Labour* II. 341 A third party entered the house,.. broke open several lockfasts, and stole the whole of the plate.

2. *Mech.* Adapted for locking something fast; fast-locking.

1881 Greener *Gun* 198 The two motions, the sliding and the drop-down, are combined in the Dougall lock-fast breech-action. **1890** *Anthony's Photogr. Bull.* III. 327 So long as there is ample bearing surface and a good lock fast attachment.

lockful ('lɒkfʊl). [f. lock *sb.*² + -ful.] As much as will fill a lock.

1811 *Two Rep. Thames Navig.* 25 The Canals, some of which have no water, pay heavily for every lockfull forced up by steam-engines. **1837** *Civil Eng. & Archit. Jrnl.* I. 44/2 Making 6740 cubic feet or 46,243⅜ gallons of water to each lockful.

Lockian ('lɒkɪən), *a.* and *sb.* [f. *Locke*, the English philosopher (1632–1704) + -ian.]

A. *adj.* Of or pertaining to Locke or his followers.

1858 W. R. Pirie *Inq. Hum. Mind* ii. ii. 80 The most eminent of the professed Lockian School. **1877** E. Caird *Philos. Kant* ii. 511 Kant was the founder of a new philosophy, which was fatal to the Leibnitzian, as well as to the Lockian, Individualism.

B. *sb.* = Lockist.

In recent Dicts.

Hence **'Lockianism**, the philosophical doctrines of Locke or his followers.

1862 *Macm. Mag.* July 201 It is here that Berkeley passes from Lockianism to Platonism. **1886** Seth in *Encycl. Brit.* XXI. 383/1 The principles of Lockianism.

locking ('lɒkɪŋ), *vbl. sb.*¹ [f. lock *v.*¹ + -ing¹.]

1. The action of lock *v.*¹ in various senses *lit.* and *fig.*; an instance of this.

1611 Shaks. *Cymb.* i. v. 41 There is No danger in what shew of death it makes, More then the locking vp the Spirits a time. **1776** G. Temple *Building in Water* 145 The locking of Headers and Stretchers together. **1835–6** Todd *Cycl. Anat.* I. 160/2 There was probably a locking of the bones with each other. **1842** Syd. Smith *Let. Locking in on Railw.* Wks. 1859 II. 322/1 We have arranged our plan upon the locking-in system. **1860** Mrs. Carlyle *Lett.* III. 53 All the hateful preparatory lockings up and packings well over. **1882** *Times* 22 Feb., Such a gigantic 'locking-up' of produce as that. **1884** F. J. Britten *Watch & Clockm.* 144 In this form of the lever escapement the pallets have not less than 10° of motion. Of this amount 2° are used for locking, and the remainder for impulse. The amount of locking is to some extent dependent on the size of the escapement... The lighter the locking the better. **1892** Zangwill *Bow Mystery* 134 The outside locking could not have been effected if it [the key] had been in the lock.

2. *concr.* A contrivance for locking: † **a.** a lock (*obs.*); **b.** the piece of machinery in a watch, serving to lock the escapement.

1632 Lithgow *Trav.* 457 Close vp sayd he, this window.. with lyme and stone, stop the holes of the doore with double Matts, hanging another locking to it. **1816** *Mechanic* I. 411 The locking may be compared to a light balance turning on fine pivots, without a pendulum-spring. **1851** *Illustr. Catal. Gt. Exhib.* 410 Patent 'diamond escapement' as intended for the use of marine chronometers... The locking is intended to be jewelled.

3. a. With *down.* The action of providing locks for lowering a vessel on a canal. **b.** The action of lowering or raising a vessel by the use of a lock or locks: also with *down, up.*

1776 in Picton *L'pool Munic. Rec.* (1886) II. 246 Concerning the locking down and making a bridge.. for the canal. **1795** J. Phillips *Hist. Inland Navig.* 361 The use, or locking down, is thus managed. *Ibid.* 362 For ascending, or locking up, the boat being in the lock, the lower gates are shut. **1840** *Evid. Hull Docks Comm.* 122 They must enter by locking.

4. *attrib.* and *Comb.*, chiefly *Mech.*, denoting appliances serving to lock or engage one portion of a machine with another, as ***locking-bolt, -box, -brace, -clutch, -pole***; **locking-bar, -frame** (see quots.); **locking-pallet, -piece**, a tooth of the detent, which engages successively the teeth of the escape-wheel; **locking-plate**, (*a*) = *count-wheel* (see count *sb.*¹ 9); (*b*) in a lock; (*c*) a plate on a vehicle to take the wear of the fore-wheel when the vehicle is turning short; a rub-plate (Knight *Dict. Mech.* 1875); (*d*) a nut-lock (*ibid.* Suppl. 1884); **locking-spring** (see quot. 1884); **locking-stone**, the 'jewel' of an escapement; **locking-wheel** = *locking-plate* (*a* and *c*).

1889 G. Findlay *Eng. Railway* 75 The '*Locking Bar'.. is chiefly applied to siding points to prevent their being moved while a train is passing over them. **1881** Greener *Gun* 206 In the snap principle, the *locking-bolt is forced into the bites or grips by a spring upon the gun being closed. **1825** J. Nicholson *Operat. Mechanic* 38 The *locking-box [in a mill governor]. **1868** *Rep. Munitions War* 284 The hammer in its fall will force the *locking-brace to enter its proper position. **1825** J. Nicholson *Operat. Mechanic* 38 A *locking clutch is fitted upon the spindle between these two wheels. **1889** G. Findlay *Eng. Railway* 71 The '*locking-frame' consists of a row of levers by means of which the signalman actuates every pair of points and every signal under his control. **1816** *Mechanic* I. 373 A semi-cylindrical pin called the *locking-pallet. *Ibid.* 194 This *locking-piece, or locking-pallet. **1879** *Cassell's Techn. Educ.* IV. 242/2 In the real lock it [the bolt] would be called the *locking-plate. **1884** F. J. Britten *Watch & Clockm.* 156 The locking plate, the earliest arrangement of striking work, is shown in the engraving of 'De Vick's clock'. **1793** *Trans. Soc. Arts* XI. 293 A cart.. with a *locking-pole fixed to the wheel. **1881** *Instr. Census Clerks* (1885) 49 Bayonet Making:..*Locking Ring Maker. **1678** *Lond. Gaz.* No. 1296/4 The *locking Spring being lost from the Watch. **1884** F. J. Britten *Watch & Clockm.* 156 [The] Locking Spring.. [is] the spring of a watch case that keeps the cover closed against the force of the fly springs. *Ibid.* 59 See that the face of the *locking stone is angled so as to give perceptible draw. **1704** Harris *Lex. Techn.*, *Count-Wheel*... It is by some called the *Locking Wheel, because it hath.. Notches in it.. in order to make the Clock strike 1, 2, 3, 4, &c. **1835** *Partington's Brit. Cycl. Arts & Sci.* I. 283 A circular horizontal locking-wheel, formed of iron, is attached to the front part of the carriage.

locking ('lɒkɪŋ), *vbl. sb.*² *Hat Manuf.* [? f. lock *sb.*¹ + -ing¹.] (See quot.)

1900 *Ann. Rep. Insp. Factories for 1898* II. 167 Locking... This is the last stage before the fur passes to the felt hat manufacturer— the trays of shaven fur.. are taken to women who remove the outer edges, leaving only the fur of the back which they compact by pressing it in the hand and place it in a bag.

Lockist ('lɒkɪst). [See Lockian and -ist. Cf. F. *lockiste.*] A follower of Locke, one of his school.

1705 Hearne *Collect.* 20 Dec. (O.H.S.) I. 134 Dr. Wynne is a great Lockist. **1856** Emerson *Eng. Traits* xiv. 239 'Tis quite certain that.. the dull men will be Lockists.

'lock-jaw. [An alteration of the older *locked jaw*: see locked *ppl. a.*] Popular name for trismus, or tonic spasm of the muscles of mastication, causing the jaws to remain rigidly closed; a variety of tetanus. 'Also extended so as to mean *Tetanus*' (*Syd. Soc. Lex.*).

1803 *Med. Jrnl.* IX. 316 One girl.. died of lock jaw. **1866** A. Flint *Princ. Med.* (1880) 841 The jaws are firmly shut by the rigid contraction of the muscles, and hence the affection is known as lock-jaw. **1874** Carpenter *Ment. Phys.* i. ii. §74 (1879) 78 Tetanus (commonly known as 'lock-jaw').

Hence **'lock-jawed** *ppl. a.*, having the jaws fixed; *fig.* unable to speak.

1801 J. Brown in *Naval Chron.* VII. 153 We were lock-jaw'd. **1809** Malkin *Gil Blas* xi. v. ¶7 On this theme you may expatiate till the populace become lock-jawed with astonishment. **1826** J. Wilson *Noct. Ambr.* Wks. 1855 I. 210, I burst out into such a torrent of indignant eloquence that the Slaves and Tyrants were all tongue-tied and lock-jawed before me.

lockless ('lɒklɪs), *a.* [f. lock *sb.*² + -less.] Having no lock (in various senses of lock *sb.*²).

1591 Florio *2nd Fruites* 99 In a lockles cheast, no man will shake his bag. **1746–74** D. Graham *Metr. Hist. Rebell.* i. Wks. 1883 I. 87 With lockless guns and rusty swords. **1821** Byron *Juan* iii. lxxi, One large gold bracelet clasp'd each

lovely arm, Lockless. **1884** HAMERTON *Hum. Interc.* xxiv, Thrust into a lockless drawer.

lockman (ˈlɒkmən). *Sc.* and *Isle of Man.* Forms: 5–6 **lokman**, 6 **loikman**, 7 **lockmane**, 7– **lockman**. [? f. LOCK *sb.*^{2} + MAN *sb.* (cf. ON. *lokusveinn* janitor); if so, the original sense would be 'turnkey, jailor'.] †**a.** In Scotland: A public executioner, hangman (*obs.*). **b.** In the Isle of Man: The coroner's summoner.

c **1470** HENRY *Wallace* XI. 1342 The lokmen than thai bur Wallace but baid On till a place, his martyrdom to tak. **1508** DUNBAR *Flyting* 174 Ay loungand, lyk ane loikman on ane ledder. *a* **1600** MONTGOMERIE *Misc. Poems* xxi. 17 Quhy hes thou me alone in langour left? Delyvring me vnto this lokman Love. **1616** *Orkney Witch Trial* in *Misc. Maitl. Club* II. 191 To be tane be the lockmane to the place of executioun. **1656** J. CHALONER *Descr. Isle of Man* in D. King *Vale-Royall* IV. 26 Either of the said Officers may give their Token for Execution to the Coroner or Lockman [*side note*, Lockman is an under-Sheriffe]. **1735** DYCHE & PARDON *Dict.*, *Lockman*, the Name of an Officer in the Isle of Man, that executes the Orders of the Governor, which at London is called a Sheriff. **1818** SCOTT *Hrt. Midl.* xiii, I wadna think of asking the lockman's place ower his head. **1863** KEBLE *Life Bp. Wilson* xix. 642 A lockman (or coroner's summoner) is presented for summoning a jury and witnesses to meet on a Sunday. **1884** C. ROGERS *Soc. Life Scotl.* II. x. 54 Every burgh lockman had his free house.

Hence ˈ**lockmanship**, the office or duties of a 'lockman'.

1500 in Pitcairn *Crim. Trials* I. *101 Gift to Adam Barde, Lockmanne, for his Service of Lokmanschip.

locko-man: see LOCOMAN^1.

lock-on (ˈlɒkɒn). [f. vbl. phr. *to lock on* (*to*): see LOCK *v.*^{1} 12.] **1.** (The commencement of) automatic tracking.

1960 *Aeroplane* 4 Mar. 278/1 The Bloodhound target radar lock-on technique will be demonstrated and a model of the missile is to be 'fired'. **1967** *Sci. Amer.* May 83 (Advt.), When an air-to-air training missile 'sees' its target, a new microminiaturized signal amplifier.. tells the pilot that lock-on has been achieved. **1971** *Time* 15 Feb. 8 As *Antares* swooped below that altitude, its radar remained inactive. 'C'mon, radar,' Mitchell implored. 'Get the lock-on.'

2. The establishment of a rigid physical connection.

1967 *Sunday Times* 23 Apr. 8 Back at the surface, a lock-on device enables divers to transfer to a larger chamber on board, releasing the sub to return to work with a fresh diving team. **1968** *New Scientist* 6 June 509/1 As it will need to contend with the underwater currents playing around the submarine, it will need extremely sensitive means of controlling its position just before lock-on. **1969** *Jane's Freight Containers 1968–69* 574/2 The top lift cradle has.. power-guided lock-on at each of the four corners. Safe lock-on indicators are monitored by the operator in the cab.

ˈ**lock-out.** Also lockout. *Pl.* lock-outs (*erron.* locks-out). [f. vbl. phr. *lock out*: see LOCK *v.* 5.] **1.** An act of 'locking out' a body of workers; *i.e.* a refusal on the part of an employer, or a number of employers acting in concert, to furnish work to their operatives until certain conditions have been assented to by the latter collectively.

1854 *Westm. Rev.* V. 120 How far the 'lock-out' has been forced upon the masters by partial 'strikes' of the men,.. what proportion of the workpeople have been victims rather than combatants 'locked-out',.. these are some among many much disputed points. **1860** *All Year Round* No. 57. 161 Lock-outs competing against operatives' intimidation. **1863** W. G. BLAIKIE *Better Days for Working People* iv. (1864) 91 Strikes on the one side have their counterpart in locks-out on the other. **1889** [see CLOSE-DOWN]. **1926** *Times* 5 May 2/1 Lord Gainford, speaking for the mine owners, said the notices which were put up were not lockout notices. **1955** *Times* 17 Aug. 7/2 The employers announced that the strike would be met by a lockout, and there seems to be no prospect that they will change their attitude. **1970** T. LUPTON *Managem. & Social Sci.* (ed. 2) iii. 62 The hidden sanction of strike or lockout always underlies bargaining. **1971** *Daily Tel.* 20 Oct. 16 It is somewhat exceptional in industrial relations for employers to resort to a lock-out in reprisal against strikes and overtime bans. **1974** *Socialist Worker* 9 Nov. 16/1 Truck workers at British Leyland's AEC plant marched through Southall last Thursday chanting and determined after the month-long lock-out.

2. *Electronics* and *Computers.* The automatic temporary prevention of the operation or use of a relay or other device. Usu. *attrib.*

1924 T. CROFT *Electr. Machinery & Control Diagrams* vii. 213 When current passes through the contactor, both the closing and the lockout portions of the switch are magnetized. **1945** '*Electr. Engineer*' *Ref. Bk.* VII. 105 When the directional relay closes contacts for fault current fed out of the feeder, the secondary coil operates the associated attracted armature relay which initiates a lock-out operation. The overcurrent relay cannot operate because the secondary coil is not connected to the series coil. **1952** I. FRAZEE et al. *Automotive Electr. Syst.* vii. 369 Vibrating and lockout circuit breakers consist of a coil winding and a set of contact points... When current in excess of the rated value flows.. a plunger.. opens the contact points. **1960** *McGraw-Hill Encycl. Sci. & Technol.* XIII. 348/2 The problem in all applications of lockout circuits is that of concurrently competing circuits, among which one has to be picked for some action. **1961** N. CHAPIN *Programming Computers for Business Applic.* viii. 198 The high-speed transfer-of-data phase during which the buffer empties into or fills from high-speed storage.. is sometimes called the lockout phase. **1972** *Computer Jrnl.* XV. 194/2 The information in the record is then read, any necessary checking done, and the update performed. The updated version of the record is then inserted in the file and finally the lockout is cancelled.

lockram^1 (ˈlɒkrəm). *Obs.* exc. *Hist.* Forms: 5 **lokerham**, 6 **locram**, **lo(c)queram**, **lockerom**, **locorum**, **lokeram**, 6–7 **locrum**, **lockrome**, 7 **lokram**, 7–9 **lock(a)rum**, 6–9 **lockeram**, 6– **lockram**. [ad. F. *locrenan*, from *Locronan* (lit. 'cell of St. Ronan'), the name of a village in Brittany, where the fabric was formerly made. For the form cf. BUCKRAM.]

1. A linen fabric of various qualities for wearing apparel and household use. Also, an article made of lockram; in *pl.*, pieces of lockram.

1483–4 in Swayne *Sarum Church-w. Acc.* (1896) 35 Pro vna vlna de lokerham ad emendand. diuersas albas, vjd. **1520** SIR R. ELYOT *Will* in *T. Elyot's Gov.* (1883) I. App. A. 313 Lynnen cloth of canvas and lokeram for shetes and smockes and shirtes. **1552** in *Surrey Church Goods* (1869) 16 One old surplice of loqueram. *a* **1592** GREENE *Jas. IV*, IV. iii, Let the linings be of tenpenny lockram. **1607** SHAKS. *Cor.* II. i. 224 The Kitchin Malkin pinnes Her richest Lockram 'bout her reechie necke. **1615** MARKHAM *Eng. Housew.* II. i. (1668) 42 Spread it thin upon new Lockram or Leather somewhat bigger than the grief. **1666** *Lond. Gaz.* No. 38/1 Two Barks of this Town laden with Lockerams from Jersey and Guernsey. **1692** *Ibid.* No. 2810/4 A considerable quantity of Locrums and Dowlas. **1719** D'URFEY *Pills* (1872) II. 245 The sisters wear Lockram, and buy it of him. **1820** SCOTT *Abbot* ii, Why should I bend to her?—is it because her kirtle is of silk, and mine of blue lockeram?

2. *attrib.*

1554 *Bury Wills* (Camden) 147 To Mother Huntman a new rayle and a lockerom kercher. **1616** R. C. *Times' Whistle* II. 755 His lockram bande sewde to his hempen shirt. **1632** BROME *North. Lasse* IV. iii. Wks. 1873 III. 74 Let all the good you intended me, be a lockram Coife, a blew Gown, a Wheel, and a clean Whip. **1640** GLAPTHORNE *Wit in a Constable* IV. Wks. 1874 I. 217 Thou thoughtst, because I did weare Lokram shirts Ide no wit. **1766** ENTICK *London* IV. 129 A lockram shift.

b. lockram jaws, jaws covered with flesh as thin as lockram. Hence **lockram-jawed** *a.*

1682 *New News fr. Bedlam* 36 Their Lockram Jaws we'l rent and tear. *a* **1700** B. E. *Dict. Cant. Crew*, *Lockram-jaw'd*, Thin, Lean, Sharp-visag'd. **1706** E. WARD *Hud. Rediv.* I. VI. 7 After he'd made a little Pause, Again he stretch'd his Lockram Jaws. **1735** DYCHE & PARDON *Dict.*, *Lockram-jaw'd*, a Person of a long, lean, meagre Visage or Countenance.

lockram^2 (ˈlɒkrəm). *dial.* and *U.S.* Also **lockum**, **lockrum**. [? Figurative use of prec.; cf. *bombast*, *fustian*.

(But cf. *logaram* dial., in the *Eng. Dial. Dict.* treated as a corruption of *logarithm*).]

A pack of gibberish. Also quasi-*adj.*

1825 J. NEAL *Bro. Jonathan* I. 157 What has all this long, lockum story to do with your trade? **1837** HALIBURTON *Clockm.*, *Slick's Let.* 8 As for that long lochrum about Mr. Everett,.. there aint a word of truth in it. **1855** —— *Nature & Hum. Nat.* I. 14 In Congress no man can speak or read an oration more than an hour long; but he can send the whole lockrum, includin' what he didn't say, to the papers. **1854** in MISS BAKER *Northants Gloss.*

lockron, corrupt form of LUCKEN-GOWAN.

lockschen, **lockshan**, **lockshen**, varr. LOKSHEN.

locksman^1 (ˈlɒksmən). [f. *lock's*, gen. of LOCK *sb.*^{2} + MAN *sb.*]

†**1.** *Sc.* A turnkey, jailor; also = LOCKMAN a.

17.. in Fountainhall *Decis.* (1759) I. 169 (Jam.) The Provosts and Baillies of Edinburgh.. do judge Alexander Cockburn their Hangman or Locksman within three suns—for [etc.]. **1820** SCOTT *Abbot* xxiii, To play the Locksman here in Lochleven, with no gayer amusement, than that of turning the key on two or three helpless women?

2. = *lock-keeper* (see LOCK *sb.*^{2}).

1846 MRS. GORE *Eng. Char.* (1852) 66 Thomas Scroggs, a locksman on the Paddington canal. **1884** *Manch. Exam.* 19 Sept. 8/4 The locksmen of the Rideau Canal have a busy time opening and shutting the 47 huge gates.

locksman^2 (ˈlɒksmən). [f. pl. of LOCK *sb.*^{1} + MAN *sb.*^{1}] In Kingston, Jamaica, a member of the Ras Tafari cult who wears his hair long and plaited as a mark of his membership.

1960 M. G. SMITH et al. *Ras Tafari Movement in Kingston, Jamaica* iv. 23 The Locksmen, whose hair is matted and plaited and never cut, neither their beards. **1966** *Guardian* 3 Feb. 8/1 The long-haired Rastas, the Locksmen, are the ones Jamaicans laugh at in the streets.

locksmith (ˈlɒksmɪθ). [f. LOCK *sb.*^{2} + SMITH.] An artificer whose occupation is to make or mend locks.

1226 in J. T. Gilbert *Hist. & Munic. Rec. Irel.* (Rolls) 87 Ricardus le lokismith de Tickehille. *c* **1440** *Promp. Parv.* 311/2 Loksmythe, *serefaber.* **1501** *Ld. Treas. Acc. Scotl.* (1900) II. 112 The lok smyth of Edinburgh. **1627** S. S. in Capt. Smith *Seaman's Gram.* a iij b, He's neither Lock-Smith, Gold-Smith, nor Black-Smith. **1707** *Lond. Gaz.* No. 4347/4 Thomas Temple the Younger, late of North-Walsham.., Lock Smith. **1872** YEATS *Techn. Hist. Comm.* 179 In the cathedrals of the period the locksmith's work was especially elaborate and ingenious.

Hence ˈ**locksmithery**, the locksmith's art.

1804–6 SYD. SMITH *Mor. Philos.* (1850) 261 Some mysteries of locksmithery.

ˈ**lockspit.** [f. LOCK *sb.*^{2} or *v.*^{1} + SPIT a turf.] (See quots.) Hence ˈ**lockspit** *v. trans.*, to mark out (ground) by a 'lockspit'; ˈ**lockspitting** *vbl. sb.*

1649–50 OGILBY tr. *Virgil* v. (1654) 319 *marg.*, Sets out the Circuit with a Plough, which we call Lock-spitting. **1704** HARRIS *Lex. Techn.*, *Lock-spit*, a Term in Fortification, signifying the small Cut or Trench made with a Spade, to mark out the first Lines of any Work that is to be made. **1753** CHAMBERS *Cycl. Supp.*, *Lockspit*, among miners, is the small cut or trench made with a spade of about a foot wide, to mark out the first lines of a work. **1889** *N.W. Linc. Gloss.*, *Lockspit*, a breadth of earth taken from the bottom of a drain of the same width as an ordinary draining tool. *Ibid.* s.v., I lockspitted her oot fra one end to t'uther.

†ˈ**lockster.** *Obs. rare*$^{-1}$. [? f. LOCK *sb.*^{1} + -STER.] ? A woman who picks yarn.

1590 *Proclam.* in Noake *Worcestersh. Relics* (1877) 61 The knitters of hose.. divers of them are common locksters and resetters of yarne.

ˈ**lock-up**, *sb.* (*a.*) [f. LOCK *v.*^{1} + UP *adv.*]

1. The action of locking up, in various senses.

a. The action of locking up a school, etc. for the night; also, the time at which this is done. Also *attrib.*

1845 T. J. GREEN *Jrnl. Texian Expedition* xvii. 300 To elude the vigilance of the officer at lock-up time. **1871** *Routledge's Ev. Boy's Ann.* Mar. 148 During the long winter's evenings, after Lock-up. **1890** M. WILLIAMS *Leaves Life* I. 16 One of the amusements of the Lower boys was, after 'lock up', to be perpetually ringing old Plumptree's bell and running away. **1910** A. HUXLEY *Let.* 5 June (1969) 37 To crown all we were 5 minutes late for lock-up! **1914** 'I. HAY' *Lighter Side School Life* iv. 104 Rules, roll-calls, bounds, lock-ups. **1968** *Eton College Chron.* 22 Mar. 6221, Sat. Mar. 23 Lock-up, 7.15 p.m.

b. The action of 'locking up' capital, or investing it so that it cannot be quickly realized; an instance of this. Also, an amount so 'locked up'. Also *attrib.*

1866 CRUMP *Banking* xi. 246 The banker continues to throw good money after bad, the termination of which.. is an indefinite lock-up. **1889** *Spectator* 9 Mar., This means a 'lock-up' of nine millions sterling. **1893** *Westm. Gaz.* 5 Apr. 6/3 To distinguish between bills and mortgages—between liquid assets and lock-ups. **1900** *Ibid.* 30 May 9/3 Those who buy such shares as a 'lock-up' may possibly be able to sell them at much higher prices. **1908** *Daily Report* 26 Aug. 5/4 As a promising speculative lock-up holding, the shares are worth buying at the present prices. **1929** *Observer* 17 Nov. 4/3 The shares may be regarded as a good lock-up investment.

c. *Printing.* The action of preparing plates or formes for printing or placing them in the press; also, a contrivance for holding the plates or formes in a press. Also *attrib.* Cf. LOCK *v.*^{1} 6.

1888 C. T. JACOBI *Printers' Vocab.* 76 Lock-up chases, special chases made in order to dispense with large quantities of furniture in filling up spare room in formes or on the press. *Lock-up iron*, the iron stick used for tightening up formes as they stand instead of laying them up. **1925** H. CRANE *Let.* 4 May (1965) 203 Lockup & Presswork.. $40.00. **1960** G. A. GLAISTER *Gloss. Bk.* 240/2 *Lock-up table*, any of several varieties of imposing surface specially equipped for the accurate imposition of formes for colour registration. **1964** *Gloss. Letterpress Rotary Printing Terms* (*B.S.I.*) 15 Lock-up. 1. A mechanical arrangement for holding the printing plates or formes on the press. 2. The action of locking the printing plates or formes on the press. **1967** KARCH & BUBER *Offset Processes* ii. 23 The form of hot type is locked up in a chase with 'furniture' (blocks of wood or metal) and quoins by the lock-up man. *Ibid.* 24 This [*sc.* preparation of printing surfaces] includes lock-up and imposition.

2. (Short for *lock-up house* or *room*: see 4.) An apartment or building that can be locked up.

a. *gen.*

1890 *Daily News* 17 Feb. 3/4 No. 126 was what builders call the 'lock up'. Tools, screws, door handles, etc., were stored in the middle room on the first floor, the door of which was kept locked.

b. A house or room for the detention (usually temporary) of offenders.

1839 *Knickerbocker* XIV. 110 He was seized, and carried to the 'lock-up'. **1859** JEPHSON *Brittany* ix. 141 Lodge me in the lock-up for the night. **1865** J. CAMERON *Malayan India* 267 In ten days.. 600 prisoners were accumulated in the lock-ups of the central police station. **1891** BARRIE *Little Minister* (1892) 65 Gavin was with the families whose breadwinners were now in the lock-up. **1972** *Police Rev.* 8 Dec. 1599/1 There would be a chance to run these establishments as if they were something more constructive than mere lock-ups. **1973** R. BUSBY *Pattern of Violence* i. 14 Sam.. was at present residing within the central lock-up in ..police headquarters, ready to appear before the court.

c. Short for *lock-up garage.*

1910 *Bradshaw's Railway Guide* Apr. 1036 Southgate Private Hotel.. Lock-up for Bicycles. *Ibid.* 1070 Motor garage, with 12 lock ups. **1973** E. LEMARCHAND *Let or Hindrance* ix. 103 'Was the car standing out while you were in Cornwall?' 'No. They gave me a lock-up.' **1974** G. MITCHELL *Javelin for Jonah* v. 68 We followed Jonah.. to the garages.. frisked him and pinched the key to his lock-up.

3. An official who locks up a building for the night.

1893 H. LE CARON *25 Yrs. in the Secret Service* (ed. 15) 165 Breslin, who was chief hospital warden, and Byrne, who was night-watchman and 'lock-up'.

4. *attrib.* passing into *adj.*, with the sense 'capable of being locked up'; as ***lock-up book***, ***coach-house***, ***cubicle***, ***garage***, ***line*** (of business), ***place***, ***prisoner***, ***room***, ***shed***; **lock-up house**, a house of detention, *spec.* (see quot. 1785); **lock-**

up shop, a detached apartment used as a shop and locked up at night.

1870 G. H. LEWES *Diary* 22 Nov. in Geo. Eliot *Lett.* (1956) V. 123 Bought Polly a *Lock-up book for her Autobiog[raphy]. **1840** DICKENS *Barn. Rudge* xxxv, Choice stabling, and a *lock-up coach-house. **1910** *Bradshaw's Railway Guide* Apr. 1019 Most up-to-date Motor Garage, with *lock-up Cubicles. **1935** *Archit. Rev.* LXXVIII. 168/1 A general garage and a number of private *lock-up garages. **1963** *Times* 21 Feb. 8/7 The rent of all council houses and lock-up garages provided by Maidstone Town Council is to be increased by 12½ per cent. **1767** *Chron.* in *Ann. Reg.* 60/2 The office keeper..found it to be a *lock-up house for recruits. **1772** *Ibid.* *72 The detestable practices carried on by kidnappers..in what are called lock-up houses. **1785** GROSE *Dict. Vulgar Tongue, Lock up house*, a spunging house ..also houses kept by agents or crimps, who inlist or rather trepan men to serve the East India, or African Company as soldiers. **1804** *Europ. Mag.* XLV. 332 *note*, Coleman-street ..had in it..a Magistrate..and a lock-up house. **1851** THACKERAY *Eng. Hum.* iii. (1876) 246 He was in hiding, or worse than in hiding, in the lock-up house. **1818** SCOTT *Hrt. Midl.* xiii, There is not a man..could be of sae muckle use ..in the..*lock-up line of business. **1809** MALKIN *Gil Blas* VI. i. ¶15 He..opened all his *lock-up places. **1846** D. CORCORAN *Pickings* 33 To the right of the column we perceived a prisoner whom we at once knew was above and beyond the ordinary class of *lock-up prisoners. **1823** *Spirit Publ. Jrnls.* (1825) I. 171 The Magistrate..was surprised to see such a figure brought out from amongst the filthy wretches..of the *lock-up room. **1880** *Daily News* 7 Oct. 4/1 Dry and clean separate lock-up rooms. **1812** COL. HAWKER *Diary* (1893) I. 54 They are under a *lock-up shed. **1897** *Daily News* 1 Dec. 3/5 The building is a *lock-up shop which was closed at about 6.30 last evening. **1906** *Daily Chron.* 10 Dec. 5/7 Many people patrolled the district in which Fell's warehouse and Beardwood's lock-up shop are situated. **1947** Lock-up shop [see AMUSEMENT 7].

locky (ˈlɒkɪ), *a.* Also 7 lockie. [f. LOCK *sb.*¹ + -Y.] Of or pertaining to locks (of hair); having locks in abundance.

1611 COTGR., *Houpelu*, lockie, tassellie, tufted. **1841** LEVER *C. O'Malley* iii. 19 Less in curls than masses of locky richness.

†ˈ**lockyer**, ˈ**locker**. *Obs.* In 4–5 lokyer(e, 5 lokere, 6 locker, lockier. [f. LOCK *sb.*² + *-yer*, -IER, -ER¹.] A locksmith.

1356 in Riley *Mem. Lond.* (1868) 282 Henry Clement, lokyer. *c* **1430** *Pilgr. Lyf Manhode* III. xvii. (1869) 144 This hand is..a fals lokyere, and a fals moneyere and a fals tellere of pens. **1481–90** *Howard Househ. Bks.* (Roxb.) 321 The same day, my Lord rekened with his lokyer..and he shall have for his wages xl.s. *c* **1532** DU WES *Introd. Fr.* in *Palsgr.* 908 The smythe or locker *le marechall ou serrurier*. **1574** HELLOWES *Gueuara's Fam. Ep.* (1577) 245 How may I make report of the euils that Vera the Lockier hath committed in Valiodolid.

loco (ˈləʊkəʊ), *sb.*¹ *U.S.* [A use of Sp. *loco* insane, mad.] **a.** One of several leguminous plants (chiefly species of *Astragalus*) found in the western and south-western U.S., which, when eaten by cattle, produce *loco-disease*. More fully ***loco-plant***, ***loco-weed***.

1879 *Special Rep. U.S. Dept. Agric.* No. 12. 211 The losses among cattle, caused by eating the poisonous loco weed, will perhaps not exceed 1 per cent. **1883** *Harper's Mag.* Mar. 503/1 The loco, or rattle-weed, met with also in California, drives them [horses] raving crazy. **1884** *Amer. Naturalist* XVIII. 1148 Experiments..prove that *Crotalaria sagittalis*, the Rattle-box, is a 'loco-plant'. **1886** *Cornh. Mag.* Sept. 297 A weed called 'loco' has of late years largely increased in some of the cattle-ranges of Texas and the Indian territory. **1889** *Science* XIII. 176/1 A curious affection which exists among horses in north-western Texas, known as 'grass-staggers', which is caused by eating the 'loco-weed', which gives rise to the saying that the horses are locoed. **1904** 'O. HENRY' in *McClure's Mag.* Apr. 617/1 If you have ever seen a horse that has eaten loco-weed you will understand what I mean when I say that the passengers get locoed. **1948** *Miami* (Okla.) *Daily News-Rec.* 30 June 8/2 Little is heard today of the once troublesome loco weed. **1955** W. FOSTER-HARRIS *Look of Old West* ix. 260 The most famous of the lethal stuff is undoubtedly loco, or crazy, weed... Loco grows all over the West, and a locoed horse is easy to spot.

b. = *loco-disease* (*Cent. Dict.*).

c. *attrib.* and *Comb.*, as ***loco-eater***, ***-intoxication***; **loco-disease**, a disease in horses, affecting the brain, caused by eating loco-weed; **loco weed** = MARIJUANA, MARIHUANA.

1884 *Pall Mall G.* 23 June 5/1 A healthy horse refuses loco; but if he once by accident acquires the taste, it grows upon him..and at last he dies of loco-intoxication. **1886** *Cornh. Mag.* Sept. 297 The animal has become a confirmed 'loco-eater'. **1889** *Syd. Soc. Lex.*, *Loco-disease*. **1935** A. J. POLLOCK *Underworld Speaks* 72/2 *Loco weed*, mariahuana; hemp; hashish. **1960** *Time* 25 Jan. 87/2 In U.S. slang marijuana is called..loco weed. **1972** *Sunday Sun* (Brisbane) 2 July 14/3 Detectives from the CIB Drug Squad in Brisbane are becoming quite familiar now with words like ..rope and locoweed.

loco, *sb.*² Short for LOCO-FOCO 2.

1841 H. CLAY *Let.* 4 July in *Private Corr.* (1855) 454 The Locos are..opposed to the scheme. **1847** EMILY DICKINSON *Lett.* (1894) I. 67 To say nothing of its falling into the merciless hands of a loco!

loco, *sb.*³ **a.** Short for LOCOMOTIVE *sb.* Also *attrib.*

1833 S. BRECK *Recoll.* (1877) App. 274 With the *loco*..he may start from one city in the morning and return again in the evening. **1869** *Bradshaw's Railway Manual* XXI. 14 Supt. of Loco. Dept., C. K. Domville, Belfast. **1898** R. KIPLING *Days Work* 215 An eight-wheeled 'American' loco. **1901** *Daily Chron.* 2 Sept. 9/6 Vertical and loco-type boilers. **1955** *Times* 28 May 10/2 The last named company received important contracts including one for 94 diesel electric locos for the Irish State Transport. **1974** A. MACLEAN *Breakheart Pass* iv. 63 To haul this heavy load with a single loco?.. Thirty hours, I'd say.

b. ˈ**loco-spotting**, train-spotting; the action of noting the numbers (and sometimes other details) of locomotives seen; so **loco-spotter**, (as back-formation) **loco-spot** *v.*

1959 *Junior Radio Times* 25 Sept. 1/1 What is the locospotter looking for? Chiefly the engine number, which normally is painted on the cab side and also on the smoke-box door; secondly, the name if the engine has one; and thirdly, the code of the shed to which the engine is allocated. *Ibid.*, One of the objects of locospotting is to see—or 'cop'—all the engines in a particular class, marking off the number of each engine as it is observed. **1960** W. E. HILDICK *Boy at Window* xvii. 131 It was a train the boy remembered well from his loco-spotting days. **1968** *Listener* 21 Mar. 368/2, I loco-spotted 45076..and 45254. **1971** *Where* Dec. 365/3 They..for many years ran the Loco Spotting Club.

loco (ˈləʊkəʊ), *a.* orig. *U.S.* [a. Sp. *loco* (see LOCO *sb.*¹). Cf. LOCOED *ppl. a.*] Mad, insane, off one's head.

1887 *Outing* X. 7/1 You won't be able to do nuthin' with 'em, sir; they'll go plumb loco. **1904** CONRAD *Notromo* I. vi. 37 He was old, ugly, learned—and a little 'loco'—mad, if not a bit of a sorcerer. **1910** C. E. MULFORD *Hopalong Cassidy* iv. 38 Are you loco? Do you mean to let th' rest of th' outfit see that? **1922** *Chambers's Jrnl.* Mar. 167/2 Some of them would be loco over it. **1929** ADE *Let.* 8 Feb. (1973) 139 We have gone a little loco on shopping, because..prices seem low. **1934** R. MACAULAY *Going Abroad* i. 13 The young people were, so far as anyone could judge, completely loco. **1965** D. FRANCIS *Odds Against* 124 He'd been quietly going loco and making hopeless decisions. **1973** 'A. HALL' *Tango Briefing* iv. 46 You heard of ergot?.. There was a case in France, remember? Half a village went loco.

loco (ˈləʊkəʊ), *adv. Mus.* [It. *al loco*, at the place.] (See quots.)

1801 BUSBY *Dict. Mus.*, *Loco*,..a word in opposition to 8*va Alta*, and signifying that the notes over which it is placed are not to be played an octave higher, but just as they are written. **1970** *Oxf. Compan. Mus.* (ed. 10) 578/2 *Loco*.., 'place', used after some sign indicating performance an octave higher or lower than written and reminding the performer that the effect of that sign now terminates. Often the expression used is *Al loco*, 'at the place'.

†**lococession**. *Obs. rare*⁻⁰. [f. L. *locō*, abl. of *locus* place + *cēssiōn-em*, n. of action from *cēdĕre* to yield.] 'A giving place' (1656 Blount *Glossogr.* citing Dr. Charleton).

ˌ**loco-deˈscriptive**, *a.* [f. *loco-* (in LOCOMOTION) erroneously taken as a combining form of L. *locus* place.] Descriptive of local scenery, etc.

1815 WORDSW. *Poems* Pref., The Epitaph, the Inscription, the Sonnet, and all loco-descriptive poetry, belong to this class [the Idyllium]. **1833** J. M. (*title*) The Invitation; a Locodescriptive Epistle, containing Sketches of Scenery in Wilts and Dorset. **1841** DISRAELI *Amen. Lit.* (1859) II. 219 These are loco-descriptive poems. Such were Denham's 'Coopers Hill', and its numerous..imitations. **1966** *English Studies* XLVII. 68 Loco-descriptive poems of and guides to the Lakes.

locoed (ˈləʊkəʊd), *ppl. a. U.S.* [f. LOCO *sb.*¹ + -ED.] Affected with or poisoned with loco; also *transf.* of a person (see quot. 1892).

1886 *Cornh. Mag.* Sept. 298 About two hundred and fifty 'locoed' horses, which had been driven in the fall from the region where 'loco' flourished... In addition to being badly locoed and half-starved, the majority suffered from Spanish itch. **1892** *Chamb. Jrnl.* 17 Dec. 816/2 In localities where loco is found,..if people are deficient in intellect, or odd and eccentric, they are designated 'locoed'.

loco-foco (ˈləʊkəʊˈfəʊkəʊ). *U.S.* [An invented word; it is not known what suggested the formation.

It has been conjectured that *loco* was taken from *locomotive*, wrongly imagined to mean 'self-moving'; *foco* may be a jingling alteration of It. *fuoco* or Sp. *fuego* fire (the inventor would hardly think of L. *focus* hearth, which is the source of the mod.Rom. words for 'fire').]

†**1.** 'A self-igniting cigar or match' (Bartlett). More fully ***loco-foco cigar***, ***match***. *Obs.*

1839 *Jrnl. Franklin Inst.* XXIV. 116 We were offered lately in the streets of Pittsburgh a kind of loco-foco matches which were new to us... They ignite by friction and burn as if containing phosphorus. **1852** BRANDE *Dict. Sci.*, etc. (ed. 2) s.v., Lucifers (which in America are termed loco-focos). **1859** BARTLETT *Dict. Amer.* s.v., In 1834 John Marck opened a store in Park Row, New York, and drew public attention to two novelties. One was champagne wine drawn like soda water from a 'fountain'; the other was a self-lighting cigar, with a match composition on the end. These he called 'Loco-foco' cigars. **1883** A. GILMAN *Amer. People* xxi. 437 When the candles had been blown out..they were lighted with matches then [1835] called 'locofocos'.

2. *U.S. Polit. Hist.* Used *attrib.* or quasi-*adj.* as the designation of the 'Equal Rights' or Radical section of the Democratic party (for the origin of the name see quot. 1842). Hence *absol.* a member of this party.

The name was given in 1835; the section originally so named soon became extinct, but the name long continued to be applied by opponents to the Democrats generally.

1837 P. HONE *Diary* 6 Sept, The President's message..is locofoco to the very core. **1838** H. CLAY *Let.* 28 Aug. in *Private Corr.* (1855) 428 The Locofocos have carried that [election] in Missouri. **1838** W. IRVING in *Life & Lett.* (1866) III. 120 Those loco foco luminaries who of late have been urging strong and sweeping measures. **1842** J. D. HAMMOND *Polit. Hist. N.Y.* II. 491–2 A very tumultuous and confused scene ensued, during which the gas-lights.. were extinguished. The Equal Rights party..had provided themselves with *loco-foco* matches and candles, and the room was re-lighted. Immediately after this outbreak at Tammany Hall, the Courier and Enquirer, a whig, and the Times, a democratic..newspaper, dubbed the anti-monopolists with the name of the Loco-Foco Party, a sort of nick-name which the whigs have since given to the whole democratic party. **1844** DICKENS *Mart. Chuz.* xvi, Here's full particulars of the patriotic loco-foco movement yesterday, in which the Whigs was so chawed up. **1850** HAWTHORNE *Scarlet L.* Introd. (1883) 23 But..you would inquire in vain for the Locofoco Surveyor. **1896** HOWELLS *Impressions & Exp.* 1 The Whig newspaper which my father edited to the confusion of the Locofocos.

Hence ˌ**locoˈfocoism**, the principles of the Loco-foco party.

1837 HAWTHORNE *Amer. Note-bks.* 27 Aug. (1883) 95 The most arrant democracy and locofocoism that I ever happened to hear. **1863** S. L. J. *Life in the South* I. i. 5 'Platforms', 'constitutions', 'compromises', 'locofocoisms', ..and 'democrats', were given up in despair.

†ˈ**locoman**¹. *Negro-English. Obs.* Also locko-. [Perh. f. some African word, possibly Aku *ológu* sorcerer (J. Platt, jun.) + MAN *sb.*] (See quots.)

1796 STEDMAN *Surinam* II. xxvi. 262 Their Locomen, or pretended prophets, find their interest in encouraging this superstition by selling them obias or amulets. *Ibid.* xxix. 359 A locko-man, or sorcerer.

locoman². [LOCO *sb.*³] A driver of a locomotive; an engine-driver.

1941 *Penguin New Writing* XII. 9 We loco-men carry on whatever the conditions overhead. **1970** *Daily Mail* 3 Mar. 1/2 Locomen at King's Cross plan a one-day stoppage today which will hit services to the North and some commuter trains. **1972** *Guardian* 14 Aug. 1/1 The locomen's union insists that drivers should be paid more money.

locomobile (ləʊkəˈməʊbɪl), *a.* and *sb.* [f. L. *locō*, abl. of *locus* place + *mōbilis* MOBILE. Cf. F. *locomobile*.] **a.** *adj.* 'Having the power to change place, partially or entirely' (*Syd. Soc. Lex.* 1889); **b.** *sb.* 'A locomobile vehicle' (Webster *Suppl.* 1902). Also *attrib.* So **locomoˈbility** [cf. F. *locomobilité*], 'the faculty of being locomobile' (*Syd. Soc. Lex.*).

1895 W. R. FISHER *Schlich's Man. Forestry* V. 748 The elevator and macerating cylinder are driven by a locomobile. **1900** *Sci. Amer.* 27 Jan. 54/1 The steam carriage which is popularly and commercially known as the 'Locomobile'. **1900** *Sun* (N.Y.) 23 May 7/6 A locomobile operator, was arraigned for driving a locomobile, which is a steam automobile. **1915** *Lit. Digest* 21 Aug. 387/2 Goodyear Cord Tires... Adopted for the new Locomobile as standard equipment. *a* **1936** KIPLING *Something of Myself* (1937) vii. 177, I bought me a steam-car called a 'Locomobile', whose nature and attributes I faithfully drew in a tale called 'Steam Tactics'. **1962** R. B. FULLER *Epic Poem on Industrialization* 169 No, the ephemeralization Of doing more with less, Took gold along with tonnage And three-ton Locomobiles.

locomote (ˈləʊkəməʊt), *v.* [Back-formation from LOCOMOTION.] *intr.* To move about from place to place.

(Originally *slang*; subsequently adopted or re-invented in biological use.)

1834 *Knickerbocker* IV. 20 Who but our author would represent him [*sc.* a bard], 'locomoting' on a long, dog-trot over the bogs of his neighborhood. **1846** *Quarter Race Kentucky* 83 He throws the galls in, and a bed too in the hay, if you git too hot to locomote. **1865** *Intell. Observ.* Sept. 83 [Snail-leeches] locomote by attaching one extremity of the body to the ground..and by drawing the other extremity up to that point. **1887** *Hardwicke's Sci.-Gossip* XXIII. 269/1 They are able to locomote very swiftly by the aid of their fins, tails and feet. **1894** *Proc. R. Soc.* LV. 163 They [*sc.* the leucocytes]..do not locomote over the floor of the counter. **1970** *Amat. Photographer* 22 Apr. 9/3 That foot..pointing daintily downward; except for a prima ballerina I've never yet seen a dame who could locomote like that. **1974** *Nature* 15 Mar. 240/1 Colchicine and vinblastine caused the ruffling activity of fibroblasts locomoting in culture to spread from a restricted area to all parts of the edge of the cells.

locomotility (ˌləʊkəməʊˈtɪlɪtɪ). *rare*⁻¹. [ad. F. *locomotilité*, f. L. *locō* (see LOCOMOTIVE) + F. *motilité* power of movement.] The faculty or power of locomotion.

1857 *Dunglison's Med. Lex.* s.v. *Locomotion*, The faculty [of locomotion] is sometimes called Locomotivity, and Locomotility.

locomotion (ləʊkəˈməʊʃən). [f. L. *locō* (see LOCOMOTIVE) + *mōtiōn-em* MOTION. Cf. F. *locomotion*, Sp. *locomocion*, It. *locomozione*.]

1. The action or power of moving from one place to another; progressive motion of an animal.

1646 SIR T. BROWNE *Pseud. Ep.* III. i. 104 All progression or animall locomotion being (as Aristotle teacheth) performed *tractu & pulsu*. **1664** POWER *Exp. Philos.* I. 39 The Animal Spirits are the Soul's immediate instrument in all Loco-motion. **1704** *New Pract. Piety* 38 He has fix'd the Laws of Loco-motion in Corporeal Substances. **1765** BLACKSTONE *Comm.* I. 134 This personal liberty consists in the power of loco-motion, of changing situation, or removing one's person to whatsoever place one's own inclination may direct; without imprisonment or restraint, unless by due course of law. **1768–74** TUCKER *Lt. Nat.* (1834) II. 395 But what is to be understood by coming to the Father? Not a locomotion surely; for..God is omnipresent.

1817 J. Evans *Excurs. Windsor*, etc. 451 The Oyster..was once thought to have no power of loco-motion, but it is now ascertained, that it can move from place to place. **1856** Sir B. Brodie *Psychol. Inq.* I. ii. 46 One office of the cerebellum is to combine the action of the voluntary muscles for the purpose of locomotion. **1872** Huxley *Physiol.* vii. 157 Movement..of the body as a whole..is termed locomotion. **1881** Burdon-Sanderson in *Nature* No. 619. 44 Those [*sc.* organs] of locomotion are no doubt more complicated than those of respiration or circulation.

2. Movement from place to place, esp. by artificial means; travel; also, the means of travelling.

1788 R. Graves *Recoll. Shenstone* 96 An excursion to London, upon the footing that loco-motion then was..was a matter of some importance. **1820** *Edin. Rev.* XXXIII. 77 Taxes upon warmth, light and locomotion. **1835** Mrs. Carlyle *Lett.* I. 31, I have no taste whatever for locomotion, by earth, air, or sea. **1849** Macaulay *Hist. Eng.* iii. I. 370 Every improvement of the means of locomotion benefits mankind morally and intellectually. **1852** H. Rogers *Ess.* I. vii. 335 He spent his days in a far greater variety of scenes than usually vary the lot of a philosopher, and indulged prodigiously in locomotion. **1874** Helps *Soc. Press.* ix. 131 Locomotion having so greatly increased and improved, the dwelling-place has become..of less importance. **1875** Jowett *Plato* (ed. 2) V. 194 The inequality of the ground in our country is more adapted to locomotion on foot.

3. Progressive movement of an inanimate body.

1851 *Illustr. Catal. Gt. Exhib.* 1234 A new system of locomotion for railways. **1854** Tomlinson tr. *Arago's Astron.* 107 We have now to inquire whether the annual revolution of the sun is real, or whether this too is not an appearance caused by the earth's locomotion.

locomotive (ləʊkə'məʊtɪv), *a.* and *sb.* [as if ad. mod.L. *lŏcōmōtīvus*, f. L. *locō*, abl. of *locus* place + *mōtīvus* motive *a.* Cf. F. *locomotif*.

Suggested by the scholastic phrase *in loco moveri* (= *moveri localiter*) to move 'locally' or by change of position in space; cf. Aristotle's ἡ κατὰ τόπον κίνησις.]

A. *adj.*

1. a. Of or pertaining to locomotion or movement from one place to another. ***locomotive faculty*** (cf. F. *faculté locomotive*), the faculty or power of movement from place to place by an act of the will; so also ***locomotive power***.

1612 W. Sclater *Chr. Strength* 12 Some kind of command over the locomotiue facultie. **1627** S. Ward *Happiness of Practice* 27 Like dying men, and sicke of Apoplexies and speech: but no faculty Loco-motiue, no power to stirre hand or foote. **1640** Bp. Reynolds *Passions* (1658) 1105 The will can hinder seeing, not immediately, but by the loco-motive power; by closing the eyes. **1646** Sir T. Browne *Pseud. Ep.* iv. vii. 196 Complaints of gravity in animated and living bodies, where the nerves subside, and the faculty locomotive seems abolished. **1649** Bulwer *Pathomyot.* i. vi. 35 To which the command of Reason and the will doe concurre with the locomotive power. **1666** Harvey *Morb. Angl.* iv. 38 The manner whereby the faculty of the brain effects a locomotive action in any muscul. **1717** Prior *Alma* i. 287 If in the night too oft he [*sc.* a child] kicks, Or shows his loco-motive tricks. **1759** Sterne *Tr. Shandy* I. ii, The Homunculus is..endow'd with the same locomotive powers and faculties with us. **1817** Coleridge *Biog. Lit.* I. iii. 62 As if the passive page of a book..instantly assumed at once loco-motive power. **1823** Bentham *Not Paul* 197 Except this exercise of the loco-motive faculty, nothing is there to distinguish him from the common stock of still-life. *a* **1862** Buckle *Civiliz.* (1869) III. v. 438 The locomotive.. functions are more active in persons of a sanguine temperament.

b. *jocular.* Of or pertaining to travel, or movement from one locality or country to another.

1771 Gray in *Corr. w. Nicholls* (1843) 120, I rejoice you have met with Froissart: he is the Herodotus of a barbarous age:..his locomotive disposition,..his religious credulity, were much like those of the old Grecian. **1786** *Observer* No. 85 III. 236 The locomotive mania of an Englishman circulates his person, and of course his cash, into every quarter of the kingdom. **1806–7** J. Beresford *Miseries Hum. Life* (1826) v. Concl., Considering them [stage coaches] as the very climax and pinnacle of locomotive griefs. **1831** Carlyle *Sart. Res.* ii. vii, We conjecture that he has known sickness; and, in spite of his locomotive habits, perhaps sickness of the chronic sort. **1850** J. Struthers *My Own Life* iv. Poet. Wks. I. p. xlvii, The young man..laid aside his locomotive dreaming, and became not only reconciled but wedded to the locality. **1874** Helps *Soc. Press.* x. (1875) 143 In these locomotive days one is too apt to forget one's neighbours.

c. Of or pertaining to vehicular locomotion. ***locomotive power***: power applied for transport purposes, as opposed to stationary power.

1825 J. Nicholson *Operat. Mechanic* 671 Engines which have a locomotive principle [*sc.* as opposed to stationary engines]. **1851** *Illustr. Catal. Gt. Exhib.* 219 Steam-engine ..adapted for stationary, locomotive, or marine purposes.

2. Having the power of locomotion. **a.** Of an animal: That moves from place to place by its own powers of locomotion.

1657 S. Purchas *Pol. Flying-Ins.* 49 They could not live and grow without food, they were not locomotive, and therefore could not go forth of their cells for it. **1709** T. Robinson *Ess. Nat. Hist. Westmld. & Cumbld.* 33 These shell Fish which were not Loco-motive were left behind. **1794** Cowper *Needless Alarm* 64 The mind He scans of every locomotive kind; Birds of all feather, beasts of every name. **1816** Kirby & Sp. *Entomol.* (1843) I. 56 A caterpillar then may be regarded as a locomotive egg. **1851–6** Woodward *Mollusca* 248 The locomotive bivalves have generally the strongest hinges. **1879** G. Allen *Colour Sense* iii. 23 The young barnacles and balani are active, locomotive animals.

b. *jocular.* Of a person: That is constantly travelling from place to place.

1732 J. Whaley *Trav. of a Shilling* 66 Poems 186 Or when my dwelling I wou'd change..My loco-motive Face was seen At Hampstead, or at Turnham-Green. **1810** Scott *Fam. Lett.* 3 Oct. (1894) I. vi. 193 You being the more locomotive persons will I trust take another peep of Scotland. **1827** *Sporting Mag.* XX. 262, I have not been much loco-motive of late. **1842** Dickens *Amer. Notes* (1850) 128/2 He had all his life been restless and locomotive, with an irresistible desire for change. **1878** C. Macgregor in *Monthly Packet* 19 Hadrian..was one of the most locomotive Emperors that Rome ever had. **1896** Farmer *Slang, Locomotive tailor*, a tramping workman.

c. Of things; *esp.* of a vehicle or piece of machinery which moves in any direction by its own mechanism.

1825 J. Nicholson *Operat. Mechanic* 670 Mr. Gordon has..taken out a patent for a locomotive carriage with the engine on springs. **1827** D. McNicoll *Wks.* (1837) 185 This new locomotive world [*sc.* a sailing-vessel]..moves onward through the ocean. **1836** E. Howard *R. Reefer* viii, Behold me..confined in a locomotive prison [*sc.* an ordinary carriage]. **1842** *Penny Cycl.* XXII. 485 Such locomotive machines, impelled by steam power, as have been contrived for use upon common roads. **1846** Greener *Sci. Gunnery* 76 You put not a locomotive train in motion at once; if attempted, you break and fracture the whole carriages. **1851** *Illustr. Catal. Gt. Exhib.* 366 Patent dibble, with locomotive machine attached. **1858** Hawthorne *Fr. & It. Jrnls.* I. 283 She looked like a locomotive mass of verdure and flowers. **1860** *All Year Round* No. 65. 352 The locomotive post-offices, with their great nets—as if they had been dragging the country for bodies.

d. spec. ***locomotive engine***, † ***locomotive steam engine***: an engine constructed for movement from place to place by its own power (as opposed to 'stationary' engine), usually by the generation of steam; *esp.* a steam engine adapted to draw a train of carriages along a railway; a railway-engine. Now generally shortened to *locomotive* (see B. 1).

1815 *Chron.* in *Ann. Reg.* 50 The proprietors had provided a powerful locomotive steam engine, for the purpose of drawing..coal-waggons. **1815** *Specif. of De Baader's Patent* No. 3959. 7 Those complicated unwieldy and dangerous machines called locomotive engines or steam horses. **1823** *Private Act* (Stockton & Darlington) 4 *Geo. IV*, c. xxxiii. §8 [To] make and erect such and so many loco-motive or moveable Engines as the said Company..shall from Time to Time think proper..for the Conveyance of Passengers. **1854** Ronalds & Richardson *Chem. Technol.* (ed. 2) I. p. x, Locomotive and marine engines. **1861** *Act 24 & 25 Vict.* c. 70 §13 Nothing in this Act contained shall authorize any Person to use upon a Highway a Locomotive Engine which shall..cause a..Nuisance.

3. Having the power to produce locomotion; adapted for or used in locomotion.

1841–71 T. R. Jones *Anim. Kingd.* (ed. 4) 207 [It] gives off minute twigs to the locomotive suckers placed on each side of its course. **1851–6** Woodward *Mollusca* 204 A cavity formed by the union of the locomotive organs.

B. *sb.*

1. a. = *locomotive engine* (see A. 2 d).

1829 J. Walker *Rep.* (7 Mar.) *to Directors L'pool & Manch. Railw. Co.* (1831) 18 The quantity of work which the locomotives are capable of performing. **1831** Booth *L'pool & Manch. Railw.* (ed. 2) 70 All established methods ..horses, locomotives, and fixed engines. **1837** Longf. in *Life* (1891) I. 258 While steamboats and locomotives traverse field and flood with the speed of light. **1849** B. Barton *Select.* etc. p. xxviii, A variety of noises, not unlike a locomotive at first starting. **1861** *Act 24 & 25 Vict.* c. 70 §8 Every Locomotive propelled by Steam or any other than Animal Power to be used on any Turnpike Road or Public Highway. **1886** *Encycl. Brit.* XX. 244/2 The two types of engines are known respectively as 'inside cylinder locomotives' and 'outside cylinder locomotives'. **1959** E. K. Wenlock *Kitchin's Road Transport Law* (ed. 12) 26/1 No one under 21 is allowed to drive a locomotive, motor tractor or heavy motor car on a road. **1971** *Morning Star* 3 July 3/3 More classes of vehicles will be able to use motorways... They include 'locomotives', which are load-carrying vehicles weighing more than 7¼ tons.

b. *slang. pl.* The legs.

1841 *Laird of Logan* 24 The disher of dainties took to her locomotives—the infuriated man with the fork at her heels. **1843** W. T. Moncrieff *Scamps of Lond.* i. i (Farmer), I will stop my locomotives directly. So now you may set your's agoing as soon as you like. **1870** *Sheffield Times* Mar. (ibid.), Having regained his freedom he again made good use of his locomotives.

c. *U.S. slang.* A cheer. Also *attrib.*

1901 *Princeton Alumni Weekly* 131/2 But he saw you trying to join in a locomotive cheer last Saturday. **1907** *Ibid.* 321/2 The boys gave a rousing locomotive and then stood in silence. **1961** Webster, *Locomotive*, a cheer characterized by a slow beginning and a progressive increase in speed and used esp. at school and college sports events.

2. An animal having powers of locomotion.

1872 Dana *Corals* i. 25 It is not a solitary case; for there are many others of Actiniæ attaching themselves to locomotives—to the claws or backs of crabs [etc.].

3. Applied to an inferior kind of needle.

1880 *Plain Hints Needlework* 95 There are a kind called 'locomotives', on which no maker will place his mark.

4. *attrib.* and *Comb.*, as ***locomotive-driver, engineer*** (also *U.S.* = -driver), ***-runner*** (*U.S.* = -driver), ***works***; **locomotive car** *U.S.*, a locomotive and a car combined in one vehicle; a dummy engine (Webster 1864–97).

1899 *Allbutt's Syst. Med.* VI. 613 *Locomotive-driver. **1889** G. Findlay *Eng. Railway* p. v, I must not omit to acknowledge my obligations to the Chief *Locomotive Engineer. **1890** M. N. Forney in *Railw. Amer.* 134 Locomotive engineers and firemen. *Ibid.* 137 *Locomotive-runners and firemen. **1848** *Mass. Private & Special Statutes* 13 Mar., A corporation, by the name of the Boston *Locomotive Works, for the purpose of manufacturing locomotive engines. **1889** G. Findlay *Working & Managem. Eng. Railway* vii. 118 Crewe, which previous to the establishment of the locomotive works was inhabited only by a few farmers and cottagers, has now developed into a flourishing town. **1966** G. F. Allen *Brit. Rail after Beeching* xii. 357 Of the Southern Region's locomotive works, Brighton had already been shut down and Ashford (Kent) had been slated for closure.

locomotively (ləʊkə'məʊtɪvlɪ), *adv.* [f. locomotive + -ly[2].] With regard to locomotion.

1861 Dickens *Gt. Expect.* xiv, He always slouched, locomotively, with his eyes on the ground. **1882** Sala *Amer. Revis.* (1883) I. iv. 63 A New York hack coupé is superior structurally, decoratively, and locomotively to one of our four-wheelers.

locomotiveness (ləʊkə'məʊtɪvnɪs). [f. as prec. + -ness.] The quality or fact of being locomotive; power of or fondness for locomotion.

1825 *Blackw. Mag.* XVII. 335 The Minuet..is..the aristocracy of locomotiveness. **1829** *Examiner* 595/1 We reduced her organ of locomotiveness. **1833** *New Monthly Mag.* XXXVIII. 308 He has the organ of locomotiveness largely developed.

locomotivity (ˌləʊkəməʊ'tɪvɪtɪ). *rare*[−1]. [ad. F. *locomotivité*, f. *locomotif, -ive*: see locomotive.] Power of locomotion; ability to move from place to place.

1792 Bryant *Authent. Script.* 4 The most superb edifice that ever was conceived or constructed, would not equal the smallest insect, blest with sight, feeling, and locomotivity. **1857** [see locomotility]. **1888** in *Syd. Soc. Lex.*

locomotor ('ləʊkəməʊtə(r)), *sb.* and *a.* [f. L. *locō* (see locomotive) + *mōtor*, agent-n. f. *movēre* to move: see motor. Cf. F. *locomoteur*, whence the adjective use B. is adopted.]

A. *sb.* One who or something which has locomotive power.

1822 Lamb *Elia* Ser. i. *Dist. Corresp.*, They [kangaroos] would show as fair a pair of hind-shifters as the expertest loco-motor in the colony. **1869** *Daily News* 2 June, There are several improved specimens of the new locomotor on view. **1883** B. W. Richardson in *Longm. Mag.* Oct. 594 [*Cycling*] Everyone his own locomotor against time. **18..** *Elect. Rev.* XXIV. 270 (Cent.) Electric locomotors.

B. *adj.* (Chiefly *Phys.*) Of, pertaining to, or concerned with locomotion. ***locomotor ataxy***: see ataxy 2.

1870 Rolleston *Anim. Life* 48 Soleshaped locomotor disc known as the 'foot'. **1877** Morley *Crit. Misc.* Ser. ii. 351 To explore our spinal cords and to observe the locomotor system of Medusæ. **1880** Bastian *Brain* 70 Animals.. devoid of..locomotor appendages. **1881** *Nature* XXIII. 280 The peculiar metamorphosis enables the larva to remain.. adapted to a locomotor life.

locomotory (ləʊkə'məʊtərɪ), *a.* [f. L. *locō* (see locomotive) + *mōtōrius* having the function of movement: see motory.] Pertaining to or having the power of locomotion.

1835–6 Todd *Cycl. Anat.* I. 701/2 Whatever the form of the locomotory organ..it is always organized in the same manner. **1892** R. L. Stevenson *Across the Plains* 292 To what passes with the anchored vermin [*sc.* plants], we have little clue... But of the locomotory, to which we ourselves belong, we can tell more.

†**loco-move**, *v. Obs. nonce-wd.* [f. move *v.*, after locomotion.] = locomote *v.*

1792 T. Twining *Let.* 16 July in *Country Clergyman 18th Cent.* (1882) 156 It is high time you should know something about us and our locomotions. To-morrow morning..we begin to loco-move towards Bitteswell. **1873** Leland *Egyptian Sk.-Bk.* 88, I only remember one instance when a man who made locomotion his business was unwilling to locomove.

locomu'tation. *nonce-wd.* [f. *loco-* (after locomotion) + mutation.] Change of place.

1886 Lowell *Progr. World* in *Latest Lit. Ess.* (1891) 184 The tendency of population towards great cities; no new thing, but intensified as never before by increased and increasing ease of locomutation.

loco-'restive, *a. nonce-wd.* [Humorous imitation of locomotive, *rest* being substituted for *mōt-*.] Inclined to rest in one place.

1796 Lamb *Corr.* Wks. 1868 I. 10 Your loco-restive and all your idle propensities, of course, have given way to the duties of providing for a family.

locorum, variant of lockram[1] *Obs.*

locoum ('ləʊkəm). Also locum, lokoum, loukoum(i. [Turk. *lokum*.] Turkish delight.

1887 F. M. Crawford *Paul Patoff* III. xxiii. 239 Two little white saucers filled with pieces of loukoum-rahat, the Turkish national sweetmeat, commonly called by school-boys fig-paste. **1894** [see delight *sb.* 4]. **1913** *Chambers's Jrnl.* Apr. 313/2 The elemes and locoums, packed respectively in layers and in cubes. **1921** S. Graham *Europe* ii. 38 Pride intervenes only to stop them begging... But you see the nicest of girls with pinched white faces trying to sell *loukoum.* **1960** *Spectator* 8 Jan. 51/1 In Istanbul,..go for Turkish delight,..a quite different confection from what

passes as Turkish delight in Britain. You ask for *lokoum*. **1962** J. FLEMING *When I grow Rich* iv. 53 A little *locum* for a friend..a present of a little Turkish delight. **1967** *Vogue* Jan. 4/2 A coral crusted dish of loukoumi. **1970** SIMON & HOWE *Dict. Gastron.*, Turkish delight, the popular English name of Turkey's sweetmeat *rahat lokum*. **1972** J. RATHBONE *Trip Trap* vi. 65 A servant poured Turkish coffee; *lokoum* was offered in tiny silver dishes.

locqueram, locram, vars. LOCKRAM[1] *Obs.*

Locrian (ˈləʊkrɪən), *a.* and *sb.* [f. L. *Locri-s* + -AN.] **a.** *adj.* Of or pertaining to the Locri, a people of Greece, or to their country Locris. ***Locrian mode***: an occasional appellation of one (not identified with certainty) of the 'modes' of ancient Greek music; in the Middle Ages applied arbitrarily to the 11th ecclesiastical mode. **b.** *sb.* One of the Locri; an inhabitant of Locris.

1598 CHAPMAN *Iliad* II. 35 Aiax the lesse, Oileus Sonne, the Locrians led to warre. **1715** POPE *Iliad* II. 630 Fierce Ajax led the Locrian Squadrons on. **1753** CHAMBERS *Cycl. Supp.*, *Locrian*, in antient music, the seventh species of the diapason. **1835** THIRLWALL *Greece* I. 99 The Locrians claimed a higher antiquity than any other branch of the Greek nation. **1836** J. GILBERT *Chr. Atonem.* vi. (1852) 179 In the fact recorded of the Locrian legislator we find [etc.]. **1880** ROCKSTRO in Grove *Dict. Mus.* II. 158/1 Locrian Mode.

So †**Loˈcrensian** [f. L. *Locrensis*].

1547 BECON *Agst. Adultery* iii, *Homilies* I. xi. (1859) 130 Among the Locrensians the adulterers had both their eyes thrust out.

loculament (ˈlɒkjʊləmənt). [ad. L. *loculāmentum*, f. *loculus* dim. of *locus* a place.] A little cell; *spec.* in *Bot.*, one of the cells or compartments of a capsule or pericarp; a loculus.

1656 BLOUNT *Glossogr.*, *Loculament*, a place of bords made with holes for Pigeons or Conies; a Coffin for a Book; also the several places wherein the seeds lye, as in Poppy heads. *Dr. Charl[eton]*. **1707** SLOANE *Jamaica* I. 18 A small pea..made up of three loculaments or cells. **1760** J. LEE *Introd. Bot.* I. vi. (1765) 13 The cells, or hollow compartments of the capsule in which the seeds are lodged, *Loculaments*. **1796** DE SERRA in *Phil. Trans.* LXXXVI. 498 A membranaceous loculament, containing the pollen. **1880** GRAY *Struct. Bot.* vii. §1. 289 The loculaments, loculi, or cells of the pericarp.

Hence **loculamentose** *a.* (*Syd. Soc. Lex.* 1889), **loculamentous** *a.* (Mayne *Expos. Lex.* 1856), full of loculaments or little cells.

locular (ˈlɒkjʊlə(r)), *a. Phys.* and *Bot.* [ad. mod.L. *loculār-is*, f. LOCULUS.] Having loculi.

1847–9 TODD *Cycl. Anat.* IV. 121/1 The locular aspect of their divided surfaces.

b. with defining prefix, as ***bi-, tri-, unilocular***, etc.

[**1783**, **1836** see BILOCULAR.] **1871** W. A. LEIGHTON *Lichen-flora* 17 Septate and murali-locular. *Ibid.* 21 Irregularly muriformi-locular. *Ibid.* 230 Spores fuscous,.. 4-locular. **1871** W. L. LINDSAY in *Q. Jrnl. Microscop. Sci.* XI. 30 The sporidia of the Biatora are..sometimes 2-locular, though also simple.

loculate (ˈlɒkjʊlət), *a.* [ad. L. *loculāt-us*, f. *loculus*: see LOCULUS and -ATE.] = LOCULAR.

1866 in *Treas. Bot.* **1889** in *Syd. Soc. Lex.*

loculated (ˈlɒkjʊleɪtɪd), *ppl. a.* [f. as prec. + -ED.] Divided into loculi; celled.

1801 HOME in *Phil. Trans.* XCII. 82 The loculated cæcum. **1859** TODD *Cycl. Anat.* V. 268/1 The infundibula of Rossignol..are loculated with the ultimate cells. **1880** BASTIAN *Brain* iv. 81 The body of the Pearly Nautilus, contained within the last chamber of its coiled and loculated shell, is [etc.]. **1897** *Allbutt's Syst. Med.* III. 894 The perityphlitic abscess is..deeply loculated.

loculation (lɒkjʊˈleɪʃən). [f. L. *loculātus*: see -ATION.] The state or condition of being loculated; development or production of loculi.

1855 in MAYNE *Expos. Lex.*

locule (ˈlɒkjuːl). [a. F. *locule*, ad. L. *loculus*, dim. of *locus*.] = LOCULUS.

1888 in *Syd. Soc. Lex.* **1953** *New Biol.* XIV. 44 The cotton fruit, called a boll, is divided into three or four locules, each with several seeds. **1967** M. E. HALE *Biol. Lichens* ii. 28 The locules in the stroma are separated by branched pseudoparaphyses.

loculicidal (ˌlɒkjʊlɪˈsaɪdəl), *a. Bot.* [f. L. *loculus*, dim. of *locus* place + *cīd-*, *cædĕre* to cut + -AL[1].] Of a carpel, etc.: That dehisces through the back or dorsal suture of the loculus.

1819 LINDLEY *Richards' Observ. Fruits & Seeds* 85 *Loculicidal*; when dehiscence takes place by the middle of the cells. **1830** —— *Nat. Syst. Bot.* 33 Dehiscence either loculicidal or septicidal. *Ibid.* 134 Capsule..with 3 loculicidal valves. **1870** HOOKER *Stud. Flora* (1884) 75 Loculicidal crustaceous or coriaceous carpels.

Hence **loculiˈcidally** *adv.*

1847 W. E. STEELE *Field Bot.* 175 Caps. separable into 3 pieces, sometimes dehiscing loculicidally. **1870** HOOKER *Stud. Flora* 46 Polygala..Capsule compressed, loculicidally splitting along the edges. *Ibid.* (1884) 413 Berry indehiscent or loculicidally 4–5-valved.

loculose (ˈlɒkjʊləʊs), *a. Bot.* [ad. L. *loculōs-us*, f. *loculus*: see -OSE.] Full of loculi or cells; divided into cells by internal partitions.

1855 in HYDE CLARKE. **1866** *Treas. Bot.*, *Loculose*, divided by internal partitions into cells, as the pith of the walnut-tree. Never applied to fruits. **1880** GRAY *Struct. Bot.* 419/1.

loculous (ˈlɒkjʊləs), *a. Bot.* [f. L. *loculōsus*: see prec. and -OUS.] = LOCULOSE.

1840 in SMART. **1900** in JACKSON *Bot. Terms.*

‖**loculus** (ˈlɒkjʊləs). Pl. **loculi** (ˈlɒkjʊlaɪ). [L. *loculus*, dim. of *locus*.]

1. A small chamber or cell in an ancient tomb for the reception of a body or an urn.

1858 CARLYLE *Fredk. Gt.* II. vi. (1872) I. 87 St. Elizabeth's loculus was put into its shrine here. **1883** *Fortn. Rev.* July 137 Another spacious cave..containing chambers and a number of loculi for corpses.

2. *Zool.*, *Anat.*, and *Bot.* One of a number of small cavities or cells separated from one another by septa.

1861 J. R. GREENE *Man. Anim. Kingd.*, *Cœlent.* 176 The number of septa in process of formation is often less than the number of loculi. **1872** NICHOLSON *Palæont.* 90 The space below the calice is broken up into a number of vertical compartments or loculi. **1873** T. H. GREEN *Introd. Pathol.* (ed. 2) 182 A simple cyst consists of a single loculus. A compound or multilocular cyst is one consisting of numerous loculi. **1880** GRAY *Struct. Bot.* 419/1 *Loculus*, the cell or cavity in an ovary or an anther. **1897** *Allbutt's Syst. Med.* III. 894 This disposition [in perityphlitic abscesses] to the formation of loculi or pockets.

ˈlocum. *colloq.* **a.** Short for LOCUM TENENS.

1901 *Scotsman* 11 Mar. 8/8 Acting..as 'locum' in Darlington place Church, Ayr (during the severe illness of the minister).

b. Short for LOCUM-TENENCY.

1903 *Lancet* 9 May 101/2 (Advt.), Hospital Locum wanted..for three weeks or less. **1946** *Ibid.* 2 Mar. 322/2 When doing a locum I attended a family of actors.

locum-tenency (ˌləʊkəmˈtiːnənsɪ). Also **-tenancy**. [f. next: see -CY. Cf. med.L. *locumtenentia*.] The position of being a *locum tenens*.

1844 G. S. FABER *Eight Dissert.* (1845) II. 343 It is not very probable that St. John..would have employed the.. word *Antichristus*, in the sense of Locum-Tenency or Usurpation of the character of Christ. **1881** *Church Bells* 19 Feb. 193 *Advt.* Curacy, or Locum Tenency, wanted by a priest. **1893** G. TRAVERS *Mona Maclean* I. 268 To look out for a practice, or a locum-tenency. **1896** *Daily News* 18 Dec. 5/2 [He] will take the locum-tenency of Berkeley Chapel, Mayfair, for at least a year.

‖**locum tenens** (ˈləʊkəm ˈtiːnɛnz). [med.L., = 'one who holds the place (of another)', a LIEUTENANT: L. *locum*, accus. of *locus* place; *tenens*, pr. pple. of *tenēre* to hold.] **a.** One who holds office temporarily in place of the person to whom the office belongs, or who undertakes another's professional duties during his absence; a deputy, substitute.

In Great Britain now chiefly applied to the deputy of a medical man or of a clergyman.

[**1463** *Rolls of Parlt.* V. 499/1, & dicti Locumtenentis mandato, declarabat, qualiter idem Locumtenens.. Parliamentum voluit prorogare.] **1641** 'SMECTYMNUUS' *Answ.* v. (1653) 22 Leaving Titus as his *Locum tenens*. **1683** in Strype *Stowe's Surv. Lond.* (1720) II. v. xviii. 391/2 The Lord Maiors *Locumtenens*. **1755** CARTE *Hist. Eng.* IV. 410 They ordered him to appoint a *locum tenens* and upon his declining to do so, they required..the three eldest aldermen, one after another, to assume the post. **1764** FOOTE *Mayor of G.* II. Wks. 1799 I. 187 D'ye mean..Master Jeremy's deputy?.. Ay, ay, his *locum tenens*. **1838** LYTTON *Alice* III. ii, The old driveller will be my *locum tenens*, till years and renown enable me to become his successor. **1883** S. C. HALL *Retrospect* I. 326 He not being on the spot, a locum tenens became a necessity.

transf. **1832** G. DOWNES *Lett. Cont. Countries* I. 461 A house wherein Petrarch was born, or perhaps its *locum-tenens*.

attrib. **1887** *Pall Mall G.* 16 Nov. 7/1 Dr. S., the *locum tenens* body physician of his Imperial and Royal Highness. **1889** *Ibid.* 13 Nov. 3/1 Young medical men..who are taking locum tenens work.

b. The post of a locum tenens; a locum-tenency.

1899 *Lancet* 5 Aug. 86/2 (Advt.), Locum Tenens or good Assistantship by doubly-qualified man. **1908** A. S. M. HUTCHINSON *Once aboard Lugger* VI. vi. §2. 437 There's this locum tenens I was going to take up in the North.

locumtenent, -tenant. [ad. late L. *locum tenent-em*: see prec.] †**a.** = LIEUTENANT. *Sc. Obs.*

1492 *Extracts Aberd. Reg.* (1844) I. 421 My lord Huntlie, locumtenant. **1544** *Ibid.* 193 For furnesing of ane thowsand horse to remain with the locumtenant on the bordouris, for resisting of our auld ennimeis of Ingland. *Ibid.* 194 And als thair was presentit in iugment twa writingis of the Erle of Huntlie, locumtenent generale of the north of Scotland.

b. = LOCUM TENENS.

1899 *Lancet* 19 Aug. 547/1, I met with a serious accident ..in consequence of which I had to engage a locum-tenent. *Ibid.*, This sort of thing should make men very careful as to locum-tenents before engaging them.

Hence †**locumtenentry** (Sc. *-tenendry*) = LIEUTENANTRY.

1544 *Extracts Aberd. Reg.* (1844) I. 194 Within the boundis of his locumtenendry.

locupletative (lɒkjuːˈpliːtətɪv), *a.* [f. L. *locuplētāre* to enrich, f. *locuplēs*: see next and -ATIVE.] Tending to enrich.

1802–12 BENTHAM *Ration. Judic. Evid.* (1812) V. 702 The distinctions of which testimony is susceptible..if servitive, exculpative, exonerative, or locupletative.

locuplete (ˈlɒkjʊpliːt), *a. rare.* [ad. L. *locuplēt-em*, *locuplēs* richly stored.] Well-stored, rich. Hence **ˈlocupletely** *adv.* *rare*$^{-1}$.

1599 NASHE *Lenten Stuffe* 21 The Digests of our English discoueries cited vp in the precedence and be documentized most locupleatly. **1656** BLOUNT *Glossogr.*, *Locuplete*, rich, wealthy, well-stored. **1864** HALDEMAN *Tours Chess Knight* Bibliogr. 3 Books..in the locuplete chess library of Professor George Allen.

‖**locus** (ˈləʊkəs), *sb.*[1] Pl. **loci** (ˈləʊsaɪ). [L. = place.]

1. a. Place in which something is situated, locality.

1715 CHEYNE *Philos. Princ. Relig.* II. 118 Yet Space is not actually to be divided; or one part of it separated from another. Since it is the universal Locus of, and penetrates all Bodies. **1874** RAYMOND *Statist. Mines & Mining* 516 These certificates were..entirely inadequate to determine the locus of the claims without parol testimony. **1876** GEO. ELIOT *Dan. Der.* v. xxxix, We all of us carry on our thinking in some habitual *locus* where there is a presence of other souls. **1889** *Syd. Soc. Lex.*, *Locus*, the whole space in or on which a thing is situated; a place. **1899** *Allbutt's Syst. Med.* VII. 395 It is even uncertain how far the writing-centre has a locus apart from the region in which impressions..are registered. **1901** *Dundee Advertiser* 10 Jan. 4 In Dundee the fish trade is divided against itself on a miserable question of the locus of its market.

b. *Genetics.* A site or position on a chromosome at which a particular gene is located; *loosely*, a gene.

1913 *Jrnl. Exper. Zoöl.* XV. 591 White and eosin are allelomorphic to each other, that is, they occupy the same locus in the sex chromosome. **1915** T. H. MORGAN et al. *Mechanism Mendelian Heredity* ii. 37 There are three pink eye colors in Drosophila, one whose locus is in the third chromosome (pink). *Ibid.* vii. 155 A mutant factor is located at a definite point in a particular chromosome; its normal allelomorph is supposed to occupy a corresponding position (locus) in the homologous chromosome. **1919** *Anatomical Rec.* XV. 358 In another case of duplication the duplication piece contains only the locus for sable as far as known. **1949** [see ALLELOMORPH]. **1962** *Lancet* 6 Jan. 10/1 The colour-blind locus is thought to be about 10 units of crossing-over from the locus for hæmophilia and about 25 units from the locus for Duchenne's type of muscular dystrophy. **1970** *Nature* 25 July 342/1 Considerable numbers of gene loci are required to code for the primary structures of the immunoglobulin molecules made in any one organism. **1971** *Ibid.* 13 Aug. 498/1 Haemoglobin type in sheep is controlled by a pair of alleles at a single locus.

c. ***locus of control*** (Psychol.) (see quot. 1972[1]).

1966 MANDLER & WATSON in C. D. Spielberger *Anxiety & Behavior* 286 A locus of control scale has been developed which differentiates individuals according to the degree to which they appraise themselves or the environment to control the occurrence of reinforcement. **1971** *Jrnl. Gen. Psychol.* LXXXV. 98 There is movement from external to internal locus of control from trial to trial. **1972** I. G. SARASON *Personality* (rev. ed.) i. 9 Locus of control refers to the degree to which an individual sees himself in control of his life and the events that influence it. **1972** *Jrnl. Social Psychol.* LXXXVI. 233 The work of Rotter and his associates on perceived locus of control has resulted in a considerable body of evidence.

2. A subject, head, topic. [So in the Latin rhetorical writers, after Gr. τόπος.]

1753 CHAMBERS *Cycl. Supp.* s.v. **1894** BRUCE *St. Paul's Concept. Chr.* vii. 155 This manner of handling the locus of justification is very open to criticism.

3. *Math.* The curve or other figure constituted by all the points which satisfy a particular equation of relation between coordinates, or generated by a point, line, or surface moving in accordance with any mathematically defined conditions.

1727–41 CHAMBERS *Cycl.* s.v., A *locus* is a line, any point of which may equally solve an indeterminate problem. *Ibid.*, All *loci* of the second degree are conic sections. **1758** LYONS *Fluxions* iv. §99 The locus of a simple equation is always a right line. **1848** SALMON *Conic Sect.* ii. §15 A single equation between the coordinates denotes a geometrical locus. **1879** CLIFFORD *Seeing & Thinking* iv. (1880) 141 When a point moves along a line, that line is the locus of the successive positions of the moving point. **1881** *Nature* XXV. 131 The locus of the centre of this extraordinary barometric depression. **1885** LEUDESDORF *Cremona's Proj. Geom.* 119 If two (non-concentric) pencils lying in the same plane are projective with one another (but not in perspective), the locus of the points of intersection of pairs of corresponding rays is a conic passing through the centres of the two pencils.

4. In Latin phrases: **locus classicus**, a standard passage (esp. one in an ancient author) which is viewed as the principal authority on a subject; **locus communis**, a COMMONPLACE; **locus desperatus** (see quot. 1966); **locus in quo**, lit. 'the place in which' (something takes place), the locality of an event, etc.; in *Law*, used to designate the land on which trespass has been committed; **locus pœnitentiæ** (after Heb. xii. 17), a place of repentance; in *Law*, an opportunity allowed by law to a person to recede from some engagement, so long as some particular step has not been taken; **locus standi**,

lit. 'place of standing'; recognized position; in *Law*, a right to appear in court. Also *genius loci* (see GENIUS 7).

1853 BAGEHOT *Coll. Works* (1965) I. 202 These lines are, as it were, the **locus classicus* of fairy literature. **1864** H. HAYMAN *Ex. Gk. & Lat. Verse* Introd. p. xxii, If a special subject has a *locus classicus*, as chariot-racing..in the *Electra* of Sophocles. **1883** *Sat. Rev.* 7 Apr. 446/1 The inclusion of honourable traffic..[was] grounded upon an utter misconception of the three *loci classici* in the Mosaic law. **1885** *Law Times* LXXIX. 328/1 His action was successful, and the report of it is now a *locus classicus* in the law of life insurance. **1531** ELYOT *Gov.* I. xiv, Hauyng almoste all the places wherof they shal fetche their raisons, called of Oratours **loci communes*, which I omitte to name. **1843** MILL *Logic* II. v. ii. 339 **Loci communes* of bad arguments on some particular subject. **1922** F. KLAEBER *Beowulf* 214 This passage remains..a '*locus desperatus'. **1966** A. J. BLISS *Dict. Foreign Words & Phrases Current Eng.* 231 *Locus desperatus*, a passage in a text transmitted by manuscript whose meaning is so corrupt as to be almost beyond conjecture. **1969** *English Studies* p. lxxv, The result is an editorial 'locus desperatus' which still to some extent defies repeated scrutiny and modern photographic aids. **1969** R. RENEHAN *Greek Textual Crit.* 2 The textual critic..must decide in each case whether the original reading..has been or can be recovered by modern conjecture or whether the passage is a *locus desperatus*. **1970** *Anglia* LXXXVIII. 367 Faced with such a *locus desperatus*, even a conscientious editor might decline to grapple afresh with the battered folio. **1717** SALKELD *King's Bench Rep.* I. 94 The Plaintiff demurred, because here are two Places alledged and the Avowant has only answered to the **locus in quo*, &c. which is but one of the two Places. **1842** DE MORGAN in Graves *Life Sir W. R. Hamilton* (1889) III. 248 Is there anything else which I ought to look at of yours on the same subject? if so, will you oblige me with a reference to the *locus in quo*. **1892** ATKINS *Kelt or Gael* i. 10 [They] suggest that the Aryan was a native of some cold part of Western Europe—Southern Scandinavia seems the latest favourite *locus in quo*. *a* **1768** ERSKINE *Instit.* III. ii. (1773) 427 The right competent to a party to resile from a bargain concerning land, before he has bound himself by writing is called in our law **locus pœnitentiæ*. **1789** *Term Rep.* III. 149 An auction is not unaptly called *locus penitentiæ*. **1855** *Newsp. Reader's Pocket Comp.* I. 68 'The doors of the institution are open to a limited number of adult male criminals, as a *locus poenitentiae*': that is to say, as a place for repentance and reformation. **1885** SIR J. PEARSON in *Law Rep.* 29 Chanc. Div. 489, I see no *locus pœnitentiæ* given to him after he has once made his election. **1835** J. W. CROKER *Ess. Fr. Rev.* vi. (1857) 342 By this daring step Robespierre acquired a kind of **locus standi*. **1886** *Law Times* LXXXII. 94/2 An expectant occupier has a *locus standi* to apply for the renewal of a public-house licence. **1911** J. WARD *Realm of Ends* x. 212 Death..means that the soul in consequence, so far as it is thus deprived of its *locus standi*, is..in the position of a deserter from the general order. **1974** *Times* 9 Feb. 20 The power of the Department [of Trade and Industry] should, of course, be discretionary but the Panel should be given a *locus standi* with the Department.

locus ('ləʊkəs), *sb.*² *slang*. Also **locust**. [As the earliest use is West Indian, the source may be Sp. *loco* lunatic (pl. *locos*): cf. LOCO *sb.*¹] Something stupefying. Also *attrib.* in **locus-ale**, an intoxicating drink made of the scum of the sugar cane.

1693 SIR T. P. BLOUNT *Nat. Hist.* 146 The first of which [*viz.* scum of sugar-cane] that ariseth is little worth; but afterwards, what is scumm'd off, they make a very good drink of, called Locus-Ale, much used by the Servants in Jamaica. **1851-61** MAYHEW *Lond. Labour* III. 387 Some of the convicts would have given me some lush with a locust in it (laudanum hocussing).

locus ('ləʊkəs), *v. slang*. [f. LOCUS *sb.*²] *trans.* To stupefy with drink. ***to locus away***: to get away under the influence of drink. Cf. HOCUS *v.*

1831 *Examiner* 764/2 May threw a glass of the gin into Bishop's tea, when the latter said, 'are you going to locus or Burke me?' Mr. Horner explained that 'locus' was a cant word to describe the act of putting a man in a state of stupidity. [The report of the same case in *John Bull* 5 Dec. 386/3 has: 'Are you going to hocus (or burk) me'.] **1868** *Temple Bar* XXIV. 539 'Locusing' is putting a chap to sleep with chloroform and 'bellowsing' is putting his light out. **1898** J. A. BARRY *S. Brown's Bunyip*, etc. 30 I've been shanghaied an' locussed away to sea, an' I wants to git back home again.

locust ('ləʊkəst), *sb.* Also (in sense 5) 7- **locus**. [a. OF. *locuste* or L. *locusta*: see LOBSTER¹. The early ME. *languste* is a. OF. *langouste* (semi-popular ad. *locusta*, through *logoste*, *longoste*).]

1. An orthopterous saltatorial insect of the family *Acridiidæ* (characterized by short horns), esp. *Œdipoda migratoria* (or *Pachytylus migratorius*), the Migratory Locust, well known for its ravages in Asia and Africa, where, migrating in countless numbers, it frequently eats up the vegetation of whole districts. Locusts are in many countries used for food.

In the Hebrew Bible there are nine different names for the insect or for particular species or varieties; in the Eng. Bible they are rendered sometimes 'locust', sometimes 'beetle', 'grasshopper', 'caterpillar', 'palmerworm', etc. The precise application of the several names is unknown. ***bald locust***: in Lev. xi. 22 used to render the Heb. *solʿām*, because the Talmud states that this word meant a locust with a smooth head.

[*c* **1200** *Trin. Coll. Hom.* 127 Wilde hunie and languste his mete.] *a* **1300** *Cursor M.* 6041 Þan sent drightin a litel beist, O toth es noght vnfelunest, Locust it hatt. *a* **1340** HAMPOLE *Psalter* lxxvii. 51 Locustis ere bestis þat fleghis & etis kornes. **1382** WYCLIF *Ps.* lxxvii[i]. 46 He ȝaf to rust the frutis of hem; and ther trauailis to a locust [COVERDALE the greshopper, **1611** the locust]. **1526** TINDALE *Matt.* iii. 4 Hys meate was locustes and wylde hony. **1611** BIBLE *Lev.* xi. 22 Euen these of them ye may eate: the Locust, after his kinde, and the Bald-locust after his kinde. **1638** WILKINS *New World* I. (1684) 184 Those great Multitudes of Locusts wherewith divers Countries have bin Destroyed. **1667** MILTON *P.L.* XII. 185. **1742** YOUNG *Nt. Th.* III. 238 Thick as the locust on the land of Nile. **1802** BINGLEY *Anim. Biog.* (1813) III. 166 The migratory locust. **1859** DARWIN *Orig. Spec.* xii. (1873) 327 Locusts are sometimes blown to great distances from the land. **1880** DISRAELI *Endym.* I. xxxi. 288 The white ant can destroy fleets and cities, and the locusts erase a province.

2. Applied to insects of other families.

a. An orthopterous saltatorial insect of the genus *Locusta* (family *Locustidæ*). **b.** A homopterous insect of the genus *Cicada* (family *Cicadidæ*); e.g. the seventeen-year locust, *C. septendecem*. **c.** *north.* and *midl. dial.* The cockchafer, *Melolontha vulgaris*.

1623 COCKERAM, *Locusts*, grashoppers. **1710** A. PHILIPS *Pastorals* vi. 29 When Locusts in the Fearny Bushes cry. **1846** J. L. STOKES *Discov. Australia* I. ix. 285 The trees swarmed with large locusts (the cicada), quite deafening us with their shrill buzzing noise. **1854** WHITTIER *Burns* vii, I hear..The locust in the haying. **1860** G. BENNETT *Gatherings of a Naturalist* xii. 270 Those noisy insects, the *Tettigoniæ* or Treehoppers, the Locusts of the colonists, are very numerous in New South Wales. **1862** JOBSON *Australia* iv. 104 We heard everywhere on the gum-trees the cricket-like insects—usually called locusts by the colonists—hissing their reed-like monotonous noise. **1899** *Daily News* 26 July 8/2 The Cicadas, of which the 17-year Locust is one, are among the noisiest of insects.

3. *fig.* (from 1). A person of devouring or destructive propensities.

1546 BALE *Eng. Votaries* I. (1560) 5 b, Theyr Byshoppes, Priestes, and Monkes, with other disguised Locustes of the same generation. **1587** FLEMING *Contn. Holinshed* III. 1323/2 Certeine locusts of the popes seminaries..arriuing in England, and dispersing themselues into such places [etc.]. **1681** DRYDEN *Sp. Fryar* III. 33 You promis'd to..bring your Regiment of Red Locusts upon me for Free-quarter. **1785** BURKE *Sp. Nabob Arcot* Wks. IV. 285 All the territorial revenues have..been covered by those locusts, the English soucars. **1826** COBBETT *Rur. Rides* (1885) II. 258 Those locusts called middle-men..who live..out of the labour of the producer and the consumer. **1840** ALISON *Europe* (1849-50) VIII. l. §8. 127 An army of locusts in the form of ..customhouse-officers..and other functionaries fell upon all the countries occupied by the French troops.

4. a. The fruit of the carob tree; a locust-bean. **b.** A cassia-pod, the fruit of *Cassia fistula*.

[The Gr. name ἀκρίς, properly denoting the insect, is applied in the Levant to the carob-pod, from some resemblance in form; and from very early times it has been believed by many that the 'locusts' eaten by John the Baptist were these pods. The application to the cassia-pod is due to confusion with the carob-pod.]

1615 G. SANDYS *Trav.* II. 121 Their fields, in which grow variety of excellent fruites; as..Dates, Almonds, Cassia fistula,..Locust, (flat, and of the forme of a cycle) [etc.]. **1718** QUINCY *Compl. Disp.* 181 Cassia, or Locust. This is a kind of Pod or Cane, which grows upon a large Tree in some parts of Brazil. **1775** *Ann. Reg.* 92 Some have called the fruit [of the algarroba tree] locusts, and supposed it was the Baptist's food in the wilderness.

5. a. = LOCUST-TREE (in its various senses).

1640 PARKINSON *Theat. Bot.* 1552 The second is called Locus by our Nation resident in Virginia. **1657** R. LIGON *Barbadoes* 74 The Locust is a tree, not unfitly to be resembled to a Tuscan Pillar. *Ibid.*, Another Locust there is, which they call the bastard Locust. **1676** T. GLOVER *Acc. Virginia* in *Phil. Trans.* XI. 628 There is likewise black Walnut,..Gum-tree, Locust. **1764** GRAINGER *Sugar Cane* I. 34 Let thy biting ax..the tough locust fell. **1775** W. EMERSON in *Harper's Mag.* (1883) Oct. 740/1 Large parks of well-regulated locusts. **1822** J. FLINT *Lett. Amer.* 229 The black locust is strong, heavy, not much subject to warping. **1858** HOMANS *Cycl. Comm.* 1272/1 There are, at least, three popular varieties of the common locust... 1. Red Locust... 2. Green, or Yellow Locust... 3. White Locust. **1869** *Rep. U.S. Commissioner Agric.* 201 Honey locust (*Gleditschia triacanthos*).

b. *U.S.* = *locust-club* (see 6).

1863 D. M. BARNES *Draft Riots N.Y.* 82 Go in they did forthwith, and, where moral suasion had failed, the locusts succeeded. **1865** G. A. SALA *My Diary in Amer.* II. 211 The New York policeman wears a handsome uniform. At his side hangs a club or bludgeon... This club is made of 'locust wood'..and by rowdies the policeman is often generically called..a 'locust'. **1882** MCCABE *New York* xxiii. 383 'Give them the locusts, men', came in sharp ringing tones from the Captain. **1904** *N.Y. Tribune* 19 June 4 The policemen did not carry their 'locusts'. **1930** E. H. LAVINE *Third Degree* 78 A detective picked out the largest and heaviest locust in the group.

6. *attrib.* and *Comb.*, as (sense 1) ***locust-army***, ***-flesh***, ***horde***, ***host***, ***legion***, ***swarm***; (senses 4, 5) ***locust fruit***, ***timber***, ***treenail***; ***locust-fashion***, ***-like*** advs.; **locust-bean**, the fruit of the carob tree; **locust-beetle** = *locust-borer*; **locust-berry**, the fruit of the West Indian locust, *Byrsonima* (*Malpighia*) *coriacea*; also, the tree itself; **locust-bird**, (*a*) a name given in S. Africa to *Creatophora carunculata*; also to *Ciconia alba* (***great locust-bird***) and *Glareola nordmanni* (***little locust-bird***); (*b*) the rose-coloured starling, *Pastor roseus*; all these birds devour locusts; **locust-borer**, a longicorn beetle, *Cyllene robiniæ*, whose larva destroys the locust-tree; **locust club**, a club made of the wood of the locust-tree, used by U.S. police; **locust-eater**, a bird of the genus *Gryllivora*; **locust-eating** *a.*, rendering mod.L. *gryllivorus*; **locust flower**, the flower of *Robinia Pseudacacia*; **locust-lobster**, a crustacean of the family *Scyllaridæ*; **locust post**, a post made of the wood of the locust-tree (*Robinia*); **locust shrimp**, the squilla or mantis-shrimp; **locust stick** = *locust club*; **locust wood**, the wood of a locust-tree; **locust years**, years of poverty and hardship (see also quot. 1962¹).

1727-46 THOMSON *Summer* 1057 Fetid fields With *locust-armies putrifying heap'd. **1847** R. W. CHURCH *Let.* 14 Feb. in *Life & Lett.* (1897) 82 The trees are very few [round Valetta]—scattered, black, shrubby carobas (or *locust-bean) are the most numerous. **1958** L. DURRELL *Balthazar* ii. 32 He would pick a stick of sugar-cane off a stall as he passed..or a sweet locust-bean. **1972** *Country Life* 30 Nov. 1481/1 Locust beans don't attack the teeth as jube-jubes did. **1756** P. BROWNE *Jamaica* 215 It seems to have a near resemblance to the *Locust-berry tree. **1776** A. RUSSELL *Aleppo* 70 The *locust-bird..is about the size and shape of a starling and seems of that species... The plumage on the body is of a flesh-colour; the head, neck, wings, and tail, are black. **1867** LAYARD *Birds S. Africa* 291 *Glareola Nordmanni*,..Small Locust-bird of Colonists. *Ibid.* 314 *Ciconia Alba*,..The White Stork, Gould..Great Locust-Bird of Colonists. **1874** FROUDE *S. Afric. Notes* 13-19 Dec., An army of locust-birds. **1884** H. B. TRISTRAM *Fauna & Flora Palestine* 73 The Rose-coloured Pastor is well known to the natives as the Locust Bird, from its habit of preying on that pest, whose flights it generally follows. **1839** H. COLMAN *2nd Rep. Agric. Mass.* (Mass. Agric. Survey) 100 *Locust-Borer... [He] washed his locust trees with spirits of turpentine, and in that way compelled the borer to leave them. **1972** SWAN & PAPP *Common Insects N. Amer.* 448 Locust borer: *Megacyllene robiniae*... The larvae bore in the sapwood of black locust. **1887** *Sat. Rev.* 9 Apr. 529 Rioters ..brained by the *locust clubs of the New York police. **1837** SWAINSON *Nat. Hist. Birds* II. 66 The resemblance between *Petroica bicolor* and the genuine *locust-eaters (*Gryllivora*) is..remarkably strong. **1802** BINGLEY *Anim. Biog.* (1813) II. 156 The *locust-eating thrush. To this new species.. Mr. Barrow has affixed the specific name of *Gryllivorus*. **1816** KIRBY & SP. *Entomol.* xvi. (1818) II. 9 The locust-eating Thrush. **1890** 'R. BOLDREWOOD' *Miner's Right* (1899) 106/2 That no hated aliens..should be suffered to..spread themselves *locust-fashion over their beloved shallow ground. **1855** BROWNING *Saul* ix, The *locust-flesh steeped in the pitcher. **1899** E. J. CHAPMAN *Drama Two Lives, Lake Scenes* 96 Pink-lipp'd *locust flowers, Hanging in thousands. **1703** DAMPIER *Voy.* III. 70 Ingwa's are a Fruit like the *Locust Fruit, 4 Inches long, and one broad. **1890** 'R. BOLDREWOOD' *Col. Reformer* (1891) 257 The *locust hordes of travelling sheep. **1812** BYRON *Ch. Har.* I. xv, With treble vengeance will his hot shafts urge Gaul's *locust host. **1884** J. S. C. ABBOTT *Napoleon* (1855) II. xviii. 334 The allied troops, in *locust legions, were pouring into Leipsic. **1602** WARNER *Alb. Eng.* x. lv. (1612) 243 Hir Guizards..into Scotland *Locusts-like in her pretext did swarme. **1855** *Cornwall* 25 Locust-like, they had devoured the edibles, and left us remains which were neither tender nor tempting. **1778** *Encycl. Brit.* (ed. 2) III. 1610/1 The locusta, or *locust-lobster. **1854** A. ADAMS, etc. *Man. Nat. Hist.* 291 Locust-Lobsters (*Scyllaridæ*). **1747** *Rhode Island Col. Rec.* (1860) V. 200 From a point where a *locust post was erected, [we] ran a line three miles north-east. **1870-80** NICHOLSON *Man. Zool.* (ed. 6) 306 The *Locust Shrimp (*Squilla mantis*). **1919** WODEHOUSE *Coming of Bill* (1920) I. i. 15 The policeman.. relieved his feelings by dispersing the crowd with well-directed prods of his *locust stick. **1795** SOUTHEY *Joan of Arc* v. 171 Who send their *locust swarms O'er ravaged realms. **1856** KANE *Arct. Expl.* I. xxiv. 321 A locust-swarm of foragers. **1858** HOMANS *Cycl. Comm.* 1271/2 The strength of *locust timber, as compared with other woods. **1866** *Treas. Bot.* 987/1 Considerable quantities of these '*locust treenails' are exported to this and other European countries. **1742** W. ELLIS *Timber-Tree Improved* II. xxxii. 166 Where the Natives can't get *Locust-wood, they use this to make their Bows. **1874** *Rep. Vermont Board Agric.* II. 777 *Clytus robiniae*. The larvae feed upon locust wood. [**1611** BIBLE Joel ii. 25 And I will restore to you the yeeres that the locust hath eaten.] **1948** W. S. CHURCHILL *Second World War* I. I. v. 52 (*heading*) The *Locust Years, 1931-1935. **1962** *Listener* 19 July 107/3 Sir Winston Churchill applied the phrase, the locust years, to the middle thirties, when vigorous rearmament should have begun. **1962** W. MCELWEE (*title*) Britain's locust years, 1918-1940. **1964** P. MAGNUS *King Edward VII* xiii. 244 (*heading*) Locust years. **1970** *Times* 27 May 8 Yet before these locust years of Labour, we had the Conservative years of rising prosperity.

'locust, *v. rare*⁻¹. [f. LOCUST *sb.*] *intr.* To swarm and devour as locusts do.

1875 TENNYSON *Q. Mary* II. i, This Philip and the black-faced swarms of Spain,..Come locusting upon us, eat us up.

locust, variant of LOCUS *sb.*²

‖**locusta** (ləʊ'kʌstə). [L.; see LOCUST *sb.*]

†**1.** A locust. *Obs.*

c **1375** *Sc. Leg. Saints* xxxvi. (*Baptista*) 281 Wyld hony wes his lyflede, & a thinge callit locusta. *c* **1380** WYCLIF *Serm.* Sel. Wks. II. 5 Sum men seien þat locusta is a litil beest good to ete. **1398** TREVISA *Barth. De P.R.* XII. xxv. (1495) 429 Locusta hathe that name for he hath longe legges as the shafte of a spere.

2. *Bot.* The spikelet of grasses. See also quot. 1727-41.

1727-41 CHAMBERS *Cycl.*, *Locustæ*, is used by botanists for the tender extremities of the branches of trees; such as, it is supposed, John the Baptist fed on in the wilderness... Some also used *locustæ* for the beards, and pendulous seeds, of oats, and of the *gramina paniculata*; to which the name is given on account of their figure, which something resembles that of a locust. **1830** LINDLEY *Nat. Syst. Bot.* 292 Flowers [of the Grass tribe] in little spikes called locustæ. **1861** BENTLEY *Man. Bot.* 192 The partial inflorescence of a Grass, which is termed a *locusta* or *spikelet*.

locustal (ləʊˈkʌstəl), *a.* [f. LOCUST *sb.* + -AL[1].] Of, pertaining to, or connected with locusts.
1891 *Chambers's Encycl.* VII. 187/1 Temperature may also have something to do with locustal migrations.

locustarian (ləʊkʌˈstɛərɪən). [f. mod.L. *Locustari-æ*, f. LOCUSTA: see -AN.] An insect of the group *Locustariæ* (in Latreille's classification) of green grasshoppers, katydids, etc.
1895 *Nature* 5 Dec. 108/1 Mr. Scudder..has given much attention to the sounds made by locustarians.

loˈcustian, *a. nonce-wd.* [f. LOCUST *sb.* + -IAN.] Pertaining to locusts.
a **1721** KEN *Hymnotheo* Poet. Wks. 1721 III. 270 Thus at his Tail he has a Scorpion's Sting, Deadly, like that of the Locustian King.

loˈcustical, *a. nonce-wd.* [f. LOCUST *sb.* + -IC + -AL[1].] Pertaining to locusts and their habits.
a **1763** BYROM *Ep. to J. Bl—k—n, Esq.* 54 Tho', all to a Man, Translators adopt the locustical Plan.

locustid (ləʊˈkʌstɪd). *Ent.* [ad. mod.L. *Locustid-æ*, f. LOCUSTA: see -ID.] An insect of the family *Locustidæ*.
1893 in Funk's *Stand. Dict.* **1899** L. N. BADENOCH *True Tales Insects* 143 The Locustids appear to show no preference for the globular galls.

ˈlocust-tree. Also 7-8 locus tree. [In sense 1 clearly f. LOCUST *sb.* In the other applications the identity of the word is somewhat doubtful, but the New World trees so called may possibly have received their name from the resemblance of their fruit either to the carob-pod (LOCUST *sb.* 4) or the insect itself.]

1. The CAROB-tree, *Ceratonia Siliqua*.
1623 JOBSON *Golden Trade* 132 They haue likewise great store of Locust trees, which growing in clusters of long cods together in the beginning of May, growes to his ripenes, which the people will feede vpon. **1775** *Ann. Reg.* II. 92 A tree growing in Spain called..carrobe or locust-tree..the fruit exactly resembles kidney-beans.

2. A well-known North American tree, *Robinia Pseudacacia*, having thorny branches and dense clusters of white heavily-scented flowers; = ACACIA[1] 2. It is used extensively for ornament and as a timber-tree, the wood being very hard and durable.
1640 PARKINSON *Theat. Bot.* 1550 *Arbor siliquosa Virginensis spinosa, Locus nostratibus dicta.* The Virginian Locus tree. **1676** S. SEWALL *Diary* 28 Sept. (1878) I. 22 Brought my Brother John going so far as the little Locust tree. **1688** R. HOLME *Armoury* II. 80/1 The [leaves of the] Locus tree, are oval leaves set on the stalk by short foot-stalks. **1775** A. BURNABY *Trav.* 69 The pseudo-acacia, or locust-tree. **1822** W. IRVING *Braceb. Hall* (1849) 389 The house stood..in the centre of a large field, with an avenue of old locust trees leading up to it. **1892** STEVENSON *Across the Plains* 8 Locust-trees..gave it a foreign grace and interest.

3. The COURBARIL of Guiana and the West Indies. Also, the West Indian *Byrsonima cinerea* and *B. coriacea* (Treas. Bot. 1866).
1629 *Plantation St. Christopher* in *J. Smith's Works* (Arb.) 905 Sugar Canes..also Masticke, and Locus Trees. **1693** S. DALE *Pharmacologia* 506 *Gummi Animi..Locus vulgò.* The Locust-Tree. *In Nova Hispania & Brasilia oritur.* **1756** P. BROWNE *Jamaica* 221 The Locus Tree. It is a spreading shady tree, and found in many parts of Liguanea. **1796** STEDMAN *Surinam* II. xxiii. 165 We saw some very fine locust-trees, being eighty or a hundred feet high, and prodigiously thick... The timber is of a beautiful cinnamon-colour,..its seeds, like beans,..enclosed in a broad light brown pod. **1838** T. THOMSON *Chem. Org. Bodies* 542 This resin [animé] is obtained from the *hymenæa courbaril*, or locust tree. **1872** OLIVER *Elem. Bot.* II. 165 The Locust-tree (*Hymenæa*) of tropical South America.. affording a very tough and close-grained wood.

4. *New Zealand.* = KOWHAI.
1872 A. DOMETT *Ranolf* VI. ii. 111 Feathery locust-trees o'erarched a little plot. **1898** MORRIS *Austral Eng.*, *Kowhai.* Maori name given to (1) Locust-tree, Yellow Kowhai *Sophora tetraptera.*

5. **African locust-tree**, *Parkia africana* (*Treas. Bot.* Suppl. 1874). **bastard locust-tree** of the West Indies, *Clethra tinifolia*. **honey locust-tree**, a North American ornamental tree, *Gleditschia triacanthos*. **swamp** or **water locust-tree**, *G. monosperma* (Treas. Bot. 1866).
1725 SLOANE *Jamaica* II. 86 Bastard Locust-tree. The berries are ripe in August. **1760** J. LEE *Introd. Bot.* App. 317 Locust-tree, Honey, *Gleditsia.*

locution (ləʊˈkjuːʃən). Also 6-7 loquution. [ad. L. *locūtiōn-em* (*loquī-*), n. of action f. *loquī* to speak. Cf. F. *locution* (14-15th c.).]

†**1.** The act of speaking, utterance. *Obs.*
c **1485** *Digby Myst.* (1882) II. 563 Of the hartes habundans the tunge makyth locucion. *c* **1500** *Melusine* 20, I wil not make grett locucion or talking. **1597** A. M. tr. *Guillemeau's Fr. Chirurg.* 23/1 A whole lippe is necessarye to the loquution and speeche. **1647** TRAPP *Comm. Acts* xviii. 24 An eloquent man... It imports, 1 skill in the words..; 2 good locution. **1666** J. SMITH *Old Age* (ed. 2) 140 Dentition and Locution are for the most part Contemporaries. **1767** LEWIS *Statius' Thebaid* XII. 1180 Should gentle Phœbus fortify my Lungs, And give Locution from a hundred Tongues.

2. Speech as the expression of thought; discourse; also, style of discourse, expression. Now *rare* or *Obs.*
1519 HORMAN *Vulg.* 98 b, Let no man call hym selfe a diuyne: that knoweth nat the figuris of construction and locucion: and specially allygoris [etc.]. *a* **1547** BALE *Image both Ch.* xv. (1550) ij, Under the shadowe of fygurate locution. **1603** H. CROSSE *Vertues Commw.* (1878) 116 To carrie the minde into sinfull thoughts, with vncleane locution, and vnchaste behauiour. **1606** MARSTON *Sophonisba* I. ii, I hate these figures in locution, These about phrases forc'd by ceremonie. **1726** AYLIFFE *Parergon* 347 A Libel may be obscure in point of Diction or Locution. **1846** GROTE *Greece* I. xxi. II. 196 The vein of Homeric feeling and the general style of locution..would be maintained. **1851** SIR F. PALGRAVE *Norm. & Eng.* I. 49 Their modes of speech accustomed every ear to their locution. **1852** FERRIER *Grk. Philos.* (1866) I. Lett. to De Quincey 483 In barbarous locution, 'the knowable alone is the ignorable'.

3. A form of expression or phraseology; a phrase, expression.
1432-50 tr. *Higden* (Rolls) I. 77 That somme men seyde Paradise to atteyn to the cercle of the moone, Alexander seythe that not to be trawthe, but after a locucion iperbolicalle. **1547** HOOPER *Answ. Bp. Winchester* D i b, Here ys a uery plain trope and figuratiue loquucion. **1555** BRADFORD in Foxe *A. & M.* (1583) II. 1616/2 Which is an hyperbolicall loquution. **1650** CHARLETON *Paradoxes* 133, I abhorre metaphoricall locutions in serious and abstruse subjects. **1654** JER. TAYLOR *Real Pres.* 140 If Testament in one place be taken for the instrument of his Testament, it is a tropical loquution. **1816** BENTHAM *Chrestom.* 146 Analysis and synthesis..are locutions which are but too frequently to be found employed. **1824** LANDOR *Imag. Conv.*, *Johnson & Tooke* Wks. 1853 I. 196/1, I cannot but think that so irregular a locution was at first occasioned by abbreviation in manuscripts. **1847** GROTE *Greece* II. ix. III. 33 It was essential to the security of the despot that..he should strike off the overtopping ears of corn in the field (to use the Greek locution). **1860** *Illustr. Lond. News* 14 July 35/3 A permanent Philological Board to watch over the introduction of new words and locutions. **1879** HOWELLS *L. Aroostook* xxvii. 319 The vigorous and imaginative locutions of the Pike language.

locutionary (ləʊˈkjuːʃənərɪ), *a. Philos.* [f. LOCUTION + -ARY[1].] Of or pertaining to an utterance by a speaker. Cf. ILLOCUTIONARY *a.*
1955 J. L. AUSTIN *How to do Things with Words* (1962) viii. 94 The act of 'saying something'..I call, i.e. dub, the performance of a locutionary act. **1962** *Times Lit. Suppl.* 21 Sept. 743/2 A locutionary act is the speaker's act of saying whatever it is he says. **1973** *Ibid.* 5 Oct. 1161/5 The locutionary act was the act of saying something—i e, the act of uttering sounds as constituting a sentence.

locutor (ləʊˈkjuːtə(r)). *rare*[−1]. [a. L. *locūtor*, f. *loquī* to speak.] A speaker.
1859 SALA *Tw. round Clock* (1861) 174 As though the whisper were of such commercial moment that the locutor feared its instantaneous transport to the ears of Rothschild.
Hence **loˈcutorship**, the office of spokesman.
a **1861** MRS. BROWNING *Lett. R. H. Horne* (1877) II. xlii. 14, I will not say that there is not some overdaring in relation to divine things, the locutorship of the Holy Ghost being among them.

locutory (ˈlɒkjʊtərɪ), *sb.* [ad. med.L. *locūtōri-um*, neut. of **locūtōri-us*, f. *locūtor*: see prec. and -ORY.] An apartment in a monastery set apart for conversation, a parlour; *occas.* a grille at which the inmates of a monastery may speak with those outside (cf. med.L. *locutoria fenestra*).
1483 CAXTON *Gold. Leg.* 242 b/1 He brouȝt hym in to the parloure or locutorye. **1534** MORE *Comf. agst. Trib.* II. Wks. 1170/1 So came she to the grate that they cal (I trowe) the locutorye. **1669** WOODHEAD *St. Teresa* II. iii. 21, I was once with him in a Locutory. **1772** NUGENT tr. *Hist. Friar Gerund* I. 557 *note*, Parlatories, or Parlours, or Locutories. **1825** SCOTT *Betrothed* xix, She left the betrothed parties in the locutory or parlour. **1841** GRESLEY *For. Arden* 60 While Latimer waited in the locutory, the compline-service, or second vespers, were prolonged beyond the usual time. **1856** R. A. VAUGHAN *Mystics* (1860) I. VI. iv. 178 Several monks in the locutory.
Also in L. form ‖**locutorium** (lɒkjuːˈtɔərɪəm).
1774 T. WEST *Antiq. Furness* (1805) 75 The times for conversation were, after dinner, in the Locutorium, or conversation-room. **1864** SKEAT tr. *Uhland's Poems* 427 The locutorium's prattle Again the convent hears. **1883** *Q. Rev.* Oct. 420 She locked up the locutoria, the parlours where visitors were received.

ˈlocutory, *a. rare*[−1]. [ad. L. **locūtōri-us* (see LOCUTORY *sb.*).] Pertaining to speech.
1828 *Harrovian* 45 Two worthies, whose locutory energies were considerably enhanced by a sapient shaking of the head.

lodam(e, variant of LOADUM *Obs.*

lodanum, obs. form of LAUDANUM.

lodberry, var. LOADBERRY.

†**ˈlodder,** *a. Obs.* [Connected with OE. *loddere* beggar, poor wretch. Cf. OHG. *lotar* adj., vain, idle (MHG. *lotar* adj., loose, unsteady, *loter*, *lotter* sb., mountebank, rogue, mod.G. dial. *lotter*, loose, exhausted; also in mod.G. *lotterbube* blackguard, and in other compounds: see Grimm). The OTeut. stem **lod-* is related by ablaut to **leuþ-* in LITHER *a.*] Wretched.
a **1400** *Minor Poems fr. Vernon MS.* (E.E.T.S.) 624/441 But a Barn be twyȝes born, Whon domus-day schal blowen his bemus, He may elles liggen loddere for-lorn.
Hence †**ˈlodderly** *adv.*, wretchedly, basely.
c **1425** *Eng. Conq. Irel.* 22 To helpe thys heyth man that ..þrogh hys owne men lodderly was of lond y-dryue.

Loddon (ˈlɒdən). The name of a tributary of the River Thames, used *attrib.*, esp. in **Loddon lily**, to designate the summer snowflake, *Leucojum æstivum*, a small, white-flowered, bulbous plant once common on the banks of this river.
1882 *Dickens's Dict. Thames* 28/3 It [*sc.* the summer snowflake] is very abundant in the meadows by the Loddon, and hence called 'Loddon lilies'. **1938** R. GATHORNE-HARDY *Wild Flowers Brit.* 53 The Loddon Lily is to be found principally on the tributaries and main river of the Thames Valley. **1971** *Country Life* 2 Sept. 575/1 On the banks of the River Loddon linger a few 2 ft.-high clumps of the snowy-white Loddon lily, or summer snowflake, *Leucojum aestivum.* **1973** *Times* 15 Dec. 10/7 The Loddon or Summer Snowflake Leucojum aestivum used to grow in great numbers on the banks of the Loddon near Reading. It has now become quite scarce.

†**loddy,** obs. slang abbreviation of LAUDANUM.
1811 L. M. HAWKINS *C'tess & Gertr.* I. 7 There are hairdressers and laundresses in London, who cannot begin their work without twopennyworth of what they call Loddy.

lode (ləʊd). Forms: 1 lád, (laad), 3 lad, 3-4 (9 *dial.*) lade, 4 lod, 6 loode, 6-9 load, 7 loade, 9 *dial.* looad, 4- lode. [OE. *lád* fem.: see LOAD *sb.*, of which *lode* is merely a graphic variant, now appropriated to certain special senses. (The obs. senses are placed under the one or the other word according to their affinity with surviving senses.)]

1. †Way, journey, course (*obs.*); *dial.* a road.
Beowulf 1987 (Gr.) Hu lomp eow on lade leofa Biowulf? *a* **1000** *Andreas* 423 (Gr.) Mycel is nu ȝena lad ofer laȝu-stream. *c* **1200** ORMIN 3455 þatt illc an shollde þrinne lac Habbenn wiþþ him o lade. *c* **1320** *Sir Tristr.* 419 He toke his lod vnliȝt, His penis wiþ him he bare. **13..** *E.E. Allit. P.* C. 156 For be monnes lode neuer so luþer, þe lyf is ay swete. **1886** *Cheshire Gloss.*, *Looad*, a lane; in Mobberley applied to the roads leading to the various moss rooms on Lindow Common.

2. A watercourse; an aqueduct, channel; an open drain in fenny districts. Now *local.*
[**789** *Grant* in Birch *Cartul. Sax.* (1885) I. 358 Mariscem ..quam circumfluit Iaeȝnlaad.] **1572** J. JONES *Bathes Buckstone* 10 b, Such evill ayre as issueth foorth of Lodes, Synckes, Sewers, and draynes. **1574** BP. COX in Ellis *Orig. Lett.* Ser. III. IV. 17 Our fennes, loodes, dykes, and banckes, being..so sore decayed. **1610** HOLLAND *Camden's Brit.* I. 491 The whole region..is overflowed by the spreading waters of the rivers..having not loades and sewers large enough to voide away. **1839** STONEHOUSE *Axholme* 376 There was formerly a small lode or gut, called Volfdyke, by which boats and small craft could sail out of the Trent. **1859** KINGSLEY *Plays & Purit.* Misc. II. 139 Down that long dark lode..he..skated home. **1865** —— *Herew.* xxi. A man cutting sedges in a punt in the lode alongside. **1893** *Northumbld. Gloss.*, *Lade, lode*, an aqueduct or channel which carries the water to a mill. **1894** *Athenæum* 5 May 587/1 A view of a fen lode or land drain in rainy weather.

†**3. a.** Leading, guidance. *Obs.*
c **1200** ORMIN 2140 Forr þatt he [*sc.* þe steoressmann] wile follȝhenn aȝȝ þat illke steorrness lade. *Ibid.* 6589 He.. Forrleoseþþ sawless soþe lihht, þatt iss Goddspelless lade. *a* **1300** *Cursor M.* 8441 Quen he cuth þe lagh o landes lade.
b. *dial.* The turn to act as pilot.
1855 *Correspondent*, When a signal is made for a pilot, at Aldeburgh, the Pilots on shore draw lots, and he, who gets the lot, or as they call it the Lode, goes off to the vessel.

4. A loadstone. Also *fig.* an object of attraction.
It is uncertain whether quot. *c* 1530 belongs to this sense; cf. 3.
1509 BARCLAY *Shyp of Folys* (1570) 211 So they that are abrode fast about may range, Rowing on the see, my selfe their lode and gyde. *c* **1530** *Hyckescorner* (ed. Manly) 84 (*Perseveraunce*), I am never varyable, but doth contynue, Still goynge upwarde the ladder of grace, And lode in me planted is so true, And fro the poore man I wyll never tourne my face. **1589** GREENE *Menaphon* (Arb.) 51 Arcadies Apollo, whose brightnesse draws euerie eye to turne as the Helitropion doth after her load. **1603** DRAYTON *Odes* vii. 34 As with the Loade The Steele we touch.

5. *Mining.* A vein of metal ore.
champion lode, the most productive lode in a district.
1602 CAREW *Cornwall* 8 They haue now two kinds of Tynne workes, Stream and Load. *Ibid.* 10 b, When they light vpon a smal veine, or chance to leese the Load which they wrought,..they begin at another place neere-hand, and so drawe by gesse to the main Load againe. **1728** NICHOLLS in *Phil. Trans.* XXXV. 402 When the Substances forming these Loads are reducible to Metal, the Loads are by the Miners said to be alive; otherwise they are term'd dead Loads. **1813** VANCOUVER *Agric. Devon* 64 In the parish of Bridestow a lode of copper has lately been discovered within six or seven fathoms of the surface. **1845** *Proc. Amer. Phil. Soc.* IV. 151 Zinc lying in two large and two smaller lodes and veins. **1866** THORNBURY *Greatheart* III. 7 The lode is a champion lode, and must run for miles, so the men tell me. **1872** RAYMOND *Statist. Mines & Mining* 93 The aggregate yield of the mines on the Comstock lode. **1881** —— *Mining Gloss.* s.v., In general miner's usage, a *lode, vein,* or *ledge* is a tabular deposit of valuable mineral between definite boundaries. **1883** STEVENSON *Silverado Sq.* 60 The lode comes to an end, and the miners move elsewhere.

6. *attrib.* and *Comb.*, as ***lode-claim, formation, -location, -mining, -ore***; **lode-light**, a light said to be seen sometimes above a vein of ore; **lode-**

plot (see quot.); †**lode-ship**, ? a pilot ship; **lode-stovvan, lodeworks** (see quots.); †**lodewort**, a name for Water Crowfoot, *Ranunculus aquatilis*, so called from its growing in watercourses.

1874 RAYMOND *Statist. Mines & Mining* 365 Brown's Gulch..contains the following *lode-claims, all claimed as silver-lodes. **1895** *Westm. Gaz.* 28 Sept. 4/2 No. 1 Shaft.. is sunk to the depth of 24 ft. on *lode formation 2 ft. 6 in. wide. **1883** *Encycl. Brit.* XVI. 443/1 The appearance of the so-called *lode-lights may be explained by the production of phosphoretted hydrogen. **1894** C. LE N. FOSTER *Ore & Stone Mining* 107 Appearances of flame above mineral veins ..are sufficiently well established to have received a special name 'lode lights' in Cornwall. **1877** RAYMOND *Statist. Mines & Mining* 328 Several lodes had in the mean time been found, or at least *load-locations [*sic*] made. **1874** *Ibid.* 363 Concerning the *lode-mining interest of the county there is but little to report. **1778** *Eng. Gazetteer* (ed. 2) s.v. *Burslem*, Its potters use almost all the *load-ore that is dug at Lawton. **1778** PRYCE *Min. Cornub.* 324 **Lode-plot*, a Lode that underlies very fast or horizontal, and may be rather called a Flat Lode. **1357** *Act 31 Edw. III*, Stat. 3. c. 2 En cas que..pesson plus grant [que] Lob soit trove en nief appelle *Lodship [*translation* has Lodeship]. **1860** *Eng. & For. Mining Gloss.* (Cornwall Terms), **Lode stovvan*, a drang driven towards rising ground on the indications of a lode in marshy ground. **1586** CAMDEN *Britannia* (1600) 148 Horum autem stannariorum, siue metallicorum operum duo sunt genera. Alterum *Lode-works, alterum streame-works vocant. **1602** CAREW *Cornwall* 8 b, To find the Loadworkes, their first labour is also imployed in seeking this Shoad, which either lieth open on the grasse, or but shallowly couered. **1727** BAILEY vol. II, *Lode works* [in the Stannaries or Tin Mines in Cornwall], Works performed in the high Grounds, by sinking deep Wells call'd Shafts. **1597** GERARDE *Herbal* App., *Lodewort is water Crowfoote.

†**lode-male.** *Obs.* In 4 loode-. [f. LODE (sense 1) + MALE *sb.*] A travelling-trunk.

13.. *Coer de Lion* 3651 Geve hym..Loode males..Ful off ryche preciouse stones.

†**lodeman.** *Obs.* Forms: 1 ládmann, 5 lodman, ladman. [OE. *ládmann*, f. *lád* LODE + *mann* MAN *sb.* Cf. LODESMAN.] In OE., a leader, guide; in later use only *spec.* a pilot.

c **1000** ÆLFRIC *Num.* x. 31 Þu canst weʒas ʒeond þæt westen; ac beo ure ladmann. *c* **1385** CHAUCER *L.G.W.* (MS. Camb. Gg. 4. 27) 1485 *Hypsip.*, If they were brokyn or ought wo begon Or haddyn nede of lodman [*MS. Arch. Seld.* ladman] or vitayle. *a* **1500** *Piers of Fullham* 260 in Hazl. *E.P.P.* II. 11 The lode man a bove that schuld sownd yerne Lakyth brayn, and also the lanterne ys owt. **1536** tr. *Laws of Oleron* in *Black Bk. Admiralty* (Rolls) I. 129 If a ship is lost by default of the lodeman, the maryners may..bring the lodeman to the windlass or any other place, and cut off his head.

lodemanage ('ləʊdmænɪdʒ). [a. AF. *lodmanage* (also *lamanage*), f. OE. *ládmann*: see prec. and -AGE.] Pilotage. ***court of lodemanage***: a court which sat at Dover for the appointment of the pilots of the Cinque Ports.

c **1386** CHAUCER *Prol.* 403 His herberwe and his moone, his lodemenage. **1412-20** LYDG. *Chron. Troy* I. iii, Maryners that..expert be of their lodmanage. **1485** *Naval Acc. Hen. VII* (1896) 24 Paid..John Henry lodesman for lodemanage of the same Ship..x^{s}. *a* **1500** *Piers of Fullham* 308 in Hazl. *E.P.P.* II. 13ef that he to long abyde To cast an anker at his tide, And faileth of his lodemonage. **1531** *Charter-party* in R. G. Marsden *Sel. Pl. Crt. Adm.* (1894) 37 All stowage lowaige wyndage pety lodmanage and averages acustomyd shalbe taken. **1616** BULLOKAR, *Lodemanage*, skill of nauigation. **1716** *Act 3 Geo. I*, c. 13 §1 A very useful.. Society or Fellowship, of Pilots of the Trinity-House of Dover [etc.], who have always had the sole Piloting and Load-manage of all Ships and Vessels from the said Places up the Rivers of Thames and Medway..Every Person must appear at a Court of Loadmanage, and be publickly examined..touching his Skill and Abilities in Pilotage, before he is to be admitted a Member of the said Society. **1755** MAGENS *Insurances* I. 72 To the petty, or accustomary Average..belong Lodemanage, Towage and Pilotage. **1873** J. LEWES 1871 *Census* 25 There was in former times a Court called the Court of Lodemanage, which seems to have been a branch of the Admiralty jurisdiction.

b. (See quot. 1607.)

1540 *Act 32 Hen. VIII*, c. 14 §2 A pece of Flemmysh monney called an Englishe for lodemanage. **1607** COWELL *Interpr.*, *Lodemanage* is the hire of a Pilot for conducting of a ship from one place to another.

loden ('ləʊdən). [a. G. *loden* thick woollen cloth.] A heavy waterproof woollen cloth. Used *attrib.* to designate garments made of this material, as ***loden cloak, cloth, coat, jacket, mantle, skirt***; also *absol.* Also, a dark green.

1911 GALSWORTHY *Little Dream* in *Plays* (1929) 204 There enters a lean, well-built, taciturn young man dressed in Loden. **1914** G. ATHERTON *Perch of Devil* II. 354 She.. wrapped herself in a dark lodenmantle, a long cape with a hood that she had worn..in Bavaria. **1916** J. BUCHAN *Greenmantle* vii. 98 Long shooting capes made of a green stuff they call *loden*. *Ibid.* xv. 196 Blue jeans, *loden* cloak. **1920** D. H. LAWRENCE *Women in Love* xxix. 450 The two.. daughters of the professor, with their plain-cut, dark blue blouses and loden skirts. **1951** V. NABOKOV *Speak, Memory* iv. 61 He wore an ulster unless the weather was very mild, when he would switch to a kind of greenish-brown woollen cloak called a *loden*. **1952** *New Yorker* 13 Dec. 128/2 A rugged coat for the country, made in Austria of greenish or brownish loden cloth and cut something like a hunting coat. **1956** *San Francisco Examiner* 9 Sept. I. 21 (Advt.), The original Alpine Lodencoat. **1957** *Times* 25 Nov. 11/1 This coat is reversible, in loden cloth and water-proofed poplin. **1964** *N.Y. Post* 4 Nov. 11 Russ Togs in black, brown, loden, navy, and menswear grey. **1966** *Listener* 3 Nov. 641/1 People dressed in green Loden jackets. **1969** R. T. WILCOX *Dict. Costume* (1970) 198/1 Loden, a waterproof cloth resembling Irish frieze, made by the Tyrolean peasants from the wool of their mountain sheep. It is woven and dyed in several colors but especially a bluish green known as loden green. **1973** *Guardian* 10 Apr. 13/1 The greatest source of inspiration is the traditional Loden coat.

†'**loder.** *Obs.* [f. LODE + -ER[1].]

1. A leader: in quot. attrib. *loder-man.*

c **1250** *Gen. & Ex.* 3723 An loder-man we wilen us sen, And wenden in-to egipte agen. *Ibid.* 4110.

2. The loadstone.

c **1400** *Beryn* 1569 The loder wherby these shipmen her cours toke echon.

†'**lodesman.** *Obs.* Also 3-6 lodes-, (4 lodez-, loodis-), 5-6 lodis-, lodys-, (5 ladis-, lods-, 6 lodse-, loades-), 6-8 loads-. [Altered form of LODEMAN, on the analogy of genitival compounds, as *doomsman.*]

1. A leader, guide.

c **1275** LAY. 6245 And solleþ habbe lodes-men [*c* **1205** lædes-men] forþ ȝou to lede. **1398** TREVISA *Barth. De P.R.* XVIII. lxxxvii. (1495) 836 Tame swyne knowe theyr owne howses and home and lerne to come therto wythout guide and lodesman. *a* **1400-50** *Alexander* 4967 Þe lede at was þar ladisman. **1482** *Monk of Evesham* (Arb.) 106 Y folowyde euermore my duke and lodisman sent Nicholas. **1528** ROY *Rede Me* (Arb.) 72 Ruffian wretches and rascall Lodes-men of all knavisshnes. *c* **1540** tr. *Pol. Verg. Eng. Hist.* (Camden 1846) I. 69 The legion whereof Manlius Valens was lodesmann. **1578** *Chr. Prayers* in *Priv. Prayers* (1851) 543 Be thou..our loadsman, guide, and captain. **1580** HOLLYBAND *Treas. Fr. Tong*, *Vne Guide qui meine autruy*, a leader, a guide, a loadesman. **1594** LATIMER *1st Serm. bef. Edw. VI* (Arb.) 21 To walke ordinatly with God and to make him his lodes man and chief guyde.

b. *spec. Mil.*

1581 STYWARD *Mart. Discipl.* I. 46 The Sergeant.. putteth them in araie that euerie man follow his lodseman, keeping his ranke fellowes iustlie on both sides. **1583** GOLDING *Calvin on Deut.* cxcix. 1241 Hee prouided them first of ye principall point, which was, y^{t} they might haue a good loadesman.

2. A pilot; a steersman.

13.. *E.E. Allit. P.* C. 179 A lodes-mon lyȝtly lep vnder hachches. *c* **1385** CHAUCER *L.G.W.* (Fairf.) 1488 *Hypsip.*, If they were broken or woo begoon Or hade nede of lodesmen [*v.rr.* lodman, ladman] or vitayle. *c* **1400** *Beryn* 1601 Sir lodis-man, Stere onys into the Costis, as wel as evir thowe can. **1513** DOUGLAS *Æneis* III. vi. 224 He..gaif ws then Gentill horsis, pilottis, and lodismen. **1530** PALSGR. 240/2 Lodes-man of a shippe, *pilotte*. *a* **1548** HALL *Chron.*, *Hen. VIII*, 22 b, The Englishe capitaines perceivyng that the haven was daungerous to entre without an expert lodesman. *a* **1571** JEWEL *Serm.*, *Luke* x. 23-4 (1611) 247 What, I pray you, betides vnto a Ship so tossed in the sea if there be no Lodes-man to steere it? **1735** DYCHE & PARDON *Dict.*, *Loadsman*, a Guide or Pilot.

fig. **1579** TOMSON *Calvin's Serm. Tim.* 61/1 If we be benighted, in deede we are glad to haue the Moone shine, or the Starres to be our Lodesmen. **1581** STUDLEY *Medea* in tr. *Seneca* 136 b, Hesperus, the loadesman of the night.

†**lodes-mate.** *Obs.* [f. LODE + MATE *sb.*, after *lodesman.*] ? A travelling companion.

1575 GASCOIGNE *Glasse Govt.* v. iii. Poems 1870 II. 77 He is their lodes mate & companion in all places.

lodestar, loadstar ('ləʊdstɑː(r)). Also 4-6 lood(e-, 5-6 lod-, 6 loade-, (lodes-); see STAR *sb.* β. *north.* and *Sc.* 5-6 lade-, 6 leid-, laidsterne, laydsterre. [f. *load*, LODE + STAR *sb.* Cf. ON. *leiðarstjarna.*]

1. A star that shows the way; *esp.* the pole star.

c **1386** CHAUCER *Knt.'s T.* 1201 Calistopee..Was turned from a womman to a Bere And after was she maad the loode sterre. **1387** TREVISA *Higden* (Rolls) I. 199 Þe sterre þat ladde þe Grees whan þey seilled þider [*sc.* to Hesperia] and was her loode sterre, Hespera, þat is Venus. **1393** LANGL. *P. Pl.* C. XVIII. 95 Wederwise sheepmen now..Han no byleyue to þe lyft ne to þe lood-sterre. ? *a* **1400** *Morte Arth.* 751 Schipe-mene..Lukkes to þe lade-sterne whene þe lyghte faillez. *c* **1400** MAUNDEV. (1839) xvii. 180 The Sterre of the See, that is unmevable and that is toward the Northe, that we clepen the Lode Sterre. *c* **1511** *1st Eng. Bk. Amer.* (Arb.) Introd. 28/1 Yat sowth layd sterre sawe we fourth with. *a* **1529** SKELTON *Col. Cloute* 1260 Tyll the cost be clere And the lode starre appere. **1535** STEWART *Cron. Scot.* (1858) I. 16 Tha had fund rycht far Furth in the north, law vnder the laid star Ane plesand yle. *a* **1571** JEWEL *On 2 Thess.* (1611) 150 The Master of the ship seemeth to be idle..Hee.. looketh vpon the load star, and in appearance doth nothing. **1594** BLUNDEVIL *Exerc.* III. I. xx. (1636) 321 The Load starre, or North starre. **1616** BULLOKAR, *Lodestar*, a Starre that guideth one. **1691** RAY *Creation* I. (1692) 183 The Load-stone and the Load-star depend both upon this [*viz.* the steadiness of the earth's axis].

2. *fig.* A 'guiding star'; that on which one's attention or hopes are fixed.

This sense appears to have been revived at the beginning of the 19th c. after a lapse of some 150 years.

c **1374** CHAUCER *Troylus* v. 1392 Biseche I yow myn hertes lady fre. That herevpon ye wolden wryte me, For loue of god my righte lode sterre. **1430-40** LYDG. *Bochas* I. iii. (1494) b ij, To the hauyn of lyf she was the lode sterre. **1500-20** DUNBAR *Poems* xxxvii. 10 O hye trivmphing peradiss of joy, Lodsteir and lamp of eivry lustines. **1509** HAWES *Past. Pleas.* XVIII. (Percy Soc.) 83 The bright lodes sterre Of my true herte. **1513** DOUGLAS *Æneis* Prol. 8 Lanterne, leid sterne, mirrour, and a *per se*. **1577-87** HOLINSHED *Chron.* (1807-8) III. 134 A paterne in princehood, a lode-starre in honour, and mirrour of magnificence. **1590** SHAKS. *Mids. N.* I. i. 183 Your eyes are loadstarres. **1641** MILTON *Reform.* I. Wks. 1851 III. 21 Since hee must needs bee the Load-starre of Reformation. **1813** SCOTT *Trierm.* Introd. v, The load-star of each heart and eye, My fair one leads the glittering ball. **1818** SHELLEY *Rev. Islam* II. xxi, An orphan with my parents lived, whose eyes Were loadstars of delight, which drew me home When I might wander forth. **1855** MACAULAY *Hist. Eng.* xix. IV. 274 The feather in the hat of Lewis was the loadstar of victory. **1861** M. ARNOLD *Pop. Educ. France* p. xxiii, The French Revolution became an historic epoch for the world, and France the lode-star of Continental democracy. **1871** ROSSETTI *Poems*, *Jenny* 18 Whose person or whose purse may be The lodestar of your reverie.

lodestone: see LOADSTONE.

lodge (lɒdʒ), *sb.* Forms: 3-6 loge, logge, (4 loghe, loȝe, *Sc.* lug), 4-6 *Sc.* luge, (5 loigge, looge, 6 loige, *Sc.* ludge), 7-8 lodg, 5- lodge. *Pl.* 4 logis, *Sc.* luggis, 4-5 loges, logges, 5 logez, loggen, loigges, loogez, 6 luges, -is. (See also LOGIS.) [ME. *loge*, *logge*, a. OF. *loge*, *loige* arbour, summerhouse, hut (F. *loge* hut, cottage, box at a theatre, etc.) = Pr. *lotja*, Pg. *loja*, It. *loggia* (dial. *lobia*):—med.L. *laubia*, *lobia* (recorded in the sense 'covered walk, cloister': hence LOBBY), a. OHG. **laubja*, later *louppea*, *lauba*, sheltered or shady place, booth, hut (glossing ***umbraculum***, ***tempes***, ***magalia***, ***mappalia***, ***proscenium***, ***propola***; MHG. *loube*, *löube* porch, balcony, hall; mod.G. *laube* arbour, summerhouse).

The derivation of the Ger. word from OTeut. **laubo*^{m} LEAF is disputed by some scholars, on the ground that the sense 'arbour' is a mod. development from compounds like *sommerlaube*, *gartenlaube*. But the Latin-OHG. glosses, and the early examples of *loge* in OF., seem to show clearly that the sense 'shelter of foliage', though not evidenced in MHG., is the primary one. Cf. LEVESEL.]

1. a. A small house or dwelling, *esp.* a temporary one; a hut or booth; a tent, arbour, or the like. Now *dial.* in specific applications.

1290 *Rolls of Parlt.* I. 29/1 Logges in quibus piscatores possent hospitari. *a* **1300** *Cursor M.* 6192 Son be a mikel wodside þai made þair loges [*Gött.* logis, *Trin.* logges] for to bide. **13..** *Sir Beues* (A.) 3622 Beues and Terri doun liȝte And wiþ here swerdes a logge piȝte. **1375** BARBOUR *Bruce* XIX. 392 Tentis and luggis als thair-by Thai gert mak. *c* **1386** CHAUCER *Nun's Pr. T.* 33 Wel sikerer was his crowyng in his logge, Than is a clokke or an abbey Orlogge. *c* **1400** *Ywaine & Gaw.* 2037 A loge of bowes sone he made. *c* **1400** MAUNDEV. (Roxb.) xxvii. 125 Þe comouns..er all hird men and lyez þeroute in logez [F. *gissent en tentis*]. *c* **1450** *Merlin* 387 A grete flame of fire..ran ouer the loigges of hem in the hoste. **1523** LD. BERNERS *Froiss.* I. xviii. 21 They cut downe bowes of trees to theyr swerdis to tye withall their horses, and to make them selfe lodges. **1575-6** *Durham Depos.* (Surtees) 278 In the plage tyme..when sick folkes had lodges maid upon the more. **1611** BIBLE *Isa.* i. 8 The daughter of Zion is left as a cottage in a vineyard, as a lodge in a garden of cucumbers. **1667** MILTON *P.L.* v. 377 So to the Silvan Lodge They came. **1748** H. ELLIS *Hudson's Bay* 177 His People..had they been furnished with large Beaver Coats, and had built Lodges in the Woods [etc.]. **1784** COWPER *Task* I. 227, I call'd the low-roof'd lodge the Peasant's Nest. **1810** SCOTT *Lady of L.* I. xxvi, Here..Some chief had framed a rustic bower. It was a lodge of ample size. **1860** DICKENS *Uncomm. Trav.* xl, Bricklayers often tramp, in twos and threes, lying by night at their 'lodges' which are scattered all over the country.

†**b.** A place of confinement; a cell, prison.

c **1290** *S. Eng. Leg.* I. 307/279 Ore louerd after is deþe In harde logge him brouȝte And teide þane schrewe faste Inovȝ. *c* **1450** *Cov. Myst.* ii. (Shaks. Soc.) 29 In helle logge thou xalt be lokyn. **1526** SKELTON *Magnyf.* 2362 Had ye not the soner ben my refuge, Of dampnacyon I had ben drawen in the luge. **1526** TINDALE *Acts* xii. 7 A light shyned in the lodge. **1676** D'URFEY *Mad. Fickle* v. ii. (1677) 59 How now! What's here one going to fire the house? Away, away with him to the Lodge. **1704** SWIFT *Tale Tub*, *Battle Bks.* 236 Books of Controversy, being of all others, haunted by the most disorderly Spirits, have always been confined in a separate Lodge from the rest.

c. A shed or out-house. *dial.*

1706 PHILLIPS (ed. Kersey), *Logium*, (in old Records) a Hovel, or Out-house, still call'd a Lodge in Kent. **1887** *Kentish Dial.*, *Lodge*, an outbuilding, a shed, with an implied notion that it is more or less of a temporary character. **1888** FENN *Dick o' the Fens* 127 The lookers-on saw that the stable and the cart lodge were doomed. **1892** R. STEAD *Bygone Kent* 201 'Lodge' means a wood or toolshed. **1901** *Daily Chron.* 20 Dec. 5/1 The Member for Carnarvon in the clothes of the average constable would be, as they say in Kent, like 'a tom-tit in a wagon-lodge'.

2. A house in a forest or other wild place, serving as a temporary abode in the hunting season; now used of the solitary houses built, e.g. in the Highlands of Scotland, for the accommodation of sportsmen during the shooting season.

1465 in *Paston Lett.* III. 437 The pullyng downe of the logge of Heylesdon. **1470-85** MALORY *Arthur* VII. xix. 242 There by was a grete lodge and there he alyghte to slepe. **1495** *Act 11 Hen. VII*, c. 33 §9 Keper of the Parke and of the Manoir or Loge there. *c* **1500** *Paston Lett.* III. 340 Writyn at the lodge in Lavenham the last day of Juylle. *a* **1586** SIDNEY *Arcadia* I. (1590) 12 He..retired himselfe, his wife, and children, into a certaine forrest..where in he hath builded two fine lodges. **1598** SHAKS. *Merry W.* I. i. 115 Knight, you haue beaten my men, kill'd my deere, and broke open my Lodge. *Fal.* But not kiss'd your Keepers daughter? **1599** —— *Much Ado* II. i. 222, I found him here as melancholy as a Lodge in a Warren. **1760-72** H. BROOKE *Foot of Qual.* (1809) II. 36 If you will give yourself the trouble to inquire out my little lodge on the hill. **1900** *Longm. Mag.* Oct. 591 The tedium of endless rain and impenetrable darkness in a Highland lodge.

3. A house or cottage, occupied by a caretaker, keeper, gardener, etc., and placed at the

entrance of a park or at some place in the grounds belonging to a mansion; the room, 'box', or the like occupied by the porter of a college, a factory, etc.

1500–20 DUNBAR *Poems* xlii. 76 Strangenes, quhar that he did ly, Wes brint in to the porter luge. **1504** *Nottingham Rec.* III. 323 For reparacion of þe logge on þe est syde [of a bridge]. **1540** *Coucher bk. of Selby* II. 356 Unam domum sive le lodge erga portas ejusdem grangiæ. *c* **1630** RISDON *Surv. Devon* §293 (1810) 301 They had a..park, the very lodge whereof hath afforded dwelling to men of good worth. **1744** OZELL tr. *Brantome's Sp. Rhodomontades* 211 Having the Lodge of the Bridge of St. Vincent at their Back. **1798** CHARLOTTE SMITH *Yng. Philos.* IV. 133 A lodge, where lived the widow of a huntsman,..gave entrance to this forest-like domain. **1827** *Oxford Guide* 27 Magdalene College, The Porter's Lodge is on the first right-hand corner of the entrance Court. **1840** DICKENS *Barn. Rudge* xxxix, As they happened to be near the Old Bailey, and Mr. Dennis knew there were turnkeys in the lodge with whom he could pass the night. **1842** TENNYSON *Audley Court* 16 We..cross'd the garden to the gardener's lodge. **1865** TROLLOPE *Belton Est.* xxvi. 319 She passed through the lodges of the park entrance. **1867** [see 8].

4. a. *gen.* A lodging, abode, esp. a temporary lodging-place, a place of sojourn; †formerly often *transf.* a place to accommodate or hold something.

1571 *Satir. Poems Reform.* xxv. 129 To saue þis noble ludge [the Castle of Edinburgh]. **1575** GASCOIGNE *Pr. Pleas. Kenilw.* (1821) 37 Nor could I see that any spark of lust A loitering lodge with her breast could find. *c* **1590** GREENE *Fr. Bacon* viii. (1630) D 3 b, If Phœbus..Come courting from the beauty of his lodge. **1594** —— *Selimus* F 3 b, Witnesse these handlesse arme, Witnesse these emptie lodges of mine eyes. **1602** MARSTON *Ant. & Mel.* IV. Wks. 1856 I. 44 The soule itself gallops along with them, As chiefetaine of this winged troope of thought, Whilst the dull lodge of spirit standeth waste. **1618** BRATHWAIT *Good Wife*, etc. E 7 b, Two empty Lodges haz he in his Head, Which had two Lights, but now his Eies be gone. **1719** WATTS *Hymns* I. xliii, Earth is our lodge, and heaven our home. **1782** COWPER *A Fable* 25 [He] long had marked her [a raven's] airy lodge. **1867** F. W. H. MYERS *St. Paul* (1898) 23 This my poor lodge, my transitory dwelling.

b. A residence or hotel. (Freq. as the second element of house- or hotel-names.)

1818 JANE AUSTEN *Persuasion* III. ii. 31 As to her young friend's health, by passing all the warm months with her at Kellynch-lodge, every danger would be avoided. *Ibid.* v. 80 Anne walked up..to the Lodge, where she was to spend the first week. **1854** DICKENS *Hard Times* I. iii. 12 To his matter of fact home, which was called Stone Lodge, Mr. Gradgrind directed his steps. He had..built Stone Lodge. **1869** *Bradshaw's Railway Manual* XXI. 307 Directors... W. C. Stobart Esq., Etherley Lodge, near Bishop Auckland. **1953** A. CHRISTIE *Pocket Full of Rye* iv. 24 *Call* it a lodge, indeed! Yew Tree Lodge!.. The house was what he..would call a mansion. **1971** *Author* LXXXII. 173 In hotels and auto lodges he listens to many a late-night argument. **1972** *Automobile Assoc. Members' Handbk. 1972–73* 154/1 Linton Lodge, Linton Road [Oxford].

†**5.** Phr. ***to take one's lodge***: to take up one's abode. (Cf. LODGING *vbl. sb.* 2.) *Obs.*

c **1475** *Partenay* 5168 Hermites Robes full faste lete doo make, In Arrygon toke hys logge and repair.

6. The workshop in which a body of 'freemasons' worked (see FREEMASON 1). *Obs.* exc. *Hist.*

1371 in Britton *Hist. Metrop. York* (1819) 80 Itte es ordayned..yat all ye Masonnes..sall..be ilk a day..atte yaire werk in ye loge yat es ordayned to ye masonnes at wyrke inwith ye close..als arly als yai may see skilfully by day lyghte for till wyrke. *c* **1430** *Freemasonry* 280 The prevetyse of the chamber telle he no mon, Ny yn the logge whatsever they donn. *Ibid.* 133. **1483** *Extracts Aberd. Reg.* (1844) I. 39 It was appoyntit..betuix the masownys of the luge. **1483** *Cath. Angl.* 223/2 A Luge for masons, *lapidicina, lapicidium*. **1483–4** *Durham Acc. Rolls* (Surtees) 415 Cum portacione eorundem [mason's tools] ad le Luge. **1870** BRENTANO *Hist. Gilds* IV. in *Eng. Gilds* (E.E.T.S.) p. cxliv, The 'lodge' itself of the architect was very similar to our factories; it consisted of one or more workshops in which the workmen worked together.

7. Among Freemasons and some other societies: The place of meeting for members of a branch; hence, the members composing a branch; also, a meeting of a 'lodge' of freemasons, etc. ***grand lodge***, the principal or governing body of the freemasons (and of some other societies), presided over by the grand-master. For *Orange lodge* see ORANGE².

1686 PLOT *Staffordsh.* 316 Into which Society when any are admitted, they call a meeting (or Lodge as they term it in some places) which must consist at lest of 5 or 6 of the Ancients of the Order. **1733** BRAMSTON *Man of Taste* 196 Next Lodge I'll be Free-Mason. **1742** in Hone *Every-day Bk.* II. 525 They..are to guard the Lodge, with a drawn Sword. **1753** *Scots Mag.* Sept. 427/1 A body of gentlemen masons belonging to foreign lodges. **1797** *Encycl. Brit.* (ed. 3) X. 625/1 It was this year [1720] agreed, that, for the future, the new grand-master shall be named and proposed to the grand lodge some time before the feast. **1813** *Gen. Hist.* in *Ann. Reg.* 93 Provisions were made for establishing district lodges [of Orangemen]: and..the masters of all regimental lodges were to make half-yearly returns..to the secretary of the grand lodge; and in these military lodges..officers and privates were to meet on terms of equality. **1845** D. JERROLD *Caudle Lect.* viii. (1846) 26, I suppose you'll be going to what you call your Lodge every night, now? **1866** LOWELL *Seward-Johnson Reaction* Pr. Wks. 1898 V. 318 Now joining a Know-Nothing 'lodge', now hanging on the outskirts of a Fenian 'circle'. **1900** MACKENZIE *Guide to Inverness* 46 The head-quarters of a lodge of Good Templars. **1969** in Halpert & Story *Christmas Mumming in Newfoundland* 181 The (Protestant) Society of United Fishermen..soon had no fewer than forty-two lodges. **1970** *Britain: Official Handbk.* (H.M.S.O.) xvi. 428 The basic unit of organisation in most British trade unions is the local branch (sometimes called a lodge). **1974** *Socialist Worker* 7 Dec. 8/3 And there were more than 30 other workplace units—such as chapels and lodges—represented.

8. At Cambridge University, the residence of the head of a college.

1769 GRAY in *Corr. w. Nicholls* (1843) 87 That Trinity Hall Lodge would be vacant..to receive Mrs. Nicholls and you. **1830** BP. MONK *Life Bentley* 115 The dean..allowed the £170 to remain in Bentley's hands..to be expended in purchasing furniture for the master's lodge. **1867** *Contemp. Rev.* IV. 529 The name 'Lodgings', as applied to the Master's House, is peculiar to Oxford. At Cambridge the word is 'The Lodge', or the Master's Lodge. At Oxford 'The Lodge' is simply the Porter's Lodge.

9. The den or lair of an animal; ? now only of a beaver or an otter.

1567 MAPLET *Gr. Forest* 6 Whilest that the Dragon is from home, these men bestrew his Lodge with certaine Graine. *Ibid.* 71 b, The Ant is called in Latine *Formica, quasi micas ferens*, carying her meale by crummes into hir Lodge. **1611** COTGR., *Reposée*,..the lodge of a Stag, &c. **1744** A. DOBBS *Hudson's Bay* 40 He has seen fifteen [Beaver] of that Colour out of one Lodge or Pond. **1756** AMORY *Buncle* (1825) I. 30 Before the beasts were roused from their lodges, or the birds had soared upwards. **1855** LONGF. *Hiaw.* Introd. 26 In the lodges of the beaver. **1897** *Encycl. Sport* I. 583/2 *Holt*, the lair of the otter... Other names for holt are Couch, Hover, Kennel, and Lodge.

10. The tent of a North American Indian; a wigwam or tepee. Also, the number of Indians accommodated in one tent as a unit of enumeration, reckoned from four to six.

1805 PIKE *Sources Mississ.* (1810) 14 Having shot at some pigeons, the report was heard at the Sioux lodges. **1807** P. GASS *Jrnl.* 45 Their lodges are about eighty in number, and contain about ten persons each. **1836** W. IRVING *Astoria* II. 204 They came to two lodges of Shoshonies. **1839** MARRYAT *Diary Amer.* Ser. I. I. 183 Wandering among the Indian Lodges (wigwams is a term not used now-a-days), I heard a sort of flute. **1855** LONGF. *Hiaw.* xvi. 12 By the shining Big-Sea-Water Stood the lodge of Pau-Puk-Keewis. **1859** MARCY *Prairie Trav.* v. 141 The usual tenement of the prairie tribes..is the Comanche lodge, which is made of eight straight peeled poles about twenty feet long, covered with hides or cloth. **1892** W. PIKE *North. Canada* 24 Four deerskin lodges made our encampment.

†**11.** A collection of objects 'lodged' or situated close to each other. *Obs. rare.*

1720 DE FOE *Capt. Singleton* xiii. (1840) 229 The Maldives, a famous lodge of islands.

12. Rendering Romanic etymological equivalents. †**a.** = LOGGIA. *Obs.*

1613–39 I. JONES in Leoni *Palladio's Archit.* (1742) II. 42 This Cornice is ⅓ part from the Lodge to the top of it. **1813** *Gentl. Mag.* LXXXIII. 226/1 Royal Military Hospital, Chelsea... Dwarf walls, having cornices, in succession, containing small door-ways. Two lodges, right and left, carry on the line, containing four compartments..each... Grounds to the dwarf-walls and lodges, brick; dressings, stone.

b. = LOGE² 2. *rare.*

1730 A. GORDON *Maffei's Amphith.* 320 A Round of large Covered Lodges, in which a great number of people were contained;..the Roofs of these Lodges were under the great Windows..in the fourth Story of the Coliseum. **1868** BROWNING *Ring & Bk.* v. 897 Where the theatre lent its lodge..Pompilia needs must find herself Launching her looks forth.

c. [? = Pg. *loja.*] A storage room for wine.

1880 VIZETELLY *Facts abt. Port*, etc. 126 We..pass through the sample and tasting rooms into the lodges. *Ibid.* 130 The Villa Nova wine-lodges. **1895** *Westm. Gaz.* 5 Apr. 1/3 We have thousands of pipes of wine at Oporto, and the lodges cover acres of ground.

13. *Mining.* **a.** 'A subterraneous reservoir for the drainage of the mine, made at the pit bottom, in the interior of the workings, or at different levels in the shaft' (Gresley *Coal-mining Gloss.* 1883).

b. A room or flat adjoining the shaft, for discharging ore, etc.

1881 in RAYMOND *Mining Gloss.*

14. A reservoir of water for mill purposes. *local.*

1853 *Gentl. Mag.* Feb. 191/1 [In the neighbourhood of Bury, Lancashire] two reservoirs..in the village of Elton, forming a 'lodge,'..for the accumulation from three narrow streams rising at Cockey Moor. **1891** *Oldham Microsc. Soc. Jrnl.* May 101 Bad smells arise from our lodges.

15. *attrib.* and *Comb.*, as ***lodge-door***, ***-keeper***, ***-man***, ***-room***; (sense 7) ***lodge-meeting***, ***official***, ***room***; (sense 10) ***lodge-cover***, ***-covering***, ***-fire***, ***-skin***, ***-trail***; **lodge-book**, a book recording the doings of a masonic lodge; **lodge-gate**, the gate of a park or the like at which there is a lodge.

1738 J. ANDERSON (*title*) The New Book of the Constitutions of the..Free and Accepted Masons, containing their History,..collected..by Order of the Grand Lodge from their old Records..and *Lodge-Books. **1878** J. H. BEADLE *Western Wilds* ix. 137 The former [*sc.* buffaloes] furnished them with food, clothing, *lodge-covers,..and a dozen other conveniences. **1847** F. PARKMAN in *Knickerbocker* XXX. 234 The squaws of each lazy warrior had made him a shelter..by stretching..the corner of a *lodge-covering upon poles. **13..** *E.E. Allit. P.* B. 784 As Loot in a *loge dor lened hym alone. **1542** *Ludlow Churchw. Acc.* (Camden) 12 For a new key to the loige dore. **1854** MRS. GASKELL *North & S.* xv, The lodge-door was like a common garden-door. **1837** W. IRVING *Capt. Bonneville* I. 111 Knots of gamblers will assemble before one of their *lodge fires, early in the evening. **1838** DICKENS *O. Twist* lii, At the *lodge gate. **1899** R. KIPLING *Stalky* i. 15 They could enter by the Lodge-gates on the upper road. **1854** MRS. GASKELL *North & S.* xv, The *lodge-keeper admitted them into a great oblong yard, on one side of which were offices for the transaction of business. **1892** *Daily News* 8 Sept. 6/4 Often in my capacity as *lodge-man have I seen a poor woman breathlessly running in order to be in the mill before 'lock-out'. **1903** C. T. BRADY *Bishop* iii. 47 Most of the Churches have a week-night prayer-meeting, and the other nights are taken up with *lodge meetings. **1926** *Scribner's Mag.* Sept. 327/2 A lodge meeting to the average negro is one of the big events of the week. **1933** J. BUCHAN *Prince of Captivity* II. i. 147 The weekly lodge meetings. **1909** *Daily Chron.* 30 Dec. 1/4 The fifteen *lodge officials and delegates prosecuted for offences against the Industrial Disputes Act. **1974** *Times* 6 Dec. 3/1 All lodge officials are completely vindicated. **1856** KANE *Arct. Expl.* I. xxxi. 421 From our *lodge-room to the forward timbers every thing is clear already. **1864** A. MCKAY *Hist. Kilmarnock* 163 The lodge-room was in Croft Street. **1911** J. C. LINCOLN *Cap'n Warren's Wards* vi. 88 I'm more used to lodge rooms than I am to clubs. *a* **1831** J. SMITH *Jrnl.* in M. S. Sullivan *Trav. J. Smith* (1934) 4 They [*sc.* Indian lodges] do not smoke except from a sudden change of wind and then no longer than it takes a squaw to spread a smoke wing of the *Lodge skin. **1891** *Century Mag.* Mar. 776 We had already devoured..a small sack made of smoked lodge skin. **1845** J. C. FRÉMONT *Rep. Exploring Expedition* 114 We resumed our journey..following an extremely good *lodge-trail.

lodge (lɒdʒ), *v.* Forms: 3–5 logge(n, 5 lodgyn, loyge, loigge, 5–6 *Sc.* luge, 5–7 loge, 6–7 *Sc.* louge, ludge, 7 lodg, 5– lodge. [ad. OF. *logier* (mod.F. *loger*), f. *loge*: see LODGE *sb.*]

I. *trans.*

†**1.** To place in tents or other temporary shelter; to encamp, station (an army). Often *refl.* to pitch one's tent, to encamp, take up a position; also in *passive*, to be encamped or stationed. *Obs.*

a **1225** *Ancr. R.* 264 *Metati sumus castra juxta lapidem adjutorii*..we beoð ilogged her bi þe, þet ert ston of help. *Ibid.*, Ismeles folc com & loggede him bi þe stone of help. *c* **1330** R. BRUNNE *Chron.* (1810) 182 Comen ere þe Inglis with pauilloun & tent, & loged þam right wele ouer alle þer þam þink. *c* **1400** *Destr. Troy* 10745 Pavilions and pure tenttes [pai] pightyn aboute, And þere logget hom to lenge, while hom lefe thoght. *a* **1400–50** *Alexander* 1952 A Messangere..him tellis, þat Alexander was at hand & had his ost loygid A-pon þe streme of Struma. *c* **1450** *Merlin* 277 Ther-of herde Gawein..that the saisnes were thus logged a-boute Bredigan. **1523** LD. BERNERS *Froiss.* I. cxciv. 231 The watchmen of saynt Quintyne..knewe that their ennemyes were natte farre lodged thense. **1568** GRAFTON *Chron.* II. 271 At night they returned and sayde, howe that the Englishmen were lodged in the fieldes. **1598** GRENEWEY *Tacitus, Ann.* XII. vii. (1622) 163 [Claudius] wrot vnto P. Attilius Histrus..to lodge a Legion, and all the aid he could leuy in the prouince, on the banke of Danubium.

†**b.** To shelter with foliage. *Obs. rare.*

c **1400** *Destr. Troy* 1140 Lurke vnder leuys logget with vines. *Ibid.* 1167 Lurkyt vnder lefe-sals loget with vines.

2. To provide with sleeping quarters or temporary habitation; to receive into one's house for the night; †to entertain, show hospitality to (guests). Also, in wider sense (cf. 7 b), to provide with a habitation; to place as a resident *in* a building; also in *passive*, to be (well or ill) accommodated with regard to dwelling.

13.. *Coer de L.* 6371 They are loggyd in this toun, I wyll goo, and aspye ther roun. *c* **1375** *Sc. Leg. Saints* xxv. (*Julian*) 624 A place quhare þat a monk lugyt wes. *c* **1386** CHAUCER *Nun's Pr. T.* 171 They ne founde as muche as o cotage, In which they bothe myghte logged bee. *a* **1420** HOCCLEVE *De Reg. Princ.* 4229 The fader logged him..In a chambre next to his joynyng. **1453** *Pol. Poems* (Rolls) II. 211 [They came] to Bedlum..Where poorly loggyd they fond the kyng of pees. **1526** TINDALE *Matt.* xxv. 35, I was herbroulesse and ye lodged me. **1535** COVERDALE *Heb.* xiii. 2 Be not forgetfull to lodge straungers. **1591** SHAKS. *Two Gent.* III. i. 35, I nightly lodge her in an vpper Towre, The key whereof, my selfe haue euer kept. **1596** DALRYMPLE tr. *Leslie's Hist. Scotland* I. 103 With glade wil and frilie thay vse to luge kin, freind and acquaintance, ȝe and strangers that turnes in to thame. **1622** BACON *Hen. VII*, 118 When hee was come to the Court of France, the King..stiled him by the name of the Duke of Yorke; lodged him, and accommodated him, in great State. **1714** SWIFT *Imit. Hor. Sat.* II. vi. 3 I've often wish'd that I had..A handsome House to lodge a Friend, A River at my garden's end. **1764** BURN *Poor Laws* 233 It is a kind of insult upon poverty, to go about to lodge poor people in a superb edifice. **1766** SMOLLETT *Trav.* I. viii. 139, I..pay at the rate of two-and-thirty livres a day, for which I am very badly lodged, and but very indifferently entertained. **1840** DICKENS *Old C. Shop* xxxi, This young lady was lodged for nothing. **1841** LYTTON *Nt. & Morn.* I. iii, You lodge your horses more magnificently than yourself. **1845** MCCULLOCH *Taxation* I. iii. (1852) 105 The latter are probably better fed, and they certainly are better clothed and better lodged than at any former period.

transf. *c* **1325** *Song, Know Thyself* 82 in *E.E.P.* (1862) 132 Preye we to god vr soules enspire Or we bene logged in eorþe lowe. *c* **1645** HABINGTON *Surv. Worcs.* in *Worcs. Hist. Soc. Proc.* I. 95 Sir Humfrey Stafford..maryed Elianor..lodged with him in thys sepulchre.

b. *refl.* To establish oneself, take up one's quarters. †In early use, = sense 7.

c **1375** BARBOUR *Bruce* II. 304 In the woud thaim logyt thai; The thrid part went to the forray. *c* **1400** MAUNDEV. (1839) xviii. 193 There ben also in that Contree a kynde of Snayles, that ben so grete, that many persones may loggen hem in here Schelles. *c* **1489** CAXTON *Sonnes of Aymon* v. 132 Reynawde sayd to his folke, 'go we lodge vs'. *a* **1533** LD. BERNERS *Huon* lxxxi. 246, I came & lodged me in the abbey. **1632** J. HAYWARD tr. *Biondi's Eromena* 108 They lodged themselves in Terranova as well as they could. **1711** *Lond. Gaz.* No. 4899/2 The Enemy..quitted the Bastion..,

where our Men..lodg'd themselves, without any Opposition.

†**c.** *fig.* To harbour, entertain (feelings, thoughts). *Obs.*

1583 BABINGTON *Commandm.* vi. (1637) 52 That say Racha, or thou foole to their brethren, that is, that..shew their hearts..to lodge an unlawfull affection towards them. 1593 SHAKS. *Rich. III*, II. i. 65 If euer any grudge were lodg'd betweene vs. 1623 PENKETHMAN *Handf. Hon.* IV. §43 Lodge not suspect, lest thou still wretched be. *a* 1708 BEVERIDGE *Thes. Theol.* (1711) III. 20 Dost thou not often lodge vain thoughts?

d. Of a chamber, house, etc.: To serve as a lodging or habitation for. Often *transf.* and *fig.* of things: To contain, be the receptacle of; in *passive*, to be contained *in* something.

c 1449 PECOCK *Repr.* v. vii. 521 Whi..ben so manye ostries clepid innes for to logge gistis, thouȝ in fewer of hem alle gestis myȝten be loggid? 1592 DAVIES *Immort. Soul* XXII. iii, The Brain doth lodge the Pow'rs of Sense. 1593 SHAKS. *Lucr.* 1530 Saying, some shape in Sinons was abusd; So faire a forme lodg'd not a mind so ill. *a* 1626 BACON *New Atl.* (1900) 6 And the other 15 Chambers were to lodge us two and two together. 1715 CHEYNE *Philos. Princ. Nat. Relig.* II. 63 The Memory [can] lodge a greater store of Images, than all the Senses can present at one time. 1729 WOODWARD *Nat. Hist. Fossils* I. I. 182 Mundick Grains..shot into several Figures; lodg'd part of them in a blueish grey, and part in a brown Stone. 1747 BERKELEY *Tarwater in Plague* Wks. 1871 III. 485 The fine oil, in which the vegetable salts are lodged. 1795 HERSCHEL in *Phil. Trans.* LXXXV. 353 As tenons of any kind, in an apparatus continually to be exposed to the open air, will bring on a premature decay, by lodging wet. 1826 LAMB *Elia* Ser. II. *Pop. Fallacies* ix, Perhaps the mind of man is not capacious enough..to lodge two puns at a time. 1830 KNOX *Béclard's Anat.* 266 The conformation of the skull, and that of the vertebral canal depend greatly upon that of the nervous centre which they lodge. 1835 S. SMITH *Philos. Health* I. v. 216 The size of the spinal canal, accurately adapted to that of the spinal cord, which it lodges and protects. 1871 R. ELLIS tr. *Catullus* lxvii. 4 Once, when his home, time was, lodged him, a master in years.

e. To receive into, or keep as an inmate of, one's house for payment; to have as a lodger.

1741 tr. *D'Argens' Chinese Lett.* i. 3 Come along with me, Sir, you shall be very welcome. I commonly lodge all Gentlemen that come to this Place. 1833 HT. MARTINEAU *Vanderput & S.* vi. 90 A peasant who had undertaken to lodge the workmen. 1884 N. HALL in *Chr. Commonw.* 6 Nov. 43/4 Lincoln, in early life, was so poor that he asked a shoe-maker to lodge him.

†**f.** ? To lay to rest (*fig.*). *Obs. rare.*

a 1658 CLEVELAND *May Day* ix, Then crown the Bowl, let every Conduit run Canary, till we lodge the reeling Sun.

3. To place, deposit.

a. To put and cause to remain in a specified place of custody or security.

1666 PEPYS *Diary* 9 Aug., Money, to enable me to pay Sir G. Carteret's 3000*l*, which he hath lodged in my hands. 1690 LOCKE *Hum. Und.* II. x. §7 (1825) 88 In this..viewing again the ideas that are lodged in the memory, the mind is oftentimes more than barely passive. 1710–11 SWIFT *Jrnl. to Stella* 25 Mar., I wish..Mrs. Brent could contrive to put up my books in boxes, and lodge them in some safe place. 1713 DERHAM *Phys.-Theol.* v. vi. (1714) 309 How could we plant the curious and great Variety of Bones..necessary..to the Support, and every Motion of the Body? where could we lodge all the Arteries and Veins to convey Nourishment? 1802 MAR. EDGEWORTH *Moral T.* (1816) I. 212 Their orders were..to lodge count L. in..a state prison. 1810 *Naval Chron.* XXIV. 459 A reward of Six Dollars will be given for apprehending and lodging him in the Cage. 1827 ROBERTS *Voy. Centr. Amer.* 52 His object was to lodge supplies of goods..at various trading depots. 1849 MACAULAY *Hist. Eng.* iv. I. 623 Soon after Monmouth had been lodged in the Tower, he was informed that [etc.]. 1866 CRUMP *Banking* ix. 177 The issue of receipts by the goldsmiths for money lodged in their hands. 1871 B. STEWART *Heat* §70 A new standard and four authorized copies were made and lodged at the office of the Exchequer. 1882 PEBODY *Eng. Journalism* xx. 149 Messrs. Stevenson and Salt are my bankers. Lodge £15,000 there to my credit, and within a week you shall have a daily evening paper.

†**b.** 'To place in the memory' (J.). *Obs.*

1622 BACON *Hen. VII*, 37 Which cunning the King would not vnderstand, though he lodged it, and noted it in some particulars, as his manner was.

c. To deposit in court or with some appointed officer a formal statement of (an information, complaint, objection, etc.). Hence, in popular language, to bring forward, allege (an objection, etc.).

1708 LD. SUNDERLAND in Ellis *Orig. Lett.* ser. II. IV. 250 Several merchants on the other side have lodged a Petition against him. 1754–62 HUME *Hist. Eng.* (1806) IV. lvii. 354 The impeachment which the king had lodged against him. 1802 MAR. EDGEWORTH *Moral T.* (1822) I. xv. 122 A magistrate, with whom informations had been lodged. 1885 CAVE in *Law Times Rep.* LII. 627/2 The objection which has been lodged against this appeal is necessarily fatal. 1888 BRYCE *Amer. Commonw.* II. xxxvi. 20 An American may..never be reminded of the Federal Government except when he..lodges a complaint against the Post-Office. 1891 *Law Times* XCII. 106/2 Persons who have any interest in land which is sought to be registered can lodge a caution with the registering officer.

d. To vest, cause to 'reside', or represent as residing, *in* a specified person or thing; to place (power, etc.) *with* or *in the hands of* a person.

1670 WALTON *Life of Hooker* 40 Acts of Parliament, intending the better preservation of the church-lands, by recalling a power which was vested in others to sell or lease them, by lodging and trusting the future care and protection of them only in the crown. *a* 1677 HALE *Prim. Orig. Man.* II. iii. 142 The Heathen Authors allow not above 1400 years at most for the continuance of the Assyrian Monarchy, and lodge the Original of it in Belus. 1712 BERKELEY *Pass. Obed.* §3 Wks. 1871 III. 108 Neither shall I consider where or in what persons the supreme or legislative power is lodged in this or that government. *a* 1715 BURNET *Own Time* (1724) I. 364 So he lodged it [*viz.* a dispute] now where he wished it might be, in a point of prerogative. 1752 YOUNG *Brothers* IV. i. Wks. 1757 II. 260 When all our hopes are lodg'd in such expedients, 'Tis as if poison were our only food. 1752 HUME *Ess.* v. *Indep. Parl.* (1768) 31 The power of the Crown is always lodged in a single person. 1804 WELLESLEY in Owen *Desp.* 277 The Peishwa's power was lodged by another train of events in the hands of Scindiah. 1817 JAS. MILL *Brit. India* III. vi. i. 52 The powers which were lodged with the Board of Control..were lodged without danger. 1818 CRUISE *Digest* VI. 381 And they could not take in that manner but by lodging an estate tail in George Grew. 1855 PRESCOTT *Philip II*, II. v. (1857) 251 Philip, on leaving the country, lodged the administration nominally in three councils. 1868 E. ARBER *Introd. to Selden's Table-T.* 11 Selden lodges the Civil Power of England in the King and the Parliament. 1869 HADDAN *Apost. Succ.* iii. (1879) 62 There can be no ministry save where the Apostles have lodged the power of appointing one. 1888 BRYCE *Amer. Commw.* II. lii. 314 The powers thus taken away from the common council, are ordinarily lodged with boards made up of the higher city officials.

e. To get (a thing) into the intended place; *esp.* to succeed in causing (a weapon, a blow) to fall and take effect where it is aimed.

1611 COTGR. s.v. *Escusson, Enter en escusson*, to lodge that bud in the bark of a tree by an incision..of the forme of a T. 1680 OTWAY *Orphan* I. i. (1691) 3 When on the brink the foaming Boar I met, And in his side thought to have lodg'd my spear. 1713 ADDISON *Cato* II. iii, O could my dying hand but lodge a sword in Cæsar's bosom. 1777 SHERIDAN *Sch. for Scandal* v. ii, Sir Peter is dangerously wounded..By a bullet lodged in the thorax. 1853 LYTTON *My Novel* xii. 50, I was shot at in cold blood, by an officer..who lodged a ball in my right shoulder.

f. *Mil.* (*a*) †To point, level (cannon). (*b*) To place (the colours) in position. (*c*) *to lodge arms* (see quot. 1867).

1627 CAPT. SMITH *Seaman's Gram.* xiii. 60 Keepe your loufe and loge your ordnance againe. 1783 *Encycl. Brit.* 8968/1 Signals by the Drum. *Two long rolls*, To bring or lodge the colours. 1802 C. JAMES *Milit. Dict.*, *To lodge arms.* 1867 SMYTH *Sailor's Word-bk.* 452 *Lodge arms*, the word of command to an armed party preparatory to their breaking off.

g. To throw (something) so that it 'lodges' or is caught in its fall (cf. sense 8); to cause to 'lodge' or be intercepted; (of a current, etc.) to deposit in passing.

1606 SHAKS. *Ant. & Cl.* IV. xii. 45 Let me lodge Licas on the hornes o' th' Moone. 1677 YARRANTON *Eng. Improv.* 41 The Stones near the Shore lay so great and thick, that they were the occasion of lodging the Sands by them. 1808 PIKE *Sources of Mississ.* (1810) III. 221 This crate or butment was filled with stone, in which the river had lodged sand, clay, &c. until it had become of a tolerable firm consistency. 1863 GEO. ELIOT *Romola* I. (1880) 21 He wore a close jerkin, a skull-cap lodged carelessly over his left ear, as if it had fallen there by chance.

†**h.** To set or fasten in a socket or the like. *Obs.*

1726 SWIFT *Gulliver* III. iii. 38 A Groove twelve Inches deep, in which the Extremities of the Axle are lodged. 1748 *Anson's Voy.* III. v. 341 The heel of the yard is always lodged in one of the sockets. 1776 G. SEMPLE *Building in water* 134 Let a Coffer..be made..and lodged upon any hard level Ground. 1792 FALCONER *Shipwr.* I. (ed. 8) 793 They lodge the bars, and wheel the engine round. 1825 E. HEWLETT *Cottage Comf.* v. 38 A scraper at each door might be furnished at no expense, and very little trouble; a bit of iron hoop lodged into two strong sticks.

4. To discover the 'lodge' of (a buck).

1576 TURBERV. *Venerie* 239 We herbor and unherbor a Harte, we lodge and rowse a Bucke. 1640 tr. *Verdere's Rom. of Rom.* II. 155, I would not walk thus with a purpose to lie all night in the wood, if it were not to lodge him Deer which to morrow he means to hunt. 1713 ADDISON *Cato* IV. ii, The deer is lodg'd. I've track'd her to her covert. 1741 *Compl. Fam.-Piece* II. i. 292 Nor is there required that Skill in lodging a Buck, as there is in harbouring a Stag. 1823 SCOTT *Peveril* vii, I thought of going to lodge a buck in the park, judging a bit of venison might be wanted.

†**b.** *transf.* ? To track (a fugitive) to his refuge.

a 1625 BEAUM. & FL. *Bonduca* IV. i, Are those come in yet that pursu'd bold Caratach? Not yet, Sir, for I think they mean to lodge him; take him I know they dare not.

5. To throw down on the ground, lay flat. Now only of rain or wind: To beat down crops. (Cf. *ledge*, LAY *v.*[1] 1 c.)

1593 SHAKS. *Rich. II*, III. iii. 162 Wee'le make foule Weather with despised Teares: Our sighes, and they, shall lodge the Summer Corne. 1605 —— *Macb.* IV. i. 55. 1621 SANDYS *Ovid's Met.* I. (1626) 7 The Corne is lodg'd, the Husband-men despaire. 1653 MILTON *Ps.* vii. 18 Let th' enemy..tread My life down to the earth and roul In the dust my glory dead, In the dust and there out spread Lodge it with dishonour foul. 1760 BROWN *Compl. Farmer* II. 72 If rye or wheat be lodged, cut it though it be not thorough ripe. 1763 *Museum Rusticum* I. 10 Land may be made too rich for flax, which will undoubtedly lodge it, that is, occasion its prematurely lying flat to the ground. 1843 *Zoologist* I. 297 Hedge-row trees..are a great nuisance, blighting the hedges, lodging the crops..and harbouring the plundering ring-dove. 1897 *Evesham Jrnl.* 24 July (E.D.D.), Winter oats lodged by the little rain.

II. *intr.*

†**6.** To encamp. *Obs.*

13.. *K. Alis.* 4098 With his ost he after ferd, And there he [Alisaunder] loggith anon, Ther Darie hadde beon erst apon. *c* 1440 LONELICH *Grail* xliv. 418 Whanne the kyng was Comen to-fore þat Castel, he gan to loggen bothe faire & wel. *c* 1500 *Melusine* xxxvi. 281 They concluded that on the morne theire oost shuld loge a leghe nygh to the Sarasyns. 1603 KNOLLES *Hist. Turks* (1621) 1251 With his armie..encamped in the self same place where the Turks armie had but the yere before lodged.

7. To remain or dwell temporarily in a place; *esp.* to pass the night, sleep. Now *rare.*

13.. *E.E. Allit. P.* B. 807 þay wolde lenge be long naȝt & logge þer-oute. *c* 1400 MAUNDEV. (Roxb.) xxv. 118 þare þer þai schall luge ilk a nyght, þai schall fynd before þam redily puruayd all maner of thinges. *c* 1470 HENRY *Wallace* I. 287 In Dunfermlyn thai lugyt all that nycht. ? *c* 1475 *Squyr lowe Degre* 180 Yf ye may no harbroughe se, Than must ye lodge under a tre. *a* 1533 LD. BERNERS *Huon* lxviii. 235 They lodged in the strete next to the palays in a good hostrye. *a* 1548 HALL *Chron.*, *Edw. IV* 228 For at the gates entered but a few that were apoynted, the remnant lodged in the feldes. 1593 SHAKS. *2 Hen. VI*, I. i. 80 Did he so often lodge in open field, In Winters cold, and Summers parching Heate, To conquer France. 1596 DALRYMPLE tr. *Leslie's Hist. Scot.* II. 124 That nycht he ludget with ane Thomas Leslie, quha maid him a saft bed, with fair coueringis dekit with al decore. 1597 A. M. tr. *Guillemeau's Fr. Chirurg* 53 b, The poore souldiours, who being wounded, must lodge on the earth. 1611 BIBLE *Job* xxiv. 7 They cause the naked to lodge without clothing, that they haue no couering in the cold. 1650 JER. TAYLOR *Holy Living* ii. §6. 139 Here thou art but a stranger travelling to thy Countrey..; it is therefore a huge folly to be much afflicted because thou hast a lesse convenient Inne to lodge in by the way. 1652–62 HEYLIN *Cosmogr.* II. (1677) 339 The extreme coldness of the Country..is so fierce that generally they lodg between two Feather-beds. 1667 MILTON *P.L.* IV. 790 Ithuriel and Zephon..Search through this Garden,..But chiefly where those two fair Creatures Lodge, Now laid perhaps asleep secure of harme. 1669 PEPYS *Diary* 19 Feb., After seeing the girls, who lodged in our bed, with their maid Martha,..I to the office. 1724 R. WODROW *Life of Jas. Wodrow* (1828) 68 He was several times forced to lodge in the open fields in the night time. 1778 MAD. D'ARBLAY *Evelina* (1791) II. 246 The Captain will lodge at the Wells. 1781 GIBBON *Decl. & F.* II. xlvi. 734 He lodged in the cottage of a peasant. 1888 *Daily News* 18 Oct. 5/3 One boy of fifteen, for example, was sent to this dismal sojourn for the offence of 'lodging in the open air'... 'Lodging', we assume, means sleeping. 1900 A. LANG in *Blackw. Mag.* Dec. 901/2 Darnley was to lodge at Craigmillar.

b. In a wider sense: To have one's abode; to dwell, reside. In later use chiefly *transf.* and *fig.* of a thing = to have its seat, 'reside', be placed. Now *rare.*

1362 LANGL. *P. Pl.* A. IX. 7 Was neuer wiht as I wente that me wisse couthe Wher this ladde loggede lasse ne more. *c* 1400 *Destr. Troy* v. 1631 Priam by purpos a pales gert make,..Louely and large to logge in hym seluyn. 1463 *Bury Wills* (Camd. Soc.) 21 He and his successours to logge there. 1567 J. MAPLET *Gr. Forest* 27 b, The bark which is the defence (and as I mought so say) their house to lodge in. 1598 YONG *Diana* 302 But he, that in high and loftie houses lodgeth (though the thunderclap smite him not) may be killed or wounded with the stones, timber, or some other thing that may fall from thence. 1602 MARSTON *Antonio's Rev.* III. ii. Wks. 1856 I. 108 O, you departed soules, That lodge in coffin'd trunkes. 1602 SHAKS. *Ham.* I. v. 87 Leaue her to heauen, And to those Thornes that in her bosome lodge, To pricke and sting her. *Ibid.* v. i. 252 She should in ground vnsanctified haue lodg'd, Till the last Trumpet. 1634 MILTON *Comus* 246 Sure something holy lodges in that brest. 1682 *Enq. Elect. Sheriffs* 31 The Right of chusing the Sheriffs of London, does by Charter,..lodg not in the Lord Mayor alone, but in him, the Court of Aldermen, and the Commons of London. *a* 1792 WOLCOT (P. Pindar) *Wks.* III. 5 The heart that lodges in that miser's breast. 1855 BAIN *Senses & Int.* II. iv. §19 (1864) 286 A strong sensibility..lodges in the lachrymal organ.

c. *spec.* To reside as an inmate in another person's house, paying a sum of money periodically in return for the accommodation afforded; to be a lodger, to live in lodgings.

1749 FIELDING *Tom Jones* XIII. v. (*heading in Contents*), The Adventure which happened to Mr. Jones at his Lodgings, with some Account of a young Gentleman who lodged there. 1858 LYTTON *What will he do* I. i, She and her grandfather lodge with me.

8. To be arrested or intercepted in fall or progress; to 'stick' in a position.

1611 COTGR., *Encrouer*, to lodge, as a cudgell in a tree; to hang on, or ledge in. 1647 COWLEY *Mistress*, '*Resolved to be Beloved*' II. iv, But if it ought that's soft and yielding hit; It lodges there, and stays in it. 1781 COWPER *Charity* 531 Worms may be caught by either head or tail;..Plunged in the stream, they lodge upon the mud. 1796 J. MORSE *Amer. Geog.* I. 480 In a freshet the flood wood frequently lodges, and in a few minutes the water rises to full banks. 1825 J. NICHOLSON *Operat. Mechanic* 374 An opening..which is nearly round or square, because if it were narrow the stuff might lodge. 1853 LYTTON *My Novel* III. xii. 125, I..who might have been shot through the lungs, only the ball lodged in the shoulder. 1885 GRANT *Pers. Mem.* I. xx. 279 A musket ball entered the room, struck the head of the sofa, passed through it and lodged in the foot.

9. *Hunting.* Of a buck: *intr.* To betake himself to his 'lodge' or lair. Also quasi-*passive*, to be in his 'lodge'.

c 1470 in *Hors, Shepe, & G.* etc. (Roxb.) 31 A bucke is logged. *c* 1486 *Bk. St. Albans* F vij b, A Bucke lodgith. 1615 [see HARBOUR *v.* 2 c]. 1801 STRUTT *Sports & Past.* I. i. 17 A hart was said to be harbored, a buck lodged [etc.]. 1888 P. LINDLEY in *Times* 16 Oct. 10/5 The hound worked on leash from the spot where the deer had lodged.

10. Of corn: = *to be lodged* (see 5).

1630 LENNARD tr. *Charron's Wisd.* III. xxxvii. (1670) 509 As corn lodgeth by too great abundance and boughs overcharged with fruit break asunder. 1731 TULL *Horse-hoeing Husb.* xiii. (1733) 151 One Argument, that it lodges for want of Nourishment is, that a rich Acre has maintain'd a Crop of Five Quarters standing. 1759 tr. *Duhamel's Husb.* I. iv. (1762) 9 It grew so rank that it lodged, and yielded but little grain. 1884 *Harper's Mag.* July 247/1 The growth had been so heavy that..it had 'lodged', or fallen.

lodgeable ('lɒdʒəb(ə)l), *a.* Also 7 **lodgable.** [f. LODGE *v.* + -ABLE.]

1. That may be lodged in; suitable for lodging or dwelling in.

1598 FLORIO, *Habitabile*, .. inhabitable, that may be dwelt in, lodgeable. *c***1630** DONNE *Serm.* xxvi. 264 The Kings presence makes a Village the Court; but he that hath service to do at Court, would be glad to finde it in a lodgeable and convenient place. **1656** FINETT *For. Ambass.* 164 The Ambassador's house was appointed, but not yet.. Lodgable. **1771** SMOLLETT *Humph. Cl.* Oct. v, The house is old-fashioned.. but lodgeable and commodious. **1794** *Stat. Acc. Scot.* XII. 22 The manse is a large lodgeable house. *a***1850** JEFFREY (Ogilvie), The lodgeable area of the earth.

2. That may be or can be lodged.

1897 WEBSTER s.v., So many persons are not lodgeable in this village.

lodged (lɒdʒd), *ppl. a.* [f. LODGE *v.* + -ED.] In senses of the vb.

1596 SHAKS. *Merch. V.* IV. i. 60 So can I giue no reason.. More than a lodg'd hate, and a certaine loathing I beare Antonio. **1607** TOPSELL *Four-f. Beasts* (1658) 120 Take a live hare, and..hide it in the earth... Your hound,..at length coming neer the lodged hare,..mendeth his pace. **1649** G. DANIEL *Trinarch., Hen. V*, clxviii, When the lodg'd Deere they Hunt. **1731** TULL *Horse-hoeing Husb.* xiii. (1733) 154 Lodg'd Ears are always lighter than those of the same Bigness which stand. **1802** A. ELLICOTT *Jrnl.* (1803) 16 My boat struck the root of a lodged tree in the river. **1854** H. MILLER *Sch. & Schm.* xiii. 287 The lodged oats and barley lay rotting on the ground.

b. *Her.* Of a buck, hart, etc.: Represented as lying on the ground.

1580 *Visit. Cheshire* (Harl. Soc. 1882) 86 Downes of Downes and Taxhall. Arms.—Sable, a buck lodged Argent. **1864** BOUTELL *Her. Hist. & Pop.* xix. 296 Each shield rests upon a white hart lodged. **1868** CUSSANS *Her.* (1882) 91.

lodgement, lodgment ('lɒdʒmənt). Also **logiament,** 8 **logement.** [a. F. *logement* (14th c. in Hatz.-Darm.), f. *loge-r* to LODGE: see -MENT.
Evelyn's form *logiament* seems to be quasi-It.; but cf. *parliament*.]

1. a. A place or building in which persons or things are lodged, located, or deposited; a place of shelter or protection; in early use *Mil.*, quarters for soldiers. ? Now *rare* or *Obs.*

1598 BARRET *Theor. Warres* I. ii. 9 The souldier giuen to this vice..doth disturbe all townes..and all lodgements. **1641** EVELYN *Diary* (1879) I. 32 It is a matchless piece of modern fortification, accom'odated with logiaments for the souldiers and magazines. **1696** C. LESLIE *Snake in Grass* (1697) 334 This, and not Prisons, had been the proper Lodgement for Fox and Muggleton. **1713** DERHAM *Phys.-Theol.* IV. xiv. (1714) 251 Such Balls, Cases, and other commodious Repositories as are an admirable Lodgment to the Eggs and Young. **1725** POPE *Odyss.* XIV. 18 Within the space were rear'd Twelve ample cells, the lodgment of his herd. **1760** STYLES in *Phil. Trans.* LI. 844 Separate lodgements, each of which contains a single bee. **1764** in PICTON *L'pool Munic. Rec.* (1886) II. 263 Design for a lodgement of fire engines. **1818** *Art Preserv. Feet* 108 The leather [of a boot] itself will form a lodgement for the corn.

b. A lodging-place; a lodging-house; lodgings. Now *rare*.

1703 MAUNDRELL *Journ. Jerus.* (1732) 2 Certain publick Lodgments founded in Charity for the use of Travellers. **1847** THACKERAY *Let.* (1887) 8 Come..and stop with me until you have found other lodgment. **1850** MAXWELL *Let.* in *Life* vi. (1882) 148 Getting room for my father (as the Bull was full) in a lodgement. **1865** BRIGHT *Sp., Reform* 18 Jan., Personages who have their lodgment higher up Whitehall. **1867** INGELOW *Dreams that came true* xxiv, Her scanty earnings, and her lodgment cold.

c. *Gunnery.* 'The hollow or cavity in the under part of the bore, where the shot rests when rammed home' (1872-6 Voyle & Stevenson *Milit. Dict.*).

d. *Mining* = LODGE *sb.* 13 a.

1883 W. S. GRESLEY *Gloss. Terms Coal Mining* 159 *Lodgment* (S[cotland]), see *sump* and *lodge*. **1886** J. BARROWMAN *Gloss. Scottish Mining Terms* 43 *Lodgment*, a reservoir or storage place underground for water for convenience of pumping.

2. *Mil.* A temporary defensive work made on a captured portion of the enemy's fortifications to make good the position of the assailants and protect them from attack.

1677 *Lond. Gaz.* No. 1187/2 We began to work for the raising a Battery, and the making a Lodgment to secure it. **1708** *Ibid.* No. 4470/3 A new Communication was made on the Grand Lodgment between the two Counterguards. **1884** *Mil. Engineering* I. II. 108 It is usually advisable to make a lodgment as quickly as possible, and for this purpose to bring up the working party rapidly.

3. The action of lodging; the fact of being lodged.

a. The action of establishing oneself or making good a position on an enemy's ground, or obtaining a foothold; hence, a stable position gained, a foothold. Chiefly in phr. *to make* or *find a lodgement*.

1702 LUTTRELL *Brief Rel.* (1857) V. 229 They were gone to Vigo,..if they found it practicable, to make a lodgment there. **1777** ROBERTSON *Hist. Amer.* II. v. 116 Cortes durst not..attempt to make a lodgment in a city. **1853** SIR H. DOUGLAS *Milit. Bridges* 209 The troops made good their landing, attacked the enemy, and established a lodgment. **1860** TYNDALL *Glac.* I. ix. 62 My friend, who had found a lodgment upon the edge of a rock. **1897** GEN. H. PORTER in *Century Mag.* Jan. 353 Many of our men succeeded in getting over the earthworks, but could not secure a lodgment which could be held.

transf. and *fig.* **1757** BURKE *Abridgm. Eng. Hist.* Wks. 1842 II. 410 But then the minister must have taken it up as a great plan of national policy, and paid with his person in every lodgment of his approach. **1824** W. IRVING *T. Trav.* I. 348, I was not perfectly sure that I had effected a lodgment in the young lady's heart. **1868** MILMAN *St. Paul's* iv. 78 Wycliffe had made a dangerous lodgment in the City of London. **1884** L. J. JENNINGS in *Croker P.* I. viii. 222 An intention which seems..never to have held more than a temporary lodgment in his mind.

b. The action of placing in position, or of providing with a receptacle.

1713 DERHAM *Phys.-Theol.* VII. ii. (1714) 355 The Structure and Lodgment of the Lungs. **1875** SIR WM. TURNER in *Encycl. Brit.* I. 827/2 The lower end of the bone ..is marked posteriorly by grooves for the lodgment of tendons passing to the back of the hand.

c. The action of depositing (a sum of money, securities, etc.); *concr.* a deposit of money. Now only *legal*.

1760-72 H. BROOKE *Fool of Qual.* (1809) II. 121 He..has entered all his lodgments in feigned names. **1825** HOR. SMITH *Gaieties & Grav.* II. 243 The lodgments made by the players. **1884** *Law Rep.* 27 Chanc. Div. 243 A decree for.. lodgment in Court of a sum then in the District Registry. **1886** *Law Times* LXXXI. 59/2 S. had gained no priority over T. by S.'s prior lodgment of the stop-order.

d. The 'lodging' of a thing or the accumulation of matter intercepted in fall or transit; *concr.* a mass of matter so lodged.

1739 S. SHARP *Surg.* (J.), An oppressed diaphragm from a mere lodgment of extravasated matter. **1767** GOOCH *Treat. Wounds* I. 98 The lodgment of blood or other fluid may easily affect the brain by compression. **1823** BUCKLAND *Reliq. Diluv.* 123 Wherever there was a ledge, or shelf or basin, however minute,..there these materials have found a lodgement. **1862** BEVERIDGE *Hist. India* III. IX. iv. 633 The plains on both sides are covered at this season by heavy lodgments of water. **1878** HUXLEY *Physiogr.* 21 Some [rain] finding lodgment in little hollows of the rock.

e. ? A body of persons established in a place.

1830 EVERETT *Orat.* (1850) I. 218 There is a great lodgment of civilized men on this continent.

4. Accommodation in a lodging-place; provision of lodgings; lodging. *rare*.

1805 W. TAYLOR in *Ann. Rev.* III. 65 The French spend less in hospitality, more in lodgement than the English. **1824** W. IRVING *T. Trav.* I. 18 The miserable lodgement and miserable fare of a provincial inn. **1853** LYTTON *My Novel* II. vii. 80 'For the board and the lodgment, good', said Riccabocca. **1858** CARLYLE *Fredk. Gt.* I. IV. ix. 477 Retinue sufficient find nooks for lodgment in the poor old Schloss.

5. **lodgement-level** (see quot. 1877).

1877 *Encycl. Brit.* VI. 63/2 Driving a gallery..along the course of the coal seam, which is known as a 'dip head level', and a lower parallel one, in which the water collects, known as a 'lodgment level'. **1886** J. BARROWMAN *Gloss. Scottish Mining Terms* 43 *Lodgment-level*, a room driven level course at a short distance to the dip of a pit and used for storage of water.

lodge-pole, *sb. N. Amer.* 1. A pole used to support a North American Indian tent.

1805 M. LEWIS in Lewis & Clark *Orig. Jrnls. Lewis & Clark Expedition* (1904) II. 88 Found a new indian lodge pole today. **1855** LONGF. *Hiaw.* ii. 171 At night Kabibonokka..Shook the lodge-poles in his fury. **1865** TYLOR *Early Hist. Man.* iii. 37 The dogs were trained to drag the lodge-poles on the march. **1903** A. ADAMS *Log of Cowboy* xxi. 330 He..with The Rebel went back about a mile to a thicket of lodge poles. **1946** G. FOREMAN *Last Trek of Indians* 242 They pulled down the lodges of three of their villages and sold the lodgepoles and lumber.

2. **lodge-pole pine,** a pine native to mountainous regions of north-west America, *Pinus contorta* var. *latifolia*.

1859 G. A. JACKSON *Diary* 9 Jan. in *Colorado Mag.* (1935) XII. 205 Cut the top off a small lodge pole pine. **1884** C. S. SARGENT *Rep. Forests N. Amer.* 564 The forests largely composed of the lodge-pole pine..cover the outlying eastern ranges of the Rocky Mountains. **1905** *N.Y. Even. Post* 29 Apr., The lodgepole pine..bears the common name of 'lodgepole' from the fact that the Indians used its long slender trunks as supports for their wigwams, or lodges. **1949** *Sierra Club Bull.* (San Francisco) June 6 Lodgepole pines, singing birds and scampering chipmunks,..all familiar elements of the mountain scenes. **1964** *N.Z. News* 24 Nov. 3/1 The lodgepole pine, becoming common on the Waiouru Plains and a cause of concern because of its possible spread in the South Island, is in fact a favoured species for pulping in U.S. **1972** *Islander* (Victoria, B.C.) 23 Jan. 6/1 Amongst the lodge-pole pines and blue spruce. **1972** *Country Life* 7 Dec. 1559/1 Foresters in Scotland can be criticized for planting an excess of sitka and Canadian lodgepole pine.

'lodge-pole, *v. U.S.* [f. prec.] *trans.* To beat with a lodge-pole. Hence **lodge-poling** *vbl. sb.*

1848 G. F. A. RUXTON in *Blackw. Mag.* LXIV. 139 Nor are they [*sc.* squaws] so schooled to perfect obedience to their lords and masters as to stand a 'lodge poling'. **1850** L. H. GARRARD *Wah-to-Yah* (1927) ix. 116 Often..their negligent spouses are lodge-poled (beaten) for such accidents. **1968** *Amer. Speech* XLIII. 218 It was customary to discipline a squaw by *lodge-poling* her, and the term became figurative for any beating.

lodger ('lɒdʒə(r)). Also 4 **loger, logger,** 6 **loghger,** *Sc.* **lugear.** [f. LODGE *v.* + -ER[1].]

†1. a. A dweller in a tent (cf. LODGE *v.* 7). *Obs.*

*a***1300** *Cursor M.* 1517 Iobal..Was first loger, and fee delt wit [*Genesis* iv. 20].

b. One who sojourns in a place, an occupant, inhabitant; also, one who sleeps or passes the night in a place. Now only *arch.*

1511 *Galway Arch.* in *10th Rep. Hist. MSS. Comm.* App. v. 394 No aliannt nor strangers shalbe loghgers ne in town nor land. **1832** SIR S. FERGUSON *Forging of Anchor* 70 O lodger in the sea-king's halls. **1834** SIR H. TAYLOR *Artevelde* II. v. i. 190 Tatterdemalions, lodgers in the hedge.

transf. **1676** WISEMAN *Surg.* VI. ii. 412 By this you..quit the Part of its troublesome Lodger [*viz.* a bullet]. **1737** POPE *Hor. Epist.* II. ii. 223 Look in that breast, most dirty D——! be fair, Say, can you find out one such lodger there? **1891** S. C. SCRIVENER *Our Fields & Cities* 147 In properly cultivated land a grub is a very rare lodger.

c. One who resides as an inmate in another person's house, paying a certain sum periodically for the accommodation.

1596 SHAKS. *Tam. Shr.* IV. iv. 5 We were lodgers, at the Pegasos. **1599** —— *Hen. V*, II. i. 33 Base Tyke, cal'st thou mee Hoste, now by this hand I sweare I scorne the terme: nor shall my Nel keep Lodgers. **1680** BAXTER *Answ. Stillingfl.* ix. 18 In London, Lodgers may change frequently. **1711** ADDISON *Spect.* No. 101 ¶7 He lived as a Lodger at the House of a Widow-Woman. **1758** JOHNSON *Idler* No. 16 ¶3 He dismissed the lodgers from the first floor. **1844** LD. BROUGHAM *Brit. Constit.* vi. 85 All lodgers and boarders, all who have no house of their own.

†2. One who lodges a person; a host. *Obs.*

1533 BELLENDEN *Livy* II. (1822) 139 Mony of thir presoneris..gaif thankis to thair lugearis for the benevolence schewin to thame during the time of thair captivite. **1632** SHERWOOD, A lodger, *hoste, qui loge, ou herberge*. **1665** BRATHWAIT *Comm. Two Tales* 8 A Lodger or Tabler of Scholars and other Artists.

3. A thing that lodges or becomes fixed in a place.

1868 *Rep. Munit. War* 17 The number of missiles discharged by these seventy-six effective rounds would be 1216 of which..443 [were] lodgers. **1880** DUNBAR *Pract. Papermaker* 24 This prevents 'lodgers', or pieces of rag not reduced to half-stuff, hanging about, which, if allowed to escape, would cause knots and grey specks in the paper.

4. *attrib.*: **lodger-franchise,** a right to vote conferred by statute in 1867 upon persons in boroughs occupying lodgings of an annual rental value of at least £10; in 1884 it was extended to counties.

1867 *Times* 20 Mar. 9/4 The total omission of the Lodger Franchise from the present multifarious and omnivorous measure. **1884** *Act 48 Vict.* c. 3 §2 A uniform household franchise and a uniform lodger franchise..shall be established in all counties and boroughs.

lodgerdom ('lɒdʒədəm). [f. LODGER + -DOM.] Lodgers collectively; the world of lodgers; a district in which lodgers are common.

1905 *Daily Chron.* 6 Mar. 4/6 Even dingy Lodgerdom would disclaim the place. **1907** *Ibid.* 23 May 3/3 A very pleasant, humorous-pathetic story of lodgerdom. **1927** *Observer* 14 Aug. 6 Discomfort..that goes with the bondage of..lodgerdom.

lodges, variant of LOGIS.

lodging ('lɒdʒɪŋ), *vbl. sb.* Forms: see LODGE *v.*; also 4 **lugyne,** 6 **loggyne,** *Sc.* **ludgene, lugin(g, lugeing;** *pl.* 5 **loggeyns,** 6 *Sc.* **luggenis.** [f. LODGE *v.* + -ING[1].]

1. The action of the verb LODGE (in various senses).

1525 *Extracts Aberd. Reg.* (1844) I. 110 The auld statut maid for the ressayt and luging of strangaris. **1576** TURBERV. *Venerie* 141 There is not so muche skill to be used in lodgyng of a Bucke as in harboring of a harte. **1652** HEYLIN *Cosmogr., Scot.* 297 The custom of the Indians in giving to the Bramines the first nights lodging with their Brides. **1726** LEONI *Alberti's Archit.* I. 95 b, Houses..for the lodging of men, animals, or tools of agriculture. **1731** TULL *Horse-hoeing Husb.* xiii. (1733) 150 One Cause is the lodging or falling of Corn. **1884** *Manch. Exam.* 30 June 5/3 That the straw is short..is a great safeguard against 'lodging' in the event of heavy rainstorms.

†2. Dwelling, abode. Phr. ***to make, take (up) one's lodging***: to take up one's (temporary) abode.

*a***1300** *Cursor M.* 6212 Þis folk..innermar þe [*Gött.* þair] loging made. **1362** LANGL. *P. Pl.* A. XII. 44 His loggyng is with Lyf that lord is of erthe. *c***1375** *Sc. Leg. Saints* iii. (*St. Andreas*) 56 Þe house..quhar þai twa þare lugyne in þe towne can ma. **1390** GOWER *Conf.* III. 62 Thei take loggynge in the toun After the disposicion Wher as him thoghte best to duelle. *c***1450** *Merlin* 44 Go to a gode town and take thy logginge. **1535** COVERDALE *Song Sol.* vii. 11 Let vs go forth in to the felde, and take oure lodginge in the vyllages. **1601** HOLLAND *Pliny* (1634) I. 126 When he [*sc.* the Ganges] is once come into the flat plains and euen countrey..he taketh vp his lodging in a certain lake. **1611** BIBLE *Isa.* x. 29 They haue taken vp their lodging at Geba.

3. a. Accommodation for rest at night or for residence; now only, accommodation in hired rooms or in a lodging-house (often in phr. ***board and lodging***).

1432-50 tr. *Higden* (Rolls) IV. 465 To ȝiffe loggenge [L. *hospitium*] and other refreschenge to theyme. **1454** in *Paston Lett.* I. 265 The Duke of Somersetes herbergeour hath taken up all the loggyng that may be goten nere the Toure. **1533** BELLENDEN *Livy* (1901) 190 He was ressauit in lugeing with Attius Tulius. **1535** COVERDALE *John* i. 38 Rabbi Where art thou at lodginge? **1588** SHAKS. *L.L.L.* v. ii. 811. **1611** BIBLE *Judg.* xix. 15 There was no man that tooke them into his house to lodging. **1668** DAVENANT *Rivals* v. 48 My lodging it is on the Cold ground. **1776** ADAM SMITH *W.N.* (1869) I. I. xi. 172 After food, clothing and lodging are the two great wants of mankind. **1849** MACAULAY *Hist. Eng.* iii. I. 327 An

ample return for his food, his lodging, and his stipend. **1859** TENNYSON *Elaine* 171 An old, dumb, myriad-wrinkled man, Who let him into lodging.

†**b.** Dwelling accommodation, house-room.

1715 LEONI *Palladio's Archit.* (1742) I. 49 One may make more or less Lodging than I have here drawn, according as ..the master shall require.

†**c.** Material to lie or sleep on. *Obs.*

1683 TRYON *Way to Health* xvii. (1697) 402 Chaff-Beds, with Ticks of Canvas, and Quilts made of Wooll or Flocks to lay on them; which..is the most easie and pleasant Lodging that can be invented. **1691** RAY *Creation* II. (1722) 371 Their Feathers serve to stuff our Beds and Pillows, yielding us soft and warm Lodging.

4. *concr.* **a.** A place or building in which a person lodges or resides; a dwelling-place, abode; †a bedroom (*obs.*); †military quarters, encampment (*obs.*). (In the sense of 'temporary lodging-place', 'hired rooms', commonly superseded by the pl. ***lodgings***: see 5 b.)

(*castle*) *of lodgings*: (one) used as a residence.

13.. *E.E. Allit. P.* B. 887 þay lest of lotez logging any lysoun to fynde. **1375** BARBOUR *Bruce* VI. 1 The King is went till his luging. *c* **1380** *Sir Ferumb.* 3063 þanne þay gunne to pryke vaste toward hure logyngge. *c* **1450** *Merlin* 43 He come in to oure loigginge in Northumberlonde while we satte at oure mete. *a* **1533** LD. BERNERS *Huon* xi. 31 He was serchyd for in his logynge. **1538** LELAND *Itin.* (1745) I. 84 Raby is the largest Castel of Logginges in al the North Cuntery. *a* **1548** HALL *Chron., Hen. VII* 23 They that went before inquyred after ynnes and lodgynges as though they woulde repose them selfes there all nighte. **1583** *Leg. Bp. St. Androis* 659 The menstrallis and the bairdis..About his ludgene loudlie played. **1588** DR. A. PERNE *Will* in Willis & Clark *Cambridge* (1886) I. 28 The Colledge Librairie..to be newe builded at the east end of the Masters Lodginge longewayes towardes the Streate. **1596** SHAKS. *Tam. Shr.* Ind. i. 49 Burne sweet Wood to make the Lodging sweete. **1604** DRAYTON *Owle* 1105 And on each small Branch of this large-limb'd Oke, Their pretty Lodgings carelessly they tooke. **1618** BEAUM. & FL. *Loyal Subj.* II. v, The rest [of the rooms] above are lodgings all. **1637** J. TAYLOR (Water-P.) (*title*) The Carriers Cosmographie: or A Briefe Relation, of The Innes, Ordinaries, Hosteries, and other lodgings in or neere London. **1712** STEELE *Spect.* No. 264 ¶1 He lives in a Lodging of Ten Shillings a Week. **1798** *Monthly Mag.* VI. 436 'A lodging all within itself, with divers easements, to set', is the common stile of a bill for letting a house in Edinburgh. **1814** SCOTT *Ld. of Isles* v. xxi, In silvan lodging close bestow'd, He placed the page. **1823** GALT *Gilhaize* I. iii. 30 Going straight up the walk to the door of a lodging, to the which this was the parterre and garden. **1849** MACAULAY *Hist. Eng.* iv. I. 479 Hacket..had already secured every inn and lodging. **1883** R. W. DIXON *Mano* II. i. 63 His eye fell fiercely on me, when my way I found into his lodging.

transf. and *fig.* *a* **1586** SIDNEY *Apol. Poetrie* (Arb.) 29 Our degenerate soules made worse by theyr clayey lodgings. **1605** SHAKS. *Lear* II. ii. 179 Not to behold This shamefull lodging [*sc.* the stocks]. **1645** WALLER *A la Malade* 23 The breaches made In that faire Lodging [the body] still more clear Make the bright Guest your Soule appear. **1646** JENKYN *Remora* 10 Without it [Religion], Kingdoms are but ..lurking places for theeves, not lodgings for the pure God. **1658** SIR T. BROWNE *Hydriot.* iii. (1736) 31 Christians.. acknowledged their Bodies to be the Lodging of Christ. **1697** DRYDEN *Virg. Georg.* IV. 64 Plaister thou their chinky Hives with Clay, And leafy Branches o'er their Lodgings lay.

†**b.** The portion of space assigned to one man in a camp. *Obs.*

1598 BARRET *Theor. Warres* 155 Vnto euery man at Armes we will allow 8 lodgings; and vnto euery roome or lodging we will give 50 superficiall foote of ground.

†**c.** A ward in a hospital; a cell in a prison.

1612 *New Life Virginia* (1897) 9 An hospital with four-score lodgings, and beds already sent to furnish them. **1679–88** *Secr. Serv. Moneys of Chas. II & Jas. II* (Camd. Soc.) 133 For strengthening divers of the prison lodgings with iron bars, bolts, and locks.

†**d.** A square on a chess-board, as being the 'place' of a particular piece. *Obs.*

1562 ROWBOTHAM *Playe Cheastes* E iv b, Thou shalte cause thy knight to retyre to the lodging of thy Quene.

†**e.** *Hunting.* The lair of a buck, stag, etc. *Obs.*

a **1586** SIDNEY *Arcadia* I. (1590) 39 b, The stagge thought it better to trust to the nimblenes of his feete, then to the slender fortification of his lodging. **1610** GUILLIM *Heraldry* III. xvi. (1611) 147 They doe readilie discover..the Tracks, Fourmes, and lodgings of beasts of chase.

5. Specialized uses of the *plural.*

†**a.** Military quarters. *Obs.*

1475 *Bk. Noblesse* 69 The duc made redy the ordenaunce wyth shot of grete gounys amongys the rebells and shot of arowes myghtelye, that they kept her loggeyns. **1548** HALL *Chron., Hen. VIII* 28 For his other lodgynges he had great and goodly tentes of blewe. **1568** GRAFTON *Chron.* I. 8 The first inventer of the Portative tents or lodgings. **1614** RALEIGH *Hist. World* v. iii. 463 [They] fell vpon him, with hope to take him vnprepared, whilest he was making his lodgings. **1665** MANLEY *Grotius' Low-C. Warres* 839 Lodgings were made for the Souldiers under Ground in the Form of Trenches. **1677** HUBBARD *Narrative* 55 Very cold Lodgings, hard Marches, Scarcity of Provision.

b. A room or rooms hired for accommodation and residence in the house of another (in mod. usage, not in an inn or hotel).

1640 D'EWES in *Lett. Lit. Men* (Camden) 165, I have promised to take lodgings close by him in the Coven Garden. **1712–14** POPE *Rape Lock* IV. 118 Sooner shall grass in Hyde-park Circus grow, And wits take lodgings in the sound of Bow. **1751** EARL ORRERY *Remarks Swift* (1752) 21 He used to lye at night in houses where he found written over the door Lodgings for a penny. **1787** CHARLOTTE SMITH *Romance Real Life* I. 220 She discharged her lodgings..and went to another part of Paris. **1849** THACKERAY *Pendennis* lxvii. (1863) 585 The house may be yours: but the lodgings are mine and you will have the goodness to leave them. **1861** MRS. J. H. RIDDELL *City & Suburb* II. vi. 107 Life in lodgings, at the best of times, is not a peculiarly exhilarating state of existence.

c. An official residence. Now the name given to the houses of the heads of certain Oxford colleges. (Cf. quot. 1588 in 4, and LODGE *sb.* 8.) Also ***Judges' lodgings***: the house which (in some assize towns) is occupied by the judges during the assizes.

1661 WOOD *Life* 3 May, They all went to the warden's lodgings, and gave him possession. **1826** *Act 7 Geo. IV*, c. 63 §1 Provisions..for providing Lodgings for the Accommodation of His Majesty's Judges of Assize. **1827** *Oxford Guide* 38 Queen's College... Over the west cloister are two stories, containing..the Provost's Lodgings [etc.]. **1895** *Strand Mag.* Mar. 320 The judge's lodgings are usually a fine old house set apart for the purpose.

6. *attrib.* and *Comb.*, as ***lodging-hunting***, ***-lease***, ***-letter***, ***-place***, ***-seeker***; **lodging-car** *U.S.*, 'a car fitted with bunks for hands at work on a railway line' (Knight *Dict. Mech., Suppl.*); †**lodging-chamber** = LODGING-ROOM b; †**lodging-fellow**, one who shares the same lodgings with another; **lodging-hall** *U.S.*, a lodging-house; **lodging-money**, an allowance made by government to all officers and soldiers for whom there is not sufficient accommodation in barracks (1872–6 Voyle *Milit. Dict.*); **lodging paper**, a handbill advertising lodgings; **lodging turn**, an occasion or period for which a railway employee has to lodge at his place of destination before returning to his place of departure. Also LODGING-HOUSE, -ROOM.

1645 EVELYN *Diary* (1879) I. 220 The hall, chapell, and great number of *lodging chambers are remarkable. **1687** DR. SMITH in *Magd. Coll.* (O.H.S.) 162 Lodging-chambers. *a* **1490** BOTONER *Itin.* (1778) 374 Sir Phelip Braunche [etc.] ..apud le sege de Roun; fuerunt le *logeyng felowys. **1860** J. G. HOLLAND *Miss Gilbert's Career* xii. 208 We left Arthur Blague..sitting on his bed in the *lodging-hall. **1879** 'EDNA LYALL' *Won by Waiting* ix, It was certainly *lodging hunting under difficulties. **1802–12** BENTHAM *Ration. Judic. Evid.* (1827) II. 483 For each distinct species of contract let a distinct species of paper be provided,..as for instance ..*lodging-lease paper. **1851** MAYHEW *Lond. Labour* I. 366 A *lodging-letter..will..drive keen bargains for plates, dishes, or wash-hand basins and jugs. **1802** C. JAMES *Milit. Dict.*, *Lodging money. **1817** JANE AUSTEN *Sanditon* vii, in *Minor Works* (1954) 402 No fewer than three *Lodging Papers staring me in the face at this very moment. **14..** *Epiph.* in *Tundale's Vis.* (1843) 116 Whyll thei slepped at her *loggyng place Ther com an angell apperyng with grette lyght. **1611** BIBLE *Josh.* iv. 3 In the lodging place where you shall lodge this night. **1878** J. BULLER *40 years in N.Z.* 70 In a small rush church we met with a lodging-place. **1885** R. L. & F. STEVENSON *Dynamiter* 99 A large number of *lodging-seekers. **1952** *Ann. Reg. 1951* 15 Economy measures, some of which (such as more *lodging turns) had caused serious strikes. **1955** *Ann. Reg. 1954* 30 About two-thirds of the.. footplate men..came out on strike against the introduction of new 'lodging turns', i.e. nights spent, usually in railway hostels, away from home.

lodging ('lɒdʒɪŋ), *ppl. a.* [f. LODGE *v.* + -ING².] That 'lodges' or rests upon something; said *Naut.* of a horizontal in contradistinction to a 'hanging' or vertical knee.

1567 TURBERV. *Ovid's Epist.* P vij b, Full oft vpon thine armes my lodging necke I lay. **1769** FALCONER *Dict. Marine* (1780) s.v. *Knee*, Knees are either said to be lodging or hanging. *Ibid.* s.v. *Decks*, The horizontal or lodging knees, which fasten the beams to the sides. **1874** THEARLE *Naval Archit.* 40 Lodging knees have not been fitted of late years to H.M. ships.

'lodging-house. A house, other than an inn or hotel, in which lodgings are let.

1766 SMOLLETT *Trav.* I. viii. 139, I was directed to a lodging house at Lyons, which being full they shewed us to a tavern. **1814** BISSET *Guide to Leamington* 23 Every house in Leamington (the Author's and two others excepted) are appropriated as Lodging or Boarding Houses. **1838** DICKENS *Nich. Nick.* xvi, One street of gloomy lodging-houses. **1891** C. JAMES *Rom. Rigmarole* 94 Elise, old, worn, haggard, and dying in a common lodging-house close by.

attrib. *c* **1815** JANE AUSTEN *Persuas.* (1833) I. xi. 300 Captain Harville did his best to supply the deficiencies of lodging-house furniture. **1848** DICKENS *Dombey* vi, Lodging-house keepers were favourable in like manner.

b. *transf.* and *fig.*

1851 BORROW *Lavengro* xcviii. (1900) 534 It seems all the drains and sewers of the place run into that same salt basin ..on which account the town is a famous lodging-house of the plague. **1858** J. MARTINEAU *Stud. Chr.* 206 Temporary settlers and mercantile agents..to whom Italy was a lodging-house rather than a home.

'lodging-room. †**a.** *nonce-use.* Space in which to dwell. **b.** A sleeping apartment, bedroom. (Now *local.*)

1571 GOLDING *Calvin on Ps.* xlvii. 4. 183 If after the bringing of the Ark into the Temple, there had appered none other hygher truth: it had bin but as a chyldish toy to lodge vp god in that narrow lodging roome [L. *in angusto illo domicilio Deum locari*]. **1615** *Manch. Crt. Leet Rec.* (1885) II. 300 One Chambʳ or lodginge Roome. **1694** DRYDEN *Love Triumph.* IV. i. 65 The Lodging Rooms are furnisht with Loam: and bare Mattresses are the Beds. **1722** DE FOE *Col. Jack* (1840) 257 She..bade her speak to the innkeeper to show her to her lodging-room. **1800** DOR. WORDSW. *Let.* 10 Sept. in Lee *Life* (1886) 66 We have one lodging-room, with two single beds. **1823** P. NICHOLSON *Pract. Builder* 438 Mezzanines..are exceedingly convenient for servants, lodging-rooms, powdering-rooms, wardrobes &c. **1849** *Ex. Doc. 31st U.S. Congress 1 Sess. House* No. 5. II. 1089 One hewed-log lodging-room for hired men. **1906** *Springfield* (Mass.) *Republ.* 7 Feb. 2 Lodging Rooms to Let.

attrib. **1885** *Sheffield Telegr.* 20 June, Lodging-room furniture.—Mahogany Dressing Table [etc.].

lodgis, -ys(e, variants of LOGIS.

‖**lodh** (ləʊd). Also 8 load. [Hindi *lodh.*] The bark of the East Indian shrub, *Symplocos racemosa*, used in dyeing. Also ***lodh-bark***.

1781 KERR in *Phil. Trans.* LXXI. 381 To make the silk hold the colour, they boil a handful of the bark called Load in water. **1848** in CRAIG.

lodicle, var. LODICULE.

lodicule ('lɒdɪkju:l). *Bot.* Also lodicle ('lɒdɪk(ə)l). [ad. L. *lōdīcul-a*, dim. of *lōdix* coverlet.] A green or white scale, the lowest part of a grass flower.

1864 OLIVER *Elem. Bot.* I. v. 53 Note also [in Wheat] 2 very minute scales, called lodicules, representing a perianth, inserted under the ovary. **1888** *Encycl. Brit.* XXIV. 531/2 Within the pale[a] are two minute, ovate, pointed, white membranous scales called 'lodicles'. **1900** L. H. BAILEY *Bot.* 146. **1968** F. W. GOULD *Grass Systematics* ii. 55 Lodicules play a role in the opening of the flower at anthesis.

lodlike, -ly, obs. forms of LOATHLY.

lodomy, obs. form of LAUDANUM.

lodsterne, obs. form of LOADSTAR.

loe, obs. form of LO, LOW.

lœllingite: see LÖLLINGITE.

lœmography, lœmology: see LOIM-.

loenge, variant of LOANGE *Obs.*

loeri, loes, var. ff. LORY, LOSE *sb.*, praise.

loerie ('lʊrɪ). *S. Afr.* Also loorie, lourie. [Afrikaans, f. Du. *lori* LORY.] = TOURACO.

1798 A. BARNARD *Jrnl.* in A. W. C. Lindsay *Lives of Lindsays* (1849) III. 408, I began to collect my Cape trifles for my friends at home,—some beautiful loories alive—some still more beautiful swallows dead. **1810** W. J. BURCHELL *Jrnl.* 7 Dec. in *Trav. S. Afr.* (1822) I. ii. 20 In the aviary, I saw the *Touracoo*, called *Loeri* by the colonists. **1812** ANNE PLUMPTRE *Lichtenstein's S. Africa* I. 195 The *cuculus persa*, a beautiful bird, called by the colonists *loeri* or *luri*. **1850** J. S. CHRISTOPHER *Natal* 33 The beautiful and soft-voiced loerie, the golden cuckoo, the green pigeon..and many others too numerous to particularise. [**1908** *East London* (Cape Province) *Dispatch* 4 Dec. 4 The *vlei-lourie*, perhaps better known hereabouts as the 'rain-bird', the natives regarding it as a weather prophet.] **1932** *Discovery* July 230/2 The Louries, magnificent in green, blue and carmine ..nest outside the door of the mission [at Kilimanjaro]. **1950** *Cape Argus Mag.* 18 Mar. 7/7 Loeries with their beautiful crimson-and-green plumage fill the air with their liquid call. **1957** V. W. TURNER *Schism & Continuity in Afr. Soc.* x. 293 The woman may dream that her dead relative has appeared to her equipped like a hunter, wearing the red wing-feather of a lourie in her hair. **1971** *Eveing Post* (Port Elizabeth, S.A.) *Suppl.* 12 June 5 When we think of birds in general, it is the pleasanter members of that enormous family that come to mind—the brilliantly-plumaged sunbird, the dove, the loerie.

loess ('ləʊɛs, Ger. lœs). *Geol.* Also löss, *erron.* loëss. [a. Ger. dial. *lösz.*] A deposit of fine yellowish-grey loam which occurs extensively from north-central Europe to eastern China, in the American mid-west, and elsewhere, esp. in the basins of large rivers, and which is usually considered to be composed of material transported by the wind during and after the Glacial Period. Also *attrib.*

1833 LYELL *Princ. Geol.* III. 151 There is a remarkable alluvium filled with land-shells of recent species..which we may refer to the newer Pliocene era. This deposit is provincially termed 'Loess'. **1873** J. GEIKIE *Gt. Ice Age* xxxii. 453 Underneath the vast deposits of löss belonging to the last cold period. **1879** LUBBOCK *Sci. Lect.* v. 141 The antiquities..are usually found in beds of gravel and loam, or, as it is technically called, 'loëss'. **1882** F. RICHTOFEN in *Geol. Mag.* IX. 302, I believe I am correct in stating that, among those who have had extensive experience in Loess regions, all who have pronounced an opinion of late years are agreed that sub-aërial deposition is the only mode of origin by which all its peculiar features can be easily explained. **1882** R. K. DOUGLAS *China* vi. 135 The huge tract of loess country in northern China. **1906** *Westm. Gaz.* 4 Dec. 2/1 North of the river [*sc.* the Hwang Ho] we come into the land of the loess, a loose light soil of prodigious fertility and the joy of the agriculturist. **1938** C. L. WHITTLES tr. *Reifenberg's Soils Palestine* ii. 25 Microscopic examination shows that loess consists mainly of extremely small particles of quartz together with calcareous particles which frequently, from their markings, etc., have been derived from fossils. **1972** J. G. CRUICKSHANK *Soil Geogr.* ii. 59 During the deglaciation phases of the Pleistocene glaciations, wind-blown silt was deposited on a spectacular scale in extensive, stoneless loess.

loessial ('lœsɪəl), *a.* [f. LOESS + -IAL.] Composed of loess.

1928 *Bull. Amer. Soil Survey Assoc.* IX. 34 These [*sc.* glacial soils] include the till, moraine, drumlin..and other typical forms and a portion of the loessial deposits. **1974** *Nature* 22 Mar. 320/2 Silt, in excess of that which could be derived from weathering of the substrata and generally considered loessial, is found in many British soils.

loessic ('lœsɪk), *a.* [f. LOESS + -IC.] = LOESSIAL *a.*

1909 in *Cent. Dict.* Suppl. **1940** *Nature* 6 July 14/1 In periglacial regions such arid episodes are represented by loessic deposits. **1952** F. E. ZEUNER *Dating Past* (ed. 3) vi. 158 The Middle Older Loess of the section is a complex of loessic hillwash material derived from higher up the slope, and of brecciated loess with large molluscan shells, interrupted by a brown soil.

lœwigite, lœwite: see LÖWIGITE, LÖWEITE.

†**lof.** *Obs.* Forms: 1 lof, loob, 2–4 lof, 3 *Orm.* loff, 3–5 lofe, 4–5 loue, 5 loff, 6 *Sc.* loif. [OE. *lof* masc. = OFris., OS. *lof* neut. (Du. *lof*), OHG. *lob* neut., masc. (MHG. *lop*, inflected *lob-*; mod.G. *lob* neut.), ON. *lof* neut. (Sw. *lof*, Da. *lov*):—OTeut. type **lobo-*, f. the root **lob-*, *lub-*: see LOVE *sb.*[1]]

1. Praise.

Beowulf 1536 Swa sceal man don, þonne he æt guðe ȝegan þenceð longsumne lof. *c* **725** *Corpus Gloss.* (Hessels) 122 *Ymnus*, loob. *c* **1175** *Lamb. Hom.* 7 Drihten þu dest þe lof of milc drinkende childre muðe. *c* **1200** ORMIN 3379 Si Drihhtin upp inn heoffness ærd Wurrþminnt & loff & wullderr. *c* **1375** *Sc. Leg. Saints* xxxvi. (*Ioh. Baptista*) 1 In lofe of patriarkes al, and of þame þat we prophetis cal. **1456** SIR G. HAYE *Law Arms* (S.T.S.) 2 Till him be gevin honoure lof and glore. *c* **1560** A. SCOTT *Poems* (S.T.S.) xxix. 18 Thair hairtis ar sett wᵗ sittelness, For loif and not for lufe. *a* **1568** *Bannatyne Poems* (Hunter. Club) 223 Leill loif, and lawte lyis behind.

2. Price, value.

c **1200** *Trin. Coll. Hom.* 213 þe sullere lat sumdel of his lofe .. þe beggere ecneð his bode [etc.]. *c* **1205** LAY. 18190 þer to he læide muchel lof.

3. *Comb.*: **lof-ȝeorn** *a.*, desirous of praise; **lof-like** *a.*, worthy of praise.

c **1175** *Lamb. Hom.* 103 þe seofeðe sunne is icweðen *Iactancia* þet is idelȝelp on englisc þenne mon bið lof-ȝeorn. *a* **1300** *E.E. Psalter* xcv[i]. 4 For mikel Laverd, swith loof-like to se; Aghfulle over alle goddes es he.

lof(e, obs. or var. ff. LOAF, LOVE, LUFF.

loff(e, obs. f. LAUGH, LOAF, LOVE, LUFF.

lo-fi ('ləʊ'faɪ). *colloq.* [Repr. *low fidelity*, after HI-FI.] Sound reproduction less good in quality than 'hi-fi'. Also *attrib.* or as *adj.*

1958 *Observer* 15 June 14/6 For heaven's sake let us have the real Bob Cats, even in lo-fi, and let the record companies make their issues under that kind of policy. **1967** *Sat. Rev.* (U.S.) 29 July 53 Despite Mr. Kolodin's warning of the 'lo-fi', we would urge the purchase of this set as a significant item in Toscanini's recorded legacy. **1968** *Which?* Oct. 312/1 You can buy your hi-fi equipment one piece at a time, and play it through the 'lo-fi' parts of, say, your old radio. **1970** *Daily Tel.* 16 Mar. 24/3 It was because of the cassette's 'lo-fi' that Philips first attacked the bottom end of the market. **1970** J. EARL *Tuners & Amplifiers* v. 100 The medium-frequency a.m. system is .. possibly adequate for 'lo-fi' reception on small transistor sets.

lofsom, -sum, obs. ff. LOVESOME.

†**'lof-song.** *Obs.* Forms: α. 1 lofsang, 2 lof-songe, 3 *Orm.* loffsang, 1–4 lof-song. β. 3 loft-song(e, 4 loft-sang. [f. LOF + SONG.] A song of praise, a hymn. Hence †**lofsonger**, a psalmist.

c **900** tr. *Bæda's Hist.* III. xii. (Schipper) 1288 Fram þære tide þæs uhtlican lofsonges. *c* **1175** *Lamb. Hom.* 99 We wurðiað þes halȝen gastes to-cume mid loftsonge seofen daȝes. *Ibid.* 153 þe lof-songere [*c* **1200** *Trin. Coll. Hom.* loft-songere] seið *Per mille meandros agitat quieta corda.* *c* **1200** ORMIN 18024 And þurrh Judea tacnedd iss Loffsang Drihhtin to wurrþenn. *a* **1240** *Sawles Warde* in *Cott. Hom.* 261 A gleadunge wið-ute met murie loft song ant liht-schipe. *c* **1320** *Cast. Love* 29 Vche mon ouȝte wᵗ al his mihte, Lof-song syngen to God ȝerne.

loft (lɒft, -ɔː-), *sb.* Also 2–7 lofte, 5–6 looft, *Sc.* loyft, 6 loaft, lofte, 7 laught. [Late OE. *loft*, a. ON. *loft* neut., air, sky, upper room (in Icel. written *lopt*; Sw., Da. *loft* upper room, garret), cognate with OE. *lyft* masc., neut., fem.: see LIFT *sb.*[1]]

†**1.** Air, sky, upper region. *Obs.*

a **1000** *Hexameron of St. Basil* (Norman 1849) 10 Heo ne lið on nanum ðinge ac on lofte heo stynt. *a* **1175** *Cotton Hom.* 217 Heo is .. loftes leom and all hiscefte ȝimston. *c* **1200** *Trin. Coll. Hom.* 222 He makeð þe fisses in þe sa, þe fueles on þe lofte. *c* **1290** *S. Eng. Leg.* 35/55 Huy comen fleo oppe in þe loft ouer þe apostle seint Ieme. *c* **1330** *King of Tars* 686 Let seche bi lofte and bi grounde, Yif eny Cristene prisoun mighte be founde. **1362** LANGL. *P. Pl.* A. I. 88 He is a-counted to þe gospel on grounde and on lofte [1377 aloft]. *c* **1400** *Destr. Troy* 3719 Two iuste goddis, Lyuond in the lofte with lordships in heuyn. **1590** SPENSER *F.Q.* I. i. 41 And ever-drizling raine upon the loft.

†**2.** Phrases. *Obs.*

a. *on, upon (the) loft*: (*a*) = ALOFT in various senses; (*b*) in a high voice, loudly.

a **1100** *O.E. Homilies* (Napier) in *Mod. Lang. Notes* (1889) May 278/2 þæt stænene cweartern stod eall on lofte fram þære eorðan. *a* **1300** *K. Horn* 974 Reynild, mi doȝter, þat sitteþ on þe lofte. *c* **1375** BARBOUR *Bruce* XIII. 652 And it, that wondir lawch wer ere, Mon lowp on loft in the contrere. *c* **1400** *Sowdone Bab.* 3250 Therfore thoue shalt be honged on lofte. *c* **1420** *Anturs of Arth.* 619 þene his lemmane one loft skrilles and skrikes. *c* **1450** *Two Cookery Bks.* 78 Couche hem in a faire chargeour, and ley the partrich on loft. *c* **1470** *Golagros & Gaw.* 875 Than said he loud vpone loft [etc.]. **1508** DUNBAR *Tua Mariit Wemen* 147 Than all thai leuch apon loft, with laitis full mery. **1535** STEWART *Cron. Scot.* II. 194 On ane litter, that buir him hie on loft. *a* **1584** MONTGOMERIE *Cherrie & Slae* 362, I luikit vp on loft.

b. *by loft*: in height.

1377 LANGL. *P. Pl.* B. XVIII. 45 And ȝit maken it .. Bothe as longe and as large bi loft [1393 aloft] & by grounde.

c. *of loft*: from above. Also used for ALOFT.

c **1375** *Cursor M.* 22143 (Fairf.) Thoner of loft falle sal he gere & trees þrali blomis bere. *a* **1400–50** *Alexander* 791* Ledes hym [the horse] forth of þat loge and þen of-lofte lepys.

d. *over loft* = ALOFT.

c **1430** LYDG. *Min. Poems* (Percy Soc.) 6 Midde of the brigge ther was a toure over loft.

3. a. An upper chamber, an attic; an apartment or chamber in general; *spec.* (see quot. 1593).

a **1300** *Cursor M.* 12277–79 In a loft was in þe tun, A child þar kest a-noiþer don, Vte of the loft vnto þe grund. *c* **1340** *Gaw. & Gr. Knt.* 1096 3e schal lenge in your lofte, & lyȝe in your ese. *c* **1385** CHAUCER *L.G.W.* 2706 *Hypermnestra*, And at the wyndow lep he fro the lofte. **1489** *Ld. Treas. Acc. Scotl.* (1877) I. 119 For the mendin of the Thesauraris houss dure and the loyft that byrnt. **1490** CAXTON *Eneydos* xxi. 77 Whan thou were in the highe lofte of thy grete towres thou sawe the see alle troubled. **1568** GRAFTON *Chron.* I. 159 While they were there .. sodeynly the Ioystes of the loft fayled, and the people fell downe. **1593** *Anc. Rites Durham* (Surtees ed. 2) 86 The mounckes dyd al dyne together at one table, in a place called yᵉ lofte, wᶜʰ was in yᵉ west end of yᵉ fratree aboue yᵉ seller. **1611** BIBLE *1 Kings* xvii. 19 He .. caried him vp into a loft, where he abode, and laide him vpon his owne bed. **1756** WESLEY *Wks.* 1872 II. 364, I preached at five in a large loft. **1874** C. GEIKIE *Life in Woods* ii. 33 One end of my sister's loft was packed .. with part of it [furniture].

b. The apartment over a stable, usually appropriated to hay and straw. (Cf. HAY-LOFT.)

1530 PALSGR. 240/2 Lofte for haye or corne, *garnier*. **1607** NORDEN *Surv. Dial.* v. 238 Some kind of loft or hay tallets, as they call them in the west. **1629** *S'hertogenbosh* 41 There was slain a Burger .. as he was a measuring the Priests Corne in the Laught. **1741** in A. Laing *Lindores Abbey*, etc. xiv. (1876) 137 *note*, [He] carried off the whole slates, lofts, jests and timber thereof. **1816** SCOTT *Old Mort.* v, A wooden bed, placed in a loft half-full of hay.

c. A pigeon-house. Hence, a flock (of pigeons).

1735 J. MOORE *Columbarium* 3 Let your Loft be large enough to contain the Number of Pigeons you intend to keep. **1876** FULTON *Bk. Pigeons* 53 We cannot advise any one to breed more than twelve pairs of Carriers in any one loft, however large. **1899** *Westm. Gaz.* 20 Nov. 8/2 A loft of the best Yorkshire racing pigeons was established at Durban some time ago.

4. A gallery in a church or public room. (Cf. *organ-loft, rood-loft.*)

1504 *Ld. Treas. Acc. Scotl.* (1900) II. 429 The loftis in the chapel of Strivelin. **1562** TURNER *Baths* 2 a, Certayn loftes shoulde be bylded ryght over som parte of the fyrst or principall bath. **1573** *Satir. Poems Reform.* xli. 92 3e Lords also, that dois frequent The loft in Sanct Geills Kirk. **1666** PEPYS *Diary* 15 Nov., I also to the ball, and with much ado got up to the loft, where with much trouble I could see very well. **1712–30** G. GUTHRIE *Memor.* (1900) 71 They provided a good large house .. and plenished it very well with Pulpit, lofts and Pews. **1849** THACKERAY *Pendennis* xv. (1885) 132 The two schools had their pews in the loft on each side of the organ. **1893** SIR A. GORDON *Earl Aberdeen* 191 The minister .. turned to the loft in which 'my Lord' was seated.

5. a. A floor or story in a house. *Obs.* exc. *U.S.* 'one of the upper floors of a warehouse' (*Cent. Dict.*).

1526 TINDALE *Acts* xx. 9 A certayne yonge man named Eutichos .. fell doune from the thyrde lofte and was taken vp deed. **1536** BELLENDEN *Cron. Scot.* (1821) II. 476 Ane woman, havand commiseratioun on this Duk, leit meill fall doun throw the loftis of the toure, be quhilkis his life wes certane dayis savit. **1600** HAKLUYT *Voy.* (1810) III. 439 The houses are very great, and the least of them with one lofte aboue head, and some of two and of three loftes. *a* **1661** FULLER *Worthies*, *Buckinghamsh.* I. 135 Our Roger .. finished the ground-room and second loft.

†**b.** The deck or half-deck of a ship. *Obs.*

c **1470** HENRY *Wallace* IX. 120 Go wndyr loft. *Ibid.* 143 Wallace .. On the our loft kest him quhar he stud.

†**c.** The ceiling or flooring of a room. *Obs.*

1596 SPENSER *F.Q.* V. vi. 27 All sodainely the bed, where she should lie, By a false trap was let adowne to fall Into a lower roome, and by and by The loft was raysd againe, that no man could it spie. **1603** OWEN *Pembrokesh.* (1891) 78 This perswadeth me to be one of the causes whie in ould buildinges are found so manye vawtes and soe few loftes, for that in these watrye walles the beames in shorte tyme doe rott & soe the loftes decaye.

d. A place where sails are manufactured; = *sail-loft*.

1938 T. NORTH *Yacht Sails* xii. 113 When a new sail leaves the loft it should be perfect. **1959** W. R. BIRD *These are Maritimes* iii. 92 He learned his trade in his father's loft in West Pubnico. .. There are only two other 'lofts' in the Maritimes. **1973** *Observer* (Colour Suppl.) 3 June 18/3 His personal sails are no better than his customers'. 'They go through the loft as part of the system.'

†**6.** A layer, stage, stratum. Also *transf.* of the lateral branches of trees at varying heights. *Obs.*

1535 COVERDALE *1 Esdras* vi. 25 With a lofte of tymbre of the same countre, yee with a new loft. **1567** MAPLET *Gr. Forest* 81 b, The Elephant espying him sitting on the loft of a tree, runneth [etc.]. **1601** HOLLAND *Pliny* I. 536 Let them climb vp higher to the vpper boughs, leauing alwaies vpon euery loft or scaffold .. one branch of the old hard wood, and another young imp or twig. **1673** MILTON *Vacat. Exerc.* 42 And hills of Snow and lofts of piled Thunder. **1686** GOAD *Celest. Bodies* II. ii. 162 We often times see Clouds as in several Stories, Lofts or Scenes, one over another.

7. *Golf.* **a.** Slope (in the head of the club) backwards from the vertical. **b.** The action of 'lofting'; also, a lofting hit or stroke. **c.** *fig.* Elevation, uplift.

1887 SIR W. G. SIMPSON *Golf* 159 A much lofted iron is very difficult to use. .. A medium amount of loft is best. **1890** HUTCHINSON *Golf* (Badm. Libr.) 200 For short approaches, there are weighty authorities who assert that the distances are most easily controlled by loft and spin. **1925** *Brit. Weekly* 12 Nov. 159/2 We need more loft in our thinking than our fathers had.

8. *attrib.* and *Comb.*, as (sense 3) *loft-floor, -room, -window*; **loft-bombing** (see quot. 1956); **loft-dried** *a.*

1956 *Time* 24 Sept. 36 Its [*sc.* a low-flying fighter-bomber's] bombing can be made extremely accurate, but if it uses any ordinary bombing system, such as dive-bombing, it is apt to be vaporized by the fireball springing up under its tail. The best way to avoid this misadventure is '*loft-bombing', which uses the speed of the airplane to make the bomb behave like an artillery shell. *Ibid.*, The main advantage of loft-bombing .. is not the range of the bomb, but the time that it spends in the air while the airplane is making its get-away. **1960** *Aeroplane* XCIX. 352/2 The first L.A.B.S. manœuvre was complete by an A3D, in which loft bombing had been pioneered by Cmdr. H. F. Lang. **1888** CROSS & BEVAN *Paper-making* 145 They are then sized, if required, by dipping them into a solution of gelatine: again slightly pressed, and hung up on lines or poles to dry. Such paper is called *loft-dried. **1419** *Mem. Ripon* (Surtees) III. 147 In grundwallyng et emend. unius *loftflore et alios defectus. **1852** DICKENS *Bleak H.* xxxi, A bed in the wholesome *loft-room by the stable. *a* **1600** in *Evergreen* (1761) I. 191 The Ladys lukit frae their *loft Windows, God bring our Men weil back again.

†**loft,** *a. Obs. rare.* [app. deduced from ALOFT, as LIVE *a.* from *alive.*] Raised aloft, elated, elevated.

The first quot. may belong to LOFTY *a.*, of which it would then be the earliest example.

14.. AUDELAY *Poems* (MS. Douce 302) lf. 29/2 Semele to se, o bold corage, Louele & lofte of his lenage. **1542** SURREY *Death Sir T. Wyatt* 27 in *Tottel's Misc.* (Arb.) 29 In neyther fortune loft, nor yet represt. **1557** *Tottel's Misc.* (Arb.) 235 Absence my frende workes wonders oft. Now bringes full low that lay full loft.

Comb. **1590** R. W. *3 Lds. & Ladies Lond.* G 2 b, Downe with your point, no loft borne Lances here By any stranger be he foe or friend.

loft (lɒft, -ɔː-), *v.* [f. LOFT *sb.*]

†**1.** *trans.* To insert a layer of planks in (a building) so as to separate the lofts or stories; to ceil or floor. Also, to furnish with a loft or upper story. *Obs.*

1563 *Stanford Chwardens' Acc.* in *Antiquary* XVII. 169/1 For Loftyng the Toure & laying the plankes beneyth. **1598** STOW *Surv.* xxx. (1603) 277 It is now lofted through, and made a store house for clothes. *a* **1615** *Brieue Cron. Erlis Ross* (1850) 20 He caused to joist and loft the chamber. **1634–5** BRERETON *Trav.* (Chetham Soc.) 43 The largest .. coy-house I have seen, lofted overhead to lay corn. **1646** *Virginia Stat.* (1823) I. 337 That they [houses] be lofted with sawne boardes and made with convenient partitions.

transf. **1601** BP. W. BARLOW *Eagle & Body* (1609) B ij b, See how many Eagles haue lofted their Ayryes .. with the gobbets and morsels pluckt and carried from those Bodies.

2. To store (goods or produce) in a loft. *rare.*

1518 *Waterf. Arch.* in *10th Rep. Hist. MSS. Comm.* App. v. 326 No freman .. shall house, loft, nor seller ony straunge marchant goods. **1785** WASHINGTON *Notes* Writings 1891 XII. 229 The remainder of the Crop which was measured and lofted must be accted. for by the Overseer. **1951** E. SEWELL in *Duckett's Reg.* July 105 Blenheims will keep till Christmas, if lofted cool and dry.

3. a. *Golf*, etc. To hit (a ball) into the air or strike it so as to lift it over an obstacle. Also, to hit the ball over (an obstacle).

1857 H. B. FARNIE *Golfer's Manual* in *Golfiana Misc.* (1887) 173 The player should practise lofting his ball directly into the hole. **1881** FORGAN *Golfer's Handbk.* 30 You may boldly take your Light Iron and try to 'loft' your ball over the other, and so drop or roll into the hole. **1887** SIR W. G. SIMPSON *Golf* 138 If there is a high face to loft. *Ibid.* 151 If taken .. too clean, it [the lofted iron] will skim it a hundred yards with the force that would have lofted it fifty. **1927** [see INFIELDER 2]. **1950** W. HAMMOND *Cricketers' School* facing p. 96 W. Hammond hits a 6; position correct for lofting the ball over mid-on. **1963** *Times* 8 June 4/2 Soon afterwards Hunte lofted Allen over mid-off for four, before Allen for the second time in the day, had the last word with a batsman trying to attack him. **1970** *Globe & Mail* (Toronto) 28 Sept. 18/6 Rookie Paul McKay lofted the final Hamilton punt, a high 47-yard spiral. **1972** J. MOSEDALE *Football* vi. 91 Tittle lofted the ball .. over the heads of the other players. **1974** *News & Reporter* (Chester, S. Carolina) 22 Apr. 10-A/6 Guy Meadow lofted a sacrifice fly and Clayton, up for the second time in the inning, singled again.

absol. **1887** *Blackw. Mag.* Nov. 697 You may loft in the sand and be little the worse. **1890** HUTCHINSON *Golf* (Badm. Libr.) 243 He takes the light iron into his hand .. to loft over .. that sluggish little burn.

b. *transf.* and *fig.*

1883 J. MARTINE *Reminisc. Haddington* 120 He [*sc.* a goat] .. thought nothing of pouting and 'lafting' folk. **1902** BARRIE *Little White Bird* xxiv. 282 We had lofted him out of the story, and did very well without him. **1948** G. H. JOHNSTON *Death takes Small Bites* v. 110 Her eyes, bright with strain, lofted above the murals to the great range behind the town. **1952** [see *day-beam* s.v. DAY *sb.* 23 a, b]. **1960** L. P. GARTNER *Jewish Immigrant* ix. 251 The banner of the Hebrew national .. renaissance was lofted. **1971** D. MEIRING *Wall of Glass* vii. 57 He would .. loft his bag up the hotel stairs himself .. instead of handing it to the orderly.

4. To keep (pigeons) in a 'loft' or flock.

1898 *Westm. Gaz.* 25 Oct. 5/1 They [pigeons] could be 'lofted' in Whitehall or in Pall-mall.

Hence **'lofter** *Golf*, a lofting-iron.

1892 *Pall Mall G.* 15 Mar. 3/1 A ridge of snow.. necessitated in many cases the use of a 'lofter' instead of the regulation 'putter'.

lofted (ˈlɒftɪd, -ɔː-), *ppl. a.* [f. LOFT *sb.* and *v.* + -ED.]

1. Of a house: †**a.** Ceiled or floored (*obs.*). **b.** (*Sc.* and *north. dial.*) Having one or more stories above the ground floor.

1549 *Compl. Scotl.* xi. 96 That na Scottis man suld duel in ane house that vas loftit, bot rather in ane litil cot house. **1639** *Declaration* in *Athenæum* 19 July (1890) 99/2 The dwelling howse of her brother..was all well lofted and boarded over wth oken boards. *c* **1730** BURT *Lett. N. Scotl.* (1760) II. xxii. 205 If any one has a Room above, it is by way of Eminence called a lofted House. **1814** SCOTT *Wav.* xix, A lofted house, that is a building of two stories. *c* **1856** *Denham Tracts* (1892) I. 343 The house being what in those districts [Northumberland] is termed lofted.

2. *Golf*, etc. **a.** Of a cleek or club: Made with a 'loft' (see LOFT *sb.* 7 a). **b.** Of a stroke: That 'lofts' the ball.

1887 SIR W. G. SIMPSON *Golf* 158 Certainly a more lofted cleek might be used. *Ibid.* 159 If a half-topped shot travels further than a lofted one over ordinary turf, the club has too much pitch. **1890** HUTCHINSON *Golf* (Badm. Libr.) 122 Using..an exceptionally lofted club to obtain the same result. *Ibid.* 200 The lofted approach is not a fancy shot.

c. Of a ball: hit into the air.

1904 *Daily Chron.* 20 Aug. 9/5, I saw a lofted ball..miss the head of a player in front by not more than six inches. **1955** *Times* 29 June 4/3 He made the winning hit, a lofted straight four, on the stroke of time. **1963** *Times* 27 May 5/3 The same player scored from a 30-yard penalty, while Ramsden replied with a well lofted hit from 40 yards.

loftily (ˈlɒftɪlɪ, -ɔː-), *adv.* [f. LOFTY *a.* + -LY².] In a lofty way or manner (see the adj.).

1548 ELYOT *Dict.*, *Elate*, proudely, loftyly. **1590** SPENSER *F.Q.* II. x. 1 Or who shall lend me wings, with which from ground My lowly verse may loftily arise, And lift it selfe vnto the highest skies? **1596** BP. W. BARLOW *Three Serm.* ii. 89 And yet they bear themselues so loftily, as if they could liue without gods blessing and help. **1607** MARKHAM *Caval.* II. (1617) 82 To ride your horse..amongst short gorsse or whinnes is exceeding good,..to make a horse trot loftilie and cleanly. **1641** BEST *Farm. Bks.* (Surtees Soc.) 4 A tuppe, if hee bee kept loftily and in lust, is sayd to be sufficient for fortie or fiftie ewes. **1665** BOYLE *Occas. Refl.* Wks. (1848) p. xxi, A Strain worthy of the same pen, that so loftily describes the Destruction of Troy. **1744** OZELL tr. *Brantome's Sp. Rhodomontades* 65 The Emperor..carried it..loftily on account of his late Victory. **1883** *Eng. Illustr. Mag.* Nov. 74/1 Ely cathedral..stands loftily grave and majestic. **1883** R. W. DIXON *Mano* II. iv. 74 We came upon him riding loftily.

loftiness (ˈlɒftɪnɪs, -ɔː-). [f. LOFTY *a.* + -NESS.] The attribute of being lofty, in senses of the adj.

1548 ELYOT *Dict.*, *Elatio*, loftynesse, hautenesse. **1560** BIBLE (*Genev.*) *Isa.* II. 17 The loftines of men shalbe abased. **1607** MARKHAM *Caval.* II. (1617) 198 Gallop the straite ring about with a little more firme loftinesse. **1610** BARROUGH *Meth. Physick* IV. ii. (1639) 219 Their face is red, and there is a loftinesse of the pulses. **1663** BUTLER *Hud.* I. i. 91 His speech, In loftiness of sound, was rich. *a* **1677** BARROW *Wks.* (1686) III. xxii. 248 He [Solomon] did himself compose above a thousand songs; whereof one yet extant declareth the loftiness of his fancy. **1781** GIBBON *Decl. & F.* xxxi. III. 218 The loftiness of these buildings..was the cause of frequent and fatal accidents. **1822** LAMB *Elia* Ser. I. *On Some Old Actors*, Bensley..threw over the part an air of Spanish loftiness. *a* **1840** J. H. NEWMAN *Hist. Sk.* Ser. III. (1873) 194 Martin gained more by loftiness than others by servility. **1884** *Manch. Exam.* 27 Nov. 5/5 A..chamber..160 feet long..and of a corresponding loftiness. **1885** SIR W. M. CONWAY in *Mag. Art* Sept. 463/1 Men..of dignity of thought and loftiness of feeling.

b. Used as a mock title of dignity.

1599 *Broughton's Let.* vii. 21 Were he so vnlearned, as your Loftines makes him.

lofting (ˈlɒftɪŋ, -ɔː-), *vbl. sb.* [f. LOFT *sb.* or *v.* + -ING¹.]

1. *concr.* A roofing, ceiling, or flooring. *Obs.* exc. *dial.* and in *Mining.*

1536 BELLENDEN *Cron. Scot.* (1821) II. 388 Quhen ony preis of horsmen come abone the said fowseis the lofting suld brek. **1603** OWEN *Pembrokesh.* (1891) 76 Tymber to serve for loftinges and roffes. **1640–1** *Kirkcudbr. War-Comm. Min. Bk.* (1855) 66 That the sklait roofe of the hows and batlement thairof be taken downe with the lofting thairof. **1851** GREENWELL *Coal-trade Terms Northumb. & Durh.* 35 *Lofting*, wood..placed upon the top of the ordinary balks or crowntrees used in timbering through a fallen place, for the purpose of keeping up the loose stones.

2. *Golf.* The action of the vb. LOFT (sense 3).

1895 *Westm. Gaz.* 4 Feb. 8/2 Golfers who can skate should be proficient at bandy, in which lofting is a most desirable accomplishment.

3. *Aeronaut.* The action of a loftsman.

1939 *Jrnl. R. Aeronaut. Soc.* XLIII. 140, I should like to mention two or three operations coming under the control of the engineering department... One of these is the mould loft. The art of lofting as it is now generally followed in American aircraft production was, of course, borrowed from the ship-building industry. **1956** W. A. HEFLIN *U.S. Air Force Dict.* 304/1 *Lofting*, as applied to airplanes, the act or process of laying out full-size drawings of an airplane that is to be built, of designing and making templates, etc. **1972** *Lebende Sprachen* XVII. 73/2 The production of aircraft part drawings, preparation of magnetic tape for machine-tool control, and many lofting, drawing and checking jobs are to be automated.

4. *attrib.* and *Comb.*: **lofting-iron**, a golf-club used to loft a ball.

1887 SIR W. G. SIMPSON *Golf* 22 Lofting irons are more light-headed. **1892** *Century Mag.* Aug. 606 The approach should always be a lofting-stroke.

lofting (ˈlɒftɪŋ), *ppl. a.* [f. LOFT *v.* + -ING².] Of a stroke in golf: that lofts.

1905 *Westm. Gaz.* 25 Aug. 3/1 Why to go for a low-running shot or for a high lofting shot, respectively.

loftless (ˈlɒftlɪs, -ɔː-), *a.* [f. LOFT *sb.* + -LESS.] That has no loft or upper story.

1891 ATKINSON *Moorland Par.* (1892) 22 These two one-roomed loftless dens.

† **ˈloftly**, *adv. Obs. rare*⁻¹. [f. LOFT *a.* + -LY².] = LOFTILY *adv.*

1598 SIDNEY *Astrophel & Stella* Song VI. v, Musicke more loftly [1591 lustie] swels In speeches nobly placed.

loftsman (ˈlɒftsmən). *Shipbuilding* and *Aeronaut.* [Cf. *mould-loft* s.v. MOULD *sb.*³ 17.] One who reproduces a draughtsman's specifications for a ship or aircraft in full size on the floor of a mould-loft.

1901 T. WALTON *Steel Ships* vii. 178 After the plans of a vessel have been prepared in the drawing office, the first man who takes her in hand is the loftsman. His domain is the mould loft, where..he proceeds to reproduce the 'lines' plan upon the loft floor to actual size. *Ibid.* 180 The loftsman's work is to rectify any..irregularities, and to produce perfect harmony and fairness in all lines which make up the form of the hull. **1909** WEBSTER, *Loftsman*, one who lays down the lines of a ship in a shipbuilding loft. **1921** *Dict. Occup. Terms* (1927) §668 s.v. *Scriever*, *Loftsman*, lays off from plans, on wooden floor,..outlines of ship frames and plates, [etc.]. **1947** *Aircraft Engin.* July 222/1 The loftsman would simply pass a curve pleasing to the eye through a few points determined by the designer. **1955** *Times* 13 July 2/5 Aircraft Loftsmen for the Aircraft Full-scale Layout Section. **1957** *Technology* Apr. 53/2 At a single step the loftsman will become a white collar worker, no longer grubbing about on hands and knees on a dirty floor marking off a life-size scrieve board. **1974** *Sci. Amer.* May 16/3, I worked for eight years..as lumberman, machinist, machine designer and loftsman before retiring to college.

lofty (ˈlɒftɪ, -ɔː-), *a.* [f. LOFT *sb.* (in *on loft, aloft*) + -Y¹.

The word occurs first in figurative applications, and even when literal has always had an emotional or rhetorical character.]

1. Extending to a great height in the air; of imposing altitude, towering.

Said of mountains, trees, buildings, rooms; not of persons, though *lofty stature* is a common phrase.

1590 SPENSER *F.Q.* I. ix. 13 Forwearied with my sportes, I did alight From loftie steed. **1593** SHAKS. *Lucr.* 1167 The Barke pild from the loftie pine, His leaues will wither, and his sap decay. **1611** BIBLE *Isa.* lvii. 7 Vpon a loftie and high mountaine hast thou set thy bed. **1646** CRASHAW *Assumpt. Our Lady* 31 Each loftyest tree Bowes low'st his leauy top, to look for thee. **1756–7** tr. *Keysler's Trav.* (1760) I. 508 The baptistery..is a large and lofty octangular structure. **1774** GOLDSM. *Nat. Hist.* (1776) I. 146 The plains are extensive; and the mountains remarkably lofty. **1791** COWPER *Iliad* II. 268 Antenor's valiant son Of loftiest stature. **1823** RUTTER *Fonthill* 19 The loftiest apartment which domestic architecture can present, probably, in the world! **1835** THIRLWALL *Greece* I. 21 The lofty and precipitous rock..on which stood the citadel of Corinth. **1884** PAE *Eustace* 6 Fading away into the loftier Highland Mountains.

†**b.** *lofty tricks*: acrobatic feats, tumbling. *Obs.*

[**1567** TURBERV. *Ovid's Epist.* P iiij b, Then did my wanton tricks and lofty mounting, more..delight thy minde.] **1603** FLORIO *Montaigne* I. xxv. **1622** B. JONSON *Masque of Augurs.*

c. Of flight: Soaring to a great height. Of the brow: Imposingly high.

1738 WESLEY *Psalms* CXLVII. ii, Ye Birds of lofty Wing, On high his Praises bear. **1798** LANDOR *Gebir* II. 154 The kingly brow, arched lofty for command.

2. In figurative and immaterial applications.

a. Haughty, overweening, proud. †Const. *of.*

c **1485** *Digby Myst.*, *Mary Magd.* 944 When I loke on þis lady, I am lofty as the lyon. **1561** T. HOBY tr. *Castiglione's Courtyer* III. (1577) Rj a, Bearing themselues lofty of their beautye and worthynesse. *c* **1586** C'TESS PEMBROKE *Ps.* CXXXI, A lofty hart, a lifted eye Lord thou dost know I never bare. **1611** BIBLE *Isa.* ii. 12 The day of the Lord of hostes shall bee vpon euery one that is proud and loftie. **1681** DRYDEN *Abs. & Achit.* 516 Cow'ring and Quaking at a Conq'ror's Sword, But Lofty to a Lawful Prince Restor'd. **1712–3** POPE *Guardian* No. 4 ¶2 A lofty gentleman, whose air and gait discovered when he had published a new book. **1787** MAD. D'ARBLAY *Diary* 21 Aug., He appeared very lofty, and highly affronted. **1868** FREEMAN *Norm. Conq.* (1876) II. App. 601 Several particulars are worked in with a lofty contempt for chronology. **1873** BLACK *Pr. Thule* viii. 123 Inclined to treat everybody..with a sort of lofty good humour.

absol. **1597** J. PAYNE *Royal Exch.* 28 Sum tymes the prowde and loftie do walke there to be sene in there heyght and braverie. **1611** BIBLE *Isa.* v. 15 The eyes of the loftie shall be humbled.

b. Exalted in dignity, rank, character, or quality. Of expectations, aims, desires: Directed to high objects.

[**14..**: see LOFT *a.*] **1548** ELYOT *Dict.*, *Excelsus*, hyghe or great, lofty, haute, noble. **1586** DAY *Eng. Secretary* (1625) 129 Their estate (being peraduenture loftie, and of power to command or sway ouer vs) will not admit by writting to intermeddle with their actions [etc.]. **1611** BIBLE *Isa.* lvii. 15 Thus saith the High and loftie One that inhabiteth eternitie. **1776** GIBBON *Decl. & F.* xii. I. 246 These lofty expectations were, however, soon disappointed. **1849** MACAULAY *Hist. Eng.* iv. I. 501 The courage of the survivor was sustained by an enthusiasm as lofty as lofty as any that is recorded in martyrology. **1857** BUCKLE *Civiliz.* I. xi. 646 How can they, constantly occupied with their lofty pursuits have leisure for such inferior matters? **1874** MAHAFFY *Soc. Life Greece* viii. 257 The moral teaching of Euripides, of Socrates, and of the more lofty Sophists, was making sure and silent progress. **1877** E. R. CONDER *Bas. Faith* v. 203 It is man's nobility, not his defect, that the most lofty and commanding part of him is his moral nature. **1878** E. JENKINS *Haverholme* 61 Heir to one of the loftiest of the English peerages.

c. Of compositions or utterances (hence occas. of writers or speakers): Elevated in style or sentiment; sublime, grandiose.

1565 COOPER *Thesaurus* s.v. *Effero*, *Elatis verbis intensa oratio*, a lofty and highe stile. **1577** J. KNEWSTUB *Confutation* (1579) **5 b, They set forth their trifling and halfepeny doctrines with loftie and high phrases of speech. **1590** SPENSER *F.Q.*, *Verses to Ld. Buckhurst*, In loftie numbers and heroicke stile. **1612** BRINSLEY *Lud. Lit.* 194 They may proceed..from the lowest kind of verse in the Eclogues, to something a loftier in the Georgics. **1637** MILTON *Lycidas* 11 He knew Himself to sing, and build the lofty rhyme. **1640** WILKINS *New Planet* (1707) I. 148 His Book [Job] is more especially remarkable for lofty Expressions. **1692** ATTERB. *On Ps. l.* 14, Serm. 1726 I. 32 Therefore is the hymn it self so lofty and moving. **1704** POPE *Windsor For.* 280 The shades where..lofty Denham sung. **1875** JOWETT *Plato* (ed. 2) III. 88 About which [astronomy] I am willing to speak in your lofty strain.

d. Of majestic sound.

1596 SHAKS. *1 Hen. IV*, v. ii. 98 Sound all the lofty Instruments of Warre. **1814** WORDSW. *White Doe Ryl.* I. 38 With one consent the people rejoice Filling the church with a lofty voice.

†**3.** Of the wind, the sea: = HIGH 10. *Obs.*

1600 HAKLUYT *Voy.* (1810) III. 236 It is very hard to find it when the wind is lofty. **1745** P. THOMAS *Jrnl. Anson's Voy.* 146 Such a lofty and dangerous Sea as I have seldom seen.

4. *dial.* 'Massive, superior' (*Eng. Dial. Dict.*, referring to Sleigh, *Derbysh. Gloss.* 1865). †Of sheep: Stout, in good condition.

1641 BEST *Farm. Bks.* (Surtees Soc.) 2 Yett is it a custome with many..to clowte their shearinges to hinder them from tuppinge, that by this meanes they may make them more lofty sheepe. **1778** PRYCE *Min. Cornub.* 324 Lofty Tin, in contradistinction to Floran Tin, for Lofty Tin is richer, massive, and rougher.

5. *Comb.* **a.** In syntactical combs. with pres. pples., as ***lofty-looking***, ***-sounding***; **b.** in parasynthetic derivatives, as ***lofty-headed***, ***-humoured***, ***-lineaged***, ***-minded***, ***-necked***, ***-paced***, ***-peaked***, ***-plumed***, ***-roofed***, ***-windowed***. Also † **lofty-like** *adv.*, as if placed on high.

1610 HOLLAND *Camden's Brit.* I. 290 That with their *loftie-headed tops reach to the cloudy skie. **1611** COTGR., *Madamoiselle de cinquante pour cent*,..may be applyed to the *loftie-humored wife of an extorting Vsurer. **1604** S. GRAHAME *Pass. Spark* E 4, Man climbes aboue the course of such conceate, That *loftie-like, they loath to look below. **1871** BROWNING *Balaust.* Wks. 1896 I. 655/1 Both..*lofty-lineaged, each of us Born of the best. **1755** SHEBBEARE *Lydia* (1769) I. 283 His great Creator..beholds with equal favour the creeping ant, and *lofty-looking Briton. **1611** COTGR., *Orgueilleux*,..hautie, *loftie-minded. **1791** BOSWELL *Johnson* I. 93 *note*, That lofty-minded man. **1697** DRYDEN *Virg. Georg.* III. 125 The Colt, that for a Stallion is design'd *loftyneck'd, Sharp headed, Barrel belly'd, broadly back'd. **1796** COLERIDGE *Lett.* (1895) 210 He does not possess opulence of imaginative *lofty-paced harmony. **1844** J. TOMLIN *Mission. Jrnls.* 272 A *lofty-peaked mountain. **1591** SHAKS. *1 Hen. VI*, v. iii. 25 Now the time is come, That France must vale her *lofty-plumed Crest. **1848** B. D. WALSH *Aristoph. Clouds* I. iv, *Lofty-roofed fanes, and marble-built portals. **1777** POTTER *Æschylus*, *Prometheus chain'd* 23 Woes like these Are earnings of the *lofty-sounding tongue. **1777** T. WARTON *Poems* 63 Along the *lofty-window'd hall The storied tapestry was hung.

†**lof-word.** *Obs.* Forms: 4 luffe-, luve-, 4–5 love-word. [f. LOF + WORD. The forms show a confusion with LOVE *sb.*¹] Praise.

a **1300** *Cursor M.* 2545 Mikel it was þat luffeword þan þat abram gat o mani man. *Ibid.* 10614 Sua wex hir loue-word and hir fame. *Ibid.* 28383, I..to gleumen cald and to ioglere, In tent þai suld me luueworde bere.

log (lɒg), *sb.*¹ Forms: 4–6 logge, 7–8 logg, 6– log. [Late ME. *logge*; of obscure origin; cf. the nearly synonymous CLOG *sb.*, which appears about the same time.

Not from ON. *lág* felled tree (f. OTeut. **lǣg-*, ablaut-variant of **leg-* LIE *v.*¹), which could only have given **low* in mod.Eng. The conjecture that the word is an adoption from a later stage of Scandinavian (mod.Norw. *laag*, Sw. dial. *låga*), due to the Norwegian timber-trade, is not without plausibility, but is open to strong objection on phonological grounds. It is most likely that *clog* and *logge* arose as attempts to express the notion of something massive by a word of appropriate sound. Cf. Du. *log* clumsy, heavy, dull; see also LUG *sb.* and *v.* In sense 6 the word has passed from Eng. into many other langs.: F. *loch*, Ger., Da. *log*, Sw. *logg*.]

I. *gen.*

1. a. A bulky mass of wood; now usually an unhewn portion of a felled tree, or a length cut off for use as firewood. *in the log*: in an unhewn condition.

1398 TREVISA *Barth. De P.R.* XVII. xlv. 630 þe frute þereof fallеþ..but he be..itrailled wt logges [L. *lignis*] & yardes as it were a vine. **1481–90** *Howard Househ. Bks.* (Roxb. Club) 355 My Lord paied..[for] iij. lodes of belet, and iij. lodes of logges..xviij. *s.* **1490** CAXTON *Eneydos* xlvi. 139 The hardy knyghtes..casted vpon theym grete logges wyth sharpe yron atte the ende. **1525** *Churchw. Acc. Heybridge, Essex* (Nicholls 1797) 173 Paide to Adrewe of Braxted, for a logge 6*d.* **1540–54** CROKE *Ps.* (Percy Soc.) 44 If one of his hate, Byfore the logge or stone wold ley, His purpose shall cumme all to late. **1545** *Rates Custom-ho.* b, Dogion logges the

hundreth peces vis. viiid. **1561** T. NORTON *Calvin's Inst.* I. 23 b, I was somtime a fig tree log, a block that serued for nought. *c* **1600** DAY *Begg. Bednall Gr.* II. ii. (1881) 38 Wol't say I lye? thou hadst as good eat a load of logs. **1610** SHAKS. *Temp.* III. i. 17, I would the lightning had Burnt vp those Logs that you are enioynd to pile. *a* **1700** DRYDEN *Ovid's Met.* VIII. *Meleager* 253 There lay a Log unlighted on the Hearth. **1800** COLQUHOUN *Comm. Thames* i. 27, 250 of the Timber Ships are laden with Logs. **1850** TENNYSON *In Mem.* cvii, Bring in great logs and let them lie, To make a solid core of heat. **1857** THOREAU *Maine W.* (1894) 196 The largest pine belonging to his firm..was worth ninety dollars in the log. **1900** *Blackw. Mag.* July 53/2 The smouldering ends of logs..gave forth a tingling smoke which filled the hovel.

b. *fig.* and in similative phrases. Said, e.g., of a vessel floating helplessly (cf. mod.G. *log sein* to float helplessly), of an inert or helpless person. †*a log in one's way*: a stumbling-block, obstacle. *to have a log to roll*: see LOG-ROLLING. *as easy* (or *simple*) *as falling* (or *rolling*) *off a log*.

1579-80 NORTH *Plutarch, Annibal* (1595) 1148 Anniball.. knew that this great ouerthrow..would also be a great logge in his way. *c* **1600** *Timon.* I. ii. (Shaks. Soc.) 7 Thou logg, thou stock, thou Arcadian beast. **1602** MARSTON *Antonio's Rev.* v. iv. Wks. 1856 I. 137 The saplesse log, that prest thy bed With an unpleasing waight. **1622** R. HAWKINS *Voy. S. Sea* 213 In this conflict, having lost all her mastes, and being no other then a logge in the sea. **1812** BYRON *Ch. Har.* II. xx, The flapping sail haul'd down to halt for logs like these! **1839** *Picayune* (New Orleans) 29 Mar. 2/2 He gradually went away from the Lubber, and won the heat, 'just as easy as falling off a log'. **1865** *Daily Tel.* 13 Nov. 5/2 The *New York Daily News* may have its log to roll and its axe to grind as well as other folks. *c* **1880** 'MARK TWAIN' *Speeches* (1923) 97 A man who could have elected himself Major-General Adam or anything else as easy as rolling off a log. **1886** STEVENSON *Treas. Isl.* II. vii. 59, I must have slept like a log. **1898** *Daily News* 19 May 7/6 Mr. Gladstone..pathetically remarked that he was now like a log. **1900** *Longm. Mag.* June 134 [He] struck Bill who fell like a log on the dusty road. **1904** 'A. DALE' *Wanted: a Cook* 207 It was so easy that the inelegant simile of 'rolling off a log' impressed me as being absolutely justifiable. **1913** F. H. BURNETT *T. Tembarom* xvii. 223, I dropped into it by accident,..and that made it as easy as falling off a log. **1949** N. MARSH *Swing, Brother, Swing* iv. 67 Don't keep asking if I can understand things that are as simple as falling off a log. **1973** *Times* 10 Feb. 11/3 Acting? said Ernest Borgnine. Why, there was nothing to it, really. 'For me,' he said, 'it's as easy as falling off a log.'

c. *Mining.* (See quot.)

1860 *Eng. & For. Mining Gloss.* (S. Staffordsh. Terms), *Log*, or *Baby*, a balance weight, placed near the end of the pit-rope, to prevent its running back over the pulley. **1881** in RAYMOND *Mining Gloss.*

†**d.** See quot. (perh. confused with LUG). *Obs.*

1669 J. WORLIDGE *Syst. Agric.* (1681) 348 *Log*, a term used in some places for a cleft of Wood, and in some places for a long piece or Pole, by some for a small Wand or Switch.

†**e.** Phr. *to hang upon the log*: ? to be slow in finding sale. *Obs.*

1655 GURNALL *Chr. in Arm.* I. 106 Something sure is in it, that Impostors finde such quick return for their ware, while Truth hangs upon the log.

†**f.** In Old St. Paul's, a block or bench on which serving-men sat. *Obs.*

1609 DEKKER *Guls Horn-bk.* iv. 18. **1639** MAYNE *City Match* III. iii. 31.

g. *Surfing.* (See quots.)

1967 J. SEVERSON *Great Surfing* Gloss., *Log*, a very heavy surfboard. **1970** *Studies in English* (Univ. of Cape Town) I. 28 His board may be described as a barge or a log, both of which describe a big cumbersome surfboard, one that is difficult to manoeuvre.

2. a. A heavy piece of wood, fastened to a man's or beast's leg, to impede his movements. †Also *fig.*

1589 *Pasquil's Return* B, Her Maiestie layeth such a logge vppon their consciences, as they ought not beare. *a* **1592** H. SMITH *Wks.* (1867) II. 483 Wedlock, with wife and children clogs, The single life, lust's heavier logs. **1837** HT. MARTINEAU *Soc. Amer.* III. 193 They [insane negroes] were kept in out-houses, chained to logs. **1843** DICKENS *Mart. Chuz.* xxviii, Here I am tied like a log to you. **1853** MARSDEN *Early Purit.* 324 W. L...was brought up before the same court with his chains and log at his heels.

b. A military punishment now abolished. (See quots.) *Obs.* exc. *Hist.*

1830 in *Rep. Commiss. Milit. Punishments* (1836) 312 The log..is a punishment..which cannot be sanctioned and is henceforth strictly forbidden. **1846** H. MARSHALL *Milit. Misc.* 205 The Log.—This punishment consisted of a log, or a large round shot, or shell, which was connected to a delinquent's leg by means of a chain; and he was obliged to drag or carry this about with him.

3. *King Log*: the log which Jupiter in the fable made king over the frogs; often used as the type of inertness on the part of rulers, as contrasted with the excess of activity typified by 'King Stork'.

1675 CROWNE *Country Wit* v. Dram. Wks. 1874 III. 114 Go, sir! manage him, whilst I handle Log, the second King of frogs, that follows him. **1761** J. WESLEY *Jrnl.* 18 Jan., The custom began in the reign of King Log. **1766** CHESTERF. *Let. to Son* 11 July, I have always owned a great regard for King Log. **1901** M. J. F. McCARTHY *Five Y. Irel.* xxiii. 320 They prefer King Log to King Stork.

4. *pl. Australian slang.* A gaol or lock-up. (Formerly built of logs. Cf. *log-house.*)

[**1802** G. BARRINGTON *Hist. N.S. Wales* 184 The governor resolved on building a large log prison both at Sydney and Paramatta.] **1888** 'ROLF BOLDREWOOD' *Robbery under Arms* xxv. (1889) 193 Let's put him in the logs. **1890** —— *Miner's Right* xxx. 273 No bail allowed either, or of course you needn't have been ten minutes in the logs.

5. A piece of quarried slate before it is split into layers.

1725 D. EATON *Let.* 13 Feb. (1971) 9 The reason why the slaters could not go on was bycause they could not run their slate out of the log for want of frost. **1939** *Evening News* 2 Feb. 8/6 When the slate is taken to the surface it is called 'log', and is then left in the 'slate-patch' to wait for the frost to break it into layers. **1946** N. WYMER *Eng. Country Crafts* x. 108 Then the props are systematically removed, and the slate is allowed to crash down, breaking up into large slabs which can be levered up and roughly broken by hammer into 'logs'. **1975** *Times* 9 Aug. 12/7 Collyweston slate is unusual in that it is produced by the action of frost on the stone logs.

II. *Naut.* and derived senses.

6. An apparatus for ascertaining the rate of a ship's motion, consisting of a thin quadrant of wood, loaded so as to float upright in the water, and fastened to a line wound on a reel. Hence in phrases *to heave, throw the log*, (*to sail* or *calculate one's way*) *by the log*. Said also of other appliances having the same object.

1574 BOURNE *Regiment for Sea* xiv. (1577) 42 b, They hale in the logge or piece of wood again, and looke how many fadome the shippe hath gone in that time. **1644** MANWAYRING *Sea-mans Dict.* s.v. *Logg-line*, One stands by with a Minut-glasse, while another out of the gallery lets fall the logg. **1669** STURMY *Mariner's Mag.* IV. ii. 146 We throw the Log every two Hours. **1686** J. DUNTON *Lett. fr. New-Eng.* (1867) 28 Being about 50 Leagues off the Lizard..we began to sail by the Log. **1719** D'URFEY *Pills* III. 305 Heave the Logg from the Poop. **1769** FALCONER *Dict. Marine* (1780) A a 4, It is usual to heave the log once every hour in ships of war. **1805** SIR E. BERRY in Nicolas *Disp. Nelson* VII. 118 *note*, During the chace we ran per log seventy miles. **1833** MARRYAT *P. Simple* (1834) I. xii. 156 It's now within five minutes of two bells, so we'll heave the log and mark the board. **1863** BARING-GOULD *Iceland* 178 Calculating their way by the log. **1876** *Catal. Sci. App. S. Kens.* 54 Patent Log, for measuring speed at sea; used in H.M. Navy.

7. a. Short for LOG-BOOK. A journal into which the contents of the log-board or log-slate are daily transcribed, together with any other circumstance deserving notice.

1825 H. B. GASCOIGNE *Nav. Fame* 79 Then down he goes his daily Log to write. **1850** SCORESBY *Cheever's Whaleman's Adv.* vi. (1859) 86 To fix the localities of whales' resorts by the comparison of the logs of a vast number of whalers. **1883** STEVENSON *Treas. Isl.* IV. xviii, The captain sat down to his log, and here is the beginning of the entry.

transf. **1875** R. F. BURTON *Gorilla L.* (1876) II. 176 Had the writers lived, they might have worked up their unfinished logs into interesting and instructive matter.

b. (See quot.)

1875 KNIGHT *Dict. Mech.*, *Log* (Steam-engine), a tabulated summary of the performance of the engines and boilers, and of the consumption of coals, tallow, oil, and other engineers' stores on board a steam-vessel.

c. = LOG-BOOK 3.

1882 in CASSELL.

d. Any record in which facts about the progress or performance of something are entered in the order in which they become known; e.g. (*a*) a record of what is found, or how some property varies, at successive depths in drilling a well; a graph or chart displaying this information; (*b*) a record kept by a lorry driver in which details of journeys are noted; (*c*) a record kept of what is broadcast by a radio or television station from moment to moment.

1913 *Jrnl. Geol.* XXI. 671 This company has prepared logs of various..salt wells. **1920** L. S. PANYITY *Prospecting for Oil & Gas* xiii. 162 It is the duty of the driller..to keep a record or log of the well. This consists in noting the various formations drilled through, the casing points, and the showings of water, oil or gas. **1924** G. W. GRUPP *Econ. Motor Transportation* ix. 187 Nothing is more interesting than..making..a motor-truck performance log. **1925** K. G. FENELON *Econ. Road Transport* 241 A daily log prepared by the driver of each vehicle, showing the nature of the work performed, the tonnage carried, the time taken, etc. **1937** *Printers' Ink Monthly* May 39/2 *Log*, an account of every minute of broadcasting, all errors being considered. An accurate journal required by law. **1956** *Nature* 21 Jan. 120/2 The study of these continuous velocity logs in conjunction with seismic reflexion records shot from the surface is leading to a better understanding of the origin of reflexions. **1957** M. R. J. WYLLIE *Fund. Electr. Log Interpretation* (ed. 2) II. 105 Even in dirty formations the neutron log can sometimes give a fairly good estimate of porosity. *Ibid.* 110 Logs which make use of the scattering of gamma-rays to determine the density of formations penetrated by boreholes..are rapidly being improved in efficiency. **1960** J. M. WELLER *Stratigr. Princ. & Pract.* xvii. 614 Electric logs consist of curves that are continuous records of self-potential and resistivity measured in wells and plotted against depth... In a general way..they indicate differences in lithologic characters of strata and many lithologic changes are shown with great precision. **1963** *Amer. Speech* XXXVIII. 44 *Log, log book*, the driver's daily report required by the I.C.C. **1965** W. S. BARRY *Airline Managem.* x. 149 Station logs report troubles that have occurred during embarkation or disembarkation. **1968** *Radio Communication Handbk.* (ed. 4) xx. 4/2 Log Keeping. The Post Office requires all amateurs to keep a log book containing full details of all transmissions... Entries must be made at the time of operation, and no gaps should be left in the log. **1974** *Sci. Amer.* May 133/3 These men filled out sleep logs (for pay) and answered many questions.

8. *Tailoring.* [*transf.* from 7] A document fixing the time to be credited to journeymen (who are paid nominally by the hour) for making each description of garment; the scale of computation embodied in this document.

1861 *Dunn's Tailor's Labour Agency Retrospect* 13 What is technically called a 'log' is agreed upon, that is a certain number of hours for every description of garment, and the wages fixed at so much per hour. **1868** *10th Rep. Trades Union Comm.* 17 We [operative tailors] wanted a uniform time-log. The masters prepared a time-log, and said to us, 'Here is the log, you must accept it as it is'.

III. *attrib.* and *Comb.*

9. a. simple attributive, as (sense 1) ***log-end***, ***-fire***, ***-mark***; (with the sense 'made of or constructed with logs') ***log barn***, ***barrack***, ***-booth***, ***-bridge***, ***building***, ***causeway***, ***-chamber***, ***chapel***, ***church***, ***city***, ***college***, ***-fence***, †***-guard***, ***heap***, ***-hut***, ***kitchen***, ***meeting-house***, ***pen***, ***pound***, ***prison***, ***-road***, ***room***, ***-shanty***, ***stable***, ***tavern***, ***tenement***, ***-tent***, ***-trap***, ***wall***, ***-way***; ('for use in dealing with logs') ***log-boom*** (BOOM *sb.*[2] 4), ***-car***, ***-chain***, ***-railway***, ***-sled***, ***-sleigh***, ***-stamp***; (sense 8) ***log prices***, ***-shop***; (in sense 'for use in dealing with logs') ***log skid***.

1795 *Pittsburgh Gaz.* 6 June 1/2 To be Sold..two cabins, a *log barn. **1845** S. JUDD *Margaret* I. iii. 12 On the east side of the road was a log barn. **1948** *Time* 11 Oct. 21/1 A country which still remembered Indians, wild turkeys, log barns, [etc.]. *a* **1861** T. WINTHROP *Life in Open Air* (1863) 32 All residents of Damville dwelt in a great *log-barrack. **1878** *Lumberman's Gaz.* 6 Apr., An addition to the wharf and a *log boom are being made. **1862** H. MARRYAT *Year in Sweden* II. 371 Two rows of weatherbeaten *log-booths. **1664** *First Cent. Hist. Springfield, Mass.* (1898) I. 316 Foure acres of low lands Northwestrly from the *logg bridge as it is called. **1806** Z. M. PIKE *Acct. Expeditions Sources Mississippi* I. App. 36 [The fur-trading establishment] at Lower Red Cedar Lake..consists of *log buildings. **1881** *Chicago Times* 11 June, The track upon which runs the *log-car. **1828** *Gore Gaz.* (Ancaster, Ontario) 18 Oct. 134/2 The stumps are all taken out—and the *log causeways, where these are necessary—are covered with a thick coat of earth. **1831** T. BUTTRICK in R. G. Thwaites *Early Western Trav.* (1904) VIII. 54 In some places, in low grounds, there would be log-causeways for a considerable distance. **1703** *Providence Rec.* (1894) VI. 224, 1 *Logg chaine. **1788** M. CUTLER in *Life* (1888) I. 401 We were turned into a hot, *log chamber, full of people. **1810** F. ASBURY *Jrnl.* (1821) III. 298 Saturday, at William Adams's *log-chapel I preached to a small assembly. **1847** F. PARKMAN in *Knickerbocker* XXIX. 313 We found the *log-church..belonging to the Methodist Shawanoe Mission. **1895** M. A. JACKSON *Mem. Stonewall Jackson* (ed. 2) 382 The little log church is..full. **1817** S. R. BROWN *Western Gaz.* 106 Vangeville,—A *log city..has fifteen or twenty old log houses. **1795** P. FRENEAU *Poems* 374 On the Demolition of a *Log-College. **1850** W. H. FOOTE *Sk. Virginia* 349 Could we..look into the school of the worthy pastor, then gaining its eminence as 'a log college'. **1659** GAUDEN *Tears Ch. Eng.* I. xiv. 122 The most heavy *log-end of Christs Cross is laid upon many of them. **1836** J. ABBOT *Way to Do Good* i. 24 They were stepping over a low place in the *log fence. **1878** BROWNING *Poets Croisic* I Praise the good *log-fire! Winter howls without. **1808** ASHE *Travels* I. 302 The town..has in its centre, the remains of an old *Log Guard. **1818** L. D. CLARKE in *Firelands Pioneer* (1920) XXI. 2324, I spread ashes where *log-heaps had been burned. **1819** E. DANA *Geogr. Sk. Western Country* 36 The Creoles never having before smelted, except by throwing the ore into log heaps. **1856** A. CARY *Married* 295 Having made a log-heap fire, Martin put the table-cloth about his shoulders. **1933** E. C. GUILLET *Early Life Upper Canada* 277 In new settlements during July the whole countryside was illuminated by the burning of log heaps. **1797** J. A. GRAHAM *Pres. State Vermont* 161 As in a former Letter I mentioned the *Log Hut, I will here.. give a short account of its construction. **1890** 'ROLF BOLDREWOOD' *Miner's Right* vi. 61 Log-huts, with the walls built American fashion of horizontal tree trunks. **1874** E. EGGLESTON *Circuit Rider* v. 56 The wide old *log-kitchen, with its loom in one corner. **1948** *Florida Hist. Q.* July 40 Close to many of the larger houses were log kitchens where cooking and eating took place. **1859** *Michigan Rep.* VI. 270 The Mill Company had given a list of *log-marks under section eight of the act. **1823** *Baptist Mag.* IV. 74 We have a good *log meeting-house on Salt Creek. **1789** M. L. WEEMS *Let.* in *M. L. Weems: Works & Ways* (1929) III. 148, I lodged in a *log-pen. **1832** *Louisville Directory* 102 The ditch was surmounted by a breast work of log pens filled with the earth obtained from the ditch. **1853** 'P. PAXTON' *Stray Yankee in Texas* 118 A fish spear is to him [*sc.* the old Texan] a groin,..a house no house, but a log-pen. **1737** in *Coll. New Hampsh. Hist. Soc.* (1863) VII. 358 A *log pound 30 ft. square, six feet high, with a good gate, and a lock and key. **1888** *Lancet* 26 May 1049/1 Tailors..obtaining '*log' prices—that is, the highest rate of wages. **1802** G. BARRINGTON *Hist. N.S. Wales* 184 (Morris), The governor resolved on building a large *log prison. **1845** C. M. KIRKLAND *Western Clearings* 212, I went to prison; nothing but a log prison. **1857** THOREAU *Maine W.* (1894) 125 A truck drawn by an ox and a horse over a rude *log-railway through the woods. **1819** F. WRIGHT *Views* (1821) 234 A *log road, or causeway, as it is denominated, is very grievous to the limbs. **1743** D. BRAINERD *Let.* 30 Apr. in J. Edwards *Acct. Life D. Brainerd* (1749) 201 It is a *Log-Room, without any Floor, that I lodge in. **1903** S. E. WHITE *Conjuror's House* x. 119 Virginia entered a small log room.. and sat down in a musty red armchair. **1847** H. HOWE *Hist. Coll. Ohio* 492 They fell to work..erecting bark huts and *log shanties. **1874** GREEN *Short Hist.* i. §3. 25 He made his way at last to a group of log-shanties in the midst of untilled solitudes. **1899** *Contemp. Rev.* Mar. 382 There are quite a number of Jewish coat makers working for 'private' or '*log' shops. **1923** *Log-skid [see BREAK-DOWN 3]. **1957** *N.Z. Timber Jrnl.* Oct. 73/2 *Log skids*, a platform on which logs are stacked in the forest to assist loading on to trucks. **1878** *Lumberman's Gaz.* 2 Feb. 89 He has constructed a road of ice ..on which the *log-sleds slip along readily. **1893** *Scribn. Mag.* June 706/2 The *log-sleighs have ten, twelve, and even fourteen-foot bunks, or cross beams, on which the load

rests. **1834** *Southern Lit. Messenger* I. 120 In the *log stable . . I saw a number of them. **1878** *Lumberman's Gaz.* 5 Jan., Wyburn's improved *log stamp is convenient for marking logs with the exact number of feet. **1810** F. CUMING *Sk. Tour Western Country* 44 We stopped to feed our horses at a small *log tavern. **1874** E. EGGLESTON *Circuit Rider* xvi. 147 Marton was conducted three miles down the river to a log tavern. **1829** J. F. COOPER *Borderers* III. i. 27 The *log tenement, the stacks, . . were sending forth clouds of murky smoke. **1841** —— *Deerslayer* (ed. 2) I. ii. 47 The furniture was of the strange mixture that it is not uncommon to find in the remotely situated log-tenements of the interior. **1748** H. ELLIS *Hudson's Bay* 154 Some of the People were employed in cutting Fire-Wood, others in building *Log-Tents. **1784** J. BELKNAP *Tour White Mts.* (1876) 13 We saw the . . *log-traps, which the hunters set for sables. **1840** *Knickerbocker* XVI. 247, I looked around on the bare *log-walls and ceiling. **1779** in F. Chase *Hist. Dartmouth Coll.* (1891) I. 562 To maintain said mills by repairing the present buildings . . and also the *log way and necessary mill houses. **1822** Logway [see *ground-hornet* (GROUND *sb.* 18 b)]. **1874** B. F. TAYLOR *World on Wheels* II. vii. 245 Days when, over the old road, ran the yellow mud-stained coach, . . pitching along its log-ways. **1973** A. PRICE in *Winter's Crimes* 5 202 The driver . . had driven the cart off the logway.

b. objective, as (sense 1) ***log-carrying, -driving, -hauling, -heaving, -raising; log-cutter, -hauler, -lumberer, -maker***; (sense 7) ***log-reading***. **c.** instrumental, as ***log-built, -lighted*** ppl. adjs. **d.** similative, as ***log-like*** adj., ***log-wise*** adv.

1835 C. F. HOFFMAN *Winter in West* I. 79 We stopped to breakfast at a low *log built shantee. **1937** *Discovery* Nov. 344/2 This sole surviving example of the log-built churches, once common in the forest region of Essex. **1898** *Daily News* 16 June 5/2 It is strange to hear that the aged poor are still at oakum-picking or *log-carrying. **1893** *Scribn. Mag.* June 710/2 At night he must get from the *log-cutters their count for the day. **1879** *Lumberman's Gaz.* 19 Dec., The dam will be used for flowage and *log-driving purposes. **1919** W. T. GRENFELL *Labrador Doctor* (1920) xiii. 233 The *log-hauler would not deliver the goods to the rotary saw. **1962** *Amer. Speech* XXXVII. 134 *Log hauler*, an engineer on a logging train. **1893** *Scribn. Mag.* June 706/2 There is great strife between the teamsters in making *log-hauling records. **1823** W. FAUX *Memorable Days Amer.* 180 *Log-heaving, that is, rolling trees together for burning, is done by the neighbours in a body, invited for the purpose. *a* **1847** ELIZA COOK *Gray-haired Dec.* iii, The *log-lighted hall. **1602** MARSTON *Antonio's Rev.* I. v. Wks. 1856 I. 86 A chaine that's fixt Onely to postes, and senselesse *log-like dolts. **1909** *Westm. Gaz.* 11 Aug. 5/1 The pulp-maker . . is not content, like the *log-lumberer, to remove the grown trees, but takes the young plants as well. **1880** *Lumberman's Gaz.* 7 Jan. 28 Next come the '*log-makers', working in gangs of three or four, each with its 'chief'. **1864** 'E. KIRKE' *Down in Tennessee* iii. 43 In April, 1862, he and his band came upon a party of neighbors collected at a *log raising in Fentress County. **1897** E. W. BRODHEAD *Bound in Shallows* 169 Law, the log-raisin's and corn-huskin's they used to have! **1901** *Blackw. Mag.* Oct. 476/1 The modern navigator has buried the best part of his astronomy under a heap of dead reckonings and *log-readings. **1879** BROWNING *Halbert & Hob* 37 So *logwise . . Was he pushed, a very log.

10. Special combs.: **log-basket**, a basket, or similar receptacle, for holding logs by a fire; **log-beam** (see quot.); **log-board**, a hinged pair of boards on which the particulars of a ship's log are noted for transcription into the log-book; **log-butter**, 'a drag-saw for butting, i.e. cutting off square the ends of logs' (Knight); **log-buttings**, the ends thus cut off; **log-camp** = *logging-camp* (see LOGGING *vbl. sb.*); **log-canoe**, one hollowed out of a single tree; **log-chip** = *log-ship*; **log-cock**, 'one of the many local names in North America of *Picus pileatus* (Woodpecker)' (Newton); **log-crop**, the quantity of logs hewn in one season; **log-deck** (see quot.); **log-drive** (see DRIVE *sb.* 3); **log-fish** a fish of the U.S. coast, *Lirus perciformis*; **log frame**, 'a name for a saw-mill' (Knight); **log-glass** (see quot. 1858); **log-head** = BLOCKHEAD 2; **log-headed** *a.*, having a head like a log; **log-house**, a house built of logs; in early use (*U.S.*) applied to a prison; also *attrib.* in *log-house quilting* (see quot.); **log-juice** *slang* [cf. LOGWOOD 2, *note*], cheap port wine; **log-knot**, a knot made in a log-line to indicate a specified length; **log-line**, a line of 100 fathoms or more to which the log is attached; also the sort of line used for this purpose; **log-man**, †(*a*) one employed to carry logs; (*b*) one employed in cutting and carrying logs to a mill (*local U.S.*); **log-paddock**, a small field fenced in with logs; **log-perch**, a freshwater fish, *Percina caprodes*, of N. America; **log-pocket**, a basin or pool in which logs collect; **log-reel** (see quot.); **log-rule** (see quot. 1905); **log-runner** *Austral.*, a ground-dwelling bird of the genus *Orthonyx* found in northern New South Wales, Queensland, and New Guinea; **log-running**, the operation of setting logs afloat down the side-streams, or conveying logs to the saw-mill; the operation of sending logs down a river; **log-scale** (see quot. 1905); **log sheet**, a log-book in which the driver of a commercial motor vehicle enters particulars of his working and rest hours; **log-ship**, also *log-chip* (see quot.); **log-slate**, a double slate used instead of the *log-board*; **log-work**, (*a*) the arrangement of logs in the walls of a house or other building; (*b*) the keeping of the log or log-book (sense 7).

1902 *Westm. Gaz.* 17 Dec. 8/2 A really nice *log-basket in wrought iron. **1972** *Country Life* 14 Dec. 1697/2 A split-willow log basket—22 in. long, 18 in. wide and 12 in. high, it costs £4.00. **1884** KNIGHT *Dict. Mech.* Suppl., **Log-Beam*, the traveling frame in which a log lies and travels in a saw-mill. **1669** STURMY *Mariner's Mag.* IV. ii. 146 Next we will work the Courses of the *Log-board. **1833** MARRYAT *P. Simple* (1834) I. xii. 156 O'Brien reported the rate of sailing to the master, marked it down on the log-board, and then returned. **1867** SMYTH *Sailor's Word-bk.*, *Log-board*. **1879** *Lumberman's Gaz.* 15 Oct., A machine that would utilize . . *Log Buttings. **1857** THOREAU *Maine W.* (1894) 180 My companion inclined to go to the *log-camp on the carry. **1752** P. STEVENS in N. D. Mereness *Trav. Amer. Colonies* (1916) 315, I . . set out . . in the morning accompanied by an officer and ten soldiers, who brought us in two *log canoes. **1788** R. PUTNAM in *M. Cutler's Life* (1888) I. 379 Our whole fleet consisted of . . three log canoes of different sizes. **1841** G. POWERS *Hist. Sk. Coos* 130 He took a log-canoe, and ascended the river to the place where Orford bridge now is. **1846** *Log-chip [see *log-ship*]. **1806** M. LEWIS in Lewis & Clark *Orig. Jrnls. Lewis & Clark Exped.* (1905) IV. 132 The large woodpecker or *log cock. **1853** 'P. PAXTON' *Stray Yankee in Texas* 58 (Th.), The log-cock, with his gaudy head-dress. **1866** *Intell. Observ.* No. 53. 333 The Log-cock (*Hylatomus Pileatus*). **1884** J. BURROUGHS in *Century Mag.* Dec. 222/2 The log-cock, or pileated woodpecker . . I have never heard drum. **1879** *Lumberman's Gaz.* 7 May, The delivery of the *log crop of Michigan. **1905** *Terms Forestry & Logging* (U.S. Dept. Agric. Bureau Forestry) 42 *Log deck*, the platform upon a loading jack. **1904** *N.Y. Even. Post* 3 May 2 The annual *log-drives have begun in the upper Hudson watershed. **1884** GOODE, etc. *Nat. Hist. Useful Aquatic Anim.* I. 334 The Black Rudder-fish—*Lirus perciformis*. This fish is also called by the fishermen '*Log-fish' and 'Barrel-fish.' *a* **1814** *Sailor's Ret.* in *New Brit. Theatre* II. 319 As sure as a can of grog, or allowance, is only left but the time of a *log-glass, so sartain [*sic*] is to be purloin'd. **1858** SIMMONDS *Dict. Trade*, *Log-glass*, a half-minute sandglass used on board ship for timing the speed of sailing, by the quantity of line run out in a given time. **1831** CARLYLE *Sart. Res.* (1858) 100 Not being born purely a *Loghead (*Dummkopf*), thou hadst no other outlook. **1571** R. EDWARDS *Damon & Pithias* E iv, The *log-headed knaue. **1926** *Spectator* 24 July 149/1 Anyone . . would have been thought log-headed or obstinate. **1662** in H. R. Shurtleff *Log Cabin Myth* (1939) 80 As fare Westwardly as the *logg house. **1669** *Maryland Archives* (1884) II. 224 That there be a Logg house Prison Twenty ffoot Square Built . . in the Baltemore County. **1680** *N. Carolina Col. Rec.* (1886) I. 300 Ye Deponent saw ye sd Mr. Miller enclosed in a Logghouse about 10 or 11 foot square purposely built for him. **1741** TAILFER, etc. *Narr. Georgia* (1835) 24 He threatned every Person . . who . . claim'd their just Rights and Privileges with the Stocks, Whipping-Post, and Logg-House. **1784** J. F. D. SMYTH *Tour U.S.A.* II. 9 Constructing temporary habitations (log houses) to reside in. **1836** *Backwoods of Canada* 46 The log-house and shanty . . [have] been supplanted by pretty frame-houses. **1879** A. W. TOURGÉE *Fool's Errand* vii. 34 This log house had . . given way to a more pretentious structure of brick. **1882** CAULFEILD & SAWARD *Dict. Needlewk.* 379 This . . pattern in Patchwork is one that in Canada is known as Loghouse Quilting. It is . . made of several coloured ribbons . . arranged so as to give the appearance of different kinds of wood formed into a succession of squares. **1965** MRS L. B. JOHNSON *White House Diary* 7 Sept. (1970) 318, I arrived at Honeymoon Cabin, a real log house. **1974** 'S. HARVESTER' *Forgotten Road* v. 54 Clusters of log houses . . formed the village. **1853** 'C. BEDE' *Verdant Green* II. iii, Mr. B. and party are discovered drinking *log-juice, and smoking cabbage-leaves. **1860** in *Merc. Marine Mag.* VII. 114 *Log knots in these . . ropes will teach the men the . . length. **1613** M. RIDLEY *Magn. Bodies* 147 Observing the way with the *logge-line. **1644** MANWAYRING *Sea-mans Dict.*, *A Logg-line*. Some call this a Minut-line. **1794** *Rigging & Seamanship* I. 94 The holes, for marling the clues of sails . . have grommets of log-line. **1867** SMYTH *Sailor's Word-bk.*, *Log-line*. **1610** SHAKS. *Temp.* III. i. 67 For your sake Am I this patient *Logge-man. **1845** C. M. KIRKLAND *Western Clearings* 175 He turned his hand to the plough, and was the 'patient log-man' of a poverty-stricken household. **1870** *Daily News* 16 Apr., The lumber business is carried on . . by the logmen. **1900** H. LAWSON *On Track* 29 He was putting up a two-rail fence along the old *log-paddock. **1882** JORDAN & GILBERT *Fishes N. Amer.* (*Bull. U.S. Nat. Mus.* III.) 499 *Percina*, *Log Perches. *Ibid.*, *P. caprodes* . . Log Perch; Rock-fish; Hog-molly; Hog-fish. **1877** *Lumberman's Gaz.* 17 Nov., A dam has been built across the river, forming a *log pocket. **1858** SIMMONDS *Dict. Trade*, **Log-reel*, the reel on which the log-line of a ship is wound. **1895** *Montgomery Ward Catal.* 369/1 *Log rules, either Scribner or Doyle scale. **1905** *Terms Forestry & Logging* (U.S. Dept. Agric. Bureau Forestry) 15 *Log rule*, 1. A tabular statement of the amount of lumber which can be sawed from logs of given lengths and diameters. 2. A graduated stick for measuring the densities of logs. The number of board feet in logs of given diameters and lengths is shown upon the stick. **1898** E. E. MORRIS *Austral Eng.* 272/1 **Log-runner*, an Australian bird, called also a Spine-tail. **1901** A. J. CAMPBELL *Nests & Eggs Austral. Birds* I. 252 A nest I found in the Big Scrub, Richmond River, which I believe belonged to the Orthonyx, or Log Runner, was in a damp situation. **1931**, **1934** [see CHOWCHILLA]. **1965** *Austral. Encycl.* V. 359/1 Log-runners construct large domed nests of leaves and moss, with a side-entrance placed usually on the ground or on the top of a low stump. **1878** *Lumberman's Gaz.* 6 Apr., The Green Bay *Advocate* of March 28 says that *log-running is commencing all around. **1901** S. E. WHITE *Westerners* xxi. 199 In the log running Michail Lafond was the man always called upon to skim over the bobbing logs. **1877** *Mich. Supreme Court Rep.* XXXVI. 168 The scale of the manufactured lumber exceeded the *log scale. **1905** *Terms Forestry & Logging* (U.S. Dept. Agric. Bureau Forestry) 42 *Log scale*, the contents of a log, or of a number of logs considered collectively. **1958** *Listener* 14 Aug. 226/2 The lights come on in the cabs [of the lorries], while the drivers make out their *log sheets. **1959** E. K. WENLOCK *Kitchin's Road Transport Law* (ed. 12) 78/2 A current record (popularly known as a log sheet) containing the prescribed particulars must be compiled by the driver of every vehicle, [etc.]. **1964** *Times* 11 Feb. 11/6 The practice of keeping duplicate sets of log sheets, . . is so common that it is hardly remarked upon. **1841** DANA *Seaman's Man.* 114 *Log*, a line with a piece of board called the *log-ship, attached to it. **1846** YOUNG *Naut. Dict.* s.v. *Log-line*, A piece of board called the Log-ship or Log-chip. *c* **1860** H. STUART *Seaman's Catech.* 43 The 'log-ship', is a flat piece of wood in the form of a quadrant, having a sufficient quantity of lead inserted in the circular edge to keep it steady and perpendicular in the water. **1834** *Knickerbocker* III. 83 Adding on the *log-slate another 'ditto' to the long column of them. **1841** DANA *Seaman's Man.* 153 It is the custom for each officer at the end of his watch to enter upon the log-slate . . the courses, distances, wind and weather during his watch, and anything of note that may have occurred. Once in twenty-four hours the mate copies from this slate into the log-book. **1721** J. BAXTER in *New Eng. Hist. & Gen. Reg.* (1867) XXI. 57 All Hands went briskly to work, to finish y^e *log-work in ye Lower Block-house. **1725** DE FOE *Voy. round World* (1840) 3 Tedious accounts of their log-work, how many leagues they sailed every day; where they had the winds [etc.]. **1856** OLMSTED *Slave States* 111 The chimney is . . commonly of lath or split sticks, laid up like log-work and plastered with mud.

‖**log** (lɒg, ləʊg), *sb.*[2] Also 6 logg. [Heb. *lōg*.] A Hebrew measure for liquids; the twelfth part of a hin; = about three quarters of a pint.

1530 TINDALE *Lev.* xiv. 24 And let the preast take . . the logge [Vulg. *sextarium*, *Wycl.* sextarie; **1611** log] of oyle. **1755** in JOHNSON; and in mod. Dicts.

log (lɒg), *sb.*[3] and *a.* Also †log. (with point). **1.** Abbrev. of LOGARITHM, LOGARITHMIC *a.*

See the last paragraph of the note to LOGARITHM; (*log* is no longer confined to a position before a number).

1631 [see LOGARITHM]. **1805** J. W. NORIE *Epitome Pract. Navigation* Expl. Tables p. xv, Thus the log. of 295 is 2·469822. **1858** I. TODHUNTER *Algebra for Schools* 308 Given log 2 find log ·0025. **1890** G. F. MATTHEWS *Man. Logarithms* 18 How many positive integers are there whose logs. to the base 3 have 6 for a characteristic? **1960** F. LAND *Lang. Math.* ix. 119 Either of the forms $1296 = 6^4$ or $4 = \log_6 1296$ describes the relationship between the number 1296, the base 6 and the index 4. **1971** *Nature* 17 Dec. 419/2 At every stage in dark adaptation, the log threshold for test flash detection . . is raised in proportion to the log brightness of the after image.

1785 C. HUTTON *Math. Tables* 150 To find the log. sine of 1° [etc.]. *Ibid.*, To find the log. tang. of 2° [etc.]. **1805** J. W. NORIE *Epitome Pract. Navigation* Expl. Tables p. xv, The log. sine of 3 points is 9·744739. **1890** G. F. MATTHEWS *Man. Logarithms* 49 The Logarithm of the sine of A is called the logarithmic sine of A and written log sin A. **1967** *Oceanogr. & Marine Biol.* V. 134 In a recent account of headland-bay beaches Yasso (1965) found that their plan geometry, which results from wave movements, closely fits a log-spiral. **1974** *Daily Tel.* 14 May 3 (Advt.), At last there's a pocket calculator which gives you log and trig functions instantly . . at a price that makes sense.

2. Special Comb.: **log log**, (*a*) *sb.*, the logarithm of the logarithm (of a number); also *attrib.*, indicating or involving such quantities; (*b*) *adj.* (usu. hyphenated), applied to a graph or to graph paper having a logarithmic scale along both axes; **log-normal** *a.* (*Statistics*), such that the logarithm of the variate is distributed according to a normal distribution; hence **log-normally** *adv.*; **log phase** *Biol.* = *logarithmic phase* s.v. LOGARITHMIC *a.*; **log table**, a table of logarithms; usu. *pl.*

1910 *Encycl. Brit.* IV. 975/1 Dr John Perry added log log scales to the ordinary slide rule in order to facilitate the calculation of a^x . . according to the formula log log a^x = log log a + log x. **1933** S. DAWSON *Introd. Computation of Statistics* i. 28 Log.-log. paper, in which both sets of values are represented by lines proportional to their logarithms. **1957** KENDALL & BUCKLAND *Dict. Statistical Terms* 169 *Loglog transformation*, the transformation of a probability P . . according to the formula $Y = \log_e(-\log_e P)$. **1962** *Lancet* 5 May 949/2 An exponential function yields a straight line when plotted on log-linear graph paper, while a power law function gives a straight line when plotted on log-log paper. **1966** D. G. BRANDON *Mod. Techniques Metallogr.* 209 The slope of the log-log plot of the current-voltage characteristic near the threshold field . . is of the order of 30. **1945** J. H. GADDUM in *Nature* 20 Oct. 465/1 It is proposed to call the distribution of x 'lognormal' when the distribution of log x is normal. *Ibid.*, Examples of lognormal distributions have been found in estimates of the numbers of plankton caught in different hauls of the net, and in the amounts of electricity used in medium-class homes in the United States. **1951** *Biometrika* XXXVIII. 434 It is assumed that the population distribution of abundance is log-normal. **1971** J. B. CARROLL et al. *Word Frequency Bk.* p. xxi, This model . . is called the lognormal model, because it postulates that the total vocabulary underlying a corpus is distributed according to the familiar 'normal distribution' when the logarithms of the frequencies are used. **1945** J. H. GADDUM in *Nature* 20 Oct. 465/1 The size of the particles of silver in a photographic emulsion were lognormally distributed. **1951** *Biometrika* XXXVIII. 427 (*heading*) The expected frequencies in a sample of an animal population in which the abundances of species are log-normally distributed. **1967** *Proc. Ussher Soc.* I. 277 Testing on a logarithmic scale, however, reveals the existence of two lognormally distributed populations with a discontinuity at about 0·15% Mg. **1938** H. L. HIND *Brewing* I. xv. 367 This method . . was termed the Log phase method because it is used to measure acidity during the logarithmic phase of the growth of the bacterium in wort. **1959** F. S. STEWART *Bigger's Handbk. Bacteriol.* (ed. 7) i. 10 The log phase is of relatively short duration, lasting at most for some hours. **1974** *Nature* 4 Jan. 67/1 Stationary and log-phase cultures of *E. coli* B, *E. coli* K

12 Sr.. and *B. subtilis* were exposed to 160° C. *c* **1935** J. A. HAMMERTON *New Popular Educator* 467/1 For practical purposes the indices of 10 have been tabulated in what are called Tables of Logarithms... The student now needs this tool, 'log tables'. **1962** R. B. FULLER *Epic Poem on Industrialization* xx. 143 Napier developed between 1614–1620 His logarithms, his complete log tables. **1969** D. C. HAGUE *Managerial Economics* vi. 132 Given time, patience and log tables, we could draw up a table like Table 7 for ourselves.

log (lɒg), *v.*[1] [f. LOG *sb.*[1]]

1. *trans.* †**a.** To bring (a tree) to the condition of a log; to deprive of branches (*obs.*). **b.** To cut (timber) into logs. **c.** To remove the logs or trees from (an area). Also const. *off, over, up.* Chiefly *N. Amer.*

1699 DAMPIER *Voy.* II. II. 80 A Tree.. so thick that after it is log'd it remains still too great a Burthen for one Man. **1717** in *Mass. House of Representatives Jrnl.* (1919) I. 272 Bridger [is trying].. to compel the Inhabitants.. to Pay Him Forty Shillings.. for each Team they send to Log and get Timber. **1818** L. D. CLARK in *Firelands Pioneer* (1920) XXI. 2322 He and Lines went logging of the land to sow with wheat. **1829** J. MACTAGGART *Three Yrs. Canada* II. 206 When the large wood is hewn down and *logged*, that is, cut into lengths and laid round these stacks in a rude pile, the fire can more readily be applied to them. **1829** in E. C. Guillet *Valley of Trent* (1957) 355 After this we logged up and cleared three acres. **1833** *Chambers's Edin. Jrnl.* II. 167/2 He.. acquaints his neighbours around him, according to the extent of the land he has to log. **1836** *Backwoods of Canada* 101 After the trees have been chopped, cut into lengths, drawn together, or logged, as we call it. **1839** A. LANGTON *Jrnl.* in *Gentlewoman Upper Canada* (1950) 114 Six or seven acres were logged up during the day. **1848** THOREAU *Maine W.* (1894) 26 Only a little spruce and hemlock beside had been logged here. **1902** S. E. WHITE *Blazed Trail* ii. 5 We own, however, five million on the Cass Branch which we would like to log on contract. **1904** —— *Blazed Trail Stories* iii. 46 Suppose you log a knoll which.. must grow at least a half million. **1919** B. W. SINCLAIR *Burned Bridges* 302 As soon as the land is logged off it is open for soldier entry. **1921** H. KEPHART *Camping & Woodcraft* (new ed.) I. 113 With this one tool a good axeman can.. quickly fell and log-up a tree large enough to keep a hot fire before his lean-to throughout the night. **1948** *Milwaukee* (Wisconsin) *Jrnl.* 18 July 6/5 By 1889 he had built a farm home and 'tourist home' from timber he had cut and logged himself. **1959** A. MCLINTOCK *Descr. Atlas N.Z.* 45 Once provisional State forest was logged over for timber it was then released for agricultural development. **1963** E. C. GUILLET *Pioneer Farmer* I. 318 Some men were known to log several acres a year entirely alone—without even oxen.

absol. **1830** GALT *Lawrie T.* III. ii. (1849) 87 The settlers.. were busy logging and burning. **1848** THOREAU *Maine W.* (1894) 97 We turned our backs on Chesuncook, which McCauslin had formerly logged on. **1878** *Michigan Rep.* XXXVII. 408 He was logging on the.. Manistee River.

d. *to log up* (see quots. 1889 and 1905). So **logging-up**. *N.Z. colloq.*

1889 *Colonia* I. I. 26 'Logging-up' is generally done in the autumn, when there are strong gales of wind blowing. The bush which has been felled in the winter, is set fire to, and after a day or two when the ground is sufficiently cool for walking on, the still-burning logs are rolled together and piled up with rubbish, so that they may be burnt clean away. **1891** R. WALLACE *Rural Econ. Austral. & N.Z.* xv. 232 When the burning is badly done the seed cannot be properly sown; the rubbish lies thick over the ground and the whole has to be gone over again and 'logged-up', else the land is thrown temporarily out of use.. while the owner waits for the remaining rubbish to decay. **1905** J. M. THOMSON *Bush Boys N.Z.* ii. 32 These [big unburned trees] are 'logged-up' afterwards, that is rolled together and piled round the stumps, so as to dry thoroughly preparatory to 'firing' them again. **1908** B. E. BAUGHAN *Shingle-Short* 84 [Trees] logged up for burning.

2. To lay *out* (a road) with a layer of logs.

1893 *Scribner's Mag.* June 706/1 Road-makers log out the road to its proper width.

3. †**a.** *trans.* Of water: To lie in (a ship) so as to reduce it to the condition of a log; in quot. *absol.*

1751 SMOLLETT *Per. Pic.* (1779) IV. lxxxvi. 10 Several feet of under-water logging in her hold.

b. *intr.* To lie like a log.

a **1813** A. WILSON *Foresters* Poet. Wks. (1846) 269 By slow degrees the sinking breezes die, And on the smooth still flood we logging lie. **1864** [see LOGGING *ppl. a.*[1]].

†**4.** *Mil.* To inflict on (a soldier) the punishment of the log (see LOG *sb.*[1] 2 b). *Obs.*

1816 C. JAMES *Milit. Dict.* (ed. 4) s.v., *To Log*.. is a punishment which is inflicted in some dragoon or hussar regiments for indisciplined and disorderly conduct. **1839** C. F. BRIGGS *Adventures Harry Franco* I. xix. 194 The captain ordered Mr. Ruffin to log me, and swore he would send me back to the States in irons.

5. a. orig. *Naut.* To enter (esp. the distance run by a ship) in a log or log-book; hence *gen.*, to record. Also with *down, up.*

1823 J. F. COOPER *Pioneers* xxxiv. (1869) 149/2 I've logged many a hard thing against your name. **1852** *Blackw. Mag.* LXXII. 94 He has just logged down, in a plain manner, what he noticed on the road. **1880** N. H. BISHOP *4 Months Sneak-Box* 106, I.. went into camp behind an island, logging with pleasure my day's run at sixty-seven miles. **1884** *Pall Mall G.* 6 Oct. 8 The weather was logged at midnight, 'Light, clear, passing showers'. **1924** J. BRUCE *Power Station Efficiency Control* v. 105 If an analysis is to be made of the boiler-room operating results, the indications from the various instruments must be carefully logged at least every half-hour. **1966** RUBIN & HALLER *Communication Switching Syst.* viii. 294 Every message which is accepted into the system is logged on a storage device. **1969** BENNISON & WRIGHT *Geol. Hist. Brit. Isles* i. 18 One further parameter of particular importance in logging bore-hole strata is the measurement of thermal conductivity. **1974** *Physics Bull.* Jan. 30/2 Up to now data from brake tests have been logged using ultraviolet recorders or human observers.

absol. **1863** W. C. BALDWIN *Afr. Hunting* 376, I have got on very slowly since logging up last.

b. Of a vessel: To traverse (a certain distance) by log-measurements. Also, to travel at (a certain speed) as measured by a log; to 'do'. Hence of an aircraft or pilot: to attain a cumulative total of (so many hours, miles, etc.) in the air. Also *transf.*, of a machine and the time spent in operation.

1883 E. F. KNIGHT *Cruise Falcon* (1887) 32 This day we logged 160 miles. **1892** *Daily Tel.* 29 Dec. 5/1 In one day she hardly logged as much as a hundred knotts. **1928** *Chambers's Jrnl.* Feb. 116/2 The liner was logging a steady seventeen knots. **1955** *Times* 22 Aug. 8/5 During the past five days.. Secretary of State for Air, who has been learning to fly, has logged 13 hours' solo flying, it was stated yesterday by an Air Ministry spokesman. **1956** *IRE Trans. Electronic Computers* V. 138/2 To date 670 hours of operation have been logged on this unit since debugging. **1966** *Listener* 4 Aug. 179/2 The *Graf Zeppelin*.. was the first aircraft to log over a million miles. **1972** *Lebende Sprachen* XVII. 73/2 Over the past two years, our HS 125s.. have proved themselves to be increasingly valuable as management tools while logging more than 1,200 trouble-free hours.

c. To enter the name of (a man as an offender) in a log-book, with a penalty attached. Hence, to fine.

1889 *Times* 10 Sept. 10/5 The understanding.. was that the penalties for logging should not be enforced. **1892** *Pall Mall G.* 30 Aug. 2/1 Taken before the captain on the bridge and 'logged' to the extent of from five to twenty shillings. **1892** *Labour Commission* Gloss., *Logging offences*, the entering.. in the 'official log' of British vessels of offences committed by members of the crew. **1899** F. T. BULLEN *Log Sea-waif* 280 I'll log ye to-morrow.

d. *to log in* or *on* (intr.), to open one's on-line access to a computer, esp. a database or other time-shared system, from a terminal; also *to log* (a person) *in* or *out*; *to log off* or *out* (intr.), to terminate one's on-line access to a computer; also *to log* (a person) *off*, *to log off* (a system). So **'log-in, -on, -out** *sbs.*, the action or an act of logging in, etc.

1963 *Compatible Time-Sharing System* (M.I.T. Computation Center) iii. 25 If the user exceeds his track quota while writing a file, there will be an automatic temporary extension of his quota... The extension will be maintained when the user issues *logout*. When he next logs in, he should relieve the excess.. by adequate deletions. **1965** *IEEE Spectrum* II. 59/1 An automatic logout of the author's problem. *Ibid.* 61/2 The total number of user-hours between logins and logouts turns out to be approximately 17 times the number of computer hours used. **1968** M. V. WILKES *Time-Sharing Computer Systems* ii. 7 The user begins a session by logging in, that is he types the command LOGIN, followed by his problem number and name. *Ibid.*, The user is logged in and the date and time are printed. *Ibid.* vii. 94 If necessary, the handshake program will log out a low priority user in favour of a high priority user who wishes to come in. **1977** *Sci. Amer.* July 65/3 (Advt.), With 300 people authorized to use the terminals,.. we now average over 400 'log-ons' a day. As many as 70 people may be online simultaneously. **1978** *Bell System Techn. Jrnl.* LVII. 1924 A user may log out simply by typing the end-of-file sequence to the shell. *Ibid.* 1925 A user has successfully logged in by supplying a name and password. **1983** *Pop. Computing* Oct. 71 Big savings come only by minimizing the time you spend actually connected to the service or database. Anything you can do off line should be done before you log on. If you get stuck on something, don't be reluctant to log off,.. and log back on. **1984** *Today in Gainesville* (Florida) Mar. 13/2 Almost everywhere, it seems, American hackers (fanatics) are 'logging on' to these computerized repositories. **1985** *Byte* Jan. 306/2 A person.. upon exiting from the program is logged off the MP/M system. **1985** *Computerworld* 29 Sept. 51/1 Allowing people to log on and leave the terminal area without logging off the system.

†**6.** *intr.* ? To be 'like a log', be sluggish. *Obs.*

1622 MABBE tr. *Aleman's Guzman d'Alf.* II. 133 Which kinde of Phrase, your old women in Spaine vse to their children, when they goe sneakingly and fearfully about any businesse. *Anda, anda, que parece que vas a hurtar*; Get thee gone, get thee gone, thou goest logging and dreamingly about it, as if thou wentest a filching.

7. Austral. Mining. *to log up*: To make a log support for the windlass.

1890 'ROLF BOLDREWOOD' *Miner's Right* v. 54 We.. had logged up and made a start with another shaft.

log (lɒg), *v.*[2] *dial.* [? Onomatopœic. Cf. *rog*, ROCK *v.*] *trans.* To rock, move to and fro. **b.** *intr.* To oscillate.

1808 POLWHELE *Cornish-Eng. Voc.* 45 *note*, This enormous mass, from its peculiarity of position, may be easily *logged* to and fro. **1880** *W. Cornwall Gloss.*, *Log*, to oscillate.

log, dial. form of LUG (worm).

log, short for LOGARITHM.

logan berry ('ləʊgən 'bɛrɪ). Also **loganberry**. [f. the name of J. H. *Logan* (1841–1928), American lawyer and horticulturist, who first cultivated it.] A fruit produced by crossing a raspberry with a blackberry, or the plant producing it. Also *attrib.*

1893 *Bull. Calif. Agric. Exper. Station* No. 103. 3 The Logan Berry.. [has] the shape of a blackberry, the color of a raspberry, and a combination of the flavors of both. **1897** *Gardeners' Chronicle* 24 July 47/1 One of the most interesting of recent contributions from American experiment-stations is Professor L. F. Kinney's bulletin on the Logan-berry. This fruit has been.. much talked of in recent years. **1900** *Speaker* 6 Oct. 11/1 Mr. Forrester.. showed me some very fine hybrids, called Logan berries, between the raspberry and the blackberry. **1902** *Daily Chron.* 28 Mar. 3/3 The blackberry, the loganberry, the wineberry, and allied fruits. **1926** *Daily Colonist* (Victoria, B.C.) 11 July 3/2 The Growers' Wine Company, with headquarters in this city, starting out this season with the objective of putting up 100,000 gallons of loganberry wine, has already more than 50 per cent. of that production. **1929** D. H. LAWRENCE *Phoenix II* (1968) 539 Women.. aren't something new on the face of the earth, like the loganberry or artificial silk. **1929** J. MASEFIELD *Hawbucks* 154 Would you care to have some loganberry plants? **1944** E. CARR *House of All Sorts* 151 The seasoned widow brought loganberry wine of her own brew. **1973** R. GENDERS *Epicure's Garden* I. 67 The loganberry.. has been widely grown for bottling and canning.

loganite ('ləʊgənaɪt). *Min.* [Named by T. S. Hunt, 1851, in honour of Sir W. *Logan*.] An altered hornblende, near penninite in composition.

1865 CARPENTER in *Intell. Observ.* No. 40. 286 *Loganite* (dark-green silicate of magnesia).

logan-stone ('lɒgənstəʊn). Also **loggan-stone, logan.** [f. *logan* = LOGGING *ppl. a.*[2] + STONE.] A rocking-stone.

1759 B. MARTIN *Nat. Hist. Eng.* I. *Cornwall* 4 This stone.. was a Logan or Rocking-stone. **1808** POLWHELE *Cornish-Eng. Voc.* 45 *Logan*, shaking. A logan stone, a rocking moving stone. [**1824**: see LOGGING *ppl. a.*[2]] **1826** CARRINGTON *Dartmoor* 66 Near the edge Of the loud brawling stream a Logan stands Haply self-poised. **1831** FONBLANQUE *Eng. under 7 Administr.* (1837) II. 79 Like the Logan stones, which the finger of a child may move. **1859** H. KINGSLEY *G. Hamlyn* xxxiv. (1900) 181/2 Strong as your famous lieutenant who capsized the logan stone. **1881** J. HAWTHORNE *Fort. Fool* I. xv, The big loggan-stone that had stood in front.. was upset, and fallen into the gulley. [**1881**: see LOGGING *ppl. a.*[2]]

logaœdic (lɒgə'iːdɪk), *a.* [ad. late L. *logaœdicus*, ad. Gr. λογαοιδικ-ός, f. λόγ-ος speech, prose + ἀοιδή song (as standing between the rhythm of prose and of poetry).] Epithet of various metres in which dactyls are combined with trochees. Also quasi-*sb.*, a logaœdic verse.

1844 MAJOR *Guide Gr. Trag.* (ed. 2) 159 The *Glyconeus*, which has a logaœdic order. **1855** LINWOOD *Greek Tragic Metres* 79 Anapæstic Logaœdics are identical in their rhythm with.. Logaœdic Dactyls. **1879** J. W. WHITE tr. *Schmidt's Rhythmic & Metric* §21. 65 Chorees and logaoedics can be extended to Series of six measures. **1883** JEBB *Œdipus Tyran.* Introd. 72 The essential difference between choreic and logaoedic rhythm is that of ictus.

†**'logarism.** *Obs.* [Corruption of LOGARITHM, after sbs. in -ISM.] = LOGARITHM (in the earlier quots. used blunderingly).

1630 BRATHWAIT *Eng. Gentlem.* (1641) Ep. Ded., If any one be minded to learn the.. art of Brachygraphie, Stenographie, Logarisme or any Art whatsoever. **1649** G. DANIEL *Trinarch., Hen. IV*, xix, Diuision (whose Arethmeticke Makes but a Logarisme to perplex The world). **1684** COCKER in *Lond. Gaz.* No. 1985/4 His Artificial Arithmetick, shewing the Genesis and Fabrick of Logarisms.

logarithm ('lɒgərɪθ(ə)m, -ɪð-). *Math.* Also 7 *erron.* **logorythm.** [ad. mod.L. *logarithm-us* (Napier, 1614), f. Gr. λόγ-ος word, proportion, ratio + ἀριθμός number.

Napier does not explain his view of the literal meaning of *logarithmus*. It is commonly taken to mean 'ratio-number', and as thus interpreted it is not inappropriate, though its fitness is not obvious without explanation. Perhaps, however, Napier may have used λόγος merely in the sense of 'reckoning', 'calculation' (cf. LOGISTIC).]

One of a particular class of arithmetical functions, invented by John Napier of Merchiston (died 1617), and tabulated for use as a means of abridging calculation. The essential property of a system of logarithms is that the sum of the logarithms of any two or more numbers is the logarithm of their product. Hence the use of a table of logarithms enables a computer to substitute addition and subtraction for the more laborious operations of multiplication and division, and likewise multiplication and division for involution and evolution.

The word is now understood to refer only to systems in which the logarithm of any number a^x is x, a being a constant which is called the *base* of the system. The logarithms (of sines) tabulated by Napier himself were not logarithms in this restricted sense, but were functions of what are now called *Napierian* (also *Neperian*), *hyperbolic*, or *natural logarithms*, the base of which, denoted by the symbol ϵ or e, is 2·71828 +. This system is still in use for analytical investigations, but for common purposes the system used is that invented by Napier's friend Henry Briggs (died 1630), the base of which is 10; the *Briggsian* or *Briggian* logarithms are also known as ***common*** or ***decimal logarithms***. For *binary, Gaussian logarithm*, see the adjs. ***logistic logarithms*** (see quot. 1795); also called ***proportional logarithms***.

In mathematical notation 'the logarithm of' is expressed by the abbreviation 'log' prefixed to numeral figures or algebraical symbols. When necessary, the base of the system is indicated by adding an inferior figure: thus '$\log_{10} a$' means 'the logarithm of a to the base 10'.

[**1614** NAPIER (*title*) Mirifici Logarithmorum Canonis descriptio...] **1615–16** H. BRIGGS in *Ussher's Lett.* (1686) 36 Napper, Lord of Markinston, hath set my Head and Hands a Work, with his new and admirable Logarithms. **1616** E. WRIGHT tr. *Napier's Logarithmus* Ded., This new course of Logarithmes doth cleane take away all the difficultye that heretofore hath beene in mathematicall calculations. **1631** H. BRIGGS *Logarithm. Arithm.* i. 1 The Logar. of 1 is 0. *Ibid.* 2 The Log. of proper fractions is Defective. **1632** B. JONSON *Magn. Lady* I. i, Sir Interest..will tell you instantly, by Logorythmes, The utmost profit of a stock imployed. **1706** W. JONES *Syn. Palmar. Matheseos* 173 Mr. Halley..has..drawn a very curious Method for Constructing Logarithms. **1795** HUTTON *Math. Dict.* s.v. *Logarithms, Logistic Logarithms*, are certain Logarithms of sexagesimal numbers or fractions, useful in astronomical calculations. **1827** SCOTT *Napoleon* VI. 80 Bonaparte said that his favourite work was a book of logarithms. *c* **1865** in *Circ. Sci.* I. 519/1 This advantage, which the base 10 has over any other, was first seen and applied by Briggs..; the logarithms are, therefore, sometimes called the 'Briggian Logarithms'.

logarithmal (lɒgəˈrɪθməl, -ɪð-), *a. rare.* [f. LOGARITHM + -AL[1].] = LOGARITHMIC.

1630 R. DELAMAIN *Grammalogia* To Rdr., To shadow out to the more learned the quintessence of this Logarythmall projection in Circles. **1849** FREESE *Comm. Class-bk.* 90 By logarithmal numbers.

†**logaˈrithmancy.** *Obs.* *rare*$^{-1}$. [f. LOGARITHM + -MANCY.] (See quot.)

1652 GAULE *Magastrom.* xix. 165 Logarithmancy, [or divining] by Logarithmes.

†**logarithˈmetic**, *a. Obs.* *rare*$^{-0}$. = next.

1721 in BAILEY. **1775** in ASH.

logarithmetical (lɒgərɪθˈmɛtɪkəl), *a.* ? *Obs.* [f. LOGARITHM, on the analogy of ARITHMETICAL.] = LOGARITHMIC.

1621 W. JAMESON (*title*) Account of John Neper's Logarithmetical Triginometriae (in *2nd Rep. Hist. MSS. Comm.* 201). **1685** J. HAWKINS *Cocker's Decimal Arith.* II. i. 205 Logarithmetical Arithmetick is an Artificial use of numbers, invented for ease in Calculation. **1690** LEYBOURN *Curs. Math.* 191 Logarithmetical or Proportional Scales. **1824** *New Monthly Mag.* XI. 416 Ye who learn logarithmetical rules at Cambridge.

Hence **logarithˈmetically** *adv.*

1775 in ASH. *c* **1850** *Rudim. Navig.* (Weale) 144 The sliding rule is..graduated logarithmetically.

logarithmic (lɒgəˈrɪθmɪk, -ɪð-), *a.* (and *sb.*) *Math.* [f. LOGARITHM + -IC. Cf. F. *logarithmique*.]

A. *adj.* **a.** Of or pertaining to logarithms. Also in ***logarithmic sine, tangent, secant***, etc., used (somewhat incorrectly) to denote the logarithm of the function named; opposed to *natural*.

logarithmic amplifier Electr., an amplifier which produces an output in logarithmic proportion to the input; ***logarithmic curve*** (or ***line***), a curve having its ordinates in geometrical progression and its abscissas in arithmetical progression, so that the abscissas are the logarithms of the corresponding ordinates; ***logarithmic decrement***: see DECREMENT 2 b; ***logarithmic ellipse, hyperbola*** (see quots. 1851); ***logarithmic phase*** Biol., the period during which the population of a culture of bacteria increases exponentially with time; ***logarithmic spiral***, a spiral which intersects all its radiants at the same angle.

1698 KEILL *Exam. Th. Earth* (1734) 243 The Applicate of the Logarithmick curve DEF. **1706** W. JONES *Syn. Palmar. Matheseos* 261 The Curve describ'd by their Intersection is called the Logarithmic Line... A Point from the Extremity thereof, moving towards the Centre with a Velocity decreasing in a Geometric Progression, will generate a Curve called the Logarithmic Spiral. **1752** ROBERTSON in *Phil. Trans.* XLVIII. 100 Now subtract the logarithmic versed sines of such degrees..as are intended to be put on the scale, from the logarithm versed sine of 180°. **1797** *Encycl. Brit.* II. 423/2 Constructing logarithmic tables to facilitate their [*sc.* astronomers] calculations. **1851** J. BOOTH *Elliptic Integrals* Pref., I have named them [two curves] the spherical parabola, and the logarithmic ellipse... The latter [may be traced] on a paraboloid of revolution. *Ibid.* 159 If a right cylinder, standing on a plane hyperbola as a base, be substituted for the elliptic cylinder, the curve of intersection with the paraboloid may be named the logarithmic hyperbola. **1878** CLIFFORD *Elem. Dynamic* I. 78 A point is said to have logarithmic motion on a straight line when the distance from a fixed point on the line is equally multiplied in equal times. **1881** MAXWELL *Electr. & Magn.* II. 347 Another point which moves with uniform angular velocity in a logarithmic spiral. **1914** *Jrnl. Hygiene* XIV. 260 This selected strain holds the field during the second or logarithmic phase. **1938** Logarithmic phase [see *log phase* s.v. LOG *sb.*[3] and *a.* 2]. **1954** C. P. SNOW *New Men* vi. 101 There was one of those counters whose ticking I had come to expect in any Barford laboratory; there was a logarithmic amplifier, a D.C. amplifier..which would give a measure..of the 'neutron flux'. **1957** C. WU in C. F. Bonilla *Nucl. Engin.* iv. 128 When a wide range of the neutron flux, as much as six to eight decades, is to be measured, a logarithmic amplifier must be used. **1971** J. S. HOUGH et al. *Malting & Brewing Sci.* xviii. 480 The next stage is the dividing of the cells at a constant rate, referred to as the 'exponential phase' or 'logarithmic phase'.

b. Pertaining to the logarithmic curve.

1875 R. F. MARTIN tr. *Havrez' Winding Mach.* 17 A round steel rope of logarithmic form..would weigh only 1594 kilogs.

B. *sb.* = *logarithmic curve* or *line*.

1753 CHAMBERS *Cycl. Supp.* s.v., Let AVD be a logarithmic, and its ordinates AB, VC, DQ. **1797** BROUGHAM in *Phil. Trans.* LXXXVIII. 396 The common logarithmic has its subtangent constant.

logarithmical (lɒgəˈrɪθmɪkəl, -ɪð-), *a.* [f. as prec. + -AL[1].] = LOGARITHMIC. ***logarithmical scales*** (see quot. 1727–41).

1631 H. BRIGGS (*title*) Logarithmicall Arithmetike. **1665–6** *Phil. Trans.* I. 215 The Logarithmical Tangent-line. **1727–41** CHAMBERS *Cycl.*, *Proportional scales*, called also *logarithmical scales*, are the artificial numbers or logarithms, placed on lines, for the ease and advantage of multiplying, dividing, &c. by means of compasses, or of sliding-rules. **1728** PEMBERTON *Newton's Philos.* 145 That line..which is now commonly known by the name of the logarithmical curve. **1799** YOUNG in *Phil. Trans.* XC. 150 The inner circle L is divided into 30103 parts, corresponding with the logarithmical parts of an octave. **1812–16** PLAYFAIR *Nat. Phil.* II. 47 Formulas..more convenient for logarithmical calculation. **1839** HALLAM *Hist. Lit.* IV. III. viii. §8. 7 Thus reducing the error, which, strictly speaking, must always exist from the principle of logarithmical construction, to an almost infinitesimal fraction.

Hence **logaˈrithmically** *adv.*, by the use of logarithms; in logarithmic proportions.

1760 PEMBERTON in *Phil. Trans.* LI. 923 The present methods of computing logarithmically an angle from the three sides of a spherical triangle given. **1828** HUTTON *Course Math.* II. 328 Expressing this equation logarithmically. **1875** JEVONS *Money* xxiv. 332 The ratios in which their gold pieces have changed would be calculated logarithmically.

†**logarithmotechny.** *Obs.* *rare*$^{-0}$. [ad. mod.L. *logarithmotechnia* (N. Mercator, 1668), f. *logarithm-us* LOGARITHM + Gr. τέχνη art.] The art of calculating or making logarithms.

1724 in BAILEY; **1775** in ASH; and in some mod. Dicts.

logatom (ˈlɒgætəm). *Telephony.* [f. Gr. λόγ-ος word + ATOM.] A meaningless syllable formed arbitrarily, usually from initial and final consonants and a vowel, for use in testing telephone systems.

1937 W. H. GRINSTED in *Siemens Mag.* (Engin. Suppl.) Jan. 4/2 Measurements are easier and more definite if one goes to the limit of intelligibility or uses nonsense syllables (logatoms). *Ibid.* 8/2 A few approximate contour curves,..for logatom articulation, have been plotted. **1942** KNIGHT & PRICKETT *Poole's Telephone Handbk.* (ed. 8) xx. 491 These syllables are composed of consonant, vowel and consonant, based on the esperanto alphabet, which are termed logatoms. **1973** D. L. RICHARDS *Telecommunication by Speech* iii. 165 Table 3.13 shows also a list of English single syllable words, which have been constructed by selecting from the English logatoms just described those that were actual English words.

Logbara, var. LUGBARA *sb.* and *a.*

ˈlog-book.

1. a. *Naut.* A book in which the particulars of a ship's voyage (including her rate of progress as indicated by the log) are entered daily from the log-board. Hence *transf.* and *fig.*, a journal of travel.

a **1679** SIR J. MOORE *Syst. Math.* (1681) I. 271 A Book called a Traverse Book or Log Book. **1753** CHAMBERS *Cycl. Supp.*, *Log-book*, at sea, a book ruled and columned like the log-board. **1779** BOSWELL *Let. to Johnson* 7 Nov., My Chester journal..is truly a log-book of felicity. **1813** *Theatrical Inquisitor* II. 362 It [*sc.* the voyage] was divested of all log-book lumber. **1821** BYRON *Diary* Wks. (1846) 677/1 This additional page of life's log-book. **1889** CLARK RUSSELL *Marooned* (1890) 146 The mate's log-book was upon the table.

b. *Aeronaut.* A book in which particulars of aircraft flights, flying hours, etc., are recorded.

1911 R. M. PIERCE *Dict. Aviation* 150 *Log-book*, a book in which the particulars of a balloon-trip or airship-flight are entered or kept. **1917** GRAHAME-WHITE & HARPER *Air Power* IV. viii. 154 Turning to his log-book, he will look up this sign, and identify the place on the coast he is approaching. **1951** O. BERTHOUD tr. *Clostermann's Big Show* 19 Flying hours..quickly mounted up in my pilot's log-book.

c. (*a*) The registration book of a motor vehicle. (*b*) (See quot. 1971.)

1958 *Listener* 20 Nov. 835/2 The internal combustion engine, or 'I.C.E.' as my log-book calls it. **1963** *Amer. Speech* XXXVIII. 44 *Log book*, the driver's daily report required by the I.C.C. **1965** *Mod. Law Rev.* XXVIII. v. 571 English lawyers will still have to admit that a car's logbook is not admissible evidence of the engine number. **1971** M. TAK *Truck Talk* 100 *Log book*, the daily log in which truckers list their activities. **1973** *Times* 28 Nov. 9 Vehicle Registration Documents (Logbooks) will be stamped by the post office to record each issue of [petrol] coupons.

2. *Tailoring.* = LOG *sb.*[1] 8.

1869 SENIOR tr. *Comte de Paris' Trades' Unions* 169 It was agreed that thenceforth payment should be by piecework, according to a tariff called the log-book.

3. A kind of journal of proceedings which the master of a public elementary school is required to keep.

1872 in Rice-Wiggin & Graves *Elem. Sch. Manager* (1879) 220 Occasional deviations from the table..should be noted by the teacher in the log-book. **1882** *Education Code* 4 The log-book..must be kept by the principal teacher, who is required to enter in it from time to time such events as the introduction of new books [etc.].

log cabin. orig. *U.S.* [LOG *sb.*[1]] A cabin, or small house, built of logs.

1770 in H. R. Shurtleff *Log Cabin Myth* (1939) 25 The court doth appoint..to agree with a workman to build a log cabbin..for a Court House. **1803** F. ASBURY *Jrnl.* (1821) III. 119 Kindness will not make a crowded log cabin, twelve feet by ten, agreeable. **1817** S. R. BROWN *Western Gaz.* 48 There are six families living in log cabins. **1835** *Southern Lit. Messenger* I. 546 Most of the log cabins have been exchanged for neat white cottages. *Ibid.* II. 53 We behold the low log-cabin of a school-house. **1850** LYELL *2nd Visit U.S.* II. 427 The husband will fell timber, run up a log cabin, and receive ready money from the steam-boats, which burn the wood. **1881** W. M. THAYER (*title*) From log-cabin to White House: the story of President Garfield's life. **1937** A. HUXLEY *Let.* 3 June (1969) 421 We have a log cabin ..on Frieda Lawrence's ranch. **1970** *Globe & Mail* (Toronto) 28 Sept. 26/6 (Advt.), Advertiser..has original log cabin for disposal. **1974** *Guardian* 23 Jan. 11/1 America has always frenetically nurtured its pioneer myths... Log cabins, and old Abe Lincoln.

attrib. **1819** R. L. MASON *Narr. in Pioneer West* (1915) 54 It is very common for a log cabin tavern without a door or window (perhaps a log out to answer both purposes) to sup and lodge twenty persons. **1840** *Nashville* (Tennessee) *Whig* 17 Aug., They are the representatives of a hardy race of honest log cabin pioneers. **1840** *Boston Atlas* 11 Sept., Crow,..For the Party laid low By the log-cabin boys Of old Tippecanoe. **1841** *Congress. Globe* 22 June 92 Mr. Clark of New York said all this log-cabin slang was quite out of date. **1887** *Harper's Mag.* Dec. 36/1 Reluctantly she slipped her book under the log-cabin quilt, and said 'Come in'. **1965** A. COLBY *Patchwork Quilts* 78 Log cabin quilts were popular in England and America from about the middle of the nineteenth century, and were so called because the square blocks were composed of a square centre patch surrounded by strips of material or 'logs'..overlapped..in much the same fashion as the log cabins were built. **1973** *Sat. Rev. World* (U.S.) 4 Dec. 46/3 Boulder Flat, a log-cabin settlement at 11,000 feet, from which the last inhabitant departed more than one hundred years ago.

†**loge**[1]. *Obs. Cant.* [? Short for HOROLOGE.] A watch.

a **1700** B. E. *Dict. Cant. Crew*, *Loge*, a Watch. I suppose from the French *Horloge*. **1725** in *New Cant. Dict.* **1785** GROSE *Dict. Vulgar Tongue* s.v., He filed a cloy of a loge,..he picked a pocket of a watch.

‖**loge**[2] (ləʊʒ). [Fr.: see LODGE *sb.*]

1. a. A booth, stall.

1749 CHESTERF. *Let.* 25 Apr., Misc. Wks. 1777 II. 357 The several *loges* are to be shops for toys, *limonades, glaces*, and other *raffraichissemens*.

b. A concierge's lodge.

1969 *Guardian* 2 Aug. 3/7 The tiny loges, ill-lit and ill-ventilated, in which too many concierges are condemned to live. **1972** R. MAYNE *Europeans* v. 72 The views of the man in the street, or the woman in the concierge's *loge*.

2. A 'box' in a theatre or opera-house.

1768 STERNE *Sent. Journ.* I. 198 (*The Rose*) He told me, it was some poor Abbe in one of the upper loges. **1818** C. CLAIRMONT in Dowden *Life Shelley* (1887) II. 192, I could not even perceive the faces of those who sat in the loge next to ours. **1848** THACKERAY *Van. Fair* xxix, George was out of the box in a moment, and he was even going to pay his respects to Rebecca in her *loge*. **1863** OUIDA *Held in Bondage* (1870) 50, I did the grand tier deliberately, going from *loge* to *loge*. **1900** ADE *More Fables* (1902) 188 When he was in a Loge at the Play-House with Exclusive Ethel and her Friends. **1904** A. BENNETT *Great Man* xxiv. 260 They occupied a 'loge' in the..Folies-Bergère. **1968** *Globe & Mail* (Toronto) 17 Feb. 24 (Advt.), Loges $5.00. **1974** *Plain Dealer* (Cleveland) 13 Oct. C2/2 The goal..is to keep the building occupied at least 300 nights a year. Naturally, it won't be completely finished for the Sinatra opener. The loges won't be ready.

-loger (lədʒə(r)), the ending of a few words which are virtually adaptations of actual or assumable Gr. words in -λόγος (L. *-logus*): see -LOGUE, -LOGY. The oldest of these is *astrologer* (14th c.); it is uncertain whether this was f. L. *astrolog-us* + -ER[1] (in which case it is an unusually early example of a type of derivation afterwards common), or whether it was f. *astrology* + -ER[1] (cf. the similar formation of *astronomyer, astronomer*). On the analogy of this word, *-loger* was applied in a few instances to form personal designations correlative with words in *-logy*, *-logic(al*, as in *chronologer*, †*geologer*, *philologer* (obsolescent), †*theologer* (*horologer* is of different formation). The suffix is no longer a living formative, being superseded by -LOGIST.

†**loges.** *Obs. Cant.* (See quot.)

1610 ROWLANDS *Martin Mark-all* E2b, *A Feager of Loges*, one that beggeth with counterfeit writings. *Ibid.* E3 *Loges*, a passe or warrant.

loggage, obs. form of LUGGAGE.

ˈloggat, ˈlogget. *Obs.* exc. *Hist.* Forms: 6–7, 9 logget, (7 logat, locket), 8–9 loggat. [app. some kind of derivative of LOG *sb.*[1]]

1. An old game (see quot. 1773); also the missile used in the game. (See LOGGERHEAD 5.)

[**1541**: Implied in LOGGATING.] **1581** LAMBARDE *Eiren.* III. ii. (1588) 353 Bowles, Closh, Coites, Loggets or other unlawfull Games. **1602** SHAKS. *Ham.* v. i. 100 Did these bones cost no more the breeding, but to play at Loggets with 'em? mine ake to thinke on't. **1612** DEKKER *If it be not good* Wks. 1873 III. 315, 200 crownes? I ha lost as much at loggets. **1705** T. BROWN *To J. Haines* in *Coll. Poems* 119 What though they ne'er broke Jest, or Pate at Lockets, They've Sence enough, for all that, in their Pockets. **1773** STEEVENS in *Shaks. Wks.* X. 315 This is a game played in several parts of England even at this time. A stake is fixed into the ground; those who play, throw loggats at it, and he that is nearest the stake, wins: I have seen it played in different counties at their sheep-shearing feasts. **1858** *Sat. Rev.* 17 Apr. 401/1 Let us take the case of a fine old English

gentleman in a country house on a wet day in the middle of the sixteenth century. After he had..played at bowls or loggats till his arms ached, how was he to pass the time till supper?

2. A pole, heavy stake.

1600 HOLLAND *Livy* XXX. x. 746 The enemies from out of the Carthaginian ships, began to cast out certaine loggets [orig. *asseres*] with yron hookes at the end (which the souldiors use to call Harpagones) for to take hold upon the Roman ships. **1613** MARKHAM *Eng. Husbandman* I. II. ix. 79 Beating of fruit downe with long poales, loggets, or such like. **1633** B. JONSON *Tale Tub* IV. vi, Now are they tossing of his legs and arms, Like loggets at a pear-tree.

3. *attrib.* and *Comb.*, as ***loggat-ground***; ***loggat-playing*** adj.

1793 BLOUNT in *Reed's Shaks.* XV. 305 *note*, A loggat-ground, like a skittle-ground, is strewed with ashes, but is more extensive. **1884** BLACK *Jud. Shakes.* iii, None of your logget-playing, tavern-jesting, come-kiss-me-Moll lovers.

†**'loggating.** *Obs.* In 6 logating. [f. prec. + -ING[1].] Playing at the game of 'loggats'.

1541 *Act 33 Hen. VIII*, c. 9 §1 Sondrie newe and crafty Games and Playes, as logatinge in the Feildes, slydethrifte otherwise called shovegrote.

logged (lɒgd), *ppl. a.* [f. LOG *v.* + -ED[1].]

a. Reduced to the condition of a log; *lit.* and *fig.* rendered incapable of action or movement. Of water: Stagnant. Of a vessel: Water-logged. **b.** Of land: Cleared by hewing the timber into logs. Also ***logged-off***.

c **1820** *N. Eng. Hist. & Gen. Register* (1891) XLV. 273 With deliberate aim, I kill one [Indian] and leave the other logg'd. **1838** *Civil Eng. & Arch. Jrnl.* I. 265/2 Should she happen to get logged, there would be perhaps a difficulty in bringing her to the proper steer again. **1880** DISRAELI *Endym.* lxiii, We should find employment..in other countries, even if the States were logged. **1889** *19th Cent.* Oct. 702 Dippers [birds] will not long stay where the water is slow or logged. **1901** *Scotsman* 29 Oct. 9/2 The assumption that the logged..areas contained the same average quantity of timber per acre as the forests still standing. **1908** *Chambers's Jrnl.* 2 May 352/1 The people who are taking up the 'logged-off' lands are usually accustomed to getting along in a small way. **1911** *U.S. Dept. Agric. Farmer's Bull.* No. 462. 5 The merchantable timber has been stripped from large areas, leaving what is known as 'logged-off' or 'cut-over' land. **1921** *Daily Colonist* (Victoria, B.C.) 25 Mar. 4/3 The report contains a great array of information referring to the sub-division of logged-off lands and expired timber licences for settlement on the coast.

logged, *a. U.S.* [f. LOG *sb.*[1] + -ED[2].] Built of logs.

1784 WASHINGTON *Diaries* (1925) II. 294 A Logged dwelling house with a punchion Roof. **1834** *Knickerbocker* III. 32 Immediately on the road, appeared a large rude double logged cabin. **1972** J. BUNTING *Lionheads* 155 The bunker, a mud carapace with logged sides, is ten meters inland.

logger ('lɒgə(r)), *sb.*[1] *N. Amer.* [f. LOG *v.* + -ER[1].] **1.** One who fells timber or cuts it into logs; a lumberman.

1734 *New Hampsh. Prov. Papers* (1870) IV. 840 Many Towns raising a generall Contribution among the Logers for him. **1827** J. F. COOPER *Prairie* II. i. 7 It will not be long before an accursed band of choppers and loggers will be following. **1890** W. J. GORDON *Foundry* 114 Life among the loggers..seems the very ideal of healthy independence. **1900** *Chamb. Jrnl.* Ser. VI. III. 681/2 One hundred and fifty-four thousand feet of timber, which an average gang of loggers would cut down in about eight days.

2. = *data logger* (DATUM 3).

1958 L. E. C. HUGHES *Electronic Engineer's Ref. Bk.* 832 Another service..by an automatic logger..is to provide the equivalent of the manuscript log of, say, temperatures in a much more useful form. **1967** *Times Rev. Industry* Apr. 63/3 The basic logger..can be connected to up to 20 data channels to monitor, for instance, the operation of a small process plant.

logger ('lɒgə(r)), *sb.*[2] *dial.* [app. a word invented as expressing by its sound the notion of something heavy and clumsy. Cf. LOG *sb.*[1] Although of late appearance in quots. it is prob. the source of LOGGERHEAD, LOGGERY.] **a.** A heavy block of wood fastened to the leg of a horse to prevent it straying (1777 in *Eng. Dial. Dict.*). **b.** Lumps of dirt on a ploughboy's feet (*Wiltsh. Gloss.* 1893). **c.** 'Meat which is sinewy, skinny, lumpy, "chunky", or not worth cooking' (*Warwicksh. Gloss.* 1896).

logger ('lɒgə(r)), *sb.*[3] In 5 logour, 9 loggar. [? f. LOGGER *v.*] In *pl.* 'Stockings without feet, tied up with garters and hanging down over the ankles' (Jam.).

1489 *Ld. Treas. Acc. Scotl.* (1877) I. 149 Item, for vii elne of quhyte to be logouris to the King, the tyme his leg wes sayre..xxviijs.

'logger, *a. Obs.* exc. *dial.* [? Back-formation from LOGGERHEAD.] Thick, heavy, stupid.

1675 COTTON *Scoffer Scoft* 9 My head too heavy was, and logger, Ever to make a Pettifogger. **1781** J. RIPLEY *Orig. Lett.* xix. 100, I would have seized you by both ears..and given your logger head forty-five severe knocks against the pavement. **1812** P. FORBES *Poems* 73 (E.D.D.) Wow, man, ye'r like Davy Spence Wi' logger head. *Ibid.* 86 They sigh, an' shake their logger head, An' cry all's over!

logger ('lɒgə(r)), *v. Sc.* and *dial.* Also *Sc.* **loggar.** [? An imitative formation; cf. LOG *v.* and -ER[5].] *intr.* **a.** 'To hang loosely and largely' (Jam.). **b.** 'To walk with a lax gait or in a loose-jointed, swaying fashion' (*Northumbld. Gloss.* 1893). **c.** To shake as a wheel which has been loosened (Forby *Voc. E. Anglia*). Hence †**'loggerand** *ppl. a.*, ? straddling.

c **1470** HENRYSON *Mor. Fab.* XIII. (*Frog & Mouse*) vii, Hir loggerand leggis and her harsky hyde.

loggerhead ('lɒgəhɛd). Also 8 (sense 3) -heat. [f. LOGGER *sb.*[2] + HEAD.]

1. a. A thick-headed or stupid person; a blockhead.

1588 SHAKS. *L.L.L.* IV. iii. 204 Ah you whoreson logger-head, you were borne to doe me shame. **1595** *Enq. Tripe-wife* (1881) 168 That shee should sweare..that she would neuer marrie with the Grocer he was such a logger-head. **1611** COTGR., *Teste de boeuf*, a ioulthead,..logerhead; one whose wit is as little as his head is great. **1708** HEARNE *Collect.* (O.H.S.) II. 107 A pitifull, sneaking, whining Puritan, related to y[e] Loggerhead at Lambeth. *a* **1754** FIELDING *Fathers* V. iv, It is almost a pity to hinder these two loggerheads from falling foul of one another. **1790** MALONE *Shaks. Wks., Twel. N.* II. iii. 17 *note*, *The picture of we three.* I believe Shakspeare had in his thoughts a common sign, in which two wooden heads are exhibited, with this inscription under it: '*We three* loggerheads be'. The spectator or reader is supposed to make the third. **1821** *Joseph the Book-Man* 25 While loggerheads, most dignified, Are soon to wealth and rank allied. **1892** *West Cumbld. Times* Christm. No. 4/1 (Cumbld. Gloss. 1899) Keep off them rods yeh gert loggerheeds.

b. A local coin or token (see quot. 1799).

1797 *Sporting Mag.* X. 222 The dollars which now circulate through that part of the country [Wales] go by the name of Loggerheads. **1799** J. CONDER *Provincial Coins* 205 [Coins issued within the last 20 years] Loggerheads (*White Metal*). O[bverse]. A Cart under a Gallows, and three Men hanging, 'The End of three Loggerheads'.

2. a. A head out of proportion to the body; a large or 'thick' head. Chiefly *fig.*; also in phr. ***to join, lay loggerheads together.*** (See also LOGGER *a.*)

1598 E. GUILPIN *Skial.* (1878) 52 His body is so fallen away and leane, That scarce it can his logger-head sustaine. **1667** DRYDEN *Sir Martin Mar-all* I. i, Now, could I break my own logger-head. **1706** [E. WARD] *Wooden World Dissected* (1708) 15 These two often join Logger-heads together, and broach more pernicious Contrivances. **1754** RICHARDSON *Grandison* (1781) I. iv. 15 Let us retire, and lay our two loggerheads together. **1816** SCOTT *Antiq.* xlii, I have been following you in fear of finding your idle loggerhead knocked against one rock or other.

b. (See quot.)

Known to be older than 1885.

1909 A. C. FOX-DAVIES *Compl. Guide Heraldry* 193 The leopard's face... For some unfathomable reason these charges when they occur in the arms of Shrewsbury are usually referred to locally as 'loggerheads'.

3. a. An iron instrument with a long handle and a ball or bulb at the end used, when heated in the fire, for melting pitch and for heating liquids.

1687 in STRYPE *Stow's Surv. Lond.* (1720) II. v. xviii. 288/2 Not to suffer Pitch, Tar, Rozin, &c. to be heated on board by Fire, Loggerhead Shot, or any other thing. **1732** *Act 5 Geo. II*, c. 20 §4 If any Master..shall..cause or permit to be heated or melted by Fire, Logger Heat, Shot..any Pitch, Tar, Rosin, Grease [etc.]. **1760** *Chron.* in *Ann. Reg.* 158/2 We put hot logger heads in buckets of tar and pitch. **1858** SIMMONDS *Dict. Trade, Logger-head*, an iron for heating tar. **1860** O. W. HOLMES *Elsie V.* v, Three or four loggerheads (long irons clubbed at the end) were always lying in the fire in the cold season, waiting to be plunged into sputtering and foaming mugs of flip. **1900** ALICE M. EARLE *Stage Coach & Tavern Days* v. 108 Into this mixture [flip] was thrust and stirred a red-hot loggerhead, made of iron and shaped like a poker.

b. (See quot.)

1904 *Athenæum* 27 Feb. 280/1 The inkstands..include many of the prototypes of the circular heavy inkstand, still used, and known to many under the old name of 'loggerheads'.

4. a. 'An upright rounded piece of wood, near the stern of a whale-boat, for catching a turn of the line to' (Smyth *Sailor's Word-bk.* 1867). Also *transf.*

1840 R. H. DANA *Bef. Mast* xiii. 30 The saddles..have large pommels or loggerheads in front, round which the 'lasso' is coiled when not in use. **1850** SCORESBY *Cheever's Whalem. Adv.* ix. (1859) 116 It passes..around a post called the loggerhead, firmly secured to the frame of the boat. **1898** F. T. BULLEN *Cruise Cachalot* 39, I looked for the rushing of the line round the loggerhead (a stout wooden post built into the boat aft).

b. (See quot.)

1836 HEBERT *Engin. & Mech. Encycl.* II. 702 The beam or loggerhead, for the purpose of transmitting the motion of the piston to the pumps in the mine.

5. ? = LOGGAT.

1871 G. R. CUTTING *Student Life Amherst Coll.* 112 The game of 'loggerheads' has become obsolete, in this part of the country... A 'loggerhead' was a spherical mass of wood, with a long handle, and the game consisted of an attempt to hurl this towards a fixed stake, in such a manner as to leave it as near as possible.

6. As the popular name of various heavy-headed animals. **a.** (Also ***loggerhead turtle***, †***tortoise***.) A species of turtle, *Thalassochelys caretta.*

1657 R. LIGON *Barbadoes* (1673) 4 The Loggerhead Turtle. **1697** DAMPIER *Voy.* (1729) I. 103 There are 4 sorts of sea turtle... The Loggerhead is so call'd, because it hath a great head. **1772–84** COOK *Voy.* (1790) I. 30 On the 24th we caught a large loggerhead tortoise. *a* **1845** HOOD *Turtles* vii, Poor loggerheads from far Ascension ferried! **1884** *Girl's Own Paper* Feb. 227/1 A rarer kind [of tortoise-shell] is derived from the loggerhead turtle, a native of the Mediterranean and the Atlantic. **1895** *Royal Nat. Hist.* V. 83 The third, and probably the largest species of turtle, is the loggerhead (*Thalassochelys caretta*), easily recognised by its enormous head. *Ibid.* 84 The Mexican loggerhead (*T. kempi*), from the Gulf of Mexico, differs in [etc.].

b. applied to (*a*) two species of tyrant-bird inhabiting Jamaica, *Pitangus caudifasciatus* and *Myiarchus validus* or *crinitus*; (*b*) a N. American shrike, *Lanius ludovicianus* or *carolinensis*; (*c*) a large duck of the Falkland Islands, *Tachyeres* or *Micropterus cinereus*, the Race-horse or Steamer-duck.

1657 S. PURCHAS *Pol. Flying-Ins.* 128 In the Island of Barbadoes, and the adjacent Islands, are certain birds bigger than Sparrows, with a very great head, called by the English Logerheads and Counsellors. **1713** RAY *Syn. Avium* 185 *Sitta seu Picus cinereus major, capite nigro.* A Loggerhead. **1725** SLOANE *Jamaica* II. 300 [*Sitta, seu picus* Ray] They.. let Men come so near them that they knock them down with Sticks, whence they have the Name of Loggerheads. **1775** CLAYTON *Falkland Islands* in *Phil. Trans.* LXVI. 104 Here is a species of ducks, called the loggerhead, from its large head. **1831** A. WILSON & BONAPARTE *Amer. Ornith.* II. 86 *Lanius carolinensis*, Wilson. *Lanius ludovicianus*, Linnæus. —Loggerhead Shrike. *Ibid.* 87 It is generally known by the name of the loggerhead. **1870** *Amer. Naturalist* III. 159, I saw a Loggerhead attack a snake. **1906** *N.Y. Even. Post* 8 Aug. 2 Charleston S.C. pet canaries are being killed by a bird that is known as the 'loggerhead'. A loggerhead strikes at the canaries through the bars of the cage. **1939** FORBUSH & MAY *Nat. Hist. Birds Amer.* 398 The Loggerhead is an indefatigable destroyer of grasshoppers, for which it seems ever on the watch.

c. *dial.* applied to various fishes, as the bullhead; also to the tadpole. (See *Eng. Dial. Dict.*)

1775 CLAYTON in *Phil. Trans.* LXVI. 102 There are three or four species of the common loggerhead, or sculpa fish, common on the English coasts. **1880–4** F. DAY *Brit. Fishes* II. 179 *Leuciscus cephalus*... Large-headed dace; loggerhead.

d. *dial.* applied to various large moths.

1847 HALLIWELL, *Loggerhead*, the large tiger moth. *North.* **1893** in *Northumbld. Gloss.* **1894** *Hetton-le-Hole Gloss.*, *Loggerhead*, a clouded butterfly. Large moths are also sometimes called 'loggerheads'. **1899** *Cumbld. Gloss.*, *Logger-heed*, any kind of moth. The Ghost Moth.

7. *dial.* A plant of the genus *Centaurea.*

1829 J. L. KNAPP *Jrnl. Nat.* 25 The crop consists almost entirely of the common field scabious (*Scabiosa succisa*), logger-heads (*Centauria nigra*) [etc.]. **1866** COCKAYNE *Leechdoms* III. 315 *Saxon Names Plants, Bolwes,* loggerheads, *centaurea nigra...* Loggerheads is a name I have often heard in Oxfordshire.

8. *pl.* in various phrases. †***to fall, get, go to loggerheads***: to come to blows. ***to be at loggerheads***: to be contending about differences of opinion; also, rarely, ***to come to loggerheads***.

[The use is of obscure origin; perh. the instrument described in 3, or something similar, may have been used as a weapon.]

1680 KIRKMAN *Eng. Rogue* IV. i. 6 They frequently quarrell'd about their Sicilian wenches, and indeed..they seem..to be worth the going to Logger-heads for. **1681** *Trial of S. Colledge* 49 So we went to loggerheads together, I think that was the word, or Fisty-cuffs. **1755** SMOLLETT *Quix.* (1803) I. 66 The others..went to loggerheads with Sancho, whom they soon overthrew. **1806** JEFFERSON *Writ.* (1830) IV. 63 In order to destroy one member of the administration, the whole were to be set to loggerheads. **1831** J. W. CROKER in *C. Papers* 25 Jan., I hear from London that our successors are at loggerheads. **1887** FRITH *Autobiog.* I. xxiv. 347 The Lord Chancellor..and the Bishop came to loggerheads in the House of Lords. **1955** *Bull. Atomic Sci.* Mar. 90/3 Uranium men and oil and gas producers had long been at loggerheads due to the fact these natural substances frequently occur on the same site, though at different horizons. **1955** *Times* 19 May 4/2 The jury would not have much difficulty in getting rid of that suggestion, because those two were obviously at loggerheads. **1975** J. GARDNER *Killer for Song* i. 13 'James, it's good to see you.' His expression was at loggerheads with the words.

9. *attrib.* or *adj.* = LOGGER-HEADED.

1684 LUTTRELL *Brief Rel.* (1857) I. 301 For sayeing col. Sidney's jury were a loggerhead jury.

10. *Comb.*: **loggerhead sponge**, a West Indian sponge of inferior quality; 'probably named from Loggerhead Key' (Webster *Suppl.* 1902).

logger-headed ('lɒgəhɛdɪd), *a.* Also 8 lugger-headed. [f. LOGGERHEAD (or parasynthetically f. LOGGER *sb.*[2]) + -ED[2].]

1. Thick-headed, stupid.

1596 SHAKS. *Tam. Shr.* IV. i. 128 You logger-headed and vnpollisht groomes. **1643** J. WHITE *1st Cent. Scandal. Priests* 44 A company of logger headed fellowes. **1667** COTTON *Scarron.* IV. 107 Like a Logger-headed Lubber. **1831** TRELAWNY *Adv. Younger Son* I. 73 You logger-headed fellow.

2. Of animals: Having a large head. ***logger-headed duck*** = LOGGER-HEAD 6 b (*c*).

1653 WALTON *Angler* ii. 62 Oh! it is a great loggerheaded Chub! **1845** DARWIN *Voy. Nat.* ix. (1852) 200 In these [Falkland] Islands a great loggerheaded duck or goose (*Anas brachyptera*)..is very abundant. **1861** *Zoologist* XIX. 7603

The loggerheaded duck, whose wings..are used as propelling fins in the water.
transf. **1728** Vanbr. & Cibber *Prov. Husb.* II. i, A great Lugger-headed Cart, with Wheels as thick as a brick Wall.

†**loggership.** *nonce-wd.* [f. LOGGER *sb.*[1] + -SHIP.] Used as a derisive title for a sluggard.
1634 W. Wood *New Eng. Prosp.* II. xx. (1865) 107 They [the Indian wives] must dresse it and..see it eaten over their shoulders; and their loggerships [*sc.* the husbands] having filled their paunches, their sweete lullabies scramble for their scrappes.

†'**loggery**, *a. Obs.* [? LOGGER *sb.*[2] + -Y[1].] Of rank growth. (Cf. LOGGY *a.*)
1641 Best *Farm. Bks.* (Surtees) 52 But 20 or 22 stookes of large or loggery haver will bee a sufficient loade. *Ibid.* 54 When barley is loggery and full of greenes.

logget: see LOGGAT.

loggeyn(g, obs. form of LODGING *vbl. sb.*

loggia ('lɒdʒɪə; It. 'lɔdʒa). Pl. loggias, It. loggie. Also 8 *erron.* log(g)io. [a. It. *loggia*: see LODGE *sb.*] A gallery or arcade having one or more of its sides open to the air.
1742 *De Foe's Tour Gt. Brit.* (ed. 3) III. 119 Temples and Loggio's, built in many delightful Recesses. **1762** Kames *Elem. Crit.* (1774) II. 459 A logio laying the house open to the north, contrived in Italy for gathering cool air. **1762–71** H. Walpole *Vertue's Anecd. Paint.* (1786) I. 250 This mansion was..much improved by Sir Francis Bacon, who added Italian porticos, and loggias. **1834** Beckford *Italy* I. 116 Carved into as many grotesque wreaths of foliage as we admire in the loggie of Raphael. **1838** *Civil Eng. & Arch. Jrnl.* I. 329/2 A small loggia, formed by three open arches resting upon coupled columns. **1851** Ruskin *Stones Ven.* I. xix. §xvi, In Italy the staircase is often in the open air, surrounding the interior court of the house, and giving access to its various galleries or loggias. **1883** —— *Art of Eng.* v. 164, I have lived in marble palaces and under frescoed loggie.

loggia'd, *a.* Provided with loggias.
1903 *Westm. Gaz.* 9 Dec. 3/1 A great loggia'd palace, gaunt, time-stained, damp-eaten.

loggin ('lɒgɪn). *dial.* A bundle (of straw).
1765 *Museum Rust.* IV. xxx. 140 A good thresher can make up his loggins of two sheaves with sufficient neatness to please the nicest keeper of racers in the north. **1855** J. C. Morton *Cycl. Agric.* II. 724/2 *Loggin* (Yorks.), a bundle of straw about 14 lbs. **1857** C. B. Robinson *Gloss. to Best's Farm. Bks.* (Surtees) 181 They set up a loggin on end.

logginess. [f. LOGGY *a.* 2.] A state of heaviness or sluggishness.
1924 *Scribner's Mag.* July 88/2 He ate sparingly..rather as insurance against any sensation of logginess. **1969** P. Highsmith *Tremor of Forgery* xxv. 237 He awakened with the now familiar logginess of brain that always took fifteen seconds to clear.

logging ('lɒgɪŋ), *vbl. sb.* [f. LOG *v.*[1] + -ING[1].] **1.** The action of felling timber or hewing it into logs. Also *concr.* A quantity of timber felled.
1706 *New Hampsh. Prov. Papers* (1869) III. 337 Those whose livelihood chiefly consists in Logging and working in the woods. **1823** J. F. Cooper *Pioneers* xvii. (1869) 74/1 His piles, or to use the language of the country, his logging. **1881** *Chicago Times* 16 Apr., It has been a hard winter for logging. **1895** Crockett *Bog-Myrtle* 400 During his student days he combined the theory of theology with the practice of 'logging'.

2. (See quot., and cf. *log-rolling* 2.)
1817 Jefferson *Let.* 16 June in *Writ.* (1830) IV. 307 The barter of votes..which with us is called 'logging', the term of the farmers for their exchanges of aid in rolling together the logs of their newly cleared grounds.

3. The process of taking and recording information about something. (Cf. LOG *v.*[1] 5, LOG *sb.*[1] 7 d.)
1941 F. H. Lahee *Field Geol.* (ed. 4) xviii. 574 For..learning more about the lithology and fluid content of rocks in the walls of a bore-hole, and..for more accurately fixing the top and bottom contacts of rocks of varying character..electrical surveying, or electrical logging..has become common practice. **1958** L. E. C. Hughes *Electronic Engineer's Ref. Bk.* 832 With the aid of the automatic logging control..the alarm circuits on each unit controller trigger off printed messages. **1965** G. J. Williams *Econ. Geol. N.Z.* xvi. 255/1 Down-hole resistivity logging..showed that the kerogen content of the shale is thin-bedded, and that it can be measured rapidly by this means. **1967** *Electronics* 6 Mar. 269/1 Suggested applications include scanning, multiplexing..data logging..and telemetering.

4. *attrib.* and *Comb.*, as ***logging-camp, -chain, company, establishment, -path, railway, -road, -shirt, -sled, swamp, wheel***; **logging-bee** *U.S.* (cf. BEE[1] 4).
1836 *Backwoods of Canada* 192 We called a *logging-bee; we had a number of settlers attend..to assist us. **1880** N. H. Bishop *4 Months in Sneak-Box* 248 Following along its bank for a mile, we arrived at the *logging-camp of Mr. Childeers. **1825** A. Anderson *Diary* 10 Sept. in G. Sellar *Narr.* (1916) vii. 103 Walked to Toronto... Am no judge of oxen... Besides them had to pay for *logging-chain and an ox-sled. **1905** *Terms Forestry & Logging* (U.S. Dept. Agric. Bureau Forestry) 36 *Dump hook*, a levered chain, grab hook attached to the evener to which a team is hitched in loading logs. A movement of the lever releases the hook from the logging chain without stopping the team. **1910** J. Hart *Vigilante Girl* xxvi. 356 He was carrying in his hand a light logging-chain which was attached to his ankles. **1949** *Sat. Even. Post* 15 Jan. 71/2, I rushed around to the toolbox, dragged out one of the heavy logging chains. **1903** A. B. Hart *Actual Govt. Amer. Colonies* 326 *Logging companies buy up immense areas of land for timber. **1948** *Time* 9 Feb. 36/3 Logging companies protested it was a poor policy to rob them of 800 loyal, trained workers when there was a shortage of labor. **1851** J. S. Springer *Forest Life & Forest Trees* 67, I have seldom taxed my judgement as severely on any subject as in judiciously locating a *logging establishment. **1857** Thoreau *Maine W.* (1894) 291 We..were soon confused by numerous *logging-paths. **1888** J. Muir *Picturesque Calif.* 460 It is moved from camp to camp by the '*logging' railway. **1926** *Daily Colonist* (Victoria, B.C.) 7 July 1/7 Construction of logging railways and similar facilities will be proceeded with..for the re-opening of the logging camps in September. **1969** *Islander* (Victoria, B.C.) 9 Mar. 12/1, I used shank's mare along the logging railway to what was referred to as Headquarters Camp. **1839** C. T. Jackson *3rd Rep. Geol. Maine* 41 We..walked along a *logging road in the forest beside the stream. **1896** R. Kipling *Seven Seas* 112 Robin down the logging-road whistles 'Come to me'. **1845** *P. Parley's Ann.* VI. 30 A coarse garment of hempen cloth, called a *logging shirt. **1741** *New Hampsh. Prov. Papers* (1872) VI. 349 Sent our Baggage on *loging sleds to Rochester from Cochecho. **1848** Bartlett *Dict. Amer.*, **Logging swamp*, in Maine, the place where pine timber is cut. **1851** J. S. Springer *Forest Life & Forest Trees* 46 We have sometimes heard the voice of prayer even in the logging swamp. **1905** *Terms Forestry & Logging* (U.S. Dept. Agric. Bureau Forestry) 42 *Logging wheels*, a pair of wheels, usually about 10 feet in diameter, for transporting logs.

logging ('lɒgɪŋ), *ppl. a.*[1] [f. LOG *v.*[1] + -ING[2].] That logs or lies like a log.
1864 Woolner *My Beautiful Lady* 6 The logging crocodiles' Outrageous bulk.

logging ('lɒgɪŋ), *ppl. a.*[2] See also LOGAN-STONE. [f. LOG *v.*[2] + -ING[2].] That rocks. Only in ***logging-rock, logging-stone***.
1818 R. P. Knight *Symbolic Lang.* (1876) 148 The rude and primitive symbol of the logging rock. **1824** Hitchins & Drew *Cornwall* I. iv. §4. 148 In the parish of Sithney..stood a celebrated logging stone. **1881** *Harper's Mag.* Nov. 803 Logging-stones whose ponderous bulk sways at the touch of a woman's hand.

logging(e, obs. form of LODGING *vbl. sb.*

†'**loggish**, *a. Obs. rare*$^{-1}$. [f. LOG *sb.*[1] + -ISH.] Heavy, sluggish.
1642 Rogers *Naaman* 2 To raise and elevate muddy and loggish spirits from the dunghill.

loggy ('lɒgɪ), *a.* [f. LOG *sb.* + -Y.]
†**1.** Of a crop: Of strong growth, rank. (Cf. LOGGERY *a.*) *Obs.*
1620 Markham *Farew. Husb.* xvi. 141 A man may well mowe of good and deepe loggy medow, or of rough vneuen medow euery day one aker. **1635** —— *Eng. Husbandman* II. II. vii. 73 The Medow or Hay which comes thereof, is so ranke, loggy, and fulsome in taste, that [etc.].

2. Heavy; sluggish in movement. (Cf. LOGY *a.*)
1847 *Illustr. Lond. News* 28 Aug. 142/1 They were beat..by their slow, loggy stroke. **1886** *Outing* VIII. 58/1 They do very well sailing free but on the wind are loggy. **1902** *Westm. Gaz.* 18 Oct. 2/2 They seemed..'loggy' and slow to get going. **1966** H. Marriott *Cariboo Cowboy* vii. 66 A fellow doing quite a bit of riding needs two or three horses at least, because riding one horse day after day makes the horse loggy and leg-weary.

3. Abounding in logs.
1851 A. O. Hall *Manhattaner* 2 The sandy, boggy, loggy, grassy, and snaggy strips of land.

loggyne, -yng, obs. forms of LODGING *vbl. sb.*

†**logh.** *Obs.* Forms: 1 lóh, 4 looȝ, loȝ. [OE. *lóh*, **lóȝ*, ? = OFris. *lôch* place, OHG. *luog*, den, cave.] Place, stead.
11.. *O.E. Chron.* an. 779 (MS. F) Her Æðelbyrht arb' forðferde & Eanbald was ȝehalȝud an his loh. *Ibid.* an. 931 On his loh. *c* **1315** Shoreham v. 260 And ȝet ne were hyt noȝt y-noȝ One to agredy hyre looȝ And heȝ ine heuene blysse. *Ibid.* VII. 436 Nou schal man be in hare loȝ, And habbe ioye and blysse y-noȝ.

logh(e, loȝe, obs. var. LOUGH, LOW.

logh(e, loȝe, obs. pa. t. of LAUGH *v.*

loȝen, obs. pa. pple. of LIE *v.*[2]

logia: plural of LOGION.

Logian ('lɒdʒɪən), *a.* [f. *logi-a* LOGION + -AN.] Containing the Logia of Jesus.
1909 V. H. Stanton *Gospels as Hist. Documents* II. 48 To call the source we are considering simply 'the Logian document' cannot, I think, be open to the same objection. **1911** J. C. Hawkins in *Stud. Synoptic Probl.* 107 The convenient practice which has grown up of calling it the 'Logian source'. **1921** *Contemp. Rev.* Mar. 263 An expanded form of the original Greek Logian document.

-logian, an ending occurring first in *theologian* (a. OF. *theologien*, f. *theologie*: see -AN, -IAN), and hence adopted in a few mod. words to form substantival personal designations correlative with the names of sciences in -LOGY. The words so formed (e.g. *geologian, philologian*) are now obs. or rare, being superseded by formations in -LOGIST.

logic ('lɒdʒɪk), *sb.* Forms: 4–5 logik, 4–6 logyk(e, 4–7 logike, logique, 6 logycke, 6–7 logicke, 7–8 logick, 6– logic. [a. F. *logique* (13th c.), ad. med.L. *logica*, ad. Gr. λογική (first found in Cicero; ellipt. for ἡ λογικὴ τέχνη, rendered in med.L. by *ars logica*), fem. of λογικός (whence L. *logicus*) pertaining to reasoning, f. λόγος word, oration, reasoning, reason, etc.: see LOGOS. The word is current in all the mod.Rom. and Teut. langs.: Sp. *lógica*, Pg., It., Du. *logica*, Sw. *logika*, Ger., Da. *logik*.
Cicero uses also *logica* neut. pl. = Gr. τὰ λογικά 'logics' (see 1 b below).]

1. a. The branch of philosophy that treats of the forms of thinking in general, and more especially of inference and of scientific method. (Prof. J. Cook Wilson.) Also, since the work of Gottlob Frege (1848–1925), a formal system using symbolic techniques and mathematical methods to establish truth-values in the physical sciences, in language, and in philosophical argument.
The proper scope of this department of study has been and is much controverted, and books on 'logic' differ widely in the range of subjects which they include. The definition formerly most commonly accepted is 'the art of reasoning'; for various modern definitions see the later quots. At all times the vulgar notion of 'logic' has been largely that it is a system of rules for convincing or confounding an opponent by argument.
In the Middle Ages logic (or DIALECTIC, q.v.) was one of the three sciences composing the 'trivium', the former of the two divisions of the seven 'liberal arts'.
1362 Langl. *P. Pl.* A. XI. 127 Lo, logyk I lered hire and al þe lawe after. *c* **1386** Chaucer *Prol.* 286 A Clerk ther was of Oxenford also, That unto logik hadde longe ygo. **1387** Trevisa *Higden* (Rolls) III. 251 Permenides satte ten ȝere on a roche, and byþouȝt hym of þe art of logik. **1390** Gower *Conf.* III. 366 Sche made him such a Silogime, That he foryat al his logique. **1481** Caxton *Myrr.* I. viii. 34 The seconde science is logyke... This science proueth the pro and the contra. **1551** T. Wilson *Logike* A 1 b, Logike is an arte to reason probablie. **1593** Nashe *Christ's T.* 49 b, Law, Logique, and the Swizers, may be hir'd to fight for any body. **1605** Bacon *Adv. Learn.* II. xviii. §5 (1891) 179 Logic differeth from rhetoric..in this, that logic handleth reason exact and in truth, and rhetoric handleth it as it is planted in popular opinions and manners. **1707** Floyer *Physic. Pulse-Watch* 12 Galen brings too much Logick into his Treatise of Pulses, and mentions the Predicaments [etc.]. **1776** Adam Smith *W.N.* v. i. (1869) II. 354 Logic, or the science of the general principles of good and bad reasoning. **1837** Sir W. Hamilton *Logic* i. (1866) I. 4 Logic is the Science of the Laws of Thought as Thought. **1843** Mill *Logic* Introd. (1846) 9 Logic is not the science of Belief, but the science of Proof, or Evidence. **1870** Jevons *Elem. Logic* i. 1 Logic may be most briefly defined as the Science of Reasoning. **1903** B. Russell *Princ. Math.* I. i. 4 But now Mathematics is able to answer, so far at least as to reduce the whole of its propositions to certain fundamental notions of logic. **1932** Lewis & Langford *Symbolic Logic* v. 118 This logistic method requires that the first branch of logic to be developed should be the calculus of propositions. **1967** A. E. Blumberg in *Encycl. Philos.* V. 13/1 What distinguishes modern from ancient and traditional logic is not only its reliance on symbolic techniques and mathematical methods but also its vastly greater formal power and range of application. **1969** F. Mondadori in R. Klibansky *Contemp. Philos.* III. 352 The phenomenological foundation of logic will make a basic use of Gödel's theorem.

b. *pl.* in the same sense. (Cf. *ethics*, etc.) Not now in general use.
1637 Gillespie *Eng. Pop. Cerem.* III. vii. 120, I remember, that I heard in the logicks, of *pars essentialis* or *Physica*. **1651** W. Jane Εικων Ακλαστος 247 The Libellers Logickes serves him to as litle purpose, as his historie. **1698** Keill *Exam. Theory Earth* (1734) 89 The Theorist in this part has endeavoured to give us a proof of his great skill in Logicks. **1862** *Dublin Univ. Cal.* 48 The following books have been appointed for the Examination for Logical and Ethical Moderatorships:—Logics. All the Logics of the Undergraduate Course.

¶**c.** Used by translators and expounders of Hegel for: The fundamental science of thought and its categories (including metaphysics or ontology).
1838 *Penny Cycl.* XII. 99/2 Hegel divides philosophy into three parts:—1. Logic, or the science of the idea in and by itself. **1854** A. Tulk tr. *Chalybäus' Speculat. Philos.* 313 Philosophy..has three cardinal divisions,—the Logic, which with Hegel, as is readily seen, implies also Metaphysics; the Philosophy of Nature; and Philosophy of Mind. **1874** W. Wallace *Logic of Hegel* i. §9 Speculative Logic contains all previous Logic and Metaphysics. **1890** W. S. Hough tr. *Erdmann's Hist. Phil.* II. 686 The fundamental science, which Hegel calls Logic, but remarks at the same time that it may equally well be called Metaphysics or Ontology.

2. a. A system or a particular exposition of logic; a treatise on logic. Also, the science or art of reasoning as applied to some particular department of knowledge or investigation.
1377 Langl. *P. Pl.* B. XII. 267 To lowe lybbyng men þe larke is resembled; Arestotle þe grete clerke suche tales he telleth; Thus he lykneth in his logyk þe leste foule oute. **1594** R. Ashley tr. *Loys le Roy* 125 b, They which write for the most part, do nothing but..heape one on another Grammars, Rhetoricks, Logicks, Institutions [etc.]. **1699** Bentley *Phal.* xi. 296 If Mr. B. had studied his new Logic more and his Phalaris less; he had made better work in the way of Reasoning. **1756** Burke *Subl. & B.* Introd., Wks. I. 96 The logick of taste, if I may be allowed the expression. **1833** Sir W. Hamilton *Discuss.* (1853) 165 The arbitrary laws of our present logics. **1838** —— *Logic* App. (1866) II. 244 The Italian and Latin Logics of Genovesi are worthy of your attention. **1880** W. Wallace in *Encycl. Brit.* XI. 619/2 The logic of Hegel is the only rival to the logic of Aristotle. ..His logic is an enumeration of the forms or categories by

which our experience exists. **1882** R. ADAMSON *ibid.* XIV. 782/1 The metaphysical logic of Hegel, the empirical logic of Mill, the formal logic of Kant. **1884** *Mind* Jan. 123 In that speculative domain [Germany], Logics swarm as bees in spring-time.

b. In phr. ***the logic of* ——**, indicating the application of logical methods to other subjects of investigation or study; the inferential procedures or structure of some field of inquiry.

1845 MILL in *Westm. Rev.* XLIII. 319 By the logic of a science we understand its method; its particular modes of investigation, and the nature of its evidence. **1882** A. BAIN *John Stuart Mill* iii. 87, I was at the meeting, and listened to Herschel's address. One notable feature in it was the allusion to the recent works on the Logic of Science, by Whewell and Mill especially. **1934** *Mind* XLIII. 101 Little puzzles about the logic of classes. **1937** A. SMEATON tr. *Carnap's Logical Syntax of Lang.* IV. §70. 256 All the foregoing systems of the logic of modalities.. have, it seems, applied the quasi-syntactical method. **1942** R. G. COLLINGWOOD *New Leviathan* xxxi. 252 As mathematics is the logic of physics, so law is the logic of politics. **1945** *Mind* LIV. 175, I now regard semantics as the fulfilment of the old search for a logic of meaning, which had not been fulfilled before in any precise and satisfactory way. **1971** KOPNIN & NARSKY in R. Klibansky *Contemp. Philos.* IV. 321 The elaboration of these problems has led to the necessity of investigating the logic of contemporary scientific knowledge.

3. a. Logical argumentation; a mode of argumentation viewed as good or bad according to its conformity or want of conformity to logical principles. *to chop logic*: see CHOP *v.*[2] 8. Also, logical pertinence or propriety.

1601 BP. W. BARLOW *Serm. Paules Crosse* Pref. 7 Malice marres logike and charitie both. **1646** SIR T. BROWNE *Pseud. Ep.* I. iv. 15 This was the Logick of the Jews, when they accused our Saviour unto Pilate. **1647** CLARENDON *Hist. Reb.* I. §150 But when they.. instead of giving were required to pay, and by a logic that left no man any thing which he might call his own. **1738** JOHNSON *London* 71, [I] A statesman's logick unconvinced can hear. **1795** *Gentl. Mag.* 541/1 You will be astonished at the logick which could draw such an inference from that address. **1830** MACAULAY *Rob. Montgomery* Ess. (1887) 140 We should be sorry to stake our faith in a higher Power on Mr. Robert Montgomery's logic. **1843** CARLYLE *Past & Pr.* III. v, Driven alike by its Logic, and its Unlogic. **1850** MRS. BROWNING *Poems* I. 4 *Gab. Depart. Luc.* And where's the logic of 'depart'? **1863** E. V. NEALE *Anal. Th. & Nat.* 33 As.. Sir William Hamilton argues with overpowering learning and logic. **1891** *Daily News* 23 Mar. 4/7 England, as Mr. Disraeli once said, is not governed by logic.

b. *transf.* A means of convincing or proving. Phr. ***the logic of the situation***, the facts which dictate what action is rationally to be taken.

1682 G. TOPHAM *Rome's Tradit.* Ep. Ded., Bonner's Logick, Fire and Faggot. **1711** ADDISON *Spect.* No. 239 ¶8 A certain Grand Monarch.. writ upon his Great Guns—*Ratio ultima Regum*, The Logick of Kings. **1816** *Sporting Mag.* XLVIII. 180 On setting to Lancaster cleanly hit Ford down; when it was loudly vociferated 'What do you think of that for logic'? **1859** E. FITZGERALD tr. *Omar* xliii. (1899) 83 The Grape that can with Logic absolute The Two-and-Seventy jarring Sects confute. **1869** J. EADIE *Comm. Gal.* 133 The logic of their facts was irresistible. **1876** W. JAMES *Coll. Ess. & Rev.* (1920) 34 The very essential logic of the situation demands that we wait not for any outward sign. **1880** *Daily Tel.* 28 Oct., The 'logic of events' may prove too strong for them, and what reason could not effect necessity may enforce. **1901** *Scotsman* 14 Mar. 7/5 Their territory.. was annexed to the British domain in consequence of the terrible logic of war. **1945** K. R. POPPER *Open Soc.* II. xiv. 90 The detailed determination of his action by what we may call the logic of the situation. **1946** E. WILSON *Mem. Hecate County* (1951) iv. 117 The logic of the situation impelled me to force her backwards, dropping one hand to her waist. **1960** *Rep. Proc. Conf. Univ. U.K.* 58 For the ambitious young man, the logic of the situation (which fortunately doesn't wholly govern his conduct) is this: time given to teaching is time taken from research; and his future depends not on teaching, but on research. **1961** *Observer* 19 Nov. 11/8 He said that Mr. Gaitskell had taken up the position of outside-right, and that the logic of the situation was for him to reorganise his team so that it would at least be facing in the same direction. **1969** H. PERKIN *Key Profession* v. 214 The logic of the situation was that the C.A.T.s should seek to complete their upgrading by seeking recognition as universities.

4. *Computers* and *Electronics*. **a.** The system or principles underlying the representation of logical operations and two-valued variables by electrical or other physical signals and their interactions; the forms and interconnections of logic elements in any particular piece of equipment, in so far as they relate to the interaction of signals and not to the physical nature of the components used; also, the actual components and circuitry; logical operations collectively, as performed by electronic or other devices.

1950 W. W. STIFLER *High-Speed Computing Devices* v. 62 For the convenient operation of a general-purpose machine, they [*sc.* Burks, Goldstine, and von Neumann] point out, it is essential that some steps be taken to translate the nonconforming command quoted above to the same stereotype form. This translation of description of all possible operations to prescribed forms has been called the logic of the machine by these authors, and the term is now in general use. **1952** *Math. Tables & Other Aids to Computation* VI. 42 It is possible, with this new approach, to obtain many of the advantages of a digital computer and also the essential advantages of an analog differential analyzer. The result is a different type of digital 'logic' from that used in the general purpose digital computer. **1954** *IRE Trans. Electronic Computers* Mar. 33/2 The authors have presented the more general aspects of the machine in block diagram form and in addition have given pertinent illustrations of the instrumentation of the logic. **1956** *Ibid.* IV. 134 (*caption*) Logic for self-timing full length carry. **1962** SIMPSON & RICHARDS *Physical Princ. Junction Transistors* xvi. 401 If we now define the most positive value of the output to represent a 'one' and the most negative value a 'zero' in a binary system of arithmetic (the positive logic system) the emitter followers form an 'AND' gate, i.e. all *n* inputs must be 'one' if the output is to be 'one'. **1967** *Electronics* 6 Mar. 26 Santa Clara was making milliwatt resistor-transistor logic for the project. **1968** *Proc. Inst. Electr. Engin.* CXV. 1385/2 He separated the ternary circuits into two sets of binary circuits, one based on a positive logic and the other on a negative one. Then he used translating circuits between the two logics and achieved a true ternary output with the aid of a combining circuit. **1970** *New Yorker* 11 Apr. 34 The computer logic is so fast that it has to loaf at several intervals while the input and output devices.. are printing information. **1971** *New Scientist* 25 Mar. 692 The technology [of fluidics] was developed basically to provide a system of control logic and power amplification in the adverse environment of space. **1973** *Nature* 20 Apr. 494/2 The transistor has endowed tremendous scope for performing electronic functions (for example switching, which permits binary logic, and amplifying, which makes possible many other forms of signal processing).

b. *attrib.*, as ***logic design, designer, diagram, function, module, network, operation, state***; **logic circuit**, a circuit for performing logical operations and consisting of one or more logic elements; **logic element**, a device (usu. electronic) for performing a logical operation, in which the past or present values of one or more inputs determine the values of one or more outputs in accordance with a simple scheme which most commonly involves, in effect, only two possible values for the signals; **logic gate**, a logic circuit that is a gate (GATE *sb.*[1] 8 g).

1953 *Communications & Electronics* (N.Y.) Nov. 593/1 The search for simple abstract techniques to be applied to the design of switching systems is still.. in its early stages. The problem in this area which has been attacked most energetically is that of the synthesis of efficient combinational that is, nonsequential, logic circuits. **1959** K. HENNEY *Radio Engin. Handbk.* (ed. 5) ix. 7 Very complicated logic circuits involving many thousands of diodes have been assembled for use in electronic computers. **1968** *Times* 18 Oct. 16/5 Computer logic circuits based on the ternary system of arithmetic have been devised by two engineers... They have devised logic circuits that perform the basic arithmetical operations in ternary numbers. **1956** *IRE Trans. Electronic Computers* V. 132/2 The evolution of a set of standard logical circuit blocks allows this design without direct reference to the circuits, thus reducing logic design to the application of a set of rules expressing the input and output capabilities of each of the logical circuit blocks. **1972** D. ZISSOS *Logic Design Algorithms* p. v, Complex switching circuits are used extensively, not only in the logic design of systems such as digital computers and message-switching networks, where they are the subject of study by specialist logic designers, but also for purposes of industrial control and automation. **1956** Logic designer [see LOGICAL *a.* 1 b]. **1962** *Gloss. Terms Automatic Data Processing* (*B.S.I.*) 59 *Logic diagram*, a graphical representation of the logic design. **1971** J. H. SMITH *Digital Logic* iv. 54 There are a number of different circuits which will carry out this function and it is normal to use the symbol of the circuit employed when drawing logic diagrams. **1959** C. V. L. SMITH *Electronic Digital Computers* iv. 106 This technique makes it possible to make large arrays of logic elements in very compact form. *Ibid.* (*heading*) Symbols for logic elements. **1969** P. B. JORDAIN *Condensed Computer Encycl.* 291 A sequential logic element has an output determined by present and past input signals: it has some degree of retention, or memory. **1971** *New Scientist* 25 Mar. 692 The technology of fluidics is divided into.. pure fluidic techniques which use a logic element with no moving parts, and the method using moving part logic. **1959** K. HENNEY *Radio Engin. Handbk.* (ed. 5) ix. 7 Since diodes have two distinctly differing impedance levels, they lend themselves to use in performing predetermined decision or logic functions just as switches or relays may. **1961** *Times* 3 Oct. (Computer Suppl.) p. v, What the technical terms (binary, logic gates, programme and many others) mean. **1967** *Electronics* 6 Mar. 45/3 Each cell will have a working structure, or 'base', of 13 logic gates, plus 13 flip-flops. **1971** J. H. SMITH *Digital Logic* iv. 40 It is usually unnecessary to design logical circuitry today, as many manufacturers supply logic modules to carry out the more common forms of logic. **1974** *Physics Bull.* Mar. 113/1 Ortec will be displaying the new fast logic modules in the M300 series. **1961** *Engineering* 17 Feb. 269/1 The first step in designing the computer was the synthesis of the logic network to perform the necessary functions. **1970** *Nature* 12 Sept. 1092/2 The most exciting possibility for these devices lies naturally in their use as shift registers and for logic operations in computers. **1973** *Sci. Amer.* Nov. 14/1 (Advt.), In a digital circuit, the important thing is to know the logic state of a node, whether it's above the threshold voltage and therefore a logic high, or below the threshold voltage and therefore a logic low.

5. *attrib.* = of or pertaining to logic.

In some of the earlier quots. possibly a real adj. (like L. *logicus*, F. *logique*) = LOGICAL 1.

1581 J. HAMILTON *Catholik & Facile Traictise* 19 Zung men neu cum out of the grammer or logic scholes. **1608** T. MORTON *Preamble Encounter* 107, I haue now my Mitigator vpon a Logicke racke. **1613** JACKSON *Creed* II. ii. §6 Most of them vsually penned in a base and barbarous Logicke phrase. **1628** T. SPENCER *Logick* 36 This distinction, is received in all the Logick schooles. **1635** PAGITT *Christianogr.* II. vii. (1636) 79 Endeavoring to enthrall us with sophisticall arguments and Logick quirks. **1652** COLLINGES *Caveat for Prof.* (1653) A iij b, They would not endure to stand in a Logicke forme. **1678** GALE *Crt. Gentiles* III. 8 Sin is not a mere nothing, but has some kind of logic positivitie or notional entitie. **1724** R. WODROW *Life J. Wodrow* (1828) 18, I had a copy of Logick and Ethick Dictates in my father's hand among his school books. **1742** YOUNG *Nt. Th.* IX. 865 Wouldst thou on metaphysic pinions soar? Or wound thy patience amid logic thorns? **1843** CARLYLE *Past & Pr.* III. v. 223 Questions insoluble, or hitherto unsolved; deeper than any of our Logic-plummets hitherto will sound. **1869** BROWNING *Ring & Bk.* VIII. 243 He'll keep clear of my cast, my logic-throw.

6. *Comb.*: ***logic-book***; (sense 3) ***logic-chopper, -chopping***; †**logic-fisted** *a.*, having the hand clenched, like Logic in personification (see Cic. *Orat.* xxxii. 113; Bacon *Adv. Learn.* II. xviii. §5); **logic-tight** *a.* [after WATERTIGHT *a.* 1], impervious to logic or reason.

1685 tr. *Arnauld & Nicole's Logic* 17 We should give a reason for omitting so many questions as are found in the common Logic-Books. **1895** W. JAMES *Coll. Ess. & Rev.* (1920) 394 An hypothesis, we are told in the logic-books, ought to propose a being that has some other constitution and definition than that of barely performing the phenomenon it is evoked to explain. **1906** *Daily Chron.* 13 Mar. 6/2 Mr. Balfour.. made his reappearance in his old part of the Logic-chopper. **1924** R. GRAVES *Mock Beggar Hall* 32 Put it another way, thou logic-chopper. **1956** J. BLISH *Earthman, Come Home* i. 33 You have no ties, no faith. You will have to excuse ours. We cannot afford to be logic-choppers. **1904** W. JAMES in *Mind* XIII. 458 This is a kind of intellectual product that never attains a classic form of expression when first promulgated. The critic ought therefore not to be too sharp and logic-chopping in his dealings with it. **1960** KOESTLER *Lotus & Robot* I. iii. 132 The Schoolmen confined themselves to verbal logic-chopping. **1683** KENNETT tr. *Erasm. on Folly* 80 One, with an open-handed freedome, spends all he lays his fingers on; another with a Logick-fisted gripingness, catches at, and grasps all he can come within the reach of. **1912** B. HART *Psychol. Insanity* vi. 82 The delusion is preserved in a logic-tight compartment. **1968** P. MCKELLAR *Experience & Behaviour* x. 269 The widespread tendency.. to surround their favourite beliefs with logic-tight compartments.

†**'logic**, *a. Obs. rare*$^{-0}$. (But see LOGIC *sb.* 5.) [ad. L. *logicus* (or F. *logique*), a. Gr. λογικός: see LOGIC *sb.*] = LOGICAL *a.*

1570 LEVINS *Manip.* 121/24 Logicke, *logicus*.

-logic ('lɒdʒɪk), **-logical** ('lɒdʒɪkəl), endings originally occurring in adaptations (through F. and L.) of Gr. adjs. in -λογικός, derived from adjs. and sbs. in -λογος, -λογον, which have derivative nouns of quality or function in -λογία, represented in Eng. by -LOGY. As the meaning of an adj. in *-logic(al)* may with substantial correctness be rendered by 'pertaining to ——logy', such adjs. are commonly apprehended as derivatives of the related sbs. (as if f. ——*logy* + -IC). In general, the existence of a sb. in *-logy* now implies the potential existence of a correlative adj. in *-logical* (the exceptions being confined to a few of the older words, such as *apology*, which have corresponding adjs. of different formation). For the difference in meaning between adjs. in *-logic* and the (now much more frequent) adjs. in *-logical*, see -ICAL, and cf. the note under GEOLOGIC 1.

logical ('lɒdʒɪkəl), *a.* (and *sb.*) [f. LOGIC *sb.* and L. *logic-us* LOGIC *a.* + -AL[1]. Cf. med.L. *logicālis* and obs. F. (16th c.) *logical.*]

1. a. Of or pertaining to logic; also, of the nature of formal argument.

1500–20 DUNBAR *Poems* lxv. 9 The curious probatioun logicall. **1588** FRAUNCE *Lawiers Log.* Ded., Since first I began to be a medler with these Logical meditations. **1626** BACON *Sylva* §98 But they are put off by the Names of Vertues, and Natures, and Actions, and Passions, and such other Logicall Words. **1646** J. HALL *Horæ Vac.* 39 A Sermon, in which there would be Ethicall Truth as well as Logicall. **1651** BAXTER *Inf. Bapt.* 212, I beg'd.. that we might keep close to the strictest Logicall Disputing. **1707** FLOYER *Physic. Pulse-Watch* 13 Galen then blam'd the School of Moses and Christ for want of Logical Demonstrations in their Discourses of Laws. **1844** WHATELY *Logic* III. Introd. (ed. 8) 156 Many Logical writers ..have undertaken to give rules 'for attaining clear ideas'. **1847** J. D. MORELL *Hist. View Philos.* (ed. 2) I. i. 95 To Logic, Hobbes devoted a considerable share of attention. The peculiarity of his logical system lies in the theory, that reasoning is merely a numerical calculation. **1851–5** G. BRIMLEY *Ess., Tennyson* 38 Our common speech, abounding in logical generalizations and names of classes. **1905** B. RUSSELL in *Mind* XIV. 490 The distinction of primary and secondary occurrences also enables us to deal with.. the logical status of denoting phrases that denote nothing. **1922** E. P. ADAMS tr. *Einstein's Meaning of Relativity* i. 1 The object of all science, whether natural science or psychology, is to co-ordinate our experiences and to bring them into a logical system. **1939** *Mind* XLVIII. 304 To say that a term is of such and such a type or category is to say something about its 'logical behaviour', namely, about the entailments and compatibilities of the propositions into which it enters. **1966** W. V. QUINE *Ways of Paradox* viii. 67 This condition is met by the usual logical languages, and presumably it can be met likewise by languages adequate to science in general.

b. *Computers* and *Electronics*. Of or pertaining to the logic (LOGIC *sb.* 4) of computers and similar equipment; designed to carry out processes on electrical or other signals analogous to the processes of reasoning, deduction, etc., employed in (formal) logic; *logical element* = *logic element* (LOGIC *sb.* 4 b);

logical operation: see 7; ***logical shift***, a displacement of the digits of a sequence by a specified number of positions in a way that is not equivalent to multiplication by an integral power of the base; *esp.* a cyclic shift, in which digits taken from one end reappear, in the same order, at the other end.

In some of the uses below *logical* can equally well be regarded as having the sense of LOGICAL *a.* 1.

1946 BURKS, GOLDSTINE, & VON NEUMANN (*title*) Preliminary discussion of the logical design of an electronic computing instrument. (Rep. submitted to U.S. Army Ordnance Dept., PB 96703.) **1946** GOLDSTINE & VON NEUMANN *Princ. Large Scale Computing Machines* in J. von Neumann *Coll. Works* (1963) V. 23 The Memory Organ.. In performing an operation (arithmetical or logical) it is usually necessary to store the quantities entering into it. **1950** [see COINCIDENCE 7 b]. **1956** *IRE Trans. Electronic Computers* V. 132/2 One of the important properties of a digital computer is that it may be assembled simply and easily from a few well-chosen functional circuits. Each of these circuits represents a logical element that is useful to the system or logic designer in planning a computer. **1958** GOTLIEB & HUME *High-Speed Data Processing* iii. 34 A concise and informative way of describing a computer is to draw its logical diagram which shows the paths and effects of the various signals through it. Logical diagrams are built up largely of gates. *Ibid.* v. 89 In a logical or cyclic shift the digits lost off one end of the number appear at the other end. **1962** *Newnes Conc. Encycl. Nucl. Energy* 671/2 Such a system is sometimes referred to as a logical switching system because the output responses are related by fixed rules to the inputs from the measurement channels. **1964** F. L. WESTWATER *Electronic Computers* iii. 49 The practical engineer must have the last word. Not infrequently, a design engineer will ask the logical designer to make alterations for various reasons. **1970** O. DOPPING *Computers & Data Processing* vii. 117 In the logical shift, all bits take part and zeroes are shifted in at one end. This kind of shift is suitable for handling non-arithmetic information. **1971** J. H. SMITH *Digital Logic* vii. 133 The reader using logical gating should analyse his specifications to eliminate the trivial and reduce the circuit as far as possible.

2. That is in accordance with the principles of logic; conformable to the laws of correct reasoning.

1588 A. FRAUNCE *Lawiers Logike* f. 120, I haue, for examples sake, put downe a Logicall Analysis of the second *Aegloge* in Virgill. **1689** PRIOR *1st Ep. Fleetwood Shephard* 39 Then he, by sequence logical, Writes best, who never thinks at all. **1814** D. STEWART *Hum. Mind* II. i. §1. 47 A process of logical reasoning has been often likened to a chain supporting a weight. **1828** MILL in *Westm. Rev.* IX. 144 Those who maintain, that to perform the logical analysis of an argument, in the manner pointed out by the syllogism, is not the best means of discovering whether it contain a flaw. **1845** COLERIDGE *Method* in *Encycl. Metrop.* I. 42 These cannot be introduced into a scientific treatise without destroying the symmetry of its parts by a suspension of the logical order. **1900** R. J. DRUMMOND *Relat. Apostol. Teach.* i. 25 He wants a logical explanation of the Christian faith. **1958** G. J. WARNOCK *Eng. Philos. since 1900* ix. 120 The narrowly logical, context-neglecting manner adopted by the practitioners of 'logical analysis'.

3. That follows as a reasonable inference or natural consequence; that is in accordance with the 'logic' of events, of human character, etc.

1860 MOTLEY *Netherl.* (1868) I. i. 11 Having the sovereignty to dispose of, it seemed logical that the Estates might keep it, if so inclined. **1874** STUBBS *Const. Hist.* I. i. 3 In France accordingly feudal government runs its logical career. **1883** tr. *Stepniak's Undergr. Russia* 121 It may be called the sign of a lofty mind to which heroism is natural and logical.

4. Of persons: Capable of reasoning correctly.

1664 PEPYS *Diary* 18 Nov., I find he is a very logicall man and a good speaker. **1712** ADDISON *Spect.* No. 291 ¶3 Nor is it sufficient, that a Man who sets up for a Judge in Criticism, should have perused the Authors above mentioned, unless he has also a clear and Logical Head. **1805** J. LEYDEN in *Scott's Prose Wks.* IV. Biographies II. (1870) 179 You logical lads of Europe will be very little disposed to admit the legitimacy of the conclusion.

Comb. **1901** *Edin. Rev.* Oct. 290 The strong and logical-minded Manning.

5. [*nonce-uses*, after Gr. λογικός.] Characterized by reason; rational, reasonable.

a **1652** J. SMITH *Sel. Disc.* I. iii. (1821) p. xxiii, We may.. be too apt to rest in a mere 'logical life', an expression of Simplicius, without any true participation of the divine life. **1768–74** TUCKER *Lt. Nat.* (1834) II. 466 The logical worship is rendered reasonable service in Rom. xii. 1.

†**6.** *sb. pl.* The subjects which are studied in a course of instruction in logic. ***little*** or ***small logicals***: certain minor questions of the science of logic, which formed the subject of the *Parva Logicalia*, a collection of treatises by Petrus Hispanus and others. *Obs.* exc. *Hist.*

1551 ROBINSON tr. *More's Utop.* II. (1895) 185 Those rules of restryctyons, amplyfycatyons, and supposytyons very wittelye inuented in the small Logycalles, whyche heare oure chyldren in euerye place do learne. **1569** J. SANFORD tr. *Arippa's Van. Artes* 22 b, Other intollerable, and vaine wordes which are writen in the little Logicals. **1691** WOOD *Ath. Oxon.* I. 10 John Colet.. after he had spent seven years in Logicals and Philosophicals, was licensed to proceed in Arts. **1716** M. DAVIES *Athen. Brit.* II. 328 He was educated in Grammaticals in Wikeham-School.. in Logicals and Philosophicals in New College Oxon.

7. Special collocations (see also sense 1 b): ***logical addition***, the formation of a logical sum; ***logical atomism*** (see ATOMISM 1 b); ***logical constant*** (see quots. 1903, 1914); ***logical construction***, an entity theoretically superfluous in that any statement referring to it can be replaced by an equivalent statement making no reference to it; ***logical empiricism***, the name given to philosophical theories which replaced those of logical positivism (see quots. 1936, 1937); so ***logical empiricist***; ***logical fiction*** = *logical construction*; ***logical form***, the form, as distinct from the content, of a proposition, argument, etc., which can be expressed in logical terms; ***logical grammar***, the rules of word-use in a proposition upon which its logical, as opposed to its purely grammatical, sense or meaning is held to depend; so ***logical-grammatical*** adj.; ***logical implication***, implication which is based on the formal and not the material relationship between propositions; ***logical machine***, an apparatus designed to facilitate logical calculations; also *transf.*; ***logical multiplication***, the formation of a logical product; ***logical operation***, an operation of the kind dealt with in logic (such as conjunction or negation); any analogous (non-arithmetical) operation on numbers, esp. binary numbers, in which each digit of the result depends on only one digit in each operand; ***logical paradox*** (see quot. 1967); ***logical positivism***, the name given to the theories and doctrines of philosophers active in Vienna in the early 1930s (the Vienna Circle), which were aimed at evolving in the language of philosophy formal methods for the verification of empirical questions similar to those of the mathematical sciences, and which therefore eliminated metaphysical and other more speculative questions as being logically ill-founded; hence ***logical positivist***; ***logical product***, the conjunction of two or more propositions, or the intersection of two or more sets (written $p \wedge q$, $p \cap q$, $p.q$, pq, p and q); ***logical structure***, the formal framework of logical rules to which a theory, language, proposition, etc., must conform in order to have truth-value; ***logical subject***, the subject which is implied in a sentence or proposition, or which exists in the deep structure of a sentence; ***logical sum***, the disjunction of two or more propositions, or the union of two or more sets (written $p \vee q$, $p \cup q$, p or q, $p + q$); ***logical syntax*** (see quot. 1934); ***logical truth***, that which is true in logical or formal terms regardless of material meaning; ***logical word***, a word of the type which gives logical context or form to a proposition but which, by itself, is non-representational and without meaning (see quot. 1940).

1868 C. S. PEIRCE in *Proc. Amer. Acad. Arts & Sci.* VII. 250 Let $a + b$ denote all the individuals contained under a and b together. The operation here performed will differ from arithmetical addition in two respects: 1st, that it has reference to identity, not to equality; and 2d, that what is common to a and b is not taken into account twice over... The process denoted by + .. I shall call the process of logical addition. **1903** B. RUSSELL *Princ. Math.* ii. 18 From this point we can prove the laws of contradiction and excluded middle and double negation, and establish all the formal properties of logical multiplication and addition—the associative, commutative and distributive laws. **1970** O. DOPPING *Computers & Data Processing* i. 23 In Boolean algebra.. instead of the usual mathematical operations, there are certain logical operations; the most common ones of these are logical addition, logical multiplication, and negation. **1914**, etc. Logical atomism [see ATOMISM 1 b]. **1973** E. GELLNER in Horton & Finnegan *Modes of Thought* 179 The.. formal fact of the existence and nature of the mosaic's framework itself. This vision is shared by classical empiricism and by doctrines such as 'logical atomism'. **1903** B. RUSSELL *Princ. Math.* i. 3 Pure Mathematics is the class of all propositions of the form 'p implies q', where p and q are propositions containing one or more variables, the same in the two propositions, and neither p nor q contains any constants except logical constants. And logical constants are all notions definable in terms of the following: Implication, the relation of a term to a class of which it is a member, the notion of *such that*, the notion of relation, and such further notions as may be involved in the general notion of propositions of the above form. **1914** —— *Our Knowl. External World* vii. 208 Such words as *or, not, if, there is, identity, greater, plus, nothing, everything, function*, and so on, are not names of definite objects, like 'John'.. but are words which require a context in order to have meaning... 'Logical constants', in short, are not entities. **1922** tr. *Wittgenstein's Tractatus* 69 My fundamental thought is that the 'logical constants' do not represent. That the *logic* of the facts cannot be represented. **1958** G. J. WARNOCK *Eng. Philos. since 1900* x. 125 We thus get a distinction between so-called 'logical constants', the irreplaceable words on which the validity of general patterns of inference depends, and items of non-logical vocabulary. **1965** B. MATES *Elem. Logic* iv. 49 The logical constants occurring in ϕ are understood in the way usual among logicians (i.e., '∨' as standing for 'or', '—' for 'not', the universal quantifier for 'all', etc.). **1883** F. H. BRADLEY *Princ. Logic* 236 To show a new relation of elements in a logical construction is demonstration in the sense of reasoning. **1914** B. RUSSELL *Our Knowl. External World* iv. 101 The only justification possible must be one which exhibits matter as a logical construction from sense-data. **1936** A. J. AYER *Lang., Truth & Logic* iii. 73 The English State.. is a logical construction out of individual people. **1956** J. O. URMSON *Philos. Analysis* iii. 36 If 'X' is an incomplete symbol then Xs are logical constructions. Thus if the expression 'the average man' is an incomplete symbol we may say that the average man is a logical construction. **1936** A. J. AYER *Lang., Truth & Logic* 10 Our own logical empiricism to be distinguished from positivism. **1937** *Mind* XLVI. 345 Logical Empiricists are not attempting to be metaphysical, when they distinguish between language and reality. On the contrary, the distinction refers only to certain rules of usage for statements and modes of speech. Since we have investigated the rules of speech in empirical sciences, we are justified in calling our viewpoint 'Logical Empiricism'. **1966** J. J. KATZ *Philos. of Lang.* iii. 16 The chief reason for this failure on the part of *logical empiricism*.. and *ordinary language philosophy* ..was that both were governed in their inferences.. by an assumption about the nature of language. **1936** *Mind* XLV. 545 J. Somerville [in] 'The Social Ideas of the Wiener Kreis's International Congress' reflects on the Paris Congress 1935, [and] announces that the 'logical positivists' desire to repudiate Comte and to be henceforth known as 'scientific' or 'logical' empiricists. **1967** *Philos.* XLII. 293 A failure to work out in detail the consequences of logical empiricist principles for ethics. **1843** MILL *Logic* I. III. v. 404 This tendency shows itself very visibly in the different logical fictions which are resorted to even by philosophers. .. Thus, rather than say that the earth causes the fall of bodies, they ascribe it to a *force* exerted by the earth, or an *attraction* by the earth. **1918** B. RUSSELL in *Monist* XXVIII. 512, I believe that series and classes are of the nature of logical fictions. **1933** L. S. STEBBING *Mod. Introd. Logic* (ed. 2) 502 To say that the table is a logical fiction (or construction) is not to say that the table is fictitious.. it is rather to deny that, in any ordinary sense, it is an object at all. *Ibid.*, 'Logical fiction' may be taken to be an unfortunate synonym for 'logical construction'. **1840** MILL in *Westm. Rev.* XXXIII. 266 A truth.. to be believed in opposition to all that appears proof to the mere understanding; nay, the more to be believed, because it cannot be put into words and into the logical form of a proposition without a contradiction in terms. **1967** A. E. BLUMBERG in *Encycl. Philos.* V. 13/2 Logic confines itself to those arguments whose validity rests exclusively on the logical form of the statements composing them... There is still no fully satisfactory account of logical form. **1922** tr. *Wittgenstein's Tractatus* 55 A symbolism.. which obeys the rules of logical grammar—of logical syntax. **1962** L. J. COHEN *Diversity of Meaning* iii. 81 The most obvious fault in the doctrine of logical grammar is that it suggests the conceptual study of meanings to be concerned with something that is timeless and unchanging. **1937** *Atlantic Monthly* CLIX. 49/2 The logical-grammatical construction involved is so commonly mishandled in current American speech and print. **1887** A. SETH *Hegelianism* v. 172 In the first sense.. development means simply logical implication. **1904** B. RUSSELL in *Mind* XIII. 209 It would seem that.. logical implication is a simple notion, into whose composition the notion of terms does not enter. **1934** COHEN & NAGEL *Introd. Logic* i. 9 (*heading*) Logical implication does not depend on the truth of our premises. **1870** W. S. JEVONS in *Proc. R. Soc.* XVIII. 167 To explain the nature of the logical machine alluded to, it may be pointed out that the third of the fundamental Laws of Thought allows us to affirm of any object one or the other of two contradictory attributes. **1883** F. H. BRADLEY *Princ. Logic* 344 We shall discuss the Indirect Method, and with it the claims of the Logical Machine. **1943** *Mind* LII. 319 He is thus stymied at the outset, and being neither a logical machine nor an esthetic idiot he is likely to feel uncomfortable about it. **1868** C. S. PEIRCE in *Proc. Amer. Acad. Arts & Sci.* VII. 251 Let a, b denote the individuals contained at once under the classes a and b... If a and b were independent events, a, b would denote the event whose probability is the product of the probabilities of each. On the strength of this analogy.. the operation indicated by the comma may be called logical multiplication. **1903, 1970** Logical multiplication [see *logical addition* above]. **1885** C. S. PEIRCE in *Amer. Jrnl. Math.* VII. 186, I prefer not to assign determinate values to **f** and **v**, nor to identify the logical operations with any special arithmetical ones. **1932** LEWIS & LANGFORD *Symbolic Logic* i. 7 It would have coincided with what we now know as symbolic logic. That is, it would have been an organon of reasoning in general, developed in ideographic symbols and enabling the logical operations to be performed according to precise rules. **1960** M. G. SAY et al. *Analogue & Digital Computers* vii. 165 A zero input digit to this unit gives a one-digit output and a one-digit input gives a zero output. This is the logical operation 'NOT'. **1970** Logical operation [see *logical addition* above]. **1904** W. JAMES *Ess. Radical Empiricism* (1912) i. 11 'Representative' theories of perception avoid the logical paradox, but on the other hand they violate the reader's sense of life, which knows no intervening mental image. **1954** I. M. COPI *Symbolic Logic* 332 These two kinds of paradoxes were first explicitly distinguished by F. P. Ramsey in 1926. Since then those of the first kind have been known as 'logical paradoxes'. **1967** J. VAN HEIJENOORT in *Encycl. Philos.* V. 45/2 In logic the word [*sc.* paradox] has taken on a more precise meaning. A logical paradox consists of two contrary, or even contradictory, propositions to which we are led by apparently sound arguments. **1931** BLUMBERG & FEIGL in *Jrnl. Philos.* XXVIII. 281 To facilitate criticism and forestall even more unfortunate attempts at labelling this aspect of contemporary European philosophy, we shall employ the term 'logical positivism'. **1934** *Philos. Rev.* XLIII. 125 The logical positivism of the Vienna Circle.. is based.. upon this consideration of empirical meaning. **1968** M. BLACK *Labyrinth of Lang.* vi. 147 Logical Positivism has seen its best days. **1931** *Jrnl. Philos.* XXVIII. 291 The principle of causality is for the logical positivist not a categorical necessity of thought. **1967** J. PASSMORE in *Encycl. Philos.* V. 55/1 The logical positivists ordinarily took for granted the substantial truth of contemporary Science. Thus, it was a matter of vital concern to them when it became apparent that the verifiability principle would rule out as meaningless all scientific laws. **1868** C. S. PEIRCE in *Proc. Amer. Acad. Arts & Sci.* VII. 411 The numerical rank of a logical product depends on the identity or diversity.. of parts of the factors. **1903** B. RUSSELL *Princ. Math.* ii. 21 Most of the propositions of the class-calculus are easily deduced from those of the propositional calculus. The logical product or common part of two classes a and b is the class of x's such that the logical product of 'x is an a' and 'x is a b' is true. Similarly we can

define the logical sum of two classes (*a* or *b*). **1955** A. N. PRIOR *Formal Logic* I. i. 7 We may also have a conjunction or logical product of more than two propositions, the analogy with arithmetical multiplication still holding. **1959** Logical product [see *logical sum* below]. **1871** A. C. FRASER *Life Berkeley* ii. 39, I have tried elsewhere..to explain the logical structure of the *Essay on Vision*. **1918** B. RUSSELL in *Monist* XXVIII. 510 The first thing to do would be to discover the kinds of atoms out of which logical structures are composed. **1943** *Mind* LII. 26 Linguistic structure, though at times it conceals or distorts, has to be taken as capable of revealing logical structure, otherwise the study of logic would be impossible. **1970** L. J. COHEN *Implications Induction* i. 6 Many propositions are never hypothesised at all, even if alike in logical structure to those that are. **1898** *Mind* VII. 34 (*heading*) On the logical subject of the proposition. **1903** B. RUSSELL *Princ. Math.* iv. 44 Every term..is a logical subject. **1933** [see GRAMMATICAL *a.* 1 b]. **1965** N. CHOMSKY *Aspects of Theory of Syntax* i. 23 In (8i) [*sc.* 'I persuaded a specialist to examine John'] the phrase 'a specialist' is the Direct-Object of the Verb Phrase and the logical Subject of the embedded sentence. *Ibid.* iv. 163 It seems that beyond the notions of surface structure..and deep structure (such as 'logical subject'), there is some still more abstract notion of 'semantic function' still unexplained. **1868** C. S. PEIRCE in *Proc. Amer. Acad. Arts & Sci.* VII. 411 The numerical rank of a logical sum depends on the identity or diversity..of the integrant parts. **1903** [see *logical product* above]. **1959** C. V. L. SMITH *Electronic Digital Computers* ii. 32 Given two binary words..it is possible to generate a third word each bit of which is the logical sum or the logical product or, indeed, any Boolean function of the bits in the corresponding position of the given words. Operations of this sort may be called 'logical operations'. **1963** G. T. KNEEBONE *Math. Logic* ii. 53 In older accounts of symbolic logic, the terms 'logical sum' and 'logical product' are often used where 'disjunction' and 'conjunction' would now be preferred. There is indeed an analogy between the arithmetical operations of addition and multiplication. **1922** Logical syntax [see *logical grammar* above]. **1934** R. CARNAP in *Philos. Sci.* I. 9 By the 'logical syntax' (or also briefly 'syntax') of a language we shall understand the system of the formal (i.e. not referring to meaning) rules of that language, as well as..the consequences of these rules. **1945** *Mind* LIV. 172 The weaknesses of the argument might be due in part at least to a certain poverty in the technical equipment of 'logical syntax'. **1970** L. J. COHEN *Implications Induction* i. 6 Some elementary principles in the logical syntax of experimental support. **1818–19** COLERIDGE *Philos. Lect.* (1949) ix. 276 This necessarily led men..to doubt whether a logical truth was necessarily an existential one, i.e. whether because a truth was logically consistent it must be necessarily existent. **1877** W. S. JEVONS *Princ. Sci.* (ed. 2) viii. 153 Nothing is more certain than logical truth. **1943** *Mind* LII. 272 An exhaustive formulation of logical truth remains a worthy undertaking. **1940** B. RUSSELL *Inquiry into Meaning & Truth* 20 We pass from the primary to the secondary language by adding what I shall call 'logical words', such as 'or', 'not', 'some', and 'all', together with the words 'true' and 'false' as applied to sentences in the object-language. **1958** S. E. TOULMIN *Uses Argument* iv. 149 The validity of syllogisms being closely bound up with the proper distribution of logical words within the statements composing them. **1972** *Sci. Amer.* Sept. 82/3 Language performs this miraculous function largely through such little particles as 'if', 'when', 'not', 'therefore', 'all' and 'some', which have been called logical words because they account for the ability of language to formulate logical inferences (also known as syllogisms).

logicalist (ˈlɒdʒɪkəlɪst). *Metaph. rare.* [f. prec. + -IST.] One who regards the categories of logic as ontologically valid.

1865 J. GROTE *Explor. Philos.* I. 210 That which the logicalist begins with, that which constitutes what I have called the *thinghood* of things, is with the phenomenalist unnoticed or treated as a delusion.

logicality (lɒdʒɪˈkælɪtɪ). [f. as prec. + -ITY.] The quality of being logical.

1847 LEWES *Hist. Philos.* (1853) 152 A fanatical logicality of mind. **1863** *Reader* 18 July 63/3 Induction, certainty, logicality,..these are some of the things which mark a science. **1873** *Athenæum* 4 Jan. 12/1 A disputative logicality inherent in the mental constitution of the people.

ˈlogicalize, *v. rare*⁻¹. [f. LOGICAL + -IZE.] *trans.* To make logical. Hence **logicaliˈzation**.

a **1849** POE *Marginalia* Wks. 1864 III. 494 The thought is logicalized by the effort at expression. *Ibid.*, The mere act of inditing tends..to the logicalization of thought.

logically (ˈlɒdʒɪkəlɪ), *adv.* [f. LOGICAL *a.* + -LY².] In a logical manner; according to the principles of logic or the laws of sound reasoning. Phr. ***a logically perfect language***: a language in which the grammatical structure of sentences would be identical with their logical structure.

1620 T. GRANGER *Div. Logike* I. xli. 143 Vpon which consideration *Ramus* most prudently, and truly logically iudgeth the nature of the argument. **1695** LD. PRESTON *Boeth.* III. 134 It is most logically and truly concluded. **1717** PRIOR *Alma* II. 109 From hence I logically gather, The woman cannot live with either. **1827** WHATELY *Logic* III. §9 (ed. 2) 163 His argument, Logically developed, will stand thus. **1836** HOR. SMITH *Tin Trump.* (1869) 255 As one of his parishioners very logically remarked. **1918** B. RUSSELL in *Monist* XXVIII. 520 In a logically perfect language the words in a proposition would correspond one by one with the components of the corresponding fact, with the exception of such words as 'or', 'not', 'if'... The language which is set forth in *Principia Mathematica*..aims at being that sort of a language that, if you add a vocabulary, would be a logically perfect language. **1922** —— in Wittgenstein *Tractatus* Introd. 7 He is concerned with the conditions which would have to be fulfilled by a logically perfect language. **1939** M. BLACK in Copi & Beard *Ess. Wittgenstein's Tractatus* (1966) 97 This view of the character of Wittgenstein's investigation..may have been suggested by Russell's own attempts to construct a logically perfect language. **1953** *Mind* LXII. 13 They have even gone so far as to suggest that philosophers should invent a logically perfect language as a substitute for ordinary speech. **1971** A. FLEW *Introd. Western Philos.* xi. 388 One..of the many projects of Leibniz..was to develop a logically perfect language in which the truth or falsity of any proposition would be obvious from the symbols alone.

logicalness (ˈlɒdʒɪkəlnɪs). [-NESS.] The quality of being logical.

1727 in BAILEY vol. II; and in recent Dicts.

†**ˈlogicaster.** *Obs. rare*⁻¹. [ad. L. type **logicaster*, f. *logicus*: see LOGIC and -ASTER.] A petty logician.

1683 O. U. *Par. Ch. no Conventicles* 7 This Logicaster will be baffled.

logician (ləˈdʒɪʃən). Forms: 4 logissian, 4–6 logicien, 5 -icion, -ycien, 6 -ecien, -yssion, 6–7 -itian, 6- logician. [a. F. *logicien* (13th c.), f. *logique* LOGIC: see -ICIAN.]

1. A writer on logic; a student of logic.

1382 WYCLIF *Pref. Ep.* 66, I holde my pees of gramariens and retorikis, filoferis, geometrers, logissians [**1388** logiciens]. **1432–50** tr. *Higden* (Rolls) III. 219 Thei be logiciones ȝiffenge reason of either thynge as Plato was and his folowers. **1474** CAXTON *Chesse* 100 Gramariens, logyciens, maysters of lawe. **1530** PALSGR. 50 If they be suche as the logiciens call abstractes. **1660** R. COKE *Justice Vind.* 18 Logicians make three necessary parts or terms in every proposition. **1736** BUTLER *Anal.* I. iii. 78 Contradictory, as the logicians speak, to virtue. **1827** WHATELY *Logic* I. §1 (ed. 2) 22 The logician's object being not to lay down principles by which one may reason, but by which all must reason. **1876** JEVONS *Logic Prim.* 7 All people are logicians in some manner or degree.

2. One skilled in reasoning.

1592 GREENE *Disput.* 15 Thou art no Logitian, thou canst not reason for thy selfe. **1630** BRATHWAIT *Eng. Gentlem.* (1641) 72 Then wee had not..a subtill Scotus to play the Logician.

†**loˈgicianer.** *Obs.* Also logicioner, -itioner, *Sc.* logicinar. [f. prec. + -ER¹. (For the form cf. *practitioner.*)] = LOGICIAN. Also, one who is studying logic.

1548 PATTEN *Exped. Scotl.* M iv, Thear is no good logicioner, but woold think [etc.]. **1549** *Compl. Scot.* xx. 183 The sophist logicinaris per chance may argou, that tua contrareis can nocht be baytht false. **1565** T. STAPLETON *Fortr. Faith* 43 b, Chose then now whether you wil be accompted a lyar or a simple logicioner. **1569** CROWLEY *Soph. Dr. Watson* i. 65 When I was a Logitioner in Oxford. **1584** *Copie of a Letter* 77 He hath store..of manie fine wittes and good Logitioners at his commandment.

logicism (ˈlɒdʒɪsɪz(ə)m). [f. LOGIC *sb.* + -ISM.] The theory of Frege that a set of axioms for mathematics could be deduced from a primitive set of purely logical axioms, so that mathematics was essentially a part of logic.

1937 A. SMEATON tr. *Carnap's Logical Syntax of Lang.* v. §84. 325 What should a logical foundation of mathematics achieve? On this question there are various views; the fundamental antithesis between them is particularly clearly brought out in two doctrines, *logicism*, which was founded by Frege (1884), and *formalism*, represented by Frege's opponents. (The designations 'logicism' and 'formalism' only appeared later.) **1970** A. E. BLUMBERG tr. *Stegmüller's Main Currents Contemp. German, Brit. & Amer. Philos.* viii. 327 The modern philosophy of mathematics is characterized by the fact that various schools have been formed to overcome the difficulties occasioned by the antinomies. The oldest of these schools is logicism and goes back to Frege. **1973** *Sci. Amer.* Apr. 103/2 Typically the choice is determined by one's degree of sympathy with one or another of three modern schools of mathematical thought: logicism, formalism and intuitionism.

logicist (ˈlɒdʒɪsɪst), *sb.* and *a.* [f. LOGIC *sb.* + -IST.] **a.** *sb.* A (formal) logician; a mathematician who uses the methods or accepts the theory of logicism. **b.** *adj.* Of or pertaining to logicism. Also occas. **logiˈcistic** *a.*

a **1910** W. JAMES *Some Probl. Philos.* (1911) v. 82 Hibben and the logicists seem to believe that conception, if only adequately attained to, might be all-sufficient. **1916** J. DEWEY *Ess. Exper. Logic* 65, I am not questioning the right of the physicist, the mathematician, or the symbolic logicist to go ahead with accepted objects and do what he can with them. **1937** A. SMEATON tr. *Carnap's Logical Syntax of Lang.* v. §84. 326 The sentence..can be derived with the help of the logicist system. **1952** S. C. KLEENE *Introd. Metamath.* I. iii. 44 The logicistic definition of natural number now becomes predicative. **1956** E. M. HUTTEN *Lang. Mod. Physics* vi. 231 Our understanding of what statistical inference can do is obscured..by the logicist scheme of taking all hypotheses as universal implications, e.g. (x) (fx⊃gx). **1973** *Sci. Amer.* Apr. 109/3 In the 'new math' the logicist theory that natural numbers are derived from the quantification of classes was at last put into educational practice.

logicize (ˈlɒdʒɪsaɪz), *v.* [f. LOGIC or L. *logic-us* + -IZE.]

1. *intr.* To use logical argument, employ logic.

1835 *Blackw. Mag.* XXXVIII. 525 *Soc.* Hast thou, tell me, the spirit of Logic within ye? *Strep.* I can't logicize—no—but I'll pilfer with any. **1844** H. P. TAPPAN *Elem. Logic* Pref. 5 Reason..is the faculty which reasons or logicizes.

2. *trans.* To turn into logic. (See also quot. 1919.)

1865 J. H. STIRLING *Secret of Hegel* I. 200 Take Hegel's widest..division of Logic, Nature, Spirit: the last subsumes the second under the first; Spirit logicises Nature. *a* **1910** W. JAMES *Mem. & Stud.* (1911) xv. 393 All these tricks for logicizing originality, self-relation, absolute process, subjective contradiction, will wither in the breath of the mystical fact. **1919** B. RUSSELL *Introd. Math. Philos.* i. 7 Frege, who first succeeded in 'logicising' mathematics, *i.e.* in reducing to logic the arithmetical notions which his predecessors had shown to be sufficient for mathematics.

Hence **ˈlogicized** *ppl. a.*, **ˈlogicizing** *vbl. sb.*

1840 CARLYLE *Heroes* vi. (1858) 348 Intellect is not speaking and logicising: it is seeing and ascertaining. **1924** C. K. OGDEN tr. *Vaihinger's Philos. of 'As If'* III. iv. 360 This creating, logicizing, arranging, falsifying, is the best guaranteed reality. **1937** [see ARITHMETIZE *v.* 2 a]. **1957** J. PASSMORE *100 Yrs. Philos.* vi. 149 It is in the writings of G. Frege that the fundamental problems of a logicised mathematics first clearly emerged.

ˈlogico-, taken as comb. form of LOGIC, LOGICAL, in the sense 'logical and...'.

Used with adjs., sbs., and occas. with advbs. as second elements.

1810 COLERIDGE in *Lit. Rem.* (1838) III. 383 Bishops, liturgies [etc.],..were,..with celestial patents, wrapped up in the womb of this or that text of Scripture to be exforcipated by the logico-obstetric skill of High Church doctors. **1858** A. DE MORGAN *On Syllogism* (1966) 89, I distinguish the two sides of logic as the *logico-mathematical* and the *logico-metaphysical*, frequently dropping the prefix *logico*. **1898** J. A. HOBSON *John Ruskin* xiii. 319 No one.. more subtly practised the vital as distinguished from the logico-mechanical method of teaching. *c* **1905** C. S. PEIRCE *Coll. Papers* (1933) IV. I. ix. 274 Dr. Georg Cantor, the great founder and *Hauptförderer* of the logico-mathematical doctrine of numbers. **1918** C. I. LEWIS *Survey Symbolic Logic* p. v, Treatises..bristling with logico-metaphysical difficulties. **1922** D. AINSLIE tr. *Croce's Aesthetic* (ed. 2) II. v. 229 The same criticism..must have extended to the logico-grammarians of Port-Royal. **1930** T. SASAKI *On Lang. R. Bridges' Poetry* 3 The following different lines of approach are possible: (1) Logico-psychological [etc.]. **1931** J. WISDOM *Interpretation & Analysis* 13 The logico-analytic philosophers are constantly asking questions such as 'What does "This is a chair" mean?' **1935** *Mind* XLV. 263 It is only from a footnote that we learn that Pareto had realized the importance (and difficulty) of the 'theorem' that 'the logico-experimental truth of a theory and its social utility are independent'. **1937** *Mind* XLVI. 253 This book should prove stimulating to scientists, methodologists, and philosophers of all kinds, speculative, critical, or logico-positivist. **1938** C. MORRIS *Found. Theory of Signs* §5. 92 The logico-grammatical structure of language. **1940** W. V. QUINE *Math. Logic* 127 The atomic formulae formed by flanking 'ε' with variables happen merely to be the ones appropriate to logico-mathematical matters. **1943** H. READ *Educ. through Art* iii. 70 What is now suggested, in opposition to the whole of the logico-rationalistic tradition, is that there exists a concrete visual mode of 'thinking'. **1946** *Mind* LV. 44 It refers only to a very small group of Logico-Analytic philosophers. **1949** *Mind* LVIII. 397 The latest logico-analysts avowedly make use of utterances that are as NonSensical as those of the metaphysician. **1951** *Mind* LX. 24 The Logico-positivist proposes not to *speak* of 'inference'. **1952** *Mind* LXI. 574 The great logico-philosophical revolution of the last half century, initiated by Frege and Russell. **1958** W. STARK *Sociol. of Knowl.* II. viii. 320 If we study social reality as all reality should be studied, namely 'logico-experimentally', i.e. truly scientifically, we find..that human action is controlled by a set of drives. **1958** *Listener* 27 Nov. 879/1 The kind of thinking which I have called metaphysical thinking can lead to positive achievements, where both the system-philosophies and logico-linguistic investigations fail. **1970** J. N. FINDLAY tr. *Husserl's Logical Investigations* II. VI. viii. 826 The purely logico-grammatical laws which, as laws of complication and modification, distinguish the spheres of sense and nonsense. **1971** P. F. STRAWSON (*title*) Logico-linguistic papers.

logie¹ (ˈlogɪ). *Sc.* [Of unknown origin.] The open space before a kiln fire; = KILLOGIE.

a **1779** D. GRAHAM *Writings* (1883) II. 215 The kill-ribs brake, and down he goes with a vengeance into the logie. *a* **1806** *Yetts of Gowrie* xi. in Child *Ballads* IV. 175/2 He's sleeping in yon logie. **1824** MACTAGGART *Gallovid. Encycl.*, *Logie*, a fire in a snug place; a snug place for a fire. **1862** HISLOP *Prov. Scot.* 143 Mak a kiln o't and creep in at the logie. **1882** J. WALKER *Jaunt to Auld Reekie* 234 Dirt-choked its loggie Nae longer reeks.

logie² (ˈləʊgɪ). *Theatr.* [Said to be named from David *Logie*, the inventor (Barrère & Leland).] An ornament made of zinc, intended to give the effect of jewellery.

1860 *Cornh. Mag.* II. 239 *note*, Bits of looking glass, not convex, but cut in facets inwards, like the theatrical ornament cast in zinc, and called a 'logie'. **1883** SALA *Living Lond.* 483 The plastering of girdles with zinc 'logies'.

ˈlogily, *adv.* [f. LOGY *a.*] In a dull or heavy manner.

1912 J. LONDON *Son of Sun* viii. 326 The schooner,..from the weight of water on her decks, behaved logily.

loging, obs. form of LODGING *vbl. sb.*

logio, erron. form of LOGGIA.

‖**logion** (ˈlɒgɪɒn). Pl. logia (ˈlɒgɪə). [Gr. λόγιον oracle, f. λόγ-ος word.] A traditional maxim of a religious teacher or sage. Chiefly used with reference to the sayings of Jesus contained in the collections supposed by some to have been among the sources of our present Gospels, or to sayings attributed to Jesus but not recorded in the Gospels.

[**1587** GOLDING *De Mornay* vi. 62 Marke what we finde in their sayings gathered by men of olde time, which are commonly called Logia, that is to say, Oracles.] **1875** M.

logical operation: see 7; ***logical shift***, a displacement of the digits of a sequence by a specified number of positions in a way that is not equivalent to multiplication by an integral power of the base; *esp.* a cyclic shift, in which digits taken from one end reappear, in the same order, at the other end.

In some of the uses below *logical* can equally well be regarded as having the sense of LOGICAL *a.* 1.

1946 BURKS, GOLDSTINE, & VON NEUMANN (*title*) Preliminary discussion of the logical design of an electronic computing instrument. (Rep. submitted to U.S. Army Ordnance Dept., PB 96703.) **1946** GOLDSTINE & VON NEUMANN *Princ. Large Scale Computing Machines* in J. von Neumann *Coll. Works* (1963) V. 23 The Memory Organ... In performing an operation (arithmetical or logical) it is usually necessary to store the quantities entering into it. **1950** [see COINCIDENCE 7b]. **1956** *IRE Trans. Electronic Computers* V. 132/2 One of the important properties of a digital computer is that it may be assembled simply and easily from a few well-chosen functional circuits. Each of these circuits represents a logical element that is useful to the system or logic designer in planning a computer. **1958** GOTLIEB & HUME *High-Speed Data Processing* iii. 34 A concise and informative way of describing a computer is to draw its logical diagram which shows the paths and effects of the various signals through it. Logical diagrams are built up largely of gates. *Ibid.* v. 89 In a logical or cyclic shift the digits lost off one end of the number appear at the other end. **1962** *Newnes Conc. Encycl. Nucl. Energy* 671/2 Such a system is sometimes referred to as a logical switching system because the output responses are related by fixed rules to the inputs from the measurement channels. **1964** F. L. WESTWATER *Electronic Computers* iii. 49 The practical engineer must have the last word. Not infrequently, a design engineer will ask the logical designer to make alterations for various reasons. **1970** O. DOPPING *Computers & Data Processing* vii. 117 In the logical shift, all bits take part and zeroes are shifted in at one end. This kind of shift is suitable for handling non-arithmetic information. **1971** J. H. SMITH *Digital Logic* vii. 133 The reader using logical gating should analyse his specifications to eliminate the trivial and reduce the circuit as far as possible.

2. That is in accordance with the principles of logic; conformable to the laws of correct reasoning.

1588 A. FRAUNCE *Lawiers Logike* f. 120, I haue, for examples sake, put downe a Logicall Analysis of the second *Aegloge* in Virgill. **1689** PRIOR *1st Ep. Fleetwood Shephard* 39 Then he, by sequence logical, Writes best, who never thinks at all. **1814** D. STEWART *Hum. Mind* II. I. § 1. 47 A process of logical reasoning has been often likened to a chain supporting a weight. **1828** MILL in *Westm. Rev.* IX. 144 Those who maintain, that to perform the logical analysis of an argument, in the manner pointed out by the syllogism, is not the best means of discovering whether it contain a flaw. **1845** COLERIDGE *Method* in *Encycl. Metrop.* I. 42 These cannot be introduced into a scientific treatise without destroying the symmetry of its parts by a suspension of the logical order. **1900** R. J. DRUMMOND *Relat. Apostol. Teach.* i. 25 He wants a logical explanation of the Christian faith. **1958** G. J. WARNOCK *Eng. Philos. since 1900* ix. 120 The narrowly logical, context-neglecting manner adopted by the practitioners of 'logical analysis'.

3. That follows as a reasonable inference or natural consequence; that is in accordance with the 'logic' of events, of human character, etc.

1860 MOTLEY *Netherl.* (1868) I. i. 11 Having the sovereignty to dispose of, it seemed logical that the Estates might keep it, if so inclined. **1874** STUBBS *Const. Hist.* I. i. 3 In France accordingly feudal government runs its logical career. **1883** tr. *Stepniak's Undergr. Russia* 121 It may be called the sign of a lofty mind to which heroism is natural and logical.

4. Of persons: Capable of reasoning correctly.

1664 PEPYS *Diary* 18 Nov., I find he is a very logicall man and a good speaker. **1712** ADDISON *Spect.* No. 291 ¶3 Nor is it sufficient, that a Man who sets up for a Judge in Criticism, should have perused the Authors above mentioned, unless he has also a clear and Logical Head. **1805** J. LEYDEN in *Scott's Prose Wks.* IV. Biographies II. (1870) 179 You logical lads of Europe will be very little disposed to admit the legitimacy of the conclusion.

Comb. **1901** *Edin. Rev.* Oct. 290 The strong and logical-minded Manning.

5. [*nonce-uses*, after Gr. λογικός.] Characterized by reason; rational, reasonable.

a **1652** J. SMITH *Sel. Disc.* I. iii. (1821) p. xxiii, We may.. be too apt to rest in a mere 'logical life', an expression of Simplicius, without any true participation of the divine life. **1768–74** TUCKER *Lt. Nat.* (1834) II. 466 The logical worship is rendered reasonable service in Rom. xii. 1.

†**6.** *sb. pl.* The subjects which are studied in a course of instruction in logic. ***little*** or ***small logicals***: certain minor questions of the science of logic, which formed the subject of the *Parva Logicalia*, a collection of treatises by Petrus Hispanus and others. *Obs.* exc. *Hist.*

1551 ROBINSON tr. *More's Utop.* II. (1895) 185 Those rules of restryctyons, amplyfycatyons, and supposytyons very wittelye inuented in the small Logycalles, whyche heare oure chyldren in euerye place do learne. **1569** J. SANFORD tr. *Arippa's Van. Artes* 22b, Other intollerable, and vaine wordes which are writen in the little Logicals. **1691** WOOD *Ath. Oxon.* I. 10 John Colet.. after he had spent seven years in Logicals and Philosophicals, was licensed to proceed in Arts. **1716** M. DAVIES *Athen. Brit.* II. 328 He was educated in Grammaticals in Wikeham-School.. in Logicals and Philosophicals in New College Oxon.

7. Special collocations (see also sense 1b): ***logical addition***, the formation of a logical sum; ***logical atomism*** (see ATOMISM 1b); ***logical constant*** (see quots. 1903, 1914); ***logical construction***, an entity theoretically superfluous in that any statement referring to it can be replaced by an equivalent statement making no reference to it; ***logical empiricism***, the name given to philosophical theories which replaced those of logical positivism (see quots. 1936, 1937); so ***logical empiricist***; ***logical fiction*** = *logical construction*; ***logical form***, the form, as distinct from the content, of a proposition, argument, etc., which can be expressed in logical terms; ***logical grammar***, the rules of word-use in a proposition upon which its logical, as opposed to its purely grammatical, sense or meaning is held to depend; so ***logical-grammatical*** adj.; ***logical implication***, implication which is based on the formal and not the material relationship between propositions; ***logical machine***, an apparatus designed to facilitate logical calculations; also *transf.*; ***logical multiplication***, the formation of a logical product; ***logical operation***, an operation of the kind dealt with in logic (such as conjunction or negation); any analogous (non-arithmetical) operation on numbers, esp. binary numbers, in which each digit of the result depends on only one digit in each operand; ***logical paradox*** (see quot. 1967); ***logical positivism***, the name given to the theories and doctrines of philosophers active in Vienna in the early 1930s (the Vienna Circle), which were aimed at evolving in the language of philosophy formal methods for the verification of empirical questions similar to those of the mathematical sciences, and which therefore eliminated metaphysical and other more speculative questions as being logically ill-founded; hence ***logical positivist***; ***logical product***, the conjunction of two or more propositions, or the intersection of two or more sets (written $p \wedge q$, $p \cap q$, $p.q$, pq, p and q); ***logical structure***, the formal framework of logical rules to which a theory, language, proposition, etc., must conform in order to have truth-value; ***logical subject***, the subject which is implied in a sentence or proposition, or which exists in the deep structure of a sentence; ***logical sum***, the disjunction of two or more propositions, or the union of two or more sets (written $p \vee q$, $p \cup q$, p or q, $p + q$); ***logical syntax*** (see quot. 1934); ***logical truth***, that which is true in logical or formal terms regardless of material meaning; ***logical word***, a word of the type which gives logical context or form to a proposition but which, by itself, is non-representational and without meaning (see quot. 1940).

1868 C. S. PEIRCE in *Proc. Amer. Acad. Arts & Sci.* VII. 250 Let $a + b$ denote all the individuals contained under a and b together. The operation here performed will differ from arithmetical addition in two respects: 1st, that it has reference to identity, not to equality; and 2d, that what is common to a and b is not taken into account twice over... The process denoted by +.. I shall call the process of logical addition. **1903** B. RUSSELL *Princ. Math.* ii. 18 From this point we can prove the laws of contradiction and excluded middle and double negation, and establish all the formal properties of logical multiplication and addition—the associative, commutative and distributive laws. **1970** O. DOPPING *Computers & Data Processing* i. 23 In Boolean algebra.. instead of the usual mathematical operations, there are certain logical operations; the most common ones of these are logical addition, logical multiplication, and negation. **1914**, etc. Logical atomism [see ATOMISM 1b]. **1973** E. GELLNER in Horton & Finnegan *Modes of Thought* 179 The.. formal fact of the existence and nature of the mosaic's framework itself. This vision is shared by classical empiricism and by doctrines such as 'logical atomism'. **1903** B. RUSSELL *Princ. Math.* i. 3 Pure Mathematics is the class of all propositions of the form 'p implies q', where p and q are propositions containing one or more variables, the same in the two propositions, and neither p nor q contains any constants except logical constants. And logical constants are all notions definable in terms of the following: Implication, the relation of a term to a class of which it is a member, the notion of *such that*, the notion of relation, and such further notions as may be involved in the general notion of propositions of the above form. **1914** —— *Our Knowl. External World* vii. 208 Such words as *or, not, if, there is, identity, greater, plus, nothing, everything, function*, and so on, are not names of definite objects, like 'John'.. but are words which require a context in order to have meaning... 'Logical constants', in short, are not entities. **1922** tr. *Wittgenstein's Tractatus* 69 My fundamental thought is that the 'logical constants' do not represent. That the *logic* of the facts cannot be represented. **1958** G. J. WARNOCK *Eng. Philos. since 1900* x. 125 We thus get a distinction between so-called 'logical constants', the irreplaceable words on which the validity of general patterns of inference depends, and items of non-logical vocabulary. **1965** B. MATES *Elem. Logic* iv. 49 The logical constants occurring in ϕ are understood in the way usual among logicians (i.e., '∨' as standing for 'or', '—' for 'not', the universal quantifier for 'all', etc.). **1883** F. H. BRADLEY *Princ. Logic* 236 To show a new relation of elements in a logical construction is demonstration in the sense of reasoning. **1914** B. RUSSELL *Our Knowl. External World* iv. 101 The only justification possible must be one which exhibits matter as a logical construction from sense-data. **1936** A. J. AYER *Lang., Truth & Logic* iii. 73 The English State.. is a logical construction out of individual people. **1956** J. O. URMSON *Philos. Analysis* iii. 36 If 'X' is an incomplete symbol then Xs are logical constructions. Thus if the expression 'the average man' is an incomplete symbol we may say that the average man is a logical construction. **1936** A. J. AYER *Lang., Truth & Logic* 10 Our own logical empiricism to be distinguished from positivism. **1937** *Mind* XLVI. 345 Logical Empiricists are not attempting to be metaphysical, when they distinguish between language and reality. On the contrary, the distinction refers only to certain rules of usage for statements and modes of speech. Since we have investigated the rules of speech in empirical sciences, we are justified in calling our viewpoint 'Logical Empiricism'. **1966** J. J. KATZ *Philos. of Lang.* iii. 16 The chief reason for this failure on the part of *logical empiricism*.. and *ordinary language philosophy*.. was that both were governed in their inferences.. by an assumption about the nature of language. **1936** *Mind* XLV. 545 J. Somerville [in] 'The Social Ideas of the Wiener Kreis's International Congress' reflects on the Paris Congress 1935, [and] announces that the 'logical positivists' desire to repudiate Comte and to be henceforth known as 'scientific' or 'logical' empiricists. **1967** *Philos.* XLII. 293 A failure to work out in detail the consequences of logical empiricist principles for ethics. **1843** MILL *Logic* I. III. v. 404 This tendency shows itself very visibly in the different logical fictions which are resorted to even by philosophers... Thus, rather than say that the earth causes the fall of bodies, they ascribe it to a *force* exerted by the earth, or an *attraction* by the earth. **1918** B. RUSSELL in *Monist* XXVIII. 512, I believe that series and classes are of the nature of logical fictions. **1933** L. S. STEBBING *Mod. Introd. Logic* (ed. 2) 502 To say that the table is a logical fiction (or construction) is not to say that the table is fictitious.. it is rather to deny that, in any ordinary sense, it is an object at all. *Ibid.*, 'Logical fiction' may be taken to be an unfortunate synonym for 'logical construction'. **1840** MILL in *Westm. Rev.* XXXIII. 266 A truth.. to be believed in opposition to all that appears proof to the mere understanding; nay, the more to be believed, because it cannot be put into words and into the logical form of a proposition without a contradiction in terms. **1967** A. E. BLUMBERG in *Encycl. Philos.* V. 13/2 Logic confines itself to those arguments whose validity rests exclusively on the logical form of the statements composing them... There is still no fully satisfactory account of logical form. **1922** tr. *Wittgenstein's Tractatus* 55 A symbolism.. which obeys the rules of logical grammar—of logical syntax. **1962** L. J. COHEN *Diversity of Meaning* iii. 81 The most obvious fault in the doctrine of logical grammar is that it suggests the conceptual study of meanings to be concerned with something that is timeless and unchanging. **1937** *Atlantic Monthly* CLIX. 49/2 The logical-grammatical construction involved is so commonly mishandled in current American speech and print. **1887** A. SETH *Hegelianism* v. 172 In the first sense.. development means simply logical implication. **1904** B. RUSSELL in *Mind* XIII. 209 It would seem that.. logical implication is a simple notion, into whose composition the notion of terms does not enter. **1934** COHEN & NAGEL *Introd. Logic* i. 9 (*heading*) Logical implication does not depend on the truth of our premises. **1870** W. S. JEVONS in *Proc. R. Soc.* XVIII. 167 To explain the nature of the logical machine alluded to, it may be pointed out that the third of the fundamental Laws of Thought allows us to affirm of any object one or the other of two contradictory attributes. **1883** F. H. BRADLEY *Princ. Logic* 344 We shall discuss the Indirect Method, and with it the claims of the Logical Machine. **1943** *Mind* LII. 319 He is thus stymied at the outset, and being neither a logical machine nor an esthetic idiot he is likely to feel uncomfortable about it. **1868** C. S. PEIRCE in *Proc. Amer. Acad. Arts & Sci.* VII. 251 Let a, b denote the individuals contained at once under the classes a and b... If a and b were independent events, a, b would denote the event whose probability is the product of the probabilities of each. On the strength of this analogy.. the operation indicated by the comma may be called logical multiplication. **1903, 1970** Logical multiplication [see *logical addition* above]. **1885** C. S. PEIRCE in *Amer. Jrnl. Math.* VII. 186, I prefer not to assign determinate values to **f** and **v**, nor to identify the logical operations with any special arithmetical ones. **1932** LEWIS & LANGFORD *Symbolic Logic* i. 7 It would have coincided with what we now know as symbolic logic. That is, it would have been an organon of reasoning in general, developed in ideographic symbols and enabling the logical operations to be performed according to precise rules. **1960** M. G. SAY et al. *Analogue & Digital Computers* vii. 165 A zero input digit to this unit gives a one-digit output and a one-digit input gives a zero output. This is the logical operation 'NOT'. **1970** Logical operation [see *logical addition* above]. **1904** W. JAMES *Ess. Radical Empiricism* (1912) i. 11 'Representative' theories of perception avoid the logical paradox, but on the other hand they violate the reader's sense of life, which knows no intervening mental image. **1954** I. M. COPI *Symbolic Logic* 332 These two kinds of paradoxes were first explicitly distinguished by F. P. Ramsey in 1926. Since then those of the first kind have been known as 'logical paradoxes'. **1967** J. VAN HEIJENOORT in *Encycl. Philos.* V. 45/2 In logic the word [*sc.* paradox] has taken on a more precise meaning. A logical paradox consists of two contrary, or even contradictory, propositions to which we are led by apparently sound arguments. **1931** BLUMBERG & FEIGL in *Jrnl. Philos.* XXVIII. 281 To facilitate criticism and forestall even more unfortunate attempts at labelling this aspect of contemporary European philosophy, we shall employ the term 'logical positivism'. **1934** *Philos. Rev.* XLIII. 125 The logical positivism of the Vienna Circle.. is based.. upon this consideration of empirical meaning. **1968** M. BLACK *Labyrinth of Lang.* vi. 147 Logical Positivism has seen its best days. **1931** *Jrnl. Philos.* XXVIII. 291 The principle of causality is for the logical positivist not a categorical necessity of thought. **1967** J. PASSMORE in *Encycl. Philos.* V. 55/1 The logical positivists ordinarily took for granted the substantial truth of contemporary Science. Thus, it was a matter of vital concern to them when it became apparent that the verifiability principle would rule out as meaningless all scientific laws. **1868** C. S. PEIRCE in *Proc. Amer. Acad. Arts & Sci.* VII. 411 The numerical rank of a logical product depends on the identity or diversity.. of parts of the factors. **1903** B. RUSSELL *Princ. Math.* ii. 21 Most of the propositions of the class-calculus are easily deduced from those of the propositional calculus. The logical product or common part of two classes a and b is the class of x's such that the logical product of 'x is an a' and 'x is a b' is true. Similarly we can

define the logical sum of two classes (*a* or *b*). **1955** A. N. Prior *Formal Logic* I. i. 7 We may also have a conjunction or logical product of more than two propositions, the analogy with arithmetical multiplication still holding. **1959** Logical product [see *logical sum* below]. **1871** A. C. Fraser *Life Berkeley* ii. 39, I have tried elsewhere..to explain the logical structure of the *Essay on Vision*. **1918** B. Russell in *Monist* XXVIII. 510 The first thing to do would be to discover the kinds of atoms out of which logical structures are composed. **1943** *Mind* LII. 26 Linguistic structure, though at times it conceals or distorts, has to be taken as capable of revealing logical structure, otherwise the study of logic would be impossible. **1970** L. J. Cohen *Implications Induction* i. 6 Many propositions are never hypothesised at all, even if alike in logical structure to those that are. **1898** *Mind* VII. 34 (*heading*) On the logical subject of the proposition. **1903** B. Russell *Princ. Math.* iv. 44 Every term..is a logical subject. **1933** [see grammatical *a.* 1 b]. **1965** N. Chomsky *Aspects of Theory of Syntax* i. 23 In (8i) [*sc.* 'I persuaded a specialist to examine John'] the phrase 'a specialist' is the Direct-Object of the Verb Phrase and the logical Subject of the embedded sentence. *Ibid.* iv. 163 It seems that beyond the notions of surface structure..and deep structure (such as 'logical subject'), there is some still more abstract notion of 'semantic function' still unexplained. **1868** C. S. Peirce in *Proc. Amer. Acad. Arts & Sci.* VII. 411 The numerical rank of a logical sum depends on the identity or diversity..of the integrant parts. **1903** [see *logical product* above]. **1959** C. V. L. Smith *Electronic Digital Computers* ii. 32 Given two binary words..it is possible to generate a third word each bit of which is the logical sum or the logical product or, indeed, any Boolean function of the bits in the corresponding position of the given words. Operations of this sort may be called 'logical operations'. **1963** G. T. Kneebone *Math. Logic* ii. 53 In older accounts of symbolic logic, the terms 'logical sum' and 'logical product' are often used where 'disjunction' and 'conjunction' would now be preferred. There is indeed an analogy between the arithmetical operations of addition and multiplication. **1922** Logical syntax [see *logical grammar* above]. **1934** R. Carnap in *Philos. Sci.* I. 9 By the 'logical syntax' (or also briefly 'syntax') of a language we shall understand the system of the formal (i.e. not referring to meaning) rules of that language, as well as..the consequences of these rules. **1945** *Mind* LIV. 172 The weaknesses of the argument might be due in part at least to a certain poverty in the technical equipment of 'logical syntax'. **1970** L. J. Cohen *Implications Induction* i. 6 Some elementary principles in the logical syntax of experimental support. **1818–19** Coleridge *Philos. Lect.* (1949) ix. 276 This necessarily led men..to doubt whether a logical truth was necessarily an existential one, i.e. whether because a truth was logically consistent it must be necessarily existent. **1877** W. S. Jevons *Princ. Sci.* (ed. 2) viii. 153 Nothing is more certain than logical truth. **1943** *Mind* LII. 272 An exhaustive formulation of logical truth remains a worthy undertaking. **1940** B. Russell *Inquiry into Meaning & Truth* 20 We pass from the primary to the secondary language by adding what I shall call 'logical words', such as 'or', 'not', 'some', and 'all', together with the words 'true' and 'false' as applied to sentences in the object-language. **1958** S. E. Toulmin *Uses Argument* iv. 149 The validity of syllogisms being closely bound up with the proper distribution of logical words within the statements composing them. **1972** *Sci. Amer.* Sept. 82/3 Language performs this miraculous function largely through such little particles as 'if', 'when', 'not', 'therefore', 'all' and 'some', which have been called logical words because they account for the ability of language to formulate logical inferences (also known as syllogisms).

logicalist (ˈlɒdʒɪkəlɪst). *Metaph. rare.* [f. prec. + -ist.] One who regards the categories of logic as ontologically valid.

1865 J. Grote *Explor. Philos.* I. 210 That which the logicalist begins with, that which constitutes what I have called the *thinghood* of things, is with the phenomenalist unnoticed or treated as a delusion.

logicality (lɒdʒɪˈkælɪtɪ). [f. as prec. + -ity.] The quality of being logical.

1847 Lewes *Hist. Philos.* (1853) 152 A fanatical logicality of mind. **1863** *Reader* 18 July 63/3 Induction, certainty, logicality,..these are some of the things which mark a science. **1873** *Athenæum* 4 Jan. 12/1 A disputative logicality inherent in the mental constitution of the people.

ˈlogicalize, *v. rare*⁻¹. [f. logical + -ize.] *trans.* To make logical. Hence **logicaliˈzation**.

a **1849** Poe *Marginalia* Wks. 1864 III. 494 The thought is logicalized by the effort at expression. *Ibid.*, The mere act of inditing tends..to the logicalization of thought.

logically (ˈlɒdʒɪkəlɪ), *adv.* [f. logical *a.* + -ly².] In a logical manner; according to the principles of logic or the laws of sound reasoning. Phr. ***a logically perfect language***: a language in which the grammatical structure of sentences would be identical with their logical structure.

1620 T. Granger *Div. Logike* I. xli. 143 Vpon which consideration *Ramus* most prudently, and truly logically iudgeth the nature of the argument. **1695** Ld. Preston *Boeth.* III. 134 It is most logically and truly concluded. **1717** Prior *Alma* II. 109 From hence I logically gather, The woman cannot live with either. **1827** Whately *Logic* III. §9 (ed. 2) 163 His argument, Logically developed, will stand thus. **1836** Hor. Smith *Tin Trump.* (1869) 255 As one of his parishioners very logically remarked. **1918** B. Russell in *Monist* XXVIII. 520 In a logically perfect language the words in a proposition would correspond one by one with the components of the corresponding fact, with the exception of such words as 'or', 'not', 'if'... The language which is set forth in *Principia Mathematica*..aims at being that sort of a language that, if you add a vocabulary, would be a logically perfect language. **1922** —— in Wittgenstein *Tractatus* Introd. 7 He is concerned with the conditions which would have to be fulfilled by a logically perfect language. **1939** M. Black in Copi & Beard *Ess. Wittgenstein's Tractatus* (1966) 97 This view of the character of Wittgenstein's investigation..may have been suggested by Russell's own attempts to construct a logically perfect language. **1953** *Mind* LXII. 13 They have even gone so far as to suggest that philosophers should invent a logically perfect language as a substitute for ordinary speech. **1971** A. Flew *Introd. Western Philos.* xi. 388 One..of the many projects of Leibniz..was to develop a logically perfect language in which the truth or falsity of any proposition would be obvious from the symbols alone.

logicalness (ˈlɒdʒɪkəlnɪs). [-ness.] The quality of being logical.

1727 in Bailey vol. II; and in recent Dicts.

†**ˈlogicaster**. *Obs. rare*⁻¹. [ad. L. type **logicaster*, f. *logicus*: see logic and -aster.] A petty logician.

1683 O. U. *Par. Ch. no Conventicles* 7 This Logicaster will be baffled.

logician (ləˈdʒɪʃən). Forms: 4 logissian, 4–6 logicien, 5 -icion, -ycien, 6 -ecien, -yssion, 6–7 -itian, 6- logician. [a. F. *logicien* (13th c.), f. *logique* logic: see -ician.]

1. A writer on logic; a student of logic.

1382 Wyclif *Pref. Ep.* 66, I holde my pees of gramariens and retorikis, filoferis, geometrers, logissians [**1388** logiciens]. **1432–50** tr. *Higden* (Rolls) III. 219 Thei be logiciones ȝiffenge reason of either thynge as Plato was and his folowers. **1474** Caxton *Chesse* 100 Gramariens, logyciens, maysters of lawe. **1530** Palsgr. 50 If they be suche as the logiciens call abstractes. **1660** R. Coke *Justice Vind.* 18 Logicians make three necessary parts or terms in every proposition. **1736** Butler *Anal.* I. iii. 78 Contradictory, as the logicians speak, to virtue. **1827** Whately *Logic* I. §1 (ed. 2) 22 The logician's object being not to lay down principles by which one may reason, but by which all must reason. **1876** Jevons *Logic Prim.* 7 All people are logicians in some manner or degree.

2. One skilled in reasoning.

1592 Greene *Disput.* 15 Thou art no Logitian, thou canst not reason for thy selfe. **1630** Brathwait *Eng. Gentlem.* (1641) 72 Then wee had not..a subtill Scotus to play the Logician.

†**loˈgicianer**. *Obs.* Also logicioner, -itioner, *Sc.* logicinar. [f. prec. + -er¹. (For the form cf. *practitioner*.)] = logician. Also, one who is studying logic.

1548 Patten *Exped. Scotl.* M iv, Thear is no good logicioner, but woold think [etc.]. **1549** *Compl. Scot.* xx. 183 The sophist logicinaris per chance may argou, that tua contrareis can nocht be baytht false. **1565** T. Stapleton *Fortr. Faith* 43 b, Chose then now whether you wil be accompted a lyar or a simple logicioner. **1569** Crowley *Soph. Dr. Watson* i. 65 When I was a Logitioner in Oxford. **1584** *Copie of a Letter* 77 He hath store..of manie fine wittes and good Logitioners at his commandment.

logicism (ˈlɒdʒɪsɪz(ə)m). [f. logic *sb.* + -ism.] The theory of Frege that a set of axioms for mathematics could be deduced from a primitive set of purely logical axioms, so that mathematics was essentially a part of logic.

1937 A. Smeaton tr. *Carnap's Logical Syntax of Lang.* v. §84. 325 What should a logical foundation of mathematics achieve? On this question there are various views; the fundamental antithesis between them is particularly clearly brought out in two doctrines, *logicism*, which was founded by Frege (1884), and *formalism*, represented by Frege's opponents. (The designations 'logicism' and 'formalism' only appeared later.) **1970** A. E. Blumberg tr. *Stegmüller's Main Currents Contemp. German, Brit. & Amer. Philos.* viii. 327 The modern philosophy of mathematics is characterized by the fact that various schools have been formed to overcome the difficulties occasioned by the antinomies. The oldest of these schools is logicism and goes back to Frege. **1973** *Sci. Amer.* Apr. 103/2 Typically the choice is determined by one's degree of sympathy with one or another of three modern schools of mathematical thought: logicism, formalism and intuitionism.

logicist (ˈlɒdʒɪsɪst), *sb.* and *a.* [f. logic *sb.* + -ist.] **a.** *sb.* A (formal) logician; a mathematician who uses the methods or accepts the theory of logicism. **b.** *adj.* Of or pertaining to logicism. Also occas. **logiˈcistic** *a.*

a **1910** W. James *Some Probl. Philos.* (1911) v. 82 Hibben and the logicists seem to believe that conception, if only adequately attained to, might be all-sufficient. **1916** J. Dewey *Ess. Exper. Logic* 65, I am not questioning the right of the physicist, the mathematician, or the symbolic logicist to go ahead with accepted objects and do what he can with them. **1937** A. Smeaton tr. *Carnap's Logical Syntax of Lang.* v. §84. 326 The sentence..can be derived with the help of the logicist system. **1952** S. C. Kleene *Introd. Metamath.* I. iii. 44 The logicistic definition of natural number now becomes predicative. **1956** E. M. Hutten *Lang. Mod. Physics* vi. 231 Our understanding of what statistical inference can do is obscured..by the logicist scheme of taking all hypotheses as universal implications, e.g. (x) (fx⊃gx). **1973** *Sci. Amer.* Apr. 109/3 In the 'new math' the logicist theory that natural numbers are derived from the quantification of classes was at last put into educational practice.

logicize (ˈlɒdʒɪsaɪz), *v.* [f. logic or L. *logic-us* + -ize.]

1. *intr.* To use logical argument, employ logic.

1835 *Blackw. Mag.* XXXVIII. 525 *Soc.* Hast thou, tell me, the spirit of Logic within ye? *Strep.* I can't logicize—no —but I'll pilfer with any. **1844** H. P. Tappan *Elem. Logic* Pref. 5 Reason..is the faculty which reasons or logicizes.

2. *trans.* To turn into logic. (See also quot. 1919.)

1865 J. H. Stirling *Secret of Hegel* I. 200 Take Hegel's widest..division of Logic, Nature, Spirit: the last subsumes the second under the first; Spirit logicises Nature. *a* **1910** W. James *Mem. & Stud.* (1911) xv. 393 All these tricks for logicizing originality, self-relation, absolute process, subjective contradiction, will wither in the breath of the mystical fact. **1919** B. Russell *Introd. Math. Philos.* i. 7 Frege, who first succeeded in 'logicising' mathematics, *i.e.* in reducing to logic the arithmetical notions which his predecessors had shown to be sufficient for mathematics.

Hence **ˈlogicized** *ppl. a.*, **ˈlogicizing** *vbl. sb.*

1840 Carlyle *Heroes* vi. (1858) 348 Intellect is not speaking and logicising: it is seeing and ascertaining. **1924** C. K. Ogden tr. *Vaihinger's Philos. of 'As If'* III. iv. 360 This creating, logicizing, arranging, falsifying, is the best guaranteed reality. **1937** [see arithmetize *v.* 2 a]. **1957** J. Passmore *100 Yrs. Philos.* vi. 149 It is in the writings of G. Frege that the fundamental problems of a logicised mathematics first clearly emerged.

ˈlogico-, taken as comb. form of logic, logical, in the sense 'logical and...'.

Used with adjs., sbs., and occas. with advbs. as second elements.

1810 Coleridge in *Lit. Rem.* (1838) III. 383 Bishops, liturgies [etc.],..were,..with celestial patents, wrapped up in the womb of this or that text of Scripture to be exforcipated by the logico-obstetric skill of High Church doctors. **1858** A. De Morgan *On Syllogism* (1966) 89, I distinguish the two sides of logic as the *logico-mathematical* and the *logico-metaphysical*, frequently dropping the prefix *logico.* **1898** J. A. Hobson *John Ruskin* xiii. 319 No one.. more subtly practised the vital as distinguished from the logico-mechanical method of teaching. *c* **1905** C. S. Peirce *Coll. Papers* (1933) IV. I. ix. 274 Dr. Georg Cantor, the great founder and *Hauptförderer* of the logico-mathematical doctrine of numbers. **1918** C. I. Lewis *Survey Symbolic Logic* p. v, Treatises..bristling with logico-metaphysical difficulties. **1922** D. Ainslie tr. *Croce's Aesthetic* (ed. 2) II. v. 229 The same criticism..must have extended to the logico-grammarians of Port-Royal. **1930** T. Sasaki *On Lang. R. Bridges' Poetry* 3 The following different lines of approach are possible: (1) Logico-psychological [etc.]. **1931** J. Wisdom *Interpretation & Analysis* 13 The logico-analytic philosophers are constantly asking questions such as 'What does "This is a chair" mean?' **1935** *Mind* XLV. 263 It is only from a footnote that we learn that Pareto had realized the importance (and difficulty) of the 'theorem' that 'the logico-experimental truth of a theory and its social utility are independent'. **1937** *Mind* XLVI. 253 This book should prove stimulating to scientists, methodologists, and philosophers of all kinds, speculative, critical, or logico-positivist. **1938** C. Morris *Found. Theory of Signs* §5. 92 The logico-grammatical structure of language. **1940** W. V. Quine *Math. Logic* 127 The atomic formulae formed by flanking 'ε' with variables happen merely to be the ones appropriate to logico-mathematical matters. **1943** H. Read *Educ. through Art* iii. 70 What is now suggested, in opposition to the whole of the logico-rationalistic tradition, is that there exists a concrete visual mode of 'thinking'. **1946** *Mind* LV. 44 It refers only to a very small group of Logico-Analytic philosophers. **1949** *Mind* LVIII. 397 The latest logico-analysts avowedly make use of utterances that are as NonSensical as those of the metaphysician. **1951** *Mind* LX. 24 The Logico-positivist proposes not to *speak* of 'inference'. **1952** *Mind* LXI. 574 The great logico-philosophical revolution of the last half century, initiated by Frege and Russell. **1958** W. Stark *Sociol. of Knowl.* II. viii. 320 If we study social reality as all reality should be studied, namely 'logico-experimentally', i.e. truly scientifically, we find..that human action is controlled by a set of drives. **1958** *Listener* 27 Nov. 879/1 The kind of thinking which I have called metaphysical thinking can lead to positive achievements, where both the system-philosophies and logico-linguistic investigations fail. **1970** J. N. Findlay tr. *Husserl's Logical Investigations* II. vi. viii. 826 The purely logico-grammatical laws which, as laws of complication and modification, distinguish the spheres of sense and nonsense. **1971** P. F. Strawson (*title*) Logico-linguistic papers.

logie¹ (ˈlogɪ). *Sc.* [Of unknown origin.] The open space before a kiln fire; = killogie.

a **1779** D. Graham *Writings* (1883) II. 215 The kill-ribs brake, and down he goes with a vengeance into the logie. *a* **1806** *Yetts of Gowrie* xi. in Child *Ballads* IV. 175/2 He's sleeping in yon logie. **1824** MacTaggart *Gallovid. Encycl.*, *Logie*, a fire in a snug place; a snug place for a fire. **1862** Hislop *Prov. Scot.* 143 Mak a kiln o't and creep in at the logie. **1882** J. Walker *Jaunt to Auld Reekie* 234 Dirt-choked its loggie Nae longer reeks.

logie² (ˈləʊgɪ). *Theatr.* [Said to be named from David *Logie*, the inventor (Barrère & Leland).] An ornament made of zinc, intended to give the effect of jewellery.

1860 *Cornh. Mag.* II. 239 *note*, Bits of looking glass, not convex, but cut in facets inwards, like the theatrical ornament cast in zinc, and called a 'logie'. **1883** Sala *Living Lond.* 483 The plastering of girdles with zinc 'logies'.

ˈlogily, *adv.* [f. logy *a.*] In a dull or heavy manner.

1912 J. London *Son of Sun* viii. 326 The schooner,..from the weight of water on her decks, behaved logily.

loging, obs. form of lodging *vbl. sb.*

logio, erron. form of loggia.

‖**logion** (ˈlɒgɪɒn). Pl. logia (ˈlɒgɪə). [Gr. λόγιον oracle, f. λόγ-ος word.] A traditional maxim of a religious teacher or sage. Chiefly used with reference to the sayings of Jesus contained in the collections supposed by some to have been among the sources of our present Gospels, or to sayings attributed to Jesus but not recorded in the Gospels.

[**1587** Golding *De Mornay* vi. 62 Marke what we finde in their sayings gathered by men of olde time, which are commonly called Logia, that is to say, Oracles.] **1875** M.

ARNOLD *God & the Bible* vi. 321 The *logion*.. is given by two out of the three Synoptics. *Ibid.*, The *logia* of the Fourth Gospel. **1879** E. A. ABBOTT in *Encycl. Brit.* X. 815/2 It may imply that he [Papias], as others had done, wrote an interpretation of the 'Logia', accompanied by comments and by supplementary traditions. **1887** H. R. HAWEIS *Light of Ages* I. i. 43 Its [Buddhism's] sacred books consisting of the words of Buddha and his exploits, the Logia and the Acta. **1889** A. B. BRUCE *Kingd. God* x. 235 The authenticity of this logion has been called in question.

†**logis.** *Obs.* (Frequent in Caxton.) In 5 **lo(d)gys(e, logise, lodgis, -es, lodygys.** [a. OF. *logis, -eis*, f. *loge-r* to LODGE.] A lodging-place; lodgings; a tent, encampment; lair (of an animal).

c **1477** CAXTON *Jason* 37b, Hering in euery logise where they descended tidinges of him. **1481** —— *Godfrey* 11 How the turkes of Anthyoche sprang out, and assaylled the lodgyses of our peple. **1484** —— *Fables of Æsop* v. ix, Nyghe to the lodgys of the lyon. *c* **1489** —— *Sonnes of Aymon* xv. 362 Goo seke hym in his lodges. *c* **1500** *Melusine* xxxvi. 291 Of them were slayn XL. M[l] & more and dured the batayll vnto euen tyme, that they withdrew them eyther other part to theire lodgyses.

†**logism.** *Obs.* [ad. Gr. λογισμ-ός calculation, reasoning, f. λογίζ-εσθαι to count, reckon, conclude by reasoning, f. λόγ-ος: see LOGOS.] Reasoning.

1656 BLOUNT *Glossogr.*, *Logism*, the due and judicious understanding of a thing, formerly considered and esteemed of, according to reason. *Cot[grave]*. **1660** JER. TAYLOR *Duct. Dubit.* II. iii. rule xiv. §5 Tell me not of your logisms and syllogisms; I rely upon Scripture alone. **1662** J. CHANDLER *Van Helmont's Oriat.* 19 Reasoning, or Logisme (from whence is a Syllogisme) is an act whereby [etc.].

†**logist.** *Obs.* [ad. L. *logist-a* or Gr. λογιστ-ής, f. λογίζ-εσθαι (see prec.).] **a.** An expert reckoner or accountant. **b.** *Gr. Hist.* One of a board of Athenian officials (see quot. 1656).

1570 DEE *Math. Pref.* 5 The common Logist, Reckenmaster, or Arithmeticien, in hys using of Numbers. **1656** BLOUNT *Glossogr.*, *Logist*, he that causeth presidents or notable sayings to be registred, a caster of accounts. The Logists among the Athenians.. were ten men.. to whom all such as had ended their Office of Magistracy.. were to render an account of all such occasions as they had then administration of. **1680** J. AUBREY in *Lett. Eminent Persons* (1813) III. 472 S[r] Jonas More was with him [W. Oughtred, mathematician] a good while, and learnt; he was but an ordinary logist before. **1735** DYCHE & PARDON *Dict.*, *Logist*, one expert in Computation, or that understands Accompts.

-logist, an ending resulting from the addition of -IST to sbs. in -LOGY, forming sbs. with the general sense 'one who is versed in ——logy'. It is now the only living formative with this function, the older equivalents *-loger, -logian, -logue* occurring only in very few words (most of which are obsolescent). The formation is mainly English, though a few examples, as *étymologiste, chronologiste*, have existed in Fr. from the 16th or 17th c., and others, as *zoologiste*, appear first in the 19th c.

logistic (lə'dʒɪstɪk), *a.* and *sb.* [ad. med.L. *logisticus* (whence F. *logistique*), ad. Gr. λογιστικός, f. λογίζεσθαι to reckon, reason, f. λόγος reckoning, account, reason: see LOGIC, LOGOS.]

A. *adj.*

†**1.** ? Pertaining to reasoning; logical. *Obs.*

1628 JACKSON *Creed* IX. vii. §6 Even the wisest.. writers oft-times swallow such fallacies in historical narrations.. as would be rejected.. were they exhibited to them in the simplicity of language or logistic form. **1644** BULWER *Chirol.* 5 Men that are borne deafe and dumbe; who can argue.. rhetorically by signes, and with a kinde of mute and logistique eloquence overcome their amaz'd opponents.

2. Pertaining to reckoning or calculation.

1706 PHILLIPS (ed. Kersey), *Logist*, one skill'd in the Logistick Science, i.e. the Art of Reckoning, or casting Account. **1732** BERKELEY *Alciphr.* II. 115 The Algebraic Mark, which denotes the Root of a negative Square, hath its Use in Logistic Operations.

3. *Math.* **a.** In ***logistic line, spiral*** = logarithmic. Also = pertaining to a logarithmic curve, e.g. ***logistic semi-ordinate***. ***logistic curve***: a logarithmic curve; also [after F. *logistique* (P.-F. Verhulst 1845, in *Nouv. Mém. de l'Acad. R. des Sci. et Belles-Lettres de Bruxelles* XVIII. 8)], a curve described by the equation $y = K/(1 + Ae^{a-bt})$, where *K, A, a,* and *b* are constants, which approximates an exponential curve for small values of *t*, has a point of inflexion at $t = a/b$, and as *t* increases approaches $y = K$ asymptotically. Hence ***logistic growth, law***, etc. **b.** ***logistic logarithms***: logarithms of sexagesimal numbers or fractions used in astronomical calculations. **c.** ***logistic numbers*** (see quot. 1882).

1727–41 CHAMBERS *Cycl.*, *Logistic*, or *Logarithmic line*, a curve so called, from its properties and uses, in constructing and explaining the nature of logarithms. *Ibid.*, There may be infinite logistic spirals. *Ibid.* s.v. *Quadrature*, The space intercepted between the two logistic semiordinates. **1785** HUTTON (*title*) Mathematical Tables; Containing the Common, Hyperbolic, and Logistic Logarithms. **1834** *Nat. Philos., Astron.* xii. 226/1 (U.K.S.) The proportional, or, as they are sometimes called, logistic logarithms. **1882** J. W. L. GLAISHER in *Encycl. Brit.* XIV. 777/1 *Logistic numbers* is the old name for what would now be called ratios or fractions. **1925** G. U. YULE in *Jrnl. R. Statistical Soc.* LXXXVIII. 11 The logistic curve implies that, if we could plot the instantaneous percentage rate of increase of the population at any moment of time against the magnitude of the population, the resulting points should lie on a straight line, a line sloping downwards from left to right, since the rate of increase falls as the population increases. **1928** R. PEARL *Rate of Living* vii. 132 The growth of the stem follows a logistic curve. **1930** W. R. INGE *Christian Ethics & Mod. Probl.* v. 252 Professor Raymond Pearl, of Baltimore,.. has evolved a theory that the growth of population follows what he calls a logistic curve, apparently independent of human volition. **1947** *Jrnl. R. Statistical Soc.* CX. 134 A most important.. paper of Feller.. on the application of Markoff processes to a series of population problems normally treated in a deterministic manner leading to exponential or logistic laws of growth. **1969** SLADEN & BANG *Biol. of Populations* vi. 72 Pearl used the logistic equation of Verhulst, which is $dN/dt = rN(K - N)/K$. The first part, $dN/dt = rN$, is the exponential equation for growth. *K* is a constant concerned with realization of the potential, and *N* is the number of individuals in the population. **1974** *Encycl. Brit. Macropædia* XIV. 831/1 (*caption*) Logistic growth of a laboratory population of the small fruit fly.

d. Of or pertaining to mathematical or symbolic logic.

1918 C. I. LEWIS *Survey Symbolic Logic* vi. 343 The logistic method is.. applicable to any sufficiently coördinated body of exact knowledge. **1934** *Mind* XLIII. 101 First, he presents 'the basic calculus of exact logic by the logistic method'. **1963** H. B. CURRY *Found. Math. Logic* i. 21, I shall discuss breifly the three principal varieties of higher-order logistic calculus.

4. Connected with or pertaining to logistics (cf. LOGISTICS *sb. pl.*[2]).

1934 in WEBSTER. **1957** *Listener* 14 Nov. 774/2 [Of local elections in Ethiopia] Everything had to be improvised; the logistic problems of this complicated terrain had to be solved as much as the psychological. **1958** *Times* 3 Nov. 11/7 When Montgomery, promised extra logistic support, fixed the date for Arnhem, Patton decided to get his forces so involved beyond the Moselle that Supreme Headquarters would find it impossible to find that extra support at his expense. **1971** *Sci. Amer.* Dec. 106/2 The Gombe Stream Centre, which arose from her work, is now a thriving institution with a dozen students and an entire little village of logistic and touristic support.

B. *sb.*

†**1.** A calculator. *Obs.*

1633 W. ROBINSON in Rigaud *Corr. Sci. Men* (1841) I. 15 A more exact way.. could not possibly be taken than by angles taken with a very large quadrant, and so good an artist and logistic as Snellius was.

2. *Math.* A logistic curve.

1727–41 CHAMBERS *Cycl.* s.v., The logistic will never concur with the axis, except at an infinite distance. *Ibid.*, Quadrature of the Logistic. **1773** HORSLEY in *Phil. Trans.* LXIV. 245 The subtangent of the atmospherical logistic, is the length of a column of such a fluid as I have supposed. **1925** G. U. YULE in *Jrnl. R. Statistical Soc.* LXXXVIII. 5, I have relegated to Appendix II some discussion of the mathematics of the curve, which, following Verhulst, we may term a 'logistic'. **1928** R. PEARL *Rate of Living* vii. 132 The seedling growth curves are slightly asymmetrical, but to a first approximation are sufficiently well graduated by the simple logistic $y = K/(1 + e^{a+bx})$. **1974** *Nature* 3 May 12/3 In the absence of competition.. the growth rate conforms to the logistic.

3. *pl.* (rarely *sing.*). **a.** The art of arithmetical calculation; the elementary processes of calculation, as addition, subtraction, multiplication, and division. **b.** Logistical or sexagesimal arithmetic.

a. 1656 BLOUNT *Glossogr.*, *Logistick*, the Art of counting or reckoning, the practice of Arithmetick, or that part thereof which contains Addition, Substraction, Multiplication and Division. **1706** PHILLIPS (ed. Kersey), *Logisticks*, the same as Logistical Arithmetick; but some apply the Term to signify the first general Rules in Algebra. **1817** COLEBROOKE *Algebra*, etc. 5 *Paricarmáshtaca*, eight operations, or modes of process: logistics or algorism. **1884** J. GOW *Hist. Gk. Math.* iii. 65 [Plato] is on many occasions careful to distinguish the vulgar *logistic* from the philosophical *arithmetic*.

b. 1801 *Encycl. Brit.* Suppl. II. 81 Logistics, or Logistical Arithmetic, a name sometimes employed for the arithmetic of sexagesimal fractions, used in astronomical computations.

c. (usu. *sing.*) Mathematical or symbolic logic (see quot. 1918).

[**1905** *Philos. Rev.* XIV. 445 A logical renaissance must be noted... I give it the name of 'logistique' from an old word which appears to be revived. *Ibid.* 453 In the 'Logistique' (the revival of the word was recognized by the congress) the presence alone of MM. Peano, Couturat, [etc.].. was sufficient to guarantee the interest and importance of the questions treated.] **1918** C. I. LEWIS *Survey Symbolic Logic* i. 3 Logistic would not have served our purpose because 'logistic' is commonly used to denote symbolic logic together with the application of its methods to other symbolic procedures. Logistic may be defined as *the science which deals with types of order as such.* It is not so much a subject as a method. **1933** *Mind.* XLII. 117 Prof. Scholz writes throughout as an enthusiastic student of symbolic logic, or—to use the name more commonly employed on the Continent—Logistic. **1936** A. J. AYER *Lang., Truth & Logic* iii. 88 The best-known example of such a symbolism [*sc.* artificial language symbolism] is the so-called system of logistic which was employed by Russell and Whitehead in their *Principia Mathematica*. **1956** A. CHURCH *Introd. Math. Logic* (rev. ed.) I. 57 The word 'logistic'.. originally meant the art of calculation or common arithmetic. Its modern use for mathematical logic dates from the International Congress of Philosophy of 1904. **1956** E. H. HUTTEN *Lang. Mod. Physics* ii. 34 There are still people who believe that Gödel's theorem represents the ultimate failure of logic and mathematics. But, to paraphrase Mark Twain, the reports of the early demise of logistic are greatly exaggerated.

lo'gistical, *a.* [f. med.L. *logisticus* (see LOGISTIC *a.*) + -AL[1].]

1. Pertaining to or based upon reasoning or disputation. (Cf. LOGISTIC 1.)

1644 BULWER *Chiron.* 3 The Logisticall motions that appear in the Hands of Disputants. **1653** R. SANDERS *Physiogn.* 214 That Logistical or rational facultie of the soul. **1833** *New Monthly Mag.* XXXVIII. 13 A question that depended upon no abstruse or logistical reasoning.

2. Pertaining to calculation. = LOGISTIC 2.

1570 BILLINGSLEY *Euclid* XI. xxxiv. 349 Ye may vse the logisticall secret of approching nere to the precise verytye. **1640** WILKINS *New Planet* x. (1707) 272 The Sacred Story.. does so exactly agree with the Conversions of Heaven, and Logistical Astronomy.

3. a. *Math.* = LOGISTIC *a.* 3 a–c.

1653 SHAKERLEY (*title*) Tabulæ Britannicæ: The British Tables: Wherein is contained Logistical Arithmetick, the Doctrine of the Sphere, Astronomicall Chronologie [etc.]. *Ibid.* 1 Chap. I. Of Logisticall Multiplication and Division. *Ibid.* 2 A new Table of Logistical Logarithmes. **1706** PHILLIPS (ed. Kersey), *Logistical Arithmetick*, was formerly the Arithmetick of Sexagesimal Fractions... It is now taken by some for the expeditious Arithmetick of Logarithms, by which all the Trouble of Multiplication and Division is sav'd. **1709–29** MANDEY *Syst. Math., Arith.* 74 Astronomical [Arithmetic], which sometimes also is called Logistical. *Ibid.* 78 Of Logistical Addition [i.e. addition of degrees, minutes, seconds, etc.; of years, days, hours, etc.]. **1777** SHUCKBURGH in *Phil. Trans.* LXVII. 586 *note*, This table bears some analogy to the tables of logistical logarithms.

b. = LOGISTIC *a.* 3 d; of or pertaining to logicism.

1932 H. W. B. JOSEPH in *Mind* XLI. 439 And it would be consonant so far with the logistical doctrine that pure mathematics is just logic, or an outgrowth of logic. **1943** *Mind* LII. 264 The 'logistical thesis' that mathematics is reducible to logic. **1966** W. V. QUINE *Ways of Paradox* viii. 64 (*heading*) A logistical approach to the ontological problem.

4. Pertaining to LOGISTICS *sb. pl.*[2]; = LOGISTIC *a.* 4.

1934 in WEBSTER. **1957** *Economist* 7 Sept. 838/3 Soldiers who can, without any lessening of their primal martial qualities, handle their logistical and procurement problems. **1966** *Listener* 13 Jan. 65/2 You would.. allow more time than six months for the 190,000 American troops to effectively dismember the 165,000 Viet Cong troops, an enemy which possesses all the strategical and logistical advantages. **1972** *Sci. Amer.* Feb. 77/3 Logistical problems such as transporting magnetic tapes and fragile equipment .. proved to be as much of a challenge as technical considerations. **1975** *Listener* 9 Jan. 41/1 Sven Hedin in 1927.. could show his journeys through East Asia, China and Mongolia with all the emphasis on the logistical dramas.

logistically (lə'dʒɪstɪkəlɪ), *adv.*

1. [f. LOGISTICAL *a.* + -LY[2].] In a logistic manner.

1932 LEWIS & LANGFORD *Symbolic Logic* v. 118 The logistically derived calculus of classes. **1933** *Mind* XLII. 32 We must hold constantly in mind that this logic is to be developed logistically.

2. [Cf. LOGISTICS *sb. pl.*[2]] Connected with or from the point of view of logistics.

1956 R. BRADDON *Nancy Wake* xviii. 212 A situation both logistically valuable and humanly comic. **1960** *Daily Tel.* 10 Oct. 24/6 The American official position has always been that it would be impractical, even logistically, to withdraw American troops from Germany and concentrate them, say, in Alsace Lorraine. **1966** M. R. D. FOOT *SOE in France* x. 308 It turned out logistically impracticable. **1971** J. B. CARROLL et al. *Word Frequency Bk.* p. xviii, Choosing *k* based on the length of individual texts was rejected as being unacceptably laborious and logistically impossible. **1971** *Physics Bull.* Dec. 726/1 If industrial work is to be done by universities, it must be set up and supported in such a way as to be logistically viable.

logistician (lɒdʒɪ'stɪʃən). [f. LOGISTIC *a.* + -IAN.] One skilled in logic or logistics.

1932 *Mind* XLI. 433 Logisticians are the last persons who should quarrel with a notational convention whereby a syllogistic 'calculus' can be simplified. **1936** OGDEN & RICHARDS *Meaning of Meaning* (ed. 4) v. 95 Logisticians will only be logical when they admit that universals are an analogous convenience. **1937** *Mind* XLVI. 244 Prof. Scholz, who is editing the series of logistical studies to which this work belongs, has the rare distinction of being both an accomplished logistician and an erudite philosophical scholar. **1966** W. V. QUINE *Ways of Paradox* viii. 65 Such conformity was the logistician's objective when he codified quantification.

logistics, *sb. pl.*[1]: see LOGISTIC B. 3.

logistics (lə'dʒɪstɪks), *sb. pl.*[2] [ad. F. *logistique*, f. *loge-r* to quarter, LODGE, or *logis* LOGIS: see -ISTIC.] The organization of supplies, stores, quarters, etc., necessary for the support of troop movements, expeditions, etc.

1879 R. TAYLOR *Destruct. & Reconstr.* v. 47, I have written of him [Johnston] as a master of logistics. **1890** *Century Mag.* Feb. 570/2 The marches of Sherman disturbed all previous axioms of logistics. **1898** *Athenæum* 10 Sept. 341 Strategy is the art of handling troops in the theatre of war; tactics that of handling them on the field of battle... The French have a third process, which they call logistics, the art of moving and quartering troops, i.e., quartermaster-general's work. **1901** *Blackw. Mag.* Jan. 3/1 To the small commandos, say of from 50 to 300 men, 'hanging about' is the beginning and end of logistics. **1944**

A. H. BURNE *Art of War on Land* i. 10 All this must be superimposed on his knowledge of the material conditions—'the logistics' of the situation, as pointed out by Lord Wavell. *Ibid.*, Logistics, the science of moving and supplying troops. The term was invented by Baron de Jomini, but is seldom used in this country. **1947** D. S. BALLANTINE (*title*) U.S. naval logistics in the Second World War. **1947** CROWTHER & WHIDDINGTON *Science at War* 117 The Americans use the word 'logistics' to describe the technique of packing stores... It is derived from the French '*maître du logie*'. **1963** MRS. L. B. JOHNSON *White House Diary* 27 Dec. (1970) 21 Bess Abell..and some Filipino stewards arrived at the Ranch yesterday and got preparations under way for Chancellor Ludwig Erhard's visit—the vast logistics of deciding who was going to stay where. **1966** *Aviation Week & Space Technol.* 5 Dec. 22/1 The new plan is to provide, essentially, separate modules for each of at least three major experimentation areas—astronomy and biology, earth resources, including meteorology, and orbital operations and logistics. **1971** *Daily Tel.* 8 May 8/6 He was responsible for the administration and logistics of the mine-sweeping forces in the operation Neptune (the invasion of North-West Europe in 1944).

logitioner, variant of LOGICIANER.

log-jam. [f. LOG *sb.*[1] + JAM *sb.*[1]]

1. An accumulation of logs in a river; a place where logs become jammed. Cf. JAM *sb.*[1] 1.

1885 E. L. DORSEY *Midshipman Bob* (1886) i. 73 His father got killed in a log-jam. **1897** KIPLING *Five Nations* (1903) 39 Do you know that racing stream With the raw, right-angled log-jam at the end? **1900** *Jrnl. School Geogr.* (U.S.) Apr. 153 The breaking of a log jam or an ice dam on one of our rivers. **1940** J. BUCHAN *Memory Hold-the-Door* v. 101 He could do what the lumberman does in a log-jam, and pick out the key log which, once moved, sets the rest going. **1957** G. E. HUTCHINSON *Treat. Limnol.* I. i. 115 The successive formation of log jams.

2. *fig.* An obstruction or blockage; a delay; a deadlock. Cf. JAM *sb.*[1] 1 b.

1890 W. JAMES *Princ. Psychol.* I. xi. 451 But at intervals an obstruction, a set-back, a log-jam occurs. **1907** *Springfield* (Mass.) *Weekly Republ.* 14 Feb. 8 The congressional log-jam which held back all legislature for nearly a week was finally broken Thursday afternoon. **1935** *Economist* 4 May 1009/1 A number of corporate refunding issues have been successfully offered.., leading the Secretary of the Treasury to affirm that the 'log-jam in the capital market' has at last been broken. **1951** M. LOWRY *Let.* 5 June (1967) 245 There is a kind of log jam in my work. **1962** *Listener* 5 Apr. 597/2 Nothing is likely to break the Arab-Israeli log-jam until the Arabs achieve a greater measure of unity. **1965** *Ibid.* 20 May 737/2 Something may have happened to show us what Mr. Ian Smith's electoral victory really means and how the political log-jam has begun to move. **1973** I. M. SINCLAIR *Vienna Convention on Law of Treaties* v. 139 Informal meetings among leading delegations failed to move the log-jam.

loglet ('lɒglɪt). [f. LOG *sb.*[1] + -LET.] A little log.

1914 W. DE MORGAN *When Ghost meets Ghost* II. vi. 504 She brought a couple of young loglets to keep a little life in the fire.

logo[1] ('lɒgəʊ). Abbrev. of LOGOGRAM 2 c or LOGOTYPE 2. Also *attrib.*

1937 *Advertising & Selling* 1 Jan. 29 He wrote the first ad ever written for that new-fangled mechanical pencil called 'Eversharp'. Designed a logo for it, too. **1960** O. SKILBECK *ABC of Film and T.V.* 79 *Logo*, the layout of a sponsor's name, brand or slogan. **1967** T. HARKNETT *Two-Way Frame* xii. 92 An eight-wheeled trailer lorry and a five-ton van, both with the company logo on the side. **1969** *Guardian* 27 May 5/8 Almost every page carries that arch public relations device, an image-making logo. **1970** *Cabinet Maker & Retail Furnisher* 25 Sept. 628 (*caption*) A stylised version of the letter A is the logo used as a feature on Arkana's fleet of vans. The van body is in silver, with the cab and the logo in blue. **1971** *B.S.I. News* Dec. 4/2 With a single gold motif drawn from the Institution's crest and logo, these ties are now available. **1975** *Times* 13 Jan. 13/4 A national airline decided..to have their logo printed on the cover of book matches.

LOGO[2] ('ləʊgəʊ). *Computing.* Also Logo. [See quot. 1980 and cf. LOGO[1].] A simple high-level programming language designed to be used by children as an educational aid.

1976 BERTONI & CASTLEMAN in J. Belzer et al. *Encycl. Computer Sci. & Technol.* III. 470 LOGO is an educational language devised..to teach school children techniques of problem solving... A most popular application of LOGO is in the programming of Irving, a turtle-like robot. **1980** S. PAPERT *Mindstorms* 210 In 1967..I began thinking about designing a computer language that would be suitable for children... The name LOGO was chosen for the new language to suggest the fact that it is primarily symbolic and only secondarily quantitative. **1984** J. HILTON *Choosing & using your Home Computer* 112 Using LOGO..a microworld can be set up in which everything behaves in true Newtonian fashion, and with the aid of tools to push objects around the screen, children soon learn all three of Newton's laws for themselves.

logocentric (lɒgəʊ'sɛntrɪk), *a.* [f. Gr. λόγο-ς reason + -CENTRIC.] Centred on reason.

1939 V. A. DEMANT *Relig. Prospect* v. 124 The connection of this biocentric dogma with a dogma of becoming is obvious. In what respects is the rational, logocentric tradition against which it revolts related to a true dogma of being? **1951** *Mind* LX. 575 Terminating in a logocentric predicament. **1952** [see BIOCENTRIC *a.*].

logocracy (lə'gɒkrəsɪ). [f. Gr. λόγο-ς word + -CRACY.] A community or system of government in which words are the ruling powers.

1804-6 SYD. SMITH *Mor. Philos.* (1850) 104 Instruments which overturn the horrible tyranny of adjectives and substantives, and free the mind from the chains of that logocracy in which it is so frequently enslaved. **1807-8** W. IRVING *Salmag.* (1824) 108 Their government is a pure unadulterated logocracy, or government of words.

logocyclic (lɒgəʊ'sɪklɪk), *a.* and *sb.* *Math.* [f. Gr. λόγο-ς ratio + κύκλ-ος circle + -IC.] **a.** *adj.* Only in ***logocyclic curve***, a crunodal circular cubic, whose equation is $(x^2 + y^2)(2a - x) = a^2x$. **b.** *sb.* A logocyclic curve.

1858 J. BOOTH in *Proc. Roy. Soc.* IX. 257 A new curve, which I have called the *Logocyclic Curve*, from the similarity of many of its properties to those of the circle, and from its use in representing numbers and their logarithms. *Ibid.* 261 The entire length of the logocyclic is equal to [etc.].

‖**logo'dædalus.** *Obs.* Pl. -i. Also in anglicized form **logodædale.** [mod.L., a. Gr. λογοδαίδαλος, f. λόγο-ς + δαίδαλος cunning.] One who is cunning in words.

1611 ? B. JONSON in *Coryat's Crudities* Charac. Authour, He is a great and bold Carpenter of Words or (to express him in one like his owne) a Logodædale. **1650** TRAPP *Comm., Song Sol.* iv. 3 (1660) III. 353 Those Logodædali, learned Asses, that prophanely disdain at the stately plainness of Gods blessed Book. **1664** EVELYN tr. *Freart's Archit.* etc. 121 Least whilest I thus discourse of the Accomplishments of our Artists..I my self be found Logodædalus.

So †**logo'dædalist.**

1727 BAILEY vol. II, *Logodædalist*, an Inventer or Forger of new Words, and strange Terms. **1806** J. LESLIE *Dict. Synon. Words* s.v. *Words*, Inventor of words, logodædalist.

logodædaly (lɒgəʊ'diːdəlɪ). *rare.* [ad. late L. *logodædalia*, a. Gr. λογοδαιδαλία, f. λογοδαίδαλος (see prec.).] Cunning in words; skill in adorning a speech; 'verbal legerdemain'.

1727 BAILEY vol. II, *Logodædaly*, a goodly shew and flourish of Words, without much matter. **1825** COLERIDGE *Aids Refl.* xliii. (1836) 114 For one instance of mere Logomachy I could bring ten instances of Logodædaly, or verbal Legerdemain.

†**logodiarrhe.** Also 8, 9 in Dicts. **logodiarrhœa.** [f. Gr. λόγο-ς word + διάρροια diarrhœa. Cf. F. *logodiarrhée.*] A flux or flow of words.

1624 BP. MOUNTAGU *Gagg* Pref. ¶¶¶4b, A rambling logodiarrhe without wit or reason. **1727** BAILEY vol. II, *Logodiarrhoea.* [**1856** MAYNE *Expos. Lex.*, *Logodiarrhœa.* So **1889** *Syd. Soc. Lex.*]

logofascinated, *ppl. a.* *nonce-wd.* [hybrid f. Gr. λόγο-ς word.] Fascinated by words.

1652 URQUHART *Jewel* Wks. (1834) 231 The logofascinated spirits of the..hearers..were so on a sudden seazed upon.

logogram ('lɒgəgræm). [f. Gr. λόγο-ς word + -GRAM.

In sense 1 substituted (owing to association with *anagram*, *lipogram*, etc.) for *logograph*, which in this sense is itself a mistake for *logogriph.*]

1. = LOGOGRIPH.

1820 HEBER *Let.* 1 Apr. in *Life* (1830) II. 19 If you are not much in the habit of composing logograms, you can hardly conceive how many words a single well-chosen noun may be coaxed into. For instance, how many are there in steam-boat? **1862** H. B. WHEATLEY (*title*) Of Anagrams,.. Lipograms, Chronograms, Logograms, Palindromes.

2. a. A sign or character representing a word; in *Phonography*, a word-letter; a single stroke which, for brevity's sake, represents a word.

1840 I. PITMAN *Man. Phonography* §159 (1845) 46 The hooked *vr* is used as a logogram for *very.* **1870** —— *Phonet. Man.* 126 The following ingenious exercise is composed entirely of Logograms.

b. *Philol.* A symbol or character used, alone or in combination, as the graphic representation of a whole word as a single letter.

1933 L. BLOOMFIELD *Lang.* 287 The Egyptians.. represented words not always by one symbol, but also by various arrangements of logograms. **1939** L. H. GRAY *Foundations of Lang.* 360 Akkadian as written contains many Sumerian logograms. **1963** BLOOMFIELD & NEWMARK *Ling. Introd. Hist. Eng.* ii. 35 Mesopotamian and Egyptian peoples developed a rebus technique by which signs for whole words (logograms) could be put together to form longer words.

c. *gen.* A symbol, as found in road-signs, advertising, &c., designed to represent in simple graphic form an object, concept, or attitude.

1966 *Sunday Times* 27 Feb. 11/2 Labour's original badge ..has progressively turned into what the trade calls a logogram.

Hence **logogra'mmatic** *a.*, pertaining to logograms (sense 1).

1820 HEBER *Let.* 1 Apr. in *Life* (1830) II. 19 The whimsical contrast which this logogrammatic Berserksgangr presented to the parallel exploit of Coleridge, who wrote his Kubla-Khan under the effects of opium.

logograph ('lɒgəgrɑːf, -æ-). [f. as prec. + -GRAPH. Cf. Gr. λογογράφος (see next).]

¶ **1.** Used erroneously for LOGOGRIPH.

Some mod. edd. of Jonson *Underwoods* lxi. have *logographes* where the original ed. has *logogriphes.*

1797 *Monthly Mag.* III. 468 The Masquerade; or, a Collection of New Epigrams, Logographs [etc.].

2. *Phonography.* A character or combination of characters representing a word; = LOGOGRAM 2.

1888 I. PITMAN *Man. Phonography* §190. 68.

3. = LOGOTYPE 1.

1872 W. SKEEN *Early Typography* 426 It is an existing book, nearly two hundred years old, one half of which is printed with movable wooden letters, logographs, and words.

4. = LOGOGRAPHER 2. *rare* (in quot. *transf.*).

1862 LATHAM *Channel Isl.* III. xviii. (ed. 2) 417 The philosophy..or mythology of the Welsh bards and logographs.

5. An instrument for giving a graphic representation of speech-sounds.

1879 G. PRESCOTT *Sp. Telephone* 295 For recording vocal impulses one of the most sensitive instruments is the logograph, invented by W. H. Barlow, F.R.S.

Hence '**logograph** *v. trans.*, to print with logotypes.

1843 *Biographical Dict.* II. II. 576 A second edition appeared in 1764 and a third in 1797-9 (which being logographed, or printed with a separately cast type for every word, was reissued in 1801).

logographer (lə'gɒgrəfə(r)). [f. late L. *logograph-us* accountant (a. Gr. λογογράφ-ος prose-writer, speech-writer, f. λόγο-ς word, speech, account + -γράφος -writer) + -ER[1]: see -GRAPHER.]

†**1.** A lawyer's clerk; an accountant. *Obs.*—[0]

1656 BLOUNT *Glossogr.*, *Logographers*, Lawyers Clerks, they that write Pleas and Causes in the Law or Books of Accompt. **1696** in PHILLIPS (ed. 5). **1735** DYCHE & PARDON *Dict.*, *Logographer*, an Accomptant or Writer of Books of Accompts.

2. *Gr. Antiq.* A writer of traditional history in prose.

1846 GROTE *Greece* I. iv. I. 117 The adventures which the ancient poets, epic, lyric, and tragic, and the logographers after them, connect with the name of the Argeian Iô. **1868** GLADSTONE *Juv. Mundi* viii. (1870) 265 Pherecydes, an Athenian logographer of the fifth century before Christ. **1875** JOWETT *Plato* (ed. 2) III. 42 After the manner of the early logographers, turning the Iliad into prose. **1880** *Encycl. Brit.* XI. 634/1 Hellanicus, the most important of the Greek logographers.

3. *Gr. Antiq.* A professional speech-writer.

1853 GROTE *Greece* II. lxxxvii. XI. 380 Before he [Demosthenes] acquired reputation as a public adviser, he was already known as a logographer, or composer of discourses to be delivered either by speakers in the public assembly or by litigants in the Dikastery. **1881** *Q. Rev.* Oct. 531 The plain man, intending to go to law, addressed himself to a professional speech-writer, or 'logographer'.

4. One who practises or is skilled in logography.

1860 in WORCESTER citing Smyth.

logographic (lɒgəʊ'græfɪk), *a.* [f. LOGOGRAPHY + -IC. Cf. Gr. λογογραφικός.]

1. Pertaining to logography (see LOGOGRAPHY 1).

1784 *Lond. Chron.* No. 4287, Logographic Office, Black Friars, April 15. By His Majesty's Royal Letters Patent for printing by words intire instead of single Letters. **1785** (*title*) Miscellanies in Prose and Verse intended as a Specimen of the Types, at the Logographic Printing Office. **1882** PEBODY *Eng. Journalism* xiii. 94 John Walter..set all the printers in London by the ears with his whim about logographic printing.

2. Consisting of characters or signs, each of which singly represents a complete word.

1801 J. HAGER *Babylon. Inscript.* 53 Goguet makes no distinction between hieroglyphic, and, as I call them, monogrammatic or logographic characters. **1828** DU PONCEAU *Chinese Syst. Writing* (1838) 110, I would not call the Chinese characters a syllabic, but a logographic system of writing. **1970** *Language* XLVI. 959 It now appears that the Proto-Indian script is a purely logographic script based on the so-called rebus principle.

So **logo'graphical** *a.*

1828-32 in WEBSTER.

logographically (lɒgəʊ'græfɪkəlɪ), *adv.* [f. prec. + -LY[2].] In a logographic manner.

1783 H. JOHNSON (*title*) An Introduction to Logography. .. Printed logographically and sold by J. Walter. **1804** W. TAYLOR in *Crit. Rev.* III. 506 The want of variety in their rhymed letter-press is so obvious that it may be thought they might print all their poetry logographically, with stereotype hemistichs. **1828** DU PONCEAU *Chinese Syst. Writing* 114 It cannot be written with the Chinese character logographically.

logography (lə'gɒgrəfɪ). [ad. Gr. λογογραφία, f. λόγο-ς speech + -γραφία writing. Cf. F. *logographie.*]

1. (See quot. 1783.)

1783 H. JOHNSON (*title*) An Introduction to Logography: or, the art of arranging and composing for printing with words intire, their radices and terminations, instead of single letters. **1796** *Mod. Gulliver's Trav.* 198, I then wrote a treatise on the beauties of Liliputian ortho and logography. **1841** *Penny Cycl.* XIX. 16/1 Logography..is merely a modification of block-printing. **1887** FOX BOURNE *Eng. Newspapers* I. 255 A new [*c* 1783] printing process known as logography.

2. A method of long-hand reporting, in which several reporters were employed, each taking down a few words in succession.

1842 BRANDE *Dict. Sci.* etc., *Logography*, a system of taking down the words of an orator without having recourse

to short-hand, which was put in practice during the French revolution.

logogriph ('lɒgəgrɪf). Forms: 6–9 logogryphe, 7–9 -iphe, 9 -iff, 7– logogriph. [ad. F. *logogriphe*, f. Gr. λόγο-ς word + γρῖφος fishing-basket, riddle.] A kind of enigma, in which a certain word, and other words that can be formed out of all or any of its letters, are to be guessed from synonyms of them introduced into a set of verses. Occasionally used for: Any anagram or puzzle involving anagrams.

1597–8 Bp. Hall *Sat.* iv. i. 33 Worse than the Logogryphes of later times, Or Hundreth Riddles shak't to sleeue-lesse rimes. *a* **1637** B. Jonson *Underwoods, Execr. upon Vulcan* 34 (1640) Bib, Had I.. weav'd fifty tomes Of Logogriphes, or curious Pallindromes. **1765** H. Walpole *Let. to Lady Hervey* 21 Nov. *Lett.* (1857) IV. 439 All I can send your ladyship is a very pretty logogriphe, made by.. Madame du Deffand. **1770** Fox in J. H. Jesse *G. Selwyn & Contemp.* (1843) II. 398, I gained great credit there by guessing a logogryphe. **1813** W. Taylor in *Monthly Mag.* XXXVI. 417 A logogriph.. describes not a word only, but all the included words, which any portion of its letters can spell. **1835** *Tait's Mag.* II. 808 A sort of logogriff not worthy of solution. **1867–77** G. F. Chambers *Astron.* i. xii. 136 The original discovery was announced to Kepler in the following logogriph. **1884** J. Payne *1001 Nts.* VII. 210 *note*, The clue to this logogriph lies in the numerical value of the letters forming the key-word.

Hence **logo'griphic** *a.*, of or pertaining to logogriphs, of the nature of a logogriph.

1814 *Q. Rev.* X. 464 By dropping *r* [from Borlase], and changing *ase* into *us*, we have the ingenious logogriphic title of Sir Bolus.

logolatry (lə'gɒlətrɪ). [f. Gr. λόγο-ς word + -latry.] 'Worship' of words; unreasonable regard for words or for verbal truth.

1810 Coleridge in *Lit. Rem.* (1839) IV. 305 [Neo-Platonism is] but one fanciful process of hypostasizing logical conceptions and generic terms. In Proclus it is Logolatry run mad. **1846** E. Miall in *Nonconf.* VI. 45 Many good people are exceedingly prone to logolatry. They get hold of a good word, representing a thing good in itself, and then conclude that every object to which that word may be applied, is a good thing. **1890** *Jrnl. Educ.* 1 Mar. 145/1 An almost morbid tendency to literal truthfulness, or, as the writer calls it, 'logolatry'.

logology (lə'gɒlədʒɪ). [f. Gr. λόγο-ς (see Logos) + -λογία discourse: see -logy.]

1. The doctrine of the Logos. (Only as the title of two books in the 18th c.)

1726 J. Jeffery (*title*) Logology, on John i. 1.

2. The science of words. *rare.*

1820 *Gentl. Mag.* XC. i. 208 Perhaps the following little attempt at Philology (Logology?) may not be deemed an inadmissable trifle. **1878** *Tinsley's Mag.* XXIII. 139 One of our most esteemed modern authorities in 'logology'. **1943** *Jrnl. R. Anthrop. Inst.* 5 Logology = the general study of linguistic elements of culture. **1961** K. Burke (*title*) The rhetoric of religion: studies in logology.

logomach ('lɒgəmæk). [ad. Gr. λογομάχ-ος adj., f. λόγος word (see Logos) + μαχ-, μάχεσθαι to fight.] One who fights about words.

1865 *Cornh. Mag.* XI. 483 The great logomach of Hippo.

logomachical (ˌlɒgəʊ'mækɪkəl), *a.* [f. as prec. + -ic + -al[1].] Disposed to logomachy.

1830 *Westm. Rev.* XII. 405 Mr. Galt.. is familiar with those.. variations from the general standard which occur among his.. logomachical countrymen.

logomachist (lə'gɒməkɪst). [f. as prec. + -ist.] One addicted to logomachy; one who disputes about verbal subtleties.

1825 Coleridge in *Lit. Rem.* (1839) IV. 272 If I met with a disputatious word-catcher or logomachist. **1882** *Pall Mall G.* 11 May 3/1 One feels inclined.. to ask like some old logomachist what he exactly means by 'is'.

logomachize (lə'gɒməkaɪz), *v.* [f. as prec. + -ize.] *intr.* To indulge in logomachy. Hence **lo'gomachizing** *ppl. a.*

1830 *Fraser's Mag.* I. 592 The.. incomprehensible cackle of logomachising ganders.

logomachy (lə'gɒməkɪ). Forms: 6–7 logomachie, 7– logomachy; also 7–8 in Latin form logomachia. *Pl.* -ies; also 8 -ys. [ad. Gr. λογομαχία, f. λόγο-ς word + -μαχία fighting.]

1. Contention about words; an instance of this.

1569 J. Sanford tr. *Agrippa's Van. Artes* 169 Of so high a science they have made a certaine Logomachie. **1675** T. Tully *Let. Baxter* 16 Which you seem to place amongst your Logomachies, or Logicall notions. **1711** tr. *Werenfels* (*title*) A Discourse of Logomachys, or Controversies about Words. **1716** M. Davies *Athen. Brit.* III. *Arianism* 25 The Sophistry call'd Logomochia [*sic*], or punning with and upon Words. **1722** Sewel *Hist. Quakers* (1795) I. ii. 122 This quarrel tending to vain logomachies.. ended in confusion. **1848** Mill *Pol. Econ.* iii. xv. §1 (1876) 341 The reproach of logomachy which is brought.. against the speculations of political economists. **1882** M. Arnold *Irish Ess.* Pref. p. xi, The barren logomachies of Plato's *Theætetus* are relieved by half a dozen immortal pages. **1901** *Contemp. Rev.* Aug. 289 It shows how much of mere logomachy there is in these disputes.

2. ? *U.S.* 'A game of cards each containing one letter with which words are formed' (*Cent. Dict.*).

†**logomacice.** *Obs. rare*[−1]. [as if ad. Gr. *λογομαχική (*sc.* τέχνη), fem. of *λογομαχικός of or pertaining to logomachy, f. λογομάχος logomach.] (See quot.)

1646 Saltmarsh *Some Drops* iii. *Smoke in Temple* 56 You criticise on words;.. I wonder you.. have leisure for that, this is logomacice, or word-fighting.

‖**logomania** (lɒgəʊ'meɪnɪə). [mod.L., f. Gr. λόγο-ς + μανία madness.] A form of insanity in which there is a great loquacity (*Syd. Soc. Lex.*).

logo'maniac. *nonce-wd.* [f. Gr. λόγο-ς word + maniac.] One who is insanely interested in words.

1870 H. Green *Shaks. & Emblem Writers* 103 We have outgrown the customs of those logo-maniacs, or word-worshippers, whom old Ralph Cudworth.. seems to have had in view.

logometer[1] (lə'gɒmɪtə(r)). [f. Gr. λόγο-ς (in the sense of ratio) + -meter.] **a.** (See quot.)

1842 De Morgan in Graves *Life Sir W. R. Hamilton* (1889) III. 248 It is of course the *à priori* introduction of what answers to the logarithm of a number, which I call the logometer of a line given in magnitude and direction. *Ibid.*, By A^B is meant the line whose logometer is $B \times$ logom. A.

b. Applied to Wollaston's 'logometric scale' for chemical equivalents.

1855 in Ogilvie, Suppl. **1860** in Worcester (citing *Gentl. Mag.*).

logometer[2] (lə'gɒmɪtə(r)). [A hybrid word f. log *sb.*[1] + -(o)meter.] A patent log for ships.

In recent Dicts.

logometric (lɒgəʊ'mɛtrɪk), *a.* [f. Gr. λόγο-ς ratio + μέτρ-ον measure + -ic.] Indicating ratios by measurement. Used by Wollaston to designate his 'scale' for the graphic representation of chemical equivalents. Hence **logo'metrical** *a.* (in the same sense), **logo'metrically** *adv.*

1813 Wollaston in *Phil. Trans.* CIV. 15 Those who are acquainted.. with the use of logarithms as measures of ratios.. will not need to be told that all the divisions are logometric. *Ibid.* 17 In the engraved scale of equivalents, the ratios of these numbers are represented by logometric intervals at which they are placed. *Ibid.*, The slider.. is logometrically divided. **1827** Faraday *Chem. Manip.* xxii. 555 The scale is the logometric line of numbers. **1855** Ogilvie, Suppl., *Logometrical.*

‖**logoneurosis** (lɒgəʊnjʊə'rəʊsɪs). [f. Gr. λόγο-ς word + neurosis.] A nervous disorder causing defective memory of words.

1857 in Dunglison *Med. Lex.* **1878** tr. *Ziemssen's Cycl. Med.* XIV. 613 The two ideas of logoneurosis and lalopathy consequently do not cover each other.

logonomy (lə'gɒnəmɪ). *nonce-wd.* [f. as prec. after astronomy.] The science of language.

1803 J. Stewart (*title*) *Opus maximum*: Logonomy; or, the science of language.

logo'pandocie. *nonce-wd.* [f. Gr. λόγο-ς word + πανδοκεία the trade of an innkeeper.] Readiness to admit words of all kinds.

1652 Urquhart *Jewel* Wks. (1834) 198 The systeme of a language, which, by reason of its logopandocie, may deservedly be intituled The Universal Tongue.

logopathy (lə'gɒpəθɪ). *Path.* [f. Gr. λόγο-ς word + -pathy.] A morbid affection of the speech (*Syd. Soc. Lex.*).

1878 tr. *Ziemssen's Cycl. Med.* XIV. 613 But as soon as the formation of thoughts is disturbed it becomes a question of dyslogia and logopathy.

logopedics (lɒgəʊ'piːdɪks), *sb. pl.* [f. Gr. λόγο-ς word, speech, after orthopædics, -ped-.] (See quot. 1951.) Also **logo'pedia** [-ia[1]], in the same sense.

1923 Dorland *Med. Dict.* (ed. 12) 622/1 Logopedia, logopedics. **1951** S. D. Robbins *Dict. Speech Path. & Therapy* (1961) 67 *Logopedia, logopedics*, the study and correction of speech and voice defects and disorders as a general field of knowledge. **1960** F. T. Wien (*title*) Current problems in phoniatrics and logopedics. **1969** J. H. van Thal *Elem. Logopedics* i. 10 Logopedics, which is widely used in many countries.. is more comprehensive.. than any other term in current use.

logophobia (lɒgə'fəʊbɪə). [mod.L., f. Gr. λόγο-ς word + -phobia.] Fear or distrust of words.

1923 [see *God-box* (god *sb.* 16a)]. **1933** H. R. Huse *Illiteracy of Literate* 48 The fear behind this logophobia is that secret names can be used in incantations. **1959** W. H. Mittins in Quirk & Smith *Teaching of English* iv. 126 The interest generated by such an approach might even help to overcome that language-resistance—the Americans call it 'logophobia'—which some teachers claim to be meeting more and more.

logopœia (lɒgə'piːjə). [a. Latinized form of Gr. λογοποιία f. λόγος word + ποιεῖν to make + -ια abstract fem. ending.] (See quot. 1929.)

1929 E. Pound in *N.Y. Herald-Tribune* 20 Jan. xi. 5/4 Logopoeia, 'the dance of the intellect among words', that is to say, it employs words not only for their direct meaning, but it takes count in a special way of habits of usage, of the context we expect to find with the word... It holds the æsthetic content which is peculiarly the domain of verbal manifestation and can not possibly be contained in plastic or in music. **1934** —— *ABC of Reading* iv. 21 You still charge words with meaning mainly in three ways, called phanopoeia, melopoeia, logopoeia. **1957** N. Frye *Anat. Crit.* 244 The context that Ezra Pound has in mind when he speaks of the three qualities of poetic creation as *melopoeia, logopoeia*, and *phanopoeia*.

logorrhœa, logorrhea (lɒgə'riːə). [f. Gr. λόγο-ς word + ῥοία flow, stream (prob. after diarrhœa).] Excessive volubility accompanying some forms of mental illness; also *gen.*, an excessive flow of words, prolixity. So **logo'rrhœic, logo'rrhœtic** *adjs.*

1902 Baldwin *Dict. Philos. & Psychol.* II. 30/1 Logorrhea refers to the excessive flow of words, a common symptom in cases of mania. **1907** *Daily Chron.* 13 Feb. 7/4 In the case of a man suffering from the insanity known as logorrhea the ideas come rapidly tumbling over each other. **1935** *Punch* 5 June 662/2, I have invented logorrhœa—or, if you prefer it, logorrhage. Like pyorrhœa.., it afflicts three out of four. **1960** *Spectator* 21 Oct. 591 Protective shields against the prevailing logorrhoeic fall-out. **1965** *Listener* 14 Jan. 62/3 No one could, or would want to, surpass that logorrhoetic master, except himself. **1965** W. R. Brain *Speech Disorders* (ed. 2) v. 56 Patients with sensory or Wernicke's aphasia or jargon aphasia include logorrhoeic patients with abundant paraphasias and serious defects of comprehension. **1970** *Daily Tel.* 5 Feb. 6/4 We are left with a tedious tale of complicated intrigues written by an author suffering from acute logorrhoea. **1970** Hinsie & Campbell *Psychiatric Dict.* (ed. 4) 751/2 Also known as *logorrhea*.. [tachylogia] is characteristic of the manic phase of manic-depressive disorder.

‖**Logos** ('lɒgɒs). *Theol.* and *Philos.* [Gr. λόγος word, speech, discourse, reason, f. λογ-, ablaut-variant of λεγ- in λέγ-ειν to say.] A term used by Greek (esp. Hellenistic and Neo-Platonist) philosophers in certain metaphysical and theological applications developed from one or both of its ordinary senses 'reason' and 'word'; also adopted in three passages of the Johannine writings of the N.T. (where the English versions render it by 'Word') as a designation of Jesus Christ; hence employed by Christian theologians, esp. those who were versed in Greek philosophy, as a title of the Second Person of the Trinity. By mod. writers the Gr. word is used untranslated in historical expositions of ancient philosophical speculation, and in discussions of the doctrine of the Trinity in its philosophical aspects.

1587 Golding *De Mornay* v. 52 We cal him Logos, which some translate word or Speech, and othersom Reason. **1647** H. More *Song of Soul* ii. i. xxiv. 79 That inward awfull Majestie Hight Logos, whom they term great sonne of God. **1720** Waterland *Eight Serm.* 243 Origen.. thence draws an Argument for the Eternity of the Logos or Word. **1831–3** E. Burton *Eccl. Hist.* xvii. (1845) 375 Plato never imagined this Logos or Mind to be a person in the sense in which Christians believe the Son of God to be a person. *a* **1834** Coleridge *Lit. Rem.* (1838) III. 158 If Christ be that Logos or Word that was in the beginning. **1882** S. D. F. Salmond in *Encycl. Brit.* XIV. 803/2 Heraclitus holds that nothing material can be thought of without this Logos, but he does not conceive the Logos itself to be immaterial. *Ibid.* 804/1 The Logos of the Stoics is a reason in the world gifted with intelligence, and analogous to the reason in man. *Ibid.*, His [Philo's] Logos is the representative of the world to God as well as of God to the world.

b. *attrib.* and *Comb.*

1839 I. Taylor *Anc. Chr.* I. ii. 150 Man.. shall.. under the conduct of the Logos-Redeemer, reascend to his source. **1865** tr. *Strauss's New Life Jesus* I. i. vi. 30 They are mere explanations of the Logos-theory. **1874** *Supernatural Relig.* II. iii. i. 340 The dogmatic system of the Logos Gospel did not admit of more than mere reference to it. **1883** Schaff *Hist. Ch.* II. lxxii. 555 This extension of the Logos revelation explains the high estimate which some of the Greek fathers.. put upon the Hellenic.. philosophy.

Hence **logos-ship**, the dignity and office of the Logos.

1895 *Expositor* Sept. 163 The logos-ship was attributed to Jesus.

logotherapy (lɒgə'θɛrəpɪ). *Psychol.* [ad. G. *logotherapie* (V. E. Frankl *Ärztliche Seelsorge* (1947)), f. Gr. λογό-ς reason + therapy.] An existential type of psychotherapy which maintains that man's mental health depends on awareness of meaning in his life.

1948 *Amer. Jrnl. Psychotherapy* 685 To help his patients in their spiritual distress the author [*sc.* Frankl] uses the art of reasoning, i.e., 'logotherapy', and as his method is principally based on an explanation of the meaning of existence, he calls it 'Existential Analysis'. **1953** *Ibid.* VII. 10 To overcome psychologism we have introduced a psychotherapeutic method which we have called *Logotherapy*, an heuristic opposite to psychotherapy in its hitherto accepted narrow psychological sense. Logotherapy is to be understood as a therapy which derives from spiritual sources, and aims toward a spiritual goal. **1964** I. Lasch tr. *Frankl's Man's Search for Meaning* ii. 98 In logotherapy the patient is actually confronted with and reoriented toward the meaning of his life. *Ibid.* 99 According to logotherapy, this striving to find a meaning in one's life is the primary motivational force in man. **1968** Reinecke & Bailey tr. *Rudin's Psychotherapy & Relig.* ix. 188 We should not bypass Viktor Frankl's logotherapy, since this is the approach which most encompasses the spiritual dimensions of man. **1972** W. C. Coe *Challenges Personal Adjustment* vi. 141 V. E. Frankl.. has developed what he calls 'logotherapy'. Its aim is to provide meaning.. to man's existential being, uniqueness, and responsibility for self-actualization.

logothete ('lɒgəθiːt). *Hist.* [ad. med.L. *logotheta*, ad. Gr. λογοθέτης, primarily 'one who audits accounts' (L. & Sc.), f. λόγο-ς account + θε-, stem of τιθέναι to set + agent-suffix -της.] The designation of various functionaries under the Byzantine emperors; applied esp. (also in the Norman kingdom of Sicily) to a high official corresponding to the 'chancellor' of Western kingdoms.

[*c* **1000** ÆLFRIC *Gloss.* in Wr.-Wülcker 164/35 *Logotheta*, ȝemotman.] **1781** GIBBON *Decl. & F.* liii. (1869) III. 286 Which the great logothete or chancellor of the empire was directed to prepare. **1862** KINGTON *Fredk. II*, II. xviii. 446 Logothete of Sicily, and Protonotary. **1864** KINGSLEY *Rom. & Teut.* viii. 217 He can talk Latin, and perhaps Greek, as well as one of those accursed man-eating Grendels, a Roman lawyer, or a logothete from Ravenna.

logotype ('lɒgətaɪp). [f. Gr. λόγο-ς word + TYPE.] **1.** *Printing.* **a.** A type containing a word, or two or more letters, cast in one piece.

a **1816** EARL STANHOPE in Hansard *Typographia* (1825) 477, I have deemed it advisable to contrive a new pair of composing cases..introducing a new set of double letters [these were *on, of, to, re, an, th, in, se*; they were not printed as ligatures], which I denominate logotypes; and rejecting altogether the double letters *ff, fi, fl, ffi, ffl, ft, ct*, formerly occupying room in the cases, but used so seldom that [etc.]. **1880** *Printing Times* 15 Feb. 41/2 The use of logotypes does rather enhance than lower the cost of printing. **1892** *Pall Mall G.* 22 Jan. 3/2 Are the Corean letters or logotypes as numerous as the Chinese?

b. *Comb.*

1824 J. JOHNSON *Typogr.* II. vi. 107 The logotype system was once attempted at the Times office, but soon abandoned. **1896** H. HART in *Collect.* Ser. III. (O.H.S.) 407 The *Times* newspaper was started in order to..show that logotype-printing was the only proper way to print!

2. = LOGOGRAM 2 c.

1957 *Archit. Rev.* CXXII. 421 These air outlet grills carry the company's loggotype [*sic*] (the three letters IBM which are the company's 'signature') in the form of magnetic plate, the position of which can be adjusted. **1968** *Heidelberg News* (Heidelberg Printing Machinery Co.) Sept. 2/2 It could concentrate its resources, as some printers have already done, on creating house styles, designing company logotypes, [etc.]. **1970** *Railway World* Apr. 166 A tatty sign affixed to the inside of the station windows (latterly in magnificent British Rail characterless logotype). **1970** *Sat. Rev.* (U.S.) 12 Sept. 94/1 The familiar *Life* logotype appears in the upper left corner. **1974** *Globe & Mail* (Toronto) 8 Feb. 12/5 The symbol was designed by Burton Kramer and Allan Fleming, authors of a number of other visual identikits including Canadian National Railways' CN logotype.

Hence **'logotypy** = LOGOGRAPHY 1.

1824 WATTS *Bibliotheca, Index Subjects, Logography*, or *Logotypy*, the art of uniting several characters into a single type.

'log-roll, *v.* [Back-formation from LOG-ROLLING.] **a.** *trans.* To procure the passing of (a bill) by log-rolling. **b.** To approach (a politician) with the view of getting his political co-operation. **c.** *intr.* To engage in log-rolling.

1835 D. CROCKETT *Tour* 120 My people don't like me to log-roll in their business, and vote away pre-emption rights to fellows in other states, that never kindle a fire on their lands. **1837** HT. MARTINEAU *Soc. Amer.* II. 279 The method of 'log rolling' bills through the legislature. **1865** *Daily Tel.* 14 Apr., The leading politicians who..log-roll the railway bills. **1876** LOWELL *Among my Bks.* Ser. II. 98 In the Greek epic, the gods..lobby and log-roll for their candidates. **1879** *Times* 19 June, To log-roll with everybody who was willing to work with him. **1888** BRYCE *Amer. Commw.* II. II. li. 286 Sometimes by express, more often by a tacit understanding, local bills are 'log-rolled' through the houses. **1896** DU MAURIER *Martian* (1898) 391 They did not log-roll Barty, whom they considered coarse and vulgar.

'log-,roller. [f. LOG *sb.*[1] + ROLLER.]

1. One who engages in political or literary 'log-rolling'.

1864 SALA in *Daily Tel.* 4 Aug., A professional politician..lobbyer and log-roller generally. **1887** *N. & Q.* 7th Ser. III. 120/1 Mr. Lang..shows what log-rollers were Hayward and Thackeray. **1897** [see BACK-SCRATCHING *vbl. sb.*]. **1900** *Author* 1 Jan. 183 In these columns notes on books are given from reviews which carry weight, and are not, so far as can be learned, logrollers. **1966** *Listener* 3 Mar. 324/1 Whether as editor,..impresario, log-roller, or friend, Ford seems to have been mixed up with almost every major writer of his time. **1968** *New Scientist* 5 Sept. 474/2 The same old professional log-rollers are going to say lightly-disguised variations of the thing they said to the same applauding audiences they met somewhere else last year. **1974** *Listener* 10 Jan. 54/3 D. G. Rossetti..would set Swinburne and the rest of his..practised log-rollers to promote his discovery.

2. *U.S.* 'A device in a saw-mill to convey logs from the log-deck or the log-way skids to the head-block' (Knight).

1884 KNIGHT *Dict. Mech.* Suppl., Fig. 1629 Emery's Log Roller.

3. One who practises the aquatic sport of 'log-rolling'.

1893 *Westm. Gaz.* 16 May 5/1 Canoes, shells, dug-outs, water-cycles, logs and log-rollers, and water-walkers, were present too in large numbers... At the start one of the log-rollers managed to drop off his log.

'log-,rolling. [f. LOG *sb.*[1] + ROLLING *vbl. sb.*]

1. *U.S.* **a.** The action of rolling logs to any required spot; a meeting for co-operation in doing this.

1848 THOREAU *Maine W.* (1894) 19 Occasionally there was a small opening on the bank, made for the purpose of log-rolling. **1859** MISS CARY *Country Life* i. (1876) 7 It was less welcome than as if it had brought a log-rolling. **1883** *Harper's Mag.* Jan. 283/1 The great festivals of Western life are camp-meetings, barbecues, and log-rollings.

b. The action of propelling over the water a log on which one is seated.

1893 *Westm. Gaz.* 16 May 5/1 For the special benefit of the distinguished spectators..an elaborate display of log-rolling was given.

2. *colloq.* (orig. *U.S.*). **a.** Combination for mutual assistance in political or other action. Also *attrib.* or as *adj.*

Suggested by the proverbial phrase 'You roll my log and I'll roll yours'.

1823 *Niles' Weekly Reg.* 7 June 210/1 That sort of 'management', now rather more fashionable, and known by the dignified appellation of 'log-rolling'—that is, a buying and selling of votes. **1838** J. A. QUITMAN *Let.* 13 Dec. in J. F. H. Claiborne *Life & Corr. J. A. Quitman* (1860) I. 165 Tending to promote combinations and log-rolling schemes. **1841-4** EMERSON *Ess., Poet* Wks. (Bohn.) I. 169 Our log-rolling, our stumps and their politics..are yet unsung. **1860** S. MORDECAI *Virginia* xxx. 303 But the log-rolling system of Virginia has diverted her energies from the completion of any one useful work. **1869** *Atlantic Monthly* Sept. 365/2 The log-rolling lobby generally exerted their powers upon objects which possessed a public character. **1879** *Times* 19 June, The bribe was political preferment, or 'log-rolling'—that is, help in passing other Bills. **1888** BRYCE *Amer. Commw.* I. I. xv. 213 Corruption..appears chiefly in the milder form of reciprocal jobbing or (as it is called) 'log-rolling'. **1889** G. B. SHAW *London Music 1888-89* (1937) 245, I received them with imprecations, having exhausted every form of words that logrolling amenity could take. **1914** W. B. YEATS *Responsibilities* 78 Log-rolling cranks and faddists. **1919** *New Statesman* 2 Aug. 437/2 There is no such thing as gratitude in politics—a fact which is perhaps the chief security we have against a universal orgie of log-rolling. **1929** A. DOUGLAS *Autobiogr.* xxxiii. 222, I was involved in half-a-dozen controversies which covered matters of principle and the welfare of letters, as opposed to log-rolling and corrupt cliques. **1932** N. M. BUTLER *Looking Forward* vi. 87 This is no time..to permit log-rolling combinations of special interests to use public authority for their own benefit. **1957** J. S. HUXLEY *Relig. without Revelation* vi. 136 Politics would degenerate into a game of log-rolling. **1967** V. NABOKOV *Speak, Memory* (ed. 2) xiv. 284 In their attitude toward literature they were curiously conservative; with them soul-saving came first, logrolling next, and art last. **1975** *N.Y. Times* 4 Mar. 33/3 In fact, a logrolling system, from which women rarely benefit, is the norm for faculty hiring.

b. Mutual puffing in literary publications.

[**1845** in *Longm. Mag.* (1900) Feb. 375 Somewhere in this book of Letters occurs, about 1845, the phrase 'literary log-rolling', the earliest instance which one has met.] **1888** J. PAYN in *Illustr. Lond. News* 7 Jan. 2 To have an eye to its [the book's] merits rather than to its defects, is obviously log-rolling. **18..** *American* XVII. 350 (Cent.) If by log-rolling is meant that reviewers praise people in hopes of being praised in turn, then the taunt is empty.

Logudoro (lɒguː'dɔərəʊ). The name of a town or area of Sardinia, used *attrib.* to designate the dialect or language used there. Hence **,Logudo'rese, ,Logudo'resian** *adjs.*

1849 J. W. TYNDALE *Island of Sardinia* II. vi. 264 (*heading*) The Logudoro dialect. **1885** R. TENNANT *Sardinia* v. 63 The rendering of the Lord's prayer in Sarde or Logudoro language, (so called to distinguish the Sarde proper from its northern and southern dialects) will give the best idea of the composite character of the language. **1946** PRIEBSCH & COLLINSON *German Lang.* (ed. 2) i. 14 The Logudoresian dialect retains certain relict-words with affinities in Basque. **1952** *Archivum Linguisticum* IV. 1. 92 Alghero, in Logodurese territory,..was an important centre of Catalan influence. **1954** PEI & GAYNOR *Dict. Ling.* 190 The most important [Sardinian dialects]..are: Campidanese..and Logudorese (Logudoresian), spoken in the southern and central parts of the island. **1965** W. S. ALLEN *Vox Latina* i. 14 The Logudoro dialect of Sardinia.

-logue (lɒg), the form assumed by the Gr. -λογος, -λογον in adapted words (most of them through Fr.), as *analogue, catalogue, dialogue.* The words with this ending which are designations of persons (in most instances repr. actual or assumed Gr. compounds of -λόγος 'speaker, discourser', and related to parallel formations in *-logy*) are now little used, derivatives in *-loger*, *-logist*, or *-logian* being commonly preferred. Examples are *Assyriologue*, †*astrologue*, *ideologue*, *philologue*, *Sinologue*, †*theologue*.

logwood ('lɒgwʊd). [f. LOG *sb.*[1] + WOOD.]

†**1.** Logs stored for fuel. *Obs.*

1666 PEPYS *Diary* 1 Dec., It seemed to be only of logwood that hath kept the fire all this while in it.

2. a. The heartwood of an American tree (*Hæmatoxylon Campechianum*) used in dyeing; so called from being imported in the form of logs.

It is used to some extent in medicine as an astringent. The alleged use of logwood in colouring spurious or adulterated port wine was at one time a frequent subject of jocular allusion.

1581 *Act 23 Eliz.* c. 9 § 1 There hathe byn brought..from beyonde the Seas..Stuffe called Logwood alias Blockewood. **1597-1602** *W. Riding Sessions Rolls* in *Yorksh. Arch. & Topogr. Assoc.* (Record Ser.) III. 174 In dying wooll & Wollen clothe Logwoodd alias Blockwood. **1641** EVELYN *Mem.* (1857) I. 25 The rasping of brasil and logwood for the dyers is very hard labour. **1703** *Lond. Gaz.* No. 3893/3 The same day arrived here the *Essex* of Boston from Campeachy, laden with Logwood. **1880** H. VIZETELLY *Facts about Port*, etc. 142 It has been often asserted that logwood is used to impart colouring matter to Port wine; and the authors of a bulky Treatise upon Wine..endorsed this preposterous assertion with their authority. **1892** WALSH *Tea* 145 A decoction..from catechu or logwood being next added to impart a tea-like color to the liquor.

b. The tree that yields this wood.

1652 WADSWORTH tr. *Colmenero's Treat. Chocolate* 15 Three Cods of the Logwood or Campeche tree. **1756** P. BROWNE *Jamaica* 221 Logwood. This shrub was first introduced to Jamaica from the main. **1785** MARTYN *Rousseau's Bot.* xix. (1794) 267 Amongst the plants with regular or equal polypetalous corollas, you will find Logwood, &c. **1834** M. G. LEWIS *Jrnl. W. Ind.* 66 The fragrance..of the delicious Logwood..composed an atmosphere.

c. *attrib.* and *Comb.*

1752 J. MACSPARRAN *Amer. Dissected* (1753) 3 A fine promising new Settlement upon the Spanish Main, mostly inhabited by the Logwood Cutters. **1833** J. RENNIE *Alph. Angling* 22 Strong tea, either with or without a few logwood scrapings. **1890** W. J. GORDON *Foundry* 165 By our side is a stack of dingy logwood red. **1900** *Daily News* 13 Feb. 9/5 A logwood ship that was about to sail for England.

3. The extract of logwood used for colouring or dyeing. Also *attrib.*

1876 [see *chrome-black*]. **1880** *Encycl. Brit.* XIII. 80/1 Such an ink is costly..on account of the concentrated condition in which the logwood must be used. **1935** C. A. MITCHELL *Documents & their Sci. Exam.* 56 Iron logwood inks have a greenish shade which gradually becomes black as the writing dries. **1966** J. S. COX *Illustr. Dict. Hairdressing & Wigmaking* 91/1 Logwood... Used in the 19th cent. for dyeing hair. **1969** T. C. THORSTENSEN *Pract. Leather Technol.* xi. 173 Logwood has been extensively applied in the development of base colors in upper leathers, particularly calf.

logy ('ləʊgɪ), *a. N. Amer.* [Of uncertain origin: cf. Du. *log* heavy, dull.] **a.** Dull and heavy in motion or thought.

1859 BARTLETT *Dict. Americanisms, Logy*, heavy, slow, stupid... He's a logy man, i.e. a slow-moving, heavy man. 'He is a logy preacher', i.e. dull. **1883** *Harper's Mag.* Aug. 452/2 Outside ballast..made boats logy. **1887** *Detroit Free Press* 21 May 2/3 He [Barnum] is heavier, and a trifle logy. **1890** in Leffingwell *Upland Shooting* 459 They [greyhounds] became 'logy' and out of heart. **1907** J. G. MILLAIS *Newfoundland* 339 *Logy*, heavy, dull. Thus, a *logy* day. **1935** H. DAVIS *Honey in Horn* iv. 37 Ordinarily he could have out-wrestled her..but he was fagged and logy. **1955** *U.S. Bureau Amer. Ethnol. Bull.* No. 159. 277 Mrs. Murphy informed me that Ute medicine men placed a root (unidentified) in the mouth of an opponent's race horse to make it logy. **1955** W. GADDIS *Recognitions* II. i. 291 And do you feel run down at the end of the day? that dull logy tired feeling that just seems to creep through you? **1973** E. PACE *Any War will Do* (1974) II. 97 The heat, the flies, the logy ground swell.

b. Used as *sb.*: A heavy fish.

1897 R. KIPLING *Captains Courageous* 61 'He's a logy. Give him room accordin' to his strength', cried Dan. 'I'll help ye. 'No, you won't', Harvey snapped, as he hung on to the line. 'It's my first fish'.

-logy (lədʒɪ), earlier written *-logie*, an ending occurring originally in words adapted from Gr. words in -λογία (the earliest examples, e.g. *theology*, having come through F. *-logie*, med.L. *-logia*). These Gr. words for the most part are parasynthetic derivatives; in some instances the terminal element is λόγος word, discourse (e.g. in τετραλογία tetralogy, τριλογία trilogy); more commonly it is the root λογ- (ablaut-variant of λεγ-, λέγειν to speak: cf. LOGOS). In the latter case, the sbs. in -λογία usually denote the character, action, or department of knowledge proper to the person who is described by an adj. or sb. in -λόγος, meaning either '(one) who speaks (in a certain way)', or '(one) who treats of (a certain subject)'. Hence the derivatives in -λογία are of two classes, (1) those which have the sense of 'saying or speaking', examples of which are the words anglicized as *battology, brachylogy, cacology, dittology, eulogy, palillogy, tautology*; and (2) names of sciences or departments of study. As the words of the last-mentioned class have always a sb. for their first element, and *o* is the combining vowel of all declensions of Gr. sbs., the ending of these compounds is in actual use always -ολογία, becoming -OLOGY in Eng. The names of sciences with this ending are very numerous: some represent words already formed in Gr., as *theology, astrology*; many represent formations which might legitimately have existed in Gr., as *geology, zoology, psychology*; others are of hybrid composition, as *sociology, terminology, insectology*. The modern formations in *-logy* follow the analogy of Gr. formations in having *o* as the combining vowel; exceptions are *petralogy* (an incorrect form which some writers prefer to *petrology* because it shows the derivation from πέτρα rock, not from πέτρος stone) and *mineralogy* (F. *minéralogie*) which may be viewed as a contraction for

mineralogy*. The suffix *-ology* is freely used in the formation of humorous nonce-wds., some of which are illustrated below. All the modern formations in *-logy* may be said to imply correlative formations in -LOGICAL and -LOGIST; in the case of some of the older words, the related personal designation ends in -LOGER or -LOGIAN. (Cf. -LOGUE.) Hence **logy *nonce-wd.* = OLOGY.

1820 W. BUCKLAND in Mrs. Gordon *Life* (1894) 40 Having allowed myself time to attend to nothing there but my undergroundology. **1837** *Fraser's Mag.* XV. 360 Hats were of scientific importance in his estimation, he had originated a system of hatology. **1853** (*title*) Chapology, or Hints about Hats. **1856** J. YOUNG *Demonol.* IV. iii. 372 The many Logies and Isms that have lately come into vogue. **1891** T. HARDY *Tess* (1900) 49/1 What are called advanced ideas are really in great part but.. a more accurate expression, by words in *logy* and *ism*, of sensations which men and women have vaguely grasped for centuries.

logyng, logyng(g)e, obs. ff. LODGING *vbl. sb.*

logyt, obs. pa. t. of LODGE *v.*

Lohan ('lohan). [Chin.] = ARHAT, ARAHAT.

1878 H. A. GILES *Gloss. Far East* 81 'Lohan cash' were cast in the reign of the Emperor K'ang Hsi, and were thus honourably named because believed to contain gold. **1880** J. EDKINS *Chinese Buddhism* 5 Among [those].. who have gone deeper than the others into the profundities of Buddhist doctrine, are included those called.. by the Chinese, P'usa and Lohan. **1905** *Daily Chron.* 26 Oct. 3/3 To call the Lohans or disciples of Buddha, 'Genii awaiting transformation into Buddhas' sounds as strange as if the twelve Apostles were described as awaiting transformation into Christs. **1936** *Discovery* Jan. 23/1 These T'ang figures and the great pottery Lohan, the Buddhist priest in contemplation, all live. **1964** M. MEDLEY *Handbk. Chinese Art* 47 They [*sc.* Arhats] are called Lohan by the Chinese. **1971** L. A. BOGER *Dict. World Pott. & Porc.* 201/2 The images of the Lohan are derived chiefly from the art work of one or two painters of the T'ang dynasty.

lohoch ('ləʊhɒk). *Med.* Forms: α. 6 loc, 6–8 loche, 6–9 loch. β. 6 lochoch, 6–8 lohoc, 7 lehoch, lohoche, 7–9 lohock, 6–9 looch, lohoch. [a. med.L. *lohoc, looch*, a. Arab. , *laᶜūq*, f. *laᶜiqa* to lick.] A linctus.

1544 PHAER *Regim. Lyfe* (1553) D j b, Take mornynge and euening, a spounefull of the syrupe of iuiubes.. in maner of a loc. **1597** GERARDE *Herbal* I. xxxiv. §2. 47 They are good in a loche or licking medicine for shortnes of breath. **1601** HOLLAND *Pliny* II. 76 This seed is passing good for lohoches or electuaries to be made thereof. **1657** W. COLES *Adam in Eden* lxxiii. 139 The Juyce of Liquorice dissolved in Rose Water, with some Gum, Tragacanth, is a fine Lohoch.. for hoarsenesse. **1753** N. TORRIANO *Sore Throat* 99, I made the Patient take.. some white Lohoc. **1781** J. MOORE *View Soc. It.* (1795) II. 222 Numerous forms of electuaries, lohochs, and linctuses. **1831** J. DAVIES *Manual Mat. Med.* 266 Dose, from gutt.xx. to gutt.xxx. a day in a looch or any mucilaginous menstruum. **1889** *Syd. Soc. Lex.*, *Looch*, a linctus, or opaque oily emulsion, which may be used as a demulcent, or as an excipient for the suspension of powders.

loiasis, var. LOAIASIS.

‖**loi-cadre** (lwa kadr). *Fr. Pol.* [Fr.] A general outline law, the principles of which can be applied by the government in succeeding parallel situations.

1953 *Ann. Reg. 1952* 202 Eight votes of confidence. On the first—to empower the Government to draw up skeleton laws (*lois cadres*) reorganizing the nationalized industries. **1957** *Observer* 27 Oct. 15/6 It was a 'Loi-Cadre' for Algeria which provoked the collapse of the French government. **1967** *Economist* 29 Apr. 435/2 The French have long used and abused the technique of decree-laws and *loi-cadres* to overcome the difficulties of inefficient rule by the assembly. **1968** *Encycl. Brit.* I 624A/1 De Gaulle ignored a *loi-cadre*, laboriously passed by the French National Assembly, which provided for the setting up of regional assemblies in Algeria.

loid (lɔɪd). *Criminals' slang.* Also 'loid. [Shortened f. CELLU)LOID *sb.*] A celluloid strip used by thieves to force open a spring lock. Also *attrib.* Also as *v. trans.*, to break open (a lock) by this method; to let (oneself) in by this method. Hence **'loiding** *vbl. sb.*

1958 M. PROCTER *Man in Ambush* xvi. 202 You said you could use a loid. Let's see you open that door. **1960** *Observer* 24 Jan. 5/5 Got yer stick (jemmy)? Got yer 'loid (celluloid strip for spring locks)? **1968** 'G. BAGBY' *Another Day* vi. 107 What point.. could there be in changing the cylinder.. when.. my visitor had managed entry by.. 'a loid job?'. He had worked a strip of heavy celluloid in over the lock tongue and pushed it back. *Ibid.* ix. 174, I loided myself into my apartment. **1968** *Observer* 10 Mar. 25/4 Mortice deadlocks with five or more levers, difficult to pick and impossible to loid. *Ibid.* 25/5 Doors are opened by picking, loiding, or using a false key. **1968** B. TURNER *Sex-Trap* xiv. 134 'Have you got keys to all Creedy's places?' 'Beatty has. I use a loid myself.' He showed a tapered wedge of blank celluloid.

loif, Sc. variant of LOF *Obs.*, praise.

loig(g)e, obs. form of LODGE *sb.* and *v.*

loig(g)inge, -ynge, obs. ff. LODGING *vbl. sb.*

loigne, var. LOIN and LOYNE. *Obs.*

loik, loikman, obs. Sc. ff. LUKE *a.*, LOCKMAN.

loimic ('lɔɪmɪk), *a.* [ad. Gr. λοιμικός, f. λοιμός plague.] Pertaining to the plague or to contagious disorders.

1842 in BRANDE *Dict. Sci.*; hence in mod. Dicts.

†**loi'mographer.** *Obs. rare*⁻⁰. [f. Gr. λοιμός plague + -GRAPHER.] 'One who writes about or describes pestilences'.

1727 BAILEY vol. II.

loimography (lɔɪ'mɒgrəfɪ). [ad. mod.L. *loimographia* (R. Lyonnet, 1639), f. as prec. + -GRAPHY. The normal form would be **lœmo-*, which is given as an alternative in some Dicts.] The descriptive science treating of pestilential diseases.

1706 in PHILLIPS (ed. Kersey). **1857** in DUNGLISON *Med. Lex.* **1864** in J. THOMAS *Med. Dict.*

loimology (lɔɪ'mɒlədʒɪ). *rare*⁻⁰. In Dicts. also lœmology. [ad. mod.L. *loimologia* (N. Hodges, 1672), f. as prec. + -LOGY.] The study of, or a treatise on, the plague or pestilential diseases.

1848 in CRAIG. **1864** in J. THOMAS *Med. Dict.*

loimous ('lɔɪməs), *a.* [f. Gr. λοιμ-ός plague + -OUS.] Having or full of the plague (Mayne *Expos. Lex.* 1856).

loin (lɔɪn), *sb.* Forms: 4–7 loyne, 6–7 loine, 6–8 loyn, (5 lony, 6 loigne, 9 *dial.* line), 7– loin. See also LUNYIE. [ad. OF. *loigne, logne*, dialectal variant of *longe* (mod.F. *longe* loin of veal) = Sp. *lonja* piece of ham:—med.L. **lumbea*, fem. of **lumbeus* adj., belonging to the loin, f. L. *lumbus* loin:—WAryan **londhwo-*: see LEND *sb.*¹]

1. a. In the living body. Chiefly *pl.* The part or parts of a human being or quadruped, situated on both sides of the vertebral column, between the false ribs and the hip-bone.

1398 TREVISA *Barth. De P.R.* v. xliii. (1495) 160 The place called the loynes is in the sydes of the joyntes of the rydge. **1541** R. COPLAND *Guydon's Quest. Chirurg.* F iij b, The loynes are musculous flesshes lyeing in the sydes of the spondyles of the backe. **1545** RAYNOLD *Byrth Mankynde* (1552) 15 b, From the ryght syde.. descendeth a braunche.. downe towardes the right loynes. **1589** PUTTENHAM *Eng. Poesie* III. xxiv. (Arb.) 290 An high paire of silke netherstocks that couered all his buttockes and loignes. **1605** SHAKS. *Lear* II. iv. 9 Horses are tide by the heads,.. Monkies, by th' loynes, and Men by th' legs. **1667** MILTON *P.L.* v. 282 The middle pair Girt like a Starrie Zone his waste, and round Skirted his loines and thighes with downie Gold. *c* **1720** W. GIBSON *Farrier's Dispens.* xiv. (1734) 269 Nothing will contribute more to strengthen a Horses Shoulders or Loyns. **1784** COWPER *Task* I. 45 But restless was the chair; the back erect Distressed the weary loins, that felt no ease. **1789** W. BUCHAN *Dom. Med.* (1790) 525 A sense of heat, weight, and dull pain in the loins. **1846** J. BAXTER *Libr. Pract. Agric.* (ed. 4) II. 135 Good hand-rubbing.. should be used.. about the loins.

b. In an animal used for food; chiefly, the joint of meat which includes the vertebræ of the loins.

c **1302** *Pol. Songs* (Camden) 191 We shule flo the Conyng, ant make roste is loyne. *c* **1440** *Promp. Parv.* 312/2 Loyne of flesche (*S.* lony), *lumbus, elumbus.* *c* **1460** *Towneley Myst.* xii. 232 Alle a hare bot the lonys. **1486** *Bk. St. Albans* C iij b, Then the loynes of the hare loke ye not forgete. **1555** in W. H. Turner *Select. Rec. Oxford* 228 Item, a loyne of vele,.. xvjᵈ. **1598** *Epulario* B j, The Loine [of a Bucke] may be rosted, and the legs baked. **1680** EARL DORSET *On C'tess Dorchester* 12 So have I seen in Larder dark Of Veal a lucid Loin,.. At once both stink and shine. **1711** SWIFT *Jrnl. to Stella* 4 Apr., I dined.. at home on a loin of mutton and half a pint of wine. **1727** W. MATHER *Yng. Man's Comp.* 30 Loyn, of Veal. **1846** J. BAXTER *Libr. Pract. Agric.* (ed. 4) II. p. xxi, The Brighton butchers sold.. loins of mutton at 6*d.* per lb. **1862** MRS. CARLYLE *Lett.* III. 101 The cookery.. would suit you:—constant loins of roast mutton.

2. Chiefly *Biblical* and *poet.* This part of the body, regarded **a.** as the part of the body that should be covered by clothing and about which the clothes are bound; so, *to gird (up) the loins* (lit. and fig.), to prepare for strenuous exertion.

1526 TINDALE *Matt.* iii. 4 This Jhon had his garment off camels heer and a gerdell off a skynne aboute his loynes. **1535** COVERDALE *Prov.* xxxi. 17 She gyrdeth hir loynes with strength. **1605** SHAKS. *Lear* II. iii. 10 My face Ile grime with filth, Blanket my loines. **1667** MILTON *P.L.* IX. 1096 Some Tree whose broad smooth Leaves together sowd, And girded on our loyns, may cover round Those middle parts. **1742** COLLINS *Ode Poet. Charac.* 21 To gird their blest prophetick loins. **1753** SMART *Hilliad* I. 27 Her loins with patch-work cincture were begirt. **1833** L. RITCHIE *Wand. by Loire* 17 It was necessary, therefore, to gird up our loins and walk. **1855** BROWNING *Statue & Bust*, The unlit lamp and the ungirt loin. **1877** BRYANT *Odyss.* v. 280 And round about her loins Wound a fair golden girdle. **1880** MRS. LYNN LINTON *Rebel of Fam.* II. v, He was standing like the impersonation of masculine punctuality with loins girded.

b. as the seat of physical strength and of generative power. †Hence occas. used as an equivalent for 'sire', 'offspring', 'descendants'. Also *fig.*

1535 COVERDALE *Gen.* xxxv. 11 Kynges shall come out of thy loynes. **1577–87** HOOKER *Chron. Irel.* 134/1 in *Holinshed*, John earle of Bath, whose ancestors were descended from out of the loines of kings. **1599** SHAKS. *Much Ado* IV. i. 137 This shame deriues it selfe from vnknowne loines. **1611** BIBLE *Job* xl. 16 Loe now, his strength is in his loynes. —— *Isa.* xlv. 1, I will loose the loines of kings. **1616** R. C. *Times' Whistle* IV. 1541 Impious villaine! to defame the fruit Of thine owne loynes. **1628** GAULE *Pract. Theory* (1629) Ep. Ded., And when it shall descend to your Loynes; may you be inuested with the Crowne, which.. fadeth not. *a* **1635** NAUNTON *Fragm. Reg.* (Arb.) 27 By inter-marriage with the Lady Iane Grey,.. to bring it [the crown] about into his [Northumberland's] loynes. **1667** MILTON *P.L.* I. 352 A multitude, like which the populous North Pour'd never from her frozen loyns. **1697** DRYDEN *Virg. Georg.* IV. 459 What boots it, that from Phœbus Loins I spring. **1786** A. GIB *Sacr. Contempl.* II. III. ii. 120 All his natural posterity, as being all in his loins. **1790** COWPER *Receipt Mother's Pict.* 109 My boast is not, that I deduce my birth From loins enthroned, and rulers of the earth. **1826** J. WILSON *Noct. Ambr.* Wks. I. 255 About a dizzen and a half—the legitimate produce o' the Eerish couple's ain fruitfu lines. **1847** TENNYSON *Princess* v. 495, I thought, can this be he From Gama's dwarfish loins? **1880** L. MORRIS *Ode of Life* 43 The Future lies within thy loins, and all the Days to be To thee Time giveth to beget.

3. *attrib.* and *Comb.*, as *loin-ache, -guard, -rag* (= *loin-cloth*), **-steak**; **loin-cloth**, a cloth worn round the loins.

1897 *Allbutt's Syst. Med.* II. 1075 This *loin ache is apt to reappear. **1859** R. F. BURTON *Centr. Afr.* in *Jrnl. Geogr. Soc.* XXIX. 324 The remainder of the dress is a *loin-cloth of white domestics or of indigo dyed cotton. **1894** *Daily News* 1 Aug. 5/5 In cold or rainy weather the cab-horses have waterproof loin-cloths. **1895** *Oracle Encycl.* I. 180/1 Brayette and *loin-guard to protect the abdomen. **1929** D. H. LAWRENCE *Escaped Cock* II. 49 He peeped round.. adjusting his *loin-rag. **1938** R. GRAVES *Coll. Poems* 184 Nor yet that brooding Hindu heat For which a loin-rag and a dish of rice Suffice until the pestilent monsoon. **1868** *Rep. Iowa Agric. Soc. 1867* 127 The reason.. is the same that persons have for preferring *loin-steaks to those cut from just aft of the horns.

†**loin**, *v.*¹ *Obs. rare*⁻¹. *trans.* The technical term for 'to carve' (a sole).

c **1486** *Bk. St. Albans* F vij b, A Sole loyned. A Gurnarde chyned. A Tenche sawced.

†**loin**, *v.*² *Obs. rare*⁻¹. [aphetic f. ALOYN.] *trans.* To keep apart.

14.. *Siege Jerus.* 63/1088 Doun þei daschen þe dores: dei scholde þe berde, þat mete yn þis meschef hadde from men loyned.

loin, obs. form of LINE *v.*¹ and *v.*³

1587 HARRISON *Descr. Brit.* III. vii. (1878) II. 49 The Indians, who tie their sault bitches often in woods, that they might be loined by tigers. **1679** WOOD *Life* 3 May (O.H.S.) II. 449 Dʳ. Michael Roberts.. died with a girdle loyned with broad gold about him (100*l.* they say).

loined (lɔɪnd), *ppl. a.* [f. LOIN *sb.* + -ED².] Having loins (of a specified kind).

1865 *Daily Tel.* 4 Mar., Headed like a snake, loined like a weasel, and breasted like a swan. **1871** *Daily News* 27 Nov., She is slack loined and light in the hindquarters. **1898** A. BALFOUR *To Arms* xv. 161 Clumsy brutes.. loose loined and shaggy fetlocked.

loiner ('lɔɪnə(r)). *slang.* [Origin uncertain.] An inhabitant of Leeds, West Yorkshire.

1950 M. MARPLES *University Slang* 180 *Loiner*,.. possibly a corruption or mispronunciation of *oiner*. **1967** P. RYAN *How I became Yorkshireman* iii. 16 The lunchtime audience of Leeds loiners applauded vociferously. *Ibid.* ix. 59, I ran through the ranks of rumbling loiners and out into the eternal, grey twilight of Leeds.

Loiolite, obs. form of LOYOLITE, a Jesuit.

loir (lɔɪə(r)). [a. F. *loir*:—pop.L. **glīrem*, for *glīr-em, glīs*.] The Fat Dormouse (*Myoxus glis*).

1774 GOLDSM. *Nat. Hist.* (1776) IV. 76 The greater dormouse, which Mr. Buffon calls the Loir. **1801** HEL. M. WILLIAMS *Sk. Fr. Rep.* I. xxi. 314, I call them rats, from their almost perfect resemblance to that animal.. but their real name is the Loir. **1884** *Evang. Mag.* Mar. 117 The Loir, or fat dormouse of France. **1885** *Riverside Nat. Hist.* (1888) V. 116 The two large European species, the Loir (*Myoxus glis*) and the Lerot (*Eliomys nitela*).

lois(s, obs. form of LOOSE, LOSE, LOSS.

loisible: see LISIBLE.

loit, dial. form of LITE, little.

loiter ('lɔɪtə(r)), *sb. rare*⁻¹. [f. LOITER *v.*] The action of loitering, an instance of this.

1876 T. HARDY *Ethelberta* (1890) 314 Picotee.. moved on in a manner intended to efface the lover's loiter of the preceding moments from her own consciousness.

loiter ('lɔɪtə(r)), *v.* Forms: 4 (? loltre or loitre), lotere, 5 loytron, 6 loyeter, loytre, lowtre, lewtre, leut(e)re, 6–8 loyter, 6– loiter. [a. MDu. *loteren* to wag about (like a loose tooth), Du. *leuteren* to shake, totter, *Naut.* (of a sail) to 'shiver'; also, to dawdle, loiter over one's work; cf. WFlem. *lutteren*, EFris. *löteren*, of similar meaning. For the development of sense cf. the fig. uses of *loose, unsteady*. The sense which the word has in Eng. has not been found in Du. earlier than the 16th c., but may be much older in slang use; the word was prob. introduced into England by foreign 'loiterers' or vagrants. The same root is found in MDu. *lutsen* to wag about.

The diphthong in the first syll. is a substitution for the unfamiliar vowel of the Du. word, which was prob. (øː) (as in mod. pronunciation) or nearly so.

In the first quot. below, the form *loltrande* may be genuine; if so it represents a distinct word, f. the root of LOLL *v.*]

1. *intr.* **a.** In early use: To idle, waste one's time in idleness. Now only with more specific meaning: To linger indolently on the way when sent on an errand or when making a journey; to linger idly about a place; to waste time when engaged in some particular task, to dawdle. Freq. in legal phr. ***to loiter with intent*** (to commit a felony).

13.. *E.E. Allit. P.* C. 458 Þenne was þe gome so glad of his gay logge, Lys loltrande [*Morris conjectures* loitrande] þer-inne, lokande to toune. *c* **1440** *Promp. Parv.* 311/1 Loytron, or byn ydyl, *ocior.* **1482** *Trevisa's Higden* (Caxton) II. v. 77 He slough caym that loyterd [*Trevisa*: loted] amonge the busshes. **1530** PALSGR. 613/1 He loytreth aboute lyke a maysterlesse hounde. *Ibid.* 613/2 And you sende hym, he wyll sure loyter somewhere by the waye. *c* **1540** *Hye way to Spyttel Ho.* 143 in Hazl. *E.P.P.* IV. 29 Lowtryng, and wandryng fro place to place. **1553** *Primer in Liturgies, etc. Edw. VI* (Parker Soc.) 472 Laboured nothing at all, but went abroad loitering idly. **1597** SHAKS. *2 Hen. IV*, II. i. 198 Sir John, you loyter heere too long. **1621** BURTON *Anat. Mel.* II. ii. IV. (1651) 277 Some of them do nought but loyter all the week long. **1660** WOOD *Life* Dec. (O.H.S.) I. 359 People might loyter about the streets in sermon time. **1697** DRYDEN *Æneid* II. 745 A Javelin threw, Which flutt'ring seemed to loiter as it flew. **1726** LEONI *Alberti's Archit.* I. 85 Nobody may loyter about in order to attempt it without instant suspicion. **1758** JOHNSON *Idler* No. 28 ¶4 That I loiter in the shop with my needle-work in my hand. **1814** SCOTT *Wav.* xxxix, Officers.. loitered in the hall, as if waiting for orders. **1855** TENNYSON *Brook* 181, I linger by my shingly bars; I loiter round my cresses. **1870** E. PEACOCK *Ralf Skirl.* III. 8 These weak old men who loitered about. **1886** *Pall Mall G.* 18 June 3/2 Cabmen have had to pay.. fines.. for 'loitering and obstructing' the roads... To loiter, in cabman's English, means to ply for hire. **1891** *Act 54 & 55 Vict.* c. 69 §7 The provisions [shall be] applied also to every suspected person or reputed thief loitering about or in any of the said places and with the said intent. **1899** C. ROOK *Hooligan Nights* i. 16 You get lagged for loiterin' wiv intent to commit a felony or some dam nonsense like that. **1952** *Economist* 26 Jan. 207/3 Montgomery is always suspected of loitering with intent. **1957** [see CASE *v.*² 5].

b. To travel or proceed indolently and with frequent pauses. With advs. or adverbial phrases.

1728 POPE *Dunc.* I. 228 Prose swell'd to verse, Verse loitring into prose. **1789** MRS. PIOZZI *Journ. France* I. 1 We have lingered and loitered.. from port to port. **1827–35** WILLIS *Florence Gray* 32, I loiter'd up the valley to a small and humbler ruin. **1850** TENNYSON *In Mem.* xxxviii, With weary steps I loiter on. **1853** KANE *Grinnell Exp.* xlviii. (1856) 445 From the 13th of July to the 13th of August we loitered along. **1860** HOLLAND *Miss Gilbert* iv. 51 He loitered thoughtfully along the uneven highway. **1863** HAWTHORNE *Our Old Home* (1879) 115 The Avon loiters past the churchyard.

2. *trans.* †**a.** To neglect (one's work). *Obs.* **b.** To allow (time, etc.) to pass idly; to waste carelessly or upon trifles. *Obs.* exc. with *away*; occas. with †*out.* †**c.** To postpone getting or giving (something). *Obs.*

c **1540** *Hye Way to Spyttel Ho.* 871 in Hazl. *E.P.P.* IV. 62 But lye in bed,.. Lewtryng theyr worke tyll it pas noone. **1549** COVERDALE, etc. *Erasm. Par. Eph.* Prol. Cij, Be not of the nombre of those men, whiche.. loyter the tyme.. and do no good at all. **1550** CROWLEY *Last Trump.* 547 When thou art determined what knowledg thou wilt most apply, then let it not be loytered, but seke to get it spedily. **1589** WARNER *Alb. Eng.* v. xxv. 111 To loyter well deserued gifts is not to giue but sell. **1680** OTWAY *Orphan* II. i. (1691) 12 Not loyter out my life at home. **1689** SHERLOCK *Death* iii. §7 (1731) 210 These Men have loitered away the Day. **1748** *Anson's Voy.* II. v. 173 It would have been extreme imprudence.. to have loitered away so much time. **1863** LYTTON *Caxtoniana* I. 50 The little lake.. on the banks of which I loitered out my schoolboy holidays. *a* **1903** *Mod.* We loitered away the rest of the day.

3. *Comb.*: †**loiter-sack**, a lazy, lumpish fellow.

1594 LYLY *Moth. Bomb.* II. ii, If the loiter-sacke bee gone springing into a taverne, I'le fetch him reeling out.

loiter, obs. form of LIGHTER *sb.*¹

loiterer ('lɔɪtərə(r)). Forms: 6 leuterar, leutterer, loitreer, loyterour, -(er)rer, 6–7 loyterar, -er, 8– loiterer. [a. Du. *leuterer*: see LOITER *v.* and -ER¹.] One who loiters (see senses of the vb.); †a vagabond, 'sturdy beggar'.

1530 PALSGR. 240/2 Loyterar, *truandeu.* **1547** *Act 1 Edw. VI*, c. 3 §1 The same Justices shall cawse such Slave, or loyterer to bee marked on the forhed. **1567** HARMAN *Caveat* (1869) 22 These lousey leuterars. *Ibid.* 27 An ydell leuterar. *Ibid.* 87 Lasy lewd Leutterers. **1588** in *Norfolk Antiq. Misc.* (1883) II. 329 Paid to Burwell and his loyterrers for vj dayes' woorke, vˢ. viijᵈ. **1612** S. RID *Art Juggling* B 1 b, Many of our English Loyterers ioined with them, and in time learned their craft and cosening. **1640–1** *Kirkcudbr. War-Comm. Min. Bk.* (1855) 84 David Macmollan, loyterar, being convenit for saying, that [etc.]. **1684** G. S. *Anglorum Spec.* 196 Th. Tusser was a Speculative Husbandman, but a Practical Loyterer in Agriculture. **1723** SWIFT *Country Life* 33 The loiterers quake, no corner hides them. **1758** JOHNSON *Idler* No. 14 ¶9 The loiterer.. makes appointments which he never keeps. **1810** SCOTT *Lady of L.* II. xxi, Come, loiterer, come! **1872** BLACK *Adv. Phaeton* ii. 14 There are still a few loiterers on the pavement. **1896** A. E. HOUSEMAN *Shropsh. Lad* xxxix. Spring will not wait the loiterer's time Who keeps so long away.

loitering ('lɔɪtərɪŋ), *vbl. sb.* [f. as prec. + -ING¹.] The action of the vb. LOITER in its various senses. †In early use, vagrancy, vagabondage.

1362 LANGL. *P. Pl.* A. v. 188 Þer was lauȝwhing and lotering and 'let go þe cuppe'. **1530** PALSGR. 240/2 Loyteryng, *truandise.* *a* **1533** LD. BERNERS *Gold. Bk. M. Aurel.* (1546) K vij, A man giuen to exercises is vertuouse, and one giuen to leutrynges is a viciouse person. **1585** FETHERSTONE tr. *Calvin's Comm. Acts* xxiii. 13 When God calleth vs expresly, our loitring is without excuse. **1612** BRINSLEY *Lud. Lit.* xxv. (1627) 270 And to see that there be no intermission, or loytering in any fourme, if the master be away. *a* **1718** PENN *Maxims* Wks. (1726) I. 854 Nor is he a good Servant.. that connives at other's Loyterings. **1822** W. IRVING *Braceb. Hall* i. 7 Should I.. in the course of my loiterings.. see.. anything curious. **1847–8** H. MILLER *First Impr.* xiii. (1857) 212 Opportunities.. which loiterings by the.. road-sides present. **1889** BROWNING *Imperante Augusto* 162 No loitering, or be sure you taste the lash.

†**b.** *attrib.*

1642 MILTON *Apol. Smect.* xi. Wks. 1851 III. 312 Were it not better to take it away soone after, as we do loitering books.. from children. **1644** —— *Areop.* (Arb.) 64 The helps of Breviaries, synopses, and other loitering gear.

loitering ('lɔɪtərɪŋ), *ppl. a.* [f. LOITER *v.* + -ING².] That loiters or idles; in early use, that leads a vagabond life.

a **1533** LD. BERNERS *Gold. Bk. M. Aurel.* (1546) Liv b, These lewtryng theues, whyche wyl not labour by daie. **1581** NOWELL & DAY in *Confer.* I. (1584) Fij b, I haue bene .. a loytering labourer in the Lords vineyarde. **1603** KNOLLES *Hist. Turks* (1638) 210 A company of loitring companions. **1671** CLARENDON *Dialogues* Tracts (1727) 346 There is no temper so much to be despised as a loitering lazy nature. **1712** STEELE *Spect.* No. 491 ¶1 After an Hour spent in this loitering way of Reading. **1784** COWPER *Task* III. 832 Herds Of fluttering, loitering, cringing.. vagrants. **1791–2** WORDSW. *Descr. Sk.* 89 The loitering traveller hence, at evening, sees From rock-hewn steps the sail between the trees. **1847** EMERSON *Poems, Musketaquid,* Loiter willing by yon loitering stream. **1865** J. H. INGRAHAM *Pillar of Fire* (1872) 110 No loitering step was permitted by the overseers.

Hence '**loiteringly** *adv.*, in a loitering manner; in early use, †like a vagabond. '**loiteringness**, the quality of being inclined to loiter.

1547 *Act 1 Edw. VI*, c. 3 §1 The said parsone so living Idelye and loyteringlie. *a* **1617** BAYNE *Lect.* (1634) 136 Not looking that loyteringly it should be atchieved. **1836** *New Monthly Mag.* XLVI. 43 He.. strolled loiteringly on. **1850** LYNCH *Theo. Trin.* vii. 135 Like a first violet of spring, Trembling downwards loiteringly. **1868** J. H. STIRLING in *N. Brit. Rev.* XLIX. 364 That inertia, that lingeringness and loiteringness, that are not unfrequent in Browning.

†'**loiterous**, *a. Obs.* In 6 loytrous. [f. LOITER *v.* + -OUS.] Inclined to loiter; sluggish.

1566 DRANT *Horace, Sat.* I. vi. Dvj b, I noynte with supple oyle My loytrous limmes.

lok, obs. form of LOCK; var. LAKE *sb.*¹ *Obs.*

c **1325** *Chron. Eng.* 445 (Ritson) In Englond he arerede a lok Of uche hous that come smok, To Rome yef a peny, y wys, That Petres peny cleped ys.

‖**lokal** (lo'ka:l). [Ger.] A local bar, a night-club.

1903 *Pop. Sci. Monthly* Dec. 126 The entire body, like a German scientific gathering, gravitated after adjournment to a summer garden or winter 'Lokal'. **1931** WYNDHAM LEWIS *Let.* 7 Feb. (1963) 200 If Miss Hamilton insists upon .. robbing the night *lokals* of Berlin of foreign custom, I at least will have nothing to do with it. **1947** L. HASTINGS *Dragons are Extra* vii. 157 Tourists were filling the *lokals* in the evenings. **1949** A. WILSON *Wrong Set* 170 Her later life of boites and lokals. **1969** A. GLYN *Dragon Variation* viii. 229 Drinking beer in a keller, singing German songs, drinking wine or apfelsaft in a Schwabing *lokal*, and singing quite different songs.

‖**lokanta** (ləʊ'kæntə). [Turk.] In Turkey: a restaurant.

1954 M. GOUGH *Plain & Rough Places* ix. 142 The courtyard.. is occupied, in summer-time, by the *lokanta*—the restaurant. **1964** D. C. HILLS *My Trav. Turkey* xi. 120 We had hardly sat down in the *lokanta* when a gendarme captain swooped on me. **1969** 'A. GARVE' *Ascent of D. 13* ii. 23 He descended the rock in time to lunch at a small *lokanta*, on watermelon, *shish kebab* and yoghurt. **1969** *Daily Tel.* 4 Jan. 15/3 There are many nearby *lokantas* where you can try Turkish food and wines.

lokart, -at, obs. forms of LOCKET.

lokdore, variant of LOCKDOR *Obs.*

loke (ləʊk). *dial.* Also loak. [repr. OE. *loca* enclosed place, also lock, f. root of LOUK *v.* to shut, lock.] A lane, a short, narrow, blind lane, a 'cul-de-sac'; a grass road; a private lane or road.

1787 MARSHALL *Norfolk* (1795) II. 383 *Gloss.*, *Loke*, a close narrow lane (common). *a* **1825** FORBY *Voc. E. Anglia*, *Loke*, a short narrow turn-again lane. **1860** GILLETT *Sng. Sol. in Norf. Dial.* iii. 2 In the lokes and causeys I'll seek him as my soul du love. **1865** W. WHITE *E. Eng.* I. 162 *Loak* means lane. **1892** P. H. EMERSON *Son of Fens* 5 We were playing down the loke, and we fell out.

attrib. **1888** *N. & Q.* Ser. VII. VI. 191/2 My house is bounded by a lokeway leading from —— to ——.

loke, variant of LAKE *sb.*¹ *Obs.*

loke, obs. form of LOCK, LOOK *sb.* and *v.*

lokecheste, variant of LOCKCHESTER.

†'**loken**, *v. Obs. rare*⁻¹. [repr. OE. *lácnian*: see LECHNE *v.*] *trans.* To heal.

c **1425** *St. Mary of Oignies* I. viii. in *Anglia* VIII. 140/24 Wiþ woundes of Criste her woundes were lokned. *Ibid.* II. v. *ibid.* 166/2 Þe inwarde esines softenyd oute warde sorowe, & sumtyme lokkenyd and cecyd þe burden of siekenesse. *Ibid.* viii. *ibid.* 175/10 In þis hir woo was lokkenyd & hir spirite strengþed.

†'**loken**, *ppl. a. Obs.* See also LUCKEN. [str. pa. pple. of LOUK *v.*¹] Locked, closed.

a **1300** *Cursor M.* 23462 Wel þan al sal þou sei, wit loken als wit open hei. **1523** FITZHERB. *Husb.* §146 One maner of linsede, called loken sede, wyll not open by the son.

loker(e, obs. form of LOCKER, LOCKYER.

loker(h)am, variant of LOCKRAM *Obs.*

†**Lokes.** *Obs. rare.* [prob. a use of the pl. of LOCK *sb.*², a transl. of OF. *closes Pentecoste*, med.L. *clausum Pentecostes*, lit. 'the close of Pentecost'.

For examples of the OFr. and med.L. terms see J. M. Manly in *Harvard Studies Philol. & Lit.* I. (1892) 88 ff. The main difficulty is that these terms appear, whenever their sense can be determined, to mean the octave of Pentecost, or Trinity Sunday. Prof. Manly, however, points out that there is evidence that 'Pentecost' was sometimes used for the season beginning at Easter and *closed* by Whitsunday, so that the transference of the name 'close of Pentecost' from Trinity Sunday to Whitsunday, though lacking direct evidence, is not improbable. The use may have been merely local English; the *Ayenbite* and Shoreham both belong to Kent.]

Whitsunday. Also **Lok-Sounday.**

c **1315** SHOREHAM (E.E.T.S.) v. 289 Al here [*sc.* the Virgin's] ioyen a lok-sounday. **1340** *Ayenbite* 213 At lokes [Fr. *a Penthecouste*]. *Ibid.* 143, 263.

†**lo'ket.** *Obs. rare*⁻¹. [Of obscure origin.

If the sense be 'lappet', the word might be a dim. of F. *loque* rag, though this has not been found earlier than the 15th c. (Cotgr. 1611 has *loquette*). A dim. of LOCK *sb.*¹ would yield an admissible sense, but a hybrid formation of this kind would be unusual at so early a period. It is not easy to see how the word can be identified with LOCKET.]

? Some part of a head-dress, ? a lappet; or ? a lovelock, curl.

c **1320** *Song* in *Harl. MS.* 2253 fo. 61 b (*Pol. Songs* Camd. 1839) Ȝef þer lyþ a loket by er ouþer eȝe þat mot wiþ worse be wet for lac [*MS.* lat] of oþer leȝe.

loket, obs. form of LOCKET.

loking, -yng(e, obs. forms of LOOKING.

lokk(e, lokked, lokkyn, obs. inf. and pa. pple. of LOCK *v.*¹

lokman, lokyer(e, obs. ff. LOCKMAN, LOCKYER.

lokoum, var. LOCOUM.

‖**Lok Sabha** (lɒk 'sɑ:bə). [Skr. *lok* people + *sabhā* assembly, council.] The lower house of the Indian parliament.

1954 BINANI & RAMA RAO *India at Glance* (rev. ed.) 178 House of the People... Called Lok Sabha with effect from May 14, 1954. **1960** *Guardian* 24 Nov. 11/5 The Loksabha .. endorsed the Indian Government's.. policies pursued during the current session of the UN. **1969** *Times* 13 Oct. (Indian Suppl.) 6/4 The fact that no Harijan or tribal member was elected to the Lok Sabha in the 1967 general election from a general seat is significant. **1971** *Femina* (Bombay) 2 Apr. 15/1 Mrs. Indira Gandhi announced the dissolution of the Lok Sabha. **1972** *Times of India* 28 Nov. 8/2 As soon as Mrs. Gandhi finished her statement in the Lok Sabha, the former minister for parliamentary affairs, Mr. Raghuramaiah, rose to seek some clarifications to assuage feelings in Andhra.

‖**lokshen** ('lɒkʃən), *sb. pl.* Also lockschen, lockshan, lockshen. [Yiddish, pl. of *loksh* noodle.] Noodles. Also *attrib.*, esp. ***lokshen soup.***

1892 [see FARFEL]. **1934** L. J. GREENBERG *Jewish Chron. Cookery Bk.* 167 Thickly grease a pudding basin and sprinkle thickly with brown sugar; then put in a layer of lockshen. **1964** G. SIMS *Terrible Door* xii. 67 Come on: the lockshan soup, the potato lutkas, are calling! **1969** *Coast to Coast 1967–68* 179 After the prayers Mrs. Katzen served traditional fare; tonight it was lokshen soup, chopped herring, [etc.]. **1973** *Jewish Chron.* 20 July 23/3 He is not a man to decry lokshen soup.

lokyn, lokyr, obs. forms of LOOK, LOCKER.

Lolar, variant of LOLLER¹ *Obs.*, Lollard.

Lolard(e, Lolart, obs. forms of LOLLARD.

‖**loligo** (ləʊ'laɪgəʊ). Also 7 lolligo. [a. L. *lolīgo.*] A genus of cephalopods; an individual of this genus, a squid. ¶ In the first quot. used *fig.* and app. by mistake for *torpedo.*

a **1626** BP. ANDREWES *96 Serm.*, *Of Holy Ghost* xv. (1629) 763 St. Paul calls them the Lolligoe's of the Land. His word is καταναρκεῖν; the six daies and the seventh, to them both alike. **1658** SIR T. BROWNE *Gard. Cyrus* v. 69 The cuttle-fish and *Loligo.* [**1706** PHILLIPS, *Loligo* (Lat.), the Calimary Fish, whose Bloud is like Ink, as well as that of the Cuttle-fish.] **1835–6** TODD *Cycl. Anat.* I. 540/1 In *Loligo* the coats of the corresponding veins.. present.. a spongy thickening. **1854** H. MILLER *Sch. & Schm.* (1858) 467 The loligo.. laid hold of the pebbles, apparently to render its abduction as difficult as possible.

[**lolion.** Error for LOTION (sense 1).

[**1549** LATIMER *6th Serm. bef. Edw. VI* Ujb, Their doctrine was vnsauery, it was but of Lotiones of decimacions of anets seade, and Cummyn and suche gere.] In ed. **1549** and later 16th c. editions 'Lotiones' is misprinted 'Loliones'. Hence in **1881** DAVIES *Suppl. Eng. Gloss.* [quoting this as 'lolions'], and in some later Dicts.]

Lolita (lə'liːtə). The name of a novel (1958) and its main character by Vladimir Nabokov (1899–1977) about a precocious schoolgirl seduced by a middle-aged man, used to designate people and situations resembling those in the book. Also *attrib.* and *Comb.*

1959 *Encounter* Feb. 31/2 The melodrama turns this country of common routines into Lolitaland. **1960** B. FRETCHMAN tr. S. de Beauvoir *(title)* Brigitte Bardot and the Lolita syndrome. **1960** *Spectator* 25 Nov. 843 A nymphomaniac launched into her life's work by a Lolitaish experience with the man who wanted to marry her mother. **1964** C. DALE *Other People* v. 113 He drew back... This was June from next door, a sweet kid but a schoolgirl... Christ, he wasn't a Lolita type! **1967** H. HUNTER *Case for Punishment* viii. 134 Jack Carter's our first assistant and he's absolutely head over heels in love with Jinnie Turner of the sixth form. A real Lolita affair. **1972** *Guardian* 25 Jan. 9/2 Louis Feraud..includes a group of dresses called schoolgirl frocks... Lolita lives again and one longs for the innocence of St Trinian's. **1975** *Listener* 6 Mar. 305/1 Chaplin had an uncontrollable infatuation with young girls... But his Lolita-like relationships in real life rarely matched the spiritual purity of love-on-the-screen.

loll (lɒl), *sb.* [f. LOLL *v.*[1]]

1. The action or posture of lolling. †Also ***at loll, upon the (high) loll.***

1709 MRS. MANLEY *Secret Mem.* (1736) I. 21 Who is that graceful Person that appears upon the high Loll in his Chariot and six Horses? *Ibid.* 152 See that beautiful Gentleman at Loll in the next Chariot. **1709** SWIFT *Tatler* No. 71 ¶7 In reading Prayers, he has such a careless Loll, that People are justly offended at his irreverent Posture. **1775** S. J. PRATT *Liberal Opin.* lxvii. (1783) II. 256 He was, in short, all laugh, loll, and liberty. **1868** BROWNING *Ring & Bk.* v. 530 The old abundant city-fare was best,..down to the loll itself O' the pot-house settle,—better such a bench Than [etc.].

2. One who lolls; an idle person. Also, a thing that lolls, e.g. a tongue.

1582 STANYHURST *Æneis* III. (Arb.) 84 Then a tayle lyke a dolphin is added Iumbled vp of sauadge fel woulfs, with grislye lol hanging. **1600** BRETON *Pasquil's Mad-cappe* 26 Then let a knaue be knowne to be a knaue,..A Lobbe a Lowte, a heavy Loll a Logge. *a* **1807** J. SKINNER *Poet. Pieces* (1809) 48 A mischievous pair O' mawten'd lolls.

3. A pet, a spoilt child. *dial.*

1728 MORGAN *Hist. Algiers* I. Pref. p. xvii, The.. Unmannerliness of this Mam's Loll. **1785** GROSE *Dict. Vulg. Tongue, Loll*, mother's loll, a favourite child, the mother's darling. **1847–78** in HALLIWELL (*Oxon.*).

loll (lɒl), *v.*[1] Also 4–6 lolle, 4, 6, 8 lull(e. [App. due to a sense of the expressiveness of the sound (with the repeated *l*) suggestive of rocking or swinging; cf. LULL *v.* and MDu. *lollen* to sleep, early mod.Du. *lollebanck* (Kilian) couch, sofa; also mod.Du. dial. *lollen* to warm oneself with a pot of charcoal placed under one's seat. With sense 3 cf. LILL *v.*]

1. *intr.* To hang down loosely; to droop, dangle. Also with *down.* ? *Obs.* or *arch.*

1362 LANGL. *P. Pl.* A. v. 110 Lyk a leþerne pors lullede [**1393** lollid] his chekes. *c* **1394** *P. Pl. Crede* 224 His chin wiþ a chol lollede As greet as a gos eye. *c* **1449** PECOCK *Repr.* III. xiv. 374 Robyn rode without stiropis, eke thanne his legge lollid. **1575** TURBERV. *Faulconrie* 339 Sometymes a hawke hathe a strype on his wing..so as..it hangeth alwayes downe and lolleth. **1578** LYTE *Dodoens* IV. xii. 465 When it rayneth muche, it maketh the leaues to loll and hang downewarde. **1845** H. B. HIRST *Poems* 75 The lady is pale —Pale as the lily that lolls on the gale. **1849** JAMES *Woodman* iv, A great white feather lolling down till it touched his left shoulder.

†**b.** To swing, hang, be suspended. *Obs.*

? *c* **1418** *Pol. Poems* (Rolls) II. 243 The game is not to lolle so hie Ther fete failen fondement.

¶**c.** Alleged by Langland to have formerly meant: To halt, be lame. *Obs.*

1393 LANGL. *P. Pl.* C. x. 215 Now kyndeliche, by crist beþ suche callyd 'lolleres', As by englisch of oure eldres of olde menne techynge. He þat lolleþ is lame oþer his leg oute of ioynte, Oþer meymed in som membre, for to meschief hit souneþ. And ryght so sothlyche suche manere eremytes Lollen aȝen þe byleyue and lawe of holy churche.

†**2.** *trans.* To let droop or dangle. Also ***to loll up***: to hang.

13.. *Minor Poems fr. Vernon MS.* (E.E.T.S.) 614/75 Mi loue i-lolled vp in þe eyr, Wiþ cradel bond I gan him bynde. Cros! he stikeþ nou on þi steir, Naked a-ȝeyn þe wylde wynde. **1377** LANGL. *P. Pl.* B. XII. 191 A meri verset, þat has take fro tybourne twenti stronge þeues; þere lewed theues ben lolled vp. **1575** TURBERV. *Faulconrie* 360 Of the Hawke that holdeth not hir wings up so well as she should do, but lolleth them. **1650** A. B. *Mutat. Polemo* 29 This made the Gallants loll their ears and laugh at one an other.

3. To thrust out (the tongue) in a pendulous manner. Also with *out.*

1611 SHAKS. *Cymb.* v. iii. 8 The Enemy full-hearted, Lolling the Tongue with slaught'ring. **1697** DRYDEN *Virg. Georg.* IV. 741 Fierce Tigers couch'd around, and loll'd their fawning Tongues. —— *Æneid* VIII. 843 The foster Dam loll'd out her fawning Tongue. **1712** ARBUTHNOT *John Bull* III. x, Then Nic. lolled out his tongue. **1746** W. HORSLEY *Fool* (1748) II. 40 Every Fool has a natural hereditary.. Right to loll out his Tongue at his Brother. **1843** LYTTON *Last Bar.* I. i, The idle apprentices..lolled out their tongues at him as he passed. **1879** BROWNING *Ivan Ivanovitch* 132 How he lolls out the length of his tongue.

b. *intr.* for *refl.* Of the tongue: To protrude. Usually with *out.*

1801 SOUTHEY *Thalaba* v. ii, His head was hanging down, His dry tongue lolling low. *a* **1845** HOOD *Captain's Cow* x, The Parching seamen stood about, Each with his tongue a-lolling out, And panting like a dog. **1900** *Longm. Mag.* June 133 His tongue lolled out in the heat like a dog's.

4. *intr.* (The chief current sense.) To lean idly; to recline or rest in a relaxed attitude, supporting oneself against something. Also with *about, back, out.*

1377 LANGL. *P. Pl.* B. XVI. 269 Or ligge þus euere Lollynge in my lappe. **1583** STUBBES *Anat. Abus.* II. (1882) 28 A sheepeheard and a dogge lolling vnder a bush. **1594** SHAKS. *Rich. III*, III. vii. 72 He is not lulling on a lewd Loue-Bed. **1635** PAGITT *Christianogr.* 30 This pope Gregory..is reported to have lulled night and day..in the armes and embracings of Matilda the countesse. **1650** SIR A. WELDON *Court & Char. Jas. I* 103 The King hung about his neck, slabboring his cheeks... For God's sake, tel me, said the King..Then lolled about his neck. **1667** PEPYS *Diary* 5 June, And, among the rest, Duncomb, lolling, with his heels upon another chair. **1674** DRYDEN *Epil. New Ho.* 9 Who lolling on our foremost benches sit. **1719** DE FOE *Crusoe* II. xiii, He sat lolling back in a great elbow-chair. **1749** LD. CHESTERF. *Lett.* cxv. (1892) I. 265, I never saw the worst bred man living guilty of lolling,..in company that he respected. **1778** W. MARSHALL *Minutes Agric.* 18 July 1774 He has good hands, but a bad head—a crazy couch, dangerous to lull upon. **1782** MISS BURNEY *Cecilia* II. iv, Lolling against the wainscoat and gaping. **1822–34** *Good's Study Med.* (ed. 4) III. 246 The complaint first shows itself by..an unwonted desire to lounge and loll about. **1833** HT. MARTINEAU *Manch. Strike* vii. 76 A knot of smokers..stood or lolled about the door of the Spread-Eagle. **1861** THACKERAY *Round. Papers, On a Chalk-mark* 115 Little boys should not loll on chairs. **1882** MISS BRADDON *Mt. Royal* III. xii. 257 The Master of the house lolled, half-dressed, in an armchair by the hearth.

b. *trans.* To allow to rest idly. *rare.* Also, to pass *away* (time) in lolling about.

1696 R. COKE *Detection Crt. & State Eng.* (1719) I. 87 The King had a loathsome Way of lolling his Arms about his Favourites Necks, and kissing them. **1709** PRIOR *When Cat is Away* 54 Whilst Fubb till ten, on silken bed, Securely lolls his drowsy head. **1784** *Unfortunate Sensibility* II. 104, I take good care that none [*sc.* no hour] shall be luxuriously lolled away in indolence. **1824** W. IRVING *T. Trav.* II. 286 Gigantic sunflowers lolled their broad jolly faces over the fences.

c. quasi-*trans.* or *refl.*; also ***to loll it.***

1796 H. HUNTER tr. *St.-Pierre's Stud. Nat.* (1799) I. 374 Others..loll it away to the opera..in magnificent equipages. **1821** CLARE *Vill. Minstr.* I. 77, I..loll'd me 'gainst a propping tree.

†**5.** *intr.* To saunter, go lazily. *Obs. rare.*

1649 G. DANIEL *Trinarch., Hen. V*, ccxliv, Hee breakes the Portall, wth vnsteddie feet, And Lolls to his owne Lamplight in coole Seas. **1678** OTWAY *Friendship in F.* III. 32 My revenge shall be to love you still; gloat on and loll after you where ere I see you.

†**6.** *Comb.*: **loll-ears**, drooping pendulous ears; **loll-eared** *a.*, having drooping ears.

1581 J. BELL *Haddon's Answ. Osor.* 109 Unlesse some Phebus have clouted upon this Mydas head..the eares of some lolleared Asse. *Ibid.* 125 b, Skill to discerne a Lyon by his pawes, or rather an Asse by his lolle-eares. **1585** HIGINS *Junius' Nomenclator* 453 *Flaccus*, that hath hanging eares: loll eared: flap eared.

Hence **lolled** (*out*) *ppl. a.*, said of the tongue.

1666 DRYDEN *Ann. Mirab.* 132 With his lolled tongue he faintly licks his prey. **1715** tr. *Pancirollus' Rerum Mem.* I. I. i. 5 The Slanderer is represented by the Picture of a Purple with its lolled-out Tongue. **1902** *Academy* 3 May 455/2 Irreverence that expressed itself in loud laughter and a lolled-out tongue.

†**loll,** *v.*[2] *Obs.* [back-formation from LOLLARD.]

a. *trans.* To call (a person) Lollard. **b.** *intr.* To act or speak as a Lollard. **c.** *trans.* To mumble (a phrase); to sing in a low tone.

c **1394** *P. Pl. Crede* 532 Whou sone þis sori men [seweden] his soule, And oueral lollede him wiþ heretykes werkes! **14..** *Pol. Poems* (Rolls) II. 245 And parde lolle thei never so longe, Yut wol lawe make hem lowte. **1655** J. COTGRAVE *Wits Interpr.* (1662) 288 The Sun-shine of the word, this he extoll'd; The Sun-shine of the word, stil this he lold.

loll, var. LULL *v. Obs.*, to pull by the ears.

lollapaloosa, etc.: see LALLAPALOOSA.

Lollar, variant of LOLLER[1] *Obs.*

Lollard ('lɒləd). Now *Hist.* Forms: 5–6 **lollarde,** 5 **loularde,** 5–6 **lolarde,** 6 **lolart, lollerd, lollord,** 7 **lolard.** See also LOLLER[1] (which occurs somewhat earlier). [a. MDu. *lollaerd*, lit. 'mumbler, mutterer', f. *lollen* to mutter, mumble (for the suffix see -ARD).

The name was orig. applied *c* 1300 to the members of a branch of the Cellite or Alexian fraternity (also called *lollebroeders*), who devoted themselves especially to the care of the sick and the providing of funeral rites for the poor. In the course of the 14th c. it was often used of other semi-monastic orders, and sometimes, by opponents, of the Franciscans. Usually it was taken to connote great pretensions to piety and humility, combined with views more or less heretical. Hence early mod.G. *lollhart*, chiefly applied to the Beghards.]

1. A name of contempt given in the 14th c. to certain heretics, who were either followers of Wyclif or held opinions similar to his.

1390 [implied in LOLLARDY]. **1415** LD. SCROPE in *43 Rep. Deputy Kpr. Rec.* 591 Yif he drue to Loulardis thai wolde subuert this londe & the chirge. *c* **1440** CAPGRAVE *Life St. Kath.* III. 327 Thow þei ȝow calle lollard, whych or elue, Beth not dysmayd. **1460** —— *Chron.* (1858) 277 In that same tyme the Lolardis set up schamful conclusiones. **1509** BARCLAY *Shyp of Folys* (1570) 74 They which to such witches will assent Are heretikes, lolardes, and false of their beleue. **1529** MORE *Dyaloge* III. Wks. 211/1 Not such men as we now speke of, lollardes & heretikes. **1571** *Satir. Poems Reform.* xxix. 43 Sa, lolarts, ȝor hypocrisy þat sa fane ȝe wald hyde, ȝe se, wyt tyme, in spyte of ȝow dois peice and peice owt slyde. **1597–8** BP. HALL *Sat.* II. i. 17 Then manie a Lollerd would in forfaitment Beare paper-fagots. **1625** in *Crt. & Times Chas. I* (1848) I. 67 Sir Edward Coke refused to take the sheriff's oath, because of the clause against Lollards. **1853** MARSDEN *Early Purit.* 144 They [Anabaptists] are said to have existed in England since the early times of the Lollards. **1876** A. LAING *Lindores Abbey*, etc. xii. 105 The opinions of the Lollards continued to spread.

attrib. and *appositive.* **1842** TODD *(title)* An Apology for Lollard Doctrines, attributed to Wicliffe. **1897** *Dict. Nat. Biog.* LI. 404/1 Jack Sharp, lollard rebel, was a weaver of Abingdon. **1901** T. G. LAW *Scots N. Test.* Introd. 13 Very little is known of the Lollard movement in Scotland.

¶**2.** [Associated with LOLL *v.*] Used for: One who lolls; an idler. *Obs. rare.*

1635 BRATHWAIT *Arcad. Pr.* I. 239 He was found choak't with meat in's mouth, Fared Lollards in each country so, I wote well how the world would go. **1659** MILTON *Hirelings* 84 A pulpited divine..a lollard indeed over his elbow-cushion.

Hence **Lo'llardian** *a.* [-IAN], of or pertaining to the Lollards. **'Lollardist** [-IST], one who holds the opinions of the Lollards; in quot. *attrib.* **'Lollardize** *v.* [-IZE], *intr.* to follow the practices of the Lollards. **'Lollardizing** *ppl. a.*

1865 S. EVANS *Bro. Fabian* 5 A lurching, lean-lipped, lollardizing loon,..No doubt hath played the spy on us and blabbed. **1882** LINDSAY in *Encycl. Brit.* XIV. 811/1 Lord Montacute..and several others had chaplains who were Lollardist preachers. **1887** H. R. HAWEIS *Light of Ages* I. 42 Everything Albigensian, or Lollardian or Lutheran was ultimately cast out of the Roman Catholic Church.

Lollardism ('lɒlədɪz(ə)m). [f. LOLLARD + -ISM.] The tenets and practice of the Lollards.

1823 LINGARD *Hist. Eng.* VI. 364 The teachers of Lollardism had awakened by their intemperance the zeal of the bishops. **1862** R. VAUGHAN *Nonconformity* 32 Lollardism was checked..but it did not die. **1882–3** SCHAFF *Encycl. Relig. Knowl.* I. 502 [Lord Cobham's] bold stand on behalf of Lollardism led to persecution.

Lollardry ('lɒlədrɪ). *Obs.* exc. *Hist.* Also 5 **lolla(r)drie,** 6 **lollerdry.** [f. LOLLARD + -RY.] *sing. collect.* and *pl.* The tenets of the Lollards.

1414 *Act 2 Hen. V*, stat. I. c. 7 Heresiez & errours appellez vulgairement Lollardrie. *c* **1425** *Hampole's Psalter* Metr. Pref. 49 Copyed has this Sauter ben of yuel men of lollardry. **1479** in *Eng. Gilds* (1870) 417, To put awey..all maner heresies and errours, clepid openly lolladries. *a* **1508** KENNEDY in *Bannatyne Poems* (Hunter. Club) 144 The schip of faith..Dryvis in the see of Lollerdry that blawis. **1651** N. BACON *Disc. Govt. Eng.* II. xvii. (1739) 94 The former opinions, then known only by the general names of Heresy, are now baptized by the new name of Lollardry. **1884** J. L. WILSON *Wycliffe* viii. 112 John of Gaunt, Lord Latimer, and the Lady Alice Perrers were all tinged with Lollardry.

Lollardy ('lɒlədɪ), *sb.* Also 4 **lollardie,** 4–5 **lollerdy,** 5 **lollardi,** 6 **lollardye.** [f. LOLLARD + -Y.] = prec.

1390 GOWER *Conf.* I. 15 This newe Secte of Lollardie. **1401** *Pol. Poems* (Rolls) II. 41 Now is oure bileve laft and Lollardi growith. **1496** *Pol. Rel. & L. Poems* 72, I was..in Englond born, & for certeyn poyntes of lollerdy I [ne] myȝt abide þer. **1554–5** *Act 1 & 2 Phil. & Mary*, c. 6 The suppression of Heresie and Lollardye. **1732** NEAL *Hist. Purit.* I. 50 They repealed..two of the Statutes against Lollardies. **1868** MILMAN *St. Paul's* 88 Accused, as a relapsed heretic, of Lollardy. **1875** STUBBS *Const. Hist.* II. xvi. 471 The reputed Lollardy at court.

'Lollardy, *a.* [f. LOLLARD + -Y[1].] Characteristic of the Lollards.

a **1529** SKELTON *Replyc.* 204 To resorte agayne To places where ye haue preched And your lollardy lernyng teched. **1888** STEVENSON *Black Arrow* 13 'John Amend-All!' A right Lollardy word.

†**'Loller**[1]. *Obs.* Forms: 4–6 **loller,** 5 **lollere, louller,** 5–6 **lollar,** 6 **lolar, loular, lowler.** [Var. of LOLLARD, with substitution of suffix -ER[1] for *-ard.*] = LOLLARD.

c **1386** CHAUCER *Shipm. Prol.* 11, I smelle a lollere in the wynde quod he. *Ibid.* 15 This lollere here wol prechen vs somwhat. **1393** LANGL. *P. Pl.* C. VI. 2 Cloþed as a lollere,.. Among lollares of london and lewede heremytes. **1426** AUDELAY *Poems* 37 And sayn hit is a lollere. *c* **1460** *Towneley Myst.* XXX. 213, I was youre chefe tollare,..Now am I master lollar. **1494** FABYAN *Chron.* VII. 600 Henry the .V... Cherysshed the churche, to Lollers gaue a fall. *c* **1515** *Cocke Lorell's B.* 11 With lollers, lordaynes, and fagot berers. **1556** *Chron. Gr. Friars* (Camden) 12 Thys yere the lorde Cobhame made a rysynge with many lollars and heryttykes. **1623** COCKERAM, *Lollar*, a breaker of fasting-daies.

loller[2] ('lɒlə(r)). [f. LOLL *v.*[1] + -ER[1].] One who lolls.

1582 STANYHURST *Æneis* III. (Arb.) 91 Thee muffe maffe loller [*sc.* the Cyclops]. **1804** MAR. EDGEWORTH *Griselda* xi, Griselda..one of the fashionable lollers by profession, established herself upon a couch. **1824** MISS MITFORD *Village* Ser. I. 18 A loller on alehouse benches.

Lollerd, Lollerdry, Lollerdy, obs. ff. LOLLARD, LOLLARDRY, LOLLARDY.

† **'Lollery.** *Obs.* Also 7 lollary. [f. LOLLER[1] + -Y.] = LOLLARDRY.

1547 BALE *Latter Exam. A. Askew* Pref. 4 These poore sowles..were put to deathe..for heresye & lollerye. **1620** J. WILKINSON *Coroners & Sherifes* 44 All manner of heresies and errors, commonly called Lollaries.

lollie, var. LOLLY[1].

,lollifi'cation. *nonce-wd.* [f. LOLL *v.*[1] + -(I)FICATION.] Lolling, lounging.

1834 BECKFORD *Italy* II. 363 A well-cushioned divan had been prepared for his lollification.

lolling ('lɒlɪŋ), *vbl. sb.*[1] [f. LOLL *v.*[1] + -ING[1].] The action of LOLL *v.*[1] **a.** Resting at one's ease, lounging. **b.** Thrusting *out* (the tongue).

a **1550** *Image Ipocr.* IV. in *Skelton's Wks.* (1843) II. 446 With bowsinge and bollinge, With lillinge and lollinge. **1699** E. WARD *Lond. Spy* VII. (1702) 3 His Graceful Lolling in his Chariot. **1770** BURKE *Corr.* (1844) I. 222 What if you gave up a few minutes of your lolling. **1872** DARWIN *Emotions* xi. 261 How it is that lolling out the tongue universally serves as a sign of contempt and hatred.

attrib. **1853** *Ecclesiologist* XIV. 114 Two huge pews for the notabilities, and within these lolling-boxes are the fireplaces which warm the church.

† **'lolling,** *vbl. sb.*[2] [f. LOLL *v.*[2] + -ING[2].] The action of LOLL *v.*[2], acting or preaching as a Lollard.

c **1418** *Pol. Poems* (Rolls) II. 247 Under colour of suiche lollynge, To shape sodeyn surreccioun Agaynst oure liege lord kynge.

lolling ('lɒlɪŋ), *ppl. a.* [f. LOLL *v.*[1] + -ING[2].] That lolls; reclining lazily; dangling, drooping. Of the tongue: Protruding and hanging down.

1567 TURBERV. *Ovid's Epist.* P v b, Marke out of order howe my lolling tresses flee. **1581** J. BELL *Haddon's Answ. Osor.* 263 He would sooner espye him to be an Asse by his lollyng eares, then a Lyon by his pawes. **1587** TURBERV. *Trag. Tales* etc. 190 None in all the land, long lolling lockes do weare. **1697** DRYDEN *Virg. Æneid* VIII. 399 The triple Porter of the Stygian Seat, With lolling Tongue, lay fawning at thy Feet. **1711** SHAFTESB. *Charac.* VI. iv. (1737) III. 371 One Hand..serving only to support, with much ado, the lolling lazy Body. **1742** POPE *Dunc.* IV. 337 A lazy, lolling sort..Of ever-listless Loit'rers. **1825** L. HUNT *Redi's Bacchus in Tuscany* 611 And now, Silenus, lend thy lolling ears. **1849** KINGSLEY *Misc.* (1860) II. 243 The silent hounds lying about.., their lolling tongues showing like bright crimson sparkles. **1850** MRS. BROWNING *Island* ix, Shut bells, that, dull with rapture, sink, And lolling buds, half shy.

b. *Her.* Of a hawk: With wings hanging down.

1688 R. HOLME *Armoury* II. xi. 230/2 When Hawks feed they do generally hang down their Wings, which the Master of such kinds of Birds of Prey term (Lolling), therefore some from thence have blazoned this an Eagle lolling and feeding on his Prey: but that is needless, seeing they feed in this posture. **1894** PARKER *Gloss. Her., Lolling*, a name rarely used for *Preying*.

löllingite ('lœlɪŋgaɪt). *Min.* [Named by Hardinger, 1845, f. name of *Lölling*, Hüttingberg, Carinthia, its locality.] Arsenide of iron, found in brilliant crystals.

1849 J. NICOL *Min.* 453 Lölingite. **1892** DANA *Min.* (ed. 6) 97 Löllingite occurs with siderite.

† **lolling-lobby.** *Obs.* [? For **loll-in-lobby*; but cf. LOOBY and *lobber* = LUBBER.] ? A derisive term for a monk.

1607 R. C[AREW] tr. *Estienne's World of Wonders* 321 A rabblement of wicked and abhominable lolling-lobbies [orig. *cafards*].

lollingly ('lɒlɪŋlɪ), *adv.* [f. LOLLING *ppl. a.* + -LY[2].] In a lolling manner.

1832 *Examiner* 516/1 Making their profession a vehicle for themselves to lollingly ride upon. **1857** BUCKLE *Civiliz.* I. ii. 128 Her tongue protrudes, and hangs lollingly from her mouth. **1865** *Athenæum* No. 1943. 83/2 To write books lollingly (if we may be allowed the expression).

lollipop ('lɒlɪpɒp), *sb. colloq.* Also **lollypop.** [Of obscure formation: cf. *lolly* (north. dial.) the tongue.]

a. *dial.* The name of a particular kind of sweetmeat, consisting chiefly of sugar or treacle, that dissolves easily in the mouth; *pl.* (formerly also *collect. sing.*) sweetmeats in general. **b.** Now, a sweet or water-ice on stick.

1784 *London Chron.* 17–20 Jan. 72/3 She confessed..that a certain person..had enticed her to commit it [*sc.* the robbery], and given her sweetmeats, called lolly-pops. **1796** GROSE *Dict. Vulg. Tongue* (ed. 3), *Lollipops*, sweet lozenges purchased by children. **1812** H. & J. SMITH *Rej. Addr.*, *Tale Drury Lane*, And buy crisp parliament with lollypops. **1835** MARRYAT *Jac. Faithf.* i, That in the petticoat age we may fearlessly indulge in lollipop. **1844** DISRAELI *Coningsby* I. ix, The irreclaimable and hopeless votary of lollypop. **1860** *All Year Round* No. 46. 459 Upright glass-cases such as country dealers keep lollypops in. **1884** SALA *Journ. due South* I. xv. (1887) 205 The consumption of lollipops [was] phenomenal. **1944** W. DE LA MARE *Coll. Rhymes & Verses* 41 A bottle of lollipops loved by Bess Stood apart on a window shelf. **1953** C. T. WILLIAMS *Chocolate & Confectionery* vi. 104 The B.C.H. Hollow Sleeve Drop Roller Machine may be augmented by a special attachment for the production of lollipops. **1959** [see BRICK *sb.*[1] 4]. **1959** N. MAILER *Advts. for Myself* (1961) 401 He is as pretentious as a rich whore, as sentimental as a lollypop. **1965** HUTTON & BODE *Simple Sweetmaking* iv. 39 The lollipops have wax or cellophane paper twisted or tied round them.

c. *fig.* 'Luscious' literary composition. Also, a showy or non-serious performance.

a **1849** [see d]. **1856** T. CHOLMONDELEY *Let.* in *Atlantic Monthly* (1893) LXXII. 750/2 There is no poetry, and very little or no literature. We are drenched with mawkish lollipops, and clothed in tawdry rags.

d. *attrib.*, as ***lollipop shop, stall, woman***, etc.; *spec.* of or pertaining to a person using a circular sign on a stick to stop traffic so that children may cross the road. Less commonly (occas. in non-attrib. use), the pole bearing a disc used by such a person.

1834 A. FONBLANQUE *Eng. under 7 Administr.* (1837) III. 13 Lollipop stalls. **1845** THACKERAY *Legend of Rhine* ix, in *George Cruikshank's Table-Bk.* Sept. 193 Ask the youth whether the lollypop-shop does not attract him? **1848** —— *Van. Fair* xxiii, Marching with great dignity towards the stall of a neighbouring lollipop-woman. *a* **1849** H. COLERIDGE *Ess.* II. 32 His [Dryden's] lolly-pop adulteration of King Lear. **1952** J. MASEFIELD *So Long to Learn* 203 Many of the speakers were of a kind that I called 'lollipop-speakers': they spoke every kind of verse as if it were a caramel to be sucked, without any glimmering of a notion that the words had any meaning. **1958** *Times* 16 Oct. 4/6 His [Beecham's] reluctance to offer 'lollipop' encores. **1959** *Courier & Advertiser* (Dundee) 28 Mar. 5/6 These old people, commonly called 'lollipop men',..do a good job. **1959** *Punch* 16 Sept. 172/2 That will be no more than the 'lollipop' innings of a Compton, the once-in-a-while reappearance of a Cotton or a Kyle. **1960** S. POTTER *Lang. in Mod. World* iv. 49 The traffic warden (or lollipop-man as the children affectionately call him) in his white overall makes himself prominent by raising his red disk on high: 'Stop, children crossing.' **1962** *Spectator* 13 Apr. 463/2 What will inevitably be known as the 'lollipop' tax. **1969** *Sunday Times* 9 Mar. 5 Top-hatted they stream from the school, one boy picks up the lollipop sign—which is hidden in a bush—and traffic is brought to a halt. **1969** *Courier-Mail* (Brisbane) 23 June 7/7 Civilian wardens to supervise school crossings..were used extensively overseas, and were known as 'lollipops' from the big discs on long poles they used to control vehicular traffic through school crossings. **1970** *Sunday Times* 25 Jan. 13 Mr. Blackmore, holding the lollipop that stops most traffic, said, 'That offside brake seems to be pulling.' **1970** P. VILLIARD *Pract. Candymaking Cookbk.* v. 62, I am going to start your candymaking career off with some recipes for lollipops... You will need a supply of lollipop sticks. **1971** *Daily Tel.* 27 July 13/1 (*heading*) Drivers must stop for lollipop men. *Ibid.*, Drivers stopped at school crossings by lollipop patrols must not proceed until the 'Stop, children crossing' sign has been taken away. **1972** *Times* 3 July 12/2 Colin Carr chose, mistakenly for a student, a lollipop, a Popper Polonaise, rather than good red meat, but it served to show off an enviable fluency on the instrument. **1972** *Sat. Titbits* 21 Oct. 20/1 Outside the school a 'lollipop lady' was holding up the traffic. **1972** *Times* 16 Dec. 12/2 We were on the lollipop patrol escorting the kids when they all scattered. **1973** *Daily Tel.* (Colour Suppl.) 16 Mar. 9/4 They watch the children in and out of school, something which on the mainland is done by a single elderly man with a 'lollipop stick'.

Hence **'lollipop** *v. trans.*, to treat to lollipops.

1837 *Fraser's Mag.* XV. 337 Mere children in matters of taste, fit only to be lollypopped by his 'lady'.

lollop ('lɒləp), *sb. colloq.* [f. next.] **1.** The action or an act of 'lolloping'.

1834 M. SCOTT *Cruise Midge* xviii. (1836) 292 Demolishing..thousands of sandflies at every lollop. **1881** BLACKMORE *Christowell* ii, The jump of the horse gave..a lollop to the near wheel.

2. A trifling lazy person.

1896 in FARMER & HENLEY *Slang* IV. 223/2. **1919** H. L. WILSON *Ma Pettengill* iv. 125 Of course the poor lollop had never been able to think under any circumstances.

lollop ('lɒləp), *v. colloq.* [Onomatopœic extension of LOLL *v.*[1] Sense 2 seems to have been evolved from a sense of the phonetic expressiveness of the word.]

1. *intr.* To lounge or sprawl; to go with a lounging gait.

1745 SIR C. H. WILLIAMS *Place Book for Year*, Next in lollop'd Sandwich with negligent grace. **1748** SMOLLETT *Rod. Rand.* xxxiv. (1804) 224 You are allowed, on pretence of sickness, to lollop at your ease. **1782** MISS BURNEY *Cecilia* II. iv, Keeping the fire from everybody!..he lollops so, that one's quite starved. **1796** GROSE *Dict. Vulg. Tongue* (ed. 3) *Lollop*, to lean with one's elbows on a table. **1825** NEAL *Bro. Jonathan* III. 314 Poor Walter felt a serious disposition to lollop and sprawl about. **1872** MISS BRADDON *To Bitter End* I. xvi. 269 Anything's better for her than lolloping over a book.

2. To bob up and down; to proceed by clumsy bounds.

1851 MAYHEW *Lond. Labour* I. 29 Its head lolloping over the end of the cart. **1878** LADY BRASSEY *Voy. Sunbeam* i. 3 For four long hours, therefore, we lolloped about in the trough of a heavy sea, the sails flapping as the vessel rolled. **1880** BLACKMORE *M. Anerley* II. xii. 217 Short, uncomfortable, clumsy waves were lolloping under the steep grey cliffs. **1887** GUILLEMARD *Cruise 'Marchesa'* (1889) 129 A young blue hare..lolloped up..to have its ears scratched.

Hence **'lolloping** *ppl. a.*

1745 *Fem. Spectator* II. 233 Many Women..when they become so [*sc.* wives], continue the same loitering, lolloping, idle Creatures they were before. **1840** MRS. F. TROLLOPE *Widow Married* xxviii, With a sort of lolloping affectation that was intended to indicate great intimacy. **1887** SAINTSBURY *Hist. Elizab. Lit.* i. 9 They [*sc.* 14-syllable verses] had an almost irresistible tendency to degenerate into a kind of lolloping amble.

lollopy ('lɒləpɪ), *a. rare.* [f. LOLLOP *v.* + -Y.] Disposed to, or characterized by, 'lolloping'.

1857 OLMSTED *Journ. Texas* 151 A free-and-easy, loloppy sort of life generally, seemed to have been adopted.

Lollord, obs. form of LOLLARD.

loll-shraub ('lɒlʃrɔːb). Also **-shrob.** ['Englishman's Hindustani *lāl-shrāb* red wine' (Yule).] 'The universal name for claret in India' (Yule).

1816 'QUIZ' *Grand Master* II. 45 Will master drink loll shraub, or beer? **1834** CAUNTER *Orient. Ann.* viii. 106 The sturdy Mussulman made no scruple of taking his bottle of loll shrob.

lolly[1] ('lɒlɪ). Also **lollie.** [short for LOLLIPOP.]

a. A sweetmeat (chiefly *Austral.* and *N.Z.*). Elsewhere now usu. = LOLLIPOP *sb.* b.

1854 C. SPENCE *Clara Morison* II. ix. 102 Fanny ran away to the nearest lolly shop, and all her brothers and sisters followed her. **1860** C. M. YONGE *Friarswood Post Office* vii. 112 You may take your choice—gingerbread-nuts, or bits of cocoa-nut; or, what's jolliest, lollies with gin inside 'em! *Ibid.* x. 189 The children..bought all the 'lollies'. **1862** *Illustr. Melbourne Post* 36 July, The gorgeous decorations at the lolly stall. **1864** H. WEATHERLEY *Treat. Art Boiling Sugar* 5 Whether they consist of the 'Loggets' or 'Cushies' of the Eastern part..the 'Humbugs' or 'Lollys' of the South ..they each have their votaries. **1871** SIMPSON *Recitat.* 24 Lollies that the children like. **1874** V. PYKE *Adventures G. W. Pratt* III. iv. 78 One of them filled her lap with cakes and 'lollies' for the 'bairnie'. **1882** A. J. BOYD *Old Colonials* 165 Cakes and lollies. **1886** A. R. BUTLER *Glimpses Maori Land* iii. 42 A friend of mine goes to the stores..and says, 'I want some lollies.' **1898** 'H.' *Grain of Gold* ii. 4 The first part of every child's education..was to catch the old man by the coat tails and get a pat on the head and a 'lollie'. **1899** *Bulletin* (Sydney) 28 Jan. 11/3 A crowd of well-dressed women amused themselves by throwing lollies, bits of ginger, and small fruits into the mouths of a straw-hat push on the other side. **1911** E. M. CLOWES *On Wallaby* v. 136 Men, when they wanted to show their appreciation of her services, sent her a box of sweets—or lollies, as they are called out here. **1915** [see CHUCK *v.*[2] 2 e]. **1935** 'G. ORWELL' *Clergyman's Daughter* ii. 131 London hawkers would come with baskets of doughnuts or water ices or 'halfpenny lollies'. **1936** C. R. ALLEN *Poor Scholar* i. 17 Even Herby fought down a longing for liquorice as they went by his favourite 'lolly' shop. **1955** *Times* 13 June 4/4 The 'real menace of sweets' to dental health was the constant sucking of lollies or other sweets, particularly at night. *Ibid.* 6 Aug. 8/4 A merry little cottage is painted in clear white and lolly pink. **1959** B. COMYNS *Vet's Daughter* xii. 100 A scraggy woman with a fringe, dressed in lolly pink. **1961** *Coast to Coast 1959–60* 161 Anyway, Vivi, you look nice in those new shoes. Here's threepence for lollies. **1964** *Weekly News* (Auckland) 10 June 3/3 The most popular event was a giant lolly scramble. Hundreds of children spent a few minutes of furious activity seizing their share of about 7000 sweets tossed among them. **1969** M. DRABBLE *Waterfall* 87 He had acquired eleven wooden lollie sticks. **1969** *Landfall* XXIII. 99 What was an award for merit promises now to become a lolly-scramble. **1972** J. WILSON *Hide & Seek* i. 8 She looked longingly at the ice-cream van... 'Can I have a lolly?'

b. In Cricket, an easy catch. Also as *adj.* Cf. DOLLY *a.* b.

1924 H. DE SÉLINCOURT *Cricket Match* v. 160 He..hit it —a 'lolly' into the hands of point. **1960** J. FINGLETON *Four Chukkas to Austral.* xv. 128 May did not last long..giving Benaud a lolly-catch at gully-slip.

c. *slang.* Money. Also *attrib.*

1943 M. HARRISON *Reported Safe Arrival* 61 This 'ere bloke touches the Guv'ment fer a nice drop er lolly. **1958** *Spectator* 14 Feb. 194/2 Next year's Budget gives fistfuls of lolly away to everybody. **1965** *Listener* 28 Oct. 677/2 A young English con-man..stands to gain lots of lovely lolly. **1971** *Ink* 12 June 14/1 Bernie's salesmen kept bringing in the lolly during the..boom. **1973** *Scotsman* 13 Feb. 8/3 The rank and file Bishops would be better off, financially, if they accepted jobs as Principals in the Egg, Poultry and Potato Division of the Ministry of Agriculture... In terms of lolly they would be better off as Senior Officers in the Land, Drainage and Water Supply Division of the Ministry. **1973** G. MOFFAT *Deviant Death* i. 14 There's only one person bringing in the lolly in that house.

lolly[2] ('lɒlɪ). *Canad.* [Shortened f. LOBLOLLY. Cf. *E.D.D.*] (See quots.)

1792 G. CARTWRIGHT *Jrnl.* I. p. xii, *Lolly*, soft ice, or congealed snow floating in the water when it first begins to freeze. **1889** W. H. WITHROW *Our own Country: Canada* 68 The distance to Cape Traverse is about nine miles, part solid ice, part drifting ice, part water, and sometimes a great deal of broken ice or 'lolly'. **1895** *Dialect Notes* I. 379 *Lolly*, ice and snow in the water along the shore... It is the hardest kind of thing to get the boat through. **1963** *Amer. Speech* XXXVIII. 299 *Lolly*, soft ice beginning to form in a harbor.

lollygag, var. LALLYGAG *v.* and *sb.*

lollypop, variant of LOLLIPOP.

Lolo ('ləʊləʊ). [Native name.] The name of an aboriginal people of south-western China, of a member of this people, and of their Tibeto-Burmese language. Also *attrib.* or as *adj.*

1736 R. BROOKES tr. *Du Halde's Gen. Hist. China* I. 59 The Nation of the Lolos rul'd in Yun nan, and was govern'd by different Sovereigns. **1878** H. A. GILES *Gloss. Far East* 81 *Lolos*, wild hill tribes of Szechuan and Yünnan. **1898** A. R. COLQUHOUN *China in Transformation* i. 24 It is clear there are but three great non-Chinese races in Southern China —the Lolo, the Shan and the Miao-tzu. **1901** E. H. PARKER *China* i. 8 Among the mountains of north-east Yün Nan and south Sz Ch'wan, the powerful confederation of so-called Lolo tribes still maintains its independence. **1933** L. BLOOMFIELD *Lang.* iv. 70 The other two groups [of *Tibeto-*

Burman], *Bodo-Naga-Kachin* and *Lo-lo*, consist of lesser dialects. **1937** E. Snow *Red Star over China* v. 194 Moving ..into Szechuan..[the Reds] soon entered the tribal country of warlike aborigines, the White and Black Lolos of Independent Lololand. **1948** D. Diringer *Alphabet* I. ix. 141 The languages of the Lolo-Mo-so group belong to the Tibeto-Burmese sub-family of the Tibeto-Chinese family of languages... Lolo is itself a sub-group of various languages, spoken by about 1,800,000 people in the south-western provinces of China. **1966** R. & D. Morris *Men & Pandas* iii. 47 Lieutenant J. W. Brooke was murdered in 1910 by the Lolos. **1968** *Encycl. Brit.* V. 567/2 The Tibeto-Burman branch of the Tibeto-Chinese language family falls into three groups: the Tibetan, the Yi (formerly called Lolo) and the Kachin.

†**lolpoop.** *Obs. rare.* [f. LOLL *v.*^{1} Cf. *liripoop* under LIRIPIPE 3.] A lazy, idle drone. Hence **lolpoop** *v. intr.*, to idle, lounge.

1661 A. Wood *Life* 3 May (O.H.S.) I. 394 They knew him to have been the very lol-poop of the University. *a* **1700** in B. E. *Dict. Cant. Crew.* **1722** *Ilias Burlesqu'd* (N.), And now to view the loggerhead, Cudgell'd and lol-pooping in bed. *a* **1825** Forby *Voc. E. Anglia*, *Loll-poop*, a sluggish sedentary lounger. Literally one who is sluggish in the stern.

loltre, *Obs.*: see LOITER *v.*

lom, obs. form of LAMB.

1506 *Inv.* in *Paston Lett.* III. 409 A gown furret with blake lom.

‖**loma** ('ləʊmə), *sb.*^{1} *Ornith.* Pl. **lomata** ('ləʊmətə). [mod.L. (Illiger), a. late Gr. λῶμα hem, fringe.] A lobe or fringe bordering the toe of a bird.

1874 in Baird etc. *N. Amer. Birds* III. 547 *Gloss.*

loma ('ləʊmə), *sb.*^{2} *U.S.* (chiefly S.-Western). [Sp., f. *lomo* back, loin, ridge.] A broad-topped hill or ridge.

1849 *Picayune* (New Orleans) 4 May 2/3 [They] were riding quietly along the Loma Blanca, (white hill,) when they came suddenly upon a party of eight or ten Indians. **1863** *Ex. Doc. 37th U.S. Congress Sp. Sess. Senate* No. 1. 20 The new road is to follow the bottom at the edge of the *lomas*. **1923** C. F. Saunders *Southern Sierras Calif.* 75 All about are rounded hills, or lomas, rising in baldness. **1941** *Harper's Mag.* Oct. 498/1 Stand on the 'knoll' at Yucca Loma, drink in the desert, and then look down at your feet.

Loma ('ləʊmə), *sb.*^{3} and *a.* Pl. **Loma, Lomas.** [Native name.] **A.** *sb.* The name of a people inhabiting the border regions of Liberia, Sierra Leone, and the Republic of Guinea, and of their language. **B.** *adj.* Of or pertaining to the Loma or their language.

1957 *Encycl. Brit.* XX. 624/1 Above the plateau surface rise many mountain ranges, the highest of which are the Loma mountains. **1964** E. A. Nida *Toward Sci. Transl.* ix. 198 In a language such as Loma, spoken in Liberia, it is impossible to duplicate these sequences. **1969** *Liberian Studies Jrnl.* I. 25 The Kpelle, Loma, Bandi and Mende are included in the Southwestern Mande group. *Ibid.* 37 The people of eastern Lukasu and Yawiyasu have several linguistic similarities to the Loma people. **1970** D. Dalby *Lang. & Hist. Afr.* 112 The Loma syllabary (with a total of at least 185 characters) was devised in the 1930's..reputedly inspired by a dream.

lomastome ('ləʊməstəʊm), *a.* and *sb. Conch.* [a. F. *lomastome* (Férussac), f. LOMA *sb.*^{1} + Gr. στόμα mouth.] **a.** *adj.* The distinctive epithet of those groups of *Helicidæ* which have the peristome reflected. **b.** *sb.* A member of any of these groups.

In recent Dicts.

lomatine ('ləʊmətɪn), *a. Ornith.* [f. Gr. λωματ-, LOMA *sb.*^{1} + -INE^1.] Having a loma, lobe, or fringe, as the toes of some birds.

1856 in Mayne *Expos. Lex.*, s.v. *Lomatinus.*

lomb, obs. form of LAMB, LOOM.

Lombard ('lɒmbəd, 'lʌmbəd), *sb.*^{1} and *a.* Forms: 4-6 **lumbarde**, 5 **lumbert**, 6 **lombarde, -berde, lumbart, -bertte**, 7 **lombart**, 8 **lombar**, 6- **lombard.** [a. F. *lombard* (whence MLG. *lombard*, MDu. *lombaert*, mod.Du. *lombard*), ad. It. *lombardo* (med.L. *lombardus*), contracted repr. late L. *Langobardus, Longobardus*, Teut. **Laŋgobardo-z, -bardon-* (OE. pl. *Langbeardas, -beardan*, ON. pl. *Langbarðar*); a compound of **laŋgo-* LONG *a.* with the proper name of the people, which appears in L. form as *Bardi*; in OE. poetry they are called *Heaðobeardan* (f. *heaðo* war).

The sense 'banker, money-lender, pawnbroker' was common in OFr., whence it passed to MLG. and MDu. The sense 'bank, pawnbroker's shop' was prob. developed in MLG. and MDu., and seems to have been adopted thence into Eng.; in this sense a fem. *lombaerde* occurs in MDu. beside the masc. *lombaert* (Du. *lombard, lommerd*). A special development of meaning belongs to the variant LUMBER *sb.*]

A. *sb.*

1. *Hist.* **a.** A person belonging to the Germanic people (L. *Langobardi*: see above) who conquered Italy in the 6th century, and from whom Lombardy received its name. **b.** A native of Lombardy.

1480 *Egerton MS.* 1765 in Gross *Gild Merch.* II. 71 No man..shall supporte nether mayntene no Lumbarde, brytton, ne Spaynnarde. **1556** *Chron. Gr. Friars* (Camden) 37 Hongyd..for kyllynge of two Lumbertes in a bote on the Temse. **1570** Levins *Manip.* 30/30 A Lumbarde, *longobardus.* **1598** Greneway *Tacitus, Ann.* II. v. (1622) 146 The King..reenforcing his army with the aide of the Lombards,..molested and annoyed the Cherusci. **1662** J. Bargrave *Pope Alex. VII* (1867) 79 Although he be a good Lumbard—which is as much as to say, an enemy to hypocrisy. **1695** Dryden *Dufresnoy's Art Painting* 94 Excepting only Titian, who, of all the Lombards has preserv'd the greatest purity in his works. **1769** Robertson *Chas. V* (1797) I. i. 74 Thither the Lombards brought the productions of India. **1841** W. Spalding *Italy & It. Isl.* II. 66 Alboin, king of the Lombards..subdued Italy without resistance. **1902** *Speaker* 10 May 167/2 A colony of Lombards should be induced to settle on the soil.

c. The language of this people. Also *attrib.* or as *adj.*

1598 Florio *Worlde of Wordes* 3 How may we ayme at the Venetian, at the Romane, at the Lombard..at so manie, and so much differing Dialects..as be used and spoken in Italie? *Ibid.* 132/2 *Fio*..In Lombard Italian for *Figlio*, a sonne, a childe. **1878**, **1880** [see EMILIAN *a.* and *sb.*]. **1936** G. F.-H. & J. Berkeley *Italy in Making* II. 353 All this he told me in Lombard dialect of which every word had to be translated into Italian by his son.

†**2.** A native of Lombardy engaged as a banker, money-changer, or pawnbroker; hence applied *gen.* to a person carrying on any of these businesses.

1377 Langl. *P. Pl.* B. v. 242, I lerned amonge Lumbardes and Iewes a lessoun, To wey pens with a peys. *c* **1386** Chaucer *Shipm. T.* 367 This Marchant..Creaunced hath ..To certeyn lumbardes..The somme of gold. **1393** Langl. *P. Pl.* C. v. 194 Lumbardes of Lukes that lyuen by lone as Iewes. **1508** Dunbar *Tua mariit wemen* 362 He was a gret goldit man,..I leit him be my lumbart. *a* **1553** Udall *Royster D.* II. ii. (Arb.) 34 If he haue not one Lumbardes touche, my lucke is bad. **1590** Greene *Mourn. Garm.* (1616) 44 They are fallen to the Lombard, left at the Brokers. **1687** Burnet *Trav.* ii. (1750) 96 They told me..that all Europe over a Lombard and a Banker signified the same thing. **1709** Steele *Tatler* No. 57 ¶2, I am an honester Man than Will. Coppersmith, for all his great Credit among the Lombards.

†**3.** The shop or place of business of a 'Lombard'; a bank, money-changer's or money-lender's office; a pawnshop, a *mont de piété*. See also the later form LUMBER. *Obs.*

1609 Markham *Famous Whore* (1868) 23 No sooner got I coine..But to the bancke or lumbard straight it went. **1620** Melton *Astrolog.* 44 It hath bin many a Gallants good fortune to haue a braue Sute of Clothes on his back on the morning, yet it hath bin his bad fortune to haue them in the Lumbard before night. **1622** T. Scott *Belg. Pismire* 79 Their Lumbards or Loane-houses are principally for the benefit of the poore, where Brokers are not suffered to take fifty, or one hundred in the hundred. **1735** Dyche & Pardon *Dict.*, *Lombar* or *Lombard*, a Bank or Place where Money is let out upon Usury and Pawns. **1764** Burn *Poor Laws* 169 The said fathers of the poor may have power to erect petty banks and lumbards for the benefit of the poor. **1799** W. Tooke *View Russian Emp.* II. 508 Her ukase concerning the imperial lombard of the year 1786. [**1849** Freese *Comm. Class-bk.* 19 Lombards was a name given formerly in the Netherlands, France and England, to loan banks or lending houses.]

†**4.** *Cookery.* [*ellipt.*: see B. 2.] Some kind of dish or culinary preparation. *Obs.*

1657 Reeve *God's Plea* 130 The Hoga's, and Olies, and Lumbards of these times.

B. *adj.*

1. a. Belonging to the Lombards or to Lombardy; Lombardic.

1500-20 Dunbar *Poems* xxxiii. 16 He fled and come in France, With littill of Lumbard leid. **1645** Milton *Tetrach.* Wks. 1851 IV. 181 (*Deut.* xxiv. 1, 2) These ages wherein Canons, and Scotisms, and Lumbard Laws..almost obliterated the lively Sculpture of ancient reason. **1664** Evelyn *Kal. Hort.* Oct. (1679) 26 Pears..Lombart-pear, Russet-pear [etc.]. **1741** Hume *Ess.* xv. *Of Liberty* 178 The Lombard School [of painting] was famous as well as the Roman. **1833** Sir S. R. Glynne *Notes Ch. Lanc.* (Chetham Soc.) 3 An inscription in Lombard letter. **1845** Graves *Rom. Law* in *Encycl. Metrop.* II. 779/1 The *Feudorum Consuetudines*,—a Lombard compilation of feudal law, formed about the middle of the 12th century. **1876** Bancroft *Hist. U.S.* I. i. 8 The marts of England were frequented by Lombard adventurers. **1882** *Garden* 14 Oct. 338/3 The Lombard Plum..holds about the same position among other varieties that the Baldwin does among Apples. **1901** *Speaker* 16 Mar. 658/1 To him the law of Justinian was 'Lombard law'.

b. ***Lombard band*** (see quots. 1959).

1936 A. W. Clapham *Romanesque Archit.* ii. 28 The so-called Lombard bands and wall-arcading..are distinctive of the first Romanesque style. **1959** *Chambers's Encycl.* I. 558/2 Shallow external pilasters cutting the wall-surface into bays and commonly called 'Lombard bands'. **1959** E. A. Fisher *Introd. Anglo-Saxon Archit. & Sculpture* 26 Lombard band ornamentation consisted of vertical pilaster strips of slight projection which divided a wall into bays.

†**2.** *Cookery.* In certain AF. names of dishes as ***leche lumbard*** (see LEACH *sb.*^{1} 2); ***frutour lumbard*** [*frutour* = FRITTER]; ***rys lumbard*** [F. *ris* sweetbread]. Also in **lombard pie** (see LUMBER-PIE).

?*c* **1390** [see LEACH *sb.*^{1} 2]. *c* **1430** *Two Cookery-bks.* 35 Leche lumbarde. **1452** *Reliq. Ant.* I. 88 Frutour lumbert.. Lesshe lumbert. **1466-7** *Durh. Acct. Rolls* (Surtees) 91 Et in 2 lib. dell powderlomberd empt. de eodem, 3*s.* 3*d.* **14..** *Anc. Cookery* in *Househ. Ord.* (1790) 438 Rys Lumbarde.—Leche Lumbarde.

†**3.** ***Lombard fever***: = FEVER-LURDEN. *Obs.* [Cf. dial. *lomber*, to idle.]

1678 Ray *Prov.* (ed. 2) 75 Sick o'th' Lombard feaver, or of the idles.

Hence †**Lombar'deer**, 'an usurer or broaker' (Blount *Glossogr.* 1656); **Lombar'desque** *a.*, resembling the Lombard school of painters; **Lom'bardian** *a.* = LOMBARDIC *a.*; †**'Lombardinian** *a.*, characteristic of a 'Lombard' or usurer; †**Lombardish** *a.*, Lombardic; **'Lombardism**, a Lombardic idiom; **Lom'bardo-**, taken as a comb. form (after It. *Lombardo-Veneto*) with the sense 'Lombardic combined with..'.

c **1489** Caxton *Fayte of A.* IV. viii. 249 Another scripture that men calle the lombardishe lawe. **1600** W. Watson *Decacordon* (1602) 36 [The Jesuits] commit extortion, symony, and all Lombardinian kind of deuises to make gain of. *c* **1645** Howell *Lett.* vi. 24 By their profession they are for the most part Broakers, and Lombardeers. **1819** W. S. Rose *Lett.* I. 232 We shall observe him [Ariosto] grafting on it a thousand Latinisms and Lombardisms not yet naturalized. **1837-9** Hallam *Hist. Lit.* I. I. viii. §7. 423 The rude Lombardisms of the Lower Po gave way to the racy idiom of Florence. **1839** *Penny Cycl.* XIV. 104/2 The Lombardo-Venetian kingdom is in a thriving and progressive condition. **1865** *Pall Mall G.* No. 81. 11/2 The Lombardian despots. **1879** Sir G. Scott *Lect. Archit.* I. 44 A style somewhat analogous to the Lombardo-Rhenish. **1894** Gould *Illustr. Dict. Med.*, *Pellagra, Ergotism, Lombardian Leprosy*, an endemic..skin-disease..due to chronic poisoning with diseased..maize. **1901** *Westm. Gaz.* 26 Mar. 4/2 Sodoma remained to the end a Lombardesque artist.

lombard ('lɒmbəd), *sb.*^{2} *Hist.* [ad. obs. Sp. *lombarda*.

The word has been supposed to be a misprint for *bombarda* BOMBARD. Cf. however the very common late Gr. λουμπάρδα, λουμπάρτα, app. synonymous with βουμβάρδα, μπουμπάρδα bombard.]

A military engine used in Spain in the 16th c.

1838 Prescott *Ferd. & Is.* (1846) I. ii. 136 A wooden fortress..was constructed by the assailants, and planted with lombards and other pieces of artillery then in use [Prescott refers to Zurita *Anales* IV. 113/1 (1610), who has: Començo se a combatir la ciudad con diuersos trabucos y lombardas]. **1849** W. Irving *Columbus* III. 55 He.. proceeded..to finish his fortress, which was defended by lombards. **1858** W. Morris *Sir P. Harpdon's End* Poems 101 Amid the crash of falling walls, And roar of lombards.

Lombardic (ləm'bɑːdɪk), *a.* [ad. med.L. *lombardicus*, f. *Lombardus* LOMBARD *sb.*^{1}: see -IC.]

Pertaining to Lombardy or the Lombards. Applied *spec.* to the style of architecture which prevailed in northern Italy from the 7th to the 13th century; to a type of handwriting common in Italian MSS. during the same period; and to the school of painters, represented esp. by Leonardo da Vinci, Mantegna, and Luini, which flourished at Milan and other Lombard cities during the 15th and 16th centuries.

1697 H. Wanley in Aubrey *Lett. Eminent Persons* (1813) I. 85 As to the Lombardic Character, we have not a book that I know of written in it, I mean agreeable to the specimens of it in *Mabillon de re Diplomatica.* **1784** Astle *Orig. Writing* v. 93 Specimen of Lombardic writing. *Ibid.*, Written in Lombardic Uncials. **1832** G. Downes *Lett. Cont. Countries* I. 479 His [St. Anthony of Padua's] church, which has six cupolas, is an admirable specimen of Lombardic architecture. **1859** J. Booker *Hist. Anc. Chapel Birch* (Chetham Soc.) 208 Legend in Lombardic capitals. **1870** Ruskin *Lect. Art* vii. §clxxvii. 180 Correggio, uniting the sensual element of the Greek schools with their gloom, and their light with their beauty, and all these with the Lombardic colour, became..the captain of the painter's art as such. **1879** Sir G. Scott *Lect. Archit.* I. 76 The Lombardic Romanesque. **1901** *Athenæum* 27 July 131/3 The..paten..in addition to the leopard's head crowned, bears a Lombardic S and a broad arrow.

b. *absol.* (quasi-*sb.*) Lombardic writing.

1893 E. M. Thompson *Gr. & Lat. Palæography* xvi. 221 The peculiar appearance which has gained for it the name of *broken* Lombardic.

'Lombard-street. Also 7 **Lumber-, Lumbard-.** The name of a street in London, so called because originally occupied by Lombard bankers, and still containing many of the principal London banks. Hence used *transf.* or *fig.* for: The 'money market'; the body of financiers.

Paris has a *Rue des Lombards*, the name of which had the same origin.

1598 Stow *Surv.* (1603) 202 Then haue ye Lombardstreete, so called of the Longobards and other Marchants, strangers of diuerse nations, assembling there twise euery day. **1645** *Ord. Lords & Com., Presb. Govt., Elect. Elders* 4 Alhallowes Lumberstreet. **1647** *N. Eng. Hist. & Gen. Register* (1885) XXXIX. 179 Mr Dixon Mcht in Lumber Street. **1721** Ramsay *Rise & Fall of Stocks* 190 Trade then shall flourish, and ilk art A lively vigour shall impart To credit languishing and famisht, And Lombard-street shall be replenisht. **1763** A. Murphy *Citizen* II. i. (1815), There we go scrambling together—reach Epsom in an hour and forty-three minutes, all Lombard-street to an egg-shell, we do. **1815** *Pancratia* (ed. 2) 367, 9th [round] —Lombard-street to a China orange; Molineux was dead beat. **1819** Moore *Tom Crib* (ed. 3) 38 All Lombard-street to nine-pence on it. *Note*, More usually 'Lombard-street to a China orange'. **1821** P. Egan *Real Life London* I. vi. 83 Beat him hollow, it was all Lombard-street to a china orange. **1849** Lytton *Caxtons* IV. iii, 'It is Lombard Street to a China orange', quoth Uncle Jack. 'Are the odds in

favour of fame against failure so great?'..answered my father. **1892** *Evening Standard* 9 Nov. 1/1 We describe the betting upon a moral certainty as being All Lombard-street to a China orange. **1902** *Speaker* 26 June 369/2 Much of the floating credit of Lombard Street is based..on loans against securities. **1974** *Times* 30 Nov. 10/5 If you didn't already know..then it's most of Lombard Street to a China Orange you'd never find out.

Lombardy. The name of a region of northern Italy, used *attrib.* in **Lombardy poplar**, to designate a columnar variety of poplar, *Populus nigra* var. *italica* (or *P. italica*), which was introduced from Italy to other countries. Also *absol.*

1766 [see POPLAR 1 b]. **1797** S. DEANE *Newengland Farmer* (ed. 2) 267 The Lombardy Poplar begins to be propagated in this country. **1799** JANE AUSTEN *Let.* 17 May (1952) 62 The drawing-room window..commands a perspective view of the left-side of Brock Street, broken by three Lombardy poplars in the garden of the last house in Queen's Parade. **1882** [see POPLAR 1 b]. **1917** L. M. MONTGOMERY *Anne's House of Dreams* vii. 58 The Lombardies down the lane, tall and sombre. **1957** M. HADFIELD *Brit. Trees* 151 The Lombardy poplar was once generally held to be a sport from the southern European black poplar. It is now said to be a true species. **1969** T. H. EVERETT *Living Trees of World* 94/1 The Berlin poplar, a tree of columnar growth and bright green foliage [is] believed to have the Lombardy poplar and *P. laurifolia* as its parents. **1974** A. MITCHELL *Field Guide to Trees of Britain* 27 A narrow, columnar or spire-like tree, like a Lombardy poplar, looks much taller than it really is.

lomber, obs. form of LUMBER.

Lombrosian (lɒmˈbrəʊzɪən), *a.* [f. the name of Cesare *Lombroso* (1836–1909), Italian physician and criminologist + -IAN.] Of or pertaining to Cesare Lombroso and to his theories of the physiology, psychology, and treatment of the criminal; also as *sb.*, an adherent or follower of Lombroso or his theories. Hence **Lomˈbrosianism**; **Lomˈbrosic** *a.*, of or pertaining to Lombrosianism.

1906 JOYCE *Let.* 19 Aug. (1966) II. 151 He was ridiculing lombrosianism and antimilitarism. **1914** *Everyman* 16 Jan. 451/2 The 'conclusions' have been so recently published that Lombrosians and anti-Lombrosians must be..excused if they ask for time. **1922** G. B. SHAW in S. & B. Webb *Eng. Prisons under Local Govt.* p. lxii, The stigmata of the Lombrosic criminal. **1973** *Listener* 8 Nov. 624/1 'We don't go in for the Lombrosian type of nonsense of measuring skulls any more,' protest our present-day criminologists.

†**lome**, *adv. Obs.* Also 4 *comparative* lomer, lommere. [aphetic form of OE. *ʒelóme* Y-LOME.] Frequently; phr. *oft and lome*.

c **1200** *Moral Ode* 11 in *Trin. Coll. Hom.* 220 Alto lome ich habbe igult a werke and a worde. **1377** LANGL. *P. Pl.* B. xx. 237 For lomer [C. xxiii. 238 lommere] he lyeth þat lyflode mote begge, þan he þat laboureth for lyflode & leneth it beggeres. *c* **1400** *Beryn* 1671 For many a tyme and offt, (I can nat sey how lome) He hath been in your marchis. *c* **1420** *Chron. Vilod.* 3887 Bot þey prey3ede so ofte & so lome, þat [etc.]. *c* **1425** *Seven Sag.* (P.) 1892 There was contek ofte and lome Bytwen Pule and the cite of Rome. *c* **1475** *Partenay* 119 So As ye may hire sondry tymes lome.

lome, obs. form of LAMB, LAME, LOAM, LOOM.

loment (ˈləʊmɛnt). [ad. L. *lōment-um* bean-meal (orig. a 'wash' or cosmetic made of bean-meal), f. *lō-*, *lavāre* to wash.]

†**1.** Bean-meal. *Obs.*

c **1420** *Pallad. on Husb.* XI. 366 The wynys browne eschaungeth into white, Yf that me putte in hit lomente of bene.

2. *Bot.* = LOMENTUM.

1814–30 *Edinb. Encycl.* IV. 45/1 *Loment* (*lomentum*), an elongated pericarp, which never bursts. It is divided into small cells, each of which contains a seed attached to the under suture. **1826–34** GOOD *Bk. Nat.* (ed. 3) I. 163 The loment..is a kind of pod..of which we have an instance in the mimosas and the cassia fistula. **1836** in LOUDON *Encycl. Plants* Gloss.

lomentaceous (ləʊmɛnˈteɪʃəs), *a. Bot.* [f. mod.L. *lōmentāce-us*, f. *lōmentum*: see prec. and -ACEOUS.] Of the nature of or resembling a lomentum; characterized by lomenta; belonging to the N.O. *Lomentaceæ*, a former sub-order of *Cruciferæ*.

1830 LINDLEY *Nat. Syst. Bot.* 88 Lomentaceous genera, such as Ornithopus. **1872** OLIVER *Elem. Bot.* II. 138 The siliqua of Radish,—an indehiscent and jointed lomentaceous siliqua.

‖**lomentum** (ləʊˈmɛntəm). *Bot.* Pl. **lomenta.** [L.; see LOMENT.] A legume which is contracted in the spaces between the seeds, breaking up when mature into one-seeded joints.

1836 *Penny Cycl.* V. 253/2. **1839** LINDLEY *Introd. Bot.* (ed. 3) 230, 236. **1847** W. E. STEELE *Field Bot.* Gloss. p. xvi. **1870** BENTLEY *Man. Bot.* (ed. 2) 305.

lomere, obs. form of LUMBER *v.*[1]

‖**lomi-lomi** (ˈləʊmɪˈləʊmɪ). [Hawaiian *lomi-lomi*, reduplication of *lomi* to rub with the hand.] The shampooing practised among the Hawaiians.

1850 W. COLTON *Deck & Port* xi. 347, I was..determined to try..the bath and the 'lomi-lomi'. **1882** HOWELLS in *Longm. Mag.* I. 51 This slippered and rhythmic pace was like a sort of Hawaiian *lomi-lomi* to our toughened sensibilities; it tickled, it lulled us. **1951** *Amer. Speech* XXVI. 23 Other common Hawaiian words are..*lomilomi* (massage).

lomme, obs. form of LAME.

Lomongo: see MONGO[1].

lomonite *Min.*: see LAUMONTITE.

lomonosovite (ləʊˈmɒnəʊsɒvaɪt). *Min.* [ad. Russ. *lomonosovit* (V. I. Gerasimovsky 1941, in *Dokl. Akad. nauk SSSR* XXXII. 498), f. the name of Michael *Lomonosov* (1711–65), Russian mineralogist: see -ITE[1].] A phosphate, silicate, and oxide of sodium and titanium, $Na_5Ti_2(Si_2O_7)(PO_4)O_2$, found as dark brown triclinic crystals in the Kola peninsula, U.S.S.R.

1941 V. I. GERASIMOVSKY in *Compt. Rend. (Doklady) de l'Acad. des Sci. de l'URSS* XXXII. 498 The pegmatite patches..are composed of hackmanite..with a very considerable content of chinglusuite and lomonosovite (a sodium phosphate-titanium silicate). **1966** *Geochem. Internat.* III. 197 It is better to interpret lomonosovite as an inorganic clathrate of murmanite structure and sodium phosphate, with the possible formation of intermediate compounds between lomonosovite and sodium-poor lomonosovite.

lomp(e, obs. form of LAMP, LUMP.

ˈ**lomper**, *v. Obs.* or *dial.* [Cf. LAMPER *v.*; also *lomber* dial., to idle, and LUMBER *v.*] *intr.* ? To idle. Hence ˈ**lompering** *vbl. sb.*, ? idleness.

The passage of Shoreham is very obscure; the text may perhaps be seriously corrupt.

c **1315** SHOREHAM iii. 277 Her hys for-bode glotenye,.. For hyt norysseþ lecherye,..And þa3 þer be alone lompryngе In lecheryes rote, All hyt destrueþ charyte. **1847** HALLIWELL, *Lomper.* (1) To idle. (2) To walk heavily.

lompet, lompish, obs. ff. LOAM-PIT, LUMPISH.

lon, lonch, obs. forms of LOAN, LAUNCH.

1449 *Paston Lett.* I. 85 They lonchyd a bote.

lonche, obs. form of LUNCH.

lonchidite (ˈlɒŋkɪdaɪt). *Min.* [ad. G. *lonchidit*, f. Gr. λογχίδιον, dim. of λόγχη spear-head (in reference to the shape of the crystals): see -ITE.] A variety of marcasite containing arsenic.

1865 WATTS *Dict. Chem.*

lond(e, obs. f. LAND; var. LAUND *Obs.*

†**Londenoys.** *Obs. rare.* [a. AF. **Londenois*, f. *London*.] A Londoner.

1387–8 T. USK *Test. Love* I. viii. (Skeat) 103 Howe should then the name of a singuler londenoys passe the glorious name of London?

Londinensian (lɒndɪˈnɛnsɪən), *a.* [f. L. type *Londinensis*, f. *Londin-ium* London: see -IAN.] Pertaining to or characteristic of London.

1891 G. MEREDITH *One of our Conq.* I. i. 13 He thinks them human in their bulk; they are Londinensian.

londisse, variant of LANDISH *Obs.*

London (ˈlʌndən), the name of the capital of England, used *attrib.* in various special collocations: †**London black**, †**London blue**, names for some particular colours of cloth; **London-bottled** *a.*, (of a wine) bottled in London; **London bridge**, a children's singing game; **London broil** *U.S.* (see quot. 1969); †**London bushel**, perhaps the same as the Winchester bushel (according to Fitzherbert it was smaller than that used in the north); †**London button(s**, the foxglove; **London clay**, an important geological formation, belonging to the lower division of the Eocene tertiary, in the south-east of England and esp. at and near London; **London fog**, a dense fog once peculiar to London and large industrial towns; **London gin**, a dry gin; **London ivy**, a fanciful name for: (*a*) the smoke of London, which 'clings' to buildings and blackens them; (*b*) a thick London fog; **London lady**, a kind of potato; †**London measure**, a former practice of London drapers of allowing something above the standard yard in their measurements; **London particular** *colloq.*, a London fog; **London paste**, a caustic composed of equal parts of quicklime and caustic soda mixed with alcohol (*Syd. Soc. Lex.* 1889); **London plane**, *Platanus* × *hispanica* (*P.* × *acerifolia*), a hybrid of *P. occidentalis* and *P. orientalis*, often planted as a street tree; **London purple**, a by-product in the manufacture of aniline dyes, consisting mainly of calcium arsenite, used as an insecticide; †**London red**, name for a particular colour of cloth; **London rocket**, the plant *Sisymbrium Irio*, which (according to Ray) sprang up abundantly on the ruins of the great fire of 1666; †**London russet**, †**London scarlet**, names for particular colours of cloth; **London shrinking**, a finishing process applied to fabric to prevent shrinkage; also **London-shrunk** *a.*; **London smoke**, a fancy name for a dull shade of grey; **London sugar**, a variety of pear; †**London tuft**, Sweet William = LONDON PRIDE (a).

c **1530** *So well ys me be-gone* in *Laneham's Let.* Pref. (1871) 130 His hoysse of *london black. **1625** MASSINGER *New Way* IV. i, One part skarlet, And the other *London-blew. **1959** *Times* 21 Sept. 13/2 *London-bottled, it costs about 10s. **1972** *Guardian* 24 Feb. 11/2 The difference between London-bottled and château or domaine-bottled wine of the same vineyard..cannot be stated in hard terms. **1972** *House & Garden* Feb. 111/1 With London-bottled clarets starting at £1.50 and château-bottled at £2.50, the prices were not excessive. [**1827** R. THOMSON *Chronicles of London Bridge* 152 'Here follows the ancient Music to the Song and Dance of London Bridge is broken down.'...'A choice piece of simple melody, indeed,' said Mr. Postern,..' but you called it also a dance, Mr. Barbican; pray was it ever adapted to the feet, as well as to the tongue?'] **1894** A. B. GOMME *Traditional Games* I. 199 It is singular that the verses of this game [*sc.* 'Hark the robbers'], also enter into the composition of 'London Bridge is broken down'. It is probable, therefore, that it may be an altered form of the game of '*London Bridge'. **1909** *Encycl. Relig. & Ethics* II. 852/1 The singing game known as 'London Bridge' has many variants in the different localities where it is played, but fundamentally the theme is the same. **1939** F. THOMPSON *Lark Rise* ix. 159 Well-known games still met with at children's parties, such as 'Oranges and Lemons', 'London Bridge'. **1969** I. & P. OPIE *Children's Games* viii. 235 A singing game such as 'London Bridge is Falling Down'. **1969** R. & D. DE SOLA *Dict. Cooking* 143/1 **London broil*, large flank steak broiled, then cut in thin slices diagonally across the grain for serving. **1973** E.-J. BAHR *Nice Neighbourhood* ii. 24 We cooked a London broil out on the grill and ate on the patio. **1974** *Columbia* (S. Carolina) *Record* 24 Apr. 14-B/1 Most steak buffs have their favorite cut, and this brings up something I haven't been able to figure out: the names they give steaks. I'm told that Britons had never heard of London broil until some Yank informed them what it was. *c* **1450** *Bk. Curtasye* 626 in *Babees Bk.*, Of a *lunden buschelle he shalle bake xx louys. **1523** [see BUSHEL *sb.*[1] 1]. **1552** ELYOT *Dict.*, *Baccharis apud Ruellium*, is supposed to be the flower called *London button. **1611** COTGR., *Gantelée*, the hearbe called Fox-gloues..and London buttons. **1830** LYELL *Princ. Geol.* I. 152 From the *London clay we have procured three or four hundred species of testacea. **1830** M. EDGEWORTH *Let.* 8 Dec. (1971) 445 It is so very dark in a thick *London fog that I can scarcely see what I write. **1887** [see FOG *sb.*[2] 2]. **1906** W. MARRIOTT *Hints to Meteorol. Observers* (ed. 6) 67/1 *London fog*, the dry, gloomy, irritating fog peculiar to London and other large towns, aggravated by smoke. **1931** E. E. CUMMINGS *Let.* 7 Jan. (1969) 120 A London fog struck the ville at the very moment of departure. **1972** E. ROUTLEY *Puritan Pleasures of Detective Story* iii. 36 Holmes..has moral status, and that makes one feel safer when one sets out with him into another London fog. **1920** G. SAINTSBURY *Notes on Cellar-Bk.* vii. 104 Gin, whether 'squareface' or *London or Plymouth, [costs] not much more than half a crown. **1954** M. SHARP *Gipsy in Parlour* xxiv. 230 'Devon cider be a powerful brew,' said my Aunt Charlotte... 'London gin's a sight worse,' retorted Clara. **1963** A. L. SIMON *Guide Good Food & Wines* 721/1 *London Gins*, which differ according to the Distilleries responsible for them. **1970** *House & Garden* Nov. 126/2 The type of gin in most general use is London Dry... Though a few countries.. deem 'London' to indicate a geographical origin,..the term London Dry Gin is mainly accepted as indicating a type of gin. **1852** DICKENS *Bleak Ho.* x, Smoke, which is the *London ivy, had so wreathed itself round Peffer's name,.. that the affectionate parasite quite overpowered the parent-tree. **1889** *Sporting Life* 4 Jan. (Farmer), A very severe cold caught by nine hours' contact with London ivy. **1780** A. YOUNG *Tour Irel.* (1892) I. 306 Of other sorts of potatoes, he finds the *London lady and the apple to be the best sorts. **1647** WARD *Simp. Cobler* 25 Whatever Christianity or Civility will allow, I can afford with *London measure. *a* **1652** BROME *Covent Gard.* Prol., 'Tis not in Book, as Cloth; we never say Make London-measure, when we buy a play. **1852** DICKENS *Bleak Ho.* iii, 'This is a *London particular'. I had never heard of such a thing. 'A fog, miss', said the young gentleman. **1860** T. RIVERS in *Gardeners' Chronicle* 21 Jan. 47/1 (*heading*) The *London Plane trees. **1885** G. S. BOULGER *Familiar Trees* 1st Ser. 23 Most of our London Plane-trees belong to an intermediate form. **1930** A. D. WEBSTER *London Trees* 92 The Maple-leaved or London Plane stands first in the list of select trees for planting in towns. **1970** *Nature* 21 Mar. 1159/2 The London plane has proved extremely valuable as a tree that will endure the difficult environments of modern cities. **1889** *Science* 24 May 394/2 The supply of powder can be regulated to such a nicety, that Mr. Leggett claims he can make half a pound of *London purple cover an acre. **1894** *Times* 16 Aug. 6/2 Paris green or London purple. **1566** A. EDWARDS in *Hakluyt's Voy.* (1599) I. 357 Your *London reds are not to be sent hither. **1837** MACGILLIVRAY *Withering's Brit. Plants* (ed. 4) 269 *S[isymbrium] Irio*, *London Rocket. **1566** A. EDWARDS in *Hakluyt's Voy.* (1599) I. 358, I wore a garment of *London russet, being much esteemed. **1501** *Ld. Treas. Acc. Scotl.* (1900) II. 30, v quarteris *Londone scarlat to lyne the samyn [doublat]. **1957** *Textile Terms & Definitions* (Textile Inst.) (ed. 3) 61 **London shrinking*, a finishing process. **1940** *Chambers's Techn. Dict.* 509/2 *London-shrunk (*Textiles*), a term used in the woollen and worsted trades to indicate that a fabric has been specially treated in order to prevent shrinkage during make-up and when worn. **1950** '*Mercury' Dict. Textile Terms* 323/2 *London shrunk.* The dry cloth to be shrunk is folded between an upper and lower layer of wet cloth. The cloth is then dried naturally, and afterwards pressed. **1968** J. IRONSIDE *Fashion Alphabet* 239 *London-shrunk*, a process for shrinking wool fabric before tailoring. **1883** *Daily News* 16 Oct. 3/1 Rich black, dark grey, and the new '*London smoke' are chosen. **1884** HOGG *Fruit Man.* (ed. 5) 605 **London Sugar*,..A small, very early pear; ripe in the end of July and beginning of August. **1597** GERARDE *Herbal* II. clxxiv. 480 Sweete Williams,

Tolmeiners, and *London Tufts. **1629** PARKINSON *Parad. in Sole* (1656) 320 We do..call the..narrower leafed kindes, Sweet Johns, and all the rest Sweet Williams; yet in some places they call the broader leafed kindes that are not spotted ..London tufts.

Londoner ('lʌndənə(r)). [see -ER[1].]

1. A native (or inhabitant) of London. (Now chiefly with some reference to the real or supposed characteristics of London people.)

c **1460** J. RUSSELL *Bk. Nurture* 1025 Hym þat hath byn meyre & a londynere. **1518** in W. H. Turner *Select. Rec. Oxford* 18 As your grace dyuysid for Londonars. **1613** SHAKS. *Hen. VIII*, I. ii. 154 The Duke..did of me demand What was the speech among the Londoners, Concerning the French Iourney. **1632** SHERWOOD (*title-p.*), Dictionaire, Anglois et François..by Robert Sherwood Londoner. **1777** SHERIDAN *Trip Scarb.* IV. i, These Londoners have got a gibberish with 'em would confound a gipsy. **1849** MACAULAY *Hist. Eng.* iii. I. 321 Towards London and Londoners he felt an aversion which more than once produced important political effects. **1884** *Contemp. Rev.* Feb. 226 The thoroughbred Londoner is seldom a perfect workman.

†**2.** A ship belonging to London. *Obs.*

1764 *Ann. Reg.* 92 Returned from the whale fishery..ten Londoners with seven fish.

Londonese (lʌndə'ni:z), *a.* and *sb.* [f. LONDON + -ESE.] **a.** *adj.* Said derisively of dialect, peculiarities of speech, etc.: Peculiar to or characteristic of London; cockney. **b.** *sb.* The 'Londonese' dialect.

In some recent Dicts.

Londonesque (lʌndə'nɛsk), *a. rare.* [-ESQUE.] Having the characteristics proper to London.

1862 MAYHEW *Crim. Prisons Lond.* 54 Is there any other sight in the Metropolis..so thoroughly Londonesque as this? **1875** *New Q. Rev.* July 477 Within this circumference ..the ideas..of the inhabitants are purely Londonesque.

Lon'donian. *rare.* [-IAN.] A Londoner.

1824 L. M. HAWKINS *Mem.* II. 41 Certainly this..would have occurred to none but a thorough-paced Londonian.

Londonish ('lʌndənɪʃ), *a.* [-ISH[1].] Pertaining to or characteristic of London; exhibiting features or aspects of London.

1838 *Civil Engin. & Arch. Jrnl.* 154/2 A modest porch below, and a *neat* viranda—something of that sort, spruce and Londonish. **1852** GEO. ELIOT *Let.* 23 June (1954) II. 37 Not that I don't like him..but I want nothing so Londonish when I go to enjoy the fields. **1922** *Sketch* 1 Nov. 194/3 A few mellow Cockney vowels to make us feel cosy—Londonish. **1925** W. DEEPING *Sorrell & Son* vi. 56, I had been getting a little—Londonish—shall we call it. **1927** *Observer* 6 Nov. 9/4 The Cromwell-road is at once the most English and the most Londonish of our thoroughfares. **1956** M. STEWART *Wildfire at Midnight* iii. 32 You look a bit Londonish, if I may say so.

Londonism ('lʌndənɪz(ə)m). [-ISM.] London habits, manners, or peculiarities of speech; a word, idiom, or pronunciation belonging to the London dialect.

1803 S. PEGGE *Anecd. Eng. Lang.* 52 The humble and accepted dialect of London, the Londonisms as I may call them. **1857** *Blackw. Mag.* LXXXI. 316 Their entire Londonism (which is not Cockneyism).

Londonize ('lʌndənaɪz), *v.* [-IZE.]

1. *trans.* To make like London or its inhabitants.

1778 MISS BURNEY *Evelina* x. (1791) I. 19 Her chief objection was to our dress, for we have had no time to Londonize ourselves. **1806** JEFFREY *Let.* in Cockburn *Life* II. lii, You try to persuade yourself that you are Londonised. **1893** J. E. RITCHIE *East Anglia* 75 The new town has spread to Kirkley, has Londonized even quiet Pakefield.

2. *intr.* To visit or frequent London. *nonce-use.*

1827 LAMB *Lett.* (1888) II. 75 (To Bernard Barton), Do you never Londonise again?.. Do your Drummonds allow no holidays?

Hence **'Londonized** *ppl. a.*; **Londoni'zation,** the action or process of Londonizing.

1832 LYTTON *Eugene A.* II. v, In our remoter roads and less Londonised districts. **1888** BLACKIE *Sp.* in *Scot. Leader* 19 Sept. 5 He did not believe in centralisation, or the Londonisation of Scotland. **1891** G. MEREDITH *One of our Conq.* III. xiii. 266 Enjoying the Londonized odour of the cab. **1959** *Daily Tel.* 21 Nov. 15/2 Mr. Grimond..said Londonisation of the whole of the country must be prevented. **1962** *Rep. Comm. Broadc. 1960* (Cmnd. 1753) xiii. 139 The dangers of Londonisation are less than those of isolation.

Londo'nologist. One learned in the history and topography of London.

1864 I. TAYLOR *Words & Places* 288 *note*, The whole tribe of modern Londonologists have followed Stow in [etc.].

'London pride. Also 7 London's Pride, Pride of London. **a.** The Sweet William, *Dianthus barbatus*, or a variety of it. Now *dial.* **b.** *Lychnis Chalcedonica.* Now *dial.* **c.** *Saxifraga umbrosa.*

a. *a* **1629** PARKINSON *Parad. in Sole* (1656) 319 Speckled Sweet Williams, or London pride. **1671** SKINNER *Etymol.* I I, Londons-Pride, or London-Tufts, *Armeria Prolifera, sic dicta, quia flores propter pulchritudinem Londini valde expetuntur.* **1672** W. Hughes *Flower Garden* 43 Sweet Williams and London-pride Flower at the same time, and are ordered as Sweet Iohns are. **1683** SUTHERLAND *Hortus Med. Edinburg.* 71 *Caryophyllus barbatus*,..Sweet Williams, or Pride of London of several colours.

b. *a* **1688** R. HOLME *Armoury* II. 64/1 The Pride of London is..of some called the Flower of Constantinople. **1886** BRITTEN & HOLLAND *Plant-names* App. (Chedworth, Glouc.).

c. **1697** MOLYNEUX in *Phil. Trans.* XIX. 510 *Cotyledon, sive Sedum serratum Latifolium Montanum guttato flore*.. vulgarly call'd by the Gardners London Pride: I suppose because of its pretty elegant Flower. **1726** THRELKELD *Synops. Stirpium Hibern.* App. 2. **1785** MARTYN *Rousseau's Bot.* xix. (1794) 270 Another species was formerly much shown out at windows and balconies in smoky towns, and hence, with its being really beautiful had the names of London Pride and None-so-pretty. **1882** *Garden* 11 Feb. 92/2 The London Pride remains fresh and bright all through the winter.

Londony ('lʌndənɪ), *a.* [-Y[1].] Suggestive of London or its characteristics.

1884 L. TROUBRIDGE *Life amongst Troubridges* (1966) 169, I thought him so very smart and Londony. **1907** D. O'CONNOR *Peter Pan Picture Bk.* 27 They made a chimney out of John's tall hat, which he had been Londony enough to bring with him. **1920** J. GALSWORTHY *In Chancery* I. x. 88 Rather pale she looked and Londony. **1949** D. SMITH *I capture Castle* xiv. 263 A cool breeze was blowing in from the Park, smelling of dry grass and petrol—a most exciting, Londony smell. **1974** C. MILNE *Enchanted Places* x. 69, I hated wearing overcoats in the country... Overcoats were Londony things.

‖**londra, luntra.** *Obs.* [Romaic λόντρα, It. *londra* 'fregata grande' (Somavera), *lontro* 'a canoa or Indian boate' (Florio). Found as med.L. *londra* A.D. 1011.] ? = FELUCCA.

1675 *Lond. Gaz.* No. 1024/1 We gave chace to a Londra, otherwise a great Sitea. **1700** RYCAUT *Hist. Turks* III. 363 Whilst an Attempt should be made to burn their Galleots, Brigantines and Londra's. **1867** SMYTH *Sailor's Word-bk.*, *Luntra*, see *Felucca*.

†**lone,** *sb. Obs.*[−1] [? a. ON. *laun* (see LAIN *v.*).] Concealment; = LAIN *sb.*[1]

a **1450** *Le Morte Arth.* 1124 The kyng than tolde wythout lone to alle hys barons..how [etc.].

lone (ləʊn), *a.* Also 7–8 loan; *Sc.* 4– lane, 6– lain, (9 *north. dial.* leane, lene). [Aphetic f. ALONE. Cf. *a lone* written for *al one* in the MSS. of R. Brunne *Handl. Synne* 2517.]

1. a. Of persons, their condition, situation, etc.: Having no fellows or companions; without company; solitary. Chiefly *poet.* and *rhetorical.*

1377 LANGL. *P. Pl.* B. XVI. 20, I..laye longe in a lone dreme. **1530** PALSGR. 317/2 Lone onely, *seul.* **1616** BULLOKAR *Eng. Expos.*, *Lone*,..single or solitarie. **1622** MABBE tr. *Aleman's Guzman d'Alf.* II. 337, I was not a lone man in this my afflictions, but had many fellowes that suffered the like torment. **1740** SHENSTONE *Judgm. Hercules* 335 When I have on those pathless wilds appear'd And the lone wand'rer with my presence cheer'd. **1747** SMOLLETT *Regicide* II. iv. (1777) 34 With not one friend his sorrows to divide, And chear his lone distress? **1764** GOLDSM. *Trav.* 51 As some lone miser, visiting his store. **1814** *Sporting Mag.* XLIII. 261, I found myself a lone man, much at a loss. **1837** DISRAELI *Venetia* I. vii. 33 She felt for this lone child. **1863** WOOLNER *My Beautiful Lady* 109 Dim in lowlands far Lone marsh-birds winged their misty flight. **1882** OUIDA *Maremma* I. 248 We trusted an old lone creature. **1901** *Blackw. Mag.* June 785/2 Two lone Englishmen in the same house, not on speaking terms.

b. *to play, hold a lone hand*: in Quadrille and Euchre, to play against all the other players, or against the opposite side without help from one's own. Hence *lone hand, lone player* are used = a person playing such a game.

1799 MRS. J. WEST *Tale of Times* I. 217 Sir Simon..was remarkably partial to holding a lone-hand [at quadrille]. **1830** R. HARDIE *Hoyle made Familiar* 37 [Quadrille.] When playing against a lone hand, never lead a king, unless you have the queen. **1886** *Euchre: how to play it* 41 Suppose a player, being four, and his adversaries nothing, plays a lone hand and makes his five tricks. *Ibid.* 108 *Lone Hand*, a hand so strong in trumps alone, or in trumps, guarded by high cards of a lay suit, that it will probably win five tricks if its holder plays alone. *Lone player*, the one playing without his partner.

fig. **1879** B. F. TAYLOR *Summer-Savory* xv. 122 In fact, in pretty nearly all his plays he had a 'lone hand'. **1888** KIPLING *Barrack-Room Ballads* (1892) 118 A lone-hand raid of the rearmost cart. *c* **1890** A. MURDOCH *Yoshiwara Episode*, etc. 81, I wasn't playing a lone hand in that game, and so I just allowed I wouldn't marry that girl just then. **1901** *Contemp. Rev.* Dec. 863, I am going to play a lone-hand, and intend being my own Commandant and Veldt Cornet and everything else. **1916** *Brit. Dominions Year Bk. 1917* 243 Lone-hand raids on Constantinople. **1922** JOYCE *Ulysses* 455 This is a lonehand fight.

c. Having a feeling of loneliness; lonesome.

a **1839** PRAED *Poems* (1864) II. 84 When the lone heart, in that long strife, Shall cling unconsciously to life. *Ibid.* 382 And there my fond mother Sits pensive and lone. **1845** HOOD *Last Man* xxxiv, I never felt so lone. **1858** LYTTON *What will He do?* I. xii, I'll rather stay with you, Grandy, you'll be so lone.

2. Unmarried; single or widowed. Now only of women, with mock-pathetic reference to sense 1.

1548 UDALL *Erasm. Par. Luke* xviii. 1–8, I am a poore wedowe and alone woman destitute of frendes. **1588** M. KYFFIN *Terence, Andria* II. iii. E ij b, This Glycerie is a lone woman. **1597** SHAKS. *2 Hen. IV*, II. i. 35, A 100. Marke is a long one, for a poore lone woman to beare. **1611** W. SCLATER *Key* (1629) 128 That is but necessarie for a master of a familie, that is superfluous for a lone man. **1642** *Title Collect. Records* (T.), Queen Elizabeth being a lone woman, and having few friends, refusing to marry. *a* **1825** FORBY *Voc. E. Anglia*, *Lone-woman*, a woman unmarried or without a male protector. **1847** HALLIWELL s.v., *Lone-man*, a man living unmarried by himself. **1859** HELPS *Friends in C.* Ser. II. I. i. 55 Men highly-placed little know..what a trouble it is for lone women [to estimate their incomes].

3. a. Standing apart from others of its kind; isolated. Formerly *esp.* in phr. *lone house* (sometimes hyphened).

1667 WOOD *Life* 1 Sept. (O.H.S.) II. 143 This Cooper's hill is a lone-house. **1717** POPE *Let. to Misses Blount* 13 Sept., No Lone-house in Wales, with a Mountain and Rookery, is more contemplative than this Court. **1722** DE FOE *Plague* (1840) 180 In a single, or, as we call it, a lone house. **1776** ADAM SMITH *W.N.* I. iii. (1869) I. 18 In the lone cottages of the Highlands. **1813** *Sketches Charac.* (ed. 2) I. 138 'Twas a lone house, in a garden, with walls round it. **1819** *Sporting Mag.* IV. 274 A little lone public-house, about a mile from our village. **1850** SCORESBY *Cheever's Whalem. Adv.* viii. (1859) 112 Dragging the lone boat quite out of sight from the mast-head. **1853** M. ARNOLD *Scholar-Gipsy* vi, At some lone ale-house in the Berkshire moors.

b. *lone star*, the single star on the state flag of Texas, hence called the ***Lone Star State.*** Also ***Lone Star Stater***, a Texan.

1843 W. B. DEWEES *Lett. from Early Settler Texas* (1852) 246 The lone star of Texas shall continue to wave proudly in the air as long as one brave Texan remains to defend it. **1845** *Congress. Globe* 28th Congress 2 Sess. App. 78/3 The 'lone star' has found a place upon the democratic banners. **1848** *Ibid.* 30th Congress 1 Sess. App. 973/1 Texas was then a 'lone star'. She is now one of thirty. **1860** *Ibid.* 5 Dec. 11/3 There is a clog in the way of the lone-star State of Texas in the person of her Governor. **1873** J. H. BEADLE *Undevel. West* 805, I am proud to find him in honor and position among the 'Lone Star Staters'. **1873** Z. N. MORRELL *Flowers & Fruits* (ed. 2) 20 Sam. Houston was then in Texas.. intending..to set in motion 'a little two-horse republic under the Lone Star'. **1886** B. P. POORE *Perley's Reminisc.* I. 315 It took him only from February 28th to April 12th to conclude the negotiation which placed the 'Lone Star' in the azure field of the ensign of the Republic. **1909** 'O. HENRY' *Roads of Destiny* xvi. 267 The Lone Star State never yet failed to grant relief, [etc.]. **1943** B. HOUSE (*title*) I give you Texas: 500 jokes of the Lone Star State. **1971** *Times* 21 Sept. (Ireland Suppl.) 1/4 Two experts from Texas are using Cork as a base..appropriate, since co Cork has always had some of the aggressive independence of the lone star state.

c. *lone wolf* (orig. *U.S.*) *fig.*, (*a*) one who mixes little with others, keeps himself to himself; (*b*) a criminal who operates alone; also *attrib.* Hence (with hyphen) as *v. intr.*, to live, work, operate, etc., alone.

1909 F. H. TILLOTSON *How to be a Detective* 130 Occasionally the police run across Panhandlers known as 'lone wolves'—that is they do not mix with others of their class. **1927** *Dialect Notes* V. 454 *Lone wolf*, a bandit or house breaker who works without confederates. **1931** *Times Lit. Suppl.* 28 May 415/3 He was the 'lone wolf' of the campaign for federation. **1938** *Amer. Speech* XIII. 195 Lone-wolf v. **1938** E. BOWEN *Death of Heart* II. iv. 249, I am quite enough of a lone wolf as it is. **1944** R. F. ADAMS *Western Words* 93/1 *Lone-wolfing*, living alone, avoiding companionship of others. **1950** 'S. RANSOME' *Deadly Miss Ashley* iii. 35 He had been given hardly a dime's worth of information by the lone-wolf doctor. **1953** A. BARON *Human Kind* xvii. 121 They despised his ignorance, his vices and his pitiless lone-wolf philosophy. **1955** *Publ. Amer. Dial. Soc.* XXIV. x. 166 She is ..a kind of *lone wolf* thief. **1955** *Times* 11 July 10/1 A 'lone wolf' terrorist. **1959** ANON. *Streetwalker* viii. 154 He's no lone wolf from Leeds or anywhere else. **1959** N. MAILER *Advts. for Myself* (1961) 408 The lone-wolf hope that we can begin to explore a little more. **1966** J. PHILIPS *Wings of Madness* II. iv. 131 You are in very serious danger if you try to lone-wolf it. **1966** G. BURNETT *Dead Account* vii. 51 Remember what I said..no lone-wolfing, no withholding information. **1970** G. F. NEWMAN *Sir, You Bastard* i. 19 An individualist to be watched unless he should develop into too much of a lone wolf. **1973** J. ROSSITER *Manipulators* ii. 21 Detective Inspector De Moro..had given him a preliminary reprimand about lone-wolfing operations.

d. *lone pair* (Physical Chem.): a pair of electrons in the outer shell of an atom which are not involved in bonding.

1923 *Chem. & Industry Rev.* 2 Nov. 1051/1 A basic substance is one which has a lone pair of electrons which may be used to complete the stable group of another atom. **1964** J. W. LINNETT *Electronic Struct. Molecules* ii. 31 In ammonia there are, therefore, three shared-pairs and one lone-pair.

4. *poet.* Of places: Lonely; unfrequented, uninhabited.

1712–14 POPE *Rape Lock* IV. 154 Oh had I rather un-admir'd remain'd In some lone isle, or distant Northern land. **1717** —— *Eloisa* 141 In these lone walls..Thy eyes diffus'd a reconciling ray. **1795** BURNS *Song*, '*Their groves o' sweet myrtles*', Far dearer to me yon lone glen o' green breckan. **1810** SCOTT *Lady of L.* I. i, In lone Glenartney's hazel shade. **1864** BROWNING *Dîs Aliter Visum* vii, We stepped O'er the lone stone fence.

†**5.** Only, sole. *Obs.*

1602 *2nd Pt. Return fr. Parnass.* II. ii. 613 Ile make it my lone request, that he wold be good to a scholler.

6. *predicatively* and quasi-*adv.*

†**a.** = ALONE; by myself, itself (etc.). *Obs.*

1613 PURCHAS *Pilgrimage, Descr. India* (1864) 156 Floris enterd lone as it were for businesse. *c* **1817** HOGG *Tales & Sk.* IV. 29 She carefully avoided meeting him lone, though often and earnestly urged to it.

b. *Sc.* and *north. dial.* with possessive pronoun prefixed, as ***my lane*** = by myself. (Cf. ALONE 3.) More recently also in form *lone* (and *lones*).

1375 *Sc. Leg. Saints* xxii. (*Laurentius*) 521 þe crystine.. Lowand god of al his lane. *a* **1584** MONTGOMERIE *Cherrie & Slae* 678 How Hope and Curage tuik the man And led him all thair lanis. *a* **1600** —— *Misc. Poems* iii. 33 And ladds vploips to lordships all thair lains. **1631** RUTHERFORD *Lett.* xiv. (1862) I. 67 He had many against Him and compeared

His lone in the fields against them all. **1725** RAMSAY *Gentle Sheph.* II. iii, When Bessy Freetock's chuffy-cheeked wean ..cou'dna stand its lane. **1788** BURNS *Let. to J. Tennant* 21 My shins, my lane, I there sit roastin'. **1894** CROCKETT *Raiders* 134 Can ye no let an auld man dee his lane? **1902** KIPLING *Just So Stories* 197 They walked in the Wet Wild Woods by their wild lones. *Ibid.* 206 This is the picture of the Cat that Walked by Himself, walking by his wild lone through the Wet Wild Woods. **1908** *Westm. Gaz.* 28 May 2/4 The roads are dusty and dry When you walk 'em all by your lone. **1910** W. M. RAINE *Bucky O'Connor* 21 But why for do they let a sick man like you travel all by his lone? **1917** W. J. LOCKE *Red Planet* vi. 75 After five minutes on my lones, I felt as if I should go off my head. **1941** W. DE LA MARE *Coll. Poems* 7 As she asks in her lone, This old, desolate crone.

7. *Comb.* (adverbial and parasynthetic).

1809–10 COLERIDGE *Friend* (1865) 215 Those loud-tongued adulators, the mob, overpowered the lone-whispered denunciations of conscience. **1887** G. MEREDITH *Ballads & P.* 141 Lycophron, this breathless, this lone-laid. **1896** *Westm. Gaz.* 15 Dec. 4/3 A man who could trust himself lone-handed in mid-ocean in such a craft.

lone, obs. form of LOAN *sb.* and *v.*

† **'lonedom.** *nonce-wd.* [f. LONE *a.* + -DOM.] Solitariness.

1612 AINSWORTH *Annot. Ps.* iv. 9 [Alone] The Hebr. phrase is, in lonedome, or in solitarines.

† **'loneful,** *a. Obs.* exc. *dial.* Also *Sc.* **lanefu'**. [f. LONE *a.* + -FUL.] Lonely, forlorn.

1565 STAPLETON tr. *Bede's Hist. Ch. Eng.* v. i. 153 b, That solytary and lonefull lyffe, which he [Aedilwalde] passed in Farne island. **1844** THOM *Rhymes* 42 The lanefu' lawyer held his breath An' word micht utter nane.

lonelihood ('ləʊnlɪhʊd). *poet.* [f. LONELY + -HOOD.] Loneliness.

1830 SCOTT *Doom Devorgoil* I. i, That fell Chief..roams through his empty halls, And mourns their wasteness and their lonelihood. **1839** BAILEY *Festus* iii. (1848) 19 Yon.. star..Making itself a lonelihood of light. **1849** A. J. SYMINGTON *Harebell Chimes* 179 The myriad stars But make us feel our lonelihood the more.

lonelily ('ləʊnlɪlɪ), *adv.* [f. LONELY + -LY².] In a lonely fashion.

1850 R. G. CUMMING *Hunter's Life S. Afr.* (ed. 2) I. 117 We lived well, but lonelily. **1852** M. ARNOLD *Tristram & Iseult*, The weird chipping of the woodpecker Rang lonelily and sharp.

loneliness ('ləʊnlɪnɪs). [f. LONELY + -NESS.] The quality or condition of being lonely.

1. Want of society or company; the condition of being alone or solitary; solitariness, loneness.

*a***1586** SIDNEY *Arcadia* I. (1590) 49 b, That huge and sportfull assemblie grewe to him a tedious lonelinesse, esteeming no body founde, since Daiphantus was lost. **1645** MILTON *Tetrach.* (*Gen.* ii. 18), It is not good for man to be alone... Loneliness is the first thing which God's eye nam'd not good. **1814** BYRON *Corsair* I. viii, That man of loneliness and mystery. **1861** GEO. ELIOT *Silas M.* i. 2 The eccentric habits which belong to a state of loneliness. **1874** GREEN *Short Hist.* vii. §3. 368 The loneliness of her [Elizabeth's] position only reflected the loneliness of her nature.

2. Uninhabited or unfrequented condition or character (of a place); desolateness.

1746–7 HERVEY *Medit.* (1818) 8 The deep silence added to the gloomy aspect, and both heightened by the loneliness of the place, greatly increased the solemnity of the scene. **1860** TYNDALL *Glac.* I. ii. 11 The loneliness of the place was very impressive. **1900** J. WATSON in *Expositor* Sept. 181 The unrelieved loneliness of mid-ocean.

b. A lonely spot. *nonce-use.*

1819 SHELLEY *Rosalind & Helen* 1029 In the bowers of mossy lonelinesses.

3. The feeling of being alone; the sense of solitude; dejection arising from want of companionship or society.

1814 WORDSW. *Excurs.* VII. 403 He grew up From year to year in loneliness of soul. **1863** J. C. MURPHY *Comm. Gen.* xxv. 1 His loneliness on the death of Sarah may have prompted him to seek a companion of his old age. **1876** MRS. WHITNEY *Sights & Ins.* II. xxx. 581 My own secret aches and lonelinesses.

† **'loneling.** *Obs.* [f. LONE *a.* + -LING.] A single child (opposed to a twin).

1579 J. JONES *Preserv. Bodie & Soule* I. xxiii. 43, I think it best that the old womans childe do sucke longer than the yong and lustie Nurce,..the twinne longer than the loneling.

lonely ('ləʊnlɪ), *a.* [f. LONE *a.* + -LY¹.]

1. a. Of persons, etc., their actions, condition, etc.: Having no companionship or society; unaccompanied, solitary, lone.

1607 SHAKS. *Cor.* IV. i. 30, I go alone Like to a lonely Dragon, that his Fenne Makes fear'd, and talk'd of more then seene. **1634** MILTON *Comus* 200 To give due light To the misled and lonely Travailer. **1667** —— *P.L.* XI. 290 Thy going is not lonely, with thee goes Thy Husband. **1708** ROWE *Roy. Convert* III. i. 27 When, fairest Princess, you avoid our Court And lonely thus from the full Pomp retire. **1750** GRAY *Elegy* 73 By Night and lonely Contemplation led. **1816** C. WOLFE *Burial Sir J. Moore* 18 As we hollow'd his narrow bed And smoothed down his lonely pillow. **1856** STANLEY *Sinai & Pal.* iii. (1858) 176 Jacob, as he wandered on his lonely exile from Beersheba to Bethel. **1859** W. COLLINS *Q. of Hearts* (1875) 1 We were three quiet, lonely old men. **1901** *Spectator* 23 Feb. 270/2 The lonely seer has his place in the vast and complex order of things, whether as philosopher or saint.

b. Colloq. or dial. phr. ***on one's lonely*(-o)**: on one's own; alone. Cf. LONE *a.* 6 b (prob. infl. by *only*).

1919 D. H. LAWRENCE *England my England* (1922) 61 Oh, I'm going home by myself to-night—all on my lonely-O. **1924** 'K. MANSFIELD' *Something Childish* 61 So you're on your lonely, missus? *a***1930** D. H. LAWRENCE *Phoenix* (1936) v. 594 A child was to be given a lump of soft clay and told to express himself, presumably in the pious hope that he might model a Tanagra figure or a Donatello plaque, all on his little lonely-o.

2. *poet.* Of things: Isolated, standing apart; = LONE 3.

1632 MILTON *Penseroso* 86 Or let my Lamp at Midnight hour, Be seen in som high lonely Towr. **1700** DRYDEN *Cock & Fox* 3 Deep in a Cell her Cottage lonely stood. **1816** BYRON *Ch. Har.* III. lxv, By a lone wall a lonelier column rears A gray and grief-worn aspect of old days. **1866** M. ARNOLD *Thyrsis* xx, That lonely tree against the western sky.

3. Of localities: Unfrequented by men; desolate.

1629 MILTON *Hymn Nativity* 181 The lonely mountains o're, And the resounding shore, A voice of weeping heard. **1749** FIELDING *Tom Jones* IX. vii, Being arrived in this lonely place, where it was very improbable he should meet with any interruption. **1798** COLERIDGE *Anc. Mar.* VII. xix, This soul hath been Alone on a wide wide sea: So lonely 'twas, that God himself Scarce seemed there to be. **1864** TENNYSON *En. Ard.* 554 An isle..the loneliest in a lonely sea. **1868** FREEMAN *Norm. Conq.* (1876) II. viii. 231 A lonely spot by the river Charenton.

4. a. Dejected because of want of company or society; sad at the thought that one is alone; having a feeling of solitariness.

1811 BYRON *'One Struggle More'* iii, Though pleasure fires the maddening soul, The heart—the heart is lonely still! **1840** BARHAM *Ingol. Leg.* Ser. I. *Look at the Clock!*, Mr. Pryce, Mrs. Winifred Pryce being dead, Felt lonely and moped. **1848** C. BRONTË *J. Eyre* vi. (1873) 51, I wandered ..among the forms and tables and laughing groups without a companion, yet not feeling lonely. **1882** OUIDA *Maremma* I. 179 'No doubt they are dead', she thought, and felt the sadder and the lonelier for the thought.

b. *poet.* Imparting a feeling of loneliness; dreary.

1813 SHELLEY *Q. Mab* ix. 98 A heap of crumbling ruins stood, and threw Year after year their stones upon the field, Wakening a lonely echo. **1863** WOOLNER *My beautiful Lady* 22 A lonely wind sighed up the pines.

† **5.** (? *adv.*) ? Alone, without counting anything else. *Obs. rare*⁻¹.

1664 in Dircks *Mrq. Worc.* xviii. (1865) 329 And above 40 others [horses] lonely worth £50 a horse.

6. *Comb.* **lonely-heart**, a sentimental name for a friendless person; so **(Miss) Lonelyhearts**, a journalist who gives advice in a newspaper or magazine to people who are lonely or in difficulties; also *transf.* and *attrib.*; also **lonely-hearted** *a.* (and *absol.*).

1863 KINGSLEY *Water-Bab.* vi. 227 He was so lonely-hearted, he thought that rough kissing was better than none. **1882** DE WINDT *Equator* 64 Sarikei, a lonely-looking place. **1904** W. DE LA MARE *Henry Brocken* 200 Criseyde..the lonely-hearted. **1931** R. CAMPBELL *Georgiad* i. 15 More lonely hearts are linked by the Reviews Than by the 'Link' or 'Matrimonial News'. **1933** 'N. WEST' (*title*) Miss Lonelyhearts. *Ibid.* 14 *Miss Lonelyhearts* tells the story of a reporter,..detailed to write an agony column and answer daily the letters desperate with human misery addressed to his paper. **1938** G. GREENE *Brighton Rock* I. i. 9 Come on over here, lonely heart. **1955** W. GADDIS *Recognitions* III. ii. 749 Down the bar, the Big Unshaven Man was offered a job writing the lonely-hearts column for a newspaper in Buffalo. **1956** A. WILSON *Anglo-Saxon Att.* I. iii. 59 You're so busy being Miss Lonelyhearts to your public. **1958** M. DICKENS *Man Overboard* ii. 31 Rose's weekly show was a toothsome mixture of soap opera and a Lonely-hearts column. **1959** 'N. BLAKE' *Widow's Cruise* 29 He might just be the fulsome, pathetic lonely-heart he appeared to be. **1959** T. GRIFFITH *Waist-High Culture* (1960) ii. 25 With a fellow lonely-heart, ..he would drive out to remote lakes. **1959** *Listener* 28 May 924/2 The office of Connie, the girl who writes the 'Lonely Hearts' column. **1975** *Times* 1 Mar. 8/4 *Music Through Midnight*..the BBC's Miss Lonelyhearts spot. The other two nights there is *Contact*, a radio advice and counselling column.

Hence **'lonelyish** *a.*, somewhat lonely.

1900 PINERO *Gay Lord Quex* II. 75 Grotto? dark I suppose, and lonelyish?

loneness ('ləʊnnɪs). Now *rare* or *dial.* Also 7 **loness, loanness(e**, 9 *Sc.* **laneness**. [f. LONE *a.* + -NESS.] The quality or condition of being lone; solitariness; loneliness; lonesomeness.

1591 PERCIVALL *Sp. Dict.*, *Desacompañamiento*, lonenesse. **1609** DANIEL *Civ. Wars* VIII. lxxi, Shee feares the fatall daunger of the place, Her loneness, and the powre of Maiestie. **1609** W. SCLATER *Threef. Preservat.* (1610) Ep. Ded., Singular I am sure I am not, Sith neyther I affect lonenesse [etc.]. **1613–16** W. BROWNE *Brit. Past.* II. iv, Yet there's in loannesse somewhat may delight. **1839** BAILEY *Festus* ii. (1852) 14 That soothing fret which makes the young untried..In dreams and loneness cry. **1844** W. HOLMES in Whitelaw *Bk. Sc. Song* (1875) 127 The laneness is gane.

loner ('ləʊnə(r)). [f. LONE *a.* + -ER¹.] A person who avoids company and prefers to be alone.

1947 *New Republic* 22 Dec. 7 Big John has decided to become a 'loner' for keeps. **1961** *Guardian* 26 Oct. 7/1 The American ex-patriates along the Seine..are what James Jones calls 'loners'. **1964** L. LINTON *Of Days & Driftwood* xviii. 88 There are many 'loners' dotted around the coastal area, only accessible by boat. **1970** *Daily Tel.* (Colour Suppl.) 3 July 7 On course, as in private life, he is a loner, a man of few words who finds it impossible to chat and joke with the crowds. **1971** *Universe* 25 June 13/5 Mr Paisley is a bit of a maverick, a loner who won't be tied by party trappings. **1971** *Country Life* 29 July 278/1 A loner done to death by his fellows for stepping out of line. **1972** *Daily Mail* 30 Oct. 7/2 By nature I'm a loner.

lonesome ('ləʊnsəm), *a.* Also 7 **loansome**, 8–9 *Sc.* **lanesome**. [f. LONE *a.* + -SOME.]

1. a. Of persons, their condition, feelings, etc.: Solitary, lonely. In later use, chiefly in emotional sense: Having a feeling of solitude or loneliness; feeling lonely or forlorn.

1647 H. MORE *Song of Soul* III. lxxvi, Where he with him the loansome night did passe. **1700** BLACKMORE *Paraphr. Isa.* xiv. 257 The lonesome Bittern shall possess This fenny seat. **1719** D'URFEY *Pills* (1872) III. 348 Again his Harp the lonesome Poet strung. **1767–95** MACNEILL *Will & Jean* VI, Light the lanesome hours gae round. **1840** DICKENS *Old C. Shop* xxii, You must keep up your spirits, mother, and not be lonesome because I'm not at home. **1876** SMILES *Sc. Natur.* iv. (ed. 4) 71 The boy began to feel very weary and lonesome.

b. ***by* (or *on*) *one's lonesome***, all alone, without company or assistance. (Cf. LONE *a.* 6 b). *colloq.*

1899 C. J. C. HYNE *Further Adventures Capt. Kettle* ii. 31 No, Kettle, if I'm to get well, some white man will have to go up by his lonesome for me, and square that witch doctor by some trick of the tongue. **1908** *Daily Chron.* 13 Aug. 5/7 Then, parting from him,..I went, all by my lonesome, along the Madeira Walk. **1920** B. CRONIN *Timber Wolves* 125 'When I marry Amelia Peters,' says George, 'you can hit the trail on your lonesome.' **1953** H. MILLER *Plexus* (1963) xii. 442 That evening I wandered off by my lonesome. **1973** G. BEARE *Snake on Grave* ii. 10 One of Rommel's 88's had taken care of his old man somewhere in the Western Desert, and that had left Latch on his lonesome.

c. ***lonesome for.***

1905 *Smart Set* Sept. 74 [He]..had become exceedingly lonesome for the nice young man. **1935** M. DE LA ROCHE *Young Renny* xi. 98 Bob has gone in to see Lizzie. She's feeling a bit lonesome for a sight of him.

2. Of localities, etc.: Solitary, unfrequented, desolate. In later use, chiefly with emotional sense: Causing feelings of loneliness, making one feel forlorn.

1647 H. MORE *Song of Soul* III. App. *Præexistency of Soul* xlix, [They] dance..Around an huge black Goat, in loansome wood. *a***1677** BARROW *Serm.* Wks. 1687 I. viii. 97 Neither shall we content our selves in lonesome tunes, and private soliloquies, to whisper out the Divine praises. **1683** TRYON *Way to Health* 495 If a man walk into loansome Fields amongst the Beasts. **1703** ROWE *Fair Penit.* II. i, An unfrequented Vale,..within whose lonesome Shade, Ravens and Birds ill omen'd, only dwell. **1798** COLERIDGE *Anc. Mar.* VI. 37 Like one that on a lonesome road Doth walk in fear and dread. **1799** WORDSW. *Infl. Nat. Objects* 18 In November days When vapours rolling down the valleys made A lonely scene more lonesome. **1850** HAWTHORNE *Scarlet L.* xiii. (1879) 186 In her lonesome cottage. **1901** *Blackw. Mag.* Jan. 60/2 This is the lonesomest place on earth.

Hence **'lonesomely** *adv.*, **'lonesomeness.**

1702 C. MATHER *Magn. Chr.* VI. i. (1852) 345 His lonesomeness was now become as much as any hermit could have wished for. **1771** MRS. GRIFFITH *Hist. Lady Barton* II. 275 Honest old Saunders,..wonders mightily at my lordship, for passing my time so lonesomely, as he phrases it. **1822** W. TAYLOR in *Monthly Mag.* LIV. 310 A shy lonesomeness of disposition. **1857** *Tait's Mag.* XXIV. 41 The gas lamps..gleam lonesomely. **1884** *Century Mag.* XXIX. 268 We would watch the lonesomeness of the river.

long (lɒŋ), *a.*¹ Forms: 1 **lang**, 4–5, *Sc.* 5–9 **lang**, (4 *Sc.* **launge**), 3 **longue**, 3–7 **longe**, (6 **lounge**), 1, 3– **long**. See also LENGER, LENGEST. [Com. Teut.: OE. *lang*, *lǫng* = OFris., OS. *lang*, *long* (MDu., MLG., Du., LG. *lang*), OHG. *lang* (MHG. *lanc*, *lang-*, mod.G. *lang*), ON. *lang-r* (Da. *lang*, Sw. *lång*), Goth. *lagg-s*:—OTeut. **laŋgo-*:—pre-Teut. **loŋgho-* (= L. *longus*, Gaulish *longo-* in proper names, ? OIrish *long-* in combination).

This is regarded by some scholars as an alteration of **dlongho-* (in OPers. *dranga*), cogn. w. **dlgho-*, **dlegho-* in OSl. *dlŭgŭ* (Russian *dolgo-*, *dolgiĭ*), Gr. δολιχός, OPers. *darga-*, Zend. *darěya*, Skr. *dīrghá*; to the same root app. belong Gr. ἐν-δελεχής perpetual, Goth. *tulgus* firm, persistent, OS. *tulgo* very; some also connect L. *indulgēre* to indulge (? orig. to be long-suffering towards).]

A. *adj.*

I. With reference to spatial measurement.

1. a. Great in measurement from end to end. Said of a line, of distance, a journey; also, of a portion of space or a material object with reference to its greatest dimension. Opposed to *short*.

Formerly often in phr. † *long and large* (see LARGE *a.* 4 b), which is sometimes applied *transf.* to immaterial things.

*c***893** K. ÆLFRED *Oros.* I. i. §13 He sæde þeah þæt land sie swiþe lang norþ þonan. *c***1200** *Trin. Coll. Hom.* 219 Foure þinges þe man find ilome on ȝerde þat he be riht and smal and long and smeþe. *c***1205** LAY. 30096 Heo breken scaftes longe. Mid longe sweorden heo smitten. **1297** R. GLOUC. (Rolls) 8481 A gyn, þat me sowe clupeþ hii made..boþe wid and long. *a***1300** *Cursor M.* 8079 Lang [*Trin.* longe] and side þair brues wern. *c***1320** *Seuyn Sag.* (W.) 577 Ac that ympe that so sprong, Hit was sschort and nothing long. *c***1386** CHAUCER *Merch. Prol.* 11 Ther is a long and large difference Bitwix Grisildis grete pacience And of my wyf the passing crueltee. *c***1400** MAUNDEV. (1839) xxv. 259 The Kyngdom of Mede..is fulle long: but it is not full large. *Ibid.* xxvi. 269 [The Griffoun] hathe his Talouns so longe and so large and grete..as though [etc.]. *c***1450** HOLLAND *Howlat* 787 Mak..

A lang sper of a betill for a berne bald. **1483** CAXTON *G. de la Tour* E ij, A long gowne, two kyrtells & two cottes hardyes. **1508** DUNBAR *Flyting w. Kennedie* 148 Thair is bot lyse, and lang nailis ȝow amang. **1530** PALSGR. 240/2 Longegonne, *flevste*. *a* **1548** HALL *Chron., Hen. IV* 31 b *note*, Midas, the Poetes faine to have longe eares. **1573** L. LLOYD *Marrow of Hist.* (1653) 207 In this play they did fight one with another at the long Spear, the long Sword. **1592** *Extracts Aberd. Reg.* (1848) II. 76 In armour, jack, steil bonat, spair, halbert, or lang gun. *a* **1614** D. DYKE *Myst. Self-Deceiving* (ed. 8) 27 To weare long haire is commonly a badge of a royster, or ruffian. **1682** T. FLATMAN *Heraclitus Ridens* No. 55 (1713) II. 93 A white Staff..would much better please the scribbling Clown; and we'll help him to a long long one. **1748** RICHARDSON *Clarissa* II. i. 5, I have not been able yet to laugh him out of his long bib and beads. **1838** *Civil Eng. & Arch. Jrnl.* I. 263/1 The Gorgon will be fitted with sixteen 32-pounders (long-guns). **1893** G. E. MATHESON *About Holland* 37 The long low line of the Dutch coast. **1899** *Allbutt's Syst. Med.* VI. 665 Many cases..yield to the long splint. **1900** *Q. Rev.* Oct. 350 These famous galleys were long low rowing boats of the ancient pattern.

b. With reference to vertical measurement: Tall. Sometimes prefixed as an epithet to proper names, e.g. *Long Meg, Tom, Will.* Now *rare* exc. in jocular use.

c **900** tr. *Bæda's Hist.* II. xvi. (Schipper) 179 Cwæþ þæt he wære se mon lang on bodiȝe. *a* **1000** *Byrhtnoth* 273 (Gr.) Ða ȝyt on orde stod Eadweard se langa. *c* **1205** LAY. 6366 Cniht he wes swiðe strong..muchel and long. **1297** R. GLOUC. (Rolls) 8526 þikke mon he was inou bote he was noȝt wel long. **1362** LANGL. *P. Pl.* A. Prol. 52 Grete lobres and longe þat loþ weore to swynke. **1377** *Ibid.* B. xv. 148, I haue lyued in londe..my name is longe wille. ? **14..** *John de Reeve* 254–5 in Furnivall *Percy Folio* (1868) II. 568 What long ffellow is yonder, quoth hee, that is soe long of lim and lyre? *c* **1420** *Pallad. on Husb.* I. 86 The treen thereon light, fertil, faire, and longe. **1430–40** LYDG. *Bochas* I. ii. (1544) 4 b, This Nembroth [Nimrod] waxe mighty, large and long. **1578** LYTE *Dodoens* VI. xv. 676 Tamarisk is a little tree or plant as long as a man. **1588** *Acc. Bk. W. Wray* in *Antiquary* XXXII. 54 Bought of lounge Tome the 23 of aprill [etc.]. **1609** BIBLE (Douay) *Deut.* ii. 21 A great and huge people, and of long stature. **1618** W. LAWSON *New Orch. & Gard.* (1623) 39 Pride of sap makes proud, long & streight growth. **1795** BURNS *Song, 'Their groves o' sweet myrtles'*, Wi' the burn stealing under the lang yellow broom. **1814** SCOTT *Wav.* xxxv, Lang John Mucklewrath the smith. **1871** R. ELLIS tr. *Catullus* lxvii. 47 Sir, 'twas a long lean suitor.

c. ***long arm, hand***: used *transf.* and *fig.* with reference to extent of reach. Also, † ***to make a long arm***: to reach out to a great distance. ***a long face*** (see FACE *sb.* 6 b) *colloq.*: an expression of countenance indicating sadness or exaggerated solemnity. ***a long head***: a head of more than ordinary length from back to front; *fig.* capacity for calculation and forethought. (Cf. LONG-HEAD, LONG-HEADED.) ***to make a long neck***: to stretch out the neck. ***to make a long nose*** (slang): to put the thumb to the nose, as a gesture of mockery. ***a long tongue***: *fig.* loquacity. ***long in the tooth***: (orig. of horses) displaying the roots of the teeth owing to the recession of the gums with increasing age; hence *gen.*, old.

c **1489** CAXTON *Sonnes of Aymon* vii. 177 Thenne he..bare his hede vp, and made a long necke. **1539** TAVERNER *Erasm. Prov.* 4 *Longae regum manus.* Kynges haue longe handes. **1599** NASHE *Lenten Stuffe* 42 Ouer that arme of the sea could be made a long arme. **1621** FLETCHER *Wildgoose Chase* v. iv, What ye have seen, be secret in;..No more of your long tongue. **1656** EARL MONM. tr. *Boccalini's Advts. fr. Parnass.* I. xxiii. (1674) 24 Potent men, who have long hands, and short consciences..would [etc.]. **1786** BURNS *Ded. to G. Hamilton* 62 Learn three-mile pray'rs, and half-mile graces, Wi' weel-spread looves, an' lang, wry faces. **1809** MALKIN *Gil Blas* IX. viii. ¶2 He had a long head, as well as a fanciful brain. **1834** HT. MARTINEAU *Farrers* i. 8 You will see long faces enough when these taxes come to be paid. **1852** THACKERAY *Esmond* I. ii. 50 She was lean, and yellow, and long in the tooth; all the red and white in all the toyshops of London could not make a beauty of her. **1854** C. M. YONGE *Heartsease* I. II. ii. 146 Rising, and making a long arm, he deposited them on the top of a high wardrobe. **1860** [see ARM *sb.*[1] 2 b]. **1868** *Routledge's Ev. Boy's Ann.* 263 Prawle made a 'long nose' in the direction of Goree Piazzas. **1879** SPURGEON *Serm.* XXV. 548 You can put on a very long face and try to scold people into religion. **1884** [see ARM *sb.*[1] 2 b]. *c* **1888** C. H. CHAMBERS *Capt. Swift* (1902) II. 29 I'm not safe here. This place is a hornet's nest. The long arm of coincidence has reached after me. **1889** J. S. WINTER *Mrs. Bob* (1891) 134 He has always had luck, and he has a long head too. **1895** G. B. SHAW *Our Theatres in Nineties* (1932) I. 229 Mr. Jerome..has discovered that in working the familiar but safe stage trick of *dénouement* by coincidence, the long arm cannot be too long. **1899** *Daily News* 15 May 3/5 The long arm of coincidence. **1919** J. C. SNAITH *Love Lane* xxi. 106 One of the youngest R.A.s on record, but a bit long in the tooth for the army. **1932** J. CONQUEST *Village Pompadour* xxv. 183 Long in the tooth, he escaped the traps laid by widow, débutante and free-lance. **1933** 'R. CROMPTON' *William—the Rebel* x. 187 They merely made long noses at the Outlaws. **1936** W. S. MAUGHAM *Cosmopolitans* 213 Go on... The long arm of coincidence was about to make a gesture. **1942** *R.A.F. Jrnl.* 27 June 20 Izzy Grant saw one [*sc.* a Gremlin]..making a long nose at him as he went into the ditch. **1951** 'E. CRISPIN' *Long Divorce* xii. 141 'That's stretching the long arm of coincidence rather far.' 'It's pulling the damned thing right out of its socket.' **1957** J. BRAINE *Room at Top* xii. 124 A trifle long in the tooth, mark you, but she has style, real style. **1963** A. HUXLEY *Let.* 17 Nov. (1969) 964 Talk about the long arm of coincidence! The mail which brought your note.. brought ..at the same time a letter from Betty Wendel. **1972** *Sunday Express* 24 Dec. 2/5 To be honest I am getting quite long in the tooth and this is a method of bringing children into my Christmas. **1973** 'B. MATHER' *Snowline* vii. 83, I made a long arm for the telephone.

d. Qualifying a sb. denoting a measure of length, to indicate an extent greater than that expressed by the sb. (Cf. 10.)

1619 in Ferguson & Nanson *Munic. Rec. Carlisle* (1887) 278 [Buying] harden cloath in the merkett with a longe yeard and selling the same againe with a short yeard. *c* **1646** *True Relation*, etc. in Glover *Hist. Derby* (1829) I. App. 63 His Major..was forced to retreate in the night to Derby, being vi. long miles. **1697** ROKEBY *Diary* 57 Att Poulston Bridge (a long mile from Launceston) we entr into Cornwall. **1790** BURNS *Tam o' Shanter* 7 We think na on the lang Scots miles ..That lie between us and our hame. **1842** BORROW *Bible in Spain* (1843) II. xi. 245, I discovered that we were still two long leagues distant from Corcuvion.

e. Of action, vision, etc.: Extending to a great distance. (Cf. *long sight*, 18.) ***at long weapons***: (fighting) at long range. Similarly, ***at long bowls*** (or ***balls***): said of ships cannonading one another at a distance. Also ***long train*** = ***long distance train***.

1604 E. G[RIMSTONE] *D'Acosta's Hist. Indies* III. xiv. 163 Man hath not so long a sight,..to transporte his eyes..in so short a time. **1715–20** POPE *Iliad* XVIII. 384 But mighty Jove cuts short, with just disdain, The long, long views of poor, designing man! **1723** *Wodrow Corr.* (1843) III. 16 This would be..liker honest men, than to keep us at long weapons, and fighting in the dark. **1840** SAUNDERS *Rep. Sel. Comm. Railways* Quest. 361 Places on the line where short and long trains are running together.

f. ***long dung, manure***: manure containing long straw undecayed; so ***long litter*** (see LITTER *sb.* 3 b, c). ***long forage***: straw and green fodder, as distinguished from hay, oats, etc.

1664 EVELYN *Kal. Hort.* Nov. (1699) 130 The Leaves fallen in the Woods, may supply for Long-dung, laid about Artichocks and other things. **1775** W. MARSHALL *Minutes Agric.* 15 Feb. (1778), It forwards the digestion of stubble, offal straw, or long dung very much. **1797** J. JAY in *Sir J. Sinclair's Corr.* (1831) II. 60 Long dung is better than rotten dung, in the furrows, for potatoes. **1812** WELLINGTON *Let. to Earl Liverpool* 11 Feb. in Gurw. *Desp.* (1838) VIII. 602 To secure a supply of long forage for the Cavalry. **1830** *Cumb. Farm. Rep.* 58 in *Husbandry* (L.U.K.) III, Long dung, that is to say, dung not fermented, may be applied to potatoes without any impropriety. **1839** J. BUEL *Farmer's Compan.* xx. 198 Great economy in dung may be effected by feeding these crops with the long manure of the yards and stables, instead of summer-yarding it.

g. ***a long beer, drink*** (colloq.): *lit.* of liquor in a long glass; hence, a large measure of liquor.

1859 TROLLOPE *W. Indies* iii. (1860) 48 A long drink is taken from a tumbler, a short one from a wine-glass. **1892** E. REEVES *Homeward Bound* 61 He stepped into a bar and called for a long beer.

2. a. Having (more or less, or a specified) extension from end to end: often with adv. or advb. phrase expressing the amount of length. ***it's as long as it is broad***: see BROAD *a.* 13. † ***through long and broad*** ——: through the length and breadth of.

c **900** tr. *Bæda's Hist.* I. iii. (Schipper) 15 þæt ealond on Wiht..is þrittiȝes mila lang east & west. *a* **1300** *Cursor M.* 1667, I sal þe tel how lang, how brade..it sal be made. *c* **1400** MAUNDEV. (Roxb.) ii. 5 þe table..was a fote and a halfe lang. **1500–20** DUNBAR *Poems* lxxii. 66 Unto the crose of breid and lenth, To gar his lymmis langar wax. *a* **1548** HALL *Chron., Edw. IV*, 233 b, No longer quantitie, then that a man myght easely put thorough his arme. **1591** SHAKS. *Two Gent.* III. i. 131 A cloake as long as thine will serue the turne. **1596** DALRYMPLE tr. *Leslie's Hist. Scot.* I. 4 The lenth..seuin hundir thousand pace lang, or thair about. **1617** MORYSON *Itin.* III. IV. iii. 195 That..each person..possessing (through long and broad Germany)..500 gold Guldens, should [etc.]. **1678** MOXON *Mech. Exerc.* 77 Four Inches broad, and seven Foot long. **1688** R. HOLME *Armoury* III. 395/2 The size for makeing of Brick are 10 Inches long, 5 broad, and 3 thick. **1840** G. V. ELLIS *Anat.* 293 The aqueduct of the cochlea is a small canal, about a quarter of an inch long. **1854** *Fraser's Mag.* XLIX. 505 A mark 30 feet long by 20. **1860** TYNDALL *Glac.* II. ii. 240 The waves which produce red [light] are longer than those which produce yellow.

¶ **b.** With mixed construction: see OF 39 b.

1535 COVERDALE *Lam.* ii. 20 Shal the women then eate their owne frute, euen children of a spanne longe?

† **c.** Extending *to. Obs.*

c **1610** *Women Saints* 148 There appeared before her a verie cleare white garment long to her foote, which she taking putt on her naked bodie.

3. With reference to shape: Having the length much greater than the breadth; elongated.

1551, etc. [see *long square* in 17]. **1826** KIRBY & SP. *Entomol.* IV. 261 Proportion..Long (*Longa*) Disproportionably long throughout. **1851** *Illustr. Catal. Gt. Exhib.* 1175 Printed long shawls. *Ibid.* 1245 French long and square cashmeres.

4. Of liquors: Ropy. ? *Obs.* [So G. *lang*.]

a **1648** DIGBY *Closet Open.* (1677) 91 There let it [the wort] stand till it begin to blink and grow long like thin Syrup. **1703** *Art & Myst. Vintners* 43 If Wine at any time grow long or lowring. *Ibid.* 65 Sack that is lumpish or long. [**1859**: cf. *long sugar* in 18 below.]

II. With reference to serial extent or duration.

5. a. Of a series, enumeration or succession, a speech, a sentence, a word, a literary work, etc.: Having a great extent from beginning to end. ***long bill***: one containing a great number of items; hence, one in which the charges are excessive. ***long hour***: one indicated by a great number of strokes. † ***long words***: long discourse.

c **1000** *Ags. Gosp.* Luke xx. 47 þa forswelȝað wydywyna hus hiwȝende lang ȝebed. *a* **1300** *Cursor M.* 791 Quat bot es lang mi tale to draw. *c* **1483** CAXTON *Dialogues* v. 16/2 Dame what shall avaylle thenne Longe wordes? *c* **1500** *Melusine* 22 What shuld auayll yf herof I shuld make a longe tale? **1585** FETHERSTONE tr. *Calvin's Acts* xiii. 42 The Jewes who made boast of their long stock and race. **1697** DRYDEN *Virg. Georg.* IV. 305 And Grandsires Grandsons the long List contains. **1712** P. STANHOPE in *Lett. C'tess Suffolk* (1824) I. 2 You do not know what you ask when you would have me write long letters. **1827** H. HEUGH *Jrnl.* in *Life* x. (1852) 203 Before the long hour of midnight all was hush. **1848** THACKERAY *Van. Fair* lx, He ain't like old Veal, who is always bragging and using such long words, don't you know? **1865** KINGSLEY *Herew.* II. vii. 106 That night the monks of Peterborough prayed in the minster till the long hours passed into the short. **1883** GILMOUR *Mongols* (1884) 157 We had to wait a long time for a poor dinner, and pay a long bill for it when it came.

b. *colloq.* Of numbers, and of things numerically estimated: Large. Chiefly in ***long family, odds, price***. Also in Card games, ***long suit*** (see quot. 1876); ***long trump*** (see quot. 1746). ***long purse***, one in which there is plenty of money; ***long shillings***, good wages.

1746 HOYLE *Whist* (ed. 6) 68 Long Trump, Means the having one or more Trumps in your Hand when all the rest are out. *Ibid.* 29 The long Trump being forced out of his Hand. **1809** M. L. WEEMS *Life F. Marion* iii. 26 Great Britain the nation of the longest purse in Europe. **1818** *Sporting Mag.* II. 22 The admirers of youth..added to the chance of long-odds proved eager takers. **1840** E. E. NAPIER *Scenes & Sports For. Lands* I. v. 140 The natives are very partial to this breed, and give long prices for them. **1849** *Chambers's Inform.* II. 720/1 Cylinder machines are only suitable for long impressions. **1858** TROLLOPE *Dr. Thorne* II. x. 177 He was a prudent, discreet man, with a long family, averse to professional hostilities. **1871** *Scribner's Monthly* II. 551 For longer purses there are hard woods in all combinations. **1876** A. CAMPBELL-WALKER *Correct Card* (1880) Gloss. 12 *Long suit*, one of which you hold originally more than three cards. The term is, therefore, indicative of strength in numbers. **1892** J. PAYN *Mod. Whittington* I. 177 He thinks I may pull off the long odds. **1910** 'SAKI' *Reginald in Russia* 105 The long arm, or perhaps one might better say the long purse, of diplomacy at last effected the release of the prisoners. **1910** *Chambers's Jrnl.* Sept. 603/2 There are 'long shillings' to be earned at the docks, but no easy ones; and the work is not only hard but dangerous. **1955** J. I. M. STEWART *Guardians* I. ix. 97 Lady Elizabeth's generalisation that here —in point of the long purse—was a particular in which Quail himself must lead any field.

c. ***long suit***, *fig.* one's strong point.

1895 W. C. GORE in *Inlander* Dec. 114 *Long suit*, something one is familiar with or expert in. **1903** A. ADAMS *Log of Cowboy* xiv. 218 Young Pete..assured our foreman that the building of bridges was his long suit. **1916** E. V. LUCAS *Vermilion Box* 26 Organizing has always been your long suit. **1923** U. L. SILBERRAD *Lett. J. Armiter* iv. 82 Charity's evidently your long suit. **1934** M. V. HUGHES *London Child of Seventies* vi. 72 'Can you do simple long division?' 'Oh, yes, Dym,' said I hopefully, for that was my long suit. **1959** N. COWARD *Look after Lulu!* II. 68 Oh Lord! That's a teaser —arithmetic's never been my long suit.

d. ***long chance***, one involving considerable uncertainty or risk.

1907 S. E. WHITE *Arizona Nights* I. xiii. 191 He's plumb scared at the prospect of suffering anything, and would rather die right off than take long chances. *Ibid.* II. iv. 262 He's one of those long-chance fellows. **1938** H. NICOLSON *Let.* 17 Feb. (1966) 322, I do not think there is going to be a war yet. Not by a long chance. **1971** D. EDEN *Afternoon Walk* ix. 125 It would be a long chance that the one I just saw was the same one.

6. a. Of a period of time, of a process, state, or action, viewed as extending over a period of time: Having a great extent in duration. ***long account***: see ACCOUNT *sb.* 8 b.

c **900** tr. *Bæda's Hist.* III. ix. (Schipper) 231 He..wæs mid langre adle laman leȝeres swiðe ȝehefiȝad. *c* **1330** *Arth. & Merl.* 6779 (Kölbing) In þis sorweful time & lange. *c* **1330** *Spec. Gy Warw.* 744 To sen..þe longe lyff, þat is so god. **1377** LANGL. *P. Pl.* B. Prol. 195 For better is a litel losse þan a longe sorwe. *c* **1475** *Rauf Coilȝear* 828 Thay maid ane lang battail, Ane hour of the day. **1500–20** DUNBAR *Poems* lxv. 21 Than in frustrar is [all] ȝour lang leirning. **1530** PALSGR. 612/2 To lyve in langour is no lyfe, but a longe dyeng. *a* **1548** HALL *Chron., Edw. IV* 229 Thus laie the englishmen in the feldes when the cold nightes began to waxe long. **1576** FLEMING *Panopl. Epist.* 348 To blesse you with the long possession of your kingdome. **1619** R. WALLER in *Lismore Papers* (1887) Ser. II. II. 228, I feare lest he be no longe lyffes man. **1667** MILTON *P.L.* IV. 535 Enjoy, till I return, Short pleasures, for long woes are to succeed. **1697** DRYDEN *Virg. Georg.* IV. 711 His long Toils were forfeit for a Look. **1727–41** CHAMBERS *Cycl.* s.v. *Bishop*, It is a long time that bishops have been distinguished from mere priests or presbyters. **1735** POPE *Prol. Sat.* 132 To help me thro' this long disease, my Life. **1759** JOHNSON *Idler* No. 45 ¶2 The general lampooner of mankind may find long exercise for his zeal. **1774** GOLDSM. *Nat. Hist.* (1776) V. 331 There was a long and earnest contention between them. **1809** SHERIDAN in *Sheridaniana* (1826) 217 Let us make a long pull, a strong pull, and a pull altogether. **1820** SCOTT *Monast.* xxxiii, The thought, that I have sent this man to a long account, unhouseled and unshrived. **1900** J. G. FRAZER *Pausanias*, etc. 52 Her brief noon of glory, and her long twilight of decrepitude and decay.

b. ***long of life***: = 'of long life'. Now *rare*.

c **1000** *Sax. Leechd.* III. 156 Gif mann bið akenned on anre nihte ealdne monan, se bið lang lifes. **1591** SPARRY tr. *Cattan's Geomancie* 97 They [children] shall be of good nature and complexion, and not long of life. **1812** MAD. D'ARBLAY *Let.* 29 May in *Diary* (1846) VI. 349 Literature, as well as astronomy, is long of life. **1821** BYRON *Foscari* IV. i. 61 Discarded princes Are seldom long of life.

¶**c.** For the use = 'occupying a long time,' 'delaying long,' see LONG *adv.* 2.

7. a. *long time, while*, etc. are often used advb. (now, exc. *poet.* and in Jamaican English (see also quot. 1961), always preceded by *a*) with the sense 'during a long time' = LONG *adv.* 1. (*Longtime, longwhile* have *occas.* been written without division.) ***this long time*** or ***while***: for a long time down to the present.

c **900** tr. *Bæda's Hist.* I. xxv. (Schipper) 54 þæt we forlætan þa wisan þe we langre tide..heoldon. *a* **1225** *Leg. Kath.* 437 He heold on to herien his heaðene maumez..long time of þe dei. *c* **1330** *Spec. Gy Warw.* 62 þe world þurw his foule gile Haþ me lad to longe while. *c* **1375** *Sc. Leg. Saints* xli. (*Agnes*) 368 A prest..paulyne..had bene chaste langtyme. *c* **1425** LYDG. *Assembly of Gods* 1417 Syth they so long tyme haue made me so madde. *c* **1470** HENRYSON *Tale of Dog* 68 They ..held ane lang quhile disputatioun. **1489** CAXTON *Blanchardyn* xxxix. 146 We..haue ben a longe espace wyth hym. **1513** MORE in Grafton *Chron.* (1568) II. 759 They.. thinke that he long time in king Edwardes life forethought to be king. **1557** GRIMALD in *Tottel's Misc.* (Arb.) 101 For if, long time, one put this yron in vre. **1640** tr. *Verdere's Rom. of Rom.* I. xxxvi. 157 Certain Magicians, whom I have long time known. **1694** L. ECHARD *Plautus's Comedies* 196, I knew th' owner o' that portmantle this long time. **1738** SWIFT *Pol. Convers.* i. 7 How has your Lordship done this long time? *a* **1849** J. C. MANGAN *Poems* (1859) 456 Dream and waking life..blended Longtime in the cavern of my soul. **1883** R. W. DIXON *Mano* I. viii. 22 So that long time he fed upon false joy. **1942** L. BENNETT *Jamaica Dial. Verses* 21 Me did tink me always hear sey Missis Queen bannish slavery lang time. **1961** F. G. CASSIDY *Jamaica Talk* vi. 107 *Long time* means long ago ('Him gone long time'). **1971** *Jamaican Weekly Gleaner* 3 Nov. 5/1 Tams are also in (well, we did have that long time).

b. Similarly with preceding prep., †*by, for*, †*in, of*. (*arch.* or *dial.*) (Now always with *a*.)

1386 *Rolls of Parlt.* III. 225/1 Many wronges..ydo to hem by longe tyme here before passed. *c* **1400** [see OF *prep.* 53]. **1440** J. SHIRLEY *Dethe K. James* (1818) 17 The Kyng, heryng of long tyme no..stirryng of the traitours,..demyd that they had all begone. *a* **1548** HALL *Chron.*, *Hen. V* 80 It is commonly sayd, that..in long tyme al thinges continue not in one estate. **1579–80** NORTH *Plutarch, Theseus* (1595) 19 Those who had hated him of a long time, had..a disdain & contempt to fear him any more. **1589** PUTTENHAM *Eng. Poesie* III. xxiv. (Arb.) 285 He had not sene him wait of long time. **1629** MAXWELL tr. *Herodian* (1635) 386 This Capellianus and Gordian had not beene friends of a long time. **1753** RICHARDSON *Grandison* (1781) V. v. 34, I have not been at church of a long time. **1833** [see OF *prep.* 53]. *Mod.* I have not seen him for a long while.

c. Colloq. phr. (orig. *U.S.*) ***long time no see***, a joc. imitation of broken English, used as a greeting after prolonged separation.

1900 W. F. DRANNAN *31 Yrs. on Plains* (1901) xxxvii. 515 When we rode up to him [*sc.* an American Indian] he said: 'Good mornin. Long time no see you.' **1939** R. CHANDLER in *Sat. Even. Post* 14 Oct. 72/4 Hi, Tony. Long time no see. **1940** [see HIYA *int.*]. **1959** D. BEATY *Cone of Silence* viii. 105 'Hello, Clive.' 'Long time no see.' **1959** C. MACINNES *Absolute Beginners* 68 Hail, squire... Long time no see. **1971** D. E. WESTLAKE *I gave at the Office* (1972) 164 'Hello, Arnold,' I said... 'Long time no see.'

8. a. Having (more or less, or a specified) extension serially or temporally. (See also LENGER, LENGEST.)

a **1300** *Cursor M.* 2173 Thare his sun liued langar lijf. *c* **1375** *Sc. Leg. Saints* iv. (*Jacobus*) 344 þai þe croice before þam set, and he bristit but langar lat. *c* **1420** *Anturs of Arth.* 314, I hafe na langare tyme mo tales to telle. **1590** SHAKS. *Mids. N.* v. i. 61 A play there is, my Lord, some ten words long. **1710** W. BISHOP in *Ballard MSS.* XXXI. 57 He read a speech an Hour & half long. **1712** STEELE *Spect.* No. 498 ¶2 Of how long standing this honour has been, I know not. **1774** J. ANDREWS *Let.* 11 Aug. (1866) 340, I shall never get the idea out of my mind the longest day I have to live. **1824** SCOTT *Redgauntlet* ch. iv, I will take such measures for silencing you as you shall remember the longest day you have to live. **1836** A. H. CLOUGH (*title*) The longest day. A poem written at Rugby School. **1838** LYTTON *Alice* iii, The lesson must be longer than usual to day. **1868** LOCKYER *Elem. Astron.* iii. §18 (1879) 100 The longest time an eclipse of the sun can be total at any place is seven minutes. **1886** SWINBURNE *Stud. Prose & Poetry* (1894) 164 The two longest of the dramatic poems..bear upon them..the sign of heroic meditation. **1911** H. S. HARRISON *Queed* xxv. 321 You'd be a marked man to the longest day you lived. **1962** *Times* 27 Sept. 16/4 Mr. Darryl Zanuck's three-hour film, *The Longest Day*,..attempts to recapture some of the immensity of the D-Day operations.

†**b.** (*all*) ***the long day, night***, etc. = 'all the day, etc. long' (see LONG *adv.* 6). Cf. LIVELONG *a.*

1297 R. GLOUC. (Rolls) 10491 þe king..hangede men gultles vor wraþþe al longe day. *c* **1375** *Cursor M.* 12624 (Fairf.) þi fader & I as many way soȝt þe a-boute þis lange day. *c* **1385** CHAUCER *L.G.W.* Prol. 50 Walking in the mede ..The longe day, thus walking in the grene. **1540–54** CROKE 13 *Ps.* (Percy Soc.) 13 To trap me, yf they coulde, They studied wiles all the longe daye. **1559** W. CUNINGHAM *Cosmogr. Glasse* 36 All sterres with in this circle included, do nether rise, nor yet set, but turne round about the pole, all the longe nyght.

¶**c.** With mixed construction: see OF 39 b.

1592 NASHE *P. Penilesse* 24 b, And hold you content, this Summer an vnder-meale of an afternoone long doth not amisse to exercise the eies withall. **1592** LYLY *Midas* III. iii, Let me heare anie woman tell a tale of x lines long without it tend to loue. **1782** MISS BURNEY *Cecilia* VI. v, A lecture of two hours long.

9. a. With implication of excessive duration: Continuing too long; lengthy, prolix, tedious; †also in phr. *it*, etc. ***were*** (***too***) ***long to***, etc. Hence occas. of a speaker or writer.

c **1175** *Lamb. Hom.* 9 Oðre godere werke þe nu were long eou to telle. *a* **1300–40** *Cursor M.* 950 (Gött.) In till þe wreched world to gang, þar þu sal thinck þi lijf ful lang. *c* **1450** HOLLAND *Howlat* 34 All thar names to nevyn..It war prolixt and lang, and lenthing of space. **1500–20** DUNBAR *Poems* xl. 5 This lang Lentern makis me lene. **1570** *Satir. Poems Reform.* x. 71 It war lang to discerne The godly giftis that this our Sone did lerne. **1573** L. LLOYD *Marrow of Hist.* (1653) 279 What should I be long in this? *a* **1586** SIDNEY *Arcadia* I. (1590) 17 b, But I am euer too long vppon him, when hee crosseth the waie of my speache. **1604** E. G[RIMSTONE] *D'Acosta's Hist. Indies* IV. xxxix. 315 It were long to report the..pleasant sportes they make. **1621** in *Crt. & Times Jas. I* (1849) II. 277 Though he were somewhat long in the explanation of these particulars, yet he had great attention. **1640** tr. *Verdere's Rom. of Rom.* III. iv. 13 He.. thought it long till hee was in the Citie, that he might be conducted to his Lady. **1661** FELTHAM *Lusoria* xli. in *Resolves* (1709) 604 A sheet of Bacon's catch'd at more, we know, Than all sad Fox, long Holinshead or Stow. **1697** DRYDEN *Virg. Georg.* I. 256, I cou'd be long in Precepts. **1704** POPE *Disc. Past. Poetry* Wks. (Globe) 11 He is apt to be too long in his descriptions. **1875** M. ARNOLD *Isa.* xl–lxvi. 31, I have been too long; but the present attempt is new, and needed explanation. **1876** TREVELYAN *Life Macaulay* I. vi. 421 He beguiled the long long languid leisure of the Calcutta afternoon.

b. Chiefly *Sc.* ***to think long***: to grow weary or impatient. Const. *for, to* (do something); also, *till* (something happens).

[*c* **1200** *Trin. Coll. Hom.* 183 Gief þe licame beð euel loð is heo þe sowle and hire þuncheð lang þat hie on him bi-lueð.] *c* **1470** HENRY *Wallace* IX. 1275 To folow him thai twa thocht neuyr lang. **1508** DUNBAR *Poems* v. 27 Sche..thoght ryght lang To se the ailhous beside, in till an euill hour. *c* **1530** LD. BERNERS *Arth. Lyt. Bryt.* 445, I shal think tyll that season be come as long or longer than ye shal do. **1586** EARL LEICESTER in *L. Corr.* (Camden) 362, I feare it be thought longe till some well-instructed come here. **1592** SHAKS. *Rom. & Jul.* IV. v. 41 Haue I thought long to see this mornings face, And doth it giue me such a sight as this? **1596** DALRYMPLE tr. *Leslie's Hist. Scot.* IX. 192 Al in Scotland thocht lang for the Gouernour. **1599** GREENE *Alphonsus* IV. Wks. (Rtldg.) 240/1 And thinking long till that we be in fight. **1628** EARL MANCHESTER in *Buccleuch MSS.* (Hist. MSS. Comm.) I. 267 The Lady mother thinks long to see them settled at their own house. *a* **1758** RAMSAY *Ep. Hamilton* ii, When kedgy carles think nae lang, When stoups and trunchers gingle. **1788** CLARA REEVE *Exiles* I. 195 We think long till we see you.

c. ***long on***: possessing a copious quantity of, having plenty of. Cf. *short on*, also *short of* (SHORT *a.* 18 e). orig. *U.S. slang*.

1913 KIPLING *Divers. Creatures* (1917) 286 He was long on Kings. And Continental crises. **1929** W. R. BURNETT *Little Caesar* IV. vi. 147 You're long on regard yourself, ain't you Rico? **1938** S. CHASE *Tyranny of Words* vii. 78 Governor Lehmann, deficient in logic but long on human understanding, commuted the sentence. **1967** 'H. HOWARD' *Routine Investigation* ix. 97 The battered Dodge may not have been long on looks, but it started first time. **1969** *Guardian* 22 Jan. 1/7 The new team is admittedly long on business management and short on statesmanship. **1973** *Good Food Guide* 429 Two inspectors describe it [*sc.* a restaurant] as long on gemütlichkeit and short on good cooking.

10. a. Qualifying a sb. denoting a period of time, a number, or quantity, to indicate an extent greater than that expressed by the sb.; also, in subjective sense, to indicate that the time is felt by the speaker to be excessive or unusual in duration. (Cf. 1 d.) ***long years***: used *rhetorically* for 'many years'. ***at*** (***the***) ***long last***: see LAST *a.* 10 b. ***long dozen, hundred, ton***: see the sbs.

1592 STOW *Ann.* (an. 1563) 1111 Continuing in fight aboue a long hower. **1676** DRYDEN *Aureng-z.* I. i. Wks. 1883 V. 207 And two long hours in close debate were spent. **1681** W. ROBERTSON *Phraseol. Gen.* 839/2 'Tis a long year since I saw you here. **1801** SCOTT *Frederick & Alice*, Seven long days, and seven long nights, Wild he wander'd. **1808** BYRON *When we two parted*, If I should meet thee After long years, How should I greet thee? **1824** —— *Juan* XVI. lxxxi, And rise at nine in lieu of long eleven. **1871** CARLYLE in *Mrs. Carlyle's Lett.* III. 175 For long years I had ceased writing in my note-books. **1883** R. W. DIXON *Mano* I. xiv. 46 Lips travelled over cheek and mouth by turn For a long hour.

b. Of the pulse: Making long beats, slow.

1898 *Allbutt's Syst. Med.* V. 929 In strict stenosis..we ordinarily have a long slow pulse.

11. a. That has continued or will continue in action, operation, or obligation for a long period. Frequently applied to feelings, dispositions, etc., e.g. enmity, friendship; hence also, to persons in whom these are exhibited. ***long memory***: one that retains the recollection of events for a long period.

c **1220** *Bestiary* 275 Ðe mire muneð vs mete to tilen, Long liuenoðe, ðis little ðe we on ðis werld wunen. **1535** COVERDALE *Jer.* xv. 15 Receaue not my cause in thy longe wrath. *a* **1548** HALL *Chron.*, *Hen. IV* 31 Havyng also approved experience that the Duke of Burgoine wolde kepe no longer promise then he him selfe listed. **1573** L. LLOYD *Marrow of Hist.* (1653) 269 Their long and great enemy, Philip King of Macedonia. **1613** SHAKS. *Hen. VIII*, III. ii. 351 A long farewell to all my Greatnesse. **1626** BACON *Sylva* §97 Juices of Stock-gilly-flowers,..applyed to the Wrests, ..have cured long Agues. **1679** EVELYN *Diary* (1827) III. 10 This most..pious Lady, my long acquaintance. **1697** DRYDEN *Æneid* IX. 102 Those Woods, that Holy Grove, my long delight. **1704** MARLBOROUGH *Lett. & Disp.* (1845) I. 238 It has been a long practice to send letters, under his covers, from unknown hands. *a* **1715** BURNET *Own Time* (1724) I. 380 He was a long, and very kind patron to me. **1726** SWIFT *Gulliver* I. viii, I had a long lease of the Black Bull in Fetter-Lane. **1733** BUDGELL *Bee* I. 37 Mr. John Mills, my long Acquaintance, living now in Drury-Lane. **1759** JOHNSON *Rasselas* xxix, Long customs are not easily broken. **1819** *Metropolis* (ed. 2) II. 228 The ridicule such conduct brought upon him among the thinking part of his long acquaintance. **1856** MRS. BROWNING *Aur. Leigh* I. 2 If her kiss Had left a longer weight upon my lips. **18..** LADY DUFFERIN *Lament Irish Emigrant* 49, I'm biddin' you a long farewell, My Mary. **1869** FREEMAN *Norm. Conq.* (1876) III. xiii. 314 The Celtic race has a long memory. **1882** T. MOZLEY *Remin. Oriel Coll.* I. 13 His recollections.. contained some novelties, not to say surprises, to his longest friends.

b. (*colloq.* or *proverbial.*) ***a long word***: one that indicates a long time.

1861 *Cornh. Mag.* Dec. 685 Ye're the biggest blag-guard my eyes have seen since I've been in London, and that's saying a long word. **1883** *Standard* 28 July 5/1 'Never' is a long word.

¶**c.** ? Used for: Long-suffering. *Obs. rare*$^{-1}$.

1483 CAXTON *Gold. Leg.* 320/1 He was a meruellous Rethour by eloquence, a susteynour and a berar up of the church by doctryne, shorte to hymself by humylyte and longe to other by charyte.

12. a. Of a point of time: Distant, remote. Now only in ***long date***, and in the legal phrase ***a long day***.

1437 *Rolls of Parlt.* IV. 509/1 Yai byen notable substance of gode to appress, and to long dayes. *c* **1449** PECOCK *Repr.* I. iv. 18 Bifore that eny positijf lawe of God..was ȝouen to the Iewis fro the long time of Adamys coming out of Paradijs into the tyme..of Abraham. *c* **1450** HOLLAND *Howlat* 425 Thar lordschipe of sa lang dait. **1596** SPENSER *Prothalamion* 144 Here fits not well Olde woes, but ioyes, to tell Against the bridale daye, which is not long. **1614** SELDEN *Titles Hon.* 261 That its deriud from *Βαρύς*, I must take long day to beleeu. **1632** MASSINGER *City Madam* I. iii, You must give me longer day. **1709** MRS. MANLEY *Secret Mem.* (1736) II. 92 Is his Punishment deferr'd to a long Hereafter? **1748** RICHARDSON *Clarissa* (1811) II. 126 A long day, I doubt, will not be permitted me. **1776** *Let.* in *Gentl. Mag.* (1792) 14/1 He has paid me with a bond..due in October 1777, which is a long date. **1787** JEFFERSON *Writ.* (1859) II. 333 To obtain on the new loans a much longer day for the reimbursement of the principal. **1846** *Daily News* 21 Jan. 4/6 Bills on Amsterdam at long, or 3 months' date, found no takers.

b. Of bills, promissory notes, etc.: Of long date, having a long time to run.

1861 GOSCHEN *For. Exch.* 87 Rates given for long paper, as compared with those for bills on demand.

13. a. *Phonetics* and *Prosody*. Applied to a vowel (in mod. use also to a consonant) when its utterance has the greater of the two measures of duration that are recognized in the ordinary classification of speech-sounds. Also, in *Prosody*, of a syllable: Belonging to that one of the two classes which is supposed to be distinguished from the other by occupying a longer time in utterance. (Opposed to *short*.) ***long mark***: the mark (¯) placed over a vowel letter to indicate long quantity.

In Greek and Latin metre, a syllable is reckoned long (1) when it contains a long vowel or a diphthong, and (2) when its vowel is followed by more than one consonant (to the latter rule there are certain exceptions). A short syllable is conventionally supposed to occupy one time-unit (*mora*) in utterance, and a long syllable two. The distinction between the two classes of syllables, with criteria nearly identical with those of Gr. and Latin, is recognized in the prosody of many other peoples; in Skr. the equivalents of 'long' and 'short' are used of vowels only, syllables being classed as 'heavy' and 'light'.

Various inaccurate uses of the terms *long* and *short* were formerly almost universal in Eng., and are still commom. (1) The vowel of a 'long' syllable, if 'naturally' short, was said to be 'long by position'. (2) By a confusion between the principles of quantitative and those of accentual verse, the stressed syllables, on the periodical recurrence of which the rhythm of English verse depends, were said to be 'long', and the unstressed syllables 'short'. (3) In ordinary language 'the long *a, e, i, o*, or *u*' denotes that sound of the letter which is used as its alphabetical name, while 'the short *a, e, i, o*, or *u*' denotes the sound which the letter most commonly has in a stressed short syllable (in the notation used in this Dictionary, respectively (æ), (ɛ), (ɪ), (ɒ), (ʌ)).

c **1000** ÆLFRIC *Gram.* iv. (Z.) 37 On langne *o* ȝeendiað grecisce naman feminini generis. **1412–20** LYDG. *Chron. Troy* ii. 184, I took none hede noþer of short ne long. **1530** PALSGR. Introd. 21 A vowell shalbe..longe or short in his pronunciation. **1575** GASCOIGNE *Eng. Verse* (Arb.) 33 The graue accent..maketh that sillable long wherevpon it is placed. **1582** STANYHURST *Æneis* (Arb.) 11 Thee first of *briefly* wyth vs must bee long. *Ibid.* 12 Although yt [*sc.* the conjunction *and*] bee long by position. **1585** JAS. I *Ess. Poesie* (Arb.) 55, I haue markit the lang fute with this mark, -. **1668** WILKINS *Real Char.* III. xi. 364 Suppose a long Vowel to be divided into two parts; as Bo-ote. **1807** ROBINSON *Archæol. Græca* v. xxiii. 535 In the Greek language every syllable was short or long. **1869** A. J. ELLIS *E.E. Pronunc.* I. 13 The use ..of the long mark (¯) for the lengthening of vowels generally short.

b. *Mus.* Of a note: Occupying a more than average time, or a specified time, in being sounded. (Cf. 6 and 8.)

1818 T. BUSBY *Grammar Mus.* 69 If a Minim is only half as long as a Semibreve, and a Crotchet but half the length of a Minim, a Crotchet is only one quarter as long as a Semibreve.

14. *Comm.* Said of the market (esp. in the cotton trade) when consumers have provided against an anticipated scarcity by large contracts in advance. See quot. 1859. Phrase, *to go* (*heavily*) *long*.

1859 Bartlett *Dict. Amer.*, *Long and short*. Broker's terms. 'Long' means when a man has bought stock on time, which he can call for at any day he chooses. He is also said to be 'long' when he holds a good deal. *Mod. Newspaper.* The spinners had gone heavily long, and consequently did not need to buy except in very small quantities. It was found that selling was impossible except at constantly declining prices; that the market was heavily long; and that there was no short interest of any moment.

III. In Combination.

15. In concord with sbs., forming combinations used attributively or quasi-adj., as ***long-berry***, ***-exposure***, ***-focus***, ***-gown***, ***-journey***, ***-period***, ***-pod***, ***-quantity***, ***-range***, ***-sentence***, ***-span***, ***-stay***; also **long-day**, (*a*) having a long working-day; (*b*) of plants, needing a long period of light each day before flowering.

1886 *Daily News* 16 Sept. 2/5 Coffee.—140 packages Mocha, *longberry, 100*s.* **1891** *Ibid.* 10 Feb. 2/8 [Wheats] To-day 39*s.* 6*d.* was required for longberry. **1892** *Labour Commission* Gloss., **Long-day men.* **1920** Garner & Allard in *Jrnl. Agric. Res.* XVIII. 559 It will be convenient to use the expressions 'long day' as meaning exposure to light for more than 12 hours and 'short day' as referring to an exposure of 12 hours or less. *Ibid.* 578 Hibiscus is a striking example of a long-day plant. **1947** *Sci. News* IV. 129 By and large, short day plants flower if they receive 8–9 hours of light a day, and long day plants flower if they receive 14–16 hours of light a day. **1966** G. E. Evans *Pattern under Plough* xiv. 146 Practical observations on a long-day plant, the lettuce. **1972** *Nature* 21 Apr. 407/1 It would be interesting to know whether other long day and short day plants exhibiting a photoperiodic response..behave in the same way as *Sinapis*. **1975** *Listener* 6 Mar. 319/1 The BBC requires Fitters (Shift-working)... The rate of pay is £62.42 p.w. for long-day shift working. **1902** *Chambers's Jrnl.* Nov. 706/2 A *long-exposure survey of the whole heavens with one of the most modern photographic telescopes would indicate, I am convinced, no fewer than five hundred million stars. **1890** *Anthony's Photogr. Bull.* III. 327 Another use of *long focus lenses is the taking of street groups from a distance. **1677** Sedley *Antony & Cl.* iv. i, Dull *long-gown statesmen. **1880** Sir E. Reed *Japan* II. 310 *Long-journey travellers. **1898** *Engineering Mag.* XVI. 80 One of the Portsmouth, or other long-journey, trains. **1903** A. M. Clerke *Probl. Astrophysics* 348 The typical *long-period variable is Mira Ceti. **1923** P. B. Ballard *New Examiner* 107 Long-period testing. **1968** R. A. Lyttleton *Mysteries Solar Syst.* iv. 109 The advent of the vast majority of comets, the so-called long-period comets, cannot be predicted. **1846** J. Baxter *Libr. Pract. Agric.* (ed. 4) I. 89 *Long-pod [Bean]—The most abundant bearer. **1872** *Young Gentleman's Mag.* 651/2 A *long-quantity monosyllable is introduced. **1854** *Long-range [see asphyxiant *a.* and *sb.*]. **1873** W. Cory *Lett. & Jrnls.* (1897) 329 An American here shouts with a long-range voice. **1902** *Edin. Rev.* Apr. 291 Into these wars long-range infantry fire seldom entered. **1932** J. Buchan *Gap in Curtain* i. 64, I..set myself..to a long-range forecast—what would be likely to happen on June 10th a year ahead. **1958** *New Statesman* 18 Jan. 59/1 Never mind your long-range missiles, Johnson said in effect. **1966** T. Pynchon *Crying of Lot 49* iii. 67 Incest or no, the marriage must be; it is vital to his long-range political plans. **1966** *Punch* 3 Aug. 186/1 According to the long-range forecast, there's a wettish month ahead. **1971** C. Bonington *Annapurna South Face* iii. 33 The Nepalese authorities..did not normally allow expeditions to use long-range radios in Nepal. **1889** 'Rolf Boldrewood' *Robbery under Arms* xxiii, We were '*long sentence men'. **1890** W. J. Gordon *Foundry* 41 Every *long-span bridge in the world. **1952** C. P. Blacker *Eugenics* xi. 316 *Long- and short-stay residential nurseries. **1970** *Guardian* 9 July 3/2 In France today..two thirds of the beds in mental hospitals are occupied permanently by long-stay patients. **1972** *Ibid.* 16 Feb. 7/3 Allegations of ill-treatment are confined to four of the long-stay wards. **1974** *Advocate-News* (Barbados) 19 Feb. 1/2 Meanwhile, during the year under review, a total of 189,000 'long-stay' visitors came to Barbados.

16. Parasynthetic derivatives in -ed[2], unlimited in number, as ***long-armed***, ***-backed***, ***-barrelled***, ***-bearded***, ***-billed***, ***-descended***, ***-grained*** (also ***-grain***), ***-lashed***, ***-leafed***, ***-leaved***, ***-rooted***, ***-skirted***, ***-sleeved***, ***-spooned***, ***-trousered***.

1774 Goldsm. *Nat. Hist.* IV. 206 The Gibbon, so called by Buffon, or the *Long Armed Ape. **1888** Barrie *Auld Licht Idylls* xii. (1902) 87/1 A lank long-armed man. **1611** Cotgr. s.v. *Eschine*, *Longue eschine*,..*long-backt, or ill shaped, loobie. **1787** 'G. Gambado' *Acad. Horsemen* (1809) 32 A long back'd horse, who throws his saddle well forward. **1837** Landor *Pentameron, 5th Day's Interview* Wks. 1853 II. 348/1 Sitting bolt-upright in that long-backed arm-chair. **1902** *Daily Chron.* 20 Mar. 3/1 The rests for the *long-barrelled muskets disappeared just at the beginning of the war. **1969** F. Wilkinson *Flintlock Pistols* 26 Pair of long-barrelled 17th century pistols of very fine quality. **1778** Da Costa *Brit. Conch.* 133 *Long-beaked Whelkes. **1573** L. Lloyd *Marrow of Hist.* (1653) 165 Those that were long haired or *long bearded. **1679** Dryden & Lee *Œdipus* ii. 18 Long-bearded Comets. *c* **1806** Mrs. Sherwood in *Life* xxi. (1847) 356 The schoolmaster..was generally a long-bearded, dry old man. **1590** Sir. J. Smyth *Disc. Weapons* 3 Verie well armed with some kind of head-peece, a collar, a deformed high and *long bellied breast. **1892** E. Reeves *Homeward Bound* 212 Dirty, dark, *long-berried wheat, 1*d.* per pound. **1594** Barnfield *Affect. Sheph.* ii. ix. 13 (Arber), Wilt thou set springes..To catch the *long-billd Woodcocke? **1822** J. Fowler *Jrnl.* (1898) 148 We thear for the first time seen the long Billed Bird;..the bill about one foot in length. **1831** A. Wilson & Bonaparte *Amer. Ornith.* III. 60 The long-billed curlew;..the bill is eight inches long. **1970** S. Trueman *Intimate Hist. New Brunswick* xi. 144 Some seafowl, like the..long-billed curlew, had become either extremely scarce, or extinct over the years. **1696** *Lond. Gaz.* No. 3163/4 W. L...low of stature, somewhat *long Bodied, and very short Legg'd. **1864** A. McKay *Hist. Kilmarnock* (1880) 299 [During a flood in a through-town river] a long-bodied cart drifted towards him. **1646–8** G. Daniel *Poems* Wks. 1878 I. 213 My *long-brail'd Pineons, (clumsye and vnapt) I cannot Spread. **1884** Bower & Scott *De Bary's Phaner. & Ferns* 388 The *long-celled initial strands of the vascular bundles. **1742** Young *Nt. Th.* ix. 1454 Ev'ry link Of that *long-chain'd succession is so frail. **1777** Pennant *Zool.* IV. 5 *Cancer*. Crab...*Cassivelaunus*. *Long-clawed. **1812** Shelley in Lady Shelley *Mem.* (1859) 44, I am one of those formidable and long-clawed animals called a man. **1813** Vancouver *Agric. Devon* 352 The washed wool of all the *Longcoated sheep, is sold from 14*d.* to 15*d.* per pound. **1861** W. F. Collier *Hist. Eng. Lit.* 123 Hordes of long-coated peasants gathered round Kilcolman. **1657** W. Coles *Adam in Eden* cxvii, After which come large and *long-crested, black-shining seed. **1847** Emerson *Poems* 53 He would come in the very hour..And tell its *long-descended race. **1866** Mrs. Gaskell *Wives & Daughters* I. xxiii. 260 Osborne was to do great things.. marry a long-descended heiress. **1892** 'Mark Twain' *Amer. Claimant* xix. 180 Every man is made up of hereditaries, long descended atoms and particles of his ancestors. **1593** Shaks. *Lucr.* cclviii, Let my unsounded self, supposed a fool, Now set thy *long-experienced wit to school. *a* **1700** Dryden *Ovid's Met.* x. *Cinyras & Myrrha* 192 My long-experienc'd Age shall be your Guide. **1591** Percivall *Sp. Dict.*, *Cariluengo*, *long faced. **1883** W. Haslam *Yet Not I* 222 He was looking well and happy, not at all long-faced and lanky. **1879** R. H. Elliot *Written on their Foreheads* I. 14 How is it..that the Scotch have got a greater amount of *long-facedness than the people of the east coast of England. **1678** *Lond. Gaz.* No. 1272/4 He is..purblind, between *long and round favoured. **1843** James *Forest Days* iv, The pen where the fat, *long-fleeced ram was confined. **1861** Miss Pratt *Flower. Pl.* V. 184 Order. *Hydrocharideæ* ..(*Long-flowered Anacharis). **1552** Huloet, *Longe foted, *compernis*. **1652** Gaule *Magastrom.* 186 The long footed are fraudulent and short footed sudden. **1832** Miss Mitford *Village* Ser. v. 60 A very *long-fronted, very regular, very ugly brick house. **1621** Wither *Motto* A 8 b, I haue no neede of these *long-gowned warriors. **1831** J. M. Peck *Guide for Emigrants* ii. 156 The *long grained Virginia corn is chiefly produced. **1970** 'D. Halliday' *Dolly & Cookie Bird* iii. 33 You all meet over the trolleys with your long-grain rice sacks at the mainline Cash & Carry. **1974** *Times* 10 Jan. 10/1 With long grain rice, when correctly cooked, the grains remain separate. **1800** tr. *Lagrange's Chem.* II. 37 Remove the oxide with a *long-handled iron spoon. **1860** Tyndall *Glac.* i. xi. 70 Simond could reach this snow with his long-handled axe. **1687** *Lond. Gaz.* No. 2292/4 A Roan Gelding..*long heel'd before. **1864** Bowen *Logic* viii. 236 Since he [negro] has many other [attributes], such as being long-heeled, &c. **1777** Pennant *Zool.* IV. 3 *Cancer*. Crab...*Longicornis*. *Longhorned. **1846** McCulloch *Acc. Brit. Empire* (1854) I. 165 The Dishly breed of long-horned cattle. **1727** Bailey vol. II, **Long Jointed* [spoken of a Horse], is one whose Pastern is slender and pliant. **1856** J. G. Whittier *Panorama* 128 A pleased surprise Looked from her *long-lashed hazel eyes. **1913** C. Mackenzie *Sinister St.* I. ii. ii. 167 The long-lashed blue eyes and rose-leaf complexion. **1963** J. Fountain in B. James *Austral. Short Stories* 277 Her long-lashed eyes modestly lowered. **1819** E. Dana *Geogr. Sk. Western Country* 173 The *long leafed pine is a stately tree, from 60 to 80 feet, clear of limbs. *c* **1605** Drayton *Man in Moone* 199 *Long leau'd willow on whose bending spray, The pide kings-fisher..sat. **1778** G. White *Let.* 3 July in *Selborne* (1789) ii. xli. 235 *Drosera rotundifolia*, round-leaved sundew. [*Drosera*] *longifolia*, long-leaved ditto. **1785** H. Marshall *Arbustrum Americanum* 83 Long-leaved Mountain Magnolia or Cucumber Tree. **1832** D. J. Browne *Sylva Amer.* 228 This invaluable tree is..called Long-leaved Pine, Yellow Pine, Pitch Pine and Broom Pine. **1861** Miss Pratt *Flower. Pl.* V. 95 Long-leaved Sallow. **1942** W. de la Mare *Songs of Childhood* 86 The twilight rain shone at its gates, Where long-leaved grass in shadow grew. **1953** E. Sitwell *Gardeners & Astronomers* 3 The long-leaved planets in our garden-shed. **1964** W. L. Goodman *Hist. Woodworking Tools* 21 Inside the court there was a long-leaved olive tree. **1838** Dickens *O. Twist* xlii, One of those *long limbed..people, to whom it is difficult to assign any precise age. **1577** tr. *Bullinger's Decades* (1592) 381 They were called Nazarites, as who should saie, *long locked or shagge haired people. **1871** R. Ellis tr. *Catullus* xxxvii. 17 Peerless paragon of the tribe long-lock'd. **1877** W. Morris in Mackail *Life* (1899) I. 359 These unreasonable Irish still remember it all, so *long-memoried they are! **1681** Grew *Musæum* 125 The *long-mouth'd Wilk, *Murex Labris parallelis*. **1685** *Lond. Gaz.* No. 2036/8 A light dapple Gray Gelding,..*long pasternd,..and a little Mare-fac'd. **1688** *Lond. Gaz.* No. 2361/4 A strawberry Mare, with a shorn Mane,..*long quarter'd, and six years old. **1693** Dryden *Persius Sat.* (1697) 414 He who in his Line, can chine the *long-ribb'd Appennine. **1820** Scott *Abbot* viii. *motto*, The long-ribb'd aisles are burst and shrunk. **1622** Drayton *Poly-olb.* xxvii. 44 That *long-ridg'd Rocke, her fathers high renowne. **1683** *Lond. Gaz.* No. 1805/4 Long Visaged, and a long ridged Nose. **1752** Fielding *Amelia* Wks. 1775 XI. 65 Women and the clergy are upon the same footing. The *long-robed gentry are exempted from the laws of honour. **1894** Safer *Persian Pict.* 158 The streets thronged with long-robed men and shrouded women. **1871** Palgrave *Lyr. Poems* 117 And *long-roof'd abbey in the dell. **1579** T. Lupton *Thousand Notable Things* ii. 28 If the disease be so *long rooted. **1902** W. James *Varieties Relig. Experience* xi. 264 It costs, then, nothing..to renounce long-rooted privileges and possessions. **1960** *Farmer & Stockbreeder* 26 Jan. Suppl. 4/1 Long-rooted carrots only grow well in deep, sandy soil. **1877** J. D. Chambers *Divine Worship* 280 Plain *long-shafted Crosses without any figure. **1601** Holland *Pliny* I. 310 Marke what *long-shanked legs above ordinary she [Nature] hath giuen vnto them [gnats]. **1835–6** Todd *Cycl. Anat.* I. 653/1 The *long-shaped dorsal vessel or heart gives off arteries to both sides. **1898** H. S. Merriman *Roden's Corner* xvii. 176 A long-shaped lantern. **1821** M. Edgeworth *Let.* 19 Dec. (1971) 296 Very *long skirted coat which he holds up often by tucking one hand under inside the bottom of the waist behind. **1921** D. H. Lawrence *Tortoises* 13 A gentleman in a long-skirted coat. **1974** R. Harris *Double Snare* xv. 105 Students..accompanied by their sandalled, long-haired, long-skirted birds. **1902** *Speaker* 25 Jan. 480/1 The Iberian was a short, dark, *long-skulled man. **1591** Percivall *Sp. Dict.*, *Mangado*, *long sleeved. *a* **1658** Cleveland *Obsequies* 105 Wks. (1687) 218 Teazers of Doctrines, which in long sleev'd Prose Run down a Sermon all upon the Nose. **1897** R. M. Gilchrist *Peakland Faggot* 95 Vignettes akin to those one sees on the porcelain faces of old Derbyshire 'long-sleeved clocks'. **1903** G. F. Abbott *Tale Tour Macedonia* 221 A long-sleeved black jacket. **1964** O. Coburn tr. *Braun-Ronsdorf's Wheel of Fashion* 263/1 The basque bodice, high-necked, long-sleeved and ever more tight-fitting. **1816** Kirby & Sp. *Entomol.* (1843) I. 378 The beautiful weevils or *long-snouted beetles. **1876** J. Macgregor *Rob Roy on Baltic* 286 A long, narrow, light racing-canoe, with a *long-spooned paddle. **1785** Martyn *Rousseau's Bot.* xxvii. (1794) 417 You may call it *long spurred, or Sweet Orchis. **1882** *Garden* 13 May 323/3 [The] Long-spurred Violet. **1791** Wolcot (P. Pindar) *Remonstrance* Wks. 1812 II. 455 Night's *long-staff'd Guardian to him steals. **1847** W. E. Steele *Field Bot.* 203 Barren spike sometimes 1; fertile *long-stalked. **1855** W. S. Dallas *Syst. Nat. Hist., Zool.* I. 314 The Long-stalked Crab (*Podophthalmus*). **1772** Jackson in *Phil. Trans.* LXIII. 6 *Long or short stapled isinglass. **1854** Hawthorne *Eng. Note-Bks.* (1883) I. 571 The long-stapled cotton. **1859** G. Meredith *R. Feverel* xxx, He strolled on beneath the *long-stemmed trees. **1898** R. Kipling in *Morn. Post* 9 Nov. 5/2 The *long-stocked port-anchor. **1863** Darwin in *Reader* 14 Feb., *Long-styled plants. **1636** C. Butler *Princ. Mus.* i. iii. §3. 53 A *long-timed Note. **1807** W. Irving *Salmag.* (1824) 313 The unseemly luxury of *long-toed shoes. **1964** *Seventeen* Jan. 46 Something very big in beach fashions—Petti's new *long-trousered Surfer! **1967** A. Wilson *No Laughing Matter* iii. 362 The long-trousered suit that he had worn this holidays. **1974** I. Murdoch *Sacred & Profane Love Machine* 104 A thin long-trousered boy. **1577** Dee *Relat. Spir.* i. (1659) 73 He is lean and *long-visaged. **1860** Dickens *Lett.* 2 Jan. (1880) II. 109 Long-visaged prophets. **1616** Surfl. & Markh. *Country Farme* 715 The *long-winged hawkes do properly belong vnto the lure. **1894** Le Conte in *Pop. Sci. Monthly* XLIV. 752 In long-winged birds..the ability to rise quickly..is sacrificed. **1805** Luccock *Nat. Wool* 184 *Long-wooled sheep. **1824** J. Symmons tr. *Æschylus' Agam.* 105 In woe deals the craft of the *long-worded lays.

17. Combinations with participles in which *long* is used as a complement, as ***long-docked***, ***-extended***, ***-grown***, ***-projected***, ***-protended***, ***-spun***, ***-thrown***; ***long-combing***, ***-descending***, ***-growing***, ***-hanging***, ***-streaming***, ***-succeeding***.

1846 McCulloch *Acc. Brit. Empire* (1854) I. 171 The native sheep of the Cotswold Hills..produce coarse *long-combing wool. **1693** J. Dryden in *D.'s Juvenal* xiv. (1697) 356 A *long-descending Healthful Progeny. **1838** Lytton *Leila* ii. iii, Long-descending robes of embroidered purple. **1688** *Lond. Gaz.* No. 2379/4 Lost.., a..Coach Gelding,.. with a *long dock'd Tail. **1718** Prior *Solomon* ii. 30 The pillars *long extended rows. **1890** W. A. Wallace *Only a Sister?* 41 A faint rumble..at *longer-growing intervals. **1757** Dyer *Fleece* ii. 446 'Tis the comber's lock, The soft, the snow-white, and the *long-grown flake. **1597** A. M. tr. *Guillemeau's Fr. Chirurg.* 25/1 The foresayed *longe hanginge pallate. **1720** Pope *Iliad* xviii. 251 With *long-projected Beams the Seas are bright. **1718** *Ibid.* xvi. 981 Euphorbus..Swift withdrew the *long-protended Wood. **1675** Cocker *Morals* 21 Which before time has run his *long-spun Race. **1761–2** Hume *Hist. Eng.* (1806) IV. lxii. 668 Long-spun allegories, distant allusions, and forced conceits. **1882** J. Walker *Jaunt to Auld Reekie*, etc. 38 He is blest wi' lang-spun tacks o' health and life. **1735** Somerville *Chase* i. 352 The panting Chace..Leaves a *long-streaming Trail behind. **1720** Pope *Iliad* xvii. 306 The *long-succeeding Numbers who can name? **1859** G. Meredith *R. Feverel* xx, Over the open, 'tis a race with the *long-thrown shadows.

18. a. Special combinations and collocations: **long-acting** *a. Pharm.*, having effects that last a long time; **long and short stitch**, in embroidery, a flat stitch used for shading; **long annuities**, a class of British Government annuities which expired in 1860; **long-arm**, (*a*) a long-barrelled gun, as a musket, rifle, etc.; (*b*) a device used as an extension of the arm, e.g. a pole fitted with a hook, shears, etc., for lifting objects to, cutting branches, etc., at a height beyond the ordinary reach of the arm; freq. *attrib.*; **long-axed** *a.*, having a long axis; **Long Bertha** = *Big Bertha* (s.v. Bertha[2]); **long blow** *Austral.* and *N.Z.* [blow *sb.*[1] 1 c], a stroke of the shears in sheep-shearing which cuts away the fleece from rump to neck; **long bond** *Comm.* (see quot. 1948); †**long-bones**, a nickname for a long-legged person; **long-bowls**, (*a*) the game of ninepins; (*b*) 'a game much used in Angus, in which heavy leaden bullets are thrown from the hand' (Jam.); hence ***long-bowling***; †**long-box**, the box formerly used by the hawkers of books; **long-bullets** = *long-bowls* (*b*); **long-butt** *Billiards*, a cue specially adapted to reach a ball lying beyond the range of the half-butt; **long card**, (*a*) (see quot. 1862); (*b*) a card of unusual length, used in conjuring tricks; (*c*) *Contract Bridge* (see quots.); **long-case clock** = *grandfather's clock* [grandfather 5], also ellipt. *long-case*; **long chain** *Chem.* [chain *sb.* 5 g], a relatively large number of atoms (usu. of carbon) linked together in a line; freq. *attrib.* (usu. hyphenated); **long chair** = chaise-longue; **long chalk** (see chalk *sb.* 6 b); **long cist** *Archæol.*, a type of megalithic tomb having a long and narrow chamber to which there is direct entry; **long clay** *colloq.* = churchwarden 3; **long clothes**, the garments of a baby in arms; also *fig.*; **long-coach** (see quot. 1807); †**long-cork** *slang*, claret, so called from the length of the corks used; **long-crop**, herbage long enough

to give an animal a good bite; **long cross,** (*a*) *Printing* (see quot. 1884); (*b*) *Numism.*, a cross of which the arms extend to the outer circle on a coin; †**long-cutler,** ? a maker of long knives; **long-dated** *a.*, †(*a*) that has existed from a remote date; (*b*) extending to a distant date in the future; chiefly of an acceptance, falling due at a distant date; **long deal,** in card-playing (see quot.); **long division** (see DIVISION 5 a); **long drawer,** a drawer which extends the full width of a chest, wardrobe, etc.; **long dress,** a floor- or ankle-length dress, usu. worn as evening dress; **long-drop,** a form of gallows in which a trap-door is withdrawn from under the feet of the person to be executed; **long ear,** a translation of the native name for a member of an extinct people which inhabited Easter Island and was distinguished by artificially lengthened ears; **long Eliza,** a 'blue and white' Chinese vase, ornamented with tall female figures; **long-ells,** a kind of coarse woollen; **long fallow** (see quots.); **long-fed** *a.* (see quot. 1969); †**long fifteens** *slang*, ? some class of lawyers; **long finger,** the middle finger; also *pl.* the three middle fingers; **long firm** (see FIRM *sb.* 2 d); **long-fly** *Baseball* (see quot.); **long Forties** *Naut.* (cf. FORTY *sb.* 4); **long-fours,** long candles, four of which went to the pound; †**Long Friday** = GOOD FRIDAY; †**long-gig,** a sort of top; **long glass,** (*a*) a full-length looking-glass; (*b*) a drinking-glass approximately three feet long for holding a yard of ale (cf. YARD *sb.*² 9 c); **long grain** = GRAIN *sb.* 15; **long grass,** used *gen.* of grass or grass-like growth, typical of certain areas in Africa, tall enough, for example, to conceal animals; **long green** *U.S. slang*, dollar-notes, money (cf. GREEN *sb.* 7 d); **long-harness** *Weaving* (see quot.); **long-haul** *attrib.* (see HAUL *sb.* 1 c); **long-home** (see HOME *sb.*¹ 4); **long-house,** †(*a*) a privy (*obs.*); (*b*) a house of unusual length, *spec.* the communal dwelling of the Iroquois and other American Indians; also, a long dwelling-house in other areas, esp. a large communal village house in certain parts of Malaysia and Indonesia; **long ink** *Printing* (see quots.); **long-jawed** *a.* (see quot.); **long john,** usu. in *pl.*, (*a*) a type of long, warm underwear; (*b*) a children's game; (*c*) (in *sing.*) a long coffee table; also *long John table*; (see also sense 18 c); **long jump** (see JUMP *sb.*¹ 1 b; esp. as one of the 'events' of an athletic contest); hence *long-jumper, long-jumping*; also (with hyphen) as vb.; **long-keeping** *a.*, able to be kept for a long time; **long lady** = *farthing-candle* (FARTHING *sb.* 5); **long-leave, -legger** (see quots.); **long legs** *W. Afr. colloq.* (see quot. 1971); **long-lick** *U.S. slang*, molasses (cf. *long-sugar*); **long-life** *a.*, remaining serviceable (quot. 1946 = remaining radioactive) for an unusually long time; †**long-little,** something very short or small; **long-lugged** *a. Sc.*, having long ears; *fig.* eager to listen to secrets or scandal; **long-lunged** *a.* = LONG-WINDED 2; †**long-man,** the middle finger; **Long March,** *spec.* the year-long retreat of the Chinese Communists across south-western China during the period of Nationalist government; also (not always with capital initials) in other contexts; **long measure,** (*a*) lineal measure, the measure of length; (*b*) a table of lineal measures; (*c*) = next; **long metre,** a hymn-stanza of four lines, each containing eight syllables; †**long-minded** *a.*, patient; **long mirror** = *long glass* (*a*); †**long-mood** *a.*, of patient mind, long-suffering; **long-nebbed** *a. Sc.*, (*a*) *lit.* long-nosed; (of a stick) long-pointed; (*b*) *fig.* curious, prying; also, making a show of learning, pedantic; **long-netting,** the process of catching fish with a long net; **long-nines,** a kind of long clay tobacco pipe; **long oyster,** the sea crayfish (Smyth *Sailor's Word-bk.*); **long paddock** *Austral.* and *N.Z. slang* (see quot.); **Long Parliament,** the Parliament which sat from Nov. 1640 to March 1653, was restored for a short time in 1659, and finally dissolved in 1660; †also, the second Parliament of Charles II (1661–1678); **long-persistence** *a.*, applied to a screen of a cathode-ray tube on which a spot remains luminous for a relatively long period after the electron beam has moved elsewhere; **long-pig,** a transl. of a cannibal's name for human flesh; also *attrib.*; **long plane** (see quot. 1842); **long prayer** in Congregational worship, the chief prayer, offered after the Scripture lessons and before the sermon; **long-primer** *Printing* (see PRIMER); **long pull,** (*a*) *Printing*, in the operation of the handpress, a pull on the bar almost to its fullest extent; (*b*) the practice in public houses of giving over-measure to attract custom; **long rains** [cf. RAIN *sb.*¹ 2 b], in tropical countries, the rainy season; **long-room,** an assembly room in a private house or public building; *spec.* in the Custom House at London, the large hall in which custom-house and other dues are paid; **long-rope,** a skipping game, in which a rope of considerable length is turned by two of the players, one at each end, while the others spring over it as it nears the ground; **long s,** a lower-case form of the letter s, printed ſ, no longer in general use; **long sauce** (see SAUCE *sb.* 4 a); **long sea,** short for *long sea passage*; also *attrib.*; **long service,** (*a*) *Naut.* (see quot.); (*b*) *Mil.*, 'the maximum period a recruit can enlist for in any branch of the service, viz. for 12 years' (Voyle); also used to denote a less specific period of service; also *attrib.*; **long-shaded, -shadowed** *adjs.*, casting a long shade or shadow, a rendering of Gr. δολιχόσκιος; **long ship,** (*a*) *Hist.*, a ship of considerable length, built to accomodate a large number of rowers; a ship of war, a galley; = L. *navis longa*; (*b*) *Naval slang* (see quots.); **long-short,** (*a*) *U.S.*, 'a gown somewhat shorter than a petticoat, worn by women when doing household work' (Bartlett); (*b*) a trochaic verse (*nonce-use*); **long short story,** a short story (see SHORT *a.* 26) of more than average length, a novella; also **long-short** *ellipt.*; **long sight,** capacity for seeing distant objects; also, the defect of sight by which only distant objects are seen distinctly; (see also SIGHT *sb.*¹); **long silk** *attrib.* of cotton, long-stapled; **long-sixes,** long candles, six of which went to the pound (cf. *long-fours*); **long sleeve,** a sleeve which extends to the wrist; also (with hyphen) *attrib.*; **long-sleever** *Austral. slang*, a tall glass; **long slide,** (*a*) *Steam-engine* (see quot.); (*b*) *Curling* (see quots.); **long-small,** a length of rod used in basket-making; **long song** (see quot.); **long-splice** *Naut.* (see quot. 1968); also as *vb.*; **long-splintery** *a.*, consisting of long splinters; †**long square** *Geom.*, an oblong rectangle; also *attrib.*; †**long-staff,** a long cudgel, ? = QUARTER-STAFF; also *attrib.*; **long-staple** *a.* (see quots.); also *ellipt.*; **long stitch** (see quot.); **long-stone,** a menhir; **long-stop** (see sense 18 d); **long-straw** *Thatching* (see quot. 1968); **long-straws,** the drawing of straws as a game; **long-stroke,** (*a*) *Naut.* (see quot. 1867); (*b*) a stroke of a piston or pump rod, which is longer than the average; also *attrib.*; **long sugar** *U.S.*, molasses; **long-sweetening** *U.S.*, (*a*) molasses; (*b*) (see quot.); **long sword** (see SWORD); **long-tackle** *Naut.* (see quot.); also *attrib.* in *long-tackle-block*; †**long-tennis,** some form of tennis (cf. F. *longue paume*, tennis played in an open court); **long-termer,** a person who is serving a long prison-sentence; **long-threads,** warp; **long-timbers** (see quot.); **long-time** *a.*, that has been such for a long time; also, extending for a long time into the future; requiring a long time; **long-timer** = *long-termer*; **long-togs** *Naut.*, landsmen's clothes (Smyth); **long twelves** *Printing*, a duodecimo (12mo) imposition scheme with the forme arranged in two rows of six long narrow type pages as opposed to three rows of four shorter and broader pages in standard 12mo schemes; **Long Vacation,** summer vacation at the Law-courts and Universities, so called in distinction from the Christmas and Easter vacations; also *attrib.*; **long verse** = LONG-LINE 3; **long voyage** (see quot.); **long-wall** *Coal-mining*, used *attrib.* (rarely *advb.*), to imply a particular method of extracting coal (see quot. 1851); **long-warped** *a.*, oblong (cf. OE. *langwyrpe* in *Techmer's Zeitschr.* II. 119); **long wave,** a wave of relatively long wavelength; *spec.* in *Broadcasting*, a radio wave with a wavelength longer than about one kilometre (but less than ten kilometres, in mod. use); freq. *attrib.* (usu. hyphenated); **long way** = *long-wall*; **long week-end,** a week-end holiday of more than the usual length; *fig.* the period between the wars of 1914–18 and 1939–45; **long whist** (see WHIST *sb.*); †**long-willed** *a.*, long suffering; **long-wool,** (*a*) long-stapled wool, suitable for combing or carding; (*b*) a long-woolled sheep; also *attrib.*; **long writ** = *prerogative writ* (see PREROGATIVE).

1951 A. GROLLMAN *Pharmacol. & Therapeutics* vi. 143 For prolonged mild sedation.. small doses of a *long-acting barbiturate are useful. **1971** D. CLARK *Sick to Death* ii. 35 Sally was on long-acting insulin. That means she only had to inject twice a day. **1848** E. C. P. in C. H. Hartshorne *Eng. Medieval Embroidery* 121 '*Long and short' stitch is employed for shading. **1960** [see *brick-stitch* (BRICK *sb.*¹ 10)]. **1967** E. SHORT *Embroidery & Fabric Collage* iv. 91 The ones in existence depict the Buddha life size, the large areas of colour being filled in solidly in chain, satin, and long-and-short stitch. **1809** R. LANGFORD *Introd. Trade* 57 *Long annuities 16½ means, that an annuity of 100l. from the present time to the year 1860, will cost.. 16½ years' purchase; at which time they will expire. This stock was originally for 99 years. **1888** BUXTON *Finance & Politics* I. 189 *note*, The 'Long Annuities' dated from 1780. Their actual amount in 1860 was £1,200,000. **1675** in *Public Rec. Colony of Connecticut* (1852) II. 270 Such Troopers as shall neglect to prouide themselues with *long armes, viz. a carbin or muskett.. shall be disbanded. **1952** GRANVILLE *Dict. Theatr. Terms* 113 *Long-arm*, a long wooden pole used for clearing borders and ceilings, that foul the lines in the flies. **1969** E. H. PINTO *Treen* 406 *Long-arms*, the trigger action, long-arm hook,.. for removing objects from crowded windows, was a useful and necessary device in Victorian times... It is still made in modified form, to assist invalids in picking up objects which are otherwise out of reach. **1972** D. W. BAILEY *Brit. Mil. Longarms 1815–65* 9 The barrels of military longarms were officially 'browned' from 1815. **1973** *Times* 14 July 12/1 Gang mowers and long-arm rotary cutters for roadside banks and verges. **1896** *Allbutt's Syst. Med.* I. 33 The deep orbit and the *long-axed eyeball going naturally with the long head. **1919** G. B. SHAW *Peace Conf. Hints* vi. 75 Within range of *Long Bertha. **1929** H. B. SMITH *Sheep & Wool Industry Austral. & N.Z.* (ed. 3) x. 77 The shearer now gets in a *long blow with the machine, running from the britch end to the top of the neck. **1949** P. NEWTON *High Country Days* v. 49 Laying his sheep full length he swung into the 'long blow'—from rump to neck. **1952** J. CLEARY *Sundowners* iii. 138 Paddy was beginning the longest cut, the 'long blow', from the flank to the top of the head. **1956** G. BOWEN *Wool Away!* (ed. 2) iii. 36 If you see a shearer with a good long blow he is usually a good shearer. **1948** G. CROWTHER *Outl. Money* (ed. 2) ii. 73 Those that mature within five years are known as Short Bonds. Medium Bonds run from five to about twenty years, and all above that are *Long Bonds. *c* **1485** *Digby Myst.* (1882) III. 190 Ye *langbaynnes, loselles, for-sake ȝe þat word! **1497** *Ld. Treas. Acc. Scotl.* (1877) I. 332 Item, the samyn nycht, in Sanctandrois, to the King to play at the *lang bowlis xviij. *s.* **1801** STRUTT *Sports & Past.* III. vii. 201 *Long-bowling .. was performed in a narrow enclosure,.. and at the further end was placed a square frame with nine small pins upon it; at these pins the players bowled in succession. **1876** *Encycl. Brit.* IV. 180/1 After the suppression of alleys 'Long bowling', or 'Dutch rubbers' was practised for a short time. *a* **1643** CARTWRIGHT *Ordinary* III. v. (1651) 52, I shall live to see thee Stand in a Play-house doore with thy *long box, Thy half-crown Library, and cry small Books. **1728** SWIFT *Past. Dialogue* 33 When you saw Tady at *long-bullets play. **1792** S. BURWOOD *Life P. Skelton* (1816) 282 He challenged any of them to play long-bullets with him... The little fellow.. took the bullet, and threw it about twice as far as Skelton. **1873** BENNETT & 'CAVENDISH' *Billiards* 27 The *long-butt is used in the same way when the ball cannot be reached with the half-butt. **1862** 'CAVENDISH' *Whist* (1870) 29 *Long cards are cards of a suit remaining in one hand after the remainder of the suit is played. **1872** *Young Gentleman's Mag.* 698/2 Packs with a long card can be obtained at many of the conjuring depôts. **1936** E. CULBERTSON *Contract Bridge Complete* i. 39 Low cards established from four-card or longer suits. They are called *long* cards. **1959** C. H. GOREN *New Contract Bridge in Nutshell* (1960) 13 What is a long card? In the trump suit, long cards start at the fifth card. In a side suit, the fourth card is considered a long card. **1892** *Long-case clock [see GRANDFATHER 5]. **1899** F. J. BRITTEN *Old Clocks & Watches* 320 Some of the earliest long-case clocks were liberally embellished with marqueterie. **1972** *Country Life* 9 Mar. 546/3 Strictly speaking, all clocks of this type should be called longcases, although since Victorian times they have been known to the general public as 'grandfathers'. **1972** B. LOOMES *Yorks. Clockmakers* 10 Very few longcase clocks were made after 1860. **1930** *Biochem. Jrnl.* XXIV. 113 A peculiar *long-chain fatty acid. *Ibid.* 114 The two long chains are connected to polar groups. **1951** *Sci. News* XXII. 98 The configuration in space of the long chains, formed by the linking together of successive amino-acids, which seem to be a common feature of all proteins. **1964** G. H. HAGGIS et al. *Introd. Molecular Biol.* ix. 216 Nucleic acids are long-chain molecules, and the individual units linked together to form these chains are called nucleotides. **1974** *Sci. Amer.* Mar. 72/3 The useful properties of a polymer depend almost entirely on the presence of long chains. **1891** KIPLING & BALESTIER *Naulahka* (1892) vi. 54 It was full of white men.. lying in the verandah in *long chairs. **1929** E. BOWEN *Last September* iv. 41 Help Uncle Richard in with the long chair. **1956** E. AMBLER *Night-comers* viii. 195 One of the long chairs was lying across the balustrade. **1925** V. G. CHILDE *Dawn European Civilization* xiii. 213 The *long cists in North France, Belgium, Hessen, and Sweden have a holed-stone for the doorway. **1963** *Field Archaeol.* (Ordnance Survey) (ed. 4) 113 In Scotland, Wales, the Isle of Man, and the South-west of England burials in long cists which are coffin-like arrangements of stone slabs are frequently met with. **1861** HUGHES *Tom Brown at Oxf.* xxi, He is churchwarden at home, and can't smoke anything but a *long clay. **1819** KEATS *Let.* 24 Sept. (1958) II. 215 A child in a[r]ms was passing by his chair.. in the nurses a[r]ms—Lamb took hold of the *long clothes saying 'Where, god bless me, Where does it leave off?' **1861** DICKENS *Gt. Expect.* II. xvi. 254 He had just finished putting somebody's hat into black long-clothes, like an African baby. **1862** SALA *Accepted Addr.* 85 It was settled almost before he was out of long-clothes, that he was to be a carpenter. **1932** *Times Lit. Suppl.* 29 Sept. 676/3 Fibonacci, the first Christian writer to give a systematic exposition of the Hindu numerals, without which analysis might still have been in its long-clothes. **1779** G. KEATE *Sketches fr. Nat.* (1790) I. 26 The Margate *Long-Coach was drawn up in the yard, and the passengers already seated in it. **1807** GOEDE *Stranger Eng.* III. 59 Stage-coaches.. others in form of a cylinder, are called long-coaches. **1829** MARRYAT *F. Mildmay* xiv, The young officer might like a drop o' *long cork; bring us.. one o' they claret bottles. **1878** J. INGLIS *Sport & W.* xi. 121 They generally betake themselves then to some patch of grass or *long-crop outside the jungle. **1683–4** J. MOXON *Mech. Exerc. Printing*

(1962) 267 Then he [sc. the Press-man] Folds a sheet of the Paper he is to Work long-ways, and broad-ways, and lays the long Crease of it upon the middle of the *Long-Cross. 1755 J. Smith Printer's Gram. 261 They [sc. compositors] lessen the Furniture on both sides the Long Cross, to enlarge the Bottom Margin. 1884 J. Gould Letter-Press Printer (ed. 3) 166/1 Longcross, the bar that divides a chase the longest way. 1904 C. L. Stainer Oxf. Silver Pennies 50 Long cross voided, each limb terminating in crescent. 1924 Southward's Mod. Printing (ed. 5) I. xl. 246 (caption) Long cross. 1972 Oxf. Univ. Gaz. CII. Suppl. No. 3. 50 A selection of 23 silver 'long-cross' pennies (1247–78) from a hoard found at Colchester. 1720 Lond. Gaz. No. 5881/5 George Cottrell, ..*Long-cuttler. 1678 Norris Coll. Misc. (1699) 213 He must be the more unwilling to break off a *long-dated Innocence, for the unsatisfying pleasure of a moment. 1866 Crump Banking vii. 153 Long-dated bills will sometimes command a higher price than shorter dates. 1883 Manch. Exam. 12 Dec. 5/1 The work-people no doubt act from a long-dated regard for their own interests. 1898 H. S. Canfield Maid of Frontier 86 It was what is termed a '*long deal', that is, no winning or losing card had slipped from the dealer's carelessly careful hands. 1827 Hutton Course Math. I. 43 Divide by the whole divisor at once, after the manner of *Long division. 1810 E. Weeton Let. 11 May (1969) I. 261 You will find the necessary keys for the three *long drawers. 1928 A. M. M. Douton Bk. with Seven Seals 19 They are in the top long drawer. 1975 Country Life 20 Feb. 426/2 The chest..has one long drawer..and below that are two deeper drawers. 1949 N. Marsh Swing, Brother, Swing iii. 40 She climbed into a *long dress, six years old. 1954 J. Masters Bhowani Junction xxxii. 275 There's a dance to-night... Please come. Long dress. 1973 H. McCloy Change of Heart ix. 102 Long dress? Surely not in these days for a family dinner at home? 1833 M. Scott Tom Cringle xi. (1859) 244 The lumbering flap of the *long drop was heard. 1891 W. J. Thomson in Rep. U.S. Nat. Museum (1889) 529 This unsatisfactory state of affairs was brought to an end..by a desperate battle, in which the '*long ears' had planned the utter annihilation of their enemies. 1919 K. Routledge Mystery of Easter Island xviii. 282 The Long Ears suddenly appear on the island at a much later time. 1958 T. Heyerdahl Aku-Aku xi. 353 The mayor ..and his ancestors who had made the great statues on Easter Island called themselves long-ears. Is it not strange that they should bother to lengthen their ears so that they hung down to their shoulders? 1884 Pall Mall G. 4 Dec. 6/1 *Long Elizas (the trade name for certain blue and white vases ornamented with figures of tall, thin China-women) is a name derived undoubtedly from the German or Dutch. 1753 Hanway Trav. (1762) I. v. lxiv. 292 From Holland they reckon one bale of maghoot, one of shalloons, and one of *long ells, to ten bales of begrest. 1843 Penny Cycl. XXVII. 555/2 Druggets and long-ells..are made in Devon and Cornwall. 1960 G. E. Evans Horse in Furrow x. 131 A bastard summer-land is so called to distinguish [it] from a true summer-land or *long fallow. 1971 World Archaeol. III. 135 They [sc. the Tifalmin] practise long-fallow cultivation, clearing a patch of forest and abandoning it after two or three years, probably for fifteen years or more. 1909 Daily Chron. 12 Oct. 4/4 *Long-fed beef, as fed by English farmers, cost 21s. 3d. 1969 Neumann & Snapp Beef Cattle (ed. 6) xi. 303 If cattle are fed finishing rations for 8 to 10 months, they are spoken of as 'long-fed' cattle. 1611 L. Barry Ram Alley ii. i. C4, Why so, these are tricks of the *long fifteenes, To giue counsell, and to take fees on both sides. c1290 S. Eng. Leg. I. 309/336 He pult forth is felawe, þe '*longue finger', þat sit him next. 1486 Bk. St. Albans Bvb, Betwene the longe fyngre and the leche fyngre. 1848 Rimbault Pianoforte 45 Every change is made by passing the thumb under the long fingers, or the long fingers over the thumb. 1891 N. Crane Baseball 81 *Long fly, a fly ball which is batted to the out-field. 1776 T. Pennant Tour in Scotl. & Voy. Hebrides 1772 II. 145 Quantities of white-fish ..might be taken on the great sand banks off this coast. The *long Fortys extend parallel to it. 1928 C. F. S. Gamble Story N. Sea Air Station xii. 183 The Grand Fleet was ordered to rendezvous in the 'Long Forties'; the Battle Cruiser Fleet to join farther south. 1832 Boston, etc. Herald 18 Sept. 1/4 Making long-sixes burn as brightly as *long-fours. c1000 Ags. Gosp. John xviii. 1 marg., Þes passio ȝebyreð on *langa frigadæȝ. c1200 Trin. Coll. Hom. 95 Crepe to cruche on lange fridai. 1636 Davenant Wits iv. ii. Dram. Wks. 1872 II. 199 When I was young, I was arrested for a stale commodity Of nut-crackers, *long-gigs, and casting-tops. 1843 C. Ridley Let. Nov. in Cecilia (1958) xii. 141 Little Matt..always gives himself a kiss in the *long glass. 1883 J. Brinsley-Richards Seven Yrs. at Eton xxix. 322 There was a way of holding the long glass at a certain angle by which catastrophes were avoided. 1942 G. Mitchell Laurels are Poison xvii. 186 Have a look at yourself in the long glass. 1953 Word for Word: Encycl. Beer (Whitbread & Co.) 37/1 Yard of ale, known also as a long glass..held between 2¾ and 3½ pints. 1884 Bower & Scott De Bary's Phaner. & Ferns 471 The longitudinal course of the single elements..appearing in the direction of the '*long grain' of the wood and bast. 1858 E. H. D. Domenech Missionary Adventures Texas & Mexico iv. 276 The way of the *long grass is not easy. 1863 Macm. Mag. Nov. 27/2 The long grass swarmed with hog-deer. 1912 D. Crawford (title) Thinking Black: 22 years without a break in the long grass of Central Africa. 1961 Listener 7 Sept. 346/1 This is the Africa of the 'long grass' such as Hyparrhenia and Echinochloa into which, half a century ago, one would have romantically disappeared. The areas of long-grass plains in the Sudan have to be experienced to be believed. 1964 C. Willock Enormous Zoo i. 14 Much of it is long-grass country. 1896 Ade Artie ix. 79, I never see him do a stroke of work, but he can always make a flash o' the *long green. 1903 A. H. Lewis Boss xiv. 174 I'd naturally s'ppose that when you went ehy on th' long green, you'd touch th' old gentleman. 1946 S. Newton Paul Bunyan x. 63 We'll be there tomorrow afternoon with Napoleon and the long green. 1782 Encycl. Brit. 6711/2 The *long-harness [of a ribbon-loom] are the front-reeds, by which the figure is raised. 1928 Electrical Communication VII. i. 62 *Long Haul Single Channel Carrier Telephone Systems Connect Melbourne with..Victoria and South Australia. 1957 [see haul sb. 1c]. 1961 Economist 11 Nov. 575/2 The [airport] buildings themselves are expected to be adequate to meet all long-haul traffic until 1970. 1974 Times 5 Jan. 9/2 Other long-haul operators to be recommended..Kenton Travel International..offer a round-the-world trip starting at £795. 1975 Islander (Victoria, B.C.) 17 Aug. 3/3 Expenses of the long-haul teamsters who rested and stabled their horses there. 1622 Mabbe tr. Aleman's Guzman d' Alf. ii. 355 To make wads and wisps for those that go to the *Long-house (you know what I meane). 1646 Sir J. Temple Irish Rebell. 4 He set up a long house, made of smoothed wattles. 1751 C. Gist Jrnls. (1893) 51 They marched in under French Colours and were conducted into the Long House. 1753 G. Washington Diaries (1925) I. 50 We met in Council at the Long House. 1774 D. Jones Jrnl. 2 Visits to Indians (1865) 76 They proceed to bind them [captives] naked to the post in the long house. 1826 J. F. Cooper Last of Mohicans Pref. (1850), Where the 'long house', or Great Council Fire, of the nation was universally admitted to be established. 1894 Fiske Hist. U.S. i. 5 Ground-plan of Iroquois Long-house. 1894 Sarawak Gaz. 1 May 67/1 The practice of herding together in 'long houses' prevents mental and moral improvement and hinders advance in gardening and planting and agricultural developement generally. 1905 Chambers's Jrnl. Oct. 714/1 The grim line of trophies hanging in the village long-house. 1912 Hose & McDougall Pagan Tribes Borneo I. iv, The Kenyah village frequently consists of a single long house. 1937 Discovery Sept. 257/1 Anga, our guide, who was head of the community on the opposite hill, invited us to visit his Longhouse... This dwelling place was cleverly constructed of bamboo and palm leaves (atap). 1949 B. A. St. J. Hepburn Handbk. Sarawak xix. 180 The 'long-house' system ensures that the individual incapacitated by illness or accident cannot be ignored or abandoned. 1961 Listener 9 Nov. 757/1, I came to my first long house after a journey of hours down the famous Rejan River, in the British territory of Sarawak in Borneo. 1965 C. Shuttleworth Malayan Safari ii. 32 The walls and roofs of the long-houses were built of palm leaves. 1966 G. E. Evans Pattern under Plough v. 72 The Welsh long-houses..with long sides and opposite doors providing a passage from side to side, and dividing the building roughly in two. 1971 Lady 15 July 88/3 The longhouse is an object lesson in community living. 1967 Karch & Buber Offset Processes 545 *Long ink, ink that can be drawn out into a long thin string—such ink has considerable tack which will pull a plate clean and sharp. 1970 E. A. D. Hutchings Survey of Printing Processes 200 Long ink, an ink which will flow freely from a knife... Such an ink will, when dabbed on a finger and thumb, stretch out without breaking as these digits are drawn apart. 1867 Smyth Sailor's Word-bk., *Long-jawed, the state of rope when its strands are straightened by being much strained and untwisted, and from its pliability will coil both ways. 1943 T. R. St. George C/o Postmaster 12 Some odd garments affectionately known as '*longjohns'. 1961 A. Smith East-Enders ix. 156 In the living room there would be ..a long John table, a small cocktail bar. 1961 Sunday Express 24 Sept. 20 'Longjohn' coffee table. 1962 W. Schirra in Into Orbit 47 We..stripped down to our long johns so that the technicians could plaster us all over with strips of wet paper. Ibid. 49 A series of waffle-weave patches on our long john underwear helps to keep the oxygen moving. 1964 Spectator 14 Feb. 217 The long john is a homely woollen undergarment of rustic provenience. 1969 J. Gardner Founder Member vii. 115 Boysie picked up the clothes... A suit of woollen long johns, a pair of heavy calf-length stockings. 1970 G. E. Evans Where Beards wag All xix. 219 The boys played Long Johns which they did as they walked along the road throwing the marbles ahead of them. 1971 New Yorker 4 Dec. 102/1 (Advt.), One-piece waist-to-toe Lightweight Long Johns with ribbed dress socks. 1972 Guardian 30 Nov. 15/6 (Advt.), Big Long John in opulent teak finish... This elegantly styled occasional table..47″ × 17″ overall width by 14¾″ high. 1882 Besant Revolt of Man vi. 160 It is better to advance the knowledge of the world one inch than to win the *long-jump with two-and-twenty feet. 1934 R. Campbell Broken Record v. 116 An Impala..can long-jump thirty-seven feet without a run. 1963 Times 4 Feb. 3/4 He long jumped 26 ft. 10 in. for a world's best indoor performance. 1887 Shearman Athletics (Badm. Libr.) 149 The *long-jumper, like the sprinter, may be a man of almost any size or weight. 1882 Society 7 Oct. 23/1 As a man he has done extraordinary work at *long-jumping, sprinting, and hurdle-racing. 1860 Trans. Mich. Agric. Soc. X. 229 That it is impossible to raise winter apples in the South, and that it is necessary to look to the North for a supply of *long-keeping varieties. 1861 Mrs. Beeton Bk. Househ. Managem. 589 As late or long-keeping potatoes, the Tartan or Red-apple stands very high in favour. 1970 Guardian 6 June 12/4 Long-keeping cream..keeps longer than fresh cream but a shorter time than sterilised cream. 1896 Farmer & Henley Slang IV. 228/2 *Long-lady, a farthing candle. 1953 A. Jobson Househ. & Country Crafts vii. 81 A farthing candle was known as a Long Lady. 1867 Smyth Sailor's Word-bk., *Long leave, permission to visit friends at a distance. 1971 A. Kirk-Greene in J. Spencer Eng. Lang. W. Afr. 144 '*Long legs' is a commonplace [in West Africa] for using influence in high places to secure a service. 1973 Listener 14 June 782/3 'Long leg' is a Nigerian colloquialism denoting corruption. 1867 Smyth Sailor's Word-bk., *Long leggers, lean schooners, longer than ordinary proportion to breadth, swift. 1898 F. T. Bullen Cruise Cachalot (1900) i. 6 A pot of something sweetened with '*longlick' (molasses) made an apology for a meal. 1928–9 T. Eaton & Co. Catal. Fall & Winter 245/2 The famous *long-life Minerva Batteries. 1946 Physical Rev. LXX. 987/1 (heading) Long-life radio-iodine. 1966 Daily Tel. 7 Nov. 17/1 The association has already announced plans to buy a half-share in a Liverpool creamery and manufacture 'long life' milk for export to the Middle East and other tropical areas. 1969 Guardian 1 Aug. 7/6 Some bread is certainly tasteless but it's the prepacked sliced long-life cotton wool wadding that most people prefer. 1971 Ibid. 9 Aug. 7/5 Children may increasingly find themselves drinking longlife or dried milk next term. 1653 Fisher Baby Baptism 7 There was but a very *long-little, in comparison of what else might have been delivered. 1815 Scott Guy M. xlv, While that *lang-lugged limmer o' a lass is gaun flisking in and out o' the room. 1901 N. Munro in Blackw. Mag. Mar. 355/1 It's a gossiping community this, long-lugged and scandal-loving. 1659 Howell Lex., Prov. Ded. to Philologers, A significant..Proverb..works upon the Intellectuals..more then a..*long-lungd Sermon. 1815 Byron To Moore 12 June, The villian is a..long-lunged orator. c1290 S. Eng. Leg. I. 308/313 '*Longueman' hatte þe midleste for he lenguest is. a1475 Pict. Voc. in Wr.-Wülcker 753/1 Hic medius, the longman. 1906 Kipling Puck of Pook's Hill 168 'Few people nowadays walk from end to end of this country.'.. 'The greater their loss. I know nothing better than the *Long March when your feet have hardened.' 1937 E. Snow Red Star over China i. i. 19 The historic Long March of 6,000 miles, in which they crossed twelve provinces of China..and triumphantly emerged at last into a powerful new base in the Northwest. Ibid. iv. vi. 180 The Long March..was begun in October 1934..the Red Army at last reached northern Shensi in October 1935. 1967 L. Deighton Expensive Place xxxvi. 217 The Long March meant the Nationalists killed two and a half million. 1970 Guardian 14 May 9/3 [Regis] Debray..overestimates the capacity of Latin Americans to envisage a 'long march'. Most Latin American revolutionaries..think mostly about the short, sharp blow that will lead to quick success. 1972 Times 23 Oct. 12/1 Mr Chou held a number of important posts and travelled widely before the Long march. Ibid. 27 Dec. 6/3 The MPLA had originally been based on the Congo (Zaire) but, after differences, had carried out the traditional 'Long March' (so beloved by revolutionaries when attempting to found a new state) to new bases in Zambia. 1973 Times 1 Oct. 6/5 The 'long march' on Besançon yesterday, organized by the leading French trade union organizations, proved a striking demonstration of the impact the six-month-old struggle of the Lip watch plant workers has had throughout France. 1709 J. Ward Yng. Math. Guide i. iii. (1734) 33 The least Part of a *Long Measure was at First a Barly Corn. 1801 W. Dupré Neolog. Fr. Dict. 131 Hectomètre..in the long measure of the new republican division, is equal to one hundred metres. 1718 *Long metre [see common a. 19b]. 1618 S. Ward Iethro's Iustice (1627) 22 [A judge] must be..*long-minded, to endure the..homelinesse of common people in giving evidence. 1869 L. M. Alcott Little Women (1871) II. i. 6 There were no..*long mirrors, or lace curtains in the little parlour. 1960 D. Lessing In Pursuit of English iv. 138 All her games were centred around the long mirror. a1300 E.E. Psalter cii. 8 Laverd..milde-herted and *lang-mode. 1720 Ramsay Rise & Fall of Stocks 32 Impos'd on by *lang-nebbit juglers Stock-jobbers, brokers [etc.]. 1823 Hogg Sheph. Cal. (1829) I. 20 A large lang nibbit staff. 1881 L. B. Walford Dick Netherby in Gd. Words 332/2 What wi' her lang-nebbit English words I kenna gif my head or my heels is boon-most. 1893 J. Watson Conf. Poacher 96 In '*long-netting' the net is dragged by a man on each side, a third wading after to lift it over the stakes. 1858 O. W. Holmes Aut. Breakf.-t. (1883) 40 They were garnered by stable-boys smoking *long-nines. 1933 L. G. D. Acland in Press (Christchurch, N.Z.) 4 Nov. 15/7 *Long paddock, the. Slang for the road. People turn stock out on it, or travel them on it, to get cheap grazing. 1659 England's Conf. 8 Their old hackney drudges of the *Long Parliament. 1678 Luttrell Brief Rel. 9 Nov. (1857) I. 3 Though this parliament [sc. that then in session] was called the long parliament, yet [etc.]. 1827 Hallam Const. Hist. (1876) II. x. 293 The long parliament, in the year 1641, had established, in its most essential parts, our existing constitution. 1960 Jrnl. Acoustical Soc. Amer. XXXII. 1065 An instrument is described which extracts from the complex speech wave.. information related to the subjective pitch of a sound. It then displays this information on the *long-persistence screen of a revolving cathode-ray tube in such a manner that a continuous graph of pitch vs. time is obtained. 1966 D. G. Brandon Mod. Techniques Metallogr. v. 236 Visual observation of the image, even on a long-persistence screen, is very difficult at small probe diameters. 1852 Mundy Our Antipodes (1857) 181 No more '*long-pig' for him [the Maori]! 1901 Westm. Gaz. 14 May 3/1 As a matter of fact, 'long-pig' orgies are not common. 1679 Moxon Mech. Exerc. 169 *Long-Plain, The same that Joyners call a Joynter. 1842 Gwilt Encycl. Archit. §2102 The long plane is..used when a piece of stuff is to be tried up very straight. It is longer and broader than the trying plane. 1897 Times 22 Apr. 12/3 The '*long prayer'..has been not only shortened but improved in quality. 1683–4 J. Moxon Mech. Exerc. Printing (1962) 261 A *long or a Soaking or Easie Pull, is when the Form feels the force of the Spindle by degrees, till the Bar comes almost to the hither Cheek of the Press, and this is also call'd a Soft Pull. 1770 P. Luckombe Conc. Hist. Printing 500 Long pull is when the bar of the Press requires to be brought close to the cheek to make a good impression. 1888 C. T. Jacobi Printers' Vocab. 77 Long pull, when the bar-handle of a press is pulled right over. 1901 Contemp. Rev. Mar. 355 The unlettered barmaid..tiring of handling the taps and the long-pull. 1909 Daily Chron. 30 Aug. 5/3 As the law stands magistrates have no power to stop the 'long pull'. 1964 New Statesman 21 Feb. 283/3 In 1921 a Licensing Act made this permanent—under the homely caption 'Long Pull Prohibited'. 1963 A. Smith Throw out Two Hands vi. 70 The plan was to take off from Zanzibar on January 1st... There was so much to be done before the *long rains began. 1970 Kenya Farmer Feb. 3/2 If the long rains fail altogether—a most unlikely event—then a shortage would follow at the end of this year. 1722 De Foe Col. Jack (1840) 19 He led me into the *long-room at the custom-house. 1759 Compl. Lett.-writer (ed. 6) 228, I hear perpetually of Miss Evelyn's praises at the long-room. 1771 Smollett Humph. Cl., To Miss Willis 6 Apr., There is a long-room for breakfasting and dancing. 1819 Gentl. Mag. 529 His regularity..extended from the Treasury to the Long-room. 1841 Knickerbocker XVII. 458 In the long room of the Village Inn. 1870 J. K. Medbery Men & Mysteries Wall St. 22 A chamber is provided at the Exchange, where members may bargain with members at any hour throughout the day. This is known as the Long Room. 1962 S. Potter in L. Frewin Boundary Bk. 21 It is not the slightest use simply making vague references to the Long Room. 1891 F. W. Newman Cardl. Newman 2 Our boys, in large bands, enjoyed *Long Rope. 1808 C. Stower Printer's Gram. vi. 143 Since the very general introduction of round, in the room of *long s's, many [type] cases have been made upon a plan different from the original ones. 1894 [see serif]. 1914 A. E. Housman Let. 8 Mar. (1971) 410 His date..cannot be much earlier than 1800, as he seems not to use the long s except when t follows. 1960 G. A. Glaister Gloss. Bk. 241/1 It was not until John Bell's edition of Shakespeare in 1775 that the long s was generally discarded. 1680 J. Aubrey in Lett. Eminent Persons (1813) III. 439 He was drowned goeing to Plymouth by *long sea. 1731 Gentl. Mag. I. 353 The Projector has already made one Trip to try Experiments, and was in his passage to London by Long-Sea to make a further Proof. 1861 Canning in Hare Two Noble Lives (1893) III. 148 In a few weeks we shall be

beginning to pack off our long-sea goods. **1830** William IV in W. A. Steward *War Medals* (1915) 348 Discharged soldiers receiving a gratuity for meritorious conduct shall be entitled to wear a medal having on one side the words For *Long Service and Good Conduct, and on the other in relief the King's Arms. **1867** Smyth *Sailor's Word-bk.*, *Long-service*, a cable properly served to prevent chafing under particular use. **1874** *Punch* 4 June 3/1 Lord Strathnairn charged the late Secretary for War with bad faith, in not enlisting men for short and long service together. **1897** *Westm. Gaz.* 27 Sept. 3/2 Had the old long-service system continued in force. **1925** A. J. Toynbee *Survey Internat. Affairs 1920–23* II. 109 Immediate legislation for the abolition of conscription and for setting up a long service army as provided in the Treaty. **1937** B. H. L. Hart *Europe in Arms* xii. 158 From that time onward the army became professional and long-service. **1675** Hobbes *Odyssey* (1677) 237 Next the dogs he went, And in his hand shook a *longshaded spear. **1848** Buckley *Iliad* 123 Brandishing his *long-shadowed spear. **1568** Grafton *Chron.* I. 96 The which [Saxons] came in three *long Shippes or Hulkes. **1799** *Naval Chron.* II. 182 Built after the model of long Ships, or Men of War. **1886** Corbett *Fall of Asgard* I. 268 A large vessel shot out from behind the point. It was a long-ship of twenty benches. **1916** M. T. Hainsselin *In Northern Mists* xvi. 63, I say, Padre, this is a pretty long ship, isn't it? .. Don't you know that 'a long ship' means one where it is a long time between drinks? **1946** J. Irving *Royal Navalese* 110 *Long ship*, a ship, or party, in which there is a long interval between .. drinks. **1840** *Knickerbocker* XVI. 22 A buxom, rosy-cheeked girl, with a blue-striped *long-short .. was busied around the fire-place. **1851** S. Judd *Margaret* I. iii. 11 Her dress was a blue-striped linen short-gown wrapper, or long-short, a coarse yellow petticoat, and checked apron. *a***1881** O. W. Holmes *Old Vol. Life* ix, The first two in iambics, or short-longs, the last in trochaics or long-shorts. **1906** J. London *Let.* 15 Dec. (1966) 235 *The Times Magazine* .. bought .. one of my best long-short-stories. **1924** F. M. Ford *Let.* 18 Sept. (1965) 162 As for the novel: Hemingway .. gave me the impression that it was a long-short story. **1942** 'G. Orwell' in *Partisan Rev.* IX. 159 The paper shortage .. may possibly bring back the 'long-short story', a form which has never had a fair deal in England. **1959** *News Chron.* 7 Oct. 8/5 Long shorts by Arthur Miller and Saul Bellow. **1844** Hoblyn *Dict. Med.*, **Long sight*, .. the *dysopia proximorum* of Cullen. **1898** Watts-Dunton *Aylwin* (1900) 109/2 His companions had the usual long-sight of agriculturists. **1870** J. Yeats *Nat. Hist. Commerce* II. ii. 200 The *long silk cotton of Algeria partakes at the same time of the character of the long silk staple of Georgia. **1802** *Sporting Mag.* XX. 15 Some have gone so far as to illuminate our discussions with tens instead of *long-sixes. **1864** Trevelyan *Compet. Wallah* (1866) 283 Peasants who had never tasted anything daintier than a rushlight now had their fill of long sixes. **1814** Jane Austen *Let.* 9 Mar. (1932) II. 93 Mrs. Tilson had *long sleeves too, & she assured me that they are worn in the evening by many. **1897** *Sears, Roebuck Catal.* 241/2 Ladies' Long Sleeve Vests .. high neck and long sleeves with elastic ribbed cuffs. **1957** M. B. Picken *Fashion Dict.* 215/2 *Long sleeve*, sleeve which ends ½ inch below wrist joint. **1888** *Cassell's Picturesque Austral.* III. 83 Their drivers had completed their regulation half-score '*long sleevers' of 'she-oak'. **1875** Knight *Dict. Mech.*, **Long-slide*, a slide-valve of such length as to govern the ports at both ends of the cylinder, and having a hollow back, which forms an eduction passage. **1962** *Canada Month* Apr. 26/3 The west .. introduced the long slide now about twice the distance the old-style curler slides before launching his stone. **1969** R. Welsh *Beginner's Guide Curling* xii. 85 The delivery called the 'Slide' or the 'Long Slide' was introduced by Canadian curlers. **1912** T. Okey *Introd. Basket-Making* vii. 76 Some Luke, *Long Small and Threepenny will be needed, and a few small two yearling sticks. **1953** A. G. Knock *Willow Basket-Work* (ed. 5) 9 The old trade names .. three feet, Tacks; four feet, Short-Small; five feet, Long-Small. **1856** *Chambers's Jrnl.* 28 June 402/1 An item in those streaming fathoms of verse technically known as '*long songs', in which as many as a hundred favourite ditties are sold for a penny. **1883** *Man. Seamanship for Boys' Training Ships R. Navy* (1886) 106 To form a *long-splice with a piece of three and four-strand rope... Unlay the ends of the two ropes to the required distance [etc.]. *Ibid.* (*heading*) How do you long-splice a three or four-strand rope together? **1968** E. Franklin *Dict. Knots* 19 *Long splice*, a splice which has no apparent thickening of the rope at the points of joining. **1796** Kirwan *Elem. Min.* (ed. 2) II. 291 Grey ore of Manganese. Fragments somewhat *long splintery. **1551** Recorde *Pathw. Knowl.* II. lxxvi, If you make a *long square of the whole line A.C, and of that parte of it that lyeth betwene the circumference and the point, .. that longe square shall be equall to the full square of the touche line A.B. **1646** Sir T. Browne *Pseud. Ep.* II. ii. 60 A Loadstone of a Parallelogram or long square figure. **1797** *Encycl. Brit.* (ed. 3) V. 18/2 Take two pieces of pasteboard .. through which you must cut long squares. **1596** Shaks. *1 Hen. IV*, II. i. 82 No *Long-staffe six-penny strikers. *a***1661** Holyday *Juvenal* 184 If thou dost carry but a little plate By night, the sword and long-staff thou fear'st straight. **1802** J. Simons *Let.* 15 Dec. in J. Steele *Papers* (1924) I. 341 *Long Staple Cotton is in demand. **1843** *Knickerbocker* XXI. 39 It is here that the most valuable product of our country, the long staple cotton, is raised. **1867** *Harper's Mag.* Aug. 349/1 A bale of uplands cotton .. demanding to be bought at the price of long-staple. **1890** *Century Dict.*, *Long-staple*, having a long fiber: a commercial term applied to cotton of a superior grade, also called *sea-island* cotton. **1882** Caulfeild & Saward *Dict. Needlewk.* 187 (Embroidery), *Long stitch, also known as Point Passé, Passé, and Au Passé. It is a name given to Satin Stitch when worked across the material without any padding. **1899** Baring-Gould *Bk. of West* I. x. 171 The menhirs, locally termed *longstones, or langstones. **1835** R. M. Bird *Hawks of Hawk-Hollow* I. ii. 33 Shall we sit down here, and play *long-straws for sweethearts? **1947** *Agriculture* LIII. 448 (*heading*) Estimate no. 1. Long straw method (unclipped surface). **1963** *Times* 22 Apr. 9/2 For the customer it means a neater job and a roof that will last anything from 35 to 60 years instead of the 10 to 20 years of the traditional long-straw thatch. **1968** J. Arnold *Shell Bk. Country Crafts* xiii. 185 One notices that long-straw has a looser, more plastic appearance, compared with the stiff, 'close cropped', brush-like texture of reed. **1867** Smyth *Sailor's Word-bk.*, **Long-stroke*, the order to a boat's crew to stretch out and hang on her. **1884** *Imp. & Mach. Rev.* 1 Dec. 6715/2 The long-stroke by which this pump is distinguished averages about one-third more. **1838** *Civil Eng. & Arch. Jrnl.* I. 394/2 The short stroke engines are propelling the boats, both sea and river class, faster than the long stroke ones. **1859** Bartlett *Dict. Amer.*, **Long sugar*, molasses, so called formerly in North Carolina from the ropiness of it. **1714** in *N. Carolina Colonial Rec.* (1886) II. 132 Let who will go unpaid, Rum, *long Sweet'n alias Molasses .. must be had. **1859** Bartlett *Dict. Amer.*, **Long sweetening*, molasses, so called formerly in New England. **1883** *Encycl. Amer.* I. 199/2 In the far West, as Down East, sugar bears the name of long and short sweetening, according as it is the product of the cane .. or of the maple tree. **1936** M. Mitchell *Gone with Wind* xxi. 352 The sorghum used for 'long sweetening' did little to improve the taste. **1794** *Rigging & Seamanship* I. 156 **Long-tackle-block*. **1867** Smyth *Sailor's Word-bk.*, *Long-tackles*, those over-hauled down for hoisting up topsails to be bent. Long-tackle blocks have two sheaves of different sizes placed one above the other, as in fiddle blocks. **1653** Urquhart *Rabelais* I. xxiii, They played at the ball, the *long-tennis [F. *à la paume*], and at the Piletrigone. **1956** B. Holiday *Lady sings Blues* (1973) xviii. 142 Quite a few girls, especially *long-termers in the joint, were lovers. **1970** Long-termer [see fantasy *v.* 1 a]. **1844** G. Dodd *Textile Manuf.* i. 36 Some [yarn] is employed as warp or *long threads for coarse goods. *c***1850** *Rudim. Navig.* (Weale) 130 **Long timbers*, those timbers afore and abaft the floors which form the floor and second futtocks in one. **1584** Cogan *Haven Health* (1636) 171 Fish of *long time salting .. is unwholsome. **1877** A. M. Sullivan *New Irel.* xv. 177 A long-time colleague and friend. **1898** *Westm. Gaz.* 21 Apr. 5/3 A long-time deacon of the Tabernacle and personal friend of the late Charles Spurgeon. **1927** Carr-Saunders & Jones *Survey Social Struct. Eng. & Wales* xx. 228 This is no indictment of the usefulness of long-time forecasts, because it is in any case impracticable to plan so far ahead. **1944** C. Sandburg in B. A. Botkin *Treas. Amer. Folklore* p. vi, A longtime book is this. One reading won't do for it. **1971** B. Malamud *Tenants* 13 Long voyage in a small room. There's a long-time book to finish. **1907** J. London *Road* (1914) v. 139, I know that the *long-timers got more substantial grub, because there was a whole row of them on the ground floor in our hall. **1952** 'J. Henry' *Who lie in Gaol* viii. 133 The long-timers are allowed to plant a few things in a plot there if they want to. **1840** R. H. Dana *Bef. Mast* xxviii. 96 His '*long togs', the half-pay, his beaver hat, white linen shirts, and everything else. **1770** P. Luckombe *Conc. Hist. Printing* 414 (*caption*) A sheet of *long twelves. **1888** C. T. Jacobi *Printers' Vocab.* 77 *Long twelves*, a plan of imposition whereby the pages are laid down in two long rows of six pages. **1972** P. Gaskell *New Introd. Bibliogr.* 81 Long twelves (long 12°), when the sheet is folded once across the shorter side and five times across the longer, again making twelve leaves, twenty-four pages. **1693** Dryden *Juvenal* VI. 100 When now the *long vacation's come The noisy hall and theatres grown dumb. **1825** Thirlwall *Lett.* (1881) 85 A most delightful fortnight which I spent last long vacation at Cambridge. **1848** Clough (*title*) The Bothie of Toper-na-Fuosich, a long-vacation pastoral. **1900** G. C. Brodrick *Mem. & Impress.* 216 Such informal arrangements suffice to create a 'Long Vacation Term'. **1871** H. Sweet in W. C. Hazlitt *Warton's Hist. Eng. Poetry* II. 3 Each *long verse has four accented syllables. **1889** C. W. Kent *Elene* 8 The so-called 'long-verse' consists of two hemistichs. **1867** Smyth *Sailor's Word-bk.*, **Long voyage*, one in which the Atlantic Ocean is crossed. **1839** Ure *Dict. Arts* 978 The fourth system of working coal, is called the long way, the *long wall, and the Shropshire method. **1851** *Illustr. Catal. Gt. Exhib.* 149 The method of working coal, adopted in the Yorkshire mines generally, is that known as the long wall, .. distinguished from the Newcastle, or pillar-and-stall method, by extracting at once all available coal. **1902** *Blackw. Mag.* Jan. 50/1, I worked the coal 'long-wall'. *c***1400** *Lanfranc's Cirurg.* 111 Þis is þe foorme of an heed weel propossiound, .. þat he be *longe warpid, hauynge tofore & bihynde eminence. **1839** *Trans. Cambr. Philos. Soc.* VII. 95 Any particle *P* revolves continually in a circular orbit... The radius of this circle, and consequently the agitation of the fluid particles, decreases very rapidly as the depth *c* increases, and much more rapidly for short than *long waves, agreeably to observation. **1895** H. Lamb *Hydrodynamics* viii. 276 Waves whose slope is gradual and whose length λ is large compared with the depth *h* of the fluid, are called 'long waves'. **1909** E. B. Titchener *Text-bk. Psychol.* I. 60 Let us take .. a chart or projection of the solar spectrum, and let us work right through it, from the left or long-wave to the right or short-wave end. **1928** D. Brunt *Meteorol.* v. 38 The term 'low temperature radiation' [is frequently used] to denote the long-wave radiation of bodies at relatively low temperature. **1928** *Chambers's Jrnl.* Jan. 79/1 Many foreign long-wave stations have also been clearly heard with this set. **1963** *Meteorol. Gloss.* (Meteorol. Office) (ed. 4) 155 *Long wave*, in synoptic meteorology, a smooth, wave-shaped contour pattern on an isobaric chart with a wavelength of the order of 2000 km... Some four or five such waves .. typically extend across a hemispherical chart. **1974** *Encycl. Brit. Macropædia* III. 311/1 [Broadcasting.] Long waves range from 30 to 300 kilohertz; medium waves from 300 kilohertz to three megahertz; and short waves from three to 30 megahertz. **1839** *Long way [see *long wall*]. **1927** M. Kennedy (*title*) A *long week-end. **1933** H. G. Wells *Shape of Things to Come* III. §8. 317 The old British institution of the *long week-end* flourishes. **1940** Graves & Hodge (*title*) The long week-end: a social history of Great Britain 1918–1939. **1944** Blunden *Cricket Country* xiv. 149 The name, 'The Long Week-End', has been devised to characterise the period between the two great wars. **1968** 'E. Peters' *Grass Widow's Tale* ii. 24, I'm heading north .. for a long week-end. *a***1340** Hampole *Psalter* cii. 8 Mercyful lord: *lang-willid [L. *longanimis*] & mykil merciful. **1694** Motteux *Rabelais* IV. vi. (1737) 21 They are *long-Wool Sheep. **1825** J. Nicholson *Operat. Mechanic* 388 Wool Manufacture. This well-known staple is .. divided into two distinct classes, long wool, or worsted spinning; and short wool, or the spinning of woollen yarn. **1835** Ure *Philos. Manuf.* 103 Long-wool yarns are numbered on the same principle. *Ibid.* 125 Long wool, called also combing wool, differs as materially in a manufacturing point of view from short or clothing wool, as flax does from cotton. *Ibid.* 130 Long wool, called also carding wool, requires length and soundness of staple. **1859** *Trans. Illinois Agric. Soc.* III. 458 The Longwools attain to greater size and shear a larger fleece. **1877** J. Darby in J. Coleman *Sheep & Pigs Gt. Brit.* II. v. 50 The best flocks of Devon Longwools are .. derived solely from Leicester and Bampton—a most valuable cross in every respect... During the past fifteen years these sheep have been designated 'Devon Longwools'. **1886** C. Scott *Sheep-farming* 57 Practically the two long-wools are equal in weight as shearlings. **1642** C. Vernon *Consid. Exch.* 18 *marg.*, The *long Writ called the Prerogative Writ, out of the Treasurers Remembrancers Office, under the Teste of the chiefe Baron.

b. In names of animals, etc., as **long-bill**, a bird with a long bill, *e.g.* a snipe; **long clam**, (*a*) *Mya arenaria* (see clam *sb.*[2] 1 d); (*b*) the razor-clam, *Ensis americana*; **long cripple** *dial.*, a slow-worm; also, a lizard; **long dog** *dial.*, a greyhound; **long-ear, long ears**, an ass; also *fig.* of a human being; **long fin** *Austral.*, a name for the fishes *Caprodon schlegelii* and *Anthias longimanus*, Günth. (Morris); †**long-fish**, ? a fish of the eel kind (cf. G. *langfisch*); **long lugs** *Sc.* = *long ears*; **long-nose**, a name for the gar-fish; **longspur**, a bunting of the genus *Calcarius*, esp. *C. lapponicus*, the Lapland bunting; **long-wing**, a name for the swift; †**long-worm**,? an adder or viper.

1884 *Times* (weekly ed.) 3 Oct. 14/1 One thousand one hundred and fifty sounds a satisfactory bag of the '*long-bills'. **1884** Goode, etc. *Nat. Hist. Useful Aquatic Anim.* I. 707 The 'Soft Clam', '*Long Clam', or 'Nanninose' (*Mya arenaria*). **1887** —— *Fisheries U.S.* II. 614 Under the name of 'long clam', 'knife-handle', and 'razor-clam', they are occasionally seen in New York market. **1758** W. Borlase *Nat. Hist. Cornw.* 284 We have a kind of viper which we call the *Long-cripple: It is the slow-worm or deaf-adder of authors. **1864** *E. Cornw. Gloss.* in *Jrnl. R. Inst. Cornw.* Mar. I. 17 *Long-cripple*, a lizard: in some parts applied to the snake. **1896** Baring-Gould *Idylls* 223 He rins away from me .. jist for all the world as if I were a long-cripple. **1847** Halliwell, **Long dog*, a greyhound. **1891** T. Hardy *Tess* (1900) 44/1 William turned, clinked off like a long-dog, and jumped safe over hedge. **1768–74** Tucker *Lt. Nat.* (1834) II. 150 The beast .. would sell for no more at a fair than his brother *Long-ear. **1845** Browning *Lett.* (1899) I. 16 This long-ears had to be 'dear-Sir'd and obedient-servanted'. **1882** J. E. Tenison-Woods *Fish N.S. Wales* 33 (Morris) The *long-fin, *Anthias longimanus*, Günth ... may be known by .. the great length of the pectoral fins. **1598** Florio, *Licostomo*, a kind of *longfish. *a***1748** Ramsay *Condemned Ass* 64 Sae poor *lang lugs man pay the kane for a'. **1836** Yarrell *Brit. Fishes* I. 391 The Garfish ... *Long-Nose. **1848** C. A. Johns *Week at Lizard* 175 A long eel-shaped fish, the gur-fish, or long-nose. **1831** A. Wilson & Bonaparte *Amer. Ornith.* IV. 121 *Emberiza Lapponica* Wilson .. Lapland *Longspur. **1893** Coues in *Lewis & Clark's Exped.* I. 349 *note*, The black-breasted lark-bunting or longspur, *Centrophanes* (*Rhynchophanes*) *maccowni*. **1894** R. B. Sharpe *Handbk. Birds Gt. Brit.* I. 77 The Long-spurs, of which the Lapland Bunting is the type, are three in number. **1917** T. G. Pearson *Birds Amer.* III. 22 Shore Larks that feed up and down the wintry seashore of New England and the middle states have also many Longspurs among them. **1953** D. A. Bannerman *Birds Brit. Is.* I. 314 While *Calcarius lapponicus* is the sole Palæarctic representative of the genus, the Nearctic fauna includes two other 'Longspurs'—as they are called in America. **1973** R. D. Symons *Where Wagon Led* I. iv. 45 The sun hit the top of the gray-green sage and the longspurs fluttered overhead. **1854** Mary Howitt *Pictor. Cal. Seasons* 390 About the 12th of August the largest of the swallow tribe, the swift or *long-wing, disappears. **1648** Gage *West Ind.* xii. 51 Moules, Rats, *Long-wormes.

c. In the names of plants or vegetable products, as †**long-bean** = kidney-bean; †**long ear**, a name for a kind of barley; **long-flax** (see quot.); **longjohn**, a tropical South American tree, *Triplaris surinamensis*, of the family Polygonaceæ; **long-leaf pine** *U.S.*, *Pinus palustris* (also *long-leafed*, *-leaved pine*: see sense 16); **long-leek**, the ordinary leek (*Allium porrum*); **long-moss** = long-beard 3; **long-pod**, a variety of broad bean which produces a very long pod; **long purples**, a local name for *Orchis mascula*, *Lythrum Salicaria*, and other plants.

1587 Mascall *Govt. Cattle* (1627) 11 Faciolia, called in .. English kidney-beane, or *long-beane. **1523** Fitzherb. *Husb.* §13 *Long-eare hath a flatte eare, halfe an inche brode, and foure inches and more of length. **1875** Knight *Dict. Mech.*, **Long-flax*, flax to be spun its natural length without cutting. **1910** *Chambers's Jrnl.* Feb. 88/2 Impenetrable jungle, consisting mostly of chinchilla or sand box-trees, with now and then a sand-cocoa or a *longjohn. **1969** S. M. Sadeek *Windswept & Other Stories* 30 We will build a nice house .. with bamboo and longjohn. *a***1816** B. Hawkins *Sk. Creek Country* (1848) 60 [On] the uplands to the south are the *long-leaf pine. **1901** [see *laurel oak* (laurel *sb.*[1] 6)]. **1904** T. E. Watson *Bethany* I. i. 8 Ours was just a plain house .. of timbers torn from the heart of the long-leaf Georgia pine. **1969** T. H. Everett *Living Trees of World* 50/2 The longleaf pine, an open-headed kind that reaches 120 feet in height and has a natural range from Virginia to Florida and Mississippi is the most important timber tree of the south-eastern United States. **1867** J. Hogg *Microsc.* II. i. 357 The young flower-stalk of the *long-leek (*Allium porrum*). **1808** T. Ashe *Trav. Amer.* I. 126 *Long Moss, *Tellandsia Usneoides*. **1833** *Penny Cycl.* I. 249/2 The long-moss region commences below 33° lat. The moss hangs in festoons from the trees. **1821** W. Cobbett *Amer. Gardening* §196 The best .. is .. the Windsor-Bean. The *Long-Pod is the next best. **1972** *Country Life* 13 Jan. 104/4 A dependable way to ensure early pickings of broad beans .. is to sow the seeds now .. for which purpose I prefer longpod varieties. **1602** Shaks. *Ham.* IV. vii. 170 There with fantasticke Garlands did she come, Of Crow-flowers,

Nettles, Daysies, and *long Purples. **1821** CLARE *Vill. Minstr.* II. 90 Gay long purple, with its tufty spike. *Ibid.* II. 210 (Gloss.), Long purples, purple loose-strife. **1830** TENNYSON *Dirge* v, Round thee blow..long purples of the dale.

d. *Cricket*: †**long ball**, a ball hit to a distance; **long field (off, on)**, the position of a fieldsman who stands at a distance behind the bowler, either to his left or right; also, one who fields in that position; also **long-fielder**, **-fieldsman**; **long-hop**, a ball bowled or thrown so that it makes a long flight after pitching; (also in *Fives*), a ball which a player has ample time to hit after it bounces; **long off, on**, short for *long field off, on*; **long-stop**, a fieldsman who stands behind the wicket-keeper to stop the balls that pass him; hence ***long-stop*** vb., to field as long-stop, whence ***long-stopping*** vbl. sb; also *fig.*, a last resort, e.g. in an emergency; also (in literal sense) **long-stopper**. Also ***long leg***, ***long slip*** (see the sbs.).

1744 J. LOVE *Cricket* (1770) III. 3 Some [fieldsmen], at a Distance, for the *Long Ball wait. **1843** *Long field [see *long on* below]. **1862** *Lond. Soc.* II. 115/2 Carpenter might have made more drives to the long field. **1816** W. LAMBERT *Cricketer's Guide* (ed. 6) iii. 44 **Long field off side* this man should stand on the off side, between the middle wicket man and bowler at a considerable distance in the Field, so as to cover them. **1850** 'BAT' *Cricketer's Man.* 43 *Long Field Off*. —— This situation demands a person who can throw well. *Long Field On* is of a character with the 'off'. **1880** *Times* 28 Sept. 11/5 Mr. Moule, long-field-off. **1897** K. S. RANJITSINHJI *Jubilee Bk. Cricket* ii. 55 Nearly all good *long-fielders take the ball, in catching, with their hands close to their bodies about chest-high. **1920** P. F. WARNER *Cricket Reminisc.* xiv. 91 Never had he been a long-fielder. **1790** *Reading Mercury* 8 Mar. 3/3 He was the swiftest bowler and best *long fieldsman at that time in the kingdom. **1837** *New Sporting Mag.* XI. 198 The lengths necessary to be pitched at that slow pace will be as good as *long hops. **1867** *Routledge's Ev. Boy's Ann.* 432 The ball should come skimming in with a long hop to the top of the bails. **1900** A. E. T. WATSON *Young Sportsman* 237 s.v. *Fives*, C..must above all avoid so returning it [*sc.* the ball] that it comes into the middle of the outer court as a long-hop. **1864** *Routledge's Ev. Boy's Ann.* 476 A drive to *long-off. **1901** I. MACLAREN *Yng. Barbarians* xv. 295 A miraculous catch which he made at long-off. **1843** 'A. WYKHAMIST' *Pract. Hints on Cricket* Frontisp., The '*long on', or long field to the on-side, is for the most part done away with. **1767** R. COTTON *Cricket Song* ix, in F. S. Ashley-Cooper *Hambledon Cricket Chron.* (1924) 184, I had almost forgot—they deserve a large bumper—Little George, the *long Stop, and Tom Sueter, the Stumper. **1797** COLMAN *Heir at Law* II. ii, I'll make you my long-stop at cricket. **1884** *Lillywhite's Cricket Ann.* 103 Reliable long-stop and very smart in the long-field. **1957** *Listener* 5 Sept. 349/1 Like all sorts of longstop laws we keep on the statute-book, but hardly ever use. **1962** *Punch* 11 Apr. 558/1 The National Assistance Board..is the long-stop of the Welfare State. **1973** *Times* 9 Nov. 1/5 The two uninvolved unions may..provide a long-stop cover. **1860** *Bailey's Mag.* I. 34 'Lords', where, in days of yore..Beagley *long stopped. **1891** W. G. GRACE *Cricket* x. 258 The most expert *long-stoppers at the time when long-stop was even of more importance than the wicket-keeper. **1832** P. EGAN *Bk. Sports* 348/2 Dick's shin-breakers stop'd them short In 'midst of their *long-stopping! **1860** *Bailey's Mag.* I. 303 The long stopping of Diver. **1871** G. MEREDITH *H. Richmond* vi, We played at catch with the Dutch cheese, and afterwards bowled it for long-stopping.

B. Quasi-*sb.* and *sb.*

I. The neuter adj. used *absol.*

1. In various phrases with preps.

†**a.** ***at long***: = 'at length'; (*a*) after a long time, in the end; (*b*) in an extended manner, in many words, fully.

a **1400–50** *Alexander* 3498 Bot lat vs leue him at longe & lende to oure hames. **1532** MORE *Confut. Tindale* Wks. 579/2, I shall purpose to treate of thys matter more at long. **1565** T. STAPLETON *Fortr. Faith* 139b, It were.. superfluous at longe to discusse.

b. ***before long***: before a long time has elapsed, soon. So ***ere long***, ERELONG.

1760–72 H. BROOKE *Fool of Qual.* (1809) IV. 69 Perhaps we may meet ere long. **1813** SOUTHEY *Nelson* II. 196 Let us hope that these islands may, ere long, be made free and independent. **1871** TROLLOPE *Ralph the Heir* xlii. 426 'Bye, bye', said Neefit, 'I'll be here again before long'. **1872** SWINBURNE *Ess. & Stud.* (1875) 28 The terror and ignorance which ere long were to impel them to the conception and perpetration of even greater crimes. **1892** *Bookman* Oct. 28/2 We expect from him before long a better novel than he has yet given us.

c. ***by long and by last*** (? dial.): in the end.

1900 *Longm. Mag.* Dec. 103 By long and by last we came to Veermut bridge.

d. ***for long***: †(*a*) long ago (*obs.*); (*b*) throughout a long period (occas. ***for long and long***, ***for long together***); also *predicatively*, destined or likely to continue long.

a **1300** *Cursor M.* 4507 For lang was said, and yeit sua bes, 'Hert sun for-gettes þat ne ei seis'. *a* **1548** HALL *Chron., Rich. III* 56 For long we have sought the furious bore, and now we have found him. **1729** B. LYNDE *Diary* 29 Dec. (1880) 35 Expecting the governor would adjourn for long the Gen'l Court. **1803** MARY CHARLTON *Wife & Mistress* IV. 171 'Well, Lord, it mayn't be for long', replied Dolly. **1839** *Spirit Metrop. Conserv. Press* (1840) II. 535 No man.. kept himself for long and long, at a fearful..speed, as did Lord Brougham. **1856** F. E. PAGET *Owlet of Owlst.* 148 Her back aches..frightfully if she sits up for long together. **1874** LD. HOUGHTON in T. W. Reid *Life* (1891) II. 300 Ripon's conversion is one of the oddest news I have heard for long.

1895 MRS. H. WARD *Bessie Costrell* 121 The children..had been restless for long.

†**e.** ***of long***: since a remote period; for a long time past. (Cf. OF 53.) *Obs.*

1583 STOCKER *Civ. Warres Lowe C.* IV. 24b, The Castle of Antwerpe..had of long been a denne of murderers. **1591** SPENSER *M. Hubberd* 1325 The Lion..gan him avize..what had of long Become of him. **1603** KNOLLES *Hist. Turks* (1638) 1 The Turks haue of long most inhabited the lesser Asia. **1615** W. LAWSON *Country Housew. Gard.* (1626) 39 Suckers of long doe not beare. **1625** BACON *Ess., Judicature* (Arb.) 453 Penall Lawes, if they haue beene Sleepers of long.

†**f.** ***on long***: in length. *Obs.*

a **1300** *Cursor M.* 21664 O four corner þe arche was made, Als has þe cros on lang and brade.

†**g.** ***umbe long***: after a long interval. *Obs.*

c **888** K. ÆLFRED *Boeth.* xxxix. §2 (Sedgefield) 125 Đa andswarode he ymbe long and cwæð. *a* **1225** *Leg. Kath.* 518 þes sondesmon, umbe long,..com, & brohte wið him fifti scolmeistres.

†**h.** ***with the longest***: for a very long time.

1636 tr. *Florus's Hist.* IV. ii. 273 When that part of his forces which was left behind..stayed with the longest [L. *moram faceret*] at Brundisium.

i. ***at (the) longest***: on the longest estimate.

1857 PUSEY *Lenten Serm.* xii. (1883) 235 Short, at the longest, were the life of man.

2. a. Without prep.: Much time. Now chiefly in ***to take long***. †***this long*** (used *advb.*): for this long time (*obs.*). ***that long*** (colloq.): that length of time.

c **1470** HENRY *Wallace* I. 262 Du sone, this lang quhar has thow beyne? **1565** T. STAPLETON tr. *Bede's Hist. Ch. Eng.* 31 Forsakyng that auncient religion whiche this longe both I and my people haue obserued. **1635** J. HAYWARD tr. *Biondi's Banish'd Virg.* 102 Otherwise he had never..this long have deferr'd its discovery. **1898** *Engineering Mag.* XVI. 67 It will take at least ten times that long to get a train ready for a return trip. **1901** A. HOPE *Tristram of Blent* xxv. 336 He had been wondering how long they would take to think of the lady who now held the title and estates. *Mod.* Don't take very long about it. I do not think it will take long to finish the work.

b. as the predicate of an impersonal clause, (*a*) ***it is (was, will be, etc.) long before, since, to*** (something); ***it will be long first; ere it be long***. †Also ***long to*** (used absol.) = 'long first'. †Also ellipt., ***though long first***.

?*c* **1000** in *Sax. Leechd.* III. 434 Næs lang to þy þæt his broþor þyses lænan lifes timan ȝeendode. *c* **1400** MAUNDEV. (Roxb.) i. 4 It es lang sen it fell oute of þe hand. **1485** CAXTON *Paris & V.* 39 It shal not be longe to but that ye shal be hyely maryed. **1540–1** ELYOT *Image Gov.* 7 There shall be or it bee longe, a more ample remembraunce. **1560** DAUS tr. *Sleidane's Comm.* 174 Leste the olde enemye of mankynde, would styre up warre..or ever it were longe. *c* **1592** MARLOWE *Massacre Paris* xx. 13 And tell him, ere it be long, I'll visit him. **1606** ROLLOCK *1 Thess.* iii. 34 Byde a little while, it is not long to. **1616** T. MATHEWS *Let.* in *Ussher's Lett.* (1686) 36 God now at last, though long first, sending so good opportunity. **1631** WEEVER *Anc. Funeral Mon.* 223 As it was long before he could be perswaded to take a Prebend of Lincolne. **1670** LADY MARY BERTIE in *12th Rep. Hist. MSS. Comm.* App. v. 22, I hope now it will not be long before I see you at Exton. **1740** tr. *De Mouhy's Fort. Country-Maid* (1741) I. 47 It will not be long first. **1824** MISS FERRIER *Inher.* lxvi, She'll bring him round to her way of thinking before it's long.

3. ***the long and the short of (it, etc.)***, less frequently ***the short and the long***: the sum total, substance, upshot. Also, ***to make short of long***: to make a long story short.

c **1500** *Merch. & Child* in Hazlitt *Early Pop. Poetry* I. 135 Thys ys the schorte and longe. **1598** SHAKS. *Merry W.* II. i. 137 There's the short and the long. **1620** SHELTON *Quix.* II. xxxix. 254 The short and the long was this. **1642** J. EATON *Honey-c. Free Justif.* 245 Whereof riseth such a necessity of beleeving..that Christ maketh this the short and long of all. **1690** W. WALKER *Idiomat. Anglo-Lat.* 412 This is the long and the short of it. **1713** ADDISON *Guardian* No. 108 ¶8 This is, sir, the long and the short of the matter. **1770** FOOTE *Lame Lover* II. Wks. 1799 II. 80 And that, Mr. John, is the long and the short on't. **1840** DICKENS *Old C. Shop* xxxv, The short and the long of it is, that [etc.]. **1883** R. W. DIXON *Mano* IV. vii. 160 There, to make short of long, was he way-laid By many knights at once. **1898** BESANT *Orange Girl* I. ix, The long and the short of it..is that you must pay me this money.

II. As *sb.* (with *a* and *plural*).

4. a. *Mus.* A long note; *spec.* in the early notation, a note equivalent to two or to three breves, according to the rhythm employed; also, the character by which it was denoted. †***long and short*** (see quot. 1597).

c **1460** *Towneley Myst.* xii. 414, It was a mery song; I dar say that he broght foure & twenty to a long. **1590** COKAINE *Treat. Hunting* D iv b, Where the Foxe is earthed, blowe for the Terriers after this manner: One long and two short. **1594** BARNFIELD *Sheph. Cont.* iii, My Prick-Song's alwayes full of Largues and Longs. **1597** MORLEY *Introd. Mus.* 78 Long and short is when we make two notes tied together, and then another of the same kinde alone. *a* **1619** FOTHERBY *Atheom.* II. xii. §1 (1622) 334 The Art of Musicke mixeth contrary sounds in her Songes: as Sharps, with flats; and briefes, with Longs. **1674** PLAYFORD *Skill Mus.* I. vii. 24 The Large contains eight Semibreves, the Long four. **1706** A. BEDFORD *Temple Mus.* xi. 227 When Musick was first invented, there were but Two Notes, viz. a Long, and a Breve. **1782** BURNEY *Hist. Mus.* II. iii. 184 The first consists of a succession of Longs and Breves. **1887** BROWNING *Parleyings w. Cert. People* Wks. 1896 II. 730/1 Larges and Longs and Breves displacing quite Crochet-and-quaver pertness. **1891** W. POLE *Philos. Mus.* 162 The breve being intended to be held about half the time of the long.

attrib. **1727–41** CHAMBERS *Cycl.* s.v. *Character*, Long Rest. **1886** W. S. ROCKSTRO *Hist. Mus.* iii. 35 Perfect Long Rest. Imperfect Long Rest.

b. In the Morse code, a dash (opp. 'short'); a long buzz, etc., sounded as a signal.

1875 W. THOMSON *Pop. Lect. & Addresses* (1891) III. 128 [It] renders quick and sure Morse signalling by longs and shorts impracticable. **1902** KIPLING *Traffics & Discov.* (1904) 192 In longs and shorts, as laid down by..Mr. Morse. **1916** [see BUZZ *v.*[1] 9]. **1926** R. W. HUTCHINSON *First Course Wireless* 112 The key in the primary circuit enables the train of sparks to be continued for a long or a short period of time, thus producing the 'longs' and 'shorts', *i.e.* the 'dashes' and 'dots' of the Morse Code. **1943** F. J. SALFELD in *Penguin New Writing* XVII. 41 The alarm sounded: a series of urgent longs on the buzzer. **1948** 'J. TEY' *Franchise Affair* x. 112 Do you know morse?.. I shall hoot the initials of your beautiful name on the horn... Two longs and three shorts. **1973** J. DRUMMOND *Bang! Bang! You're Dead!* xxxviii. 134 A buzzer sounded..two longs, two shorts, another long.

5. *Prosody.* A long syllable. ***longs and shorts***: quantitative (esp. Latin or Greek) verses or versification. Hence (*nonce-use*) **long-and-short** *v.*, to make Greek or Latin verses.

a **1548** HALL *Chron., Rich. III* 42 This poeticall schoole-mayster corrector of breves and longes, caused Collyngborne to be abbreviate shorter by the hed. **1811** BYRON *Hints from Hor.* 514 Whom public schools compel To 'long and short' before they're taught to spell. **1851** CARLYLE *Sterling* I. iv. (1872) 29 Classicality,..greatly distinguishable from..death in longs and shorts. **1871** M. ARNOLD *Friendship's Garland* vi. 51, 'I have seen some longs and shorts of Hittall's', said I, 'about the Calydonian Boar, which were not bad'. **1872** *Young Gentleman's Mag.* 23/1 As two shorts are supposed to equal one long, you may..put a dactyl for a spondee.

6. Building. ***longs and shorts***: long and short blocks placed alternately in a vertical line; the style of masonry characterized by this arrangement. Also *attrib.*, as in ***long-and-short work***, ***masonry***.

1845 PETRIE *Round Towers Irel.* II. iii. 188 Long and short. .. This masonry consists of alternate long and short blocks of ashlar, or hewn stone, bonding into the wall. **1863** G. G. SCOTT *Westm. Abbey* (ed. 2) 11 A small loop window..with long-and-short work in the jambs. **1884** EARLE *Ags. Lit.* 54 Of Saxon construction a chief peculiarity is that which is called 'longs and shorts'. It occurs in coins of towers, in panelling work, and sometimes in door jambs.

7. = *Long Vacation* (A. 18).

1848 J. H. NEWMAN *Loss & Gain* I. x. 71 'Reding ought to live here all through the Long,' said Tenby: 'does any one live through the Vacation, sir, in Oxford?' **1852** C. A. BRISTED *Five Yrs. in Eng. Univ.* (ed. 2) 37 For a month or six weeks in the 'Long' they rambled off to see the sights of Paris. **1857** MRS. GASKELL *Let.* 7 Dec. (1966) 490 Arthur Stanley..has just been spending the 'Long' at Moscow. **1861** D. G. ROSSETTI *Let.* June (1965) II. 406 Amateur workmen..offered on all hands, chiefly university men who stayed in Oxford that 'Long' for the purpose. **1863** G. M. HOPKINS *Let.* 22 Mar. (1956) 15 The probability is I shall not see you for an age, unless we manage to meet in the Long. **1885** M. PATTISON *Mem.* 149, I began the Long in the belief that I was going in for my degree in November. **1888** *Echoes Oxford Mag.* (1890) 111 If you dare to come up in the Long. **1891** *Daily News* 25 Oct. 2/3 [Oxford] had not yet awakened from the lethargy of the 'Long'. **1920** G. SAINTSBURY *Notes on Cellar-Bk.* x. 158 A mixture..first imparted to me..by a very amiable Dorsetshire farmer whom I met while walking from Sherborne to Blandford in my first Oxford 'long'.

8. *pl.* **a.** = *long-clothes.*

1841 J. T. HEWLETT *Parish Clerk* II. 63 A baby in longs.

b. Long trousers. *colloq.*

1928 *T. Eaton & Co. Catal.* Spring & Summer 219/3 Flannel longs..boy's long trousers made from grey union flannel. **1947** D. M. DAVIN *Gorse blooms Pale* 57 His first suit of longs, all nearly pressed. **1954** 'A. GARVE' *Riddle of Samson* i. 15 A pair of grey flannel shorts that looked as though they'd been cut down from 'longs'. **1962** B. HARRISSON *Orang-Utan* i. 37 They wanted to buy smart shorts (or, better still, longs), shirts and tie, a radio.

9. *pl.* Long whist. (See WHIST *sb.*) *rare.*

1841 J. T. HEWLETT *Parish Clerk* II. 29 Shilling points at longs..were the fashion. **1850** *Bohn's Handbk. Games* 162.

10. *Comm.* **a.** One who has purchased in expectation of future demand.

1881 *Chicago Times* 12 Mar., Under negotiations by the 'longs'..the market [i.e. for pork] fell back 5c. **1890** *Daily News* 2 Sept. 2/5 Wheat..fell off owing to longs unloading. **1897** *Westm. Gaz.* 23 Aug. 5/1 'Longs' circulating sensational accounts of damage done to the spring wheat crop.

b. *pl.* Long-term stocks.

1964 *Financial Times* 12 Mar. 21/1 Partly reflecting technical influences, gilt-edged continued to gain ground, with the 'longs' closing up to $\frac{7}{16}$ better. **1969** *Daily Tel.* 16 Sept. 2 The 'longs' and undated stocks were particularly prominent and Treasury $6\frac{3}{4}$ p.c. 1995–98 rose a full point. **1972** *Times* 17 June 23/3 The 'longs'..closed 'uneasily steady', dealers said.

long (lɒŋ), *a.*[2] Also 3–5, *north. dial.* 8–9 lang, 4–5 lange, 5–6 longe. [Aphetic f. ME. *ilong*, OE. *ȝelang* ALONG *a.*[1]] Phr. ***long of*** (†***long on***): attributable to, owing to, on account of, because of, 'along of'. Now *arch.* and *dial.*

c **1200** ORMIN 13377 All Crisstene follkess hald Iss lang o Cristess hellpe. *c* **1275** LAY. 15886 Sai waren [= whereon] hit his lang þat þe wal falleþ. *a* **1300** *Cursor M.* 6030 Al þis wrak on me es lang [*Fairf.* lange, *Trin.* longe]. *c* **1330** *Spec. Gy Warw.* 750 Here ȝe muwen se þe wrong And knowe, wher-on hit is long [*v.r.* alange]. *c* **1350** *St. Mary Magd.* 464 in Horstm. *Altengl. Leg.* (1881) 86 All my los es lang on þe. *a* **1400–50** *Alexander* 4606 Slik lust is lang on þe leuir &

likand spices. *c* **1489** CAXTON *Sonnes of Aymon* i. 50 Neuer we shall faylle you but if it be longe of you. **1494** FABYAN *Chron.* VII. 535 Whether it were of the Englysshmen longe or of the Portyngaleys, moche harme was done to the Spaynyardys. **1549** COVERDALE *Erasm. Par. 1 John* 44 All is long of the darkenes of the hate of his brother, that hath so blynded his eyes. **1583** STUBBES *Anat. Abus.* II. (1882) 33 Who is it long of, can you tell? **1591** FLORIO *2nd Fruites* 51, I wot not what it is long of, but I haue no stomack. **1602** *2nd Pt. Return fr. Parnass.* Prol. (Arb.) 3 Its all long on you, I could not get my part a night or two before. **1651** BAXTER *Saints' Rest* I. v. §2. 61 That the very Damned live, is to be ascribed to him; That they live in misery, is long of themselves. **1705** J. BLAIR in Perry *Hist. Coll. Am. Col. Ch.* I. 148, I do again assure you it shall not be long of me if our differences be long lived. **1749** CHESTERFIELD *Lett.* 24 Nov. (1892) I. 377, I have told the French Minister, *as how, that if* that affair be not soon concluded, your Lordship would think it *all long of him.* **1881** SWINBURNE *Mary Stuart* III. i. 113 That all these Have fallen out profitless, 'tis long of you.

long (lɒŋ), *adv.* Compared **longer** ('lɒŋgə(r)), **longest** ('lɒŋgɪst). Forms: 1 **lange, longe,** 2 **lange,** *Orm.* **lannge,** 3–5, *Sc.* 6–9 **lang,** 3–5 **longe,** 5– **long.** See also LENG, LENGER, LENGEST. [OE. *lange, lǫnge,* = OFris. *lang(e, long(e,* OS. *lango* (Du. *lang*), OHG. *lango* (MHG., mod.G. *lange*):—OTeut. **laŋgô,* f. **laŋgo-* LONG *a.*]

1. a. For or during a long time.

† ***long a day*** (Spenser): for a long time. [Prob. for *long of the day*; cf. 'long time of þe dei,' quot. *a* 1225 in A. 7. Possibly the rare phrase *long the day* may have had this origin; but see 6 below.]

Beowulf (Z.) 2344 Þeah ðe hord-welan heolde lange. *c* **888** K. ÆLFRED *Boeth.* (Sedgefield) xxxv. §7 Ða he ða longe and longe hearpode, ða cleopode se hellwara cyning. *c* **1175** *Lamb. Hom.* 25 Ȝet ic mei longe libben. *c* **1200** ORMIN 219 Forrwhi þe preost swa lannge wass þatt daȝȝ att Godess allterr. *c* **1250** *Owl & Night.* 466 He nis nother ȝep ne wis, That longe abid war him nod nis. *a* **1300** *Cursor M.* 169 Iesus quen he lang had fast Was fondid wit þe wik gast. **1340** *Ayenb.* 205 A roted eppel amang þe holen, makeþ rotie þe yzounde, yef he is longe þer amange. *c* **1400** MAUNDEV. (Roxb.) ii. 5 Þai wald þat it schuld hafe lang lasted. **1495** *Act 11 Hen. VII*, c. 22 §4 Laborers..longe sitting at ther brekfast at ther dyner and nonemete. *a* **1548** HALL *Chron., Edw. IV* 192 b, This matter..hangyng long in consultacion. **1562** PILKINGTON *Expos. Abdyas* Pref. 9 Tyrannes raygne not long. **1590** SPENSER *F.Q.* I. x. 9 Most vertuous virgin.. That..hast wandered through the world now long a day. **1596** *Ibid.* VI. iii. 4 Is this the timely joy, which I expected long. *c* **1605** *Acc. Bk. W. Wray* in *Antiquary* XXXII. 178, 1469. K. henry 6 proclamed kinge, but continued not longe. **1659** *Burton's Diary* (1828) IV. 372 If they could spare members, they must attend long. **1697** DRYDEN *Æneid* x. 501 They long suspend the Fortune of the Field. **1721** RAMSAY *Prospect Plenty* vii, Lang have they ply'd that trade. **1766** GOLDSM. *Hermit* viii, Man wants but little here below, Nor wants that little long. **1787** JEFFERSON *Writ.* (1859) II. 322 We have long been expecting a packet. **1844** THIRLWALL *Greece* VIII. 115 The principle, which had long been generally admitted in the Greek republics, that [etc.]. **1883** R. W. DIXON *Mano* I. i. 1 Gerbert's disciple once, but long a monk Of Sant Evreult. **1895** F. HARRISON in *19th Cent.* Aug. 215 Many of his criticisms of modern scientific philosophy are precisely those which I have long urged.

b. In the comparative and superlative, or preceded by advs. of comparison (*as, how, so, thus, too,* etc.), the adv. indicates amount of relative duration. (Cf. LONG *a.* 8.) *so* (or ***as***) ***long as***: often nearly equivalent to 'provided that', 'if only'. Also, ***long as***, ellipt. for *so* (or *as*) *long as.*

c **900** tr. *Bæda's Hist.* IV. xxv. (Schipper) 496 Ic..þe ..ætywde..hu lange þu on hreowe awunian sceole. **971** *Blickl. Hom.* 169 Swa lange swa ȝe ðisdydon ðara anum ðe on me ȝelyfdon. *a* **1225** *Leg. Kath.* 1816 To longe we habbeð idriuen ure dusischipes. *c* **1375** *Sc. Leg. Saints* vii. (*Jacobus Minor*) 623 Ay þe langare he sat sa, þe mare grew his sorow & va. *c* **1400** *Lanfranc's Cirurg.* 37 If þat a wounde haþ be to longe in þe eir open..þanne [etc.]. **1433** *Rolls of Parlt.* IV. 424/1 Whiles and as longe as hit is or shall be soo. *c* **1500** *Melusine* lv. 331 So long rode geffray that he came to the Castel. **1513** MORE in Grafton *Chron.* (1568) II. 775 The Cardinall perceyved that the Queene waxed ever the longer the farther of. *c* **1560** A. SCOTT *Poems* (S.T.S.) xix. 13 How lang sall I this lyfe inleid. **1567** *Gude & Godlie Ball.* (S.T.S.) 27 Als lang as I leue on this eird. **1568** TILNEY *Disc. Mariage* C viij b, I have alreadie troubled them to long. **1590** SPENSER *F.Q.* II. viii. 28 The guilt, which if he liued had thus long, His life for dew reuenge should deare abye. **1631** GOUGE *God's Arrows* III. lxv. 304 A liquour..which kept them from rotting, and made them last the longer. **1642** J. SHUTE *Sarah & Hagar* (1649) 171 Absalon..kept his wrath so long; until it burst out into blood. *c* **1680** BEVERIDGE *Serm.* (1729) I. 68 So long as there are devils in hell. **1715** ATTERBURY *On Matt.* xxvii. 25 in *Serm.* (1734) I. 127 Thus long have they [Jews] been no Nation. **1732** BERKELEY *Alciphr.* II. §20 The world ..always will be the same, as long as men are men. **1776** *Trial of Nundocomar* 29/2 How long did you live with Sielabut at Delhi? **1807** WORDSWORTH *To Small Celandine* in *Poems* I. 22 Long as there's a sun that sets Primroses will have their glory. **1825** THIRLWALL *Lett.* (1881) 85 To cling to your profession as long as you can. **1834** SOUTHEY *Lett.* (1856) IV. 391 God has mercifully supported me thus long. **1846** BROWNING *Lost Mistress* v, I will hold your hand but as long as all may, Or so very little longer. **1863** H. COX *Instit.* III. ix. 730 One-third who have been longest in office retire annually. **1870** MORRIS *Earthly Par.* I. I. 394 She stood so long that she forgot to weep. **1887** L. CARROLL *Game of Logic* Pref., Is there any great harm in that, so long as you get plenty of amusement? **1938** G. GREENE *Brighton Rock* I. i. 22 'It's all right,' he said, 'long as you are here.'

c. colloq. *so* ***long***: good-bye, 'au revoir'. [Cf. G. *so lange.*]

1865 F. H. NIXON *P. Perfume* 8 Will wish you 'ta ta'— gentle reader—'So long!' *a* **1868** W. WHITMAN *Poems* 398, I whisper So long! And take the young woman's hand..for the last time. **1889** *Chamb. Jrnl.* 22 June 397 'When shall we see you again? Not for another six months I s'pose. So long'. **1894** A. ROBERTSON *Nuggets*, etc. 199 'So long then; wish you luck'.

d. ***I, you,*** etc. ***may*** (do something) ***long enough***: a colloquial phrase expressing hopelessness of result. Now usually followed by *before* conj.

1530 PALSGR. 616/2, I may do a thing longe ynough, which sayeng we use whan we signyfye our labour to be in vayne. .. Thou maye krye longe ynough: *tu as beau braire.* **1871** BROWNING *Hervé Riel* xi, Search the heroes flung pell-mell On the Louvre, face and flank; You shall look long enough ere you come to Hervé Riel.

2. a. The suppression of the qualified adj., adv., or phrase, in expressions like ***to be long about one's work***, causes the adv. *long* to assume the character of a quasi-adjectival predicate = 'occupying a long time', 'delaying long'. Const. *in,* †*of,* †*a* (with gerund; the prep. is now often omitted *colloq.*), also followed by conj. *ere, or, before.*

The originally advb. character of the word in this use is shown by the form *longe* (riming with *fonge*) in the first example, and by the analogy of the similar use of the advb. phrase in ***to be a long time***. Cf. however F. *être long à.*

c **1290** *S. Eng. Leg.* I. 145/1368 Sumdel þe pope was anuyd þat he hadde i-beo so longe. **1479** *Paston Lett.* III. 258 Let myn oncle..kepe the patent..tyll he have hys mone, and that shall not be longe to. **1530** TINDALE *Num.* xiv. 18 The Lorde is longe yer he be angrye, and full of mercy. **1539** *Cranmer's Bible* Matt. xxiv. 48 My lord will be long a commyng. **1542** UDALL *Erasm. Apoph.* 268 Whiche thyng forasmuch as it was veray slacke and longe in dooyng..he assaied to passe ouer the sea of Adria. **1560** J. DAUS tr. *Sleidane's Comm.* 86 b, Went to mete..the Emperour, but they were longe or they myght be suffered to come to his speche. **1606** G. W[OODCOCKE] *Hist. Ivstine* VI. 31 That the Empire which was so long a getting..might not come to wracke. **1611** SHAKS. *Wint. T.* III. iii. 8 Ile not be long before I call vpon thee. **1612** CHAPMAN *Widdowes Teares* I. Dram. Wks. 1873 III. 19 Goe, Ile not be long. **1637** EARL MONM. tr. *Malvezzi's Romulus & Tarquin* 294 The witchcraft of Rhetorique being ended, which is not long a doing. **1671** H. M. tr. *Erasm. Colloq.* 545, I advise to be long a chusing a kind of life. **1780** H. WALPOLE *Lett.* (1902) 26 It is from Glasgow, whence I am still longer before I believe. **1796** MRS. E. PARSONS *Myst. Warning* IV. 242 You shall..remain ..till I have discovered the whole of your vile plot, which will not be long first. **1799** ANNA SEWARD *Lett.* (1811) V. 257 The real author cannot be long of being déterré. **1803** *Loriman* II. 57 The wound was long before it was healed. *a* **1814** *Last Act* II. i. in *New Brit. Theatre* II. 381 Is not our old gentleman rather beyond his time? in truth, I think him long. **1829** SCOTT *Anne of G.* ix, They were not long of discovering the *tête-du-pont.* **1880** FROUDE *Bunyan* 53 His remarkable ability was not long in showing itself. **1894** *Pall Mall Mag.* Mar. II. 740 The opportunity was not long in coming.

b. ***not to be long for this world***: to have only a short time to live.

1822 BYRON *Let. to J. Murray* 23 Sept., If it is, I cannot be long for this world. **1849** THACKERAY *Pendennis* I. xxv. 239 She fairly told Pen one day..that she felt herself breaking, and not long for this world. **1933** J. MASEFIELD *Bird of Dawning* 43 He was shocked by the roaring wash of the water coming into the after hold. 'She's not long for this world,' he muttered. **1968** L. GOODMAN *Sun Signs* (1970) 193 These people either radiate incredible vitality or else complain that they're not long for this world.

3. With an agent-noun, as ***long-liver***. Also ***longer, longest liver***, in legal use for 'the survivor, the last survivor'.

1485 *Rolls of Parlt.* VI. 271/2 The longest liver of them. **1522** in *Eng. Gilds* (1870) 237 The sayd Elizabethe nowe hys wyffe yf she be longer lyuer. **1530** PALSGR. 317/2 Longe taryer. **1602** *Narcissus* (1893) 241 Why am I longer liver? **1662** BP. HOPKINS *Funeral Serm.* (1685) 13 The longest liver hath no more but that he is longer a dying than others. **1781** MAD. D'ARBLAY *Diary* Aug., He is strong-built,..I dare say he will be a very long liver. **1818** CRUISE *Digest* (ed. 2) II. 311 For and during the term of their natural lives, and the life of the longer liver of them. **1869** HUGHES *Alfred Gt.* iv. 53 The longest liver..should take land and treasure. **1873** H. SPENCER *Stud. Sociol.* (1882) 94 The qualities which make him likely to be a long-liver.

4. Followed by *after, before,* †*eft, ere,* †*or,* or *since* (advs., conjs., or preps.): At, from, or to a point of time far distant from the time indicated.

a **1300** *Cursor M.* 5259 Sun i wend, lang siþengan, þat wild beistes had þe slain. *Ibid.* 15938 Him..i sagh lang ar wit him in rute. *c* **1425** WYNTOUN *Cron.* III. iii. 598 Scotland was dyssawarra left And wast nere lyand lang thare eft. *a* **1400–50** *Alexander* 1145 Þare he lies with his ledis lang or he foundes. **1470–85** MALORY *Arthur* I. iii, Alle the estates were longe or day in the chirche for to praye. **1513** MORE in Grafton *Chron.* (1568) II. 759 One Mistlebrooke long before morning came in great haste. **1523** LD. BERNERS *Froiss.* I. vii. 5 The kyng sawe his suster, whom he had nat sene long before. *c* **1530** TINDALE *Prol. to Jonah* (1551), Wycleffe preached repentaunce vnto our fathers not longe sence. **1560** DAUS tr. *Sleidane's Comm.* 26 b, And so not longe after they burned Luthers workes. *a* **1649** DRUMM. OF HAWTH. *Poems* Wks. (1711) 25 The long-since dead from bursted graves arise. **1662** STILLINGFL. *Orig. Sacr.* III. iv. §1 If there were persons existent in the World long before Adam was. *a* **1774** GOLDSM. *Surv. Exp. Philos.* (1776) I. 9 Wanting the basis of reason, the whole fabric has long since fallen to the ground. **1816** SOUTHEY *Ess.* (1832) I. 331 They ought, long ere this, to have been prevented. **1845** M. PATTISON *Ess.* (1889) I. 28 A prison..the ruins of which long after remained on the left bank of the Seine. **1861** *Ibid.* 47 Protestant and peaceful times, long after London had ceased to fear a foreign foe. **1860** READE *Cloister & H.* xxx, He and I were born the same year, but he cut his teeth long before me. **1889** SWINBURNE *Stud. Prose & Poetry* (1894) 269 Such is life—as Mrs. Harris long since observed. **1897** *Outing* (U.S.) XXX. 167/2 You are hemmed in on every side by the long-since past.

5. The comparative is used (chiefly with qualifying adv., as *any, no, much, a little,* etc.) in the sense: After the point of time indicated by the context (= L. *amplius,* F. *plus* with negative, G. *mehr*). ***no longer***: not now as formerly.

a **1300** *Cursor M.* 1300 To liue moght he na langar drei. **1423** JAS. I *Kingis Q.* xi, Vp I rase, no langer wald I lye. **1594** SHAKS. *Rich. III,* I. iii. 157, I can no longer hold me patient. **1662** STILLINGFL. *Orig. Sacr.* II. vii. §7 There should a time come when the Ceremoniall Law should oblige no longer. **1766** GOLDSM. *Vic. W.* xxviii, Happiness I fear is no longer reserved for me here. **1802** *Hatred* I. 126, I could no longer dissemble with myself. **1894** HALL CAINE *Manxman* III. xix. 190 There was no longer any room for doubt.

6. Subjoined to expressions designating a period of time, with the sense: Throughout the length of (the period specified). [Cf. G. *sein leben lang.*] †Also rarely *poet.* in reversed order, as ***long the day*** (cf. *long a day* under 1).

c **1290** *S. Eng. Leg.* I. 264/122 Heore ȝat was swiþe faste i-mad: þoruȝ al þe ȝere longue. **1530** TINDALE *Answ. More* IV. xi. Wks. (1573) 332 There were martyrs that suffered martyrdome for the name of Christ all the yeare long. **1568** GRAFTON *Chron.* I. 169 He traveyled all night long to Winchester warde. *c* **1586** C'TESS PEMBROKE *Ps.* LXXI. v, Thy gratious glory Was my ditty long the day. **1590** SPENSER *F.Q.* I. i. 32 The Sunne that measures heaven all day long. *a* **1641** BP. MOUNTAGU *Acts & Mon.* (1642) 478 Without any change or alteration all the Sabbath long. **1650** TRAPP *Comm. Num.* xxiii. 10 Carnall men..live all their lives-long in Dalilah's lap. **1659** H. L'ESTRANGE *Alliance Div. Off.* 154 All Lent long..the very faithful themselves were cast upon their knees. **1720** T. GORDON *Humourist* I. 158 In Scotland ..a Man must be all Sunday long tied either to the Kirk or his Chamber. **1825** THIRLWALL *Crit. Ess.* 36 Accustomed to pass their nights the whole summer long in the open air. **1849** HELPS *Friends in C.* II. iv. 92 You are out all day long with the sheep. **1875** BROWNING *Aristoph. Apol.* 1064 While ..the lesson long, No learner ever dared to cross his legs. **1875** JOWETT *Plato* (ed. 2) III. 245 He was to continue working all his life long at that and at no other.

†**7.** At or to a great or a specified distance in space; far. *Obs. rare.*

c **1250** *Gen. & Ex.* 2485 So longe he hauen ðeðen numen To flum iurdon ðat he ben cumen. **13..** in *Minor P. Vern. MS.* 502 Two wyues sat ȝonder, langare. *c* **1450** *Merlin* 155 Thei smyten..so vigorously that oon myght here the crassinge of speres half a myle longe. **1523** BERNERS tr. *Froissart* I. ix. 7 She..rode to warde Heynaulte, and so long she rode that she came to Cambresys. **1532** in More *Confut. Barnes* VIII. *M.'s Wks.* (1557) 782/2 The church through oute all the worlde scattered farre and long. **1542** *Lam. & Piteous Treat.* in *Harl. Misc.* (1809) IV. 535 His gallyes.. were harboured fyue legges longe frome the sayde towne of Argiere. **1586** D. ROWLAND *Lazarillo* II. (1672) R viij, All the way long did I nothing but think upon my good Gypseys. **1887** W. MORRIS tr. *Homer's Odyssey* XII. 251 As the fisher sits on the headland with a rod that reaches long.

†**8.** With a long step. *Obs.*

1705 *Lond. Gaz.* No. 4116/4 Paces and gallops well, trots a little long.

9. *Comb.* **a.** When qualifying a ppl. adj. used attrib., the word, like most other advs., is commonly hyphened, forming innumerable quasi-compounds with the sense 'for a long time': as ***long-accustomed, -awaited, -borne, -dead, -departed, -expected, -felt, -gone, -held, -lost,*** (as *sb.*), ***-waited, -wearing,*** etc. Also LONG-CONTINUED, LONG-LASTING, LONG-LIVING.

1540 COVERDALE *Fruitf. Less.* To Rdr. (1593) ¶2 b, After *long accustomate doing of vertuous deeds. **1711** SHAFTESB. *Charac.* (1737) II. 64 The abject and compliant state of *long-accustom'd slaves. **1789** COWPER *Annus Mirab.* 47 Our Queen's *long-agitated breast. **1914** *Times* 25 Aug. 6/4 The *long-awaited battle is begun. **1974** *Melody Maker* 23 Mar. 19/3 The release of Jackson Browne's long awaited album 'For Everyman'. *c* **1620** S. A. GORGES *To the King* in Farr *S.P. Jas. I* (1847) 315 Yet in my *long-borne zeale Time's chaunge Can make no chaunge appeare. **1817** LADY MORGAN *France* (1818) I. 194 The sudden resurrection of a *long-buried aristocracy. **1833** J. H. NEWMAN *Arians* v. ii. (1876) 381 That resurrection which now awaited the long-buried truths of the Gospel. **1725** POPE *Odyss.* xx. 400 The *long-contended prize. **1905** *Daily Chron.* 14 Nov. 3/4 The old Franciscan..mourned frantically for his *long-dead brother. **1937** AUDEN in Auden & MacNeice *Lett. from Iceland* i. 21 Scribbling to a long-dead poet. **1974** A. PRICE *Other Paths to Glory* I. vii. 79 The two long-dead riflemen. **1868** LIGHTFOOT *Comm. Philipp.* (1873) 199 The *long-delayed judgment of God. *c* **1838** E. BRONTË *Compl. Poems* (1941) 77 Old Hall of Elbë, ruined, lonely now;..Home of the departed, the *long-departed dead. **1869** 'MARK TWAIN' *Innoc. Abr.* xi. 102 Their long-departed owners seemed to throng the gloomy cells. **1952** R. CAMPBELL tr. *Baudelaire's Poems* 19 Sweeping the far-off skylines with a gaze Regretful of Chimeras long-departed. **1570** J. PHILLIP *Frendly Larum* in Farr *S.P. Eliz.* (1845) II. 526 And eke enioy, as wee doo wish, Our *long-desired masse. **1877** BRYANT *Odyss.* v. 534 To thee, the long-desired, I come. **1533** ELYOT *Cast. Helthe* II. xxxiv. (1541) 52 These exercises,..may put out of the body, all *long duryng sicknesses. **1588** SHAKS. *L.L.L.* IV. iii. 307 As motion and long during action tyres The sinnowy vigour of the trauailer. **1567** TURBERV. *Ovid's Epist.* Q ij, And all my wit is me bereft by *long enduring smart. **1876** GEO. ELIOT *Dan. Der.* IV. lxiii. 251 The long-enduring watcher. **1640** WALLER *Sp. Ho. Com.* 22 Apr., Wks. (1729) 406 A *long-establish'd government. **1837** HT. MARTINEAU *Soc. Amer.* III. 124 A long-established and very eminent lawyer of Boston. **1622** DRAYTON *Poly-olb.* XXII. 929 Their *long expected hopes were vtterly forlorne. **1878** BOSW. SMITH *Carthage* 302 They..balked their Roman conquerors of their long-expected revenge. **1862** A. LINCOLN *Ann. Message to Congress* in *Evening Star* (Washington, D.C.) 1 Dec. 1/2 The judicious legislation of

Congress.. has satisfied.. the *long felt want of an uniform circulating medium. **1936** *Discovery* Mar. 83/2 To satisfy a long-felt want on the part of the serious student. ?**1605** DRAYTON *Eclogue* I. xii, And that all-searching and impartiall Fate Shall take account of *long-forgotten dust. **1725** POPE *Odyss.* XIX. 191 Tears repeat their long-forgotten course. **1950** W. DE LA MARE *Inward Compan.* 25 A happy house in that *long-gone sunshine. **1943** D. GASCOYNE *Poems 1937–42* 33 With *long-held burning breath. **1960** R. W. MARKS *Dymaxion World of B. Fuller* 117/2 Fuller's long-held theory that energy in gases evolves unique local patternings. **1593** SHAKS. *Lucr.* 1816 Now he.. armed his *long-hid wits advisedly. **1843** BROWNING *Return Druses* I. 229 Tell them the *long-kept secret. **1590** SPENSER *F.Q.* I. iii. 27 Ah my *long-lacked lord, Where have ye bene thus long out of my sight? **1860** PUSEY *Min. Proph.* 483 He, the *long-longed for, the chosen of God. **1606** DAY *Ile of Guls* D iij, *Long lookt for comes at last. **1848** DICKENS *Dombey* i, Exulting in the long-looked-for event. **1738** GRAY *Propertius* iii. 83 To Chiron Phœnix owed his *long-lost Sight. **1853** MRS. GASKELL *Cranford* xv. 308, I could no longer confirm her belief that the long-lost was really here. **1887** BESANT *The World went*, etc. xi. 87 The safe return of the long-lost sailor. **1920** M. BEERBOHM *And Even Now* 80, I was always in hope that when next the long-lost turned up.. I should *see* him. **1760–72** H. BROOKE *Fool of Qual.* (1809) IV. 156 The images of his *long-parted friends. **1870** J. H. NEWMAN *Gram. Assent* II. x. 481 During His *long-past sojourn upon earth. **1792** BURKE *Corr.* (1844) III. 388 The solid, permanent, *long-possessed property of the country. **1725** POPE *Odyss.* IV. 9 Hermione.. Was sent to crown the *long-protracted joy. **1715** —— *Iliad* II. 185 With *long-resounding Cries they urge the Train To fit the Ships, and launch into the Main. **1822** SCOTT *Pirate* v, The groans of the mountains, and the long-resounding shores. **1862** H. SPENCER *First Princ.* II. xvi. §134 (1875) 373 Its *long-settled political organization. *a* **1649** DRUMM. OF HAWTH. *Poems* Wks. (1711) 9 With *long-shut eyes I shun the irksome light. **1729** LAW *Serious C.* 299 [He] triumphantly entered that *long-shut-up paradise. **1622** DRAYTON *Poly-olb.* ix. 319 Ere the Iberian Powers had toucht the *long-sought Bay. **1760–72** H. BROOKE *Fool of Qual.* (1809) IV. 74 My long-lost, my long-sought brother! **1643** MILTON *Divorce* To Parl., To be acquitted from the *long-suffer'd ungodly attribute of patronizing Adultery. **1636** B. JONSON *Discov.*, *Homeri Ulysses* (1640) 93 Vlysses, in Homer, is made a *long thinking man, before hee speaks. **1671** MILTON *P.R.* I. 59 We Must bide the stroke of that *long-threatened wound. **1760–72** H. BROOKE *Fool of Qual.* (1809) IV. 149 *Long-toiled mariners, whom storms have at length compelled to seek a final port. **1928** *Publisher's Weekly* 16 June 2425 The *long-waited reminiscences of the British Prime Minister. **1972** *Buenos Aires Herald* 4 Feb. 6/4 The long-waited inauguration in July of the Peligre Hydroelectric Dam. **1590** SPENSER *F.Q.* I. iii. 21 That *long-wandring Greeke, That for his love refused deitye. **1908** *Westm. Gaz.* 16 Apr. 4/2 Greasers are fitted everywhere to.. add to the *long-wearing life of the parts. **1963** *New Yorker* 23 Nov. 15 (Advt.), Our famous shirts.. are made.. of exclusively woven, long-wearing materials. **1975** *Country Life* 2 Jan. 32/1 The engine is.. low-revving and long-wearing. **1693** CONGREVE in *Dryden's Juvenal* (1697) 293 The dry Embraces of *long-wedded Love. **1570** J. PHILLIP *Frendly Larum* in Farr *S.P. Eliz.* (1845) II. 533 And keepe the cruell papists still From their *longe-wished day. *a* **1649** DRUMM. OF HAWTH. *Poems* Wks. (1711) 6 That day, long-wished day. **1748** *Anson's Voy.* I. x. 107 We at last discovered the long-wished for Island. **1857** RUSKIN *Pol. Econ. Art* 38 The *long-withheld sympathy is given at last.

b. With the sense 'to or at a great distance'; in a few nonce-words, chiefly *poet.*, as ***long-destroying, -travelled, wandered, -withdrawing.***

1632 LITHGOW *Trav.* VII. 326 Our long-reaching Ordonance. *a* **1649** DRUMM. OF HAWTH. *Poems* Wks. (1711) 2 The palm her love with long-stretch'd arms embraces. **1667** MILTON *P.L.* XII. 313 Who shall.. bring back Through the worlds wilderness long wanderd man Safe to eternal Paradise of rest. **1681** T. FLATMAN *Heraclitus Ridens* No. 31 (1713) I. 200 A sad Experiment I have made Of the long-reaching Arm of Kings. **1715** POPE *Iliad* VIII. 265 They shake the brands, and threat With long-destroying flames the hostile fleet. **1728–46** THOMSON *Spring* 67 O'er your hills and long-withdrawing vales, Let Autumn spread his treasures. **1870** HAWTHORNE *Eng. Note-Bks.* (1879) II. 23 He is a.. widely and long travelled man.

long (lɒŋ), *v.*[1] Forms: 1 langian, 3–4 longen, 3–6 longe, *north.* lang, (3 longy, 3, 6 longue, 4 loungy, 5 lung, longyn), 3– long. [OE. *langian* = OS. *langôn* impers. = sense 5 below (MDu. *langen* to be or seem long; to 'think long', desire; to extend, hold out, offer, Du. *langen* to offer, present), OHG. *langên* impers. = sense 5 (MHG., G. *langen* to reach, extend, suffice), ON. *langa* impers. and pers. to desire, long:—OTeut. **laŋgôjan*, **laŋgǽjan* f. **laŋgo-* LONG *a.*[1]]

†**I. 1.** *intr.* To grow longer; to lengthen. *Obs.*

c **1000** *Sax. Leechd.* III. 250 Þonne se dæȝ langað þonne gæð seo sunne norðweard. **13..** *K. Alis.* 139 Averil is meory, and longith the day. *c* **1325** *Song on Passion* 2 in *O.E. Misc.* 197 Somer is comen.. þis day biginniz to longe. **1422** tr. *Secreta Secret.*, *Priv. Priv.* 245 The dayes longyth fro equinoccium forth, and the nyghtes shortith.

†**2.** *trans.* To lengthen, prolong. *Obs.*

1382 WYCLIF *Eccl.* viii. 12 Be ther not good to the vnpitouse, ne be ther aferr longid the daȝes of hym. **1422** tr. *Secreta Secret.*, *Priv. Priv.* 202 Prayer longyth a mannys lyue. ?*a* **1500** *Roberd of Cysille* 32 in Hazl. *E.P.P.* I. 271 Hys dwellynge thoȝt he there to longe.

†**3.** *to long away* [used to tr. L. *ēlongāre*].

a. *trans.* To put far away. **b.** *intr.* To depart. *Obs.*

1382 WYCLIF *Ps.* lxxxvii. 19 Thou longedest awei [Vulg. *elongasti*] fro me frend and neȝhebore. —— *Ecclus.* xxxv. 22 The Lord shal not longen awey [Vulg. *elongabit*].

4. *trans.* To cause to pass over a certain distance (see quots.). *dial.*

1674 RAY *S. & E.C. Words* 71 *Long it hither*: Reach it hither. Suffolk. *a* **1825** FORBY *Voc. E. Anglia*, *Long*, to forward to a distance, from one hand to another, in succession.

II. †**5.** *impers.* with accus. ***me longs*** (***longeth***): I have a yearning desire; I long. Const. *after*, or *to* with sb. or inf. *Obs.* (Cf. *to think long*, LONG *a.* 9 b.)

c **893** K. ÆLFRED *Oros.* II. xi. §1 Þæt us nu æfter swelcum longian mæȝe swelce þa wæron. *c* **1200** *Trin. Coll. Hom.* 149 Him wile sone longe þar after. *c* **1290** *S. Eng. Leg.* I. 199/14 Hire longuede with hire broþer to speke. *a* **1300** *Cursor M.* 20141 Hir langed sare hir sun cum to. *a* **1340** HAMPOLE *Psalter* cxxxix. 9 Vs langis eftire a thynge of þe warld. **1406** HOCCLEVE *La Male Regle* 38 Me longed aftir nouelrie.

6. To have a yearning desire; to wish earnestly. Const. *for* (†*after*, occas. †*at*, †*to*), or *to* with inf. (The only current sense.) †Also, to be restless or impatient *till* (something is attained).

a **1300** *Cursor M.* 10548 (Cott.) Þan sal þou find þin husband þar, þat þou has langed efter sare. *c* **1386–90** CHAUCER *Prol.* 12 Thanne longen folk to goon on pilgrimages. *c* **1470** HENRY *Wallace* III. 352 Rycht sar he langyt the toune of Ayr to se. *c* **1500** *Melusine* xix. 72 For therat I lang moche. **1509** HAWES *Past. Pleas.* XXIX. (Percy Soc.) 138 You knowe well that some women do long After nyce thynges, be it ryght or wrong. **1530** PALSGR. 614/1, I longe, as a woman with chylde longeth, or lusteth for a thynge that she wolde eate or drinke of. *a* **1584** MONTGOMERIE *Cherrie & Slae* 177, I langt in Luiffis bow to shute. **1590** MARLOWE *Edw. II*, II. i. 82 Come, leade the way, I long till I am there. **1611** BIBLE *Ps.* cxix. 40, I haue longed after thy precepts. **1632** LITHGOW *Trav.* x. 480 He longed for day, and it being come,.. hee quietly left his Lodging. **1667** MILTON *P.L.* IX. 593 All other Beasts that saw, with like desire Longing and envying stood. **1738** SWIFT *Pol. Conversat.* ii. 129 But what if any of the Ladies should long? Well, here take it, and the D——l do you good with it. **1786** MAD. D'ARBLAY *Diary* 8 Nov., Though she gave me a thousand small distresses, I longed to kiss her for every one of them. **1816** J. WILSON *City of Plague* I. ii. 51 As the cold grave that longeth for its coffin. **1855** KINGSLEY *Heroes, Theseus* I. 197 He longed to ask his mother the meaning of that stone. **1865** TROLLOPE *Belton Est.* xxviii. 338 This man longed for her,—desired to call her his own. **1884** F. TEMPLE *Relat. Relig. & Sci.* viii. (1885) 239 Believers in all ages have longed for external support to their faith.

†**7.** Const. an adv. or advb. phr. with a verb of motion implied: To long to go. *Obs.*

c **1175** *Lamb. Hom.* 157 Him wile sone longe þiderward. *a* **1225** *Leg. Kath.* 1915 Mi longeð heonneward. **1297** R. GLOUC. (Rolls) 3649 Þo þe king hurde þis, him longede þuder sore. *c* **1400** *Destr. Troy* 2914 So longid this lady with lust to the temple. **1548** HALL *Chron.*, *Rich. III* 27 The man had an high harte and sore longed upwarde, not risyng yet so fast as he had hoped.

†**8.** To grow weary. *Sc. Obs.*

1606 ROLLOCK *1 Thess.* xxiii. 293 Let vs not wearie in doing good, and he addes to the promise, we shall reape the frute of our good deeds in our owne tyme, if we long not, but goe forward ay to the end.

long (lɒŋ), *v.*[2] *arch.* Also 3 *north.* lang. [f. *lang*, *long* (not recorded in OE.), aphetic f. OE. *ȝelang* at hand, dependent on, ALONG *a.*[1] (= OHG. *gilang*, *kalang* akin). The simple vb. is now superseded in general use by the compound BELONG *v.*]

1. *intr.* To be appropriate *to* (†occas. *for*); to pertain *to* (†rarely with simple dative); to refer or relate to; to belong, as a member of a family or the like, a native, adherent, or dependent; to be a part, appendage, or dependency. Now only *poet.* as a rare archaism (written *'long* as if short for *belong*).

?*a* **1200** *Charter Edw. Conf.* in Kemble *Cod. Dipl.* (1846) IV. 215 Alle ða land ðe longen into ðare halaȝen stowe. *a* **1300** *Cursor M.* 2808 Has þou her.. ani man.. to þe langand, or hei or lau. *c* **1330** R. BRUNNE *Chron.* (1810) 82 Unto þe Marche gan long an erle, Wolnot he hight. *c* **1386** CHAUCER *Miller's T.* 23 His astrelabie longinge for his Art. —— *Sqr.'s T.* 8 Hym lakked noght that longeth to a kyng. *a* **1400** *Prymer* (1891) 73 God to wham it longeth alone to haue mercy. *c* **1430** LYDG. *Min. Poems* (Percy Soc.) 19 Withe observaunces longyng for a kyng. **1432–50** tr. *Higden* (Rolls) V. 277 A swyneherde longynge to the kynge. *c* **1489** CAXTON *Faytes of A.* IV. x. 258 It is a thinge wherof the knowledge longeth unto him. **1508** DUNBAR *Tua mariit wemen* 407 For neuer I likit a leid that langit till his blude. **1508** FISHER 7 *Penit. Ps.* xxxviii. Wks. (1876) 82 Yf the thynge asked of almyghty god be longynge and not contrary to the soules helth. *a* **1548** HALL *Chron.*, *Hen. V* 70 Their.. fraunchises longyng or dewe to them in all maner of places. **1596** SHAKS. *Tam. Shr.* IV. iv. 6 With such austeritie as longeth to a father. **1600** HOLLAND *Livy* v. xxi. 194 But hereto longeth a tale. **1605** BACON *Adv. Learn.* II. viii. §3 (1873) 124 Such mechanique as longeth to the production of the natures afore rehearsed. **1647** H. MORE *Song of Soul* II. i. II. xlvii, But that full grasp of vast Eternitie 'Longs not to beings simply vegetive. **1650** FULLER *Pisgah* III. iii. 383 West-gate where Shuppim and Hosah were Porters. To them also longed the gate Shallecheth. **1868–70** MORRIS *Earthly Par.* I. 240 He will give thee everything That 'longs unto the daughter of a King.

†**b.** To concern (a person); hence, to be fitting, befit, beseem. *Obs.*

?*a* **1366** CHAUCER *Rom. Rose* 1222 She durste never seyn ne do But that thing that hir longed to. *c* **1380** WYCLIF *Sel. Wks.* III. 146 Hit longis to knyghtis to deffende hom. **1387** TREVISA *Higden* (Rolls) I. 237 In towne, as it longes, þe osul twyterеþ mery songes. *c* **1440** *Gesta Rom.* xxxvi. 140 (Add. MS.) Alle Ioye and gladnesse, as longeth to a maiden for to have. **1450–80** tr. *Secreta Secret.* 5 That, þat longith not to be knowe. *a* **1548** HALL *Chron.*, *Hen. V* 64 It longeth not to clerkes to intermele of them. **1564** tr. *P. Martyr's Comm. Judges* 211 b, That longeth to reason to seeke and search out.

†**2.** (Const. *to*, *unto*.) To be the property or rightful possession of; = BELONG *v.* 3. *Obs.*

1389 in *Eng. Gilds* (1870) 11 Þe catel longynge to þe companye. *c* **1450** *St. Cuthbert* (Surtees) 4818 The maners that to the bischop langed. *c* **1450** *Merlin* 140 All the londe that longeth to the crowne. *a* **1548** HALL *Chron.*, *Hen. V* 63 Any hous or edefice or place of ground longyng to any of the saied citezens. *a* **1552** LELAND *Collect.* I. 235 Fulco had robbid Ruyton a castle longging to Straunge. **1608** DAY *Law-Trickes* v. (1881) 79 Unto what great Prince, Christian or Pagan, longs this mansion?

long, obs. form of LUNG; aphetic f. ALONG.

-long (lɒŋ), †**-longs** *suffix*, forming advs. The earliest instance is *endlong*, from ON. *endlang-r* adj., 'extending from end to end', 'the whole length of'. The word is properly a compound of LONG *a.*; but in Eng. it was principally used as adv., and developed the sense 'end-wise', 'end foremost', so that it became parallel in meaning to words like *sideling*, *headling*, *backling*. The ending *-long* thus came to be regarded as a variant of -LING *suffix*[2]. Hence, on the one hand, the occasional 14th c. form *endelyng* for *endlong*, and, on the other hand, the substitution of *headlong(s*, *sidelong(s*, *flatlong(s* for the earlier *headling(s*, *sideling(s*, *flatling(s*.

‖**longa** ('lɒŋgə). *Mus.* Also 7 longo. [It., a. med.L. *longa* (sc. *nota*), fem. of *longus* long.] = LONG *sb.* 4.

c **1648–50** BRATHWAIT *Barnabees Jrnl.* (1818) 181 What though brieves too be made longo's? **1753** in CHAMBERS *Cycl. Supp.* **1893** SHEDLOCK tr. *Riemann's Dict. Mus.*, *Longa* (▭), the second longest note of mensurable music = $\frac{1}{2}$ or $\frac{1}{3}$ *Maxima*.

longable, obs. form of LAND-GAVEL.

1407 *Waterf. Arch.* in *10th Rep. Hist. MSS. Comm.* App. v. 329 The Kings chief rent called *Longable*.

longabo, longacion: see LONGANON.

†**long-acre.** *Obs.* Apparently a usual proper name for a long narrow field containing an acre. (Now preserved as the name of a well-known London street.) In quots. *allusive* = one's estate or patrimony.

1607 MIDDLETON *Trick to catch the Old One* I. i, But where's Long-acre? in my vncle's conscience, which is 3 yeares voyage about. **1608** *Yorksh. Trag.* I. ix, In a word, Sir, I have consumed all, played away long-acre. **1659** *Lady Alimony* II. i. B 3 b, It will run like Quicksilver over all their Husbands Demains: and in very short time make a quick dispatch of all his Long acre.

long-a'cuminate, *a. Bot.* [f. L. *long-us* long + ACUMINATE.] Having a long tapering point.

1870 HOOKER *Stud. Flora* 336 *Salix fragilis*; leaves lanceolate long-acuminate.

longæval, etc., var. or obs. ff. LONGEVAL, etc.

long-ago. Attrib. use of the advb. phrase *long ago* (see AGO): That has long gone by; that belongs to the distant past. Also quasi-*sb.* and *sb.*, the distant past or its events; rarely in *pl.*

a **1834** COLERIDGE in *Blackw. Mag.* CXXXI. (1882) 116/2 My long, long-ago theory of volition as a mode of double-touch. **1851** LONGF. *Gold. Leg.* I. *Castle Vautsberg*, The shapes of joy and woe, The airy crowds of long-ago. **1861** A. A. PROCTER *Leg. & Lyr.* 205, I have buried grief and sorrow In the depths of Long-ago. **1872** LEVER *Ld. Kilgobbin* ix. (1875) 56 Desultory thoughts.. with 'long-agoes'. **1889** *Chicago Advance* 24 Jan., A book, the long-ago gift of his dead mother. **1896** HARE *Story of my Life* I. Pref. 6 Time is always apt to paint the long-ago in fresh colours. **1896** *Spectator* 7 Mar. 338 In spite of his wide severance from the ways of that long-ago time. **1900** *Pall Mall Mag.* May 77 The long-ago silk gown of a long-ago lady.

longan ('lɒŋgən). Also 8 lungung, 9 lungan, lung-yen. [Chinese *lung-yen*, lit. 'dragon's eye', f. *lung* dragon + *yen* eye.] The fruit of an evergreen tree, *Nephelium Longanum*, cultivated in China and the East Indies; also, the tree itself.

1732 S. BARON *Descript. Tonqueen* in *Churchill's Voy.* III. 4 The fruit called Jean or Lungung (that is, Dragon's eggs [*sic*]) by the Chinese. **1846** LINDLEY *Veg. Kingd.* 383 Thus the Longan, the Litchi, and the Rambutan, fruits among the more delicious of the Indian archipelago, are the produce of different species of Nephelium. **1869** I. BURNS *Life W.C. Burns* xix. (1870) 502 No house could be had for divine service, and they had to gather under the shade of a magnificent lung-yen tree. **1874** S. W. WILLIAMS *Dict. Chinese* 567 *Lung-yen*, the longan fruit (*Nephelium Longan*).

longanimity (lɒŋgə'nɪmɪtɪ). Now *rare*; formerly common in religious use. Also 5 -yte, 6–7 -itie, -ye. [ad. late L. *longanimitāt-em* (occurring, e.g., in Vulg. 2 Pet. iii. 15), f. *longanimus* (see next), after Gr. μακροθυμία. Cf. F. *longanimité*.] Long-suffering; forbearance or patience (e.g. under provocation). (See also quot. 1656.)

c **1450** tr. *De Imitatione* I. xiii. 14 Thou shalt ouercome hem [temptacions] better litel & litel by pacience & longanimyte. **1552** LATIMER *Serm. Lincoln.* viii. 131 Hys

longanimity and long tarying for our amendment. *a* **1600** HOOKER *Serm. Pride* Wks. 1888 III. 614 In Isaac such simplicity, such longanimity in Jacob. **1652** HOWELL *Giraffi's Rev. Naples* II. 198 The staidnesse, longanimity and constancy of the Spaniard. **1656** BLOUNT *Glossogr.* s.v., In Divinity it is thus defined; Longanimity is an untired confidence of mind in expecting the good things of the life to come. **1682** SIR T. BROWNE *Chr. Mor.* III. §1 The Longanimity of God would no longer endure such vivacious abominations. **1724** WARBURTON *Tracts* (1789) 14 Constancy is a Word too weak to express so extraordinary a Behaviour, 'twas Patience, 'twas Longanimity. **1813** MAR. EDGEWORTH *Patronage* (1832) III. xxxviii. 71 The same penetration, the same longanimity, which enabled him to govern the affairs of a great nation, gave him a foresight for his own happiness. **1868** E. EDWARDS *Ralegh* I. xi. 217 In true generosity of soul, he [Essex] was as little a match for Ralegh as in longanimity. **1890** *Spectator* 11 Jan., His longanimity under the foolishness of the young woman is really marvellous.

¶ *erron.* Length (of time); also, prolixity.

1607 [see LONGINQUITY 2, quot. 1658]. **1854** LOWELL *Cambridge 30 Yrs. Ago* Pr. Wks. 1890 I. 83 He is expected to ask a blessing and return thanks at the dinner, a function which he performs with centenarian longanimity, as if he reckoned the ordinary life of man to be fivescore years. **1861** —— *Biglow P.* Ser. II. i. Poet. Wks. 1890 II. 216 A catalogue ..emulous in longanimity of Homer's list of ships.

longanimous (lɒŋ'gænɪməs), *a. rare.* [f. L. *longanim-us* (f. *long-us* LONG + *animus* mind, after Gr. μακρόθυμος) + -OUS.] Long-suffering; enduring, patient.

1620 C. RAWLINSON *Confess. St. Augustine* 45 Thou seest these thinges, O Lord, and thou holdest thy peace, being longanimous, and full of mercy, and truth. **1849** LOWELL *Biglow P.* Ser. I. Introd., Poet. Wks. 1890 II. 35 The present Yankee, full of shifts..longanimous, good at patching.

†'**longanon.** *Med. Obs.* Also 5 langaon, 6 longanum, 6–7 longaon, 8 longano(n, longabo; also 6 *corruptly* longacion, -ation. [Late L. *longano(n, -gabo, -gavo, -gao.*] The rectum.

c **1400** *Lanfranc's Cirurg.* 168 And aftir þis gutt [colon] comeþ langaon, & is þe eende of alle. **1547** BOORDE *Brev. Health* xxv, The longation which is the ars gut. *Ibid.* cccIxiv, They [the wormes] be in a gutte named the longacion. **1548** VICARY *Anat.* viii. 66 The syxte and last is called Rectum or Longaon. **1597** A. M. tr. *Guillemeau's Fr. Chirurg.* 2 b/2 The gutte Ileon..and the Longanum. **1601** HOLLAND *Pliny* I. 343 Those creatures..whose meat passes immediatly..into the straight gut Longaon, or the Tiwill. **1706** PHILLIPS (ed. Kersey), *Longano, Longanon,* or *Longabo*, the Straight Gut, in the Fundament. [In BAILEY, MAYNE *Expos. Lex., Syd. Soc. Lex.*]

longart, variant of LONQUHARD *Sc. Obs.*

†**lon'gation.** *Obs.* [ad. med.L. **longātiōn-em*, n. of action f. *longāre* to prolong, f. *longus* LONG *a.*]

1. Lengthening, elongation.

1597 A. M. tr. *Guillemeau's Fr. Chirurg.* 38/1 Strippe vp the skinne and the muscles, as well for the longation of the skinne, as lengtheninge of the Vaynes and Arteryes.

2. The longer process for transmuting metals.

1584 R. SCOT *Discov. Witchcr.* XIV. v. (1886) 301 In this art [Alcumystrie] there are two waies, the one called longation, the other curtation. **1606** N. BRETON *Sir P. Sydney's Ourânia* K 2 b, With great expence and longation, Must come this metals alteration. **1671** H. M. tr. *Erasm. Colloq.* 259 Longation, and..Curtation.

longation, corrupt form of LONGANON.

†**longayne.** *Obs. rare*⁻¹. [a. OF. *longayne, longaigne* latrina, filthy place.] A filthy place.

1340 *Ayenb.* 212 Me ssel bidde ine oneste stedes naȝt ine longaynes ase doþ þe ypocrites. [An odd misapprehension of the point of Matt. vi. 5.]

'**long-beard.**

1. A man with a long beard.

1786 tr. *Beckford's Vathek* (1883) 128 Loud must have been the sound of the tymbals to overpower the blubbering of the Emir and his longbeards.

¶ **b.** A pseudo-etymol. rendering of LOMBARD.

1647–8 COTTERELL *Davila's Hist. Fr.* (1678) 3 Famous incursions of the Longbeards. **1889** [see LONGOBARDIAN].

2. An epiphytic plant, *Tillandsia usneoides*, found in the forests of the southern United States: also called *long-moss, Spanish moss.*

1858 SIMMONDS *Dict. Trade, Long-beard*, a name for a kind of moss or epiphyte brought down the Mississippi. **1866** in *Treas. Bot.*

3. A bellarmine.

1878 JEWITT *Ceramic Art Gt. Brit.* I. 92 The Bellarmine, or Grey Beard, or Long Beard, as it was commonly called.

'**long-boat.** The largest boat belonging to a sailing vessel.

c **1515** *Cocke Lorell's B.* 12 Some yᵉ longe bote dyde launce. **1578** in G. T. Clarke *Cartæ Glamorgan* (1890) II. 348 And that the..Greene Dragon sent certaine in her longe boate and prayed the said Rich. to come abourde her who so did in the said longe boate. **1593** SHAKS. *2 Hen. VI*, IV. i. 68 Conuey him hence, and on our long boats side, Strike off his head. **1626** CAPT. SMITH *Accid. Yng. Seamen* 3 The Boteswaine..his Mate [is to haue] the command of the long boate, for the setting forth of Anchors. **1694** tr *Milton's Lett. State* Wks. 1851 VIII. 410 Our Long-boats sent to take in fresh Water, were assail'd in the Port. **1702** *Eng. Theophrast.* 130 When they find themselves sinking they save themselves in the long-boat. **1769** FALCONER *Dict. Marine* (1780) F 4, The largest boat that usually accompanies a ship is the long-boat,..which is generally furnished with a mast and sails. **1814** SCOTT *Wav.* lix, The vessel is going to pieces, and it is full time for all who can, to get into the long-boat and leave her. **1840** R. H. DANA *Bef. Mast* xiv. 33 All hands are sent ashore with an officer in the long-boat. **1867** SMYTH *Sailor's Word-bk., Long Boat*, is carvel-built, full, flat, and high.

long-bow ('lɒŋbəʊ). [See BOW *sb.*¹ 4.]

1. The name given to the bow drawn by hand and discharging a long feathered arrow (and so distinguished from CROSS-BOW), the national arm of England from the 14th c. till the introduction of firearms. † *occas.* A soldier armed with a long-bow.

1500 *Robin Hood* (Ritson) II. xx. 75 With a long bow they shot a fat doe. *c* **1511** *1st Eng. Bk. Amer.* (Arb.) Introd. 34/2, .xv. M. longe bowes and .xl. M. othere men. **1530** PALSGR. 240/2 Long bowe, *arc.* **1590** SIR J. SMYTH *Disc. Conc. Weapons* 38 The excellencie of our Long-bowes and Archers. **1598** HAKLUYT *Voy.* I. 63 They..must..discharge at the enemie with long bowes and cros-bowes. **1630** *R. Johnson's Kingd. & Commw.* II. 186 The long Bow (the ancient glory of our English service). **1801** STRUTT *Sports & Past.* II. i. 46 The long-bow, so called, to distinguish it from the arbalist, or cross-bow. **1820** SCOTT *Abbot* iv, Shooting with hand-gun, cross-bow, or long-bow. **1868** MISS YONGE *Cameos* I. xxxix. 334 The fatal power of the English long-bow was..well known to the Scots.

2. Phr. *to draw* or *pull the* (or *a*) *long-bow,* occas. *to draw with the long-bow*: to make exaggerated statements (*colloq.*).

1668 R. L'ESTRANGE *Vis. Quev.* (ed. 3) 8 There came to us several Tradesmen; the first of them a Poor Rogue that made profession of drawing the long Bow. **1809** MALKIN *Gil Blas* I. v. ¶4 My grandfather set me the example of drawing the long bow. **1823** BYRON *Juan* VIII. cxxxviii, I have drawn much less with a long bow Than my forerunners. **1824** *Ibid.* XVI. i, At speaking truth perhaps they are less clever, But draw the long bow better now than ever. **1860** THACKERAY *Lovel* ii, I dare say I drew a number of long bows about her. **1888** INGLIS *Tent Life Tigerland* 97 Critics, who have twitted me with 'drawing the long bow'.

3. *attrib.*: †**long-bow man** (see sense 2).

1678 RAY *Prov.* (ed. 2) 89 A Lier..He's a long-bow-man. **1694** MOTTEUX *Rabelais* v. xxx. 153 Tho' 'twere Ælian that Long-Bow-man that told you so, never believe him.

long-breathed (-brɛθt), *a.* [See BREATHED II.] Long of breath. *lit.* and *fig.*

1568 GRAFTON *Chron.* I. 132 His knightes were leane, pale, and long brethed, so that they might endure to fight long. *a* **1628** F. GREVIL *Sidney* iv. (1652) 49 To negotiate with that long-breathed Nation [the Germans] proves commonly a work in steel, where many stroaks hardly leave any print. **1694** F. BRAGGE *Disc. Parables* xiii. 433 Whole armies of words, and legions of long-breath'd petitions. **1816, 1884** [see BREATHED *ppl. a.* 6]. **1878** O. W. HOLMES *Motley* i. 8 The long-breathed tenacity of purpose, which in after years gave effect to his brilliant mental endowments.

long cloth, 'long-cloth. A kind of cotton cloth or calico manufactured in long pieces; *esp.* cloth of this kind made in India.

1545 *Rates Custom-ho.* d iij, One long cloth makyth one shorte cloth and .vii. yardes. **1622** MALYNES *Anc. Law-Merch.* 57 An allowance or abatement for Draped, Dressed, Rowed, and Sheared Clothes, which is foure ℔ in a Long-cloth, and foure ℔ in a Broad-cloth. **1670** *Let.* 9 Nov. in *Notes & Extr. Govt. Rec. Fort St. George* No. I. (1871) 2 We have continued to supply you with the great stock..in reguard ye Dutch do so fully fall in with the Calicoe trade that they had the last year 50,000 pieces of Long-cloth. **1696** J. F. *Merchant's Ware-ho.* 26. **1720** *Lond. Gaz.* No. 5815/3 A Parcel of long Cloaths white. **1721** C. KING *Brit. Merch.* I. 313 The Long-Cloths exported in that Year make 10,000 of the Pieces. **1851** *Illustr. Catal. Gt. Exhib.* 1195 Samples of thick calicoes (called long cloths and Wigans) woven by hand. **1864** J. S. BUCKLE *Manuf. Compend.* p. ix, 39 inches wide Long Cloth, 36 yards long. **1882** FLOYER *Unexpl. Balūchistan* 46 Long cloths from Dizzak are much prized. **1898** *Globe* 28 Oct. 1/5 Long-cloth! What you make night-gowns of!

long coat, 'long-coat. a. A coat reaching to the ankles; also in *pl.* (= *long-clothes*) the garments of a baby in arms. Also *attrib.* **b.** One who wears a long coat.

1603 DEKKER *Grissil* II. i. (Shaks. Soc.) 18 Yet he doth but as many of his brother knights do, keep an ordinary table for him and his long coat follower. That long coat makes the master a little king. **1614** R. TAILOR *Hog hath lost his Pearl* III. E 2 Ile laugh shalt see enough, and thou shalt weepe Softly, good long coate, softly. **1614** B. JONSON *Barth. Fair* I. i, And where hee spi'd a Parrat, or a Monkey, there hee was pitch'd, with all the little-long-coats about him male and female. **1625** —— *Staple of News* III. i, A Cabal..set out by Archie, Or some such head, of whose long coat they haue heard, And, being black, desire it. **1667** EVELYN *Diary* 29 Jan., Not as yet 13 years old. He was newly out of long coates. **1840** THACKERAY *Catherine* vii, Master Thomas Billings..was in his long-coats fearfully passionate.

long-con'tinued, *a.* [LONG *adv.*] Continued or that has continued for a long period or space.

1478 *Will R. Verney* in *Verney Papers* (1853) 28, I biqueth to Alice Wetherhede, my long-continued seruaunt, xls. **1570** T. NORTON *Nowels Catech.* (1853) 131 Long-continued age in such a miserable and wicked life. **1596** DRAYTON *Leg. Robt. Norm.* cxxii, But now to end this long-continued Strife. **1725** POPE *Odyss.* VII. 127 Day following day, a long-continued feast. *Ibid.* XIII. 233 Long-continu'd ways, and winding floods. **1876** BRISTOWE *Th. & Pract. Med.* (1878) 667 Worn out by..long-continued pain.

longdebefe, -bieffe, var. LANGUE DE BŒUF.

1472–3 *Rolls of Parlt.* VI. 51/2 Bowes, Arrowes and Longdebieffes.

long distance. [LONG *a.*¹ + DISTANCE *sb.*]

1. *attrib.* or as quasi-*adj.* (With hyphen.) Over a relatively great distance; between distant places; used esp. (*a*) of a telephone call; (*b*) of a race; (*c*) of a journey.

1884 *Whitaker's Almanack* 385/1 In America some remarkable trials of long distance telephoning have taken place. **1886** *Sci. Amer.* 2 Oct. 208/2 There is a popular belief that the long distance telephone is crowding the telegraph to the wall. **1887** SHEARMAN *Athletics* (Badm. Libr.) 101 In training for long-distance races, in which category we should place those at a mile and upwards, [etc.]. *Ibid.* 103 The long-distance runner is rarely over middle height. **1897** [see CENTURION 3]. **1908** *Sat. Even. Post* 26 Sept. 15/3 A long distance line can only be used by one person at a time. **1919** [see CEILING *vbl. sb.* 6 b]. **1923** [see *all-red* adj. (ALL E. III. 13)]. **1925** W. J. BRYAN *Mem.* 487 After the meal he made several long distance telephone calls. **1926** *Times* 6 May 3/4 The following other long-distance trains will also run, calling at the principal stations. **1929** *Daily Express* 7 Nov. 2/5 A Socialist member's resolution urging the nationalisation of railways and long-distance road transport was debated. *Ibid.* 11/3 The airship has now to compete with the flying boat as a long-distance craft. **1933** *Discovery* Apr. 131/2 The 'bypath' system gives faster service on local and long-distance calls. **1934** *Ibid.* Nov. 316/2 This railcar recently set up a world's record for long-distance running. **1934** [see *door-to-door* attrib. (DOOR 8)]. **1935** *Discovery* Dec. 352/1 Long-distance flight. **1935** G. GREENE *England made Me* ii. 47 Put through any long-distance calls. **1959** A. SILLITOE (*title*) The loneliness of the long-distance runner. **1960** *Guardian* 13 June 3/3 Walking down a long-distance Russian train is apt to be..dull. **1961** *Times* 3 Oct. (Computer Suppl.) p. vi/4 Long-distance telephone calls. **1961** L. VAN DER POST *Heart of Hunter* I. i. 25 The men sat with their heads bowed over arms clasped round their knees like long-distance runners from the race of their lives. **1968** *National Fisherman* Aug. 15-A/3 Formosa and South Korea started long-distance tuna fishing later than Japan. **1975** J. RATHBONE *Kill Cure* II. i. 53 A long distance call from Ankara to Istanbul involved time and trouble.

2. A long-distance telephone (call). Also as *adv.*, by long-distance telephone.

1904 'MARK TWAIN' *$30,000 Bequest* (1906) viii. 44 Aleck's imaginary brokers were shouting frantically by imaginary long-distance, 'Sell! sell!' **1920** WODEHOUSE *Jill the Reckless* (1921) xx. 295 Calling Izzy on the long distance. **1923** —— *Inimitable Jeeves* xv. 196 He became a sort of Voice Heard Off, developing a habit of ringing me up on long-distance. **1961** WEBSTER s.v., Called her up long-distance. **1969** A. GLYN *Dragon Variation* v. 147 He went straight to the telephone and called New York long-distance.

B. As *v. trans.* To make a long-distance telephone call to (a person); to report by means of such a call.

1945 *Time* 6 Aug. 79/1 Henry J. Kaiser last week long-distanced an old friend. **1950** *Newsweek* 30 Oct. 61 A UP staffer simply copied the story as it came in, went to an open phone, and long-distanced it to UP in San Francisco in a few seconds. **1965** E. LACY *Double Trouble* viii. 79 My own family is down in the Bahamas, and I long-distanced them.

long-drawn, *a.*

1. Prolonged to a great or inordinate length. Also ***long-drawn-out.***

[**1632** MILTON *L'Allegro* 140 In notes, with many a winding bout Of lincked sweetnes long drawn out.] **1646** CRASHAW *Delights Muses* (1652) 88 Now negligently rash He throws his arm, and with a long-drawn dash Blends all together. **1770** GOLDSM. *Des. Vill.* 317 While the proud their long-drawn pomps display. **1832** TENNYSON *Lady of Shalott* iv. 28 A longdrawn carol, mournful, holy. **1842** MANNING *Serm.* (1848) I. 138 Long-drawn schemes of action. **1851** H. MELVILLE *Whale* x. 54 A long-drawn, gurgling whistle. **1883** STEVENSON *Treas. Isl.* III. xiv, Far away out in the marsh there arose one horrid, long-drawn scream. **1891** T. R. LOUNSBURY *Stud. Chaucer* III. viii. 331 The long-drawn-out romances which had been the favorites of the generations preceding his own [*sc.* Fielding's]. **1897** SIR E. WOOD *Achievem. Cavalry* ii. 20 The long-drawn-out battle [Marengo], which lasted over fourteen hours.

2. Having great longitudinal extension. Chiefly *poet.*

1750 GRAY *Elegy* 39 The long-drawn Isle and fretted Vault. **1804** J. GRAHAME *Sabbath* 69 The long-drawn aisles, At every close, the lingering strain prolong. **1851** MRS. BROWNING *Casa Guidi W.* II. 299 The long-drawn street. **1871** R. ELLIS tr. *Catullus* lxiv. 333 Trail ye a long-drawn thread and run with eddying, spindles. **1888** INGLIS *Tent Life Tigerland* 282 A long-drawn, thin echelon.

longe, obs. form of LONG, LUNG.

longe, obs. f. LUNGE *sb.*¹, *v.*¹; var. LUNGE *sb.*², *v.*²

long-eared, *a.*

1. Having long ears; used *spec.* in the names of some animals.

1591 PERCIVALL *Sp. Dict., Orejudo*, long eared. **1646** G. DANIEL *Poems* Wks. 1878 I. 60 With long-eard Caps, and Bells to make a noise. **1752** J. HILL *Hist. Animals* 582 The long-eared, Syrian Goat. **1807** HOME in *Phil. Trans.* XCVII. 176 The stomach of the long-eared bat. **1831** A. WILSON & BONAPARTE *Amer. Ornith.* I. 104 The long-eared owl is fourteen inches and a half long. **187.** *Cassell's Nat. Hist.* II. 96 The Long-eared Fox (*Megalotis*).

2. In allusion to the ass's ears: Asinine.

1605 CAMDEN *Rem.* (1637) 340 They are counted long eared which delight in them. **1789** WOLCOT (P. Pindar) *Subj. for Paint.* iii, And like some long-ear'd creatures, bray 'what art?' **1850** CARLYLE *Latter-d. Pamph.* i. 12 You are fallen in an evil, heavy-laden, long-eared age. **1901** *Scotsman* 3 Oct. 4/2 The feeling of weariness with the war.. is getting the better of the long-eared multitude.

longebeff, obs. var. LANGUE DE BŒUF.

c **1430** *Two Cookery-bks.* 5.

longed (lɒŋd), *ppl. a.* [f. LONG *v.* + -ED[1].] Earnestly desired. Now always ***longed-for***; formerly also (*poet.*) without the adv., as if from a transitive use of the vb.

1526 TINDALE *Phil.* iv. i, Brethren dearly beloved and longed for. *a* **1592** H. SMITH *6 Serm.* (1618) C 7 b, May not the fastned Ship in a strange Land desire to bee loosed, to hasten to his longed for Port at home? **1595** SHAKS. *John* IV. ii. 8 Fresh expectation troubled not the Land With any long'd for change, or better State. **1601** BRETON *Longing Blessed Heart* (Grosart) 10/2 She went all weeping..And would not cease vntill her loue might haue Her longèd fruite. **1721** RAMSAY *Content* 206 Our long'd-for bliss. *c* **1800** H. K. WHITE *Poems* (1830) 134, I..will smile With joy that I have got my long'd release. **1876** GEO. ELIOT *Dan. Der.* IV. li. 19 The longed-for mother. **1898** W. K. JOHNSON *Terra Tenebr.* 120 She sees the longed-for strand.

†**longee.** *Obs.* = LUNGE *sb.*[1]

1678 BUTLER *Hud.* III. i. 159 After Longees Of humble, and submissive Congees. *a* **1680** —— *Rem.* (1759) II. 92 When he accosts a Lady, he stamps with his Foot, like a French Fencer, and makes a Longee at her.

longee, obs. form of LUNGI *Anglo-Indian.*

longen, obs. pl. form of LUNG.

longer (ˈlɒŋə(r)), *sb.*[1] [f. LONG *v.* + -ER[1].] One who longs.

1435 MISYN *Fire of Love* (1896) 78 Meditacion of þe longar to his lufe & forsakynge of felyschip. **1622** T. SCOTT *Belg. Pismire* 10 Surely he is a longer, that is never satisfied.

longer (ˈlɒŋgə(r)), *sb.*[2] *Naut.* [? a. F. *longueur* length.] **a.** A row of casks stored next to the keelson. Also *pl.* **b.** 'The fore and aft space allotted to a hammock' (Smyth *Sailor's Word-bk.* 1867).

1730 CAPT. W. WRIGLESWORTH *MS. Log-bk. of the Lyell* 12 June, Yesterday..sent the Long Boat for Water, and stowed a Longer of emty Butts. **1841** DANA *Seaman's Man.* Gloss., *Longers*, the longest casks, stowed next the keelson.

longer (ˈlɒŋgə(r)), *sb.*[3] *Canad.* (Atlantic Provinces). [f. LONG *a.*[1] + -ER[1].] A long pole or piece of timber used for fencing, a fishing stage, etc.

1772 G. CARTWRIGHT *Jrnl.* 17 Apr. (1792) I. 216 At noon I..searched the woods..where I found some good longers, and boat-hook staffs. **1837** *Times* (Halifax, Nova Scotia) 25 July 235/1 The skeleton of a man was found in the woods..by a man and boy who were cutting longers. **1878** *North Star* (St. John's, Newfoundland) 30 Mar. 3/2 On the afternoon of their death, the deceased..left home for the woods to draw 'longers' across the pond. **1973** *Canad. Antiques Collector* Jan.–Feb. 13/2 Fences of longers made from spruce or marsh juniper meet and sometimes mingle with the hedgerows.

†ˈ**longer,** *v. Obs. intr.* To linger.

1576–87 TURBERV. *Trag. Tales* vii. 97 My absence is the cause of care, Thou doest accuse thy friend Of longring.

longeron (ˈlɒndʒərɒn). [a. F. *longeron* stringer, beam, (longitudinal) member.] A frame member running lengthways along a fuselage.

1912 *Flight* 13 July 626/1 In front, the four longerons are assembled into a specially designed pressed-steel housing. **1915** W. E. DOMMETT *Aeroplanes & Airships* ii. 26 The framework has as its ground-work four members running fore and aft known as 'longerons'. **1931** J. E. YOUNGER *Airplane Construction & Repair* viii. 130 Longerons are usually made of ash. **1962** F. I. ORDWAY et al. *Basic Astronautics* xi. 444 (*caption*) Space frame and longerons. **1966** E. V. RICKENBACKER *Rickenbacker* (1968) vi. 107 The explosive bullet had hit the longeron just behind me.

longesought, var. LUNGSOUGHT. *Obs.*

longethebeve, var. LANGUE DE BŒUF *Obs.*

1485 *Rolls of Parlt.* VI. 295/1 Bows, Arrows, Speares, and Longethebeves.

longeur: see LONGUEUR.

longeval, longæval (lɒnˈdʒiːvəl), *a.* [f. L. *longæv-us* LONGEVOUS + -AL[1].] Long-lived, long-lasting.

1597 A. M. tr. *Guillemeau's Fr. Chirurg.* 48 b/1 A longevalle or longe-continuinge Dysenterye. **1597** M. BOWMAN *ibid.* Ded. ij, The omnipotent and Longevalle Emperioure of the Caelestialle influences. *c* **1714** ARBUTHNOT & POPE *Mem. Mart. Scriblerus, Ess. Orig. Sci.* P.'s Prose Wks. 1741 II. 246 What prodigies may we not conceive of those primitive Longæval and Antediluvian man-tigers, who first taught sciences to the world? **1856** GRINDON *Life* viii. (1875) 97 Did man's daily bread grow on longæval trees, like acorns. **1871** J. PHILLIPS *Geol. Oxford* 249 Bones..quietly reposing in their 'longæval' graves.

†**lonˈgeve, longæve,** *a. Obs.* [ad. L. *longæv-us* LONGEVOUS.] = prec.

1673–4 GREW *Veget. Trunks* iii. §15 According as the Tree is less or more Longæve. **1678** CUDWORTH *Intell. Syst.* I. iv. §18. 345 Demons having Bodies as well as men, (though of a different kind from them and much more longeve).

longevity (lɒnˈdʒɛvɪtɪ). Also 7 -ævitie, -evitie, 7–8 -ævity, 8 -ivity. [ad. L. *longævitātem, f. longæv-us* LONGEVOUS. Cf. F. *longévité*.] Long life; long duration of existence.

1615 A. STAFFORD *Heav. Dogge* 105 He beleeued the longeuity of the soule, and not the eternity. **1621** S. WARD *Life Faith* xiii. 109 The longæuity of those that liued before the Floud. **1692** BENTLEY *Boyle Serm.* iii. 90 He hath not extended the period of our Lives to the Longævity of the Antediluvians. **1751** JOHNSON *Rambler* No. 169 ¶1 Animals generally exceed each other in longevity, in proportion to the time between their conception and their birth. **1756** C. LUCAS *Ess. Waters* III. 43 The town is..remarkable for the health and longævity of its inhabitants. **1813** BINGLEY *Anim. Biog.* (ed. 4) I. 40 The longevity of fish is far superior to that of other creatures. **1862** LYTTON *Str. Story* I. 180 Is it a sign of longevity when a man looks much younger than he is? **1873** HAMERTON *Intell. Life* I. vii. (1875) 41 Young men are careless of longevity.

longevous, -ævous (lɒnˈdʒiːvəs), *a.* Now *rare.* [f. L. *longæv-us*, f. *long-us* LONG *a.* + *æv-um* age.] Long-lived; living or having lived to a great age.

1680 AUBREY *Let.* in *Lives* (1813) II. 198, I come of a longævous race. **1682** SIR T. BROWNE *Chr. Mor.* III. §1 The ..Element of Water..so shut up the first Windows of Time, leaving no Histories of those longevous generations. **1699** EVELYN *Acetaria* 138 The longævous Elephant. **1701** GREW *Cosm. Sacra* IV. viii. 263 Cedar wood..is longevous, and an Evergreen. **1768–74** TUCKER *Lt. Nat.* (1834) I. 391 The longevous antediluvian. **1860** READE *Cloister & H.* IV. 432 Eli and Catherine lived to a great age... Giles also was longævous. **1878** STEVENSON *Inland Voy.* 198 He begins to feel dignified and longævous like a tree.

longewoo, var. LUNG-WOE *Obs.*

ˈ**longful,** *a.*[1] *dial.* [f. LONG *a.* + -FUL.] Long.

1798 J. JEFFERSON *Let. to Rev. J. Boucher* 19 Mar. (MS.), A longful time, is a curious kind of Hampshire Paragoge —for a long time. *a* **1825** FORBY *Voc. E. Anglia, Longful*, very long; full long. **1860** READE *Cloister & H.* IV. 179 Bless you, they left this a longful while ago.

ˈ**longful,** *a.*[2] *dial.* [f. LONG *v.*[1] + -FUL.] Longing. (See Eng. Dial. Dict.)

longfully (ˈlɒŋfʊlɪ), *adv. rare.* [f. LONGFUL *a.*[2] + -LY[2].] With longing looks, longingly.

1849 MITCHELL *Battle Summer* (1852) 251 The idle garçons lean upon the marble-topped tables..looking longfully at the passers-by. **1862** MAYHEW *Dogs* 107 They will eat greedily what they do not want if the cat looks longfully at that..which no coaxing could induce them to swallow.

ˈ**long-hair,** *sb.* Also longhair. [f. LONG *a.*[1] + HAIR *sb.*] **1.** A cat with long fur. Also *attrib.*

1893 J. JENNINGS *Domestic or Fancy Cats* ii. 6 The several varieties which range under Long-hair embrace Persian, Angora, Chinese, Indian, French, and Russian. **1935** E. B. SIMMONS *Cats* xxviii. 143 The long-hair standard demands a body that is low on the legs. **1948** P. M. SODERBERG *Cat Breeding* 78 Long-hairs need constant attention from the brush. **1958** *Listener* 28 Aug. 298/2 Pedigree cats are divided into two categories: long-hairs and short-hairs. **1972** M. BABSON *Murder on Show* viii. 94, I was in the Cream and Blue-Cream Longhair aisle, cheering the lot of a lonely little Cream Longhair.

2. a. A 'brainy' person, an æsthete, an intellectual; also, a devotee of classical (as opp. to popular) music. (Freq. used contemptuously.) Also *attrib.*

1920 S. LEWIS *Main St.* xxiii. 281 I'm surprised to find you talking like a New York Russian Jew, or one of these long-hairs! **1930** E. FERBER *Cimarron* xxiv. 378 These were the reformers—the long-hairs—fanatics. **1936** *Amer. Mercury* XXXVIII. x/2 *Long hair*, a symphony man. **1938** *Manch. Guardian Weekly* 2 Sept. 188/4 Very few [swing players] are 'long hairs' (people who like classical music). **1950** BLESH & JANIS *They all played Ragtime* (1958) x. 208 Victor has withheld the records..because of fear of insulting the long-hairs. **1955** R. BLESH *Shining Trumpets* (ed. 3) xiii. 314 One can understand why Scott Joplin..could praise ragtime..and could heap fiery denunciation on its 'long-hair' detractors. **1957** O. NASH *You can't get there from Here* 84 So what do you want on yours—a lot of pinko longhairs, or red-blooded athletes and drum majorettes? **1958** OSBORNE & CREIGHTON *Epitaph G. Dillon* II. 57 Intense students, incompetent longhairs, and rather flashy deadbeats. **1960** 'W. HAGGARD' *Closed Circuit* xvi. 192 All those longhairs advising us. **1967** *Listener* 16 Feb. 236/3 He planned to become a 'long hair' musician... He wanted to be a composer of symphonies.

b. A hippie, a beatnik.

1969 *Rolling Stone* 17 May 6/1 Would hippies and long-hairs sit on the youth commission? **1972** *Last Whole Earth Catalog* (Portola Inst.) 215/1 Long-hairs are doing new stuff with their bodies and nervous systems that occasionally needs medical attention or perspective. **1972** 'R. LLEWELLYN' *Night is Child* (1974) i. 13 The noise of the band, a group of longhairs in..girlish duds, velvets, silks and falderals.

long-haired, *a.* (Stress variable.) Also long haired, longhaired. [f. LONG *a.*[1] + HAIRED *a.*] Having long hair; *spec.* applied, at various times, (*a*) to Merovingians; (*b*) (freq. derog.) to æsthetes and intellectuals; (*c*) to cats with long fur; (*d*) to classical (as opposed to popular) music and musicians; (*e*) to beatniks and hippies. Sometimes without reference to the actual length of the hair: with or of intellectual or æsthetic pretensions. Spec. ***long-haired chum*** (see quot. 1890).

1552 HULOET, Longe heared, *acrocomus.* **1781** GIBBON *Decl. & F.* xxx. III. 150 A military council was assembled of the long-haired chiefs of the Gothic nation. **1871** FREEMAN *Norm. Conq.* (1876) IV. xvii. 92 The..long-haired children of the north. **1872** GEO. ELIOT *Middlem.* I. II. xix. 340 Romanticism..was fermenting still..in certain long-haired German artists at Rome. **1881** W. S. GILBERT *Patience* I. 11 The peripatetics Of long haired aesthetics Are very much more to their taste. **1889** H. WEIR *Our Cats* 16 Long-haired cats..are very diversified, both in form, colour, and the quality of the hair. **1890** BARRÈRE & LELAND *Dict. Slang* II. 27/2 *Long-haired chum* (tailors), a young woman, a young lady friend. **1914** C. MACKENZIE *Sinister St.* II. xiii. 769 After a year with long-haired students I want a change. **1915** J. E. PATTERSON *Epistles from Deep Seas* 262 Goin' to have a 'long-haired chum', are we. **1917** 'TAFFRAIL' *Off Shore* 92 Some sort of a friendship, platonic or otherwise, with a 'long-haired' pal. **1922** S. LEWIS *Babbitt* xiv. 184 The long-haired gentry who call themselves 'liberals'..and 'intelligentsia'... Irresponsible teachers and professors constitute the worst of this whole gang. **1935** *Vanity Fair* (N.Y.) Nov. 71/3 Straight or commercial musicians are often derisively called *salon-men* or *long-haired boys.* **1943** G. W. WILLIS *Tangleweed* xii. 174 It ain't a song. It's a composition. Long-haired. **1955** J. CANNAN *Long Shadows* iii. 33 The long-haired fraternity hold the art of the camera in contempt—it rivals their daubs. **1959** C. MACINNES *Absolute Beginners* 157 Archeology, and long-haired music, and all those sorts of thing. **1959** *Times* 22 Nov. 5/6 Since the result of the general election..some of the long-haired boys in our movement have been holding inquiries and assessing blame for our defeat on everyone but themselves. **1962** J. M. WALLACE-HADRILL (*title*) The long-haired kings. **1963** *Listener* 7 Feb. 264/2 It [*sc.* jazz] has begun an unwise flirtation with 'long-haired music'. **1965** M. MORSE *Unattached* i. 59 Howard..found the atmosphere so sombre, long-haired and tedious that he quickly left. **1972** ING & POND *Champion Cats of World* 73 A definite breeding programme has begun in an endeavour to popularize once more the original long-haired cats. **1975** J. SYMONS *Three Pipe Problem* ii. 15 Sir Pountney was..opposed..to long-haired students, and to spineless intellectuals.

ˈ**long-hand,** ˈ**longhand.** Handwriting of the ordinary character (in which words are written in full), as distinguished from shorthand.

1666 PEPYS *Diary* 17 Nov., So as I can read it [a shorthand memorandum] to-morrow to Sir W. Coventry, and then come home, and Hewer read it to me while I take it in long-hand. **1712** F. I. *Shorthand* 25 Even in Long-Hand oftentimes equivocal abbreviations are often written. **1864** *Social Sci. Rev.* 224 Many years must necessarily elapse before phonography will entirely supersede the longhand now in use. **1888** *Times* (weekly ed.) 7 Dec. 20/3 Did you take notes in longhand of the speeches?

attrib. **1884** *Law Times* 24 May 55/2 There are obvious reasons why a longhand note cannot always be relied upon to contain every material point in the evidence. **1897** *Westm. Gaz.* 22 Jan. 7/1 Sir Isaac Pitman's efforts in the cause of the reform of longhand spelling.

longhe, obs. f. LUNG; var. LUNYIE (loin). *Obs.*

long-head. [f. LONG *a.*]

†**1.** *nonce-use.* One who wears his hair long; opposed to ROUNDHEAD. *Obs.*

1642 (*title*) Description of Round-Heads and Long Heads.

2. One who has a skull of more than average length; in mod. scientific language *spec.* one the breadth of whose head is less than four-fifths of its length; a dolichocephalic person.

1650 BULWER *Anthropomet.* 2 There were found many Macrocephali among them, that is, such Long-heads as no other Nation had the like. **1704** SWIFT *Mech. Operat. Spirit* Misc. (1711) 282 Hippocrates tells us that among our Ancestors the Scythians there was a Nation, called Longheads. **1890** HUXLEY in *19th Cent.* Nov. 757 The tall blond long-heads practically disappear. **1900** *Daily News* 31 July 6/5 The wanderings of the long heads over the Western hemisphere are traced by their monuments.

long-headed, *a.*

1. Having a long head: **a.** of persons, dolichocephalic; **b.** of things.

1875 DARWIN *Insectiv. Plants* ii. 24, I experimented on both the oval and long-headed glands. **1888** *Pall Mall G.* 13 Sept. 11/2 The men, who are wont to claim superior business cunning, are literally more long-headed ('dolichocephalic'). **1890** HUXLEY in *19th Cent.* Nov. 757 People who are as regularly broad-headed as the Swedes and Germans are long-headed. **1900** *Daily News* 31 July 6/5 The long-headed Neolithic man.

2. Of great discernment or foresight; discerning, shrewd, far-seeing.

a **1700** B. E. *Dict. Cant. Crew, Long-headed*, wise, of great reach and foresight. **1711** STEELE *Spect.* No. 52 ¶3 Being a long-headed Gentlewoman, I am apt to imagine she has some further Design than you have yet penetrated. **1721** AMHERST *Terræ Fil.* x. 49 The heads of colleges, d'ye see, being, most of them, long-headed men, argue logically upon this point. **1735** DYCHE & PARDON *Dict., Long-headed*, cunning, subtle, wise, artful. **1815** MAD. D'ARBLAY *Diary* (1876) IV. 301 Madame..was a woman that the Scotch would call long-headed. **1840** DICKENS *Old C. Shop* lxvi, Men of the world, long-headed customers, knowing dogs. **1864** LOWELL *McClellan or Lincoln?* Pr. Wks. (1890) V. 173 Mr. Lincoln is a long-headed and long-purposed man.

Hence **longˈheadedness.**

1863 LYTTON *Caxtoniana* I. xi. 188 The practical long-headedness, the ready adaptation of shrewd wit to immediate circumstance. **1866** LOWELL *Swinburne's Trag.* Pr. Wks. (1890) II. 128 Ulysses was the type of long-headedness. **1880** DAWKINS *Early Man in Brit.* ix. 324 The Iberic element in the population of Spain has mainly contributed to the long-headedness of the modern Spaniard.

long-horn. [LONG *a.*[1] + HORN *sb.*] **1.** A breed of beef cattle, orig. English, now common in the U.S., raised especially in the south-western states. Also *attrib.* and *transf.*

1834 YOUATT *Cattle* 188 The long horns seem to have first appeared in Craven. **1879** JEFFERIES *Wild Life in S. Co.* 130 The cows in the field used to be longhorns, much more hardy. **1901** W. A. WHITE in *McClure's Mag.* Dec. 145/2

The picture of Tom Platt..standing at the head of a drove of wild-eyed human long-horns, as if to keep them from a stampede. **1903** A. ADAMS *Log of Cowboy* xxii. 353 There were lots of old long-horn cowmen living in the town. *Ibid.* 356 Some of those old long-horns didn't think any more of a twenty-dollar gold piece than I do of a white chip. **1949** O. NASH *Versus* 24 The big dog is to her Like a scarlet rag to a Longhorn. **1955** *Sci. News Let.* 22 Jan. 61/1 The longhorn first landed in this country when the animals were brought to America in 1521 by Gregorio Vallalobos, a governor-general sent to 'New Spain'. **1972** *Sat. Rev.* (U.S.) 6 May 20/3 Those are white-faced Herefords and black Angus... Don't see many longhorns anymore. **1974** *Sunday Times* (Colour Suppl.) 28 July 18 (*caption*) Longhorn Bull Hillpatrick at Cotswold Farm Park, near Cheltenham: a survivor from the Stone Age?

2. long-horn(ed) beetle = LONGICORN *sb.*

1840 J. & M. LOUDON tr. *Köllar's Treat. Insects* 15 The family of the long-horned beetles, (*Cerambycidæ*). **1894** *Insect Life* VI. 219 A Cerambycid or long-horned beetle; in pods of Enterolobium from Paraguay. **1936** *Forestry* X. 49 Longhorn beetles—Cerambycidae..are large, conspicuous, and easily recognized by their long horns or antennae. **1966** A. W. LEWIS *Gloss. Woodworking Terms* 5 Longhorn beetle. Black and grey beetle about 1 in. long which sometimes attacks the softwoods used in buildings. **1968** R. D. MARTIN tr. *Wickler's Mimicry in Plants & Animals* viii. 86 The long-horned beetle *Erythrus rotundicollis* also resembles the same bug.

3. The long-eared owl, *Asio otus*.

1856 YARRELL *Brit. Birds* I. 131 *Otus vulgaris*, the Long-horn.

4. long-horn(ed) grasshopper, a grasshopper of the family Tettigoniidæ (formerly called Locustidæ), having very long antennæ.

1893 *Insect Life* V. 271 The large Locustidæ, or long-horn grasshoppers, are very appropriately called 'cradlers' from the resemblance of the ovipositor of the female to a grain cradle. **1920** W. J. LUCAS *Monogr. Brit. Orthoptera* 5 Locustodea (Long-horned Grasshoppers). **1972** L. E. CHADWICK tr. *Linsenmaier's Insects of World* 80/2 In contrast with ordinary grasshoppers, most of which live on the ground, the long-horned grasshoppers do more climbing. **1972** SWAN & PAPP *Common Insects N. Amer.* 74 The tettigoniids, or longhorn grasshoppers, may be distinguished from the acridids, or grasshoppers, by their long filamentous antennae.

longi, obs. form of LUNGI.

longi- ('lɒndʒɪ), comb. form of L. *longus* LONG, in many scientific terms: **longi'caudal, -'caudate** *adjs.* [L. *cauda* tail], long-tailed (Mayne *Expos. Lex.* 1856). **longicauline** (-'kɔːlaɪn) *a.* [Gr. καυλός stem], long-stemmed (*Syd. Soc. Lex.* 1889). **longicollous** (-'kɒləs) *a.* [L. *collum* neck], *Bot.* 'applied to mosses that have urns in the form of a very elongated pear'; *Ent.* 'having the neck or the corselet long' (*ibid.*). **'longicone** *a. Conch.* [CONE], having a long cone, said of certain cephalopods; also as *sb.* **longilabrous** (-'leɪbrəs) *a.* [LABRUM], having a long labrum, as some *Hemiptera* (Mayne). †**longi'lateral** *a.* [LATERAL], long-sided; of the form of a long parallelogram. **longi'lingual** *a. Zool.* [LINGUAL], having a long tongue (*Cent. Dict.*). **longipalp** ('lɒndʒɪpælp) *sb.* and *a. Zool.* [PALP], *sb.* one of the *Longipalpi*, a group of beetles having long maxillary feelers (Brande *Dict. Sci.*, etc. 1842); *adj.* pertaining to the *Longipalpi* (Cassell 1884). So **longi'palpate, -'palpous** *adjs.*, having long palps (*Syd. Soc. Lex.*). **longipedate** (lɒn'dʒɪpɪdət), **longipede** (-piːd) *adjs.* [L. *pēs, pedis* foot], long-footed (*Syd. Soc. Lex.*). **longipennate** (-'pɛnət) *a. Ornith.* [PENNATE] = next (Ogilvie, *Suppl.* 1855). **longipennine** (-'pɛnɪn) *a. Ornith.* [mod.L. *Longipennes*; L. *penna* wing], long-winged; pertaining to the *Longipennes* or long-winged natatorial birds (*Cent. Dict.*). **longiroster** (-'rɒstə(r)) *Ornith.* [mod.L. *Longirostres*; L. *rostrum* beak], one of the *Longirostres*, a family of wading birds distinguished by the length and tenuity of the bill (Brande *Dict. Sci.*, etc. 1842). **longi'rostral** *a.* [see prec.], pertaining to or resembling the *Longirostres*; also **longi'rostrate** *a.*, in same sense (Mayne). **longisect** ('lɒndʒɪsɛkt) *v.* [L. *sect-, secāre* to cut], to bisect lengthwise and horizontally (*Cent. Dict.*). **longi'section** [SECTION], longitudinal division of the body in a plane parallel with the axis and at right angles to the meson (*ibid.*). **longi'tarsal** *a.* [TARSAL], having a long tarsus (*Syd. Soc. Lex.*).

1884 *Proc. Boston Soc. Nat. Hist.* XXII. 275 Kionoceras, nobis, includes the *longicones in which the longitudinal ridges are more prominent than the transverse striae or ridges. *Ibid.* 276 All those longicone species. **1658** SIR T. BROWNE *Gard. Cyrus* i. 37 The decussis is made within a *longilateral square, with opposite angles. *Ibid.* ii. 44 Nineveh..was of a longilateral figure. **1855** OGILVIE, Suppl., **Longirostral*. **1890** COUES *Field & Gen. Ornithol.* II. 149 The longirostral [type],..best exhibited in the great snipe family.

longicorn ('lɒndʒɪkɔːn), *a.* and *sb. Zool.* [ad. mod.L. *longicornis*, f. L. *long-us* LONG *a.* + *cornū* horn.] **a.** *adj.* Pertaining to the *Longicornes* or *Longicornia*, a group of coleopterous beetles having very long filiform antennæ. **b.** *sb.* A beetle of this group.

1848 CRAIG, *Longicornes, Longecorns*. **1855** OGILVIE, Suppl., *Longicorn*, pertaining to the longicornes. **1856** BATES in *Zoologist* XV. 5659 You take a dozen Longicorns one day, and they are sure to be of eight or ten distinct species. **1874** WOOD *Nat. Hist.* 675 We now come to the Longicorn Beetles. **1882** *Garden* 27 May 370/2 The common Longicorn Pine borer (*Monohammus confusor*). **1897** MARY KINGSLEY *W. Africa* 585 There were quantities of large longicorn beetles about during the night.

longie ('lʌŋɪ), *Sc.* Also **lungie, lungy**. [ad. Norw. dial. *lomgivie*, f. *lom* LOOM *sb.*^{2}] The guillemot, *Lomvia troile*.

1802 G. MONTAGU *Ornith. Dict.* (1833) 545. **1809** EDMONSTON *Zetland* II. 276 Longie,..Guillemot, Foolish Guillemot, Sea Hen. **1816** SCOTT *Antiq.* vii, Mony a..lungie's nest hae I harried up amang thae very black rocks.

longifolene (lɒndʒɪ'fəʊliːn). *Chem.* [f. mod.L. *longifol-ia*, specific epithet of the pine *Pinus longifolia* from which the oil was first isolated (f. LONGI- + *-folia*, f. L. *folium* leaf) + -ENE.] A colourless, somewhat viscous oil that is present in the turpentine oil from some species of pine and is a tricyclic sesquiterpene, $C_{15}H_{24}$.

1920 J. L. SIMONSEN in *Jrnl. Chem. Soc.* CXVII. 573 The sesquiterpene for which the name longifolene is proposed has..only been cursorily examined. **1962** E. L. ELIEL *Stereochem. Carbon Compounds* x. 298 Among natural products, polycyclic bridged systems are exemplified by..the sesquiterpenoids longifolene and cedrene.

longiloquence (lɒn'dʒɪləkwəns). *rare.* [f. L. *long-us* LONG *a.* + *loquentia* speaking.] Speaking at great length.

1836 COCKBURN *Jrnl.* I. 114 The quantity they have to get through..makes longiloquence impossible. **1887** *Sat. Rev.* 21 May 730 Longiloquence, if we may coin a new word for a very familiar thing, is neither their forte nor their foible. **18..** F. HALL (cited in Webster, 1897), American longiloquence in oratory.

longimanous (lɒn'dʒɪmənəs), *a.* [f. late L. *longiman-us* (f. *long-us* LONG *a.* + *manus* hand) + -OUS.] Long-handed; *Zool.* applied to certain apes. †*fig.* Far-reaching. *Obs.*

1646 SIR T. BROWNE *Pseud. Ep.* VII. xix. 384 The villany of this Christian exceeded the persecution of Heathens, whose malice was never so Longimanous as to reach the soul of their enemies. **1650** CHARLETON *Van Helmont's Tern. Paradoxes* Prol. Djb, Whether the Sanative Faculty of Vitriol, may not be conceded so longimanous and extensive, as to produce the same effect, at distance. **1856** in MAYNE *Expos. Lex.*

longimetry (lɒn'dʒɪmɪtrɪ). ? *Obs.* [ad. mod.L. **longimetria*, f. *longus* LONG *a.* + Gr. -μετρία measurement, -METRY. Cf. F. *longimétrie*.] The art or process of measuring distances.

1674 in *Phil. Trans.* IX. 85 In *Longimetry*, the Art of Levelling, the Measuring of Hights or Distances unapproachable. **1715** CHEYNE *Philos. Princ. Relig.* I. 350 Our two Eyes are like two different Stations in Longimetry by the assistance of which, the distance between two Objects is measured. **1727** J. DOUGLAS (*title*) The Art of Planometry, Longemetry, and Altemetry, brought to Perfection by the Instrument called the Infallible.

Hence **longi'metric** *a.*, pertaining to longimetry.

In recent Dicts.

longing ('lɒŋɪŋ), *vbl. sb.*^{1} Also 3-6 *north.* **langing**. [OE. *langung*, f. *langian* LONG *v.*]

1. The action of LONG *v.*^{1}; yearning desire; an instance of this. Const. *for, after,* †*to,* †*of*; also with *inf.*

971 *Blickl. Hom.* 131 Ne mæȝ þæt na beon þæt þa bearn þe unbliþran ne syn, & langunga nabban æfter þæm freondum. *c* **1200** *Trin. Coll. Hom.* 27 þe godfrihte..habbeð longinge to heuene. *a* **1225** *Ancr. R.* 190 Oðer one deies longunge, oðer a sicnesse of ane stunde. **1390** GOWER *Conf.* III. 309 Youre oghne liege men..That live in longinge and desir Til ye be come ayein to Tyr. *c* **1400** *Destr. Troy* 9154 A fell arow..of loue..Made hym langwys in Loue & Longynges grete. *c* **1500** *Melusine* xxi. 119, I haue grete langyng to approche nygh the paynemys. **1598** BACON *Relig. Medit.* Ess. (Arb.) 113 As if they were euer children and beginners, they are still in longing for things to come. **1606** SHAKS. *Ant. & Cl.* v. ii. 284 Giue me my Robe, put on my Crowne, I haue Immortall longings in me. **1611** BIBLE *Ps.* cxix. 20 My soule breaketh for the longing: that it hath vnto thy iudgements at all times. **1667** MILTON *P.L.* IV. 511 Fierce desire,..Still unfulfill'd with pain of longing pines. **1713** ADDISON *Cato* v. i, Whence this pleasing hope, this fond desire, This longing after immortality? **1748** *Anson's Voy.* II. xiii. 378 Our native country, for which many of us by this time began to have great longings. **1860** TYNDALL *Glac.* I. xxii. 160 Sometimes..when a guide was in front of me, I have felt an extreme longing to have a second one behind me. **1866** GEO. ELIOT *F. Holt* (1868) 22 The return was still looked for with longing. **1875** JOWETT *Plato* (ed. 2) III. 436 They will have a fierce secret longing after gold and silver.

2. *spec.* in *Path.* The fanciful cravings incident to women during pregnancy. Chiefly *pl.*

1552 ELYOT *Dict.*, *Citta*, is also the affection of longing in women with childe. **1594** T. B. *La Primaud. Fr. Acad.* II. 157 The longings and imaginations of women with childe. **1606** SHAKS. *Tr. & Cr.* III. iii. 237, I haue a womans longing, An appetite that I am sicke withall. **1799** M. UNDERWOOD *Dis. Children* (ed. 4) II. 227 There is certainly nothing that we know of in a fright or longing that can produce such a change in organized matter. **1812** *Sporting Mag.* XXXIX. 7 He had..a pregnant wife, to satisfy whose longings, and to prevent any deformity of the child, he had ventured to trespass by shooting a hare.

b. *attrib.*: **longing mark**, a birth-mark, nævus (popularly supposed to be the impressed image of some object 'longed for' by the mother).

1644 DIGBY *Nat. Bodies* xxxviii. 335 The longing markes which are often times seene in children, and do remaine with them all their life.

†**'longing**, *vbl. sb.*^{2} *Obs.* [f. LONG *v.*^{2} + -ING^1.] *pl.* Belongings; appurtenances.

c **1449** PECOCK *Repr.* I. iii. 15 And so forth of manie purtenauncis and longingis to matrimonye. *a* **1470** GREGORY in *Hist. Collect. Lond. Cit.* (Camden) 196 They dyspoylyd the placys and longgynges of many dyvers lordys. [But possibly this should read *louggynges* = lodgings.]

'longing, *ppl. a.*^{1} [f. LONG *v.*^{1} + -ING^2.] That longs; characterized by yearning desire.

1509 FISHER *Funeral Serm. C'tess. Richmond* Wks. (1876) 303 A grete comforte then it is vnto the soule that hath so longynge desyre vnto the body to here that the body shal ryse agayne. **1567** *Gude & Godlie B.* (S.T.S.) 219 Gif..we ..leif this art of langing lust. **1611** BIBLE *Ps.* cvii. 9. **1667** MILTON *P.L.* IX. 743 That Fruit, which with desire,.. Sollicited her longing eye. **1697** DRYDEN *Virg. Georg.* iii. (1721) 425 Of Love defrauded in their longing Hour. **1750** GRAY *Elegy* 88 Nor cast one longing ling'ring Look behind! **1868** J. H. BLUNT *Ref. Ch. Eng.* I. 87 Wolsey had longing visions of the great work that might be effected if he could become pope. **1875** JOWETT *Plato* (ed. 2) III. 55 He felt a longing desire to see them.

Hence **'longingness**.

1651 DAVENANT *Gondibert* III. VI. lxxi, And now his Eyes even ake with longingness.

†**'longing**, *ppl. a.*^{2} *Obs.* [f. LONG *v.*^{2} + -ING^2.] Belonging.

13.. *E.E. Allit. P.* A. 462 So is vcha krysten sawle, A longande lym to þe mayster of myste.

longingly ('lɒŋɪŋlɪ), *adv.* [f. LONGING *ppl. a.* + -LY^2.] In a longing manner; with yearning desire.

1435 MISYN *Fire of Love* II. 103. **1634** W. TIRWHYT tr. *Balzac's Lett.* 374 The most zealous among them [Our Doctors] longingly expect a more quiet season. **1682** DRYDEN *Medal* 5 To his first byass, longingly he leans. **1861** SMILES *Engineers* (1862) III. 247 No wonder that in the midst of these troubles he should longingly speak of returning to his native land. **1881** *Macm. Mag.* XLIV. 51/1 She whispered longingly, 'If I had only had your first love!' **1885** *Manch. Exam.* 10 July 4/7 Mexican parties who look longingly upon the surplus of the American treasury.

†**longinque**, *a. Obs.* [ad. L. *longinqu-us* long, distant, f. *longus* LONG *a.*] Distant.

1614 RALEIGH *Hist. World* I. I. viii. §3. 132 Of the antiquitie of Longinque Nauigation.

longinquity (lɒn'dʒɪŋkwɪtɪ). Now *rare.* [ad. L. *longinquitās*, f. *longinquus* (see prec.).]

1. Long distance; remoteness.

1549 *Compl. Scot.* Ded. Ep. 4 The longinquite of his martial voyaige. **1613** PURCHAS *Pilgrimage* IV. xii. 411 There may shine a Tartarian sunne in Cathay, when as a darke night in this longinquitie of distance hideth him from our eyes. **1665** MANLEY *Grotius's Low C. Warres* 343 Many famous Miracles have been done by them, as is believed with great facility from confident Asseverations; for that the Longinquity of places excludes further Tryals. **1831** T. L. PEACOCK *Crotchet Cast.* ii. 34, I think the proximity of wine a matter of much more importance than the longinquity of water.

2. Remoteness, long continuance (of time). Also, (? *erron.*) prolixity (of discourse).

1623 COCKERAM, *Longinquitie*, distance of time. **1658** TOPSELL *Four-f. Beasts* 556 The bones of the head—some of which are so affected by longinquity [ed. 1607 longanimity] of time that [etc.]. **1669** GALE *Crt. Gentiles* I. III. ii. 30 Thucydides..could know nothing..of things before the Peloponnesian war, by reason of the Longinquitie of Time. **1879** G. MEREDITH *Egoist* Prel., Inordinate unvaried length, sheer longinquity.

†**lon'ginquous**, *a. Obs.* [f. L. *longinqu-us* (see LONGINQUE) + -OUS.] Long.

1666 HARVEY *Morb. Angl.* iv. 32 By..every ordinate longinquous propulsion or pulsation of the blood.

longipalp, -pennate *a.*, etc.: see LONGI-.

longis, variant of LUNGIS *Obs.*

longish ('lɒŋɪʃ), *a.* [f. LONG *a.* + -ISH.] Somewhat long (in various senses).

1611 COTGR., *Longuet*, longish, or somewhat long. *a* **1637** B. JONSON *Eng. Gram.* I. iii. (1640) 36, E..where it endeth a former Syllabe, it soundeth longish, but flat: as in *dérive prépare, résolve*. **1719** QUINCY *Lex. Physico-Med.* (ed. 2) 348 Such as have a longish Seed swelling out in the middle. **1794** MRS. RADCLIFFE *Myst. Udolpho* xxv, A tall signor, with a longish face. **1884** *Illustr. Lond. News* 30 Aug. 199/1, I'll lay longish odds I know Squire Cowcumber's way. **1889** 'ROLF BOLDREWOOD' *Robbery under Arms* xxxiv, They'd had a longish day and a fast ride.

Comb. **1691** *Lond. Gaz.* No. 2666/4 A black brown Mare, ..round and longish Bodied. **1709** *Ibid.* No. 4526/4 She is of a middle Stature, somewhat thin and longish-Favour'd. ? **1855** CHR. ROSSETTI in *Ruskin, Rossetti*, etc. (1899) 49 Three white longish-haired dogs.

longitude (ˈlɒndʒɪtjuːd, ˈlɒŋgɪtjuːd). Also 7 **-tud**. [ad. L. *longitūdo*, f. *longus* LONG *a*. Cf. F. *longitude*.]

1. Length, longitudinal extent; *occas.* an instance of this; a length; a long figure. †Also, tallness, height. Now chiefly *jocular*.

1398 TREVISA *Barth. De P.R.* VIII. xxiv. (1495) 335 Orion ..his lengthe and longitude stretchyth nyghe to the brede and latitude of thre synges. *c* **1420** *Pallad. on Husb.* IV. 431 And of the claue Is best an handful greet in crassitude And cubital let make her longitude. *c* **1470** *MS. Lambeth No.* 306 in *Rel. Ant.* I. 200 The longitude of men folowyng. Moyses xiij. fote and viij. ynches and half [etc.]. **1589** PUTTENHAM *Eng. Poesie* II. xi[i]. (Arb.) 114 A bastard or imperfect rounde declining toward a longitude. **1607** ROWLANDS *Famous Hist.* 64 Thy Giants longitude shall shorter shrink. **1653** R. SANDERS *Physiogn.* 161 The forehead..its.. Longitude is from one temple to the other. **1669** STURMY *Mariner's Mag.* I. 23 A Superficies is a Longitude, having only Latitude. **1784** COWPER *Task* V. 11 Mine [*sc.* a shadow] spindling into longitude immense. **1814** SCOTT *Wav.* xviii, A petticoat, of scanty longitude. **1824** —— *St. Ronan's* xvii, The direct longitude of their promenade never exceeded a hundred yards. **1824** *Examiner* 555/2 A longitude of beard that would honour a pubescent Jew. **1867** HOWELLS *Ital. Journ.* iii. 23 One may walk long through the longitude and rectitude of many of her streets. **1869** ROGERS *Pref. Adam Smith's W. Nat.* I. 11 The wisdom of government is to limit that border land to the narrowest possible longitude.

2. Length (in immaterial senses, *esp.* of time); long continuance. Now *rare*.

1607 TOPSELL *Four-f. Beasts* (1658) 499 The curing of a Horse waxing hot with weariness and longitude of the way. **1613** M. RIDLEY *Magn. Bodies* Pref. Magn. 5 These men have found insteed of the longitude of places, a longitude of unprofitable labors. *a* **1626** BP. ANDREWES *Serm.* (1661) 15 The longitude, or continuance of the joy. **1661** LOVELL *Hist. Anim. & Min.* 437 Of longitude or brevity of a disease. **1692** BENTLEY *Boyle Lect.* 226 According to quantity of matter and longitude of distance. **1902** *N. & Q.* 9th Ser. IX. 198/2 The life of the artist is all too brief for the exacting longitude of art.

3. *Geog.* †**a.** The extent lengthwise (i.e. from east to west) of the habitable world as known to the ancients (*obs.*). **b.** Distance east or west on the earth's surface, measured by the angle which the meridian of a particular place makes with some standard meridian, as (in England) that of Greenwich. It is reckoned to 180° east or west, and is expressed either in degrees, minutes, and seconds, or in time (15° being equivalent to 1 hour). Abbreviated *long.* †**c.** *occas.* = Difference of longitude (between two places). †**d.** In the 18th c. sometimes confusedly used for: The method of ascertaining longitude at sea. *Obs.*

For the origin of the term see LATITUDE 4. ***circle of longitude***: see CIRCLE *sb.* 2.

c **1391** CHAUCER *Astrol.* II. §39 The arch of the equinoxial, that is conteyned or bounded by-twixe the 2 meridians, is cleped the longitude of the toun. **1432-50** tr. *Higden* (Rolls) I. 45 The longitude of the erthe habitable from the este to the weste..hath viij[the] tymes v. tymes a clxx[ti] myles and viij[the]. **1527** R. THORNE *His Booke* in *Hakluyt* (1589) 253 The longitude..is counted from West to East. **1551** ROBINSON tr. *More's Utop.* (1895) p. xcix (Giles to Buslyde), I will be hable..to instructe you..in the longitude or true meridian of the ylande. **1594** J. DAVIS *Seaman's Secr.* (1880) 284 The longitude between place and place, is the portion of the Equator, which is contained betweene the Meridians of the same places. **1625** N. CARPENTER *Geog. Del.* I. xi. (1635) 235 Places inioying the same Longitude are not alwayes equally distant from the first Meridian. **1712** STEELE *Spect.* No. 428 ¶1 The late noble Inventor of the Longitude. **1791** BOSWELL *Johnson* an. 1755 (1847) 99/1 Mr. Williams..had made many ingenious advances towards a discovery of the longitude. **1812-16** PLAYFAIR *Nat. Phil.* II. 61 The hour, as reckoned under any two meridians, is different, and the difference is proportional to the difference of longitude. **1831** BREWSTER *Newton* (1855) I. xiii. 350 The determination of the longitude at sea by observing the distance of the moon from the stars. **1841** ELPHINSTONE *Hist. India* II. 197 About the middle of the seventy-sixth degree of east longitude. **1878** HUXLEY *Physiogr.* xix. (ed. 2) 329 All lines of longitude form circles which have the earth's centre as their centre.

fig. **1852** MRS. STOWE *Uncle Tom's C.* xvi. 143 As if determined fully to ascertain her longitude and position, before she committed herself.

4. *Astron.* The distance in degrees reckoned eastward on the ecliptic from the vernal equinoctial point to a circle at right angles to the ecliptic through the heavenly body (or the point on the celestial sphere) whose longitude is required. (See also GEOCENTRIC, HELIOCENTRIC, HELIOGRAPHIC.) †Also *occas.* in the etymologically prior sense: The length or total extent of the ecliptic or of the sun's annual course.

The use of *latitude* (see LATITUDE 5) to denote distance from the ecliptic determined the astronomical application of the corresponding term *longitude*. ***circle of longitude***: see CIRCLE *sb.* 2.

c **1391** CHAUCER *Astrol.* II. §40 Knowe by thyn almenak the degree of the ecliptik of any signe in which that the planete is rekned for to be, and that is cleped the degree of his longitude. **1551** RECORDE *Cast. Knowl.* (1556) 176 So doo they call the motion of them [the Planetes] in Longitude, theyr distaunce by theyr naturall course from the beginninge of Aries. **1594** BLUNDEVIL *Exerc.* Introd. (1636) 435 The Ecliptique line containeth 360 degrees, which is the Longitude of Heaven, and the first degree of the Longitude of any Starre beginneth at the first point of Aries. **1667** MILTON *P.L.* VII. 373 The glorious Lamp,..Regent of Day,..jocond to run His Longitude through Heav'n his high rode. **1725** POPE *Odyss.* XIX. 350 Before the sun His annual longitude of heav'n shall run. **1834** MRS. SOMERVILLE *Connex. Phys. Sci.* (1849) 11 The mean or circular motion of a body estimated from the vernal equinox, is its mean longitude; and its elliptical, or true motion, reckoned from that point, is its true longitude. **1867** DENISON *Astron. without Math.* 270 Geocentric or common celestial longitude.

5. *Comb.*, as ***longitude-table***; †**longitude hunter**, one bent on inventing a method for ascertaining the longitude; **longitude star** (see quot.); **longitude watch**, a chronometer for use in ascertaining the longitude.

1738 WEDDELL *Voy. up Thames* 64 At College they had been pestered with so many crack-brain'd *Longitude-Hunters. **1842** G. W. FRANCIS *Dict. Arts*, etc., **Longitude Stars*, a term frequently used to denote those fixed stars which have been selected for the purpose of finding the longitude by lunar observations. The chief of these are as follows:—Aldebaran, Pollux, Regulus, Spica Virginis, Antares, Formanault, and the largest star in Aquila. **1790** MARGETTS (*title*) *Longitude Tables. **1763** *Ann. Reg., Chron.* 100 The trial of Mr. Harrison's *longitude watch.

longitudinal (lɒndʒɪˈtjuːdɪnəl), *a.* and *sb.* [f. L. *longitūdin-*, *longitūdo* LONGITUDE + -AL[1].]

A. *adj.*

1. Of or pertaining to length as a dimension; (extent) in length.

1765 BLACKSTONE *Comm.* I. 275 Our antient historians inform us, that a new standard of longitudinal measure was ascertained by king Henry the first. **1796** MORSE *Amer. Geog.* II. 270 The real depth, or longitudinal extent of the mine. **1810** D. STEWART *Philos. Ess.* II. I. i. 223 To express a limited portion of longitudinal extension in general. **1818** COBBETT *Pol. Reg.* XXXIII. 182 The number of longitudinal inches of the foot measure.

2. a. Extending or proceeding in the direction of the length of a body; running lengthwise.

longitudinal elevation: one showing the side of a structure, as distinguished from an end view; a side elevation.

1715 CHEYNE *Philos. Princ. Relig.* I. (ed. 2) 134 These Vesiculæ are distended, and their Longitudinal Diameters ..straitned, and so the length of the whole Muscle shortned. *Ibid.* 518 The oblique Fibres which make but few turns serve to propagate gently the included Fluid, the Longitudinal ones to move the Vessel. **1794** SULLIVAN *View Nat.* II. 3 The great longitudinal vallies of the Alps. **1807** M. BAILLIE *Morb. Anat.* (ed. 7) 394 A longitudinal section was made with a saw completely through its substance. **1822** CONYBEARE & PHILLIPS *Outl. Geol. Eng. & Wales* p. xxiv, The longitudinal valleys are those which pursue a course parallel to the direction of the chains [of hills] which bound them. **1825** J. NICHOLSON *Operat. Mechanic* 564 If two pieces of timber are connected, so that the joint runs parallel with the fibres of both, it is called a longitudinal joint. **1839** MURCHISON *Silur. Syst.* I. xxviii. 529 By longitudinal valleys is meant those which range parallel to the ridges or general strike of the mountains. **1845** DARWIN *Voy. Nat.* ii. (1879) 7 Several of the species are beautifully coloured with longitudinal stripes. **1860** TYNDALL *Glac.* I. xii. 88 The glacier..is in a state of longitudinal strain. **1861** BERESF. HOPE *Eng. Cathedr. 19th C.* 81, I have selected..the longitudinal elevation and the longitudinal and transverse sections..for their intrinsic merit. **1924** *Bull. Seismol. Soc. Amer.* XIV. 28 Tectonic earthquakes have also been divided into longitudinal and transverse earthquakes according as they are associated with the strike or transverse faults of a district. **1937** [see CONCORDANT *a.* 4]. **1937** WOOLDRIDGE & MORGAN *Physical Basis Geogr.* xxi. 354 The conception of truly longitudinal coasts as characteristic of the Pacific Basin breaks down on the coasts of Eastern Asia. **1971** C. R. TWIDALE *Structural Landforms* i. 11 Cross joints which cut vertically across the lineation or foliation of the rock; and longitudinal joints, which run parallel to such textural features in a vertical plane.

b. *Anat.* and *Zool.*

1706 PHILLIPS (ed. Kersey), *Longitudinal Suture* (in *Anat.*), the cross Seam of the Scull, that goes from one Side to the other. **1826** KIRBY & SP. *Entomol.* IV. 298. **1840** W. J. E. WILSON *Anat. Vade M.* 361 The longitudinal fissure is the space separating the two hemispheres. **1854** OWEN *Skel. & Teeth* (1855) 3 The head of the sturgeon is defended by a case of superficial bony plates, and the body by five longitudinal rows of similar plates. **1863** HUXLEY *Man's Place Nat.* iii. 142 The two depressions for the lateral sinuses, sweeping inwards towards the middle line of the roof of the skull, to form the longitudinal sinus. **1870** ROLLESTON *Anim. Life* 1 The longitudinal fissure in which is lodged the longitudinal sinus.

c. *Bot.*

longitudinal system, 'an old term for fibro-vascular system' (Jackson *Bot. Terms* 1900).

1787 *Linnæus' Fam. Plants* I. 76 Petals four, egg'd, sessile, with a longitudinal pit at the base. **1884** BOWER & SCOTT *De Bary's Phaner.* 565 The beginning of the formation of lenticels takes place..before longitudinal extension is complete. **1888** *Syd. Soc. Lex.*, *Longitudinal system*.

d. *Acoustics.* Of vibrations: Produced in the direction of the length of the vibrating body; also (see quot. 1869).

1867 TYNDALL *Sound* v. 159 The sounds produced by the longitudinal vibrations of a string are, as a general rule, much more acute than those produced by its transverse vibrations. **1869** —— in *Fortn. Rev.* 1 Feb. 239 In the case of sound, the vibrations of the air-particles are executed in the direction in which the sound travels. They are therefore called longitudinal vibrations. **1879** W. H. STONE *Sound* 13 Longitudinal Vibrations. Every string which vibrates transversely between two points must also vibrate longitudinally.

3. Pertaining to longitude; measured from east to west.

1874 COUES *Birds N.W.* 360 Its longitudinal dispersion is thus quite restricted, contrary to the rule among our birds of this..continent.

4. Involving information about an individual or group at different times throughout a long period (obtained by repeated examination or by eliciting recall on one occasion).

1949 B. J. UNDERWOOD *Exper. Psychol.* v. 117 Most researches in the past have been concerned with cross-sectional analyses of the organism, i.e., the capacity of the organism at the moment. When we study the influence of learning on these processes we are interested in the longitudinal aspects, i.e., how they developed. **1958** M. ARGYLE *Relig. Behaviour* vi. 59 These longitudinal studies can supply important supplementary information. **1962** *Arch. Gen. Psychiatry* VI. 328/1 Longitudinal studies of the urinary excretions of tryptamine and total indole-3-acetic acid..were made on 20 male schizophrenic patients. **1973** *Sci. Amer.* Sept. 35/3 Mathematical curves have been fitted with great success to measurements of individuals followed during the adolescent spurt... Such serial studies of individuals are called longitudinal, as opposed to the studies of populations called cross-sectional, in which each child is measured only once.

B. *sb.*

†**1.** *Anat.* A name for two muscles of the epigastrium. *Obs.*

1541 [see LATITUDINAL *sb.*].

2. a. *Ship-building.* In iron and steel ships, a plate parallel or nearly so to the vertical keel.

1869 SIR E. REED *Shipbuild.* i. 10 To preserve the continuity of their longitudinals. **1883** NARES *Constr. Ironclad* 5 *Longitudinals* are plates of iron, which run fore and aft between the frames, to strengthen the ship lengthways. **1900** *Engineering Mag.* 678 The stiffening angles for longitudinals.

b. *Aeronaut.* A longeron, esp. one in an airship.

1911 *Aero* May 38/1 There are three main longitudinals, which are of ash rebated for the reception of the diagonal cross-pieces. **1914** H. M. BUIST *Aircraft in German War* i. 21 (*in figure*) Longitudinal. **1919** *Jane's All the World's Aircraft* 37a/1 Fuselage longitudinals and struts have sections of I-shape. **1950** *Gloss. Aeronaut. Terms (B.S.I.)* I. 50 *Longitudinal*, a girder on the outside of the hull structure running fore and aft. **1973** D. H. ROBINSON *Giants in Sky* ii. 31 The hull was identical with that of the LZ 2, the dimensions, the number of longitudinals and ring frames being identical with those of the ships lost at Kisslegg.

3. A railway sleeper lying parallel with the rail (Webster 1864).

longitudinally (lɒndʒɪˈtjuːdɪnəlɪ), *adv.* [f. prec. + -LY[2].] In a longitudinal direction; in the direction of the length of an object; lengthways.

1724 in BAILEY. **1779** MRS. BOSCAWEN in *Mrs. Delany's Lett.* Ser. II. II. 489 The seeds are..somewhat flat, and situated longitudinally. **1787** *Linnæus' Fam. Plants* I. 4 Style ..slit longitudinally. **1834** MRS. SOMERVILLE *Connex. Phys. Sci.* xvii. (1849) 159 The air also vibrates longitudinally. **1868** *Rep. to Govt. U.S. Munitions War* App. 284 The locking device combined with a longitudinally moving breech-block. **1870** ROLLESTON *Anim. Life* 15 The longitudinally-fissured..pancreas. **1880** HAUGHTON *Phys. Geog.* vi. 303 A broad band of latitude, extending longitudinally from the Pyrenees to the east Coast of China. **1897** MARY KINGSLEY *W. Africa* 540 His body..was slit all over longitudinally with long cuts on the face, head, legs, and arms.

longitudinarian (ˌlɒndʒɪtjuːdɪˈnɛərɪən), *a.* and *sb. rare.* [f. L. *longitūdin-* (see LONGITUDE) + *-arian* as in *latitudinarian*.]

A. *adj.* Pertaining to longitude.

1853 DE QUINCEY *Autobiog. Sk.* Wks. I. 186 What was the centre of London for any purpose whatever—latitudinarian or longitudinarian—literary, social, or mercantile?

†**B.** *sb.* A student of longitude. *Obs.*

1754 *Stow's Surv. Lond.* I. I. xxiv. 178/2 Aristotelians, Cartesians, Adepts, Astrologers and common Longitudinarians.

longiˈtudinated, *a.* *rare*[−1]. [f. L. *longitūdin-* (see LONGITUDE) + -ATE + -ED.] Placed longitudinally.

1774 GOLDSM. *Nat. Hist.* III. iii. 71 Their [*sc.* Gazelles'] horns are..annulated or ringed round, at the same time, that there are longitudinated depressions running from the bottom to the point.

†**longiturnity.** *Obs.*[−0] [ad. late L. *longiturnitās*, f. *longiturn-us*, f. *longus* LONG.] Long duration or continuance.

1727 BAILEY vol. II, *Longiturnity*, continuance of Space.

†**ˈlongity.** *Obs. rare*[−1]. [ad. L. *longitās*, f. *longus* LONG.] Length.

1664 POWER *Exp. Philos.* I. 12 [House-spiders' eyes] in some were four..and in some eight, according to the proportion of their bulk, and longity of their legs.

longivity, obs. form of LONGEVITY.

long knife. [f. LONG *a.*[1] + KNIFE *sb.*]

1. *N. Amer. Hist.* (Freq. *pl.*, and with capital initials.) A name given by North American Indians to white settlers, esp. of Virginia, or white soldiers. In Canada, *spec.* a citizen of the United States.

1774 J. R. PEYTON *Let.* 10 Oct. in J. L. Peyton *Adventures my Grandfather* (1867) 143 The white troops, or 'Long Knives',..imagined no enemy was near. **1784** D. BOON in J. Filson *Discovery Kentucke* 62 The savages now learned the superiority of the long knife, as they call the Virginians, by

experience. **1827** J. F. COOPER *Prairie* I. v. 135 If the Tetons lose their great chief by the hands of the Long-knives, old shall die as well as young! **1838** A. JAMESON *Winter Stud. & Summer Rambles Canada* III. 55 A distinguished Pottowottomie warrior.. was.. a good friend to the Long-knives, (The Americans). *Ibid.* 142 The Indians gave the name of Cheemokomaun (Long Knives, or *Big Knives*) to the Americans at the time they were defeated by General Wayne.. in 1795, and suffered so severely from the *sabres* of the cavalry. **1908** W. R. NURSEY *Story Isaac Brock* xviii. 100 'My object,' said Brock, addressing the Indians, 'is to assist you to drive the "Long-knives" from the frontier.' **1959** R. GANT *World in Jug* 38 Paleface, hear me. Do not send pony soldiers and long knives against my nation. **1959** N. SLUMAN *Blackfoot Crossing* 33 Crowfoot says that the border—the medicine line—protects his people from the Long Knives. **1972** J. MOSHER *Some would call it Adultery* III. xvi. 147 Brought General Terry and his 'Long Knives', as the Indians called U.S. Cavalry, 'up across the border, Mounted Police or no'.

2. Phr. ***(night of) the long knives***: a treacherous massacre (as, according to legend, of the Britons by Hengist in 472, or of Ernst Roehm and his associates by Hitler on 29–30 June 1934); hence used allusively of any similarly decisive or ruthless action.

The massacre of the Britons is described by Geoffrey of Monmouth in *Historia Regum Britanniæ* Bk. VI. xv.

1862 BORROW *Wild Wales* II. xx. 226 Hengist had commanded.. that.. each Saxon should draw his long sax, or knife,.. and should plunge it into the throat of his neighbour... This infernal carnage the Welsh have appropriately denominated the treachery of the long knives. **1891** E. C. BREWER *Historic Note-Bk.* 531/2 *Long Knives (The Plot or Treachery of the)*. This was a treacherous conference to which Geoffrey of Monmouth tells us the chief Britons were invited by Hengist at Ambresbury; others say by Vortigern. Beside each Briton a Saxon was seated, armed with a long knife; and, at a given signal, each Saxon slew the Briton seated by his side. Geoffrey tells us the signal was the utterance of these words: *Nemet oure Saxas*, and that the number massacred was 460. **1936** R. OLDEN *Hitler the Pawn* xvi. 378 The consequence is massacre, 'the night of the long knives', a St. Bartholomew's night. **1937** S. H. ROBERTS *House Hitler Built* II. iii. 114 Such seem to have been the facts of this 'Night of the Long Knives' (the name given to it by Hitler and taken from one of the earliest marching songs of the Nazis). **1960** 'W. HAGGARD' *Closed Circuit* iii. 29 Many would die in any night of the long knives. **1961** G. THOMAS *Keep* in *Plays of Year* XXIV. 217 This is the night of the long knives and they all landed on Con. **1967** W. R. MANCHESTER *Death of President* I. i. 93 His popularity margin with state voters was.. wider than those of Connally or Kennedy-Johnson... He could be fairly confident of surviving the long knives of Austin. **1967** *Economist* 22 July 313/2 A government that can provide some degree of stability may be forgiven its day of the long knives—if the exercise is not repeated. **1968** J. BINGHAM *I love, I Kill* iv. 44 There was not the 'night of the long knives' feeling you get when a commercial management has ten thousand smackers at stake. **1968** *Sunday Times* 1 Dec. 11/5 The Long Knives flashed last week at Bush House. **1973** *Times* 18 June 1/7 They both lost their jobs last April 30, the night of the long knives when a whole series of officials suddenly resigned. **1973** R. PAYNE *Life & Death of Hitler* 274 The historical event known as the Night of the Long Knives took place in broad daylight.

† **longlasting**, *sb. Obs.* [f. LONG *adv.* + LASTING *vbl. sb.*] The fact of lasting a long time.

c **1400** tr. *Secreta Secret., Gov. Lordsh.* 67 þis sentence, þat all delitable þinges of þys world.. ben alle for longlastynge of durabilyte.

long-lasting, *a.* [See LONG *adv.* 9.] That lasts a long time.

1530 PALSGR. 317/2 Longe lastyng, *perdurable*. **1587** GOLDING *De Mornay* xxx. (1617) 483 That when he had giuen his life in sacrifice for sin, he might see a longlasting seede. **1669** WORLIDGE *Syst. Agric.* (1681) 282 Gather not long-lasting Fruit till after Michaelmas. **1677** GILPIN *Demonol.* (1867) 217 When their sorrows are long-lasting and deep. **1886** C. SCOTT *Sheep-farming* 182 Long-lasting storms of frost and snow.

Hence **long-lastingness**. *rare*$^{-1}$.

1598 FLORIO, *Longinquita*,.. a length of time, long lastingnes.

'long-leg.

† **1.** = BUPRESTIS 1. *Obs.*$^{-0}$

1585 HIGINS *Junius' Nomencl.* 76 *Buprestis*,.. a venemous flie like a beetle, and hurtfull to cattell: a longe legge: a wag-leg. **1611** COTGR. s.v. *Bupreste*. **1783** AINSWORTH *Lat. Dict.* (Morell) I. s.v. *Beetle*.

2. long-legs. a. The stilt; the 'long-legged plover'.

1713 RAY *Syn. Avium* 190 *Himantopus Plinii* Aldrov... Long-legs. **1802** G. MONTAGU *Ornith. Dict.* (1833) 496 Black-winged Stilt, *Himantopus melanopterus*.. Longlegs, Longshanks.

b. = DADDY-LONG-LEGS.

1806 SHAW *Gen. Zool.* VI. II. 374 This [*Tipula*] is popularly known by the title of Long-Legs.

longleg (*Cricket*): see LEG *sb.* 6 c.

long-legged, *a.* **a.** Having long legs: used *spec.* in the names of some animals.

1590 SHAKS. *Mids. N.* II. ii. 21 Hence you long-leg'd Spinners, hence. **1592** CHETTLE *Kinde-harts Dr.* (1841) 18 Is it not absurde to see a long legd lubber pinned in a chayre [etc.]? **1676** *Lond. Gaz.* No. 1079/4 They are shaped like a Moscovy Mallard, but larger and longer legg'd. **1717** BERKELEY *Jrnl. Tour Italy* 30 May in Fraser *Life* (1871) 555 All the spiders except the long-legged ones bite. **1828** SCOTT *F.M. Perth* xix, What could have brought down the lang-legged loons to do their bloody wark within burgh? **1831** A. WILSON & BONAPARTE *Amer. Ornith.* III. 75 *Recurvirostra himantopus*.. Long-legged plover. **1848** JOHNSTON in *Proc. Berw. Nat. Club* II. No. 6. 292 The Phalangia,.. or long-legged spiders. **1875** W. S. HAYWARD *Love agst. World* 14 A long-legged puppy.

b. *Naut.* Of a ship: Drawing a great deal of water. Hence ***long leg*** (see quots.) (*slang*).

1802 *Naval Chron.* VIII. 83 Those ships being, to make use of a nautical phrase, too long legged for the eastern yard. **1867** in SMYTH *Sailor's Word-bk.* **1929** F. C. BOWEN *Sea Slang* 85 *Long leg*, a big difference in the draught forward and aft in a sailing ship. **1961** F. H. BURGESS *Dict. Sailing* 137 Any sailing vessel that draws a lot of water is said to have a long leg.

long-line, long line.

1. A deep-sea fishing-line.

1876 *Rep. Crab & Lobster Fisheries Scot.* App. I. 15 Every third hook on the long lines is baited with crabs. **1883** *Fisheries Exhib. Catal.* (ed. 4) 176 Long Lines, Hand Lines, .. Deep Sea Lines. **1883** G. B. GOODE *Fish. Industry U.S.A.* 13 (Fish. Exhib. Publ.) The much more general use of the trawl-line or long-line.

b. *attrib.* Furnished with or using long-lines.

1877 HOLDSWORTH *Sea Fisheries* 79 Dog-fish are the great enemies of the long-line fishermen. **1894** *Pall Mall G.* 5 Dec. 3/1 Scotch long-line boats were lent early this year to the Donegal fishermen, who were encouraged to fish further out.

2. A line of manuscript or type that runs across the page without columnar division. Also (with hyphen) *attrib.*

1755 *Advt.* in *Whole Duty Man*, A Long-line Octavo Common-Prayer. **1849** TICKNOR *Sp. Lit.* III. 16 The old long-line stanza. **1914** E. A. LOEW *Beneventan Script* xi. 289 The oldest extant Beneventan MSS. are written in long lines and not in two or more columns. **1939** W. H. P. HATCH *Princ. Uncial Manuscripts New Testament* 17 It was soon found that a wide column and a long line are more convenient for the reader. **1964** DEAN & LEGGE *Rule of St. Benedict* p. xviii, The Douce Rule has thirty long lines to the page.

3. In Old English verse, two half-lines considered as a unit. Cf. G. *langzeile*.

1868 W. W. SKEAT in Hales & Furnivall *Bp. Percy's Folio MS.* III. p. xxiv, There has been much discussion as to whether alliterative poems should be printed in couplets of short lines, or in long lines comprising two sections. **1877** H. REHRMANN *Essay concerning Anglo-Saxon Poetry* 9 All words of a long line are fit for alliteration that distinguish themselves in the verse by natural gravity or grammatical accent. **1929** W. E. LEONARD in Malone & Ruud *Studies Eng. Philol. in Honor of F. Klaeber* 7 The law of the meter remains, an eight-beat long-line. **1970** *Rev. Eng. Studies* XXI. 133 The metrical division between two verses (hemistichs) of an alliterative long line.

Hence **long-lining**, fishing with long-lines.

1877 HOLDSWORTH *Sea Fisheries* 71 Long-lining from Grimsby is worked by means of large smacks. **1885** *St. James's Gaz.* 28 Feb. 4/2 Three fishermen have been drowned at Scarborough while long-lining.

'longliner. Chiefly *N. Amer.* Also **long-liner**. [f. LONG-LINE 1 + -ER[1].] One who fishes with a long-line; a fishing vessel which uses longlines.

1909 *Westm. Gaz.* 3 June 14/3 Dog-fish, these terrors to netsmen and long-liners. **1919** W. T. GRENFELL *Labrador Doctor* (1920) x. 183 The Hearn long-liners and trawlers, who were just beginning their vast fishery in those waters. **1955** *Fishermen's Advocate* (Port Union, Newfoundland) 14 Jan. 10/5 Three new longliners are now under construction. **1959** *Globe Mag.* (Toronto) 12 Sept. 21/2 Groundfishing operations—draggers with their great, bottom-scraping nets, and longliners with multiple lines armed with hundreds of baited hooks—were the principal targets. **1969** *Guardian* 8 Mar. 7/5 Off this place the professional Japanese long-liners have taken swordfish in excess of a thousand pounds. **1974** *Nat. Geographic* Jan. 114/2 The boat is of the type still called a long-liner, from a time when the crews of such boats fished with lines and hooks. **1974** *Sci. Amer.* Mar. 119/1 The yellowfin-tuna fishery on the Pacific Equator, worked only recently by American and Japanese long-liners, is plainly disclosed in the Nantucketers' logbooks.

Hence **longlinerman**, a member of the crew of a longliner.

1955 *Fishermen's Advocate* (Port Union, Newfoundland) 14 Jan. 7/3 The courses, while aimed at longlinermen, were made available to all who wished to attend.

long-lived (-laɪvd), *a.* Also 7 -lif't. [f. LONG *a.* + *live*, LIFE *sb.* + -ED[2]. Often pronounced (lɒŋlɪvd), as if etymologically parallel to *smooth-spoken*, etc.] Having a long life or existence; living or lasting a long time; longeval.

a **1420** HOCCLEVE *De Reg. Princ.* 570 Fader and moder honoure, That thow maist be longe lyved. *c* **1425** *Cursor M.* 1268 (Trin.) Longe lyued am I in elde. **1553** EDEN *Treat. Newe Ind.* (Arb.) 22 They are long lyued and lyue euen vntyl an hundreth yeares of age. **1607** WALKINGTON *Opt. Glasse* 41 Little eyes denotate a large cheverill conscience.. spacious breasted, long-lif't. **1609** BIBLE (Douay) *Exod.* xx. 12 Honour thy father and thy mother, that thou mayest be long-lived upon the earth. **1633** EARL MANCH. *Al Mondo* (1636) 176 Seldom is excellencie in any kinde long lived. **1653** WALTON *Angler* vii. 142 Bacon observes the Pike to be the longest lived of any fresh water fish. **1707** *Curios. in Husb. & Gard.* 171 The Sea.. produces Animals.. more sound, and longer-liv'd, than any of the other Elements. **1774** GOLDSM. *Nat. Hist.* (1776) III. 230 The lion.. is a very long-lived animal. **1883** JEFFERIES *Story Heart* i. (1891) 13 The long-lived summer days dried and warmed the turf in the meadows. **1899** *Allbutt's Syst. Med.* VIII. 374 Chronic uncured melancholics.. are often long-lived.

Hence **long'livedness**, longevity.

1872 *Echo* 27 Sept., The long-livedness of the Mastai family. **1882** R. ADAMSON in *Encycl. Brit.* XIV. 789/2 If.. there can be discovered a reciprocating relation between the want of gall in animals and longlivedness.

long-living, *a.* [See LONG *adv.* 9.] That lives for a long time.

1382 WYCLIF *Isa.* ix. 15 The longe lyuende and the wrshepefull. *c* **1500** in *Q. Eliz. Acad.* 94 The langest leving men. **1677** GALE *Crt. Gentiles* II. III. 157 The admired Wisdome of the long-living Fathers of the elder world. *a* **1680** BUTLER *Rem.* (1759) X. 8 Another.. That.. in the Register of Fame Had enter'd his long-living Name. **1899** *Daily News* 24 May, Her Majesty comes.. of a long-living stock.

longly ('lɒŋlɪ), *adv.* Also 5 **langly**, 6–7 **longely**. [f. LONG *a.* + -LY[2].]

† **1.** For a long while. = LONG *adv.* 1. *Obs.*

1340 HAMPOLE *Pr. Consc.* 3188 þe mast veniel syns sal þar bryn langly, Als wodde brinnes, þat es sadde and hevy. *a* **1400** *Ipomedon* (ed. Kölbing) 327/8 And whan they departed, eithre loked on othre so longly, that they left not, whilles oon might see that othre. **14..** *Life Alexander* MS. Linc. A. i. 17 lf. 1 (Halliw.) He knelid doune on his kneesse, and bihelde Alexander in the vesage langly. **1502** *Ord. Crysten Men* (W. de W. 1506) v. vii. 415 A man may desyre for to lyue longely for too amende his lyfe. **1506** *Kalender of Sheph.* F vij b, Father & mother thou shalt honour, end shalt lyue longely. **1581** DEE *Diary* (Camden) 11 Somewhat like the shrich of an owle but more longly drawn. **1596** SHAKS. *Tam. Shr.* I. i. 170 Master, you look'd so longly on the maide, Perhaps you mark'd not what's the pith of all. **1605** SIR E. WATSON in *Buccleuch MSS.* (Hist. MSS. Comm.) I. 238, I pray you.. deliver it to.. the Earl of Exceter with speed, for he longely looketh for it.

2. At considerable length: said of speech or writing. Now *Sc.*

c **1330** R. BRUNNE *Chron.* (1810) 222 To say longly or schorte, alle armes bare. **1553** *Reg. Privy Council Scot.* Ser. I. 140 Lyk as the said artikill mair langlie proportis. **1850** MRS. CARLYLE *Lett.* II. 121 Don't mind length, at least only write longly about yourself.

3. To a considerable length (in space). *rare*.

1662 J. CHANDLER *Van Helmont's Oriat.* 54 The bottom of the Sea, hath the Sand *Quellem* longly and largely laying open. **1871** COOKE *Handbk. Brit. Fungi* II. 761 Asci clavate, obtuse, longly pedicellate.

Longmyndian (lɒŋ'mɪndɪən), *a. Geol.* [f. *Long Mynd* (see def.) + -IAN.] Applied to a thick series of non-fossiliferous sedimentary rocks in the west Midlands, now believed to be of Pre-Cambrian age, whose main outcrop forms the hills of the Long Mynd in southern Shropshire (Salop). Also *absol.*

1888 C. CALLAWAY in *Trans. Shrops. Archæol. & Nat. Hist. Soc.* XI. 239 We are able to determine the relative ages of the three most ancient rock-systems in the region, viz., the Malvernian, the Uriconian, and the Longmyndian... The great series which forms the Longmynd Hills was referred.. to the Lower Cambrian; but until good evidence of its age is obtained, I have thought it better to use a local designation. *Ibid.* 240 The Longmyndian conglomerates are largely derived from the Uriconian. **1929** EVANS & STUBBLEFIELD *Handbk. Geol. Gt. Brit.* iii. 20 The outcrop of the Longmyndian Rocks at Church Stretton forms the wild, moorland tract called the Longmynd. **1967** D. H. RAYNER *Stratigr. Brit. Isles* ii. 45 The structures in the Longmyndian pediments.. suggest strongly that the western part of the Wentnor outcrops are inverted. **1969** BENNISON & WRIGHT *Geol. Hist. Brit. Isles* iii. 67 The Longmyndian is in the form of a very large syncline.

'long-neck.

† **1.** An earthenware retort or still with a long neck. *Obs.*

1662 R. MATHEW *Unl. Alch.* cxii. 183 Take good Copperas.. beat it to powder, put it in long necks, lute fast, and draw it with judgement. **1684** BOYLE *Porousn. Anim. & Solid Bod.* v. 90. **1734** P. SHAW *Chem. Lect.* (1755) 432 This Matter may now be put into a well coated Long-Neck, and worked with care in a Reverberatory Furnace. **1763** W. LEWIS *Comm. Phil. Techn.* 13 Distillation in coated glass retorts, earthen retorts, or longnecks.

2. a. A local name for birds having a long neck, e.g. the bittern, the heron, the pin-tailed duck.

1864 ATKINSON *Prov. Names Birds*, *Long-neck*,.. Common Bittern. *Botarus stellaris*. **1882** *Field Naturalist* 44 Locally, the heron is called 'crane' or 'long-neck'. **1890** *Century Dict.* (citing G. Trumbull 1888), *Longneck*, the pintail duck, *Dafila acuta*.

b. In full, ***long-neck clam***. An elongated, thin-shelled clam, *Mya arenaria*, found on the eastern coast of North America; = *long clam* (LONG *a.*[1] A. 18 b).

1905 *Bull N.Y. State Mus.* No. 71. 22 The soft or long-neck clam, Mya, is capable of locomotion only when very small. **1910** J. L. KELLOGG *Shell-Fish Industries* 281 Mya, in different localities, is known as the clam, the soft clam, the long neck, long clam, squirt clam. **1923** D. K. TRESSLER *Marine Products of Commerce* 533 *Mya arenaria* commonly called soft clam, long clam, long neck.. is found from South Carolina to the Arctic Ocean. **1970** R. LOWELL *Notebk.* 200 File upon file, the beds of long-neck clams.

long-necked, *a.* Having a long neck (in various senses): used *spec.* in the names of some animals.

c **1605** DRAYTON *Man in Moone* 203 The long neck'd Heron there watching by the brim. **1689** *Lond. Gaz.* No. 2422/4 A slender Horse, 5 years old,.. long neck'd, thick jaw'd. **1707** *Curios. in Husb. & Gard.* 337 A long-neck'd Vial, like a Matrass. **1835** MRS. CARLYLE *Lett.* I. 27 The thing goes off with small damage to even a long-necked purse. **1854** A. ADAMS, etc. *Man. Nat. Hist.* 69 Long-necked Tortoises (*Chelydidæ*). **1890** *Daily News* 27 Sept. 2/1 The long-necked will rejoice to learn that collars are higher than

ever. **1894** *Cosmopolitan* XVI. 344 Gracefully long-necked plesiosauri.

longness ('lɒŋnɪs). Now *rare*. [OE. *langnys*, f. *lang* LONG *a.* + *-nys* -NESS.] Length (in various senses); long continuance; †protractedness, delay.

c **1000** ÆLFRIC *Hom.* II. 408 Bradnyss, langnyss, heahnyss and deopnyss. **1340** *Ayenb.* 105 Þet uerste word ous ssewep þe langnesse of his eurebleuinge. **1398** TREVISA *Barth. De P.R.* XVIII. xxi. (1495) 781 The Camelion is a beest lyke to the Cocadryll and is dyuers oonly in crokydnesse of the backe and in longnesse of the tayll. **1486** *Bk. St. Albans, Her.* C vij b, And it be dyuidid after the longnes or after the brodenes. **1579** FENTON *Guicciard.* (1618) 250 The affaires betweene Cæsar and the French King proceeded with so great a longnesse. **1587** GOLDING *De Mornay* Pref. 9, I shall sometimes be long, and peradventure tedious to the Reader, . . But . . in this longnesse of mine, I straine my nature to apply myselfe to all men. **1616** SURFL. & MARKH. *Country Farme* 475 The longnesse of time will become tedious. **1668** CULPEPPER & COLE *Barthol. Anat.* III. viii. 148 It is shineing, indifferently hard, round behind, with some longness. **1684** H. MORE *Answer* 254 The longness of the time. **1841** LATHAM *Eng. Lang.* vi. 128 The Longness or Shortness of a Vowel or Syllable is said to be its Quantity. **1890** *Temple Bar* July 431 She had a curious, opium-like perception of time's longness.

†**long nine.** *Obs. U.S.* [f. LONG *a.*[1] I + NINE *sb.* 4 b.] A kind of cheap cigar.

1830 N. DANA *Mariner's Sk.* 213 (Th.), The fourfold row of long-nine-smoking beaux, that are regularly drawn up on Sunday forenoon in Market Square. **1835** *Harvardiana* I. 157 (Th.), He unfolded the wrapper; it contained two long-nine segars. **1851** *Yale Lit. Mag.* June 315 Pete had, as he always had after breakfast, a cigar in his mouth, a long nine. **1879** *Bradstreet's* 31 Dec. 3/3 Boys smoke 'long nines' while they still wear jackets.

long-nosed, *a.* Having a long nose: used *spec.* in the names of some animals.

1552 HULOET, Longe nosed, *acronasus*. **1591** PERCIVALL *Sp. Dict., Narigudo*, long nosed, *Nasutus*. **1680** WOOD *Life* 14 June, The servitor is tall, long-nosed, flowing hair and slow speech. **1712** ARBUTHNOT *John Bull* III. vi, A little long-nosed thin man. **1802** BINGLEY *Anim. Biog.* (1813) I. 508 The Long-nosed Tapir. **187.** *Cassell's Nat. Hist.* I. 88 The Long-nosed Monkey. **1897** *Outing* (U.S.) XXIX. 327/1 Copious draughts of saki, which steamed in a long-nosed pot overlaid with dragons.

Longobard ('lɒŋgəbɑːd), *sb.* and *a.* [ad. L. *Longobard-ī* (see LOMBARD).] = LOMBARD.

1598 GRENEWEY *Tacitus' Ann.* II. x. (1622) 48 The Semnones and the Longobards tooke part. **1644** EVELYN *Mem.* (1857) I. 155 The barbarous Goths and Longobards. **1707** CHAMBERLAYNE *St. Gt. Brit.* III. iii. 274 The Laws of the Longobards. **1839** *Penny Cycl.* XIV. 147 Luitprandus . . the most illustrious of the Longobard kings. **1902** *Union Mag.* May 214/2 There is no single trace of the real Gothic or Longobard style.

So **Longo'bardian** *sb.*, Lombard; **Longo'bardic** *a.*, Lombardic.

1846 GROTE *Greece* II. I. xx. 113 *note*, The Longobardic law is the most copious of all the barbaric codes in its provisions respecting marriage. **1877** W. JONES *Finger-ring* 85 A large gold thumb-ring . . on which is engraved the letter E of Longobardic form. **1889** R. R. ANDERSON tr. *Rydberg's Teut. Mythol.* 67 From that day the Vinnillians were called Longobardians—that is to say long-beards.

‖**longo intervallo** ('lɒŋgəʊ ɪntə'vælәʊ). [Lat., lit. 'at a great distance'.] At some remove, though there is a gulf between them (of two persons, places, etc., being compared).

1693 DRYDEN tr. *Juvenal's Satires* (Dedication) p. iii, The most Vain, and the most Ambitious . . have yielded the first place without dispute; and have been arrogantly content, to be esteem'd as second to your Lordship, and even that also, with a *Longo, sed proximi Intervallo*. **1890** W. JAMES *Princ. Psychol.* II. xx. 227 Almost all subsequent progress has been made in Germany, Holland, and, *longo intervallo*, America. **1923** *Spectator* 17 Feb. 294/1 In casual passages *The Orissers* may seem dull, pompous and even ridiculous; but as a whole it has a strange power, a conviction and an intensity of imagination that mark it off from other novels and link it, *longo intervallo*, with *Moby Dick* and *Wuthering Heights*. **1935** J. C. MASTERMAN *Fate cannot harm Me* ii. 44, I remember asking him once . . who were his literary idols among the moderns. 'Well,' he said, 'Max Beerbohm of course . . and then, but *longo intervallo*, P. G. Wodehouse.'

long-playing, *a.* [LONG *adv.* 9 a.] That plays for a long time; *spec.* designating or pertaining to a microgroove gramophone record designed to be played at $33\frac{1}{3}$ revolutions per minute. Cf. *L.P.* (L 7).

1912 *Talking Machine News & Jrnl. Amusements* Nov. 529/1 The Petmecky Needle, which plays ten times, is the subject of an interesting little leaflet. . . Users interested in this long-playing needle should ask their dealers for full particulars. **1929** *Wireless Mag.* Oct. 252 (*heading*) Long-playing dance records. **1931** *Electronics* Dec. 236/1 Long-playing records. . . Already announced is a phonograph record that will play for 15 minutes. **1948** *Electronic Engin.* XX. 333 A new library of recorded music has been announced . . which consists of a series of long-playing 10 and 12 in. records run at $33\frac{1}{3}$ r.p.m. **1951** *Ann. Reg. 1950* 386 An important advance was made by the introduction of 'long-playing' records containing about 20 minutes of music in place of the $4\frac{1}{2}$ minutes hitherto available. **1958** V. BELLERBY in P. Gammond *Duke Ellington* II. 151 With the advent of the Long Playing record he has shown himself ready to compose well outside his former 'three-minute' form. **1968** P. OLIVER *Screening Blues* ii. 81 Singers who have been recently recorded under the more liberal circumstances of the long-playing era. **1972** *Gramophone* Oct. 834/2 (Advt.), Trade in your unwanted classical long-playing records . . for guaranteed unplayed new records.

So **long-play** *a.* = LONG-PLAYING *a.*; also *ellipt.* as *sb.*, long-playing records collectively; **long-player**, a long-playing record.

1954 F. RAMSEY (*title*) A guide to longplay jazz records. **1957** M. GOFF (*title*) Short guide to Long Play. **1958** *Times* 19 Apr. 7/3 Already tape recording is hard on the heels of the long-play record and stereophonic reproduction promises to invade both. **1958** *New Statesman* 3 May 580/2 The Rank Organisation . . has decided to start a record club . . which will issue long-players. **1958** I. MURDOCH *Bell* xiv. 187 I'll . . put on my new long-player. **1962** A. NISBETT *Technique Sound Studio* 273 Long Play tape gives 50% more recording time on a spool than standard play. **1962** R. DOUGLAS-HOME *Sinatra* i. 8 The buying of long-players was (and still is) an expensive pursuit. **1968** *Blues Unlimited* Sept. 26 Phillips was introduced to long-play by Origin with two of his less impressive pieces. **1975** M. KENYON *Mr Big* ii. 18 He chose a long-player of Carroll Gibbons and his Savoy Orpheans.

long robe. [Cf. F. '*gens de robbe longue*, Lawyers, Clerkes, Professors of Artes, &c.' (Cotgr.).] Put symbolically for: The legal profession; esp. in ***gentlemen, men, members of the long robe*** = lawyers, barristers. Also *occas.* = The priesthood or ministry. (Cf. GOWN *sb.* 4 b.)

1601 HOLLAND *Pliny* I. 231 The first man of the long robe that deuised parks as well for these bores, as for other deere and sauage beasts, was Fulvius Lippinus. **1642** G. MOUNTAGU in *Buccleuch MSS.* (Hist. MSS. Comm.) I. 292 The Houses . . have likewise appointed a Committee of the long robe to declare how the King ought . . by the law to pass those Ordinances. **1680** *Honest Cavalier* 6, I believe there never was more worthy and Loyal Men under the Long Robe, than there is in this Age. **1712** ARBUTHNOT *John Bull* I. xii, They were the aversion of the Gentlemen of the Long Robe, and at perpetual war with all the country attorneys. **1762** FOOTE *Orators* I. Wks. 1799 I. 200 The two orders of the long robe next demand our attention. **1812** *Sporting Mag.* XXXIX. 42 A source of much profit to the gentlemen of the long robe. **1875** *Punch* 25 Dec. 266/2 The long-lived gentlemen of the surplice and the long robe.

†**b. long-robe-man**, a lawyer, barrister. *Obs.*

1654 GAYTON *Pleas. Notes* IV. xv. 251 He . . entertaines a Justice of grave carriage, . . Perswading the Long-robe-men, and his daughter. **1659** *Burton's Diary* (1828) IV. 434 All the eminent long-robe-men, except Turner and Terrill, were absent, in respect of the change of the Chair.

long run, 'long-run, *sb.* and *a.* (Also *Sc.* **lang run, langrin.**) **A.** *sb.* **1.** Phr. ***in the long run***, in earliest use †***at (the) long run***, occas. †***on***, †***upon the long run***: in the end; when things have run their full course; as the ultimate outcome of a series of vicissitudes. (Cf. F. *à la longue*.) In the Sc. examples: At last, at the end.

1627 J. CARTER *Plain Expos.* 117 (F. Hall) At the long run. **1656** CROMWELL *Speech* 17 Sept., They [the discontented] must end at the interest of the Cavalier at the long run. **1669** R. MONTAGU in *Buccleuch MSS.* (Hist. MSS. Comm.) I. 459 At long run he will make his fortune. **1681** T. FLATMAN *Heraclitus Ridens* No. 1 (1713) I. 4 There is neither Honour nor Estate to be got by Rebellion at the long run. **1722** RAMSAY *Three Bonnets* III. 31 At langrun Bawsy raik'd his een. **1768** TUCKER *Lt. Nat.* I. II. xxviii. 205 Prudence and steddiness will always succeed in the long run better than folly and inconsiderateness. **1771** SMOLLETT *Humph. Cl.* 18 July i, Humphry is certainly the north star to which the needle of her affection would have pointed at the long run. **1804** MAR. EDGEWORTH *Contrast* ix, At the long run, these fellows never thrive. **1806** *Jamieson's Pop. Ball.* I. 295 At langrin, wi' waxin and fleechin', . . She knit up her thrum to his wab. *a* **1814** *Manœuvring* II. i. in *New Brit. Theatre* II. 89 That is but a bad way on the long run. **1818** COLEBROOKE *Import Colon. Corn* 101 Upon the long run, a mean value is received for the average of crops. **1824** BENTHAM *Bk. Fallacies* Wks. 1843 II. 426 To labour at the long-run under an imputation that is not just. **1842** MRS. CARLYLE *Lett.* I. 156 Compromises never are found to answer, I think, in the long run. **1853** 'C. BEDE' *Verdant Green* I. vii, He'll find it all right in the long-run. **1898** L. STEPHEN *Stud. Biogr.* I. v. 178 To speak freely and openly is no doubt the best rule in the long-run.

2. *Theatr.* A long period of being presented on the stage; a play or entertainment presented for a long period. Also *attrib.*

1714 [see RUN *sb.*[1] 18]. **1883** D. COOK *On Stage* I. ix. 203 These are the days of 'long runs', when but one or two plays can be produced in a season. **1896** [see RUN *sb.*[1] 18]. **1901** BEERBOHM *Around Theatres* (1924) I. 320 The long-run system is often deplored on the ground that the mimes 'walk through' their parts. **1909** *Westm. Gaz.* 22 Apr. 2/3 Half the week is to be given to 'long-run' plays; the other half to new plays, revivals, and the classical drama. **1967** *Oxf. Compan. Theatre* (ed. 3) 195/2 Alfred Butt presented Laurette Taylor in *Peg o' My Heart*. This had a long run and was then transferred to the Globe.

B. *adj.* Taken or considered in the long run; = LONG-TERM *a.*

1904 W. JAMES *Meaning of Truth* (1909) iii. 89 Abstract truth, truth verified by the long run, and abstract satisfactoriness, long-run satisfactoriness, coincide. **1931** A. L. ROWSE *Politics & Younger Generation* 7, I have had in mind the necessity of a long-run view of politics. **1946** J. S. HUXLEY *Unesco* i. 19 Long-run human progress. **1957** K. R. POPPER *Poverty of Historicism* I. i. 6 There is no long-run uniformity in society on which long-term generalizations could be based. **1969** D. C. HAGUE *Managerial Econ.* II. iii. 61 With many industrial goods, long-run costs will be constant or falling. **1975** *Times* 6 Jan. 12/6 We need . . restraint from business and labour in which their longrun interests are elevated over . . shortrun interests.

So †**long-running** (in sense 1 of the sb.).

1528 ROY *Rede Me* (Arb.) 48 Their interrupcion Shall tourne to their destruccion At longe runnynge fynally. **1661** BAXTER *Mor. Prognost.* I. xcv. 25 As knowing, that at long-running, its only Truth that will stand upper-most. **1670** —— *Cure Ch. Div.* 150 At the long running, the wound will be found to be increased, and the cure the harder because of the delay.

long-running, *a.* [LONG *adv.* 9 a.] Continuing for a relatively long period of time; *spec.* of a play: having a large number of consecutive performances.

1956 *Nature* 21 Jan 142/1 This is precisely the case in a long-running crossing experiment with strains *H* . . and *O*. **1968** G. C. RAMSEY *Agatha Christie* iv. 50 It is . . poetic justice that the most famous play in the English language should have supplied the title for the longest-running play in England. **1972** *Guinness Bk. Records* (ed. 19) 98/2 The longest-running musical show ever performed in Britain was *The Black and White Minstrel Show*. **1975** *Listener* 6 Feb. 166/2 A long-running and repetitive weekly discussion.

longs, *adv.* and *prep.* Now *Sc.* or *dial.* Also 5 **longes,** 6 *Sc.* **langis, -ous,** 9 *Sc.* **langs.** [f. LONG + adverbial *s*. Cf. MHG. *langes* some time before; Du. *langs* prep., along.]

†**A.** *adv.* Long (ago). *Obs.*

c **1450** LONELICH *Grail* lii. 748, I Entrede Into ȝowre Castel Not longes Agon.

B. *prep.* Along, alongside.

[*c* **1275** LAY. 19677 In langes [*c* 1205 on longen] þane strete.] **1513** DOUGLAS *Æneis* III. iv. 134 And, langis the channel, . . The Actiane gemmis and sportis did assay. *Ibid.* VII. xii. 100 Thai that duellis langis the chyll river Of Anyene. **1535** *Aberdeen Reg.* XV. 639 (Jam.) Als gud hagyng throucht the cloiss & langous the hous syd. **18..** D. NICOLSON *MS. Coll. Caithness Words* (E.D.D.), *Langs*, along.

longsaddle, -settle, vars. LANGSETTLE *dial.*

longsaugh, variant of LUNGSOUGHT.

Longshanks ('lɒŋʃæŋks). [See SHANK *sb.*]

1. A nickname given to Edward I of England on account of his long legs.

[**13..** P. DE LANGTOFT *Chron.* (Rolls) II. 284 Lewelin . . & David son frere, unt perdu manantie, Cil od le lunge jambes de tut est seisie. ? **1306** *Pol. Songs* (Camden) 223 Whil him lasteth the lyf with the longe shonkes. **1556** *Chron. Gr. Friars* (Camden) 4 Kynge Edward the furst, that was callyd kinge Edward with the longshangkes.] **1590** MARLOWE *Edw. II*, III. ii. 12 Great Edward Longshanks' issue. **1596** DALRYMPLE tr. *Leslie's Hist. Scot.* VI. 342 Edward King of England frome his lang leggis callid Lang-schankis. **1603** DRAYTON *Barons' Wars* II. xxx. 34 Great Lancaster . . Canst thou thy oath to Longshancks thus forget? *a* **1661** FULLER *Worthies, Westminster* (1811) II. 104 He was surnamed Longshanks, his step being another man's stride.

b. Hence applied generally to a tall or long-legged person, often as a term of derision.

1699 B. E. *New Dict. Canting Crew, Long-shanks*, long-legged. **1915** *Dialect Notes* IV. 206 There comes long-shanks across the fields. **1939** F. THOMPSON *Lark Rise* ii. 32 The two tamer children . . would make a dash on their long stalky legs for their own garden gate followed by . . cries of 'Long-shanks! Cowardy, cowardy custards.' **1954** J. R. R. TOLKIEN *Fellowship of Ring* xi. 193 He was smoking a short black pipe. As they approached he took it out of his mouth and spat. 'Morning, Longshanks!' he said. **1959** I. & P. OPIE *Lore & Lang. Schoolch.* ix. 169 In the following [terms] the chief emphasis is on height, 'Lofty' being the most popular nickname, followed by 'Longshanks'.

2. A stilt or long-legged plover.

1817 T. FORSTER *Observ. Nat. Hist. Swallow* 86 *Charadrius himantopus*, Longleggedplover, Longshanks, or Longlegs. **1831** A. WILSON & BONAPARTE *Amer. Ornith.* III. 77 The name by which this bird is known on the sea-coast is the stilt or tilt, or long-shanks.

'long-shore, *attrib. phr.* (*sb.*) Also **longshore, 'longshore.** [Aphetic f. ALONGSHORE.]

1. a. Existing on or frequenting the shore; found or employed along the shore.

Often contemptuous as applied to men.

1822 *Blackw. Mag.* XI. 432 *note*, The functions of a Long-shore lawyer. **1837** MARRYAT *Dog-fiend* xiv, Sort of half-bred, long-shore chap. **1855** KINGSLEY *Westw. Ho!* i. (1881) I. 11 Your rascally longshore vermin, who get five pounds out of this captain, and ten out of that, and let him sail without them after all. **1888** *Argosy* Apr. 277 Within easy reach of the coast, where the 'long shore' herrings abound.

b. *Physical Geogr.* Moving, taking place, or laid down more or less parallel to a shore.

1837 *Lett. fr. Madras* (1843) 72 St. Thomé is not thought healthy the whole year through, because the 'long-shore winds' . . are more felt. **1910** V. CORNISH *Waves of Sea* vi. 179 When, at sea, the wind is obliquely on-shore there is not only a 'longshore current . . , but waves also break obliquely. Their effect to drive shingle along the shore is then obvious to the eye. **1952** R. F. PEEL *Physical Geogr.* xv. 253 Longshore drift . . is often the main factor controlling the supply of shingle to beaches. **1964** V. J. CHAPMAN *Coastal Vegetation* viii. 193 Long-shore movement of beach material takes place . . at the upper limit of the waves. **1968** R. W. FAIRBRIDGE *Encycl. Geomorphol.* 58/1 Currents from both flanks later build up the long-shore bar, both trough and bars being affected by long-shore currents, and the troughs are scoured by water escaping laterally behind the bars from the beach zone and longshore drift-currents bringing sand.

2. *sb.* A longshoreman. *rare.*

1857 KINGSLEY *Two Y. Ago* I. 82 Out of the way you loafing long-shores!

'longshoreman. [f. prec. + MAN *sb.*] One who frequents, or is employed along, the shore; e.g.

a man engaged in loading and unloading cargoes, or in fishing for oysters, etc. along the shore.

18.. MRS. H. E. SPOFFORD *Pilot's Wife*, He would sooner turn longshoreman and sweep a crossing. **1883** *Chamb. Jrnl.* 20 Jan. 33/2 His [the old-fashioned sailor's] oaths were appalling to 'long-shore men. **1888** BRYCE *Amer. Commw.* III. xc. 234 The longshore men,..an important element in this great port, and a dangerous element wherever one finds them.

'longshoring. [f. LONG-SHORE *attrib. phr.* (*sb.*) + -ING[1].] The type of work done at a port; the occupation of a longshoreman.

1926 *Daily Colonist* (Victoria, B.C.) 1 July 7/1 Two men were injured while doing longshoring work on Monday. **1930** C. S. JOHNSON *Negro in Amer. Civilization* (1931) iv. 53 In a study of the conditions of the longshoring industry of the Chicago port in 1915 by Charles B. Barnes, 100 workmen were interviewed.

long shot. Also long-shot, longshot. [f. LONG *a.*[1] + SHOT *sb.*[1]] **1.** A shot fired at a distance; a distant range; also *attrib.*

1791 *Hist. Eur.* in *Ann. Reg.* 185/1 What our sea men call a long shot fire is the most destructive of any to the rigging of ships. **1814** SCOTT *Let. to Southey* 17 June, I should be tempted to take a long shot at him [Buonaparte] in his retreat to Elba. **1853** KANE *Grinnell Exp.* xl. (1856) 362, I ventured the ice, crawled on my belly, and reached long-shot distance. **1867** SMYTH *Sailor's Word-bk.*, *Long-shot*, a distant range. It is also used to express a long way; a far-fetched explanation; something incredible. **1873** *Young Gentl. Mag.* July 490 This did not, however, suit her long-shot tactics.

2. Something incredible or very unlikely; a far-fetched explanation; a wild guess; *spec.* a bet laid against considerable odds; = OUTSIDER 1 b. See also SHOT *sb.*[1] 9 d. Also *attrib.*

1867 [see sense 1 above]. **1869** *Leisure Hour* May 326/1 He may also..learn to systematise his turf speculations, may know when it is prudent to 'back a jockey' or a long shot. **1906** 'O. HENRY' *Four Million* (1916) 33 A few long-shot winners at the New Orleans race-track. **1939** *Sun* (Baltimore) 30 Nov. 24/7 The long shots won the first and second races. **1955** *Sci. Amer.* Feb. 47/2, I made the first test very simple, because the whole idea seemed a long shot. **1970** *Globe & Mail* (Toronto) 26 Sept. 38/1 The other sign that fall has arrived is a sudden surge of long-shots from Western Canada speeding across the finish line in first place. **1971** *Publishers' Weekly* 23 Aug. 45/2 Since establishing his company nine years ago, Grossman has played hunches and longshots. **1975** *New Yorker* 20 Jan. 81/1 It was a day for long-shot players.

3. A cinema or television shot which includes figures or scenery at a distance; opp. CLOSE-UP. orig. *U.S.*

1922 *Sci. Amer.* Sept. 177/1 A quarter of a mile away, from which distance some of the so-called 'long shots' were filmed by the cameraman. **1930** *Sunday Times* 12 Oct. 4/3 Some of the close-ups are brilliantly clear and fascinating in detail, some of the long shots blurred and vague. **1934** *B.B.C. Year-Bk.* 58 The first television programme was transmitted... New ways of using photo cells enabled artists to be followed from 'long shot' to 'close up' and vice versa. **1962** *Movie* Sept. 7/3 The last shot of the film is a longshot of a general advance. **1974** *Times* 19 Jan. 9/7 We got Griffith in long shot winding up like a clock gone haywire.

†long-side, *a. Obs.* [For earlier *long and side*; cf. SIDE *a.*] Of garments: Long and sweeping.

1599 MASSINGER, etc. *Old Law* II. i, Thast beene so us'd to wide long side things, that..I shall have the waste of my Dublet lie upon my buttocks. *a* **1653** GOUGE *Comm. Heb.* vii. (1655) 150 Runners..use to gird up their long-side garments.

†long-sided, *a. Obs.* Having long sides.

14.. *Ragman Roll* 72 in Hazlitt *E.P.P.* (1864) 72 And at revell for to se yow hoope, Ys joy y-now so ye your lyggus streyne; Ye lade longe sydyde as a loppe. **1664** BUTLER *Hud.* II. i. 45 There is a tall long-sided Dame (But wondrous light) ycleped Fame.

long-sighted, *a.*

1. Having 'long sight' (see LONG *a.* 18); capable of distinguishing objects clearly at a distance but not close at hand; hypermetropic.

c **1790** IMISON *Sch. Art* I. 208 The short-sighted..can distinguish much smaller objects than long-sighted people. **1829** *Nat. Philos., Optics* xvii. 46 (U.K.S.) When the eye loses the power of accommodating itself to near objects, the person is said to be longsighted. **1833** N. ARNOTT *Physics* (ed. 5) II. 228 After middle age, most persons become more or less long-sighted. **1869** H. USSHER in *Eng. Mech.* 10 Dec. 295/2 He is long-sighted looking forward and short-sighted looking upward.

2. *fig.* Able to see far ahead; having great foresight; far-seeing.

1791 GIBBON *Autobiog.* (1896) 341 *note*, The judicious lines in which Pope answers the objection of his long-sighted friend. **1855** GROTE *Greece* II. xcv. XII. 443 Throughout the whole career of Demosthenes..we trace the same combination of earnest patriotism with wise and long-sighted policy. **1901** *Speaker* 3 Nov. 204/2 Such a city would have been distinguished for long-sighted prudence.

Hence **long'sightedness.**

1794 G. ADAMS *Nat. & Exp. Philos.* II. xvii. 295 Long-sightedness may be acquired: for..those that are habituated to look at remote objects, are generally long-sighted. **1832** *Nat. Philos., Acc. Newt. Opt.* i. 3 (U.K.S.) He showed that those defects which are called long-sightedness, and short-sightedness, proceeded from too small or too great a refracting power in the eye. **1864** PUSEY *Lect. Daniel* vii. 423 To discern their [events] purport and tendencies from the first, is the province of human long-sightedness.

longsome ('lɒŋsəm), *a.* Now chiefly *dial.* and *arch.* Forms: 1 longsum, 1–4, 6 *Sc.* langsum, (2 lonsum, 6 *Sc.* layngsum, 7 longsom), 6– longsome, *Sc.* langsome. [OE. *langsum*, f. *lang* LONG *a.* + *-sum* -SOME. Cf. OS. *langsam* (Du. *langzaam*), OHG., MHG. *lancsam* (G. *langsam*).] Long, lengthy; long-lasting; *esp.* tediously long; †tardy, dilatory, slow.

Beowulf (Gr.) 134 Wæs þæt ȝewin to strang, lað and longsum. *c* **1000** *Sax. Leechd.* II. 210 Þonne seo unȝefelde aheardung þære lifre to langsum wyrð. *c* **1175** *Lamb. Hom.* 111 Þa dusian him sculen efre adredan elles ne bið his rixlunge ne fest ne lonsum. *c* **1300** *Cursor M.* 28471, I haue halden quen i was sett langsum setes at my mete. *c* **1375** *Sc. Leg. Saints* xxvii. (*Machor*) 1237 It ware langsum for to say the wondir þat god in þe way wrocht. **1513** DOUGLAS *Æneis* IV. Prol. 133 Quhat is, bot turment, all his langsum fair, Begun with feir, and endit in dispair? **1535** STEWART *Cron. Scot.* (1858) II. 3 With soir travell than baith with barne and wyfe, Richt mony da leidand ane langsum lyfe. **1563** WINȜET *Four Scoir Thre Quest.* Wks. 1888 I. 60 We ar offendit be his layngsum delay. **1575** GASCOIGNE *Dan Bartholomew* Posies 99 A Lampe..With oyle and weecke to last the longsome night. **1599** JAS. I *Βασιλ. Δωρον* (1603) 118 Take no longsome workes in hande, for distracting you from your calling. *a* **1656** BP. HALL *Rem. Wks.* (1660) 401 To demonstrate this in particulars, were a long-some task. **1661–2** MARVELL *Corr.* xxxiv. Wks. 1872–5 II. 78 You may perhaps think us longsome in giuing you an account of your businesse. *c* **1704** PRIOR *Henry & Emma* 371 We tread with weary steps the longsome plain. **1728** RAMSAY *Lure* 55 She is not langsome In taking captives. **1842** MRS. F. TROLLOPE *Visit Italy* I. i. 4 The longsome interval between leaving Paris and arriving at Lyons. **1859** HELPS *Friends in C.* Ser. II. II. ii. 27 Men contrive to make their pleasures as dull, longsome, and laborious as any part of their daily task-work. **1861** W. BARNES in *Macm. Mag.* June 135 Many a cheek has been paled..by longsome hours of over-work. **1893** STEVENSON *Catriona* 87 The way there was a little longsome.

longsomely ('lɒŋsəmlɪ), *adv.* [f. prec. + -LY[2]. OE. *langsumlice* (Sweet).] †For long; †tardily; lengthily and tediously.

1456 SIR G. HAYE *Law of Arms* (S.T.S.) 301 That thai may nocht endure the weris langsumly. *c* **1610** SIR J. MELVIL *Mem.* (1683) 155 As he was making his preparations too longsomly and slowly in Dundie. **1834** *Q. Rev.* L. 527 [They] expatiate so 'longsomely' on corn, currency, or corporations, that [etc.].

'longsomeness. [f. as prec. + -NESS.] Tedious lengthiness; †tardiness (*Sc.*).

a **1000** *Ags. Ps.* xx. 4 (Spelman) Langsumnysse daȝa. **1597** JAS. I *Dæmonol.* 18 Considering the long-somenesse of the labour [etc.]. **1601** J. WHEELER *Treat. Comm.* 57 Such was the longsomenes of Returne, and the badness of the time at that instant. **1687** in Shields *Faithf. Contend.* (1780) 289 We ..must intreat your favour..for our longsomeness in sending. **1834** *Q. Rev.* L. 527 The first..of these objections is the length of the Sunday morning service—the 'longsomeness', as Archdeacon Berens terms it. **1887** *Sat. Rev.* 1 Jan. 19 A pretty scene, but superfluous, and producing no other effect than that of longsomeness.

longsought, variant of LUNGSOUGHT.

†longst, *prep. Obs.* Also 6 longest, *Sc.* langest. [Aphetic f. ALONGST.] Along.

a **1578** LINDESAY (Pitscottie) *Chron. Scot.* (S.T.S.) II. 165 They sould..gang langest the cost to Sanctandrois and syne to Couper. **1585** BURROGH *Jrnl.* in *Leycester Corr.* (Camden) 464 With these 4 vessells my lord and the rest passed from Flushinge..longest by 2 fly-boates of warr,..into Midlebroughe havon. **1591** GREENE *Farew. to Folly* (1617) D 3 b, Her shape was passing tall, Diana-like, when longst the Lawnes she goes. **1591** SYLVESTER *Du Bartas* I. i. 16 But 'longst the shore with sails of Faith must coast. *a* **1649** DRUMM. OF HAWTH. *Poems* Wks. (1711) 22 When Venus, longst that plain, This Parian Adon saw.

long standing.

[The origin of this phrase seems to be illustrated by the following passage:–*a* 1568 ASCHAM *Scholem.* I. (Arb.) 34 Except a verie fewe, to whom peraduenture blood and happie parentage, may perchance purchase a long standing vpon the stage.]

1. Continuance for a long time in a settled and recognized position, rank, etc. Chiefly in phr. ***of long standing.***

1601 SIR W. CORNWALLIS *Ess.* II. xxix. (1631) 36 Their discent..from families of long standings. **1678** BUNYAN *Pilgr.* I. (C.P.S.) 83 This Fair therefore is an Ancient thing, of long standing. **1713** *Guardian* (1756) I. xxix. 124 Mothers of long standing, undesigning maids, and contented widows. **1833** HT. MARTINEAU *Berkeley* I. ii. 24 A favorite of longer standing was in everybody's thoughts for at least three weeks. **1844** DICKENS *Mart. Chuz.* xxiv, Thomas is a friend of mine, of rather long-standing. **1855** MACAULAY *Hist. Eng.* xix. IV. 353 Between him and the licensers there was a feud of long standing.

2. *attrib.* or *compound adj.* (hyphened).

1814 JANE AUSTEN *Mansf. Park* II. ix. 196 In spite of every long-standing expectation. **1848** MILL *Pol. Econ.* I. xi. 208 A long-standing and hereditary confidence in the safety of funds when trusted out of the owner's hands. **1871** JAMES *Duty & Doctrine* 20 The afflictions of many upright, deserving, poor, long-standing curates. **1878** BROWNING *Poets Croisic* cxxxii, La Rogue..Had a long-standing little debt to pay. **1888** BURGON *Twelve Gd. Men* II. xi. 336 He determined to carry into effect a long-standing wish to have a parish 'Mission'. **1898** *Allbutt's Syst. Med.* V. 655 It [i.e. splenic enlargement] is greatest in long-standing cases. **1900** *Longman's Mag.* Dec. 139 They had a long-standing account to settle with these bush heathen. **1975** *Times* 15 Jan. 14/1 The holing of the Japanese supertanker, Showa Maru, on a rock off Singapore last week is bound to reactivate sharply a long-standing conflict of views over control of the nearby Malacca Straits.

longstwayes, -wise: see LONGWAYS, -WISE.

long sufferance. *arch.* = next.

1526 *Pilgr. Perf.* (W. de W. 1531) 109 Longanimitie, yt is longe suffraunce. **1526** TINDALE *Rom.* ii. 4 Despisest thou the riches off his..longe sufferance [1611 long suffering]? **1548–9** (Mar.) *Bk. Com. Prayer, Commination*, Obstinate synners..which despised the goodnesse, pacience, & long sufferaunce of god [so in **1552–1662**]. **1621** AINSWORTH *Annot. Pentat., Gen.* vi. 3 This long-sufferance of God the Apostle mentioneth in 1 Pet. 3. 19, 20. **1667** MILTON *P.L.* III. 198 This my long sufferance and my day of grace. *c* **1776** WASHINGTON in Bancroft *Hist. U.S.* (1876) VI. lvii. 496 The long-sufferance of the army is almost exhausted. **1813** SCOTT *Rokeby* IV. xxiv, Long-sufferance is one path to heaven. **1864** TENNYSON *En. Arden* 467 Trying his truth and his long-sufferance.

long-suffering, *sb.* Patient endurance of provocation or trial; longanimity.

1526 TINDALE *Gal.* v. 22 The frute off the sprete is, love, ioye, peace, longe sufferynge [so Coverdale; Luther has *langmüthigkeit*]. ? **1529** —— *Prol. to Exod.* (1884) 162 Marke the longesoferinge and softe pacience of Moses. **1597** J. PAYNE *Royal Exch.* 39 Cease thy admirations on Gods longe suffrings and providens, neyther mervell..why God delayeth his help. **1611** BIBLE *Rom.* ii. 4. *a* **1729** J. ROGERS 19 *Serm.* (1735) 351 His Forbearance and Long-suffering will not endure for ever. **1854** J. S. C. ABBOTT *Napoleon* (1855) I. viii. 154 Napoleon, who was by no means distinguished for meekness and long-suffering. **1860** TRENCH *Serm. Westm. Abb.* xxx. 339 Long-suffering, or slowness to anger.

long-suffering, *a.* Bearing provocation or trial with patience.

1535 COVERDALE *Exod.* xxxiv. 6 Lorde Lorde, God, mercifull and gracious, and longe sufferinge. **1611** BIBLE 2 *Pet.* iii. 9 The Lorde..is long-suffring to vs-ward. **1687** DRYDEN *Hind. & P.* III. 276 And grant ungrateful friends a lengthened space To implore the remnants of long-suffering grace. **1837** W. IRVING *Capt. Bonneville* I. 269 They showed them-selves..as brave and skilful in war as they had been mild and long-suffering in peace. **1860** PUSEY *Min. Proph.* 374 God can be long-suffering, because He can, whenever He sees good, punish. **1900** *Speaker* 8 Sept. 615/1 Henry the Sixth's longsuffering Queen rested here awhile.

Hence **long'sufferingly** *adv.*

1891 L. KEITH *Lost Illusion* I. iii. 54 Priscilla bore..long-sufferingly with this mild pursuit.

long sword. *Obs.* exc. *Hist.* A sword with a long cutting blade. Often *fig.* or *allusive*. Also transl. of the cognomen (AF. *Longespei*) of William, son of Henry II and Fair Rosamond.

1593 G. HARVEY *Pierce's Super.* Wks. (Grosart) II. 129 Shall I..tell thee, where thy slashing Long-sword commeth short? **1599** MASSINGER, etc. *Old Law* III. ii, Here's long-sword, your last weapon. **1607** MIDDLETON *Phoenix* F 1 b, A Writ of Delay, Long-sword. Scandala Magnatum, Backesword. **1612** DRAYTON *Poly-olb.* XVIII. 170 With Long-sword the braue sonne of beautious Rosamond. *a* **1616** BEAUM. & FL. *Coxcomb* v. i, Provide pen and inke to take their Confessions, and my long sword, I cannot tell what danger wee may meete with.

'long-tail.

1. a. A long-tailed animal, formerly a dog or horse with the tail uncut; *spec.* a greyhound. Also *attrib.* ***cut and long-tail***: see CUT *ppl. a.* 9; *fig.* in the sense 'riff-raff' (cf. quot. *a* 1700 and BOB-TAIL).

1575–1699 [see CUT *ppl. a.* 9]. **1602** *2nd Pt. Return fr. Parnass.* IV. i. 1509 He hath bestowed an ounce of Tobacco vpon vs, and as long as it lasts, come cut and long-taile, weele spend it as liberally for his sake. *a* **1700** B. E. *Dict. Cant. Crew*, *Riff-raff*,..Tagrag and Long-tail. **1865** *Daily Tel.* 17 Oct. 5/1 Ten brace more or less of 'longtails' [= pheasants]. **1876** *Coursing Calendar* 12 The former Duke of Hamilton.. and others of their day, were followers of the 'long tails' on the very same ground. **1900** *Westm. Gaz.* 20 June 4/2 The farmer wants to sell his horse as a 'long-tail', and the military authorities would prefer not to receive it till it is five or six. **1927** *Daily Express* 25 May 12 A little more foresight.. might have made 'rag running' a very popular entertainment, commanding as much notice as the sport of long-tail racing. **1930** BILLIS & KENYON *Pastures New* vi. 102 Some high-priced coursing dogs,—longtails as they were called—were brought into the colony.

b. The long-tailed duck, *Clangula hyemalis*.

1837 SWAINSON *Nat. Hist. Birds* II. 189 *Heralda*, or the long-tails. **1919** J. MASEFIELD *Reynard* 93 Some longtails prinking. **1958** D. A. BANNERMAN *Birds Brit. Isles* VII. 141 A number of immature long-tails may be seen in the Channel from November onwards.

c. The white-tailed tropic bird, *Phaëthon lepturus*.

1905 *Chambers's Jrnl.* May 367/1 The tropic bird commonly called 'longtail'. **1960** J. BOND *Birds W. Indies* 22 White-tailed Tropicbird... Local names:..Boatswain Bird; Long-tail.

2. A nickname for: **†a.** A native of Kent. *Obs.*

In allusion to the jocular imputation that the people of Kent had tails (cf. quot. *a* 1661); the French made the same accusation against Englishmen generally.

[**1617** MORYSON *Itin.* III. 53 The Kentish men of old were sayd to have tayles, because trafficking in the Low-Countries, they never paid full..but still left some part unpaid.] **1628** *Robin Goodfellow, his mad Prankes* (Percy Soc.) 4 They ever after were called Kentish Long-tayles. *Ibid.* 5 Truly, sir, sayd my hoastesse, I thinke we are called Long-tayles, by reason our tales are long, that we use to passe the time withall, and make our selves merry. **1656** SIR J. MENNIS & J. SMITH *Musarum Deliciæ* 7 Which still stands as a Monument, Call'd Long-taile, from the Man of Kent. **1659** HOWELL *Lex., Eng. Prov.* 21 Essex Calfs, Kentish Long-tails, Yorkshire Tikes. *a* **1661** FULLER *Worthies, Kent* (1811) I. 486 '*Kentish Long-Tailes*'... It happened in an English Village where Saint Austin was preaching, that the

Pagans therein did beat and abuse both him and his associates, opprobriously tying Fish-tails to their backsides; in revenge whereof an impudent Author relateth.. how such Appendants grew to the hind-parts of all that Generation. **1701** T. BROWN *Advice* in *Coll. Poems* 104 We, the Long Heads of Gotham,.. To the Long-Tails of Kent, by these Presents send Greeting.

b. A Chinaman.

1867 in SMYTH *Sailor's Word-bk.*

3. *Tobacco-manuf.*

1839 'JOSEPH FUME' *Paper on Tobacco* 119 The manufacturers tried them with a sample of returns under the name of long-tails.

4. *attrib.* = LONG-TAILED. **long-tail pair** *Electronics* = *long-tailed pair* (LONG-TAILED *a.* 3).

1848 C. A. JOHNS *Week at Lizard* 327 Longtail Tit (*Parus Caudatus*). **1855** OGILVIE, Suppl., *Long-tail*, a. Having the tail uncut, as a dog. **1946** *Electronic Engin.* XVIII. 298/2 Each of the amplifiers.. embodies a 3-stage network, employing valves (EF. 50) in a long-tail pair connexion... The circuiting is such that the amplifiers respond to difference of signal potential between the input terminals, being several hundred times less sensitive to variations of the potential of the two terminals together with respect to ground. **1971** J. H. SMITH *Digital Logic* iv. 70 Transistors T_2 and T_3 form a long tail pair where a fixed current is passed through R_3 into either T_2 or T_3, so that either one or the other transistor will conduct, but not both.

long-tailed, *a.*

1. a. Having a long tail.

1500–20 DUNBAR *Poems* xxxii. 17 Ane lang taild beist and grit with all. **1567** *Gude & Godlie Ball.* (S.T.S.) 202 Thair land taillit gowne. **1718** PRIOR *Solomon* I. 178 The crested snake, and long-tailed crocodile. **1859** GEO. ELIOT *A. Bede* v, The striped waistcoat, long-tailed coat, and low top-boots. **1896** *Peterson Mag.* Jan. 62/1, I shall have it printed in the old-fashioned way, long-tailed s and all. **1897** MARY KINGSLEY *W. Africa* 198 Long-tailed Adooma canoes.

b. *spec.* in names of animals.

1752 J. HILL *Hist. Animals* 544 The long-tailed Felis, with pencilled ears. **1766** PENNANT *Zool.* (1776) II. 507 Long tailed Duck. **1774** G. WHITE *Selborne* xli. 106 The delicate long-tailed titmouse. **1831** A. WILSON & BONAPARTE *Amer. Ornith.* III. 233 *Anas glacialis*.. Long-tailed duck. **1868** WOOD *Homes without H.* xiii. 232 Long-tailed Humming Bird (*Trochilus polytmus*). **1899** *Westm. Gaz.* 13 Sept. 1/3 Another beautiful butterfly—the long-tailed blue.

2. Of words: Having a long termination. †Also applied to a long-winded speech. *jocular.*

1549 *Compl. Scot.* Prol. 16 Thir lang tailit vordis, *conturbabuntur*,.. *innumerabilibus*. *a* **1670** SPALDING *Troub. Chas. I* (Spalding Club 1851) II. 262 It is said this long taillit supplicatioun wes weill hard of by the bretheren of the general assembly. **1767** A. CAMPBELL *Lexiph.* (1774) 87 Hard long-tailed words drawn from the Greek and Latin languages. **1817** J. H. FRERE *K. Arthur* I. vi, With long-tailed words in *osity* and *ation*. **1854** MRS. M. HOLMES *Tempest & Sunshine* 20 She was so heartily tired of its long tailed verbs. **1902** *Pall Mall G.* 4 Jan. 6/3 Would not the combination—Demont-Breton-Worms-Baretta—be a little long-tailed, say, for a visiting card?

3. long-tailed pair *Electronics*, a pair of identical valves (or transistors) with their cathodes (or emitters) connected together to a large resistor and usu. with their anodes (or collectors) connected to equal loads. Cf. *long-tail pair*.

1947 *Electronic Engin.* XIX. 272/1 The type of circuit used is based on what is generally referred to as the 'long-tailed pair' and owes its inception to the late A. D. Blumlein. **1970** J. SHEPHERD et al. *Higher Electr. Engin.* (ed. 2) xxii. 713 Drift [in a d.c. amplifier] cannot be reduced by straightforward feedback since this reduces the gain in proportion; the technique of compensation may however be employed. In this method drift in one part of a circuit is balanced against drift in another part. The long-tailed or emitter-coupled pair circuit.. is an example.

long-term, *a.* [f. LONG *a.*[1] + TERM *sb.*] Lasting for, pertaining to, or involving a relatively long period of time; maturing or becoming effective only after a long period. Also quasi-*advb.*

1908 *Daily Chron.* 24 July 1/6 The long-term men, who wore blue cotton overalls marked with the broad arrows, were in the rear. **1909** *Westm. Gaz.* 2 June 5/2 Mr. Fielding was able to place a 2½ per cent., long-term loan in London. **1937** *Discovery* June 178/1 A long-term programme of development. **1942** C. S. LEWIS *Screwtape Lett.* xiv. 73 It is His long-term policy.. to restore to them a new kind of self-love. **1956** C. AUERBACH *Genetics in Atomic Age* 65 Thus each species has to strike a balance between the short-term requirement for a low frequency of mutation and the long-term requirement for an ample store of mutant genes. **1956** *Planning* XXII. 38 The more specific the investment the greater the need for forecasting, especially long-term. **1959** A. LEJEUNE *Crowded & Dangerous* xii. 134 The long-term future could look after itself. **1969** *Listener* 5 June 786/3 The difficulty in getting both politicians and the bureaucracy to think long-term, particularly on financial affairs. **1971** *Jrnl. Gen. Psychol.* LXXXV. 51 Short-term memory is required to act as.. a cue to recall data from long-term storage. *Ibid.*, The effectiveness of extracting information from long-term memory may depend on short-term load. **1972** *Accountant* 23 Mar. 383/2 Valuation of long-term contracts. **1972** *Listener* 21 Dec. 854/2 Courses of action are followed without regard for their long-term consequences. **1974** *Times* 28 Dec. 9/6 Ordinary table wines.. must not be kept long-term in the refrigerator.

Long Tom.

1. A name for a gun of large size and long range.

1832 M. SCOTT *Tom Cringle's Log* xi, in *Blackw. Mag.* July 27/2 The long Tom must be a tearer to pitch its mouthful of iron this length. **1867** SMYTH *Sailor's Word-bk.*, *Long Tom*, or *Long Tom Turks*, pieces of lengthy ordnance for chasers, &c. **1897** *Westm. Gaz.* 13 Apr. 5/1 One of the white twins, familiarly known as 'Long Toms', from the *Camperdown* barbette. **1900** *Daily News* 7 Mar. 2/6 Four 'Long Toms', or Canet guns of the type known as the '155 long'.

2. A kind of gold-washing cradle.

1839 *Amer. Railroad Jrnl.* VIII. 98 The Long Tom.. consists merely of a trough. **1852** *Elora* (Ontario) *Backwoodsman* 17 June 2/4 The plough is a far more profitable instrument than 'the long Tom' or 'the rocker'. **1855** F. MARRYAT *Mtns. & Molehills* xiv. 262 They [miners] return to their camps and long toms [*foot-n.* gold washers]. **1874** RAYMOND *Statist. Mines & Mining* 18. **1890** *Golden South* 166 The real 'Long Tom' or cradle was a narrow trough filled with earth, into which water flowed; the cradle was rocked, and the gold washed from the earth fell into a tin dish.

3. *dial.* A name for certain animals (see quot.).

1854 MISS BAKER *Northampt. Gloss.*, *Long Tom*, the long-tailed titmouse, *Parvus caudatus*.

4. *Austral.* A marine fish of the family Belonidæ.

1883 E. P. RAMSAY *Food Fishes N.S. Wales* 29 (Fish. Exhib. Publ.) There are three or four species of *Belone* on our coast, all known under the name of 'Long Toms' by the fishermen. **1908** E. J. BANFIELD *Confessions of Beachcomber* I. iv. 154 The 'long tom' (*Zylosurus*, sp.) or alligator-pike, which shoots from the water. **1934** *Bulletin* (Sydney) 24 Jan. 20/2 The slender Long Tom must in future be known as *Lewinichthys ferox*... On the other hand the stout Long Tom is to be styled *Lhotskia macleayana*. **1965** *Austral. Encycl.* V. 362/2 Long toms or Needle-fish, members of the family Belonidae, in England and America called garfish... Long toms have the habit of leaping from the water, when either pursuing or being pursued.

5. *slang.* A particularly high-powered telephoto camera lens.

1968 'J. WELCOME' *Hell is where you find It* iv. 58 There were Rollieflexes, a Leica, a Long Tom for peeping, a couple of polaroids. **1968** 'O. MILLS' *Sundry Fell Designs* xiii. 142 Russ, grinning, remembered a Long Tom lens he had seen in the hands of one of the photographers. **1973** R. BUSBY *Pattern of Violence* x. 165 The long tom lenses and the barrels of the TV cameras peering down into the cleared arena.

'long-tongue. A person or thing with a 'long tongue'.

1. a. A small bird of the Cape of Good Hope. ? *Obs.* **b.** *dial.* The wryneck.

1731 MEDLEY *Kolben's Cape G. Hope* II. 155 There is a little bird at the Cape for which I know no other name than what the Cape Europeans give it, which is Long Tongue. **1772–84** COOK *Voy.* (1790) III. 937 The long-tongue is about the size of a bull-finch, and his tongue is not only very long, but said to be as hard as iron. **1837** MACGILLIVRAY *Hist. Brit. Birds* III. 100 The Wryneck. Emmet-hunter. Long-tongue. **1843** *Penny Cycl.* XXVII. 592/2 The Wryneck is the.. Long-Tongue.. of the modern British.

2. A chatterer, blab.

1847 in HALLIWELL. **1877** *N.W. Linc. Gloss.*, *Long-tongue*, (1) a tale-bearer.

long-tongued, *a.* Having a 'long tongue'; having much to say; chattering, babbling.

1553 *Respublica* (Brandl) III. vi. 84 A daughter eke he hath .. As vnhappie a longtounged girle as can be. **1593** SHAKS. *3 Hen. VI*, II. ii. 102 Why how now long-tongu'd Warwick, dare you speak? **1602** *How Choose Good Wife* G 3, She blusht & said that long tongu'd men would tell. **1737** RAMSAY *Sc. Prov.* (1797) 56 Lang tongu'd wives gae lang wi' bairn. **1818** SCOTT *Old Mort.* vi, The foul fa' ye.. for a lang-tongued wife. **1880** MISS BRADDON *Just as I am* xii, You didn't ought to give heed to a long-tongued fellow like Jebb, a man that must be talking.

Longton Hall ('lɒŋtən hɔːl). The name of a house in Staffordshire where the first Staffordshire porcelain was manufactured; hence *attrib.* of the porcelain manufactured there. Also *ellipt.* Longton.

1757 *Public Advertiser* 4 Apr. 3/3 A Quantity of new and curious Porcelain or China, both useful and ornamental, of the Longton-Hall Manufactory, which has never been exposed to public View. **1885** C. SCHREIBER *Jrnl.* 27 Feb. (1911) II. 469 A certain Longton Teapot, which we had discovered among her china. **1925** W. W. WORSTER tr. *Hannover's Pott. & Porc.* III. xx. 533 A mode of decoration probably peculiar to Longton Hall is the application of designs like those on Battersea or Staffordshire enamels, in white enamel pigment on a strong blue ground. **1961** *Connoisseur* Dec. p. xiv (Advt.), A rare Longton Hall Vase finely painted with flowers. **1973** *Times* 14 Nov. 21/5 For Longton Hall a small melon tureen.. made a record price at £4,000.

longue, obs. form of LUNG.

longuette (lɒŋ'gɛt). [f. F. *longuette* somewhat long, longish.] A midi dress, a midi skirt.

1970 *New Yorker* 10 Oct. 167/1 A photographer hopped among them adding to the bulging dossier of *Women's Wear Daily* evidence of the arrival of its 'longuette'. **1971** *Time* 29 Mar. 29 Along Belgrade's Terazije, maxicoats and Longuettes, velvet knickers and leather gaucho pants abound.

‖**longueur** (lɔ̃gœr). [Fr. = length.] A lengthy or tedious passage of writing. Also in extended use, of music, etc.

The form *longeur* in quots. 1959 and 1970 is *erron.*

1791 H. WALPOLE *Let.* 26 May (1905) XIV. 437 Boswell's book is gossiping;.. but there are woful longueurs, both about his hero and himself. **1821** BYRON *Juan* III. xcvii, I know that what our neighbours call 'longueurs', (We've not so good a word, but have the thing),.. Form not the true temptation which allures The reader. **1866** *Nation* (N.Y.) 16 Aug. 127/2 In what other writer than George Eliot could we forgive so rusty a plot, and such *langueurs* [sic] of exposition? **1887** DOWDEN *Life Shelley* I. v. 183 Admirable moralists, no doubt, were Fenelon and Marmontel, but there are longueurs in their writings. **1892** I. ZANGWILL *Childr. Ghetto* I. 5 The terrible *longueurs* induced by the meaningless ministerial repetition of prayers already said by the congregation. **1950** 'G. ORWELL' *Shooting Elephant* 41 A kind of pattern.. survives the complications and the *longueurs* [in *King Lear*]. **1952** 'M. COST' *Hour Awaits* 251 This sense of impending pause in herself—this *longueur* of spirit. **1958** *Times* 22 Dec. 5/5 Should the recitalist be an imperfect executant, the audience must listen for much too long a period, with only one interval to alleviate the *longueurs*. **1959** *Guardian* 2 Nov. 7/1 One was aware of extensive stretches in which nothing historically worth while seemed to be going on—longeurs which the Director of History.. would not have tolerated in his scenario. **1963** *Times Lit. Suppl.* 18 Jan. 40/3 Some of his own early experiences were clearly embedded: the longueurs of the middle-class Sunday, the deadly frustrations of office routine. **1970** *Times* 29 May 7/2 Despite the show's contradictions and longeurs, it does at least attempt something audacious and original. **1971** *Guardian* 18 Feb. 9/8 There are so many longueurs in most of the originals that one can hardly jib at Miss Wilson's frequent condensations. **1974** *Times* 6 Mar. 14/8 A perfect committee man, he would remain wholly silent—and even asleep—during the *longueurs* not unknown in university meetings.

Longueville (lɔ̃gviːl). Also **Longevil**. [Prob. from the surname *Longueville*; for its existence in Scotland cf. Henry's *Wallace* x. 789.] The name of a kind of pear.

1683 J. REID *Scots Gardener* (1756) 101 No Pear holds well on it [the quince], that I have tried, excepting the Red Pear, Achan, and Longevil. **1817** P. NEILL *Horticulture* in *Edin. Encycl.* (1830) XI. 211/2 The Longueville is very generally spread over the northern part of Britain, where aged trees of it exist in the neighbourhood of ancient monasteries.

long-waisted, *a.*

1. Having a long waist, as a person, a ship, etc.

1653 R. SANDERS *Physiogn.* 183 Slender, long-wasted, and not corpulent. **1676** ETHEREDGE *Man of Mode* III. ii, It makes me show long-waisted, and, I think, slender. **1694** *Lond. Gaz.* No. 2965/4 A young Bay Mare,.. long-waisted and weak Pasturn. **1826** MISS MITFORD *Village* Ser. II. 214 Her long-waisted pigeon-breasted gown. **1897** *Allbutt's Syst. Med.* III. 589 The thorax appears to be unduly long and narrow, and the patients describe themselves as 'long-waisted'.

†**2.** *fig.* Easy; loose. *Obs.*

1647 WARD *Simp. Cobler* 24, I shall.. borrow a little of their [women's] loose tongue Liberty, and mispend a word or two upon their long-wasted, but short-skirted patience. *a* **1658** CLEVELAND *Lenten Litany* I. iv, From a Parliament long-wasted Conscience, *Libera nos*, &c. —— *Square Cap* iv, Next comes the Puritan in a Wrought-Cap, With a long-wasted Conscience towards a Sister.

longward(s ('lɒŋwəd(z)), *adv.* [f. LONG *a.*[1] + -WARD, or -WARDS.] Towards longer wavelengths; on the long-wavelength side *of*.

1971 D. W. SCIAMA *Mod. Cosmol.* ix. 132 Because of the red shift the emission is spread out longwards of 21 cm. **1974** *Nature* 22 Feb. 513/1 Since the first report of a diffuse ultraviolet background, there have been several measurements attempted, both longward and shortward of Lyman α.

†**longway.** *Obs. rare.* [f. LONG *a.* + WAY.] A long road or causeway.

1627 in *Crt. & Times Chas. I* (1848) I. 293 They took the English at an advantage, when they were engaged in a narrow longway, going towards the bridge of the Isle de l'Oye.

longways ('lɒŋweɪz), *adv.* Also 7 **longstwayes**. [f. LONG *a.* + WAY *sb.* with adverbial *s*.] In the direction of the length of a thing; longwise, lengthways; longitudinally.

1588 A. PERNE *Will* in Willis & Clark *Cambridge* (1886) I. 28 The Colledge Librairie.. to be newe builded at the east end of the Masters Lodginge longewayes towardes the Streate. **1601** SIR W. CORNWALLIS *Ess.* II. xli. (1631) 181 Man.. his definition must be a creature with two legs made long-wayes. **1639** T. DE GRAY *Compl. Horsem.* 91 Give fire to the spaven both longst-wayes and crosse-wayes. **1683** MOXON *Mech. Exerc.*, *Printing* xxiv. ¶7 He Folds a sheet of the Paper he is to Work long-ways, and broad-ways. **1705** A. VAN LEUWENHOEK in *Phil. Trans.* XXV. 1844 The Bark of the said Wood can't be stripp'd off longways. **1831** T. HOPE *Ess. Origin Man* II. 399 Uneven bearing of the sole both longways and broadways. **1847** GROTE *Greece* II. liii. (1862) IV. 486 A channel through it long-ways from end to end. **1899** *Daily News* 13 Dec. 8/3 To have alternately to hold the book up longways and sideways.

†**b.** quasi-*prep.* *Obs.*

1656 FINETT *For. Ambass.* 11 Another Table placed long-wayes the chamber.

long-winded, *a.*

1. Capable of continuing in action for a long time without being out of breath; long-breathed.

1596 SHAKS. *1 Hen. IV*, III. iii. 181 One poore peny-worth of Sugar-candie to make thee long-winded. **1608** DAY *Humour out of breath* IV. G, *Pa.* Are you in breath my Lord? *Hort.* As a bruers horse, and as long-winded. **1728** POPE *Dunc.* II. 300 A cold, long-winded native of the deep. **1758** *Mickmakis & Maricheets* 37 Men that pretend to foretel futurity.. by frightful and long-winded howlings. **1870** DICKENS *E. Drood* xii, I am younger and longer-winded than you. **1870** EMERSON *Soc. & Solit.*, *Farming* Wks. (Bohn) III. 57 This hard work will always be done by.. men of endurance,—deep-chested, long-winded, tough.

fig. **1708** OCKLEY *Saracens* (1848) 322 That every one might make preparation for a war which..would be more long-winded than the former.

b. *Naut.* (See quot.)

1867 SMYTH *Sailor's Word-bk., Long-winded Whistlers*, chase-guns.

2. Of persons: Given to lengthy speaking or writing; characterized by tedious lengthiness in speech, or dilatoriness in action. Of their speech, etc.: Tediously long; of a tedious or wearisome length.

1589 *Hay any Work* 48 Thou are longer winded then Deane Iohn is. **1652** COTTERELL tr. *Cassandra* III. (1676) 41 Such a long-winded Discourse. **1696** PRIOR *Secretary* 8 For her, neither visits, nor parties at tea, Nor the long-winded cant of a dull refugee. *a* **1700** B. E. *Dict. Cant. Crew, Long-winded Pay-master*, one that very slowly..Paies. **1741** tr. *D'Argens' Chinese Lett.* iv. 22 The French Tradesmen are incapable of entering upon such long-winded Methods to favour their Commerce. **1764** *Mem. G. Psalmanazar* 230 A long-winded and multifarious dissimulation. **1769** BURKE *Corr.* (1844) I. 171, I am no great friend, in general, of long-winded performances. **1884** *Century Mag.* XXVIII. 589 The long-winded old salts who come here to report their wrecks. **1891** *Law Times* XCII. 106/2 Complicated provisions to suit the varying tastes of different owners..make conveyancing often seem long-winded.

Hence **long'windedly** *adv.*, **long'windedness**.

1837 CARLYLE *Fr. Rev.* I. v. ii, [They] make known, not without longwindedness, the determinations of the royal breast. **1866** G. MACDONALD *Ann. Q. Neighb.* xi. (1878) 213, I may speak long-windedly and even inconsiderately as regards my young readers. **1874** HELPS *Soc. Press.* vii. (1875) 82, I hate long-windedness as much as you do..; but I cannot call good similes and metaphors padding. **1885** *Athenæum* 12 Dec. 766/1 The longwindedness of narrative and dialogue only increases the insipidity of the whole.

longwise ('lɒŋwaɪz), *adv.* (*a.*) Also 6-7 **longst wise**. [f. LONG *a.* + -WISE.] Lengthwise, longitudinally, longways.

1544 W. PATTEN *Exped. Scotl.* C ij, Dunbar, a toun standing longwise vpon yᵉ seasyde. **1580** BLUNDEVILLE *Curing Horses Dis.* 54 Laurentius Russius would haue the splent to be cured by fiering it longst wise & ouerthwart. **1657** R. LIGON *Barbadoes* (1673) 67 That kernel..as our Hazle-nuts in England, will part in the middle long-wise. **1715** LEONI *Palladio's Archit.* (1742) I. 86 Upon which..are laid other beams longwise. **1848** DICKENS *Dombey* xxii, Standing it [a letter] long-wise and broad-wise on his table. **1865** —— *Mut. Fr.* I. xvi, Too much of him longwise, too little of him broadwise, and too many sharp angles of him anglewise.

†**b.** Used as *adj.*: Oblong. *Obs. rare.*

1600 HOLLAND tr. *Marlianus' Topogr. Rome* 1348 The Viminall hill... The forme thereof is longwise [L. *oblongam*].

longwort: see LUNGWORT.

longyi, var. LUNGI.

‖**lonicera** (ləʊ'nɪsərə). *Bot.* [mod.L., f. name of Adam *Lonicer* (1528-86), a German botanist.] A genus of caprifoliaceous plants consisting of the honeysuckles; a plant of this genus.

1863 *Life in South* II. 329 The..scarlet lonicera, with vines and other climbers, reached the tops of the tallest trees. **1882** *Garden* 11 Mar. 170/3 The two early flowering Loniceras..are just now in perfection. **1882** HARDY in *Proc. Berw. Nat. Club* IX. No. 3. 434 A wide spreading Lonicera helped to cover the walls.

loning, obs. form of LOANING *sb.*

†'**lonish**, *a. Obs.* [f. LONE *a.* + -ISH.] Lonely.

1653 WOOD *Life* Sept. (O.H.S.) I. 181 After he had spent the summer at Cassington in a lonish and retir'd condition, he return'd to Oxon.

Lonk (lɒŋk). [dial. var. of *Lank*, the first syllable of *Lancashire*: see *E.D.D.*] A large-sized variety of mountain sheep which originated in Lancashire or Yorkshire; the wool of this variety of sheep.

1863 in W. Fream *Youatt's Compl. Grazier* (1893) 473 If the Lonks be as hardy as they are good, they must be the most valuable sheep for the hills that we have at present. **1866** *Jrnl. R. Agric. Soc.* II. 367 The hill ranges of Yorkshire and Lancashire are believed to be the earliest home of the Lonks. **1911** *Chambers's Jrnl.* Dec. 778/2 The lonk is believed to have come originally from the Yorkshire hills. **1940** *Chambers's Techn. Dict.* 510/2 *Lonk*, wool that comes from the large type of mountain sheep of the same name, reared on the Lancashire and Yorkshire moorlands. **1968** FRASER & STAMP *Sheep Husbandry* (ed. 5) ii. 110 The Lonk. Another horned and black-faced breed is native to a rather confined hill district of Lancashire and Yorkshire. It is a big sheep, handsome, with very clearly differentiated black-and-white markings on face and legs, strong-boned and active. **1972** J. WAINWRIGHT *Night is Time to Die* 7 The dark patch could be a sheep... Ye-es—it *could* be some stupid, wandering Lonk. **1974** *Times* 23 Feb. 14 Several farmers may turn out their Swaledale or Scottish Blackface, Herdwick or Lonk sheep onto one moor.

lonnin(g, var. LOANING *sb.*

†**lonquhard**. *Sc. Obs.* Also 4 **longart**, 7 **lonckart**. [app. a. Gael. *longphort*.] A temporary cottage or hut; a 'shieling'. ? *Sc.* or *dial.*

c **1375** *Sc. Leg. Saints* xix. (*Cristofore*) 269 Ore he 3ed his longart to. **1618** J. TAYLOR (Water P.) *Pennyles Pilgr.* F, There were small cottages built on purpose to lodge in, which they call Lonquhards. **1632** in *4th Rep. Hist. MSS. Comm.* I. (1874) 533/2 [Vassals] sall caus big and put up our lonckartis for the hunting. **1771** PENNANT *Tour Scotl.* in 1769 (1790) 125 They lived in temporary cottages called Lonquhards.

Lonsdale ('lɒnzdeɪl). The title of Hugh Cecil Lowther (1857-1944), fifth earl of *Lonsdale*, used *attrib.* to denote any of various belts conferred upon professional boxing champions of the United Kingdom. Also *transf.* So ***to give*** (someone) ***the Lonsdale*** (slang), to dismiss, repudiate, 'throw out' (cf. BELT *sb.*^{4}).

1910 *Daily Graphic* 18 Oct. 10/4 At the National Sporting Club..last evening, the contest was decided for the Bantam-weight Championship of Great Britain, the winner of which also holds the Lonsdale belt for that weight. **1914** *Boxing's Bk. Records* 9 (*caption*) Lonsdale Belt Holders. **1958** F. NORMAN *Bang to Rights* III. 167, I can always give her the Lonsdale after a week or two. **1959** C. MACINNES *Absolute Beginners* 77 The Wiz was wearing a gladiator Lonsdale belt with studs on it. **1973** *Country Life* 26 July 249/1 The traditional Lonsdale Belt..with its enamel portrait of the 5th Earl.

lont, rare obs. form of LAND *sb.*^{1}

†**lontaigne**, *a. Obs. rare*$^{-1}$. [a. F. *lointaine*, fem. of *lointain*:—pop.L. **longitānum*, f. *longe* far off, f. *long-us* LONG *a.*] Distant.

c **1450** *Mirour Saluacioun* 4187 A man weending in til a Regionne lontaigne.

lontar ('lɒntɑː(r)). [Malay.] = PALMYRA; also, a manuscript written on leaves of this palm.

1820 J. CRAWFURD *Hist. Indian Archip.* I. IV. 443 The *Lontar*, (*Borassus flabellifer*), the *Tar*, or Tal of Western India, grows abundantly in the Indian islands. **1935** I. H. BURKILL *Dict. Econ. Products Malay Peninsula* I. 348 Lontar is also the best-known Malayan name. **1937** M. COVARRUBIAS *Island of Bali* (1972) vii. 193 In Singaradja there is a library of these manuscripts,..where are preserved some splendid old *lontars* with illustrations... These are masterpieces of the art of illustration, with miniature pictures incised with an iron style on the blades of the *lontar* palm. **1952** 'W. MARCH' *October Island* i. 11 He moved majestically towards the four tall lontar palms. **1953** C. A. GIBSON-HILL *Malay Arts & Crafts* §Hats & Dish-covers. Other fibres are employed, including strips from the Lontar Palm. **1961** P. KEMP *Alms for Oblivion* ix. 152 You know about *lontars*? Good. Well, in one important *lontar* is written, 'It is fair to lie to wifes [*sic*] and enemies.'

lonys, obs. pl. of LOIN.

loo (luː), *sb.*^{1} Also 6, 8 **lu**, 8 **liew**, **lue**. [abbreviated f. LANTERLOO.]

1. A round card-game played by a varying number of players. The cards in three-card loo have the same value as in whist; in five-card loo the Jack of Clubs ('Pam') is the highest card. A player who fails to take a trick or breaks any of the laws of the game is 'looed', i.e. required to pay a certain sum, or 'loo', to the pool. ***limited, unlimited loo***: see quots. 1830, 1883. **b.** The fact of being looed. **c.** The sum deposited in the pool by a player who is looed.

1675 WYCHERLEY *Country Wife* Epil., They..May kiss the Cards at Picquet, Hombre,—Lu, And so he thought to kiss the Lady too. **1680** COTTON *Compl. Gamester* (ed. 2) xx. Lanterloo 102 If three, four, five or six play, they may lay out the threes, fours, fives, sixes and sevens to the intent they may not be quickly loo'd; but if they would have the loos come fast about then play with the whole pack. *Ibid.* 104 If any be loo'd he must lay down so much for his loo as his five Cards amount to. **1710** *Brit. Apollo* III. No. 5. 2/2 A. gives B. 3*s.* 6*d.* to Play for him at Liew... B. had lost all but 5*d.* and there was a Liew down of 2*s.* 6*d.* **1712-14** POPE *Rape Lock* III. 62 Ev'n mighty Pam, that Kings and Queens o'erthrew And mow'd down armies in the fights of Lu. **1731** SWIFT *To Dr. Helsham* 16 Yet, ladies are seldom at ombre or lue sick. **1777** COLMAN *Epil. Sch. Scand.* in *Prose on Sev. Occas.* (1787) III. 215 And as Backgammon mortify my soul That pants for Lu, or flutters at a Vole. **1796** JANE AUSTEN *Pride & Prej.* (1885) I. viii. 30 On entering the drawing room, she found the party at loo. **1823** SOUTHEY in *Life* (1849) I. 89 In the evening my aunt and I generally played at five-card loo with him. **1830** R. HARDIE *Hoyle made familiar* 70 At Limited Loo those who play and do not get a trick pay into the pool only the price of the deal, while at Unlimited Loo they pay the whole amount that happens to be in the pool at the time. *a* **1845** BARHAM *Ingol. Leg., Ld. Thoulouse* xii, I should like to see you Try to *sauter le coup* With this chap at short whist, or unlimited loo. **1861** HUGHES *Tom Brown at Oxf.* i. (1889) 2 They..played billiards until the gates closed, and then were ready for..unlimited loo..in their own rooms. **1883** H. JONES in *Encycl. Brit.* XV. 1/1 If there is a loo in the last deal of a round, the game continues till there is a hand without a loo. *Ibid.* 1/2 At *unlimited loo* each player looed has to put in the amount there was in the pool. But it is generally agreed to *limit* the loo, so that it shall not exceed a certain fixed sum. Thus, at eighteen-penny loo, the loo is generally limited to half a guinea. **1885** FARJEON *Sacred Nugget* xv, The game being loo, six shillings 'tit-up', limited to two guineas. *Ibid.*, 'Let it be club law'... So club law it was, and the loos became more frequent.

2. A party playing at loo.

1760 H. WALPOLE *Let. to G. Montagu* 7 Jan., There were two tables at loo, two at whist, and a quadrille. I was commanded to the duke's loo. *Mod.* (*Ireland*) Are you coming to my loo?

†**3.** Party, set. Phr. ***for the good of the loo***: 'for the benefit of the company or community' (Grose *Dict. Vulg. Tongue* 1785). *Obs.*

1764 H. WALPOLE *Let. to Hertford* 27 May, Lady Falkener's daughter is to be married to..Mr. Crewe, a Maccarone and of our loo. **1774** *Association Delegates Colonies* 12 They shall be..sold Auction-wise, for the Good of the Loo.

4. *attrib.* and *Comb.*, as **loo club**; **loo-table**, a table for playing loo upon; now the trade designation of a particular form of round table, originally devised for this purpose.

1789 CHARLOTTE SMITH *Ethelinde* (1814) II. 130 Dinner was no sooner over, than the loo-table was introduced into the drawing-room. **1830** R. HARDIE *Hoyle made familiar* 72 The following [laws] are those observed at the Loo Clubs. **1862** TROLLOPE *Orley F.* I. vi. 46 A round loo-table.

†**loo**, *sb.*^{2} *Obs.* exc. *Hist.* [F. *loup*: see LOUP.] A velvet mask partly covering the face, worn by females in the 17th century to protect the complexion. Chiefly *attrib.* in ***loo mask***.

1690 EVELYN *Ladies Dressing-R.* 10 Loo Masks, and whole, as wind does blow, And Miss abroad's dispos'd to go. —— *Fops Dict.* 18 *Loo Mask*, an half Mask. **1839** W. H. AINSWORTH *Jack Sheppard* I. ii, Blueskin..turning..beheld a young female, whose features were partially concealed by a loo, or half mask, standing beside him.

loo (luː), *sb.*^{3} [Hind., f. Skr. *ulkā* flame.] The name given in Bihar and the Punjab to a hot dust-laden wind.

1888 KIPLING *Phantom 'Rickshaw* 78 The *loo*, the red-hot wind from the westward, was booming among the tinder-dry trees. *a* **1936** —— *Something of Myself* (1937) iv. 98 A hot wind, like the *loo* of the Punjab. **1954** O. H. K. SPATE *India & Pakistan* ii. 55 In the NW hot weather depressions generally take the form of violent dust-storms... Such dust-storms are distinct from the *loo*, a very hot dust-laden wind which may blow for days on end. **1965** E. AHMAD *Bihar* iv. 45 The hot scorching 'loo' winds of the Bihar plains during late April and May have an average velocity of 5-10 miles per hour. **1974** M. PEISSEL *Great Himalayan Passage* xi. 175 The Loo is caused by the hot expanding air of the Indian plains rushing into the cool hills.

loo (luː), *sb.*^{4} [Etym. obscure.] A privy, a lavatory. Also *attrib.* and *Comb.*

A. S. C. Ross's examination of possible sources in *Blackw. Mag.* (1974) Oct. 309-16 is inconclusive: he favours derivation, in some manner that cannot be demonstrated, from *Waterloo*.

[**1922** JOYCE *Ulysses* 556 O yes, *mon loup*. How much cost? Waterloo. Watercloset. **1932** N. MITFORD *Christmas Pudding* ix. 137 The absence in his speech of such expressions as 'O.K. loo'..'we'll call it a day'.] **1940** —— *Pigeon Pie* ii. 27 In the night when you want to go to the loo. **1943** C. BEATON in *Horizon* Jan. 37 They had dressed, teeth brushed, breakfasted, had visited the loo, and were on their precarious journey all in a question of fifteen minutes. **1944** AUDEN *For Time Being* (1945) 20 Between the bottle and the 'loo' A lost thing looks for a lost name. **1954** KOESTLER *Invis. Writing* xxxix. 419 The story of 'the loo-tank papers'..is another instance of the cloak-and-dagger atmosphere. **1955** G. FREEMAN *Liberty Man* II. vi. 113 Johnnie, do take him to the loo, there's a good boy. **1957** P. WILDEBLOOD *Main Chance* 57 The loo's on the landing, if you want to spend a penny. **1960** C. MACKENZIE *Greece in my Life* 23, I think I should sigh for the old Grande Bretagne Hotel in spite of the squalor of the loo which was no paradise for dysentery. **1971** *Petticoat* 17 July 31/2 You can wait until he goes to the loo or, if he appears to have a bladder like an ox, send him to the kitchen for more coffee. **1972** *Guardian* 23 Feb. 18/5 Matching bathmats (£2.20)..and loo seat covers (£1.80 and £1.12). **1973** E. MCGIRR *Bardel's Murder* iv. 85 A neighbouring cat had come through the window and made away with the loo brush. **1974** *Observer* 28 Apr. 28/6 The loo rolls unfurling across the pitch.

loo (luː), *v.*^{1} [f. LOO *sb.*^{1}] *trans.* To subject to a forfeit at loo (see LOO *sb.*^{1} 1). ***to loo the board*** (see quot. 1883).

1680 COTTON *Compl. Gamester* (ed. 2) xx. 102 If you play and are loo'd (that is, win never a trick). *Ibid.* 103 He who hath five Cards of a suit in his hand loos all the Gamesters then playing,..and sweeps the board. *c* **1750** SHENSTONE *To a Friend*, I'll play the cards come next my fingers—Fortune cou'd never let Ned loo her, When she had left it wholly to her. **1797** *Sporting Mag.* X. 304 The whole sum which happens to be down at the time when he is looed. **1862** H. KINGSLEY *Ravenshoe* III. 240 General Mainwaring had been looed in miss four times running. **1883** H. JONES in *Encycl. Brit.* XV. 1/2 A flush..*loos the board*, i.e., the holder receives the amount of a loo from every one, and the hand is not played. **1885** FARJEON *Sacred Nugget* xv, [He] suggested that 'black Jack should loo the board'..so black Jack looed the board, and the loos became more frequent still. *Ibid.* xvi, It was proposed that the stakes should be raised to five guineas unlimited... Each player put in five guineas, making a total of twenty-five guineas, which sum represented the amount a player would be looed for. **1886** D. C. MURRAY *First Person Singular* xviii. 134 To hold King, Knave, nine, and get looed on it.

b. *transf.* and *fig.* (See quots.) Now *dial.*

1706 ESTCOURT *Fair Examp.* I. i. 10 For let me tell ye, Madam, Scandal is the very Pam in Conversation, and you shou'd always lead it about for the good of the Board; spare no body, every one's pleas'd to see their Neighbour Loo'd. *a* **1845** HOOD *Storm at Hastings* v, No living luck could loo him! Sir Stamford would have lost his Raffles to him! **1859** BARTLETT *Dict. Amer., Looed*, defeated. A term borrowed from the game called *loo*. **1879** MISS JACKSON *Shropsh. Word-bk., Looed*, thwarted, 'check-mated'. **1888** *Sheffield Gloss.* s.v., When a cutler agrees to make a number of knives for a fixed sum and has not finished them when pay-time comes he is said to be *lood*.

†**loo**, *v.*^{2} *Obs.* exc. *dial.* [aphet. f. HALLOO *v.* Cf. LOO *int.*] *trans.* To incite by shouting 'halloo'; to urge *on* by shouts; = HALLOO *v.* 1 b. Const. *at*, *upon*, or inf.

1666-7 DENHAM *Direct. Paint.* ii. 15 And therefore next uncouple either Hound, And loo them at two Hares ere one be found. **1681** T. FLATMAN *Heraclitus Ridens* No. 40 (1713)

II. 8 The Rabble 'lood to worry it [*sc.* the Government] as tyrannical and unjust. **1682** SHADWELL *Medal of John Bayes* Ep. A i j, Young fellows, (who clap him on the back,..and loo him on upon the Whiggs, as they call 'em). **1689** *State Eur.* in *Harl. Misc.* I. 195 England and Holland are desperately bruised through mutual buffetings, to which France cunningly looed them on. **1711** *Vind. Sacheverell* 9 Ben was pitch'd upon..to hollow the Hounds together, to looe them full cry at Monarchy.

loo (luː), *int.* Also written 'loo; in 7 lo, lowe. [abbreviated f. HALLOO.] A cry to incite a dog to the chase; = HALLOO. Also *loo in!* Also quasi-*sb.*

1605 SHAKS. *Lear* III. iv. 79 Alow: alow, loo, loo. **1606**—— *Tr. & Cr.* v. vii. 10 Now bull, now dogge, lowe, Paris, lowe. **1681** T. FLATMAN *Heraclitus Ridens* No. 4 (1713) I. 19 Ho loo Bob! Loo Crop, Loo, Loo, Loo, Smug! *Ibid.* No. 39 I. 255 'Loo my Dog Tutty..speak to 'em Tutty. **1718** BP. HUTCHINSON *Witchcraft* 266 Presently a Hare did rise very near before him, at the Sight whereof he cried Loo, Loo, Loo; but the Dogs would not run. **1810** J. WOOD *Let.* 27 May in *Life of S. Butler* (1896) I. 61 The youths are brought up with a rooted objection to St. John's, and, like bull-dogs of true breed, are always ready to fall upon us at the loo of their seniors. **1830** R. EGERTON-WARBURTON *Hunt. Songs* I. i. (1883) 1 His cheer by the echo repeated, 'Loo in! little dearies! 'loo in! **1853** 'C. BEDE' *Verdant Green* I. ix, A perfect pack in full cry, with a human chorus of 'Hoo rat! Too loo! loo dog!' **1881** JEFFERIES *Wood Magic* I. i. 19 Bevis..called 'Loo! Loo!' urging the dog on.

loo, var. LEW, and LOOR *dial.*; Sc. form of LOVE.

looard, var. LEEWARD *a.* (*sb.*) and *adv.*

loob (luːb). *Tin-mining.*
  1. (See quot.)
  1674 RAY *Collect. Words, Prepar. Tin* 121 The dross and earth..is carried all along the trough to a pit or vessel, into which the trough delivers it, called a loob.
  2. *pl.* (See quots.)
  1778 PRYCE *Min. Cornub.* 324 Loobs, tin slime or sludge of the after leavings, or leavings slime. **1860** *Eng. & For. Mining Gloss.* (Cornwall mines), Loobs, slime containing ore.

loobel, variant of LOWBELL *Obs.*

†**'loobily**, *a. Obs.* [f. LOOBY + -LY¹.] Looby-like; awkward, clumsy, lubberly.
  1655 FULLER *Ch. Hist.* VI. v. *False Miracles* §12 There was in Wales a great and Loobily Image, called Darvell Gatherne. **1756** TOLDERVY *Hist. 2 Orphans* III. 148 Talked politicks with the landlord, and disputed about religion with three loobily farmers. **1777** H. CAREY *Honest Yorkshirem.* 13 It's enough to put any young lady in the pouts, to .. force her to marry a great loobily Yorkshire tike.

†**'loobish**, *a. Obs. rare*—¹. In 7 loubish. [? f. LOOBY + -ISH.] = prec.
  1648 HEXHAM *Dutch Dict.*, *Onbelompen*, Clomnish [*sic*], or Loubish.

looby ('luːbɪ). Now chiefly *dial.* Forms: 4-6 loby, -ie, 6 loubie, lowbie, -ye, 7 lubby, loubee, 7-looby. [Cf. LOB *sb.*, LUBBER, and the Teut. cognates mentioned under those words.] A lazy hulking fellow; a lout; an awkward, stupid, clownish person.
  1377 LANGL. *P. Pl.* B. Prol. 55 Grete lobyes and longe that loth were to swynke. **1529** S. FISH *Supplic. Beggars* (E.E.T.S.) 14 Set these sturdy lobies a brode in the world.. to get theire liuing with their laboure. *a* **1550** *Image Ipocr.* IV. 129 in *Skelton's Wks.* (1843) II. 440 With priors of like place.. Great lobyes and lompes. **1577-87** STANYHURST *Descr. Irel.* 17/2 in Holinshed, Sir, you take me verie short, as long and as verie a lowbie as you imagine to make me.

1629 SYMMER *Spir. Posie* I. ix. 30 What is the state then of the sluggard, the lazie Lizzard, and the luskish Lubby? **1681** T. FLATMAN *Heraclitus Ridens* No. 41 (1713) I. 15 This is but like a great Looby at School, who [etc.]. **1696** PHILLIPS s.v. *Lob*, A great heavy sluggish Fellow is called a Lob, *Loubee* [**1706** *Looby*], or *Lob-cock*. **1705** HICKERINGILL *Priest-cr.* II. Pref. A iv, Homer—Achilles makes a great strong Looby. **1713** STEELE *Englishman* No. 24. 158 [These] are all convincing Arguments to a Country Looby. **1783** JOHNSON in *Boswell* 20 Apr., A savage, when he is hungry, will not carry about with him a looby of nine years old, who cannot help himself. **1821** CLARE *Vill. Minstr.* I. 159 A good-for-nought looby, he nettled me sore. **1845** DISRAELI *Sybil* (1863) 207, I went once and stayed a week at Lady Jenny Spinner's to gain her looby of a son and his eighty thousand a-year. **1871** R. ELLIS tr. *Catullus* xxii. 11 No ditcher e'er appeared more rude, No looby coarser. **1872** GEO. ELIOT *Middlem.* xxxv. (1873) 213 While I tell the truth about loobies, my reader's imagination need not be entirely excluded from an occupation with lords. **1886** in ELWORTHY *W. Somerset Word-bk.*

  b. *attrib.* and *appositive*, passing into *adj.* Also in comb. *looby-like.*
  1582 STANYHURST *Æneis* III. (Arb.) 91 Al wee see the giaunt, with his hole flock lowbylyke hagling. **1679** LD. ROCHESTER *Epigr. Ld. All-Pride* in *Roxb. Ballads* (1883) IV. 567 A plowman's looby meen, face all awry. **1687** *Advise to Pestholders* ii. 1 in *Third Collect. Poems* (1689) 21/1 That Looby Duke. **1771** T. HULL *Sir W. Harrington* (1797) I. 143 A country squire, of the looby kind. **1830** J. BEE *Ess.* in *Dram. Wks. Foote* I. (Cent.), This great, big, overgrown metropolis .. like a looby son who has outgrown his stamina.

looce, obs. form of LOOSE.

looch, variant of LOHOCH.

loode, lood(e)sterre, obs. ff. LODE, -STAR.

looder, var. LOWDER.

looe, variant of LEW *a.*¹, *sb.*², and *v.*

looer ('luːə(r)). *rare*—¹. [f. LOO *sb.*¹ or *v.*¹ + -ER¹.] A player at loo.
  1770 FOOTE *Lame Lover* II. 50 There is Mrs. Allspice.. has six tables every Sunday, besides looers, and braggers.

looer, variant of LOWER *sb. Obs.*, LURE *sb.*²

looey ('luːɪ). *N. Amer. slang.* Also looie, louie. [f. LIEU(TENANT with pronunc. (luː) + -Y⁶, -IE.] A lieutenant.
  1916 *Rio Grande Rattler* 11 Oct. 5 The 'Looey' gaily saunters from his tent. **1920** J. DOS PASSOS *One Man's Initiation: 1917* vii. 86 Our louie's name's Duval. **1928** W. H. UPSON *Me & Henry & Artillery* 120 Then the looeys started hollering to the sergeants. **1935** A. J. POLLOCK *Underworld Speaks* 73/1 *Looie*, a police lieutenant. **1942** M. HARGROVE *See Here, Private Hargrove* lxiii. 182 How would you like a second looey's commission? **1967** I. A. BARAKA in W. King *Black Short Story Anthol.* (1972) 119 Jimmy Lassiter, first looie. **1974** *Weekend Mag.* (Montreal) 27 Apr. 10/1 One scrap of the rarely-talked-about reality: after being a private 14 months, Angus was commissioned in the field as second looey.

loof (luf), *sb.*¹ Sc. and *north. dial.* Forms: 4-5 lofe, love, loove, 5-6 luif(f, 6 luyff, luff, loofe, 7 luve, 4- lufe, 7- loof. (See also E.D.D.) [a. ON. *lófe* wk. masc. = Goth. *lófa*; related by ablaut to OHG. *laffa* blade of an oar, OSl. (Polish, Russian) *lapa* paw, Lettish *lēpa* paw.] The palm

---

of the hand. *to creesh one's loof*: see CREESH *v. aff loof* adv. phr. = off hand.
  13.. *E.E. Allit. P.* B. 987 Wyth lyȝt louez vplyfte þay loued hym swype. **13..** *S. Erkenwolde* 349 in Horstm. *Altengl. Leg.* (1881) 274 þene wos lounyge oure lorde with loves vp haldene. *c* **1400** MAUNDEV. (Roxb.) vii. 26 Take a litill bawme and lay it on þe lufe of þi hand. *a* **1400-50** *Alexander* 2569 (Ashm. MS.) þe licor in þis awen looue [*Dublin MS.* lofe], þe lettir in þe tothire. *c* **1460** *Towneley Myst.* iii. 462 Noe. I may towch with my lufe the grownd evyn here. *c* **1470** HENRYSON *Mor. Fables* 2072 in *Anglia* IX. 466, I sall of it mak mittenis to my luffis, Till hald my handis hait quhair euer I be. **1513** DOUGLAS *Æneis* VIII. ii. 5 And in the holl luffis of his hand, quhair he stude, Dewly the wattir hynt he fra the flude. **1562** TURNER *Herbal* II. 108 They be as big as a man may grype in the palm or loofe of his hande. **1573** *Satir. Poems Reform.* xxxix. 203 The suddartis luiffis wes as ouirlaid wᵗ lyme. *c* **1620** Z. BOYD *Zion's Flowers* (1855) 54 If in your loof yee all this silver had. **1637** RUTHERFORD *Lett.* (1862) I. 198 We are fools to see browden and fond of a pawn in the loof of our hand. **1721** RAMSAY *Lucky Spence* xii, Wi' well-creesh'd loofs I hae been canty. **1728**—— *Rob. Rich. & Sandy* 62 (1877) II. 8 A canty tale he'd tell aff loof. **1792** BURNS *Willie's Wife* vi, Auld baudrons by the ingle sits, An' wi' her loof her face a-washin. **1830** GALT *Lawrie T.* VII. vii. (1849) 335 Though the case were as plain as my loofe. **1855** ROBINSON *Whitby Gloss.* s.v., Give us thy lufe, not thy fist. **1896** BARRIE *Sentim. Tommy* xix. 215 Using the loof of his hand as a spoon.
  Hence **loof-ful** *Sc.*, a handful.
  c **1540** LYNDESAY *Kittie's Conf.* 90 Curnis of meil, and luffillis of Malt. **1728** P. WALKER *Life Peden* (1827) 61 Waving his Hand to the West, from whence he desired the Wind, said, Lord, give us a Loof-full of Wind.

loof, *sb.*² and *v.* See LUFF *sb.* and *v.*

loof (luːf), *sb.*³ Also louff, lough. [a. Arab. *lúf* (see LOOFAH).] = LOOFAH.
  1865 *Pall Mall G.* 4 Aug. 3/2 A good rough Baden-Baden towel, or the Lough used in the Turkish bath. **1870** *Treas. Bot.*, Louff. *Luffa ægyptiaca.* **1897** WEBSTER, *Loof.*

†**loof**, *adv. Obs.* = ALOOF, at a distance.
  1555-8 PHAER *Æneid* I. A j, There was a towne of auncient tyme Carthago of old it hight, Against Italia and Tybers mouthe laie lord afar at seas aright. *Ibid.* III. F i j j, There lieth a lond far loof at seas, wher Mars is lord. **1557-8** *Ibid.* VII. U j b, Him wandring loof astray.

loof, obs. form of LOAF *sb.*¹

loofah ('luːfə). [a. Egyptian Arabic *lúfaʰ*, a plant of this species, which collectively is called *lúf.*] The fibrous substance of the pod of the plant *Luffa ægyptiaca*, used as a sponge or flesh-brush. Also *attrib.*, as *loofah-tree.*
  1887 MOLONEY *Forestry W. Afr.* 356 Loofah, Konyikon, or Native Sponge of Western Africa. **1889** C. D. BELL *Winter Nile* xxvi. 231 The loofah tree bears a long green pod. **1889** *Pall Mall G.* 7 Oct. 3/3 Rubbing myself well with a well-soaped loofah.

loogan ('luːgən). *U.S. slang.* [Etym. unknown.] In derogatory use: a fellow, a 'fool'.
  1929 D. RUNYON in *Hearst's International* July 126/3 The poor loogan she is marrying will never have enough dough to buy her such a rock. **1932** J. T. FARRELL *Young Lonigan* ii. 86 Bill's a loogin who always tries to wise-crack. **1933** 'P. CAIN' *Fast One* 200 There's Rose, with his syndicate behind him, and all the loogans he's imported from back East.

looge, obs. form of LODGE *sb.*

looie, var. LOOEY.

1995-96 SUZUKI MANUAL TRANSMISSIONS

Vehicle Application	Transmission Model
Swift	[1] Suzuki 5-Speed
Sidekick	[2] Suzuki 5-Speed
Samurai	Suzuki Samurai 5-Speed
X90	[2] Suzuki 5-Speed

[1] – See GEO METRO & SUZUKI SWIFT transmission article.
[2] – See GEO TRACKER & SUZUKI SIDEKICK transmission article.

1995-96 TOYOTA MANUAL TRANSMISSIONS

Vehicle Application	Transmission Model
Camry	
4-Cylinder	S51
V6	E53
Celica	
1.8L (7A-FE)	C52
2.2L (5S-FE)	S54
Corolla	
1.6L	C50
1.8L	C52
MR2	
Turbo (1995)	E153
Non-Turbo (1995)	S54
Paseo (1.5L)	C150
Pickup (1995)	
4-Cylinder (22R-E)	
2WD	G58 Or W55
4WD	G58 Or W56
V6	
2WD	R150
4WD	R150F
RAV4 (1996)	E250F
Supra (3.0L)	W58
T100	
2.7L 4-Cylinder	
1995	W56
1996	W59
V6	
2WD	R150
4WD	R150F

1995-96 TOYOTA MANUAL TRANSMISSIONS (Cont.)

Vehicle Application	Transmission Model
Tacoma	
1995	
2WD	R150
4WD	R150F
1996	W59
4Runner	
1995	
2.4L 4-Cylinder	G58
V6	R150F
1996	
2.7L 4-Cylinder	W59
V6	R150F
Tercel (1.5L)	
4-Speed	C141
5-Speed	C151

[1] – Overhaul information is not available.

1995-96 VOLKSWAGEN MANUAL TRANSMISSIONS

Vehicle Application	Transmission Model
4-Cylinder	
Golf III, Cabriolet & Jetta III	VAG 020
V6	
GTI VR6, Jetta & Passat	02A

1995-96 VOLVO MANUAL TRANSMISSIONS

Vehicle Application	Transmission Model
850	[1] M56

[1] – Overhaul information is not available.

Transfer Cases

1995-96 ACURA TRANSFER CASE APPLICATIONS

Vehicle Model	Transfer Case Model
SLX	See ISUZU

1995-96 GEO TRANSFER CASE APPLICATIONS

Vehicle Application	Transfer Case Model
Geo & Suzuki	[1]

[1] – Transfer case model number is not available.

1995-96 HONDA TRANSFER CASE APPLICATIONS

Vehicle Model	Transfer Case Model
Passport	See ISUZU

1995-96 LEXUS TRANSFER CASE APPLICATIONS

Vehicle Application	Transfer Case Model
LX450	Toyota HF2AV

1995-96 MAZDA TRANSFER CASE APPLICATIONS

Vehicle Application	Transfer Case Model
MPV	RA4AX-EL
Pickup Models	[1] BW 1354

[1] – See article in MITCHELL® 1995-96 TRANSMISSION SERVICE & REPAIR manual for DOMESTIC CARS, LIGHT TRUCKS & VANS.

1995-96 MITSUBISHI TRANSFER CASE APPLICATIONS

Vehicle Application	Transfer Case Model
Montero	[1]
Pickup	[1]

[1] – Transfer case model number not available from manufacturer.